THE GENERAL COUNCIL OF THE BAR™

THE BAR
DIRECTORY

Sweet & Maxwell
2000 EDITION

Published by Sweet & Maxwell Limited of
100 Avenue Road
London NW3 3PF

Set by AMA DataSet Ltd, Preston
Printed in Great Britain by The Bath Press, Bath

A CIP catalogue record for this book
is available from the British Library

ISBN 0421 674504

The information in this Directory was supplied in part by chambers
and individual barristers directly to the publishers (for Parts A, B, G
and I), and in part by the General Council of the Bar Records
Office (for Parts E and F). Part H was supplied by the Institute of
Barristers' Clerks. Parts C and D were drawn from information
supplied by the Bar Council in the first instance and supplemented
with information from chambers and individual barristers.

The General Council of the Bar information on chambers dates up
to 31 March 1999. Sweet & Maxwell accepted applications for
bronze, silver and gold chambers entries up to 28 May 1999.

The General Council of the Bar information on individual
barristers in private practice dates up to 31 March 1999. Sweet &
Maxwell accepted bronze entries up to 4 May 1999, and silver and
gold entries up to 28 May 1999.

A copy of the full Bar Directory Terms and Conditions is available
from Sweet & Maxwell upon request. The publishers have
attempted to ensure accuracy of all entries in this Directory, but
cannot accept responsibility for any errors, inconsistencies or
omissions.

No natural forests were destroyed to make this product, only
naturally farmed timber was used and replanted.

CONTENTS

Foreword by the Chairman of the Bar   iv

Guide to Using the Directory   v

Telephone Number Changes   ix

The Bar of England and Wales   xi

The General Council of the Bar   xiii

Circuits of the Bar   xv

Specialist Bar Associations   xvii

Direct Professional Access   xxiii

Advertised Services   xxvii

Part A   Types of Work by Chambers   A3

Part B   Types of Work by Individual Barristers   B3

Part C   Chambers by Location   C3

Part D   Individual Barristers in Private Practice   D3

Part E   Individual Barristers in Employment and Non-practising   E3

Part F   Individual Barristers Overseas   F3

Part G   Index of Languages Spoken   G3

Part H   Qualified Members of the Institute of Barristers' Clerks   H3

Part I   A–Z of Chambers   I3

THE SERVICES PROVIDED BY THE BAR EVOLVE AND EXPAND CONTINUOUSLY IN RESPONSE TO THE DEMANDS OF A MODERN SOCIETY. IT IS INCREASINGLY IMPORTANT TO BE ABLE TO IDENTIFY READILY THE SOURCES OF APPROPRIATE SPECIALIST ADVICE AND ADVOCACY.

THIS DIRECTORY CONTAINS COMPREHENSIVE INFORMATION ON CHAMBERS AND BARRISTERS. THE ASSOCIATED WEBSITE SETS OUT SIMILAR DETAILS, AND BOTH ALLOW THE READER TO SEARCH IN TERMS OF SPECIALISATION, GEOGRAPHIC AREA AND LANGUAGES SPOKEN.

I COMMEND THIS DIRECTORY TO ALL THOSE SEEKING TO USE THE BAR'S SERVICES.

DAN BRENNAN QC

CHAIRMAN OF THE BAR 1999

This Directory has been compiled from information supplied by chambers and individual barristers directly to the publishers (for Parts A, B, G and I), and by the General Council of the Bar Records Office (for Parts E and F). Part H was supplied by the Institute of Barristers' Clerks. Information in Parts C and D was supplied by the Bar Council in the first instance and supplemented with information from chambers and individual barristers.

The General Council of the Bar information on chambers dates up to 31 March 1999. Sweet & Maxwell accepted applications for bronze, silver and gold chambers entries up to 28 May 1999. The General Council of the Bar information on individual barristers dates up to 31 March 1999. Sweet & Maxwell accepted bronze entries up to 4 May 1999 and silver and gold entries up to 28 May 1999.

The introductory pages include information on the Bar of England and Wales, the General Council of the Bar, the Circuits of the Bar, Specialist Bar Associations and Direct Professional Access. This information was supplied by the General Council of the Bar. The Directory is divided into nine parts as follows:

Part A Types of Work by Chambers

Part A lists chambers by the type of work they do and by the town or city where they are located. The types of work undertaken by chambers are listed in alphabetical order. Within these main categories, chambers are listed alphabetically under the town or city in which they practise. For example, a reader wishing to locate a Birmingham-based chambers specialising in trademarks would be able to look under 'T' for Trademarks and find under that heading the details of any chambers in Birmingham which offer their services in this field. A complete list of the types of work can be found at the front of Part A.

Each listing provides the chambers' name and telephone number. The first point of contact in each instance will be the clerk. (Details of clerks can be found in *Part C Chambers by Location*).

Please note that chambers are only listed in this section if information on specialisms has been supplied by them.

The symbol • indicates that chambers have an expanded entry in *Part C Chambers by Location*.

Part B Types of Work by Individual Barristers

Part B lists individual barristers by the types of work in which they specialise. The areas of work are listed in alphabetical order. Within these main categories, individual barristers are listed alphabetically by surname. For example, a reader wishing to locate a particular barrister specialising in trademarks would be able to look under 'T' for Trademarks and find under that heading those barristers who offer their services in this field. A complete list of the types of work can be found at the front of Part B.

Each listing provides the name of the individual barrister, their chambers' address and chambers' telephone number. The first point of contact in each instance will be the clerk. (Details of clerks can be found in *Part C Chambers by Location*)

Please note that barristers are only listed in this section if information on specialisms has been supplied by them.

The symbol • indicates that a barrister has an expanded entry in *Part D Individual Barristers in Private Practice*.

Part C Chambers by Location

Part C lists chambers in England and Wales by the town or city in which they are located. The town/city names are in alphabetical order and under those main headings chambers are listed alphabetically, thus 7 King's Bench Walk would be listed before 4 Pump Court under London.

Information for each set of chambers includes full contact details. Some chambers have opted to include additional information about themselves in this part of the Directory. Additional information includes the names of barristers practising from that chambers, date chambers were established, opening times, chambers' facilities, languages spoken, details regarding fees and a list of the types of work undertaken including details of the number of counsel practising in each area. Please note that details of the types of work undertaken by those chambers which have chosen not to include this information in Part C may be found in *Part A Types of Work by Chambers*.

The following symbols indicate that barristers are:

† Recorders
‡ Assistant Recorders
* Door Tenants

Part D Individual Barristers in Private Practice

Part D lists barristers in private practice. Individuals are listed alphabetically by surname, and details include the chambers at which they practise, year of call to the Bar, Inn of Court and academic qualifications.

Some individual barristers have opted to include additional information about themselves in this part of the Directory, such as other qualifications, membership of foreign bars, other professional experience, languages spoken, publications, reported cases and a list of the types of work they undertake. Please note that details of the types of work undertaken by individual barristers who have chosen not to include this information in Part D may be found in *Part B Types of Work by Individual Barristers*.

Part E Individual Barristers in Employment and Non-Practising

Part E lists those barristers who are in employment and those who do not practise. Barristers are listed alphabetically by surname, and details include their date of call to the Bar and academic qualifications. Barristers who are currently employed have details of their position of employment with a full address.

The symbol • indicates that a barrister is in employment.

Part F Individual Barristers Overseas

Part F lists barristers who are based overseas. Barristers are listed alphabetically by surname and details include their membership of other Bars where appropriate, date of call to the Bar, their Inn of Court and academic qualifications.

Part G Index of Languages Spoken

Part G is an index of languages spoken by chambers and individual barristers. The languages are listed alphabetically, as are chambers and individuals.

All chambers in this section have an expanded entry in *Part C Chambers by Location* and all individual barristers in this section have an expanded entry in *Part D Individual Barristers in Private Practice*.

Part H Qualified Members of the Institute of Barristers' Clerks

Part H lists all qualified members of the Institute of Barristers' Clerks. The listings are divided into four sections: Senior Clerks, Junior Clerks, Senior Associates and Junior Associates. The information in this section was supplied by the Institute of Barristers' Clerks. The year of qualification, if supplied, is shown in brackets. Management Committee Members and Executive Committee Members are identified by the following symbols:

* Management Committee Members
** Executive Committee Members

Part I A-Z Index of Chambers

Part I lists all the chambers from *Part C Chambers by Location* alphabetically with the Part C page reference.

Bar Directory Website

Information in Parts A, B, C and D of the book is also available on the Internet at: http://www.smlawpub.co.uk/bar

Updating of Information

Information about chambers or individual barristers which needs updating should in the first instance be discussed with the Records Office at the Bar Council on the following number:

Tel: 0171 242 0934

Any comments regarding *The Bar Directory* or requests for updating on *The Bar Directory* website should be directed in the first instance to:

The Bar Directory
The Directories Unit
Sweet & Maxwell
100 Avenue Road
London NW3 3PF
Tel: 0171 393 7000

Six geographic areas of the UK are to be assigned new 02 codes and numbers: Cardiff, Coventry, London, Northern Ireland, Portsmouth and Southampton. All six areas will have a three-digit code followed by an eight-digit number. Portsmouth and Southampton will share the same code. There will be one code for Northern Ireland. The London 0171 and 0181 areas will share the same code.

The new area codes can be used with the new local numbers from 1 June 1999. Callers will be able to use either the new area code and new local number, or the existing area code and existing local number, until Autumn 2000. Before the changeover day on 22 April 2000, callers will need to use the existing local number when dialling locally. From 22 April 2000 only the new local number will work.

Cardiff

The area code will change from (01222) to (029). The new local number will be formed by the addition of '20' to the front of the existing six-digit local number.

For example: (01222) XXXXXX will become (029) 20XX XXXX

Coventry

The area code will change from (01203) to (024). The new local number will be formed by the addition of '76' to the front of the existing six-digit local number.

For example:(01203) XXXXXX will become (024) 76XX XXXX

London

London's existing area codes will change from (0171) or (0181) to (020). The new local numbers will be created by the addition of '7' or '8' to the front of the existing local number, depending on whether they are in the existing 0171 or 0181 area.

For example: (0171) XXX XXXX will become (020) 7XXX XXXX, (0181) XXX XXXX will become (020) 8XXX XXXX

Portsmouth

The area code will change from (01705) to (023). The new local number will be formed by the addition of '92' to the front of the existing six-digit local number.

For example: (01705) XXXXXX will become (023) 92XX XXXX

Southampton

The area code will change from (01703) to (023). The new local number will be formed by the addition of '80' to the front of the existing six-digit local number.

For example: (01703) XXXXXX will become (023) 80XX XXXX

More information about these changes can be found on the Big Number website at:
http://www.numberchange.org

Barristers are independent and objective. Their highly competitive training in litigation and advocacy, together with their specialist knowledge and experience in and out of court, can make a substantial difference to the outcome of a case, whether criminal or civil. Whatever the nature of the legal problem, it is important at an early stage to decide whether to bring in a barrister.

There are some 9,000 barristers in independent private practice in England and Wales. Through them the Bar offers unparalleled expertise. Broad areas of specialisation include: Building and Construction, Commercial, Company, Criminal (including extradition), Defamation, Employment, Environment, Family, Housing, Immigration, Insolvency, Insurance, Liquidation, Personal Injury, Property, Taxation and Trusts, Wills and Estates. These can be subdivided further into more than 300 categories of expertise.

Through their grouping in chambers, or in some cases working as sole practitioners, barristers are able to operate with low overheads and to offer competitive rates. Legal Aid will often cover the services of a barrister and sometimes a Queen's Counsel; for those not eligible for Legal Aid, solicitors can help the lay client by negotiating an affordable fee which in some cases can be on a 'no win, no fee' basis (conditional fee agreements).

The Bar remains a referral profession, usually instructed by solicitors. However, members of certain professional bodies (see *Direct Professional Access* on page xxiii) are able to seek advice direct from Counsel or may instruct counsel in non-court litigation. In some cases, members of the Bar provide their services *pro bono*, for example through Free Representation Units or the Bar Pro Bono Unit. *Pro bono* work has been undertaken also in humanitarian cases.

The era of the quill pen has gone. The Bar recognises that it must offer excellence not only in its advocacy and specialist advisory work, but through the efficiency with which it provides its services.

Time was when everyone was expected to attend in chambers upon the barrister, however inconvenient or expensive that was. The modern Bar is very different. Conferences with lay and professional clients in their own premises are becoming the norm. 'Have brief, will travel' is the motto of today's barrister.

Now, modern technology allows an approach which makes the delivery of our services even more efficient and economical: video conferencing.

Video conferencing allows people to communicate with each other face-to-face from different sites across the country. An expert in Cheltenham, a lay client in Liverpool, a solicitor in Manchester and a barrister in London can all hold a conference together by video link. The Bar Council's Practice Management and Development Committee has compiled a Video Conferencing Directory, which meets the demand for a nationwide index of video conferencing centres. The Bar Council has been at the forefront of the development and legal application of video conferencing since it first became available.

The substantial increase in the size of the Bar in recent years has been accompanied by an increase in the size of chambers, as well as in their number. This reflects the need to accommodate an increasing range of specialisation. A majority of the profession continues to practise from London, but about 3,000 barristers practise from major cities and in some cases small towns outside London, offering a wide range and depth of expertise.

The Inns of Court developed when lawyers took over the Inner and Middle Temples from the Order of Knights Templar, a Common Bench having been established at Westminster in the late 13th and early 14th century. Lincoln's and Gray's Inn grew from association with Henry de Lacy, Earl of Lincoln and the de Gray family respectively. From the 17th century onward, the right to practise as an advocate in the Royal Courts was restricted to members of the Inns, the Bar becoming firmly a referral profession acting on the instructions of solicitors in the 19th century.

Discipline over the Bar has, since the reign of Edward I been the responsibility of the judges, in practice carried out by the Benchers of the Inns but subject to the visitorial jurisdiction of the judges. The General Council of the Bar® (Bar Council®) was formed in 1894 to deal with matters of professional etiquette. In 1974, the Bar Council and the governing body of the Inns, the Senate, combined to form the Senate of the Inns of Court and the Bar. However, on 1 January 1987, in line with the recommendations of a report on the Constitution of the Senate by Lord Rawlinson QC, a Council of the Inns of Court was re-established separately and the Courts and Legal Services Act 1990 designated the General Council of the Bar as the authorised body for the profession.

The Courts and Legal Services Act 1990 requires the exercise of rights of audience to be dependent upon membership of a professional body which has rules governing the conduct of its members, has an effective mechanism for enforcing those rules and is likely to enforce them. Accordingly, the General Council of the Bar provides a regulatory framework, requiring compliance on complaints and discipline, ethics and standards, education and training, equal opportunities and pupillage. It also publishes guidance on a range of other subjects such as practice management standards and certification, health and safety within chambers, and taxation of barristers' income.

The Council has representational responsibilities in many areas including the administration of justice, relations with government, the European Union, legal professions in other countries, and other professional organisations with common interests. It participates in the negotiation of publicly funded fees and provides advice on legal aid matters, in addition to law reform consultation. Over 300 barristers serve on a range of committees contributing to the well-being of the profession, and of the public interest, through the quality of service the profession

provides. The positive involvement of so many practitioners also promotes accountability, both generally and
within the work of the Secretariat.

The General Council of the Bar

Main Offices: 3 Bedford Row London WC1R 4DB,
Telephone 0171 242 0082

Records Office: Telephone 0171 242 0934,
Fax 0171 831 9217, DX 240 LDE

Complaints, Education & Training Departments:
2/3 Cursitor Street, London EC4A 1NE,
Telephone 0171 440 4000, DX 325 LDE
Fax: (Complaints) 0171 440 4001
Fax: (Education & Training) 0171 440 4002

Chief Executive: Niall Morison

CIRCUITS OF THE BAR

There are six Circuits covering England and Wales evolving from the Assize system and they form the framework for the administration of courts and the Bar of England and Wales.

The Circuits are, alphabetically, Midland & Oxford, Northern, North-Eastern, South-Eastern, Wales & Chester and Western. Midland and Oxford Circuit covers central England from the east to Wales. Northern covers northern England to the west of the Pennines and North Eastern the east of that area. Wales and Chester covers the whole of Wales and Cheshire. South Eastern encompasses London, the Home Counties and East Anglia and Western from just west of Guildford to Truro and includes Winchester, Bristol and Exeter. Each of the Circuits is separately administered on the court side by a circuit administrator and office under the Court Service and on the Bar side by circuit officers, including a circuit leader and junior, and in the case of the larger Circuits, a circuit committee.

Each Circuit has its own presiding High Court judge who, with resident circuit judges, takes responsibility for every aspect of the administration of the court system. Long gone are the days of Judges travelling between towns on Circuit. In consultation with the Bar, courts administrators have been able to design 'user-friendly' courts with major cases being held on Circuit instead of having to be limited to London hearings. There is an English/Welsh translation service in Welsh courts, with extensive use of information technology. The Bar in many courts are now able to take notes direct to lap-top computers and one Circuit has been invited to develop computer training by distance-learning by video conference. Circuit meetings can be held by video conference from centres 100 miles apart.

The Bar and the administration have made great strides recently in co-operation and communication even though there has been a huge increase in numbers at the Bar. Setting up and maintaining lines of communication with all parts of the legal system, including the courts administration, the Lord Chancellor's Department, the judiciary and The Law Society, is an important aspect of the work of the Circuits on the Bar side. As a result of this rise in numbers many more barristers now practise on Circuit and work very effectively. Circuits provide a wide range of services for their members, including continuing education seminars, advocacy courses, new practitioner programmes and efficient information.

The circuit leaders are consulted by the Lord Chancellor on the appointment of part- and full-time judges and Queen's Counsel, and the Circuits still play an important part in the maintenance of professional standards. As constraints on public funds increase, the Circuits have assisted in the setting-up and extension of free representation schemes in different parts of the country. Citizens' Advice Bureaux and solicitors have shown great appreciation for this invaluable service and it has provided a springboard for pupil training.

Circuits have proved their capacity to accommodate change. In this momentous year and at a time of fundamental alteration in the legal profession, they continue to thrive. Regardless of changes, every member of the Bar will still maintain, in Lord Denning's words, that they belong to: 'My Circuit – the best of Circuits'.

Leaders of the Circuits

South Eastern Circuit
Michael Lawson QC
23 Essex Street, London WC2R 3AS
(telephone 0171 413 0353)

Midland & Oxford Circuit
Rex Tedd QC
St Philip's Chambers, Fountain Court, Steelhouse Lane, Birmingham B4 6DR
(telephone 0121 246 7000)

Northern Circuit
Peter Birkett QC
18 St. John Street, Manchester, M3 4EA
(telephone 0161 278 1800)

North Eastern Circuit
Malcolm Swift QC
Park Court Chambers, 16 Park Place, Leeds LS1 1SJ
(telephone 0113 243 3277)

Wales & Chester Circuit
J. Christopher Pitchford QC
Farrar's Building, Temple, London EC4Y 7BL
(telephone 0171 583 9241)

Western Circuit
R. John Royce QC
Guildhall Chambers, 22–26 Broad Street, Bristol BS1 2HG
(telephone 0117 927 3366)

SPECIALIST BAR ASSOCIATIONS

These associations are groups of barristers in independent practice in specialist fields. Their memberships often overlap. The associations concern themselves with the law and procedure in their fields, advise on law reform, look after their members interests and help them to keep up to date with new developments. Many also provide extensive continuing professional education and many publish their own directories.

Administrative Law Bar Association (ALBA)

Members provide specialist advice to public bodies (and those who have dealings with them) on their duties and powers and the exercise of them, in the light of both the general law and the specifically applicable provisions, and also of practice. They also act as specialist advocates for and against public authorities, including the government, particularly in judicial review proceedings and on appeal.

Secretary: *Owen Davies QC, 2 Garden Court, 1st Floor, Middle Temple, London EC4Y 9BL (telephone 0171 353 1633)*

Bar European Group

Set up to promote interest in, and knowledge of, Community law, this group holds a yearly conference in a European country and a number of other conferences and day educational courses in the UK. Open to all interested barristers or Bar students, membership includes specialist community law barristers advising and appearing here or before the Luxembourg Court and the Commission.

Chairman: *Nicholas Green QC, Brick Court Chambers, 7/8 Essex Street, London WC2R 3LD (telephone 0171 379 3550)*

Hon Secretary: *Julie Anderson, Litmann Chambers, 12 Grey's Inn Square, London WC1R 5JP (telephone 0171 831 0861)*

Chancery Bar Association

The work of the Chancery Bar involves property, business and commercial disputes, trusts and connected tax matters. It encompasses litigation, drafting, and advice covering a wide field including mortgages, landlord and tenant, companies and partnerships, insolvency, probate, pensions, intellectual property and professional negligence in these areas.

Hon Secretary: *Anthony Trace QC, 13 Old Square, Lincoln's Inn, London WC2A 3UA (telephone 0171 404 4800)*

Bristol and Cardiff Chancery Bar Association

The Association was formed in 1990. It is open to all members of the Bar who undertake work of a Chancery or commercial nature in the west of England and South Wales.

Chairman: *Winston Roddick QC, 10 Kings Bench Walk, Temple, London EC4 7EB (telephone 0171 353 2501)*

Hon Secretary: *Paul French, Guildhall Chambers, 23 Broad Street, Bristol BS1 2HG (telephone 0117 927 3366)*

Assistant Secretary: *Andrew Keyser 9 Park Place, Cardiff CF1 3DP (telephone 01222 382731)*

Northern Chancery Bar Association

Set up in 1987 as part of the lobbying exercise which led to the appointment of a full High Court judge as Vice-Chancellor of the County Palatine of Lancaster, the Association represents barristers practising on the Northern and North-Eastern Circuits doing Chancery work. The membership is just over 100. It is not always appreciated that one in four trials in the Chancery Division takes place on circuit. Membership varies from those with highly litigious practices to those who deal with the more traditional drafting and advisory work.

Secretary: *Julie Case, Exchange Chambers, Pearl Assurance House, Derby Square, Liverpool L2 9XX (telephone 0151 236 7747)*

Commercial Bar Association (COMBAR)

COMBAR was founded in 1989 to represent and promote the interests of commercial barristers serving the specialist needs of commerce, including international commercial litigation and arbitration. Its membership comprises leading commercial chambers and individual practitioners at the Commercial Bar whose expertise extends across the fields of international trade, shipping and aviation, banking and financial services, insurance and reinsurance, commodity transactions, insolvency, oil & gas/energy law, mergers and acquisitions, competition law, intellectual property, professional negligence, licensing, judicial review of government acts, employment, European Community matters and public international law. COMBAR represents its members on the Bar Council, liaises with other specialist Bar associations on matters of common interest, comments on proposed legislation affecting the commercial field, contributes to the debate concerning the reform of the English civil justice system and offers a continuing programme of lectures and seminars and links with international Bar associations. An annual directory is published in January. COMBAR actively encourages close working links with lawyers practising in other jurisdictions, particularly in Europe, North America and the Far East.

Secretary: *Timothy Howe, The Commercial Bar Association, 222–225 Strand, The Outer Temple, London WC2R 1ND (telephone 0171 353 3502)*

Criminal Bar Association

The largest Specialist Bar Association with over 2,500 members who cover all criminal cases plus extradition and human rights. The Association is consulted on issues of law reform and matters of public interest. It runs a series of seven winter lectures on law and procedure. There is also an annual conference dedicated to a specific subject, eg forensic science or recent developments in the law.

Secretary: *Nick Wood, 3rd Floor, Queen Elizabeth Building, Temple, London EC4Y 9BS (telephone 0171 583 5766; fax 0171 353 0339; website www.criminalbar.co.uk)*

Employment Law Bar Association

The Employment Law Bar Association was formed in April 1994. The principal aim is to be a forum of consultation on behalf of those barristers throughout the UK, in private and employed practice, who work in employment law; to assist Free Representation Units; to be consulted on Tribunal and High Court Rules and on appointments; to sit on Tribunal User Groups; to help with pupils seeking to specialise, and to be the official organ of the Bar for barristers in this field.

Secretary: *Jenny Eady, Old Square Chambers, 1 Verulam Buildings, Grays Inn, London WC1R 5LR (telephone 0171 831 0801; e-mail: jeady@compuserve.com)*

Family Law Bar Association

Members include all barristers with any degree of family work. This includes public and private work in connection with children, financial disputes between spouses, claims of cohabitees and Inheritance Act claims, covering all courts including magistrates courts.

Secretary: *Pamela Scriven QC, 1 Kings Bench Walk, Temple, London EC4Y 9DB (telephone 0171 936 1500)*

Bar Association for Local Government and the Public Service

The main objectives of the association include the protection and promotion of the professional rights and interests of barristers employed in the public sector by giving advice to barristers seeking a career in the public sector, making representations to the Bar Council and elsewhere relating to training, rights of audience, direct access to counsel and by promoting professional knowledge. Details about the Association and application forms for membership can be obtained from the Chairman.

Chairman: *Mirza F N Ahmad, Assistant Director of Legal Services, Bolton Metropolitan Borough Council, Town Hall, Bolton BL1 1RU (telephone 01204 522311 ext 1111; website www.balgps.freeeserve.co.uk; email chairman@balgps.freeserve.co.uk)*

IP Bar Association (formerly Patent Bar Association)

Members cover all kinds of intellectual property work, including patents, trademarks, copyright, registered designs, passing-off and breach of confidence. They appear mainly in the High Court and the Patents County Court. The main patent chambers belong en bloc and there are a number of individuals from elsewhere.

Secretary: *Dr Heather Lawrence, 11 South Square, Grays Inn, London WC1R 5EU (telephone 0171 405 1222)*

London Common Law and Commercial Bar Association

The Association was formed about 30 years ago. As its name suggests, it represents London common law and commercial practitioners. Its membership stands at well over 1,000 barristers.

Secretary: *David Melville, 39 Essex Street, London WC2R 3AT (telephone 0171 832 1111)*

Parliamentary Bar Mess

Members of this long-standing association appear before parliamentary committees at the committee stage of private and hybrid bills, either for local authorities or others promoting the bills, or for petitioners against them. Members also appear at inquiries held under the Transport and Works Act 1992. In addition most members do town and country planning work. The association has assisted in the debate on the parliamentary committee procedure.

Treasurer: *Timothy Comyn, 2 Harcourt Buildings, Temple, London EC4Y 9DB (telephone 0171 353 8415)*

Personal Injuries Bar Association (PIBA)

PIBA was established in March 1995. Its members provide specialist advice across the entire field of personal injuries, from road traffic accidents to industrial disease and multi-party drugs cases. PIBA currently has a membership of 1,000 spread throughout England and Wales. PIBA responds on behalf of the Personal Injuries Bar to government consultative documents, Law Commission papers and represents the Personal Injury Bar in its dealings with other bodies. The Association conducts a programme of continuing education for its members. Its members represent both plaintiffs and defendants.

Secretary: *Matthias Kelly, Old Square Chambers, 1 Verulam Buildings, Grays Inn, London WC1R 5LQ (telephone 0171 831 0801)*

Planning and Environment Bar Association (PEBA)

The Associations members regularly appear at public inquiries held under legislation dealing with town and country planning, compulsory purchase, highways, housing, local government, rating and related matters. Members' specialist practices frequently require them also to appear in the courts, principally in the High Court of Justice, on matters of law arising from ministerial decisions. The Lands Tribunal is also a regular forum on rating and compulsory purchase matters.

Secretary: *Douglas Edwards, 2 Harcourt Buildings, Temple, London EC4Y 9DB (telephone 0171 353 8415)*

Professional Negligence Bar Association

Formed in November 1990 to promote the idea of a professional negligence speciality, this Association is concerned mostly with lectures, seminars and continuing professional education generally. Members are recruited from widely different parts of the Bar, as the Association covers medical, financial, construction and legal professional negligence.

Secretary: *Andrew Goodman, 199 Strand, London WC2R 1DR (telephone 0171 379 9779)*

Revenue Bar Association

Over half the members are Chancery people who do capital taxes work. The others are pure tax specialists covering all kinds of taxation, offering advice on tax claims and problems and tax planning and appearing before General and Special Commissioners and VAT Tribunals as well as in the High Court and beyond.

Secretary: *Hugh McKay, Grays Inn Tax Chambers, Grays Inn, London WC1R 5JA (telephone 0171 242 2642)*

Technology and Construction Bar Association (TECBAR)

The members appear regularly in the Technology and Construction Court where the judges specialise in building, civil engineering and other disputes whose subject-matter is technical, eg disputes about ships, aircraft, chemical plant and computers. In addition to advising and drafting pleadings, members appear in disputes in litigation, arbitration (both domestic and international) and adjudications and act variously for employers, contractors and professionals, eg architects, engineers, etc.

Secretary: *Chantal-Aime Doerries, 1 Atkin Building, Grays Inn, London WC1R 5AT (telephone 0171 404 0102)*

DIRECT PROFESSIONAL ACCESS

Direct Professional Access (DPA) has been in existence for more than seven years. Prior to April 1989 only solicitors and a few notable exceptions, such as patent and trademark agents, could instruct counsel direct.

Members of the professional bodies listed below are now able to seek advice direct from counsel or may instruct counsel in non-court litigation. DPA does not include instructing barristers to appear in the higher courts or the county courts of Employment Appeal Tribunal. Nor is DPA allowed if at any stage a barrister considers that the interests of the lay client or the administration of justice require that a solicitor be instructed.

BarDirect

The Bar Council has approved a six-month pilot scheme to explore the extension of access to the Bar's services by means of an extension of the existing DPA Rules. It is intended that BarDirect work should cover not only advisory and other non-contentious work but also contentious matters. The scheme will operate through a licensing system. Queries regarding the scheme should be addressed to: Ms Jan Bye, The General Council of the Bar, 3 Bedford Row, London WC1R 4DB, telephone 0171 242 0082.

Approved list of DPA Bodies (as of May 1999)

The Architects Registration Council of the UK
73 Hallam Street
London W1N 6EE
(Approved November 1989)

The Architects and Surveyors Institute
St Mary House
15 St Mary Street
Chippenham
Wiltshire SN15 3WD
(Approved September 1995)

The Association of Authorised Public Accountants
10 Cornfield Road
Eastbourne
East Sussex BN21 4QE
(Approved September 1989)

The Association of Average Adjusters
HQS 'Wellington'
Temple Stairs
Victoria Embankment
London WC2R 2PN
(Approved June 1989)

Association of Consultant Architects
7 Park Street
Bristol BS1 5NF
(Approved November 1989)

Association of Taxation Technicians
12 Upper Belgrave Street
London SW1X 8BB
(Approved September 1996)

Banking Ombudsman
70 Grays Inn Road
London WC1X 8NB
(Approved March 1990)

Building Society Ombudsman
Grosvenor Gardens House
35-37 Grosvenor Gardens
London SW1
(Approved March 1990)

The Chartered Association of Certified Accountants
29 Lincoln's Inn Fields
London WC2A 3EE
(Approved April 1989)

The Chartered Institute of Loss Adjusters
Mansfield House
376 Strand
London WC2R 0LR
(Approved July 1990)

The Chartered Institute of Management Accountants
63 Portland Place
London W1N 4AB
(Approved September 1989)

The Chartered Insurance Institute
20 Aldermanbury
London EC2V 7HY
(Approved May 1990)

*Commissioner for Local Administration
in England and Wales*
21 Queen Anne's Gate
London SW1
(Approved March 1990)

*Commissioner for Local Administration
in England and Wales*
Derwen House
Bridge End
Mid Glamorgan CF31 1BN
(Approved March 1990)

The Faculty of Actuaries
23 St Andrews Square
Edinburgh EH2 1AQ
(Approved November 1989)

Health Service Commissioner
Church House
Great Smith Street
London SW1P 3BW
(Approved March 1990)

*The Incorporated Society of Valuers &
Auctioneers*
3 Cadogan Gate
London SW1X 0AS
(Approved July 1989)

*Insolvency Practitioners Association
Buchlet Phillips & Co*
43/44 Albermarle Street
Mayfair
London W1N 4AB
(Approved September 1989)

Institute of Actuaries
Staple Inn Hall
High Holborn
London WC1V 7QJ
(Approved November 1989)

*Institute of Chartered Accountants in
England and Wales*
PO Box 433
Chartered Accountants Hall
London EC2P 2BY
(Approved April 1989)

*The Institute of Chartered Accountants
in Ireland*
Chartered Accountants House
87/89 Pembroke Road
Dublin 4
Ireland
(Approved July 1989)

*Institute of Chartered Accountants in
Scotland*
27 Queen Street
Edinburgh EH2 1LA
(Approved July 1989)

*The Institute of Chartered Secretaries
and Administrators*
19 Park Crescent
London W1N 4AH
(Approved July 1989)

The Chartered Institute of Taxation
12 Upper Belgrave Street
London SW1X 8BB
(Approved July 1989)

The Institution of Chemical Engineers
George E Davis Building
165-171 Railway Terrace
Rugby CV21 3HQ
(Approved July 1989)

*The Institution of Civil Engineering
Surveyors*
26 Market Street,
Altrincham, Cheshire WA14 1PF
(Approved November 1997)

The Institute of Civil Engineers
Great George Street
Westminster
London SW1P 3AA
(Approved November 1989)

The Institute of Electrical Engineers
Savoy Place
London WC2R 0BL
(Approved November 1991)

The Institute of Financial Accountants
Burford House
44 London Road
Sevenoaks
Kent TN13 1AS
(Approved January 1995)

The Institute of Indirect Taxation
PO Box 96
Oxted
Surrey RH8 0FX
(Approved May 1999)

Institution of Mechanical Engineers
1 Birdcage Walk
London SW1H 9JJ
(Approved July 1989)

The Institution of Structural Engineers
11 Upper Belgrave Street
London SW1X 8BH
(Approved July 1991)

Insurance Ombudsman Bureau
City Gate One
135 Park Street
London SE1
(Approved July 1990)

*Parliamentary Commissioner for
Administration*
Church House
Great Smith Street
London SW1P 3BW
(Approved March 1990)

*The Personal Investment Authority
Ombudsman Bureau Ltd*
Hertsmere House,
Hertsmere Road,
London E14 4AB
(Approved January 1998)

The Royal Institute of British Architects
66 Portland Place
London W1N 4AD
(Approved September 1989)

*The Royal Institution of Chartered
Surveyors*
12 Great George Street
Parliament Square
London SW1P 3AD
(Approved April 1989)

The Royal Town Planning Institute
26 Portland Place
London W1N 4BE
(Approved April 1989)

EQUITY BARRISTERS' CHAMBERS

The Chambers of Dr K Glah, LL.M. [London]; Ph.D. [London]; of the Inner Temple, Barrister.

Administrative Law	International Courts and Tribunals Advocates
Administration of Estates	International Law
Banking	Judicial Review
Company Commercial	Land Law Planning and Housing
Competition	Local Government
Constitutional Law	Medical Negligence
Employment	Personal Injury
Human Rights	Professional Negligence
Immigrations & Asylum	Public Law
Insurance and Reinsurance	Trusts
Intellectual Property Rights	United Nations Law

PUBLICATIONS IN PROGRESS

Universal Human Rights Advocate Handbook
Hard Cover 1,350 pp (approx.) - £205.00 - ISBN 1 902698 00 2 Millennium Edition Equitylaw Limited

By Robert K Glah, LL.M [London]; Ph.D [London]; of the Inner Temple, Barrister; of the Ghana Bar Association, Solicitor and Advocate of the Superior Court of the Judicature, Ghana and Afolake Jaja, LL.M [London]; of Gray's Inn, Barrister.

This reference book offers an authorative text covering a wide range of practical tools for under standing the elements of the universal human rights and the fundamental freedoms and their interplay with other areas of international and transnational law, where a legal duty of care is owed. The book explains that public authorities, governments, and corporations, which abuse their dominant relation are the barriers to the social and economic achievement of individuals, corporations and nations and liberalisation of world trade, finance and competition world wide. Finally, it concludes that the universal human and the fundamental freedoms are the wealth of every individual, corporation and nation and absence of recognition is the cause of lack in the world and that lack can be overcome through tolerance and the rule of law.

The target audience includes practising lawyers, judges, corporate lawyers, diplomats, academics, employers, directors, executives, trade unions, advocates before international courts, tribunals and conferences and progressive individuals worldwide.

Judicial Review of Immigration and Asylum Decisions
Soft Cover 1,350 pp (approx.) – £50.00 Millennium Edition Equitylaw Limited

By Robert K Glah, et al supra

This authoritative text offers a comprehensive understanding of judicial review of immigration and asylum decisions in English Courts and in the European Court of Human Rights in Strasbourg. The book draws on the jurisprudence of foreign juridictions in order to offer alternative tools as persuasive guidelines. The target audience includes practising lawyers and judges.

CHAMBERS FEES STATEMENT
Fees are negotiated with the Clerk for every case. As a general guide, our fees are competitive and range from £300.00 to £5,000.00 per day depending on time engaged, turnaround, urgency, complexity, priority and importance of the case to the client.

LANGUAGES
Ewe, French, German, and Yoruba

CONTACT
Dr K Glah (24 Hours)
Tel: 0181 558 8336   **Fax:** 0181 558 6757
Website: http://www.equitybar.co.uk   **E-mail:** equitylawyer@equitybar.co.uk

EQUITY BARRRISTERS' CHAMBERS
Temple Chambers, Second Floor Room 152-153, 3/7 Temple Avenue, London EC4Y 0NP

Types of Work by Chambers

This section lists chambers by the type of work they do and by the town or city where they are located. The types of work undertaken by chambers are listed in alphabetical order. Within these main categories, chambers are listed alphabetically under the town or city in which they practise. For example, a reader wishing to locate a Birmingham-based chambers specialising in trademarks would be able to look under 'T' for Trademarks and find under that heading the details of any chambers in Birmingham which offer their services in this field. A complete list of the types of work can be found overleaf.

Each listing provides the chambers' name and chambers' telephone number. The first point of contact in each instance will be the clerk. (Details of clerks can be found in *Part C Chambers by Location*)

Please note that chambers are only listed in this section if information on specialisms has been supplied by them.

The symbol • indicates that chambers have an expanded entry in *Part C Chambers by Location.*

Types of Work

A

Adjudication	A4
Administrative	A4
Admiralty	A6
ADR	A6
Agriculture	A6
American law	A7
Ancillary relief	A7
Arbitration	A7
Asset finance	A9
Asset forfeiture and money laundering	A9
Aviation	A9

B

Bahamas law	A10
Banking	A10
Bankruptcy	A11
Breach of confidence	A14
Building	A14

C

Care proceedings	A14
Chancery (commercial)	A17
Chancery (general)	A17
Chancery land law	A20
Charities	A21
Children	A22
Civil actions against the police	A22
Civil actions involving the police	A22
Civil fraud	A22
Civil jury actions for police authorities	A22
Civil liberties	A22
Clinical negligence	A24
Club law	A24
Commercial	A24
Commercial litigation	A25
Commercial planning	A27
Commercial property	A27
Commodities	A29
Common land	A29
Common law (general)	A30
Company and commercial	A34
Competition	A37
Compulsory purchase	A37
Confiscation	A37
Constitutional law	A37
Construction	A37
Consumer law	A39
Contract	A40
Conveyancing	A40
Copyright	A41
Corporate finance	A42
Corporate insolvency	A42
Costs	A42
Court of Protection	A42
Courts martial	A43
Crime	A44
Crime – corporate fraud	A48
Crime – corporate manslaughter	A51
Customs & Excise – serious fraud	A51

D

Damages	A51
Defamation	A51
Disciplinary tribunals	A52
Discrimination	A52
Drink and driving	A54

E

E-Commerce	A54
EC and competition law	A54
EC law	A55
Ecclesiastical	A55
Education	A56
Employment	A57
Energy	A61
Entertainment	A62
Environment	A62
Environmental law and pollution	A64
Equity, wills and trusts	A64
European law	A66
Extradition	A66

F

Factoring	A66
Family	A66
Family – child abduction	A70
Family provision	A70
Film, cable, TV	A74
Financial provision	A74
Financial services	A74
Food	A75
Foreign law	A75
Franchising	A76
Fraud	A76
FSA related work	A76

H

Health & safety	A77
Highways	A77
Housing	A77
Human rights	A79

I

Immigration	A80
Information technology	A82
Inquests	A83
Insolvency	A83
Insurance	A85
Insurance/reinsurance	A87
Intellectual property	A88
International law	A89
International trade	A89
Internet law	A90
Islamic law	A90

J

Judicial review	A90

A

L

Land law	A90
Landlord and tenant	A90
Licensing	A94
Local Authority claims	A97
Local government	A97

M

Malicious prosecution	A99
Markets and fairs	A99
Matrimonial	A99
Media	A99
Mediation	A99
Medical law	A99
Medical negligence	A100
Mental health	A103
Middle East/Pakistani/Islamic law	A104
Mines and minerals	A105
Mortgages	A105
Mortgages and borrowers	A105
Motoring law	A105

N

National Insurance	A105

O

Official referee	A105

P

Parliamentary	A105
Partnerships	A105
Patents	A107
Pensions	A108
Personal injury	A108
Planning	A113
Police discipline	A113
Police law	A113
Prison law	A113
Prisoners' rights	A113
Private client	A113
Private international	A114
Privy Council Appeals	A114
Probate and administration	A114
Procurement	A116
Product liability	A116
Professional disciplinary matters (sols) – CICB	A116
Professional negligence	A116
Property	A120
Public childcare	A120
Public inquiries	A120
Public international	A120
Public law	A121
Public procurement	A121

R

Rating and CPO	A121
Regulatory work	A121
Rights of light	A121

S

Sale and carriage of goods	A121
Share options	A123
Shipping	A124
Shipping, admiralty	A124
Social security	A124
Social Services	A124
South Asian law	A124
Sports	A124

T

Tax	A125
Tax – capital and income	A125
Tax – corporate	A126
Taxation and costs	A127
Telecommunications	A127
Timeshare	A127
Town and country planning	A127
Trade Descriptions Act and allied legislation	A129
Trademarks	A129
Trading standards	A130
Travel and holiday law	A130

U

Unfair dismissal	A130
Unit trusts	A130
Utilities	A130

V

VAT	A130
VAT and Customs & Excise	A130

W

Welfare	A130

A

ADJUDICATION

Malvern	Resolution Chambers	01684 561279

ADMINISTRATIVE

Birmingham	• 5 Fountain Court	0121 606 0500
	• St Philip's Chambers	0121 246 7000
Bristol	Guildhall Chambers	0117 9273366
	Old Square Chambers	0117 9277111
	St John's Chambers	0117 9213456/298514
Cambridge	Fenners Chambers	01223 368761
Cardiff	9 Park Place	01222 382731
	30 Park Place	01222 398421
Chester	Nicholas Street Chambers	01244 323886
Chichester	Chichester Chambers	01243 784538
Durham	Durham Barristers' Chambers	0191 386 9199
Exeter	Cathedral Chambers (Jan Wood Independent Barristers' Clerk)	01392 210900
Leeds	The Chambers of Philip Raynor QC	0113 242 1123
	• 9 Woodhouse Square	0113 2451986
Leicester	Chambers of Michael Pert QC	0116 249 2020
Liverpool	25-27 Castle Street	0151 227 5661/051 236 5072
	• Exchange Chambers	0151 236 7747
	India Buildings Chambers	0151 243 6000
London	Albany Chambers	0171 485 5736/5758
	• Arden Chambers	020 7242 4244
	• Chambers of Michael Pert QC	0171 421 8000
	• 9-12 Bell Yard	0171 400 1800
	Bell Yard Chambers	0171 306 9292
	• Blackstone Chambers	0171 583 1770
	11 Bolt Court (also at 7 Stone Buildings – 1st Floor)	0171 353 2300
	• 4 Breams Buildings	0171 353 5835/430 1221
	Brick Court Chambers	0171 379 3550
	Bridewell Chambers	020 7797 8800
	Cloisters	0171 827 4000
	• 1 Crown Office Row, Ground Floor	0171 797 7500
	1 Crown Office Row, 3rd Floor	0171 583 9292
	• Devereux Chambers	0171 353 7534
	• Doughty Street Chambers	0171 404 1313
	1 Dr Johnson's Buildings	0171 353 9328
	Equity Barristers' Chambers	0181 558 8336
	• One Essex Court, Ground Floor	020 7583 2000
	• One Essex Court, 1st Floor	0171 936 3030
	• Essex Court Chambers	0171 813 8000
	• 20 Essex Street	0171 583 9294
	• 39 Essex Street	0171 832 1111
	• Farrar's Building	0171 583 9241
	• Chambers of Norman Palmer	0171 405 6114
	Chambers of Wilfred Forster-Jones	0171 353 0853/4/7222
	• Fountain Court	0171 583 3335
	• 2nd Floor, Francis Taylor Building	0171 353 9942/3157
	• Two Garden Court	0171 353 1633
	• Gough Square Chambers	0171 353 0924
	• Gray's Inn Chambers, The Chambers of Norman Patterson	0171 831 5344
	Gray's Inn Chambers	0171 831 7888 (Chambers)/ 0171 831 7904 (Mr M Ullah)
	• 2-3 Gray's Inn Square	0171 242 4986
	• 4-5 Gray's Inn Square	0171 404 5252
	Counsels' Chambers	0171 405 2576
	• 2 Harcourt Buildings, Ground Floor/Left	0171 583 9020

• Expanded entry in Part C

A

● 2 Harcourt Buildings, 2nd Floor	020 7353 8415
● Harcourt Chambers	0171 353 6961
● Hardwicke Building	020 7242 2523
● One Hare Court	020 7353 3171
● 3 Hare Court	0171 395 2000
Chambers of Harjit Singh	0171 353 1356 (4 Lines)
● Harrow on the Hill Chambers	0181 423 7444
John Street Chambers	0171 242 1911
● One King's Bench Walk	0171 936 1500
2 King's Bench Walk	0171 353 1746
6 King's Bench Walk	0171 353 4931/583 0695
8 King's Bench Walk	0171 797 8888
9 King's Bench Walk	0171 353 7202/3909
● 11 King's Bench Walk,	0171 632 8500/583 0610
11 King's Bench Walk, 1st Floor	0171 353 3337
2 King's Bench Walk Chambers	020 7353 9276
Lamb Chambers	020 7797 8300
● Littman Chambers	020 7404 4866
2 Mitre Court Buildings, 1st Floor	0171 353 1353
2 Mitre Court Buildings, 2nd Floor	0171 583 1380
● Mitre House Chambers	0171 583 8233
● Monckton Chambers	0171 405 7211
● Chambers of John L Powell QC	0171 797 8000
● 12 New Square	0171 419 1212
● 22 Old Buildings	0171 831 0222
● 9 Old Square	0171 405 4682
11 Old Square	0171 242 5022/405 1074
● Old Square Chambers	0171 269 0300
● 4 Paper Buildings	0171 353 3366/583 7155
● 5 Paper Buildings	0171 583 9275/583 4555
Five Paper Buildings	0171 583 6117
● 1 Pump Court	0171 583 2012/353 4341
● 5 Pump Court	020 7353 2532
6 Pump Court	0171 797 8400
● 3 Raymond Buildings	020 7831 3833
No. 1 Serjeants' Inn	0171 415 6666
1 Serjeants' Inn	0171 583 1355
● Stanbrook & Henderson	0171 353 0101
7 Stone Buildings (also at 11 Bolt Court)	0171 242 0961
● 1 Temple Gardens	0171 583 1315/353 0407
● 14 Tooks Court	0171 405 8828
3 Verulam Buildings	0171 831 8441
Virtual Chambers	07071 244 944
Warwick House Chambers	0171 430 2323

Maidstone	6-8 Mill Street	01622 688094
Manchester	● Central Chambers	0161 236 1133
	● Cobden House Chambers	0161 833 6000
	● 40 King Street	0161 832 9082
	● 8 King Street Chambers	0161 834 9560
	Lincoln House Chambers	0161 832 5701
	● Chambers of Ian Macdonald QC (In Association with Two Garden Court, Temple, London)	0161 236 1840
	● St James's Chambers	0161 834 7000
Northampton	Chambers of Michael Pert QC	01604 602333
Nottingham	Ropewalk Chambers	0115 9472581
Oxford	Harcourt Chambers	01865 791559
	King's Bench Chambers	01865 311066
Peterborough	Fenners Chambers	01733 562030
Pontypridd	● Windsor Chambers	01443 402067
Preston	New Bailey Chambers	01772 258087

● Expanded entry in Part C

Redhill	Redhill Chambers	01737 780781
Slough	Slough Chamber	01753 553806/817989
Wolverhampton	Claremont Chambers	01902 426222

ADMIRALTY

Leeds	Chambers of Andrew Campbell QC	0113 2455438
Liverpool	• Corn Exchange Chambers	0151 227 1081/5009
London	Brick Court Chambers	0171 379 3550
	• 4 Essex Court	020 7797 7970
	• Essex Court Chambers	0171 813 8000
	• 20 Essex Street	0171 583 9294
	• 4 Field Court	0171 440 6900
	• Goldsmith Building	0171 353 7881
	• 9 Gough Square	020 7832 0500
	S Tomlinson QC	0171 583 0404
Plymouth	Devon Chambers	01752 661659

ADR

London	• Littleton Chambers	0171 797 8600

AGRICULTURE

Birmingham	1 Fountain Court	0121 236 5721
	• 5 Fountain Court	0121 606 0500
Bristol	St John's Chambers	0117 9213456/298514
Cambridge	Fenners Chambers	01223 368761
Chester	Nicholas Street Chambers	01244 323886
	Sedan House	01244 320480/348282
Exeter	Cathedral Chambers (Jan Wood Independent Barristers' Clerk)	01392 210900
Leeds	• Chancery House Chambers	0113 244 6691
	• 37 Park Square Chambers	0113 2439422
Leicester	Chambers of Michael Pert QC	0116 249 2020
Liverpool	India Buildings Chambers	0151 243 6000
London	• Chambers of Michael Pert QC	0171 421 8000
	• 4 Breams Buildings	0171 353 5835/430 1221
	Brick Court Chambers	0171 379 3550
	• Essex Court Chambers	0171 813 8000
	Falcon Chambers	0171 353 2484
	• Farrar's Building	0171 583 9241
	• 2 Harcourt Buildings	020 7353 8415
	2 Mitre Court Buildings	0171 583 1380
	• Monckton Chambers	0171 405 7211
	• Chambers of Lord Goodhart QC	0171 405 5577
	• 9 Old Square	0171 405 4682
	• 11 Old Square	020 7430 0341
	• 4 Paper Buildings	0171 353 3366/583 7155
	1 Serjeants' Inn	0171 583 1355
	• 9 Stone Buildings	0171 404 5055
	3 Verulam Buildings	0171 831 8441
Manchester	• Cobden House Chambers	0161 833 6000
	• St James's Chambers	0161 834 7000
Northampton	Chambers of Michael Pert QC	01604 602333
Nottingham	Ropewalk Chambers	0115 9472581
Peterborough	Fenners Chambers	01733 562030
Plymouth	Devon Chambers	01752 661659
Preston	New Bailey Chambers	01772 258087
	15 Winckley Square	01772 252828
Sheffield	Paradise Chambers	0114 2738951
Swansea	Iscoed Chambers	01792 652988/9/330

A

AMERICAN LAW
London	• 11 Old Square	020 7430 0341

ANCILLARY RELIEF
Leeds	• 9 Woodhouse Square	0113 2451986
Liverpool	• Oriel Chambers	0151 236 7191/236 4321

ARBITRATION
Birmingham	1 Fountain Court	0121 236 5721
	• 5 Fountain Court	0121 606 0500
	• 8 Fountain Court	0121 236 5514/5
	• St Philip's Chambers	0121 246 7000
Bristol	Old Square Chambers	0117 9277111
	St John's Chambers	0117 9213456/298514
Cambridge	Fenners Chambers	01223 368761
Cardiff	30 Park Place	01222 398421
	• 33 Park Place	02920 233313
Chester	Nicholas Street Chambers	01244 323886
	Sedan House	01244 320480/348282
	White Friars Chambers	01244 323070
Chesterfield	26 Morley Avenue	01246 234790/01298 871350
Colchester	East Anglian Chambers	01206 572756
Consett	6 Ascot Road	01207 507785
Exeter	Cathedral Chambers (Jan Wood Independent Barristers' Clerk)	01392 210900
Guildford	• Guildford Chambers	01483 539131
Ipswich	East Anglian Chambers	01473 214481
Leeds	Chambers of Andrew Campbell QC	0113 2455438
	11 King's Bench Walk	0113 297 1200
	The Chambers of Philip Raynor QC	0113 242 1123
	• 30 Park Square	0113 2436388
	• Sovereign Chambers	0113 2451841/2/3
	• 9 Woodhouse Square	0113 2451986
Liverpool	25-27 Castle Street	0151 227 5661/051 236 5072
	19 Castle Street Chambers	0151 236 9402
	Chavasse Court Chambers	0151 707 1191
	India Buildings Chambers	0151 243 6000
London	• Arbitration Chambers	020 7267 2137
	Atkin Chambers	020 7404 0102
	9 Bedford Row	0171 242 3555
	33 Bedford Row	0171 242 6476
	• Blackstone Chambers	0171 583 1770
	11 Bolt Court (also at 7 Stone Buildings – 1st Floor)	0171 353 2300
	Bracton Chambers	0171 242 4248
	• 4 Breams Buildings	0171 353 5835/430 1221
	Brick Court Chambers	0171 379 3550
	• Chambers of Mr Peter Crampin QC	020 7831 0081
	1 Crown Office Row	0171 583 9292
	• Devereux Chambers	0171 353 7534
	• Enterprise Chambers	0171 405 9471
	• One Essex Court, Ground Floor	020 7583 2000
	• One Essex Court, 1st Floor	0171 936 3030
	• 4 Essex Court	020 7797 7970
	• Essex Court Chambers	0171 813 8000
	• 20 Essex Street	0171 583 9294
	• 35 Essex Street	0171 353 6381
	• 39 Essex Street	0171 832 1111
	Chambers of Geoffrey Hawker	0171 583 8899
	Falcon Chambers	0171 353 2484
	• 4 Field Court	0171 440 6900

• Expanded entry in Part C

• Fountain Court	0171 583 3335
Francis Taylor Building	0171 353 7768/7769/2711
• Goldsmith Building	0171 353 7881
• Gray's Inn Chambers, The Chambers of	0171 831 5344
Norman Patterson	
96 Gray's Inn Road	0171 405 0585
• 4-5 Gray's Inn Square	0171 404 5252
• 2 Harcourt Buildings	0171 583 9020
• Hardwicke Building	020 7242 2523
• One Hare Court	020 7353 3171
John Street Chambers	0171 242 1911
• Keating Chambers	0171 544 2600
S Tomlinson QC	0171 583 0404
• 12 King's Bench Walk	0171 583 0811
• 13 King's Bench Walk	0171 353 7204
2 King's Bench Walk Chambers	020 7353 9276
• Lamb Building	020 7797 7788
Lamb Chambers	020 7797 8300
• Littleton Chambers	0171 797 8600
• Littman Chambers	020 7404 4866
2 Mitre Court Buildings	0171 353 1353
• Monckton Chambers	0171 405 7211
• 1 New Square	0171 405 0884/5/6/7
• 3 New Square	0171 405 1111
• Chambers of John L Powell QC	0171 797 8000
5 New Square	020 7404 0404
• 12 New Square	0171 419 1212
• 9 Old Square	0171 405 4682
11 Old Square, Ground Floor	0171 242 5022/405 1074
• 11 Old Square, Ground Floor	020 7430 0341
13 Old Square	0171 404 4800
• Old Square Chambers	0171 269 0300
• 3 Paper Buildings	020 7583 8055
• 4 Paper Buildings, Ground Floor	0171 353 3366/583 7155
• 4 Paper Buildings, 1st Floor	0171 583 0816/353 1131
Pepys' Chambers	0171 936 2710
Phoenix Chambers	0171 404 7888
2 Pump Court	0171 353 5597
• 4 Pump Court	020 7842 5555
• 5 Pump Court	020 7353 2532
No. 1 Serjeants' Inn	0171 415 6666
• 3 Serjeants' Inn	0171 353 5537
• 3/4 South Square	0171 696 9900
• Stanbrook & Henderson	0171 353 0101
Staple Inn Chambers	0171 242 5240
• 5 Stone Buildings	0171 242 6201
• 7 Stone Buildings	0171 405 3886/242 3546
7 Stone Buildings (also at 11 Bolt Court)	0171 242 0961
• 9 Stone Buildings	0171 404 5055
• 2 Temple Gardens	0171 583 6041
3 Verulam Buildings	0171 831 8441
Verulam Chambers	0171 813 2400
Warwick House Chambers	0171 430 2323
Resolution Chambers	01684 561279
• Byrom Street Chambers	0161 829 2100
• Cobden House Chambers	0161 833 6000
Deans Court Chambers	0161 214 6000
• 40 King Street	0161 832 9082
• 8 King Street Chambers	0161 834 9560
Lincoln House Chambers	0161 832 5701
• St James's Chambers	0161 834 7000

Malvern
Manchester

• Expanded entry in Part C

Meopham	West Lodge Farm	01474 812280
Middlesbrough	Baker Street Chambers	01642 873873
Newcastle upon Tyne	• Broad Chare	0191 232 0541
	Cathedral Chambers	0191 232 1311
	• Trinity Chambers	0191 232 1927
Northampton	Chartlands Chambers	01604 603322
	Northampton Chambers	01604 636271
Norwich	East Anglian Chambers	01603 617351
	Octagon House	01603 623186
	Sackville Chambers	01603 613516/616221
Nottingham	Ropewalk Chambers	0115 9472581
Oxford	King's Bench Chambers	01865 311066
	3 Paper Buildings (Oxford)	01865 793736
Peterborough	Fenners Chambers	01733 562030
Plymouth	Devon Chambers	01752 661659
Pontypridd	• Windsor Chambers	01443 402067
Portsmouth	• Portsmouth Barristers' Chambers	023 92 831292/811811
Preston	Deans Court Chambers	01772 555163
	New Bailey Chambers	01772 258087
Reading	Wessex Chambers	0118 956 8856
Redhill	Redhill Chambers	01737 780781
Saint Albans	St Albans Chambers	01727 843383
Slough	Slough Chamber	01753 553806/817989
Southampton	• 17 Carlton Crescent	023 8032 0320/0823 2003
	• Eighteen Carlton Crescent	01703 639001
Stoke On Trent	Regent Chambers	01782 286666
Swansea	Angel Chambers	01792 464623/464648
Winchester	3 Paper Buildings (Winchester)	01962 868884
Wolverhampton	Claremont Chambers	01902 426222

ASSET FINANCE

Birmingham	• 5 Fountain Court	0121 606 0500
Liverpool	• Exchange Chambers	0151 236 7747
	• Oriel Chambers	0151 236 7191/236 4321
London	Brick Court Chambers	0171 379 3550
	1 Crown Office Row	0171 583 9292
	• One Essex Court	020 7583 2000
	• Chambers of Norman Palmer	0171 405 6114
	• 2 Harcourt Buildings	0171 583 9020
	• One Hare Court	020 7353 3171
	Chambers of John Gardiner QC	0171 242 4017
	• 3/4 South Square	0171 696 9900
	• Stanbrook & Henderson	0171 353 0101
	Verulam Chambers	0171 813 2400
Pontypridd	• Windsor Chambers	01443 402067

ASSET FORFEITURE AND MONEY LAUNDERING

London	• Furnival Chambers	0171 405 3232

AVIATION

Birmingham	• St Philip's Chambers	0121 246 7000
Bristol	Assize Court Chambers	0117 9264587
Exeter	Cathedral Chambers (Jan Wood Independent Barristers' Clerk)	01392 210900
Leeds	• 9 Woodhouse Square	0113 2451986
London	11 Bolt Court (also at 7 Stone Buildings – 1st Floor)	0171 353 2300
	• Dr Johnson's Chambers	0171 353 4716
	• 4 Essex Court	020 7797 7970
	• Essex Court Chambers	0171 813 8000
	• 20 Essex Street	0171 583 9294

• Expanded entry in Part C

	• 4 Field Court	0171 440 6900
	• Fountain Court	0171 583 3335
	• 4-5 Gray's Inn Square	0171 404 5252
	2 Harcourt Buildings	020 7353 2112
	S Tomlinson QC	0171 583 0404
	2 King's Bench Walk Chambers	020 7353 9276
	• Monckton Chambers	0171 405 7211
	• Twenty-Four Old Buildings	0171 404 0946
	• 4 Pump Court	020 7842 5555
	7 Stone Buildings (also at 11 Bolt Court)	0171 242 0961
	• 2 Temple Gardens	0171 583 6041
Manchester	• St James's Chambers	0161 834 7000
Redhill	Redhill Chambers	01737 780781

BAHAMAS LAW

London	• 11 Old Square	020 7430 0341

BANKING

Birmingham	1 Fountain Court	0121 236 5721
	• 3 Fountain Court	0121 236 5854
	• 5 Fountain Court	0121 606 0500
	• St Philip's Chambers	0121 246 7000
Bristol	Guildhall Chambers	0117 9273366
	St John's Chambers	0117 9213456/298514
Cardiff	9 Park Place	01222 382731
	30 Park Place	01222 398421
Chester	White Friars Chambers	01244 323070
Exeter	Cathedral Chambers (Jan Wood Independent Barristers' Clerk)	01392 210900
Leeds	Chambers of Andrew Campbell QC	0113 2455438
	• Chancery House Chambers	0113 244 6691
	Enterprise Chambers	0113 246 0391
	The Chambers of Philip Raynor QC	0113 242 1123
Liverpool	• Exchange Chambers	0151 236 7747
	• Oriel Chambers	0151 236 7191/236 4321
London	Barristers' Common Law Chambers	0171 375 3012
	17 Bedford Row	0171 831 7314
	• Blackstone Chambers	0171 583 1770
	Bracton Chambers	0171 242 4248
	Brick Court Chambers	0171 379 3550
	Cloisters	0171 827 4000
	• Chambers of Mr Peter Crampin QC	020 7831 0081
	1 Crown Office Row	0171 583 9292
	• Enterprise Chambers	0171 405 9471
	Equity Barristers' Chambers	0181 558 8336
	• Erskine Chambers	0171 242 5532
	• One Essex Court	020 7583 2000
	• 4 Essex Court	020 7797 7970
	• Essex Court Chambers	0171 813 8000
	• 20 Essex Street	0171 583 9294
	• Chambers of Norman Palmer	0171 405 6114
	• 4 Field Court	0171 440 6900
	• Fountain Court	0171 583 3335
	Francis Taylor Building	0171 353 7768/7769/2711
	• 2nd Floor, Francis Taylor Building	0171 353 9942/3157
	• Gough Square Chambers	0171 353 0924
	• 2-3 Gray's Inn Square	0171 242 4986
	• 4-5 Gray's Inn Square	0171 404 5252
	• 1 Harcourt Buildings	0171 353 9421/0375
	• Hardwicke Building	020 7242 2523
	• One Hare Court	020 7353 3171

A

● Harrow on the Hill Chambers	0181 423 7444
● 4 King's Bench Walk	0171 822 8822
S Tomlinson QC	0171 583 0404
● 12 King's Bench Walk	0171 583 0811
● 13 King's Bench Walk	0171 353 7204
2 King's Bench Walk Chambers	020 7353 9276
● Lamb Building	020 7797 7788
Lamb Chambers	020 7797 8300
● Littleton Chambers	0171 797 8600
● Littman Chambers	020 7404 4866
● Monckton Chambers	0171 405 7211
● New Court	0171 583 5123/0510
● 1 New Square	0171 405 0884/5/6/7
● Chambers of Lord Goodhart QC	0171 405 5577
● Chambers of John L Powell QC	0171 797 8000
5 New Square	020 7404 0404
● 12 New Square	0171 419 1212
● Twenty-Four Old Buildings	0171 404 0946
● 9 Old Square	0171 405 4682
The Chambers of Leolin Price CBE, QC	0171 405 0758
11 Old Square, Ground Floor	0171 242 5022/405 1074
● 11 Old Square, Ground Floor	020 7430 0341
13 Old Square	0171 404 4800
● 4 Paper Buildings	0171 583 0816/353 1131
● 5 Paper Buildings	0171 583 9275/583 4555
● Pump Court Chambers	0171 353 0711
● 4 Pump Court	020 7842 5555
● 3/4 South Square	0171 696 9900
● Stanbrook & Henderson	0171 353 0101
● 3 Stone Buildings	0171 242 4937
4 Stone Buildings	0171 242 5524
● 5 Stone Buildings	0171 242 6201
● 7 Stone Buildings	0171 405 3886/242 3546
● 9 Stone Buildings	0171 404 5055
55 Temple Chambers	0171 353 7400
● 2 Temple Gardens	0171 583 6041
3 Verulam Buildings	0171 831 8441
Verulam Chambers	0171 813 2400
Warwick House Chambers	0171 430 2323

Manchester	● Byrom Street Chambers	0161 829 2100
	● Cobden House Chambers	0161 833 6000
	Deans Court Chambers	0161 214 6000
	● 40 King Street	0161 832 9082
	● 8 King Street Chambers	0161 834 9560
	● Merchant Chambers	0161 839 7070
	● St James's Chambers	0161 834 7000
Newcastle upon Tyne	Enterprise Chambers	0191 222 3344
	● Trinity Chambers	0191 232 1927
	Westgate Chambers	0191 261 4407/2329785
Oxford	King's Bench Chambers	01865 311066
Preston	New Bailey Chambers	01772 258087
Reading	Wessex Chambers	0118 956 8856
Swindon	Pump Court Chambers, 5 Temple Chambers	01793 539899
Winchester	Pump Court Chambers, 31 Southgate Street	01962 868161
Wolverhampton	Claremont Chambers	01902 426222

BANKRUPTCY

Birmingham	1 Fountain Court	0121 236 5721
	● 3 Fountain Court	0121 236 5854
	● 5 Fountain Court	0121 606 0500
	● 8 Fountain Court	0121 236 5514/5

● Expanded entry in Part C

	• St Philip's Chambers	0121 246 7000
Bradford	Broadway House Chambers	01274 722560
Brighton	Crown Office Row Chambers	01273 625625
Bristol	Guildhall Chambers	0117 9273366
	St John's Chambers	0117 9213456/298514
Cambridge	Fenners Chambers	01223 368761
Canterbury	• Becket Chambers	01227 786331
Cardiff	9 Park Place	01222 382731
	30 Park Place	01222 398421
Chester	White Friars Chambers	01244 323070
Chichester	Chichester Chambers	01243 784538
Guildford	• Guildford Chambers	01483 539131
Leeds	Chambers of Andrew Campbell QC	0113 2455438
	Broadway House Chambers	0113 246 2600
	• Chancery House Chambers	0113 244 6691
	Enterprise Chambers	0113 246 0391
	No. 6	0113 2459763
	The Chambers of Philip Raynor QC	0113 242 1123
	• 30 Park Square	0113 2436388
	• 9 Woodhouse Square	0113 2451986
Leicester	Chambers of Michael Pert QC	0116 249 2020
Liverpool	• Exchange Chambers	0151 236 7747
	India Buildings Chambers	0151 243 6000
	• Oriel Chambers	0151 236 7191/236 4321
London	Barnard's Inn Chambers	0171 369 6969
	9 Bedford Row	0171 242 3555
	17 Bedford Row	0171 831 7314
	33 Bedford Row	0171 242 6476
	• Chambers of Michael Pert QC	0171 421 8000
	11 Bolt Court (also at 7 Stone Buildings – 1st Floor)	0171 353 2300
	Bracton Chambers	0171 242 4248
	Bridewell Chambers	020 7797 8800
	• Chambers of Mr Peter Crampin QC	020 7831 0081
	1 Crown Office Row	0171 583 9292
	• Enterprise Chambers	0171 405 9471
	• One Essex Court, Ground Floor	020 7583 2000
	• One Essex Court, 1st Floor	0171 936 3030
	• Essex Court Chambers	0171 813 8000
	• Chambers of Norman Palmer	0171 405 6114
	• 4 Field Court	0171 440 6900
	Francis Taylor Building	0171 353 7768/7769/2711
	• 2nd Floor, Francis Taylor Building	0171 353 9942/3157
	• Goldsmith Building	0171 353 7881
	Gray's Inn Chambers	0171 831 7888 (Chambers)/ 0171 831 7904 (Mr M Ullah)
	• 2-3 Gray's Inn Square	0171 242 4986
	Counsels' Chambers	0171 405 2576
	• 1 Harcourt Buildings	0171 353 9421/0375
	• Hardwicke Building	020 7242 2523
	• One Hare Court	020 7353 3171
	Chambers of Harjit Singh	0171 353 1356 (4 Lines)
	• Harrow on the Hill Chambers	0181 423 7444
	• 4 King's Bench Walk	0171 822 8822
	9 King's Bench Walk	0171 353 7202/3909
	10 King's Bench Walk	0171 353 7742
	• 11 King's Bench Walk,	0171 632 8500/583 0610
	11 King's Bench Walk, 1st Floor	0171 353 3337
	• 13 King's Bench Walk	0171 353 7204
	2 King's Bench Walk Chambers	020 7353 9276
	• Lamb Building	020 7797 7788

• Expanded entry in Part C

A

	Lamb Chambers	020 7797 8300
	Lion Court	0171 404 6565
	• Littleton Chambers	0171 797 8600
	• Littman Chambers	020 7404 4866
	2 Mitre Court Buildings	0171 353 1353
	• Mitre Court Chambers	0171 353 9394
	• New Court	0171 583 5123/0510
	• 1 New Square	0171 405 0884/5/6/7
	• Chambers of Lord Goodhart QC	0171 405 5577
	5 New Square	020 7404 0404
	• 12 New Square	0171 419 1212
	• 22 Old Buildings	0171 831 0222
	• Twenty-Four Old Buildings	0171 404 0946
	• 9 Old Square	0171 405 4682
	The Chambers of Leolin Price CBE, QC	0171 405 0758
	11 Old Square, Ground Floor	0171 242 5022/405 1074
	• 11 Old Square, Ground Floor	020 7430 0341
	13 Old Square	0171 404 4800
	• 3 Paper Buildings	020 7583 8055
	• 4 Paper Buildings	0171 583 0816/353 1131
	• 5 Paper Buildings	0171 583 9275/583 4555
	2 Pump Court	0171 353 5597
	• 5 Pump Court	020 7353 2532
	• 3/4 South Square	0171 696 9900
	Staple Inn Chambers	0171 242 5240
	• 3 Stone Buildings	0171 242 4937
	4 Stone Buildings	0171 242 5524
	• 5 Stone Buildings	0171 242 6201
	• 7 Stone Buildings	0171 405 3886/242 3546
	7 Stone Buildings (also at 11 Bolt Court)	0171 242 0961
	• 9 Stone Buildings	0171 404 5055
	55 Temple Chambers	0171 353 7400
	• 2 Temple Gardens	0171 583 6041
	• Thomas More Chambers	0171 404 7000
	Verulam Chambers	0171 813 2400
	Warwick House Chambers	0171 430 2323
Manchester	• Cobden House Chambers	0161 833 6000
	• 40 King Street	0161 832 9082
	• Merchant Chambers	0161 839 7070
	• St James's Chambers	0161 834 7000
Newcastle upon Tyne	• Broad Chare	0191 232 0541
	Enterprise Chambers	0191 222 3344
	• Trinity Chambers	0191 232 1927
	Westgate Chambers	0191 261 4407/2329785
Northampton	Chambers of Michael Pert QC	01604 602333
	Northampton Chambers	01604 636271
Nottingham	King Charles House	0115 9418851
	Ropewalk Chambers	0115 9472581
Oxford	King's Bench Chambers	01865 311066
	3 Paper Buildings (Oxford)	01865 793736
Peterborough	Fenners Chambers	01733 562030
Plymouth	Devon Chambers	01752 661659
Pontypridd	• Windsor Chambers	01443 402067
Portsmouth	• Portsmouth Barristers' Chambers	023 92 831292/811811
Preston	New Bailey Chambers	01772 258087
	Queens Chambers	01772 828300
	15 Winckley Square	01772 252828
Reading	Wessex Chambers	0118 956 8856
Redhill	Redhill Chambers	01737 780781
Saint Albans	St Albans Chambers	01727 843383
Southampton	• Eighteen Carlton Crescent	01703 639001

• Expanded entry in Part C

Swansea	Angel Chambers	01792 464623/464648
	Iscoed Chambers	01792 652988/9/330
Winchester	3 Paper Buildings (Winchester)	01962 868884
Wolverhampton	Claremont Chambers	01902 426222

BREACH OF CONFIDENCE

London	• 8 New Square	0171 405 4321

BUILDING

Leeds	• 37 Park Square Chambers	0113 2439422

CARE PROCEEDINGS

Birmingham	Coleridge Chambers	0121 233 8500
	1 Fountain Court	0121 236 5721
	• 3 Fountain Court	0121 236 5854
	• 5 Fountain Court	0121 606 0500
	6 Fountain Court	0121 233 3282
	• 8 Fountain Court	0121 236 5514/5
	New Court Chambers	0121 693 6656
	St Ive's Chambers	0121 236 0863/5720
	• St Philip's Chambers	0121 246 7000
Bournemouth	3 Paper Buildings (Bournemouth)	01202 292102
Bradford	Broadway House Chambers	01274 722560
Brighton	Crown Office Row Chambers	01273 625625
Bristol	Assize Court Chambers	0117 9264587
	Guildhall Chambers	0117 9273366
	St John's Chambers	0117 9213456/298514
Cambridge	Fenners Chambers	01223 368761
Canterbury	• Becket Chambers	01227 786331
	Stour Chambers	01227 764899
Cardiff	30 Park Place	01222 398421
	32 Park Place	01222 397364
	• 33 Park Place	02920 233313
Chester	Nicholas Street Chambers	01244 323886
	Sedan House	01244 320480/348282
	White Friars Chambers	01244 323070
Chesterfield	26 Morley Avenue	01246 234790/01298 871350
Chichester	Chichester Chambers	01243 784538
Colchester	East Anglian Chambers	01206 572756
Durham	Durham Barristers' Chambers	0191 386 9199
Exeter	Cathedral Chambers (Jan Wood Independent Barristers' Clerk)	01392 210900
	Southernhay Chambers	01392 255777
	Walnut House	01392 279751
Guildford	• Guildford Chambers	01483 539131
Hull	Wilberforce Chambers	01482 323264
Ipswich	East Anglian Chambers	01473 214481
Leatherhead	Pembroke House	01372 376160/376493
Leeds	Chambers of Andrew Campbell QC	0113 2455438
	Broadway House Chambers	0113 246 2600
	11 King's Bench Walk	0113 297 1200
	No. 6	0113 2459763
	Park Lane Chambers	0113 2285000
	The Chambers of Philip Raynor QC	0113 242 1123
	• 30 Park Square	0113 2436388
	• 37 Park Square Chambers	0113 2439422
	• Sovereign Chambers	0113 2451841/2/3
	• St Paul's House	0113 2455866
	• 9 Woodhouse Square	0113 2451986
Leicester	Chambers of Michael Pert QC	0116 249 2020
Liverpool	25-27 Castle Street	0151 227 5661/051 236 5072

• Expanded entry in Part C

A

London

Chavasse Court Chambers	0151 707 1191
• Corn Exchange Chambers	0151 227 1081/5009
• Exchange Chambers	0151 236 7747
First National Chambers	0151 236 2098
India Buildings Chambers	0151 243 6000
• Oriel Chambers	0151 236 7191/236 4321
Arlington Chambers	0171 580 9188
Barristers' Common Law Chambers	0171 375 3012
9 Bedford Row	0171 242 3555
17 Bedford Row	0171 831 7314
33 Bedford Row	0171 242 6476
• Chambers of Michael Pert QC	0171 421 8000
Bell Yard Chambers	0171 306 9292
11 Bolt Court (also at 7 Stone Buildings – 1st Floor)	0171 353 2300
Bridewell Chambers	020 7797 8800
Britton Street Chambers	0171 608 3765
Cloisters	0171 827 4000
1 Crown Office Row	0171 583 9292
1 Dr Johnson's Buildings	0171 353 9328
• 3 Dr Johnson's Buildings	0171 353 4854
• One Essex Court	0171 936 3030
• 35 Essex Street	0171 353 6381
Chambers of Geoffrey Hawker	0171 583 8899
• Chambers of Norman Palmer	0171 405 6114
Francis Taylor Building	0171 353 7768/7769/2711
• 2nd Floor, Francis Taylor Building	0171 353 9942/3157
One Garden Court Family Law Chambers	0171 797 7900
• Two Garden Court	0171 353 1633
• Goldsmith Building	0171 353 7881
Goldsmith Chambers	0171 353 6802/3/4/5
• 9 Gough Square	020 7832 0500
• Gray's Inn Chambers, The Chambers of Norman Patterson	0171 831 5344
Gray's Inn Chambers	0171 831 7888 (Chambers)/ 0171 831 7904 (Mr M Ullah)
96 Gray's Inn Road	0171 405 0585
2 Gray's Inn Square Chambers	020 7242 0328
6 Gray's Inn Square	0171 242 1052
Counsels' Chambers	0171 405 2576
14 Gray's Inn Square	0171 242 0858
• 1 Harcourt Buildings	0171 353 9421/0375
• 2 Harcourt Buildings	0171 583 9020
• Harcourt Chambers	0171 353 6961
• Hardwicke Building	020 7242 2523
• 1 Inner Temple Lane	020 7353 0933
John Street Chambers	0171 242 1911
Justice Court Chambers	0181 830 7786
• 4 King's Bench Walk, Ground/First Floor/ Basement	0171 822 8822
4 King's Bench Walk, 2nd Floor	020 7353 3581
6 King's Bench Walk	0171 353 4931/583 0695
8 King's Bench Walk	0171 797 8888
9 King's Bench Walk	0171 353 7202/3909
10 King's Bench Walk	0171 353 7742
11 King's Bench Walk	0171 353 3337
• 13 King's Bench Walk	0171 353 7204
2 King's Bench Walk Chambers	020 7353 9276
• Lamb Building	020 7797 7788
Lamb Chambers	020 7797 8300
Lion Court	0171 404 6565

A

• Littleton Chambers	0171 797 8600
1 Mitre Court Buildings	0171 797 7070
2 Mitre Court Buildings	0171 353 1353
• Mitre Court Chambers	0171 353 9394
• Mitre House Chambers	0171 583 8233
• New Court	0171 583 5123/0510
• New Court Chambers	0171 831 9500
• 22 Old Buildings	0171 831 0222
11 Old Square	0171 242 5022/405 1074
• 3 Paper Buildings	020 7583 8055
Phoenix Chambers	0171 404 7888
Plowden Buildings	0171 583 0808
• 1 Pump Court	0171 583 2012/353 4341
2 Pump Court	0171 353 5597
• Pump Court Chambers	0171 353 0711
• 5 Pump Court	020 7353 2532
• Chambers of Kieran Coonan QC	0171 583 6013/2510
6 Pump Court	0171 797 8400
Queen Elizabeth Building	0171 797 7837
Somersett Chambers	0171 404 6701
• Stanbrook & Henderson	0171 353 0101
Staple Inn Chambers	0171 242 5240
7 Stone Buildings (also at 11 Bolt Court)	0171 242 0961
55 Temple Chambers	0171 353 7400
• 3 Temple Gardens	0171 353 3102/5/9297
• Thomas More Chambers	0171 404 7000
• 14 Tooks Court	0171 405 8828
Verulam Chambers	0171 813 2400
Warwick House Chambers	0171 430 2323
Maidstone Earl Street Chambers	01622 671222
• Maidstone Chambers	01622 688592
6-8 Mill Street	01622 688094
Manchester • Central Chambers	0161 236 1133
• Cobden House Chambers	0161 833 6000
Deans Court Chambers	0161 214 6000
Kenworthy's Chambers	0161 832 4036/834 6954
• 40 King Street	0161 832 9082
• 8 King Street Chambers	0161 834 9560
58 King Street Chambers	0161 831 7477
Lincoln House Chambers	0161 832 5701
• Chambers of Ian Macdonald QC (In Association with Two Garden Court, Temple, London)	0161 236 1840
Peel Court Chambers	0161 832 3791
• Queen's Chambers	0161 834 6875/4738
• St James's Chambers	0161 834 7000
18 St John Street	0161 278 1800
24a St John Street	0161 833 9628
• 28 St John Street	0161 834 8418
Young Street Chambers	0161 833 0489
Middlesbrough Baker Street Chambers	01642 873873
Newcastle upon Tyne • Broad Chare	0191 232 0541
Cathedral Chambers	0191 232 1311
• Trinity Chambers	0191 232 1927
Northampton Chartlands Chambers	01604 603322
Chambers of Michael Pert QC	01604 602333
Northampton Chambers	01604 636271
Norwich East Anglian Chambers	01603 617351
Octagon House	01603 623186
Sackville Chambers	01603 613516/616221
Nottingham King Charles House	0115 9418851

• Expanded entry in Part C

	Ropewalk Chambers	0115 9472581
	St Mary's Chambers	0115 9503503
Oxford	Harcourt Chambers	01865 791559
	King's Bench Chambers	01865 311066
	3 Paper Buildings (Oxford)	01865 793736
	28 Western Road	01865 204911
Peterborough	Fenners Chambers	01733 562030
Plymouth	Devon Chambers	01752 661659
Pontypridd	• Windsor Chambers	01443 402067
Preston	Deans Court Chambers	01772 555163
	New Bailey Chambers	01772 258087
	Queens Chambers	01772 828300
	15 Winckley Square	01772 252828
Reading	Wessex Chambers	0118 956 8856
Redhill	Redhill Chambers	01737 780781
Rugby	Merriemore Cottage	01788 891832
Saint Albans	St Albans Chambers	01727 843383
Sheffield	Paradise Chambers	0114 2738951
Southampton	• 17 Carlton Crescent	023 8032 0320/0823 2003
	• College Chambers	01703 230338
	• Eighteen Carlton Crescent	01703 639001
Stoke On Trent	Regent Chambers	01782 286666
Swansea	Angel Chambers	01792 464623/464648
	Iscoed Chambers	01792 652988/9/330
Swindon	Pump Court Chambers	01793 539899
Taunton	South Western Chambers	01823 331919 (24 hrs)
Winchester	3 Paper Buildings (Winchester)	01962 868884
	Pump Court Chambers	01962 868161
Wolverhampton	Claremont Chambers	01902 426222
Woodford Green	1 Wensley Avenue	0181 505 9259
York	• York Chambers	01904 620048

CHANCERY (COMMERCIAL)

London	• Serle Court Chambers	0171 242 6105

CHANCERY (GENERAL)

Birmingham	1 Fountain Court	0121 236 5721
	• 3 Fountain Court	0121 236 5854
	• 5 Fountain Court	0121 606 0500
	• 8 Fountain Court	0121 236 5514/5
	• St Philip's Chambers	0121 246 7000
Bournemouth	3 Paper Buildings (Bournemouth)	01202 292102
Bristol	Assize Court Chambers	0117 9264587
	Guildhall Chambers	0117 9273366
	Old Square Chambers	0117 9277111
	St John's Chambers	0117 9213456/298514
Cambridge	Fenners Chambers	01223 368761
Canterbury	Stour Chambers	01227 764899
Cardiff	30 Park Place	01222 398421
	• 33 Park Place	02920 233313
Chichester	Chichester Chambers	01243 784538
Eastbourne	King's Chambers	01323 416053
Exeter	Cathedral Chambers (Jan Wood Independent Barristers' Clerk)	01392 210900
	Southernhay Chambers	01392 255777
	Walnut House	01392 279751
Guildford	• Guildford Chambers	01483 539131
Leeds	Chambers of Andrew Campbell QC	0113 2455438
	• Chancery House Chambers	0113 244 6691
	11 King's Bench Walk	0113 297 1200
	• Mercury Chambers	0113 234 2265

• Expanded entry in Part C

Liverpool
London

No. 6	0113 2459763
The Chambers of Philip Raynor QC	0113 242 1123
• Sovereign Chambers	0113 2451841/2/3
• St Paul's House	0113 2455866
• 9 Woodhouse Square	0113 2451986
• Exchange Chambers	0151 236 7747
Barnard's Inn Chambers	0171 369 6969
Barristers' Common Law Chambers	0171 375 3012
17 Bedford Row	0171 831 7314
33 Bedford Row	0171 242 6476
• 9-12 Bell Yard	0171 400 1800
• Blackstone Chambers	0171 583 1770
11 Bolt Court (also at 7 Stone Buildings – 1st Floor)	0171 353 2300
Bracton Chambers	0171 242 4248
• 4 Breams Buildings	0171 353 5835/430 1221
Brick Court Chambers	0171 379 3550
Bridewell Chambers	020 7797 8800
Cardinal Chambers	020 7353 2622
• Chambers of Mr Peter Crampin QC	020 7831 0081
1 Crown Office Row	0171 583 9292
• Dr Johnson's Chambers	0171 353 4716
• Enterprise Chambers	0171 405 9471
• One Essex Court	0171 936 3030
Chambers of Geoffrey Hawker	0171 583 8899
• Farrar's Building	0171 583 9241
• Chambers of Norman Palmer	0171 405 6114
Chambers of Wilfred Forster-Jones	0171 353 0853/4/7222
• Fountain Court	0171 583 3335
Francis Taylor Building	0171 353 7768/7769/2711
• 2nd Floor, Francis Taylor Building	0171 353 9942/3157
• Goldsmith Building	0171 353 7881
• Gough Square Chambers	0171 353 0924
• Gray's Inn Chambers, The Chambers of Norman Patterson	0171 831 5344
Gray's Inn Chambers	0171 831 7888 (Chambers)/ 0171 831 7904 (Mr M Ullah)
96 Gray's Inn Road	0171 405 0585
8 Gray's Inn Square	0171 242 3529
Counsels' Chambers	0171 405 2576
• 1 Harcourt Buildings	0171 353 9421/0375
• 2 Harcourt Buildings	0171 583 9020
• Hardwicke Building	020 7242 2523
• One Hare Court	020 7353 3171
Chambers of Harjit Singh	0171 353 1356 (4 Lines)
• Harrow on the Hill Chambers	0181 423 7444
Justice Court Chambers	0181 830 7786
• 4 King's Bench Walk	0171 822 8822
6 King's Bench Walk	0171 353 4931/583 0695
8 King's Bench Walk	0171 797 8888
9 King's Bench Walk	0171 353 7202/3909
11 King's Bench Walk	0171 353 3337
• 13 King's Bench Walk	0171 353 7204
• Lamb Building	020 7797 7788
Lamb Chambers	020 7797 8300
Lion Court	0171 404 6565
• Littleton Chambers	0171 797 8600
• Littman Chambers	020 7404 4866
2 Mitre Court Buildings	0171 353 1353
• Mitre Court Chambers	0171 353 9394
• Mitre House Chambers	0171 583 8233

• Expanded entry in Part C

A

	• New Court	0171 583 5123/0510
	• 1 New Square	0171 405 0884/5/6/7
	• Chambers of Lord Goodhart QC	0171 405 5577
	• Chambers of John L Powell QC	0171 797 8000
	5 New Square	020 7404 0404
	• 12 New Square	0171 419 1212
	• 22 Old Buildings	0171 831 0222
	• Twenty-Four Old Buildings	0171 404 0946
	• 9 Old Square	0171 405 4682
	The Chambers of Leolin Price CBE, QC	0171 405 0758
	11 Old Square, Ground Floor	0171 242 5022/405 1074
	• 11 Old Square, Ground Floor	020 7430 0341
	13 Old Square	0171 404 4800
	• Old Square Chambers	0171 269 0300
	• 3 Paper Buildings	020 7583 8055
	• 4 Paper Buildings	0171 583 0816/353 1131
	Phoenix Chambers	0171 404 7888
	Plowden Buildings	0171 583 0808
	• 1 Pump Court	0171 583 2012/353 4341
	2 Pump Court	0171 353 5597
	• 5 Pump Court	020 7353 2532
	No. 1 Serjeants' Inn	0171 415 6666
	• Serle Court Chambers	0171 242 6105
	• 3/4 South Square	0171 696 9900
	• Stanbrook & Henderson	0171 353 0101
	Staple Inn Chambers	0171 242 5240
	• 3 Stone Buildings	0171 242 4937
	• 5 Stone Buildings	0171 242 6201
	• 7 Stone Buildings	0171 405 3886/242 3546
	7 Stone Buildings (also at 11 Bolt Court)	0171 242 0961
	• 9 Stone Buildings	0171 404 5055
	11 Stone Buildings	+44 (0)207 831 6381
	• 2 Temple Gardens	0171 583 6041
	• 3 Temple Gardens	0171 353 3102/5/9297
	Verulam Chambers	0171 813 2400
	Warwick House Chambers	0171 430 2323
	• Wilberforce Chambers	0171 306 0102
Maidstone	Earl Street Chambers	01622 671222
Manchester	• Cobden House Chambers	0161 833 6000
	Deans Court Chambers	0161 214 6000
	• 40 King Street	0161 832 9082
	• 8 King Street Chambers	0161 834 9560
	58 King Street Chambers	0161 831 7477
	• Merchant Chambers	0161 839 7070
	• Queen's Chambers	0161 834 6875/4738
	• St James's Chambers	0161 834 7000
	18 St John Street	0161 278 1800
	• 28 St John Street	0161 834 8418
	Young Street Chambers	0161 833 0489
Milton Keynes	Milton Keynes Chambers	01908 664 128
Newcastle upon Tyne	• Broad Chare	0191 232 0541
	• Trinity Chambers	0191 232 1927
	Westgate Chambers	0191 261 4407/2329785
Norwich	Octagon House	01603 623186
Nottingham	King Charles House	0115 9418851
	Ropewalk Chambers	0115 9472581
	St Mary's Chambers	0115 9503503
Oxford	King's Bench Chambers	01865 311066
	3 Paper Buildings (Oxford)	01865 793736
	28 Western Road	01865 204911
Peterborough	Fenners Chambers	01733 562030

• Expanded entry in Part C

Portsmouth	• Portsmouth Barristers' Chambers	023 92 831292/811811
Preston	Deans Court Chambers	01772 555163
	New Bailey Chambers	01772 258087
	Queens Chambers	01772 828300
	15 Winckley Square	01772 252828
Reading	Wessex Chambers	0118 956 8856
Redhill	Redhill Chambers	01737 780781
Saint Albans	St Albans Chambers	01727 843383
Sheffield	Paradise Chambers	0114 2738951
Southampton	• 17 Carlton Crescent	023 8032 0320/0823 2003
	• College Chambers	01703 230338
	• Eighteen Carlton Crescent	01703 639001
Stoke On Trent	Regent Chambers	01782 286666
Swansea	Iscoed Chambers	01792 652988/9/330
Winchester	3 Paper Buildings (Winchester)	01962 868884
Wolverhampton	Claremont Chambers	01902 426222

CHANCERY LAND LAW

Birmingham	• 3 Fountain Court	0121 236 5854
	• 5 Fountain Court	0121 606 0500
	• 8 Fountain Court	0121 236 5514/5
	• St Philip's Chambers	0121 246 7000
Bristol	Assize Court Chambers	0117 9264587
	Guildhall Chambers	0117 9273366
	St John's Chambers	0117 9213456/298514
Cambridge	Fenners Chambers	01223 368761
Cardiff	9 Park Place	01222 382731
	• 33 Park Place	02920 233313
Exeter	Southernhay Chambers	01392 255777
	Walnut House	01392 279751
Guildford	• Guildford Chambers	01483 539131
Leeds	Chambers of Andrew Campbell QC	0113 2455438
	• Chancery House Chambers	0113 244 6691
	11 King's Bench Walk	0113 297 1200
	No. 6	0113 2459763
	The Chambers of Philip Raynor QC	0113 242 1123
	• Sovereign Chambers	0113 2451841/2/3
	• 9 Woodhouse Square	0113 2451986
Liverpool	• Exchange Chambers	0151 236 7747
London	Barnard's Inn Chambers	0171 369 6969
	33 Bedford Row	0171 242 6476
	Bracton Chambers	0171 242 4248
	• 4 Breams Buildings	0171 353 5835/430 1221
	• Chambers of Mr Peter Crampin QC	020 7831 0081
	• Dr Johnson's Chambers	0171 353 4716
	• One Essex Court	0171 936 3030
	Falcon Chambers	0171 353 2484
	• Chambers of Norman Palmer	0171 405 6114
	• Fountain Court	0171 583 3335
	• 2nd Floor, Francis Taylor Building	0171 353 9942/3157
	96 Gray's Inn Road	0171 405 0585
	• 1 Harcourt Buildings	0171 353 9421/0375
	• Harcourt Chambers	0171 353 6961
	• Harrow on the Hill Chambers	0181 423 7444
	Justice Court Chambers	0181 830 7786
	6 King's Bench Walk	0171 353 4931/583 0695
	• 13 King's Bench Walk	0171 353 7204
	• Lamb Building	020 7797 7788
	Lamb Chambers	020 7797 8300
	• Littman Chambers	020 7404 4866
	• Mitre Court Chambers	0171 353 9394

• Expanded entry in Part C

A

	• Mitre House Chambers	0171 583 8233
	• 1 New Square	0171 405 0884/5/6/7
	• Chambers of Lord Goodhart QC	0171 405 5577
	5 New Square	020 7404 0404
	• 12 New Square	0171 419 1212
	• 22 Old Buildings	0171 831 0222
	• Twenty-Four Old Buildings	0171 404 0946
	• 9 Old Square	0171 405 4682
	The Chambers of Leolin Price CBE, QC	0171 405 0758
	11 Old Square, Ground Floor	0171 242 5022/405 1074
	• 11 Old Square, Ground Floor	020 7430 0341
	13 Old Square	0171 404 4800
	• 3 Paper Buildings	020 7583 8055
	• 4 Paper Buildings	0171 583 0816/353 1131
	• 1 Pump Court	0171 583 2012/353 4341
	• 5 Pump Court	020 7353 2532
	No. 1 Serjeants' Inn	0171 415 6666
	Staple Inn Chambers	0171 242 5240
	• 3 Stone Buildings	0171 242 4937
	• 5 Stone Buildings	0171 242 6201
	• 7 Stone Buildings	0171 405 3886/242 3546
	• 9 Stone Buildings	0171 404 5055
	• 199 Strand	0171 379 9779
	• Wilberforce Chambers	0171 306 0102
Manchester	• Cobden House Chambers	0161 833 6000
	Deans Court Chambers	0161 214 6000
	• 40 King Street	0161 832 9082
	• 8 King Street Chambers	0161 834 9560
	58 King Street Chambers	0161 831 7477
	• Merchant Chambers	0161 839 7070
	• Queen's Chambers	0161 834 6875/4738
	• St James's Chambers	0161 834 7000
Milton Keynes	Milton Keynes Chambers	01908 664 128
Newcastle upon Tyne	• Broad Chare	0191 232 0541
	• Trinity Chambers	0191 232 1927
	Westgate Chambers	0191 261 4407/2329785
Northampton	Northampton Chambers	01604 636271
Nottingham	Ropewalk Chambers	0115 9472581
	St Mary's Chambers	0115 9503503
Oxford	Harcourt Chambers	01865 791559
	King's Bench Chambers	01865 311066
	3 Paper Buildings (Oxford)	01865 793736
Peterborough	Fenners Chambers	01733 562030
Portsmouth	• Portsmouth Barristers' Chambers	023 92 831292/811811
Preston	Deans Court Chambers	01772 555163
	New Bailey Chambers	01772 258087
	15 Winckley Square	01772 252828
Reading	Wessex Chambers	0118 956 8856
Southampton	• 17 Carlton Crescent	023 8032 0320/0823 2003
Stoke On Trent	Regent Chambers	01782 286666
Swansea	Angel Chambers	01792 464623/464648
Winchester	3 Paper Buildings (Winchester)	01962 868884
Wolverhampton	Claremont Chambers	01902 426222

CHARITIES

Birmingham	• St Philip's Chambers	0121 246 7000
Bristol	St John's Chambers	0117 9213456/298514
Leeds	The Chambers of Philip Raynor QC	0113 242 1123
	• 9 Woodhouse Square	0113 2451986
Liverpool	• Exchange Chambers	0151 236 7747
	First National Chambers	0151 236 2098

• Expanded entry in Part C

A

London	Barnard's Inn Chambers	0171 369 6969
	Bracton Chambers	0171 242 4248
	• 4 Breams Buildings	0171 353 5835/430 1221
	• Chambers of Mr Peter Crampin QC	020 7831 0081
	• Chambers of Norman Palmer	0171 405 6114
	• Fountain Court	0171 583 3335
	Chambers of Harjit Singh	0171 353 1356 (4 Lines)
	Justice Court Chambers	0181 830 7786
	9 King's Bench Walk	0171 353 7202/3909
	11 King's Bench Walk	0171 353 3337
	• Mitre House Chambers	0171 583 8233
	• 1 New Square	0171 405 0884/5/6/7
	• Chambers of Lord Goodhart QC	0171 405 5577
	5 New Square	020 7404 0404
	• 12 New Square	0171 419 1212
	24 Old Buildings	020 7242 2744
	• 9 Old Square	0171 405 4682
	The Chambers of Leolin Price CBE, QC	0171 405 0758
	11 Old Square, Ground Floor	0171 242 5022/405 1074
	• 11 Old Square, Ground Floor	020 7430 0341
	13 Old Square	0171 404 4800
	• 3 Stone Buildings	0171 242 4937
	• 5 Stone Buildings	0171 242 6201
	• 7 Stone Buildings	0171 405 3886/242 3546
	• 9 Stone Buildings	0171 404 5055
	• Wilberforce Chambers	0171 306 0102
	Wynne Chambers	0181 961 6144
Manchester	• Cobden House Chambers	0161 833 6000
	• 40 King Street	0161 832 9082
	• St James's Chambers	0161 834 7000
Newcastle upon Tyne	• Trinity Chambers	0191 232 1927
	Westgate Chambers	0191 261 4407/2329785
Pontypridd	• Windsor Chambers	01443 402067
Wolverhampton	Claremont Chambers	01902 426222

CHILDREN

| London | • One King's Bench Walk | 0171 936 1500 |

CIVIL ACTIONS AGAINST THE POLICE

London	• 9 Gough Square	020 7832 0500
	• 3 Serjeants' Inn	0171 353 5537
	Somersett Chambers	0171 404 6701
Manchester	• Queen's Chambers	0161 834 6875/4738
Reading	Wessex Chambers	0118 956 8856

CIVIL ACTIONS INVOLVING THE POLICE

| Manchester | • Queen's Chambers | 0161 834 6875/4738 |

CIVIL FRAUD

| London | • Serle Court Chambers | 0171 242 6105 |

CIVIL JURY ACTIONS FOR POLICE AUTHORITIES

| London | 5 Essex Court | 0171 410 2000 |

CIVIL LIBERTIES

Birmingham	• 5 Fountain Court	0121 606 0500
	• 8 Fountain Court	0121 236 5514/5
	New Court Chambers	0121 693 6656
Bristol	Old Square Chambers	0117 9277111
	St John's Chambers	0117 9213456/298514
	Veritas Chambers	0117 930 8802

• Expanded entry in Part C

A

Chichester	Chichester Chambers	01243 784538
Leeds	• Sovereign Chambers	0113 2451841/2/3
	• 9 Woodhouse Square	0113 2451986
Liverpool	25-27 Castle Street	0151 227 5661/051 236 5072
	19 Castle Street Chambers	0151 236 9402
	• Corn Exchange Chambers	0151 227 1081/5009
	India Buildings Chambers	0151 243 6000
London	Acre Lane Neighbourhood Chambers	0171 274 4400
	Barristers' Common Law Chambers	0171 375 3012
	Bell Yard Chambers	0171 306 9292
	• Blackstone Chambers	0171 583 1770
	Bridewell Chambers	020 7797 8800
	Britton Street Chambers	0171 608 3765
	Cloisters	0171 827 4000
	• Devereux Chambers	0171 353 7534
	• Doughty Street Chambers	0171 404 1313
	1 Dr Johnson's Buildings	0171 353 9328
	• One Essex Court	0171 936 3030
	• Essex Court Chambers	0171 813 8000
	• 20 Essex Street	0171 583 9294
	• 39 Essex Street	0171 832 1111
	• Farrar's Building	0171 583 9241
	• Chambers of Norman Palmer	0171 405 6114
	Chambers of Wilfred Forster-Jones	0171 353 0853/4/7222
	• Two Garden Court	0171 353 1633
	• Gray's Inn Chambers, The Chambers of Norman Patterson	0171 831 5344
	• 2-3 Gray's Inn Square	0171 242 4986
	• 4-5 Gray's Inn Square	0171 404 5252
	Counsels' Chambers	0171 405 2576
	• One Hare Court	020 7353 3171
	• 1 Inner Temple Lane	020 7353 0933
	John Street Chambers	0171 242 1911
	Justice Court Chambers	0181 830 7786
	• 4 King's Bench Walk	0171 822 8822
	8 King's Bench Walk	0171 797 8888
	10 King's Bench Walk	0171 353 7742
	• 11 King's Bench Walk	0171 632 8500/583 0610
	• Mitre House Chambers	0171 583 8233
	• Monckton Chambers	0171 405 7211
	• New Court Chambers	0171 831 9500
	• 12 New Square	0171 419 1212
	• Old Square Chambers	0171 269 0300
	• 2 Paper Buildings	020 7556 5500
	• 4 Paper Buildings	0171 353 3366/583 7155
	Five Paper Buildings	0171 583 6117
	• 1 Pump Court	0171 583 2012/353 4341
	• 3 Raymond Buildings	020 7831 3833
	55 Temple Chambers	0171 353 7400
	• 2 Temple Gardens	0171 583 6041
	• Thomas More Chambers	0171 404 7000
	• 14 Tooks Court	0171 405 8828
	• 2-4 Tudor Street	0171 797 7111
	Verulam Chambers	0171 813 2400
	Virtual Chambers	07071 244 944
	Warwick House Chambers	0171 430 2323
Manchester	• Central Chambers	0161 236 1133
	• Chambers of Ian Macdonald QC (In Association with Two Garden Court, Temple, London)	0161 236 1840
	• St James's Chambers	0161 834 7000

• Expanded entry in Part C

Middlesbrough	Young Street Chambers	0161 833 0489
Norwich	Baker Street Chambers	01642 873873
Nottingham	Sackville Chambers	01603 613516/616221
Oxford	Ropewalk Chambers	0115 9472581
Plymouth	King's Bench Chambers	01865 311066
Pontypridd	Devon Chambers	01752 661659
Preston	• Windsor Chambers	01443 402067
	New Bailey Chambers	01772 258087
	15 Winckley Square	01772 252828
Slough	Slough Chamber	01753 553806/817989
Wolverhampton	Claremont Chambers	01902 426222
Woodford Green	1 Wensley Avenue	0181 505 9259

CLINICAL NEGLIGENCE

Bristol	Old Square Chambers	0117 9277111
London	• Hardwicke Building	020 7242 2523
	• 12 King's Bench Walk	0171 583 0811
	• Mitre Court Chambers	0171 353 9394
	• Old Square Chambers	0171 269 0300
	One Paper Buildings	0171 583 7355
Maidstone	• Maidstone Chambers	01622 688592

CLUB LAW

London	• 13 King's Bench Walk	0171 353 7204
Oxford	King's Bench Chambers	01865 311066

COMMERCIAL

Birmingham	1 Fountain Court	0121 236 5721
	• 5 Fountain Court	0121 606 0500
	St Ive's Chambers	0121 236 0863/5720
Bristol	Guildhall Chambers	0117 9273366
	St John's Chambers	0117 9213456/298514
Canterbury	• Becket Chambers	01227 786331
Colchester	East Anglian Chambers	01206 572756
Eastbourne	King's Chambers	01323 416053
Ipswich	East Anglian Chambers	01473 214481
Leeds	• Mercury Chambers	0113 234 2265
	No. 6	0113 2459763
	• 37 Park Square Chambers	0113 2439422
	• Sovereign Chambers	0113 2451841/2/3
Leicester	Chambers of Michael Pert QC	0116 249 2020
Liverpool	• Exchange Chambers	0151 236 7747
	India Buildings Chambers	0151 243 6000
London	Alban Chambers	0171 419 5051
	Atkin Chambers	020 7404 0102
	33 Bedford Row	0171 242 6476
	• Chambers of Michael Pert QC	0171 421 8000
	Bell Yard Chambers	0171 306 9292
	• Blackstone Chambers	0171 583 1770
	Bridewell Chambers	020 7797 8800
	Cardinal Chambers	020 7353 2622
	Cloisters	0171 827 4000
	• One Essex Court	0171 936 3030
	• 35 Essex Street	0171 353 6381
	• 4-5 Gray's Inn Square	0171 404 5252
	• Hardwicke Building	020 7242 2523
	• One Hare Court	020 7353 3171
	• Harrow on the Hill Chambers	0181 423 7444
	John Street Chambers	0171 242 1911
	Justice Court Chambers	0181 830 7786
	4 King's Bench Walk	020 7353 3581

• Expanded entry in Part C

A

	S Tomlinson QC	0171 583 0404
	● 13 King's Bench Walk	0171 353 7204
	● Monckton Chambers	0171 405 7211
	● New Court Chambers	0171 831 9500
	7 New Square	020 7404 5484
	13 Old Square	0171 404 4800
	● 3 Paper Buildings	020 7583 8055
	● 4 Paper Buildings	0171 353 3366/583 7155
	Phoenix Chambers	0171 404 7888
	Plowden Buildings	0171 583 0808
	● Pump Court Chambers	0171 353 0711
	● 5 Pump Court	020 7353 2532
	11 Stone Buildings	+44 (0)207 831 6381
	● Thomas More Chambers	0171 404 7000
	Virtual Chambers	07071 244 944
	● Wilberforce Chambers	0171 306 0102
Luton	Beresford Chambers	01582 429111
Manchester	● Byrom Street Chambers	0161 829 2100
	● Merchant Chambers	0161 839 7070
	● Queen's Chambers	0161 834 6875/4738
Newcastle upon Tyne	Westgate Chambers	0191 261 4407/2329785
Northampton	Chambers of Michael Pert QC	01604 602333
Norwich	East Anglian Chambers	01603 617351
Oxford	3 Paper Buildings (Oxford)	01865 793736
Pontypridd	● Windsor Chambers	01443 402067
Swindon	Pump Court Chambers	01793 539899
Winchester	3 Paper Buildings (Winchester)	01962 868884
	Pump Court Chambers	01962 868161

COMMERCIAL LITIGATION

Birmingham	1 Fountain Court	0121 236 5721
	● 3 Fountain Court	0121 236 5854
	● 5 Fountain Court	0121 606 0500
	● 8 Fountain Court	0121 236 5514/5
	New Court Chambers	0121 693 6656
	● St Philip's Chambers	0121 246 7000
Bournemouth	3 Paper Buildings (Bournemouth)	01202 292102
Bradford	Broadway House Chambers	01274 722560
Bristol	Guildhall Chambers	0117 9273366
	Old Square Chambers	0117 9277111
	St John's Chambers	0117 9213456/298514
Cambridge	Fenners Chambers	01223 368761
Cardiff	30 Park Place	01222 398421
	● 33 Park Place	02920 233313
Exeter	Cathedral Chambers (Jan Wood Independent Barristers' Clerk)	01392 210900
Leeds	Chambers of Andrew Campbell QC	0113 2455438
	Broadway House Chambers	0113 246 2600
	● Chancery House Chambers	0113 244 6691
	● Mercury Chambers	0113 234 2265
	No. 6	0113 2459763
	The Chambers of Philip Raynor QC	0113 242 1123
	● 9 Woodhouse Square	0113 2451986
Liverpool	● Corn Exchange Chambers	0151 227 1081/5009
	● Exchange Chambers	0151 236 7747
	India Buildings Chambers	0151 243 6000
	● Oriel Chambers	0151 236 7191/236 4321
London	Alban Chambers	0171 419 5051
	Atkin Chambers	020 7404 0102
	9 Bedford Row	0171 242 3555
	33 Bedford Row	0171 242 6476

● Expanded entry in Part C

• 9-12 Bell Yard	0171 400 1800
11 Bolt Court (also at 7 Stone Buildings – 1st Floor)	0171 353 2300
Bracton Chambers	0171 242 4248
Brick Court Chambers	0171 379 3550
Bridewell Chambers	020 7797 8800
39 Windsor Road	0181 349 9194
Cloisters	0171 827 4000
1 Crown Office Row	0171 583 9292
• Two Crown Office Row	020 7797 8100
• Devereux Chambers	0171 353 7534
• Enterprise Chambers	0171 405 9471
• Erskine Chambers	0171 242 5532
• One Essex Court, Ground Floor	020 7583 2000
• One Essex Court, 1st Floor	0171 936 3030
• 4 Essex Court	020 7797 7970
• Essex Court Chambers	0171 813 8000
• 20 Essex Street	0171 583 9294
• 35 Essex Street	0171 353 6381
• 39 Essex Street	0171 832 1111
Chambers of Geoffrey Hawker	0171 583 8899
• Farrar's Building	0171 583 9241
• Chambers of Norman Palmer	0171 405 6114
• Fountain Court	0171 583 3335
Francis Taylor Building	0171 353 7768/7769/2711
• Goldsmith Building	0171 353 7881
• 9 Gough Square	020 7832 0500
• Gough Square Chambers	0171 353 0924
• 2-3 Gray's Inn Square	0171 242 4986
Counsels' Chambers	0171 405 2576
• 1 Harcourt Buildings	0171 353 9421/0375
• 2 Harcourt Buildings	0171 583 9020
• Harrow on the Hill Chambers	0181 423 7444
John Street Chambers	0171 242 1911
Justice Court Chambers	0181 830 7786
• Keating Chambers	0171 544 2600
• 4 King's Bench Walk	0171 822 8822
S Tomlinson QC	0171 583 0404
9 King's Bench Walk	0171 353 7202/3909
10 King's Bench Walk	0171 353 7742
• 11 King's Bench Walk,	0171 632 8500/583 0610
11 King's Bench Walk, 1st Floor	0171 353 3337
• 12 King's Bench Walk	0171 583 0811
• 13 King's Bench Walk	0171 353 7204
Lamb Chambers	020 7797 8300
• Littleton Chambers	0171 797 8600
• Littman Chambers	020 7404 4866
• Monckton Chambers	0171 405 7211
• Chambers of John L Powell QC	0171 797 8000
5 New Square	020 7404 0404
• 12 New Square	0171 419 1212
• Twenty-Four Old Buildings	0171 404 0946
The Chambers of Leolin Price CBE, QC	0171 405 0758
13 Old Square	0171 404 4800
• Old Square Chambers	0171 269 0300
One Paper Buildings	0171 583 7355
• 3 Paper Buildings	020 7583 8055
• 5 Paper Buildings	0171 583 9275/583 4555
Five Paper Buildings	0171 583 6117
Phoenix Chambers	0171 404 7888
Plowden Buildings	0171 583 0808

• Expanded entry in Part C

A

• Pump Court Chambers	0171 353 0711
• 5 Raymond Buildings	0171 242 2902
• 3 Serjeants' Inn	0171 353 5537
• Serle Court Chambers	0171 242 6105
• 3/4 South Square	0171 696 9900
• Stanbrook & Henderson	0171 353 0101
• 3 Stone Buildings	0171 242 4937
4 Stone Buildings	0171 242 5524
• 5 Stone Buildings	0171 242 6201
• 7 Stone Buildings	0171 405 3886/242 3546
7 Stone Buildings (also at 11 Bolt Court)	0171 242 0961
• 9 Stone Buildings	0171 404 5055
11 Stone Buildings	+44 (0)207 831 6381
• 199 Strand	0171 379 9779
• 2 Temple Gardens	0171 583 6041
3 Verulam Buildings	0171 831 8441
Verulam Chambers	0171 813 2400
Warwick House Chambers	0171 430 2323
• Wilberforce Chambers	0171 306 0102

Manchester	• Cobden House Chambers	0161 833 6000
	Deans Court Chambers	0161 214 6000
	Kenworthy's Chambers	0161 832 4036/834 6954
	• 40 King Street	0161 832 9082
	• Queen's Chambers	0161 834 6875/4738
	18 St John Street	0161 278 1800
	Young Street Chambers	0161 833 0489
Milton Keynes	Milton Keynes Chambers	01908 664 128
Newcastle upon Tyne	• Trinity Chambers	0191 232 1927
	Westgate Chambers	0191 261 4407/2329785
Nottingham	St Mary's Chambers	0115 9503503
Oxford	King's Bench Chambers	01865 311066
	3 Paper Buildings (Oxford)	01865 793736
Peterborough	Fenners Chambers	01733 562030
Pontypridd	• Windsor Chambers	01443 402067
Portsmouth	• Portsmouth Barristers' Chambers	023 92 831292/811811
Preston	Deans Court Chambers	01772 555163
	Queens Chambers	01772 828300
Reading	Wessex Chambers	0118 956 8856
Redhill	Redhill Chambers	01737 780781
Saint Albans	St Albans Chambers	01727 843383
Swindon	Pump Court Chambers	01793 539899
Winchester	3 Paper Buildings (Winchester)	01962 868884
	Pump Court Chambers	01962 868161
York	• York Chambers	01904 620048

COMMERCIAL PLANNING

Liverpool	• Exchange Chambers	0151 236 7747

COMMERCIAL PROPERTY

Birmingham	1 Fountain Court	0121 236 5721
	• 5 Fountain Court	0121 606 0500
	• 8 Fountain Court	0121 236 5514/5
	• St Philip's Chambers	0121 246 7000
Bristol	Guildhall Chambers	0117 9273366
	St John's Chambers	0117 9213456/298514
Cambridge	Fenners Chambers	01223 368761
Cardiff	9 Park Place	01222 382731
	• 33 Park Place	02920 233313
Chester	Nicholas Street Chambers	01244 323886
Exeter	Cathedral Chambers (Jan Wood Independent Barristers' Clerk)	01392 210900

Leeds

Leicester
Liverpool

London

Southernhay Chambers	01392 255777
Chambers of Andrew Campbell QC	0113 2455438
• Chancery House Chambers	0113 244 6691
• Mercury Chambers	0113 234 2265
No. 6	0113 2459763
• 37 Park Square Chambers	0113 2439422
• Sovereign Chambers	0113 2451841/2/3
Chambers of Michael Pert QC	0116 249 2020
• Exchange Chambers	0151 236 7747
India Buildings Chambers	0151 243 6000
Barnard's Inn Chambers	0171 369 6969
17 Bedford Row	0171 831 7314
33 Bedford Row	0171 242 6476
• Chambers of Michael Pert QC	0171 421 8000
Bracton Chambers	0171 242 4248
• 4 Breams Buildings	0171 353 5835/430 1221
Bridewell Chambers	020 7797 8800
• Chambers of Mr Peter Crampin QC	020 7831 0081
• Devereux Chambers	0171 353 7534
• Enterprise Chambers	0171 405 9471
• One Essex Court	0171 936 3030
Chambers of Geoffrey Hawker	0171 583 8899
Falcon Chambers	0171 353 2484
• Chambers of Norman Palmer	0171 405 6114
• 4 Field Court	0171 440 6900
Francis Taylor Building	0171 353 7768/7769/2711
• 2nd Floor, Francis Taylor Building	0171 353 9942/3157
• Goldsmith Building	0171 353 7881
• 9 Gough Square	020 7832 0500
2 Gray's Inn Square Chambers	020 7242 0328
Counsels' Chambers	0171 405 2576
• 1 Harcourt Buildings	0171 353 9421/0375
• Harrow on the Hill Chambers	0181 423 7444
Justice Court Chambers	0181 830 7786
9 King's Bench Walk	0171 353 7202/3909
10 King's Bench Walk	0171 353 7742
11 King's Bench Walk	0171 353 3337
• 13 King's Bench Walk	0171 353 7204
Lamb Chambers	020 7797 8300
• Littman Chambers	020 7404 4866
2 Mitre Court Buildings	0171 353 1353
• Mitre Court Chambers	0171 353 9394
• New Court Chambers	0171 831 9500
• 1 New Square	0171 405 0884/5/6/7
• Chambers of Lord Goodhart QC	0171 405 5577
• 12 New Square	0171 419 1212
• Twenty-Four Old Buildings	0171 404 0946
• 9 Old Square	0171 405 4682
The Chambers of Leolin Price CBE, QC	0171 405 0758
• 11 Old Square	020 7430 0341
13 Old Square	0171 404 4800
• 3 Paper Buildings	020 7583 8055
• 4 Paper Buildings	0171 583 0816/353 1131
• 5 Pump Court	020 7353 2532
No. 1 Serjeants' Inn	0171 415 6666
• 3/4 South Square	0171 696 9900
• 3 Stone Buildings	0171 242 4937
• 5 Stone Buildings	0171 242 6201
• 7 Stone Buildings	0171 405 3886/242 3546
• 9 Stone Buildings	0171 404 5055
11 Stone Buildings	+44 (0)207 831 6381

• Expanded entry in Part C

A

	• 199 Strand	0171 379 9779
	• 2 Temple Gardens	0171 583 6041
	3 Verulam Buildings	0171 831 8441
	Verulam Chambers	0171 813 2400
	Warwick House Chambers	0171 430 2323
	• Wilberforce Chambers	0171 306 0102
Manchester	• Cobden House Chambers	0161 833 6000
	Kenworthy's Chambers	0161 832 4036/834 6954
	• Merchant Chambers	0161 839 7070
	• Queen's Chambers	0161 834 6875/4738
	• St James's Chambers	0161 834 7000
Newcastle upon Tyne	Westgate Chambers	0191 261 4407/2329785
Northampton	Chambers of Michael Pert QC	01604 602333
Nottingham	King Charles House	0115 9418851
	Ropewalk Chambers	0115 9472581
Oxford	3 Paper Buildings (Oxford)	01865 793736
Peterborough	Fenners Chambers	01733 562030
Preston	New Bailey Chambers	01772 258087
Reading	Wessex Chambers	0118 956 8856
Saint Albans	St Albans Chambers	01727 843383
Swansea	Angel Chambers	01792 464623/464648
	Iscoed Chambers	01792 652988/9/330
Winchester	3 Paper Buildings (Winchester)	01962 868884
Wolverhampton	Claremont Chambers	01902 426222

COMMODITIES

Exeter	Cathedral Chambers (Jan Wood Independent Barristers' Clerk)	01392 210900
London	• Blackstone Chambers	0171 583 1770
	Brick Court Chambers	0171 379 3550
	• 4 Essex Court	020 7797 7970
	• Essex Court Chambers	0171 813 8000
	• 20 Essex Street	0171 583 9294
	• One Hare Court	020 7353 3171
	S Tomlinson QC	0171 583 0404
	• Mitre Court Chambers	0171 353 9394
	• 4 Paper Buildings	0171 353 3366/583 7155
	• 3/4 South Square	0171 696 9900
	• 9 Stone Buildings	0171 404 5055
	3 Verulam Buildings	0171 831 8441

COMMON LAND

Birmingham	• 5 Fountain Court	0121 606 0500
Bristol	Assize Court Chambers	0117 9264587
	Guildhall Chambers	0117 9273366
	St John's Chambers	0117 9213456/298514
Cambridge	Fenners Chambers	01223 368761
Cardiff	9 Park Place	01222 382731
Chester	Nicholas Street Chambers	01244 323886
Exeter	Walnut House	01392 279751
Leeds	Chambers of Andrew Campbell QC	0113 2455438
	• 9 Woodhouse Square	0113 2451986
Leicester	Chambers of Michael Pert QC	0116 249 2020
Liverpool	• Exchange Chambers	0151 236 7747
London	• Chambers of Michael Pert QC	0171 421 8000
	• 4 Breams Buildings	0171 353 5835/430 1221
	• Chambers of Mr Peter Crampin QC	020 7831 0081
	• One Essex Court	0171 936 3030
	Chambers of Geoffrey Hawker	0171 583 8899
	• Chambers of Norman Palmer	0171 405 6114
	• 2-3 Gray's Inn Square	0171 242 4986

• Expanded entry in Part C

	2 Gray's Inn Square Chambers	020 7242 0328
	Counsels' Chambers	0171 405 2576
	• 2 Harcourt Buildings	020 7353 8415
	• Harrow on the Hill Chambers	0181 423 7444
	Justice Court Chambers	0181 830 7786
	Lamb Chambers	020 7797 8300
	2 Mitre Court Buildings	0171 583 1380
	• Mitre Court Chambers	0171 353 9394
	• 1 New Square	0171 405 0884/5/6/7
	• Chambers of Lord Goodhart QC	0171 405 5577
	5 New Square	020 7404 0404
	• 12 New Square	0171 419 1212
	• Twenty-Four Old Buildings	0171 404 0946
	• 9 Old Square	0171 405 4682
	• Pump Court Chambers	0171 353 0711
	• 5 Stone Buildings	0171 242 6201
	• 7 Stone Buildings	0171 405 3886/242 3546
	• 9 Stone Buildings	0171 404 5055
	• 199 Strand	0171 379 9779
Manchester	• Cobden House Chambers	0161 833 6000
	• St James's Chambers	0161 834 7000
Newcastle upon Tyne	• Trinity Chambers	0191 232 1927
Northampton	Chambers of Michael Pert QC	01604 602333
Nottingham	Ropewalk Chambers	0115 9472581
Peterborough	Fenners Chambers	01733 562030
Plymouth	Devon Chambers	01752 661659
Preston	New Bailey Chambers	01772 258087
Saint Albans	St Albans Chambers	01727 843383
Sheffield	Paradise Chambers	0114 2738951
Southampton	• 17 Carlton Crescent	023 8032 0320/0823 2003
Stoke On Trent	Regent Chambers	01782 286666
Swansea	Angel Chambers	01792 464623/464648
	Iscoed Chambers	01792 652988/9/330
Swindon	Pump Court Chambers, 5 Temple Chambers	01793 539899
Winchester	Pump Court Chambers, 31 Southgate Street	01962 868161
York	• York Chambers	01904 620048

COMMON LAW (GENERAL)

Birmingham	Coleridge Chambers	0121 233 8500
	1 Fountain Court	0121 236 5721
	• 3 Fountain Court	0121 236 5854
	• 5 Fountain Court	0121 606 0500
	6 Fountain Court	0121 233 3282
	• 8 Fountain Court	0121 236 5514/5
	New Court Chambers	0121 693 6656
	St Ive's Chambers	0121 236 0863/5720
	• St Philip's Chambers	0121 246 7000
Bournemouth	3 Paper Buildings (Bournemouth)	01202 292102
Bradford	Broadway House Chambers	01274 722560
Brighton	Crown Office Row Chambers	01273 625625
Bristol	Assize Court Chambers	0117 9264587
	Guildhall Chambers	0117 9273366
	St John's Chambers	0117 9213456/298514
Cambridge	Fenners Chambers	01223 368761
Canterbury	• Becket Chambers	01227 786331
	Stour Chambers	01227 764899
Cardiff	9 Park Place	01222 382731
	30 Park Place	01222 398421
	32 Park Place	01222 397364
	• 33 Park Place	02920 233313
Chester	Nicholas Street Chambers	01244 323886

A

	Sedan House	01244 320480/348282
	White Friars Chambers	01244 323070
	26 Morley Avenue	01246 234790/01298 871350
Chesterfield		
Chichester	Chichester Chambers	01243 784538
Colchester	East Anglian Chambers	01206 572756
Consett	6 Ascot Road	01207 507785
Durham	Durham Barristers' Chambers	0191 386 9199
Exeter	Cathedral Chambers (Jan Wood Independent Barristers' Clerk)	01392 210900
	Southernhay Chambers	01392 255777
	Walnut House	01392 279751
Guildford	• Guildford Chambers	01483 539131
Hull	Wilberforce Chambers	01482 323264
Ipswich	East Anglian Chambers	01473 214481
Leatherhead	Pembroke House	01372 376160/376493
Leeds	Chambers of Andrew Campbell QC	0113 2455438
	Broadway House Chambers	0113 246 2600
	• Chancery House Chambers	0113 244 6691
	11 King's Bench Walk	0113 297 1200
	Park Lane Chambers	0113 2285000
	The Chambers of Philip Raynor QC	0113 242 1123
	• 30 Park Square	0113 2436388
	• St Paul's House	0113 2455866
	• 9 Woodhouse Square	0113 2451986
Leicester	Chambers of Michael Pert QC	0116 249 2020
Liverpool	25-27 Castle Street	0151 227 5661/051 236 5072
	19 Castle Street Chambers	0151 236 9402
	Chavasse Court Chambers	0151 707 1191
	• Corn Exchange Chambers	0151 227 1081/5009
	• Exchange Chambers	0151 236 7747
	First National Chambers	0151 236 2098
	India Buildings Chambers	0151 243 6000
	• Oriel Chambers	0151 236 7191/236 4321
London	Alban Chambers	0171 419 5051
	Albany Chambers	0171 485 5736/5758
	Arlington Chambers	0171 580 9188
	Barnard's Inn Chambers	0171 369 6969
	Barristers' Common Law Chambers	0171 375 3012
	9 Bedford Row	0171 242 3555
	17 Bedford Row	0171 831 7314
	33 Bedford Row	0171 242 6476
	• Chambers of Michael Pert QC	0171 421 8000
	• 9-12 Bell Yard	0171 400 1800
	Bell Yard Chambers	0171 306 9292
	11 Bolt Court (also at 7 Stone Buildings – 1st Floor)	0171 353 2300
	Bracton Chambers	0171 242 4248
	• 4 Brick Court	0171 797 8910
	Brick Court Chambers	0171 379 3550
	Bridewell Chambers	020 7797 8800
	Britton Street Chambers	0171 608 3765
	39 Windsor Road	0181 349 9194
	Cloisters	0171 827 4000
	• 1 Crown Office Row, Ground Floor	0171 797 7500
	1 Crown Office Row, 3rd Floor	0171 583 9292
	• Two Crown Office Row	020 7797 8100
	• Devereux Chambers	0171 353 7534
	• Doughty Street Chambers	0171 404 1313
	1 Dr Johnson's Buildings	0171 353 9328
	• 3 Dr Johnson's Buildings	0171 353 4854
	• Dr Johnson's Chambers	0171 353 4716

• Expanded entry in Part C

• One Essex Court	0171 936 3030
5 Essex Court	0171 410 2000
23 Essex Street	0171 413 0353/836 8366
• 35 Essex Street	0171 353 6381
• 39 Essex Street	0171 832 1111
Chambers of Geoffrey Hawker	0171 583 8899
• Farrar's Building	0171 583 9241
• Chambers of Norman Palmer	0171 405 6114
Fleet Chambers	0171 936 3707
Chambers of Wilfred Forster-Jones	0171 353 0853/4/7222
• Fountain Court	0171 583 3335
Francis Taylor Building	0171 353 7768/7769/2711
• 2nd Floor, Francis Taylor Building	0171 353 9942/3157
Goldsmith Chambers	0171 353 6802/3/4/5
• 9 Gough Square	020 7832 0500
• Gray's Inn Chambers, The Chambers of	0171 831 5344
Norman Patterson	
Gray's Inn Chambers	0171 831 7888 (Chambers)/
	0171 831 7904 (Mr M Ullah)
96 Gray's Inn Road	0171 405 0585
• 2-3 Gray's Inn Square	0171 242 4986
2 Gray's Inn Square Chambers	020 7242 0328
Counsels' Chambers	0171 405 2576
14 Gray's Inn Square	0171 242 0858
• 1 Harcourt Buildings	0171 353 9421/0375
• 2 Harcourt Buildings	0171 583 9020
• Hardwicke Building	020 7242 2523
• One Hare Court	020 7353 3171
Chambers of Harjit Singh	0171 353 1356 (4 Lines)
• Harrow on the Hill Chambers	0181 423 7444
• 1 Inner Temple Lane	020 7353 0933
John Street Chambers	0171 242 1911
Justice Court Chambers	0181 830 7786
• One King's Bench Walk	0171 936 1500
2 King's Bench Walk	0171 353 1746
• 4 King's Bench Walk, Ground/First Floor/	0171 822 8822
Basement	
4 King's Bench Walk, 2nd Floor	020 7353 3581
6 King's Bench Walk	0171 353 4931/583 0695
8 King's Bench Walk	0171 797 8888
9 King's Bench Walk	0171 353 7202/3909
10 King's Bench Walk	0171 353 7742
11 King's Bench Walk	0171 353 3337
• 13 King's Bench Walk	0171 353 7204
2 King's Bench Walk Chambers	020 7353 9276
• Lamb Building	020 7797 7788
Lamb Chambers	020 7797 8300
Leone Chambers	0181 200 4020
Lion Court	0171 404 6565
• Littleton Chambers	0171 797 8600
22 Melcombe Regis Court	0171 487 5589
• Mitre Court Chambers	0171 353 9394
• Mitre House Chambers	0171 583 8233
• New Court	0171 583 5123/0510
• New Court Chambers	0171 831 9500
• 1 New Square	0171 405 0884/5/6/7
• Chambers of John L Powell QC	0171 797 8000
5 New Square	020 7404 0404
• 22 Old Buildings	0171 831 0222
• 9 Old Square	0171 405 4682
11 Old Square, Ground Floor	0171 242 5022/405 1074

A

• 11 Old Square, Ground Floor	020 7430 0341
• 2 Paper Buildings	020 7556 5500
• 3 Paper Buildings	020 7583 8055
Five Paper Buildings	0171 583 6117
Phoenix Chambers	0171 404 7888
Plowden Buildings	0171 583 0808
• 1 Pump Court	0171 583 2012/353 4341
2 Pump Court	0171 353 5597
• 4 Pump Court	020 7842 5555
• 5 Pump Court	020 7353 2532
• Chambers of Kieran Coonan QC	0171 583 6013/2510
6 Pump Court	0171 797 8400
• Queen Elizabeth Building, Ground Floor	0171 353 7181 (12 Lines)
Queen Elizabeth Building, 2nd Floor	0171 797 7837
• 3 Raymond Buildings	020 7831 3833
No. 1 Serjeants' Inn	0171 415 6666
• 3 Serjeants' Inn	0171 353 5537
Somersett Chambers	0171 404 6701
• 3/4 South Square	0171 696 9900
• Stanbrook & Henderson	0171 353 0101
Staple Inn Chambers	0171 242 5240
7 Stone Buildings (also at 11 Bolt Court)	0171 242 0961
8 Stone Buildings	0171 831 9881
• 199 Strand	0171 379 9779
55 Temple Chambers	0171 353 7400
• 1 Temple Gardens	0171 583 1315/353 0407
• 2 Temple Gardens	0171 583 6041
• 3 Temple Gardens	0171 353 3102/5/9297
• Thomas More Chambers	0171 404 7000
Tollgate Mews Chambers	0171 511 1838
• 14 Tooks Court	0171 405 8828
3 Verulam Buildings	0171 831 8441
Verulam Chambers	0171 813 2400
Warwick House Chambers	0171 430 2323

Maidstone	Earl Street Chambers	01622 671222
	• Maidstone Chambers	01622 688592
	6-8 Mill Street	01622 688094
Malvern	Resolution Chambers	01684 561279
Manchester	• Byrom Street Chambers	0161 829 2100
	• Cobden House Chambers	0161 833 6000
	Deans Court Chambers	0161 214 6000
	Kenworthy's Chambers	0161 832 4036/834 6954
	• 40 King Street	0161 832 9082
	• 8 King Street Chambers	0161 834 9560
	58 King Street Chambers	0161 831 7477
	• Chambers of Ian Macdonald QC (In Association with Two Garden Court, Temple, London)	0161 236 1840
	Peel Court Chambers	0161 832 3791
	• St James's Chambers	0161 834 7000
	18 St John Street	0161 278 1800
	24a St John Street	0161 833 9628
	• 28 St John Street	0161 834 8418
	Young Street Chambers	0161 833 0489
Meopham	West Lodge Farm	01474 812280
Middlesbrough	Baker Street Chambers	01642 873873
Newcastle upon Tyne	• Broad Chare	0191 232 0541
	Cathedral Chambers	0191 232 1311
	• Trinity Chambers	0191 232 1927
	Westgate Chambers	0191 261 4407/2329785
Northampton	Chambers of Michael Pert QC	01604 602333

• Expanded entry in Part C

	Northampton Chambers	01604 636271
Norwich	East Anglian Chambers	01603 617351
	Octagon House	01603 623186
	Sackville Chambers	01603 613516/616221
Nottingham	King Charles House	0115 9418851
	Ropewalk Chambers	0115 9472581
	St Mary's Chambers	0115 9503503
Oxford	King's Bench Chambers	01865 311066
	3 Paper Buildings (Oxford)	01865 793736
	28 Western Road	01865 204911
Peterborough	Fenners Chambers	01733 562030
Plymouth	Devon Chambers	01752 661659
Pontypridd	•Windsor Chambers	01443 402067
Portsmouth	•Portsmouth Barristers' Chambers	023 92 831292/811811
Preston	Deans Court Chambers	01772 555163
	New Bailey Chambers	01772 258087
	Queens Chambers	01772 828300
	15 Winckley Square	01772 252828
Reading	Wessex Chambers	0118 956 8856
Redhill	Redhill Chambers	01737 780781
Saint Albans	St Albans Chambers	01727 843383
Sheffield	Bank House Chambers	0114 2751223
	Paradise Chambers	0114 2738951
Slough	Slough Chamber	01753 553806/817989
Southampton	•17 Carlton Crescent	023 8032 0320/0823 2003
	•College Chambers	01703 230338
	•Eighteen Carlton Crescent	01703 639001
Stoke On Trent	Regent Chambers	01782 286666
Swansea	Angel Chambers	01792 464623/464648
	Iscoed Chambers	01792 652988/9/330
Taunton	South Western Chambers	01823 331919 (24 hrs)
Winchester	3 Paper Buildings (Winchester)	01962 868884
Wolverhampton	Claremont Chambers	01902 426222
Woodford Green	1 Wensley Avenue	0181 505 9259
York	•York Chambers	01904 620048

COMPANY AND COMMERCIAL

Birmingham	1 Fountain Court	0121 236 5721
	•3 Fountain Court	0121 236 5854
	•5 Fountain Court	0121 606 0500
	•8 Fountain Court	0121 236 5514/5
	•St Philip's Chambers	0121 246 7000
Bournemouth	3 Paper Buildings (Bournemouth)	01202 292102
Bristol	Assize Court Chambers	0117 9264587
	Guildhall Chambers	0117 9273366
	St John's Chambers	0117 9213456/298514
Cambridge	Fenners Chambers	01223 368761
Cardiff	9 Park Place	01222 382731
	30 Park Place	01222 398421
	•33 Park Place	02920 233313
Chester	Nicholas Street Chambers	01244 323886
Exeter	Cathedral Chambers (Jan Wood Independent Barristers' Clerk)	01392 210900
	Southernhay Chambers	01392 255777
	Walnut House	01392 279751
Leeds	Chambers of Andrew Campbell QC	0113 2455438
	•Chancery House Chambers	0113 244 6691
	Enterprise Chambers	0113 246 0391
	11 King's Bench Walk	0113 297 1200
	•Mercury Chambers	0113 234 2265
	No. 6	0113 2459763

• Expanded entry in Part C

	• Park Court Chambers	0113 2433277
	The Chambers of Philip Raynor QC	0113 242 1123
	• 30 Park Square	0113 2436388
	• Sovereign Chambers	0113 2451841/2/3
	• St Paul's House	0113 2455866
Liverpool	25-27 Castle Street	0151 227 5661/051 236 5072
	• Exchange Chambers	0151 236 7747
	India Buildings Chambers	0151 243 6000
London	Barnard's Inn Chambers	0171 369 6969
	17 Bedford Row	0171 831 7314
	33 Bedford Row	0171 242 6476
	Bell Yard Chambers	0171 306 9292
	• Blackstone Chambers	0171 583 1770
	11 Bolt Court (also at 7 Stone Buildings – 1st Floor)	0171 353 2300
	Bracton Chambers	0171 242 4248
	Brick Court Chambers	0171 379 3550
	Bridewell Chambers	020 7797 8800
	Cloisters	0171 827 4000
	• Chambers of Mr Peter Crampin QC	020 7831 0081
	1 Crown Office Row	0171 583 9292
	• Devereux Chambers	0171 353 7534
	• Enterprise Chambers	0171 405 9471
	Equity Barristers' Chambers	0181 558 8336
	• Erskine Chambers	0171 242 5532
	• One Essex Court, Ground Floor	020 7583 2000
	• One Essex Court, 1st Floor	0171 936 3030
	• Essex Court Chambers	0171 813 8000
	Chambers of Geoffrey Hawker	0171 583 8899
	• Chambers of Norman Palmer	0171 405 6114
	• 4 Field Court	0171 440 6900
	• Fountain Court	0171 583 3335
	• 2nd Floor, Francis Taylor Building	0171 353 9942/3157
	• Goldsmith Building	0171 353 7881
	• 9 Gough Square	020 7832 0500
	• Gough Square Chambers	0171 353 0924
	96 Gray's Inn Road	0171 405 0585
	• 2-3 Gray's Inn Square	0171 242 4986
	2 Gray's Inn Square Chambers	020 7242 0328
	8 Gray's Inn Square	0171 242 3529
	Counsels' Chambers	0171 405 2576
	• 1 Harcourt Buildings	0171 353 9421/0375
	• 2 Harcourt Buildings	0171 583 9020
	• Harcourt Chambers	0171 353 6961
	• Hardwicke Building	020 7242 2523
	• One Hare Court	020 7353 3171
	• Harrow on the Hill Chambers	0181 423 7444
	John Street Chambers	0171 242 1911
	Justice Court Chambers	0181 830 7786
	• 4 King's Bench Walk	0171 822 8822
	9 King's Bench Walk	0171 353 7202/3909
	11 King's Bench Walk	0171 353 3337
	• 13 King's Bench Walk	0171 353 7204
	• Lamb Building	020 7797 7788
	Lamb Chambers	020 7797 8300
	Leone Chambers	0181 200 4020
	• Littleton Chambers	0171 797 8600
	• Littman Chambers	020 7404 4866
	2 Mitre Court Buildings	0171 353 1353
	• Mitre Court Chambers	0171 353 9394
	• Monckton Chambers	0171 405 7211

• 1 New Square	0171 405 0884/5/6/7
• Chambers of Lord Goodhart QC	0171 405 5577
• Chambers of John L Powell QC	0171 797 8000
5 New Square	020 7404 0404
• 12 New Square	0171 419 1212
• 22 Old Buildings	0171 831 0222
• Twenty-Four Old Buildings	0171 404 0946
• 9 Old Square	0171 405 4682
The Chambers of Leolin Price CBE, QC	0171 405 0758
• 11 Old Square	020 7430 0341
13 Old Square	0171 404 4800
• 3 Paper Buildings	020 7583 8055
• 4 Paper Buildings	0171 583 0816/353 1131
• 5 Paper Buildings	0171 583 9275/583 4555
Phoenix Chambers	0171 404 7888
Plowden Buildings	0171 583 0808
• 5 Pump Court	020 7353 2532
No. 1 Serjeants' Inn	0171 415 6666
• Serle Court Chambers	0171 242 6105
• 3/4 South Square	0171 696 9900
• Stanbrook & Henderson	0171 353 0101
• 3 Stone Buildings	0171 242 4937
4 Stone Buildings	0171 242 5524
• 7 Stone Buildings	0171 405 3886/242 3546
7 Stone Buildings (also at 11 Bolt Court)	0171 242 0961
• 9 Stone Buildings	0171 404 5055
11 Stone Buildings	+44 (0)207 831 6381
• 2 Temple Gardens	0171 583 6041
• Thomas More Chambers	0171 404 7000
3 Verulam Buildings	0171 831 8441
Verulam Chambers	0171 813 2400
Warwick House Chambers	0171 430 2323
• Wilberforce Chambers	0171 306 0102
Maidstone — Earl Street Chambers	01622 671222
Manchester — • Cobden House Chambers	0161 833 6000
Kenworthy's Chambers	0161 832 4036/834 6954
• 40 King Street	0161 832 9082
• 8 King Street Chambers	0161 834 9560
• Merchant Chambers	0161 839 7070
• Queen's Chambers	0161 834 6875/4738
• St James's Chambers	0161 834 7000
• 28 St John Street	0161 834 8418
Newcastle upon Tyne — Enterprise Chambers	0191 222 3344
• Trinity Chambers	0191 232 1927
Westgate Chambers	0191 261 4407/2329785
Nottingham — Ropewalk Chambers	0115 9472581
St Mary's Chambers	0115 9503503
Oxford — Harcourt Chambers	01865 791559
King's Bench Chambers	01865 311066
3 Paper Buildings (Oxford)	01865 793736
Peterborough — Fenners Chambers	01733 562030
Pontypridd — • Windsor Chambers	01443 402067
Portsmouth — • Portsmouth Barristers' Chambers	023 92 831292/811811
Preston — New Bailey Chambers	01772 258087
Queens Chambers	01772 828300
Reading — Wessex Chambers	0118 956 8856
Redhill — Redhill Chambers	01737 780781
Saint Albans — St Albans Chambers	01727 843383
Southampton — • College Chambers	01703 230338
• Eighteen Carlton Crescent	01703 639001
Swansea — Angel Chambers	01792 464623/464648

A

Winchester	3 Paper Buildings (Winchester)	01962 868884
Wolverhampton	Claremont Chambers	01902 426222
York	• York Chambers	01904 620048

COMPETITION

Birmingham	1 Fountain Court	0121 236 5721
	• 5 Fountain Court	0121 606 0500
Bournemouth	3 Paper Buildings (Bournemouth)	01202 292102
Bristol	St John's Chambers	0117 9213456/298514
Guildford	• Guildford Chambers	01483 539131
Leeds	• Sovereign Chambers	0113 2451841/2/3
London	Bell Yard Chambers	0171 306 9292
	• Blackstone Chambers	0171 583 1770
	Brick Court Chambers	0171 379 3550
	Equity Barristers' Chambers	0181 558 8336
	• One Essex Court	020 7583 2000
	• Essex Court Chambers	0171 813 8000
	• 20 Essex Street	0171 583 9294
	• 4 Field Court	0171 440 6900
	• Fountain Court	0171 583 3335
	Francis Taylor Building	0171 353 7768/7769/2711
	• 4-5 Gray's Inn Square	0171 404 5252
	• 2 Harcourt Buildings	0171 583 9020
	• One Hare Court	020 7353 3171
	• Harrow on the Hill Chambers	0181 423 7444
	Lamb Chambers	020 7797 8300
	• Littleton Chambers	0171 797 8600
	• Littman Chambers	020 7404 4866
	• Monckton Chambers	0171 405 7211
	• 1 New Square	0171 405 0884/5/6/7
	• 8 New Square	0171 405 4321
	19 Old Buildings	0171 405 2001
	13 Old Square	0171 404 4800
	• 4 Paper Buildings	0171 353 3366/583 7155
	• 5 Paper Buildings	0171 583 9275/583 4555
	• Stanbrook & Henderson	0171 353 0101
Manchester	• Cobden House Chambers	0161 833 6000
	• 8 King Street Chambers	0161 834 9560
	Peel Court Chambers	0161 832 3791
Newcastle upon Tyne	Westgate Chambers	0191 261 4407/2329785
Pontypridd	• Windsor Chambers	01443 402067
Preston	New Bailey Chambers	01772 258087

COMPULSORY PURCHASE

London	• 2 Harcourt Buildings	020 7353 8415

CONFISCATION

London	• Furnival Chambers	0171 405 3232

CONSTITUTIONAL LAW

London	Equity Barristers' Chambers	0181 558 8336

CONSTRUCTION

Birmingham	1 Fountain Court	0121 236 5721
	• 5 Fountain Court	0121 606 0500
	• 8 Fountain Court	0121 236 5514/5
	• St Philip's Chambers	0121 246 7000
Bournemouth	3 Paper Buildings (Bournemouth)	01202 292102
Bristol	Assize Court Chambers	0117 9264587
	St John's Chambers	0117 9213456/298514
Cambridge	Fenners Chambers	01223 368761

• Expanded entry in Part C

Cardiff	9 Park Place	01222 382731
	30 Park Place	01222 398421
	• 33 Park Place	02920 233313
Colchester	East Anglian Chambers	01206 572756
Exeter	Cathedral Chambers (Jan Wood	01392 210900
	Independent Barristers' Clerk)	
Ipswich	East Anglian Chambers	01473 214481
Leeds	• Chancery House Chambers	0113 244 6691
	The Chambers of Philip Raynor QC	0113 242 1123
	• Sovereign Chambers	0113 2451841/2/3
	• 9 Woodhouse Square	0113 2451986
	25-27 Castle Street	0151 227 5661/051 236 5072
Liverpool	• Corn Exchange Chambers	0151 227 1081/5009
	India Buildings Chambers	0151 243 6000
	• Oriel Chambers	0151 236 7191/236 4321
London	• Arbitration Chambers	020 7267 2137
	Atkin Chambers	020 7404 0102
	9 Bedford Row	0171 242 3555
	• 4 Breams Buildings	0171 353 5835/430 1221
	Brick Court Chambers	0171 379 3550
	Bridewell Chambers	020 7797 8800
	• 1 Crown Office Row, Ground Floor	0171 797 7500
	1 Crown Office Row, 3rd Floor	0171 583 9292
	• Two Crown Office Row	020 7797 8100
	• Devereux Chambers	0171 353 7534
	• One Essex Court	0171 936 3030
	• 4 Essex Court	020 7797 7970
	• Essex Court Chambers	0171 813 8000
	• 35 Essex Street	0171 353 6381
	• 39 Essex Street	0171 832 1111
	Chambers of Geoffrey Hawker	0171 583 8899
	• Farrar's Building	0171 583 9241
	• Chambers of Norman Palmer	0171 405 6114
	• 4 Field Court	0171 440 6900
	• Fountain Court	0171 583 3335
	Francis Taylor Building	0171 353 7768/7769/2711
	• Goldsmith Building	0171 353 7881
	• 2-3 Gray's Inn Square	0171 242 4986
	Counsels' Chambers	0171 405 2576
	• 1 Harcourt Buildings	0171 353 9421/0375
	• 2 Harcourt Buildings	0171 583 9020
	• Hardwicke Building	020 7242 2523
	• One Hare Court	020 7353 3171
	• Harrow on the Hill Chambers	0181 423 7444
	Justice Court Chambers	0181 830 7786
	• Keating Chambers	0171 544 2600
	S Tomlinson QC	0171 583 0404
	9 King's Bench Walk	0171 353 7202/3909
	10 King's Bench Walk	0171 353 7742
	• 12 King's Bench Walk	0171 583 0811
	• 13 King's Bench Walk	0171 353 7204
	• Lamb Building	020 7797 7788
	Lamb Chambers	020 7797 8300
	• Littleton Chambers	0171 797 8600
	• Littman Chambers	020 7404 4866
	• Mitre Court Chambers	0171 353 9394
	• Mitre House Chambers	0171 583 8233
	• Monckton Chambers	0171 405 7211
	• Chambers of John L Powell QC	0171 797 8000
	• 22 Old Buildings	0171 831 0222
	The Chambers of Leolin Price CBE, QC	0171 405 0758

• Expanded entry in Part C

	11 Old Square	0171 242 5022/405 1074
	● Old Square Chambers	0171 269 0300
	One Paper Buildings	0171 583 7355
	● 3 Paper Buildings	020 7583 8055
	● 4 Paper Buildings, Ground Floor	0171 353 3366/583 7155
	● 4 Paper Buildings, 1st Floor	0171 583 0816/353 1131
	● 5 Paper Buildings	0171 583 9275/583 4555
	Pepys' Chambers	0171 936 2710
	Phoenix Chambers	0171 404 7888
	Plowden Buildings	0171 583 0808
	● Pump Court Chambers	0171 353 0711
	● 4 Pump Court	020 7842 5555
	● 5 Pump Court	020 7353 2532
	No. 1 Serjeants' Inn	0171 415 6666
	● 3 Serjeants' Inn	0171 353 5537
	● Stanbrook & Henderson	0171 353 0101
	55 Temple Chambers	0171 353 7400
	● 2 Temple Gardens	0171 583 6041
	3 Verulam Buildings	0171 831 8441
Malvern	Resolution Chambers	01684 561279
Manchester	● Byrom Street Chambers	0161 829 2100
	Deans Court Chambers	0161 214 6000
	● 40 King Street	0161 832 9082
	● 8 King Street Chambers	0161 834 9560
	● Merchant Chambers	0161 839 7070
	Peel Court Chambers	0161 832 3791
	● Queen's Chambers	0161 834 6875/4738
	● St James's Chambers	0161 834 7000
	Young Street Chambers	0161 833 0489
Meopham	West Lodge Farm	01474 812280
Newcastle upon Tyne	● Trinity Chambers	0191 232 1927
	Westgate Chambers	0191 261 4407/2329785
Norwich	East Anglian Chambers	01603 617351
Nottingham	Ropewalk Chambers	0115 9472581
Oxford	King's Bench Chambers	01865 311066
	3 Paper Buildings (Oxford)	01865 793736
Peterborough	Fenners Chambers	01733 562030
Pontypridd	● Windsor Chambers	01443 402067
Portsmouth	● Portsmouth Barristers' Chambers	023 92 831292/811811
Preston	Deans Court Chambers	01772 555163
	15 Winckley Square	01772 252828
Reading	Wessex Chambers	0118 956 8856
Sheffield	Paradise Chambers	0114 2738951
Stoke On Trent	Regent Chambers	01782 286666
Swansea	Iscoed Chambers	01792 652988/9/330
Swindon	Pump Court Chambers	01793 539899
Winchester	3 Paper Buildings (Winchester)	01962 868884
	Pump Court Chambers	01962 868161
Wolverhampton	Claremont Chambers	01902 426222

CONSUMER LAW

Birmingham	1 Fountain Court	0121 236 5721
	● 5 Fountain Court	0121 606 0500
	● St Philip's Chambers	0121 246 7000
Bristol	Guildhall Chambers	0117 9273366
	St John's Chambers	0117 9213456/298514
Cambridge	Fenners Chambers	01223 368761
Canterbury	● Becket Chambers	01227 786331
Chester	Sedan House	01244 320480/348282
Leeds	No. 6	0113 2459763
Liverpool	India Buildings Chambers	0151 243 6000

● Expanded entry in Part C

A

London	Barristers' Common Law Chambers	0171 375 3012
	• Devereux Chambers	0171 353 7534
	• Fountain Court	0171 583 3335
	• 2nd Floor, Francis Taylor Building	0171 353 9942/3157
	• Gough Square Chambers	0171 353 0924
	• Harrow on the Hill Chambers	0181 423 7444
	John Street Chambers	0171 242 1911
	• 13 King's Bench Walk	0171 353 7204
	22 Melcombe Regis Court	0171 487 5589
	• Monckton Chambers	0171 405 7211
	• 4 Paper Buildings	0171 353 3366/583 7155
	Phoenix Chambers	0171 404 7888
	Queen Elizabeth Building	0171 797 7837
	• 199 Strand	0171 379 9779
	• Thomas More Chambers	0171 404 7000
	Warwick House Chambers	0171 430 2323
Manchester	• Chambers of Ian Macdonald QC (In Association with Two Garden Court, Temple, London)	0161 236 1840
	• Queen's Chambers	0161 834 6875/4738
Peterborough	Fenners Chambers	01733 562030
Pontypridd	• Windsor Chambers	01443 402067
Preston	15 Winckley Square	01772 252828
Reading	Wessex Chambers	0118 956 8856
Slough	Slough Chamber	01753 553806/817989

CONTRACT

Leeds	• 37 Park Square Chambers	0113 2439422
London	• Hardwicke Building	020 7242 2523
	4 King's Bench Walk	020 7353 3581
	• Thomas More Chambers	0171 404 7000
Manchester	Lincoln House Chambers	0161 832 5701

CONVEYANCING

Birmingham	• 5 Fountain Court	0121 606 0500
	• 8 Fountain Court	0121 236 5514/5
	• St Philip's Chambers	0121 246 7000
Bristol	Guildhall Chambers	0117 9273366
Cambridge	Fenners Chambers	01223 368761
Cardiff	9 Park Place	01222 382731
	30 Park Place	01222 398421
Exeter	Southernhay Chambers	01392 255777
Leeds	Chambers of Andrew Campbell QC	0113 2455438
	Enterprise Chambers	0113 246 0391
	The Chambers of Philip Raynor QC	0113 242 1123
	• 37 Park Square Chambers	0113 2439422
Liverpool	• Exchange Chambers	0151 236 7747
	India Buildings Chambers	0151 243 6000
London	11 Bolt Court (also at 7 Stone Buildings – 1st Floor)	0171 353 2300
	• 4 Breams Buildings	0171 353 5835/430 1221
	• Chambers of Mr Peter Crampin QC	020 7831 0081
	• Enterprise Chambers	0171 405 9471
	Falcon Chambers	0171 353 2484
	• Chambers of Norman Palmer	0171 405 6114
	Counsels' Chambers	0171 405 2576
	• Hardwicke Building	020 7242 2523
	• Harrow on the Hill Chambers	0181 423 7444
	9 King's Bench Walk	0171 353 7202/3909
	• 13 King's Bench Walk	0171 353 7204
	• Littman Chambers	020 7404 4866

• Expanded entry in Part C

A

• 1 New Square	0171 405 0884/5/6/7
• Chambers of Lord Goodhart QC	0171 405 5577
5 New Square	020 7404 0404
• 12 New Square	0171 419 1212
• 22 Old Buildings	0171 831 0222
• Twenty-Four Old Buildings	0171 404 0946
• 9 Old Square	0171 405 4682
The Chambers of Leolin Price CBE, QC	0171 405 0758
11 Old Square, Ground Floor	0171 242 5022/405 1074
• 11 Old Square, Ground Floor	020 7430 0341
13 Old Square	0171 404 4800
• 3 Stone Buildings	0171 242 4937
• 5 Stone Buildings	0171 242 6201
7 Stone Buildings (also at 11 Bolt Court)	0171 242 0961
• 9 Stone Buildings	0171 404 5055
55 Temple Chambers	0171 353 7400
Warwick House Chambers	0171 430 2323

Manchester	• Cobden House Chambers	0161 833 6000
	• 40 King Street	0161 832 9082
	• St James's Chambers	0161 834 7000
	• 28 St John Street	0161 834 8418
Newcastle upon Tyne	Enterprise Chambers	0191 222 3344
	• Trinity Chambers	0191 232 1927
Nottingham	Ropewalk Chambers	0115 9472581
Oxford	King's Bench Chambers	01865 311066
Peterborough	Fenners Chambers	01733 562030
Redhill	Redhill Chambers	01737 780781
Southampton	• 17 Carlton Crescent	023 8032 0320/0823 2003

COPYRIGHT

Birmingham	1 Fountain Court	0121 236 5721
	• 5 Fountain Court	0121 606 0500
Bristol	St John's Chambers	0117 9213456/298514
Cardiff	9 Park Place	01222 382731
Chester	Nicholas Street Chambers	01244 323886
Leeds	Chambers of Andrew Campbell QC	0113 2455438
	• Chancery House Chambers	0113 244 6691
	11 King's Bench Walk	0113 297 1200
	The Chambers of Philip Raynor QC	0113 242 1123
	• Sovereign Chambers	0113 2451841/2/3
London	17 Bedford Row	0171 831 7314
	• Blackstone Chambers	0171 583 1770
	• Doughty Street Chambers	0171 404 1313
	• One Essex Court	020 7583 2000
	• 35 Essex Street	0171 353 6381
	• Chambers of Norman Palmer	0171 405 6114
	• 4 Field Court	0171 440 6900
	Francis Taylor Building	0171 353 7768/7769/2711
	• Furnival Chambers	0171 405 3232
	• 2 Harcourt Buildings	0171 583 9020
	9 King's Bench Walk	0171 353 7202/3909
	Lamb Chambers	020 7797 8300
	• Littleton Chambers	0171 797 8600
	2 Mitre Court Buildings	0171 353 1353
	• Mitre Court Chambers	0171 353 9394
	• Monckton Chambers	0171 405 7211
	• 3 New Square	0171 405 1111
	5 New Square	020 7404 0404
	7 New Square	020 7404 5484
	• 8 New Square	0171 405 4321
	19 Old Buildings	0171 405 2001

• Expanded entry in Part C

The Chambers of Leolin Price CBE, QC	0171 405 0758
• 11 Old Square	020 7430 0341
13 Old Square	0171 404 4800
• 5 Paper Buildings	0171 583 9275/583 4555
Five Paper Buildings	0171 583 6117
• 5 Raymond Buildings	0171 242 2902
• 11 South Square	0171 405 1222 (24hr messaging service)
• Stanbrook & Henderson	0171 353 0101
• 3 Stone Buildings	0171 242 4937
• 9 Stone Buildings	0171 404 5055

Manchester	• Cobden House Chambers	0161 833 6000
	• 40 King Street	0161 832 9082
	• Merchant Chambers	0161 839 7070
	• St James's Chambers	0161 834 7000
Newcastle upon Tyne	• Broad Chare	0191 232 0541
Nottingham	King Charles House	0115 9418851
	Ropewalk Chambers	0115 9472581
Oxford	King's Bench Chambers	01865 311066
Pontypridd	• Windsor Chambers	01443 402067
Preston	New Bailey Chambers	01772 258087
Reading	Wessex Chambers	0118 956 8856

CORPORATE FINANCE

Birmingham	• 5 Fountain Court	0121 606 0500
Chester	Nicholas Street Chambers	01244 323886
Leeds	Chambers of Andrew Campbell QC	0113 2455438
	• Chancery House Chambers	0113 244 6691
	11 King's Bench Walk	0113 297 1200
	The Chambers of Philip Raynor QC	0113 242 1123
Liverpool	• Exchange Chambers	0151 236 7747
London	• Blackstone Chambers	0171 583 1770
	1 Crown Office Row	0171 583 9292
	• Erskine Chambers	0171 242 5532
	• One Essex Court	020 7583 2000
	• Essex Court Chambers	0171 813 8000
	• Chambers of Norman Palmer	0171 405 6114
	• One Hare Court	020 7353 3171
	• 4 King's Bench Walk	0171 822 8822
	• 1 New Square	0171 405 0884/5/6/7
	Chambers of John Gardiner QC	0171 242 4017
	• 12 New Square	0171 419 1212
	24 Old Buildings	020 7242 2744
	The Chambers of Leolin Price, QC	0171 405 0758
	• 3/4 South Square	0171 696 9900
	4 Stone Buildings	0171 242 5524
	• 7 Stone Buildings	0171 405 3886/242 3546
	• 9 Stone Buildings	0171 404 5055
Manchester	• 40 King Street	0161 832 9082
	• Merchant Chambers	0161 839 7070
Pontypridd	• Windsor Chambers	01443 402067

CORPORATE INSOLVENCY

London	S Tomlinson QC	0171 583 0404

COSTS

London	• 1 Temple Gardens	0171 583 1315/353 0407

COURT OF PROTECTION

London	• Chambers of Mr Peter Crampin QC	020 7831 0081

• Expanded entry in Part C

COURTS MARTIAL

Birmingham	• 5 Fountain Court	0121 606 0500
	• St Philip's Chambers	0121 246 7000
Bournemouth	3 Paper Buildings (Bournemouth)	01202 292102
Bristol	St John's Chambers	0117 9213456/298514
	Veritas Chambers	0117 930 8802
Cambridge	Fenners Chambers	01223 368761
Cardiff	30 Park Place	01222 398421
	32 Park Place	01222 397364
Chichester	Chichester Chambers	01243 784538
Colchester	East Anglian Chambers	01206 572756
Exeter	Walnut House	01392 279751
Guildford	• Guildford Chambers	01483 539131
Ipswich	East Anglian Chambers	01473 214481
Leeds	Chambers of Andrew Campbell QC	0113 2455438
	11 King's Bench Walk	0113 297 1200
	No. 6	0113 2459763
	• 30 Park Square	0113 2436388
	• St Paul's House	0113 2455866
Leicester	Chambers of Michael Pert QC	0116 249 2020
Liverpool	25-27 Castle Street	0151 227 5661/051 236 5072
	First National Chambers	0151 236 2098
London	9 Bedford Row	0171 242 3555
	33 Bedford Row	0171 242 6476
	• Chambers of Michael Pert QC	0171 421 8000
	• 9-12 Bell Yard	0171 400 1800
	11 Bolt Court (also at 7 Stone Buildings – 1st Floor)	0171 353 2300
	• 4 Brick Court, Chambers of Anne Rafferty QC	0171 583 8455
	Bridewell Chambers	020 7797 8800
	• Devereux Chambers	0171 353 7534
	1 Dr Johnson's Buildings	0171 353 9328
	• Dr Johnson's Chambers	0171 353 4716
	23 Essex Street	0171 413 0353/836 8366
	• Farrar's Building	0171 583 9241
	Francis Taylor Building	0171 353 7768/7769/2711
	• Furnival Chambers	0171 405 3232
	• Goldsmith Building	0171 353 7881
	• Gray's Inn Chambers, The Chambers of Norman Patterson	0171 831 5344
	Counsels' Chambers	0171 405 2576
	• 2 Harcourt Buildings, Ground Floor/Left	0171 583 9020
	2 Harcourt Buildings, 1st Floor	020 7353 2112
	• 1 Hare Court	0171 353 3982/5324
	• 3 Hare Court	0171 395 2000
	• One King's Bench Walk	0171 936 1500
	• 4 King's Bench Walk	0171 822 8822
	8 King's Bench Walk	0171 797 8888
	9 King's Bench Walk	0171 353 7202/3909
	• Lamb Building	020 7797 7788
	Lamb Chambers	020 7797 8300
	• Mitre House Chambers	0171 583 8233
	• 2 Paper Buildings	020 7556 5500
	• 3 Paper Buildings	020 7583 8055
	2 Pump Court	0171 353 5597
	• Pump Court Chambers	0171 353 0711
	• Hollis Whiteman Chambers	020 7583 5766
	• 3 Raymond Buildings	020 7831 3833
	• Stanbrook & Henderson	0171 353 0101
	7 Stone Buildings (also at 11 Bolt Court)	0171 242 0961

• Expanded entry in Part C

	• 3 Temple Gardens	0171 353 3102/5/9297
	• Thomas More Chambers	0171 404 7000
	• 2-4 Tudor Street	0171 797 7111
	Warwick House Chambers	0171 430 2323
Maidstone	Earl Street Chambers	01622 671222
	• Maidstone Chambers	01622 688592
Manchester	• Cobden House Chambers	0161 833 6000
	• 8 King Street Chambers	0161 834 9560
	• Chambers of Ian Macdonald QC (In Association with Two Garden Court, Temple, London)	0161 236 1840
	Young Street Chambers	0161 833 0489
Middlesbrough	Baker Street Chambers	01642 873873
Newcastle upon Tyne	• Broad Chare	0191 232 0541
	Westgate Chambers	0191 261 4407/2329785
Northampton	Chambers of Michael Pert QC	01604 602333
Norwich	East Anglian Chambers	01603 617351
Nottingham	King Charles House	0115 9418851
Oxford	3 Paper Buildings (Oxford)	01865 793736
Peterborough	Fenners Chambers	01733 562030
Plymouth	Devon Chambers	01752 661659
Preston	15 Winckley Square	01772 252828
Redhill	Redhill Chambers	01737 780781
Sheffield	Paradise Chambers	0114 2738951
Southampton	• Eighteen Carlton Crescent	01703 639001
Swindon	Pump Court Chambers	01793 539899
Taunton	South Western Chambers	01823 331919 (24 hrs)
Winchester	3 Paper Buildings (Winchester)	01962 868884
	Pump Court Chambers	01962 868161
York	• York Chambers	01904 620048

CRIME

Birmingham	Coleridge Chambers	0121 233 8500
	1 Fountain Court	0121 236 5721
	• 3 Fountain Court	0121 236 5854
	• 5 Fountain Court	0121 606 0500
	6 Fountain Court	0121 233 3282
	• 8 Fountain Court	0121 236 5514/5
	St Ive's Chambers	0121 236 0863/5720
	• St Philip's Chambers	0121 246 7000
Bournemouth	3 Paper Buildings (Bournemouth)	01202 292102
Bradford	Broadway House Chambers	01274 722560
Brighton	Crown Office Row Chambers	01273 625625
Bristol	Assize Court Chambers	0117 9264587
	Guildhall Chambers	0117 9273366
	St John's Chambers	0117 9213456/298514
	Veritas Chambers	0117 930 8802
Cambridge	Fenners Chambers	01223 368761
Canterbury	• Becket Chambers	01227 786331
	Stour Chambers	01227 764899
Cardiff	9 Park Place	01222 382731
	30 Park Place	01222 398421
	32 Park Place	01222 397364
	• 33 Park Place	02920 233313
Chester	Nicholas Street Chambers	01244 323886
	Sedan House	01244 320480/348282
	White Friars Chambers	01244 323070
Chesterfield	26 Morley Avenue	01246 234790/01298 871350
Chichester	Chichester Chambers	01243 784538
Colchester	East Anglian Chambers	01206 572756
Consett	6 Ascot Road	01207 507785

                                  • Expanded entry in Part C

Durham	Durham Barristers' Chambers	0191 386 9199
Eastbourne	King's Chambers	01323 416053
Exeter	Cathedral Chambers (Jan Wood	01392 210900
	Independent Barristers' Clerk)	
	Walnut House	01392 279751
Guildford	• Guildford Chambers	01483 539131
Hull	Wilberforce Chambers	01482 323264
Ipswich	East Anglian Chambers	01473 214481
Leeds	Chambers of Andrew Campbell QC	0113 2455438
	Broadway House Chambers	0113 246 2600
	11 King's Bench Walk	0113 297 1200
	No. 6	0113 2459763
	• Park Court Chambers	0113 2433277
	The Chambers of Philip Raynor QC	0113 242 1123
	• 30 Park Square	0113 2436388
	• 37 Park Square Chambers	0113 2439422
	• Sovereign Chambers	0113 2451841/2/3
	• St Paul's House	0113 2455866
	• 9 Woodhouse Square	0113 2451986
Leicester	Chambers of Michael Pert QC	0116 249 2020
Liverpool	25-27 Castle Street	0151 227 5661/051 236 5072
	19 Castle Street Chambers	0151 236 9402
	Chavasse Court Chambers	0151 707 1191
	• Corn Exchange Chambers	0151 227 1081/5009
	• Exchange Chambers	0151 236 7747
	First National Chambers	0151 236 2098
	India Buildings Chambers	0151 243 6000
	• Oriel Chambers	0151 236 7191/236 4321
London	ACHMA Chambers	0171 639 7817/0171 635 7904
	Acre Lane Neighbourhood Chambers	0171 274 4400
	Albany Chambers	0171 485 5736/5758
	Barristers' Common Law Chambers	0171 375 3012
	9 Bedford Row	0171 242 3555
	17 Bedford Row	0171 831 7314
	33 Bedford Row	0171 242 6476
	• Chambers of Michael Pert QC	0171 421 8000
	• 9-12 Bell Yard	0171 400 1800
	Bell Yard Chambers	0171 306 9292
	11 Bolt Court (also at 7 Stone Buildings –	0171 353 2300
	1st Floor)	
	• 4 Brick Court	0171 797 8910
	Bridewell Chambers	020 7797 8800
	Britton Street Chambers	0171 608 3765
	Cardinal Chambers	020 7353 2622
	Cloisters	0171 827 4000
	• 1 Crown Office Row	0171 797 7500
	• Doughty Street Chambers	0171 404 1313
	1 Dr Johnson's Buildings	0171 353 9328
	• 3 Dr Johnson's Buildings	0171 353 4854
	• Dr Johnson's Chambers	0171 353 4716
	2 Dyers Buildings	0171 404 1881
	• One Essex Court	0171 936 3030
	5 Essex Court	0171 410 2000
	23 Essex Street	0171 413 0353/836 8366
	• 35 Essex Street	0171 353 6381
	Chambers of Geoffrey Hawker	0171 583 8899
	• Farrar's Building	0171 583 9241
	Fleet Chambers	0171 936 3707
	Chambers of Wilfred Forster-Jones	0171 353 0853/4/7222
	Francis Taylor Building	0171 353 7768/7769/2711
	• 2nd Floor, Francis Taylor Building	0171 353 9942/3157

• Expanded entry in Part C

A

• Furnival Chambers	0171 405 3232
• Two Garden Court	0171 353 1633
• Goldsmith Building	0171 353 7881
Goldsmith Chambers	0171 353 6802/3/4/5
• 9 Gough Square	020 7832 0500
• Gray's Inn Chambers, The Chambers of	0171 831 5344
Norman Patterson	
Gray's Inn Chambers	0171 831 7888 (Chambers)/
	0171 831 7904 (Mr M Ullah)
96 Gray's Inn Road	0171 405 0585
• 2-3 Gray's Inn Square	0171 242 4986
2 Gray's Inn Square Chambers	020 7242 0328
• 3 Gray's Inn Square	0171 520 5600
6 Gray's Inn Square	0171 242 1052
Counsels' Chambers	0171 405 2576
Chambers of Helen Grindrod QC	0171 583 2792
• 1 Harcourt Buildings	0171 353 9421/0375
• 2 Harcourt Buildings, Ground Floor/Left	0171 583 9020
2 Harcourt Buildings, 1st Floor	020 7353 2112
• Harcourt Chambers	0171 353 6961
• Hardwicke Building	020 7242 2523
• 1 Hare Court	0171 353 3982/5324
• 3 Hare Court	0171 395 2000
Chambers of Harjit Singh	0171 353 1356 (4 Lines)
• Harrow on the Hill Chambers	0181 423 7444
• 1 Inner Temple Lane	020 7353 0933
John Street Chambers	0171 242 1911
• One King's Bench Walk	0171 936 1500
2 King's Bench Walk	0171 353 1746
• 4 King's Bench Walk, Ground/First Floor/	0171 822 8822
Basement	
4 King's Bench Walk, 2nd Floor	020 7353 3581
• 6 King's Bench Walk, Ground Floor	0171 583 0410
6 King's Bench Walk, Ground, Third &	0171 353 4931/583 0695
Fourth Floors	
8 King's Bench Walk	0171 797 8888
9 King's Bench Walk	0171 353 7202/3909
10 King's Bench Walk	0171 353 7742
11 King's Bench Walk	0171 353 3337
• 13 King's Bench Walk	0171 353 7204
• Lamb Building	020 7797 7788
Leone Chambers	0181 200 4020
Lion Court	0171 404 6565
• 1 Middle Temple Lane	0171 583 0659 (12 Lines)
2 Mitre Court Buildings	0171 353 1353
• Mitre Court Chambers	0171 353 9394
• Mitre House Chambers	0171 583 8233
• New Court	0171 583 5123/0510
11 Old Square	0171 242 5022/405 1074
• 2 Paper Buildings	020 7556 5500
2 Paper Buildings, Basement North	0171 936 2613
• 3 Paper Buildings	020 7583 8055
Five Paper Buildings	0171 583 6117
Pepys' Chambers	0171 936 2710
Phoenix Chambers	0171 404 7888
Plowden Buildings	0171 583 0808
• 1 Pump Court	0171 583 2012/353 4341
2 Pump Court	0171 353 5597
• Pump Court Chambers	0171 353 0711
• 5 Pump Court	020 7353 2532
6 Pump Court	0171 797 8400

• Expanded entry in Part C

A

• Queen Elizabeth Building	0171 353 7181 (12 Lines)
• Hollis Whiteman Chambers	020 7583 5766
• 3 Raymond Buildings	020 7831 3833
• 18 Red Lion Court	0171 520 6000
• 3 Serjeants' Inn	0171 353 5537
Somersett Chambers	0171 404 6701
• Stanbrook & Henderson	0171 353 0101
Staple Inn Chambers	0171 242 5240
7 Stone Buildings (also at 11 Bolt Court)	0171 242 0961
55 Temple Chambers	0171 353 7400
• 1 Temple Gardens	0171 583 1315/353 0407
• 3 Temple Gardens	0171 353 3102/5/9297
• Thomas More Chambers	0171 404 7000
Tollgate Mews Chambers	0171 511 1838
• 14 Tooks Court	0171 405 8828
Tower Hamlets Barristers Chambers	0171 377 8090
• 2-4 Tudor Street	0171 797 7111
Verulam Chambers	0171 813 2400
Virtual Chambers	07071 244 944
Warwick House Chambers	0171 430 2323

Luton	Beresford Chambers	01582 429111
Maidstone	Earl Street Chambers	01622 671222
	• Maidstone Chambers	01622 688592
	6-8 Mill Street	01622 688094
Manchester	• Byrom Street Chambers	0161 829 2100
	• Central Chambers	0161 236 1133
	• Cobden House Chambers	0161 833 6000
	Deans Court Chambers	0161 214 6000
	Kenworthy's Chambers	0161 832 4036/834 6954
	• 40 King Street	0161 832 9082
	• 8 King Street Chambers	0161 834 9560
	58 King Street Chambers	0161 831 7477
	Lincoln House Chambers	0161 832 5701
	• Chambers of Ian Macdonald QC (In Association with Two Garden Court, Temple, London)	0161 236 1840
	Peel Court Chambers	0161 832 3791
	• Queen's Chambers	0161 834 6875/4738
	• St James's Chambers	0161 834 7000
	18 St John Street	0161 278 1800
	24a St John Street	0161 833 9628
	• 28 St John Street	0161 834 8418
	Young Street Chambers	0161 833 0489
Middlesbrough	Baker Street Chambers	01642 873873
Newcastle upon Tyne	• Broad Chare	0191 232 0541
	Cathedral Chambers	0191 232 1311
	• Trinity Chambers	0191 232 1927
	Westgate Chambers	0191 261 4407/2329785
Northampton	Chartlands Chambers	01604 603322
	Chambers of Michael Pert QC	01604 602333
	Northampton Chambers	01604 636271
Norwich	East Anglian Chambers	01603 617351
	Octagon House	01603 623186
	Sackville Chambers	01603 613516/616221
Nottingham	High Pavement Chambers	0115 9418218
	King Charles House	0115 9418851
	St Mary's Chambers	0115 9503503
Oxford	Harcourt Chambers	01865 791559
	King's Bench Chambers	01865 311066
	3 Paper Buildings (Oxford)	01865 793736
Peterborough	Fenners Chambers	01733 562030

• Expanded entry in Part C

Plymouth	Devon Chambers	01752 661659
Pontyclun	Everest	01443 229850
Pontypridd	• Windsor Chambers	01443 402067
Preston	Deans Court Chambers	01772 555163
	New Bailey Chambers	01772 258087
	Queens Chambers	01772 828300
	15 Winckley Square	01772 252828
Reading	Wessex Chambers	0118 956 8856
Redhill	Redhill Chambers	01737 780781
Saint Albans	New Chambers	0966 212126
	St Albans Chambers	01727 843383
Sheffield	Bank House Chambers	0114 2751223
	Paradise Chambers	0114 2738951
Slough	Slough Chamber	01753 553806/817989
Southampton	• 17 Carlton Crescent	023 8032 0320/0823 2003
	• College Chambers	01703 230338
	• Eighteen Carlton Crescent	01703 639001
Stoke On Trent	Regent Chambers	01782 286666
Swansea	Angel Chambers	01792 464623/464648
	Chambers of Davina Gammon	01792 480770
	Iscoed Chambers	01792 652988/9/330
Swindon	Pump Court Chambers	01793 539899
Taunton	South Western Chambers	01823 331919 (24 hrs)
Winchester	3 Paper Buildings (Winchester)	01962 868884
	Pump Court Chambers	01962 868161
Wolverhampton	Claremont Chambers	01902 426222
Woodford Green	1 Wensley Avenue	0181 505 9259
York	• York Chambers	01904 620048

CRIME – CORPORATE FRAUD

Birmingham	Coleridge Chambers	0121 233 8500
	1 Fountain Court	0121 236 5721
	• 3 Fountain Court	0121 236 5854
	• 5 Fountain Court	0121 606 0500
	New Court Chambers	0121 693 6656
	• St Philip's Chambers	0121 246 7000
Brighton	Crown Office Row Chambers	01273 625625
Bristol	Guildhall Chambers	0117 9273366
	St John's Chambers	0117 9213456/298514
	Veritas Chambers	0117 930 8802
Cambridge	Fenners Chambers	01223 368761
Cardiff	9 Park Place	01222 382731
	30 Park Place	01222 398421
	32 Park Place	01222 397364
	• 33 Park Place	02920 233313
Chester	Nicholas Street Chambers	01244 323886
	Sedan House	01244 320480/348282
	White Friars Chambers	01244 323070
Chichester	Chichester Chambers	01243 784538
Exeter	Walnut House	01392 279751
Guildford	• Guildford Chambers	01483 539131
Leeds	11 King's Bench Walk	0113 297 1200
	No. 6	0113 2459763
	Park Lane Chambers	0113 2285000
	The Chambers of Philip Raynor QC	0113 242 1123
	• 30 Park Square	0113 2436388
	• 37 Park Square Chambers	0113 2439422
	• Sovereign Chambers	0113 2451841/2/3
	• St Paul's House	0113 2455866
Leicester	Chambers of Michael Pert QC	0116 249 2020
Liverpool	25-27 Castle Street	0151 227 5661/051 236 5072

• Expanded entry in Part C

London

• Corn Exchange Chambers	0151 227 1081/5009
• Exchange Chambers	0151 236 7747
India Buildings Chambers	0151 243 6000
9 Bedford Row	0171 242 3555
33 Bedford Row	0171 242 6476
• Chambers of Michael Pert QC	0171 421 8000
• 9-12 Bell Yard	0171 400 1800
Bell Yard Chambers	0171 306 9292
• Blackstone Chambers	0171 583 1770
11 Bolt Court (also at 7 Stone Buildings – 1st Floor)	0171 353 2300
Bracton Chambers	0171 242 4248
• 4 Brick Court, Chambers of Anne Rafferty QC	0171 583 8455
Bridewell Chambers	020 7797 8800
Cardinal Chambers	020 7353 2622
Cloisters	0171 827 4000
• 1 Crown Office Row, Ground Floor	0171 797 7500
1 Crown Office Row, 3rd Floor	0171 583 9292
• Devereux Chambers	0171 353 7534
• Doughty Street Chambers	0171 404 1313
1 Dr Johnson's Buildings	0171 353 9328
2 Dyers Buildings	0171 404 1881
• One Essex Court	0171 936 3030
23 Essex Street	0171 413 0353/836 8366
• 35 Essex Street	0171 353 6381
Chambers of Geoffrey Hawker	0171 583 8899
Chambers of Wilfred Forster-Jones	0171 353 0853/4/7222
Francis Taylor Building	0171 353 7768/7769/2711
• Furnival Chambers	0171 405 3232
• Two Garden Court	0171 353 1633
• Goldsmith Building	0171 353 7881
Goldsmith Chambers	0171 353 6802/3/4/5
• 9 Gough Square	020 7832 0500
• Gough Square Chambers	0171 353 0924
• Gray's Inn Chambers, The Chambers of Norman Patterson	0171 831 5344
• 2-3 Gray's Inn Square	0171 242 4986
2 Gray's Inn Square Chambers	020 7242 0328
• 3 Gray's Inn Square	0171 520 5600
• 4-5 Gray's Inn Square	0171 404 5252
6 Gray's Inn Square	0171 242 1052
Counsels' Chambers	0171 405 2576
• 1 Harcourt Buildings	0171 353 9421/0375
• 2 Harcourt Buildings, Ground Floor/Left	0171 583 9020
2 Harcourt Buildings, 1st Floor	020 7353 2112
• Hardwicke Building	020 7242 2523
• 1 Hare Court	0171 353 3982/5324
• One Hare Court	020 7353 3171
• 3 Hare Court	0171 395 2000
• Harrow on the Hill Chambers	0181 423 7444
John Street Chambers	0171 242 1911
• One King's Bench Walk	0171 936 1500
• 4 King's Bench Walk	0171 822 8822
• 6 King's Bench Walk, Ground Floor	0171 583 0410
6 King's Bench Walk, Ground, Third & Fourth Floors	0171 353 4931/583 0695
8 King's Bench Walk	0171 797 8888
9 King's Bench Walk	0171 353 7202/3909
10 King's Bench Walk	0171 353 7742
11 King's Bench Walk	0171 353 3337

• 13 King's Bench Walk	0171 353 7204
• Lamb Building	020 7797 7788
Lion Court	0171 404 6565
• Littleton Chambers	0171 797 8600
• 1 Middle Temple Lane	0171 583 0659 (12 Lines)
• Mitre Court Chambers	0171 353 9394
• Mitre House Chambers	0171 583 8233
• Monckton Chambers	0171 405 7211
• New Court	0171 583 5123/0510
• 12 New Square	0171 419 1212
11 Old Square	0171 242 5022/405 1074
• 2 Paper Buildings	020 7556 5500
• 3 Paper Buildings	020 7583 8055
• 4 Paper Buildings	0171 583 0816/353 1131
Five Paper Buildings	0171 583 6117
Phoenix Chambers	0171 404 7888
• 1 Pump Court	0171 583 2012/353 4341
2 Pump Court	0171 353 5597
• Pump Court Chambers	0171 353 0711
• Chambers of Kieran Coonan QC	0171 583 6013/2510
6 Pump Court	0171 797 8400
• Queen Elizabeth Building	0171 353 7181 (12 Lines)
• Hollis Whiteman Chambers	020 7583 5766
• 3 Raymond Buildings	020 7831 3833
• 18 Red Lion Court	0171 520 6000
No. 1 Serjeants' Inn	0171 415 6666
• Stanbrook & Henderson	0171 353 0101
7 Stone Buildings (also at 11 Bolt Court)	0171 242 0961
• 9 Stone Buildings	0171 404 5055
11 Stone Buildings	+44 (0)207 831 6381
• 199 Strand	0171 379 9779
55 Temple Chambers	0171 353 7400
• 3 Temple Gardens	0171 353 3102/5/9297
• Thomas More Chambers	0171 404 7000
• 2-4 Tudor Street	0171 797 7111
Virtual Chambers	07071 244 944
Warwick House Chambers	0171 430 2323

Maidstone

6-8 Mill Street	01622 688094

Manchester

• Central Chambers	0161 236 1133
• Cobden House Chambers	0161 833 6000
Deans Court Chambers	0161 214 6000
Kenworthy's Chambers	0161 832 4036/834 6954
• 40 King Street	0161 832 9082
• 8 King Street Chambers	0161 834 9560
58 King Street Chambers	0161 831 7477
Lincoln House Chambers	0161 832 5701
• Chambers of Ian Macdonald QC (In Association with Two Garden Court, Temple, London)	0161 236 1840
Peel Court Chambers	0161 832 3791
• St James's Chambers	0161 834 7000
18 St John Street	0161 278 1800
24a St John Street	0161 833 9628
• 28 St John Street	0161 834 8418
Young Street Chambers	0161 833 0489

Northampton

Chambers of Michael Pert QC	01604 602333

Nottingham

High Pavement Chambers	0115 9418218
St Mary's Chambers	0115 9503503

Oxford

King's Bench Chambers	01865 311066
3 Paper Buildings (Oxford)	01865 793736

Peterborough

Fenners Chambers	01733 562030

• Expanded entry in Part C

Plymouth	Devon Chambers	01752 661659
Pontyclun	Everest	01443 229850
Pontypridd	● Windsor Chambers	01443 402067
Preston	Deans Court Chambers	01772 555163
	New Bailey Chambers	01772 258087
	Queens Chambers	01772 828300
	15 Winckley Square	01772 252828
Redhill	Redhill Chambers	01737 780781
Saint Albans	New Chambers	0966 212126
	St Albans Chambers	01727 843383
Slough	Slough Chamber	01753 553806/817989
Southampton	● 17 Carlton Crescent	023 8032 0320/0823 2003
Swansea	Angel Chambers	01792 464623/464648
	Iscoed Chambers	01792 652988/9/330
Swindon	Pump Court Chambers	01793 539899
Taunton	South Western Chambers	01823 331919 (24 hrs)
Winchester	3 Paper Buildings (Winchester)	01962 868884
	Pump Court Chambers	01962 868161
Wolverhampton	Claremont Chambers	01902 426222

CRIME – CORPORATE MANSLAUGHTER

London	● Hardwicke Building	020 7242 2523

CUSTOMS & EXCISE – SERIOUS FRAUD

London	5 Essex Court	0171 410 2000

DAMAGES

London	● 4 Paper Buildings	0171 353 3366/583 7155

DEFAMATION

Birmingham	● 5 Fountain Court	0121 606 0500
Bristol	St John's Chambers	0117 9213456/298514
Cardiff	30 Park Place	01222 398421
	32 Park Place	01222 397364
Chester	Nicholas Street Chambers	01244 323886
	White Friars Chambers	01244 323070
Leeds	11 King's Bench Walk	0113 297 1200
	The Chambers of Philip Raynor QC	0113 242 1123
	● 37 Park Square Chambers	0113 2439422
Liverpool	25-27 Castle Street	0151 227 5661/051 236 5072
	● Corn Exchange Chambers	0151 227 1081/5009
	India Buildings Chambers	0151 243 6000
London	Barristers' Common Law Chambers	0171 375 3012
	9 Bedford Row	0171 242 3555
	17 Bedford Row	0171 831 7314
	● Blackstone Chambers	0171 583 1770
	1 Brick Court	0171 353 8845
	Brick Court Chambers	0171 379 3550
	Cloisters	0171 827 4000
	1 Crown Office Row	0171 583 9292
	● Devereux Chambers	0171 353 7534
	● Doughty Street Chambers	0171 404 1313
	1 Dr Johnson's Buildings	0171 353 9328
	● One Essex Court	0171 936 3030
	23 Essex Street	0171 413 0353/836 8366
	● Farrar's Building	0171 583 9241
	● Chambers of Norman Palmer	0171 405 6114
	● 4 Field Court	0171 440 6900
	● Fountain Court	0171 583 3335
	Francis Taylor Building	0171 353 7768/7769/2711
	● Goldsmith Building	0171 353 7881

● Expanded entry in Part C

	• 4-5 Gray's Inn Square	0171 404 5252
	• Hardwicke Building	020 7242 2523
	• Harrow on the Hill Chambers	0181 423 7444
	John Street Chambers	0171 242 1911
	9 King's Bench Walk	0171 353 7202/3909
	• 11 King's Bench Walk,	0171 632 8500/583 0610
	11 King's Bench Walk, 1st Floor	0171 353 3337
	2 King's Bench Walk Chambers	020 7353 9276
	• Littleton Chambers	0171 797 8600
	2 Mitre Court Buildings	0171 353 1353
	• New Court Chambers	0171 831 9500
	7 New Square	020 7404 5484
	The Chambers of Leolin Price CBE, QC	0171 405 0758
	• 4 Paper Buildings	0171 353 3366/583 7155
	Five Paper Buildings	0171 583 6117
	• Pump Court Chambers	0171 353 0711
	• 5 Raymond Buildings	0171 242 2902
	No. 1 Serjeants' Inn	0171 415 6666
	• 3 Serjeants' Inn	0171 353 5537
	• Thomas More Chambers	0171 404 7000
	• 14 Tooks Court	0171 405 8828
	• 2-4 Tudor Street	0171 797 7111
	Warwick House Chambers	0171 430 2323
Manchester	• Cobden House Chambers	0161 833 6000
	Kenworthy's Chambers	0161 832 4036/834 6954
	• 40 King Street	0161 832 9082
	Lincoln House Chambers	0161 832 5701
	• Queen's Chambers	0161 834 6875/4738
	• St James's Chambers	0161 834 7000
Newcastle upon Tyne	• Broad Chare	0191 232 0541
Northampton	Chartlands Chambers	01604 603322
Oxford	King's Bench Chambers	01865 311066
Pontypridd	• Windsor Chambers	01443 402067
Preston	Queens Chambers	01772 828300
Sheffield	Paradise Chambers	0114 2738951
Stoke On Trent	Regent Chambers	01782 286666
Swindon	Pump Court Chambers, 5 Temple Chambers	01793 539899
Winchester	Pump Court Chambers, 31 Southgate Street	01962 868161

DISCIPLINARY TRIBUNALS

Leeds	• 37 Park Square Chambers	0113 2439422
London	6 Gray's Inn Square	0171 242 1052

DISCRIMINATION

Birmingham	• 5 Fountain Court	0121 606 0500
	• 8 Fountain Court	0121 236 5514/5
	• St Philip's Chambers	0121 246 7000
Bradford	Broadway House Chambers	01274 722560
Bristol	Guildhall Chambers	0117 9273366
	Old Square Chambers	0117 9277111
	St John's Chambers	0117 9213456/298514
Cambridge	Fenners Chambers	01223 368761
Cardiff	30 Park Place	01222 398421
Chester	Nicholas Street Chambers	01244 323886
	White Friars Chambers	01244 323070
Exeter	Walnut House	01392 279751
Leeds	Chambers of Andrew Campbell QC	0113 2455438
	Broadway House Chambers	0113 246 2600
	The Chambers of Philip Raynor QC	0113 242 1123
	• 37 Park Square Chambers	0113 2439422
Leicester	Chambers of Michael Pert QC	0116 249 2020

• Expanded entry in Part C

A

Liverpool	25-27 Castle Street	0151 227 5661/051 236 5072
	• Corn Exchange Chambers	0151 227 1081/5009
	India Buildings Chambers	0151 243 6000
	• Oriel Chambers	0151 236 7191/236 4321
London	Barnard's Inn Chambers	0171 369 6969
	Barristers' Common Law Chambers	0171 375 3012
	• Chambers of Michael Pert QC	0171 421 8000
	• Blackstone Chambers	0171 583 1770
	11 Bolt Court (also at 7 Stone Buildings – 1st Floor)	0171 353 2300
	Bridewell Chambers	020 7797 8800
	39 Windsor Road	0181 349 9194
	Cloisters	0171 827 4000
	1 Crown Office Row	0171 583 9292
	• Devereux Chambers	0171 353 7534
	• Doughty Street Chambers	0171 404 1313
	• Essex Court Chambers	0171 813 8000
	• 39 Essex Street	0171 832 1111
	• Chambers of Norman Palmer	0171 405 6114
	• 4 Field Court	0171 440 6900
	Chambers of Wilfred Forster-Jones	0171 353 0853/4/7222
	• Fountain Court	0171 583 3335
	• Two Garden Court	0171 353 1633
	• Gray's Inn Chambers, The Chambers of Norman Patterson	0171 831 5344
	2 Gray's Inn Square Chambers	020 7242 0328
	• 4-5 Gray's Inn Square	0171 404 5252
	Counsels' Chambers	0171 405 2576
	• One Hare Court	020 7353 3171
	• Harrow on the Hill Chambers	0181 423 7444
	John Street Chambers	0171 242 1911
	Justice Court Chambers	0181 830 7786
	6 King's Bench Walk	0171 353 4931/583 0695
	8 King's Bench Walk	0171 797 8888
	• 11 King's Bench Walk,	0171 632 8500/583 0610
	11 King's Bench Walk, 1st Floor	0171 353 3337
	• 13 King's Bench Walk	0171 353 7204
	• Littleton Chambers	0171 797 8600
	• Littman Chambers	020 7404 4866
	• Mitre Court Chambers	0171 353 9394
	• Mitre House Chambers	0171 583 8233
	• New Court Chambers	0171 831 9500
	• Chambers of John L Powell QC	0171 797 8000
	• Old Square Chambers	0171 269 0300
	• 4 Paper Buildings	0171 583 0816/353 1131
	Five Paper Buildings	0171 583 6117
	• 1 Pump Court	0171 583 2012/353 4341
	Somersett Chambers	0171 404 6701
	7 Stone Buildings (also at 11 Bolt Court)	0171 242 0961
	• 9 Stone Buildings	0171 404 5055
	• 199 Strand	0171 379 9779
	55 Temple Chambers	0171 353 7400
	• Thomas More Chambers	0171 404 7000
	• 14 Tooks Court	0171 405 8828
	Wynne Chambers	0181 961 6144
Manchester	• Central Chambers	0161 236 1133
	• 40 King Street	0161 832 9082
	• 8 King Street Chambers	0161 834 9560
	Lincoln House Chambers	0161 832 5701
	•	

	Chambers of Ian Macdonald QC (In Association with Two Garden Court, Temple, London)	0161 236 1840
	• Queen's Chambers	0161 834 6875/4738
	• St James's Chambers	0161 834 7000
Middlesbrough	Baker Street Chambers	01642 873873
Newcastle upon Tyne	Milburn House Chambers	0191 230 5511
Northampton	Chambers of Michael Pert QC	01604 602333
Norwich	Sackville Chambers	01603 613516/616221
Peterborough	Fenners Chambers	01733 562030
Pontypridd	• Windsor Chambers	01443 402067
Preston	New Bailey Chambers	01772 258087
	Queens Chambers	01772 828300
Redhill	Redhill Chambers	01737 780781
Slough	Slough Chamber	01753 553806/817989
Swansea	Angel Chambers	01792 464623/464648
Wolverhampton	Claremont Chambers	01902 426222

DRINK AND DRIVING

London	Gray's Inn Chambers	0171 831 7888 (Chambers)/ 0171 831 7904 (Mr M Ullah)

E-COMMERCE

London	Virtual Chambers	07071 244 944

EC AND COMPETITION LAW

Birmingham	1 Fountain Court	0121 236 5721
	• 5 Fountain Court	0121 606 0500
	• St Philip's Chambers	0121 246 7000
Bournemouth	3 Paper Buildings (Bournemouth)	01202 292102
Bristol	Old Square Chambers	0117 9277111
	St John's Chambers	0117 9213456/298514
Guildford	• Guildford Chambers	01483 539131
Leeds	• Chancery House Chambers	0113 244 6691
	The Chambers of Philip Raynor QC	0113 242 1123
	• Sovereign Chambers	0113 2451841/2/3
London	• Arden Chambers	020 7242 4244
	• Blackstone Chambers	0171 583 1770
	11 Bolt Court (also at 7 Stone Buildings – 1st Floor)	0171 353 2300
	• 4 Breams Buildings	0171 353 5835/430 1221
	• 4 Brick Court	0171 797 8910
	Brick Court Chambers	0171 379 3550
	Bridewell Chambers	020 7797 8800
	Cloisters	0171 827 4000
	• One Essex Court	020 7583 2000
	• 4 Essex Court	020 7797 7970
	• Essex Court Chambers	0171 813 8000
	• 20 Essex Street	0171 583 9294
	• 39 Essex Street	0171 832 1111
	Falcon Chambers	0171 353 2484
	• 4 Field Court	0171 440 6900
	• Fountain Court	0171 583 3335
	Francis Taylor Building	0171 353 7768/7769/2711
	• Two Garden Court	0171 353 1633
	96 Gray's Inn Road	0171 405 0585
	• 4-5 Gray's Inn Square	0171 404 5252
	Counsels' Chambers	0171 405 2576
	• 1 Harcourt Buildings	0171 353 9421/0375
	• 2 Harcourt Buildings	020 7353 8415
	• One Hare Court	020 7353 3171

• Expanded entry in Part C

A

Chambers of Harjit Singh	0171 353 1356 (4 Lines)
John Street Chambers	0171 242 1911
• Keating Chambers	0171 544 2600
• 4 King's Bench Walk	0171 822 8822
S Tomlinson QC	0171 583 0404
• 11 King's Bench Walk	0171 632 8500/583 0610
Lamb Chambers	020 7797 8300
• Littleton Chambers	0171 797 8600
• Littman Chambers	020 7404 4866
• Mitre House Chambers	0171 583 8233
• Monckton Chambers	0171 405 7211
• 3 New Square	0171 405 1111
5 New Square	020 7404 0404
• 8 New Square	0171 405 4321
19 Old Buildings	0171 405 2001
24 Old Buildings	020 7242 2744
The Chambers of Leolin Price CBE, QC	0171 405 0758
13 Old Square	0171 404 4800
• Old Square Chambers	0171 269 0300
• 4 Paper Buildings	0171 353 3366/583 7155
• 5 Paper Buildings	0171 583 9275/583 4555
• 5 Pump Court	020 7353 2532
No. 1 Serjeants' Inn	0171 415 6666
7 Stone Buildings (also at 11 Bolt Court)	0171 242 0961
• 9 Stone Buildings	0171 404 5055
• 2 Temple Gardens	0171 583 6041
3 Verulam Buildings	0171 831 8441
Verulam Chambers	0171 813 2400

Manchester	• 40 King Street	0161 832 9082
	• 8 King Street Chambers	0161 834 9560
	Peel Court Chambers	0161 832 3791
	• 28 St John Street	0161 834 8418
Pontypridd	• Windsor Chambers	01443 402067
Portsmouth	• Portsmouth Barristers' Chambers	023 92 831292/811811
Preston	New Bailey Chambers	01772 258087
Redhill	Redhill Chambers	01737 780781

EC LAW

Cardiff	30 Park Place	01222 398421
London	• Thomas More Chambers	0171 404 7000

ECCLESIASTICAL

Birmingham	1 Fountain Court	0121 236 5721
Bournemouth	3 Paper Buildings (Bournemouth)	01202 292102
Bristol	Guildhall Chambers	0117 9273366
	St John's Chambers	0117 9213456/298514
	Veritas Chambers	0117 930 8802
Durham	Durham Barristers' Chambers	0191 386 9199
Leeds	• 30 Park Square	0113 2436388
London	Francis Taylor Building	0171 353 7768/7769/2711
	• 2 Harcourt Buildings, Ground Floor/Left	0171 583 9020
	• 2 Harcourt Buildings, 2nd Floor	020 7353 8415
	• Harcourt Chambers	0171 353 6961
	• Mitre Court Chambers	0171 353 9394
	• Twenty-Four Old Buildings	0171 404 0946
	The Chambers of Leolin Price CBE, QC	0171 405 0758
	11 Old Square, Ground Floor	0171 242 5022/405 1074
	• 11 Old Square, Ground Floor	020 7430 0341
	• 3 Paper Buildings	020 7583 8055
	• Pump Court Chambers	0171 353 0711
	• Stanbrook & Henderson	0171 353 0101

• Expanded entry in Part C

Newcastle upon Tyne	
Oxford	
Swindon	
Winchester	

8 Stone Buildings	0171 831 9881
Verulam Chambers	0171 813 2400
• Wilberforce Chambers	0171 306 0102
• Broad Chare	0191 232 0541
Harcourt Chambers	01865 791559
3 Paper Buildings (Oxford)	01865 793736
28 Western Road	01865 204911
Pump Court Chambers	01793 539899
3 Paper Buildings (Winchester)	01962 868884
Pump Court Chambers	01962 868161

EDUCATION

Birmingham	
Bristol	
Cardiff	
Chesterfield	
Guildford	
Leeds	
Liverpool	
London	

• 3 Fountain Court	0121 236 5854
• 5 Fountain Court	0121 606 0500
• St Philip's Chambers	0121 246 7000
Old Square Chambers	0117 9277111
St John's Chambers	0117 9213456/298514
30 Park Place	01222 398421
26 Morley Avenue	01246 234790/01298 871350
• Guildford Chambers	01483 539131
• Chancery House Chambers	0113 244 6691
The Chambers of Philip Raynor QC	0113 242 1123
25-27 Castle Street	0151 227 5661/051 236 5072
India Buildings Chambers	0151 243 6000
Barristers' Common Law Chambers	0171 375 3012
9 Bedford Row	0171 242 3555
11 Bolt Court (also at 7 Stone Buildings – 1st Floor)	0171 353 2300
• 4 Breams Buildings	0171 353 5835/430 1221
Cardinal Chambers	020 7353 2622
Cloisters	0171 827 4000
• Devereux Chambers	0171 353 7534
• Doughty Street Chambers	0171 404 1313
1 Dr Johnson's Buildings	0171 353 9328
• 39 Essex Street	0171 832 1111
Chambers of Geoffrey Hawker	0171 583 8899
• Chambers of Norman Palmer	0171 405 6114
One Garden Court Family Law Chambers	0171 797 7900
• Two Garden Court	0171 353 1633
• 4-5 Gray's Inn Square	0171 404 5252
Counsels' Chambers	0171 405 2576
• 2 Harcourt Buildings, Ground Floor/Left	0171 583 9020
• 2 Harcourt Buildings, 2nd Floor	020 7353 8415
• Harcourt Chambers	0171 353 6961
• One Hare Court	020 7353 3171
• Harrow on the Hill Chambers	0181 423 7444
Justice Court Chambers	0181 830 7786
• One King's Bench Walk	0171 936 1500
2 King's Bench Walk	0171 353 1746
4 King's Bench Walk	020 7353 3581
6 King's Bench Walk	0171 353 4931/583 0695
8 King's Bench Walk	0171 797 8888
• 11 King's Bench Walk	0171 632 8500/583 0610
2 King's Bench Walk Chambers	020 7353 9276
• Littleton Chambers	0171 797 8600
2 Mitre Court Buildings	0171 583 1380
• Mitre House Chambers	0171 583 8233
• Chambers of John L Powell QC	0171 797 8000
• 22 Old Buildings	0171 831 0222
The Chambers of Leolin Price CBE, QC	0171 405 0758
11 Old Square	0171 242 5022/405 1074

• Expanded entry in Part C

A

	• Old Square Chambers	0171 269 0300
	• 5 Paper Buildings	0171 583 9275/583 4555
	Phoenix Chambers	0171 404 7888
	• 1 Pump Court	0171 583 2012/353 4341
	• Queen Elizabeth Building	0171 353 7181 (12 Lines)
	No. 1 Serjeants' Inn	0171 415 6666
	7 Stone Buildings (also at 11 Bolt Court)	0171 242 0961
	• 199 Strand	0171 379 9779
	55 Temple Chambers	0171 353 7400
	• 3 Temple Gardens	0171 353 3102/5/9297
	• 14 Tooks Court	0171 405 8828
Manchester	• Central Chambers	0161 236 1133
	• 40 King Street	0161 832 9082
	• 8 King Street Chambers	0161 834 9560
	• Chambers of Ian Macdonald QC (In Association with Two Garden Court, Temple, London)	0161 236 1840
	• St James's Chambers	0161 834 7000
	Young Street Chambers	0161 833 0489
Middlesbrough	Baker Street Chambers	01642 873873
Nottingham	Ropewalk Chambers	0115 9472581
Oxford	Harcourt Chambers	01865 791559
Plymouth	Devon Chambers	01752 661659
Redhill	Redhill Chambers	01737 780781
Slough	Slough Chamber	01753 553806/817989
Southampton	• 17 Carlton Crescent	023 8032 0320/0823 2003
York	• York Chambers	01904 620048

EMPLOYMENT

Birmingham	Coleridge Chambers	0121 233 8500
	1 Fountain Court	0121 236 5721
	• 3 Fountain Court	0121 236 5854
	• 5 Fountain Court	0121 606 0500
	6 Fountain Court	0121 233 3282
	• 8 Fountain Court	0121 236 5514/5
	New Court Chambers	0121 693 6656
	• St Philip's Chambers	0121 246 7000
Bournemouth	3 Paper Buildings (Bournemouth)	01202 292102
Bradford	Broadway House Chambers	01274 722560
Brighton	Crown Office Row Chambers	01273 625625
Bristol	Assize Court Chambers	0117 9264587
	Guildhall Chambers	0117 9273366
	Old Square Chambers	0117 9277111
	St John's Chambers	0117 9213456/298514
Cambridge	Fenners Chambers	01223 368761
Canterbury	• Becket Chambers	01227 786331
	Stour Chambers	01227 764899
Cardiff	9 Park Place	01222 382731
	30 Park Place	01222 398421
	32 Park Place	01222 397364
	• 33 Park Place	02920 233313
Chester	Nicholas Street Chambers	01244 323886
	Sedan House	01244 320480/348282
	White Friars Chambers	01244 323070
Chichester	Chichester Chambers	01243 784538
Colchester	East Anglian Chambers	01206 572756
Consett	6 Ascot Road	01207 507785
Eastbourne	King's Chambers	01323 416053
Exeter	Cathedral Chambers (Jan Wood Independent Barristers' Clerk)	01392 210900
	Walnut House	01392 279751

• Expanded entry in Part C

A

Guildford
Hull
Ipswich
Leatherhead
Leeds

• Guildford Chambers	01483 539131
Wilberforce Chambers	01482 323264
East Anglian Chambers	01473 214481
Pembroke House	01372 376160/376493
Chambers of Andrew Campbell QC	0113 2455438
Broadway House Chambers	0113 246 2600
• Chancery House Chambers	0113 244 6691
Enterprise Chambers	0113 246 0391
11 King's Bench Walk	0113 297 1200
• Mercury Chambers	0113 234 2265
No. 6	0113 2459763
Park Lane Chambers	0113 2285000
The Chambers of Philip Raynor QC	0113 242 1123
• 30 Park Square	0113 2436388
• 37 Park Square Chambers	0113 2439422
• Sovereign Chambers	0113 2451841/2/3
• St Paul's House	0113 2455866
• 9 Woodhouse Square	0113 2451986

Leicester
Liverpool

Chambers of Michael Pert QC	0116 249 2020
25-27 Castle Street	0151 227 5661/051 236 5072
19 Castle Street Chambers	0151 236 9402
Chavasse Court Chambers	0151 707 1191
• Corn Exchange Chambers	0151 227 1081/5009
• Exchange Chambers	0151 236 7747
First National Chambers	0151 236 2098
India Buildings Chambers	0151 243 6000
• Oriel Chambers	0151 236 7191/236 4321

London

Acre Lane Neighbourhood Chambers	0171 274 4400
Albany Chambers	0171 485 5736/5758
Arlington Chambers	0171 580 9188
Barnard's Inn Chambers	0171 369 6969
Barristers' Common Law Chambers	0171 375 3012
9 Bedford Row	0171 242 3555
17 Bedford Row	0171 831 7314
33 Bedford Row	0171 242 6476
• Chambers of Michael Pert QC	0171 421 8000
Bell Yard Chambers	0171 306 9292
• Blackstone Chambers	0171 583 1770
11 Bolt Court (also at 7 Stone Buildings – 1st Floor)	0171 353 2300
Bracton Chambers	0171 242 4248
• 4 Breams Buildings	0171 353 5835/430 1221
Brick Court Chambers	0171 379 3550
Bridewell Chambers	020 7797 8800
Britton Street Chambers	0171 608 3765
39 Windsor Road	0181 349 9194
Cloisters	0171 827 4000
1 Crown Office Row	0171 583 9292
• Devereux Chambers	0171 353 7534
• Doughty Street Chambers	0171 404 1313
1 Dr Johnson's Buildings	0171 353 9328
• Dr Johnson's Chambers	0171 353 4716
• Enterprise Chambers	0171 405 9471
Equity Barristers' Chambers	0181 558 8336
• One Essex Court	0171 936 3030
• 4 Essex Court	020 7797 7970
• Essex Court Chambers	0171 813 8000
23 Essex Street	0171 413 0353/836 8366
• 35 Essex Street	0171 353 6381
• 39 Essex Street	0171 832 1111
Chambers of Geoffrey Hawker	0171 583 8899

• Expanded entry in Part C

A

• Farrar's Building	0171 583 9241
• Chambers of Norman Palmer	0171 405 6114
• 4 Field Court	0171 440 6900
Chambers of Wilfred Forster-Jones	0171 353 0853/4/7222
• Fountain Court	0171 583 3335
Francis Taylor Building	0171 353 7768/7769/2711
• 2nd Floor, Francis Taylor Building	0171 353 9942/3157
• Two Garden Court	0171 353 1633
• Goldsmith Building	0171 353 7881
Goldsmith Chambers	0171 353 6802/3/4/5
• 9 Gough Square	020 7832 0500
• Gough Square Chambers	0171 353 0924
• Gray's Inn Chambers, The Chambers of Norman Patterson	0171 831 5344
96 Gray's Inn Road	0171 405 0585
• 2-3 Gray's Inn Square	0171 242 4986
2 Gray's Inn Square Chambers	020 7242 0328
• 4-5 Gray's Inn Square	0171 404 5252
6 Gray's Inn Square	0171 242 1052
Counsels' Chambers	0171 405 2576
• 1 Harcourt Buildings	0171 353 9421/0375
• 2 Harcourt Buildings	0171 583 9020
• Harcourt Chambers	0171 353 6961
• Hardwicke Building	020 7242 2523
Chambers of Harjit Singh	0171 353 1356 (4 Lines)
• Harrow on the Hill Chambers	0181 423 7444
• 1 Inner Temple Lane	020 7353 0933
John Street Chambers	0171 242 1911
Justice Court Chambers	0181 830 7786
2 King's Bench Walk	0171 353 1746
• 4 King's Bench Walk, Ground/First Floor/ Basement	0171 822 8822
4 King's Bench Walk, 2nd Floor	020 7353 3581
6 King's Bench Walk	0171 353 4931/583 0695
8 King's Bench Walk	0171 797 8888
9 King's Bench Walk	0171 353 7202/3909
10 King's Bench Walk	0171 353 7742
• 11 King's Bench Walk,	0171 632 8500/583 0610
11 King's Bench Walk, 1st Floor	0171 353 3337
• 12 King's Bench Walk	0171 583 0811
• 13 King's Bench Walk	0171 353 7204
2 King's Bench Walk Chambers	020 7353 9276
• Lamb Building	020 7797 7788
Lamb Chambers	020 7797 8300
Leone Chambers	0181 200 4020
• Littleton Chambers	0171 797 8600
• Littman Chambers	020 7404 4866
22 Melcombe Regis Court	0171 487 5589
2 Mitre Court Buildings, 1st Floor	0171 353 1353
2 Mitre Court Buildings, 2nd Floor	0171 583 1380
• Mitre Court Chambers	0171 353 9394
• Mitre House Chambers	0171 583 8233
• Monckton Chambers	0171 405 7211
• New Court	0171 583 5123/0510
• New Court Chambers	0171 831 9500
• 1 New Square	0171 405 0884/5/6/7
• Chambers of John L Powell QC	0171 797 8000
• 22 Old Buildings	0171 831 0222
The Chambers of Leolin Price CBE, QC	0171 405 0758
11 Old Square	0171 242 5022/405 1074
• Old Square Chambers	0171 269 0300

A

2 Paper Buildings, Basement North	0171 936 2613
• 3 Paper Buildings	020 7583 8055
• 4 Paper Buildings	0171 583 0816/353 1131
• 5 Paper Buildings	0171 583 9275/583 4555
Pepys' Chambers	0171 936 2710
Phoenix Chambers	0171 404 7888
Plowden Buildings	0171 583 0808
• 1 Pump Court	0171 583 2012/353 4341
2 Pump Court	0171 353 5597
• Pump Court Chambers	0171 353 0711
• 4 Pump Court	020 7842 5555
• 5 Pump Court	020 7353 2532
• Chambers of Kieran Coonan QC	0171 583 6013/2510
Queen Elizabeth Building	0171 797 7837
No. 1 Serjeants' Inn	0171 415 6666
• 3 Serjeants' Inn	0171 353 5537
Somersett Chambers	0171 404 6701
• Stanbrook & Henderson	0171 353 0101
Staple Inn Chambers	0171 242 5240
7 Stone Buildings (also at 11 Bolt Court)	0171 242 0961
8 Stone Buildings	0171 831 9881
• 9 Stone Buildings	0171 404 5055
• 199 Strand	0171 379 9779
55 Temple Chambers	0171 353 7400
• 1 Temple Gardens	0171 583 1315/353 0407
• 2 Temple Gardens	0171 583 6041
• 3 Temple Gardens	0171 353 3102/5/9297
• Thomas More Chambers	0171 404 7000
• 14 Tooks Court	0171 405 8828
Tower Hamlets Barristers Chambers	0171 377 8090
3 Verulam Buildings	0171 831 8441
Verulam Chambers	0171 813 2400
Warwick House Chambers	0171 430 2323
Wynne Chambers	0181 961 6144

Maidstone

Earl Street Chambers	01622 671222
• Maidstone Chambers	01622 688592

Manchester

• Central Chambers	0161 236 1133
• Cobden House Chambers	0161 833 6000
Deans Court Chambers	0161 214 6000
Kenworthy's Chambers	0161 832 4036/834 6954
• 40 King Street	0161 832 9082
• 8 King Street Chambers	0161 834 9560
58 King Street Chambers	0161 831 7477
Lincoln House Chambers	0161 832 5701
• Chambers of Ian Macdonald QC (In Association with Two Garden Court, Temple, London)	0161 236 1840
• Merchant Chambers	0161 839 7070
Peel Court Chambers	0161 832 3791
• Queen's Chambers	0161 834 6875/4738
• St James's Chambers	0161 834 7000
24a St John Street	0161 833 9628
• 28 St John Street	0161 834 8418

Middlesbrough

Baker Street Chambers	01642 873873

Newcastle upon Tyne

• Broad Chare	0191 232 0541
Cathedral Chambers	0191 232 1311
Enterprise Chambers	0191 222 3344
Milburn House Chambers	0191 230 5511
• Trinity Chambers	0191 232 1927
Westgate Chambers	0191 261 4407/2329785

Northampton

Chartlands Chambers	01604 603322

• Expanded entry in Part C

A

	Chambers of Michael Pert QC	01604 602333
	Northampton Chambers	01604 636271
Norwich	East Anglian Chambers	01603 617351
	Octagon House	01603 623186
	Sackville Chambers	01603 613516/616221
Nottingham	King Charles House	0115 9418851
	Ropewalk Chambers	0115 9472581
	St Mary's Chambers	0115 9503503
Oxford	Harcourt Chambers	01865 791559
	King's Bench Chambers	01865 311066
	3 Paper Buildings (Oxford)	01865 793736
Peterborough	Fenners Chambers	01733 562030
Plymouth	Devon Chambers	01752 661659
Pontypridd	• Windsor Chambers	01443 402067
Portsmouth	• Portsmouth Barristers' Chambers	023 92 831292/811811
Preston	Deans Court Chambers	01772 555163
	New Bailey Chambers	01772 258087
	Queens Chambers	01772 828300
	15 Winckley Square	01772 252828
Reading	Wessex Chambers	0118 956 8856
Redhill	Redhill Chambers	01737 780781
Saint Albans	St Albans Chambers	01727 843383
Sheffield	Paradise Chambers	0114 2738951
Slough	Slough Chamber	01753 553806/817989
Southampton	• 17 Carlton Crescent	023 8032 0320/0823 2003
	• College Chambers	01703 230338
	• Eighteen Carlton Crescent	01703 639001
Stoke On Trent	Regent Chambers	01782 286666
Swansea	Angel Chambers	01792 464623/464648
	Chambers of Davina Gammon	01792 480770
	Iscoed Chambers	01792 652988/9/330
Swindon	Pump Court Chambers	01793 539899
Taunton	South Western Chambers	01823 331919 (24 hrs)
Winchester	3 Paper Buildings (Winchester)	01962 868884
	Pump Court Chambers	01962 868161
Wolverhampton	Claremont Chambers	01902 426222
York	• York Chambers	01904 620048

ENERGY

Bristol	St John's Chambers	0117 9213456/298514
London	Atkin Chambers	020 7404 0102
	• Blackstone Chambers	0171 583 1770
	• 4 Breams Buildings	0171 353 5835/430 1221
	• One Essex Court	020 7583 2000
	• Essex Court Chambers	0171 813 8000
	• 20 Essex Street	0171 583 9294
	• 39 Essex Street	0171 832 1111
	• Fountain Court	0171 583 3335
	Francis Taylor Building	0171 353 7768/7769/2711
	2 Gray's Inn Square Chambers	020 7242 0328
	• 2 Harcourt Buildings	020 7353 8415
	• Hardwicke Building	020 7242 2523
	• One Hare Court	020 7353 3171
	S Tomlinson QC	0171 583 0404
	• Littman Chambers	020 7404 4866
	2 Mitre Court Buildings	0171 583 1380
	• 9 Old Square	0171 405 4682
	1 Serjeants' Inn	0171 583 1355
	• 7 Stone Buildings	0171 405 3886/242 3546
	• Wilberforce Chambers	0171 306 0102
Nottingham	Ropewalk Chambers	0115 9472581

• Expanded entry in Part C

A

Swansea	Iscoed Chambers	01792 652988/9/330

ENTERTAINMENT

Birmingham	1 Fountain Court	0121 236 5721
	• 5 Fountain Court	0121 606 0500
	• St Philip's Chambers	0121 246 7000
London	17 Bedford Row	0171 831 7314
	• Blackstone Chambers	0171 583 1770
	11 Bolt Court (also at 7 Stone Buildings – 1st Floor)	0171 353 2300
	Brick Court Chambers	0171 379 3550
	Cardinal Chambers	020 7353 2622
	Cloisters	0171 827 4000
	1 Crown Office Row	0171 583 9292
	• Devereux Chambers	0171 353 7534
	• 4 Essex Court	020 7797 7970
	• Essex Court Chambers	0171 813 8000
	• 39 Essex Street	0171 832 1111
	• Chambers of Norman Palmer	0171 405 6114
	• 4 Field Court	0171 440 6900
	• Fountain Court	0171 583 3335
	Francis Taylor Building	0171 353 7768/7769/2711
	2 Gray's Inn Square Chambers	020 7242 0328
	• Hardwicke Building	020 7242 2523
	• One Hare Court	020 7353 3171
	• 11 King's Bench Walk	0171 632 8500/583 0610
	Lion Court	0171 404 6565
	• Littleton Chambers	0171 797 8600
	• 1 New Square	0171 405 0884/5/6/7
	• 3 New Square	0171 405 1111
	5 New Square	020 7404 0404
	7 New Square	020 7404 5484
	• 8 New Square	0171 405 4321
	• 12 New Square	0171 419 1212
	19 Old Buildings	0171 405 2001
	• Twenty-Four Old Buildings	0171 404 0946
	The Chambers of Leolin Price CBE, QC	0171 405 0758
	Five Paper Buildings	0171 583 6117
	Phoenix Chambers	0171 404 7888
	• 4 Pump Court	020 7842 5555
	• 5 Raymond Buildings	0171 242 2902
	No. 1 Serjeants' Inn	0171 415 6666
	• 3 Stone Buildings	0171 242 4937
	• 7 Stone Buildings	0171 405 3886/242 3546
	7 Stone Buildings (also at 11 Bolt Court)	0171 242 0961
	• 9 Stone Buildings	0171 404 5055
	3 Verulam Buildings	0171 831 8441
	Verulam Chambers	0171 813 2400
Redhill	Redhill Chambers	01737 780781
Wolverhampton	Claremont Chambers	01902 426222

ENVIRONMENT

Birmingham	1 Fountain Court	0121 236 5721
	• 3 Fountain Court	0121 236 5854
	• 5 Fountain Court	0121 606 0500
	St Ive's Chambers	0121 236 0863/5720
	• St Philip's Chambers	0121 246 7000
Bradford	Broadway House Chambers	01274 722560
Bristol	Old Square Chambers	0117 9277111
	St John's Chambers	0117 9213456/298514
Cambridge	Fenners Chambers	01223 368761

• Expanded entry in Part C

A

Canterbury	• Becket Chambers	01227 786331
Cardiff	9 Park Place	01222 382731
	30 Park Place	01222 398421
	• 33 Park Place	02920 233313
Chesterfield	26 Morley Avenue	01246 234790/01298 871350
Durham	Durham Barristers' Chambers	0191 386 9199
Exeter	Walnut House	01392 279751
Leeds	Chambers of Andrew Campbell QC	0113 2455438
	Broadway House Chambers	0113 246 2600
	11 King's Bench Walk	0113 297 1200
	No. 6	0113 2459763
	The Chambers of Philip Raynor QC	0113 242 1123
	• Sovereign Chambers	0113 2451841/2/3
	• 9 Woodhouse Square	0113 2451986
Leicester	Chambers of Michael Pert QC	0116 249 2020
Liverpool	• Corn Exchange Chambers	0151 227 1081/5009
	• Exchange Chambers	0151 236 7747
	India Buildings Chambers	0151 243 6000
	• Oriel Chambers	0151 236 7191/236 4321
London	• Arden Chambers	020 7242 4244
	Atkin Chambers	020 7404 0102
	Barnard's Inn Chambers	0171 369 6969
	9 Bedford Row	0171 242 3555
	• Chambers of Michael Pert QC	0171 421 8000
	• Blackstone Chambers	0171 583 1770
	11 Bolt Court (also at 7 Stone Buildings – 1st Floor)	0171 353 2300
	• 4 Breams Buildings	0171 353 5835/430 1221
	Brick Court Chambers	0171 379 3550
	• 1 Crown Office Row	0171 797 7500
	• Devereux Chambers	0171 353 7534
	• Doughty Street Chambers	0171 404 1313
	• 4 Essex Court	020 7797 7970
	• Essex Court Chambers	0171 813 8000
	• 20 Essex Street	0171 583 9294
	• 39 Essex Street	0171 832 1111
	• 4 Field Court	0171 440 6900
	• Two Garden Court	0171 353 1633
	• Goldsmith Building	0171 353 7881
	• Gough Square Chambers	0171 353 0924
	• 2-3 Gray's Inn Square	0171 242 4986
	• 4-5 Gray's Inn Square	0171 404 5252
	Counsels' Chambers	0171 405 2576
	• 1 Harcourt Buildings	0171 353 9421/0375
	• 2 Harcourt Buildings, Ground Floor/Left	0171 583 9020
	2 Harcourt Buildings, 1st Floor	020 7353 2112
	• 2 Harcourt Buildings, 2nd Floor	020 7353 8415
	• One Hare Court	020 7353 3171
	• One King's Bench Walk	0171 936 1500
	• 4 King's Bench Walk	0171 822 8822
	8 King's Bench Walk	0171 797 8888
	10 King's Bench Walk	0171 353 7742
	• 11 King's Bench Walk	0171 632 8500/583 0610
	• 12 King's Bench Walk	0171 583 0811
	• 13 King's Bench Walk	0171 353 7204
	Lamb Chambers	020 7797 8300
	• Littman Chambers	020 7404 4866
	2 Mitre Court Buildings	0171 583 1380
	• Mitre House Chambers	0171 583 8233
	• Monckton Chambers	0171 405 7211
	• 3 New Square	0171 405 1111

A

	• Chambers of John L Powell QC	0171 797 8000
	• 12 New Square	0171 419 1212
	• 22 Old Buildings	0171 831 0222
	• 9 Old Square	0171 405 4682
	• Old Square Chambers	0171 269 0300
	Five Paper Buildings	0171 583 6117
	• 1 Pump Court	0171 583 2012/353 4341
	• Pump Court Chambers	0171 353 0711
	• 4 Pump Court	020 7842 5555
	• 5 Pump Court	020 7353 2532
	6 Pump Court	0171 797 8400
	• 3 Raymond Buildings	020 7831 3833
	1 Serjeants' Inn	0171 583 1355
	• 3 Serjeants' Inn	0171 353 5537
	• Stanbrook & Henderson	0171 353 0101
	7 Stone Buildings (also at 11 Bolt Court)	0171 242 0961
	• 199 Strand	0171 379 9779
	• 2 Temple Gardens	0171 583 6041
	• 3 Temple Gardens	0171 353 3102/5/9297
	3 Verulam Buildings	0171 831 8441
	Verulam Chambers	0171 813 2400
Maidstone	• Maidstone Chambers	01622 688592
	6-8 Mill Street	01622 688094
Manchester	• Cobden House Chambers	0161 833 6000
	Deans Court Chambers	0161 214 6000
	• 40 King Street	0161 832 9082
	• 8 King Street Chambers	0161 834 9560
	Lincoln House Chambers	0161 832 5701
	• Queen's Chambers	0161 834 6875/4738
	• St James's Chambers	0161 834 7000
	• 28 St John Street	0161 834 8418
Newcastle upon Tyne	• Broad Chare	0191 232 0541
Northampton	Chambers of Michael Pert QC	01604 602333
Nottingham	Ropewalk Chambers	0115 9472581
Peterborough	Fenners Chambers	01733 562030
Plymouth	Devon Chambers	01752 661659
Pontypridd	• Windsor Chambers	01443 402067
Preston	Deans Court Chambers	01772 555163
	New Bailey Chambers	01772 258087
	Queens Chambers	01772 828300
Redhill	Redhill Chambers	01737 780781
Slough	Slough Chamber	01753 553806/817989
Southampton	• 17 Carlton Crescent	023 8032 0320/0823 2003
	• College Chambers	01703 230338
Swansea	Angel Chambers	01792 464623/464648
	Iscoed Chambers	01792 652988/9/330
Swindon	Pump Court Chambers	01793 539899
Taunton	South Western Chambers	01823 331919 (24 hrs)
Winchester	Pump Court Chambers	01962 868161
Wolverhampton	Claremont Chambers	01902 426222
York	• York Chambers	01904 620048

ENVIRONMENTAL LAW AND POLLUTION

Leeds	• 37 Park Square Chambers	0113 2439422

EQUITY, WILLS AND TRUSTS

Birmingham	• 3 Fountain Court	0121 236 5854
	• 5 Fountain Court	0121 606 0500
	• 8 Fountain Court	0121 236 5514/5
	• St Philip's Chambers	0121 246 7000
Bradford	Broadway House Chambers	01274 722560

• Expanded entry in Part C

A

Bristol	Guildhall Chambers	0117 9273366
	St John's Chambers	0117 9213456/298514
Cambridge	Fenners Chambers	01223 368761
Cardiff	9 Park Place	01222 382731
	30 Park Place	01222 398421
	• 33 Park Place	02920 233313
Chester	White Friars Chambers	01244 323070
Eastbourne	King's Chambers	01323 416053
Exeter	Southernhay Chambers	01392 255777
Leeds	Chambers of Andrew Campbell QC	0113 2455438
	Broadway House Chambers	0113 246 2600
	• Chancery House Chambers	0113 244 6691
	Enterprise Chambers	0113 246 0391
	11 King's Bench Walk	0113 297 1200
	No. 6	0113 2459763
	The Chambers of Philip Raynor QC	0113 242 1123
	• Sovereign Chambers	0113 2451841/2/3
	• 9 Woodhouse Square	0113 2451986
Liverpool	• Exchange Chambers	0151 236 7747
	First National Chambers	0151 236 2098
London	Barnard's Inn Chambers	0171 369 6969
	11 Bolt Court (also at 7 Stone Buildings – 1st Floor)	0171 353 2300
	Bracton Chambers	0171 242 4248
	• 4 Breams Buildings	0171 353 5835/430 1221
	Bridewell Chambers	020 7797 8800
	• Chambers of Mr Peter Crampin QC	020 7831 0081
	• Enterprise Chambers	0171 405 9471
	Equity Barristers' Chambers	0181 558 8336
	• One Essex Court	0171 936 3030
	Chambers of Geoffrey Hawker	0171 583 8899
	• Chambers of Norman Palmer	0171 405 6114
	Francis Taylor Building	0171 353 7768/7769/2711
	• Gough Square Chambers	0171 353 0924
	8 Gray's Inn Square	0171 242 3529
	Counsels' Chambers	0171 405 2576
	• 1 Harcourt Buildings	0171 353 9421/0375
	• 2 Harcourt Buildings	0171 583 9020
	• Harcourt Chambers	0171 353 6961
	• Hardwicke Building	020 7242 2523
	Chambers of Harjit Singh	0171 353 1356 (4 Lines)
	• Harrow on the Hill Chambers	0181 423 7444
	Justice Court Chambers	0181 830 7786
	9 King's Bench Walk	0171 353 7202/3909
	11 King's Bench Walk	0171 353 3337
	• Lamb Building	020 7797 7788
	Lamb Chambers	020 7797 8300
	Lion Court	0171 404 6565
	• Littman Chambers	020 7404 4866
	• Mitre Court Chambers	0171 353 9394
	• Mitre House Chambers	0171 583 8233
	• 1 New Square	0171 405 0884/5/6/7
	• Chambers of Lord Goodhart QC	0171 405 5577
	5 New Square	020 7404 0404
	• 12 New Square	0171 419 1212
	• Twenty-Four Old Buildings	0171 404 0946
	24 Old Buildings	020 7242 2744
	• 9 Old Square	0171 405 4682
	The Chambers of Leolin Price CBE, QC	0171 405 0758
	11 Old Square, Ground Floor	0171 242 5022/405 1074
	• 11 Old Square, Ground Floor	020 7430 0341

• Expanded entry in Part C

	13 Old Square	0171 404 4800
	• 5 Paper Buildings	0171 583 9275/583 4555
	• 1 Pump Court	0171 583 2012/353 4341
	• Pump Court Chambers	0171 353 0711
	No. 1 Serjeants' Inn	0171 415 6666
	• Stanbrook & Henderson	0171 353 0101
	• 3 Stone Buildings	0171 242 4937
	4 Stone Buildings	0171 242 5524
	• 5 Stone Buildings	0171 242 6201
	• 7 Stone Buildings	0171 405 3886/242 3546
	7 Stone Buildings (also at 11 Bolt Court)	0171 242 0961
	• 9 Stone Buildings	0171 404 5055
	11 Stone Buildings	+44 (0)207 831 6381
	55 Temple Chambers	0171 353 7400
	Verulam Chambers	0171 813 2400
	• Wilberforce Chambers	0171 306 0102
Manchester	• Cobden House Chambers	0161 833 6000
	• 40 King Street	0161 832 9082
	58 King Street Chambers	0161 831 7477
	• Merchant Chambers	0161 839 7070
	• St James's Chambers	0161 834 7000
Milton Keynes	Milton Keynes Chambers	01908 664 128
Newcastle upon Tyne	• Broad Chare	0191 232 0541
	Enterprise Chambers	0191 222 3344
	• Trinity Chambers	0191 232 1927
	Westgate Chambers	0191 261 4407/2329785
Nottingham	King Charles House	0115 9418851
	Ropewalk Chambers	0115 9472581
	St Mary's Chambers	0115 9503503
Oxford	Harcourt Chambers	01865 791559
	28 Western Road	01865 204911
Peterborough	Fenners Chambers	01733 562030
Pontypridd	• Windsor Chambers	01443 402067
Portsmouth	• Portsmouth Barristers' Chambers	023 92 831292/811811
Preston	New Bailey Chambers	01772 258087
	15 Winckley Square	01772 252828
Reading	Wessex Chambers	0118 956 8856
Redhill	Redhill Chambers	01737 780781
Saint Albans	St Albans Chambers	01727 843383
Swansea	Iscoed Chambers	01792 652988/9/330
Swindon	Pump Court Chambers	01793 539899
Taunton	South Western Chambers	01823 331919 (24 hrs)
Winchester	Pump Court Chambers	01962 868161
Wolverhampton	Claremont Chambers	01902 426222
Woodford Green	1 Wensley Avenue	0181 505 9259
York	• York Chambers	01904 620048

EUROPEAN LAW

Stoke On Trent	Regent Chambers	01782 286666

EXTRADITION

London	• 4 Brick Court	0171 797 8910

FACTORING

Liverpool	• Oriel Chambers	0151 236 7191/236 4321

FAMILY

Birmingham	Coleridge Chambers	0121 233 8500
	1 Fountain Court	0121 236 5721
	• 3 Fountain Court	0121 236 5854
	• 5 Fountain Court	0121 606 0500

• Expanded entry in Part C

	6 Fountain Court	0121 233 3282
	• 8 Fountain Court	0121 236 5514/5
	New Court Chambers	0121 693 6656
	St Ive's Chambers	0121 236 0863/5720
	• St Philip's Chambers	0121 246 7000
Bournemouth	3 Paper Buildings (Bournemouth)	01202 292102
Bradford	Broadway House Chambers	01274 722560
Brighton	Crown Office Row Chambers	01273 625625
Bristol	Assize Court Chambers	0117 9264587
	Guildhall Chambers	0117 9273366
	St John's Chambers	0117 9213456/298514
	29 Gwilliam Street	0117 966 8997
Cambridge	Fenners Chambers	01223 368761
Canterbury	• Becket Chambers	01227 786331
	Stour Chambers	01227 764899
Cardiff	9 Park Place	01222 382731
	30 Park Place	01222 398421
	32 Park Place	01222 397364
	• 33 Park Place	02920 233313
Chester	Nicholas Street Chambers	01244 323886
	Sedan House	01244 320480/348282
	White Friars Chambers	01244 323070
Chichester	Chichester Chambers	01243 784538
Colchester	East Anglian Chambers	01206 572756
Durham	Durham Barristers' Chambers	0191 386 9199
Eastbourne	King's Chambers	01323 416053
Exeter	Cathedral Chambers (Jan Wood Independent Barristers' Clerk)	01392 210900
	Southernhay Chambers	01392 255777
	Walnut House	01392 279751
Guildford	• Guildford Chambers	01483 539131
Hull	Wilberforce Chambers	01482 323264
Ipswich	East Anglian Chambers	01473 214481
Leatherhead	Pembroke House	01372 376160/376493
Leeds	Chambers of Andrew Campbell QC	0113 2455438
	Broadway House Chambers	0113 246 2600
	11 King's Bench Walk	0113 297 1200
	No. 6	0113 2459763
	• Park Court Chambers	0113 2433277
	Park Lane Chambers	0113 2285000
	The Chambers of Philip Raynor QC	0113 242 1123
	• 30 Park Square	0113 2436388
	• 37 Park Square Chambers	0113 2439422
	• Sovereign Chambers	0113 2451841/2/3
	• St Paul's House	0113 2455866
	• 9 Woodhouse Square	0113 2451986
Leicester	Chambers of Michael Pert QC	0116 249 2020
Liverpool	25-27 Castle Street	0151 227 5661/051 236 5072
	19 Castle Street Chambers	0151 236 9402
	Chavasse Court Chambers	0151 707 1191
	• Corn Exchange Chambers	0151 227 1081/5009
	• Exchange Chambers	0151 236 7747
	First National Chambers	0151 236 2098
	India Buildings Chambers	0151 243 6000
	• Oriel Chambers	0151 236 7191/236 4321
London	ACHMA Chambers	0171 639 7817/0171 635 7904
	Acre Lane Neighbourhood Chambers	0171 274 4400
	Albany Chambers	0171 485 5736/5758
	Arlington Chambers	0171 580 9188
	Barristers' Common Law Chambers	0171 375 3012
	9 Bedford Row	0171 242 3555

17 Bedford Row	0171 831 7314
33 Bedford Row	0171 242 6476
• Chambers of Michael Pert QC	0171 421 8000
Bell Yard Chambers	0171 306 9292
11 Bolt Court (also at 7 Stone Buildings – 1st Floor)	0171 353 2300
Bracton Chambers	0171 242 4248
• 4 Brick Court	0171 797 8910
Bridewell Chambers	020 7797 8800
Cloisters	0171 827 4000
• 1 Crown Office Row, Ground Floor	0171 797 7500
1 Crown Office Row, 3rd Floor	0171 583 9292
1 Dr Johnson's Buildings	0171 353 9328
• 3 Dr Johnson's Buildings	0171 353 4854
• Dr Johnson's Chambers	0171 353 4716
• One Essex Court	0171 936 3030
23 Essex Street	0171 413 0353/836 8366
• 35 Essex Street	0171 353 6381
Chambers of Geoffrey Hawker	0171 583 8899
• Chambers of Norman Palmer	0171 405 6114
Fleet Chambers	0171 936 3707
Chambers of Wilfred Forster-Jones	0171 353 0853/4/7222
Francis Taylor Building	0171 353 7768/7769/2711
• 2nd Floor, Francis Taylor Building	0171 353 9942/3157
One Garden Court Family Law Chambers	0171 797 7900
• Two Garden Court	0171 353 1633
• Goldsmith Building	0171 353 7881
Goldsmith Chambers	0171 353 6802/3/4/5
• 9 Gough Square	020 7832 0500
• Gray's Inn Chambers, The Chambers of Norman Patterson	0171 831 5344
96 Gray's Inn Road	0171 405 0585
2 Gray's Inn Square Chambers	020 7242 0328
6 Gray's Inn Square	0171 242 1052
Counsels' Chambers	0171 405 2576
14 Gray's Inn Square	0171 242 0858
• 1 Harcourt Buildings	0171 353 9421/0375
• 2 Harcourt Buildings	0171 583 9020
• Harcourt Chambers	0171 353 6961
• Hardwicke Building	020 7242 2523
Chambers of Harjit Singh	0171 353 1356 (4 Lines)
• Harrow on the Hill Chambers	0181 423 7444
• 1 Inner Temple Lane	020 7353 0933
John Street Chambers	0171 242 1911
Justice Court Chambers	0181 830 7786
• One King's Bench Walk	0171 936 1500
2 King's Bench Walk	0171 353 1746
• 4 King's Bench Walk, Ground/First Floor/ Basement	0171 822 8822
4 King's Bench Walk, 2nd Floor	020 7353 3581
6 King's Bench Walk	0171 353 4931/583 0695
8 King's Bench Walk	0171 797 8888
9 King's Bench Walk	0171 353 7202/3909
10 King's Bench Walk	0171 353 7742
11 King's Bench Walk	0171 353 3337
• 13 King's Bench Walk	0171 353 7204
2 King's Bench Walk Chambers	020 7353 9276
• Lamb Building	020 7797 7788
Lamb Chambers	020 7797 8300
Leone Chambers	0181 200 4020
Lion Court	0171 404 6565

• Expanded entry in Part C

• Littleton Chambers	0171 797 8600
22 Melcombe Regis Court	0171 487 5589
1 Mitre Court Buildings	0171 797 7070
2 Mitre Court Buildings	0171 353 1353
• Mitre Court Chambers	0171 353 9394
• Mitre House Chambers	0171 583 8233
• New Court	0171 583 5123/0510
• New Court Chambers	0171 831 9500
• 1 New Square	0171 405 0884/5/6/7
• 22 Old Buildings	0171 831 0222
• Twenty-Four Old Buildings	0171 404 0946
The Chambers of Leolin Price CBE, QC	0171 405 0758
11 Old Square	0171 242 5022/405 1074
• 2 Paper Buildings	020 7556 5500
2 Paper Buildings, Basement North	0171 936 2613
• 3 Paper Buildings	020 7583 8055
• 4 Paper Buildings	0171 583 0816/353 1131
• 5 Paper Buildings	0171 583 9275/583 4555
Pepys' Chambers	0171 936 2710
Phoenix Chambers	0171 404 7888
Plowden Buildings	0171 583 0808
• 1 Pump Court	0171 583 2012/353 4341
2 Pump Court	0171 353 5597
• Pump Court Chambers	0171 353 0711
• 5 Pump Court	020 7353 2532
• Chambers of Kieran Coonan QC	0171 583 6013/2510
6 Pump Court	0171 797 8400
• Queen Elizabeth Building, Ground Floor	0171 353 7181 (12 Lines)
Queen Elizabeth Building, 2nd Floor	0171 797 7837
No. 1 Serjeants' Inn	0171 415 6666
Somersett Chambers	0171 404 6701
• Stanbrook & Henderson	0171 353 0101
Staple Inn Chambers	0171 242 5240
7 Stone Buildings (also at 11 Bolt Court)	0171 242 0961
55 Temple Chambers	0171 353 7400
• 3 Temple Gardens	0171 353 3102/5/9297
• Thomas More Chambers	0171 404 7000
Tollgate Mews Chambers	0171 511 1838
• 14 Tooks Court	0171 405 8828
Tower Hamlets Barristers Chambers	0171 377 8090
Verulam Chambers	0171 813 2400
Warwick House Chambers	0171 430 2323

Maidstone

Earl Street Chambers	01622 671222
• Maidstone Chambers	01622 688592
6-8 Mill Street	01622 688094

Manchester

• Central Chambers	0161 236 1133
• Cobden House Chambers	0161 833 6000
Deans Court Chambers	0161 214 6000
Kenworthy's Chambers	0161 832 4036/834 6954
• 40 King Street	0161 832 9082
• 8 King Street Chambers	0161 834 9560
58 King Street Chambers	0161 831 7477
Lincoln House Chambers	0161 832 5701
• Chambers of Ian Macdonald QC (In Association with Two Garden Court, Temple, London)	0161 236 1840
Peel Court Chambers	0161 832 3791
• Queen's Chambers	0161 834 6875/4738
• St James's Chambers	0161 834 7000
18 St John Street	0161 278 1800
24a St John Street	0161 833 9628

• Expanded entry in Part C

	• 28 St John Street	0161 834 8418
	Young Street Chambers	0161 833 0489
Middlesbrough	Baker Street Chambers	01642 873873
Newcastle upon Tyne	• Broad Chare	0191 232 0541
	Cathedral Chambers	0191 232 1311
	Westgate Chambers	0191 261 4407/2329785
Northampton	Chartlands Chambers	01604 603322
	Chambers of Michael Pert QC	01604 602333
	Northampton Chambers	01604 636271
Norwich	East Anglian Chambers	01603 617351
	Octagon House	01603 623186
	Sackville Chambers	01603 613516/616221
Nottingham	King Charles House	0115 9418851
	Ropewalk Chambers	0115 9472581
	St Mary's Chambers	0115 9503503
Oxford	Harcourt Chambers	01865 791559
	King's Bench Chambers	01865 311066
	3 Paper Buildings (Oxford)	01865 793736
	28 Western Road	01865 204911
Peterborough	Fenners Chambers	01733 562030
Plymouth	Devon Chambers	01752 661659
Pontypridd	• Windsor Chambers	01443 402067
Portsmouth	• Portsmouth Barristers' Chambers	023 92 831292/811811
Preston	Deans Court Chambers	01772 555163
	New Bailey Chambers	01772 258087
	Queens Chambers	01772 828300
	15 Winckley Square	01772 252828
Reading	Wessex Chambers	0118 956 8856
Redhill	Redhill Chambers	01737 780781
Rugby	Merriemore Cottage	01788 891832
Saint Albans	St Albans Chambers	01727 843383
Sheffield	Bank House Chambers	0114 2751223
	Paradise Chambers	0114 2738951
Slough	Slough Chamber	01753 553806/817989
Southampton	• 17 Carlton Crescent	023 8032 0320/0823 2003
	• College Chambers	01703 230338
	• Eighteen Carlton Crescent	01703 639001
Stoke On Trent	Regent Chambers	01782 286666
Swansea	Angel Chambers	01792 464623/464648
	Chambers of Davina Gammon	01792 480770
	Iscoed Chambers	01792 652988/9/330
Swindon	Pump Court Chambers	01793 539899
Taunton	South Western Chambers	01823 331919 (24 hrs)
Winchester	3 Paper Buildings (Winchester)	01962 868884
	Pump Court Chambers	01962 868161
Wolverhampton	Claremont Chambers	01902 426222
Woodford Green	1 Wensley Avenue	0181 505 9259
York	• York Chambers	01904 620048

FAMILY – CHILD ABDUCTION

London	• Hardwicke Building	020 7242 2523

FAMILY PROVISION

Birmingham	Coleridge Chambers	0121 233 8500
	1 Fountain Court	0121 236 5721
	• 3 Fountain Court	0121 236 5854
	• 5 Fountain Court	0121 606 0500
	• 8 Fountain Court	0121 236 5514/5
	• St Philip's Chambers	0121 246 7000
Bradford	Broadway House Chambers	01274 722560
Brighton	Crown Office Row Chambers	01273 625625

• Expanded entry in Part C

Bristol	Assize Court Chambers	0117 9264587
	Guildhall Chambers	0117 9273366
	St John's Chambers	0117 9213456/298514
Cambridge	Fenners Chambers	01223 368761
Canterbury	● Becket Chambers	01227 786331
	Stour Chambers	01227 764899
Cardiff	9 Park Place	01222 382731
	30 Park Place	01222 398421
	32 Park Place	01222 397364
	● 33 Park Place	02920 233313
Chester	Nicholas Street Chambers	01244 323886
	White Friars Chambers	01244 323070
Chichester	Chichester Chambers	01243 784538
Colchester	East Anglian Chambers	01206 572756
Exeter	Cathedral Chambers (Jan Wood	01392 210900
	Independent Barristers' Clerk)	
	Southernhay Chambers	01392 255777
	Walnut House	01392 279751
Guildford	● Guildford Chambers	01483 539131
Hull	Wilberforce Chambers	01482 323264
Ipswich	East Anglian Chambers	01473 214481
Leatherhead	Pembroke House	01372 376160/376493
Leeds	Chambers of Andrew Campbell QC	0113 2455438
	Broadway House Chambers	0113 246 2600
	11 King's Bench Walk	0113 297 1200
	● Mercury Chambers	0113 234 2265
	No. 6	0113 2459763
	The Chambers of Philip Raynor QC	0113 242 1123
	● 30 Park Square	0113 2436388
	● 37 Park Square Chambers	0113 2439422
	● Sovereign Chambers	0113 2451841/2/3
	● St Paul's House	0113 2455866
	● 9 Woodhouse Square	0113 2451986
Leicester	Chambers of Michael Pert QC	0116 249 2020
Liverpool	25-27 Castle Street	0151 227 5661/051 236 5072
	Chavasse Court Chambers	0151 707 1191
	● Corn Exchange Chambers	0151 227 1081/5009
	● Exchange Chambers	0151 236 7747
	India Buildings Chambers	0151 243 6000
London	Arlington Chambers	0171 580 9188
	9 Bedford Row	0171 242 3555
	33 Bedford Row	0171 242 6476
	● Chambers of Michael Pert QC	0171 421 8000
	Bell Yard Chambers	0171 306 9292
	11 Bolt Court (also at 7 Stone Buildings –	0171 353 2300
	1st Floor)	
	Bracton Chambers	0171 242 4248
	Bridewell Chambers	020 7797 8800
	● Chambers of Mr Peter Crampin QC	020 7831 0081
	● 1 Crown Office Row, Ground Floor	0171 797 7500
	1 Crown Office Row, 3rd Floor	0171 583 9292
	1 Dr Johnson's Buildings	0171 353 9328
	● 3 Dr Johnson's Buildings	0171 353 4854
	● Dr Johnson's Chambers	0171 353 4716
	● One Essex Court	0171 936 3030
	Chambers of Geoffrey Hawker	0171 583 8899
	● Chambers of Norman Palmer	0171 405 6114
	Francis Taylor Building	0171 353 7768/7769/2711
	● 2nd Floor, Francis Taylor Building	0171 353 9942/3157
	One Garden Court Family Law Chambers	0171 797 7900
	● Two Garden Court	0171 353 1633

● Expanded entry in Part C

• Goldsmith Building	0171 353 7881
• 9 Gough Square	020 7832 0500
96 Gray's Inn Road	0171 405 0585
2 Gray's Inn Square Chambers	020 7242 0328
6 Gray's Inn Square	0171 242 1052
14 Gray's Inn Square	0171 242 0858
• 1 Harcourt Buildings	0171 353 9421/0375
• 2 Harcourt Buildings	0171 583 9020
• Harcourt Chambers	0171 353 6961
• Harrow on the Hill Chambers	0181 423 7444
• 1 Inner Temple Lane	020 7353 0933
John Street Chambers	0171 242 1911
Justice Court Chambers	0181 830 7786
• One King's Bench Walk	0171 936 1500
• 4 King's Bench Walk	0171 822 8822
6 King's Bench Walk	0171 353 4931/583 0695
8 King's Bench Walk	0171 797 8888
9 King's Bench Walk	0171 353 7202/3909
10 King's Bench Walk	0171 353 7742
11 King's Bench Walk	0171 353 3337
• 13 King's Bench Walk	0171 353 7204
• Lamb Building	020 7797 7788
Lamb Chambers	020 7797 8300
1 Mitre Court Buildings	0171 797 7070
2 Mitre Court Buildings	0171 353 1353
• Mitre Court Chambers	0171 353 9394
• Mitre House Chambers	0171 583 8233
• New Court	0171 583 5123/0510
• New Court Chambers	0171 831 9500
• Chambers of Lord Goodhart QC	0171 405 5577
5 New Square	020 7404 0404
• 12 New Square	0171 419 1212
• 22 Old Buildings	0171 831 0222
• Twenty-Four Old Buildings	0171 404 0946
• 9 Old Square	0171 405 4682
The Chambers of Leolin Price CBE, QC	0171 405 0758
11 Old Square, Ground Floor	0171 242 5022/405 1074
• 11 Old Square, Ground Floor	020 7430 0341
13 Old Square	0171 404 4800
• 3 Paper Buildings	020 7583 8055
• 4 Paper Buildings	0171 583 0816/353 1131
• 5 Paper Buildings	0171 583 9275/583 4555
Phoenix Chambers	0171 404 7888
• 1 Pump Court	0171 583 2012/353 4341
2 Pump Court	0171 353 5597
• Pump Court Chambers	0171 353 0711
• 4 Pump Court	020 7842 5555
• 5 Pump Court	020 7353 2532
• Chambers of Kieran Coonan QC	0171 583 6013/2510
6 Pump Court	0171 797 8400
Queen Elizabeth Building	0171 797 7837
No. 1 Serjeants' Inn	0171 415 6666
• Stanbrook & Henderson	0171 353 0101
• 3 Stone Buildings	0171 242 4937
• 5 Stone Buildings	0171 242 6201
7 Stone Buildings (also at 11 Bolt Court)	0171 242 0961
8 Stone Buildings	0171 831 9881
• 9 Stone Buildings	0171 404 5055
55 Temple Chambers	0171 353 7400
• 3 Temple Gardens	0171 353 3102/5/9297
• Thomas More Chambers	0171 404 7000

• Expanded entry in Part C

A

	Tollgate Mews Chambers	0171 511 1838
	Tower Hamlets Barristers Chambers	0171 377 8090
	Verulam Chambers	0171 813 2400
	Warwick House Chambers	0171 430 2323
Maidstone	● Maidstone Chambers	01622 688592
	6-8 Mill Street	01622 688094
Manchester	● Central Chambers	0161 236 1133
	● Cobden House Chambers	0161 833 6000
	Deans Court Chambers	0161 214 6000
	Kenworthy's Chambers	0161 832 4036/834 6954
	● 40 King Street	0161 832 9082
	● 8 King Street Chambers	0161 834 9560
	● Chambers of Ian Macdonald QC (In	0161 236 1840
	Association with Two Garden Court,	
	Temple, London)	
	Peel Court Chambers	0161 832 3791
	● Queen's Chambers	0161 834 6875/4738
	● St James's Chambers	0161 834 7000
	24a St John Street	0161 833 9628
	● 28 St John Street	0161 834 8418
	Young Street Chambers	0161 833 0489
Middlesbrough	Baker Street Chambers	01642 873873
Newcastle upon Tyne	● Broad Chare	0191 232 0541
	Cathedral Chambers	0191 232 1311
	● Trinity Chambers	0191 232 1927
	Westgate Chambers	0191 261 4407/2329785
Northampton	Chartlands Chambers	01604 603322
	Chambers of Michael Pert QC	01604 602333
Norwich	East Anglian Chambers	01603 617351
	Octagon House	01603 623186
Nottingham	King Charles House	0115 9418851
	Ropewalk Chambers	0115 9472581
	St Mary's Chambers	0115 9503503
Oxford	Harcourt Chambers	01865 791559
	King's Bench Chambers	01865 311066
	3 Paper Buildings (Oxford)	01865 793736
	28 Western Road	01865 204911
Peterborough	Fenners Chambers	01733 562030
Plymouth	Devon Chambers	01752 661659
Pontypridd	● Windsor Chambers	01443 402067
Portsmouth	● Portsmouth Barristers' Chambers	023 92 831292/811811
Preston	Deans Court Chambers	01772 555163
	New Bailey Chambers	01772 258087
	Queens Chambers	01772 828300
	15 Winckley Square	01772 252828
Reading	Wessex Chambers	0118 956 8856
Redhill	Redhill Chambers	01737 780781
Saint Albans	St Albans Chambers	01727 843383
Sheffield	Paradise Chambers	0114 2738951
Southampton	● 17 Carlton Crescent	023 8032 0320/0823 2003
	● Eighteen Carlton Crescent	01703 639001
Stoke On Trent	Regent Chambers	01782 286666
Swansea	Angel Chambers	01792 464623/464648
	Chambers of Davina Gammon	01792 480770
	Iscoed Chambers	01792 652988/9/330
Swindon	Pump Court Chambers	01793 539899
Taunton	South Western Chambers	01823 331919 (24 hrs)
Winchester	3 Paper Buildings (Winchester)	01962 868884
	Pump Court Chambers	01962 868161
Wolverhampton	Claremont Chambers	01902 426222
York	● York Chambers	01904 620048

● Expanded entry in Part C

FILM, CABLE, TV

Birmingham	1 Fountain Court	0121 236 5721
	● 8 Fountain Court	0121 236 5514/5
	● St Philip's Chambers	0121 246 7000
London	● Blackstone Chambers	0171 583 1770
	11 Bolt Court (also at 7 Stone Buildings – 1st Floor)	0171 353 2300
	Brick Court Chambers	0171 379 3550
	● Doughty Street Chambers	0171 404 1313
	● Essex Court Chambers	0171 813 8000
	● 39 Essex Street	0171 832 1111
	● 4 Field Court	0171 440 6900
	● Fountain Court	0171 583 3335
	● One Hare Court	020 7353 3171
	● Littleton Chambers	0171 797 8600
	● Monckton Chambers	0171 405 7211
	● 3 New Square	0171 405 1111
	5 New Square	020 7404 0404
	7 New Square	020 7404 5484
	● 8 New Square	0171 405 4321
	19 Old Buildings	0171 405 2001
	● 5 Raymond Buildings	0171 242 2902
	● 3 Stone Buildings	0171 242 4937
	7 Stone Buildings (also at 11 Bolt Court)	0171 242 0961
	● 9 Stone Buildings	0171 404 5055
Redhill	Redhill Chambers	01737 780781

FINANCIAL PROVISION

Rugby	Merriemore Cottage	01788 891832

FINANCIAL SERVICES

Birmingham	● 5 Fountain Court	0121 606 0500
Bristol	Guildhall Chambers	0117 9273366
	St John's Chambers	0117 9213456/298514
Cambridge	Fenners Chambers	01223 368761
Exeter	Walnut House	01392 279751
Leeds	Chambers of Andrew Campbell QC	0113 2455438
	The Chambers of Philip Raynor QC	0113 242 1123
London	Barnard's Inn Chambers	0171 369 6969
	9 Bedford Row	0171 242 3555
	17 Bedford Row	0171 831 7314
	● Blackstone Chambers	0171 583 1770
	Bracton Chambers	0171 242 4248
	Brick Court Chambers	0171 379 3550
	Cloisters	0171 827 4000
	1 Crown Office Row	0171 583 9292
	● Erskine Chambers	0171 242 5532
	● One Essex Court, Ground Floor	020 7583 2000
	● One Essex Court, 1st Floor	0171 936 3030
	● Essex Court Chambers	0171 813 8000
	● 20 Essex Street	0171 583 9294
	● 35 Essex Street	0171 353 6381
	● Chambers of Norman Palmer	0171 405 6114
	● 4 Field Court	0171 440 6900
	● Fountain Court	0171 583 3335
	● 1 Harcourt Buildings	0171 353 9421/0375
	● 2 Harcourt Buildings	0171 583 9020
	● Hardwicke Building	020 7242 2523
	● One Hare Court	020 7353 3171
	● Harrow on the Hill Chambers	0181 423 7444
	● 4 King's Bench Walk	0171 822 8822

● Expanded entry in Part C

	S Tomlinson QC	0171 583 0404
	Lamb Chambers	020 7797 8300
	• Littleton Chambers	0171 797 8600
	• Mitre Court Chambers	0171 353 9394
	• Chambers of Lord Goodhart QC	0171 405 5577
	• Chambers of John L Powell QC	0171 797 8000
	• 12 New Square	0171 419 1212
	• Twenty-Four Old Buildings	0171 404 0946
	• 9 Old Square	0171 405 4682
	The Chambers of Leolin Price CBE, QC	0171 405 0758
	• 11 Old Square	020 7430 0341
	13 Old Square	0171 404 4800
	• 5 Paper Buildings	0171 583 9275/583 4555
	Five Paper Buildings	0171 583 6117
	• 4 Pump Court	020 7842 5555
	• Hollis Whiteman Chambers	020 7583 5766
	No. 1 Serjeants' Inn	0171 415 6666
	• 3/4 South Square	0171 696 9900
	• Stanbrook & Henderson	0171 353 0101
	• 3 Stone Buildings	0171 242 4937
	4 Stone Buildings	0171 242 5524
	• 5 Stone Buildings	0171 242 6201
	• 7 Stone Buildings	0171 405 3886/242 3546
	• 9 Stone Buildings	0171 404 5055
	• 2 Temple Gardens	0171 583 6041
	• Thomas More Chambers	0171 404 7000
	3 Verulam Buildings	0171 831 8441
	Verulam Chambers	0171 813 2400
	• Wilberforce Chambers	0171 306 0102
Manchester	• 40 King Street	0161 832 9082
	• 8 King Street Chambers	0161 834 9560
	• Merchant Chambers	0161 839 7070
	• St James's Chambers	0161 834 7000
Nottingham	Ropewalk Chambers	0115 9472581
Oxford	King's Bench Chambers	01865 311066
Peterborough	Fenners Chambers	01733 562030
Pontypridd	• Windsor Chambers	01443 402067
Portsmouth	• Portsmouth Barristers' Chambers	023 92 831292/811811
Preston	New Bailey Chambers	01772 258087
Saint Albans	New Chambers	0966 212126
Swansea	Iscoed Chambers	01792 652988/9/330
Wolverhampton	Claremont Chambers	01902 426222

FOOD

London	• Gough Square Chambers	0171 353 0924

FOREIGN LAW

Birmingham	• 5 Fountain Court	0121 606 0500
Bournemouth	3 Paper Buildings (Bournemouth)	01202 292102
Leicester	Chambers of Michael Pert QC	0116 249 2020
London	Barristers' Common Law Chambers	0171 375 3012
	• Chambers of Michael Pert QC	0171 421 8000
	• Blackstone Chambers	0171 583 1770
	Brick Court Chambers	0171 379 3550
	1 Crown Office Row	0171 583 9292
	• Essex Court Chambers	0171 813 8000
	Chambers of Geoffrey Hawker	0171 583 8899
	• Chambers of Norman Palmer	0171 405 6114
	• Two Garden Court	0171 353 1633
	Counsels' Chambers	0171 405 2576
	• One Hare Court	020 7353 3171

	• 3 Hare Court	0171 395 2000
	Chambers of Harjit Singh	0171 353 1356 (4 Lines)
	John Street Chambers	0171 242 1911
	• Lamb Building	020 7797 7788
	• Mitre House Chambers	0171 583 8233
	• New Court	0171 583 5123/0510
	• 12 New Square	0171 419 1212
	• 2 Paper Buildings	020 7556 5500
	• 3 Paper Buildings	020 7583 8055
	• 4 Paper Buildings, Ground Floor	0171 353 3366/583 7155
	• 4 Paper Buildings, 1st Floor	0171 583 0816/353 1131
	• 5 Paper Buildings	0171 583 9275/583 4555
	• Pump Court Chambers	0171 353 0711
	• 9 Stone Buildings	0171 404 5055
	Tollgate Mews Chambers	0171 511 1838
	Tower Hamlets Barristers Chambers	0171 377 8090
	Verulam Chambers	0171 813 2400
	Warwick House Chambers	0171 430 2323
	Wynne Chambers	0181 961 6144
Northampton	Chambers of Michael Pert QC	01604 602333
Oxford	3 Paper Buildings (Oxford)	01865 793736
Swindon	Pump Court Chambers	01793 539899
Winchester	3 Paper Buildings (Winchester)	01962 868884
	Pump Court Chambers	01962 868161

FRANCHISING

Birmingham	1 Fountain Court	0121 236 5721
	• 5 Fountain Court	0121 606 0500
	• St Philip's Chambers	0121 246 7000
Bristol	St John's Chambers	0117 9213456/298514
Cardiff	30 Park Place	01222 398421
Leeds	• 37 Park Square Chambers	0113 2439422
London	1 Crown Office Row	0171 583 9292
	• One Essex Court	020 7583 2000
	• Essex Court Chambers	0171 813 8000
	Francis Taylor Building	0171 353 7768/7769/2711
	• Gough Square Chambers	0171 353 0924
	• 2 Harcourt Buildings	0171 583 9020
	• One Hare Court	020 7353 3171
	• Harrow on the Hill Chambers	0181 423 7444
	11 King's Bench Walk	0171 353 3337
	• 3 New Square	0171 405 1111
	7 New Square	020 7404 5484
	19 Old Buildings	0171 405 2001
	• Stanbrook & Henderson	0171 353 0101
	• 199 Strand	0171 379 9779
Manchester	• 8 King Street Chambers	0161 834 9560
	• Merchant Chambers	0161 839 7070
	• St James's Chambers	0161 834 7000
Nottingham	King Charles House	0115 9418851
	Ropewalk Chambers	0115 9472581
Pontypridd	• Windsor Chambers	01443 402067
Preston	New Bailey Chambers	01772 258087
Swansea	Iscoed Chambers	01792 652988/9/330

FRAUD

Leeds	• 37 Park Square Chambers	0113 2439422
London	• Thomas More Chambers	0171 404 7000

FSA RELATED WORK

Portsmouth	• Portsmouth Barristers' Chambers	023 92 831292/811811

• Expanded entry in Part C

A

HEALTH & SAFETY

London	• Devereux Chambers	0171 353 7534
	One Paper Buildings	0171 583 7355
	No. 1 Serjeants' Inn	0171 415 6666
	8 Stone Buildings	0171 831 9881
	• 1 Temple Gardens	0171 583 1315/353 0407
Slough	Slough Chamber	01753 553806/817989

HIGHWAYS

London	11 Bolt Court (also at 7 Stone Buildings – 1st Floor)	0171 353 2300
	7 Stone Buildings (also at 11 Bolt Court)	0171 242 0961
Redhill	Redhill Chambers	01737 780781

HOUSING

Birmingham	1 Fountain Court	0121 236 5721
	• 5 Fountain Court	0121 606 0500
	• 8 Fountain Court	0121 236 5514/5
	New Court Chambers	0121 693 6656
	• St Philip's Chambers	0121 246 7000
Bradford	Broadway House Chambers	01274 722560
Cambridge	Fenners Chambers	01223 368761
Cardiff	30 Park Place	01222 398421
	• 33 Park Place	02920 233313
Chester	Nicholas Street Chambers	01244 323886
	White Friars Chambers	01244 323070
Chichester	Chichester Chambers	01243 784538
Eastbourne	King's Chambers	01323 416053
Exeter	Southernhay Chambers	01392 255777
	Walnut House	01392 279751
Guildford	• Guildford Chambers	01483 539131
Leeds	Chambers of Andrew Campbell QC	0113 2455438
	Broadway House Chambers	0113 246 2600
	Enterprise Chambers	0113 246 0391
	No. 6	0113 2459763
	The Chambers of Philip Raynor QC	0113 242 1123
	• 37 Park Square Chambers	0113 2439422
	• Sovereign Chambers	0113 2451841/2/3
	• 9 Woodhouse Square	0113 2451986
Leicester	Chambers of Michael Pert QC	0116 249 2020
Liverpool	25-27 Castle Street	0151 227 5661/051 236 5072
	Chavasse Court Chambers	0151 707 1191
	• Corn Exchange Chambers	0151 227 1081/5009
	• Exchange Chambers	0151 236 7747
	India Buildings Chambers	0151 243 6000
	• Oriel Chambers	0151 236 7191/236 4321
London	Albany Chambers	0171 485 5736/5758
	• Arden Chambers	020 7242 4244
	Barnard's Inn Chambers	0171 369 6969
	Barristers' Common Law Chambers	0171 375 3012
	17 Bedford Row	0171 831 7314
	33 Bedford Row	0171 242 6476
	• Chambers of Michael Pert QC	0171 421 8000
	Bell Yard Chambers	0171 306 9292
	11 Bolt Court (also at 7 Stone Buildings – 1st Floor)	0171 353 2300
	• 4 Breams Buildings	0171 353 5835/430 1221
	Bridewell Chambers	020 7797 8800
	Britton Street Chambers	0171 608 3765
	• Chambers of Mr Peter Crampin QC	020 7831 0081
	• Devereux Chambers	0171 353 7534

• Doughty Street Chambers	0171 404 1313
1 Dr Johnson's Buildings	0171 353 9328
• 3 Dr Johnson's Buildings	0171 353 4854
• Enterprise Chambers	0171 405 9471
Equity Barristers' Chambers	0181 558 8336
• One Essex Court	0171 936 3030
Chambers of Geoffrey Hawker	0171 583 8899
Falcon Chambers	0171 353 2484
• Chambers of Norman Palmer	0171 405 6114
• 4 Field Court	0171 440 6900
Chambers of Wilfred Forster-Jones	0171 353 0853/4/7222
Francis Taylor Building	0171 353 7768/7769/2711
• 2nd Floor, Francis Taylor Building	0171 353 9942/3157
• Two Garden Court	0171 353 1633
Goldsmith Chambers	0171 353 6802/3/4/5
• Gray's Inn Chambers, The Chambers of	0171 831 5344
Norman Patterson	
Gray's Inn Chambers	0171 831 7888 (Chambers)/
	0171 831 7904 (Mr M Ullah)
96 Gray's Inn Road	0171 405 0585
• 2-3 Gray's Inn Square	0171 242 4986
2 Gray's Inn Square Chambers	020 7242 0328
• 4-5 Gray's Inn Square	0171 404 5252
6 Gray's Inn Square	0171 242 1052
Counsels' Chambers	0171 405 2576
14 Gray's Inn Square	0171 242 0858
• 1 Harcourt Buildings	0171 353 9421/0375
• 2 Harcourt Buildings	0171 583 9020
• Hardwicke Building	020 7242 2523
Chambers of Harjit Singh	0171 353 1356 (4 Lines)
• Harrow on the Hill Chambers	0181 423 7444
• 1 Inner Temple Lane	020 7353 0933
John Street Chambers	0171 242 1911
Justice Court Chambers	0181 830 7786
• 4 King's Bench Walk	0171 822 8822
6 King's Bench Walk	0171 353 4931/583 0695
8 King's Bench Walk	0171 797 8888
9 King's Bench Walk	0171 353 7202/3909
10 King's Bench Walk	0171 353 7742
• 11 King's Bench Walk	0171 632 8500/583 0610
• 12 King's Bench Walk	0171 583 0811
2 King's Bench Walk Chambers	020 7353 9276
• Lamb Building	020 7797 7788
Lamb Chambers	020 7797 8300
Lion Court	0171 404 6565
2 Mitre Court Buildings	0171 353 1353
• Mitre Court Chambers	0171 353 9394
• Mitre House Chambers	0171 583 8233
• New Court	0171 583 5123/0510
• 1 New Square	0171 405 0884/5/6/7
• 22 Old Buildings	0171 831 0222
11 Old Square, Ground Floor	0171 242 5022/405 1074
• 11 Old Square, Ground Floor	020 7430 0341
• 2 Paper Buildings	020 7556 5500
• 4 Paper Buildings	0171 353 3366/583 7155
Phoenix Chambers	0171 404 7888
• 1 Pump Court	0171 583 2012/353 4341
2 Pump Court	0171 353 5597
• 5 Pump Court	020 7353 2532
• Chambers of Kieran Coonan QC	0171 583 6013/2510
1 Serjeants' Inn	0171 583 1355

• Expanded entry in Part C

A

	Somersett Chambers	0171 404 6701
	• Stanbrook & Henderson	0171 353 0101
	Staple Inn Chambers	0171 242 5240
	7 Stone Buildings (also at 11 Bolt Court)	0171 242 0961
	• 9 Stone Buildings	0171 404 5055
	• 199 Strand	0171 379 9779
	55 Temple Chambers	0171 353 7400
	• 3 Temple Gardens	0171 353 3102/5/9297
	• Thomas More Chambers	0171 404 7000
	• 14 Tooks Court	0171 405 8828
	Verulam Chambers	0171 813 2400
	Warwick House Chambers	0171 430 2323
Manchester	• Central Chambers	0161 236 1133
	• Cobden House Chambers	0161 833 6000
	Kenworthy's Chambers	0161 832 4036/834 6954
	• 40 King Street	0161 832 9082
	• 8 King Street Chambers	0161 834 9560
	58 King Street Chambers	0161 831 7477
	• Chambers of Ian Macdonald QC (In Association with Two Garden Court, Temple, London)	0161 236 1840
	• Merchant Chambers	0161 839 7070
	Peel Court Chambers	0161 832 3791
	• Queen's Chambers	0161 834 6875/4738
	• St James's Chambers	0161 834 7000
	24a St John Street	0161 833 9628
	Young Street Chambers	0161 833 0489
Middlesbrough	Baker Street Chambers	01642 873873
Newcastle upon Tyne	Cathedral Chambers	0191 232 1311
	Enterprise Chambers	0191 222 3344
	• Trinity Chambers	0191 232 1927
	Westgate Chambers	0191 261 4407/2329785
Northampton	Chambers of Michael Pert QC	01604 602333
	Northampton Chambers	01604 636271
Nottingham	King Charles House	0115 9418851
	Ropewalk Chambers	0115 9472581
Oxford	King's Bench Chambers	01865 311066
	28 Western Road	01865 204911
Peterborough	Fenners Chambers	01733 562030
Plymouth	Devon Chambers	01752 661659
Pontypridd	• Windsor Chambers	01443 402067
Preston	New Bailey Chambers	01772 258087
	Queens Chambers	01772 828300
	15 Winckley Square	01772 252828
Reading	Wessex Chambers	0118 956 8856
Redhill	Redhill Chambers	01737 780781
Saint Albans	St Albans Chambers	01727 843383
Slough	Slough Chamber	01753 553806/817989
Southampton	• 17 Carlton Crescent	023 8032 0320/0823 2003
Stoke On Trent	Regent Chambers	01782 286666
Swansea	Angel Chambers	01792 464623/464648
	Chambers of Davina Gammon	01792 480770
	Iscoed Chambers	01792 652988/9/330
Wolverhampton	Claremont Chambers	01902 426222

HUMAN RIGHTS

London	17 Bedford Row	0171 831 7314
	Equity Barristers' Chambers	0181 558 8336
	• 20 Essex Street	0171 583 9294
	2 King's Bench Walk	0171 353 1746
	10 King's Bench Walk	0171 353 7742

	6 Pump Court	0171 797 8400
	• Thomas More Chambers	0171 404 7000
Maidstone	6-8 Mill Street	01622 688094
Slough	Slough Chamber	01753 553806/817989

IMMIGRATION

Birmingham	Coleridge Chambers	0121 233 8500
	1 Fountain Court	0121 236 5721
	• 5 Fountain Court	0121 606 0500
	• 8 Fountain Court	0121 236 5514/5
	New Court Chambers	0121 693 6656
	• St Philip's Chambers	0121 246 7000
Bradford	Broadway House Chambers	01274 722560
Cardiff	30 Park Place	01222 398421
Chester	White Friars Chambers	01244 323070
Eastbourne	King's Chambers	01323 416053
Leeds	Chambers of Andrew Campbell QC	0113 2455438
	Broadway House Chambers	0113 246 2600
	Park Lane Chambers	0113 2285000
	The Chambers of Philip Raynor QC	0113 242 1123
	• 37 Park Square Chambers	0113 2439422
	• Sovereign Chambers	0113 2451841/2/3
	• 9 Woodhouse Square	0113 2451986
Liverpool	India Buildings Chambers	0151 243 6000
London	ACHMA Chambers	0171 639 7817/0171 635 7904
	Acre Lane Neighbourhood Chambers	0171 274 4400
	Albany Chambers	0171 485 5736/5758
	Barnard's Inn Chambers	0171 369 6969
	Barristers' Common Law Chambers	0171 375 3012
	33 Bedford Row	0171 242 6476
	Bell Yard Chambers	0171 306 9292
	• Blackstone Chambers	0171 583 1770
	11 Bolt Court (also at 7 Stone Buildings – 1st Floor)	0171 353 2300
	Bracton Chambers	0171 242 4248
	• 4 Breams Buildings	0171 353 5835/430 1221
	• 4 Brick Court	0171 797 8910
	Bridewell Chambers	020 7797 8800
	Britton Street Chambers	0171 608 3765
	• Doughty Street Chambers	0171 404 1313
	1 Dr Johnson's Buildings	0171 353 9328
	• One Essex Court	0171 936 3030
	• Essex Court Chambers	0171 813 8000
	• 20 Essex Street	0171 583 9294
	• 39 Essex Street	0171 832 1111
	Chambers of Geoffrey Hawker	0171 583 8899
	• Chambers of Norman Palmer	0171 405 6114
	Fleet Chambers	0171 936 3707
	Chambers of Wilfred Forster-Jones	0171 353 0853/4/7222
	Francis Taylor Building	0171 353 7768/7769/2711
	• Two Garden Court	0171 353 1633
	• Goldsmith Building	0171 353 7881
	Goldsmith Chambers	0171 353 6802/3/4/5
	• Gray's Inn Chambers, The Chambers of Norman Patterson	0171 831 5344
	Gray's Inn Chambers	0171 831 7888 (Chambers)/ 0171 831 7904 (Mr M Ullah)
	96 Gray's Inn Road	0171 405 0585
	2 Gray's Inn Square Chambers	020 7242 0328
	• 4-5 Gray's Inn Square	0171 404 5252
	6 Gray's Inn Square	0171 242 1052

• Expanded entry in Part C

A

Counsels' Chambers	0171 405 2576
• 1 Harcourt Buildings	0171 353 9421/0375
2 Harcourt Buildings	020 7353 2112
• One Hare Court	020 7353 3171
Chambers of Harjit Singh	0171 353 1356 (4 Lines)
• Harrow on the Hill Chambers	0181 423 7444
• 1 Inner Temple Lane	020 7353 0933
John Street Chambers	0171 242 1911
Justice Court Chambers	0181 830 7786
• One King's Bench Walk	0171 936 1500
• 4 King's Bench Walk, Ground/First Floor/ Basement	0171 822 8822
4 King's Bench Walk, 2nd Floor	020 7353 3581
6 King's Bench Walk	0171 353 4931/583 0695
8 King's Bench Walk	0171 797 8888
9 King's Bench Walk	0171 353 7202/3909
10 King's Bench Walk	0171 353 7742
• 11 King's Bench Walk	0171 632 8500/583 0610
• 13 King's Bench Walk	0171 353 7204
2 King's Bench Walk Chambers	020 7353 9276
• Lamb Building	020 7797 7788
Leone Chambers	0181 200 4020
Lion Court	0171 404 6565
• Littman Chambers	020 7404 4866
• 1 Middle Temple Lane	0171 583 0659 (12 Lines)
2 Mitre Court Buildings	0171 353 1353
• Mitre Court Chambers	0171 353 9394
• Mitre House Chambers	0171 583 8233
• Monckton Chambers	0171 405 7211
11 Old Square	0171 242 5022/405 1074
• 2 Paper Buildings	020 7556 5500
• 5 Paper Buildings	0171 583 9275/583 4555
Pepys' Chambers	0171 936 2710
Phoenix Chambers	0171 404 7888
Plowden Buildings	0171 583 0808
• 1 Pump Court	0171 583 2012/353 4341
2 Pump Court	0171 353 5597
Staple Inn Chambers	0171 242 5240
7 Stone Buildings (also at 11 Bolt Court)	0171 242 0961
8 Stone Buildings	0171 831 9881
55 Temple Chambers	0171 353 7400
• 1 Temple Gardens	0171 583 1315/353 0407
• Thomas More Chambers	0171 404 7000
Tollgate Mews Chambers	0171 511 1838
• 14 Tooks Court	0171 405 8828
Tower Hamlets Barristers Chambers	0171 377 8090
Verulam Chambers	0171 813 2400
Virtual Chambers	07071 244 944
Warwick House Chambers	0171 430 2323

Maidstone

Earl Street Chambers	01622 671222
• Maidstone Chambers	01622 688592

Manchester

• Central Chambers	0161 236 1133
Kenworthy's Chambers	0161 832 4036/834 6954
• 40 King Street	0161 832 9082
Lincoln House Chambers	0161 832 5701
• Chambers of Ian Macdonald QC (In Association with Two Garden Court, Temple, London)	0161 236 1840
24a St John Street	0161 833 9628
Young Street Chambers	0161 833 0489

Middlesbrough

Baker Street Chambers	01642 873873

• Expanded entry in Part C

Nottingham	Ropewalk Chambers	0115 9472581
Oxford	King's Bench Chambers	01865 311066
	28 Western Road	01865 204911
Plymouth	Devon Chambers	01752 661659
Pontypridd	• Windsor Chambers	01443 402067
Preston	New Bailey Chambers	01772 258087
Reading	Wessex Chambers	0118 956 8856
Redhill	Redhill Chambers	01737 780781
Saint Albans	St Albans Chambers	01727 843383
Sheffield	Bank House Chambers	0114 2751223
Slough	Slough Chamber	01753 553806/817989
Stoke On Trent	Regent Chambers	01782 286666
Swansea	Angel Chambers	01792 464623/464648
Wolverhampton	Claremont Chambers	01902 426222
Woodford Green	1 Wensley Avenue	0181 505 9259
York	• York Chambers	01904 620048

INFORMATION TECHNOLOGY

Birmingham	• 3 Fountain Court	0121 236 5854
	• 5 Fountain Court	0121 606 0500
Cardiff	30 Park Place	01222 398421
Leeds	11 King's Bench Walk	0113 297 1200
	The Chambers of Philip Raynor QC	0113 242 1123
	• Sovereign Chambers	0113 2451841/2/3
London	Atkin Chambers	020 7404 0102
	9 Bedford Row	0171 242 3555
	Brick Court Chambers	0171 379 3550
	• Devereux Chambers	0171 353 7534
	• Essex Court Chambers	0171 813 8000
	• 35 Essex Street	0171 353 6381
	• 4 Field Court	0171 440 6900
	• Fountain Court	0171 583 3335
	Francis Taylor Building	0171 353 7768/7769/2711
	• Two Garden Court	0171 353 1633
	• 2-3 Gray's Inn Square	0171 242 4986
	• 2 Harcourt Buildings	0171 583 9020
	• One Hare Court	020 7353 3171
	• Keating Chambers	0171 544 2600
	• Littleton Chambers	0171 797 8600
	• Littman Chambers	020 7404 4866
	• Mitre Court Chambers	0171 353 9394
	• New Court Chambers	0171 831 9500
	• 3 New Square	0171 405 1111
	5 New Square	020 7404 0404
	7 New Square	020 7404 5484
	• 8 New Square	0171 405 4321
	• 12 New Square	0171 419 1212
	19 Old Buildings	0171 405 2001
	• 3 Paper Buildings	020 7583 8055
	• 4 Paper Buildings	0171 353 3366/583 7155
	• 4 Pump Court	020 7842 5555
	• 5 Raymond Buildings	0171 242 2902
	• 11 South Square	0171 405 1222 (24hr messaging service)
	• Stanbrook & Henderson	0171 353 0101
	• 9 Stone Buildings	0171 404 5055
	• 199 Strand	0171 379 9779
	• 2 Temple Gardens	0171 583 6041
	3 Verulam Buildings	0171 831 8441
	Virtual Chambers	07071 244 944
	Warwick House Chambers	0171 430 2323

• Expanded entry in Part C

A

Luton	Beresford Chambers	01582 429111
Manchester	• Cobden House Chambers	0161 833 6000
	Deans Court Chambers	0161 214 6000
	• 40 King Street	0161 832 9082
	• St James's Chambers	0161 834 7000
Nottingham	Ropewalk Chambers	0115 9472581
Oxford	3 Paper Buildings (Oxford)	01865 793736
Plymouth	Devon Chambers	01752 661659
Pontypridd	• Windsor Chambers	01443 402067
Preston	Deans Court Chambers	01772 555163
	New Bailey Chambers	01772 258087
Southampton	• Eighteen Carlton Crescent	01703 639001
Winchester	3 Paper Buildings (Winchester)	01962 868884

INQUESTS

Leeds	• 37 Park Square Chambers	0113 2439422
London	• Dr Johnson's Chambers	0171 353 4716
	• 14 Tooks Court	0171 405 8828

INSOLVENCY

Birmingham	1 Fountain Court	0121 236 5721
	• 3 Fountain Court	0121 236 5854
	• 5 Fountain Court	0121 606 0500
	6 Fountain Court	0121 233 3282
	• 8 Fountain Court	0121 236 5514/5
	• St Philip's Chambers	0121 246 7000
Brighton	Crown Office Row Chambers	01273 625625
Bristol	Guildhall Chambers	0117 9273366
	St John's Chambers	0117 9213456/298514
Cambridge	Fenners Chambers	01223 368761
Cardiff	9 Park Place	01222 382731
	30 Park Place	01222 398421
	• 33 Park Place	02920 233313
Chester	Nicholas Street Chambers	01244 323886
Chichester	Chichester Chambers	01243 784538
Colchester	East Anglian Chambers	01206 572756
Exeter	Cathedral Chambers (Jan Wood Independent Barristers' Clerk)	01392 210900
Ipswich	East Anglian Chambers	01473 214481
Leeds	Chambers of Andrew Campbell QC	0113 2455438
	• Chancery House Chambers	0113 244 6691
	Enterprise Chambers	0113 246 0391
	11 King's Bench Walk	0113 297 1200
	• Mercury Chambers	0113 234 2265
	No. 6	0113 2459763
	Park Lane Chambers	0113 2285000
	The Chambers of Philip Raynor QC	0113 242 1123
	• 30 Park Square	0113 2436388
	• Sovereign Chambers	0113 2451841/2/3
	• St Paul's House	0113 2455866
Liverpool	• Exchange Chambers	0151 236 7747
	• Oriel Chambers	0151 236 7191/236 4321
London	Barnard's Inn Chambers	0171 369 6969
	17 Bedford Row	0171 831 7314
	33 Bedford Row	0171 242 6476
	11 Bolt Court (also at 7 Stone Buildings – 1st Floor)	0171 353 2300
	Bracton Chambers	0171 242 4248
	Bridewell Chambers	020 7797 8800
	Cloisters	0171 827 4000
	• Chambers of Mr Peter Crampin QC	020 7831 0081

• Expanded entry in Part C

1 Crown Office Row	0171 583 9292
• Dr Johnson's Chambers	0171 353 4716
• Enterprise Chambers	0171 405 9471
• Erskine Chambers	0171 242 5532
• One Essex Court	020 7583 2000
• Essex Court Chambers	0171 813 8000
• Chambers of Norman Palmer	0171 405 6114
• 4 Field Court	0171 440 6900
• Fountain Court	0171 583 3335
Francis Taylor Building	0171 353 7768/7769/2711
• 2nd Floor, Francis Taylor Building	0171 353 9942/3157
• Goldsmith Building	0171 353 7881
• Gough Square Chambers	0171 353 0924
96 Gray's Inn Road	0171 405 0585
Counsels' Chambers	0171 405 2576
• 1 Harcourt Buildings	0171 353 9421/0375
• Hardwicke Building	020 7242 2523
• One Hare Court	020 7353 3171
• 3 Hare Court	0171 395 2000
• Harrow on the Hill Chambers	0181 423 7444
• 4 King's Bench Walk	0171 822 8822
9 King's Bench Walk	0171 353 7202/3909
11 King's Bench Walk	0171 353 3337
• 13 King's Bench Walk	0171 353 7204
• Lamb Building	020 7797 7788
Lamb Chambers	020 7797 8300
Lion Court	0171 404 6565
• Littleton Chambers	0171 797 8600
• Littman Chambers	020 7404 4866
• Mitre Court Chambers	0171 353 9394
• Monckton Chambers	0171 405 7211
• New Court	0171 583 5123/0510
• 1 New Square	0171 405 0884/5/6/7
• Chambers of Lord Goodhart QC	0171 405 5577
• Chambers of John L Powell QC	0171 797 8000
5 New Square	020 7404 0404
• 12 New Square	0171 419 1212
• 22 Old Buildings	0171 831 0222
• Twenty-Four Old Buildings	0171 404 0946
• 9 Old Square	0171 405 4682
The Chambers of Leolin Price CBE, QC	0171 405 0758
11 Old Square, Ground Floor	0171 242 5022/405 1074
• 11 Old Square, Ground Floor	020 7430 0341
13 Old Square	0171 404 4800
• 3 Paper Buildings	020 7583 8055
• 4 Paper Buildings	0171 583 0816/353 1131
• 5 Paper Buildings	0171 583 9275/583 4555
Phoenix Chambers	0171 404 7888
Plowden Buildings	0171 583 0808
• Pump Court Chambers	0171 353 0711
• 5 Pump Court	020 7353 2532
Queen Elizabeth Building	0171 797 7837
• Serle Court Chambers	0171 242 6105
• 3/4 South Square	0171 696 9900
Staple Inn Chambers	0171 242 5240
• 3 Stone Buildings	0171 242 4937
4 Stone Buildings	0171 242 5524
• 5 Stone Buildings	0171 242 6201
• 7 Stone Buildings	0171 405 3886/242 3546
7 Stone Buildings (also at 11 Bolt Court)	0171 242 0961
• 9 Stone Buildings	0171 404 5055

• Expanded entry in Part C

	11 Stone Buildings	+44 (0)207 831 6381
	• 199 Strand	0171 379 9779
	55 Temple Chambers	0171 353 7400
	• 2 Temple Gardens	0171 583 6041
	• Thomas More Chambers	0171 404 7000
	3 Verulam Buildings	0171 831 8441
	Warwick House Chambers	0171 430 2323
	• Wilberforce Chambers	0171 306 0102
Manchester	• Cobden House Chambers	0161 833 6000
	Deans Court Chambers	0161 214 6000
	• 40 King Street	0161 832 9082
	• 8 King Street Chambers	0161 834 9560
	58 King Street Chambers	0161 831 7477
	• Merchant Chambers	0161 839 7070
	• Queen's Chambers	0161 834 6875/4738
	• St James's Chambers	0161 834 7000
	Young Street Chambers	0161 833 0489
Newcastle upon Tyne	• Broad Chare	0191 232 0541
	Enterprise Chambers	0191 222 3344
	• Trinity Chambers	0191 232 1927
	Westgate Chambers	0191 261 4407/2329785
Northampton	Northampton Chambers	01604 636271
Norwich	East Anglian Chambers	01603 617351
Nottingham	King Charles House	0115 9418851
	Ropewalk Chambers	0115 9472581
	St Mary's Chambers	0115 9503503
Oxford	King's Bench Chambers	01865 311066
	3 Paper Buildings (Oxford)	01865 793736
Plymouth	Devon Chambers	01752 661659
Pontypridd	• Windsor Chambers	01443 402067
Portsmouth	• Portsmouth Barristers' Chambers	023 92 831292/811811
Preston	Deans Court Chambers	01772 555163
	New Bailey Chambers	01772 258087
	Queens Chambers	01772 828300
	15 Winckley Square	01772 252828
Reading	Wessex Chambers	0118 956 8856
Redhill	Redhill Chambers	01737 780781
Saint Albans	St Albans Chambers	01727 843383
Slough	Slough Chamber	01753 553806/817989
Southampton	• College Chambers	01703 230338
	• Eighteen Carlton Crescent	01703 639001
Stoke On Trent	Regent Chambers	01782 286666
Swansea	Angel Chambers	01792 464623/464648
	Iscoed Chambers	01792 652988/9/330
Swindon	Pump Court Chambers	01793 539899
Winchester	3 Paper Buildings (Winchester)	01962 868884
	Pump Court Chambers	01962 868161
Wolverhampton	Claremont Chambers	01902 426222

INSURANCE

Birmingham	1 Fountain Court	0121 236 5721
	• 5 Fountain Court	0121 606 0500
	• 8 Fountain Court	0121 236 5514/5
	• St Philip's Chambers	0121 246 7000
Bristol	St John's Chambers	0117 9213456/298514
Cardiff	9 Park Place	01222 382731
	30 Park Place	01222 398421
	• 33 Park Place	02920 233313
Chichester	Chichester Chambers	01243 784538
Leeds	Chambers of Andrew Campbell QC	0113 2455438
	• Chancery House Chambers	0113 244 6691

Liverpool

London

The Chambers of Philip Raynor QC	0113 242 1123
• Exchange Chambers	0151 236 7747
• Oriel Chambers	0151 236 7191/236 4321
9 Bedford Row	0171 242 3555
• Blackstone Chambers	0171 583 1770
Bracton Chambers	0171 242 4248
Brick Court Chambers	0171 379 3550
• 1 Crown Office Row, Ground Floor	0171 797 7500
1 Crown Office Row, 3rd Floor	0171 583 9292
• Two Crown Office Row	020 7797 8100
• Devereux Chambers	0171 353 7534
• One Essex Court, Ground Floor	020 7583 2000
• One Essex Court, 1st Floor	0171 936 3030
• 4 Essex Court	020 7797 7970
• Essex Court Chambers	0171 813 8000
• 20 Essex Street	0171 583 9294
• 39 Essex Street	0171 832 1111
• Chambers of Norman Palmer	0171 405 6114
• 4 Field Court	0171 440 6900
• Fountain Court	0171 583 3335
• Goldsmith Building	0171 353 7881
96 Gray's Inn Road	0171 405 0585
• 4-5 Gray's Inn Square	0171 404 5252
• 1 Harcourt Buildings	0171 353 9421/0375
• 2 Harcourt Buildings	0171 583 9020
• Hardwicke Building	020 7242 2523
• One Hare Court	020 7353 3171
• Harrow on the Hill Chambers	0181 423 7444
Justice Court Chambers	0181 830 7786
• 4 King's Bench Walk	0171 822 8822
S Tomlinson QC	0171 583 0404
8 King's Bench Walk	0171 797 8888
11 King's Bench Walk	0171 353 3337
• 12 King's Bench Walk	0171 583 0811
• 13 King's Bench Walk	0171 353 7204
Lamb Chambers	020 7797 8300
Leone Chambers	0181 200 4020
• Littleton Chambers	0171 797 8600
• Littman Chambers	020 7404 4866
• Mitre Court Chambers	0171 353 9394
• Chambers of John L Powell QC	0171 797 8000
• 12 New Square	0171 419 1212
• 22 Old Buildings	0171 831 0222
11 Old Square	0171 242 5022/405 1074
13 Old Square	0171 404 4800
One Paper Buildings	0171 583 7355
• 4 Paper Buildings	0171 353 3366/583 7155
• 4 Pump Court	020 7842 5555
• 5 Pump Court	020 7353 2532
No. 1 Serjeants' Inn	0171 415 6666
• 3/4 South Square	0171 696 9900
• Stanbrook & Henderson	0171 353 0101
• 3 Stone Buildings	0171 242 4937
4 Stone Buildings	0171 242 5524
8 Stone Buildings	0171 831 9881
• 9 Stone Buildings	0171 404 5055
• 199 Strand	0171 379 9779
55 Temple Chambers	0171 353 7400
• 1 Temple Gardens	0171 583 1315/353 0407
• 2 Temple Gardens	0171 583 6041
3 Verulam Buildings	0171 831 8441

• Expanded entry in Part C

A

Manchester	• Byrom Street Chambers	0161 829 2100
	Deans Court Chambers	0161 214 6000
	• 40 King Street	0161 832 9082
	• 8 King Street Chambers	0161 834 9560
	• Merchant Chambers	0161 839 7070
	• St James's Chambers	0161 834 7000
Newcastle upon Tyne	• Trinity Chambers	0191 232 1927
Nottingham	Ropewalk Chambers	0115 9472581
Oxford	King's Bench Chambers	01865 311066
Pontypridd	• Windsor Chambers	01443 402067
Preston	Deans Court Chambers	01772 555163
	New Bailey Chambers	01772 258087
	15 Winckley Square	01772 252828
Wolverhampton	Claremont Chambers	01902 426222

INSURANCE/REINSURANCE

Birmingham	• 5 Fountain Court	0121 606 0500
Bristol	Guildhall Chambers	0117 9273366
Exeter	Cathedral Chambers (Jan Wood Independent Barristers' Clerk)	01392 210900
Leeds	Chambers of Andrew Campbell QC	0113 2455438
Liverpool	• Exchange Chambers	0151 236 7747
London	Atkin Chambers	020 7404 0102
	9 Bedford Row	0171 242 3555
	17 Bedford Row	0171 831 7314
	• Blackstone Chambers	0171 583 1770
	Brick Court Chambers	0171 379 3550
	• 1 Crown Office Row, Ground Floor	0171 797 7500
	1 Crown Office Row, 3rd Floor	0171 583 9292
	• Two Crown Office Row	020 7797 8100
	• Devereux Chambers	0171 353 7534
	Equity Barristers' Chambers	0181 558 8336
	• One Essex Court	020 7583 2000
	• 4 Essex Court	020 7797 7970
	• Essex Court Chambers	0171 813 8000
	• 20 Essex Street	0171 583 9294
	• 39 Essex Street	0171 832 1111
	• Chambers of Norman Palmer	0171 405 6114
	• 4 Field Court	0171 440 6900
	• Fountain Court	0171 583 3335
	• 9 Gough Square	020 7832 0500
	• 4-5 Gray's Inn Square	0171 404 5252
	• 2 Harcourt Buildings	0171 583 9020
	• One Hare Court	020 7353 3171
	• Keating Chambers	0171 544 2600
	• 4 King's Bench Walk	0171 822 8822
	S Tomlinson QC	0171 583 0404
	8 King's Bench Walk	0171 797 8888
	• 11 King's Bench Walk,	0171 632 8500/583 0610
	11 King's Bench Walk, 1st Floor	0171 353 3337
	• 12 King's Bench Walk	0171 583 0811
	• Mitre Court Chambers	0171 353 9394
	• Monckton Chambers	0171 405 7211
	• 1 New Square	0171 405 0884/5/6/7
	• Chambers of John L Powell QC	0171 797 8000
	• 12 New Square	0171 419 1212
	11 Old Square	0171 242 5022/405 1074
	13 Old Square	0171 404 4800
	One Paper Buildings	0171 583 7355
	• 4 Pump Court	020 7842 5555
	• 5 Raymond Buildings	0171 242 2902

• Expanded entry in Part C

	No. 1 Serjeants' Inn	0171 415 6666
	● 3/4 South Square	0171 696 9900
	● Stanbrook & Henderson	0171 353 0101
	● 3 Stone Buildings	0171 242 4937
	● 9 Stone Buildings	0171 404 5055
	● 2 Temple Gardens	0171 583 6041
	3 Verulam Buildings	0171 831 8441
Manchester	● 8 King Street Chambers	0161 834 9560
	● Merchant Chambers	0161 839 7070
Nottingham	Ropewalk Chambers	0115 9472581
Preston	New Bailey Chambers	01772 258087
Wolverhampton	Claremont Chambers	01902 426222

INTELLECTUAL PROPERTY

Birmingham	1 Fountain Court	0121 236 5721
	● 3 Fountain Court	0121 236 5854
	● 5 Fountain Court	0121 606 0500
Bristol	St John's Chambers	0117 9213456/298514
Cardiff	9 Park Place	01222 382731
Chichester	Chichester Chambers	01243 784538
Leeds	Chambers of Andrew Campbell QC	0113 2455438
	● Chancery House Chambers	0113 244 6691
	The Chambers of Philip Raynor QC	0113 242 1123
	● Sovereign Chambers	0113 2451841/2/3
	● 9 Woodhouse Square	0113 2451986
London	17 Bedford Row	0171 831 7314
	● Blackstone Chambers	0171 583 1770
	Britton Street Chambers	0171 608 3765
	1 Crown Office Row	0171 583 9292
	● Doughty Street Chambers	0171 404 1313
	Equity Barristers' Chambers	0181 558 8336
	● One Essex Court	020 7583 2000
	● Essex Court Chambers	0171 813 8000
	● 20 Essex Street	0171 583 9294
	● 35 Essex Street	0171 353 6381
	● 4 Field Court	0171 440 6900
	● Fountain Court	0171 583 3335
	Francis Taylor Building	0171 353 7768/7769/2711
	● Gough Square Chambers	0171 353 0924
	Counsels' Chambers	0171 405 2576
	● 2 Harcourt Buildings	0171 583 9020
	● Hardwicke Building	020 7242 2523
	● One Hare Court	020 7353 3171
	9 King's Bench Walk	0171 353 7202/3909
	● 11 King's Bench Walk,	0171 632 8500/583 0610
	11 King's Bench Walk, 1st Floor	0171 353 3337
	Lamb Chambers	020 7797 8300
	● Littleton Chambers	0171 797 8600
	2 Mitre Court Buildings	0171 353 1353
	● Monckton Chambers	0171 405 7211
	● 1 New Square	0171 405 0884/5/6/7
	● 3 New Square	0171 405 1111
	5 New Square	020 7404 0404
	7 New Square	020 7404 5484
	● 8 New Square	0171 405 4321
	● 12 New Square	0171 419 1212
	19 Old Buildings	0171 405 2001
	● 11 Old Square	020 7430 0341
	● 3 Paper Buildings	020 7583 8055
	Phoenix Chambers	0171 404 7888
	● 5 Raymond Buildings	0171 242 2902

● Expanded entry in Part C

A

	• 11 South Square	0171 405 1222 (24hr messaging service)
	• Stanbrook & Henderson	0171 353 0101
	• 7 Stone Buildings	0171 405 3886/242 3546
	• 9 Stone Buildings	0171 404 5055
	11 Stone Buildings	+44 (0)207 831 6381
	3 Verulam Buildings	0171 831 8441
Manchester	• Byrom Street Chambers	0161 829 2100
	• Cobden House Chambers	0161 833 6000
	• 40 King Street	0161 832 9082
	• 8 King Street Chambers	0161 834 9560
	• Merchant Chambers	0161 839 7070
	• Queen's Chambers	0161 834 6875/4738
	• St James's Chambers	0161 834 7000
	18 St John Street	0161 278 1800
Newcastle upon Tyne	Westgate Chambers	0191 261 4407/2329785
Nottingham	King Charles House	0115 9418851
	Ropewalk Chambers	0115 9472581
Oxford	King's Bench Chambers	01865 311066
	3 Paper Buildings (Oxford)	01865 793736
Preston	New Bailey Chambers	01772 258087
	15 Winckley Square	01772 252828
Reading	Wessex Chambers	0118 956 8856
Southampton	• Eighteen Carlton Crescent	01703 639001
Swansea	Angel Chambers	01792 464623/464648
Winchester	3 Paper Buildings (Winchester)	01962 868884
Wolverhampton	Claremont Chambers	01902 426222

INTERNATIONAL LAW

London	Equity Barristers' Chambers	0181 558 8336

INTERNATIONAL TRADE

Birmingham	• 5 Fountain Court	0121 606 0500
Bristol	Guildhall Chambers	0117 9273366
Leeds	• Chancery House Chambers	0113 244 6691
Liverpool	• Exchange Chambers	0151 236 7747
London	• Blackstone Chambers	0171 583 1770
	Brick Court Chambers	0171 379 3550
	1 Crown Office Row	0171 583 9292
	• 4 Essex Court	020 7797 7970
	• Essex Court Chambers	0171 813 8000
	• 20 Essex Street	0171 583 9294
	• Chambers of Norman Palmer	0171 405 6114
	• 4 Field Court	0171 440 6900
	• Fountain Court	0171 583 3335
	• 2 Harcourt Buildings	0171 583 9020
	• One Hare Court	020 7353 3171
	John Street Chambers	0171 242 1911
	• 4 King's Bench Walk	0171 822 8822
	S Tomlinson QC	0171 583 0404
	• 11 King's Bench Walk	0171 632 8500/583 0610
	Lamb Chambers	020 7797 8300
	• Littleton Chambers	0171 797 8600
	• Littman Chambers	020 7404 4866
	• Monckton Chambers	0171 405 7211
	7 New Square	020 7404 5484
	• 12 New Square	0171 419 1212
	• 5 Paper Buildings	0171 583 9275/583 4555
	• 5 Raymond Buildings	0171 242 2902
	• 3/4 South Square	0171 696 9900
	• Stanbrook & Henderson	0171 353 0101

	• 9 Stone Buildings	0171 404 5055
	3 Verulam Buildings	0171 831 8441
	Warwick House Chambers	0171 430 2323
Manchester	• Byrom Street Chambers	0161 829 2100
Pontypridd	• Windsor Chambers	01443 402067
Preston	New Bailey Chambers	01772 258087

INTERNET LAW

Luton	Beresford Chambers	01582 429111

ISLAMIC LAW

London	Chambers of Dr Jamal Nasir	0171 405 3818/9
	Wynne Chambers	0181 961 6144

JUDICIAL REVIEW

Leeds	• 37 Park Square Chambers	0113 2439422
Liverpool	India Buildings Chambers	0151 243 6000
	• Oriel Chambers	0151 236 7191/236 4321
London	8 Gray's Inn Square	0171 242 3529
	Chambers of Harjit Singh	0171 353 1356 (4 Lines)
	• Hollis Whiteman Chambers	020 7583 5766
	• Thomas More Chambers	0171 404 7000
Manchester	• Central Chambers	0161 236 1133
	Lincoln House Chambers	0161 832 5701
Slough	Slough Chamber	01753 553806/817989

LAND LAW

London	Equity Barristers' Chambers	0181 558 8336

LANDLORD AND TENANT

Birmingham	1 Fountain Court	0121 236 5721
	• 3 Fountain Court	0121 236 5854
	• 5 Fountain Court	0121 606 0500
	• 8 Fountain Court	0121 236 5514/5
	New Court Chambers	0121 693 6656
	St Ive's Chambers	0121 236 0863/5720
	• St Philip's Chambers	0121 246 7000
Bournemouth	3 Paper Buildings (Bournemouth)	01202 292102
Bradford	Broadway House Chambers	01274 722560
Brighton	Crown Office Row Chambers	01273 625625
Bristol	Guildhall Chambers	0117 9273366
	Old Square Chambers	0117 9277111
	St John's Chambers	0117 9213456/298514
Cambridge	Fenners Chambers	01223 368761
Canterbury	• Becket Chambers	01227 786331
	Stour Chambers	01227 764899
Cardiff	9 Park Place	01222 382731
	30 Park Place	01222 398421
	32 Park Place	01222 397364
	• 33 Park Place	02920 233313
Chester	Nicholas Street Chambers	01244 323886
	Sedan House	01244 320480/348282
	White Friars Chambers	01244 323070
Chichester	Chichester Chambers	01243 784538
Colchester	East Anglian Chambers	01206 572756
Eastbourne	King's Chambers	01323 416053
Exeter	Cathedral Chambers (Jan Wood Independent Barristers' Clerk)	01392 210900
	Southernhay Chambers	01392 255777
	Walnut House	01392 279751
Guildford	• Guildford Chambers	01483 539131

• Expanded entry in Part C

A

Hull	Wilberforce Chambers	01482 323264
Ipswich	East Anglian Chambers	01473 214481
Leatherhead	Pembroke House	01372 376160/376493
Leeds	Chambers of Andrew Campbell QC	0113 2455438
	Broadway House Chambers	0113 246 2600
	• Chancery House Chambers	0113 244 6691
	Enterprise Chambers	0113 246 0391
	11 King's Bench Walk	0113 297 1200
	No. 6	0113 2459763
	• Park Court Chambers	0113 2433277
	Park Lane Chambers	0113 2285000
	The Chambers of Philip Raynor QC	0113 242 1123
	• 37 Park Square Chambers	0113 2439422
	• Sovereign Chambers	0113 2451841/2/3
	• St Paul's House	0113 2455866
	• 9 Woodhouse Square	0113 2451986
Leicester	Chambers of Michael Pert QC	0116 249 2020
Liverpool	25-27 Castle Street	0151 227 5661/051 236 5072
	19 Castle Street Chambers	0151 236 9402
	Chavasse Court Chambers	0151 707 1191
	• Corn Exchange Chambers	0151 227 1081/5009
	• Exchange Chambers	0151 236 7747
	First National Chambers	0151 236 2098
	India Buildings Chambers	0151 243 6000
	• Oriel Chambers	0151 236 7191/236 4321
London	Alban Chambers	0171 419 5051
	Albany Chambers	0171 485 5736/5758
	• Arden Chambers	020 7242 4244
	Barnard's Inn Chambers	0171 369 6969
	Barristers' Common Law Chambers	0171 375 3012
	9 Bedford Row	0171 242 3555
	17 Bedford Row	0171 831 7314
	33 Bedford Row	0171 242 6476
	• Chambers of Michael Pert QC	0171 421 8000
	Bell Yard Chambers	0171 306 9292
	11 Bolt Court (also at 7 Stone Buildings – 1st Floor)	0171 353 2300
	Bracton Chambers	0171 242 4248
	• 4 Breams Buildings	0171 353 5835/430 1221
	• 4 Brick Court	0171 797 8910
	Bridewell Chambers	020 7797 8800
	Britton Street Chambers	0171 608 3765
	39 Windsor Road	0181 349 9194
	• Chambers of Mr Peter Crampin QC	020 7831 0081
	• 1 Crown Office Row, Ground Floor	0171 797 7500
	1 Crown Office Row, 3rd Floor	0171 583 9292
	• Devereux Chambers	0171 353 7534
	• Doughty Street Chambers	0171 404 1313
	1 Dr Johnson's Buildings	0171 353 9328
	• 3 Dr Johnson's Buildings	0171 353 4854
	• Dr Johnson's Chambers	0171 353 4716
	• Enterprise Chambers	0171 405 9471
	• One Essex Court	0171 936 3030
	5 Essex Court	0171 410 2000
	• 35 Essex Street	0171 353 6381
	Chambers of Geoffrey Hawker	0171 583 8899
	Falcon Chambers	0171 353 2484
	• Farrar's Building	0171 583 9241
	• Chambers of Norman Palmer	0171 405 6114
	• 4 Field Court	0171 440 6900
	Fleet Chambers	0171 936 3707

• Expanded entry in Part C

Chambers of Wilfred Forster-Jones	0171 353 0853/4/7222
• Fountain Court	0171 583 3335
Francis Taylor Building	0171 353 7768/7769/2711
• 2nd Floor, Francis Taylor Building	0171 353 9942/3157
• Two Garden Court	0171 353 1633
• Goldsmith Building	0171 353 7881
Goldsmith Chambers	0171 353 6802/3/4/5
• 9 Gough Square	020 7832 0500
• Gough Square Chambers	0171 353 0924
• Gray's Inn Chambers, The Chambers of Norman Patterson	0171 831 5344
Gray's Inn Chambers	0171 831 7888 (Chambers)/ 0171 831 7904 (Mr M Ullah)
96 Gray's Inn Road	0171 405 0585
• 2-3 Gray's Inn Square	0171 242 4986
2 Gray's Inn Square Chambers	020 7242 0328
• 4-5 Gray's Inn Square	0171 404 5252
6 Gray's Inn Square	0171 242 1052
Counsels' Chambers	0171 405 2576
14 Gray's Inn Square	0171 242 0858
• 1 Harcourt Buildings	0171 353 9421/0375
• 2 Harcourt Buildings	0171 583 9020
• Hardwicke Building	020 7242 2523
• One Hare Court	020 7353 3171
Chambers of Harjit Singh	0171 353 1356 (4 Lines)
• Harrow on the Hill Chambers	0181 423 7444
• 1 Inner Temple Lane	020 7353 0933
John Street Chambers	0171 242 1911
Justice Court Chambers	0181 830 7786
• Keating Chambers	0171 544 2600
• 4 King's Bench Walk, Ground/First Floor/ Basement	0171 822 8822
4 King's Bench Walk, 2nd Floor	020 7353 3581
6 King's Bench Walk	0171 353 4931/583 0695
8 King's Bench Walk	0171 797 8888
9 King's Bench Walk	0171 353 7202/3909
10 King's Bench Walk	0171 353 7742
11 King's Bench Walk	0171 353 3337
• 12 King's Bench Walk	0171 583 0811
• 13 King's Bench Walk	0171 353 7204
2 King's Bench Walk Chambers	020 7353 9276
• Lamb Building	020 7797 7788
Lamb Chambers	020 7797 8300
Leone Chambers	0181 200 4020
Lion Court	0171 404 6565
• Littleton Chambers	0171 797 8600
• Littman Chambers	020 7404 4866
22 Melcombe Regis Court	0171 487 5589
2 Mitre Court Buildings, 1st Floor	0171 353 1353
2 Mitre Court Buildings, 2nd Floor	0171 583 1380
• Mitre Court Chambers	0171 353 9394
• Mitre House Chambers	0171 583 8233
• New Court	0171 583 5123/0510
• New Court Chambers	0171 831 9500
• 1 New Square	0171 405 0884/5/6/7
• Chambers of Lord Goodhart QC	0171 405 5577
• Chambers of John L Powell QC	0171 797 8000
5 New Square	020 7404 0404
• 12 New Square	0171 419 1212
• 22 Old Buildings	0171 831 0222
• Twenty-Four Old Buildings	0171 404 0946

• Expanded entry in Part C

A

• 9 Old Square	0171 405 4682
The Chambers of Leolin Price CBE, QC	0171 405 0758
11 Old Square, Ground Floor	0171 242 5022/405 1074
• 11 Old Square, Ground Floor	020 7430 0341
13 Old Square	0171 404 4800
• 2 Paper Buildings	020 7556 5500
• 3 Paper Buildings	020 7583 8055
• 4 Paper Buildings, Ground Floor	0171 353 3366/583 7155
• 4 Paper Buildings, 1st Floor	0171 583 0816/353 1131
• 5 Paper Buildings	0171 583 9275/583 4555
Phoenix Chambers	0171 404 7888
• 1 Pump Court	0171 583 2012/353 4341
2 Pump Court	0171 353 5597
• Pump Court Chambers	0171 353 0711
• 5 Pump Court	020 7353 2532
• Chambers of Kieran Coonan QC	0171 583 6013/2510
6 Pump Court	0171 797 8400
Queen Elizabeth Building	0171 797 7837
No. 1 Serjeants' Inn	0171 415 6666
Somersett Chambers	0171 404 6701
• Stanbrook & Henderson	0171 353 0101
Staple Inn Chambers	0171 242 5240
• 3 Stone Buildings	0171 242 4937
• 5 Stone Buildings	0171 242 6201
• 7 Stone Buildings	0171 405 3886/242 3546
7 Stone Buildings (also at 11 Bolt Court)	0171 242 0961
• 9 Stone Buildings	0171 404 5055
• 199 Strand	0171 379 9779
55 Temple Chambers	0171 353 7400
• 1 Temple Gardens	0171 583 1315/353 0407
• 2 Temple Gardens	0171 583 6041
• Thomas More Chambers	0171 404 7000
Tollgate Mews Chambers	0171 511 1838
• 14 Tooks Court	0171 405 8828
3 Verulam Buildings	0171 831 8441
Verulam Chambers	0171 813 2400
Warwick House Chambers	0171 430 2323
• Wilberforce Chambers	0171 306 0102

Maidstone

• Maidstone Chambers	01622 688592
6-8 Mill Street	01622 688094

Manchester

• Central Chambers	0161 236 1133
• Cobden House Chambers	0161 833 6000
Deans Court Chambers	0161 214 6000
Kenworthy's Chambers	0161 832 4036/834 6954
• 40 King Street	0161 832 9082
• 8 King Street Chambers	0161 834 9560
58 King Street Chambers	0161 831 7477
• Chambers of Ian Macdonald QC (In Association with Two Garden Court, Temple, London)	0161 236 1840
• Merchant Chambers	0161 839 7070
Peel Court Chambers	0161 832 3791
• Queen's Chambers	0161 834 6875/4738
• St James's Chambers	0161 834 7000
18 St John Street	0161 278 1800
24a St John Street	0161 833 9628
• 28 St John Street	0161 834 8418
Young Street Chambers	0161 833 0489

Middlesbrough

Baker Street Chambers	01642 873873

Milton Keynes

Milton Keynes Chambers	01908 664 128

Newcastle upon Tyne

• Broad Chare	0191 232 0541

• Expanded entry in Part C

	Cathedral Chambers	0191 232 1311
	Enterprise Chambers	0191 222 3344
	• Trinity Chambers	0191 232 1927
	Westgate Chambers	0191 261 4407/2329785
Northampton	Chartlands Chambers	01604 603322
	Chambers of Michael Pert QC	01604 602333
	Northampton Chambers	01604 636271
Norwich	East Anglian Chambers	01603 617351
	Octagon House	01603 623186
	Sackville Chambers	01603 613516/616221
Nottingham	King Charles House	0115 9418851
	Ropewalk Chambers	0115 9472581
Oxford	King's Bench Chambers	01865 311066
	3 Paper Buildings (Oxford)	01865 793736
	28 Western Road	01865 204911
Plymouth	Devon Chambers	01752 661659
Pontypridd	• Windsor Chambers	01443 402067
Portsmouth	• Portsmouth Barristers' Chambers	023 92 831292/811811
Preston	Deans Court Chambers	01772 555163
	New Bailey Chambers	01772 258087
	Queens Chambers	01772 828300
	15 Winckley Square	01772 252828
Reading	Wessex Chambers	0118 956 8856
Redhill	Redhill Chambers	01737 780781
Saint Albans	St Albans Chambers	01727 843383
Sheffield	Paradise Chambers	0114 2738951
Slough	Slough Chamber	01753 553806/817989
Southampton	• 17 Carlton Crescent	023 8032 0320/0823 2003
	• College Chambers	01703 230338
	• Eighteen Carlton Crescent	01703 639001
Stoke On Trent	Regent Chambers	01782 286666
Swansea	Angel Chambers	01792 464623/464648
	Iscoed Chambers	01792 652988/9/330
Swindon	Pump Court Chambers	01793 539899
Taunton	South Western Chambers	01823 331919 (24 hrs)
Winchester	3 Paper Buildings (Winchester)	01962 868884
	Pump Court Chambers	01962 868161
Wolverhampton	Claremont Chambers	01902 426222
Woodford Green	1 Wensley Avenue	0181 505 9259
York	• York Chambers	01904 620048

LICENSING

Birmingham	Coleridge Chambers	0121 233 8500
	1 Fountain Court	0121 236 5721
	• 3 Fountain Court	0121 236 5854
	• 5 Fountain Court	0121 606 0500
	6 Fountain Court	0121 233 3282
	• St Philip's Chambers	0121 246 7000
Bournemouth	3 Paper Buildings (Bournemouth)	01202 292102
Bradford	Broadway House Chambers	01274 722560
Brighton	Crown Office Row Chambers	01273 625625
Bristol	Guildhall Chambers	0117 9273366
	St John's Chambers	0117 9213456/298514
	Veritas Chambers	0117 930 8802
Cambridge	Fenners Chambers	01223 368761
Canterbury	• Becket Chambers	01227 786331
Cardiff	30 Park Place	01222 398421
	• 33 Park Place	02920 233313
Chester	Nicholas Street Chambers	01244 323886
	Sedan House	01244 320480/348282
Chichester	Chichester Chambers	01243 784538

• Expanded entry in Part C

A

Colchester	East Anglian Chambers	01206 572756
Exeter	Cathedral Chambers (Jan Wood Independent Barristers' Clerk)	01392 210900
	Walnut House	01392 279751
Guildford	• Guildford Chambers	01483 539131
Ipswich	East Anglian Chambers	01473 214481
Leeds	Chambers of Andrew Campbell QC	0113 2455438
	Broadway House Chambers	0113 246 2600
	11 King's Bench Walk	0113 297 1200
	• Park Court Chambers	0113 2433277
	The Chambers of Philip Raynor QC	0113 242 1123
	• 30 Park Square	0113 2436388
	• 37 Park Square Chambers	0113 2439422
	• Sovereign Chambers	0113 2451841/2/3
	• 9 Woodhouse Square	0113 2451986
Leicester	Chambers of Michael Pert QC	0116 249 2020
Liverpool	25-27 Castle Street	0151 227 5661/051 236 5072
	Chavasse Court Chambers	0151 707 1191
	• Corn Exchange Chambers	0151 227 1081/5009
	• Exchange Chambers	0151 236 7747
	First National Chambers	0151 236 2098
	India Buildings Chambers	0151 243 6000
London	Acre Lane Neighbourhood Chambers	0171 274 4400
	Barnard's Inn Chambers	0171 369 6969
	9 Bedford Row	0171 242 3555
	17 Bedford Row	0171 831 7314
	33 Bedford Row	0171 242 6476
	• Chambers of Michael Pert QC	0171 421 8000
	• 9-12 Bell Yard	0171 400 1800
	Bell Yard Chambers	0171 306 9292
	11 Bolt Court (also at 7 Stone Buildings – 1st Floor)	0171 353 2300
	Bracton Chambers	0171 242 4248
	• 4 Brick Court	0171 797 8910
	Bridewell Chambers	020 7797 8800
	1 Crown Office Row	0171 583 9292
	1 Dr Johnson's Buildings	0171 353 9328
	• One Essex Court, Ground Floor	020 7583 2000
	• One Essex Court, 1st Floor	0171 936 3030
	23 Essex Street	0171 413 0353/836 8366
	Chambers of Geoffrey Hawker	0171 583 8899
	• Chambers of Norman Palmer	0171 405 6114
	• 4 Field Court	0171 440 6900
	Chambers of Wilfred Forster-Jones	0171 353 0853/4/7222
	Francis Taylor Building	0171 353 7768/7769/2711
	• 2nd Floor, Francis Taylor Building	0171 353 9942/3157
	• Goldsmith Building	0171 353 7881
	Goldsmith Chambers	0171 353 6802/3/4/5
	• Gough Square Chambers	0171 353 0924
	• Gray's Inn Chambers, The Chambers of Norman Patterson	0171 831 5344
	96 Gray's Inn Road	0171 405 0585
	• 2-3 Gray's Inn Square	0171 242 4986
	2 Gray's Inn Square Chambers	020 7242 0328
	6 Gray's Inn Square	0171 242 1052
	Counsels' Chambers	0171 405 2576
	• 1 Harcourt Buildings	0171 353 9421/0375
	2 Harcourt Buildings, 1st Floor	020 7353 2112
	• 2 Harcourt Buildings, 2nd Floor	020 7353 8415
	• Hardwicke Building	020 7242 2523
	• 1 Hare Court	0171 353 3982/5324

• Expanded entry in Part C

A

● 3 Hare Court	0171 395 2000
Chambers of Harjit Singh	0171 353 1356 (4 Lines)
● Harrow on the Hill Chambers	0181 423 7444
● 1 Inner Temple Lane	020 7353 0933
John Street Chambers	0171 242 1911
● 4 King's Bench Walk	0171 822 8822
8 King's Bench Walk	0171 797 8888
9 King's Bench Walk	0171 353 7202/3909
10 King's Bench Walk	0171 353 7742
11 King's Bench Walk	0171 353 3337
● 13 King's Bench Walk	0171 353 7204
2 King's Bench Walk Chambers	020 7353 9276
● Lamb Building	020 7797 7788
Lion Court	0171 404 6565
● 1 Middle Temple Lane	0171 583 0659 (12 Lines)
2 Mitre Court Buildings	0171 583 1380
● Mitre Court Chambers	0171 353 9394
● Mitre House Chambers	0171 583 8233
● New Court	0171 583 5123/0510
● 3 New Square	0171 405 1111
● 22 Old Buildings	0171 831 0222
11 Old Square	0171 242 5022/405 1074
● 2 Paper Buildings	020 7556 5500
● 3 Paper Buildings	020 7583 8055
● 4 Paper Buildings	0171 353 3366/583 7155
Five Paper Buildings	0171 583 6117
Phoenix Chambers	0171 404 7888
● 1 Pump Court	0171 583 2012/353 4341
2 Pump Court	0171 353 5597
● Pump Court Chambers	0171 353 0711
● 4 Pump Court	020 7842 5555
● 5 Pump Court	020 7353 2532
6 Pump Court	0171 797 8400
● Queen Elizabeth Building	0171 353 7181 (12 Lines)
● Hollis Whiteman Chambers	020 7583 5766
● 3 Raymond Buildings	020 7831 3833
Staple Inn Chambers	0171 242 5240
7 Stone Buildings (also at 11 Bolt Court)	0171 242 0961
55 Temple Chambers	0171 353 7400
● 3 Temple Gardens	0171 353 3102/5/9297
● Thomas More Chambers	0171 404 7000
● 2-4 Tudor Street	0171 797 7111
Verulam Chambers	0171 813 2400
Warwick House Chambers	0171 430 2323

Maidstone

Earl Street Chambers	01622 671222
● Maidstone Chambers	01622 688592
6-8 Mill Street	01622 688094

Manchester

● Cobden House Chambers	0161 833 6000
Deans Court Chambers	0161 214 6000
Kenworthy's Chambers	0161 832 4036/834 6954
● 40 King Street	0161 832 9082
● 8 King Street Chambers	0161 834 9560
Lincoln House Chambers	0161 832 5701
● Chambers of Ian Macdonald QC (In Association with Two Garden Court, Temple, London)	0161 236 1840
Peel Court Chambers	0161 832 3791
● St James's Chambers	0161 834 7000
● 28 St John Street	0161 834 8418

Middlesbrough

Baker Street Chambers	01642 873873

Newcastle upon Tyne

● Broad Chare	0191 232 0541

● Expanded entry in Part C

A

	Cathedral Chambers	0191 232 1311
	• Trinity Chambers	0191 232 1927
	Westgate Chambers	0191 261 4407/2329785
Northampton	Chartlands Chambers	01604 603322
	Chambers of Michael Pert QC	01604 602333
	Northampton Chambers	01604 636271
Norwich	East Anglian Chambers	01603 617351
	Octagon House	01603 623186
	Sackville Chambers	01603 613516/616221
Nottingham	High Pavement Chambers	0115 9418218
	King Charles House	0115 9418851
	Ropewalk Chambers	0115 9472581
	St Mary's Chambers	0115 9503503
Oxford	King's Bench Chambers	01865 311066
	3 Paper Buildings (Oxford)	01865 793736
Peterborough	Fenners Chambers	01733 562030
Plymouth	Devon Chambers	01752 661659
Pontypridd	• Windsor Chambers	01443 402067
Preston	Deans Court Chambers	01772 555163
	New Bailey Chambers	01772 258087
	Queens Chambers	01772 828300
	15 Winckley Square	01772 252828
Reading	Wessex Chambers	0118 956 8856
Redhill	Redhill Chambers	01737 780781
Saint Albans	St Albans Chambers	01727 843383
Sheffield	Paradise Chambers	0114 2738951
Slough	Slough Chamber	01753 553806/817989
Southampton	• College Chambers	01703 230338
	• Eighteen Carlton Crescent	01703 639001
Stoke On Trent	Regent Chambers	01782 286666
Swansea	Angel Chambers	01792 464623/464648
	Iscoed Chambers	01792 652988/9/330
Swindon	Pump Court Chambers	01793 539899
Winchester	3 Paper Buildings (Winchester)	01962 868884
	Pump Court Chambers	01962 868161
Wolverhampton	Claremont Chambers	01902 426222
York	• York Chambers	01904 620048

LOCAL AUTHORITY CLAIMS
London	No. 1 Serjeants' Inn	0171 415 6666

LOCAL GOVERNMENT
Birmingham	• 3 Fountain Court	0121 236 5854
	• 5 Fountain Court	0121 606 0500
Bristol	Assize Court Chambers	0117 9264587
	St John's Chambers	0117 9213456/298514
Cambridge	Fenners Chambers	01223 368761
Canterbury	• Becket Chambers	01227 786331
Cardiff	30 Park Place	01222 398421
	• 33 Park Place	02920 233313
Chester	Nicholas Street Chambers	01244 323886
	Sedan House	01244 320480/348282
Chesterfield	26 Morley Avenue	01246 234790/01298 871350
Colchester	East Anglian Chambers	01206 572756
Durham	Durham Barristers' Chambers	0191 386 9199
Exeter	Cathedral Chambers (Jan Wood Independent Barristers' Clerk)	01392 210900
	Walnut House	01392 279751
Guildford	• Guildford Chambers	01483 539131
Ipswich	East Anglian Chambers	01473 214481
Leeds	Chambers of Andrew Campbell QC	0113 2455438

• Expanded entry in Part C

Leicester
Liverpool

London

The Chambers of Philip Raynor QC	0113 242 1123
• 37 Park Square Chambers	0113 2439422
• Sovereign Chambers	0113 2451841/2/3
Chambers of Michael Pert QC	0116 249 2020
25-27 Castle Street	0151 227 5661/051 236 5072
19 Castle Street Chambers	0151 236 9402
• Exchange Chambers	0151 236 7747
First National Chambers	0151 236 2098
Albany Chambers	0171 485 5736/5758
• Arden Chambers	020 7242 4244
Barnard's Inn Chambers	0171 369 6969
Barristers' Common Law Chambers	0171 375 3012
• Chambers of Michael Pert QC	0171 421 8000
• 9-12 Bell Yard	0171 400 1800
11 Bolt Court (also at 7 Stone Buildings – 1st Floor)	0171 353 2300
Bracton Chambers	0171 242 4248
• 4 Breams Buildings	0171 353 5835/430 1221
Brick Court Chambers	0171 379 3550
Cardinal Chambers	020 7353 2622
Cloisters	0171 827 4000
• Chambers of Mr Peter Crampin QC	020 7831 0081
• Devereux Chambers	0171 353 7534
• Doughty Street Chambers	0171 404 1313
1 Dr Johnson's Buildings	0171 353 9328
• Dr Johnson's Chambers	0171 353 4716
Equity Barristers' Chambers	0181 558 8336
• One Essex Court	0171 936 3030
23 Essex Street	0171 413 0353/836 8366
• 35 Essex Street	0171 353 6381
• 39 Essex Street	0171 832 1111
Chambers of Geoffrey Hawker	0171 583 8899
• Chambers of Norman Palmer	0171 405 6114
• 4 Field Court	0171 440 6900
• 2nd Floor, Francis Taylor Building	0171 353 9942/3157
One Garden Court Family Law Chambers	0171 797 7900
• Two Garden Court	0171 353 1633
Gray's Inn Chambers	0171 831 7888 (Chambers)/ 0171 831 7904 (Mr M Ullah)
• 2-3 Gray's Inn Square	0171 242 4986
• 4-5 Gray's Inn Square	0171 404 5252
Counsels' Chambers	0171 405 2576
• 1 Harcourt Buildings	0171 353 9421/0375
• 2 Harcourt Buildings, Ground Floor/Left	0171 583 9020
• 2 Harcourt Buildings, 2nd Floor	020 7353 8415
• Harcourt Chambers	0171 353 6961
• One Hare Court	020 7353 3171
• 3 Hare Court	0171 395 2000
• Harrow on the Hill Chambers	0181 423 7444
• Keating Chambers	0171 544 2600
• One King's Bench Walk	0171 936 1500
8 King's Bench Walk	0171 797 8888
10 King's Bench Walk	0171 353 7742
• 11 King's Bench Walk,	0171 632 8500/583 0610
11 King's Bench Walk, 1st Floor	0171 353 3337
• 13 King's Bench Walk	0171 353 7204
2 King's Bench Walk Chambers	020 7353 9276
• Lamb Building	020 7797 7788
Lamb Chambers	020 7797 8300
2 Mitre Court Buildings	0171 583 1380
• Mitre Court Chambers	0171 353 9394

• Expanded entry in Part C

A

	• Mitre House Chambers	0171 583 8233
	• 1 New Square	0171 405 0884/5/6/7
	• 12 New Square	0171 419 1212
	• 22 Old Buildings	0171 831 0222
	• 9 Old Square	0171 405 4682
	11 Old Square	0171 242 5022/405 1074
	• 1 Pump Court	0171 583 2012/353 4341
	6 Pump Court	0171 797 8400
	1 Serjeants' Inn	0171 583 1355
	• Stanbrook & Henderson	0171 353 0101
	7 Stone Buildings (also at 11 Bolt Court)	0171 242 0961
	• 3 Temple Gardens	0171 353 3102/5/9297
Maidstone	6-8 Mill Street	01622 688094
Manchester	• 40 King Street	0161 832 9082
	• 8 King Street Chambers	0161 834 9560
	• Chambers of Ian Macdonald QC (In Association with Two Garden Court, Temple, London)	0161 236 1840
	• Queen's Chambers	0161 834 6875/4738
	24a St John Street	0161 833 9628
Middlesbrough	Baker Street Chambers	01642 873873
Newcastle upon Tyne	Cathedral Chambers	0191 232 1311
	Milburn House Chambers	0191 230 5511
	• Trinity Chambers	0191 232 1927
	Westgate Chambers	0191 261 4407/2329785
Northampton	Chambers of Michael Pert QC	01604 602333
Norwich	East Anglian Chambers	01603 617351
Nottingham	Ropewalk Chambers	0115 9472581
Oxford	Harcourt Chambers	01865 791559
Peterborough	Fenners Chambers	01733 562030
Plymouth	Devon Chambers	01752 661659
Pontypridd	• Windsor Chambers	01443 402067
Preston	New Bailey Chambers	01772 258087
	Queens Chambers	01772 828300
Reading	Wessex Chambers	0118 956 8856
Redhill	Redhill Chambers	01737 780781
Saint Albans	St Albans Chambers	01727 843383
Slough	Slough Chamber	01753 553806/817989
Southampton	• 17 Carlton Crescent	023 8032 0320/0823 2003
Swansea	Iscoed Chambers	01792 652988/9/330
Taunton	South Western Chambers	01823 331919 (24 hrs)
Wolverhampton	Claremont Chambers	01902 426222

MALICIOUS PROSECUTION

London	• Dr Johnson's Chambers	0171 353 4716

MARKETS AND FAIRS

London	11 Stone Buildings	+44 (0)207 831 6381

MATRIMONIAL

London	Chambers of Harjit Singh	0171 353 1356 (4 Lines)

MEDIA

London	1 Brick Court	0171 353 8845
	13 Old Square	0171 404 4800

MEDIATION

Malvern	Resolution Chambers	01684 561279

MEDICAL LAW

Leeds	• 37 Park Square Chambers	0113 2439422

• Expanded entry in Part C

MEDICAL NEGLIGENCE

Ampthill	Bedford Chambers	0870 7337333
Birmingham	Coleridge Chambers	0121 233 8500
	1 Fountain Court	0121 236 5721
	• 3 Fountain Court	0121 236 5854
	• 5 Fountain Court	0121 606 0500
	• 8 Fountain Court	0121 236 5514/5
	New Court Chambers	0121 693 6656
	• St Philip's Chambers	0121 246 7000
Bournemouth	3 Paper Buildings (Bournemouth)	01202 292102
Bradford	Broadway House Chambers	01274 722560
Brighton	Crown Office Row Chambers	01273 625625
Bristol	Assize Court Chambers	0117 9264587
	Guildhall Chambers	0117 9273366
	St John's Chambers	0117 9213456/298514
Cambridge	Fenners Chambers	01223 368761
Canterbury	Stour Chambers	01227 764899
Cardiff	9 Park Place	01222 382731
	30 Park Place	01222 398421
	32 Park Place	01222 397364
	• 33 Park Place	02920 233313
Chester	Nicholas Street Chambers	01244 323886
	Sedan House	01244 320480/348282
	White Friars Chambers	01244 323070
Chichester	Chichester Chambers	01243 784538
Colchester	East Anglian Chambers	01206 572756
Durham	Durham Barristers' Chambers	0191 386 9199
Exeter	Cathedral Chambers (Jan Wood Independent Barristers' Clerk)	01392 210900
	Walnut House	01392 279751
Guildford	• Guildford Chambers	01483 539131
Ipswich	East Anglian Chambers	01473 214481
Leatherhead	Pembroke House	01372 376160/376493
Leeds	Chambers of Andrew Campbell QC	0113 2455438
	Broadway House Chambers	0113 246 2600
	• Chancery House Chambers	0113 244 6691
	11 King's Bench Walk	0113 297 1200
	No. 6	0113 2459763
	Park Lane Chambers	0113 2285000
	The Chambers of Philip Raynor QC	0113 242 1123
	• 30 Park Square	0113 2436388
	• 37 Park Square Chambers	0113 2439422
	• Sovereign Chambers	0113 2451841/2/3
	• St Paul's House	0113 2455866
	• 9 Woodhouse Square	0113 2451986
Leicester	Chambers of Michael Pert QC	0116 249 2020
Liverpool	25-27 Castle Street	0151 227 5661/051 236 5072
	19 Castle Street Chambers	0151 236 9402
	Chavasse Court Chambers	0151 707 1191
	• Corn Exchange Chambers	0151 227 1081/5009
	• Exchange Chambers	0151 236 7747
	First National Chambers	0151 236 2098
	India Buildings Chambers	0151 243 6000
	• Oriel Chambers	0151 236 7191/236 4321
London	Barnard's Inn Chambers	0171 369 6969
	9 Bedford Row	0171 242 3555
	17 Bedford Row	0171 831 7314
	33 Bedford Row	0171 242 6476
	• Chambers of Michael Pert QC	0171 421 8000
	11 Bolt Court (also at 7 Stone Buildings – 1st Floor)	0171 353 2300

• Expanded entry in Part C

A

• 4 Brick Court	0171 797 8910
Bridewell Chambers	020 7797 8800
Britton Street Chambers	0171 608 3765
Cloisters	0171 827 4000
• 1 Crown Office Row, Ground Floor	0171 797 7500
1 Crown Office Row, 3rd Floor	0171 583 9292
• Two Crown Office Row	020 7797 8100
• Devereux Chambers	0171 353 7534
• Doughty Street Chambers	0171 404 1313
1 Dr Johnson's Buildings	0171 353 9328
• Dr Johnson's Chambers	0171 353 4716
Equity Barristers' Chambers	0181 558 8336
• One Essex Court	0171 936 3030
5 Essex Court	0171 410 2000
• 35 Essex Street	0171 353 6381
• 39 Essex Street	0171 832 1111
Chambers of Geoffrey Hawker	0171 583 8899
• Farrar's Building	0171 583 9241
• Chambers of Norman Palmer	0171 405 6114
• 4 Field Court	0171 440 6900
• Fountain Court	0171 583 3335
Francis Taylor Building	0171 353 7768/7769/2711
• 2nd Floor, Francis Taylor Building	0171 353 9942/3157
• Two Garden Court	0171 353 1633
• Goldsmith Building	0171 353 7881
Goldsmith Chambers	0171 353 6802/3/4/5
• 9 Gough Square	020 7832 0500
• Gough Square Chambers	0171 353 0924
• Gray's Inn Chambers, The Chambers of	0171 831 5344
Norman Patterson	
Gray's Inn Chambers	0171 831 7888 (Chambers)/
	0171 831 7904 (Mr M Ullah)
96 Gray's Inn Road	0171 405 0585
2 Gray's Inn Square Chambers	020 7242 0328
Counsels' Chambers	0171 405 2576
• 1 Harcourt Buildings	0171 353 9421/0375
• 2 Harcourt Buildings	0171 583 9020
• Harcourt Chambers	0171 353 6961
• Harrow on the Hill Chambers	0181 423 7444
John Street Chambers	0171 242 1911
Justice Court Chambers	0181 830 7786
• One King's Bench Walk	0171 936 1500
• 4 King's Bench Walk	0171 822 8822
8 King's Bench Walk	0171 797 8888
9 King's Bench Walk	0171 353 7202/3909
10 King's Bench Walk	0171 353 7742
11 King's Bench Walk	0171 353 3337
• 13 King's Bench Walk	0171 353 7204
• Lamb Building	020 7797 7788
Lamb Chambers	020 7797 8300
Lion Court	0171 404 6565
• Littleton Chambers	0171 797 8600
• 1 Middle Temple Lane	0171 583 0659 (12 Lines)
• Mitre House Chambers	0171 583 8233
• New Court	0171 583 5123/0510
• New Court Chambers	0171 831 9500
• Chambers of John L Powell QC	0171 797 8000
• 12 New Square	0171 419 1212
• 22 Old Buildings	0171 831 0222
• 3 Paper Buildings	020 7583 8055
• 4 Paper Buildings, Ground Floor	0171 353 3366/583 7155

• 4 Paper Buildings, 1st Floor	0171 583 0816/353 1131
• 5 Paper Buildings	0171 583 9275/583 4555
Phoenix Chambers	0171 404 7888
Plowden Buildings	0171 583 0808
• 1 Pump Court	0171 583 2012/353 4341
2 Pump Court	0171 353 5597
• Pump Court Chambers	0171 353 0711
• 4 Pump Court	020 7842 5555
• 5 Pump Court	020 7353 2532
• Chambers of Kieran Coonan QC	0171 583 6013/2510
6 Pump Court	0171 797 8400
Queen Elizabeth Building	0171 797 7837
No. 1 Serjeants' Inn	0171 415 6666
• 3 Serjeants' Inn	0171 353 5537
• Stanbrook & Henderson	0171 353 0101
7 Stone Buildings (also at 11 Bolt Court)	0171 242 0961
8 Stone Buildings	0171 831 9881
• 9 Stone Buildings	0171 404 5055
• 199 Strand	0171 379 9779
• 1 Temple Gardens	0171 583 1315/353 0407
• 2 Temple Gardens	0171 583 6041
• Thomas More Chambers	0171 404 7000
• 14 Tooks Court	0171 405 8828
3 Verulam Buildings	0171 831 8441
Verulam Chambers	0171 813 2400
Warwick House Chambers	0171 430 2323

Maidstone
Manchester

6-8 Mill Street	01622 688094
• Byrom Street Chambers	0161 829 2100
• Central Chambers	0161 236 1133
• Cobden House Chambers	0161 833 6000
Deans Court Chambers	0161 214 6000
Kenworthy's Chambers	0161 832 4036/834 6954
• 40 King Street	0161 832 9082
• 8 King Street Chambers	0161 834 9560
58 King Street Chambers	0161 831 7477
Lincoln House Chambers	0161 832 5701
• Chambers of Ian Macdonald QC (In Association with Two Garden Court, Temple, London)	0161 236 1840
• Merchant Chambers	0161 839 7070
Peel Court Chambers	0161 832 3791
• Queen's Chambers	0161 834 6875/4738
• St James's Chambers	0161 834 7000
18 St John Street	0161 278 1800
• 28 St John Street	0161 834 8418
Young Street Chambers	0161 833 0489

Middlesbrough
Milton Keynes
Newcastle upon Tyne

Baker Street Chambers	01642 873873
Milton Keynes Chambers	01908 664 128
• Broad Chare	0191 232 0541
Cathedral Chambers	0191 232 1311
• Trinity Chambers	0191 232 1927
Westgate Chambers	0191 261 4407/2329785

Northampton

Chambers of Michael Pert QC	01604 602333
Northampton Chambers	01604 636271

Norwich
Nottingham

East Anglian Chambers	01603 617351
King Charles House	0115 9418851
Ropewalk Chambers	0115 9472581
St Mary's Chambers	0115 9503503

Oxford

Harcourt Chambers	01865 791559
King's Bench Chambers	01865 311066
3 Paper Buildings (Oxford)	01865 793736

• Expanded entry in Part C

A

Peterborough	Fenners Chambers	01733 562030
Plymouth	Devon Chambers	01752 661659
Pontypridd	● Windsor Chambers	01443 402067
Portsmouth	● Portsmouth Barristers' Chambers	023 92 831292/811811
Preston	Deans Court Chambers	01772 555163
	New Bailey Chambers	01772 258087
	Queens Chambers	01772 828300
	15 Winckley Square	01772 252828
Reading	Wessex Chambers	0118 956 8856
Redhill	Redhill Chambers	01737 780781
Saint Albans	St Albans Chambers	01727 843383
Sheffield	Paradise Chambers	0114 2738951
Slough	Slough Chamber	01753 553806/817989
Southampton	● 17 Carlton Crescent	023 8032 0320/0823 2003
	● College Chambers	01703 230338
	● Eighteen Carlton Crescent	01703 639001
Stoke On Trent	Regent Chambers	01782 286666
Swansea	Angel Chambers	01792 464623/464648
	Iscoed Chambers	01792 652988/9/330
Swindon	Pump Court Chambers	01793 539899
Taunton	South Western Chambers	01823 331919 (24 hrs)
Winchester	3 Paper Buildings (Winchester)	01962 868884
	Pump Court Chambers	01962 868161
Wolverhampton	Claremont Chambers	01902 426222
Woodford Green	1 Wensley Avenue	0181 505 9259
York	● York Chambers	01904 620048

MENTAL HEALTH

Birmingham	Coleridge Chambers	0121 233 8500
	● 5 Fountain Court	0121 606 0500
	● 8 Fountain Court	0121 236 5514/5
Bradford	Broadway House Chambers	01274 722560
Bristol	St John's Chambers	0117 9213456/298514
	Veritas Chambers	0117 930 8802
Cardiff	32 Park Place	01222 397364
Chester	Nicholas Street Chambers	01244 323886
Guildford	● Guildford Chambers	01483 539131
Leeds	Broadway House Chambers	0113 246 2600
	No. 6	0113 2459763
	● 30 Park Square	0113 2436388
	● St Paul's House	0113 2455866
	● 9 Woodhouse Square	0113 2451986
Leicester	Chambers of Michael Pert QC	0116 249 2020
Liverpool	● Corn Exchange Chambers	0151 227 1081/5009
	● Exchange Chambers	0151 236 7747
	India Buildings Chambers	0151 243 6000
London	ACHMA Chambers	0171 639 7817/0171 635 7904
	Barnard's Inn Chambers	0171 369 6969
	9 Bedford Row	0171 242 3555
	● Chambers of Michael Pert QC	0171 421 8000
	● 4 Breams Buildings	0171 353 5835/430 1221
	Bridewell Chambers	020 7797 8800
	1 Crown Office Row	0171 583 9292
	● Devereux Chambers	0171 353 7534
	● Doughty Street Chambers	0171 404 1313
	1 Dr Johnson's Buildings	0171 353 9328
	5 Essex Court	0171 410 2000
	● 39 Essex Street	0171 832 1111
	● Chambers of Norman Palmer	0171 405 6114
	Francis Taylor Building	0171 353 7768/7769/2711
	One Garden Court Family Law Chambers	0171 797 7900

● Expanded entry in Part C

	• Two Garden Court	0171 353 1633
	• Goldsmith Building	0171 353 7881
	Goldsmith Chambers	0171 353 6802/3/4/5
	• Gray's Inn Chambers, The Chambers of	0171 831 5344
	Norman Patterson	
	96 Gray's Inn Road	0171 405 0585
	6 Gray's Inn Square	0171 242 1052
	Counsels' Chambers	0171 405 2576
	14 Gray's Inn Square	0171 242 0858
	2 Harcourt Buildings	020 7353 2112
	John Street Chambers	0171 242 1911
	• One King's Bench Walk	0171 936 1500
	8 King's Bench Walk	0171 797 8888
	9 King's Bench Walk	0171 353 7202/3909
	10 King's Bench Walk	0171 353 7742
	• 13 King's Bench Walk	0171 353 7204
	• Lamb Building	020 7797 7788
	Lamb Chambers	020 7797 8300
	• Mitre Court Chambers	0171 353 9394
	• Mitre House Chambers	0171 583 8233
	• New Court	0171 583 5123/0510
	• 12 New Square	0171 419 1212
	• 22 Old Buildings	0171 831 0222
	13 Old Square	0171 404 4800
	• 4 Paper Buildings	0171 353 3366/583 7155
	Phoenix Chambers	0171 404 7888
	• 1 Pump Court	0171 583 2012/353 4341
	• Chambers of Kieran Coonan QC	0171 583 6013/2510
	• 3 Serjeants' Inn	0171 353 5537
	Somersett Chambers	0171 404 6701
	Staple Inn Chambers	0171 242 5240
	• 5 Stone Buildings	0171 242 6201
	55 Temple Chambers	0171 353 7400
	• 1 Temple Gardens	0171 583 1315/353 0407
	• 3 Temple Gardens	0171 353 3102/5/9297
	• 14 Tooks Court	0171 405 8828
	Warwick House Chambers	0171 430 2323
Manchester	• Central Chambers	0161 236 1133
	Kenworthy's Chambers	0161 832 4036/834 6954
	• 8 King Street Chambers	0161 834 9560
	Lincoln House Chambers	0161 832 5701
	• Chambers of Ian Macdonald QC (In	0161 236 1840
	Association with Two Garden Court,	
	Temple, London)	
	• St James's Chambers	0161 834 7000
Middlesbrough	Baker Street Chambers	01642 873873
Northampton	Chartlands Chambers	01604 603322
	Chambers of Michael Pert QC	01604 602333
Nottingham	King Charles House	0115 9418851
Oxford	King's Bench Chambers	01865 311066
Plymouth	Devon Chambers	01752 661659
Pontypridd	• Windsor Chambers	01443 402067
Preston	Queens Chambers	01772 828300
	15 Winckley Square	01772 252828
Saint Albans	St Albans Chambers	01727 843383
Southampton	• College Chambers	01703 230338
Taunton	South Western Chambers	01823 331919 (24 hrs)
York	• York Chambers	01904 620048

MIDDLE EAST/PAKISTANI/ISLAMIC LAW

London	Justice Court Chambers	0181 830 7786

• Expanded entry in Part C

A

MINES AND MINERALS
London	• Chambers of Mr Peter Crampin QC	020 7831 0081
	• 11 Old Square	020 7430 0341

MORTGAGES
London	11 Stone Buildings	+44 (0)207 831 6381

MORTGAGES AND BORROWERS
Milton Keynes	Milton Keynes Chambers	01908 664 128

MOTORING LAW
London	22 Melcombe Regis Court	0171 487 5589

NATIONAL INSURANCE
London	Prince Henry's Chambers	0171 713 0376

OFFICIAL REFEREE
Manchester	Lincoln House Chambers	0161 832 5701

PARLIAMENTARY
Leeds	The Chambers of Philip Raynor QC	0113 242 1123
London	• 4 Breams Buildings	0171 353 5835/430 1221
	• Fountain Court	0171 583 3335
	• 4-5 Gray's Inn Square	0171 404 5252
	• 2 Harcourt Buildings, Ground Floor/Left	0171 583 9020
	• 2 Harcourt Buildings, 2nd Floor	020 7353 8415
	• One Hare Court	020 7353 3171
	• One King's Bench Walk	0171 936 1500
	• Littleton Chambers	0171 797 8600
	2 Mitre Court Buildings	0171 583 1380
	• 12 New Square	0171 419 1212
	• 4 Paper Buildings	0171 353 3366/583 7155
	6 Pump Court	0171 797 8400
	1 Serjeants' Inn	0171 583 1355
	• Stanbrook & Henderson	0171 353 0101
Maidstone	6-8 Mill Street	01622 688094
Manchester	• 40 King Street	0161 832 9082

PARTNERSHIPS
Birmingham	1 Fountain Court	0121 236 5721
	• 3 Fountain Court	0121 236 5854
	• 5 Fountain Court	0121 606 0500
	• 8 Fountain Court	0121 236 5514/5
	• St Philip's Chambers	0121 246 7000
Bradford	Broadway House Chambers	01274 722560
Bristol	Guildhall Chambers	0117 9273366
	St John's Chambers	0117 9213456/298514
Cambridge	Fenners Chambers	01223 368761
Canterbury	• Becket Chambers	01227 786331
	Stour Chambers	01227 764899
Cardiff	9 Park Place	01222 382731
	30 Park Place	01222 398421
	• 33 Park Place	02920 233313
Chester	Nicholas Street Chambers	01244 323886
Chichester	Chichester Chambers	01243 784538
Exeter	Cathedral Chambers (Jan Wood Independent Barristers' Clerk)	01392 210900
	Southernhay Chambers	01392 255777
Leeds	Chambers of Andrew Campbell QC	0113 2455438
	Broadway House Chambers	0113 246 2600
	• Chancery House Chambers	0113 244 6691

• Expanded entry in Part C

Liverpool

London

Enterprise Chambers	0113 246 0391
11 King's Bench Walk	0113 297 1200
No. 6	0113 2459763
The Chambers of Philip Raynor QC	0113 242 1123
• 30 Park Square	0113 2436388
• 37 Park Square Chambers	0113 2439422
• Sovereign Chambers	0113 2451841/2/3
• Corn Exchange Chambers	0151 227 1081/5009
• Exchange Chambers	0151 236 7747
India Buildings Chambers	0151 243 6000
Barnard's Inn Chambers	0171 369 6969
Barristers' Common Law Chambers	0171 375 3012
9 Bedford Row	0171 242 3555
17 Bedford Row	0171 831 7314
48 Bedford Row	0171 430 2005
• Blackstone Chambers	0171 583 1770
11 Bolt Court (also at 7 Stone Buildings – 1st Floor)	0171 353 2300
• 4 Breams Buildings	0171 353 5835/430 1221
Bridewell Chambers	020 7797 8800
• Chambers of Mr Peter Crampin QC	020 7831 0081
1 Crown Office Row	0171 583 9292
• Enterprise Chambers	0171 405 9471
• Erskine Chambers	0171 242 5532
• One Essex Court	020 7583 2000
• Essex Court Chambers	0171 813 8000
• 35 Essex Street	0171 353 6381
Chambers of Geoffrey Hawker	0171 583 8899
• Chambers of Norman Palmer	0171 405 6114
• 4 Field Court	0171 440 6900
• Fountain Court	0171 583 3335
• 2nd Floor, Francis Taylor Building	0171 353 9942/3157
• Goldsmith Building	0171 353 7881
Counsels' Chambers	0171 405 2576
• 1 Harcourt Buildings	0171 353 9421/0375
• 2 Harcourt Buildings	0171 583 9020
• Hardwicke Building	020 7242 2523
• One Hare Court	020 7353 3171
• Harrow on the Hill Chambers	0181 423 7444
11 King's Bench Walk	0171 353 3337
• 13 King's Bench Walk	0171 353 7204
• Lamb Building	020 7797 7788
Lamb Chambers	020 7797 8300
• Littleton Chambers	0171 797 8600
• Littman Chambers	020 7404 4866
2 Mitre Court Buildings	0171 353 1353
• Mitre Court Chambers	0171 353 9394
• 1 New Square	0171 405 0884/5/6/7
• Chambers of Lord Goodhart QC	0171 405 5577
• Chambers of John L Powell QC	0171 797 8000
5 New Square	020 7404 0404
• 12 New Square	0171 419 1212
• 22 Old Buildings	0171 831 0222
• Twenty-Four Old Buildings	0171 404 0946
• 9 Old Square	0171 405 4682
The Chambers of Leolin Price CBE, QC	0171 405 0758
• 11 Old Square	020 7430 0341
13 Old Square	0171 404 4800
• 4 Paper Buildings, Ground Floor	0171 353 3366/583 7155
• 4 Paper Buildings, 1st Floor	0171 583 0816/353 1131
Phoenix Chambers	0171 404 7888

• Expanded entry in Part C

A

• Serle Court Chambers	0171 242 6105
• 3/4 South Square	0171 696 9900
• Stanbrook & Henderson	0171 353 0101
• 3 Stone Buildings	0171 242 4937
4 Stone Buildings	0171 242 5524
• 5 Stone Buildings	0171 242 6201
• 7 Stone Buildings	0171 405 3886/242 3546
7 Stone Buildings (also at 11 Bolt Court)	0171 242 0961
• 9 Stone Buildings	0171 404 5055
• 199 Strand	0171 379 9779
• Thomas More Chambers	0171 404 7000
3 Verulam Buildings	0171 831 8441
Verulam Chambers	0171 813 2400

Manchester
• Cobden House Chambers	0161 833 6000
• 40 King Street	0161 832 9082
• 8 King Street Chambers	0161 834 9560
• Merchant Chambers	0161 839 7070
• St James's Chambers	0161 834 7000
Young Street Chambers	0161 833 0489

Milton Keynes Milton Keynes Chambers — 01908 664 128
Newcastle upon Tyne Enterprise Chambers — 0191 222 3344
• Trinity Chambers — 0191 232 1927
Westgate Chambers — 0191 261 4407/2329785
Northampton Northampton Chambers — 01604 636271
Nottingham King Charles House — 0115 9418851
Ropewalk Chambers — 0115 9472581
St Mary's Chambers — 0115 9503503
Oxford King's Bench Chambers — 01865 311066
Peterborough Fenners Chambers — 01733 562030
Portsmouth • Portsmouth Barristers' Chambers — 023 92 831292/811811
Preston New Bailey Chambers — 01772 258087
15 Winckley Square — 01772 252828
Reading Wessex Chambers — 0118 956 8856
Redhill Redhill Chambers — 01737 780781
Southampton • 17 Carlton Crescent — 023 8032 0320/0823 2003
• Eighteen Carlton Crescent — 01703 639001
Swansea Iscoed Chambers — 01792 652988/9/330
Wolverhampton Claremont Chambers — 01902 426222

PATENTS

Birmingham 1 Fountain Court — 0121 236 5721
• 5 Fountain Court — 0121 606 0500
Bristol St John's Chambers — 0117 9213456/298514
Leeds Chambers of Andrew Campbell QC — 0113 2455438
• Sovereign Chambers — 0113 2451841/2/3
London • Fountain Court — 0171 583 3335
Francis Taylor Building — 0171 353 7768/7769/2711
• 2 Harcourt Buildings — 0171 583 9020
• One Hare Court — 020 7353 3171
9 King's Bench Walk — 0171 353 7202/3909
11 King's Bench Walk — 0171 353 3337
2 Mitre Court Buildings — 0171 353 1353
• 3 New Square — 0171 405 1111
5 New Square — 020 7404 0404
7 New Square — 020 7404 5484
• 8 New Square — 0171 405 4321
19 Old Buildings — 0171 405 2001
• 11 South Square — 0171 405 1222 (24hr messaging service)
• Stanbrook & Henderson — 0171 353 0101
Manchester • Cobden House Chambers — 0161 833 6000

• Expanded entry in Part C

A

	• St James's Chambers	0161 834 7000
Pontypridd	• Windsor Chambers	01443 402067
Preston	New Bailey Chambers	01772 258087
	Queens Chambers	01772 828300
Reading	Wessex Chambers	0118 956 8856
Wolverhampton	Claremont Chambers	01902 426222

PENSIONS

Birmingham	• 5 Fountain Court	0121 606 0500
	• St Philip's Chambers	0121 246 7000
Bristol	Guildhall Chambers	0117 9273366
	St John's Chambers	0117 9213456/298514
Cambridge	Fenners Chambers	01223 368761
Chester	White Friars Chambers	01244 323070
Leeds	Chambers of Andrew Campbell QC	0113 2455438
	11 King's Bench Walk	0113 297 1200
	The Chambers of Philip Raynor QC	0113 242 1123
	• Sovereign Chambers	0113 2451841/2/3
Liverpool	• Exchange Chambers	0151 236 7747
London	9 Bedford Row	0171 242 3555
	• Chambers of Mr Peter Crampin QC	020 7831 0081
	• Devereux Chambers	0171 353 7534
	• 35 Essex Street	0171 353 6381
	11 King's Bench Walk	0171 353 3337
	• Mitre House Chambers	0171 583 8233
	• Monckton Chambers	0171 405 7211
	• 1 New Square	0171 405 0884/5/6/7
	• Chambers of Lord Goodhart QC	0171 405 5577
	• 12 New Square	0171 419 1212
	• Twenty-Four Old Buildings	0171 404 0946
	24 Old Buildings	020 7242 2744
	The Chambers of Leolin Price CBE, QC	0171 405 0758
	• 11 Old Square	020 7430 0341
	13 Old Square	0171 404 4800
	• 3/4 South Square	0171 696 9900
	• 3 Stone Buildings	0171 242 4937
	• 5 Stone Buildings	0171 242 6201
	• 7 Stone Buildings	0171 405 3886/242 3546
	• 9 Stone Buildings	0171 404 5055
	Tower Hamlets Barristers Chambers	0171 377 8090
	3 Verulam Buildings	0171 831 8441
	Verulam Chambers	0171 813 2400
	• Wilberforce Chambers	0171 306 0102
Manchester	• Cobden House Chambers	0161 833 6000
	• 40 King Street	0161 832 9082
	• 8 King Street Chambers	0161 834 9560
	• St James's Chambers	0161 834 7000
	• 28 St John Street	0161 834 8418
Milton Keynes	Milton Keynes Chambers	01908 664 128
Peterborough	Fenners Chambers	01733 562030
Pontypridd	• Windsor Chambers	01443 402067
Portsmouth	• Portsmouth Barristers' Chambers	023 92 831292/811811
Rugby	Merriemore Cottage	01788 891832
Southampton	• Eighteen Carlton Crescent	01703 639001
Taunton	South Western Chambers	01823 331919 (24 hrs)

PERSONAL INJURY

Ampthill	Bedford Chambers	0870 7337333
Birmingham	Coleridge Chambers	0121 233 8500
	1 Fountain Court	0121 236 5721
	• 3 Fountain Court	0121 236 5854

• Expanded entry in Part C

	• 5 Fountain Court	0121 606 0500
	• 8 Fountain Court	0121 236 5514/5
	New Court Chambers	0121 693 6656
	St Ive's Chambers	0121 236 0863/5720
	• St Philip's Chambers	0121 246 7000
Bournemouth	3 Paper Buildings (Bournemouth)	01202 292102
Bradford	Broadway House Chambers	01274 722560
Brighton	Crown Office Row Chambers	01273 625625
Bristol	Assize Court Chambers	0117 9264587
	Guildhall Chambers	0117 9273366
	Old Square Chambers	0117 9277111
	St John's Chambers	0117 9213456/298514
Cambridge	Fenners Chambers	01223 368761
Canterbury	• Becket Chambers	01227 786331
	Stour Chambers	01227 764899
Cardiff	9 Park Place	01222 382731
	30 Park Place	01222 398421
	32 Park Place	01222 397364
	• 33 Park Place	02920 233313
Chester	Nicholas Street Chambers	01244 323886
	Sedan House	01244 320480/348282
	White Friars Chambers	01244 323070
Chichester	Chichester Chambers	01243 784538
Colchester	East Anglian Chambers	01206 572756
Consett	6 Ascot Road	01207 507785
Durham	Durham Barristers' Chambers	0191 386 9199
Eastbourne	King's Chambers	01323 416053
Exeter	Cathedral Chambers (Jan Wood Independent Barristers' Clerk)	01392 210900
	Southernhay Chambers	01392 255777
	Walnut House	01392 279751
Guildford	• Guildford Chambers	01483 539131
Hull	Wilberforce Chambers	01482 323264
Ipswich	East Anglian Chambers	01473 214481
Leatherhead	Pembroke House	01372 376160/376493
Leeds	Chambers of Andrew Campbell QC	0113 2455438
	Broadway House Chambers	0113 246 2600
	• Chancery House Chambers	0113 244 6691
	11 King's Bench Walk	0113 297 1200
	• Mercury Chambers	0113 234 2265
	No. 6	0113 2459763
	• Park Court Chambers	0113 2433277
	Park Lane Chambers	0113 2285000
	The Chambers of Philip Raynor QC	0113 242 1123
	• 30 Park Square	0113 2436388
	• 37 Park Square Chambers	0113 2439422
	• Sovereign Chambers	0113 2451841/2/3
	• St Paul's House	0113 2455866
	• 9 Woodhouse Square	0113 2451986
Leicester	Chambers of Michael Pert QC	0116 249 2020
Liverpool	25-27 Castle Street	0151 227 5661/051 236 5072
	19 Castle Street Chambers	0151 236 9402
	Chavasse Court Chambers	0151 707 1191
	• Corn Exchange Chambers	0151 227 1081/5009
	• Exchange Chambers	0151 236 7747
	First National Chambers	0151 236 2098
	India Buildings Chambers	0151 243 6000
	• Oriel Chambers	0151 236 7191/236 4321
London	Acre Lane Neighbourhood Chambers	0171 274 4400
	Albany Chambers	0171 485 5736/5758
	Barnard's Inn Chambers	0171 369 6969

• Expanded entry in Part C

A

Barristers' Common Law Chambers	0171 375 3012
9 Bedford Row	0171 242 3555
17 Bedford Row	0171 831 7314
33 Bedford Row	0171 242 6476
• Chambers of Michael Pert QC	0171 421 8000
• 9-12 Bell Yard	0171 400 1800
Bell Yard Chambers	0171 306 9292
11 Bolt Court (also at 7 Stone Buildings – 1st Floor)	0171 353 2300
Bracton Chambers	0171 242 4248
• 4 Brick Court	0171 797 8910
Bridewell Chambers	020 7797 8800
Britton Street Chambers	0171 608 3765
Cloisters	0171 827 4000
• 1 Crown Office Row, Ground Floor	0171 797 7500
1 Crown Office Row, 3rd Floor	0171 583 9292
• Two Crown Office Row	020 7797 8100
• Devereux Chambers	0171 353 7534
• Doughty Street Chambers	0171 404 1313
1 Dr Johnson's Buildings	0171 353 9328
• Dr Johnson's Chambers	0171 353 4716
Equity Barristers' Chambers	0181 558 8336
• 4 Essex Court	020 7797 7970
5 Essex Court	0171 410 2000
23 Essex Street	0171 413 0353/836 8366
• 35 Essex Street	0171 353 6381
• 39 Essex Street	0171 832 1111
Chambers of Geoffrey Hawker	0171 583 8899
• Farrar's Building	0171 583 9241
• Chambers of Norman Palmer	0171 405 6114
• 4 Field Court	0171 440 6900
Chambers of Wilfred Forster-Jones	0171 353 0853/4/7222
• Fountain Court	0171 583 3335
Francis Taylor Building	0171 353 7768/7769/2711
• 2nd Floor, Francis Taylor Building	0171 353 9942/3157
• Two Garden Court	0171 353 1633
• Goldsmith Building	0171 353 7881
Goldsmith Chambers	0171 353 6802/3/4/5
• 9 Gough Square	020 7832 0500
• Gough Square Chambers	0171 353 0924
• Gray's Inn Chambers, The Chambers of Norman Patterson	0171 831 5344
96 Gray's Inn Road	0171 405 0585
• 2-3 Gray's Inn Square	0171 242 4986
2 Gray's Inn Square Chambers	020 7242 0328
6 Gray's Inn Square	0171 242 1052
Counsels' Chambers	0171 405 2576
14 Gray's Inn Square	0171 242 0858
• 1 Harcourt Buildings	0171 353 9421/0375
• 2 Harcourt Buildings	0171 583 9020
• Harcourt Chambers	0171 353 6961
• Hardwicke Building	020 7242 2523
• 1 Hare Court	0171 353 3982/5324
Chambers of Harjit Singh	0171 353 1356 (4 Lines)
• Harrow on the Hill Chambers	0181 423 7444
• 1 Inner Temple Lane	020 7353 0933
John Street Chambers	0171 242 1911
Justice Court Chambers	0181 830 7786
• One King's Bench Walk	0171 936 1500
• 4 King's Bench Walk, Ground/First Floor/ Basement	0171 822 8822

• Expanded entry in Part C

A

4 King's Bench Walk, 2nd Floor	020 7353 3581
6 King's Bench Walk	0171 353 4931/583 0695
8 King's Bench Walk	0171 797 8888
9 King's Bench Walk	0171 353 7202/3909
10 King's Bench Walk	0171 353 7742
11 King's Bench Walk	0171 353 3337
• 12 King's Bench Walk	0171 583 0811
• 13 King's Bench Walk	0171 353 7204
2 King's Bench Walk Chambers	020 7353 9276
Lamb Chambers	020 7797 8300
Lion Court	0171 404 6565
• Littleton Chambers	0171 797 8600
• 1 Middle Temple Lane	0171 583 0659 (12 Lines)
2 Mitre Court Buildings	0171 353 1353
• Mitre Court Chambers	0171 353 9394
• Mitre House Chambers	0171 583 8233
• New Court	0171 583 5123/0510
• New Court Chambers	0171 831 9500
• 1 New Square	0171 405 0884/5/6/7
• Chambers of John L Powell QC	0171 797 8000
• 22 Old Buildings	0171 831 0222
11 Old Square	0171 242 5022/405 1074
• Old Square Chambers	0171 269 0300
One Paper Buildings	0171 583 7355
2 Paper Buildings, Basement North	0171 936 2613
• 3 Paper Buildings	020 7583 8055
• 4 Paper Buildings, Ground Floor	0171 353 3366/583 7155
• 4 Paper Buildings, 1st Floor	0171 583 0816/353 1131
• 5 Paper Buildings	0171 583 9275/583 4555
Pepys' Chambers	0171 936 2710
Phoenix Chambers	0171 404 7888
Plowden Buildings	0171 583 0808
• 1 Pump Court	0171 583 2012/353 4341
2 Pump Court	0171 353 5597
• Pump Court Chambers	0171 353 0711
• 4 Pump Court	020 7842 5555
• 5 Pump Court	020 7353 2532
• Chambers of Kieran Coonan QC	0171 583 6013/2510
6 Pump Court	0171 797 8400
Queen Elizabeth Building	0171 797 7837
No. 1 Serjeants' Inn	0171 415 6666
• 3 Serjeants' Inn	0171 353 5537
Somersett Chambers	0171 404 6701
• Stanbrook & Henderson	0171 353 0101
Staple Inn Chambers	0171 242 5240
7 Stone Buildings (also at 11 Bolt Court)	0171 242 0961
8 Stone Buildings	0171 831 9881
• 9 Stone Buildings	0171 404 5055
• 199 Strand	0171 379 9779
55 Temple Chambers	0171 353 7400
• 1 Temple Gardens	0171 583 1315/353 0407
• 2 Temple Gardens	0171 583 6041
• 3 Temple Gardens	0171 353 3102/5/9297
• Thomas More Chambers	0171 404 7000
• 14 Tooks Court	0171 405 8828
Verulam Chambers	0171 813 2400
Warwick House Chambers	0171 430 2323

Maidstone

• Maidstone Chambers	01622 688592
6-8 Mill Street	01622 688094

Manchester

• Byrom Street Chambers	0161 829 2100
• Central Chambers	0161 236 1133

• Expanded entry in Part C

	• Cobden House Chambers	0161 833 6000
	Deans Court Chambers	0161 214 6000
	Kenworthy's Chambers	0161 832 4036/834 6954
	• 40 King Street	0161 832 9082
	• 8 King Street Chambers	0161 834 9560
	58 King Street Chambers	0161 831 7477
	Lincoln House Chambers	0161 832 5701
	• Chambers of Ian Macdonald QC (In Association with Two Garden Court, Temple, London)	0161 236 1840
	Peel Court Chambers	0161 832 3791
	• Queen's Chambers	0161 834 6875/4738
	• St James's Chambers	0161 834 7000
	18 St John Street	0161 278 1800
	24a St John Street	0161 833 9628
	• 28 St John Street	0161 834 8418
	Young Street Chambers	0161 833 0489
Middlesbrough	Baker Street Chambers	01642 873873
Milton Keynes	Milton Keynes Chambers	01908 664 128
Newcastle upon Tyne	• Broad Chare	0191 232 0541
	Cathedral Chambers	0191 232 1311
	• Trinity Chambers	0191 232 1927
	Westgate Chambers	0191 261 4407/2329785
Northampton	Chartlands Chambers	01604 603322
	Chambers of Michael Pert QC	01604 602333
	Northampton Chambers	01604 636271
Norwich	East Anglian Chambers	01603 617351
	Octagon House	01603 623186
	Sackville Chambers	01603 613516/616221
Nottingham	King Charles House	0115 9418851
	Ropewalk Chambers	0115 9472581
	St Mary's Chambers	0115 9503503
Oxford	Harcourt Chambers	01865 791559
	King's Bench Chambers	01865 311066
	3 Paper Buildings (Oxford)	01865 793736
Peterborough	Fenners Chambers	01733 562030
Plymouth	Devon Chambers	01752 661659
Pontypridd	• Windsor Chambers	01443 402067
Portsmouth	• Portsmouth Barristers' Chambers	023 92 831292/811811
Preston	Deans Court Chambers	01772 555163
	New Bailey Chambers	01772 258087
	Queens Chambers	01772 828300
	15 Winckley Square	01772 252828
Reading	Wessex Chambers	0118 956 8856
Redhill	Redhill Chambers	01737 780781
Saint Albans	St Albans Chambers	01727 843383
Sheffield	Bank House Chambers	0114 2751223
	Paradise Chambers	0114 2738951
Slough	Slough Chamber	01753 553806/817989
Southampton	• 17 Carlton Crescent	023 8032 0320/0823 2003
	• College Chambers	01703 230338
	• Eighteen Carlton Crescent	01703 639001
Stoke On Trent	Regent Chambers	01782 286666
Swansea	Angel Chambers	01792 464623/464648
	Chambers of Davina Gammon	01792 480770
	Iscoed Chambers	01792 652988/9/330
Swindon	Pump Court Chambers	01793 539899
Taunton	South Western Chambers	01823 331919 (24 hrs)
Winchester	3 Paper Buildings (Winchester)	01962 868884
	Pump Court Chambers	01962 868161
Wolverhampton	Claremont Chambers	01902 426222

• Expanded entry in Part C

York

• York Chambers   01904 620048

A

PLANNING

Birmingham	1 Fountain Court	0121 236 5721
	• 5 Fountain Court	0121 606 0500
	• St Philip's Chambers	0121 246 7000
Bristol	St John's Chambers	0117 9213456/298514
Cardiff	32 Park Place	01222 397364
Chester	Sedan House	01244 320480/348282
Colchester	East Anglian Chambers	01206 572756
Durham	Durham Barristers' Chambers	0191 386 9199
Ipswich	East Anglian Chambers	01473 214481
Leeds	• 30 Park Square	0113 2436388
	• Sovereign Chambers	0113 2451841/2/3
Liverpool	25-27 Castle Street	0151 227 5661/051 236 5072
	• Exchange Chambers	0151 236 7747
	India Buildings Chambers	0151 243 6000
London	Atkin Chambers	020 7404 0102
	33 Bedford Row	0171 242 6476
	• 4 Breams Buildings	0171 353 5835/430 1221
	1 Dr Johnson's Buildings	0171 353 9328
	• Hardwicke Building	020 7242 2523
	• Harrow on the Hill Chambers	0181 423 7444
	4 King's Bench Walk	020 7353 3581
	• 3 Paper Buildings	020 7583 8055
	• Pump Court Chambers	0171 353 0711
	1 Serjeants' Inn	0171 583 1355
	• Thomas More Chambers	0171 404 7000
Maidstone	6-8 Mill Street	01622 688094
Norwich	East Anglian Chambers	01603 617351
Oxford	3 Paper Buildings (Oxford)	01865 793736
Plymouth	Devon Chambers	01752 661659
Pontypridd	• Windsor Chambers	01443 402067
Preston	New Bailey Chambers	01772 258087
Slough	Slough Chamber	01753 553806/817989
Swindon	Pump Court Chambers	01793 539899
Taunton	South Western Chambers	01823 331919 (24 hrs)
Winchester	3 Paper Buildings (Winchester)	01962 868884
	Pump Court Chambers	01962 868161

POLICE DISCIPLINE

Leeds	• 37 Park Square Chambers	0113 2439422
	• Sovereign Chambers	0113 2451841/2/3

POLICE LAW

Leeds	• 37 Park Square Chambers	0113 2439422
London	No. 1 Serjeants' Inn	0171 415 6666

PRISON LAW

London	• 14 Tooks Court	0171 405 8828
Manchester	• Chambers of Ian Macdonald QC (In Association with Two Garden Court, Temple, London)	0161 236 1840

PRISONERS' RIGHTS

Manchester	• Central Chambers	0161 236 1133

PRIVATE CLIENT

Oxford	28 Western Road	01865 204911

• Expanded entry in Part C

PRIVATE INTERNATIONAL

Bournemouth	3 Paper Buildings (Bournemouth)	01202 292102
Cardiff	• 33 Park Place	02920 233313
Leeds	• 9 Woodhouse Square	0113 2451986
London	Barristers' Common Law Chambers	0171 375 3012
	• Blackstone Chambers	0171 583 1770
	11 Bolt Court (also at 7 Stone Buildings – 1st Floor)	0171 353 2300
	Brick Court Chambers	0171 379 3550
	1 Crown Office Row	0171 583 9292
	• 4 Essex Court	020 7797 7970
	• Essex Court Chambers	0171 813 8000
	• 20 Essex Street	0171 583 9294
	• Chambers of Norman Palmer	0171 405 6114
	• Fountain Court	0171 583 3335
	8 Gray's Inn Square	0171 242 3529
	• Hardwicke Building	020 7242 2523
	• One Hare Court	020 7353 3171
	Chambers of Harjit Singh	0171 353 1356 (4 Lines)
	Justice Court Chambers	0181 830 7786
	• 4 King's Bench Walk	0171 822 8822
	• 11 King's Bench Walk	0171 632 8500/583 0610
	• Littman Chambers	020 7404 4866
	• Monckton Chambers	0171 405 7211
	Chambers of Dr Jamal Nasir	0171 405 3818/9
	• Chambers of John L Powell QC	0171 797 8000
	• 12 New Square	0171 419 1212
	The Chambers of Leolin Price CBE, QC	0171 405 0758
	13 Old Square	0171 404 4800
	• 4 Paper Buildings	0171 353 3366/583 7155
	• 5 Paper Buildings	0171 583 9275/583 4555
	Queen Elizabeth Building	0171 797 7837
	No. 1 Serjeants' Inn	0171 415 6666
	• 3 Stone Buildings	0171 242 4937
	• 7 Stone Buildings	0171 405 3886/242 3546
	7 Stone Buildings (also at 11 Bolt Court)	0171 242 0961
	• 9 Stone Buildings	0171 404 5055
	3 Verulam Buildings	0171 831 8441
	Verulam Chambers	0171 813 2400
	Warwick House Chambers	0171 430 2323
Manchester	• 28 St John Street	0161 834 8418
Oxford	King's Bench Chambers	01865 311066
Pontypridd	• Windsor Chambers	01443 402067
Redhill	Redhill Chambers	01737 780781

PRIVY COUNCIL APPEALS

London	• Thomas More Chambers	0171 404 7000

PROBATE AND ADMINISTRATION

Birmingham	• 5 Fountain Court	0121 606 0500
	• 8 Fountain Court	0121 236 5514/5
	• St Philip's Chambers	0121 246 7000
Bristol	Guildhall Chambers	0117 9273366
	St John's Chambers	0117 9213456/298514
Cambridge	Fenners Chambers	01223 368761
Canterbury	• Becket Chambers	01227 786331
Cardiff	9 Park Place	01222 382731
	30 Park Place	01222 398421
	• 33 Park Place	02920 233313
Chester	White Friars Chambers	01244 323070
Exeter	Southernhay Chambers	01392 255777

• Expanded entry in Part C

A

Leeds	Chambers of Andrew Campbell QC	0113 2455438
	Enterprise Chambers	0113 246 0391
	11 King's Bench Walk	0113 297 1200
	No. 6	0113 2459763
	The Chambers of Philip Raynor QC	0113 242 1123
	• 9 Woodhouse Square	0113 2451986
Liverpool	• Exchange Chambers	0151 236 7747
London	33 Bedford Row	0171 242 6476
	Bell Yard Chambers	0171 306 9292
	Bridewell Chambers	020 7797 8800
	• Chambers of Mr Peter Crampin QC	020 7831 0081
	• Enterprise Chambers	0171 405 9471
	• One Essex Court	0171 936 3030
	• Chambers of Norman Palmer	0171 405 6114
	Francis Taylor Building	0171 353 7768/7769/2711
	8 Gray's Inn Square	0171 242 3529
	Counsels' Chambers	0171 405 2576
	• 1 Harcourt Buildings	0171 353 9421/0375
	• 2 Harcourt Buildings	0171 583 9020
	• Hardwicke Building	020 7242 2523
	• Harrow on the Hill Chambers	0181 423 7444
	John Street Chambers	0171 242 1911
	4 King's Bench Walk	020 7353 3581
	9 King's Bench Walk	0171 353 7202/3909
	11 King's Bench Walk	0171 353 3337
	• Lamb Building	020 7797 7788
	Lion Court	0171 404 6565
	• Littman Chambers	020 7404 4866
	• Mitre Court Chambers	0171 353 9394
	• New Court	0171 583 5123/0510
	• New Court Chambers	0171 831 9500
	• 1 New Square	0171 405 0884/5/6/7
	• Chambers of Lord Goodhart QC	0171 405 5577
	5 New Square	020 7404 0404
	• 12 New Square	0171 419 1212
	• Twenty-Four Old Buildings	0171 404 0946
	• 9 Old Square	0171 405 4682
	The Chambers of Leolin Price CBE, QC	0171 405 0758
	11 Old Square, Ground Floor	0171 242 5022/405 1074
	• 11 Old Square, Ground Floor	020 7430 0341
	13 Old Square	0171 404 4800
	• 5 Paper Buildings	0171 583 9275/583 4555
	• 5 Pump Court	020 7353 2532
	Queen Elizabeth Building	0171 797 7837
	No. 1 Serjeants' Inn	0171 415 6666
	• Stanbrook & Henderson	0171 353 0101
	• 3 Stone Buildings	0171 242 4937
	• 5 Stone Buildings	0171 242 6201
	• 9 Stone Buildings	0171 404 5055
	11 Stone Buildings	+44 (0)207 831 6381
	Tollgate Mews Chambers	0171 511 1838
	Verulam Chambers	0171 813 2400
	• Wilberforce Chambers	0171 306 0102
Manchester	• Cobden House Chambers	0161 833 6000
	• 40 King Street	0161 832 9082
	• 8 King Street Chambers	0161 834 9560
	• Queen's Chambers	0161 834 6875/4738
	• St James's Chambers	0161 834 7000
Newcastle upon Tyne	Enterprise Chambers	0191 222 3344
	• Trinity Chambers	0191 232 1927
Northampton	Chartlands Chambers	01604 603322

• Expanded entry in Part C

Oxford	28 Western Road	01865 204911
Peterborough	Fenners Chambers	01733 562030
Preston	New Bailey Chambers	01772 258087
	15 Winckley Square	01772 252828
Reading	Wessex Chambers	0118 956 8856
Saint Albans	St Albans Chambers	01727 843383
Southampton	• 17 Carlton Crescent	023 8032 0320/0823 2003
	• Eighteen Carlton Crescent	01703 639001
Stoke On Trent	Regent Chambers	01782 286666
Swansea	Iscoed Chambers	01792 652988/9/330
Taunton	South Western Chambers	01823 331919 (24 hrs)
Wolverhampton	Claremont Chambers	01902 426222

PROCUREMENT

London	Atkin Chambers	020 7404 0102

PRODUCT LIABILITY

Bristol	Old Square Chambers, Hanover House	0117 9277111
London	• Old Square Chambers, 1 Verulam Buildings	0171 269 0300

PROFESSIONAL DISCIPLINARY MATTERS (SOLS) – CICB

London	• Mitre House Chambers	0171 583 8233

PROFESSIONAL NEGLIGENCE

Birmingham	Coleridge Chambers	0121 233 8500
	1 Fountain Court	0121 236 5721
	• 3 Fountain Court	0121 236 5854
	• 5 Fountain Court	0121 606 0500
	• 8 Fountain Court	0121 236 5514/5
	New Court Chambers	0121 693 6656
	• St Philip's Chambers	0121 246 7000
Bournemouth	3 Paper Buildings (Bournemouth)	01202 292102
Bradford	Broadway House Chambers	01274 722560
Brighton	Crown Office Row Chambers	01273 625625
Bristol	Guildhall Chambers	0117 9273366
	Old Square Chambers	0117 9277111
	St John's Chambers	0117 9213456/298514
Cambridge	Fenners Chambers	01223 368761
Canterbury	• Becket Chambers	01227 786331
	Stour Chambers	01227 764899
Cardiff	9 Park Place	01222 382731
	30 Park Place	01222 398421
	• 33 Park Place	02920 233313
Chester	Nicholas Street Chambers	01244 323886
	Sedan House	01244 320480/348282
	White Friars Chambers	01244 323070
Chichester	Chichester Chambers	01243 784538
Colchester	East Anglian Chambers	01206 572756
Durham	Durham Barristers' Chambers	0191 386 9199
Exeter	Cathedral Chambers (Jan Wood Independent Barristers' Clerk)	01392 210900
	Southernhay Chambers	01392 255777
	Walnut House	01392 279751
Guildford	• Guildford Chambers	01483 539131
Ipswich	East Anglian Chambers	01473 214481
Leatherhead	Pembroke House	01372 376160/376493
Leeds	Chambers of Andrew Campbell QC	0113 2455438
	Broadway House Chambers	0113 246 2600
	• Chancery House Chambers	0113 244 6691
	Enterprise Chambers	0113 246 0391
	11 King's Bench Walk	0113 297 1200

• Expanded entry in Part C

A

• Mercury Chambers	0113 234 2265
No. 6	0113 2459763
Park Lane Chambers	0113 2285000
The Chambers of Philip Raynor QC	0113 242 1123
• 30 Park Square	0113 2436388
• 37 Park Square Chambers	0113 2439422
• Sovereign Chambers	0113 2451841/2/3
• St Paul's House	0113 2455866
• 9 Woodhouse Square	0113 2451986

Leicester

Chambers of Michael Pert QC	0116 249 2020

Liverpool

25-27 Castle Street	0151 227 5661/051 236 5072
19 Castle Street Chambers	0151 236 9402
Chavasse Court Chambers	0151 707 1191
• Corn Exchange Chambers	0151 227 1081/5009
• Exchange Chambers	0151 236 7747
India Buildings Chambers	0151 243 6000
• Oriel Chambers	0151 236 7191/236 4321

London

Atkin Chambers	020 7404 0102
Barnard's Inn Chambers	0171 369 6969
Barristers' Common Law Chambers	0171 375 3012
9 Bedford Row	0171 242 3555
17 Bedford Row	0171 831 7314
33 Bedford Row	0171 242 6476
• Chambers of Michael Pert QC	0171 421 8000
• 9-12 Bell Yard	0171 400 1800
• Blackstone Chambers	0171 583 1770
11 Bolt Court (also at 7 Stone Buildings – 1st Floor)	0171 353 2300
Bracton Chambers	0171 242 4248
• 4 Breams Buildings	0171 353 5835/430 1221
Brick Court Chambers	0171 379 3550
Bridewell Chambers	020 7797 8800
Cloisters	0171 827 4000
• Chambers of Mr Peter Crampin QC	020 7831 0081
• 1 Crown Office Row, Ground Floor	0171 797 7500
1 Crown Office Row, 3rd Floor	0171 583 9292
• Two Crown Office Row	020 7797 8100
• Devereux Chambers	0171 353 7534
• Doughty Street Chambers	0171 404 1313
• Dr Johnson's Chambers	0171 353 4716
• Enterprise Chambers	0171 405 9471
Equity Barristers' Chambers	0181 558 8336
• Erskine Chambers	0171 242 5532
• One Essex Court, Ground Floor	020 7583 2000
• One Essex Court, 1st Floor	0171 936 3030
• 4 Essex Court	020 7797 7970
5 Essex Court	0171 410 2000
• Essex Court Chambers	0171 813 8000
• 20 Essex Street	0171 583 9294
• 35 Essex Street	0171 353 6381
• 39 Essex Street	0171 832 1111
Chambers of Geoffrey Hawker	0171 583 8899
Falcon Chambers	0171 353 2484
• Farrar's Building	0171 583 9241
• Chambers of Norman Palmer	0171 405 6114
• 4 Field Court	0171 440 6900
Chambers of Wilfred Forster-Jones	0171 353 0853/4/7222
• Fountain Court	0171 583 3335
Francis Taylor Building	0171 353 7768/7769/2711
• 2nd Floor, Francis Taylor Building	0171 353 9942/3157
• Two Garden Court	0171 353 1633

• Expanded entry in Part C

• Goldsmith Building	0171 353 7881
Goldsmith Chambers	0171 353 6802/3/4/5
• Gough Square Chambers	0171 353 0924
• Gray's Inn Chambers, The Chambers of Norman Patterson	0171 831 5344
Gray's Inn Chambers	0171 831 7888 (Chambers)/ 0171 831 7904 (Mr M Ullah)
96 Gray's Inn Road	0171 405 0585
• 2-3 Gray's Inn Square	0171 242 4986
2 Gray's Inn Square Chambers	020 7242 0328
• 4-5 Gray's Inn Square	0171 404 5252
Counsels' Chambers	0171 405 2576
• 1 Harcourt Buildings	0171 353 9421/0375
• 2 Harcourt Buildings, Ground Floor/Left	0171 583 9020
• 2 Harcourt Buildings, 2nd Floor	020 7353 8415
• Harcourt Chambers	0171 353 6961
• Hardwicke Building	020 7242 2523
• 1 Hare Court	0171 353 3982/5324
• One Hare Court	020 7353 3171
Chambers of Harjit Singh	0171 353 1356 (4 Lines)
• Harrow on the Hill Chambers	0181 423 7444
John Street Chambers	0171 242 1911
Justice Court Chambers	0181 830 7786
• One King's Bench Walk	0171 936 1500
• 4 King's Bench Walk, Ground/First Floor/ Basement	0171 822 8822
4 King's Bench Walk, 2nd Floor	020 7353 3581
S Tomlinson QC	0171 583 0404
8 King's Bench Walk	0171 797 8888
9 King's Bench Walk	0171 353 7202/3909
10 King's Bench Walk	0171 353 7742
• 11 King's Bench Walk,	0171 632 8500/583 0610
11 King's Bench Walk, 1st Floor	0171 353 3337
• 12 King's Bench Walk	0171 583 0811
• 13 King's Bench Walk	0171 353 7204
2 King's Bench Walk Chambers	020 7353 9276
• Lamb Building	020 7797 7788
Lamb Chambers	020 7797 8300
• Littleton Chambers	0171 797 8600
• Littman Chambers	020 7404 4866
1 Mitre Court Buildings	0171 797 7070
2 Mitre Court Buildings	0171 353 1353
• Mitre Court Chambers	0171 353 9394
• Mitre House Chambers	0171 583 8233
• Monckton Chambers	0171 405 7211
• New Court	0171 583 5123/0510
• New Court Chambers	0171 831 9500
• 1 New Square	0171 405 0884/5/6/7
• Chambers of Lord Goodhart QC	0171 405 5577
• 3 New Square	0171 405 1111
• Chambers of John L Powell QC	0171 797 8000
5 New Square	020 7404 0404
• 12 New Square	0171 419 1212
• 22 Old Buildings	0171 831 0222
• Twenty-Four Old Buildings	0171 404 0946
• 9 Old Square	0171 405 4682
The Chambers of Leolin Price CBE, QC	0171 405 0758
• 11 Old Square	020 7430 0341
13 Old Square	0171 404 4800
• Old Square Chambers	0171 269 0300
One Paper Buildings	0171 583 7355

• Expanded entry in Part C

A

• 3 Paper Buildings	020 7583 8055
• 4 Paper Buildings, Ground Floor	0171 353 3366/583 7155
• 4 Paper Buildings, 1st Floor	0171 583 0816/353 1131
• 5 Paper Buildings	0171 583 9275/583 4555
Phoenix Chambers	0171 404 7888
• 1 Pump Court	0171 583 2012/353 4341
2 Pump Court	0171 353 5597
• Pump Court Chambers	0171 353 0711
• 4 Pump Court	020 7842 5555
• 5 Pump Court	020 7353 2532
• Chambers of Kieran Coonan QC	0171 583 6013/2510
6 Pump Court	0171 797 8400
Queen Elizabeth Building	0171 797 7837
• 5 Raymond Buildings	0171 242 2902
No. 1 Serjeants' Inn	0171 415 6666
• 3 Serjeants' Inn	0171 353 5537
• Serle Court Chambers	0171 242 6105
• 3/4 South Square	0171 696 9900
• Stanbrook & Henderson	0171 353 0101
• 3 Stone Buildings	0171 242 4937
4 Stone Buildings	0171 242 5524
• 5 Stone Buildings	0171 242 6201
• 7 Stone Buildings	0171 405 3886/242 3546
7 Stone Buildings (also at 11 Bolt Court)	0171 242 0961
8 Stone Buildings	0171 831 9881
• 9 Stone Buildings	0171 404 5055
11 Stone Buildings	+44 (0)207 831 6381
• 199 Strand	0171 379 9779
55 Temple Chambers	0171 353 7400
• 1 Temple Gardens	0171 583 1315/353 0407
• 2 Temple Gardens	0171 583 6041
• Thomas More Chambers	0171 404 7000
• 14 Tooks Court	0171 405 8828
3 Verulam Buildings	0171 831 8441
Verulam Chambers	0171 813 2400
Warwick House Chambers	0171 430 2323
• Wilberforce Chambers	0171 306 0102
Maidstone • Maidstone Chambers	01622 688592
6-8 Mill Street	01622 688094
Malvern Resolution Chambers	01684 561279
Manchester • Byrom Street Chambers	0161 829 2100
• Central Chambers	0161 236 1133
• Cobden House Chambers	0161 833 6000
Deans Court Chambers	0161 214 6000
Kenworthy's Chambers	0161 832 4036/834 6954
• 40 King Street	0161 832 9082
• 8 King Street Chambers	0161 834 9560
Lincoln House Chambers	0161 832 5701
• Chambers of Ian Macdonald QC (In Association with Two Garden Court, Temple, London)	0161 236 1840
• Merchant Chambers	0161 839 7070
• St James's Chambers	0161 834 7000
18 St John Street	0161 278 1800
24a St John Street	0161 833 9628
• 28 St John Street	0161 834 8418
Young Street Chambers	0161 833 0489
Meopham West Lodge Farm	01474 812280
Middlesbrough Baker Street Chambers	01642 873873
Milton Keynes Milton Keynes Chambers	01908 664 128
Newcastle upon Tyne Cathedral Chambers	0191 232 1311

• Expanded entry in Part C

A

	Enterprise Chambers	0191 222 3344
	Milburn House Chambers	0191 230 5511
	• Trinity Chambers	0191 232 1927
	Westgate Chambers	0191 261 4407/2329785
Northampton	Chartlands Chambers	01604 603322
	Chambers of Michael Pert QC	01604 602333
	Northampton Chambers	01604 636271
Norwich	East Anglian Chambers	01603 617351
	Sackville Chambers	01603 613516/616221
Nottingham	King Charles House	0115 9418851
	Ropewalk Chambers	0115 9472581
	St Mary's Chambers	0115 9503503
Oxford	Harcourt Chambers	01865 791559
	King's Bench Chambers	01865 311066
	3 Paper Buildings (Oxford)	01865 793736
Peterborough	Fenners Chambers	01733 562030
Plymouth	Devon Chambers	01752 661659
Pontypridd	• Windsor Chambers	01443 402067
Portsmouth	• Portsmouth Barristers' Chambers	023 92 831292/811811
Preston	Deans Court Chambers	01772 555163
	New Bailey Chambers	01772 258087
	Queens Chambers	01772 828300
	15 Winckley Square	01772 252828
Reading	Wessex Chambers	0118 956 8856
Redhill	Redhill Chambers	01737 780781
Saint Albans	St Albans Chambers	01727 843383
Sheffield	Paradise Chambers	0114 2738951
Slough	Slough Chamber	01753 553806/817989
Southampton	• 17 Carlton Crescent	023 8032 0320/0823 2003
	• College Chambers	01703 230338
	• Eighteen Carlton Crescent	01703 639001
Stoke On Trent	Regent Chambers	01782 286666
Swansea	Angel Chambers	01792 464623/464648
	Iscoed Chambers	01792 652988/9/330
Swindon	Pump Court Chambers	01793 539899
Taunton	South Western Chambers	01823 331919 (24 hrs)
Winchester	3 Paper Buildings (Winchester)	01962 868884
	Pump Court Chambers	01962 868161
Wolverhampton	Claremont Chambers	01902 426222
York	• York Chambers	01904 620048

PROPERTY

London	Falcon Chambers	0171 353 2484
	• Serle Court Chambers	0171 242 6105

PUBLIC CHILDCARE

Bristol	29 Gwilliam Street	0117 966 8997

PUBLIC INQUIRIES

Leeds	• 30 Park Square	0113 2436388
	• 37 Park Square Chambers	0113 2439422
London	One Paper Buildings	0171 583 7355
	• 14 Tooks Court	0171 405 8828

PUBLIC INTERNATIONAL

Leeds	• 9 Woodhouse Square	0113 2451986
London	Acre Lane Neighbourhood Chambers	0171 274 4400
	• Blackstone Chambers	0171 583 1770
	Brick Court Chambers	0171 379 3550
	Cloisters	0171 827 4000
	1 Crown Office Row	0171 583 9292

• Expanded entry in Part C

A

• Essex Court Chambers	0171 813 8000
• 20 Essex Street	0171 583 9294
• Chambers of Norman Palmer	0171 405 6114
• Fountain Court	0171 583 3335
• 4-5 Gray's Inn Square	0171 404 5252
• Hardwicke Building	020 7242 2523
• One Hare Court	020 7353 3171
10 King's Bench Walk	0171 353 7742
• Monckton Chambers	0171 405 7211
Chambers of Dr Jamal Nasir	0171 405 3818/9
• 12 New Square	0171 419 1212
3 Verulam Buildings	0171 831 8441

PUBLIC LAW
London

Equity Barristers' Chambers	0181 558 8336
4 King's Bench Walk	020 7353 3581

PUBLIC PROCUREMENT
Cardiff

30 Park Place	01222 398421

RATING AND CPO
London

2 Mitre Court Buildings	0171 583 1380

REGULATORY WORK
London

23 Essex Street	0171 413 0353/836 8366

RIGHTS OF LIGHT
London

• Chambers of Mr Peter Crampin QC	020 7831 0081

SALE AND CARRIAGE OF GOODS

Birmingham	• 3 Fountain Court	0121 236 5854
	• 5 Fountain Court	0121 606 0500
	• 8 Fountain Court	0121 236 5514/5
	• St Philip's Chambers	0121 246 7000
Bournemouth	3 Paper Buildings (Bournemouth)	01202 292102
Bradford	Broadway House Chambers	01274 722560
Bristol	Guildhall Chambers	0117 9273366
	St John's Chambers	0117 9213456/298514
Cambridge	Fenners Chambers	01223 368761
Cardiff	30 Park Place	01222 398421
	32 Park Place	01222 397364
Chester	White Friars Chambers	01244 323070
Chichester	Chichester Chambers	01243 784538
Exeter	Cathedral Chambers (Jan Wood Independent Barristers' Clerk)	01392 210900
Leeds	Chambers of Andrew Campbell QC	0113 2455438
	Broadway House Chambers	0113 246 2600
	• Chancery House Chambers	0113 244 6691
	The Chambers of Philip Raynor QC	0113 242 1123
	• 37 Park Square Chambers	0113 2439422
	• 9 Woodhouse Square	0113 2451986
Liverpool	25-27 Castle Street	0151 227 5661/051 236 5072
	• Corn Exchange Chambers	0151 227 1081/5009
	• Exchange Chambers	0151 236 7747
	India Buildings Chambers	0151 243 6000
	• Oriel Chambers	0151 236 7191/236 4321
London	Barnard's Inn Chambers	0171 369 6969
	9 Bedford Row	0171 242 3555
	17 Bedford Row	0171 831 7314
	• Blackstone Chambers	0171 583 1770
	Bracton Chambers	0171 242 4248

Brick Court Chambers	0171 379 3550
Bridewell Chambers	020 7797 8800
• Chambers of Mr Peter Crampin QC	020 7831 0081
• 1 Crown Office Row, Ground Floor	0171 797 7500
1 Crown Office Row, 3rd Floor	0171 583 9292
• Two Crown Office Row	020 7797 8100
• Devereux Chambers	0171 353 7534
1 Dr Johnson's Buildings	0171 353 9328
• Dr Johnson's Chambers	0171 353 4716
• One Essex Court	0171 936 3030
• 4 Essex Court	020 7797 7970
• Essex Court Chambers	0171 813 8000
• 20 Essex Street	0171 583 9294
• 35 Essex Street	0171 353 6381
• 39 Essex Street	0171 832 1111
Chambers of Geoffrey Hawker	0171 583 8899
• Farrar's Building	0171 583 9241
• Chambers of Norman Palmer	0171 405 6114
• 4 Field Court	0171 440 6900
• Fountain Court	0171 583 3335
Francis Taylor Building	0171 353 7768/7769/2711
• 2nd Floor, Francis Taylor Building	0171 353 9942/3157
• Goldsmith Building	0171 353 7881
Goldsmith Chambers	0171 353 6802/3/4/5
• Gough Square Chambers	0171 353 0924
• 2-3 Gray's Inn Square	0171 242 4986
2 Gray's Inn Square Chambers	020 7242 0328
• 1 Harcourt Buildings	0171 353 9421/0375
• 2 Harcourt Buildings, Ground Floor/Left	0171 583 9020
2 Harcourt Buildings, 1st Floor	020 7353 2112
• Hardwicke Building	020 7242 2523
• One Hare Court	020 7353 3171
• Harrow on the Hill Chambers	0181 423 7444
S Tomlinson QC	0171 583 0404
9 King's Bench Walk	0171 353 7202/3909
10 King's Bench Walk	0171 353 7742
• 11 King's Bench Walk,	0171 632 8500/583 0610
11 King's Bench Walk, 1st Floor	0171 353 3337
• 12 King's Bench Walk	0171 583 0811
• 13 King's Bench Walk	0171 353 7204
• Lamb Building	020 7797 7788
Lamb Chambers	020 7797 8300
Lion Court	0171 404 6565
• Littleton Chambers	0171 797 8600
• Littman Chambers	020 7404 4866
• Mitre Court Chambers	0171 353 9394
• Monckton Chambers	0171 405 7211
• 3 New Square	0171 405 1111
• Chambers of John L Powell QC	0171 797 8000
• 12 New Square	0171 419 1212
• 22 Old Buildings	0171 831 0222
The Chambers of Leolin Price CBE, QC	0171 405 0758
• 3 Paper Buildings	020 7583 8055
• 4 Paper Buildings, Ground Floor	0171 353 3366/583 7155
• 4 Paper Buildings, 1st Floor	0171 583 0816/353 1131
• 5 Paper Buildings	0171 583 9275/583 4555
2 Pump Court	0171 353 5597
• 4 Pump Court	020 7842 5555
• 5 Pump Court	020 7353 2532
• 5 Raymond Buildings	0171 242 2902
No. 1 Serjeants' Inn	0171 415 6666

       • Expanded entry in Part C

	• 3 Serjeants' Inn	0171 353 5537
	• 3/4 South Square	0171 696 9900
	• Stanbrook & Henderson	0171 353 0101
	• 199 Strand	0171 379 9779
	• 1 Temple Gardens	0171 583 1315/353 0407
	• 2 Temple Gardens	0171 583 6041
	• Thomas More Chambers	0171 404 7000
	3 Verulam Buildings	0171 831 8441
	Warwick House Chambers	0171 430 2323
Manchester	• Cobden House Chambers	0161 833 6000
	Deans Court Chambers	0161 214 6000
	• 40 King Street	0161 832 9082
	• 8 King Street Chambers	0161 834 9560
	• Merchant Chambers	0161 839 7070
	• Queen's Chambers	0161 834 6875/4738
	• St James's Chambers	0161 834 7000
	Young Street Chambers	0161 833 0489
Middlesbrough	Baker Street Chambers	01642 873873
Newcastle upon Tyne	• Broad Chare	0191 232 0541
	• Trinity Chambers	0191 232 1927
	Westgate Chambers	0191 261 4407/2329785
Northampton	Chartlands Chambers	01604 603322
	Northampton Chambers	01604 636271
Norwich	Sackville Chambers	01603 613516/616221
Nottingham	King Charles House	0115 9418851
	Ropewalk Chambers	0115 9472581
Oxford	King's Bench Chambers	01865 311066
	3 Paper Buildings (Oxford)	01865 793736
Peterborough	Fenners Chambers	01733 562030
Plymouth	Devon Chambers	01752 661659
Pontypridd	• Windsor Chambers	01443 402067
Portsmouth	• Portsmouth Barristers' Chambers	023 92 831292/811811
Preston	Deans Court Chambers	01772 555163
	New Bailey Chambers	01772 258087
	Queens Chambers	01772 828300
	15 Winckley Square	01772 252828
Reading	Wessex Chambers	0118 956 8856
Saint Albans	St Albans Chambers	01727 843383
Southampton	• Eighteen Carlton Crescent	01703 639001
Stoke On Trent	Regent Chambers	01782 286666
Swansea	Iscoed Chambers	01792 652988/9/330
Winchester	3 Paper Buildings (Winchester)	01962 868884
Wolverhampton	Claremont Chambers	01902 426222
York	• York Chambers	01904 620048

SHARE OPTIONS

Birmingham	• 5 Fountain Court	0121 606 0500
Bristol	Guildhall Chambers	0117 9273366
Leeds	Chambers of Andrew Campbell QC	0113 2455438
Liverpool	• Exchange Chambers	0151 236 7747
London	• Erskine Chambers	0171 242 5532
	• One Essex Court	020 7583 2000
	• Essex Court Chambers	0171 813 8000
	• Chambers of Norman Palmer	0171 405 6114
	• Fountain Court	0171 583 3335
	• One Hare Court	020 7353 3171
	• Harrow on the Hill Chambers	0181 423 7444
	• 11 King's Bench Walk,	0171 632 8500/583 0610
	11 King's Bench Walk, 1st Floor	0171 353 3337
	• Littleton Chambers	0171 797 8600
	• 1 New Square	0171 405 0884/5/6/7

• Expanded entry in Part C

	5 New Square	020 7404 0404
	Chambers of John Gardiner QC	0171 242 4017
	• Twenty-Four Old Buildings	0171 404 0946
	• 3/4 South Square	0171 696 9900
	• 9 Stone Buildings	0171 404 5055
Manchester	• 8 King Street Chambers	0161 834 9560
	• Merchant Chambers	0161 839 7070
	• St James's Chambers	0161 834 7000
Preston	New Bailey Chambers	01772 258087

SHIPPING

Manchester	• Byrom Street Chambers	0161 829 2100

SHIPPING, ADMIRALTY

Exeter	Cathedral Chambers (Jan Wood	01392 210900
	Independent Barristers' Clerk)	
Leeds	Chambers of Andrew Campbell QC	0113 2455438
Liverpool	• Corn Exchange Chambers	0151 227 1081/5009
	• Exchange Chambers	0151 236 7747
London	Brick Court Chambers	0171 379 3550
	Bridewell Chambers	020 7797 8800
	• One Essex Court	020 7583 2000
	• 4 Essex Court	020 7797 7970
	• Essex Court Chambers	0171 813 8000
	• 20 Essex Street	0171 583 9294
	• 4 Field Court	0171 440 6900
	• Fountain Court	0171 583 3335
	• Goldsmith Building	0171 353 7881
	• 4-5 Gray's Inn Square	0171 404 5252
	• 4 King's Bench Walk	0171 822 8822
	S Tomlinson QC	0171 583 0404
	• 11 King's Bench Walk	0171 632 8500/583 0610
	2 King's Bench Walk Chambers	020 7353 9276
	• Littman Chambers	020 7404 4866
	3 Verulam Buildings	0171 831 8441
	Verulam Chambers	0171 813 2400
	Warwick House Chambers	0171 430 2323
Plymouth	Devon Chambers	01752 661659
Portsmouth	• Portsmouth Barristers' Chambers	023 92 831292/811811

SOCIAL SECURITY

Bristol	Veritas Chambers	0117 930 8802
Consett	6 Ascot Road	01207 507785
London	Acre Lane Neighbourhood Chambers	0171 274 4400
	Tower Hamlets Barristers Chambers	0171 377 8090

SOCIAL SERVICES

Slough	Slough Chamber	01753 553806/817989

SOUTH ASIAN LAW

London	• Essex Court Chambers	0171 813 8000

SPORTS

Birmingham	• 5 Fountain Court	0121 606 0500
	• 8 Fountain Court	0121 236 5514/5
Bristol	Old Square Chambers	0117 9277111
	St John's Chambers	0117 9213456/298514
Leeds	Park Lane Chambers	0113 2285000
	• Sovereign Chambers	0113 2451841/2/3
Leicester	Chambers of Michael Pert QC	0116 249 2020
Liverpool	25-27 Castle Street	0151 227 5661/051 236 5072

A

	• Corn Exchange Chambers	0151 227 1081/5009
	• Oriel Chambers	0151 236 7191/236 4321
London	Barnard's Inn Chambers	0171 369 6969
	9 Bedford Row	0171 242 3555
	• Chambers of Michael Pert QC	0171 421 8000
	•9-12 Bell Yard	0171 400 1800
	• Blackstone Chambers	0171 583 1770
	Brick Court Chambers	0171 379 3550
	Cardinal Chambers	020 7353 2622
	Cloisters	0171 827 4000
	• Devereux Chambers	0171 353 7534
	• Essex Court Chambers	0171 813 8000
	• 39 Essex Street	0171 832 1111
	• Farrar's Building	0171 583 9241
	• 4 Field Court	0171 440 6900
	• Fountain Court	0171 583 3335
	Francis Taylor Building	0171 353 7768/7769/2711
	• Goldsmith Building	0171 353 7881
	•4-5 Gray's Inn Square	0171 404 5252
	• 2 Harcourt Buildings	0171 583 9020
	• Hardwicke Building	020 7242 2523
	• 3 Hare Court	0171 395 2000
	Chambers of Harjit Singh	0171 353 1356 (4 Lines)
	• Harrow on the Hill Chambers	0181 423 7444
	• One King's Bench Walk	0171 936 1500
	2 King's Bench Walk Chambers	020 7353 9276
	• Littleton Chambers	0171 797 8600
	• Mitre Court Chambers	0171 353 9394
	• Monckton Chambers	0171 405 7211
	• New Court Chambers	0171 831 9500
	• 1 New Square	0171 405 0884/5/6/7
	• 12 New Square	0171 419 1212
	•9 Old Square	0171 405 4682
	11 Old Square	0171 242 5022/405 1074
	13 Old Square	0171 404 4800
	• Old Square Chambers	0171 269 0300
	• 2 Paper Buildings	020 7556 5500
	• 4 Paper Buildings	0171 353 3366/583 7155
	Five Paper Buildings	0171 583 6117
	• Pump Court Chambers	0171 353 0711
	• 4 Pump Court	020 7842 5555
	Queen Elizabeth Building	0171 797 7837
	• 5 Raymond Buildings	0171 242 2902
	No. 1 Serjeants' Inn	0171 415 6666
	• Stanbrook & Henderson	0171 353 0101
	• 3 Stone Buildings	0171 242 4937
	11 Stone Buildings	+44 (0)207 831 6381
	• 199 Strand	0171 379 9779
	• 2-4 Tudor Street	0171 797 7111
Northampton	Chambers of Michael Pert QC	01604 602333
Nottingham	Ropewalk Chambers	0115 9472581
Plymouth	Devon Chambers	01752 661659
Swindon	Pump Court Chambers, 5 Temple Chambers	01793 539899
Winchester	Pump Court Chambers, 31 Southgate Street	01962 868161

TAX

Leeds	• Park Court Chambers	0113 2433277

TAX – CAPITAL AND INCOME

Birmingham	• 5 Fountain Court	0121 606 0500
	• St Philip's Chambers	0121 246 7000

• Expanded entry in Part C

A

Bradford	Broadway House Chambers	01274 722560
Exeter	Cathedral Chambers (Jan Wood Independent Barristers' Clerk)	01392 210900
Leeds	Chambers of Andrew Campbell QC	0113 2455438
	Broadway House Chambers	0113 246 2600
	• Chancery House Chambers	0113 244 6691
	11 King's Bench Walk	0113 297 1200
	The Chambers of Philip Raynor QC	0113 242 1123
	• 9 Woodhouse Square	0113 2451986
Liverpool	• Exchange Chambers	0151 236 7747
London	Bracton Chambers	0171 242 4248
	• 4 Breams Buildings	0171 353 5835/430 1221
	• Devereux Chambers	0171 353 7534
	• Fountain Court	0171 583 3335
	96 Gray's Inn Road	0171 405 0585
	8 Gray's Inn Square	0171 242 3529
	Counsels' Chambers	0171 405 2576
	Gray's Inn Tax Chambers	0171 242 2642
	• 2 Harcourt Buildings	0171 583 9020
	11 King's Bench Walk	0171 353 3337
	• Chambers of Lord Goodhart QC	0171 405 5577
	Chambers of John Gardiner QC	0171 242 4017
	• 12 New Square	0171 419 1212
	24 Old Buildings	020 7242 2744
	• 9 Old Square	0171 405 4682
	The Chambers of Leolin Price CBE, QC	0171 405 0758
	• 11 Old Square	020 7430 0341
	13 Old Square	0171 404 4800
	• 5 Paper Buildings	0171 583 9275/583 4555
	Plowden Buildings	0171 583 0808
	Prince Henry's Chambers	0171 713 0376
	Pump Court Tax Chambers	0171 414 8080
	• Hollis Whiteman Chambers	020 7583 5766
	• Stanbrook & Henderson	0171 353 0101
	• 3 Stone Buildings	0171 242 4937
	• 5 Stone Buildings	0171 242 6201
	• 9 Stone Buildings	0171 404 5055
	11 Stone Buildings	+44 (0)207 831 6381
	Temple Gardens Tax Chambers	0171 353 7884/5 8982/3
	• Wilberforce Chambers	0171 306 0102
Manchester	• Cobden House Chambers	0161 833 6000
	• 40 King Street	0161 832 9082
	• St James's Chambers	0161 834 7000
	• 28 St John Street	0161 834 8418
Newcastle upon Tyne	Westgate Chambers	0191 261 4407/2329785
Reading	Wessex Chambers	0118 956 8856

TAX – CORPORATE

Birmingham	• 5 Fountain Court	0121 606 0500
	• St Philip's Chambers	0121 246 7000
Bradford	Broadway House Chambers	01274 722560
Exeter	Cathedral Chambers (Jan Wood Independent Barristers' Clerk)	01392 210900
Leeds	Chambers of Andrew Campbell QC	0113 2455438
	Broadway House Chambers	0113 246 2600
	11 King's Bench Walk	0113 297 1200
	The Chambers of Philip Raynor QC	0113 242 1123
Liverpool	• Exchange Chambers	0151 236 7747
London	Bracton Chambers	0171 242 4248
	• 4 Breams Buildings	0171 353 5835/430 1221
	• One Essex Court	020 7583 2000

             • Expanded entry in Part C

A

• 4 Field Court	0171 440 6900
96 Gray's Inn Road	0171 405 0585
8 Gray's Inn Square	0171 242 3529
Gray's Inn Tax Chambers	0171 242 2642
• 2 Harcourt Buildings	0171 583 9020
11 King's Bench Walk	0171 353 3337
Chambers of John Gardiner QC	0171 242 4017
• 12 New Square	0171 419 1212
24 Old Buildings	020 7242 2744
The Chambers of Leolin Price CBE, QC	0171 405 0758
13 Old Square	0171 404 4800
Prince Henry's Chambers	0171 713 0376
Pump Court Tax Chambers	0171 414 8080
• Hollis Whiteman Chambers	020 7583 5766
• 3/4 South Square	0171 696 9900
• Stanbrook & Henderson	0171 353 0101
• 3 Stone Buildings	0171 242 4937
• 9 Stone Buildings	0171 404 5055
11 Stone Buildings	+44 (0)207 831 6381
Temple Gardens Tax Chambers	0171 353 7884/5 8982/3

Manchester   • 40 King Street   0161 832 9082
            • St James's Chambers   0161 834 7000
Newcastle upon Tyne   Westgate Chambers   0191 261 4407/2329785

TAXATION AND COSTS

London   • Farrar's Building   0171 583 9241

TELECOMMUNICATIONS

London

Atkin Chambers	020 7404 0102
11 Bolt Court (also at 7 Stone Buildings – 1st Floor)	0171 353 2300
Brick Court Chambers	0171 379 3550
• Devereux Chambers	0171 353 7534
• One Essex Court	020 7583 2000
• Essex Court Chambers	0171 813 8000
• Fountain Court	0171 583 3335
Francis Taylor Building	0171 353 7768/7769/2711
• 4-5 Gray's Inn Square	0171 404 5252
• 2 Harcourt Buildings	0171 583 9020
• Hardwicke Building	020 7242 2523
S Tomlinson QC	0171 583 0404
• Littman Chambers	020 7404 4866
• Mitre Court Chambers	0171 353 9394
• Monckton Chambers	0171 405 7211
• 3 New Square	0171 405 1111
• 8 New Square	0171 405 4321
13 Old Square	0171 404 4800
• 5 Raymond Buildings	0171 242 2902
1 Serjeants' Inn	0171 583 1355
• Stanbrook & Henderson	0171 353 0101
7 Stone Buildings (also at 11 Bolt Court)	0171 242 0961

Manchester   • St James's Chambers   0161 834 7000
Pontypridd   • Windsor Chambers   01443 402067
Redhill   Redhill Chambers   01737 780781

TIMESHARE

Exeter   Cathedral Chambers (Jan Wood Independent Barristers' Clerk)   01392 210900

TOWN AND COUNTRY PLANNING

Birmingham   1 Fountain Court   0121 236 5721

• Expanded entry in Part C

• 3 Fountain Court	0121 236 5854
• 5 Fountain Court	0121 606 0500
• 8 Fountain Court	0121 236 5514/5
St Ive's Chambers	0121 236 0863/5720
• St Philip's Chambers	0121 246 7000

Bournemouth	3 Paper Buildings (Bournemouth)	01202 292102
Bristol	St John's Chambers	0117 9213456/298514
Cambridge	Fenners Chambers	01223 368761
Canterbury	• Becket Chambers	01227 786331
Cardiff	9 Park Place	01222 382731
	30 Park Place	01222 398421
	• 33 Park Place	02920 233313
Chesterfield	26 Morley Avenue	01246 234790/01298 871350
Colchester	East Anglian Chambers	01206 572756
Durham	Durham Barristers' Chambers	0191 386 9199
Exeter	Cathedral Chambers (Jan Wood Independent Barristers' Clerk)	01392 210900
	Southernhay Chambers	01392 255777
	Walnut House	01392 279751
Guildford	• Guildford Chambers	01483 539131
Henley-in-Arden	Berkeley Chambers	01564 795546
Ipswich	East Anglian Chambers	01473 214481
Leeds	Chambers of Andrew Campbell QC	0113 2455438
	11 King's Bench Walk	0113 297 1200
	The Chambers of Philip Raynor QC	0113 242 1123
	• 30 Park Square	0113 2436388
	• 37 Park Square Chambers	0113 2439422
	• Sovereign Chambers	0113 2451841/2/3
	• 9 Woodhouse Square	0113 2451986
Leicester	Chambers of Michael Pert QC	0116 249 2020
Liverpool	• Exchange Chambers	0151 236 7747
London	• Arden Chambers	020 7242 4244
	9 Bedford Row	0171 242 3555
	• Chambers of Michael Pert QC	0171 421 8000
	11 Bolt Court (also at 7 Stone Buildings – 1st Floor)	0171 353 2300
	• 4 Breams Buildings	0171 353 5835/430 1221
	• Chambers of Mr Peter Crampin QC	020 7831 0081
	• 1 Crown Office Row	0171 797 7500
	1 Dr Johnson's Buildings	0171 353 9328
	Chambers of Geoffrey Hawker	0171 583 8899
	Falcon Chambers	0171 353 2484
	• Chambers of Norman Palmer	0171 405 6114
	Francis Taylor Building	0171 353 7768/7769/2711
	• 2nd Floor, Francis Taylor Building	0171 353 9942/3157
	96 Gray's Inn Road	0171 405 0585
	• 2-3 Gray's Inn Square	0171 242 4986
	• 4-5 Gray's Inn Square	0171 404 5252
	Counsels' Chambers	0171 405 2576
	• 2 Harcourt Buildings	020 7353 8415
	• Harcourt Chambers	0171 353 6961
	• Harrow on the Hill Chambers	0181 423 7444
	6 King's Bench Walk	0171 353 4931/583 0695
	• 11 King's Bench Walk,	0171 632 8500/583 0610
	11 King's Bench Walk, 1st Floor	0171 353 3337
	• Lamb Building	020 7797 7788
	Lamb Chambers	020 7797 8300
	• Littman Chambers	020 7404 4866
	2 Mitre Court Buildings, 1st Floor	0171 353 1353
	2 Mitre Court Buildings, 2nd Floor	0171 583 1380
	• Mitre Court Chambers	0171 353 9394

• Expanded entry in Part C

A

	• Chambers of John L Powell QC	0171 797 8000
	• 12 New Square	0171 419 1212
	• 22 Old Buildings	0171 831 0222
	• Twenty-Four Old Buildings	0171 404 0946
	The Chambers of Leolin Price CBE, QC	0171 405 0758
	11 Old Square	0171 242 5022/405 1074
	• 3 Paper Buildings	020 7583 8055
	• 5 Pump Court	020 7353 2532
	6 Pump Court	0171 797 8400
	1 Serjeants' Inn	0171 583 1355
	7 Stone Buildings (also at 11 Bolt Court)	0171 242 0961
	• 9 Stone Buildings	0171 404 5055
	55 Temple Chambers	0171 353 7400
	• 3 Temple Gardens	0171 353 3102/5/9297
	• Thomas More Chambers	0171 404 7000
	Warwick House Chambers	0171 430 2323
Maidstone	• Maidstone Chambers	01622 688592
	6-8 Mill Street	01622 688094
Manchester	• 40 King Street	0161 832 9082
	• Queen's Chambers	0161 834 6875/4738
	• 28 St John Street	0161 834 8418
Newcastle upon Tyne	• Trinity Chambers	0191 232 1927
Northampton	Chambers of Michael Pert QC	01604 602333
Norwich	East Anglian Chambers	01603 617351
	Sackville Chambers	01603 613516/616221
Nottingham	King Charles House	0115 9418851
	Ropewalk Chambers	0115 9472581
Oxford	Harcourt Chambers	01865 791559
	3 Paper Buildings (Oxford)	01865 793736
Peterborough	Fenners Chambers	01733 562030
Plymouth	Devon Chambers	01752 661659
Pontypridd	• Windsor Chambers	01443 402067
Preston	Queens Chambers	01772 828300
	15 Winckley Square	01772 252828
Redhill	Redhill Chambers	01737 780781
Saint Albans	St Albans Chambers	01727 843383
Sheffield	Paradise Chambers	0114 2738951
Slough	Slough Chamber	01753 553806/817989
Southampton	• 17 Carlton Crescent	023 8032 0320/0823 2003
	• College Chambers	01703 230338
	• Eighteen Carlton Crescent	01703 639001
Stoke On Trent	Regent Chambers	01782 286666
Swansea	Angel Chambers	01792 464623/464648
	Iscoed Chambers	01792 652988/9/330
Taunton	South Western Chambers	01823 331919 (24 hrs)
Winchester	3 Paper Buildings (Winchester)	01962 868884
Wolverhampton	Claremont Chambers	01902 426222

TRADE DESCRIPTIONS ACT AND ALLIED LEGISLATION

London	22 Melcombe Regis Court	0171 487 5589

TRADEMARKS

Birmingham	1 Fountain Court	0121 236 5721
	• 5 Fountain Court	0121 606 0500
	St Ive's Chambers	0121 236 0863/5720
Bristol	St John's Chambers	0117 9213456/298514
Leeds	Chambers of Andrew Campbell QC	0113 2455438
	• Chancery House Chambers	0113 244 6691
	• Sovereign Chambers	0113 2451841/2/3
London	• One Essex Court	020 7583 2000
	• 4 Field Court	0171 440 6900

● Fountain Court	0171 583 3335
Francis Taylor Building	0171 353 7768/7769/2711
9 King's Bench Walk	0171 353 7202/3909
11 King's Bench Walk	0171 353 3337
Lamb Chambers	020 7797 8300
● Littleton Chambers	0171 797 8600
2 Mitre Court Buildings	0171 353 1353
● Monckton Chambers	0171 405 7211
● 3 New Square	0171 405 1111
5 New Square	020 7404 0404
7 New Square	020 7404 5484
● 8 New Square	0171 405 4321
19 Old Buildings	0171 405 2001
● 11 Old Square	020 7430 0341
● 11 South Square	0171 405 1222 (24hr messaging service)

Manchester	● Cobden House Chambers	0161 833 6000
	● St James's Chambers	0161 834 7000
Preston	New Bailey Chambers	01772 258087
Reading	Wessex Chambers	0118 956 8856

TRADING STANDARDS

London	● Thomas More Chambers	0171 404 7000

TRAVEL AND HOLIDAY LAW

London	Barnard's Inn Chambers	0171 369 6969
	● New Court Chambers	0171 831 9500

UNFAIR DISMISSAL

London	Chambers of Harjit Singh	0171 353 1356 (4 Lines)

UNIT TRUSTS

Birmingham	● 5 Fountain Court	0121 606 0500
Leeds	Chambers of Andrew Campbell QC	0113 2455438
London	● Erskine Chambers	0171 242 5532
	11 King's Bench Walk	0171 353 3337
	Leone Chambers	0181 200 4020
	● Chambers of John L Powell QC	0171 797 8000
	Chambers of John Gardiner QC	0171 242 4017
	● 12 New Square	0171 419 1212

UTILITIES

London	● 199 Strand	0171 379 9779

VAT

Leeds	11 King's Bench Walk	0113 297 1200
London	Chambers of Geoffrey Hawker	0171 583 8899
	Chambers of John Gardiner QC	0171 242 4017

VAT AND CUSTOMS & EXCISE

London	● 39 Essex Street	0171 832 1111
	● Monckton Chambers	0171 405 7211

WELFARE

London	Tower Hamlets Barristers Chambers	0171 377 8090

Types of Work by Individual Barristers

This section lists individual barristers by the types of work in which they specialise. The areas of work are listed in alphabetical order. Within these main categories, individual barristers are listed alphabetically by surname. For example, a reader wishing to locate a particular barrister specialising in trademarks would be able to look under 'T' for Trademarks and find under that heading those barristers who offer their services in this field. A complete list of the types of work can be found overleaf.

Each listing provides the name of the individual barrister, their chambers' address and chambers' telephone number. The first point of contact in each instance will be the clerk. (Details of clerks can be found in *Part C Chambers by Location*)

Please note that barristers are only listed in this section if information on specialisms has been supplied by them.

The symbol • indicates that a barrister has an expanded entry in *Part D Individual Barristers in Private Practice*.

B

Type of Work

A

Accountancy	B5
Actions against the police	B5
Actions involving the police	B5
Adjudication	B5
Administrative	B5
Admiralty	B10
ADR	B10
Agency	B10
Agriculture	B10
Animal welfare	B11
Arab laws	B11
Arab World contracts	B11
Arbitration	B12
Asset finance	B17
Aviation	B17

B

Banking	B18
Bankruptcy	B22
Breach of confidence	B26
Building societies	B26

C

Capital taxes/estate planning	B26
Care proceedings	B26
Chancery (commercial)	B32
Chancery (general)	B33
Chancery land law	B40
Charities	B46
Child abduction	B47
Child care law	B47
Children	B47
Civil actions against prisons	B47
Civil actions against the police	B48
Civil actions involving the police	B48
Civil fraud	B48
Civil jury actions	B48
Civil jury actions for police authorities	B48
Civil liberties	B48
Clinical negligence	B51
Club law	B51
Commercial	B52
Commercial fraud	B57
Commercial litigation	B58
Commercial property	B69
Commodities	B73
Common land	B74
Common law (general)	B75
Commons	B88
Community care	B88
Companies investigations	B88
Company and commercial	B88
Competition	B94
Competitive tendering/public procurement	B95
Compulsory purchase	B95
Computer litigation	B95

Computer systems procurement	B95
Construction	B95
Consumer credit	B99
Consumer law	B99
Contract	B101
Conveyancing	B101
Copyright	B104
Copyright theft	B105
Copyright tribunal	B105
Coroners inquests	B105
Corporate finance	B105
Corporate manslaughter	B106
Costs	B106
Court of Protection	B106
Courts martial	B106
Credit hire	B108
Crime	B109
Crime – corporate fraud	B124

D

Damages	B131
Defamation	B131
Directors' disqualification	B132
Disciplinary (nurses)	B132
Disciplinary tribunals	B132
Discrimination	B132
Domestic violence injunctions	B135
Drink and driving	B135

E

E-Commerce	B135
EC and competition law	B135
EC law	B137
Ecclesiastical	B137
ECHR	B138
Education	B138
Election law	B139
Employment	B139
Energy	B148
Entertainment	B149
Environment	B150
Equestrian	B153
Equine law	B153
Equity, wills and trusts	B153
European law	B158
Extradition	B158

F

Family	B158
Family mediation	B168
Family provision	B168
Field sports	B176
Film, cable, TV	B176
Financial provision	B177
Financial services	B177
Fine art	B179
Fisheries	B179
Food law	B179
Food poisoning	B179
Foreign law	B179
Franchising	B179

B

H

Hague Convention – Children	B180
Health & safety	B180
Healthcare administration and contracting	B180
Highways	B180
Hong Kong law	B180
Housing	B180
Human rights	B184

I

Immigration	B184
Industrial Tribunals	B186
Information technology	B186
Inquests	B188
Insolvency	B188
Insurance	B195
Insurance/reinsurance	B199
Intellectual property	B202
International child abduction	B204
International family law	B204
International loan documentation	B204
International trade	B204
Irish law	B206
Islamic law	B206
Italian law	B206

J

Judicial review	B206
Jurisdiction	B206

L

Labour arbitration	B206
Landlord and tenant	B207
Licensing	B216
Limited partnerships	B220
Local authority claims	B220
Local government	B220

M

Media	B223
Mediation	B223
Medical inquiries	B223
Medical law	B224
Medical negligence	B224
Medical/dental disciplinary work	B231
Mental health	B231
Mobile homes	B233
Mortgages and borrowers	B233
Motor vehicles	B233
Motoring law	B233
Music, film and tv	B233

N

National Insurance contributions	B233
New York law	B233

P

Parliamentary	B233
Partnerships	B234
Patents	B239

Pensions	B239
Personal injury	B241
Pharmaceuticals	B255
Pharmacy	B256
Planning	B256
Police actions	B258
Police discipline	B258
Police law	B258
Prison law	B258
Prisoners' rights	B258
Private client	B258
Private international	B258
Privy Council	B260
Probate and administration	B260
Product liability	B263
Professional disciplinary tribunals	B263
Professional negligence	B263
Public inquiries	B280
Public international	B280
Public procurement	B280
Public rights of way	B280

R

Regulatory tribunals	B280
Restitution	B280
Rights of way	B280
Road traffic	B281
Road Traffic Offences	B281

S

Sale and carriage of goods	B281
School sites	B285
Scientific and technical disputes	B285
Share options	B285
Shipping	B286
Shipping, admiralty	B286
Social security	B287
Society of Lloyd's	B287
Solicitors' costs and taxation	B287
South African law	B287
Spanish law	B287
Sports	B287
Sports medicine	B289
Sports – motor racing law	B289

T

Takeovers and mergers	B289
Tax – capital and income	B289
Tax – corporate	B290
Tax investigations	B291
Telecommunications	B291
Town and country planning	B292
Trademarks	B294
Travel and holiday law	B294
Tribunals/inquiries	B295

U

Unit trusts	B295
Utilities	B295

B

V

VAT	B295
VAT and Customs & Excise	B295
VAT fraud	B295

W

Warranty claims	B295
Waste management	B295
Welfare	B296

B

ACCOUNTANCY

Barker Simon George Harry	• 13 Old Square, London	0171 404 4800

ACTIONS AGAINST THE POLICE

Abbott Francis Arthur	Pump Court Chambers, Winchester	01962 868161
	Pump Court Chambers, London	0171 353 0711
	Pump Court Chambers, Swindon	01793 539899
Barton Hugh Geoffrey	Doughty Street Chambers, London	0171 404 1313
Bentley Stephen	1 Gray's Inn Square, London	0171 405 8946/7/8
Brown Miss Althea Sonia	Doughty Street Chambers, London	0171 404 1313
Denney Stuart Henry Macdonald	Deans Court Chambers, Manchester	0161 214 6000
	Deans Court Chambers, Preston	01772 555163
McCluggage Brian Thomas	Chambers of John Hand QC, Manchester	0161 955 9000
Paul Nicholas Martin	Doughty Street Chambers, London	0171 404 1313
	Westgate Chambers, Lewes	01273 480510
Rees Edward Parry	Doughty Street Chambers, London	0171 404 1313
Thornton Peter Ribblesdale	Doughty Street Chambers, London	0171 404 1313
Whitaker Ms Quincy Rachel Suzy	Doughty Street Chambers, London	0171 404 1313
Wood James Alexander Douglas	Doughty Street Chambers, London	0171 404 1313

ACTIONS INVOLVING THE POLICE

Stevens Howard Linton	1 Crown Office Row, London	0171 583 9292

ADJUDICATION

Franklin Miss Kim	• One Paper Buildings, London	0171 583 7355

ADMINISTRATIVE

Akiwumi Anthony Sebastian Akitayo	Pump Court Chambers, London	0171 353 0711
	Pump Court Chambers, Winchester	01962 868161
	Pump Court Chambers, Swindon	01793 539899
Aldous Grahame Linley	9 Gough Square, London	020 7832 0500
Alesbury Alun	2 Mitre Court Buildings, London	0171 583 1380
Allfrey Richard Forbes	Doughty Street Chambers, London	0171 404 1313
Anderson Anthony John	2 Mitre Court Buildings, London	0171 583 1380
Anderson Miss Julie	• Littman Chambers, London	020 7404 4866
Barlow Craig Martin	29 Bedford Row Chambers, London	0171 831 2626
Beard Daniel Matthew	Monckton Chambers, London	0171 405 7211
Beard Mark Christopher	6 Pump Court, London	0171 797 8400
	6-8 Mill Street, Maidstone	01622 688094
Beaumont Marc Clifford	• Harrow on the Hill Chambers, Harrow-on-the-Hill	0181 423 7444
	Windsor Barristers' Chambers, Windsor	01753 648899
	Pump Court Chambers, London	0171 353 0711
Bhanji Shiraz Musa	4 Bingham Place, London	0171 486 5347/071 487 5910
Birtles William	Old Square Chambers, London	0171 269 0300
	Old Square Chambers, Bristol	0117 9277111
Blake Arthur Joseph	13 King's Bench Walk, London	0171 353 7204
	King's Bench Chambers, Oxford	01865 311066
Bowen Paul Edward	4 King's Bench Walk, London	0171 822 8822
Boyle Christopher Alexander David	2 Mitre Court Buildings, London	0171 583 1380
Broatch Michael Donald	5 Paper Buildings, London	0171 583 9275/583 4555
Brockley Nigel Simon	Bracton Chambers, London	0171 242 4248
Brown Miss Althea Sonia	Doughty Street Chambers, London	0171 404 1313
Burton Nicholas Anthony	2 Mitre Court Buildings, London	0171 583 1380
Butcher Christopher John	S Tomlinson QC, London	0171 583 0404
Butt Michael Robert	Pump Court Chambers, Swindon	01793 539899
	Pump Court Chambers, London	0171 353 0711
	Pump Court Chambers, Winchester	01962 868161
Cakebread Stuart Alan Charles	• 2nd Floor, Francis Taylor Building, London	0171 353 9942/3157
Catchpole Stuart Paul	• 39 Essex Street, London	0171 832 1111

Cavanagh John Patrick	11 King's Bench Walk, London	0171 632 8500/583 0610
Cheshire Anthony Peter	199 Strand, London	0171 379 9779
Cox Bryan Richard	9 Woodhouse Square, Leeds	0113 2451986
Craig Alistair Trevor	Chambers of Mr Peter Crampin QC, London	020 7831 0081
Daly David	Francis Taylor Building, London	0171 797 7250
Daniel Leon Roger	6 King's Bench Walk, London	0171 353 4931/583 0695
Dodd Christopher John Nicholas	9 Woodhouse Square, Leeds	0113 2451986
Dolan Dr Bridget Maura	3 Serjeants' Inn, London	0171 353 5537
Dowley Dominic Myles	One Hare Court, London	020 7353 3171
Druce Michael James	2 Mitre Court Buildings, London	0171 583 1380
Duddridge Robert James	2 Gray's Inn Square Chambers, London	020 7242 0328
Eadie James Raymond	One Hare Court, London	020 7353 3171
Eccles David Thomas	8 King Street Chambers, Manchester	0161 834 9560
Edge Timothy Richard	Deans Court Chambers, Preston	01772 555163
	Deans Court Chambers, Manchester	0161 214 6000
Edusei Francis Victor Burg	Chambers of Ian Macdonald QC (In Association with Two Garden Court, Temple, London), Manchester	0161 236 1840
Emmerson (Michael) Benedict	Doughty Street Chambers, London	0171 404 1313
Farbey Miss Judith Sarah	Plowden Buildings, London	0171 583 0808
Firth Miss Georgina Elizabeth	Chambers of Ian Macdonald QC (In Association with Two Garden Court, Temple, London), Manchester	0161 236 1840
Fisher Jonathan Simon	• 18 Red Lion Court, London	0171 520 6000
	Thornwood House, Chelmsford	01245 280880
Fitzgerald Edward Hamilton	Doughty Street Chambers, London	0171 404 1313
Fitzgerald Michael Frederick Clive	2 Mitre Court Buildings, London	0171 583 1380
Flaux Julian Martin	S Tomlinson QC, London	0171 583 0404
Fookes Robert Lawrence	2 Mitre Court Buildings, London	0171 583 1380
Ford Gerard James	Baker Street Chambers, Middlesbrough	01642 873873
Ford Michael David	Doughty Street Chambers, London	0171 404 1313
Forte Mark Julian Carmino	8 King Street Chambers, Manchester	0161 834 9560
Foster Miss Alison Lee Caroline	39 Essex Street, London	0171 832 1111
Fowler Richard Nicholas	Monckton Chambers, London	0171 405 7211
Freeland Simon Dennis Marsden	5 Essex Court, London	0171 410 2000
Fullwood Adam Garrett	Chambers of Ian Macdonald QC (In Association with Two Garden Court, Temple, London), Manchester	0161 236 1840
Garlick Paul Richard	Pump Court Chambers, London	0171 353 0711
	Pump Court Chambers, Winchester	01962 868161
	Pump Court Chambers, Swindon	01793 539899
Gasztowicz Steven	2-3 Gray's Inn Square, London	0171 242 4986
	2 New Street, Leicester	0116 2625906
Gau Justin Charles	Pump Court Chambers, London	0171 353 0711
	Pump Court Chambers, Winchester	01962 868161
	Pump Court Chambers, Swindon	01793 539899
Gledhill Kris	Camberwell Chambers, London	0171 274 0830
Glover Richard Michael	2 Mitre Court Buildings, London	0171 583 1380
Gordon Richard John Francis	Brick Court Chambers, London	0171 379 3550
Goudie James	• 11 King's Bench Walk, London	0171 632 8500/583 0610
Grace John Oliver Bowman	3 Serjeants' Inn, London	0171 353 5537
Grayson Edward	• 9-12 Bell Yard, London	0171 400 1800
Grey Miss Eleanor Mary Grace	39 Essex Street, London	0171 832 1111
Grodzinski Samuel Marc	39 Essex Street, London	0171 832 1111
Hall Mrs Melanie Ruth	Monckton Chambers, London	0171 405 7211
Harington Michael Kenneth	6 Pump Court, London	0171 797 8400
	6-8 Mill Street, Maidstone	01622 688094
Harris Paul Best	Monckton Chambers, London	0171 405 7211
Harrison Peter John	6 Pump Court, London	0171 797 8400
	6-8 Mill Street, Maidstone	01622 688094

• Expanded entry in Part D

Harwood Richard John	1 Serjeants' Inn, London	0171 583 1355
Hatfield Ms Sally Anne	Doughty Street Chambers, London	0171 404 1313
Haynes Miss Rebecca	Monckton Chambers, London	0171 405 7211
Henderson (Anthony) Mark	Doughty Street Chambers, London	0171 404 1313
Henderson Roger Anthony	2 Harcourt Buildings, London	0171 583 9020
Henderson Miss Sophie	Plowden Buildings, London	0171 583 0808
Hershman David Allan	St Philip's Chambers, Birmingham	0121 246 7000
	1 Mitre Court Buildings, London	0171 797 7070
Hill Nicholas Mark	• Pump Court Chambers, London	0171 353 0711
	Pump Court Chambers, Winchester	01962 868161
	Pump Court Chambers, Swindon	01793 539899
Hill Raymond	Monckton Chambers, London	0171 405 7211
Hockman Stephen Alexander	• 6 Pump Court, London	0171 797 8400
	6-8 Mill Street, Maidstone	01622 688094
Hogg The Hon Douglas Martin	37 Park Square Chambers, Leeds	0113 2439422
	Cathedral Chambers (Jan Wood Independent Barristers' Clerk), Exeter	01392 210900
Horton Matthew Bethell	2 Mitre Court Buildings, London	0171 583 1380
Hudson Anthony Sean	Doughty Street Chambers, London	0171 404 1313
Humphries Michael John	2 Mitre Court Buildings, London	0171 583 1380
Hunter William Quigley	No. 1 Serjeants' Inn, London	0171 415 6666
Hyams Oliver Marks	5 Paper Buildings, London	0171 583 9275/583 4555
Irwin Stephen John	Doughty Street Chambers, London	0171 404 1313
Ivimy Ms Cecilia Rachel	11 King's Bench Walk, London	0171 632 8500/583 0610
Jay Robert Maurice	39 Essex Street, London	0171 832 1111
Jones Clive Hugh	1 New Square, London	0171 405 0884/5/6/7
Jones Philip John	Serle Court Chambers, London	0171 242 6105
Jones Sean William Paul	11 King's Bench Walk, London	0171 632 8500/583 0610
Jones Timothy Arthur	• St Philip's Chambers, Birmingham	0121 246 7000
	Arden Chambers, London	020 7242 4244
Kaufmann Ms Phillippa Jane	Doughty Street Chambers, London	0171 404 1313
Keane Desmond St John	Pendragon Chambers, Swansea	01792 411188
Kent Miss Georgina	5 Essex Court, London	0171 410 2000
Kent Michael Harcourt	Two Crown Office Row, London	020 7797 8100
Kenward Timothy David Nelson	25-27 Castle Street, Liverpool	0151 227 5661/051 236 5072
King Neil Gerald Alexander	2 Mitre Court Buildings, London	0171 583 1380
Kovats Steven Laszlo	39 Essex Street, London	0171 832 1111
Laing Miss Elisabeth Mary Caroline	11 King's Bench Walk, London	0171 632 8500/583 0610
Langham Richard Geoffrey	1 Serjeants' Inn, London	0171 583 1355
Lasok Karol Paul Edward	Monckton Chambers, London	0171 405 7211
Lavender Nicholas	One Hare Court, London	020 7353 3171
Leigh Kevin	6 Pump Court, London	0171 797 8400
	Regency Chambers, Peterborough	01733 315215
	Westgate Chambers, Lewes	01273 480510
	6-8 Mill Street, Maidstone	01622 688094
Leiper Richard Thomas	11 King's Bench Walk, London	0171 632 8500/583 0610
Lewis Robert	11 Bolt Court (also at 7 Stone Buildings – 1st Floor), London	0171 353 2300
	7 Stone Buildings (also at 11 Bolt Court), London	0171 242 0961
	Redhill Chambers, Redhill	01737 780781
Maclean Alan John	39 Essex Street, London	0171 832 1111
Macpherson The Hon Mary Stewart	2 Mitre Court Buildings, London	0171 583 1380
Mainwaring [Robert] Paul Clason	Carmarthen Chambers, Carmarthen	01267 234410
Malecka Dr Mary Margaret	• 3 Temple Gardens, London	0171 353 0832
	65-67 King Street, Leicester	0116 2547710
Markus Ms Kate	Doughty Street Chambers, London	0171 404 1313
McCafferty Miss Lynne	5 Paper Buildings, London	0171 583 9275/583 4555
Mercer Hugh Charles	• Essex Court Chambers, London	0171 813 8000
Middleton Joseph	Doughty Street Chambers, London	0171 404 1313
Millar Gavin James	Doughty Street Chambers, London	0171 404 1313

• Expanded entry in Part D

B

Moore Professor Victor William Edward	2 Mitre Court Buildings, London	0171 583 1380
Moran Andrew John	One Hare Court, London	020 7353 3171
Morgan (Thomas) Jeremy	39 Essex Street, London	0171 832 1111
Moriarty Gerald Evelyn	2 Mitre Court Buildings, London	0171 583 1380
Morris Miss Fenella	39 Essex Street, London	0171 832 1111
Morris Stephen Nathan	20 Essex Street, London	0171 583 9294
Mulholland Michael	St James's Chambers, Manchester	0161 834 7000
Nardell Gordon Lawrence	6 Pump Court, London	0171 797 8400
	6-8 Mill Street, Maidstone	01622 688094
Neill of Bladen Lord	One Hare Court, London	020 7353 3171
Neville-Clarke Sebastian Adrian Bennett	1 Crown Office Row, London	0171 583 9292
Newcombe Andrew Bennett	2 Harcourt Buildings, London	020 7353 8415
Nicol Andrew George Lindsay	Doughty Street Chambers, London	0171 404 1313
Nicol Nicholas Keith	1 Pump Court, London	0171 583 2012/353 4341
O'Neill Tadhg Joseph	1 Crown Office Row, London	0171 583 9292
Ornsby Miss Suzanne Doreen	2 Harcourt Buildings, London	020 7353 8415
Outhwaite Mrs Wendy-Jane Tivnan	2 Harcourt Buildings, London	0171 583 9020
Owen Timothy Wynn	Doughty Street Chambers, London	0171 404 1313
Padfield Nicholas David	One Hare Court, London	020 7353 3171
Page Howard William Barrett	One Hare Court, London	020 7353 3171
Paines Nicholas Paul Billot	Monckton Chambers, London	0171 405 7211
Panford Frank Haig	•Doughty Street Chambers, London	0171 404 1313
Parker Kenneth Blades	Monckton Chambers, London	0171 405 7211
Patel Parishil Jayantilal	39 Essex Street, London	0171 832 1111
Paul Nicholas Martin	Doughty Street Chambers, London	0171 404 1313
	Westgate Chambers, Lewes	01273 480510
Pereira James Alexander	2 Harcourt Buildings, London	020 7353 8415
Peretz George Michael John	Monckton Chambers, London	0171 405 7211
Phillpot Hereward Lindon	2 Harcourt Buildings, London	020 7353 8415
Pitt-Payne Timothy Sheridan	•11 King's Bench Walk, London	0171 632 8500/583 0610
Pleming Nigel Peter	39 Essex Street, London	0171 832 1111
Plender Richard Owen	•20 Essex Street, London	0171 583 9294
Pomeroy Toby	Barristers' Common Law Chambers, London	0171 375 3012
	Virtual Chambers, London	07071 244 944
Price Albert John	23 Essex Street, London	0171 413 0353/836 8366
Price John Scott	10 Launceston Avenue, Reading	01189 479548
	Southsea Chambers, Portsmouth	01705 291261
	Cathedral Chambers, Newcastle upon Tyne	0191 232 1311
Purchas Robin Michael	•2 Harcourt Buildings, London	020 7353 8415
Randall John Yeoman	St Philip's Chambers, Birmingham	0121 246 7000
	7 Stone Buildings, London	0171 405 3886/242 3546
Readhead Simon John Howard	No. 1 Serjeants' Inn, London	0171 415 6666
Rhodes Robert Elliott	4 King's Bench Walk, London	0171 822 8822
Richards Miss Jennifer	39 Essex Street, London	0171 832 1111
Richardson David John	13 King's Bench Walk, London	0171 353 7204
	King's Bench Chambers, Oxford	01865 311066
Robb Adam Duncan	39 Essex Street, London	0171 832 1111
Roberts Miss Clare Justine	•2nd Floor, Francis Taylor Building, London	0171 353 9942/3157
Robertson Geoffrey Ronald	Doughty Street Chambers, London	0171 404 1313
Rogers Ian Paul	1 Crown Office Row, London	0171 583 9292
Roots Guy Robert Godfrey	2 Mitre Court Buildings, London	0171 583 1380
Roth Peter Marcel	Monckton Chambers, London	0171 405 7211
Rumney Conrad William Arthur	St Philip's Chambers, Birmingham	0121 246 7000
Ryder Ernest Nigel	Deans Court Chambers, Manchester	0161 214 6000
	Deans Court Chambers, Preston	01772 555163
	1 Mitre Court Buildings, London	0171 797 7070

• Expanded entry in Part D

Sharpston Miss Eleanor Veronica Elizabeth	4 Paper Buildings, London	0171 353 3366/583 7155
Sheldon Clive David	11 King's Bench Walk, London	0171 632 8500/583 0610
Sheppard Timothy Derie	Bracton Chambers, London	0171 242 4248
Shrimpton Michael	Francis Taylor Building, London	0171 797 7250
Shukla Ms Vina	New Court Chambers, London	0171 831 9500
Silsoe The Lord	2 Mitre Court Buildings, London	0171 583 1380
Silvester Bruce Ross	Lamb Chambers, London	020 7797 8300
Simor Miss Jessica Margaret Poppaea	Monckton Chambers, London	0171 405 7211
Sinclair Graham Kelso	East Anglian Chambers, Norwich	01603 617351
	East Anglian Chambers, Colchester	01206 572756
	East Anglian Chambers, Ipswich	01473 214481
Singh Kuldip	Five Paper Buildings, London	0171 583 6117
Skilbeck Mrs Jennifer Seth	Monckton Chambers, London	0171 405 7211
Smith Ms Katherine Emma	Monckton Chambers, London	0171 405 7211
Smith Michael Joseph	8 King Street Chambers, Manchester	0161 834 9560
Smith Paul Andrew	One Hare Court, London	020 7353 3171
Southwell Richard Charles	One Hare Court, London	020 7353 3171
Stark James Hayden Alexander	Chambers of Ian Macdonald QC (In Association with Two Garden Court, Temple, London), Manchester	0161 236 1840
Starmer Keir	Doughty Street Chambers, London	0171 404 1313
Stern Dr Kristina Anne	39 Essex Street, London	0171 832 1111
Stewart Nicholas John Cameron	Hardwicke Building, London	020 7242 2523
Stilitz Daniel Malachi	11 King's Bench Walk, London	0171 632 8500/583 0610
Stone Gregory	• 4-5 Gray's Inn Square, London	0171 404 5252
Straker Timothy Derrick	• 4-5 Gray's Inn Square, London	0171 404 5252
Supperstone Michael Alan	11 King's Bench Walk, London	0171 632 8500/583 0610
Tait Andrew Charles Gordon	2 Harcourt Buildings, London	020 7353 8415
Taylor John Charles	2 Mitre Court Buildings, London	0171 583 1380
Taylor Reuben Mallinson	2 Mitre Court Buildings, London	0171 583 1380
Thomas Miss Megan Moira	1 Serjeants' Inn, London	0171 583 1355
Thompson Rhodri William Ralph	Monckton Chambers, London	0171 405 7211
Travers David	• 3 Fountain Court, Birmingham	0121 236 5854
Tucker Dr Peter Louis	Leone Chambers, London	0181 200 4020
	12 Old Square, London	0171 404 0875
Turner Adrian John	Eastbourne Chambers, Eastbourne	01323 642102
Turner Jonathan Richard	Monckton Chambers, London	0171 405 7211
Vajda Christopher Stephen	Monckton Chambers, London	0171 405 7211
Wadsworth James Patrick	4 Paper Buildings, London	0171 353 3366/583 7155
Wald Richard Daniel	2 Mitre Court Buildings, London	0171 583 1380
Wallington Peter Thomas	11 King's Bench Walk, London	0171 632 8500/583 0610
Ward Timothy Justin	Monckton Chambers, London	0171 405 7211
Warren Rupert Miles	2 Mitre Court Buildings, London	0171 583 1380
Waters Julian William Penrose	No. 1 Serjeants' Inn, London	0171 415 6666
Weatherby Peter Francis	Two Garden Court, London	0171 353 1633
	Chambers of Ian Macdonald QC (In Association with Two Garden Court, Temple, London), Manchester	0161 236 1840
Weereratne Ms Rufina Aswini	Doughty Street Chambers, London	0171 404 1313
Westgate Martin Trevor	Doughty Street Chambers, London	0171 404 1313
Weston Ms Amanda	Chambers of Ian Macdonald QC (In Association with Two Garden Court, Temple, London), Manchester	0161 236 1840
Whipple Mrs Philippa Jane Edwards	1 Crown Office Row, London	0171 797 7500
Whybrow Christopher John	1 Serjeants' Inn, London	0171 583 1355
Widdicombe David Graham	2 Mitre Court Buildings, London	0171 583 1380
Wilken Sean David Henry	39 Essex Street, London	0171 832 1111
Williams Ms Heather Jean	Doughty Street Chambers, London	0171 404 1313
Williams Dr Jason Scott	• 3 Dr Johnson's Buildings, London	0171 353 4854

Williams Rhodri John	30 Park Place, Cardiff	01222 398421
	2 Harcourt Buildings, London	0171 583 9020
Williams Wyn Lewis	39 Essex Street, London	0171 832 1111
	33 Park Place, Cardiff	02920 233313
Wise Ian	Doughty Street Chambers, London	0171 404 1313
Zwart Auberon Christiaan Conrad	1 Serjeants' Inn, London	0171 583 1355

ADMIRALTY

Ambrose Miss Clare Mary Geneste	20 Essex Street, London	0171 583 9294
Blackburn Mrs Elizabeth	4 Field Court, London	0171 440 6900
Blackwood Andrew Guy	4 Field Court, London	0171 440 6900
Brenton Timothy Deane	4 Essex Court, London	020 7797 7970
Brice Geoffrey James Barrington	4 Field Court, London	0171 440 6900
Buckingham Stewart John	4 Essex Court, London	020 7797 7970
Chambers Jonathan	4 Essex Court, London	020 7797 7970
Collett Michael John	20 Essex Street, London	0171 583 9294
Davey Michael Philip	4 Field Court, London	0171 440 6900
Davies Dr Charles Edward	4 Field Court, London	0171 440 6900
Gee Steven Mark	4 Field Court, London	0171 440 6900
Ghaffar Arshad	4 Field Court, London	0171 440 6900
Goldstone David Julian	4 Field Court, London	0171 440 6900
Hill Timothy John	4 Field Court, London	0171 440 6900
Howard Michael Newman	4 Essex Court, London	020 7797 7970
Kay Robert Jervis	4 Field Court, London	0171 440 6900
Kverndal Simon Richard	4 Essex Court, London	020 7797 7970
Macdonald Charles Adam	4 Essex Court, London	020 7797 7970
Males Stephen Martin	20 Essex Street, London	0171 583 9294
Masters Miss Sara Alayna	20 Essex Street, London	0171 583 9294
Meeson Nigel Keith	4 Field Court, London	0171 440 6900
Milligan Iain Anstruther	20 Essex Street, London	0171 583 9294
Nolan Michael Alfred Anthony	4 Essex Court, London	020 7797 7970
O'Shea Eoin Finbarr	4 Field Court, London	0171 440 6900
Persey Lionel Edward	● 4 Field Court, London	0171 440 6900
Reeder John	4 Field Court, London	0171 440 6900
Russell Jeremy Jonathan	● 4 Essex Court, London	020 7797 7970
Saunders Nicholas Joseph	4 Field Court, London	0171 440 6900
Selvaratnam Miss Vasanti Emily Indrani	4 Field Court, London	0171 440 6900
Smith Christopher Frank	Essex Court Chambers, London	0171 813 8000
Stone Richard Frederick	4 Field Court, London	0171 440 6900
Teare Nigel John Martin	4 Essex Court, London	020 7797 7970
Turner James Michael	● 4 Essex Court, London	020 7797 7970
Waller Richard Beaumont	S Tomlinson QC, London	0171 583 0404
Whitehouse-Vaux William Edward	4 Field Court, London	0171 440 6900
Wright Colin John	4 Field Court, London	0171 440 6900

ADR

Behrens James Nicholas Edward	Serle Court Chambers, London	0171 242 6105

AGENCY

Reynolds Professor Francis Martin Baillie	S Tomlinson QC, London	0171 583 0404
Segal Oliver Leon	Old Square Chambers, London	0171 269 0300
	Old Square Chambers, Bristol	0117 9277111

AGRICULTURE

Aldous Robert John	Octagon House, Norwich	01603 623186
Ambrose Miss Clare Mary Geneste	20 Essex Street, London	0171 583 9294
Baxter-Phillips Miss Felicity Dawn	Becket Chambers, Canterbury	01227 786331
Behrens James Nicholas Edward	Serle Court Chambers, London	0171 242 6105

● Expanded entry in Part D

Berry Nicholas Michael	Southernhay Chambers, Exeter	01392 255777
	1 Gray's Inn Square, London	0171 405 8946/7/8
	22 Old Buildings, London	0171 831 0222
Cranfield Peter Anthony	3 Verulam Buildings, London	0171 831 8441
De Freitas Anthony Peter Stanley	4 Paper Buildings, London	0171 353 3366/583 7155
Denbin Jack Arnold	Greenway, Sonning-on-Thames	0118 969 2484
Fookes Robert Lawrence	2 Mitre Court Buildings, London	0171 583 1380
Fryer-Spedding James Walter	St James's Chambers, Manchester	0161 834 7000
Garner Miss Sophie Jane	199 Strand, London	0171 379 9779
Gregory John Raymond	Deans Court Chambers, Manchester	0161 214 6000
	Deans Court Chambers, Preston	01772 555163
Haynes Miss Rebecca	Monckton Chambers, London	0171 405 7211
Hill Raymond	Monckton Chambers, London	0171 405 7211
Hogg The Hon Douglas Martin	37 Park Square Chambers, Leeds	0113 2439422
	Cathedral Chambers (Jan Wood	01392 210900
	Independent Barristers' Clerk), Exeter	
Howarth Simon Stuart	Two Crown Office Row, London	020 7797 8100
Jackson Dirik George Allan	Chambers of Mr Peter Crampin QC,	020 7831 0081
	London	
Lamont Miss Camilla Rose	Chambers of Lord Goodhart QC, London	0171 405 5577
Lasok Karol Paul Edward	Monckton Chambers, London	0171 405 7211
Legge Henry	5 Stone Buildings, London	0171 242 6201
Mainwaring [Robert] Paul Clason	Carmarthen Chambers, Carmarthen	01267 234410
McAllister Miss Elizabeth Ann	Enterprise Chambers, London	0171 405 9471
	Enterprise Chambers, Leeds	0113 246 0391
	Enterprise Chambers, Newcastle upon	0191 222 3344
	Tyne	
Mercer Hugh Charles	• Essex Court Chambers, London	0171 813 8000
Paines Nicholas Paul Billot	Monckton Chambers, London	0171 405 7211
Parker Kenneth Blades	Monckton Chambers, London	0171 405 7211
Peacocke Mrs Teresa Anne Rosen	Enterprise Chambers, London	0171 405 9471
	Enterprise Chambers, Leeds	0113 246 0391
	Enterprise Chambers, Newcastle upon	0191 222 3344
	Tyne	
Roth Peter Marcel	Monckton Chambers, London	0171 405 7211
Rowell David Stewart	Chambers of Lord Goodhart QC, London	0171 405 5577
Sheridan Maurice Bernard Gerard	• 3 Verulam Buildings, London	0171 831 8441
Simor Miss Jessica Margaret	Monckton Chambers, London	0171 405 7211
Poppaea		
Skilbeck Mrs Jennifer Seth	Monckton Chambers, London	0171 405 7211
Smith Ms Katherine Emma	Monckton Chambers, London	0171 405 7211
Start Miss Angharad Jocelyn	3 Verulam Buildings, London	0171 831 8441
Talbot Patrick John	Serle Court Chambers, London	0171 242 6105
Taylor Reuben Mallinson	2 Mitre Court Buildings, London	0171 583 1380
Thomas Nigel Matthew	13 Old Square, London	0171 404 4800
Thompson Rhodri William Ralph	Monckton Chambers, London	0171 405 7211
Turner Jonathan Richard	Monckton Chambers, London	0171 405 7211
Vajda Christopher Stephen	Monckton Chambers, London	0171 405 7211

ANIMAL WELFARE

Brunton Sean Alexander McKay	Pump Court Chambers, Winchester	01962 868161
	Pump Court Chambers, London	0171 353 0711
	Pump Court Chambers, Swindon	01793 539899
Mainwaring [Robert] Paul Clason	Carmarthen Chambers, Carmarthen	01267 234410

ARAB LAWS

Ballantyne Professor William Morris	One Hare Court, London	020 7353 3171

ARAB WORLD CONTRACTS

El-Falahi Sami David	International Law Chambers, London	0171 221 5684/5/4840

B

ARBITRATION

Abbott Francis Arthur	Pump Court Chambers, Winchester	01962 868161
	Pump Court Chambers, London	0171 353 0711
	Pump Court Chambers, Swindon	01793 539899
Akenhead Robert	Atkin Chambers, London	020 7404 0102
Aldous Robert John	Octagon House, Norwich	01603 623186
Ali Miss Huma	Eastbourne Chambers, Eastbourne	01323 642102
Allen Michael David Prior	S Tomlinson QC, London	0171 583 0404
Allingham-Nicholson Mrs Elizabeth Sarah	2 New Street, Leicester	0116 2625906
Atherton Ian David	Enterprise Chambers, London	0171 405 9471
	Enterprise Chambers, Newcastle upon Tyne	0191 222 3344
	Enterprise Chambers, Leeds	0113 246 0391
Auckland Miss Elizabeth Rachel	30 Park Square, Leeds	0113 2436388
Baatz Nicholas Stephen	Atkin Chambers, London	020 7404 0102
Bailey David John	S Tomlinson QC, London	0171 583 0404
Bailey Edward Henry	Monckton Chambers, London	0171 405 7211
Baldry Antony Brian	No. 1 Serjeants' Inn, London	0171 415 6666
Barker Simon George Harry	• 13 Old Square, London	0171 404 4800
Barnett Andrew John	Pump Court Chambers, Winchester	01962 868161
	Pump Court Chambers, London	0171 353 0711
	Pump Court Chambers, Swindon	01793 539899
Barwise Miss Stephanie Nicola	Atkin Chambers, London	020 7404 0102
Bean Matthew Allen	11 King's Bench Walk, Leeds	0113 297 1200
	11 King's Bench Walk, London	0171 353 3337
Behrens James Nicholas Edward	Serle Court Chambers, London	0171 242 6105
Bellamy Jonathan Mark	39 Essex Street, London	0171 832 1111
Bignall John Francis	S Tomlinson QC, London	0171 583 0404
Birch Miss Elizabeth Blanche	3 Verulam Buildings, London	0171 831 8441
Blackburn Mrs Elizabeth	4 Field Court, London	0171 440 6900
Blackburn John	Atkin Chambers, London	020 7404 0102
Blackwood Andrew Guy	4 Field Court, London	0171 440 6900
Blair William James Lynton	3 Verulam Buildings, London	0171 831 8441
Blunt David John	4 Pump Court, London	020 7842 5555
Bowdery Martin	Atkin Chambers, London	020 7404 0102
Brannigan Peter John Sean	4 Pump Court, London	020 7842 5555
Brent Richard	3 Verulam Buildings, London	0171 831 8441
Brice Geoffrey James Barrington	4 Field Court, London	0171 440 6900
Bridgman David Martin	No. 1 Serjeants' Inn, London	0171 415 6666
Bright Robert Graham	S Tomlinson QC, London	0171 583 0404
Brodie (James) Bruce	39 Essex Street, London	0171 832 1111
Browne-Wilkinson Simon	Serle Court Chambers, London	0171 242 6105
Burnett Harold Wallace	4 Paper Buildings, London	0171 353 3366/583 7155
Burr Andrew Charles	Atkin Chambers, London	020 7404 0102
Butcher Christopher John	S Tomlinson QC, London	0171 583 0404
Butterworth Paul Anthony	Octagon House, Norwich	01603 623186
Cameron Jonathan James O'Grady	3 Verulam Buildings, London	0171 831 8441
Castle Peter Bolton	Chambers of Mr Peter Crampin QC, London	020 7831 0081
Catchpole Stuart Paul	• 39 Essex Street, London	0171 832 1111
Challenger Colin Westcott	Bridewell Chambers, London	020 7797 8800
Chambers Jonathan	4 Essex Court, London	020 7797 7970
Clarke Miss Alison Lee	No. 1 Serjeants' Inn, London	0171 415 6666
Clay Robert Charles	Atkin Chambers, London	020 7404 0102
Collard Michael David	5 Pump Court, London	020 7353 2532
Collett Ivor William	No. 1 Serjeants' Inn, London	0171 415 6666
Collett Michael John	20 Essex Street, London	0171 583 9294
Collings Nicholas Stewart	Atkin Chambers, London	020 7404 0102
Cooke Jeremy Lionel	S Tomlinson QC, London	0171 583 0404
Cooper Nigel Stuart	4 Essex Court, London	020 7797 7970

• Expanded entry in Part D

Corbett James Patrick	St Philip's Chambers, Birmingham	0121 246 7000
	Chambers of Andrew Campbell QC, Leeds	0113 2455438
Cranfield Peter Anthony	3 Verulam Buildings, London	0171 831 8441
Crawford Professor James Richard	3 Verulam Buildings, London	0171 831 8441
Curtis Michael Alexander	Two Crown Office Row, London	020 7797 8100
Davey Michael Philip	4 Field Court, London	0171 440 6900
Davies Miss Carol Elizabeth	2 New Street, Leicester	0116 2625906
Davies Dr Charles Edward	4 Field Court, London	0171 440 6900
Davies Stephen Richard	8 King Street Chambers, Manchester	0161 834 9560
de Lacy Richard Michael	3 Verulam Buildings, London	0171 831 8441
Dempsey Brian Paul	Lancaster Building, Manchester	0161 661 4444/0171 649 9872
Denbin Jack Arnold	Greenway, Sonning-on-Thames	0118 969 2484
Dennison Stephen Randell	Atkin Chambers, London	020 7404 0102
Dennys Nicholas Charles Jonathan	Atkin Chambers, London	020 7404 0102
Dillon Thomas William Matthew	1 Fountain Court, Birmingham	0121 236 5721
Dodd Christopher John Nicholas	9 Woodhouse Square, Leeds	0113 2451986
Doerries Miss Chantal-Aimee Renee Aemelia Annemarie	Atkin Chambers, London	020 7404 0102
Doig Mrs Jeanetta Rose	Neston Home Chambers, Corsham	01225 811909
Dowley Dominic Myles	One Hare Court, London	020 7353 3171
Dumaresq Ms Delia Jane	Atkin Chambers, London	020 7404 0102
Dyer David Roger	St Philip's Chambers, Birmingham	0121 246 7000
Eadie James Raymond	One Hare Court, London	020 7353 3171
Edey Philip David	20 Essex Street, London	0171 583 9294
Edwards David Leslie	S Tomlinson QC, London	0171 583 0404
Edwards-Stuart Antony James Cobham	Two Crown Office Row, London	020 7797 8100
El-Falahi Sami David	International Law Chambers, London	0171 221 5684/5/4840
Evans James Frederick Meurig	3 Verulam Buildings, London	0171 831 8441
Faluyi Albert Osamudiamen	Chambers of Martin Burr, London	0171 353 4636
Faulks Edward Peter Lawless	No. 1 Serjeants' Inn, London	0171 415 6666
Fenton Adam Timothy Downs	S Tomlinson QC, London	0171 583 0404
Fieldsend James William	2nd Floor, Francis Taylor Building, London	0171 353 9942/3157
Finn Terence	Chambers of Martin Burr, London	0171 353 4636
Flaux Julian Martin	S Tomlinson QC, London	0171 583 0404
Fletcher Christopher Michael	Octagon House, Norwich	01603 623186
Franklin Miss Kim	• One Paper Buildings, London	0171 583 7355
Fraser Peter Donald	Atkin Chambers, London	020 7404 0102
Freedman Sampson Clive	3 Verulam Buildings, London	0171 831 8441
Friedman David Peter	4 Pump Court, London	020 7842 5555
Gaisman Jonathan Nicholas Crispin	S Tomlinson QC, London	0171 583 0404
Geary Gavin John	S Tomlinson QC, London	0171 583 0404
Gee Steven Mark	4 Field Court, London	0171 440 6900
Ghaffar Arshad	4 Field Court, London	0171 440 6900
Gilmore Ian Martin	30 Park Square, Leeds	0113 2436388
Goddard Andrew Stephen	Atkin Chambers, London	020 7404 0102
Godwin William George Henry	Atkin Chambers, London	020 7404 0102
Goldstone David Julian	4 Field Court, London	0171 440 6900
Gore-Andrews Gavin Angus Russell	2 Harcourt Buildings, London	0171 583 9020
Grantham Andrew Timothy	• Deans Court Chambers, Manchester	0161 214 6000
	Deans Court Chambers, Preston	01772 555163
Gray Richard Paul	39 Essex Street, London	0171 832 1111
Green Miss Jane Elizabeth	Design Chambers, London	0171 353 0747
	Chambers of Martin Burr, London	0171 353 4636
Grime Mark Stephen Eastburn	Deans Court Chambers, Manchester	0161 214 6000
	2 Pump Court, London	0171 353 5597
	Deans Court Chambers, Preston	01772 555163
Grodzinski Samuel Marc	39 Essex Street, London	0171 832 1111
Guggenheim Miss Anna Maeve	Two Crown Office Row, London	020 7797 8100

Guy John David Colin	Francis Taylor Building, London	0171 797 7250
Hamilton Adrian Walter	S Tomlinson QC, London	0171 583 0404
Hamilton Graeme Montagu	Two Crown Office Row, London	020 7797 8100
Hammerton Miss Veronica Lesley	No. 1 Serjeants' Inn, London	0171 415 6666
Harris Paul Best	Monckton Chambers, London	0171 405 7211
Harvey Michael Llewellyn Tucker	Two Crown Office Row, London	020 7797 8100
Havelock-Allan Anthony Mark David	20 Essex Street, London	0171 583 9294
Hayward Peter Michael	The Outer Temple, London	0171 353 4647
Healy Miss Sioban	S Tomlinson QC, London	0171 583 0404
Henley Raymond Francis St Luke	Lancaster Building, Manchester	0161 661 4444/0171 649 9872
Higgins Rupert James Hale	Littman Chambers, London	020 7404 4866
Hill Timothy John	4 Field Court, London	0171 440 6900
Hofmeyr Stephen Murray	S Tomlinson QC, London	0171 583 0404
Holdsworth James Arthur	Two Crown Office Row, London	020 7797 8100
Holroyd Charles Wilfrid	S Tomlinson QC, London	0171 583 0404
Hossain Ajmalul	• 29 Bedford Row Chambers, London	0171 831 2626
Howard Michael Newman	4 Essex Court, London	020 7797 7970
Howells James Richard	Atkin Chambers, London	020 7404 0102
Hughes Adrian Warwick	4 Pump Court, London	020 7842 5555
Jarvis John Manners	3 Verulam Buildings, London	0171 831 8441
Jess Digby Charles	8 King Street Chambers, Manchester	0161 834 9560
Jones Miss Gillian Hunter	18 Red Lion Court, London	0171 520 6000
	Thornwood House, Chelmsford	01245 280880
Jones Miss Susannah Lucy	Octagon House, Norwich	01603 623186
Kay Robert Jervis	4 Field Court, London	0171 440 6900
Kealey Gavin Sean James	S Tomlinson QC, London	0171 583 0404
Kendrick Dominic John	S Tomlinson QC, London	0171 583 0404
Kenefick Timothy	S Tomlinson QC, London	0171 583 0404
Kenny Stephen Charles Wilfrid	S Tomlinson QC, London	0171 583 0404
Kerr Simon Alexander	S Tomlinson QC, London	0171 583 0404
Khurshid Jawdat	S Tomlinson QC, London	0171 583 0404
Kolodziej Andrzej Jozef	• Littman Chambers, London	020 7404 4866
Kverndal Simon Richard	4 Essex Court, London	020 7797 7970
Leech Brian Walter Thomas	No. 1 Serjeants' Inn, London	0171 415 6666
Lindqvist Andrew Nils Gunnar	Octagon House, Norwich	01603 623186
Littman Mark	Littman Chambers, London	020 7404 4866
Lofthouse Simon Timothy	Atkin Chambers, London	020 7404 0102
Lowenstein Paul David	Littleton Chambers, London	0171 797 8600
Macdonald Charles Adam	4 Essex Court, London	020 7797 7970
Macnab Alexander Andrew	Monckton Chambers, London	0171 405 7211
Malek Ali	3 Verulam Buildings, London	0171 831 8441
Males Stephen Martin	20 Essex Street, London	0171 583 9294
Malhotra Miss Mehtab Roshan	2 Middle Temple Lane, London	0171 583 4540
Malins Julian Henry	One Hare Court, London	020 7353 3171
Mantle Peter John	Monckton Chambers, London	0171 405 7211
Manzoni Charles Peter	39 Essex Street, London	0171 832 1111
Marshall-Andrews Robert Graham	37 Park Square Chambers, Leeds	0113 2439422
	2-4 Tudor Street, London	0171 797 7111
Masters Miss Sara Alayna	20 Essex Street, London	0171 583 9294
Matthews Duncan Henry Rowland	20 Essex Street, London	0171 583 9294
Mauleverer Peter Bruce	4 Pump Court, London	020 7842 5555
May Miss Juliet Mary	3 Verulam Buildings, London	0171 831 8441
McCahill Patrick Gerard	St Philip's Chambers, Birmingham	0121 246 7000
	Chambers of Andrew Campbell QC, Leeds	0113 2455438
McClure Brian David	Littman Chambers, London	020 7404 4866
McGregor Harvey	4 Paper Buildings, London	0171 353 3366/583 7155
McMullan Manus Anthony	Atkin Chambers, London	020 7404 0102
Meeson Nigel Keith	4 Field Court, London	0171 440 6900
Mellor John Walter	30 Park Square, Leeds	0113 2436388
Mendoza Neil David Pereira	Hardwicke Building, London	020 7242 2523

Mercer Hugh Charles	• Essex Court Chambers, London	0171 813 8000
Merriman Nicholas Flavelle	3 Verulam Buildings, London	0171 831 8441
Milligan Iain Anstruther	20 Essex Street, London	0171 583 9294
Milne Michael	Resolution Chambers, Malvern	01684 561279
	Chambers of Geoffrey Hawker, London	0171 583 8899
Moran Andrew John	One Hare Court, London	020 7353 3171
Morgan Dr Austen Jude	3 Temple Gardens, London	0171 353 0832
Morgan Charles James Arthur	Enterprise Chambers, London	0171 405 9471
	Enterprise Chambers, Newcastle upon Tyne	0191 222 3344
	Enterprise Chambers, Leeds	0113 246 0391
Morgan Richard Hugo Lyndon	13 Old Square, London	0171 404 4800
Mortimer Miss Sophie Kate	No. 1 Serjeants' Inn, London	0171 415 6666
Myers Allan James	4 Field Court, London	0171 440 6900
Naidoo Sean Van	Littman Chambers, London	020 7404 4866
Nash Jonathan Scott	3 Verulam Buildings, London	0171 831 8441
Naughton Philip Anthony	3 Serjeants' Inn, London	0171 353 5537
Neill of Bladen Lord	One Hare Court, London	020 7353 3171
Neville-Clarke Sebastian Adrian Bennett	1 Crown Office Row, London	0171 583 9292
Nolan Michael Alfred Anthony	4 Essex Court, London	020 7797 7970
Norman Christopher John George	No. 1 Serjeants' Inn, London	0171 415 6666
Norris Alastair Hubert	5 Stone Buildings, London	0171 242 6201
	Southernhay Chambers, Exeter	01392 255777
O'Donoghue Florence	2 Mitre Court Buildings, London	0171 353 1353
O'Shea Eoin Finbarr	4 Field Court, London	0171 440 6900
O'Toole Simon Gerard	2 Mitre Court Buildings, London	0171 353 1353
Oliver Andrew James	Octagon House, Norwich	01603 623186
Ough Dr Richard Norman	• Hardwicke Building, London	020 7242 2523
Owen David Christopher	20 Essex Street, London	0171 583 9294
Padfield Nicholas David	One Hare Court, London	020 7353 3171
Page Howard William Barrett	One Hare Court, London	020 7353 3171
Parker Matthew Richard	3 Verulam Buildings, London	0171 831 8441
Parkin Miss Fiona Jane	Atkin Chambers, London	020 7404 0102
Patchett-Joyce Michael Thurston	Monckton Chambers, London	0171 405 7211
Patterson Stewart	Pump Court Chambers, Winchester	01962 868161
	Pump Court Chambers, London	0171 353 0711
	Pump Court Chambers, Swindon	01793 539899
Pelling (Philip) Mark	Monckton Chambers, London	0171 405 7211
Persey Lionel Edward	• 4 Field Court, London	0171 440 6900
Pershad Rohan	Two Crown Office Row, London	020 7797 8100
Phillips S J	S Tomlinson QC, London	0171 583 0404
Phillips Stephen Edmund	3 Verulam Buildings, London	0171 831 8441
Picken Simon Derek	S Tomlinson QC, London	0171 583 0404
	30 Park Place, Cardiff	01222 398421
Pilling Benjamin	4 Pump Court, London	020 7842 5555
Pittaway David Michael	No. 1 Serjeants' Inn, London	0171 415 6666
Plender Richard Owen	• 20 Essex Street, London	0171 583 9294
Power Lawrence Imam	4 King's Bench Walk, London	0171 822 8822
Prasad Krishna	21 Craven Road, Kingston-Upon-Thames	0181 974 6799
Priday Charles Nicholas Bruton	S Tomlinson QC, London	0171 583 0404
Quest David Charles	3 Verulam Buildings, London	0171 831 8441
Qureshi Khawar Mehmood	One Hare Court, London	020 7353 3171
Raeside Mark Andrew	Atkin Chambers, London	020 7404 0102
Rainey Philip Carslake	2nd Floor, Francis Taylor Building, London	0171 353 9942/3157
Rashid Omar	Chambers of Mr Peter Crampin QC, London	020 7831 0081
Rawley Miss Dominique Jane	Atkin Chambers, London	020 7404 0102
Readhead Simon John Howard	No. 1 Serjeants' Inn, London	0171 415 6666
Reeder John	4 Field Court, London	0171 440 6900

B

B

Reese Colin Edward	Atkin Chambers, London	020 7404 0102
Restell Thomas George	Granary Chambers, Bexhill-On-Sea	01424 733008
Reynolds Professor Francis Martin Baillie	S Tomlinson QC, London	0171 583 0404
Ross John Graffin	No. 1 Serjeants' Inn, London	0171 415 6666
Ross Martyn John Greaves	• 5 New Square, London	020 7404 0404
Rowland John Peter	4 Pump Court, London	020 7842 5555
Rowlands Marc Humphreys	4 Pump Court, London	020 7842 5555
Royce Darryl Fraser	Atkin Chambers, London	020 7404 0102
Russell Jeremy Jonathan	• 4 Essex Court, London	020 7797 7970
Sabben-Clare Miss Rebecca Mary	S Tomlinson QC, London	0171 583 0404
Salmon Jonathan Carl	1 Fountain Court, Birmingham	0121 236 5721
Saloman Timothy Peter (Dayrell)	S Tomlinson QC, London	0171 583 0404
Salter Richard Stanley	3 Verulam Buildings, London	0171 831 8441
Sands Mr Philippe Joseph	3 Verulam Buildings, London	0171 831 8441
Schaff Alistair Graham	S Tomlinson QC, London	0171 583 0404
Sears Robert David Murray	4 Pump Court, London	020 7842 5555
Selvaratnam Miss Vasanti Emily Indrani	4 Field Court, London	0171 440 6900
Seymour Richard William	Monckton Chambers, London	0171 405 7211
Smith Christopher Frank	Essex Court Chambers, London	0171 813 8000
Smith Paul Andrew	One Hare Court, London	020 7353 3171
Smith Warwick Timothy Cresswell	Deans Court Chambers, Manchester	0161 214 6000
	Deans Court Chambers, Preston	01772 555163
Southern Richard Michael	S Tomlinson QC, London	0171 583 0404
Southwell Richard Charles	One Hare Court, London	020 7353 3171
Sparrow Miss Claire Louise	Eastbourne Chambers, Eastbourne	01323 642102
Stagg Paul Andrew	No. 1 Serjeants' Inn, London	0171 415 6666
Sterling Robert Alan	St James's Chambers, Manchester	0161 834 7000
	12 New Square, London	0171 419 1212
	Park Lane Chambers, Leeds	0113 2285000
Stevenson John Melford	Two Crown Office Row, London	020 7797 8100
Stewart Ms Alexandra Mary Hamilton	30 Park Square, Leeds	0113 2436388
Stewart Nicholas John Cameron	Hardwicke Building, London	020 7242 2523
Storey Jeremy Brian	4 Pump Court, London	020 7842 5555
Streatfeild-James David Stewart	Atkin Chambers, London	020 7404 0102
Symons Christopher John Maurice	3 Verulam Buildings, London	0171 831 8441
Tackaberry John Antony	Arbitration Chambers, London	020 7267 2137
	40 King Street, Manchester	0161 832 9082
	Assize Court Chambers, Bristol	0117 9264587
	Littman Chambers, London	020 7404 4866
Teare Nigel John Martin	4 Essex Court, London	020 7797 7970
Tecks Jonathan Howard	Littman Chambers, London	020 7404 4866
Temple Anthony Dominic	4 Pump Court, London	020 7842 5555
Terry Robert Jeffrey	8 King Street Chambers, Manchester	0161 834 9560
Thomas (Robert) Neville	3 Verulam Buildings, London	0171 831 8441
Tomlinson Stephen Miles	S Tomlinson QC, London	0171 583 0404
Trace Anthony John	• 13 Old Square, London	0171 404 4800
Travers Hugh	Pump Court Chambers, London	0171 353 0711
	Pump Court Chambers, Winchester	01962 868161
	Pump Court Chambers, Swindon	01793 539899
Tregilgas-Davey Marcus Ian	Pump Court Chambers, Swindon	01793 539899
	Pump Court Chambers, London	0171 353 0711
	Pump Court Chambers, Winchester	01962 868161
Trotman Timothy Oliver	Deans Court Chambers, Manchester	0161 214 6000
	Deans Court Chambers, Preston	01772 555163
Tselentis Michael	• 20 Essex Street, London	0171 583 9294
Tucker David William	Two Crown Office Row, London	020 7797 8100
Tully Ms Anne Margaret	Eastbourne Chambers, Eastbourne	01323 642102
Turner Adrian John	Eastbourne Chambers, Eastbourne	01323 642102
Turner James Michael	• 4 Essex Court, London	020 7797 7970

Turner Miss Janet Mary	3 Verulam Buildings, London	0171 831 8441
Tyler William John	30 Park Square, Leeds	0113 2436388
Ullstein Augustus Rupert Patrick A	• 29 Bedford Row Chambers, London	0171 831 2626
Valentine Donald Graham	Atkin Chambers, London	020 7404 0102
Wales Andrew Nigel Malcolm	S Tomlinson QC, London	0171 583 0404
Walker Steven John	Atkin Chambers, London	020 7404 0102
Wallace Ian Norman Duncan	Atkin Chambers, London	020 7404 0102
Waller Richard Beaumont	S Tomlinson QC, London	0171 583 0404
Weatherill Bernard Richard	Chambers of Lord Goodhart QC, London	0171 405 5577
Weitzman Thomas Edward Benjamin	3 Verulam Buildings, London	0171 831 8441
Wheetman Alan	East Anglian Chambers, Norwich	01603 617351
	East Anglian Chambers, Colchester	01206 572756
	East Anglian Chambers, Ipswich	01473 214481
White Andrew	Atkin Chambers, London	020 7404 0102
Whitehouse-Vaux William Edward	4 Field Court, London	0171 440 6900
Williams Leigh Michael	S Tomlinson QC, London	0171 583 0404
Wilmot-Smith Richard James Crosbie	39 Essex Street, London	0171 832 1111
Wood Richard Gillies	20 Essex Street, London	0171 583 9294
	Cathedral Chambers (Jan Wood Independent Barristers' Clerk), Exeter	01392 210900
Wright Colin John	4 Field Court, London	0171 440 6900
Yell Nicholas Anthony	No. 1 Serjeants' Inn, London	0171 415 6666

ASSET FINANCE

Ayliffe James Justin Barnett	• Wilberforce Chambers, London	0171 306 0102
Ayres Andrew John William	13 Old Square, London	0171 404 4800
de Lacy Richard Michael	3 Verulam Buildings, London	0171 831 8441
Hodgkinson Tristram Patrick	• 5 Pump Court, London	020 7353 2532
Lazarus Michael Steven	1 Crown Office Row, London	0171 583 9292
Pearson Thomas Adam Spenser	Pump Court Chambers, London	0171 353 0711
	Pump Court Chambers, Winchester	01962 868161
	Pump Court Chambers, Swindon	01793 539899

AVIATION

Bailey Edward Henry	Monckton Chambers, London	0171 405 7211
Boswell Miss Lindsay Alice	4 Pump Court, London	020 7842 5555
Browne-Wilkinson Simon	Serle Court Chambers, London	0171 242 6105
Davey Michael Philip	4 Field Court, London	0171 440 6900
Dean Paul Benjamin	Two Crown Office Row, London	020 7797 8100
Dugdale Nicholas	4 Field Court, London	0171 440 6900
Fowler Richard Nicholas	Monckton Chambers, London	0171 405 7211
Gee Steven Mark	4 Field Court, London	0171 440 6900
Ghaffar Arshad	4 Field Court, London	0171 440 6900
Gibbs Patrick Michael Evan	2 Harcourt Buildings, London	020 7353 2112
Hill Timothy John	4 Field Court, London	0171 440 6900
Hofmeyr Stephen Murray	S Tomlinson QC, London	0171 583 0404
Howard Michael Newman	4 Essex Court, London	020 7797 7970
Lawson Robert John	4 Essex Court, London	020 7797 7970
Meeson Nigel Keith	4 Field Court, London	0171 440 6900
Milligan Iain Anstruther	20 Essex Street, London	0171 583 9294
Morgan Dr Austen Jude	3 Temple Gardens, London	0171 353 0832
Ng Ray Kian Hin	Two Crown Office Row, London	020 7797 8100
Nolan Michael Alfred Anthony	4 Essex Court, London	020 7797 7970
O'Shea Eoin Finbarr	4 Field Court, London	0171 440 6900
Persey Lionel Edward	• 4 Field Court, London	0171 440 6900
Puckrin Cedric Eldred	19 Old Buildings, London	0171 405 2001
Russell Jeremy Jonathan	• 4 Essex Court, London	020 7797 7970
Sabben-Clare Miss Rebecca Mary	S Tomlinson QC, London	0171 583 0404
Saunders Nicholas Joseph	4 Field Court, London	0171 440 6900
Symons Christopher John Maurice	3 Verulam Buildings, London	0171 831 8441

• Expanded entry in Part D

Tedd Rex Hilary	• St Philip's Chambers, Birmingham	0121 246 7000
	De Montfort Chambers, Leicester	0116 254 8686
	Northampton Chambers, Northampton	01604 636271
Vaughan-Neil Miss Catherine Mary Bernardine	4 Pump Court, London	020 7842 5555
Waller Richard Beaumont	S Tomlinson QC, London	0171 583 0404
Wood Richard Gillies	20 Essex Street, London	0171 583 9294
	Cathedral Chambers (Jan Wood Independent Barristers' Clerk), Exeter	01392 210900

BANKING

Acton Stephen Neil	11 Old Square, London	020 7430 0341
Adkin Jonathan William	One Hare Court, London	020 7353 3171
Ambrose Miss Clare Mary Geneste	20 Essex Street, London	0171 583 9294
Arden Peter Leonard	Enterprise Chambers, London	0171 405 9471
	Enterprise Chambers, Leeds	0113 246 0391
	Enterprise Chambers, Newcastle upon Tyne	0191 222 3344
Ashton David Sambrook	13 King's Bench Walk, London	0171 353 7204
	King's Bench Chambers, Oxford	01865 311066
Ayliffe James Justin Barnett	• Wilberforce Chambers, London	0171 306 0102
Ayres Andrew John William	13 Old Square, London	0171 404 4800
Bailey David John	S Tomlinson QC, London	0171 583 0404
Bailey Edward Henry	Monckton Chambers, London	0171 405 7211
Barker James Sebastian	Enterprise Chambers, London	0171 405 9471
	Enterprise Chambers, Leeds	0113 246 0391
	Enterprise Chambers, Newcastle upon Tyne	0191 222 3344
Barker Simon George Harry	• 13 Old Square, London	0171 404 4800
Baylis Ms Natalie Jayne	3 Verulam Buildings, London	0171 831 8441
Beltrami Adrian Joseph	3 Verulam Buildings, London	0171 831 8441
Birch Miss Elizabeth Blanche	3 Verulam Buildings, London	0171 831 8441
Blair William James Lynton	3 Verulam Buildings, London	0171 831 8441
Brent Richard	3 Verulam Buildings, London	0171 831 8441
Bright Robert Graham	S Tomlinson QC, London	0171 583 0404
Brockley Nigel Simon	Bracton Chambers, London	0171 242 4248
Browne-Wilkinson Simon	Serle Court Chambers, London	0171 242 6105
Butcher Christopher John	S Tomlinson QC, London	0171 583 0404
Castle Peter Bolton	Chambers of Mr Peter Crampin QC, London	020 7831 0081
Cawley Neil Robert Loudoun	169 Temple Chambers, London	0171 583 7644
	Milton Keynes Chambers, Milton Keynes	01908 664 128
Cawson Peter Mark	St James's Chambers, Manchester	0161 834 7000
	12 New Square, London	0171 419 1212
	Park Lane Chambers, Leeds	0113 2285000
Chalmers Miss Suzanne Frances	Two Crown Office Row, London	020 7797 8100
Charman Andrew Julian	St Philip's Chambers, Birmingham	0121 246 7000
Chivers (Tom) David	Erskine Chambers, London	0171 242 5532
Clegg Sebastian James Barwick	Deans Court Chambers, Manchester	0161 214 6000
	Deans Court Chambers, Preston	01772 555163
Collett Michael John	20 Essex Street, London	0171 583 9294
Cooke Jeremy Lionel	S Tomlinson QC, London	0171 583 0404
Craig Alistair Trevor	Chambers of Mr Peter Crampin QC, London	020 7831 0081
Cranfield Peter Anthony	3 Verulam Buildings, London	0171 831 8441
Crawford Grant	11 Old Square, London	020 7430 0341
Davey Benjamin Nicholas	11 Old Square, London	020 7430 0341
Davies Stephen Richard	8 King Street Chambers, Manchester	0161 834 9560
Davies-Jones Jonathan	3 Verulam Buildings, London	0171 831 8441
de Lacy Richard Michael	3 Verulam Buildings, London	0171 831 8441
Dillon Thomas William Matthew	1 Fountain Court, Birmingham	0121 236 5721

• Expanded entry in Part D

Dougherty Nigel Peter	Erskine Chambers, London	0171 242 5532
Dowley Dominic Myles	One Hare Court, London	020 7353 3171
Eadie James Raymond	One Hare Court, London	020 7353 3171
Eaton Turner David Murray	1 New Square, London	0171 405 0884/5/6/7
Edwards David Leslie	S Tomlinson QC, London	0171 583 0404
Edwards Richard Julian Henshaw	3 Verulam Buildings, London	0171 831 8441
Elliott Nicholas Blethyn	3 Verulam Buildings, London	0171 831 8441
Ellis Roger John	13 King's Bench Walk, London	0171 353 7204
	King's Bench Chambers, Oxford	01865 311066
Etherton Terence Michael Elkan Barnet	• Wilberforce Chambers, London	0171 306 0102
Evans James Frederick Meurig	3 Verulam Buildings, London	0171 831 8441
Evans Richard Gareth	5 Paper Buildings, London	0171 583 9275/583 4555
Eyre Stephen John Arthur	1 Fountain Court, Birmingham	0121 236 5721
Farber James Henry Martin	5 Stone Buildings, London	0171 242 6201
Feltham Piers Jonathan	Chambers of Mr Peter Crampin QC, London	020 7831 0081
Fenton Adam Timothy Downs	S Tomlinson QC, London	0171 583 0404
Flaux Julian Martin	S Tomlinson QC, London	0171 583 0404
Fletcher Andrew Fitzroy Stephen	4 Pump Court, London	020 7842 5555
Forte Mark Julian Carmino	8 King Street Chambers, Manchester	0161 834 9560
Francis Andrew James	Chambers of Mr Peter Crampin QC, London	020 7831 0081
Freedman Sampson Clive	3 Verulam Buildings, London	0171 831 8441
Gaisman Jonathan Nicholas Crispin	S Tomlinson QC, London	0171 583 0404
Garcia-Miller Miss Laura	Enterprise Chambers, London	0171 405 9471
	Enterprise Chambers, Leeds	0113 246 0391
	Enterprise Chambers, Newcastle upon Tyne	0191 222 3344
Geary Gavin John	S Tomlinson QC, London	0171 583 0404
Gee Steven Mark	4 Field Court, London	0171 440 6900
Geering Ian Walter	3 Verulam Buildings, London	0171 831 8441
Gibaud Miss Catherine Alison Annetta	3 Verulam Buildings, London	0171 831 8441
Gibson Martin John	Littman Chambers, London	020 7404 4866
Gore-Andrews Gavin Angus Russell	2 Harcourt Buildings, London	0171 583 9020
Grantham Andrew Timothy	• Deans Court Chambers, Manchester	0161 214 6000
	Deans Court Chambers, Preston	01772 555163
Green Miss Amanda Jane	3 Verulam Buildings, London	0171 831 8441
Hamilton Adrian Walter	S Tomlinson QC, London	0171 583 0404
Hantusch Robert Anthony	• 3 Stone Buildings, London	0171 242 4937
Hardwick Matthew Richard	Enterprise Chambers, London	0171 405 9471
	Enterprise Chambers, Leeds	0113 246 0391
	Enterprise Chambers, Newcastle upon Tyne	0191 222 3344
Havelock-Allan Anthony Mark David	20 Essex Street, London	0171 583 9294
Head David Ian	3 Verulam Buildings, London	0171 831 8441
Hirst William Timothy John	Park Court Chambers, Leeds	0113 2433277
Hockaday Miss Annie	3 Verulam Buildings, London	0171 831 8441
Hodgkinson Tristram Patrick	• 5 Pump Court, London	020 7353 2532
Hofmeyr Stephen Murray	S Tomlinson QC, London	0171 583 0404
Hossain Ajmalul	• 29 Bedford Row Chambers, London	0171 831 2626
Howard Michael Newman	4 Essex Court, London	020 7797 7970
Ife Miss Linden Elizabeth	Enterprise Chambers, London	0171 405 9471
	Enterprise Chambers, Leeds	0113 246 0391
	Enterprise Chambers, Newcastle upon Tyne	0191 222 3344
Jarvis John Manners	3 Verulam Buildings, London	0171 831 8441

B

Jory Robert John Hugh	Enterprise Chambers, London	0171 405 9471
	Enterprise Chambers, Leeds	0113 246 0391
	Enterprise Chambers, Newcastle upon Tyne	0191 222 3344
Kay Michael Jack David	3 Verulam Buildings, London	0171 831 8441
	Park Lane Chambers, Leeds	0113 2285000
Kealey Gavin Sean James	S Tomlinson QC, London	0171 583 0404
Kendrick Dominic John	S Tomlinson QC, London	0171 583 0404
Kenny Stephen Charles Wilfrid	S Tomlinson QC, London	0171 583 0404
Kolodziej Andrzej Jozef	• Littman Chambers, London	020 7404 4866
Kynoch Duncan Stuart Sanderson	29 Bedford Row Chambers, London	0171 831 2626
Lamont Miss Camilla Rose	Chambers of Lord Goodhart QC, London	0171 405 5577
Lavender Nicholas	One Hare Court, London	020 7353 3171
Lazarus Michael Steven	1 Crown Office Row, London	0171 583 9292
Lennard Stephen Charles	Hardwicke Building, London	020 7242 2523
Lowenstein Paul David	Littleton Chambers, London	0171 797 8600
Malek Ali	3 Verulam Buildings, London	0171 831 8441
Males Stephen Martin	20 Essex Street, London	0171 583 9294
Mann George Anthony	Enterprise Chambers, London	0171 405 9471
	Enterprise Chambers, Leeds	0113 246 0391
	Enterprise Chambers, Newcastle upon Tyne	0191 222 3344
Marks Jonathan Harold	3 Verulam Buildings, London	0171 831 8441
Marquand Charles Nicholas Hilary	Chambers of Lord Goodhart QC, London	0171 405 5577
Marshall Philip Scott	Serle Court Chambers, London	0171 242 6105
Matthews Duncan Henry Rowland	20 Essex Street, London	0171 583 9294
May Miss Juliet Mary	3 Verulam Buildings, London	0171 831 8441
Maynard-Connor Giles	St James's Chambers, Manchester	0161 834 7000
McClure Brian David	Littman Chambers, London	020 7404 4866
McDonnell John Beresford William	1 New Square, London	0171 405 0884/5/6/7
McHugh Denis David	Bracton Chambers, London	0171 242 4248
McQuater Ewan Alan	3 Verulam Buildings, London	0171 831 8441
Meeson Nigel Keith	4 Field Court, London	0171 440 6900
Mendoza Neil David Pereira	Hardwicke Building, London	020 7242 2523
Merriman Nicholas Flavelle	3 Verulam Buildings, London	0171 831 8441
Metzer Anthony David Erwin	Doughty Street Chambers, London	0171 404 1313
Milligan Iain Anstruther	20 Essex Street, London	0171 583 9294
Mitchell Gregory Charles Mathew	3 Verulam Buildings, London	0171 831 8441
Moran Andrew John	One Hare Court, London	020 7353 3171
Morgan Dr Austen Jude	3 Temple Gardens, London	0171 353 0832
Morgan Richard Hugo Lyndon	13 Old Square, London	0171 404 4800
Naidoo Sean Van	Littman Chambers, London	020 7404 4866
Nash Jonathan Scott	3 Verulam Buildings, London	0171 831 8441
Neill of Bladen Lord	One Hare Court, London	020 7353 3171
Neville Stephen John	Gough Square Chambers, London	0171 353 0924
Neville-Clarke Sebastian Adrian Bennett	1 Crown Office Row, London	0171 583 9292
O'Leary Robert Michael	33 Park Place, Cardiff	02920 233313
O'Neill Tadhg Joseph	1 Crown Office Row, London	0171 583 9292
Odgers John Arthur	3 Verulam Buildings, London	0171 831 8441
Ohrenstein Dov	Chambers of Lord Goodhart QC, London	0171 405 5577
Onslow Andrew George	3 Verulam Buildings, London	0171 831 8441
Owen David Christopher	20 Essex Street, London	0171 583 9294
Padfield Nicholas David	One Hare Court, London	020 7353 3171
Page Howard William Barrett	One Hare Court, London	020 7353 3171
Parker Matthew Richard	3 Verulam Buildings, London	0171 831 8441
Patchett-Joyce Michael Thurston	Monckton Chambers, London	0171 405 7211
Pelling (Philip) Mark	Monckton Chambers, London	0171 405 7211
Perkoff Richard Michael	Littleton Chambers, London	0171 797 8600
Pershad Rohan	Two Crown Office Row, London	020 7797 8100
Phillips Jonathan Mark	3 Verulam Buildings, London	0171 831 8441

         • Expanded entry in Part D

Phillips S J	S Tomlinson QC, London	0171 583 0404
Phillips Stephen Edmund	3 Verulam Buildings, London	0171 831 8441
Piper Angus Richard	No. 1 Serjeants' Inn, London	0171 415 6666
Pope David James	3 Verulam Buildings, London	0171 831 8441
Potts Robin	Erskine Chambers, London	0171 242 5532
Power Lawrence Imam	4 King's Bench Walk, London	0171 822 8822
Priday Charles Nicholas Bruton	S Tomlinson QC, London	0171 583 0404
Proudman Miss Sonia Rosemary Susan	Chambers of Mr Peter Crampin QC, London	020 7831 0081
Purves Gavin Bowman	Swan House, London	0181 998 3035
Quest David Charles	3 Verulam Buildings, London	0171 831 8441
Qureshi Khawar Mehmood	One Hare Court, London	020 7353 3171
Rainey Philip Carslake	2nd Floor, Francis Taylor Building, London	0171 353 9942/3157
Rich Jonathan Bernard George	5 Paper Buildings, London	0171 583 9275/583 4555
Rogers Ian Paul	1 Crown Office Row, London	0171 583 9292
Sabben-Clare Miss Rebecca Mary	S Tomlinson QC, London	0171 583 0404
Salmon Jonathan Carl	1 Fountain Court, Birmingham	0121 236 5721
Saloman Timothy Peter (Dayrell)	S Tomlinson QC, London	0171 583 0404
Salter Richard Stanley	3 Verulam Buildings, London	0171 831 8441
Sandells Ms Nicole	11 Old Square, London	020 7430 0341
Schaff Alistair Graham	S Tomlinson QC, London	0171 583 0404
Selvaratnam Miss Vasanti Emily Indrani	4 Field Court, London	0171 440 6900
Selway Dr Katherine Emma	11 Old Square, London	020 7430 0341
Seymour Richard William	Monckton Chambers, London	0171 405 7211
Sheridan Maurice Bernard Gerard	• 3 Verulam Buildings, London	0171 831 8441
Singh Kuldip	Five Paper Buildings, London	0171 583 6117
Smith Howard James	Chambers of Mr Peter Crampin QC, London	020 7831 0081
Smith Paul Andrew	One Hare Court, London	020 7353 3171
Snowden Richard Andrew	Erskine Chambers, London	0171 242 5532
Southall Richard Anthony	• 17 Bedford Row, London	0171 831 7314
Southern David Boardman	• Temple Gardens Tax Chambers, London	0171 353 7884/5 8982/3
Southern Richard Michael	S Tomlinson QC, London	0171 583 0404
Southwell Richard Charles	One Hare Court, London	020 7353 3171
Start Miss Angharad Jocelyn	3 Verulam Buildings, London	0171 831 8441
Staunton (Thomas) Ulick (Patrick)	Chambers of Mr Peter Crampin QC, London	020 7831 0081
	65-67 King Street, Leicester	0116 2547710
Storey Jeremy Brian	4 Pump Court, London	020 7842 5555
Sutcliffe Andrew Harold Wentworth	3 Verulam Buildings, London	0171 831 8441
Swerling Robert Harry	13 Old Square, London	0171 404 4800
Sykes (James) Richard	Erskine Chambers, London	0171 242 5532
Tedd Rex Hilary	• St Philip's Chambers, Birmingham	0121 246 7000
	De Montfort Chambers, Leicester	0116 254 8686
	Northampton Chambers, Northampton	01604 636271
Terry Robert Jeffrey	8 King Street Chambers, Manchester	0161 834 9560
Thomas (Robert) Neville	3 Verulam Buildings, London	0171 831 8441
Todd Michael Alan	Erskine Chambers, London	0171 242 5532
Tolaney Miss Sonia	3 Verulam Buildings, London	0171 831 8441
Tomlinson Stephen Miles	S Tomlinson QC, London	0171 583 0404
Trace Anthony John	• 13 Old Square, London	0171 404 4800
Vaughan-Neil Miss Catherine Mary Bernardine	4 Pump Court, London	020 7842 5555
Wales Andrew Nigel Malcolm	S Tomlinson QC, London	0171 583 0404
Waters Malcolm Ian	• 11 Old Square, London	020 7430 0341
Watson-Gandy Mark	• Plowden Buildings, London	0171 583 0808
Wilson Ian Robert	3 Verulam Buildings, London	0171 831 8441
Wilson-Barnes Miss Lucy Emma	St James's Chambers, Manchester	0161 834 7000
Wood Ian Robert	8 King Street Chambers, Manchester	0161 834 9560

• Expanded entry in Part D

Wright Colin John	4 Field Court, London	0171 440 6900
Wyvill Alistair	St Philip's Chambers, Birmingham	0121 246 7000
Yell Nicholas Anthony	No. 1 Serjeants' Inn, London	0171 415 6666
Zelin Geoffrey Andrew	Enterprise Chambers, London	0171 405 9471
	Enterprise Chambers, Leeds	0113 246 0391
	Enterprise Chambers, Newcastle upon Tyne	0191 222 3344

BANKRUPTCY

Acton Stephen Neil	11 Old Square, London	020 7430 0341
Angus Miss Tracey Anne	5 Stone Buildings, London	0171 242 6201
Arden Peter Leonard	Enterprise Chambers, London	0171 405 9471
	Enterprise Chambers, Leeds	0113 246 0391
	Enterprise Chambers, Newcastle upon Tyne	0191 222 3344
Ashton David Sambrook	13 King's Bench Walk, London	0171 353 7204
	King's Bench Chambers, Oxford	01865 311066
Ayres Andrew John William	13 Old Square, London	0171 404 4800
Bailey Edward Henry	Monckton Chambers, London	0171 405 7211
Barker James Sebastian	Enterprise Chambers, London	0171 405 9471
	Enterprise Chambers, Leeds	0113 246 0391
	Enterprise Chambers, Newcastle upon Tyne	0191 222 3344
Barker Simon George Harry	• 13 Old Square, London	0171 404 4800
Baylis Ms Natalie Jayne	3 Verulam Buildings, London	0171 831 8441
Behrens James Nicholas Edward	Serle Court Chambers, London	0171 242 6105
Berry Nicholas Michael	Southernhay Chambers, Exeter	01392 255777
	1 Gray's Inn Square, London	0171 405 8946/7/8
	22 Old Buildings, London	0171 831 0222
Bleasdale Miss Marie-Claire	Chambers of Mr Peter Crampin QC, London	020 7831 0081
Bowker Robert James	2nd Floor, Francis Taylor Building, London	0171 353 9942/3157
Bowmer Michael Paul	11 Old Square, London	020 7430 0341
Buck Dr Andrew Theodore	Chambers of Martin Burr, London	0171 353 4636
Burr Martin John	Chambers of Martin Burr, London	0171 353 4636
	7 New Square, London	0171 430 1660
Butler Andrew	2nd Floor, Francis Taylor Building, London	0171 353 9942/3157
Capon Philip Christopher William	St Philip's Chambers, Birmingham	0121 246 7000
Castle Peter Bolton	Chambers of Mr Peter Crampin QC, London	020 7831 0081
Cawson Peter Mark	St James's Chambers, Manchester	0161 834 7000
	12 New Square, London	0171 419 1212
	Park Lane Chambers, Leeds	0113 2285000
Chapman Michael Andrew	Barnard's Inn Chambers, London	0171 369 6969
Charman Andrew Julian	St Philip's Chambers, Birmingham	0121 246 7000
Chesner Howard Michael	Bracton Chambers, London	0171 242 4248
Clark Andrew Richard	Manchester House Chambers, Manchester	0161 834 7007
	8 King Street Chambers, Manchester	0161 834 9560
Clarke Miss Anna Victoria	5 Stone Buildings, London	0171 242 6201
Clarke Ian James	Hardwicke Building, London	020 7242 2523
Clegg Sebastian James Barwick	Deans Court Chambers, Manchester	0161 214 6000
	Deans Court Chambers, Preston	01772 555163
Cole Robert Ian Gawain	30 Park Square, Leeds	0113 2436388
Cook Christopher Graham	St James's Chambers, Manchester	0161 834 7000
Cooper Gilead Patrick	Chambers of Mr Peter Crampin QC, London	020 7831 0081

Corbett James Patrick	St Philip's Chambers, Birmingham	0121 246 7000
	Chambers of Andrew Campbell QC, Leeds	0113 2455438
Craig Alistair Trevor	Chambers of Mr Peter Crampin QC, London	020 7831 0081
Craig Kenneth Allen	Hardwicke Building, London	020 7242 2523
Crail Miss (Elspeth) Ross	12 New Square, London	0171 419 1212
	Sovereign Chambers, Leeds	0113 2451841/2/3
Crawford Grant	11 Old Square, London	020 7430 0341
Cunningham Miss Claire Louise	St Philip's Chambers, Birmingham	0121 246 7000
Davey Benjamin Nicholas	11 Old Square, London	020 7430 0341
Davies Miss (Susan) Louise	12 New Square, London	0171 419 1212
	Sovereign Chambers, Leeds	0113 2451841/2/3
de Lacy Richard Michael	3 Verulam Buildings, London	0171 831 8441
Dedezade Taner	Tindal Chambers, Chelmsford	01245 267742
Dillon Thomas William Matthew	1 Fountain Court, Birmingham	0121 236 5721
Dixon Philip John	2nd Floor, Francis Taylor Building, London	0171 353 9942/3157
Dodge Peter Clive	11 Old Square, London	020 7430 0341
Dooher Miss Nancy Helen	St James's Chambers, Manchester	0161 834 7000
Duddridge Robert James	2 Gray's Inn Square Chambers, London	020 7242 0328
Elleray Anthony John	• St James's Chambers, Manchester	0161 834 7000
	12 New Square, London	0171 419 1212
	Park Lane Chambers, Leeds	0113 2285000
Ellis Roger John	13 King's Bench Walk, London	0171 353 7204
	King's Bench Chambers, Oxford	01865 311066
Evans Richard Gareth	5 Paper Buildings, London	0171 583 9275/583 4555
Fadipe Gabriel Charles	• Wilberforce Chambers, London	0171 306 0102
Faluyi Albert Osamudiamen	Chambers of Martin Burr, London	0171 353 4636
Fieldsend James William	2nd Floor, Francis Taylor Building, London	0171 353 9942/3157
Francis Andrew James	Chambers of Mr Peter Crampin QC, London	020 7831 0081
Francis Edward Gerald Francis	Enterprise Chambers, London	0171 405 9471
	Enterprise Chambers, Leeds	0113 246 0391
	Enterprise Chambers, Newcastle upon Tyne	0191 222 3344
Franco Gianpiero	2 Middle Temple Lane, London	0171 583 4540
Fryer-Spedding James Walter	St James's Chambers, Manchester	0161 834 7000
Gasztowicz Steven	2-3 Gray's Inn Square, London	0171 242 4986
	2 New Street, Leicester	0116 2625906
Gibaud Miss Catherine Alison Annetta	3 Verulam Buildings, London	0171 831 8441
Gifford Andrew James Morris	7 New Square, London	0171 430 1660
Graham Thomas Patrick Henry	1 New Square, London	0171 405 0884/5/6/7
Grantham Andrew Timothy	• Deans Court Chambers, Manchester	0161 214 6000
	Deans Court Chambers, Preston	01772 555163
Green David Cameron	Adrian Lyon's Chambers, Liverpool	0151 236 4421/8240
Green Miss Jane Elizabeth	Design Chambers, London	0171 353 0747
	Chambers of Martin Burr, London	0171 353 4636
Gregory John Raymond	Deans Court Chambers, Manchester	0161 214 6000
	Deans Court Chambers, Preston	01772 555163
Groves Hugo Gerard	Enterprise Chambers, London	0171 405 9471
	Enterprise Chambers, Leeds	0113 246 0391
	Enterprise Chambers, Newcastle upon Tyne	0191 222 3344
Hall Taylor Alexander Edward	11 Old Square, London	020 7430 0341
Halpern David Anthony	Enterprise Chambers, London	0171 405 9471
	Enterprise Chambers, Leeds	0113 246 0391
	Enterprise Chambers, Newcastle upon Tyne	0191 222 3344

Hantusch Robert Anthony	• 3 Stone Buildings, London	0171 242 4937
Harding Dr Gladys Modwyn Cicely	Leone Chambers, London	0181 200 4020
Hardwick Matthew Richard	Enterprise Chambers, London	0171 405 9471
	Enterprise Chambers, Leeds	0113 246 0391
	Enterprise Chambers, Newcastle upon Tyne	0191 222 3344
Harris Melvyn	7 New Square, London	0171 430 1660
Henley Mark Robert Daniel	9 Woodhouse Square, Leeds	0113 2451986
Henley Raymond Francis St Luke	Lancaster Building, Manchester	0161 661 4444/0171 649 9872
Higgo Justin Beresford	Serle Court Chambers, London	0171 242 6105
Hill Robert Douglas	Pump Court Chambers, Winchester	01962 868161
	Pump Court Chambers, London	0171 353 0711
	Pump Court Chambers, Swindon	01793 539899
Hockaday Miss Annie	3 Verulam Buildings, London	0171 831 8441
Hoffmann Miss Jocelyn Clare	Serle Court Chambers, London	0171 242 6105
Hoser Philip Jacob	Serle Court Chambers, London	0171 242 6105
Ife Miss Linden Elizabeth	Enterprise Chambers, London	0171 405 9471
	Enterprise Chambers, Leeds	0113 246 0391
	Enterprise Chambers, Newcastle upon Tyne	0191 222 3344
Jack Adrian Laurence Robert	Enterprise Chambers, London	0171 405 9471
	Enterprise Chambers, Newcastle upon Tyne	0191 222 3344
	Enterprise Chambers, Leeds	0113 246 0391
Jackson Hugh Woodward	Hardwicke Building, London	020 7242 2523
Jackson Nicholas David Kingsley	Adrian Lyon's Chambers, Liverpool	0151 236 4421/8240
James-Stadden Miss Jodie Cara	Westgate Chambers, Newcastle upon Tyne	0191 261 4407/2329785
Jefferis Arthur Michael Quentin	Chambers of Mr Peter Crampin QC, London	020 7831 0081
Jones Philip John	Serle Court Chambers, London	0171 242 6105
Jory Robert John Hugh	Enterprise Chambers, London	0171 405 9471
	Enterprise Chambers, Leeds	0113 246 0391
	Enterprise Chambers, Newcastle upon Tyne	0191 222 3344
King-Smith James	1 Crown Office Row, London	0171 797 7500
	Crown Office Row Chambers, Brighton	01273 625625
Kremen Philip Michael	Hardwicke Building, London	020 7242 2523
Kynoch Duncan Stuart Sanderson	29 Bedford Row Chambers, London	0171 831 2626
Lamont Miss Camilla Rose	Chambers of Lord Goodhart QC, London	0171 405 5577
Landes Miss Anna-Rose	St Philip's Chambers, Birmingham	0121 246 7000
Lightman Daniel	Serle Court Chambers, London	0171 242 6105
Lloyd Stephen James George	Chambers of Mr Peter Crampin QC, London	020 7831 0081
Lo Bernard Norman	17 Bedford Row, London	0171 831 7314
Lowenstein Paul David	Littleton Chambers, London	0171 797 8600
Lucas Miss Bridget Ann	Serle Court Chambers, London	0171 242 6105
	Fountain Court, London	0171 583 3335
Machell John William	Serle Court Chambers, London	0171 242 6105
Mandalia Vinesh Lalji	Harrow on the Hill Chambers, Harrow-on-the-Hill	0181 423 7444
Mann George Anthony	Enterprise Chambers, London	0171 405 9471
	Enterprise Chambers, Leeds	0113 246 0391
	Enterprise Chambers, Newcastle upon Tyne	0191 222 3344
Marshall Philip Scott	Serle Court Chambers, London	0171 242 6105
Mauger Miss Claire Shanti Andrea	Enterprise Chambers, London	0171 405 9471
	Enterprise Chambers, Newcastle upon Tyne	0191 222 3344
	Enterprise Chambers, Leeds	0113 246 0391
Maynard-Connor Giles	St James's Chambers, Manchester	0161 834 7000

• Expanded entry in Part D

McAlinden Barry O'Neill	17 Bedford Row, London	0171 831 7314
McKinnell Miss Soraya Jane	Enterprise Chambers, London	0171 405 9471
	Enterprise Chambers, Newcastle upon Tyne	0191 222 3344
	Enterprise Chambers, Leeds	0113 246 0391
McQuail Ms Katherine Emma	11 Old Square, London	020 7430 0341
McQuater Ewan Alan	3 Verulam Buildings, London	0171 831 8441
Mendoza Neil David Pereira	Hardwicke Building, London	020 7242 2523
Metzer Anthony David Erwin	Doughty Street Chambers, London	0171 404 1313
Morgan Andrew James	St Philip's Chambers, Birmingham	0121 246 7000
Morgan Richard Hugo Lyndon	13 Old Square, London	0171 404 4800
Oakley Paul James	1 Gray's Inn Square, London	0171 405 8946/7/8
Ohrenstein Dov	Chambers of Lord Goodhart QC, London	0171 405 5577
Patchett-Joyce Michael Thurston	Monckton Chambers, London	0171 405 7211
Patel Bhavin Vinubhai	Chambers of Martin Burr, London	0171 353 4636
Peacock Nicholas Christopher	13 Old Square, London	0171 404 4800
Perkoff Richard Michael	Littleton Chambers, London	0171 797 8600
Pershad Rohan	Two Crown Office Row, London	020 7797 8100
Phillips Jonathan Mark	3 Verulam Buildings, London	0171 831 8441
Pickering James Patrick	Enterprise Chambers, London	0171 405 9471
	Enterprise Chambers, Leeds	0113 246 0391
	Enterprise Chambers, Newcastle upon Tyne	0191 222 3344
Poyer-Sleeman Ms Patricia	Pump Court Chambers, London	0171 353 0711
	Pump Court Chambers, Winchester	01962 868161
	Pump Court Chambers, Swindon	01793 539899
Prentis Sebastian Hugh Runton	1 New Square, London	0171 405 0884/5/6/7
Preston Nicholas John Holman	Bracton Chambers, London	0171 242 4248
Rai Amarjit Singh	St Philip's Chambers, Birmingham	0121 246 7000
Rainey Philip Carslake	2nd Floor, Francis Taylor Building, London	0171 353 9942/3157
Rashid Omar	Chambers of Mr Peter Crampin QC, London	020 7831 0081
Rees David Benjamin	5 Stone Buildings, London	0171 242 6201
Richardson Giles John	Serle Court Chambers, London	0171 242 6105
Ross Martyn John Greaves	• 5 New Square, London	020 7404 0404
Rowley Keith Nigel	11 Old Square, London	020 7430 0341
Salter Richard Stanley	3 Verulam Buildings, London	0171 831 8441
Sartin Leon James	5 Stone Buildings, London	0171 242 6201
Sellers Graham	Adrian Lyon's Chambers, Liverpool	0151 236 4421/8240
Shuman Miss Karen Ann Elizabeth	Bracton Chambers, London	0171 242 4248
Sinclair Miss Lisa Anne	7 New Square, London	0171 430 1660
Skelly Andrew Jon	1 Gray's Inn Square, London	0171 405 8946/7/8
Smith Howard James	Chambers of Mr Peter Crampin QC, London	020 7831 0081
Southall Richard Anthony	• 17 Bedford Row, London	0171 831 7314
Staddon Miss Claire Ann	12 New Square, London	0171 419 1212
	Sovereign Chambers, Leeds	0113 2451841/2/3
Start Miss Angharad Jocelyn	3 Verulam Buildings, London	0171 831 8441
Staunton (Thomas) Ulick (Patrick)	Chambers of Mr Peter Crampin QC, London	020 7831 0081
	65-67 King Street, Leicester	0116 2547710
Sterling Robert Alan	St James's Chambers, Manchester	0161 834 7000
	12 New Square, London	0171 419 1212
	Park Lane Chambers, Leeds	0113 2285000
Sullivan Scott	Barnard's Inn Chambers, London	0171 369 6969
Szanto Gregory John Michael	Eastbourne Chambers, Eastbourne	01323 642102
Teeman Miss Miriam Joy	30 Park Square, Leeds	0113 2436388
Thomas (Robert) Neville	3 Verulam Buildings, London	0171 831 8441
Tidmarsh Christopher Ralph Francis	5 Stone Buildings, London	0171 242 6201
Tipples Miss Amanda Jane	13 Old Square, London	0171 404 4800

Trace Anthony John	• 13 Old Square, London	0171 404 4800
Tully Ms Anne Margaret	Eastbourne Chambers, Eastbourne	01323 642102
Van Tonder Gerard Dirk	1 New Square, London	0171 405 0884/5/6/7
Walker Andrew Greenfield	Chambers of Lord Goodhart QC, London	0171 405 5577
Weatherill Bernard Richard	Chambers of Lord Goodhart QC, London	0171 405 5577
West Mark	• 11 Old Square, London	020 7430 0341
Williams Andrew Arthur	Adrian Lyon's Chambers, Liverpool	0151 236 4421/8240
Williamson Miss Bridget Susan	Enterprise Chambers, London	0171 405 9471
	Enterprise Chambers, Leeds	0113 246 0391
	Enterprise Chambers, Newcastle upon Tyne	0191 222 3344
Wilson Ian Robert	3 Verulam Buildings, London	0171 831 8441
Wilson-Barnes Miss Lucy Emma	St James's Chambers, Manchester	0161 834 7000
Zelin Geoffrey Andrew	Enterprise Chambers, London	0171 405 9471
	Enterprise Chambers, Leeds	0113 246 0391
	Enterprise Chambers, Newcastle upon Tyne	0191 222 3344

BREACH OF CONFIDENCE

Abrahams James	8 New Square, London	0171 405 4321
Alexander Daniel Sakyi	8 New Square, London	0171 405 4321
Baldwin John Paul	8 New Square, London	0171 405 4321
Clark Miss Fiona Jane Stewart	8 New Square, London	0171 405 4321
Fysh Michael	8 New Square, London	0171 405 4321
Hamer George Clemens	8 New Square, London	0171 405 4321
Howe Martin Russell Thomson	8 New Square, London	0171 405 4321
Kitchin David James Tyson	8 New Square, London	0171 405 4321
Lane Ms Lindsay Ruth Busfield	8 New Square, London	0171 405 4321
May Miss Charlotte Louisa	8 New Square, London	0171 405 4321
Meade Richard David	8 New Square, London	0171 405 4321
Mellor Edward James Wilson	8 New Square, London	0171 405 4321
Moody-Stuart Thomas	8 New Square, London	0171 405 4321
Onslow Robert Denzil	8 New Square, London	0171 405 4321
Platts-Mills Mark Fortescue	8 New Square, London	0171 405 4321
Prescott Peter Richard Kyle	8 New Square, London	0171 405 4321
Speck Adrian	8 New Square, London	0171 405 4321
St Ville Laurence James	8 New Square, London	0171 405 4321
Tappin Michael John	8 New Square, London	0171 405 4321
Vitoria Miss Mary Christine	8 New Square, London	0171 405 4321

BUILDING SOCIETIES

Ovey Miss Elizabeth Helen	11 Old Square, London	020 7430 0341
Waters Malcolm Ian	• 11 Old Square, London	020 7430 0341

CAPITAL TAXES/ESTATE PLANNING

Shillingford George Miles	Chambers of Mr Peter Crampin QC, London	020 7831 0081

CARE PROCEEDINGS

Adams Christopher Alan	St Philip's Chambers, Birmingham	0121 246 7000
Adams Miss Lorraine Joan	Pulteney Chambers, Bath	01225 723987
Adejumo Mrs Hilda Ekpo	Temple Chambers, London	0171 583 1001 (2 lines)
Ahmed Farooq Tahir	8 King Street Chambers, Manchester	0161 834 9560
	3 Dr Johnson's Buildings, London	0171 353 4854
Ahmed Miss Jacqueline Michelle	Southernhay Chambers, Exeter	01392 255777
Akerman Miss Kate Louise	Queen's Chambers, Manchester	0161 834 6875/4738
	Queens Chambers, Preston	01772 828300
Aldous Robert John	Octagon House, Norwich	01603 623186
Alford Robert John	Southernhay Chambers, Exeter	01392 255777

Allardice Miss Miranda Jane	Pump Court Chambers, London	0171 353 0711
	Pump Court Chambers, Winchester	01962 868161
	Pump Court Chambers, Swindon	01793 539899
Allingham-Nicholson Mrs Elizabeth Sarah	2 New Street, Leicester	0116 2625906
Amaouche Miss Sassa-Ann	One Garden Court Family Law Chambers, London	0171 797 7900
Amiraftabi Miss Roshanak	Hardwicke Building, London	020 7242 2523
Ancliffe Mrs Shiva Edwina	Francis Taylor Building, London	0171 353 7768/7769/2711
Atherton Miss Sally	Bridewell Chambers, London	020 7797 8800
Auckland Miss Elizabeth Rachel	30 Park Square, Leeds	0113 2436388
Bancroft Miss Anna Louise	Deans Court Chambers, Manchester	0161 214 6000
	Deans Court Chambers, Preston	01772 555163
Banks Francis Andrew	Adrian Lyon's Chambers, Liverpool	0151 236 4421/8240
Barker John Steven Roy	Queen's Chambers, Manchester	0161 834 6875/4738
	Queens Chambers, Preston	01772 828300
Barker Nicholas	30 Park Square, Leeds	0113 2436388
Barnett Miss Sally Louise	2 New Street, Leicester	0116 2625906
Barry Miss Kirsten Lesley	8 King Street Chambers, Manchester	0161 834 9560
Bassa Yousef	St Albans Chambers, St Albans	01727 843383
	Tindal Chambers, Chelmsford	01245 267742
Bazley Miss Janet Clare	One Garden Court Family Law Chambers, London	0171 797 7900
Beasley-Murray Mrs Caroline Wynne	Fenners Chambers, Cambridge	01223 368761
	Fenners Chambers, Peterborough	01733 562030
Bedingfield David Herbert	• 14 Gray's Inn Square, London	0171 242 0858
Bennett John Martyn	• Oriel Chambers, Liverpool	0151 236 7191/236 4321
Bergin Timothy William	Crown Office Row Chambers, Brighton	01273 625625
Birk Miss Dewinder	2 New Street, Leicester	0116 2625906
Bishop Miss Keeley Susan	1 Crown Office Row, London	0171 797 7500
	Crown Office Row Chambers, Brighton	01273 625625
Black Mrs Jill Margaret	30 Park Square, Leeds	0113 2436388
Bloom-Davis Desmond Niall Laurence	Pump Court Chambers, Winchester	01962 868161
	Pump Court Chambers, London	0171 353 0711
	Pump Court Chambers, Swindon	01793 539899
Boothroyd Miss Susan Elizabeth	Westgate Chambers, Newcastle upon Tyne	0191 261 4407/2329785
Bradshaw Howard Sydney	Queen's Chambers, Manchester	0161 834 6875/4738
	Queens Chambers, Preston	01772 828300
Brereton Mrs Fiorella	Peel Court Chambers, Manchester	0161 832 3791
Brodwell John Shenton	9 Woodhouse Square, Leeds	0113 2451986
Brown Miss Althea Sonia	Doughty Street Chambers, London	0171 404 1313
Brown Miss Joanne	2 Gray's Inn Square Chambers, London	020 7242 0328
Buck Dr Andrew Theodore	Chambers of Martin Burr, London	0171 353 4636
Buckingham Mrs Kathleen Rosemary Bernadette	30 Park Square, Leeds	0113 2436388
Budaly Miss Susan	One Garden Court Family Law Chambers, London	0171 797 7900
Bugg Ian Stephen	Crown Office Row Chambers, Brighton	01273 625625
Burden Miss Emma Louise Verena	2 New Street, Leicester	0116 2625906
	Sovereign Chambers, Leeds	0113 2451841/2/3
Burdon Michael Stewart	37 Park Square Chambers, Leeds	0113 2439422
Butler Simon David	10 King's Bench Walk, London	0171 353 7742
Butterworth Paul Anthony	Octagon House, Norwich	01603 623186
Buxton Miss Sarah Ruth	1 Fountain Court, Birmingham	0121 236 5721
Cains Ms Linda Hilary	37 Park Square Chambers, Leeds	0113 2439422
Calvert David Edward	St James's Chambers, Manchester	0161 834 7000
Campbell Miss Alexis Anne	Hardwicke Building, London	020 7242 2523
Campbell Miss Susan Claire	Southernhay Chambers, Exeter	01392 255777
Campbell-Brown Miss Anne Louise	Bracton Chambers, London	0171 242 4248

B

Carpenter Miss Jane Patricia Anne	2nd Floor, Francis Taylor Building, London	0171 353 9942/3157
Carr Simon Andrew	9 Gough Square, London	020 7832 0500
Carter Miss Holly Eugenie Sophia	3 Dr Johnson's Buildings, London	0171 353 4854
Carter Miss Rosalyn Frances	St Philip's Chambers, Birmingham	0121 246 7000
Chandler Alexander Charles Ross	One Garden Court Family Law Chambers, London	0171 797 7900
Clark Timothy Noel	2 New Street, Leicester	0116 2625906
Cobb Stephen William Scott	One Garden Court Family Law Chambers, London	0171 797 7900
Cole Robert Ian Gawain	30 Park Square, Leeds	0113 2436388
Collier Peter Neville	30 Park Square, Leeds	0113 2436388
Collins Miss Jennifer Clair	Eastbourne Chambers, Eastbourne	01323 642102
Compton Gareth Francis Thomas	22 Old Buildings, London	0171 831 0222
Conrath Philip Bernard	2nd Floor, Francis Taylor Building, London	0171 353 9942/3157
Cook Miss Alison Noele	St Philip's Chambers, Birmingham	0121 246 7000
Cotterill Miss Susan Amanda	Lamb Building, London	020 7797 7788
Crawford Miss Marie-Bernadette Claire	Eastbourne Chambers, Eastbourne	01323 642102
Crawforth Miss Emma	Southernhay Chambers, Exeter	01392 255777
Crawley Gary Thomas Bernard	One Garden Court Family Law Chambers, London	0171 797 7900
Cross Mrs Joanna	9 Woodhouse Square, Leeds	0113 2451986
Cruickshank Miss Cynthia Marilyn Benton	1 Gray's Inn Square, London	0171 405 8946/7/8
Da Costa Miss Elissa Josephine	• Arlington Chambers, London	0171 580 9188
Date Julian Richard	17 Bedford Row, London	0171 831 7314
Davies Miss Carol Elizabeth	2 New Street, Leicester	0116 2625906
Davies Miss Lindsay Jane	Fenners Chambers, Cambridge	01223 368761
	Fenners Chambers, Peterborough	01733 562030
De Zonie Miss Jane	14 Gray's Inn Square, London	0171 242 0858
Dodson Miss Joanna	14 Gray's Inn Square, London	0171 242 0858
	Park Court Chambers, Leeds	0113 2433277
Doig Mrs Jeanetta Rose	Neston Home Chambers, Corsham	01225 811909
Dubbery Mark Edward	Pump Court Chambers, London	0171 353 0711
	Pump Court Chambers, Winchester	01962 868161
	Pump Court Chambers, Swindon	01793 539899
Edge Timothy Richard	Deans Court Chambers, Preston	01772 555163
	Deans Court Chambers, Manchester	0161 214 6000
Eley Miss Joanne Mary	Trinity Chambers, Chelmsford	01245 605040
Evans Miss Lisa Claire	St Philip's Chambers, Birmingham	0121 246 7000
Faluyi Albert Osamudiamen	Chambers of Martin Burr, London	0171 353 4636
Farquharson Jonathan	Colleton Chambers, Exeter	01392 274898/9
Fenston Miss Felicia Donovan	2 Harcourt Buildings, London	0171 583 9020
Fields Miss Helen Sarah	Pump Court Chambers, Winchester	01962 868161
	Pump Court Chambers, London	0171 353 0711
	Pump Court Chambers, Swindon	01793 539899
Fieldsend James William	2nd Floor, Francis Taylor Building, London	0171 353 9942/3157
Finch Mrs Nadine Elizabeth	Doughty Street Chambers, London	0171 404 1313
Finn Terence	Chambers of Martin Burr, London	0171 353 4636
Fletcher Christopher Michael	Octagon House, Norwich	01603 623186
Forbes Peter George	6 Pump Court, London	0171 797 8400
	6-8 Mill Street, Maidstone	01622 688094
Ford Miss Caroline Emma	37 Park Square Chambers, Leeds	0113 2439422
Ford Gerard James	Baker Street Chambers, Middlesbrough	01642 873873
Ford Miss Monica Dorothy Patience	14 Gray's Inn Square, London	0171 242 0858
Forshaw Miss Sarah Anne	5 King's Bench Walk, London	0171 353 5638
Foster Miss Juliet Kate	Southernhay Chambers, Exeter	01392 255777

• Expanded entry in Part D

Fox Miss Nicola Susan	One Garden Court Family Law Chambers, London	0171 797 7900
Freeston Miss Lynn Roberta	Hardwicke Building, London	020 7242 2523
Fricker Mrs Marilyn Ann	Sovereign Chambers, Leeds	0113 2451841/2/3
	Farrar's Building, London	0171 583 9241
Frith Nicholas John	30 Park Square, Leeds	0113 2436388
Gardner Miss Eilidh Anne Mairi	22 Old Buildings, London	0171 831 0222
Geekie Charles Nairn	One Garden Court Family Law Chambers, London	0171 797 7900
Gibbons Mrs Sarah Isobel	13 King's Bench Walk, London	0171 353 7204
	King's Bench Chambers, Oxford	01865 311066
Gillibrand Philip Martin Mangnall	Pump Court Chambers, Winchester	01962 868161
	Pump Court Chambers, London	0171 353 0711
	Pump Court Chambers, Swindon	01793 539899
Gilmore Ian Martin	30 Park Square, Leeds	0113 2436388
Ginsburg Mrs Amanda	37 Park Square Chambers, Leeds	0113 2439422
Godfrey Christopher Nicholas	Queen's Chambers, Manchester	0161 834 6875/4738
	Queens Chambers, Preston	01772 828300
Gordon-Saker Mrs Liza Helen	Fenners Chambers, Cambridge	01223 368761
	Fenners Chambers, Peterborough	01733 562030
Gore Andrew Julian Mark	37 Park Square Chambers, Leeds	0113 2439422
Gray Miss Nichola Jayne	29 Bedford Row Chambers, London	0171 831 2626
Greenan Miss Sarah Octavia	9 Woodhouse Square, Leeds	0113 2451986
Gresty Miss Denise Lynn	Sovereign Chambers, Leeds	0113 2451841/2/3
Grocott Miss Susan	Queen's Chambers, Manchester	0161 834 6875/4738
	Queens Chambers, Preston	01772 828300
Haigh Martin James	30 Park Square, Leeds	0113 2436388
Hall Jeremy John	Becket Chambers, Canterbury	01227 786331
Hallam Miss Rona Mary Louise	30 Park Square, Leeds	0113 2436388
Hamilton-Hague Miss Rachael Elizabeth	8 King Street Chambers, Manchester	0161 834 9560
Hanson Timothy Vincent Richard	St Philip's Chambers, Birmingham	0121 246 7000
Hargan James John	30 Park Square, Leeds	0113 2436388
Harrison Ms Averil	Chambers of Averil Harrison, London	0181 692 4949
Hay Miss Fiona Ruth	13 King's Bench Walk, London	0171 353 7204
	King's Bench Chambers, Oxford	01865 311066
Heaton Miss Frances Margaret	Deans Court Chambers, Manchester	0161 214 6000
	Deans Court Chambers, Preston	01772 555163
	4 Brick Court, London	0171 797 7766
Heppenstall Miss Rachael Elizabeth	Sovereign Chambers, Leeds	0113 2451841/2/3
Hershman David Allan	St Philip's Chambers, Birmingham	0121 246 7000
	1 Mitre Court Buildings, London	0171 797 7070
Hill Miss Catherine Louise	30 Park Square, Leeds	0113 2436388
Hobson Miss Heather Fiona	Queen's Chambers, Manchester	0161 834 6875/4738
	Queens Chambers, Preston	01772 828300
Hodgson Ms Jane	9 Woodhouse Square, Leeds	0113 2451986
Hogg The Hon Douglas Martin	37 Park Square Chambers, Leeds	0113 2439422
	Cathedral Chambers (Jan Wood Independent Barristers' Clerk), Exeter	01392 210900
Holland William	2nd Floor, Francis Taylor Building, London	0171 353 9942/3157
Holroyd Ms Joanne	37 Park Square Chambers, Leeds	0113 2439422
Horton Mark Varney	Colleton Chambers, Exeter	01392 274898/9
Howard Graham John	Pump Court Chambers, Winchester	01962 868161
	Pump Court Chambers, London	0171 353 0711
	Pump Court Chambers, Swindon	01793 539899
Howe Miss Penelope Anne Macgregor	Pump Court Chambers, London	0171 353 0711
	Pump Court Chambers, Winchester	01962 868161
	Pump Court Chambers, Swindon	01793 539899
Hoyal Ms Jane	• 1 Pump Court, London	0171 583 2012/353 4341

Hughes Miss Kathryn Ann	Iscoed Chambers, Swansea	01792 652988/9/330
James Miss Rachael Elizabeth	33 Bedford Row, London	0171 242 6476
Jarman Mark Christopher	14 Gray's Inn Square, London	0171 242 0858
Johnson Miss Christine Margaret	Adrian Lyon's Chambers, Liverpool	0151 236 4421/8240
Jones Miss Carolyn Nerys	1 Fountain Court, Birmingham	0121 236 5721
	Clock Chambers, Wolverhampton	01902 313444
Jones Huw Michael Rees	St Albans Chambers, St Albans	01727 843383
Jones Miss Susannah Lucy	Octagon House, Norwich	01603 623186
Kelleher Keith Roy	3 Wellington Road, Poole	07771 905671 (Mobile)
	Bell Yard Chambers, London	0171 306 9292
Kenward Timothy David Nelson	25-27 Castle Street, Liverpool	0151 227 5661/051 236 5072
Ker-Reid John	Pump Court Chambers, London	0171 353 0711
	Pump Court Chambers, Winchester	01962 868161
	Pump Court Chambers, Swindon	01793 539899
Khan Miss Helen Mary Grace	Pump Court Chambers, London	0171 353 0711
	Pump Court Chambers, Winchester	01962 868161
	Pump Court Chambers, Swindon	01793 539899
Langridge Ms Nicola Dawn	Hardwicke Building, London	020 7242 2523
Latimer-Sayer William Laurence	2 Mitre Court Buildings, London	0171 353 1353
Lee Miss Taryn Jane	37 Park Square Chambers, Leeds	0113 2439422
Lewis Hugh Wilson	Southernhay Chambers, Exeter	01392 255777
Liebrecht John Michael	One Garden Court Family Law Chambers, London	0171 797 7900
Lindqvist Andrew Nils Gunnar	Octagon House, Norwich	01603 623186
Lochrane Damien Horatio Ross	Pump Court Chambers, London	0171 353 0711
	Pump Court Chambers, Winchester	01962 868161
	Pump Court Chambers, Swindon	01793 539899
Lockhart Andrew William Jardine	St Philip's Chambers, Birmingham	0121 246 7000
Lunt Steven	9 Woodhouse Square, Leeds	0113 2451986
MacDonald Alistair William Orchard	St Philip's Chambers, Birmingham	0121 246 7000
MacLaren Miss Catriona Longueville	2nd Floor, Francis Taylor Building, London	0171 353 9942/3157
Mainwaring [Robert] Paul Clason	Carmarthen Chambers, Carmarthen	01267 234410
Mandalia Vinesh Lalji	Harrow on the Hill Chambers, Harrow-on-the-Hill	0181 423 7444
Manuel Miss Elizabeth	Eighteen Carlton Crescent, Southampton	01703 639001
Marks Miss Jacqueline Stephanie	2 Gray's Inn Square Chambers, London	020 7242 0328
Marley Miss Sarah Anne	5 Pump Court, London	020 7353 2532
Mathew Miss Nergis-Anne	2 Gray's Inn Square Chambers, London	020 7242 0328
	St Philip's Chambers, Birmingham	0121 246 7000
McAllister Miss Eimear Jane	9 Woodhouse Square, Leeds	0113 2451986
McCabe Miss Louise Anne	St Philip's Chambers, Birmingham	0121 246 7000
McCandless Paul James	2 New Street, Leicester	0116 2625906
McCourt Christopher	22 Old Buildings, London	0171 831 0222
McCullough Miss Louise Clare	Lion Court, London	0171 404 6565
McGrath Miss Elizabeth Ann	St Philip's Chambers, Birmingham	0121 246 7000
McHugh Denis David	Bracton Chambers, London	0171 242 4248
Meachin Miss (Sarah) Vanessa Veronica	St Philip's Chambers, Birmingham	0121 246 7000
Mehendale Ms Neelima Krishna	2 Mitre Court Buildings, London	0171 353 1353
Melly Miss Kama Louise	37 Park Square Chambers, Leeds	0113 2439422
Mercer David Paul	Queen's Chambers, Manchester	0161 834 6875/4738
	Queens Chambers, Preston	01772 828300
Meredith George Hubbard	Southernhay Chambers, Exeter	01392 255777
Merry Hugh Gairns	17 Carlton Crescent, Southampton	023 8032 0320/0823 2003
Messling Lawrence David	St Philip's Chambers, Birmingham	0121 246 7000
Miller Miss Jane Elizabeth Mackay	Pump Court Chambers, London	0171 353 0711
	Pump Court Chambers, Winchester	01962 868161
	Pump Court Chambers, Swindon	01793 539899
Mills Corey Arthur	Becket Chambers, Canterbury	01227 786331
Moseley Miss Julie Ruth	St Philip's Chambers, Birmingham	0121 246 7000

Naish Christopher John	Southernhay Chambers, Exeter	01392 255777
Newton Philip	Becket Chambers, Canterbury	01227 786331
Niblett Anthony Ian	1 Crown Office Row, London	0171 797 7500
	Crown Office Row Chambers, Brighton	01273 625625
Nuvoloni Stefano Vincenzo	• 22 Old Buildings, London	0171 831 0222
O'Donoghue Florence	2 Mitre Court Buildings, London	0171 353 1353
O'Donovan Ronan Daniel James	14 Gray's Inn Square, London	0171 242 0858
O'Sullivan Michael Neil	5 King's Bench Walk, London	0171 353 5638
Ogle Miss Rebecca Theodosia Abigail	Southernhay Chambers, Exeter	01392 255777
Osman Robert Walter	Queen's Chambers, Manchester	0161 834 6875/4738
	Queens Chambers, Preston	01772 828300
Owens Mrs Lucy Isabel	13 King's Bench Walk, London	0171 353 7204
	King's Bench Chambers, Oxford	01865 311066
Parker John	2 Mitre Court Buildings, London	0171 353 1353
Parry Simon Edward	White Friars Chambers, Chester	01244 323070
Peacock Miss Lisa Jayne	3 Dr Johnson's Buildings, London	0171 353 4854
Pears Derrick Allan	2nd Floor, Francis Taylor Building, London	0171 353 9942/3157
Peel Robert Roger	29 Bedford Row Chambers, London	0171 831 2626
Pema Anes Bhumin Laloo	9 Woodhouse Square, Leeds	0113 2451986
Platt Miss Eleanor Frances	One Garden Court Family Law Chambers, London	0171 797 7900
Portnoy Leslie Reuben	Chambers of John Hand QC, Manchester	0161 955 9000
Pote Andrew Thomas	13 King's Bench Walk, London	0171 353 7204
	King's Bench Chambers, Oxford	01865 311066
Pounder Gerard	5 Essex Court, London	0171 410 2000
Poyer-Sleeman Ms Patricia	Pump Court Chambers, London	0171 353 0711
	Pump Court Chambers, Winchester	01962 868161
	Pump Court Chambers, Swindon	01793 539899
Prasad Krishna	21 Craven Road, Kingston-Upon-Thames	0181 974 6799
Price Miss Collette	St James's Chambers, Manchester	0161 834 7000
Prinn Miss Helen Elizabeth	Octagon House, Norwich	01603 623186
Purdie Robert Anthony James	28 Western Road, Oxford	01865 204911
Pye Miss Margaret Jane	Sovereign Chambers, Leeds	0113 2451841/2/3
Ramsahoye Miss Indira Kim	Hardwicke Building, London	020 7242 2523
Redford Miss Jessica Kate	3 Dr Johnson's Buildings, London	0171 353 4854
Reid Paul William	13 King's Bench Walk, London	0171 353 7204
	King's Bench Chambers, Oxford	01865 311066
Renfree Peter Gerald Stanley	Harbour Court Chambers, Fareham	01329 827828
Richards Jeremy Simon	Octagon House, Norwich	01603 623186
Rigby Miss Charity Elizabeth	Sovereign Chambers, Leeds	0113 2451841/2/3
Rosenblatt Jeremy George	4 Paper Buildings, London	0171 583 0816/353 1131
Ross Miss Jacqueline Gordon	Crown Office Row Chambers, Brighton	01273 625625
Rothery Peter	Queen's Chambers, Manchester	0161 834 6875/4738
	Queens Chambers, Preston	01772 828300
Rowe Miss Judith May	• One Garden Court Family Law Chambers, London	0171 797 7900
Rudd Matthew Allan	11 Bolt Court (also at 7 Stone Buildings – 1st Floor), London	0171 353 2300
	Redhill Chambers, Redhill	01737 780781
	7 Stone Buildings (also at 11 Bolt Court), London	0171 242 0961
Ryan Miss Eithne Mary Catherine	Hardwicke Building, London	020 7242 2523
Ryder Ernest Nigel	Deans Court Chambers, Manchester	0161 214 6000
	Deans Court Chambers, Preston	01772 555163
	1 Mitre Court Buildings, London	0171 797 7070
Rylands Miss Margaret Elizabeth	8 King Street Chambers, Manchester	0161 834 9560
Samuels Leslie John	Pump Court Chambers, London	0171 353 0711
	Pump Court Chambers, Winchester	01962 868161
	Pump Court Chambers, Swindon	01793 539899

• Expanded entry in Part D

Sandbrook-Hughes Stewert Karl Anthony	Iscoed Chambers, Swansea	01792 652988/9/330
Scott Miss Alexandra Elisabeth	2 New Street, Leicester	0116 2625906
Searle Barrie	St James's Chambers, Manchester	0161 834 7000
Sheldrake Miss Christine Anne	3 Dr Johnson's Buildings, London	0171 353 4854
Shenton Miss Suzanne Helene	One Garden Court Family Law Chambers, London	0171 797 7900
Shield Miss Deborah	White Friars Chambers, Chester	01244 323070
Shiels Ian	30 Park Square, Leeds	0113 2436388
Slaughter Andrew Francis	Bridewell Chambers, London	020 7797 8800
Small Mrs Arlene Ann-Marie	Francis Taylor Building, London	0171 353 7768/7769/2711
Smith Adam John	Crown Office Row Chambers, Brighton	01273 625625
Smith Matthew Robert	Sovereign Chambers, Leeds	0113 2451841/2/3
Smith Miss Sally-Ann	Crown Office Row Chambers, Brighton	01273 625625
Spollon Guy Merton	St Philip's Chambers, Birmingham	0121 246 7000
Stewart Ms Alexandra Mary Hamilton	30 Park Square, Leeds	0113 2436388
Stone Miss Sally Victoria	One Garden Court Family Law Chambers, London	0171 797 7900
Styles Clive Richard	Becket Chambers, Canterbury	01227 786331
Tankel Mrs Ruth Shoshana	St James's Chambers, Manchester	0161 834 7000
Teeman Miss Miriam Joy	30 Park Square, Leeds	0113 2436388
Thain Miss Ashley	East Anglian Chambers, Colchester	01206 572756
	East Anglian Chambers, Ipswich	01473 214481
	East Anglian Chambers, Norwich	01603 617351
Thompson Jonathan Richard	8 King Street Chambers, Manchester	0161 834 9560
Tighe Miss Dawn	37 Park Square Chambers, Leeds	0113 2439422
Travers Hugh	Pump Court Chambers, London	0171 353 0711
	Pump Court Chambers, Winchester	01962 868161
	Pump Court Chambers, Swindon	01793 539899
Tucker Miss Katherine Jane Greening	St Philip's Chambers, Birmingham	0121 246 7000
Turner Adrian John	Eastbourne Chambers, Eastbourne	01323 642102
Turner David George Patrick	14 Gray's Inn Square, London	0171 242 0858
Tyack David Guy	St Philip's Chambers, Birmingham	0121 246 7000
Tyler William John	30 Park Square, Leeds	0113 2436388
Tyzack David Ian Heslop	Southernhay Chambers, Exeter	01392 255777
	1 Mitre Court Buildings, London	0171 797 7070
Waddicor Miss Janet	1 Crown Office Row, London	0171 797 7500
	Crown Office Row Chambers, Brighton	01273 625625
Waddington Mrs Anne Louise	Pump Court Chambers, London	0171 353 0711
	Pump Court Chambers, Winchester	01962 868161
	Pump Court Chambers, Swindon	01793 539899
Walker Mrs Susannah Mary	One Garden Court Family Law Chambers, London	0171 797 7900
Ward Simon John	1 Fountain Court, Birmingham	0121 236 5721
Warrender Miss Nichola Mary	New Court Chambers, London	0171 831 9500
Webb Stanley George	The Chambers of Mr Ali Mohammed Azhar, London	0171 353 9564
	Bracton Chambers, London	0171 242 4248
Wenlock Miss Heather	13 King's Bench Walk, London	0171 353 7204
	King's Bench Chambers, Oxford	01865 311066
White Timothy Richard	30 Park Square, Leeds	0113 2436388
Williams Hugh David Haydn	St Philip's Chambers, Birmingham	0121 246 7000
Wills Miss Janice Marie	St James's Chambers, Manchester	0161 834 7000
Wilson Gerald Simon John	2nd Floor, Francis Taylor Building, London	0171 353 9942/3157
Worrall Miss Shirley Vera Frances	8 King Street Chambers, Manchester	0161 834 9560
Wyatt Mark	2 New Street, Leicester	0116 2625906

CHANCERY (COMMERCIAL)

Davidson Edward Alan	11 Old Square, London	020 7430 0341

• Expanded entry in Part D

CHANCERY (GENERAL)

Acton Stephen Neil	11 Old Square, London	020 7430 0341
Adamyk Simon Charles	12 New Square, London	0171 419 1212
Adejumo Mrs Hilda Ekpo	Temple Chambers, London	0171 583 1001 (2 lines)
Aldous Robert John	Octagon House, Norwich	01603 623186
Anderson Miss Julie	• Littman Chambers, London	020 7404 4866
Angus Miss Tracey Anne	5 Stone Buildings, London	0171 242 6201
Ash Edward William	3 Temple Gardens, London	0171 353 0832
Asplin Miss Sarah Jane	• 3 Stone Buildings, London	0171 242 4937
Asprey Nicholas	Serle Court Chambers, London	0171 242 6105
Ayliffe James Justin Barnett	• Wilberforce Chambers, London	0171 306 0102
Ayres Andrew John William	13 Old Square, London	0171 404 4800
Bacon Francis Michael	4 Paper Buildings, London	0171 353 3366/583 7155
Baker Stuart Christopher	1 Fountain Court, Birmingham	0121 236 5721
Barker James Sebastian	Enterprise Chambers, London	0171 405 9471
	Enterprise Chambers, Leeds	0113 246 0391
	Enterprise Chambers, Newcastle upon Tyne	0191 222 3344
Barraclough Richard Michael	6 Pump Court, London	0171 797 8400
	6-8 Mill Street, Maidstone	01622 688094
Barton Alan John	Lamb Building, London	020 7797 7788
Beever Edmund Damian	St Philip's Chambers, Birmingham	0121 246 7000
Behrens James Nicholas Edward	Serle Court Chambers, London	0171 242 6105
Bennett Gordon Irvine	12 New Square, London	0171 419 1212
Berry Nicholas Michael	Southernhay Chambers, Exeter	01392 255777
	1 Gray's Inn Square, London	0171 405 8946/7/8
	22 Old Buildings, London	0171 831 0222
Birch Roger Allen	Sovereign Chambers, Leeds	0113 2451841/2/3
	12 New Square, London	0171 419 1212
Blayney David James	Serle Court Chambers, London	0171 242 6105
Bleasdale Miss Marie-Claire	Chambers of Mr Peter Crampin QC, London	020 7831 0081
Bourne Geoffrey Robert	4 Field Court, London	0171 440 6900
Bowker Robert James	2nd Floor, Francis Taylor Building, London	0171 353 9942/3157
Bowmer Michael Paul	11 Old Square, London	020 7430 0341
Bredemear Zachary Charles	Barnard's Inn Chambers, London	0171 369 6969
Briggs Michael Townley Featherstone	Serle Court Chambers, London	0171 242 6105
Brockley Nigel Simon	Bracton Chambers, London	0171 242 4248
Bryant Miss Judith Anne	• Wilberforce Chambers, London	0171 306 0102
Buck Dr Andrew Theodore	Chambers of Martin Burr, London	0171 353 4636
Burr Martin John	Chambers of Martin Burr, London	0171 353 4636
	7 New Square, London	0171 430 1660
Butler Andrew	2nd Floor, Francis Taylor Building, London	0171 353 9942/3157
Butterworth Paul Anthony	Octagon House, Norwich	01603 623186
Campbell Miss Emily Charlotte	• Wilberforce Chambers, London	0171 306 0102
Castle Peter Bolton	Chambers of Mr Peter Crampin QC, London	020 7831 0081
Cawson Peter Mark	St James's Chambers, Manchester	0161 834 7000
	12 New Square, London	0171 419 1212
	Park Lane Chambers, Leeds	0113 2285000
Challenger Colin Westcott	Bridewell Chambers, London	020 7797 8800
Charman Andrew Julian	St Philip's Chambers, Birmingham	0121 246 7000
Clark Andrew Richard	Manchester House Chambers, Manchester	0161 834 7007
	8 King Street Chambers, Manchester	0161 834 9560
Clarke Miss Anna Victoria	5 Stone Buildings, London	0171 242 6201
Clarke Ian James	Hardwicke Building, London	020 7242 2523
Clegg Sebastian James Barwick	Deans Court Chambers, Manchester	0161 214 6000
	Deans Court Chambers, Preston	01772 555163

• Expanded entry in Part D

B

Close Douglas Jonathan	Serle Court Chambers, London	0171 242 6105
Collingwood Timothy Donald	Serle Court Chambers, London	0171 242 6105
Cook Christopher Graham	St James's Chambers, Manchester	0161 834 7000
Cooper Gilead Patrick	Chambers of Mr Peter Crampin QC, London	020 7831 0081
Corbett James Patrick	St Philip's Chambers, Birmingham	0121 246 7000
	Chambers of Andrew Campbell QC, Leeds	0113 2455438
Cosedge Andrew John	3 Stone Buildings, London	0171 242 4937
Cowen Timothy Arieh	Barnard's Inn Chambers, London	0171 369 6969
Craig Alistair Trevor	Chambers of Mr Peter Crampin QC, London	020 7831 0081
Craig Kenneth Allen	Hardwicke Building, London	020 7242 2523
Crail Miss (Elspeth) Ross	12 New Square, London	0171 419 1212
	Sovereign Chambers, Leeds	0113 2451841/2/3
Crampin Peter	Chambers of Mr Peter Crampin QC, London	020 7831 0081
Cranfield Peter Anthony	3 Verulam Buildings, London	0171 831 8441
Crawford Grant	11 Old Square, London	020 7430 0341
Croxford Ian Lionel	• Wilberforce Chambers, London	0171 306 0102
Cunningham Miss Claire Louise	St Philip's Chambers, Birmingham	0121 246 7000
Davey Benjamin Nicholas	11 Old Square, London	020 7430 0341
Davidson Edward Alan	11 Old Square, London	020 7430 0341
Davies Miss (Susan) Louise	12 New Square, London	0171 419 1212
	Sovereign Chambers, Leeds	0113 2451841/2/3
Dean Peter Thomas	1 Crown Office Row, London	0171 583 9292
Dempsey Brian Paul	Lancaster Building, Manchester	0161 661 4444/0171 649 9872
Denbin Jack Arnold	Greenway, Sonning-on-Thames	0118 969 2484
Dineen Michael Laurence	Pump Court Chambers, Winchester	01962 868161
	Pump Court Chambers, London	0171 353 0711
	Queens Square Chambers, Bristol	0117 921 1966
	Pump Court Chambers, Swindon	01793 539899
Dodge Peter Clive	11 Old Square, London	020 7430 0341
Dooher Miss Nancy Helen	St James's Chambers, Manchester	0161 834 7000
Dowley Dominic Myles	One Hare Court, London	020 7353 3171
Drake David Christopher	Serle Court Chambers, London	0171 242 6105
Driscoll Miss Lynn	Sovereign Chambers, Leeds	0113 2451841/2/3
Duddridge Robert James	2 Gray's Inn Square Chambers, London	020 7242 0328
Dumont Thomas Julian Bradley	Chambers of Mr Peter Crampin QC, London	020 7831 0081
Dutton Timothy Christopher	Barnard's Inn Chambers, London	0171 369 6969
Eadie James Raymond	One Hare Court, London	020 7353 3171
Eaton Turner David Murray	1 New Square, London	0171 405 0884/5/6/7
Elleray Anthony John	• St James's Chambers, Manchester	0161 834 7000
	12 New Square, London	0171 419 1212
	Park Lane Chambers, Leeds	0113 2285000
Ellis Roger John	13 King's Bench Walk, London	0171 353 7204
	King's Bench Chambers, Oxford	01865 311066
Evans Jonathan Edward	• Wilberforce Chambers, London	0171 306 0102
Eyre Stephen John Arthur	1 Fountain Court, Birmingham	0121 236 5721
Fadipe Gabriel Charles	• Wilberforce Chambers, London	0171 306 0102
Farber James Henry Martin	5 Stone Buildings, London	0171 242 6201
Farrow Kenneth John	Serle Court Chambers, London	0171 242 6105
Fawls Richard Granville	5 Stone Buildings, London	0171 242 6201
Feltham Piers Jonathan	Chambers of Mr Peter Crampin QC, London	020 7831 0081
Fieldsend James William	2nd Floor, Francis Taylor Building, London	0171 353 9942/3157
Finlay Darren	Sovereign Chambers, Leeds	0113 2451841/2/3
Finn Terence	Chambers of Martin Burr, London	0171 353 4636
Fletcher Christopher Michael	Octagon House, Norwich	01603 623186

• Expanded entry in Part D

Forte Mark Julian Carmino	8 King Street Chambers, Manchester	0161 834 9560
Foster Brian Ian	St James's Chambers, Manchester	0161 834 7000
	Park Lane Chambers, Leeds	0113 2285000
Francis Andrew James	Chambers of Mr Peter Crampin QC, London	020 7831 0081
Francis Edward Gerald Francis	Enterprise Chambers, London	0171 405 9471
	Enterprise Chambers, Leeds	0113 246 0391
	Enterprise Chambers, Newcastle upon Tyne	0191 222 3344
Fryer-Spedding James Walter	St James's Chambers, Manchester	0161 834 7000
Furness Michael James	• Wilberforce Chambers, London	0171 306 0102
Furze Miss Caroline Mary	• Wilberforce Chambers, London	0171 306 0102
Garcia-Miller Miss Laura	Enterprise Chambers, London	0171 405 9471
	Enterprise Chambers, Leeds	0113 246 0391
	Enterprise Chambers, Newcastle upon Tyne	0191 222 3344
Garner Miss Sophie Jane	199 Strand, London	0171 379 9779
Gasztowicz Steven	2-3 Gray's Inn Square, London	0171 242 4986
	2 New Street, Leicester	0116 2625906
Gee Steven Mark	4 Field Court, London	0171 440 6900
Geering Ian Walter	3 Verulam Buildings, London	0171 831 8441
George Miss Judith Sarah	St Philip's Chambers, Birmingham	0121 246 7000
Gerald Nigel Mortimer	Enterprise Chambers, London	0171 405 9471
	Enterprise Chambers, Leeds	0113 246 0391
	Enterprise Chambers, Newcastle upon Tyne	0191 222 3344
Gibaud Miss Catherine Alison Annetta	3 Verulam Buildings, London	0171 831 8441
Gibbons James Francis	3 Stone Buildings, London	0171 242 4937
Gibson Miss Jill Maureen	Chambers of Mr Peter Crampin QC, London	020 7831 0081
Gibson Martin John	Littman Chambers, London	020 7404 4866
Gifford Andrew James Morris	7 New Square, London	0171 430 1660
Graham Thomas Patrick Henry	1 New Square, London	0171 405 0884/5/6/7
Grantham Andrew Timothy	• Deans Court Chambers, Manchester	0161 214 6000
	Deans Court Chambers, Preston	01772 555163
Grayson Edward	• 9-12 Bell Yard, London	0171 400 1800
Green Brian Russell	Wilberforce Chambers, London	0171 306 0102
Green David Cameron	Adrian Lyon's Chambers, Liverpool	0151 236 4421/8240
Green Miss Jane Elizabeth	Design Chambers, London	0171 353 0747
	Chambers of Martin Burr, London	0171 353 4636
Greenhill Julian Rutherford	• Wilberforce Chambers, London	0171 306 0102
Gregory John Raymond	Deans Court Chambers, Manchester	0161 214 6000
	Deans Court Chambers, Preston	01772 555163
Groves Hugo Gerard	Enterprise Chambers, London	0171 405 9471
	Enterprise Chambers, Leeds	0113 246 0391
	Enterprise Chambers, Newcastle upon Tyne	0191 222 3344
Hall Taylor Alexander Edward	11 Old Square, London	020 7430 0341
Halpern David Anthony	Enterprise Chambers, London	0171 405 9471
	Enterprise Chambers, Leeds	0113 246 0391
	Enterprise Chambers, Newcastle upon Tyne	0191 222 3344
Ham Robert Wallace	• Wilberforce Chambers, London	0171 306 0102
Hamilton Eben William	1 New Square, London	0171 405 0884/5/6/7
Hantusch Robert Anthony	• 3 Stone Buildings, London	0171 242 4937
Hardwick Matthew Richard	Enterprise Chambers, London	0171 405 9471
	Enterprise Chambers, Leeds	0113 246 0391
	Enterprise Chambers, Newcastle upon Tyne	0191 222 3344
Harries Raymond Elwyn	Bracton Chambers, London	0171 242 4248

• Expanded entry in Part D

Harris Melvyn	7 New Square, London	0171 430 1660
Harrod Henry Mark	5 Stone Buildings, London	0171 242 6201
Henderson Launcelot Dinadan James	5 Stone Buildings, London	0171 242 6201
Henderson William Hugo	Serle Court Chambers, London	0171 242 6105
Henley Raymond Francis St Luke	Lancaster Building, Manchester	0161 661 4444/0171 649 9872
Herbert Mark Jeremy	• 5 Stone Buildings, London	0171 242 6201
Higgo Justin Beresford	Serle Court Chambers, London	0171 242 6105
Hindmarsh Miss Elizabeth	Plowden Buildings, London	0171 583 0808
Hodgson Timothy Paul	8 King Street Chambers, Manchester	0161 834 9560
Hoffman David Alexander	8 King Street Chambers, Manchester	0161 834 9560
Hoffmann Miss Jocelyn Clare	Serle Court Chambers, London	0171 242 6105
Hollington Robin Frank	1 New Square, London	0171 405 0884/5/6/7
Holmes-Milner James Neil	2 Mitre Court Buildings, London	0171 353 1353
Horne Roger Cozens-Hardy	Chambers of Mr Peter Crampin QC, London	020 7831 0081
Hoser Philip Jacob	Serle Court Chambers, London	0171 242 6105
Hughes Miss Anna Gabriel	• Wilberforce Chambers, London	0171 306 0102
Hunter William Quigley	No. 1 Serjeants' Inn, London	0171 415 6666
Ife Miss Linden Elizabeth	Enterprise Chambers, London	0171 405 9471
	Enterprise Chambers, Leeds	0113 246 0391
	Enterprise Chambers, Newcastle upon Tyne	0191 222 3344
Jackson Dirik George Allan	Chambers of Mr Peter Crampin QC, London	020 7831 0081
James-Stadden Miss Jodie Cara	Westgate Chambers, Newcastle upon Tyne	0191 261 4407/2329785
Jarron Miss Stephanie Allan	Westgate Chambers, Newcastle upon Tyne	0191 261 4407/2329785
Jefferis Arthur Michael Quentin	Chambers of Mr Peter Crampin QC, London	020 7831 0081
Johnston Anthony Paul	1 Fountain Court, Birmingham	0121 236 5721
Jones Miss Elizabeth Sian	Serle Court Chambers, London	0171 242 6105
Jones Philip John	Serle Court Chambers, London	0171 242 6105
Jory Robert John Hugh	Enterprise Chambers, London	0171 405 9471
	Enterprise Chambers, Leeds	0113 246 0391
	Enterprise Chambers, Newcastle upon Tyne	0191 222 3344
Kennedy Michael Kirk Inches	1 New Square, London	0171 405 0884/5/6/7
Kirby Peter John	Hardwicke Building, London	020 7242 2523
Kolodziej Andrzej Jozef	• Littman Chambers, London	020 7404 4866
Kremen Philip Michael	Hardwicke Building, London	020 7242 2523
Kynoch Duncan Stuart Sanderson	29 Bedford Row Chambers, London	0171 831 2626
Lamacraft Ian Richard	Bracton Chambers, London	0171 242 4248
Lamb Robert Glasson	13 King's Bench Walk, London	0171 353 7204
	King's Bench Chambers, Oxford	01865 311066
Lambert John	Lancaster Building, Manchester	0161 661 4444/0171 649 9872
Lamont Miss Camilla Rose	Chambers of Lord Goodhart QC, London	0171 405 5577
Landes Miss Anna-Rose	St Philip's Chambers, Birmingham	0121 246 7000
Lavender Nicholas	One Hare Court, London	020 7353 3171
Legge Henry	5 Stone Buildings, London	0171 242 6201
Levene Victor	1 Gray's Inn Square, London	0171 405 8946/7/8
Levin Craig Michael	Lancaster Building, Manchester	0161 661 4444/0171 649 9872
Levy Benjamin Keith	Enterprise Chambers, London	0171 405 9471
	Enterprise Chambers, Leeds	0113 246 0391
	Enterprise Chambers, Newcastle upon Tyne	0191 222 3344
Lloyd Stephen James George	Chambers of Mr Peter Crampin QC, London	020 7831 0081
Lowe David Alexander	• Wilberforce Chambers, London	0171 306 0102
Lowe Thomas William Gordon	• Wilberforce Chambers, London	0171 306 0102

Lucas Miss Bridget Ann	Serle Court Chambers, London	0171 242 6105
	Fountain Court, London	0171 583 3335
Machell John William	Serle Court Chambers, London	0171 242 6105
Macpherson Duncan Charles Stewart	Bracton Chambers, London	0171 242 4248
Mainwaring [Robert] Paul Clason	Carmarthen Chambers, Carmarthen	01267 234410
Malecka Dr Mary Margaret	• 3 Temple Gardens, London	0171 353 0832
	65-67 King Street, Leicester	0116 2547710
Malins Julian Henry	One Hare Court, London	020 7353 3171
Mandalia Vinesh Lalji	Harrow on the Hill Chambers, Harrow-on-the-Hill	0181 423 7444
Mann George Anthony	Enterprise Chambers, London	0171 405 9471
	Enterprise Chambers, Leeds	0113 246 0391
	Enterprise Chambers, Newcastle upon Tyne	0191 222 3344
Margolin Daniel George	Chambers of Mr Peter Crampin QC, London	020 7831 0081
Marshall Philip Scott	Serle Court Chambers, London	0171 242 6105
Martin Mrs Jill Elizabeth	Barnard's Inn Chambers, London	0171 369 6969
Martin John Vandeleur	• Wilberforce Chambers, London	0171 306 0102
Mason Miss Alexandra	3 Stone Buildings, London	0171 242 4937
Mauger Miss Claire Shanti Andrea	Enterprise Chambers, London	0171 405 9471
	Enterprise Chambers, Newcastle upon Tyne	0191 222 3344
	Enterprise Chambers, Leeds	0113 246 0391
Maynard-Connor Giles	St James's Chambers, Manchester	0161 834 7000
McAlinden Barry O'Neill	17 Bedford Row, London	0171 831 7314
McAllister Miss Elizabeth Ann	Enterprise Chambers, London	0171 405 9471
	Enterprise Chambers, Leeds	0113 246 0391
	Enterprise Chambers, Newcastle upon Tyne	0191 222 3344
McCulloch Ian	Bracton Chambers, London	0171 242 4248
	Lloyds House Chambers, Manchester	0161 839 3371
	Claremont Chambers, Wolverhampton	01902 426222
McDonnell John Beresford William	1 New Square, London	0171 405 0884/5/6/7
McKinnell Miss Soraya Jane	Enterprise Chambers, London	0171 405 9471
	Enterprise Chambers, Newcastle upon Tyne	0191 222 3344
	Enterprise Chambers, Leeds	0113 246 0391
McQuail Ms Katherine Emma	11 Old Square, London	020 7430 0341
Mendoza Neil David Pereira	Hardwicke Building, London	020 7242 2523
Moran Andrew John	One Hare Court, London	020 7353 3171
Morgan Andrew James	St Philip's Chambers, Birmingham	0121 246 7000
Morgan Edward Patrick	Deans Court Chambers, Manchester	0161 214 6000
	Deans Court Chambers, Preston	01772 555163
Morgan Richard Hugo Lyndon	13 Old Square, London	0171 404 4800
Munby James Lawrence	1 New Square, London	0171 405 0884/5/6/7
Murray-Smith James Michael	8 King's Bench Walk, London	0171 797 8888
	8 King's Bench Walk North, Leeds	0113 2439797
Neill of Bladen Lord	One Hare Court, London	020 7353 3171
Neville-Clarke Sebastian Adrian Bennett	1 Crown Office Row, London	0171 583 9292
Newman Miss Catherine Mary	• 13 Old Square, London	0171 404 4800
Newman Ms Ingrid	Hardwicke Building, London	020 7242 2523
Newman Paul Lance	• Wilberforce Chambers, London	0171 306 0102
Nicholls John Peter	13 Old Square, London	0171 404 4800
Norbury Hugh Robert	Serle Court Chambers, London	0171 242 6105
Norris Alastair Hubert	5 Stone Buildings, London	0171 242 6201
	Southernhay Chambers, Exeter	01392 255777
Nugee Christopher George	• Wilberforce Chambers, London	0171 306 0102
Nugee Edward George	• Wilberforce Chambers, London	0171 306 0102

• Expanded entry in Part D

Nurse Gordon Bramwell William	11 Old Square, London	020 7430 0341
O'Leary Robert Michael	33 Park Place, Cardiff	02920 233313
O'Sullivan Michael Morton	5 Stone Buildings, London	0171 242 6201
Oakley Anthony James	• 11 Old Square, London	020 7430 0341
Oakley Paul James	1 Gray's Inn Square, London	0171 405 8946/7/8
Ohrenstein Dov	Chambers of Lord Goodhart QC, London	0171 405 5577
Osman Robert Walter	Queen's Chambers, Manchester	0161 834 6875/4738
	Queens Chambers, Preston	01772 828300
Ovey Miss Elizabeth Helen	11 Old Square, London	020 7430 0341
Owens Miss Hilary Jane	St Philip's Chambers, Birmingham	0121 246 7000
Padfield Nicholas David	One Hare Court, London	020 7353 3171
Page Howard William Barrett	One Hare Court, London	020 7353 3171
Peacocke Mrs Teresa Anne Rosen	Enterprise Chambers, London	0171 405 9471
	Enterprise Chambers, Leeds	0113 246 0391
	Enterprise Chambers, Newcastle upon Tyne	0191 222 3344
Pearce Robert Edgar	Chambers of Mr Peter Crampin QC, London	020 7831 0081
Perkins Miss Marianne Yvette	7 New Square, London	0171 430 1660
Perkoff Richard Michael	Littleton Chambers, London	0171 797 8600
Phillips David John	199 Strand, London	0171 379 9779
	30 Park Place, Cardiff	01222 398421
Pilkington Mrs Mavis Patricia	9 Woodhouse Square, Leeds	0113 2451986
Pimentel Carlos de Serpa Alberto Legg	3 Stone Buildings, London	0171 242 4937
Porter David Leonard	St James's Chambers, Manchester	0161 834 7000
	Park Lane Chambers, Leeds	0113 2285000
Potts Warren Nigel	Queen's Chambers, Manchester	0161 834 6875/4738
	Queens Chambers, Preston	01772 828300
Prasad Krishna	21 Craven Road, Kingston-Upon-Thames	0181 974 6799
Prentis Sebastian Hugh Runton	1 New Square, London	0171 405 0884/5/6/7
Proudman Miss Sonia Rosemary Susan	Chambers of Mr Peter Crampin QC, London	020 7831 0081
Purdie Robert Anthony James	28 Western Road, Oxford	01865 204911
Purkis Ms Kathryn Miranda	Serle Court Chambers, London	0171 242 6105
Purves Gavin Bowman	Swan House, London	0181 998 3035
Qureshi Khawar Mehmood	One Hare Court, London	020 7353 3171
Randall John Yeoman	St Philip's Chambers, Birmingham	0121 246 7000
	7 Stone Buildings, London	0171 405 3886/242 3546
Rashid Omar	Chambers of Mr Peter Crampin QC, London	020 7831 0081
Read Simon Eric	8 King's Bench Walk, London	0171 797 8888
	8 King's Bench Walk North, Leeds	0113 2439797
Reed John William Rupert	• Wilberforce Chambers, London	0171 306 0102
Rees David Benjamin	5 Stone Buildings, London	0171 242 6201
Rich Miss Ann Barbara	5 Stone Buildings, London	0171 242 6201
Richardson Giles John	Serle Court Chambers, London	0171 242 6105
Rogers Miss Beverly-Ann	Serle Court Chambers, London	0171 242 6105
Rolfe Patrick John Benedict	5 Stone Buildings, London	0171 242 6201
Ross Martyn John Greaves	• 5 New Square, London	020 7404 0404
Rowell David Stewart	Chambers of Lord Goodhart QC, London	0171 405 5577
Rowntree Edward John Pickering	Hardwicke Building, London	020 7242 2523
Rumney Conrad William Arthur	St Philip's Chambers, Birmingham	0121 246 7000
Russell Christopher Garnet	• 12 New Square, London	0171 419 1212
	Sovereign Chambers, Leeds	0113 2451841/2/3
Sagar (Edward) Leigh	12 New Square, London	0171 419 1212
	Newport Chambers, Newport	01633 267403/255855
	Sovereign Chambers, Leeds	0113 2451841/2/3
Salmon Jonathan Carl	1 Fountain Court, Birmingham	0121 236 5721
Salter Charles Philip Arthur	8 King's Bench Walk, London	0171 797 8888
	8 King's Bench Walk North, Leeds	0113 2439797

• Expanded entry in Part D

Sandells Ms Nicole	11 Old Square, London	020 7430 0341
Sartin Leon James	5 Stone Buildings, London	0171 242 6201
Seal Julius Damien	189 Randolph Avenue, London	0171 624 9139
Sellers Graham	Adrian Lyon's Chambers, Liverpool	0151 236 4421/8240
Selway Dr Katherine Emma	11 Old Square, London	020 7430 0341
Semken Christopher Richard	1 New Square, London	0171 405 0884/5/6/7
Seymour Thomas Oliver	• Wilberforce Chambers, London	0171 306 0102
Shepherd Nigel Patrick	8 King's Bench Walk North, Leeds	0113 2439797
	8 King's Bench Walk, London	0171 797 8888
Sheppard Timothy Derie	Bracton Chambers, London	0171 242 4248
Sher Jules	• Wilberforce Chambers, London	0171 306 0102
Shillingford George Miles	Chambers of Mr Peter Crampin QC, London	020 7831 0081
Shuman Miss Karen Ann Elizabeth	Bracton Chambers, London	0171 242 4248
Siddiqi Faizul Aqtab	Justice Court Chambers, London	0181 830 7786
Simmonds Andrew John	5 Stone Buildings, London	0171 242 6201
Simpson Ian	Bracton Chambers, London	0171 242 4248
Skelly Andrew Jon	1 Gray's Inn Square, London	0171 405 8946/7/8
Smith Howard James	Chambers of Mr Peter Crampin QC, London	020 7831 0081
Smith Miss Joanna Angela	• Wilberforce Chambers, London	0171 306 0102
Smith Paul Andrew	One Hare Court, London	020 7353 3171
Southall Richard Anthony	• 17 Bedford Row, London	0171 831 7314
Southwell Richard Charles	One Hare Court, London	020 7353 3171
Staddon Miss Claire Ann	12 New Square, London	0171 419 1212
	Sovereign Chambers, Leeds	0113 2451841/2/3
Start Miss Angharad Jocelyn	3 Verulam Buildings, London	0171 831 8441
Staunton (Thomas) Ulick (Patrick)	Chambers of Mr Peter Crampin QC, London	020 7831 0081
	65-67 King Street, Leicester	0116 2547710
Sterling Robert Alan	St James's Chambers, Manchester	0161 834 7000
	12 New Square, London	0171 419 1212
	Park Lane Chambers, Leeds	0113 2285000
Stevenson John Melford	Two Crown Office Row, London	020 7797 8100
Stewart Nicholas John Cameron	Hardwicke Building, London	020 7242 2523
Stewart-Smith William Rodney	1 New Square, London	0171 405 0884/5/6/7
Studer Mark Edgar Walter	Chambers of Mr Peter Crampin QC, London	020 7831 0081
Sutcliffe Andrew Harold Wentworth	3 Verulam Buildings, London	0171 831 8441
Swerling Robert Harry	13 Old Square, London	0171 404 4800
Swindells Miss Heather Hughson	Chambers of Michael Pert QC, London	0171 421 8000
	Chambers of Michael Pert QC, Leicester	0116 249 2020
	Chambers of Michael Pert QC, Northampton	01604 602333
	St Philip's Chambers, Birmingham	0121 246 7000
Szanto Gregory John Michael	Eastbourne Chambers, Eastbourne	01323 642102
Talbot Patrick John	Serle Court Chambers, London	0171 242 6105
Tedd Rex Hilary	• St Philip's Chambers, Birmingham	0121 246 7000
	De Montfort Chambers, Leicester	0116 254 8686
	Northampton Chambers, Northampton	01604 636271
Templeman Michael Richard	Southernhay Chambers, Exeter	01392 255777
	5 Stone Buildings, London	0171 242 6201
Tennet Michael John	• Wilberforce Chambers, London	0171 306 0102
Terry Robert Jeffrey	8 King Street Chambers, Manchester	0161 834 9560
Thomas Nigel Matthew	13 Old Square, London	0171 404 4800
Tidmarsh Christopher Ralph Francis	5 Stone Buildings, London	0171 242 6201
Tipples Miss Amanda Jane	13 Old Square, London	0171 404 4800
Trace Anthony John	• 13 Old Square, London	0171 404 4800
Tucker Miss Katherine Jane Greening	St Philip's Chambers, Birmingham	0121 246 7000
Tully Ms Anne Margaret	Eastbourne Chambers, Eastbourne	01323 642102
Turnbull Charles Emerson Lovett	• Wilberforce Chambers, London	0171 306 0102

Ullstein Augustus Rupert Patrick A	• 29 Bedford Row Chambers, London	0171 831 2626
Van Tonder Gerard Dirk	1 New Square, London	0171 405 0884/5/6/7
Verduyn Dr Anthony James	St Philip's Chambers, Birmingham	0121 246 7000
Vickery Neil Michael	13 King's Bench Walk, London	0171 353 7204
	King's Bench Chambers, Oxford	01865 311066
Walden-Smith Miss Karen Jane	5 Stone Buildings, London	0171 242 6201
Walford Richard Henry Howard	Serle Court Chambers, London	0171 242 6105
Walker Andrew Greenfield	Chambers of Lord Goodhart QC, London	0171 405 5577
Warner David Alexander	1 New Square, London	0171 405 0884/5/6/7
Warnock-Smith Mrs Shan	5 Stone Buildings, London	0171 242 6201
Warren Nicholas Roger	• Wilberforce Chambers, London	0171 306 0102
Waters Malcolm Ian	• 11 Old Square, London	020 7430 0341
Watkin Toby Paul	22 Old Buildings, London	0171 831 0222
Weatherill Bernard Richard	Chambers of Lord Goodhart QC, London	0171 405 5577
West Mark	• 11 Old Square, London	020 7430 0341
Whittaker John Percival	Serle Court Chambers, London	0171 242 6105
Wicks Ms Joanne	• Wilberforce Chambers, London	0171 306 0102
Wilkins Mrs Colette Ann	1 New Square, London	0171 405 0884/5/6/7
Willer Robert Michael	Hardwicke Building, London	020 7242 2523
Williams Andrew Arthur	Adrian Lyon's Chambers, Liverpool	0151 236 4421/8240
Williams Dr Jason Scott	• 3 Dr Johnson's Buildings, London	0171 353 4854
Williams Thomas Christopher Charles	1 Fountain Court, Birmingham	0121 236 5721
Williamson Miss Bridget Susan	Enterprise Chambers, London	0171 405 9471
	Enterprise Chambers, Leeds	0113 246 0391
	Enterprise Chambers, Newcastle upon Tyne	0191 222 3344
Wilson-Barnes Miss Lucy Emma	St James's Chambers, Manchester	0161 834 7000
Wright Colin John	4 Field Court, London	0171 440 6900
Zelin Geoffrey Andrew	Enterprise Chambers, London	0171 405 9471
	Enterprise Chambers, Leeds	0113 246 0391
	Enterprise Chambers, Newcastle upon Tyne	0191 222 3344

CHANCERY LAND LAW

Acton Stephen Neil	11 Old Square, London	020 7430 0341
Adamyk Simon Charles	12 New Square, London	0171 419 1212
Angus Miss Tracey Anne	5 Stone Buildings, London	0171 242 6201
Asplin Miss Sarah Jane	• 3 Stone Buildings, London	0171 242 4937
Asprey Nicholas	Serle Court Chambers, London	0171 242 6105
Atherton Ian David	Enterprise Chambers, London	0171 405 9471
	Enterprise Chambers, Newcastle upon Tyne	0191 222 3344
	Enterprise Chambers, Leeds	0113 246 0391
Ayliffe James Justin Barnett	• Wilberforce Chambers, London	0171 306 0102
Ayres Andrew John William	13 Old Square, London	0171 404 4800
Baker Miss Anne Jacqueline	Enterprise Chambers, London	0171 405 9471
	Enterprise Chambers, Leeds	0113 246 0391
	Enterprise Chambers, Newcastle upon Tyne	0191 222 3344
Barker James Sebastian	Enterprise Chambers, London	0171 405 9471
	Enterprise Chambers, Leeds	0113 246 0391
	Enterprise Chambers, Newcastle upon Tyne	0191 222 3344
Barton Alan John	Lamb Building, London	020 7797 7788
Bates John Hayward	Old Square Chambers, London	0171 269 0300
	Old Square Chambers, Bristol	0117 9277111
Beaumont Marc Clifford	• Harrow on the Hill Chambers, Harrow-on-the-Hill	0181 423 7444
	Windsor Barristers' Chambers, Windsor	01753 648899
	Pump Court Chambers, London	0171 353 0711

• Expanded entry in Part D

Behrens James Nicholas Edward	Serle Court Chambers, London	0171 242 6105
Berry Nicholas Michael	Southernhay Chambers, Exeter	01392 255777
	1 Gray's Inn Square, London	0171 405 8946/7/8
	22 Old Buildings, London	0171 831 0222
Bhaloo Miss Zia Kurban	Enterprise Chambers, London	0171 405 9471
	Enterprise Chambers, Leeds	0113 246 0391
	Enterprise Chambers, Newcastle upon Tyne	0191 222 3344
Birtles William	Old Square Chambers, London	0171 269 0300
	Old Square Chambers, Bristol	0117 9277111
Blackett-Ord Mark	• 5 Stone Buildings, London	0171 242 6201
Blayney David James	Serle Court Chambers, London	0171 242 6105
Bleasdale Miss Marie-Claire	Chambers of Mr Peter Crampin QC, London	020 7831 0081
Bowker Robert James	2nd Floor, Francis Taylor Building, London	0171 353 9942/3157
Bowmer Michael Paul	11 Old Square, London	020 7430 0341
Boyd Stephen James Harvey	29 Bedford Row Chambers, London	0171 831 2626
Briggs Michael Townley Featherstone	Serle Court Chambers, London	0171 242 6105
Browne James William	96 Gray's Inn Road, London	0171 405 0585
Bruce Andrew Jonathan	Serle Court Chambers, London	0171 242 6105
Bryant John Malcolm Cornelius	Barnard's Inn Chambers, London	0171 369 6969
Buck Dr Andrew Theodore	Chambers of Martin Burr, London	0171 353 4636
Burr Martin John	Chambers of Martin Burr, London	0171 353 4636
	7 New Square, London	0171 430 1660
Butler Andrew	2nd Floor, Francis Taylor Building, London	0171 353 9942/3157
Campbell Miss Emily Charlotte	• Wilberforce Chambers, London	0171 306 0102
Cannon Adam Richard	96 Gray's Inn Road, London	0171 405 0585
Chan Miss Susan	13 King's Bench Walk, London	0171 353 7204
	King's Bench Chambers, Oxford	01865 311066
Charman Andrew Julian	St Philip's Chambers, Birmingham	0121 246 7000
Clark Andrew Richard	Manchester House Chambers, Manchester	0161 834 7007
	8 King Street Chambers, Manchester	0161 834 9560
Clarke Miss Anna Victoria	5 Stone Buildings, London	0171 242 6201
Clarke Ian James	Hardwicke Building, London	020 7242 2523
Clarke Peter John	St Philip's Chambers, Birmingham	0121 246 7000
	Harcourt Chambers, London	0171 353 6961
	Harcourt Chambers, Oxford	01865 791559
Clegg Sebastian James Barwick	Deans Court Chambers, Manchester	0161 214 6000
	Deans Court Chambers, Preston	01772 555163
Cooper Gilead Patrick	Chambers of Mr Peter Crampin QC, London	020 7831 0081
Cosedge Andrew John	3 Stone Buildings, London	0171 242 4937
Craig Kenneth Allen	Hardwicke Building, London	020 7242 2523
Crail Miss (Elspeth) Ross	12 New Square, London	0171 419 1212
	Sovereign Chambers, Leeds	0113 2451841/2/3
Crampin Peter	Chambers of Mr Peter Crampin QC, London	020 7831 0081
Cramsie James Sinclair Beresford	13 King's Bench Walk, London	0171 353 7204
	King's Bench Chambers, Oxford	01865 311066
Cranfield Peter Anthony	3 Verulam Buildings, London	0171 831 8441
Crawford Grant	11 Old Square, London	020 7430 0341
Davey Benjamin Nicholas	11 Old Square, London	020 7430 0341
Davidson Edward Alan	11 Old Square, London	020 7430 0341
Davies Miss (Susan) Louise	12 New Square, London	0171 419 1212
	Sovereign Chambers, Leeds	0113 2451841/2/3
de Lacy Richard Michael	3 Verulam Buildings, London	0171 831 8441
de Waal John Henry Lowndes	St Philip's Chambers, Birmingham	0121 246 7000
Dean Peter Thomas	1 Crown Office Row, London	0171 583 9292

Dodd Christopher John Nicholas	9 Woodhouse Square, Leeds	0113 2451986
Dodge Peter Clive	11 Old Square, London	020 7430 0341
Dooher Miss Nancy Helen	St James's Chambers, Manchester	0161 834 7000
Duddridge Robert James	2 Gray's Inn Square Chambers, London	020 7242 0328
Dumont Thomas Julian Bradley	Chambers of Mr Peter Crampin QC, London	020 7831 0081
Eadie James Raymond	One Hare Court, London	020 7353 3171
Eidinow John Samuel Christopher	1 New Square, London	0171 405 0884/5/6/7
Elleray Anthony John	•St James's Chambers, Manchester	0161 834 7000
	12 New Square, London	0171 419 1212
	Park Lane Chambers, Leeds	0113 2285000
Ellis Roger John	13 King's Bench Walk, London	0171 353 7204
	King's Bench Chambers, Oxford	01865 311066
Eyre Stephen John Arthur	1 Fountain Court, Birmingham	0121 236 5721
Farrow Kenneth John	Serle Court Chambers, London	0171 242 6105
Feltham Piers Jonathan	Chambers of Mr Peter Crampin QC, London	020 7831 0081
Finn Terence	Chambers of Martin Burr, London	0171 353 4636
Foster Brian Ian	St James's Chambers, Manchester	0161 834 7000
	Park Lane Chambers, Leeds	0113 2285000
Francis Andrew James	Chambers of Mr Peter Crampin QC, London	020 7831 0081
Francis Edward Gerald Francis	Enterprise Chambers, London	0171 405 9471
	Enterprise Chambers, Leeds	0113 246 0391
	Enterprise Chambers, Newcastle upon Tyne	0191 222 3344
Fryer-Spedding James Walter	St James's Chambers, Manchester	0161 834 7000
Furber (Robert) John	•Wilberforce Chambers, London	0171 306 0102
Furze Miss Caroline Mary	•Wilberforce Chambers, London	0171 306 0102
Gasztowicz Steven	2-3 Gray's Inn Square, London	0171 242 4986
	2 New Street, Leicester	0116 2625906
Gee Steven Mark	4 Field Court, London	0171 440 6900
Gerald Nigel Mortimer	Enterprise Chambers, London	0171 405 9471
	Enterprise Chambers, Leeds	0113 246 0391
	Enterprise Chambers, Newcastle upon Tyne	0191 222 3344
Gibbons James Francis	3 Stone Buildings, London	0171 242 4937
Gibson Miss Jill Maureen	Chambers of Mr Peter Crampin QC, London	020 7831 0081
Gifford Andrew James Morris	7 New Square, London	0171 430 1660
Green David Cameron	Adrian Lyon's Chambers, Liverpool	0151 236 4421/8240
Green Miss Jane Elizabeth	Design Chambers, London	0171 353 0747
	Chambers of Martin Burr, London	0171 353 4636
Greenan Miss Sarah Octavia	9 Woodhouse Square, Leeds	0113 2451986
Gregory John Raymond	Deans Court Chambers, Manchester	0161 214 6000
	Deans Court Chambers, Preston	01772 555163
Grime John Andrew	Pump Court Chambers, Swindon	01793 539899
	Pump Court Chambers, London	0171 353 0711
	Pump Court Chambers, Winchester	01962 868161
Hall Taylor Alexander Edward	11 Old Square, London	020 7430 0341
Halpern David Anthony	Enterprise Chambers, London	0171 405 9471
	Enterprise Chambers, Leeds	0113 246 0391
	Enterprise Chambers, Newcastle upon Tyne	0191 222 3344
Hantusch Robert Anthony	•3 Stone Buildings, London	0171 242 4937
Harris Melvyn	7 New Square, London	0171 430 1660
Harrod Henry Mark	5 Stone Buildings, London	0171 242 6201
Henderson William Hugo	Serle Court Chambers, London	0171 242 6105
Higgins Adrian John	13 King's Bench Walk, London	0171 353 7204
	King's Bench Chambers, Oxford	01865 311066
Higgins Rupert James Hale	Littman Chambers, London	020 7404 4866

• Expanded entry in Part D

Higgo Justin Beresford	Serle Court Chambers, London	0171 242 6105
Hinks Frank Peter	Serle Court Chambers, London	0171 242 6105
Hoffman David Alexander	8 King Street Chambers, Manchester	0161 834 9560
Holland David Moore	29 Bedford Row Chambers, London	0171 831 2626
Horne Roger Cozens-Hardy	Chambers of Mr Peter Crampin QC, London	020 7831 0081
Hoser Philip Jacob	Serle Court Chambers, London	0171 242 6105
Hubbard Mark Iain	1 New Square, London	0171 405 0884/5/6/7
Hunter William Quigley	No. 1 Serjeants' Inn, London	0171 415 6666
Hutchings Martin Anthony	199 Strand, London	0171 379 9779
Iles Adrian	5 Paper Buildings, London	0171 583 9275/583 4555
Jack Adrian Laurence Robert	Enterprise Chambers, London	0171 405 9471
	Enterprise Chambers, Newcastle upon Tyne	0191 222 3344
	Enterprise Chambers, Leeds	0113 246 0391
Jackson Dirik George Allan	Chambers of Mr Peter Crampin QC, London	020 7831 0081
Jackson Hugh Woodward	Hardwicke Building, London	020 7242 2523
Jackson Nicholas David Kingsley	Adrian Lyon's Chambers, Liverpool	0151 236 4421/8240
James-Stadden Miss Jodie Cara	Westgate Chambers, Newcastle upon Tyne	0191 261 4407/2329785
Jefferis Arthur Michael Quentin	Chambers of Mr Peter Crampin QC, London	020 7831 0081
Jones Philip John	Serle Court Chambers, London	0171 242 6105
Karas Jonathan Marcus	● Wilberforce Chambers, London	0171 306 0102
King Charles Granville	96 Gray's Inn Road, London	0171 405 0585
Kremen Philip Michael	Hardwicke Building, London	020 7242 2523
Kynoch Duncan Stuart Sanderson	29 Bedford Row Chambers, London	0171 831 2626
Lamb Robert Glasson	13 King's Bench Walk, London	0171 353 7204
	King's Bench Chambers, Oxford	01865 311066
Lamont Miss Camilla Rose	Chambers of Lord Goodhart QC, London	0171 405 5577
Landes Miss Anna-Rose	St Philip's Chambers, Birmingham	0121 246 7000
Legge Henry	5 Stone Buildings, London	0171 242 6201
Leigh Kevin	6 Pump Court, London	0171 797 8400
	Regency Chambers, Peterborough	01733 315215
	Westgate Chambers, Lewes	01273 480510
	6-8 Mill Street, Maidstone	01622 688094
Levy Benjamin Keith	Enterprise Chambers, London	0171 405 9471
	Enterprise Chambers, Leeds	0113 246 0391
	Enterprise Chambers, Newcastle upon Tyne	0191 222 3344
Lloyd Stephen James George	Chambers of Mr Peter Crampin QC, London	020 7831 0081
Lochrane Damien Horatio Ross	Pump Court Chambers, London	0171 353 0711
	Pump Court Chambers, Winchester	01962 868161
	Pump Court Chambers, Swindon	01793 539899
Lowry Charles Stephen	Colleton Chambers, Exeter	01392 274898/9
Machell John William	Serle Court Chambers, London	0171 242 6105
Mainwaring [Robert] Paul Clason	Carmarthen Chambers, Carmarthen	01267 234410
Majumdar Shantanu	Lamb Chambers, London	020 7797 8300
Mann George Anthony	Enterprise Chambers, London	0171 405 9471
	Enterprise Chambers, Leeds	0113 246 0391
	Enterprise Chambers, Newcastle upon Tyne	0191 222 3344
Margolin Daniel George	Chambers of Mr Peter Crampin QC, London	020 7831 0081
Martin John Vandeleur	● Wilberforce Chambers, London	0171 306 0102
Mason Miss Alexandra	3 Stone Buildings, London	0171 242 4937
Maynard-Connor Giles	St James's Chambers, Manchester	0161 834 7000
McAlinden Barry O'Neill	17 Bedford Row, London	0171 831 7314
McQuail Ms Katherine Emma	11 Old Square, London	020 7430 0341

Mehendale Ms Neelima Krishna	2 Mitre Court Buildings, London	0171 353 1353
Mendoza Neil David Pereira	Hardwicke Building, London	020 7242 2523
Morgan Richard Hugo Lyndon	13 Old Square, London	0171 404 4800
Munby James Lawrence	1 New Square, London	0171 405 0884/5/6/7
Newman Miss Catherine Mary	• 13 Old Square, London	0171 404 4800
Norbury Hugh Robert	Serle Court Chambers, London	0171 242 6105
Norris Alastair Hubert	5 Stone Buildings, London	0171 242 6201
	Southernhay Chambers, Exeter	01392 255777
Nugee Christopher George	• Wilberforce Chambers, London	0171 306 0102
Nugee Edward George	• Wilberforce Chambers, London	0171 306 0102
Nurse Gordon Bramwell William	11 Old Square, London	020 7430 0341
O'Leary Robert Michael	33 Park Place, Cardiff	02920 233313
O'Sullivan Michael Morton	5 Stone Buildings, London	0171 242 6201
Oakley Anthony James	• 11 Old Square, London	020 7430 0341
Oakley Paul James	1 Gray's Inn Square, London	0171 405 8946/7/8
Ohrenstein Dov	Chambers of Lord Goodhart QC, London	0171 405 5577
Ovey Miss Elizabeth Helen	11 Old Square, London	020 7430 0341
Panesar Deshpal Singh	13 King's Bench Walk, London	0171 353 7204
	King's Bench Chambers, Oxford	01865 311066
Peacock Nicholas Christopher	13 Old Square, London	0171 404 4800
Pearce Robert Edgar	Chambers of Mr Peter Crampin QC, London	020 7831 0081
Pereira James Alexander	2 Harcourt Buildings, London	020 7353 8415
Phillpot Hereward Lindon	2 Harcourt Buildings, London	020 7353 8415
Pilkington Mrs Mavis Patricia	9 Woodhouse Square, Leeds	0113 2451986
Pimentel Carlos de Serpa Alberto Legg	3 Stone Buildings, London	0171 242 4937
Porter David Leonard	St James's Chambers, Manchester	0161 834 7000
	Park Lane Chambers, Leeds	0113 2285000
Potts Warren Nigel	Queen's Chambers, Manchester	0161 834 6875/4738
	Queens Chambers, Preston	01772 828300
Proudman Miss Sonia Rosemary Susan	Chambers of Mr Peter Crampin QC, London	020 7831 0081
Purkis Ms Kathryn Miranda	Serle Court Chambers, London	0171 242 6105
Radevsky Anthony Eric	Falcon Chambers, London	0171 353 2484
Rainey Philip Carslake	2nd Floor, Francis Taylor Building, London	0171 353 9942/3157
Rashid Omar	Chambers of Mr Peter Crampin QC, London	020 7831 0081
Raybaud Mrs June Rose	96 Gray's Inn Road, London	0171 405 0585
Reed John William Rupert	• Wilberforce Chambers, London	0171 306 0102
Rich Miss Ann Barbara	5 Stone Buildings, London	0171 242 6201
Richardson Giles John	Serle Court Chambers, London	0171 242 6105
Rogers Miss Beverly-Ann	Serle Court Chambers, London	0171 242 6105
Rolfe Patrick John Benedict	5 Stone Buildings, London	0171 242 6201
Ross Martyn John Greaves	• 5 New Square, London	020 7404 0404
Rowell David Stewart	Chambers of Lord Goodhart QC, London	0171 405 5577
Rowley Keith Nigel	11 Old Square, London	020 7430 0341
Rumney Conrad William Arthur	St Philip's Chambers, Birmingham	0121 246 7000
Russell Christopher Garnet	• 12 New Square, London	0171 419 1212
	Sovereign Chambers, Leeds	0113 2451841/2/3
Salmon Jonathan Carl	1 Fountain Court, Birmingham	0121 236 5721
Sandells Ms Nicole	11 Old Square, London	020 7430 0341
Sartin Leon James	5 Stone Buildings, London	0171 242 6201
Sellers Graham	Adrian Lyon's Chambers, Liverpool	0151 236 4421/8240
Selway Dr Katherine Emma	11 Old Square, London	020 7430 0341
Semken Christopher Richard	1 New Square, London	0171 405 0884/5/6/7
Sheehan Malcolm Peter	2 Harcourt Buildings, London	0171 583 9020
Shillingford George Miles	Chambers of Mr Peter Crampin QC, London	020 7831 0081
Siddiqi Faizul Aqtab	Justice Court Chambers, London	0181 830 7786

• Expanded entry in Part D

Simmonds Andrew John	5 Stone Buildings, London	0171 242 6201
Sinclair Graham Kelso	East Anglian Chambers, Norwich	01603 617351
	East Anglian Chambers, Colchester	01206 572756
	East Anglian Chambers, Ipswich	01473 214481
Sinclair Miss Lisa Anne	7 New Square, London	0171 430 1660
Smith Howard James	Chambers of Mr Peter Crampin QC, London	020 7831 0081
Staddon Miss Claire Ann	12 New Square, London	0171 419 1212
	Sovereign Chambers, Leeds	0113 2451841/2/3
Staddon Paul	2nd Floor, Francis Taylor Building, London	0171 353 9942/3157
Staunton (Thomas) Ulick (Patrick)	Chambers of Mr Peter Crampin QC, London	020 7831 0081
	65-67 King Street, Leicester	0116 2547710
Sterling Robert Alan	St James's Chambers, Manchester	0161 834 7000
	12 New Square, London	0171 419 1212
	Park Lane Chambers, Leeds	0113 2285000
Stevens-Hoare Miss Michelle	Hardwicke Building, London	020 7242 2523
Stewart-Smith William Rodney	1 New Square, London	0171 405 0884/5/6/7
Talbot Patrick John	Serle Court Chambers, London	0171 242 6105
Templeman Michael Richard	Southernhay Chambers, Exeter	01392 255777
	5 Stone Buildings, London	0171 242 6201
Terry Robert Jeffrey	8 King Street Chambers, Manchester	0161 834 9560
Thom James Alexander Francis	4 Field Court, London	0171 440 6900
Thomas Nigel Matthew	13 Old Square, London	0171 404 4800
Tidmarsh Christopher Ralph Francis	5 Stone Buildings, London	0171 242 6201
Tipples Miss Amanda Jane	13 Old Square, London	0171 404 4800
Trace Anthony John	• 13 Old Square, London	0171 404 4800
Tully Ms Anne Margaret	Eastbourne Chambers, Eastbourne	01323 642102
Van Tonder Gerard Dirk	1 New Square, London	0171 405 0884/5/6/7
Vickery Neil Michael	13 King's Bench Walk, London	0171 353 7204
	King's Bench Chambers, Oxford	01865 311066
Wagner Mrs Linda Ann	96 Gray's Inn Road, London	0171 405 0585
Walden-Smith Miss Karen Jane	5 Stone Buildings, London	0171 242 6201
Walker Andrew Greenfield	Chambers of Lord Goodhart QC, London	0171 405 5577
Walters Edmund John	13 King's Bench Walk, London	0171 353 7204
	King's Bench Chambers, Oxford	01865 311066
Warner David Alexander	1 New Square, London	0171 405 0884/5/6/7
Warnock-Smith Mrs Shan	5 Stone Buildings, London	0171 242 6201
Warren Nicholas Roger	• Wilberforce Chambers, London	0171 306 0102
Waters Malcolm Ian	• 11 Old Square, London	020 7430 0341
Weatherill Bernard Richard	Chambers of Lord Goodhart QC, London	0171 405 5577
West Mark	• 11 Old Square, London	020 7430 0341
Westgate Martin Trevor	Doughty Street Chambers, London	0171 404 1313
Whitaker Steven Dixon	199 Strand, London	0171 379 9779
	Queens Square Chambers, Bristol	0117 921 1966
Whittaker John Percival	Serle Court Chambers, London	0171 242 6105
Wicks Ms Joanne	• Wilberforce Chambers, London	0171 306 0102
Williams Andrew Arthur	Adrian Lyon's Chambers, Liverpool	0151 236 4421/8240
Williamson Miss Bridget Susan	Enterprise Chambers, London	0171 405 9471
	Enterprise Chambers, Leeds	0113 246 0391
	Enterprise Chambers, Newcastle upon Tyne	0191 222 3344
Wilson-Barnes Miss Lucy Emma	St James's Chambers, Manchester	0161 834 7000
Zelin Geoffrey Andrew	Enterprise Chambers, London	0171 405 9471
	Enterprise Chambers, Leeds	0113 246 0391
	Enterprise Chambers, Newcastle upon Tyne	0191 222 3344
Zwart Auberon Christiaan Conrad	1 Serjeants' Inn, London	0171 583 1355

B

CHARITIES

Angus Miss Tracey Anne	5 Stone Buildings, London	0171 242 6201
Asplin Miss Sarah Jane	• 3 Stone Buildings, London	0171 242 4937
Asprey Nicholas	Serle Court Chambers, London	0171 242 6105
Ayres Andrew John William	13 Old Square, London	0171 404 4800
Bleasdale Miss Marie-Claire	Chambers of Mr Peter Crampin QC, London	020 7831 0081
Bryant Miss Judith Anne	• Wilberforce Chambers, London	0171 306 0102
Buck Dr Andrew Theodore	Chambers of Martin Burr, London	0171 353 4636
Burr Martin John	Chambers of Martin Burr, London	0171 353 4636
	7 New Square, London	0171 430 1660
Campbell Miss Emily Charlotte	• Wilberforce Chambers, London	0171 306 0102
Child John Frederick	• Wilberforce Chambers, London	0171 306 0102
Clarke Miss Anna Victoria	5 Stone Buildings, London	0171 242 6201
Cracknell Douglas George	23 Warham Road, Sevenoaks	01959 522325
Crampin Peter	Chambers of Mr Peter Crampin QC, London	020 7831 0081
Crawford Grant	11 Old Square, London	020 7430 0341
Davidson Edward Alan	11 Old Square, London	020 7430 0341
Davies Miss (Susan) Louise	12 New Square, London	0171 419 1212
	Sovereign Chambers, Leeds	0113 2451841/2/3
Dodge Peter Clive	11 Old Square, London	020 7430 0341
Dumont Thomas Julian Bradley	Chambers of Mr Peter Crampin QC, London	020 7831 0081
Elleray Anthony John	• St James's Chambers, Manchester	0161 834 7000
	12 New Square, London	0171 419 1212
	Park Lane Chambers, Leeds	0113 2285000
Farrow Kenneth John	Serle Court Chambers, London	0171 242 6105
Feltham Piers Jonathan	Chambers of Mr Peter Crampin QC, London	020 7831 0081
Foster Brian Ian	St James's Chambers, Manchester	0161 834 7000
	Park Lane Chambers, Leeds	0113 2285000
Francis Andrew James	Chambers of Mr Peter Crampin QC, London	020 7831 0081
Fryer-Spedding James Walter	St James's Chambers, Manchester	0161 834 7000
Furness Michael James	• Wilberforce Chambers, London	0171 306 0102
Furze Miss Caroline Mary	• Wilberforce Chambers, London	0171 306 0102
Gibson Miss Jill Maureen	Chambers of Mr Peter Crampin QC, London	020 7831 0081
Green David Cameron	Adrian Lyon's Chambers, Liverpool	0151 236 4421/8240
Green Miss Jane Elizabeth	Design Chambers, London	0171 353 0747
	Chambers of Martin Burr, London	0171 353 4636
Gregory John Raymond	Deans Court Chambers, Manchester	0161 214 6000
	Deans Court Chambers, Preston	01772 555163
Hall Taylor Alexander Edward	11 Old Square, London	020 7430 0341
Ham Robert Wallace	• Wilberforce Chambers, London	0171 306 0102
Harrod Henry Mark	5 Stone Buildings, London	0171 242 6201
Henderson Launcelot Dinadan James	5 Stone Buildings, London	0171 242 6201
Henderson William Hugo	Serle Court Chambers, London	0171 242 6105
Horne Roger Cozens-Hardy	Chambers of Mr Peter Crampin QC, London	020 7831 0081
Kennedy Michael Kirk Inches	1 New Square, London	0171 405 0884/5/6/7
Lamont Miss Camilla Rose	Chambers of Lord Goodhart QC, London	0171 405 5577
Legge Henry	5 Stone Buildings, London	0171 242 6201
Lloyd Stephen James George	Chambers of Mr Peter Crampin QC, London	020 7831 0081
Lowe David Alexander	• Wilberforce Chambers, London	0171 306 0102
Mainwaring [Robert] Paul Clason	Carmarthen Chambers, Carmarthen	01267 234410
Margolin Daniel George	Chambers of Mr Peter Crampin QC, London	020 7831 0081

B

• Expanded entry in Part D

Martin Mrs Jill Elizabeth	Barnard's Inn Chambers, London	0171 369 6969
Mason Miss Alexandra	3 Stone Buildings, London	0171 242 4937
McQuail Ms Katherine Emma	11 Old Square, London	020 7430 0341
Minhas Ms Rafhat	Leone Chambers, London	0181 200 4020
Norris Alastair Hubert	5 Stone Buildings, London	0171 242 6201
	Southernhay Chambers, Exeter	01392 255777
Nugee Edward George	• Wilberforce Chambers, London	0171 306 0102
Nurse Gordon Bramwell William	11 Old Square, London	020 7430 0341
Oakley Anthony James	• 11 Old Square, London	020 7430 0341
Ohrenstein Dov	Chambers of Lord Goodhart QC, London	0171 405 5577
Ovey Miss Elizabeth Helen	11 Old Square, London	020 7430 0341
Pearce Robert Edgar	Chambers of Mr Peter Crampin QC, London	020 7831 0081
Pilkington Mrs Mavis Patricia	9 Woodhouse Square, Leeds	0113 2451986
Proudman Miss Sonia Rosemary Susan	Chambers of Mr Peter Crampin QC, London	020 7831 0081
Rashid Omar	Chambers of Mr Peter Crampin QC, London	020 7831 0081
Rees David Benjamin	5 Stone Buildings, London	0171 242 6201
Rogers Miss Beverly-Ann	Serle Court Chambers, London	0171 242 6105
Ross Martyn John Greaves	• 5 New Square, London	020 7404 0404
Rowell David Stewart	Chambers of Lord Goodhart QC, London	0171 405 5577
Sartin Leon James	5 Stone Buildings, London	0171 242 6201
Selway Dr Katherine Emma	11 Old Square, London	020 7430 0341
Shillingford George Miles	Chambers of Mr Peter Crampin QC, London	020 7831 0081
Siddiqi Faizul Aqtab	Justice Court Chambers, London	0181 830 7786
Smith Howard James	Chambers of Mr Peter Crampin QC, London	020 7831 0081
Staunton (Thomas) Ulick (Patrick)	Chambers of Mr Peter Crampin QC, London	020 7831 0081
	65-67 King Street, Leicester	0116 2547710
Sterling Robert Alan	St James's Chambers, Manchester	0161 834 7000
	12 New Square, London	0171 419 1212
	Park Lane Chambers, Leeds	0113 2285000
Stewart-Smith William Rodney	1 New Square, London	0171 405 0884/5/6/7
Studer Mark Edgar Walter	Chambers of Mr Peter Crampin QC, London	020 7831 0081
Talbot Patrick John	Serle Court Chambers, London	0171 242 6105
Thomson Martin Haldane Ahmad	Wynne Chambers, London	0181 961 6144
Turnbull Charles Emerson Lovett	• Wilberforce Chambers, London	0171 306 0102
Warnock-Smith Mrs Shan	5 Stone Buildings, London	0171 242 6201
Waters Malcolm Ian	• 11 Old Square, London	020 7430 0341
West Mark	• 11 Old Square, London	020 7430 0341

CHILD ABDUCTION

Ramsahoye Miss Indira Kim	Hardwicke Building, London	020 7242 2523

CHILD CARE LAW

deSouza Mrs Josephine Claudia	Chancery Chambers, London	0171 405 6879/6870

CHILDREN

Malecka Dr Mary Margaret	• 3 Temple Gardens, London	0171 353 0832
	65-67 King Street, Leicester	0116 2547710

CIVIL ACTIONS AGAINST PRISONS

Firth Miss Georgina Elizabeth	Chambers of Ian Macdonald QC (In Association with Two Garden Court, Temple, London), Manchester	0161 236 1840

CIVIL ACTIONS AGAINST THE POLICE

Bailey John Charles Williams	Queen's Chambers, Manchester	0161 834 6875/4738
	Queens Chambers, Preston	01772 828300
Barker John Steven Roy	Queen's Chambers, Manchester	0161 834 6875/4738
	Queens Chambers, Preston	01772 828300
Beer Jason Barrington	5 Essex Court, London	0171 410 2000
Bradley Miss Clodagh Maria	3 Serjeants' Inn, London	0171 353 5537
Courtney Nicholas Piers	Queen's Chambers, Manchester	0161 834 6875/4738
	Queens Chambers, Preston	01772 828300
Eccles David Thomas	8 King Street Chambers, Manchester	0161 834 9560
Firth Miss Georgina Elizabeth	Chambers of Ian Macdonald QC (In Association with Two Garden Court, Temple, London), Manchester	0161 236 1840
Freeland Simon Dennis Marsden	5 Essex Court, London	0171 410 2000
Mercer David Paul	Queen's Chambers, Manchester	0161 834 6875/4738
	Queens Chambers, Preston	01772 828300
Ryder Timothy Robert	Queen's Chambers, Manchester	0161 834 6875/4738
	Queens Chambers, Preston	01772 828300
Shannon Thomas Eric	Queen's Chambers, Manchester	0161 834 6875/4738
	Queens Chambers, Preston	01772 828300
Smith Michael Joseph	8 King Street Chambers, Manchester	0161 834 9560
Thompson Patrick Miles	Queen's Chambers, Manchester	0161 834 6875/4738
	Queens Chambers, Preston	01772 828300

CIVIL ACTIONS INVOLVING THE POLICE

Barton Miss Fiona	5 Essex Court, London	0171 410 2000
Hall David Percy	9 Woodhouse Square, Leeds	0113 2451986
Jackson Anthony Warren	3 Serjeants' Inn, London	0171 353 5537
Wakeham Philip John Le Messurier	Hardwicke Building, London	020 7242 2523

CIVIL FRAUD

Geering Ian Walter	3 Verulam Buildings, London	0171 831 8441
Green Miss Amanda Jane	3 Verulam Buildings, London	0171 831 8441
Parker Matthew Richard	3 Verulam Buildings, London	0171 831 8441

CIVIL JURY ACTIONS

Challenger Colin Westcott	Bridewell Chambers, London	020 7797 8800

CIVIL JURY ACTIONS FOR POLICE AUTHORITIES

Kent Miss Georgina	5 Essex Court, London	0171 410 2000

CIVIL LIBERTIES

Akiwumi Anthony Sebastian Akitayo	Pump Court Chambers, London	0171 353 0711
	Pump Court Chambers, Winchester	01962 868161
	Pump Court Chambers, Swindon	01793 539899
Alty Andrew Stephen John	Deans Court Chambers, Manchester	0161 214 6000
	Deans Court Chambers, Preston	01772 555163
Anderson Miss Julie	• Littman Chambers, London	020 7404 4866
Banks Francis Andrew	Adrian Lyon's Chambers, Liverpool	0151 236 4421/8240
Bassett John Stewart Britten	5 Essex Court, London	0171 410 2000
Beer Jason Barrington	5 Essex Court, London	0171 410 2000
Bhanji Shiraz Musa	4 Bingham Place, London	0171 486 5347/071 487 5910
Birch Roger Allen	Sovereign Chambers, Leeds	0113 2451841/2/3
	12 New Square, London	0171 419 1212
Blake Arthur Joseph	13 King's Bench Walk, London	0171 353 7204
	King's Bench Chambers, Oxford	01865 311066
Blom-Cooper Sir Louis Jacques	Doughty Street Chambers, London	0171 404 1313
Bogan Paul Simon	Doughty Street Chambers, London	0171 404 1313
Booth Nicholas John	Old Square Chambers, London	0171 269 0300
	Old Square Chambers, Bristol	0117 9277111
Bowen Paul Edward	4 King's Bench Walk, London	0171 822 8822

• Expanded entry in Part D

Brooks Mr Paul Anthony	Doughty Street Chambers, London	0171 404 1313
Brown Miss Althea Sonia	Doughty Street Chambers, London	0171 404 1313
Burrows Simon Paul	Peel Court Chambers, Manchester	0161 832 3791
Carter Peter	• 18 Red Lion Court, London	0171 520 6000
	Thornwood House, Chelmsford	01245 280880
Cavanagh John Patrick	11 King's Bench Walk, London	0171 632 8500/583 0610
Clover (Thomas) Anthony	New Court Chambers, London	0171 831 9500
Crampin Paul	Lamb Building, London	020 7797 7788
Daniel Leon Roger	6 King's Bench Walk, London	0171 353 4931/583 0695
Dingemans James Michael	1 Crown Office Row, London	0171 583 9292
Dobbs Miss Linda Penelope	18 Red Lion Court, London	0171 520 6000
	Thornwood House, Chelmsford	01245 280880
Dolan Dr Bridget Maura	3 Serjeants' Inn, London	0171 353 5537
Dunn Christopher	Sovereign Chambers, Leeds	0113 2451841/2/3
Eccles David Thomas	8 King Street Chambers, Manchester	0161 834 9560
Edusei Francis Victor Burg	Chambers of Ian Macdonald QC (In	0161 236 1840
	Association with Two Garden Court,	
	Temple, London), Manchester	
Ellin Miss Nina Caroline	6 Pump Court, London	0171 797 8400
	6-8 Mill Street, Maidstone	01622 688094
Emmerson (Michael) Benedict	Doughty Street Chambers, London	0171 404 1313
Featherstone Jason Neil	Virtual Chambers, London	07071 244 944
	Barristers' Common Law Chambers,	0171 375 3012
	London	
Field Rory Dominic	Hardwicke Building, London	020 7242 2523
Finch Mrs Nadine Elizabeth	Doughty Street Chambers, London	0171 404 1313
Firth Miss Georgina Elizabeth	Chambers of Ian Macdonald QC (In	0161 236 1840
	Association with Two Garden Court,	
	Temple, London), Manchester	
Fitzgerald Edward Hamilton	Doughty Street Chambers, London	0171 404 1313
Fitzpatrick Edward James	8 King's Bench Walk, London	0171 797 8888
Ford Michael David	Doughty Street Chambers, London	0171 404 1313
Foster Miss Alison Lee Caroline	39 Essex Street, London	0171 832 1111
Freeland Simon Dennis Marsden	5 Essex Court, London	0171 410 2000
Gannon Kevin Francis	8 King's Bench Walk, London	0171 797 8888
	8 King's Bench Walk North, Leeds	0113 2439797
Gibson Arthur George Adrian	Adrian Lyon's Chambers, Liverpool	0151 236 4421/8240
Gifford Lord Anthony Maurice	8 King's Bench Walk, London	0171 797 8888
	8 King's Bench Walk North, Leeds	0113 2439797
Gill Ms Sarah Teresa	• Old Square Chambers, London	0171 269 0300
	Old Square Chambers, Bristol	0117 9277111
Gledhill Kris	Camberwell Chambers, London	0171 274 0830
Gordon Richard John Francis	Brick Court Chambers, London	0171 379 3550
Grey Miss Eleanor Mary Grace	39 Essex Street, London	0171 832 1111
Grieve Michael Robertson Crichton	Doughty Street Chambers, London	0171 404 1313
Haji Miss Shaheen	Bell Yard Chambers, London	0171 306 9292
Hall Jonathan Rupert	5 King's Bench Walk, London	0171 353 5638
Hatfield Ms Sally Anne	Doughty Street Chambers, London	0171 404 1313
Henderson Miss Sophie	Plowden Buildings, London	0171 583 0808
Hermer Richard Simon	Doughty Street Chambers, London	0171 404 1313
	30 Park Place, Cardiff	01222 398421
Hogg The Hon Douglas Martin	37 Park Square Chambers, Leeds	0113 2439422
	Cathedral Chambers (Jan Wood	01392 210900
	Independent Barristers' Clerk), Exeter	
Hoyal Ms Jane	• 1 Pump Court, London	0171 583 2012/353 4341
Hudson Anthony Sean	Doughty Street Chambers, London	0171 404 1313
Jackson Anthony Warren	3 Serjeants' Inn, London	0171 353 5537
Jay Robert Maurice	39 Essex Street, London	0171 832 1111
Jones Martin Wynne	8 King's Bench Walk, London	0171 797 8888
	8 King's Bench Walk North, Leeds	0113 2439797
Kaufmann Ms Phillippa Jane	Doughty Street Chambers, London	0171 404 1313

Keeley James Francis	Sovereign Chambers, Leeds	0113 2451841/2/3
Kent Miss Georgina	5 Essex Court, London	0171 410 2000
Keogh Andrew John	8 King's Bench Walk, London	0171 797 8888
	8 King's Bench Walk North, Leeds	0113 2439797
Khan Anwar William	Eastbourne Chambers, Eastbourne	01323 642102
	Wessex Chambers, Reading	0118 956 8856
Kovats Steven Laszlo	39 Essex Street, London	0171 832 1111
Maclean Alan John	39 Essex Street, London	0171 832 1111
Macleod Duncan	9 Gough Square, London	020 7832 0500
Marks Jonathan Clive	4 Pump Court, London	020 7842 5555
Markus Ms Kate	Doughty Street Chambers, London	0171 404 1313
Marshall-Andrews Robert Graham	37 Park Square Chambers, Leeds	0113 2439422
	2-4 Tudor Street, London	0171 797 7111
McCrindell James Derrey	Mitre House Chambers, London	0171 583 8233
McMullen Jeremy John	• Old Square Chambers, London	0171 269 0300
	Old Square Chambers, Bristol	0117 9277111
Metzer Anthony David Erwin	Doughty Street Chambers, London	0171 404 1313
Millar Gavin James	Doughty Street Chambers, London	0171 404 1313
Morris Miss Fenella	39 Essex Street, London	0171 832 1111
Murray-Smith James Michael	8 King's Bench Walk, London	0171 797 8888
	8 King's Bench Walk North, Leeds	0113 2439797
Nardell Gordon Lawrence	6 Pump Court, London	0171 797 8400
	6-8 Mill Street, Maidstone	01622 688094
Newman Austin Eric	9 Woodhouse Square, Leeds	0113 2451986
Nicol Andrew George Lindsay	Doughty Street Chambers, London	0171 404 1313
Omambala Miss Ijeoma Chinyelu	Old Square Chambers, London	0171 269 0300
	Old Square Chambers, Bristol	0117 9277111
Owen Timothy Wynn	Doughty Street Chambers, London	0171 404 1313
Panford Frank Haig	• Doughty Street Chambers, London	0171 404 1313
Parker Kenneth Blades	Monckton Chambers, London	0171 405 7211
Parry Simon Edward	White Friars Chambers, Chester	01244 323070
Paul Nicholas Martin	Doughty Street Chambers, London	0171 404 1313
	Westgate Chambers, Lewes	01273 480510
Peterson Miss Geraldine Shelda	Lamb Building, London	020 7797 7788
Pickersgill David William	Bell Yard Chambers, London	0171 306 9292
Pirani Rohan Carl	Old Square Chambers, Bristol	0117 9277111
	Old Square Chambers, London	0171 269 0300
Pleming Nigel Peter	39 Essex Street, London	0171 832 1111
Plender Richard Owen	• 20 Essex Street, London	0171 583 9294
Plimmer Miss Melanie Ann	Chambers of Ian Macdonald QC (In Association with Two Garden Court, Temple, London), Manchester	0161 236 1840
Pomeroy Toby	Barristers' Common Law Chambers, London	0171 375 3012
	Virtual Chambers, London	07071 244 944
Qureshi Khawar Mehmood	One Hare Court, London	020 7353 3171
Rees Edward Parry	Doughty Street Chambers, London	0171 404 1313
Robb Adam Duncan	39 Essex Street, London	0171 832 1111
Robertson Geoffrey Ronald	Doughty Street Chambers, London	0171 404 1313
Roebuck Roy Delville	Bell Yard Chambers, London	0171 306 9292
Rogers Ian Paul	1 Crown Office Row, London	0171 583 9292
Roth Peter Marcel	Monckton Chambers, London	0171 405 7211
Sallon Christopher Robert	Doughty Street Chambers, London	0171 404 1313
	Westgate Chambers, Lewes	01273 480510
Salter Charles Philip Arthur	8 King's Bench Walk, London	0171 797 8888
	8 King's Bench Walk North, Leeds	0113 2439797
Sethi Mohinderpal Singh	Barnard's Inn Chambers, London	0171 369 6969
Shale Justin Anton	4 King's Bench Walk, London	0171 822 8822
	King's Bench Chambers, Bournemouth	01202 250025
Shepherd Nigel Patrick	8 King's Bench Walk North, Leeds	0113 2439797
	8 King's Bench Walk, London	0171 797 8888

• Expanded entry in Part D

Shrimpton Michael	Francis Taylor Building, London	0171 797 7250
Shukla Ms Vina	New Court Chambers, London	0171 831 9500
Siddiqi Faizul Aqtab	Justice Court Chambers, London	0181 830 7786
Simor Miss Jessica Margaret Poppaea	Monckton Chambers, London	0171 405 7211
Singh Kuldip	Five Paper Buildings, London	0171 583 6117
Smith Michael Joseph	8 King Street Chambers, Manchester	0161 834 9560
Staddon Paul	2nd Floor, Francis Taylor Building, London	0171 353 9942/3157
Stark James Hayden Alexander	Chambers of Ian Macdonald QC (In Association with Two Garden Court, Temple, London), Manchester	0161 236 1840
Starmer Keir	Doughty Street Chambers, London	0171 404 1313
Stevens Howard Linton	1 Crown Office Row, London	0171 583 9292
Stewart Nicholas John Cameron	Hardwicke Building, London	020 7242 2523
Straker Timothy Derrick	• 4-5 Gray's Inn Square, London	0171 404 5252
Szanto Gregory John Michael	Eastbourne Chambers, Eastbourne	01323 642102
Taylor Paul Richard	Doughty Street Chambers, London	0171 404 1313
Tehrani Christopher	8 King's Bench Walk North, Leeds	0113 2439797
	8 King's Bench Walk, London	0171 797 8888
Thorne Timothy Peter	33 Bedford Row, London	0171 242 6476
Thornley David	Chambers of Martin Burr, London	0171 353 4636
Thornton Peter Ribblesdale	Doughty Street Chambers, London	0171 404 1313
Tizzano Franco Salvatore	8 King's Bench Walk, London	0171 797 8888
	8 King's Bench Walk North, Leeds	0113 2439797
Ward Timothy Justin	Monckton Chambers, London	0171 405 7211
Weatherby Peter Francis	Two Garden Court, London	0171 353 1633
	Chambers of Ian Macdonald QC (In Association with Two Garden Court, Temple, London), Manchester	0161 236 1840
West Ian Stuart	Fountain Chambers, Middlesbrough	01642 804040
Westgate Martin Trevor	Doughty Street Chambers, London	0171 404 1313
Weston Ms Amanda	Chambers of Ian Macdonald QC (In Association with Two Garden Court, Temple, London), Manchester	0161 236 1840
Whitaker Ms Quincy Rachel Suzy	Doughty Street Chambers, London	0171 404 1313
Wilken Sean David Henry	39 Essex Street, London	0171 832 1111
Williams Ms Heather Jean	Doughty Street Chambers, London	0171 404 1313
Williams Ms Nicola Egersis	8 King's Bench Walk, London	0171 797 8888
Williams Paul Robert	8 King's Bench Walk North, Leeds	0113 2439797
	8 King's Bench Walk, London	0171 797 8888
Wise Ian	Doughty Street Chambers, London	0171 404 1313
Wood James Alexander Douglas	Doughty Street Chambers, London	0171 404 1313

CLINICAL NEGLIGENCE

Brough Alasdair Matheson	13 King's Bench Walk, London	0171 353 7204
	King's Bench Chambers, Oxford	01865 311066
Cameron Miss Barbara Alexander	• 2 Harcourt Buildings, London	0171 583 9020
Cramsie James Sinclair Beresford	13 King's Bench Walk, London	0171 353 7204
	King's Bench Chambers, Oxford	01865 311066
Dawson Alexander William	13 King's Bench Walk, London	0171 353 7204
	King's Bench Chambers, Oxford	01865 311066
Majumdar Shantanu	Lamb Chambers, London	020 7797 8300
Ough Dr Richard Norman	• Hardwicke Building, London	020 7242 2523
Panesar Deshpal Singh	13 King's Bench Walk, London	0171 353 7204
	King's Bench Chambers, Oxford	01865 311066
Wood Simon Edward	Plowden Buildings, London	0171 583 0808

CLUB LAW

Reid Paul William	13 King's Bench Walk, London	0171 353 7204
	King's Bench Chambers, Oxford	01865 311066

COMMERCIAL

Adkin Jonathan William	One Hare Court, London	020 7353 3171
Allen Michael David Prior	S Tomlinson QC, London	0171 583 0404
Ambrose Miss Clare Mary Geneste	20 Essex Street, London	0171 583 9294
Anderson Miss Julie	• Littman Chambers, London	020 7404 4866
Arden Peter Leonard	Enterprise Chambers, London	0171 405 9471
	Enterprise Chambers, Leeds	0113 246 0391
	Enterprise Chambers, Newcastle upon Tyne	0191 222 3344
Ashton David Sambrook	13 King's Bench Walk, London	0171 353 7204
	King's Bench Chambers, Oxford	01865 311066
Asprey Nicholas	Serle Court Chambers, London	0171 242 6105
Ayres Andrew John William	13 Old Square, London	0171 404 4800
Bailey David John	S Tomlinson QC, London	0171 583 0404
Bailey Edward Henry	Monckton Chambers, London	0171 405 7211
Basu Dr Dijendra Bhushan	Devereux Chambers, London	0171 353 7534
Behrens James Nicholas Edward	Serle Court Chambers, London	0171 242 6105
Beltrami Adrian Joseph	3 Verulam Buildings, London	0171 831 8441
Berry Nicholas Michael	Southernhay Chambers, Exeter	01392 255777
	1 Gray's Inn Square, London	0171 405 8946/7/8
	22 Old Buildings, London	0171 831 0222
Bignall John Francis	S Tomlinson QC, London	0171 583 0404
Birch Miss Elizabeth Blanche	3 Verulam Buildings, London	0171 831 8441
Birtles William	Old Square Chambers, London	0171 269 0300
	Old Square Chambers, Bristol	0117 9277111
Blackburn Mrs Elizabeth	4 Field Court, London	0171 440 6900
Blackwood Andrew Guy	4 Field Court, London	0171 440 6900
Blair William James Lynton	3 Verulam Buildings, London	0171 831 8441
Boyd James Andrew Donaldson	8 King Street Chambers, Manchester	0161 834 9560
Brace Michael Wesley	33 Park Place, Cardiff	02920 233313
Brannigan Peter John Sean	4 Pump Court, London	020 7842 5555
Brent Richard	3 Verulam Buildings, London	0171 831 8441
Brice Geoffrey James Barrington	4 Field Court, London	0171 440 6900
Bright Robert Graham	S Tomlinson QC, London	0171 583 0404
Brodie (James) Bruce	39 Essex Street, London	0171 832 1111
Brown Geoffrey Barlow	39 Essex Street, London	0171 832 1111
Browne-Wilkinson Simon	Serle Court Chambers, London	0171 242 6105
Bruce Andrew Jonathan	Serle Court Chambers, London	0171 242 6105
Buckingham Stewart John	4 Essex Court, London	020 7797 7970
Burnett Harold Wallace	4 Paper Buildings, London	0171 353 3366/583 7155
Butcher Christopher John	S Tomlinson QC, London	0171 583 0404
Butler Andrew	2nd Floor, Francis Taylor Building, London	0171 353 9942/3157
Calvert David Edward	St James's Chambers, Manchester	0161 834 7000
Castle Peter Bolton	Chambers of Mr Peter Crampin QC, London	020 7831 0081
Chalmers Miss Suzanne Frances	Two Crown Office Row, London	020 7797 8100
Chambers Jonathan	4 Essex Court, London	020 7797 7970
Charlton Alexander Murray	4 Pump Court, London	020 7842 5555
Compton Gareth Francis Thomas	22 Old Buildings, London	0171 831 0222
Cook Christopher Graham	St James's Chambers, Manchester	0161 834 7000
Cory-Wright Charles Alexander	39 Essex Street, London	0171 832 1111
Craig Alistair Trevor	Chambers of Mr Peter Crampin QC, London	020 7831 0081
Cranfield Peter Anthony	3 Verulam Buildings, London	0171 831 8441
Croxon Raymond Patrick	8 King's Bench Walk, London	0171 797 8888
	Regency Chambers, Peterborough	01733 315215
	Regency Chambers, Cambridge	01223 301517
Datta Mrs Wendy Patricia Mizal	Alban Chambers, London	0171 419 5051
Davey Michael Philip	4 Field Court, London	0171 440 6900
Davies Dr Charles Edward	4 Field Court, London	0171 440 6900

• Expanded entry in Part D

Davies-Jones Jonathan	3 Verulam Buildings, London	0171 831 8441
de Lacy Richard Michael	3 Verulam Buildings, London	0171 831 8441
Dempsey Brian Paul	Lancaster Building, Manchester	0161 661 4444/0171 649 9872
Dillon Thomas William Matthew	1 Fountain Court, Birmingham	0121 236 5721
Dingemans James Michael	1 Crown Office Row, London	0171 583 9292
Doherty Bernard James	39 Essex Street, London	0171 832 1111
Dooher Miss Nancy Helen	St James's Chambers, Manchester	0161 834 7000
Douglas Michael John	4 Pump Court, London	020 7842 5555
Dowley Dominic Myles	One Hare Court, London	020 7353 3171
Dunn Christopher	Sovereign Chambers, Leeds	0113 2451841/2/3
Eadie James Raymond	One Hare Court, London	020 7353 3171
Edwards David Leslie	S Tomlinson QC, London	0171 583 0404
Edwards Richard Julian Henshaw	3 Verulam Buildings, London	0171 831 8441
Ekins Charles Wareing	Sovereign Chambers, Leeds	0113 2451841/2/3
El-Falahi Sami David	International Law Chambers, London	0171 221 5684/5/4840
Elliott Nicholas Blethyn	3 Verulam Buildings, London	0171 831 8441
Ellis Roger John	13 King's Bench Walk, London	0171 353 7204
	King's Bench Chambers, Oxford	01865 311066
Evans James Frederick Meurig	3 Verulam Buildings, London	0171 831 8441
Evans Richard Gareth	5 Paper Buildings, London	0171 583 9275/583 4555
Faluyi Albert Osamudiamen	Chambers of Martin Burr, London	0171 353 4636
Farrer Adam Michael	4 Fountain Court, Birmingham	0121 236 3476
Featherstone Jason Neil	Virtual Chambers, London	07071 244 944
	Barristers' Common Law Chambers, London	0171 375 3012
Feltham Piers Jonathan	Chambers of Mr Peter Crampin QC, London	020 7831 0081
Fenton Adam Timothy Downs	S Tomlinson QC, London	0171 583 0404
Finlay Darren	Sovereign Chambers, Leeds	0113 2451841/2/3
Flaux Julian Martin	S Tomlinson QC, London	0171 583 0404
Fletcher Andrew Fitzroy Stephen	4 Pump Court, London	020 7842 5555
Forte Mark Julian Carmino	8 King Street Chambers, Manchester	0161 834 9560
Freedman Sampson Clive	3 Verulam Buildings, London	0171 831 8441
Fryer-Spedding James Walter	St James's Chambers, Manchester	0161 834 7000
Gaisman Jonathan Nicholas Crispin	S Tomlinson QC, London	0171 583 0404
Gardner Miss Eilidh Anne Mairi	22 Old Buildings, London	0171 831 0222
Gasztowicz Steven	2-3 Gray's Inn Square, London	0171 242 4986
	2 New Street, Leicester	0116 2625906
Gatt Ian Andrew	Littleton Chambers, London	0171 797 8600
Geary Gavin John	S Tomlinson QC, London	0171 583 0404
Gee Steven Mark	4 Field Court, London	0171 440 6900
Gerald Nigel Mortimer	Enterprise Chambers, London	0171 405 9471
	Enterprise Chambers, Leeds	0113 246 0391
	Enterprise Chambers, Newcastle upon Tyne	0191 222 3344
Ghaffar Arshad	4 Field Court, London	0171 440 6900
Gibaud Miss Catherine Alison Annetta	3 Verulam Buildings, London	0171 831 8441
Gibson Martin John	Littman Chambers, London	020 7404 4866
Goldstone David Julian	4 Field Court, London	0171 440 6900
Graham Thomas Patrick Henry	1 New Square, London	0171 405 0884/5/6/7
Grantham Andrew Timothy	•Deans Court Chambers, Manchester	0161 214 6000
	Deans Court Chambers, Preston	01772 555163
Green Miss Alison Anne	4 Field Court, London	0171 440 6900
Green Miss Amanda Jane	3 Verulam Buildings, London	0171 831 8441
Green Miss Jane Elizabeth	Design Chambers, London	0171 353 0747
	Chambers of Martin Burr, London	0171 353 4636
Gregory John Raymond	Deans Court Chambers, Manchester	0161 214 6000
	Deans Court Chambers, Preston	01772 555163
Gunning Alexander Rupert	4 Pump Court, London	020 7842 5555
Hall Mrs Melanie Ruth	Monckton Chambers, London	0171 405 7211

B

Hall Taylor Alexander Edward	11 Old Square, London	020 7430 0341
Hamilton Adrian Walter	S Tomlinson QC, London	0171 583 0404
Hamilton Graeme Montagu	Two Crown Office Row, London	020 7797 8100
Hantusch Robert Anthony	• 3 Stone Buildings, London	0171 242 4937
Harries Raymond Elwyn	Bracton Chambers, London	0171 242 4248
Harris Melvyn	7 New Square, London	0171 430 1660
Harris Paul Best	Monckton Chambers, London	0171 405 7211
Harvey Michael Llewellyn Tucker	Two Crown Office Row, London	020 7797 8100
Hatch Miss Lisa Sharmila	4 King's Bench Walk, London	0171 822 8822
Havelock-Allan Anthony Mark David	20 Essex Street, London	0171 583 9294
Healy Miss Sioban	S Tomlinson QC, London	0171 583 0404
Henley Raymond Francis St Luke	Lancaster Building, Manchester	0161 661 4444/0171 649 9872
Higgo Justin Beresford	Serle Court Chambers, London	0171 242 6105
Hill Timothy John	4 Field Court, London	0171 440 6900
Hirst William Timothy John	Park Court Chambers, Leeds	0113 2433277
Hockaday Miss Annie	3 Verulam Buildings, London	0171 831 8441
Hoffman David Alexander	8 King Street Chambers, Manchester	0161 834 9560
Hofmeyr Stephen Murray	S Tomlinson QC, London	0171 583 0404
Holroyd Charles Wilfrid	S Tomlinson QC, London	0171 583 0404
Hossain Ajmalul	• 29 Bedford Row Chambers, London	0171 831 2626
Howarth Simon Stuart	Two Crown Office Row, London	020 7797 8100
Hughes Adrian Warwick	4 Pump Court, London	020 7842 5555
Hurd James Robert	St James's Chambers, Manchester	0161 834 7000
Ivimy Ms Cecilia Rachel	11 King's Bench Walk, London	0171 632 8500/583 0610
Jabati Miss Maria Hannah	2 Middle Temple Lane, London	0171 583 4540
Jacobson Lawrence	5 Paper Buildings, London	0171 583 9275/583 4555
Jarron Miss Stephanie Allan	Westgate Chambers, Newcastle upon Tyne	0191 261 4407/2329785
Kay Robert Jervis	4 Field Court, London	0171 440 6900
Kealey Gavin Sean James	S Tomlinson QC, London	0171 583 0404
Kendrick Dominic John	S Tomlinson QC, London	0171 583 0404
Kenefick Timothy	S Tomlinson QC, London	0171 583 0404
Kenny Julian Hector Marriott	20 Essex Street, London	0171 583 9294
Kenny Stephen Charles Wilfrid	S Tomlinson QC, London	0171 583 0404
Kerr Simon Alexander	S Tomlinson QC, London	0171 583 0404
Khokhar Mushtaq Ahmed	Sovereign Chambers, Leeds	0113 2451841/2/3
Khurshid Jawdat	S Tomlinson QC, London	0171 583 0404
Kremen Philip Michael	Hardwicke Building, London	020 7242 2523
Kynoch Duncan Stuart Sanderson	29 Bedford Row Chambers, London	0171 831 2626
Lamb Robert Glasson	13 King's Bench Walk, London	0171 353 7204
	King's Bench Chambers, Oxford	01865 311066
Lambert John	Lancaster Building, Manchester	0161 661 4444/0171 649 9872
Lamont Miss Camilla Rose	Chambers of Lord Goodhart QC, London	0171 405 5577
Lavender Nicholas	One Hare Court, London	020 7353 3171
Lawson Robert John	4 Essex Court, London	020 7797 7970
Leason Ms Karen Dawn	St Philip's Chambers, Birmingham	0121 246 7000
Leiper Richard Thomas	11 King's Bench Walk, London	0171 632 8500/583 0610
Levin Craig Michael	Lancaster Building, Manchester	0161 661 4444/0171 649 9872
Lewis Andrew William	Sovereign Chambers, Leeds	0113 2451841/2/3
Littman Mark	Littman Chambers, London	020 7404 4866
Lowenstein Paul David	Littleton Chambers, London	0171 797 8600
Lumley Nicholas James Henry	Sovereign Chambers, Leeds	0113 2451841/2/3
Macdonald Charles Adam	4 Essex Court, London	020 7797 7970
Maclean Alan John	39 Essex Street, London	0171 832 1111
Macnab Alexander Andrew	Monckton Chambers, London	0171 405 7211
Malek Ali	3 Verulam Buildings, London	0171 831 8441
Males Stephen Martin	20 Essex Street, London	0171 583 9294
Malins Julian Henry	One Hare Court, London	020 7353 3171
Mandalia Vinesh Lalji	Harrow on the Hill Chambers, Harrow-on-the-Hill	0181 423 7444

• Expanded entry in Part D

Mann George Anthony	Enterprise Chambers, London	0171 405 9471
	Enterprise Chambers, Leeds	0113 246 0391
	Enterprise Chambers, Newcastle upon Tyne	0191 222 3344
Mantle Peter John	Monckton Chambers, London	0171 405 7211
Marks Jonathan Harold	3 Verulam Buildings, London	0171 831 8441
Marquand Charles Nicholas Hilary	Chambers of Lord Goodhart QC, London	0171 405 5577
Marshall Philip Scott	Serle Court Chambers, London	0171 242 6105
Matthews Duncan Henry Rowland	20 Essex Street, London	0171 583 9294
Maudslay Miss Diana Elizabeth	Sovereign Chambers, Leeds	0113 2451841/2/3
May Miss Juliet Mary	3 Verulam Buildings, London	0171 831 8441
Maynard-Connor Giles	St James's Chambers, Manchester	0161 834 7000
McClure Brian David	Littman Chambers, London	020 7404 4866
McCourt Christopher	22 Old Buildings, London	0171 831 0222
McGregor Harvey	4 Paper Buildings, London	0171 353 3366/583 7155
McKendrick Ewan Gordon	3 Verulam Buildings, London	0171 831 8441
McMaster Peter	Serle Court Chambers, London	0171 242 6105
McQuater Ewan Alan	3 Verulam Buildings, London	0171 831 8441
Meeson Nigel Keith	4 Field Court, London	0171 440 6900
Melville Richard David	● 39 Essex Street, London	0171 832 1111
Mercer Hugh Charles	● Essex Court Chambers, London	0171 813 8000
Merriman Nicholas Flavelle	3 Verulam Buildings, London	0171 831 8441
Metzer Anthony David Erwin	Doughty Street Chambers, London	0171 404 1313
Milligan Iain Anstruther	20 Essex Street, London	0171 583 9294
Moger Christopher Richard Derwent	4 Pump Court, London	020 7842 5555
Moran Andrew John	One Hare Court, London	020 7353 3171
Morgan Edward Patrick	Deans Court Chambers, Manchester	0161 214 6000
	Deans Court Chambers, Preston	01772 555163
Morgan Richard Hugo Lyndon	13 Old Square, London	0171 404 4800
Moser Philip Curt Harold	4 Paper Buildings, London	0171 353 3366/583 7155
Myers Allan James	4 Field Court, London	0171 440 6900
Naidoo Sean Van	Littman Chambers, London	020 7404 4866
Neill of Bladen Lord	One Hare Court, London	020 7353 3171
Nelson Vincent Leonard	39 Essex Street, London	0171 832 1111
Neville Stephen John	Gough Square Chambers, London	0171 353 0924
Neville-Clarke Sebastian Adrian Bennett	1 Crown Office Row, London	0171 583 9292
Newman Miss Catherine Mary	● 13 Old Square, London	0171 404 4800
Nicholls John Peter	13 Old Square, London	0171 404 4800
Nolan Michael Alfred Anthony	4 Essex Court, London	020 7797 7970
O'Leary Robert Michael	33 Park Place, Cardiff	02920 233313
O'Neill Tadhg Joseph	1 Crown Office Row, London	0171 583 9292
O'Shea Eoin Finbarr	4 Field Court, London	0171 440 6900
Odgers John Arthur	3 Verulam Buildings, London	0171 831 8441
Ohrenstein Dov	Chambers of Lord Goodhart QC, London	0171 405 5577
Onslow Andrew George	3 Verulam Buildings, London	0171 831 8441
Osman Robert Walter	Queen's Chambers, Manchester	0161 834 6875/4738
	Queens Chambers, Preston	01772 828300
Owen David Christopher	20 Essex Street, London	0171 583 9294
Padfield Nicholas David	One Hare Court, London	020 7353 3171
Page Howard William Barrett	One Hare Court, London	020 7353 3171
Parker Matthew Richard	3 Verulam Buildings, London	0171 831 8441
Parkin Jonathan	● Chambers of John Hand QC, Manchester	0161 955 9000
Patchett-Joyce Michael Thurston	Monckton Chambers, London	0171 405 7211
Patel Parishil Jayantilal	39 Essex Street, London	0171 832 1111
Pelling (Philip) Mark	Monckton Chambers, London	0171 405 7211
Pepperall Edward Brian	St Philip's Chambers, Birmingham	0121 246 7000
Perkins Miss Marianne Yvette	7 New Square, London	0171 430 1660
Persey Lionel Edward	● 4 Field Court, London	0171 440 6900
Pershad Rohan	Two Crown Office Row, London	020 7797 8100
Phillips Jonathan Mark	3 Verulam Buildings, London	0171 831 8441

Phillips S J	S Tomlinson QC, London	0171 583 0404
Phillips Stephen Edmund	3 Verulam Buildings, London	0171 831 8441
Picken Simon Derek	S Tomlinson QC, London	0171 583 0404
	30 Park Place, Cardiff	01222 398421
Pickersgill David William	Bell Yard Chambers, London	0171 306 9292
Pipi Chukwuemeka Ezekiel	Chambers of Martin Burr, London	0171 353 4636
Pirani Rohan Carl	Old Square Chambers, Bristol	0117 9277111
	Old Square Chambers, London	0171 269 0300
Plender Richard Owen	• 20 Essex Street, London	0171 583 9294
Pope David James	3 Verulam Buildings, London	0171 831 8441
Potts Warren Nigel	Queen's Chambers, Manchester	0161 834 6875/4738
	Queens Chambers, Preston	01772 828300
Priday Charles Nicholas Bruton	S Tomlinson QC, London	0171 583 0404
Quest David Charles	3 Verulam Buildings, London	0171 831 8441
Qureshi Khawar Mehmood	One Hare Court, London	020 7353 3171
Rankin Andrew	4 Field Court, London	0171 440 6900
Rashid Omar	Chambers of Mr Peter Crampin QC, London	020 7831 0081
Readings Douglas George	St Philip's Chambers, Birmingham	0121 246 7000
Reed John William Rupert	• Wilberforce Chambers, London	0171 306 0102
Reeder John	4 Field Court, London	0171 440 6900
Reynolds Professor Francis Martin Baillie	S Tomlinson QC, London	0171 583 0404
Richardson Giles John	Serle Court Chambers, London	0171 242 6105
Romney Miss Daphne Irene	4 Field Court, London	0171 440 6900
Russell Christopher Garnet	• 12 New Square, London	0171 419 1212
	Sovereign Chambers, Leeds	0113 2451841/2/3
Russell Jeremy Jonathan	• 4 Essex Court, London	020 7797 7970
Ryder Timothy Robert	Queen's Chambers, Manchester	0161 834 6875/4738
	Queens Chambers, Preston	01772 828300
Sabben-Clare Miss Rebecca Mary	S Tomlinson QC, London	0171 583 0404
Saloman Timothy Peter (Dayrell)	S Tomlinson QC, London	0171 583 0404
Salter Richard Stanley	3 Verulam Buildings, London	0171 831 8441
Sandells Ms Nicole	11 Old Square, London	020 7430 0341
Saunders Nicholas Joseph	4 Field Court, London	0171 440 6900
Schaff Alistair Graham	S Tomlinson QC, London	0171 583 0404
Seligman Matthew Thomas Arthur	39 Essex Street, London	0171 832 1111
Sellers Graham	Adrian Lyon's Chambers, Liverpool	0151 236 4421/8240
Selvaratnam Miss Vasanti Emily Indrani	4 Field Court, London	0171 440 6900
Selway Dr Katherine Emma	11 Old Square, London	020 7430 0341
Sephton Craig Gardner	Deans Court Chambers, Manchester	0161 214 6000
	Deans Court Chambers, Preston	01772 555163
Seymour Richard William	Monckton Chambers, London	0171 405 7211
Shannon Thomas Eric	Queen's Chambers, Manchester	0161 834 6875/4738
	Queens Chambers, Preston	01772 828300
Sheridan Maurice Bernard Gerard	• 3 Verulam Buildings, London	0171 831 8441
Siddiqi Faizul Aqtab	Justice Court Chambers, London	0181 830 7786
Simpson Mark Taylor	4 Paper Buildings, London	0171 353 3366/583 7155
Skelly Andrew Jon	1 Gray's Inn Square, London	0171 405 8946/7/8
Smail Alastair Harold Kurt	St Philip's Chambers, Birmingham	0121 246 7000
Smith Christopher Frank	Essex Court Chambers, London	0171 813 8000
Smith Paul Andrew	One Hare Court, London	020 7353 3171
Smith Warwick Timothy Cresswell	Deans Court Chambers, Manchester	0161 214 6000
	Deans Court Chambers, Preston	01772 555163
Southern Richard Michael	S Tomlinson QC, London	0171 583 0404
Southwell Richard Charles	One Hare Court, London	020 7353 3171
Spicer Robert Haden	Frederick Place Chambers, Bristol	0117 9738667
Staddon Miss Claire Ann	12 New Square, London	0171 419 1212
	Sovereign Chambers, Leeds	0113 2451841/2/3

• Expanded entry in Part D

Staunton (Thomas) Ulick (Patrick)	Chambers of Mr Peter Crampin QC, London	020 7831 0081
	65-67 King Street, Leicester	0116 2547710
Sterling Robert Alan	St James's Chambers, Manchester	0161 834 7000
	12 New Square, London	0171 419 1212
	Park Lane Chambers, Leeds	0113 2285000
Stevenson John Melford	Two Crown Office Row, London	020 7797 8100
Stilitz Daniel Malachi	11 King's Bench Walk, London	0171 632 8500/583 0610
Stokell Robert	Two Crown Office Row, London	020 7797 8100
Storey Jeremy Brian	4 Pump Court, London	020 7842 5555
Swindells Miss Heather Hughson	Chambers of Michael Pert QC, London	0171 421 8000
	Chambers of Michael Pert QC, Leicester	0116 249 2020
	Chambers of Michael Pert QC, Northampton	01604 602333
	St Philip's Chambers, Birmingham	0121 246 7000
Symons Christopher John Maurice	3 Verulam Buildings, London	0171 831 8441
Szanto Gregory John Michael	Eastbourne Chambers, Eastbourne	01323 642102
Tackaberry John Antony	Arbitration Chambers, London	020 7267 2137
	40 King Street, Manchester	0161 832 9082
	Assize Court Chambers, Bristol	0117 9264587
	Littman Chambers, London	020 7404 4866
Taft Christopher Heiton	St James's Chambers, Manchester	0161 834 7000
Tatton-Brown Daniel Nicholas	Littleton Chambers, London	0171 797 8600
Temple Anthony Dominic	4 Pump Court, London	020 7842 5555
Tolaney Miss Sonia	3 Verulam Buildings, London	0171 831 8441
Tomlinson Stephen Miles	S Tomlinson QC, London	0171 583 0404
Trace Anthony John	• 13 Old Square, London	0171 404 4800
Tselentis Michael	• 20 Essex Street, London	0171 583 9294
Tucker David William	Two Crown Office Row, London	020 7797 8100
Tully Ms Anne Margaret	Eastbourne Chambers, Eastbourne	01323 642102
Turner James Michael	• 4 Essex Court, London	020 7797 7970
Turner Miss Janet Mary	3 Verulam Buildings, London	0171 831 8441
Verduyn Dr Anthony James	St Philip's Chambers, Birmingham	0121 246 7000
Vickery Neil Michael	13 King's Bench Walk, London	0171 353 7204
	King's Bench Chambers, Oxford	01865 311066
Vineall Nicholas Edward John	4 Pump Court, London	020 7842 5555
Waller Richard Beaumont	S Tomlinson QC, London	0171 583 0404
Ward Timothy Justin	Monckton Chambers, London	0171 405 7211
Warrender Miss Nichola Mary	New Court Chambers, London	0171 831 9500
Watson-Gandy Mark	• Plowden Buildings, London	0171 583 0808
Weatherill Bernard Richard	Chambers of Lord Goodhart QC, London	0171 405 5577
Weitzman Thomas Edward Benjamin	3 Verulam Buildings, London	0171 831 8441
Whitehouse-Vaux William Edward	4 Field Court, London	0171 440 6900
Wilken Sean David Henry	39 Essex Street, London	0171 832 1111
Williams Andrew Arthur	Adrian Lyon's Chambers, Liverpool	0151 236 4421/8240
Williams Leigh Michael	S Tomlinson QC, London	0171 583 0404
Wilmot-Smith Richard James Crosbie	39 Essex Street, London	0171 832 1111
Wilson Ian Robert	3 Verulam Buildings, London	0171 831 8441
Wilson Peter Julian	Sovereign Chambers, Leeds	0113 2451841/2/3
Wood Richard Gillies	20 Essex Street, London	0171 583 9294
	Cathedral Chambers (Jan Wood Independent Barristers' Clerk), Exeter	01392 210900
Wynter Colin Peter	Devereux Chambers, London	0171 353 7534
Wyvill Alistair	St Philip's Chambers, Birmingham	0121 246 7000
Young Alastair Angus McLeod	St Philip's Chambers, Birmingham	0121 246 7000
Zaman Mohammed Khalil	St Philip's Chambers, Birmingham	0121 246 7000

COMMERCIAL FRAUD

Baylis Ms Natalie Jayne	3 Verulam Buildings, London	0171 831 8441
Beltrami Adrian Joseph	3 Verulam Buildings, London	0171 831 8441

Blair William James Lynton	3 Verulam Buildings, London	0171 831 8441
Davies-Jones Jonathan	3 Verulam Buildings, London	0171 831 8441
Hockaday Miss Annie	3 Verulam Buildings, London	0171 831 8441
Jarvis John Manners	3 Verulam Buildings, London	0171 831 8441
Kay Michael Jack David	3 Verulam Buildings, London	0171 831 8441
	Park Lane Chambers, Leeds	0113 2285000
Malek Ali	3 Verulam Buildings, London	0171 831 8441
May Miss Juliet Mary	3 Verulam Buildings, London	0171 831 8441
Nash Jonathan Scott	3 Verulam Buildings, London	0171 831 8441
Odgers John Arthur	3 Verulam Buildings, London	0171 831 8441
Onslow Andrew George	3 Verulam Buildings, London	0171 831 8441
Phillips Jonathan Mark	3 Verulam Buildings, London	0171 831 8441
Phillips S J	S Tomlinson QC, London	0171 583 0404
Phillips Stephen Edmund	3 Verulam Buildings, London	0171 831 8441
Pope David James	3 Verulam Buildings, London	0171 831 8441
Sutcliffe Andrew Harold Wentworth	3 Verulam Buildings, London	0171 831 8441
Tolaney Miss Sonia	3 Verulam Buildings, London	0171 831 8441

COMMERCIAL LITIGATION

Acton Stephen Neil	11 Old Square, London	020 7430 0341
Acton Davis Jonathan James	4 Pump Court, London	020 7842 5555
Adamyk Simon Charles	12 New Square, London	0171 419 1212
Adkin Jonathan William	One Hare Court, London	020 7353 3171
Akenhead Robert	Atkin Chambers, London	020 7404 0102
Allen Michael David Prior	S Tomlinson QC, London	0171 583 0404
Althaus Antony Justin	No. 1 Serjeants' Inn, London	0171 415 6666
Ambrose Miss Clare Mary Geneste	20 Essex Street, London	0171 583 9294
Anderson Miss Julie	• Littman Chambers, London	020 7404 4866
Ansell Miss Rachel Louise	4 Pump Court, London	020 7842 5555
Arden Peter Leonard	Enterprise Chambers, London	0171 405 9471
	Enterprise Chambers, Leeds	0113 246 0391
	Enterprise Chambers, Newcastle upon Tyne	0191 222 3344
Arentsen Andrew Nicholas	33 Park Place, Cardiff	02920 233313
Ashworth Lance Dominic Piers	St Philip's Chambers, Birmingham	0121 246 7000
	2 Harcourt Buildings, London	0171 583 9020
Ashworth Piers	2 Harcourt Buildings, London	0171 583 9020
Atherton Ian David	Enterprise Chambers, London	0171 405 9471
	Enterprise Chambers, Newcastle upon Tyne	0191 222 3344
	Enterprise Chambers, Leeds	0113 246 0391
Ayliffe James Justin Barnett	• Wilberforce Chambers, London	0171 306 0102
Ayres Andrew John William	13 Old Square, London	0171 404 4800
Baatz Nicholas Stephen	Atkin Chambers, London	020 7404 0102
Bacon Francis Michael	4 Paper Buildings, London	0171 353 3366/583 7155
Bailey David John	S Tomlinson QC, London	0171 583 0404
Bailey Edward Henry	Monckton Chambers, London	0171 405 7211
Baldock Nicholas John	6 Pump Court, London	0171 797 8400
	6-8 Mill Street, Maidstone	01622 688094
Baldry Antony Brian	No. 1 Serjeants' Inn, London	0171 415 6666
Barker James Sebastian	Enterprise Chambers, London	0171 405 9471
	Enterprise Chambers, Leeds	0113 246 0391
	Enterprise Chambers, Newcastle upon Tyne	0191 222 3344
Barker Simon George Harry	• 13 Old Square, London	0171 404 4800
Barlow Craig Martin	29 Bedford Row Chambers, London	0171 831 2626
Barwise Miss Stephanie Nicola	Atkin Chambers, London	020 7404 0102
Bather Miss Victoria Maclean	Littleton Chambers, London	0171 797 8600
Baylis Ms Natalie Jayne	3 Verulam Buildings, London	0171 831 8441
Beal Kieron Conrad	4 Paper Buildings, London	0171 353 3366/583 7155
Beard Daniel Matthew	Monckton Chambers, London	0171 405 7211

• Expanded entry in Part D

Beaumont Marc Clifford	• Harrow on the Hill Chambers, Harrow-on-the-Hill	0181 423 7444
	Windsor Barristers' Chambers, Windsor	01753 648899
	Pump Court Chambers, London	0171 353 0711
Beever Edmund Damian	St Philip's Chambers, Birmingham	0121 246 7000
Behrens James Nicholas Edward	Serle Court Chambers, London	0171 242 6105
Bellamy Jonathan Mark	39 Essex Street, London	0171 832 1111
Beltrami Adrian Joseph	3 Verulam Buildings, London	0171 831 8441
Bennett Gordon Irvine	12 New Square, London	0171 419 1212
Berry Nicholas Michael	Southernhay Chambers, Exeter	01392 255777
	1 Gray's Inn Square, London	0171 405 8946/7/8
	22 Old Buildings, London	0171 831 0222
Bignall John Francis	S Tomlinson QC, London	0171 583 0404
Birch Miss Elizabeth Blanche	3 Verulam Buildings, London	0171 831 8441
Birtles William	Old Square Chambers, London	0171 269 0300
	Old Square Chambers, Bristol	0117 9277111
Bishop Edward James	No. 1 Serjeants' Inn, London	0171 415 6666
Blackburn Mrs Elizabeth	4 Field Court, London	0171 440 6900
Blackburn John	Atkin Chambers, London	020 7404 0102
Blair William James Lynton	3 Verulam Buildings, London	0171 831 8441
Blakesley Patrick James	Two Crown Office Row, London	020 7797 8100
Blayney David James	Serle Court Chambers, London	0171 242 6105
Boswell Miss Lindsay Alice	4 Pump Court, London	020 7842 5555
Bourne Geoffrey Robert	4 Field Court, London	0171 440 6900
Bowdery Martin	Atkin Chambers, London	020 7404 0102
Bowker Robert James	2nd Floor, Francis Taylor Building, London	0171 353 9942/3157
Bowmer Michael Paul	11 Old Square, London	020 7430 0341
Boyd Stephen James Harvey	29 Bedford Row Chambers, London	0171 831 2626
Boyle Gerard James	No. 1 Serjeants' Inn, London	0171 415 6666
Brannigan Peter John Sean	4 Pump Court, London	020 7842 5555
Brent Richard	3 Verulam Buildings, London	0171 831 8441
Brenton Timothy Deane	4 Essex Court, London	020 7797 7970
Brice Geoffrey James Barrington	4 Field Court, London	0171 440 6900
Bridgman David Martin	No. 1 Serjeants' Inn, London	0171 415 6666
Briggs Michael Townley Featherstone	Serle Court Chambers, London	0171 242 6105
Bright Robert Graham	S Tomlinson QC, London	0171 583 0404
Browne-Wilkinson Simon	Serle Court Chambers, London	0171 242 6105
Bruce Andrew Jonathan	Serle Court Chambers, London	0171 242 6105
Bryant Keith	Devereux Chambers, London	0171 353 7534
Buck Dr Andrew Theodore	Chambers of Martin Burr, London	0171 353 4636
Buckingham Stewart John	4 Essex Court, London	020 7797 7970
Burden Edward Angus	St Philip's Chambers, Birmingham	0121 246 7000
Burnett Harold Wallace	4 Paper Buildings, London	0171 353 3366/583 7155
Burns Peter Richard	Deans Court Chambers, Manchester	0161 214 6000
	Deans Court Chambers, Preston	01772 555163
Burr Andrew Charles	Atkin Chambers, London	020 7404 0102
Butcher Christopher John	S Tomlinson QC, London	0171 583 0404
Butler Andrew	2nd Floor, Francis Taylor Building, London	0171 353 9942/3157
Cakebread Stuart Alan Charles	• 2nd Floor, Francis Taylor Building, London	0171 353 9942/3157
Campbell Stephen Gordon	St Philip's Chambers, Birmingham	0121 246 7000
Capon Philip Christopher William	St Philip's Chambers, Birmingham	0121 246 7000
Carr Bruce Conrad	Devereux Chambers, London	0171 353 7534
Castle Peter Bolton	Chambers of Mr Peter Crampin QC, London	020 7831 0081
Catchpole Stuart Paul	• 39 Essex Street, London	0171 832 1111
Cavanagh John Patrick	11 King's Bench Walk, London	0171 632 8500/583 0610
Chalmers Miss Suzanne Frances	Two Crown Office Row, London	020 7797 8100
Chambers Jonathan	4 Essex Court, London	020 7797 7970

• Expanded entry in Part D

Chapple James Malcolm Dundas	1 New Square, London	0171 405 0884/5/6/7
Charman Andrew Julian	St Philip's Chambers, Birmingham	0121 246 7000
Christie Aidan Patrick	4 Pump Court, London	020 7842 5555
Clark Andrew Richard	Manchester House Chambers, Manchester	0161 834 7007
	8 King Street Chambers, Manchester	0161 834 9560
Clarke Miss Alison Lee	No. 1 Serjeants' Inn, London	0171 415 6666
Clarke Ian James	Hardwicke Building, London	020 7242 2523
Clay Robert Charles	Atkin Chambers, London	020 7404 0102
Clegg Sebastian James Barwick	Deans Court Chambers, Manchester	0161 214 6000
	Deans Court Chambers, Preston	01772 555163
Close Douglas Jonathan	Serle Court Chambers, London	0171 242 6105
Collett Ivor William	No. 1 Serjeants' Inn, London	0171 415 6666
Collett Michael John	20 Essex Street, London	0171 583 9294
Collings Nicholas Stewart	Atkin Chambers, London	020 7404 0102
Conlon Michael Anthony	● One Essex Court, London	020 7583 2000
Cook Christopher Graham	St James's Chambers, Manchester	0161 834 7000
Cook Jeremy David	Lamb Building, London	020 7797 7788
Cooke Jeremy Lionel	S Tomlinson QC, London	0171 583 0404
Cooper Gilead Patrick	Chambers of Mr Peter Crampin QC, London	020 7831 0081
Cooper Nigel Stuart	4 Essex Court, London	020 7797 7970
Corbett James Patrick	St Philip's Chambers, Birmingham	0121 246 7000
	Chambers of Andrew Campbell QC, Leeds	0113 2455438
Craig Alistair Trevor	Chambers of Mr Peter Crampin QC, London	020 7831 0081
Craig Kenneth Allen	Hardwicke Building, London	020 7242 2523
Cranfield Peter Anthony	3 Verulam Buildings, London	0171 831 8441
Crawford Grant	11 Old Square, London	020 7430 0341
Cunningham Miss Claire Louise	St Philip's Chambers, Birmingham	0121 246 7000
Curtis Michael Alexander	Two Crown Office Row, London	020 7797 8100
Datta Mrs Wendy Patricia Mizal	Alban Chambers, London	0171 419 5051
Davey Benjamin Nicholas	11 Old Square, London	020 7430 0341
Davey Michael Philip	4 Field Court, London	0171 440 6900
Davidson Nicholas Ranking	4 Paper Buildings, London	0171 353 3366/583 7155
Davie Michael James	4 Pump Court, London	020 7842 5555
Davies Andrew Christopher	New Court Chambers, London	0171 831 9500
Davies Dr Charles Edward	4 Field Court, London	0171 440 6900
Davies Stephen Richard	8 King Street Chambers, Manchester	0161 834 9560
Davies Miss (Susan) Louise	12 New Square, London	0171 419 1212
	Sovereign Chambers, Leeds	0113 2451841/2/3
Davies-Jones Jonathan	3 Verulam Buildings, London	0171 831 8441
de Lacy Richard Michael	3 Verulam Buildings, London	0171 831 8441
de Waal John Henry Lowndes	St Philip's Chambers, Birmingham	0121 246 7000
Dean Brian John Anthony	St Philip's Chambers, Birmingham	0121 246 7000
Dennison Stephen Randell	Atkin Chambers, London	020 7404 0102
Dennys Nicholas Charles Jonathan	Atkin Chambers, London	020 7404 0102
Dillon Thomas William Matthew	1 Fountain Court, Birmingham	0121 236 5721
Dingemans James Michael	1 Crown Office Row, London	0171 583 9292
Doerries Miss Chantal-Aimee Renee Aemelia Annemarie	Atkin Chambers, London	020 7404 0102
Dooher Miss Nancy Helen	St James's Chambers, Manchester	0161 834 7000
Dougherty Nigel Peter	Erskine Chambers, London	0171 242 5532
Dowley Dominic Myles	One Hare Court, London	020 7353 3171
Drake David Christopher	Serle Court Chambers, London	0171 242 6105
Drake James Frederick	S Tomlinson QC, London	0171 583 0404
Dugdale Nicholas	4 Field Court, London	0171 440 6900
Dumaresq Ms Delia Jane	Atkin Chambers, London	020 7404 0102
Dyer Allen Gordon	4 Pump Court, London	020 7842 5555
Eadie James Raymond	One Hare Court, London	020 7353 3171

         ● Expanded entry in Part D

Edey Philip David	20 Essex Street, London	0171 583 9294
Edwards David Leslie	S Tomlinson QC, London	0171 583 0404
Edwards Richard Julian Henshaw	3 Verulam Buildings, London	0171 831 8441
Edwards-Stuart Antony James Cobham	Two Crown Office Row, London	020 7797 8100
Elleray Anthony John	• St James's Chambers, Manchester	0161 834 7000
	12 New Square, London	0171 419 1212
	Park Lane Chambers, Leeds	0113 2285000
Elliott Nicholas Blethyn	3 Verulam Buildings, London	0171 831 8441
Ellis Dr Peter Simon	7 New Square, London	0171 430 1660
Ellis Roger John	13 King's Bench Walk, London	0171 353 7204
	King's Bench Chambers, Oxford	01865 311066
Etherton Terence Michael Elkan Barnet	• Wilberforce Chambers, London	0171 306 0102
Evans James Frederick Meurig	3 Verulam Buildings, London	0171 831 8441
Evans Jonathan Edward	• Wilberforce Chambers, London	0171 306 0102
Evans Stephen James	8 King's Bench Walk, London	0171 797 8888
	8 King's Bench Walk North, Leeds	0113 2439797
Evans-Tovey Jason Robert	Two Crown Office Row, London	020 7797 8100
Eyre Stephen John Arthur	1 Fountain Court, Birmingham	0121 236 5721
Fadipe Gabriel Charles	• Wilberforce Chambers, London	0171 306 0102
Farber James Henry Martin	5 Stone Buildings, London	0171 242 6201
Faulks Edward Peter Lawless	No. 1 Serjeants' Inn, London	0171 415 6666
Feltham Piers Jonathan	Chambers of Mr Peter Crampin QC, London	020 7831 0081
Fenton Adam Timothy Downs	S Tomlinson QC, London	0171 583 0404
Fieldsend James William	2nd Floor, Francis Taylor Building, London	0171 353 9942/3157
Flaux Julian Martin	S Tomlinson QC, London	0171 583 0404
Fletcher Andrew Fitzroy Stephen	4 Pump Court, London	020 7842 5555
Forte Mark Julian Carmino	8 King Street Chambers, Manchester	0161 834 9560
Foster Brian Ian	St James's Chambers, Manchester	0161 834 7000
	Park Lane Chambers, Leeds	0113 2285000
Francis Edward Gerald Francis	Enterprise Chambers, London	0171 405 9471
	Enterprise Chambers, Leeds	0113 246 0391
	Enterprise Chambers, Newcastle upon Tyne	0191 222 3344
Franco Gianpiero	2 Middle Temple Lane, London	0171 583 4540
Fraser Peter Donald	Atkin Chambers, London	020 7404 0102
Freedman Sampson Clive	3 Verulam Buildings, London	0171 831 8441
Fryer-Spedding James Walter	St James's Chambers, Manchester	0161 834 7000
Furze Miss Caroline Mary	• Wilberforce Chambers, London	0171 306 0102
Gaisman Jonathan Nicholas Crispin	S Tomlinson QC, London	0171 583 0404
Garcia-Miller Miss Laura	Enterprise Chambers, London	0171 405 9471
	Enterprise Chambers, Leeds	0113 246 0391
	Enterprise Chambers, Newcastle upon Tyne	0191 222 3344
Garner Miss Sophie Jane	199 Strand, London	0171 379 9779
Gasztowicz Steven	2-3 Gray's Inn Square, London	0171 242 4986
	2 New Street, Leicester	0116 2625906
Gatt Ian Andrew	Littleton Chambers, London	0171 797 8600
Geary Gavin John	S Tomlinson QC, London	0171 583 0404
Gee Steven Mark	4 Field Court, London	0171 440 6900
Geering Ian Walter	3 Verulam Buildings, London	0171 831 8441
George Miss Judith Sarah	St Philip's Chambers, Birmingham	0121 246 7000
Gerald Nigel Mortimer	Enterprise Chambers, London	0171 405 9471
	Enterprise Chambers, Leeds	0113 246 0391
	Enterprise Chambers, Newcastle upon Tyne	0191 222 3344
Ghaffar Arshad	4 Field Court, London	0171 440 6900

B

• Expanded entry in Part D

Gibaud Miss Catherine Alison Annetta	3 Verulam Buildings, London	0171 831 8441
Gibson Martin John	Littman Chambers, London	020 7404 4866
Glasgow Edwin John	39 Essex Street, London	0171 832 1111
Goddard Andrew Stephen	Atkin Chambers, London	020 7404 0102
Godwin William George Henry	Atkin Chambers, London	020 7404 0102
Goldblatt Simon	39 Essex Street, London	0171 832 1111
Goldstone David Julian	4 Field Court, London	0171 440 6900
Gordon-Saker Andrew Stephen	Fenners Chambers, Cambridge	01223 368761
	Fenners Chambers, Peterborough	01733 562030
Goudie James	● 11 King's Bench Walk, London	0171 632 8500/583 0610
Graham Thomas Patrick Henry	1 New Square, London	0171 405 0884/5/6/7
Grantham Andrew Timothy	● Deans Court Chambers, Manchester	0161 214 6000
	Deans Court Chambers, Preston	01772 555163
Green Miss Alison Anne	4 Field Court, London	0171 440 6900
Green Miss Amanda Jane	3 Verulam Buildings, London	0171 831 8441
Green Miss Jane Elizabeth	Design Chambers, London	0171 353 0747
	Chambers of Martin Burr, London	0171 353 4636
Greenbourne John Hugo	Two Crown Office Row, London	020 7797 8100
Greenhill Julian Rutherford	● Wilberforce Chambers, London	0171 306 0102
Gregory John Raymond	Deans Court Chambers, Manchester	0161 214 6000
	Deans Court Chambers, Preston	01772 555163
Grime Mark Stephen Eastburn	Deans Court Chambers, Manchester	0161 214 6000
	2 Pump Court, London	0171 353 5597
	Deans Court Chambers, Preston	01772 555163
Grodzinski Samuel Marc	39 Essex Street, London	0171 832 1111
Guggenheim Miss Anna Maeve	Two Crown Office Row, London	020 7797 8100
Gun Cuninghame Julian Arthur	Gough Square Chambers, London	0171 353 0924
Gunning Alexander Rupert	4 Pump Court, London	020 7842 5555
Guy John David Colin	Francis Taylor Building, London	0171 797 7250
Hall Mrs Melanie Ruth	Monckton Chambers, London	0171 405 7211
Hall Taylor Alexander Edward	11 Old Square, London	020 7430 0341
Halpern David Anthony	Enterprise Chambers, London	0171 405 9471
	Enterprise Chambers, Leeds	0113 246 0391
	Enterprise Chambers, Newcastle upon Tyne	0191 222 3344
Hamilton Adrian Walter	S Tomlinson QC, London	0171 583 0404
Hamilton Graeme Montagu	Two Crown Office Row, London	020 7797 8100
Hammerton Alastair Rolf	No. 1 Serjeants' Inn, London	0171 415 6666
Hammerton Miss Veronica Lesley	No. 1 Serjeants' Inn, London	0171 415 6666
Hantusch Robert Anthony	● 3 Stone Buildings, London	0171 242 4937
Hardwick Matthew Richard	Enterprise Chambers, London	0171 405 9471
	Enterprise Chambers, Leeds	0113 246 0391
	Enterprise Chambers, Newcastle upon Tyne	0191 222 3344
Harris Melvyn	7 New Square, London	0171 430 1660
Harris Paul Best	Monckton Chambers, London	0171 405 7211
Harvey Michael Llewellyn Tucker	Two Crown Office Row, London	020 7797 8100
Havelock-Allan Anthony Mark David	20 Essex Street, London	0171 583 9294
Haynes Miss Rebecca	Monckton Chambers, London	0171 405 7211
Hayward Peter Michael	The Outer Temple, London	0171 353 4647
Healy Miss Sioban	S Tomlinson QC, London	0171 583 0404
Heather Christopher Mark	● 2nd Floor, Francis Taylor Building, London	0171 353 9942/3157
Hegarty Kevin John	St Philip's Chambers, Birmingham	0121 246 7000
Henderson Simon Alexander	4 Pump Court, London	020 7842 5555
Henley Raymond Francis St Luke	Lancaster Building, Manchester	0161 661 4444/0171 649 9872
Hibbert William John	Gough Square Chambers, London	0171 353 0924
Higgo Justin Beresford	Serle Court Chambers, London	0171 242 6105

● Expanded entry in Part D

Hill Robert Douglas	Pump Court Chambers, Winchester	01962 868161
	Pump Court Chambers, London	0171 353 0711
	Pump Court Chambers, Swindon	01793 539899
Hill Timothy John	4 Field Court, London	0171 440 6900
Hockaday Miss Annie	3 Verulam Buildings, London	0171 831 8441
Hodgkinson Tristram Patrick	• 5 Pump Court, London	020 7353 2532
Hodgson Timothy Paul	8 King Street Chambers, Manchester	0161 834 9560
Hofmeyr Stephen Murray	S Tomlinson QC, London	0171 583 0404
Holdsworth James Arthur	Two Crown Office Row, London	020 7797 8100
Holmes Philip John	8 King Street Chambers, Manchester	0161 834 9560
Holroyd Charles Wilfrid	S Tomlinson QC, London	0171 583 0404
Hoser Philip Jacob	Serle Court Chambers, London	0171 242 6105
Hossain Ajmalul	• 29 Bedford Row Chambers, London	0171 831 2626
Houghton Miss Kirsten Annette	4 Pump Court, London	020 7842 5555
Howard Michael Newman	4 Essex Court, London	020 7797 7970
Howells James Richard	Atkin Chambers, London	020 7404 0102
Hughes Adrian Warwick	4 Pump Court, London	020 7842 5555
Hunter William Quigley	No. 1 Serjeants' Inn, London	0171 415 6666
Hutchings Martin Anthony	199 Strand, London	0171 379 9779
Hutton Miss Caroline	Enterprise Chambers, London	0171 405 9471
	Enterprise Chambers, Leeds	0113 246 0391
	Enterprise Chambers, Newcastle upon Tyne	0191 222 3344
James Michael Frank	Enterprise Chambers, London	0171 405 9471
	Enterprise Chambers, Leeds	0113 246 0391
	Enterprise Chambers, Newcastle upon Tyne	0191 222 3344
Jefferis Arthur Michael Quentin	Chambers of Mr Peter Crampin QC, London	020 7831 0081
Jess Digby Charles	8 King Street Chambers, Manchester	0161 834 9560
Joffe Victor Howard	Serle Court Chambers, London	0171 242 6105
Johnston Anthony Paul	1 Fountain Court, Birmingham	0121 236 5721
Jones Clive Hugh	1 New Square, London	0171 405 0884/5/6/7
Jones Miss Elizabeth Sian	Serle Court Chambers, London	0171 242 6105
Jones Philip John	Serle Court Chambers, London	0171 242 6105
Jory Robert John Hugh	Enterprise Chambers, London	0171 405 9471
	Enterprise Chambers, Leeds	0113 246 0391
	Enterprise Chambers, Newcastle upon Tyne	0191 222 3344
Kay Michael Jack David	3 Verulam Buildings, London	0171 831 8441
	Park Lane Chambers, Leeds	0113 2285000
Kay Robert Jervis	4 Field Court, London	0171 440 6900
Kealey Gavin Sean James	S Tomlinson QC, London	0171 583 0404
Kendrick Dominic John	S Tomlinson QC, London	0171 583 0404
Kenefick Timothy	S Tomlinson QC, London	0171 583 0404
Kenny Julian Hector Marriott	20 Essex Street, London	0171 583 9294
Kenny Stephen Charles Wilfrid	S Tomlinson QC, London	0171 583 0404
Kent Michael Harcourt	Two Crown Office Row, London	020 7797 8100
Kerr Simon Alexander	S Tomlinson QC, London	0171 583 0404
Khurshid Jawdat	S Tomlinson QC, London	0171 583 0404
Kolodziej Andrzej Jozef	• Littman Chambers, London	020 7404 4866
Kremen Philip Michael	Hardwicke Building, London	020 7242 2523
Kuschke Leon Siegfried	Erskine Chambers, London	0171 242 5532
Kverndal Simon Richard	4 Essex Court, London	020 7797 7970
Kynoch Duncan Stuart Sanderson	29 Bedford Row Chambers, London	0171 831 2626
Laing Miss Elisabeth Mary Caroline	11 King's Bench Walk, London	0171 632 8500/583 0610
Lamb Robert Glasson	13 King's Bench Walk, London	0171 353 7204
	King's Bench Chambers, Oxford	01865 311066
Lamont Miss Camilla Rose	Chambers of Lord Goodhart QC, London	0171 405 5577
Landes Miss Anna-Rose	St Philip's Chambers, Birmingham	0121 246 7000
Lavender Nicholas	One Hare Court, London	020 7353 3171

Lawrence The Hon Patrick John Tristram	4 Paper Buildings, London	0171 353 3366/583 7155
Lazarus Michael Steven	1 Crown Office Row, London	0171 583 9292
Leech Brian Walter Thomas	No. 1 Serjeants' Inn, London	0171 415 6666
Lennard Stephen Charles	Hardwicke Building, London	020 7242 2523
Levene Victor	1 Gray's Inn Square, London	0171 405 8946/7/8
Levin Craig Michael	Lancaster Building, Manchester	0161 661 4444/0171 649 9872
Levy Benjamin Keith	Enterprise Chambers, London	0171 405 9471
	Enterprise Chambers, Leeds	0113 246 0391
	Enterprise Chambers, Newcastle upon Tyne	0191 222 3344
Lightman Daniel	Serle Court Chambers, London	0171 242 6105
Littman Mark	Littman Chambers, London	020 7404 4866
Lo Bernard Norman	17 Bedford Row, London	0171 831 7314
Lowe David Alexander	• Wilberforce Chambers, London	0171 306 0102
Lowe Thomas William Gordon	• Wilberforce Chambers, London	0171 306 0102
Lowenstein Paul David	Littleton Chambers, London	0171 797 8600
Lucas Miss Bridget Ann	Serle Court Chambers, London	0171 242 6105
	Fountain Court, London	0171 583 3335
Lynagh Richard Dudley	Two Crown Office Row, London	020 7797 8100
Macdonald Charles Adam	4 Essex Court, London	020 7797 7970
Macnab Alexander Andrew	Monckton Chambers, London	0171 405 7211
Malek Ali	3 Verulam Buildings, London	0171 831 8441
Males Stephen Martin	20 Essex Street, London	0171 583 9294
Malins Julian Henry	One Hare Court, London	020 7353 3171
Mandalia Vinesh Lalji	Harrow on the Hill Chambers, Harrow-on-the-Hill	0181 423 7444
Mann George Anthony	Enterprise Chambers, London	0171 405 9471
	Enterprise Chambers, Leeds	0113 246 0391
	Enterprise Chambers, Newcastle upon Tyne	0191 222 3344
Mantle Peter John	Monckton Chambers, London	0171 405 7211
Manzoni Charles Peter	39 Essex Street, London	0171 832 1111
Marks Jonathan Clive	4 Pump Court, London	020 7842 5555
Marks Jonathan Harold	3 Verulam Buildings, London	0171 831 8441
Marquand Charles Nicholas Hilary	Chambers of Lord Goodhart QC, London	0171 405 5577
Marshall Philip Scott	Serle Court Chambers, London	0171 242 6105
Martin John Vandeleur	• Wilberforce Chambers, London	0171 306 0102
Masters Miss Sara Alayna	20 Essex Street, London	0171 583 9294
Matthews Duncan Henry Rowland	20 Essex Street, London	0171 583 9294
Maxwell-Scott James Herbert	Two Crown Office Row, London	020 7797 8100
Maynard-Connor Giles	St James's Chambers, Manchester	0161 834 7000
McAlinden Barry O'Neill	17 Bedford Row, London	0171 831 7314
McCahill Patrick Gerard	St Philip's Chambers, Birmingham	0121 246 7000
	Chambers of Andrew Campbell QC, Leeds	0113 2455438
McCall Duncan James	4 Pump Court, London	020 7842 5555
McClure Brian David	Littman Chambers, London	020 7404 4866
McGregor Harvey	4 Paper Buildings, London	0171 353 3366/583 7155
McKinnell Miss Soraya Jane	Enterprise Chambers, London	0171 405 9471
	Enterprise Chambers, Newcastle upon Tyne	0191 222 3344
	Enterprise Chambers, Leeds	0113 246 0391
McMaster Peter	Serle Court Chambers, London	0171 242 6105
McMullan Manus Anthony	Atkin Chambers, London	020 7404 0102
McQuater Ewan Alan	3 Verulam Buildings, London	0171 831 8441
Meeson Nigel Keith	4 Field Court, London	0171 440 6900
Melville Richard David	• 39 Essex Street, London	0171 832 1111
Mendoza Neil David Pereira	Hardwicke Building, London	020 7242 2523
Mercer Hugh Charles	• Essex Court Chambers, London	0171 813 8000
Merriman Nicholas Flavelle	3 Verulam Buildings, London	0171 831 8441

• **Expanded entry in Part D**

Milligan Iain Anstruther	20 Essex Street, London	0171 583 9294
Mitchell Gregory Charles Mathew	3 Verulam Buildings, London	0171 831 8441
Mitropoulos Christos	Chambers of Geoffrey Hawker, London	0171 583 8899
Moger Christopher Richard Derwent	4 Pump Court, London	020 7842 5555
Moran Andrew John	One Hare Court, London	020 7353 3171
Morgan Andrew James	St Philip's Chambers, Birmingham	0121 246 7000
Morgan Charles James Arthur	Enterprise Chambers, London	0171 405 9471
	Enterprise Chambers, Newcastle upon Tyne	0191 222 3344
	Enterprise Chambers, Leeds	0113 246 0391
Morgan Richard Hugo Lyndon	13 Old Square, London	0171 404 4800
Morris Stephen Nathan	20 Essex Street, London	0171 583 9294
Mortimer Miss Sophie Kate	No. 1 Serjeants' Inn, London	0171 415 6666
Mulcahy Miss Leigh-Ann Maria	Chambers of John L Powell QC, London	0171 797 8000
Mulholland Michael	St James's Chambers, Manchester	0161 834 7000
Myers Allan James	4 Field Court, London	0171 440 6900
Naidoo Sean Van	Littman Chambers, London	020 7404 4866
Nardell Gordon Lawrence	6 Pump Court, London	0171 797 8400
	6-8 Mill Street, Maidstone	01622 688094
Nash Jonathan Scott	3 Verulam Buildings, London	0171 831 8441
Naughton Philip Anthony	3 Serjeants' Inn, London	0171 353 5537
Naylor Dr Kevin Michael Thomas	8 King Street Chambers, Manchester	0161 834 9560
Neill of Bladen Lord	One Hare Court, London	020 7353 3171
Neish Andrew Graham	4 Pump Court, London	020 7842 5555
Nesbitt Timothy John Robert	199 Strand, London	0171 379 9779
Neville Stephen John	Gough Square Chambers, London	0171 353 0924
Neville-Clarke Sebastian Adrian Bennett	1 Crown Office Row, London	0171 583 9292
Newman Miss Catherine Mary	• 13 Old Square, London	0171 404 4800
Newman Ms Ingrid	Hardwicke Building, London	020 7242 2523
Nicholls John Peter	13 Old Square, London	0171 404 4800
Nolan Michael Alfred Anthony	4 Essex Court, London	020 7797 7970
Norbury Hugh Robert	Serle Court Chambers, London	0171 242 6105
Norman Christopher John George	No. 1 Serjeants' Inn, London	0171 415 6666
Nugee Christopher George	• Wilberforce Chambers, London	0171 306 0102
Nurse Gordon Bramwell William	11 Old Square, London	020 7430 0341
O'Connor Andrew McDougal	Two Crown Office Row, London	020 7797 8100
O'Leary Robert Michael	33 Park Place, Cardiff	02920 233313
O'Shea Eoin Finbarr	4 Field Court, London	0171 440 6900
O'Sullivan Thomas Sean Patrick	4 Pump Court, London	020 7842 5555
Oakley Paul James	1 Gray's Inn Square, London	0171 405 8946/7/8
Odgers John Arthur	3 Verulam Buildings, London	0171 831 8441
Ohrenstein Dov	Chambers of Lord Goodhart QC, London	0171 405 5577
Onslow Andrew George	3 Verulam Buildings, London	0171 831 8441
Osman Robert Walter	Queen's Chambers, Manchester	0161 834 6875/4738
	Queens Chambers, Preston	01772 828300
Owen David Christopher	20 Essex Street, London	0171 583 9294
Padfield Ms Alison Mary	Devereux Chambers, London	0171 353 7534
Padfield Nicholas David	One Hare Court, London	020 7353 3171
Page Howard William Barrett	One Hare Court, London	020 7353 3171
Paneth Miss Sarah Ruth	No. 1 Serjeants' Inn, London	0171 415 6666
Parker Matthew Richard	3 Verulam Buildings, London	0171 831 8441
Parkin Miss Fiona Jane	Atkin Chambers, London	020 7404 0102
Patchett-Joyce Michael Thurston	Monckton Chambers, London	0171 405 7211
Patten Benedict Joseph	Two Crown Office Row, London	020 7797 8100
Peacock Nicholas Christopher	13 Old Square, London	0171 404 4800
Peacocke Mrs Teresa Anne Rosen	Enterprise Chambers, London	0171 405 9471
	Enterprise Chambers, Leeds	0113 246 0391
	Enterprise Chambers, Newcastle upon Tyne	0191 222 3344
Pearson Christopher	• Bridewell Chambers, London	020 7797 8800

Pelling (Philip) Mark	Monckton Chambers, London	0171 405 7211
Peretz George Michael John	Monckton Chambers, London	0171 405 7211
Perkoff Richard Michael	Littleton Chambers, London	0171 797 8600
Persey Lionel Edward	• 4 Field Court, London	0171 440 6900
Pershad Rohan	Two Crown Office Row, London	020 7797 8100
Phillips Andrew Charles	Two Crown Office Row, London	020 7797 8100
Phillips David John	199 Strand, London	0171 379 9779
	30 Park Place, Cardiff	01222 398421
Phillips Jonathan Mark	3 Verulam Buildings, London	0171 831 8441
Phillips S J	S Tomlinson QC, London	0171 583 0404
Phillips Stephen Edmund	3 Verulam Buildings, London	0171 831 8441
Picken Simon Derek	S Tomlinson QC, London	0171 583 0404
	30 Park Place, Cardiff	01222 398421
Pickering James Patrick	Enterprise Chambers, London	0171 405 9471
	Enterprise Chambers, Leeds	0113 246 0391
	Enterprise Chambers, Newcastle upon Tyne	0191 222 3344
Pinder Miss Mary Elizabeth	No. 1 Serjeants' Inn, London	0171 415 6666
Piper Angus Richard	No. 1 Serjeants' Inn, London	0171 415 6666
Pirani Rohan Carl	Old Square Chambers, Bristol	0117 9277111
	Old Square Chambers, London	0171 269 0300
Pitt-Payne Timothy Sheridan	• 11 King's Bench Walk, London	0171 632 8500/583 0610
Pittaway David Michael	No. 1 Serjeants' Inn, London	0171 415 6666
Pliener David Jonathan	New Court Chambers, London	0171 831 9500
Pope David James	3 Verulam Buildings, London	0171 831 8441
Porter David Leonard	St James's Chambers, Manchester	0161 834 7000
	Park Lane Chambers, Leeds	0113 2285000
Potts Robin	Erskine Chambers, London	0171 242 5532
Potts Warren Nigel	Queen's Chambers, Manchester	0161 834 6875/4738
	Queens Chambers, Preston	01772 828300
Power Lawrence Imam	4 King's Bench Walk, London	0171 822 8822
Price Richard Mervyn	Littleton Chambers, London	0171 797 8600
Priday Charles Nicholas Bruton	S Tomlinson QC, London	0171 583 0404
Quest David Charles	3 Verulam Buildings, London	0171 831 8441
Qureshi Khawar Mehmood	One Hare Court, London	020 7353 3171
Raeside Mark Andrew	Atkin Chambers, London	020 7404 0102
Rankin Andrew	4 Field Court, London	0171 440 6900
Rashid Omar	Chambers of Mr Peter Crampin QC, London	020 7831 0081
Rawley Miss Dominique Jane	Atkin Chambers, London	020 7404 0102
Readhead Simon John Howard	No. 1 Serjeants' Inn, London	0171 415 6666
Reed John William Rupert	• Wilberforce Chambers, London	0171 306 0102
Reeder John	4 Field Court, London	0171 440 6900
Reese Colin Edward	Atkin Chambers, London	020 7404 0102
Reid Sebastian Peter Scott	2nd Floor, Francis Taylor Building, London	0171 353 9942/3157
Renfree Peter Gerald Stanley	Harbour Court Chambers, Fareham	01329 827828
Rich Jonathan Bernard George	5 Paper Buildings, London	0171 583 9275/583 4555
Richardson Giles John	Serle Court Chambers, London	0171 242 6105
Rigney Andrew James	Two Crown Office Row, London	020 7797 8100
Rivalland Marc-Edouard	No. 1 Serjeants' Inn, London	0171 415 6666
Robb Adam Duncan	39 Essex Street, London	0171 832 1111
Roberts Miss Catherine Ann	Erskine Chambers, London	0171 242 5532
Rochford Thomas Nicholas Beverley	St Philip's Chambers, Birmingham	0121 246 7000
Rogers Miss Beverly-Ann	Serle Court Chambers, London	0171 242 6105
Rogers Ian Paul	1 Crown Office Row, London	0171 583 9292
Rolfe Patrick John Benedict	5 Stone Buildings, London	0171 242 6201
Romney Miss Daphne Irene	4 Field Court, London	0171 440 6900
Ross John Graffin	No. 1 Serjeants' Inn, London	0171 415 6666
Roth Peter Marcel	Monckton Chambers, London	0171 405 7211
Rowlands Marc Humphreys	4 Pump Court, London	020 7842 5555

Rowley Keith Nigel	11 Old Square, London	020 7430 0341
Royce Darryl Fraser	Atkin Chambers, London	020 7404 0102
Rumney Conrad William Arthur	St Philip's Chambers, Birmingham	0121 246 7000
Russell Christopher Garnet	• 12 New Square, London	0171 419 1212
	Sovereign Chambers, Leeds	0113 2451841/2/3
Russell Jeremy Jonathan	• 4 Essex Court, London	020 7797 7970
Ryder Timothy Robert	Queen's Chambers, Manchester	0161 834 6875/4738
	Queens Chambers, Preston	01772 828300
Sabben-Clare Miss Rebecca Mary	S Tomlinson QC, London	0171 583 0404
Salmon Jonathan Carl	1 Fountain Court, Birmingham	0121 236 5721
Saloman Timothy Peter (Dayrell)	S Tomlinson QC, London	0171 583 0404
Salter Richard Stanley	3 Verulam Buildings, London	0171 831 8441
Sandbrook-Hughes Stewert Karl Anthony	Iscoed Chambers, Swansea	01792 652988/9/330
Sandells Ms Nicole	11 Old Square, London	020 7430 0341
Saunders Nicholas Joseph	4 Field Court, London	0171 440 6900
Schaff Alistair Graham	S Tomlinson QC, London	0171 583 0404
Scorah Christopher James	8 King Street Chambers, Manchester	0161 834 9560
Seal Julius Damien	189 Randolph Avenue, London	0171 624 9139
Sears Robert David Murray	4 Pump Court, London	020 7842 5555
Segal Oliver Leon	Old Square Chambers, London	0171 269 0300
	Old Square Chambers, Bristol	0117 9277111
Sellers Graham	Adrian Lyon's Chambers, Liverpool	0151 236 4421/8240
Selvaratnam Miss Vasanti Emily Indrani	4 Field Court, London	0171 440 6900
Selway Dr Katherine Emma	11 Old Square, London	020 7430 0341
Sendall Antony John Christmas	Littleton Chambers, London	0171 797 8600
Seymour Richard William	Monckton Chambers, London	0171 405 7211
Shannon Thomas Eric	Queen's Chambers, Manchester	0161 834 6875/4738
	Queens Chambers, Preston	01772 828300
Sheehan Malcolm Peter	2 Harcourt Buildings, London	0171 583 9020
Sheldon Clive David	11 King's Bench Walk, London	0171 632 8500/583 0610
Sher Jules	• Wilberforce Chambers, London	0171 306 0102
Sheridan Maurice Bernard Gerard	• 3 Verulam Buildings, London	0171 831 8441
Shrimpton Michael	Francis Taylor Building, London	0171 797 7250
Shukla Ms Vina	New Court Chambers, London	0171 831 9500
Siddiqi Faizul Aqtab	Justice Court Chambers, London	0181 830 7786
Simor Miss Jessica Margaret Poppaea	Monckton Chambers, London	0171 405 7211
Singh Kuldip	Five Paper Buildings, London	0171 583 6117
Skelly Andrew Jon	1 Gray's Inn Square, London	0171 405 8946/7/8
Skilbeck Mrs Jennifer Seth	Monckton Chambers, London	0171 405 7211
Smith Christopher Frank	Essex Court Chambers, London	0171 813 8000
Smith Ms Katherine Emma	Monckton Chambers, London	0171 405 7211
Smith Michael Joseph	8 King Street Chambers, Manchester	0161 834 9560
Smith Paul Andrew	One Hare Court, London	020 7353 3171
Smith Warwick Timothy Cresswell	Deans Court Chambers, Manchester	0161 214 6000
	Deans Court Chambers, Preston	01772 555163
Snowden John Stevenson	Two Crown Office Row, London	020 7797 8100
Snowden Richard Andrew	Erskine Chambers, London	0171 242 5532
Southall Richard Anthony	• 17 Bedford Row, London	0171 831 7314
Southern Richard Michael	S Tomlinson QC, London	0171 583 0404
Southwell Richard Charles	One Hare Court, London	020 7353 3171
Staddon Miss Claire Ann	12 New Square, London	0171 419 1212
	Sovereign Chambers, Leeds	0113 2451841/2/3
Stagg Paul Andrew	No. 1 Serjeants' Inn, London	0171 415 6666
Starcevic Petar	St Philip's Chambers, Birmingham	0121 246 7000
Stark James Hayden Alexander	Chambers of Ian Macdonald QC (In Association with Two Garden Court, Temple, London), Manchester	0161 236 1840
Start Miss Angharad Jocelyn	3 Verulam Buildings, London	0171 831 8441

B

Staunton (Thomas) Ulick (Patrick)	Chambers of Mr Peter Crampin QC, London	020 7831 0081
	65-67 King Street, Leicester	0116 2547710
Sterling Robert Alan	St James's Chambers, Manchester	0161 834 7000
	12 New Square, London	0171 419 1212
	Park Lane Chambers, Leeds	0113 2285000
Stevens Howard Linton	1 Crown Office Row, London	0171 583 9292
Stewart Nicholas John Cameron	Hardwicke Building, London	020 7242 2523
Stilitz Daniel Malachi	11 King's Bench Walk, London	0171 632 8500/583 0610
Stokes Miss Mary Elizabeth	Erskine Chambers, London	0171 242 5532
Storey Jeremy Brian	4 Pump Court, London	020 7842 5555
Streatfeild-James David Stewart	Atkin Chambers, London	020 7404 0102
Sutcliffe Andrew Harold Wentworth	3 Verulam Buildings, London	0171 831 8441
Swan Ian Christopher	Two Crown Office Row, London	020 7797 8100
Swerling Robert Harry	13 Old Square, London	0171 404 4800
Symons Christopher John Maurice	3 Verulam Buildings, London	0171 831 8441
Szanto Gregory John Michael	Eastbourne Chambers, Eastbourne	01323 642102
Talbot Patrick John	Serle Court Chambers, London	0171 242 6105
Taylor Miss Deborah Frances	Two Crown Office Row, London	020 7797 8100
Teare Nigel John Martin	4 Essex Court, London	020 7797 7970
Tecks Jonathan Howard	Littman Chambers, London	020 7404 4866
Tedd Rex Hilary	• St Philip's Chambers, Birmingham	0121 246 7000
	De Montfort Chambers, Leicester	0116 254 8686
	Northampton Chambers, Northampton	01604 636271
Temple Anthony Dominic	4 Pump Court, London	020 7842 5555
Tennet Michael John	• Wilberforce Chambers, London	0171 306 0102
Ter Haar Roger Eduard Lound	Two Crown Office Row, London	020 7797 8100
Terry Robert Jeffrey	8 King Street Chambers, Manchester	0161 834 9560
Thom James Alexander Francis	4 Field Court, London	0171 440 6900
Thompson Andrew Richard	Erskine Chambers, London	0171 242 5532
Thompson Rhodri William Ralph	Monckton Chambers, London	0171 405 7211
Tolaney Miss Sonia	3 Verulam Buildings, London	0171 831 8441
Tomlinson Stephen Miles	S Tomlinson QC, London	0171 583 0404
Tozzi Nigel Kenneth	4 Pump Court, London	020 7842 5555
Trace Anthony John	• 13 Old Square, London	0171 404 4800
Tselentis Michael	• 20 Essex Street, London	0171 583 9294
Tucker David William	Two Crown Office Row, London	020 7797 8100
Tucker Miss Katherine Jane Greening	St Philip's Chambers, Birmingham	0121 246 7000
Tully Ms Anne Margaret	Eastbourne Chambers, Eastbourne	01323 642102
Turner James Michael	• 4 Essex Court, London	020 7797 7970
Turner Miss Janet Mary	3 Verulam Buildings, London	0171 831 8441
Turner Jonathan Richard	Monckton Chambers, London	0171 405 7211
Ullstein Augustus Rupert Patrick A	• 29 Bedford Row Chambers, London	0171 831 2626
Valentine Donald Graham	Atkin Chambers, London	020 7404 0102
Van Tonder Gerard Dirk	1 New Square, London	0171 405 0884/5/6/7
Vaughan-Neil Miss Catherine Mary Bernardine	4 Pump Court, London	020 7842 5555
Vickery Neil Michael	13 King's Bench Walk, London	0171 353 7204
	King's Bench Chambers, Oxford	01865 311066
Wadsworth James Patrick	4 Paper Buildings, London	0171 353 3366/583 7155
Walden-Smith Miss Karen Jane	5 Stone Buildings, London	0171 242 6201
Wales Andrew Nigel Malcolm	S Tomlinson QC, London	0171 583 0404
Walford Richard Henry Howard	Serle Court Chambers, London	0171 242 6105
Walker Steven John	Atkin Chambers, London	020 7404 0102
Wallace Ian Norman Duncan	Atkin Chambers, London	020 7404 0102
Waller Richard Beaumont	S Tomlinson QC, London	0171 583 0404
Warnock Andrew Ronald	No. 1 Serjeants' Inn, London	0171 415 6666
Warrender Miss Nichola Mary	New Court Chambers, London	0171 831 9500
Waters Julian William Penrose	No. 1 Serjeants' Inn, London	0171 415 6666
Watson-Gandy Mark	• Plowden Buildings, London	0171 583 0808
Weatherill Bernard Richard	Chambers of Lord Goodhart QC, London	0171 405 5577

       • Expanded entry in Part D

Weitzman Thomas Edward Benjamin	3 Verulam Buildings, London	0171 831 8441
West Mark	• 11 Old Square, London	020 7430 0341
West-Knights Laurence James	4 Paper Buildings, London	0171 353 3366/583 7155
Westgate Martin Trevor	Doughty Street Chambers, London	0171 404 1313
Weston Clive Aubrey Richard	Two Crown Office Row, London	020 7797 8100
White Andrew	Atkin Chambers, London	020 7404 0102
Whitehouse-Vaux William Edward	4 Field Court, London	0171 440 6900
Whittaker John Percival	Serle Court Chambers, London	0171 242 6105
Wicks Ms Joanne	• Wilberforce Chambers, London	0171 306 0102
Wilby David Christopher	• 199 Strand, London	0171 379 9779
	Park Lane Chambers, Leeds	0113 2285000
Wilkins Mrs Colette Ann	1 New Square, London	0171 405 0884/5/6/7
Williams Andrew Arthur	Adrian Lyon's Chambers, Liverpool	0151 236 4421/8240
Williams Leigh Michael	S Tomlinson QC, London	0171 583 0404
Wilson Ian Robert	3 Verulam Buildings, London	0171 831 8441
Wilson-Barnes Miss Lucy Emma	St James's Chambers, Manchester	0161 834 7000
Wood Ian Robert	8 King Street Chambers, Manchester	0161 834 9560
Wood Richard Gillies	20 Essex Street, London	0171 583 9294
	Cathedral Chambers (Jan Wood Independent Barristers' Clerk), Exeter	01392 210900
Wright Colin John	4 Field Court, London	0171 440 6900
Wynter Colin Peter	Devereux Chambers, London	0171 353 7534
Yell Nicholas Anthony	No. 1 Serjeants' Inn, London	0171 415 6666
Zaman Mohammed Khalil	St Philip's Chambers, Birmingham	0121 246 7000
Zelin Geoffrey Andrew	Enterprise Chambers, London	0171 405 9471
	Enterprise Chambers, Leeds	0113 246 0391
	Enterprise Chambers, Newcastle upon Tyne	0191 222 3344

COMMERCIAL PROPERTY

Acton Stephen Neil	11 Old Square, London	020 7430 0341
Asprey Nicholas	Serle Court Chambers, London	0171 242 6105
Atherton Ian David	Enterprise Chambers, London	0171 405 9471
	Enterprise Chambers, Newcastle upon Tyne	0191 222 3344
	Enterprise Chambers, Leeds	0113 246 0391
Ayliffe James Justin Barnett	• Wilberforce Chambers, London	0171 306 0102
Ayres Andrew John William	13 Old Square, London	0171 404 4800
Baker Miss Anne Jacqueline	Enterprise Chambers, London	0171 405 9471
	Enterprise Chambers, Leeds	0113 246 0391
	Enterprise Chambers, Newcastle upon Tyne	0191 222 3344
Baldry Antony Brian	No. 1 Serjeants' Inn, London	0171 415 6666
Barker James Sebastian	Enterprise Chambers, London	0171 405 9471
	Enterprise Chambers, Leeds	0113 246 0391
	Enterprise Chambers, Newcastle upon Tyne	0191 222 3344
Barnes (David) Michael (William)	• Wilberforce Chambers, London	0171 306 0102
Beaumont Marc Clifford	• Harrow on the Hill Chambers, Harrow-on-the-Hill	0181 423 7444
	Windsor Barristers' Chambers, Windsor	01753 648899
	Pump Court Chambers, London	0171 353 0711
Behrens James Nicholas Edward	Serle Court Chambers, London	0171 242 6105
Berry Nicholas Michael	Southernhay Chambers, Exeter	01392 255777
	1 Gray's Inn Square, London	0171 405 8946/7/8
	22 Old Buildings, London	0171 831 0222
Bhaloo Miss Zia Kurban	Enterprise Chambers, London	0171 405 9471
	Enterprise Chambers, Leeds	0113 246 0391
	Enterprise Chambers, Newcastle upon Tyne	0191 222 3344
Blayney David James	Serle Court Chambers, London	0171 242 6105

Bourne Geoffrey Robert	4 Field Court, London	0171 440 6900
Bowker Robert James	2nd Floor, Francis Taylor Building, London	0171 353 9942/3157
Bowmer Michael Paul	11 Old Square, London	020 7430 0341
Boyd Stephen James Harvey	29 Bedford Row Chambers, London	0171 831 2626
Bredemear Zachary Charles	Barnard's Inn Chambers, London	0171 369 6969
Briggs Michael Townley Featherstone	Serle Court Chambers, London	0171 242 6105
Bruce Andrew Jonathan	Serle Court Chambers, London	0171 242 6105
Buckpitt Michael David	2nd Floor, Francis Taylor Building, London	0171 353 9942/3157
Butler Andrew	2nd Floor, Francis Taylor Building, London	0171 353 9942/3157
Castle Peter Bolton	Chambers of Mr Peter Crampin QC, London	020 7831 0081
Challenger Colin Westcott	Bridewell Chambers, London	020 7797 8800
Chan Miss Susan	13 King's Bench Walk, London	0171 353 7204
	King's Bench Chambers, Oxford	01865 311066
Charman Andrew Julian	St Philip's Chambers, Birmingham	0121 246 7000
Clarke Ian James	Hardwicke Building, London	020 7242 2523
Clegg Sebastian James Barwick	Deans Court Chambers, Manchester	0161 214 6000
	Deans Court Chambers, Preston	01772 555163
Collard Michael David	5 Pump Court, London	020 7353 2532
Cooke Jeremy Lionel	S Tomlinson QC, London	0171 583 0404
Cooper Gilead Patrick	Chambers of Mr Peter Crampin QC, London	020 7831 0081
Cowen Timothy Arieh	Barnard's Inn Chambers, London	0171 369 6969
Craig Alistair Trevor	Chambers of Mr Peter Crampin QC, London	020 7831 0081
Crawford Grant	11 Old Square, London	020 7430 0341
Davey Benjamin Nicholas	11 Old Square, London	020 7430 0341
Davies Miss (Susan) Louise	12 New Square, London	0171 419 1212
	Sovereign Chambers, Leeds	0113 2451841/2/3
Dillon Thomas William Matthew	1 Fountain Court, Birmingham	0121 236 5721
Dixon Philip John	2nd Floor, Francis Taylor Building, London	0171 353 9942/3157
Dodd Christopher John Nicholas	9 Woodhouse Square, Leeds	0113 2451986
Dooher Miss Nancy Helen	St James's Chambers, Manchester	0161 834 7000
Duddridge Robert James	2 Gray's Inn Square Chambers, London	020 7242 0328
Dugdale Nicholas	4 Field Court, London	0171 440 6900
Dumont Thomas Julian Bradley	Chambers of Mr Peter Crampin QC, London	020 7831 0081
Dutton Timothy Christopher	Barnard's Inn Chambers, London	0171 369 6969
Elleray Anthony John	• St James's Chambers, Manchester	0161 834 7000
	12 New Square, London	0171 419 1212
	Park Lane Chambers, Leeds	0113 2285000
Ellis Roger John	13 King's Bench Walk, London	0171 353 7204
	King's Bench Chambers, Oxford	01865 311066
Etherton Terence Michael Elkan Barnet	• Wilberforce Chambers, London	0171 306 0102
Evans Jonathan Edward	• Wilberforce Chambers, London	0171 306 0102
Farrow Kenneth John	Serle Court Chambers, London	0171 242 6105
Feltham Piers Jonathan	Chambers of Mr Peter Crampin QC, London	020 7831 0081
Fieldsend James William	2nd Floor, Francis Taylor Building, London	0171 353 9942/3157
Flenley William David Wingate	4 Paper Buildings, London	0171 353 3366/583 7155
Forte Mark Julian Carmino	8 King Street Chambers, Manchester	0161 834 9560
Foster Brian Ian	St James's Chambers, Manchester	0161 834 7000
	Park Lane Chambers, Leeds	0113 2285000
Francis Andrew James	Chambers of Mr Peter Crampin QC, London	020 7831 0081

• Expanded entry in Part D

Francis Edward Gerald Francis	Enterprise Chambers, London	0171 405 9471
	Enterprise Chambers, Leeds	0113 246 0391
	Enterprise Chambers, Newcastle upon Tyne	0191 222 3344
Furber (Robert) John	• Wilberforce Chambers, London	0171 306 0102
Gasztowicz Steven	2-3 Gray's Inn Square, London	0171 242 4986
	2 New Street, Leicester	0116 2625906
Gerald Nigel Mortimer	Enterprise Chambers, London	0171 405 9471
	Enterprise Chambers, Leeds	0113 246 0391
	Enterprise Chambers, Newcastle upon Tyne	0191 222 3344
Green David Cameron	Adrian Lyon's Chambers, Liverpool	0151 236 4421/8240
Gregory John Raymond	Deans Court Chambers, Manchester	0161 214 6000
	Deans Court Chambers, Preston	01772 555163
Hall Taylor Alexander Edward	11 Old Square, London	020 7430 0341
Halpern David Anthony	Enterprise Chambers, London	0171 405 9471
	Enterprise Chambers, Leeds	0113 246 0391
	Enterprise Chambers, Newcastle upon Tyne	0191 222 3344
Hammerton Alastair Rolf	No. 1 Serjeants' Inn, London	0171 415 6666
Hardwick Matthew Richard	Enterprise Chambers, London	0171 405 9471
	Enterprise Chambers, Leeds	0113 246 0391
	Enterprise Chambers, Newcastle upon Tyne	0191 222 3344
Harris Melvyn	7 New Square, London	0171 430 1660
Heather Christopher Mark	• 2nd Floor, Francis Taylor Building, London	0171 353 9942/3157
Higgins Rupert James Hale	Littman Chambers, London	020 7404 4866
Holland David Moore	29 Bedford Row Chambers, London	0171 831 2626
Horne Roger Cozens-Hardy	Chambers of Mr Peter Crampin QC, London	020 7831 0081
Hoser Philip Jacob	Serle Court Chambers, London	0171 242 6105
Hughes Miss Anna Gabriel	• Wilberforce Chambers, London	0171 306 0102
Hunter William Quigley	No. 1 Serjeants' Inn, London	0171 415 6666
Hutchings Martin Anthony	199 Strand, London	0171 379 9779
Hutton Miss Caroline	Enterprise Chambers, London	0171 405 9471
	Enterprise Chambers, Leeds	0113 246 0391
	Enterprise Chambers, Newcastle upon Tyne	0191 222 3344
Ife Miss Linden Elizabeth	Enterprise Chambers, London	0171 405 9471
	Enterprise Chambers, Leeds	0113 246 0391
	Enterprise Chambers, Newcastle upon Tyne	0191 222 3344
Jackson Dirik George Allan	Chambers of Mr Peter Crampin QC, London	020 7831 0081
Jackson Nicholas David Kingsley	Adrian Lyon's Chambers, Liverpool	0151 236 4421/8240
James-Stadden Miss Jodie Cara	Westgate Chambers, Newcastle upon Tyne	0191 261 4407/2329785
Jefferis Arthur Michael Quentin	Chambers of Mr Peter Crampin QC, London	020 7831 0081
Jennings Timothy Robin Finnegan	Enterprise Chambers, London	0171 405 9471
	Enterprise Chambers, Leeds	0113 246 0391
	Enterprise Chambers, Newcastle upon Tyne	0191 222 3344
Jones Philip John	Serle Court Chambers, London	0171 242 6105
Karas Jonathan Marcus	• Wilberforce Chambers, London	0171 306 0102
Kremen Philip Michael	Hardwicke Building, London	020 7242 2523
Kynoch Duncan Stuart Sanderson	29 Bedford Row Chambers, London	0171 831 2626
Lamb Robert Glasson	13 King's Bench Walk, London	0171 353 7204
	King's Bench Chambers, Oxford	01865 311066
Lamont Miss Camilla Rose	Chambers of Lord Goodhart QC, London	0171 405 5577

• Expanded entry in Part D

Lampard Miss Kathryn Felice	1 New Square, London	0171 405 0884/5/6/7
Levy Benjamin Keith	Enterprise Chambers, London	0171 405 9471
	Enterprise Chambers, Leeds	0113 246 0391
	Enterprise Chambers, Newcastle upon Tyne	0191 222 3344
Lloyd Stephen James George	Chambers of Mr Peter Crampin QC, London	020 7831 0081
Lofthouse Simon Timothy	Atkin Chambers, London	020 7404 0102
Lowe David Alexander	•Wilberforce Chambers, London	0171 306 0102
Lowenstein Paul David	Littleton Chambers, London	0171 797 8600
Macpherson Duncan Charles Stewart	Bracton Chambers, London	0171 242 4248
Malins Julian Henry	One Hare Court, London	020 7353 3171
Mann George Anthony	Enterprise Chambers, London	0171 405 9471
	Enterprise Chambers, Leeds	0113 246 0391
	Enterprise Chambers, Newcastle upon Tyne	0191 222 3344
Martin John Vandeleur	•Wilberforce Chambers, London	0171 306 0102
McAllister Miss Elizabeth Ann	Enterprise Chambers, London	0171 405 9471
	Enterprise Chambers, Leeds	0113 246 0391
	Enterprise Chambers, Newcastle upon Tyne	0191 222 3344
McQuail Ms Katherine Emma	11 Old Square, London	020 7430 0341
Mendoza Neil David Pereira	Hardwicke Building, London	020 7242 2523
Norman Christopher John George	No. 1 Serjeants' Inn, London	0171 415 6666
Norris Alastair Hubert	5 Stone Buildings, London	0171 242 6201
	Southernhay Chambers, Exeter	01392 255777
Nugee Christopher George	•Wilberforce Chambers, London	0171 306 0102
Nugee Edward George	•Wilberforce Chambers, London	0171 306 0102
Ohrenstein Dov	Chambers of Lord Goodhart QC, London	0171 405 5577
Osman Robert Walter	Queen's Chambers, Manchester	0161 834 6875/4738
	Queens Chambers, Preston	01772 828300
Padfield Nicholas David	One Hare Court, London	020 7353 3171
Palfrey Montague Mark	Hardwicke Building, London	020 7242 2523
Panesar Deshpal Singh	13 King's Bench Walk, London	0171 353 7204
	King's Bench Chambers, Oxford	01865 311066
Peacock Nicholas Christopher	13 Old Square, London	0171 404 4800
Peacocke Mrs Teresa Anne Rosen	Enterprise Chambers, London	0171 405 9471
	Enterprise Chambers, Leeds	0113 246 0391
	Enterprise Chambers, Newcastle upon Tyne	0191 222 3344
Pearce Robert Edgar	Chambers of Mr Peter Crampin QC, London	020 7831 0081
Purkis Ms Kathryn Miranda	Serle Court Chambers, London	0171 242 6105
Radevsky Anthony Eric	Falcon Chambers, London	0171 353 2484
Rainey Philip Carslake	2nd Floor, Francis Taylor Building, London	0171 353 9942/3157
Rashid Omar	Chambers of Mr Peter Crampin QC, London	020 7831 0081
Reed John William Rupert	•Wilberforce Chambers, London	0171 306 0102
Rees David Benjamin	5 Stone Buildings, London	0171 242 6201
Reid Sebastian Peter Scott	2nd Floor, Francis Taylor Building, London	0171 353 9942/3157
Roberts Michael Charles	1 New Square, London	0171 405 0884/5/6/7
Rolfe Patrick John Benedict	5 Stone Buildings, London	0171 242 6201
Ross Martyn John Greaves	•5 New Square, London	020 7404 0404
Rowley Keith Nigel	11 Old Square, London	020 7430 0341
Rumney Conrad William Arthur	St Philip's Chambers, Birmingham	0121 246 7000
Russell Christopher Garnet	•12 New Square, London	0171 419 1212
	Sovereign Chambers, Leeds	0113 2451841/2/3
Sandells Ms Nicole	11 Old Square, London	020 7430 0341

Seitler Jonathan Simon	• Wilberforce Chambers, London	0171 306 0102
Sellers Graham	Adrian Lyon's Chambers, Liverpool	0151 236 4421/8240
Selway Dr Katherine Emma	11 Old Square, London	020 7430 0341
Seymour Thomas Oliver	• Wilberforce Chambers, London	0171 306 0102
Sheehan Malcolm Peter	2 Harcourt Buildings, London	0171 583 9020
Shillingford George Miles	Chambers of Mr Peter Crampin QC, London	020 7831 0081
Sinclair Miss Lisa Anne	7 New Square, London	0171 430 1660
Skelly Andrew Jon	1 Gray's Inn Square, London	0171 405 8946/7/8
Smith Howard James	Chambers of Mr Peter Crampin QC, London	020 7831 0081
Smith Miss Julia Mair Wheldon	Gough Square Chambers, London	0171 353 0924
Southwell Richard Charles	One Hare Court, London	020 7353 3171
Staddon Paul	2nd Floor, Francis Taylor Building, London	0171 353 9942/3157
Staunton (Thomas) Ulick (Patrick)	Chambers of Mr Peter Crampin QC, London	020 7831 0081
	65-67 King Street, Leicester	0116 2547710
Sterling Robert Alan	St James's Chambers, Manchester	0161 834 7000
	12 New Square, London	0171 419 1212
	Park Lane Chambers, Leeds	0113 2285000
Stevens-Hoare Miss Michelle	Hardwicke Building, London	020 7242 2523
Stewart-Smith William Rodney	1 New Square, London	0171 405 0884/5/6/7
Swerling Robert Harry	13 Old Square, London	0171 404 4800
Szanto Gregory John Michael	Eastbourne Chambers, Eastbourne	01323 642102
Talbot Patrick John	Serle Court Chambers, London	0171 242 6105
Tecks Jonathan Howard	Littman Chambers, London	020 7404 4866
Tennet Michael John	• Wilberforce Chambers, London	0171 306 0102
Thom James Alexander Francis	4 Field Court, London	0171 440 6900
Tidmarsh Christopher Ralph Francis	5 Stone Buildings, London	0171 242 6201
Tipples Miss Amanda Jane	13 Old Square, London	0171 404 4800
Trace Anthony John	• 13 Old Square, London	0171 404 4800
Tully Ms Anne Margaret	Eastbourne Chambers, Eastbourne	01323 642102
Turnbull Charles Emerson Lovett	• Wilberforce Chambers, London	0171 306 0102
Van Tonder Gerard Dirk	1 New Square, London	0171 405 0884/5/6/7
Vickery Neil Michael	13 King's Bench Walk, London	0171 353 7204
	King's Bench Chambers, Oxford	01865 311066
Walden-Smith Miss Karen Jane	5 Stone Buildings, London	0171 242 6201
Wales Andrew Nigel Malcolm	S Tomlinson QC, London	0171 583 0404
Walker Andrew Greenfield	Chambers of Lord Goodhart QC, London	0171 405 5577
Warwick Mark Granville	• 29 Bedford Row Chambers, London	0171 831 2626
West Mark	• 11 Old Square, London	020 7430 0341
Whitaker Steven Dixon	199 Strand, London	0171 379 9779
	Queens Square Chambers, Bristol	0117 921 1966
Whittaker John Percival	Serle Court Chambers, London	0171 242 6105
Wicks Ms Joanne	• Wilberforce Chambers, London	0171 306 0102
Wilson-Barnes Miss Lucy Emma	St James's Chambers, Manchester	0161 834 7000
Yoxall Basil Joshua	Francis Taylor Building, London	0171 797 7250
Zelin Geoffrey Andrew	Enterprise Chambers, London	0171 405 9471
	Enterprise Chambers, Leeds	0113 246 0391
	Enterprise Chambers, Newcastle upon Tyne	0191 222 3344

COMMODITIES

Ambrose Miss Clare Mary Geneste	20 Essex Street, London	0171 583 9294
Birch Miss Elizabeth Blanche	3 Verulam Buildings, London	0171 831 8441
Blackburn Mrs Elizabeth	4 Field Court, London	0171 440 6900
Bright Robert Graham	S Tomlinson QC, London	0171 583 0404
Collett Michael John	20 Essex Street, London	0171 583 9294
Davey Michael Philip	4 Field Court, London	0171 440 6900
Drake James Frederick	S Tomlinson QC, London	0171 583 0404

• Expanded entry in Part D

Edey Philip David	20 Essex Street, London	0171 583 9294
Gee Steven Mark	4 Field Court, London	0171 440 6900
Havelock-Allan Anthony Mark David	20 Essex Street, London	0171 583 9294
Healy Miss Sioban	S Tomlinson QC, London	0171 583 0404
Hofmeyr Stephen Murray	S Tomlinson QC, London	0171 583 0404
Kverndal Simon Richard	4 Essex Court, London	020 7797 7970
Malek Ali	3 Verulam Buildings, London	0171 831 8441
Males Stephen Martin	20 Essex Street, London	0171 583 9294
Marquand Charles Nicholas Hilary	Chambers of Lord Goodhart QC, London	0171 405 5577
Masters Miss Sara Alayna	20 Essex Street, London	0171 583 9294
Matthews Duncan Henry Rowland	20 Essex Street, London	0171 583 9294
McClure Brian David	Littman Chambers, London	020 7404 4866
Meeson Nigel Keith	4 Field Court, London	0171 440 6900
Milligan Iain Anstruther	20 Essex Street, London	0171 583 9294
O'Shea Eoin Finbarr	4 Field Court, London	0171 440 6900
Owen David Christopher	20 Essex Street, London	0171 583 9294
Perkoff Richard Michael	Littleton Chambers, London	0171 797 8600
Persey Lionel Edward	• 4 Field Court, London	0171 440 6900
Priday Charles Nicholas Bruton	S Tomlinson QC, London	0171 583 0404
Rowland John Peter	4 Pump Court, London	020 7842 5555
Salter Richard Stanley	3 Verulam Buildings, London	0171 831 8441
Selvaratnam Miss Vasanti Emily Indrani	4 Field Court, London	0171 440 6900
Teare Nigel John Martin	4 Essex Court, London	020 7797 7970
Thomas (Robert) Neville	3 Verulam Buildings, London	0171 831 8441
Tselentis Michael	• 20 Essex Street, London	0171 583 9294
Wood Richard Gillies	20 Essex Street, London	0171 583 9294
	Cathedral Chambers (Jan Wood Independent Barristers' Clerk), Exeter	01392 210900
Wright Colin John	4 Field Court, London	0171 440 6900

COMMON LAND

Alesbury Alun	2 Mitre Court Buildings, London	0171 583 1380
Anderson Anthony John	2 Mitre Court Buildings, London	0171 583 1380
Ayres Andrew John William	13 Old Square, London	0171 404 4800
Boyle Christopher Alexander David	2 Mitre Court Buildings, London	0171 583 1380
Burr Martin John	Chambers of Martin Burr, London	0171 353 4636
	7 New Square, London	0171 430 1660
Burton Nicholas Anthony	2 Mitre Court Buildings, London	0171 583 1380
Cooper Gilead Patrick	Chambers of Mr Peter Crampin QC, London	020 7831 0081
Crail Miss (Elspeth) Ross	12 New Square, London	0171 419 1212
	Sovereign Chambers, Leeds	0113 2451841/2/3
Dineen Michael Laurence	Pump Court Chambers, Winchester	01962 868161
	Pump Court Chambers, London	0171 353 0711
	Queens Square Chambers, Bristol	0117 921 1966
	Pump Court Chambers, Swindon	01793 539899
Druce Michael James	2 Mitre Court Buildings, London	0171 583 1380
Fairbank Nicholas James	Becket Chambers, Canterbury	01227 786331
Farrow Kenneth John	Serle Court Chambers, London	0171 242 6105
Fitzgerald Michael Frederick Clive	2 Mitre Court Buildings, London	0171 583 1380
Fookes Robert Lawrence	2 Mitre Court Buildings, London	0171 583 1380
Foster Brian Ian	St James's Chambers, Manchester	0161 834 7000
	Park Lane Chambers, Leeds	0113 2285000
Francis Andrew James	Chambers of Mr Peter Crampin QC, London	020 7831 0081
Fryer-Spedding James Walter	St James's Chambers, Manchester	0161 834 7000
Gerald Nigel Mortimer	Enterprise Chambers, London	0171 405 9471
	Enterprise Chambers, Leeds	0113 246 0391
	Enterprise Chambers, Newcastle upon Tyne	0191 222 3344

• Expanded entry in Part D

Glover Richard Michael	2 Mitre Court Buildings, London	0171 583 1380
Green David Cameron	Adrian Lyon's Chambers, Liverpool	0151 236 4421/8240
Hall Taylor Alexander Edward	11 Old Square, London	020 7430 0341
Harrod Henry Mark	5 Stone Buildings, London	0171 242 6201
Harwood Richard John	1 Serjeants' Inn, London	0171 583 1355
Hinks Frank Peter	Serle Court Chambers, London	0171 242 6105
Horne Roger Cozens-Hardy	Chambers of Mr Peter Crampin QC, London	020 7831 0081
Horton Matthew Bethell	2 Mitre Court Buildings, London	0171 583 1380
Humphries Michael John	2 Mitre Court Buildings, London	0171 583 1380
Jackson Dirik George Allan	Chambers of Mr Peter Crampin QC, London	020 7831 0081
King Neil Gerald Alexander	2 Mitre Court Buildings, London	0171 583 1380
Kynoch Duncan Stuart Sanderson	29 Bedford Row Chambers, London	0171 831 2626
Lamont Miss Camilla Rose	Chambers of Lord Goodhart QC, London	0171 405 5577
Levy Benjamin Keith	Enterprise Chambers, London	0171 405 9471
	Enterprise Chambers, Leeds	0113 246 0391
	Enterprise Chambers, Newcastle upon Tyne	0191 222 3344
Macpherson The Hon Mary Stewart	2 Mitre Court Buildings, London	0171 583 1380
Mainwaring [Robert] Paul Clason	Carmarthen Chambers, Carmarthen	01267 234410
Moore Professor Victor William Edward	2 Mitre Court Buildings, London	0171 583 1380
Moriarty Gerald Evelyn	2 Mitre Court Buildings, London	0171 583 1380
Nugee Edward George	• Wilberforce Chambers, London	0171 306 0102
Pearce Robert Edgar	Chambers of Mr Peter Crampin QC, London	020 7831 0081
Renfree Peter Gerald Stanley	Harbour Court Chambers, Fareham	01329 827828
Roots Guy Robert Godfrey	2 Mitre Court Buildings, London	0171 583 1380
Ross Martyn John Greaves	• 5 New Square, London	020 7404 0404
Rowell David Stewart	Chambers of Lord Goodhart QC, London	0171 405 5577
Shale Justin Anton	4 King's Bench Walk, London	0171 822 8822
	King's Bench Chambers, Bournemouth	01202 250025
Shillingford George Miles	Chambers of Mr Peter Crampin QC, London	020 7831 0081
Siddiqi Faizul Aqtab	Justice Court Chambers, London	0181 830 7786
Silsoe The Lord	2 Mitre Court Buildings, London	0171 583 1380
Sterling Robert Alan	St James's Chambers, Manchester	0161 834 7000
	12 New Square, London	0171 419 1212
	Park Lane Chambers, Leeds	0113 2285000
Stewart-Smith William Rodney	1 New Square, London	0171 405 0884/5/6/7
Szanto Gregory John Michael	Eastbourne Chambers, Eastbourne	01323 642102
Taylor John Charles	2 Mitre Court Buildings, London	0171 583 1380
Taylor Reuben Mallinson	2 Mitre Court Buildings, London	0171 583 1380
Thomas Nigel Matthew	13 Old Square, London	0171 404 4800
Turnbull Charles Emerson Lovett	• Wilberforce Chambers, London	0171 306 0102
Wald Richard Daniel	2 Mitre Court Buildings, London	0171 583 1380
Warren Rupert Miles	2 Mitre Court Buildings, London	0171 583 1380
Whybrow Christopher John	1 Serjeants' Inn, London	0171 583 1355
Widdicombe David Graham	2 Mitre Court Buildings, London	0171 583 1380

COMMON LAW (GENERAL)

Acton Davis Jonathan James	4 Pump Court, London	020 7842 5555
Adkin Jonathan William	One Hare Court, London	020 7353 3171
Ahmed Miss Jacqueline Michelle	Southernhay Chambers, Exeter	01392 255777
Akerman Miss Kate Louise	Queen's Chambers, Manchester	0161 834 6875/4738
	Queens Chambers, Preston	01772 828300
Aldous Robert John	Octagon House, Norwich	01603 623186
Aldridge James William	199 Strand, London	0171 379 9779
Alford Robert John	Southernhay Chambers, Exeter	01392 255777
Ali Miss Huma	Eastbourne Chambers, Eastbourne	01323 642102

B

Allen Nicholas Paul	29 Bedford Row Chambers, London	0171 831 2626
Allingham-Nicholson Mrs Elizabeth Sarah	2 New Street, Leicester	0116 2625906
Allsop Alexander Nigel Mark	3 Temple Gardens, London	0171 353 0832
Althaus Antony Justin	No. 1 Serjeants' Inn, London	0171 415 6666
Ancliffe Mrs Shiva Edwina	Francis Taylor Building, London	0171 353 7768/7769/2711
Arentsen Andrew Nicholas	33 Park Place, Cardiff	02920 233313
Ash Edward William	3 Temple Gardens, London	0171 353 0832
Ashley Mark Robert	Pump Court Chambers, Swindon	01793 539899
	Pump Court Chambers, London	0171 353 0711
	Pump Court Chambers, Winchester	01962 868161
Atherton Peter	Deans Court Chambers, Manchester	0161 214 6000
	Deans Court Chambers, Preston	01772 555163
Bacon Francis Michael	4 Paper Buildings, London	0171 353 3366/583 7155
Baker Ms Rachel Mary Theresa	Hardwicke Building, London	020 7242 2523
Baker Stuart Christopher	1 Fountain Court, Birmingham	0121 236 5721
Balchin Richard Alexander	Crown Office Row Chambers, Brighton	01273 625625
Baldock Nicholas John	6 Pump Court, London	0171 797 8400
	6-8 Mill Street, Maidstone	01622 688094
Baldry Antony Brian	No. 1 Serjeants' Inn, London	0171 415 6666
Banks Francis Andrew	Adrian Lyon's Chambers, Liverpool	0151 236 4421/8240
Barker Nicholas	30 Park Square, Leeds	0113 2436388
Barnett Daniel Alexander	2 Gray's Inn Square Chambers, London	020 7242 0328
Barraclough Richard Michael	6 Pump Court, London	0171 797 8400
	6-8 Mill Street, Maidstone	01622 688094
Barton Alan John	Lamb Building, London	020 7797 7788
Bash-Taqi Mrs Shahineh	Leone Chambers, London	0181 200 4020
Bassa Yousef	St Albans Chambers, St Albans	01727 843383
	Tindal Chambers, Chelmsford	01245 267742
Bassett John Stewart Britten	5 Essex Court, London	0171 410 2000
Bastin Alexander Charles	2nd Floor, Francis Taylor Building, London	0171 353 9942/3157
Basu Dr Dijendra Bhushan	Devereux Chambers, London	0171 353 7534
Bather Miss Victoria Maclean	Littleton Chambers, London	0171 797 8600
Baxter-Phillips Miss Felicity Dawn	Becket Chambers, Canterbury	01227 786331
Bean Matthew Allen	11 King's Bench Walk, Leeds	0113 297 1200
	11 King's Bench Walk, London	0171 353 3337
Beard Mark Christopher	6 Pump Court, London	0171 797 8400
	6-8 Mill Street, Maidstone	01622 688094
Beaumont Marc Clifford	• Harrow on the Hill Chambers, Harrow-on-the-Hill	0181 423 7444
	Windsor Barristers' Chambers, Windsor	01753 648899
	Pump Court Chambers, London	0171 353 0711
Beer Jason Barrington	5 Essex Court, London	0171 410 2000
Bellamy Jonathan Mark	39 Essex Street, London	0171 832 1111
Bergin Timothy William	Crown Office Row Chambers, Brighton	01273 625625
Bevis Dominic Joseph	10 King's Bench Walk, London	0171 353 7742
Bhanji Shiraz Musa	4 Bingham Place, London	0171 486 5347/071 487 5910
Bidder Neil	33 Park Place, Cardiff	02920 233313
	Goldsmith Building, London	0171 353 7881
Birtles William	Old Square Chambers, London	0171 269 0300
	Old Square Chambers, Bristol	0117 9277111
Birts Peter William	Farrar's Building, London	0171 583 9241
	St Philip's Chambers, Birmingham	0121 246 7000
Bishop Edward James	No. 1 Serjeants' Inn, London	0171 415 6666
Blackburn Mrs Elizabeth	4 Field Court, London	0171 440 6900
Blakesley Patrick James	Two Crown Office Row, London	020 7797 8100
Blom-Cooper Sir Louis Jacques	Doughty Street Chambers, London	0171 404 1313

• Expanded entry in Part D

Bloom-Davis Desmond Niall Laurence	Pump Court Chambers, Winchester	01962 868161
	Pump Court Chambers, London	0171 353 0711
	Pump Court Chambers, Swindon	01793 539899
Blower Matthew John	3 Temple Gardens, London	0171 353 0832
Blunt David John	4 Pump Court, London	020 7842 5555
Booth Alan James	Deans Court Chambers, Manchester	0161 214 6000
	Deans Court Chambers, Preston	01772 555163
Booth Richard John	1 Crown Office Row, London	0171 797 7500
Boothroyd Miss Susan Elizabeth	Westgate Chambers, Newcastle upon Tyne	0191 261 4407/2329785
Boswell Miss Lindsay Alice	4 Pump Court, London	020 7842 5555
Bourne Geoffrey Robert	4 Field Court, London	0171 440 6900
Boyd James Andrew Donaldson	8 King Street Chambers, Manchester	0161 834 9560
Boydell Edward Patrick Stirrup	Pump Court Chambers, London	0171 353 0711
	Pump Court Chambers, Winchester	01962 868161
	Pump Court Chambers, Swindon	01793 539899
Boyle David Stuart	Deans Court Chambers, Manchester	0161 214 6000
	Deans Court Chambers, Preston	01772 555163
Boyle Gerard James	No. 1 Serjeants' Inn, London	0171 415 6666
Brace Michael Wesley	33 Park Place, Cardiff	02920 233313
Bradley Miss Clodagh Maria	3 Serjeants' Inn, London	0171 353 5537
Brennan John David	4 Fountain Court, Birmingham	0121 236 3476
Bresler Fenton Shea	22 Melcombe Regis Court, London	0171 487 5589
Bridgman David Martin	No. 1 Serjeants' Inn, London	0171 415 6666
Brockley Nigel Simon	Bracton Chambers, London	0171 242 4248
Brough Alasdair Matheson	13 King's Bench Walk, London	0171 353 7204
	King's Bench Chambers, Oxford	01865 311066
Brown Miss Althea Sonia	Doughty Street Chambers, London	0171 404 1313
Brunton Sean Alexander McKay	Pump Court Chambers, Winchester	01962 868161
	Pump Court Chambers, London	0171 353 0711
	Pump Court Chambers, Swindon	01793 539899
Bryant John Malcolm Cornelius	Barnard's Inn Chambers, London	0171 369 6969
Buck Dr Andrew Theodore	Chambers of Martin Burr, London	0171 353 4636
Burbidge James Michael	St Philip's Chambers, Birmingham	0121 246 7000
Burns Peter Richard	Deans Court Chambers, Manchester	0161 214 6000
	Deans Court Chambers, Preston	01772 555163
Butler Andrew	2nd Floor, Francis Taylor Building, London	0171 353 9942/3157
Butler Simon David	10 King's Bench Walk, London	0171 353 7742
Butterworth Paul Anthony	Octagon House, Norwich	01603 623186
Calvert David Edward	St James's Chambers, Manchester	0161 834 7000
Cameron Miss Barbara Alexander	● 2 Harcourt Buildings, London	0171 583 9020
Campbell Miss Susan Claire	Southernhay Chambers, Exeter	01392 255777
Campbell-Brown Miss Anne Louise	Bracton Chambers, London	0171 242 4248
Capon Philip Christopher William	St Philip's Chambers, Birmingham	0121 246 7000
Carr Bruce Conrad	Devereux Chambers, London	0171 353 7534
Carr Simon Andrew	9 Gough Square, London	020 7832 0500
Carrasco Glenn Lawrence	3 Temple Gardens, London	0171 353 0832
Carroll Jonathan Neil	9 Woodhouse Square, Leeds	0113 2451986
Carvalho Gomes Miss Ana Alexandra	St Albans Chambers, St Albans	01727 843383
Catchpole Stuart Paul	● 39 Essex Street, London	0171 832 1111
Cave Jeremy Stephen	1 Crown Office Row, London	0171 797 7500
	Crown Office Row Chambers, Brighton	01273 625625
Challenger Colin Westcott	Bridewell Chambers, London	020 7797 8800
Chalmers Miss Suzanne Frances	Two Crown Office Row, London	020 7797 8100
Chan Miss Susan	13 King's Bench Walk, London	0171 353 7204
	King's Bench Chambers, Oxford	01865 311066
Chapman Matthew James	Barnard's Inn Chambers, London	0171 369 6969
Chapman Michael Andrew	Barnard's Inn Chambers, London	0171 369 6969

Charles Ms Deborah Ann	6 Pump Court, London	0171 797 8400
	6-8 Mill Street, Maidstone	01622 688094
Charlton Alexander Murray	4 Pump Court, London	020 7842 5555
Charlwood Spike Llewellyn	4 Paper Buildings, London	0171 353 3366/583 7155
Chesner Howard Michael	Bracton Chambers, London	0171 242 4248
Christie-Brown Miss Sarah Louise	4 Paper Buildings, London	0171 353 3366/583 7155
Clark Christopher Harvey	Pump Court Chambers, Winchester	01962 868161
	Pump Court Chambers, London	0171 353 0711
	Westgate Chambers, Lewes	01273 480510
	Pump Court Chambers, Swindon	01793 539899
	Harrow on the Hill Chambers, Harrow-on-the-Hill	0181 423 7444
Clarke Miss Alison Lee	No. 1 Serjeants' Inn, London	0171 415 6666
Clegg Sebastian James Barwick	Deans Court Chambers, Manchester	0161 214 6000
	Deans Court Chambers, Preston	01772 555163
Clover (Thomas) Anthony	New Court Chambers, London	0171 831 9500
Coghlan Terence	1 Crown Office Row, London	0171 797 7500
	Crown Office Row Chambers, Brighton	01273 625625
Colbey Richard (Alan)	• Francis Taylor Building, London	0171 797 7250
	Guildhall Chambers Portsmouth, Portsmouth	01705 752400
Cole Robert Ian Gawain	30 Park Square, Leeds	0113 2436388
Colin Giles David	Crown Office Row Chambers, Brighton	01273 625625
Collard Michael David	5 Pump Court, London	020 7353 2532
Collett Ivor William	No. 1 Serjeants' Inn, London	0171 415 6666
Collins Miss Jennifer Clair	Eastbourne Chambers, Eastbourne	01323 642102
Collins Kenneth Guy Wyndham	3 Dr Johnson's Buildings, London	0171 353 4854
Collins Michael Antony	37 Park Square Chambers, Leeds	0113 2439422
Compton Gareth Francis Thomas	22 Old Buildings, London	0171 831 0222
Conry Michael Harvey	1 Fountain Court, Birmingham	0121 236 5721
Cook Miss Alison Noele	St Philip's Chambers, Birmingham	0121 246 7000
Cook Jeremy David	Lamb Building, London	020 7797 7788
Cooper Alan George	39 Essex Street, London	0171 832 1111
Cooper Mark Anthony John	2 Mitre Court Buildings, London	0171 353 1353
Craig Kenneth Allen	Hardwicke Building, London	020 7242 2523
Cramsie James Sinclair Beresford	13 King's Bench Walk, London	0171 353 7204
	King's Bench Chambers, Oxford	01865 311066
Crawforth Miss Emma	Southernhay Chambers, Exeter	01392 255777
Crossley Simon Justin	9 Woodhouse Square, Leeds	0113 2451986
Crossley Steven Richard	37 Park Square Chambers, Leeds	0113 2439422
Crowley John Desmond	Two Crown Office Row, London	020 7797 8100
Croxford Ian Lionel	• Wilberforce Chambers, London	0171 306 0102
Cunningham Miss Claire Louise	St Philip's Chambers, Birmingham	0121 246 7000
Curtis Michael Alexander	Two Crown Office Row, London	020 7797 8100
Curwen Michael Jonathan	Chambers of Kieran Coonan QC, London	0171 583 6013/2510
Da Costa Miss Elissa Josephine	• Arlington Chambers, London	0171 580 9188
Daniel Leon Roger	6 King's Bench Walk, London	0171 353 4931/583 0695
Date Julian Richard	17 Bedford Row, London	0171 831 7314
Datta Mrs Wendy Patricia Mizal	Alban Chambers, London	0171 419 5051
Davey Benjamin Nicholas	11 Old Square, London	020 7430 0341
Davidson Dr Ranald Dunbar	3 Serjeants' Inn, London	0171 353 5537
Davie Michael James	4 Pump Court, London	020 7842 5555
Davies Andrew Christopher	New Court Chambers, London	0171 831 9500
Davies Miss Carol Elizabeth	2 New Street, Leicester	0116 2625906
Davies Dr Charles Edward	4 Field Court, London	0171 440 6900
Davies Stephen Richard	8 King Street Chambers, Manchester	0161 834 9560
Davis Andrew Paul	Two Crown Office Row, London	020 7797 8100
Dean Paul Benjamin	Two Crown Office Row, London	020 7797 8100
Dean Peter Thomas	1 Crown Office Row, London	0171 583 9292
Dedezade Taner	Tindal Chambers, Chelmsford	01245 267742
Denbin Jack Arnold	Greenway, Sonning-on-Thames	0118 969 2484

• Expanded entry in Part D

deSouza Mrs Josephine Claudia	Chancery Chambers, London	0171 405 6879/6870
Devine Michael Buxton	95A Chancery Lane, London	0171 405 3101
Devlin Jonathan Nicholas Ponton	Park Court Chambers, Leeds	0113 2433277
Dineen Michael Laurence	Pump Court Chambers, Winchester	01962 868161
	Pump Court Chambers, London	0171 353 0711
	Queens Square Chambers, Bristol	0117 921 1966
	Pump Court Chambers, Swindon	01793 539899
Dixon Philip John	2nd Floor, Francis Taylor Building, London	0171 353 9942/3157
Dodd Christopher John Nicholas	9 Woodhouse Square, Leeds	0113 2451986
Dodge Peter Clive	11 Old Square, London	020 7430 0341
Doig Mrs Jeanetta Rose	Neston Home Chambers, Corsham	01225 811909
Dolan Dr Bridget Maura	3 Serjeants' Inn, London	0171 353 5537
Douglas Michael John	4 Pump Court, London	020 7842 5555
Dowley Dominic Myles	One Hare Court, London	020 7353 3171
Dubbery Mark Edward	Pump Court Chambers, London	0171 353 0711
	Pump Court Chambers, Winchester	01962 868161
	Pump Court Chambers, Swindon	01793 539899
Duddridge Robert James	2 Gray's Inn Square Chambers, London	020 7242 0328
Dudley Michael John	1 Fountain Court, Birmingham	0121 236 5721
Dunning Francis John Grove	37 Park Square Chambers, Leeds	0113 2439422
Eadie James Raymond	One Hare Court, London	020 7353 3171
Eastman Roger	2 Harcourt Buildings, London	0171 583 9020
Eccles David Thomas	8 King Street Chambers, Manchester	0161 834 9560
Edge Timothy Richard	Deans Court Chambers, Preston	01772 555163
	Deans Court Chambers, Manchester	0161 214 6000
Edis Angus William Butler	1 Crown Office Row, London	0171 797 7500
Edwards-Stuart Antony James Cobham	Two Crown Office Row, London	020 7797 8100
Eldridge Mark	3 Temple Gardens, London	0171 353 0832
	114 Liverpool Road, London	0171 226 9863
Elfield Miss Laura Elaine	5 Pump Court, London	020 7353 2532
Ellin Miss Nina Caroline	6 Pump Court, London	0171 797 8400
	6-8 Mill Street, Maidstone	01622 688094
Ellis Miss Catherine Anne	Derby Square Chambers, Liverpool	0151 709 4222
Emmerson (Michael) Benedict	Doughty Street Chambers, London	0171 404 1313
Evans Miss Claire Louise	Peel Court Chambers, Manchester	0161 832 3791
Evans-Tovey Jason Robert	Two Crown Office Row, London	020 7797 8100
Ewins Miss Catherine Jane	4 Paper Buildings, London	0171 353 3366/583 7155
Eyre Stephen John Arthur	1 Fountain Court, Birmingham	0121 236 5721
Fairbank Nicholas James	Becket Chambers, Canterbury	01227 786331
Faluyi Albert Osamudiamen	Chambers of Martin Burr, London	0171 353 4636
Farquharson Jonathan	Colleton Chambers, Exeter	01392 274898/9
Faul Miss Anne Frances Louise	Lamb Building, London	020 7797 7788
Faulks Edward Peter Lawless	No. 1 Serjeants' Inn, London	0171 415 6666
Ferm Rodney Eric	37 Park Square Chambers, Leeds	0113 2439422
Field Patrick John	Deans Court Chambers, Manchester	0161 214 6000
	Deans Court Chambers, Preston	01772 555163
Fieldsend James William	2nd Floor, Francis Taylor Building, London	0171 353 9942/3157
Finn Terence	Chambers of Martin Burr, London	0171 353 4636
Fisher Jonathan Simon	• 18 Red Lion Court, London	0171 520 6000
	Thornwood House, Chelmsford	01245 280880
Fitzgerald Edward Hamilton	Doughty Street Chambers, London	0171 404 1313
Fleming Paul Stephen	37 Park Square Chambers, Leeds	0113 2439422
Fletcher Christopher Michael	Octagon House, Norwich	01603 623186
Flockhart Miss Sharon Linda	3 Serjeants' Inn, London	0171 353 5537
Forbes Peter George	6 Pump Court, London	0171 797 8400
	6-8 Mill Street, Maidstone	01622 688094
Ford Gerard James	Baker Street Chambers, Middlesbrough	01642 873873
Forte Mark Julian Carmino	8 King Street Chambers, Manchester	0161 834 9560

Foster Charles Andrew	• Chambers of Kieran Coonan QC, London	0171 583 6013/2510
Foster Miss Juliet Kate	Southernhay Chambers, Exeter	01392 255777
Foy John Leonard	9 Gough Square, London	020 7832 0500
Franco Gianpiero	2 Middle Temple Lane, London	0171 583 4540
Francois Herbert Dolton	Chambers of Herbert Francois, Mitcham	0181 640 4529
Frith Nicholas John	30 Park Square, Leeds	0113 2436388
Gabb Charles Henry Escott	Pump Court Chambers, Winchester	01962 868161
	Pump Court Chambers, London	0171 353 0711
	Pump Court Chambers, Swindon	01793 539899
Gadney George Munro	Two Crown Office Row, London	020 7797 8100
Gardner Miss Eilidh Anne Mairi	22 Old Buildings, London	0171 831 0222
Garner Graham Howard	Southsea Chambers, Portsmouth	01705 291261
Garner Miss Sophie Jane	199 Strand, London	0171 379 9779
Gasztowicz Steven	2-3 Gray's Inn Square, London	0171 242 4986
	2 New Street, Leicester	0116 2625906
Gee Steven Mark	4 Field Court, London	0171 440 6900
Gersch Adam Nissen	Trafalgar Chambers, London	0171 583 5858
Gibbons James Francis	3 Stone Buildings, London	0171 242 4937
Gifford Andrew James Morris	7 New Square, London	0171 430 1660
Gilmore Ian Martin	30 Park Square, Leeds	0113 2436388
Glasson Jonathan Joseph	Doughty Street Chambers, London	0171 404 1313
Gledhill Kris	Camberwell Chambers, London	0171 274 0830
Glennie Andrew David	13 King's Bench Walk, London	0171 353 7204
	King's Bench Chambers, Oxford	01865 311066
Glover Stephen Julian	37 Park Square Chambers, Leeds	0113 2439422
Glynn Stephen Peter	9 Gough Square, London	020 7832 0500
Goodwin Miss Deirdre Evelyn	13 King's Bench Walk, London	0171 353 7204
	King's Bench Chambers, Oxford	01865 311066
Gordon Donald Cameron	3 Temple Gardens, London	0171 353 0832
Gordon-Saker Andrew Stephen	Fenners Chambers, Cambridge	01223 368761
	Fenners Chambers, Peterborough	01733 562030
Gore Andrew Julian Mark	37 Park Square Chambers, Leeds	0113 2439422
Gore-Andrews Gavin Angus Russell	2 Harcourt Buildings, London	0171 583 9020
Gow Miss Elizabeth Suzanne	Iscoed Chambers, Swansea	01792 652988/9/330
Grace Timothy Michael	Adrian Lyon's Chambers, Liverpool	0151 236 4421/8240
Grant David Euan Barron	13 King's Bench Walk, London	0171 353 7204
	King's Bench Chambers, Oxford	01865 311066
Gray Richard Paul	39 Essex Street, London	0171 832 1111
Grayson Edward	• 9-12 Bell Yard, London	0171 400 1800
Greatorex Ms Helen Louise	9 Woodhouse Square, Leeds	0113 2451986
Greenan Miss Sarah Octavia	9 Woodhouse Square, Leeds	0113 2451986
Greenbourne John Hugo	Two Crown Office Row, London	020 7797 8100
Grieve Michael Robertson Crichton	Doughty Street Chambers, London	0171 404 1313
Grime John Andrew	Pump Court Chambers, Swindon	01793 539899
	Pump Court Chambers, London	0171 353 0711
	Pump Court Chambers, Winchester	01962 868161
Grime Mark Stephen Eastburn	Deans Court Chambers, Manchester	0161 214 6000
	2 Pump Court, London	0171 353 5597
	Deans Court Chambers, Preston	01772 555163
Grodzinski Samuel Marc	39 Essex Street, London	0171 832 1111
Guggenheim Miss Anna Maeve	Two Crown Office Row, London	020 7797 8100
Guirguis Miss Sheren	White Friars Chambers, Chester	01244 323070
Gunning Alexander Rupert	4 Pump Court, London	020 7842 5555
Gunther Miss Elizabeth Ann	Pump Court Chambers, Winchester	01962 868161
	Pump Court Chambers, London	0171 353 0711
	Pump Court Chambers, Swindon	01793 539899
Guy John David Colin	Francis Taylor Building, London	0171 797 7250
Haigh Martin James	30 Park Square, Leeds	0113 2436388
Hall David Percy	9 Woodhouse Square, Leeds	0113 2451986
Hall Jonathan Rupert	5 King's Bench Walk, London	0171 353 5638
Hall Taylor Alexander Edward	11 Old Square, London	020 7430 0341

• Expanded entry in Part D

Hamilton Graeme Montagu	Two Crown Office Row, London	020 7797 8100
Hammerton Alastair Rolf	No. 1 Serjeants' Inn, London	0171 415 6666
Hammerton Miss Veronica Lesley	No. 1 Serjeants' Inn, London	0171 415 6666
Hanson Timothy Vincent Richard	St Philip's Chambers, Birmingham	0121 246 7000
Harding Dr Gladys Modwyn Cicely	Leone Chambers, London	0181 200 4020
Hargan James John	30 Park Square, Leeds	0113 2436388
Haring Simon Nicholas	30 Park Square, Leeds	0113 2436388
Harington Michael Kenneth	6 Pump Court, London	0171 797 8400
	6-8 Mill Street, Maidstone	01622 688094
Harper Miss Victoria Jane Tryphosa	3 Temple Gardens, London	0171 353 0832
Harries Raymond Elwyn	Bracton Chambers, London	0171 242 4248
Harris David Robert	St Albans Chambers, St Albans	01727 843383
Harrison Gordon William	3 Temple Gardens, London	0171 353 0832
Hartley Robert Edward	3 Temple Gardens, London	0171 353 0832
Harvey Michael Llewellyn Tucker	Two Crown Office Row, London	020 7797 8100
Hassall James Christopher	Southernhay Chambers, Exeter	01392 255777
Hatch Miss Lisa Sharmila	4 King's Bench Walk, London	0171 822 8822
Heather Christopher Mark	• 2nd Floor, Francis Taylor Building, London	0171 353 9942/3157
Henderson Roger Anthony	2 Harcourt Buildings, London	0171 583 9020
Henderson Simon Alexander	4 Pump Court, London	020 7842 5555
Henley Mark Robert Daniel	9 Woodhouse Square, Leeds	0113 2451986
Herbert Mrs Rebecca Mary	2 New Street, Leicester	0116 2625906
Higgins Adrian John	13 King's Bench Walk, London	0171 353 7204
	King's Bench Chambers, Oxford	01865 311066
Hignett Richard James	St Albans Chambers, St Albans	01727 843383
Hill Robert Douglas	Pump Court Chambers, Winchester	01962 868161
	Pump Court Chambers, London	0171 353 0711
	Pump Court Chambers, Swindon	01793 539899
Hockman Stephen Alexander	• 6 Pump Court, London	0171 797 8400
	6-8 Mill Street, Maidstone	01622 688094
Hodgson Timothy Paul	8 King Street Chambers, Manchester	0161 834 9560
Hodson Peter David	Chambers of Ian Macdonald QC (In Association with Two Garden Court, Temple, London), Manchester	0161 236 1840
Hoffman David Alexander	8 King Street Chambers, Manchester	0161 834 9560
Hofmeyr Stephen Murray	S Tomlinson QC, London	0171 583 0404
Hogg The Hon Douglas Martin	37 Park Square Chambers, Leeds	0113 2439422
	Cathedral Chambers (Jan Wood Independent Barristers' Clerk), Exeter	01392 210900
Hogg Miss Katharine Elizabeth	1 Crown Office Row, London	0171 797 7500
Holdsworth James Arthur	Two Crown Office Row, London	020 7797 8100
Holland David Moore	29 Bedford Row Chambers, London	0171 831 2626
Holmes-Milner James Neil	2 Mitre Court Buildings, London	0171 353 1353
Holroyd Ms Joanne	37 Park Square Chambers, Leeds	0113 2439422
Howard Graham John	Pump Court Chambers, Winchester	01962 868161
	Pump Court Chambers, London	0171 353 0711
	Pump Court Chambers, Swindon	01793 539899
Howarth Simon Stuart	Two Crown Office Row, London	020 7797 8100
Hudson Anthony Sean	Doughty Street Chambers, London	0171 404 1313
Hunter William Quigley	No. 1 Serjeants' Inn, London	0171 415 6666
Hurd James Robert	St James's Chambers, Manchester	0161 834 7000
Hutchin Edward Alister David	Bracton Chambers, London	0171 242 4248
Jabati Miss Maria Hannah	2 Middle Temple Lane, London	0171 583 4540
Jacobson Lawrence	5 Paper Buildings, London	0171 583 9275/583 4555
Johnston Anthony Paul	1 Fountain Court, Birmingham	0121 236 5721
Johnston Miss Justine Jane	4 Paper Buildings, London	0171 583 0816/353 1131
Jones Miss Susannah Lucy	Octagon House, Norwich	01603 623186
Karas Jonathan Marcus	• Wilberforce Chambers, London	0171 306 0102
Kaufmann Ms Phillippa Jane	Doughty Street Chambers, London	0171 404 1313
Keane Desmond St John	Pendragon Chambers, Swansea	01792 411188

Kent Miss Georgina	5 Essex Court, London	0171 410 2000
Kent Michael Harcourt	Two Crown Office Row, London	020 7797 8100
Kenward Timothy David Nelson	25-27 Castle Street, Liverpool	0151 227 5661/051 236 5072
King Peter Duncan	Fenners Chambers, Cambridge	01223 368761
	5 Pump Court, London	020 7353 2532
	Fenners Chambers, Peterborough	01733 562030
King-Smith James	1 Crown Office Row, London	0171 797 7500
	Crown Office Row Chambers, Brighton	01273 625625
Kinnier Andrew John	2 Harcourt Buildings, London	0171 583 9020
Kirby Peter John	Hardwicke Building, London	020 7242 2523
Knowles Graham Roy	Peel Court Chambers, Manchester	0161 832 3791
Kolodziej Andrzej Jozef	• Littman Chambers, London	020 7404 4866
Kremen Philip Michael	Hardwicke Building, London	020 7242 2523
Kynoch Duncan Stuart Sanderson	29 Bedford Row Chambers, London	0171 831 2626
Lambert Miss Sarah Katrina	1 Crown Office Row, London	0171 797 7500
Latimer-Sayer William Laurence	2 Mitre Court Buildings, London	0171 353 1353
Lavender Nicholas	One Hare Court, London	020 7353 3171
Leech Brian Walter Thomas	No. 1 Serjeants' Inn, London	0171 415 6666
Lennard Stephen Charles	Hardwicke Building, London	020 7242 2523
Levene Victor	1 Gray's Inn Square, London	0171 405 8946/7/8
Lewis Jeffrey Allan	9 Woodhouse Square, Leeds	0113 2451986
Lindqvist Andrew Nils Gunnar	Octagon House, Norwich	01603 623186
Lloyd Stephen James George	Chambers of Mr Peter Crampin QC, London	020 7831 0081
Lo Bernard Norman	17 Bedford Row, London	0171 831 7314
Lowry Charles Stephen	Colleton Chambers, Exeter	01392 274898/9
Lynagh Richard Dudley	Two Crown Office Row, London	020 7797 8100
MacDonald Alistair William Orchard	St Philip's Chambers, Birmingham	0121 246 7000
Machell Raymond Donatus	Deans Court Chambers, Manchester	0161 214 6000
	2 Pump Court, London	0171 353 5597
	Deans Court Chambers, Preston	01772 555163
Mackay Colin Crichton	39 Essex Street, London	0171 832 1111
Macleod Duncan	9 Gough Square, London	020 7832 0500
Mainwaring [Robert] Paul Clason	Carmarthen Chambers, Carmarthen	01267 234410
Majumdar Shantanu	Lamb Chambers, London	020 7797 8300
Malecka Dr Mary Margaret	• 3 Temple Gardens, London	0171 353 0832
	65-67 King Street, Leicester	0116 2547710
Malek Ali	3 Verulam Buildings, London	0171 831 8441
Malins Julian Henry	One Hare Court, London	020 7353 3171
Mandalia Vinesh Lalji	Harrow on the Hill Chambers, Harrow-on-the-Hill	0181 423 7444
Mann George Anthony	Enterprise Chambers, London	0171 405 9471
	Enterprise Chambers, Leeds	0113 246 0391
	Enterprise Chambers, Newcastle upon Tyne	0191 222 3344
Marks Jonathan Clive	4 Pump Court, London	020 7842 5555
Marley Miss Sarah Anne	5 Pump Court, London	020 7353 2532
Marsh Laurence John	4 Pump Court, London	020 7842 5555
Marshall-Andrews Robert Graham	37 Park Square Chambers, Leeds	0113 2439422
	2-4 Tudor Street, London	0171 797 7111
Mauleverer Peter Bruce	4 Pump Court, London	020 7842 5555
Maxwell Richard	Ropewalk Chambers, Nottingham	0115 9472581
	Doughty Street Chambers, London	0171 404 1313
Maxwell-Scott James Herbert	Two Crown Office Row, London	020 7797 8100
May Miss Juliet Mary	3 Verulam Buildings, London	0171 831 8441
McAlinden Barry O'Neill	17 Bedford Row, London	0171 831 7314
McAllister Miss Eimear Jane	9 Woodhouse Square, Leeds	0113 2451986
McCafferty Miss Lynne	5 Paper Buildings, London	0171 583 9275/583 4555
McCahill Patrick Gerard	St Philip's Chambers, Birmingham	0121 246 7000
	Chambers of Andrew Campbell QC, Leeds	0113 2455438

• Expanded entry in Part D

McCann Simon Howard	Deans Court Chambers, Manchester	0161 214 6000
	Deans Court Chambers, Preston	01772 555163
McCullough Miss Louise Clare	Lion Court, London	0171 404 6565
McGregor Harvey	4 Paper Buildings, London	0171 353 3366/583 7155
McGuinness-Way Andrew Jeffrey Sebastian B	3 Temple Gardens, London	0171 353 0832
McHugh Denis David	Bracton Chambers, London	0171 242 4248
McKechnie Stuart Iain William	2 Gray's Inn Square Chambers, London	020 7242 0328
McLean Mrs Mandy Rachel	5 Essex Court, London	0171 410 2000
Mead John Philip	Old Square Chambers, London	0171 269 0300
	Old Square Chambers, Bristol	0117 9277111
Meeson Nigel Keith	4 Field Court, London	0171 440 6900
Mehendale Ms Neelima Krishna	2 Mitre Court Buildings, London	0171 353 1353
Melly Miss Kama Louise	37 Park Square Chambers, Leeds	0113 2439422
Melville Richard David	• 39 Essex Street, London	0171 832 1111
Mendoza Neil David Pereira	Hardwicke Building, London	020 7242 2523
Meredith George Hubbard	Southernhay Chambers, Exeter	01392 255777
Metzer Anthony David Erwin	Doughty Street Chambers, London	0171 404 1313
Middleton Joseph	Doughty Street Chambers, London	0171 404 1313
Mills Corey Arthur	Becket Chambers, Canterbury	01227 786331
Mitchell Miss Julianna Marie	2 Harcourt Buildings, London	0171 583 9020
Mitropoulos Christos	Chambers of Geoffrey Hawker, London	0171 583 8899
Moger Christopher Richard Derwent	4 Pump Court, London	020 7842 5555
Mohabir Gerald Yogin	3 Temple Gardens, London	0171 353 0832
Moore Mr Craig Ian	Barnard's Inn Chambers, London	0171 369 6969
	Park Lane Chambers, Leeds	0113 2285000
Moran Andrew John	One Hare Court, London	020 7353 3171
Morgan Andrew James	St Philip's Chambers, Birmingham	0121 246 7000
Morris Miss Antonia Louise	Trafalgar Chambers, London	0171 583 5858
Mortimer Miss Sophie Kate	No. 1 Serjeants' Inn, London	0171 415 6666
Mulcahy Miss Leigh-Ann Maria	Chambers of John L Powell QC, London	0171 797 8000
Mulholland Michael	St James's Chambers, Manchester	0161 834 7000
Mundy Robert Geoffrey	St James's Chambers, Manchester	0161 834 7000
Murphy Miss Nicola Jane	4 King's Bench Walk, London	0171 822 8822
Naish Christopher John	Southernhay Chambers, Exeter	01392 255777
Naughton Philip Anthony	3 Serjeants' Inn, London	0171 353 5537
Neill of Bladen Lord	One Hare Court, London	020 7353 3171
Nesbitt Timothy John Robert	199 Strand, London	0171 379 9779
Neville-Clarke Sebastian Adrian Bennett	1 Crown Office Row, London	0171 583 9292
Newbury Richard Lennox	Sovereign Chambers, Leeds	0113 2451841/2/3
Newman Austin Eric	9 Woodhouse Square, Leeds	0113 2451986
Newman Ms Ingrid	Hardwicke Building, London	020 7242 2523
Newton-Price James Edward	Pump Court Chambers, London	0171 353 0711
	Pump Court Chambers, Winchester	01962 868161
	Pump Court Chambers, Swindon	01793 539899
Ng Ray Kian Hin	Two Crown Office Row, London	020 7797 8100
Niblett Anthony Ian	1 Crown Office Row, London	0171 797 7500
	Crown Office Row Chambers, Brighton	01273 625625
Nicol Andrew George Lindsay	Doughty Street Chambers, London	0171 404 1313
Nicol Stuart Henry David	3 Temple Gardens, London	0171 353 0832
Nisbett James Theophilus	7 Westmeath Avenue, Leicester	0116 2412003
	Victoria Chambers, Birmingham	0121 236 9900
Norman Christopher John George	No. 1 Serjeants' Inn, London	0171 415 6666
O'Connor Andrew McDougal	Two Crown Office Row, London	020 7797 8100
O'Donoghue Florence	2 Mitre Court Buildings, London	0171 353 1353
O'Donovan Ronan Daniel James	14 Gray's Inn Square, London	0171 242 0858
O'Leary Robert Michael	33 Park Place, Cardiff	02920 233313
O'Shea Eoin Finbarr	4 Field Court, London	0171 440 6900
O'Sullivan Michael Neil	5 King's Bench Walk, London	0171 353 5638

Ogle Miss Rebecca Theodosia Abigail	Southernhay Chambers, Exeter	01392 255777
Oliver Andrew James	Octagon House, Norwich	01603 623186
Ough Dr Richard Norman	• Hardwicke Building, London	020 7242 2523
Outhwaite Mrs Wendy-Jane Tivnan	2 Harcourt Buildings, London	0171 583 9020
Owen Timothy Wynn	Doughty Street Chambers, London	0171 404 1313
Packman Miss Claire Geraldine Vance	4 Pump Court, London	020 7842 5555
Padfield Nicholas David	One Hare Court, London	020 7353 3171
Page Howard William Barrett	One Hare Court, London	020 7353 3171
Paget Michael Rodborough	Bracton Chambers, London	0171 242 4248
Palfrey Montague Mark	Hardwicke Building, London	020 7242 2523
Palmer Patrick John Steven	Sovereign Chambers, Leeds	0113 2451841/2/3
Panesar Deshpal Singh	13 King's Bench Walk, London	0171 353 7204
	King's Bench Chambers, Oxford	01865 311066
Paneth Miss Sarah Ruth	No. 1 Serjeants' Inn, London	0171 415 6666
Panford Frank Haig	• Doughty Street Chambers, London	0171 404 1313
Parker John	2 Mitre Court Buildings, London	0171 353 1353
Parr John Edward	8 King Street Chambers, Manchester	0161 834 9560
Patel Bhavin Vinubhai	Chambers of Martin Burr, London	0171 353 4636
Paul Nicholas Martin	Doughty Street Chambers, London	0171 404 1313
	Westgate Chambers, Lewes	01273 480510
Pawson Robert Edward Cruickshank	Pump Court Chambers, Winchester	01962 868161
	Pump Court Chambers, London	0171 353 0711
	Pump Court Chambers, Swindon	01793 539899
Pearce Richard William	Peel Court Chambers, Manchester	0161 832 3791
Pears Derrick Allan	2nd Floor, Francis Taylor Building, London	0171 353 9942/3157
Pearson Christopher	• Bridewell Chambers, London	020 7797 8800
Pearson Michael	30 Park Square, Leeds	0113 2436388
Peirson Oliver James	Pump Court Chambers, London	0171 353 0711
	Pump Court Chambers, Winchester	01962 868161
	Pump Court Chambers, Swindon	01793 539899
Pema Anes Bhumin Laloo	9 Woodhouse Square, Leeds	0113 2451986
Pereira James Alexander	2 Harcourt Buildings, London	020 7353 8415
Perkoff Richard Michael	Littleton Chambers, London	0171 797 8600
Peterson Miss Geraldine Shelda	Lamb Building, London	020 7797 7788
Phillips Andrew Charles	Two Crown Office Row, London	020 7797 8100
Phillips David John	199 Strand, London	0171 379 9779
	30 Park Place, Cardiff	01222 398421
Phillpot Hereward Lindon	2 Harcourt Buildings, London	020 7353 8415
Picton Julian Mark	4 Paper Buildings, London	0171 353 3366/583 7155
Pilkington Mrs Mavis Patricia	9 Woodhouse Square, Leeds	0113 2451986
Pinder Miss Mary Elizabeth	No. 1 Serjeants' Inn, London	0171 415 6666
Pinter Joseph Philip	3 Temple Gardens, London	0171 353 0832
Piper Angus Richard	No. 1 Serjeants' Inn, London	0171 415 6666
Pipi Chukwuemeka Ezekiel	Chambers of Martin Burr, London	0171 353 4636
Pirani Rohan Carl	Old Square Chambers, Bristol	0117 9277111
	Old Square Chambers, London	0171 269 0300
Pittaway David Michael	No. 1 Serjeants' Inn, London	0171 415 6666
Pliener David Jonathan	New Court Chambers, London	0171 831 9500
Portnoy Leslie Reuben	Chambers of John Hand QC, Manchester	0161 955 9000
Powell Miss Debra Ann	3 Serjeants' Inn, London	0171 353 5537
Prasad Krishna	21 Craven Road, Kingston-Upon-Thames	0181 974 6799
Price Albert John	23 Essex Street, London	0171 413 0353/836 8366
Price Miss Collette	St James's Chambers, Manchester	0161 834 7000
Price John Scott	10 Launceston Avenue, Reading	01189 479548
	Southsea Chambers, Portsmouth	01705 291261
	Cathedral Chambers, Newcastle upon Tyne	0191 232 1311
Price Richard Mervyn	Littleton Chambers, London	0171 797 8600

• Expanded entry in Part D

Prinn Miss Helen Elizabeth	Octagon House, Norwich	01603 623186
Pulling Dean	Iscoed Chambers, Swansea	01792 652988/9/330
Purchas Christopher Patrick Brooks	Two Crown Office Row, London	020 7797 8100
Purdie Robert Anthony James	28 Western Road, Oxford	01865 204911
Purves Gavin Bowman	Swan House, London	0181 998 3035
Pusey William James	St Philip's Chambers, Birmingham	0121 246 7000
Qureshi Khawar Mehmood	One Hare Court, London	020 7353 3171
Rampersad Devan	St Philip's Chambers, Birmingham	0121 246 7000
Rasul Miss Lubna	St Albans Chambers, St Albans	01727 843383
Readhead Simon John Howard	No. 1 Serjeants' Inn, London	0171 415 6666
Rector Miss Penelope Jane	• Five Paper Buildings, London	0171 583 6117
Redford Miss Jessica Kate	3 Dr Johnson's Buildings, London	0171 353 4854
Rees David Benjamin	5 Stone Buildings, London	0171 242 6201
Reid Paul William	13 King's Bench Walk, London	0171 353 7204
	King's Bench Chambers, Oxford	01865 311066
Reid Sebastian Peter Scott	2nd Floor, Francis Taylor Building, London	0171 353 9942/3157
Restell Thomas George	Granary Chambers, Bexhill-On-Sea	01424 733008
Rhodes Robert Elliott	4 King's Bench Walk, London	0171 822 8822
Rich Jonathan Bernard George	5 Paper Buildings, London	0171 583 9275/583 4555
Rivalland Marc-Edouard	No. 1 Serjeants' Inn, London	0171 415 6666
Roberts Stuart Royd	37 Park Square Chambers, Leeds	0113 2439422
Robertson Geoffrey Ronald	Doughty Street Chambers, London	0171 404 1313
Robinson Simon Robert	Chambers of Ian Macdonald QC (In Association with Two Garden Court, Temple, London), Manchester	0161 236 1840
Robinson Ms Tanya Lin	6 Pump Court, London	0171 797 8400
	6-8 Mill Street, Maidstone	01622 688094
Rochford Thomas Nicholas Beverley	St Philip's Chambers, Birmingham	0121 246 7000
Roebuck Roy Delville	Bell Yard Chambers, London	0171 306 9292
Rogers Ian Paul	1 Crown Office Row, London	0171 583 9292
Ronksley Andrew Peter	3 Temple Gardens, London	0171 353 0832
Ross John Graffin	No. 1 Serjeants' Inn, London	0171 415 6666
Rudd Matthew Allan	11 Bolt Court (also at 7 Stone Buildings – 1st Floor), London	0171 353 2300
	Redhill Chambers, Redhill	01737 780781
	7 Stone Buildings (also at 11 Bolt Court), London	0171 242 0961
Rumney Conrad William Arthur	St Philip's Chambers, Birmingham	0121 246 7000
Russell Anthony Patrick	Peel Court Chambers, Manchester	0161 832 3791
Saggerson Alan David	Barnard's Inn Chambers, London	0171 369 6969
Salmon Jonathan Carl	1 Fountain Court, Birmingham	0121 236 5721
Samuel Glyn Ross	St Philip's Chambers, Birmingham	0121 246 7000
Samuels Leslie John	Pump Court Chambers, London	0171 353 0711
	Pump Court Chambers, Winchester	01962 868161
	Pump Court Chambers, Swindon	01793 539899
Scott Matthew John	Pump Court Chambers, London	0171 353 0711
	Pump Court Chambers, Winchester	01962 868161
	Pump Court Chambers, Swindon	01793 539899
Seal Julius Damien	189 Randolph Avenue, London	0171 624 9139
Searle Barrie	St James's Chambers, Manchester	0161 834 7000
Sears Robert David Murray	4 Pump Court, London	020 7842 5555
Selway Dr Katherine Emma	11 Old Square, London	020 7430 0341
Semple Andrew Blair	Sovereign Chambers, Leeds	0113 2451841/2/3
Shale Justin Anton	4 King's Bench Walk, London	0171 822 8822
	King's Bench Chambers, Bournemouth	01202 250025
Shaw Mrs Gabriele	3 Temple Gardens, London	0171 353 0832
Sheehan Malcolm Peter	2 Harcourt Buildings, London	0171 583 9020
Shepherd Miss Joanne Elizabeth	St Albans Chambers, St Albans	01727 843383
	Tindal Chambers, Chelmsford	01245 267742
	New Bailey Chambers, Preston	01772 258087

Shiels Ian	30 Park Square, Leeds	0113 2436388
Short Miss Anna Louise	Barnard's Inn Chambers, London	0171 369 6969
Shrimpton Michael	Francis Taylor Building, London	0171 797 7250
Shukla Ms Vina	New Court Chambers, London	0171 831 9500
Siddiqi Faizul Aqtab	Justice Court Chambers, London	0181 830 7786
Simpson Ian	Bracton Chambers, London	0171 242 4248
Sinclair Graham Kelso	East Anglian Chambers, Norwich	01603 617351
	East Anglian Chambers, Colchester	01206 572756
	East Anglian Chambers, Ipswich	01473 214481
Singh Kuldip	Five Paper Buildings, London	0171 583 6117
Sinnatt Simon Peter Randall	Crown Office Row Chambers, Brighton	01273 625625
Skelly Andrew Jon	1 Gray's Inn Square, London	0171 405 8946/7/8
Slaughter Andrew Francis	Bridewell Chambers, London	020 7797 8800
Sleightholme John Trevor	37 Park Square Chambers, Leeds	0113 2439422
Smith Andrew Duncan	1 Fountain Court, Birmingham	0121 236 5721
Smith Michael Joseph	8 King Street Chambers, Manchester	0161 834 9560
Smith Nicholas Martin	1 Fountain Court, Birmingham	0121 236 5721
Smith Paul Andrew	One Hare Court, London	020 7353 3171
Smith Ms Rachel Catherine	Peel Court Chambers, Manchester	0161 832 3791
Smith Miss Sally-Ann	Crown Office Row Chambers, Brighton	01273 625625
Smith Warwick Timothy Cresswell	Deans Court Chambers, Manchester	0161 214 6000
	Deans Court Chambers, Preston	01772 555163
Snowden John Stevenson	Two Crown Office Row, London	020 7797 8100
Southwell Richard Charles	One Hare Court, London	020 7353 3171
Sparrow Miss Claire Louise	Eastbourne Chambers, Eastbourne	01323 642102
Spencer Martin Benedict	4 Paper Buildings, London	0171 353 3366/583 7155
Spicer Robert Haden	Frederick Place Chambers, Bristol	0117 9738667
Spinks Roderick Cameron	Fenners Chambers, Cambridge	01223 368761
	Fenners Chambers, Peterborough	01733 562030
Spollon Guy Merton	St Philip's Chambers, Birmingham	0121 246 7000
St Louis Brian Lloyd	Hardwicke Building, London	020 7242 2523
Staddon Paul	2nd Floor, Francis Taylor Building, London	0171 353 9942/3157
Stagg Paul Andrew	No. 1 Serjeants' Inn, London	0171 415 6666
Starcevic Petar	St Philip's Chambers, Birmingham	0121 246 7000
Stark James Hayden Alexander	Chambers of Ian Macdonald QC (In Association with Two Garden Court, Temple, London), Manchester	0161 236 1840
Starmer Keir	Doughty Street Chambers, London	0171 404 1313
Stavros Ms Evanthia	3 Temple Gardens, London	0171 353 0832
Stevens Howard Linton	1 Crown Office Row, London	0171 583 9292
Stevenson John Melford	Two Crown Office Row, London	020 7797 8100
Stewart Ms Alexandra Mary Hamilton	30 Park Square, Leeds	0113 2436388
Stewart Nicholas John Cameron	Hardwicke Building, London	020 7242 2523
Stockdale David Andrew	Deans Court Chambers, Manchester	0161 214 6000
	Deans Court Chambers, Preston	01772 555163
	9 Bedford Row, London	0171 242 3555
Storey Jeremy Brian	4 Pump Court, London	020 7842 5555
Strange Ms (Karen) Michelle	Doughty Street Chambers, London	0171 404 1313
Styles Clive Richard	Becket Chambers, Canterbury	01227 786331
Sullivan Scott	Barnard's Inn Chambers, London	0171 369 6969
Sutcliffe Andrew Harold Wentworth	3 Verulam Buildings, London	0171 831 8441
Swan Ian Christopher	Two Crown Office Row, London	020 7797 8100
Swift Malcolm Robin	Park Court Chambers, Leeds	0113 2433277
	6 Gray's Inn Square, London	0171 242 1052
Syed Mohammad Ali	39 Park Avenue, Mitcham	0181 648 1684
	Tower Hamlets Barristers Chambers, London	0171 247 9825
Szanto Gregory John Michael	Eastbourne Chambers, Eastbourne	01323 642102
Taft Christopher Heiton	St James's Chambers, Manchester	0161 834 7000
Tatton-Brown Daniel Nicholas	Littleton Chambers, London	0171 797 8600

• Expanded entry in Part D

Taylor Miss Deborah Frances	Two Crown Office Row, London	020 7797 8100
Taylor Paul Richard	Doughty Street Chambers, London	0171 404 1313
Tedd Rex Hilary	• St Philip's Chambers, Birmingham	0121 246 7000
	De Montfort Chambers, Leicester	0116 254 8686
	Northampton Chambers, Northampton	01604 636271
Teeman Miss Miriam Joy	30 Park Square, Leeds	0113 2436388
Temple Anthony Dominic	4 Pump Court, London	020 7842 5555
Ter Haar Roger Eduard Lound	Two Crown Office Row, London	020 7797 8100
Thain Miss Ashley	East Anglian Chambers, Colchester	01206 572756
	East Anglian Chambers, Ipswich	01473 214481
	East Anglian Chambers, Norwich	01603 617351
Thomson Dr David James Ramsay Gibb	Barnard's Inn Chambers, London	0171 369 6969
Thornley David	Chambers of Martin Burr, London	0171 353 4636
Thornton Peter Ribblesdale	Doughty Street Chambers, London	0171 404 1313
Tozzi Nigel Kenneth	4 Pump Court, London	020 7842 5555
Travers Hugh	Pump Court Chambers, London	0171 353 0711
	Pump Court Chambers, Winchester	01962 868161
	Pump Court Chambers, Swindon	01793 539899
Treasure Francis Seton	199 Strand, London	0171 379 9779
Trippier Lady	Deans Court Chambers, Manchester	0161 214 6000
	Deans Court Chambers, Preston	01772 555163
Trotman Timothy Oliver	Deans Court Chambers, Manchester	0161 214 6000
	Deans Court Chambers, Preston	01772 555163
Tucker David William	Two Crown Office Row, London	020 7797 8100
Tucker Miss Katherine Jane Greening	St Philip's Chambers, Birmingham	0121 246 7000
Tucker Dr Peter Louis	Leone Chambers, London	0181 200 4020
	12 Old Square, London	0171 404 0875
Tully Ms Anne Margaret	Eastbourne Chambers, Eastbourne	01323 642102
Tyack David Guy	St Philip's Chambers, Birmingham	0121 246 7000
Tyler William John	30 Park Square, Leeds	0113 2436388
Tyzack David Ian Heslop	Southernhay Chambers, Exeter	01392 255777
	1 Mitre Court Buildings, London	0171 797 7070
Ullstein Augustus Rupert Patrick A	• 29 Bedford Row Chambers, London	0171 831 2626
Underhill Miss Alison	Tindal Chambers, Chelmsford	01245 267742
Van Hagen Christopher Seymour Nigel	4 King's Bench Walk, London	0171 822 8822
	King's Bench Chambers, Bournemouth	01202 250025
Vickery Neil Michael	13 King's Bench Walk, London	0171 353 7204
	King's Bench Chambers, Oxford	01865 311066
Vineall Nicholas Edward John	4 Pump Court, London	020 7842 5555
Waddicor Miss Janet	1 Crown Office Row, London	0171 797 7500
	Crown Office Row Chambers, Brighton	01273 625625
Walsh Simon	Bridewell Chambers, London	020 7797 8800
Walters Edmund John	13 King's Bench Walk, London	0171 353 7204
	King's Bench Chambers, Oxford	01865 311066
Ward Mrs Annie Frances	Pump Court Chambers, London	0171 353 0711
	Pump Court Chambers, Swindon	01793 539899
	Pump Court Chambers, Winchester	01962 868161
Ward Simon John	1 Fountain Court, Birmingham	0121 236 5721
Warner David Alexander	1 New Square, London	0171 405 0884/5/6/7
Warnock Andrew Ronald	No. 1 Serjeants' Inn, London	0171 415 6666
Warren Miss Sasha	3 Temple Gardens, London	0171 353 0832
Warrender Miss Nichola Mary	New Court Chambers, London	0171 831 9500
Waters Julian William Penrose	No. 1 Serjeants' Inn, London	0171 415 6666
Watkin Toby Paul	22 Old Buildings, London	0171 831 0222
Watson James Vernon	3 Serjeants' Inn, London	0171 353 5537
Watson Mark	6 Pump Court, London	0171 797 8400
	6-8 Mill Street, Maidstone	01622 688094

Webb Stanley George	The Chambers of Mr Ali Mohammed Azhar, London	0171 353 9564
	Bracton Chambers, London	0171 242 4248
Wedderspoon Miss Rachel Leone	Chambers of John Hand QC, Manchester	0161 955 9000
Weddle Steven Edgar	Hardwicke Building, London	020 7242 2523
Weeden Ross Charles	Bell Yard Chambers, London	0171 306 9292
West Mark	• 11 Old Square, London	020 7430 0341
West-Knights Laurence James	4 Paper Buildings, London	0171 353 3366/583 7155
Weston Clive Aubrey Richard	Two Crown Office Row, London	020 7797 8100
Whipple Mrs Philippa Jane Edwards	1 Crown Office Row, London	0171 797 7500
White Matthew James	13 King's Bench Walk, London	0171 353 7204
	King's Bench Chambers, Oxford	01865 311066
Whitfield Adrian	3 Serjeants' Inn, London	0171 353 5537
Wickens Simon	Maidstone Chambers, Maidstone	01622 688592
Wilkinson Nigel Vivian Marshall	Two Crown Office Row, London	020 7797 8100
Willer Robert Michael	Hardwicke Building, London	020 7242 2523
Williams A John	13 King's Bench Walk, London	0171 353 7204
	King's Bench Chambers, Oxford	01865 311066
Williams Miss Caroline Sarah	Maidstone Chambers, Maidstone	01622 688592
Williams Dr Jason Scott	• 3 Dr Johnson's Buildings, London	0171 353 4854
Williams Thomas Christopher Charles	1 Fountain Court, Birmingham	0121 236 5721
Wilson Andrew Robert	9 Woodhouse Square, Leeds	0113 2451986
Wilson Myles Brennand	White Friars Chambers, Chester	01244 323070
Wilton Simon Daniel	4 Paper Buildings, London	0171 353 3366/583 7155
Winzer Benjamin Charles	Southernhay Chambers, Exeter	01392 255777
Wood James Alexander Douglas	Doughty Street Chambers, London	0171 404 1313
Woods Jonathan	Two Crown Office Row, London	020 7797 8100
Woolf Steven Jeremy	Hardwicke Building, London	020 7242 2523
Worrall Miss Shirley Vera Frances	8 King Street Chambers, Manchester	0161 834 9560
Wright Miss Clare Elizabeth	6 Pump Court, London	0171 797 8400
	6-8 Mill Street, Maidstone	01622 688094
Yell Nicholas Anthony	No. 1 Serjeants' Inn, London	0171 415 6666
Yoxall Basil Joshua	Francis Taylor Building, London	0171 797 7250

COMMONS
Purchas Robin Michael	• 2 Harcourt Buildings, London	020 7353 8415

COMMUNITY CARE
Nicol Nicholas Keith	1 Pump Court, London	0171 583 2012/353 4341

COMPANIES INVESTIGATIONS
Rector Miss Penelope Jane	• Five Paper Buildings, London	0171 583 6117

COMPANY AND COMMERCIAL
Acton Stephen Neil	11 Old Square, London	020 7430 0341
Adamyk Simon Charles	12 New Square, London	0171 419 1212
Adejumo Mrs Hilda Ekpo	Temple Chambers, London	0171 583 1001 (2 lines)
Arden Peter Leonard	Enterprise Chambers, London	0171 405 9471
	Enterprise Chambers, Leeds	0113 246 0391
	Enterprise Chambers, Newcastle upon Tyne	0191 222 3344
Ashton David Sambrook	13 King's Bench Walk, London	0171 353 7204
	King's Bench Chambers, Oxford	01865 311066
Asprey Nicholas	Serle Court Chambers, London	0171 242 6105
Ayliffe James Justin Barnett	• Wilberforce Chambers, London	0171 306 0102
Ayres Andrew John William	13 Old Square, London	0171 404 4800
Barker James Sebastian	Enterprise Chambers, London	0171 405 9471
	Enterprise Chambers, Leeds	0113 246 0391
	Enterprise Chambers, Newcastle upon Tyne	0191 222 3344

Barker Simon George Harry	• 13 Old Square, London	0171 404 4800
Behrens James Nicholas Edward	Serle Court Chambers, London	0171 242 6105
Birch Roger Allen	Sovereign Chambers, Leeds	0113 2451841/2/3
	12 New Square, London	0171 419 1212
Blayney David James	Serle Court Chambers, London	0171 242 6105
Bowmer Michael Paul	11 Old Square, London	020 7430 0341
Briden Richard John	96 Gray's Inn Road, London	0171 405 0585
Briggs Michael Townley Featherstone	Serle Court Chambers, London	0171 242 6105
Brockley Nigel Simon	Bracton Chambers, London	0171 242 4248
Bryant Miss Ceri Jane	Erskine Chambers, London	0171 242 5532
Bryant John Malcolm Cornelius	Barnard's Inn Chambers, London	0171 369 6969
Butler Andrew	2nd Floor, Francis Taylor Building, London	0171 353 9942/3157
Cannan Jonathan Michael	St James's Chambers, Manchester	0161 834 7000
	Broadway House Chambers, Bradford	01274 722560
	Broadway House Chambers, Leeds	0113 246 2600
Capon Philip Christopher William	St Philip's Chambers, Birmingham	0121 246 7000
Castle Peter Bolton	Chambers of Mr Peter Crampin QC, London	020 7831 0081
Cawson Peter Mark	St James's Chambers, Manchester	0161 834 7000
	12 New Square, London	0171 419 1212
	Park Lane Chambers, Leeds	0113 2285000
Charman Andrew Julian	St Philip's Chambers, Birmingham	0121 246 7000
Chesner Howard Michael	Bracton Chambers, London	0171 242 4248
Chivers (Tom) David	Erskine Chambers, London	0171 242 5532
Clarke Ian James	Hardwicke Building, London	020 7242 2523
Clegg Sebastian James Barwick	Deans Court Chambers, Manchester	0161 214 6000
	Deans Court Chambers, Preston	01772 555163
Cole Robert Ian Gawain	30 Park Square, Leeds	0113 2436388
Collingwood Timothy Donald	Serle Court Chambers, London	0171 242 6105
Cone John Crawford	Erskine Chambers, London	0171 242 5532
Cook Christopher Graham	St James's Chambers, Manchester	0161 834 7000
Cooper Gilead Patrick	Chambers of Mr Peter Crampin QC, London	020 7831 0081
Corbett James Patrick	St Philip's Chambers, Birmingham	0121 246 7000
	Chambers of Andrew Campbell QC, Leeds	0113 2455438
Corbett Mrs Sandra Margaret	1 New Square, London	0171 405 0884/5/6/7
Craig Alistair Trevor	Chambers of Mr Peter Crampin QC, London	020 7831 0081
Craig Kenneth Allen	Hardwicke Building, London	020 7242 2523
Crail Miss (Elspeth) Ross	12 New Square, London	0171 419 1212
	Sovereign Chambers, Leeds	0113 2451841/2/3
Cranfield Peter Anthony	3 Verulam Buildings, London	0171 831 8441
Crawford Grant	11 Old Square, London	020 7430 0341
Dalby Joseph Francis	Portsmouth Barristers' Chambers, Winchester	01962 863222
	Portsmouth Barristers' Chambers, Portsmouth	023 92 831292/811811
Davey Benjamin Nicholas	11 Old Square, London	020 7430 0341
Davies Philip Edward Hamilton	Erskine Chambers, London	0171 242 5532
de Lacy Richard Michael	3 Verulam Buildings, London	0171 831 8441
Dillon Thomas William Matthew	1 Fountain Court, Birmingham	0121 236 5721
Dodge Peter Clive	11 Old Square, London	020 7430 0341
Dooher Miss Nancy Helen	St James's Chambers, Manchester	0161 834 7000
Dougherty Nigel Peter	Erskine Chambers, London	0171 242 5532
Dowley Dominic Myles	One Hare Court, London	020 7353 3171
Driscoll Miss Lynn	Sovereign Chambers, Leeds	0113 2451841/2/3
Duddridge Robert James	2 Gray's Inn Square Chambers, London	020 7242 0328
Eaton Turner David Murray	1 New Square, London	0171 405 0884/5/6/7

Elleray Anthony John	• St James's Chambers, Manchester	0161 834 7000
	12 New Square, London	0171 419 1212
	Park Lane Chambers, Leeds	0113 2285000
Ellis Roger John	13 King's Bench Walk, London	0171 353 7204
	King's Bench Chambers, Oxford	01865 311066
Evans James Frederick Meurig	3 Verulam Buildings, London	0171 831 8441
Evans Richard Gareth	5 Paper Buildings, London	0171 583 9275/583 4555
Farber James Henry Martin	5 Stone Buildings, London	0171 242 6201
Farrow Kenneth John	Serle Court Chambers, London	0171 242 6105
Fawls Richard Granville	5 Stone Buildings, London	0171 242 6201
Feltham Piers Jonathan	Chambers of Mr Peter Crampin QC, London	020 7831 0081
Fletcher Andrew Fitzroy Stephen	4 Pump Court, London	020 7842 5555
Francis Edward Gerald Francis	Enterprise Chambers, London	0171 405 9471
	Enterprise Chambers, Leeds	0113 246 0391
	Enterprise Chambers, Newcastle upon Tyne	0191 222 3344
Freedman Sampson Clive	3 Verulam Buildings, London	0171 831 8441
Garcia-Miller Miss Laura	Enterprise Chambers, London	0171 405 9471
	Enterprise Chambers, Leeds	0113 246 0391
	Enterprise Chambers, Newcastle upon Tyne	0191 222 3344
Garner Miss Sophie Jane	199 Strand, London	0171 379 9779
Gasztowicz Steven	2-3 Gray's Inn Square, London	0171 242 4986
	2 New Street, Leicester	0116 2625906
Gee Steven Mark	4 Field Court, London	0171 440 6900
George Miss Judith Sarah	St Philip's Chambers, Birmingham	0121 246 7000
Gerald Nigel Mortimer	Enterprise Chambers, London	0171 405 9471
	Enterprise Chambers, Leeds	0113 246 0391
	Enterprise Chambers, Newcastle upon Tyne	0191 222 3344
Gibaud Miss Catherine Alison Annetta	3 Verulam Buildings, London	0171 831 8441
Gillyon Philip Jeffrey	Erskine Chambers, London	0171 242 5532
Graham Thomas Patrick Henry	1 New Square, London	0171 405 0884/5/6/7
Grantham Andrew Timothy	• Deans Court Chambers, Manchester	0161 214 6000
	Deans Court Chambers, Preston	01772 555163
Green David Cameron	Adrian Lyon's Chambers, Liverpool	0151 236 4421/8240
Green Miss Jane Elizabeth	Design Chambers, London	0171 353 0747
	Chambers of Martin Burr, London	0171 353 4636
Gregory John Raymond	Deans Court Chambers, Manchester	0161 214 6000
	Deans Court Chambers, Preston	01772 555163
Groves Hugo Gerard	Enterprise Chambers, London	0171 405 9471
	Enterprise Chambers, Leeds	0113 246 0391
	Enterprise Chambers, Newcastle upon Tyne	0191 222 3344
Hall Taylor Alexander Edward	11 Old Square, London	020 7430 0341
Halpern David Anthony	Enterprise Chambers, London	0171 405 9471
	Enterprise Chambers, Leeds	0113 246 0391
	Enterprise Chambers, Newcastle upon Tyne	0191 222 3344
Hamilton Eben William	1 New Square, London	0171 405 0884/5/6/7
Hantusch Robert Anthony	• 3 Stone Buildings, London	0171 242 4937
Harries Raymond Elwyn	Bracton Chambers, London	0171 242 4248
Harris Melvyn	7 New Square, London	0171 430 1660
Henley Raymond Francis St Luke	Lancaster Building, Manchester	0161 661 4444/0171 649 9872
Hibbert William John	Gough Square Chambers, London	0171 353 0924
Hoffman David Alexander	8 King Street Chambers, Manchester	0161 834 9560
Hoffmann Miss Jocelyn Clare	Serle Court Chambers, London	0171 242 6105
Hollington Robin Frank	1 New Square, London	0171 405 0884/5/6/7
Hornett Stuart Ian	29 Bedford Row Chambers, London	0171 831 2626

• Expanded entry in Part D

Hoser Philip Jacob	Serle Court Chambers, London	0171 242 6105
Hossain Ajmalul	• 29 Bedford Row Chambers, London	0171 831 2626
Hubbard Mark Iain	1 New Square, London	0171 405 0884/5/6/7
Ife Miss Linden Elizabeth	Enterprise Chambers, London	0171 405 9471
	Enterprise Chambers, Leeds	0113 246 0391
	Enterprise Chambers, Newcastle upon Tyne	0191 222 3344
Jackson Dirik George Allan	Chambers of Mr Peter Crampin QC, London	020 7831 0081
Jarvis John Manners	3 Verulam Buildings, London	0171 831 8441
Jefferis Arthur Michael Quentin	Chambers of Mr Peter Crampin QC, London	020 7831 0081
Joffe Victor Howard	Serle Court Chambers, London	0171 242 6105
Jones Clive Hugh	1 New Square, London	0171 405 0884/5/6/7
Jones Philip John	Serle Court Chambers, London	0171 242 6105
Jory Robert John Hugh	Enterprise Chambers, London	0171 405 9471
	Enterprise Chambers, Leeds	0113 246 0391
	Enterprise Chambers, Newcastle upon Tyne	0191 222 3344
Kennedy Michael Kirk Inches	1 New Square, London	0171 405 0884/5/6/7
Kinnier Andrew John	2 Harcourt Buildings, London	0171 583 9020
Kolodziej Andrzej Jozef	• Littman Chambers, London	020 7404 4866
Kosmin Leslie Gordon	Erskine Chambers, London	0171 242 5532
Kremen Philip Michael	Hardwicke Building, London	020 7242 2523
Kuschke Leon Siegfried	Erskine Chambers, London	0171 242 5532
Kynoch Duncan Stuart Sanderson	29 Bedford Row Chambers, London	0171 831 2626
Lamacraft Ian Richard	Bracton Chambers, London	0171 242 4248
Lamb Robert Glasson	13 King's Bench Walk, London	0171 353 7204
	King's Bench Chambers, Oxford	01865 311066
Lamont Miss Camilla Rose	Chambers of Lord Goodhart QC, London	0171 405 5577
Lampard Miss Kathryn Felice	1 New Square, London	0171 405 0884/5/6/7
Levin Craig Michael	Lancaster Building, Manchester	0161 661 4444/0171 649 9872
Lightman Daniel	Serle Court Chambers, London	0171 242 6105
Littman Mark	Littman Chambers, London	020 7404 4866
Lloyd Stephen James George	Chambers of Mr Peter Crampin QC, London	020 7831 0081
Lowenstein Paul David	Littleton Chambers, London	0171 797 8600
Lucas Miss Bridget Ann	Serle Court Chambers, London	0171 242 6105
	Fountain Court, London	0171 583 3335
Mabb David Michael	Erskine Chambers, London	0171 242 5532
Macpherson Duncan Charles Stewart	Bracton Chambers, London	0171 242 4248
Malek Ali	3 Verulam Buildings, London	0171 831 8441
Mandalia Vinesh Lalji	Harrow on the Hill Chambers, Harrow-on-the-Hill	0181 423 7444
Mann George Anthony	Enterprise Chambers, London	0171 405 9471
	Enterprise Chambers, Leeds	0113 246 0391
	Enterprise Chambers, Newcastle upon Tyne	0191 222 3344
Marquand Charles Nicholas Hilary	Chambers of Lord Goodhart QC, London	0171 405 5577
Marshall Philip Scott	Serle Court Chambers, London	0171 242 6105
Martin John Vandeleur	• Wilberforce Chambers, London	0171 306 0102
Masters Miss Sara Alayna	20 Essex Street, London	0171 583 9294
Mauger Miss Claire Shanti Andrea	Enterprise Chambers, London	0171 405 9471
	Enterprise Chambers, Newcastle upon Tyne	0191 222 3344
	Enterprise Chambers, Leeds	0113 246 0391
Maynard-Connor Giles	St James's Chambers, Manchester	0161 834 7000
McCafferty Miss Lynne	5 Paper Buildings, London	0171 583 9275/583 4555
McClure Brian David	Littman Chambers, London	020 7404 4866

McCulloch Ian	Bracton Chambers, London	0171 242 4248
	Lloyds House Chambers, Manchester	0161 839 3371
	Claremont Chambers, Wolverhampton	01902 426222
McDonnell John Beresford William	1 New Square, London	0171 405 0884/5/6/7
McHugh Denis David	Bracton Chambers, London	0171 242 4248
Mendoza Neil David Pereira	Hardwicke Building, London	020 7242 2523
Merriman Nicholas Flavelle	3 Verulam Buildings, London	0171 831 8441
Milligan Iain Anstruther	20 Essex Street, London	0171 583 9294
Mitchell Gregory Charles Mathew	3 Verulam Buildings, London	0171 831 8441
Moore Mr Craig Ian	Barnard's Inn Chambers, London	0171 369 6969
	Park Lane Chambers, Leeds	0113 2285000
Moore Martin Luke	Erskine Chambers, London	0171 242 5532
Moran Andrew John	One Hare Court, London	020 7353 3171
Morgan Richard Hugo Lyndon	13 Old Square, London	0171 404 4800
Munby James Lawrence	1 New Square, London	0171 405 0884/5/6/7
Neville Stephen John	Gough Square Chambers, London	0171 353 0924
Newman Miss Catherine Mary	• 13 Old Square, London	0171 404 4800
Nicholls John Peter	13 Old Square, London	0171 404 4800
Norbury Hugh Robert	Serle Court Chambers, London	0171 242 6105
O'Leary Robert Michael	33 Park Place, Cardiff	02920 233313
O'Toole Simon Gerard	2 Mitre Court Buildings, London	0171 353 1353
Odgers John Arthur	3 Verulam Buildings, London	0171 831 8441
Ohrenstein Dov	Chambers of Lord Goodhart QC, London	0171 405 5577
Owens Miss Hilary Jane	St Philip's Chambers, Birmingham	0121 246 7000
Patchett-Joyce Michael Thurston	Monckton Chambers, London	0171 405 7211
Peacocke Mrs Teresa Anne Rosen	Enterprise Chambers, London	0171 405 9471
	Enterprise Chambers, Leeds	0113 246 0391
	Enterprise Chambers, Newcastle upon Tyne	0191 222 3344
Pearce Robert Edgar	Chambers of Mr Peter Crampin QC, London	020 7831 0081
Pelling (Philip) Mark	Monckton Chambers, London	0171 405 7211
Perkoff Richard Michael	Littleton Chambers, London	0171 797 8600
Phillips Stephen Edmund	3 Verulam Buildings, London	0171 831 8441
Piper Angus Richard	No. 1 Serjeants' Inn, London	0171 415 6666
Potts James Rupert	Erskine Chambers, London	0171 242 5532
Potts Robin	Erskine Chambers, London	0171 242 5532
Prentice Professor Daniel David	Erskine Chambers, London	0171 242 5532
Prentis Sebastian Hugh Runton	1 New Square, London	0171 405 0884/5/6/7
Proudman Miss Sonia Rosemary Susan	Chambers of Mr Peter Crampin QC, London	020 7831 0081
Prudhoe Timothy Nixon	Queen's Chambers, Manchester	0161 834 6875/4738
	Queens Chambers, Preston	01772 828300
Rai Amarjit Singh	St Philip's Chambers, Birmingham	0121 246 7000
Randall John Yeoman	St Philip's Chambers, Birmingham	0121 246 7000
	7 Stone Buildings, London	0171 405 3886/242 3546
Rashid Omar	Chambers of Mr Peter Crampin QC, London	020 7831 0081
Reed John William Rupert	• Wilberforce Chambers, London	0171 306 0102
Reid Graham Matthew	4 Paper Buildings, London	0171 353 3366/583 7155
Richardson Giles John	Serle Court Chambers, London	0171 242 6105
Rivalland Marc-Edouard	No. 1 Serjeants' Inn, London	0171 415 6666
Roberts Miss Catherine Ann	Erskine Chambers, London	0171 242 5532
Roberts Jeremy Michael Graham	9 Gough Square, London	020 7832 0500
Roberts Michael Charles	1 New Square, London	0171 405 0884/5/6/7
Rowley Keith Nigel	11 Old Square, London	020 7430 0341
Rowntree Edward John Pickering	Hardwicke Building, London	020 7242 2523
Ryder Timothy Robert	Queen's Chambers, Manchester	0161 834 6875/4738
	Queens Chambers, Preston	01772 828300

Sagar (Edward) Leigh	12 New Square, London	0171 419 1212
	Newport Chambers, Newport	01633 267403/255855
	Sovereign Chambers, Leeds	0113 2451841/2/3
Saggerson Alan David	Barnard's Inn Chambers, London	0171 369 6969
Salter Richard Stanley	3 Verulam Buildings, London	0171 831 8441
Seal Julius Damien	189 Randolph Avenue, London	0171 624 9139
Sellers Graham	Adrian Lyon's Chambers, Liverpool	0151 236 4421/8240
Seymour Richard William	Monckton Chambers, London	0171 405 7211
Shuman Miss Karen Ann Elizabeth	Bracton Chambers, London	0171 242 4248
Siddiqi Faizul Aqtab	Justice Court Chambers, London	0181 830 7786
Simpson Ian	Bracton Chambers, London	0171 242 4248
Smith Paul Andrew	One Hare Court, London	020 7353 3171
Snowden Richard Andrew	Erskine Chambers, London	0171 242 5532
Southall Richard Anthony	• 17 Bedford Row, London	0171 831 7314
Staddon Miss Claire Ann	12 New Square, London	0171 419 1212
	Sovereign Chambers, Leeds	0113 2451841/2/3
Staddon Paul	2nd Floor, Francis Taylor Building, London	0171 353 9942/3157
Start Miss Angharad Jocelyn	3 Verulam Buildings, London	0171 831 8441
Staunton (Thomas) Ulick (Patrick)	Chambers of Mr Peter Crampin QC, London	020 7831 0081
	65-67 King Street, Leicester	0116 2547710
	St James's Chambers, Manchester	0161 834 7000
Sterling Robert Alan	12 New Square, London	0171 419 1212
	Park Lane Chambers, Leeds	0113 2285000
Stewart Nicholas John Cameron	Hardwicke Building, London	020 7242 2523
Stockdale Sir Thomas Minshull	Erskine Chambers, London	0171 242 5532
Stokes Miss Mary Elizabeth	Erskine Chambers, London	0171 242 5532
Stubbs William Frederick	Erskine Chambers, London	0171 242 5532
Sullivan Scott	Barnard's Inn Chambers, London	0171 369 6969
Swerling Robert Harry	13 Old Square, London	0171 404 4800
Sykes (James) Richard	Erskine Chambers, London	0171 242 5532
Szanto Gregory John Michael	Eastbourne Chambers, Eastbourne	01323 642102
Talbot Patrick John	Serle Court Chambers, London	0171 242 6105
Tedd Rex Hilary	• St Philip's Chambers, Birmingham	0121 246 7000
	De Montfort Chambers, Leicester	0116 254 8686
	Northampton Chambers, Northampton	01604 636271
Terry Robert Jeffrey	8 King Street Chambers, Manchester	0161 834 9560
Thomas (Robert) Neville	3 Verulam Buildings, London	0171 831 8441
Thompson Andrew Richard	Erskine Chambers, London	0171 242 5532
Thornton Andrew James	Erskine Chambers, London	0171 242 5532
Tipples Miss Amanda Jane	13 Old Square, London	0171 404 4800
Todd Michael Alan	Erskine Chambers, London	0171 242 5532
Tolaney Miss Sonia	3 Verulam Buildings, London	0171 831 8441
Trace Anthony John	• 13 Old Square, London	0171 404 4800
Tselentis Michael	• 20 Essex Street, London	0171 583 9294
Tucker Miss Katherine Jane Greening	St Philip's Chambers, Birmingham	0121 246 7000
Tully Ms Anne Margaret	Eastbourne Chambers, Eastbourne	01323 642102
Van Tonder Gerard Dirk	1 New Square, London	0171 405 0884/5/6/7
Vines Anthony Robert Francis	Gough Square Chambers, London	0171 353 0924
Walford Richard Henry Howard	Serle Court Chambers, London	0171 242 6105
Walker Andrew Greenfield	Chambers of Lord Goodhart QC, London	0171 405 5577
Watson-Gandy Mark	• Plowden Buildings, London	0171 583 0808
Weatherill Bernard Richard	Chambers of Lord Goodhart QC, London	0171 405 5577
West Mark	• 11 Old Square, London	020 7430 0341
Wilkins Mrs Colette Ann	1 New Square, London	0171 405 0884/5/6/7
Williams Dr Jason Scott	• 3 Dr Johnson's Buildings, London	0171 353 4854
Williamson Miss Bridget Susan	Enterprise Chambers, London	0171 405 9471
	Enterprise Chambers, Leeds	0113 246 0391
	Enterprise Chambers, Newcastle upon Tyne	0191 222 3344

B

• Expanded entry in Part D

Wilson Ian Robert	3 Verulam Buildings, London	0171 831 8441
Wilson-Barnes Miss Lucy Emma	St James's Chambers, Manchester	0161 834 7000
Wood Ian Robert	8 King Street Chambers, Manchester	0161 834 9560
Woolf Steven Jeremy	Hardwicke Building, London	020 7242 2523
Worster David James Stewart	St Philip's Chambers, Birmingham	0121 246 7000
Wyatt Michael Christopher	10 Winterbourne Grove, Weybridge	0181 941 3939
Zelin Geoffrey Andrew	Enterprise Chambers, London	0171 405 9471
	Enterprise Chambers, Leeds	0113 246 0391
	Enterprise Chambers, Newcastle upon Tyne	0191 222 3344

COMPETITION

Abrahams James	8 New Square, London	0171 405 4321
Alexander Daniel Sakyi	8 New Square, London	0171 405 4321
Anderson Miss Julie	• Littman Chambers, London	020 7404 4866
Anderson Rupert John	Monckton Chambers, London	0171 405 7211
Baldwin John Paul	8 New Square, London	0171 405 4321
Beal Kieron Conrad	4 Paper Buildings, London	0171 353 3366/583 7155
Beard Daniel Matthew	Monckton Chambers, London	0171 405 7211
Beaumont Marc Clifford	• Harrow on the Hill Chambers, Harrow-on-the-Hill	0181 423 7444
	Windsor Barristers' Chambers, Windsor	01753 648899
	Pump Court Chambers, London	0171 353 0711
Buck Dr Andrew Theodore	Chambers of Martin Burr, London	0171 353 4636
Clark Miss Fiona Jane Stewart	8 New Square, London	0171 405 4321
Driscoll Miss Lynn	Sovereign Chambers, Leeds	0113 2451841/2/3
Fowler Richard Nicholas	Monckton Chambers, London	0171 405 7211
Fysh Michael	8 New Square, London	0171 405 4321
Ghaffar Arshad	4 Field Court, London	0171 440 6900
Gore-Andrews Gavin Angus Russell	2 Harcourt Buildings, London	0171 583 9020
Green Miss Jane Elizabeth	Design Chambers, London	0171 353 0747
	Chambers of Martin Burr, London	0171 353 4636
Gregory John Raymond	Deans Court Chambers, Manchester	0161 214 6000
	Deans Court Chambers, Preston	01772 555163
Hamer George Clemens	8 New Square, London	0171 405 4321
Harris Paul Best	Monckton Chambers, London	0171 405 7211
Haynes Miss Rebecca	Monckton Chambers, London	0171 405 7211
Henley Raymond Francis St Luke	Lancaster Building, Manchester	0161 661 4444/0171 649 9872
Hicks Michael Charles	• 19 Old Buildings, London	0171 405 2001
Hill Raymond	Monckton Chambers, London	0171 405 7211
Holman Miss Tamsin Perdita	19 Old Buildings, London	0171 405 2001
Howe Martin Russell Thomson	8 New Square, London	0171 405 4321
Jones Philip John	Serle Court Chambers, London	0171 242 6105
Kitchin David James Tyson	8 New Square, London	0171 405 4321
Lambert John	Lancaster Building, Manchester	0161 661 4444/0171 649 9872
Lane Ms Lindsay Ruth Busfield	8 New Square, London	0171 405 4321
Lasok Karol Paul Edward	Monckton Chambers, London	0171 405 7211
Lever Jeremy Frederick	Monckton Chambers, London	0171 405 7211
Macnab Alexander Andrew	Monckton Chambers, London	0171 405 7211
Mantle Peter John	Monckton Chambers, London	0171 405 7211
May Miss Charlotte Louisa	8 New Square, London	0171 405 4321
McClure Brian David	Littman Chambers, London	020 7404 4866
Meade Richard David	8 New Square, London	0171 405 4321
Mellor Edward James Wilson	8 New Square, London	0171 405 4321
Mercer Hugh Charles	• Essex Court Chambers, London	0171 813 8000
Mitropoulos Christos	Chambers of Geoffrey Hawker, London	0171 583 8899
Moody-Stuart Thomas	8 New Square, London	0171 405 4321
Morris Stephen Nathan	20 Essex Street, London	0171 583 9294
O'Shea Eoin Finbarr	4 Field Court, London	0171 440 6900
Onslow Robert Denzil	8 New Square, London	0171 405 4321
Padfield Nicholas David	One Hare Court, London	020 7353 3171

• Expanded entry in Part D

Page Howard William Barrett	One Hare Court, London	020 7353 3171
Paines Nicholas Paul Billot	Monckton Chambers, London	0171 405 7211
Parker Kenneth Blades	Monckton Chambers, London	0171 405 7211
Pelling (Philip) Mark	Monckton Chambers, London	0171 405 7211
Peretz George Michael John	Monckton Chambers, London	0171 405 7211
Pickford Anthony James	Prince Henry's Chamber, London	0171 834 2572
Platts-Mills Mark Fortescue	8 New Square, London	0171 405 4321
Pope David James	3 Verulam Buildings, London	0171 831 8441
Prescott Peter Richard Kyle	8 New Square, London	0171 405 4321
Reed Jeremy Nigel	19 Old Buildings, London	0171 405 2001
Roth Peter Marcel	Monckton Chambers, London	0171 405 7211
Shipley Norman Graham	• 19 Old Buildings, London	0171 405 2001
Simor Miss Jessica Margaret Poppaea	Monckton Chambers, London	0171 405 7211
Skilbeck Mrs Jennifer Seth	Monckton Chambers, London	0171 405 7211
Smith Ms Katherine Emma	Monckton Chambers, London	0171 405 7211
Speck Adrian	8 New Square, London	0171 405 4321
St Ville Laurence James	8 New Square, London	0171 405 4321
Sullivan Rory Myles	19 Old Buildings, London	0171 405 2001
Swift John Anthony	Monckton Chambers, London	0171 405 7211
Tappin Michael John	8 New Square, London	0171 405 4321
Thompson Rhodri William Ralph	Monckton Chambers, London	0171 405 7211
Turner Jonathan Richard	Monckton Chambers, London	0171 405 7211
Vajda Christopher Stephen	Monckton Chambers, London	0171 405 7211
Vitoria Miss Mary Christine	8 New Square, London	0171 405 4321
Wilson Alastair James Drysdale	• 19 Old Buildings, London	0171 405 2001

COMPETITIVE TENDERING/PUBLIC PROCUREMENT

Dalby Joseph Francis	Portsmouth Barristers' Chambers, Winchester	01962 863222
	Portsmouth Barristers' Chambers, Portsmouth	023 92 831292/811811

COMPULSORY PURCHASE

Purchas Robin Michael	• 2 Harcourt Buildings, London	020 7353 8415
Straker Timothy Derrick	• 4-5 Gray's Inn Square, London	0171 404 5252

COMPUTER LITIGATION

Boyd James Andrew Donaldson	8 King Street Chambers, Manchester	0161 834 9560
Guy John David Colin	Francis Taylor Building, London	0171 797 7250

COMPUTER SYSTEMS PROCUREMENT

Lambert John	Lancaster Building, Manchester	0161 661 4444/0171 649 9872

CONSTRUCTION

Acton Davis Jonathan James	4 Pump Court, London	020 7842 5555
Akenhead Robert	Atkin Chambers, London	020 7404 0102
Allen Michael David Prior	S Tomlinson QC, London	0171 583 0404
Ansell Miss Rachel Louise	4 Pump Court, London	020 7842 5555
Atherton Ian David	Enterprise Chambers, London	0171 405 9471
	Enterprise Chambers, Newcastle upon Tyne	0191 222 3344
	Enterprise Chambers, Leeds	0113 246 0391
Ayres Andrew John William	13 Old Square, London	0171 404 4800
Baatz Nicholas Stephen	Atkin Chambers, London	020 7404 0102
Bailey Edward Henry	Monckton Chambers, London	0171 405 7211
Baldry Antony Brian	No. 1 Serjeants' Inn, London	0171 415 6666
Banks Francis Andrew	Adrian Lyon's Chambers, Liverpool	0151 236 4421/8240
Barker Simon George Harry	• 13 Old Square, London	0171 404 4800
Barraclough Richard Michael	6 Pump Court, London	0171 797 8400
	6-8 Mill Street, Maidstone	01622 688094

B

Barwise Miss Stephanie Nicola	Atkin Chambers, London	020 7404 0102
Bellamy Jonathan Mark	39 Essex Street, London	0171 832 1111
Blackburn John	Atkin Chambers, London	020 7404 0102
Blakesley Patrick James	Two Crown Office Row, London	020 7797 8100
Blunt David John	4 Pump Court, London	020 7842 5555
Boswell Miss Lindsay Alice	4 Pump Court, London	020 7842 5555
Bowdery Martin	Atkin Chambers, London	020 7404 0102
Brannigan Peter John Sean	4 Pump Court, London	020 7842 5555
Browne-Wilkinson Simon	Serle Court Chambers, London	0171 242 6105
Burns Peter Richard	Deans Court Chambers, Manchester	0161 214 6000
	Deans Court Chambers, Preston	01772 555163
Burns Miss Susan Linda	3 Serjeants' Inn, London	0171 353 5537
Burr Andrew Charles	Atkin Chambers, London	020 7404 0102
Catchpole Stuart Paul	• 39 Essex Street, London	0171 832 1111
Challenger Colin Westcott	Bridewell Chambers, London	020 7797 8800
Chalmers Miss Suzanne Frances	Two Crown Office Row, London	020 7797 8100
Charlton Alexander Murray	4 Pump Court, London	020 7842 5555
Clark Andrew Richard	Manchester House Chambers, Manchester	0161 834 7007
	8 King Street Chambers, Manchester	0161 834 9560
Clark Christopher Harvey	Pump Court Chambers, Winchester	01962 868161
	Pump Court Chambers, London	0171 353 0711
	Westgate Chambers, Lewes	01273 480510
	Pump Court Chambers, Swindon	01793 539899
	Harrow on the Hill Chambers, Harrow-on-the-Hill	0181 423 7444
Clay Robert Charles	Atkin Chambers, London	020 7404 0102
Clegg Sebastian James Barwick	Deans Court Chambers, Manchester	0161 214 6000
	Deans Court Chambers, Preston	01772 555163
Collard Michael David	5 Pump Court, London	020 7353 2532
Collings Nicholas Stewart	Atkin Chambers, London	020 7404 0102
Cory-Wright Charles Alexander	39 Essex Street, London	0171 832 1111
Cross James Edward Michael	4 Pump Court, London	020 7842 5555
Crowley John Desmond	Two Crown Office Row, London	020 7797 8100
Croxford Ian Lionel	• Wilberforce Chambers, London	0171 306 0102
Curtis Michael Alexander	Two Crown Office Row, London	020 7797 8100
Dalby Joseph Francis	Portsmouth Barristers' Chambers, Winchester	01962 863222
	Portsmouth Barristers' Chambers, Portsmouth	023 92 831292/811811
Davies Stephen Richard	8 King Street Chambers, Manchester	0161 834 9560
DeCamp Miss Jane Louise	Two Crown Office Row, London	020 7797 8100
Dempsey Brian Paul	Lancaster Building, Manchester	0161 661 4444/0171 649 9872
Denbin Jack Arnold	Greenway, Sonning-on-Thames	0118 969 2484
Dennison Stephen Randell	Atkin Chambers, London	020 7404 0102
Dennys Nicholas Charles Jonathan	Atkin Chambers, London	020 7404 0102
Dingemans James Michael	1 Crown Office Row, London	0171 583 9292
Dixon Philip John	2nd Floor, Francis Taylor Building, London	0171 353 9942/3157
Dodd Christopher John Nicholas	9 Woodhouse Square, Leeds	0113 2451986
Doerries Miss Chantal-Aimee Renee Aemelia Annemarie	Atkin Chambers, London	020 7404 0102
Douglas Michael John	4 Pump Court, London	020 7842 5555
Dumaresq Ms Delia Jane	Atkin Chambers, London	020 7404 0102
Dyer Allen Gordon	4 Pump Court, London	020 7842 5555
Dyer David Roger	St Philip's Chambers, Birmingham	0121 246 7000
Eastman Roger	2 Harcourt Buildings, London	0171 583 9020
Edwards-Stuart Antony James Cobham	Two Crown Office Row, London	020 7797 8100
Evans-Tovey Jason Robert	Two Crown Office Row, London	020 7797 8100
Farrow Kenneth John	Serle Court Chambers, London	0171 242 6105

Fletcher Andrew Fitzroy Stephen	4 Pump Court, London	020 7842 5555
Franklin Miss Kim	• One Paper Buildings, London	0171 583 7355
Fraser Peter Donald	Atkin Chambers, London	020 7404 0102
Freedman Sampson Clive	3 Verulam Buildings, London	0171 831 8441
Friedman David Peter	4 Pump Court, London	020 7842 5555
Gerald Nigel Mortimer	Enterprise Chambers, London	0171 405 9471
	Enterprise Chambers, Leeds	0113 246 0391
	Enterprise Chambers, Newcastle upon Tyne	0191 222 3344
Gibson Martin John	Littman Chambers, London	020 7404 4866
Goddard Andrew Stephen	Atkin Chambers, London	020 7404 0102
Godwin William George Henry	Atkin Chambers, London	020 7404 0102
Goldblatt Simon	39 Essex Street, London	0171 832 1111
Grant David Euan Barron	13 King's Bench Walk, London	0171 353 7204
	King's Bench Chambers, Oxford	01865 311066
Grantham Andrew Timothy	• Deans Court Chambers, Manchester	0161 214 6000
	Deans Court Chambers, Preston	01772 555163
Gray Richard Paul	39 Essex Street, London	0171 832 1111
Greenbourne John Hugo	Two Crown Office Row, London	020 7797 8100
Grime Mark Stephen Eastburn	Deans Court Chambers, Manchester	0161 214 6000
	2 Pump Court, London	0171 353 5597
	Deans Court Chambers, Preston	01772 555163
Guggenheim Miss Anna Maeve	Two Crown Office Row, London	020 7797 8100
Gunning Alexander Rupert	4 Pump Court, London	020 7842 5555
Hall Mrs Melanie Ruth	Monckton Chambers, London	0171 405 7211
Hamilton Graeme Montagu	Two Crown Office Row, London	020 7797 8100
Hamilton Peter Bernard	4 Pump Court, London	020 7842 5555
Hantusch Robert Anthony	• 3 Stone Buildings, London	0171 242 4937
Harris Paul Best	Monckton Chambers, London	0171 405 7211
Harvey Michael Llewellyn Tucker	Two Crown Office Row, London	020 7797 8100
Henderson Simon Alexander	4 Pump Court, London	020 7842 5555
Higgins Rupert James Hale	Littman Chambers, London	020 7404 4866
Holdsworth James Arthur	Two Crown Office Row, London	020 7797 8100
Houghton Miss Kirsten Annette	4 Pump Court, London	020 7842 5555
Howarth Simon Stuart	Two Crown Office Row, London	020 7797 8100
Howells James Richard	Atkin Chambers, London	020 7404 0102
Hughes Adrian Warwick	4 Pump Court, London	020 7842 5555
Jess Digby Charles	8 King Street Chambers, Manchester	0161 834 9560
Kay Michael Jack David	3 Verulam Buildings, London	0171 831 8441
	Park Lane Chambers, Leeds	0113 2285000
Kent Michael Harcourt	Two Crown Office Row, London	020 7797 8100
Kolodziej Andrzej Jozef	• Littman Chambers, London	020 7404 4866
Lavender Nicholas	One Hare Court, London	020 7353 3171
Lofthouse Simon Timothy	Atkin Chambers, London	020 7404 0102
Lowenstein Paul David	Littleton Chambers, London	0171 797 8600
Lynagh Richard Dudley	Two Crown Office Row, London	020 7797 8100
Maclean Alan John	39 Essex Street, London	0171 832 1111
Majumdar Shantanu	Lamb Chambers, London	020 7797 8300
Mantle Peter John	Monckton Chambers, London	0171 405 7211
Manzoni Charles Peter	39 Essex Street, London	0171 832 1111
Marks Jonathan Clive	4 Pump Court, London	020 7842 5555
Mauleverer Peter Bruce	4 Pump Court, London	020 7842 5555
McCall Duncan James	4 Pump Court, London	020 7842 5555
McClure Brian David	Littman Chambers, London	020 7404 4866
McGregor Harvey	4 Paper Buildings, London	0171 353 3366/583 7155
McKinnell Miss Soraya Jane	Enterprise Chambers, London	0171 405 9471
	Enterprise Chambers, Newcastle upon Tyne	0191 222 3344
	Enterprise Chambers, Leeds	0113 246 0391
McMullan Manus Anthony	Atkin Chambers, London	020 7404 0102
Meeson Nigel Keith	4 Field Court, London	0171 440 6900

Mendoza Neil David Pereira	Hardwicke Building, London	020 7242 2523
Milne Michael	Resolution Chambers, Malvern	01684 561279
	Chambers of Geoffrey Hawker, London	0171 583 8899
Moger Christopher Richard Derwent	4 Pump Court, London	020 7842 5555
Morgan Charles James Arthur	Enterprise Chambers, London	0171 405 9471
	Enterprise Chambers, Newcastle upon Tyne	0191 222 3344
	Enterprise Chambers, Leeds	0113 246 0391
Mulcahy Miss Leigh-Ann Maria	Chambers of John L Powell QC, London	0171 797 8000
Naidoo Sean Van	Littman Chambers, London	020 7404 4866
Naughton Philip Anthony	3 Serjeants' Inn, London	0171 353 5537
Neville-Clarke Sebastian Adrian Bennett	1 Crown Office Row, London	0171 583 9292
Nicholson Jeremy Mark	4 Pump Court, London	020 7842 5555
Norman Christopher John George	No. 1 Serjeants' Inn, London	0171 415 6666
O'Sullivan Thomas Sean Patrick	4 Pump Court, London	020 7842 5555
O'Toole Simon Gerard	2 Mitre Court Buildings, London	0171 353 1353
Ohrenstein Dov	Chambers of Lord Goodhart QC, London	0171 405 5577
Packman Miss Claire Geraldine Vance	4 Pump Court, London	020 7842 5555
Padfield Ms Alison Mary	Devereux Chambers, London	0171 353 7534
Panesar Deshpal Singh	13 King's Bench Walk, London	0171 353 7204
	King's Bench Chambers, Oxford	01865 311066
Parkin Miss Fiona Jane	Atkin Chambers, London	020 7404 0102
Patchett-Joyce Michael Thurston	Monckton Chambers, London	0171 405 7211
Patten Benedict Joseph	Two Crown Office Row, London	020 7797 8100
Patterson Stewart	Pump Court Chambers, Winchester	01962 868161
	Pump Court Chambers, London	0171 353 0711
	Pump Court Chambers, Swindon	01793 539899
Pearson Christopher	• Bridewell Chambers, London	020 7797 8800
Pelling (Philip) Mark	Monckton Chambers, London	0171 405 7211
Persey Lionel Edward	• 4 Field Court, London	0171 440 6900
Pershad Rohan	Two Crown Office Row, London	020 7797 8100
Phillips Andrew Charles	Two Crown Office Row, London	020 7797 8100
Pilling Benjamin	4 Pump Court, London	020 7842 5555
Pleming Nigel Peter	39 Essex Street, London	0171 832 1111
Raeside Mark Andrew	Atkin Chambers, London	020 7404 0102
Rawley Miss Dominique Jane	Atkin Chambers, London	020 7404 0102
Reese Colin Edward	Atkin Chambers, London	020 7404 0102
Reid Sebastian Peter Scott	2nd Floor, Francis Taylor Building, London	0171 353 9942/3157
Richards Miss Jennifer	39 Essex Street, London	0171 832 1111
Richardson David John	13 King's Bench Walk, London	0171 353 7204
	King's Bench Chambers, Oxford	01865 311066
Rigney Andrew James	Two Crown Office Row, London	020 7797 8100
Robb Adam Duncan	39 Essex Street, London	0171 832 1111
Ross John Graffin	No. 1 Serjeants' Inn, London	0171 415 6666
Roth Peter Marcel	Monckton Chambers, London	0171 405 7211
Rowland John Peter	4 Pump Court, London	020 7842 5555
Rowlands Marc Humphreys	4 Pump Court, London	020 7842 5555
Royce Darryl Fraser	Atkin Chambers, London	020 7404 0102
Rumney Conrad William Arthur	St Philip's Chambers, Birmingham	0121 246 7000
Ryder Timothy Robert	Queen's Chambers, Manchester	0161 834 6875/4738
	Queens Chambers, Preston	01772 828300
Salmon Jonathan Carl	1 Fountain Court, Birmingham	0121 236 5721
Salter Richard Stanley	3 Verulam Buildings, London	0171 831 8441
Sears Robert David Murray	4 Pump Court, London	020 7842 5555
Seymour Richard William	Monckton Chambers, London	0171 405 7211
Siddiqi Faizul Aqtab	Justice Court Chambers, London	0181 830 7786
Smith Miss Joanna Angela	• Wilberforce Chambers, London	0171 306 0102
Smith Ms Katherine Emma	Monckton Chambers, London	0171 405 7211

• Expanded entry in Part D

Smith Warwick Timothy Cresswell	Deans Court Chambers, Manchester	0161 214 6000
	Deans Court Chambers, Preston	01772 555163
Snowden John Stevenson	Two Crown Office Row, London	020 7797 8100
Starcevic Petar	St Philip's Chambers, Birmingham	0121 246 7000
Stevenson John Melford	Two Crown Office Row, London	020 7797 8100
Storey Jeremy Brian	4 Pump Court, London	020 7842 5555
Streatfeild-James David Stewart	Atkin Chambers, London	020 7404 0102
Swan Ian Christopher	Two Crown Office Row, London	020 7797 8100
Tackaberry John Antony	Arbitration Chambers, London	020 7267 2137
	40 King Street, Manchester	0161 832 9082
	Assize Court Chambers, Bristol	0117 9264587
	Littman Chambers, London	020 7404 4866
Tecks Jonathan Howard	Littman Chambers, London	020 7404 4866
Tedd Rex Hilary	• St Philip's Chambers, Birmingham	0121 246 7000
	De Montfort Chambers, Leicester	0116 254 8686
	Northampton Chambers, Northampton	01604 636271
Temple Anthony Dominic	4 Pump Court, London	020 7842 5555
Ter Haar Roger Eduard Lound	Two Crown Office Row, London	020 7797 8100
Travers Hugh	Pump Court Chambers, London	0171 353 0711
	Pump Court Chambers, Winchester	01962 868161
	Pump Court Chambers, Swindon	01793 539899
Trotman Timothy Oliver	Deans Court Chambers, Manchester	0161 214 6000
	Deans Court Chambers, Preston	01772 555163
Tucker David William	Two Crown Office Row, London	020 7797 8100
Valentine Donald Graham	Atkin Chambers, London	020 7404 0102
Vaughan-Neil Miss Catherine Mary Bernardine	4 Pump Court, London	020 7842 5555
Vineall Nicholas Edward John	4 Pump Court, London	020 7842 5555
Walker Steven John	Atkin Chambers, London	020 7404 0102
Wallace Ian Norman Duncan	Atkin Chambers, London	020 7404 0102
Ward Timothy Justin	Monckton Chambers, London	0171 405 7211
Weston Clive Aubrey Richard	Two Crown Office Row, London	020 7797 8100
White Andrew	Atkin Chambers, London	020 7404 0102
Wilken Sean David Henry	39 Essex Street, London	0171 832 1111
Wilkinson Nigel Vivian Marshall	Two Crown Office Row, London	020 7797 8100
Williams A John	13 King's Bench Walk, London	0171 353 7204
	King's Bench Chambers, Oxford	01865 311066
Wilmot-Smith Richard James Crosbie	39 Essex Street, London	0171 832 1111
Wood Ian Robert	8 King Street Chambers, Manchester	0161 834 9560
Wyvill Alistair	St Philip's Chambers, Birmingham	0121 246 7000

CONSUMER CREDIT

Butler Andrew	2nd Floor, Francis Taylor Building, London	0171 353 9942/3157
Hibbert William John	Gough Square Chambers, London	0171 353 0924
Hodgkinson Tristram Patrick	• 5 Pump Court, London	020 7353 2532
Neville Stephen John	Gough Square Chambers, London	0171 353 0924
Philpott Frederick Alan	Gough Square Chambers, London	0171 353 0924
Sayer Mr Peter Edwin	Gough Square Chambers, London	0171 353 0924
Smith Miss Julia Mair Wheldon	Gough Square Chambers, London	0171 353 0924

CONSUMER LAW

Althaus Antony Justin	No. 1 Serjeants' Inn, London	0171 415 6666
Andrews Miss Claire Marguerite	Gough Square Chambers, London	0171 353 0924
Ayres Andrew John William	13 Old Square, London	0171 404 4800
Basu Dr Dijendra Bhushan	Devereux Chambers, London	0171 353 7534
Bean Matthew Allen	11 King's Bench Walk, Leeds	0113 297 1200
	11 King's Bench Walk, London	0171 353 3337

Beaumont Marc Clifford	• Harrow on the Hill Chambers, Harrow-on-the-Hill	0181 423 7444
	Windsor Barristers' Chambers, Windsor	01753 648899
	Pump Court Chambers, London	0171 353 0711
Blakesley Patrick James	Two Crown Office Row, London	020 7797 8100
Bourne Geoffrey Robert	4 Field Court, London	0171 440 6900
Bowmer Michael Paul	11 Old Square, London	020 7430 0341
Bresler Fenton Shea	22 Melcombe Regis Court, London	0171 487 5589
Buck Dr Andrew Theodore	Chambers of Martin Burr, London	0171 353 4636
Burden Edward Angus	St Philip's Chambers, Birmingham	0121 246 7000
Burns Peter Richard	Deans Court Chambers, Manchester	0161 214 6000
	Deans Court Chambers, Preston	01772 555163
Cawley Neil Robert Loudoun	169 Temple Chambers, London	0171 583 7644
	Milton Keynes Chambers, Milton Keynes	01908 664 128
Chalmers Miss Suzanne Frances	Two Crown Office Row, London	020 7797 8100
Cogswell Miss Frederica Natasha	Gough Square Chambers, London	0171 353 0924
Colbey Richard (Alan)	• Francis Taylor Building, London	0171 797 7250
	Guildhall Chambers Portsmouth, Portsmouth	01705 752400
Cole Richard John	Lancaster Building, Manchester	0161 661 4444/0171 649 9872
Cook Jeremy David	Lamb Building, London	020 7797 7788
Cotter Barry Paul	Old Square Chambers, Bristol	0117 9277111
	Old Square Chambers, London	0171 269 0300
Davey Benjamin Nicholas	11 Old Square, London	020 7430 0341
Dillon Thomas William Matthew	1 Fountain Court, Birmingham	0121 236 5721
Ellin Miss Nina Caroline	6 Pump Court, London	0171 797 8400
	6-8 Mill Street, Maidstone	01622 688094
Ellis Dr Peter Simon	7 New Square, London	0171 430 1660
Evans Miss Claire Louise	Peel Court Chambers, Manchester	0161 832 3791
Finn Terence	Chambers of Martin Burr, London	0171 353 4636
Ford Gerard James	Baker Street Chambers, Middlesbrough	01642 873873
Forte Mark Julian Carmino	8 King Street Chambers, Manchester	0161 834 9560
Glennie Andrew David	13 King's Bench Walk, London	0171 353 7204
	King's Bench Chambers, Oxford	01865 311066
Goulding Jonathan Steven	Gough Square Chambers, London	0171 353 0924
Grantham Andrew Timothy	• Deans Court Chambers, Manchester	0161 214 6000
	Deans Court Chambers, Preston	01772 555163
Grime John Andrew	Pump Court Chambers, Swindon	01793 539899
	Pump Court Chambers, London	0171 353 0711
	Pump Court Chambers, Winchester	01962 868161
Hanson Timothy Vincent Richard	St Philip's Chambers, Birmingham	0121 246 7000
Harris Melvyn	7 New Square, London	0171 430 1660
Harvey Michael Llewellyn Tucker	Two Crown Office Row, London	020 7797 8100
Hibbert William John	Gough Square Chambers, London	0171 353 0924
Hodgkinson Tristram Patrick	• 5 Pump Court, London	020 7353 2532
Holmes-Milner James Neil	2 Mitre Court Buildings, London	0171 353 1353
Howarth Simon Stuart	Two Crown Office Row, London	020 7797 8100
Hulme Miss Amanda Claire	Gough Square Chambers, London	0171 353 0924
Kynoch Duncan Stuart Sanderson	29 Bedford Row Chambers, London	0171 831 2626
Lo Bernard Norman	17 Bedford Row, London	0171 831 7314
MacDonald Iain	Gough Square Chambers, London	0171 353 0924
Macleod Duncan	9 Gough Square, London	020 7832 0500
Mainwaring [Robert] Paul Clason	Carmarthen Chambers, Carmarthen	01267 234410
Mandalia Vinesh Lalji	Harrow on the Hill Chambers, Harrow-on-the-Hill	0181 423 7444
Mantle Peter John	Monckton Chambers, London	0171 405 7211
Maxwell-Scott James Herbert	Two Crown Office Row, London	020 7797 8100
McAlinden Barry O'Neill	17 Bedford Row, London	0171 831 7314
McAllister Miss Eimear Jane	9 Woodhouse Square, Leeds	0113 2451986
Mercer David Paul	Queen's Chambers, Manchester	0161 834 6875/4738
	Queens Chambers, Preston	01772 828300

B

• Expanded entry in Part D

Mills Corey Arthur	Becket Chambers, Canterbury	01227 786331
Morgan Andrew James	St Philip's Chambers, Birmingham	0121 246 7000
Mulholland Michael	St James's Chambers, Manchester	0161 834 7000
Murray-Smith James Michael	8 King's Bench Walk, London	0171 797 8888
	8 King's Bench Walk North, Leeds	0113 2439797
Nardell Gordon Lawrence	6 Pump Court, London	0171 797 8400
	6-8 Mill Street, Maidstone	01622 688094
Neville Stephen John	Gough Square Chambers, London	0171 353 0924
Ohrenstein Dov	Chambers of Lord Goodhart QC, London	0171 405 5577
Outhwaite Mrs Wendy-Jane Tivnan	2 Harcourt Buildings, London	0171 583 9020
Pearce Richard William	Peel Court Chambers, Manchester	0161 832 3791
Pears Derrick Allan	2nd Floor, Francis Taylor Building, London	0171 353 9942/3157
Pearson Christopher	• Bridewell Chambers, London	020 7797 8800
Peirson Oliver James	Pump Court Chambers, London	0171 353 0711
	Pump Court Chambers, Winchester	01962 868161
	Pump Court Chambers, Swindon	01793 539899
Peretz George Michael John	Monckton Chambers, London	0171 405 7211
Perkins Miss Marianne Yvette	7 New Square, London	0171 430 1660
Pershad Rohan	Two Crown Office Row, London	020 7797 8100
Philpott Frederick Alan	Gough Square Chambers, London	0171 353 0924
Potts Warren Nigel	Queen's Chambers, Manchester	0161 834 6875/4738
	Queens Chambers, Preston	01772 828300
Renfree Peter Gerald Stanley	Harbour Court Chambers, Fareham	01329 827828
Rigney Andrew James	Two Crown Office Row, London	020 7797 8100
Roth Peter Marcel	Monckton Chambers, London	0171 405 7211
Sayer Mr Peter Edwin	Gough Square Chambers, London	0171 353 0924
Seymour Richard William	Monckton Chambers, London	0171 405 7211
Shale Justin Anton	4 King's Bench Walk, London	0171 822 8822
	King's Bench Chambers, Bournemouth	01202 250025
Sheehan Malcolm Peter	2 Harcourt Buildings, London	0171 583 9020
Skelly Andrew Jon	1 Gray's Inn Square, London	0171 405 8946/7/8
Smith Miss Julia Mair Wheldon	Gough Square Chambers, London	0171 353 0924
Staddon Paul	2nd Floor, Francis Taylor Building, London	0171 353 9942/3157
Szanto Gregory John Michael	Eastbourne Chambers, Eastbourne	01323 642102
Taft Christopher Heiton	St James's Chambers, Manchester	0161 834 7000
Tracy Forster Miss Jane Elizabeth	13 King's Bench Walk, London	0171 353 7204
	King's Bench Chambers, Oxford	01865 311066
Travers David	• 3 Fountain Court, Birmingham	0121 236 5854
Tregilgas-Davey Marcus Ian	Pump Court Chambers, Swindon	01793 539899
	Pump Court Chambers, London	0171 353 0711
	Pump Court Chambers, Winchester	01962 868161
Tucker Miss Katherine Jane Greening	St Philip's Chambers, Birmingham	0121 246 7000
Tully Ms Anne Margaret	Eastbourne Chambers, Eastbourne	01323 642102
Tyack David Guy	St Philip's Chambers, Birmingham	0121 246 7000
Verduyn Dr Anthony James	St Philip's Chambers, Birmingham	0121 246 7000
Vines Anthony Robert Francis	Gough Square Chambers, London	0171 353 0924
Westgate Martin Trevor	Doughty Street Chambers, London	0171 404 1313

CONTRACT

Crossley Steven Richard	37 Park Square Chambers, Leeds	0113 2439422
Ferm Rodney Eric	37 Park Square Chambers, Leeds	0113 2439422
Glover Stephen Julian	37 Park Square Chambers, Leeds	0113 2439422

CONVEYANCING

Acton Stephen Neil	11 Old Square, London	020 7430 0341
Angus Miss Tracey Anne	5 Stone Buildings, London	0171 242 6201
Asprey Nicholas	Serle Court Chambers, London	0171 242 6105
Ayres Andrew John William	13 Old Square, London	0171 404 4800
Barton Alan John	Lamb Building, London	020 7797 7788

Bash-Taqi Mrs Shahineh	Leone Chambers, London	0181 200 4020
Beaumont Marc Clifford	• Harrow on the Hill Chambers, Harrow-on-the-Hill	0181 423 7444
	Windsor Barristers' Chambers, Windsor	01753 648899
	Pump Court Chambers, London	0171 353 0711
Behrens James Nicholas Edward	Serle Court Chambers, London	0171 242 6105
Blackett-Ord Mark	• 5 Stone Buildings, London	0171 242 6201
Burr Martin John	Chambers of Martin Burr, London	0171 353 4636
	7 New Square, London	0171 430 1660
Chan Miss Susan	13 King's Bench Walk, London	0171 353 7204
	King's Bench Chambers, Oxford	01865 311066
Clarke Peter John	St Philip's Chambers, Birmingham	0121 246 7000
	Harcourt Chambers, London	0171 353 6961
	Harcourt Chambers, Oxford	01865 791559
Cosedge Andrew John	3 Stone Buildings, London	0171 242 4937
Craig Alistair Trevor	Chambers of Mr Peter Crampin QC, London	020 7831 0081
Crampin Peter	Chambers of Mr Peter Crampin QC, London	020 7831 0081
Cranfield Peter Anthony	3 Verulam Buildings, London	0171 831 8441
Crawford Grant	11 Old Square, London	020 7430 0341
Dodge Peter Clive	11 Old Square, London	020 7430 0341
Ellis Roger John	13 King's Bench Walk, London	0171 353 7204
	King's Bench Chambers, Oxford	01865 311066
Farrow Kenneth John	Serle Court Chambers, London	0171 242 6105
Feltham Piers Jonathan	Chambers of Mr Peter Crampin QC, London	020 7831 0081
Flenley William David Wingate	4 Paper Buildings, London	0171 353 3366/583 7155
Foster Brian Ian	St James's Chambers, Manchester	0161 834 7000
	Park Lane Chambers, Leeds	0113 2285000
Francis Andrew James	Chambers of Mr Peter Crampin QC, London	020 7831 0081
Fryer-Spedding James Walter	St James's Chambers, Manchester	0161 834 7000
Gerald Nigel Mortimer	Enterprise Chambers, London	0171 405 9471
	Enterprise Chambers, Leeds	0113 246 0391
	Enterprise Chambers, Newcastle upon Tyne	0191 222 3344
Gibson Miss Jill Maureen	Chambers of Mr Peter Crampin QC, London	020 7831 0081
Gifford Andrew James Morris	7 New Square, London	0171 430 1660
Green David Cameron	Adrian Lyon's Chambers, Liverpool	0151 236 4421/8240
Gregory John Raymond	Deans Court Chambers, Manchester	0161 214 6000
	Deans Court Chambers, Preston	01772 555163
Hall Taylor Alexander Edward	11 Old Square, London	020 7430 0341
Halpern David Anthony	Enterprise Chambers, London	0171 405 9471
	Enterprise Chambers, Leeds	0113 246 0391
	Enterprise Chambers, Newcastle upon Tyne	0191 222 3344
Hantusch Robert Anthony	• 3 Stone Buildings, London	0171 242 4937
Harrod Henry Mark	5 Stone Buildings, London	0171 242 6201
Henderson William Hugo	Serle Court Chambers, London	0171 242 6105
Higgins Adrian John	13 King's Bench Walk, London	0171 353 7204
	King's Bench Chambers, Oxford	01865 311066
Hill Piers Nicholas	37 Park Square Chambers, Leeds	0113 2439422
Horne Roger Cozens-Hardy	Chambers of Mr Peter Crampin QC, London	020 7831 0081
Hoser Philip Jacob	Serle Court Chambers, London	0171 242 6105
Jackson Dirik George Allan	Chambers of Mr Peter Crampin QC, London	020 7831 0081
Jefferis Arthur Michael Quentin	Chambers of Mr Peter Crampin QC, London	020 7831 0081

B

         • Expanded entry in Part D

Karas Jonathan Marcus	• Wilberforce Chambers, London	0171 306 0102
Kremen Philip Michael	Hardwicke Building, London	020 7242 2523
Lamb Robert Glasson	13 King's Bench Walk, London	0171 353 7204
	King's Bench Chambers, Oxford	01865 311066
Lamont Miss Camilla Rose	Chambers of Lord Goodhart QC, London	0171 405 5577
Legge Henry	5 Stone Buildings, London	0171 242 6201
Levy Benjamin Keith	Enterprise Chambers, London	0171 405 9471
	Enterprise Chambers, Leeds	0113 246 0391
	Enterprise Chambers, Newcastle upon Tyne	0191 222 3344
Lloyd Stephen James George	Chambers of Mr Peter Crampin QC, London	020 7831 0081
Mainwaring [Robert] Paul Clason	Carmarthen Chambers, Carmarthen	01267 234410
Mann George Anthony	Enterprise Chambers, London	0171 405 9471
	Enterprise Chambers, Leeds	0113 246 0391
	Enterprise Chambers, Newcastle upon Tyne	0191 222 3344
Mason Miss Alexandra	3 Stone Buildings, London	0171 242 4937
McAllister Miss Elizabeth Ann	Enterprise Chambers, London	0171 405 9471
	Enterprise Chambers, Leeds	0113 246 0391
	Enterprise Chambers, Newcastle upon Tyne	0191 222 3344
McQuail Ms Katherine Emma	11 Old Square, London	020 7430 0341
Mendoza Neil David Pereira	Hardwicke Building, London	020 7242 2523
Norris Alastair Hubert	5 Stone Buildings, London	0171 242 6201
	Southernhay Chambers, Exeter	01392 255777
Nugee Edward George	• Wilberforce Chambers, London	0171 306 0102
Nurse Gordon Bramwell William	11 Old Square, London	020 7430 0341
O'Sullivan Michael Morton	5 Stone Buildings, London	0171 242 6201
Oakley Anthony James	• 11 Old Square, London	020 7430 0341
Ohrenstein Dov	Chambers of Lord Goodhart QC, London	0171 405 5577
Ovey Miss Elizabeth Helen	11 Old Square, London	020 7430 0341
Panesar Deshpal Singh	13 King's Bench Walk, London	0171 353 7204
	King's Bench Chambers, Oxford	01865 311066
Pearce Robert Edgar	Chambers of Mr Peter Crampin QC, London	020 7831 0081
Pilkington Mrs Mavis Patricia	9 Woodhouse Square, Leeds	0113 2451986
Purkis Ms Kathryn Miranda	Serle Court Chambers, London	0171 242 6105
Radevsky Anthony Eric	Falcon Chambers, London	0171 353 2484
Rashid Omar	Chambers of Mr Peter Crampin QC, London	020 7831 0081
Rich Miss Ann Barbara	5 Stone Buildings, London	0171 242 6201
Rogers Miss Beverly-Ann	Serle Court Chambers, London	0171 242 6105
Ross Martyn John Greaves	• 5 New Square, London	020 7404 0404
Rowell David Stewart	Chambers of Lord Goodhart QC, London	0171 405 5577
Sellers Graham	Adrian Lyon's Chambers, Liverpool	0151 236 4421/8240
Selway Dr Katherine Emma	11 Old Square, London	020 7430 0341
Shale Justin Anton	4 King's Bench Walk, London	0171 822 8822
	King's Bench Chambers, Bournemouth	01202 250025
Shillingford George Miles	Chambers of Mr Peter Crampin QC, London	020 7831 0081
Sinclair Miss Lisa Anne	7 New Square, London	0171 430 1660
Smith Howard James	Chambers of Mr Peter Crampin QC, London	020 7831 0081
Southall Richard Anthony	• 17 Bedford Row, London	0171 831 7314
Staddon Paul	2nd Floor, Francis Taylor Building, London	0171 353 9942/3157
Sterling Robert Alan	St James's Chambers, Manchester	0161 834 7000
	12 New Square, London	0171 419 1212
	Park Lane Chambers, Leeds	0113 2285000
Stewart-Smith William Rodney	1 New Square, London	0171 405 0884/5/6/7

Studer Mark Edgar Walter	Chambers of Mr Peter Crampin QC, London	020 7831 0081
Tipples Miss Amanda Jane	13 Old Square, London	0171 404 4800
Turnbull Charles Emerson Lovett	• Wilberforce Chambers, London	0171 306 0102
Vickery Neil Michael	13 King's Bench Walk, London	0171 353 7204
	King's Bench Chambers, Oxford	01865 311066
Walker Andrew Greenfield	Chambers of Lord Goodhart QC, London	0171 405 5577
Warnock-Smith Mrs Shan	5 Stone Buildings, London	0171 242 6201
Waters Malcolm Ian	• 11 Old Square, London	020 7430 0341
West Mark	• 11 Old Square, London	020 7430 0341
White Matthew James	13 King's Bench Walk, London	0171 353 7204
	King's Bench Chambers, Oxford	01865 311066
Zelin Geoffrey Andrew	Enterprise Chambers, London	0171 405 9471
	Enterprise Chambers, Leeds	0113 246 0391
	Enterprise Chambers, Newcastle upon Tyne	0191 222 3344

B

COPYRIGHT

Abrahams James	8 New Square, London	0171 405 4321
Alexander Daniel Sakyi	8 New Square, London	0171 405 4321
Anderson Rupert John	Monckton Chambers, London	0171 405 7211
Ayres Andrew John William	13 Old Square, London	0171 404 4800
Baldwin John Paul	8 New Square, London	0171 405 4321
Barker Simon George Harry	• 13 Old Square, London	0171 404 4800
Bevis Dominic Joseph	10 King's Bench Walk, London	0171 353 7742
Chapple James Malcolm Dundas	1 New Square, London	0171 405 0884/5/6/7
Clark Miss Fiona Jane Stewart	8 New Square, London	0171 405 4321
Cole Richard John	Lancaster Building, Manchester	0161 661 4444/0171 649 9872
Colley Dr Peter McLean	• 19 Old Buildings, London	0171 405 2001
Cook Christopher Graham	St James's Chambers, Manchester	0161 834 7000
Coulthard Alan Terence	33 Park Place, Cardiff	02920 233313
Dillon Thomas William Matthew	1 Fountain Court, Birmingham	0121 236 5721
Driscoll Miss Lynn	Sovereign Chambers, Leeds	0113 2451841/2/3
Edwards Richard Julian Henshaw	3 Verulam Buildings, London	0171 831 8441
Elleray Anthony John	• St James's Chambers, Manchester	0161 834 7000
	12 New Square, London	0171 419 1212
	Park Lane Chambers, Leeds	0113 2285000
Emmerson (Michael) Benedict	Doughty Street Chambers, London	0171 404 1313
Fysh Michael	8 New Square, London	0171 405 4321
Gibaud Miss Catherine Alison Annetta	3 Verulam Buildings, London	0171 831 8441
Grayson Edward	• 9-12 Bell Yard, London	0171 400 1800
Greatorex Ms Helen Louise	9 Woodhouse Square, Leeds	0113 2451986
Green Miss Jane Elizabeth	Design Chambers, London	0171 353 0747
	Chambers of Martin Burr, London	0171 353 4636
Gregory John Raymond	Deans Court Chambers, Manchester	0161 214 6000
	Deans Court Chambers, Preston	01772 555163
Hamer George Clemens	8 New Square, London	0171 405 4321
Heal Mrs Madeleine	4 Field Court, London	0171 440 6900
Henley Raymond Francis St Luke	Lancaster Building, Manchester	0161 661 4444/0171 649 9872
Hicks Michael Charles	• 19 Old Buildings, London	0171 405 2001
Hilton Alan John Howard	Hollis Whiteman Chambers, London	020 7583 5766
Holman Miss Tamsin Perdita	19 Old Buildings, London	0171 405 2001
Howe Martin Russell Thomson	8 New Square, London	0171 405 4321
Hudson Anthony Sean	Doughty Street Chambers, London	0171 404 1313
Jefferis Arthur Michael Quentin	Chambers of Mr Peter Crampin QC, London	020 7831 0081
Kelman Alistair Bruce	Lancaster Building, Manchester	0161 661 4444/0171 649 9872
Kitchin David James Tyson	8 New Square, London	0171 405 4321
Lambert John	Lancaster Building, Manchester	0161 661 4444/0171 649 9872
Lane Ms Lindsay Ruth Busfield	8 New Square, London	0171 405 4321

• Expanded entry in Part D

Langdale Timothy James	Hollis Whiteman Chambers, London	020 7583 5766
May Miss Charlotte Louisa	8 New Square, London	0171 405 4321
Meade Richard David	8 New Square, London	0171 405 4321
Mellor Edward James Wilson	8 New Square, London	0171 405 4321
Metzer Anthony David Erwin	Doughty Street Chambers, London	0171 404 1313
Moody-Stuart Thomas	8 New Square, London	0171 405 4321
Nicol Andrew George Lindsay	Doughty Street Chambers, London	0171 404 1313
Onslow Robert Denzil	8 New Square, London	0171 405 4321
Peretz George Michael John	Monckton Chambers, London	0171 405 7211
Pickering James Patrick	Enterprise Chambers, London	0171 405 9471
	Enterprise Chambers, Leeds	0113 246 0391
	Enterprise Chambers, Newcastle upon Tyne	0191 222 3344
Pickford Anthony James	Prince Henry's Chamber, London	0171 834 2572
Platts-Mills Mark Fortescue	8 New Square, London	0171 405 4321
Prescott Peter Richard Kyle	8 New Square, London	0171 405 4321
Price Richard Mervyn	Littleton Chambers, London	0171 797 8600
Puckrin Cedric Eldred	19 Old Buildings, London	0171 405 2001
Purves Gavin Bowman	Swan House, London	0181 998 3035
Reed Jeremy Nigel	19 Old Buildings, London	0171 405 2001
Reid Brian Christopher	19 Old Buildings, London	0171 405 2001
Renfree Peter Gerald Stanley	Harbour Court Chambers, Fareham	01329 827828
Robertson Geoffrey Ronald	Doughty Street Chambers, London	0171 404 1313
Shipley Norman Graham	• 19 Old Buildings, London	0171 405 2001
Speck Adrian	8 New Square, London	0171 405 4321
St Ville Laurence James	8 New Square, London	0171 405 4321
Sterling Robert Alan	St James's Chambers, Manchester	0161 834 7000
	12 New Square, London	0171 419 1212
	Park Lane Chambers, Leeds	0113 2285000
Sullivan Rory Myles	19 Old Buildings, London	0171 405 2001
Sutcliffe Andrew Harold Wentworth	3 Verulam Buildings, London	0171 831 8441
Tappin Michael John	8 New Square, London	0171 405 4321
Vitoria Miss Mary Christine	8 New Square, London	0171 405 4321
Wilson Alastair James Drysdale	• 19 Old Buildings, London	0171 405 2001

COPYRIGHT THEFT

Strudwick Miss Linda Diane	Hollis Whiteman Chambers, London	020 7583 5766

COPYRIGHT TRIBUNAL

Barker Simon George Harry	• 13 Old Square, London	0171 404 4800

CORONERS INQUESTS

Davidson Dr Ranald Dunbar	3 Serjeants' Inn, London	0171 353 5537
McCahill Patrick Gerard	St Philip's Chambers, Birmingham	0121 246 7000
	Chambers of Andrew Campbell QC, Leeds	0113 2455438
Newton-Price James Edward	Pump Court Chambers, London	0171 353 0711
	Pump Court Chambers, Winchester	01962 868161
	Pump Court Chambers, Swindon	01793 539899
Wheetman Alan	East Anglian Chambers, Norwich	01603 617351
	East Anglian Chambers, Colchester	01206 572756
	East Anglian Chambers, Ipswich	01473 214481

CORPORATE FINANCE

Ayres Andrew John William	13 Old Square, London	0171 404 4800
Barker Simon George Harry	• 13 Old Square, London	0171 404 4800
Bryant Miss Ceri Jane	Erskine Chambers, London	0171 242 5532
Chivers (Tom) David	Erskine Chambers, London	0171 242 5532
Cone John Crawford	Erskine Chambers, London	0171 242 5532
de Lacy Richard Michael	3 Verulam Buildings, London	0171 831 8441
Dougherty Nigel Peter	Erskine Chambers, London	0171 242 5532

Dowley Dominic Myles	One Hare Court, London	020 7353 3171
Garcia-Miller Miss Laura	Enterprise Chambers, London	0171 405 9471
	Enterprise Chambers, Leeds	0113 246 0391
	Enterprise Chambers, Newcastle upon Tyne	0191 222 3344
Gillyon Philip Jeffrey	Erskine Chambers, London	0171 242 5532
Green Miss Jane Elizabeth	Design Chambers, London	0171 353 0747
	Chambers of Martin Burr, London	0171 353 4636
Halpern David Anthony	Enterprise Chambers, London	0171 405 9471
	Enterprise Chambers, Leeds	0113 246 0391
	Enterprise Chambers, Newcastle upon Tyne	0191 222 3344
Jones Philip John	Serle Court Chambers, London	0171 242 6105
Lazarus Michael Steven	1 Crown Office Row, London	0171 583 9292
Legge Henry	5 Stone Buildings, London	0171 242 6201
Lowenstein Paul David	Littleton Chambers, London	0171 797 8600
Mabb David Michael	Erskine Chambers, London	0171 242 5532
Malek Ali	3 Verulam Buildings, London	0171 831 8441
Marquand Charles Nicholas Hilary	Chambers of Lord Goodhart QC, London	0171 405 5577
Moore Martin Luke	Erskine Chambers, London	0171 242 5532
Naidoo Sean Van	Littman Chambers, London	020 7404 4866
Potts Robin	Erskine Chambers, London	0171 242 5532
Roberts Miss Catherine Ann	Erskine Chambers, London	0171 242 5532
Salter Richard Stanley	3 Verulam Buildings, London	0171 831 8441
Southern David Boardman	• Temple Gardens Tax Chambers, London	0171 353 7884/5 8982/3
Stockdale Sir Thomas Minshull	Erskine Chambers, London	0171 242 5532
Stokes Miss Mary Elizabeth	Erskine Chambers, London	0171 242 5532
Stubbs William Frederick	Erskine Chambers, London	0171 242 5532
Sykes (James) Richard	Erskine Chambers, London	0171 242 5532
Thornton Andrew James	Erskine Chambers, London	0171 242 5532
Todd Michael Alan	Erskine Chambers, London	0171 242 5532
Walford Richard Henry Howard	Serle Court Chambers, London	0171 242 6105
Watson-Gandy Mark	• Plowden Buildings, London	0171 583 0808

CORPORATE MANSLAUGHTER

Forlin Gerard Emlyn	Hardwicke Building, London	020 7242 2523

COSTS

Morgan Richard Hugo Lyndon	13 Old Square, London	0171 404 4800
Morgan (Thomas) Jeremy	39 Essex Street, London	0171 832 1111
Post Andrew John	Chambers of Kieran Coonan QC, London	0171 583 6013/2510
Van Tonder Gerard Dirk	1 New Square, London	0171 405 0884/5/6/7
Williams Dr Jason Scott	• 3 Dr Johnson's Buildings, London	0171 353 4854

COURT OF PROTECTION

Angus Miss Tracey Anne	5 Stone Buildings, London	0171 242 6201
Mason Miss Alexandra	3 Stone Buildings, London	0171 242 4937
Warnock-Smith Mrs Shan	5 Stone Buildings, London	0171 242 6201

COURTS MARTIAL

Aldred Mark Steven	Hollis Whiteman Chambers, London	020 7583 5766
Barker Nicholas	30 Park Square, Leeds	0113 2436388
Barnard Jonathan James	Hollis Whiteman Chambers, London	020 7583 5766
Barnett Andrew John	Pump Court Chambers, Winchester	01962 868161
	Pump Court Chambers, London	0171 353 0711
	Pump Court Chambers, Swindon	01793 539899
Barnfather Miss Lydia Helen	Hollis Whiteman Chambers, London	020 7583 5766
Barraclough Nicholas Maylin	2nd Floor, Francis Taylor Building, London	0171 353 9942/3157
Bennetts Philip James	Hollis Whiteman Chambers, London	020 7583 5766
Bergin Timothy William	Crown Office Row Chambers, Brighton	01273 625625

• Expanded entry in Part D

Blackburn Luke Sebastian	Pump Court Chambers, London	0171 353 0711
	Pump Court Chambers, Winchester	01962 868161
	Pump Court Chambers, Swindon	01793 539899
Boyce William	Hollis Whiteman Chambers, London	020 7583 5766
Brodwell John Shenton	9 Woodhouse Square, Leeds	0113 2451986
Brown Edward Francis Trevenen	Hollis Whiteman Chambers, London	020 7583 5766
Burbidge James Michael	St Philip's Chambers, Birmingham	0121 246 7000
Burn Colin Richard	30 Park Square, Leeds	0113 2436388
Butt Michael Robert	Pump Court Chambers, Swindon	01793 539899
	Pump Court Chambers, London	0171 353 0711
	Pump Court Chambers, Winchester	01962 868161
Cawley Neil Robert Loudoun	169 Temple Chambers, London	0171 583 7644
	Milton Keynes Chambers, Milton Keynes	01908 664 128
Coward Miss Victoria Jane	Hollis Whiteman Chambers, London	020 7583 5766
Darbishire Adrian Munro	Hollis Whiteman Chambers, London	020 7583 5766
Donne Jeremy Nigel	Hollis Whiteman Chambers, London	020 7583 5766
Ellison Mark Christopher	Hollis Whiteman Chambers, London	020 7583 5766
Emlyn Jones William Nicholas	2 Harcourt Buildings, London	020 7353 2112
Evans Julian Jacob	Hollis Whiteman Chambers, London	020 7583 5766
Farrer Paul Ainsworth	1 Fountain Court, Birmingham	0121 236 5721
Finnigan Peter Anthony	Hollis Whiteman Chambers, London	020 7583 5766
Gabb Charles Henry Escott	Pump Court Chambers, Winchester	01962 868161
	Pump Court Chambers, London	0171 353 0711
	Pump Court Chambers, Swindon	01793 539899
Gibbs Patrick Michael Evan	2 Harcourt Buildings, London	020 7353 2112
Gore-Andrews Gavin Angus Russell	2 Harcourt Buildings, London	0171 583 9020
Grey Robin Douglas	Hollis Whiteman Chambers, London	020 7583 5766
Gunther Miss Elizabeth Ann	Pump Court Chambers, Winchester	01962 868161
	Pump Court Chambers, London	0171 353 0711
	Pump Court Chambers, Swindon	01793 539899
Harris Ms Rebecca Elizabeth	Hollis Whiteman Chambers, London	020 7583 5766
Henry Edward Joseph Aloysius	Hollis Whiteman Chambers, London	020 7583 5766
Herbert David Richard	2 New Street, Leicester	0116 2625906
Hill Robert Douglas	Pump Court Chambers, Winchester	01962 868161
	Pump Court Chambers, London	0171 353 0711
	Pump Court Chambers, Swindon	01793 539899
Hodson Peter David	Chambers of Ian Macdonald QC (In Association with Two Garden Court, Temple, London), Manchester	0161 236 1840
Hogg The Hon Douglas Martin	37 Park Square Chambers, Leeds	0113 2439422
	Cathedral Chambers (Jan Wood Independent Barristers' Clerk), Exeter	01392 210900
Horwell Richard Eric	Hollis Whiteman Chambers, London	020 7583 5766
Johnson Miss Zoe Elisabeth	Hollis Whiteman Chambers, London	020 7583 5766
Jones Huw Michael Rees	St Albans Chambers, St Albans	01727 843383
Josse David Benjamin	Bridewell Chambers, London	020 7797 8800
Kark Thomas Victor William	Hollis Whiteman Chambers, London	020 7583 5766
Keane Michael Leo	4 Paper Buildings, London	0171 353 3366/583 7155
Kelsey-Fry John	Hollis Whiteman Chambers, London	020 7583 5766
Large Alan Macdonald	South Western Chambers, Taunton	01823 331919 (24 hrs)
Larkin Sean	Hollis Whiteman Chambers, London	020 7583 5766
Longden Anthony Gordon	Hollis Whiteman Chambers, London	020 7583 5766
Lowry Miss Emma Margaret Collins	Hollis Whiteman Chambers, London	020 7583 5766
Marshall-Andrews Robert Graham	37 Park Square Chambers, Leeds	0113 2439422
	2-4 Tudor Street, London	0171 797 7111
McCrindell James Derrey	Mitre House Chambers, London	0171 583 8233
McEvilly Gerard Martin	Furnival Chambers, London	0171 405 3232
Mitchell Christopher Richard	Hollis Whiteman Chambers, London	020 7583 5766
Newton-Price James Edward	Pump Court Chambers, London	0171 353 0711
	Pump Court Chambers, Winchester	01962 868161
	Pump Court Chambers, Swindon	01793 539899

● Expanded entry in Part D

Niblett Anthony Ian	1 Crown Office Row, London	0171 797 7500
	Crown Office Row Chambers, Brighton	01273 625625
Oliver Michael Richard	Hardwicke Building, London	020 7242 2523
Parr John Edward	8 King Street Chambers, Manchester	0161 834 9560
Parry Charles Robert	Pump Court Chambers, Swindon	01793 539899
	Pump Court Chambers, London	0171 353 0711
	Pump Court Chambers, Winchester	01962 868161
Parry Simon Edward	White Friars Chambers, Chester	01244 323070
Pascoe Nigel Spencer Knight	Pump Court Chambers, Winchester	01962 868161
	Pump Court Chambers, London	0171 353 0711
	Queens Square Chambers, Bristol	0117 921 1966
	Pump Court Chambers, Swindon	01793 539899
Paton Ian Francis	Hollis Whiteman Chambers, London	020 7583 5766
Pawson Robert Edward Cruickshank	Pump Court Chambers, Winchester	01962 868161
	Pump Court Chambers, London	0171 353 0711
	Pump Court Chambers, Swindon	01793 539899
Peirson Oliver James	Pump Court Chambers, London	0171 353 0711
	Pump Court Chambers, Winchester	01962 868161
	Pump Court Chambers, Swindon	01793 539899
Phillips Simon David	1 Fountain Court, Birmingham	0121 236 5721
Plaschkes Ms Sarah Georgina	Hollis Whiteman Chambers, London	020 7583 5766
Ramasamy Selvaraju	Hollis Whiteman Chambers, London	020 7583 5766
Roebuck Roy Delville	Bell Yard Chambers, London	0171 306 9292
Rogers Paul John	1 Crown Office Row, London	0171 797 7500
	Crown Office Row Chambers, Brighton	01273 625625
Ryan Timothy John	8 King's Bench Walk, London	0171 797 8888
	8 King's Bench Walk North, Leeds	0113 2439797
Ryder Ernest Nigel	Deans Court Chambers, Manchester	0161 214 6000
	Deans Court Chambers, Preston	01772 555163
	1 Mitre Court Buildings, London	0171 797 7070
Shrimpton Michael	Francis Taylor Building, London	0171 797 7250
Sibson Mrs Clare Adele	Hollis Whiteman Chambers, London	020 7583 5766
Stewart Neill Alastair	Hollis Whiteman Chambers, London	020 7583 5766
Still Geoffrey John Churchill	Pump Court Chambers, Swindon	01793 539899
	Pump Court Chambers, London	0171 353 0711
	Pump Court Chambers, Winchester	01962 868161
Sullivan Ms Jane Teresa	Hollis Whiteman Chambers, London	020 7583 5766
Summers Benjamin Dylan James	Hollis Whiteman Chambers, London	020 7583 5766
Swift Malcolm Robin	Park Court Chambers, Leeds	0113 2433277
	6 Gray's Inn Square, London	0171 242 1052
Thompson Miss Blondelle Marguerite	1 Fountain Court, Birmingham	0121 236 5721
Thompson Miss Sally	2 Harcourt Buildings, London	020 7353 2112
Thorne Timothy Peter	33 Bedford Row, London	0171 242 6476
Tregilgas-Davey Marcus Ian	Pump Court Chambers, Swindon	01793 539899
	Pump Court Chambers, London	0171 353 0711
	Pump Court Chambers, Winchester	01962 868161
Verduyn Dr Anthony James	St Philip's Chambers, Birmingham	0121 246 7000
Wakeham Philip John Le Messurier	Hardwicke Building, London	020 7242 2523
Warne Peter Lawrence	Hollis Whiteman Chambers, London	020 7583 5766
Wastie William Granville	Hollis Whiteman Chambers, London	020 7583 5766
Wilcken Anthony David Felix	Hollis Whiteman Chambers, London	020 7583 5766
Williams Neal Martin	1 Fountain Court, Birmingham	0121 236 5721
Wing Christopher John	Eighteen Carlton Crescent, Southampton	01703 639001
Winter Ian David	Hollis Whiteman Chambers, London	020 7583 5766

CREDIT HIRE

Boyle David Stuart	Deans Court Chambers, Manchester	0161 214 6000
	Deans Court Chambers, Preston	01772 555163
McCann Simon Howard	Deans Court Chambers, Manchester	0161 214 6000
	Deans Court Chambers, Preston	01772 555163

• Expanded entry in Part D

CRIME

Abbott Francis Arthur	Pump Court Chambers, Winchester	01962 868161
	Pump Court Chambers, London	0171 353 0711
	Pump Court Chambers, Swindon	01793 539899
Abel Miss Ann Petrina	3 Temple Gardens, London	0171 353 0832
Agnew Miss Christine	3 Hare Court, London	0171 395 2000
Ainsworth Mark Justin Simon	Peel Court Chambers, Manchester	0161 832 3791
Akiwumi Anthony Sebastian Akitayo	Pump Court Chambers, London	0171 353 0711
	Pump Court Chambers, Winchester	01962 868161
	Pump Court Chambers, Swindon	01793 539899
Alcock Peter Michael	6 Pump Court, London	0171 797 8400
	6-8 Mill Street, Maidstone	01622 688094
Aldred Mark Steven	Hollis Whiteman Chambers, London	020 7583 5766
Ali Miss Huma	Eastbourne Chambers, Eastbourne	01323 642102
Ali Zafar	• 1 Gray's Inn Square, London	0171 405 8946/7/8
	Cardinal Chambers, London	020 7353 2622
Allingham-Nicholson Mrs Elizabeth Sarah	2 New Street, Leicester	0116 2625906
Allsop Alexander Nigel Mark	3 Temple Gardens, London	0171 353 0832
Altman Brian	• 3 Hare Court, London	0171 395 2000
Alty Andrew Stephen John	Deans Court Chambers, Manchester	0161 214 6000
	Deans Court Chambers, Preston	01772 555163
Apfel Freddy	37 Park Square Chambers, Leeds	0113 2439422
Archer John Francis Ashweek	Two Crown Office Row, London	020 7797 8100
Arlow Ms Ruth Marian	Pump Court Chambers, London	0171 353 0711
	Pump Court Chambers, Swindon	01793 539899
	Pump Court Chambers, Winchester	01962 868161
Ashley Mark Robert	Pump Court Chambers, Swindon	01793 539899
	Pump Court Chambers, London	0171 353 0711
	Pump Court Chambers, Winchester	01962 868161
Ashman Peter Michael	Colleton Chambers, Exeter	01392 274898/9
Aston Maurice Charles	Five Paper Buildings, London	0171 583 6117
Atkins Richard Paul	1 Fountain Court, Birmingham	0121 236 5721
Auckland Miss Elizabeth Rachel	30 Park Square, Leeds	0113 2436388
Ayers Guy Russell	Octagon House, Norwich	01603 623186
	1 Paper Buildings, London	0171 353 3728/4953
Azam Javaid	Plowden Buildings, London	0171 583 0808
Bailey John Charles Williams	Queen's Chambers, Manchester	0161 834 6875/4738
	Queens Chambers, Preston	01772 828300
Bajwa Ali Naseem	Plowden Buildings, London	0171 583 0808
Baker Andrew James	7 New Square, London	0171 430 1660
	Richmond Green Chambers, Richmond-upon-Thames	0181 940 1841
	5 Fountain Court, Birmingham	0121 606 0500
Baker Stuart Christopher	1 Fountain Court, Birmingham	0121 236 5721
Baker William Arthur	Peel Court Chambers, Manchester	0161 832 3791
Balchin Richard Alexander	Crown Office Row Chambers, Brighton	01273 625625
Banks Robert James	100e Great Portland Street, London	0171 636 6323
Barker Brian John	Hollis Whiteman Chambers, London	020 7583 5766
Barker Nicholas	30 Park Square, Leeds	0113 2436388
Barnard Jonathan James	Hollis Whiteman Chambers, London	020 7583 5766
Barnes Miss Margaret Susanne	3 Hare Court, London	0171 395 2000
Barnett Andrew John	Pump Court Chambers, Winchester	01962 868161
	Pump Court Chambers, London	0171 353 0711
	Pump Court Chambers, Swindon	01793 539899
Barnfather Miss Lydia Helen	Hollis Whiteman Chambers, London	020 7583 5766
Barr Edward Robert	2 New Street, Leicester	0116 2625906
Barraclough Nicholas Maylin	2nd Floor, Francis Taylor Building, London	0171 353 9942/3157
Bart Delano Frank	8 King's Bench Walk, London	0171 797 8888
	8 King's Bench Walk North, Leeds	0113 2439797

• Expanded entry in Part D

Barton Alan John	Lamb Building, London	020 7797 7788
Barton Hugh Geoffrey	Doughty Street Chambers, London	0171 404 1313
Bash-Taqi Mrs Shahineh	Leone Chambers, London	0181 200 4020
Bassano Alaric Julian	Chambers of John Hand QC, Manchester	0161 955 9000
Bate David Christopher	Hollis Whiteman Chambers, London	020 7583 5766
Baughan Julian James	13 King's Bench Walk, London	0171 353 7204
	King's Bench Chambers, Oxford	01865 311066
Baxter-Phillips Miss Felicity Dawn	Becket Chambers, Canterbury	01227 786331
Bean Matthew Allen	11 King's Bench Walk, Leeds	0113 297 1200
	11 King's Bench Walk, London	0171 353 3337
Bedeau Stephen	Sovereign Chambers, Leeds	0113 2451841/2/3
	Lancaster Building, Manchester	0161 661 4444/0171 649 9872
Bennett Richard John	15 Winckley Square, Preston	01772 252828
Bennetts Philip James	Hollis Whiteman Chambers, London	020 7583 5766
Bentham Howard Lownds	Peel Court Chambers, Manchester	0161 832 3791
Bentley David Neil	Doughty Street Chambers, London	0171 404 1313
Bentley Stephen	1 Gray's Inn Square, London	0171 405 8946/7/8
Bergin Timothy William	Crown Office Row Chambers, Brighton	01273 625625
Bevan Edward Julian	Hollis Whiteman Chambers, London	020 7583 5766
Bexley Simon Mark	3 Temple Gardens, London	0171 353 0832
Bhanji Shiraz Musa	4 Bingham Place, London	0171 486 5347/071 487 5910
Bidder Neil	33 Park Place, Cardiff	02920 233313
	Goldsmith Building, London	0171 353 7881
Birch Roger Allen	Sovereign Chambers, Leeds	0113 2451841/2/3
	12 New Square, London	0171 419 1212
Birts Peter William	Farrar's Building, London	0171 583 9241
	St Philip's Chambers, Birmingham	0121 246 7000
Bitmead Paul Graham	Lamb Building, London	020 7797 7788
Blackburn Luke Sebastian	Pump Court Chambers, London	0171 353 0711
	Pump Court Chambers, Winchester	01962 868161
	Pump Court Chambers, Swindon	01793 539899
Blackshaw Henry William Randle	Peel Court Chambers, Manchester	0161 832 3791
Blake Arthur Joseph	13 King's Bench Walk, London	0171 353 7204
	King's Bench Chambers, Oxford	01865 311066
Blom-Cooper Sir Louis Jacques	Doughty Street Chambers, London	0171 404 1313
Blower Matthew John	3 Temple Gardens, London	0171 353 0832
Boateng Paul Yaw	8 King's Bench Walk, London	0171 797 8888
	8 King's Bench Walk North, Leeds	0113 2439797
Bogan Paul Simon	Doughty Street Chambers, London	0171 404 1313
Boney Guy Thomas Knowles	Pump Court Chambers, Winchester	01962 868161
	Pump Court Chambers, London	0171 353 0711
	Harrow on the Hill Chambers, Harrow-on-the-Hill	0181 423 7444
	Pump Court Chambers, Swindon	01793 539899
	Eighteen Carlton Crescent, Southampton	01703 639001
Boothroyd Miss Susan Elizabeth	Westgate Chambers, Newcastle upon Tyne	0191 261 4407/2329785
Bowen Paul Edward	4 King's Bench Walk, London	0171 822 8822
Boyce William	Hollis Whiteman Chambers, London	020 7583 5766
Bradshaw Howard Sydney	Queen's Chambers, Manchester	0161 834 6875/4738
	Queens Chambers, Preston	01772 828300
Brennan John David	4 Fountain Court, Birmingham	0121 236 3476
Brereton Mrs Fiorella	Peel Court Chambers, Manchester	0161 832 3791
Bright David Reginald	13 King's Bench Walk, London	0171 353 7204
	King's Bench Chambers, Oxford	01865 311066
Broatch Michael Donald	5 Paper Buildings, London	0171 583 9275/583 4555
Brodwell John Shenton	9 Woodhouse Square, Leeds	0113 2451986
Bromley-Davenport John	Deans Court Chambers, Manchester	0161 214 6000
	Deans Court Chambers, Preston	01772 555163
Brook Ian Stuart	Hardwicke Building, London	020 7242 2523
Brooks Mr Paul Anthony	Doughty Street Chambers, London	0171 404 1313

             • Expanded entry in Part D

Brown Miss Althea Sonia	Doughty Street Chambers, London	0171 404 1313
Brown Andrew Charles	Queen's Chambers, Manchester	0161 834 6875/4738
	Queens Chambers, Preston	01772 828300
Brown Edward Francis Trevenen	Hollis Whiteman Chambers, London	020 7583 5766
Browne James William	96 Gray's Inn Road, London	0171 405 0585
Brunton Sean Alexander McKay	Pump Court Chambers, Winchester	01962 868161
	Pump Court Chambers, London	0171 353 0711
	Pump Court Chambers, Swindon	01793 539899
Buckingham Mrs Kathleen Rosemary Bernadette	30 Park Square, Leeds	0113 2436388
Buckley Peter Evered	Queen's Chambers, Manchester	0161 834 6875/4738
	Queens Chambers, Preston	01772 828300
Burbidge James Michael	St Philip's Chambers, Birmingham	0121 246 7000
Burn Colin Richard	30 Park Square, Leeds	0113 2436388
Busby Thomas Andrew	1 Fountain Court, Birmingham	0121 236 5721
Butler Miss Judith Jane Scott	6 Pump Court, London	0171 797 8400
	6-8 Mill Street, Maidstone	01622 688094
Butt Michael Robert	Pump Court Chambers, Swindon	01793 539899
	Pump Court Chambers, London	0171 353 0711
	Pump Court Chambers, Winchester	01962 868161
Calvert David Edward	St James's Chambers, Manchester	0161 834 7000
Cannon Adam Richard	96 Gray's Inn Road, London	0171 405 0585
Carpenter Miss Jane Patricia Anne	2nd Floor, Francis Taylor Building, London	0171 353 9942/3157
Carr Simon Andrew	9 Gough Square, London	020 7832 0500
Carrasco Glenn Lawrence	3 Temple Gardens, London	0171 353 0832
Carroll Jonathan Neil	9 Woodhouse Square, Leeds	0113 2451986
Carter Peter	• 18 Red Lion Court, London	0171 520 6000
	Thornwood House, Chelmsford	01245 280880
Carter Miss Rosalyn Frances	St Philip's Chambers, Birmingham	0121 246 7000
Cartwright John Martin	Francis Taylor Building, London	0171 353 7768/7769/2711
Cartwright Nicholas Frederick	St Philip's Chambers, Birmingham	0121 246 7000
Carvalho Gomes Miss Ana Alexandra	St Albans Chambers, St Albans	01727 843383
Caswell Timothy Charles	8 King's Bench Walk North, Leeds	0113 2439797
	8 King's Bench Walk, London	0171 797 8888
Cave Jeremy Stephen	1 Crown Office Row, London	0171 797 7500
	Crown Office Row Chambers, Brighton	01273 625625
Chadd Paul	Theatre House, Bristol	0117 974 1553
	Colleton Chambers, Exeter	01392 274898/9
Charles Ms Deborah Ann	6 Pump Court, London	0171 797 8400
	6-8 Mill Street, Maidstone	01622 688094
Clare Michael Christopher	Octagon House, Norwich	01603 623186
	1 Paper Buildings, London	0171 353 3728/4953
Clark Christopher Harvey	Pump Court Chambers, Winchester	01962 868161
	Pump Court Chambers, London	0171 353 0711
	Westgate Chambers, Lewes	01273 480510
	Pump Court Chambers, Swindon	01793 539899
	Harrow on the Hill Chambers, Harrow-on-the-Hill	0181 423 7444
Clarke Peter William	Hollis Whiteman Chambers, London	020 7583 5766
Clemes Andrew John	Angel Chambers, Swansea	01792 464623/464648
Cliff Graham Hilton	St Philip's Chambers, Birmingham	0121 246 7000
Clover (Thomas) Anthony	New Court Chambers, London	0171 831 9500
Cole Robert Ian Gawain	30 Park Square, Leeds	0113 2436388
Colin Giles David	Crown Office Row Chambers, Brighton	01273 625625
Collier Peter Neville	30 Park Square, Leeds	0113 2436388
Collins Miss Jennifer Clair	Eastbourne Chambers, Eastbourne	01323 642102
Collins Michael Antony	37 Park Square Chambers, Leeds	0113 2439422

B

Conlon Michael John Patrick	4 Overdale Road, Leicester	0116 2883930
	St Albans Chambers, St Albans	01727 843383
	Tindal Chambers, Chelmsford	01245 267742
Conrath Philip Bernard	2nd Floor, Francis Taylor Building, London	0171 353 9942/3157
Conry Michael Harvey	1 Fountain Court, Birmingham	0121 236 5721
Coode Jonathan Graham	13 King's Bench Walk, London	0171 353 7204
	King's Bench Chambers, Oxford	01865 311066
Coombe Peter Michael Aeneas	2 Harcourt Buildings, London	020 7353 2112
Cooper Mark Anthony John	2 Mitre Court Buildings, London	0171 353 1353
Cooper Morris	St Philip's Chambers, Birmingham	0121 246 7000
Corkery Michael	Five Paper Buildings, London	0171 583 6117
Cotton Miss Diana Rosemary	Devereux Chambers, London	0171 353 7534
Courtney Nicholas Piers	Queen's Chambers, Manchester	0161 834 6875/4738
	Queens Chambers, Preston	01772 828300
Coward Miss Victoria Jane	Hollis Whiteman Chambers, London	020 7583 5766
Cox Bryan Richard	9 Woodhouse Square, Leeds	0113 2451986
Cox Miss Catherine Ailsa	St Philip's Chambers, Birmingham	0121 246 7000
Cox James Duncan Malcom	13 King's Bench Walk, London	0171 353 7204
	King's Bench Chambers, Oxford	01865 311066
Crampin Paul	Lamb Building, London	020 7797 7788
Crawford Miss Marie-Bernadette Claire	Eastbourne Chambers, Eastbourne	01323 642102
Crigman David Ian	1 Fountain Court, Birmingham	0121 236 5721
Crossley Simon Justin	9 Woodhouse Square, Leeds	0113 2451986
Crossley Steven Richard	37 Park Square Chambers, Leeds	0113 2439422
Crowley John Desmond	Two Crown Office Row, London	020 7797 8100
Cruickshank Miss Cynthia Marilyn Benton	1 Gray's Inn Square, London	0171 405 8946/7/8
Dale Julian Charles Rigby	Eastbourne Chambers, Eastbourne	01323 642102
Daly Nigel Jonathan	13 King's Bench Walk, London	0171 353 7204
	King's Bench Chambers, Oxford	01865 311066
Daniel Leon Roger	6 King's Bench Walk, London	0171 353 4931/583 0695
Daniells-Smith Roger Charles	8 King's Bench Walk, London	0171 797 8888
	8 King's Bench Walk North, Leeds	0113 2439797
Darbishire Adrian Munro	Hollis Whiteman Chambers, London	020 7583 5766
Davies Miss Carol Elizabeth	2 New Street, Leicester	0116 2625906
Davies The Rt Hon David John Denzil	96 Gray's Inn Road, London	0171 405 0585
	8 Gray's Inn Square, London	0171 242 3529
Davis William Easthope	St Philip's Chambers, Birmingham	0121 246 7000
Dean Brian John Anthony	St Philip's Chambers, Birmingham	0121 246 7000
Dedezade Taner	Tindal Chambers, Chelmsford	01245 267742
Dempster Dr Tina Doreen Anne	11 King's Bench Walk, London	0171 353 3337
	11 King's Bench Walk, Leeds	0113 297 1200
Denney Stuart Henry Macdonald	Deans Court Chambers, Manchester	0161 214 6000
	Deans Court Chambers, Preston	01772 555163
deSouza Mrs Josephine Claudia	Chancery Chambers, London	0171 405 6879/6870
Devlin Jonathan Nicholas Ponton	Park Court Chambers, Leeds	0113 2433277
Dixon David Steven	Sovereign Chambers, Leeds	0113 2451841/2/3
Dobbs Miss Linda Penelope	18 Red Lion Court, London	0171 520 6000
	Thornwood House, Chelmsford	01245 280880
Doig Mrs Jeanetta Rose	Neston Home Chambers, Corsham	01225 811909
Donne Jeremy Nigel	Hollis Whiteman Chambers, London	020 7583 5766
Draycott Simon Douglas	13 King's Bench Walk, London	0171 353 7204
Drinkwater Philip Murray	Colleton Chambers, Exeter	01392 274898/9
Dubbery Mark Edward	Pump Court Chambers, London	0171 353 0711
	Pump Court Chambers, Winchester	01962 868161
	Pump Court Chambers, Swindon	01793 539899
Dudley Michael John	1 Fountain Court, Birmingham	0121 236 5721
Dunn Alexander	8 King's Bench Walk, London	0171 797 8888
	8 King's Bench Walk North, Leeds	0113 2439797

• Expanded entry in Part D

Dunn Christopher	Sovereign Chambers, Leeds	0113 2451841/2/3
Dunning Francis John Grove	37 Park Square Chambers, Leeds	0113 2439422
Dyer Simon Christopher	Plowden Buildings, London	0171 583 0808
Eastman Roger	2 Harcourt Buildings, London	0171 583 9020
Edginton Horace Ronald	Becket Chambers, Canterbury	01227 786331
	Westgate Chambers, Lewes	01273 480510
Edis Andrew Jeremy Coulter	• Adrian Lyon's Chambers, Liverpool	0151 236 4421/8240
Edusei Francis Victor Burg	Chambers of Ian Macdonald QC (In Association with Two Garden Court, Temple, London), Manchester	0161 236 1840
Edwards John David	St Philip's Chambers, Birmingham	0121 246 7000
Eldridge Mark	3 Temple Gardens, London	0171 353 0832
	114 Liverpool Road, London	0171 226 9863
Eley Miss Joanne Mary	Trinity Chambers, Chelmsford	01245 605040
Ellin Miss Nina Caroline	6 Pump Court, London	0171 797 8400
	6-8 Mill Street, Maidstone	01622 688094
Ellis Miss Catherine Anne	Derby Square Chambers, Liverpool	0151 709 4222
Ellison Mark Christopher	Hollis Whiteman Chambers, London	020 7583 5766
Emlyn Jones William Nicholas	2 Harcourt Buildings, London	020 7353 2112
Emmerson (Michael) Benedict	Doughty Street Chambers, London	0171 404 1313
English Miss Caroline Frances	Francis Taylor Building, London	0171 353 7768/7769/2711
Enoch Dafydd Huw	Bridewell Chambers, London	020 7797 8800
Evans Andrew Sutherland	10 King's Bench Walk, London	0171 353 7742
	2 Paper Buildings, Basement North, London	0171 936 2613
Evans David Howard	Hollis Whiteman Chambers, London	020 7583 5766
Evans Ms Jill Annaliese	Doughty Street Chambers, London	0171 404 1313
Evans John Wainwright	1 Fountain Court, Birmingham	0121 236 5721
Evans Julian Jacob	Hollis Whiteman Chambers, London	020 7583 5766
Fairbank Nicholas James	Becket Chambers, Canterbury	01227 786331
Faluyi Albert Osamudiamen	Chambers of Martin Burr, London	0171 353 4636
Farrer Adam Michael	4 Fountain Court, Birmingham	0121 236 3476
Farrer Paul Ainsworth	1 Fountain Court, Birmingham	0121 236 5721
Faul Miss Anne Frances Louise	Lamb Building, London	020 7797 7788
Featherstone Jason Neil	Virtual Chambers, London	07071 244 944
	Barristers' Common Law Chambers, London	0171 375 3012
Ferm Rodney Eric	37 Park Square Chambers, Leeds	0113 2439422
Fessal Ignatius	8 King's Bench Walk, London	0171 797 8888
	8 King's Bench Walk North, Leeds	0113 2439797
Field Rory Dominic	Hardwicke Building, London	020 7242 2523
Fields Miss Helen Sarah	Pump Court Chambers, Winchester	01962 868161
	Pump Court Chambers, London	0171 353 0711
	Pump Court Chambers, Swindon	01793 539899
Finnigan Peter Anthony	Hollis Whiteman Chambers, London	020 7583 5766
Firth Miss Georgina Elizabeth	Chambers of Ian Macdonald QC (In Association with Two Garden Court, Temple, London), Manchester	0161 236 1840
Fish David Thomas	Deans Court Chambers, Manchester	0161 214 6000
	Deans Court Chambers, Preston	01772 555163
	Goldsmith Chambers, London	0171 353 6802/3/4/5
Fisher Jonathan Simon	• 18 Red Lion Court, London	0171 520 6000
	Thornwood House, Chelmsford	01245 280880
Fisher Richard Alan	Francis Taylor Building, London	0171 353 7768/7769/2711
Fitzgerald Edward Hamilton	Doughty Street Chambers, London	0171 404 1313
Flahive Daniel Michael	Hardwicke Building, London	020 7242 2523
Fleming Paul Stephen	37 Park Square Chambers, Leeds	0113 2439422
Flockhart Miss Sharon Linda	3 Serjeants' Inn, London	0171 353 5537
Forbes Peter George	6 Pump Court, London	0171 797 8400
	6-8 Mill Street, Maidstone	01622 688094
Ford Miss Caroline Emma	37 Park Square Chambers, Leeds	0113 2439422

Forlin Gerard Emlyn	Hardwicke Building, London	020 7242 2523
Forshall Ms Isabella Louise	Doughty Street Chambers, London	0171 404 1313
Forshaw Miss Sarah Anne	5 King's Bench Walk, London	0171 353 5638
Francois Herbert Dolton	Chambers of Herbert Francois, Mitcham	0181 640 4529
Frith Nicholas John	30 Park Square, Leeds	0113 2436388
Fryer Anthony James	St Philip's Chambers, Birmingham	0121 246 7000
Fryman Neil	Peel Court Chambers, Manchester	0161 832 3791
Gabb Charles Henry Escott	Pump Court Chambers, Winchester	01962 868161
	Pump Court Chambers, London	0171 353 0711
	Pump Court Chambers, Swindon	01793 539899
Garlick Paul Richard	Pump Court Chambers, London	0171 353 0711
	Pump Court Chambers, Winchester	01962 868161
	Pump Court Chambers, Swindon	01793 539899
Garrett Michael Owen	St Philip's Chambers, Birmingham	0121 246 7000
Garth Steven David	Sovereign Chambers, Leeds	0113 2451841/2/3
Gassman Miss Caroline Dora	8 King's Bench Walk, London	0171 797 8888
	8 King's Bench Walk North, Leeds	0113 2439797
Gatto Miss Nicola Esterina	8 King's Bench Walk, London	0171 797 8888
	8 King's Bench Walk North, Leeds	0113 2439797
Gau Justin Charles	Pump Court Chambers, London	0171 353 0711
	Pump Court Chambers, Winchester	01962 868161
	Pump Court Chambers, Swindon	01793 539899
Geekie Charles Nairn	One Garden Court Family Law Chambers, London	0171 797 7900
George Donald Eric Joseph	Leone Chambers, London	0181 200 4020
Gerry Miss Felicity Ruth	2 New Street, Leicester	0116 2625906
Gersch Adam Nissen	Trafalgar Chambers, London	0171 583 5858
Gibbs Mrs Jocelyn Ida	8 King's Bench Walk, London	0171 797 8888
Gibbs Patrick Michael Evan	2 Harcourt Buildings, London	020 7353 2112
Gibson Arthur George Adrian	Adrian Lyon's Chambers, Liverpool	0151 236 4421/8240
Gifford Lord Anthony Maurice	8 King's Bench Walk, London	0171 797 8888
	8 King's Bench Walk North, Leeds	0113 2439797
Gillibrand Philip Martin Mangnall	Pump Court Chambers, Winchester	01962 868161
	Pump Court Chambers, London	0171 353 0711
	Pump Court Chambers, Swindon	01793 539899
Gilmore Ian Martin	30 Park Square, Leeds	0113 2436388
Glass Anthony Trevor	Hollis Whiteman Chambers, London	020 7583 5766
Gledhill Kris	Camberwell Chambers, London	0171 274 0830
Glenn Paul Anthony	4 Fountain Court, Birmingham	0121 236 3476
Goddard Harold Keith	Deans Court Chambers, Manchester	0161 214 6000
	Deans Court Chambers, Preston	01772 555163
	4 Paper Buildings, London	0171 353 3366/583 7155
Godfrey Christopher Nicholas	Queen's Chambers, Manchester	0161 834 6875/4738
	Queens Chambers, Preston	01772 828300
Goodwin Michael Gary	2 Mitre Court Buildings, London	0171 353 1353
Gopinathan Miss Anupama	Harrow on the Hill Chambers, Harrow-on-the-Hill	0181 423 7444
	Windsor Barristers' Chambers, Windsor	01753 648899
Gordon Ms Clare	8 King's Bench Walk, London	0171 797 8888
Gordon David Myer	Sovereign Chambers, Leeds	0113 2451841/2/3
Gordon Donald Cameron	3 Temple Gardens, London	0171 353 0832
Gordon John Sandford	New Court, London	0171 583 5123/0510
Gore Andrew Julian Mark	37 Park Square Chambers, Leeds	0113 2439422
Gow Miss Elizabeth Suzanne	Iscoed Chambers, Swansea	01792 652988/9/330
Goymer Andrew Alfred	6 Pump Court, London	0171 797 8400
	6-8 Mill Street, Maidstone	01622 688094
Graham John Malcolm	37 Park Square Chambers, Leeds	0113 2439422
	11 King's Bench Walk, London	0171 353 3337
Grant Edward William	6 Pump Court, London	0171 797 8400
	6-8 Mill Street, Maidstone	01622 688094
Grant Gary Steven	3 Temple Gardens, London	0171 583 1155

• Expanded entry in Part D

Granville-Fall Anthony	30 Park Square, Leeds	0113 2436388
Grayson Edward	• 9-12 Bell Yard, London	0171 400 1800
Green Miss Jane Elizabeth	Design Chambers, London	0171 353 0747
	Chambers of Martin Burr, London	0171 353 4636
Green Jonathan Paul	2nd Floor, Francis Taylor Building, London	0171 353 9942/3157
Green Roger John Bailey	Queen's Chambers, Manchester	0161 834 6875/4738
	Queens Chambers, Preston	01772 828300
Gresty Miss Denise Lynn	Sovereign Chambers, Leeds	0113 2451841/2/3
Grey Philip John	Hardwicke Building, London	020 7242 2523
Grey Robin Douglas	Hollis Whiteman Chambers, London	020 7583 5766
Grieve Michael Robertson Crichton	Doughty Street Chambers, London	0171 404 1313
Griffith-Jones Richard Haydn	1 Fountain Court, Birmingham	0121 236 5721
Grime John Andrew	Pump Court Chambers, Swindon	01793 539899
	Pump Court Chambers, London	0171 353 0711
	Pump Court Chambers, Winchester	01962 868161
Grout-Smith Jeremy Gaywood	Peel Court Chambers, Manchester	0161 832 3791
Gubbay Jeffrey	3 Temple Gardens, London	0171 353 0832
Guirguis Miss Sheren	White Friars Chambers, Chester	01244 323070
Gunther Miss Elizabeth Ann	Pump Court Chambers, Winchester	01962 868161
	Pump Court Chambers, London	0171 353 0711
	Pump Court Chambers, Swindon	01793 539899
Haigh Martin James	30 Park Square, Leeds	0113 2436388
Haji Miss Shaheen	Bell Yard Chambers, London	0171 306 9292
Hall Andrew Joseph	Doughty Street Chambers, London	0171 404 1313
Hall David Percy	9 Woodhouse Square, Leeds	0113 2451986
Hall Jonathan Rupert	5 King's Bench Walk, London	0171 353 5638
Hallowes Rupert John Michael	Britton Street Chambers, London	0171 608 3765
Harding Mrs Christine Lauretta Ayodele	Leone Chambers, London	0181 200 4020
Harding Dr Gladys Modwyn Cicely	Leone Chambers, London	0181 200 4020
Hargan James John	30 Park Square, Leeds	0113 2436388
Haring Simon Nicholas	30 Park Square, Leeds	0113 2436388
Harington Michael Kenneth	6 Pump Court, London	0171 797 8400
	6-8 Mill Street, Maidstone	01622 688094
Harounoff David	4 King's Bench Walk, London	0171 822 8822
Harper Miss Victoria Jane Tryphosa	3 Temple Gardens, London	0171 353 0832
Harris David Robert	St Albans Chambers, St Albans	01727 843383
Harris Ms Rebecca Elizabeth	Hollis Whiteman Chambers, London	020 7583 5766
Harrison Gordon William	3 Temple Gardens, London	0171 353 0832
Hart-Leverton Colin Allen	8 King's Bench Walk, London	0171 797 8888
	8 King's Bench Walk North, Leeds	0113 2439797
Hartley Robert Edward	3 Temple Gardens, London	0171 353 0832
Haslam Andrew Peter	Sovereign Chambers, Leeds	0113 2451841/2/3
Hawkesworth (Walter) Gareth	Fenners Chambers, Cambridge	01223 368761
	Fenners Chambers, Peterborough	01733 562030
	Five Paper Buildings, London	0171 583 6117
Hayhow Mrs Lyndsay Jill	5 Essex Court, London	0171 410 2000
Hayne Miss Janette Elizabeth	Tindal Chambers, Chelmsford	01245 267742
	St Albans Chambers, St Albans	01727 843383
Haynes Peter	St Philip's Chambers, Birmingham	0121 246 7000
Hayton Michael Pearson	Deans Court Chambers, Manchester	0161 214 6000
	Deans Court Chambers, Preston	01772 555163
Heer Miss Deanna Mary	Hardwicke Building, London	020 7242 2523
Hegarty Kevin John	St Philip's Chambers, Birmingham	0121 246 7000
Henderson Ian Francis	8 King's Bench Walk, London	0171 797 8888
	8 King's Bench Walk North, Leeds	0113 2439797
Hennell Peter Gordon	Queen's Chambers, Manchester	0161 834 6875/4738
	Queens Chambers, Preston	01772 828300
Henry Edward Joseph Aloysius	Hollis Whiteman Chambers, London	020 7583 5766
Herbert David Richard	2 New Street, Leicester	0116 2625906

• Expanded entry in Part D

B

Herbert Mrs Rebecca Mary	2 New Street, Leicester	0116 2625906
Hershman David Allan	St Philip's Chambers, Birmingham	0121 246 7000
	1 Mitre Court Buildings, London	0171 797 7070
Hignett Richard James	St Albans Chambers, St Albans	01727 843383
Hill Andrew Charles Rowland	8 King's Bench Walk, London	0171 797 8888
	Harrow on the Hill Chambers, Harrow-on-the-Hill	0181 423 7444
	8 King's Bench Walk North, Leeds	0113 2439797
Hilton Alan John Howard	Hollis Whiteman Chambers, London	020 7583 5766
Hockman Stephen Alexander	• 6 Pump Court, London	0171 797 8400
	6-8 Mill Street, Maidstone	01622 688094
Hodson Peter David	Chambers of Ian Macdonald QC (In Association with Two Garden Court, Temple, London), Manchester	0161 236 1840
Hogg The Hon Douglas Martin	37 Park Square Chambers, Leeds	0113 2439422
	Cathedral Chambers (Jan Wood Independent Barristers' Clerk), Exeter	01392 210900
Holroyd Ms Joanne	37 Park Square Chambers, Leeds	0113 2439422
Horgan Peter Thomas	Queen's Chambers, Manchester	0161 834 6875/4738
	Queens Chambers, Preston	01772 828300
Horwell Richard Eric	Hollis Whiteman Chambers, London	020 7583 5766
Howard Graham John	Pump Court Chambers, Winchester	01962 868161
	Pump Court Chambers, London	0171 353 0711
	Pump Court Chambers, Swindon	01793 539899
Hudson Anthony Sean	Doughty Street Chambers, London	0171 404 1313
Hudson Christopher John	Deans Court Chambers, Manchester	0161 214 6000
	Deans Court Chambers, Preston	01772 555163
Humpage Miss Heather June	9 Woodhouse Square, Leeds	0113 2451986
Humphries Paul Benedict	Deans Court Chambers, Manchester	0161 214 6000
	Deans Court Chambers, Preston	01772 555163
Hurd Mark Dunsdon	2 New Street, Leicester	0116 2625906
Hussain Miss Frida Khanam	17 Carlton Crescent, Southampton	023 8032 0320/0823 2003
Hutchin Edward Alister David	Bracton Chambers, London	0171 242 4248
Igori Kingsley Izehiuwa	8 King's Bench Walk, London	0171 797 8888
Inman Melbourne Donald	1 Fountain Court, Birmingham	0121 236 5721
Ironfield Miss Janet Ruth	Deans Court Chambers, Manchester	0161 214 6000
	Deans Court Chambers, Preston	01772 555163
Irwin Stephen John	Doughty Street Chambers, London	0171 404 1313
Ivens Ms Jemima	8 King's Bench Walk, London	0171 797 8888
	8 King's Bench Walk North, Leeds	0113 2439797
Jackson Anthony Warren	3 Serjeants' Inn, London	0171 353 5537
Jafferjee Aftab Asger	2 Harcourt Buildings, London	020 7353 2112
James Ian Frederick	Octagon House, Norwich	01603 623186
	1 Paper Buildings, London	0171 353 3728/4953
Jeffreys David Alfred	Hollis Whiteman Chambers, London	020 7583 5766
Jenkins Dr Janet Caroline	Chambers of Kieran Coonan QC, London	0171 583 6013/2510
Johnson Alan Michael Borthwick	1 Gray's Inn Square, London	0171 405 8946/7/8
Johnson Miss Christine Margaret	Adrian Lyon's Chambers, Liverpool	0151 236 4421/8240
Johnson Miss Zoe Elisabeth	Hollis Whiteman Chambers, London	020 7583 5766
Johnston Anthony Paul	1 Fountain Court, Birmingham	0121 236 5721
Jones Miss Carolyn Nerys	1 Fountain Court, Birmingham	0121 236 5721
	Clock Chambers, Wolverhampton	01902 313444
Jones Miss Gillian Hunter	18 Red Lion Court, London	0171 520 6000
	Thornwood House, Chelmsford	01245 280880
Jones Howard Peter	2nd Floor, Francis Taylor Building, London	0171 353 9942/3157
Jones Martin Wynne	8 King's Bench Walk, London	0171 797 8888
	8 King's Bench Walk North, Leeds	0113 2439797
Jones Miss Susannah Lucy	Octagon House, Norwich	01603 623186
Josse David Benjamin	Bridewell Chambers, London	020 7797 8800
Kadri Sadakat	Doughty Street Chambers, London	0171 404 1313

• Expanded entry in Part D

Kark Thomas Victor William	Hollis Whiteman Chambers, London	020 7583 5766
Keane Desmond St John	Pendragon Chambers, Swansea	01792 411188
Keane Michael Leo	4 Paper Buildings, London	0171 353 3366/583 7155
Keating Dermot John	8 King's Bench Walk, London	0171 797 8888
Keeley James Francis	Sovereign Chambers, Leeds	0113 2451841/2/3
Kelbrick Anthony Michael	37 Park Square Chambers, Leeds	0113 2439422
Kelleher Keith Roy	3 Wellington Road, Poole	07771 905671 (Mobile)
	Bell Yard Chambers, London	0171 306 9292
Kelsey-Fry John	Hollis Whiteman Chambers, London	020 7583 5766
Kennedy of the Shaws Baroness	Doughty Street Chambers, London	0171 404 1313
Kenward Timothy David Nelson	25-27 Castle Street, Liverpool	0151 227 5661/051 236 5072
Keogh Andrew John	8 King's Bench Walk, London	0171 797 8888
	8 King's Bench Walk North, Leeds	0113 2439797
Kerner Mrs Angela	Bell Yard Chambers, London	0171 306 9292
Kerr Derek William	Francis Taylor Building, London	0171 353 7768/7769/2711
Kershaw Andrew	30 Park Square, Leeds	0113 2436388
Khan Anwar William	Eastbourne Chambers, Eastbourne	01323 642102
	Wessex Chambers, Reading	0118 956 8856
Khan Miss Helen Mary Grace	Pump Court Chambers, London	0171 353 0711
	Pump Court Chambers, Winchester	01962 868161
	Pump Court Chambers, Swindon	01793 539899
Khokhar Mushtaq Ahmed	Sovereign Chambers, Leeds	0113 2451841/2/3
Khubber Ranjiv	3 Temple Gardens, London	0171 353 0832
King Charles Granville	96 Gray's Inn Road, London	0171 405 0585
King Peter Duncan	Fenners Chambers, Cambridge	01223 368761
	5 Pump Court, London	020 7353 2532
	Fenners Chambers, Peterborough	01733 562030
Knight Miss Jennifer Claudia	2 Harcourt Buildings, London	020 7353 2112
Knowles Graham Roy	Peel Court Chambers, Manchester	0161 832 3791
Kramer Stephen Ernest	• 1 Hare Court, London	0171 353 3982/5324
Kulatilake Indra Semage	52 Wembley Park Drive, Wembley	0181 902 5629
Kyte Peter Eric	Hollis Whiteman Chambers, London	020 7583 5766
Lamberty Mark Julian Harker	Queen's Chambers, Manchester	0161 834 6875/4738
	Queens Chambers, Preston	01772 828300
Landaw John Nicholas	Hardwicke Building, London	020 7242 2523
Langdale Timothy James	Hollis Whiteman Chambers, London	020 7583 5766
Lanlehin Olajide Adebola	Britton Street Chambers, London	0171 608 3765
Large Alan Macdonald	South Western Chambers, Taunton	01823 331919 (24 hrs)
Larkin Sean	Hollis Whiteman Chambers, London	020 7583 5766
Latimer-Sayer William Laurence	2 Mitre Court Buildings, London	0171 353 1353
Lawson Miss Sara Lucy Jane	18 Red Lion Court, London	0171 520 6000
	Thornwood House, Chelmsford	01245 280880
Le Cornu Philip John	St Philip's Chambers, Birmingham	0121 246 7000
Leason Ms Karen Dawn	St Philip's Chambers, Birmingham	0121 246 7000
Leigh Kevin	6 Pump Court, London	0171 797 8400
	Regency Chambers, Peterborough	01733 315215
	Westgate Chambers, Lewes	01273 480510
	6-8 Mill Street, Maidstone	01622 688094
Levene Victor	1 Gray's Inn Square, London	0171 405 8946/7/8
Lever The Hon Bernard Lewis	Peel Court Chambers, Manchester	0161 832 3791
	Harcourt Chambers, London	0171 353 6961
Lewis Edward Trevor Gwyn	Francis Taylor Building, London	0171 353 7768/7769/2711
Lewis Jeffrey Allan	9 Woodhouse Square, Leeds	0113 2451986
Lewis Thomas Robin Arwel	St Philip's Chambers, Birmingham	0121 246 7000
Lindsay Jeremy Mark Henry	37 Park Square Chambers, Leeds	0113 2439422
Lloyd-Smith Miss Rebecca Jane	Peel Court Chambers, Manchester	0161 832 3791
Lockhart Andrew William Jardine	St Philip's Chambers, Birmingham	0121 246 7000
Lodder Peter Norman	3 Hare Court, London	0171 395 2000
Long Tobias Charles	8 King's Bench Walk, London	0171 797 8888
	8 King's Bench Walk North, Leeds	0113 2439797
Longden Anthony Gordon	Hollis Whiteman Chambers, London	020 7583 5766

Lowry Miss Emma Margaret Collins	Hollis Whiteman Chambers, London	020 7583 5766
Lumley Gerald	9 Woodhouse Square, Leeds	0113 2451986
Lumley Nicholas James Henry	Sovereign Chambers, Leeds	0113 2451841/2/3
Lunt Steven	9 Woodhouse Square, Leeds	0113 2451986
Lynagh Richard Dudley	Two Crown Office Row, London	020 7797 8100
Macadam Jason Angus Alaister Robert L	37 Park Square Chambers, Leeds	0113 2439422
MacKinnon Thomas Joseph	8 King's Bench Walk, London	0171 797 8888
	8 King's Bench Walk North, Leeds	0113 2439797
Maidment Kieran Francis	Doughty Street Chambers, London	0171 404 1313
Mainwaring [Robert] Paul Clason	Carmarthen Chambers, Carmarthen	01267 234410
Malhotra Miss Mehtab Roshan	2 Middle Temple Lane, London	0171 583 4540
Mallison Miss Catherine Mary Helen	2nd Floor, Francis Taylor Building, London	0171 353 9942/3157
Mandalia Vinesh Lalji	Harrow on the Hill Chambers, Harrow-on-the-Hill	0181 423 7444
Mann Jonathan Simon	8 King's Bench Walk, London	0171 797 8888
	8 King's Bench Walk North, Leeds	0113 2439797
Mansoor Miss Parveen	8 King's Bench Walk, London	0171 797 8888
Marks Richard Leon	Peel Court Chambers, Manchester	0161 832 3791
Marshall-Andrews Robert Graham	37 Park Square Chambers, Leeds	0113 2439422
	2-4 Tudor Street, London	0171 797 7111
Marson Geoffrey Charles	Sovereign Chambers, Leeds	0113 2451841/2/3
Matthews Phillip Rowland	2nd Floor, Francis Taylor Building, London	0171 353 9942/3157
Maudslay Miss Diana Elizabeth	Sovereign Chambers, Leeds	0113 2451841/2/3
Maxwell Richard	Ropewalk Chambers, Nottingham	0115 9472581
	Doughty Street Chambers, London	0171 404 1313
Mazzag Anthony James	Peel Court Chambers, Manchester	0161 832 3791
Mbatha Mrs Myrtle	54 Anne Way, Ilford	0181 501 4311
McBride Gavin John	Peel Court Chambers, Manchester	0161 832 3791
McCahey Miss Catherine Anne Mary	St Philip's Chambers, Birmingham	0121 246 7000
McCahill Patrick Gerard	St Philip's Chambers, Birmingham	0121 246 7000
	Chambers of Andrew Campbell QC, Leeds	0113 2455438
McCarthy Martin Raymond	8 King's Bench Walk, London	0171 797 8888
	8 King's Bench Walk North, Leeds	0113 2439797
McCartney Peter	St Philip's Chambers, Birmingham	0121 246 7000
McCrindell James Derrey	Mitre House Chambers, London	0171 583 8233
McCullough Miss Judith Ann	Queen's Chambers, Manchester	0161 834 6875/4738
	Queens Chambers, Preston	01772 828300
McCullough Miss Louise Clare	Lion Court, London	0171 404 6565
McEvilly Gerard Martin	Furnival Chambers, London	0171 405 3232
McGeorge Anthony William	13 King's Bench Walk, London	0171 353 7204
	King's Bench Chambers, Oxford	01865 311066
McGonigal David Ambrose	30 Park Square, Leeds	0113 2436388
	Broadway House Chambers, Bradford	01274 722560
McGregor Miss Helen Margaret	Eastern Chambers, Oxford	0118 972 3722
McGuinness-Way Andrew Jeffrey Sebastian B	3 Temple Gardens, London	0171 353 0832
McHugh Denis David	Bracton Chambers, London	0171 242 4248
McKechnie Stuart Iain William	2 Gray's Inn Square Chambers, London	020 7242 0328
McKone Mark Desmond	Sovereign Chambers, Leeds	0113 2451841/2/3
McLaughlin Miss Elaine	8 King's Bench Walk, London	0171 797 8888
McLean Mrs Mandy Rachel	5 Essex Court, London	0171 410 2000
Meachin Miss (Sarah) Vanessa Veronica	St Philip's Chambers, Birmingham	0121 246 7000
Mehendale Ms Neelima Krishna	2 Mitre Court Buildings, London	0171 353 1353
Mellor John Walter	30 Park Square, Leeds	0113 2436388
Melly Miss Kama Louise	37 Park Square Chambers, Leeds	0113 2439422
Metzer Anthony David Erwin	Doughty Street Chambers, London	0171 404 1313

• Expanded entry in Part D

Middleton Joseph	Doughty Street Chambers, London	0171 404 1313
Miller Miss Jane Elizabeth Mackay	Pump Court Chambers, London	0171 353 0711
	Pump Court Chambers, Winchester	01962 868161
	Pump Court Chambers, Swindon	01793 539899
Milliken-Smith Mark Gordon	3 Hare Court, London	0171 395 2000
Millington Christopher John	1 Fountain Court, Birmingham	0121 236 5721
Minhas Ms Rafhat	Leone Chambers, London	0181 200 4020
Mitchell Brenton Ballingtine	Bell Yard Chambers, London	0171 306 9292
Mitchell Christopher Richard	Hollis Whiteman Chambers, London	020 7583 5766
Mitchell Keith Arno	3 Hare Court, London	0171 395 2000
Mitchell Paul	13 King's Bench Walk, London	0171 353 7204
	King's Bench Chambers, Oxford	01865 311066
Mitropoulos Christos	Chambers of Geoffrey Hawker, London	0171 583 8899
Mohabir Gerald Yogin	3 Temple Gardens, London	0171 353 0832
Monk David Kenneth	2 New Street, Leicester	0116 2625906
Moore Roderick Andrew McGowan	3 Temple Gardens, London	0171 353 0832
Morgan Andrew James	St Philip's Chambers, Birmingham	0121 246 7000
Morley Stephen Douglas	Bridewell Chambers, London	020 7797 8800
Morse Malcolm George McEwan	1 Fountain Court, Birmingham	0121 236 5721
Moses Miss Rebecca	Virtual Chambers, London	07071 244 944
	Barristers' Common Law Chambers, London	0171 375 3012
Muller Antonie Sean	4 Fountain Court, Birmingham	0121 236 3476
Munday Miss Anne Margaret	8 King's Bench Walk North, Leeds	0113 2439797
	8 King's Bench Walk, London	0171 797 8888
Murphy Mrs Catriona Anne	1 Gray's Inn Square, London	0171 405 8946/7/8
Murphy Miss Nicola Jane	4 King's Bench Walk, London	0171 822 8822
Murray-Smith James Michael	8 King's Bench Walk, London	0171 797 8888
	8 King's Bench Walk North, Leeds	0113 2439797
Myatt Charles Edward	Fenners Chambers, Cambridge	01223 368761
	Fenners Chambers, Peterborough	01733 562030
Newbury Richard Lennox	Sovereign Chambers, Leeds	0113 2451841/2/3
Newman Austin Eric	9 Woodhouse Square, Leeds	0113 2451986
Newton-Price James Edward	Pump Court Chambers, London	0171 353 0711
	Pump Court Chambers, Winchester	01962 868161
	Pump Court Chambers, Swindon	01793 539899
Niblett Anthony Ian	1 Crown Office Row, London	0171 797 7500
	Crown Office Row Chambers, Brighton	01273 625625
Nicholls Christopher Benjamin	1 Fountain Court, Birmingham	0121 236 5721
Nicholson Pratt Thomas Hycy	Hardwicke Building, London	020 7242 2523
Nicol Stuart Henry David	3 Temple Gardens, London	0171 353 0832
Nisbett James Theophilus	7 Westmeath Avenue, Leicester	0116 2412003
	Victoria Chambers, Birmingham	0121 236 9900
Nsugbe Oba Eric	Pump Court Chambers, London	0171 353 0711
	Pump Court Chambers, Winchester	01962 868161
	Pump Court Chambers, Swindon	01793 539899
O'Donoghue Florence	2 Mitre Court Buildings, London	0171 353 1353
O'Sullivan Michael Neil	5 King's Bench Walk, London	0171 353 5638
Oakley Paul James	1 Gray's Inn Square, London	0171 405 8946/7/8
Ofori George Edward	ACHMA Chambers, London	0171 639 7817/0171 635 7904
	Chancery Chambers, London	0171 405 6879/6870
Oke Olanrewaju Oladipupo	Kingsway Chambers, London	07000 653529
Oliver Andrew James	Octagon House, Norwich	01603 623186
Oliver Miss Juliet Dianne	Bridewell Chambers, London	020 7797 8800
Oliver Michael Richard	Hardwicke Building, London	020 7242 2523
Orme Richard Andrew	Peel Court Chambers, Manchester	0161 832 3791
Owen Timothy Wynn	Doughty Street Chambers, London	0171 404 1313
Palmer Patrick John Steven	Sovereign Chambers, Leeds	0113 2451841/2/3
Paneth Miss Sarah Ruth	No. 1 Serjeants' Inn, London	0171 415 6666
Panton William Dwight	Britton Street Chambers, London	0171 608 3765

B

Parry Charles Robert	Pump Court Chambers, Swindon	01793 539899
	Pump Court Chambers, London	0171 353 0711
	Pump Court Chambers, Winchester	01962 868161
Parry Simon Edward	White Friars Chambers, Chester	01244 323070
Parry Evans Ms Mary Alethea	33 Park Place, Cardiff	02920 233313
Pascoe Nigel Spencer Knight	Pump Court Chambers, Winchester	01962 868161
	Pump Court Chambers, London	0171 353 0711
	Queens Square Chambers, Bristol	0117 921 1966
	Pump Court Chambers, Swindon	01793 539899
Patel Bhavin Vinubhai	Chambers of Martin Burr, London	0171 353 4636
Paton Ian Francis	Hollis Whiteman Chambers, London	020 7583 5766
Patterson Stewart	Pump Court Chambers, Winchester	01962 868161
	Pump Court Chambers, London	0171 353 0711
	Pump Court Chambers, Swindon	01793 539899
Paul Nicholas Martin	Doughty Street Chambers, London	0171 404 1313
	Westgate Chambers, Lewes	01273 480510
Pawson Robert Edward Cruickshank	Pump Court Chambers, Winchester	01962 868161
	Pump Court Chambers, London	0171 353 0711
	Pump Court Chambers, Swindon	01793 539899
Pearson Michael	30 Park Square, Leeds	0113 2436388
Peel Stuart James	Bell Yard Chambers, London	0171 306 9292
Peet Andrew Geraint	2 New Street, Leicester	0116 2625906
Peirson Oliver James	Pump Court Chambers, London	0171 353 0711
	Pump Court Chambers, Winchester	01962 868161
	Pump Court Chambers, Swindon	01793 539899
Pema Anes Bhumin Laloo	9 Woodhouse Square, Leeds	0113 2451986
Penn Jonathan Peter Robert	8 King's Bench Walk, London	0171 797 8888
Phillips Simon David	1 Fountain Court, Birmingham	0121 236 5721
Pickersgill David William	Bell Yard Chambers, London	0171 306 9292
Pinter Joseph Philip	3 Temple Gardens, London	0171 353 0832
Pipi Chukwuemeka Ezekiel	Chambers of Martin Burr, London	0171 353 4636
Plaschkes Ms Sarah Georgina	Hollis Whiteman Chambers, London	020 7583 5766
Pomeroy Toby	Barristers' Common Law Chambers, London	0171 375 3012
	Virtual Chambers, London	07071 244 944
Portnoy Leslie Reuben	Chambers of John Hand QC, Manchester	0161 955 9000
Potts Richard Andrew	Octagon House, Norwich	01603 623186
	1 Paper Buildings, London	0171 353 3728/4953
Poulet Mrs Rebecca Maria	Hollis Whiteman Chambers, London	020 7583 5766
Pounder Gerard	5 Essex Court, London	0171 410 2000
Powis Miss Samantha Inez	St Philip's Chambers, Birmingham	0121 246 7000
Prasad Krishna	21 Craven Road, Kingston-Upon-Thames	0181 974 6799
Price Miss Collette	St James's Chambers, Manchester	0161 834 7000
Price John Charles	St Philip's Chambers, Birmingham	0121 246 7000
Pringle Gordon Alexander	Bridewell Chambers, London	020 7797 8800
Prudhoe Timothy Nixon	Queen's Chambers, Manchester	0161 834 6875/4738
	Queens Chambers, Preston	01772 828300
Pulling Dean	Iscoed Chambers, Swansea	01792 652988/9/330
Pulman George Frederick	Hardwicke Building, London	020 7242 2523
	Stour Chambers, Canterbury	01227 764899
Purves Gavin Bowman	Swan House, London	0181 998 3035
Pusey William James	St Philip's Chambers, Birmingham	0121 246 7000
Puzey James Roderick	1 Fountain Court, Birmingham	0121 236 5721
Ramasamy Selvaraju	Hollis Whiteman Chambers, London	020 7583 5766
Rampersad Devan	St Philip's Chambers, Birmingham	0121 246 7000
Rankin Andrew	4 Field Court, London	0171 440 6900
Rector Miss Penelope Jane	•Five Paper Buildings, London	0171 583 6117
Redgrave Adrian Robert Frank	No. 1 Serjeants' Inn, London	0171 415 6666
Rees Edward Parry	Doughty Street Chambers, London	0171 404 1313
Rees Gareth David	Hollis Whiteman Chambers, London	020 7583 5766

Reid Paul William	13 King's Bench Walk, London	0171 353 7204
	King's Bench Chambers, Oxford	01865 311066
Restell Thomas George	Granary Chambers, Bexhill-On-Sea	01424 733008
Richardson Paul Brayshaw	Peel Court Chambers, Manchester	0161 832 3791
Roberts Jeremy Michael Graham	9 Gough Square, London	020 7832 0500
Roberts Stuart Royd	37 Park Square Chambers, Leeds	0113 2439422
Robertson Geoffrey Ronald	Doughty Street Chambers, London	0171 404 1313
Robins Miss Alison Elizabeth	2 Paper Buildings, Basement North, London	0171 936 2613
Robinson Ms Tanya Lin	6 Pump Court, London	0171 797 8400
	6-8 Mill Street, Maidstone	01622 688094
Robinson Vivian	Hollis Whiteman Chambers, London	020 7583 5766
Robotham John Ansel	St Philip's Chambers, Birmingham	0121 246 7000
Rodger Mark Stuart	30 Park Square, Leeds	0113 2436388
Roebuck Roy Delville	Bell Yard Chambers, London	0171 306 9292
Rogers Paul John	1 Crown Office Row, London	0171 797 7500
	Crown Office Row Chambers, Brighton	01273 625625
Ronksley Andrew Peter	3 Temple Gardens, London	0171 353 0832
Rose Miss Pamela Susan	8 King's Bench Walk, London	0171 797 8888
	8 King's Bench Walk North, Leeds	0113 2439797
Rothery Peter	Queen's Chambers, Manchester	0161 834 6875/4738
	Queens Chambers, Preston	01772 828300
Rowe John Jermyn	• 8 King Street Chambers, Manchester	0161 834 9560
Rubery Philip Alan	8 King's Bench Walk, London	0171 797 8888
	8 King's Bench Walk North, Leeds	0113 2439797
Rudd Matthew Allan	11 Bolt Court (also at 7 Stone Buildings – 1st Floor), London	0171 353 2300
	Redhill Chambers, Redhill	01737 780781
	7 Stone Buildings (also at 11 Bolt Court), London	0171 242 0961
Russell Anthony Patrick	Peel Court Chambers, Manchester	0161 832 3791
Ryan Timothy John	8 King's Bench Walk, London	0171 797 8888
	8 King's Bench Walk North, Leeds	0113 2439797
Ryan William	8 King's Bench Walk, London	0171 797 8888
	8 King's Bench Walk North, Leeds	0113 2439797
Rylands Miss Margaret Elizabeth	8 King Street Chambers, Manchester	0161 834 9560
Sallon Christopher Robert	Doughty Street Chambers, London	0171 404 1313
	Westgate Chambers, Lewes	01273 480510
Salmon Jonathan Carl	1 Fountain Court, Birmingham	0121 236 5721
Salter Charles Philip Arthur	8 King's Bench Walk, London	0171 797 8888
	8 King's Bench Walk North, Leeds	0113 2439797
Salter Miss Sibby Anne Victoria	1 Gray's Inn Square, London	0171 405 8946/7/8
Samuel Glyn Ross	St Philip's Chambers, Birmingham	0121 246 7000
Savill Mark Ashley	Deans Court Chambers, Manchester	0161 214 6000
	Deans Court Chambers, Preston	01772 555163
Saxby Oliver Charles John	• 6 Pump Court, London	0171 797 8400
	6-8 Mill Street, Maidstone	01622 688094
Scobie James Timothy Norman	Francis Taylor Building, London	0171 353 7768/7769/2711
Scott Matthew John	Pump Court Chambers, London	0171 353 0711
	Pump Court Chambers, Winchester	01962 868161
	Pump Court Chambers, Swindon	01793 539899
Seal Julius Damien	189 Randolph Avenue, London	0171 624 9139
Sells Oliver Matthew	Five Paper Buildings, London	0171 583 6117
	Fenners Chambers, Cambridge	01223 368761
Semple Andrew Blair	Sovereign Chambers, Leeds	0113 2451841/2/3
Shale Justin Anton	4 King's Bench Walk, London	0171 822 8822
	King's Bench Chambers, Bournemouth	01202 250025
Shaw Mrs Gabriele	3 Temple Gardens, London	0171 353 0832
Shenton Miss Rachel Claire	White Friars Chambers, Chester	01244 323070

Shepherd Miss Joanne Elizabeth	St Albans Chambers, St Albans	01727 843383
	Tindal Chambers, Chelmsford	01245 267742
	New Bailey Chambers, Preston	01772 258087
Shepherd Nigel Patrick	8 King's Bench Walk North, Leeds	0113 2439797
	8 King's Bench Walk, London	0171 797 8888
Shiels Ian	30 Park Square, Leeds	0113 2436388
Shoker Makkan Singh	St Philip's Chambers, Birmingham	0121 246 7000
Shorrock John Michael	Peel Court Chambers, Manchester	0161 832 3791
Shrimpton Michael	Francis Taylor Building, London	0171 797 7250
Sibson Mrs Clare Adele	Hollis Whiteman Chambers, London	020 7583 5766
Simmonds Nicholas Harold	Peel Court Chambers, Manchester	0161 832 3791
Singh Kuldip	Five Paper Buildings, London	0171 583 6117
Slaughter Andrew Francis	Bridewell Chambers, London	020 7797 8800
Sleightholme John Trevor	37 Park Square Chambers, Leeds	0113 2439422
Small Mrs Arlene Ann-Marie	Francis Taylor Building, London	0171 353 7768/7769/2711
Smith Andrew Duncan	1 Fountain Court, Birmingham	0121 236 5721
Smith Nicholas Martin	1 Fountain Court, Birmingham	0121 236 5721
Smith Ms Rachel Catherine	Peel Court Chambers, Manchester	0161 832 3791
Smith Sean David	St Albans Chambers, St Albans	01727 843383
Smith Ms Zoe Philippa	Hardwicke Building, London	020 7242 2523
Sparrow Miss Claire Louise	Eastbourne Chambers, Eastbourne	01323 642102
Spence Simon Peter	18 Red Lion Court, London	0171 520 6000
	Thornwood House, Chelmsford	01245 280880
Spencer Paul Anthony	2 New Street, Leicester	0116 2625906
Spinks Roderick Cameron	Fenners Chambers, Cambridge	01223 368761
	Fenners Chambers, Peterborough	01733 562030
Spollon Guy Merton	St Philip's Chambers, Birmingham	0121 246 7000
St Louis Brian Lloyd	Hardwicke Building, London	020 7242 2523
Starmer Keir	Doughty Street Chambers, London	0171 404 1313
Stavros Ms Evanthia	3 Temple Gardens, London	0171 353 0832
Stern Ian Michael	Hollis Whiteman Chambers, London	020 7583 5766
Stewart Ms Alexandra Mary Hamilton	30 Park Square, Leeds	0113 2436388
Stewart Neill Alastair	Hollis Whiteman Chambers, London	020 7583 5766
Still Geoffrey John Churchill	Pump Court Chambers, Swindon	01793 539899
	Pump Court Chambers, London	0171 353 0711
	Pump Court Chambers, Winchester	01962 868161
Stokes Michael George Thomas	Chambers of Michael Pert QC, London	0171 421 8000
	Chambers of Michael Pert QC, Leicester	0116 249 2020
	Chambers of Michael Pert QC, Northampton	01604 602333
	St Philip's Chambers, Birmingham	0121 246 7000
Strange Ms (Karen) Michelle	Doughty Street Chambers, London	0171 404 1313
Strudwick Miss Linda Diane	Hollis Whiteman Chambers, London	020 7583 5766
Suckling Alan Blair	Hollis Whiteman Chambers, London	020 7583 5766
Sullivan Ms Jane Teresa	Hollis Whiteman Chambers, London	020 7583 5766
Summers Benjamin Dylan James	Hollis Whiteman Chambers, London	020 7583 5766
Sutton Philip Julian	Bell Yard Chambers, London	0171 306 9292
Swift Malcolm Robin	Park Court Chambers, Leeds	0113 2433277
	6 Gray's Inn Square, London	0171 242 1052
Syed Mohammad Ali	39 Park Avenue, Mitcham	0181 648 1684
	Tower Hamlets Barristers Chambers, London	0171 247 9825
Syfret Nicholas	13 King's Bench Walk, London	0171 353 7204
	King's Bench Chambers, Oxford	01865 311066
Szanto Gregory John Michael	Eastbourne Chambers, Eastbourne	01323 642102
Talbot Richard Kevin Kent	Deans Court Chambers, Manchester	0161 214 6000
	Deans Court Chambers, Preston	01772 555163
Tapsell Paul Richard	Becket Chambers, Canterbury	01227 786331
Taylor David Edward	37 Park Square Chambers, Leeds	0113 2439422
Taylor Julian Richard	Peel Court Chambers, Manchester	0161 832 3791
Taylor Paul Richard	Doughty Street Chambers, London	0171 404 1313

     • Expanded entry in Part D

Taylor-Camara Alexander Abdu Rahman	8 King's Bench Walk, London	0171 797 8888
Tedd Rex Hilary	• St Philip's Chambers, Birmingham	0121 246 7000
	De Montfort Chambers, Leicester	0116 254 8686
	Northampton Chambers, Northampton	01604 636271
Teeman Miss Miriam Joy	30 Park Square, Leeds	0113 2436388
Tehrani Christopher	8 King's Bench Walk North, Leeds	0113 2439797
	8 King's Bench Walk, London	0171 797 8888
Terry Miss Michelle Jane Evelyn	Lamb Building, London	020 7797 7788
Thain Miss Ashley	East Anglian Chambers, Colchester	01206 572756
	East Anglian Chambers, Ipswich	01473 214481
	East Anglian Chambers, Norwich	01603 617351
Thomas Stephen Edward Owen	St Philip's Chambers, Birmingham	0121 246 7000
Thompson Andrew Ian	1 Inner Temple Lane, London	020 7353 0933
Thompson Miss Blondelle Marguerite	1 Fountain Court, Birmingham	0121 236 5721
Thompson Lyall Norris	Tindal Chambers, Chelmsford	01245 267742
Thompson Patrick Miles	Queen's Chambers, Manchester	0161 834 6875/4738
	Queens Chambers, Preston	01772 828300
Thompson Miss Sally	2 Harcourt Buildings, London	020 7353 2112
Thorne Timothy Peter	33 Bedford Row, London	0171 242 6476
Thornley David	Chambers of Martin Burr, London	0171 353 4636
Thornton Peter Ribblesdale	Doughty Street Chambers, London	0171 404 1313
Tizzano Franco Salvatore	8 King's Bench Walk, London	0171 797 8888
	8 King's Bench Walk North, Leeds	0113 2439797
Travers Hugh	Pump Court Chambers, London	0171 353 0711
	Pump Court Chambers, Winchester	01962 868161
	Pump Court Chambers, Swindon	01793 539899
Tregilgas-Davey Marcus Ian	Pump Court Chambers, Swindon	01793 539899
	Pump Court Chambers, London	0171 353 0711
	Pump Court Chambers, Winchester	01962 868161
Turner Adrian John	Eastbourne Chambers, Eastbourne	01323 642102
Tyler William John	30 Park Square, Leeds	0113 2436388
Underhill Miss Alison	Tindal Chambers, Chelmsford	01245 267742
Vine James Peter Stockman	Hardwicke Building, London	020 7242 2523
Wakeham Philip John Le Messurier	Hardwicke Building, London	020 7242 2523
Walden-Smith David Edward	6 Pump Court, London	0171 797 8400
	6-8 Mill Street, Maidstone	01622 688094
Walker Paul Christopher	Bridewell Chambers, London	020 7797 8800
Walker-Smith Sir John Jonah	Doughty Street Chambers, London	0171 404 1313
	De Montfort Chambers, Leicester	0116 254 8686
Wall Mark Arthur	4 Fountain Court, Birmingham	0121 236 3476
Wallbanks Miss Joanne	1 Fountain Court, Birmingham	0121 236 5721
	Rowchester Chambers, Birmingham	0121 233 2327/2361951
Walsh Martin Fraser	Peel Court Chambers, Manchester	0161 832 3791
Walshe Ms Annie Patricia	Chambers of Geoffrey Hawker, London	0171 583 8899
Walters Gareth Rupel	St Philip's Chambers, Birmingham	0121 246 7000
Walters Geraint Wyn	Angel Chambers, Swansea	01792 464623/464648
Walters Miss Vivian Irene Elizabeth	13 King's Bench Walk, London	0171 353 7204
	King's Bench Chambers, Oxford	01865 311066
Ward Simon John	1 Fountain Court, Birmingham	0121 236 5721
Warne Peter Lawrence	Hollis Whiteman Chambers, London	020 7583 5766
Warren Philip David Charles	Pump Court Chambers, Swindon	01793 539899
	Pump Court Chambers, London	0171 353 0711
	Pump Court Chambers, Winchester	01962 868161
Warren Miss Sasha	3 Temple Gardens, London	0171 353 0832
Wastie William Granville	Hollis Whiteman Chambers, London	020 7583 5766
Watson Mark	6 Pump Court, London	0171 797 8400
	6-8 Mill Street, Maidstone	01622 688094
Watts Lawrence Peter	St Philip's Chambers, Birmingham	0121 246 7000
Wayne Nicholas	1 Gray's Inn Square, London	0171 405 8946/7/8

Weatherby Peter Francis	Two Garden Court, London	0171 353 1633
	Chambers of Ian Macdonald QC (In Association with Two Garden Court, Temple, London), Manchester	0161 236 1840
Webster Miss Elizabeth Jane	18 Red Lion Court, London	0171 520 6000
	Thornwood House, Chelmsford	01245 280880
Weeden Ross Charles	Bell Yard Chambers, London	0171 306 9292
West Ian Stuart	Fountain Chambers, Middlesbrough	01642 804040
West Michael Charles Beresford	3 & 4 Farnham Hall, Saxmundham	01728 602758
	8 Lambert Jones Mews, London	0171 638 8804
Wheetman Alan	East Anglian Chambers, Norwich	01603 617351
	East Anglian Chambers, Colchester	01206 572756
	East Anglian Chambers, Ipswich	01473 214481
Whitaker Ms Quincy Rachel Suzy	Doughty Street Chambers, London	0171 404 1313
White Timothy Richard	30 Park Square, Leeds	0113 2436388
Wickens Simon	Maidstone Chambers, Maidstone	01622 688592
Wilcken Anthony David Felix	Hollis Whiteman Chambers, London	020 7583 5766
Wilding Miss Lisa Marie	2 Harcourt Buildings, London	020 7353 2112
Williams Alan Ronald	8 King's Bench Walk, London	0171 797 8888
	8 King's Bench Walk North, Leeds	0113 2439797
Williams Miss Caroline Sarah	Maidstone Chambers, Maidstone	01622 688592
Williams Hugh David Haydn	St Philip's Chambers, Birmingham	0121 246 7000
Williams Neal Martin	1 Fountain Court, Birmingham	0121 236 5721
Williams Ms Nicola Egersis	8 King's Bench Walk, London	0171 797 8888
Williams Paul Robert	8 King's Bench Walk North, Leeds	0113 2439797
	8 King's Bench Walk, London	0171 797 8888
Williams Richard Evan Huw	Queens Square Chambers, Bristol	0117 921 1966
Williams Thomas Christopher Charles	1 Fountain Court, Birmingham	0121 236 5721
Wilson (Alan) Martin	9 Bedford Row, London	0171 242 3555
	St Philip's Chambers, Birmingham	0121 246 7000
Wilson Andrew Robert	9 Woodhouse Square, Leeds	0113 2451986
Wilson Myles Brennand	White Friars Chambers, Chester	01244 323070
Wilson Peter Julian	Sovereign Chambers, Leeds	0113 2451841/2/3
Wing Christopher John	Eighteen Carlton Crescent, Southampton	01703 639001
Winter Ian David	Hollis Whiteman Chambers, London	020 7583 5766
Wiseman Adam Philip Pasternak	18 Red Lion Court, London	0171 520 6000
	Thornwood House, Chelmsford	01245 280880
Wolchover Chaim David Hirsch	Ridgeway Chambers, London	0181 455 2939
	Virtual Chambers, London	07071 244 944
	Lion Court, London	0171 404 6565
Wood Guy Nicholas Marshall	Hollis Whiteman Chambers, London	020 7583 5766
Wood James Alexander Douglas	Doughty Street Chambers, London	0171 404 1313
Wood Percy	St James's Chambers, Manchester	0161 834 7000
Woodhall Gary	Chambers of John Hand QC, Manchester	0161 955 9000
Woodhouse Charles Philip	Bridewell Chambers, London	020 7797 8800
Woodley Leonard Gaston	8 King's Bench Walk, London	0171 797 8888
	8 King's Bench Walk North, Leeds	0113 2439797
Wyatt Mark	2 New Street, Leicester	0116 2625906
Yearwood Jeffrey Ryeburn	8 King's Bench Walk, London	0171 797 8888
	8 King's Bench Walk North, Leeds	0113 2439797
Young Alastair Angus McLeod	St Philip's Chambers, Birmingham	0121 246 7000

CRIME – CORPORATE FRAUD

Abbott Francis Arthur	Pump Court Chambers, Winchester	01962 868161
	Pump Court Chambers, London	0171 353 0711
	Pump Court Chambers, Swindon	01793 539899
Ainsworth Mark Justin Simon	Peel Court Chambers, Manchester	0161 832 3791
Aldred Mark Steven	Hollis Whiteman Chambers, London	020 7583 5766
Altman Brian	• 3 Hare Court, London	0171 395 2000
Andrews Miss Claire Marguerite	Gough Square Chambers, London	0171 353 0924

Atkins Richard Paul	1 Fountain Court, Birmingham	0121 236 5721
Azam Javaid	Plowden Buildings, London	0171 583 0808
Bacon Francis Michael	4 Paper Buildings, London	0171 353 3366/583 7155
Bailey Edward Henry	Monckton Chambers, London	0171 405 7211
Baker William Arthur	Peel Court Chambers, Manchester	0161 832 3791
Banks Robert James	100e Great Portland Street, London	0171 636 6323
Barker Brian John	Hollis Whiteman Chambers, London	020 7583 5766
Barnard Jonathan James	Hollis Whiteman Chambers, London	020 7583 5766
Barnes Miss Margaret Susanne	3 Hare Court, London	0171 395 2000
Barnett Andrew John	Pump Court Chambers, Winchester	01962 868161
	Pump Court Chambers, London	0171 353 0711
	Pump Court Chambers, Swindon	01793 539899
Barnfather Miss Lydia Helen	Hollis Whiteman Chambers, London	020 7583 5766
Barraclough Nicholas Maylin	2nd Floor, Francis Taylor Building, London	0171 353 9942/3157
Bart Delano Frank	8 King's Bench Walk, London	0171 797 8888
	8 King's Bench Walk North, Leeds	0113 2439797
Barton Alan John	Lamb Building, London	020 7797 7788
Barton Hugh Geoffrey	Doughty Street Chambers, London	0171 404 1313
Bate David Christopher	Hollis Whiteman Chambers, London	020 7583 5766
Baughan Julian James	13 King's Bench Walk, London	0171 353 7204
	King's Bench Chambers, Oxford	01865 311066
Bennetts Philip James	Hollis Whiteman Chambers, London	020 7583 5766
Bentham Howard Lownds	Peel Court Chambers, Manchester	0161 832 3791
Bentley David Neil	Doughty Street Chambers, London	0171 404 1313
Bevan Edward Julian	Hollis Whiteman Chambers, London	020 7583 5766
Bidder Neil	33 Park Place, Cardiff	02920 233313
	Goldsmith Building, London	0171 353 7881
Birch Roger Allen	Sovereign Chambers, Leeds	0113 2451841/2/3
	12 New Square, London	0171 419 1212
Blackburn Luke Sebastian	Pump Court Chambers, London	0171 353 0711
	Pump Court Chambers, Winchester	01962 868161
	Pump Court Chambers, Swindon	01793 539899
Blair William James Lynton	3 Verulam Buildings, London	0171 831 8441
Blom-Cooper Sir Louis Jacques	Doughty Street Chambers, London	0171 404 1313
Boateng Paul Yaw	8 King's Bench Walk, London	0171 797 8888
	8 King's Bench Walk North, Leeds	0113 2439797
Bogan Paul Simon	Doughty Street Chambers, London	0171 404 1313
Boney Guy Thomas Knowles	Pump Court Chambers, Winchester	01962 868161
	Pump Court Chambers, London	0171 353 0711
	Harrow on the Hill Chambers, Harrow-on-the-Hill	0181 423 7444
	Pump Court Chambers, Swindon	01793 539899
	Eighteen Carlton Crescent, Southampton	01703 639001
Boyce William	Hollis Whiteman Chambers, London	020 7583 5766
Broatch Michael Donald	5 Paper Buildings, London	0171 583 9275/583 4555
Bromley-Davenport John	Deans Court Chambers, Manchester	0161 214 6000
	Deans Court Chambers, Preston	01772 555163
Brooks Mr Paul Anthony	Doughty Street Chambers, London	0171 404 1313
Brown Miss Althea Sonia	Doughty Street Chambers, London	0171 404 1313
Brown Edward Francis Trevenen	Hollis Whiteman Chambers, London	020 7583 5766
Buckingham Mrs Kathleen Rosemary Bernadette	30 Park Square, Leeds	0113 2436388
Burbidge James Michael	St Philip's Chambers, Birmingham	0121 246 7000
Burn Colin Richard	30 Park Square, Leeds	0113 2436388
Carter Peter	• 18 Red Lion Court, London	0171 520 6000
	Thornwood House, Chelmsford	01245 280880

Clark Christopher Harvey	Pump Court Chambers, Winchester	01962 868161
	Pump Court Chambers, London	0171 353 0711
	Westgate Chambers, Lewes	01273 480510
	Pump Court Chambers, Swindon	01793 539899
	Harrow on the Hill Chambers,	0181 423 7444
	Harrow-on-the-Hill	
Clarke Peter William	Hollis Whiteman Chambers, London	020 7583 5766
Cole Robert Ian Gawain	30 Park Square, Leeds	0113 2436388
Collier Peter Neville	30 Park Square, Leeds	0113 2436388
Conry Michael Harvey	1 Fountain Court, Birmingham	0121 236 5721
Cook Jeremy David	Lamb Building, London	020 7797 7788
Corkery Michael	Five Paper Buildings, London	0171 583 6117
Coward Miss Victoria Jane	Hollis Whiteman Chambers, London	020 7583 5766
Crawford Miss Marie-Bernadette	Eastbourne Chambers, Eastbourne	01323 642102
Claire		
Dale Julian Charles Rigby	Eastbourne Chambers, Eastbourne	01323 642102
Daniells-Smith Roger Charles	8 King's Bench Walk, London	0171 797 8888
	8 King's Bench Walk North, Leeds	0113 2439797
Darbishire Adrian Munro	Hollis Whiteman Chambers, London	020 7583 5766
Davis William Easthope	St Philip's Chambers, Birmingham	0121 246 7000
Dedazade Taner	Tindal Chambers, Chelmsford	01245 267742
Denney Stuart Henry Macdonald	Deans Court Chambers, Manchester	0161 214 6000
	Deans Court Chambers, Preston	01772 555163
Dobbs Miss Linda Penelope	18 Red Lion Court, London	0171 520 6000
	Thornwood House, Chelmsford	01245 280880
Donne Jeremy Nigel	Hollis Whiteman Chambers, London	020 7583 5766
Draycott Simon Douglas	13 King's Bench Walk, London	0171 353 7204
Dunn Alexander	8 King's Bench Walk, London	0171 797 8888
	8 King's Bench Walk North, Leeds	0113 2439797
Edis Andrew Jeremy Coulter	● Adrian Lyon's Chambers, Liverpool	0151 236 4421/8240
Edusei Francis Victor Burg	Chambers of Ian Macdonald QC (In	0161 236 1840
	Association with Two Garden Court,	
	Temple, London), Manchester	
Ekins Charles Wareing	Sovereign Chambers, Leeds	0113 2451841/2/3
Ellison Mark Christopher	Hollis Whiteman Chambers, London	020 7583 5766
Emlyn Jones William Nicholas	2 Harcourt Buildings, London	020 7353 2112
Enoch Dafydd Huw	Bridewell Chambers, London	020 7797 8800
Evans David Howard	Hollis Whiteman Chambers, London	020 7583 5766
Evans Ms Jill Annaliese	Doughty Street Chambers, London	0171 404 1313
Evans John Wainwright	1 Fountain Court, Birmingham	0121 236 5721
Evans Julian Jacob	Hollis Whiteman Chambers, London	020 7583 5766
Farrer Paul Ainsworth	1 Fountain Court, Birmingham	0121 236 5721
Ferm Rodney Eric	37 Park Square Chambers, Leeds	0113 2439422
Fessal Ignatius	8 King's Bench Walk, London	0171 797 8888
	8 King's Bench Walk North, Leeds	0113 2439797
Field Rory Dominic	Hardwicke Building, London	020 7242 2523
Finnigan Peter Anthony	Hollis Whiteman Chambers, London	020 7583 5766
Fisher Jonathan Simon	● 18 Red Lion Court, London	0171 520 6000
	Thornwood House, Chelmsford	01245 280880
Flahive Daniel Michael	Hardwicke Building, London	020 7242 2523
Forshall Ms Isabella Louise	Doughty Street Chambers, London	0171 404 1313
Garlick Paul Richard	Pump Court Chambers, London	0171 353 0711
	Pump Court Chambers, Winchester	01962 868161
	Pump Court Chambers, Swindon	01793 539899
Garrett Michael Owen	St Philip's Chambers, Birmingham	0121 246 7000
Gassman Miss Caroline Dora	8 King's Bench Walk, London	0171 797 8888
	8 King's Bench Walk North, Leeds	0113 2439797
Gatt Ian Andrew	Littleton Chambers, London	0171 797 8600
Gatto Miss Nicola Esterina	8 King's Bench Walk, London	0171 797 8888
	8 King's Bench Walk North, Leeds	0113 2439797

       ● Expanded entry in Part D

Gau Justin Charles	Pump Court Chambers, London	0171 353 0711
	Pump Court Chambers, Winchester	01962 868161
	Pump Court Chambers, Swindon	01793 539899
Gibbs Mrs Jocelyn Ida	8 King's Bench Walk, London	0171 797 8888
Gibbs Patrick Michael Evan	2 Harcourt Buildings, London	020 7353 2112
Gibson Arthur George Adrian	Adrian Lyon's Chambers, Liverpool	0151 236 4421/8240
Gifford Lord Anthony Maurice	8 King's Bench Walk, London	0171 797 8888
	8 King's Bench Walk North, Leeds	0113 2439797
Gillibrand Philip Martin Mangnall	Pump Court Chambers, Winchester	01962 868161
	Pump Court Chambers, London	0171 353 0711
	Pump Court Chambers, Swindon	01793 539899
Glass Anthony Trevor	Hollis Whiteman Chambers, London	020 7583 5766
Gledhill Kris	Camberwell Chambers, London	0171 274 0830
Gordon Ms Clare	8 King's Bench Walk, London	0171 797 8888
Gordon John Sandford	New Court, London	0171 583 5123/0510
Goulding Jonathan Steven	Gough Square Chambers, London	0171 353 0924
Grant Edward William	6 Pump Court, London	0171 797 8400
	6-8 Mill Street, Maidstone	01622 688094
Grant Gary Steven	3 Temple Gardens, London	0171 583 1155
Green Jonathan Paul	2nd Floor, Francis Taylor Building, London	0171 353 9942/3157
Grey Robin Douglas	Hollis Whiteman Chambers, London	020 7583 5766
Grieve Michael Robertson Crichton	Doughty Street Chambers, London	0171 404 1313
Griffith-Jones Richard Haydn	1 Fountain Court, Birmingham	0121 236 5721
Grout-Smith Jeremy Gaywood	Peel Court Chambers, Manchester	0161 832 3791
Hall Andrew Joseph	Doughty Street Chambers, London	0171 404 1313
Hamilton Graeme Montagu	Two Crown Office Row, London	020 7797 8100
Harris Ms Rebecca Elizabeth	Hollis Whiteman Chambers, London	020 7583 5766
Hart-Leverton Colin Allen	8 King's Bench Walk, London	0171 797 8888
	8 King's Bench Walk North, Leeds	0113 2439797
Hawkesworth (Walter) Gareth	Fenners Chambers, Cambridge	01223 368761
	Fenners Chambers, Peterborough	01733 562030
	Five Paper Buildings, London	0171 583 6117
Hayhow Mrs Lyndsay Jill	5 Essex Court, London	0171 410 2000
Haynes Peter	St Philip's Chambers, Birmingham	0121 246 7000
Hayton Michael Pearson	Deans Court Chambers, Manchester	0161 214 6000
	Deans Court Chambers, Preston	01772 555163
Hegarty Kevin John	St Philip's Chambers, Birmingham	0121 246 7000
Henderson Ian Francis	8 King's Bench Walk, London	0171 797 8888
	8 King's Bench Walk North, Leeds	0113 2439797
Henry Edward Joseph Aloysius	Hollis Whiteman Chambers, London	020 7583 5766
Hibbert William John	Gough Square Chambers, London	0171 353 0924
Hilton Alan John Howard	Hollis Whiteman Chambers, London	020 7583 5766
Hockman Stephen Alexander	•6 Pump Court, London	0171 797 8400
	6-8 Mill Street, Maidstone	01622 688094
Hodgson Martin Derrick	8 King's Bench Walk, London	0171 797 8888
	8 King's Bench Walk North, Leeds	0113 2439797
Horwell Richard Eric	Hollis Whiteman Chambers, London	020 7583 5766
Hudson Anthony Sean	Doughty Street Chambers, London	0171 404 1313
Igori Kingsley Izehiuwa	8 King's Bench Walk, London	0171 797 8888
Inman Melbourne Donald	1 Fountain Court, Birmingham	0121 236 5721
Ivens Ms Jemima	8 King's Bench Walk, London	0171 797 8888
	8 King's Bench Walk North, Leeds	0113 2439797
Jafferjee Aftab Asger	2 Harcourt Buildings, London	020 7353 2112
Jeffreys David Alfred	Hollis Whiteman Chambers, London	020 7583 5766
Johnson Miss Zoe Elisabeth	Hollis Whiteman Chambers, London	020 7583 5766
Jones Martin Wynne	8 King's Bench Walk, London	0171 797 8888
	8 King's Bench Walk North, Leeds	0113 2439797
Josse David Benjamin	Bridewell Chambers, London	020 7797 8800
Kadri Sadakat	Doughty Street Chambers, London	0171 404 1313
Kark Thomas Victor William	Hollis Whiteman Chambers, London	020 7583 5766

B

• Expanded entry in Part D

Keating Dermot John	8 King's Bench Walk, London	0171 797 8888
Keeley James Francis	Sovereign Chambers, Leeds	0113 2451841/2/3
Kelman Alistair Bruce	Lancaster Building, Manchester	0161 661 4444/0171 649 9872
Kelsey-Fry John	Hollis Whiteman Chambers, London	020 7583 5766
Keogh Andrew John	8 King's Bench Walk, London	0171 797 8888
	8 King's Bench Walk North, Leeds	0113 2439797
Kershaw Andrew	30 Park Square, Leeds	0113 2436388
Khan Anwar William	Eastbourne Chambers, Eastbourne	01323 642102
	Wessex Chambers, Reading	0118 956 8856
Khan Miss Helen Mary Grace	Pump Court Chambers, London	0171 353 0711
	Pump Court Chambers, Winchester	01962 868161
	Pump Court Chambers, Swindon	01793 539899
Khokhar Mushtaq Ahmed	Sovereign Chambers, Leeds	0113 2451841/2/3
Kramer Stephen Ernest	• 1 Hare Court, London	0171 353 3982/5324
Kyte Peter Eric	Hollis Whiteman Chambers, London	020 7583 5766
Langdale Timothy James	Hollis Whiteman Chambers, London	020 7583 5766
Large Alan Macdonald	South Western Chambers, Taunton	01823 331919 (24 hrs)
Larkin Sean	Hollis Whiteman Chambers, London	020 7583 5766
Lawson Miss Sara Lucy Jane	18 Red Lion Court, London	0171 520 6000
	Thornwood House, Chelmsford	01245 280880
Levene Victor	1 Gray's Inn Square, London	0171 405 8946/7/8
Lever The Hon Bernard Lewis	Peel Court Chambers, Manchester	0161 832 3791
	Harcourt Chambers, London	0171 353 6961
Lodder Peter Norman	3 Hare Court, London	0171 395 2000
Long Tobias Charles	8 King's Bench Walk, London	0171 797 8888
	8 King's Bench Walk North, Leeds	0113 2439797
Longden Anthony Gordon	Hollis Whiteman Chambers, London	020 7583 5766
Lowry Miss Emma Margaret Collins	Hollis Whiteman Chambers, London	020 7583 5766
MacKinnon Thomas Joseph	8 King's Bench Walk, London	0171 797 8888
	8 King's Bench Walk North, Leeds	0113 2439797
Maidment Kieran Francis	Doughty Street Chambers, London	0171 404 1313
Mann Jonathan Simon	8 King's Bench Walk, London	0171 797 8888
	8 King's Bench Walk North, Leeds	0113 2439797
Marks Richard Leon	Peel Court Chambers, Manchester	0161 832 3791
Marshall-Andrews Robert Graham	37 Park Square Chambers, Leeds	0113 2439422
	2-4 Tudor Street, London	0171 797 7111
Marson Geoffrey Charles	Sovereign Chambers, Leeds	0113 2451841/2/3
McCahill Patrick Gerard	St Philip's Chambers, Birmingham	0121 246 7000
	Chambers of Andrew Campbell QC, Leeds	0113 2455438
McCarthy Martin Raymond	8 King's Bench Walk, London	0171 797 8888
	8 King's Bench Walk North, Leeds	0113 2439797
McCourt Christopher	22 Old Buildings, London	0171 831 0222
McCrindell James Derrey	Mitre House Chambers, London	0171 583 8233
McDonnell John Beresford William	1 New Square, London	0171 405 0884/5/6/7
McEvilly Gerard Martin	Furnival Chambers, London	0171 405 3232
McLaughlin Miss Elaine	8 King's Bench Walk, London	0171 797 8888
Middleton Joseph	Doughty Street Chambers, London	0171 404 1313
Miller Miss Jane Elizabeth Mackay	Pump Court Chambers, London	0171 353 0711
	Pump Court Chambers, Winchester	01962 868161
	Pump Court Chambers, Swindon	01793 539899
Milliken-Smith Mark Gordon	3 Hare Court, London	0171 395 2000
Millington Christopher John	1 Fountain Court, Birmingham	0121 236 5721
Mitchell Christopher Richard	Hollis Whiteman Chambers, London	020 7583 5766
Mitchell Keith Arno	3 Hare Court, London	0171 395 2000
Morse Malcolm George McEwan	1 Fountain Court, Birmingham	0121 236 5721
Muller Antonie Sean	4 Fountain Court, Birmingham	0121 236 3476
Munday Miss Anne Margaret	8 King's Bench Walk North, Leeds	0113 2439797
	8 King's Bench Walk, London	0171 797 8888
Newbury Richard Lennox	Sovereign Chambers, Leeds	0113 2451841/2/3
Newman Miss Catherine Mary	• 13 Old Square, London	0171 404 4800

• Expanded entry in Part D

Nicholls Christopher Benjamin	1 Fountain Court, Birmingham	0121 236 5721
Nicholson Pratt Thomas Hycy	Hardwicke Building, London	020 7242 2523
Nsugbe Oba Eric	Pump Court Chambers, London	0171 353 0711
	Pump Court Chambers, Winchester	01962 868161
	Pump Court Chambers, Swindon	01793 539899
O'Donoghue Florence	2 Mitre Court Buildings, London	0171 353 1353
O'Sullivan Michael Neil	5 King's Bench Walk, London	0171 353 5638
Oliver Michael Richard	Hardwicke Building, London	020 7242 2523
Orme Richard Andrew	Peel Court Chambers, Manchester	0161 832 3791
Palmer Patrick John Steven	Sovereign Chambers, Leeds	0113 2451841/2/3
Parry Charles Robert	Pump Court Chambers, Swindon	01793 539899
	Pump Court Chambers, London	0171 353 0711
	Pump Court Chambers, Winchester	01962 868161
Pascoe Nigel Spencer Knight	Pump Court Chambers, Winchester	01962 868161
	Pump Court Chambers, London	0171 353 0711
	Queens Square Chambers, Bristol	0117 921 1966
	Pump Court Chambers, Swindon	01793 539899
Paton Ian Francis	Hollis Whiteman Chambers, London	020 7583 5766
Paul Nicholas Martin	Doughty Street Chambers, London	0171 404 1313
	Westgate Chambers, Lewes	01273 480510
Pearson Michael	30 Park Square, Leeds	0113 2436388
Pelling (Philip) Mark	Monckton Chambers, London	0171 405 7211
Penn Jonathan Peter Robert	8 King's Bench Walk, London	0171 797 8888
Plaschkes Ms Sarah Georgina	Hollis Whiteman Chambers, London	020 7583 5766
Pomeroy Toby	Barristers' Common Law Chambers, London	0171 375 3012
	Virtual Chambers, London	07071 244 944
Portnoy Leslie Reuben	Chambers of John Hand QC, Manchester	0161 955 9000
Poulet Mrs Rebecca Maria	Hollis Whiteman Chambers, London	020 7583 5766
Pounder Gerard	5 Essex Court, London	0171 410 2000
Powis Miss Samantha Inez	St Philip's Chambers, Birmingham	0121 246 7000
Prasad Krishna	21 Craven Road, Kingston-Upon-Thames	0181 974 6799
Pringle Gordon Alexander	Bridewell Chambers, London	020 7797 8800
Ramasamy Selvaraju	Hollis Whiteman Chambers, London	020 7583 5766
Randall John Yeoman	St Philip's Chambers, Birmingham	0121 246 7000
	7 Stone Buildings, London	0171 405 3886/242 3546
Rankin Andrew	4 Field Court, London	0171 440 6900
Rector Miss Penelope Jane	• Five Paper Buildings, London	0171 583 6117
Redgrave Adrian Robert Frank	No. 1 Serjeants' Inn, London	0171 415 6666
Rees Edward Parry	Doughty Street Chambers, London	0171 404 1313
Rees Gareth David	Hollis Whiteman Chambers, London	020 7583 5766
Rhodes Robert Elliott	4 King's Bench Walk, London	0171 822 8822
Roberts Jeremy Michael Graham	9 Gough Square, London	020 7832 0500
Robertson Geoffrey Ronald	Doughty Street Chambers, London	0171 404 1313
Robinson Vivian	Hollis Whiteman Chambers, London	020 7583 5766
Rose Miss Pamela Susan	8 King's Bench Walk, London	0171 797 8888
	8 King's Bench Walk North, Leeds	0113 2439797
Rowe John Jermyn	• 8 King Street Chambers, Manchester	0161 834 9560
Rubery Philip Alan	8 King's Bench Walk, London	0171 797 8888
	8 King's Bench Walk North, Leeds	0113 2439797
Russell Anthony Patrick	Peel Court Chambers, Manchester	0161 832 3791
Ryan Timothy John	8 King's Bench Walk, London	0171 797 8888
	8 King's Bench Walk North, Leeds	0113 2439797
Ryan William	8 King's Bench Walk, London	0171 797 8888
	8 King's Bench Walk North, Leeds	0113 2439797
Sallon Christopher Robert	Doughty Street Chambers, London	0171 404 1313
	Westgate Chambers, Lewes	01273 480510
Salmon Jonathan Carl	1 Fountain Court, Birmingham	0121 236 5721
Salter Charles Philip Arthur	8 King's Bench Walk, London	0171 797 8888
	8 King's Bench Walk North, Leeds	0113 2439797

B

Scott Matthew John	Pump Court Chambers, London	0171 353 0711
	Pump Court Chambers, Winchester	01962 868161
	Pump Court Chambers, Swindon	01793 539899
Seal Julius Damien	189 Randolph Avenue, London	0171 624 9139
Sells Oliver Matthew	Five Paper Buildings, London	0171 583 6117
	Fenners Chambers, Cambridge	01223 368761
Seymour Richard William	Monckton Chambers, London	0171 405 7211
Shale Justin Anton	4 King's Bench Walk, London	0171 822 8822
	King's Bench Chambers, Bournemouth	01202 250025
Shepherd Nigel Patrick	8 King's Bench Walk North, Leeds	0113 2439797
	8 King's Bench Walk, London	0171 797 8888
Shorrock John Michael	Peel Court Chambers, Manchester	0161 832 3791
Sibson Mrs Clare Adele	Hollis Whiteman Chambers, London	020 7583 5766
Singh Kuldip	Five Paper Buildings, London	0171 583 6117
Smith Ms Zoe Philippa	Hardwicke Building, London	020 7242 2523
Spence Simon Peter	18 Red Lion Court, London	0171 520 6000
	Thornwood House, Chelmsford	01245 280880
Staddon Miss Claire Ann	12 New Square, London	0171 419 1212
	Sovereign Chambers, Leeds	0113 2451841/2/3
Stancombe Barry Terrence	Gough Square Chambers, London	0171 353 0924
Stern Ian Michael	Hollis Whiteman Chambers, London	020 7583 5766
Stewart Neill Alastair	Hollis Whiteman Chambers, London	020 7583 5766
Still Geoffrey John Churchill	Pump Court Chambers, Swindon	01793 539899
	Pump Court Chambers, London	0171 353 0711
	Pump Court Chambers, Winchester	01962 868161
Stokes Michael George Thomas	Chambers of Michael Pert QC, London	0171 421 8000
	Chambers of Michael Pert QC, Leicester	0116 249 2020
	Chambers of Michael Pert QC, Northampton	01604 602333
	St Philip's Chambers, Birmingham	0121 246 7000
Strange Ms (Karen) Michelle	Doughty Street Chambers, London	0171 404 1313
Strudwick Miss Linda Diane	Hollis Whiteman Chambers, London	020 7583 5766
Suckling Alan Blair	Hollis Whiteman Chambers, London	020 7583 5766
Sullivan Ms Jane Teresa	Hollis Whiteman Chambers, London	020 7583 5766
Summers Benjamin Dylan James	Hollis Whiteman Chambers, London	020 7583 5766
Sutton Philip Julian	Bell Yard Chambers, London	0171 306 9292
Swift Malcolm Robin	Park Court Chambers, Leeds	0113 2433277
	6 Gray's Inn Square, London	0171 242 1052
Szanto Gregory John Michael	Eastbourne Chambers, Eastbourne	01323 642102
Taylor David Edward	37 Park Square Chambers, Leeds	0113 2439422
Taylor Julian Richard	Peel Court Chambers, Manchester	0161 832 3791
Taylor Paul Richard	Doughty Street Chambers, London	0171 404 1313
Taylor-Camara Alexander Abdu Rahman	8 King's Bench Walk, London	0171 797 8888
Tedd Rex Hilary	• St Philip's Chambers, Birmingham	0121 246 7000
	De Montfort Chambers, Leicester	0116 254 8686
	Northampton Chambers, Northampton	01604 636271
Teeman Miss Miriam Joy	30 Park Square, Leeds	0113 2436388
Tehrani Christopher	8 King's Bench Walk North, Leeds	0113 2439797
	8 King's Bench Walk, London	0171 797 8888
Terry Miss Michelle Jane Evelyn	Lamb Building, London	020 7797 7788
Thornton Peter Ribblesdale	Doughty Street Chambers, London	0171 404 1313
Tizzano Franco Salvatore	8 King's Bench Walk, London	0171 797 8888
	8 King's Bench Walk North, Leeds	0113 2439797
Travers Hugh	Pump Court Chambers, London	0171 353 0711
	Pump Court Chambers, Winchester	01962 868161
	Pump Court Chambers, Swindon	01793 539899
Turner Adrian John	Eastbourne Chambers, Eastbourne	01323 642102
Van Hagen Christopher Seymour Nigel	4 King's Bench Walk, London	0171 822 8822
	King's Bench Chambers, Bournemouth	01202 250025

• Expanded entry in Part D

Vine James Peter Stockman	Hardwicke Building, London	020 7242 2523
Vines Anthony Robert Francis	Gough Square Chambers, London	0171 353 0924
Wakeham Philip John Le Messurier	Hardwicke Building, London	020 7242 2523
Walsh Martin Fraser	Peel Court Chambers, Manchester	0161 832 3791
Walters Gareth Rupel	St Philip's Chambers, Birmingham	0121 246 7000
Walters Miss Vivian Irene Elizabeth	13 King's Bench Walk, London	0171 353 7204
	King's Bench Chambers, Oxford	01865 311066
Ward Simon John	1 Fountain Court, Birmingham	0121 236 5721
Warne Peter Lawrence	Hollis Whiteman Chambers, London	020 7583 5766
Wastie William Granville	Hollis Whiteman Chambers, London	020 7583 5766
Watts Lawrence Peter	St Philip's Chambers, Birmingham	0121 246 7000
Weatherby Peter Francis	Two Garden Court, London	0171 353 1633
	Chambers of Ian Macdonald QC (In Association with Two Garden Court, Temple, London), Manchester	0161 236 1840
West Ian Stuart	Fountain Chambers, Middlesbrough	01642 804040
Whitaker Ms Quincy Rachel Suzy	Doughty Street Chambers, London	0171 404 1313
Wilby David Christopher	• 199 Strand, London	0171 379 9779
	Park Lane Chambers, Leeds	0113 2285000
Wilcken Anthony David Felix	Hollis Whiteman Chambers, London	020 7583 5766
Williams Alan Ronald	8 King's Bench Walk, London	0171 797 8888
	8 King's Bench Walk North, Leeds	0113 2439797
Williams Ms Nicola Egersis	8 King's Bench Walk, London	0171 797 8888
Williams Paul Robert	8 King's Bench Walk North, Leeds	0113 2439797
	8 King's Bench Walk, London	0171 797 8888
Wilson (Alan) Martin	9 Bedford Row, London	0171 242 3555
	St Philip's Chambers, Birmingham	0121 246 7000
Winter Ian David	Hollis Whiteman Chambers, London	020 7583 5766
Wood Guy Nicholas Marshall	Hollis Whiteman Chambers, London	020 7583 5766
Wood James Alexander Douglas	Doughty Street Chambers, London	0171 404 1313
Woodley Leonard Gaston	8 King's Bench Walk, London	0171 797 8888
	8 King's Bench Walk North, Leeds	0113 2439797
Yearwood Jeffrey Ryeburn	8 King's Bench Walk, London	0171 797 8888
	8 King's Bench Walk North, Leeds	0113 2439797

DAMAGES

McGregor Harvey	4 Paper Buildings, London	0171 353 3366/583 7155

DEFAMATION

Barca Manuel David	1 Brick Court, London	0171 353 8845
Basu Dr Dijendra Bhushan	Devereux Chambers, London	0171 353 7534
Buckley Peter Evered	Queen's Chambers, Manchester	0161 834 6875/4738
	Queens Chambers, Preston	01772 828300
Cakebread Stuart Alan Charles	• 2nd Floor, Francis Taylor Building, London	0171 353 9942/3157
Craig Kenneth Allen	Hardwicke Building, London	020 7242 2523
Date Julian Richard	17 Bedford Row, London	0171 831 7314
Emmerson (Michael) Benedict	Doughty Street Chambers, London	0171 404 1313
Evans Ms Catrin Miranda	1 Brick Court, London	0171 353 8845
Ferm Rodney Eric	37 Park Square Chambers, Leeds	0113 2439422
Foster Charles Andrew	• Chambers of Kieran Coonan QC, London	0171 583 6013/2510
Gee Steven Mark	4 Field Court, London	0171 440 6900
Grieve Michael Robertson Crichton	Doughty Street Chambers, London	0171 404 1313
Hermer Richard Simon	Doughty Street Chambers, London	0171 404 1313
	30 Park Place, Cardiff	01222 398421
Hogg The Hon Douglas Martin	37 Park Square Chambers, Leeds	0113 2439422
	Cathedral Chambers (Jan Wood Independent Barristers' Clerk), Exeter	01392 210900
Hudson Anthony Sean	Doughty Street Chambers, London	0171 404 1313
Keane Desmond St John	Pendragon Chambers, Swansea	01792 411188
Kolodziej Andrzej Jozef	• Littman Chambers, London	020 7404 4866

Levene Victor	1 Gray's Inn Square, London	0171 405 8946/7/8
Lewis Edward Trevor Gwyn	Francis Taylor Building, London	0171 353 7768/7769/2711
Maidment Kieran Francis	Doughty Street Chambers, London	0171 404 1313
Markus Ms Kate	Doughty Street Chambers, London	0171 404 1313
Marshall-Andrews Robert Graham	37 Park Square Chambers, Leeds	0113 2439422
	2-4 Tudor Street, London	0171 797 7111
McCahey Miss Catherine Anne Mary	St Philip's Chambers, Birmingham	0121 246 7000
Metzer Anthony David Erwin	Doughty Street Chambers, London	0171 404 1313
Millar Gavin James	Doughty Street Chambers, London	0171 404 1313
Nicol Andrew George Lindsay	Doughty Street Chambers, London	0171 404 1313
Oppenheim Robin Frank	Doughty Street Chambers, London	0171 404 1313
Panford Frank Haig	• Doughty Street Chambers, London	0171 404 1313
Pascoe Nigel Spencer Knight	Pump Court Chambers, Winchester	01962 868161
	Pump Court Chambers, London	0171 353 0711
	Queens Square Chambers, Bristol	0117 921 1966
	Pump Court Chambers, Swindon	01793 539899
Pearson Thomas Adam Spenser	Pump Court Chambers, London	0171 353 0711
	Pump Court Chambers, Winchester	01962 868161
	Pump Court Chambers, Swindon	01793 539899
Pershad Rohan	Two Crown Office Row, London	020 7797 8100
Price Richard Mervyn	Littleton Chambers, London	0171 797 8600
Robertson Geoffrey Ronald	Doughty Street Chambers, London	0171 404 1313
Shannon Thomas Eric	Queen's Chambers, Manchester	0161 834 6875/4738
	Queens Chambers, Preston	01772 828300
Singh Kuldip	Five Paper Buildings, London	0171 583 6117
Skinner Miss Lorna Jane	1 Brick Court, London	0171 353 8845
Starmer Keir	Doughty Street Chambers, London	0171 404 1313
Stewart Nicholas John Cameron	Hardwicke Building, London	020 7242 2523
Temple Anthony Dominic	4 Pump Court, London	020 7842 5555
Terry Robert Jeffrey	8 King Street Chambers, Manchester	0161 834 9560
Waters Julian William Penrose	No. 1 Serjeants' Inn, London	0171 415 6666
Williams Ms Heather Jean	Doughty Street Chambers, London	0171 404 1313

DIRECTORS' DISQUALIFICATION

Lucas Miss Bridget Ann	Serle Court Chambers, London	0171 242 6105
	Fountain Court, London	0171 583 3335

DISCIPLINARY (NURSES)

Christie-Brown Miss Sarah Louise	4 Paper Buildings, London	0171 353 3366/583 7155

DISCIPLINARY TRIBUNALS

Apfel Freddy	37 Park Square Chambers, Leeds	0113 2439422
Bennetts Philip James	Hollis Whiteman Chambers, London	020 7583 5766
Ewins Miss Catherine Jane	4 Paper Buildings, London	0171 353 3366/583 7155
Kark Thomas Victor William	Hollis Whiteman Chambers, London	020 7583 5766
Kelbrick Anthony Michael	37 Park Square Chambers, Leeds	0113 2439422
Lindsay Jeremy Mark Henry	37 Park Square Chambers, Leeds	0113 2439422
Macadam Jason Angus Alaister Robert L	37 Park Square Chambers, Leeds	0113 2439422
Mitchell Christopher Richard	Hollis Whiteman Chambers, London	020 7583 5766
Stern Ian Michael	Hollis Whiteman Chambers, London	020 7583 5766
Sullivan Ms Jane Teresa	Hollis Whiteman Chambers, London	020 7583 5766
Winter Ian David	Hollis Whiteman Chambers, London	020 7583 5766

DISCRIMINATION

Anderson Miss Julie	• Littman Chambers, London	020 7404 4866
Barker John Steven Roy	Queen's Chambers, Manchester	0161 834 6875/4738
	Queens Chambers, Preston	01772 828300
Barnett Daniel Alexander	2 Gray's Inn Square Chambers, London	020 7242 0328
Barry Miss Kirsten Lesley	8 King Street Chambers, Manchester	0161 834 9560
Basu Dr Dijendra Bhushan	Devereux Chambers, London	0171 353 7534

       • Expanded entry in Part D

Bather Miss Victoria Maclean	Littleton Chambers, London	0171 797 8600
Benson John Trevor	Adrian Lyon's Chambers, Liverpool	0151 236 4421/8240
Birtles William	Old Square Chambers, London	0171 269 0300
	Old Square Chambers, Bristol	0117 9277111
Booth Nicholas John	Old Square Chambers, London	0171 269 0300
	Old Square Chambers, Bristol	0117 9277111
Broatch Michael Donald	5 Paper Buildings, London	0171 583 9275/583 4555
Brown Miss Althea Sonia	Doughty Street Chambers, London	0171 404 1313
Brown Damian Robert	• Old Square Chambers, London	0171 269 0300
	Old Square Chambers, Bristol	0117 9277111
Bryant Keith	Devereux Chambers, London	0171 353 7534
Buck Dr Andrew Theodore	Chambers of Martin Burr, London	0171 353 4636
Burrows Simon Paul	Peel Court Chambers, Manchester	0161 832 3791
Carr Bruce Conrad	Devereux Chambers, London	0171 353 7534
Cavanagh John Patrick	11 King's Bench Walk, London	0171 632 8500/583 0610
Chudleigh Miss Louise Katrina	Old Square Chambers, London	0171 269 0300
	Old Square Chambers, Bristol	0117 9277111
Connolly Miss Joanne Marie	8 King Street Chambers, Manchester	0161 834 9560
Cook Miss Alison Noele	St Philip's Chambers, Birmingham	0121 246 7000
Daly David	Francis Taylor Building, London	0171 797 7250
Dedezade Taner	Tindal Chambers, Chelmsford	01245 267742
Dolan Dr Bridget Maura	3 Serjeants' Inn, London	0171 353 5537
Donovan Joel	New Court Chambers, London	0171 831 9500
Doughty Peter	17 Carlton Crescent, Southampton	023 8032 0320/0823 2003
Eady Miss Jennifer Jane	Old Square Chambers, London	0171 269 0300
	Old Square Chambers, Bristol	0117 9277111
Edge Timothy Richard	Deans Court Chambers, Preston	01772 555163
	Deans Court Chambers, Manchester	0161 214 6000
Elfield Miss Laura Elaine	5 Pump Court, London	020 7353 2532
Ferm Rodney Eric	37 Park Square Chambers, Leeds	0113 2439422
Garner Miss Sophie Jane	199 Strand, London	0171 379 9779
George Miss Judith Sarah	St Philip's Chambers, Birmingham	0121 246 7000
Gill Ms Sarah Teresa	• Old Square Chambers, London	0171 269 0300
	Old Square Chambers, Bristol	0117 9277111
Goudie James	• 11 King's Bench Walk, London	0171 632 8500/583 0610
Gower Miss Helen Clare	Old Square Chambers, Bristol	0117 9277111
	Old Square Chambers, London	0171 269 0300
Green Roger John Bailey	Queen's Chambers, Manchester	0161 834 6875/4738
	Queens Chambers, Preston	01772 828300
Harris Melvyn	7 New Square, London	0171 430 1660
Harrison Ms Averil	Chambers of Averil Harrison, London	0181 692 4949
Hermer Richard Simon	Doughty Street Chambers, London	0171 404 1313
	30 Park Place, Cardiff	01222 398421
Hudson Anthony Sean	Doughty Street Chambers, London	0171 404 1313
Hyams Oliver Marks	5 Paper Buildings, London	0171 583 9275/583 4555
Ivimy Ms Cecilia Rachel	11 King's Bench Walk, London	0171 632 8500/583 0610
Johnston Anthony Paul	1 Fountain Court, Birmingham	0121 236 5721
Jones Sean William Paul	11 King's Bench Walk, London	0171 632 8500/583 0610
Kaufmann Ms Phillippa Jane	Doughty Street Chambers, London	0171 404 1313
Kempster Ivor Toby Chalmers	Old Square Chambers, Bristol	0117 9277111
	Old Square Chambers, London	0171 269 0300
Kenward Timothy David Nelson	25-27 Castle Street, Liverpool	0151 227 5661/051 236 5072
Korn Anthony Henry	Barnard's Inn Chambers, London	0171 369 6969
Leiper Richard Thomas	11 King's Bench Walk, London	0171 632 8500/583 0610
Lennard Stephen Charles	Hardwicke Building, London	020 7242 2523
Lewis Professor Roy Malcolm	Old Square Chambers, London	0171 269 0300
	Old Square Chambers, Bristol	0117 9277111
Malecka Dr Mary Margaret	• 3 Temple Gardens, London	0171 353 0832
	65-67 King Street, Leicester	0116 2547710
McCafferty Miss Lynne	5 Paper Buildings, London	0171 583 9275/583 4555
McCluggage Brian Thomas	Chambers of John Hand QC, Manchester	0161 955 9000

McMullen Jeremy John	• Old Square Chambers, London	0171 269 0300
	Old Square Chambers, Bristol	0117 9277111
Melville Miss Elizabeth Emma Jane	Old Square Chambers, London	0171 269 0300
	Old Square Chambers, Bristol	0117 9277111
Millar Gavin James	Doughty Street Chambers, London	0171 404 1313
Mitropoulos Christos	Chambers of Geoffrey Hawker, London	0171 583 8899
Moor Miss Sarah Kathryn	Old Square Chambers, London	0171 269 0300
	Old Square Chambers, Bristol	0117 9277111
Nardell Gordon Lawrence	6 Pump Court, London	0171 797 8400
	6-8 Mill Street, Maidstone	01622 688094
Newman Austin Eric	9 Woodhouse Square, Leeds	0113 2451986
Nicol Andrew George Lindsay	Doughty Street Chambers, London	0171 404 1313
Nicol Nicholas Keith	1 Pump Court, London	0171 583 2012/353 4341
O'Neill Tadhg Joseph	1 Crown Office Row, London	0171 583 9292
Oppenheim Robin Frank	Doughty Street Chambers, London	0171 404 1313
Panton William Dwight	Britton Street Chambers, London	0171 608 3765
Parkin Jonathan	• Chambers of John Hand QC, Manchester	0161 955 9000
Pirani Rohan Carl	Old Square Chambers, Bristol	0117 9277111
	Old Square Chambers, London	0171 269 0300
Pitt-Payne Timothy Sheridan	• 11 King's Bench Walk, London	0171 632 8500/583 0610
Plimmer Miss Melanie Ann	Chambers of Ian Macdonald QC (In Association with Two Garden Court, Temple, London), Manchester	0161 236 1840
Rees Professor William Michael	Barnard's Inn Chambers, London	0171 369 6969
Robinson Simon Robert	Chambers of Ian Macdonald QC (In Association with Two Garden Court, Temple, London), Manchester	0161 236 1840
Roebuck Roy Delville	Bell Yard Chambers, London	0171 306 9292
Rogers Ian Paul	1 Crown Office Row, London	0171 583 9292
Rose Paul Telfer	Old Square Chambers, London	0171 269 0300
	Old Square Chambers, Bristol	0117 9277111
Salmon Jonathan Carl	1 Fountain Court, Birmingham	0121 236 5721
Segal Oliver Leon	Old Square Chambers, London	0171 269 0300
	Old Square Chambers, Bristol	0117 9277111
Sendall Antony John Christmas	Littleton Chambers, London	0171 797 8600
Sethi Mohinderpal Singh	Barnard's Inn Chambers, London	0171 369 6969
Shale Justin Anton	4 King's Bench Walk, London	0171 822 8822
	King's Bench Chambers, Bournemouth	01202 250025
Shannon Thomas Eric	Queen's Chambers, Manchester	0161 834 6875/4738
	Queens Chambers, Preston	01772 828300
Shukla Ms Vina	New Court Chambers, London	0171 831 9500
Siddiqi Faizul Aqtab	Justice Court Chambers, London	0181 830 7786
Slade Miss Elizabeth Ann	11 King's Bench Walk, London	0171 632 8500/583 0610
Smail Alastair Harold Kurt	St Philip's Chambers, Birmingham	0121 246 7000
Smith Miss Emma Louise	Old Square Chambers, London	0171 269 0300
	Old Square Chambers, Bristol	0117 9277111
Spicer Robert Haden	Frederick Place Chambers, Bristol	0117 9738667
Stark James Hayden Alexander	Chambers of Ian Macdonald QC (In Association with Two Garden Court, Temple, London), Manchester	0161 236 1840
Stilitz Daniel Malachi	11 King's Bench Walk, London	0171 632 8500/583 0610
Straker Timothy Derrick	• 4-5 Gray's Inn Square, London	0171 404 5252
Supperstone Michael Alan	11 King's Bench Walk, London	0171 632 8500/583 0610
Tatton-Brown Daniel Nicholas	Littleton Chambers, London	0171 797 8600
Tether Ms Melanie Georgia Kim	Old Square Chambers, London	0171 269 0300
	Old Square Chambers, Bristol	0117 9277111
Thomson Martin Haldane Ahmad	Wynne Chambers, London	0181 961 6144
Tucker Miss Katherine Jane Greening	St Philip's Chambers, Birmingham	0121 246 7000
Tucker Dr Peter Louis	Leone Chambers, London	0181 200 4020
	12 Old Square, London	0171 404 0875
Wallington Peter Thomas	11 King's Bench Walk, London	0171 632 8500/583 0610

• Expanded entry in Part D

Wayne Nicholas	1 Gray's Inn Square, London	0171 405 8946/7/8
Westgate Martin Trevor	Doughty Street Chambers, London	0171 404 1313
Weston Ms Amanda	Chambers of Ian Macdonald QC (In Association with Two Garden Court, Temple, London), Manchester	0161 236 1840
Whitcombe Mark David	Old Square Chambers, Bristol	0117 9277111
	Old Square Chambers, London	0171 269 0300
Williams Ms Heather Jean	Doughty Street Chambers, London	0171 404 1313
Wilson Stephen Mark	4 Field Court, London	0171 440 6900
Wood Ian Robert	8 King Street Chambers, Manchester	0161 834 9560
Worrall Miss Shirley Vera Frances	8 King Street Chambers, Manchester	0161 834 9560
Zaman Mohammed Khalil	St Philip's Chambers, Birmingham	0121 246 7000

DOMESTIC VIOLENCE INJUNCTIONS

Chandler Alexander Charles Ross	One Garden Court Family Law Chambers, London	0171 797 7900

DRINK AND DRIVING

Ley Nigel Joseph	Gray's Inn Chambers, London	0171 831 7888 (Chambers)/ 0171 831 7904 (Mr M Ullah)

E-COMMERCE

Featherstone Jason Neil	Virtual Chambers, London	07071 244 944
	Barristers' Common Law Chambers, London	0171 375 3012

EC AND COMPETITION LAW

Abrahams James	8 New Square, London	0171 405 4321
Alexander Daniel Sakyi	8 New Square, London	0171 405 4321
Anderson Miss Julie	• Littman Chambers, London	020 7404 4866
Anderson Rupert John	Monckton Chambers, London	0171 405 7211
Baldwin John Paul	8 New Square, London	0171 405 4321
Beal Kieron Conrad	4 Paper Buildings, London	0171 353 3366/583 7155
Beard Daniel Matthew	Monckton Chambers, London	0171 405 7211
Brent Richard	3 Verulam Buildings, London	0171 831 8441
Buck Dr Andrew Theodore	Chambers of Martin Burr, London	0171 353 4636
Burnett Harold Wallace	4 Paper Buildings, London	0171 353 3366/583 7155
Butcher Christopher John	S Tomlinson QC, London	0171 583 0404
Cavanagh John Patrick	11 King's Bench Walk, London	0171 632 8500/583 0610
Cawley Neil Robert Loudoun	169 Temple Chambers, London	0171 583 7644
	Milton Keynes Chambers, Milton Keynes	01908 664 128
Clark Miss Fiona Jane Stewart	8 New Square, London	0171 405 4321
Colley Dr Peter McLean	• 19 Old Buildings, London	0171 405 2001
Conlon Michael Anthony	• One Essex Court, London	020 7583 2000
Cooper Nigel Stuart	4 Essex Court, London	020 7797 7970
Craig Alistair Trevor	Chambers of Mr Peter Crampin QC, London	020 7831 0081
Cranfield Peter Anthony	3 Verulam Buildings, London	0171 831 8441
Dalby Joseph Francis	Portsmouth Barristers' Chambers, Winchester	01962 863222
	Portsmouth Barristers' Chambers, Portsmouth	023 92 831292/811811
Davies The Rt Hon David John Denzil	96 Gray's Inn Road, London	0171 405 0585
	8 Gray's Inn Square, London	0171 242 3529
Devine Michael Buxton	95A Chancery Lane, London	0171 405 3101
Fowler Richard Nicholas	Monckton Chambers, London	0171 405 7211
Fysh Michael	8 New Square, London	0171 405 4321
Gasztowicz Steven	2-3 Gray's Inn Square, London	0171 242 4986
	2 New Street, Leicester	0116 2625906
Ghaffar Arshad	4 Field Court, London	0171 440 6900
Gore-Andrews Gavin Angus Russell	2 Harcourt Buildings, London	0171 583 9020

• Expanded entry in Part D

Grayson Edward	• 9-12 Bell Yard, London	0171 400 1800
Green Miss Jane Elizabeth	Design Chambers, London	0171 353 0747
	Chambers of Martin Burr, London	0171 353 4636
Hamer George Clemens	8 New Square, London	0171 405 4321
Harris Paul Best	Monckton Chambers, London	0171 405 7211
Haynes Miss Rebecca	Monckton Chambers, London	0171 405 7211
Heal Mrs Madeleine	4 Field Court, London	0171 440 6900
Henderson Roger Anthony	2 Harcourt Buildings, London	0171 583 9020
Henley Raymond Francis St Luke	Lancaster Building, Manchester	0161 661 4444/0171 649 9872
Hicks Michael Charles	• 19 Old Buildings, London	0171 405 2001
Hill Raymond	Monckton Chambers, London	0171 405 7211
Holman Miss Tamsin Perdita	19 Old Buildings, London	0171 405 2001
Howe Martin Russell Thomson	8 New Square, London	0171 405 4321
Jabati Miss Maria Hannah	2 Middle Temple Lane, London	0171 583 4540
Jones Philip John	Serle Court Chambers, London	0171 242 6105
Jones Sean William Paul	11 King's Bench Walk, London	0171 632 8500/583 0610
Kenefick Timothy	S Tomlinson QC, London	0171 583 0404
Kerr Simon Alexander	S Tomlinson QC, London	0171 583 0404
Kinnier Andrew John	2 Harcourt Buildings, London	0171 583 9020
Kitchin David James Tyson	8 New Square, London	0171 405 4321
Kolodziej Andrzej Jozef	• Littman Chambers, London	020 7404 4866
Lambert John	Lancaster Building, Manchester	0161 661 4444/0171 649 9872
Lane Ms Lindsay Ruth Busfield	8 New Square, London	0171 405 4321
Lasok Karol Paul Edward	Monckton Chambers, London	0171 405 7211
Lever Jeremy Frederick	Monckton Chambers, London	0171 405 7211
Macnab Alexander Andrew	Monckton Chambers, London	0171 405 7211
Mantle Peter John	Monckton Chambers, London	0171 405 7211
Marquand Charles Nicholas Hilary	Chambers of Lord Goodhart QC, London	0171 405 5577
Masters Miss Sara Alayna	20 Essex Street, London	0171 583 9294
May Miss Charlotte Louisa	8 New Square, London	0171 405 4321
McClure Brian David	Littman Chambers, London	020 7404 4866
Meade Richard David	8 New Square, London	0171 405 4321
Mellor Edward James Wilson	8 New Square, London	0171 405 4321
Mercer Hugh Charles	• Essex Court Chambers, London	0171 813 8000
Minhas Ms Rafhat	Leone Chambers, London	0181 200 4020
Mitropoulos Christos	Chambers of Geoffrey Hawker, London	0171 583 8899
Moody-Stuart Thomas	8 New Square, London	0171 405 4321
Morgan Dr Austen Jude	3 Temple Gardens, London	0171 353 0832
Morris Stephen Nathan	20 Essex Street, London	0171 583 9294
Moser Philip Curt Harold	4 Paper Buildings, London	0171 353 3366/583 7155
Nardell Gordon Lawrence	6 Pump Court, London	0171 797 8400
	6-8 Mill Street, Maidstone	01622 688094
O'Shea Eoin Finbarr	4 Field Court, London	0171 440 6900
Onslow Robert Denzil	8 New Square, London	0171 405 4321
Outhwaite Mrs Wendy-Jane Tivnan	2 Harcourt Buildings, London	0171 583 9020
Padfield Ms Alison Mary	Devereux Chambers, London	0171 353 7534
Paines Nicholas Paul Billot	Monckton Chambers, London	0171 405 7211
Parker Kenneth Blades	Monckton Chambers, London	0171 405 7211
Peretz George Michael John	Monckton Chambers, London	0171 405 7211
Persey Lionel Edward	• 4 Field Court, London	0171 440 6900
Pickersgill David William	Bell Yard Chambers, London	0171 306 9292
Pickup David Michael Walker	Peel Court Chambers, Manchester	0161 832 3791
Platts-Mills Mark Fortescue	8 New Square, London	0171 405 4321
Plender Richard Owen	• 20 Essex Street, London	0171 583 9294
Pope David James	3 Verulam Buildings, London	0171 831 8441
Power Lawrence Imam	4 King's Bench Walk, London	0171 822 8822
Prescott Peter Richard Kyle	8 New Square, London	0171 405 4321
Raybaud Mrs June Rose	96 Gray's Inn Road, London	0171 405 0585
Reed Jeremy Nigel	19 Old Buildings, London	0171 405 2001
Roth Peter Marcel	Monckton Chambers, London	0171 405 7211

       • Expanded entry in Part D

Sharpston Miss Eleanor Veronica Elizabeth	4 Paper Buildings, London	0171 353 3366/583 7155
Shipley Norman Graham	• 19 Old Buildings, London	0171 405 2001
Shrimpton Michael	Francis Taylor Building, London	0171 797 7250
Simor Miss Jessica Margaret Poppaea	Monckton Chambers, London	0171 405 7211
Skilbeck Mrs Jennifer Seth	Monckton Chambers, London	0171 405 7211
Smith Ms Katherine Emma	Monckton Chambers, London	0171 405 7211
Speck Adrian	8 New Square, London	0171 405 4321
St Ville Laurence James	8 New Square, London	0171 405 4321
Stewart Nicholas John Cameron	Hardwicke Building, London	020 7242 2523
Sullivan Rory Myles	19 Old Buildings, London	0171 405 2001
Swift John Anthony	Monckton Chambers, London	0171 405 7211
Tappin Michael John	8 New Square, London	0171 405 4321
Thompson Rhodri William Ralph	Monckton Chambers, London	0171 405 7211
Thornley David	Chambers of Martin Burr, London	0171 353 4636
Tucker Miss Katherine Jane Greening	St Philip's Chambers, Birmingham	0121 246 7000
Tully Ms Anne Margaret	Eastbourne Chambers, Eastbourne	01323 642102
Turner Jonathan David Chattyn	• 4 Field Court, London	0171 440 6900
Turner Jonathan Richard	Monckton Chambers, London	0171 405 7211
Vajda Christopher Stephen	Monckton Chambers, London	0171 405 7211
Vitoria Miss Mary Christine	8 New Square, London	0171 405 4321
Williams Rhodri John	30 Park Place, Cardiff	01222 398421
	2 Harcourt Buildings, London	0171 583 9020
Wilson Alastair James Drysdale	• 19 Old Buildings, London	0171 405 2001
Yell Nicholas Anthony	No. 1 Serjeants' Inn, London	0171 415 6666

EC LAW

Cameron Jonathan James O'Grady	3 Verulam Buildings, London	0171 831 8441
Marks Jonathan Harold	3 Verulam Buildings, London	0171 831 8441
Mercer Hugh Charles	• Essex Court Chambers, London	0171 813 8000
Sands Mr Philippe Joseph	3 Verulam Buildings, London	0171 831 8441
Sheridan Maurice Bernard Gerard	• 3 Verulam Buildings, London	0171 831 8441
Southern David Boardman	• Temple Gardens Tax Chambers, London	0171 353 7884/5 8982/3

ECCLESIASTICAL

Behrens James Nicholas Edward	Serle Court Chambers, London	0171 242 6105
Briden Timothy John	• 8 Stone Buildings, London	0171 831 9881
Burr Martin John	Chambers of Martin Burr, London	0171 353 4636
	7 New Square, London	0171 430 1660
Campbell Miss Emily Charlotte	• Wilberforce Chambers, London	0171 306 0102
Clark Christopher Harvey	Pump Court Chambers, Winchester	01962 868161
	Pump Court Chambers, London	0171 353 0711
	Westgate Chambers, Lewes	01273 480510
	Pump Court Chambers, Swindon	01793 539899
	Harrow on the Hill Chambers, Harrow-on-the-Hill	0181 423 7444
Collier Peter Neville	30 Park Square, Leeds	0113 2436388
Finn Terence	Chambers of Martin Burr, London	0171 353 4636
Green Miss Jane Elizabeth	Design Chambers, London	0171 353 0747
	Chambers of Martin Burr, London	0171 353 4636
Hill Nicholas Mark	• Pump Court Chambers, London	0171 353 0711
	Pump Court Chambers, Winchester	01962 868161
	Pump Court Chambers, Swindon	01793 539899
Newcombe Andrew Bennett	2 Harcourt Buildings, London	020 7353 8415
Nugee Edward George	• Wilberforce Chambers, London	0171 306 0102
Ough Dr Richard Norman	• Hardwicke Building, London	020 7242 2523
Pulman George Frederick	Hardwicke Building, London	020 7242 2523
	Stour Chambers, Canterbury	01227 764899
Purdie Robert Anthony James	28 Western Road, Oxford	01865 204911
Turner David George Patrick	14 Gray's Inn Square, London	0171 242 0858

• Expanded entry in Part D

ECHR

Anderson Miss Julie	• Littman Chambers, London	020 7404 4866
Daniel Leon Roger	6 King's Bench Walk, London	0171 353 4931/583 0695
Emmerson (Michael) Benedict	Doughty Street Chambers, London	0171 404 1313
Fitzgerald Edward Hamilton	Doughty Street Chambers, London	0171 404 1313
Hoyal Ms Jane	• 1 Pump Court, London	0171 583 2012/353 4341
Hudson Anthony Sean	Doughty Street Chambers, London	0171 404 1313
Jones Timothy Arthur	• St Philip's Chambers, Birmingham	0121 246 7000
	Arden Chambers, London	020 7242 4244
Markus Ms Kate	Doughty Street Chambers, London	0171 404 1313
Mercer Hugh Charles	• Essex Court Chambers, London	0171 813 8000
Owen Timothy Wynn	Doughty Street Chambers, London	0171 404 1313
Sharpston Miss Eleanor Veronica Elizabeth	4 Paper Buildings, London	0171 353 3366/583 7155
Starmer Keir	Doughty Street Chambers, London	0171 404 1313

EDUCATION

Allfrey Richard Forbes	Doughty Street Chambers, London	0171 404 1313
Bancroft Miss Anna Louise	Deans Court Chambers, Manchester	0161 214 6000
	Deans Court Chambers, Preston	01772 555163
Beaumont Marc Clifford	• Harrow on the Hill Chambers, Harrow-on-the-Hill	0181 423 7444
	Windsor Barristers' Chambers, Windsor	01753 648899
	Pump Court Chambers, London	0171 353 0711
Bedingfield David Herbert	• 14 Gray's Inn Square, London	0171 242 0858
Brooks Mr Paul Anthony	Doughty Street Chambers, London	0171 404 1313
Bryant Keith	Devereux Chambers, London	0171 353 7534
Buck Dr Andrew Theodore	Chambers of Martin Burr, London	0171 353 4636
Cavanagh John Patrick	11 King's Bench Walk, London	0171 632 8500/583 0610
Cawley Neil Robert Loudoun	169 Temple Chambers, London	0171 583 7644
	Milton Keynes Chambers, Milton Keynes	01908 664 128
Cole-Wilson Miss Yatoni Iyamide Elizabeth	Lancaster Building, Manchester	0161 661 4444/0171 649 9872
Cooper Mark Anthony John	2 Mitre Court Buildings, London	0171 353 1353
Cotton Miss Diana Rosemary	Devereux Chambers, London	0171 353 7534
Cox Bryan Richard	9 Woodhouse Square, Leeds	0113 2451986
Edge Timothy Richard	Deans Court Chambers, Preston	01772 555163
	Deans Court Chambers, Manchester	0161 214 6000
Faulks Edward Peter Lawless	No. 1 Serjeants' Inn, London	0171 415 6666
Ford Michael David	Doughty Street Chambers, London	0171 404 1313
Foster Miss Alison Lee Caroline	39 Essex Street, London	0171 832 1111
Gordon Richard John Francis	Brick Court Chambers, London	0171 379 3550
Goudie James	• 11 King's Bench Walk, London	0171 632 8500/583 0610
Grey Miss Eleanor Mary Grace	39 Essex Street, London	0171 832 1111
Hermer Richard Simon	Doughty Street Chambers, London	0171 404 1313
	30 Park Place, Cardiff	01222 398421
Hunter William Quigley	No. 1 Serjeants' Inn, London	0171 415 6666
Hyams Oliver Marks	5 Paper Buildings, London	0171 583 9275/583 4555
Kaufmann Ms Phillippa Jane	Doughty Street Chambers, London	0171 404 1313
Kenward Timothy David Nelson	25-27 Castle Street, Liverpool	0151 227 5661/051 236 5072
Lewis Robert	11 Bolt Court (also at 7 Stone Buildings – 1st Floor), London	0171 353 2300
	7 Stone Buildings (also at 11 Bolt Court), London	0171 242 0961
	Redhill Chambers, Redhill	01737 780781
Maclean Alan John	39 Essex Street, London	0171 832 1111
Macpherson The Hon Mary Stewart	2 Mitre Court Buildings, London	0171 583 1380
Mainwaring [Robert] Paul Clason	Carmarthen Chambers, Carmarthen	01267 234410
Malecka Dr Mary Margaret	• 3 Temple Gardens, London	0171 353 0832
	65-67 King Street, Leicester	0116 2547710
Markus Ms Kate	Doughty Street Chambers, London	0171 404 1313

• Expanded entry in Part D

McCafferty Miss Lynne	5 Paper Buildings, London	0171 583 9275/583 4555
Messling Lawrence David	St Philip's Chambers, Birmingham	0121 246 7000
Morris Miss Fenella	39 Essex Street, London	0171 832 1111
O'Donovan Ronan Daniel James	14 Gray's Inn Square, London	0171 242 0858
Oke Olanrewaju Oladipupo	Kingsway Chambers, London	07000 653529
Outhwaite Mrs Wendy-Jane Tivnan	2 Harcourt Buildings, London	0171 583 9020
Pleming Nigel Peter	39 Essex Street, London	0171 832 1111
Richards Miss Jennifer	39 Essex Street, London	0171 832 1111
Sheldon Clive David	11 King's Bench Walk, London	0171 632 8500/583 0610
Shillingford George Miles	Chambers of Mr Peter Crampin QC, London	020 7831 0081
Siddiqi Faizul Aqtab	Justice Court Chambers, London	0181 830 7786
Smail Alastair Harold Kurt	St Philip's Chambers, Birmingham	0121 246 7000
Straker Timothy Derrick	• 4-5 Gray's Inn Square, London	0171 404 5252
Supperstone Michael Alan	11 King's Bench Walk, London	0171 632 8500/583 0610
Tedd Rex Hilary	• St Philip's Chambers, Birmingham	0121 246 7000
	De Montfort Chambers, Leicester	0116 254 8686
	Northampton Chambers, Northampton	01604 636271
Tether Ms Melanie Georgia Kim	Old Square Chambers, London	0171 269 0300
	Old Square Chambers, Bristol	0117 9277111
Walker Mrs Susannah Mary	One Garden Court Family Law Chambers, London	0171 797 7900
Wallington Peter Thomas	11 King's Bench Walk, London	0171 632 8500/583 0610
Warren Rupert Miles	2 Mitre Court Buildings, London	0171 583 1380
Westgate Martin Trevor	Doughty Street Chambers, London	0171 404 1313
Weston Ms Amanda	Chambers of Ian Macdonald QC (In Association with Two Garden Court, Temple, London), Manchester	0161 236 1840
Whybrow Christopher John	1 Serjeants' Inn, London	0171 583 1355
Williams Ms Heather Jean	Doughty Street Chambers, London	0171 404 1313
Wing Christopher John	Eighteen Carlton Crescent, Southampton	01703 639001
Wise Ian	Doughty Street Chambers, London	0171 404 1313

ELECTION LAW

Price Richard Mervyn	Littleton Chambers, London	0171 797 8600

EMPLOYMENT

Acton Davis Jonathan James	4 Pump Court, London	020 7842 5555
Adams Miss Lorraine Joan	Pulteney Chambers, Bath	01225 723987
Adejumo Mrs Hilda Ekpo	Temple Chambers, London	0171 583 1001 (2 lines)
Akerman Miss Kate Louise	Queen's Chambers, Manchester	0161 834 6875/4738
	Queens Chambers, Preston	01772 828300
Aldous Robert John	Octagon House, Norwich	01603 623186
Allingham-Nicholson Mrs Elizabeth Sarah	2 New Street, Leicester	0116 2625906
Althaus Antony Justin	No. 1 Serjeants' Inn, London	0171 415 6666
Anderson Miss Julie	• Littman Chambers, London	020 7404 4866
Andrews Miss Claire Marguerite	Gough Square Chambers, London	0171 353 0924
Ash Edward William	3 Temple Gardens, London	0171 353 0832
Atherton Peter	Deans Court Chambers, Manchester	0161 214 6000
	Deans Court Chambers, Preston	01772 555163
Bailey Edward Henry	Monckton Chambers, London	0171 405 7211
Baker Stuart Christopher	1 Fountain Court, Birmingham	0121 236 5721
Barnett Daniel Alexander	2 Gray's Inn Square Chambers, London	020 7242 0328
Barr Edward Robert	2 New Street, Leicester	0116 2625906
Barraclough Nicholas Maylin	2nd Floor, Francis Taylor Building, London	0171 353 9942/3157
Barraclough Richard Michael	6 Pump Court, London	0171 797 8400
	6-8 Mill Street, Maidstone	01622 688094
Barry Miss Kirsten Lesley	8 King Street Chambers, Manchester	0161 834 9560
Bash-Taqi Mrs Shahineh	Leone Chambers, London	0181 200 4020

Bassa Yousef	St Albans Chambers, St Albans	01727 843383
	Tindal Chambers, Chelmsford	01245 267742
Bastin Alexander Charles	2nd Floor, Francis Taylor Building, London	0171 353 9942/3157
Basu Dr Dijendra Bhushan	Devereux Chambers, London	0171 353 7534
Bather Miss Victoria Maclean	Littleton Chambers, London	0171 797 8600
Beard Daniel Matthew	Monckton Chambers, London	0171 405 7211
Beaumont Marc Clifford	• Harrow on the Hill Chambers, Harrow-on-the-Hill	0181 423 7444
	Windsor Barristers' Chambers, Windsor	01753 648899
	Pump Court Chambers, London	0171 353 0711
Bedeau Stephen	Sovereign Chambers, Leeds	0113 2451841/2/3
	Lancaster Building, Manchester	0161 661 4444/0171 649 9872
Bedingfield David Herbert	• 14 Gray's Inn Square, London	0171 242 0858
Beever Edmund Damian	St Philip's Chambers, Birmingham	0121 246 7000
Bennett John Martyn	• Oriel Chambers, Liverpool	0151 236 7191/236 4321
Benson John Trevor	Adrian Lyon's Chambers, Liverpool	0151 236 4421/8240
Bentley Stephen	1 Gray's Inn Square, London	0171 405 8946/7/8
Berry Nicholas Michael	Southernhay Chambers, Exeter	01392 255777
	1 Gray's Inn Square, London	0171 405 8946/7/8
	22 Old Buildings, London	0171 831 0222
Birtles William	Old Square Chambers, London	0171 269 0300
	Old Square Chambers, Bristol	0117 9277111
Booth Nicholas John	Old Square Chambers, London	0171 269 0300
	Old Square Chambers, Bristol	0117 9277111
Booth Richard John	1 Crown Office Row, London	0171 797 7500
Boyd James Andrew Donaldson	8 King Street Chambers, Manchester	0161 834 9560
Boyle Gerard James	No. 1 Serjeants' Inn, London	0171 415 6666
Bradley Miss Clodagh Maria	3 Serjeants' Inn, London	0171 353 5537
Bresler Fenton Shea	22 Melcombe Regis Court, London	0171 487 5589
Bridgman David Martin	No. 1 Serjeants' Inn, London	0171 415 6666
Broatch Michael Donald	5 Paper Buildings, London	0171 583 9275/583 4555
Brockley Nigel Simon	Bracton Chambers, London	0171 242 4248
Brown Damian Robert	• Old Square Chambers, London	0171 269 0300
	Old Square Chambers, Bristol	0117 9277111
Browne-Wilkinson Simon	Serle Court Chambers, London	0171 242 6105
Bruce Andrew Jonathan	Serle Court Chambers, London	0171 242 6105
Bryant John Malcolm Cornelius	Barnard's Inn Chambers, London	0171 369 6969
Bryant Keith	Devereux Chambers, London	0171 353 7534
Buck Dr Andrew Theodore	Chambers of Martin Burr, London	0171 353 4636
Burden Edward Angus	St Philip's Chambers, Birmingham	0121 246 7000
Burrows Simon Paul	Peel Court Chambers, Manchester	0161 832 3791
Butler Andrew	2nd Floor, Francis Taylor Building, London	0171 353 9942/3157
Butterworth Paul Anthony	Octagon House, Norwich	01603 623186
Buxton Miss Sarah Ruth	1 Fountain Court, Birmingham	0121 236 5721
Calvert David Edward	St James's Chambers, Manchester	0161 834 7000
Carr Bruce Conrad	Devereux Chambers, London	0171 353 7534
Carr Simon Andrew	9 Gough Square, London	020 7832 0500
Cavanagh John Patrick	11 King's Bench Walk, London	0171 632 8500/583 0610
Chan Miss Susan	13 King's Bench Walk, London	0171 353 7204
	King's Bench Chambers, Oxford	01865 311066
Chapman Matthew James	Barnard's Inn Chambers, London	0171 369 6969
Cheshire Anthony Peter	199 Strand, London	0171 379 9779
Chudleigh Miss Louise Katrina	Old Square Chambers, London	0171 269 0300
	Old Square Chambers, Bristol	0117 9277111
Clark Andrew Richard	Manchester House Chambers, Manchester	0161 834 7007
	8 King Street Chambers, Manchester	0161 834 9560
Clarke Miss Alison Lee	No. 1 Serjeants' Inn, London	0171 415 6666

                 • Expanded entry in Part D

Clegg Sebastian James Barwick	Deans Court Chambers, Manchester	0161 214 6000
	Deans Court Chambers, Preston	01772 555163
Colbey Richard (Alan)	• Francis Taylor Building, London	0171 797 7250
	Guildhall Chambers Portsmouth, Portsmouth	01705 752400
Cole Robert Ian Gawain	30 Park Square, Leeds	0113 2436388
Cole-Wilson Miss Yatoni Iyamide Elizabeth	Lancaster Building, Manchester	0161 661 4444/0171 649 9872
Colin Giles David	Crown Office Row Chambers, Brighton	01273 625625
Collett Ivor William	No. 1 Serjeants' Inn, London	0171 415 6666
Compton Gareth Francis Thomas	22 Old Buildings, London	0171 831 0222
Connolly Miss Joanne Marie	8 King Street Chambers, Manchester	0161 834 9560
Cook Miss Alison Noele	St Philip's Chambers, Birmingham	0121 246 7000
Corbett James Patrick	St Philip's Chambers, Birmingham	0121 246 7000
	Chambers of Andrew Campbell QC, Leeds	0113 2455438
Cotton Miss Diana Rosemary	Devereux Chambers, London	0171 353 7534
Craig Kenneth Allen	Hardwicke Building, London	020 7242 2523
Crossley Steven Richard	37 Park Square Chambers, Leeds	0113 2439422
Croxon Raymond Patrick	8 King's Bench Walk, London	0171 797 8888
	Regency Chambers, Peterborough	01733 315215
	Regency Chambers, Cambridge	01223 301517
Curtis Michael Alexander	Two Crown Office Row, London	020 7797 8100
Da Costa Miss Elissa Josephine	• Arlington Chambers, London	0171 580 9188
Dalby Joseph Francis	Portsmouth Barristers' Chambers, Winchester	01962 863222
	Portsmouth Barristers' Chambers, Portsmouth	023 92 831292/811811
Daly David	Francis Taylor Building, London	0171 797 7250
Daniells-Smith Roger Charles	8 King's Bench Walk, London	0171 797 8888
	8 King's Bench Walk North, Leeds	0113 2439797
Davies Miss Carol Elizabeth	2 New Street, Leicester	0116 2625906
Davies Dr Charles Edward	4 Field Court, London	0171 440 6900
Dean Paul Benjamin	Two Crown Office Row, London	020 7797 8100
Dedezade Taner	Tindal Chambers, Chelmsford	01245 267742
Dineen Michael Laurence	Pump Court Chambers, Winchester	01962 868161
	Pump Court Chambers, London	0171 353 0711
	Queens Square Chambers, Bristol	0117 921 1966
	Pump Court Chambers, Swindon	01793 539899
Dixon David Steven	Sovereign Chambers, Leeds	0113 2451841/2/3
Dixon Philip John	2nd Floor, Francis Taylor Building, London	0171 353 9942/3157
Dolan Dr Bridget Maura	3 Serjeants' Inn, London	0171 353 5537
Donovan Joel	New Court Chambers, London	0171 831 9500
Doughty Peter	17 Carlton Crescent, Southampton	023 8032 0320/0823 2003
Downs Martin John	1 Crown Office Row, London	0171 797 7500
	Crown Office Row Chambers, Brighton	01273 625625
Dubbery Mark Edward	Pump Court Chambers, London	0171 353 0711
	Pump Court Chambers, Winchester	01962 868161
	Pump Court Chambers, Swindon	01793 539899
Dudley Michael John	1 Fountain Court, Birmingham	0121 236 5721
Dugdale Nicholas	4 Field Court, London	0171 440 6900
Dunn Christopher	Sovereign Chambers, Leeds	0113 2451841/2/3
Eady Miss Jennifer Jane	Old Square Chambers, London	0171 269 0300
	Old Square Chambers, Bristol	0117 9277111
Eastman Roger	2 Harcourt Buildings, London	0171 583 9020
Edge Timothy Richard	Deans Court Chambers, Preston	01772 555163
	Deans Court Chambers, Manchester	0161 214 6000
Edis Angus William Butler	1 Crown Office Row, London	0171 797 7500
Elfield Miss Laura Elaine	5 Pump Court, London	020 7353 2532
Elliott Nicholas Blethyn	3 Verulam Buildings, London	0171 831 8441

Ellis Dr Peter Simon	7 New Square, London	0171 430 1660
Fairbank Nicholas James	Becket Chambers, Canterbury	01227 786331
Farrer Adam Michael	4 Fountain Court, Birmingham	0121 236 3476
Fieldsend James William	2nd Floor, Francis Taylor Building, London	0171 353 9942/3157
Finlay Darren	Sovereign Chambers, Leeds	0113 2451841/2/3
Fitzpatrick Edward James	8 King's Bench Walk, London	0171 797 8888
Fletcher Christopher Michael	Octagon House, Norwich	01603 623186
Ford Michael David	Doughty Street Chambers, London	0171 404 1313
Freedman Sampson Clive	3 Verulam Buildings, London	0171 831 8441
Frith Nicholas John	30 Park Square, Leeds	0113 2436388
Fullwood Adam Garrett	Chambers of Ian Macdonald QC (In Association with Two Garden Court, Temple, London), Manchester	0161 236 1840
Gardner Miss Eilidh Anne Mairi	22 Old Buildings, London	0171 831 0222
Garner Miss Sophie Jane	199 Strand, London	0171 379 9779
Gasztowicz Steven	2-3 Gray's Inn Square, London	0171 242 4986
	2 New Street, Leicester	0116 2625906
Gatt Ian Andrew	Littleton Chambers, London	0171 797 8600
George Donald Eric Joseph	Leone Chambers, London	0181 200 4020
George Miss Judith Sarah	St Philip's Chambers, Birmingham	0121 246 7000
Gersch Adam Nissen	Trafalgar Chambers, London	0171 583 5858
Gibbons James Francis	3 Stone Buildings, London	0171 242 4937
Gifford Lord Anthony Maurice	8 King's Bench Walk, London	0171 797 8888
	8 King's Bench Walk North, Leeds	0113 2439797
Gill Ms Sarah Teresa	• Old Square Chambers, London	0171 269 0300
	Old Square Chambers, Bristol	0117 9277111
Ginniff Nigel Thomas	Adrian Lyon's Chambers, Liverpool	0151 236 4421/8240
Glennie Andrew David	13 King's Bench Walk, London	0171 353 7204
	King's Bench Chambers, Oxford	01865 311066
Goldman Mrs Linda	7 New Square, London	0171 430 1660
Goudie James	• 11 King's Bench Walk, London	0171 632 8500/583 0610
Gow Miss Elizabeth Suzanne	Iscoed Chambers, Swansea	01792 652988/9/330
Gower Miss Helen Clare	Old Square Chambers, Bristol	0117 9277111
	Old Square Chambers, London	0171 269 0300
Grace Timothy Michael	Adrian Lyon's Chambers, Liverpool	0151 236 4421/8240
Graham Thomas Patrick Henry	1 New Square, London	0171 405 0884/5/6/7
Grant David Euan Barron	13 King's Bench Walk, London	0171 353 7204
	King's Bench Chambers, Oxford	01865 311066
Green Miss Jane Elizabeth	Design Chambers, London	0171 353 0747
	Chambers of Martin Burr, London	0171 353 4636
Green Roger John Bailey	Queen's Chambers, Manchester	0161 834 6875/4738
	Queens Chambers, Preston	01772 828300
Guirguis Miss Sheren	White Friars Chambers, Chester	01244 323070
Haigh Martin James	30 Park Square, Leeds	0113 2436388
Hall Jeremy John	Becket Chambers, Canterbury	01227 786331
Hall Mrs Melanie Ruth	Monckton Chambers, London	0171 405 7211
Hand John Lester	Chambers of John Hand QC, Manchester	0161 955 9000
	Old Square Chambers, London	0171 269 0300
	Old Square Chambers, Bristol	0117 9277111
Hardwick Matthew Richard	Enterprise Chambers, London	0171 405 9471
	Enterprise Chambers, Leeds	0113 246 0391
	Enterprise Chambers, Newcastle upon Tyne	0191 222 3344
Harris Melvyn	7 New Square, London	0171 430 1660
Harris Paul Best	Monckton Chambers, London	0171 405 7211
Harrison Ms Averil	Chambers of Averil Harrison, London	0181 692 4949
Haslam Andrew Peter	Sovereign Chambers, Leeds	0113 2451841/2/3
Hassall James Christopher	Southernhay Chambers, Exeter	01392 255777
Hawkes Miss Naomi Nanteza Astrid Wallusimbi	22 Old Buildings, London	0171 831 0222

                  • Expanded entry in Part D

Haynes Miss Rebecca	Monckton Chambers, London	0171 405 7211
Hendy John Giles	• Old Square Chambers, London	0171 269 0300
	Old Square Chambers, Bristol	0117 9277111
Henley Mark Robert Daniel	9 Woodhouse Square, Leeds	0113 2451986
Herbert Mrs Rebecca Mary	2 New Street, Leicester	0116 2625906
Hermer Richard Simon	Doughty Street Chambers, London	0171 404 1313
	30 Park Place, Cardiff	01222 398421
Hignett Richard James	St Albans Chambers, St Albans	01727 843383
Hill Raymond	Monckton Chambers, London	0171 405 7211
Hofmeyr Stephen Murray	S Tomlinson QC, London	0171 583 0404
Hogg Miss Katharine Elizabeth	1 Crown Office Row, London	0171 797 7500
Holl-Allen Jonathan Guy	3 Serjeants' Inn, London	0171 353 5537
Holmes-Milner James Neil	2 Mitre Court Buildings, London	0171 353 1353
Horgan Peter Thomas	Queen's Chambers, Manchester	0161 834 6875/4738
	Queens Chambers, Preston	01772 828300
Hornett Stuart Ian	29 Bedford Row Chambers, London	0171 831 2626
Hossain Ajmalul	• 29 Bedford Row Chambers, London	0171 831 2626
Howe Miss Penelope Anne Macgregor	Pump Court Chambers, London	0171 353 0711
	Pump Court Chambers, Winchester	01962 868161
	Pump Court Chambers, Swindon	01793 539899
Hudson Anthony Sean	Doughty Street Chambers, London	0171 404 1313
Hurd James Robert	St James's Chambers, Manchester	0161 834 7000
Hurd Mark Dunsdon	2 New Street, Leicester	0116 2625906
Hyams Oliver Marks	5 Paper Buildings, London	0171 583 9275/583 4555
Iles Adrian	5 Paper Buildings, London	0171 583 9275/583 4555
Ivimy Ms Cecilia Rachel	11 King's Bench Walk, London	0171 632 8500/583 0610
Jabati Miss Maria Hannah	2 Middle Temple Lane, London	0171 583 4540
Jack Adrian Laurence Robert	Enterprise Chambers, London	0171 405 9471
	Enterprise Chambers, Newcastle upon Tyne	0191 222 3344
	Enterprise Chambers, Leeds	0113 246 0391
James Michael Frank	Enterprise Chambers, London	0171 405 9471
	Enterprise Chambers, Leeds	0113 246 0391
	Enterprise Chambers, Newcastle upon Tyne	0191 222 3344
Jess Digby Charles	8 King Street Chambers, Manchester	0161 834 9560
Johnston Anthony Paul	1 Fountain Court, Birmingham	0121 236 5721
Jones Miss (Catherine) Charlotte	Two Crown Office Row, London	020 7797 8100
Jones Martin Wynne	8 King's Bench Walk, London	0171 797 8888
	8 King's Bench Walk North, Leeds	0113 2439797
Jones Sean William Paul	11 King's Bench Walk, London	0171 632 8500/583 0610
Jones Miss Susannah Lucy	Octagon House, Norwich	01603 623186
Kay Michael Jack David	3 Verulam Buildings, London	0171 831 8441
	Park Lane Chambers, Leeds	0113 2285000
Kempster Ivor Toby Chalmers	Old Square Chambers, Bristol	0117 9277111
	Old Square Chambers, London	0171 269 0300
Kenny Julian Hector Marriott	20 Essex Street, London	0171 583 9294
Kent Miss Georgina	5 Essex Court, London	0171 410 2000
Kenward Timothy David Nelson	25-27 Castle Street, Liverpool	0151 227 5661/051 236 5072
Kerr Derek William	Francis Taylor Building, London	0171 353 7768/7769/2711
Khan Saadallah Frans Hassan	55 Temple Chambers, London	0171 353 7400
King Charles Granville	96 Gray's Inn Road, London	0171 405 0585
Kinnier Andrew John	2 Harcourt Buildings, London	0171 583 9020
Kirby Peter John	Hardwicke Building, London	020 7242 2523
Kirtley Paul George	37 Park Square Chambers, Leeds	0113 2439422
Kolodziej Andrzej Jozef	• Littman Chambers, London	020 7404 4866
Korn Anthony Henry	Barnard's Inn Chambers, London	0171 369 6969
Kynoch Duncan Stuart Sanderson	29 Bedford Row Chambers, London	0171 831 2626
Laing Miss Elisabeth Mary Caroline	11 King's Bench Walk, London	0171 632 8500/583 0610
Lambert Miss Sarah Katrina	1 Crown Office Row, London	0171 797 7500

• Expanded entry in Part D

B

Leiper Richard Thomas	11 King's Bench Walk, London	0171 632 8500/583 0610
Lennard Stephen Charles	Hardwicke Building, London	020 7242 2523
Lewis Jeffrey Allan	9 Woodhouse Square, Leeds	0113 2451986
Lewis Robert	11 Bolt Court (also at 7 Stone Buildings – 1st Floor), London	0171 353 2300
	7 Stone Buildings (also at 11 Bolt Court), London	0171 242 0961
	Redhill Chambers, Redhill	01737 780781
Lewis Professor Roy Malcolm	Old Square Chambers, London	0171 269 0300
	Old Square Chambers, Bristol	0117 9277111
Lewis Thomas Robin Arwel	St Philip's Chambers, Birmingham	0121 246 7000
Lo Bernard Norman	17 Bedford Row, London	0171 831 7314
MacLaren Miss Catriona Longueville	2nd Floor, Francis Taylor Building, London	0171 353 9942/3157
Macpherson The Hon Mary Stewart	2 Mitre Court Buildings, London	0171 583 1380
Mainwaring [Robert] Paul Clason	Carmarthen Chambers, Carmarthen	01267 234410
Makey Christopher Douglas	Old Square Chambers, London	0171 269 0300
	Old Square Chambers, Bristol	0117 9277111
Malecka Dr Mary Margaret	• 3 Temple Gardens, London	0171 353 0832
	65-67 King Street, Leicester	0116 2547710
Matthews Dennis Roland	Two Crown Office Row, London	020 7797 8100
Maudslay Miss Diana Elizabeth	Sovereign Chambers, Leeds	0113 2451841/2/3
May Miss Juliet Mary	3 Verulam Buildings, London	0171 831 8441
McCafferty Miss Lynne	5 Paper Buildings, London	0171 583 9275/583 4555
McCluggage Brian Thomas	Chambers of John Hand QC, Manchester	0161 955 9000
McDermott Gerard Francis	8 King Street Chambers, Manchester	0161 834 9560
	2 Pump Court, London	0171 353 5597
McHugh Denis David	Bracton Chambers, London	0171 242 4248
McMaster Peter	Serle Court Chambers, London	0171 242 6105
McMullen Jeremy John	• Old Square Chambers, London	0171 269 0300
	Old Square Chambers, Bristol	0117 9277111
McNeill Miss Elizabeth Jane	• Old Square Chambers, London	0171 269 0300
	Old Square Chambers, Bristol	0117 9277111
Mead John Philip	Old Square Chambers, London	0171 269 0300
	Old Square Chambers, Bristol	0117 9277111
Mehendale Ms Neelima Krishna	2 Mitre Court Buildings, London	0171 353 1353
Melville Miss Elizabeth Emma Jane	Old Square Chambers, London	0171 269 0300
	Old Square Chambers, Bristol	0117 9277111
Melville Richard David	• 39 Essex Street, London	0171 832 1111
Mercer David Paul	Queen's Chambers, Manchester	0161 834 6875/4738
	Queens Chambers, Preston	01772 828300
Millar Gavin James	Doughty Street Chambers, London	0171 404 1313
Minhas Ms Rafhat	Leone Chambers, London	0181 200 4020
Mitropoulos Christos	Chambers of Geoffrey Hawker, London	0171 583 8899
Monk David Kenneth	2 New Street, Leicester	0116 2625906
Moor Miss Sarah Kathryn	Old Square Chambers, London	0171 269 0300
	Old Square Chambers, Bristol	0117 9277111
Moore Roderick Andrew McGowan	3 Temple Gardens, London	0171 353 0832
Moriarty Gerald Evelyn	2 Mitre Court Buildings, London	0171 583 1380
Mortimer Miss Sophie Kate	No. 1 Serjeants' Inn, London	0171 415 6666
Murphy Mrs Catriona Anne	1 Gray's Inn Square, London	0171 405 8946/7/8
Naidoo Sean Van	Littman Chambers, London	020 7404 4866
Nesbitt Timothy John Robert	199 Strand, London	0171 379 9779
Neville Stephen John	Gough Square Chambers, London	0171 353 0924
Neville-Clarke Sebastian Adrian Bennett	1 Crown Office Row, London	0171 583 9292
Newman Austin Eric	9 Woodhouse Square, Leeds	0113 2451986
Newton Philip	Becket Chambers, Canterbury	01227 786331
Nicol Nicholas Keith	1 Pump Court, London	0171 583 2012/353 4341
O'Donoghue Florence	2 Mitre Court Buildings, London	0171 353 1353
O'Neill Tadhg Joseph	1 Crown Office Row, London	0171 583 9292

• Expanded entry in Part D

Omambala Miss Ijeoma Chinyelu	Old Square Chambers, London	0171 269 0300
	Old Square Chambers, Bristol	0117 9277111
Packman Miss Claire Geraldine Vance	4 Pump Court, London	020 7842 5555
Padfield Ms Alison Mary	Devereux Chambers, London	0171 353 7534
Pain Kenneth William	College Chambers, Southampton	01703 230338
Paines Nicholas Paul Billot	Monckton Chambers, London	0171 405 7211
Panesar Deshpal Singh	13 King's Bench Walk, London	0171 353 7204
	King's Bench Chambers, Oxford	01865 311066
Panton William Dwight	Britton Street Chambers, London	0171 608 3765
Parkin Jonathan	• Chambers of John Hand QC, Manchester	0161 955 9000
Patchett-Joyce Michael Thurston	Monckton Chambers, London	0171 405 7211
Patten Benedict Joseph	Two Crown Office Row, London	020 7797 8100
Peirson Oliver James	Pump Court Chambers, London	0171 353 0711
	Pump Court Chambers, Winchester	01962 868161
	Pump Court Chambers, Swindon	01793 539899
Pema Anes Bhumin Laloo	9 Woodhouse Square, Leeds	0113 2451986
Pepperall Edward Brian	St Philip's Chambers, Birmingham	0121 246 7000
Pershad Rohan	Two Crown Office Row, London	020 7797 8100
Phillpot Hereward Lindon	2 Harcourt Buildings, London	020 7353 8415
Pickup David Michael Walker	Peel Court Chambers, Manchester	0161 832 3791
Pinder Miss Mary Elizabeth	No. 1 Serjeants' Inn, London	0171 415 6666
Piper Angus Richard	No. 1 Serjeants' Inn, London	0171 415 6666
Pirani Rohan Carl	Old Square Chambers, Bristol	0117 9277111
	Old Square Chambers, London	0171 269 0300
Pitt-Payne Timothy Sheridan	• 11 King's Bench Walk, London	0171 632 8500/583 0610
Pliener David Jonathan	New Court Chambers, London	0171 831 9500
Plimmer Miss Melanie Ann	Chambers of Ian Macdonald QC (In Association with Two Garden Court, Temple, London), Manchester	0161 236 1840
Powell Miss Debra Ann	3 Serjeants' Inn, London	0171 353 5537
Price Miss Collette	St James's Chambers, Manchester	0161 834 7000
Prinn Miss Helen Elizabeth	Octagon House, Norwich	01603 623186
Prudhoe Timothy Nixon	Queen's Chambers, Manchester	0161 834 6875/4738
	Queens Chambers, Preston	01772 828300
Purves Gavin Bowman	Swan House, London	0181 998 3035
Pusey William James	St Philip's Chambers, Birmingham	0121 246 7000
Rai Amarjit Singh	St Philip's Chambers, Birmingham	0121 246 7000
Readings Douglas George	St Philip's Chambers, Birmingham	0121 246 7000
Rees Professor William Michael	Barnard's Inn Chambers, London	0171 369 6969
Reid Sebastian Peter Scott	2nd Floor, Francis Taylor Building, London	0171 353 9942/3157
Renfree Peter Gerald Stanley	Harbour Court Chambers, Fareham	01329 827828
Richards Jeremy Simon	Octagon House, Norwich	01603 623186
Richardson David John	13 King's Bench Walk, London	0171 353 7204
	King's Bench Chambers, Oxford	01865 311066
Roberts Stuart Royd	37 Park Square Chambers, Leeds	0113 2439422
Robinson Simon Robert	Chambers of Ian Macdonald QC (In Association with Two Garden Court, Temple, London), Manchester	0161 236 1840
Rochford Thomas Nicholas Beverley	St Philip's Chambers, Birmingham	0121 246 7000
Roebuck Roy Delville	Bell Yard Chambers, London	0171 306 9292
Rogers Ian Paul	1 Crown Office Row, London	0171 583 9292
Rogers Paul John	1 Crown Office Row, London	0171 797 7500
	Crown Office Row Chambers, Brighton	01273 625625
Romney Miss Daphne Irene	4 Field Court, London	0171 440 6900
Rose Paul Telfer	Old Square Chambers, London	0171 269 0300
	Old Square Chambers, Bristol	0117 9277111

Rudd Matthew Allan	11 Bolt Court (also at 7 Stone Buildings – 1st Floor), London	0171 353 2300
	Redhill Chambers, Redhill	01737 780781
	7 Stone Buildings (also at 11 Bolt Court), London	0171 242 0961
Salmon Jonathan Carl	1 Fountain Court, Birmingham	0121 236 5721
Samuels Leslie John	Pump Court Chambers, London	0171 353 0711
	Pump Court Chambers, Winchester	01962 868161
	Pump Court Chambers, Swindon	01793 539899
Scott Ian Richard	Old Square Chambers, London	0171 269 0300
	Old Square Chambers, Bristol	0117 9277111
Scott Matthew John	Pump Court Chambers, London	0171 353 0711
	Pump Court Chambers, Winchester	01962 868161
	Pump Court Chambers, Swindon	01793 539899
Segal Oliver Leon	Old Square Chambers, London	0171 269 0300
	Old Square Chambers, Bristol	0117 9277111
Semple Andrew Blair	Sovereign Chambers, Leeds	0113 2451841/2/3
Sendall Antony John Christmas	Littleton Chambers, London	0171 797 8600
Sethi Mohinderpal Singh	Barnard's Inn Chambers, London	0171 369 6969
Shale Justin Anton	4 King's Bench Walk, London	0171 822 8822
	King's Bench Chambers, Bournemouth	01202 250025
Shannon Thomas Eric	Queen's Chambers, Manchester	0161 834 6875/4738
	Queens Chambers, Preston	01772 828300
Sheehan Malcolm Peter	2 Harcourt Buildings, London	0171 583 9020
Sheldon Clive David	11 King's Bench Walk, London	0171 632 8500/583 0610
Shiels Ian	30 Park Square, Leeds	0113 2436388
Shrimpton Michael	Francis Taylor Building, London	0171 797 7250
Shukla Ms Vina	New Court Chambers, London	0171 831 9500
Siddiqi Faizul Aqtab	Justice Court Chambers, London	0181 830 7786
Simor Miss Jessica Margaret Poppaea	Monckton Chambers, London	0171 405 7211
Skelly Andrew Jon	1 Gray's Inn Square, London	0171 405 8946/7/8
Slade Miss Elizabeth Ann	11 King's Bench Walk, London	0171 632 8500/583 0610
Smail Alastair Harold Kurt	St Philip's Chambers, Birmingham	0121 246 7000
Smith Miss Emma Louise	Old Square Chambers, London	0171 269 0300
	Old Square Chambers, Bristol	0117 9277111
Smith Miss Joanna Angela	•Wilberforce Chambers, London	0171 306 0102
Smith Ms Katherine Emma	Monckton Chambers, London	0171 405 7211
Sparrow Miss Claire Louise	Eastbourne Chambers, Eastbourne	01323 642102
Spencer Paul Anthony	2 New Street, Leicester	0116 2625906
Spicer Robert Haden	Frederick Place Chambers, Bristol	0117 9738667
St Louis Brian Lloyd	Hardwicke Building, London	020 7242 2523
Staddon Paul	2nd Floor, Francis Taylor Building, London	0171 353 9942/3157
Stagg Paul Andrew	No. 1 Serjeants' Inn, London	0171 415 6666
Stancombe Barry Terrence	Gough Square Chambers, London	0171 353 0924
Starcevic Petar	St Philip's Chambers, Birmingham	0121 246 7000
Stark James Hayden Alexander	Chambers of Ian Macdonald QC (In Association with Two Garden Court, Temple, London), Manchester	0161 236 1840
Stavros Ms Evanthia	3 Temple Gardens, London	0171 353 0832
Stilitz Daniel Malachi	11 King's Bench Walk, London	0171 632 8500/583 0610
Sullivan Scott	Barnard's Inn Chambers, London	0171 369 6969
Supperstone Michael Alan	11 King's Bench Walk, London	0171 632 8500/583 0610
Swerling Robert Harry	13 Old Square, London	0171 404 4800
Szanto Gregory John Michael	Eastbourne Chambers, Eastbourne	01323 642102
Taft Christopher Heiton	St James's Chambers, Manchester	0161 834 7000
Tapsell Paul Richard	Becket Chambers, Canterbury	01227 786331
Tatton-Brown Daniel Nicholas	Littleton Chambers, London	0171 797 8600

• Expanded entry in Part D

Tedd Rex Hilary	• St Philip's Chambers, Birmingham	0121 246 7000
	De Montfort Chambers, Leicester	0116 254 8686
	Northampton Chambers, Northampton	01604 636271
Tether Ms Melanie Georgia Kim	Old Square Chambers, London	0171 269 0300
	Old Square Chambers, Bristol	0117 9277111
Thain Miss Ashley	East Anglian Chambers, Colchester	01206 572756
	East Anglian Chambers, Ipswich	01473 214481
	East Anglian Chambers, Norwich	01603 617351
Thompson Patrick Miles	Queen's Chambers, Manchester	0161 834 6875/4738
	Queens Chambers, Preston	01772 828300
Thomson Martin Haldane Ahmad	Wynne Chambers, London	0181 961 6144
Tizzano Franco Salvatore	8 King's Bench Walk, London	0171 797 8888
	8 King's Bench Walk North, Leeds	0113 2439797
Tracy Forster Miss Jane Elizabeth	13 King's Bench Walk, London	0171 353 7204
	King's Bench Chambers, Oxford	01865 311066
Tregilgas-Davey Marcus Ian	Pump Court Chambers, Swindon	01793 539899
	Pump Court Chambers, London	0171 353 0711
	Pump Court Chambers, Winchester	01962 868161
Truscott Ian Derek	Old Square Chambers, London	0171 269 0300
	Old Square Chambers, Bristol	0117 9277111
Tucker Miss Katherine Jane Greening	St Philip's Chambers, Birmingham	0121 246 7000
Tully Ms Anne Margaret	Eastbourne Chambers, Eastbourne	01323 642102
Vajda Christopher Stephen	Monckton Chambers, London	0171 405 7211
Vaughan-Neil Miss Catherine Mary Bernardine	4 Pump Court, London	020 7842 5555
Vickers Miss Rachel Clare	199 Strand, London	0171 379 9779
Vickery Neil Michael	13 King's Bench Walk, London	0171 353 7204
	King's Bench Chambers, Oxford	01865 311066
Walden-Smith Miss Karen Jane	5 Stone Buildings, London	0171 242 6201
Walker Christopher David Bestwick	Old Square Chambers, Bristol	0117 9277111
	Old Square Chambers, London	0171 269 0300
Wallington Peter Thomas	11 King's Bench Walk, London	0171 632 8500/583 0610
Warnock Andrew Ronald	No. 1 Serjeants' Inn, London	0171 415 6666
Warren Rupert Miles	2 Mitre Court Buildings, London	0171 583 1380
Warrender Miss Nichola Mary	New Court Chambers, London	0171 831 9500
Watkin Toby Paul	22 Old Buildings, London	0171 831 0222
Wayne Nicholas	1 Gray's Inn Square, London	0171 405 8946/7/8
Webb Stanley George	The Chambers of Mr Ali Mohammed Azhar, London	0171 353 9564
	Bracton Chambers, London	0171 242 4248
	Old Square Chambers, London	0171 269 0300
	Old Square Chambers, Bristol	0117 9277111
Wedderburn of Charlton Lord		
Wedderspoon Miss Rachel Leone	Chambers of John Hand QC, Manchester	0161 955 9000
Wenlock Miss Heather	13 King's Bench Walk, London	0171 353 7204
	King's Bench Chambers, Oxford	01865 311066
Westgate Martin Trevor	Doughty Street Chambers, London	0171 404 1313
Whipple Mrs Philippa Jane Edwards	1 Crown Office Row, London	0171 797 7500
Whitcombe Mark David	Old Square Chambers, Bristol	0117 9277111
	Old Square Chambers, London	0171 269 0300
Williams Ms Heather Jean	Doughty Street Chambers, London	0171 404 1313
Wilson Peter Julian	Sovereign Chambers, Leeds	0113 2451841/2/3
Wilson Stephen Mark	4 Field Court, London	0171 440 6900
Winzer Benjamin Charles	Southernhay Chambers, Exeter	01392 255777
Wood Ian Robert	8 King Street Chambers, Manchester	0161 834 9560
Worrall Miss Shirley Vera Frances	8 King Street Chambers, Manchester	0161 834 9560
Wyatt Mark	2 New Street, Leicester	0116 2625906
Wynter Colin Peter	Devereux Chambers, London	0171 353 7534
Yell Nicholas Anthony	No. 1 Serjeants' Inn, London	0171 415 6666
Zaman Mohammed Khalil	St Philip's Chambers, Birmingham	0121 246 7000

• Expanded entry in Part D

ENERGY

Akenhead Robert	Atkin Chambers, London	020 7404 0102
Alesbury Alun	2 Mitre Court Buildings, London	0171 583 1380
Anderson Anthony John	2 Mitre Court Buildings, London	0171 583 1380
Baatz Nicholas Stephen	Atkin Chambers, London	020 7404 0102
Bailey David John	S Tomlinson QC, London	0171 583 0404
Barwise Miss Stephanie Nicola	Atkin Chambers, London	020 7404 0102
Blackburn John	Atkin Chambers, London	020 7404 0102
Bowdery Martin	Atkin Chambers, London	020 7404 0102
Boyle Christopher Alexander David	2 Mitre Court Buildings, London	0171 583 1380
Bright Robert Graham	S Tomlinson QC, London	0171 583 0404
Burr Andrew Charles	Atkin Chambers, London	020 7404 0102
Burton Nicholas Anthony	2 Mitre Court Buildings, London	0171 583 1380
Butcher Christopher John	S Tomlinson QC, London	0171 583 0404
Clay Robert Charles	Atkin Chambers, London	020 7404 0102
Collings Nicholas Stewart	Atkin Chambers, London	020 7404 0102
Cooke Jeremy Lionel	S Tomlinson QC, London	0171 583 0404
Dennison Stephen Randell	Atkin Chambers, London	020 7404 0102
Dennys Nicholas Charles Jonathan	Atkin Chambers, London	020 7404 0102
Doerries Miss Chantal-Aimee Renee Aemelia Annemarie	Atkin Chambers, London	020 7404 0102
Druce Michael James	2 Mitre Court Buildings, London	0171 583 1380
Dumaresq Ms Delia Jane	Atkin Chambers, London	020 7404 0102
Edwards David Leslie	S Tomlinson QC, London	0171 583 0404
Fitzgerald Michael Frederick Clive	2 Mitre Court Buildings, London	0171 583 1380
Flaux Julian Martin	S Tomlinson QC, London	0171 583 0404
Fookes Robert Lawrence	2 Mitre Court Buildings, London	0171 583 1380
Fraser Peter Donald	Atkin Chambers, London	020 7404 0102
Gaisman Jonathan Nicholas Crispin	S Tomlinson QC, London	0171 583 0404
Gee Steven Mark	4 Field Court, London	0171 440 6900
Glover Richard Michael	2 Mitre Court Buildings, London	0171 583 1380
Goddard Andrew Stephen	Atkin Chambers, London	020 7404 0102
Godwin William George Henry	Atkin Chambers, London	020 7404 0102
Hamilton Adrian Walter	S Tomlinson QC, London	0171 583 0404
Horton Matthew Bethell	2 Mitre Court Buildings, London	0171 583 1380
Howells James Richard	Atkin Chambers, London	020 7404 0102
Humphries Michael John	2 Mitre Court Buildings, London	0171 583 1380
Kendrick Dominic John	S Tomlinson QC, London	0171 583 0404
King Neil Gerald Alexander	2 Mitre Court Buildings, London	0171 583 1380
Lever Jeremy Frederick	Monckton Chambers, London	0171 405 7211
Lofthouse Simon Timothy	Atkin Chambers, London	020 7404 0102
Macpherson The Hon Mary Stewart	2 Mitre Court Buildings, London	0171 583 1380
Manzoni Charles Peter	39 Essex Street, London	0171 832 1111
McMaster Peter	Serle Court Chambers, London	0171 242 6105
McMullan Manus Anthony	Atkin Chambers, London	020 7404 0102
Mercer Hugh Charles	● Essex Court Chambers, London	0171 813 8000
Milligan Iain Anstruther	20 Essex Street, London	0171 583 9294
Moore Professor Victor William Edward	2 Mitre Court Buildings, London	0171 583 1380
Moriarty Gerald Evelyn	2 Mitre Court Buildings, London	0171 583 1380
Parkin Miss Fiona Jane	Atkin Chambers, London	020 7404 0102
Raeside Mark Andrew	Atkin Chambers, London	020 7404 0102
Rawley Miss Dominique Jane	Atkin Chambers, London	020 7404 0102
Reese Colin Edward	Atkin Chambers, London	020 7404 0102
Royce Darryl Fraser	Atkin Chambers, London	020 7404 0102
Sabben-Clare Miss Rebecca Mary	S Tomlinson QC, London	0171 583 0404
Schaff Alistair Graham	S Tomlinson QC, London	0171 583 0404
Silsoe The Lord	2 Mitre Court Buildings, London	0171 583 1380
Southern Richard Michael	S Tomlinson QC, London	0171 583 0404
Streatfeild-James David Stewart	Atkin Chambers, London	020 7404 0102
Swift John Anthony	Monckton Chambers, London	0171 405 7211

● Expanded entry in Part D

Taylor John Charles	2 Mitre Court Buildings, London	0171 583 1380
Taylor Reuben Mallinson	2 Mitre Court Buildings, London	0171 583 1380
Tomlinson Stephen Miles	S Tomlinson QC, London	0171 583 0404
Tucker David William	Two Crown Office Row, London	020 7797 8100
Valentine Donald Graham	Atkin Chambers, London	020 7404 0102
Wald Richard Daniel	2 Mitre Court Buildings, London	0171 583 1380
Wales Andrew Nigel Malcolm	S Tomlinson QC, London	0171 583 0404
Walker Steven John	Atkin Chambers, London	020 7404 0102
Wallace Ian Norman Duncan	Atkin Chambers, London	020 7404 0102
Warren Rupert Miles	2 Mitre Court Buildings, London	0171 583 1380
White Andrew	Atkin Chambers, London	020 7404 0102
Whybrow Christopher John	1 Serjeants' Inn, London	0171 583 1355
Widdicombe David Graham	2 Mitre Court Buildings, London	0171 583 1380
Wilken Sean David Henry	39 Essex Street, London	0171 832 1111
Wilmot-Smith Richard James Crosbie	39 Essex Street, London	0171 832 1111

ENTERTAINMENT

Abrahams James	8 New Square, London	0171 405 4321
Alexander Daniel Sakyi	8 New Square, London	0171 405 4321
Ayres Andrew John William	13 Old Square, London	0171 404 4800
Baldwin John Paul	8 New Square, London	0171 405 4321
Barker Simon George Harry	• 13 Old Square, London	0171 404 4800
Baylis Ms Natalie Jayne	3 Verulam Buildings, London	0171 831 8441
Bennett Gordon Irvine	12 New Square, London	0171 419 1212
Brodie (James) Bruce	39 Essex Street, London	0171 832 1111
Burnett Harold Wallace	4 Paper Buildings, London	0171 353 3366/583 7155
Charlton Alexander Murray	4 Pump Court, London	020 7842 5555
Clark Miss Fiona Jane Stewart	8 New Square, London	0171 405 4321
Cole Richard John	Lancaster Building, Manchester	0161 661 4444/0171 649 9872
Cooke Jeremy Lionel	S Tomlinson QC, London	0171 583 0404
Coulthard Alan Terence	33 Park Place, Cardiff	02920 233313
Craig Kenneth Allen	Hardwicke Building, London	020 7242 2523
De Freitas Anthony Peter Stanley	4 Paper Buildings, London	0171 353 3366/583 7155
Dillon Thomas William Matthew	1 Fountain Court, Birmingham	0121 236 5721
Edwards Richard Julian Henshaw	3 Verulam Buildings, London	0171 831 8441
Elliott Nicholas Blethyn	3 Verulam Buildings, London	0171 831 8441
Faulks Edward Peter Lawless	No. 1 Serjeants' Inn, London	0171 415 6666
Fysh Michael	8 New Square, London	0171 405 4321
Gibaud Miss Catherine Alison Annetta	3 Verulam Buildings, London	0171 831 8441
Goudie James	• 11 King's Bench Walk, London	0171 632 8500/583 0610
Hamer George Clemens	8 New Square, London	0171 405 4321
Hardwick Matthew Richard	Enterprise Chambers, London	0171 405 9471
	Enterprise Chambers, Leeds	0113 246 0391
	Enterprise Chambers, Newcastle upon Tyne	0191 222 3344
Head David Ian	3 Verulam Buildings, London	0171 831 8441
Hicks Michael Charles	• 19 Old Buildings, London	0171 405 2001
Hofmeyr Stephen Murray	S Tomlinson QC, London	0171 583 0404
Holman Miss Tamsin Perdita	19 Old Buildings, London	0171 405 2001
Howe Martin Russell Thomson	8 New Square, London	0171 405 4321
Jones Miss Elizabeth Sian	Serle Court Chambers, London	0171 242 6105
Kelman Alistair Bruce	Lancaster Building, Manchester	0161 661 4444/0171 649 9872
Kitchin David James Tyson	8 New Square, London	0171 405 4321
Lambert John	Lancaster Building, Manchester	0161 661 4444/0171 649 9872
Lane Ms Lindsay Ruth Busfield	8 New Square, London	0171 405 4321
Lowenstein Paul David	Littleton Chambers, London	0171 797 8600
Malecka Dr Mary Margaret	• 3 Temple Gardens, London	0171 353 0832
	65-67 King Street, Leicester	0116 2547710
Marks Jonathan Harold	3 Verulam Buildings, London	0171 831 8441

May Miss Charlotte Louisa	8 New Square, London	0171 405 4321
Meade Richard David	8 New Square, London	0171 405 4321
Mellor Edward James Wilson	8 New Square, London	0171 405 4321
Merriman Nicholas Flavelle	3 Verulam Buildings, London	0171 831 8441
Millar Gavin James	Doughty Street Chambers, London	0171 404 1313
Moody-Stuart Thomas	8 New Square, London	0171 405 4321
Munby James Lawrence	1 New Square, London	0171 405 0884/5/6/7
Neish Andrew Graham	4 Pump Court, London	020 7842 5555
Nelson Vincent Leonard	39 Essex Street, London	0171 832 1111
Newman Ms Ingrid	Hardwicke Building, London	020 7242 2523
Newton John Simon	Derby Square Chambers, Liverpool	0151 709 4222
Ng Ray Kian Hin	Two Crown Office Row, London	020 7797 8100
Nicol Andrew George Lindsay	Doughty Street Chambers, London	0171 404 1313
Onslow Robert Denzil	8 New Square, London	0171 405 4321
Pain Kenneth William	College Chambers, Southampton	01703 230338
Panford Frank Haig	• Doughty Street Chambers, London	0171 404 1313
Pershad Rohan	Two Crown Office Row, London	020 7797 8100
Platts-Mills Mark Fortescue	8 New Square, London	0171 405 4321
Prescott Peter Richard Kyle	8 New Square, London	0171 405 4321
Price Albert John	23 Essex Street, London	0171 413 0353/836 8366
Price Richard Mervyn	Littleton Chambers, London	0171 797 8600
Purves Gavin Bowman	Swan House, London	0181 998 3035
Reed Jeremy Nigel	19 Old Buildings, London	0171 405 2001
Shipley Norman Graham	• 19 Old Buildings, London	0171 405 2001
Speck Adrian	8 New Square, London	0171 405 4321
St Ville Laurence James	8 New Square, London	0171 405 4321
Sullivan Rory Myles	19 Old Buildings, London	0171 405 2001
Sutcliffe Andrew Harold Wentworth	3 Verulam Buildings, London	0171 831 8441
Talbot Patrick John	Serle Court Chambers, London	0171 242 6105
Tappin Michael John	8 New Square, London	0171 405 4321
Tozzi Nigel Kenneth	4 Pump Court, London	020 7842 5555
Tucker David William	Two Crown Office Row, London	020 7797 8100
Vitoria Miss Mary Christine	8 New Square, London	0171 405 4321
Wilson Alastair James Drysdale	• 19 Old Buildings, London	0171 405 2001

ENVIRONMENT

Akenhead Robert	Atkin Chambers, London	020 7404 0102
Alesbury Alun	2 Mitre Court Buildings, London	0171 583 1380
Allardice Miss Miranda Jane	Pump Court Chambers, London	0171 353 0711
	Pump Court Chambers, Winchester	01962 868161
	Pump Court Chambers, Swindon	01793 539899
Anderson Anthony John	2 Mitre Court Buildings, London	0171 583 1380
Anderson Miss Julie	• Littman Chambers, London	020 7404 4866
Ashworth Piers	2 Harcourt Buildings, London	0171 583 9020
Atherton Peter	Deans Court Chambers, Manchester	0161 214 6000
	Deans Court Chambers, Preston	01772 555163
Baatz Nicholas Stephen	Atkin Chambers, London	020 7404 0102
Baldry Antony Brian	No. 1 Serjeants' Inn, London	0171 415 6666
Barwise Miss Stephanie Nicola	Atkin Chambers, London	020 7404 0102
Bates John Hayward	Old Square Chambers, London	0171 269 0300
	Old Square Chambers, Bristol	0117 9277111
Beard Mark Christopher	6 Pump Court, London	0171 797 8400
	6-8 Mill Street, Maidstone	01622 688094
Bellamy Jonathan Mark	39 Essex Street, London	0171 832 1111
Birtles William	Old Square Chambers, London	0171 269 0300
	Old Square Chambers, Bristol	0117 9277111
Blackburn John	Atkin Chambers, London	020 7404 0102
Blackford Simon John	Barnard's Inn Chambers, London	0171 369 6969
Booth Nicholas John	Old Square Chambers, London	0171 269 0300
	Old Square Chambers, Bristol	0117 9277111
Booth Richard John	1 Crown Office Row, London	0171 797 7500

• Expanded entry in Part D

Bowdery Martin	Atkin Chambers, London	020 7404 0102
Boyle Christopher Alexander David	2 Mitre Court Buildings, London	0171 583 1380
Brent Richard	3 Verulam Buildings, London	0171 831 8441
Buck Dr Andrew Theodore	Chambers of Martin Burr, London	0171 353 4636
Burr Andrew Charles	Atkin Chambers, London	020 7404 0102
Burton Nicholas Anthony	2 Mitre Court Buildings, London	0171 583 1380
Butler Simon David	10 King's Bench Walk, London	0171 353 7742
Cameron Jonathan James O'Grady	3 Verulam Buildings, London	0171 831 8441
Cameron Neil St Clair	1 Serjeants' Inn, London	0171 583 1355
Carter Peter	• 18 Red Lion Court, London	0171 520 6000
	Thornwood House, Chelmsford	01245 280880
Clay Robert Charles	Atkin Chambers, London	020 7404 0102
Collings Nicholas Stewart	Atkin Chambers, London	020 7404 0102
DeCamp Miss Jane Louise	Two Crown Office Row, London	020 7797 8100
Dennison Stephen Randell	Atkin Chambers, London	020 7404 0102
Dennys Nicholas Charles Jonathan	Atkin Chambers, London	020 7404 0102
Doerries Miss Chantal-Aimee Renee Aemelia Annemarie	Atkin Chambers, London	020 7404 0102
Druce Michael James	2 Mitre Court Buildings, London	0171 583 1380
Dumaresq Ms Delia Jane	Atkin Chambers, London	020 7404 0102
Edis Angus William Butler	1 Crown Office Row, London	0171 797 7500
Edwards-Stuart Antony James Cobham	Two Crown Office Row, London	020 7797 8100
Fitzgerald Michael Frederick Clive	2 Mitre Court Buildings, London	0171 583 1380
Fookes Robert Lawrence	2 Mitre Court Buildings, London	0171 583 1380
Francis Andrew James	Chambers of Mr Peter Crampin QC, London	020 7831 0081
Fraser Peter Donald	Atkin Chambers, London	020 7404 0102
Gibbs Patrick Michael Evan	2 Harcourt Buildings, London	020 7353 2112
Gifford Andrew James Morris	7 New Square, London	0171 430 1660
Gill Ms Sarah Teresa	• Old Square Chambers, London	0171 269 0300
	Old Square Chambers, Bristol	0117 9277111
Glover Richard Michael	2 Mitre Court Buildings, London	0171 583 1380
Goddard Andrew Stephen	Atkin Chambers, London	020 7404 0102
Godwin William George Henry	Atkin Chambers, London	020 7404 0102
Gordon Richard John Francis	Brick Court Chambers, London	0171 379 3550
Goudie James	• 11 King's Bench Walk, London	0171 632 8500/583 0610
Goulding Jonathan Steven	Gough Square Chambers, London	0171 353 0924
Hall Mrs Melanie Ruth	Monckton Chambers, London	0171 405 7211
Hand John Lester	Chambers of John Hand QC, Manchester	0161 955 9000
	Old Square Chambers, London	0171 269 0300
	Old Square Chambers, Bristol	0117 9277111
Harington Michael Kenneth	6 Pump Court, London	0171 797 8400
	6-8 Mill Street, Maidstone	01622 688094
Harrison Peter John	6 Pump Court, London	0171 797 8400
	6-8 Mill Street, Maidstone	01622 688094
Harwood Richard John	1 Serjeants' Inn, London	0171 583 1355
Haynes Peter	St Philip's Chambers, Birmingham	0121 246 7000
Haynes Miss Rebecca	Monckton Chambers, London	0171 405 7211
Hockman Stephen Alexander	• 6 Pump Court, London	0171 797 8400
	6-8 Mill Street, Maidstone	01622 688094
Horton Matthew Bethell	2 Mitre Court Buildings, London	0171 583 1380
Howard Michael Newman	4 Essex Court, London	020 7797 7970
Howell Williams Craig	2 Harcourt Buildings, London	020 7353 8415
Howells James Richard	Atkin Chambers, London	020 7404 0102
Hughes Adrian Warwick	4 Pump Court, London	020 7842 5555
Humphries Michael John	2 Mitre Court Buildings, London	0171 583 1380
Jefferis Arthur Michael Quentin	Chambers of Mr Peter Crampin QC, London	020 7831 0081
Jones Timothy Arthur	• St Philip's Chambers, Birmingham	0121 246 7000
	Arden Chambers, London	020 7242 4244

King Neil Gerald Alexander	2 Mitre Court Buildings, London	0171 583 1380
Langham Richard Geoffrey	1 Serjeants' Inn, London	0171 583 1355
Leigh Kevin	6 Pump Court, London	0171 797 8400
	Regency Chambers, Peterborough	01733 315215
	Westgate Chambers, Lewes	01273 480510
	6-8 Mill Street, Maidstone	01622 688094
Lewis Robert	11 Bolt Court (also at 7 Stone Buildings – 1st Floor), London	0171 353 2300
	7 Stone Buildings (also at 11 Bolt Court), London	0171 242 0961
	Redhill Chambers, Redhill	01737 780781
Lofthouse Simon Timothy	Atkin Chambers, London	020 7404 0102
Lyness Scott Edward	1 Serjeants' Inn, London	0171 583 1355
MacDonald Iain	Gough Square Chambers, London	0171 353 0924
Macnab Alexander Andrew	Monckton Chambers, London	0171 405 7211
Macpherson The Hon Mary Stewart	2 Mitre Court Buildings, London	0171 583 1380
Mainwaring [Robert] Paul Clason	Carmarthen Chambers, Carmarthen	01267 234410
Malecka Dr Mary Margaret	● 3 Temple Gardens, London	0171 353 0832
	65-67 King Street, Leicester	0116 2547710
Manzoni Charles Peter	39 Essex Street, London	0171 832 1111
Marks Jonathan Harold	3 Verulam Buildings, London	0171 831 8441
Markus Ms Kate	Doughty Street Chambers, London	0171 404 1313
McCullough Miss Judith Ann	Queen's Chambers, Manchester	0161 834 6875/4738
	Queens Chambers, Preston	01772 828300
McMullan Manus Anthony	Atkin Chambers, London	020 7404 0102
Mead John Philip	Old Square Chambers, London	0171 269 0300
	Old Square Chambers, Bristol	0117 9277111
Mehendale Ms Neelima Krishna	2 Mitre Court Buildings, London	0171 353 1353
Melville Miss Elizabeth Emma Jane	Old Square Chambers, London	0171 269 0300
	Old Square Chambers, Bristol	0117 9277111
Moger Christopher Richard Derwent	4 Pump Court, London	020 7842 5555
Moor Miss Sarah Kathryn	Old Square Chambers, London	0171 269 0300
	Old Square Chambers, Bristol	0117 9277111
Moore Professor Victor William Edward	2 Mitre Court Buildings, London	0171 583 1380
Morgan Charles James Arthur	Enterprise Chambers, London	0171 405 9471
	Enterprise Chambers, Newcastle upon Tyne	0191 222 3344
	Enterprise Chambers, Leeds	0113 246 0391
Moriarty Gerald Evelyn	2 Mitre Court Buildings, London	0171 583 1380
Muller Antonie Sean	4 Fountain Court, Birmingham	0121 236 3476
Nardell Gordon Lawrence	6 Pump Court, London	0171 797 8400
	6-8 Mill Street, Maidstone	01622 688094
Nesbitt Timothy John Robert	199 Strand, London	0171 379 9779
Newcombe Andrew Bennett	2 Harcourt Buildings, London	020 7353 8415
Newton Philip	Becket Chambers, Canterbury	01227 786331
Ornsby Miss Suzanne Doreen	2 Harcourt Buildings, London	020 7353 8415
Palfrey Montague Mark	Hardwicke Building, London	020 7242 2523
Parker Kenneth Blades	Monckton Chambers, London	0171 405 7211
Parkin Miss Fiona Jane	Atkin Chambers, London	020 7404 0102
Pereira James Alexander	2 Harcourt Buildings, London	020 7353 8415
Phillpot Hereward Lindon	2 Harcourt Buildings, London	020 7353 8415
Philpott Frederick Alan	Gough Square Chambers, London	0171 353 0924
Pickles Simon Robert	1 Serjeants' Inn, London	0171 583 1355
Pickup David Michael Walker	Peel Court Chambers, Manchester	0161 832 3791
Pirani Rohan Carl	Old Square Chambers, Bristol	0117 9277111
	Old Square Chambers, London	0171 269 0300
Price Albert John	23 Essex Street, London	0171 413 0353/836 8366

● Expanded entry in Part D

Price John Scott	10 Launceston Avenue, Reading	01189 479548
	Southsea Chambers, Portsmouth	01705 291261
	Cathedral Chambers, Newcastle upon Tyne	0191 232 1311
Pugh Michael Charles	Old Square Chambers, London	0171 269 0300
	Old Square Chambers, Bristol	0117 9277111
Purchas Robin Michael	• 2 Harcourt Buildings, London	020 7353 8415
Purves Gavin Bowman	Swan House, London	0181 998 3035
Raeside Mark Andrew	Atkin Chambers, London	020 7404 0102
Rawley Miss Dominique Jane	Atkin Chambers, London	020 7404 0102
Reese Colin Edward	Atkin Chambers, London	020 7404 0102
Roots Guy Robert Godfrey	2 Mitre Court Buildings, London	0171 583 1380
Royce Darryl Fraser	Atkin Chambers, London	020 7404 0102
Salmon Jonathan Carl	1 Fountain Court, Birmingham	0121 236 5721
Sands Mr Philippe Joseph	3 Verulam Buildings, London	0171 831 8441
Selvaratnam Miss Vasanti Emily Indrani	4 Field Court, London	0171 440 6900
Sheridan Maurice Bernard Gerard	• 3 Verulam Buildings, London	0171 831 8441
Silsoe The Lord	2 Mitre Court Buildings, London	0171 583 1380
Simor Miss Jessica Margaret Poppaea	Monckton Chambers, London	0171 405 7211
Skelly Andrew Jon	1 Gray's Inn Square, London	0171 405 8946/7/8
Smith Ms Katherine Emma	Monckton Chambers, London	0171 405 7211
Stone Gregory	• 4-5 Gray's Inn Square, London	0171 404 5252
Streatfeild-James David Stewart	Atkin Chambers, London	020 7404 0102
Symons Christopher John Maurice	3 Verulam Buildings, London	0171 831 8441
Tait Andrew Charles Gordon	2 Harcourt Buildings, London	020 7353 8415
Taylor John Charles	2 Mitre Court Buildings, London	0171 583 1380
Taylor Reuben Mallinson	2 Mitre Court Buildings, London	0171 583 1380
Thomas Miss Megan Moira	1 Serjeants' Inn, London	0171 583 1355
Thomas Stephen Edward Owen	St Philip's Chambers, Birmingham	0121 246 7000
Travers David	• 3 Fountain Court, Birmingham	0121 236 5854
Tucker Miss Katherine Jane Greening	St Philip's Chambers, Birmingham	0121 246 7000
Turner Jonathan Richard	Monckton Chambers, London	0171 405 7211
Tyack David Guy	St Philip's Chambers, Birmingham	0121 246 7000
Valentine Donald Graham	Atkin Chambers, London	020 7404 0102
Wald Richard Daniel	2 Mitre Court Buildings, London	0171 583 1380
Walker Steven John	Atkin Chambers, London	020 7404 0102
Wallace Ian Norman Duncan	Atkin Chambers, London	020 7404 0102
Ward Trevor Robert Edward	17 Carlton Crescent, Southampton	023 8032 0320/0823 2003
Warren Rupert Miles	2 Mitre Court Buildings, London	0171 583 1380
White Andrew	Atkin Chambers, London	020 7404 0102
Whittaker John Percival	Serle Court Chambers, London	0171 242 6105
Whybrow Christopher John	1 Serjeants' Inn, London	0171 583 1355
Widdicombe David Graham	2 Mitre Court Buildings, London	0171 583 1380
Wilby David Christopher	• 199 Strand, London	0171 379 9779
	Park Lane Chambers, Leeds	0113 2285000
Williams A John	13 King's Bench Walk, London	0171 353 7204
	King's Bench Chambers, Oxford	01865 311066
Williams The Hon John Melville	Old Square Chambers, London	0171 269 0300
	Old Square Chambers, Bristol	0117 9277111
Zwart Auberon Christiaan Conrad	1 Serjeants' Inn, London	0171 583 1355

EQUESTRIAN

Cotterill Miss Susan Amanda	Lamb Building, London	020 7797 7788

EQUINE LAW

Keane Michael Leo	4 Paper Buildings, London	0171 353 3366/583 7155

EQUITY, WILLS AND TRUSTS

Acton Stephen Neil	11 Old Square, London	020 7430 0341

• Expanded entry in Part D

B

Adamyk Simon Charles	12 New Square, London	0171 419 1212
Allingham-Nicholson Mrs Elizabeth Sarah	2 New Street, Leicester	0116 2625906
Anderson Miss Julie	● Littman Chambers, London	020 7404 4866
Angus Miss Tracey Anne	5 Stone Buildings, London	0171 242 6201
Asplin Miss Sarah Jane	● 3 Stone Buildings, London	0171 242 4937
Asprey Nicholas	Serle Court Chambers, London	0171 242 6105
Ayres Andrew John William	13 Old Square, London	0171 404 4800
Barton Alan John	Lamb Building, London	020 7797 7788
Bedingfield David Herbert	● 14 Gray's Inn Square, London	0171 242 0858
Behrens James Nicholas Edward	Serle Court Chambers, London	0171 242 6105
Blackett-Ord Mark	● 5 Stone Buildings, London	0171 242 6201
Blayney David James	Serle Court Chambers, London	0171 242 6105
Bleasdale Miss Marie-Claire	Chambers of Mr Peter Crampin QC, London	020 7831 0081
Bowmer Michael Paul	11 Old Square, London	020 7430 0341
Briggs Michael Townley Featherstone	Serle Court Chambers, London	0171 242 6105
Bryant Miss Judith Anne	● Wilberforce Chambers, London	0171 306 0102
Buck Dr Andrew Theodore	Chambers of Martin Burr, London	0171 353 4636
Burr Martin John	Chambers of Martin Burr, London	0171 353 4636
	7 New Square, London	0171 430 1660
Cameron Miss Barbara Alexander	● 2 Harcourt Buildings, London	0171 583 9020
Campbell Miss Emily Charlotte	● Wilberforce Chambers, London	0171 306 0102
Cannan Jonathan Michael	St James's Chambers, Manchester	0161 834 7000
	Broadway House Chambers, Bradford	01274 722560
	Broadway House Chambers, Leeds	0113 246 2600
Castle Peter Bolton	Chambers of Mr Peter Crampin QC, London	020 7831 0081
Charman Andrew Julian	St Philip's Chambers, Birmingham	0121 246 7000
Child John Frederick	● Wilberforce Chambers, London	0171 306 0102
Clarke Miss Anna Victoria	5 Stone Buildings, London	0171 242 6201
Clarke Ian James	Hardwicke Building, London	020 7242 2523
Clarke Peter John	St Philip's Chambers, Birmingham	0121 246 7000
	Harcourt Chambers, London	0171 353 6961
	Harcourt Chambers, Oxford	01865 791559
Clegg Sebastian James Barwick	Deans Court Chambers, Manchester	0161 214 6000
	Deans Court Chambers, Preston	01772 555163
Close Douglas Jonathan	Serle Court Chambers, London	0171 242 6105
Cooper Gilead Patrick	Chambers of Mr Peter Crampin QC, London	020 7831 0081
Corbett Mrs Sandra Margaret	1 New Square, London	0171 405 0884/5/6/7
Cosedge Andrew John	3 Stone Buildings, London	0171 242 4937
Craig Alistair Trevor	Chambers of Mr Peter Crampin QC, London	020 7831 0081
Crail Miss (Elspeth) Ross	12 New Square, London	0171 419 1212
	Sovereign Chambers, Leeds	0113 2451841/2/3
Crampin Peter	Chambers of Mr Peter Crampin QC, London	020 7831 0081
Cranfield Peter Anthony	3 Verulam Buildings, London	0171 831 8441
Crawford Grant	11 Old Square, London	020 7430 0341
Cunningham Miss Claire Louise	St Philip's Chambers, Birmingham	0121 246 7000
Davey Benjamin Nicholas	11 Old Square, London	020 7430 0341
Davidson Edward Alan	11 Old Square, London	020 7430 0341
Davies Miss (Susan) Louise	12 New Square, London	0171 419 1212
	Sovereign Chambers, Leeds	0113 2451841/2/3
Dean Peter Thomas	1 Crown Office Row, London	0171 583 9292
Dodge Peter Clive	11 Old Square, London	020 7430 0341
Dooher Miss Nancy Helen	St James's Chambers, Manchester	0161 834 7000
Dumont Thomas Julian Bradley	Chambers of Mr Peter Crampin QC, London	020 7831 0081
Eidinow John Samuel Christopher	1 New Square, London	0171 405 0884/5/6/7

       ● Expanded entry in Part D

Elleray Anthony John	• St James's Chambers, Manchester	0161 834 7000
	12 New Square, London	0171 419 1212
	Park Lane Chambers, Leeds	0113 2285000
Etherton Terence Michael Elkan Barnet	• Wilberforce Chambers, London	0171 306 0102
Eyre Stephen John Arthur	1 Fountain Court, Birmingham	0121 236 5721
Fadipe Gabriel Charles	• Wilberforce Chambers, London	0171 306 0102
Faluyi Albert Osamudiamen	Chambers of Martin Burr, London	0171 353 4636
Farrow Kenneth John	Serle Court Chambers, London	0171 242 6105
Fawls Richard Granville	5 Stone Buildings, London	0171 242 6201
Feltham Piers Jonathan	Chambers of Mr Peter Crampin QC, London	020 7831 0081
Francis Andrew James	Chambers of Mr Peter Crampin QC, London	020 7831 0081
Francis Edward Gerald Francis	Enterprise Chambers, London	0171 405 9471
	Enterprise Chambers, Leeds	0113 246 0391
	Enterprise Chambers, Newcastle upon Tyne	0191 222 3344
Fryer-Spedding James Walter	St James's Chambers, Manchester	0161 834 7000
Furness Michael James	• Wilberforce Chambers, London	0171 306 0102
Furze Miss Caroline Mary	• Wilberforce Chambers, London	0171 306 0102
Garcia-Miller Miss Laura	Enterprise Chambers, London	0171 405 9471
	Enterprise Chambers, Leeds	0113 246 0391
	Enterprise Chambers, Newcastle upon Tyne	0191 222 3344
Gasztowicz Steven	2-3 Gray's Inn Square, London	0171 242 4986
	2 New Street, Leicester	0116 2625906
Gee Steven Mark	4 Field Court, London	0171 440 6900
Gerald Nigel Mortimer	Enterprise Chambers, London	0171 405 9471
	Enterprise Chambers, Leeds	0113 246 0391
	Enterprise Chambers, Newcastle upon Tyne	0191 222 3344
Gibson Miss Jill Maureen	Chambers of Mr Peter Crampin QC, London	020 7831 0081
Gifford Andrew James Morris	7 New Square, London	0171 430 1660
Grantham Andrew Timothy	• Deans Court Chambers, Manchester	0161 214 6000
	Deans Court Chambers, Preston	01772 555163
Green Brian Russell	Wilberforce Chambers, London	0171 306 0102
Green David Cameron	Adrian Lyon's Chambers, Liverpool	0151 236 4421/8240
Gregory John Raymond	Deans Court Chambers, Manchester	0161 214 6000
	Deans Court Chambers, Preston	01772 555163
Hall Taylor Alexander Edward	11 Old Square, London	020 7430 0341
Halpern David Anthony	Enterprise Chambers, London	0171 405 9471
	Enterprise Chambers, Leeds	0113 246 0391
	Enterprise Chambers, Newcastle upon Tyne	0191 222 3344
Ham Robert Wallace	• Wilberforce Chambers, London	0171 306 0102
Hantusch Robert Anthony	• 3 Stone Buildings, London	0171 242 4937
Harris Melvyn	7 New Square, London	0171 430 1660
Harrod Henry Mark	5 Stone Buildings, London	0171 242 6201
Henderson Launcelot Dinadan James	5 Stone Buildings, London	0171 242 6201
Henderson William Hugo	Serle Court Chambers, London	0171 242 6105
Herbert Mark Jeremy	• 5 Stone Buildings, London	0171 242 6201
Higgo Justin Beresford	Serle Court Chambers, London	0171 242 6105
Hindmarsh Miss Elizabeth	Plowden Buildings, London	0171 583 0808
Hinks Frank Peter	Serle Court Chambers, London	0171 242 6105
Hoffman David Alexander	8 King Street Chambers, Manchester	0161 834 9560
Horne Roger Cozens-Hardy	Chambers of Mr Peter Crampin QC, London	020 7831 0081
Hoser Philip Jacob	Serle Court Chambers, London	0171 242 6105

B

• Expanded entry in Part D

Hubbard Mark Iain	1 New Square, London	0171 405 0884/5/6/7
Hughes Miss Anna Gabriel	•Wilberforce Chambers, London	0171 306 0102
Hunter William Quigley	No. 1 Serjeants' Inn, London	0171 415 6666
Jackson Dirik George Allan	Chambers of Mr Peter Crampin QC, London	020 7831 0081
Jackson Nicholas David Kingsley	Adrian Lyon's Chambers, Liverpool	0151 236 4421/8240
James-Stadden Miss Jodie Cara	Westgate Chambers, Newcastle upon Tyne	0191 261 4407/2329785
Jefferis Arthur Michael Quentin	Chambers of Mr Peter Crampin QC, London	020 7831 0081
Johnston Anthony Paul	1 Fountain Court, Birmingham	0121 236 5721
Jones Miss Elizabeth Sian	Serle Court Chambers, London	0171 242 6105
Kremen Philip Michael	Hardwicke Building, London	020 7242 2523
Kynoch Duncan Stuart Sanderson	29 Bedford Row Chambers, London	0171 831 2626
Lamont Miss Camilla Rose	Chambers of Lord Goodhart QC, London	0171 405 5577
Lampard Miss Kathryn Felice	1 New Square, London	0171 405 0884/5/6/7
Landes Miss Anna-Rose	St Philip's Chambers, Birmingham	0121 246 7000
Legge Henry	5 Stone Buildings, London	0171 242 6201
Levy Benjamin Keith	Enterprise Chambers, London	0171 405 9471
	Enterprise Chambers, Leeds	0113 246 0391
	Enterprise Chambers, Newcastle upon Tyne	0191 222 3344
Lindqvist Andrew Nils Gunnar	Octagon House, Norwich	01603 623186
Lloyd Stephen James George	Chambers of Mr Peter Crampin QC, London	020 7831 0081
Lowe David Alexander	•Wilberforce Chambers, London	0171 306 0102
Lowry Charles Stephen	Colleton Chambers, Exeter	01392 274898/9
Machell John William	Serle Court Chambers, London	0171 242 6105
Mann George Anthony	Enterprise Chambers, London	0171 405 9471
	Enterprise Chambers, Leeds	0113 246 0391
	Enterprise Chambers, Newcastle upon Tyne	0191 222 3344
Margolin Daniel George	Chambers of Mr Peter Crampin QC, London	020 7831 0081
Martin Mrs Jill Elizabeth	Barnard's Inn Chambers, London	0171 369 6969
Martin John Vandeleur	•Wilberforce Chambers, London	0171 306 0102
Mason Miss Alexandra	3 Stone Buildings, London	0171 242 4937
Maynard-Connor Giles	St James's Chambers, Manchester	0161 834 7000
McDonnell John Beresford William	1 New Square, London	0171 405 0884/5/6/7
McQuail Ms Katherine Emma	11 Old Square, London	020 7430 0341
Mehendale Ms Neelima Krishna	2 Mitre Court Buildings, London	0171 353 1353
Metzer Anthony David Erwin	Doughty Street Chambers, London	0171 404 1313
Morgan Richard Hugo Lyndon	13 Old Square, London	0171 404 4800
Newman Miss Catherine Mary	•13 Old Square, London	0171 404 4800
Newman Paul Lance	•Wilberforce Chambers, London	0171 306 0102
Norris Alastair Hubert	5 Stone Buildings, London	0171 242 6201
	Southernhay Chambers, Exeter	01392 255777
Nugee Edward George	•Wilberforce Chambers, London	0171 306 0102
Nurse Gordon Bramwell William	11 Old Square, London	020 7430 0341
O'Leary Robert Michael	33 Park Place, Cardiff	02920 233313
O'Sullivan Michael Morton	5 Stone Buildings, London	0171 242 6201
Oakley Anthony James	•11 Old Square, London	020 7430 0341
Ohrenstein Dov	Chambers of Lord Goodhart QC, London	0171 405 5577
Ovey Miss Elizabeth Helen	11 Old Square, London	020 7430 0341
Pearce Robert Edgar	Chambers of Mr Peter Crampin QC, London	020 7831 0081
Peel Robert Roger	29 Bedford Row Chambers, London	0171 831 2626
Pilkington Mrs Mavis Patricia	9 Woodhouse Square, Leeds	0113 2451986
Pimentel Carlos de Serpa Alberto Legg	3 Stone Buildings, London	0171 242 4937

     • Expanded entry in Part D

Porter David Leonard	St James's Chambers, Manchester	0161 834 7000
	Park Lane Chambers, Leeds	0113 2285000
Prasad Krishna	21 Craven Road, Kingston-Upon-Thames	0181 974 6799
Prentis Sebastian Hugh Runton	1 New Square, London	0171 405 0884/5/6/7
Proudman Miss Sonia Rosemary Susan	Chambers of Mr Peter Crampin QC, London	020 7831 0081
Purdie Robert Anthony James	28 Western Road, Oxford	01865 204911
Purkis Ms Kathryn Miranda	Serle Court Chambers, London	0171 242 6105
Purves Gavin Bowman	Swan House, London	0181 998 3035
Radevsky Anthony Eric	Falcon Chambers, London	0171 353 2484
Randall John Yeoman	St Philip's Chambers, Birmingham	0121 246 7000
	7 Stone Buildings, London	0171 405 3886/242 3546
Rashid Omar	Chambers of Mr Peter Crampin QC, London	020 7831 0081
Reed John William Rupert	• Wilberforce Chambers, London	0171 306 0102
Rees David Benjamin	5 Stone Buildings, London	0171 242 6201
Renfree Peter Gerald Stanley	Harbour Court Chambers, Fareham	01329 827828
Rich Miss Ann Barbara	5 Stone Buildings, London	0171 242 6201
Richardson Giles John	Serle Court Chambers, London	0171 242 6105
Rogers Miss Beverly-Ann	Serle Court Chambers, London	0171 242 6105
Ross Martyn John Greaves	• 5 New Square, London	020 7404 0404
Rowell David Stewart	Chambers of Lord Goodhart QC, London	0171 405 5577
Rumney Conrad William Arthur	St Philip's Chambers, Birmingham	0121 246 7000
Russell Christopher Garnet	• 12 New Square, London	0171 419 1212
	Sovereign Chambers, Leeds	0113 2451841/2/3
Sagar (Edward) Leigh	12 New Square, London	0171 419 1212
	Newport Chambers, Newport	01633 267403/255855
	Sovereign Chambers, Leeds	0113 2451841/2/3
Sandells Ms Nicole	11 Old Square, London	020 7430 0341
Sartin Leon James	5 Stone Buildings, London	0171 242 6201
Sellers Graham	Adrian Lyon's Chambers, Liverpool	0151 236 4421/8240
Selway Dr Katherine Emma	11 Old Square, London	020 7430 0341
Semken Christopher Richard	1 New Square, London	0171 405 0884/5/6/7
Seymour Thomas Oliver	• Wilberforce Chambers, London	0171 306 0102
Sher Jules	• Wilberforce Chambers, London	0171 306 0102
Shillingford George Miles	Chambers of Mr Peter Crampin QC, London	020 7831 0081
Simmonds Andrew John	5 Stone Buildings, London	0171 242 6201
Smith Howard James	Chambers of Mr Peter Crampin QC, London	020 7831 0081
Spicer Robert Haden	Frederick Place Chambers, Bristol	0117 9738667
Staddon Miss Claire Ann	12 New Square, London	0171 419 1212
	Sovereign Chambers, Leeds	0113 2451841/2/3
Staddon Paul	2nd Floor, Francis Taylor Building, London	0171 353 9942/3157
Staunton (Thomas) Ulick (Patrick)	Chambers of Mr Peter Crampin QC, London	020 7831 0081
	65-67 King Street, Leicester	0116 2547710
Sterling Robert Alan	St James's Chambers, Manchester	0161 834 7000
	12 New Square, London	0171 419 1212
	Park Lane Chambers, Leeds	0113 2285000
Stevens-Hoare Miss Michelle	Hardwicke Building, London	020 7242 2523
Stewart Nicholas John Cameron	Hardwicke Building, London	020 7242 2523
Stewart-Smith William Rodney	1 New Square, London	0171 405 0884/5/6/7
Studer Mark Edgar Walter	Chambers of Mr Peter Crampin QC, London	020 7831 0081
Swerling Robert Harry	13 Old Square, London	0171 404 4800
Talbot Patrick John	Serle Court Chambers, London	0171 242 6105
Taussig Anthony Christopher	• Wilberforce Chambers, London	0171 306 0102
Templeman Michael Richard	Southernhay Chambers, Exeter	01392 255777
	5 Stone Buildings, London	0171 242 6201

• Expanded entry in Part D

Terry Robert Jeffrey	8 King Street Chambers, Manchester	0161 834 9560
Thomas Nigel Matthew	13 Old Square, London	0171 404 4800
Tidmarsh Christopher Ralph Francis	5 Stone Buildings, London	0171 242 6201
Tipples Miss Amanda Jane	13 Old Square, London	0171 404 4800
Trace Anthony John	• 13 Old Square, London	0171 404 4800
Tully Ms Anne Margaret	Eastbourne Chambers, Eastbourne	01323 642102
Walker Andrew Greenfield	Chambers of Lord Goodhart QC, London	0171 405 5577
Warner David Alexander	1 New Square, London	0171 405 0884/5/6/7
Warnock-Smith Mrs Shan	5 Stone Buildings, London	0171 242 6201
Warren Nicholas Roger	• Wilberforce Chambers, London	0171 306 0102
Waters Malcolm Ian	• 11 Old Square, London	020 7430 0341
Weatherill Bernard Richard	Chambers of Lord Goodhart QC, London	0171 405 5577
West Mark	• 11 Old Square, London	020 7430 0341
Whittaker John Percival	Serle Court Chambers, London	0171 242 6105
Williams Andrew Arthur	Adrian Lyon's Chambers, Liverpool	0151 236 4421/8240
Wilson-Barnes Miss Lucy Emma	St James's Chambers, Manchester	0161 834 7000
Wyvill Alistair	St Philip's Chambers, Birmingham	0121 246 7000
Zelin Geoffrey Andrew	Enterprise Chambers, London	0171 405 9471
	Enterprise Chambers, Leeds	0113 246 0391
	Enterprise Chambers, Newcastle upon Tyne	0191 222 3344

EUROPEAN LAW

Mercer Hugh Charles	• Essex Court Chambers, London	0171 813 8000

EXTRADITION

Enoch Dafydd Huw	Bridewell Chambers, London	020 7797 8800

FAMILY

Adams Christopher Alan	St Philip's Chambers, Birmingham	0121 246 7000
Adams Miss Lorraine Joan	Pulteney Chambers, Bath	01225 723987
Adejumo Mrs Hilda Ekpo	Temple Chambers, London	0171 583 1001 (2 lines)
Ahmed Farooq Tahir	8 King Street Chambers, Manchester	0161 834 9560
	3 Dr Johnson's Buildings, London	0171 353 4854
Ahmed Miss Jacqueline Michelle	Southernhay Chambers, Exeter	01392 255777
Akerman Miss Kate Louise	Queen's Chambers, Manchester	0161 834 6875/4738
	Queens Chambers, Preston	01772 828300
Aldous Robert John	Octagon House, Norwich	01603 623186
Alford Robert John	Southernhay Chambers, Exeter	01392 255777
Ali Miss Huma	Eastbourne Chambers, Eastbourne	01323 642102
Allardice Miss Miranda Jane	Pump Court Chambers, London	0171 353 0711
	Pump Court Chambers, Winchester	01962 868161
	Pump Court Chambers, Swindon	01793 539899
Allen Nicholas Paul	29 Bedford Row Chambers, London	0171 831 2626
Allingham-Nicholson Mrs Elizabeth Sarah	2 New Street, Leicester	0116 2625906
Amaouche Miss Sassa-Ann	One Garden Court Family Law Chambers, London	0171 797 7900
Amiraftabi Miss Roshanak	Hardwicke Building, London	020 7242 2523
Ancliffe Mrs Shiva Edwina	Francis Taylor Building, London	0171 353 7768/7769/2711
Arlow Ms Ruth Marian	Pump Court Chambers, London	0171 353 0711
	Pump Court Chambers, Swindon	01793 539899
	Pump Court Chambers, Winchester	01962 868161
Ashley Mark Robert	Pump Court Chambers, Swindon	01793 539899
	Pump Court Chambers, London	0171 353 0711
	Pump Court Chambers, Winchester	01962 868161
Atherton Miss Sally	Bridewell Chambers, London	020 7797 8800
Atkins Charles Edward Spencer	29 Bedford Row Chambers, London	0171 831 2626
Auckland Miss Elizabeth Rachel	30 Park Square, Leeds	0113 2436388
Bagchi Andrew Kumar	One Garden Court Family Law Chambers, London	0171 797 7900

• Expanded entry in Part D

Baker Ms Rachel Mary Theresa	Hardwicke Building, London	020 7242 2523
Baker Stuart Christopher	1 Fountain Court, Birmingham	0121 236 5721
Balchin Richard Alexander	Crown Office Row Chambers, Brighton	01273 625625
Baldock Nicholas John	6 Pump Court, London	0171 797 8400
	6-8 Mill Street, Maidstone	01622 688094
Bancroft Miss Anna Louise	Deans Court Chambers, Manchester	0161 214 6000
	Deans Court Chambers, Preston	01772 555163
Banks Francis Andrew	Adrian Lyon's Chambers, Liverpool	0151 236 4421/8240
Barker John Steven Roy	Queen's Chambers, Manchester	0161 834 6875/4738
	Queens Chambers, Preston	01772 828300
Barker Nicholas	30 Park Square, Leeds	0113 2436388
Barnett Miss Adrienne Elise	8 King's Bench Walk, London	0171 797 8888
	8 King's Bench Walk North, Leeds	0113 2439797
Barnett Miss Sally Louise	2 New Street, Leicester	0116 2625906
Barraclough Richard Michael	6 Pump Court, London	0171 797 8400
	6-8 Mill Street, Maidstone	01622 688094
Barry Miss Kirsten Lesley	8 King Street Chambers, Manchester	0161 834 9560
Barton Alan John	Lamb Building, London	020 7797 7788
Bash-Taqi Mrs Shahineh	Leone Chambers, London	0181 200 4020
Bassa Yousef	St Albans Chambers, St Albans	01727 843383
	Tindal Chambers, Chelmsford	01245 267742
Bastin Alexander Charles	2nd Floor, Francis Taylor Building, London	0171 353 9942/3157
Bazley Miss Janet Clare	One Garden Court Family Law Chambers, London	0171 797 7900
Beasley-Murray Mrs Caroline Wynne	Fenners Chambers, Cambridge	01223 368761
	Fenners Chambers, Peterborough	01733 562030
Bedingfield David Herbert	• 14 Gray's Inn Square, London	0171 242 0858
Bennett John Martyn	• Oriel Chambers, Liverpool	0151 236 7191/236 4321
Bensted Miss Rebecca Claire	Bracton Chambers, London	0171 242 4248
Bergin Timothy William	Crown Office Row Chambers, Brighton	01273 625625
Birk Miss Dewinder	2 New Street, Leicester	0116 2625906
Bishop Miss Keeley Susan	1 Crown Office Row, London	0171 797 7500
	Crown Office Row Chambers, Brighton	01273 625625
Bitmead Paul Graham	Lamb Building, London	020 7797 7788
Black Mrs Jill Margaret	30 Park Square, Leeds	0113 2436388
Blom-Cooper Sir Louis Jacques	Doughty Street Chambers, London	0171 404 1313
Bloom-Davis Desmond Niall Laurence	Pump Court Chambers, Winchester	01962 868161
	Pump Court Chambers, London	0171 353 0711
	Pump Court Chambers, Swindon	01793 539899
Boney Guy Thomas Knowles	Pump Court Chambers, Winchester	01962 868161
	Pump Court Chambers, London	0171 353 0711
	Harrow on the Hill Chambers, Harrow-on-the-Hill	0181 423 7444
	Pump Court Chambers, Swindon	01793 539899
	Eighteen Carlton Crescent, Southampton	01703 639001
Booth Alan James	Deans Court Chambers, Manchester	0161 214 6000
	Deans Court Chambers, Preston	01772 555163
Boothroyd Miss Susan Elizabeth	Westgate Chambers, Newcastle upon Tyne	0191 261 4407/2329785
Boyd Miss Kerstin Margaret	2nd Floor, Francis Taylor Building, London	0171 353 9942/3157
Boydell Edward Patrick Stirrup	Pump Court Chambers, London	0171 353 0711
	Pump Court Chambers, Winchester	01962 868161
	Pump Court Chambers, Swindon	01793 539899
Boyle David Stuart	Deans Court Chambers, Manchester	0161 214 6000
	Deans Court Chambers, Preston	01772 555163
Bradshaw Howard Sydney	Queen's Chambers, Manchester	0161 834 6875/4738
	Queens Chambers, Preston	01772 828300

• Expanded entry in Part D

Breese-Laughran Ms Eleanore   8 King's Bench Walk, London   0171 797 8888
Delphine

                                         8 King's Bench Walk North, Leeds   0113 2439797
Brereton Mrs Fiorella   Peel Court Chambers, Manchester   0161 832 3791
Bresler Fenton Shea   22 Melcombe Regis Court, London   0171 487 5589
Brodwell John Shenton   9 Woodhouse Square, Leeds   0113 2451986
Brody Miss Karen Rachel   Deans Court Chambers, Manchester   0161 214 6000
                                         Deans Court Chambers, Preston   01772 555163
Brown Miss Althea Sonia   Doughty Street Chambers, London   0171 404 1313
Brown Miss Joanne   2 Gray's Inn Square Chambers, London   020 7242 0328
Brunton Sean Alexander McKay   Pump Court Chambers, Winchester   01962 868161
                                         Pump Court Chambers, London   0171 353 0711
                                         Pump Court Chambers, Swindon   01793 539899
Buck Dr Andrew Theodore   Chambers of Martin Burr, London   0171 353 4636
Buckingham Mrs Kathleen   30 Park Square, Leeds   0113 2436388
Rosemary Bernadette
Buckley Peter Evered   Queen's Chambers, Manchester   0161 834 6875/4738
                                         Queens Chambers, Preston   01772 828300
Budaly Miss Susan   One Garden Court Family Law   0171 797 7900
                                            Chambers, London

Bugg Ian Stephen   Crown Office Row Chambers, Brighton   01273 625625
Burden Miss Emma Louise Verena   2 New Street, Leicester   0116 2625906
                                         Sovereign Chambers, Leeds   0113 2451841/2/3
Burdon Michael Stewart   37 Park Square Chambers, Leeds   0113 2439422
Butler Miss Judith Jane Scott   6 Pump Court, London   0171 797 8400
                                         6-8 Mill Street, Maidstone   01622 688094
Butterworth Paul Anthony   Octagon House, Norwich   01603 623186
Buxton Miss Sarah Ruth   1 Fountain Court, Birmingham   0121 236 5721
Cains Ms Linda Hilary   37 Park Square Chambers, Leeds   0113 2439422
Calvert David Edward   St James's Chambers, Manchester   0161 834 7000
Cameron Miss Barbara Alexander   • 2 Harcourt Buildings, London   0171 583 9020
Campbell Miss Alexis Anne   Hardwicke Building, London   020 7242 2523
Campbell Miss Susan Claire   Southernhay Chambers, Exeter   01392 255777
Campbell-Brown Miss Anne Louise   Bracton Chambers, London   0171 242 4248
Cannon Adam Richard   96 Gray's Inn Road, London   0171 405 0585
Carpenter Miss Jane Patricia Anne   2nd Floor, Francis Taylor Building,   0171 353 9942/3157
                                            London

Carr Simon Andrew   9 Gough Square, London   020 7832 0500
Carter Miss Holly Eugenie Sophia   3 Dr Johnson's Buildings, London   0171 353 4854
Carter Miss Rosalyn Frances   St Philip's Chambers, Birmingham   0121 246 7000
Cave Jeremy Stephen   1 Crown Office Row, London   0171 797 7500
                                         Crown Office Row Chambers, Brighton   01273 625625
Chandler Alexander Charles Ross   One Garden Court Family Law   0171 797 7900
                                            Chambers, London

Charles Ms Deborah Ann   6 Pump Court, London   0171 797 8400
                                         6-8 Mill Street, Maidstone   01622 688094
Clark Timothy Noel   2 New Street, Leicester   0116 2625906
Clarke Ms Joanne Elizabeth   33 Bedford Row, London   0171 242 6476
Cobb Stephen William Scott   One Garden Court Family Law   0171 797 7900
                                            Chambers, London

Cole Robert Ian Gawain   30 Park Square, Leeds   0113 2436388
Collier Peter Neville   30 Park Square, Leeds   0113 2436388
Collins Miss Jennifer Clair   Eastbourne Chambers, Eastbourne   01323 642102
Collins Kenneth Guy Wyndham   3 Dr Johnson's Buildings, London   0171 353 4854
Compton Gareth Francis Thomas   22 Old Buildings, London   0171 831 0222
Conrath Philip Bernard   2nd Floor, Francis Taylor Building,   0171 353 9942/3157
                                            London

Cook Miss Alison Noele   St Philip's Chambers, Birmingham   0121 246 7000
Cotterill Miss Susan Amanda   Lamb Building, London   020 7797 7788
Crawford Miss Marie-Bernadette   Eastbourne Chambers, Eastbourne   01323 642102
Claire

• Expanded entry in Part D

Crawforth Miss Emma	Southernhay Chambers, Exeter	01392 255777
Crawley Gary Thomas Bernard	One Garden Court Family Law Chambers, London	0171 797 7900
Cross Mrs Joanna	9 Woodhouse Square, Leeds	0113 2451986
Cruickshank Miss Cynthia Marilyn Benton	1 Gray's Inn Square, London	0171 405 8946/7/8
Da Costa Miss Elissa Josephine	• Arlington Chambers, London	0171 580 9188
Date Julian Richard	17 Bedford Row, London	0171 831 7314
Davies Miss Carol Elizabeth	2 New Street, Leicester	0116 2625906
Davies Miss Lindsay Jane	Fenners Chambers, Cambridge	01223 368761
	Fenners Chambers, Peterborough	01733 562030
De Zonie Miss Jane	14 Gray's Inn Square, London	0171 242 0858
Dean Brian John Anthony	St Philip's Chambers, Birmingham	0121 246 7000
Dean Peter Thomas	1 Crown Office Row, London	0171 583 9292
Dedezade Taner	Tindal Chambers, Chelmsford	01245 267742
deSouza Mrs Josephine Claudia	Chancery Chambers, London	0171 405 6879/6870
Devlin Jonathan Nicholas Ponton	Park Court Chambers, Leeds	0113 2433277
Dodson Miss Joanna	14 Gray's Inn Square, London	0171 242 0858
	Park Court Chambers, Leeds	0113 2433277
Doig Mrs Jeanetta Rose	Neston Home Chambers, Corsham	01225 811909
Downs Martin John	1 Crown Office Row, London	0171 797 7500
	Crown Office Row Chambers, Brighton	01273 625625
Dubbery Mark Edward	Pump Court Chambers, London	0171 353 0711
	Pump Court Chambers, Winchester	01962 868161
	Pump Court Chambers, Swindon	01793 539899
Edge Timothy Richard	Deans Court Chambers, Preston	01772 555163
	Deans Court Chambers, Manchester	0161 214 6000
Edginton Horace Ronald	Becket Chambers, Canterbury	01227 786331
	Westgate Chambers, Lewes	01273 480510
Evans Miss Lisa Claire	St Philip's Chambers, Birmingham	0121 246 7000
Fairbank Nicholas James	Becket Chambers, Canterbury	01227 786331
Faluyi Albert Osamudiamen	Chambers of Martin Burr, London	0171 353 4636
Farquharson Jonathan	Colleton Chambers, Exeter	01392 274898/9
Fenston Miss Felicia Donovan	2 Harcourt Buildings, London	0171 583 9020
Fields Miss Helen Sarah	Pump Court Chambers, Winchester	01962 868161
	Pump Court Chambers, London	0171 353 0711
	Pump Court Chambers, Swindon	01793 539899
Fieldsend James William	2nd Floor, Francis Taylor Building, London	0171 353 9942/3157
Finch Mrs Nadine Elizabeth	Doughty Street Chambers, London	0171 404 1313
Finn Terence	Chambers of Martin Burr, London	0171 353 4636
Fletcher Christopher Michael	Octagon House, Norwich	01603 623186
Forbes Peter George	6 Pump Court, London	0171 797 8400
	6-8 Mill Street, Maidstone	01622 688094
Ford Miss Caroline Emma	37 Park Square Chambers, Leeds	0113 2439422
Ford Gerard James	Baker Street Chambers, Middlesbrough	01642 873873
Ford Miss Monica Dorothy Patience	14 Gray's Inn Square, London	0171 242 0858
Forshaw Miss Sarah Anne	5 King's Bench Walk, London	0171 353 5638
Foster Miss Juliet Kate	Southernhay Chambers, Exeter	01392 255777
Foudy Miss Kim Frances	8 King Street Chambers, Manchester	0161 834 9560
Fox Miss Nicola Susan	One Garden Court Family Law Chambers, London	0171 797 7900
Freeston Miss Lynn Roberta	Hardwicke Building, London	020 7242 2523
Fricker Mrs Marilyn Ann	Sovereign Chambers, Leeds	0113 2451841/2/3
	Farrar's Building, London	0171 583 9241
Frith Nicholas John	30 Park Square, Leeds	0113 2436388
Gardner Miss Eilidh Anne Mairi	22 Old Buildings, London	0171 831 0222
Garner Graham Howard	Southsea Chambers, Portsmouth	01705 291261
Geekie Charles Nairn	One Garden Court Family Law Chambers, London	0171 797 7900
George Donald Eric Joseph	Leone Chambers, London	0181 200 4020

George Miss Susan Deborah	8 King's Bench Walk, London	0171 797 8888
	8 King's Bench Walk North, Leeds	0113 2439797
Gibbons Mrs Sarah Isobel	13 King's Bench Walk, London	0171 353 7204
	King's Bench Chambers, Oxford	01865 311066
Gillibrand Philip Martin Mangnall	Pump Court Chambers, Winchester	01962 868161
	Pump Court Chambers, London	0171 353 0711
	Pump Court Chambers, Swindon	01793 539899
Gilmore Ian Martin	30 Park Square, Leeds	0113 2436388
Ginsburg Mrs Amanda	37 Park Square Chambers, Leeds	0113 2439422
Godfrey Christopher Nicholas	Queen's Chambers, Manchester	0161 834 6875/4738
	Queens Chambers, Preston	01772 828300
Gordon-Saker Mrs Liza Helen	Fenners Chambers, Cambridge	01223 368761
	Fenners Chambers, Peterborough	01733 562030
Gore Andrew Julian Mark	37 Park Square Chambers, Leeds	0113 2439422
Gow Miss Elizabeth Suzanne	Iscoed Chambers, Swansea	01792 652988/9/330
Gray Miss Nichola Jayne	29 Bedford Row Chambers, London	0171 831 2626
Greenan Miss Sarah Octavia	9 Woodhouse Square, Leeds	0113 2451986
Gresty Miss Denise Lynn	Sovereign Chambers, Leeds	0113 2451841/2/3
Grocott Miss Susan	Queen's Chambers, Manchester	0161 834 6875/4738
	Queens Chambers, Preston	01772 828300
Guirguis Miss Sheren	White Friars Chambers, Chester	01244 323070
Haigh Martin James	30 Park Square, Leeds	0113 2436388
Hall Jeremy John	Becket Chambers, Canterbury	01227 786331
Hallam Miss Rona Mary Louise	30 Park Square, Leeds	0113 2436388
Hallowes Rupert John Michael	Britton Street Chambers, London	0171 608 3765
Hamilton-Hague Miss Rachael Elizabeth	8 King Street Chambers, Manchester	0161 834 9560
Hammerton Miss Veronica Lesley	No. 1 Serjeants' Inn, London	0171 415 6666
Hanson Timothy Vincent Richard	St Philip's Chambers, Birmingham	0121 246 7000
Harding Mrs Christine Lauretta Ayodele	Leone Chambers, London	0181 200 4020
Harding Dr Gladys Modwyn Cicely	Leone Chambers, London	0181 200 4020
Hargan James John	30 Park Square, Leeds	0113 2436388
Harington Michael Kenneth	6 Pump Court, London	0171 797 8400
	6-8 Mill Street, Maidstone	01622 688094
Harper Miss Victoria Jane Tryphosa	3 Temple Gardens, London	0171 353 0832
Harrill Miss Jayne Anne	8 King's Bench Walk, London	0171 797 8888
	8 King's Bench Walk North, Leeds	0113 2439797
Harris Melvyn	7 New Square, London	0171 430 1660
Harrison Ms Averil	Chambers of Averil Harrison, London	0181 692 4949
Hassall James Christopher	Southernhay Chambers, Exeter	01392 255777
Hay Miss Fiona Ruth	13 King's Bench Walk, London	0171 353 7204
	King's Bench Chambers, Oxford	01865 311066
Hay Malcolm John Marshall	3 Dr Johnson's Buildings, London	0171 353 4854
Healy Brian Patrick James	St Philip's Chambers, Birmingham	0121 246 7000
Heaton Miss Frances Margaret	Deans Court Chambers, Manchester	0161 214 6000
	Deans Court Chambers, Preston	01772 555163
	4 Brick Court, London	0171 797 7766
Henderson Ian Francis	8 King's Bench Walk, London	0171 797 8888
	8 King's Bench Walk North, Leeds	0113 2439797
Heppenstall Miss Rachael Elizabeth	Sovereign Chambers, Leeds	0113 2451841/2/3
Hershman David Allan	St Philip's Chambers, Birmingham	0121 246 7000
	1 Mitre Court Buildings, London	0171 797 7070
Hill Miss Catherine Louise	30 Park Square, Leeds	0113 2436388
Hobson Miss Heather Fiona	Queen's Chambers, Manchester	0161 834 6875/4738
	Queens Chambers, Preston	01772 828300
Hodgson Ms Jane	9 Woodhouse Square, Leeds	0113 2451986
Hodgson Martin Derrick	8 King's Bench Walk, London	0171 797 8888
	8 King's Bench Walk North, Leeds	0113 2439797

Hogg The Hon Douglas Martin	37 Park Square Chambers, Leeds	0113 2439422
	Cathedral Chambers (Jan Wood	01392 210900
	Independent Barristers' Clerk), Exeter	
Hogg Miss Katharine Elizabeth	1 Crown Office Row, London	0171 797 7500
Holland William	2nd Floor, Francis Taylor Building,	0171 353 9942/3157
	London	
Hollow Paul John	Fenners Chambers, Cambridge	01223 368761
	Fenners Chambers, Peterborough	01733 562030
Holroyd Ms Joanne	37 Park Square Chambers, Leeds	0113 2439422
Horgan Peter Thomas	Queen's Chambers, Manchester	0161 834 6875/4738
	Queens Chambers, Preston	01772 828300
Horton Miss Caroline Ann	Fenners Chambers, Cambridge	01223 368761
	Fenners Chambers, Peterborough	01733 562030
Horton Mark Varney	Colleton Chambers, Exeter	01392 274898/9
Howard Graham John	Pump Court Chambers, Winchester	01962 868161
	Pump Court Chambers, London	0171 353 0711
	Pump Court Chambers, Swindon	01793 539899
Howe Miss Carole Anne	8 King's Bench Walk North, Leeds	0113 2439797
	8 King's Bench Walk, London	0171 797 8888
Howe Miss Penelope Anne Macgregor	Pump Court Chambers, London	0171 353 0711
	Pump Court Chambers, Winchester	01962 868161
	Pump Court Chambers, Swindon	01793 539899
Hoyal Ms Jane	• 1 Pump Court, London	0171 583 2012/353 4341
Huda Miss Abida Alia Jehan	8 King's Bench Walk, London	0171 797 8888
	8 King's Bench Walk North, Leeds	0113 2439797
Hughes Miss Kathryn Ann	Iscoed Chambers, Swansea	01792 652988/9/330
Hutchin Edward Alister David	Bracton Chambers, London	0171 242 4248
Ivens Ms Jemima	8 King's Bench Walk, London	0171 797 8888
	8 King's Bench Walk North, Leeds	0113 2439797
Jackson Peter Arthur Brian	4 Paper Buildings, London	0171 583 0816/353 1131
James Miss Rachael Elizabeth	33 Bedford Row, London	0171 242 6476
Jarman Mark Christopher	14 Gray's Inn Square, London	0171 242 0858
Johnston Miss Justine Jane	4 Paper Buildings, London	0171 583 0816/353 1131
Jones Miss Carolyn Nerys	1 Fountain Court, Birmingham	0121 236 5721
	Clock Chambers, Wolverhampton	01902 313444
Jones Huw Michael Rees	St Albans Chambers, St Albans	01727 843383
Kelly Geoffrey Robert	Pump Court Chambers, London	0171 353 0711
	Pump Court Chambers, Winchester	01962 868161
	Pump Court Chambers, Swindon	01793 539899
Kent Miss Georgina	5 Essex Court, London	0171 410 2000
Kenward Timothy David Nelson	25-27 Castle Street, Liverpool	0151 227 5661/051 236 5072
Ker-Reid John	Pump Court Chambers, London	0171 353 0711
	Pump Court Chambers, Winchester	01962 868161
	Pump Court Chambers, Swindon	01793 539899
Khan Miss Helen Mary Grace	Pump Court Chambers, London	0171 353 0711
	Pump Court Chambers, Winchester	01962 868161
	Pump Court Chambers, Swindon	01793 539899
Khan Saadallah Frans Hassan	55 Temple Chambers, London	0171 353 7400
King-Smith James	1 Crown Office Row, London	0171 797 7500
	Crown Office Row Chambers, Brighton	01273 625625
Kynoch Duncan Stuart Sanderson	29 Bedford Row Chambers, London	0171 831 2626
Ladak Miss Tahera	8 King's Bench Walk, London	0171 797 8888
	8 King's Bench Walk North, Leeds	0113 2439797
Lambert Miss Sarah Katrina	1 Crown Office Row, London	0171 797 7500
Lamberty Mark Julian Harker	Queen's Chambers, Manchester	0161 834 6875/4738
	Queens Chambers, Preston	01772 828300
Langridge Ms Nicola Dawn	Hardwicke Building, London	020 7242 2523
Latimer-Sayer William Laurence	2 Mitre Court Buildings, London	0171 353 1353
Leason Ms Karen Dawn	St Philip's Chambers, Birmingham	0121 246 7000
Lee Miss Taryn Jane	37 Park Square Chambers, Leeds	0113 2439422

Leech Brian Walter Thomas	No. 1 Serjeants' Inn, London	0171 415 6666
Lewis Hugh Wilson	Southernhay Chambers, Exeter	01392 255777
Lewis Jeffrey Allan	9 Woodhouse Square, Leeds	0113 2451986
Lewis Thomas Robin Arwel	St Philip's Chambers, Birmingham	0121 246 7000
Liebrecht John Michael	One Garden Court Family Law Chambers, London	0171 797 7900
Lindqvist Andrew Nils Gunnar	Octagon House, Norwich	01603 623186
Lo Bernard Norman	17 Bedford Row, London	0171 831 7314
Lochrane Damien Horatio Ross	Pump Court Chambers, London	0171 353 0711
	Pump Court Chambers, Winchester	01962 868161
	Pump Court Chambers, Swindon	01793 539899
Lockhart Andrew William Jardine	St Philip's Chambers, Birmingham	0121 246 7000
Lunt Steven	9 Woodhouse Square, Leeds	0113 2451986
MacDonald Alistair William Orchard	St Philip's Chambers, Birmingham	0121 246 7000
Mackenzie Miss Julie Fiona	Colleton Chambers, Exeter	01392 274898/9
	Colleton Chambers, Taunton	01823 324252
	Pump Court Chambers, Swindon	01793 539899
	Pump Court Chambers, London	0171 353 0711
	Pump Court Chambers, Winchester	01962 868161
MacLaren Miss Catriona Longueville	2nd Floor, Francis Taylor Building, London	0171 353 9942/3157
Mainwaring [Robert] Paul Clason	Carmarthen Chambers, Carmarthen	01267 234410
Malhotra Miss Mehtab Roshan	2 Middle Temple Lane, London	0171 583 4540
Mandalia Vinesh Lalji	Harrow on the Hill Chambers, Harrow-on-the-Hill	0181 423 7444
Manuel Miss Elizabeth	Eighteen Carlton Crescent, Southampton	01703 639001
Marks Miss Jacqueline Stephanie	2 Gray's Inn Square Chambers, London	020 7242 0328
Marley Miss Sarah Anne	5 Pump Court, London	020 7353 2532
Mathew Miss Nergis-Anne	2 Gray's Inn Square Chambers, London	020 7242 0328
	St Philip's Chambers, Birmingham	0121 246 7000
McAlinden Barry O'Neill	17 Bedford Row, London	0171 831 7314
McAllister Miss Eimear Jane	9 Woodhouse Square, Leeds	0113 2451986
McBride Gavin John	Peel Court Chambers, Manchester	0161 832 3791
McCabe Miss Louise Anne	St Philip's Chambers, Birmingham	0121 246 7000
McCahey Miss Catherine Anne Mary	St Philip's Chambers, Birmingham	0121 246 7000
McCourt Christopher	22 Old Buildings, London	0171 831 0222
McGrath Miss Elizabeth Ann	St Philip's Chambers, Birmingham	0121 246 7000
McHugh Denis David	Bracton Chambers, London	0171 242 4248
Meachin Miss (Sarah) Vanessa Veronica	St Philip's Chambers, Birmingham	0121 246 7000
Mehendale Ms Neelima Krishna	2 Mitre Court Buildings, London	0171 353 1353
Melly Miss Kama Louise	37 Park Square Chambers, Leeds	0113 2439422
Mercer David Paul	Queen's Chambers, Manchester	0161 834 6875/4738
	Queens Chambers, Preston	01772 828300
Meredith George Hubbard	Southernhay Chambers, Exeter	01392 255777
Merry Hugh Gairns	17 Carlton Crescent, Southampton	023 8032 0320/0823 2003
Messling Lawrence David	St Philip's Chambers, Birmingham	0121 246 7000
Mills Corey Arthur	Becket Chambers, Canterbury	01227 786331
Minhas Ms Rafhat	Leone Chambers, London	0181 200 4020
Mitropoulos Christos	Chambers of Geoffrey Hawker, London	0171 583 8899
Moat Frank Robert	Pump Court Chambers, London	0171 353 0711
	Pump Court Chambers, Winchester	01962 868161
	Pump Court Chambers, Swindon	01793 539899
Moore Roderick Andrew McGowan	3 Temple Gardens, London	0171 353 0832
Moseley Miss Julie Ruth	St Philip's Chambers, Birmingham	0121 246 7000
Mulholland Michael	St James's Chambers, Manchester	0161 834 7000
Munby James Lawrence	1 New Square, London	0171 405 0884/5/6/7
Munday Miss Anne Margaret	8 King's Bench Walk North, Leeds	0113 2439797
	8 King's Bench Walk, London	0171 797 8888
Murphy Miss Nicola Jane	4 King's Bench Walk, London	0171 822 8822
Murray Miss Judith Rowena	4 Paper Buildings, London	0171 583 0816/353 1131

Naish Christopher John	Southernhay Chambers, Exeter	01392 255777
Newbold Ronald Edgar	St Philip's Chambers, Birmingham	0121 246 7000
Newton Philip	Becket Chambers, Canterbury	01227 786331
Newton-Price James Edward	Pump Court Chambers, London	0171 353 0711
	Pump Court Chambers, Winchester	01962 868161
	Pump Court Chambers, Swindon	01793 539899
Niblett Anthony Ian	1 Crown Office Row, London	0171 797 7500
	Crown Office Row Chambers, Brighton	01273 625625
Nuvoloni Stefano Vincenzo	• 22 Old Buildings, London	0171 831 0222
O'Donoghue Florence	2 Mitre Court Buildings, London	0171 353 1353
O'Donovan Ronan Daniel James	14 Gray's Inn Square, London	0171 242 0858
O'Flynn Timothy James	Pump Court Chambers, Winchester	01962 868161
	Pump Court Chambers, London	0171 353 0711
	Pump Court Chambers, Swindon	01793 539899
O'Sullivan Michael Neil	5 King's Bench Walk, London	0171 353 5638
Ofori George Edward	ACHMA Chambers, London	0171 639 7817/0171 635 7904
	Chancery Chambers, London	0171 405 6879/6870
Ogle Miss Rebecca Theodosia Abigail	Southernhay Chambers, Exeter	01392 255777
Oliver Miss Juliet Dianne	Bridewell Chambers, London	020 7797 8800
Osman Robert Walter	Queen's Chambers, Manchester	0161 834 6875/4738
	Queens Chambers, Preston	01772 828300
Owens Mrs Lucy Isabel	13 King's Bench Walk, London	0171 353 7204
	King's Bench Chambers, Oxford	01865 311066
Panton William Dwight	Britton Street Chambers, London	0171 608 3765
Parker John	2 Mitre Court Buildings, London	0171 353 1353
Parry Simon Edward	White Friars Chambers, Chester	01244 323070
Pawson Robert Edward Cruickshank	Pump Court Chambers, Winchester	01962 868161
	Pump Court Chambers, London	0171 353 0711
	Pump Court Chambers, Swindon	01793 539899
Peacock Miss Lisa Jayne	3 Dr Johnson's Buildings, London	0171 353 4854
Pears Derrick Allan	2nd Floor, Francis Taylor Building, London	0171 353 9942/3157
Peirson Oliver James	Pump Court Chambers, London	0171 353 0711
	Pump Court Chambers, Winchester	01962 868161
	Pump Court Chambers, Swindon	01793 539899
Pema Anes Bhumin Laloo	9 Woodhouse Square, Leeds	0113 2451986
Pipi Chukwuemeka Ezekiel	Chambers of Martin Burr, London	0171 353 4636
Platt Miss Eleanor Frances	One Garden Court Family Law Chambers, London	0171 797 7900
Plimmer Miss Melanie Ann	Chambers of Ian Macdonald QC (In Association with Two Garden Court, Temple, London), Manchester	0161 236 1840
Portnoy Leslie Reuben	Chambers of John Hand QC, Manchester	0161 955 9000
Pote Andrew Thomas	13 King's Bench Walk, London	0171 353 7204
	King's Bench Chambers, Oxford	01865 311066
Pounder Gerard	5 Essex Court, London	0171 410 2000
Poyer-Sleeman Ms Patricia	Pump Court Chambers, London	0171 353 0711
	Pump Court Chambers, Winchester	01962 868161
	Pump Court Chambers, Swindon	01793 539899
Prasad Krishna	21 Craven Road, Kingston-Upon-Thames	0181 974 6799
Price Miss Collette	St James's Chambers, Manchester	0161 834 7000
Price John Scott	10 Launceston Avenue, Reading	01189 479548
	Southsea Chambers, Portsmouth	01705 291261
	Cathedral Chambers, Newcastle upon Tyne	0191 232 1311
Prinn Miss Helen Elizabeth	Octagon House, Norwich	01603 623186
Prudhoe Timothy Nixon	Queen's Chambers, Manchester	0161 834 6875/4738
	Queens Chambers, Preston	01772 828300
Pulling Dean	Iscoed Chambers, Swansea	01792 652988/9/330

Pulman George Frederick	Hardwicke Building, London	020 7242 2523
	Stour Chambers, Canterbury	01227 764899
Purdie Robert Anthony James	28 Western Road, Oxford	01865 204911
Pye Miss Margaret Jane	Sovereign Chambers, Leeds	0113 2451841/2/3
Ramsahoye Miss Indira Kim	Hardwicke Building, London	020 7242 2523
Ratcliffe Miss Anne Kirkpatrick	5 Pump Court, London	020 7353 2532
Raybaud Mrs June Rose	96 Gray's Inn Road, London	0171 405 0585
Rayson Miss Jane Vivienne	2 Gray's Inn Square Chambers, London	020 7242 0328
Redford Miss Jessica Kate	3 Dr Johnson's Buildings, London	0171 353 4854
Reid Paul William	13 King's Bench Walk, London	0171 353 7204
	King's Bench Chambers, Oxford	01865 311066
Reid Sebastian Peter Scott	2nd Floor, Francis Taylor Building, London	0171 353 9942/3157
Renfree Peter Gerald Stanley	Harbour Court Chambers, Fareham	01329 827828
Richards Jeremy Simon	Octagon House, Norwich	01603 623186
Rigby Miss Charity Elizabeth	Sovereign Chambers, Leeds	0113 2451841/2/3
Robinson Ms Tanya Lin	6 Pump Court, London	0171 797 8400
	6-8 Mill Street, Maidstone	01622 688094
Rogers Paul John	1 Crown Office Row, London	0171 797 7500
	Crown Office Row Chambers, Brighton	01273 625625
Rosenblatt Jeremy George	4 Paper Buildings, London	0171 583 0816/353 1131
Ross Miss Jacqueline Gordon	Crown Office Row Chambers, Brighton	01273 625625
Rothery Peter	Queen's Chambers, Manchester	0161 834 6875/4738
	Queens Chambers, Preston	01772 828300
Rowe Miss Judith May	• One Garden Court Family Law Chambers, London	0171 797 7900
Rudd Matthew Allan	11 Bolt Court (also at 7 Stone Buildings – 1st Floor), London	0171 353 2300
	Redhill Chambers, Redhill	01737 780781
	7 Stone Buildings (also at 11 Bolt Court), London	0171 242 0961
Ryan Miss Eithne Mary Catherine	Hardwicke Building, London	020 7242 2523
Ryder Ernest Nigel	Deans Court Chambers, Manchester	0161 214 6000
	Deans Court Chambers, Preston	01772 555163
	1 Mitre Court Buildings, London	0171 797 7070
Rylands Miss Margaret Elizabeth	8 King Street Chambers, Manchester	0161 834 9560
Samuels Leslie John	Pump Court Chambers, London	0171 353 0711
	Pump Court Chambers, Winchester	01962 868161
	Pump Court Chambers, Swindon	01793 539899
Sandbrook-Hughes Stewert Karl Anthony	Iscoed Chambers, Swansea	01792 652988/9/330
Sapnara Miss Khatun	8 King's Bench Walk, London	0171 797 8888
	8 King's Bench Walk North, Leeds	0113 2439797
Scott Miss Alexandra Elisabeth	2 New Street, Leicester	0116 2625906
Scott-Manderson Marcus Charles William	4 Paper Buildings, London	0171 583 0816/353 1131
Shale Justin Anton	4 King's Bench Walk, London	0171 822 8822
	King's Bench Chambers, Bournemouth	01202 250025
Sheldrake Miss Christine Anne	3 Dr Johnson's Buildings, London	0171 353 4854
Shield Miss Deborah	White Friars Chambers, Chester	01244 323070
Shiels Ian	30 Park Square, Leeds	0113 2436388
Shoker Makkan Singh	St Philip's Chambers, Birmingham	0121 246 7000
Shuman Miss Karen Ann Elizabeth	Bracton Chambers, London	0171 242 4248
Siddiqi Faizul Aqtab	Justice Court Chambers, London	0181 830 7786
Slaughter Andrew Francis	Bridewell Chambers, London	020 7797 8800
Slowe Miss Emily Jane	Chancery Chambers, London	0171 405 6879/6870
Small Mrs Arlene Ann-Marie	Francis Taylor Building, London	0171 353 7768/7769/2711
Smith Adam John	Crown Office Row Chambers, Brighton	01273 625625
Smith Matthew Robert	Sovereign Chambers, Leeds	0113 2451841/2/3
Smith Nicholas Martin	1 Fountain Court, Birmingham	0121 236 5721
Smith Miss Sally-Ann	Crown Office Row Chambers, Brighton	01273 625625

B

                                           • Expanded entry in Part D

Solomons Mrs Ellen Betty	One Garden Court Family Law Chambers, London	0171 797 7900
Spinks Roderick Cameron	Fenners Chambers, Cambridge	01223 368761
	Fenners Chambers, Peterborough	01733 562030
Spollon Guy Merton	St Philip's Chambers, Birmingham	0121 246 7000
Sternberg Michael Vivian	• 4 Paper Buildings, London	0171 583 0816/353 1131
Stewart Ms Alexandra Mary Hamilton	30 Park Square, Leeds	0113 2436388
Stocker John Crispin	One Garden Court Family Law Chambers, London	0171 797 7900
Stone Miss Sally Victoria	One Garden Court Family Law Chambers, London	0171 797 7900
Styles Clive Richard	Becket Chambers, Canterbury	01227 786331
Swindells Miss Heather Hughson	Chambers of Michael Pert QC, London	0171 421 8000
	Chambers of Michael Pert QC, Leicester	0116 249 2020
	Chambers of Michael Pert QC, Northampton	01604 602333
	St Philip's Chambers, Birmingham	0121 246 7000
Syed Mohammad Ali	39 Park Avenue, Mitcham	0181 648 1684
	Tower Hamlets Barristers Chambers, London	0171 247 9825
Szanto Gregory John Michael	Eastbourne Chambers, Eastbourne	01323 642102
Taft Christopher Heiton	St James's Chambers, Manchester	0161 834 7000
Tankel Mrs Ruth Shoshana	St James's Chambers, Manchester	0161 834 7000
Teeman Miss Miriam Joy	30 Park Square, Leeds	0113 2436388
Thain Miss Ashley	East Anglian Chambers, Colchester	01206 572756
	East Anglian Chambers, Ipswich	01473 214481
	East Anglian Chambers, Norwich	01603 617351
Thomas Stephen Edward Owen	St Philip's Chambers, Birmingham	0121 246 7000
Thompson Miss Blondelle Marguerite	1 Fountain Court, Birmingham	0121 236 5721
Thompson Jonathan Richard	8 King Street Chambers, Manchester	0161 834 9560
Tighe Miss Dawn	37 Park Square Chambers, Leeds	0113 2439422
Townshend Timothy John Hume	Octagon House, Norwich	01603 623186
Travers Hugh	Pump Court Chambers, London	0171 353 0711
	Pump Court Chambers, Winchester	01962 868161
	Pump Court Chambers, Swindon	01793 539899
Turner David George Patrick	14 Gray's Inn Square, London	0171 242 0858
Tyack David Guy	St Philip's Chambers, Birmingham	0121 246 7000
Tyler William John	30 Park Square, Leeds	0113 2436388
Tyzack David Ian Heslop	Southernhay Chambers, Exeter	01392 255777
	1 Mitre Court Buildings, London	0171 797 7070
Ullstein Augustus Rupert Patrick A	• 29 Bedford Row Chambers, London	0171 831 2626
Underhill Miss Alison	Tindal Chambers, Chelmsford	01245 267742
Waddicor Miss Janet	1 Crown Office Row, London	0171 797 7500
	Crown Office Row Chambers, Brighton	01273 625625
Waddington Mrs Anne Louise	Pump Court Chambers, London	0171 353 0711
	Pump Court Chambers, Winchester	01962 868161
	Pump Court Chambers, Swindon	01793 539899
Wagstaffe Christopher David	New Court Chambers, London	0171 831 9500
Walker Mrs Elizabeth Mary	St Philip's Chambers, Birmingham	0121 246 7000
Walker Mrs Susannah Mary	One Garden Court Family Law Chambers, London	0171 797 7900
Wallbanks Miss Joanne	1 Fountain Court, Birmingham	0121 236 5721
	Rowchester Chambers, Birmingham	0121 233 2327/2361951
Ward Mrs Annie Frances	Pump Court Chambers, London	0171 353 0711
	Pump Court Chambers, Swindon	01793 539899
	Pump Court Chambers, Winchester	01962 868161
Ward Simon John	1 Fountain Court, Birmingham	0121 236 5721
Warrender Miss Nichola Mary	New Court Chambers, London	0171 831 9500
Watkin Toby Paul	22 Old Buildings, London	0171 831 0222

B

• Expanded entry in Part D

Webb Stanley George	The Chambers of Mr Ali Mohammed Azhar, London	0171 353 9564
	Bracton Chambers, London	0171 242 4248
Wenlock Miss Heather	13 King's Bench Walk, London	0171 353 7204
	King's Bench Chambers, Oxford	01865 311066
Wheeldon Miss Sarah Helen Elizabeth	St James's Chambers, Manchester	0161 834 7000
White Timothy Richard	30 Park Square, Leeds	0113 2436388
Williams Miss Caroline Sarah	Maidstone Chambers, Maidstone	01622 688592
Williams Hugh David Haydn	St Philip's Chambers, Birmingham	0121 246 7000
Williams Paul Robert	8 King's Bench Walk North, Leeds	0113 2439797
	8 King's Bench Walk, London	0171 797 8888
Wills Miss Janice Marie	St James's Chambers, Manchester	0161 834 7000
Wilson Gerald Simon John	2nd Floor, Francis Taylor Building, London	0171 353 9942/3157
Wilson Myles Brennand	White Friars Chambers, Chester	01244 323070
Winzer Benjamin Charles	Southernhay Chambers, Exeter	01392 255777
Worrall Miss Shirley Vera Frances	8 King Street Chambers, Manchester	0161 834 9560
Wright Miss Clare Elizabeth	6 Pump Court, London	0171 797 8400
	6-8 Mill Street, Maidstone	01622 688094
Wyatt Mark	2 New Street, Leicester	0116 2625906
Young Alastair Angus McLeod	St Philip's Chambers, Birmingham	0121 246 7000

FAMILY MEDIATION

Hall Jeremy John	Becket Chambers, Canterbury	01227 786331

FAMILY PROVISION

Acton Stephen Neil	11 Old Square, London	020 7430 0341
Adams Miss Lorraine Joan	Pulteney Chambers, Bath	01225 723987
Akerman Miss Kate Louise	Queen's Chambers, Manchester	0161 834 6875/4738
	Queens Chambers, Preston	01772 828300
Aldous Robert John	Octagon House, Norwich	01603 623186
Alford Robert John	Southernhay Chambers, Exeter	01392 255777
Allardice Miss Miranda Jane	Pump Court Chambers, London	0171 353 0711
	Pump Court Chambers, Winchester	01962 868161
	Pump Court Chambers, Swindon	01793 539899
Allen Nicholas Paul	29 Bedford Row Chambers, London	0171 831 2626
Allingham-Nicholson Mrs Elizabeth Sarah	2 New Street, Leicester	0116 2625906
Amaouche Miss Sassa-Ann	One Garden Court Family Law Chambers, London	0171 797 7900
Amiraftabi Miss Roshanak	Hardwicke Building, London	020 7242 2523
Angus Miss Tracey Anne	5 Stone Buildings, London	0171 242 6201
Asprey Nicholas	Serle Court Chambers, London	0171 242 6105
Atherton Miss Sally	Bridewell Chambers, London	020 7797 8800
Atkins Charles Edward Spencer	29 Bedford Row Chambers, London	0171 831 2626
Auckland Miss Elizabeth Rachel	30 Park Square, Leeds	0113 2436388
Ayres Andrew John William	13 Old Square, London	0171 404 4800
Baker Ms Rachel Mary Theresa	Hardwicke Building, London	020 7242 2523
Baldock Nicholas John	6 Pump Court, London	0171 797 8400
	6-8 Mill Street, Maidstone	01622 688094
Banks Francis Andrew	Adrian Lyon's Chambers, Liverpool	0151 236 4421/8240
Barker Nicholas	30 Park Square, Leeds	0113 2436388
Barker Simon George Harry	• 13 Old Square, London	0171 404 4800
Barnett Miss Adrienne Elise	8 King's Bench Walk, London	0171 797 8888
	8 King's Bench Walk North, Leeds	0113 2439797
Barnett Miss Sally Louise	2 New Street, Leicester	0116 2625906
Barry Miss Kirsten Lesley	8 King Street Chambers, Manchester	0161 834 9560
Barton Alan John	Lamb Building, London	020 7797 7788
Bazley Miss Janet Clare	One Garden Court Family Law Chambers, London	0171 797 7900

• Expanded entry in Part D

Beasley-Murray Mrs Caroline Wynne	Fenners Chambers, Cambridge	01223 368761
	Fenners Chambers, Peterborough	01733 562030
Beaumont Marc Clifford	• Harrow on the Hill Chambers, Harrow-on-the-Hill	0181 423 7444
	Windsor Barristers' Chambers, Windsor	01753 648899
	Pump Court Chambers, London	0171 353 0711
Bedingfield David Herbert	• 14 Gray's Inn Square, London	0171 242 0858
Behrens James Nicholas Edward	Serle Court Chambers, London	0171 242 6105
Bennett John Martyn	• Oriel Chambers, Liverpool	0151 236 7191/236 4321
Birk Miss Dewinder	2 New Street, Leicester	0116 2625906
Bishop Miss Keeley Susan	1 Crown Office Row, London	0171 797 7500
	Crown Office Row Chambers, Brighton	01273 625625
Black Mrs Jill Margaret	30 Park Square, Leeds	0113 2436388
Blackett-Ord Mark	• 5 Stone Buildings, London	0171 242 6201
Bloom-Davis Desmond Niall Laurence	Pump Court Chambers, Winchester	01962 868161
	Pump Court Chambers, London	0171 353 0711
	Pump Court Chambers, Swindon	01793 539899
Booth Alan James	Deans Court Chambers, Manchester	0161 214 6000
	Deans Court Chambers, Preston	01772 555163
Boothroyd Miss Susan Elizabeth	Westgate Chambers, Newcastle upon Tyne	0191 261 4407/2329785
Boyd Miss Kerstin Margaret	2nd Floor, Francis Taylor Building, London	0171 353 9942/3157
Boydell Edward Patrick Stirrup	Pump Court Chambers, London	0171 353 0711
	Pump Court Chambers, Winchester	01962 868161
	Pump Court Chambers, Swindon	01793 539899
Bradshaw Howard Sydney	Queen's Chambers, Manchester	0161 834 6875/4738
	Queens Chambers, Preston	01772 828300
Breese-Laughran Ms Eleanore Delphine	8 King's Bench Walk, London	0171 797 8888
	8 King's Bench Walk North, Leeds	0113 2439797
Brereton Mrs Fiorella	Peel Court Chambers, Manchester	0161 832 3791
Brodwell John Shenton	9 Woodhouse Square, Leeds	0113 2451986
Brody Miss Karen Rachel	Deans Court Chambers, Manchester	0161 214 6000
	Deans Court Chambers, Preston	01772 555163
Brown Miss Joanne	2 Gray's Inn Square Chambers, London	020 7242 0328
Bryant Miss Judith Anne	• Wilberforce Chambers, London	0171 306 0102
Buck Dr Andrew Theodore	Chambers of Martin Burr, London	0171 353 4636
Buckley Peter Evered	Queen's Chambers, Manchester	0161 834 6875/4738
	Queens Chambers, Preston	01772 828300
Budaly Miss Susan	One Garden Court Family Law Chambers, London	0171 797 7900
Burden Miss Emma Louise Verena	2 New Street, Leicester	0116 2625906
	Sovereign Chambers, Leeds	0113 2451841/2/3
Burdon Michael Stewart	37 Park Square Chambers, Leeds	0113 2439422
Burr Martin John	Chambers of Martin Burr, London	0171 353 4636
	7 New Square, London	0171 430 1660
Butterworth Paul Anthony	Octagon House, Norwich	01603 623186
Buxton Miss Sarah Ruth	1 Fountain Court, Birmingham	0121 236 5721
Cains Ms Linda Hilary	37 Park Square Chambers, Leeds	0113 2439422
Calvert David Edward	St James's Chambers, Manchester	0161 834 7000
Cameron Miss Barbara Alexander	• 2 Harcourt Buildings, London	0171 583 9020
Campbell Miss Alexis Anne	Hardwicke Building, London	020 7242 2523
Cannon Adam Richard	96 Gray's Inn Road, London	0171 405 0585
Carr Simon Andrew	9 Gough Square, London	020 7832 0500
Carter Miss Holly Eugenie Sophia	3 Dr Johnson's Buildings, London	0171 353 4854
Carter Miss Rosalyn Frances	St Philip's Chambers, Birmingham	0121 246 7000
Cave Jeremy Stephen	1 Crown Office Row, London	0171 797 7500
	Crown Office Row Chambers, Brighton	01273 625625

Chandler Alexander Charles Ross	One Garden Court Family Law Chambers, London	0171 797 7900
Clark Timothy Noel	2 New Street, Leicester	0116 2625906
Clarke Miss Anna Victoria	5 Stone Buildings, London	0171 242 6201
Clarke Ms Joanne Elizabeth	33 Bedford Row, London	0171 242 6476
Clarke Peter John	St Philip's Chambers, Birmingham	0121 246 7000
	Harcourt Chambers, London	0171 353 6961
	Harcourt Chambers, Oxford	01865 791559
Cobb Stephen William Scott	One Garden Court Family Law Chambers, London	0171 797 7900
Cole Robert Ian Gawain	30 Park Square, Leeds	0113 2436388
Collins Kenneth Guy Wyndham	3 Dr Johnson's Buildings, London	0171 353 4854
Conrath Philip Bernard	2nd Floor, Francis Taylor Building, London	0171 353 9942/3157
Cook Miss Alison Noele	St Philip's Chambers, Birmingham	0121 246 7000
Cooper Gilead Patrick	Chambers of Mr Peter Crampin QC, London	020 7831 0081
Crail Miss (Elspeth) Ross	12 New Square, London	0171 419 1212
	Sovereign Chambers, Leeds	0113 2451841/2/3
Crawford Grant	11 Old Square, London	020 7430 0341
Crawford Miss Marie-Bernadette Claire	Eastbourne Chambers, Eastbourne	01323 642102
Crawley Gary Thomas Bernard	One Garden Court Family Law Chambers, London	0171 797 7900
Cross Mrs Joanna	9 Woodhouse Square, Leeds	0113 2451986
Cruickshank Miss Cynthia Marilyn Benton	1 Gray's Inn Square, London	0171 405 8946/7/8
Da Costa Miss Elissa Josephine	• Arlington Chambers, London	0171 580 9188
Date Julian Richard	17 Bedford Row, London	0171 831 7314
Davies Miss Carol Elizabeth	2 New Street, Leicester	0116 2625906
Davies Miss Lindsay Jane	Fenners Chambers, Cambridge	01223 368761
	Fenners Chambers, Peterborough	01733 562030
De Zonie Miss Jane	14 Gray's Inn Square, London	0171 242 0858
Devlin Jonathan Nicholas Ponton	Park Court Chambers, Leeds	0113 2433277
Dodge Peter Clive	11 Old Square, London	020 7430 0341
Dooher Miss Nancy Helen	St James's Chambers, Manchester	0161 834 7000
Dubbery Mark Edward	Pump Court Chambers, London	0171 353 0711
	Pump Court Chambers, Winchester	01962 868161
	Pump Court Chambers, Swindon	01793 539899
Dumont Thomas Julian Bradley	Chambers of Mr Peter Crampin QC, London	020 7831 0081
Eccles David Thomas	8 King Street Chambers, Manchester	0161 834 9560
Eley Miss Joanne Mary	Trinity Chambers, Chelmsford	01245 605040
Elleray Anthony John	• St James's Chambers, Manchester	0161 834 7000
	12 New Square, London	0171 419 1212
	Park Lane Chambers, Leeds	0113 2285000
Evans Miss Lisa Claire	St Philip's Chambers, Birmingham	0121 246 7000
Farrow Kenneth John	Serle Court Chambers, London	0171 242 6105
Fawls Richard Granville	5 Stone Buildings, London	0171 242 6201
Feltham Piers Jonathan	Chambers of Mr Peter Crampin QC, London	020 7831 0081
Fenston Miss Felicia Donovan	2 Harcourt Buildings, London	0171 583 9020
Ferm Rodney Eric	37 Park Square Chambers, Leeds	0113 2439422
Fields Miss Helen Sarah	Pump Court Chambers, Winchester	01962 868161
	Pump Court Chambers, London	0171 353 0711
	Pump Court Chambers, Swindon	01793 539899
Fieldsend James William	2nd Floor, Francis Taylor Building, London	0171 353 9942/3157
Finn Terence	Chambers of Martin Burr, London	0171 353 4636
Fletcher Christopher Michael	Octagon House, Norwich	01603 623186
Ford Miss Caroline Emma	37 Park Square Chambers, Leeds	0113 2439422

• Expanded entry in Part D

Ford Gerard James	Baker Street Chambers, Middlesbrough	01642 873873
Ford Miss Monica Dorothy Patience	14 Gray's Inn Square, London	0171 242 0858
Foster Brian Ian	St James's Chambers, Manchester	0161 834 7000
	Park Lane Chambers, Leeds	0113 2285000
Fox Miss Nicola Susan	One Garden Court Family Law Chambers, London	0171 797 7900
Francis Andrew James	Chambers of Mr Peter Crampin QC, London	020 7831 0081
Freeston Miss Lynn Roberta	Hardwicke Building, London	020 7242 2523
Fricker Mrs Marilyn Ann	Sovereign Chambers, Leeds	0113 2451841/2/3
	Farrar's Building, London	0171 583 9241
Frith Nicholas John	30 Park Square, Leeds	0113 2436388
Furze Miss Caroline Mary	• Wilberforce Chambers, London	0171 306 0102
Garner Graham Howard	Southsea Chambers, Portsmouth	01705 291261
Gasztowicz Steven	2-3 Gray's Inn Square, London	0171 242 4986
	2 New Street, Leicester	0116 2625906
George Miss Susan Deborah	8 King's Bench Walk, London	0171 797 8888
	8 King's Bench Walk North, Leeds	0113 2439797
Gerald Nigel Mortimer	Enterprise Chambers, London	0171 405 9471
	Enterprise Chambers, Leeds	0113 246 0391
	Enterprise Chambers, Newcastle upon Tyne	0191 222 3344
Gibbons Mrs Sarah Isobel	13 King's Bench Walk, London	0171 353 7204
	King's Bench Chambers, Oxford	01865 311066
Gibson Miss Jill Maureen	Chambers of Mr Peter Crampin QC, London	020 7831 0081
Glover Stephen Julian	37 Park Square Chambers, Leeds	0113 2439422
Goddard Harold Keith	Deans Court Chambers, Manchester	0161 214 6000
	Deans Court Chambers, Preston	01772 555163
	4 Paper Buildings, London	0171 353 3366/583 7155
Gordon-Saker Mrs Liza Helen	Fenners Chambers, Cambridge	01223 368761
	Fenners Chambers, Peterborough	01733 562030
Gore Andrew Julian Mark	37 Park Square Chambers, Leeds	0113 2439422
Gray Miss Nichola Jayne	29 Bedford Row Chambers, London	0171 831 2626
Green David Cameron	Adrian Lyon's Chambers, Liverpool	0151 236 4421/8240
Gregory John Raymond	Deans Court Chambers, Manchester	0161 214 6000
	Deans Court Chambers, Preston	01772 555163
Gresty Miss Denise Lynn	Sovereign Chambers, Leeds	0113 2451841/2/3
Grocott Miss Susan	Queen's Chambers, Manchester	0161 834 6875/4738
	Queens Chambers, Preston	01772 828300
Haigh Martin James	30 Park Square, Leeds	0113 2436388
Hall Jeremy John	Becket Chambers, Canterbury	01227 786331
Hall Taylor Alexander Edward	11 Old Square, London	020 7430 0341
Hallam Miss Rona Mary Louise	30 Park Square, Leeds	0113 2436388
Hamilton-Hague Miss Rachael Elizabeth	8 King Street Chambers, Manchester	0161 834 9560
Hammerton Miss Veronica Lesley	No. 1 Serjeants' Inn, London	0171 415 6666
Hargan James John	30 Park Square, Leeds	0113 2436388
Harington Michael Kenneth	6 Pump Court, London	0171 797 8400
	6-8 Mill Street, Maidstone	01622 688094
Harrap Giles Thresher	• Pump Court Chambers, Winchester	01962 868161
	Pump Court Chambers, London	0171 353 0711
	Pump Court Chambers, Swindon	01793 539899
Harrill Miss Jayne Anne	8 King's Bench Walk, London	0171 797 8888
	8 King's Bench Walk North, Leeds	0113 2439797
Harris Melvyn	7 New Square, London	0171 430 1660
Harrod Henry Mark	5 Stone Buildings, London	0171 242 6201
Hay Miss Fiona Ruth	13 King's Bench Walk, London	0171 353 7204
	King's Bench Chambers, Oxford	01865 311066
Hay Malcolm John Marshall	3 Dr Johnson's Buildings, London	0171 353 4854
Healy Brian Patrick James	St Philip's Chambers, Birmingham	0121 246 7000

• Expanded entry in Part D

Heaton Miss Frances Margaret	Deans Court Chambers, Manchester	0161 214 6000
	Deans Court Chambers, Preston	01772 555163
	4 Brick Court, London	0171 797 7766
Henderson William Hugo	Serle Court Chambers, London	0171 242 6105
Henley Mark Robert Daniel	9 Woodhouse Square, Leeds	0113 2451986
Heppenstall Miss Rachael Elizabeth	Sovereign Chambers, Leeds	0113 2451841/2/3
Hill Miss Catherine Louise	30 Park Square, Leeds	0113 2436388
Hindmarsh Miss Elizabeth	Plowden Buildings, London	0171 583 0808
Hirst William Timothy John	Park Court Chambers, Leeds	0113 2433277
Hobson Miss Heather Fiona	Queen's Chambers, Manchester	0161 834 6875/4738
	Queens Chambers, Preston	01772 828300
Hodgson Martin Derrick	8 King's Bench Walk, London	0171 797 8888
	8 King's Bench Walk North, Leeds	0113 2439797
Holland William	2nd Floor, Francis Taylor Building, London	0171 353 9942/3157
Hollow Paul John	Fenners Chambers, Cambridge	01223 368761
	Fenners Chambers, Peterborough	01733 562030
Holroyd Ms Joanne	37 Park Square Chambers, Leeds	0113 2439422
Horne Roger Cozens-Hardy	Chambers of Mr Peter Crampin QC, London	020 7831 0081
Howard Graham John	Pump Court Chambers, Winchester	01962 868161
	Pump Court Chambers, London	0171 353 0711
	Pump Court Chambers, Swindon	01793 539899
Howe Miss Penelope Anne Macgregor	Pump Court Chambers, London	0171 353 0711
	Pump Court Chambers, Winchester	01962 868161
	Pump Court Chambers, Swindon	01793 539899
Huda Miss Abida Alia Jehan	8 King's Bench Walk, London	0171 797 8888
	8 King's Bench Walk North, Leeds	0113 2439797
Hughes Miss Kathryn Ann	Iscoed Chambers, Swansea	01792 652988/9/330
Iles Adrian	5 Paper Buildings, London	0171 583 9275/583 4555
Jackson Dirik George Allan	Chambers of Mr Peter Crampin QC, London	020 7831 0081
James Miss Rachael Elizabeth	33 Bedford Row, London	0171 242 6476
Jarman Mark Christopher	14 Gray's Inn Square, London	0171 242 0858
Jefferis Arthur Michael Quentin	Chambers of Mr Peter Crampin QC, London	020 7831 0081
Johnson Miss Christine Margaret	Adrian Lyon's Chambers, Liverpool	0151 236 4421/8240
Johnston Miss Justine Jane	4 Paper Buildings, London	0171 583 0816/353 1131
Jones Miss Carolyn Nerys	1 Fountain Court, Birmingham	0121 236 5721
	Clock Chambers, Wolverhampton	01902 313444
Kenward Timothy David Nelson	25-27 Castle Street, Liverpool	0151 227 5661/051 236 5072
Ker-Reid John	Pump Court Chambers, London	0171 353 0711
	Pump Court Chambers, Winchester	01962 868161
	Pump Court Chambers, Swindon	01793 539899
Kirtley Paul George	37 Park Square Chambers, Leeds	0113 2439422
Kynoch Duncan Stuart Sanderson	29 Bedford Row Chambers, London	0171 831 2626
Ladak Miss Tahera	8 King's Bench Walk, London	0171 797 8888
	8 King's Bench Walk North, Leeds	0113 2439797
Lambert Miss Sarah Katrina	1 Crown Office Row, London	0171 797 7500
Langridge Ms Nicola Dawn	Hardwicke Building, London	020 7242 2523
Latimer-Sayer William Laurence	2 Mitre Court Buildings, London	0171 353 1353
Lee Miss Taryn Jane	37 Park Square Chambers, Leeds	0113 2439422
Legge Henry	5 Stone Buildings, London	0171 242 6201
Lewis Jeffrey Allan	9 Woodhouse Square, Leeds	0113 2451986
Lindqvist Andrew Nils Gunnar	Octagon House, Norwich	01603 623186
Lloyd Stephen James George	Chambers of Mr Peter Crampin QC, London	020 7831 0081
Lowry Charles Stephen	Colleton Chambers, Exeter	01392 274898/9
Lucas Miss Bridget Ann	Serle Court Chambers, London	0171 242 6105
	Fountain Court, London	0171 583 3335

● Expanded entry in Part D

MacDonald Alistair William Orchard	St Philip's Chambers, Birmingham	0121 246 7000
MacLaren Miss Catriona Longueville	2nd Floor, Francis Taylor Building, London	0171 353 9942/3157
Mandalia Vinesh Lalji	Harrow on the Hill Chambers, Harrow-on-the-Hill	0181 423 7444
Manuel Miss Elizabeth	Eighteen Carlton Crescent, Southampton	01703 639001
Marks Miss Jacqueline Stephanie	2 Gray's Inn Square Chambers, London	020 7242 0328
Marks Jonathan Clive	4 Pump Court, London	020 7842 5555
Marley Miss Sarah Anne	5 Pump Court, London	020 7353 2532
Mason Miss Alexandra	3 Stone Buildings, London	0171 242 4937
Mathew Miss Nergis-Anne	2 Gray's Inn Square Chambers, London	020 7242 0328
	St Philip's Chambers, Birmingham	0121 246 7000
Maynard-Connor Giles	St James's Chambers, Manchester	0161 834 7000
McAlinden Barry O'Neill	17 Bedford Row, London	0171 831 7314
McAllister Miss Eimear Jane	9 Woodhouse Square, Leeds	0113 2451986
McGrath Miss Elizabeth Ann	St Philip's Chambers, Birmingham	0121 246 7000
McQuail Ms Katherine Emma	11 Old Square, London	020 7430 0341
Meachin Miss (Sarah) Vanessa Veronica	St Philip's Chambers, Birmingham	0121 246 7000
Mehendale Ms Neelima Krishna	2 Mitre Court Buildings, London	0171 353 1353
Melly Miss Kama Louise	37 Park Square Chambers, Leeds	0113 2439422
Mercer David Paul	Queen's Chambers, Manchester	0161 834 6875/4738
	Queens Chambers, Preston	01772 828300
Merry Hugh Gairns	17 Carlton Crescent, Southampton	023 8032 0320/0823 2003
Mills Corey Arthur	Becket Chambers, Canterbury	01227 786331
Moseley Miss Julie Ruth	St Philip's Chambers, Birmingham	0121 246 7000
Mulholland Michael	St James's Chambers, Manchester	0161 834 7000
Murray Miss Judith Rowena	4 Paper Buildings, London	0171 583 0816/353 1131
Newton Philip	Becket Chambers, Canterbury	01227 786331
Norris Alastair Hubert	5 Stone Buildings, London	0171 242 6201
	Southernhay Chambers, Exeter	01392 255777
Nuvoloni Stefano Vincenzo	• 22 Old Buildings, London	0171 831 0222
O'Donovan Ronan Daniel James	14 Gray's Inn Square, London	0171 242 0858
Oakley Anthony James	• 11 Old Square, London	020 7430 0341
Osman Robert Walter	Queen's Chambers, Manchester	0161 834 6875/4738
	Queens Chambers, Preston	01772 828300
Ovey Miss Elizabeth Helen	11 Old Square, London	020 7430 0341
Owens Mrs Lucy Isabel	13 King's Bench Walk, London	0171 353 7204
	King's Bench Chambers, Oxford	01865 311066
Parker John	2 Mitre Court Buildings, London	0171 353 1353
Peacock Miss Lisa Jayne	3 Dr Johnson's Buildings, London	0171 353 4854
Pearce Robert Edgar	Chambers of Mr Peter Crampin QC, London	020 7831 0081
Pears Derrick Allan	2nd Floor, Francis Taylor Building, London	0171 353 9942/3157
Peel Robert Roger	29 Bedford Row Chambers, London	0171 831 2626
Pimentel Carlos de Serpa Alberto Legg	3 Stone Buildings, London	0171 242 4937
Platt Miss Eleanor Frances	One Garden Court Family Law Chambers, London	0171 797 7900
Porter David Leonard	St James's Chambers, Manchester	0161 834 7000
	Park Lane Chambers, Leeds	0113 2285000
Pote Andrew Thomas	13 King's Bench Walk, London	0171 353 7204
	King's Bench Chambers, Oxford	01865 311066
Poyer-Sleeman Ms Patricia	Pump Court Chambers, London	0171 353 0711
	Pump Court Chambers, Winchester	01962 868161
	Pump Court Chambers, Swindon	01793 539899
Price Miss Collette	St James's Chambers, Manchester	0161 834 7000
Price John Charles	St Philip's Chambers, Birmingham	0121 246 7000
Prinn Miss Helen Elizabeth	Octagon House, Norwich	01603 623186

B

Proudman Miss Sonia Rosemary Susan	Chambers of Mr Peter Crampin QC, London	020 7831 0081
Prudhoe Timothy Nixon	Queen's Chambers, Manchester	0161 834 6875/4738
	Queens Chambers, Preston	01772 828300
Pulman George Frederick	Hardwicke Building, London	020 7242 2523
	Stour Chambers, Canterbury	01227 764899
Purdie Robert Anthony James	28 Western Road, Oxford	01865 204911
Purkis Ms Kathryn Miranda	Serle Court Chambers, London	0171 242 6105
Purves Gavin Bowman	Swan House, London	0181 998 3035
Pye Miss Margaret Jane	Sovereign Chambers, Leeds	0113 2451841/2/3
Rashid Omar	Chambers of Mr Peter Crampin QC, London	020 7831 0081
Raybaud Mrs June Rose	96 Gray's Inn Road, London	0171 405 0585
Redford Miss Jessica Kate	3 Dr Johnson's Buildings, London	0171 353 4854
Reed John William Rupert	•Wilberforce Chambers, London	0171 306 0102
Rees David Benjamin	5 Stone Buildings, London	0171 242 6201
Reid Paul William	13 King's Bench Walk, London	0171 353 7204
	King's Bench Chambers, Oxford	01865 311066
Renfree Peter Gerald Stanley	Harbour Court Chambers, Fareham	01329 827828
Rich Miss Ann Barbara	5 Stone Buildings, London	0171 242 6201
Richards Jeremy Simon	Octagon House, Norwich	01603 623186
Rigby Miss Charity Elizabeth	Sovereign Chambers, Leeds	0113 2451841/2/3
Rogers Miss Beverly-Ann	Serle Court Chambers, London	0171 242 6105
Rosenblatt Jeremy George	4 Paper Buildings, London	0171 583 0816/353 1131
Ross Miss Jacqueline Gordon	Crown Office Row Chambers, Brighton	01273 625625
Ross Martyn John Greaves	•5 New Square, London	020 7404 0404
Rowe Miss Judith May	•One Garden Court Family Law Chambers, London	0171 797 7900
Rowell David Stewart	Chambers of Lord Goodhart QC, London	0171 405 5577
Rudd Matthew Allan	11 Bolt Court (also at 7 Stone Buildings – 1st Floor), London	0171 353 2300
	Redhill Chambers, Redhill	01737 780781
	7 Stone Buildings (also at 11 Bolt Court), London	0171 242 0961
Ryan Miss Eithne Mary Catherine	Hardwicke Building, London	020 7242 2523
Ryder Ernest Nigel	Deans Court Chambers, Manchester	0161 214 6000
	Deans Court Chambers, Preston	01772 555163
	1 Mitre Court Buildings, London	0171 797 7070
Rylands Miss Margaret Elizabeth	8 King Street Chambers, Manchester	0161 834 9560
Salmon Jonathan Carl	1 Fountain Court, Birmingham	0121 236 5721
Samuels Leslie John	Pump Court Chambers, London	0171 353 0711
	Pump Court Chambers, Winchester	01962 868161
	Pump Court Chambers, Swindon	01793 539899
Sandbrook-Hughes Stewert Karl Anthony	Iscoed Chambers, Swansea	01792 652988/9/330
Sandells Ms Nicole	11 Old Square, London	020 7430 0341
Sapnara Miss Khatun	8 King's Bench Walk, London	0171 797 8888
	8 King's Bench Walk North, Leeds	0113 2439797
Scott Miss Alexandra Elisabeth	2 New Street, Leicester	0116 2625906
Searle Barrie	St James's Chambers, Manchester	0161 834 7000
Sellers Graham	Adrian Lyon's Chambers, Liverpool	0151 236 4421/8240
Selway Dr Katherine Emma	11 Old Square, London	020 7430 0341
Seymour Thomas Oliver	•Wilberforce Chambers, London	0171 306 0102
Shale Justin Anton	4 King's Bench Walk, London	0171 822 8822
	King's Bench Chambers, Bournemouth	01202 250025
Sheldrake Miss Christine Anne	3 Dr Johnson's Buildings, London	0171 353 4854
Shenton Miss Suzanne Helene	One Garden Court Family Law Chambers, London	0171 797 7900
Shield Miss Deborah	White Friars Chambers, Chester	01244 323070
Shiels Ian	30 Park Square, Leeds	0113 2436388

Shillingford George Miles	Chambers of Mr Peter Crampin QC, London	020 7831 0081
Siddiqi Faizul Aqtab	Justice Court Chambers, London	0181 830 7786
Silvester Bruce Ross	Lamb Chambers, London	020 7797 8300
Small Mrs Arlene Ann-Marie	Francis Taylor Building, London	0171 353 7768/7769/2711
Smith Adam John	Crown Office Row Chambers, Brighton	01273 625625
Smith Howard James	Chambers of Mr Peter Crampin QC, London	020 7831 0081
Smith Matthew Robert	Sovereign Chambers, Leeds	0113 2451841/2/3
Smith Miss Sally-Ann	Crown Office Row Chambers, Brighton	01273 625625
Solomons Mrs Ellen Betty	One Garden Court Family Law Chambers, London	0171 797 7900
Spollon Guy Merton	St Philip's Chambers, Birmingham	0121 246 7000
Staddon Miss Claire Ann	12 New Square, London	0171 419 1212
	Sovereign Chambers, Leeds	0113 2451841/2/3
Staunton (Thomas) Ulick (Patrick)	Chambers of Mr Peter Crampin QC, London	020 7831 0081
	65-67 King Street, Leicester	0116 2547710
Sterling Robert Alan	St James's Chambers, Manchester	0161 834 7000
	12 New Square, London	0171 419 1212
	Park Lane Chambers, Leeds	0113 2285000
Sternberg Michael Vivian	• 4 Paper Buildings, London	0171 583 0816/353 1131
Stewart Ms Alexandra Mary Hamilton	30 Park Square, Leeds	0113 2436388
Stewart Nicholas John Cameron	Hardwicke Building, London	020 7242 2523
Stewart-Smith William Rodney	1 New Square, London	0171 405 0884/5/6/7
Stone Miss Sally Victoria	One Garden Court Family Law Chambers, London	0171 797 7900
Studer Mark Edgar Walter	Chambers of Mr Peter Crampin QC, London	020 7831 0081
Styles Clive Richard	Becket Chambers, Canterbury	01227 786331
Szanto Gregory John Michael	Eastbourne Chambers, Eastbourne	01323 642102
Talbot Richard Kevin Kent	Deans Court Chambers, Manchester	0161 214 6000
	Deans Court Chambers, Preston	01772 555163
Tankel Mrs Ruth Shoshana	St James's Chambers, Manchester	0161 834 7000
Teeman Miss Miriam Joy	30 Park Square, Leeds	0113 2436388
Thomas Nigel Matthew	13 Old Square, London	0171 404 4800
Thompson Miss Blondelle Marguerite	1 Fountain Court, Birmingham	0121 236 5721
Thompson Jonathan Richard	8 King Street Chambers, Manchester	0161 834 9560
Townshend Timothy John Hume	Octagon House, Norwich	01603 623186
Travers Hugh	Pump Court Chambers, London	0171 353 0711
	Pump Court Chambers, Winchester	01962 868161
	Pump Court Chambers, Swindon	01793 539899
Tucker Miss Katherine Jane Greening	St Philip's Chambers, Birmingham	0121 246 7000
Tully Ms Anne Margaret	Eastbourne Chambers, Eastbourne	01323 642102
Turner Adrian John	Eastbourne Chambers, Eastbourne	01323 642102
Turner David George Patrick	14 Gray's Inn Square, London	0171 242 0858
Tyler William John	30 Park Square, Leeds	0113 2436388
Ullstein Augustus Rupert Patrick A	• 29 Bedford Row Chambers, London	0171 831 2626
Waddicor Miss Janet	1 Crown Office Row, London	0171 797 7500
	Crown Office Row Chambers, Brighton	01273 625625
Waddington Mrs Anne Louise	Pump Court Chambers, London	0171 353 0711
	Pump Court Chambers, Winchester	01962 868161
	Pump Court Chambers, Swindon	01793 539899
Wagstaffe Christopher David	New Court Chambers, London	0171 831 9500
Ward Mrs Annie Frances	Pump Court Chambers, London	0171 353 0711
	Pump Court Chambers, Swindon	01793 539899
	Pump Court Chambers, Winchester	01962 868161
Ward Simon John	1 Fountain Court, Birmingham	0121 236 5721
Warner David Alexander	1 New Square, London	0171 405 0884/5/6/7
Warnock-Smith Mrs Shan	5 Stone Buildings, London	0171 242 6201
Warrender Miss Nichola Mary	New Court Chambers, London	0171 831 9500

B

Weatherill Bernard Richard	Chambers of Lord Goodhart QC, London	0171 405 5577
Wenlock Miss Heather	13 King's Bench Walk, London	0171 353 7204
	King's Bench Chambers, Oxford	01865 311066
West Mark	• 11 Old Square, London	020 7430 0341
Wheeldon Miss Sarah Helen Elizabeth	St James's Chambers, Manchester	0161 834 7000
White Timothy Richard	30 Park Square, Leeds	0113 2436388
Wilby David Christopher	• 199 Strand, London	0171 379 9779
	Park Lane Chambers, Leeds	0113 2285000
Williams Andrew Arthur	Adrian Lyon's Chambers, Liverpool	0151 236 4421/8240
Wilson Gerald Simon John	2nd Floor, Francis Taylor Building, London	0171 353 9942/3157
Wilson Myles Brennand	White Friars Chambers, Chester	01244 323070
Wilson-Barnes Miss Lucy Emma	St James's Chambers, Manchester	0161 834 7000
Wright Miss Clare Elizabeth	6 Pump Court, London	0171 797 8400
	6-8 Mill Street, Maidstone	01622 688094
Wyatt Mark	2 New Street, Leicester	0116 2625906

FIELD SPORTS

Dineen Michael Laurence	Pump Court Chambers, Winchester	01962 868161
	Pump Court Chambers, London	0171 353 0711
	Queens Square Chambers, Bristol	0117 921 1966
	Pump Court Chambers, Swindon	01793 539899

FILM, CABLE, TV

Abrahams James	8 New Square, London	0171 405 4321
Alexander Daniel Sakyi	8 New Square, London	0171 405 4321
Baldwin John Paul	8 New Square, London	0171 405 4321
Beard Daniel Matthew	Monckton Chambers, London	0171 405 7211
Charlton Alexander Murray	4 Pump Court, London	020 7842 5555
Clark Miss Fiona Jane Stewart	8 New Square, London	0171 405 4321
Cole Richard John	Lancaster Building, Manchester	0161 661 4444/0171 649 9872
Dillon Thomas William Matthew	1 Fountain Court, Birmingham	0121 236 5721
Evans Ms Catrin Miranda	1 Brick Court, London	0171 353 8845
Fowler Richard Nicholas	Monckton Chambers, London	0171 405 7211
Fysh Michael	8 New Square, London	0171 405 4321
Hamer George Clemens	8 New Square, London	0171 405 4321
Henley Raymond Francis St Luke	Lancaster Building, Manchester	0161 661 4444/0171 649 9872
Hicks Michael Charles	• 19 Old Buildings, London	0171 405 2001
Holman Miss Tamsin Perdita	19 Old Buildings, London	0171 405 2001
Howe Martin Russell Thomson	8 New Square, London	0171 405 4321
Kitchin David James Tyson	8 New Square, London	0171 405 4321
Lane Ms Lindsay Ruth Busfield	8 New Square, London	0171 405 4321
Lever Jeremy Frederick	Monckton Chambers, London	0171 405 7211
May Miss Charlotte Louisa	8 New Square, London	0171 405 4321
Meade Richard David	8 New Square, London	0171 405 4321
Mellor Edward James Wilson	8 New Square, London	0171 405 4321
Mercer Hugh Charles	• Essex Court Chambers, London	0171 813 8000
Millar Gavin James	Doughty Street Chambers, London	0171 404 1313
Moody-Stuart Thomas	8 New Square, London	0171 405 4321
Nelson Vincent Leonard	39 Essex Street, London	0171 832 1111
Ng Ray Kian Hin	Two Crown Office Row, London	020 7797 8100
Onslow Robert Denzil	8 New Square, London	0171 405 4321
Parker Kenneth Blades	Monckton Chambers, London	0171 405 7211
Peel Stuart James	Bell Yard Chambers, London	0171 306 9292
Platts-Mills Mark Fortescue	8 New Square, London	0171 405 4321
Prescott Peter Richard Kyle	8 New Square, London	0171 405 4321
Price Richard Mervyn	Littleton Chambers, London	0171 797 8600
Reed Jeremy Nigel	19 Old Buildings, London	0171 405 2001
Shipley Norman Graham	• 19 Old Buildings, London	0171 405 2001
Speck Adrian	8 New Square, London	0171 405 4321

• Expanded entry in Part D

St Ville Laurence James	8 New Square, London	0171 405 4321
Sullivan Rory Myles	19 Old Buildings, London	0171 405 2001
Sutton Philip Julian	Bell Yard Chambers, London	0171 306 9292
Swift John Anthony	Monckton Chambers, London	0171 405 7211
Tappin Michael John	8 New Square, London	0171 405 4321
Tedd Rex Hilary	• St Philip's Chambers, Birmingham	0121 246 7000
	De Montfort Chambers, Leicester	0116 254 8686
	Northampton Chambers, Northampton	01604 636271
Thompson Rhodri William Ralph	Monckton Chambers, London	0171 405 7211
Turner Jonathan Richard	Monckton Chambers, London	0171 405 7211
Vitoria Miss Mary Christine	8 New Square, London	0171 405 4321
Wilson Alastair James Drysdale	• 19 Old Buildings, London	0171 405 2001

FINANCIAL PROVISION

Howe Miss Carole Anne	8 King's Bench Walk North, Leeds	0113 2439797
	8 King's Bench Walk, London	0171 797 8888

FINANCIAL SERVICES

Adkin Jonathan William	One Hare Court, London	020 7353 3171
Ayliffe James Justin Barnett	• Wilberforce Chambers, London	0171 306 0102
Ayres Andrew John William	13 Old Square, London	0171 404 4800
Baylis Ms Natalie Jayne	3 Verulam Buildings, London	0171 831 8441
Birch Miss Elizabeth Blanche	3 Verulam Buildings, London	0171 831 8441
Blair William James Lynton	3 Verulam Buildings, London	0171 831 8441
Browne-Wilkinson Simon	Serle Court Chambers, London	0171 242 6105
Burnett Harold Wallace	4 Paper Buildings, London	0171 353 3366/583 7155
Cawley Neil Robert Loudoun	169 Temple Chambers, London	0171 583 7644
	Milton Keynes Chambers, Milton Keynes	01908 664 128
Chivers (Tom) David	Erskine Chambers, London	0171 242 5532
Cone John Crawford	Erskine Chambers, London	0171 242 5532
Cooke Jeremy Lionel	S Tomlinson QC, London	0171 583 0404
Davey Benjamin Nicholas	11 Old Square, London	020 7430 0341
de Lacy Richard Michael	3 Verulam Buildings, London	0171 831 8441
Dedezade Taner	Tindal Chambers, Chelmsford	01245 267742
Dougherty Nigel Peter	Erskine Chambers, London	0171 242 5532
Dowley Dominic Myles	One Hare Court, London	020 7353 3171
Eadie James Raymond	One Hare Court, London	020 7353 3171
Edwards-Stuart Antony James Cobham	Two Crown Office Row, London	020 7797 8100
Etherton Terence Michael Elkan Barnet	• Wilberforce Chambers, London	0171 306 0102
Evans David Howard	Hollis Whiteman Chambers, London	020 7583 5766
Fisher Jonathan Simon	• 18 Red Lion Court, London	0171 520 6000
	Thornwood House, Chelmsford	01245 280880
Flaux Julian Martin	S Tomlinson QC, London	0171 583 0404
Fletcher Andrew Fitzroy Stephen	4 Pump Court, London	020 7842 5555
Freedman Sampson Clive	3 Verulam Buildings, London	0171 831 8441
Gaisman Jonathan Nicholas Crispin	S Tomlinson QC, London	0171 583 0404
Garcia-Miller Miss Laura	Enterprise Chambers, London	0171 405 9471
	Enterprise Chambers, Leeds	0113 246 0391
	Enterprise Chambers, Newcastle upon Tyne	0191 222 3344
Gibaud Miss Catherine Alison Annetta	3 Verulam Buildings, London	0171 831 8441
Gillyon Philip Jeffrey	Erskine Chambers, London	0171 242 5532
Grantham Andrew Timothy	• Deans Court Chambers, Manchester	0161 214 6000
	Deans Court Chambers, Preston	01772 555163
Guy John David Colin	Francis Taylor Building, London	0171 797 7250
Hall Taylor Alexander Edward	11 Old Square, London	020 7430 0341
Hamilton Adrian Walter	S Tomlinson QC, London	0171 583 0404
Hamilton Peter Bernard	4 Pump Court, London	020 7842 5555

Hantusch Robert Anthony	• 3 Stone Buildings, London	0171 242 4937
Harvey Michael Llewellyn Tucker	Two Crown Office Row, London	020 7797 8100
Head David Ian	3 Verulam Buildings, London	0171 831 8441
Hodgkinson Tristram Patrick	• 5 Pump Court, London	020 7353 2532
Jones Philip John	Serle Court Chambers, London	0171 242 6105
Kealey Gavin Sean James	S Tomlinson QC, London	0171 583 0404
Kennedy Michael Kirk Inches	1 New Square, London	0171 405 0884/5/6/7
Lavender Nicholas	One Hare Court, London	020 7353 3171
Lowe Thomas William Gordon	• Wilberforce Chambers, London	0171 306 0102
Mabb David Michael	Erskine Chambers, London	0171 242 5532
Marquand Charles Nicholas Hilary	Chambers of Lord Goodhart QC, London	0171 405 5577
McQuater Ewan Alan	3 Verulam Buildings, London	0171 831 8441
Merriman Nicholas Flavelle	3 Verulam Buildings, London	0171 831 8441
Milligan Iain Anstruther	20 Essex Street, London	0171 583 9294
Mitchell Gregory Charles Mathew	3 Verulam Buildings, London	0171 831 8441
Moore Martin Luke	Erskine Chambers, London	0171 242 5532
Moran Andrew John	One Hare Court, London	020 7353 3171
Morgan Richard Hugo Lyndon	13 Old Square, London	0171 404 4800
Naidoo Sean Van	Littman Chambers, London	020 7404 4866
Nardell Gordon Lawrence	6 Pump Court, London	0171 797 8400
	6-8 Mill Street, Maidstone	01622 688094
Neill of Bladen Lord	One Hare Court, London	020 7353 3171
Newman Miss Catherine Mary	• 13 Old Square, London	0171 404 4800
Newman Paul Lance	• Wilberforce Chambers, London	0171 306 0102
Nugee Edward George	• Wilberforce Chambers, London	0171 306 0102
Onslow Andrew George	3 Verulam Buildings, London	0171 831 8441
Owen David Christopher	20 Essex Street, London	0171 583 9294
Padfield Nicholas David	One Hare Court, London	020 7353 3171
Page Howard William Barrett	One Hare Court, London	020 7353 3171
Peacock Nicholas Christopher	13 Old Square, London	0171 404 4800
Pearson Thomas Adam Spenser	Pump Court Chambers, London	0171 353 0711
	Pump Court Chambers, Winchester	01962 868161
	Pump Court Chambers, Swindon	01793 539899
Perkoff Richard Michael	Littleton Chambers, London	0171 797 8600
Phillips S J	S Tomlinson QC, London	0171 583 0404
Pimentel Carlos de Serpa Alberto Legg	3 Stone Buildings, London	0171 242 4937
Potts Robin	Erskine Chambers, London	0171 242 5532
Prentice Professor Daniel David	Erskine Chambers, London	0171 242 5532
Quest David Charles	3 Verulam Buildings, London	0171 831 8441
Qureshi Khawar Mehmood	One Hare Court, London	020 7353 3171
Rector Miss Penelope Jane	• Five Paper Buildings, London	0171 583 6117
Rees Professor William Michael	Barnard's Inn Chambers, London	0171 369 6969
Rhodes Robert Elliott	4 King's Bench Walk, London	0171 822 8822
Rivalland Marc-Edouard	No. 1 Serjeants' Inn, London	0171 415 6666
Roberts Miss Catherine Ann	Erskine Chambers, London	0171 242 5532
Saloman Timothy Peter (Dayrell)	S Tomlinson QC, London	0171 583 0404
Salter Richard Stanley	3 Verulam Buildings, London	0171 831 8441
Selway Dr Katherine Emma	11 Old Square, London	020 7430 0341
Singh Kuldip	Five Paper Buildings, London	0171 583 6117
Smith Paul Andrew	One Hare Court, London	020 7353 3171
Snowden Richard Andrew	Erskine Chambers, London	0171 242 5532
Southwell Richard Charles	One Hare Court, London	020 7353 3171
Stockdale Sir Thomas Minshull	Erskine Chambers, London	0171 242 5532
Stokes Miss Mary Elizabeth	Erskine Chambers, London	0171 242 5532
Stubbs William Frederick	Erskine Chambers, London	0171 242 5532
Sykes (James) Richard	Erskine Chambers, London	0171 242 5532
Temple Anthony Dominic	4 Pump Court, London	020 7842 5555
Tennet Michael John	• Wilberforce Chambers, London	0171 306 0102
Thomas (Robert) Neville	3 Verulam Buildings, London	0171 831 8441
Ullstein Augustus Rupert Patrick A	• 29 Bedford Row Chambers, London	0171 831 2626

     • Expanded entry in Part D

Vineall Nicholas Edward John	4 Pump Court, London	020 7842 5555
Walford Richard Henry Howard	Serle Court Chambers, London	0171 242 6105

FINE ART

Peterson Miss Geraldine Shelda	Lamb Building, London	020 7797 7788

FISHERIES

Davey Michael Philip	4 Field Court, London	0171 440 6900

FOOD LAW

Andrews Miss Claire Marguerite	Gough Square Chambers, London	0171 353 0924
Brown Edward Francis Trevenen	Hollis Whiteman Chambers, London	020 7583 5766
Hulme Miss Amanda Claire	Gough Square Chambers, London	0171 353 0924
MacDonald Iain	Gough Square Chambers, London	0171 353 0924
Macleod Duncan	9 Gough Square, London	020 7832 0500
Vines Anthony Robert Francis	Gough Square Chambers, London	0171 353 0924

FOOD POISONING

Colbey Richard (Alan)	• Francis Taylor Building, London	0171 797 7250
	Guildhall Chambers Portsmouth, Portsmouth	01705 752400

FOREIGN LAW

El-Falahi Sami David	International Law Chambers, London	0171 221 5684/5/4840
Franco Gianpiero	2 Middle Temple Lane, London	0171 583 4540
Gee Steven Mark	4 Field Court, London	0171 440 6900
Hossain Ajmalul	• 29 Bedford Row Chambers, London	0171 831 2626
Lowenstein Paul David	Littleton Chambers, London	0171 797 8600
McGregor Harvey	4 Paper Buildings, London	0171 353 3366/583 7155
Melville Richard David	• 39 Essex Street, London	0171 832 1111
Mercer Hugh Charles	• Essex Court Chambers, London	0171 813 8000
Middleton Joseph	Doughty Street Chambers, London	0171 404 1313
Naidoo Sean Van	Littman Chambers, London	020 7404 4866
Nsugbe Oba Eric	Pump Court Chambers, London	0171 353 0711
	Pump Court Chambers, Winchester	01962 868161
	Pump Court Chambers, Swindon	01793 539899
Oakley Anthony James	• 11 Old Square, London	020 7430 0341
Qureshi Khawar Mehmood	One Hare Court, London	020 7353 3171
Smith Christopher Frank	Essex Court Chambers, London	0171 813 8000
Thomson Martin Haldane Ahmad	Wynne Chambers, London	0181 961 6144
Tselentis Michael	• 20 Essex Street, London	0171 583 9294
Ullstein Augustus Rupert Patrick A	• 29 Bedford Row Chambers, London	0171 831 2626

FRANCHISING

Beaumont Marc Clifford	• Harrow on the Hill Chambers, Harrow-on-the-Hill	0181 423 7444
	Windsor Barristers' Chambers, Windsor	01753 648899
	Pump Court Chambers, London	0171 353 0711
Cogswell Miss Frederica Natasha	Gough Square Chambers, London	0171 353 0924
Gore-Andrews Gavin Angus Russell	2 Harcourt Buildings, London	0171 583 9020
Grantham Andrew Timothy	• Deans Court Chambers, Manchester	0161 214 6000
	Deans Court Chambers, Preston	01772 555163
Henley Raymond Francis St Luke	Lancaster Building, Manchester	0161 661 4444/0171 649 9872
Hicks Michael Charles	• 19 Old Buildings, London	0171 405 2001
Holman Miss Tamsin Perdita	19 Old Buildings, London	0171 405 2001
Kolodziej Andrzej Jozef	• Littman Chambers, London	020 7404 4866
Marquand Charles Nicholas Hilary	Chambers of Lord Goodhart QC, London	0171 405 5577
Ohrenstein Dov	Chambers of Lord Goodhart QC, London	0171 405 5577
Philpott Frederick Alan	Gough Square Chambers, London	0171 353 0924
Pickford Anthony James	Prince Henry's Chamber, London	0171 834 2572
Reed Jeremy Nigel	19 Old Buildings, London	0171 405 2001

• Expanded entry in Part D

Terry Robert Jeffrey	8 King Street Chambers, Manchester	0161 834 9560
Thompson Rhodri William Ralph	Monckton Chambers, London	0171 405 7211
Wilson Alastair James Drysdale	• 19 Old Buildings, London	0171 405 2001

HAGUE CONVENTION – CHILDREN

Rylands Miss Margaret Elizabeth	8 King Street Chambers, Manchester	0161 834 9560

HEALTH & SAFETY

Bevan Edward Julian	Hollis Whiteman Chambers, London	020 7583 5766
Donne Jeremy Nigel	Hollis Whiteman Chambers, London	020 7583 5766
Eastman Roger	2 Harcourt Buildings, London	0171 583 9020
Gibbs Patrick Michael Evan	2 Harcourt Buildings, London	020 7353 2112
Pringle Gordon Alexander	Bridewell Chambers, London	020 7797 8800
Pugh Michael Charles	Old Square Chambers, London	0171 269 0300
	Old Square Chambers, Bristol	0117 9277111
Richardson David John	13 King's Bench Walk, London	0171 353 7204
	King's Bench Chambers, Oxford	01865 311066
Tracy Forster Miss Jane Elizabeth	13 King's Bench Walk, London	0171 353 7204
	King's Bench Chambers, Oxford	01865 311066
Waters Julian William Penrose	No. 1 Serjeants' Inn, London	0171 415 6666

HEALTHCARE ADMINISTRATION AND CONTRACTING

Cole-Wilson Miss Yatoni Iyamide Elizabeth	Lancaster Building, Manchester	0161 661 4444/0171 649 9872

HIGHWAYS

Birts Peter William	Farrar's Building, London	0171 583 9241
	St Philip's Chambers, Birmingham	0121 246 7000
Ward Trevor Robert Edward	17 Carlton Crescent, Southampton	023 8032 0320/0823 2003

HONG KONG LAW

Wilson (Alan) Martin	9 Bedford Row, London	0171 242 3555
	St Philip's Chambers, Birmingham	0121 246 7000

HOUSING

Adams Miss Lorraine Joan	Pulteney Chambers, Bath	01225 723987
Akerman Miss Kate Louise	Queen's Chambers, Manchester	0161 834 6875/4738
	Queens Chambers, Preston	01772 828300
Baker Stuart Christopher	1 Fountain Court, Birmingham	0121 236 5721
Barry Miss Kirsten Lesley	8 King Street Chambers, Manchester	0161 834 9560
Bastin Alexander Charles	2nd Floor, Francis Taylor Building, London	0171 353 9942/3157
Bedeau Stephen	Sovereign Chambers, Leeds	0113 2451841/2/3
	Lancaster Building, Manchester	0161 661 4444/0171 649 9872
Berry Nicholas Michael	Southernhay Chambers, Exeter	01392 255777
	1 Gray's Inn Square, London	0171 405 8946/7/8
	22 Old Buildings, London	0171 831 0222
Bhaloo Miss Zia Kurban	Enterprise Chambers, London	0171 405 9471
	Enterprise Chambers, Leeds	0113 246 0391
	Enterprise Chambers, Newcastle upon Tyne	0191 222 3344
Birtles William	Old Square Chambers, London	0171 269 0300
	Old Square Chambers, Bristol	0117 9277111
Bloom Ms Tracey Dora	Doughty Street Chambers, London	0171 404 1313
Bowker Robert James	2nd Floor, Francis Taylor Building, London	0171 353 9942/3157
Bredemear Zachary Charles	Barnard's Inn Chambers, London	0171 369 6969
Broatch Michael Donald	5 Paper Buildings, London	0171 583 9275/583 4555
Brockley Nigel Simon	Bracton Chambers, London	0171 242 4248
Buck Dr Andrew Theodore	Chambers of Martin Burr, London	0171 353 4636

Buckpitt Michael David	2nd Floor, Francis Taylor Building, London	0171 353 9942/3157
Burden Edward Angus	St Philip's Chambers, Birmingham	0121 246 7000
Butler Simon David	10 King's Bench Walk, London	0171 353 7742
Cains Ms Linda Hilary	37 Park Square Chambers, Leeds	0113 2439422
Campbell-Brown Miss Anne Louise	Bracton Chambers, London	0171 242 4248
Carroll Jonathan Neil	9 Woodhouse Square, Leeds	0113 2451986
Cawley Neil Robert Loudoun	169 Temple Chambers, London	0171 583 7644
	Milton Keynes Chambers, Milton Keynes	01908 664 128
Cheshire Anthony Peter	199 Strand, London	0171 379 9779
Clarke Miss Anna Victoria	5 Stone Buildings, London	0171 242 6201
Clegg Sebastian James Barwick	Deans Court Chambers, Manchester	0161 214 6000
	Deans Court Chambers, Preston	01772 555163
Collard Michael David	5 Pump Court, London	020 7353 2532
Compton Gareth Francis Thomas	22 Old Buildings, London	0171 831 0222
Cooper Mark Anthony John	2 Mitre Court Buildings, London	0171 353 1353
Cowen Timothy Arieh	Barnard's Inn Chambers, London	0171 369 6969
Crossley Simon Justin	9 Woodhouse Square, Leeds	0113 2451986
Daly David	Francis Taylor Building, London	0171 797 7250
Daniel Leon Roger	6 King's Bench Walk, London	0171 353 4931/583 0695
Daniells-Smith Roger Charles	8 King's Bench Walk, London	0171 797 8888
	8 King's Bench Walk North, Leeds	0113 2439797
Davies Miss Carol Elizabeth	2 New Street, Leicester	0116 2625906
Davies Dr Charles Edward	4 Field Court, London	0171 440 6900
Dedezade Taner	Tindal Chambers, Chelmsford	01245 267742
Dixon Philip John	2nd Floor, Francis Taylor Building, London	0171 353 9942/3157
Dodd Christopher John Nicholas	9 Woodhouse Square, Leeds	0113 2451986
Duddridge Robert James	2 Gray's Inn Square Chambers, London	020 7242 0328
Dugdale Nicholas	4 Field Court, London	0171 440 6900
Dunn Christopher	Sovereign Chambers, Leeds	0113 2451841/2/3
Evans Richard Gareth	5 Paper Buildings, London	0171 583 9275/583 4555
Evans Stephen James	8 King's Bench Walk, London	0171 797 8888
	8 King's Bench Walk North, Leeds	0113 2439797
Faluyi Albert Osamudiamen	Chambers of Martin Burr, London	0171 353 4636
Farquharson Jonathan	Colleton Chambers, Exeter	01392 274898/9
Fieldsend James William	2nd Floor, Francis Taylor Building, London	0171 353 9942/3157
Finn Terence	Chambers of Martin Burr, London	0171 353 4636
Fitzpatrick Edward James	8 King's Bench Walk, London	0171 797 8888
Ford Gerard James	Baker Street Chambers, Middlesbrough	01642 873873
Francis Edward Gerald Francis	Enterprise Chambers, London	0171 405 9471
	Enterprise Chambers, Leeds	0113 246 0391
	Enterprise Chambers, Newcastle upon Tyne	0191 222 3344
Francois Herbert Dolton	Chambers of Herbert Francois, Mitcham	0181 640 4529
Fullwood Adam Garrett	Chambers of Ian Macdonald QC (In Association with Two Garden Court, Temple, London), Manchester	0161 236 1840
Gannon Kevin Francis	8 King's Bench Walk, London	0171 797 8888
	8 King's Bench Walk North, Leeds	0113 2439797
Gardner Miss Eilidh Anne Mairi	22 Old Buildings, London	0171 831 0222
Garner Miss Sophie Jane	199 Strand, London	0171 379 9779
George Donald Eric Joseph	Leone Chambers, London	0181 200 4020
Gifford Andrew James Morris	7 New Square, London	0171 430 1660
Glasson Jonathan Joseph	Doughty Street Chambers, London	0171 404 1313
Glen Philip Alexander	17 Carlton Crescent, Southampton	023 8032 0320/0823 2003
Greenan Miss Sarah Octavia	9 Woodhouse Square, Leeds	0113 2451986
Gregory John Raymond	Deans Court Chambers, Manchester	0161 214 6000
	Deans Court Chambers, Preston	01772 555163
Haji Miss Shaheen	Bell Yard Chambers, London	0171 306 9292

B

Harding Dr Gladys Modwyn Cicely	Leone Chambers, London	0181 200 4020
Harwood Richard John	1 Serjeants' Inn, London	0171 583 1355
Hassall James Christopher	Southernhay Chambers, Exeter	01392 255777
Hatfield Ms Sally Anne	Doughty Street Chambers, London	0171 404 1313
Hawkes Miss Naomi Nanteza Astrid Wallusimbi	22 Old Buildings, London	0171 831 0222
Heather Christopher Mark	• 2nd Floor, Francis Taylor Building, London	0171 353 9942/3157
Henderson Roger Anthony	2 Harcourt Buildings, London	0171 583 9020
Henley Mark Robert Daniel	9 Woodhouse Square, Leeds	0113 2451986
Higgins Rupert James Hale	Littman Chambers, London	020 7404 4866
Hodgson Ms Jane	9 Woodhouse Square, Leeds	0113 2451986
Hodgson Martin Derrick	8 King's Bench Walk, London	0171 797 8888
	8 King's Bench Walk North, Leeds	0113 2439797
Hodgson Timothy Paul	8 King Street Chambers, Manchester	0161 834 9560
Holmes-Milner James Neil	2 Mitre Court Buildings, London	0171 353 1353
Hutchings Martin Anthony	199 Strand, London	0171 379 9779
James-Stadden Miss Jodie Cara	Westgate Chambers, Newcastle upon Tyne	0191 261 4407/2329785
Johnston Anthony Paul	1 Fountain Court, Birmingham	0121 236 5721
Jones Clive Hugh	1 New Square, London	0171 405 0884/5/6/7
Jones Martin Wynne	8 King's Bench Walk, London	0171 797 8888
	8 King's Bench Walk North, Leeds	0113 2439797
Kenward Timothy David Nelson	25-27 Castle Street, Liverpool	0151 227 5661/051 236 5072
Keogh Andrew John	8 King's Bench Walk, London	0171 797 8888
	8 King's Bench Walk North, Leeds	0113 2439797
Kynoch Duncan Stuart Sanderson	29 Bedford Row Chambers, London	0171 831 2626
Latham Robert James	Doughty Street Chambers, London	0171 404 1313
Lewis Robert	11 Bolt Court (also at 7 Stone Buildings – 1st Floor), London	0171 353 2300
	7 Stone Buildings (also at 11 Bolt Court), London	0171 242 0961
	Redhill Chambers, Redhill	01737 780781
Lo Bernard Norman	17 Bedford Row, London	0171 831 7314
Mainwaring [Robert] Paul Clason	Carmarthen Chambers, Carmarthen	01267 234410
Malhotra Miss Mehtab Roshan	2 Middle Temple Lane, London	0171 583 4540
Mandalia Vinesh Lalji	Harrow on the Hill Chambers, Harrow-on-the-Hill	0181 423 7444
Markus Ms Kate	Doughty Street Chambers, London	0171 404 1313
McAllister Miss Eimear Jane	9 Woodhouse Square, Leeds	0113 2451986
McHugh Denis David	Bracton Chambers, London	0171 242 4248
McKinnell Miss Soraya Jane	Enterprise Chambers, London	0171 405 9471
	Enterprise Chambers, Newcastle upon Tyne	0191 222 3344
	Enterprise Chambers, Leeds	0113 246 0391
McLean Mrs Mandy Rachel	5 Essex Court, London	0171 410 2000
Mehendale Ms Neelima Krishna	2 Mitre Court Buildings, London	0171 353 1353
Middleton Joseph	Doughty Street Chambers, London	0171 404 1313
Mitchell Miss Julianna Marie	2 Harcourt Buildings, London	0171 583 9020
Mitropoulos Christos	Chambers of Geoffrey Hawker, London	0171 583 8899
Morgan (Thomas) Jeremy	39 Essex Street, London	0171 832 1111
Murray-Smith James Michael	8 King's Bench Walk, London	0171 797 8888
	8 King's Bench Walk North, Leeds	0113 2439797
Nesbitt Timothy John Robert	199 Strand, London	0171 379 9779
Nicol Nicholas Keith	1 Pump Court, London	0171 583 2012/353 4341
O'Donovan Ronan Daniel James	14 Gray's Inn Square, London	0171 242 0858
O'Leary Robert Michael	33 Park Place, Cardiff	02920 233313
O'Shea Eoin Finbarr	4 Field Court, London	0171 440 6900
Paget Michael Rodborough	Bracton Chambers, London	0171 242 4248
Palfrey Montague Mark	Hardwicke Building, London	020 7242 2523
Peacock Miss Lisa Jayne	3 Dr Johnson's Buildings, London	0171 353 4854

Pearce Richard William	Peel Court Chambers, Manchester	0161 832 3791
Pema Anes Bhumin Laloo	9 Woodhouse Square, Leeds	0113 2451986
Price John Scott	10 Launceston Avenue, Reading	01189 479548
	Southsea Chambers, Portsmouth	01705 291261
	Cathedral Chambers, Newcastle upon Tyne	0191 232 1311
Purdie Robert Anthony James	28 Western Road, Oxford	01865 204911
Purkis Ms Kathryn Miranda	Serle Court Chambers, London	0171 242 6105
Radevsky Anthony Eric	Falcon Chambers, London	0171 353 2484
Rainey Philip Carslake	2nd Floor, Francis Taylor Building, London	0171 353 9942/3157
Read Simon Eric	8 King's Bench Walk, London	0171 797 8888
	8 King's Bench Walk North, Leeds	0113 2439797
Redford Miss Jessica Kate	3 Dr Johnson's Buildings, London	0171 353 4854
Reeder Stephen	Doughty Street Chambers, London	0171 404 1313
Reid Sebastian Peter Scott	2nd Floor, Francis Taylor Building, London	0171 353 9942/3157
Roberts Miss Clare Justine	• 2nd Floor, Francis Taylor Building, London	0171 353 9942/3157
Robinson Simon Robert	Chambers of Ian Macdonald QC (In Association with Two Garden Court, Temple, London), Manchester	0161 236 1840
Salmon Jonathan Carl	1 Fountain Court, Birmingham	0121 236 5721
Salter Charles Philip Arthur	8 King's Bench Walk, London	0171 797 8888
	8 King's Bench Walk North, Leeds	0113 2439797
Sellers Graham	Adrian Lyon's Chambers, Liverpool	0151 236 4421/8240
Selway Dr Katherine Emma	11 Old Square, London	020 7430 0341
Shale Justin Anton	4 King's Bench Walk, London	0171 822 8822
	King's Bench Chambers, Bournemouth	01202 250025
Sheehan Malcolm Peter	2 Harcourt Buildings, London	0171 583 9020
Shepherd Nigel Patrick	8 King's Bench Walk North, Leeds	0113 2439797
	8 King's Bench Walk, London	0171 797 8888
Sheppard Timothy Derie	Bracton Chambers, London	0171 242 4248
Short Miss Anna Louise	Barnard's Inn Chambers, London	0171 369 6969
Shuman Miss Karen Ann Elizabeth	Bracton Chambers, London	0171 242 4248
Siddiqi Faizul Aqtab	Justice Court Chambers, London	0181 830 7786
Simpson Ian	Bracton Chambers, London	0171 242 4248
Skelly Andrew Jon	1 Gray's Inn Square, London	0171 405 8946/7/8
Slaughter Andrew Francis	Bridewell Chambers, London	020 7797 8800
Smith Nicholas Martin	1 Fountain Court, Birmingham	0121 236 5721
Sparrow Miss Claire Louise	Eastbourne Chambers, Eastbourne	01323 642102
Staddon Paul	2nd Floor, Francis Taylor Building, London	0171 353 9942/3157
Stagg Paul Andrew	No. 1 Serjeants' Inn, London	0171 415 6666
Stark James Hayden Alexander	Chambers of Ian Macdonald QC (In Association with Two Garden Court, Temple, London), Manchester	0161 236 1840
Straker Timothy Derrick	• 4-5 Gray's Inn Square, London	0171 404 5252
Szanto Gregory John Michael	Eastbourne Chambers, Eastbourne	01323 642102
Thomas Miss Megan Moira	1 Serjeants' Inn, London	0171 583 1355
Tizzano Franco Salvatore	8 King's Bench Walk, London	0171 797 8888
	8 King's Bench Walk North, Leeds	0113 2439797
Tully Ms Anne Margaret	Eastbourne Chambers, Eastbourne	01323 642102
Tyack David Guy	St Philip's Chambers, Birmingham	0121 246 7000
Verduyn Dr Anthony James	St Philip's Chambers, Birmingham	0121 246 7000
Walden-Smith Miss Karen Jane	5 Stone Buildings, London	0171 242 6201
Ward Trevor Robert Edward	17 Carlton Crescent, Southampton	023 8032 0320/0823 2003
Warner David Alexander	1 New Square, London	0171 405 0884/5/6/7
Watkin Toby Paul	22 Old Buildings, London	0171 831 0222
Wayne Nicholas	1 Gray's Inn Square, London	0171 405 8946/7/8

• Expanded entry in Part D

Webb Stanley George	The Chambers of Mr Ali Mohammed Azhar, London	0171 353 9564
	Bracton Chambers, London	0171 242 4248
Westgate Martin Trevor	Doughty Street Chambers, London	0171 404 1313
Whybrow Christopher John	1 Serjeants' Inn, London	0171 583 1355
Williams Ms Heather Jean	Doughty Street Chambers, London	0171 404 1313
Wilson Gerald Simon John	2nd Floor, Francis Taylor Building, London	0171 353 9942/3157
Woolf Steven Jeremy	Hardwicke Building, London	020 7242 2523
Yoxall Basil Joshua	Francis Taylor Building, London	0171 797 7250

HUMAN RIGHTS

Butler Simon David	10 King's Bench Walk, London	0171 353 7742
Eadie James Raymond	One Hare Court, London	020 7353 3171
Elfield Miss Laura Elaine	5 Pump Court, London	020 7353 2532
Field Rory Dominic	Hardwicke Building, London	020 7242 2523
Lavender Nicholas	One Hare Court, London	020 7353 3171
Mercer Hugh Charles	• Essex Court Chambers, London	0171 813 8000
Newton Philip	Becket Chambers, Canterbury	01227 786331
Outhwaite Mrs Wendy-Jane Tivnan	2 Harcourt Buildings, London	0171 583 9020
Pomeroy Toby	Barristers' Common Law Chambers, London	0171 375 3012
	Virtual Chambers, London	07071 244 944
Shukla Ms Vina	New Court Chambers, London	0171 831 9500
Simor Miss Jessica Margaret Poppaea	Monckton Chambers, London	0171 405 7211
Thorne Timothy Peter	33 Bedford Row, London	0171 242 6476
Wilson (Alan) Martin	9 Bedford Row, London	0171 242 3555
	St Philip's Chambers, Birmingham	0121 246 7000

IMMIGRATION

Akiwumi Anthony Sebastian Akitayo	Pump Court Chambers, London	0171 353 0711
	Pump Court Chambers, Winchester	01962 868161
	Pump Court Chambers, Swindon	01793 539899
Ali Miss Huma	Eastbourne Chambers, Eastbourne	01323 642102
Bash-Taqi Mrs Shahineh	Leone Chambers, London	0181 200 4020
Bazini Daniel	8 King's Bench Walk, London	0171 797 8888
	8 King's Bench Walk North, Leeds	0113 2439797
Bedeau Stephen	Sovereign Chambers, Leeds	0113 2451841/2/3
	Lancaster Building, Manchester	0161 661 4444/0171 649 9872
Bevis Dominic Joseph	10 King's Bench Walk, London	0171 353 7742
Bhanji Shiraz Musa	4 Bingham Place, London	0171 486 5347/071 487 5910
Birtles William	Old Square Chambers, London	0171 269 0300
	Old Square Chambers, Bristol	0117 9277111
Blake Arthur Joseph	13 King's Bench Walk, London	0171 353 7204
	King's Bench Chambers, Oxford	01865 311066
Briden Richard John	96 Gray's Inn Road, London	0171 405 0585
Broatch Michael Donald	5 Paper Buildings, London	0171 583 9275/583 4555
Buck Dr Andrew Theodore	Chambers of Martin Burr, London	0171 353 4636
Catchpole Stuart Paul	• 39 Essex Street, London	0171 832 1111
Daniel Leon Roger	6 King's Bench Walk, London	0171 353 4931/583 0695
Davies The Rt Hon David John Denzil	96 Gray's Inn Road, London	0171 405 0585
	8 Gray's Inn Square, London	0171 242 3529
Dean Peter Thomas	1 Crown Office Row, London	0171 583 9292
deSouza Mrs Josephine Claudia	Chancery Chambers, London	0171 405 6879/6870
Faluyi Albert Osamudiamen	Chambers of Martin Burr, London	0171 353 4636
Farbey Miss Judith Sarah	Plowden Buildings, London	0171 583 0808
Featherstone Jason Neil	Virtual Chambers, London	07071 244 944
	Barristers' Common Law Chambers, London	0171 375 3012
Finch Mrs Nadine Elizabeth	Doughty Street Chambers, London	0171 404 1313

Foster Miss Alison Lee Caroline	39 Essex Street, London	0171 832 1111
Francois Herbert Dolton	Chambers of Herbert Francois, Mitcham	0181 640 4529
Gannon Kevin Francis	8 King's Bench Walk, London	0171 797 8888
	8 King's Bench Walk North, Leeds	0113 2439797
George Donald Eric Joseph	Leone Chambers, London	0181 200 4020
Gordon Donald Cameron	3 Temple Gardens, London	0171 353 0832
Grodzinski Samuel Marc	39 Essex Street, London	0171 832 1111
Haji Miss Shaheen	Bell Yard Chambers, London	0171 306 9292
Haynes Miss Rebecca	Monckton Chambers, London	0171 405 7211
Henderson (Anthony) Mark	Doughty Street Chambers, London	0171 404 1313
Henderson Miss Sophie	Plowden Buildings, London	0171 583 0808
Huda Miss Abida Alia Jehan	8 King's Bench Walk, London	0171 797 8888
	8 King's Bench Walk North, Leeds	0113 2439797
Jabati Miss Maria Hannah	2 Middle Temple Lane, London	0171 583 4540
Johnston Anthony Paul	1 Fountain Court, Birmingham	0121 236 5721
Jones David James	8 King's Bench Walk, London	0171 797 8888
	8 King's Bench Walk North, Leeds	0113 2439797
Jones Martin Wynne	8 King's Bench Walk, London	0171 797 8888
	8 King's Bench Walk North, Leeds	0113 2439797
Khan Anwar William	Eastbourne Chambers, Eastbourne	01323 642102
	Wessex Chambers, Reading	0118 956 8856
Khan Saadallah Frans Hassan	55 Temple Chambers, London	0171 353 7400
Khubber Ranjiv	3 Temple Gardens, London	0171 353 0832
King Peter Duncan	Fenners Chambers, Cambridge	01223 368761
	5 Pump Court, London	020 7353 2532
	Fenners Chambers, Peterborough	01733 562030
Kulatilake Indra Semage	52 Wembley Park Drive, Wembley	0181 902 5629
Malecka Dr Mary Margaret	• 3 Temple Gardens, London	0171 353 0832
	65-67 King Street, Leicester	0116 2547710
Malhotra Miss Mehtab Roshan	2 Middle Temple Lane, London	0171 583 4540
Mandalia Vinesh Lalji	Harrow on the Hill Chambers, Harrow-on-the-Hill	0181 423 7444
Mansoor Miss Parveen	8 King's Bench Walk, London	0171 797 8888
McCafferty Miss Lynne	5 Paper Buildings, London	0171 583 9275/583 4555
McCullough Miss Louise Clare	Lion Court, London	0171 404 6565
Middleton Joseph	Doughty Street Chambers, London	0171 404 1313
Morley Stephen Douglas	Bridewell Chambers, London	020 7797 8800
Moses Miss Rebecca	Virtual Chambers, London	07071 244 944
	Barristers' Common Law Chambers, London	0171 375 3012
Murphy Mrs Catriona Anne	1 Gray's Inn Square, London	0171 405 8946/7/8
Newman Austin Eric	9 Woodhouse Square, Leeds	0113 2451986
Nicol Andrew George Lindsay	Doughty Street Chambers, London	0171 404 1313
Nisbett James Theophilus	7 Westmeath Avenue, Leicester	0116 2412003
	Victoria Chambers, Birmingham	0121 236 9900
Ofori George Edward	ACHMA Chambers, London	0171 639 7817/0171 635 7904
	Chancery Chambers, London	0171 405 6879/6870
Panford Frank Haig	• Doughty Street Chambers, London	0171 404 1313
Peterson Miss Geraldine Shelda	Lamb Building, London	020 7797 7788
Pipi Chukwuemeka Ezekiel	Chambers of Martin Burr, London	0171 353 4636
Pleming Nigel Peter	39 Essex Street, London	0171 832 1111
Plender Richard Owen	• 20 Essex Street, London	0171 583 9294
Plimmer Miss Melanie Ann	Chambers of Ian Macdonald QC (In Association with Two Garden Court, Temple, London), Manchester	0161 236 1840
Pomeroy Toby	Barristers' Common Law Chambers, London	0171 375 3012
	Virtual Chambers, London	07071 244 944
Purdie Robert Anthony James	28 Western Road, Oxford	01865 204911
Puzey James Roderick	1 Fountain Court, Birmingham	0121 236 5721
Qureshi Khawar Mehmood	One Hare Court, London	020 7353 3171

• Expanded entry in Part D

Rosenblatt Jeremy George	4 Paper Buildings, London	0171 583 0816/353 1131
Sheppard Timothy Derie	Bracton Chambers, London	0171 242 4248
Shoker Makkan Singh	St Philip's Chambers, Birmingham	0121 246 7000
Shrimpton Michael	Francis Taylor Building, London	0171 797 7250
Siddiqi Faizul Aqtab	Justice Court Chambers, London	0181 830 7786
Smith Ms Katherine Emma	Monckton Chambers, London	0171 405 7211
Supperstone Michael Alan	11 King's Bench Walk, London	0171 632 8500/583 0610
Syed Mohammad Ali	39 Park Avenue, Mitcham	0181 648 1684
	Tower Hamlets Barristers Chambers, London	0171 247 9825
Taylor Paul Richard	Doughty Street Chambers, London	0171 404 1313
Terry Miss Michelle Jane Evelyn	Lamb Building, London	020 7797 7788
Thornley David	Chambers of Martin Burr, London	0171 353 4636
Tucker Dr Peter Louis	Leone Chambers, London	0181 200 4020
	12 Old Square, London	0171 404 0875
Walters Edmund John	13 King's Bench Walk, London	0171 353 7204
	King's Bench Chambers, Oxford	01865 311066
Weereratne Ms Rufina Aswini	Doughty Street Chambers, London	0171 404 1313
Weston Ms Amanda	Chambers of Ian Macdonald QC (In Association with Two Garden Court, Temple, London), Manchester	0161 236 1840

INDUSTRIAL TRIBUNALS

Frith Nicholas John	30 Park Square, Leeds	0113 2436388
Shiels Ian	30 Park Square, Leeds	0113 2436388

INFORMATION TECHNOLOGY

Abrahams James	8 New Square, London	0171 405 4321
Akenhead Robert	Atkin Chambers, London	020 7404 0102
Alexander Daniel Sakyi	8 New Square, London	0171 405 4321
Ayres Andrew John William	13 Old Square, London	0171 404 4800
Baatz Nicholas Stephen	Atkin Chambers, London	020 7404 0102
Baldwin John Paul	8 New Square, London	0171 405 4321
Barwise Miss Stephanie Nicola	Atkin Chambers, London	020 7404 0102
Behrens James Nicholas Edward	Serle Court Chambers, London	0171 242 6105
Bevis Dominic Joseph	10 King's Bench Walk, London	0171 353 7742
Blackburn John	Atkin Chambers, London	020 7404 0102
Blunt David John	4 Pump Court, London	020 7842 5555
Boswell Miss Lindsay Alice	4 Pump Court, London	020 7842 5555
Bowdery Martin	Atkin Chambers, London	020 7404 0102
Boyd James Andrew Donaldson	8 King Street Chambers, Manchester	0161 834 9560
Burr Andrew Charles	Atkin Chambers, London	020 7404 0102
Chapple James Malcolm Dundas	1 New Square, London	0171 405 0884/5/6/7
Charlton Alexander Murray	4 Pump Court, London	020 7842 5555
Clark Miss Fiona Jane Stewart	8 New Square, London	0171 405 4321
Clay Robert Charles	Atkin Chambers, London	020 7404 0102
Cole Richard John	Lancaster Building, Manchester	0161 661 4444/0171 649 9872
Collings Nicholas Stewart	Atkin Chambers, London	020 7404 0102
Cook Christopher Graham	St James's Chambers, Manchester	0161 834 7000
Davidson Nicholas Ranking	4 Paper Buildings, London	0171 353 3366/583 7155
Davis Andrew Paul	Two Crown Office Row, London	020 7797 8100
Dennison Stephen Randell	Atkin Chambers, London	020 7404 0102
Dennys Nicholas Charles Jonathan	Atkin Chambers, London	020 7404 0102
Doerries Miss Chantal-Aimee Renee Aemelia Annemarie	Atkin Chambers, London	020 7404 0102
Dumaresq Ms Delia Jane	Atkin Chambers, London	020 7404 0102
Featherstone Jason Neil	Virtual Chambers, London	07071 244 944
	Barristers' Common Law Chambers, London	0171 375 3012
Fletcher Andrew Fitzroy Stephen	4 Pump Court, London	020 7842 5555
Fraser Peter Donald	Atkin Chambers, London	020 7404 0102

● Expanded entry in Part D

Freedman Sampson Clive	3 Verulam Buildings, London	0171 831 8441
Friedman David Peter	4 Pump Court, London	020 7842 5555
Fysh Michael	8 New Square, London	0171 405 4321
Gee Steven Mark	4 Field Court, London	0171 440 6900
Goddard Andrew Stephen	Atkin Chambers, London	020 7404 0102
Godwin William George Henry	Atkin Chambers, London	020 7404 0102
Green Miss Jane Elizabeth	Design Chambers, London	0171 353 0747
	Chambers of Martin Burr, London	0171 353 4636
Guy John David Colin	Francis Taylor Building, London	0171 797 7250
Hamer George Clemens	8 New Square, London	0171 405 4321
Henley Raymond Francis St Luke	Lancaster Building, Manchester	0161 661 4444/0171 649 9872
Hill Miss Carol Jane	● 22 Old Buildings, London	0171 831 0222
Hofmeyr Stephen Murray	S Tomlinson QC, London	0171 583 0404
Holman Miss Tamsin Perdita	19 Old Buildings, London	0171 405 2001
Horne Roger Cozens-Hardy	Chambers of Mr Peter Crampin QC, London	020 7831 0081
Howe Martin Russell Thomson	8 New Square, London	0171 405 4321
Howells James Richard	Atkin Chambers, London	020 7404 0102
Jackson Hugh Woodward	Hardwicke Building, London	020 7242 2523
Jones Sean William Paul	11 King's Bench Walk, London	0171 632 8500/583 0610
Kelman Alistair Bruce	Lancaster Building, Manchester	0161 661 4444/0171 649 9872
Kitchin David James Tyson	8 New Square, London	0171 405 4321
Lambert John	Lancaster Building, Manchester	0161 661 4444/0171 649 9872
Lane Ms Lindsay Ruth Busfield	8 New Square, London	0171 405 4321
Lofthouse Simon Timothy	Atkin Chambers, London	020 7404 0102
Lowenstein Paul David	Littleton Chambers, London	0171 797 8600
Manzoni Charles Peter	39 Essex Street, London	0171 832 1111
Mauleverer Peter Bruce	4 Pump Court, London	020 7842 5555
May Miss Charlotte Louisa	8 New Square, London	0171 405 4321
McCall Duncan James	4 Pump Court, London	020 7842 5555
McClure Brian David	Littman Chambers, London	020 7404 4866
McMullan Manus Anthony	Atkin Chambers, London	020 7404 0102
Meade Richard David	8 New Square, London	0171 405 4321
Mellor Edward James Wilson	8 New Square, London	0171 405 4321
Moger Christopher Richard Derwent	4 Pump Court, London	020 7842 5555
Moody-Stuart Thomas	8 New Square, London	0171 405 4321
Morgan Richard Hugo Lyndon	13 Old Square, London	0171 404 4800
Onslow Robert Denzil	8 New Square, London	0171 405 4321
Parkin Miss Fiona Jane	Atkin Chambers, London	020 7404 0102
Pearson Christopher	● Bridewell Chambers, London	020 7797 8800
Pema Anes Bhumin Laloo	9 Woodhouse Square, Leeds	0113 2451986
Pilling Benjamin	4 Pump Court, London	020 7842 5555
Platts-Mills Mark Fortescue	8 New Square, London	0171 405 4321
Power Lawrence Imam	4 King's Bench Walk, London	0171 822 8822
Prescott Peter Richard Kyle	8 New Square, London	0171 405 4321
Raeside Mark Andrew	Atkin Chambers, London	020 7404 0102
Rawley Miss Dominique Jane	Atkin Chambers, London	020 7404 0102
Reed Jeremy Nigel	19 Old Buildings, London	0171 405 2001
Reese Colin Edward	Atkin Chambers, London	020 7404 0102
Reid Graham Matthew	4 Paper Buildings, London	0171 353 3366/583 7155
Renfree Peter Gerald Stanley	Harbour Court Chambers, Fareham	01329 827828
Rowlands Marc Humphreys	4 Pump Court, London	020 7842 5555
Royce Darryl Fraser	Atkin Chambers, London	020 7404 0102
Salter Richard Stanley	3 Verulam Buildings, London	0171 831 8441
Shipley Norman Graham	● 19 Old Buildings, London	0171 405 2001
Speck Adrian	8 New Square, London	0171 405 4321
Spencer Martin Benedict	4 Paper Buildings, London	0171 353 3366/583 7155
St Ville Laurence James	8 New Square, London	0171 405 4321
Stewart Nicholas John Cameron	Hardwicke Building, London	020 7242 2523
Storey Jeremy Brian	4 Pump Court, London	020 7842 5555
Streatfeild-James David Stewart	Atkin Chambers, London	020 7404 0102

Sullivan Rory Myles	19 Old Buildings, London	0171 405 2001
Tappin Michael John	8 New Square, London	0171 405 4321
Turner Jonathan David Chattyn	• 4 Field Court, London	0171 440 6900
Valentine Donald Graham	Atkin Chambers, London	020 7404 0102
Vitoria Miss Mary Christine	8 New Square, London	0171 405 4321
Wadsworth James Patrick	4 Paper Buildings, London	0171 353 3366/583 7155
Walker Steven John	Atkin Chambers, London	020 7404 0102
Wallace Ian Norman Duncan	Atkin Chambers, London	020 7404 0102
West-Knights Laurence James	4 Paper Buildings, London	0171 353 3366/583 7155
White Andrew	Atkin Chambers, London	020 7404 0102
Williams Andrew Arthur	Adrian Lyon's Chambers, Liverpool	0151 236 4421/8240
Wilson Alastair James Drysdale	• 19 Old Buildings, London	0171 405 2001

INQUESTS

Breese-Laughran Ms Eleanore Delphine	8 King's Bench Walk, London	0171 797 8888
	8 King's Bench Walk North, Leeds	0113 2439797
Croxon Raymond Patrick	8 King's Bench Walk, London	0171 797 8888
	Regency Chambers, Peterborough	01733 315215
	Regency Chambers, Cambridge	01223 301517
Jenkins Dr Janet Caroline	Chambers of Kieran Coonan QC, London	0171 583 6013/2510
Pirani Rohan Carl	Old Square Chambers, Bristol	0117 9277111
	Old Square Chambers, London	0171 269 0300
Tizzano Franco Salvatore	8 King's Bench Walk, London	0171 797 8888
	8 King's Bench Walk North, Leeds	0113 2439797
Wastie William Granville	Hollis Whiteman Chambers, London	020 7583 5766

INSOLVENCY

Acton Stephen Neil	11 Old Square, London	020 7430 0341
Adamyk Simon Charles	12 New Square, London	0171 419 1212
Angus Miss Tracey Anne	5 Stone Buildings, London	0171 242 6201
Arden Peter Leonard	Enterprise Chambers, London	0171 405 9471
	Enterprise Chambers, Leeds	0113 246 0391
	Enterprise Chambers, Newcastle upon Tyne	0191 222 3344
Ashton David Sambrook	13 King's Bench Walk, London	0171 353 7204
	King's Bench Chambers, Oxford	01865 311066
Ashworth Lance Dominic Piers	St Philip's Chambers, Birmingham	0121 246 7000
	2 Harcourt Buildings, London	0171 583 9020
Ayliffe James Justin Barnett	• Wilberforce Chambers, London	0171 306 0102
Ayres Andrew John William	13 Old Square, London	0171 404 4800
Bailey Edward Henry	Monckton Chambers, London	0171 405 7211
Barker James Sebastian	Enterprise Chambers, London	0171 405 9471
	Enterprise Chambers, Leeds	0113 246 0391
	Enterprise Chambers, Newcastle upon Tyne	0191 222 3344
Basu Dr Dijendra Bhushan	Devereux Chambers, London	0171 353 7534
Baylis Ms Natalie Jayne	3 Verulam Buildings, London	0171 831 8441
Behrens James Nicholas Edward	Serle Court Chambers, London	0171 242 6105
Beltrami Adrian Joseph	3 Verulam Buildings, London	0171 831 8441
Berry Nicholas Michael	Southernhay Chambers, Exeter	01392 255777
	1 Gray's Inn Square, London	0171 405 8946/7/8
	22 Old Buildings, London	0171 831 0222
Birch Roger Allen	Sovereign Chambers, Leeds	0113 2451841/2/3
	12 New Square, London	0171 419 1212
Blair William James Lynton	3 Verulam Buildings, London	0171 831 8441
Bowker Robert James	2nd Floor, Francis Taylor Building, London	0171 353 9942/3157
Bowmer Michael Paul	11 Old Square, London	020 7430 0341
Briden Richard John	96 Gray's Inn Road, London	0171 405 0585
Briggs Michael Townley Featherstone	Serle Court Chambers, London	0171 242 6105

Bryant Miss Ceri Jane	Erskine Chambers, London	0171 242 5532
Buck Dr Andrew Theodore	Chambers of Martin Burr, London	0171 353 4636
Burr Martin John	Chambers of Martin Burr, London	0171 353 4636
	7 New Square, London	0171 430 1660
Butler Andrew	2nd Floor, Francis Taylor Building, London	0171 353 9942/3157
Capon Philip Christopher William	St Philip's Chambers, Birmingham	0121 246 7000
Castle Peter Bolton	Chambers of Mr Peter Crampin QC, London	020 7831 0081
Chapman Matthew James	Barnard's Inn Chambers, London	0171 369 6969
Chapman Michael Andrew	Barnard's Inn Chambers, London	0171 369 6969
Charman Andrew Julian	St Philip's Chambers, Birmingham	0121 246 7000
Chesner Howard Michael	Bracton Chambers, London	0171 242 4248
Chivers (Tom) David	Erskine Chambers, London	0171 242 5532
Clark Andrew Richard	Manchester House Chambers, Manchester	0161 834 7007
	8 King Street Chambers, Manchester	0161 834 9560
Clarke Miss Anna Victoria	5 Stone Buildings, London	0171 242 6201
Clarke Ian James	Hardwicke Building, London	020 7242 2523
Clegg Sebastian James Barwick	Deans Court Chambers, Manchester	0161 214 6000
	Deans Court Chambers, Preston	01772 555163
Cole Robert Ian Gawain	30 Park Square, Leeds	0113 2436388
Collingwood Timothy Donald	Serle Court Chambers, London	0171 242 6105
Cone John Crawford	Erskine Chambers, London	0171 242 5532
Cook Christopher Graham	St James's Chambers, Manchester	0161 834 7000
Cook Jeremy David	Lamb Building, London	020 7797 7788
Cooper Gilead Patrick	Chambers of Mr Peter Crampin QC, London	020 7831 0081
Corbett James Patrick	St Philip's Chambers, Birmingham	0121 246 7000
	Chambers of Andrew Campbell QC, Leeds	0113 2455438
Corbett Mrs Sandra Margaret	1 New Square, London	0171 405 0884/5/6/7
Craig Alistair Trevor	Chambers of Mr Peter Crampin QC, London	020 7831 0081
Craig Kenneth Allen	Hardwicke Building, London	020 7242 2523
Crail Miss (Elspeth) Ross	12 New Square, London	0171 419 1212
	Sovereign Chambers, Leeds	0113 2451841/2/3
Cranfield Peter Anthony	3 Verulam Buildings, London	0171 831 8441
Crawford Grant	11 Old Square, London	020 7430 0341
Cunningham Miss Claire Louise	St Philip's Chambers, Birmingham	0121 246 7000
Davey Benjamin Nicholas	11 Old Square, London	020 7430 0341
Davies Philip Edward Hamilton	Erskine Chambers, London	0171 242 5532
Davies Miss (Susan) Louise	12 New Square, London	0171 419 1212
	Sovereign Chambers, Leeds	0113 2451841/2/3
de Lacy Richard Michael	3 Verulam Buildings, London	0171 831 8441
Dedezade Taner	Tindal Chambers, Chelmsford	01245 267742
Dillon Thomas William Matthew	1 Fountain Court, Birmingham	0121 236 5721
Dineen Michael Laurence	Pump Court Chambers, Winchester	01962 868161
	Pump Court Chambers, London	0171 353 0711
	Queens Square Chambers, Bristol	0117 921 1966
	Pump Court Chambers, Swindon	01793 539899
Dixon Philip John	2nd Floor, Francis Taylor Building, London	0171 353 9942/3157
Dodge Peter Clive	11 Old Square, London	020 7430 0341
Dooher Miss Nancy Helen	St James's Chambers, Manchester	0161 834 7000
Dougherty Nigel Peter	Erskine Chambers, London	0171 242 5532
Drake David Christopher	Serle Court Chambers, London	0171 242 6105
Duddridge Robert James	2 Gray's Inn Square Chambers, London	020 7242 0328
Eaton Turner David Murray	1 New Square, London	0171 405 0884/5/6/7

Elleray Anthony John	• St James's Chambers, Manchester	0161 834 7000
	12 New Square, London	0171 419 1212
	Park Lane Chambers, Leeds	0113 2285000
Elliott Nicholas Blethyn	3 Verulam Buildings, London	0171 831 8441
Evans Richard Gareth	5 Paper Buildings, London	0171 583 9275/583 4555
Fadipe Gabriel Charles	• Wilberforce Chambers, London	0171 306 0102
Faluyi Albert Osamudiamen	Chambers of Martin Burr, London	0171 353 4636
Farber James Henry Martin	5 Stone Buildings, London	0171 242 6201
Farrow Kenneth John	Serle Court Chambers, London	0171 242 6105
Fawls Richard Granville	5 Stone Buildings, London	0171 242 6201
Feltham Piers Jonathan	Chambers of Mr Peter Crampin QC, London	020 7831 0081
Fieldsend James William	2nd Floor, Francis Taylor Building, London	0171 353 9942/3157
Finlay Darren	Sovereign Chambers, Leeds	0113 2451841/2/3
Fletcher Andrew Fitzroy Stephen	4 Pump Court, London	020 7842 5555
Francis Andrew James	Chambers of Mr Peter Crampin QC, London	020 7831 0081
Francis Edward Gerald Francis	Enterprise Chambers, London	0171 405 9471
	Enterprise Chambers, Leeds	0113 246 0391
	Enterprise Chambers, Newcastle upon Tyne	0191 222 3344
Fryer-Spedding James Walter	St James's Chambers, Manchester	0161 834 7000
Garcia-Miller Miss Laura	Enterprise Chambers, London	0171 405 9471
	Enterprise Chambers, Leeds	0113 246 0391
	Enterprise Chambers, Newcastle upon Tyne	0191 222 3344
Gasztowicz Steven	2-3 Gray's Inn Square, London	0171 242 4986
	2 New Street, Leicester	0116 2625906
George Miss Judith Sarah	St Philip's Chambers, Birmingham	0121 246 7000
Gerald Nigel Mortimer	Enterprise Chambers, London	0171 405 9471
	Enterprise Chambers, Leeds	0113 246 0391
	Enterprise Chambers, Newcastle upon Tyne	0191 222 3344
Gibaud Miss Catherine Alison Annetta	3 Verulam Buildings, London	0171 831 8441
Gifford Andrew James Morris	7 New Square, London	0171 430 1660
Gillyon Philip Jeffrey	Erskine Chambers, London	0171 242 5532
Graham Thomas Patrick Henry	1 New Square, London	0171 405 0884/5/6/7
Grantham Andrew Timothy	• Deans Court Chambers, Manchester	0161 214 6000
	Deans Court Chambers, Preston	01772 555163
Green Miss Amanda Jane	3 Verulam Buildings, London	0171 831 8441
Green David Cameron	Adrian Lyon's Chambers, Liverpool	0151 236 4421/8240
Green Miss Jane Elizabeth	Design Chambers, London	0171 353 0747
	Chambers of Martin Burr, London	0171 353 4636
Gregory John Raymond	Deans Court Chambers, Manchester	0161 214 6000
	Deans Court Chambers, Preston	01772 555163
Groves Hugo Gerard	Enterprise Chambers, London	0171 405 9471
	Enterprise Chambers, Leeds	0113 246 0391
	Enterprise Chambers, Newcastle upon Tyne	0191 222 3344
Hall Taylor Alexander Edward	11 Old Square, London	020 7430 0341
Halpern David Anthony	Enterprise Chambers, London	0171 405 9471
	Enterprise Chambers, Leeds	0113 246 0391
	Enterprise Chambers, Newcastle upon Tyne	0191 222 3344
Hamilton Eben William	1 New Square, London	0171 405 0884/5/6/7
Hantusch Robert Anthony	• 3 Stone Buildings, London	0171 242 4937

          • Expanded entry in Part D

Hardwick Matthew Richard	Enterprise Chambers, London	0171 405 9471
	Enterprise Chambers, Leeds	0113 246 0391
	Enterprise Chambers, Newcastle upon Tyne	0191 222 3344
Harris Melvyn	7 New Square, London	0171 430 1660
Hawkes Miss Naomi Nanteza Astrid Wallusimbi	22 Old Buildings, London	0171 831 0222
Head David Ian	3 Verulam Buildings, London	0171 831 8441
Heather Christopher Mark	• 2nd Floor, Francis Taylor Building, London	0171 353 9942/3157
Henley Mark Robert Daniel	9 Woodhouse Square, Leeds	0113 2451986
Henley Raymond Francis St Luke	Lancaster Building, Manchester	0161 661 4444/0171 649 9872
Hibbert William John	Gough Square Chambers, London	0171 353 0924
Higgo Justin Beresford	Serle Court Chambers, London	0171 242 6105
Hockaday Miss Annie	3 Verulam Buildings, London	0171 831 8441
Hoffman David Alexander	8 King Street Chambers, Manchester	0161 834 9560
Hoffmann Miss Jocelyn Clare	Serle Court Chambers, London	0171 242 6105
Holland David Moore	29 Bedford Row Chambers, London	0171 831 2626
Hollington Robin Frank	1 New Square, London	0171 405 0884/5/6/7
Holmes-Milner James Neil	2 Mitre Court Buildings, London	0171 353 1353
Hornett Stuart Ian	29 Bedford Row Chambers, London	0171 831 2626
Hoser Philip Jacob	Serle Court Chambers, London	0171 242 6105
Hossain Ajmalul	• 29 Bedford Row Chambers, London	0171 831 2626
Hubbard Mark Iain	1 New Square, London	0171 405 0884/5/6/7
Ife Miss Linden Elizabeth	Enterprise Chambers, London	0171 405 9471
	Enterprise Chambers, Leeds	0113 246 0391
	Enterprise Chambers, Newcastle upon Tyne	0191 222 3344
Jackson Dirik George Allan	Chambers of Mr Peter Crampin QC, London	020 7831 0081
Jackson Hugh Woodward	Hardwicke Building, London	020 7242 2523
Jackson Nicholas David Kingsley	Adrian Lyon's Chambers, Liverpool	0151 236 4421/8240
James Michael Frank	Enterprise Chambers, London	0171 405 9471
	Enterprise Chambers, Leeds	0113 246 0391
	Enterprise Chambers, Newcastle upon Tyne	0191 222 3344
James-Stadden Miss Jodie Cara	Westgate Chambers, Newcastle upon Tyne	0191 261 4407/2329785
Jarron Miss Stephanie Allan	Westgate Chambers, Newcastle upon Tyne	0191 261 4407/2329785
Jefferis Arthur Michael Quentin	Chambers of Mr Peter Crampin QC, London	020 7831 0081
Joffe Victor Howard	Serle Court Chambers, London	0171 242 6105
Jones Clive Hugh	1 New Square, London	0171 405 0884/5/6/7
Jones Philip John	Serle Court Chambers, London	0171 242 6105
Jory Robert John Hugh	Enterprise Chambers, London	0171 405 9471
	Enterprise Chambers, Leeds	0113 246 0391
	Enterprise Chambers, Newcastle upon Tyne	0191 222 3344
Kay Michael Jack David	3 Verulam Buildings, London	0171 831 8441
	Park Lane Chambers, Leeds	0113 2285000
Kendrick Dominic John	S Tomlinson QC, London	0171 583 0404
Kennedy Michael Kirk Inches	1 New Square, London	0171 405 0884/5/6/7
Kerr Simon Alexander	S Tomlinson QC, London	0171 583 0404
Kosmin Leslie Gordon	Erskine Chambers, London	0171 242 5532
Kremen Philip Michael	Hardwicke Building, London	020 7242 2523
Kuschke Leon Siegfried	Erskine Chambers, London	0171 242 5532
Kynoch Duncan Stuart Sanderson	29 Bedford Row Chambers, London	0171 831 2626
Lamacraft Ian Richard	Bracton Chambers, London	0171 242 4248
Lamont Miss Camilla Rose	Chambers of Lord Goodhart QC, London	0171 405 5577
Lampard Miss Kathryn Felice	1 New Square, London	0171 405 0884/5/6/7

• Expanded entry in Part D

Landes Miss Anna-Rose	St Philip's Chambers, Birmingham	0121 246 7000
Levene Victor	1 Gray's Inn Square, London	0171 405 8946/7/8
Levin Craig Michael	Lancaster Building, Manchester	0161 661 4444/0171 649 9872
Lightman Daniel	Serle Court Chambers, London	0171 242 6105
Lloyd Stephen James George	Chambers of Mr Peter Crampin QC, London	020 7831 0081
Lo Bernard Norman	17 Bedford Row, London	0171 831 7314
Lowe Thomas William Gordon	• Wilberforce Chambers, London	0171 306 0102
Lowenstein Paul David	Littleton Chambers, London	0171 797 8600
Lucas Miss Bridget Ann	Serle Court Chambers, London	0171 242 6105
	Fountain Court, London	0171 583 3335
Mabb David Michael	Erskine Chambers, London	0171 242 5532
Machell John William	Serle Court Chambers, London	0171 242 6105
Macpherson Duncan Charles Stewart	Bracton Chambers, London	0171 242 4248
Mann George Anthony	Enterprise Chambers, London	0171 405 9471
	Enterprise Chambers, Leeds	0113 246 0391
	Enterprise Chambers, Newcastle upon Tyne	0191 222 3344
Marks Jonathan Harold	3 Verulam Buildings, London	0171 831 8441
Marquand Charles Nicholas Hilary	Chambers of Lord Goodhart QC, London	0171 405 5577
Marshall Philip Scott	Serle Court Chambers, London	0171 242 6105
Mauger Miss Claire Shanti Andrea	Enterprise Chambers, London	0171 405 9471
	Enterprise Chambers, Newcastle upon Tyne	0191 222 3344
	Enterprise Chambers, Leeds	0113 246 0391
Maynard-Connor Giles	St James's Chambers, Manchester	0161 834 7000
McAlinden Barry O'Neill	17 Bedford Row, London	0171 831 7314
McCahill Patrick Gerard	St Philip's Chambers, Birmingham	0121 246 7000
	Chambers of Andrew Campbell QC, Leeds	0113 2455438
McClure Brian David	Littman Chambers, London	020 7404 4866
McCulloch Ian	Bracton Chambers, London	0171 242 4248
	Lloyds House Chambers, Manchester	0161 839 3371
	Claremont Chambers, Wolverhampton	01902 426222
McKinnell Miss Soraya Jane	Enterprise Chambers, London	0171 405 9471
	Enterprise Chambers, Newcastle upon Tyne	0191 222 3344
	Enterprise Chambers, Leeds	0113 246 0391
McQuail Ms Katherine Emma	11 Old Square, London	020 7430 0341
McQuater Ewan Alan	3 Verulam Buildings, London	0171 831 8441
Mendoza Neil David Pereira	Hardwicke Building, London	020 7242 2523
Merriman Nicholas Flavelle	3 Verulam Buildings, London	0171 831 8441
Metzer Anthony David Erwin	Doughty Street Chambers, London	0171 404 1313
Mitchell Gregory Charles Mathew	3 Verulam Buildings, London	0171 831 8441
Moore Mr Craig Ian	Barnard's Inn Chambers, London	0171 369 6969
	Park Lane Chambers, Leeds	0113 2285000
Moore Martin Luke	Erskine Chambers, London	0171 242 5532
Morgan Andrew James	St Philip's Chambers, Birmingham	0121 246 7000
Morgan Richard Hugo Lyndon	13 Old Square, London	0171 404 4800
Murray-Smith James Michael	8 King's Bench Walk, London	0171 797 8888
	8 King's Bench Walk North, Leeds	0113 2439797
Nash Jonathan Scott	3 Verulam Buildings, London	0171 831 8441
Neville Stephen John	Gough Square Chambers, London	0171 353 0924
Newman Miss Catherine Mary	• 13 Old Square, London	0171 404 4800
Nicholls John Peter	13 Old Square, London	0171 404 4800
O'Leary Robert Michael	33 Park Place, Cardiff	02920 233313
Odgers John Arthur	3 Verulam Buildings, London	0171 831 8441
Ohrenstein Dov	Chambers of Lord Goodhart QC, London	0171 405 5577
Osman Robert Walter	Queen's Chambers, Manchester	0161 834 6875/4738
	Queens Chambers, Preston	01772 828300

• Expanded entry in Part D

Patchett-Joyce Michael Thurston	Monckton Chambers, London	0171 405 7211
Patel Bhavin Vinubhai	Chambers of Martin Burr, London	0171 353 4636
Peacock Nicholas Christopher	13 Old Square, London	0171 404 4800
Peacocke Mrs Teresa Anne Rosen	Enterprise Chambers, London	0171 405 9471
	Enterprise Chambers, Leeds	0113 246 0391
	Enterprise Chambers, Newcastle upon Tyne	0191 222 3344
Pearce Robert Edgar	Chambers of Mr Peter Crampin QC, London	020 7831 0081
Pearson Christopher	• Bridewell Chambers, London	020 7797 8800
Pelling (Philip) Mark	Monckton Chambers, London	0171 405 7211
Pepperall Edward Brian	St Philip's Chambers, Birmingham	0121 246 7000
Perkins Miss Marianne Yvette	7 New Square, London	0171 430 1660
Perkoff Richard Michael	Littleton Chambers, London	0171 797 8600
Phillips Jonathan Mark	3 Verulam Buildings, London	0171 831 8441
Phillips Stephen Edmund	3 Verulam Buildings, London	0171 831 8441
Pickering James Patrick	Enterprise Chambers, London	0171 405 9471
	Enterprise Chambers, Leeds	0113 246 0391
	Enterprise Chambers, Newcastle upon Tyne	0191 222 3344
Pope David James	3 Verulam Buildings, London	0171 831 8441
Porter David Leonard	St James's Chambers, Manchester	0161 834 7000
	Park Lane Chambers, Leeds	0113 2285000
Potts James Rupert	Erskine Chambers, London	0171 242 5532
Potts Robin	Erskine Chambers, London	0171 242 5532
Potts Warren Nigel	Queen's Chambers, Manchester	0161 834 6875/4738
	Queens Chambers, Preston	01772 828300
Power Lawrence Imam	4 King's Bench Walk, London	0171 822 8822
Poyer-Sleeman Ms Patricia	Pump Court Chambers, London	0171 353 0711
	Pump Court Chambers, Winchester	01962 868161
	Pump Court Chambers, Swindon	01793 539899
Prentice Professor Daniel David	Erskine Chambers, London	0171 242 5532
Prentis Sebastian Hugh Runton	1 New Square, London	0171 405 0884/5/6/7
Preston Nicholas John Holman	Bracton Chambers, London	0171 242 4248
Purves Gavin Bowman	Swan House, London	0181 998 3035
Qureshi Khawar Mehmood	One Hare Court, London	020 7353 3171
Rai Amarjit Singh	St Philip's Chambers, Birmingham	0121 246 7000
Rainey Philip Carslake	2nd Floor, Francis Taylor Building, London	0171 353 9942/3157
Randall John Yeoman	St Philip's Chambers, Birmingham	0121 246 7000
	7 Stone Buildings, London	0171 405 3886/242 3546
Rashid Omar	Chambers of Mr Peter Crampin QC, London	020 7831 0081
Reed John William Rupert	• Wilberforce Chambers, London	0171 306 0102
Rees David Benjamin	5 Stone Buildings, London	0171 242 6201
Rees Professor William Michael	Barnard's Inn Chambers, London	0171 369 6969
Richardson Giles John	Serle Court Chambers, London	0171 242 6105
Roberts Miss Catherine Ann	Erskine Chambers, London	0171 242 5532
Roberts Michael Charles	1 New Square, London	0171 405 0884/5/6/7
Ross Martyn John Greaves	• 5 New Square, London	020 7404 0404
Rowley Keith Nigel	11 Old Square, London	020 7430 0341
Russell Christopher Garnet	• 12 New Square, London	0171 419 1212
	Sovereign Chambers, Leeds	0113 2451841/2/3
Ryder Timothy Robert	Queen's Chambers, Manchester	0161 834 6875/4738
	Queens Chambers, Preston	01772 828300
Salter Richard Stanley	3 Verulam Buildings, London	0171 831 8441
Sartin Leon James	5 Stone Buildings, London	0171 242 6201
Sellers Graham	Adrian Lyon's Chambers, Liverpool	0151 236 4421/8240
Seymour Richard William	Monckton Chambers, London	0171 405 7211
Seymour Thomas Oliver	• Wilberforce Chambers, London	0171 306 0102

B

• Expanded entry in Part D

Shannon Thomas Eric	Queen's Chambers, Manchester	0161 834 6875/4738
	Queens Chambers, Preston	01772 828300
Shillingford George Miles	Chambers of Mr Peter Crampin QC, London	020 7831 0081
Shuman Miss Karen Ann Elizabeth	Bracton Chambers, London	0171 242 4248
Sinclair Graham Kelso	East Anglian Chambers, Norwich	01603 617351
	East Anglian Chambers, Colchester	01206 572756
	East Anglian Chambers, Ipswich	01473 214481
Sinclair Miss Lisa Anne	7 New Square, London	0171 430 1660
Skelly Andrew Jon	1 Gray's Inn Square, London	0171 405 8946/7/8
Smith Howard James	Chambers of Mr Peter Crampin QC, London	020 7831 0081
Snowden Richard Andrew	Erskine Chambers, London	0171 242 5532
Southall Richard Anthony	• 17 Bedford Row, London	0171 831 7314
Staddon Miss Claire Ann	12 New Square, London	0171 419 1212
	Sovereign Chambers, Leeds	0113 2451841/2/3
Staddon Paul	2nd Floor, Francis Taylor Building, London	0171 353 9942/3157
Start Miss Angharad Jocelyn	3 Verulam Buildings, London	0171 831 8441
Staunton (Thomas) Ulick (Patrick)	Chambers of Mr Peter Crampin QC, London	020 7831 0081
	65-67 King Street, Leicester	0116 2547710
Sterling Robert Alan	St James's Chambers, Manchester	0161 834 7000
	12 New Square, London	0171 419 1212
	Park Lane Chambers, Leeds	0113 2285000
Stewart Nicholas John Cameron	Hardwicke Building, London	020 7242 2523
Stockdale Sir Thomas Minshull	Erskine Chambers, London	0171 242 5532
Stokes Miss Mary Elizabeth	Erskine Chambers, London	0171 242 5532
Stubbs William Frederick	Erskine Chambers, London	0171 242 5532
Sullivan Scott	Barnard's Inn Chambers, London	0171 369 6969
Swerling Robert Harry	13 Old Square, London	0171 404 4800
Sykes (James) Richard	Erskine Chambers, London	0171 242 5532
Szanto Gregory John Michael	Eastbourne Chambers, Eastbourne	01323 642102
Talbot Patrick John	Serle Court Chambers, London	0171 242 6105
Tedd Rex Hilary	• St Philip's Chambers, Birmingham	0121 246 7000
	De Montfort Chambers, Leicester	0116 254 8686
	Northampton Chambers, Northampton	01604 636271
Thomas (Robert) Neville	3 Verulam Buildings, London	0171 831 8441
Thompson Andrew Richard	Erskine Chambers, London	0171 242 5532
Thornton Andrew James	Erskine Chambers, London	0171 242 5532
Tidmarsh Christopher Ralph Francis	5 Stone Buildings, London	0171 242 6201
Tipples Miss Amanda Jane	13 Old Square, London	0171 404 4800
Todd Michael Alan	Erskine Chambers, London	0171 242 5532
Tolaney Miss Sonia	3 Verulam Buildings, London	0171 831 8441
Trace Anthony John	• 13 Old Square, London	0171 404 4800
Tucker Miss Katherine Jane Greening	St Philip's Chambers, Birmingham	0121 246 7000
Tully Ms Anne Margaret	Eastbourne Chambers, Eastbourne	01323 642102
Van Tonder Gerard Dirk	1 New Square, London	0171 405 0884/5/6/7
Walford Richard Henry Howard	Serle Court Chambers, London	0171 242 6105
Walker Andrew Greenfield	Chambers of Lord Goodhart QC, London	0171 405 5577
Waller Richard Beaumont	S Tomlinson QC, London	0171 583 0404
Weatherill Bernard Richard	Chambers of Lord Goodhart QC, London	0171 405 5577
West Mark	• 11 Old Square, London	020 7430 0341
Wilkins Mrs Colette Ann	1 New Square, London	0171 405 0884/5/6/7
Williams Leigh Michael	S Tomlinson QC, London	0171 583 0404
Williamson Miss Bridget Susan	Enterprise Chambers, London	0171 405 9471
	Enterprise Chambers, Leeds	0113 246 0391
	Enterprise Chambers, Newcastle upon Tyne	0191 222 3344
Wilson Ian Robert	3 Verulam Buildings, London	0171 831 8441
Wilson-Barnes Miss Lucy Emma	St James's Chambers, Manchester	0161 834 7000

• Expanded entry in Part D

Wood Ian Robert	8 King Street Chambers, Manchester	0161 834 9560
Worster David James Stewart	St Philip's Chambers, Birmingham	0121 246 7000
Wyvill Alistair	St Philip's Chambers, Birmingham	0121 246 7000
Zelin Geoffrey Andrew	Enterprise Chambers, London	0171 405 9471
	Enterprise Chambers, Leeds	0113 246 0391
	Enterprise Chambers, Newcastle upon Tyne	0191 222 3344

INSURANCE

Adkin Jonathan William	One Hare Court, London	020 7353 3171
Allen Michael David Prior	S Tomlinson QC, London	0171 583 0404
Ambrose Miss Clare Mary Geneste	20 Essex Street, London	0171 583 9294
Anderson Miss Julie	• Littman Chambers, London	020 7404 4866
Ashton David Sambrook	13 King's Bench Walk, London	0171 353 7204
	King's Bench Chambers, Oxford	01865 311066
Ashworth Lance Dominic Piers	St Philip's Chambers, Birmingham	0121 246 7000
	2 Harcourt Buildings, London	0171 583 9020
Ashworth Piers	2 Harcourt Buildings, London	0171 583 9020
Ayres Andrew John William	13 Old Square, London	0171 404 4800
Bailey David John	S Tomlinson QC, London	0171 583 0404
Basu Dr Dijendra Bhushan	Devereux Chambers, London	0171 353 7534
Baylis Ms Natalie Jayne	3 Verulam Buildings, London	0171 831 8441
Beaumont Marc Clifford	• Harrow on the Hill Chambers, Harrow-on-the-Hill	0181 423 7444
	Windsor Barristers' Chambers, Windsor	01753 648899
	Pump Court Chambers, London	0171 353 0711
Bellamy Jonathan Mark	39 Essex Street, London	0171 832 1111
Bignall John Francis	S Tomlinson QC, London	0171 583 0404
Birch Miss Elizabeth Blanche	3 Verulam Buildings, London	0171 831 8441
Bishop Edward James	No. 1 Serjeants' Inn, London	0171 415 6666
Blackburn Mrs Elizabeth	4 Field Court, London	0171 440 6900
Blakesley Patrick James	Two Crown Office Row, London	020 7797 8100
Block Neil Selwyn	39 Essex Street, London	0171 832 1111
Boyle Gerard James	No. 1 Serjeants' Inn, London	0171 415 6666
Brannigan Peter John Sean	4 Pump Court, London	020 7842 5555
Brent Richard	3 Verulam Buildings, London	0171 831 8441
Brenton Timothy Deane	4 Essex Court, London	020 7797 7970
Brice Geoffrey James Barrington	4 Field Court, London	0171 440 6900
Briden Richard John	96 Gray's Inn Road, London	0171 405 0585
Briden Timothy John	• 8 Stone Buildings, London	0171 831 9881
Bright Robert Graham	S Tomlinson QC, London	0171 583 0404
Brockley Nigel Simon	Bracton Chambers, London	0171 242 4248
Brodie (James) Bruce	39 Essex Street, London	0171 832 1111
Brown Geoffrey Barlow	39 Essex Street, London	0171 832 1111
Browne-Wilkinson Simon	Serle Court Chambers, London	0171 242 6105
Burnett Harold Wallace	4 Paper Buildings, London	0171 353 3366/583 7155
Burns Peter Richard	Deans Court Chambers, Manchester	0161 214 6000
	Deans Court Chambers, Preston	01772 555163
Butcher Christopher John	S Tomlinson QC, London	0171 583 0404
Butler Philip Andrew	Deans Court Chambers, Manchester	0161 214 6000
	Deans Court Chambers, Preston	01772 555163
Catchpole Stuart Paul	• 39 Essex Street, London	0171 832 1111
Cawson Peter Mark	St James's Chambers, Manchester	0161 834 7000
	12 New Square, London	0171 419 1212
	Park Lane Chambers, Leeds	0113 2285000
Chalmers Miss Suzanne Frances	Two Crown Office Row, London	020 7797 8100
Charlton Alexander Murray	4 Pump Court, London	020 7842 5555
Charlwood Spike Llewellyn	4 Paper Buildings, London	0171 353 3366/583 7155
Christie Aidan Patrick	4 Pump Court, London	020 7842 5555
Clegg Sebastian James Barwick	Deans Court Chambers, Manchester	0161 214 6000
	Deans Court Chambers, Preston	01772 555163

• Expanded entry in Part D

Colbey Richard (Alan)	• Francis Taylor Building, London	0171 797 7250
	Guildhall Chambers Portsmouth, Portsmouth	01705 752400
Collett Michael John	20 Essex Street, London	0171 583 9294
Cooke Jeremy Lionel	S Tomlinson QC, London	0171 583 0404
Cory-Wright Charles Alexander	39 Essex Street, London	0171 832 1111
Crowley John Desmond	Two Crown Office Row, London	020 7797 8100
Croxon Raymond Patrick	8 King's Bench Walk, London	0171 797 8888
	Regency Chambers, Peterborough	01733 315215
	Regency Chambers, Cambridge	01223 301517
Curtis Michael Alexander	Two Crown Office Row, London	020 7797 8100
Davey Michael Philip	4 Field Court, London	0171 440 6900
Davie Michael James	4 Pump Court, London	020 7842 5555
Davies Dr Charles Edward	4 Field Court, London	0171 440 6900
Davies Stephen Richard	8 King Street Chambers, Manchester	0161 834 9560
Davies-Jones Jonathan	3 Verulam Buildings, London	0171 831 8441
Davis Andrew Paul	Two Crown Office Row, London	020 7797 8100
De Freitas Anthony Peter Stanley	4 Paper Buildings, London	0171 353 3366/583 7155
Dean Peter Thomas	1 Crown Office Row, London	0171 583 9292
DeCamp Miss Jane Louise	Two Crown Office Row, London	020 7797 8100
Doherty Bernard James	39 Essex Street, London	0171 832 1111
Douglas Michael John	4 Pump Court, London	020 7842 5555
Dowley Dominic Myles	One Hare Court, London	020 7353 3171
Eadie James Raymond	One Hare Court, London	020 7353 3171
Eastman Roger	2 Harcourt Buildings, London	0171 583 9020
Edey Philip David	20 Essex Street, London	0171 583 9294
Edwards David Leslie	S Tomlinson QC, London	0171 583 0404
Edwards-Stuart Antony James Cobham	Two Crown Office Row, London	020 7797 8100
Elliott Nicholas Blethyn	3 Verulam Buildings, London	0171 831 8441
Evans-Tovey Jason Robert	Two Crown Office Row, London	020 7797 8100
Fadipe Gabriel Charles	• Wilberforce Chambers, London	0171 306 0102
Farrow Kenneth John	Serle Court Chambers, London	0171 242 6105
Faulks Edward Peter Lawless	No. 1 Serjeants' Inn, London	0171 415 6666
Fenton Adam Timothy Downs	S Tomlinson QC, London	0171 583 0404
Field Patrick John	Deans Court Chambers, Manchester	0161 214 6000
	Deans Court Chambers, Preston	01772 555163
Finn Terence	Chambers of Martin Burr, London	0171 353 4636
Flaux Julian Martin	S Tomlinson QC, London	0171 583 0404
Fletcher Andrew Fitzroy Stephen	4 Pump Court, London	020 7842 5555
Forte Mark Julian Carmino	8 King Street Chambers, Manchester	0161 834 9560
Freedman Sampson Clive	3 Verulam Buildings, London	0171 831 8441
Gadney George Munro	Two Crown Office Row, London	020 7797 8100
Gaisman Jonathan Nicholas Crispin	S Tomlinson QC, London	0171 583 0404
Garcia-Miller Miss Laura	Enterprise Chambers, London	0171 405 9471
	Enterprise Chambers, Leeds	0113 246 0391
	Enterprise Chambers, Newcastle upon Tyne	0191 222 3344
Gasztowicz Steven	2-3 Gray's Inn Square, London	0171 242 4986
	2 New Street, Leicester	0116 2625906
Geary Gavin John	S Tomlinson QC, London	0171 583 0404
Gee Steven Mark	4 Field Court, London	0171 440 6900
Gibaud Miss Catherine Alison Annetta	3 Verulam Buildings, London	0171 831 8441
Glasgow Edwin John	39 Essex Street, London	0171 832 1111
Goldblatt Simon	39 Essex Street, London	0171 832 1111
Goldstone David Julian	4 Field Court, London	0171 440 6900
Grace Jonathan Robert	Deans Court Chambers, Manchester	0161 214 6000
	Deans Court Chambers, Preston	01772 555163
Grantham Andrew Timothy	• Deans Court Chambers, Manchester	0161 214 6000
	Deans Court Chambers, Preston	01772 555163

• Expanded entry in Part D

Green Miss Alison Anne	4 Field Court, London	0171 440 6900
Grimshaw Nicholas Edward	Deans Court Chambers, Manchester	0161 214 6000
	Deans Court Chambers, Preston	01772 555163
Guggenheim Miss Anna Maeve	Two Crown Office Row, London	020 7797 8100
Gunning Alexander Rupert	4 Pump Court, London	020 7842 5555
Hamilton Adrian Walter	S Tomlinson QC, London	0171 583 0404
Hamilton Graeme Montagu	Two Crown Office Row, London	020 7797 8100
Hammerton Alastair Rolf	No. 1 Serjeants' Inn, London	0171 415 6666
Harris Melvyn	7 New Square, London	0171 430 1660
Harvey Michael Llewellyn Tucker	Two Crown Office Row, London	020 7797 8100
Healy Miss Sioban	S Tomlinson QC, London	0171 583 0404
Henderson Simon Alexander	4 Pump Court, London	020 7842 5555
Hill Timothy John	4 Field Court, London	0171 440 6900
Hoffman David Alexander	8 King Street Chambers, Manchester	0161 834 9560
Hofmeyr Stephen Murray	S Tomlinson QC, London	0171 583 0404
Holdsworth James Arthur	Two Crown Office Row, London	020 7797 8100
Holroyd Charles Wilfrid	S Tomlinson QC, London	0171 583 0404
Howard Michael Newman	4 Essex Court, London	020 7797 7970
Howarth Simon Stuart	Two Crown Office Row, London	020 7797 8100
Hughes Adrian Warwick	4 Pump Court, London	020 7842 5555
Jackson Matthew David Everard	4 Paper Buildings, London	0171 353 3366/583 7155
Jarvis John Manners	3 Verulam Buildings, London	0171 831 8441
Jess Digby Charles	8 King Street Chambers, Manchester	0161 834 9560
Kay Robert Jervis	4 Field Court, London	0171 440 6900
Kealey Gavin Sean James	S Tomlinson QC, London	0171 583 0404
Kendrick Dominic John	S Tomlinson QC, London	0171 583 0404
Kenefick Timothy	S Tomlinson QC, London	0171 583 0404
Kenny Stephen Charles Wilfrid	S Tomlinson QC, London	0171 583 0404
Kent Michael Harcourt	Two Crown Office Row, London	020 7797 8100
Kenward Timothy David Nelson	25-27 Castle Street, Liverpool	0151 227 5661/051 236 5072
Kerr Simon Alexander	S Tomlinson QC, London	0171 583 0404
Khurshid Jawdat	S Tomlinson QC, London	0171 583 0404
Kolodziej Andrzej Jozef	• Littman Chambers, London	020 7404 4866
Kremen Philip Michael	Hardwicke Building, London	020 7242 2523
Lavender Nicholas	One Hare Court, London	020 7353 3171
Levin Craig Michael	Lancaster Building, Manchester	0161 661 4444/0171 649 9872
Lowenstein Paul David	Littleton Chambers, London	0171 797 8600
MacDonald Alistair William Orchard	St Philip's Chambers, Birmingham	0121 246 7000
Machell Raymond Donatus	Deans Court Chambers, Manchester	0161 214 6000
	2 Pump Court, London	0171 353 5597
	Deans Court Chambers, Preston	01772 555163
Mackay Colin Crichton	39 Essex Street, London	0171 832 1111
Males Stephen Martin	20 Essex Street, London	0171 583 9294
Manzoni Charles Peter	39 Essex Street, London	0171 832 1111
Marquand Charles Nicholas Hilary	Chambers of Lord Goodhart QC, London	0171 405 5577
Masters Miss Sara Alayna	20 Essex Street, London	0171 583 9294
Matthews Dennis Roland	Two Crown Office Row, London	020 7797 8100
Matthews Duncan Henry Rowland	20 Essex Street, London	0171 583 9294
Mauleverer Peter Bruce	4 Pump Court, London	020 7842 5555
Maxwell-Scott James Herbert	Two Crown Office Row, London	020 7797 8100
May Miss Juliet Mary	3 Verulam Buildings, London	0171 831 8441
McAlinden Barry O'Neill	17 Bedford Row, London	0171 831 7314
McCahill Patrick Gerard	St Philip's Chambers, Birmingham	0121 246 7000
	Chambers of Andrew Campbell QC, Leeds	0113 2455438
McClure Brian David	Littman Chambers, London	020 7404 4866
Meeson Nigel Keith	4 Field Court, London	0171 440 6900
Melville Richard David	• 39 Essex Street, London	0171 832 1111
Merriman Nicholas Flavelle	3 Verulam Buildings, London	0171 831 8441
Milligan Iain Anstruther	20 Essex Street, London	0171 583 9294
Minhas Ms Rafhat	Leone Chambers, London	0181 200 4020

Mishcon Miss Jane Malca	4 Paper Buildings, London	0171 353 3366/583 7155
Moger Christopher Richard Derwent	4 Pump Court, London	020 7842 5555
Moran Andrew John	One Hare Court, London	020 7353 3171
Morgan Dr Austen Jude	3 Temple Gardens, London	0171 353 0832
Mulcahy Miss Leigh-Ann Maria	Chambers of John L Powell QC, London	0171 797 8000
Naidoo Sean Van	Littman Chambers, London	020 7404 4866
Nash Jonathan Scott	3 Verulam Buildings, London	0171 831 8441
Neill of Bladen Lord	One Hare Court, London	020 7353 3171
Neish Andrew Graham	4 Pump Court, London	020 7842 5555
Nelson Vincent Leonard	39 Essex Street, London	0171 832 1111
Neville-Clarke Sebastian Adrian Bennett	1 Crown Office Row, London	0171 583 9292
Nolan Michael Alfred Anthony	4 Essex Court, London	020 7797 7970
Norman Christopher John George	No. 1 Serjeants' Inn, London	0171 415 6666
O'Leary Robert Michael	33 Park Place, Cardiff	02920 233313
O'Shea Eoin Finbarr	4 Field Court, London	0171 440 6900
O'Sullivan Thomas Sean Patrick	4 Pump Court, London	020 7842 5555
Packman Miss Claire Geraldine Vance	4 Pump Court, London	020 7842 5555
Page Howard William Barrett	One Hare Court, London	020 7353 3171
Pearson Christopher	• Bridewell Chambers, London	020 7797 8800
Perkins Miss Marianne Yvette	7 New Square, London	0171 430 1660
Persey Lionel Edward	• 4 Field Court, London	0171 440 6900
Pershad Rohan	Two Crown Office Row, London	020 7797 8100
Phillips Andrew Charles	Two Crown Office Row, London	020 7797 8100
Phillips Rory Andrew Livingstone	3 Verulam Buildings, London	0171 831 8441
Phillips S J	S Tomlinson QC, London	0171 583 0404
Phillips Stephen Edmund	3 Verulam Buildings, London	0171 831 8441
Picken Simon Derek	S Tomlinson QC, London	0171 583 0404
	30 Park Place, Cardiff	01222 398421
Picton Julian Mark	4 Paper Buildings, London	0171 353 3366/583 7155
Pilling Benjamin	4 Pump Court, London	020 7842 5555
Piper Angus Richard	No. 1 Serjeants' Inn, London	0171 415 6666
Pittaway David Michael	No. 1 Serjeants' Inn, London	0171 415 6666
Pooles Michael Philip Holmes	4 Paper Buildings, London	0171 353 3366/583 7155
Priday Charles Nicholas Bruton	S Tomlinson QC, London	0171 583 0404
Pulman George Frederick	Hardwicke Building, London	020 7242 2523
	Stour Chambers, Canterbury	01227 764899
Purves Gavin Bowman	Swan House, London	0181 998 3035
Quest David Charles	3 Verulam Buildings, London	0171 831 8441
Qureshi Khawar Mehmood	One Hare Court, London	020 7353 3171
Readhead Simon John Howard	No. 1 Serjeants' Inn, London	0171 415 6666
Reeder John	4 Field Court, London	0171 440 6900
Reid Graham Matthew	4 Paper Buildings, London	0171 353 3366/583 7155
Rich Jonathan Bernard George	5 Paper Buildings, London	0171 583 9275/583 4555
Rigney Andrew James	Two Crown Office Row, London	020 7797 8100
Rivalland Marc-Edouard	No. 1 Serjeants' Inn, London	0171 415 6666
Robb Adam Duncan	39 Essex Street, London	0171 832 1111
Ross John Graffin	No. 1 Serjeants' Inn, London	0171 415 6666
Sabben-Clare Miss Rebecca Mary	S Tomlinson QC, London	0171 583 0404
Saloman Timothy Peter (Dayrell)	S Tomlinson QC, London	0171 583 0404
Salter Richard Stanley	3 Verulam Buildings, London	0171 831 8441
Saunt Thomas William Gatty	Two Crown Office Row, London	020 7797 8100
Schaff Alistair Graham	S Tomlinson QC, London	0171 583 0404
Sellers Graham	Adrian Lyon's Chambers, Liverpool	0151 236 4421/8240
Selvaratnam Miss Vasanti Emily Indrani	4 Field Court, London	0171 440 6900
Sephton Craig Gardner	Deans Court Chambers, Manchester	0161 214 6000
	Deans Court Chambers, Preston	01772 555163
Sheehan Malcolm Peter	2 Harcourt Buildings, London	0171 583 9020
Siddiqi Faizul Aqtab	Justice Court Chambers, London	0181 830 7786

• Expanded entry in Part D

Sinclair Graham Kelso	East Anglian Chambers, Norwich	01603 617351
	East Anglian Chambers, Colchester	01206 572756
	East Anglian Chambers, Ipswich	01473 214481
Smith Michael Joseph	8 King Street Chambers, Manchester	0161 834 9560
Smith Paul Andrew	One Hare Court, London	020 7353 3171
Smith Warwick Timothy Cresswell	Deans Court Chambers, Manchester	0161 214 6000
	Deans Court Chambers, Preston	01772 555163
Snowden John Stevenson	Two Crown Office Row, London	020 7797 8100
Southern Richard Michael	S Tomlinson QC, London	0171 583 0404
Southwell Richard Charles	One Hare Court, London	020 7353 3171
Spencer Martin Benedict	4 Paper Buildings, London	0171 353 3366/583 7155
Stewart Nicholas John Cameron	Hardwicke Building, London	020 7242 2523
Stockdale David Andrew	Deans Court Chambers, Manchester	0161 214 6000
	Deans Court Chambers, Preston	01772 555163
	9 Bedford Row, London	0171 242 3555
Stokell Robert	Two Crown Office Row, London	020 7797 8100
Storey Jeremy Brian	4 Pump Court, London	020 7842 5555
Swan Ian Christopher	Two Crown Office Row, London	020 7797 8100
Symons Christopher John Maurice	3 Verulam Buildings, London	0171 831 8441
Taylor Miss Deborah Frances	Two Crown Office Row, London	020 7797 8100
Teare Nigel John Martin	4 Essex Court, London	020 7797 7970
Temple Anthony Dominic	4 Pump Court, London	020 7842 5555
Ter Haar Roger Eduard Lound	Two Crown Office Row, London	020 7797 8100
Terry Robert Jeffrey	8 King Street Chambers, Manchester	0161 834 9560
Tolaney Miss Sonia	3 Verulam Buildings, London	0171 831 8441
Tomlinson Stephen Miles	S Tomlinson QC, London	0171 583 0404
Tozzi Nigel Kenneth	4 Pump Court, London	020 7842 5555
Turner Miss Janet Mary	3 Verulam Buildings, London	0171 831 8441
Turner Mark George	Deans Court Chambers, Manchester	0161 214 6000
	Deans Court Chambers, Preston	01772 555163
Ullstein Augustus Rupert Patrick A	● 29 Bedford Row Chambers, London	0171 831 2626
Wadsworth James Patrick	4 Paper Buildings, London	0171 353 3366/583 7155
Wales Andrew Nigel Malcolm	S Tomlinson QC, London	0171 583 0404
Waller Richard Beaumont	S Tomlinson QC, London	0171 583 0404
Ward Timothy Justin	Monckton Chambers, London	0171 405 7211
Warnock Andrew Ronald	No. 1 Serjeants' Inn, London	0171 415 6666
Waters Julian William Penrose	No. 1 Serjeants' Inn, London	0171 415 6666
Weddle Steven Edgar	Hardwicke Building, London	020 7242 2523
Weitzman Thomas Edward Benjamin	3 Verulam Buildings, London	0171 831 8441
Weston Clive Aubrey Richard	Two Crown Office Row, London	020 7797 8100
Whitehouse-Vaux William Edward	4 Field Court, London	0171 440 6900
Wilken Sean David Henry	39 Essex Street, London	0171 832 1111
Wilkinson Nigel Vivian Marshall	Two Crown Office Row, London	020 7797 8100
Williams Leigh Michael	S Tomlinson QC, London	0171 583 0404
Wilson Ian Robert	3 Verulam Buildings, London	0171 831 8441
Wood Richard Gillies	20 Essex Street, London	0171 583 9294
	Cathedral Chambers (Jan Wood Independent Barristers' Clerk), Exeter	01392 210900
Woods Jonathan	Two Crown Office Row, London	020 7797 8100
Wright Colin John	4 Field Court, London	0171 440 6900
Wynter Colin Peter	Devereux Chambers, London	0171 353 7534
Wyvill Alistair	St Philip's Chambers, Birmingham	0121 246 7000
Yell Nicholas Anthony	No. 1 Serjeants' Inn, London	0171 415 6666

INSURANCE/REINSURANCE

Adkin Jonathan William	One Hare Court, London	020 7353 3171
Allen Michael David Prior	S Tomlinson QC, London	0171 583 0404
Ambrose Miss Clare Mary Geneste	20 Essex Street, London	0171 583 9294
Ashworth Piers	2 Harcourt Buildings, London	0171 583 9020
Ayres Andrew John William	13 Old Square, London	0171 404 4800
Bailey David John	S Tomlinson QC, London	0171 583 0404

Bailey Edward Henry	Monckton Chambers, London	0171 405 7211
Baylis Ms Natalie Jayne	3 Verulam Buildings, London	0171 831 8441
Bignall John Francis	S Tomlinson QC, London	0171 583 0404
Birch Miss Elizabeth Blanche	3 Verulam Buildings, London	0171 831 8441
Blakesley Patrick James	Two Crown Office Row, London	020 7797 8100
Blunt David John	4 Pump Court, London	020 7842 5555
Brent Richard	3 Verulam Buildings, London	0171 831 8441
Brice Geoffrey James Barrington	4 Field Court, London	0171 440 6900
Bright Robert Graham	S Tomlinson QC, London	0171 583 0404
Browne-Wilkinson Simon	Serle Court Chambers, London	0171 242 6105
Bryant Keith	Devereux Chambers, London	0171 353 7534
Burns Peter Richard	Deans Court Chambers, Manchester	0161 214 6000
	Deans Court Chambers, Preston	01772 555163
Butcher Christopher John	S Tomlinson QC, London	0171 583 0404
Castle Peter Bolton	Chambers of Mr Peter Crampin QC, London	020 7831 0081
Christie Aidan Patrick	4 Pump Court, London	020 7842 5555
Clegg Sebastian James Barwick	Deans Court Chambers, Manchester	0161 214 6000
	Deans Court Chambers, Preston	01772 555163
Cooke Jeremy Lionel	S Tomlinson QC, London	0171 583 0404
Cross James Edward Michael	4 Pump Court, London	020 7842 5555
Crowley John Desmond	Two Crown Office Row, London	020 7797 8100
Davey Michael Philip	4 Field Court, London	0171 440 6900
Davies Dr Charles Edward	4 Field Court, London	0171 440 6900
Dowley Dominic Myles	One Hare Court, London	020 7353 3171
Drake James Frederick	S Tomlinson QC, London	0171 583 0404
Eadie James Raymond	One Hare Court, London	020 7353 3171
Edey Philip David	20 Essex Street, London	0171 583 9294
Edwards David Leslie	S Tomlinson QC, London	0171 583 0404
Edwards-Stuart Antony James Cobham	Two Crown Office Row, London	020 7797 8100
Elliott Nicholas Blethyn	3 Verulam Buildings, London	0171 831 8441
Evans-Tovey Jason Robert	Two Crown Office Row, London	020 7797 8100
Fenton Adam Timothy Downs	S Tomlinson QC, London	0171 583 0404
Flaux Julian Martin	S Tomlinson QC, London	0171 583 0404
Freedman Sampson Clive	3 Verulam Buildings, London	0171 831 8441
Gaisman Jonathan Nicholas Crispin	S Tomlinson QC, London	0171 583 0404
Garcia-Miller Miss Laura	Enterprise Chambers, London	0171 405 9471
	Enterprise Chambers, Leeds	0113 246 0391
	Enterprise Chambers, Newcastle upon Tyne	0191 222 3344
Geary Gavin John	S Tomlinson QC, London	0171 583 0404
Gee Steven Mark	4 Field Court, London	0171 440 6900
Ghaffar Arshad	4 Field Court, London	0171 440 6900
Gibaud Miss Catherine Alison Annetta	3 Verulam Buildings, London	0171 831 8441
Grantham Andrew Timothy	• Deans Court Chambers, Manchester	0161 214 6000
	Deans Court Chambers, Preston	01772 555163
Green Miss Alison Anne	4 Field Court, London	0171 440 6900
Greenbourne John Hugo	Two Crown Office Row, London	020 7797 8100
Guggenheim Miss Anna Maeve	Two Crown Office Row, London	020 7797 8100
Hamilton Adrian Walter	S Tomlinson QC, London	0171 583 0404
Hamilton Graeme Montagu	Two Crown Office Row, London	020 7797 8100
Hammerton Alastair Rolf	No. 1 Serjeants' Inn, London	0171 415 6666
Harvey Michael Llewellyn Tucker	Two Crown Office Row, London	020 7797 8100
Havelock-Allan Anthony Mark David	20 Essex Street, London	0171 583 9294
Hayward Peter Michael	The Outer Temple, London	0171 353 4647
Head David Ian	3 Verulam Buildings, London	0171 831 8441
Healy Miss Sioban	S Tomlinson QC, London	0171 583 0404
Henderson Simon Alexander	4 Pump Court, London	020 7842 5555
Hill Timothy John	4 Field Court, London	0171 440 6900

• Expanded entry in Part D

Hofmeyr Stephen Murray	S Tomlinson QC, London	0171 583 0404
Holdsworth James Arthur	Two Crown Office Row, London	020 7797 8100
Holroyd Charles Wilfrid	S Tomlinson QC, London	0171 583 0404
Houghton Miss Kirsten Annette	4 Pump Court, London	020 7842 5555
Howard Michael Newman	4 Essex Court, London	020 7797 7970
Howarth Simon Stuart	Two Crown Office Row, London	020 7797 8100
Hughes Adrian Warwick	4 Pump Court, London	020 7842 5555
Jarvis John Manners	3 Verulam Buildings, London	0171 831 8441
Jess Digby Charles	8 King Street Chambers, Manchester	0161 834 9560
Kay Robert Jervis	4 Field Court, London	0171 440 6900
Kealey Gavin Sean James	S Tomlinson QC, London	0171 583 0404
Kenefick Timothy	S Tomlinson QC, London	0171 583 0404
Kenny Stephen Charles Wilfrid	S Tomlinson QC, London	0171 583 0404
Kerr Simon Alexander	S Tomlinson QC, London	0171 583 0404
Khurshid Jawdat	S Tomlinson QC, London	0171 583 0404
Lavender Nicholas	One Hare Court, London	020 7353 3171
Lawrence The Hon Patrick John Tristram	4 Paper Buildings, London	0171 353 3366/583 7155
Lynagh Richard Dudley	Two Crown Office Row, London	020 7797 8100
Manzoni Charles Peter	39 Essex Street, London	0171 832 1111
Masters Miss Sara Alayna	20 Essex Street, London	0171 583 9294
Matthews Duncan Henry Rowland	20 Essex Street, London	0171 583 9294
May Miss Juliet Mary	3 Verulam Buildings, London	0171 831 8441
McClure Brian David	Littman Chambers, London	020 7404 4866
Meeson Nigel Keith	4 Field Court, London	0171 440 6900
Merriman Nicholas Flavelle	3 Verulam Buildings, London	0171 831 8441
Milligan Iain Anstruther	20 Essex Street, London	0171 583 9294
Moger Christopher Richard Derwent	4 Pump Court, London	020 7842 5555
Moran Andrew John	One Hare Court, London	020 7353 3171
Morgan Dr Austen Jude	3 Temple Gardens, London	0171 353 0832
Morgan Edward Patrick	Deans Court Chambers, Manchester	0161 214 6000
	Deans Court Chambers, Preston	01772 555163
Morris Stephen Nathan	20 Essex Street, London	0171 583 9294
Naidoo Sean Van	Littman Chambers, London	020 7404 4866
Nash Jonathan Scott	3 Verulam Buildings, London	0171 831 8441
Neill of Bladen Lord	One Hare Court, London	020 7353 3171
Neish Andrew Graham	4 Pump Court, London	020 7842 5555
Ng Ray Kian Hin	Two Crown Office Row, London	020 7797 8100
Noble Roderick Grant	39 Essex Street, London	0171 832 1111
Nolan Michael Alfred Anthony	4 Essex Court, London	020 7797 7970
Norman Christopher John George	No. 1 Serjeants' Inn, London	0171 415 6666
O'Shea Eoin Finbarr	4 Field Court, London	0171 440 6900
O'Sullivan Thomas Sean Patrick	4 Pump Court, London	020 7842 5555
O'Toole Simon Gerard	2 Mitre Court Buildings, London	0171 353 1353
Owen David Christopher	20 Essex Street, London	0171 583 9294
Padfield Ms Alison Mary	Devereux Chambers, London	0171 353 7534
Page Howard William Barrett	One Hare Court, London	020 7353 3171
Pelling (Philip) Mark	Monckton Chambers, London	0171 405 7211
Persey Lionel Edward	• 4 Field Court, London	0171 440 6900
Pershad Rohan	Two Crown Office Row, London	020 7797 8100
Phillips Andrew Charles	Two Crown Office Row, London	020 7797 8100
Phillips Rory Andrew Livingstone	3 Verulam Buildings, London	0171 831 8441
Phillips S J	S Tomlinson QC, London	0171 583 0404
Picken Simon Derek	S Tomlinson QC, London	0171 583 0404
	30 Park Place, Cardiff	01222 398421
Pittaway David Michael	No. 1 Serjeants' Inn, London	0171 415 6666
Priday Charles Nicholas Bruton	S Tomlinson QC, London	0171 583 0404
Pulman George Frederick	Hardwicke Building, London	020 7242 2523
	Stour Chambers, Canterbury	01227 764899
Quest David Charles	3 Verulam Buildings, London	0171 831 8441
Qureshi Khawar Mehmood	One Hare Court, London	020 7353 3171

• Expanded entry in Part D

Reeder John	4 Field Court, London	0171 440 6900
Rich Jonathan Bernard George	5 Paper Buildings, London	0171 583 9275/583 4555
Rigney Andrew James	Two Crown Office Row, London	020 7797 8100
Ross John Graffin	No. 1 Serjeants' Inn, London	0171 415 6666
Rowland John Peter	4 Pump Court, London	020 7842 5555
Russell Jeremy Jonathan	• 4 Essex Court, London	020 7797 7970
Sabben-Clare Miss Rebecca Mary	S Tomlinson QC, London	0171 583 0404
Saloman Timothy Peter (Dayrell)	S Tomlinson QC, London	0171 583 0404
Salter Richard Stanley	3 Verulam Buildings, London	0171 831 8441
Saunders Nicholas Joseph	4 Field Court, London	0171 440 6900
Schaff Alistair Graham	S Tomlinson QC, London	0171 583 0404
Selvaratnam Miss Vasanti Emily Indrani	4 Field Court, London	0171 440 6900
Smith Christopher Frank	Essex Court Chambers, London	0171 813 8000
Smith Paul Andrew	One Hare Court, London	020 7353 3171
Snowden John Stevenson	Two Crown Office Row, London	020 7797 8100
Southern Richard Michael	S Tomlinson QC, London	0171 583 0404
Southwell Richard Charles	One Hare Court, London	020 7353 3171
Storey Jeremy Brian	4 Pump Court, London	020 7842 5555
Swan Ian Christopher	Two Crown Office Row, London	020 7797 8100
Symons Christopher John Maurice	3 Verulam Buildings, London	0171 831 8441
Taylor Miss Deborah Frances	Two Crown Office Row, London	020 7797 8100
Temple Anthony Dominic	4 Pump Court, London	020 7842 5555
Ter Haar Roger Eduard Lound	Two Crown Office Row, London	020 7797 8100
Terry Robert Jeffrey	8 King Street Chambers, Manchester	0161 834 9560
Thomas (Robert) Neville	3 Verulam Buildings, London	0171 831 8441
Tolaney Miss Sonia	3 Verulam Buildings, London	0171 831 8441
Tomlinson Stephen Miles	S Tomlinson QC, London	0171 583 0404
Trace Anthony John	• 13 Old Square, London	0171 404 4800
Tselentis Michael	• 20 Essex Street, London	0171 583 9294
Tucker David William	Two Crown Office Row, London	020 7797 8100
Turner Miss Janet Mary	3 Verulam Buildings, London	0171 831 8441
Wales Andrew Nigel Malcolm	S Tomlinson QC, London	0171 583 0404
Walford Richard Henry Howard	Serle Court Chambers, London	0171 242 6105
Waller Richard Beaumont	S Tomlinson QC, London	0171 583 0404
Weitzman Thomas Edward Benjamin	3 Verulam Buildings, London	0171 831 8441
Weston Clive Aubrey Richard	Two Crown Office Row, London	020 7797 8100
Wicks Ms Joanne	• Wilberforce Chambers, London	0171 306 0102
Wilkinson Nigel Vivian Marshall	Two Crown Office Row, London	020 7797 8100
Williams Leigh Michael	S Tomlinson QC, London	0171 583 0404
Wilson Ian Robert	3 Verulam Buildings, London	0171 831 8441
Wright Colin John	4 Field Court, London	0171 440 6900
Wynter Colin Peter	Devereux Chambers, London	0171 353 7534

INTELLECTUAL PROPERTY

Baldwin John Paul	8 New Square, London	0171 405 4321
Barton Alan John	Lamb Building, London	020 7797 7788
Bevis Dominic Joseph	10 King's Bench Walk, London	0171 353 7742
Chapple James Malcolm Dundas	1 New Square, London	0171 405 0884/5/6/7
Clarke Ian James	Hardwicke Building, London	020 7242 2523
Clegg Sebastian James Barwick	Deans Court Chambers, Manchester	0161 214 6000
	Deans Court Chambers, Preston	01772 555163
Cole Richard John	Lancaster Building, Manchester	0161 661 4444/0171 649 9872
Cole-Wilson Miss Yatoni Iyamide Elizabeth	Lancaster Building, Manchester	0161 661 4444/0171 649 9872
Colley Dr Peter McLean	• 19 Old Buildings, London	0171 405 2001
Cook Christopher Graham	St James's Chambers, Manchester	0161 834 7000
Corbett James Patrick	St Philip's Chambers, Birmingham	0121 246 7000
	Chambers of Andrew Campbell QC, Leeds	0113 2455438
Coulthard Alan Terence	33 Park Place, Cardiff	02920 233313

         • Expanded entry in Part D

Dalby Joseph Francis	Portsmouth Barristers' Chambers, Winchester	01962 863222
	Portsmouth Barristers' Chambers, Portsmouth	023 92 831292/811811
Dillon Thomas William Matthew	1 Fountain Court, Birmingham	0121 236 5721
Driscoll Miss Lynn	Sovereign Chambers, Leeds	0113 2451841/2/3
Edwards Richard Julian Henshaw	3 Verulam Buildings, London	0171 831 8441
Elleray Anthony John	• St James's Chambers, Manchester	0161 834 7000
	12 New Square, London	0171 419 1212
	Park Lane Chambers, Leeds	0113 2285000
Farrow Kenneth John	Serle Court Chambers, London	0171 242 6105
Feltham Piers Jonathan	Chambers of Mr Peter Crampin QC, London	020 7831 0081
Fysh Michael	8 New Square, London	0171 405 4321
Gee Steven Mark	4 Field Court, London	0171 440 6900
Grayson Edward	• 9-12 Bell Yard, London	0171 400 1800
Greatorex Ms Helen Louise	9 Woodhouse Square, Leeds	0113 2451986
Green Miss Jane Elizabeth	Design Chambers, London	0171 353 0747
	Chambers of Martin Burr, London	0171 353 4636
Gregory John Raymond	Deans Court Chambers, Manchester	0161 214 6000
	Deans Court Chambers, Preston	01772 555163
Hamer George Clemens	8 New Square, London	0171 405 4321
Heal Mrs Madeleine	4 Field Court, London	0171 440 6900
Henley Raymond Francis St Luke	Lancaster Building, Manchester	0161 661 4444/0171 649 9872
Hicks Michael Charles	• 19 Old Buildings, London	0171 405 2001
Hoffman David Alexander	8 King Street Chambers, Manchester	0161 834 9560
Holman Miss Tamsin Perdita	19 Old Buildings, London	0171 405 2001
Howe Martin Russell Thomson	8 New Square, London	0171 405 4321
Hudson Anthony Sean	Doughty Street Chambers, London	0171 404 1313
Kelman Alistair Bruce	Lancaster Building, Manchester	0161 661 4444/0171 649 9872
Lambert John	Lancaster Building, Manchester	0161 661 4444/0171 649 9872
Littman Mark	Littman Chambers, London	020 7404 4866
McClure Brian David	Littman Chambers, London	020 7404 4866
Merriman Nicholas Flavelle	3 Verulam Buildings, London	0171 831 8441
Nicol Andrew George Lindsay	Doughty Street Chambers, London	0171 404 1313
Page Howard William Barrett	One Hare Court, London	020 7353 3171
Peel Stuart James	Bell Yard Chambers, London	0171 306 9292
Pickering James Patrick	Enterprise Chambers, London	0171 405 9471
	Enterprise Chambers, Leeds	0113 246 0391
	Enterprise Chambers, Newcastle upon Tyne	0191 222 3344
Pickford Anthony James	Prince Henry's Chamber, London	0171 834 2572
Platts-Mills Mark Fortescue	8 New Square, London	0171 405 4321
Power Lawrence Imam	4 King's Bench Walk, London	0171 822 8822
Prescott Peter Richard Kyle	8 New Square, London	0171 405 4321
Price Richard Mervyn	Littleton Chambers, London	0171 797 8600
Puckrin Cedric Eldred	19 Old Buildings, London	0171 405 2001
Purves Gavin Bowman	Swan House, London	0181 998 3035
Reed Jeremy Nigel	19 Old Buildings, London	0171 405 2001
Reid Brian Christopher	19 Old Buildings, London	0171 405 2001
Shannon Thomas Eric	Queen's Chambers, Manchester	0161 834 6875/4738
	Queens Chambers, Preston	01772 828300
Shipley Norman Graham	• 19 Old Buildings, London	0171 405 2001
Staddon Paul	2nd Floor, Francis Taylor Building, London	0171 353 9942/3157
Sterling Robert Alan	St James's Chambers, Manchester	0161 834 7000
	12 New Square, London	0171 419 1212
	Park Lane Chambers, Leeds	0113 2285000
Stevens-Hoare Miss Michelle	Hardwicke Building, London	020 7242 2523
Sullivan Rory Myles	19 Old Buildings, London	0171 405 2001
Sutcliffe Andrew Harold Wentworth	3 Verulam Buildings, London	0171 831 8441

B

• Expanded entry in Part D

Turner Jonathan David Chattyn	• 4 Field Court, London	0171 440 6900
Vitoria Miss Mary Christine	8 New Square, London	0171 405 4321
Wilson Alastair James Drysdale	• 19 Old Buildings, London	0171 405 2001

INTERNATIONAL CHILD ABDUCTION

Scott-Manderson Marcus Charles William	4 Paper Buildings, London	0171 583 0816/353 1131

INTERNATIONAL FAMILY LAW

Sternberg Michael Vivian	• 4 Paper Buildings, London	0171 583 0816/353 1131

INTERNATIONAL LOAN DOCUMENTATION

Gore-Andrews Gavin Angus Russell	2 Harcourt Buildings, London	0171 583 9020

INTERNATIONAL TRADE

Allen Michael David Prior	S Tomlinson QC, London	0171 583 0404
Ambrose Miss Clare Mary Geneste	20 Essex Street, London	0171 583 9294
Ayres Andrew John William	13 Old Square, London	0171 404 4800
Bailey David John	S Tomlinson QC, London	0171 583 0404
Bignall John Francis	S Tomlinson QC, London	0171 583 0404
Birch Miss Elizabeth Blanche	3 Verulam Buildings, London	0171 831 8441
Blackburn Mrs Elizabeth	4 Field Court, London	0171 440 6900
Blair William James Lynton	3 Verulam Buildings, London	0171 831 8441
Bright Robert Graham	S Tomlinson QC, London	0171 583 0404
Browne-Wilkinson Simon	Serle Court Chambers, London	0171 242 6105
Buckingham Stewart John	4 Essex Court, London	020 7797 7970
Burnett Harold Wallace	4 Paper Buildings, London	0171 353 3366/583 7155
Butcher Christopher John	S Tomlinson QC, London	0171 583 0404
Chambers Jonathan	4 Essex Court, London	020 7797 7970
Collett Michael John	20 Essex Street, London	0171 583 9294
Cooke Jeremy Lionel	S Tomlinson QC, London	0171 583 0404
Cooper Nigel Stuart	4 Essex Court, London	020 7797 7970
Davey Michael Philip	4 Field Court, London	0171 440 6900
Davies Dr Charles Edward	4 Field Court, London	0171 440 6900
Driscoll Miss Lynn	Sovereign Chambers, Leeds	0113 2451841/2/3
Edey Philip David	20 Essex Street, London	0171 583 9294
Edwards David Leslie	S Tomlinson QC, London	0171 583 0404
Evans James Frederick Meurig	3 Verulam Buildings, London	0171 831 8441
Flaux Julian Martin	S Tomlinson QC, London	0171 583 0404
Franco Gianpiero	2 Middle Temple Lane, London	0171 583 4540
Freedman Sampson Clive	3 Verulam Buildings, London	0171 831 8441
Gaisman Jonathan Nicholas Crispin	S Tomlinson QC, London	0171 583 0404
Geary Gavin John	S Tomlinson QC, London	0171 583 0404
Gee Steven Mark	4 Field Court, London	0171 440 6900
Ghaffar Arshad	4 Field Court, London	0171 440 6900
Goldstone David Julian	4 Field Court, London	0171 440 6900
Grantham Andrew Timothy	• Deans Court Chambers, Manchester	0161 214 6000
	Deans Court Chambers, Preston	01772 555163
Green Miss Jane Elizabeth	Design Chambers, London	0171 353 0747
	Chambers of Martin Burr, London	0171 353 4636
Havelock-Allan Anthony Mark David	20 Essex Street, London	0171 583 9294
Healy Miss Sioban	S Tomlinson QC, London	0171 583 0404
Hofmeyr Stephen Murray	S Tomlinson QC, London	0171 583 0404
Holroyd Charles Wilfrid	S Tomlinson QC, London	0171 583 0404
Hossain Ajmalul	• 29 Bedford Row Chambers, London	0171 831 2626
Howard Michael Newman	4 Essex Court, London	020 7797 7970
Hughes Adrian Warwick	4 Pump Court, London	020 7842 5555
Jabati Miss Maria Hannah	2 Middle Temple Lane, London	0171 583 4540

• Expanded entry in Part D

James Michael Frank	Enterprise Chambers, London	0171 405 9471
	Enterprise Chambers, Leeds	0113 246 0391
	Enterprise Chambers, Newcastle upon Tyne	0191 222 3344
Kay Robert Jervis	4 Field Court, London	0171 440 6900
Kealey Gavin Sean James	S Tomlinson QC, London	0171 583 0404
Kendrick Dominic John	S Tomlinson QC, London	0171 583 0404
Kenefick Timothy	S Tomlinson QC, London	0171 583 0404
Kenny Julian Hector Marriott	20 Essex Street, London	0171 583 9294
Kenny Stephen Charles Wilfrid	S Tomlinson QC, London	0171 583 0404
Kerr Simon Alexander	S Tomlinson QC, London	0171 583 0404
Khurshid Jawdat	S Tomlinson QC, London	0171 583 0404
Kolodziej Andrzej Jozef	• Littman Chambers, London	020 7404 4866
Kverndal Simon Richard	4 Essex Court, London	020 7797 7970
Lowenstein Paul David	Littleton Chambers, London	0171 797 8600
Macdonald Charles Adam	4 Essex Court, London	020 7797 7970
Malek Ali	3 Verulam Buildings, London	0171 831 8441
Males Stephen Martin	20 Essex Street, London	0171 583 9294
Masters Miss Sara Alayna	20 Essex Street, London	0171 583 9294
Matthews Duncan Henry Rowland	20 Essex Street, London	0171 583 9294
McClure Brian David	Littman Chambers, London	020 7404 4866
Meeson Nigel Keith	4 Field Court, London	0171 440 6900
Melville Richard David	• 39 Essex Street, London	0171 832 1111
Mercer Hugh Charles	• Essex Court Chambers, London	0171 813 8000
Merriman Nicholas Flavelle	3 Verulam Buildings, London	0171 831 8441
Milligan Iain Anstruther	20 Essex Street, London	0171 583 9294
Morgan Richard Hugo Lyndon	13 Old Square, London	0171 404 4800
Morris Stephen Nathan	20 Essex Street, London	0171 583 9294
Neville-Clarke Sebastian Adrian Bennett	1 Crown Office Row, London	0171 583 9292
Nolan Michael Alfred Anthony	4 Essex Court, London	020 7797 7970
O'Shea Eoin Finbarr	4 Field Court, London	0171 440 6900
Owen David Christopher	20 Essex Street, London	0171 583 9294
Pelling (Philip) Mark	Monckton Chambers, London	0171 405 7211
Persey Lionel Edward	• 4 Field Court, London	0171 440 6900
Pershad Rohan	Two Crown Office Row, London	020 7797 8100
Phillips S J	S Tomlinson QC, London	0171 583 0404
Phillips Stephen Edmund	3 Verulam Buildings, London	0171 831 8441
Picken Simon Derek	S Tomlinson QC, London	0171 583 0404
	30 Park Place, Cardiff	01222 398421
Power Lawrence Imam	4 King's Bench Walk, London	0171 822 8822
Reeder John	4 Field Court, London	0171 440 6900
Russell Jeremy Jonathan	• 4 Essex Court, London	020 7797 7970
Sabben-Clare Miss Rebecca Mary	S Tomlinson QC, London	0171 583 0404
Saloman Timothy Peter (Dayrell)	S Tomlinson QC, London	0171 583 0404
Salter Richard Stanley	3 Verulam Buildings, London	0171 831 8441
Sands Mr Philippe Joseph	3 Verulam Buildings, London	0171 831 8441
Saunders Nicholas Joseph	4 Field Court, London	0171 440 6900
Schaff Alistair Graham	S Tomlinson QC, London	0171 583 0404
Selvaratnam Miss Vasanti Emily Indrani	4 Field Court, London	0171 440 6900
Smith Christopher Frank	Essex Court Chambers, London	0171 813 8000
Southern Richard Michael	S Tomlinson QC, London	0171 583 0404
Teare Nigel John Martin	4 Essex Court, London	020 7797 7970
Thomas (Robert) Neville	3 Verulam Buildings, London	0171 831 8441
Tomlinson Stephen Miles	S Tomlinson QC, London	0171 583 0404
Tselentis Michael	• 20 Essex Street, London	0171 583 9294
Turner James Michael	• 4 Essex Court, London	020 7797 7970
Wales Andrew Nigel Malcolm	S Tomlinson QC, London	0171 583 0404
Walford Richard Henry Howard	Serle Court Chambers, London	0171 242 6105
Waller Richard Beaumont	S Tomlinson QC, London	0171 583 0404

• Expanded entry in Part D

Williams Leigh Michael	S Tomlinson QC, London	0171 583 0404
Wood Richard Gillies	20 Essex Street, London	0171 583 9294
	Cathedral Chambers (Jan Wood Independent Barristers' Clerk), Exeter	01392 210900
Wright Colin John	4 Field Court, London	0171 440 6900

IRISH LAW

O'Donoghue Florence	2 Mitre Court Buildings, London	0171 353 1353

ISLAMIC LAW

Syed Mohammad Ali	39 Park Avenue, Mitcham	0181 648 1684
	Tower Hamlets Barristers Chambers, London	0171 247 9825
Thomson Martin Haldane Ahmad	Wynne Chambers, London	0181 961 6144

ITALIAN LAW

Franco Gianpiero	2 Middle Temple Lane, London	0171 583 4540

JUDICIAL REVIEW

Bate David Christopher	Hollis Whiteman Chambers, London	020 7583 5766
Blackford Simon John	Barnard's Inn Chambers, London	0171 369 6969
Boyce William	Hollis Whiteman Chambers, London	020 7583 5766
Clarke Peter William	Hollis Whiteman Chambers, London	020 7583 5766
Ellison Mark Christopher	Hollis Whiteman Chambers, London	020 7583 5766
Finnigan Peter Anthony	Hollis Whiteman Chambers, London	020 7583 5766
Glass Anthony Trevor	Hollis Whiteman Chambers, London	020 7583 5766
Henry Edward Joseph Aloysius	Hollis Whiteman Chambers, London	020 7583 5766
Horwell Richard Eric	Hollis Whiteman Chambers, London	020 7583 5766
Jeffreys David Alfred	Hollis Whiteman Chambers, London	020 7583 5766
Johnson Miss Zoe Elisabeth	Hollis Whiteman Chambers, London	020 7583 5766
Khan Saadallah Frans Hassan	55 Temple Chambers, London	0171 353 7400
Kyte Peter Eric	Hollis Whiteman Chambers, London	020 7583 5766
Larkin Sean	Hollis Whiteman Chambers, London	020 7583 5766
Longden Anthony Gordon	Hollis Whiteman Chambers, London	020 7583 5766
Moser Philip Curt Harold	4 Paper Buildings, London	0171 353 3366/583 7155
Paton Ian Francis	Hollis Whiteman Chambers, London	020 7583 5766
Plaschkes Ms Sarah Georgina	Hollis Whiteman Chambers, London	020 7583 5766
Poulet Mrs Rebecca Maria	Hollis Whiteman Chambers, London	020 7583 5766
Rees Gareth David	Hollis Whiteman Chambers, London	020 7583 5766
Robinson Vivian	Hollis Whiteman Chambers, London	020 7583 5766
Stewart Neill Alastair	Hollis Whiteman Chambers, London	020 7583 5766
Suckling Alan Blair	Hollis Whiteman Chambers, London	020 7583 5766
Weston Ms Amanda	Chambers of Ian Macdonald QC (In Association with Two Garden Court, Temple, London), Manchester	0161 236 1840
Wilcken Anthony David Felix	Hollis Whiteman Chambers, London	020 7583 5766
Wood Guy Nicholas Marshall	Hollis Whiteman Chambers, London	020 7583 5766

JURISDICTION

Gaisman Jonathan Nicholas Crispin	S Tomlinson QC, London	0171 583 0404
Kerr Simon Alexander	S Tomlinson QC, London	0171 583 0404
Priday Charles Nicholas Bruton	S Tomlinson QC, London	0171 583 0404
Saloman Timothy Peter (Dayrell)	S Tomlinson QC, London	0171 583 0404
Southern Richard Michael	S Tomlinson QC, London	0171 583 0404
Tomlinson Stephen Miles	S Tomlinson QC, London	0171 583 0404

LABOUR ARBITRATION

Lewis Professor Roy Malcolm	Old Square Chambers, London	0171 269 0300
	Old Square Chambers, Bristol	0117 9277111

• Expanded entry in Part D

LANDLORD AND TENANT

Abbott Francis Arthur	Pump Court Chambers, Winchester	01962 868161
	Pump Court Chambers, London	0171 353 0711
	Pump Court Chambers, Swindon	01793 539899
Acton Stephen Neil	11 Old Square, London	020 7430 0341
Adams Miss Lorraine Joan	Pulteney Chambers, Bath	01225 723987
Adamyk Simon Charles	12 New Square, London	0171 419 1212
Adejumo Mrs Hilda Ekpo	Temple Chambers, London	0171 583 1001 (2 lines)
Akerman Miss Kate Louise	Queen's Chambers, Manchester	0161 834 6875/4738
	Queens Chambers, Preston	01772 828300
Aldous Robert John	Octagon House, Norwich	01603 623186
Allen Nicholas Paul	29 Bedford Row Chambers, London	0171 831 2626
Allingham-Nicholson Mrs Elizabeth Sarah	2 New Street, Leicester	0116 2625906
Althaus Antony Justin	No. 1 Serjeants' Inn, London	0171 415 6666
Andrews Miss Claire Marguerite	Gough Square Chambers, London	0171 353 0924
Angus Miss Tracey Anne	5 Stone Buildings, London	0171 242 6201
Ash Edward William	3 Temple Gardens, London	0171 353 0832
Ashworth Lance Dominic Piers	St Philip's Chambers, Birmingham	0121 246 7000
	2 Harcourt Buildings, London	0171 583 9020
Atherton Ian David	Enterprise Chambers, London	0171 405 9471
	Enterprise Chambers, Newcastle upon Tyne	0191 222 3344
	Enterprise Chambers, Leeds	0113 246 0391
Ayliffe James Justin Barnett	• Wilberforce Chambers, London	0171 306 0102
Ayres Andrew John William	13 Old Square, London	0171 404 4800
Baker Miss Anne Jacqueline	Enterprise Chambers, London	0171 405 9471
	Enterprise Chambers, Leeds	0113 246 0391
	Enterprise Chambers, Newcastle upon Tyne	0191 222 3344
Baker Stuart Christopher	1 Fountain Court, Birmingham	0121 236 5721
Balchin Richard Alexander	Crown Office Row Chambers, Brighton	01273 625625
Barker James Sebastian	Enterprise Chambers, London	0171 405 9471
	Enterprise Chambers, Leeds	0113 246 0391
	Enterprise Chambers, Newcastle upon Tyne	0191 222 3344
Barker John Steven Roy	Queen's Chambers, Manchester	0161 834 6875/4738
	Queens Chambers, Preston	01772 828300
Barlow Craig Martin	29 Bedford Row Chambers, London	0171 831 2626
Barnes (David) Michael (William)	• Wilberforce Chambers, London	0171 306 0102
Barnett Daniel Alexander	2 Gray's Inn Square Chambers, London	020 7242 0328
Barraclough Richard Michael	6 Pump Court, London	0171 797 8400
	6-8 Mill Street, Maidstone	01622 688094
Barton Alan John	Lamb Building, London	020 7797 7788
Bash-Taqi Mrs Shahineh	Leone Chambers, London	0181 200 4020
Bassa Yousef	St Albans Chambers, St Albans	01727 843383
	Tindal Chambers, Chelmsford	01245 267742
Bastin Alexander Charles	2nd Floor, Francis Taylor Building, London	0171 353 9942/3157
Basu Dr Dijendra Bhushan	Devereux Chambers, London	0171 353 7534
Beard Mark Christopher	6 Pump Court, London	0171 797 8400
	6-8 Mill Street, Maidstone	01622 688094
Beaumont Marc Clifford	• Harrow on the Hill Chambers, Harrow-on-the-Hill	0181 423 7444
	Windsor Barristers' Chambers, Windsor	01753 648899
	Pump Court Chambers, London	0171 353 0711
Beer Jason Barrington	5 Essex Court, London	0171 410 2000
Beever Edmund Damian	St Philip's Chambers, Birmingham	0121 246 7000
Behrens James Nicholas Edward	Serle Court Chambers, London	0171 242 6105
Bennett Gordon Irvine	12 New Square, London	0171 419 1212

• Expanded entry in Part D

Berry Nicholas Michael	Southernhay Chambers, Exeter	01392 255777
	1 Gray's Inn Square, London	0171 405 8946/7/8
	22 Old Buildings, London	0171 831 0222
Bevis Dominic Joseph	10 King's Bench Walk, London	0171 353 7742
Bhaloo Miss Zia Kurban	Enterprise Chambers, London	0171 405 9471
	Enterprise Chambers, Leeds	0113 246 0391
	Enterprise Chambers, Newcastle upon Tyne	0191 222 3344
Birtles William	Old Square Chambers, London	0171 269 0300
	Old Square Chambers, Bristol	0117 9277111
Blackett-Ord Mark	• 5 Stone Buildings, London	0171 242 6201
Blayney David James	Serle Court Chambers, London	0171 242 6105
Bleasdale Miss Marie-Claire	Chambers of Mr Peter Crampin QC, London	020 7831 0081
Blom-Cooper Sir Louis Jacques	Doughty Street Chambers, London	0171 404 1313
Bowker Robert James	2nd Floor, Francis Taylor Building, London	0171 353 9942/3157
Bowmer Michael Paul	11 Old Square, London	020 7430 0341
Boyd Stephen James Harvey	29 Bedford Row Chambers, London	0171 831 2626
Bredemear Zachary Charles	Barnard's Inn Chambers, London	0171 369 6969
Bresler Fenton Shea	22 Melcombe Regis Court, London	0171 487 5589
Briggs Michael Townley Featherstone	Serle Court Chambers, London	0171 242 6105
Broatch Michael Donald	5 Paper Buildings, London	0171 583 9275/583 4555
Brockley Nigel Simon	Bracton Chambers, London	0171 242 4248
Browne James William	96 Gray's Inn Road, London	0171 405 0585
Bruce Andrew Jonathan	Serle Court Chambers, London	0171 242 6105
Bryant John Malcolm Cornelius	Barnard's Inn Chambers, London	0171 369 6969
Buck Dr Andrew Theodore	Chambers of Martin Burr, London	0171 353 4636
Buckley Peter Evered	Queen's Chambers, Manchester	0161 834 6875/4738
	Queens Chambers, Preston	01772 828300
Buckpitt Michael David	2nd Floor, Francis Taylor Building, London	0171 353 9942/3157
Burden Edward Angus	St Philip's Chambers, Birmingham	0121 246 7000
Burr Martin John	Chambers of Martin Burr, London	0171 353 4636
	7 New Square, London	0171 430 1660
Burton Nicholas Anthony	2 Mitre Court Buildings, London	0171 583 1380
Butler Andrew	2nd Floor, Francis Taylor Building, London	0171 353 9942/3157
Butler Simon David	10 King's Bench Walk, London	0171 353 7742
Butterworth Paul Anthony	Octagon House, Norwich	01603 623186
Buxton Miss Sarah Ruth	1 Fountain Court, Birmingham	0121 236 5721
Cakebread Stuart Alan Charles	• 2nd Floor, Francis Taylor Building, London	0171 353 9942/3157
Campbell-Brown Miss Anne Louise	Bracton Chambers, London	0171 242 4248
Cannon Adam Richard	96 Gray's Inn Road, London	0171 405 0585
Carroll Jonathan Neil	9 Woodhouse Square, Leeds	0113 2451986
Cave Jeremy Stephen	1 Crown Office Row, London	0171 797 7500
	Crown Office Row Chambers, Brighton	01273 625625
Cawley Neil Robert Loudoun	169 Temple Chambers, London	0171 583 7644
	Milton Keynes Chambers, Milton Keynes	01908 664 128
Chan Miss Susan	13 King's Bench Walk, London	0171 353 7204
	King's Bench Chambers, Oxford	01865 311066
Charlwood Spike Llewellyn	4 Paper Buildings, London	0171 353 3366/583 7155
Christie-Brown Miss Sarah Louise	4 Paper Buildings, London	0171 353 3366/583 7155
Clark Andrew Richard	Manchester House Chambers, Manchester	0161 834 7007
	8 King Street Chambers, Manchester	0161 834 9560
Clarke Miss Anna Victoria	5 Stone Buildings, London	0171 242 6201
Clarke Ian James	Hardwicke Building, London	020 7242 2523
Clarke Ms Joanne Elizabeth	33 Bedford Row, London	0171 242 6476

       • Expanded entry in Part D

Clegg Sebastian James Barwick	Deans Court Chambers, Manchester	0161 214 6000
	Deans Court Chambers, Preston	01772 555163
Cogswell Miss Frederica Natasha	Gough Square Chambers, London	0171 353 0924
Colbey Richard (Alan)	• Francis Taylor Building, London	0171 797 7250
	Guildhall Chambers Portsmouth, Portsmouth	01705 752400
Colin Giles David	Crown Office Row Chambers, Brighton	01273 625625
Collard Michael David	5 Pump Court, London	020 7353 2532
Compton Gareth Francis Thomas	22 Old Buildings, London	0171 831 0222
Cooper Gilead Patrick	Chambers of Mr Peter Crampin QC, London	020 7831 0081
Cooper Mark Anthony John	2 Mitre Court Buildings, London	0171 353 1353
Corbett Mrs Sandra Margaret	1 New Square, London	0171 405 0884/5/6/7
Cowen Timothy Arieh	Barnard's Inn Chambers, London	0171 369 6969
Craig Alistair Trevor	Chambers of Mr Peter Crampin QC, London	020 7831 0081
Craig Kenneth Allen	Hardwicke Building, London	020 7242 2523
Crail Miss (Elspeth) Ross	12 New Square, London	0171 419 1212
	Sovereign Chambers, Leeds	0113 2451841/2/3
Cramsie James Sinclair Beresford	13 King's Bench Walk, London	0171 353 7204
	King's Bench Chambers, Oxford	01865 311066
Cranfield Peter Anthony	3 Verulam Buildings, London	0171 831 8441
Crawford Grant	11 Old Square, London	020 7430 0341
Crossley Simon Justin	9 Woodhouse Square, Leeds	0113 2451986
Daly David	Francis Taylor Building, London	0171 797 7250
Datta Mrs Wendy Patricia Mizal	Alban Chambers, London	0171 419 5051
Davey Benjamin Nicholas	11 Old Square, London	020 7430 0341
Davies Miss Carol Elizabeth	2 New Street, Leicester	0116 2625906
Davies Dr Charles Edward	4 Field Court, London	0171 440 6900
Davies Miss (Susan) Louise	12 New Square, London	0171 419 1212
	Sovereign Chambers, Leeds	0113 2451841/2/3
De Freitas Anthony Peter Stanley	4 Paper Buildings, London	0171 353 3366/583 7155
de Waal John Henry Lowndes	St Philip's Chambers, Birmingham	0121 246 7000
Dean Peter Thomas	1 Crown Office Row, London	0171 583 9292
Dedezade Taner	Tindal Chambers, Chelmsford	01245 267742
Denbin Jack Arnold	Greenway, Sonning-on-Thames	0118 969 2484
deSouza Mrs Josephine Claudia	Chancery Chambers, London	0171 405 6879/6870
Dillon Thomas William Matthew	1 Fountain Court, Birmingham	0121 236 5721
Dineen Michael Laurence	Pump Court Chambers, Winchester	01962 868161
	Pump Court Chambers, London	0171 353 0711
	Queens Square Chambers, Bristol	0117 921 1966
	Pump Court Chambers, Swindon	01793 539899
Dixon Philip John	2nd Floor, Francis Taylor Building, London	0171 353 9942/3157
Dodd Christopher John Nicholas	9 Woodhouse Square, Leeds	0113 2451986
Dodge Peter Clive	11 Old Square, London	020 7430 0341
Dooher Miss Nancy Helen	St James's Chambers, Manchester	0161 834 7000
Douglas Michael John	4 Pump Court, London	020 7842 5555
Duddridge Robert James	2 Gray's Inn Square Chambers, London	020 7242 0328
Dudley Michael John	1 Fountain Court, Birmingham	0121 236 5721
Dugdale Nicholas	4 Field Court, London	0171 440 6900
Dunn Christopher	Sovereign Chambers, Leeds	0113 2451841/2/3
Dutton Timothy Christopher	Barnard's Inn Chambers, London	0171 369 6969
Eidinow John Samuel Christopher	1 New Square, London	0171 405 0884/5/6/7
Elleray Anthony John	• St James's Chambers, Manchester	0161 834 7000
	12 New Square, London	0171 419 1212
	Park Lane Chambers, Leeds	0113 2285000
Ellis Miss Catherine Anne	Derby Square Chambers, Liverpool	0151 709 4222
Ellis Roger John	13 King's Bench Walk, London	0171 353 7204
	King's Bench Chambers, Oxford	01865 311066
Evans Jonathan Edward	• Wilberforce Chambers, London	0171 306 0102

Evans Richard Gareth	5 Paper Buildings, London	0171 583 9275/583 4555
Evans Stephen James	8 King's Bench Walk, London	0171 797 8888
	8 King's Bench Walk North, Leeds	0113 2439797
Eyre Stephen John Arthur	1 Fountain Court, Birmingham	0121 236 5721
Fadipe Gabriel Charles	• Wilberforce Chambers, London	0171 306 0102
Fairbank Nicholas James	Becket Chambers, Canterbury	01227 786331
Faluyi Albert Osamudiamen	Chambers of Martin Burr, London	0171 353 4636
Farquharson Jonathan	Colleton Chambers, Exeter	01392 274898/9
Farrow Kenneth John	Serle Court Chambers, London	0171 242 6105
Feltham Piers Jonathan	Chambers of Mr Peter Crampin QC, London	020 7831 0081
Fenston Miss Felicia Donovan	2 Harcourt Buildings, London	0171 583 9020
Fieldsend James William	2nd Floor, Francis Taylor Building, London	0171 353 9942/3157
Finn Terence	Chambers of Martin Burr, London	0171 353 4636
Fitzpatrick Edward James	8 King's Bench Walk, London	0171 797 8888
Fletcher Christopher Michael	Octagon House, Norwich	01603 623186
Ford Gerard James	Baker Street Chambers, Middlesbrough	01642 873873
Foster Brian Ian	St James's Chambers, Manchester	0161 834 7000
	Park Lane Chambers, Leeds	0113 2285000
Francis Andrew James	Chambers of Mr Peter Crampin QC, London	020 7831 0081
Francis Edward Gerald Francis	Enterprise Chambers, London	0171 405 9471
	Enterprise Chambers, Leeds	0113 246 0391
	Enterprise Chambers, Newcastle upon Tyne	0191 222 3344
Francois Herbert Dolton	Chambers of Herbert Francois, Mitcham	0181 640 4529
Fryer-Spedding James Walter	St James's Chambers, Manchester	0161 834 7000
Furber (Robert) John	• Wilberforce Chambers, London	0171 306 0102
Gannon Kevin Francis	8 King's Bench Walk, London	0171 797 8888
	8 King's Bench Walk North, Leeds	0113 2439797
Garner Miss Sophie Jane	199 Strand, London	0171 379 9779
Gasztowicz Steven	2-3 Gray's Inn Square, London	0171 242 4986
	2 New Street, Leicester	0116 2625906
George Donald Eric Joseph	Leone Chambers, London	0181 200 4020
Gerald Nigel Mortimer	Enterprise Chambers, London	0171 405 9471
	Enterprise Chambers, Leeds	0113 246 0391
	Enterprise Chambers, Newcastle upon Tyne	0191 222 3344
Gibaud Miss Catherine Alison Annetta	3 Verulam Buildings, London	0171 831 8441
Gibson Miss Jill Maureen	Chambers of Mr Peter Crampin QC, London	020 7831 0081
Gifford Andrew James Morris	7 New Square, London	0171 430 1660
Glen Philip Alexander	17 Carlton Crescent, Southampton	023 8032 0320/0823 2003
Glynn Stephen Peter	9 Gough Square, London	020 7832 0500
Gow Miss Elizabeth Suzanne	Iscoed Chambers, Swansea	01792 652988/9/330
Green David Cameron	Adrian Lyon's Chambers, Liverpool	0151 236 4421/8240
Green Miss Jane Elizabeth	Design Chambers, London	0171 353 0747
	Chambers of Martin Burr, London	0171 353 4636
Greenan Miss Sarah Octavia	9 Woodhouse Square, Leeds	0113 2451986
Gregory John Raymond	Deans Court Chambers, Manchester	0161 214 6000
	Deans Court Chambers, Preston	01772 555163
Grime John Andrew	Pump Court Chambers, Swindon	01793 539899
	Pump Court Chambers, London	0171 353 0711
	Pump Court Chambers, Winchester	01962 868161
Haji Miss Shaheen	Bell Yard Chambers, London	0171 306 9292
Hall Taylor Alexander Edward	11 Old Square, London	020 7430 0341

Halpern David Anthony	Enterprise Chambers, London	0171 405 9471
	Enterprise Chambers, Leeds	0113 246 0391
	Enterprise Chambers, Newcastle upon Tyne	0191 222 3344
Hantusch Robert Anthony	• 3 Stone Buildings, London	0171 242 4937
Harding Dr Gladys Modwyn Cicely	Leone Chambers, London	0181 200 4020
Hardwick Matthew Richard	Enterprise Chambers, London	0171 405 9471
	Enterprise Chambers, Leeds	0113 246 0391
	Enterprise Chambers, Newcastle upon Tyne	0191 222 3344
Harper Miss Victoria Jane Tryphosa	3 Temple Gardens, London	0171 353 0832
Harris Melvyn	7 New Square, London	0171 430 1660
Harrod Henry Mark	5 Stone Buildings, London	0171 242 6201
Hassall James Christopher	Southernhay Chambers, Exeter	01392 255777
Hawkes Miss Naomi Nanteza Astrid Wallusimbi	22 Old Buildings, London	0171 831 0222
Heather Christopher Mark	• 2nd Floor, Francis Taylor Building, London	0171 353 9942/3157
Henley Mark Robert Daniel	9 Woodhouse Square, Leeds	0113 2451986
Higgins Adrian John	13 King's Bench Walk, London	0171 353 7204
	King's Bench Chambers, Oxford	01865 311066
Higgins Rupert James Hale	Littman Chambers, London	020 7404 4866
Higgo Justin Beresford	Serle Court Chambers, London	0171 242 6105
Hill Piers Nicholas	37 Park Square Chambers, Leeds	0113 2439422
Hinks Frank Peter	Serle Court Chambers, London	0171 242 6105
Hodgson Ms Jane	9 Woodhouse Square, Leeds	0113 2451986
Hodgson Martin Derrick	8 King's Bench Walk, London	0171 797 8888
	8 King's Bench Walk North, Leeds	0113 2439797
Hodgson Timothy Paul	8 King Street Chambers, Manchester	0161 834 9560
Holland David Moore	29 Bedford Row Chambers, London	0171 831 2626
Holmes Philip John	8 King Street Chambers, Manchester	0161 834 9560
Hornett Stuart Ian	29 Bedford Row Chambers, London	0171 831 2626
Horton Matthew Bethell	2 Mitre Court Buildings, London	0171 583 1380
Howarth Simon Stuart	Two Crown Office Row, London	020 7797 8100
Hunter William Quigley	No. 1 Serjeants' Inn, London	0171 415 6666
Hutchin Edward Alister David	Bracton Chambers, London	0171 242 4248
Hutchings Martin Anthony	199 Strand, London	0171 379 9779
Hutton Miss Caroline	Enterprise Chambers, London	0171 405 9471
	Enterprise Chambers, Leeds	0113 246 0391
	Enterprise Chambers, Newcastle upon Tyne	0191 222 3344
Ife Miss Linden Elizabeth	Enterprise Chambers, London	0171 405 9471
	Enterprise Chambers, Leeds	0113 246 0391
	Enterprise Chambers, Newcastle upon Tyne	0191 222 3344
Iles Adrian	5 Paper Buildings, London	0171 583 9275/583 4555
Jack Adrian Laurence Robert	Enterprise Chambers, London	0171 405 9471
	Enterprise Chambers, Newcastle upon Tyne	0191 222 3344
	Enterprise Chambers, Leeds	0113 246 0391
Jackson Dirik George Allan	Chambers of Mr Peter Crampin QC, London	020 7831 0081
Jackson Hugh Woodward	Hardwicke Building, London	020 7242 2523
Jackson Nicholas David Kingsley	Adrian Lyon's Chambers, Liverpool	0151 236 4421/8240
James-Stadden Miss Jodie Cara	Westgate Chambers, Newcastle upon Tyne	0191 261 4407/2329785
Jefferis Arthur Michael Quentin	Chambers of Mr Peter Crampin QC, London	020 7831 0081
Johnston Anthony Paul	1 Fountain Court, Birmingham	0121 236 5721
Jones Martin Wynne	8 King's Bench Walk, London	0171 797 8888
	8 King's Bench Walk North, Leeds	0113 2439797

B

Jones Philip John	Serle Court Chambers, London	0171 242 6105
Jones Miss Susannah Lucy	Octagon House, Norwich	01603 623186
Karas Jonathan Marcus	• Wilberforce Chambers, London	0171 306 0102
Keane Michael Leo	4 Paper Buildings, London	0171 353 3366/583 7155
Kenward Timothy David Nelson	25-27 Castle Street, Liverpool	0151 227 5661/051 236 5072
Keogh Andrew John	8 King's Bench Walk, London	0171 797 8888
	8 King's Bench Walk North, Leeds	0113 2439797
Kerr Derek William	Francis Taylor Building, London	0171 353 7768/7769/2711
King Charles Granville	96 Gray's Inn Road, London	0171 405 0585
Kinnier Andrew John	2 Harcourt Buildings, London	0171 583 9020
Kremen Philip Michael	Hardwicke Building, London	020 7242 2523
Kynoch Duncan Stuart Sanderson	29 Bedford Row Chambers, London	0171 831 2626
Lamb Robert Glasson	13 King's Bench Walk, London	0171 353 7204
	King's Bench Chambers, Oxford	01865 311066
Lamont Miss Camilla Rose	Chambers of Lord Goodhart QC, London	0171 405 5577
Leason Ms Karen Dawn	St Philip's Chambers, Birmingham	0121 246 7000
Levy Benjamin Keith	Enterprise Chambers, London	0171 405 9471
	Enterprise Chambers, Leeds	0113 246 0391
	Enterprise Chambers, Newcastle upon Tyne	0191 222 3344
Lightman Daniel	Serle Court Chambers, London	0171 242 6105
Lindqvist Andrew Nils Gunnar	Octagon House, Norwich	01603 623186
Lloyd Stephen James George	Chambers of Mr Peter Crampin QC, London	020 7831 0081
Lo Bernard Norman	17 Bedford Row, London	0171 831 7314
Lochrane Damien Horatio Ross	Pump Court Chambers, London	0171 353 0711
	Pump Court Chambers, Winchester	01962 868161
	Pump Court Chambers, Swindon	01793 539899
Lowry Charles Stephen	Colleton Chambers, Exeter	01392 274898/9
MacDonald Alistair William Orchard	St Philip's Chambers, Birmingham	0121 246 7000
Macpherson Duncan Charles Stewart	Bracton Chambers, London	0171 242 4248
Mainwaring [Robert] Paul Clason	Carmarthen Chambers, Carmarthen	01267 234410
Majumdar Shantanu	Lamb Chambers, London	020 7797 8300
Mandalia Vinesh Lalji	Harrow on the Hill Chambers, Harrow-on-the-Hill	0181 423 7444
Mann George Anthony	Enterprise Chambers, London	0171 405 9471
	Enterprise Chambers, Leeds	0113 246 0391
	Enterprise Chambers, Newcastle upon Tyne	0191 222 3344
Margolin Daniel George	Chambers of Mr Peter Crampin QC, London	020 7831 0081
Markus Ms Kate	Doughty Street Chambers, London	0171 404 1313
Martin Mrs Jill Elizabeth	Barnard's Inn Chambers, London	0171 369 6969
Martin John Vandeleur	• Wilberforce Chambers, London	0171 306 0102
Mauger Miss Claire Shanti Andrea	Enterprise Chambers, London	0171 405 9471
	Enterprise Chambers, Newcastle upon Tyne	0191 222 3344
	Enterprise Chambers, Leeds	0113 246 0391
Maynard-Connor Giles	St James's Chambers, Manchester	0161 834 7000
McAlinden Barry O'Neill	17 Bedford Row, London	0171 831 7314
McAllister Miss Eimear Jane	9 Woodhouse Square, Leeds	0113 2451986
McAllister Miss Elizabeth Ann	Enterprise Chambers, London	0171 405 9471
	Enterprise Chambers, Leeds	0113 246 0391
	Enterprise Chambers, Newcastle upon Tyne	0191 222 3344
McCahey Miss Catherine Anne Mary	St Philip's Chambers, Birmingham	0121 246 7000
McHugh Denis David	Bracton Chambers, London	0171 242 4248
McKechnie Stuart Iain William	2 Gray's Inn Square Chambers, London	020 7242 0328

          • Expanded entry in Part D

McKinnell Miss Soraya Jane	Enterprise Chambers, London	0171 405 9471
	Enterprise Chambers, Newcastle upon Tyne	0191 222 3344
	Enterprise Chambers, Leeds	0113 246 0391
McQuail Ms Katherine Emma	11 Old Square, London	020 7430 0341
Mehendale Ms Neelima Krishna	2 Mitre Court Buildings, London	0171 353 1353
Mendoza Neil David Pereira	Hardwicke Building, London	020 7242 2523
Middleton Joseph	Doughty Street Chambers, London	0171 404 1313
Mitchell Brenton Ballingtine	Bell Yard Chambers, London	0171 306 9292
Mitchell Miss Julianna Marie	2 Harcourt Buildings, London	0171 583 9020
Mitropoulos Christos	Chambers of Geoffrey Hawker, London	0171 583 8899
Morgan Andrew James	St Philip's Chambers, Birmingham	0121 246 7000
Morgan Charles James Arthur	Enterprise Chambers, London	0171 405 9471
	Enterprise Chambers, Newcastle upon Tyne	0191 222 3344
	Enterprise Chambers, Leeds	0113 246 0391
Morgan Richard Hugo Lyndon	13 Old Square, London	0171 404 4800
Morgan (Thomas) Jeremy	39 Essex Street, London	0171 832 1111
Murray-Smith James Michael	8 King's Bench Walk, London	0171 797 8888
	8 King's Bench Walk North, Leeds	0113 2439797
Nesbitt Timothy John Robert	199 Strand, London	0171 379 9779
Norris Alastair Hubert	5 Stone Buildings, London	0171 242 6201
	Southernhay Chambers, Exeter	01392 255777
Nugee Christopher George	• Wilberforce Chambers, London	0171 306 0102
Nugee Edward George	• Wilberforce Chambers, London	0171 306 0102
Nurse Gordon Bramwell William	11 Old Square, London	020 7430 0341
O'Donovan Ronan Daniel James	14 Gray's Inn Square, London	0171 242 0858
O'Leary Robert Michael	33 Park Place, Cardiff	02920 233313
O'Shea Eoin Finbarr	4 Field Court, London	0171 440 6900
Oakley Paul James	1 Gray's Inn Square, London	0171 405 8946/7/8
Ohrenstein Dov	Chambers of Lord Goodhart QC, London	0171 405 5577
Osman Robert Walter	Queen's Chambers, Manchester	0161 834 6875/4738
	Queens Chambers, Preston	01772 828300
Paget Michael Rodborough	Bracton Chambers, London	0171 242 4248
Palfrey Montague Mark	Hardwicke Building, London	020 7242 2523
Panesar Deshpal Singh	13 King's Bench Walk, London	0171 353 7204
	King's Bench Chambers, Oxford	01865 311066
Parker John	2 Mitre Court Buildings, London	0171 353 1353
Patel Bhavin Vinubhai	Chambers of Martin Burr, London	0171 353 4636
Peacock Miss Lisa Jayne	3 Dr Johnson's Buildings, London	0171 353 4854
Peacock Nicholas Christopher	13 Old Square, London	0171 404 4800
Peacocke Mrs Teresa Anne Rosen	Enterprise Chambers, London	0171 405 9471
	Enterprise Chambers, Leeds	0113 246 0391
	Enterprise Chambers, Newcastle upon Tyne	0191 222 3344
Pearce Robert Edgar	Chambers of Mr Peter Crampin QC, London	020 7831 0081
Pears Derrick Allan	2nd Floor, Francis Taylor Building, London	0171 353 9942/3157
Pearson Christopher	• Bridewell Chambers, London	020 7797 8800
Peirson Oliver James	Pump Court Chambers, London	0171 353 0711
	Pump Court Chambers, Winchester	01962 868161
	Pump Court Chambers, Swindon	01793 539899
Pema Anes Bhumin Laloo	9 Woodhouse Square, Leeds	0113 2451986
Perkins Miss Marianne Yvette	7 New Square, London	0171 430 1660
Pickering James Patrick	Enterprise Chambers, London	0171 405 9471
	Enterprise Chambers, Leeds	0113 246 0391
	Enterprise Chambers, Newcastle upon Tyne	0191 222 3344
Pilkington Mrs Mavis Patricia	9 Woodhouse Square, Leeds	0113 2451986

Pimentel Carlos de Serpa Alberto Legg	3 Stone Buildings, London	0171 242 4937
Pliener David Jonathan	New Court Chambers, London	0171 831 9500
Pomeroy Toby	Barristers' Common Law Chambers, London	0171 375 3012
	Virtual Chambers, London	07071 244 944
Post Andrew John	Chambers of Kieran Coonan QC, London	0171 583 6013/2510
Potts Warren Nigel	Queen's Chambers, Manchester	0161 834 6875/4738
	Queens Chambers, Preston	01772 828300
Price John Scott	10 Launceston Avenue, Reading	01189 479548
	Southsea Chambers, Portsmouth	01705 291261
	Cathedral Chambers, Newcastle upon Tyne	0191 232 1311
Prinn Miss Helen Elizabeth	Octagon House, Norwich	01603 623186
Purdie Robert Anthony James	28 Western Road, Oxford	01865 204911
Purkis Ms Kathryn Miranda	Serle Court Chambers, London	0171 242 6105
Purves Gavin Bowman	Swan House, London	0181 998 3035
Radevsky Anthony Eric	Falcon Chambers, London	0171 353 2484
Rai Amarjit Singh	St Philip's Chambers, Birmingham	0121 246 7000
Rainey Philip Carslake	2nd Floor, Francis Taylor Building, London	0171 353 9942/3157
Rashid Omar	Chambers of Mr Peter Crampin QC, London	020 7831 0081
Raybaud Mrs June Rose	96 Gray's Inn Road, London	0171 405 0585
Read Simon Eric	8 King's Bench Walk, London	0171 797 8888
	8 King's Bench Walk North, Leeds	0113 2439797
Readings Douglas George	St Philip's Chambers, Birmingham	0121 246 7000
Reed John William Rupert	• Wilberforce Chambers, London	0171 306 0102
Reeder Stephen	Doughty Street Chambers, London	0171 404 1313
Rees David Benjamin	5 Stone Buildings, London	0171 242 6201
Reid Sebastian Peter Scott	2nd Floor, Francis Taylor Building, London	0171 353 9942/3157
Renfree Peter Gerald Stanley	Harbour Court Chambers, Fareham	01329 827828
Rich Jonathan Bernard George	5 Paper Buildings, London	0171 583 9275/583 4555
Richardson Giles John	Serle Court Chambers, London	0171 242 6105
Roberts Michael Charles	1 New Square, London	0171 405 0884/5/6/7
Robinson Simon Robert	Chambers of Ian Macdonald QC (In Association with Two Garden Court, Temple, London), Manchester	0161 236 1840
Rochford Thomas Nicholas Beverley	St Philip's Chambers, Birmingham	0121 246 7000
Rogers Miss Beverly-Ann	Serle Court Chambers, London	0171 242 6105
Rolfe Patrick John Benedict	5 Stone Buildings, London	0171 242 6201
Ronksley Andrew Peter	3 Temple Gardens, London	0171 353 0832
Ross Martyn John Greaves	• 5 New Square, London	020 7404 0404
Rothery Peter	Queen's Chambers, Manchester	0161 834 6875/4738
	Queens Chambers, Preston	01772 828300
Rowell David Stewart	Chambers of Lord Goodhart QC, London	0171 405 5577
Rowley Keith Nigel	11 Old Square, London	020 7430 0341
Rowntree Edward John Pickering	Hardwicke Building, London	020 7242 2523
Rumney Conrad William Arthur	St Philip's Chambers, Birmingham	0121 246 7000
Russell Christopher Garnet	• 12 New Square, London	0171 419 1212
	Sovereign Chambers, Leeds	0113 2451841/2/3
Ryder Timothy Robert	Queen's Chambers, Manchester	0161 834 6875/4738
	Queens Chambers, Preston	01772 828300
Salmon Jonathan Carl	1 Fountain Court, Birmingham	0121 236 5721
Salter Charles Philip Arthur	8 King's Bench Walk, London	0171 797 8888
	8 King's Bench Walk North, Leeds	0113 2439797
Sartin Leon James	5 Stone Buildings, London	0171 242 6201
Seal Julius Damien	189 Randolph Avenue, London	0171 624 9139
Seitler Jonathan Simon	• Wilberforce Chambers, London	0171 306 0102
Sellers Graham	Adrian Lyon's Chambers, Liverpool	0151 236 4421/8240

                            • Expanded entry in Part D

Selway Dr Katherine Emma	11 Old Square, London	020 7430 0341
Semken Christopher Richard	1 New Square, London	0171 405 0884/5/6/7
Seymour Thomas Oliver	• Wilberforce Chambers, London	0171 306 0102
Shale Justin Anton	4 King's Bench Walk, London	0171 822 8822
	King's Bench Chambers, Bournemouth	01202 250025
Sheehan Malcolm Peter	2 Harcourt Buildings, London	0171 583 9020
Shepherd Nigel Patrick	8 King's Bench Walk North, Leeds	0113 2439797
	8 King's Bench Walk, London	0171 797 8888
Sheppard Timothy Derie	Bracton Chambers, London	0171 242 4248
Sher Jules	• Wilberforce Chambers, London	0171 306 0102
Shillingford George Miles	Chambers of Mr Peter Crampin QC, London	020 7831 0081
Short Miss Anna Louise	Barnard's Inn Chambers, London	0171 369 6969
Shuman Miss Karen Ann Elizabeth	Bracton Chambers, London	0171 242 4248
Siddiqi Faizul Aqtab	Justice Court Chambers, London	0181 830 7786
Simpson Ian	Bracton Chambers, London	0171 242 4248
Sinclair Graham Kelso	East Anglian Chambers, Norwich	01603 617351
	East Anglian Chambers, Colchester	01206 572756
	East Anglian Chambers, Ipswich	01473 214481
Sinclair Miss Lisa Anne	7 New Square, London	0171 430 1660
Sinnatt Simon Peter Randall	Crown Office Row Chambers, Brighton	01273 625625
Skelly Andrew Jon	1 Gray's Inn Square, London	0171 405 8946/7/8
Slaughter Andrew Francis	Bridewell Chambers, London	020 7797 8800
Smith Howard James	Chambers of Mr Peter Crampin QC, London	020 7831 0081
Smith Miss Julia Mair Wheldon	Gough Square Chambers, London	0171 353 0924
Smith Nicholas Martin	1 Fountain Court, Birmingham	0121 236 5721
Sparrow Miss Claire Louise	Eastbourne Chambers, Eastbourne	01323 642102
Staddon Paul	2nd Floor, Francis Taylor Building, London	0171 353 9942/3157
Stagg Paul Andrew	No. 1 Serjeants' Inn, London	0171 415 6666
Starcevic Petar	St Philip's Chambers, Birmingham	0121 246 7000
Stark James Hayden Alexander	Chambers of Ian Macdonald QC (In Association with Two Garden Court, Temple, London), Manchester	0161 236 1840
Start Miss Angharad Jocelyn	3 Verulam Buildings, London	0171 831 8441
Staunton (Thomas) Ulick (Patrick)	Chambers of Mr Peter Crampin QC, London	020 7831 0081
	65-67 King Street, Leicester	0116 2547710
Sterling Robert Alan	St James's Chambers, Manchester	0161 834 7000
	12 New Square, London	0171 419 1212
	Park Lane Chambers, Leeds	0113 2285000
Stevens-Hoare Miss Michelle	Hardwicke Building, London	020 7242 2523
Stevens-Hoare Miss Michelle	Hardwicke Building, London	020 7242 2523
Stewart Nicholas John Cameron	Hardwicke Building, London	020 7242 2523
Stewart-Smith William Rodney	1 New Square, London	0171 405 0884/5/6/7
Sullivan Scott	Barnard's Inn Chambers, London	0171 369 6969
Szanto Gregory John Michael	Eastbourne Chambers, Eastbourne	01323 642102
Talbot Patrick John	Serle Court Chambers, London	0171 242 6105
Thain Miss Ashley	East Anglian Chambers, Colchester	01206 572756
	East Anglian Chambers, Ipswich	01473 214481
	East Anglian Chambers, Norwich	01603 617351
Thom James Alexander Francis	4 Field Court, London	0171 440 6900
Thomas Nigel Matthew	13 Old Square, London	0171 404 4800
Tipples Miss Amanda Jane	13 Old Square, London	0171 404 4800
Tizzano Franco Salvatore	8 King's Bench Walk, London	0171 797 8888
	8 King's Bench Walk North, Leeds	0113 2439797
Trace Anthony John	• 13 Old Square, London	0171 404 4800
Tully Ms Anne Margaret	Eastbourne Chambers, Eastbourne	01323 642102
Turnbull Charles Emerson Lovett	• Wilberforce Chambers, London	0171 306 0102
Tyack David Guy	St Philip's Chambers, Birmingham	0121 246 7000

• Expanded entry in Part D

Van Tonder Gerard Dirk	1 New Square, London	0171 405 0884/5/6/7
Vaughan-Neil Miss Catherine Mary Bernardine	4 Pump Court, London	020 7842 5555
Verduyn Dr Anthony James	St Philip's Chambers, Birmingham	0121 246 7000
Vickery Neil Michael	13 King's Bench Walk, London	0171 353 7204
	King's Bench Chambers, Oxford	01865 311066
Wagner Mrs Linda Ann	96 Gray's Inn Road, London	0171 405 0585
Walden-Smith Miss Karen Jane	5 Stone Buildings, London	0171 242 6201
Walker Andrew Greenfield	Chambers of Lord Goodhart QC, London	0171 405 5577
Walsh Simon	Bridewell Chambers, London	020 7797 8800
Walters Edmund John	13 King's Bench Walk, London	0171 353 7204
	King's Bench Chambers, Oxford	01865 311066
Warner David Alexander	1 New Square, London	0171 405 0884/5/6/7
Warrender Miss Nichola Mary	New Court Chambers, London	0171 831 9500
Warwick Mark Granville	• 29 Bedford Row Chambers, London	0171 831 2626
Waters Julian William Penrose	No. 1 Serjeants' Inn, London	0171 415 6666
Watkin Toby Paul	22 Old Buildings, London	0171 831 0222
Wayne Nicholas	1 Gray's Inn Square, London	0171 405 8946/7/8
Weatherill Bernard Richard	Chambers of Lord Goodhart QC, London	0171 405 5577
Webb Stanley George	The Chambers of Mr Ali Mohammed Azhar, London	0171 353 9564
	Bracton Chambers, London	0171 242 4248
West Mark	• 11 Old Square, London	020 7430 0341
Westgate Martin Trevor	Doughty Street Chambers, London	0171 404 1313
Whitaker Steven Dixon	199 Strand, London	0171 379 9779
	Queens Square Chambers, Bristol	0117 921 1966
White Matthew James	13 King's Bench Walk, London	0171 353 7204
	King's Bench Chambers, Oxford	01865 311066
Wicks Ms Joanne	• Wilberforce Chambers, London	0171 306 0102
Williams Andrew Arthur	Adrian Lyon's Chambers, Liverpool	0151 236 4421/8240
Williams Ms Heather Jean	Doughty Street Chambers, London	0171 404 1313
Williams Dr Jason Scott	• 3 Dr Johnson's Buildings, London	0171 353 4854
Williams Thomas Christopher Charles	1 Fountain Court, Birmingham	0121 236 5721
Wilson Gerald Simon John	2nd Floor, Francis Taylor Building, London	0171 353 9942/3157
Wilson-Barnes Miss Lucy Emma	St James's Chambers, Manchester	0161 834 7000
Wilton Simon Daniel	4 Paper Buildings, London	0171 353 3366/583 7155
Woolf Steven Jeremy	Hardwicke Building, London	020 7242 2523
Young Alastair Angus McLeod	St Philip's Chambers, Birmingham	0121 246 7000
Yoxall Basil Joshua	Francis Taylor Building, London	0171 797 7250
Zaman Mohammed Khalil	St Philip's Chambers, Birmingham	0121 246 7000
Zelin Geoffrey Andrew	Enterprise Chambers, London	0171 405 9471
	Enterprise Chambers, Leeds	0113 246 0391
	Enterprise Chambers, Newcastle upon Tyne	0191 222 3344
Zwart Auberon Christiaan Conrad	1 Serjeants' Inn, London	0171 583 1355

LICENSING

Aldred Mark Steven	Hollis Whiteman Chambers, London	020 7583 5766
Allingham-Nicholson Mrs Elizabeth Sarah	2 New Street, Leicester	0116 2625906
Aston Maurice Charles	Five Paper Buildings, London	0171 583 6117
Atkins Richard Paul	1 Fountain Court, Birmingham	0121 236 5721
Ayers Guy Russell	Octagon House, Norwich	01603 623186
	1 Paper Buildings, London	0171 353 3728/4953
Barnard Jonathan James	Hollis Whiteman Chambers, London	020 7583 5766
Barnfather Miss Lydia Helen	Hollis Whiteman Chambers, London	020 7583 5766
Barr Edward Robert	2 New Street, Leicester	0116 2625906
Bennetts Philip James	Hollis Whiteman Chambers, London	020 7583 5766

• Expanded entry in Part D

Birch Roger Allen	Sovereign Chambers, Leeds	0113 2451841/2/3
	12 New Square, London	0171 419 1212
Boyce William	Hollis Whiteman Chambers, London	020 7583 5766
Briden Richard John	96 Gray's Inn Road, London	0171 405 0585
Brodwell John Shenton	9 Woodhouse Square, Leeds	0113 2451986
Bromley-Davenport John	Deans Court Chambers, Manchester	0161 214 6000
	Deans Court Chambers, Preston	01772 555163
Brown Edward Francis Trevenen	Hollis Whiteman Chambers, London	020 7583 5766
Capon Philip Christopher William	St Philip's Chambers, Birmingham	0121 246 7000
Chapman Matthew James	Barnard's Inn Chambers, London	0171 369 6969
Chapman Michael Andrew	Barnard's Inn Chambers, London	0171 369 6969
Cheshire Anthony Peter	199 Strand, London	0171 379 9779
Clare Michael Christopher	Octagon House, Norwich	01603 623186
	1 Paper Buildings, London	0171 353 3728/4953
Collier Peter Neville	30 Park Square, Leeds	0113 2436388
Collins Robert Urquhart	8 King's Bench Walk North, Leeds	0113 2439797
	8 King's Bench Walk, London	0171 797 8888
Conry Michael Harvey	1 Fountain Court, Birmingham	0121 236 5721
Cooper Morris	St Philip's Chambers, Birmingham	0121 246 7000
Corkery Michael	Five Paper Buildings, London	0171 583 6117
Coward Miss Victoria Jane	Hollis Whiteman Chambers, London	020 7583 5766
Darbishire Adrian Munro	Hollis Whiteman Chambers, London	020 7583 5766
Davies Miss Carol Elizabeth	2 New Street, Leicester	0116 2625906
Dedezade Taner	Tindal Chambers, Chelmsford	01245 267742
Denney Stuart Henry Macdonald	Deans Court Chambers, Manchester	0161 214 6000
	Deans Court Chambers, Preston	01772 555163
Devlin Jonathan Nicholas Ponton	Park Court Chambers, Leeds	0113 2433277
Dineen Michael Laurence	Pump Court Chambers, Winchester	01962 868161
	Pump Court Chambers, London	0171 353 0711
	Queens Square Chambers, Bristol	0117 921 1966
	Pump Court Chambers, Swindon	01793 539899
Doig Mrs Jeanetta Rose	Neston Home Chambers, Corsham	01225 811909
Donne Jeremy Nigel	Hollis Whiteman Chambers, London	020 7583 5766
Drinkwater Philip Murray	Colleton Chambers, Exeter	01392 274898/9
Edge Timothy Richard	Deans Court Chambers, Preston	01772 555163
	Deans Court Chambers, Manchester	0161 214 6000
Ellison Mark Christopher	Hollis Whiteman Chambers, London	020 7583 5766
Evans Julian Jacob	Hollis Whiteman Chambers, London	020 7583 5766
Evans Stephen James	8 King's Bench Walk, London	0171 797 8888
	8 King's Bench Walk North, Leeds	0113 2439797
Faluyi Albert Osamudiamen	Chambers of Martin Burr, London	0171 353 4636
Farrer Adam Michael	4 Fountain Court, Birmingham	0121 236 3476
Faul Miss Anne Frances Louise	Lamb Building, London	020 7797 7788
Field Rory Dominic	Hardwicke Building, London	020 7242 2523
Finnigan Peter Anthony	Hollis Whiteman Chambers, London	020 7583 5766
Fish David Thomas	Deans Court Chambers, Manchester	0161 214 6000
	Deans Court Chambers, Preston	01772 555163
	Goldsmith Chambers, London	0171 353 6802/3/4/5
Flahive Daniel Michael	Hardwicke Building, London	020 7242 2523
Foudy Miss Kim Frances	8 King Street Chambers, Manchester	0161 834 9560
Freedman Jeremy Stuart	New Court Chambers, Newcastle upon Tyne	0191 232 1980
	Plowden Buildings, London	0171 583 0808
Garrett Michael Owen	St Philip's Chambers, Birmingham	0121 246 7000
Glenn Paul Anthony	4 Fountain Court, Birmingham	0121 236 3476
Goodwin Michael Gary	2 Mitre Court Buildings, London	0171 353 1353
Grime John Andrew	Pump Court Chambers, Swindon	01793 539899
	Pump Court Chambers, London	0171 353 0711
	Pump Court Chambers, Winchester	01962 868161
Harris Ms Rebecca Elizabeth	Hollis Whiteman Chambers, London	020 7583 5766

Hawkesworth (Walter) Gareth	Fenners Chambers, Cambridge	01223 368761
	Fenners Chambers, Peterborough	01733 562030
	Five Paper Buildings, London	0171 583 6117
Haynes Peter	St Philip's Chambers, Birmingham	0121 246 7000
Henry Edward Joseph Aloysius	Hollis Whiteman Chambers, London	020 7583 5766
Herbert David Richard	2 New Street, Leicester	0116 2625906
Herbert Mrs Rebecca Mary	2 New Street, Leicester	0116 2625906
Hodgson Martin Derrick	8 King's Bench Walk, London	0171 797 8888
	8 King's Bench Walk North, Leeds	0113 2439797
Horton Matthew Bethell	2 Mitre Court Buildings, London	0171 583 1380
Horwell Richard Eric	Hollis Whiteman Chambers, London	020 7583 5766
James Ian Frederick	Octagon House, Norwich	01603 623186
	1 Paper Buildings, London	0171 353 3728/4953
Johnson Miss Zoe Elisabeth	Hollis Whiteman Chambers, London	020 7583 5766
Jones Martin Wynne	8 King's Bench Walk, London	0171 797 8888
	8 King's Bench Walk North, Leeds	0113 2439797
Kark Thomas Victor William	Hollis Whiteman Chambers, London	020 7583 5766
Keane Desmond St John	Pendragon Chambers, Swansea	01792 411188
Kelsey-Fry John	Hollis Whiteman Chambers, London	020 7583 5766
Kenward Timothy David Nelson	25-27 Castle Street, Liverpool	0151 227 5661/051 236 5072
Kershaw Andrew	30 Park Square, Leeds	0113 2436388
Khan Anwar William	Eastbourne Chambers, Eastbourne	01323 642102
	Wessex Chambers, Reading	0118 956 8856
Kynoch Duncan Stuart Sanderson	29 Bedford Row Chambers, London	0171 831 2626
Larkin Sean	Hollis Whiteman Chambers, London	020 7583 5766
Lewis Edward Trevor Gwyn	Francis Taylor Building, London	0171 353 7768/7769/2711
Lo Bernard Norman	17 Bedford Row, London	0171 831 7314
Longden Anthony Gordon	Hollis Whiteman Chambers, London	020 7583 5766
Lowry Miss Emma Margaret Collins	Hollis Whiteman Chambers, London	020 7583 5766
Lumley Gerald	9 Woodhouse Square, Leeds	0113 2451986
Mainwaring [Robert] Paul Clason	Carmarthen Chambers, Carmarthen	01267 234410
Marks Jonathan Clive	4 Pump Court, London	020 7842 5555
Marson Geoffrey Charles	Sovereign Chambers, Leeds	0113 2451841/2/3
McAlinden Barry O'Neill	17 Bedford Row, London	0171 831 7314
McCahill Patrick Gerard	St Philip's Chambers, Birmingham	0121 246 7000
	Chambers of Andrew Campbell QC, Leeds	0113 2455438
McCrindell James Derrey	Mitre House Chambers, London	0171 583 8233
McCullough Miss Louise Clare	Lion Court, London	0171 404 6565
McHugh Denis David	Bracton Chambers, London	0171 242 4248
Mehendale Ms Neelima Krishna	2 Mitre Court Buildings, London	0171 353 1353
Mellor John Walter	30 Park Square, Leeds	0113 2436388
Messling Lawrence David	St Philip's Chambers, Birmingham	0121 246 7000
Millington Christopher John	1 Fountain Court, Birmingham	0121 236 5721
Mitchell Brenton Ballingtine	Bell Yard Chambers, London	0171 306 9292
Mitchell Christopher Richard	Hollis Whiteman Chambers, London	020 7583 5766
Mitropoulos Christos	Chambers of Geoffrey Hawker, London	0171 583 8899
Moger Christopher Richard Derwent	4 Pump Court, London	020 7842 5555
Monk David Kenneth	2 New Street, Leicester	0116 2625906
Moore Mr Craig Ian	Barnard's Inn Chambers, London	0171 369 6969
	Park Lane Chambers, Leeds	0113 2285000
Morse Malcolm George McEwan	1 Fountain Court, Birmingham	0121 236 5721
Muller Antonie Sean	4 Fountain Court, Birmingham	0121 236 3476
Niblett Anthony Ian	1 Crown Office Row, London	0171 797 7500
	Crown Office Row Chambers, Brighton	01273 625625
Oakley Paul James	1 Gray's Inn Square, London	0171 405 8946/7/8
Oliver Miss Juliet Dianne	Bridewell Chambers, London	020 7797 8800
Pain Kenneth William	College Chambers, Southampton	01703 230338
Parr John Edward	8 King Street Chambers, Manchester	0161 834 9560

• Expanded entry in Part D

Parry Charles Robert	Pump Court Chambers, Swindon	01793 539899
	Pump Court Chambers, London	0171 353 0711
	Pump Court Chambers, Winchester	01962 868161
Paton Ian Francis	Hollis Whiteman Chambers, London	020 7583 5766
Pearce Richard William	Peel Court Chambers, Manchester	0161 832 3791
Peel Stuart James	Bell Yard Chambers, London	0171 306 9292
Pickup David Michael Walker	Peel Court Chambers, Manchester	0161 832 3791
Plaschkes Ms Sarah Georgina	Hollis Whiteman Chambers, London	020 7583 5766
Potts Richard Andrew	Octagon House, Norwich	01603 623186
	1 Paper Buildings, London	0171 353 3728/4953
Price Albert John	23 Essex Street, London	0171 413 0353/836 8366
Price John Charles	St Philip's Chambers, Birmingham	0121 246 7000
Price John Scott	10 Launceston Avenue, Reading	01189 479548
	Southsea Chambers, Portsmouth	01705 291261
	Cathedral Chambers, Newcastle upon Tyne	0191 232 1311
Purchas Robin Michael	• 2 Harcourt Buildings, London	020 7353 8415
Ramasamy Selvaraju	Hollis Whiteman Chambers, London	020 7583 5766
Rankin Andrew	4 Field Court, London	0171 440 6900
Rees Gareth David	Hollis Whiteman Chambers, London	020 7583 5766
Reid Sebastian Peter Scott	2nd Floor, Francis Taylor Building, London	0171 353 9942/3157
Restell Thomas George	Granary Chambers, Bexhill-On-Sea	01424 733008
Roebuck Roy Delville	Bell Yard Chambers, London	0171 306 9292
Russell Anthony Patrick	Peel Court Chambers, Manchester	0161 832 3791
Saggerson Alan David	Barnard's Inn Chambers, London	0171 369 6969
Salter Charles Philip Arthur	8 King's Bench Walk, London	0171 797 8888
	8 King's Bench Walk North, Leeds	0113 2439797
Samuel Glyn Ross	St Philip's Chambers, Birmingham	0121 246 7000
Sandbrook-Hughes Stewert Karl Anthony	Iscoed Chambers, Swansea	01792 652988/9/330
Sells Oliver Matthew	Five Paper Buildings, London	0171 583 6117
	Fenners Chambers, Cambridge	01223 368761
Sibson Mrs Clare Adele	Hollis Whiteman Chambers, London	020 7583 5766
Silvester Bruce Ross	Lamb Chambers, London	020 7797 8300
Singh Kuldip	Five Paper Buildings, London	0171 583 6117
Skelly Andrew Jon	1 Gray's Inn Square, London	0171 405 8946/7/8
Slaughter Andrew Francis	Bridewell Chambers, London	020 7797 8800
Sleightholme John Trevor	37 Park Square Chambers, Leeds	0113 2439422
Sparrow Miss Claire Louise	Eastbourne Chambers, Eastbourne	01323 642102
Spence Simon Peter	18 Red Lion Court, London	0171 520 6000
	Thornwood House, Chelmsford	01245 280880
Spencer Paul Anthony	2 New Street, Leicester	0116 2625906
St Louis Brian Lloyd	Hardwicke Building, London	020 7242 2523
Stern Ian Michael	Hollis Whiteman Chambers, London	020 7583 5766
Stewart Neill Alastair	Hollis Whiteman Chambers, London	020 7583 5766
Strudwick Miss Linda Diane	Hollis Whiteman Chambers, London	020 7583 5766
Sullivan Ms Jane Teresa	Hollis Whiteman Chambers, London	020 7583 5766
Sullivan Scott	Barnard's Inn Chambers, London	0171 369 6969
Summers Benjamin Dylan James	Hollis Whiteman Chambers, London	020 7583 5766
Szanto Gregory John Michael	Eastbourne Chambers, Eastbourne	01323 642102
Tapsell Paul Richard	Becket Chambers, Canterbury	01227 786331
Temple Anthony Dominic	4 Pump Court, London	020 7842 5555
Thain Miss Ashley	East Anglian Chambers, Colchester	01206 572756
	East Anglian Chambers, Ipswich	01473 214481
	East Anglian Chambers, Norwich	01603 617351
Thompson Andrew Ian	1 Inner Temple Lane, London	020 7353 0933
Thompson Lyall Norris	Tindal Chambers, Chelmsford	01245 267742
Tizzano Franco Salvatore	8 King's Bench Walk, London	0171 797 8888
	8 King's Bench Walk North, Leeds	0113 2439797
Tucker David William	Two Crown Office Row, London	020 7797 8100

B

Turner Adrian John	Eastbourne Chambers, Eastbourne	01323 642102
Tyack David Guy	St Philip's Chambers, Birmingham	0121 246 7000
Wakeham Philip John Le Messurier	Hardwicke Building, London	020 7242 2523
Walsh Martin Fraser	Peel Court Chambers, Manchester	0161 832 3791
Warne Peter Lawrence	Hollis Whiteman Chambers, London	020 7583 5766
Wastie William Granville	Hollis Whiteman Chambers, London	020 7583 5766
Watkin Toby Paul	22 Old Buildings, London	0171 831 0222
Wayne Nicholas	1 Gray's Inn Square, London	0171 405 8946/7/8
Weeden Ross Charles	Bell Yard Chambers, London	0171 306 9292
Wheetman Alan	East Anglian Chambers, Norwich	01603 617351
	East Anglian Chambers, Colchester	01206 572756
	East Anglian Chambers, Ipswich	01473 214481
Wilcken Anthony David Felix	Hollis Whiteman Chambers, London	020 7583 5766
Williams A John	13 King's Bench Walk, London	0171 353 7204
	King's Bench Chambers, Oxford	01865 311066
Winter Ian David	Hollis Whiteman Chambers, London	020 7583 5766
Wood Guy Nicholas Marshall	Hollis Whiteman Chambers, London	020 7583 5766
Wood Ian Robert	8 King Street Chambers, Manchester	0161 834 9560
Woodhouse Charles Philip	Bridewell Chambers, London	020 7797 8800
Worrall Miss Shirley Vera Frances	8 King Street Chambers, Manchester	0161 834 9560

LIMITED PARTNERSHIPS

Banks Roderick Charles l'Anson	• 48 Bedford Row, London	0171 430 2005

LOCAL AUTHORITY CLAIMS

Boyle Gerard James	No. 1 Serjeants' Inn, London	0171 415 6666
Faulks Edward Peter Lawless	No. 1 Serjeants' Inn, London	0171 415 6666
Ross John Graffin	No. 1 Serjeants' Inn, London	0171 415 6666
Warnock Andrew Ronald	No. 1 Serjeants' Inn, London	0171 415 6666

LOCAL GOVERNMENT

Alesbury Alun	2 Mitre Court Buildings, London	0171 583 1380
Allingham-Nicholson Mrs Elizabeth Sarah	2 New Street, Leicester	0116 2625906
Anderson Anthony John	2 Mitre Court Buildings, London	0171 583 1380
Bagchi Andrew Kumar	One Garden Court Family Law Chambers, London	0171 797 7900
Barnes (David) Michael (William)	• Wilberforce Chambers, London	0171 306 0102
Basu Dr Dijendra Bhushan	Devereux Chambers, London	0171 353 7534
Bates John Hayward	Old Square Chambers, London	0171 269 0300
	Old Square Chambers, Bristol	0117 9277111
Baxter-Phillips Miss Felicity Dawn	Becket Chambers, Canterbury	01227 786331
Beard Mark Christopher	6 Pump Court, London	0171 797 8400
	6-8 Mill Street, Maidstone	01622 688094
Beaumont Marc Clifford	• Harrow on the Hill Chambers, Harrow-on-the-Hill	0181 423 7444
	Windsor Barristers' Chambers, Windsor	01753 648899
	Pump Court Chambers, London	0171 353 0711
Bedingfield David Herbert	• 14 Gray's Inn Square, London	0171 242 0858
Birtles William	Old Square Chambers, London	0171 269 0300
	Old Square Chambers, Bristol	0117 9277111
Blackford Simon John	Barnard's Inn Chambers, London	0171 369 6969
Blom-Cooper Sir Louis Jacques	Doughty Street Chambers, London	0171 404 1313
Boyle Christopher Alexander David	2 Mitre Court Buildings, London	0171 583 1380
Broatch Michael Donald	5 Paper Buildings, London	0171 583 9275/583 4555
Bryant Keith	Devereux Chambers, London	0171 353 7534
Buck Dr Andrew Theodore	Chambers of Martin Burr, London	0171 353 4636
Burton Nicholas Anthony	2 Mitre Court Buildings, London	0171 583 1380
Butler Simon David	10 King's Bench Walk, London	0171 353 7742
Cakebread Stuart Alan Charles	• 2nd Floor, Francis Taylor Building, London	0171 353 9942/3157

        • Expanded entry in Part D

Cavanagh John Patrick	11 King's Bench Walk, London	0171 632 8500/583 0610
Chapman Matthew James	Barnard's Inn Chambers, London	0171 369 6969
Cheshire Anthony Peter	199 Strand, London	0171 379 9779
Clarkson Patrick Robert James	• 1 Serjeants' Inn, London	0171 583 1355
Cobb Stephen William Scott	One Garden Court Family Law Chambers, London	0171 797 7900
Compton Gareth Francis Thomas	22 Old Buildings, London	0171 831 0222
Corbett Mrs Sandra Margaret	1 New Square, London	0171 405 0884/5/6/7
Craig Alistair Trevor	Chambers of Mr Peter Crampin QC, London	020 7831 0081
Curtis Michael Alexander	Two Crown Office Row, London	020 7797 8100
Daly David	Francis Taylor Building, London	0171 797 7250
Daniel Leon Roger	6 King's Bench Walk, London	0171 353 4931/583 0695
Drinkwater Philip Murray	Colleton Chambers, Exeter	01392 274898/9
Druce Michael James	2 Mitre Court Buildings, London	0171 583 1380
Dugdale Nicholas	4 Field Court, London	0171 440 6900
Fitzgerald Michael Frederick Clive	2 Mitre Court Buildings, London	0171 583 1380
Fookes Robert Lawrence	2 Mitre Court Buildings, London	0171 583 1380
Ford Gerard James	Baker Street Chambers, Middlesbrough	01642 873873
Ford Michael David	Doughty Street Chambers, London	0171 404 1313
Gardner Miss Eilidh Anne Mairi	22 Old Buildings, London	0171 831 0222
Gasztowicz Steven	2-3 Gray's Inn Square, London	0171 242 4986
	2 New Street, Leicester	0116 2625906
Geekie Charles Nairn	One Garden Court Family Law Chambers, London	0171 797 7900
Glover Richard Michael	2 Mitre Court Buildings, London	0171 583 1380
Gordon Richard John Francis	Brick Court Chambers, London	0171 379 3550
Goudie James	• 11 King's Bench Walk, London	0171 632 8500/583 0610
Grey Miss Eleanor Mary Grace	39 Essex Street, London	0171 832 1111
Harrison Peter John	6 Pump Court, London	0171 797 8400
	6-8 Mill Street, Maidstone	01622 688094
Harwood Richard John	1 Serjeants' Inn, London	0171 583 1355
Haynes Peter	St Philip's Chambers, Birmingham	0121 246 7000
Heather Christopher Mark	• 2nd Floor, Francis Taylor Building, London	0171 353 9942/3157
Henderson Roger Anthony	2 Harcourt Buildings, London	0171 583 9020
Hermer Richard Simon	Doughty Street Chambers, London	0171 404 1313
	30 Park Place, Cardiff	01222 398421
Hill Piers Nicholas	37 Park Square Chambers, Leeds	0113 2439422
Hockman Stephen Alexander	• 6 Pump Court, London	0171 797 8400
	6-8 Mill Street, Maidstone	01622 688094
Horton Matthew Bethell	2 Mitre Court Buildings, London	0171 583 1380
Humphries Michael John	2 Mitre Court Buildings, London	0171 583 1380
Hyams Oliver Marks	5 Paper Buildings, London	0171 583 9275/583 4555
Ivimy Ms Cecilia Rachel	11 King's Bench Walk, London	0171 632 8500/583 0610
Jefferis Arthur Michael Quentin	Chambers of Mr Peter Crampin QC, London	020 7831 0081
Jones Clive Hugh	1 New Square, London	0171 405 0884/5/6/7
Jones Sean William Paul	11 King's Bench Walk, London	0171 632 8500/583 0610
Jones Timothy Arthur	• St Philip's Chambers, Birmingham	0121 246 7000
	Arden Chambers, London	020 7242 4244
Karas Jonathan Marcus	• Wilberforce Chambers, London	0171 306 0102
Keane Desmond St John	Pendragon Chambers, Swansea	01792 411188
Kenward Timothy David Nelson	25-27 Castle Street, Liverpool	0151 227 5661/051 236 5072
King Neil Gerald Alexander	2 Mitre Court Buildings, London	0171 583 1380
Kovats Steven Laszlo	39 Essex Street, London	0171 832 1111
Laing Miss Elisabeth Mary Caroline	11 King's Bench Walk, London	0171 632 8500/583 0610
Langham Richard Geoffrey	1 Serjeants' Inn, London	0171 583 1355

• Expanded entry in Part D

Leigh Kevin

6 Pump Court, London	0171 797 8400
Regency Chambers, Peterborough	01733 315215
Westgate Chambers, Lewes	01273 480510
6-8 Mill Street, Maidstone	01622 688094

Leiper Richard Thomas — 11 King's Bench Walk, London — 0171 632 8500/583 0610

Lewis Robert

11 Bolt Court (also at 7 Stone Buildings – 1st Floor), London	0171 353 2300
7 Stone Buildings (also at 11 Bolt Court), London	0171 242 0961
Redhill Chambers, Redhill	01737 780781

Lyness Scott Edward — 1 Serjeants' Inn, London — 0171 583 1355

Maclean Alan John — 39 Essex Street, London — 0171 832 1111

Macpherson The Hon Mary Stewart — 2 Mitre Court Buildings, London — 0171 583 1380

Mainwaring [Robert] Paul Clason — Carmarthen Chambers, Carmarthen — 01267 234410

Malecka Dr Mary Margaret

• 3 Temple Gardens, London	0171 353 0832
65-67 King Street, Leicester	0116 2547710

Markus Ms Kate — Doughty Street Chambers, London — 0171 404 1313

McCafferty Miss Lynne — 5 Paper Buildings, London — 0171 583 9275/583 4555

McCahill Patrick Gerard

St Philip's Chambers, Birmingham	0121 246 7000
Chambers of Andrew Campbell QC, Leeds	0113 2455438

Millar Gavin James — Doughty Street Chambers, London — 0171 404 1313

Moore Professor Victor William Edward — 2 Mitre Court Buildings, London — 0171 583 1380

Morgan (Thomas) Jeremy — 39 Essex Street, London — 0171 832 1111

Moriarty Gerald Evelyn — 2 Mitre Court Buildings, London — 0171 583 1380

Morris Miss Fenella — 39 Essex Street, London — 0171 832 1111

Nardell Gordon Lawrence

6 Pump Court, London	0171 797 8400
6-8 Mill Street, Maidstone	01622 688094

Newcombe Andrew Bennett — 2 Harcourt Buildings, London — 020 7353 8415

Ornsby Miss Suzanne Doreen — 2 Harcourt Buildings, London — 020 7353 8415

Osman Robert Walter

Queen's Chambers, Manchester	0161 834 6875/4738
Queens Chambers, Preston	01772 828300

Pain Kenneth William — College Chambers, Southampton — 01703 230338

Pereira James Alexander — 2 Harcourt Buildings, London — 020 7353 8415

Phillpot Hereward Lindon — 2 Harcourt Buildings, London — 020 7353 8415

Pickles Simon Robert — 1 Serjeants' Inn, London — 0171 583 1355

Pickup David Michael Walker — Peel Court Chambers, Manchester — 0161 832 3791

Pitt-Payne Timothy Sheridan — • 11 King's Bench Walk, London — 0171 632 8500/583 0610

Pleming Nigel Peter — 39 Essex Street, London — 0171 832 1111

Price Albert John — 23 Essex Street, London — 0171 413 0353/836 8366

Price John Scott

10 Launceston Avenue, Reading	01189 479548
Southsea Chambers, Portsmouth	01705 291261
Cathedral Chambers, Newcastle upon Tyne	0191 232 1311

Purchas Robin Michael — • 2 Harcourt Buildings, London — 020 7353 8415

Reid Sebastian Peter Scott — 2nd Floor, Francis Taylor Building, London — 0171 353 9942/3157

Richards Miss Jennifer — 39 Essex Street, London — 0171 832 1111

Roberts Miss Clare Justine — • 2nd Floor, Francis Taylor Building, London — 0171 353 9942/3157

Robertson Geoffrey Ronald — Doughty Street Chambers, London — 0171 404 1313

Roots Guy Robert Godfrey — 2 Mitre Court Buildings, London — 0171 583 1380

Rumney Conrad William Arthur — St Philip's Chambers, Birmingham — 0121 246 7000

Ryder Ernest Nigel

Deans Court Chambers, Manchester	0161 214 6000
Deans Court Chambers, Preston	01772 555163
1 Mitre Court Buildings, London	0171 797 7070

Salmon Jonathan Carl — 1 Fountain Court, Birmingham — 0121 236 5721

Salter Charles Philip Arthur

8 King's Bench Walk, London	0171 797 8888
8 King's Bench Walk North, Leeds	0113 2439797

Seligman Matthew Thomas Arthur — 39 Essex Street, London — 0171 832 1111

• Expanded entry in Part D

Shannon Thomas Eric	Queen's Chambers, Manchester	0161 834 6875/4738
	Queens Chambers, Preston	01772 828300
Sheldon Clive David	11 King's Bench Walk, London	0171 632 8500/583 0610
Shukla Ms Vina	New Court Chambers, London	0171 831 9500
Silsoe The Lord	2 Mitre Court Buildings, London	0171 583 1380
Silvester Bruce Ross	Lamb Chambers, London	020 7797 8300
Slaughter Andrew Francis	Bridewell Chambers, London	020 7797 8800
Stark James Hayden Alexander	Chambers of Ian Macdonald QC (In Association with Two Garden Court, Temple, London), Manchester	0161 236 1840
Stilitz Daniel Malachi	11 King's Bench Walk, London	0171 632 8500/583 0610
Stone Gregory	• 4-5 Gray's Inn Square, London	0171 404 5252
Straker Timothy Derrick	• 4-5 Gray's Inn Square, London	0171 404 5252
Supperstone Michael Alan	11 King's Bench Walk, London	0171 632 8500/583 0610
Swindells Miss Heather Hughson	Chambers of Michael Pert QC, London	0171 421 8000
	Chambers of Michael Pert QC, Leicester	0116 249 2020
	Chambers of Michael Pert QC, Northampton	01604 602333
	St Philip's Chambers, Birmingham	0121 246 7000
Tait Andrew Charles Gordon	2 Harcourt Buildings, London	020 7353 8415
Tapsell Paul Richard	Becket Chambers, Canterbury	01227 786331
Taylor John Charles	2 Mitre Court Buildings, London	0171 583 1380
Taylor Reuben Mallinson	2 Mitre Court Buildings, London	0171 583 1380
Thomas Miss Megan Moira	1 Serjeants' Inn, London	0171 583 1355
Travers David	• 3 Fountain Court, Birmingham	0121 236 5854
Tucker Miss Katherine Jane Greening	St Philip's Chambers, Birmingham	0121 246 7000
Wald Richard Daniel	2 Mitre Court Buildings, London	0171 583 1380
Walker Mrs Susannah Mary	One Garden Court Family Law Chambers, London	0171 797 7900
Wallington Peter Thomas	11 King's Bench Walk, London	0171 632 8500/583 0610
Ward Timothy Justin	Monckton Chambers, London	0171 405 7211
Ward Trevor Robert Edward	17 Carlton Crescent, Southampton	023 8032 0320/0823 2003
Warner David Alexander	1 New Square, London	0171 405 0884/5/6/7
Warren Rupert Miles	2 Mitre Court Buildings, London	0171 583 1380
Westgate Martin Trevor	Doughty Street Chambers, London	0171 404 1313
Weston Ms Amanda	Chambers of Ian Macdonald QC (In Association with Two Garden Court, Temple, London), Manchester	0161 236 1840
Whybrow Christopher John	1 Serjeants' Inn, London	0171 583 1355
Widdicombe David Graham	2 Mitre Court Buildings, London	0171 583 1380
Wilkins Mrs Colette Ann	1 New Square, London	0171 405 0884/5/6/7
Williams Ms Heather Jean	Doughty Street Chambers, London	0171 404 1313
Williams Rhodri John	30 Park Place, Cardiff	01222 398421
	2 Harcourt Buildings, London	0171 583 9020
Wise Ian	Doughty Street Chambers, London	0171 404 1313
Zaman Mohammed Khalil	St Philip's Chambers, Birmingham	0121 246 7000
Zwart Auberon Christiaan Conrad	1 Serjeants' Inn, London	0171 583 1355

MEDIA

Barca Manuel David	1 Brick Court, London	0171 353 8845
Barker Simon George Harry	• 13 Old Square, London	0171 404 4800
Evans Ms Catrin Miranda	1 Brick Court, London	0171 353 8845

MEDIATION

Cooper Nigel Stuart	4 Essex Court, London	020 7797 7970
Ough Dr Richard Norman	• Hardwicke Building, London	020 7242 2523

MEDICAL INQUIRIES

Ritchie Miss Jean Harris	4 Paper Buildings, London	0171 353 3366/583 7155

• Expanded entry in Part D

MEDICAL LAW

Melton Christopher   Peel Court Chambers, Manchester   0161 832 3791
                                199 Strand, London   0171 379 9779

MEDICAL NEGLIGENCE

Abbott Francis Arthur   Pump Court Chambers, Winchester   01962 868161
                                Pump Court Chambers, London   0171 353 0711
                                Pump Court Chambers, Swindon   01793 539899
Aldous Grahame Linley   9 Gough Square, London   020 7832 0500
Aldridge James William   199 Strand, London   0171 379 9779
Allfrey Richard Forbes   Doughty Street Chambers, London   0171 404 1313
Allingham-Nicholson Mrs Elizabeth   2 New Street, Leicester   0116 2625906
  Sarah
Andrews Peter John   • 199 Strand, London   0171 379 9779
                                3 Fountain Court, Birmingham   0121 236 5854
Archer John Francis Ashweek Two Crown Office Row, London   020 7797 8100
Armitage Ernest Keith   8 King Street Chambers, Manchester   0161 834 9560
Ashworth Piers   2 Harcourt Buildings, London   0171 583 9020
Atherton Peter   Deans Court Chambers, Manchester   0161 214 6000
                                Deans Court Chambers, Preston   01772 555163
Badenoch (Ian) James Forster 1 Crown Office Row, London   0171 797 7500
                                Crown Office Row Chambers, Brighton   01273 625625
Bailey Edward Henry   Monckton Chambers, London   0171 405 7211
Baker Andrew James   7 New Square, London   0171 430 1660
                                Richmond Green Chambers,   0181 940 1841
                                  Richmond-upon-Thames
                                5 Fountain Court, Birmingham   0121 606 0500
Baker Stuart Christopher   1 Fountain Court, Birmingham   0121 236 5721
Baldock Nicholas John   6 Pump Court, London   0171 797 8400
                                6-8 Mill Street, Maidstone   01622 688094
Barker John Steven Roy   Queen's Chambers, Manchester   0161 834 6875/4738
                                Queens Chambers, Preston   01772 828300
Barnett Andrew John   Pump Court Chambers, Winchester   01962 868161
                                Pump Court Chambers, London   0171 353 0711
                                Pump Court Chambers, Swindon   01793 539899
Barnett Daniel Alexander   2 Gray's Inn Square Chambers, London   020 7242 0328
Barraclough Richard Michael 6 Pump Court, London   0171 797 8400
                                6-8 Mill Street, Maidstone   01622 688094
Bassa Yousef   St Albans Chambers, St Albans   01727 843383
                                Tindal Chambers, Chelmsford   01245 267742
Bassett John Stewart Britten 5 Essex Court, London   0171 410 2000
Beever Edmund Damian   St Philip's Chambers, Birmingham   0121 246 7000
Bellamy Jonathan Mark   39 Essex Street, London   0171 832 1111
Bennett John Martyn   • Oriel Chambers, Liverpool   0151 236 7191/236 4321
Benson John Trevor   Adrian Lyon's Chambers, Liverpool   0151 236 4421/8240
Berry Nicholas Michael   Southernhay Chambers, Exeter   01392 255777
                                1 Gray's Inn Square, London   0171 405 8946/7/8
                                22 Old Buildings, London   0171 831 0222
Bidder Neil   33 Park Place, Cardiff   02920 233313
                                Goldsmith Building, London   0171 353 7881
Bishop Edward James   No. 1 Serjeants' Inn, London   0171 415 6666
Blakesley Patrick James   Two Crown Office Row, London   020 7797 8100
Block Neil Selwyn   39 Essex Street, London   0171 832 1111
Bloom-Davis Desmond Niall   Pump Court Chambers, Winchester   01962 868161
  Laurence
                                Pump Court Chambers, London   0171 353 0711
                                Pump Court Chambers, Swindon   01793 539899
Blunt David John   4 Pump Court, London   020 7842 5555
Booth Alan James   Deans Court Chambers, Manchester   0161 214 6000
                                Deans Court Chambers, Preston   01772 555163
Booth Richard John   1 Crown Office Row, London   0171 797 7500

Boyd Stephen James Harvey	29 Bedford Row Chambers, London	0171 831 2626
Boydell Edward Patrick Stirrup	Pump Court Chambers, London	0171 353 0711
	Pump Court Chambers, Winchester	01962 868161
	Pump Court Chambers, Swindon	01793 539899
Bradley Miss Clodagh Maria	3 Serjeants' Inn, London	0171 353 5537
Bradly David Lawrence	39 Essex Street, London	0171 832 1111
Brahams Mrs Diana Joyce	Old Square Chambers, London	0171 269 0300
	Old Square Chambers, Bristol	0117 9277111
Braithwaite William Thomas Scatchard	Exchange Chambers, Liverpool	0151 236 7747
Breese-Laughran Ms Eleanore Delphine	8 King's Bench Walk, London	0171 797 8888
	8 King's Bench Walk North, Leeds	0113 2439797
Brennan Daniel Joseph	39 Essex Street, London	0171 832 1111
	18 St John Street, Manchester	0161 278 1800
Briden Richard John	96 Gray's Inn Road, London	0171 405 0585
Briden Timothy John	• 8 Stone Buildings, London	0171 831 9881
Bridgman David Martin	No. 1 Serjeants' Inn, London	0171 415 6666
Broatch Michael Donald	5 Paper Buildings, London	0171 583 9275/583 4555
Brown (Geoffrey) Charles	39 Essex Street, London	0171 832 1111
Browne James William	96 Gray's Inn Road, London	0171 405 0585
Brunton Sean Alexander McKay	Pump Court Chambers, Winchester	01962 868161
	Pump Court Chambers, London	0171 353 0711
	Pump Court Chambers, Swindon	01793 539899
Bryant John Malcolm Cornelius	Barnard's Inn Chambers, London	0171 369 6969
Buck Dr Andrew Theodore	Chambers of Martin Burr, London	0171 353 4636
Buckley Peter Evered	Queen's Chambers, Manchester	0161 834 6875/4738
	Queens Chambers, Preston	01772 828300
Burden Miss Susan Jane	Chambers of Kieran Coonan QC, London	0171 583 6013/2510
Burns Peter Richard	Deans Court Chambers, Manchester	0161 214 6000
	Deans Court Chambers, Preston	01772 555163
Burns Miss Susan Linda	3 Serjeants' Inn, London	0171 353 5537
Burrows Simon Paul	Peel Court Chambers, Manchester	0161 832 3791
Butler Philip Andrew	Deans Court Chambers, Manchester	0161 214 6000
	Deans Court Chambers, Preston	01772 555163
Butler Simon David	10 King's Bench Walk, London	0171 353 7742
Butterworth Paul Anthony	Octagon House, Norwich	01603 623186
Cannon Adam Richard	96 Gray's Inn Road, London	0171 405 0585
Carling Christopher James	Old Square Chambers, London	0171 269 0300
	Old Square Chambers, Bristol	0117 9277111
Carr Simon Andrew	9 Gough Square, London	020 7832 0500
Cartwright John Martin	Francis Taylor Building, London	0171 353 7768/7769/2711
Cawley Neil Robert Loudoun	169 Temple Chambers, London	0171 583 7644
	Milton Keynes Chambers, Milton Keynes	01908 664 128
Cheshire Anthony Peter	199 Strand, London	0171 379 9779
Christie-Brown Miss Sarah Louise	4 Paper Buildings, London	0171 353 3366/583 7155
Clarke Miss Alison Lee	No. 1 Serjeants' Inn, London	0171 415 6666
Clarke Jonathan Christopher St John	Old Square Chambers, Bristol	0117 9277111
	Old Square Chambers, London	0171 269 0300
Clegg Sebastian James Barwick	Deans Court Chambers, Manchester	0161 214 6000
	Deans Court Chambers, Preston	01772 555163
Cliff Graham Hilton	St Philip's Chambers, Birmingham	0121 246 7000
Clover (Thomas) Anthony	New Court Chambers, London	0171 831 9500
Coghlan Terence	1 Crown Office Row, London	0171 797 7500
	Crown Office Row Chambers, Brighton	01273 625625
Collett Ivor William	No. 1 Serjeants' Inn, London	0171 415 6666
Collins Miss Jennifer Clair	Eastbourne Chambers, Eastbourne	01323 642102
Connolly Miss Joanne Marie	8 King Street Chambers, Manchester	0161 834 9560
Cook Jeremy David	Lamb Building, London	020 7797 7788
Cooksley Nigel James	Old Square Chambers, London	0171 269 0300
	Old Square Chambers, Bristol	0117 9277111

Cooper Alan George	39 Essex Street, London	0171 832 1111
Cotter Barry Paul	Old Square Chambers, Bristol	0117 9277111
	Old Square Chambers, London	0171 269 0300
Cotton Miss Diana Rosemary	Devereux Chambers, London	0171 353 7534
Cross Mrs Joanna	9 Woodhouse Square, Leeds	0113 2451986
Crowley John Desmond	Two Crown Office Row, London	020 7797 8100
Croxon Raymond Patrick	8 King's Bench Walk, London	0171 797 8888
	Regency Chambers, Peterborough	01733 315215
	Regency Chambers, Cambridge	01223 301517
Curwen Michael Jonathan	Chambers of Kieran Coonan QC, London	0171 583 6013/2510
Daniells-Smith Roger Charles	8 King's Bench Walk, London	0171 797 8888
	8 King's Bench Walk North, Leeds	0113 2439797
Davidson Dr Ranald Dunbar	3 Serjeants' Inn, London	0171 353 5537
Davies Miss Carol Elizabeth	2 New Street, Leicester	0116 2625906
Davies The Rt Hon David John Denzil	96 Gray's Inn Road, London	0171 405 0585
	8 Gray's Inn Square, London	0171 242 3529
Davis Andrew Paul	Two Crown Office Row, London	020 7797 8100
Davis William Easthope	St Philip's Chambers, Birmingham	0121 246 7000
Dean Paul Benjamin	Two Crown Office Row, London	020 7797 8100
Dean Peter Thomas	1 Crown Office Row, London	0171 583 9292
DeCamp Miss Jane Louise	Two Crown Office Row, London	020 7797 8100
Devlin Jonathan Nicholas Ponton	Park Court Chambers, Leeds	0113 2433277
Dolan Dr Bridget Maura	3 Serjeants' Inn, London	0171 353 5537
Donovan Joel	New Court Chambers, London	0171 831 9500
Du Cann Christian Dillon Lott	39 Essex Street, London	0171 832 1111
Dudley Michael John	1 Fountain Court, Birmingham	0121 236 5721
Eastman Roger	2 Harcourt Buildings, London	0171 583 9020
Eccles David Thomas	8 King Street Chambers, Manchester	0161 834 9560
Edis Andrew Jeremy Coulter	• Adrian Lyon's Chambers, Liverpool	0151 236 4421/8240
Edis Angus William Butler	1 Crown Office Row, London	0171 797 7500
Ekins Charles Wareing	Sovereign Chambers, Leeds	0113 2451841/2/3
Ellis Dr Peter Simon	7 New Square, London	0171 430 1660
Evans Miss Claire Louise	Peel Court Chambers, Manchester	0161 832 3791
Evans Stephen James	8 King's Bench Walk, London	0171 797 8888
	8 King's Bench Walk North, Leeds	0113 2439797
Ewins Miss Catherine Jane	4 Paper Buildings, London	0171 353 3366/583 7155
Fairbank Nicholas James	Becket Chambers, Canterbury	01227 786331
Faluyi Albert Osamudiamen	Chambers of Martin Burr, London	0171 353 4636
Faul Miss Anne Frances Louise	Lamb Building, London	020 7797 7788
Faulks Edward Peter Lawless	No. 1 Serjeants' Inn, London	0171 415 6666
Ferm Rodney Eric	37 Park Square Chambers, Leeds	0113 2439422
Fieldsend James William	2nd Floor, Francis Taylor Building, London	0171 353 9942/3157
Finlay Darren	Sovereign Chambers, Leeds	0113 2451841/2/3
Fitzpatrick Edward James	8 King's Bench Walk, London	0171 797 8888
Fletcher Christopher Michael	Octagon House, Norwich	01603 623186
Flockhart Miss Sharon Linda	3 Serjeants' Inn, London	0171 353 5537
Ford Gerard James	Baker Street Chambers, Middlesbrough	01642 873873
Formby Ms Emily Jane	Hardwicke Building, London	020 7242 2523
Forte Mark Julian Carmino	8 King Street Chambers, Manchester	0161 834 9560
Foster Charles Andrew	• Chambers of Kieran Coonan QC, London	0171 583 6013/2510
Foudy Miss Kim Frances	8 King Street Chambers, Manchester	0161 834 9560
Fox Dr Simon James	Exchange Chambers, Liverpool	0151 236 7747
	St Philip's Chambers, Birmingham	0121 246 7000
Foy John Leonard	9 Gough Square, London	020 7832 0500
Freedman Jeremy Stuart	New Court Chambers, Newcastle upon Tyne	0191 232 1980
	Plowden Buildings, London	0171 583 0808
Friston Dr Mark Harpham	Chambers of Kieran Coonan QC, London	0171 583 6013/2510

• Expanded entry in Part D

Gabb Charles Henry Escott	Pump Court Chambers, Winchester	01962 868161
	Pump Court Chambers, London	0171 353 0711
	Pump Court Chambers, Swindon	01793 539899
Gadney George Munro	Two Crown Office Row, London	020 7797 8100
Gibson Arthur George Adrian	Adrian Lyon's Chambers, Liverpool	0151 236 4421/8240
Glasson Jonathan Joseph	Doughty Street Chambers, London	0171 404 1313
Glover Stephen Julian	37 Park Square Chambers, Leeds	0113 2439422
Glynn Stephen Peter	9 Gough Square, London	020 7832 0500
Goddard Harold Keith	Deans Court Chambers, Manchester	0161 214 6000
	Deans Court Chambers, Preston	01772 555163
	4 Paper Buildings, London	0171 353 3366/583 7155
Goldman Mrs Linda	7 New Square, London	0171 430 1660
Goodwin Miss Deirdre Evelyn	13 King's Bench Walk, London	0171 353 7204
	King's Bench Chambers, Oxford	01865 311066
Grace John Oliver Bowman	3 Serjeants' Inn, London	0171 353 5537
Grace Timothy Michael	Adrian Lyon's Chambers, Liverpool	0151 236 4421/8240
Grayson Edward	• 9-12 Bell Yard, London	0171 400 1800
Greenbourne John Hugo	Two Crown Office Row, London	020 7797 8100
Grime Mark Stephen Eastburn	Deans Court Chambers, Manchester	0161 214 6000
	2 Pump Court, London	0171 353 5597
	Deans Court Chambers, Preston	01772 555163
Grimshaw Nicholas Edward	Deans Court Chambers, Manchester	0161 214 6000
	Deans Court Chambers, Preston	01772 555163
Grodzinski Samuel Marc	39 Essex Street, London	0171 832 1111
Gulliver Miss Alison Louise	4 Paper Buildings, London	0171 353 3366/583 7155
Haigh Martin James	30 Park Square, Leeds	0113 2436388
Hamey John Anthony	East Anglian Chambers, Norwich	01603 617351
	East Anglian Chambers, Colchester	01206 572756
	East Anglian Chambers, Ipswich	01473 214481
Hamilton Graeme Montagu	Two Crown Office Row, London	020 7797 8100
Harrap Giles Thresher	• Pump Court Chambers, Winchester	01962 868161
	Pump Court Chambers, London	0171 353 0711
	Pump Court Chambers, Swindon	01793 539899
Harvey Michael Llewellyn Tucker	Two Crown Office Row, London	020 7797 8100
Haslam Andrew Peter	Sovereign Chambers, Leeds	0113 2451841/2/3
Hatfield Ms Sally Anne	Doughty Street Chambers, London	0171 404 1313
Henderson Roger Anthony	2 Harcourt Buildings, London	0171 583 9020
Hendy John Giles	• Old Square Chambers, London	0171 269 0300
	Old Square Chambers, Bristol	0117 9277111
Herbert Mrs Rebecca Mary	2 New Street, Leicester	0116 2625906
Hermer Richard Simon	Doughty Street Chambers, London	0171 404 1313
	30 Park Place, Cardiff	01222 398421
Hewitson William Andrew	1 Crown Office Row, London	0171 583 9292
Hill Nicholas Mark	• Pump Court Chambers, London	0171 353 0711
	Pump Court Chambers, Winchester	01962 868161
	Pump Court Chambers, Swindon	01793 539899
Hill Robert Douglas	Pump Court Chambers, Winchester	01962 868161
	Pump Court Chambers, London	0171 353 0711
	Pump Court Chambers, Swindon	01793 539899
Hillier Nicolas Peter	9 Gough Square, London	020 7832 0500
Hockman Stephen Alexander	• 6 Pump Court, London	0171 797 8400
	6-8 Mill Street, Maidstone	01622 688094
Hodgson Martin Derrick	8 King's Bench Walk, London	0171 797 8888
	8 King's Bench Walk North, Leeds	0113 2439797
Hodson Peter David	Chambers of Ian Macdonald QC (In Association with Two Garden Court, Temple, London), Manchester	0161 236 1840
Hogg The Hon Douglas Martin	37 Park Square Chambers, Leeds	0113 2439422
	Cathedral Chambers (Jan Wood Independent Barristers' Clerk), Exeter	01392 210900
Hogg Miss Katharine Elizabeth	1 Crown Office Row, London	0171 797 7500

Holdsworth James Arthur	Two Crown Office Row, London	020 7797 8100
Holl-Allen Jonathan Guy	3 Serjeants' Inn, London	0171 353 5537
Hollow Paul John	Fenners Chambers, Cambridge	01223 368761
	Fenners Chambers, Peterborough	01733 562030
Holmes Philip John	8 King Street Chambers, Manchester	0161 834 9560
Holwill Derek Paul Winsor	4 Paper Buildings, London	0171 353 3366/583 7155
Horne Michael Andrew	3 Serjeants' Inn, London	0171 353 5537
Howarth Simon Stuart	Two Crown Office Row, London	020 7797 8100
Hudson Anthony Sean	Doughty Street Chambers, London	0171 404 1313
Hurd Mark Dunsdon	2 New Street, Leicester	0116 2625906
Hutchin Edward Alister David	Bracton Chambers, London	0171 242 4248
Inman Melbourne Donald	1 Fountain Court, Birmingham	0121 236 5721
Irwin Stephen John	Doughty Street Chambers, London	0171 404 1313
Jackson Anthony Warren	3 Serjeants' Inn, London	0171 353 5537
Jackson Matthew David Everard	4 Paper Buildings, London	0171 353 3366/583 7155
Jacobson Lawrence	5 Paper Buildings, London	0171 583 9275/583 4555
Jenkins Dr Janet Caroline	Chambers of Kieran Coonan QC, London	0171 583 6013/2510
Johnston Anthony Paul	1 Fountain Court, Birmingham	0121 236 5721
Jones Miss (Catherine) Charlotte	Two Crown Office Row, London	020 7797 8100
Katrak Cyrus Pesi	Gough Square Chambers, London	0171 353 0924
Kelly Geoffrey Robert	Pump Court Chambers, London	0171 353 0711
	Pump Court Chambers, Winchester	01962 868161
	Pump Court Chambers, Swindon	01793 539899
Kelly Matthias John	Old Square Chambers, London	0171 269 0300
	Old Square Chambers, Bristol	0117 9277111
Kempster Ivor Toby Chalmers	Old Square Chambers, Bristol	0117 9277111
	Old Square Chambers, London	0171 269 0300
Kent Michael Harcourt	Two Crown Office Row, London	020 7797 8100
Khokhar Mushtaq Ahmed	Sovereign Chambers, Leeds	0113 2451841/2/3
Kirtley Paul George	37 Park Square Chambers, Leeds	0113 2439422
Knowles Graham Roy	Peel Court Chambers, Manchester	0161 832 3791
Kynoch Duncan Stuart Sanderson	29 Bedford Row Chambers, London	0171 831 2626
Lambert Miss Sarah Katrina	1 Crown Office Row, London	0171 797 7500
Lamberty Mark Julian Harker	Queen's Chambers, Manchester	0161 834 6875/4738
	Queens Chambers, Preston	01772 828300
Latimer-Sayer William Laurence	2 Mitre Court Buildings, London	0171 353 1353
Leech Brian Walter Thomas	No. 1 Serjeants' Inn, London	0171 415 6666
Lewis Andrew William	Sovereign Chambers, Leeds	0113 2451841/2/3
Lewis Charles James	Old Square Chambers, London	0171 269 0300
	Old Square Chambers, Bristol	0117 9277111
Lindqvist Andrew Nils Gunnar	Octagon House, Norwich	01603 623186
Lochrane Damien Horatio Ross	Pump Court Chambers, London	0171 353 0711
	Pump Court Chambers, Winchester	01962 868161
	Pump Court Chambers, Swindon	01793 539899
Lynagh Richard Dudley	Two Crown Office Row, London	020 7797 8100
MacDonald Alistair William Orchard	St Philip's Chambers, Birmingham	0121 246 7000
Machell Raymond Donatus	Deans Court Chambers, Manchester	0161 214 6000
	2 Pump Court, London	0171 353 5597
	Deans Court Chambers, Preston	01772 555163
Mackay Colin Crichton	39 Essex Street, London	0171 832 1111
Macleod Duncan	9 Gough Square, London	020 7832 0500
Main Peter Ramsay	Deans Court Chambers, Manchester	0161 214 6000
	Deans Court Chambers, Preston	01772 555163
Mainwaring [Robert] Paul Clason	Carmarthen Chambers, Carmarthen	01267 234410
Mandalia Vinesh Lalji	Harrow on the Hill Chambers, Harrow-on-the-Hill	0181 423 7444
Mangat Dr Tejina Kiran	New Court Chambers, London	0171 831 9500
Marks Jonathan Clive	4 Pump Court, London	020 7842 5555
Marks Peter	3 Temple Gardens, London	0171 353 0832
Matthews Dennis Roland	Two Crown Office Row, London	020 7797 8100

B

           ● Expanded entry in Part D

Maxwell Richard	Ropewalk Chambers, Nottingham	0115 9472581
	Doughty Street Chambers, London	0171 404 1313
McCahill Patrick Gerard	St Philip's Chambers, Birmingham	0121 246 7000
	Chambers of Andrew Campbell QC, Leeds	0113 2455438
McCann Simon Howard	Deans Court Chambers, Manchester	0161 214 6000
	Deans Court Chambers, Preston	01772 555163
McCaul Colin Brownlie	39 Essex Street, London	0171 832 1111
McDermott Gerard Francis	8 King Street Chambers, Manchester	0161 834 9560
	2 Pump Court, London	0171 353 5597
McGregor Harvey	4 Paper Buildings, London	0171 353 3366/583 7155
McNeill Miss Elizabeth Jane	• Old Square Chambers, London	0171 269 0300
	Old Square Chambers, Bristol	0117 9277111
Mehendale Ms Neelima Krishna	2 Mitre Court Buildings, London	0171 353 1353
Melton Christopher	Peel Court Chambers, Manchester	0161 832 3791
	199 Strand, London	0171 379 9779
Melville Miss Elizabeth Emma Jane	Old Square Chambers, London	0171 269 0300
	Old Square Chambers, Bristol	0117 9277111
Melville Richard David	• 39 Essex Street, London	0171 832 1111
Mercer David Paul	Queen's Chambers, Manchester	0161 834 6875/4738
	Queens Chambers, Preston	01772 828300
Metzer Anthony David Erwin	Doughty Street Chambers, London	0171 404 1313
Michael Simon Laurence	• Bedford Chambers, Ampthill	0870 7337333
Millar Gavin James	Doughty Street Chambers, London	0171 404 1313
Mishcon Miss Jane Malca	4 Paper Buildings, London	0171 353 3366/583 7155
Moat Frank Robert	Pump Court Chambers, London	0171 353 0711
	Pump Court Chambers, Winchester	01962 868161
	Pump Court Chambers, Swindon	01793 539899
Moore Mr Craig Ian	Barnard's Inn Chambers, London	0171 369 6969
	Park Lane Chambers, Leeds	0113 2285000
Morgan Andrew James	St Philip's Chambers, Birmingham	0121 246 7000
Mortimer Miss Sophie Kate	No. 1 Serjeants' Inn, London	0171 415 6666
Mulcahy Miss Leigh-Ann Maria	Chambers of John L Powell QC, London	0171 797 8000
Mulholland Michael	St James's Chambers, Manchester	0161 834 7000
Murphy Miss Nicola Jane	4 King's Bench Walk, London	0171 822 8822
Naughton Philip Anthony	3 Serjeants' Inn, London	0171 353 5537
Naylor Dr Kevin Michael Thomas	8 King Street Chambers, Manchester	0161 834 9560
Neale Miss Fiona Rosalind	3 Serjeants' Inn, London	0171 353 5537
Neville-Clarke Sebastian Adrian Bennett	1 Crown Office Row, London	0171 583 9292
Newman Austin Eric	9 Woodhouse Square, Leeds	0113 2451986
Ng Ray Kian Hin	Two Crown Office Row, London	020 7797 8100
Noble Roderick Grant	39 Essex Street, London	0171 832 1111
O'Connor Andrew McDougal	Two Crown Office Row, London	020 7797 8100
Oppenheim Robin Frank	Doughty Street Chambers, London	0171 404 1313
Outhwaite Mrs Wendy-Jane Tivnan	2 Harcourt Buildings, London	0171 583 9020
Paneth Miss Sarah Ruth	No. 1 Serjeants' Inn, London	0171 415 6666
Pearce Richard William	Peel Court Chambers, Manchester	0161 832 3791
Pearson Christopher	• Bridewell Chambers, London	020 7797 8800
Perry Miss Jacqueline Anne	• Lamb Building, London	020 7797 7788
Pershad Rohan	Two Crown Office Row, London	020 7797 8100
Picton Julian Mark	4 Paper Buildings, London	0171 353 3366/583 7155
Pinder Miss Mary Elizabeth	No. 1 Serjeants' Inn, London	0171 415 6666
Pirani Rohan Carl	Old Square Chambers, Bristol	0117 9277111
	Old Square Chambers, London	0171 269 0300
Pittaway David Michael	No. 1 Serjeants' Inn, London	0171 415 6666
Pliener David Jonathan	New Court Chambers, London	0171 831 9500
Pooles Michael Philip Holmes	4 Paper Buildings, London	0171 353 3366/583 7155
Portnoy Leslie Reuben	Chambers of John Hand QC, Manchester	0161 955 9000
Post Andrew John	Chambers of Kieran Coonan QC, London	0171 583 6013/2510
Pounder Gerard	5 Essex Court, London	0171 410 2000

• Expanded entry in Part D

Powell Miss Debra Ann	3 Serjeants' Inn, London	0171 353 5537
Pratt Allan Duncan	New Court Chambers, London	0171 831 9500
Price Miss Katharine Clare Harding	4 Paper Buildings, London	0171 353 3366/583 7155
Price Richard Mervyn	Littleton Chambers, London	0171 797 8600
Prinn Miss Helen Elizabeth	Octagon House, Norwich	01603 623186
Pulman George Frederick	Hardwicke Building, London	020 7242 2523
	Stour Chambers, Canterbury	01227 764899
Purchas Christopher Patrick Brooks	Two Crown Office Row, London	020 7797 8100
Pusey William James	St Philip's Chambers, Birmingham	0121 246 7000
Rankin Andrew	4 Field Court, London	0171 440 6900
Raybaud Mrs June Rose	96 Gray's Inn Road, London	0171 405 0585
Readhead Simon John Howard	No. 1 Serjeants' Inn, London	0171 415 6666
Renfree Peter Gerald Stanley	Harbour Court Chambers, Fareham	01329 827828
Richardson David John	13 King's Bench Walk, London	0171 353 7204
	King's Bench Chambers, Oxford	01865 311066
Rigney Andrew James	Two Crown Office Row, London	020 7797 8100
Ritchie Andrew George	9 Gough Square, London	020 7832 0500
Ritchie Miss Jean Harris	4 Paper Buildings, London	0171 353 3366/583 7155
Rivalland Marc-Edouard	No. 1 Serjeants' Inn, London	0171 415 6666
Rogers Paul John	1 Crown Office Row, London	0171 797 7500
	Crown Office Row Chambers, Brighton	01273 625625
Romney Miss Daphne Irene	4 Field Court, London	0171 440 6900
Rose Paul Telfer	Old Square Chambers, London	0171 269 0300
	Old Square Chambers, Bristol	0117 9277111
Ross John Graffin	No. 1 Serjeants' Inn, London	0171 415 6666
Rowe John Jermyn	• 8 King Street Chambers, Manchester	0161 834 9560
Ryder Timothy Robert	Queen's Chambers, Manchester	0161 834 6875/4738
	Queens Chambers, Preston	01772 828300
Saggerson Alan David	Barnard's Inn Chambers, London	0171 369 6969
Salmon Jonathan Carl	1 Fountain Court, Birmingham	0121 236 5721
Samuel Glyn Ross	St Philip's Chambers, Birmingham	0121 246 7000
Samuels Leslie John	Pump Court Chambers, London	0171 353 0711
	Pump Court Chambers, Winchester	01962 868161
	Pump Court Chambers, Swindon	01793 539899
Saunt Thomas William Gatty	Two Crown Office Row, London	020 7797 8100
Scorah Christopher James	8 King Street Chambers, Manchester	0161 834 9560
Searle Barrie	St James's Chambers, Manchester	0161 834 7000
Shale Justin Anton	4 King's Bench Walk, London	0171 822 8822
	King's Bench Chambers, Bournemouth	01202 250025
Shannon Thomas Eric	Queen's Chambers, Manchester	0161 834 6875/4738
	Queens Chambers, Preston	01772 828300
Shiels Ian	30 Park Square, Leeds	0113 2436388
Shorrock John Michael	Peel Court Chambers, Manchester	0161 832 3791
Siddiqi Faizul Aqtab	Justice Court Chambers, London	0181 830 7786
Silvester Bruce Ross	Lamb Chambers, London	020 7797 8300
Smail Alastair Harold Kurt	St Philip's Chambers, Birmingham	0121 246 7000
Smith Miss Emma Louise	Old Square Chambers, London	0171 269 0300
	Old Square Chambers, Bristol	0117 9277111
Smith Michael Joseph	8 King Street Chambers, Manchester	0161 834 9560
Smith Ms Rachel Catherine	Peel Court Chambers, Manchester	0161 832 3791
Smith Warwick Timothy Cresswell	Deans Court Chambers, Manchester	0161 214 6000
	Deans Court Chambers, Preston	01772 555163
Snowden John Stevenson	Two Crown Office Row, London	020 7797 8100
Spencer Martin Benedict	4 Paper Buildings, London	0171 353 3366/583 7155
Stern Dr Kristina Anne	39 Essex Street, London	0171 832 1111
Stevens Howard Linton	1 Crown Office Row, London	0171 583 9292
Stevenson John Melford	Two Crown Office Row, London	020 7797 8100
Stockdale David Andrew	Deans Court Chambers, Manchester	0161 214 6000
	Deans Court Chambers, Preston	01772 555163
	9 Bedford Row, London	0171 242 3555
Storey Jeremy Brian	4 Pump Court, London	020 7842 5555

• Expanded entry in Part D

B

Swan Ian Christopher	Two Crown Office Row, London	020 7797 8100
Syed Mohammad Ali	39 Park Avenue, Mitcham	0181 648 1684
	Tower Hamlets Barristers Chambers, London	0171 247 9825
Szanto Gregory John Michael	Eastbourne Chambers, Eastbourne	01323 642102
Taft Christopher Heiton	St James's Chambers, Manchester	0161 834 7000
Taylor Miss Deborah Frances	Two Crown Office Row, London	020 7797 8100
Temple Anthony Dominic	4 Pump Court, London	020 7842 5555
Thompson Patrick Miles	Queen's Chambers, Manchester	0161 834 6875/4738
	Queens Chambers, Preston	01772 828300
Thomson Dr David James Ramsay Gibb	Barnard's Inn Chambers, London	0171 369 6969
Thorold Oliver	Doughty Street Chambers, London	0171 404 1313
Tracy Forster Miss Jane Elizabeth	13 King's Bench Walk, London	0171 353 7204
	King's Bench Chambers, Oxford	01865 311066
Treasure Francis Seton	199 Strand, London	0171 379 9779
Trippier Lady	Deans Court Chambers, Manchester	0161 214 6000
	Deans Court Chambers, Preston	01772 555163
Trotman Timothy Oliver	Deans Court Chambers, Manchester	0161 214 6000
	Deans Court Chambers, Preston	01772 555163
Tucker David William	Two Crown Office Row, London	020 7797 8100
Tully Ms Anne Margaret	Eastbourne Chambers, Eastbourne	01323 642102
Ullstein Augustus Rupert Patrick A	• 29 Bedford Row Chambers, London	0171 831 2626
Vickers Miss Rachel Clare	199 Strand, London	0171 379 9779
Wadsworth James Patrick	4 Paper Buildings, London	0171 353 3366/583 7155
Walker Christopher David Bestwick	Old Square Chambers, Bristol	0117 9277111
	Old Square Chambers, London	0171 269 0300
Warrender Miss Nichola Mary	New Court Chambers, London	0171 831 9500
Waters Julian William Penrose	No. 1 Serjeants' Inn, London	0171 415 6666
Watson James Vernon	3 Serjeants' Inn, London	0171 353 5537
Weddle Steven Edgar	Hardwicke Building, London	020 7242 2523
Weereratne Ms Rufina Aswini	Doughty Street Chambers, London	0171 404 1313
Weston Clive Aubrey Richard	Two Crown Office Row, London	020 7797 8100
Whipple Mrs Philippa Jane Edwards	1 Crown Office Row, London	0171 797 7500
Whitfield Adrian	3 Serjeants' Inn, London	0171 353 5537
Wilby David Christopher	• 199 Strand, London	0171 379 9779
	Park Lane Chambers, Leeds	0113 2285000
Wilkinson Nigel Vivian Marshall	Two Crown Office Row, London	020 7797 8100
Willer Robert Michael	Hardwicke Building, London	020 7242 2523
Williams Graeme	13 King's Bench Walk, London	0171 353 7204
	King's Bench Chambers, Oxford	01865 311066
Williams Hugh David Haydn	St Philip's Chambers, Birmingham	0121 246 7000
Williams The Hon John Melville	Old Square Chambers, London	0171 269 0300
	Old Square Chambers, Bristol	0117 9277111
Williams Thomas Christopher Charles	1 Fountain Court, Birmingham	0121 236 5721
Williams Wyn Lewis	39 Essex Street, London	0171 832 1111
	33 Park Place, Cardiff	02920 233313
Wilson Peter Julian	Sovereign Chambers, Leeds	0113 2451841/2/3
Wilton Simon Daniel	4 Paper Buildings, London	0171 353 3366/583 7155
Witcomb Henry James	199 Strand, London	0171 379 9779
Yell Nicholas Anthony	No. 1 Serjeants' Inn, London	0171 415 6666

MEDICAL/DENTAL DISCIPLINARY WORK

Burden Miss Susan Jane	Chambers of Kieran Coonan QC, London	0171 583 6013/2510

MENTAL HEALTH

Barlow Craig Martin	29 Bedford Row Chambers, London	0171 831 2626
Beasley-Murray Mrs Caroline Wynne	Fenners Chambers, Cambridge	01223 368761
	Fenners Chambers, Peterborough	01733 562030
Bowen Paul Edward	4 King's Bench Walk, London	0171 822 8822

Brodwell John Shenton	9 Woodhouse Square, Leeds	0113 2451986
Brook Ian Stuart	Hardwicke Building, London	020 7242 2523
Bugg Ian Stephen	Crown Office Row Chambers, Brighton	01273 625625
Burrows Simon Paul	Peel Court Chambers, Manchester	0161 832 3791
Campbell Miss Alexis Anne	Hardwicke Building, London	020 7242 2523
Campbell Miss Emily Charlotte	• Wilberforce Chambers, London	0171 306 0102
Cannon Adam Richard	96 Gray's Inn Road, London	0171 405 0585
Cawley Neil Robert Loudoun	169 Temple Chambers, London	0171 583 7644
	Milton Keynes Chambers, Milton Keynes	01908 664 128
Coghlan Terence	1 Crown Office Row, London	0171 797 7500
	Crown Office Row Chambers, Brighton	01273 625625
Curwen Michael Jonathan	Chambers of Kieran Coonan QC, London	0171 583 6013/2510
Daniel Leon Roger	6 King's Bench Walk, London	0171 353 4931/583 0695
Davidson Dr Ranald Dunbar	3 Serjeants' Inn, London	0171 353 5537
De Zonie Miss Jane	14 Gray's Inn Square, London	0171 242 0858
Dolan Dr Bridget Maura	3 Serjeants' Inn, London	0171 353 5537
Edis Angus William Butler	1 Crown Office Row, London	0171 797 7500
Ellis Dr Peter Simon	7 New Square, London	0171 430 1660
English Miss Caroline Frances	Francis Taylor Building, London	0171 353 7768/7769/2711
Fitzgerald Edward Hamilton	Doughty Street Chambers, London	0171 404 1313
Flahive Daniel Michael	Hardwicke Building, London	020 7242 2523
Foudy Miss Kim Frances	8 King Street Chambers, Manchester	0161 834 9560
Francis Andrew James	Chambers of Mr Peter Crampin QC, London	020 7831 0081
Friston Dr Mark Harpham	Chambers of Kieran Coonan QC, London	0171 583 6013/2510
Fullwood Adam Garrett	Chambers of Ian Macdonald QC (In Association with Two Garden Court, Temple, London), Manchester	0161 236 1840
Gledhill Kris	Camberwell Chambers, London	0171 274 0830
Gordon Richard John Francis	Brick Court Chambers, London	0171 379 3550
Grace John Oliver Bowman	3 Serjeants' Inn, London	0171 353 5537
Grey Miss Eleanor Mary Grace	39 Essex Street, London	0171 832 1111
Hargan James John	30 Park Square, Leeds	0113 2436388
Hatfield Ms Sally Anne	Doughty Street Chambers, London	0171 404 1313
Irwin Stephen John	Doughty Street Chambers, London	0171 404 1313
Jackson Anthony Warren	3 Serjeants' Inn, London	0171 353 5537
Jackson Dirik George Allan	Chambers of Mr Peter Crampin QC, London	020 7831 0081
Jenkins Dr Janet Caroline	Chambers of Kieran Coonan QC, London	0171 583 6013/2510
Kaufmann Ms Phillippa Jane	Doughty Street Chambers, London	0171 404 1313
Khan Anwar William	Eastbourne Chambers, Eastbourne	01323 642102
	Wessex Chambers, Reading	0118 956 8856
Kovats Steven Laszlo	39 Essex Street, London	0171 832 1111
Lunt Steven	9 Woodhouse Square, Leeds	0113 2451986
Marks Peter	3 Temple Gardens, London	0171 353 0832
Markus Ms Kate	Doughty Street Chambers, London	0171 404 1313
Melton Christopher	Peel Court Chambers, Manchester	0161 832 3791
	199 Strand, London	0171 379 9779
Messling Lawrence David	St Philip's Chambers, Birmingham	0121 246 7000
Morris Miss Fenella	39 Essex Street, London	0171 832 1111
Ofori George Edward	ACHMA Chambers, London	0171 639 7817/0171 635 7904
	Chancery Chambers, London	0171 405 6879/6870
Ogle Miss Rebecca Theodosia Abigail	Southernhay Chambers, Exeter	01392 255777
Oliver Michael Richard	Hardwicke Building, London	020 7242 2523
Oppenheim Robin Frank	Doughty Street Chambers, London	0171 404 1313
Pearce Robert Edgar	Chambers of Mr Peter Crampin QC, London	020 7831 0081
Pleming Nigel Peter	39 Essex Street, London	0171 832 1111
Powell Miss Debra Ann	3 Serjeants' Inn, London	0171 353 5537
Price Miss Katharine Clare Harding	4 Paper Buildings, London	0171 353 3366/583 7155

       • Expanded entry in Part D

Raybaud Mrs June Rose	96 Gray's Inn Road, London	0171 405 0585
Richards Miss Jennifer	39 Essex Street, London	0171 832 1111
Ryder Ernest Nigel	Deans Court Chambers, Manchester	0161 214 6000
	Deans Court Chambers, Preston	01772 555163
	1 Mitre Court Buildings, London	0171 797 7070
Shale Justin Anton	4 King's Bench Walk, London	0171 822 8822
	King's Bench Chambers, Bournemouth	01202 250025
Teeman Miss Miriam Joy	30 Park Square, Leeds	0113 2436388
Thorne Timothy Peter	33 Bedford Row, London	0171 242 6476
Thorold Oliver	Doughty Street Chambers, London	0171 404 1313
Wakeham Philip John Le Messurier	Hardwicke Building, London	020 7242 2523
Wallbanks Miss Joanne	1 Fountain Court, Birmingham	0121 236 5721
	Rowchester Chambers, Birmingham	0121 233 2327/2361951
Weereratne Ms Rufina Aswini	Doughty Street Chambers, London	0171 404 1313
Weston Ms Amanda	Chambers of Ian Macdonald QC (In Association with Two Garden Court, Temple, London), Manchester	0161 236 1840
Williams Graeme	13 King's Bench Walk, London	0171 353 7204
	King's Bench Chambers, Oxford	01865 311066
Wise Ian	Doughty Street Chambers, London	0171 404 1313

MOBILE HOMES

Foster Brian Ian	St James's Chambers, Manchester	0161 834 7000
	Park Lane Chambers, Leeds	0113 2285000

MORTGAGES AND BORROWERS

Cawley Neil Robert Loudoun	169 Temple Chambers, London	0171 583 7644
	Milton Keynes Chambers, Milton Keynes	01908 664 128
Hodgkinson Tristram Patrick	• 5 Pump Court, London	020 7353 2532
Sandells Ms Nicole	11 Old Square, London	020 7430 0341
Southall Richard Anthony	• 17 Bedford Row, London	0171 831 7314

MOTOR VEHICLES

Spollon Guy Merton	St Philip's Chambers, Birmingham	0121 246 7000

MOTORING LAW

Bresler Fenton Shea	22 Melcombe Regis Court, London	0171 487 5589

MUSIC, FILM AND TV

Barker Simon George Harry	• 13 Old Square, London	0171 404 4800

NATIONAL INSURANCE CONTRIBUTIONS

Harris David Raymond	Prince Henry's Chambers, London	0171 713 0376

NEW YORK LAW

Sagar (Edward) Leigh	12 New Square, London	0171 419 1212
	Newport Chambers, Newport	01633 267403/255855
	Sovereign Chambers, Leeds	0113 2451841/2/3

PARLIAMENTARY

Alesbury Alun	2 Mitre Court Buildings, London	0171 583 1380
Asprey Nicholas	Serle Court Chambers, London	0171 242 6105
Boyle Christopher Alexander David	2 Mitre Court Buildings, London	0171 583 1380
Burton Nicholas Anthony	2 Mitre Court Buildings, London	0171 583 1380
Cameron Neil St Clair	1 Serjeants' Inn, London	0171 583 1355
Clarkson Patrick Robert James	• 1 Serjeants' Inn, London	0171 583 1355
Druce Michael James	2 Mitre Court Buildings, London	0171 583 1380
Farrer Adam Michael	4 Fountain Court, Birmingham	0121 236 3476
Fitzgerald Michael Frederick Clive	2 Mitre Court Buildings, London	0171 583 1380
Fookes Robert Lawrence	2 Mitre Court Buildings, London	0171 583 1380
Ford Michael David	Doughty Street Chambers, London	0171 404 1313

• Expanded entry in Part D

Glover Richard Michael	2 Mitre Court Buildings, London	0171 583 1380
Harwood Richard John	1 Serjeants' Inn, London	0171 583 1355
Henderson Roger Anthony	2 Harcourt Buildings, London	0171 583 9020
Hockman Stephen Alexander	• 6 Pump Court, London	0171 797 8400
	6-8 Mill Street, Maidstone	01622 688094
Hogg The Hon Douglas Martin	37 Park Square Chambers, Leeds	0113 2439422
	Cathedral Chambers (Jan Wood Independent Barristers' Clerk), Exeter	01392 210900
Horton Matthew Bethell	2 Mitre Court Buildings, London	0171 583 1380
Humphries Michael John	2 Mitre Court Buildings, London	0171 583 1380
King Neil Gerald Alexander	2 Mitre Court Buildings, London	0171 583 1380
Macpherson The Hon Mary Stewart	2 Mitre Court Buildings, London	0171 583 1380
Markus Ms Kate	Doughty Street Chambers, London	0171 404 1313
Millar Gavin James	Doughty Street Chambers, London	0171 404 1313
Moore Professor Victor William Edward	2 Mitre Court Buildings, London	0171 583 1380
Moriarty Gerald Evelyn	2 Mitre Court Buildings, London	0171 583 1380
Nardell Gordon Lawrence	6 Pump Court, London	0171 797 8400
	6-8 Mill Street, Maidstone	01622 688094
Newcombe Andrew Bennett	2 Harcourt Buildings, London	020 7353 8415
Purchas Robin Michael	• 2 Harcourt Buildings, London	020 7353 8415
Roots Guy Robert Godfrey	2 Mitre Court Buildings, London	0171 583 1380
Shrimpton Michael	Francis Taylor Building, London	0171 797 7250
Silsoe The Lord	2 Mitre Court Buildings, London	0171 583 1380
Stone Gregory	• 4-5 Gray's Inn Square, London	0171 404 5252
Tait Andrew Charles Gordon	2 Harcourt Buildings, London	020 7353 8415
Taylor John Charles	2 Mitre Court Buildings, London	0171 583 1380
Taylor Reuben Mallinson	2 Mitre Court Buildings, London	0171 583 1380
Thomas Miss Megan Moira	1 Serjeants' Inn, London	0171 583 1355
Wald Richard Daniel	2 Mitre Court Buildings, London	0171 583 1380
Warren Rupert Miles	2 Mitre Court Buildings, London	0171 583 1380
Whybrow Christopher John	1 Serjeants' Inn, London	0171 583 1355
Widdicombe David Graham	2 Mitre Court Buildings, London	0171 583 1380

PARTNERSHIPS

Acton Stephen Neil	11 Old Square, London	020 7430 0341
Adamyk Simon Charles	12 New Square, London	0171 419 1212
Ashton David Sambrook	13 King's Bench Walk, London	0171 353 7204
	King's Bench Chambers, Oxford	01865 311066
Asplin Miss Sarah Jane	• 3 Stone Buildings, London	0171 242 4937
Asprey Nicholas	Serle Court Chambers, London	0171 242 6105
Ayres Andrew John William	13 Old Square, London	0171 404 4800
Banks Roderick Charles l'Anson	• 48 Bedford Row, London	0171 430 2005
Barker Simon George Harry	• 13 Old Square, London	0171 404 4800
Barton Alan John	Lamb Building, London	020 7797 7788
Beaumont Marc Clifford	• Harrow on the Hill Chambers, Harrow-on-the-Hill	0181 423 7444
	Windsor Barristers' Chambers, Windsor	01753 648899
	Pump Court Chambers, London	0171 353 0711
Behrens James Nicholas Edward	Serle Court Chambers, London	0171 242 6105
Berry Nicholas Michael	Southernhay Chambers, Exeter	01392 255777
	1 Gray's Inn Square, London	0171 405 8946/7/8
	22 Old Buildings, London	0171 831 0222
Blackett-Ord Mark	• 5 Stone Buildings, London	0171 242 6201
Briggs Michael Townley Featherstone	Serle Court Chambers, London	0171 242 6105
Buck Dr Andrew Theodore	Chambers of Martin Burr, London	0171 353 4636
Burr Martin John	Chambers of Martin Burr, London	0171 353 4636
	7 New Square, London	0171 430 1660
Butler Andrew	2nd Floor, Francis Taylor Building, London	0171 353 9942/3157

• Expanded entry in Part D

Castle Peter Bolton	Chambers of Mr Peter Crampin QC, London	020 7831 0081
Cawley Neil Robert Loudoun	169 Temple Chambers, London	0171 583 7644
	Milton Keynes Chambers, Milton Keynes	01908 664 128
Charman Andrew Julian	St Philip's Chambers, Birmingham	0121 246 7000
Chesner Howard Michael	Bracton Chambers, London	0171 242 4248
Chivers (Tom) David	Erskine Chambers, London	0171 242 5532
Clark Andrew Richard	Manchester House Chambers, Manchester	0161 834 7007
	8 King Street Chambers, Manchester	0161 834 9560
Clarke Miss Anna Victoria	5 Stone Buildings, London	0171 242 6201
Clarke Ian James	Hardwicke Building, London	020 7242 2523
Clegg Sebastian James Barwick	Deans Court Chambers, Manchester	0161 214 6000
	Deans Court Chambers, Preston	01772 555163
Close Douglas Jonathan	Serle Court Chambers, London	0171 242 6105
Cole Robert Ian Gawain	30 Park Square, Leeds	0113 2436388
Cook Jeremy David	Lamb Building, London	020 7797 7788
Cooper Gilead Patrick	Chambers of Mr Peter Crampin QC, London	020 7831 0081
Corbett James Patrick	St Philip's Chambers, Birmingham	0121 246 7000
	Chambers of Andrew Campbell QC, Leeds	0113 2455438
Cosedge Andrew John	3 Stone Buildings, London	0171 242 4937
Craig Alistair Trevor	Chambers of Mr Peter Crampin QC, London	020 7831 0081
Crampin Peter	Chambers of Mr Peter Crampin QC, London	020 7831 0081
Cranfield Peter Anthony	3 Verulam Buildings, London	0171 831 8441
Davey Benjamin Nicholas	11 Old Square, London	020 7430 0341
Davidson Edward Alan	11 Old Square, London	020 7430 0341
Dedezade Taner	Tindal Chambers, Chelmsford	01245 267742
Dodd Christopher John Nicholas	9 Woodhouse Square, Leeds	0113 2451986
Dodge Peter Clive	11 Old Square, London	020 7430 0341
Dooher Miss Nancy Helen	St James's Chambers, Manchester	0161 834 7000
Dougherty Nigel Peter	Erskine Chambers, London	0171 242 5532
Elleray Anthony John	● St James's Chambers, Manchester	0161 834 7000
	12 New Square, London	0171 419 1212
	Park Lane Chambers, Leeds	0113 2285000
Eyre Stephen John Arthur	1 Fountain Court, Birmingham	0121 236 5721
Fadipe Gabriel Charles	● Wilberforce Chambers, London	0171 306 0102
Farrow Kenneth John	Serle Court Chambers, London	0171 242 6105
Fawls Richard Granville	5 Stone Buildings, London	0171 242 6201
Feltham Piers Jonathan	Chambers of Mr Peter Crampin QC, London	020 7831 0081
Finn Terence	Chambers of Martin Burr, London	0171 353 4636
Foster Brian Ian	St James's Chambers, Manchester	0161 834 7000
	Park Lane Chambers, Leeds	0113 2285000
Francis Andrew James	Chambers of Mr Peter Crampin QC, London	020 7831 0081
Fryer-Spedding James Walter	St James's Chambers, Manchester	0161 834 7000
Garcia-Miller Miss Laura	Enterprise Chambers, London	0171 405 9471
	Enterprise Chambers, Leeds	0113 246 0391
	Enterprise Chambers, Newcastle upon Tyne	0191 222 3344
Gasztowicz Steven	2-3 Gray's Inn Square, London	0171 242 4986
	2 New Street, Leicester	0116 2625906
Gee Steven Mark	4 Field Court, London	0171 440 6900
Gerald Nigel Mortimer	Enterprise Chambers, London	0171 405 9471
	Enterprise Chambers, Leeds	0113 246 0391
	Enterprise Chambers, Newcastle upon Tyne	0191 222 3344

● Expanded entry in Part D

B

Gifford Andrew James Morris	7 New Square, London	0171 430 1660
Gillyon Philip Jeffrey	Erskine Chambers, London	0171 242 5532
Graham Thomas Patrick Henry	1 New Square, London	0171 405 0884/5/6/7
Grantham Andrew Timothy	• Deans Court Chambers, Manchester	0161 214 6000
	Deans Court Chambers, Preston	01772 555163
Green David Cameron	Adrian Lyon's Chambers, Liverpool	0151 236 4421/8240
Gregory John Raymond	Deans Court Chambers, Manchester	0161 214 6000
	Deans Court Chambers, Preston	01772 555163
Groves Hugo Gerard	Enterprise Chambers, London	0171 405 9471
	Enterprise Chambers, Leeds	0113 246 0391
	Enterprise Chambers, Newcastle upon Tyne	0191 222 3344
Hall Taylor Alexander Edward	11 Old Square, London	020 7430 0341
Halpern David Anthony	Enterprise Chambers, London	0171 405 9471
	Enterprise Chambers, Leeds	0113 246 0391
	Enterprise Chambers, Newcastle upon Tyne	0191 222 3344
Hamilton Eben William	1 New Square, London	0171 405 0884/5/6/7
Hantusch Robert Anthony	• 3 Stone Buildings, London	0171 242 4937
Harrod Henry Mark	5 Stone Buildings, London	0171 242 6201
Henley Mark Robert Daniel	9 Woodhouse Square, Leeds	0113 2451986
Henley Raymond Francis St Luke	Lancaster Building, Manchester	0161 661 4444/0171 649 9872
Hill Robert Douglas	Pump Court Chambers, Winchester	01962 868161
	Pump Court Chambers, London	0171 353 0711
	Pump Court Chambers, Swindon	01793 539899
Hinks Frank Peter	Serle Court Chambers, London	0171 242 6105
Hirst William Timothy John	Park Court Chambers, Leeds	0113 2433277
Hodgson Martin Derrick	8 King's Bench Walk, London	0171 797 8888
	8 King's Bench Walk North, Leeds	0113 2439797
Hollington Robin Frank	1 New Square, London	0171 405 0884/5/6/7
Horne Roger Cozens-Hardy	Chambers of Mr Peter Crampin QC, London	020 7831 0081
Hoser Philip Jacob	Serle Court Chambers, London	0171 242 6105
Jackson Dirik George Allan	Chambers of Mr Peter Crampin QC, London	020 7831 0081
Jackson Nicholas David Kingsley	Adrian Lyon's Chambers, Liverpool	0151 236 4421/8240
Jacobson Lawrence	5 Paper Buildings, London	0171 583 9275/583 4555
James-Stadden Miss Jodie Cara	Westgate Chambers, Newcastle upon Tyne	0191 261 4407/2329785
Jefferis Arthur Michael Quentin	Chambers of Mr Peter Crampin QC, London	020 7831 0081
Jennings Timothy Robin Finnegan	Enterprise Chambers, London	0171 405 9471
	Enterprise Chambers, Leeds	0113 246 0391
	Enterprise Chambers, Newcastle upon Tyne	0191 222 3344
Joffe Victor Howard	Serle Court Chambers, London	0171 242 6105
Jones Philip John	Serle Court Chambers, London	0171 242 6105
Jory Robert John Hugh	Enterprise Chambers, London	0171 405 9471
	Enterprise Chambers, Leeds	0113 246 0391
	Enterprise Chambers, Newcastle upon Tyne	0191 222 3344
Kosmin Leslie Gordon	Erskine Chambers, London	0171 242 5532
Kremen Philip Michael	Hardwicke Building, London	020 7242 2523
Kynoch Duncan Stuart Sanderson	29 Bedford Row Chambers, London	0171 831 2626
Lamont Miss Camilla Rose	Chambers of Lord Goodhart QC, London	0171 405 5577
Landes Miss Anna-Rose	St Philip's Chambers, Birmingham	0121 246 7000
Levy Benjamin Keith	Enterprise Chambers, London	0171 405 9471
	Enterprise Chambers, Leeds	0113 246 0391
	Enterprise Chambers, Newcastle upon Tyne	0191 222 3344

Lloyd Stephen James George	Chambers of Mr Peter Crampin QC, London	020 7831 0081
Lowenstein Paul David	Littleton Chambers, London	0171 797 8600
Mabb David Michael	Erskine Chambers, London	0171 242 5532
Machell John William	Serle Court Chambers, London	0171 242 6105
Mann George Anthony	Enterprise Chambers, London	0171 405 9471
	Enterprise Chambers, Leeds	0113 246 0391
	Enterprise Chambers, Newcastle upon Tyne	0191 222 3344
Marquand Charles Nicholas Hilary	Chambers of Lord Goodhart QC, London	0171 405 5577
Maynard-Connor Giles	St James's Chambers, Manchester	0161 834 7000
McAlinden Barry O'Neill	17 Bedford Row, London	0171 831 7314
McClure Brian David	Littman Chambers, London	020 7404 4866
McDonnell John Beresford William	1 New Square, London	0171 405 0884/5/6/7
McQuail Ms Katherine Emma	11 Old Square, London	020 7430 0341
Mendoza Neil David Pereira	Hardwicke Building, London	020 7242 2523
Milligan Iain Anstruther	20 Essex Street, London	0171 583 9294
Morgan Dr Austen Jude	3 Temple Gardens, London	0171 353 0832
Morgan Charles James Arthur	Enterprise Chambers, London	0171 405 9471
	Enterprise Chambers, Newcastle upon Tyne	0191 222 3344
	Enterprise Chambers, Leeds	0113 246 0391
Morgan Richard Hugo Lyndon	13 Old Square, London	0171 404 4800
Naidoo Sean Van	Littman Chambers, London	020 7404 4866
Neville Stephen John	Gough Square Chambers, London	0171 353 0924
Neville-Clarke Sebastian Adrian Bennett	1 Crown Office Row, London	0171 583 9292
Newman Miss Catherine Mary	• 13 Old Square, London	0171 404 4800
Nicholls John Peter	13 Old Square, London	0171 404 4800
Norris Alastair Hubert	5 Stone Buildings, London	0171 242 6201
	Southernhay Chambers, Exeter	01392 255777
Nugee Edward George	• Wilberforce Chambers, London	0171 306 0102
O'Leary Robert Michael	33 Park Place, Cardiff	02920 233313
Ohrenstein Dov	Chambers of Lord Goodhart QC, London	0171 405 5577
Ovey Miss Elizabeth Helen	11 Old Square, London	020 7430 0341
Peacocke Mrs Teresa Anne Rosen	Enterprise Chambers, London	0171 405 9471
	Enterprise Chambers, Leeds	0113 246 0391
	Enterprise Chambers, Newcastle upon Tyne	0191 222 3344
Pearce Robert Edgar	Chambers of Mr Peter Crampin QC, London	020 7831 0081
Pearson Christopher	• Bridewell Chambers, London	020 7797 8800
Perkoff Richard Michael	Littleton Chambers, London	0171 797 8600
Pickering James Patrick	Enterprise Chambers, London	0171 405 9471
	Enterprise Chambers, Leeds	0113 246 0391
	Enterprise Chambers, Newcastle upon Tyne	0191 222 3344
Porter David Leonard	St James's Chambers, Manchester	0161 834 7000
	Park Lane Chambers, Leeds	0113 2285000
Potts James Rupert	Erskine Chambers, London	0171 242 5532
Potts Robin	Erskine Chambers, London	0171 242 5532
Prentice Professor Daniel David	Erskine Chambers, London	0171 242 5532
Purves Gavin Bowman	Swan House, London	0181 998 3035
Randall John Yeoman	St Philip's Chambers, Birmingham	0121 246 7000
	7 Stone Buildings, London	0171 405 3886/242 3546
Rashid Omar	Chambers of Mr Peter Crampin QC, London	020 7831 0081
Reed John William Rupert	• Wilberforce Chambers, London	0171 306 0102
Rees Professor William Michael	Barnard's Inn Chambers, London	0171 369 6969
Renfree Peter Gerald Stanley	Harbour Court Chambers, Fareham	01329 827828

B

Richardson David John	13 King's Bench Walk, London	0171 353 7204
	King's Bench Chambers, Oxford	01865 311066
Richardson Giles John	Serle Court Chambers, London	0171 242 6105
Roberts Miss Catherine Ann	Erskine Chambers, London	0171 242 5532
Rogers Miss Beverly-Ann	Serle Court Chambers, London	0171 242 6105
Rolfe Patrick John Benedict	5 Stone Buildings, London	0171 242 6201
Ross Martyn John Greaves	• 5 New Square, London	020 7404 0404
Rowell David Stewart	Chambers of Lord Goodhart QC, London	0171 405 5577
Russell Christopher Garnet	• 12 New Square, London	0171 419 1212
	Sovereign Chambers, Leeds	0113 2451841/2/3
Sandbrook-Hughes Stewert Karl Anthony	Iscoed Chambers, Swansea	01792 652988/9/330
Sandells Ms Nicole	11 Old Square, London	020 7430 0341
Sellers Graham	Adrian Lyon's Chambers, Liverpool	0151 236 4421/8240
Selway Dr Katherine Emma	11 Old Square, London	020 7430 0341
Semken Christopher Richard	1 New Square, London	0171 405 0884/5/6/7
Seymour Thomas Oliver	• Wilberforce Chambers, London	0171 306 0102
Shale Justin Anton	4 King's Bench Walk, London	0171 822 8822
	King's Bench Chambers, Bournemouth	01202 250025
Shepherd Nigel Patrick	8 King's Bench Walk North, Leeds	0113 2439797
	8 King's Bench Walk, London	0171 797 8888
Skelly Andrew Jon	1 Gray's Inn Square, London	0171 405 8946/7/8
Snowden Richard Andrew	Erskine Chambers, London	0171 242 5532
Staddon Paul	2nd Floor, Francis Taylor Building, London	0171 353 9942/3157
Start Miss Angharad Jocelyn	3 Verulam Buildings, London	0171 831 8441
Staunton (Thomas) Ulick (Patrick)	Chambers of Mr Peter Crampin QC, London	020 7831 0081
	65-67 King Street, Leicester	0116 2547710
Sterling Robert Alan	St James's Chambers, Manchester	0161 834 7000
	12 New Square, London	0171 419 1212
	Park Lane Chambers, Leeds	0113 2285000
Stevens-Hoare Miss Michelle	Hardwicke Building, London	020 7242 2523
Stewart Nicholas John Cameron	Hardwicke Building, London	020 7242 2523
Stewart-Smith William Rodney	1 New Square, London	0171 405 0884/5/6/7
Stokes Miss Mary Elizabeth	Erskine Chambers, London	0171 242 5532
Sutcliffe Andrew Harold Wentworth	3 Verulam Buildings, London	0171 831 8441
Swerling Robert Harry	13 Old Square, London	0171 404 4800
Szanto Gregory John Michael	Eastbourne Chambers, Eastbourne	01323 642102
Talbot Patrick John	Serle Court Chambers, London	0171 242 6105
Tedd Rex Hilary	• St Philip's Chambers, Birmingham	0121 246 7000
	De Montfort Chambers, Leicester	0116 254 8686
	Northampton Chambers, Northampton	01604 636271
Thomas Nigel Matthew	13 Old Square, London	0171 404 4800
Thompson Andrew Richard	Erskine Chambers, London	0171 242 5532
Thornton Andrew James	Erskine Chambers, London	0171 242 5532
Tipples Miss Amanda Jane	13 Old Square, London	0171 404 4800
Trace Anthony John	• 13 Old Square, London	0171 404 4800
Tully Ms Anne Margaret	Eastbourne Chambers, Eastbourne	01323 642102
Van Tonder Gerard Dirk	1 New Square, London	0171 405 0884/5/6/7
Walker Andrew Greenfield	Chambers of Lord Goodhart QC, London	0171 405 5577
Weatherill Bernard Richard	Chambers of Lord Goodhart QC, London	0171 405 5577
West Mark	• 11 Old Square, London	020 7430 0341
Whittaker John Percival	Serle Court Chambers, London	0171 242 6105
Wilson-Barnes Miss Lucy Emma	St James's Chambers, Manchester	0161 834 7000
Wood Ian Robert	8 King Street Chambers, Manchester	0161 834 9560
Zaman Mohammed Khalil	St Philip's Chambers, Birmingham	0121 246 7000
Zelin Geoffrey Andrew	Enterprise Chambers, London	0171 405 9471
	Enterprise Chambers, Leeds	0113 246 0391
	Enterprise Chambers, Newcastle upon Tyne	0191 222 3344

• Expanded entry in Part D

PATENTS

Abrahams James	8 New Square, London	0171 405 4321
Alexander Daniel Sakyi	8 New Square, London	0171 405 4321
Baldwin John Paul	8 New Square, London	0171 405 4321
Clark Miss Fiona Jane Stewart	8 New Square, London	0171 405 4321
Cole Richard John	Lancaster Building, Manchester	0161 661 4444/0171 649 9872
Colley Dr Peter McLean	• 19 Old Buildings, London	0171 405 2001
Cook Christopher Graham	St James's Chambers, Manchester	0161 834 7000
Fysh Michael	8 New Square, London	0171 405 4321
Gee Steven Mark	4 Field Court, London	0171 440 6900
Greatorex Ms Helen Louise	9 Woodhouse Square, Leeds	0113 2451986
Green Miss Jane Elizabeth	Design Chambers, London	0171 353 0747
	Chambers of Martin Burr, London	0171 353 4636
Hamer George Clemens	8 New Square, London	0171 405 4321
Heal Mrs Madeleine	4 Field Court, London	0171 440 6900
Henley Raymond Francis St Luke	Lancaster Building, Manchester	0161 661 4444/0171 649 9872
Hicks Michael Charles	• 19 Old Buildings, London	0171 405 2001
Holman Miss Tamsin Perdita	19 Old Buildings, London	0171 405 2001
Howe Martin Russell Thomson	8 New Square, London	0171 405 4321
Kelman Alistair Bruce	Lancaster Building, Manchester	0161 661 4444/0171 649 9872
Kitchin David James Tyson	8 New Square, London	0171 405 4321
Lambert John	Lancaster Building, Manchester	0161 661 4444/0171 649 9872
Lane Ms Lindsay Ruth Busfield	8 New Square, London	0171 405 4321
May Miss Charlotte Louisa	8 New Square, London	0171 405 4321
Meade Richard David	8 New Square, London	0171 405 4321
Mellor Edward James Wilson	8 New Square, London	0171 405 4321
Moody-Stuart Thomas	8 New Square, London	0171 405 4321
Onslow Robert Denzil	8 New Square, London	0171 405 4321
Pickford Anthony James	Prince Henry's Chamber, London	0171 834 2572
Platts-Mills Mark Fortescue	8 New Square, London	0171 405 4321
Prescott Peter Richard Kyle	8 New Square, London	0171 405 4321
Puckrin Cedric Eldred	19 Old Buildings, London	0171 405 2001
Reed Jeremy Nigel	19 Old Buildings, London	0171 405 2001
Reid Brian Christopher	19 Old Buildings, London	0171 405 2001
Shipley Norman Graham	• 19 Old Buildings, London	0171 405 2001
Speck Adrian	8 New Square, London	0171 405 4321
St Ville Laurence James	8 New Square, London	0171 405 4321
Sullivan Rory Myles	19 Old Buildings, London	0171 405 2001
Tappin Michael John	8 New Square, London	0171 405 4321
Vitoria Miss Mary Christine	8 New Square, London	0171 405 4321
Wilson Alastair James Drysdale	• 19 Old Buildings, London	0171 405 2001

PENSIONS

Angus Miss Tracey Anne	5 Stone Buildings, London	0171 242 6201
Asplin Miss Sarah Jane	• 3 Stone Buildings, London	0171 242 4937
Bryant Miss Judith Anne	• Wilberforce Chambers, London	0171 306 0102
Buck Dr Andrew Theodore	Chambers of Martin Burr, London	0171 353 4636
Campbell Miss Alexis Anne	Hardwicke Building, London	020 7242 2523
Campbell Miss Emily Charlotte	• Wilberforce Chambers, London	0171 306 0102
Clarke Miss Anna Victoria	5 Stone Buildings, London	0171 242 6201
Cosedge Andrew John	3 Stone Buildings, London	0171 242 4937
Crampin Peter	Chambers of Mr Peter Crampin QC, London	020 7831 0081
Cranfield Peter Anthony	3 Verulam Buildings, London	0171 831 8441
Dodge Peter Clive	11 Old Square, London	020 7430 0341
Etherton Terence Michael Elkan Barnet	• Wilberforce Chambers, London	0171 306 0102
Evans Jonathan Edward	• Wilberforce Chambers, London	0171 306 0102
Fadipe Gabriel Charles	• Wilberforce Chambers, London	0171 306 0102
Fricker Mrs Marilyn Ann	Sovereign Chambers, Leeds	0113 2451841/2/3
	Farrar's Building, London	0171 583 9241

• Expanded entry in Part D

Furness Michael James	• Wilberforce Chambers, London	0171 306 0102
Furze Miss Caroline Mary	• Wilberforce Chambers, London	0171 306 0102
Garcia-Miller Miss Laura	Enterprise Chambers, London	0171 405 9471
	Enterprise Chambers, Leeds	0113 246 0391
	Enterprise Chambers, Newcastle upon Tyne	0191 222 3344
Gibaud Miss Catherine Alison Annetta	3 Verulam Buildings, London	0171 831 8441
Gill Ms Sarah Teresa	• Old Square Chambers, London	0171 269 0300
	Old Square Chambers, Bristol	0117 9277111
Ginniff Nigel Thomas	Adrian Lyon's Chambers, Liverpool	0151 236 4421/8240
Green Brian Russell	Wilberforce Chambers, London	0171 306 0102
Hall Taylor Alexander Edward	11 Old Square, London	020 7430 0341
Halpern David Anthony	Enterprise Chambers, London	0171 405 9471
	Enterprise Chambers, Leeds	0113 246 0391
	Enterprise Chambers, Newcastle upon Tyne	0191 222 3344
Ham Robert Wallace	• Wilberforce Chambers, London	0171 306 0102
Harris Melvyn	7 New Square, London	0171 430 1660
Henderson Launcelot Dinadan James	5 Stone Buildings, London	0171 242 6201
Herbert Mark Jeremy	• 5 Stone Buildings, London	0171 242 6201
Hill Raymond	Monckton Chambers, London	0171 405 7211
Horne Roger Cozens-Hardy	Chambers of Mr Peter Crampin QC, London	020 7831 0081
Hughes Miss Anna Gabriel	• Wilberforce Chambers, London	0171 306 0102
Jackson Dirik George Allan	Chambers of Mr Peter Crampin QC, London	020 7831 0081
Jones Sean William Paul	11 King's Bench Walk, London	0171 632 8500/583 0610
Lamont Miss Camilla Rose	Chambers of Lord Goodhart QC, London	0171 405 5577
Legge Henry	5 Stone Buildings, London	0171 242 6201
Lindqvist Andrew Nils Gunnar	Octagon House, Norwich	01603 623186
Lowe David Alexander	• Wilberforce Chambers, London	0171 306 0102
Lowenstein Paul David	Littleton Chambers, London	0171 797 8600
Marquand Charles Nicholas Hilary	Chambers of Lord Goodhart QC, London	0171 405 5577
McQuail Ms Katherine Emma	11 Old Square, London	020 7430 0341
Mehendale Ms Neelima Krishna	2 Mitre Court Buildings, London	0171 353 1353
Newman Paul Lance	• Wilberforce Chambers, London	0171 306 0102
Norris Alastair Hubert	5 Stone Buildings, London	0171 242 6201
	Southernhay Chambers, Exeter	01392 255777
Nugee Christopher George	• Wilberforce Chambers, London	0171 306 0102
Nugee Edward George	• Wilberforce Chambers, London	0171 306 0102
Oakley Anthony James	• 11 Old Square, London	020 7430 0341
Ovey Miss Elizabeth Helen	11 Old Square, London	020 7430 0341
Paines Nicholas Paul Billot	Monckton Chambers, London	0171 405 7211
Reed John William Rupert	• Wilberforce Chambers, London	0171 306 0102
Rees David Benjamin	5 Stone Buildings, London	0171 242 6201
Rich Miss Ann Barbara	5 Stone Buildings, London	0171 242 6201
Ross Martyn John Greaves	• 5 New Square, London	020 7404 0404
Rowley Keith Nigel	11 Old Square, London	020 7430 0341
Seymour Thomas Oliver	• Wilberforce Chambers, London	0171 306 0102
Shale Justin Anton	4 King's Bench Walk, London	0171 822 8822
	King's Bench Chambers, Bournemouth	01202 250025
Sher Jules	• Wilberforce Chambers, London	0171 306 0102
Simmonds Andrew John	5 Stone Buildings, London	0171 242 6201
Taussig Anthony Christopher	• Wilberforce Chambers, London	0171 306 0102
Tennet Michael John	• Wilberforce Chambers, London	0171 306 0102
Thomas Stephen Edward Owen	St Philip's Chambers, Birmingham	0121 246 7000
Tidmarsh Christopher Ralph Francis	5 Stone Buildings, London	0171 242 6201
Turnbull Charles Emerson Lovett	• Wilberforce Chambers, London	0171 306 0102
Walker Andrew Greenfield	Chambers of Lord Goodhart QC, London	0171 405 5577

Wallington Peter Thomas	11 King's Bench Walk, London	0171 632 8500/583 0610
Warnock-Smith Mrs Shan	5 Stone Buildings, London	0171 242 6201
Warren Nicholas Roger	• Wilberforce Chambers, London	0171 306 0102
Wicks Ms Joanne	• Wilberforce Chambers, London	0171 306 0102

PERSONAL INJURY

Abbott Francis Arthur	Pump Court Chambers, Winchester	01962 868161
	Pump Court Chambers, London	0171 353 0711
	Pump Court Chambers, Swindon	01793 539899
Adams Miss Lorraine Joan	Pulteney Chambers, Bath	01225 723987
Ahmed Farooq Tahir	8 King Street Chambers, Manchester	0161 834 9560
	3 Dr Johnson's Buildings, London	0171 353 4854
Akerman Miss Kate Louise	Queen's Chambers, Manchester	0161 834 6875/4738
	Queens Chambers, Preston	01772 828300
Aldous Grahame Linley	9 Gough Square, London	020 7832 0500
Aldous Robert John	Octagon House, Norwich	01603 623186
Aldridge James William	199 Strand, London	0171 379 9779
Alford Robert John	Southernhay Chambers, Exeter	01392 255777
Ali Miss Huma	Eastbourne Chambers, Eastbourne	01323 642102
Allen Nicholas Paul	29 Bedford Row Chambers, London	0171 831 2626
Allfrey Richard Forbes	Doughty Street Chambers, London	0171 404 1313
Allingham-Nicholson Mrs Elizabeth Sarah	2 New Street, Leicester	0116 2625906
Althaus Antony Justin	No. 1 Serjeants' Inn, London	0171 415 6666
Ancliffe Mrs Shiva Edwina	Francis Taylor Building, London	0171 353 7768/7769/2711
Andrews Peter John	• 199 Strand, London	0171 379 9779
	3 Fountain Court, Birmingham	0121 236 5854
Archer John Francis Ashweek	Two Crown Office Row, London	020 7797 8100
Arentsen Andrew Nicholas	33 Park Place, Cardiff	02920 233313
Arlow Ms Ruth Marian	Pump Court Chambers, London	0171 353 0711
	Pump Court Chambers, Swindon	01793 539899
	Pump Court Chambers, Winchester	01962 868161
Armitage Ernest Keith	8 King Street Chambers, Manchester	0161 834 9560
Ashley Mark Robert	Pump Court Chambers, Swindon	01793 539899
	Pump Court Chambers, London	0171 353 0711
	Pump Court Chambers, Winchester	01962 868161
Ashworth Lance Dominic Piers	St Philip's Chambers, Birmingham	0121 246 7000
	2 Harcourt Buildings, London	0171 583 9020
Ashworth Piers	2 Harcourt Buildings, London	0171 583 9020
Atherton Peter	Deans Court Chambers, Manchester	0161 214 6000
	Deans Court Chambers, Preston	01772 555163
Azam Javaid	Plowden Buildings, London	0171 583 0808
Badenoch (Ian) James Forster	1 Crown Office Row, London	0171 797 7500
	Crown Office Row Chambers, Brighton	01273 625625
Baker Ms Rachel Mary Theresa	Hardwicke Building, London	020 7242 2523
Baker Stuart Christopher	1 Fountain Court, Birmingham	0121 236 5721
Baldock Nicholas John	6 Pump Court, London	0171 797 8400
	6-8 Mill Street, Maidstone	01622 688094
Baldry Antony Brian	No. 1 Serjeants' Inn, London	0171 415 6666
Banks Francis Andrew	Adrian Lyon's Chambers, Liverpool	0151 236 4421/8240
Barker John Steven Roy	Queen's Chambers, Manchester	0161 834 6875/4738
	Queens Chambers, Preston	01772 828300
Barker Nicholas	30 Park Square, Leeds	0113 2436388
Barnett Andrew John	Pump Court Chambers, Winchester	01962 868161
	Pump Court Chambers, London	0171 353 0711
	Pump Court Chambers, Swindon	01793 539899
Barnett Daniel Alexander	2 Gray's Inn Square Chambers, London	020 7242 0328
Barr Edward Robert	2 New Street, Leicester	0116 2625906
Barraclough Richard Michael	6 Pump Court, London	0171 797 8400
	6-8 Mill Street, Maidstone	01622 688094
Barry Miss Kirsten Lesley	8 King Street Chambers, Manchester	0161 834 9560

• Expanded entry in Part D

Bassa Yousef	St Albans Chambers, St Albans	01727 843383
	Tindal Chambers, Chelmsford	01245 267742
Bassett John Stewart Britten	5 Essex Court, London	0171 410 2000
Bastin Alexander Charles	2nd Floor, Francis Taylor Building, London	0171 353 9942/3157
Baxter-Phillips Miss Felicity Dawn	Becket Chambers, Canterbury	01227 786331
Bean Matthew Allen	11 King's Bench Walk, Leeds	0113 297 1200
	11 King's Bench Walk, London	0171 353 3337
Beard Mark Christopher	6 Pump Court, London	0171 797 8400
	6-8 Mill Street, Maidstone	01622 688094
Bedeau Stephen	Sovereign Chambers, Leeds	0113 2451841/2/3
	Lancaster Building, Manchester	0161 661 4444/0171 649 9872
Beer Jason Barrington	5 Essex Court, London	0171 410 2000
Beever Edmund Damian	St Philip's Chambers, Birmingham	0121 246 7000
Bellamy Jonathan Mark	39 Essex Street, London	0171 832 1111
Benson John Trevor	Adrian Lyon's Chambers, Liverpool	0151 236 4421/8240
Bensted Miss Rebecca Claire	Bracton Chambers, London	0171 242 4248
Bentley Stephen	1 Gray's Inn Square, London	0171 405 8946/7/8
Bhanji Shiraz Musa	4 Bingham Place, London	0171 486 5347/071 487 5910
Bidder Neil	33 Park Place, Cardiff	02920 233313
	Goldsmith Building, London	0171 353 7881
Bishop Edward James	No. 1 Serjeants' Inn, London	0171 415 6666
Blakesley Patrick James	Two Crown Office Row, London	020 7797 8100
Block Neil Selwyn	39 Essex Street, London	0171 832 1111
Bloom-Davis Desmond Niall Laurence	Pump Court Chambers, Winchester	01962 868161
	Pump Court Chambers, London	0171 353 0711
	Pump Court Chambers, Swindon	01793 539899
Blunt David John	4 Pump Court, London	020 7842 5555
Boney Guy Thomas Knowles	Pump Court Chambers, Winchester	01962 868161
	Pump Court Chambers, London	0171 353 0711
	Harrow on the Hill Chambers, Harrow-on-the-Hill	0181 423 7444
	Pump Court Chambers, Swindon	01793 539899
	Eighteen Carlton Crescent, Southampton	01703 639001
Booth Alan James	Deans Court Chambers, Manchester	0161 214 6000
	Deans Court Chambers, Preston	01772 555163
Booth Nicholas John	Old Square Chambers, London	0171 269 0300
	Old Square Chambers, Bristol	0117 9277111
Booth Richard John	1 Crown Office Row, London	0171 797 7500
Boothroyd Miss Susan Elizabeth	Westgate Chambers, Newcastle upon Tyne	0191 261 4407/2329785
Boyd James Andrew Donaldson	8 King Street Chambers, Manchester	0161 834 9560
Boyd Miss Kerstin Margaret	2nd Floor, Francis Taylor Building, London	0171 353 9942/3157
Boyd Stephen James Harvey	29 Bedford Row Chambers, London	0171 831 2626
Boydell Edward Patrick Stirrup	Pump Court Chambers, London	0171 353 0711
	Pump Court Chambers, Winchester	01962 868161
	Pump Court Chambers, Swindon	01793 539899
Boyle David Stuart	Deans Court Chambers, Manchester	0161 214 6000
	Deans Court Chambers, Preston	01772 555163
Boyle Gerard James	No. 1 Serjeants' Inn, London	0171 415 6666
Brace Michael Wesley	33 Park Place, Cardiff	02920 233313
Bradley Miss Clodagh Maria	3 Serjeants' Inn, London	0171 353 5537
Bradly David Lawrence	39 Essex Street, London	0171 832 1111
Bradshaw Howard Sydney	Queen's Chambers, Manchester	0161 834 6875/4738
	Queens Chambers, Preston	01772 828300
Brahams Mrs Diana Joyce	Old Square Chambers, London	0171 269 0300
	Old Square Chambers, Bristol	0117 9277111
Braithwaite William Thomas Scatchard	Exchange Chambers, Liverpool	0151 236 7747

● Expanded entry in Part D

Brennan Daniel Joseph	39 Essex Street, London	0171 832 1111
	18 St John Street, Manchester	0161 278 1800
Briden Richard John	96 Gray's Inn Road, London	0171 405 0585
Briden Timothy John	• 8 Stone Buildings, London	0171 831 9881
Bridgman David Martin	No. 1 Serjeants' Inn, London	0171 415 6666
Broatch Michael Donald	5 Paper Buildings, London	0171 583 9275/583 4555
Brockley Nigel Simon	Bracton Chambers, London	0171 242 4248
Brough Alasdair Matheson	13 King's Bench Walk, London	0171 353 7204
	King's Bench Chambers, Oxford	01865 311066
Brown Andrew Charles	Queen's Chambers, Manchester	0161 834 6875/4738
	Queens Chambers, Preston	01772 828300
Brown Geoffrey Barlow	39 Essex Street, London	0171 832 1111
Brown (Geoffrey) Charles	39 Essex Street, London	0171 832 1111
Brown Miss Joanne	2 Gray's Inn Square Chambers, London	020 7242 0328
Browne James William	96 Gray's Inn Road, London	0171 405 0585
Brunton Sean Alexander McKay	Pump Court Chambers, Winchester	01962 868161
	Pump Court Chambers, London	0171 353 0711
	Pump Court Chambers, Swindon	01793 539899
Bryant John Malcolm Cornelius	Barnard's Inn Chambers, London	0171 369 6969
Bryant Keith	Devereux Chambers, London	0171 353 7534
Buck Dr Andrew Theodore	Chambers of Martin Burr, London	0171 353 4636
Buckley Peter Evered	Queen's Chambers, Manchester	0161 834 6875/4738
	Queens Chambers, Preston	01772 828300
Burden Edward Angus	St Philip's Chambers, Birmingham	0121 246 7000
Burden Miss Susan Jane	Chambers of Kieran Coonan QC, London	0171 583 6013/2510
Burns Peter Richard	Deans Court Chambers, Manchester	0161 214 6000
	Deans Court Chambers, Preston	01772 555163
Burrows Simon Paul	Peel Court Chambers, Manchester	0161 832 3791
Butler Andrew	2nd Floor, Francis Taylor Building, London	0171 353 9942/3157
Butler Philip Andrew	Deans Court Chambers, Manchester	0161 214 6000
	Deans Court Chambers, Preston	01772 555163
Butler Simon David	10 King's Bench Walk, London	0171 353 7742
Butterworth Paul Anthony	Octagon House, Norwich	01603 623186
Cains Ms Linda Hilary	37 Park Square Chambers, Leeds	0113 2439422
Calvert David Edward	St James's Chambers, Manchester	0161 834 7000
Cameron Miss Barbara Alexander	• 2 Harcourt Buildings, London	0171 583 9020
Campbell Stephen Gordon	St Philip's Chambers, Birmingham	0121 246 7000
Campbell-Brown Miss Anne Louise	Bracton Chambers, London	0171 242 4248
Cannon Adam Richard	96 Gray's Inn Road, London	0171 405 0585
Capon Philip Christopher William	St Philip's Chambers, Birmingham	0121 246 7000
Carling Christopher James	Old Square Chambers, London	0171 269 0300
	Old Square Chambers, Bristol	0117 9277111
Carr Bruce Conrad	Devereux Chambers, London	0171 353 7534
Carr Simon Andrew	9 Gough Square, London	020 7832 0500
Carroll Jonathan Neil	9 Woodhouse Square, Leeds	0113 2451986
Cartwright John Martin	Francis Taylor Building, London	0171 353 7768/7769/2711
Cave Jeremy Stephen	1 Crown Office Row, London	0171 797 7500
	Crown Office Row Chambers, Brighton	01273 625625
Cawley Neil Robert Loudoun	169 Temple Chambers, London	0171 583 7644
	Milton Keynes Chambers, Milton Keynes	01908 664 128
Challenger Colin Westcott	Bridewell Chambers, London	020 7797 8800
Chalmers Miss Suzanne Frances	Two Crown Office Row, London	020 7797 8100
Chambers Jonathan	4 Essex Court, London	020 7797 7970
Chan Miss Susan	13 King's Bench Walk, London	0171 353 7204
	King's Bench Chambers, Oxford	01865 311066
Chapman Matthew James	Barnard's Inn Chambers, London	0171 369 6969
Chapman Michael Andrew	Barnard's Inn Chambers, London	0171 369 6969
Charlton Alexander Murray	4 Pump Court, London	020 7842 5555
Cheshire Anthony Peter	199 Strand, London	0171 379 9779
Christie-Brown Miss Sarah Louise	4 Paper Buildings, London	0171 353 3366/583 7155

Chudleigh Miss Louise Katrina	Old Square Chambers, London	0171 269 0300
	Old Square Chambers, Bristol	0117 9277111
Clark Andrew Richard	Manchester House Chambers, Manchester	0161 834 7007
	8 King Street Chambers, Manchester	0161 834 9560
Clark Christopher Harvey	Pump Court Chambers, Winchester	01962 868161
	Pump Court Chambers, London	0171 353 0711
	Westgate Chambers, Lewes	01273 480510
	Pump Court Chambers, Swindon	01793 539899
	Harrow on the Hill Chambers, Harrow-on-the-Hill	0181 423 7444
Clarke Miss Alison Lee	No. 1 Serjeants' Inn, London	0171 415 6666
Clarke Jonathan Christopher St John	Old Square Chambers, Bristol	0117 9277111
	Old Square Chambers, London	0171 269 0300
Clegg Sebastian James Barwick	Deans Court Chambers, Manchester	0161 214 6000
	Deans Court Chambers, Preston	01772 555163
Clemes Andrew John	Angel Chambers, Swansea	01792 464623/464648
Cliff Graham Hilton	St Philip's Chambers, Birmingham	0121 246 7000
Clover (Thomas) Anthony	New Court Chambers, London	0171 831 9500
Coghlan Terence	1 Crown Office Row, London	0171 797 7500
	Crown Office Row Chambers, Brighton	01273 625625
Colbey Richard (Alan)	• Francis Taylor Building, London	0171 797 7250
	Guildhall Chambers Portsmouth, Portsmouth	01705 752400
Cole Robert Ian Gawain	30 Park Square, Leeds	0113 2436388
Colin Giles David	Crown Office Row Chambers, Brighton	01273 625625
Collett Ivor William	No. 1 Serjeants' Inn, London	0171 415 6666
Collins Miss Jennifer Clair	Eastbourne Chambers, Eastbourne	01323 642102
Compton Gareth Francis Thomas	22 Old Buildings, London	0171 831 0222
Connolly Miss Joanne Marie	8 King Street Chambers, Manchester	0161 834 9560
Conry Michael Harvey	1 Fountain Court, Birmingham	0121 236 5721
Cook Jeremy David	Lamb Building, London	020 7797 7788
Cooksley Nigel James	Old Square Chambers, London	0171 269 0300
	Old Square Chambers, Bristol	0117 9277111
Cooper Alan George	39 Essex Street, London	0171 832 1111
Cooper Mark Anthony John	2 Mitre Court Buildings, London	0171 353 1353
Cory-Wright Charles Alexander	39 Essex Street, London	0171 832 1111
Cotter Barry Paul	Old Square Chambers, Bristol	0117 9277111
	Old Square Chambers, London	0171 269 0300
Cotton Miss Diana Rosemary	Devereux Chambers, London	0171 353 7534
Courtney Nicholas Piers	Queen's Chambers, Manchester	0161 834 6875/4738
	Queens Chambers, Preston	01772 828300
Cox Bryan Richard	9 Woodhouse Square, Leeds	0113 2451986
Cramsie James Sinclair Beresford	13 King's Bench Walk, London	0171 353 7204
	King's Bench Chambers, Oxford	01865 311066
Crawforth Miss Emma	Southernhay Chambers, Exeter	01392 255777
Cross Mrs Joanna	9 Woodhouse Square, Leeds	0113 2451986
Crossley Simon Justin	9 Woodhouse Square, Leeds	0113 2451986
Crossley Steven Richard	37 Park Square Chambers, Leeds	0113 2439422
Crowley John Desmond	Two Crown Office Row, London	020 7797 8100
Croxon Raymond Patrick	8 King's Bench Walk, London	0171 797 8888
	Regency Chambers, Peterborough	01733 315215
	Regency Chambers, Cambridge	01223 301517
Curtis Michael Alexander	Two Crown Office Row, London	020 7797 8100
Curwen Michael Jonathan	Chambers of Kieran Coonan QC, London	0171 583 6013/2510
Daniells-Smith Roger Charles	8 King's Bench Walk, London	0171 797 8888
	8 King's Bench Walk North, Leeds	0113 2439797
Davidson Nicholas Ranking	4 Paper Buildings, London	0171 353 3366/583 7155
Davidson Dr Ranald Dunbar	3 Serjeants' Inn, London	0171 353 5537
Davies Miss Carol Elizabeth	2 New Street, Leicester	0116 2625906

         • Expanded entry in Part D

Davies The Rt Hon David John Denzil	96 Gray's Inn Road, London	0171 405 0585
	8 Gray's Inn Square, London	0171 242 3529
Davis Andrew Paul	Two Crown Office Row, London	020 7797 8100
Davis William Easthope	St Philip's Chambers, Birmingham	0121 246 7000
Dawson Alexander William	13 King's Bench Walk, London	0171 353 7204
	King's Bench Chambers, Oxford	01865 311066
Dean Paul Benjamin	Two Crown Office Row, London	020 7797 8100
Dean Peter Thomas	1 Crown Office Row, London	0171 583 9292
DeCamp Miss Jane Louise	Two Crown Office Row, London	020 7797 8100
Dedezade Taner	Tindal Chambers, Chelmsford	01245 267742
Denney Stuart Henry Macdonald	Deans Court Chambers, Manchester	0161 214 6000
	Deans Court Chambers, Preston	01772 555163
Devlin Jonathan Nicholas Ponton	Park Court Chambers, Leeds	0113 2433277
Dingemans James Michael	1 Crown Office Row, London	0171 583 9292
Dixon David Steven	Sovereign Chambers, Leeds	0113 2451841/2/3
Dixon Philip John	2nd Floor, Francis Taylor Building, London	0171 353 9942/3157
Doherty Bernard James	39 Essex Street, London	0171 832 1111
Dolan Dr Bridget Maura	3 Serjeants' Inn, London	0171 353 5537
Donovan Joel	New Court Chambers, London	0171 831 9500
Douglas Michael John	4 Pump Court, London	020 7842 5555
Du Cann Christian Dillon Lott	39 Essex Street, London	0171 832 1111
Dubbery Mark Edward	Pump Court Chambers, London	0171 353 0711
	Pump Court Chambers, Winchester	01962 868161
	Pump Court Chambers, Swindon	01793 539899
Dudley Michael John	1 Fountain Court, Birmingham	0121 236 5721
Dunning Francis John Grove	37 Park Square Chambers, Leeds	0113 2439422
Dyer Simon Christopher	Plowden Buildings, London	0171 583 0808
Eastman Roger	2 Harcourt Buildings, London	0171 583 9020
Eccles David Thomas	8 King Street Chambers, Manchester	0161 834 9560
Edge Timothy Richard	Deans Court Chambers, Preston	01772 555163
	Deans Court Chambers, Manchester	0161 214 6000
Edis Andrew Jeremy Coulter	● Adrian Lyon's Chambers, Liverpool	0151 236 4421/8240
Edis Angus William Butler	1 Crown Office Row, London	0171 797 7500
Ekins Charles Wareing	Sovereign Chambers, Leeds	0113 2451841/2/3
Elfield Miss Laura Elaine	5 Pump Court, London	020 7353 2532
Ellis Miss Catherine Anne	Derby Square Chambers, Liverpool	0151 709 4222
Ellis Dr Peter Simon	7 New Square, London	0171 430 1660
Evans Andrew Sutherland	10 King's Bench Walk, London	0171 353 7742
	2 Paper Buildings, Basement North, London	0171 936 2613
Evans Miss Claire Louise	Peel Court Chambers, Manchester	0161 832 3791
Evans John Wainwright	1 Fountain Court, Birmingham	0121 236 5721
Evans Miss Lisa Claire	St Philip's Chambers, Birmingham	0121 246 7000
Evans Stephen James	8 King's Bench Walk, London	0171 797 8888
	8 King's Bench Walk North, Leeds	0113 2439797
Evans-Tovey Jason Robert	Two Crown Office Row, London	020 7797 8100
Ewins Miss Catherine Jane	4 Paper Buildings, London	0171 353 3366/583 7155
Eyre Stephen John Arthur	1 Fountain Court, Birmingham	0121 236 5721
Fairbank Nicholas James	Becket Chambers, Canterbury	01227 786331
Faluyi Albert Osamudiamen	Chambers of Martin Burr, London	0171 353 4636
Farquharson Jonathan	Colleton Chambers, Exeter	01392 274898/9
Farrer Adam Michael	4 Fountain Court, Birmingham	0121 236 3476
Faul Miss Anne Frances Louise	Lamb Building, London	020 7797 7788
Faulks Edward Peter Lawless	No. 1 Serjeants' Inn, London	0171 415 6666
Ferm Rodney Eric	37 Park Square Chambers, Leeds	0113 2439422
Field Patrick John	Deans Court Chambers, Manchester	0161 214 6000
	Deans Court Chambers, Preston	01772 555163
Fieldsend James William	2nd Floor, Francis Taylor Building, London	0171 353 9942/3157
Finlay Darren	Sovereign Chambers, Leeds	0113 2451841/2/3

Finn Terence	Chambers of Martin Burr, London	0171 353 4636
Fitzpatrick Edward James	8 King's Bench Walk, London	0171 797 8888
Fleming Paul Stephen	37 Park Square Chambers, Leeds	0113 2439422
Flenley William David Wingate	4 Paper Buildings, London	0171 353 3366/583 7155
Fletcher Christopher Michael	Octagon House, Norwich	01603 623186
Flockhart Miss Sharon Linda	3 Serjeants' Inn, London	0171 353 5537
Forbes Peter George	6 Pump Court, London	0171 797 8400
	6-8 Mill Street, Maidstone	01622 688094
Ford Gerard James	Baker Street Chambers, Middlesbrough	01642 873873
Ford Michael David	Doughty Street Chambers, London	0171 404 1313
Formby Ms Emily Jane	Hardwicke Building, London	020 7242 2523
Forte Mark Julian Carmino	8 King Street Chambers, Manchester	0161 834 9560
Foster Charles Andrew	• Chambers of Kieran Coonan QC, London	0171 583 6013/2510
Foster Miss Juliet Kate	Southernhay Chambers, Exeter	01392 255777
Foudy Miss Kim Frances	8 King Street Chambers, Manchester	0161 834 9560
Fox Dr Simon James	Exchange Chambers, Liverpool	0151 236 7747
	St Philip's Chambers, Birmingham	0121 246 7000
Foy John Leonard	9 Gough Square, London	020 7832 0500
Francois Herbert Dolton	Chambers of Herbert Francois, Mitcham	0181 640 4529
Freedman Jeremy Stuart	New Court Chambers, Newcastle upon Tyne	0191 232 1980
	Plowden Buildings, London	0171 583 0808
Freeland Simon Dennis Marsden	5 Essex Court, London	0171 410 2000
Friston Dr Mark Harpham	Chambers of Kieran Coonan QC, London	0171 583 6013/2510
Frith Nicholas John	30 Park Square, Leeds	0113 2436388
Gabb Charles Henry Escott	Pump Court Chambers, Winchester	01962 868161
	Pump Court Chambers, London	0171 353 0711
	Pump Court Chambers, Swindon	01793 539899
Gadney George Munro	Two Crown Office Row, London	020 7797 8100
Gardner Miss Eilidh Anne Mairi	22 Old Buildings, London	0171 831 0222
Gasztowicz Steven	2-3 Gray's Inn Square, London	0171 242 4986
	2 New Street, Leicester	0116 2625906
Gersch Adam Nissen	Trafalgar Chambers, London	0171 583 5858
Gibbons James Francis	3 Stone Buildings, London	0171 242 4937
Gibson Arthur George Adrian	Adrian Lyon's Chambers, Liverpool	0151 236 4421/8240
Gifford Andrew James Morris	7 New Square, London	0171 430 1660
Gill Ms Sarah Teresa	• Old Square Chambers, London	0171 269 0300
	Old Square Chambers, Bristol	0117 9277111
Gilmore Ian Martin	30 Park Square, Leeds	0113 2436388
Glasgow Edwin John	39 Essex Street, London	0171 832 1111
Glasson Jonathan Joseph	Doughty Street Chambers, London	0171 404 1313
Glennie Andrew David	13 King's Bench Walk, London	0171 353 7204
	King's Bench Chambers, Oxford	01865 311066
Glover Stephen Julian	37 Park Square Chambers, Leeds	0113 2439422
Glynn Stephen Peter	9 Gough Square, London	020 7832 0500
Goddard Harold Keith	Deans Court Chambers, Manchester	0161 214 6000
	Deans Court Chambers, Preston	01772 555163
	4 Paper Buildings, London	0171 353 3366/583 7155
Godfrey Christopher Nicholas	Queen's Chambers, Manchester	0161 834 6875/4738
	Queens Chambers, Preston	01772 828300
Goldman Mrs Linda	7 New Square, London	0171 430 1660
Goodwin Miss Deirdre Evelyn	13 King's Bench Walk, London	0171 353 7204
	King's Bench Chambers, Oxford	01865 311066
Gordon-Saker Andrew Stephen	Fenners Chambers, Cambridge	01223 368761
	Fenners Chambers, Peterborough	01733 562030
Gore-Andrews Gavin Angus Russell	2 Harcourt Buildings, London	0171 583 9020
Gow Miss Elizabeth Suzanne	Iscoed Chambers, Swansea	01792 652988/9/330
Gower Miss Helen Clare	Old Square Chambers, Bristol	0117 9277111
	Old Square Chambers, London	0171 269 0300
Grace John Oliver Bowman	3 Serjeants' Inn, London	0171 353 5537

• Expanded entry in Part D

Grace Jonathan Robert	Deans Court Chambers, Manchester	0161 214 6000
	Deans Court Chambers, Preston	01772 555163
Grace Timothy Michael	Adrian Lyon's Chambers, Liverpool	0151 236 4421/8240
Grant David Euan Barron	13 King's Bench Walk, London	0171 353 7204
	King's Bench Chambers, Oxford	01865 311066
Grayson Edward	• 9-12 Bell Yard, London	0171 400 1800
Greatorex Ms Helen Louise	9 Woodhouse Square, Leeds	0113 2451986
Green Roger John Bailey	Queen's Chambers, Manchester	0161 834 6875/4738
	Queens Chambers, Preston	01772 828300
Greenan Miss Sarah Octavia	9 Woodhouse Square, Leeds	0113 2451986
Greenbourne John Hugo	Two Crown Office Row, London	020 7797 8100
Grey Miss Eleanor Mary Grace	39 Essex Street, London	0171 832 1111
Grime John Andrew	Pump Court Chambers, Swindon	01793 539899
	Pump Court Chambers, London	0171 353 0711
	Pump Court Chambers, Winchester	01962 868161
Grime Mark Stephen Eastburn	Deans Court Chambers, Manchester	0161 214 6000
	2 Pump Court, London	0171 353 5597
	Deans Court Chambers, Preston	01772 555163
Grimshaw Nicholas Edward	Deans Court Chambers, Manchester	0161 214 6000
	Deans Court Chambers, Preston	01772 555163
Grocott Miss Susan	Queen's Chambers, Manchester	0161 834 6875/4738
	Queens Chambers, Preston	01772 828300
Grodzinski Samuel Marc	39 Essex Street, London	0171 832 1111
Guggenheim Miss Anna Maeve	Two Crown Office Row, London	020 7797 8100
Guirguis Miss Sheren	White Friars Chambers, Chester	01244 323070
Gulliver Miss Alison Louise	4 Paper Buildings, London	0171 353 3366/583 7155
Gunther Miss Elizabeth Ann	Pump Court Chambers, Winchester	01962 868161
	Pump Court Chambers, London	0171 353 0711
	Pump Court Chambers, Swindon	01793 539899
Haigh Martin James	30 Park Square, Leeds	0113 2436388
Hall David Percy	9 Woodhouse Square, Leeds	0113 2451986
Hall Jeremy John	Becket Chambers, Canterbury	01227 786331
Hamey John Anthony	East Anglian Chambers, Norwich	01603 617351
	East Anglian Chambers, Colchester	01206 572756
	East Anglian Chambers, Ipswich	01473 214481
Hamilton Graeme Montagu	Two Crown Office Row, London	020 7797 8100
Hamilton-Hague Miss Rachael Elizabeth	8 King Street Chambers, Manchester	0161 834 9560
Hammerton Miss Veronica Lesley	No. 1 Serjeants' Inn, London	0171 415 6666
Hand John Lester	Chambers of John Hand QC, Manchester	0161 955 9000
	Old Square Chambers, London	0171 269 0300
	Old Square Chambers, Bristol	0117 9277111
Harding Dr Gladys Modwyn Cicely	Leone Chambers, London	0181 200 4020
Hargan James John	30 Park Square, Leeds	0113 2436388
Harrap Giles Thresher	• Pump Court Chambers, Winchester	01962 868161
	Pump Court Chambers, London	0171 353 0711
	Pump Court Chambers, Swindon	01793 539899
Harvey Michael Llewellyn Tucker	Two Crown Office Row, London	020 7797 8100
Haslam Andrew Peter	Sovereign Chambers, Leeds	0113 2451841/2/3
Hassall James Christopher	Southernhay Chambers, Exeter	01392 255777
Hatfield Ms Sally Anne	Doughty Street Chambers, London	0171 404 1313
Hawkes Miss Naomi Nanteza Astrid Wallusimbi	22 Old Buildings, London	0171 831 0222
Henderson Roger Anthony	2 Harcourt Buildings, London	0171 583 9020
Hendy John Giles	• Old Square Chambers, London	0171 269 0300
	Old Square Chambers, Bristol	0117 9277111
Henley Mark Robert Daniel	9 Woodhouse Square, Leeds	0113 2451986
Herbert Mrs Rebecca Mary	2 New Street, Leicester	0116 2625906
Hermer Richard Simon	Doughty Street Chambers, London	0171 404 1313
	30 Park Place, Cardiff	01222 398421
Hewitson William Andrew	1 Crown Office Row, London	0171 583 9292

• Expanded entry in Part D

Higgins Adrian John	13 King's Bench Walk, London	0171 353 7204
	King's Bench Chambers, Oxford	01865 311066
Hignett Richard James	St Albans Chambers, St Albans	01727 843383
Hill Nicholas Mark	• Pump Court Chambers, London	0171 353 0711
	Pump Court Chambers, Winchester	01962 868161
	Pump Court Chambers, Swindon	01793 539899
Hill Robert Douglas	Pump Court Chambers, Winchester	01962 868161
	Pump Court Chambers, London	0171 353 0711
	Pump Court Chambers, Swindon	01793 539899
Hillier Nicolas Peter	9 Gough Square, London	020 7832 0500
Hobson Miss Heather Fiona	Queen's Chambers, Manchester	0161 834 6875/4738
	Queens Chambers, Preston	01772 828300
Hockman Stephen Alexander	• 6 Pump Court, London	0171 797 8400
	6-8 Mill Street, Maidstone	01622 688094
Hodgson Martin Derrick	8 King's Bench Walk, London	0171 797 8888
	8 King's Bench Walk North, Leeds	0113 2439797
Hodgson Timothy Paul	8 King Street Chambers, Manchester	0161 834 9560
Hodson Peter David	Chambers of Ian Macdonald QC (In	0161 236 1840
	Association with Two Garden Court,	
	Temple, London), Manchester	
Hoffman David Alexander	8 King Street Chambers, Manchester	0161 834 9560
Hogg The Hon Douglas Martin	37 Park Square Chambers, Leeds	0113 2439422
	Cathedral Chambers (Jan Wood	01392 210900
	Independent Barristers' Clerk), Exeter	
Hogg Miss Katharine Elizabeth	1 Crown Office Row, London	0171 797 7500
Holdsworth James Arthur	Two Crown Office Row, London	020 7797 8100
Holl-Allen Jonathan Guy	3 Serjeants' Inn, London	0171 353 5537
Hollow Paul John	Fenners Chambers, Cambridge	01223 368761
	Fenners Chambers, Peterborough	01733 562030
Holmes Philip John	8 King Street Chambers, Manchester	0161 834 9560
Holmes-Milner James Neil	2 Mitre Court Buildings, London	0171 353 1353
Holwill Derek Paul Winsor	4 Paper Buildings, London	0171 353 3366/583 7155
Horgan Peter Thomas	Queen's Chambers, Manchester	0161 834 6875/4738
	Queens Chambers, Preston	01772 828300
Hornett Stuart Ian	29 Bedford Row Chambers, London	0171 831 2626
Howarth Simon Stuart	Two Crown Office Row, London	020 7797 8100
Hudson Anthony Sean	Doughty Street Chambers, London	0171 404 1313
Humpage Miss Heather June	9 Woodhouse Square, Leeds	0113 2451986
Hunter William Quigley	No. 1 Serjeants' Inn, London	0171 415 6666
Hurd James Robert	St James's Chambers, Manchester	0161 834 7000
Hurd Mark Dunsdon	2 New Street, Leicester	0116 2625906
Hutchin Edward Alister David	Bracton Chambers, London	0171 242 4248
Inman Melbourne Donald	1 Fountain Court, Birmingham	0121 236 5721
Irwin Stephen John	Doughty Street Chambers, London	0171 404 1313
Jackson Matthew David Everard	4 Paper Buildings, London	0171 353 3366/583 7155
Jacobson Lawrence	5 Paper Buildings, London	0171 583 9275/583 4555
Jay Robert Maurice	39 Essex Street, London	0171 832 1111
Jenkins Dr Janet Caroline	Chambers of Kieran Coonan QC, London	0171 583 6013/2510
Johnston Anthony Paul	1 Fountain Court, Birmingham	0121 236 5721
Johnston Miss Justine Jane	4 Paper Buildings, London	0171 583 0816/353 1131
Jones Martin Wynne	8 King's Bench Walk, London	0171 797 8888
	8 King's Bench Walk North, Leeds	0113 2439797
Jones Miss Susannah Lucy	Octagon House, Norwich	01603 623186
Katrak Cyrus Pesi	Gough Square Chambers, London	0171 353 0924
Kay Robert Jervis	4 Field Court, London	0171 440 6900
Kelly Geoffrey Robert	Pump Court Chambers, London	0171 353 0711
	Pump Court Chambers, Winchester	01962 868161
	Pump Court Chambers, Swindon	01793 539899
Kelly Matthias John	Old Square Chambers, London	0171 269 0300
	Old Square Chambers, Bristol	0117 9277111

        • Expanded entry in Part D

Kempster Ivor Toby Chalmers	Old Square Chambers, Bristol	0117 9277111
	Old Square Chambers, London	0171 269 0300
Kent Miss Georgina	5 Essex Court, London	0171 410 2000
Kent Michael Harcourt	Two Crown Office Row, London	020 7797 8100
Kenward Timothy David Nelson	25-27 Castle Street, Liverpool	0151 227 5661/051 236 5072
Kerr Derek William	Francis Taylor Building, London	0171 353 7768/7769/2711
Khokhar Mushtaq Ahmed	Sovereign Chambers, Leeds	0113 2451841/2/3
King Peter Duncan	Fenners Chambers, Cambridge	01223 368761
	5 Pump Court, London	020 7353 2532
	Fenners Chambers, Peterborough	01733 562030
King-Smith James	1 Crown Office Row, London	0171 797 7500
	Crown Office Row Chambers, Brighton	01273 625625
Kirtley Paul George	37 Park Square Chambers, Leeds	0113 2439422
Knowles Graham Roy	Peel Court Chambers, Manchester	0161 832 3791
Kynoch Duncan Stuart Sanderson	29 Bedford Row Chambers, London	0171 831 2626
Lambert Miss Sarah Katrina	1 Crown Office Row, London	0171 797 7500
Lamberty Mark Julian Harker	Queen's Chambers, Manchester	0161 834 6875/4738
	Queens Chambers, Preston	01772 828300
Latimer-Sayer William Laurence	2 Mitre Court Buildings, London	0171 353 1353
Le Cornu Philip John	St Philip's Chambers, Birmingham	0121 246 7000
Leason Ms Karen Dawn	St Philip's Chambers, Birmingham	0121 246 7000
Leech Brian Walter Thomas	No. 1 Serjeants' Inn, London	0171 415 6666
Lewis Andrew William	Sovereign Chambers, Leeds	0113 2451841/2/3
Lewis Jeffrey Allan	9 Woodhouse Square, Leeds	0113 2451986
Lewis Robert	11 Bolt Court (also at 7 Stone Buildings – 1st Floor), London	0171 353 2300
	7 Stone Buildings (also at 11 Bolt Court), London	0171 242 0961
	Redhill Chambers, Redhill	01737 780781
Lindqvist Andrew Nils Gunnar	Octagon House, Norwich	01603 623186
Lo Bernard Norman	17 Bedford Row, London	0171 831 7314
Lochrane Damien Horatio Ross	Pump Court Chambers, London	0171 353 0711
	Pump Court Chambers, Winchester	01962 868161
	Pump Court Chambers, Swindon	01793 539899
Lumley Nicholas James Henry	Sovereign Chambers, Leeds	0113 2451841/2/3
Lynagh Richard Dudley	Two Crown Office Row, London	020 7797 8100
MacDonald Alistair William Orchard	St Philip's Chambers, Birmingham	0121 246 7000
Machell Raymond Donatus	Deans Court Chambers, Manchester	0161 214 6000
	2 Pump Court, London	0171 353 5597
	Deans Court Chambers, Preston	01772 555163
Mackay Colin Crichton	39 Essex Street, London	0171 832 1111
MacLaren Miss Catriona Longueville	2nd Floor, Francis Taylor Building, London	0171 353 9942/3157
Macleod Duncan	9 Gough Square, London	020 7832 0500
Main Peter Ramsay	Deans Court Chambers, Manchester	0161 214 6000
	Deans Court Chambers, Preston	01772 555163
Mainwaring [Robert] Paul Clason	Carmarthen Chambers, Carmarthen	01267 234410
Majumdar Shantanu	Lamb Chambers, London	020 7797 8300
Makey Christopher Douglas	Old Square Chambers, London	0171 269 0300
	Old Square Chambers, Bristol	0117 9277111
Malecka Dr Mary Margaret	• 3 Temple Gardens, London	0171 353 0832
	65-67 King Street, Leicester	0116 2547710
Mandalia Vinesh Lalji	Harrow on the Hill Chambers, Harrow-on-the-Hill	0181 423 7444
Mangat Dr Tejina Kiran	New Court Chambers, London	0171 831 9500
Marks Jonathan Clive	4 Pump Court, London	020 7842 5555
Marks Peter	3 Temple Gardens, London	0171 353 0832
Marley Miss Sarah Anne	5 Pump Court, London	020 7353 2532
Marsh Laurence John	4 Pump Court, London	020 7842 5555
Marshall-Andrews Robert Graham	37 Park Square Chambers, Leeds	0113 2439422
	2-4 Tudor Street, London	0171 797 7111

• Expanded entry in Part D

Matthews Dennis Roland	Two Crown Office Row, London	020 7797 8100
Maudslay Miss Diana Elizabeth	Sovereign Chambers, Leeds	0113 2451841/2/3
Maxwell Richard	Ropewalk Chambers, Nottingham	0115 9472581
	Doughty Street Chambers, London	0171 404 1313
Maxwell-Scott James Herbert	Two Crown Office Row, London	020 7797 8100
Mazzag Anthony James	Peel Court Chambers, Manchester	0161 832 3791
McAlinden Barry O'Neill	17 Bedford Row, London	0171 831 7314
McCabe Miss Louise Anne	St Philip's Chambers, Birmingham	0121 246 7000
McCahey Miss Catherine Anne Mary	St Philip's Chambers, Birmingham	0121 246 7000
McCahill Patrick Gerard	St Philip's Chambers, Birmingham	0121 246 7000
	Chambers of Andrew Campbell QC, Leeds	0113 2455438
McCann Simon Howard	Deans Court Chambers, Manchester	0161 214 6000
	Deans Court Chambers, Preston	01772 555163
McCaul Colin Brownlie	39 Essex Street, London	0171 832 1111
McCluggage Brian Thomas	Chambers of John Hand QC, Manchester	0161 955 9000
McCourt Christopher	22 Old Buildings, London	0171 831 0222
McCullough Miss Judith Ann	Queen's Chambers, Manchester	0161 834 6875/4738
	Queens Chambers, Preston	01772 828300
McCullough Miss Louise Clare	Lion Court, London	0171 404 6565
McDermott Gerard Francis	8 King Street Chambers, Manchester	0161 834 9560
	2 Pump Court, London	0171 353 5597
McGrath Miss Elizabeth Ann	St Philip's Chambers, Birmingham	0121 246 7000
McGregor Harvey	4 Paper Buildings, London	0171 353 3366/583 7155
McHugh Denis David	Bracton Chambers, London	0171 242 4248
McKechnie Stuart Iain William	2 Gray's Inn Square Chambers, London	020 7242 0328
McLean Mrs Mandy Rachel	5 Essex Court, London	0171 410 2000
McNeill Miss Elizabeth Jane	• Old Square Chambers, London	0171 269 0300
	Old Square Chambers, Bristol	0117 9277111
Mead John Philip	Old Square Chambers, London	0171 269 0300
	Old Square Chambers, Bristol	0117 9277111
Melton Christopher	Peel Court Chambers, Manchester	0161 832 3791
	199 Strand, London	0171 379 9779
Melville Miss Elizabeth Emma Jane	Old Square Chambers, London	0171 269 0300
	Old Square Chambers, Bristol	0117 9277111
Melville Richard David	• 39 Essex Street, London	0171 832 1111
Mercer David Paul	Queen's Chambers, Manchester	0161 834 6875/4738
	Queens Chambers, Preston	01772 828300
Metzer Anthony David Erwin	Doughty Street Chambers, London	0171 404 1313
Michael Simon Laurence	• Bedford Chambers, Ampthill	0870 7337333
Mishcon Miss Jane Malca	4 Paper Buildings, London	0171 353 3366/583 7155
Mitchell Miss Julianna Marie	2 Harcourt Buildings, London	0171 583 9020
Mitropoulos Christos	Chambers of Geoffrey Hawker, London	0171 583 8899
Moat Frank Robert	Pump Court Chambers, London	0171 353 0711
	Pump Court Chambers, Winchester	01962 868161
	Pump Court Chambers, Swindon	01793 539899
Moger Christopher Richard Derwent	4 Pump Court, London	020 7842 5555
Moore Mr Craig Ian	Barnard's Inn Chambers, London	0171 369 6969
	Park Lane Chambers, Leeds	0113 2285000
Morgan Andrew James	St Philip's Chambers, Birmingham	0121 246 7000
Mortimer Miss Sophie Kate	No. 1 Serjeants' Inn, London	0171 415 6666
Mulcahy Miss Leigh-Ann Maria	Chambers of John L Powell QC, London	0171 797 8000
Mulholland Michael	St James's Chambers, Manchester	0161 834 7000
Murphy Miss Nicola Jane	4 King's Bench Walk, London	0171 822 8822
Murray-Smith James Michael	8 King's Bench Walk, London	0171 797 8888
	8 King's Bench Walk North, Leeds	0113 2439797
Naish Christopher John	Southernhay Chambers, Exeter	01392 255777
Naylor Dr Kevin Michael Thomas	8 King Street Chambers, Manchester	0161 834 9560
Nesbitt Timothy John Robert	199 Strand, London	0171 379 9779
Newman Austin Eric	9 Woodhouse Square, Leeds	0113 2451986
Newton John Simon	Derby Square Chambers, Liverpool	0151 709 4222

• Expanded entry in Part D

Ng Ray Kian Hin	Two Crown Office Row, London	020 7797 8100
Niblett Anthony Ian	1 Crown Office Row, London	0171 797 7500
	Crown Office Row Chambers, Brighton	01273 625625
Nisbett James Theophilus	7 Westmeath Avenue, Leicester	0116 2412003
	Victoria Chambers, Birmingham	0121 236 9900
Noble Roderick Grant	39 Essex Street, London	0171 832 1111
Norman Christopher John George	No. 1 Serjeants' Inn, London	0171 415 6666
O'Connor Andrew McDougal	Two Crown Office Row, London	020 7797 8100
O'Donovan Ronan Daniel James	14 Gray's Inn Square, London	0171 242 0858
O'Leary Robert Michael	33 Park Place, Cardiff	02920 233313
O'Sullivan Derek Anthony	• 5 Pump Court, London	020 7353 2532
Oakley Paul James	1 Gray's Inn Square, London	0171 405 8946/7/8
Omambala Miss Ijeoma Chinyelu	Old Square Chambers, London	0171 269 0300
	Old Square Chambers, Bristol	0117 9277111
Oppenheim Robin Frank	Doughty Street Chambers, London	0171 404 1313
Ough Dr Richard Norman	• Hardwicke Building, London	020 7242 2523
Outhwaite Mrs Wendy-Jane Tivnan	2 Harcourt Buildings, London	0171 583 9020
Owens Mrs Lucy Isabel	13 King's Bench Walk, London	0171 353 7204
	King's Bench Chambers, Oxford	01865 311066
Paget Michael Rodborough	Bracton Chambers, London	0171 242 4248
Palmer Patrick John Steven	Sovereign Chambers, Leeds	0113 2451841/2/3
Panesar Deshpal Singh	13 King's Bench Walk, London	0171 353 7204
	King's Bench Chambers, Oxford	01865 311066
Paneth Miss Sarah Ruth	No. 1 Serjeants' Inn, London	0171 415 6666
Panton William Dwight	Britton Street Chambers, London	0171 608 3765
Parker John	2 Mitre Court Buildings, London	0171 353 1353
Parr John Edward	8 King Street Chambers, Manchester	0161 834 9560
Patel Bhavin Vinubhai	Chambers of Martin Burr, London	0171 353 4636
Patel Parishil Jayantilal	39 Essex Street, London	0171 832 1111
Pawson Robert Edward Cruickshank	Pump Court Chambers, Winchester	01962 868161
	Pump Court Chambers, London	0171 353 0711
	Pump Court Chambers, Swindon	01793 539899
Pearce Richard William	Peel Court Chambers, Manchester	0161 832 3791
Pears Derrick Allan	2nd Floor, Francis Taylor Building, London	0171 353 9942/3157
Pearson Christopher	• Bridewell Chambers, London	020 7797 8800
Pearson Thomas Adam Spenser	Pump Court Chambers, London	0171 353 0711
	Pump Court Chambers, Winchester	01962 868161
	Pump Court Chambers, Swindon	01793 539899
Peirson Oliver James	Pump Court Chambers, London	0171 353 0711
	Pump Court Chambers, Winchester	01962 868161
	Pump Court Chambers, Swindon	01793 539899
Pema Anes Bhumin Laloo	9 Woodhouse Square, Leeds	0113 2451986
Pepperall Edward Brian	St Philip's Chambers, Birmingham	0121 246 7000
Perkins Miss Marianne Yvette	7 New Square, London	0171 430 1660
Perry Miss Jacqueline Anne	• Lamb Building, London	020 7797 7788
Pershad Rohan	Two Crown Office Row, London	020 7797 8100
Phillips Andrew Charles	Two Crown Office Row, London	020 7797 8100
Phillips David John	199 Strand, London	0171 379 9779
	30 Park Place, Cardiff	01222 398421
Picton Julian Mark	4 Paper Buildings, London	0171 353 3366/583 7155
Pinder Miss Mary Elizabeth	No. 1 Serjeants' Inn, London	0171 415 6666
Piper Angus Richard	No. 1 Serjeants' Inn, London	0171 415 6666
Pirani Rohan Carl	Old Square Chambers, Bristol	0117 9277111
	Old Square Chambers, London	0171 269 0300
Pittaway David Michael	No. 1 Serjeants' Inn, London	0171 415 6666
Pliener David Jonathan	New Court Chambers, London	0171 831 9500
Pooles Michael Philip Holmes	4 Paper Buildings, London	0171 353 3366/583 7155
Portnoy Leslie Reuben	Chambers of John Hand QC, Manchester	0161 955 9000
Pounder Gerard	5 Essex Court, London	0171 410 2000
Powell Miss Debra Ann	3 Serjeants' Inn, London	0171 353 5537

B

B

Pratt Allan Duncan	New Court Chambers, London	0171 831 9500
Price Miss Collette	St James's Chambers, Manchester	0161 834 7000
Price John Charles	St Philip's Chambers, Birmingham	0121 246 7000
Price Miss Katharine Clare Harding	4 Paper Buildings, London	0171 353 3366/583 7155
Prinn Miss Helen Elizabeth	Octagon House, Norwich	01603 623186
Prudhoe Timothy Nixon	Queen's Chambers, Manchester	0161 834 6875/4738
	Queens Chambers, Preston	01772 828300
Pugh Michael Charles	Old Square Chambers, London	0171 269 0300
	Old Square Chambers, Bristol	0117 9277111
Pulling Dean	Iscoed Chambers, Swansea	01792 652988/9/330
Pulman George Frederick	Hardwicke Building, London	020 7242 2523
	Stour Chambers, Canterbury	01227 764899
Purchas Christopher Patrick Brooks	Two Crown Office Row, London	020 7797 8100
Purves Gavin Bowman	Swan House, London	0181 998 3035
Pusey William James	St Philip's Chambers, Birmingham	0121 246 7000
Puzey James Roderick	1 Fountain Court, Birmingham	0121 236 5721
Rankin Andrew	4 Field Court, London	0171 440 6900
Raybaud Mrs June Rose	96 Gray's Inn Road, London	0171 405 0585
Readhead Simon John Howard	No. 1 Serjeants' Inn, London	0171 415 6666
Reid Paul William	13 King's Bench Walk, London	0171 353 7204
	King's Bench Chambers, Oxford	01865 311066
Reid Sebastian Peter Scott	2nd Floor, Francis Taylor Building, London	0171 353 9942/3157
Renfree Peter Gerald Stanley	Harbour Court Chambers, Fareham	01329 827828
Richards Miss Jennifer	39 Essex Street, London	0171 832 1111
Richardson David John	13 King's Bench Walk, London	0171 353 7204
	King's Bench Chambers, Oxford	01865 311066
Rigney Andrew James	Two Crown Office Row, London	020 7797 8100
Ritchie Andrew George	9 Gough Square, London	020 7832 0500
Ritchie Miss Jean Harris	4 Paper Buildings, London	0171 353 3366/583 7155
Rivalland Marc-Edouard	No. 1 Serjeants' Inn, London	0171 415 6666
Roberts Jeremy Michael Graham	9 Gough Square, London	020 7832 0500
Robins Miss Alison Elizabeth	2 Paper Buildings, Basement North, London	0171 936 2613
Rochford Thomas Nicholas Beverley	St Philip's Chambers, Birmingham	0121 246 7000
Roebuck Roy Delville	Bell Yard Chambers, London	0171 306 9292
Rogers Ian Paul	1 Crown Office Row, London	0171 583 9292
Rogers Paul John	1 Crown Office Row, London	0171 797 7500
	Crown Office Row Chambers, Brighton	01273 625625
Romney Miss Daphne Irene	4 Field Court, London	0171 440 6900
Ronksley Andrew Peter	3 Temple Gardens, London	0171 353 0832
Rose Paul Telfer	Old Square Chambers, London	0171 269 0300
	Old Square Chambers, Bristol	0117 9277111
Ross John Graffin	No. 1 Serjeants' Inn, London	0171 415 6666
Rothery Peter	Queen's Chambers, Manchester	0161 834 6875/4738
	Queens Chambers, Preston	01772 828300
Rowe John Jermyn	• 8 King Street Chambers, Manchester	0161 834 9560
Ryder Timothy Robert	Queen's Chambers, Manchester	0161 834 6875/4738
	Queens Chambers, Preston	01772 828300
Saggerson Alan David	Barnard's Inn Chambers, London	0171 369 6969
Salmon Jonathan Carl	1 Fountain Court, Birmingham	0121 236 5721
Samuel Glyn Ross	St Philip's Chambers, Birmingham	0121 246 7000
Samuels Leslie John	Pump Court Chambers, London	0171 353 0711
	Pump Court Chambers, Winchester	01962 868161
	Pump Court Chambers, Swindon	01793 539899
Sandbrook-Hughes Stewert Karl Anthony	Iscoed Chambers, Swansea	01792 652988/9/330
Saunt Thomas William Gatty	Two Crown Office Row, London	020 7797 8100
Scorah Christopher James	8 King Street Chambers, Manchester	0161 834 9560
Scott Ian Richard	Old Square Chambers, London	0171 269 0300
	Old Square Chambers, Bristol	0117 9277111

        • Expanded entry in Part D

Searle Barrie	St James's Chambers, Manchester	0161 834 7000
Seligman Matthew Thomas Arthur	39 Essex Street, London	0171 832 1111
Semple Andrew Blair	Sovereign Chambers, Leeds	0113 2451841/2/3
Sephton Craig Gardner	Deans Court Chambers, Manchester	0161 214 6000
	Deans Court Chambers, Preston	01772 555163
Sethi Mohinderpal Singh	Barnard's Inn Chambers, London	0171 369 6969
Shale Justin Anton	4 King's Bench Walk, London	0171 822 8822
	King's Bench Chambers, Bournemouth	01202 250025
Shannon Thomas Eric	Queen's Chambers, Manchester	0161 834 6875/4738
	Queens Chambers, Preston	01772 828300
Sheehan Malcolm Peter	2 Harcourt Buildings, London	0171 583 9020
Shepherd Nigel Patrick	8 King's Bench Walk North, Leeds	0113 2439797
	8 King's Bench Walk, London	0171 797 8888
Sheppard Timothy Derie	Bracton Chambers, London	0171 242 4248
Shield Miss Deborah	White Friars Chambers, Chester	01244 323070
Shiels Ian	30 Park Square, Leeds	0113 2436388
Shorrock John Michael	Peel Court Chambers, Manchester	0161 832 3791
Shukla Ms Vina	New Court Chambers, London	0171 831 9500
Silvester Bruce Ross	Lamb Chambers, London	020 7797 8300
Simpson Ian	Bracton Chambers, London	0171 242 4248
Skelly Andrew Jon	1 Gray's Inn Square, London	0171 405 8946/7/8
Slaughter Andrew Francis	Bridewell Chambers, London	020 7797 8800
Sleightholme John Trevor	37 Park Square Chambers, Leeds	0113 2439422
Smail Alastair Harold Kurt	St Philip's Chambers, Birmingham	0121 246 7000
Smith Andrew Duncan	1 Fountain Court, Birmingham	0121 236 5721
Smith Miss Emma Louise	Old Square Chambers, London	0171 269 0300
	Old Square Chambers, Bristol	0117 9277111
Smith Matthew Robert	Sovereign Chambers, Leeds	0113 2451841/2/3
Smith Michael Joseph	8 King Street Chambers, Manchester	0161 834 9560
Smith Nicholas Martin	1 Fountain Court, Birmingham	0121 236 5721
Smith Ms Rachel Catherine	Peel Court Chambers, Manchester	0161 832 3791
Smith Miss Sally-Ann	Crown Office Row Chambers, Brighton	01273 625625
Smith Warwick Timothy Cresswell	Deans Court Chambers, Manchester	0161 214 6000
	Deans Court Chambers, Preston	01772 555163
Snowden John Stevenson	Two Crown Office Row, London	020 7797 8100
Solomons Mrs Ellen Betty	One Garden Court Family Law Chambers, London	0171 797 7900
Spencer Martin Benedict	4 Paper Buildings, London	0171 353 3366/583 7155
Spicer Robert Haden	Frederick Place Chambers, Bristol	0117 9738667
Spinks Roderick Cameron	Fenners Chambers, Cambridge	01223 368761
	Fenners Chambers, Peterborough	01733 562030
Spollon Guy Merton	St Philip's Chambers, Birmingham	0121 246 7000
St Louis Brian Lloyd	Hardwicke Building, London	020 7242 2523
Staddon Paul	2nd Floor, Francis Taylor Building, London	0171 353 9942/3157
Stagg Paul Andrew	No. 1 Serjeants' Inn, London	0171 415 6666
Starcevic Petar	St Philip's Chambers, Birmingham	0121 246 7000
Stark James Hayden Alexander	Chambers of Ian Macdonald QC (In Association with Two Garden Court, Temple, London), Manchester	0161 236 1840
Stavros Ms Evanthia	3 Temple Gardens, London	0171 353 0832
Stern Dr Kristina Anne	39 Essex Street, London	0171 832 1111
Stevens Howard Linton	1 Crown Office Row, London	0171 583 9292
Stevenson John Melford	Two Crown Office Row, London	020 7797 8100
Stewart Ms Alexandra Mary Hamilton	30 Park Square, Leeds	0113 2436388
Stockdale David Andrew	Deans Court Chambers, Manchester	0161 214 6000
	Deans Court Chambers, Preston	01772 555163
	9 Bedford Row, London	0171 242 3555
Stokell Robert	Two Crown Office Row, London	020 7797 8100

B

Stokes Michael George Thomas	Chambers of Michael Pert QC, London	0171 421 8000
	Chambers of Michael Pert QC, Leicester	0116 249 2020
	Chambers of Michael Pert QC, Northampton	01604 602333
	St Philip's Chambers, Birmingham	0121 246 7000
Storey Jeremy Brian	4 Pump Court, London	020 7842 5555
Styles Clive Richard	Becket Chambers, Canterbury	01227 786331
Sullivan Scott	Barnard's Inn Chambers, London	0171 369 6969
Swan Ian Christopher	Two Crown Office Row, London	020 7797 8100
Swift Malcolm Robin	Park Court Chambers, Leeds	0113 2433277
	6 Gray's Inn Square, London	0171 242 1052
Szanto Gregory John Michael	Eastbourne Chambers, Eastbourne	01323 642102
Taft Christopher Heiton	St James's Chambers, Manchester	0161 834 7000
Tankel Mrs Ruth Shoshana	St James's Chambers, Manchester	0161 834 7000
Tarbitt Nicholas Edward Henry	6 Fountain Court, Birmingham	0121 233 3282
Taylor Miss Deborah Frances	Two Crown Office Row, London	020 7797 8100
Tedd Rex Hilary	• St Philip's Chambers, Birmingham	0121 246 7000
	De Montfort Chambers, Leicester	0116 254 8686
	Northampton Chambers, Northampton	01604 636271
Temple Anthony Dominic	4 Pump Court, London	020 7842 5555
Ter Haar Roger Eduard Lound	Two Crown Office Row, London	020 7797 8100
Thompson Jonathan Richard	8 King Street Chambers, Manchester	0161 834 9560
Thompson Patrick Miles	Queen's Chambers, Manchester	0161 834 6875/4738
	Queens Chambers, Preston	01772 828300
Thomson Dr David James Ramsay Gibb	Barnard's Inn Chambers, London	0171 369 6969
Thorold Oliver	Doughty Street Chambers, London	0171 404 1313
Ticciati Oliver	4 Pump Court, London	020 7842 5555
Tillett Michael Burn	39 Essex Street, London	0171 832 1111
Tizzano Franco Salvatore	8 King's Bench Walk, London	0171 797 8888
	8 King's Bench Walk North, Leeds	0113 2439797
Tracy Forster Miss Jane Elizabeth	13 King's Bench Walk, London	0171 353 7204
	King's Bench Chambers, Oxford	01865 311066
Treasure Francis Seton	199 Strand, London	0171 379 9779
Tregilgas-Davey Marcus Ian	Pump Court Chambers, Swindon	01793 539899
	Pump Court Chambers, London	0171 353 0711
	Pump Court Chambers, Winchester	01962 868161
Trippier Lady	Deans Court Chambers, Manchester	0161 214 6000
	Deans Court Chambers, Preston	01772 555163
Trotman Timothy Oliver	Deans Court Chambers, Manchester	0161 214 6000
	Deans Court Chambers, Preston	01772 555163
Tucker David William	Two Crown Office Row, London	020 7797 8100
Tucker Miss Katherine Jane Greening	St Philip's Chambers, Birmingham	0121 246 7000
Tully Ms Anne Margaret	Eastbourne Chambers, Eastbourne	01323 642102
Turner Mark George	Deans Court Chambers, Manchester	0161 214 6000
	Deans Court Chambers, Preston	01772 555163
Tyack David Guy	St Philip's Chambers, Birmingham	0121 246 7000
Tyler William John	30 Park Square, Leeds	0113 2436388
Tyzack David Ian Heslop	Southernhay Chambers, Exeter	01392 255777
	1 Mitre Court Buildings, London	0171 797 7070
Ullstein Augustus Rupert Patrick A	• 29 Bedford Row Chambers, London	0171 831 2626
Vaughan-Neil Miss Catherine Mary Bernardine	4 Pump Court, London	020 7842 5555
Verduyn Dr Anthony James	St Philip's Chambers, Birmingham	0121 246 7000
Vickers Miss Rachel Clare	199 Strand, London	0171 379 9779
Vickery Neil Michael	13 King's Bench Walk, London	0171 353 7204
	King's Bench Chambers, Oxford	01865 311066
Waddicor Miss Janet	1 Crown Office Row, London	0171 797 7500
	Crown Office Row Chambers, Brighton	01273 625625
Wadsworth James Patrick	4 Paper Buildings, London	0171 353 3366/583 7155

• Expanded entry in Part D

Walker Christopher David Bestwick	Old Square Chambers, Bristol	0117 9277111
	Old Square Chambers, London	0171 269 0300
Walsh Simon	Bridewell Chambers, London	020 7797 8800
Walters Edmund John	13 King's Bench Walk, London	0171 353 7204
	King's Bench Chambers, Oxford	01865 311066
Warnock Andrew Ronald	No. 1 Serjeants' Inn, London	0171 415 6666
Warren Miss Sasha	3 Temple Gardens, London	0171 353 0832
Warrender Miss Nichola Mary	New Court Chambers, London	0171 831 9500
Waters Julian William Penrose	No. 1 Serjeants' Inn, London	0171 415 6666
Webb Stanley George	The Chambers of Mr Ali Mohammed Azhar, London	0171 353 9564
Wedderspoon Miss Rachel Leone	Bracton Chambers, London	0171 242 4248
Weddle Steven Edgar	Chambers of John Hand QC, Manchester	0161 955 9000
West-Knights Laurence James	Hardwicke Building, London	020 7242 2523
Weston Clive Aubrey Richard	4 Paper Buildings, London	0171 353 3366/583 7155
Wheeldon Miss Sarah Helen Elizabeth	Two Crown Office Row, London	020 7797 8100
	St James's Chambers, Manchester	0161 834 7000
Whipple Mrs Philippa Jane Edwards	1 Crown Office Row, London	0171 797 7500
Whitcombe Mark David	Old Square Chambers, Bristol	0117 9277111
	Old Square Chambers, London	0171 269 0300
White Matthew James	13 King's Bench Walk, London	0171 353 7204
	King's Bench Chambers, Oxford	01865 311066
Whitfield Adrian	3 Serjeants' Inn, London	0171 353 5537
Wilby David Christopher	• 199 Strand, London	0171 379 9779
	Park Lane Chambers, Leeds	0113 2285000
Wilkinson Nigel Vivian Marshall	Two Crown Office Row, London	020 7797 8100
Willer Robert Michael	Hardwicke Building, London	020 7242 2523
Williams A John	13 King's Bench Walk, London	0171 353 7204
	King's Bench Chambers, Oxford	01865 311066
Williams Graeme	13 King's Bench Walk, London	0171 353 7204
	King's Bench Chambers, Oxford	01865 311066
Williams Hugh David Haydn	St Philip's Chambers, Birmingham	0121 246 7000
Williams Dr Jason Scott	• 3 Dr Johnson's Buildings, London	0171 353 4854
Williams The Hon John Melville	Old Square Chambers, London	0171 269 0300
	Old Square Chambers, Bristol	0117 9277111
Williams Thomas Christopher Charles	1 Fountain Court, Birmingham	0121 236 5721
Williams Wyn Lewis	39 Essex Street, London	0171 832 1111
	33 Park Place, Cardiff	02920 233313
Wilson Andrew Robert	9 Woodhouse Square, Leeds	0113 2451986
Wilson Gerald Simon John	2nd Floor, Francis Taylor Building, London	0171 353 9942/3157
Wilson Peter Julian	Sovereign Chambers, Leeds	0113 2451841/2/3
Wilton Simon Daniel	4 Paper Buildings, London	0171 353 3366/583 7155
Winzer Benjamin Charles	Southernhay Chambers, Exeter	01392 255777
Witcomb Henry James	199 Strand, London	0171 379 9779
Wood Ian Robert	8 King Street Chambers, Manchester	0161 834 9560
Wood Simon Edward	Plowden Buildings, London	0171 583 0808
Woodhouse Charles Philip	Bridewell Chambers, London	020 7797 8800
Woods Jonathan	Two Crown Office Row, London	020 7797 8100
Worrall Miss Shirley Vera Frances	8 King Street Chambers, Manchester	0161 834 9560
Worster David James Stewart	St Philip's Chambers, Birmingham	0121 246 7000
Yell Nicholas Anthony	No. 1 Serjeants' Inn, London	0171 415 6666
Young Alastair Angus McLeod	St Philip's Chambers, Birmingham	0121 246 7000
Yoxall Basil Joshua	Francis Taylor Building, London	0171 797 7250

PHARMACEUTICALS

Brennan Daniel Joseph	39 Essex Street, London	0171 832 1111
	18 St John Street, Manchester	0161 278 1800

PHARMACY

Fisher Jonathan Simon	• 18 Red Lion Court, London	0171 520 6000
	Thornwood House, Chelmsford	01245 280880

PLANNING

Alesbury Alun	2 Mitre Court Buildings, London	0171 583 1380
Anderson Anthony John	2 Mitre Court Buildings, London	0171 583 1380
Barraclough Richard Michael	6 Pump Court, London	0171 797 8400
	6-8 Mill Street, Maidstone	01622 688094
Birtles William	Old Square Chambers, London	0171 269 0300
	Old Square Chambers, Bristol	0117 9277111
Blackford Simon John	Barnard's Inn Chambers, London	0171 369 6969
Boyle Christopher Alexander David	2 Mitre Court Buildings, London	0171 583 1380
Buck Dr Andrew Theodore	Chambers of Martin Burr, London	0171 353 4636
Burton Nicholas Anthony	2 Mitre Court Buildings, London	0171 583 1380
Butterworth Paul Anthony	Octagon House, Norwich	01603 623186
Cameron Neil St Clair	1 Serjeants' Inn, London	0171 583 1355
Campbell Miss Susan Claire	Southernhay Chambers, Exeter	01392 255777
Chadd Paul	Theatre House, Bristol	0117 974 1553
	Colleton Chambers, Exeter	01392 274898/9
Clarkson Patrick Robert James	• 1 Serjeants' Inn, London	0171 583 1355
Compton Gareth Francis Thomas	22 Old Buildings, London	0171 831 0222
Daly David	Francis Taylor Building, London	0171 797 7250
Dodd Christopher John Nicholas	9 Woodhouse Square, Leeds	0113 2451986
Driscoll Miss Lynn	Sovereign Chambers, Leeds	0113 2451841/2/3
Druce Michael James	2 Mitre Court Buildings, London	0171 583 1380
Finlay Darren	Sovereign Chambers, Leeds	0113 2451841/2/3
Fitzgerald Michael Frederick Clive	2 Mitre Court Buildings, London	0171 583 1380
Fookes Robert Lawrence	2 Mitre Court Buildings, London	0171 583 1380
Francis Andrew James	Chambers of Mr Peter Crampin QC, London	020 7831 0081
Gardner Miss Eilidh Anne Mairi	22 Old Buildings, London	0171 831 0222
Gasztowicz Steven	2-3 Gray's Inn Square, London	0171 242 4986
	2 New Street, Leicester	0116 2625906
Glover Richard Michael	2 Mitre Court Buildings, London	0171 583 1380
Haigh Martin James	30 Park Square, Leeds	0113 2436388
Harrison Peter John	6 Pump Court, London	0171 797 8400
	6-8 Mill Street, Maidstone	01622 688094
Harwood Richard John	1 Serjeants' Inn, London	0171 583 1355
Hassall James Christopher	Southernhay Chambers, Exeter	01392 255777
Hill Nicholas Mark	• Pump Court Chambers, London	0171 353 0711
	Pump Court Chambers, Winchester	01962 868161
	Pump Court Chambers, Swindon	01793 539899
Hockman Stephen Alexander	• 6 Pump Court, London	0171 797 8400
	6-8 Mill Street, Maidstone	01622 688094
Hodgson Timothy Paul	8 King Street Chambers, Manchester	0161 834 9560
Horton Matthew Bethell	2 Mitre Court Buildings, London	0171 583 1380
Howell Williams Craig	2 Harcourt Buildings, London	020 7353 8415
Humphries Michael John	2 Mitre Court Buildings, London	0171 583 1380
Jefferis Arthur Michael Quentin	Chambers of Mr Peter Crampin QC, London	020 7831 0081
Keane Desmond St John	Pendragon Chambers, Swansea	01792 411188
King Neil Gerald Alexander	2 Mitre Court Buildings, London	0171 583 1380
Langham Richard Geoffrey	1 Serjeants' Inn, London	0171 583 1355
Leigh Kevin	6 Pump Court, London	0171 797 8400
	Regency Chambers, Peterborough	01733 315215
	Westgate Chambers, Lewes	01273 480510
	6-8 Mill Street, Maidstone	01622 688094

• Expanded entry in Part D

Lewis Robert	11 Bolt Court (also at 7 Stone Buildings – 1st Floor), London	0171 353 2300
	7 Stone Buildings (also at 11 Bolt Court), London	0171 242 0961
	Redhill Chambers, Redhill	01737 780781
Lumley Gerald	9 Woodhouse Square, Leeds	0113 2451986
Macpherson The Hon Mary Stewart	2 Mitre Court Buildings, London	0171 583 1380
Mainwaring [Robert] Paul Clason	Carmarthen Chambers, Carmarthen	01267 234410
Markus Ms Kate	Doughty Street Chambers, London	0171 404 1313
McCahill Patrick Gerard	St Philip's Chambers, Birmingham	0121 246 7000
	Chambers of Andrew Campbell QC, Leeds	0113 2455438
McCullough Miss Judith Ann	Queen's Chambers, Manchester	0161 834 6875/4738
	Queens Chambers, Preston	01772 828300
Moore Professor Victor William Edward	2 Mitre Court Buildings, London	0171 583 1380
Moriarty Gerald Evelyn	2 Mitre Court Buildings, London	0171 583 1380
Nall-Cain The Hon Richard Christopher Philip	St Albans Chambers, St Albans	01727 843383
Nardell Gordon Lawrence	6 Pump Court, London	0171 797 8400
	6-8 Mill Street, Maidstone	01622 688094
Newcombe Andrew Bennett	2 Harcourt Buildings, London	020 7353 8415
Newton Philip	Becket Chambers, Canterbury	01227 786331
Ornsby Miss Suzanne Doreen	2 Harcourt Buildings, London	020 7353 8415
Pearson Thomas Adam Spenser	Pump Court Chambers, London	0171 353 0711
	Pump Court Chambers, Winchester	01962 868161
	Pump Court Chambers, Swindon	01793 539899
Pereira James Alexander	2 Harcourt Buildings, London	020 7353 8415
Phillpot Hereward Lindon	2 Harcourt Buildings, London	020 7353 8415
Purchas Robin Michael	• 2 Harcourt Buildings, London	020 7353 8415
Readings Douglas George	St Philip's Chambers, Birmingham	0121 246 7000
Roots Guy Robert Godfrey	2 Mitre Court Buildings, London	0171 583 1380
Salmon Jonathan Carl	1 Fountain Court, Birmingham	0121 236 5721
Sellers Graham	Adrian Lyon's Chambers, Liverpool	0151 236 4421/8240
Sheppard Timothy Derie	Bracton Chambers, London	0171 242 4248
Silsoe The Lord	2 Mitre Court Buildings, London	0171 583 1380
Spencer Paul Anthony	2 New Street, Leicester	0116 2625906
Spicer Robert Haden	Frederick Place Chambers, Bristol	0117 9738667
Stokes Michael George Thomas	Chambers of Michael Pert QC, London	0171 421 8000
	Chambers of Michael Pert QC, Leicester	0116 249 2020
	Chambers of Michael Pert QC, Northampton	01604 602333
	St Philip's Chambers, Birmingham	0121 246 7000
Straker Timothy Derrick	• 4-5 Gray's Inn Square, London	0171 404 5252
Swindells Miss Heather Hughson	Chambers of Michael Pert QC, London	0171 421 8000
	Chambers of Michael Pert QC, Leicester	0116 249 2020
	Chambers of Michael Pert QC, Northampton	01604 602333
	St Philip's Chambers, Birmingham	0121 246 7000
Tait Andrew Charles Gordon	2 Harcourt Buildings, London	020 7353 8415
Tapsell Paul Richard	Becket Chambers, Canterbury	01227 786331
Taylor John Charles	2 Mitre Court Buildings, London	0171 583 1380
Taylor Reuben Mallinson	2 Mitre Court Buildings, London	0171 583 1380
Thomas Miss Megan Moira	1 Serjeants' Inn, London	0171 583 1355
Travers David	• 3 Fountain Court, Birmingham	0121 236 5854
Wald Richard Daniel	2 Mitre Court Buildings, London	0171 583 1380
Walden-Smith Miss Karen Jane	5 Stone Buildings, London	0171 242 6201
Ward Trevor Robert Edward	17 Carlton Crescent, Southampton	023 8032 0320/0823 2003
Warren Rupert Miles	2 Mitre Court Buildings, London	0171 583 1380
Widdicombe David Graham	2 Mitre Court Buildings, London	0171 583 1380
Young Alastair Angus McLeod	St Philip's Chambers, Birmingham	0121 246 7000

B

• Expanded entry in Part D

Zwart Auberon Christiaan Conrad · 1 Serjeants' Inn, London · 0171 583 1355

POLICE ACTIONS
Barraclough Nicholas Maylin · 2nd Floor, Francis Taylor Building, London · 0171 353 9942/3157
Crampin Paul · Lamb Building, London · 020 7797 7788
Walsh Simon · Bridewell Chambers, London · 020 7797 8800

POLICE DISCIPLINE
Dunn Christopher · Sovereign Chambers, Leeds · 0113 2451841/2/3
Searle Barrie · St James's Chambers, Manchester · 0161 834 7000
Sleightholme John Trevor · 37 Park Square Chambers, Leeds · 0113 2439422

POLICE LAW
Powell Miss Debra Ann · 3 Serjeants' Inn, London · 0171 353 5537
Samuel Glyn Ross · St Philip's Chambers, Birmingham · 0121 246 7000
Sleightholme John Trevor · 37 Park Square Chambers, Leeds · 0113 2439422
Young Alastair Angus McLeod · St Philip's Chambers, Birmingham · 0121 246 7000

PRISON LAW
Banks Robert James · 100e Great Portland Street, London · 0171 636 6323
Hall Jonathan Rupert · 5 King's Bench Walk, London · 0171 353 5638
Kaufmann Ms Phillippa Jane · Doughty Street Chambers, London · 0171 404 1313
Parry Simon Edward · White Friars Chambers, Chester · 01244 323070
Weatherby Peter Francis · Two Garden Court, London · 0171 353 1633
Chambers of Ian Macdonald QC (In Association with Two Garden Court, Temple, London), Manchester · 0161 236 1840

PRISONERS' RIGHTS
Blake Arthur Joseph · 13 King's Bench Walk, London · 0171 353 7204
King's Bench Chambers, Oxford · 01865 311066
Williams Graeme · 13 King's Bench Walk, London · 0171 353 7204
King's Bench Chambers, Oxford · 01865 311066

PRIVATE CLIENT
Purdie Robert Anthony James · 28 Western Road, Oxford · 01865 204911

PRIVATE INTERNATIONAL
Allen Nicholas Paul · 29 Bedford Row Chambers, London · 0171 831 2626
Ambrose Miss Clare Mary Geneste · 20 Essex Street, London · 0171 583 9294
Beal Kieron Conrad · 4 Paper Buildings, London · 0171 353 3366/583 7155
Bevis Dominic Joseph · 10 King's Bench Walk, London · 0171 353 7742
Blackburn Mrs Elizabeth · 4 Field Court, London · 0171 440 6900
Blair William James Lynton · 3 Verulam Buildings, London · 0171 831 8441
Burnett Harold Wallace · 4 Paper Buildings, London · 0171 353 3366/583 7155
Campbell Miss Emily Charlotte · •Wilberforce Chambers, London · 0171 306 0102
Castle Peter Bolton · Chambers of Mr Peter Crampin QC, London · 020 7831 0081
Child John Frederick · •Wilberforce Chambers, London · 0171 306 0102
Collett Michael John · 20 Essex Street, London · 0171 583 9294
Cooper Nigel Stuart · 4 Essex Court, London · 020 7797 7970
Cosedge Andrew John · 3 Stone Buildings, London · 0171 242 4937
Crawford Professor James Richard · 3 Verulam Buildings, London · 0171 831 8441
Davey Michael Philip · 4 Field Court, London · 0171 440 6900
Davie Michael James · 4 Pump Court, London · 020 7842 5555
Dowley Dominic Myles · One Hare Court, London · 020 7353 3171
Drake James Frederick · S Tomlinson QC, London · 0171 583 0404
Eadie James Raymond · One Hare Court, London · 020 7353 3171
Edwards-Stuart Antony James Cobham · Two Crown Office Row, London · 020 7797 8100

• Expanded entry in Part D

Evans James Frederick Meurig	3 Verulam Buildings, London	0171 831 8441
Fawls Richard Granville	5 Stone Buildings, London	0171 242 6201
Francis Andrew James	Chambers of Mr Peter Crampin QC, London	020 7831 0081
Franco Gianpiero	2 Middle Temple Lane, London	0171 583 4540
Freedman Sampson Clive	3 Verulam Buildings, London	0171 831 8441
Ghaffar Arshad	4 Field Court, London	0171 440 6900
Goldstone David Julian	4 Field Court, London	0171 440 6900
Grantham Andrew Timothy	• Deans Court Chambers, Manchester	0161 214 6000
	Deans Court Chambers, Preston	01772 555163
Green Miss Jane Elizabeth	Design Chambers, London	0171 353 0747
	Chambers of Martin Burr, London	0171 353 4636
Gun Cuninghame Julian Arthur	Gough Square Chambers, London	0171 353 0924
Hamilton Adrian Walter	S Tomlinson QC, London	0171 583 0404
Harvey Michael Llewellyn Tucker	Two Crown Office Row, London	020 7797 8100
Havelock-Allan Anthony Mark David	20 Essex Street, London	0171 583 9294
Haynes Miss Rebecca	Monckton Chambers, London	0171 405 7211
Hossain Ajmalul	• 29 Bedford Row Chambers, London	0171 831 2626
Hoyal Ms Jane	• 1 Pump Court, London	0171 583 2012/353 4341
Hughes Adrian Warwick	4 Pump Court, London	020 7842 5555
Jabati Miss Maria Hannah	2 Middle Temple Lane, London	0171 583 4540
James Michael Frank	Enterprise Chambers, London	0171 405 9471
	Enterprise Chambers, Leeds	0113 246 0391
	Enterprise Chambers, Newcastle upon Tyne	0191 222 3344
Jarvis John Manners	3 Verulam Buildings, London	0171 831 8441
Kolodziej Andrzej Jozef	• Littman Chambers, London	020 7404 4866
Kverndal Simon Richard	4 Essex Court, London	020 7797 7970
Lasok Karol Paul Edward	Monckton Chambers, London	0171 405 7211
Lavender Nicholas	One Hare Court, London	020 7353 3171
Lazarus Michael Steven	1 Crown Office Row, London	0171 583 9292
Lever Jeremy Frederick	Monckton Chambers, London	0171 405 7211
Littman Mark	Littman Chambers, London	020 7404 4866
Lowenstein Paul David	Littleton Chambers, London	0171 797 8600
Macdonald Charles Adam	4 Essex Court, London	020 7797 7970
Malek Ali	3 Verulam Buildings, London	0171 831 8441
Marquand Charles Nicholas Hilary	Chambers of Lord Goodhart QC, London	0171 405 5577
Marshall Philip Scott	Serle Court Chambers, London	0171 242 6105
Masters Miss Sara Alayna	20 Essex Street, London	0171 583 9294
Matthews Duncan Henry Rowland	20 Essex Street, London	0171 583 9294
McClure Brian David	Littman Chambers, London	020 7404 4866
McGregor Harvey	4 Paper Buildings, London	0171 353 3366/583 7155
Mead John Philip	Old Square Chambers, London	0171 269 0300
	Old Square Chambers, Bristol	0117 9277111
Meeson Nigel Keith	4 Field Court, London	0171 440 6900
Melville Richard David	• 39 Essex Street, London	0171 832 1111
Mercer Hugh Charles	• Essex Court Chambers, London	0171 813 8000
Milligan Iain Anstruther	20 Essex Street, London	0171 583 9294
Morgan Dr Austen Jude	3 Temple Gardens, London	0171 353 0832
Morgan Richard Hugo Lyndon	13 Old Square, London	0171 404 4800
Morris Stephen Nathan	20 Essex Street, London	0171 583 9294
Moser Philip Curt Harold	4 Paper Buildings, London	0171 353 3366/583 7155
Naidoo Sean Van	Littman Chambers, London	020 7404 4866
Neill of Bladen Lord	One Hare Court, London	020 7353 3171
Nolan Michael Alfred Anthony	4 Essex Court, London	020 7797 7970
O'Shea Eoin Finbarr	4 Field Court, London	0171 440 6900
Owen David Christopher	20 Essex Street, London	0171 583 9294
Padfield Nicholas David	One Hare Court, London	020 7353 3171
Page Howard William Barrett	One Hare Court, London	020 7353 3171
Paines Nicholas Paul Billot	Monckton Chambers, London	0171 405 7211
Panford Frank Haig	• Doughty Street Chambers, London	0171 404 1313

• Expanded entry in Part D

Parker Kenneth Blades	Monckton Chambers, London	0171 405 7211
Pearce Robert Edgar	Chambers of Mr Peter Crampin QC, London	020 7831 0081
Perkoff Richard Michael	Littleton Chambers, London	0171 797 8600
Persey Lionel Edward	● 4 Field Court, London	0171 440 6900
Pickup David Michael Walker	Peel Court Chambers, Manchester	0161 832 3791
Plender Richard Owen	● 20 Essex Street, London	0171 583 9294
Pope David James	3 Verulam Buildings, London	0171 831 8441
Qureshi Khawar Mehmood	One Hare Court, London	020 7353 3171
Rashid Omar	Chambers of Mr Peter Crampin QC, London	020 7831 0081
Rosenblatt Jeremy George	4 Paper Buildings, London	0171 583 0816/353 1131
Roth Peter Marcel	Monckton Chambers, London	0171 405 7211
Russell Jeremy Jonathan	● 4 Essex Court, London	020 7797 7970
Sagar (Edward) Leigh	12 New Square, London	0171 419 1212
	Newport Chambers, Newport	01633 267403/255855
	Sovereign Chambers, Leeds	0113 2451841/2/3
Salter Richard Stanley	3 Verulam Buildings, London	0171 831 8441
Saunders Nicholas Joseph	4 Field Court, London	0171 440 6900
Scott-Manderson Marcus Charles William	4 Paper Buildings, London	0171 583 0816/353 1131
Selvaratnam Miss Vasanti Emily Indrani	4 Field Court, London	0171 440 6900
Sheridan Maurice Bernard Gerard	● 3 Verulam Buildings, London	0171 831 8441
Shillingford George Miles	Chambers of Mr Peter Crampin QC, London	020 7831 0081
Siddiqi Faizul Aqtab	Justice Court Chambers, London	0181 830 7786
Smith Christopher Frank	Essex Court Chambers, London	0171 813 8000
Southwell Richard Charles	One Hare Court, London	020 7353 3171
Stewart Nicholas John Cameron	Hardwicke Building, London	020 7242 2523
Teare Nigel John Martin	4 Essex Court, London	020 7797 7970
Tselentis Michael	● 20 Essex Street, London	0171 583 9294
Tucker David William	Two Crown Office Row, London	020 7797 8100
Turner James Michael	● 4 Essex Court, London	020 7797 7970
Vajda Christopher Stephen	Monckton Chambers, London	0171 405 7211
Vaughan-Neil Miss Catherine Mary Bernardine	4 Pump Court, London	020 7842 5555
Walford Richard Henry Howard	Serle Court Chambers, London	0171 242 6105
Watson-Gandy Mark	● Plowden Buildings, London	0171 583 0808
Williams The Hon John Melville	Old Square Chambers, London	0171 269 0300
	Old Square Chambers, Bristol	0117 9277111

PRIVY COUNCIL

Elfield Miss Laura Elaine	5 Pump Court, London	020 7353 2532

PROBATE AND ADMINISTRATION

Acton Stephen Neil	11 Old Square, London	020 7430 0341
Adamyk Simon Charles	12 New Square, London	0171 419 1212
Anderson Miss Julie	● Littman Chambers, London	020 7404 4866
Angus Miss Tracey Anne	5 Stone Buildings, London	0171 242 6201
Asplin Miss Sarah Jane	● 3 Stone Buildings, London	0171 242 4937
Ayres Andrew John William	13 Old Square, London	0171 404 4800
Barraclough Richard Michael	6 Pump Court, London	0171 797 8400
	6-8 Mill Street, Maidstone	01622 688094
Behrens James Nicholas Edward	Serle Court Chambers, London	0171 242 6105
Blackett-Ord Mark	● 5 Stone Buildings, London	0171 242 6201
Bowmer Michael Paul	11 Old Square, London	020 7430 0341
Bryant John Malcolm Cornelius	Barnard's Inn Chambers, London	0171 369 6969
Bryant Miss Judith Anne	● Wilberforce Chambers, London	0171 306 0102
Buck Dr Andrew Theodore	Chambers of Martin Burr, London	0171 353 4636

Burr Martin John	Chambers of Martin Burr, London	0171 353 4636
	7 New Square, London	0171 430 1660
Castle Peter Bolton	Chambers of Mr Peter Crampin QC, London	020 7831 0081
Charman Andrew Julian	St Philip's Chambers, Birmingham	0121 246 7000
Child John Frederick	•Wilberforce Chambers, London	0171 306 0102
Clarke Miss Anna Victoria	5 Stone Buildings, London	0171 242 6201
Clarke Peter John	St Philip's Chambers, Birmingham	0121 246 7000
	Harcourt Chambers, London	0171 353 6961
	Harcourt Chambers, Oxford	01865 791559
Clegg Sebastian James Barwick	Deans Court Chambers, Manchester	0161 214 6000
	Deans Court Chambers, Preston	01772 555163
Cooper Gilead Patrick	Chambers of Mr Peter Crampin QC, London	020 7831 0081
Cosedge Andrew John	3 Stone Buildings, London	0171 242 4937
Craig Kenneth Allen	Hardwicke Building, London	020 7242 2523
Crail Miss (Elspeth) Ross	12 New Square, London	0171 419 1212
	Sovereign Chambers, Leeds	0113 2451841/2/3
Crampin Peter	Chambers of Mr Peter Crampin QC, London	020 7831 0081
Crawford Grant	11 Old Square, London	020 7430 0341
Davey Benjamin Nicholas	11 Old Square, London	020 7430 0341
Dodge Peter Clive	11 Old Square, London	020 7430 0341
Dooher Miss Nancy Helen	St James's Chambers, Manchester	0161 834 7000
Farrow Kenneth John	Serle Court Chambers, London	0171 242 6105
Fawls Richard Granville	5 Stone Buildings, London	0171 242 6201
Feltham Piers Jonathan	Chambers of Mr Peter Crampin QC, London	020 7831 0081
Foster Brian Ian	St James's Chambers, Manchester	0161 834 7000
	Park Lane Chambers, Leeds	0113 2285000
Francis Andrew James	Chambers of Mr Peter Crampin QC, London	020 7831 0081
Fryer-Spedding James Walter	St James's Chambers, Manchester	0161 834 7000
Furze Miss Caroline Mary	•Wilberforce Chambers, London	0171 306 0102
Gifford Andrew James Morris	7 New Square, London	0171 430 1660
Green David Cameron	Adrian Lyon's Chambers, Liverpool	0151 236 4421/8240
Gregory John Raymond	Deans Court Chambers, Manchester	0161 214 6000
	Deans Court Chambers, Preston	01772 555163
Hall Taylor Alexander Edward	11 Old Square, London	020 7430 0341
Halpern David Anthony	Enterprise Chambers, London	0171 405 9471
	Enterprise Chambers, Leeds	0113 246 0391
	Enterprise Chambers, Newcastle upon Tyne	0191 222 3344
Ham Robert Wallace	•Wilberforce Chambers, London	0171 306 0102
Hantusch Robert Anthony	•3 Stone Buildings, London	0171 242 4937
Harris Melvyn	7 New Square, London	0171 430 1660
Harrod Henry Mark	5 Stone Buildings, London	0171 242 6201
Henderson William Hugo	Serle Court Chambers, London	0171 242 6105
Herbert Mark Jeremy	•5 Stone Buildings, London	0171 242 6201
Hinks Frank Peter	Serle Court Chambers, London	0171 242 6105
Hoffman David Alexander	8 King Street Chambers, Manchester	0161 834 9560
Horne Roger Cozens-Hardy	Chambers of Mr Peter Crampin QC, London	020 7831 0081
Hoser Philip Jacob	Serle Court Chambers, London	0171 242 6105
Hunter William Quigley	No. 1 Serjeants' Inn, London	0171 415 6666
Jackson Dirik George Allan	Chambers of Mr Peter Crampin QC, London	020 7831 0081
James-Stadden Miss Jodie Cara	Westgate Chambers, Newcastle upon Tyne	0191 261 4407/2329785
Jefferis Arthur Michael Quentin	Chambers of Mr Peter Crampin QC, London	020 7831 0081

B

• Expanded entry in Part D

Jennings Timothy Robin Finnegan	Enterprise Chambers, London	0171 405 9471
	Enterprise Chambers, Leeds	0113 246 0391
	Enterprise Chambers, Newcastle upon Tyne	0191 222 3344
Lamont Miss Camilla Rose	Chambers of Lord Goodhart QC, London	0171 405 5577
Legge Henry	5 Stone Buildings, London	0171 242 6201
Levy Benjamin Keith	Enterprise Chambers, London	0171 405 9471
	Enterprise Chambers, Leeds	0113 246 0391
	Enterprise Chambers, Newcastle upon Tyne	0191 222 3344
Lloyd Stephen James George	Chambers of Mr Peter Crampin QC, London	020 7831 0081
Lowry Charles Stephen	Colleton Chambers, Exeter	01392 274898/9
Mann George Anthony	Enterprise Chambers, London	0171 405 9471
	Enterprise Chambers, Leeds	0113 246 0391
	Enterprise Chambers, Newcastle upon Tyne	0191 222 3344
Mason Miss Alexandra	3 Stone Buildings, London	0171 242 4937
Maynard-Connor Giles	St James's Chambers, Manchester	0161 834 7000
McQuail Ms Katherine Emma	11 Old Square, London	020 7430 0341
Morgan Richard Hugo Lyndon	13 Old Square, London	0171 404 4800
Newman Miss Catherine Mary	• 13 Old Square, London	0171 404 4800
Norris Alastair Hubert	5 Stone Buildings, London	0171 242 6201
	Southernhay Chambers, Exeter	01392 255777
Nugee Edward George	• Wilberforce Chambers, London	0171 306 0102
Nurse Gordon Bramwell William	11 Old Square, London	020 7430 0341
O'Leary Robert Michael	33 Park Place, Cardiff	02920 233313
O'Sullivan Michael Morton	5 Stone Buildings, London	0171 242 6201
Oakley Anthony James	• 11 Old Square, London	020 7430 0341
Ohrenstein Dov	Chambers of Lord Goodhart QC, London	0171 405 5577
Ovey Miss Elizabeth Helen	11 Old Square, London	020 7430 0341
Pearce Robert Edgar	Chambers of Mr Peter Crampin QC, London	020 7831 0081
Pilkington Mrs Mavis Patricia	9 Woodhouse Square, Leeds	0113 2451986
Pimentel Carlos de Serpa Alberto Legg	3 Stone Buildings, London	0171 242 4937
Porter David Leonard	St James's Chambers, Manchester	0161 834 7000
	Park Lane Chambers, Leeds	0113 2285000
Proudman Miss Sonia Rosemary Susan	Chambers of Mr Peter Crampin QC, London	020 7831 0081
Purdie Robert Anthony James	28 Western Road, Oxford	01865 204911
Rashid Omar	Chambers of Mr Peter Crampin QC, London	020 7831 0081
Reed John William Rupert	• Wilberforce Chambers, London	0171 306 0102
Rees David Benjamin	5 Stone Buildings, London	0171 242 6201
Rich Miss Ann Barbara	5 Stone Buildings, London	0171 242 6201
Rogers Miss Beverly-Ann	Serle Court Chambers, London	0171 242 6105
Ross Martyn John Greaves	• 5 New Square, London	020 7404 0404
Sandells Ms Nicole	11 Old Square, London	020 7430 0341
Sartin Leon James	5 Stone Buildings, London	0171 242 6201
Sellers Graham	Adrian Lyon's Chambers, Liverpool	0151 236 4421/8240
Selway Dr Katherine Emma	11 Old Square, London	020 7430 0341
Shillingford George Miles	Chambers of Mr Peter Crampin QC, London	020 7831 0081
Smith Howard James	Chambers of Mr Peter Crampin QC, London	020 7831 0081
Spicer Robert Haden	Frederick Place Chambers, Bristol	0117 9738667
Staunton (Thomas) Ulick (Patrick)	Chambers of Mr Peter Crampin QC, London	020 7831 0081
	65-67 King Street, Leicester	0116 2547710

       • Expanded entry in Part D

Sterling Robert Alan	St James's Chambers, Manchester	0161 834 7000
	12 New Square, London	0171 419 1212
	Park Lane Chambers, Leeds	0113 2285000
Stewart-Smith William Rodney	1 New Square, London	0171 405 0884/5/6/7
Studer Mark Edgar Walter	Chambers of Mr Peter Crampin QC, London	020 7831 0081
Talbot Patrick John	Serle Court Chambers, London	0171 242 6105
Templeman Michael Richard	Southernhay Chambers, Exeter	01392 255777
	5 Stone Buildings, London	0171 242 6201
Terry Robert Jeffrey	8 King Street Chambers, Manchester	0161 834 9560
Thomas Nigel Matthew	13 Old Square, London	0171 404 4800
Tidmarsh Christopher Ralph Francis	5 Stone Buildings, London	0171 242 6201
Trace Anthony John	• 13 Old Square, London	0171 404 4800
Tully Ms Anne Margaret	Eastbourne Chambers, Eastbourne	01323 642102
Walker Andrew Greenfield	Chambers of Lord Goodhart QC, London	0171 405 5577
Warner David Alexander	1 New Square, London	0171 405 0884/5/6/7
Warnock-Smith Mrs Shan	5 Stone Buildings, London	0171 242 6201
Weatherill Bernard Richard	Chambers of Lord Goodhart QC, London	0171 405 5577
West Mark	• 11 Old Square, London	020 7430 0341
Wicks Ms Joanne	• Wilberforce Chambers, London	0171 306 0102
Williams Dr Jason Scott	• 3 Dr Johnson's Buildings, London	0171 353 4854
Wilson-Barnes Miss Lucy Emma	St James's Chambers, Manchester	0161 834 7000
Zelin Geoffrey Andrew	Enterprise Chambers, London	0171 405 9471
	Enterprise Chambers, Leeds	0113 246 0391
	Enterprise Chambers, Newcastle upon Tyne	0191 222 3344

PRODUCT LIABILITY

Brahams Mrs Diana Joyce	Old Square Chambers, London	0171 269 0300
	Old Square Chambers, Bristol	0117 9277111
Cotter Barry Paul	Old Square Chambers, Bristol	0117 9277111
	Old Square Chambers, London	0171 269 0300
Weitzman Thomas Edward Benjamin	3 Verulam Buildings, London	0171 831 8441
Williams The Hon John Melville	Old Square Chambers, London	0171 269 0300
	Old Square Chambers, Bristol	0117 9277111

PROFESSIONAL DISCIPLINARY TRIBUNALS

Dobbs Miss Linda Penelope	18 Red Lion Court, London	0171 520 6000
	Thornwood House, Chelmsford	01245 280880

PROFESSIONAL NEGLIGENCE

Abbott Francis Arthur	Pump Court Chambers, Winchester	01962 868161
	Pump Court Chambers, London	0171 353 0711
	Pump Court Chambers, Swindon	01793 539899
Acton Stephen Neil	11 Old Square, London	020 7430 0341
Acton Davis Jonathan James	4 Pump Court, London	020 7842 5555
Adamyk Simon Charles	12 New Square, London	0171 419 1212
Adkin Jonathan William	One Hare Court, London	020 7353 3171
Akenhead Robert	Atkin Chambers, London	020 7404 0102
Akerman Miss Kate Louise	Queen's Chambers, Manchester	0161 834 6875/4738
	Queens Chambers, Preston	01772 828300
Aldous Grahame Linley	9 Gough Square, London	020 7832 0500
Allen Michael David Prior	S Tomlinson QC, London	0171 583 0404
Allingham-Nicholson Mrs Elizabeth Sarah	2 New Street, Leicester	0116 2625906
Althaus Antony Justin	No. 1 Serjeants' Inn, London	0171 415 6666
Ambrose Miss Clare Mary Geneste	20 Essex Street, London	0171 583 9294
Angus Miss Tracey Anne	5 Stone Buildings, London	0171 242 6201
Ansell Miss Rachel Louise	4 Pump Court, London	020 7842 5555
Archer John Francis Ashweek	Two Crown Office Row, London	020 7797 8100

• Expanded entry in Part D

Arden Peter Leonard	Enterprise Chambers, London	0171 405 9471
	Enterprise Chambers, Leeds	0113 246 0391
	Enterprise Chambers, Newcastle upon Tyne	0191 222 3344
Ashton David Sambrook	13 King's Bench Walk, London	0171 353 7204
	King's Bench Chambers, Oxford	01865 311066
Ashworth Lance Dominic Piers	St Philip's Chambers, Birmingham	0121 246 7000
	2 Harcourt Buildings, London	0171 583 9020
Ashworth Piers	2 Harcourt Buildings, London	0171 583 9020
Asplin Miss Sarah Jane	• 3 Stone Buildings, London	0171 242 4937
Asprey Nicholas	Serle Court Chambers, London	0171 242 6105
Atherton Ian David	Enterprise Chambers, London	0171 405 9471
	Enterprise Chambers, Newcastle upon Tyne	0191 222 3344
	Enterprise Chambers, Leeds	0113 246 0391
Atherton Peter	Deans Court Chambers, Manchester	0161 214 6000
	Deans Court Chambers, Preston	01772 555163
Ayliffe James Justin Barnett	• Wilberforce Chambers, London	0171 306 0102
Ayres Andrew John William	13 Old Square, London	0171 404 4800
Baatz Nicholas Stephen	Atkin Chambers, London	020 7404 0102
Bacon Francis Michael	4 Paper Buildings, London	0171 353 3366/583 7155
Badenoch (Ian) James Forster	1 Crown Office Row, London	0171 797 7500
	Crown Office Row Chambers, Brighton	01273 625625
Bailey David John	S Tomlinson QC, London	0171 583 0404
Bailey Edward Henry	Monckton Chambers, London	0171 405 7211
Baker Miss Anne Jacqueline	Enterprise Chambers, London	0171 405 9471
	Enterprise Chambers, Leeds	0113 246 0391
	Enterprise Chambers, Newcastle upon Tyne	0191 222 3344
Baker Stuart Christopher	1 Fountain Court, Birmingham	0121 236 5721
Baldock Nicholas John	6 Pump Court, London	0171 797 8400
	6-8 Mill Street, Maidstone	01622 688094
Banks Francis Andrew	Adrian Lyon's Chambers, Liverpool	0151 236 4421/8240
Barker James Sebastian	Enterprise Chambers, London	0171 405 9471
	Enterprise Chambers, Leeds	0113 246 0391
	Enterprise Chambers, Newcastle upon Tyne	0191 222 3344
Barker John Steven Roy	Queen's Chambers, Manchester	0161 834 6875/4738
	Queens Chambers, Preston	01772 828300
Barker Simon George Harry	• 13 Old Square, London	0171 404 4800
Barnett Daniel Alexander	2 Gray's Inn Square Chambers, London	020 7242 0328
Barraclough Richard Michael	6 Pump Court, London	0171 797 8400
	6-8 Mill Street, Maidstone	01622 688094
Barton Alan John	Lamb Building, London	020 7797 7788
Barwise Miss Stephanie Nicola	Atkin Chambers, London	020 7404 0102
Bassett John Stewart Britten	5 Essex Court, London	0171 410 2000
Bather Miss Victoria Maclean	Littleton Chambers, London	0171 797 8600
Beal Kieron Conrad	4 Paper Buildings, London	0171 353 3366/583 7155
Beard Daniel Matthew	Monckton Chambers, London	0171 405 7211
Beaumont Marc Clifford	• Harrow on the Hill Chambers, Harrow-on-the-Hill	0181 423 7444
	Windsor Barristers' Chambers, Windsor	01753 648899
	Pump Court Chambers, London	0171 353 0711
Beer Jason Barrington	5 Essex Court, London	0171 410 2000
Behrens James Nicholas Edward	Serle Court Chambers, London	0171 242 6105
Bellamy Jonathan Mark	39 Essex Street, London	0171 832 1111
Beltrami Adrian Joseph	3 Verulam Buildings, London	0171 831 8441
Bennett John Martyn	• Oriel Chambers, Liverpool	0151 236 7191/236 4321
Berry Nicholas Michael	Southernhay Chambers, Exeter	01392 255777
	1 Gray's Inn Square, London	0171 405 8946/7/8
	22 Old Buildings, London	0171 831 0222

Bignall John Francis	S Tomlinson QC, London	0171 583 0404
Birtles William	Old Square Chambers, London	0171 269 0300
	Old Square Chambers, Bristol	0117 9277111
Birts Peter William	Farrar's Building, London	0171 583 9241
	St Philip's Chambers, Birmingham	0121 246 7000
Bishop Edward James	No. 1 Serjeants' Inn, London	0171 415 6666
Blackburn Mrs Elizabeth	4 Field Court, London	0171 440 6900
Blackburn John	Atkin Chambers, London	020 7404 0102
Blackett-Ord Mark	• 5 Stone Buildings, London	0171 242 6201
Blakesley Patrick James	Two Crown Office Row, London	020 7797 8100
Blayney David James	Serle Court Chambers, London	0171 242 6105
Bleasdale Miss Marie-Claire	Chambers of Mr Peter Crampin QC, London	020 7831 0081
Block Neil Selwyn	39 Essex Street, London	0171 832 1111
Bloom-Davis Desmond Niall Laurence	Pump Court Chambers, Winchester	01962 868161
	Pump Court Chambers, London	0171 353 0711
	Pump Court Chambers, Swindon	01793 539899
Blunt David John	4 Pump Court, London	020 7842 5555
Booth Alan James	Deans Court Chambers, Manchester	0161 214 6000
	Deans Court Chambers, Preston	01772 555163
Booth Richard John	1 Crown Office Row, London	0171 797 7500
Boswell Miss Lindsay Alice	4 Pump Court, London	020 7842 5555
Bourne Geoffrey Robert	4 Field Court, London	0171 440 6900
Bowdery Martin	Atkin Chambers, London	020 7404 0102
Bowker Robert James	2nd Floor, Francis Taylor Building, London	0171 353 9942/3157
Boyd Stephen James Harvey	29 Bedford Row Chambers, London	0171 831 2626
Boydell Edward Patrick Stirrup	Pump Court Chambers, London	0171 353 0711
	Pump Court Chambers, Winchester	01962 868161
	Pump Court Chambers, Swindon	01793 539899
Boyle David Stuart	Deans Court Chambers, Manchester	0161 214 6000
	Deans Court Chambers, Preston	01772 555163
Boyle Gerard James	No. 1 Serjeants' Inn, London	0171 415 6666
Bradly David Lawrence	39 Essex Street, London	0171 832 1111
Brannigan Peter John Sean	4 Pump Court, London	020 7842 5555
Brent Richard	3 Verulam Buildings, London	0171 831 8441
Briden Richard John	96 Gray's Inn Road, London	0171 405 0585
Briden Timothy John	• 8 Stone Buildings, London	0171 831 9881
Bridgman David Martin	No. 1 Serjeants' Inn, London	0171 415 6666
Briggs Michael Townley Featherstone	Serle Court Chambers, London	0171 242 6105
Bright Robert Graham	S Tomlinson QC, London	0171 583 0404
Broatch Michael Donald	5 Paper Buildings, London	0171 583 9275/583 4555
Brockley Nigel Simon	Bracton Chambers, London	0171 242 4248
Brodie (James) Bruce	39 Essex Street, London	0171 832 1111
Brough Alasdair Matheson	13 King's Bench Walk, London	0171 353 7204
	King's Bench Chambers, Oxford	01865 311066
Brown Geoffrey Barlow	39 Essex Street, London	0171 832 1111
Brown (Geoffrey) Charles	39 Essex Street, London	0171 832 1111
Browne James William	96 Gray's Inn Road, London	0171 405 0585
Browne-Wilkinson Simon	Serle Court Chambers, London	0171 242 6105
Bruce Andrew Jonathan	Serle Court Chambers, London	0171 242 6105
Brunton Sean Alexander McKay	Pump Court Chambers, Winchester	01962 868161
	Pump Court Chambers, London	0171 353 0711
	Pump Court Chambers, Swindon	01793 539899
Bryant Miss Judith Anne	• Wilberforce Chambers, London	0171 306 0102
Bryant Keith	Devereux Chambers, London	0171 353 7534
Buck Dr Andrew Theodore	Chambers of Martin Burr, London	0171 353 4636
Buckley Peter Evered	Queen's Chambers, Manchester	0161 834 6875/4738
	Queens Chambers, Preston	01772 828300
Burden Miss Susan Jane	Chambers of Kieran Coonan QC, London	0171 583 6013/2510

B

Burnett Harold Wallace	4 Paper Buildings, London	0171 353 3366/583 7155
Burns Peter Richard	Deans Court Chambers, Manchester	0161 214 6000
	Deans Court Chambers, Preston	01772 555163
Burns Miss Susan Linda	3 Serjeants' Inn, London	0171 353 5537
Burr Andrew Charles	Atkin Chambers, London	020 7404 0102
Burrows Simon Paul	Peel Court Chambers, Manchester	0161 832 3791
Butler Andrew	2nd Floor, Francis Taylor Building, London	0171 353 9942/3157
Butler Philip Andrew	Deans Court Chambers, Manchester	0161 214 6000
	Deans Court Chambers, Preston	01772 555163
Cameron Miss Barbara Alexander	• 2 Harcourt Buildings, London	0171 583 9020
Campbell Miss Emily Charlotte	• Wilberforce Chambers, London	0171 306 0102
Campbell Stephen Gordon	St Philip's Chambers, Birmingham	0121 246 7000
Cannan Jonathan Michael	St James's Chambers, Manchester	0161 834 7000
	Broadway House Chambers, Bradford	01274 722560
	Broadway House Chambers, Leeds	0113 246 2600
Cannon Adam Richard	96 Gray's Inn Road, London	0171 405 0585
Carr Bruce Conrad	Devereux Chambers, London	0171 353 7534
Carr Simon Andrew	9 Gough Square, London	020 7832 0500
Castle Peter Bolton	Chambers of Mr Peter Crampin QC, London	020 7831 0081
Catchpole Stuart Paul	• 39 Essex Street, London	0171 832 1111
Cawson Peter Mark	St James's Chambers, Manchester	0161 834 7000
	12 New Square, London	0171 419 1212
	Park Lane Chambers, Leeds	0113 2285000
Challenger Colin Westcott	Bridewell Chambers, London	020 7797 8800
Chalmers Miss Suzanne Frances	Two Crown Office Row, London	020 7797 8100
Chan Miss Susan	13 King's Bench Walk, London	0171 353 7204
	King's Bench Chambers, Oxford	01865 311066
Charlton Alexander Murray	4 Pump Court, London	020 7842 5555
Charlwood Spike Llewellyn	4 Paper Buildings, London	0171 353 3366/583 7155
Charman Andrew Julian	St Philip's Chambers, Birmingham	0121 246 7000
Christie Aidan Patrick	4 Pump Court, London	020 7842 5555
Christie-Brown Miss Sarah Louise	4 Paper Buildings, London	0171 353 3366/583 7155
Clark Andrew Richard	Manchester House Chambers, Manchester	0161 834 7007
	8 King Street Chambers, Manchester	0161 834 9560
Clarke Miss Alison Lee	No. 1 Serjeants' Inn, London	0171 415 6666
Clarke Jonathan Christopher St John	Old Square Chambers, Bristol	0117 9277111
	Old Square Chambers, London	0171 269 0300
Clay Robert Charles	Atkin Chambers, London	020 7404 0102
Clegg Sebastian James Barwick	Deans Court Chambers, Manchester	0161 214 6000
	Deans Court Chambers, Preston	01772 555163
Cliff Graham Hilton	St Philip's Chambers, Birmingham	0121 246 7000
Coghlan Terence	1 Crown Office Row, London	0171 797 7500
	Crown Office Row Chambers, Brighton	01273 625625
Colbey Richard (Alan)	• Francis Taylor Building, London	0171 797 7250
	Guildhall Chambers Portsmouth, Portsmouth	01705 752400
Collard Michael David	5 Pump Court, London	020 7353 2532
Collett Ivor William	No. 1 Serjeants' Inn, London	0171 415 6666
Collings Nicholas Stewart	Atkin Chambers, London	020 7404 0102
Cook Jeremy David	Lamb Building, London	020 7797 7788
Cooke Jeremy Lionel	S Tomlinson QC, London	0171 583 0404
Cooksley Nigel James	Old Square Chambers, London	0171 269 0300
	Old Square Chambers, Bristol	0117 9277111
Cooper Gilead Patrick	Chambers of Mr Peter Crampin QC, London	020 7831 0081
Corbett James Patrick	St Philip's Chambers, Birmingham	0121 246 7000
	Chambers of Andrew Campbell QC, Leeds	0113 2455438

       • Expanded entry in Part D

Cory-Wright Charles Alexander	39 Essex Street, London	0171 832 1111
Cotton Miss Diana Rosemary	Devereux Chambers, London	0171 353 7534
Craig Alistair Trevor	Chambers of Mr Peter Crampin QC, London	020 7831 0081
Craig Kenneth Allen	Hardwicke Building, London	020 7242 2523
Crail Miss (Elspeth) Ross	12 New Square, London	0171 419 1212
	Sovereign Chambers, Leeds	0113 2451841/2/3
Crampin Peter	Chambers of Mr Peter Crampin QC, London	020 7831 0081
Cramsie James Sinclair Beresford	13 King's Bench Walk, London	0171 353 7204
	King's Bench Chambers, Oxford	01865 311066
Cranfield Peter Anthony	3 Verulam Buildings, London	0171 831 8441
Crawford Grant	11 Old Square, London	020 7430 0341
Cross James Edward Michael	4 Pump Court, London	020 7842 5555
Crossley Simon Justin	9 Woodhouse Square, Leeds	0113 2451986
Crowley John Desmond	Two Crown Office Row, London	020 7797 8100
Croxford Ian Lionel	• Wilberforce Chambers, London	0171 306 0102
Croxon Raymond Patrick	8 King's Bench Walk, London	0171 797 8888
	Regency Chambers, Peterborough	01733 315215
	Regency Chambers, Cambridge	01223 301517
Curtis Michael Alexander	Two Crown Office Row, London	020 7797 8100
Curwen Michael Jonathan	Chambers of Kieran Coonan QC, London	0171 583 6013/2510
Dalby Joseph Francis	Portsmouth Barristers' Chambers, Winchester	01962 863222
	Portsmouth Barristers' Chambers, Portsmouth	023 92 831292/811811
Davidson Edward Alan	11 Old Square, London	020 7430 0341
Davidson Nicholas Ranking	4 Paper Buildings, London	0171 353 3366/583 7155
Davie Michael James	4 Pump Court, London	020 7842 5555
Davies Andrew Christopher	New Court Chambers, London	0171 831 9500
Davies Miss Carol Elizabeth	2 New Street, Leicester	0116 2625906
Davies The Rt Hon David John Denzil	96 Gray's Inn Road, London	0171 405 0585
	8 Gray's Inn Square, London	0171 242 3529
Davies Stephen Richard	8 King Street Chambers, Manchester	0161 834 9560
Davies Miss (Susan) Louise	12 New Square, London	0171 419 1212
	Sovereign Chambers, Leeds	0113 2451841/2/3
Davies-Jones Jonathan	3 Verulam Buildings, London	0171 831 8441
Davis Andrew Paul	Two Crown Office Row, London	020 7797 8100
Dawson Alexander William	13 King's Bench Walk, London	0171 353 7204
	King's Bench Chambers, Oxford	01865 311066
De Freitas Anthony Peter Stanley	4 Paper Buildings, London	0171 353 3366/583 7155
de Lacy Richard Michael	3 Verulam Buildings, London	0171 831 8441
Dean Peter Thomas	1 Crown Office Row, London	0171 583 9292
DeCamp Miss Jane Louise	Two Crown Office Row, London	020 7797 8100
Dennison Stephen Randell	Atkin Chambers, London	020 7404 0102
Dennys Nicholas Charles Jonathan	Atkin Chambers, London	020 7404 0102
Dillon Thomas William Matthew	1 Fountain Court, Birmingham	0121 236 5721
Dingemans James Michael	1 Crown Office Row, London	0171 583 9292
Dodge Peter Clive	11 Old Square, London	020 7430 0341
Doerries Miss Chantal-Aimee Renee Aemelia Annemarie	Atkin Chambers, London	020 7404 0102
Donovan Joel	New Court Chambers, London	0171 831 9500
Dooher Miss Nancy Helen	St James's Chambers, Manchester	0161 834 7000
Dougherty Nigel Peter	Erskine Chambers, London	0171 242 5532
Douglas Michael John	4 Pump Court, London	020 7842 5555
Dowley Dominic Myles	One Hare Court, London	020 7353 3171
Drake David Christopher	Serle Court Chambers, London	0171 242 6105
Dubbery Mark Edward	Pump Court Chambers, London	0171 353 0711
	Pump Court Chambers, Winchester	01962 868161
	Pump Court Chambers, Swindon	01793 539899
Duddridge Robert James	2 Gray's Inn Square Chambers, London	020 7242 0328

Dugdale Nicholas	4 Field Court, London	0171 440 6900
Dumaresq Ms Delia Jane	Atkin Chambers, London	020 7404 0102
Dumont Thomas Julian Bradley	Chambers of Mr Peter Crampin QC, London	020 7831 0081
Dutton Timothy Christopher	Barnard's Inn Chambers, London	0171 369 6969
Dyer Allen Gordon	4 Pump Court, London	020 7842 5555
Eadie James Raymond	One Hare Court, London	020 7353 3171
Eastman Roger	2 Harcourt Buildings, London	0171 583 9020
Eccles David Thomas	8 King Street Chambers, Manchester	0161 834 9560
Edge Timothy Richard	Deans Court Chambers, Preston	01772 555163
	Deans Court Chambers, Manchester	0161 214 6000
Edis Andrew Jeremy Coulter	• Adrian Lyon's Chambers, Liverpool	0151 236 4421/8240
Edis Angus William Butler	1 Crown Office Row, London	0171 797 7500
Edwards David Leslie	S Tomlinson QC, London	0171 583 0404
Edwards Richard Julian Henshaw	3 Verulam Buildings, London	0171 831 8441
Edwards-Stuart Antony James Cobham	Two Crown Office Row, London	020 7797 8100
Eidinow John Samuel Christopher	1 New Square, London	0171 405 0884/5/6/7
Elleray Anthony John	• St James's Chambers, Manchester	0161 834 7000
	12 New Square, London	0171 419 1212
	Park Lane Chambers, Leeds	0113 2285000
Elliott Nicholas Blethyn	3 Verulam Buildings, London	0171 831 8441
Ellis Roger John	13 King's Bench Walk, London	0171 353 7204
	King's Bench Chambers, Oxford	01865 311066
Etherton Terence Michael Elkan Barnet	• Wilberforce Chambers, London	0171 306 0102
Evans Miss Claire Louise	Peel Court Chambers, Manchester	0161 832 3791
Evans James Frederick Meurig	3 Verulam Buildings, London	0171 831 8441
Evans Jonathan Edward	• Wilberforce Chambers, London	0171 306 0102
Evans Stephen James	8 King's Bench Walk, London	0171 797 8888
	8 King's Bench Walk North, Leeds	0113 2439797
Evans-Tovey Jason Robert	Two Crown Office Row, London	020 7797 8100
Ewins Miss Catherine Jane	4 Paper Buildings, London	0171 353 3366/583 7155
Eyre Stephen John Arthur	1 Fountain Court, Birmingham	0121 236 5721
Fadipe Gabriel Charles	• Wilberforce Chambers, London	0171 306 0102
Fairbank Nicholas James	Becket Chambers, Canterbury	01227 786331
Farrow Kenneth John	Serle Court Chambers, London	0171 242 6105
Faulks Edward Peter Lawless	No. 1 Serjeants' Inn, London	0171 415 6666
Fawls Richard Granville	5 Stone Buildings, London	0171 242 6201
Feltham Piers Jonathan	Chambers of Mr Peter Crampin QC, London	020 7831 0081
Fenton Adam Timothy Downs	S Tomlinson QC, London	0171 583 0404
Ferm Rodney Eric	37 Park Square Chambers, Leeds	0113 2439422
Field Patrick John	Deans Court Chambers, Manchester	0161 214 6000
	Deans Court Chambers, Preston	01772 555163
Fieldsend James William	2nd Floor, Francis Taylor Building, London	0171 353 9942/3157
Finn Terence	Chambers of Martin Burr, London	0171 353 4636
Flaux Julian Martin	S Tomlinson QC, London	0171 583 0404
Flenley William David Wingate	4 Paper Buildings, London	0171 353 3366/583 7155
Fletcher Andrew Fitzroy Stephen	4 Pump Court, London	020 7842 5555
Ford Michael David	Doughty Street Chambers, London	0171 404 1313
Forte Mark Julian Carmino	8 King Street Chambers, Manchester	0161 834 9560
Foster Brian Ian	St James's Chambers, Manchester	0161 834 7000
	Park Lane Chambers, Leeds	0113 2285000
Foster Charles Andrew	• Chambers of Kieran Coonan QC, London	0171 583 6013/2510
Foy John Leonard	9 Gough Square, London	020 7832 0500
Francis Andrew James	Chambers of Mr Peter Crampin QC, London	020 7831 0081
Franklin Miss Kim	• One Paper Buildings, London	0171 583 7355
Fraser Peter Donald	Atkin Chambers, London	020 7404 0102

B

• Expanded entry in Part D

Freedman Sampson Clive	3 Verulam Buildings, London	0171 831 8441
Freeland Simon Dennis Marsden	5 Essex Court, London	0171 410 2000
Friedman David Peter	4 Pump Court, London	020 7842 5555
Fryer-Spedding James Walter	St James's Chambers, Manchester	0161 834 7000
Furness Michael James	• Wilberforce Chambers, London	0171 306 0102
Furze Miss Caroline Mary	• Wilberforce Chambers, London	0171 306 0102
Gadney George Munro	Two Crown Office Row, London	020 7797 8100
Gaisman Jonathan Nicholas Crispin	S Tomlinson QC, London	0171 583 0404
Garcia-Miller Miss Laura	Enterprise Chambers, London	0171 405 9471
	Enterprise Chambers, Leeds	0113 246 0391
	Enterprise Chambers, Newcastle upon Tyne	0191 222 3344
Garner Miss Sophie Jane	199 Strand, London	0171 379 9779
Gasztowicz Steven	2-3 Gray's Inn Square, London	0171 242 4986
	2 New Street, Leicester	0116 2625906
Gatt Ian Andrew	Littleton Chambers, London	0171 797 8600
Geary Gavin John	S Tomlinson QC, London	0171 583 0404
Gee Steven Mark	4 Field Court, London	0171 440 6900
Geering Ian Walter	3 Verulam Buildings, London	0171 831 8441
Gerald Nigel Mortimer	Enterprise Chambers, London	0171 405 9471
	Enterprise Chambers, Leeds	0113 246 0391
	Enterprise Chambers, Newcastle upon Tyne	0191 222 3344
Gibaud Miss Catherine Alison Annetta	3 Verulam Buildings, London	0171 831 8441
Gibson Arthur George Adrian	Adrian Lyon's Chambers, Liverpool	0151 236 4421/8240
Gibson Martin John	Littman Chambers, London	020 7404 4866
Gifford Andrew James Morris	7 New Square, London	0171 430 1660
Glasson Jonathan Joseph	Doughty Street Chambers, London	0171 404 1313
Glover Stephen Julian	37 Park Square Chambers, Leeds	0113 2439422
Goddard Andrew Stephen	Atkin Chambers, London	020 7404 0102
Goddard Harold Keith	Deans Court Chambers, Manchester	0161 214 6000
	Deans Court Chambers, Preston	01772 555163
	4 Paper Buildings, London	0171 353 3366/583 7155
Godwin William George Henry	Atkin Chambers, London	020 7404 0102
Gordon-Saker Andrew Stephen	Fenners Chambers, Cambridge	01223 368761
	Fenners Chambers, Peterborough	01733 562030
Gore-Andrews Gavin Angus Russell	2 Harcourt Buildings, London	0171 583 9020
Grace Jonathan Robert	Deans Court Chambers, Manchester	0161 214 6000
	Deans Court Chambers, Preston	01772 555163
Grace Timothy Michael	Adrian Lyon's Chambers, Liverpool	0151 236 4421/8240
Grantham Andrew Timothy	• Deans Court Chambers, Manchester	0161 214 6000
	Deans Court Chambers, Preston	01772 555163
Gray Richard Paul	39 Essex Street, London	0171 832 1111
Green Miss Alison Anne	4 Field Court, London	0171 440 6900
Green Miss Amanda Jane	3 Verulam Buildings, London	0171 831 8441
Green Brian Russell	Wilberforce Chambers, London	0171 306 0102
Green David Cameron	Adrian Lyon's Chambers, Liverpool	0151 236 4421/8240
Greenbourne John Hugo	Two Crown Office Row, London	020 7797 8100
Gregory John Raymond	Deans Court Chambers, Manchester	0161 214 6000
	Deans Court Chambers, Preston	01772 555163
Grime Mark Stephen Eastburn	Deans Court Chambers, Manchester	0161 214 6000
	2 Pump Court, London	0171 353 5597
	Deans Court Chambers, Preston	01772 555163
Grimshaw Nicholas Edward	Deans Court Chambers, Manchester	0161 214 6000
	Deans Court Chambers, Preston	01772 555163
Grodzinski Samuel Marc	39 Essex Street, London	0171 832 1111
Guggenheim Miss Anna Maeve	Two Crown Office Row, London	020 7797 8100
Gulliver Miss Alison Louise	4 Paper Buildings, London	0171 353 3366/583 7155
Gun Cuninghame Julian Arthur	Gough Square Chambers, London	0171 353 0924
Gunning Alexander Rupert	4 Pump Court, London	020 7842 5555

B

Guy John David Colin	Francis Taylor Building, London	0171 797 7250
Haigh Martin James	30 Park Square, Leeds	0113 2436388
Hall David Percy	9 Woodhouse Square, Leeds	0113 2451986
Hall Mrs Melanie Ruth	Monckton Chambers, London	0171 405 7211
Hall Taylor Alexander Edward	11 Old Square, London	020 7430 0341
Halpern David Anthony	Enterprise Chambers, London	0171 405 9471
	Enterprise Chambers, Leeds	0113 246 0391
	Enterprise Chambers, Newcastle upon Tyne	0191 222 3344
Hamilton Adrian Walter	S Tomlinson QC, London	0171 583 0404
Hamilton Graeme Montagu	Two Crown Office Row, London	020 7797 8100
Hamilton Peter Bernard	4 Pump Court, London	020 7842 5555
Hammerton Alastair Rolf	No. 1 Serjeants' Inn, London	0171 415 6666
Hammerton Miss Veronica Lesley	No. 1 Serjeants' Inn, London	0171 415 6666
Hantusch Robert Anthony	• 3 Stone Buildings, London	0171 242 4937
Hardwick Matthew Richard	Enterprise Chambers, London	0171 405 9471
	Enterprise Chambers, Leeds	0113 246 0391
	Enterprise Chambers, Newcastle upon Tyne	0191 222 3344
Harrap Giles Thresher	• Pump Court Chambers, Winchester	01962 868161
	Pump Court Chambers, London	0171 353 0711
	Pump Court Chambers, Swindon	01793 539899
Harris Paul Best	Monckton Chambers, London	0171 405 7211
Harrod Henry Mark	5 Stone Buildings, London	0171 242 6201
Harvey Michael Llewellyn Tucker	Two Crown Office Row, London	020 7797 8100
Hawkes Miss Naomi Nanteza Astrid Wallusimbi	22 Old Buildings, London	0171 831 0222
Head David Ian	3 Verulam Buildings, London	0171 831 8441
Healy Miss Sioban	S Tomlinson QC, London	0171 583 0404
Heather Christopher Mark	• 2nd Floor, Francis Taylor Building, London	0171 353 9942/3157
Henderson Roger Anthony	2 Harcourt Buildings, London	0171 583 9020
Henderson Simon Alexander	4 Pump Court, London	020 7842 5555
Hermer Richard Simon	Doughty Street Chambers, London	0171 404 1313
	30 Park Place, Cardiff	01222 398421
Hershman David Allan	St Philip's Chambers, Birmingham	0121 246 7000
	1 Mitre Court Buildings, London	0171 797 7070
Hewitson William Andrew	1 Crown Office Row, London	0171 583 9292
Higgins Adrian John	13 King's Bench Walk, London	0171 353 7204
	King's Bench Chambers, Oxford	01865 311066
Higgo Justin Beresford	Serle Court Chambers, London	0171 242 6105
Hill Nicholas Mark	• Pump Court Chambers, London	0171 353 0711
	Pump Court Chambers, Winchester	01962 868161
	Pump Court Chambers, Swindon	01793 539899
Hirst William Timothy John	Park Court Chambers, Leeds	0113 2433277
Hockaday Miss Annie	3 Verulam Buildings, London	0171 831 8441
Hockman Stephen Alexander	• 6 Pump Court, London	0171 797 8400
	6-8 Mill Street, Maidstone	01622 688094
Hodgkinson Tristram Patrick	• 5 Pump Court, London	020 7353 2532
Hodson Peter David	Chambers of Ian Macdonald QC (In Association with Two Garden Court, Temple, London), Manchester	0161 236 1840
Hoffman David Alexander	8 King Street Chambers, Manchester	0161 834 9560
Hoffmann Miss Jocelyn Clare	Serle Court Chambers, London	0171 242 6105
Hofmeyr Stephen Murray	S Tomlinson QC, London	0171 583 0404
Hogg The Hon Douglas Martin	37 Park Square Chambers, Leeds	0113 2439422
	Cathedral Chambers (Jan Wood Independent Barristers' Clerk), Exeter	01392 210900
Hogg Miss Katharine Elizabeth	1 Crown Office Row, London	0171 797 7500
Holdsworth James Arthur	Two Crown Office Row, London	020 7797 8100
Holland David Moore	29 Bedford Row Chambers, London	0171 831 2626

• Expanded entry in Part D

Hollington Robin Frank	1 New Square, London	0171 405 0884/5/6/7
Holmes Philip John	8 King Street Chambers, Manchester	0161 834 9560
Holmes-Milner James Neil	2 Mitre Court Buildings, London	0171 353 1353
Holwill Derek Paul Winsor	4 Paper Buildings, London	0171 353 3366/583 7155
Hornett Stuart Ian	29 Bedford Row Chambers, London	0171 831 2626
Hoser Philip Jacob	Serle Court Chambers, London	0171 242 6105
Houghton Miss Kirsten Annette	4 Pump Court, London	020 7842 5555
Howarth Simon Stuart	Two Crown Office Row, London	020 7797 8100
Howells James Richard	Atkin Chambers, London	020 7404 0102
Hubbard Mark Iain	1 New Square, London	0171 405 0884/5/6/7
Hughes Adrian Warwick	4 Pump Court, London	020 7842 5555
Hunter William Quigley	No. 1 Serjeants' Inn, London	0171 415 6666
Ife Miss Linden Elizabeth	Enterprise Chambers, London	0171 405 9471
	Enterprise Chambers, Leeds	0113 246 0391
	Enterprise Chambers, Newcastle upon Tyne	0191 222 3344
Iles Adrian	5 Paper Buildings, London	0171 583 9275/583 4555
Irwin Stephen John	Doughty Street Chambers, London	0171 404 1313
Jack Adrian Laurence Robert	Enterprise Chambers, London	0171 405 9471
	Enterprise Chambers, Newcastle upon Tyne	0191 222 3344
	Enterprise Chambers, Leeds	0113 246 0391
Jackson Dirik George Allan	Chambers of Mr Peter Crampin QC, London	020 7831 0081
Jackson Hugh Woodward	Hardwicke Building, London	020 7242 2523
Jackson Matthew David Everard	4 Paper Buildings, London	0171 353 3366/583 7155
Jackson Nicholas David Kingsley	Adrian Lyon's Chambers, Liverpool	0151 236 4421/8240
Jacobson Lawrence	5 Paper Buildings, London	0171 583 9275/583 4555
James Michael Frank	Enterprise Chambers, London	0171 405 9471
	Enterprise Chambers, Leeds	0113 246 0391
	Enterprise Chambers, Newcastle upon Tyne	0191 222 3344
Jarvis John Manners	3 Verulam Buildings, London	0171 831 8441
Jefferis Arthur Michael Quentin	Chambers of Mr Peter Crampin QC, London	020 7831 0081
Jess Digby Charles	8 King Street Chambers, Manchester	0161 834 9560
Johnston Anthony Paul	1 Fountain Court, Birmingham	0121 236 5721
Jones Martin Wynne	8 King's Bench Walk, London	0171 797 8888
	8 King's Bench Walk North, Leeds	0113 2439797
Jones Philip John	Serle Court Chambers, London	0171 242 6105
Jory Robert John Hugh	Enterprise Chambers, London	0171 405 9471
	Enterprise Chambers, Leeds	0113 246 0391
	Enterprise Chambers, Newcastle upon Tyne	0191 222 3344
Kay Michael Jack David	3 Verulam Buildings, London	0171 831 8441
	Park Lane Chambers, Leeds	0113 2285000
Kay Robert Jervis	4 Field Court, London	0171 440 6900
Kealey Gavin Sean James	S Tomlinson QC, London	0171 583 0404
Kelly Geoffrey Robert	Pump Court Chambers, London	0171 353 0711
	Pump Court Chambers, Winchester	01962 868161
	Pump Court Chambers, Swindon	01793 539899
Kendrick Dominic John	S Tomlinson QC, London	0171 583 0404
Kenny Stephen Charles Wilfrid	S Tomlinson QC, London	0171 583 0404
Kent Michael Harcourt	Two Crown Office Row, London	020 7797 8100
King-Smith James	1 Crown Office Row, London	0171 797 7500
	Crown Office Row Chambers, Brighton	01273 625625
Kirby Peter John	Hardwicke Building, London	020 7242 2523
Kirtley Paul George	37 Park Square Chambers, Leeds	0113 2439422
Knowles Graham Roy	Peel Court Chambers, Manchester	0161 832 3791
Kolodziej Andrzej Jozef	• Littman Chambers, London	020 7404 4866
Kosmin Leslie Gordon	Erskine Chambers, London	0171 242 5532

B

Kremen Philip Michael	Hardwicke Building, London	020 7242 2523
Kuschke Leon Siegfried	Erskine Chambers, London	0171 242 5532
Kynoch Duncan Stuart Sanderson	29 Bedford Row Chambers, London	0171 831 2626
Lamb Robert Glasson	13 King's Bench Walk, London	0171 353 7204
	King's Bench Chambers, Oxford	01865 311066
Lambert Miss Sarah Katrina	1 Crown Office Row, London	0171 797 7500
Lamberty Mark Julian Harker	Queen's Chambers, Manchester	0161 834 6875/4738
	Queens Chambers, Preston	01772 828300
Lamont Miss Camilla Rose	Chambers of Lord Goodhart QC, London	0171 405 5577
Latimer-Sayer William Laurence	2 Mitre Court Buildings, London	0171 353 1353
Lavender Nicholas	One Hare Court, London	020 7353 3171
Lawrence The Hon Patrick John Tristram	4 Paper Buildings, London	0171 353 3366/583 7155
Lazarus Michael Steven	1 Crown Office Row, London	0171 583 9292
Leech Brian Walter Thomas	No. 1 Serjeants' Inn, London	0171 415 6666
Legge Henry	5 Stone Buildings, London	0171 242 6201
Lennard Stephen Charles	Hardwicke Building, London	020 7242 2523
Levy Benjamin Keith	Enterprise Chambers, London	0171 405 9471
	Enterprise Chambers, Leeds	0113 246 0391
	Enterprise Chambers, Newcastle upon Tyne	0191 222 3344
Lewis Andrew William	Sovereign Chambers, Leeds	0113 2451841/2/3
Lloyd Stephen James George	Chambers of Mr Peter Crampin QC, London	020 7831 0081
Lochrane Damien Horatio Ross	Pump Court Chambers, London	0171 353 0711
	Pump Court Chambers, Winchester	01962 868161
	Pump Court Chambers, Swindon	01793 539899
Lofthouse Simon Timothy	Atkin Chambers, London	020 7404 0102
Lowe Thomas William Gordon	•Wilberforce Chambers, London	0171 306 0102
Lowenstein Paul David	Littleton Chambers, London	0171 797 8600
Lowry Charles Stephen	Colleton Chambers, Exeter	01392 274898/9
Lynagh Richard Dudley	Two Crown Office Row, London	020 7797 8100
Machell Raymond Donatus	Deans Court Chambers, Manchester	0161 214 6000
	2 Pump Court, London	0171 353 5597
	Deans Court Chambers, Preston	01772 555163
Mackay Colin Crichton	39 Essex Street, London	0171 832 1111
Macleod Duncan	9 Gough Square, London	020 7832 0500
Macnab Alexander Andrew	Monckton Chambers, London	0171 405 7211
Main Peter Ramsay	Deans Court Chambers, Manchester	0161 214 6000
	Deans Court Chambers, Preston	01772 555163
Mainwaring [Robert] Paul Clason	Carmarthen Chambers, Carmarthen	01267 234410
Malek Ali	3 Verulam Buildings, London	0171 831 8441
Malins Julian Henry	One Hare Court, London	020 7353 3171
Mandalia Vinesh Lalji	Harrow on the Hill Chambers, Harrow-on-the-Hill	0181 423 7444
Mann George Anthony	Enterprise Chambers, London	0171 405 9471
	Enterprise Chambers, Leeds	0113 246 0391
	Enterprise Chambers, Newcastle upon Tyne	0191 222 3344
Mantle Peter John	Monckton Chambers, London	0171 405 7211
Manzoni Charles Peter	39 Essex Street, London	0171 832 1111
Margolin Daniel George	Chambers of Mr Peter Crampin QC, London	020 7831 0081
Marks Jonathan Clive	4 Pump Court, London	020 7842 5555
Marks Jonathan Harold	3 Verulam Buildings, London	0171 831 8441
Markus Ms Kate	Doughty Street Chambers, London	0171 404 1313
Marquand Charles Nicholas Hilary	Chambers of Lord Goodhart QC, London	0171 405 5577
Marsh Laurence John	4 Pump Court, London	020 7842 5555
Marshall Philip Scott	Serle Court Chambers, London	0171 242 6105
Marshall-Andrews Robert Graham	37 Park Square Chambers, Leeds	0113 2439422
	2-4 Tudor Street, London	0171 797 7111

• Expanded entry in Part D

Martin John Vandeleur	•Wilberforce Chambers, London	0171 306 0102
Masters Miss Sara Alayna	20 Essex Street, London	0171 583 9294
Matthews Dennis Roland	Two Crown Office Row, London	020 7797 8100
Matthews Duncan Henry Rowland	20 Essex Street, London	0171 583 9294
Mauleverer Peter Bruce	4 Pump Court, London	020 7842 5555
Maxwell Richard	Ropewalk Chambers, Nottingham	0115 9472581
	Doughty Street Chambers, London	0171 404 1313
Maxwell-Scott James Herbert	Two Crown Office Row, London	020 7797 8100
May Miss Juliet Mary	3 Verulam Buildings, London	0171 831 8441
Maynard-Connor Giles	St James's Chambers, Manchester	0161 834 7000
McAlinden Barry O'Neill	17 Bedford Row, London	0171 831 7314
McAllister Miss Elizabeth Ann	Enterprise Chambers, London	0171 405 9471
	Enterprise Chambers, Leeds	0113 246 0391
	Enterprise Chambers, Newcastle upon Tyne	0191 222 3344
McCafferty Miss Lynne	5 Paper Buildings, London	0171 583 9275/583 4555
McCahill Patrick Gerard	St Philip's Chambers, Birmingham	0121 246 7000
	Chambers of Andrew Campbell QC, Leeds	0113 2455438
McCall Duncan James	4 Pump Court, London	020 7842 5555
McCann Simon Howard	Deans Court Chambers, Manchester	0161 214 6000
	Deans Court Chambers, Preston	01772 555163
McCaul Colin Brownlie	39 Essex Street, London	0171 832 1111
McClure Brian David	Littman Chambers, London	020 7404 4866
McCourt Christopher	22 Old Buildings, London	0171 831 0222
McCulloch Ian	Bracton Chambers, London	0171 242 4248
	Lloyds House Chambers, Manchester	0161 839 3371
	Claremont Chambers, Wolverhampton	01902 426222
McDermott Gerard Francis	8 King Street Chambers, Manchester	0161 834 9560
	2 Pump Court, London	0171 353 5597
McGregor Harvey	4 Paper Buildings, London	0171 353 3366/583 7155
McKendrick Ewan Gordon	3 Verulam Buildings, London	0171 831 8441
McMullan Manus Anthony	Atkin Chambers, London	020 7404 0102
McQuail Ms Katherine Emma	11 Old Square, London	020 7430 0341
McQuater Ewan Alan	3 Verulam Buildings, London	0171 831 8441
Meeson Nigel Keith	4 Field Court, London	0171 440 6900
Mehendale Ms Neelima Krishna	2 Mitre Court Buildings, London	0171 353 1353
Melton Christopher	Peel Court Chambers, Manchester	0161 832 3791
	199 Strand, London	0171 379 9779
Melville Richard David	• 39 Essex Street, London	0171 832 1111
Mendoza Neil David Pereira	Hardwicke Building, London	020 7242 2523
Mercer David Paul	Queen's Chambers, Manchester	0161 834 6875/4738
	Queens Chambers, Preston	01772 828300
Merriman Nicholas Flavelle	3 Verulam Buildings, London	0171 831 8441
Metzer Anthony David Erwin	Doughty Street Chambers, London	0171 404 1313
Millar Gavin James	Doughty Street Chambers, London	0171 404 1313
Milligan Iain Anstruther	20 Essex Street, London	0171 583 9294
Mills Corey Arthur	Becket Chambers, Canterbury	01227 786331
Milne Michael	Resolution Chambers, Malvern	01684 561279
	Chambers of Geoffrey Hawker, London	0171 583 8899
Mishcon Miss Jane Malca	4 Paper Buildings, London	0171 353 3366/583 7155
Mitchell Gregory Charles Mathew	3 Verulam Buildings, London	0171 831 8441
Mitropoulos Christos	Chambers of Geoffrey Hawker, London	0171 583 8899
Moger Christopher Richard Derwent	4 Pump Court, London	020 7842 5555
Morgan Charles James Arthur	Enterprise Chambers, London	0171 405 9471
	Enterprise Chambers, Newcastle upon Tyne	0191 222 3344
	Enterprise Chambers, Leeds	0113 246 0391
Morgan Richard Hugo Lyndon	13 Old Square, London	0171 404 4800
Morgan (Thomas) Jeremy	39 Essex Street, London	0171 832 1111
Mortimer Miss Sophie Kate	No. 1 Serjeants' Inn, London	0171 415 6666

Moser Philip Curt Harold	4 Paper Buildings, London	0171 353 3366/583 7155
Mulcahy Miss Leigh-Ann Maria	Chambers of John L Powell QC, London	0171 797 8000
Mulholland Michael	St James's Chambers, Manchester	0161 834 7000
Nardell Gordon Lawrence	6 Pump Court, London	0171 797 8400
	6-8 Mill Street, Maidstone	01622 688094
Nash Jonathan Scott	3 Verulam Buildings, London	0171 831 8441
Naughton Philip Anthony	3 Serjeants' Inn, London	0171 353 5537
Neill of Bladen Lord	One Hare Court, London	020 7353 3171
Neish Andrew Graham	4 Pump Court, London	020 7842 5555
Nesbitt Timothy John Robert	199 Strand, London	0171 379 9779
Neville Stephen John	Gough Square Chambers, London	0171 353 0924
Neville-Clarke Sebastian Adrian Bennett	1 Crown Office Row, London	0171 583 9292
Newman Miss Catherine Mary	● 13 Old Square, London	0171 404 4800
Newman Ms Ingrid	Hardwicke Building, London	020 7242 2523
Newman Paul Lance	● Wilberforce Chambers, London	0171 306 0102
Ng Ray Kian Hin	Two Crown Office Row, London	020 7797 8100
Nicholls John Peter	13 Old Square, London	0171 404 4800
Nicholson Jeremy Mark	4 Pump Court, London	020 7842 5555
Nicol Stuart Henry David	3 Temple Gardens, London	0171 353 0832
Noble Roderick Grant	39 Essex Street, London	0171 832 1111
Nolan Michael Alfred Anthony	4 Essex Court, London	020 7797 7970
Norman Christopher John George	No. 1 Serjeants' Inn, London	0171 415 6666
Norris Alastair Hubert	5 Stone Buildings, London	0171 242 6201
	Southernhay Chambers, Exeter	01392 255777
Nugee Christopher George	● Wilberforce Chambers, London	0171 306 0102
Nurse Gordon Bramwell William	11 Old Square, London	020 7430 0341
O'Connor Andrew McDougal	Two Crown Office Row, London	020 7797 8100
O'Donoghue Florence	2 Mitre Court Buildings, London	0171 353 1353
O'Leary Robert Michael	33 Park Place, Cardiff	02920 233313
O'Neill Tadhg Joseph	1 Crown Office Row, London	0171 583 9292
O'Shea Eoin Finbarr	4 Field Court, London	0171 440 6900
O'Sullivan Michael Morton	5 Stone Buildings, London	0171 242 6201
O'Sullivan Thomas Sean Patrick	4 Pump Court, London	020 7842 5555
O'Toole Simon Gerard	2 Mitre Court Buildings, London	0171 353 1353
Oakley Anthony James	● 11 Old Square, London	020 7430 0341
Odgers John Arthur	3 Verulam Buildings, London	0171 831 8441
Ohrenstein Dov	Chambers of Lord Goodhart QC, London	0171 405 5577
Onslow Andrew George	3 Verulam Buildings, London	0171 831 8441
Osman Robert Walter	Queen's Chambers, Manchester	0161 834 6875/4738
	Queens Chambers, Preston	01772 828300
Ovey Miss Elizabeth Helen	11 Old Square, London	020 7430 0341
Packman Miss Claire Geraldine Vance	4 Pump Court, London	020 7842 5555
Padfield Ms Alison Mary	Devereux Chambers, London	0171 353 7534
Padfield Nicholas David	One Hare Court, London	020 7353 3171
Page Howard William Barrett	One Hare Court, London	020 7353 3171
Paneth Miss Sarah Ruth	No. 1 Serjeants' Inn, London	0171 415 6666
Parker Matthew Richard	3 Verulam Buildings, London	0171 831 8441
Parkin Miss Fiona Jane	Atkin Chambers, London	020 7404 0102
Parkin Jonathan	● Chambers of John Hand QC, Manchester	0161 955 9000
Patchett-Joyce Michael Thurston	Monckton Chambers, London	0171 405 7211
Patel Parishil Jayantilal	39 Essex Street, London	0171 832 1111
Patten Benedict Joseph	Two Crown Office Row, London	020 7797 8100
Peacock Nicholas Christopher	13 Old Square, London	0171 404 4800
Peacocke Mrs Teresa Anne Rosen	Enterprise Chambers, London	0171 405 9471
	Enterprise Chambers, Leeds	0113 246 0391
	Enterprise Chambers, Newcastle upon Tyne	0191 222 3344
Pearce Richard William	Peel Court Chambers, Manchester	0161 832 3791

● Expanded entry in Part D

Pearce Robert Edgar	Chambers of Mr Peter Crampin QC, London	020 7831 0081
Pears Derrick Allan	2nd Floor, Francis Taylor Building, London	0171 353 9942/3157
Pearson Christopher	• Bridewell Chambers, London	020 7797 8800
Pelling (Philip) Mark	Monckton Chambers, London	0171 405 7211
Pema Anes Bhumin Laloo	9 Woodhouse Square, Leeds	0113 2451986
Pepperall Edward Brian	St Philip's Chambers, Birmingham	0121 246 7000
Perkoff Richard Michael	Littleton Chambers, London	0171 797 8600
Perry Miss Jacqueline Anne	• Lamb Building, London	020 7797 7788
Pershad Rohan	Two Crown Office Row, London	020 7797 8100
Phillips Andrew Charles	Two Crown Office Row, London	020 7797 8100
Phillips David John	199 Strand, London	0171 379 9779
	30 Park Place, Cardiff	01222 398421
Phillips Jonathan Mark	3 Verulam Buildings, London	0171 831 8441
Phillips Rory Andrew Livingstone	3 Verulam Buildings, London	0171 831 8441
Phillips S J	S Tomlinson QC, London	0171 583 0404
Phillips Stephen Edmund	3 Verulam Buildings, London	0171 831 8441
Picken Simon Derek	S Tomlinson QC, London	0171 583 0404
	30 Park Place, Cardiff	01222 398421
Pickering James Patrick	Enterprise Chambers, London	0171 405 9471
	Enterprise Chambers, Leeds	0113 246 0391
	Enterprise Chambers, Newcastle upon Tyne	0191 222 3344
Picton Julian Mark	4 Paper Buildings, London	0171 353 3366/583 7155
Pilkington Mrs Mavis Patricia	9 Woodhouse Square, Leeds	0113 2451986
Pilling Benjamin	4 Pump Court, London	020 7842 5555
Pimentel Carlos de Serpa Alberto Legg	3 Stone Buildings, London	0171 242 4937
Pinder Miss Mary Elizabeth	No. 1 Serjeants' Inn, London	0171 415 6666
Piper Angus Richard	No. 1 Serjeants' Inn, London	0171 415 6666
Pirani Rohan Carl	Old Square Chambers, Bristol	0117 9277111
	Old Square Chambers, London	0171 269 0300
Pittaway David Michael	No. 1 Serjeants' Inn, London	0171 415 6666
Pliener David Jonathan	New Court Chambers, London	0171 831 9500
Pooles Michael Philip Holmes	4 Paper Buildings, London	0171 353 3366/583 7155
Pope David James	3 Verulam Buildings, London	0171 831 8441
Porter David Leonard	St James's Chambers, Manchester	0161 834 7000
	Park Lane Chambers, Leeds	0113 2285000
Portnoy Leslie Reuben	Chambers of John Hand QC, Manchester	0161 955 9000
Post Andrew John	Chambers of Kieran Coonan QC, London	0171 583 6013/2510
Potts Warren Nigel	Queen's Chambers, Manchester	0161 834 6875/4738
	Queens Chambers, Preston	01772 828300
Pounder Gerard	5 Essex Court, London	0171 410 2000
Pratt Allan Duncan	New Court Chambers, London	0171 831 9500
Price Miss Katharine Clare Harding	4 Paper Buildings, London	0171 353 3366/583 7155
Price Richard Mervyn	Littleton Chambers, London	0171 797 8600
Priday Charles Nicholas Bruton	S Tomlinson QC, London	0171 583 0404
Proudman Miss Sonia Rosemary Susan	Chambers of Mr Peter Crampin QC, London	020 7831 0081
Pulman George Frederick	Hardwicke Building, London	020 7242 2523
	Stour Chambers, Canterbury	01227 764899
Purchas Christopher Patrick Brooks	Two Crown Office Row, London	020 7797 8100
Purchas Robin Michael	• 2 Harcourt Buildings, London	020 7353 8415
Purkis Ms Kathryn Miranda	Serle Court Chambers, London	0171 242 6105
Purves Gavin Bowman	Swan House, London	0181 998 3035
Pusey William James	St Philip's Chambers, Birmingham	0121 246 7000
Quest David Charles	3 Verulam Buildings, London	0171 831 8441
Qureshi Khawar Mehmood	One Hare Court, London	020 7353 3171
Radevsky Anthony Eric	Falcon Chambers, London	0171 353 2484
Raeside Mark Andrew	Atkin Chambers, London	020 7404 0102

• Expanded entry in Part D

Rai Amarjit Singh	St Philip's Chambers, Birmingham	0121 246 7000
Rainey Philip Carslake	2nd Floor, Francis Taylor Building, London	0171 353 9942/3157
Randall John Yeoman	St Philip's Chambers, Birmingham	0121 246 7000
	7 Stone Buildings, London	0171 405 3886/242 3546
Rashid Omar	Chambers of Mr Peter Crampin QC, London	020 7831 0081
Rawley Miss Dominique Jane	Atkin Chambers, London	020 7404 0102
Raybaud Mrs June Rose	96 Gray's Inn Road, London	0171 405 0585
Readhead Simon John Howard	No. 1 Serjeants' Inn, London	0171 415 6666
Readings Douglas George	St Philip's Chambers, Birmingham	0121 246 7000
Rees David Benjamin	5 Stone Buildings, London	0171 242 6201
Reese Colin Edward	Atkin Chambers, London	020 7404 0102
Reid Graham Matthew	4 Paper Buildings, London	0171 353 3366/583 7155
Reid Paul William	13 King's Bench Walk, London	0171 353 7204
	King's Bench Chambers, Oxford	01865 311066
Renfree Peter Gerald Stanley	Harbour Court Chambers, Fareham	01329 827828
Reynolds Professor Francis Martin Baillie	S Tomlinson QC, London	0171 583 0404
Rich Miss Ann Barbara	5 Stone Buildings, London	0171 242 6201
Rich Jonathan Bernard George	5 Paper Buildings, London	0171 583 9275/583 4555
Richardson David John	13 King's Bench Walk, London	0171 353 7204
	King's Bench Chambers, Oxford	01865 311066
Richardson Giles John	Serle Court Chambers, London	0171 242 6105
Rigney Andrew James	Two Crown Office Row, London	020 7797 8100
Ritchie Andrew George	9 Gough Square, London	020 7832 0500
Rivalland Marc-Edouard	No. 1 Serjeants' Inn, London	0171 415 6666
Roberts Jeremy Michael Graham	9 Gough Square, London	020 7832 0500
Rogers Miss Beverly-Ann	Serle Court Chambers, London	0171 242 6105
Rolfe Patrick John Benedict	5 Stone Buildings, London	0171 242 6201
Ross John Graffin	No. 1 Serjeants' Inn, London	0171 415 6666
Ross Martyn John Greaves	• 5 New Square, London	020 7404 0404
Roth Peter Marcel	Monckton Chambers, London	0171 405 7211
Rothery Peter	Queen's Chambers, Manchester	0161 834 6875/4738
	Queens Chambers, Preston	01772 828300
Rowland John Peter	4 Pump Court, London	020 7842 5555
Rowlands Marc Humphreys	4 Pump Court, London	020 7842 5555
Rowley Keith Nigel	11 Old Square, London	020 7430 0341
Royce Darryl Fraser	Atkin Chambers, London	020 7404 0102
Rumney Conrad William Arthur	St Philip's Chambers, Birmingham	0121 246 7000
Russell Christopher Garnet	• 12 New Square, London	0171 419 1212
	Sovereign Chambers, Leeds	0113 2451841/2/3
Ryder Ernest Nigel	Deans Court Chambers, Manchester	0161 214 6000
	Deans Court Chambers, Preston	01772 555163
	1 Mitre Court Buildings, London	0171 797 7070
Ryder Timothy Robert	Queen's Chambers, Manchester	0161 834 6875/4738
	Queens Chambers, Preston	01772 828300
Sabben-Clare Miss Rebecca Mary	S Tomlinson QC, London	0171 583 0404
Saggerson Alan David	Barnard's Inn Chambers, London	0171 369 6969
Salmon Jonathan Carl	1 Fountain Court, Birmingham	0121 236 5721
Saloman Timothy Peter (Dayrell)	S Tomlinson QC, London	0171 583 0404
Salter Richard Stanley	3 Verulam Buildings, London	0171 831 8441
Samuels Leslie John	Pump Court Chambers, London	0171 353 0711
	Pump Court Chambers, Winchester	01962 868161
	Pump Court Chambers, Swindon	01793 539899
Sandbrook-Hughes Stewert Karl Anthony	Iscoed Chambers, Swansea	01792 652988/9/330
Sandells Ms Nicole	11 Old Square, London	020 7430 0341
Saunt Thomas William Gatty	Two Crown Office Row, London	020 7797 8100
Schaff Alistair Graham	S Tomlinson QC, London	0171 583 0404
Searle Barrie	St James's Chambers, Manchester	0161 834 7000

• Expanded entry in Part D

Sears Robert David Murray	4 Pump Court, London	020 7842 5555
Seitler Jonathan Simon	• Wilberforce Chambers, London	0171 306 0102
Sellers Graham	Adrian Lyon's Chambers, Liverpool	0151 236 4421/8240
Semken Christopher Richard	1 New Square, London	0171 405 0884/5/6/7
Sendall Antony John Christmas	Littleton Chambers, London	0171 797 8600
Sephton Craig Gardner	Deans Court Chambers, Manchester	0161 214 6000
	Deans Court Chambers, Preston	01772 555163
Seymour Richard William	Monckton Chambers, London	0171 405 7211
Seymour Thomas Oliver	• Wilberforce Chambers, London	0171 306 0102
Shale Justin Anton	4 King's Bench Walk, London	0171 822 8822
	King's Bench Chambers, Bournemouth	01202 250025
Shannon Thomas Eric	Queen's Chambers, Manchester	0161 834 6875/4738
	Queens Chambers, Preston	01772 828300
Sheehan Malcolm Peter	2 Harcourt Buildings, London	0171 583 9020
Shepherd Nigel Patrick	8 King's Bench Walk North, Leeds	0113 2439797
	8 King's Bench Walk, London	0171 797 8888
Sher Jules	• Wilberforce Chambers, London	0171 306 0102
Shiels Ian	30 Park Square, Leeds	0113 2436388
Shillingford George Miles	Chambers of Mr Peter Crampin QC, London	020 7831 0081
Shukla Ms Vina	New Court Chambers, London	0171 831 9500
Shuman Miss Karen Ann Elizabeth	Bracton Chambers, London	0171 242 4248
Siddiqi Faizul Aqtab	Justice Court Chambers, London	0181 830 7786
Silvester Bruce Ross	Lamb Chambers, London	020 7797 8300
Simmonds Andrew John	5 Stone Buildings, London	0171 242 6201
Simpson Mark Taylor	4 Paper Buildings, London	0171 353 3366/583 7155
Sinclair Graham Kelso	East Anglian Chambers, Norwich	01603 617351
	East Anglian Chambers, Colchester	01206 572756
	East Anglian Chambers, Ipswich	01473 214481
Sinclair Miss Lisa Anne	7 New Square, London	0171 430 1660
Singh Kuldip	Five Paper Buildings, London	0171 583 6117
Skelly Andrew Jon	1 Gray's Inn Square, London	0171 405 8946/7/8
Smith Christopher Frank	Essex Court Chambers, London	0171 813 8000
Smith Howard James	Chambers of Mr Peter Crampin QC, London	020 7831 0081
Smith Miss Joanna Angela	• Wilberforce Chambers, London	0171 306 0102
Smith Ms Katherine Emma	Monckton Chambers, London	0171 405 7211
Smith Michael Joseph	8 King Street Chambers, Manchester	0161 834 9560
Smith Paul Andrew	One Hare Court, London	020 7353 3171
Smith Warwick Timothy Cresswell	Deans Court Chambers, Manchester	0161 214 6000
	Deans Court Chambers, Preston	01772 555163
Snowden John Stevenson	Two Crown Office Row, London	020 7797 8100
Southall Richard Anthony	• 17 Bedford Row, London	0171 831 7314
Southern Richard Michael	S Tomlinson QC, London	0171 583 0404
Southwell Richard Charles	One Hare Court, London	020 7353 3171
Spencer Martin Benedict	4 Paper Buildings, London	0171 353 3366/583 7155
Staddon Miss Claire Ann	12 New Square, London	0171 419 1212
	Sovereign Chambers, Leeds	0113 2451841/2/3
Staddon Paul	2nd Floor, Francis Taylor Building, London	0171 353 9942/3157
Stagg Paul Andrew	No. 1 Serjeants' Inn, London	0171 415 6666
Start Miss Angharad Jocelyn	3 Verulam Buildings, London	0171 831 8441
Staunton (Thomas) Ulick (Patrick)	Chambers of Mr Peter Crampin QC, London	020 7831 0081
	65-67 King Street, Leicester	0116 2547710
Sterling Robert Alan	St James's Chambers, Manchester	0161 834 7000
	12 New Square, London	0171 419 1212
	Park Lane Chambers, Leeds	0113 2285000
Stevens Howard Linton	1 Crown Office Row, London	0171 583 9292
Stevens-Hoare Miss Michelle	Hardwicke Building, London	020 7242 2523
Stevenson John Melford	Two Crown Office Row, London	020 7797 8100

• Expanded entry in Part D

Stewart Nicholas John Cameron	Hardwicke Building, London	020 7242 2523
Stewart-Smith William Rodney	1 New Square, London	0171 405 0884/5/6/7
Stockdale David Andrew	Deans Court Chambers, Manchester	0161 214 6000
	Deans Court Chambers, Preston	01772 555163
	9 Bedford Row, London	0171 242 3555
Stokell Robert	Two Crown Office Row, London	020 7797 8100
Storey Jeremy Brian	4 Pump Court, London	020 7842 5555
Streatfeild-James David Stewart	Atkin Chambers, London	020 7404 0102
Studer Mark Edgar Walter	Chambers of Mr Peter Crampin QC, London	020 7831 0081
Styles Clive Richard	Becket Chambers, Canterbury	01227 786331
Sutcliffe Andrew Harold Wentworth	3 Verulam Buildings, London	0171 831 8441
Swan Ian Christopher	Two Crown Office Row, London	020 7797 8100
Swerling Robert Harry	13 Old Square, London	0171 404 4800
Swindells Miss Heather Hughson	Chambers of Michael Pert QC, London	0171 421 8000
	Chambers of Michael Pert QC, Leicester	0116 249 2020
	Chambers of Michael Pert QC, Northampton	01604 602333
	St Philip's Chambers, Birmingham	0121 246 7000
Symons Christopher John Maurice	3 Verulam Buildings, London	0171 831 8441
Szanto Gregory John Michael	Eastbourne Chambers, Eastbourne	01323 642102
Taft Christopher Heiton	St James's Chambers, Manchester	0161 834 7000
Talbot Patrick John	Serle Court Chambers, London	0171 242 6105
Tatton-Brown Daniel Nicholas	Littleton Chambers, London	0171 797 8600
Taylor Miss Deborah Frances	Two Crown Office Row, London	020 7797 8100
Tedd Rex Hilary	• St Philip's Chambers, Birmingham	0121 246 7000
	De Montfort Chambers, Leicester	0116 254 8686
	Northampton Chambers, Northampton	01604 636271
Temple Anthony Dominic	4 Pump Court, London	020 7842 5555
Templeman Michael Richard	Southernhay Chambers, Exeter	01392 255777
	5 Stone Buildings, London	0171 242 6201
Tennet Michael John	• Wilberforce Chambers, London	0171 306 0102
Ter Haar Roger Eduard Lound	Two Crown Office Row, London	020 7797 8100
Terry Robert Jeffrey	8 King Street Chambers, Manchester	0161 834 9560
Thom James Alexander Francis	4 Field Court, London	0171 440 6900
Thomas Nigel Matthew	13 Old Square, London	0171 404 4800
Thompson Andrew Richard	Erskine Chambers, London	0171 242 5532
Thompson Patrick Miles	Queen's Chambers, Manchester	0161 834 6875/4738
	Queens Chambers, Preston	01772 828300
Ticciati Oliver	4 Pump Court, London	020 7842 5555
Tidmarsh Christopher Ralph Francis	5 Stone Buildings, London	0171 242 6201
Tillett Michael Burn	39 Essex Street, London	0171 832 1111
Tipples Miss Amanda Jane	13 Old Square, London	0171 404 4800
Todd Michael Alan	Erskine Chambers, London	0171 242 5532
Tolaney Miss Sonia	3 Verulam Buildings, London	0171 831 8441
Tomlinson Stephen Miles	S Tomlinson QC, London	0171 583 0404
Tozzi Nigel Kenneth	4 Pump Court, London	020 7842 5555
Trace Anthony John	• 13 Old Square, London	0171 404 4800
Travers Hugh	Pump Court Chambers, London	0171 353 0711
	Pump Court Chambers, Winchester	01962 868161
	Pump Court Chambers, Swindon	01793 539899
Treasure Francis Seton	199 Strand, London	0171 379 9779
Trippier Lady	Deans Court Chambers, Manchester	0161 214 6000
	Deans Court Chambers, Preston	01772 555163
Trotman Timothy Oliver	Deans Court Chambers, Manchester	0161 214 6000
	Deans Court Chambers, Preston	01772 555163
Tucker David William	Two Crown Office Row, London	020 7797 8100
Tully Ms Anne Margaret	Eastbourne Chambers, Eastbourne	01323 642102
Turnbull Charles Emerson Lovett	• Wilberforce Chambers, London	0171 306 0102
Turner Miss Janet Mary	3 Verulam Buildings, London	0171 831 8441

       • Expanded entry in Part D

Turner Mark George	Deans Court Chambers, Manchester	0161 214 6000
	Deans Court Chambers, Preston	01772 555163
Tyack David Guy	St Philip's Chambers, Birmingham	0121 246 7000
Ullstein Augustus Rupert Patrick A	• 29 Bedford Row Chambers, London	0171 831 2626
Valentine Donald Graham	Atkin Chambers, London	020 7404 0102
Van Tonder Gerard Dirk	1 New Square, London	0171 405 0884/5/6/7
Vaughan-Neil Miss Catherine Mary Bernardine	4 Pump Court, London	020 7842 5555
Vickers Miss Rachel Clare	199 Strand, London	0171 379 9779
Vickery Neil Michael	13 King's Bench Walk, London	0171 353 7204
	King's Bench Chambers, Oxford	01865 311066
Vineall Nicholas Edward John	4 Pump Court, London	020 7842 5555
Wadsworth James Patrick	4 Paper Buildings, London	0171 353 3366/583 7155
Walden-Smith Miss Karen Jane	5 Stone Buildings, London	0171 242 6201
Wales Andrew Nigel Malcolm	S Tomlinson QC, London	0171 583 0404
Walford Richard Henry Howard	Serle Court Chambers, London	0171 242 6105
Walker Steven John	Atkin Chambers, London	020 7404 0102
Wallace Ian Norman Duncan	Atkin Chambers, London	020 7404 0102
Warner David Alexander	1 New Square, London	0171 405 0884/5/6/7
Warnock Andrew Ronald	No. 1 Serjeants' Inn, London	0171 415 6666
Warnock-Smith Mrs Shan	5 Stone Buildings, London	0171 242 6201
Warren Nicholas Roger	• Wilberforce Chambers, London	0171 306 0102
Warrender Miss Nichola Mary	New Court Chambers, London	0171 831 9500
Waters Julian William Penrose	No. 1 Serjeants' Inn, London	0171 415 6666
Waters Malcolm Ian	• 11 Old Square, London	020 7430 0341
Watson James Vernon	3 Serjeants' Inn, London	0171 353 5537
Weatherill Bernard Richard	Chambers of Lord Goodhart QC, London	0171 405 5577
Weitzman Thomas Edward Benjamin	3 Verulam Buildings, London	0171 831 8441
West Mark	• 11 Old Square, London	020 7430 0341
West-Knights Laurence James	4 Paper Buildings, London	0171 353 3366/583 7155
Westgate Martin Trevor	Doughty Street Chambers, London	0171 404 1313
Weston Clive Aubrey Richard	Two Crown Office Row, London	020 7797 8100
Whipple Mrs Philippa Jane Edwards	1 Crown Office Row, London	0171 797 7500
Whitaker Steven Dixon	199 Strand, London	0171 379 9779
	Queens Square Chambers, Bristol	0117 921 1966
White Andrew	Atkin Chambers, London	020 7404 0102
White Matthew James	13 King's Bench Walk, London	0171 353 7204
	King's Bench Chambers, Oxford	01865 311066
Whitfield Adrian	3 Serjeants' Inn, London	0171 353 5537
Wicks Ms Joanne	• Wilberforce Chambers, London	0171 306 0102
Wilby David Christopher	• 199 Strand, London	0171 379 9779
	Park Lane Chambers, Leeds	0113 2285000
Wilkinson Nigel Vivian Marshall	Two Crown Office Row, London	020 7797 8100
Willer Robert Michael	Hardwicke Building, London	020 7242 2523
Williams Andrew Arthur	Adrian Lyon's Chambers, Liverpool	0151 236 4421/8240
Williams Ms Heather Jean	Doughty Street Chambers, London	0171 404 1313
Williamson Miss Bridget Susan	Enterprise Chambers, London	0171 405 9471
	Enterprise Chambers, Leeds	0113 246 0391
	Enterprise Chambers, Newcastle upon Tyne	0191 222 3344
Wilmot-Smith Richard James Crosbie	39 Essex Street, London	0171 832 1111
Wilson Ian Robert	3 Verulam Buildings, London	0171 831 8441
Wilson Stephen Mark	4 Field Court, London	0171 440 6900
Wilson-Barnes Miss Lucy Emma	St James's Chambers, Manchester	0161 834 7000
Wilton Simon Daniel	4 Paper Buildings, London	0171 353 3366/583 7155
Wood Ian Robert	8 King Street Chambers, Manchester	0161 834 9560
Wood Richard Gillies	20 Essex Street, London	0171 583 9294
	Cathedral Chambers (Jan Wood Independent Barristers' Clerk), Exeter	01392 210900
Wood Simon Edward	Plowden Buildings, London	0171 583 0808

Woods Jonathan	Two Crown Office Row, London	020 7797 8100
Woolf Steven Jeremy	Hardwicke Building, London	020 7242 2523
Worster David James Stewart	St Philip's Chambers, Birmingham	0121 246 7000
Wynter Colin Peter	Devereux Chambers, London	0171 353 7534
Wyvill Alistair	St Philip's Chambers, Birmingham	0121 246 7000
Yell Nicholas Anthony	No. 1 Serjeants' Inn, London	0171 415 6666
Yoxall Basil Joshua	Francis Taylor Building, London	0171 797 7250
Zaman Mohammed Khalil	St Philip's Chambers, Birmingham	0121 246 7000
Zelin Geoffrey Andrew	Enterprise Chambers, London	0171 405 9471
	Enterprise Chambers, Leeds	0113 246 0391
	Enterprise Chambers, Newcastle upon Tyne	0191 222 3344

PUBLIC INQUIRIES

Barker Brian John	Hollis Whiteman Chambers, London	020 7583 5766
Black Mrs Jill Margaret	30 Park Square, Leeds	0113 2436388

PUBLIC INTERNATIONAL

Cameron Jonathan James O'Grady	3 Verulam Buildings, London	0171 831 8441
Crawford Professor James Richard	3 Verulam Buildings, London	0171 831 8441
Evans James Frederick Meurig	3 Verulam Buildings, London	0171 831 8441
Gee Steven Mark	4 Field Court, London	0171 440 6900
Ghaffar Arshad	4 Field Court, London	0171 440 6900
Haynes Miss Rebecca	Monckton Chambers, London	0171 405 7211
Hughes Adrian Warwick	4 Pump Court, London	020 7842 5555
Jabati Miss Maria Hannah	2 Middle Temple Lane, London	0171 583 4540
Lasok Karol Paul Edward	Monckton Chambers, London	0171 405 7211
Lavender Nicholas	One Hare Court, London	020 7353 3171
Lever Jeremy Frederick	Monckton Chambers, London	0171 405 7211
Meeson Nigel Keith	4 Field Court, London	0171 440 6900
Nardell Gordon Lawrence	6 Pump Court, London	0171 797 8400
	6-8 Mill Street, Maidstone	01622 688094
Padfield Nicholas David	One Hare Court, London	020 7353 3171
Paines Nicholas Paul Billot	Monckton Chambers, London	0171 405 7211
Parker Kenneth Blades	Monckton Chambers, London	0171 405 7211
Pickup David Michael Walker	Peel Court Chambers, Manchester	0161 832 3791
Plender Richard Owen	• 20 Essex Street, London	0171 583 9294
Rashid Omar	Chambers of Mr Peter Crampin QC, London	020 7831 0081
Roth Peter Marcel	Monckton Chambers, London	0171 405 7211
Salter Richard Stanley	3 Verulam Buildings, London	0171 831 8441
Sands Mr Philippe Joseph	3 Verulam Buildings, London	0171 831 8441
Starmer Keir	Doughty Street Chambers, London	0171 404 1313
Vajda Christopher Stephen	Monckton Chambers, London	0171 405 7211

PUBLIC PROCUREMENT

Skilbeck Mrs Jennifer Seth	Monckton Chambers, London	0171 405 7211

PUBLIC RIGHTS OF WAY

Adamyk Simon Charles	12 New Square, London	0171 419 1212

REGULATORY TRIBUNALS

Marquand Charles Nicholas Hilary	Chambers of Lord Goodhart QC, London	0171 405 5577

RESTITUTION

West Mark	• 11 Old Square, London	020 7430 0341
Williams Leigh Michael	S Tomlinson QC, London	0171 583 0404

RIGHTS OF WAY

Davies Miss (Susan) Louise	12 New Square, London	0171 419 1212
	Sovereign Chambers, Leeds	0113 2451841/2/3

• Expanded entry in Part D

ROAD TRAFFIC

Dale Julian Charles Rigby	Eastbourne Chambers, Eastbourne	01323 642102
Thompson Lyall Norris	Tindal Chambers, Chelmsford	01245 267742

ROAD TRAFFIC OFFENCES

Grant Gary Steven	3 Temple Gardens, London	0171 583 1155

SALE AND CARRIAGE OF GOODS

Acton Stephen Neil	11 Old Square, London	020 7430 0341
Adkin Jonathan William	One Hare Court, London	020 7353 3171
Ali Miss Huma	Eastbourne Chambers, Eastbourne	01323 642102
Allen Michael David Prior	S Tomlinson QC, London	0171 583 0404
Althaus Antony Justin	No. 1 Serjeants' Inn, London	0171 415 6666
Ambrose Miss Clare Mary Geneste	20 Essex Street, London	0171 583 9294
Andrews Miss Claire Marguerite	Gough Square Chambers, London	0171 353 0924
Ashton David Sambrook	13 King's Bench Walk, London	0171 353 7204
	King's Bench Chambers, Oxford	01865 311066
Ashworth Piers	2 Harcourt Buildings, London	0171 583 9020
Ayres Andrew John William	13 Old Square, London	0171 404 4800
Bailey David John	S Tomlinson QC, London	0171 583 0404
Barker John Steven Roy	Queen's Chambers, Manchester	0161 834 6875/4738
	Queens Chambers, Preston	01772 828300
Basu Dr Dijendra Bhushan	Devereux Chambers, London	0171 353 7534
Bellamy Jonathan Mark	39 Essex Street, London	0171 832 1111
Berry Nicholas Michael	Southernhay Chambers, Exeter	01392 255777
	1 Gray's Inn Square, London	0171 405 8946/7/8
	22 Old Buildings, London	0171 831 0222
Bignall John Francis	S Tomlinson QC, London	0171 583 0404
Birch Miss Elizabeth Blanche	3 Verulam Buildings, London	0171 831 8441
Blackburn Mrs Elizabeth	4 Field Court, London	0171 440 6900
Blackwood Andrew Guy	4 Field Court, London	0171 440 6900
Blakesley Patrick James	Two Crown Office Row, London	020 7797 8100
Bowker Robert James	2nd Floor, Francis Taylor Building, London	0171 353 9942/3157
Boyd Stephen James Harvey	29 Bedford Row Chambers, London	0171 831 2626
Boyle Gerard James	No. 1 Serjeants' Inn, London	0171 415 6666
Brent Richard	3 Verulam Buildings, London	0171 831 8441
Bright Robert Graham	S Tomlinson QC, London	0171 583 0404
Browne-Wilkinson Simon	Serle Court Chambers, London	0171 242 6105
Bruce Andrew Jonathan	Serle Court Chambers, London	0171 242 6105
Bryant John Malcolm Cornelius	Barnard's Inn Chambers, London	0171 369 6969
Buck Dr Andrew Theodore	Chambers of Martin Burr, London	0171 353 4636
Buckingham Stewart John	4 Essex Court, London	020 7797 7970
Burnett Harold Wallace	4 Paper Buildings, London	0171 353 3366/583 7155
Burns Peter Richard	Deans Court Chambers, Manchester	0161 214 6000
	Deans Court Chambers, Preston	01772 555163
Butcher Christopher John	S Tomlinson QC, London	0171 583 0404
Butler Andrew	2nd Floor, Francis Taylor Building, London	0171 353 9942/3157
Calvert David Edward	St James's Chambers, Manchester	0161 834 7000
Cawley Neil Robert Loudoun	169 Temple Chambers, London	0171 583 7644
	Milton Keynes Chambers, Milton Keynes	01908 664 128
Chambers Jonathan	4 Essex Court, London	020 7797 7970
Collett Michael John	20 Essex Street, London	0171 583 9294
Collins Miss Jennifer Clair	Eastbourne Chambers, Eastbourne	01323 642102
Cooke Jeremy Lionel	S Tomlinson QC, London	0171 583 0404
Cooper Nigel Stuart	4 Essex Court, London	020 7797 7970
Corbett James Patrick	St Philip's Chambers, Birmingham	0121 246 7000
	Chambers of Andrew Campbell QC, Leeds	0113 2455438
Curtis Michael Alexander	Two Crown Office Row, London	020 7797 8100

● Expanded entry in Part D

Dalby Joseph Francis	Portsmouth Barristers' Chambers, Winchester	01962 863222
	Portsmouth Barristers' Chambers, Portsmouth	023 92 831292/811811
Davey Benjamin Nicholas	11 Old Square, London	020 7430 0341
Davey Michael Philip	4 Field Court, London	0171 440 6900
Davies Dr Charles Edward	4 Field Court, London	0171 440 6900
Davies Stephen Richard	8 King Street Chambers, Manchester	0161 834 9560
Davies-Jones Jonathan	3 Verulam Buildings, London	0171 831 8441
Dean Peter Thomas	1 Crown Office Row, London	0171 583 9292
Dillon Thomas William Matthew	1 Fountain Court, Birmingham	0121 236 5721
Dodd Christopher John Nicholas	9 Woodhouse Square, Leeds	0113 2451986
Dowley Dominic Myles	One Hare Court, London	020 7353 3171
Dugdale Nicholas	4 Field Court, London	0171 440 6900
Eadie James Raymond	One Hare Court, London	020 7353 3171
Eaton Turner David Murray	1 New Square, London	0171 405 0884/5/6/7
Edey Philip David	20 Essex Street, London	0171 583 9294
Edwards Richard Julian Henshaw	3 Verulam Buildings, London	0171 831 8441
Edwards-Stuart Antony James Cobham	Two Crown Office Row, London	020 7797 8100
Elliott Nicholas Blethyn	3 Verulam Buildings, London	0171 831 8441
Evans James Frederick Meurig	3 Verulam Buildings, London	0171 831 8441
Farber James Henry Martin	5 Stone Buildings, London	0171 242 6201
Farquharson Jonathan	Colleton Chambers, Exeter	01392 274898/9
Fenton Adam Timothy Downs	S Tomlinson QC, London	0171 583 0404
Fieldsend James William	2nd Floor, Francis Taylor Building, London	0171 353 9942/3157
Finn Terence	Chambers of Martin Burr, London	0171 353 4636
Flaux Julian Martin	S Tomlinson QC, London	0171 583 0404
Ford Gerard James	Baker Street Chambers, Middlesbrough	01642 873873
Forte Mark Julian Carmino	8 King Street Chambers, Manchester	0161 834 9560
Franco Gianpiero	2 Middle Temple Lane, London	0171 583 4540
Freedman Sampson Clive	3 Verulam Buildings, London	0171 831 8441
Gadney George Munro	Two Crown Office Row, London	020 7797 8100
Gaisman Jonathan Nicholas Crispin	S Tomlinson QC, London	0171 583 0404
Gasztowicz Steven	2-3 Gray's Inn Square, London	0171 242 4986
	2 New Street, Leicester	0116 2625906
Geary Gavin John	S Tomlinson QC, London	0171 583 0404
Gee Steven Mark	4 Field Court, London	0171 440 6900
Geering Ian Walter	3 Verulam Buildings, London	0171 831 8441
Gerald Nigel Mortimer	Enterprise Chambers, London	0171 405 9471
	Enterprise Chambers, Leeds	0113 246 0391
	Enterprise Chambers, Newcastle upon Tyne	0191 222 3344
Ghaffar Arshad	4 Field Court, London	0171 440 6900
Gibaud Miss Catherine Alison Annetta	3 Verulam Buildings, London	0171 831 8441
Goldstone David Julian	4 Field Court, London	0171 440 6900
Graham Thomas Patrick Henry	1 New Square, London	0171 405 0884/5/6/7
Grantham Andrew Timothy	• Deans Court Chambers, Manchester	0161 214 6000
	Deans Court Chambers, Preston	01772 555163
Green Miss Jane Elizabeth	Design Chambers, London	0171 353 0747
	Chambers of Martin Burr, London	0171 353 4636
Greenbourne John Hugo	Two Crown Office Row, London	020 7797 8100
Grodzinski Samuel Marc	39 Essex Street, London	0171 832 1111
Hamilton Adrian Walter	S Tomlinson QC, London	0171 583 0404
Hanson Timothy Vincent Richard	St Philip's Chambers, Birmingham	0121 246 7000
Hantusch Robert Anthony	• 3 Stone Buildings, London	0171 242 4937
Harris Melvyn	7 New Square, London	0171 430 1660
Harvey Michael Llewellyn Tucker	Two Crown Office Row, London	020 7797 8100
Havelock-Allan Anthony Mark David	20 Essex Street, London	0171 583 9294

     • Expanded entry in Part D

Hayward Peter Michael	The Outer Temple, London	0171 353 4647
Healy Miss Sioban	S Tomlinson QC, London	0171 583 0404
Hibbert William John	Gough Square Chambers, London	0171 353 0924
Higgins Adrian John	13 King's Bench Walk, London	0171 353 7204
	King's Bench Chambers, Oxford	01865 311066
Hodgkinson Tristram Patrick	• 5 Pump Court, London	020 7353 2532
Hodgson Timothy Paul	8 King Street Chambers, Manchester	0161 834 9560
Hofmeyr Stephen Murray	S Tomlinson QC, London	0171 583 0404
Holroyd Charles Wilfrid	S Tomlinson QC, London	0171 583 0404
Howard Michael Newman	4 Essex Court, London	020 7797 7970
Howarth Simon Stuart	Two Crown Office Row, London	020 7797 8100
Hurd James Robert	St James's Chambers, Manchester	0161 834 7000
James Michael Frank	Enterprise Chambers, London	0171 405 9471
	Enterprise Chambers, Leeds	0113 246 0391
	Enterprise Chambers, Newcastle upon Tyne	0191 222 3344
Kay Michael Jack David	3 Verulam Buildings, London	0171 831 8441
	Park Lane Chambers, Leeds	0113 2285000
Kay Robert Jervis	4 Field Court, London	0171 440 6900
Kealey Gavin Sean James	S Tomlinson QC, London	0171 583 0404
Kendrick Dominic John	S Tomlinson QC, London	0171 583 0404
Kenefick Timothy	S Tomlinson QC, London	0171 583 0404
Kenny Stephen Charles Wilfrid	S Tomlinson QC, London	0171 583 0404
Kerr Simon Alexander	S Tomlinson QC, London	0171 583 0404
Khan Anwar William	Eastbourne Chambers, Eastbourne	01323 642102
	Wessex Chambers, Reading	0118 956 8856
Khurshid Jawdat	S Tomlinson QC, London	0171 583 0404
Kolodziej Andrzej Jozef	• Littman Chambers, London	020 7404 4866
Kremen Philip Michael	Hardwicke Building, London	020 7242 2523
Kverndal Simon Richard	4 Essex Court, London	020 7797 7970
Kynoch Duncan Stuart Sanderson	29 Bedford Row Chambers, London	0171 831 2626
Lavender Nicholas	One Hare Court, London	020 7353 3171
Lowenstein Paul David	Littleton Chambers, London	0171 797 8600
Macdonald Charles Adam	4 Essex Court, London	020 7797 7970
MacDonald Iain	Gough Square Chambers, London	0171 353 0924
Malek Ali	3 Verulam Buildings, London	0171 831 8441
Males Stephen Martin	20 Essex Street, London	0171 583 9294
Mandalia Vinesh Lalji	Harrow on the Hill Chambers, Harrow-on-the-Hill	0181 423 7444
Marquand Charles Nicholas Hilary	Chambers of Lord Goodhart QC, London	0171 405 5577
Marshall Philip Scott	Serle Court Chambers, London	0171 242 6105
Marshall-Andrews Robert Graham	37 Park Square Chambers, Leeds	0113 2439422
	2-4 Tudor Street, London	0171 797 7111
Masters Miss Sara Alayna	20 Essex Street, London	0171 583 9294
Matthews Duncan Henry Rowland	20 Essex Street, London	0171 583 9294
Maynard-Connor Giles	St James's Chambers, Manchester	0161 834 7000
McClure Brian David	Littman Chambers, London	020 7404 4866
McGregor Harvey	4 Paper Buildings, London	0171 353 3366/583 7155
Meeson Nigel Keith	4 Field Court, London	0171 440 6900
Melville Richard David	• 39 Essex Street, London	0171 832 1111
Mercer David Paul	Queen's Chambers, Manchester	0161 834 6875/4738
	Queens Chambers, Preston	01772 828300
Milligan Iain Anstruther	20 Essex Street, London	0171 583 9294
Moore Mr Craig Ian	Barnard's Inn Chambers, London	0171 369 6969
	Park Lane Chambers, Leeds	0113 2285000
Moran Andrew John	One Hare Court, London	020 7353 3171
Morgan Richard Hugo Lyndon	13 Old Square, London	0171 404 4800
Naidoo Sean Van	Littman Chambers, London	020 7404 4866
Neville Stephen John	Gough Square Chambers, London	0171 353 0924
Neville-Clarke Sebastian Adrian Bennett	1 Crown Office Row, London	0171 583 9292

Nolan Michael Alfred Anthony	4 Essex Court, London	020 7797 7970
O'Shea Eoin Finbarr	4 Field Court, London	0171 440 6900
Ohrenstein Dov	Chambers of Lord Goodhart QC, London	0171 405 5577
Onslow Andrew George	3 Verulam Buildings, London	0171 831 8441
Owen David Christopher	20 Essex Street, London	0171 583 9294
Padfield Nicholas David	One Hare Court, London	020 7353 3171
Page Howard William Barrett	One Hare Court, London	020 7353 3171
Patchett-Joyce Michael Thurston	Monckton Chambers, London	0171 405 7211
Pearson Christopher	• Bridewell Chambers, London	020 7797 8800
Peirson Oliver James	Pump Court Chambers, London	0171 353 0711
	Pump Court Chambers, Winchester	01962 868161
	Pump Court Chambers, Swindon	01793 539899
Pelling (Philip) Mark	Monckton Chambers, London	0171 405 7211
Peretz George Michael John	Monckton Chambers, London	0171 405 7211
Persey Lionel Edward	• 4 Field Court, London	0171 440 6900
Pershad Rohan	Two Crown Office Row, London	020 7797 8100
Peterson Miss Geraldine Shelda	Lamb Building, London	020 7797 7788
Phillips Andrew Charles	Two Crown Office Row, London	020 7797 8100
Phillips S J	S Tomlinson QC, London	0171 583 0404
Picken Simon Derek	S Tomlinson QC, London	0171 583 0404
	30 Park Place, Cardiff	01222 398421
Piper Angus Richard	No. 1 Serjeants' Inn, London	0171 415 6666
Pirani Rohan Carl	Old Square Chambers, Bristol	0117 9277111
	Old Square Chambers, London	0171 269 0300
Pittaway David Michael	No. 1 Serjeants' Inn, London	0171 415 6666
Pope David James	3 Verulam Buildings, London	0171 831 8441
Price Albert John	23 Essex Street, London	0171 413 0353/836 8366
Price John Scott	10 Launceston Avenue, Reading	01189 479548
	Southsea Chambers, Portsmouth	01705 291261
	Cathedral Chambers, Newcastle upon Tyne	0191 232 1311
Qureshi Khawar Mehmood	One Hare Court, London	020 7353 3171
Reeder John	4 Field Court, London	0171 440 6900
Reid Graham Matthew	4 Paper Buildings, London	0171 353 3366/583 7155
Reynolds Professor Francis Martin Baillie	S Tomlinson QC, London	0171 583 0404
Richardson David John	13 King's Bench Walk, London	0171 353 7204
	King's Bench Chambers, Oxford	01865 311066
Richardson Giles John	Serle Court Chambers, London	0171 242 6105
Rigney Andrew James	Two Crown Office Row, London	020 7797 8100
Rogers Ian Paul	1 Crown Office Row, London	0171 583 9292
Rolfe Patrick John Benedict	5 Stone Buildings, London	0171 242 6201
Russell Jeremy Jonathan	• 4 Essex Court, London	020 7797 7970
Sabben-Clare Miss Rebecca Mary	S Tomlinson QC, London	0171 583 0404
Saggerson Alan David	Barnard's Inn Chambers, London	0171 369 6969
Salmon Jonathan Carl	1 Fountain Court, Birmingham	0121 236 5721
Saloman Timothy Peter (Dayrell)	S Tomlinson QC, London	0171 583 0404
Salter Richard Stanley	3 Verulam Buildings, London	0171 831 8441
Saunders Nicholas Joseph	4 Field Court, London	0171 440 6900
Schaff Alistair Graham	S Tomlinson QC, London	0171 583 0404
Scorah Christopher James	8 King Street Chambers, Manchester	0161 834 9560
Selvaratnam Miss Vasanti Emily Indrani	4 Field Court, London	0171 440 6900
Seymour Richard William	Monckton Chambers, London	0171 405 7211
Shale Justin Anton	4 King's Bench Walk, London	0171 822 8822
	King's Bench Chambers, Bournemouth	01202 250025
Skelly Andrew Jon	1 Gray's Inn Square, London	0171 405 8946/7/8
Smith Christopher Frank	Essex Court Chambers, London	0171 813 8000
Smith Miss Julia Mair Wheldon	Gough Square Chambers, London	0171 353 0924
Smith Michael Joseph	8 King Street Chambers, Manchester	0161 834 9560
Smith Paul Andrew	One Hare Court, London	020 7353 3171

• Expanded entry in Part D

Smith Warwick Timothy Cresswell	Deans Court Chambers, Manchester	0161 214 6000
	Deans Court Chambers, Preston	01772 555163
Snowden John Stevenson	Two Crown Office Row, London	020 7797 8100
Southall Richard Anthony	• 17 Bedford Row, London	0171 831 7314
Southern Richard Michael	S Tomlinson QC, London	0171 583 0404
Staddon Paul	2nd Floor, Francis Taylor Building, London	0171 353 9942/3157
Staunton (Thomas) Ulick (Patrick)	Chambers of Mr Peter Crampin QC, London	020 7831 0081
	65-67 King Street, Leicester	0116 2547710
Storey Jeremy Brian	4 Pump Court, London	020 7842 5555
Sullivan Scott	Barnard's Inn Chambers, London	0171 369 6969
Sutcliffe Andrew Harold Wentworth	3 Verulam Buildings, London	0171 831 8441
Swan Ian Christopher	Two Crown Office Row, London	020 7797 8100
Szanto Gregory John Michael	Eastbourne Chambers, Eastbourne	01323 642102
Taft Christopher Heiton	St James's Chambers, Manchester	0161 834 7000
Teare Nigel John Martin	4 Essex Court, London	020 7797 7970
Terry Robert Jeffrey	8 King Street Chambers, Manchester	0161 834 9560
Thomas (Robert) Neville	3 Verulam Buildings, London	0171 831 8441
Thornley David	Chambers of Martin Burr, London	0171 353 4636
Tomlinson Stephen Miles	S Tomlinson QC, London	0171 583 0404
Tselentis Michael	• 20 Essex Street, London	0171 583 9294
Tucker David William	Two Crown Office Row, London	020 7797 8100
Tully Ms Anne Margaret	Eastbourne Chambers, Eastbourne	01323 642102
Turner James Michael	• 4 Essex Court, London	020 7797 7970
Turner Miss Janet Mary	3 Verulam Buildings, London	0171 831 8441
Tyack David Guy	St Philip's Chambers, Birmingham	0121 246 7000
Vines Anthony Robert Francis	Gough Square Chambers, London	0171 353 0924
Wales Andrew Nigel Malcolm	S Tomlinson QC, London	0171 583 0404
Walford Richard Henry Howard	Serle Court Chambers, London	0171 242 6105
Waller Richard Beaumont	S Tomlinson QC, London	0171 583 0404
West-Knights Laurence James	4 Paper Buildings, London	0171 353 3366/583 7155
Weston Clive Aubrey Richard	Two Crown Office Row, London	020 7797 8100
Whitehouse-Vaux William Edward	4 Field Court, London	0171 440 6900
Williams Leigh Michael	S Tomlinson QC, London	0171 583 0404
Wilson Ian Robert	3 Verulam Buildings, London	0171 831 8441
Wood Ian Robert	8 King Street Chambers, Manchester	0161 834 9560
Wright Colin John	4 Field Court, London	0171 440 6900
Wynter Colin Peter	Devereux Chambers, London	0171 353 7534
Yoxall Basil Joshua	Francis Taylor Building, London	0171 797 7250
Zaman Mohammed Khalil	St Philip's Chambers, Birmingham	0121 246 7000

SCHOOL SITES

Turnbull Charles Emerson Lovett	• Wilberforce Chambers, London	0171 306 0102

SCIENTIFIC AND TECHNICAL DISPUTES

Colley Dr Peter McLean	• 19 Old Buildings, London	0171 405 2001

SHARE OPTIONS

Dougherty Nigel Peter	Erskine Chambers, London	0171 242 5532
Jones Philip John	Serle Court Chambers, London	0171 242 6105
Mandalia Vinesh Lalji	Harrow on the Hill Chambers, Harrow-on-the-Hill	0181 423 7444
Marquand Charles Nicholas Hilary	Chambers of Lord Goodhart QC, London	0171 405 5577
Milligan Iain Anstruther	20 Essex Street, London	0171 583 9294
Nugee Edward George	• Wilberforce Chambers, London	0171 306 0102
Potts Robin	Erskine Chambers, London	0171 242 5532
Sterling Robert Alan	St James's Chambers, Manchester	0161 834 7000
	12 New Square, London	0171 419 1212
	Park Lane Chambers, Leeds	0113 2285000
Sykes (James) Richard	Erskine Chambers, London	0171 242 5532

Terry Robert Jeffrey	8 King Street Chambers, Manchester	0161 834 9560
Walford Richard Henry Howard	Serle Court Chambers, London	0171 242 6105
Wyatt Michael Christopher	10 Winterbourne Grove, Weybridge	0181 941 3939

SHIPPING

McClure Brian David	Littman Chambers, London	020 7404 4866
Wood Richard Gillies	20 Essex Street, London	0171 583 9294
	Cathedral Chambers (Jan Wood	01392 210900
	Independent Barristers' Clerk), Exeter	

SHIPPING, ADMIRALTY

Allen Michael David Prior	S Tomlinson QC, London	0171 583 0404
Ambrose Miss Clare Mary Geneste	20 Essex Street, London	0171 583 9294
Bailey David John	S Tomlinson QC, London	0171 583 0404
Bignall John Francis	S Tomlinson QC, London	0171 583 0404
Birch Miss Elizabeth Blanche	3 Verulam Buildings, London	0171 831 8441
Blackburn Mrs Elizabeth	4 Field Court, London	0171 440 6900
Blackwood Andrew Guy	4 Field Court, London	0171 440 6900
Brenton Timothy Deane	4 Essex Court, London	020 7797 7970
Brice Geoffrey James Barrington	4 Field Court, London	0171 440 6900
Bright Robert Graham	S Tomlinson QC, London	0171 583 0404
Browne-Wilkinson Simon	Serle Court Chambers, London	0171 242 6105
Buckingham Stewart John	4 Essex Court, London	020 7797 7970
Butcher Christopher John	S Tomlinson QC, London	0171 583 0404
Chambers Jonathan	4 Essex Court, London	020 7797 7970
Collett Michael John	20 Essex Street, London	0171 583 9294
Cooke Jeremy Lionel	S Tomlinson QC, London	0171 583 0404
Cooper Nigel Stuart	4 Essex Court, London	020 7797 7970
Davey Michael Philip	4 Field Court, London	0171 440 6900
Davies Dr Charles Edward	4 Field Court, London	0171 440 6900
Drake James Frederick	S Tomlinson QC, London	0171 583 0404
Edey Philip David	20 Essex Street, London	0171 583 9294
Fenton Adam Timothy Downs	S Tomlinson QC, London	0171 583 0404
Flaux Julian Martin	S Tomlinson QC, London	0171 583 0404
Gaisman Jonathan Nicholas Crispin	S Tomlinson QC, London	0171 583 0404
Geary Gavin John	S Tomlinson QC, London	0171 583 0404
Gee Steven Mark	4 Field Court, London	0171 440 6900
Ghaffar Arshad	4 Field Court, London	0171 440 6900
Goldstone David Julian	4 Field Court, London	0171 440 6900
Hamilton Adrian Walter	S Tomlinson QC, London	0171 583 0404
Havelock-Allan Anthony Mark David	20 Essex Street, London	0171 583 9294
Healy Miss Sioban	S Tomlinson QC, London	0171 583 0404
Hill Timothy John	4 Field Court, London	0171 440 6900
Hofmeyr Stephen Murray	S Tomlinson QC, London	0171 583 0404
Holroyd Charles Wilfrid	S Tomlinson QC, London	0171 583 0404
Howard Michael Newman	4 Essex Court, London	020 7797 7970
Hughes Adrian Warwick	4 Pump Court, London	020 7842 5555
Kay Robert Jervis	4 Field Court, London	0171 440 6900
Kealey Gavin Sean James	S Tomlinson QC, London	0171 583 0404
Kendrick Dominic John	S Tomlinson QC, London	0171 583 0404
Kenefick Timothy	S Tomlinson QC, London	0171 583 0404
Kenny Stephen Charles Wilfrid	S Tomlinson QC, London	0171 583 0404
Kerr Simon Alexander	S Tomlinson QC, London	0171 583 0404
Khurshid Jawdat	S Tomlinson QC, London	0171 583 0404
Kverndal Simon Richard	4 Essex Court, London	020 7797 7970
Macdonald Charles Adam	4 Essex Court, London	020 7797 7970
Males Stephen Martin	20 Essex Street, London	0171 583 9294
Masters Miss Sara Alayna	20 Essex Street, London	0171 583 9294
Matthews Duncan Henry Rowland	20 Essex Street, London	0171 583 9294
Meeson Nigel Keith	4 Field Court, London	0171 440 6900
Melville Richard David	• 39 Essex Street, London	0171 832 1111

Milligan Iain Anstruther	20 Essex Street, London	0171 583 9294
Morgan Dr Austen Jude	3 Temple Gardens, London	0171 353 0832
Nolan Michael Alfred Anthony	4 Essex Court, London	020 7797 7970
O'Shea Eoin Finbarr	4 Field Court, London	0171 440 6900
Owen David Christopher	20 Essex Street, London	0171 583 9294
Persey Lionel Edward	• 4 Field Court, London	0171 440 6900
Phillips S J	S Tomlinson QC, London	0171 583 0404
Picken Simon Derek	S Tomlinson QC, London	0171 583 0404
	30 Park Place, Cardiff	01222 398421
Priday Charles Nicholas Bruton	S Tomlinson QC, London	0171 583 0404
Reeder John	4 Field Court, London	0171 440 6900
Reynolds Professor Francis Martin Baillie	S Tomlinson QC, London	0171 583 0404
Russell Jeremy Jonathan	• 4 Essex Court, London	020 7797 7970
Sabben-Clare Miss Rebecca Mary	S Tomlinson QC, London	0171 583 0404
Saloman Timothy Peter (Dayrell)	S Tomlinson QC, London	0171 583 0404
Saunders Nicholas Joseph	4 Field Court, London	0171 440 6900
Schaff Alistair Graham	S Tomlinson QC, London	0171 583 0404
Selvaratnam Miss Vasanti Emily Indrani	4 Field Court, London	0171 440 6900
Smith Christopher Frank	Essex Court Chambers, London	0171 813 8000
Southern Richard Michael	S Tomlinson QC, London	0171 583 0404
Stone Richard Frederick	4 Field Court, London	0171 440 6900
Teare Nigel John Martin	4 Essex Court, London	020 7797 7970
Thomas (Robert) Neville	3 Verulam Buildings, London	0171 831 8441
Tomlinson Stephen Miles	S Tomlinson QC, London	0171 583 0404
Tselentis Michael	• 20 Essex Street, London	0171 583 9294
Turner James Michael	• 4 Essex Court, London	020 7797 7970
Wales Andrew Nigel Malcolm	S Tomlinson QC, London	0171 583 0404
Waller Richard Beaumont	S Tomlinson QC, London	0171 583 0404
Whitehouse-Vaux William Edward	4 Field Court, London	0171 440 6900
Williams Leigh Michael	S Tomlinson QC, London	0171 583 0404
Wright Colin John	4 Field Court, London	0171 440 6900

SOCIAL SECURITY

Francois Herbert Dolton	Chambers of Herbert Francois, Mitcham	0181 640 4529
Mitchell Brenton Ballingtine	Bell Yard Chambers, London	0171 306 9292
Stagg Paul Andrew	No. 1 Serjeants' Inn, London	0171 415 6666

SOCIETY OF LLOYD'S

Child John Frederick	• Wilberforce Chambers, London	0171 306 0102

SOLICITORS' COSTS AND TAXATION

Lloyd Stephen James George	Chambers of Mr Peter Crampin QC, London	020 7831 0081

SOUTH AFRICAN LAW

Levin Craig Michael	Lancaster Building, Manchester	0161 661 4444/0171 649 9872

SPANISH LAW

Oakley Anthony James	• 11 Old Square, London	020 7430 0341

SPORTS

Akiwumi Anthony Sebastian Akitayo	Pump Court Chambers, London	0171 353 0711
	Pump Court Chambers, Winchester	01962 868161
	Pump Court Chambers, Swindon	01793 539899
Allen Michael David Prior	S Tomlinson QC, London	0171 583 0404
Anderson Rupert John	Monckton Chambers, London	0171 405 7211
Badenoch (Ian) James Forster	1 Crown Office Row, London	0171 797 7500
	Crown Office Row Chambers, Brighton	01273 625625

Baldock Nicholas John	6 Pump Court, London	0171 797 8400
	6-8 Mill Street, Maidstone	01622 688094
Beard Daniel Matthew	Monckton Chambers, London	0171 405 7211
Bellamy Jonathan Mark	39 Essex Street, London	0171 832 1111
Block Neil Selwyn	39 Essex Street, London	0171 832 1111
Booth Richard John	1 Crown Office Row, London	0171 797 7500
Boyd Stephen James Harvey	29 Bedford Row Chambers, London	0171 831 2626
Brodie (James) Bruce	39 Essex Street, London	0171 832 1111
Cakebread Stuart Alan Charles	• 2nd Floor, Francis Taylor Building, London	0171 353 9942/3157
Charlton Alexander Murray	4 Pump Court, London	020 7842 5555
Chudleigh Miss Louise Katrina	Old Square Chambers, London	0171 269 0300
	Old Square Chambers, Bristol	0117 9277111
Coghlan Terence	1 Crown Office Row, London	0171 797 7500
	Crown Office Row Chambers, Brighton	01273 625625
Driscoll Miss Lynn	Sovereign Chambers, Leeds	0113 2451841/2/3
Eastman Roger	2 Harcourt Buildings, London	0171 583 9020
Eccles David Thomas	8 King Street Chambers, Manchester	0161 834 9560
Fowler Richard Nicholas	Monckton Chambers, London	0171 405 7211
Gillibrand Philip Martin Mangnall	Pump Court Chambers, Winchester	01962 868161
	Pump Court Chambers, London	0171 353 0711
	Pump Court Chambers, Swindon	01793 539899
Glasgow Edwin John	39 Essex Street, London	0171 832 1111
Goudie James	• 11 King's Bench Walk, London	0171 632 8500/583 0610
Grayson Edward	• 9-12 Bell Yard, London	0171 400 1800
Harris Paul Best	Monckton Chambers, London	0171 405 7211
Haynes Miss Rebecca	Monckton Chambers, London	0171 405 7211
Hill Raymond	Monckton Chambers, London	0171 405 7211
Holdsworth James Arthur	Two Crown Office Row, London	020 7797 8100
Kay Robert Jervis	4 Field Court, London	0171 440 6900
Kempster Ivor Toby Chalmers	Old Square Chambers, Bristol	0117 9277111
	Old Square Chambers, London	0171 269 0300
Lasok Karol Paul Edward	Monckton Chambers, London	0171 405 7211
Lennard Stephen Charles	Hardwicke Building, London	020 7242 2523
Mackay Colin Crichton	39 Essex Street, London	0171 832 1111
Makey Christopher Douglas	Old Square Chambers, London	0171 269 0300
	Old Square Chambers, Bristol	0117 9277111
Malecka Dr Mary Margaret	• 3 Temple Gardens, London	0171 353 0832
	65-67 King Street, Leicester	0116 2547710
Marshall-Andrews Robert Graham	37 Park Square Chambers, Leeds	0113 2439422
	2-4 Tudor Street, London	0171 797 7111
Maxwell Richard	Ropewalk Chambers, Nottingham	0115 9472581
	Doughty Street Chambers, London	0171 404 1313
Melton Christopher	Peel Court Chambers, Manchester	0161 832 3791
	199 Strand, London	0171 379 9779
Mercer Hugh Charles	• Essex Court Chambers, London	0171 813 8000
Moore Mr Craig Ian	Barnard's Inn Chambers, London	0171 369 6969
	Park Lane Chambers, Leeds	0113 2285000
Morgan Richard Hugo Lyndon	13 Old Square, London	0171 404 4800
Nurse Gordon Bramwell William	11 Old Square, London	020 7430 0341
Oke Olanrewaju Oladipupo	Kingsway Chambers, London	07000 653529
Parker Kenneth Blades	Monckton Chambers, London	0171 405 7211
Patterson Stewart	Pump Court Chambers, Winchester	01962 868161
	Pump Court Chambers, London	0171 353 0711
	Pump Court Chambers, Swindon	01793 539899
Pershad Rohan	Two Crown Office Row, London	020 7797 8100
Rankin Andrew	4 Field Court, London	0171 440 6900
Rashid Omar	Chambers of Mr Peter Crampin QC, London	020 7831 0081
Roberts Michael Charles	1 New Square, London	0171 405 0884/5/6/7
Sendall Antony John Christmas	Littleton Chambers, London	0171 797 8600

Singh Kuldip	Five Paper Buildings, London	0171 583 6117
Stewart Nicholas John Cameron	Hardwicke Building, London	020 7242 2523
Talbot Patrick John	Serle Court Chambers, London	0171 242 6105
Thom James Alexander Francis	4 Field Court, London	0171 440 6900
Thompson Rhodri William Ralph	Monckton Chambers, London	0171 405 7211
Tillett Michael Burn	39 Essex Street, London	0171 832 1111
Trace Anthony John	• 13 Old Square, London	0171 404 4800
Trippier Lady	Deans Court Chambers, Manchester	0161 214 6000
	Deans Court Chambers, Preston	01772 555163
Tucker David William	Two Crown Office Row, London	020 7797 8100
Turner Jonathan Richard	Monckton Chambers, London	0171 405 7211
Ullstein Augustus Rupert Patrick A	• 29 Bedford Row Chambers, London	0171 831 2626
Vajda Christopher Stephen	Monckton Chambers, London	0171 405 7211
Weddle Steven Edgar	Hardwicke Building, London	020 7242 2523
Whitehouse-Vaux William Edward	4 Field Court, London	0171 440 6900
Wilson Stephen Mark	4 Field Court, London	0171 440 6900

SPORTS MEDICINE

Grayson Edward	• 9-12 Bell Yard, London	0171 400 1800

SPORTS – MOTOR RACING LAW

Gillibrand Philip Martin Mangnall	Pump Court Chambers, Winchester	01962 868161
	Pump Court Chambers, London	0171 353 0711
	Pump Court Chambers, Swindon	01793 539899

TAKEOVERS AND MERGERS

Wales Andrew Nigel Malcolm	S Tomlinson QC, London	0171 583 0404

TAX – CAPITAL AND INCOME

Akin Barrie Simon	Gray's Inn Tax Chambers, London	0171 242 2642
Anderson Miss Julie	• Littman Chambers, London	020 7404 4866
Angus Miss Tracey Anne	5 Stone Buildings, London	0171 242 6201
Baker Philip Woolf	Gray's Inn Tax Chambers, London	0171 242 2642
Birch Roger Allen	Sovereign Chambers, Leeds	0113 2451841/2/3
	12 New Square, London	0171 419 1212
Briden Richard John	96 Gray's Inn Road, London	0171 405 0585
Bryant Miss Judith Anne	• Wilberforce Chambers, London	0171 306 0102
Buck Dr Andrew Theodore	Chambers of Martin Burr, London	0171 353 4636
Burr Martin John	Chambers of Martin Burr, London	0171 353 4636
	7 New Square, London	0171 430 1660
Campbell Miss Emily Charlotte	• Wilberforce Chambers, London	0171 306 0102
Cannan Jonathan Michael	St James's Chambers, Manchester	0161 834 7000
	Broadway House Chambers, Bradford	01274 722560
	Broadway House Chambers, Leeds	0113 246 2600
Child John Frederick	• Wilberforce Chambers, London	0171 306 0102
Cosedge Andrew John	3 Stone Buildings, London	0171 242 4937
Crawford Grant	11 Old Square, London	020 7430 0341
Cullen Mrs Felicity Ann	Gray's Inn Tax Chambers, London	0171 242 2642
Davies The Rt Hon David John Denzil	96 Gray's Inn Road, London	0171 405 0585
	8 Gray's Inn Square, London	0171 242 3529
Farrow Kenneth John	Serle Court Chambers, London	0171 242 6105
Flesch Michael Charles	Gray's Inn Tax Chambers, London	0171 242 2642
Ginniff Nigel Thomas	Adrian Lyon's Chambers, Liverpool	0151 236 4421/8240
Goldberg David Gerard	Gray's Inn Tax Chambers, London	0171 242 2642
Goy David John Lister	Gray's Inn Tax Chambers, London	0171 242 2642
Green Brian Russell	Wilberforce Chambers, London	0171 306 0102
Grundy James Milton	Gray's Inn Tax Chambers, London	0171 242 2642
Harries Raymond Elwyn	Bracton Chambers, London	0171 242 4248
Harris David Raymond	Prince Henry's Chambers, London	0171 713 0376
Harrod Henry Mark	5 Stone Buildings, London	0171 242 6201

• Expanded entry in Part D

Henderson Launcelot Dinadan James	5 Stone Buildings, London	0171 242 6201
Herbert Mark Jeremy	• 5 Stone Buildings, London	0171 242 6201
Horne Roger Cozens-Hardy	Chambers of Mr Peter Crampin QC, London	020 7831 0081
Legge Henry	5 Stone Buildings, London	0171 242 6201
Mason Miss Alexandra	3 Stone Buildings, London	0171 242 4937
McDonnell Conrad Mortimer	Gray's Inn Tax Chambers, London	0171 242 2642
McKay Hugh Joseph Peter	Gray's Inn Tax Chambers, London	0171 242 2642
Nathan Miss Aparna	Gray's Inn Tax Chambers, London	0171 242 2642
Nugee Edward George	• Wilberforce Chambers, London	0171 306 0102
Oakley Anthony James	• 11 Old Square, London	020 7430 0341
Pearce Robert Edgar	Chambers of Mr Peter Crampin QC, London	020 7831 0081
Pilkington Mrs Mavis Patricia	9 Woodhouse Square, Leeds	0113 2451986
Rich Miss Ann Barbara	5 Stone Buildings, London	0171 242 6201
Rowell David Stewart	Chambers of Lord Goodhart QC, London	0171 405 5577
Shaw Miss Nicola Jane	Gray's Inn Tax Chambers, London	0171 242 2642
Southern David Boardman	• Temple Gardens Tax Chambers, London	0171 353 7884/5 8982/3
Tedd Rex Hilary	• St Philip's Chambers, Birmingham	0121 246 7000
	De Montfort Chambers, Leicester	0116 254 8686
	Northampton Chambers, Northampton	01604 636271
Thomas Nigel Matthew	13 Old Square, London	0171 404 4800
Tidmarsh Christopher Ralph Francis	5 Stone Buildings, London	0171 242 6201
Walters John Latimer	Gray's Inn Tax Chambers, London	0171 242 2642
Warnock-Smith Mrs Shan	5 Stone Buildings, London	0171 242 6201
Warren Nicholas Roger	• Wilberforce Chambers, London	0171 306 0102
Whiteman Peter George	Hollis Whiteman Chambers, London	020 7583 5766
Wyatt Michael Christopher	10 Winterbourne Grove, Weybridge	0181 941 3939

TAX – CORPORATE

Akin Barrie Simon	Gray's Inn Tax Chambers, London	0171 242 2642
Baker Philip Woolf	Gray's Inn Tax Chambers, London	0171 242 2642
Birch Roger Allen	Sovereign Chambers, Leeds	0113 2451841/2/3
	12 New Square, London	0171 419 1212
Briden Richard John	96 Gray's Inn Road, London	0171 405 0585
Burr Martin John	Chambers of Martin Burr, London	0171 353 4636
	7 New Square, London	0171 430 1660
Campbell Miss Emily Charlotte	• Wilberforce Chambers, London	0171 306 0102
Cannan Jonathan Michael	St James's Chambers, Manchester	0161 834 7000
	Broadway House Chambers, Bradford	01274 722560
	Broadway House Chambers, Leeds	0113 246 2600
Conlon Michael Anthony	• One Essex Court, London	020 7583 2000
Cullen Mrs Felicity Ann	Gray's Inn Tax Chambers, London	0171 242 2642
Davies The Rt Hon David John Denzil	96 Gray's Inn Road, London	0171 405 0585
	8 Gray's Inn Square, London	0171 242 3529
Flesch Michael Charles	Gray's Inn Tax Chambers, London	0171 242 2642
Ginniff Nigel Thomas	Adrian Lyon's Chambers, Liverpool	0151 236 4421/8240
Goldberg David Gerard	Gray's Inn Tax Chambers, London	0171 242 2642
Goy David John Lister	Gray's Inn Tax Chambers, London	0171 242 2642
Grundy James Milton	Gray's Inn Tax Chambers, London	0171 242 2642
Harries Raymond Elwyn	Bracton Chambers, London	0171 242 4248
Harris David Raymond	Prince Henry's Chambers, London	0171 713 0376
McDonnell Conrad Mortimer	Gray's Inn Tax Chambers, London	0171 242 2642
McKay Hugh Joseph Peter	Gray's Inn Tax Chambers, London	0171 242 2642
Nathan Miss Aparna	Gray's Inn Tax Chambers, London	0171 242 2642
Shaw Miss Nicola Jane	Gray's Inn Tax Chambers, London	0171 242 2642
Southern David Boardman	• Temple Gardens Tax Chambers, London	0171 353 7884/5 8982/3
Tedd Rex Hilary	• St Philip's Chambers, Birmingham	0121 246 7000
	De Montfort Chambers, Leicester	0116 254 8686
	Northampton Chambers, Northampton	01604 636271

• Expanded entry in Part D

Walters John Latimer	Gray's Inn Tax Chambers, London	0171 242 2642
Whiteman Peter George	Hollis Whiteman Chambers, London	020 7583 5766
Wyatt Michael Christopher	10 Winterbourne Grove, Weybridge	0181 941 3939

TAX INVESTIGATIONS

Rhodes Robert Elliott	4 King's Bench Walk, London	0171 822 8822

TELECOMMUNICATIONS

Abrahams James	8 New Square, London	0171 405 4321
Akenhead Robert	Atkin Chambers, London	020 7404 0102
Alexander Daniel Sakyi	8 New Square, London	0171 405 4321
Baatz Nicholas Stephen	Atkin Chambers, London	020 7404 0102
Baldwin John Paul	8 New Square, London	0171 405 4321
Barwise Miss Stephanie Nicola	Atkin Chambers, London	020 7404 0102
Blackburn John	Atkin Chambers, London	020 7404 0102
Bowdery Martin	Atkin Chambers, London	020 7404 0102
Briggs Michael Townley Featherstone	Serle Court Chambers, London	0171 242 6105
Burr Andrew Charles	Atkin Chambers, London	020 7404 0102
Clark Miss Fiona Jane Stewart	8 New Square, London	0171 405 4321
Clay Robert Charles	Atkin Chambers, London	020 7404 0102
Cole Richard John	Lancaster Building, Manchester	0161 661 4444/0171 649 9872
Collings Nicholas Stewart	Atkin Chambers, London	020 7404 0102
Dennison Stephen Randell	Atkin Chambers, London	020 7404 0102
Dennys Nicholas Charles Jonathan	Atkin Chambers, London	020 7404 0102
Doerries Miss Chantal-Aimee Renee Aemelia Annemarie	Atkin Chambers, London	020 7404 0102
Dumaresq Ms Delia Jane	Atkin Chambers, London	020 7404 0102
Fowler Richard Nicholas	Monckton Chambers, London	0171 405 7211
Fraser Peter Donald	Atkin Chambers, London	020 7404 0102
Fysh Michael	8 New Square, London	0171 405 4321
Goddard Andrew Stephen	Atkin Chambers, London	020 7404 0102
Godwin William George Henry	Atkin Chambers, London	020 7404 0102
Hamer George Clemens	8 New Square, London	0171 405 4321
Henderson Roger Anthony	2 Harcourt Buildings, London	0171 583 9020
Henley Raymond Francis St Luke	Lancaster Building, Manchester	0161 661 4444/0171 649 9872
Hofmeyr Stephen Murray	S Tomlinson QC, London	0171 583 0404
Howe Martin Russell Thomson	8 New Square, London	0171 405 4321
Howells James Richard	Atkin Chambers, London	020 7404 0102
Kelman Alistair Bruce	Lancaster Building, Manchester	0161 661 4444/0171 649 9872
Kitchin David James Tyson	8 New Square, London	0171 405 4321
Lambert John	Lancaster Building, Manchester	0161 661 4444/0171 649 9872
Lane Ms Lindsay Ruth Busfield	8 New Square, London	0171 405 4321
Lasok Karol Paul Edward	Monckton Chambers, London	0171 405 7211
Lazarus Michael Steven	1 Crown Office Row, London	0171 583 9292
Lever Jeremy Frederick	Monckton Chambers, London	0171 405 7211
Lofthouse Simon Timothy	Atkin Chambers, London	020 7404 0102
May Miss Charlotte Louisa	8 New Square, London	0171 405 4321
McCall Duncan James	4 Pump Court, London	020 7842 5555
McMullan Manus Anthony	Atkin Chambers, London	020 7404 0102
Meade Richard David	8 New Square, London	0171 405 4321
Mellor Edward James Wilson	8 New Square, London	0171 405 4321
Moody-Stuart Thomas	8 New Square, London	0171 405 4321
Nicholls John Peter	13 Old Square, London	0171 404 4800
Onslow Robert Denzil	8 New Square, London	0171 405 4321
Parkin Miss Fiona Jane	Atkin Chambers, London	020 7404 0102
Platts-Mills Mark Fortescue	8 New Square, London	0171 405 4321
Prescott Peter Richard Kyle	8 New Square, London	0171 405 4321
Raeside Mark Andrew	Atkin Chambers, London	020 7404 0102
Rawley Miss Dominique Jane	Atkin Chambers, London	020 7404 0102
Reese Colin Edward	Atkin Chambers, London	020 7404 0102
Roth Peter Marcel	Monckton Chambers, London	0171 405 7211

B

• Expanded entry in Part D

Royce Darryl Fraser	Atkin Chambers, London	020 7404 0102
Speck Adrian	8 New Square, London	0171 405 4321
St Ville Laurence James	8 New Square, London	0171 405 4321
Streatfeild-James David Stewart	Atkin Chambers, London	020 7404 0102
Swift John Anthony	Monckton Chambers, London	0171 405 7211
Tappin Michael John	8 New Square, London	0171 405 4321
Turner Jonathan Richard	Monckton Chambers, London	0171 405 7211
Valentine Donald Graham	Atkin Chambers, London	020 7404 0102
Vitoria Miss Mary Christine	8 New Square, London	0171 405 4321
Walker Steven John	Atkin Chambers, London	020 7404 0102
Wallace Ian Norman Duncan	Atkin Chambers, London	020 7404 0102
White Andrew	Atkin Chambers, London	020 7404 0102
Wilson Alastair James Drysdale	• 19 Old Buildings, London	0171 405 2001

TOWN AND COUNTRY PLANNING

Alesbury Alun	2 Mitre Court Buildings, London	0171 583 1380
Anderson Anthony John	2 Mitre Court Buildings, London	0171 583 1380
Barker John Steven Roy	Queen's Chambers, Manchester	0161 834 6875/4738
	Queens Chambers, Preston	01772 828300
Barnes (David) Michael (William)	•Wilberforce Chambers, London	0171 306 0102
Bates John Hayward	Old Square Chambers, London	0171 269 0300
	Old Square Chambers, Bristol	0117 9277111
Beard Mark Christopher	6 Pump Court, London	0171 797 8400
	6-8 Mill Street, Maidstone	01622 688094
Birtles William	Old Square Chambers, London	0171 269 0300
	Old Square Chambers, Bristol	0117 9277111
Boyle Christopher Alexander David	2 Mitre Court Buildings, London	0171 583 1380
Buck Dr Andrew Theodore	Chambers of Martin Burr, London	0171 353 4636
Burton Nicholas Anthony	2 Mitre Court Buildings, London	0171 583 1380
Cameron Neil St Clair	1 Serjeants' Inn, London	0171 583 1355
Clarkson Patrick Robert James	• 1 Serjeants' Inn, London	0171 583 1355
Daly David	Francis Taylor Building, London	0171 797 7250
Devlin Jonathan Nicholas Ponton	Park Court Chambers, Leeds	0113 2433277
Dineen Michael Laurence	Pump Court Chambers, Winchester	01962 868161
	Pump Court Chambers, London	0171 353 0711
	Queens Square Chambers, Bristol	0117 921 1966
	Pump Court Chambers, Swindon	01793 539899
Druce Michael James	2 Mitre Court Buildings, London	0171 583 1380
Fitzgerald Michael Frederick Clive	2 Mitre Court Buildings, London	0171 583 1380
Fookes Robert Lawrence	2 Mitre Court Buildings, London	0171 583 1380
Francis Andrew James	Chambers of Mr Peter Crampin QC, London	020 7831 0081
Furber (Robert) John	•Wilberforce Chambers, London	0171 306 0102
Gasztowicz Steven	2-3 Gray's Inn Square, London	0171 242 4986
	2 New Street, Leicester	0116 2625906
Glover Richard Michael	2 Mitre Court Buildings, London	0171 583 1380
Haigh Martin James	30 Park Square, Leeds	0113 2436388
Harrison Peter John	6 Pump Court, London	0171 797 8400
	6-8 Mill Street, Maidstone	01622 688094
Harwood Richard John	1 Serjeants' Inn, London	0171 583 1355
Hill Nicholas Mark	•Pump Court Chambers, London	0171 353 0711
	Pump Court Chambers, Winchester	01962 868161
	Pump Court Chambers, Swindon	01793 539899
Hill Piers Nicholas	37 Park Square Chambers, Leeds	0113 2439422
Hockman Stephen Alexander	•6 Pump Court, London	0171 797 8400
	6-8 Mill Street, Maidstone	01622 688094
Hodgson Timothy Paul	8 King Street Chambers, Manchester	0161 834 9560
Horton Matthew Bethell	2 Mitre Court Buildings, London	0171 583 1380
Howell Williams Craig	2 Harcourt Buildings, London	020 7353 8415
Humphries Michael John	2 Mitre Court Buildings, London	0171 583 1380
Jackson Nicholas David Kingsley	Adrian Lyon's Chambers, Liverpool	0151 236 4421/8240

• Expanded entry in Part D

Jefferis Arthur Michael Quentin	Chambers of Mr Peter Crampin QC, London	020 7831 0081
Jones Timothy Arthur	• St Philip's Chambers, Birmingham	0121 246 7000
	Arden Chambers, London	020 7242 4244
Karas Jonathan Marcus	• Wilberforce Chambers, London	0171 306 0102
King Neil Gerald Alexander	2 Mitre Court Buildings, London	0171 583 1380
Kremen Philip Michael	Hardwicke Building, London	020 7242 2523
Langham Richard Geoffrey	1 Serjeants' Inn, London	0171 583 1355
Leigh Kevin	6 Pump Court, London	0171 797 8400
	Regency Chambers, Peterborough	01733 315215
	Westgate Chambers, Lewes	01273 480510
	6-8 Mill Street, Maidstone	01622 688094
Lewis Robert	11 Bolt Court (also at 7 Stone Buildings – 1st Floor), London	0171 353 2300
	7 Stone Buildings (also at 11 Bolt Court), London	0171 242 0961
	Redhill Chambers, Redhill	01737 780781
Lyness Scott Edward	1 Serjeants' Inn, London	0171 583 1355
Macpherson The Hon Mary Stewart	2 Mitre Court Buildings, London	0171 583 1380
Mainwaring [Robert] Paul Clason	Carmarthen Chambers, Carmarthen	01267 234410
Maxwell Richard	Ropewalk Chambers, Nottingham	0115 9472581
	Doughty Street Chambers, London	0171 404 1313
Moore Professor Victor William Edward	2 Mitre Court Buildings, London	0171 583 1380
Moriarty Gerald Evelyn	2 Mitre Court Buildings, London	0171 583 1380
Nall-Cain The Hon Richard Christopher Philip	St Albans Chambers, St Albans	01727 843383
Newcombe Andrew Bennett	2 Harcourt Buildings, London	020 7353 8415
Ornsby Miss Suzanne Doreen	2 Harcourt Buildings, London	020 7353 8415
Pereira James Alexander	2 Harcourt Buildings, London	020 7353 8415
Phillpot Hereward Lindon	2 Harcourt Buildings, London	020 7353 8415
Pickles Simon Robert	1 Serjeants' Inn, London	0171 583 1355
Purchas Robin Michael	• 2 Harcourt Buildings, London	020 7353 8415
Randall John Yeoman	St Philip's Chambers, Birmingham	0121 246 7000
	7 Stone Buildings, London	0171 405 3886/242 3546
Raybaud Mrs June Rose	96 Gray's Inn Road, London	0171 405 0585
Roots Guy Robert Godfrey	2 Mitre Court Buildings, London	0171 583 1380
Rumney Conrad William Arthur	St Philip's Chambers, Birmingham	0121 246 7000
Salmon Jonathan Carl	1 Fountain Court, Birmingham	0121 236 5721
Sellers Graham	Adrian Lyon's Chambers, Liverpool	0151 236 4421/8240
Shannon Thomas Eric	Queen's Chambers, Manchester	0161 834 6875/4738
	Queens Chambers, Preston	01772 828300
Silsoe The Lord	2 Mitre Court Buildings, London	0171 583 1380
Spencer Paul Anthony	2 New Street, Leicester	0116 2625906
Spicer Robert Haden	Frederick Place Chambers, Bristol	0117 9738667
Stone Gregory	• 4-5 Gray's Inn Square, London	0171 404 5252
Straker Timothy Derrick	• 4-5 Gray's Inn Square, London	0171 404 5252
Symons Christopher John Maurice	3 Verulam Buildings, London	0171 831 8441
Tait Andrew Charles Gordon	2 Harcourt Buildings, London	020 7353 8415
Taylor John Charles	2 Mitre Court Buildings, London	0171 583 1380
Taylor Reuben Mallinson	2 Mitre Court Buildings, London	0171 583 1380
Tedd Rex Hilary	• St Philip's Chambers, Birmingham	0121 246 7000
	De Montfort Chambers, Leicester	0116 254 8686
	Northampton Chambers, Northampton	01604 636271
Thomas Miss Megan Moira	1 Serjeants' Inn, London	0171 583 1355
Wald Richard Daniel	2 Mitre Court Buildings, London	0171 583 1380
Walden-Smith Miss Karen Jane	5 Stone Buildings, London	0171 242 6201
Ward Trevor Robert Edward	17 Carlton Crescent, Southampton	023 8032 0320/0823 2003
Warren Rupert Miles	2 Mitre Court Buildings, London	0171 583 1380
Whybrow Christopher John	1 Serjeants' Inn, London	0171 583 1355
Widdicombe David Graham	2 Mitre Court Buildings, London	0171 583 1380

• Expanded entry in Part D

Wyatt Mark	2 New Street, Leicester	0116 2625906
Zwart Auberon Christiaan Conrad	1 Serjeants' Inn, London	0171 583 1355

TRADEMARKS

Abrahams James	8 New Square, London	0171 405 4321
Alexander Daniel Sakyi	8 New Square, London	0171 405 4321
Anderson Rupert John	Monckton Chambers, London	0171 405 7211
Baldwin John Paul	8 New Square, London	0171 405 4321
Bevis Dominic Joseph	10 King's Bench Walk, London	0171 353 7742
Chapple James Malcolm Dundas	1 New Square, London	0171 405 0884/5/6/7
Clark Miss Fiona Jane Stewart	8 New Square, London	0171 405 4321
Cogswell Miss Frederica Natasha	Gough Square Chambers, London	0171 353 0924
Cole Richard John	Lancaster Building, Manchester	0161 661 4444/0171 649 9872
Colley Dr Peter McLean	• 19 Old Buildings, London	0171 405 2001
Cook Christopher Graham	St James's Chambers, Manchester	0161 834 7000
Coulthard Alan Terence	33 Park Place, Cardiff	02920 233313
Dillon Thomas William Matthew	1 Fountain Court, Birmingham	0121 236 5721
Driscoll Miss Lynn	Sovereign Chambers, Leeds	0113 2451841/2/3
Fysh Michael	8 New Square, London	0171 405 4321
Gee Steven Mark	4 Field Court, London	0171 440 6900
Greatorex Ms Helen Louise	9 Woodhouse Square, Leeds	0113 2451986
Green Miss Jane Elizabeth	Design Chambers, London	0171 353 0747
	Chambers of Martin Burr, London	0171 353 4636
Hamer George Clemens	8 New Square, London	0171 405 4321
Heal Mrs Madeleine	4 Field Court, London	0171 440 6900
Henley Raymond Francis St Luke	Lancaster Building, Manchester	0161 661 4444/0171 649 9872
Hicks Michael Charles	• 19 Old Buildings, London	0171 405 2001
Holman Miss Tamsin Perdita	19 Old Buildings, London	0171 405 2001
Howe Martin Russell Thomson	8 New Square, London	0171 405 4321
Kelman Alistair Bruce	Lancaster Building, Manchester	0161 661 4444/0171 649 9872
Kitchin David James Tyson	8 New Square, London	0171 405 4321
Lambert John	Lancaster Building, Manchester	0161 661 4444/0171 649 9872
Lane Ms Lindsay Ruth Busfield	8 New Square, London	0171 405 4321
May Miss Charlotte Louisa	8 New Square, London	0171 405 4321
Meade Richard David	8 New Square, London	0171 405 4321
Mellor Edward James Wilson	8 New Square, London	0171 405 4321
Moody-Stuart Thomas	8 New Square, London	0171 405 4321
Onslow Robert Denzil	8 New Square, London	0171 405 4321
Pickering James Patrick	Enterprise Chambers, London	0171 405 9471
	Enterprise Chambers, Leeds	0113 246 0391
	Enterprise Chambers, Newcastle upon Tyne	0191 222 3344
Pickford Anthony James	Prince Henry's Chamber, London	0171 834 2572
Platts-Mills Mark Fortescue	8 New Square, London	0171 405 4321
Prescott Peter Richard Kyle	8 New Square, London	0171 405 4321
Puckrin Cedric Eldred	19 Old Buildings, London	0171 405 2001
Purves Gavin Bowman	Swan House, London	0181 998 3035
Reed Jeremy Nigel	19 Old Buildings, London	0171 405 2001
Reid Brian Christopher	19 Old Buildings, London	0171 405 2001
Shipley Norman Graham	• 19 Old Buildings, London	0171 405 2001
Speck Adrian	8 New Square, London	0171 405 4321
St Ville Laurence James	8 New Square, London	0171 405 4321
Sullivan Rory Myles	19 Old Buildings, London	0171 405 2001
Tappin Michael John	8 New Square, London	0171 405 4321
Vitoria Miss Mary Christine	8 New Square, London	0171 405 4321
Wilson Alastair James Drysdale	• 19 Old Buildings, London	0171 405 2001

TRAVEL AND HOLIDAY LAW

Chapman Matthew James	Barnard's Inn Chambers, London	0171 369 6969
Chapman Michael Andrew	Barnard's Inn Chambers, London	0171 369 6969
Saggerson Alan David	Barnard's Inn Chambers, London	0171 369 6969

• Expanded entry in Part D

Sethi Mohinderpal Singh	Barnard's Inn Chambers, London	0171 369 6969
Short Miss Anna Louise	Barnard's Inn Chambers, London	0171 369 6969
Sullivan Scott	Barnard's Inn Chambers, London	0171 369 6969
Thomson Dr David James Ramsay Gibb	Barnard's Inn Chambers, London	0171 369 6969
Warrender Miss Nichola Mary	New Court Chambers, London	0171 831 9500

TRIBUNALS/INQUIRIES

Ryder Ernest Nigel	Deans Court Chambers, Manchester	0161 214 6000
	Deans Court Chambers, Preston	01772 555163
	1 Mitre Court Buildings, London	0171 797 7070

UNIT TRUSTS

Burr Martin John	Chambers of Martin Burr, London	0171 353 4636
	7 New Square, London	0171 430 1660
Jones Philip John	Serle Court Chambers, London	0171 242 6105
Marquand Charles Nicholas Hilary	Chambers of Lord Goodhart QC, London	0171 405 5577
Minhas Ms Rafhat	Leone Chambers, London	0181 200 4020
Nugee Edward George	• Wilberforce Chambers, London	0171 306 0102
Potts Robin	Erskine Chambers, London	0171 242 5532
Sykes (James) Richard	Erskine Chambers, London	0171 242 5532

UTILITIES

Fowler Richard Nicholas	Monckton Chambers, London	0171 405 7211
Lever Jeremy Frederick	Monckton Chambers, London	0171 405 7211
Swift John Anthony	Monckton Chambers, London	0171 405 7211
Turner Jonathan Richard	Monckton Chambers, London	0171 405 7211

VAT

Gresty Miss Denise Lynn	Sovereign Chambers, Leeds	0113 2451841/2/3
Kent Michael Harcourt	Two Crown Office Row, London	020 7797 8100
Southern David Boardman	• Temple Gardens Tax Chambers, London	0171 353 7884/5 8982/3
Whipple Mrs Philippa Jane Edwards	1 Crown Office Row, London	0171 797 7500

VAT AND CUSTOMS & EXCISE

Anderson Rupert John	Monckton Chambers, London	0171 405 7211
Conlon Michael Anthony	• One Essex Court, London	020 7583 2000
Hall Mrs Melanie Ruth	Monckton Chambers, London	0171 405 7211
Harris Paul Best	Monckton Chambers, London	0171 405 7211
Haynes Miss Rebecca	Monckton Chambers, London	0171 405 7211
Hill Raymond	Monckton Chambers, London	0171 405 7211
Lasok Karol Paul Edward	Monckton Chambers, London	0171 405 7211
Macnab Alexander Andrew	Monckton Chambers, London	0171 405 7211
Mantle Peter John	Monckton Chambers, London	0171 405 7211
Paines Nicholas Paul Billot	Monckton Chambers, London	0171 405 7211
Parker Kenneth Blades	Monckton Chambers, London	0171 405 7211
Peretz George Michael John	Monckton Chambers, London	0171 405 7211
Smith Ms Katherine Emma	Monckton Chambers, London	0171 405 7211
Vajda Christopher Stephen	Monckton Chambers, London	0171 405 7211

VAT FRAUD

West Ian Stuart	Fountain Chambers, Middlesbrough	01642 804040

WARRANTY CLAIMS

Barker Simon George Harry	• 13 Old Square, London	0171 404 4800

WASTE MANAGEMENT

Sheridan Maurice Bernard Gerard	• 3 Verulam Buildings, London	0171 831 8441
Travers David	• 3 Fountain Court, Birmingham	0121 236 5854

• Expanded entry in Part D

WELFARE

Nicol Nicholas Keith	1 Pump Court, London	0171 583 2012/353 4341
Robinson Simon Robert	Chambers of Ian Macdonald QC (In	0161 236 1840
	Association with Two Garden Court,	
	Temple, London), Manchester	

• Expanded entry in Part D

Chambers of
Christopher Lockhart-Mummery QC

Property, Planning and Public Law

We aim to provide a consistently high quality of service to a wide range of clients in the private and public sectors in those areas of law in which we specialise.

Christopher Lockhart-Mummery QC	The Rt. Hon. Viscount Dilhorne
Nigel Macleod QC	David Smith
John Cherryman QC	Anne Seifert
David Hands QC	Anne Williams
The Rt. Hon. Lord Kingsland QC	Alice Robinson
Joseph Harper QC	David Elvin
John Howell QC	Timothy Mould
Richard Drabble QC	Nathalie Lieven
David Holgate QC	John Litton
Christopher Katkowski QC	Nicholas Taggart
Colin Sydenham	Karen McHugh
Stephen Bickford-Smith QC	David Forsdick
Eian Caws	Timothy Morshead
Robert Bailey-King	Graeme Keen
Christopher Lewsley	James Maurici
John Male	Alison Oakes

4 Breams Buildings
London EC4A 1AQ

Telephone: (0171) 430 1221, (0171) 353 5835
Fax: (0171) 430 1677

Email: breams@4breamsbuildings.law.co.uk
DX: 1042 Chancery Lane

Clerks: Stephen Graham and Jay Fullilove

2 PAPER BUILDINGS
BARRISTERS
Chambers of Desmond de Silva QC

Chambers of Desmond de Silva QC,' is one of the largest and longest-established sets in the Temple, specialising in criminal work and providing a complete service from the Magistrates Court upwards. This service includes the provision of counsel for overnight cases and cases at weekends and Bank Holidays. This service can be arranged by ringing an out of hours number (07860-416061 24 Hours).

Work Undertaken
Chambers is a specialist Criminal Defence set practising principally in white-collar fraud, terrorist cases, major drugs, sexual abuse and extradition cases. This set has a very long-standing Commonwealth connection acting in appeals to the Privy Council. The international flavour of Chambers is reflected in its diverse membership.

Members practice primarily within the criminal field, at all levels. Several members of Chambers also practice in the civil, family and immigration courts. This is a set that has always had a strong civil liberties tradition. In particular, several members of Chambers specialise in civil actions against the police, some of which have arisen out of criminal matters conducted by Chambers. The set is one of the very few Chambers in which the same barrister who conducted the criminal trial will deal with any subsequent civil action against the police.

Seminars
'2 Paper Buildings, Chambers of Desmond de Silva QC,' also present seminars on specialist areas of criminal law and these are open to all solicitors. Chambers is an accredited Law Society Course Provider. Recent topics have included: Human Rights Legislation, Disclosure and Civil Actions against the Police. Seminars are provided on suggested topics to individual firms of Solicitors.

'2 Paper Buildings, Chambers of Desmond de Silva QC,' aim to continue to improve the efficiency of their service for both lay and professional clients. Though a traditional Chambers they are approachable and at the forefront of the modernisation and technological changes that the Bar has experienced in recent times.

Senior Clerk: Robin Driscoll

Clerks: Stephen Ball, Lynn Pilkington and Joel Mason

Chambers Administrator and Fees Clerk: Marc Jennings
2 Paper Buildings, Temple, London EC4Y 7ET

Tel: 020 7556 5500 **Fax:** 020 7583 3423. **DX:** LDE 494
OUT OF HOURS 07860-416061

E-mail: clerks@2pbbarristers.co.uk
Internet: www.2pbbarristers.co.uk

Chambers by Location

This section lists chambers in England and Wales by the town or city in which they are located. The town/city names are in alphabetical order and under those main headings chambers are listed alphabetically, thus 7 King's Bench Walk would be listed before 4 Pump Court under London.

Information for each set of chambers includes full contact details. Some chambers have opted to include additional information about themselves in this part of the Directory. Additional information includes the names of barristers practising from that chambers, date chambers were established, opening times, chambers' facilities, languages spoken, details regarding fees and a list of the types of work undertaken including details of the number of counsel practising in each area. Please note that details of the types of work undertaken by those chambers which have chosen not to include this information in Part C may be found in *Part A Types of Work by Chambers*.

Note: For those chambers listed in this section, information has been supplied by the Bar Council and supplemented with information from chambers.

The following symbols indicate that barristers are:

† Recorders
‡ Assistant Recorders
* Door Tenants

C

C

CHAMBERS OF THELMA OSBORNE-HALSEY

North Eastern Law Chambers, 19 Augustus Drive, Alcester, Warwickshire B49 5HH
01789 766206
Fax: 01789 766211

Chambers of Mrs T E Osborne-Halsey

PRIMROSE CHAMBERS

5 Primrose Way, Alperton, Middlesex HA0 1DS
0181 998 1806

Chambers of Mr B P Sharma

BEDFORD CHAMBERS

2 Park Hill, Ampthill, Bedford MK45 2LW
0870 7337333
Fax: 0870 7337331; DX 36901 Ampthill
E-mail:
simonmichael@pilawyer.demon.co.uk
Out of hours telephone: 070 500 99557

Chambers of Simon Michael
Clerk: Elaine Duncan

Michael, Simon *1978*

CHAMBERS OF PAUL HOGBEN

199 Kingsworth Road, Ashford, Kent TN23 6NB
01233 645805
Fax: 01233 645805

Chambers of Mr P R Hogben

PULTENEY CHAMBERS

14 Johnstone Street, Bath, BA2 4DH
01225 723987
Fax: 01225 723989

Chambers of Miss L J Adams

GRANARY CHAMBERS

4 Glenleigh Park Road, Bexhill-On-Sea, East Sussex TN39 4EH
01424 733008
Fax: 01424 220064

Chambers of Mr T G Restell

COLERIDGE CHAMBERS

COLERIDGE Chambers

Citadel, 190 Corporation Street, Birmingham, B4 6QD
0121 233 8500
Fax: 0121 233 8501; DX 23503 Birmingham 3

Chambers of Mr S D Brand
Clerks: Bill Maynard, David Dobson

Brand, Simon *1973*	**Stelling,** Nigel *1987*
Andreae-Jones, William QC *1965*†	**Bond,** Richard *1988*
	Forsyth, Samantha *1988*
Clough, Geoffrey *1961*	**Hankin,** Jonas *1994*
Seconde, David *1968*	**Jenkins,** Martin *1994*
Grey, Michael *1975*	**Parker,** Alan *1995*
Morris, Christopher *1977*	**Loram,** Mary *1995*
Fisher, Andrew *1980*	**Jones,** Nicola *1996*
Brand, Rachel *1981*	**Western,** Adam *1997*
Nawaz, Amjad *1983*	**Harrington,** Timothy Mark *1997*
Butterworth, Martin *1985*	
Williams, Jeanette *1985*	**Knotts,** Carol Elaine *1996*

COMMONWEALTH CHAMBERS

354 Moseley Road, Birmingham, B12 9AZ
0121 446 5732

Chambers of Mr M A Rashid

C

EQUITY CHAMBERS

3rd Floor, 153a Corporation Street,
Birmingham, B4 6PH
0121 233 2100
Fax: 0121 233 2102; DX 23531 Birmingham
3

Chambers of Mohammed Latif

1 FOUNTAIN COURT

Steelhouse Lane, Birmingham, B4 6DR
0121 236 5721
Fax: 0121 236 3639; DX 16077 Birmingham
Out of hours telephone: 0836 322733

Chambers of D Crigman QC
Clerks: C T Hayfield, G Williams, P McNab,
P Jones

Crigman, David QC 1969†	**Ward**, Simon 1986
Morse, Malcolm 1967†	**Salmon**, Jonathan 1987
Hodgkinson, John 1968	**Thompson**, Blondelle 1987
Dudley, Michael 1972†	**Buxton**, Sarah 1988
Griffith-Jones, Richard 1974†	**Farrer**, Paul 1988
	Quirke, Gerard 1988
Busby, Thomas 1975	**Atkins**, Richard 1989
Millington, Christopher 1976†	**Puzey**, James 1990
	Thornett, Gary 1991
Harrison-Hall, Giles 1977	**Considine**, Paul 1992
Nicholls, Christopher 1978	**Johnston**, Anthony 1993
Conry, Michael 1979	**Smith**, Nicholas 1994
Inman, Melbourne QC 1979†	**Williams**, Thomas 1995
	Baker, Stuart 1995
Eyre, Stephen 1981	**Jones**, Carolyn 1995
Dillon, Thomas 1983	**Phillips**, Simon 1996
Evans, John 1983	**Smith**, Andrew 1997
Williams, Neal 1984	**Wallbanks**, Joanne 1997

3 FOUNTAIN COURT

Steelhouse Lane, Birmingham, B4 6DR
0121 236 5854
Fax: 0121 236 7008; DX 16079 Birmingham

Chambers of C M Treacy QC
Clerks: Jonathan Maskew (Senior Clerk),
Justin Luckman, Carl Streeting, Alex
Brown; Administrator: Jackie McNab

Treacy, Colman QC 1971†	**Jones**, David 1967†
Palmer, Anthony QC 1962†	**Faber**, Trevor 1970†
Andrews, Peter QC 1970†	**Chavasse**, Anne 1971
Juckes, Robert QC 1974†	**Arnold**, Peter 1972
McConville, Donald 1963	**Challinor**, Michael 1974†
Calderwood, Patricia 1964	**Parker**, Philip 1976‡

Thomas, Sybil 1976‡	**Hilder**, Carolyn 1991
Perks, Richard 1977	**Bailey**, Steven 1992
Darby, Patrick 1978	**Barnes**, Matthew 1992
Burrows, Michael 1979	**Lattimer**, Justine 1992
Warner, Anthony 1979	**Todd**, Susan Margaret 1991
Linnemann, Bernard 1980	**Kubik**, Heidi 1993
Engel, Anthony 1965	**Montgomery**, Kristina 1993
Travers, David 1981	**Harvey**, Simon 1994
Anderson, Mark 1983	**Jones**, Jonathan 1994
Bright, Christopher 1985	**Leader**, Tim 1994
Wall, Daryl 1985	**Butterfield**, John 1995
Jackson, Andrew 1986	**Chatterjee**, Adreeja 1997
Laird, Francis 1986	**Green**, Timothy Sinclair 1996
Mason, David 1986	
Duck, Michael 1988	**Isaacs**, Elizabeth 1998
Wallace, Andrew 1988	**Raggatt**, Timothy QC 1972*
Keeling, Adrian 1990	**Escott-Cox**, Brian QC 1954*

Types of work (and number of counsel practising in that area if supplied)
Banking 3 · Bankruptcy 3 · Care
proceedings 8 · Chancery (general) 3 ·
Chancery land law 3 · Commercial
litigation 6 · Common law (general) 12 ·
Company and commercial 6 · Crime 20 ·
Crime – corporate fraud 9 · Education 3 ·
Employment 5 · Environment 6 · Equity,
wills and trusts 6 · Family 8 · Family
provision 8 · Information technology 2 ·
Insolvency 6 · Intellectual property 3 ·
Landlord and tenant 4 · Licensing 3 · Local
government 3 · Medical negligence 6 ·
Partnerships 3 · Personal injury 12 ·
Professional negligence 6 · Sale and
carriage of goods 8 · Town and country
planning 4

Chambers established: 1913
Opening times: 8.30 am-6 pm

Chambers' facilities
Conference rooms, Disabled access

Languages spoken
French, German

Fees policy
Fees will be negotiated with the clerk
depending on the case but as a general
guide: under three years call £50–75 per
hour, three to five years call £50–100 per
hour, five to ten years £70–125 per hour.
Fees are negotiable with the clerk on a case
by case basis.

Bar Directory on the Internet
The Bar Directory is also available on
the Internet at the following address:
http://www.smlawpub.co.uk/bar

---

4 FOUNTAIN COURT

Steelhouse Lane, Birmingham, B4 6DR
0121 236 3476
Fax: 0121 200 1214; DX 16074 Birmingham

Chambers of Mr R M Wakerley QC

5 FOUNTAIN COURT

Steelhouse Lane, Birmingham, B4 6DR
0121 606 0500
Fax: 0121 606 1501; DX 16075 Birmingham
E-mail: clerks@5fountaincourt.law.co.uk
URL: http://www.5fountaincourt.law.co.uk
Out of hours telephone: 0374 298047

Chambers of Mr Anthony Barker QC, Mr Gareth Evans QC (Deputy Head)
Clerks: Tony McDaid (Practice Director), Sandra Astbury (PA); Practice Managers: Alan Smith, Patrick Hawkins (Senior Practice Managers)

Barker, Anthony QC 1966†
Stembridge, David QC 1955†
Kingston, Martin QC 1972†
Linehan, Stephen QC 1970†
Evans, Gareth QC 1973†
Oliver-Jones, Stephen QC 1970†
Wood, William QC 1970†
Lewis, Ralph QC 1978‡
West, John 1965
Whitaker, Stephen 1970
Dooley, Allan 1991†
Elsom, Michael 1972‡
Harvey, John 1973
Eades, Mark 1974‡
Cahill, Jeremy 1975
Giles, Roger 1976
Bealby, Walter 1976
Smallwood, Anne 1977
Rowland, Robin 1977
James, Christopher 1977
Iles, David 1977
O'Donovan, Kevin 1978
Bleasdale, Paul 1978†
Bush, Rosalind 1978
Draycott, Jean 1980
Newman, Timothy 1981

Brown, Stephanie 1982
Thompson, Neil 1982
Stephens, Michael 1983
McGrath, Andrew 1983
Hunjan, Satinder 1984
Stockill, David 1985
Lee, Richard 1993
Moat, Richard 1985
Dove, Ian 1986
Meyer, Lorna 1986
Thorogood, Bernard 1986
Heywood, Mark 1986
Drew, Simon 1987
Craig, Aubrey 1987
Oyebanji, Adam 1987
Crean, Anthony 1987
Hickey, Eugene 1988
Baker, Caroline 1988
Chadwick, Joanna 1988
Williams, Sara 1989
Duthie, Malcolm 1989
Liddiard, Martin 1989
Bedford, Becket 1989
Anning, Michael 1990
McDonald, Melanie 1990
Wynne, Ashley 1990
Bennett, Mary 1990
Baker, Andrew 1990

Radburn, Mark 1991
Friel, Michele 1991
Jones, Jennifer 1991
Wilson, Marion 1991
Reid, Howard 1991
O'Brien-Quinn, Hugh 1992
Park, David 1992
Goatley, Peter 1992
Xydias, Nicholas 1992
Wilkinson, Marc 1992
Preston, Nicola 1992
Richards, Hugh 1992
Hitching, Isabel 1992
Down, Jonathan 1993
Taylor, David 1993

Clover, Sarah 1993
Khalique, Nageena 1994
Price, Rachael 1994
Smallwood, Robert 1994
Cotter, Rachel 1994
Duffy, Joanne 1994
Potter, Anthony 1994
Diamond, Anna 1995
Mitchell, David 1995
Gilchrist, Naomi 1996
Wright, Jeremy 1996
Hogan, Emma 1996
Walsh, Michael 1996
Mayer, Tim 1997

Types of work (and number of counsel practising in that area if supplied)
Administrative · Agriculture · Arbitration · Asset finance · Banking · Bankruptcy · Care proceedings · Chancery (general) · Chancery land law · Civil liberties · Commercial · Commercial litigation · Commercial property · Common land · Common law (general) · Company and commercial · Competition · Construction · Consumer law · Conveyancing · Copyright · Corporate finance · Courts martial · Crime · Crime – corporate fraud · Defamation · Discrimination · EC and competition law · Education · Employment · Entertainment · Environment · Equity, wills and trusts · Family · Family provision · Financial services · Foreign law · Franchising · Housing · Immigration · Information technology · Insolvency · Insurance · Insurance/reinsurance · Intellectual property · International trade · Landlord and tenant · Licensing · Local government · Medical negligence · Mental health · Partnerships · Patents · Pensions · Personal injury · Planning · Probate and administration · Professional negligence · Sale and carriage of goods · Share options · Sports · Tax – capital and income · Tax – corporate · Town and country planning · Trademarks · Unit trusts

Opening times: 7.30 am-6.30 pm (Monday-Friday) (24-hour mobile phone answer-phone)

Chambers' facilities
Conference rooms, Video conferences, Disks accepted, Disabled access, Seminar suite

Languages spoken
French, German, Spanish

Fees policy

Up to five years call £65–100, Up to ten years call £100–125, Over ten years call £125–300. Chambers operate a flexible charging policy regularly agreeing pre-fixed budgets prior to work being undertaken for both advisory and court work. Chambers also offers competitive rates for Queens Counsel in civil work.

Additional information

5 Fountain Court, Birmingham is the largest set of barristers' chambers in the UK, with 83 members including nine Queen's Counsel. Within chambers we have six specialist practice groups, each with its own membership, group identity and head of group, co-ordinated under one administration team. Video conferencing and arbitration facilities are available within chambers, which is also committed to alternative dispute resolution.

Crime and licensing

The criminal group covers a broad area of criminal, licensing and administrative law, ranging from appearances before magistrates' courts and Crown Courts in England and Wales, to the specific demands of disciplinary, regulatory and appellate tribunals and to offering specialist skills in defence and prosecution cases involving complex fraud.

Planning

The town and country planning group has expanded from its Midlands base to its present nationwide client base which includes local planning, mineral and highway authorities, airport authorities, employed solicitors and barristers, planning consultancies, government agencies, foreign lawyers and governments in respect of overseas work. Chambers is instructed directly by members of The Royal Institution of Chartered Surveyors, The Royal Institute of British Architects and the Architects Registration Council of the UK.

Personal injury and medical negligence (including disaster injuries)

Members undertake litigation on behalf of plaintiffs and defendants and have extensive experience of asbestos-related injury, repetitive strain injury, industrial deafness, occupational asthma and respiratory disease, occupational cancer, dermatitis, vibration white finger as well as industrial accident claims, tetraplegic and paraplegic claims and those involving brain damage, major spinal injury and other injuries of the utmost severity. Counsel are also experienced in health and safety at work and medical negligence litigation on behalf of both plaintiffs and defendants.

Family

Counsel have considerable experience in financial provision on divorce, matrimonial finance, custody and access, co-habitation, family provision on death, adoption and wardship, property disputes between unmarried couples and registered homes tribunals.

Commercial and Chancery

Eighteen specialist counsel, virtually all commercial and Chancery work, contentious and non-contentious, including: general commercial litigation, real and personal property, probate, trusts, tax, banking, intellectual property, competition, EU, US commercial, competition and intellectual property law, emergency interlocutory applications, drafting applications and settling affidavits, advice upon enforcement and strategy, non-contentious drafting and consultative work.

Employment

Counsel specialise in matters involving redundancy, harassment, disablement and industrial injury, restraint of trade and safety of confidential information and wrongful and unfair dismissal, representing both employers and employees before tribunals and courts.

6 FOUNTAIN COURT

Steelhouse Lane, Birmingham, B4 6DR
0121 233 3282
Fax: 0121 236 3600; DX 16076 Birmingham
E-mail: clerks@sixfountain.co.uk

Chambers of Roger Smith QC

Clerk: M Harris

Smith, Roger QC 1972†	Desmond, Denis 1974
Hutt, Michael 1968	Quirke, James 1974
Mason, John 1971	Seddon, Dorothy 1974
Bown, Philip 1974	Gregory, Philip 1975‡

† Recorder ‡ Assistant Recorder *Door Tenant

Rickarby, William *1975*
Lowe, Anthony *1976*
Pitt-Lewis, Janet *1976*
Tucker, Andrew *1977*
Pittaway, Amanda *1980*
Somerville, Bryce *1980*
Davis, Jonathan *1983*
Cooke, Peter *1985*
Khangure, Avtar *1985‡*
Stenhouse, John *1986*
Tarbitt, Nicholas *1988*
Attwood, John *1989*
Davis, Simon *1990*

Price, Robert *1990*
Cadwaladr, Stephen *1992*
Shakoor, Tariq *1992*
Egan, Caroline *1993*
Marklew, Lee *1993*
Watson, David *1994*
Dunstan, James *1995*
Bushell, Terence *1982*
Swinnerton, David *1995*
Walker, Jane *1974**
Sapwell, Timothy *1997*
Borthwick, Lorna *1997*

wills and trusts 3 · Family 12 · Family provision 11 · Film, cable, TV 1 · Housing 1 · Immigration 2 · Insolvency 1 · Insurance 1 · Landlord and tenant 3 · Medical negligence 3 · Mental health 2 · Partnerships 3 · Personal injury 9 · Probate and administration 2 · Professional negligence 4 · Sale and carriage of goods 2 · Sports 1 · Town and country planning 1

Chambers established: 1974
Opening times: 8.30 am-6 pm

Chambers' facilities
Conference rooms, E-mail

Languages spoken
Bengali, Hindi, Punjabi, Urdu

Fees policy
Chambers offer very competitive rates, negotiated by experienced and efficient clerks of 25 years' standing.

8 FOUNTAIN COURT

Steelhouse Lane, Birmingham, B4 6DR
0121 236 5514/5
Fax: 0121 236 8225; DX 16078 Birmingham
E-mail: clerks@no8chambers.co.uk
URL: http://www.no8chambers.co.uk
Out of hours telephone: Emergency no: 01426 129889

Chambers of Ian Strongman TD
Clerks: Christina Maloney, Rosemarie Maloney

Strongman, Ian *1981*
Vaughan, Keith *1968*
Pirotta, Monica *1976*
White, Amanda *1976*
Murray, Stephen *1986*
Hickman, Sally *1987*
Starks, Nicholas *1989*
Hartley, Antony *1991*
Cowley, Robert *1992*
Sparrow, Julie *1992*

Mahmood, Abid *1992*
Dutta, Nandini *1993*
Clarke, Timothy *1992*
Mathews, Deni *1996*
Bugeja, Evelyn *1997*
Archer of Sandwell, Lord QC *1952**
Thomas of Gresford, Lord QC *1967**
Jones, Richard *1979**

Types of work (and number of counsel practising in that area if supplied)
Arbitration 4 · Bankruptcy 2 · Care proceedings 6 · Chancery (general) 1 · Chancery land law 1 · Civil liberties 1 · Commercial litigation 2 · Commercial property 1 · Common law (general) 11 · Company and commercial 3 · Construction 2 · Conveyancing 1 · Crime 8 · Discrimination 1 · Employment 3 · Equity,

NEW COURT CHAMBERS

Gazette Building, 168 Corporation Street, Birmingham, B4 6TZ
0121 693 6656
Fax: 0121 693 6657; DX 23533 Birmingham 3

Chambers of Thomas Kenning
Clerks: Patricia Walker (Senior Clerk), Zoe Owen (Junior Clerk); Chairman of Management Committee: Thomas Kenning

Kenning, Thomas *1989*
Birnbaum, Michael QC *1969**
Twana, Ekwall *1988*
Dhaliwal, Davinder *1990*
Billingham, Rex *1990*
Russell, Jenny *1990*
Sidhu-Brar, Nishan *1991*
Kalsi, Maninder *1992*

Kolodynski, Stefan *1993*
Brotherton, John *1994*
Ashton, Raglan *1994*
Crane, Suzanne *1995*
Kelly, Emma *1997*
Ranauta, Mani *1997*
de Mello, Rambert *1983**
Nduka-Eze, Chuck *1990**

ROWCHESTER CHAMBERS

4 Rowchester Court, Whittall Street, Birmingham, B4 6DH
0121 233 2327/2361951
Fax: 0121 236 7645; DX 16080 Birmingham

Chambers of Mr W A Harris

C

85 SPRINGFIELD ROAD

King's Heath, Birmingham, B14 7DU
0121 444 2818
Fax: 0121 247 6935; DX 10795 Moseley 1

Chambers of Mr A S J Bean

ST IVE'S CHAMBERS

Whittall Street, Birmingham, B4 6DH
0121 236 0863/5720
Fax: 0121 236 6961; DX 16072 Birmingham
E-mail:
stives.headofchambers@btinternet.com

Chambers of Mr E P Coke
*Clerks: Craig Jeavons (Senior Clerk),
Linda Butler (Senior Clerk);
Administrator: Lyndsey Hyde*

Coke, Edward *1976*	Mullen, Jayne *1989*
Macur, Julia QC *1979*	Maguire, Andrew *1988*
Hodgson, Margaret *1975*	Starks, Nicholas *1989*
Carr, Peter *1976*	Newman, Janet *1990*
Henderson, Roderick *1978*	Weston, Jeremy *1991*
Bladon, Kenneth *1980*	Haynes, Matthew *1991*
Berlin, Barry *1981*	Rogers, Gregory *1992*
Anthony, Peter *1981*	Dewsbery, Richard *1992*
Lopez, Paul *1982*	Schenkenberg, Barbara *1993*
Keehan, Michael *1982*	
Dismorr, Edward *1983*	Cole, Nicholas *1993*
McCann, John *1983*	Thomas, Ian *1993*
Grice, Peter *1984*	Hawkins, Lucy *1994*
Clarkson, Stuart *1987*	Cooper, Peter *1996*
Singleton, Michael *1987*	Walsh, Michael *1996*
Jackson, David *1986*	Pritchard, Sarah *1997*
Preen, Catherine *1988*	

ST PHILIP'S CHAMBERS

ST. PHILIP'S CHAMBERS

*Fountain Court, Steelhouse Lane,
Birmingham, B4 6DR*
0121 246 7000
Fax: 0121 246 7001; DX 16073 Birmingham

E-mail: clerks@st-philips.co.uk
URL: http://www.st-philips.co.uk
Out of hours telephone: A/A will divert to
clerk on duty

**Chambers of Rex Tedd QC, Deputies: John
Randall QC and Patrick McCahill QC**
*Clerks: Vincent Denham (Chief Executive),
Clive Witcomb (Chief Clerk), Matthew
Fleming, Richard Fowler, David Partridge
(Senior Clerks), Jenny Culligan, Su Gilbert,
Charles Jones, Marguerite Lawrence
(Clerks); Administrator: Linda Taylor*

Tedd, Rex QC *1970†*	Watts, Lawrence *1988*
Randall, John QC *1978†*	Cook, Alison *1989*
McCahill, Patrick QC *1975†*	Cox, Ailsa *1989*
Swindells, Heather QC *1974†*	Hanson, Timothy *1989*
	Pepperall, Edward *1989*
Davis, William QC *1975†*	Rai, Amarjit *1989*
Corbett, James QC *1975‡*	Beever, Edmund *1990*
Wilson, Martin QC *1963†*	Capon, Philip *1990*
Birts, Peter QC *1968†*	Meachin, Vanessa *1990*
Stokes, Michael QC *1971†*	Robotham, John *1990*
Newbold, Ronald *1965*	Lockhart, Andrew *1991*
Garrett, Michael *1967*	Evans, Lisa *1991*
Healy, Brian *1967*	George, Sarah *1991*
Price, John *1969†*	Lewis, Robin *1991*
Clarke, Peter *1970*	Samuel, Glyn *1991*
Readings, Douglas *1972‡*	Starkie, Claire *1991*
Cliff, Graham *1973*	Williams, Hugh *1992*
Jones, Timothy *1975*	de Waal, John *1992*
Spollon, Guy *1976*	Le Cornu, Philip *1992*
Pusey, William *1977*	Moseley, Julie *1992*
Cooper, Morris *1979*	Tucker, Katherine *1993*
Burbidge, James *1979‡*	Verduyn, Anthony *1993*
Thomas, Stephen *1980*	Owens, Jane *1994*
Dyer, Roger *1980*	Charman, Andrew *1994*
Worster, David *1980*	Rampersad, Devan *1994*
Shoker, Makhan *1981*	Walker, Elizabeth *1994*
Hershman, David *1981*	Burden, Angus *1994*
Mathew, Nergis-Anne *1981*	Carter, Rosalyn *1994*
Campbell, Stephen *1982*	Tyack, David *1994*
Hegarty, Kevin *1982*	Dean, Brian *1994*
Messling, Lawrence *1983*	Fox, Simon *1994*
Edwards, John *1983*	Fryer, Anthony *1995*
Haynes, Peter *1983*	MacDonald, Alistair *1995*
Starcevic, Petar *1983*	McCahey, Catherine *1996*
McCartney, Peter *1983*	Morgan, James *1996*
Rochford, Thomas *1984*	Cunningham, Claire *1996*
Powis, Samantha *1985*	McCabe, Louise *1996*
Zaman, Mohammed *1985*	Young, Alastair *1997*
Adams, Christopher *1986*	Leason, Karen *1997*
Cartwright, Nicolas *1986*	Wyvill, Alistair *1998*
Landes, Anna-Rose *1986*	Hotten, Christopher QC *1972**
Walters, Gareth *1986*	
Ashworth, Lance *1987*	McFarlane, Andrew QC *1977**
McGrath, Elizabeth *1987*	
Smail, Alastair *1987*	Lock, David MP *1985**
Rumney, Conrad *1988*	

Types of work (and number of counsel practising in that area if supplied)

Administrative 6 · Arbitration 2 · Aviation 1 · Banking 5 · Bankruptcy 13 · Care proceedings 21 · Chancery (general) 20 · Chancery land law 5 · Charities 1 · Commercial litigation 28 · Commercial property 5 · Common law (general) 28 · Company and commercial 17 · Construction 7 · Consumer law 5 · Conveyancing 1 · Courts martial 2 · Crime 44 · Crime – corporate fraud 16 · Discrimination 5 · EC and competition law 1 · Education 2 · Employment 16 · Entertainment 1 · Environment 8 · Equity, wills and trusts 8 · Family 29 · Family provision 18 · Film, cable, TV 1 · Franchising 2 · Housing 8 · Immigration 2 · Insolvency 19 · Insurance 16 · Landlord and tenant 14 · Licensing 11 · Medical negligence 30 · Partnerships 11 · Pensions 1 · Personal injury 33 · Planning 8 · Probate and administration 5 · Professional negligence 28 · Sale and carriage of goods 11 · Tax – capital and income 1 · Tax – corporate 1 · Town and country planning 9

Chambers established: 1998
Opening times: 8 am-6 pm

Chambers' facilities
Conference rooms, Disks accepted

Languages spoken
French, German, Italian, Punjabi, Spanish, Welsh

Additional information
St Philip's is the largest set of chambers in the country and is one of the UK's most broadly based set of chambers with considerable strength and depth. It has six practice groups, these being:

Chancery and Commercial
Criminal
Employment
Family
Personal Injury and Clinical Negligence
Property, Planning and Public Law

St Philip's also has expertise in a wide range of subjects including Licensing and General Common Law.

The combined premises at Fountain Court have been extensively refurbished to provide purpose-built conference rooms and arbitration facilities. These are complemented by extensive IT facilities. St Philip's provides a friendly service of the highest quality, and to this end our clerking team will always be pleased to assist with detailed information on the specialisations and availability of individual members of chambers. Chambers appointed a chief executive at the beginning of this year whose role is to ensure that all members and staff within chambers are responsive to the changing needs of our clients and committed to delivering the highest quality of service.

The large number of members and experience available means that we can offer flexibility without sacrificing the assurance of the case being dealt with in an appropriate manner by a specialist practitioner. Members have been involved in a large number of significant court cases.

Several members are active in academic writing and regular continuing education sessions are provided by the individual practice groups, both for members and others who wish to attend. Many carry solicitors' continuing professional development points.

VICTORIA CHAMBERS

3rd Floor, 177 Corporation Street, Birmingham, B4 6RG
0121 236 9900
Fax: 0121 233 0675; DX 23520 Birmingham 3
E-mail: viccham@aol.com

Chambers of Lee Masters
Clerks: Lisa Clarke, Patricia Venables

Masters, Lee *1984*	**Slater,** Julie *1988*
Nisbett, James *1973*	**Cook,** Gary *1989*
Migdal, Stephen *1974*	**Powell,** Richard *1991*
Pearson, David *1983*	**Thomas,** Dorothy *1991*
O'Gorman, Christopher *1987*	**Rowlands,** Catherine *1992*
	Lakin, Tracy *1993*

Garside, Mark *1993*
Thomas, Kate *1994*
Hawthorne, Patricia *1995*
Woolhouse, Oliver *1996*
Dubb, Tarlowchan *1997*
Beese, Nicola *1998*

KING'S BENCH CHAMBERS

Wellington House, 175 Holdenhurst Road, Bournemouth, Dorset BH8 8DQ
01202 250025
Fax: 01202 250026; DX 7617 Bournemouth

Chambers of William Andreae-Jones QC, Kenneth Cameron

3 PAPER BUILDINGS (BOURNEMOUTH)

THE CHAMBERS OF MICHAEL PARROY Q.C.

20 Lorne Park Road, Bournemouth, Dorset BH1 1JN
01202 292102
Fax: 01202 298498; DX 7612 Bournemouth
E-mail: Bournemouth@3paper.com

Chambers of M P Parroy QC
Clerks: Stephen Clark (Senior Clerk), Robert Leonard, Debbie Smyth, Hannah Stone

Annexe of: 3 Paper Buildings, Temple, London, EC4Y 7EU
Tel: 020 7583 8055
Fax: 020 7353 6271

Parroy, Michael QC *1969*
Harris, David QC *1969†*
Hughes, Peter QC *1971*
Jones, Stewart QC *1972†*
Aspinall, John QC *1971*
Parrish, Samuel *1962*
Solomon, Susan *1967*
Trevethan, Susan *1967*
Haynes, John *1968*
Swinstead, David *1970*
Aylwin, Christopher *1970*
Hope, Derwin *1970†*
Norman, Michael *1971†*
Curran, Leo *1972*
Jennings, Peter *1972*
Coleman, Anthony *1973*
Stephenson, Ben *1973*
Litchfield, Linda *1974*
Bartlett, David *1975†*
Richardson, Garth *1975*
Tyson, Richard *1975‡*
Henry, Peter *1977*
Mitchell, Nigel *1978*
Seed, Nigel *1978‡*
Kent, Peter *1978*
Partridge, Ian *1979*
Grey, Robert *1979*
Leviseur, Nicholas *1979*
Coombes, Timothy *1980*
Cairnes, Paul *1980*
Marshall, David *1981*
Edge, Ian *1981*
Strutt, Martin *1981*
Lickley, Nigel *1983*
Lomas, Mark *1983*
Maccabe, Irvine *1983*
Branigan, Kate *1984*
O'Hara, Sarah *1984*

Chamberlain, Francis *1985*
Sanderson, David *1985*
Bailey, Russell *1985*
Parker, Christopher *1986*
Hudson, Elisabeth *1987*
Letman, Paul *1987*
Rowland, Nicholas *1988*
Kelly, Patricia *1988*
Woolgar, Dermot *1988*
Hester, Paul *1989*
Opperman, Guy *1989*
Bradbury, Timothy *1989*
Killen, Geoffrey *1990*
Kilpatrick, Jean *1990*
Buckley-Clarke, Amanda *1991*
Ross, Iain *1991*
Steenson, David *1991*
Sweeney, Christian *1992*
Bingham, Tony *1992*
Kirkpatrick, Krystyna *1965*
Fitzharris, Ginnette *1993*
Clargo, John *1994*
Earle, Judy *1994*
Walter, Francesca *1994*
Reid, David *1994*
Williams, Ben *1994*
Sutherland Williams, Mark *1995*
Hughes, Melanie *1995*
McIlroy, David *1995*
Strachan, Elaine *1995*
Case, Richard *1996*
Kay, Dominic *1997*
Leech, Ben *1997*
Purdy, Catherine *1997*
Sullivan, Mark *1997*

BROADWAY HOUSE CHAMBERS

Broadway House, 9 Bank Street, Bradford, West Yorkshire BD1 1TW
01274 722560
Fax: 01274 370708; DX 11746 Bradford 1
E-mail: clerks@broadwayhouse.co.uk

Chambers of J Graham K Hyland QC
Clerk: Neil Appleyard

Also at: Broadway House Chambers, 31 Park Square West, Leeds LS1 2PF Tel: 0113 246 2600 Fax: 0113 246 2609

Hyland, Graham QC *1978†*
Mitchell, David *1972**
Wood, Martin *1973*
Topham, John *1970*
Thomas, Roger *1976†*
Newbon, Ian *1977*
Kelly, David *1980*
Shelton, Gordon *1981‡*
Gibson, Jonathan *1982‡*
McGonigal, David *1982*
Walker, Brian *1985*
Jones, David *1985*
Birkby, Peter *1987*
Howard, Ian *1987*
Askins, Nicholas *1989*
Wilson, Paul *1989*
Drake, Sophie *1990*
Fletton, Mark *1991*
Wood, Stephen *1991*
Khan, Tahir *1986*
Crosland, Ben *1993*
Hendron, Gerald *1992*
Colborne, Michelle *1993*
Nelson, Julia *1993*
Jamil, Aisha *1995*
Chaplain, Jayne *1995*
Peers, Nicola *1996*
Morland, Camille *1996*
Anderson, Simon Peter Bede *1997*
Blantern, Robert *1996*
Brown, Ian Keith Rae *1971*
Cannan, Jonathan *1989**

† Recorder ‡ Assistant Recorder *Door Tenant

THETFORD LODGE FARM

*Santon Downham, Brandon, Suffolk
IP27 OTU*
01842 813132

Chambers of J H Barnett

CHAMBERS OF LESLEY MITCHELL

*Stapleton Lodge, 71 Hamilton Road,
Brentford, Middlesex TW8 0QJ*
0181 568 2164
Fax: 0181 560 2798

Chambers of Ms L Mitchell

CROWN OFFICE ROW CHAMBERS

*Blenheim House, 120 Church Street,
Brighton, Sussex BN1 1WH*
01273 625625
Fax: 01273 698888; DX 36670 Brighton 2
E-mail: crownofficerow@clara.net
URL: http://www.onecrownofficerow.com

Chambers of R J Seabrook QC
*Clerks: Matthew Phipps, Jenny Lewis,
Natasha Brind; Chambers Director: Bob
Wilson*

Annexe of: 1 Crown Office Row, Ground
Floor, Temple, London, EC4Y 7HH
Tel: 0171 797 7500
Fax: 0171 797 7550

Seabrook, Robert QC 1964†	**Hart**, David 1982
Owen, Robert QC 1968†	**Garnham**, Neil 1982
Matheson, Duncan QC 1965†	**Waddicor**, Janet 1985
Badenoch, James QC 1968†	**Ross**, Jacqueline 1985
Miller, Stephen QC 1971†	**Smith**, Adam 1987
Coghlan, Terence QC 1968†	**Bergin**, Timothy 1987
Havers, Philip QC 1974†	**Rogers**, Paul 1989
Chambers, Gregory 1973	**Bishop**, Keeley 1990
Niblett, Anthony 1976†	**Downs**, Martin 1990
Bowron, Margaret 1978†	**Cave**, Jeremy 1992
Balcombe, David 1980	**Bugg**, Ian 1992
King-Smith, James 1980	**Colin**, Giles 1994
	Sinnatt, Simon 1993
	Smith, Sally-Ann 1996
	Balchin, Richard 1997

CHAMBERS OF DOMINIC DUDKOWSKI

7 White Street, Brighton, Sussex BN2 2JH
0973 314252
Fax: 01273 270599

Chambers of Mr D C Dudkowski

CHAMBERS OF ELIZABETH STEVENTON

50 Firle Road, Brighton, Sussex BN2 2YH
01273 670394
Fax: 01273 670394

Chambers of Mrs E A Steventon

SUSSEX CHAMBERS

9 Old Steine, Brighton, Sussex BN1 1FJ
01273 607953
Fax: 01273 571839; DX 2724 Brighton 1

Chambers of Mr P M Ashwell

ALBION CHAMBERS

Broad Street, Bristol, BS1 1DR
0117 9272144
Fax: 0117 9262569; DX 7822 Bristol

Chambers of Mr J C T Barton QC

ASSIZE COURT CHAMBERS

14 Small Street, Bristol, BS1 1DE
0117 9264587
Fax: 0117 9226835; DX 78134 Bristol
E-mail:
chambers@assize-court-chambers.co.uk

Chambers of J S Isherwood
*Clerks: Peter Nixon (Senior Clerk), Judith
Taylor (Junior Clerk)*

Tackaberry, John QC 1967*	**Robson**, John 1974*
Vere-Hodge, Michael QC 1970*†	**Waley**, Eric 1976
Isherwood, John 1978	**Ferguson**, Christopher 1979
Wood, Graeme 1968	**Rea**, Karen 1980
Wyatt, Jonathan 1973	**Evans**, Timothy 1982
	Curwen, David 1982
	Howells, Julian 1985

Wightwick, Iain *1985*
Sproston-Matthews, Lynne *1987*
Austins, Christopher *1988*
Levy, Robert *1988*
Halliday, Ian Nicolas *1989*
Ralph, Caroline *1990*
Langlois, Peter *1991*

Halliwell, Toby *1992*
Stanniland, Jonathan *1993*
Dawson, Judy *1993*
Hufford, Victoria *1994*
Marven, Robert *1994*
Atkinson, Jodie *1996*
Dawar, Archna *1996*
Currie, Fergus *1997*

THE CLOVE HITCH

High Street, Iron Acton, Bristol, BS37 9UG
01454 228243

Chambers of Mr H W Aplin

FREDERICK PLACE CHAMBERS

9 Frederick Place, Clifton, Bristol, BS8 1AS
0117 9738667
Fax: 0117 9738667

Chambers of Mr R H Spicer

GUILDHALL CHAMBERS

GUILDHALL
CHAMBERS

22-26 Broad Street, Bristol, BS1 2HG
0117 9273366
Fax: 0117 9303800; DX 7823 Bristol
E-mail:
civil.clerks@guildhallchambers.co.uk and
criminal.clerks@guildhallchambers.co.uk
Out of hours telephone: 0468 651334

Chambers of Mr A O Palmer QC
Clerks: Paul Fletcher (Head Clerk), James Turner, Justin Emmett, Lucy Northeast; Practice Manager: Robert Thomas (robert.thomas@guildhallchambers.co.uk)

Palmer, Adrian QC *1972†*
Royce, R John QC *1970†*
Glen, Ian QC *1973‡*
Gosland, Christopher *1966*
Barker, Kerry *1972*
Price, Louise *1972*
Newsom, George *1973*
Chippindall, Adam *1975†*

Corfield, Sheelagh *1975*
Barrie, Peter *1976‡*
Fenny, Ian *1978*
Watson, Brian *1978*
Pringle, Ian *1979‡*
Warner, Malcolm *1979*
Townsend, James *1980*
Duthie, Catriona *1981*

Wynne-Griffiths, Ralph *1981*
Blair, Peter *1983‡*
Davies, Stephen *1983*
Virgo, John *1983*
Langdon, Andrew *1986*
Smith, Richard *1986*
Maher, Martha *1987*
Bamford, Jeremy *1989*
French, Paul *1989*
Patrick, James *1989*
Davies, Robert *1990*
Dent, Stephen *1991*
Reddiford, Anthony *1991*

Peers, Heather *1991*
Ambrose, Euan *1992*
Quinlan, Christopher *1992*
Wales, Matthew *1993*
Miller, Nicholas *1994*
Farmer, Gabriel *1994*
Macfarlane, Andrew *1995*
Vigars, Anna Lilian *1996*
McMeel, Gerard Patrick *1993*
Worsley, Mark Indra *1994*
Collins, Rosaleen *1996*
Paton, Ewan William *1996*

OLD SQUARE CHAMBERS

OLD SQUARE CHAMBERS

Hanover House, 47 Corn Street, Bristol, BS1 1HT
0117 9277111
Fax: 0117 9273478; DX 78229 Bristol
E-mail: oldsqbri@globalnet.co.uk
URL: http://www.oldsquarechambers.co.uk
Out of hours telephone: 0973 330793

Chambers of Hon John Melville Williams QC, (John Hendy QC from Jan 2000)
Clerks: John Taylor, William Meade, Andrew York, Robert Bocock, Oliver Parkhouse, David Portch; Bristol Administrator: Sarah Hassall

Williams, The Hon John QC *1955†*
Hendy, John QC *1972*
Hand, John QC *1972†*
Wedderburn of Charlton, Lord QC *1953*
McMullen, Jeremy QC *1971‡*
Truscott, Ian QC (Scot) *1995*
Kelly, Matthias QC *1979*
Lewis, Charles *1963*
Carling, Christopher *1969*
Birtles, William *1970†*
Brahams, Diana *1972*
Bates, John *1973*
Cooksley, Nigel *1975*
Makey, Christopher *1975*
Pugh, Charles *1975*
Kempster, Toby *1980*
Rose, Paul *1981*

McNeill, Jane *1982*
Cotter, Barry *1985*
Chudleigh, Louise *1987*
Omambala, Ijeoma *1989*
Eady, Jennifer *1989*
Mead, Philip *1989*
Brown, Damian *1989*
Clarke, Jonathan *1990*
Gill, Tess *1990*
Walker, Christopher *1990*
Booth, Nicholas *1991*
Moor, Sarah *1991*
Scott, Ian *1991*
Segal, Oliver *1992*
Gower, Helen *1992*
Lewis, Prof Roy *1992*
Whitcombe, Mark *1994*
Melville, Elizabeth *1994*
Tether, Melanie *1995*
Smith, Emma *1995*
Pirani, Rohan *1995*

QUEEN SQUARE CHAMBERS

56 Queen Square, Bristol, BS1 4PR
0117 921 1966
Fax: 0117 927 6493; DX 7870 Bristol

Chambers of Mr T A Jenkins QC

ST JOHN'S CHAMBERS

Small Street, Bristol, BS1 1DW
0117 9213456/298514
Fax: 0117 9294821; DX 78138 Bristol
Other comms: Video Conference Number:
0117 922 1586
E-mail: @stjohnschambers.co.uk

Chambers of R L Denyer QC
Clerks: Richard Hyde, Maureen Rowe,
Annette Moles

Denyer, Roderick QC 1970†	**Duval,** Robert 1979
Hamilton, Nigel QC 1965	**Dixon,** Ralph 1980
Mann, Martin QC 1968	**Jacklin,** Susan 1980‡
Kaye, Roger QC 1970†	**Auld,** Charles 1980
Grumbar, Paul 1974	**Wadsley,** Peter 1984
Sharp, Christopher QC 1975	**Dixey,** Ian 1984
Bullock, Ian 1975	**Bromilow,** Richard 1977‡
Marston, Nicholas 1975‡	**Blohm,** Leslie 1982
Grice, Timothy 1975	**Hunter,** Susan 1985
Horton, Mark 1976‡	**Edwards,** Glyn 1987
Blackmore, John 1983	**Morgan,** Simon 1988
Longman, Michael 1978	**O'Neill,** Louise 1989
Stead, Richard 1979‡	**Corston,** Jean 1991

Levy, Neil 1986	**Humphreys,** Jacqueline 1994
Adams, Guy 1989	**Walker,** Bruce 1994
Evans, Susan 1989	**Doig,** Gavin 1995
Hopkins, Andrea 1992	**Lebasci,** Jetsun 1995
Sharples, John 1992	**Dickinson,** John 1995
Martin, Dianne 1992	**Evans,** Judi 1996
Light, Prof Roy 1992	**Goodman,** Simon 1996
Bateman, Christine 1992	**Das,** Kamala 1975
Burgess, Edward 1993	**Asplin,** Patrick Christopher 1997
Skellorn, Kathryn 1993	
Maunder, David 1993	**Lowe,** Prof Nigel 1972*
McLaughlin, Andrew 1993	

THEATRE HOUSE

Percival Road, Clifton, Bristol, BS8 3LE
0117 974 1553
Fax: 0117 974 1554

Chambers of Mr P Chadd QC

29 GWILLIAM STREET

Bristol, BS3 4LT
0117 966 8997
Fax: 0117 966 8997
E-mail: tthornhill@freeuk.com

Chambers of T Thornhill
Clerk: Self

Thornhill, Teresa 1986

VERITAS CHAMBERS

33 Corn Street, Bristol, BS1 1HT
0117 930 8802
Fax: 0117 930 8834; DX 133602 Bristol 1

Chambers of Mr N C Sweeney
Clerk: S Winschief

Sweeney, Noël 1975	**Hunter,** William Edward Henry 1982
Best, Stanley P 1989	
Penny, John Cornelius 1995	**Boyd,** Roland Philip 1997

HERONS REST

Parkham Lane, Brixham, Devon TQ5 9JR
01803 882293
Fax: 01803 852168

Chambers of Mr M A Furminger

C

BROMLEY CHAMBERS

39 Durham Road, Bromley, Kent BR2 OSN
0181 325 0863
Fax: 0181 325 1431; DX 40604 Beckenham

Chambers of E Georghiades

27 ROSE GROVE

Bury, Greater Manchester BL8 2UJ
0161 763 4739
Fax: 0161 763 4739

Chambers of Mr F A Chaudhry

PHYDEAUX CHAMBERS

*Dunelm, Mount Pleasant Road,
Camborne, Cornwall TR14 7RJ*
01209 715285
Fax: 01209 715285

Chambers of Mr A R Jopling

FENNERS CHAMBERS

3 Madingley Road, Cambridge, CB3 0EE
01223 368761
Fax: 01223 313007; DX 5809 Cambridge 1
E-mail: clerks@fennerschambers.co.uk
URL: http://www.fennerschambers.co.uk

Chambers of Lindsay Davies
*Clerks: Mark Springham, Louis Rankin,
Ian Spencer, Joanna Gray; Administrator:
Jane Longhurst*

Also at: Fenners Chambers, 8-12 Priestgate,
Peterborough PE1 1JA Tel: 01733 562030

Davies, Lindsay 1975‡	Brown, T C E 1980
Stokes, David QC 1968*†	Crimp, Michael 1980
King, Peter 1970	Hollow, Paul 1981
Sells, Oliver QC 1972*†	Gordon-Saker, Andrew
Hawkesworth, Gareth	1981
1972†	Bridge, Stuart 1981
Jones, Geraint 1972	Collier, Martin 1982
Gore, Andrew 1973	Gordon-Saker, Liza 1982
Franklin, Stephen 1974	Hughes, Meryl 1987
Espley, Susan 1976	Foxwell, George 1987
Pointon, Caroline 1976	Wilson, Alasdair 1988
Heald, Oliver 1977	Beasley-Murray, Caroline
Tattersall, Simon 1977	1988
Leigh-Morgan, Paul 1978	Pithers, Clive 1989

Meakin, Timothy 1989	Ferguson, Katharine 1995
Taylor, Andrew 1989	Josling, William 1995
Hobson, Sally 1991	Magee, Mike 1997
Horton, Caroline 1993	Spinks, Roderick 1997
Myatt, Charles 1993	

REGENCY CHAMBERS

*Sheraton House, Castle Park, Cambridge,
CB3 0AX*
01223 301517
Fax: 01223 359267; DX 12349
Peterborough 1

Chambers of R P Croxon QC

BECKET CHAMBERS

*17 New Dover Road, Canterbury, Kent
CT1 3AS*
01227 786331
Fax: 01227 786329; DX 5330 Canterbury

*Clerks: Miss Julie Lewis-Mackay, Miss Ellen
Maxwell*

Newton, Philip 1984	Tapsell, Paul 1991
Edginton, Ronald 1984	Adamson, Lilias Louisa
Jackson, Kevin Roy 1984	1994
Mills, Corey Arthur 1987	Fairbank, Nicholas 1996
Wall, Christopher 1987	Baxter-Phillips, Felicity
Hall, Jeremy John 1988	Dawn 1964
Styles, Clive Richard 1990	

**Types of work (and number of counsel practising in
that area if supplied)**
Bankruptcy 1 · Care proceedings 9 ·
Commercial 1 · Common law (general) 7 ·
Consumer law 2 · Crime 5 · Employment 4
· Environment 1 · Family 9 · Family
provision 7 · Landlord and tenant 4 ·
Licensing 2 · Local government 5 ·
Partnerships 1 · Personal injury 7 · Probate
and administration 2 · Professional

negligence 1 · Town and country planning 2

Chambers established: 1993
Opening times: Mon-Thurs: 8.30 am-5.45 pm, Fri: 8.30 am-5.30 pm

Chambers' facilities
Conference rooms, Disks accepted

Languages spoken
French

Fees policy
Up to five years call £50–75, Up to ten years call £65–100, Over ten years call £85–130. Chambers has a flexible approach to fees. For further information please discuss with the clerks.

STOUR CHAMBERS

Barton Mill House, Barton Mill Road, Canterbury, Kent CT1 1BP
01227 764899
Fax: 01227 764941; DX 5342 Canterbury
E-mail: clerks@stourchambers.co.uk
URL: http://www.stourchambers.co.uk

Chambers of Simon Johnson
Clerk: Neil Terry

Johnson, Simon 1987	**Buckley**, Gerardine 1991
Warne, Roy 1979	**Clegg**, Adam 1994
Kirwan, Helen 1983	**Pulman**, George QC 1971*†
Cox, Sita 1987	**Pines-Richman**, Helene
Batey, Michael 1989	1992*

9 PARK PLACE

Cardiff, CF1 3DP
01222 382731
Fax: 01222 222542; DX 50751 Cardiff 2
Out of hours telephone: 01222 382731

Chambers of I Murphy QC
Clerk: James Williams

Murphy, Ian QC 1972†	**Thomas**, Keith 1977‡
Thomas, Roger QC 1969†	**Davies**, Philip 1978
Cooke, Nicholas QC 1977‡	**Parry**, Isabel 1979‡
Rees, Phillip 1965†	**Morris**, Ieuan 1979
Kelly, Martyn 1972	**Jarman**, Milwyn 1980
Taylor, Gregory 1974	**Williams**, Karl 1982
Francis, Richard 1974	**McDonald**, Janet 1984
Williams, David 1975	**Lewis**, Owen 1985
Jones, Geraint 1976	**Ferrier**, Susan 1985
Twomlow, Richard 1976‡	**Keyser**, Andrew 1986

Brooks, Peter 1986	**Edwards**, Richard 1997
Hopkins, Paul 1989	**Lewis**, Kynric QC 1954*
Reed, Julian 1991	**Llewellyn-Jones**,
Jones, Brian 1992	‾Christopher QC 1965*†
Donoghue, Steven 1992	**Elias**, Gerard QC 1968*†
Wallace, Hugh 1993	**Roddick**, Winston QC
Hardy, David 1993	1968*†
Elias, David 1994	**Davies**, Leighton QC
Hughes, Gwydion 1994	1975*‡
Thomas, Owen 1994	**George**, Gareth 1977*
Edwards, Heath 1996	**Abbott**, Helen 1988*
Davies, Manon 1997	

30 PARK PLACE

Cardiff, CF1 3BA
01222 398421
Fax: 01222 398725; DX 50756 Cardiff 2
E-mail: 100757.1456@compuserve.com

Chambers of P B Richards
Clerks: Huw Davies, Phillip Griffiths, Catherine Spencer

Richards, Philip 1969‡	**Coombes Davies**, Mair
Bishop, Malcolm QC 1968‡	1988
Jenkins, John QC 1970†	**Austin**, Jonathan 1991
Griffiths, Peter QC 1970†	**Buckland**, Robert 1991
Venmore, John 1971	**John**, Catrin 1992
Curran, Patrick QC 1972*†	**Baker**, Harry 1992
Hopkins, Stephen 1973†	**Hermer**, Richard 1993*
Green, Andrew 1974	**Crowther**, Tom 1993
Morgan, David Wynn 1976†	**Egan**, Eugene 1993
Crowley, Jane QC 1976†	**McGahey**, Elizabeth 1994
Hartley-Davies, Paul 1977	**Hughes**, Hywel 1995
Bush, Keith 1977†	**Jones**, Andrew 1996
Lewis, Marian 1977	**Williams**, Thomas 1996
Tillyard, James 1978‡	**Jayanathan**, Shamini 1996
Davies, Huw 1978‡	**Edmondson**, Harriet Jane
Furness, Jonathan 1979‡	1997
Murphy, Peter 1980‡	**Pitchford**, Christopher QC
Williams, Lloyd 1981	1969*
Lewis, Paul 1981‡	**Harrington**, Patrick QC
Allen, Mark 1981	1973*
Mifflin, Helen 1982	**Phillips**, David QC 1976*
Rees, Ieuan 1982	**Picken**, Simon 1989*
Williams, Rhodri 1987	**Harpwood**, Vivienne 1969
Harrison, Robert 1988	

32 PARK PLACE

Cardiff, CF1 3BA
01222 397364
Fax: 01222 238423; DX 50769 Cardiff 2

Chambers of David Aubrey QC
Clerks: David Brinning, Craig Mansfield

Aubrey, David QC 1976†   Jonathan-Jones, Gareth
Williams, Christopher 1972   1991
Evans, Jane 1971   Kember, Richard 1993
Christie, Ronald 1974   Webster, David 1993
Davies, John Meirion 1975   Lewis, Raymond 1994
Jones, Guy 1975   Gibbon, Juliet 1994
Harris, David 1979   Sprunks, James 1995
Price, Wayne 1982   Thomas, David 1975
Griffiths, Roger 1983   Thomas, Stephen 1993
Morgan, Lynne 1984   Ingham, R Lee 1994
Evans, Huw 1985   Seal, Kevin Paul 1998
Jeary, Stephen 1987   Foulser, Jane 1994
Smith, Ruth 1987   Parry, Sian 1994
Jenkins, D Morgan 1990   Barnett, Joanne 1989
   Jones, Carwyn 1989

33 PARK PLACE

Cardiff, CF1 3BA
02920 233313
Fax: 02920 228294; DX 50755 Cardiff
URL: http://www.33parkplace.co.uk

Chambers of John Charles Rees QC
*Clerks: Graham Barrett, Stephen Price,
Sandra Williams*

Williams, Wyn QC 1974*†   Williams, Daniel 1993
Griffith Williams, John QC   Rees, Caroline 1994
 1968*†   Parry Evans, Mary 1953†
Pugh, Vernon QC 1969*†   Howells, Cenydd 1964*†
Rees, John QC 1972‡   Garfield, Roger 1965
Price, Gerald QC 1969†   Jones, Richard 1969
Davies, Peter 1996   Jones, Nicholas Gareth
Cook, Charles 1966†   1970‡
Davies, Colin 1973   Parsley, Charles 1973
Bidder, Neil QC 1976‡   Price Lewis, Rhodri 1975*
Bull, Gregory 1976‡   Treharne, Jennet 1975
Walters, Jill 1979   Harris, Russell 1986*
Evans, Timothy 1984   Arentsen, Andrew 1995
Walters, Jonathan 1984   Jenkins, Jeremy 1984
Huckle, Theodore 1985   Rees, Christopher 1996
Walters, Graham 1986   Taylor, Rhys 1996
Jones, Nicholas David 1987 Taylor, Andrew 1984
Bennett, Ieuan 1989   Edwards, Helen 1995
O'Leary, Robert 1990   Coulthard, Alan 1987*
Brace, Michael 1991   Campbell, Joan Carolyn
Harris, Nicola 1992   1996
Higginson, Lucy 1992   Thomas, Bryan 1978
Jones, Gareth 1992   Troy, Alan 1990
Osborne, Nigel 1993

**Types of work (and number of counsel practising in
that area if supplied)**
Arbitration · Care proceedings · Chancery
(general) · Chancery land law ·
Commercial litigation · Commercial
property · Common law (general) ·
Company and commercial · Construction ·

Crime · Crime – corporate fraud ·
Employment · Environment · Equity, wills
and trusts · Family · Family provision ·
Housing · Insolvency · Insurance ·
Landlord and tenant · Licensing · Local
government · Medical negligence ·
Partnerships · Personal injury · Private
international · Probate and administration ·
Professional negligence · Town and
country planning

Opening times: 8.30 am-6.15 pm

Chambers' facilities
Video conferences, Disks accepted

Additional information
33 Park Place offers a comprehensive
service in the traditional areas of work
undertaken by an established provincial set
of chambers, namely crime, general
common law and family.

Additionally, however, individuals and
groups within chambers have particular
specialisations which are in the fields of
Chancery, company, construction, employment, local government, personal injury
(including medical negligence) and town
and country planning.

The work undertaken by chambers covers
the whole of Wales and work is also undertaken in the West Midlands and the West
Country.

A number of members of chambers operate
direct access to recognised professional
bodies.

CARMARTHEN CHAMBERS

*30 Spilman Street, Carmarthen, Dyfed
SA31 1LQ*
01267 234410
Fax: 01267 223397

Chambers of Mr R S Griffiths

146 CARSHALTON PARK ROAD

Carshalton, Surrey SM5 3SG
0181 773 0531
Fax: 0181 773 0531

Chambers of Mr B S Mustafa

THE RALEK

66 Carshalton Park Road, Carshalton,
Surrey SM5 3SS
0181 669 1777
Fax: 0181 669 1777

Chambers of Mr R K Tay

THORNWOOD HOUSE

102 New London Road, Chelmsford, Essex
CM2 0RG
01245 280880
Fax: 01245 280882; DX 89706 Chelmsford
2

Chambers of A Arlidge QC

TINDAL CHAMBERS

3/5 New Street, Chelmsford, Essex
CM1 1NT
01245 267742
Fax: 01245 359766; DX 3358 Chelmsford

Chambers of Mr G J Nixon-Moss

TRINITY CHAMBERS

140 New London Road, Chelmsford, Essex
CM2 0AW
01245 605040
Fax: 01245 605041; DX 89725 Chelmsford
2

Chambers of Mr R W J Howard

CHAMBERS OF ROBERT SMITH

16 Wilson Road, Chessington, Surrey
KT9 2HE
0181 288 2594
Fax: 0181 288 2594

Chambers of Mr R A Smith

Bar Directory on the Internet
The Bar Directory is also available on
the Internet at the following address:
http://www.smlawpub.co.uk/bar

NICHOLAS STREET CHAMBERS

22 Nicholas Street, Chester, CH1 2NX
01244 323886
Fax: 01244 347732; DX 22154 Chester
E-mail: clerks@40king.co.uk

Chambers of Janet Case
*Clerks: Robert King, Angela Malcolmson,
Gareth Stickels*

Case, Janet 1975†	Drummond, Bruce 1992
Hughes, Peter QC 1971†	Medland, Simon 1991
Hughes, Merfyn QC 1971†	Jarvis, Oliver 1992
Teague, Edward 1977†	Dunford, Matthew 1992
Trevor-Jones, Robert 1977‡	Jebb, Andrew 1993
	Jesudason, Christine 1993
Lever, John 1978	O'Toole, Anthony 1993‡
Le Brocq, Mark 1982	Abberton, David 1994
Ganner, Joseph 1983	Hewitt, Alexandra 1995
Leigh, Sarah 1983	Parry, Desmond 1995
Bould, Duncan 1984	Price, Anna 1996
Mason, Nicholas 1984	Anderson, Brendan 1985*
Clarke, Jeffrey 1985	Campbell, Gayle 1997
Billington, Moira 1988	Bolton, Sally Ann 1997
Swallow, Jodie 1989	

SEDAN HOUSE

Stanley Place, Chester, CH1 2LU
01244 320480/348282
Fax: 01244 342336; DX 19984 Chester
Out of hours telephone: Pager:
04325565003

Chambers of M Lewis-Jones
Clerk: Gavin James Reeves

Lewis-Jones, Meirion 1971	Hornby, Robert 1990
Thomas of Gresford, Lord QC 1967	Morris, Shân 1991
	Lloyd, Gaynor 1992
Carlile, Alex QC 1970	Edwards, Owen 1992
Farmer, Michael QC 1972†	Williams, John 1992
Spencer, Robin QC 1978‡	Stanton, Carolyn 1993
Little, Geoffrey 1973‡	Roberts, Huw 1993
Jones, I W L 1979	Mullan, Richard 1994
Chambers, Michael 1980‡	Clarke, Andrew 1996
Moss, Peter 1980	Llwyd, Elfyn 1997
Rowlands, Rhys 1986	Japheth, Bethan 1997
Everett, Steven 1989‡	Waller, Helen Margaret 1997
Thomas, Andrew 1989	

---

† Recorder   ‡ Assistant Recorder   *Door Tenant

WHITE FRIARS CHAMBERS

WHITE FRIARS CHAMBERS

21 White Friars, Chester, CH1 1NZ
01244 323070
Fax: 01244 42930; DX 19979 Chester
E-mail:
whitefriarschambers@btinternet.com
Out of hours telephone: 0973 766550

Chambers of John Hedgecoe
*Clerks: Robin Whinnett (Senior Clerk),
Mark Robinson*

Hedgecoe, John *1972*	Roberts, Mark *1991*
Jamieson, Anthony *1974*	Shield, Deborah *1991*
Woodward, Nicholas *1975‡*	Green, Andrew *1992*
Garside, David *1982*	Unsworth, Ian *1992*
Shaw, Richard *1984*	Pates, Richard *1993*
Lloyd, Julian *1985*	Wilson, Myles *1993*
Mills, Simon *1986*	Connor, Mark *1994*
Oates, John *1987*	Shenton, Rachel *1993*
Britcliffe, Anne *1989*	Guirguis, Sheren *1996*
Potter, David *1990*	Parry, Simon Edward *1997*

26 MORLEY AVENUE

Ashgate, Chesterfield, S40 4DA
01246 234790/01298 871350

Chambers of N R Grainger
Clerk: Mrs D M Grainger

Grainger, Norman *1973*

CHICHESTER CHAMBERS

*12 North Pallant, Chichester, West Sussex
PO19 1TQ*
01243 784538
Fax: 01243 780861; DX 30303 Chichester

E-mail:
clerks@chichesterchambers.law.co.uk
Out of hours telephone: 0836 600508

**Chambers of Michael Beckman QC, Charles
Taylor (Executive Head)**
Clerk: Jonathan Kay

Also at: Ground Floor Chambers, 11 Stone
Buildings, London WC2A 3TG Tel: 0171
8316381, Fax 0171 8312575

Beckman, Michael QC *1954*	Regan, David *1994*
Taylor, Charles *1974*	Mogridge, Fraser *1995*
Davis, Lucinda *1981*	Whitehead, Darron *1995*
Rowlinson, Wendy *1981*	Cherrill, Beverley *1996*
Darton, Clifford *1988*	Barker, Charles *1997*
Morgan, Colin *1989*	Cousins, Edward *1971**
Loosemore, Mary *1992*	Salter, Adrian *1973**
Emerson, William *1992*	Deacon, Robert *1976**
Burgess, Emma *1995*	Giret, Jane *1981**
Magee, Rosein *1994*	Dight, Marc *1984**

2 SOUTH AVENUE

Cleverley, Lancashire

Chambers of Mr R A Burgess

EAST ANGLIAN CHAMBERS

52 North Hill, Colchester, Essex CO1 1PY
01206 572756
Fax: 01206 562447; DX 3611 Colchester
E-mail: colchester@ealaw.co.uk
Out of hours telephone: 0585 505333

Chambers of Roderick Newton
*Clerk: Fraser McLaren (Senior Clerk);
Administrator: Carol Bull*

Also at: 5 Museum Street, Ipswich, Suffolk
IP1 1HQ Tel: 01473 214481 Fax: 01473
231388; 57 London Street, Norwich,
Norfolk NR2 1HL Tel: 01603 617351 Fax:
01603 633589

Newton, Roderick *1982‡*	Hamey, John *1979*
Akast, John *1968†*	Sinclair, Graham *1979*
Wardlow, John *1971†*	Kefford, Anthony *1980*
Pearce, Marcus *1972*	Brooke-Smith, John *1981‡*
Wain, Peter *1972*	Parnell, Graham *1982*
Marsden, Andrew *1975‡*	Redmayne, Simon *1982*
Bryant, Caroline *1976*	Davies, Jane *1983*
Levett, Martyn *1978*	Lane, Michael *1983*
McLoughlin, Timothy *1978*	Vass, Hugh *1983*
Miller, Celia *1978*	Cox, Lindsay *1984*
Pugh, David *1978*	Shadarevian, Paul *1984*

Bettle, Janet *1985*
Dyble, Steven *1986*
Bate, Anthony *1987*
Degel, Rebecca *1987*
Elcombe, Nicholas *1987*
Mandil-Wade, Rosalyne *1988*
Richards, David *1989*
Greaves, Ann *1989*
Greenwood, John *1990*
Jackson, Andrew *1990*
Bell, Marika *1991*
Bundell, Katharine *1991*
Smith, Raymond *1991*
Barratt, Dominic *1992*
Parry-Jones, Carole *1992*
Rippon, Amanda *1993*
Walsh, Patricia *1993*

Gilbertson, Helen *1993*
Hanlon, Jacqueline *1994*
Phelps, Mark *1994*
Kelly, Richard *1994*
Preston, Hugh *1994*
Wheetman, Alan *1995*
Freeman, Sally *1995*
Leigh, Samantha *1995*
Durr, Jude *1995*
Wilson, David *1996*
Baruah, Fiona *1996*
Thain, Ashley *1996*
Morgans, John *1996*
Rauf, Saqib *1996*
McArdle, Martin *1996*
Ivory, Martin *1996*
Cannatella, Marc *1997*
Pugh-Smith, John *1977**

6 ASCOT ROAD

Shotley Bridge, Consett, County Durham DH8 0NU
01207 507785
Fax: 01207 507785

Chambers of Mr J Winch
Clerk: Mrs Angela Grogan, FILEX

Also at: 11 King's Bench Walk, The Temple, London EC4 7EQ Tel: 0171 353 3337 Fax: 0171 583 2190

Winch, John *1973*

ADVOLEX CHAMBERS

70 Coulsdon Road, Coulsdon, Surrey CR5 2LB
0181 763 2345
Fax: 0870 742 1151

Chambers of Geoffrey Leech

26 SHAFTESBURY ROAD

Earlsdon, Coventry, Warwickshire CV5 6FN
01203 677337
Fax: 01203 677337

Chambers of Dr B A Brobbey

SPON CHAMBERS

13 Spon Street, Coventry, Warwickshire CV1 3BA
01203 632977
Fax: 01203 632108; DX 11257 Coventry

Chambers of Mr A Sharpe

BRENTWOOD CHAMBERS

Denton, North Yorkshire LS29 0HE
01943 817230
Fax: 01943 817230

Chambers of Miss S I Bedell-Pearce

DEVIZES CHAMBERS

11 High Street, Potterne, Devizes, Wiltshire SN10 5PY
01380 724896

Chambers of Mr P F T L Codner

3 AISBY DRIVE

Rossington, Doncaster, DN11 0YY
01302 866495

Chambers of Mr W A P O'Reilly

3 ATHOL STREET

Douglas, Isle of Man
01624 897 420
Fax: 01624 897 420

Chambers of Mr J A Nutter

DURHAM BARRISTERS' CHAMBERS

27 Old Elvet, Durham, DH1 3HN
0191 386 9199
Fax: 0191 384 6020; DX 60229 Durham 1
Out of hours telephone: 01913 869199

Chambers of C L Roy-Toole
Clerk: Iain Johnston Dip Law

Roy-Toole, Christopher *1990*
Morrison, Christopher *1986*
Powell, Jonathan *1984*

C

Towers, Martin *1996*   **Kilgour**, Peter *1984*
MacFaul, Donald *1998*   **Bloomfield**, Richard *1984*

EASTBOURNE CHAMBERS

*15 Hyde Gardens, Eastbourne, East Sussex
BN21 4PR*
01323 642102
Fax: 01323 641402; DX 6925 Eastbourne

Chambers of Mr A W Khan

KING'S CHAMBERS

*5a Gildredge Road, Eastbourne, East
Sussex BN21 4RB*
01323 416053
Fax: 01323 416110; DX 6931 Eastbourne 1

Chambers of P G Doggart
Administrator: Sharon Longhurst

Doggart, Piers *1991*   **Chadwick**, Emma Jane
Nicol-Gent, Philip *1991*   *1996*
Valks, Michael *1994*   **Claridge**, Rachael Sarah
Naylor, Jonathan *1995*   *1996*

CATHEDRAL CHAMBERS, ELY

P O Box 24, Ely, Cambridgeshire CB6 1SL
01353 666775
Fax: 01353 666776; DX 41010 Ely

Chambers of Mr Michael Duffy

12 PAGE COURT

Ely, Cambridgeshire CB7 4SD
01353 669213
Fax: 01353 669213

Chambers of Mr G Goodwill

ENFIELD CHAMBERS

*First Floor, Refuge House, 9-10 River Front,
Enfield, Middlesex EN1 3SZ*
0181 364 5627
Fax: 0181 364 5973; DX 90638 Enfield 1

Chambers of Mr Adrian Hall

CHAMBERS OF CHRISTOPHER J MORRISON

*2 Brook Mead, Ewell Court, Epsom, Surrey
KT19 0BD*
0181 393 8376
Fax: 0181 873 8219

Chambers of Mr C J Morrison

CATHEDRAL CHAMBERS (JAN WOOD INDEPENDENT BARRISTERS' CLERK)

1 Maple Road, Exeter, Devon EX4 1BN
01392 210900
Fax: 01392 210901; DX 89855 Exeter (St
Thomas)
E-mail: cathedral.chambers@eclipse.co.uk
Out of hours telephone: 01392 204259

Clerk: Jan Wood

Gorna, Christina *1960*   **Gray**, Robert *1993*
Leckie, James *1964*   **White**, Darren *1996*
Wood, Richard *1975*   **Hogg**, The Rt Hon Douglas
Hayward, James *1985*   QC MP *1968**
Vaughan-Williams,
   Laurence *1988*

COLLETON CHAMBERS

Colleton Crescent, Exeter, Devon EX2 4DG
01392 274898/9
Fax: 01392 412368; DX 8330 Exeter

Chambers of R M J Meeke

ROUGEMONT CHAMBERS

*8 Colleton Crescent, Exeter, Devon
EX1 1RR*
01392 208484
Fax: 01392 208204; DX 8396 Exeter 1

Chambers of Michael Berkley

† Recorder ‡ Assistant Recorder *Door Tenant

SOUTHERNHAY CHAMBERS

33 Southernhay East, Exeter, Devon
EX1 1NX
01392 255777
Fax: 01392 412021; DX 8353 Exeter
E-mail:
southernhay.chambers@lineone.net
Out of hours telephone: 01837 840765

Chambers of D I H Tyzack QC
Clerks: J Daniell, A Choules

Tyzack, David QC *1970*‡	**Naish**, Christopher *1980*
Posnansky, Jeremy QC *1972**‡	**Campbell**, Susan *1986*
	Berry, Nicholas *1988*
Norris, Alastair QC *1973**‡	**Ahmed**, Jacqueline *1988*
Meredith, George *1969*	**Ogle**, Rebecca *1989*
Alford, Robert *1970*	**Foster**, Juliet *1989*
Ward, Anthony *1971*	**Crawforth**, Emma *1992*
Lewis, Hugh *1970*	**Hassall**, James *1995*
Templeman, Michael *1973*	**Winzer**, Benjamin Charles
Le Grice, Valentine *1977**	*1997*

WALNUT HOUSE

63 St David's Hill, Exeter, Devon EX4 4DW
01392 279751
Fax: 01392 412080; DX 115582 Exeter St
Davids
E-mail: 106627.2451@compuserve.com
Out of hours telephone: 0467 790471

Chambers of Francis Gilbert QC
Clerk: Chris Doe (Senior Clerk)

Gilbert, Francis QC *1970*†	**Treneer**, Mark *1987*
Dunkels, Paul QC *1972*†	**Eaton Hart**, Andrew *1989*
Burkett, Francis *1969*	**Ingham**, Elizabeth *1989*
Barnes, Jonathan *1970*†	**MacRae**, Robert *1990*
Mercer, Geoffrey *1975*†	**Oldland**, Andrew *1990*
Leadbetter, Iain *1975*	**Laws**, Simon *1991*
Searle, Corinne *1982*	**Lyon**, Shane *1976*
Munro, Sarah *1984*‡	**McCarthy**, Mary *1994*
Edmunds, Martin *1983*‡	**Evans**, David *1996*
Melville-Shreeve, Michael *1986*	**Vaitilingam**, Adam *1987*

HARBOUR COURT CHAMBERS

11 William Price Gardens, Fareham,
Hampshire PO16 7PD
01329 827828
Fax: 01329 829282; DX 40835 Fareham

Chambers of Mr P G S Renfree

45 GREENWAY

Frinton-on-Sea, Essex CO13 9AJ
01255 670699
Fax: 01255 670699

Chambers of Miss S M Murphy

HIGH STREET CHAMBERS

102 High Street, Godalming, Surrey
GU7 1DS
01483 861170
Fax: 01483 861171; DX 58320 Godalming

Chambers of Mr S Shapiro

GUILDFORD CHAMBERS

Stoke House, Leapale Lane, Guildford,
Surrey GU1 4LY
01483 539131
Fax: 01483 300542; DX 97863 Guildford 5
E-mail:
guildford.barristers@btinternet.com
URL: http://www.guildfordbarristers.com

Chambers of S J P Widdup
Clerks: Richard Moore (Senior Clerk),
Pippa Sherriff (Assistant Clerk)

Widdup, Stanley Jeffrey *1973*†	**Coates**, George *1990*
	Watson-Hopkinson,
Matthews, Suzan QC *1974*†	Ghislaine *1991*
Oliver, Simon *1981*	**Ward**, Martin *1992*
Shrimpton, Claire *1983*	**Mawson**, Stephen *1994*
Pascall, Matthew *1984*	**Sellers**, Robin *1994*
Clements, Paula *1985*	**Moulder**, Paul John *1997*
Haywood, Janet *1985*	**Gillan**, Dominique Lye-Ping
Blatch, Francesca *1987*	*1998*
Wilcox, Jerome *1988*	**Bamford**, Ronald *1972*
Flood, Diarmuid *1989*	**Korah**, Valentine *1952*

**Types of work (and number of counsel practising in
that area if supplied)**
Arbitration · Bankruptcy · Care
proceedings · Chancery (general) ·
Chancery land law · Common law
(general) · Competition · Courts martial ·
Crime · Crime – corporate fraud · EC and
competition law · Education · Employment

· Family · Family provision · Housing · Landlord and tenant · Licensing · Local government · Medical negligence · Mental health · Personal injury · Professional negligence · Town and country planning

Chambers established: 1976

Chambers' facilities
Conference rooms, Disks accepted, Disabled access

Languages spoken
Cantonese, French, Malay

ST JOHN'S CHAMBERS

One High Elm Drive, Hale Barns, Cheshire WA15 0JD
0161 980 7379
Fax: 0161 980 7379

Chambers of Miss M Logan

10 KINGSFIELD AVENUE

Harrow, Middlesex HA2 6AH
0181 427 8709/081 248 4943
Fax: 0181 427 8709

Chambers of Mr N Alsolaimani

WESTGATE CHAMBERS

16-17 Wellington Square, Hastings, East Sussex TN34 1PB
01424 432105
Fax: 01424 717850; DX 7062 Hastings

Chambers of Mr J J Collins

HELIONS CHAMBERS

Pilgrims' Way, Camps Road, Helions Bumpstead, Haverhill, Suffolk CB9 7AS
01440 730523
Fax: 01440 730523

Chambers of Mr M H M Hely

23 HARRIES ROAD

Hayes, Middlesex UB4 9DD
0181 841 8236

Chambers of Mr B Esprit

BERKELEY CHAMBERS

1st Floor, 52 High Street, Henley-in-Arden, Warwickshire B95 5AN
01564 795546
Fax: 01564 795549

Chambers of A T Smith QC
Clerk: Mrs Julia Meehan

Sharif, Nadia *1985*   **Smith,** Anthony QC *1958*†

HICKSTEAD COTTAGE

Brighton Road, Hickstead, West Sussex RH17 5NU
01444 881182

Chambers of Mr N J Perry

CHAMBERS OF ALAN HARLE

19 Summerhouse Farm, East Rainton, Houghton-le-Spring, Tyne & Wear DH5 9QQ
0191 5844604

Chambers of Mr A Harle

A K CHAMBERS

19 Headlands Drive, Hessle, Hull, HU13 0JP
01482 641180
Fax: 01482 642275

Chambers of Mr A Khan

WILBERFORCE CHAMBERS

7 Bishop Lane, Hull, East Yorkshire HU1 1PA
01482 323264
Fax: 01482 325533; DX 11940 Hull
E-mail: clerks@hullbar.demon.co.uk

     † Recorder ‡ Assistant Recorder *Door Tenant

URL: http://www.hullbar.demon.co.uk

Chambers of J B Gateshill

Clerks: John M Kennedy, Frances Sheard

Gateshill, Bernard *1972‡*	Shaw, Elizabeth *1986*
Cole, Lorna *1950*	Wray, Nigel *1986*
Bevan, Hugh *1959**	Comaish, Andrew *1989*
Stevenson, Robert *1972*	Murray, Anil *1989*
Miller, Paul *1974‡*	Golder-Welby, Andrew *1992*
Genney, Paul *1976*	
Hands, Jane *1978*	Woolfall, Richard *1992*
Cameron, Neil *1984*	Trimmer, Carol *1993*
Godfrey, John *1985*	Hirst, Simon *1993*
Sampson, James *1985*	Thackray, John *1994*
Tremberg, David *1985*	Bryan, Jayne *1994*
Bury, Mark *1986*	Pickering, Simon *1996*

54 ANNE WAY

Ilford, Essex IG6 2RL
0181 501 4311
Fax: 0181 501 4311

Chambers of Mrs M Mbatha

EAST ANGLIAN CHAMBERS

Gresham House, 5 Museum Street, Ipswich, Suffolk IP1 1HQ
01473 214481
Fax: 01473 231388; DX 3227 Ipswich
E-mail: ipswich@ealaw.co.uk

Chambers of Roderick Newton
Clerk: Peter Hall (Senior Clerk); Administrator: Carol Bull

Also at: 52 North Hill, Colchester, Essex CO1 1PY; 57 London Street, Norwich, Norfolk NR2 1HL

Newton, Roderick *1982‡*	Redmayne, Simon *1982*
Akast, John *1968†*	Davies, Jane *1983*
Wardlow, John *1971†*	Lane, Michael *1983*
Pearce, Marcus *1972*	Vass, Hugh *1983*
Wain, Peter *1972*	Cox, Lindsay *1984*
Marsden, Andrew *1975‡*	Shadarevian, Paul *1984*
Bryant, Caroline *1976*	Richards, David *1989*
Levett, Martyn *1978*	Bettle, Janet *1985*
McLoughlin, Timothy *1978*	Dyble, Steven *1986*
Miller, Celia *1978*	Bate, Anthony *1987*
Pugh, David *1978*	Degel, Rebecca *1987*
Hamey, John *1979*	Elcombe, Nicholas *1987*
Sinclair, Graham *1979*	Mandil-Wade, Rosalyne *1988*
Kefford, Anthony *1980*	
Brooke-Smith, John *1981‡*	Greaves, Ann *1989*
Parnell, Graham *1982*	Greenwood, John *1990*

Jackson, Andrew *1990*	Wheetman, Alan *1995*
Bell, Marika *1991*	Freeman, Sally *1995*
Bundell, Katharine *1991*	Leigh, Samantha *1995*
Smith, Raymond *1991*	Durr, Jude *1995*
Barratt, Dominic *1992*	Wilson, David *1996*
Parry-Jones, Carole *1992*	Baruah, Fiona *1996*
Rippon, Amanda *1993*	Thain, Ashley *1996*
Walsh, Patricia *1993*	Morgans, John *1996*
Gilbertson, Helen *1993*	Ivory, Martin *1996*
Hanlon, Jacqueline *1994*	Rauf, Saqib *1996*
Phelps, Mark *1994*	McArdle, Martin *1996*
Kelly, Richard *1994*	Cannatella, Marc *1997*
Preston, Hugh *1994*	Pugh-Smith, John *1977**

21 CRAVEN ROAD

Kingston-Upon-Thames, Surrey KT2 6LW
0181 974 6799
Fax: 0181 287 5466

Chambers of Mr K Prasad

66 WORTHINGTON ROAD

Surbiton, Kingston-Upon-Thames, Surrey KT6

Chambers of Mr O G Hinds

WESTLEIGH CHAMBERS

Westleigh Wiltown, Curry Rivel, Langport, Somerset TA10 0JE
01458 251261
Fax: 01458 251261

Chambers of Mr J H L Leckie

PEMBROKE HOUSE

18 The Crescent, Leatherhead, Surrey KT22 8EE
01372 376160/376493
Fax: 01372 376188; DX 7301 Leatherhead 1
Other comms: Mobile: 0973 346693
Out of hours telephone: 01372 376493

Chambers of P J White, T White
Clerks: P J White, T White

White, Peter-John *1977*   White, Tanya *1983*

CHAMBERS OF ANDREW CAMPBELL QC

10 Park Square, Leeds, LS1 2LH
0113 2455438
Fax: 0113 2423515; DX 26412 Leeds
E-mail: clerks@10pksq.co.uk
Out of hours telephone: 07000 781576

Chambers of A N Campbell QC
*Clerks: Robin Butchard (Senior Clerk),
Phillip Paxton (First Junior Clerk), Clive
Taylor (First Junior Clerk)*

Campbell, Andrew QC 1972†	**Waley**, Simon 1988
McCahill, Patrick QC 1975*	**Reevell**, Simon 1990
Corbett, James QC 1975*	**Hookway**, Aelred 1990
Munkman, John 1948	**Kealey**, Simon 1991
Kealy, Charles 1965†	**Exall**, Gordon 1991
Sutton, Richard 1968	**Moulson**, Peter 1991
Woolman, Andrew 1973†	**Heaton**, Clive 1992
Bradshaw, David 1975†	**Hayes**, John 1992
Rudland, Martin 1977†	**Bindloss**, Edward 1993
Dallas, Andrew 1978‡	**Storey**, Tom 1993
Davies, Felicity 1980‡	**Iqbal**, Abdul 1994
Clappison, William 1981	**Clarke**, Sarah 1994
Goose, Julian 1984‡	**Wordsworth**, Philippa 1995
Hajimitsis, Anthony 1984	**Kelly**, Geraldine 1996
Worrall, John 1984	**Yates**, Sean 1996
Hickey, Simon 1985	**Branchflower**, George 1997
Brook, Paul 1986	**Madan**, Pankaj 1997

BROADWAY HOUSE CHAMBERS

31 Park Square West, Leeds, LS1 2PF
0113 246 2600
Fax: 0113 246 2609; DX 26403 Leeds Park
Square

Chambers of J Graham K Hyland QC
Clerk: Neil Appleyard

Hyland, Graham QC 1978†	**Fletton**, Mark 1991
Mitchell, David 1972*†	**Wood**, Stephen 1991
Wood, Martin 1973	**Khan**, Tahir 1986
Topham, John 1970	**Crosland**, Ben 1993
Thomas, Roger 1976†	**Hendron**, Gerald 1992
Newbon, Ian 1977	**Colborne**, Michelle 1993
Kelly, David 1980	**Nelson**, Julia 1993
Shelton, Gordon 1981‡	**Jamil**, Aisha 1995
Gibson, Jonathan 1982‡	**Chaplain**, Jayne 1995
Walker, Brian 1985	**Peers**, Nicola 1996
Jones, David 1985	**Morland**, Camille 1996
Birkby, Peter 1987	**Anderson**, Simon Peter Bede 1997
Howard, Ian 1987	
Askins, Nicholas 1989	**Brown**, Ian Keith Rae 1971
Wilson, Paul 1989	**Cannan**, Jonathan 1989*
Drake, Sophie 1990	

CHANCERY HOUSE CHAMBERS

7 Lisbon Square, Leeds, LS1 4LY
0113 244 6691
Fax: 0113 244 6766; DX 26421 Leeds
E-mail: chanceryhouse@btinternet.com
Out of hours telephone: 0370 624448

Chambers of James H Allen QC
Clerk: Colin Hedley

Allen, James QC 1973†	**Williamson**, Melanie 1990
Dent, Adrian 1974	**Klein**, Jonathan 1992
Emm, Roger 1977	**Pipe**, Gregory 1995
Walker, Patrick 1979	**Linklater**, Lisa 1995
Carpenter, Richard 1981	**French**, Jonathan Gabriel 1997
Walker, Mark 1986	
Partington, David 1987	**Wilson**, Richard 1996*
Howd, Stephen 1989	

Types of work (and number of counsel practising in that area if supplied)
Agriculture 2 · Banking 3 · Bankruptcy 3 ·
Chancery (general) 4 · Chancery land law 4
· Commercial litigation 7 · Commercial
property 4 · Common law (general) 9 ·
Company and commercial 4 · Construction
3 · Copyright 2 · Corporate finance 3 · EC
and competition law 1 · Education 3 ·
Employment 3 · Equity, wills and trusts 3 ·
Insolvency 3 · Insurance 3 · Intellectual
property 2 · International trade 3 ·
Landlord and tenant 4 · Medical
negligence 3 · Partnerships 4 · Personal
injury 4 · Professional negligence 4 · Sale
and carriage of goods 4 · Tax – capital and
income · Trademarks 1

Chambers established: 1996
Opening times: 8 am-6 pm (weekdays)

Chambers' facilities
Conference   rooms,   Disks accepted,
Disabled access, E-mail

Languages spoken
Dutch, French, German

Fees policy

Chambers adopts a flexible and open approach to fees and indeed, all areas of administration. Fees are charged either on a time–costed or inclusive 'global' basis. In appropriate cases estimates can be provided or limits agreed prior to work being undertaken.

ENTERPRISE CHAMBERS

38 Park Square, Leeds, LS1 2PA
0113 246 0391
Fax: 0113 242 4802; DX 26448 Leeds
E-mail: enterprise.leeds@dial.pipex.com
URL: http://www.enterprisechambers.com

Chambers of Anthony Mann QC

Clerks: Joanne Glew, Barry Clayton;
Chambers Director: Elspeth Mills Rendall;
Accounts Administrator: Hannah
Steininger-Nath

Mann, Anthony QC *1974*	**Jack**, Adrian *1986*
Levy, Benjamin *1956*	**Groves**, Hugo *1980*
Jennings, Timothy *1962*	**Atherton**, Ian *1988*
Halpern, David *1978*	**Garcia-Miller**, Laura *1989*
Morgan, Charles *1978*	**Bhaloo**, Zia *1990*
Hutton, Caroline *1979*	**Pickering**, James *1991*
James, Michael *1976*	**McKinnell**, Soraya *1991*
Peacocke, Teresa *1982*	**Jory**, Hugh *1992*
Ife, Linden *1982*	**Williamson**, Bridget *1993*
McAllister, Ann *1982*	**Richardson**, Sarah *1993*
Arden, Peter *1983*	**Hardwick**, Matthew *1994*
Zelin, Geoffrey *1984*	**Francis**, Edward *1995*
Baker, Jacqueline *1985*	**Mauger**, Shanti *1996*
Gerald, Nigel *1985*	
Barker, James *1984*	

Types of Work

Use the types of work listings in Parts A and B to locate chambers and individual barristers who specialise in particular areas of work.

11 KING'S BENCH WALK

3 Park Court, Park Cross Street, Leeds,
LS1 2QH
0113 297 1200
Fax: 0113 297 1201; DX Leeds 26433; DX Sheffield 10621
Out of hours telephone: 01423 359252

Chambers of F J Muller QC

Clerks: A T Blaney, A P Dunstone

Annexe of: 11 King's Bench Walk, 1st Floor, Temple, London, EC4Y 7EQ
Tel: 0171 353 3337
Fax: 0171 583 2190

Muller, Franz QC *1961*†	**Swain**, Fiona *1983*
Spencer, James QC *1975*†	**Reeds**, Graham *1984*
Robertson, Andrew QC *1975*†	**Cooper**, John *1985*
	Mallett, Simon *1986*
Radcliffe, Francis *1962*	**Waterman**, Adrian *1988*
Caswell, Matthew *1968*	**Brooke**, David *1990*
Barlow, Richard *1970*	**Toone**, Robert *1993*
Campbell, Nicholas *1978*	**Skelt**, Ian *1994*
O'Neill, Michael *1979*	**Mitchell**, Tom *1995*
Richardson, Jeremy *1980*	**Antrobus**, Simon *1995*
Attwooll, Christopher *1980*	**Margree**, Sarah *1996*
Sylvester, Mio *1980*	**Dempster**, Tina *1997*
Wynn, Toby *1982*	**Bean**, Matthew *1997*
Caswell, Rebecca *1983*	

8 KING'S BENCH WALK NORTH

1 Park Square East, Leeds, LS1 2NE
0113 2439797
Fax: 0113 2457215; DX 713111 Leeds Park Square

Chambers of Mr L G Woodley QC

C

MERCURY CHAMBERS

MERCURY CHAMBERS

Mercury House, 33-35 Clarendon Road, Leeds, LS2 9NZ
0113 234 2265
Fax: 0113 244 4243; DX 713115 Leeds Park Square
E-mail: cdexter@mercurychambers.co.uk

Chambers of Mr Benjamin Nolan QC
Clerk: Miss Carole Dexter

Nolan, Benjamin QC *1971†*
Horowitz, Michael QC *1968*†*
Upward, Patrick QC *1972*‡*
Isaacs, Paul *1974†*
Cohen, Raphael *1981*
Heap, Gerard *1985*
Stiles, John *1986*
Walling, Philip *1986*
Baltaian, Anna *1995*
Smith, Robert *1995*
Serr, Ashley *1996*

Types of work (and number of counsel practising in that area if supplied)
Chancery (general) · Commercial · Commercial litigation · Commercial property · Company and commercial · Employment · Family provision · Insolvency · Personal injury · Professional negligence

Chambers established: 1998
Opening times: 8.30 am-6 pm Mon-Fri

Chambers' facilities
Conference rooms, Video conferences, Disks accepted, Disabled access, Lecture theatre

Fees policy
Fees discussed in confidence with clerk to Chambers.

Languages
See the Index of Languages Spoken in Part G to locate a chambers where a particular language is spoken, or find an individual who speaks a particular language.

NO. 6

6 Park Square, Leeds, LS1 2LW
0113 2459763
Fax: 0113 2424395; DX 26402 Leeds
E-mail: chambers@no6.co.uk
URL: http://www.no6.co.uk

Chambers of Shaun Spencer QC
Clerks: Andrea Nettleton, Kate Birkbeck, Richard Sadler; Practice Director: Tim Collins

Spencer, Shaun QC *1968†*
Williamson, Stephen QC *1964†*
Lawler, Simon QC *1971*
Goss, James QC *1975†*
Kershaw, Jennifer QC *1974‡*
Hamilton, Eleanor QC *1979‡*
Hitchen, John *1961†*
Winteler, John *1969*
Lakin, Gordon *1972*
Clayson, Timothy *1974†*
Shipley, Jane *1974†*
Jameson, Rodney *1976‡*
Rose, David *1977*
Stead, Timothy *1979*
Smith, Michael *1980*
Gargan, Mark *1983*
Hill-Baker, Jeremy *1983*
Morris, Sean *1983*
Frieze, Robin *1985*
Capstick, Timothy *1986*
Clews, Richard *1986*
Troy, Jill *1986*
Clark, Neil *1987*
Reeds, Madeleine *1988*
Smales, Suzanne *1990*
Mansell, Richard *1991*
Mitchell, Andrew *1991*
Gioserano, Richard *1992*
Caswell, Benjamin *1993*
Hill, Nicholas *1993*
Valli, Yunus *1994*
Wilson, Adam *1994*
Batiste, Simon *1995*
Munsi, Ayshea Khatune *1997*
Wright, Richard *1998*

PARK COURT CHAMBERS

16 Park Place, Leeds, LS1 2SJ
0113 2433277
Fax: 0113 2421285; DX 26401 Leeds Park Square

Chambers of Mr J S H Stewart QC, Mr R S Smith QC
Clerk: Roy Kemp

Steer, Wilfred QC *1950*
Chadwin, James QC *1958*

† Recorder ‡ Assistant Recorder *Door Tenant

Stewart, James QC *1966*†
Smith, Robert QC *1971*†
Harrison, Michael QC *1969*†
Swift, Malcolm QC *1970*†
Lodge, Anton QC *1966*†
Worsley, Paul QC *1970*†
Godfrey, Louise QC *1972*†
Bourne-Arton, Simon QC *1975*†
Hatton, David QC *1976*†
Prosser, Henry *1969*†
Hirst, Tim *1970*†
Hartley, Timothy *1970*
Addleman, Andrea *1977*
Bayliss, Thomas *1977*‡
Devlin, Jonathan *1978*
Robinson, Adrian *1981*
Lodge, John *1980*
Taylor, Michael *1980*
Jackson, Simon *1982*
MacDonald, Alistair *1983*‡
Wigin, Caroline *1984*
Phillips, Simon *1985*

Beattie, Sharon *1986*
Myerson, Simon *1986*
Bashir, Nadim *1988*
Turner, Taryn *1990*
Thompson, Andrew *1989*
Davies, Maria *1988*
Patel, Elyas *1991*
Tucker, Ashley *1990*
Greaney, Paul *1993*
Johnson, Nicholas *1994*
Kent, Jenny *1993*
Pitter, Jason *1994*
Widdett, Ceri Louise *1994*
Rajgopal, Uthra Devi *1998*
Sterling, Valerie *1981*
Taylor, Alan *1986*
Michaelson, Justin *1997*
Gray, Gilbert QC *1953**
Dodson, Joanna QC *1970**
Feinberg, Peter QC *1972**
Thornhill, Andrew QC *1969**
Thomas, Roger *1979**
Woolf, Jeremy *1986**

Types of work (and number of counsel practising in that area if supplied)
Company and commercial 6 · Crime 34 · Family 8 · Landlord and tenant 6 · Licensing 4 · Personal injury 31 · Tax 3

Chambers' facilities
Conference rooms, Disks accepted

Languages spoken
French, German, Hindi, Urdu

Additional information
Park Court Chambers is one of the largest sets of chambers outside London, having 11 silks and 30 juniors. It is a long-established but modern and expanding set based in the thriving commercial centre of Leeds. It offers a wide range of services. Specialist areas of practice include crime, corporate fraud, personal injury, general commercial, family, landlord and tenant and licensing.

PARK LANE CHAMBERS

19 Westgate, Leeds, LS1 2RD
0113 2285000
Fax: 0113 2281500; DX 26404 Leeds
E-mail: clerks@parklanechambers.co.uk

Chambers of Stuart Brown QC
Clerks: Mr John Payne, Mr Andy Gray, Mr Jason Middlewood; Administrator: Mrs Dawn Bell (Fees)

Zucker, David Graham *1986*
Bethel, Martin QC *1965*†
Brown, Stuart QC *1974*†
Storey, Christopher QC *1979*‡
Wilby, David QC *1974*‡
Dalziel, Alaric *1967*†
Elgot, Howard *1974*
Finnerty, Angela *1976*†
Cahill, Sally *1978*‡
O'Hare, Elizabeth *1980*
Sigsworth, George *1977*
Kay, Michael *1981*
Armitage, Lindy *1985*‡
Hanbury, William *1985*
Thorp, Simon *1988*
Astbury, Joanne *1989*
Moore, Craig I *1989*

Copnall, Richard *1990*
Nazir, Kaiser *1991*
Swiffen, Guy *1991*
Axon, Andrew *1992*
Korn, Adam *1992*
Murphy, James *1993*
Furness, Corin *1994*
Turner, Steven *1993*
Whittaker, Dornier *1994*
Anning, Sara *1995*
Friday, Stephen *1996*
Plaut, Simon Michael *1997*
Cawson, Mark *1982**
Elleray, Anthony QC *1977**
Sterling, Robert *1970**
Foster, Ian *1988**
Porter, David *1980**

THE CHAMBERS OF PHILIP RAYNOR QC

40 KING STREET
MANCHESTER

5 PARK PLACE
LEEDS

5 Park Place, Leeds, LS1 2RU
0113 242 1123
Fax: 0113 242 1124; DX 713113 Leeds Park Square

Chambers of Philip Raynor QC
Clerks: William Brown, Colin Griffin, Michael Stubbs, Lisa Rogers (Assistant Clerk), Paul Clarke (Assistant Clerk); Administrator: Gina Pinkerton

Also at: 40 King Street, Manchester, M2 6BA Tel: 0161 832 9085 Fax: 0161 835 2139

Raynor, Philip QC *1973*†
Macleod, Nigel QC *1961*†
Hoggett, John QC *1969*†
Gilbart, Andrew QC *1972*†

Smith, Peter QC *1975*†
Farley, Roger QC *1974*†
Sauvain, Stephen QC *1977*

Patterson, Frances QC 1977‡
Booth, Michael QC 1981
Braslavsky, Nicholas QC 1983
Owen, Eric 1969
Jackson, John 1970
Halliday, Harold 1972
Pass, Geoffrey 1975
Evans, Alan 1978
Khan, Shokat 1979
Fraser, Vincent 1981
Manley, David 1981
Barrett, John 1982
Chaisty, Paul 1982
Halliwell, Mark 1985
Dunn, Katherine 1987
Hilton, Simon 1987
Ashworth, Fiona 1988
Stockley, Ruth 1988

Pritchett, Stephen 1989
Anderson, Lesley 1989
Campbell, John QC QC (Scot) 1990
Singer, Andrew 1990
Tucker, Paul 1990
Smith, Matthew 1991
Carter, Martin 1992
Horne, Wilson 1992
Powis, Lucy 1992
Ghosh, Julian 1993
Harper, Mark 1993
Lander, Richard 1993
Pritchard, Sarah 1993
Latimer, Andrew 1995
Doyle, Louis 1996
Berridge, Elizabeth 1996
Nowell, Katie 1996
Siddall, Nicholas 1997
Crawford, Colin 1997

30 PARK SQUARE

Leeds, LS1 2PF
0113 2436388
Fax: 0113 2423510; DX 26411 Leeds
E-mail: clerks@30parksquare.co.uk
URL: http://www.30parksquare.co.uk

Chambers of J W Mellor
Clerks: Jennifer Thompson, Claudine Hinchliffe, Andrew Thornton; Fees Administrator: Amanda Kershaw

Mellor, John 1953
Collier, Peter QC 1970†
Black, Jill QC 1976†
Kershaw, Andrew 1975
McGonigal, David 1982
Haigh, Martin 1970
Haring, Simon 1982
Rodger, Mark 1983
Hallam, Louise 1984‡
Buckingham, Kate 1986
Hill, Louise 1988
Burn, Colin 1985
Pearson, Michael 1984

Granville-Fall, Anthony 1990
Hargan, James 1990
Cole, Robert 1991
Frith, Nicholas 1992
Teeman, Miriam 1993
White, Timothy 1993
Shiels, Ian 1992
Barker, Nicholas 1994
Auckland, Elizabeth 1995
Gilmore, Ian 1996
Tyler, William 1996
Stewart, Alexandra 1997

Types of work (and number of counsel practising in that area if supplied)
Arbitration 5 · Bankruptcy 2 · Care proceedings 17 · Common law (general) 12 · Company and commercial 1 · Courts martial 2 · Crime 22 · Crime – corporate fraud 7 · Ecclesiastical 1 · Employment 4 · Family 17 · Family provision 14 · Insolvency 1 · Licensing 3 · Medical negligence 2 · Mental health 2 · Partnerships 1 · Personal injury 9 · Planning 1 · Professional negligence 2 · Public inquiries · Town and country planning 1

Chambers established: 1984
Opening times: 8.30 am-6 pm Monday to Thursday, 8.30 am-5.30 pm Friday

Chambers' facilities
Conference rooms, Disks accepted

Languages spoken
French, German, Icelandic, Japanese

Fees policy
Chambers operates a flexible and open policy towards the negotiation of fees.

39 PARK SQUARE

Leeds, LS1 2NU
0113 2456633
Fax: 0113 2421567; DX 26407 Leeds 1

Chambers of Mr T M A Bubb

37 PARK SQUARE CHAMBERS

37 Park Square, Leeds, LS1 2NY
0113 2439422
Fax: 0113 2424229; DX 26405 Leeds
E-mail: chambers@no37.co.uk

† Recorder ‡ Assistant Recorder *Door Tenant

Chambers of Mr S J Glover, Mr P G Kirtley
Clerk: Mrs Ann Fothergill (Senior Clerk)

Glover, Stephen *1978*	Tighe, Dawn *1989*
Kirtley, Paul *1982*	Kelbrick, Anthony *1992*
Hogg, The Rt Hon Douglas QC MP *1968*	Cains, Linda *1990*
	Crossley, Steven *1992*
Marshall-Andrews, Robert QC MP *1967*	Ford, Caroline *1993*
	Hill, Piers *1987*
Graham, John *1955*	Gore, Mark *1994*
Wootliff, Barbara *1956*	Taylor, David *1995*
Ferm, Rodney *1972*	Holroyd, Joanne *1994*
Sleightholme, John *1982*	Lee, Taryn *1992*
Dunning, John *1973*	Roberts, Stuart *1994*
Fleming, Paul *1983*	Macadam, Jason *1990*
Apfel, Freddy *1986*	Burdon, Michael *1993*
Lindsay, Jeremy *1986*	Melly, Kama *1997*
Ginsburg, Amanda *1986*	Collins, Michael *1998*

Types of work (and number of counsel practising in that area if supplied)
Agriculture · Building · Care proceedings · Commercial · Commercial property · Contract · Conveyancing · Crime · Crime – corporate fraud · Defamation · Disciplinary tribunals · Discrimination · Employment · Environmental law and pollution · Family · Family provision · Franchising · Fraud · Housing · Immigration · Inquests · Judicial review · Landlord and Tenant · Licensing · Local government · Medical law · Medical negligence · Partnerships · Personal injury · Police discipline · Police law · Professional negligence · Public inquiries · Sale and carriage of goods · Town and country planning

Chambers' facilities
Conference rooms, Video conferences, Disks accepted

Languages spoken
French, German, Hebrew

SOVEREIGN CHAMBERS

SOVEREIGN
C H A M B E R S

25 Park Square, Leeds, LS1 2PW
0113 2451841/2/3
Fax: 0113 2420194; DX 26408 Leeds Park Square

E-mail: sovereignchambers@btinternet.com
URL: http://www.sovereignchambers.co.uk
Out of hours telephone: Home phone: 01977 620780 Mobile: 07775 615580

Chambers of G C Marson QC
Practice Manager: S Paul Slater (Practice and Finance Manager); Administrator: Chris Dixon

Also at: 12 New Square, Lincoln's Inn, London, WC2A 3SW Tel: 0171 419 1212, Fax: 0171 419 1313

Marson, Geoffrey QC *1975*†	Wilson, Peter *1995*
Newbury, Richard *1976*	Maudslay, Diana *1997*
Palmer, Patrick *1978*‡	Heppenstall, Rachael *1997*
Ekins, Charles *1980*†	Mowbray, John QC *1953**
Khokhar, Mushtaq *1982*‡	Macdonald, John QC *1955**
Garth, Steven *1983*	Purle, Charles QC *1970**
Gordon, David *1984*‡	Laurence, George QC *1972**‡
Fricker, Marilyn *1969*	
Driscoll, Lynn *1981*	Tucker, Lynton *1971**
Lewis, Andrew *1985*	Braham, Colin *1971**
McKone, Mark *1988*	Russell, Christopher *1971**
Bedeau, Stephen *1980*	Le Poidevin, Nicholas *1975**
Gresty, Denise *1990*	
Haslam, Andrew *1991*	Barber, Stuart *1979**
Birch, Roger *1979*	Hargreaves, Sara *1979**
Dixon, David *1992*	Bridge, Jane *1981**
Lumley, Nicholas *1992*	McCabe, Margaret *1981**
Rigby, Charity *1993*	Smith, Stephen *1983**
Semple, Andrew *1993*	Sagar, Leigh *1983**
Pye, Jayne *1995*	Staddon, Claire *1985**
Finlay, Darren *1994*	Crail, Ross *1986**
Burden, Emma *1994*	Peacock, Ian *1990**
Smith, Matthew *1996*	Evans-Gordon, Jane *1992**
Dunn, Christopher *1996*	Terras, Nicholas *1993**
Keeley, James *1993*	Davies, Louise *1995**

Types of work (and number of counsel practising in that area if supplied)
Arbitration · Care proceedings · Chancery (general) · Chancery land law · Civil liberties · Commercial · Commercial property · Company and commercial · Competition · Construction · Copyright · Crime · Crime – corporate fraud · EC and competition law · Employment · Environment · Equity, wills and trusts · Family · Family provision · Housing · Immigration · Information technology · Insolvency · Intellectual property · Landlord and tenant · Licensing · Local government · Medical negligence · Partnerships · Patents · Pensions · Personal injury · Planning · Police discipline · Professional negligence · Sports · Town and country planning · Trademarks

C

Chambers established: 1925
Opening times: 8.45 am-6 pm

Chambers' facilities
Conference rooms, Disks accepted, Work returned via e-mail

Languages spoken
Czech, French, German, Italian, Punjabi, Russian, Spanish

Fees policy
Please refer to Practice and Finance Manager. (Can be charged on a time–costed or inclusive 'global' basis.)

ST PAUL'S HOUSE

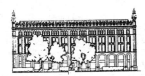

5th Floor, St Paul's House, 23 Park Square South, Leeds, LS1 2ND
0113 2455866
Fax: 0113 2455807; DX 26410 Leeds
E-mail: catherinegrimshaw@stpauls- chambers.demon.co.uk
Out of hours telephone: 0113 250 9857 (Senior Clerk)

Chambers of Nigel Sangster QC
Clerks: Catherine J Grimshaw (Senior Clerk), Bridget Heyhirst, David Haslam; Administrator: Vine Pemberton Joss

Sangster, Nigel QC *1976*‡	Foster, Francis *1990*
Newcombe, Timothy *1972*	Godfrey, Jonathan *1990*
Benson, Peter *1975*†	Sandiford, Jonathan *1992*
Harvey, Colin *1975*	Mairs, Robin *1992*
Barnett, Jeremy *1980*	Saxton, Nicola *1992*
Standfast, Philip *1980*	Barlow, Sarah *1993*
Rose, Jonathan *1981*	Wilson, Scott *1993*
Kearl, Guy *1982*	Bassra, Sukhbir *1993*
Lees, Andrew *1984*	Bates, Alexander *1994*
Hunt, Alison *1986*	Harrison, John *1994*
Dix-Dyer, Fiona *1986*	Watson, Kirstie *1995*
Crowson, Howard *1987*	Edwards, Nigel *1995*
Bickler, Simon *1988*	Dry, Nicholas David *1996*
de Jehan, David *1988*	Duffy, Derek *1997*
Stubbs, Andrew *1988*	Wood, Natasha *1997*
Batty, Christopher *1989*	

Types of work (and number of counsel practising in that area if supplied)
Care proceedings 7 · Chancery (general) 6 · Common law (general) 15 · Company and commercial 9 · Courts martial 1 · Crime 17 · Crime – corporate fraud 6 · Employment 6 · Family 7 · Family provision 7 · Insolvency 8 · Landlord and tenant 8 · Medical negligence 9 · Mental health 9 · Personal injury 15 · Professional negligence 10

Chambers established: 1982
Opening times: 8.30 am-6 pm

Chambers' facilities
Conference rooms, Disks accepted

Languages spoken
French, Hindi, Italian, Urdu

Fees policy
Chambers undertakes all types of legal aid work. Private fees are negotiated with the clerk depending on the case and the experience of counsel instructed.

9 WOODHOUSE SQUARE

Nine Woodhouse Square

Leeds, LS3 1AD
0113 2451986
Fax: 0113 2448623; DX 26406 Leeds
E-mail: clerks@9woodhouse.co.uk

Chambers of John M Collins
Clerks: Samantha Ashford, Helen Dring; Fees Administrators: Erica Newby, Veronica Cliffe

Collins, John *1956**†	Holroyd, John *1989*
Sinclair-Morris, Charles *1966*	Pilkington, Mavis *1990*
	Lunt, Steven *1991*
Muir, John *1969*	Cross, Joanna *1992*
Lumley, Gerald *1972*	McAllister, Eimear *1992*
Jack, Simon *1974*†	Crossley, Justin *1993*
Thornton, Rebecca *1976*	Pema, Anesh *1994*
Lewis, Jeffrey *1978*†	Carroll, Jonathan *1994*
Cox, Bryan *1979*	Henley, Mark *1994*
Hall, David *1980*	Wilson, Andrew *1995*
Hendry, Helen *1983*	Humpage, Heather *1996*
Dodd, Christopher *1984*	Greatorex, Helen Louise *1997*
Greenan, Sarah *1987*	
Newman, Austin *1987*	Brodwell, John Shenton *1998*
Bickerdike, Roger *1986*	
Hodgson, Jane *1989*	Lowe, William QC *1972**

Types of work (and number of counsel practising in that area if supplied)

Administrative 1 · Ancillary relief 9 · Arbitration 1 · Aviation 1 · Bankruptcy 1 · Care proceedings 7 · Chancery (general) 1 · Chancery land law 2 · Charities 1 · Civil liberties 3 · Commercial litigation 4 · Common land 2 · Common law (general) 5 · Construction 1 · Crime 12 · Employment 4 · Environment 1 · Equity, wills and trusts 2 · Family 11 · Family provision 5 · Housing 8 · Immigration 8 · Intellectual property 1 · Landlord and tenant 7 · Licensing 1 · Medical negligence 4 · Mental health 1 · Personal injury 13 · Private international 1 · Probate and administration 2 · Professional negligence 5 · Public international 1 · Sale and carriage of goods 1 · Tax – capital and income 1 · Town and country planning 1

Chambers established: 1928
Opening times: 8.30 am-6 pm (Monday to Friday)

Chambers' facilities

Conference rooms, Disks accepted, Disabled access

Languages spoken

French, German, Spanish

Fees policy

Up to five years call £25–75, Up to ten years call £60–85, Over ten years call £75–125. Fees should be negotiated with the clerks depending upon the complexity of the case, together with the expertise of counsel. Financial limits can be agreed before work is undertaken and an estimate of fees provided if required.

DE MONTFORT CHAMBERS

95 Princess Road East, Leicester, LE1 7DQ
0116 254 8686
Fax: 0116 254 8684; DX 10843 Leicester 1
E-mail: dmcbar@aol.com

Chambers of Mr G J Buchanan
Clerk: Jeanette Petty

Buchanan, Graham *1971*	Gibbs, Philip *1991*
Cursham, Geoffrey *1964*	House, James *1995*
Krone, Maxine *1980*	Power, Elizabeth Joanne *1996*
Smith, Leonard *1991*	
Lucking, Adrienne *1989*	Walker-Smith, Jonah *1963*
Harper, Andrew *1989*	Tedd, Rex QC *1970*

CHAMBERS OF MICHAEL PERT QC

104 New Walk, Leicester, LE1 7EA
0116 249 2020
Fax: 0116 255 0885; MDX 28816 Leicester 2

Chambers of Michael Pert QC
Clerks: Martin Poulter (Senior Clerk), Graeme Logan (Silks Clerk), Joanne Pickersgill (Senior Criminal Clerk), Harri Bennetts (Criminal Clerk), Richard Cade (Civil and Family Clerk), Everton Wedderburn (Civil and Family Clerk), Lynne Edmond (Senior Fees Clerk); Practice Manager: Peter Bennett FCCA MCIM; Administrator: Louise West

Also at: 36 Bedford Row, London WC1R 4JH Tel: 0171 421 8000 Fax: 0171 421 8080; 24 Albion Place, Northampton NN1 1UD Tel: 01604 602333 Fax: 01604 601600

Pert, Michael QC *1970†*	Tayton, Lynn *1981*
Escott-Cox, Brian QC *1954*	Farrell, Edmund *1981*
Bowley, Martin QC *1962*	Wilson, Richard *1981*
Hunt, James QC *1968†*	Akman, Mercy *1982*
Raggatt, Timothy QC *1972†*	Plunkett, Christopher *1983*
Stokes, Michael QC *1971†*	Harbage, William *1983*
Oldham, Frances QC *1977†*	Bull, Simon *1984*
Browne, Nicholas QC *1971†*	Ecob, Joanne *1985*
	Underwood, Robert *1986*
Benson, Richard QC *1974†*	Gumpert, Benjamin *1987*
Swindells, Heather QC *1974†*	Malik, Amjad *1987*
	Pryce, Gregory *1988*
Walker, Annabel QC *1976†*	Aspden, Gordon *1988*
Weekes, Anesta QC *1981‡*	Howarth, Andrew *1988*
Urquhart, Andrew *1963*	Johnson, Amanda *1990*
Waine, Stephen *1969†*	Gibson, John *1991*
Altaras, David *1969†*	Lowe, Matthew *1991*
Metcalf, Christopher *1972†*	Alford, Stuart *1992*
Lee, David *1973*	Gaunt, Sarah *1992*
de Burgos, Jamie *1973*	Dean, Rosa *1993*
Fowler, Michael *1974‡*	Lloyd-Jones, John *1993*
Solomons, Geoffrey *1974*	Johnston, Karen *1994*
Greaves, Michael *1976*	Jupp, Jeffrey *1994*
Mainds, Allan *1977†*	Bojarski, Andrzej *1995*
Lewis, Charles *1977*	Kirk, Jonathan *1995*
Neaves, Andrew *1977*	Ferguson, Niall *1996*
Morrison, Howard OBE *1977†*	Skilbeck, Rupert *1996*
Farrell, David *1978‡*	Connolly, Oliver *1997*
Gargan, Catherine *1978*	Brunner, Kate *1997*
Beddoe, Martin *1979*	Barry, Kevin *1997*
Kushner, Martine *1980*	Joyce, Peter QC *1968**†
Donnellan, Christopher *1981*	Treacy, Colman QC *1971**†
	Ingham, Elizabeth *1989**
	Payne, Richard *1964**

C

65-67 KING STREET

Leicester, LE1 6RP
0116 2547710
Fax: 0116 2470145; DX 10873 Leicester 1

Chambers of Mr W S Bach

MELBURY HOUSE

55 Manor Road, Oadby, Leicester, LE2 2LL
0116 2711848
Fax: 0116 2711848

Chambers of Mr M T Khan

2 NEW STREET

Leicester, LE1 5NA
0116 2625906
Fax: 0116 2512023; DX 10849 Leicester 1

Chambers of Mr Paul Spencer

NEW WALK CHAMBERS

27 New Walk, Leicester, LE1 6TE
0116 2559144
Fax: 0116 2559084; DX 10872 Leicester 1

Chambers of Mr J Snell

4 OVERDALE ROAD

Knighton, Leicester, LE2 3YH
0116 2883930
Fax: 0116 2883930

Chambers of Mr M J P Conlon

21 PORTLAND ROAD

Clarendon Park, Leicester, LE2 3AB
0116 2706235
Fax: 0116 2705532

Chambers of Mr J Whitmore

7 WESTMEATH AVENUE

Evington, Leicester, LE5 6SS
0116 2412003

Chambers of Mr J T Nisbett

WESTGATE CHAMBERS

144 High Street, Lewes, East Sussex BN7 1XT
01273 480510
Fax: 01273 483179; DX 50250 Lewes 2

Chambers of Mr J J Collins

25-27 CASTLE STREET

1st Floor, Liverpool, L2 4TA
0151 227 5661/051 236 5072
Fax: 0151 236 4054; DX 14224 Liverpool
Out of hours telephone: 0151 201 2516

Chambers of S V Riordan QC
Clerk: Joanne Stapley (Senior Clerk)

Riordan, Stephen QC 1972†	**Haygarth**, Edmund 1988
Wright, Gerard QC 1954	**Smith**, Jason 1989
Baxter, Gerald 1971	**Carter**, Lesley 1990
Badley, Pamela 1974†	**Harris**, Ian 1990
Biddle, Neville 1974‡	**Driver**, Simon 1991
Barraclough, Anthony 1978	**Horwood**, Anya 1991
Goff, Anthony 1978	**Power**, Nigel 1992
Carville, Brendan 1980	**Lander**, Charles 1993
Owen, David 1981	**Nolan**, Damian 1994
Lloyd, Wendy-Jane 1983	**Loftus**, Teresa 1995
Price Rowlands, Gwynn 1985	**McLachlan**, David 1996
	Morris, Ben 1996
Lennon, Desmond 1986	**Grant**, Kenneth 1998
Johnson, Nicholas 1987	**Bisarya**, Neil 1998
Kenward, Tim 1987	**Jones**, Michael 1999

19 CASTLE STREET CHAMBERS

Liverpool, L2 4SX
0151 236 9402
Fax: 0151 231 1296; DX 14193 Liverpool
E-mail: DBrei16454@aol.com
Out of hours telephone: 0151 220 1521/
07957 633421

Chambers of Vincent Deane
*Clerks: Jennie Connor (Senior Clerk),
Damien Breingan (Junior Clerk)*

Deane, Vincent 1976	**Polglase**, David 1993
Hope, Nadine 1988	**Gow**, Henry 1995
Flood, Diarmuid 1989	**Morris**, Ben 1996
Slater, Iain 1991	**Woosey**, Jane 1993
Sinker, Andrew 1991	**Askey**, Robert 1998
Ackerley, David 1992	**Parkinson**, William 1997
Burke, Brendan 1995	

† Recorder ‡ Assistant Recorder *Door Tenant

CASTLE STREET CHAMBERS

*2nd Floor, 42 Castle Street, Liverpool,
L2 7LD*
0151 242 0500
Fax: 0151 242 0505; DX 14169 Liverpool

Chambers of Mr C S Feeny

CHAVASSE COURT CHAMBERS

*2nd Floor, Chavasse Court, 24 Lord Street,
Liverpool, L2 1TA*
0151 707 1191
Fax: 0151 707 1189; DX 14223 Liverpool

Chambers of Miss Theresa Pepper
*Clerks: Colin Cubley (Senior Clerk),
Sandra McConnell (Civil Clerk)*

Pepper, Theresa *1973‡*	**Bagley**, Michael *1984*
Mattison, Andrew *1963*	**Connolly**, Michael *1985*
Limont, William *1964*	**Christie**, Simon *1988*
Noble, Arthur *1965*	**Williams**, David *1990‡*
Hall, Philip *1973*	**Watson**, Tom *1990*
Pickavance, Graham *1973*	**Crallan**, Richard *1991*
Cliff, Elizabeth *1975*	**Becker**, Paul *1990*
McDermott, John *1976*	**Greenwood**, Celestine *1991*
Simms, Alan *1976*	**McNeill**, Fiona *1992*
Rose, Anthony *1978*	**Sherman**, Susan *1993*
Lloyd, Heather *1979*	**Mintz**, Simon *1996*
Forsyth, Julie *1983*	**Povoas**, Simon *1996*
O'Donohoe, Anthony *1983*	**Biswas**, Nisha *1996*

CORN EXCHANGE CHAMBERS

*5th Floor, Fenwick Street, Liverpool,
L2 7QS*
0151 227 1081/5009
Fax: 0151 236 1120; DX 14221/14240
Liverpool

**Chambers of David Steer QC, I S Goldrein QC -
Corn Exchange**
*Clerks: Alex Keith, Rachel Kehoe, Kate
Masher; Practice Manager: Alex Keith;
Administrator: Pauline Haines; Other
Admin: Marna Jones*

Steer, David QC *1974†*	**Goldrein**, Iain QC *1975‡*

Aubrey, David QC *1974†*	**Killeen**, Simon *1984*
Bellis, Gordon *1972*	**Knifton**, David *1986*
Pickavance, Michael *1974*	**Khan**, Jamil *1986*
de Haas, Margaret QC *1977‡*	**Davies**, Peter *1986*
	Reaney, Janet *1987*
Gilchrist, Nicholas *1975†*	**Parker**, Steven *1987*
Brown, Mark *1975†*	**Sutton**, Keith *1988*
Grice, Kevin *1977‡*	**Bispham**, Christine *1991*
Pratt, Richard *1980‡*	**Parry-Jones**, Trevor *1992*
Flewitt, Neil *1981‡*	**Altham**, Rob *1993*
Riding, Henry *1981*	**Jones**, Elaine *1984*
Lazarus, Grant *1981*	**Baker**, Clive *1995*
Loveridge, Andrew *1983*	**Clare**, Stuart *1997*
O'Neill, Philip *1983*	**Arkush**, Jonathan *1977*

**Types of work (and number of counsel practising in
that area if supplied)**
Admiralty 1 · Care proceedings 10 · Civil
liberties 2 · Commercial litigation 7 ·
Common law (general) 31 · Construction 5
· Crime 28 · Crime – corporate fraud 28 ·
Defamation 5 · Discrimination 5 ·
Employment 5 · Environment 3 · Family 15
· Family provision 15 · Housing 3 ·
Landlord and tenant 3 · Licensing 7 ·
Medical negligence 8 · Mental health 3 ·
Partnerships 4 · Personal injury 18 ·
Professional negligence 10 · Sale and
carriage of goods 10 · Shipping, admiralty
1 · Sports 1

Opening times: 9 am-6.30 pm

Chambers' facilities
Conference rooms, Disabled access

Areas of practice
These chambers have their work-base in
the North but with established contacts in
Cheshire and North Wales. The size of
chambers has enabled a broad basis of
specialisations to be developed especially
in the following fields: crime, family law,
personal injuries (including catastrophic
injuries and multi-party actions), professional negligence (in particular medical,
legal and surveyors'), all forms of local
government work and general common
law work.
Specialists are also available in the
following fields: employment, mental
health, commercial work, licensing,
housing and general landlord and tenant
law. Major claims handling: Ian S Goldrein
QC and Margaret R de Haas QC (authors
and editors of the *Butterworths Personal
Injury Litigation Service*) operate the Corn
Exchange Chambers major claims handling
unit.

DERBY SQUARE CHAMBERS

Merchants Court, Derby Square, Liverpool, L2 1TS
0151 709 4222
Fax: 0151 708 6311; DX 14213 Liverpool 1

Chambers of Mr J S Newton

EXCHANGE CHAMBERS

Pearl Assurance House, Derby Square, Liverpool, L2 9XX
0151 236 7747
Fax: 0151 236 3433; DX 14207 Liverpool
E-mail: exchangechambers@btinternet.com
URL: http://www.exchangechambers.co.uk
Out of hours telephone: 017048 77272

Chambers of William Waldron QC
Clerks: Roy Finney, Barbara Jones;
Practice Manager: Tom Handley;
Administrator: Sally Smylie

Waldron, William QC *1970*†	**Clark**, Paul *1994*
Turner, David QC *1971**†	**Jones**, Gerald *1995*
Braithwaite, William QC *1970*†	**Berkson**, Simon *1986*
	James, Alun *1986*
Globe, Henry QC *1972*†	**Waldron**, William *1986*
Morrow, Graham QC *1974*‡	**McCarroll**, John *1988*
Holroyde, Timothy QC *1977*‡	**Cummings**, Brian *1988*
	Mulrooney, Mark *1988*
Bartley Jones, Edward QC *1975*‡	**Clark**, Rebecca *1989*
	Howells, Catherine *1989*
Smith, Peter *1954*	**Wood**, Michael *1989*
Nance, Francis *1970*	**Stables**, Christopher *1990*
Cornwall, Christopher *1975*†	**Case**, Julie *1990*
	Philpotts, John *1990*
Earlam, Simon *1975*‡	**Yip**, Amanda *1991*
Lamb, Eric *1975*	**Casement**, David *1992*
Rae, James *1976*	**Evans**, Paul *1992*
Martin, Gerard *1978*‡	**Dudley**, Robert *1993*
Fordham, Judith *1991*	**Kenny**, Charlotte *1993*
Cole, Gordon *1979*	**Fox**, Simon *1994*
Griffiths, Tania *1982*	**Pennifer**, Kelly *1994*
Hillman, Roger *1983*	**Silverbeck**, Rachel *1996*
Cadwallader, Neil *1984*	**Slack**, Kevin John *1997*
Gregory, Karen *1985*	**Gourley**, Claire *1996*
Talbot, Dennis *1985*	**Metcalf**, Louise *1997*

Types of work (and number of counsel practising in that area if supplied)
Administrative · Asset finance · Banking · Bankruptcy · Care proceedings · Chancery (general) · Chancery land law · Charities · Commercial · Commercial litigation · Commercial planning · Commercial property · Common land · Common law (general) · Company and commercial · Conveyancing · Corporate finance · Crime · Crime – corporate fraud · Employment · Environment · Equity, wills and trusts · Family · Family provision · Housing · Insolvency · Insurance · Insurance/reinsurance · International trade · Landlord and tenant · Licensing · Local government · Medical negligence · Mental health · Partnerships · Pensions · Personal injury · Planning · Probate and administration · Professional negligence · Sale and carriage of goods · Share options · Shipping, admiralty · Tax – capital and income · Tax – corporate · Town and country planning

Opening times: 8 am-7 pm

Chambers' facilities
Conference rooms, Disks accepted, Disabled access, E-mail

Languages spoken
French

Fees policy
Chambers adopts a flexible and open approach to fees. Estimates can be provided prior to work being undertaken. Fees are charged on an agreed hourly rate or inclusive global basis. Please feel free to discuss this with the clerks.

The Chambers: An established set undertaking a wide variety of work with individual members working in specialist teams. Direct Professional Access work is undertaken.

The Personal Injury Team consists of 21 members of chambers of all ranges of seniority. All types of personal injury claims are dealt with, especially catastrophic injuries to brain and spine where Bill Braithwaite QC (the Consultant Editor of Kemp & Kemp on *The Quantum of Damages*) is highly regarded. Several members of this team offer a very quick turnaround of RTA papers. Several members of the team specialise particularly in medical negligence work. There is a fairly even split between plaintiff and defence work. All members of the team accept work on a conditional fee basis.

The Criminal Team consists of 22 barristers, five of which are Silks. There is an even balance between prosecution and defence work. The criminal team prosecutes for several specialist agencies, for example Customs and Excise, Health and Safety Executive, DTI and DSS. The team also specialises in fraud work, having prosecuted and defended in SFO cases.

The Commercial Team practises within all aspects of commercial and chancery law. This incorporates professional negligence, commercial arbitrations, property, mortgages, commercial landlord and tenant, planning, banking, insolvency, tax/VAT, copyright, wills, administration of estates, trusts, insurance and reinsurance, sale of goods, construction law, shipping law, carriage of goods, international trade and EC law.

The Family Team practises in all areas of family law. They deal with cases involving ancillary relief, inheritance law, children and family law, and education law.

The Civil Team contains individual counsel of all ranges of seniority and experience. The team is able to deal with all the main fields of work that fall within this wide sector. These areas include, licensing, employment matters and local government.

Recruitment and Training: One or two pupillages with financial support are offered each year. Guaranteed earnings of £10,000 the first year with a guarantee of £50,000 in the first two years. Chambers is a member of PACH.

FIRST NATIONAL CHAMBERS

2nd Floor, First National Building, 24 Fenwick Street, Liverpool, L2 7NE
0151 236 2098
Fax: 0151 255 0484; DX 14167 Liverpool 1

Clerk: Mark Bloor

Barnes, Ashley *1990*	**Iro**, Augustine *1995*
Beeson, Nigel *1983*	**Mills**, Stuart *1992*
Crean, Mary *1996*	**O'Halloran**, Jill *1994*
Gatenby, James *1994*	**Simpson**, Paul *1980*
Gray, Mark *1996*	**Stephenson**, Anthony Mark
Holt, Margaret *1978*	*1997*

INDIA BUILDINGS CHAMBERS

Water Street, Liverpool, L2 0XG
0151 243 6000
Fax: 0151 243 6040; DX 14227 Liverpool
E-mail: clerks@chambers.u-net.com

Chambers of D M Harris QC
Clerks: Robert Moss (Senior Clerk/Practice Manager), Helen Southworth, Gail Curran, Alastair Webster, Neil McHugh

Harris, David QC *1969*†	**Holder**, Simon *1989*
Briggs, John *1953*	**Andrews**, Rachel *1989*
Wolff, Michael *1964*	**Browne**, Louis *1988*
Atherton, Robert *1970*†	**Gould**, Deborah *1990*
Byrne, Michael *1971*†	**Chaudhry**, Zia *1991*
Herman, Raymond *1972*†	**Taylor**, Jonathan *1991*
Brittain, Richard *1971*†	**Pratt**, Patricia *1991*
Bedford, Stephen *1974*‡	**Swift**, Steven *1991*
Lowe, Geoffrey *1975*	**Butler**, Jonathan *1992*
Roddy, Maureen *1977*†	**Gibson**, John *1993*
Duggan, James *1978*†	**Jones**, Ben *1993*
Wood, Graham *1979**‡	**Flood**, David *1993*
Owen, Gail *1980*‡	**Harrison**, Leona *1993*
Jones, Gareth *1984*	**Mann**, Sara *1994*
Kennedy, Michael *1985*	**Scholes**, Michael *1996*
Wall, Jacqueline *1986*	**Dixon**, John *1995*
France-Hayhurst, Jean *1972*	**Chukwuemeka**, John *1994*
Davey, Charles *1989*	**Barron-Eaves**, Emma Lorraine *1998*
Sanders, Damian *1988*	

JOHN PUGH'S CHAMBERS

3rd Floor, 14 Castle Street, Liverpool, L2 0NE
0151 236 5415
Fax: 0151 227 5468; DX 14182 Liverpool 1

Chambers of Mr J B Pugh

ADRIAN LYON'S CHAMBERS

14 Castle Street, Liverpool, L2 0NE
0151 236 4421/8240
Fax: 0151 236 1559; DX 14176 Liverpool 1

Chambers of Adrian Lyon

MARTINS BUILDING

2nd Floor, No 4 Water Street, Liverpool, L2 3SP
0151 236 5818/4919
Fax: 0151 236 2800; DX 14232 Liverpool

Chambers of R A Fordham QC

C

ORIEL CHAMBERS

14 Water Street, Liverpool, L2 8TD
0151 236 7191/236 4321
Fax: 0151 227 5909/236 3332; DX 14106
Liverpool
E-mail: clerks@oriel-chambers.co.uk

Chambers of A T Sander

Clerks: Sarah Cavanagh (Chambers Director), Paul Thompson (Practice Manager), Andrew Hampton, Mark Shannon, Ian Pitt (Clerks); Michael Gray, Wendy O'Donnell (Administration)

Sander, Andrew *1970*†	**Lewthwaite**, Joanne *1990*
Gilmour, Nigel QC *1970*†	**Rahman**, Yaqub *1991*
Bennett, Martyn *1969*	**Gruffydd**, John *1992*
Alldis, Christopher *1970*†	**Belbin**, Heather *1992*
Edwards, Anthony *1972*†	**Foster**, Peter *1992*
Rankin, William *1972*	**Brant**, Paul *1993*
Murray, Ashley *1974*†	**Brandon**, Helen *1993*
Wright, Norman *1974*†	**Dawson**, James *1994*
Bradley, Richard *1978*	**Somerset-Jones**, Felicity
Somerville, Thomas *1979*	*1994*
Cowan, Peter *1980*‡	**Rankin**, William K *1994*
Gibson, Titus *1981*	**Whitehurst**, Ian *1994*
Fogarty, Peter *1982*	**Kemp**, Stephen *1995*
Bundred, Gillian *1982*	**Hughes**, Rachel *1995*
Evans, Suzanne *1985*	**Cottrell**, Matthew *1996*
Fox, Anna *1986*	**Frodsham**, Alexander *1996*
Goodbody, Peter *1986*	**Sawyer**, John *1978*
Breheny, Mark *1986*	**Clarke**, Susan *1996*
Nicholls, Jane *1989*	**Close**, Jon *1997*
Baldwin, John *1990*	

Types of work (and number of counsel practising in that area if supplied)

Ancillary relief · Asset finance · Banking · Bankruptcy · Care proceedings · Commercial litigation · Common law (general) · Construction · Crime · Discrimination · Employment · Environment · Factoring · Family · Housing · Insolvency · Insurance · Judicial review · Landlord and tenant · Medical negligence · Personal injury · Professional negligence · Sale and carriage of goods · Sports

Chambers established: 1965
Opening times: 8.30 am-6 pm

Chambers' facilities
Conference rooms, Disks accepted, Disabled access, E-mail

Languages spoken
Afrikaans, French, German, Spanish

Fees policy
Fee information and structuring can be obtained through the clerks. Direct professional access and conditional fee agreements accepted.

Additional information
The clerks and members of Oriel Chambers aim to provide a friendly, professional and efficient service to complement the very highest standards of advocacy, drafting and advice.

Recent expansion in members of chambers has strengthened the existing specialist groups, which provide expertise at all levels.

Members of chambers regularly lecture and have the benefit of CPD Law Society Accreditation.

The UK College of Family Mediators Directory & Handbook 1999/2000

- provides expert commentary on family mediation training and professional development and includes contributions by leading family mediation professionals
- lists over 130 family mediation groups/services and over 1000 individual family mediators by location and alphabetically
- gives details of all Members and Associates of the UK College of Family Mediators
- includes the UK College of Family Mediators Standards and Code of Practice
- gives details of all the family mediation bodies which make up the UK College of Family Mediators.

For more information call Sweet & Maxwell on 0171 449 1111.

---

† Recorder ‡ Assistant Recorder *Door Tenant

WESTMINSTER CHAMBERS

3 Crosshall Street, Liverpool, L1 6DQ
0151 236 4774
Fax: 0151 236 4774

Chambers of Miss L Brown

ACHMA CHAMBERS

44 Yarnfield Square, Clayton Road,
London, SE15 5JD
0171 639 7817/0171 635 7904
Fax: 0171 635 7904
Out of hours telephone: 0958 301089

Chambers of George Edward Ofori
Clerk: Lucy Akua Ofori; Administrator:
Lucy Akua Ofori

Ofori, George *1982*

ACRE LANE NEIGHBOURHOOD CHAMBERS

30A Acre Lane, London, SW2 5SG
0171 274 4400
Fax: 0171 274 4333; DX 58782 Brixton
E-mail:
barristerschambers@acrelane.demon.co.uk

Chambers of Ms N Sultan

Roach, Jacqueline Alison *1996*	**Monteith,** Keir *1994*
Pedro, Terry Adebisi *1996*	**Kaur,** Rani *1993**
Taylor, Sue *1996*	**Sultan,** Neelim *1993*
Horstead, Sean Kevan *1996*	**Cooper,** Nicholas *1997*
Sekar, Chandra *1996*	**Reid,** Silas *1995*
Hyams-Parish, Antony Robert *1995*	**Tavener,** Lucinda *1997*
	Simms, Sonia *1993**
	Rohard, Adrian *1993*

ALBAN CHAMBERS

Alban Chambers

27 Old Gloucester Street, London,
WC1N 3XX
0171 419 5051
Fax: 0181 858 3533; DX 35209 Greenwich
2
E-mail: wpmd@clara.net
URL: http://www.wpdm.clara.net
Out of hours telephone: 0385 564775

Chambers of Mrs W P M Datta

Datta, Mrs Wendy Patricia
Mizal *1990*

ALBANY CHAMBERS

91 Kentish Town Road, London, NW1 8NY
0171 485 5736/5758
Fax: 0171 485 6752
E-mail: albany91.freeserve.co.uk
URL: http://www.eyerhyme.demon.co.uk/
albany/
Out of hours telephone: 0171 435 8533

Chambers of P A Lawrence
Clerk: Daniel Currie

Lawrence, Pamela *1975*	**Kavanagh,** Jennifer *1993*
Omideyi, Christina *1987*	**Martin,** Philip *1995*
Martins, Yetunde *1989*	**Molloy,** Philippa *1995*
Babajide, Ibukun *1990*	

ALEXANDRA CHAMBERS

163 Albert Road, London, N22 7AQ
0181 881 8523
Fax: 0181 881 8523; DX 35650 Wood
Green

Chambers of Mr J D Hunter

AMHURST CHAMBERS

76 Amhurst Park, London, N16 5AR
0181 800 5817
Fax: DX 58061 Stoke Newington

Chambers of Mr F L Caramazza

CHAMBERS OF GAMINI ANGAMMANA

'Woodcroft', 13 Woodend, Upper Norwood,
London, SE19 3NU
0181 240 7476
Fax: 0181 571 5205

Chambers of Mr G B Angammana

C

---

† Recorder ‡ Assistant Recorder *Door Tenant

CHAMBERS OF JAMES APEA

11 Helix Road, London, SW2 2JR
0181 244 5545

Chambers of Mr J B Apea

ARBITRATION CHAMBERS

22 Willes Road, London, NW5 3DS
020 7267 2137
Fax: 020 7267 2137; DX 46454 Kentish Town
E-mail: jatqc@atack.demon.co.uk
Out of hours telephone: 020 7267 2137

Chambers of J A Tackaberry QC
Clerk: Pearl O'Brien

Tackaberry, John QC 1967†	**Morris**, Derrick *1983*
	Gough, Karen *1983*

Types of work (and number of counsel practising in that area if supplied)
Arbitration 6 · Construction

John Tackaberry: Queen's Counsel (since 1982), Recorder (since 1988) UN Commissioner (1998) During his career at the Bar, Mr Tackaberry has undertaken a wide range of work. In more recent years as an advocate he has had a substantial degree of experience in building and civil engineering work.

As well as work in the UK, counsel has a great deal of expertise in international disputes throughout Europe, the USA, the West Indies, Africa, Hong Kong, Singapore, Malaysia, and, more recently, India and South America.
He is spending an increasing amount of time as arbitrator both within the UK and overseas. In this context Mr Tackaberry was the first QC to appear on the list of all three of the following organisations: the Institute of Civil Engineers; the Royal Institute of British Architects; and the Chartered Institute of Arbitrators.

He is or has been a member of, and/or on the arbitration panels of, the American Arbitration Association, the Los Angeles Center for Commercial Arbitration, the Chartered Institute of Arbitrators (past chairman), the Society of Construction Law (past president), the Indian Council of Arbitrators and its panel of international arbitrators, the Association of Arbitrators in South Africa, the Singapore International Arbitration Council, the Hong Kong Centre for International Arbitration, Mauritius Chamber of Commerce and Industry and the Institute for Transnational Arbitration and the Advisory Board thereof of the South Western Legal Foundation Texas.

Mr Tackaberry is a member of, or has been admitted *ad hoc*, to the Bars of California, Ireland, Hong Kong, Malaysia, and New South Wales, and is heavily involved in ICC arbitrations.

He has written and contributed to many books and conferences over the years.

Mr Tackaberry is also associated with the following chambers:
Assize Court Chambers, Small Street, Bristol BS1 1DE (telephone: 01272 264587); Chambers of Philip Raynor QC, 40 King Street, Manchester M2 6BA (telephone: 0161 832 9082). Littman Chambers, 12 Gray's Inn Square, Gray's Inn, London, WC1R 5JP (telephone: 0171 404 4866).

Derrick Morris: Prior to being called to the Bar, Mr Morris had a comprehensive career in the building and civil engineering industries. Since his call to the Bar he has had substantial experience as an advocate in building and civil engineering particularly in the field of arbitrations. A great deal of Mr Morris's experience has been gained in arbitration work in South East Asia and the Far East as well as in England and Wales.

Mr Morris has written and contributed articles and papers to a number of journals and conferences – particularly on legal matters in the construction and engineering field in South East Asia and the Far East.

Both members undertake direct professional access work. A full CV and a copy of terms of engagement are available.

ARCADIA CHAMBERS

P O Box 16674, 18 Kensington Court, London, W8 5DW
0171 938 1285
Fax: 0171 938 1285

Chambers of Mr J P A L Fernandes

ARDEN CHAMBERS

27 John Street, London, WC1N 2BL
020 7242 4244
Fax: 0171 242 3224; DX 29 Chancery Lane
E-mail: clerks@arden-chambers.law.co.uk
URL:
http://www.arden-chambers.lawco.uk/
arden chambers

Chambers of A P R Arden QC
Clerk: Barry Landa (Senior Clerk)

Arden, Andrew QC *1974*
Carter, David *1971*
Jones, Timothy *1975*
Hayton, Linda *1975*
Partington, Prof Martin *1984*
Baker, Christopher *1984*
Balogh, Christopher *1984*
Hunter, Caroline *1985*
Manning, Jonathan *1989*
Colville, Iain *1989*
Okoya, William *1989*
Kilcoyne, Desmond *1990*
Henderson, Josephine *1990*
Jenrick, Kate *1990*

Kilpatrick, Alyson *1991*
Dymond, Andrew *1991*
Bretherton, Kerry *1992*
Moore, Arthur *1992*
Halloran, Celidh *1992**
Collins, Scott *1994*
Preston, Dominic *1995*
Challen, Lydia *1995*
Pengelly, Sarah *1996*
Rowley, Alison *1987*
Waritay, Samuel *1993*
Gallagher, Stanley *1994*
McGrath, Siobhan *1982**
Saunders, Emma *1994**
Thomas, Gareth MP *1977*

Types of work (and number of counsel practising in that area if supplied)
Administrative 3 · EC and competition law 1 · Environment 10 · Housing 16 · Landlord and tenant 16 · Local government 5 · Town and country planning 1

Chambers established: 1993
Opening times: 9 am-6 pm

Chambers' facilities
Disks accepted

Languages spoken
French

Fees policy
Fees will be negotiated with the clerk depending on the case. The range of fees is available in writing from the clerks.

ARLINGTON CHAMBERS

5 Park Crescent Mews East, Great Portland Street, London, W1N 5HB
0171 580 9188
Fax: 0171 580 9189

E-mail: ejdc1@aol.com
Out of hours telephone: 0831 777477

Chambers of Miss E J Da Costa
Clerk: Self

Da Costa, Elissa *1990*

CHAMBERS OF DR MICHAEL ARNHEIM

101 Queen Alexandra Mansions, Judd Street, London, WC1H 9DP
0171 833 5093
Fax: 0171 916 0962; DX 330 London Chancery Lane

Chambers of Dr M T W Arnheim

ATKIN CHAMBERS

ATKIN CHAMBERS
Barristers

1 Atkin Building, Gray's Inn, London, WC1R 5AT
020 7404 0102
Fax: 020 7405 7456; DX 1033 London
E-mail: clerks@atkin-chambers.co.uk

Chambers of Mr J Blackburn QC
Clerks: S Goldsmith, D Barnes

Wallace, Ian QC *1948*
Blackburn, John QC *1969*
Reese, Colin QC *1973†*
Akenhead, Robert QC *1972†*
Dennys, Nicholas QC *1975‡*
White, Andrew QC *1980*
Baatz, Nicholas QC *1978*
Valentine, Donald *1956*
Royce, Darryl *1976*
Bowdery, Martin *1980*
Burr, Andrew *1981*
Raeside, Mark *1982*
Dumaresq, Delia *1984*
Dennison, Stephen *1985*
Goddard, Andrew *1985*

Streatfeild-James, David *1986*
Godwin, William *1986*
Barwise, Stephanie *1988*
Lofthouse, Simon *1988*
Clay, Robert *1989*
Fraser, D Peter *1989*
Rawley, Dominique *1991*
Doerries, Chantal-Aimée *1992*
Parkin, Fiona *1993*
Walker, Steven *1993*
McMullan, Manus *1994*
Howells, James *1995*
Collings, Nicholas Stewart *1997*
Lane, Patrick *1997**

AVONDALE CHAMBERS

2 Avondale Avenue, London, N12 8EJ
0181 445 9984

Chambers of Eur Ing Christopher Shaikh

BALHAM CHAMBERS

*82 Balham High Road, London,
SW12 9AG*
0181 675 4609
Fax: 0181 675 4920; DX 34002 Tooting
North

Chambers of Mr R S Sukul

47 BANBURY HOUSE

Banbury Road, London, E9 7EB
0181 985 8716

Chambers of Ms L Longhurst-Woods

BARCLAY CHAMBERS

*2a Barclay Road, Leytonstone, London,
E11 3DG*
0181 558 2289/925 0688
Fax: 0181 558 2289

Chambers of Mr A S Qureshi

BARNARD'S INN CHAMBERS

*6th Floor, Halton House, 20-23 Holborn,
London, EC1N 2JD*
0171 369 6969

Fax: 0171 404 3139; DX 336 Chancery Lane
E-mail: clerks@biclaw.co.uk

Chambers of Alan Saggerson
Clerks: Andrew Flanagan, Toby Eales

Saggerson, Alan *1981*	**Cowen**, Timothy *1993*
Rees, William *1973*	**Elliott**, Jason *1993*
Bryant, John *1976*	**Thomson**, David *1994*
Korn, Anthony *1978*	**Chapman**, Michael *1994*
Blackford, Simon *1979*	**Chapman**, Matthew *1994*
Dutton, Timothy *1985*	**Bredemear**, Zachary *1996*
Moore, Craig I *1989*	**Sethi**, Mohinderpal *1996*
Sullivan, Scott *1991*	**Short**, Anna *1997*
Martin, Jill *1993*	

BARRISTERS' COMMON LAW CHAMBERS

*57 Whitechapel Road, Aldgate East,
London, E1 1DU*
0171 375 3012
Fax: 0171 375 3068
E-mail: barristers@hotmail.com and barristers@lawchambers.freeserve.co.uk
Out of hours telephone: Mobile: 07931
748320; Mobile: 07957 515570

Chambers of Muhammad Altafur Rahman
*Clerks: M D Abul Kalam, Ms Hafsa
Rahman Khan, Ms Sarah Rahman
Hussain; Administrator: M D Sohul
Ahmed*

Rahman, Muhammad *1970*	**Moses**, Rebecca *1996*
Abrahams, Jonathan David *1976*	**Halsall**, Stephen James *1997*
Featherstone, Jason *1995*	**Pomeroy**, Toby *1997*
Stead, Kate *1996*	

9 BEDFORD ROW

London, WC1R 4AZ
0171 242 3555
Fax: 0171 242 2511; DX 347 London
E-mail: clerks@9br.co.uk
Out of hours telephone: Answering
machine gives emergency number

Chambers of John Goldring QC
*Clerks: Chris Owen (Senior Clerk), Perry
Allen (Senior Civil Clerk), Wayne King
(Senior Criminal Clerk); Administrator:
Don Seligmann*

Goldring, John QC *1969*†	**Coward**, Stephen QC *1964*†
Wilson, Martin QC *1963*	**Farrer**, David QC *1967*†

Barnes, Timothy QC 1968†
Baker, Nigel QC 1969†
Latham, Richard QC 1971†
Hotten, Christopher QC 1972†
Coker, William QC 1973†
Rumfitt, Nigel QC 1974†
Wide, Charles QC 1974†
Shears, Philip QC 1972†
Thompson, Collingwood QC 1975†
Maskrey, Simeon QC 1977†
Butler, Joan QC 1977†
Pawlak, Witold 1970†
Christie, David 1973
Head, Philip 1976‡
Matthews, Julian 1979
Wheatley, Simon 1979
Godsmark, Nigel 1979
Pendlebury, Jeremy 1980
Pini, John 1981
Spencer, Timothy 1982
Thirlwall, Kate QC 1982‡
Coen, Yvonne 1982‡
Dean, Nicholas 1982
Sweeting, Derek 1983
Mooncey, Ebraham 1983
Reed, Susan 1984
Baker, Maureen 1984
Connolly, Barbara 1986

Varty, Louise 1986
King, Simon 1987
Matthew, David 1987
Mayo, Rupert 1987
Baker, Stephen 1989
Roche, Brendan 1989
Langdale, Rachel 1990
McGahey, Cathryn 1990
Ford, Steven 1992
Dakyns, Isabel 1992
Weitzman, Adam 1993
Marshall, Vanessa 1994
Jowitt, Matthew 1994
Rawat, Bilal 1995
Redgrave, William 1995
Nashashibi, Anwar 1995
Johnson, Susannah 1996
Thomas, Simon 1995
Allan, David 1998
Ellison, Anthony (Bermuda) 1957*
Milmo, John QC 1966*
Birt, Michael (Jersey) 1970*
Bach, William 1972*
Aiken, Nigel SC (Hong Kong) 1974*
Stockdale, David QC 1975*
Murray, Virginia (Greece) 1991*

McLinden, John (1974, NZ) 1991
Sharpe, Dennis 1976
Huyton, Brian 1977
Russell, Martin 1977
Belson, Jane 1978
Callaway, Anthony 1978
Reza, Hashim 1981
Hurst, Brian 1983
Southall, Richard 1983
Critchley, John 1985

Croally, Miles 1987
Date, Julian 1988
Raffray, Frederic 1991
Lo, Bernard 1991
McAlinden, Barry 1993
Michalos, Christina 1994
Crosfill, John 1995
Hamilton, Carolyn 1996
Joy, Michael 1997
Bevan, Hugh 1959*
Chapman, James 1987*

33 BEDFORD ROW

London, WC1R 4JH
0171 242 6476
Fax: 0171 831 6065; DX 75 London
E-mail:
clerks@bedfordrow33.demon.co.uk
URL:
http://www.bedfordrow33.demon.co.uk

Chambers of David Barnard
Clerks: Alastair Roberts, Spencer Payne, Helen d'Agostino; Practice Manager: Michael Lieberman

Barnard, David 1967†
Kogan, Barry 1973‡
May, Nigel 1974‡
Zeidman, Martyn QC 1974†
Whippman, Constance 1978
Bendall, Richard 1979
Stanton, David 1979
Webber, Gary 1979
Galberg, Marc 1982
Burke, Michael 1985
Castle, Susan 1986
Fitzgibbon, Francis 1986
Spratt, Christopher 1986
Thorne, Timothy 1987

Lonsdale, David 1988
Oxlade, Joanne 1988
Soor, Smair 1988
Sinclair, Jean-Paul 1989
Jones, Rhys 1990
James, Rachael 1992
Clarke, Joanne 1993
Cleeve, Thomas 1993
Pullen, Timothy 1993
Boyd, Tom 1995
Armstrong, Stuart 1995
Law, John 1996
Harrison, Piers 1997
Houghton, Mark 1980*
Leader, Sheldon 1980*

17 BEDFORD ROW

London, WC1R 4EB
0171 831 7314
Fax: 0171 831 0061; DX 370 London, Chancery Lane
Other comms: Mobile: 0831 234861
E-mail: iboard7314@aol.com
Out of hours telephone: 01494 676504

Chambers of Allan Levy QC
Clerk: Ian D Boardman

Levy, Allan QC 1969†
Jennings, Nigel 1967

Gill, Jane 1973

CHAMBERS OF MICHAEL PERT QC

Formerly 1 King's Bench Walk

36 Bedford Row, London, WC1R 4JH
0171 421 8000
Fax: 0171 421 8080; DX LDE 360
Other comms: Link: 36bedfordrow
E-mail: 36bedfordrow@link.org
URL: http://www.36bedfordrow.co.uk

Chambers of Michael Pert QC

Clerks: Martin Poulter (Senior Clerk), Graeme Logan (Silks Clerk), Joanne Pickersgill (Senior Criminal Clerk), Harri Bennetts (Criminal Clerk), Richard Cade (Civil and Family Clerk), Everton Wedderburn (Civil and Family Clerk), Lynne Edmond (Senior Fees Clerk); Practice Manager: Peter Bennett FCCA MCIM; Administrator: Louise West

Also at: 24 Albion Place, Northampton NN1 1UD Tel: 01604 602333 Fax: 01604 601600; 104 New Walk, Leicester LE1 7EA Tel: 0116 2492020 Fax: 0116 2550885

Pert, Michael QC *1970*†	**Tayton,** Lynn *1981*
Escott-Cox, Brian QC *1954*	**Farrell,** Edmund *1981*
Bowley, Martin QC *1962*	**Wilson,** Richard *1981*
Hunt, James QC *1968*†	**Akman,** Mercy *1982*
Raggatt, Timothy QC *1972*†	**Plunkett,** Christopher *1983*
Stokes, Michael QC *1971*†	**Harbage,** William *1983*
Oldham, Frances QC *1977*†	**Bull,** Simon *1984*
Browne, Nicholas QC *1971*†	**Ecob,** Joanne *1985*
Benson, Richard QC *1974*†	**Underwood,** Robert *1986*
Swindells, Heather QC *1974*†	**Gumpert,** Benjamin *1987*
	Malik, Amjad *1987*
Walker, Annabel QC *1976*†	**Pryce,** Gregory *1988*
Weekes, Anesta QC *1981*‡	**Aspden,** Gordon *1988*
Urquhart, Andrew *1963*	**Howarth,** Andrew *1988*
Waine, Stephen *1969*†	**Johnson,** Amanda *1990*
Altaras, David *1969*†	**Gibson,** John *1991*
Metcalf, Christopher *1972*†	**Lowe,** Matthew *1991*
Lee, David *1973*	**Alford,** Stuart *1992*
de Burgos, Jamie *1973*	**Gaunt,** Sarah *1992*
Fowler, Michael *1974*‡	**Dean,** Rosa *1993*
Solomons, Geoffrey *1974*	**Lloyd-Jones,** John *1993*
Greaves, Michael *1976*	**Johnston,** Karen *1994*
Mainds, Allan *1977*†	**Jupp,** Jeffrey *1994*
Lewis, Charles *1977*	**Bojarski,** Andrzej *1995*
Neaves, Andrew *1977*	**Kirk,** Jonathan *1995*
Morrison, Howard OBE *1977*†	**Ferguson,** Niall *1996*
Farrell, David *1978*‡	**Skilbeck,** Rupert *1996*
Gargan, Catherine *1978*	**Connolly,** Oliver *1997*
Beddoe, Martin *1979*	**Brunner,** Kate *1997*
Kushner, Martine *1980*	**Barry,** Kevin *1997*
Donnellan, Christopher *1981*	**Joyce,** Peter QC *1968**†
	Treacy, Colman QC *1971**†
	Ingham, Elizabeth *1989**
	Payne, Richard *1964**

Types of work (and number of counsel practising in that area if supplied)

Administrative 3 · Agriculture 2 · Bankruptcy 2 · Care proceedings 20 · Commercial 14 · Commercial property 2 · Common land 1 · Common law (general) 10 · Courts martial 1 · Crime 41 · Crime – corporate fraud 17 · Discrimination 2 · Employment 8 · Environment 2 · Family 20 · Family provision 20 · Foreign law 1 · Housing 2 · Landlord and tenant 6 · Licensing 1 · Local government 2 · Medical negligence 14 · Mental health 1 · Personal injury 25 · Professional negligence 14 · Sports 1 · Town and country planning 3

Chambers established: 1890
Opening times: 8.30 am-6.30 pm

Chambers' facilities

Conference rooms, Video conferences, Disks accepted, Disabled access, E-mail, Also at Northampton and Leicester annexe, ISO 9002 quality accredited chambers, web site at http://www.36bedfordrow.co.uk, Conditional fees, Direct Professional Access

Languages spoken

French, German, Polish, Serbo-Croat, Spanish, Urdu

Fees policy

We are a large set with low overheads which allows good barristers to be charged at competitive rates. Fee rates are available to clients.

Chambers of Michael Pert QC

Chambers is a progressive, London based, Midland and Oxford Circuit set, founded 1890.

Sixty members including twelve Silks operate within three specialist teams: **crime, civil and commercial, and family.** Among these are thirteen Recorders or Assistant Recorders. James Hunt QC was elected Leader of the Circuit in 1996.

A full list of our specialities is given above. We have a brochure for chambers generally, for each team and for our commercial and fraud expertise. All of these are available on request and are available, together with a short CV for every Barrister, on our world wide web site.

Each team has the strength and depth to handle cases of the utmost complexity or sensitivity. Recent cases include Matrix Churchill, the Herald of Free Enterprise, Ruth Neave murder trial and the Twyford Down M3 motorway planning inquiry. Teams follow published standards, including maximum response times, for briefs and other communications.

Annexes in Northampton and Leicester are fully staffed, have computer links to chambers and have good video conferencing facilities, offered at no charge to clients.

Through our compliance with the Bar Practice Management Standard and Equality Code we are the **only chambers to have been awarded ISO 9002 quality accreditation.** We see this as indicative of our commitment to a modern approach, which treats instructing solicitors as valued clients.

48 BEDFORD ROW

London, WC1R 4LR
0171 430 2005
Fax: 0171 831 4885; DX 284 London
Out of hours telephone: 0181 857 5418

Chambers of Roderick I'Anson Banks
Practice Manager: Mrs K E Pangratis

Banks, Roderick *1974*

29 BEDFORD ROW CHAMBERS

London, WC1R 4HE
0171 831 2626
Fax: 0171 831 0626; DX 1044 London

Chambers of Peter Ralls QC

9-12 BELL YARD

London, WC2A 2LF
0171 400 1800
Fax: 0171 404 1405; DX 390 London
E-mail: clerks@bellyard.co.uk
URL: http://www.bellyard.co.uk
Out of hours telephone: 01702 200838

Chambers of D Anthony Evans QC
Clerk: Gary Reed (Senior Clerk)

Evans, Anthony QC *1965*†   Lawson, Edmund QC *1971*

Carlile, Alex QC *1970*†
Birnbaum, Michael QC *1969*†
Carter-Manning, Jeremy QC *1975*†
Curran, Patrick QC *1972*†
Woodley, Sonia QC *1968*†
Rouch, Peter QC *1972*†
Spencer, Robin QC *1978*†
Kerrigan, Herbert QC (Scot) *1990*
Grayson, Edward *1948*
Caton, Peter *1963*
Cherrill, Richard *1965*
Field, Martin *1966*†
Phelvin, Bernard *1971*
Merz, Richard *1972*
Barker, Alison *1973*
Greaves, John *1973*
Heaton-Armstrong, Anthony *1973*
Owen, Tudor *1974*†
Cranbrook, Alexander *1975*
Doyle, Peter *1975*
John, Stephen *1975*
Harwood-Stevenson, John *1975*
Katz, Philip *1976*
Moss, Peter *1976*

Spencer, Timothy *1976*
Hadrill, Keith *1977*
Orsulik, Michael *1978*
Chan, Dianne *1979*
Williams, John *1979*
McGuinness, John *1980*
Egan, Michael *1981*
Davies, Jonathan N *1981*
Enright, Sean *1982*
Chawla, Mukul *1983*
Laing, Christine *1984*
Khamisa, Mohammed *1985*
McAtasney, Philippa *1985*
Bryant-Heron, Mark *1986*
Hughes, William *1989*
Ellis, Sarah *1989*
Chaplin, Adrian *1990*
Healy, Alexandra *1992*
Seymour, Mark *1992*
Jory, Richard *1993*
Reeve, Suzanne *1993*
Tatford, Warwick *1993*
Kinnear, Jonathan *1994*
Russell, Christina *1994*
Davey, Tina *1993*
Gavron, Jessica *1995*
Denton, Michelle *1996*
Griffin, Neil *1996*

Types of work (and number of counsel practising in that area if supplied)
Administrative 10 · Chancery (general) 10 · Commercial litigation 10 · Common law (general) 27 · Courts martial 1 · Crime 49 · Crime – corporate fraud 25 · Licensing 17 · Local government 32 · Personal injury 20 · Professional negligence 10 · Sports 1

Opening times: 8 am-6.30 pm

Chambers' facilities
Conference rooms, Video conferences, Disks accepted, Disabled access, Chambers is fully computerised

Languages spoken
French, German, Hindi, Italian, Russian, Spanish, Urdu

Fees policy
Further information, including fees rates, can be obtained from the clerks.

Additional information
9-12 Bell Yard is one of the largest criminal and common law Chambers in the country. Established over 30 years ago, it has continually developed to meet the demands within its focused areas of expertise. It has

C

recently acquired substantial additional accommodation at 5 Bell Yard. Members of Chambers have been involved in some of the most widely reported cases including Blue Arrow, Maxwell, BCCI, the Marchioness disaster, the criminal trials following the Guildford Four and Birmingham Six Appeals and the Stephen Lawrence Public Inquiry. The ability and expertise of members is widely recognised. A number of members have been recognised by their appointment to judicial and other legal positions.

Criminal litigation: From the largest of City firms to the smallest of High Street practices, advocacy and advisory work is undertaken at all levels. Professional clients include in-house lawyers of major companies, local authorities, government departments and professional institutions. Chambers welcomes Direct Professional Instructions. Prosecution work is undertaken on behalf of prosecuting authorities, public and private, local and national. Chambers has a particular established expertise in fraud (including corporate and commercial fraud and cases with an international dimension); drugs and money laundering (both prosecuting and defending); sexual offences (wide experience combined with sensitivity); judicial review (a growing and more varied field arising from criminal cases); environment (members increasingly engaged in litigation concerning the enforcement of environmental legislation).

Civil litigation: Both leading and junior members advise and appear in cases concerning company law, consumer credit, contract, employment, landlord and tenant, personal injury, professional negligence and sports law. Members also undertake cases before Tribunals in connection with professional disciplinary proceedings and planning issues.

Other areas of practice: Arbitration, comparative law, criminal injuries compensation, environment, inquests, judicial review, licensing and self-regulatory tribunals.

Recruitment: Tenancy applications to D Anthony Evans QC. On average, there are six pupillages in Chambers at any one time. Pupillage applications are only accepted if made through PACH. Further enquiries can be made to William Hughes.

BELL YARD CHAMBERS

116/118 Chancery Lane, London, WC2A 1PP
0171 306 9292
Fax: 0171 404 5143; DX 0075 London
Out of hours telephone: 0181 290 5129

Clerks: Mrs Karen Bardens, Mr Philip Bishop

Lee, John *1960*	**Robinson,** Daniel *1993*
Kerner, Angela *1965*	**Stirling,** Christopher *1993*
Brigden, Anthony *1967†*	**Peel,** Stuart *1994*
Gibson-Lee, David *1970*	**Sheehan,** Anne-Marie *1994*
Sutton, Philip *1971*	**Siva,** Kannan *1996*
Mitchell, Brenton *1973*	**Pickersgill,** David *1996*
Roebuck, Roy *1974*	**Weeden,** Ross *1996*
Guy-Davies, Judith *1976*	**Haji,** Shaheen *1997*
Clarke, Michelle *1988*	**Booth,** Roger *1966**
Beard, David *1990*	**Fridd,** Nicholas *1975**
Simpson, James *1990*	**Kelleher,** Keith *1987**
Twomey, Mark *1990*	**Marlow,** Patricia *1988**
Salmon, Louise *1991*	**Dunn,** Timothy *1996**
Wright, Trevor *1992*	**Prentice,** Dorothy *1983**
Richardson, Paul *1993*	**Taylor,** Ross *1984**

BELMARSH CHAMBERS

20 Warland Road, London, SE18 2EU
0181 316 7322

Chambers of Miss V C Cameron

4 BINGHAM PLACE

London, W1M 3FF
0171 486 5347/071 487 5910
Fax: 0171 224 6057

Chambers of Mr S M Bhanji

BLACKSTONE CHAMBERS

Blackstone House, Temple, London, EC4Y 9BW
0171 583 1770

† Recorder ‡ Assistant Recorder *Door Tenant

Fax: 0171 822 7222; DX 281 London
E-mail: clerks@blackstonechambers.com
URL: http://www.blackstonechambers.com
Out of hours telephone: 0171 822 7272

Chambers of Presiley Baxendale QC, Charles Flint QC

Clerks: Martin Smith, Gary Oliver;
Practice Manager: Julia Hornor

Ross-Munro, Colin QC *1951*	Beale, Judith *1978*
Brodie, Stanley QC *1954*	Lang, Beverley *1978*
Lester of Herne Hill, Lord QC *1963*	Beazley, Thomas *1979*
Sinclair, Sir Ian QC *1952*	Goulding, Paul *1984*
Brownlie, Ian QC *1958*	Carss-Frisk, Monica *1985*
Donaldson, David QC *1968†*	Lewis, Adam *1985*
Englehart, Robert QC *1969†*	Peto, Anthony *1985*
Hunt, David QC *1969†*	Anderson, Robert *1986*
Dohmann, Barbara QC *1971†*	Clarke, Gerard *1986*
Pugh, Andrew QC *1961†*	Shaw, Mark *1987*
Forrester, Ian QC (Scot) *1996*	Green, Andrew *1988*
Goode, Roy QC *1988*	Howe, Robert *1988*
Mendelson, Maurice QC *1965*	Briggs, Adrian *1989*
Harvie, Jonathan QC *1973‡*	Rose, Dinah *1989*
Baxendale, Presiley QC *1974*	Fordham, Michael *1990*
Pannick, David QC *1979†*	Saini, Pushpinder *1991*
Jowell, Jeffrey QC *1965*	Croxford, Thomas *1992*
Nathan, Stephen QC *1969‡*	Herberg, Javan *1992*
Flint, Charles QC *1975*	Hunter, Andrew *1993*
Hepple, Bob QC *1966*	Pollard, Joanna *1993*
Mill, Ian QC *1981*	Collier, Jane *1994*
Levy, Gerald *1964*	Dixon, Emma *1994*
Oliver, Dawn *1965*	White, Gemma *1994*
Sutton, Alastair *1972*	de la Mare, Thomas *1995*
Page, Hugo *1977*	Mulcahy, Jane *1995*
	Weisselberg, Tom *1995*
	Ellins, Julia *1994*
	Gallafent, Kate *1997*
	George, Andrew *1997*
	Fitzmaurice, Maurice *1969**
	Morse, Christopher *1972**

Types of work (and number of counsel practising in that area if supplied)

Administrative · Arbitration · Banking · Chancery (general) · Civil liberties · Commercial · Commodities · Company and commercial · Competition · Copyright · Corporate finance · Crime – corporate fraud · Defamation · Discrimination · EC and competition law · Employment · Energy · Entertainment · Environment · Film, cable, TV · Financial services · Foreign law · Immigration · Insurance · Insurance/reinsurance · Intellectual property · International trade · Partnerships · Private international · Professional negligence · Public

international · Sale and carriage of goods · Sports

Opening times: 8.15 am-7 pm; out of hours contact always available.

Chambers' facilities

Conference rooms, Disks accepted, Disabled access, E-mail

Languages spoken

Dutch, Finnish, French, German, Hindi, Italian, Japanese, Norwegian, Portuguese, Russian, Spanish, Swedish, Urdu

Additional information

The reputation of Blackstone Chambers (formerly 2 Hare Court) is founded on its special mix of commercial and public law work.

Commercial work covers a wide range of general contract and business law including international trade, banking, insurance, shipping, conflict of laws, financial services, media and entertainment, intellectual property, sports law and professional negligence. Members of chambers appear regularly in all divisions of the High Court. Instructions are undertaken in arbitrations, both domestic and international, and in proceedings before different types of tribunals. Blackstone Chambers has a strong specialist practice, experienced in advising and litigating on public international law disputes.

The public law work undertaken by chambers covers the human rights arena and judicial review work both for and against public bodies arising from decisions in many and varied areas. Such areas include freedom of expression, immigration, education, social security, housing, planning, and local government.

A team of employment law specialists offers advice and representation in all relevant tribunals and the High Court covering all aspects of employment law, including sex, race and disability discrimination.

Members appear not only in the English courts but also before the European Court of Justice, the European Court of Human Rights and in other Commonwealth jurisdictions.

Within these broad categories individual members of chambers offer advice and representation over a wide range of commercial and public law topics. Reference should be made to the clerks for further details.

11 BOLT COURT (ALSO AT 7 STONE BUILDINGS - 1ST FLOOR)

London, EC4A 3DQ
0171 353 2300
Fax: 0171 353 1878; DX 0022 London
E-mail: boltct11@aol.com
Out of hours telephone: 01737 814 791

Clerks: John Lister (Director of Chambers), Scott Savage; Practice Manager: (Redhill Chambers) Jan Rogers

Also at: Redhill Chambers, Seloduct House, 30 Station Road, Redhill RH1 1NF
Tel: 01737 780781, Fax: 01737 761760

Alexander, Ian QC *1964*†	**Tod,** Jonathan *1990*
Ashmore, Terence *1961*	**Murch,** Stephen *1991*
Bishop, John *1970*	**Benner,** Lucinda *1992*
Martin, Gay *1970*	**Carron,** Richard *1992*
Wood, Penelope (formerly a	**Burrington,** Richard *1993*
solicitor) *1999*	**Gerrish,** Simon *1993*
Conway, Robert *1974*	**Le Quesne,** Catherine *1993*
Lynch, Julian *1976*	**Linstead,** Peter *1994*
Lewis, Robert (formerly a	**Mathias,** Anna *1994*
solicitor) *1996*	**Papazian,** Cliona *1994*
Temple-Bone, Gillian *1978*	**Rudd,** Matthew *1994*
Birks, Simon *1981*	**Casey,** Noel *1995*
Randle, Simon *1982*	**Ellis,** Jonathan *1995*
Jenkala, Adrian *1984*	**Simkin,** Iain *1995*
Manson, Juliann *1985*	**Badenoch,** Tony *1996*
Pyle, Susan *1985*	**Islam-Choudhury,** Mugni
Owens, Matthew *1988*	*1996*
Porter, Geoffrey *1988*	**McGregor,** Alexander *1996*
Airey, Simon *1989*	**Porter,** Sarah *1996*
Cave, Patricia *1989*	**Harris,** Richard *1997*
Lakha, Shabbir *1989*	**Husain,** Laureen *1997*
Swirsky, Adam *1989*	**Langton,** Steven *1998*
Gordon, Mark *1990*	**Moys,** Clive *1998*
Livingstone, Simon *1990*	

BOND STREET CHAMBERS

Standbrook House, 2-5 Old Bond Street, Mayfair, London, W1X 3TB
01932 342951
Fax: 01932 336176

Chambers of Mr R T F Turrall-Clarke

23 BRACKEN GARDENS

Barnes, London, SW13 9HW
0181 748 4924
Fax: 0181 741 4814

Chambers of Mr A T Nicolson

BRACTON CHAMBERS

95a Chancery Lane, London, WC2A 1DT
0171 242 4248
Fax: 0171 242 4232; DX 416 London
Other comms: Mobile: 0421 866858
Out of hours telephone: 0421 866858

Chambers of Ian McCulloch
Clerks: Ian Hogg (Senior Clerk), John Crimmins (Junior Clerk), David Hogg (Junior Clerk)

McCulloch, Ian *1951*	**Webb,** Stanley *1993*
Bailey, Thomas *1984*	**Macpherson,** Duncan *1994*
Preston, Nicholas *1986*	**McHugh,** David *1994*
Harries, Raymond *1988*	**Thorndike,** Tony *1994*
Iyer, Sunil *1988*	**Chesner,** Howard *1995*
Lamacraft, Ian *1989*	**Sheppard,** Timothy *1995*
Shuman, Karen *1991*	**Paget,** Michael *1995*
Brockley, Nigel *1992*	**Hutchin,** Edward *1996*
Bensted, Rebecca *1993*	**Simpson,** Ian *1997*
Campbell-Brown, Louise	
1993	

4 BREAMS BUILDINGS

London, EC4A 1AQ
0171 353 5835/430 1221
Fax: 0171 430 1677; DX 1042 London
E-mail:
breams@4breamsbuildings.law.co.uk
URL:
http://www.4breamsbuildings.law.co.uk

Chambers of C J Lockhart-Mummery QC
Clerks: S Graham, J Fullilove

Lockhart-Mummery, Christopher QC *1971*
Macleod, Nigel QC *1961†*
Cherryman, John QC *1955†*
Hands, David QC *1965*
Kingsland, Lord QC *1972*
Gilbart, Andrew QC *1972*†*
Harper, Joseph QC *1970*
Howell, John QC *1979*
Drabble, Richard QC *1975*
Holgate, David QC *1978*
Katkowski, Christopher QC *1982*
Sydenham, Colin *1963*
Owen, Eric *1969**
Bickford-Smith, Stephen *1972*
Caws, Eian *1974*
Bailey-King, Robert *1975*
Seifert, Anne *1975*

Lewsley, Christopher *1976*
Male, John *1976*
Dilhorne, The Rt Hon Viscount *1979*
Smith, David *1980*
Williams, Anne *1980*
Barrett, John *1982**
Elvin, David *1983*
Robinson, Alice *1983*
Mould, Timothy *1987*
Lieven, Nathalie *1989*
Litton, John *1989*
Taggart, Nicholas *1991*
McHugh, Karen *1992*
Forsdick, David *1993*
Morshead, Timothy *1995*
Keen, Graeme *1995*
Maurici, James *1996*
Oakes, Alison *1996*

Types of work (and number of counsel practising in that area if supplied)

Administrative 25 · Agriculture 7 · Arbitration 4 · Chancery (general) 2 · Chancery land law 12 · Charities 1 · Commercial property 17 · Common land 7 · Construction 1 · Conveyancing 2 · EC and competition law 1 · Education 4 · Employment 3 · Energy 6 · Environment 31 · Equity, wills and trusts 1 · Housing 8 · Immigration 2 · Landlord and tenant 24 · Local government 32 · Mental health 1 · Parliamentary 20 · Partnerships 1 · Planning 39 · Professional negligence 8 · Tax – capital and income 1 · Tax – corporate 1 · Town and country planning 29

Chambers established: 1945
Opening times: 9 am-6.15 pm

Chambers' facilities

Conference rooms, Disks accepted, Disabled access, Air conditioning

Languages spoken

French

Additional information

This is a long-established chambers which formerly practised at 2 Paper Buildings. It provides experience and expertise in advocacy, drafting and advisory work, and specialised fields include public and property law, all aspects of local government law, planning, judicial review and landlord and tenant.

Members act for a wide range of clients including individuals (some of whom may be legally aided), companies, local authorities and government agencies. It also accepts direct instructions from other professions in accordance with the Bar Council direct professional access arrangements. In addition, special expertise in taxation, social security law and European law is available within chambers.

Being a new building, facilities have been tailored to the precise requirements of chambers' practice. It provides four fully-equipped conference rooms, air conditioning, and computer network links enabling the facility for rapid drafting and finalisation of documents. For further information contact the clerks.

Published works include:

Hill's Law of Town & Country Planning (4th edn)
Town Planning Law Handbook & Casebook
Atkins Court Forms: Town & Country Planning
Halsbury's Laws: Town & Country Planning (edited entirely within chambers)
Hill & Redman's Law of Landlord & Tenant
Halsbury's Laws: Landlord & Tenant Encyclopaedia of Rating & Local Taxation
Atkins Court Forms: Rating & Local Taxation
Corfield & Carnwath's Compulsory Acquisition & Compensation
Unlawful Interference with Land
Emdens Building Contracts & Practice
Halsbury's Laws: European Communities
Halsbury's Laws: Compulsory Purchase
Party Walls: The New Law

1 BRICK COURT

1st Floor, Temple, London, EC4Y 9BY
0171 353 8845
Fax: 0171 583 9144; DX 468 London
E-mail: clerks@1brickcourt.co.uk

Chambers of R L C Hartley QC

Clerks: J Woodcock, D Mace, E Billimore

Hartley, Richard QC *1956*
Rampton, Richard QC *1965*
Shaw, Geoffrey QC *1968*
Shields, Thomas QC *1973*
Caldecott, Andrew QC *1975*
Garnier, Edward QC *1976‡*
Boggis-Rolfe, Harry *1969*

Moloney, Patrick QC *1976‡*
Sharp, Victoria *1979‡*
Suttle, Stephen *1980*
Starte, Harvey *1985*
Barca, Manuel *1986*
Atkinson, Timothy *1988*
Elliott, Rupert *1988*

C

Phillips, Jane *1989*
Addy, Caroline *1991*
Hinchliff, Benjamin *1992*

Crown, Giles *1993*
Evans, Catrin *1994*
Skinner, Lorna *1997*

4 BRICK COURT

Temple, London, EC4Y 9AD
0171 797 8910
Fax: 0171 797 8929; DX 491 London
E-mail: medhurst@dial.pipex.com

Chambers of D C Medhurst
Clerk: Michael Corrigan

Medhurst, David *1969*
Chatterjee, Mira *1973*
Burgess, David *1975*
Colover, Robert *1975*
Hildyard, Marianna *1977*
Mitchell, Janet *1978*
Haynes, Michael *1979*
Quinn, Susan *1983*
St Clair Gainer, Richard *1983*
Roberts, Marc *1984*
Lynch, Peter *1985*
Bell, Anthony *1985*
Molyneux, Simon *1986*
Mylonas-Widdall, Michael *1988*

Ishmael, Colin *1989*
Sheppard, Abigail *1990*
Storey-Rea, Alexa *1990*
Wentworth, Annabel *1990*
Cooper, Penelope *1990*
Knapp, Edward *1992*
Simon, Michael *1992*
Knowles, Gwynneth *1993*
Peter, Levi *1993*
Sumeray, Caroline *1993*
Piyadasa, Sue *1994*
Perks, Jolyon *1994*
Pritchard, Teresa *1994*
Morton, Rachael *1995*
Morris, Sarah *1996*
Griffin, Ian *1997*

Types of work (and number of counsel practising in that area if supplied)
Common law (general) 9 · Crime 16 · EC and competition law 4 · Extradition 2 · Family 14 · Immigration 4 · Landlord and tenant 5 · Licensing 3 · Medical negligence 2 · Personal injury 4

Chambers established: 1977
Opening times: 8.30 am-6.30 pm

Chambers' facilities
Conference rooms, Video conferences

Languages spoken
French, Greek, Hebrew, Hindi, Italian, Mandarin Chinese, Russian, Spanish

Fees policy
Please refer to clerks.

4 BRICK COURT

Ground Floor, Temple, London, EC4Y 9AD
0171 797 7766
Fax: 0171 797 7700; DX 404 London

Chambers of A M N Shaw QC

4 BRICK COURT, CHAMBERS OF ANNE RAFFERTY QC

BRICK | COURT

1st Floor, Temple, London, EC4Y 9AD
0171 583 8455
Fax: 0171 353 1699; DX 453 London, Chancery Lane

Chambers of Anne J Rafferty QC
Clerk: Michael Eves

Rafferty, Anne QC *1973*†
Berry, Anthony QC *1976*‡
Garside, Charles QC *1971*†
Marsh, Elizabeth QC *1979*
Colton, Mary *1955*†
May, Patricia *1965*†
Germain, Richard *1968*
Carne, Roger *1969*
Lockyer, Jane *1970*
Chinn, Antony *1972*‡
Williams, David *1972*
Bright, Andrew *1973*‡
Sheridan, Shane *1973*
Mirwitch, Jane *1974*
Williams, Owen *1974*
Testar, Peter *1974*‡
Zeitlin, Derek James *1977*
Pitts, Anthony *1975*‡
Jones, Nicholas *1975*†
Fortune, Robert *1976*
Carey-Hughes, Richard *1977*‡
Traversi, John *1977*

French, Louis *1979*
Markson, Jonathan *1980*
Kennedy, Matthew *1981*
Rouse, Justin *1982*
Speak, Michael *1983*
Henderson, James *1984*
Lakha, Abbas *1984*
Monro Davies, Tiffany *1984*
Whittaker, David *1986*
Young, David *1986*
Cammegh, John *1987*
D'Arcy, Louise *1988*
Stirling, Simon *1989*
Smart, Roger *1989*
Wicks, Iain *1990*
Akinsanya, Jonathan *1993*
Mackeson-Sandbach, Antoinette *1993*
Arora, Anita *1994*
Rappo, Patrick *1995*
Cohen, Samantha *1995*
Maher, Michael *1995*

Types of work (and number of counsel practising in that area if supplied)
Courts martial · Crime – corporate fraud

Opening times: 8.30 am-7 pm

Chambers' facilities
Conference rooms

Languages spoken
French, Hindi, Italian, Spanish

† Recorder ‡ Assistant Recorder *Door Tenant

Additional information

This is a large set of chambers with 43 members which undertakes all aspects of criminal law in courts ranging from the magistrates and crown courts through to the Court of Appeal (Criminal Division), the House of Lords and the Privy Council. The set undertakes a well-balanced mixture of prosecution and defence cases which encompasses all areas of criminal work, including serious fraud matters. In addition, members regularly undertake a wide range of work in courts martial, police disciplinary hearings and licensing applications.

As the turn of the century approaches chambers is in a position to deal with the changes imposed on the Criminal Bar. Our Head of Chambers, the former Chairman of the Criminal Bar Association, and other members serving on that and other committees are instrumental in protecting the interests of the Bar and those we represent.

Barling, Gerald QC 1972*†	Quigley, Conor 1985
Simon, Peregrine QC 1973‡	Garland, David 1986
Charlton, Timothy QC 1974	Calver, Neil 1987
Hapgood, Mark QC 1979	Chambers, Dominic 1987
Gordon, Richard QC 1972	Slade, Richard 1987
Howard, Mark QC 1980	Matovu, Harry 1988
Ruttle, Stephen QC 1976	Kinsky, Cyril 1988
Popplewell, Andrew QC 1981	Wright, Paul 1990
	Lee, Sarah 1990
Leggatt, George QC 1983	Davies, Helen 1991
Wood, William QC 1980	Adam, Tom 1991
Green, Nicholas QC 1986	Hoskins, Mark 1991
Jones, David QC 1975†	Roxburgh, Alan 1992
Hollander, Charles QC 1978	Stratford, Jemima 1993
Walker, Paul QC 1979	Haydon, Alec 1993
Anderson, David QC 1985	Bools, Michael 1991
Irvin, Peter 1972	Masefield, Roger 1994
Brunner, Peter 1971	Robertson, Aidan 1995
Flynn, James 1978	Salzedo, Simon 1995
Lydiard, Andrew 1980	Dhillon, Jasbir 1996
Lord, Richard 1981	Thomas, Andrew 1996
Otton-Goulder, Catharine 1963	Jolowicz, John QC 1952*
	MacRory, Richard 1974*
Brealey, Mark 1984	Muchlinski, Peter 1981*
Swainston, Michael 1985	Wyatt, Derrick QC 1972*
Randolph, Fergus 1985	Andenas, Mads 1997*

BRICK COURT CHAMBERS

BRICK COURT CHAMBERS

BARRISTERS

7-8 Essex Street, London, WC2R 3LD
0171 379 3550
Fax: 0171 379 3558; DX 302 London
Other comms: Mobiles: 0468 614183 J Hawes and 0468 614193 I Moyler
E-mail: [surname]@brickcourt.co.uk
URL: http://www.brickcourt.co.uk

Chambers of C S Clarke QC
Clerks: Julian Hawes, Ian Moyler;
Administrator: Nancy Lockwood

Also at: 36 Avenue D'Augerham, B 1040 Brussels Tel: 00322 230 3161, Fax: 00322 230 03347

Clarke, Christopher QC 1969†	Chambers, Nicholas QC 1966†
Lyell, Sir Nicholas QC PC, MP 1965	Sumption, Jonathan QC 1975†
Owen, Philip QC 1949	Heilbron, Hilary QC 1971
Kentridge, Sir Sydney QC 1977	Forwood, Nicholas QC 1970
	Cran, Mark QC 1973
Vaughan, David QC 1963†	Hirst, Jonathan QC 1975

BRIDEWELL CHAMBERS

BRIDEWELL
CHAMBERS

2 Bridewell Place, London, EC4V 6AP
020 7797 8800
Fax: 020 7797 8801; DX 383 London
E-mail: HughesGage@bridewell.law.co.uk
URL: http://www.bridewell.law.co.uk
Out of hours telephone: 01708 640863/ 07957 295669

Chambers of C W Challenger
Clerk: Lee Hughes-Gage (Senior Clerk)

Challenger, Colin 1970	Clemens, Adam 1985
Boothby, Joseph 1972†	Doyle, James 1985
Pringle, Gordon 1973	Enoch, Dafydd 1985
Oliver, Juliet 1974	Josse, David 1985
James, Ernest 1977	Lawrie, Ian 1985
Knight, Adrienne 1981	Walsh, Simon 1987
Gray, Peter 1984	Atherton, Sally 1987

Michell, Paul *1991*
Rothwell, Carolyn *1991*
Walmsley, Alan *1991*
Cummins, Brian *1992*
Sefton-Smith, Lloyd *1993*
Slaughter, Andrew *1993*

Walker, Paul *1993*
Scotland, Maria *1995*
Pearson, Christopher *1995*
Morley, Stephen *1996*
Chandran, Parosha *1997*
Woodhouse, Charles *1997*

BRITTON STREET CHAMBERS

1st Floor, 20 Britton Street, London,
EC1M 5NQ
0171 608 3765
Fax: 0171 608 3746; DX 53329 Clerkenwell
Out of hours telephone: 0410 684776

Chambers of M T Gederon
Clerk: Ms R M Phillips

Gederon, Marvin *1979*
Rafique, Tariq *1961*
Aslangul, Michel *1978*
Ramdeen, Kamala *1978*
Lovell, Jeanette *1976*
Panton, William *1977*
Sheikh, Amjad *1988*
Atunwa, Razak *1994*
Desouza, Esperanza *1994*

Lanlehin, Olajide *1994*
Maciel, Kareena *1994*
Hallowes, Rupert *1995*
Carrington, Dominic *1996*
Al-Ani, Abdul-Haq *1996*
Bibi, Samiyya *1996*
Adamson, Alan *1997*
Pepper, Dr William *1991**

517 BUNYAN COURT

Barbican, London, EC2Y 8DH
0171 638 5076

Chambers of Mr R H Temblett

CHAMBERS OF MARTIN BURR

Fourth Floor, Eldon Chambers, 30/32 Fleet
Street, London, EC4Y 1AA
0171 353 4636
Fax: 0171 353 4637; DX 146 Chancery Lane

Chambers of Mr M J Burr

CAMBERWELL CHAMBERS

66 Grove Park, Camberwell, London,
SE5 8LF
0171 274 0830
Fax: 0171 274 0830

Chambers of Mr K Gledhill

16A CAMPDEN HILL COURT

Campden Hill Road, London, W8 7HS
0171 937 3492
Fax: 0171 937 3492

Chambers of Mr J W Rae

CARDINAL CHAMBERS

4 Old Mitre Court, 4th Floor, Temple,
London, EC4Y 7BP
020 7353 2622
Fax: 020 7353 2722; DX 138301 London
Chancery Lane
E-mail: admin@cardinal-chambers.co.uk
Out of hours telephone: 0468 003 779/
0797 0252 196

Chambers of Philip Engleman
Practice Managers: Michael Martin, Rod
McGurk (Practice Directors)

Engelman, Philip *1979*
Horgan, Timothy *1982*
King, John *1983*
Power, Lewis *1990*
Ali, Zafar *1994*

Lane-Smith, Zoe *1997*
Afeeva, Mark *1997*
Pezzani, Roger *1997*
Briggs, Joanne *1993**

55B CAVENDISH ROAD

Brondesbury, London, NW2 3TN
0181 830 1495

Chambers of Miss V K Nassar

39 WINDSOR ROAD

London, N3 3SN
0181 349 9194
Fax: 0181 346 8506
E-mail: lindacohen@cobeck.clara.net
Out of hours telephone: 0181 349 9194

Chambers of Linda Cohen
Clerk: J F Beckett

Cohen, Linda *1985*

Bar Directory on the Internet
The Bar Directory is also available on
the Internet at the following address:
http://www.smlawpub.co.uk/bar

---

† Recorder ‡ Assistant Recorder *Door Tenant

CHANCERY CHAMBERS

1st Floor Offices, 70/72 Chancery Lane,
London, WC2A 1AB
0171 405 6879/6870
Fax: 0171 430 0502

Chambers of Mr L A I St Ville

74 CHANCERY LANE

First Floor, London, WC2A 1AA
0171 430 0667
Fax: 0171 430 1358

Chambers of Mr E M Yakubu

95A CHANCERY LANE

London, WC2A 1DT
0171 405 3101
Fax: 0171 405 3112

Chambers of Mrs M Sparrow

CLAPHAM CHAMBERS

21-25 Bedford Road, Clapham North,
London, SW4 7SH
0171 978 8482/642 5777
Fax: 0171 642 5777; DX 53263 Clapham
Common

Chambers of Mrs B N Hamid

CLOISTERS

1 Pump Court, Temple, London, EC4Y 7AA
0171 827 4000
Fax: 0171 827 4100; DX 452 Chancery Lane
E-mail: clerks@cloisters.com

Chambers of Laura Cox QC
Chambers Director: Vanessa Peters

Cox, Laura QC *1975†*	Solley, Stephen QC *1969*
Platts-Mills, John QC *1932*	Kershen, Lawrence QC
Worrall, Anna QC *1959†*	*1967*
Newman, Alan QC *1968*	Langstaff, Brian QC *1971†*
Lawson, Elizabeth QC *1969*	Davidson, Arthur QC *1953*

Allen, Robin QC *1974*	Monaghan, Karon *1989*
McCarthy, Roger QC *1975*	Galbraith-Marten, Jason
Price, Roderick *1971*	*1991*
Montrose, Stuart *1972*	Quinn, Christopher *1992*
Crystal, Jonathan *1972*	Ryder, Matthew *1992*
Guest, Peter *1975*	Shaw, Peter *1992*
Culver, Thomas *1976†*	Glyn, Caspar *1992*
Algazy, Jacques *1980*	D'Cruz, Rufus *1993*
Buchan, Andrew *1981*	Sidhu, Navjot *1993*
Turner, Michael *1981*	Brooks, Louise *1994*
White, Antony *1983*	Crasnow, Rachel *1994*
Lynch, Jerome *1983*	Robertson, Sally *1995*
Taylor, Dr Simon *1984*	Laddie, James *1995*
Hendy, Pauline *1985*	Burnham, Ulele *1997*
Bradley, Anthony *1989*	Hill, Henrietta *1997*
Hitchcock, Patricia *1988*	Coghlin, Thomas *1998*
Epstein, Paul *1988*	Thomas, David QC *1992**
Spencer, Paul *1988*	Pimm, Peter *1991**
Kibling, Thomas *1990*	Whitmore, John *1976**

CHAMBERS OF MR PETER CRAMPIN QC

Ground Floor, 11 New Square, Lincoln's
Inn, London, WC2A 3QB
020 7831 0081
Fax: 020 7405 2560/0798; DX 319 London
E-mail: 11newsquare.co.uk
Out of hours telephone: Michael Gibbs,
Home: 01233 840237 Mobile: 0860
737668, Gary Ventura, Home: 01708
384106

Chambers of Peter Crampin QC
Clerks: M J Gibbs (Senior Clerk), G Ventura
(Assistant Senior Clerk)

Crampin, Peter QC *1976†*	Francis, Andrew *1977*
Proudman, Sonia QC *1972*	Dumont, Thomas *1979*
Shillingford, Miles *1964*	Craig, Alistair *1983*
Horne, Roger *1967*	Cooper, Gilead *1983*
Jackson, Dirik *1969†*	Staunton, Ulick *1984*
Castle, Peter *1970*	Feltham, Piers *1985*
Lloyd, Stephen *1971*	Smith, Howard *1986*
Gibson, Jill *1972*	Bleasdale, Marie-Claire
Jefferis, Michael *1976*	*1993*
Studer, Mark *1976*	Margolin, Daniel *1995*
Pearce, Robert *1977*	Rashid, Omar *1997*

**Types of work (and number of counsel practising in
that area if supplied)**
Arbitration · Banking · Bankruptcy ·
Chancery (general) · Chancery land law ·
Charities · Commercial property ·
Common land · Company and commercial
· Conveyancing · Court of Protection ·
Equity, wills and trusts · Family provision ·
Housing · Insolvency · Landlord and tenant
· Local government · Mines and minerals ·

Partnerships · Pensions · Probate and administration · Professional negligence · Rights of light · Sale and carriage of goods · Town and country planning

Opening times: 8.45 am-6.45 pm

Chambers' facilities
Conference rooms, Disks accepted

Languages spoken
French, German, Italian

CRAWFORD CHAMBERS

7 Gerrard House, 23-25 Crawford Place, London, W1H 1HY
0171 724 0835
Fax: 0171 724 0835; DX 94255 Marylebone 2

Chambers of Mr M P W Rattigan

CROMWELL-AYEH-KUMI CHAMBERS

1st Floor Suite, 119 Cricklewood Broadway, London, NW2 3JG
0181 450 6620
Fax: 0181 450 6620; DX 35364 Cricklewood

Chambers of Mr I J Kumi

1 CROWN OFFICE ROW

ONE CROWN OFFICE ROW

Ground Floor, Temple, London, EC4Y 7HH
0171 797 7500
Fax: 0171 797 7550; DX 1020 London, Chancery Lane
E-mail: mail@onecrownofficerow.com

Chambers of Robert J Seabrook QC
Clerks: Matthew Phipps (Senior Clerk), Nick Rees

Annexe: Crown Office Row Chambers, Blenheim House, 120 Church Street, Brighton, Sussex BN1 1WH
Tel: 01273 625625
Fax: 01273 698888

Seabrook, Robert QC 1964†
Owen, Robert QC 1968†
Matheson, Duncan QC 1965†
Vallance, Philip QC 1968
Badenoch, James QC 1968†
Miller, Stephen QC 1971†
Foskett, David QC 1972†
Coghlan, Terence QC 1968†
Mansfield, Guy QC 1972†
Havers, Philip QC 1974†
Smith, Sally QC 1977
Chambers, Gregory 1973
Niblett, Anthony 1976†
Bowron, Margaret 1978†
Rees, Paul 1980
Balcombe, David 1980
King-Smith, James 1980
Hart, David 1982
Garnham, Neil 1982

Forde, Martin 1984
Edis, William 1985
Waddicor, Janet 1985
Freeman, Keith 1985
Gimlette, John 1986
Evans, David 1988
Grant, Kim 1988
Rogers, Paul 1989
McCullough, Angus 1990
Bishop, Keeley 1990
Whitting, John 1991
Downs, Martin 1990
Cave, Jeremy 1992
Booth, Richard 1993
Whipple, Philippa 1994
Chawatama, Sydney 1994
Lambert, Sarah 1994
Thomas, William 1995
Hyam, Jeremy 1995
Hogg, Katharine 1996
Collins, Ben 1996
Rahman, Shaheen 1996

Types of work (and number of counsel practising in that area if supplied)
Administrative 9 · Common law (general) 41 · Construction 10 · Crime 23 · Crime – corporate fraud 8 · Environment 10 · Family 18 · Family provision 18 · Insurance 40 · Insurance/reinsurance 41 · Landlord and tenant 12 · Medical negligence 41 · Personal injury 41 · Professional negligence 41 · Sale and carriage of goods 41 · Town and country planning 9

Chambers' facilities
Conference rooms, Disks accepted

Languages spoken
French, Spanish

Additional information
Chambers' history dates from 1925 when it was established in Fig Tree Court. Following the Second World War, the set moved to Crown Office Row.

This is a common law set now predominantly undertaking civil work with a strong emphasis on all areas of professional negligence work especially medical negligence. Chambers also offers particular expertise in the fields of commercial contract work, personal injury, administrative law, matrimonial finance, environmental pollution, building law and insurance law.

Advocacy is complemented by advisory work. By virtue of its size – 41 barristers of whom 11 are QCs – and the nature of individuals' practices, chambers can offer considerable expertise in specialist areas of the common law.

Chambers insists on the highest professional standards and has a long tradition of providing a thorough training in pupillage, being one of the first sets to organise structured tuition and funding for pupils. As a result, chambers has always been able to select new tenants from among the very ablest candidates.

1 CROWN OFFICE ROW

3rd Floor, Temple, London, EC4Y 7HH
0171 583 9292
Fax: 0171 353 9292; DX 212 London
E-mail: onecor@link.org
URL: http://www.crownofficerow.co.uk
Out of hours telephone: 0956 498217

Chambers of Mark Strachan QC
Clerks: James Donovan, Michael Couser, David Thomas; Administrator: Michael Oliver

Strachan, Mark QC *1969*†	**Lazarus**, Michael *1987*
Le Quesne, Sir Godfray QC *1947*	**Dean**, Peter *1987*
Guthrie, James QC *1975*†	**O'Neill**, Joseph *1987*
Jones, Richard QC *1972*‡	**Stevens**, Howard *1990*
Irvine, Michael *1964*	**Boadita-Cormican**, Aedeen *1990*
McLeod, Iain *1969*†	**Marshall**, Paul *1991*
Neville-Clarke, Sebastian *1973*	**Casey**, Aidan *1992*
Walker, Terence *1973*	**Aslam**, Farzana *1993*
Hewitson, William *1975*	**Dignum**, Marcus *1994*
Young, Andrew *1977*	**Rogers**, Ian *1995*
Janusz, Pierre *1979*	**Kumar**, Umesh *1995*
Knox, Peter *1983*	**Deal**, Katherine Alison Frances *1997*
Dingemans, James *1987*	

TWO CROWN OFFICE ROW

TWO CROWN
OFFICE ROW

Ground Floor, Temple, London, EC4Y 7HJ
020 7797 8100
Fax: 020 7797 8101; DX 344 London

E-mail: mail@2cor.co.uk, or to individual barristers at: [barrister's surname] @2cor.co.uk
URL: http://www.2cor.co.uk

Chambers of Christopher Purchas QC
Clerks: David Newcomb, Nick Hamilton, Jon Miller, Greg Frewin; Administration: Yvonne Probert; Accounts: Sandra Gidaree

Purchas, Christopher QC *1966*†	**Curtis**, Michael *1982*
	Dean, Paul *1982*
Archer, John QC *1950*	**Jones**, Charlotte *1982*
Hamilton, Graeme QC *1959*	**Taylor**, Deborah *1983*
Crowley, John QC *1962*†	**Swan**, Ian *1985*
Harvey, Michael QC *1966*†	**Patten**, Ben *1986*
Wilkinson, Nigel QC *1972*†	**DeCamp**, Jane *1987*
Edwards-Stuart, Antony QC *1976*‡	**Ng**, Ray *1987*
	Snowden, Steven *1989*
Ter Haar, Roger QC *1974*	**Evans-Tovey**, Jason *1990*
Lynagh, Richard QC *1975*	**Howarth**, Simon *1991*
Kent, Michael QC *1975*	**Pershad**, Rohan *1991*
Woods, Jonathan *1965*†	**Rigney**, Andrew *1992*
Tucker, David *1973*‡	**Blakesley**, Patrick *1993*
Matthews, Dennis *1973*	**Weston**, Clive *1993*
Gadney, George *1974*	**Maxwell-Scott**, James *1995*
Saunt, Thomas *1974*	
Stevenson, John *1975*	**Stokell**, Robert *1995*
Holdsworth, James *1977*	**Chalmers**, Suzanne *1995*
Greenbourne, John *1978*	**O'Connor**, Andrew *1996*
Phillips, Andrew *1978*	**Davis**, Andrew *1996*
Guggenheim, Anna *1982*	

Types of work (and number of counsel practising in that area if supplied)
Commercial litigation · Common law (general) · Construction · Insurance · Insurance/reinsurance · Medical negligence · Personal injury · Professional negligence · Sale and carriage of goods

Chambers established: 1940s
Opening times: 8 am-7.30 pm

Chambers' facilities
Conference rooms, Disks accepted, Disabled access, E-mail

Languages spoken
French, Italian

Fees policy
Up to five years call £35–100 per hour. Five to ten years call £75–150 per hour. Over ten years call £100–350 per hour. Hourly rates are intended as a guide and will vary according to the nature and complexity of the work involved. The senior clerk is always happy to discuss rates for particular

cases and suggest counsel who can undertake the work at a range of fee rates.

CRYSTAL CHAMBERS

25A Cintra Park, London, SE19 2LH
0181 402 5801
Fax: 0181 289 8401

Chambers of Mr A Padman

DEAL CHAMBERS

60 Moordown, Shooters Hill, London, SE18 3NG
0181 856 8738
Fax: 0181 856 3888

Chambers of Mr T J Deal

DESIGN CHAMBERS

30 Fleet Street, London, EC4Y 1AA
0171 353 0747
Fax: 0171 353 0722; DX 59 LDE

Chambers of Mr R A Hodgson

DEVEREUX CHAMBERS

DEVEREUX CHAMBERS

Devereux Court, London, WC2R 3JJ
0171 353 7534
Fax: 0171 353 1724; DX 349 London, Chancery Lane
E-mail: mailbox@devchambers.co.uk
URL: http://www.devchambers.co.uk
Out of hours telephone: 0171 353 7534

Chambers of Jeffrey Burke QC
Clerk: Elton Maryon (Senior Clerk); Practice Manager: Clifford Holland, Andrew Frankland; Practice Development Manager: Angela Griffiths

Burke, Jeffrey QC *1964*†	**Glancy**, Robert QC *1972*†
Cotton, Diana QC *1964*†	**Lemon**, Roy *1970*
Pardoe, Alan QC *1971*†	**Wulwik**, Peter *1972*‡
Edelman, Colin QC *1977*†	**Smith**, Prof Ian *1972*

Rabie, Gerald *1973*	**Thornton**, Philip *1988*
Goddard, Christopher *1973*	**Tayler**, James *1989*
Lee, Ian *1973*	**Randall**, Nicholas *1990*
Andrew, Elizabeth *1974*†	**Bryant**, Keith *1991*
Greening, Richard *1975*	**Harrison**, Richard *1991*
Griffith-Jones, David *1975*†	**Joffe**, Natasha *1992*
Clayton, Richard *1977*	**Padfield**, Alison *1992*
Downing, Ruth *1978*‡	**Weir**, Robert *1992*
Bard, Nicholas *1979*	**Burns**, Andrew *1993*
Brennan, Timothy *1981*‡	**Edwards**, Peter *1992*
Killalea, Stephen *1981*	**Basu**, Dijen *1994*
Read, Graham *1981*	**Craig**, David *1997*
Wynter, Colin *1984*	**Seymour**, Lydia *1997*
Carr, Bruce *1986*‡	**Herbert**, Douglas *1973**
Simler, Ingrid *1987*	**Butler**, Christopher *1972**
Heal, Joanna *1988*	

Types of work (and number of counsel practising in that area if supplied)
Administrative · Arbitration · Civil liberties · Commercial litigation · Commercial property · Common law (general) · Company and commercial · Construction · Consumer law · Courts martial · Crime – corporate fraud · Defamation · Discrimination · Education · Employment · Entertainment · Environment · Health & safety · Housing · Information technology · Insurance · Insurance/reinsurance · Landlord and tenant · Local government · Medical negligence · Mental health · Pensions · Personal injury · Professional negligence · Sale and carriage of goods · Sports · Tax – capital and income · Telecommunications

Chambers established: 1948
Opening times: 8.30 am-6.30 pm (24-hr answering service available)

Chambers' facilities
Conference rooms, Video conferences, Disks accepted, Disabled access, Law Society accredited seminar programme, Fully networked IT system, e-mail, Instructions accepted on a conditional fee basis in accordance with recommended conditional fee agreements

Languages spoken
French, German

Fees policy
Devereux Chambers aims to offer competitive rates which the senior clerk will be happy to discuss. Estimates of fees will be given on request.

Devereux Chambers – Chambers of Jeffrey Burke QC

Devereux Chambers offers a comprehensive inter-disciplinary service to its clients. Areas of special expertise include administrative and local government law, commercial litigation, employment law, insurance and reinsurance, professional negligence, personal injury and medical negligence.

Chambers has a wide client base ranging from public companies, underwriters and brokers to local authorities, government departments, trades unions and individual litigants.

All Members of Chambers are advocates making regular appearances before Judges, Tribunals and Arbitrators.

A number of senior Members of Chambers serve as Deputy High Court Judges, Recorders and Assistant Recorders. Members of Chambers sit on the Criminal Injuries Compensation Board, Criminal Injuries Compensation Appeals Panel and Mental Health Independent Review Tribunal and Rent Assessment Panel. They also chair Tribunals and Inquiries.

The junior Members of Chambers include the Junior Counsel to the Inland Revenue and members of the Supplementary Panel of Treasury Counsel, Common Law. Members of Chambers play a prominent role in the Bar's professional bodies and associations and Chambers includes members of the Bar Council and its Professional Conduct Committee and other Bar Council committees.

Chambers also includes founders, committee members and members of COMBAR, the London Common Law and Commercial Bar Association, the Employment Law Bar Association, the Personal Injuries Bar Association, the Association of Personal Injuries Lawyers, the Industrial Law Society, the British Association for Sport and Law, the Revenue Bar Association, the London Maritime Association and CENTREBAR.

Members of Chambers regularly appear in leading cases and have written or co-written prominent text and practitioners books in their specialist fields.

Three Members of Chambers: Professor Ian Smith, Christopher Goddard and Nicholas Randall co-wrote *Health and Safety the New Legal Framework* published by Butterworths. Ian Smith also co-wrote *Smith and Wood on Industrial Law* and is the author of the Employment Law and Social Security titles in Halsbury's Laws. He and Nicholas Randall are editors of *Harvey on Industrial Relations and Employment Law*.

Members of Chambers have also written the *Personal Injury Factbook* (Gee). Richard Clayton is the author of *Practice and Procedure in Industrial Tribunals* (LAG 1986) and co-author of *Civil Actions against the Police* (Sweet & Maxwell 2nd edn 1992), *Judicial Review Procedure* (Wiley 2nd edition 1997) and, in preparation, co-author of *The Bill of Rights in English Law* (Oxford University Press), *Judicial Review of Local Government Decisions* (Wiley) and *Commercial Judicial Review* (Wiley).

David Griffith-Jones is the author of *Law and the Business of Sport* (Butterworths).

Bruce Carr is a contributing author to FT Law & Tax, *Litigation Practice* ('Emergency Procedures'). Ingrid Simler is a contributing author to Tolley's *Employment Law* (1994).

James Tayler is a contributor to *Dix on Employment Law* (Butterworths) and Nicholas Randall is the author of the Pensions title in Halsbury's Laws. Alison Padfield is the co-author of the Contempt of Court title in Halsbury's Laws.

Members of Chambers also write for legal publications and give lectures and seminars both externally and as part of Chambers' own continuing education programme which is fully accredited by the Law Society.

Great emphasis is placed on the calibre of pupils recruited to ensure that the high standards are maintained and generous pupillage awards are offered.

Additional Specialisms:
Civil liberties and human rights • Community Care • Consumer and business credit • Contempt • Electoral and Parliamentary Law • Europe • Health and Safety • Industrial injury and disease • Judicial review • Mortgage and guarantee litigation • Police complaints • Product liability • Property • Public interest immunity • Revenue • Tribunals and Inquiries • VAT/customs and excise.

C

DOUGHTY STREET CHAMBERS

11 Doughty Street, London, WC1N 2PG
0171 404 1313
Fax: 0171 404 2283/4; DX 223 Chancery Lane
E-mail: enquiries@doughtystreet.co.uk
URL: Video No: 0171 831 1694; Website: http://www.doughtystreet.co.uk
Out of hours telephone: 0171 404 1313 (24 hours with emergency no's)

Chambers of Geoffrey Robertson QC, Peter Thornton QC (Deputy)

Clerks: Michelle Simpson, Richard Bayliss, Paul Friend, Melanie Stephenson, Elly Foster, Stuart Hinton; Practice Manager: Christine Kings; Administrator: Steffan Roberts (Administration & IT Manager); Finance Manager: Kevin Hooper

Robertson, Geoffrey QC *1973*†	**Starmer,** Keir *1987*
Blom-Cooper, Louis QC *1952*	**Hatfield,** Sally *1988*
	Oppenheim, Robin *1988*
Maxwell, Richard QC *1968*†	**Strange,** Michelle *1989*
Thornton, Peter QC *1969*‡	**Maidment,** Kieran *1989*
Kennedy of the Shaws, Helena QC *1972*	**Taylor,** Paul *1989*
	Barton, Hugh *1989*
Sallon, Christopher QC *1973*†	**Brooks,** Paul *1989*
Nicol, Andrew QC *1978*‡	**Kadri,** Sadakat *1989*
Fitzgerald, Edward QC *1978*	**Hislop,** David *1989*
	Hall, Andrew *1991*
Irwin, Stephen QC *1976*‡	**Kaufmann,** Phillippa *1991*
Rees, Edward QC *1973*	**Whitaker,** Quincy *1991*
Grieve, Michael QC *1975*‡	**Finch,** Nadine *1991*
Panford, Frank QC *1972*	**Reeder,** Stephen *1991*
Wood, James QC *1975*‡	**Ford,** Michael *1992*
Walker-Smith, Jonah *1963*‡	**Wise,** Ian *1992*
	Hermer, Richard *1993*
Thorold, Oliver *1971*	**Henderson,** Mark *1994*
Allfrey, Richard *1974*	**Brown,** Althea *1995*
Latham, Robert *1976*	**Trowler,** Rebecca *1995*
Paul, Nicholas *1980*	**Glasson,** Jonathan *1996*
Millar, Gavin *1981*	**Hudson,** Anthony *1996*
Markus, Kate *1981*	**Middleton,** Joseph *1997*
Hough, Christopher *1981*	**Mahomed,** Ismail SC *1984***
Forshall, Isabella *1982*	**Ollivry,** Guy QC *1957***
Bogan, Paul *1983*	**Ramsahoye,** Fenton SC *1953***
Owen, Timothy *1983*	**Hardiman,** Adrian SC *1988***
Mendoza, Colin *1983*	
Bentley, David *1984*	**Boyle,** Kevin *1992***
Bloom, Tracey *1984*	**Booker,** Christine *1978***
Williams, Heather *1985*	**Fulbrook,** Julian *1977***
Westgate, Martin *1985*	**Van Bueren,** Geraldine *1979***
Emmerson, Ben *1986*	**Marcus,** Gilbert SC *1999***
Weereratne, Aswini *1986*	**Peay,** Jill *1991***
Evans, Jill *1986*	**Cooper,** Jonathan *1992***
Metzer, Anthony *1987*	

Types of work (and number of counsel practising in that area if supplied)

Administrative 29 · Civil liberties 46 · Common law (general) 31 · Copyright 4 · Crime 30 · Crime – corporate fraud 22 · Defamation 11 · Discrimination 11 · Education 8 · Employment 13 · Environment 6 · Film, cable, TV 10 · Housing 13 · Immigration 7 · Intellectual property 3 · Landlord and tenant 12 · Local government 8 · Medical negligence 12 · Mental health 10 · Personal injury 12 · Professional negligence 10

Chambers established: 1990
Opening times: 8.30 am-6.30 pm

Chambers' facilities

Conference rooms, Video conferences, Disks accepted, Disabled access, CD Roms accepted, Telephone and video conferencing, E-mail, Internet access

Languages spoken

British Sign Language, French, German, Greek, Hebrew, Italian, Russian, Spanish

Fees policy

Up to five years call £50–80 per hour. Five to ten years call £70–100 per hour. Ten to fifteen years call £100–130 per hour. Fifteen to twenty years call £130–160 per hour. Silks £200–500 per hour.

The clerks will be pleased to discuss fees appropriate to your case within these general fee bands, arrangements for volume work, and subsidised/pro bono work. Fee notes will itemise work done and time spent.

Additional information

Chambers offers a wide range of experience and specialisations, notably in the advocacy of civil liberties and human rights. Individual practitioners specialise in criminal law, media law and defamation, public and administrative law, prisoners' rights and cases involving issues of mental health, discrimination, immigration, employment and housing, personal injury and medical negligence.

The emphasis in chambers is on customer care and a friendly but professional service. Doughty Street Chambers was awarded Chambers of the Year in 1995 and 1996 by *The Lawyer*, received the Bronze Law Firm Management Award in 1997, and the Silver Chambers of the Year award in 1998.

† Recorder ‡ Assistant Recorder *Door Tenant

Details of specialist teams are available on request.

1 DR JOHNSON'S BUILDINGS

Ground Floor, Temple, London, EC4Y 7AX
0171 353 9328
Fax: 0171 353 4410; DX 297 London
E-mail: OneDr.Johnsons@btinternet.com
Out of hours telephone: 01474 872071

Chambers of Lord Thomas OBE QC
Clerks: J Francis, T McBennett, Chris Mitchell

Annexe: Dr Johnson's Chambers, The Atrium Court, Apex Plaza, Reading, Berkshire RG1 1AX
Tel: 01734 254221
Fax: 01734 560380

Granville, Alexander *1978*	Mackie, Jeannie *1995*
Thomas of Gresford, Lord QC *1967†*	Hickman, Claire *1994*
	Levinson, Justin *1994*
Oldland, Jennifer *1978*	Pollock, Hilary *1993*
Sabido, John *1976*	Kane, Adam *1993*
Britton, Robert *1973†*	Habboo, Camille *1987*
Hamblin, Nicholas *1981*	Anderson, Brendan *1985*
Wernham, Stewart *1984*	Brodie, Graham *1989*
Digney, Peter *1968†*	Gill, Pamilla *1989*
Dean, James *1977*	Mailer, Clifford *1987*
Colvin, Andrew *1972*	Wignall, Gordon *1987*
Clark, Dingle *1981*	McIlwain, Sylvester *1985*
Nott, Emma *1995*	Jay, Elizabeth *1996*

3 DR JOHNSON'S BUILDINGS

THREE
DR JOHNSON'S
BUILDINGS

Ground Floor, Temple, London, EC4Y 7BA
0171 353 4854
Fax: 0171 583 8784; DX 1009 London
E-mail: clerks@3djb.co.uk

Chambers of J A Hodgson
Clerk: J E Hubbard

Hodgson, John *1963*	Toch, Joanna *1988*
Vain, Richard *1970*	Chisholm, Malcolm *1989*
Hay, Malcolm *1972*	Heppenstall, Claire *1990*
Houston, Russell *1973*	Peacock, Lisa *1992*
Harris, Annmarie *1975*	Carter, Holly *1993*
Sheldrake, Christine *1977*	Abey, Mahie *1993*
King, Barbara *1980*	Erwood, Heather *1993*
Ahmed, Farooq *1983*	Redford, Jessica *1994*
Daniels, Nicholas *1988*	Williams, Jason *1995*
Hasan, Ayesha *1987*	Barnes, Luke *1996*
Hames, Christopher *1987*	Collins, Ken *1996*
Gillman, Rachel *1988*	Blackwood, Francesca *1997*
Moore, Finola *1988*	

Types of work (and number of counsel practising in that area if supplied)
Care proceedings 22 · Common law (general) 18 · Crime 6 · Family 23 · Family provision 23 · Housing 10 · Landlord and tenant 14

Chambers established: 1946
Opening times: 8.45 am-6.15 pm

Languages spoken
French, Urdu

Additional information
This set of chambers was established 50 years ago at this address. Throughout its history most of the members of chambers have specialised in family law and that continues to be the case today. The building has recently been renovated and refurbished. We have taken on extra accommodation at this address and we are now the only set of chambers at No 3. In answer to the question 'What do you particularly value about the service you obtain from Chambers?' contained in a questionnaire sent recently to our regular instructing solicitors, the most popular answers were 'friendliness' and 'efficiency'.

Although nearly all members specialise in family work there are individuals who practise in other areas such as real property, landlord and tenant, common law and crime.

Types of Work
Use the types of work listings in Parts A and B to locate chambers and individual barristers who specialise in particular areas of work.

DR JOHNSON'S CHAMBERS

Two Dr Johnson's Buildings, Temple, London, EC4Y 7AY
0171 353 4716
Fax: 0171 334 0242; DX 429 London, Chancery Lane
E-mail: clerks@2djb.freeserve.co.uk

Chambers of David J Batcup

Clerks: Patrick Duane (Senior Clerk), Kevin Crawley, Ashley Baum, Claire Wright, Chris Blake, Jonathan Spanjar; Administrator: Nick Pickels; Administrative Support Clerk: Jean Brown

Batcup, David *1974‡*	**Taylor**, David *1986*
Bishop, Malcolm QC *1968*	**Buck**, John *1987*
Bayliss, Alan *1966†*	**Hamilton-Shield**, Anna-
Fogg, Anthony *1970*	Maria *1989*
Davies, Graham J *1971*	**Hawes**, Neil *1989*
Bruce, Richard *1974*	**Fraser**, Alan *1990*
Wurtzel, David *1974*	**Lavers**, Michael *1990*
Higginson, Peter *1975*	**Williams**, David *1990*
Sherman, Robert *1977*	**Deignan**, Dr Mary-Teresa
Wheatly, Ian *1977*	*1991*
Armstrong, Grant *1978*	**Phillips**, Paul *1991*
Mejzner, Stephen *1978*	**Robinson**, Claire *1991*
Davey, Roger *1978*	**Benzynie**, Robert *1992*
Williams, Susan *1978*	**Edwards**, Jennifer *1992*
Paltenghi, Mark *1979*	**Hale**, Charles *1992*
Rhodes, Nicholas *1981*	**Flanagan**, Julia *1993*
Tomassi, Mark *1981*	**Grey**, Siobhan *1994*
Oon, Pamela *1982*	**McCalla**, Tarquin *1994*
Buxton, Thomas *1983*	**Raudnitz**, Paul *1994*
Belger, Tyrone *1984*	**Jones**, Daniel *1994*
Tetlow, Bernard *1984*	**Goudie**, Martin *1996*
Marsh, Carolyn *1985*	**Morgan**, Adam *1996*
Davies, Graham B *1986*	**Bowyer**, Juliet Elizabeth
Rose, Jonathan *1986*	Catherine *1997*

Types of work (and number of counsel practising in that area if supplied)
Aviation 1 · Chancery (general) 1 · Chancery land law 2 · Common law (general) 12 · Courts martial 1 · Crime 42 · Employment 2 · Family 15 · Family provision 5 · Inquests 8 · Insolvency 1 ·

Landlord and tenant 4 · Local government 2 · Malicious prosecution 8 · Medical negligence 2 · Personal injury 13 · Professional negligence 3 · Sale and carriage of goods 1

Opening times: 8.30 am-6.30 pm

Chambers' facilities
Conference rooms, Video conferences, Disks accepted

Languages spoken
French, Spanish

2 DYERS BUILDINGS

2
DYERS
BUILDINGS

London, EC1N 2JT
0171 404 1881
Fax: 0171 404 1991; DX 175 London, Chancery Lane
Out of hours telephone: 0956 985929

Chambers of Mrs N P Radford QC

Clerks: Graham Islin, Dave Scothern

Radford, Nadine QC *1974†*	**Kitchen**, Simon *1988*
Gledhill, Michael *1976†*	**Stein**, Sam *1988*
Campbell-Tiech, Andrew	**Jefferies**, Andrew *1990*
1978	**Bell**, Dominic *1992*
Munro, Sanderson *1981*	**Tolhurst**, Robert *1992*
Jobling, Ian *1982*	**Forte**, Timothy Axel *1994*
Postill, Julia *1982*	**Bsis**, Ibtihal *1995*
Burton, Charles *1983*	**Caldwell**, Peter *1995*
Davis, Adam *1985*	**Irwin**, Gavin David *1996*
Boulter, Terence *1986*	**Fishwick**, Gregory David
Black, Harriette *1986*	Philip Kyle *1996*
Magarian, Michael *1988*	

43 EGLANTINE ROAD

London, SW18 2DE
0181 874 3469

Chambers of Miss J S Walker

† Recorder ‡ Assistant Recorder *Door Tenant

38 ELDON CHAMBERS

30 Fleet Street, London, EC4Y 1AA
0171 353 8822
Fax: 0171 353 8811

Chambers of Mr A L de Moller

197 ELLESMERE ROAD

London, NW10 1LG
0181 208 1663
Fax: 0181 208 1663

Chambers of Mr G M G Haque

EMMANUEL CHAMBERS

259 Gray's Inn Road, London, WC1X 8QT
0171 713 7772
Fax: 0171 713 6894

Chambers of Mrs E A A Joseph

ENTERPRISE CHAMBERS

9 Old Square, Lincoln's Inn, London, WC2A 3SR
0171 405 9471
Fax: 0171 242 1447; DX 301 London
E-mail: enterprise.london@dial.pipex.com
URL: http://www.enterprisechambers.com

Chambers of Anthony Mann QC
Clerks: Barry Clayton, Tony Armstrong, Dylan Wendleken; Chambers Director: Elspeth Mills Rendall; Accounts Administrator: Hannah Steininger-Nath

Also at: 38 Park Square, Leeds LS1 2PA; 65 Quayside, Newcastle upon Tyne NE1 3DS

Mann, Anthony QC *1974*	**Halpern**, David *1978*
Levy, Benjamin *1956*	**Morgan**, Charles *1978*
Jennings, Timothy *1962*	**Hutton**, Caroline *1979*

James, Michael *1976*	**Atherton**, Ian *1988*
Peacocke, Teresa *1982*	**Garcia-Miller**, Laura *1989*
Ife, Linden *1982*	**Bhaloo**, Zia *1990*
McAllister, Ann *1982*	**Pickering**, James *1991*
Arden, Peter *1983*	**McKinnell**, Soraya *1991*
Zelin, Geoffrey *1984*	**Jory**, Hugh *1992*
Baker, Jacqueline *1985*	**Williamson**, Bridget *1993*
Gerald, Nigel *1985*	**Richardson**, Sarah *1993*
Barker, James *1984*	**Hardwick**, Matthew *1994*
Jack, Adrian *1986*	**Francis**, Edward *1995*
Groves, Hugo *1980*	**Mauger**, Shanti *1996*

Types of work (and number of counsel practising in that area if supplied)
Arbitration 7 · Banking 8 · Bankruptcy 13 · Chancery (general) 17 · Commercial litigation 28 · Commercial property 16 · Company and commercial 20 · Conveyancing 6 · Employment 3 · Equity, wills and trusts 7 · Housing 3 · Insolvency 17 · Landlord and tenant 18 · Partnerships 12 · Probate and administration 5 · Professional negligence 20

Chambers established: 1964
Opening times: 8.45 am-7 pm

Chambers' facilities
Disks accepted, Conference rooms, Video conferencing and out of hours contact/accessibility, E-mail, Website

Languages spoken
French, German, Italian, Portuguese, Spanish

Fees policy
Fees are negotiated with the clerk depending on the case, but as a general guide, charge out rates are as follows: Up to five years call £300–750 per day, six to ten years call £600–900 per day, over ten years call £650–1,500 per day, QC £1,500–2,500 per day. The chambers was the *first* set to publish charge out rates for all members and we are happy to provide estimates of fees before any work starts.

EQUITY BARRISTERS' CHAMBERS

Temple Chambers, Second Floor rooms 152-153, 3-7 Temple Avenue, London, EC4Y 0NP
0181 558 8336

---

† Recorder ‡ Assistant Recorder *Door Tenant

Fax: 0181 558 6757
E-mail: equitylawyer@equitybar.co.uk
URL: http://www.equitybar.co.uk
Out of hours telephone: 0181 558 8336

Chambers of Dr K Glah
Clerk: Richard Glah; Practice Manager:
Tres-Ann Cooke BSc (Hons)

Glah, Dr Kwao *1971*

ERSKINE CHAMBERS

30 Lincoln's Inn Fields, Lincoln's Inn,
London, WC2A 3PF
0171 242 5532
Fax: 0171 831 0125; DX 308 London
E-mail: clerks@erskine-chambers.co.uk
Out of hours telephone: Emergency no's
available on Answerphone via main no.

Chambers of Richard Sykes QC
Clerk: Mike Hannibal; Administrator:
Nicola Pettenuzzo

Sykes, Richard QC *1958*	**Bryant**, Ceri *1984*
Stubbs, William QC *1957*	**Snowden**, Richard *1986*
Stockdale, Sir Thomas *1966*	**Roberts**, Catherine *1986*
	Gillyon, Philip *1988*
Potts, Robin QC *1968*	**Stokes**, Mary *1989*
Richards, David QC *1974*	**Thompson**, Andrew *1991*
Cone, John *1975*	**Prentice**, Prof Daniel *1982*
Kosmin, Leslie QC *1976*	**Dougherty**, Nigel *1993*
Todd, Michael QC *1977*	**Kuschke**, Leon *1993*
Mabb, David *1979*	**Potts**, James *1994*
Moore, Martin *1982*	**Thornton**, Andrew *1994*
Chivers, David *1983*	**Davies**, Edward *1998*

**Types of work (and number of counsel practising in
that area if supplied)**
Banking · Commercial litigation · Company
and commercial · Corporate finance ·
Financial services · Insolvency ·
Partnerships · Professional negligence ·
Share options · Unit trusts

Opening times: 8.30 am-7 pm

Chambers' facilities
Conference   rooms,   Disks   accepted,
Disabled access, E-mail

Types of Work
Use the types of work listings in Parts
A and B to locate chambers and indi-
vidual barristers who specialise in
particular areas of work.

ONE ESSEX COURT

Ground Floor, Temple, London, EC4Y 9AR
020 7583 2000
Fax: 020 7583 0118; DX 430 London
E-mail: clerks@oneessexcourt.co.uk
URL: http://www.oneessexcourt.co.uk

Chambers of Lord Grabiner QC
Clerks: Robert Ralphs, Paul Shrubsall MBE;
Administrator: Joanne Huxley

Grabiner, Lord QC *1968*†	**Reffin**, Clare *1981*
Butler, Gerald QC *1955*	**McCaughran**, John *1982*
Burnton, Stanley QC *1965*‡	**Gillis**, Richard *1982*
Aaronson, Graham QC *1966*	**Lenon**, Andrew *1982*
Carr, Christopher QC *1968*	**Sullivan**, Michael *1983*
Strauss, Nicholas QC *1965*‡	**MacLean**, Kenneth *1985*
	Graham, Charles *1986*
Thomas, Roydon QC *1960*†	**de Garr Robinson**, Anthony *1987*
Leaver, Peter QC *1967*‡	
Glick, Ian QC *1970*	**Rabinowitz**, Laurence *1987*
Gloster, Elizabeth QC *1971*†	**Kitchener**, Neil *1991*
Hobbs, Geoffrey QC *1977*	**Choo Choy**, Alain *1991*
Barnes, Mark QC *1974*	**Brown**, Hannah *1992*
MacGregor, Alastair QC *1974*	**Rollason**, Michael *1992*
	Wolfson, David *1992*
Sharpe, Thomas QC *1976*	**Cavender**, David *1993*
Mowschenson, Terence QC *1977*	**Toledano**, Daniel *1993*
	O'Sullivan, Zoë *1993*
Gruder, Jeffrey QC *1977*	**Himsworth**, Emma *1993*
Ivory, Thomas QC *1978*	**Grierson**, Jacob *1993*
Bloch, Michael QC *1979*	**Lake**, Lisa *1994*
Onions, Jeffery QC *1981*	**Nourse**, Edmund *1994*
FitzGerald, Susanna QC *1973*	**Halkerston**, Graeme *1994*
	Hossain, Sa'ad *1995*
Auld, Stephen QC *1979*	**Jowell**, Daniel *1995*
Davies, Rhodri QC *1979*	**Bingham**, Camilla *1996*
Redfern, Alan *1995*	**Roberts**, Philip *1996*
Behar, Richard *1965*†	**Fealy**, Michael *1997*
Conlon, Michael *1974*	**Rosen**, Anushka *1997*
Gammie, Malcolm *1997*	**Gledhill**, Orlando John *1998*
Malone, Michael *1975*	**Abrams**, Neill *1998*
Grainger, Ian *1978*	**Lamb**, Sophie Jane *1998*
Griffiths, Alan *1981*	

† Recorder ‡ Assistant Recorder *Door Tenant

Types of work (and number of counsel practising in that area if supplied)

Administrative 4 · Arbitration 12 · Asset finance 10 · Banking 23 · Bankruptcy 15 · Commercial litigation 45 · Company and commercial 30 · Competition 3 · Copyright 4 · Corporate finance 12 · EC and competition law 3 · Energy 20 · Financial services 20 · Franchising 1 · Insolvency 20 · Insurance 20 · Insurance/reinsurance 20 · Intellectual property 4 · Licensing 1 · Partnerships 10 · Professional negligence 21 · Share options 10 · Shipping, admiralty 6 · Tax – corporate 1 · Telecommunications 3 · Trademarks 4

Chambers established: 1966
Opening times: 8 am-10 pm

Chambers' facilities
Disks accepted, E-mail

Languages spoken
Arabic, French, German, Hebrew, Italian, Spanish

Fees policy
Fees will be negotiated with the clerk depending on the case but as a general guide:
Advisory work at One Essex Court is in most cases time costed. Charge rates range, in the main, from £20 to £200 per hour for junior counsel and from £240 per hour upwards for Queen's Counsel. If requested, charge rates and times spent will be shown on fee notes. In appropriate cases charge rates can be negotiated prior to the commencement of work. Currently hourly charge rates for individuals or groups of individuals will be faxed on request.

Additional information
One Essex Court is among the largest sets of commercial barristers' chambers in Great Britain. It occupies 1, 2, and 3 Essex Court, a site which has historically been synonymous with commercial law. The range of work carried out embraces almost every aspect of domestic and international commerce and finance.

ONE ESSEX COURT

1st Floor, Temple, London, EC4Y 9AR
0171 936 3030
Fax: 0171 583 1606; DX 371 London
E-mail: one.essex_court@virgin.net

Out of hours telephone: 07957 303647

Chambers of Sir Ivan Lawrence QC
Clerk: Christopher J Doe (Senior Clerk)

Lawrence, Ivan QC 1962†	Gursoy, Ramiz 1991
Norris, Paul 1963†	Lawrence, Rachel 1992
Benedict, John 1963	Farquharson, Jane 1993
Mullen, Patrick 1967	Grundy, Nicholas 1993
Bull, Roger 1974	Mills, Simon 1994
Bhalla, Bitu 1978	Milsom, Catherine 1994
Lyne, Mark 1981	Sleeman, Rachel 1996
Joss, Norman 1982	Miller, Jonathan 1996
Coulter, Barry 1985	Brownhill, Joanna 1997
Ong, Grace 1985	Rooney, Adam Charles 1997
John, Peter 1989	
Wilson, Elizabeth 1989	Mew, Graeme 1982*
Benson, Julian 1991	

Types of work (and number of counsel practising in that area if supplied)

Administrative · Arbitration · Bankruptcy · Care proceedings · Chancery (general) · Chancery land law · Civil liberties · Commercial · Commercial litigation · Commercial property · Common land · Common law (general) · Company and commercial · Construction · Crime · Crime – corporate fraud · Defamation · Employment · Equity, wills and trusts · Family · Family provision · Financial services · Housing · Immigration · Insurance · Landlord and tenant · Licensing · Local government · Medical negligence · Probate and administration · Professional negligence · Sale and carriage of goods

Chambers established: 1947
Opening times: 8 am-6.30 pm

Chambers' facilities
Conference rooms, Disks accepted, E-mail

Languages spoken
Cantonese, French, Turkish

Fees policy
Chambers adopts an open policy to the agreement of fees by the clerks. Estimates can be provided prior to the commencement of work. Fees are agreed at an hourly rate or on an overall basis.

Bar Directory on the Internet
The Bar Directory is also available on the Internet at the following address:
http://www.smlawpub.co.uk/bar

---

† Recorder ‡ Assistant Recorder *Door Tenant

4 ESSEX COURT

Temple, London, EC4Y 9AJ
020 7797 7970
Fax: 020 7353 0998; DX 292 Chancery Lane
E-mail: clerks@4essexcourt.law.co.uk
URL: http://www.4essexcourt.law.co.uk
Out of hours telephone: Dial as above for
answerphone message

Chambers of Nigel Teare QC
Clerk: Gordon Armstrong

Teare, Nigel QC *1974†*	Croall, Simon *1986*
Howard, M N QC *1971†*	Cooper, Nigel *1987*
Bucknall, Belinda QC *1974†*	Reeve, Matthew *1987*
Macdonald, Charles QC *1972‡*	Melwani, Poonam *1989*
	Lawson, Robert *1989*
Russell, Jeremy QC *1975*	Turner, James M *1990*
Brenton, Timothy QC *1981*	Thomas, Robert *1992*
Haddon-Cave, Charles QC *1978‡*	Phillips, Nevil *1992*
	Russell, John *1993*
de Cotta, John *1955*	Macey-Dare, Thomas *1994*
Economou, George *1965*	Kimbell, John *1995*
Gault, Simon *1970†*	Chambers, Jonathan *1996*
Kinley, Geoffrey *1970*	Buckingham, Stewart *1996*
Caldin, Giles *1974*	Ribeiro, Robert QC *1978*
Griffin, Paul *1979*	Gaskell, Nicholas Joseph James *1976*
Nolan, Michael *1981*	
Smith, Marion *1981*	Gardiner, Richard *1969*
Rainey, Simon *1982*	Rose, Francis Dennis *1983*
Kverndal, Simon *1982*	Qureshi, Asif Hasan *1978*
Jacobs, Nigel *1983*	Caplan, Harold *1955*
Parsons, Luke *1985*	

Types of work (and number of counsel practising in that area if supplied)
Admiralty 21 · Arbitration 28 · Aviation 9 ·
Banking 8 · Commercial litigation 28 ·
Commodities 4 · Construction 9 · EC and
competition law 4 · Employment 6 ·
Entertainment 3 · Environment 9 ·
Insurance 28 · Insurance/reinsurance 28 ·
International trade 27 · Personal injury 5 ·
Private international 25 · Professional
negligence 8 · Sale and carriage of goods
28 · Shipping, admiralty 23

Opening times: 8 am-7 pm

Chambers' facilities
Conference rooms, Disks accepted, Arbitration room

Languages spoken
Dutch, French, German, Greek, Italian,
Portuguese, Spanish

Fees policy
Fees charged are generally tied to the time
spent on (or allocated to) each item of
work. There is, however, a wide measure of
flexibility in the arrangements that will be
agreed.

Types of work undertaken: Most of the work at 4
Essex Court is for international clients and/
or involves international commercial law.
Individual members will act as advocates,
legal advisers, arbitrators, and expert
witnesses. They will also draft and prepare
commercial contracts and other instruments. Many of the barristers have
membership of overseas Bars including
America (NY), Hong Kong, New South
Wales, Spain, Greece and Cyprus.

Several members are authors or editors of
or contributors to a wide variety of publications. For further information contact
Gordon Armstrong.

The main telephone number provides an
alternative service for out-of-hours emergencies.

5 ESSEX COURT

1st Floor, Temple, London, EC4Y 9AH
0171 410 2000
Fax: 0171 410 2010; DX 1048 Chancery
Lane
E-mail: barristers@5essexcourt.co.uk
Out of hours telephone: 0370 533599

Chambers of A J J Gompertz QC
Clerks: Michael Dean, Mark Waller, Rachel Shepherd

Gompertz, Jeremy QC *1962†*	Roberts, Mervyn *1963†*
	Catterson, Marie *1972†*

† Recorder ‡ Assistant Recorder *Door Tenant

Moss, Christopher QC 1972†	Kerr, Christopher 1988	Stanley, Paul 1993	Scorey, David 1997
Ainley, Nicholas 1973‡	Kent, Georgina 1989	Hunter, Martin 1994	Wordsworth, Sam 1997
Bassett, John 1975	Powell, Giles 1990	Hopkins, Philippa 1994	Pillow, Nathan 1997
Freeland, Simon 1978‡	Hayhow, Lyn 1990	McGrath, Paul 1994	Gearty, Conor 1995*
Wilcox, Nicholas 1977	Buckingham, Sarah 1991	Collins, James 1995	Moollan, Salim 1998
Pounder, Gerard 1980	Pollock, Dr Evelyn 1991	Eicke, Tim 1993	Diwan, Ricky 1998
Apthorp, Charles 1983	Beer, Jason 1992	Houseman, Stephen 1995	Hart, Neil 1998
Butcher, John 1984	Leek, Samantha 1993	Key, Paul 1997	O'Reilly, James 1983*
Barton, Fiona 1986	Akinsanya, Stephen 1993	Lau, Martin 1996*	
Davenport, Simon 1987	Johnson, Jeremy 1994		
Waters, Andrew 1987	Virdi, Prabjhot 1995		
Farrimond, Stephanie 1987	Rose, Stephen 1995		
Walbank, David 1987	Ahmad, Nadeem 1996		
Studd, Anne 1988	McLean, Mandy 1996		

ESSEX COURT CHAMBERS

24 Lincoln's Inn Fields, London,
WC2A 3ED
0171 813 8000
Fax: 0171 813 8080; DX 320 London,
Chancery Lane
E-mail:
clerksroom@essexcourt-chambers.co.uk
URL:
http://www.essexcourt-chambers.co.uk

Chambers of Gordon Pollock QC
Clerks: David Grief, Joe Ferrigno, Nigel Jones, Sam Biggerstaff, Mathew Kesby, Ben Perry, Tim Rycroft; Administrator: Jean T Muircroft

Pollock, Gordon QC 1968	Prevezer, Sue 1983
Thomas, Michael QC 1955	Berry, Steven 1984
Hunter, Ian QC 1967†	Joseph, David 1984
Boyd, Stewart QC 1967†	Millett, Richard 1985
Veeder, VV QC 1971‡	Davies, Huw 1985
Collins, Michael QC 1971†	Smouha, Joe 1986
Siberry, Richard QC 1974‡	Watson, Philippa 1988
Gilman, Jonathan QC 1965	Mercer, Hugh 1985
Eder, Bernard QC 1975‡	Griffiths, Martin 1986
Cordara, Roderick QC 1975	Troy-Davies, Karen 1981
Crookenden, Simon QC 1975‡	Lockey, John 1987
	Bryan, Simon 1988
Hochhauser, Andrew QC 1977	Foxton, David 1989
Beatson, Jack QC 1972†	Smith, Christopher 1989
Jacobs, Richard QC 1979	Shaw, Malcolm 1988
Greenwood, Christopher QC 1978	Cockerill, Sara 1990
	Snider, John 1982
Dicks, Anthony 1961	Flynn, James 1991
Mildon, David 1980	Dye, Brian 1991
Lyon, Victor 1980	Eaton, Nigel 1991
Smith, Mark 1981	Blanchard, Claire 1992
Andrews, Geraldine 1981	Cargill-Thompson, Perdita 1993
Dunning, Graham 1982	Lowe, Vaughan 1993
Templeman, Mark 1981	Landau, Toby 1993

Types of work (and number of counsel practising in that area if supplied)
Administrative · Admiralty · Agriculture · Arbitration · Aviation · Banking · Bankruptcy · Civil liberties · Commercial litigation · Commodities · Company and commercial · Competition · Construction · Corporate finance · Discrimination · EC and competition law · Employment · Energy · Entertainment · Environment · Film, cable, TV · Financial services · Foreign law · Franchising · Immigration · Information technology · Insolvency · Insurance · Insurance/reinsurance · Intellectual property · International trade · Partnerships · Private international · Professional negligence · Public international · Sale and carriage of goods · Share options · Shipping, admiralty · South Asian law · Sports · Telecommunications

Chambers established: 1961
Opening times: 7.45 am-7 pm

Chambers' facilities
Conference rooms, Video conferences, Disks accepted, Disabled access, E-mail, Website

Languages spoken
Chinese, French, German, Italian, Spanish

Additional information
A full-service commercial set, acting for clients ranging from major institutions and multi-national corporations to private companies and individuals. Members advise across the whole spectrum of international, commercial and European law, and act as advocates in litigation and commercial arbitration worldwide.

The set: Essex Court Chambers, called Four Essex Court until its relocation to Lincoln's Inn Fields in 1994, was formed as a separate chambers in 1961, when the set at Three Essex Court split into two sets. The founding members of Four Essex Court were Michael Kerr (later Lord Justice Kerr), Robert MacCrindle, Michael Mustill (later

Lord Mustill), Anthony Evans (later Lord Justice Evans), and Anthony Diamond (later Judge Diamond). Chambers grew rapidly in the late 1960s and 1970s, developing a reputation as one of the leading sets of commercial barristers in England, during which time Mark Saville (later Lord Saville), Johan Steyn (later Lord Steyn), Anthony Colman (later Mr Justice Colman) and John Thomas (later Mr Justice Thomas) joined.

Types of work undertaken: The work of chambers covers the entire range of international and commercial litigation and arbitration. The fields of work for which chambers is best known are: Administrative Law and Judicial Review, Agriculture and Farming, Arbitration, Australian Trade Practices Law, Aviation, Banking, Chinese Law, Company Law and Insolvency, Conflict of Laws, Construction and Engineering, Commodity Transactions, Computer Law, Custom Duty, Employment Law, Energy and Utilities Law, Entertainment and Sports Law, Environmental Law, European Law, Financial Services, Hong Kong Law, Human Rights, Immigration and Nationality Law, Injunctions and Arrests, Insurance and Reinsurance, International Commercial Fraud, International Trade and Transport, Professional Negligence, Public International Law, Public Law, Rail Disputes, Sale of Goods and Product Liability, Shipping, South Asian Law, VAT and Excise. Also members act as arbitrators and mediators in domestic and international disputes when invited to do so by the parties concerned, or by the person or body named in the contract.

Several members have written or co-operated on legal works. These include: *Arnould on Marine Insurance* (co-editor: Jonathan Gilman QC); *Mustill & Boyd on Commercial Arbitration* (co-author: Stewart Boyd QC); *Scrutton on Charterparties* (co-editors: Stewart Boyd QC and David Foxton); *Chitty on Contracts* (co-editor: Jack Beatson QC); *Anson's Law of Contract* 27th edition (editor Jack Beatson QC) *International Law* (Professor Malcolm Shaw); *The Law of Guarantees* (Geraldine Andrews and Richard Millett) and *International Commercial Arbitration* (co-author: Martin Hunter); *The Law of the Sea* co-author: Vaughan Lowe), *Commercial Debt in Europe: Recovery and Remedies* (Hugh Mercer); *Cross Border litigation within ASEAN: The Prospects for Harmonization*

of Civil and Commercial Litigation, by Kluwer Law Intl (1997); *Various legal complexities of syndicated loans* (Malek & Ong).

The international nature of chambers' practice is underlined by the fact that French, German, Italian, Spanish and Chinese are spoken within chambers. Members have appeared as advocates in the European Commission, European Court of Justice, and European Court of Human Rights; International Court of Justice in the Courts of jurisdictions including Hong Kong, Malaysia, Australia, Belfast, Dublin, Gibraltar, St Vincent, Brunei, Kenya and the Cayman Islands; and in arbitrations in places such as Paris, Geneva, Singapore, New Orleans and Beijing.

ESSEX HOUSE CHAMBERS

Unit 6 (Part 2nd Floor South), Stratford Office Village, 14-30 Romford Road, London, E15 4BZ
0181 536 1077
Fax: 0181 555 7135

Chambers of Mr Y N K S Serugo-Lugo

20 ESSEX STREET

20 Essex Street

London, WC2R 3AL
0171 583 9294
Fax: 0171 583 1341 Gp.2 & 3; DX 0009 Chancery Lane
E-mail: clerks@20essexst.com
URL: http://www.20essexst.com

Chambers of Iain Milligan QC
Clerks: Neil Palmer, Brian Lee

Milligan, Iain QC *1973*	**Gross,** Peter QC *1977†*
Johnson, David QC *1967†*	**Havelock-Allan,** Mark QC
Lauterpacht, Sir Elihu QC	*1974‡*
1950	**Young,** Timothy Nicholas
Watts, Sir Arthur QC *1957*	QC *1977*
Pickering, Murray QC	**Hamblen,** Nicholas QC
1963†	*1981*
Legh-Jones, Nicholas QC	**Cooke,** Julian *1965*
1968	**Wood,** Richard *1975*
Plender, Richard QC *1972†*	**Males,** Stephen QC *1978*
Glennie, Angus QC *1974*	**Tselentis,** Michael SC *1995*

Broadbent, Edmund *1980*	**Charkham**, Graham *1993*	**Kinch**, Christopher QC	**Carter**, William *1989*
Morris, Stephen *1981‡*	**Masters**, Sara *1993*	*1976†*	**Hotten**, Keith *1990*
Hancock, Christopher *1983*	**Edey**, Philip *1994*	**Davis**, Simon *1978‡*	**Griffin**, Lynn *1991*
Owen, David *1983*	**Kimmins**, Charles *1994*	**James**, Roderick *1979*	**Ascherson**, Isobel *1991*
Matthews, Duncan *1986*	**Collett**, Michael *1995*	**Causer**, John *1979*	**Medland**, Simon *1991*
Baker, Andrew *1988*	**Ashcroft**, Michael *1997*	**Janner**, Daniel *1980*	**Acheson**, Ian *1992*
Bethlehem, Daniel *1988*	**Swaroop**, Sudhanshu *1997*	**Russell Flint**, Simon *1980‡*	**Fenhalls**, Mark *1992*
Coburn, Michael *1990*	**Kenny**, Julian Hector	**Price**, John *1982*	**Hurst**, Andrew *1992*
Akka, Lawrence *1991*	Marriott *1997*	**Del Fabbro**, Oscar *1982*	**Milne**, Richard *1992*
Morpuss, Guy *1991*	**Collier**, John *1961**	**Cooke**, Graham *1983*	**Horlick**, Fiona *1992*
Ambrose, Clare *1992*	**Allott**, Philip *1960**	**Glynn**, Joanna *1983‡*	**Curtis-Raleigh**, Giles *1992*
Maxwell, Karen *1992*		**Claxton**, Elroy *1983‡*	**Marshall**, Eloise *1994*
		Pardoe, Rupert *1984*	**Swain**, Hannah *1994*

Types of work (and number of counsel practising in that area if supplied)

Administrative · Admiralty · Arbitration · Aviation · Banking · Civil liberties · Commercial litigation · Commodities · Competition · EC and competition law · Energy · Environment · Financial services · Human rights · Immigration · Insurance · Insurance/reinsurance · Intellectual property · International trade · Private international · Professional negligence · Public international · Sale and carriage of goods · Shipping, admiralty

Carnes, Andrew *1984*	**Stilgoe**, Rufus *1994*
Kent, Alan *1986*	**Durran**, Alexia *1995*
Cutts, Johannah *1986*	**Strickland**, Clare *1995*
Cranston-Morris, Wayne *1986*	**May**, Alan *1995*
Byrne, Garrett *1986*	**Belson**, Emily Elizabeth *1997*
Ozin, Paul *1987*	**Campbell**, Sarah Jane *1997*
Norton, Heather *1988*	**Goldsworthy**, Ian QC *1968**
Morley, Iain *1988*	**Jones**, Alison *1988**

Opening times: 8.15 am-6.45 pm

Chambers' facilities
Conference rooms, Disks accepted

Languages spoken
French, German, Italian, Spanish

35 ESSEX STREET

Temple, London, WC2R 3AR
0171 353 6381
Fax: 0171 583 1786; DX 351 London
Other comms: Link: 35 Essex Street
E-mail: derek_jenkins@link.org
URL: http://www.35-essex-street.com

23 ESSEX STREET

23 ESSEX STREET
LONDON WC2R 3AS

London, WC2R 3AS
0171 413 0353/836 8366
Fax: 0171 413 0374; DX 148 London
E-mail: clerks@essexstreet23.demon.co.uk
Out of hours telephone: on answerphone

Chambers of M H Lawson QC
Clerks: Nicholas Hopgood, Daren Milton, Nicole Kansley, Robert Mayes; Practice Manager: Nicholas Hopgood; Administrator: Sheona Taylor

Lawson, Michael QC *1969†*	**Lawson Rogers**, Stuart QC *1969†*
Hill, Michael QC *1958*	**Miskin**, Charles QC *1975†*
Purnell, Nicholas QC *1968†*	**Sangster**, Nigel QC *1976**
Austin-Smith, Michael QC *1969†*	**Richardson**, James *1975*
Edwards, Susan QC *1972†*	**Wood**, Michael QC *1976†*
	Finucane, Brendan *1976*

Chambers of Nigel Inglis-Jones QC
Clerk: Derek Jenkins

Inglis-Jones, Nigel QC *1959*	**Mawhinney**, Richard *1977‡*
Rawley, Alan QC *1958†*	**Coley**, William *1980*
Calcutt, David QC *1955*	**Tolson**, Robin *1980‡*
Wilson-Smith, Christopher QC *1965†*	**Climie**, Stephen *1982‡*
Mott, Philip QC *1970†*	**Westcott**, David *1982*
Sullivan, Linda QC *1973†*	**Kemp**, Christopher *1984*
Gibbons, Jeremy QC *1973*†*	**Spink**, Andrew *1985*
Lissack, Richard QC *1978†*	**Trusted**, Harry *1985*
Rains, Richard *1963**	**McCormick**, Alison *1988*
Jenkins, Hywel *1974*	**Freeborn**, Susan *1989*
Stephens, John *1975*	**Hitchcock**, Richard *1989*
	Hand, Jonathan *1990*
	Leeper, Thomas *1991*

† Recorder   ‡ Assistant Recorder   *Door Tenant

Tavares, Nathan *1992*	**Temmink,** Robert-Jan *1996*
Malden, Grace *1993*	**Vines,** Clare *1997*
Phillips, Matthew *1993*	**Skelton,** Peter *1997*
Stallworthy, Nicolas *1993*	**Jerram,** Harriet *1998*
Willmot, Rachel *1994*	

Types of work (and number of counsel practising in that area if supplied)
Arbitration 2 · Care proceedings 6 · Commercial · Commercial litigation 2 · Common law (general) 20 · Construction 2 · Copyright 2 · Crime 5 · Crime – corporate fraud 7 · Employment 6 · Family 4 · Financial services · Information technology 2 · Intellectual property 2 · Landlord and tenant 6 · Local government 6 · Medical negligence 10 · Partnerships · Pensions 5 · Personal injury 20 · Professional negligence 20 · Sale and carriage of goods 20

Opening times: 9 am-6 pm

Chambers' facilities
Conference rooms, Disks accepted, Disabled access, E-mail, Disabled toilets

Languages spoken
French, German, Italian

Fees policy
Up to five years call £25–75, Up to ten years call £75–125, Over ten years call £125–200

Types of work undertaken
35 Essex Street is primarily a commercial and common law set of chambers. It offers clients experienced representation and advice covering a wide range of legal work and the aim is to provide these services in an accessible manner at both a general and a specialist level.

The past decade has seen a shift in emphasis in the types of work undertaken. Historically, a large proportion of work was carried out on the Western Circuit and emphasis was placed on advocacy and the ability to deal with varied general common law work. Today, much of the work under-taken by chambers is based in and around central London and is of a commercial and, in particular, City-based nature. It now involves considerable specialist expertise which is able to be provided at all levels.

However, the importance that was tradi-tionally attached to the art of advocacy and the provision of a general service has not been lost but combined with the ability to provide a real range of specialisations. As such, many members are also active in areas of law outside the fields in which they have particular expertise.

Various members serve on the committees of the Bar Council and the Inns of Court. One is a former chairman of the Bar Council and is the chairman of the Take-over Panel.

Six members of chambers are Recorders of the Crown Court and three are Assistant Recorders.

Additional specialisations: The areas of practice in which individual members have partic-ular expertise and experience are as follows: commercial fraud, company and commercial contract, employment, intel-lectual property, landlord and tenant, local government law, medical negligence, occu-pational pension schemes and trusts, personal injury, professional negligence, property law, and sale and carriage of goods. A brochure is available on request.

Please see web site 35-essex-street.com. for list of all practice areas and barristers within the various groups.

39 ESSEX STREET

39 ESSEX STREET
LONDON WC2R 3AT

London, WC2R 3AT
0171 832 1111
Fax: 0171 353 3978; DX 298 London
E-mail: clerks@39essex.co.uk
Out of hours telephone: 01730 263 631/ 01634 262 332

Chambers of Edwin Glasgow QC
Clerks: Nigel Connor, Michael Phipps (Assistant), David Smith (Assistant), Sandie Smith (Assistant), Stuart Ritchie (Assistant); Administrator: Susan Rice; Fees Manager: Nigel Cheshire

Glasgow, Edwin QC *1969*	**Gray,** Richard QC *1970*
Mackay, Colin QC *1967*†	**Pleming,** Nigel QC *1971*
Goldblatt, Simon QC *1953*	**Williams,** Wyn QC *1974*
Brennan, Daniel QC *1967*†	**Davies,** Richard QC *1973*

† Recorder ‡ Assistant Recorder *Door Tenant

Wilmot-Smith, Richard QC *1978*
Tillett, Michael QC *1965*†
Jay, Robert QC *1981*
Cooper, Alan *1969*
Melville, David *1975*
Brown, Charles *1976*
Noble, Roderick *1977*
McCaul, Colin *1978*
Block, Neil *1980*
Brown, Geoffrey *1981*
Du Cann, Christian *1982*
Cory-Wright, Charles *1984*
Foster, Alison *1984*
Bellamy, Jonathan *1986*
Catchpole, Stuart *1987*
Bradly, David *1987*

Manzoni, Charles *1988*
Morgan, Jeremy *1989*
Kovats, Steven *1989*
Grey, Eleanor *1990*
Doherty, Bernard *1990*
Nelson, Vincent *1980*
Morris, Fenella *1990*
Richards, Jennifer *1991*
Wilken, Sean *1991*
Brodie, Bruce *1993*
Maclean, Alan *1993*
Seligman, Matthew *1994*
Robb, Adam *1995*
Grodzinski, Samuel *1996*
Patel, Parishil *1996*
Stern, Kristina *1996*

Types of work (and number of counsel practising in that area if supplied)
Administrative · Arbitration · Civil liberties · Commercial litigation · Common law (general) · Construction · Discrimination · EC and competition law · Education · Employment · Energy · Entertainment · Environment · Film, cable, TV · Immigration · Insurance · Insurance/reinsurance · Local government · Medical negligence · Mental health · Personal injury · Professional negligence · Sale and carriage of goods · Sports · VAT and Customs & Excise

Chambers established: 1796
Opening times: 8 am-7 pm

Chambers' facilities
Conference rooms, Video conferences, Disks accepted, E-mail

Languages spoken
French, German, Gujarati, Italian, Spanish

CHAMBERS OF GEOFFREY HAWKER

46/48 Essex Street, London, WC2R 3GH
0171 583 8899

Fax: 0171 583 8800; DX 1014 London, Chancery Lane
Other comms: Mobile: 07957 830811

Chambers of G F Hawker TD
Clerks: Stephen English (Senior Clerk), Samantha Gibbs (1st Jnr Clerk), Louise Bearman (2nd Jnr Clerk)

Hawker, Geoffrey *1970*
Sofer, Jonathan *1942*
Clarke, Ivan *1973*
Goh, Allan *1984*
Lonsdale, Marion *1984*
Turner, Alan *1984*
Ryan, David *1985*
Toussaint, Deborah *1988*
Mitropoulos, Georgia *1989*
Cheah, Albert *1989*
Aeberli, Peter *1990*†
Sliwinski, Robert *1990*
Candlin, James *1991*
Keogh, Richard *1991*
Copeland, Andrew *1992*

Peglow, Michael *1993*
Bagnall, Matthew *1993*
Walshe, Annie *1993*
Volz, Karl *1993*
Bentwood, Richard *1994*
Tobin, Daniel *1994*
Cowen, Sally *1995*
Woodruff, Sarah *1996*
Mitropoulos, Chris *1997*
Storr, Honourable Mr Justice Philip (Bermuda) *1990**
Milne, Michael *1987**
Chapman, Peter *1991**
Marks, Medina *1992**

EUROLAWYER CHAMBERS

PO Box 3621, London, N7 0BQ
0171 607 0075
Fax: 0171 607 2081

Chambers of Mr O G Ernstzen

16 FAIRHAZEL GARDENS

London, NW6 3SJ
0171 328 5486
Fax: 0171 328 5486

Chambers of Mr E M G Soden-Bird

FALCON CHAMBERS

 Falcon Chambers

Falcon Court, London, EC4Y 1AA
0171 353 2484
Fax: 0171 353 1261; DX 408 London
E-mail: clerks@falcon-chambers.com
URL: http://www.falcon-chambers.com

Chambers of Jonathan Gaunt QC, Kim Lewison QC

Clerks: Mark Clewley, Steven Francis;
Administrator: Tarlika Patel

Wood, Derek QC CBE *1964*†   **Rodger,** Martin *1986*
Gaunt, Jonathan QC *1972*   **Fancourt,** Timothy *1987*
Lewison, Kim QC *1975*†   **Denyer-Green,** Barry *1972*
Morgan, Paul QC *1975*   **Jourdan,** Stephen *1989*
Reynolds, Kirk QC *1974*   **Cowen,** Gary *1990*
Brock, Jonathan QC *1977*†   **Small,** Jonathan *1990*
Dowding, Nicholas QC *1979*   **Bignell,** Janet *1992*
Prince, Edwin *1955*   **Dray,** Martin *1992*
de la Piquerie, Paul *1966*†   **Shea,** Caroline *1994*
Moss, Joanne R *1976*   **Tanney,** Anthony *1994*
Radevsky, Anthony *1978*   **Taskis,** Catherine *1995*
Cole, Edward *1980*   **Windsor,** Emily *1995*
Clark, Wayne *1982*   **Peters,** Edward *1998*
Fetherstonhaugh, Guy   **Astill,** Katherine *1998*
1983

FARRAR'S BUILDING

Temple, London, EC4Y 7BD
0171 583 9241
Fax: 0171 583 0090; DX 406 London
E-mail: chambers@farrarsbuilding.co.uk
Out of hours telephone: Home: 01245
601710, Mobile: 0468 366558

Chambers of Gerard Elias QC

Clerk: Alan Kilbey (Senior Clerk and
Practice Manager)

Elias, Gerard QC *1968*†   **Treverton-Jones,** Gregory
Lewer, Michael QC *1958*†   *1977*‡
Williams, John QC *1964*†   **Jones,** Stephen *1978*
Pitchford, Christopher QC   **McDermott,** Thomas *1980*
  1969†   **Browne,** Simon *1982*
Day, Douglas QC *1967*†   **Ayling,** Tracy *1983*
Birts, Peter QC *1968*†   **Matovu,** Daniel *1985*
Nice, Geoffrey QC *1971*†   **Ley,** Spencer *1985*
Harrington, Patrick QC   **Peebles,** Andrew *1987*
  1973†   **Watt-Pringle,** Jonathan
Davies, Leighton QC *1975*†   *1987*
Jeffreys, Alan QC *1970*†   **Wicks,** David *1989*
Norris, William QC *1974*   **Middleton,** Georgina *1989*
Dutton, Timothy QC *1979*‡   **Todd,** Alan *1990*
Southwell, Edward *1970*†   **Hobhouse,** Helen *1990*
Nussey, Richard *1971*   **Moorman,** Lucinda *1992*
Seys Llewellyn, Anthony   **Cash,** Joanne *1994*
  1972†   **Pack,** Melissa *1995*
Rubin, Stephen *1977*   **Allen,** Darryl *1995*

Evans, Lee *1996*   **Morgan,** David Wynn
Garfield, Roger *1965**   *1976**†
Thomas, Roger QC *1969**   **Lewis,** Marian *1977**
Rees, Phillip *1965**   **Vosper,** Christopher
Fricker, Marilyn *1969**   *1977**‡
Jones, Richard *1969**   **Davies,** Huw *1978**‡
Murphy, Ian QC *1972**   **Thomas,** Paul *1979**
Jenkins, James *1974**‡   **Barnett,** Jeremy *1980**
Marshall, Philip *1975**‡   **Gilroy,** Paul *1985**
Brabin, Michael *1976**   **Tillyard,** James *1978**
Jones, Geraint *1976**   **Cooke,** Nicholas QC *1977**

**Types of work (and number of counsel practising in
that area if supplied)**
Administrative · Agriculture · Chancery
(general) · Civil liberties · Commercial
litigation · Common law (general) ·
Construction · Courts martial · Crime ·
Defamation · Employment · Landlord and
tenant · Medical negligence · Personal
injury · Professional negligence · Sale and
carriage of goods · Sports · Taxation and
costs

Chambers' facilities
Conference rooms, Disks accepted,
Disabled access

Languages spoken
French

Fees policy
Up to five years call £50–75, Up to ten years
call £75–100, Over ten years call £85–250.
Fees are assessed to take account of a
number of factors and are not charged
purely on an hourly rate basis. The Senior
Clerk Alan Kilbey is happy to give an indication as to the likely fee range on inquiry.

Additional information
Farrar's Building is a long-established set of
common law chambers with an excellent
reputation built up over many years. Areas
of practice fall within the broad categorisa-
tion 'General Common Law' but members
of chambers have particular specialities in
Administrative and Public Law, Contract
and Commercial Litigation, Criminal Law,
Defamation and Media Law, Disciplinary
Tribunals, Employment, Environmental
and Agricultural Law, Health and Safety,
Insurance Litigation, Landlord and Tenant,
Licensing, Medical Law, Personal Injury,
Police Actions and Civil Liberties, Product
Liability, Public Inquiries and Tribunals,
Professional Negligence, Solicitors' Costs
and Taxation, Sports and Competition Law.

CHAMBERS OF NORMAN PALMER

2 Field Court, Gray's Inn, London,
WC1R 5BB
0171 405 6114
Fax: 0171 831 6112; DX 457 London
E-mail: fieldct2@netcomuk.co.uk

Chambers of Ashley Underwood
Clerk: Michael Clark

Underwood, Ashley *1976*	**Swirsky,** Joshua *1987*
Bowring, William *1974*	**Hamilton,** John *1988*
Palmer, Norman *1973*	**Lewis,** Eleri *1989*
Jones, Kay *1974*	**Rutledge,** Kelvin *1989*
Littman, Jeffrey *1974*	**Youll,** Joanna *1989*
Harrop-Griffiths, Hilton *1978*	**Champion,** Rowena *1990*
	Deighton, Richard *1990*
Bennington, Jane *1981*	**Fox,** Ian *1990*
Evans, Franklin *1981*	**Giovannetti,** Lisa *1990*
Theis, Lucy *1982‡*	**Howling,** Rex *1991*
McGuire, Bryan *1983*	**Nicholson,** Michael *1993*
Carlisle, Timothy *1984*	**Tyson,** Thomas *1995*
Presland, Frederick *1985*	**Godfrey,** Emma *1995*
Stevenson-Watt, Neville *1985*	**Davis,** Adrian *1996*

Types of work (and number of counsel practising in that area if supplied)
Administrative 5 · Asset finance 9 · Banking 5 · Bankruptcy 5 · Care proceedings 11 · Chancery (general) 6 · Chancery land law 4 · Charities 2 · Civil liberties 6 · Commercial litigation 4 · Commercial property 4 · Common land 4 · Common law (general) 10 · Company and commercial 6 · Construction 6 · Conveyancing 3 · Copyright 2 · Corporate finance 6 · Defamation 4 · Discrimination 5 · Education 2 · Employment 7 · Entertainment 2 · Equity, wills and trusts 2 · Family 12 · Family provision 10 · Financial services 5 · Foreign law 2 · Housing 6 · Immigration 4 · Insolvency 6 · Insurance 2 · Insurance/reinsurance 2 · International trade 2 · Landlord and tenant 2 · Licensing 3 · Local government 2 · Medical negligence 5 · Mental health 2 · Partnerships 3 · Personal injury 5 · Private international 2 · Probate and administration 2 · Professional negligence 7 · Public international 1 · Sale and carriage of goods 4 · Share options · Town and country planning 2

Chambers established: 1976
Opening times: 8.30 am-6.30 pm

Chambers' facilities
Conference rooms, Disks accepted, E-mail

Languages spoken
French, German, Hebrew, Italian, Mandarin Chinese, Russian, Serbo-Croat, Spanish

Fees policy
Speak to clerks.

4 FIELD COURT

Gray's Inn, London, WC1R 5EA
0171 440 6900
Fax: 0171 242 0197; DX 483 London
E-mail: chambers@4fieldcourt.co.uk
Out of hours telephone: Paul Coveney 0181 886 3801 or 0468 404562, Christopher James 01428 727360 or 0468 404463

Chambers of Steven Gee QC
Clerks: Paul Coveney, Christopher James,
Toni McKenna, Jean-Pierre Schulz, Venetia
Jeffcock

Gee, Steven QC *1975*	**Meeson,** Nigel *1982*
Rankin, Andrew QC *1950†*	**Selvaratnam,** Vasanti *1983*
Stone, Richard QC *1952*	**Sutton,** Mark *1982*
Brice, Geoffrey QC *1960†*	**Turner,** Jonathan D C *1982*
Reeder, John QC *1971*	**Goldstone,** David *1986*
Kay, Jervis QC *1972*	**Wright,** Colin *1987*
Persey, Lionel QC *1981*	**Saunders,** Nicholas *1989*
Blackburn, Elizabeth QC *1978*	**Wilson,** Stephen *1990*
	Davey, Michael *1990*
Myers, Allan QC (Aus) *1988*	**Hill,** Timothy *1990*
Miller, Sarah *1971*	**Ghaffar,** Arshad *1991*
Lloyd, Lloyd *1973*	**Dugdale,** Nicholas *1992*
Green, Alison *1974*	**Davies,** Charles *1995*
Thom, James *1974*	**Heal,** Madeleine *1996*
Whitehouse-Vaux, William *1977*	**O'Shea,** Eoin *1996*
	Blackwood, Andrew Guy *1997*
Bourne, Robert *1978*	
Romney, Daphne *1979*	

Types of work (and number of counsel practising in that area if supplied)
Admiralty 19 · Arbitration 33 · Aviation 4 · Banking 10 · Bankruptcy 5 · Commercial property 4 · Company and commercial 8 · Competition 4 · Construction 10 ·

Copyright 2 · Defamation 1 · Discrimination 4 · EC and competition law 4 · Employment 3 · Entertainment 2 · Environment 10 · Film, cable, TV 1 · Financial services 5 · Housing 3 · Information technology 1 · Insolvency 4 · Insurance 33 · Insurance/reinsurance 25 · Intellectual property 2 · International trade 20 · Landlord and tenant 5 · Licensing 1 · Local government 3 · Medical negligence 2 · Partnerships 1 · Personal injury 10 · Professional negligence 12 · Sale and carriage of goods 32 · Shipping, admiralty 20 · Sports 4 · Tax – corporate 1 · Trademarks 2

Chambers established: 1920s
Opening times: 8.30 am-7 pm Monday to Friday

Chambers' facilities
Conference rooms, Disks accepted, E-mail

Languages spoken
French, German, Italian, Persian, Urdu

Additional information
Established in the 1920s, 4 Field Court is a commercial set. Barristers at 4 Field Court offer advocacy and advisory expertise and experience in many aspects of commercial, chancery/commercial and civil law.

Members appear before all courts and tribunals in England and Wales, as well as in the European Court and a range of overseas courts and tribunals. Members of Chambers also act as arbitrators, as mediators in Alternative Dispute Resolution and as expert witnesses.

The breadth of expertise and experience within Chambers is such that Members are able to deal with a very wide range of civil litigation and other matters.

Particular areas of practice include: Shipping and Maritime law; Commercial Contracts; Insurance and Reinsurance; Banking and Financial Services; Road, Rail and Air law; Professional Negligence; Employment law; Property law; Intellectual Property; EC, Free Trade and Competition; Public, Administrative and Local Government; Licensing.

Barristers at 4 Field Court are members of the Bars of Antigua, California, Gibraltar, New South Wales, New York, New Zealand, Papua New Guinea, St Vincent and the Grenadines and Victoria.

Some members are contributors to various works: Geoffrey Brice, author of *The Maritime Law of Salvage* and contributor to *Lloyd's Maritime Law Quarterly*, as are Elizabeth Blackburn, Nigel Meeson; Allan Myers, editor *Australian Taxation Review*; Jervis Kay, editor *Atkin's Court Forms (Admiralty)*; James Thom, co-editor *Handbook of Dilapidations*; Alison Green, editorial adviser *Insurance Contract Law* (Kluwer) and EC editor *Current Law*; Robert Bourne has edited the Admiralty section of *The Civil Court Practice*; Nigel Meeson, author of *Practice and Procedure of the Admiralty Court, Ship and Aircraft Mortgages, Admiralty Jurisdiction and Practice* and contributor to *Ship Sale and Purchase* (2nd edition); Daphne Romney is a libel reader for the *Observer*. Jonathan D C Turner, co-author of *Vaughan's Law of the EC* and *Halsbury's Laws* (on EC competition law), *Countdown to 2000 – A Guide to the Legal Issues, Melville's Forms and Agreements on Intellectual Property and International Licensing*, co-editor *European Patent Office Reports*.

Direct professional access work and matters relating to the Overseas Practice Rules are accepted. A brochure is available.

FIELD COURT CHAMBERS

2nd Floor, 3 Field Court, Gray's Inn, London, WC1R 5EP
0171 404 7474
Fax: 0171 404 7475; DX 136 Chancery Lane

Chambers of Miss M D Spencer

FLEET CHAMBERS

Mitre House, 44-46 Fleet Street, London, EC4Y 1BN
0171 936 3707
Fax: 0171 936 3708; DX 274 Chancery Lane
E-mail: rr@fleetchambers.demon.co.uk
Out of hours telephone: 0171 936 3707

Chambers of Mr J D C Cartwright
Clerks: Robert Ruegg, Brian Newton

Cartwright, James 1968		Jones, Cheryl 1996	
Montgomery, Tony 1987		Halstead, Robin 1996	
Procter, Michael 1993		Sidhu, Sukhwant Singh	
Cornford, Hugh 1994		1996	
Frymann, Andrew 1995		Hall, Michael 1996	
Daniels, Philippa 1995		Onuaguluchi, Jones 1971	
Panton, Alastair 1996			

† Recorder ‡ Assistant Recorder *Door Tenant

FOREST HOUSE CHAMBERS

15 Granville Road, Walthamstow, London,
E17 9BS
0181 925 2240
Fax: 0181 556 6125

Chambers of Mr H D Singer

CHAMBERS OF WILFRED FORSTER-JONES

New Court, 1st Floor South, Temple,
London, EC4Y 9BE
0171 353 0853/4/7222
Fax: 0171 583 2823; DX 0008 Chancery
Lane
E-mail: chambers@newcourt.net
URL: http://www.newcourt.net

Chambers of W J E Forster-Jones
Clerks: Brian Peters, Alvin Stefanopulos

Forster-Jones, Wilfred *1976*	Thompson, Glenna *1993*
Roberts, Dominic *1977*	Sharma, Suman *1994*
Macaulay, Donora *1982*	Fell, Alistair *1994*
Metzger, Kevin *1984*	Palmer, Nathan *1994*
Aderemi, Adedamola *1992*	Stevens, Nina *1994*
Kivdeh, Shahrokh-Sean *1992*	Lams, Barnabas *1995*
	Dajani, Rafeef *1996*
Owusu-Yianoma, David *1992*	Daneshyar, Osama *1996*
	Hewitt, Susan *1997*

FOUNTAIN COURT

Fountain Court
CHAMBERS

Temple, London, EC4Y 9DH
0171 583 3335
Fax: 0171 353 0329/1794; DX 5 London
E-mail: chambers@fountaincourt.co.uk
Out of hours telephone: 0831 465 305

Chambers of A Boswood QC
Clerks: Mark Watson (Head of Clerking),
Michael Couling, Vince Plant, Danny
Wilkinson, Rob Smith; Practice Manager:
Ric Martin (Chambers Director);
Administrator: Prue Woodbridge

Dehn, Conrad QC *1952†*	Scott, Peter QC *1960*
Bathurst, Christopher QC *1959*	Boswood, Anthony QC *1970*
	Goldsmith, Lord QC *1972†*

Philipson, Trevor QC *1972*	Thanki, Bankim *1988*
Lerego, Michael QC *1972*	Robertson, Patricia *1988*
Smith, Andrew QC *1974†*	Chapman, Jeffrey *1989*
Brindle, Michael QC *1975*	Lucas, Bridget *1989*
Crane, Michael QC *1975*	Napier, Brian *1990*
Underhill, Nicholas QC *1976†*	Dale, Derrick *1990*
	Shah, Akhil *1990*
Stadlen, Nicholas QC *1976‡*	Smith, Marcus *1991*
	Gott, Paul *1991*
Railton, David QC *1979*	Buehrlen, Veronique *1991*
Moriarty, Stephen QC *1986*	Mitchell, Andrew *1992*
Doctor, Brian QC *1991*	Handyside, Richard *1993*
Wormington, Timothy *1977*	Taylor, John *1993*
Keene, Gillian *1980*	Coleman, Richard *1994*
McLaren, Michael *1981*	Tolley, Adam *1994*
Brook Smith, Philip *1982*	Merrett, Louise *1995*
Cox, Raymond *1982*	Hamilton, Philippa *1996*
Waksman, David *1982*	Sinclair, Paul *1997*
Martino, Anthony *1982*	Goodall, Patrick John *1998*
Keith, Thomas *1983*	Carter, Peter QC *1947**
Shanks, Murray *1984*	Sinan, Izzet *1981**
Philipps, Guy *1986*	Hooley, Richard *1984**
Orr, Craig *1986*	Li, Gladys SC (Hong Kong) *1971**
Green, Michael *1987*	
Howe, Timothy *1987*	

Types of work (and number of counsel practising in that area if supplied)
Administrative · Arbitration · Aviation · Banking · Chancery (general) · Chancery land law · Charities · Commercial litigation · Common law (general) · Company and commercial · Competition · Construction · Consumer law · Defamation · Discrimination · EC and competition law · Employment · Energy · Entertainment · Film, cable, TV · Financial services · Information technology · Insolvency · Insurance · Insurance/reinsurance · Intellectual property · International trade · Landlord and tenant · Medical negligence · Parliamentary · Partnerships · Patents · Personal injury · Private international · Professional negligence · Public international · Sale and carriage of goods · Share options · Shipping, admiralty · Sports · Tax – capital and income · Telecommunications · Trademarks

Chambers established: 1939
Opening times: 8 am-9 pm (Monday to Friday), 8 am-1 pm (Saturday)

Chambers' facilities
Conference rooms, Disks accepted, Catering for conferences, including light lunches, E-mail

Languages spoken
Afrikaans, French, German, Greek, Italian, Russian

C

---

† Recorder   ‡ Assistant Recorder   *Door Tenant

FRANCIS TAYLOR BUILDING

Ground Floor, Temple, London, EC4Y 7BY
0171 353 7768/7769/2711
Fax: 0171 353 0659; DX 441 London, Chancery Lane
E-mail:
clerks@francistaylorbuilding.law.co.uk
Out of hours telephone: 0831 635683

Chambers of N P Valios QC
Clerk: David Green; Practice Manager: David Green; Administrator: Janet P Clark

Valios, Nicholas QC *1964†*	**Ingram**, Jonathan *1984*
Lewis, Peter *1964*	**McFarlane**, Alastair *1985*
Cartwright, John *1964*	**Giret**, Joseph *1985*
Rylance, John *1968†*	**Bermingham**, Gerald *1985*
Mason, James *1969*	**Lewis**, Andrew *1986*
Lodge, Graham *1971*	**Braithwaite**, Garfield *1987*
Lewis, Edward *1972*	**English**, Caroline *1989*
Piercy, Mark *1976*	**Ancliffe**, Shiva *1991*
Cunningham, Graham *1976*	**Watson**, Isabelle *1991*
Parker, Wendy *1978*	**Taylor**, Simon *1993*
Mayall, David *1979*	**Vaughan**, Kieran *1993*
Cheves, Simon *1980*	**McLoughlin**, Ian *1993*
Tapson, Lesley *1982*	**Kerr**, Derek *1994*
Brown, Roy *1983*	**Fisher**, Richard *1994*
Rimmer, Anthony *1983*	**Small**, Arlene Ann-Marie
Jones, Richard *1984*	*1997*
Scobie, James *1984*	**Smith**, Christopher *1997*

2ND FLOOR, FRANCIS TAYLOR BUILDING

SECOND FLOOR

FRANCIS TAYLOR BUILDING

barristers chambers

Temple, London, EC4Y 7BY
0171 353 9942/3157
Fax: 0171 353 9924; DX 211 London

Chambers of D A Pears
Clerks: Kevin Moore (Senior Clerk), Kathryn Thornton, Ryan Bartlett, Susan Yacoub (Fees Clerk)

Williamson, Stephen QC   *1964†*

Lethbridge, Nemone *1956*	**Wilson**, Gerald *1989*
Merrylees, Gavin *1964*	**Rainey**, Philip *1990*
Naish, Dennis *1966*	**Barraclough**, Nicholas
Conrath, Philip *1972*	*1990*
Matthews, Phillip *1974†*	**Brimelow**, Kirsty *1991*
Mallison, Kate *1974*	**Heath**, Stephen *1992*
Pears, Derrick *1975*	**Jones**, Howard *1992*
Staddon, Paul *1976*	**Green**, Jonathan Paul *1993*
Cakebread, Stuart *1978*	**MacLaren**, Catriona *1993*
Dencer, Mark *1978*	**Butler**, Andrew *1993*
Boyd, Kerstin *1979*	**Aleeson**, Warwick *1994*
Manners, Henrietta *1981*	**Bastin**, Alexander *1995*
Holland, William *1982*	**Heather**, Christopher Mark
Reid, Sebastian *1982*	*1995*
Clarke, Kevin *1983*	**Bowker**, Robert *1995*
Carpenter, Jane *1984*	**Fieldsend**, James William
Matthews-Stroud,	*1997*
Jacqueline *1984*	**Cook**, Wendy *1997*
Dixon, Philip *1986*	**Selwyn Sharpe**, Richard
Buckpitt, Michael *1988*	*1985**
Roberts, Clare *1988*	**Chirimuuta**, Gilbert *1990**

Types of work (and number of counsel practising in that area if supplied)
Administrative · Banking · Bankruptcy · Care proceedings · Chancery (general) · Chancery land law · Commercial property · Common law (general) · Company and commercial · Consumer law · Crime · Employment · Family · Family provision · Housing · Insolvency · Landlord and tenant · Licensing · Local government · Medical negligence · Partnerships · Personal injury · Professional negligence · Sale and carriage of goods · Town and country planning

Opening times: 8.30 am-6.30 pm

Chambers' facilities
Conference rooms, Disks accepted

Languages spoken
French

Fees policy
Fees vary according to case, client and counsel: refer for details to clerks.

FRANCIS TAYLOR BUILDING

3rd Floor, Temple, London, EC4Y 7BY
0171 797 7250
Fax: 0171 797 7299; DX 46 London

Chambers of Mr J D C Guy

55 FRITH ROAD

Leytonstone, London, E11 4EX

Chambers of Mr K B K Mayo

FURNIVAL CHAMBERS

32 Furnival Street, London, EC4A 1JQ
0171 405 3232
Fax: 0171 405 3322; DX 72 London, Chancery Lane
E-mail: clerks@furnivallaw.co.uk
URL: http://www.furnivallaw.co.uk
Out of hours telephone: 0831 230 420

Chambers of Andrew Mitchell QC
Clerks: John Gutteridge, Joanne Thomas

Mitchell, Andrew QC *1976†*	Sherrard, Charles *1986*
Blunt, Oliver QC *1974†*	Romans, Philip *1982*
O'Neill, Sally QC *1976*	Gregory, Barry *1987*
Griffiths, Hugh *1972*	Lees, Patricia *1988*
Baur, Christopher *1972*	Gerasimidis, Nicolas *1988*
Connor, Gino *1974*	Earnshaw, Stephen *1990*
Matthews, Lisa *1974*	Hurtley, Diane *1990*
Latham, Michael *1975*	Forster, Timothy *1990*
Clompus, Joel *1976*	Woolls, Tanya *1991*
Henson, Graham *1976*	Patel, Sandip *1991*
Holt, Stephen *1978*	de Costa, Leon *1992*
Coughlin, Vincent *1980*	Henley, Andrew *1992*
Sheridan, Francis *1980*	Panayiotou, Lefi *1992*
Mytton, Paul *1982*	Giuliani, Mark *1993*
Whittam, Richard *1983*	Pearce, Ivan *1994*
Merrick, Nicola *1983*	McEvilly, Gerard *1994*
Swain, Jon *1983*	Winship, Julian *1995*
Caddle, Sherrie *1983*	Cockings, Giles *1996*
Headlam, Roy *1983*	Convey, Christopher *1994*
Carmichael, John *1984*	Coughlin, Elizabeth *1989**
Talbot, Kennedy *1984*	Candler, Linda *1997**
Blore, Carolyn *1985*	Fitzpatrick, Edward *1985**

Types of work (and number of counsel practising in that area if supplied)
Asset forfeiture and money laundering · Confiscation 6 · Copyright 4 · Courts

martial 4 · Crime 41 · Crime – corporate fraud 6

Chambers established: 1985
Opening times: 8.15 am-6.45 pm

Chambers' facilities
Conference rooms, Disks accepted, Disabled access, E-mail

Languages spoken
French, German, Greek, Italian, Portuguese, Serbo-Croat, Spanish

Additional information
Established in 1985, Furnival Chambers offers expertise in all areas of criminal law. Chambers' practice ranges from the most complex and involved commercial fraud to minor driving cases. Expertise is available for matters of fraud, sexual offences including rape and child abuse, Customs and Excise offences, drugs-related cases and crimes of violence including murder and terrorism. In addition chambers has a specialist team that deals with criminal confiscation proceedings in the Crown, High Court and Court of Appeal. The team offers a comprehensive range of services in this field including drafting of all relevant documentation and representation.

Asset Forfeiture and Money Laundering
Furnival Chambers has a specialist team which deals with confiscation, asset forfeiture and money laundering. Members of the team have appeared in the vast majority of the leading cases in the High Court and Court of Appeal.

Furnival Chambers recognises that urgent advice is often required and so informal telephone contact from solicitors and professional clients is welcomed.

Mitchell Taylor and Talbot on Confiscation and Proceeds of Crime, published by Sweet & Maxwell, 2nd Edition, 1996.

Languages
See the Index of Languages Spoken in Part G to locate a chambers where a particular language is spoken, or find an individual who speaks a particular language.

ONE GARDEN COURT FAMILY LAW CHAMBERS

Ground Floor, Temple, London, EC4Y 9BJ
0171 797 7900
Fax: 0171 797 7929; DX 1034 London
E-mail: clerks@onegardencourt.co.uk

Chambers of Eleanor F Platt QC, Alison Ball QC
Clerks: Howard Rayner (Senior Clerk), Dennis Davies (Fees Clerk), Chris Ferrison, Paul Harris, James Mitchell (Junior Clerks); Chief Executive: Nicholas Martin

Annexe of: Brentwood Chambers, Denton, North Yorkshire LS29 OHE
Tel: 01943 817230
Fax: 01943 817230

Platt, Eleanor QC *1960†*	**Cobb**, Stephen *1985*
Ball, Alison QC *1972†*	**Stocker**, John *1985*
Peddie, Ian QC *1971†*	**Geekie**, Charles *1985*
Solomons, Ellen *1964*	**Cleave**, Gillian *1988*
Willbourne, Caroline *1970*	**Crawley**, Gary *1988*
Coleman, Bruce *1972‡*	**Morgan**, Sarah *1988*
Nathan, Peter *1973*	**Inglis**, Alan *1989*
Shenton, Suzanne *1973*	**Bagchi**, Andrew *1989*
Szwed, Elizabeth *1974*	**Liebrecht**, Michael *1989*
Crowley, Jane QC *1976†*	**Jenkins**, Catherine *1990*
Horrocks, Peter *1977*	**Rozhan**, Ariff *1990*
Bedell-Pearce, Sheron *1978*	**Robbins**, Ian *1991*
O'Dwyer, Martin *1978‡*	**Krishnadasan**, Doushka *1991*
Wicherek, Ann *1978*	**Geddes**, Joanna *1992*
Scarratt, Richard *1979*	**Norton**, Andrew *1992*
Rowe, Judith *1979‡*	**Budaly**, Susan *1994*
Halkyard, Kay *1980*	**Stone**, Sally *1994*
Bazley, Janet *1980*	**Hudson**, Emma *1995*
Shackleford, Susan *1980*	**Chandler**, Alexander *1995*
Lachkovic, Veronica *1982*	**Fox**, Nicola *1996*
Hely Hutchinson, Caroline *1983*	**Amaouche**, Sassa-Ann *1996*
Rippon, Paul *1985*	**Yaqub**, Omar *1997*
Walker, Susannah *1985*	

TWO GARDEN COURT

CHAMBERS

1st Floor, Middle Temple, London, EC4Y 9BL
0171 353 1633
Fax: 0171 353 4621; DX 34 London, Chancery Lane
E-mail: barristers@2gardenct.law.co.uk
URL: http://www.2gardenct.law.co.uk

Chambers of Ian Macdonald QC, Owen Davies QC
Clerk: Colin Cook MBA; Administrator: Judy Ware

Macdonald, Ian QC *1963*	**Meusz**, Amanda *1986*
Davies, Owen QC *1973*	**Scannell**, Richard *1986*
Blake, Nicholas QC *1974‡*	**Veats**, Elizabeth *1986*
Macdonald, Kenneth QC *1978*	**Dias**, Dexter *1988*
	Eissa, Adrian *1988*
Griffiths, Courtenay QC *1980‡*	**Thomas**, Leslie *1988*
House, Michael *1972*	**Khan**, Judy *1989*
Munyard, Terry *1972*	**Grief**, Alison *1990*
Russell, Marguerite *1972*	**Harris**, Bethan *1990*
Watkinson, David *1972*	**Hutchinson**, Colin *1990*
George, Mark *1976*	**Jones**, Maggie *1990*
Blaxland, Henry *1978*	**Chahall**, Jasbinder *1991*
de Kauwe, Lalith *1978*	**Genn**, Yvette *1991*
Peart, Icah *1978‡*	**Harris**, Joanne *1991*
Webber, Frances *1978*	**Harrison**, Stephanie *1991*
Fransman, Laurens *1979*	**Holbrook**, Jon *1991*
Luba, Jan *1980*	**Naik**, Sonali *1991*
Graves, Celia *1981*	**Simblet**, Stephen *1991*
Jessup, Anne *1981*	**Easty**, Valerie *1992*
Williams, Cheryl *1982*	**Edie**, Alastair *1992*
Cudby, Markanza *1983*	**Weatherby**, Pete *1992*
Farrell, Simon *1983*	**Husain**, Raza *1993*
Hall, Michael *1983*	**Littlewood**, Robert *1993*
Jennings, Anthony *1983*	**Menon**, Rajiv *1993*
Rahal, Ravinder *1983*	**Davies**, Liz *1994*
Cottle, Stephen *1984*	**Seddon**, Duran *1994*
Harford-Bell, Nerida *1984*	**Cragg**, Stephen *1996*
Gold, Debra *1985*	**Friedman**, Daniel *1996*
Prevatt, Beatrice *1985*	**Lewis**, Anya *1997*
McKeone, Mary *1986*	**Lewis**, Patrick John *1997*
	Sikand, Maya *1997*

Types of work (and number of counsel practising in that area if supplied)

Administrative 25 · Care proceedings 10 · Civil liberties 19 · Crime 25 · Crime – corporate fraud 4 · Discrimination 4 · EC and competition law 3 · Education 4 · Employment 4 · Environment 2 · Family 11 · Family provision 10 · Foreign law 2 · Housing 10 · Immigration 12 · Information technology 2 · Landlord and tenant 10 · Local government 3 · Medical negligence 4 · Mental health 3 · Personal injury 5 · Professional negligence 3

Chambers established: 1974
Opening times: 8.45 am-6.15 pm

Chambers' facilities
Conference rooms, Disks accepted, E-mail

Languages spoken
Afrikaans, Dutch, French, German, Hindi, Sinhala, Spanish, Urdu

Fees policy
Open to discussion with clients.

Additional information
Since its inception 25 years ago this set of chambers has grown to make it one of the largest in the Temple. In the areas in which members specialise, a complete range of services can be provided, with professional and efficient back-up from the clerks and other supporting staff. The reputation of chambers rests on its high-profile public law cases, its criminal defence work and its immigration, family and housing law practices. The commitment of chambers to fostering a multi-disciplinary set has enabled it to benefit from cross-fertilisation of ideas between colleagues.

This is of particular benefit for some of the more unusual cases undertaken, but helps all practitioners to remain fresh, innovative and enthusiastic about their work. The civil team has been strengthened in order to fill a gap in demand for such work as civil actions against public authorities, cases for employees and personal injury work.
The atmosphere in chambers and its client care are friendly and informal. The facilities are second to none and up-to-date; the premises have been refurbished inside and out and the latest technology is fully utilised by the administration and counsel. The demands of looking after the library have led to the employment of a librarian. The appointment of an administrator has enabled our clerks to concentrate exclu-sively on client care and the clerks' room has been reorganised to provide teams of clerks dedicated to the specialised areas of work.

THE GARDEN HOUSE

14 New Square, Lincoln's Inn, London, WC2A 3SH
0171 404 6150
Fax: 0171 404 7395; DX 227 Chancery Lane

Chambers of Miss J M A Maxwell

1 GARFIELD ROAD

Battersea, London, SW11 5PL
0171 228 1137
Fax: 0171 228 1137

Chambers of Mr F Shah

159 GLENEAGLE ROAD

Streatham, London, SW16 6AZ
0181 769 3063
Fax: 0181 480 7208

Chambers of Mr A K Sharda

GOLDSMITH BUILDING

GOLDSMITH BUILDING

1st Floor, Temple, London, EC4Y 7BL
0171 353 7881
Fax: 0171 353 5319; DX 435 London
E-mail:
clerks@goldsmith-building.law.co.uk
URL:
http://www.goldsmith-building.law.co.uk

Chambers of John Griffith Williams QC
Clerks: Edith A Robertson (Senior Clerk), Danny O'Brien (First Junior Clerk)

Griffith Williams, John QC 1968†
Maguire, Michael QC 1949
Somerset Jones, Eric QC 1952†
Llewellyn-Jones, Christopher QC 1965†
Hughes, Merfyn QC 1971†
Farmer, Michael QC 1972†
Hay, Robin 1964†

Martineau, Henry 1966†
Hall-Smith, Martin 1972
Morris-Coole, Christopher 1974†
Gallagher, John 1974‡
Friel, John 1974
Calvert, Charles 1975
Leonard, Robert 1976
Routley, Patrick 1979
Higgins, Anthony 1978
Maitland Jones, Mark 1986
Burles, David 1984
Browne, Julie 1989
Hay, Deborah 1991
Newton, Claire 1992
Knowles, Linda 1993
Lawson, Daniel 1994

Wright, Sadie 1994
Bloom, Margaret 1994
Rawlings, Clive 1994
Roe, Thomas 1995
Mayhew, Jerome 1995
Fane, Angela 1992
Scolding, Fiona Kate 1996
Lewis, David Nicholas 1997
Price, Gerald QC 1969*†
Aubrey, David QC 1976*
Bidder, Neil QC 1976
Jones, Nicholas Gareth 1970*
Sander, Andrew 1970*†
Parsley, Charles 1973*
Brunnen, David 1976
Dawes, Gordon 1989

Types of work (and number of counsel practising in that area if supplied)
Admiralty 1 · Arbitration 6 · Bankruptcy 4 · Care proceedings 7 · Chancery (general) 5 · Commercial litigation 17 · Commercial property 10 · Company and commercial 6 · Construction 2 · Courts martial 2 · Crime 12 · Crime – corporate fraud 6 · Defamation 3 · Employment 10 · Environment 1 · Family 11 · Family provision 9 · Immigration 4 · Insolvency 4 · Insurance 4 · Landlord and tenant 10 · Licensing 4 · Medical negligence 6 · Mental health 3 · Partnerships 6 · Personal injury 21 · Professional negligence 19 · Sale and carriage of goods 6 · Shipping, admiralty 1 · Sports 4

Opening times: 8.30 am-6.30 pm

Chambers' facilities
Conference rooms, Disks accepted, E-mail, Link, Internet

Languages spoken
French

Additional information
Goldsmith Building is an established set of chambers which is able to provide individuals or teams of Counsel to undertake a wide variety of litigation, arbitration and advisory work. The traditional strength of chambers has been its high standard of advocacy. Chambers' work is centred on London and the South Eastern Circuit, with strong senior connections on the Wales and Chester and Northern Circuits. We provide an efficient, flexible and comprehensive legal service with established specialist practice groups.

Chambers has eight Practice Groups, namely, Personal Injury, Professional Negligence, Crime, Family, Business Law, Property and Landlord and Tenant, Public and Administrative Law and Employment. These groups form the core of the infrastructure of chambers. The groups meet on a regular basis and continuing education is one of their objectives. In addition to the practice groups, chambers also has specialists in the areas of environmental law, insolvency, and commercial fraud.

Goldsmith Building has developed a programme to provide seminars on a range of legal topics, and as authorised providers of continuing education by the Law Society and Institute of Legal Executives, all seminars carry a CPD rating. Chambers publishes a range of newsletters, which contain news and information about chambers and comments on current developments in the law.

Chambers has an experienced clerking team and the clerks are always ready to advise on suitable counsel and fee levels along with liaising with courts on the listing of cases. Members of chambers and the clerks are aware of the needs of clients and strive to give the highest quality of service. A Chambers Charter has been adopted which details the level of service you can expect when you instruct a member of chambers or deal with the clerks. More specific information, fee levels, chambers brochures and other chambers publications are available from the clerks.

GOLDSMITH CHAMBERS

Ground Floor, Goldsmith Building, Temple, London, EC4Y 7BL
0171 353 6802/3/4/5
Fax: 0171 583 5255; DX 376 London
E-mail:
clerks@goldsmithchambers.law.co.uk

Out of hours telephone: 0836 265096

Chambers of Philip Sapsford QC
Clerk: Celia Monksfield

Sapsford, Philip QC 1974‡	Day, Dorian 1987
Hall, Jonathan D QC	Smith, David 1988
1975*†	Evans, Charles 1988
Morrish, Peter 1962	Williams, Richard 1988
Torrance, Hugh 1956	Calway, Mark 1989
Meikle, Robert 1970	James, Grahame 1989
Easterman, Nicholas 1975	Singh, Gurdial 1989
Harkus, George 1975	FitzGibbon, Neil 1989
Leigh, Edward 1977	Hargreaves, Ben 1989
Barnett, Diane 1978	Katan, Jonathan 1990
Burrow, John 1980	Moss, Norman 1990
Woodall, Peter 1983	George, Michael 1990
Hulme, John 1983	McLevy, Tracey 1993
O'Leary, Michele 1983	Brennan, Christopher 1995
Markham, David 1983	Allen, Douglas 1995
Whelan, Roma 1984	Foster, Julien 1995
Norris, James 1984	Cadman, David 1996
Dabbs, David 1984	Jones, Mark 1997
Morris, Michael 1984	Ford, Andrew 1997
Wehrle, Jacqueline 1984	Middleton, Dianne 1997
Buswell, Richard 1985	Fish, David QC 1973*
Munonyedi, Ifey 1985	Jakens, Claire 1988*
Szerard, Andrei 1986	

GOLDSWORTH CHAMBERS

1st Floor, 11 Gray's Inn Square, London, WC1R 5JD
0171 405 7117
Fax: 0171 831 8308; DX 1057 London

---

9 GOUGH SQUARE

GOUGH
SQUARE

London, EC4A 3DE
020 7832 0500
Fax: 020 7353 1344; DX 439 Chancery Lane
E-mail: clerks@9goughsq.co.uk
URL: http://www.9goughsq.co.uk

Chambers of Jeremy Roberts QC
Practice Director: Joanna Poulton

Roberts, Jeremy QC 1965†	Verdan, Alexander 1987
Brent, Michael QC 1961†	Buckett, Edwin 1988
Upward, Patrick QC 1972‡	Wheeler, Andrew 1988
Burrell, Gary QC 1977†	Hales, Sally-Ann 1988
Foy, John QC 1969‡	Cottage, Rosina 1988
Reddihough, John 1969†	Glynn, Stephen 1990
Baillie, Andrew 1970†	Sinclair, Jane 1990
Gerrey, David 1975†	Jones, Philip 1990
Joyce, Michael 1976	Padley, Clare 1991
Davies, Trevor 1978	Tughan, John 1991
Ferguson, Frederick 1978	Crowther, Jeremy 1991
Aldous, Grahame 1979‡	Downey, Aileen 1991
Macleod, Duncan 1980	Begley, Laura 1993
Wilson, Christopher 1980	Neilson, Louise 1994
Hillier, Nicolas 1982	Stephenson, Christopher
Hiorns, Roger 1983	1994
Carr, Simon 1984	Vindis, Tara 1996
Ritchie, Andrew 1985	Little, Tom Charles 1997
Naik, Gaurang 1985	Palmer, Anthony QC 1962*
Fisher, David 1985	Harrington, Tina 1985*
Levy, Jacob 1986	Graffy, Prof Coleen 1991*
Loades, Jonathan 1986	Williams, Vincent 1985

Types of work (and number of counsel practising in that area if supplied)
Admiralty 1 · Care proceedings 9 · Civil actions against the police 8 · Commercial litigation 6 · Commercial property 8 · Common law (general) 34 · Company and commercial 8 · Crime 15 · Crime – corporate fraud 10 · Employment · Family 9 · Family provision 9 · Insurance/ reinsurance · Landlord and tenant 8 · Medical negligence 12 · Personal injury 30

Chambers established: approx 1940
Opening times: 8.15 am-6.45 pm

Chambers' facilities
Conference rooms, Disks accepted, Disabled access, E-mail

Languages spoken
French, Hebrew

Fees policy
Fee levels depend upon seniority, complexity of work and availability. It is our policy to charge a reasonable fee for all work reasonably undertaken. We are always prepared to discuss fee levels and give an estimate of likely cost before instructions are taken on. Any enquiries should first be directed to the clerks. Thereafter our Practice Director would be pleased to assist.

Additional information
The chambers: We are a long-established general common law set specialising in particular in personal injury, clinical and

C

professional negligence, serious fraud and family work.

We are noted for our friendly yet commercial approach which we believe enhances our ability to provide realistic advice to our clients. Focused along the lines of specialist teams, we draw upon the considerable depth of knowledge and expertise held in chambers through regular team meetings.

Our facilities are modern and up-to-date, including disabled facilities, large dedicated conference rooms and full computerisation. We are professionally managed by a qualified Practice Director who is happy to discuss any aspects of our service and in particular to recommend suitable counsel. A brochure is available on request.

Work undertaken:
Personal injury: We can offer experts in complex multi-party actions, industrial diseases, RSI, deafness, lifting, marine accidents, etc, representing either plaintiffs or defendants. Special payment terms are negotiable for union or insurance-backed claims. All members of chambers have agreed to accept conditional fee work and where appropriate single agreements covering individual firms can be negotiated.

Clinical negligence: We can offer true experts who are renowned for being sensitive to the issues in these cases yet are tenacious advocates and negotiators. Our experience for both plaintiffs and defendants includes brain injuries, birth defects, failed sterilisations, surgical and non-surgical maltreatment.

Professional negligence: Members of our professional negligence team regularly advise on and appear in cases involving all aspects of professional negligence, but in particular actions involving solicitors, accountants, insurance brokers and surveyors.

Serious fraud: Chambers has some of the country's leading fraud practitioners. More than 12 members of chambers regularly prosecute for the SFO and for CPS HQ, as well as defending some of the most complex fraud cases such as Blue Arrow and Nissan. We can provide experts on advance fee frauds, city frauds, pension frauds, customs and excise and revenue fraud etc.

General crime: The crime team has established an enviable reputation in both prosecuting and defending general crime on the M and O Circuit, in particular at Northampton, Luton, St Albans, Aylesbury and Birmingham Crown Courts. In addition, members of chambers regularly appear in the major London Crown Courts.

Family: A full range of family work is undertaken including care proceedings, adoption, residence and contact applications, domestic violence injunctions and ancillary relief. We have particular expertise in local authority child care work and regularly appear in the High Courts on contested family matters. Work is also undertaken in the related areas of mental health and community care.

Landlord and Tenant: Members appear for Landlords and Tenants in both commercial and residential disputes at all court levels. Advisory work before and after litigation has commenced is commonly undertaken often with tight deadlines imposed. As editors of the Sweet & Maxwell *Landlord and Tenant Law Reports* chambers is able to provide up-to-the minute thinking in all aspects of this area of law.

Other work: Chambers also has smaller specialist groups working in such areas as insurance, contract, civil actions against police, employment, judicial review and inheritance.

Publications:
a) *Landlord and Tenant Law Reports* (Sweet & Maxwell Series). Christopher Wilson and Clare Padley
b) *Medical Evidence in Whiplash Cases* (Sweet & Maxwell 1998). Andrew Ritchie
c) *Applications for Judicial Review* (Butterworths). Grahame Aldous
d) *Housing Law for the Elderly* (Oyez). Grahame Aldous.

Languages
See the Index of Languages Spoken in Part G to locate a chambers where a particular language is spoken, or find an individual who speaks a particular language.

† Recorder ‡ Assistant Recorder *Door Tenant

GOUGH SQUARE CHAMBERS

6-7 Gough Square, London, EC4A 3DE
0171 353 0924
Fax: 0171 353 2221; DX 476 London
E-mail: gsc@goughsq.co.uk
URL: http://www.goughsq.co.uk
Out of hours telephone: 0860 219162

Chambers of Fred Philpott
Clerks: Bob Weekes (Senior Clerk), Paul Messenger; Administrator: Elizabeth Owen-Ward

Philpott, Fred *1974*	**Gun Cuninghame**, Julian *1989*
Sayer, Peter *1975*	
Andrews, Claire *1979*	**Katrak**, Cyrus *1991*
Hibbert, William *1979*	**Vines**, Anthony *1993*
Stancombe, Barry *1983*	**Cogswell**, Frederica *1995*
Goulding, Jonathan *1984*	**MacDonald**, Iain *1996*
Neville, Stephen *1986*	**Hulme**, Amanda *1997*
Smith, Julia *1988*	

Types of work (and number of counsel practising in that area if supplied)
Administrative 4 · Banking 4 · Chancery (general) 4 · Commercial litigation 5 · Company and commercial 5 · Consumer law 14 · Crime – corporate fraud 8 · Employment 3 · Environment 5 · Equity, wills and trusts 3 · Food 7 · Franchising 4 · Insolvency 4 · Intellectual property 2 · Landlord and tenant 6 · Licensing 5 · Medical negligence 1 · Personal injury 3 · Professional negligence 3 · Sale and carriage of goods 10

Chambers established: 1986
Opening times: 8.45 am-6.15 pm

Chambers' facilities
Conference rooms, Disks accepted, Disabled access, E-mail

Languages spoken
French

Fees policy
The senior clerk will be pleased to provide an indication of fees in advance and will negotiate the fees depending upon each case. A flexible approach is maintained and, if preferred, hourly rates can be agreed.

GRAY'S INN CHAMBERS, THE CHAMBERS OF NORMAN PATTERSON

First Floor, Gray's Inn Chambers, Gray's Inn, London, WC1R 5JA
0171 831 5344
Fax: 0171 242 7799; DX 182 Chancery Lane
E-mail: s.mcblain@btinternet.com
URL: http://www.barristers-chambers.co.uk
Out of hours telephone: 0973 132347

Chambers of Norman Patterson
Clerks: Spencer McBlain (01245 280 213) (Senior Clerk), James Parker (07931 939701)

Patterson, Norman *1971*	**Akinsanya**, Stephen *1993*
Mier, Andrew *1973*	**Kashmiri**, Sophia *1994*
Dickens, Andrew *1983*	**Owen**, Helen *1994*
Deal, Timothy *1988**	**Millard**, Martin *1995*
Dowell, Gregory *1990*	**Savage**, Ayisha *1995*
O'Sullivan, Michael *1991**	**Rahman**, Sami *1996*
Burnett, Iain *1993*	**Myers**, Keith *1996*
Bergenthal, Ronnie *1993*	**Selby**, Lawrence *1997*

Types of work (and number of counsel practising in that area if supplied)
Administrative · Arbitration · Care proceedings · Chancery (general) · Civil liberties · Common law (general) · Courts martial · Crime · Crime – corporate fraud · Discrimination · Employment · Family · Housing · Immigration · Landlord and tenant · Licensing · Medical negligence · Mental health · Personal injury · Professional negligence

C

Chambers' facilities
Conference rooms, Disks accepted

Languages spoken
French, German, Hebrew, Hindi, Italian, Spanish, Urdu, Yoruba

GRAY'S INN CHAMBERS

Chambers of Nigel Ley (2nd Floor), Gray's Inn, London, WC1R 5JA
0171 831 7888 (Chambers)
0171 831 7904 (Mr M Ullah)
Fax: 0171 831 7227

Chambers of Mr N J Ley

Ley, Nigel *1969*	**Orme,** John *1995*
Ullah, Mohammed Hashmot *1989*	

GRAY'S INN CHAMBERS

5th Floor, Gray's Inn, London, WC1R 5JA
0171 404 1111
Fax: 0171 430 1522; DX 0074 London

Chambers of Brian P Jubb

96 GRAY'S INN ROAD

London, WC1X 8AL
0171 405 0585
Fax: 0171 405 0586; DX 214 Chancery Lane
Out of hours telephone: 0498 751877

Chambers of The Rt Hon D J D Davies
Clerk: Philip Havelock

Davies, The Rt Hon Denzil MP *1965*	**Browne,** James *1994*
Briden, Richard *1982*	**Gray,** Kären *1995*
Wagner, Linda *1990*	**King,** Charles *1995*
Raybaud, June *1990*	**Cannon,** Adam Richard *1997*

1 GRAY'S INN SQUARE, CHAMBERS OF THE BARONESS SCOTLAND OF ASTHAL QC

1st Floor, London, WC1R 5AG
0171 405 3000
Fax: 0171 405 9942; LDE 238

Chambers of The Baroness Scotland of Asthal QC

1 GRAY'S INN SQUARE

Ground Floor, London, WC1R 5AA
0171 405 8946/7/8
Fax: 0171 405 1617; DX 1013 Chancery Lane

Chambers of C W Teper

2-3 GRAY'S INN SQUARE

Gray's Inn, London, WC1R 5JH
0171 242 4986
Fax: 0171 405 1166; DX 316 London
E-mail: chambers@2-3graysinnsquare.co.uk

Chambers of Anthony F B Scrivener QC
Clerks: Martin Hart, Stuart Pullum, Robert Barrow; Chambers Director: Douglas Lewis CBE

Scrivener, Anthony QC *1958†*	**Haines,** John *1967†*
	Rundell, Richard *1971†*
Eyre, Sir Graham QC *1954†*	**Stephenson,** Geoffrey *1971*
Spence, Malcolm QC *1958†*	**Lamming,** David *1972*
Ground, Patrick QC *1960*	**Thomas,** Adrian Trevelyan *1974*
Cochrane, Christopher QC *1965†*	
	Nardecchia, Nicholas *1974*
Porten, Anthony QC *1969†*	**Davey,** Tobias *1977*
Dinkin, Anthony QC *1968†*	**Stoker,** Graham *1977*
Pugh, Vernon QC *1969†*	**Albutt,** Ian *1981*
Wolton, Harry QC *1969†*	**Gasztowicz,** Steven *1981*
Lowe, Mark QC *1972*	**Cook,** Mary *1982*

Ellis, Morag *1984*
Findlay, James *1984*
Astaniotis, Katerine *1985*
Bedford, Michael *1985*
Kolvin, Philip *1985*
Bird, Simon *1987*
Bhose, Ranjit *1989*
Clay, Jonathan *1990*
Colquhoun, Celina *1990*
Carrington, Gillian *1990*
Green, Robin *1992*

Murray, Harriet *1992*
Miller, Peter *1993*
Ponter, Ian *1993*
Coppel, Philip *1994*
Cosgrove, Thomas *1994*
Ground, Richard *1994*
Beglan, Wayne *1996*
Lintott, David *1996*
Easton, Jonathan *1996*
Clarke, Rory James *1996*

Types of work (and number of counsel practising in that area if supplied)
Administrative 8 · Banking 2 · Bankruptcy 5 · Civil liberties 1 · Commercial litigation 12 · Common land 3 · Common law (general) 8 · Company and commercial 2 · Construction 7 · Crime 8 · Crime – corporate fraud 3 · Employment 9 · Environment 3 · Housing 11 · Information technology 1 · Landlord and tenant 6 · Licensing 3 · Local government 22 · Personal injury 5 · Professional negligence 5 · Sale and carriage of goods 4 · Town and country planning 22

Chambers established: Before 1914
Opening times: 8 am-7 pm

Chambers' facilities
Conference rooms, Video conferences, Disks accepted, Disabled access, Direct-dial telephone, Voice-mail, Individual E-mail boxes

Languages spoken
French, German, Greek, Italian

Fees policy
Fees will be negotiated with the clerks depending on the case and the seniority and experience of the selected counsel. The clerks will always strive to accommodate the particular requirements of each client, and flexible terms, including all–in fees, fixed rates and bulk billing can be arranged.

The Chambers
2-3 Gray's Inn Square is a long-established set of Chambers. It provides a comprehensive, in-depth service in all areas relating to local government and planning, including common law actions involving government agencies.

Specialisms covered by various members of Chambers:

1. Planning, including all types of planning and highway inquiries.

2. Administrative law, including judicial review applications and tribunal hearings.

3. Environmental and public health law, including EPA hearings, waste and pollution control, and statutory nuisances.

4. Other local government matters, including public health, compulsory purchase, highways, local government finance, housing law and rating.

5. Prosecuting and defending local government prosecutions, including breach of planning/listed building control, EPA enforcement, and offences relating to pollution, trade descriptions, weights and measures, food safety and building regulations.

6. Contractual claims and tortious disputes involving governmental bodies, including building and computing claims and arbitrations, and sale of goods/services contracts.

7. Employment law including unfair and wrongful dismissal claims, discrimination claims and professional disciplinary hearings (doctors, dentists *etc*).

8. Landlord and tenant law, particularly leases under the *Housing Act 1985* and restraint of unneighbourly conduct.

9. Personal injury actions.

10. Privy Council appeals.

Counsel are available at all levels of experience. Junior tenants are available at short notice for all magistrates' court, county court and tribunal hearings, as well as for procedural applications. Members of Chambers work in all parts of England and Wales. Various members of Chambers also practise or are admitted in other jurisdictions.

Work will be provided on diskette or to an e-mail address where requested. Chambers can provide documents in most word-processing formats.

Further details about Chambers and its members are set out in its brochure: the clerks will send a copy on request.

2 GRAY'S INN SQUARE CHAMBERS

2nd Floor, Gray's Inn, London, WC1R 5AA
020 7242 0328
Fax: 020 7405 3082; DX 43 London
Chancery Lane
E-mail: clerks@2gis.co.uk
URL: http://www.2gis.co.uk

Chambers of Giles Eyre
*Clerks: Bill Harris (Senior Clerk), Sue
Reding, Michael Goodridge; Practice
Manager: Paul Simpson; Fees: Paul Hughes*

Eyre, Giles *1974*	**Collaco Moraes**, Francis *1985*
Leighton, Peter *1966*	
Knight, Keith *1969*	**Bhakar**, Surinder *1986*
Robson, John *1974*	**Dixon**, Sorrel *1987*
Cross, Edward *1975*	**Baldock**, Susan *1988*
Robinson, Richard *1977*	**Roberts**, Adrian *1988*
Fortune, Peter *1978*	**Whalan**, Mark *1988*
McConnell, Christopher *1979*	**Woods**, Terence *1989*
Hughes, David *1980*	**Brown**, Joanne *1990*
Mathew, Nergis-Anne *1981*	**Watkins**, Myles *1990*
Dulovic, Milan *1982*	**Rice**, Christopher *1991*
Rayson, Jane *1982*	**Arney**, James *1992*
Haven, Kevin *1982*	**Duddridge**, Robert *1992*
Church, John *1984*	**Priestley**, Rebecca *1989*
Marks, Jacqueline *1984*	**Drayton**, Henry *1993*
Moore, Anthony *1984*	**Barnett**, Daniel *1993*
Posner, Gabrielle *1984*	**Parr**, Judith *1994*
King, Fawzia *1985*	**Hepher**, Paul *1994*
	McKechnie, Stuart Iain William *1997*

Languages
See the Index of Languages Spoken in
Part G to locate a chambers where a
particular language is spoken, or find
an individual who speaks a particular
language.

3 GRAY'S INN SQUARE

Ground Floor, London, WC1R 5AH
0171 520 5600
Fax: 0171 520 5607; DX 1043 Chancery
Lane
E-mail: clerks@3gis.co.uk
Out of hours telephone: 0410 354598

Chambers of Rock Tansey QC
*Clerks: Guy Williams (Senior Clerk), Marc
King, Stephen Lucas; Administrator: Jacky
Chase*

Tansey, Rock QC *1966*†	**Barrett**, Penelope *1982*
Perry, John QC *1975*†	**Dein**, Jeremy *1982*
Kay, Steven QC *1977*‡	**Pentol**, Simon *1982*
Carter-Stephenson, George QC *1975*	**Maley**, Bill *1982*
	Redhead, Leroy *1982*
Taylor, William QC QC (Scot) *1990*	**Cooper**, John *1983*
	Wells, Colin *1987*
Hooper, David *1971*	**Hynes**, Paul *1987*
Allan, Colin *1971*	**Levitt**, Alison *1988*
Farrington, David *1972*	**Kayne**, Adrian *1989*
Jaffa, Ronald *1974*	**Stone**, Joseph *1989*
Keany, Brendan *1974*	**Valley**, Helen *1990*
Mitchell, Jonathan *1974*	**Piercy**, Arlette *1990*
Statman, Philip *1975*‡	**Akuwudike**, Emma *1992*
Fortson, Rudi *1976*	**De Bertodano**, Sylvia *1993*
Ellis, Diana *1978*‡	**Potter**, Harry *1993*
Offenbach, Roger *1978*	**Furlong**, Richard *1994*
Beyts, Chester *1978*	**Byrnes**, Aisling *1994*
Bott, Charles *1979*	**Smith**, Tyrone *1994*
Keleher, Paul *1980*	**Howard**, Nicola *1995*
Mendelle, Paul *1981*	**Gardiner**, Sebastian *1997*

Types of work (and number of counsel practising in that area if supplied)
Crime 40 · Crime – corporate fraud 40

Chambers established: 1975
Opening times: 8.30 am-6 pm

Chambers' facilities
Conference rooms, Video conferences,
Disks accepted, E-mail, Voice-mail for all
Members of Chambers

Chambers

3 Gray's Inn Square is a specialist Criminal Defence Set which aims to ensure that everyone has equal access to the best representation.

Chambers has earned a reputation as a leader in its field by maintaining the highest standards of professionalism, integrity, commitment and both accessibility and approachability.

First-class representation is provided at every level of seniority by practitioners who appear regularly in 'high profile cases' and who offer experience in the conduct of all categories of criminal case including European Human Rights, International Criminal Tribunal, (International) Terrorism and War Crimes, Murder, Serious Fraud, Organised Crime, International Drugs Trafficking/allied Money Laundering and offences of Extreme/Sexual Violence.

Within this framework there is a positive commitment to legally aided clients and where appropriate, pro bono work is undertaken.

Particular expertise is provided in all aspects of Appellate Work, including Judicial Review and Privy Council. Further, there is experience in the conduct of Civil Cases, especially Actions against the Police and allied issues and Mental Health Review Tribunals.

In recent years Chambers has presented lectures to solicitors and practitioners generally, concerning the effect of significant changes in Criminal Legislation. Some members have also lectured nationally and internationally to and on behalf of Legal/Human Rights organisations on Drug Trafficking and International War Crimes.

Publications

Rudi Forston: *Law on the Misuse of Drugs*; Sweet & Maxwell Practical Research Papers – Crime:
(a) *Pre-Trial Disclosure* – Rock Tansey QC and Paul Keleher
(b) *Identification by Police Officers* – Ronald Jaffa
(c) *Pre-Trial Disclosure* – Colin Wells
(d) *Tape Recording of Interviews* – John Cooper

Foreign connections

Rock Tansey QC and Steven Kay QC have founded the European Criminal Bar Association in order to advance issues of mutual concern for European Criminal Defence Lawyers.

Rock Tansey QC is the First Chairman of the ECBA and organised its inaugural conference at the European Commission for Human Rights, Strasbourg.

Steven Kay QC, Defence Counsel in the first International Criminal Tribunal for the former Yugoslavia, undertakes European Human Rights cases.

John Perry QC also practises in Bermuda and is a member of the West Indian Bar.

4-5 GRAY'S INN SQUARE

Ground Floor, Gray's Inn, London, WC1R 5JP
0171 404 5252
Fax: 0171 242 7803; DX 1029 London
E-mail: chambers@4-5graysinnsquare.co.uk
URL: http://www.4-5graysinnsquare.co.uk

Chambers of Miss Elizabeth Appleby QC, The Hon Michael J Beloff QC

Chambers Director: Anthony Wells; Clerks: Michael Kaplan, Mark Regan, Amanda Campbell; Chambers Administrator: Barbara Morris; Operations Manager: Miriam Don

Appleby, Elizabeth QC *1965†*	**Steel,** John QC *1978‡*
	Stone, Gregory QC *1976‡*
Beloff, Michael QC *1967†*	**Booth,** Cherie QC *1976†*
Wade, William QC *1946*	**Spearman,** Richard QC *1977*
Flather, Gary QC *1962†*	
Mole, David QC *1970†*	**Straker,** Timothy QC *1977‡*
Ash, Brian QC *1975*	**Bean,** David QC *1976‡*
Isaacs, Stuart QC *1975‡*	**McManus,** Richard QC *1982*
Ouseley, Duncan QC *1973†*	
Fox, Hazel QC *1950*	**Malek,** Hodge QC *1983*
Griffiths, Robert QC *1974*	**Aaron,** Sam SC *1986*

Campbell, Robin *1967*
Huskinson, Nicholas *1971*†
Chichester, Julian *1977*
Hobson, John *1980*‡
Corner, Timothy *1981*
Kerr, Tim *1983*
Village, Peter *1983*
Havey, Peter *1984*
Oldham, Jane *1985*
Stinchcombe, Paul *1985*
Humphreys, Richard *1986*
Lewis, Clive *1987*
Ramsden, James *1987*
Hill, Thomas *1988*
Clark, Geraldine *1988*
Singh, Rabinder *1989*
Linden, Thomas *1989*
Moore, Sarah *1990*
Brown, Paul *1991*
Mountfield, Helen *1991*
Tabachnik, Andrew *1991*
Hunt, Murray *1992*
Wolfe, David *1992*
Fraser-Urquhart, Andrew *1993*
Barav, Amihud *1993*
Steyn, Karen *1995*
Demetriou, Marie-Eleni *1995*
Davies, Sarah-Jane *1996*
Moffett, Jonathan *1996*
Sharland, Andrew *1996*
Strachan, James *1996*
Chamberlain, Martin *1997*
Palmer, Robert *1998*
Rhee, Deok-Joo *1998*
Harris, Brian QC *1960**

Types of work (and number of counsel practising in that area if supplied)

Administrative 35 · Arbitration 8 · Aviation 6 · Banking 8 · Civil liberties 6 · Commercial 20 · Competition 3 · Crime – corporate fraud 4 · Defamation 4 · Discrimination 21 · EC and competition law 10 · Education 15 · Employment 21 · Environment 10 · Housing 26 · Immigration 5 · Insurance 10 · Insurance/reinsurance 20 · Landlord and tenant 3 · Local government 33 · Parliamentary 10 · Professional negligence 6 · Public international 2 · Shipping, admiralty 3 · Sports 5 · Telecommunications 2 · Town and country planning 26

Chambers established: 1936
Opening times: 8 am-7 pm

Chambers' facilities

Conference rooms, Disks accepted, E-mail, Facilities for the disabled

Languages spoken

French, German, Greek, Spanish

Fees policy

Clerk will quote fees on request.

The Chambers

4-5 Gray's Inn Square is regarded as one of the leading Chambers in London and its pre-eminence has been recognised for many years in various independent legal publications.

Members of Chambers possess expertise and experience of the highest quality in the fields of public law and judicial review, planning and environmental law, commercial law, European Community law, human rights, employment law and sports law. The intersection of these specialisations within Chambers allows collaboration between members on complex litigation.

Many members hold part-time judicial appointments in England, as well as overseas. The joint Heads of Chambers are Elizabeth Appleby QC, the first woman to head a leading set of chambers, and Michael Beloff QC, now also President of Trinity College, Oxford. Several of the present juniors are on the Treasury Panels of Counsel instructed on behalf of the Crown.

Foreign Connections:

Members of Chambers have appeared at the Privy Council, the European Court of Justice and of Human Rights, international arbitration tribunals and other courts worldwide, including in the Far East, the Caribbean, Cyprus, Gibraltar, Belfast and Bermuda. One member is a former Judge of the Court of Appeal in Swaziland and a current Judge of the Court of Appeal in Lesotho. Another is a Judge of the Court of Appeal of Jersey and Guernsey and one a Member of the Court of Arbitration for Sport. Several are Recorders.

Recent and Forthcoming Publications:

Books
Michael Beloff QC, Tim Kerr and Marie Demetriou, *Sports Law* (forthcoming 1999); Richard McManus QC, *Education and the Courts* (1998); Hodge Malek QC and Paul Matthews, *Discovery* (3rd edn, forthcoming 1999); Clive Lewis, *Judicial Remedies in Public Law* (2nd edn, forthcoming 1999); Murray Hunt and Rabinder Singh eds, *A Practitioner's Guide to the Impact of the Human Rights Act* (forthcoming 1999); Helen Mountfield and John Wadham, *The Blackstone Guide to the Human Rights Act 1998* (1999); Rabinder Singh, *The Future of Human Rights in the United Kingdom* (1997); Murray Hunt, *Using Human Rights in English Courts* (1997); A Nicol, G Millar and Andrew Sharland, *Blackstone's Guide to Media Law and the Human Rights Act 1998* (forthcoming 1999).

Chapters and Articles
Michael Beloff QC, *What does it all mean? How to interpret the Human Rights Act*

(Lasok Lecture 1998); Michael Beloff QC, 'Community Law in the UK and European Courts' in *European Community Law in the English Courts* (Andenas and Jacobs eds, 1998); Clive Lewis, 'Judicial Review and the Role of the English Court on European Community Disputes' in *European Community Law in the English Courts* (Andenas and Jacobs eds, (1998); Clive Lewis, 'Damages and the Right to an Effective Remedy for Breach of European Community Law' in *The Golden Metwand and the Crooked Cord: Essays in Honour of Sir William Wade QC* (1998); Geraldine Clark, 'Composite Policies: a Trap for Unwary Insurers', *Kluwer Insurance and Reinsurance Law Briefing*, 13 April 1999; Rabinder Singh, Murray Hunt and Marie Demetriou, 'Is There a Role for the "Margin of Appreciation" in National Law After the Human Rights Act?' (1999) EHRLR 15; Rabinder Singh, 'Privacy and the Media after the Human Rights Act' (1998) EHRLR 712; Murray Hunt, 'Annual Survey of the European Convention on Human Rights' *1997 Yearbook of European Law* (1999); Murray Hunt, 'The 'Horizontal Effect' of the Human Rights Act' [1998] Public Law 423; Michael Beloff QC and Helen Mountfield 'Leave it to the Lords' Judicial Review (Pt III) 119; Michael Beloff QC and Sarah Jane Davies, *Halsbury's Laws 4th Edn*, Time, (forthcoming) (1999).

Former Members:
The Right Honourable Lord Justice Schiemann; the Honourable Mr Justice Keene; The Honourable Mr Justice Collins; The Honourable Mr Justice Moses; The Honourable Mr Justice Sullivan; Richard Yorke QC (1956) (QC – 1971); Sir Douglas Frank QC, former President of the Lands Tribunal; His Honour Judge Marder QC, President of the Lands Tribunal; His Honour Judge Barratt QC, Victor Wellings QC, former President of the Lands Tribunal.

Associate Tenants:
Professor Sir G H Treitel QC; Professor E P Ellinger; Lord Borrie QC; Sir John Freeland QC (1952) (QC – 1987); Marc Dassesse (Brussels Bar); Professor Sir D G T Williams QC; Patrick Patelin (Juriste d'Enterprise, Paris); Edmund McGovern (also in Brussels); Narinder Hargun (Bermuda); Brian Harris QC; Jeremy Gauntlett (SC) (South Africa); John Sacker QC (NSW); Mansoor Jamal Malik (Oman).

Other Matters:
The Chambers has been the first set to appoint an academic panel as a research and advisory facility. Its members are Professor Craig (Administrative), Professor M Grant (Local government and planning), Professor P Davies (Employment), Professor J Usher (EU), Professor E Barendt (Media, Human Rights, Welfare), Professor A Arnull, Professor David Harris (International Law and Human Rights). The Chambers now publishes a journal covering areas of work in which members practise and recent developments in the law.

6 GRAY'S INN SQUARE

Ground Floor, Gray's Inn, London, WC1R 5AZ
0171 242 1052
Fax: 0171 405 4934; DX 224 London
E-mail: 6graysinn@clara.co.uk
Out of hours telephone: 0961 128858

Chambers of M L Boardman
Clerks: Russell Kinsley, Matthew Corrigan; Other Admin: Colin Sartain, Jai Roff

Boardman, Michael *1979*	**Lobbenberg**, Nicholas *1987*
Thomas, David Owen QC *1952*†	**Minihan**, Sean *1988*
	Van Stone, Grant *1988*
Chadwin, James QC *1958*†	**Bromfield**, Colin *1988*
Swift, Malcolm QC *1970*†	**O'Connor**, Maureen *1988*
Yajnik, Ram *1965*	**Bickerstaff**, Jane *1989*
Addezio, Mario *1971*	**Hunter**, Win *1990*
Gordon, Ashley *1973*	**Sims**, Paul *1990*
Landsbury, Alan *1975*	**Smith**, Helen *1990*
Trimmer, Stuart *1977*	**McKay**, Annmarie *1992*
Heimler, George *1978*	**McAulay**, Mark *1993*
Barker, John *1982*	**Alderson**, Pippa *1993*
Kopieczek, Louis *1983*	**Spiro**, Dafna *1994*
Evans, Ann *1983*	**Crook**, Adam *1994*
Misner, Philip *1984*	**Harries**, Mark *1995*
Price, Tom *1985*	**Evans**, Philip *1995*

8 GRAY'S INN SQUARE

Gray's Inn, London, WC1R 5AZ
0171 242 3529
Fax: 0171 404 0395; DX 411 Chancery Lane

Chambers of Patrick C Soares
Clerk: Miss Jane Fullbrook

Soares, Patrick *1983*	**Chamberlain**, Emma *1998*
McCutcheon, Barry *1975*	**Ferrier**, Ian *1976**
Brownbill, David *1989*	**Davies**, The Rt Hon Denzil
Way, Patrick *1994*	MP *1965**
Whitehouse, Chris *1972*	

COUNSELS' CHAMBERS

2nd Floor, 10-11 Gray's Inn Square,
London, WC1R 5JD
0171 405 2576
Fax: 0171 831 2430; DX 484 London
E-mail: clerks@10-11graysinnsquare.co.uk
URL:
http://www.10-11graysinnsquare.co.uk
Out of hours telephone: 01428 644863/
0802 217096/01708 473715/07930 230539

Chambers of Mark Muller
Clerks: Richard Loasby, Sarah Gregory
(First Junior), Claire Campbell (Second
Junior); Administrator: Conrad
Blanchard

Muller, Mark 1991	Baruah, Rima 1994
McCreath, Jean 1978	Moore, Alison 1994
Masters, Alan 1979	O'Connor, Mark 1994
Donnelly, John 1983	Ojutiku, Kemi 1994
Magill, Ciaran 1988	Thorne, Katie 1994
Williams, Chris 1988	Hughes, Mary 1994
Trevis, Robert 1990	Darroch, Fiona Culverwell 1994
Amin, Farah 1991	
Ivers, Michael 1991	Edwards, Richard John 1994
Eldergill, Edmund 1991	
Dixon, Anne 1991	Grieves, Edward James 1996
McCrimmon, Kate 1991	
Pardoe, Matthew 1992	Rowe, Freya Emily Beatrice 1996
Solari, Yolanda 1992	
Wray, Nigel 1993	Ham, Nicholas Treharne 1997
Morel, Peter 1993	
Rai, Rajesh 1993	Jack, Andrew Michael 1997
Field, Stephen 1993	Davidson, Tom 1973*
Painter, Ian 1993	Mitchell, Sally 1990*

14 GRAY'S INN SQUARE

Gray's Inn, London, WC1R 5JP
0171 242 0858
Fax: 0171 242 5434; DX 399 London, Chancery Lane
E-mail: 100712.2134@compuserve.com

Chambers of J Dodson QC
Clerk: Jonathan Cue

Dodson, Joanna QC 1970	Warner, Pamela 1985
Godfrey, Louise QC 1972†	Sutton, Karoline 1986
Kushner, Lindsey QC 1974†	Corbett, Michelle 1987
Dangor, Patricia 1970†	Lyon, Stephen 1987
Hall, Joanna 1973	Roberts, Patricia 1987
McNab, Mhairi 1974	Brown, Rebecca 1989
Forster, Sarah 1976	Jarman, Mark 1989
Slomnicka, Barbara 1976	King, Samantha 1990
Turner, David GP 1976‡	Alomo, Richard 1990
Brasse, Gillian 1977	Bedingfield, David 1991
Morris, Brenda 1978	Vavrecka, David 1992
Hudson, Kathryn 1981	De Zonie, Jane 1993
McLaughlin, Karen 1982	Brazil, Dominic 1995
Reid, Caroline 1982	Whittam, Samantha 1995
Ford, Monica 1984	O'Donovan, Ronan Daniel James 1995
Emanuel, Mark 1985	
Buswell, Richard 1985	

GRAY'S INN TAX CHAMBERS

3rd Floor, Gray's Inn Chambers, Gray's Inn, London, WC1R 5JA
0171 242 2642
Fax: 0171 831 9017/405 4078; DX 352 London
E-mail: clerks@taxbar.com
URL: http://www.taxbar.com
Out of hours telephone: 0956 144042

Chambers of J M Grundy
Clerk: Chris Broom (Senior Clerk)

Grundy, Milton 1954	Akin, Barrie 1976
Flesch, Michael QC 1963	McKay, Hugh 1990
Goldberg, David QC 1971	Nathan, Aparna 1994
Goy, David QC 1973	McDonnell, Conrad 1994
Walters, John QC 1977	Shaw, Nicola 1995
Cullen, Felicity 1985	Swersky, Abe 1996*
Baker, Philip 1979	Wilson, Graham 1975*

100E GREAT PORTLAND STREET

London, W1N 5PD
0171 636 6323
Fax: 0171 436 3544

Chambers of Robert Banks

> **Bar Directory on the Internet**
> *The Bar Directory* is also available on the Internet at the following address:
> http://www.smlawpub.co.uk/bar

CHAMBERS OF HELEN GRINDROD QC

15-19
DEVEREUX COURT

*4th Floor, 15-19 Devereux Court, London,
WC2R 3JJ*
0171 583 2792
Fax: 0171 353 0608; DX 425 Lon Chancery
Lane
Out of hours telephone: 0777 556 7949

Chambers of H M Grindrod QC
Clerks: Mark Auger, Reg Harris

Grindrod, Helen QC *1966*	Anders, Jonathan *1990*
Rowling, Fiona *1980*	Adkin, Tana *1992*
Blake, Richard *1982*	Keigan, Linda *1992*
Johnston, Christopher *1983*	Fuad, Kerim *1992*
Manley, Lesley *1983*	West, Stephanie *1993*
Gedge, Simon *1984*	Gatley, Mark *1993*
Brain, Pamela *1985*	Maylin, Kerry *1994*
Smullen, Marion *1985*	Walker, Andrew *1994*
O'Higgins, John *1990*	Inyundo, Kwame *1997*

CHAMBERS OF BEVERLEY GUTTERIDGE

*36 Dunmore Road, Wimbledon, London,
SW20 8TN*
0181 947 0717

Chambers of Miss B J Gutteridge

1 HARCOURT BUILDINGS

2nd Floor, Temple, London, EC4Y 9DA
0171 353 9421/0375
Fax: 0171 353 4170; DX 417 London

E-mail:
clerks@1harcourtbuildings.law.co.uk
Out of hours telephone: Emergency 24-
hour mobile: 0973 675 426

Chambers of Simon Buckhaven
*Clerks: William Lavell, Gary Norton,
Theresa Burke, Keith Sharman*

Buckhaven, Simon *1970*	Knight, Caroline *1985*
Walker, Raymond QC *1966*†	Rupasinha, Sunil *1983*
Bartlett, Roger *1968*	Bird, Andrew *1987*
Glossop, Willliam *1969*	Munir, Edward *1956*
Gratwicke, Charles *1974*‡	Connolly, Dominic *1989*
Ross, David *1974*	Dunlop, Hamish *1991*
Hungerford, Guy *1971*	Hewitt, David *1991*
Bennett, Charles *1972*	McLaren, Nicola *1991*
Van Der Bijl, Nigel *1973*†	Lundie, Christopher *1991*
Harris, James *1975*	Eilledge, Amanda *1991*
Griffith, Martin *1977*	Goldring, Jenny *1993*
Coggins, Jonathan *1980*	Baum, Victoria *1993*
Devlin, Bernard *1980*	Valder, Paul *1994*
Sampson, Graeme *1981*	Mullins, Mark *1995*
Richards, David *1981*	Blakemore, Jessica *1995*
May, Christopher *1983*	Musgrave, Kerry *1992*
Prosser, Anthony *1985*	Payne, Alan *1996*
Foinette, Ian *1986*	Webster, Robert *1979**
	Beecroft, Robert *1977**

**Types of work (and number of counsel practising in
that area if supplied)**
Banking 7 · Bankruptcy 3 · Care
proceedings 2 · Chancery (general) 7 ·
Chancery land law 7 · Commercial
litigation 7 · Commercial property 4 ·
Common law (general) 30 · Company and
commercial 5 · Construction 4 · Crime 21 ·
Crime – corporate fraud 15 · EC and
competition law 2 · Employment 5 ·
Environment 5 · Equity, wills and trusts 5 ·
Family 3 · Family provision 3 · Financial
services 3 · Housing 5 · Immigration 2 ·
Insolvency 3 · Insurance 5 · Landlord and
tenant 5 · Licensing 4 · Local government 8
· Medical negligence 10 · Partnerships 3 ·
Personal injury 15 · Probate and
administration 5 · Professional negligence
10 · Sale and carriage of goods 10

Chambers established: 1950
Opening times: 9 am-6 pm

Chambers' facilities
Conference rooms, Disks accepted,
Disabled access

Languages spoken
French, German, Spanish

C

---

† Recorder ‡ Assistant Recorder *Door Tenant

Additional information

This is a common law set of chambers, in which members appear before a wide range of courts and tribunals, and advise on questions in most areas of the law. Civil and criminal work is undertaken at all levels. Some members tend to specialise in particular fields.

On the civil side, members undertake work in all divisions of the High Court and in the county courts. They appear in commercial arbitrations and building disputes. The work includes contract, negligence (including professional negligence), personal property, and land law (including easements and boundary disputes). Family Division work undertaken includes matrimonial finance, wardship and other child cases. A particular area is that of interests in land and trusts for sale, and the rights of banks under mortgages: Simon Buckhaven and Bernard Devlin represented the successful wife in *Barclays Bank v O'Brien* in the House of Lords.

The criminal work undertaken involves all kinds of crime including fraud, drugs, health and safety at work, and proceedings before disciplinary tribunals. All criminal practitioners both prosecute and defend. Some are on the approved lists for HM Customs and Excise, the Department of Social Security, the Health and Safety Executive and the Department of Trade and Industry. Some prosecute on behalf of local authorities. Raymond Walker QC represented the Appellant in *R v Associated Octel Ltd* in the House of Lords.

In addition to the general work undertaken, particular members can offer individual specialisations in a number of areas.

Direct professional access work is accepted. Documents and pleadings can be produced on disk or sent by E-mail if required.

In view of the wide area of litigation undertaken by chambers, members tend to specialise in different fields. The clerks are available to offer advice. A brochure is available on request.

Bar Directory on the Internet

The Bar Directory is also available on the Internet at the following address: http://www.smlawpub.co.uk/bar

2 HARCOURT BUILDINGS

Ground Floor/Left, Temple, London, EC4Y 9DB
0171 583 9020
Fax: 0171 583 2686; DX 1039 London, Chancery Lane
E-mail: clerks@harcourt.co.uk

Chambers of Roger Henderson QC

Clerks: John White, Simon Boutwood; Chambers Development Manager: Martin Dyke

Henderson, Roger QC 1964†	**Battcock**, Benjamin 1987
	Wheeler, Marina 1987
Ashworth, Piers QC 1956†	**Williams**, Rhodri 1987
Mawrey, Richard QC 1964†	**Outhwaite**, Wendy-Jane 1990
Brunner, Adrian QC 1968†	
Powles, Stephen QC 1972†	**Green**, Patrick 1990
Prynne, Andrew QC 1975	**Bourne**, Charles 1991
Iwi, Quintin 1956	**Popat**, Prashant 1992
Dashwood, Prof Alan 1969	**Campbell**, Oliver 1992
Cooper, Adrian 1970‡	**Zornoza**, Isabelle 1993
O'Sullivan, Bernard 1971	**Sheehan**, Malcolm 1993
Gore-Andrews, Gavin 1972	**Fenston**, Felicia 1994
Jordan, Andrew 1973	**Webb**, Geraint 1995
Harvey, Jonathan 1974	**Riley-Smith**, Toby 1995
Hamer, Kenneth 1975‡	**Mitchell**, Julianna 1994
West, Lawrence 1979‡	**Kinnier**, Andrew 1996
Eastman, Roger 1978	**Martin-Jenkins**, James 1997
Staite, Sara 1979‡	
Cameron, Barbara 1979	**Ashworth**, Lance 1987*
Palmer, James 1983	**Garner**, Adrian John Robinson 1985*
Gibson, Charles 1984	
Alliott, George 1981	**Schoneveld**, Frank 1992*
Griffiths, Conrad 1986	

Types of work (and number of counsel practising in that area if supplied)

Administrative · Arbitration · Asset finance · Care proceedings · Chancery (general) · Commercial litigation · Common law (general) · Company and commercial · Competition · Construction · Copyright · Courts martial · Crime · Crime – corporate fraud · Ecclesiastical · Education · Employment · Environment · Equity, wills and trusts · Family · Family provision · Financial services · Franchising · Housing · Information technology · Insurance · Insurance/reinsurance · Intellectual property · International trade · Landlord and tenant · Local government · Medical negligence · Parliamentary · Partnerships · Patents · Personal injury · Probate and administration · Professional negligence · Sale and carriage of goods · Sports · Tax – capital and income · Tax – corporate · Telecommunications

Chambers established: 1954

Chambers' facilities
Conference rooms, Disks accepted, E-mail

Languages spoken
French, Italian, Japanese, Spanish

Fees policy
Fees are negotiated with the senior clerk: our aim is that fees will be reasonable and competitive, depending on the importance and nature of the work and the expertise and seniority of Counsel.

2 HARCOURT BUILDINGS

1st Floor, Temple, London, EC4Y 9DB
020 7353 2112
Fax: 020 7353 8339; DX 489 London

Chambers of N Atkinson QC, J Bevan QC
Clerks: Michael Watts, Simon Butler, Michael Bazeley, Bernard Hayward; Chambers Development Executive: Sue Watt

Atkinson, Nicholas QC 1971†	Darling, Ian 1985
	Gibbs, Patrick 1986
Bevan, John QC 1970†	Whittle-Martin, Lucia 1985
Mylne, Nigel QC 1963†	Rees, Jonathan 1987
Cooper, Peter QC 1974†	Clement, Peter 1988
Williams, John 1973	Cobbs, Laura 1989
Smyth, Stephen 1974‡	Hamblin, Stewart 1990
Clayton, Stephen 1973	Fitzgerald, Toby 1993
Loraine-Smith, Nicholas 1977‡	Coombe, Peter 1993
	Wilkins, Thomas 1993
Shorrock, Philip 1978	Wilding, Lisa 1993
Adlard, William 1978	Dawes, James 1993*
Leach, Robin 1979	Halkerston, Sally 1994*
Gadsden, Mark 1980	Farmer, Matthew 1987
Jafferjee, Aftab 1980	Thompson, Sally 1994
Probert-Wood, Timothy 1983	Kelleher, Benedict 1994
	Emlyn Jones, William 1996
Willis, Rhyddian 1984	Knight, Jennifer 1996

2 HARCOURT BUILDINGS

2 HARCOURT BUILDINGS

2nd Floor, Temple, London, EC4Y 9DB
020 7353 8415
Fax: 020 7353 7622; DX 402 London, Chancery Lane
E-mail: clerks@2hb.law.co.uk

Chambers of Gerard Ryan QC
Clerks: Allen Collier (Senior Clerk), Paul Munday (First Junior Clerk), Andrew Briton (Second Junior Clerk)

Ryan, Gerard QC 1955	Howell Williams, Craig 1983
Cameron, Sheila QC 1957†	
Purchas, Robin QC 1968†	Ornsby, Suzanne 1986
Phillips, Richard QC 1970	Lewis, Meyric 1986
George, Charles QC 1974†	Newcombe, Andrew 1987
Newberry, Clive QC 1978	Mynors, Charles 1988
Lindblom, Keith QC 1980	Jones, Gregory 1991
McCracken, Robert 1973	Edwards, Douglas 1992
Petchey, Philip 1976	Burrows, Euan 1995
Milner, Jonathan 1977	Clayton, Joanna 1995
Kelly, Andrew 1978	Pereira, James 1996
Comyn, Timothy 1980	Phillpot, Hereward Lindon 1997
Tait, Andrew 1981	

Types of work (and number of counsel practising in that area if supplied)
Administrative · Agriculture · Common land · Compulsory purchase · EC and competition law · Ecclesiastical · Education · Energy · Environment · Licensing · Local government · Parliamentary · Professional negligence · Town and country planning

Languages spoken
French, German

The Chambers: A specialist chambers for more than half a century with particular expertise in planning, environmental, energy and utilities, property and administrative law. Disabled conference facilities are available by prior arrangement. Members accept Direct Professional Access from the approved professions. A chambers brochure is available on request.

All members of chambers belong to the Planning and Environment Bar Association of which Douglas Edwards is Secretary. Members of chambers also belong to the Administrative Law Bar Association, the Education Law Society, the Bar European Group, the Association for Regulated Procurement, the United Kingdom

Environmental Law Association, JUSTICE, the Ecclesiastical Law Society and the Parliamentary Bar.

Two members of chambers are Deputy High Court Judges, three are Recorders of the Crown Court and three are Diocesan Chancellors. Craig Howell Williams and Meyric Lewis are members of the Supplementary Panel of Junior Counsel to the Crown. Gerard Ryan QC chaired the Tribunal of Inquiry into the gas explosion at Loscoe, Derbyshire. Charles George QC conducted the Independent Inquiry into Planning Decisions in the London Borough of Brent. Robert McCracken was Chairman of the United Kingdom Environmental Law Association. Sheila Cameron QC is Vicar General of the Province of Canterbury and was a Parliamentary Boundary Commissioner for England. Richard Phillips QC is an assistant Parliamentary Commissioner for England. Takis Tridimas, an Associate Member of Chambers, is Professor of European Law at the University of Southampton and an advocate of the Bar of Athens.

Publications include: *Education Case Reports* (editor-in-chief), *Journal of Planning and Environment Law* (editorial board), *Planning Appeal Decisions* (joint editor), *Planning and Environmental Law Bulletin* (joint editor), *Journal of Architectural Conservation* (editorial board), *Yearbook of European Law* (co-editor), *The Company Lawyer* (editorial board) and *European Financial Services Law* (advisory board). Charles Mynors is the author of *Planning Applications and Appeals* (1987), *Planning Control and the Display of Advertisements* (1992) and *Listed Buildings and Conservation Areas* (3ed.1999). Takis Tridimas is the author of *The General Principles of EC Law* (1999), and co-author of Ellis and Tridimas, *Public Law of the European Community: Cases, materials and commentary* (1995), and a co-editor of Beatson and Tridimas, *New Directions in European Public Law* (1998).

Work undertaken:
Main Areas of Work: planning, environmental, compulsory purchase, administrative, local government finance, public procurement, parliamentary, transport and works, energy, utilities, education, highways, licensing, housing, human rights (European Convention) and European Community law.
Additional Areas: ecclesiastical law, land-lord and tenant, the law of commons and that relating to easements, agricultural tenancies, rating and restrictive covenants.

Foreign Connections: Chambers includes members called to the Dublin, Northern Ireland and Greek Bars.

Former Members of Chambers include: Roy Vandermeer QC, inspector at the Terminal Five inquiry; Peter Boydell QC, Leader of the Parliamentary Bar and first Chairman of what is now the Planning and Environment Bar Association; Michael Harrison QC, now Mr Justice Harrison, Michael Mann QC, later Lord Justice Mann and Sir John Drinkwater QC.

HARCOURT CHAMBERS

HARCOURT CHAMBERS

1st Floor, 2 Harcourt Buildings, Temple, London, EC4Y 9DB
0171 353 6961
Fax: 0171 353 6968; DX 373 London, Chancery Lane
E-mail:
clerks@harcourtchambers.law.co.uk
URL:
http://www.harcourtchambers.law.co.uk
Out of hours telephone: 0973 316959

Chambers of Patrick Eccles QC
Clerks: Brian Wheeler, Timothy Wheeler, Judith Partington

Annexe: Harcourt Chambers, Churchill House, 3 St Aldate's Courtyard, St Aldate's, Oxford, OX1 1BN
Tel: 01865 791559
Fax: 01865 791585

Eccles, Patrick QC *1968*†	**Blackwood**, Clive *1986*
Evans, Roger *1970*‡	**Brett**, Matthew *1987*
Rodgers, June *1971*†	**Miles**, Edward *1989*
Sefi, Benedict *1972*	**Clarke**, Peter *1970**
Arthur, Gavyn *1975*	**Pressdee**, Piers *1990*
Dixon, John *1975*‡	**Granshaw**, Sara *1991*
Lever, Bernard *1975**†	**Max**, Sally *1991*
Barstow, Stephen *1976*	**Auld**, Rohan *1992*
Baker, Jonathan *1978*‡	**Vater**, John *1995*
Collinson, Alicia *1982*	**Goodwin**, Nicholas *1995*
Frazer, Christopher *1983*	**Vine**, Aidan *1995*
Judd, Frances *1984*	**Sampson**, Jonathan *1997*
Hess, Edward *1985*	**Daley**, Howard *1997*

† Recorder ‡ Assistant Recorder *Door Tenant

Types of work (and number of counsel practising in that area if supplied)
Administrative 4 · Care proceedings 17 · Chancery land law 8 · Company and commercial 8 · Crime 3 · Ecclesiastical 1 · Education 4 · Employment 16 · Equity, wills and trusts 8 · Family 17 · Family provision 17 · Local government 4 · Medical negligence 9 · Personal injury 9 · Professional negligence 13 · Town and country planning 8

Opening times: 24 Hrs on 0973 316959

Chambers' facilities
Conference rooms, Disks accepted, Disabled access, Annexe in Oxford

Languages spoken
French, German

HARDWICKE BUILDING

HARDWICKE BUILDING

New Square, Lincoln's Inn, London, WC2A 3SB
020 7242 2523
Fax: 020 7691 1234; DX 393 London
E-mail: clerks@hardwicke.co.uk
URL: http://www.hardwicke.co.uk
Out of hours telephone: 07771 603609 - civil & 07771 603613 - crime

Chambers of Walter Aylen QC
Clerks: Kevin Mitchell, Greg Piner, Gary Brown, Lloyd Smith, Jason Housden; Chief Executive: Hilary Mundella; Business Manager: Peter Clark; Admin Manager: Lesley Richardson

Aylen, Walter QC *1962*†
Stewart, Nicholas QC *1971*†
Pulman, George QC *1971*†
Tager, Romie QC *1970*†
Jones, Nigel QC *1976*
Raynor, Philip QC *1973*†
Smith, Zoe *1970*†
Willer, Robert *1970*
Hopmeier, Michael *1974*†
Craig, Kenneth *1975*
Kremen, Philip *1975*
Lennard, Stephen *1976*‡
Warner, Stephen *1976*‡
Landaw, John *1976*
Vine, James *1977*

Weddle, Steven *1977*
Oliver, Michael *1977*
Wakeham, Philip *1978*
Baker, Nicholas *1980*
Field, Rory *1980*
Matthias, David *1980*
Ramsahoye, Indira *1980*
Aaronberg, David *1981*
Jackson, Hugh *1981*
Smith, Alan *1981*
Mendoza, Neil *1982*
Flahive, Daniel *1982*
Bojczuk, William *1983*
Brook, Ian *1983*
Banks, Timothy *1983*
Forlin, Gerard *1984*
Greenan, John *1984*
Taylor, Debbie *1984*
Briefel, Charles *1984*
MacDonald, Lindsey *1985*
Ough, Richard *1985*
King, Karl *1985*
Palfrey, Monty *1985*
Whitfield, Jonathan *1985*
Stevens-Hoare, Michelle *1986*
Nicholson Pratt, Tom *1986*
Mulholland, James *1986*
Lloyd, Francis *1987*
Spooner, Judith *1987*
Reed, Paul *1988*
Kirby, Peter *1989*

Mulligan, Ann *1989*
Woolf, Steven *1989*
Hallissey, Caroline *1990*
Campbell, Alexis *1990*
Benbow, Sara *1990*
Baker, Rachel *1990*
Ryan, Eithne *1990*
Clarke, Ian *1990*
Argyropoulos, Kyriakos *1991*
McCartney, Kevin *1991*
Newman, Ingrid *1992*
Nugent, Colm *1992*
Bates, Richard *1992*
Preston, David *1993*
Jarzabkowski, Julia *1993*
Formby, Emily *1993*
Amiraftabi, Roshi *1993*
Chaudhry, Sabuhi *1993*
Langridge, Niki *1993*
St Louis, Brian *1994*
Goold, Alexander *1994*
Leckie, David *1994*
Heer, Deanna *1994*
Freeston, Lynn *1996*
Grey, Philip *1996*
Rowntree, Edward *1996*
Bagot, Charles *1997*
Mosteshar, Sa'id *1975**
Treharne, Jennet *1975**
Joelson, Stephen *1980**
Gray, Pauline *1980**

Types of work (and number of counsel practising in that area if supplied)
Administrative · Arbitration · Banking · Bankruptcy · Care proceedings · Chancery (general) · Clinical negligence · Commercial · Common law (general) · Company and commercial · Construction · Contract · Conveyancing · Crime · Crime – corporate fraud · Crime – corporate manslaughter · Defamation · Employment · Energy · Entertainment · Equity, wills and trusts · Family · Family – child abduction · Financial services · Housing · Insolvency · Insurance · Intellectual property · Landlord and tenant · Licensing · Partnerships · Personal injury · Planning · Private international · Probate and administration · Professional negligence · Public international · Sale and carriage of goods · Sports · Telecommunications

Chambers established: 1991
Opening times: 8.30 am-6.30 pm

Languages spoken
Farsi, French, German, Greek, Hindi, Italian, Portuguese, Punjabi, Spanish, Urdu

C

† Recorder   ‡ Assistant Recorder   *Door Tenant

Hardwicke Building

The success and continued growth of this progressive, established set is attributable to expertise and specialisation in all ares of civil litigation, cime and family law.

The benefits derived from Chambers of this size include the availability of counsel at all levels of seniority to provide comprehensive advice from informal telephone guidance to advice and representation in the most complex cases. Members of Chambers act as arbitrators and mediators and, when advising clients, provide clear and concise advice.

Hardwicke Building's modern facilities and outlook provide an atmosphere conducive to a professional service.

Cost effective and innovative legal solutions are promoted to meet the needs of both professional and lay clients. A similar flexible and practical approach is applied to the negotiation of fees. In addition to privately funded work, conditional fee arrangements, publicly funded litigation and block – and bulk – contracting are welcomed.

A strategic approach to Information Technology is reflected in the investment in e-mail, video conferencing and Internet services, all of which promote the accessibility of barristers to clients throughout the UK and overseas.

The wide range of expertise within the specialist groups is demonstrated in the programme of in-house seminars for professional clients which are CPD accredited.

Types of work undertaken: The main groups are civil, crime and family.

Civil:

Whilst acting in a broad range of commercial work, barristers work in specialist teams, in particular:
• **Real Property and Landlord and Tenant** – The Property Group specialises in all aspects of the law relating to real property, landlord and tenant, and housing.
• **Professional negligence** – The Professional Negligence Team is at the forefront of lenders', solicitors' and valuers' litigation and the recent development of legal principles involved; in addition claims against accountants and other financial advisers are undertaken.
• **Personal injury** – The Injury Litigation Team undertakes a broad range of personal injury, clinical and medical negligence cases.
• **Employment** – The Employment Team offers specialist advocacy, drafting and advisory services for employees and employers.

Crime:

The team of 30 barristers offers a comprehensive service of defence and prosecution work including:
• **Serious fraud**
• **Corporate manslaughter**
• **Licensing**
• **Health and safety**
• **Human rights**
• **Local authority**
• **Professional offences.**

Family:

The Family Team of 16 members receive instructions in all family and matrimonial work including:-
• **Financial cases**
• **Children**
• **International child abduction.**

Other specialist ares include:
• **Construction law** – Defects and loss and expense claims, negligence of construction professionals, domestic and international arbitrations.
• **Public law** – Judicial review, local government and environmental law.
• **Insurance** – Drafting and advising on insurance policies, coverage issues and associated litigation, with particular emphasis on public liability, product liability, professional indemnity and construction/engineering.
• **Company, insolvency and partnership** – Shareholders' disputes, issues concerning directors' duties and disqualification; partnership matters and all aspects of insolvency, bankruptcy and voluntary arrangements.
• **Intellectual property and media law** – Passing off, breach of copyright, confidentiality and music business agreements.

Languages
See the Index of Languages Spoken in Part G to locate a chambers where a particular language is spoken, or find an individual who speaks a particular language.

† Recorder ‡ Assistant Recorder *Door Tenant

1 HARE COURT

Ground Floor, Temple, London, EC4Y 7BE
0171 353 3982/5324
Fax: 0171 353 0667; DX 444 London, Chancery Lane

Chambers of Stephen Kramer QC
Clerks: Deryk Butler, Ian Fitzgerald; Administrator: Stephen Wall

Kramer, Stephen QC *1970†*
Green, Sir Allan QC *1959*
Worsley, Paul QC *1970*†
Heslop, Martin QC *1972†*
Salmon, Charles QC *1972†*
Waters, David QC *1973†*
Warner, Brian *1969†*
Samuel, Jacqueline *1971*
Jones, John *1972†*
Kamill, Louise *1974†*
Dodgson, Paul *1975†*
Pownall, Orlando *1975†*
Radcliffe, Andrew *1975‡*
Hicks, Martin *1977*
Benson, Jeremy *1978†*
Lloyd-Eley, Andrew *1979*
Colman, Andrew *1980*
Leist, Ian *1981*
Howker, David *1982‡*
Laidlaw, Jonathan *1982‡*
Howes, Sally *1983*

Bennett Jenkins, Sallie *1984‡*
Dawson, James *1984*
Holland, Michael *1984*
Barnes, Shani *1986‡*
O'Neill, Brian *1987*
Kelly, Brendan *1988*
Logsdon, Michael *1988*
Millett, Kenneth *1988*
Cheema, Parmjit *1989*
Lambis, Marios *1989*
Hehir, Christopher *1990*
Lewis, Alex *1990*
Bex, Kate *1992*
Ferguson, Craig *1992*
Grahame, Nina *1993*
Foulkes, Christopher *1994*
Glasgow, Oliver *1995*
Karmy-Jones, Riel *1995*
Lowe, Emma *1996*

Types of work (and number of counsel practising in that area if supplied)
Courts martial 40 · Crime 40 · Crime – corporate fraud 40 · Licensing 40 · Personal injury 1 · Professional negligence 1

Opening times: 8.30 am-6.30 pm

Chambers' facilities
Conference rooms

Languages spoken
French, Greek, Hindi, Spanish, Urdu

Additional information
Chambers is a leading set specialising in criminal law. We prosecute and defend at all levels, in London and throughout England and Wales.

In recent years, chambers has increasingly specialised in commercial fraud and corruption cases.

We also offer expertise in related fields including extradition, courts martial, coroners' inquests, immigration, food and drugs and trade descriptions.

A brochure is available on request.

ONE HARE COURT

ONE HARE COURT

1st Floor, Temple, London, EC4Y 7BE
020 7353 3171
Fax: 020 7583 9127; DX 0065 Chancery Lane
E-mail:
admin-oneharecourt@btinternet.com
Out of hours telephone: 01474 812778

Chambers of Lord Neill of Bladen QC, Richard Southwell QC
Clerks: Barry Ellis, Paul Ballard

Neill of Bladen, Lord QC *1951*
Southwell, Richard QC *1959†*
Page, Howard QC *1967*
Padfield, Nicholas QC *1972†*
Malins, Julian QC *1972*
Ballantyne, William *1977*
Smith, Paul *1978*

Dowley, Dominic *1983*
Eadie, James *1984*
Lavender, Nicholas *1989*
Moran, Andrew *1989*
Qureshi, Khawar *1990*
Adkin, Jonathan W *1997*
Braithwaite, Thomas James *1998*
Detter de Lupis Frankopan, Prof Ingrid *1977**

Types of work (and number of counsel practising in that area if supplied)
Administrative · Arbitration · Asset finance · Banking · Bankruptcy · Chancery (general) · Civil liberties · Commercial · Commodities · Common law (general) · Company and commercial · Competition · Construction · Corporate finance · Crime – corporate fraud · Discrimination · EC and competition law · Education · Energy · Entertainment · Environment · Film, cable,

TV · Financial services · Foreign law · Franchising · Immigration · Information technology · Insolvency · Insurance · Insurance/reinsurance · Intellectual property · International trade · Landlord and tenant · Local government · Parliamentary · Partnerships · Patents · Private international · Professional negligence · Public international · Sale and carriage of goods · Share options

Opening times: 8.30 am-6.30 pm

Chambers' facilities
Video conferences, Disks accepted, E-mail

Languages spoken
Arabic, French

Fees policy
Fees are available on enquiry to the clerks.

Types of work undertaken: One Hare Court is a long-established, small set of chambers which specialises in commercial and international work and other related fields of litigation, arbitration and legal advice.

Litigation work is undertaken in the High Court (with the emphasis on Commercial Court litigation) and in international and domestic arbitrations. Junior members also undertake work in the county courts and in tribunals.

Individual practices vary from one member to another; however, together they cover the following areas of law: commercial contracts, international trade and carriage of goods, commodities, sale of goods, insurance and reinsurance, banking and negotiable instruments, commercial aspects of company and insolvency law, commercial fraud claims, intellectual property, public international law, constitutional law and administrative law. Also undertaken are arbitration, both international and domestic, construction and engineering, private international law, competition, regulation of trade, insurance and financial markets, financial services, European Community law, professional negligence, professional regulatory and disciplinary proceedings, and Privy Council appeals.

A high proportion of chambers' work originates from overseas and, subject to admission to local Bars, instructions are accepted to appear in the courts of Hong Kong,

Singapore, Malaysia, Caribbean and other foreign jurisdictions.

Arbitration: Members of chambers are highly experienced in the field of arbitration, (international commercial and construction: ICC, LCIA, Lloyd's, UNCITRAL, amongst others).

Chambers is a founder member of the London Court of International Arbitration and is a member of the Commercial Bar Association (COMBAR).

All members of chambers accept instructions under the direct professional access arrangements.

Additional specialisations: Arab Laws (Prof Ballantyne, formerly solicitor 1949); Scandinavian and environmental law (Prof De Lupis Frankopan).
Richard Southwell QC and Nicholas Padfield QC are members of the Executive Committee of COMBAR.
Richard Southwell QC (who sits as a Deputy High Court Judge) is President and Howard Page QC is Deputy President of Lloyd's Appeal Tribunal. Mr Nicholas Lavender and Mr Khawar Qureshi are both appointed to the Junior Counsel to the Crown (B Panel).

Former Members: Sir Henry Fisher, President of Wolfson College, Oxford 1975-85, Arbitrator; Lord Slynn of Hadley, Lord of Appeal in Ordinary (former Judge of the Court of Justice of the European Communities); Sir Roger Parker, former Lord Justice of Appeal, Arbitrator; Sir Mark Waller, a Lord Justice of the High Court; HH Judge Raymond Jack QC, Circuit Mercantile Judge of the Bristol Mercantile Court; Sir Nicolas Bratza, a High Court Judge and UK Representative for the European Court of Human Rights.

Languages
See the Index of Languages Spoken in Part G to locate a chambers where a particular language is spoken, or find an individual who speaks a particular language.

---

       † Recorder ‡ Assistant Recorder *Door Tenant

3 HARE COURT

HARE COURT

1 Little Essex Street, London, WC2R 3LD
0171 395 2000
Fax: 0171 240 8711; DX 17 London,
Chancery Lane
Out of hours telephone: 0956 243560/0181
886 4772

Chambers of William Clegg QC
Clerk: John Grimmer

Clegg, William QC *1972†*	Mitchell, Keith *1981*
Lewis, Michael QC *1956†*	Sturman, James *1982*
Morris, The Rt Hon John QC *1954†*	McIvor, Jane *1983*
	King, Gelaga *1985*
Godfrey, Howard QC *1970†*	Kendall, Timothy *1985*
Munday, Andrew QC *1973‡*	Milliken-Smith, Mark *1986*
Lithman, Nigel QC *1976‡*	Campbell-Clyne,
Jenkins, Alun QC *1972**	Christopher *1988*
Griffiths, Peter QC *1970*	Matthews, Richard *1989*
Flach, Robert *1950*	Ashley-Norman, Jonathan
Conway, Charles *1969*	*1989*
Champion, Deborah *1970†*	Derbyshire, Tom *1989*
Ingram, Nigel *1974*	Rush, Craig *1989*
Halsey, Mark *1974*	Ageros, James *1990*
Neill, Robert *1975*	Agnew, Christine *1992*
Barnes, Margaret *1976*	Budworth, Adam *1992*
Caudle, John *1976*	Epstein, Michael *1992*
Abell, Anthony *1977*	Charbit, Valerie *1992*
Hackett, Philip QC *1978*	Hurlock, John *1993*
Dodd, John *1979*	Pople, Alison *1993*
Dodd, Margaret *1979**	Henson, Christine *1994*
Levy, Michael *1979*	Galvin, Kieran *1996*
Livingston, Richard *1980*	Dineen, Maria *1997*
McGowan, Maura *1980‡*	Daruwalla, Navaz *1997*
Altman, Brian *1981*	Trott, Ronald *1956**
Lodder, Peter *1981*	

Types of work (and number of counsel practising in that area if supplied)
Administrative · Courts martial · Crime ·
Crime – corporate fraud · Foreign law ·
Insolvency · Licensing · Local government ·
Sports

Opening times: 8 am-7 pm

Languages spoken
Dutch, French, German, Hebrew, Italian,
Krio (Sierra Leone), Serbo-Croat

Additional information
3 Hare Court is long established as a
leading Chambers specialising in criminal
law and related areas of practice.

Building on this tradition of both prosecuting and defending in all types of criminal work Chambers has developed to meet
the demands of modern practices by
providing a broad range of experience in
general criminal matters as well as in a
number of specialist areas.
Chambers presently consists of Queen's
Counsel and Juniors. Members include the
Attorney-General, Treasury Counsel at the
Central Criminal Court, standing members
of Counsel to the Department of Trade and
Industry and standing Counsel to H M
Customs and Exise. Additionally, a number
of members of Chambers hold office as
Recorders or Assistant Recorders of the
Crown Court.

In general criminal practice, the size and
varied experience of Chambers enables it
to offer practitioners at all levels and for all
types of cases. Members of Chambers
appear in all criminal matters from the
Magistrates' Court to the House of Lords
and also before international bodies such
as the International War Crimes Tribunal at
the Hague. Members of Chambers have
appeared in many leading cases including
R v Colin Stagg, *R v Michael Stone*, *R v
Corporal Lee Clegg*, *R v Tadic*, *R v Serafino-
wicz*, *R v Sawoniuk*. There is considerable
experience in confiscation and forfeiture
proceedings, including interim orders.
Individual members of Chambers are experienced in Judicial Review, Extradition and
Immigration as well as challenges to search
and the exercise of privilege, all of which
arise in conjunction with the criminal practice.

A particular specialisation of Chambers is in
advising and acting in relation to the investigation and prosecution of allegations of
financial offences. As well as acting in the
normal range of Revenue, VAT and Diver-
sion frauds members have experience in
the full range of commercial cases
including issues of auditing, banking and
regulatory breaches. There is particular
experience in investigations and prosecutions brought by the Serious Fraud Office

C

and in advising parties from the commencement of the investigation, including issues arising from international judicial assistance. Examples of cases in which members of Chambers have acted include *R v Maxwell and Ors, BCCI, Polly Peck, Resort Hotels, Bute Mining* and *Wallace Smith*. There is also considerable experience in related areas of regulatory and disciplinary work, including investigations and tribunals under the jurisdiction of the SFA, Lloyds, the Department of Trade and Industry (including directors' disqualification) and the disciplinary tribunals of professional bodies.

Developing areas of criminal practices such as Health and Safety, manslaughter by gross negligence following accidents and environmental pollution are ones in which members of Chambers have acted in numerous cases for both the Prosecution and Defence.

CHAMBERS OF HARJIT SINGH

Ground Floor, 2 Middle Temple Lane, Temple, London, EC4Y 9AA
0171 353 1356 (4 Lines)
Fax: 0171 583 4928; DX 0072 LDE

Chambers of Mr Harjit Singh
Clerk: Mr Matthew Jones

Singh, Harjit *1956*	**Leslie**, Nigel *1994*
Lakha, Murtaza *1961*	**Noble**, Antonia *1995*
O'Brien, John *1976*	**Davies**, Penny *1995*
Calder, Renée *1978*	**Ward**, Peter *1996*
Bulloch, Anne *1989*	**Record**, Celia *1998*
Qazi, M Ayaz *1993*	**Vanhegan**, Toby *1996*
Dogra, Tanyia *1994*	**Jafferji**, Zainul *1999*
Miszkiel, Ursula *1994*	

CHAMBERS OF AVERIL HARRISON

7 King George Street, Greenwich, London, SE10 8QJ
0181 692 4949
Fax: 0181 491 9559

Chambers of Averil Harrison

HARROW ON THE HILL CHAMBERS

60 High Street, Harrow-on-the-Hill, Middlesex HA1 3LL
0181 423 7444
Fax: 0181 423 7368; DX 130112 Slough 6

Chambers of M C Beaumont
*Practice Manager: Mrs Ann Kenyon;
Chambers Manager: Michèle Acton*

Also at: Windsor Barristers' Chambers, Tel: 01753 648899, Fax: 01753 648877

Boney, Guy QC *1968**†	**Whitley**, Jonathan *1993*
Clark, Christopher QC *1969**†	**Green**, Victoria *1994*
	Nugent, Peter *1994*
Beaumont, Marc *1985*	**Simpson**, Graeme *1994*
Hill, Andrew *1982**	**Gopinathan**, Anu *1994*
Kimsey, Mark *1990*	**Wilkins**, Andrew *1995*
Bergin, Terence *1985**	**Sheikh**, Khalid *1993*
Swift, Antony *1984*	**Al-Yunusi**, Abdullah *1994*
Bridges, Dr Paul *1984**	**Mandalia**, Vinesh *1997*
Dowden, Andrew *1991*	**Steele**, Laura *1997*
Bearman, Justin *1992*	

Types of work (and number of counsel practising in that area if supplied)
Administrative · Banking · Bankruptcy · Chancery (general) · Chancery land law · Commercial · Commercial litigation · Commercial property · Common land · Common law (general) · Company and commercial · Competition · Construction · Consumer law · Conveyancing · Crime · Crime – corporate fraud · Defamation · Discrimination · Education · Employment · Equity, wills and trusts · Family · Family provision · Financial services · Franchising · Housing · Immigration · Insolvency · Insurance · Landlord and tenant · Licensing · Local government · Medical negligence · Partnerships · Personal injury · Planning · Probate and administration · Professional negligence · Sale and carriage of goods · Share options · Sports · Town and country planning

Chambers established: 1990
Opening times: 9 am-6 pm

Chambers' facilities
Conference rooms, Disks accepted

Languages spoken
French, Gujarati, Hindi

Fees policy
Our fees are designed to be competitive, whilst reflecting the complexity and importance of the case and the seniority of counsel. Specific requests for information should be made to the chambers manager.

10 HIGHLEVER ROAD

North Kensington, London, W10 6PS
0181 969 8514
Fax: 0181 969 8514

Chambers of Mr M A Sayeed

HOLBORN CHAMBERS

6 Gate Street, Lincoln's Inn Fields, London, WC2A 3HP
0171 242 6060
Fax: 0171 242 2777; DX 159 London

Chambers of Mr S S Stevens

HORIZON CHAMBERS

95a Chancery Lane, London, WC2A 1DT
0171 242 2440
Fax: 0171 242 2443; DX 275 LDE

1 INNER TEMPLE LANE

Temple, London, EC4Y 1AF
020 7353 0933
Fax: 020 7353 0937; DX LDE 286 Chancery Lane
Out of hours telephone: 07967 033884

Chambers of S F Hadley
Clerk: Neville Ackerley

Hadley, Steven *1987*	**McCann**, Catryn *1988*
Adonis, George *1973*	**Etherton**, Gillian *1988*
Sheikh, Irshad *1983*	**Lindop**, Sarah *1989*
Baylis, Christopher *1986*	**Le Foe**, Sarah *1989*

Rhodes, Karen *1990*	**Hart**, Jenny *1993*
Cornwall, Virginia *1990*	**Whaites**, Louise *1994*
Thompson, Andrew *1991*	**McDonagh**, Matthew *1994*
Tedore, Amanda *1992*	**Baughan**, Andrew *1994*
McNiff, Matthew *1992*	**Connell**, Edward *1996*
Baker, William *1992*	**Goodall**, Emma *1996*
Clark, Timothy *1993*	

Types of work (and number of counsel practising in that area if supplied)
Care proceedings 6 · Civil liberties 4 · Common law (general) 8 · Crime 21 · Employment 4 · Family 6 · Family provision 6 · Housing 4 · Immigration 1 · Landlord and tenant 4 · Licensing 6 · Personal injury 6

Chambers established: 1991
Opening times: 8.30 am-6.30 pm

Chambers' facilities
Conference rooms, Disks accepted

Languages spoken
French, German, Greek, Italian

INTERNATIONAL LAW CHAMBERS

ILC House, 77/79 Chepstow Road, Bayswater, London, W2 5QR
0171 221 5684/5/4840
Fax: 0171 221 5685 Gps12&3

Chambers of Mr S D El-Falahi

JOHN STREET CHAMBERS

2 John Street, London, WC1N 2HJ
0171 242 1911
Fax: 0171 242 2515; DX 1000 Chancery Lane
E-mail: john.street_chambers@virgin.net

Chambers of Mr Jean-Gilles Raymond
Clerk: Sheila Doyle

Raymond, Jean-Gilles *1982*	**Richards**, Joanne *1992*
Bignall, Paula *1988*	**Sternberg**, Lesli *1994*
Hopewell, Gregory *1992*	**Foster**, Margaret *1993*
Cheltenham, Jacqueline *1992**	**Heller**, Anne *1995*
	Gladwell, Simon M *1996*
Labelle, Jean-Marie *1992*	**Balancy**, Alex Jacques *1992*
Oji, Atim *1992*	**Gamble**, Neil *1998*

JUSTICE COURT CHAMBERS

75 *Kendal Road, Willesden Green,*
London, NW10 1JE
0181 830 7786
Fax: 0181 830 7787
E-mail: faiz@ndirect.co.uk
Out of hours telephone: 0973 617277

Chambers of Mr F A Siddiqi
Clerks: Mr M Amir, Mr M Ammar

Siddiqi, Faizul *1990*

KEATING CHAMBERS

10 Essex Street, Outer Temple, London,
WC2R 3AA
0171 544 2600
Fax: 0171 240 7722; DX 1045 London

Chambers of Richard Fernyhough QC
Clerks: Barry Bridgman (Senior Clerk),
Philip Goldsmith, John Munton, Nick
McCarron-Child

Fernyhough, Richard QC *1970*†	**O'Farrell**, Finola *1983*
Uff, John QC *1970*‡	**Williamson**, Adrian *1983*
Collins, Martin QC *1952*	**Nissen**, Alexander *1985*
Thomas, Christopher QC *1973*‡	**Bowsher**, Michael *1985*
Marrin, John QC *1974*†	**Jefford**, Nerys *1986*
Furst, Stephen QC *1975*†	**Randall**, Louise *1988*
Elliott, Timothy QC *1975*	**Evans**, Robert *1989*
Ramsey, Vivian QC *1979*‡	**Hannaford**, Sarah *1989*
Gaitskell, Robert QC *1978*‡	**Hargreaves**, Simon *1991*
Boulding, Philip QC *1979*	**Harding**, Richard *1992*
Darling, Paul QC *1983*	**Lemon**, Jane *1993*
Steynor, Alan *1975*†	**Stansfield**, Piers *1993*
Jackson, Rosemary *1981*	**Lee**, Jonathan *1993*
Taverner, Marcus *1981*	**Hughes**, Simon *1995*
Coulson, Peter *1982*	**Jinadu**, Abdul-Lateef *1995*
Pennicott, Ian *1982*	**Coplin**, Richard James *1997*

Types of work (and number of counsel practising in that area if supplied)
Arbitration 32 · Commercial litigation 32 · Construction 32 · EC and competition law 3 · Information technology · Insurance/reinsurance · Landlord and tenant 3 · Local government

Opening times: 8 am-6.45 pm

Chambers' facilities
Conference rooms, Disks accepted, E-mail

Languages spoken
Arabic, French, German, Spanish

Fees policy
Estimates for members of chambers are available on request from the Senior Clerk or his assistants.

Additional information
This set specialises in building and all kinds of engineering matters in the UK and abroad, acting for employers, contractors, sub-contractors and consultants. These specialisations include contractual claims, development contracts, claims in respect of defective buildings and structures and the professional negligence of architects, surveyors, valuers, engineers and other consultants concerned with building and engineering matters. Other areas include local authority work (including building control work), environmental law and EC law (in particular, public procurement).

Members of chambers also undertake work relating to information technology, commercial and insurance contracts, performance bonds and warranties and freezing and other types of injunction. Some members also practise in landlord and tenant, planning, other property-related matters and competition law.

Members of chambers act and advise in litigation, arbitration, adjudication and all forms of ADR. Their work abroad includes ICC and FIDIC arbitrations and other arbitral work, particularly in Paris, Hong Kong, Singapore and the Middle East. Senior members act as arbitrators, legal assessors, adjudicators, mediators and conciliators in the UK and internationally.

ONE KING'S BENCH WALK

1st Floor, Temple, London, EC4Y 7DB
0171 936 1500
Fax: 0171 936 1590; DX LDE 20 (Delivery only)
E-mail: ddear@1kbw.co.uk
URL: http://www.1kbw.co.uk
Out of hours telephone: 0831 339391

Chambers of A Hacking QC
Clerks: David Dear, Nicola Cade, Tim Madden, David McDonald; Practice Manager: Lisa Pavlovsky; Administrators: Jud Lisette, Paul Rudd; Other Administration: Sonia Khan

Also at: Kings Bench Chambers, 174 High Street, Lewes, East Sussex BN7 1YE Tel: 01273 402600, Fax: 01273 402609

Townend, James QC 1962†	Kirk, Anthony 1981
Hacking, Anthony QC 1965†	Maidment, Susan 1968‡
	Woodbridge, Julian 1981
Hayward-Smith, Rodger QC 1967†	Pocock, Christopher 1984
	Shay, Stephen 1984
Singleton, Barry QC 1968	Eaton, Deborah 1985
Parker, Judith QC 1973‡	O'Connor, Sarah 1986
Pratt, Camden QC 1970†	Cellan-Jones, Deiniol 1988
Scriven, Pamela QC 1970‡	Marshall, Philip 1989
Anelay, Richard QC 1970†	Selman, Elizabeth 1989
Wood, Roderic QC 1974‡	Barton, Richard 1990
Bellamy, Stephen QC 1974†	Fletcher, Marcus 1990
	Gibson, Caroline 1990
Gale, Michael QC 1957	Grice, Joanna 1991
Turner, James QC 1976	Harrison, Richard 1993
McFarlane, Andrew QC 1977†	Roberts, James 1993
	Cook, Ian 1994
Newton, Clive 1968	Mulholland, Shona 1994
Warren, Michael 1971	Crosthwaite, Graham 1995
Reddish, John 1973	Jay, Adam 1995
Tanzer, John 1975‡	Rayment, Benedick 1996
Rennie, David 1976‡	Esprit, Shaun 1996
Budden, Caroline 1977‡	Gardner, Alan 1997
Lister, Caroline 1980	Jackson, Gordon 1989

Types of work (and number of counsel practising in that area if supplied)
Administrative · Children · Common law (general) · Courts martial · Crime · Crime – corporate fraud · Education · Environment · Family · Family provision · Immigration · Local government · Medical negligence · Mental health · Parliamentary · Personal injury · Professional negligence · Sports

Chambers established: 1962
Opening times: 8.30 am-7 pm

Chambers' facilities
Conference rooms, Disks accepted, Disabled access, E-mail, Telephone conferences

Languages spoken
French, German, Hebrew, Portuguese, Spanish

2 KING'S BENCH WALK

Ground Floor, Temple, London, EC4Y 7DE
0171 353 1746
Fax: 0171 583 2051; DX 1032 London
E-mail: 2kbw@atlas.co.uk

Chambers of Mr A M Donne QC
Clerk: R Plager; Administrator: Mrs J Garforth

Also at: 115 North Hill, Plymouth

Onslow, Richard 1982	Amis, Christopher 1991
Zimbler, Alexia 1993	Darwall-Smith, Belinda
Bailey, Anthony 1972	Claire 1997
Robertshaw, Miranda-Louise 1985	Brown, Richard Gordon 1997
Crozier, Rawdon 1984	Selwood, Dominic Kim 1997
Counsell, James 1984	
Burwin, Heather 1983	Jones, Sarah 1996
Mousley, Timothy 1979	Start, Victoria 1996
Selfe, Michael 1965†	Oulton, Richard 1995
Wright, Jeremy 1970†	Weston, Louis 1994
Vere-Hodge, Michael QC 1970†	Rees, James 1994
	Russell, Fern 1994
Stopa, Christopher 1976	Feest, Adam 1994
Sellick, William 1973†	Rafati, Ali 1993
Sayers, Michael QC 1970†	Lumsdon, Katherine 1993
Rowsell, Paul 1971	Beal, Jason 1993
Sharp, Jonathan 1987	Mousley, William 1986
Maddick, Francis 1970	Bailey, Edward 1990
Bebb, Gordon 1975	Holmes, Susan 1989
Bowes, Michael 1980	Lewin, Nicholas 1989
Brennan, Janice 1980	Griffiths, John 1948*
Compton-Welstead, Benjamin 1979	Meredith-Hardy, John 1989
	Leonard, James 1989
Donne, Anthony QC 1973†	Trafford, Mark 1992
Miller, Robin 1960†	Bolton, Robert 1987
Fuller, Jonathan 1977	Fleming, Adrian 1991
Paterson, David 1961	Dugdale, Paul 1990
Jenkins, David 1967	Cadin, David 1990
Lofthouse, John 1979	Page, David 1984
Maitland, Andrew 1970†	Pyne, Russell 1991
Parish, Stephen 1966†	Small, Gina 1991
Parker, Hugh 1973	Jones, Elisabeth Barbara 1997
Blair, Ruth 1987	
Foster, Simon 1982	Weddell, Geoffrey 1989

C

4 KING'S BENCH WALK

Ground/First Floor/Basement, Temple, London, EC4Y 7DL
0171 822 8822
Fax: 0171 822 8844; DX 422 London, Chancery Lane
E-mail: 4kbw@barristersatlaw.com
URL: http://www.barristersatlaw.com
Out of hours telephone: Available on request

Chambers of Chamber of Robert Rhodes QC
Clerks: Ian Lee (Senior Clerk), Edward Holland, Robert Bryant, Glen Swift; Receptionist: Lisa Frangimore

Also at: Kings Bench Chambers, 175 Holdenhurst Road, Bournemouth, Dorset BN8 8DQ Tel: 01202 250025, Fax: 01202 250026

Rhodes, Robert QC *1968*†	**Jarman**, Samuel *1989*
Toogood, John *1957*	**Stern**, David *1989*
Evans, Keith *1962*	**Huston**, Graham *1991*
Cattle, David *1975*	**Nelson**, Michael *1992*
Anderson, Clive *1976*	**Bowen**, Paul *1993*
Davis, Greville *1976*	**Maxwell**, Adrian *1993*
Howard, Margaret *1977*	**Dunn**, Katherine *1993*
Hulme, Graham *1977*	**Crossfield**, Anne *1993*
Stuart, Bruce *1977*	**Edhem**, Emma *1993*
Van Hagen, Christopher *1980*	**Hood**, Nigel *1993*
	Mishcon, Oliver *1993*
Shale, Justin *1982*	**Yazawa**, Yutaka *1994*
Jones, John Evan *1982*	**Murphy**, Nicola *1995*
Stafford-Michael, Simon *1982*	**Power**, Lawrence *1995*
	Hatch, Lisa *1995*
Harounoff, David *1984*	**Aiken**, Kimberley *1995*
Hurst, Martin *1985*	**Farmer**, Kimberly *1997*

Types of work (and number of counsel practising in that area if supplied)
Banking 5 · Bankruptcy 6 · Care proceedings 4 · Chancery (general) 4 · Civil liberties 2 · Commercial litigation 14 · Common law (general) 20 · Company and commercial 16 · Corporate finance 4 · Courts martial 2 · Crime 20 · Crime – corporate fraud 14 · EC and competition law 2 · Employment 2 · Environment 8 · Family 4 · Family provision 4 · Financial services 10 · Housing 2 · Immigration 1 · Insolvency 6 · Insurance 10 · Insurance/reinsurance 10 · International trade 10 · Landlord and tenant 8 · Licensing 10 ·

Medical negligence 8 · Personal injury 14 · Private international 8 · Professional negligence 10 · Shipping, admiralty 2

Chambers established: 1920
Opening times: 8.45 am-6.30 pm

Chambers' facilities
Conference rooms, Video conferences, LAN, E-mail, Audio-visual deposition taking, Court news service

Languages spoken
French, German, Japanese, Spanish, Turkish

Fees policy
Information on individual areas of practice, fees and hourly charging rates is available from the Senior Clerk.

Additional information
4 Kings Bench Walk is an established set of chambers in the heart of the Temple. Accommodation is basement, ground and first floors. Cutting-edge IT systems, high standards of advocacy and advisory work, integrated communications and a flexible approach to litigation management mean a first-class service nationally and internationally.

In all areas of the criminal and civil law chambers is able to provide a rapid response in any jurisdiction worldwide. 4 Kings Bench Walk is in the vanguard of applying information technology to the business of law.

Principle Areas of Practice
Criminal defence in all courts (extensive experience in confiscation, drugs, firearms, murder and sexual offences), white collar crime (VAT, Inland Revenue and commercial fraud), commercial litigation (global – chambers has established links in the Far East and North America), commercial regulation, financial regulation, insurance and re-insurance, judicial review, matrimonial (and family), personal injury (including disaster litigation) and professional negligence.

Other Areas of Practice
Property disputes, partnership law, engineering and building contracts.

Tenancy applications should be made to the head of chambers, Robert RHODES QC. Chambers is in the PACH scheme. Pupilage enquiries should be made to Katherine DUNN. All other matters should be addressed to the Senior Clerk, Ian LEE. A chambers brochure is available but an ideal first point of contact is the chambers web site.

4 KING'S BENCH WALK

2nd Floor, Temple, London, EC4Y 7DL
020 7353 3581
Fax: 020 7583 2257; DX 1050 London
E-mail: clerks@4kbw.co.uk
URL: http://www.4kbw.co.uk
Out of hours telephone: 0378 192960 or 01920 831142

Chambers of N F B Jarman QC
Clerks: Lee Cook, Philip Burnell, Jayne Barnes

Jarman, Nicholas QC 1965†	Metcalf, John 1990
Hillman, Basil 1968	Wakerley, Paul 1990
Spencer Bernard, Robert 1969†	Mather, Kate 1990
Cousins, Christopher 1969	Murphy, Cressida 1991
Denniss, John 1974	Skelley, Michael 1991
Pooley, Moira 1974	Preston, Kim 1991
Evans, Barnaby 1978	McCreath, Fiona 1991
Riley, John 1983	Ashmole, Timothy 1992
Arkhurst, Reginald 1984	Ruffell, Mark 1992
Alt, Jane 1984	Simpson, Jonathan 1993
Stanfield, Sandra 1984	Hurworth, Jillian 1993
Goddard, Philip 1985	Davis, Brendan 1994
Nightingale, Peter 1986	Maguire, Benn 1994
Granville Stafford, Andrew 1987	Phillimore, Sarah 1994
Jacobs, Claire 1989	McGee, Tamala 1995
	Drane, Amanda 1996
	Blake, Alan 1997

5 KING'S BENCH WALK

Temple, London, EC4Y 7DN
0171 353 5638
Fax: 0171 353 6166; DX 367 London, Chancery Lane

Chambers of Mr B J Higgs QC

6 KING'S BENCH WALK

Ground Floor, Temple, London, EC4Y 7DR
0171 583 0410
Fax: 0171 353 8791; DX 26 London, Chancery Lane
E-mail: worsley@6kbw.freeserve.co.uk

Chambers of M D L Worsley QC
Clerk: David Garstang

Worsley, Michael QC 1955	Ryder, John 1980‡
Curnow, Ann QC 1957†	Hilliard, Nicholas 1981
Mallalieu, Ann QC 1970	Wass, Sasha 1981‡
Amlot, Roy QC 1963	Bowyer, Martin 1984
Curtis, James QC 1970†	Brierley, Andrew 1984
Lovell-Pank, Dorian QC 1971†	Denison, Simon 1984
	Armstrong, Dean 1985
Temple, Victor QC 1971†	Broadbent, Emma 1986
Korner, Joanna QC 1974†	Cray, Timothy 1989
Houlder, Bruce QC 1969†	Grieves-Smith, Peter 1989
Spens, David QC 1973†	Ray-Crosby, Irena 1990
Fisher, David QC 1973†	Oldland, Andrew 1990*
Joseph, Wendy QC 1975†	Laws, Simon 1991*
Leonard, Anthony QC 1978‡	Dunn-Shaw, Jason 1992
	Penny, Duncan 1992
Turner, David QC 1971*†	Darlow, Annabel 1993
Turner, Jonathan 1974‡	Whitehouse, Sarah 1993
Vagg, Howard 1974†	Atkinson, Duncan 1995
Sweeney, Nigel 1976†	Pilling, Annabel 1995
Dennis, Mark 1977‡	Hallam, Jacob 1996
Jessel, Philippa 1978	Ezekiel, Adina 1997
Moore, Marks 1979‡	Foulkes, Alison 1997
Perry, David 1980	Mably, Louis 1997

Types of work (and number of counsel practising in that area if supplied)
Crime 41 · Crime – corporate fraud 41

Opening times: 8.30 am-7 pm

Chambers' facilities
Conference rooms, Video conferences, Disks accepted

Languages spoken
French, German, Italian, Spanish

Additional information
The chambers of Michael Worsley QC at 6 King's Bench Walk is recognised as one of the leading sets in the field of criminal law with strength at all levels of seniority. There are at present 41 members including 13 QCs and four Treasury Counsel.

Chambers' practice covers all aspects of criminal law and members specialise in advocacy in the higher courts in both defence and prosecution work. Senior members have participated in many of the major criminal trials in recent years.

In particular, members of chambers defend and prosecute in a large number of commercial crime, fraud and regulatory cases. All aspects of work in the field of financial services are undertaken.

C

Individual members also appear in libel, licensing, extradition and trade description cases; before coroners' courts, inquiries, disciplinary and industrial tribunals; and undertake work involving human rights.

6 KING'S BENCH WALK

Ground, Third & Fourth Floors, Temple, London, EC4Y 7DR
0171 353 4931/583 0695
Fax: 0171 353 1726; DX 471 London

Chambers of S Kadri QC
Clerks: Gary Jeffery, Ms Janet McGlasson, Philip Bampfylde

Kadri, Sibghatullah QC 1969	**Clarke**, Helen 1988
Rafique, Tariq 1961	**Driver**, Emily 1988
Geldart, William 1975	**Dias**, Asoka 1989
Bowen, James 1979	**Giz**, Alev 1988
Carrott, Sylvester 1980	**Juss**, Satvinder 1989
Grewal, Harjit 1980	**Panesar**, Manjit 1989
Gallivan, Terence 1981	**Tagliavini**, Lorna 1989
Gill, Manjit 1982	**Neathey**, Rona 1990
Pearce, Linda 1982	**Wan Daud**, Malek 1991
Fielden, Christa 1982	**Daniel**, Leon 1992
de Mello, Rambert 1983	**Braganza**, Nicola 1992
Joseph, Elizabeth 1983	**Knafler**, Stephen 1993
Gumbiti-Zimuto, Andrew 1983	**Rothwell**, Joanne 1993
	Najand, Maryam 1993
Cogan, Michael 1986	**Taghavi**, Shahram 1994
Howat, Robin 1986	**Browne**, Shereener 1996
Taylor, Martin 1988	**Adedeji**, Yinka 1997

S TOMLINSON QC

KING'S BENCH WALK

7 King's Bench Walk, Temple, London, EC4Y 7DS
0171 583 0404
Fax: 0171 583 0950/353 2455; DX 239 London
E-mail: clerks@7kbw.law.co.uk
Out of hours telephone: 0831 394225

Chambers of Stephen Tomlinson QC
Clerks: Bernie Hyatt, Greg Leyden; Administrator: Sue Luxford

Tomlinson, Stephen QC 1974†	**Bright**, Robert 1987
Hamilton, Adrian QC 1949	**Geary**, Gavin 1989
Cooke, Jeremy QC 1976‡	**Bailey**, David 1989
Saloman, Timothy QC 1975‡	**Edwards**, David 1989
	Allen, David 1990
Reynolds, Prof Francis QC 1961	**Picken**, Simon 1989
Kealey, Gavin QC 1977	**Wales**, Andrew 1992
Flaux, Julian QC 1978	**Healy**, Siobán 1993
Gaisman, Jonathan QC 1979	**Phillips**, S J 1993
	Sabben-Clare, Rebecca 1993
Kendrick, Dominic QC 1981	**Khurshid**, Jawdat 1994
Schaff, Alistair QC 1983	**Waller**, Richard 1994
Priday, Charles 1982	**Williams**, Leigh 1996
Fenton, Adam 1984	**Kenefick**, Timothy 1996
Hofmeyr, Stephen 1982	**Bignall**, John 1996
Butcher, Christopher 1986	**Kerr**, Simon 1997
Kenny, Stephen 1987	**Holroyd**, Charles Wilfrid 1997
Southern, Richard 1987	**Drake**, James 1998

8 KING'S BENCH WALK

CHAMBERS OF
LEONARD WOODLEY Q.C.

EIGHT KING'S BENCH WALK

2nd Floor, Temple, London, EC4Y 7DU
0171 797 8888
Fax: 0171 797 8880/8854; DX 195 Chancery Lane
Out of hours telephone: Mobiles: 07771 845605 (Marc Foss) 07771 845606 (Del Edgeler) 07771 845607 (Tony Burton) 07771 845608 (Scott Haley)

Chambers of L G Woodley QC
Clerks: Marc Foss, Del Edgeler, Tony Burton, Scott Haley; Accountant: St Hilliare Bastien

Woodley, Leonard QC 1963†	**Gifford**, Lord Anthony QC 1962
Croxon, Raymond QC 1960	**Paulusz**, Jan 1957†
Hart-Leverton, Colin QC 1957	**Allum**, Desmond SC 1962
	Gibbs, Jocelyn 1972
	Rubery, Philip 1973

     † Recorder ‡ Assistant Recorder *Door Tenant

Shepherd, Nigel *1973*
Gassman, Caroline *1974*
Daniells-Smith, Roger *1974*
Yearwood, Jeffrey *1975‡*
Bart, Delano *1977*
Jones, Martin Wynne *1977*
Keogh, Andrew *1978*
Williams, Alan *1978*
Collins, Robert *1978*
Howe, Carole *1984*
Rose, Pamela *1980*
Hodgson, Martin *1980*
Salter, Charles *1981*
Fessal, Ignatius *1981*
Barnett, Adrienne *1981*
MacKinnon, Tom *1982*
Hill, Andrew *1982*
Dunn, Alex *1985*
Williams, Nicola *1985*
Fraser, Nigel *1986*
Ladak, Tahera *1986*
Gatto, Nicola *1987*
Long, Tobias *1988*
Boateng, Paul *1989*
Read, Simon *1989*
Tizzano, Franco *1989*
Huda, Abida *1989*
Mann, Jonathan *1989*

Taylor-Camara, Alex *1989*
Murray-Smith, James *1990*
George, Susan *1990*
Harrill, Jayne *1990*
Henderson, Ian *1990*
Tehrani, Christopher *1990*
Sapnara, Khatun *1990*
Fitzpatrick, Edward *1990*
Ryan, Timothy *1991*
Breese-Laughran, Delphine *1991*
Evans, Stephen *1992*
Bazini, Danny *1992*
Igori, Kingsly *1993*
McLaughlin, Elaine *1993*
Gannon, Kevin *1993*
Taylor, Steven *1992*
Williams, Paul *1994*
Ivens, Jemma *1994*
Ryan, William *1994*
Jones, David *1994*
Munday, Anne *1994*
McCarthy, Martin *1994*
Caswell, Timothy Charles *1994*
Gordon, Clare *1995*
Penn, John Peter *1996*
Mansoor, Parveen *1996*
Keating, Dermot *1997*

9 KING'S BENCH WALK

Ground Floor, Temple, London, EC4Y 7DX
0171 353 7202/3909
Fax: 0171 583 2030; DX 472 London
E-mail: 9kbw@compuserve.com
URL: http://freespace.virgin.net/nine.kbw
Out of hours telephone: 0171 353 7202 (24 hours)

Chambers of Mr P J Gribble
Clerks: Gary Morgan (Senior Clerk), Gary Nichols (Junior Clerk), Adam Murray (Junior Clerk)

Gribble, Peter *1972*
Popat, Surendra *1969‡*
Marsh, Peter *1975*
Stones, Keith *1975*
Deschampsneufs, Alice *1976*
Greenslade, Henry *1982*
Delamere, Isabel *1985*
McGivern, William *1987*
Trigg, Miles *1987*
Brown, Susan *1989*
Miah, Zacharias *1990*
Sheffi, Bosmath *1991*

Bankole-Jones, Gwen *1991*
Howe, Peter *1992*
Murphy, Michael *1992*
Obuka, Obijuo *1993*
Pavlou, Paul *1993*
Jacobs, Christopher *1994*
Sneller, Elaine *1994*
Lowry, Anne-Marie *1995*
Villarosa, Annunziata *1995*
Jackson, Myles *1995*
Wood, Joanna *1996*
Vallejo, Jacqueline *1997*

THE CHAMBERS OF MR ALI MOHAMMED AZHAR

Basement, 9 King's Bench Walk, Temple, London, EC4Y 7DX
0171 353 9564
Fax: 0171 353 7943; DX 118 Chancery Lane

Chambers of A M Azhar

10 KING'S BENCH WALK

$$10$$
KING'S BENCH
WALK

Ground Floor, Temple, London, EC4Y 7EB
0171 353 7742
Fax: 0171 583 0579; DX 24 London
E-mail: 10kbw@lineone.net

Chambers of Claudius John Algar
Clerks: Alan Curtis, Mathew Harper, Colin Middleton, Terry Lee

Algar, Claudius *1972*
Hare, Rosina QC *1956†*
Hart, Colin *1966*
Vaudin D'Imecourt, Charles *1971*
Powell, William *1971*
Tapping, Susan *1975†*
Boston, Janet *1976*
Christensen, Carlton *1977*
Pearce, Reid *1979*
Hedworth, Leonard *1979*
Miscampbell, Bernadette *1980*
Lanigan, William *1980*
Powell, Dean *1982*
Gibbons, Orlando *1982*
Evans, Andrew *1984*
Talacchi, Carlo *1986*
Thompson, Simon *1988*
Williams, David *1989*
Crallan, Richard *1991*

Bogle, James *1991*
Johal, Suki *1991*
Serle, Diana *1992*
Noble, Andrew *1992*
Harris, Michael *1993*
Hurworth, Jillian *1993*
Swainson, Richard *1994*
Harding, Patricia *1994*
Martin, Jonathan *1994*
Bailey, Rosana *1994*
O'Callaghan, Declan *1995*
Galpin, Diana *1995*
Ramzan, Mohammed *1995*
Butler, Simon *1996*
Bui, Victoria *1996*
McNally, John *1996*
Bevis, Dominic *1996*
Nabijou, Sharifeh *1996*
Back, Patrick QC *1940*†
Habib, Mustafa *1980**

C

10 KING'S BENCH WALK

1st Floor, Temple, London, EC4Y 7EB
0171 353 2501
Fax: 0171 353 0658; DX 294 London

Chambers of Mr R Thwaites QC

11 KING'S BENCH WALK

Temple, London, EC4Y 7EQ
0171 632 8500/583 0610
Fax: 0171 583 9123/3690; DX 368 London
E-mail: clerksroom@11kbw.com
URL: http://www.11kbw.com
Out of hours telephone: 0171 632 8500

Chambers of Eldred Tabachnik and James Goudie QC
Clerks: Philip Monham, Nicholas Hill, Stephen Penson, Andrew Monks

Tabachnik, Eldred QC 1970‡	**Wallington**, Peter 1987
Goudie, James QC 1970†	**Pitt-Payne**, Timothy 1989
Field, Richard QC 1977†	**Swift**, Jonathan 1989
Supperstone, Michael QC 1973†	**Oldham**, Peter 1990
Slade, Elizabeth QC 1972†	**Jones**, Sean 1991
McGregor, Alistair QC 1974	**Sheldon**, Clive 1991
Jeans, Christopher QC 1980	**Choudhury**, Akhlaq 1992
Sales, Philip 1985‡	**Nicholls**, Paul 1992
Hillier, Andrew 1972	**Stilitz**, Daniel 1992
Laing, Elisabeth 1980‡	**Coppel**, Jason 1994
Lynch, Adrian 1983	**Porter**, Nigel 1994
Ward, Siobhan 1984	**Ivimy**, Cecilia 1995
Cavanagh, John 1985	**Restrick**, Tom 1995
Bear, Charles 1986	**Leiper**, Richard 1996
Giffin, Nigel 1986	**Wilson**, Julian 1997
	Morris, Gillian 1997*

Types of work (and number of counsel practising in that area if supplied)
Administrative 19 · Bankruptcy 5 · Civil liberties 12 · Commercial litigation 17 · Defamation 2 · Discrimination 23 · EC and competition law 7 · Education 12 · Employment 26 · Entertainment 3 · Environment 5 · Housing 5 · Immigration 3 · Insurance/reinsurance 5 · Intellectual property 3 · International trade 7 · Local government 20 · Private international 7 · Professional negligence 9 · Sale and carriage of goods 13 · Share options 6 · Shipping, admiralty 3 · Town and country planning 2

Chambers established: 1981
Opening times: 8 am-7 pm

Chambers' facilities
Conference rooms, Disks accepted, E-mail

Languages spoken
French, Italian, Spanish

11 KING'S BENCH WALK

1st Floor, Temple, London, EC4Y 7EQ
0171 353 3337
Fax: 0171 583 2190; DX 389 London, Chancery Lane/ 26433 Leeds/ 10621 Sheffield
E-mail: fmuller11@aol.com

Chambers of F J Muller QC
Clerks: A T Blaney (London), A Dunstone (Leeds)

Annexe: 11 King's Bench Walk, 3 Park Court, Park Cross Street, Leeds, LS1 2QH
Tel: 0113 297 1200
Fax: 0113 297 1201

Muller, Franz QC 1961†	**Sylvester**, Mio 1980
Robson, David QC 1965†	**Wynn**, Toby 1982
Spencer, James QC 1975†	**Caswell**, Rebecca 1983
Lawler, Simon QC 1971*	**Swain**, Fiona 1983
Batty, Paul QC 1975†	**Reeds**, Graham 1984
Robertson, Andrew QC 1975†	**Cooper**, John 1985
Graham, John 1955	**Mallett**, Simon 1986
Collins, John 1956*†	**Waterman**, Adrian 1988
Radcliffe, Francis 1962	**Brooke**, David 1990
Caswell, Matthew 1968	**Toone**, Robert 1993
Barlow, Richard 1970	**Skelt**, Ian 1994
Winch, John 1973*	**Mitchell**, Tom 1995
Adams, James 1978*	**Antrobus**, Simon 1995
Campbell, Nicholas 1978	**Margree**, Sarah 1996
O'Neill, Michael 1979	**Dempster**, Tina 1997
Richardson, Jeremy 1980	**Bean**, Matthew 1997
Attwooll, Christopher 1980	**Hedworth**, Alan QC 1975*
	Spencer, Shaun QC 1968*

12 KING'S BENCH WALK

Temple, London, EC4Y 7EL
0171 583 0811
Fax: 0171 583 7228; DX 1037 London
E-mail: chambers@12kbw.co.uk
URL: http://www.12kbw.co.uk

Chambers of T Stow QC
Clerks: John Cooper, Nicholas Clark

Stow, Timothy QC 1965†	Hill-Smith, Alexander 1978
Whitby, Charles QC 1952†	Featherby, William 1978
Walker, Ronald QC 1962†	Rodway, Susan 1981
Goldstaub, Anthony QC 1972	Howard, Jonathan 1983
	Russell, Paul 1984
Speaight, Anthony QC 1973	Lewers, Nigel 1986
Methuen, Richard QC 1972	Newbery, Freya 1986
Goldrein, Iain QC 1975‡	Pickering, Andrew 1987
de Haas, Margaret QC 1977†	Hamill, Hugh 1988
	Chambers, Adam 1989
Burton, Frank QC 1982‡	Brown, Catherine 1990
Grobel, Peter 1967†	Chandler, Kate 1990
Dedman, Peter 1968†	Evans, Caroline 1991
Spencer-Lewis, Neville 1970	Moran, Vincent 1991
	Audland, William 1992
Hooper, Toby 1973‡	Vincent, Patrick 1992
King, John 1973	Jackson, Stephanie 1992
Hogarth, Andrew 1974	Kendall, Joel 1993
Gallagher, Brian 1975	Viney, Richard 1994
Williams, Nicholas 1976‡	D'Souza, Carolyn 1994
Worthington, Stephen 1976	Peck, Catherine 1995
Crawford, Lincoln 1977†	Petts, Timothy 1996
Gore, Allan 1977‡	Steinberg, Harry 1997

Types of work (and number of counsel practising in that area if supplied)
Arbitration 7 · Banking 4 · Clinical negligence 19 · Commercial litigation 12 · Construction 11 · Employment 12 · Environment 4 · Housing 6 · Insurance 20 · Insurance/reinsurance 16 · Landlord and tenant 13 · Personal injury 38 · Professional negligence 34 · Sale and carriage of goods 10

Chambers' facilities
Conference rooms, Disks accepted, E-mail

Languages spoken
French, Italian, Portuguese, Spanish

Fees policy
Chambers is always willing to negotiate fees on a basis suitable to the client.

Additional information
This established civil and commercial set of chambers has specialist groups of barristers with particular expertise in the fields of Construction and Employment law. Chambers has a progressive outlook: it has modern staffing arrangements and is equipped with the latest computerisation, thus ensuring that the work is dealt with quickly and efficiently with the needs of each individual client in mind.

Work undertaken
Personal Injury: includes all industrial disease claims, particularly asbestos, VWF and RSI; brain damage; spinal injuries; all employers', public and product liability claims; all road traffic related work.
Professional Negligence: includes solicitors' and barristers' negligence in addition to those mentioned below.
Clinical Negligence: includes injuries at birth; catastrophic brain damage; all other cases involving complex medical and scientific issues.
Insurance: includes drafting and construction of policies; material damage; motor policy claims.
Construction: includes all standard form building contracts; engineering, mining and computer contracts; architects', engineers' and surveyors' negligence.
Property: includes landlord and tenant; housing.
Employment: includes race relations; equal opportunity; trade union work; restrictive covenants; transfers of undertakings; wrongful and unfair dismissal; equal pay; bonus and pension schemes; EC employment law.
Commercial: includes banking and credit transactions; sale and carriage of goods; accountants' and bankers' negligence.
Public Law: includes judicial review; disaster inquiries; planning enforcement; local government law.
Environmental: includes pollution of land by chemicals and nuclear matter; pollution-related criminal charges.

Publications:
Members of chambers have written, edited or contributed to a significant number of publications, including: Walker & Walker:

---

† Recorder ‡ Assistant Recorder *Door Tenant

The English Legal System; Bullen & Leake &
Jacob's *Precedents of Pleadings*; *Master
and Servant*, in *Halsbury's Laws of
England*, 3rd edition; *Atkins Court Forms*,
2nd edition; *Law of Defective Premises*;
Architects' Journal Legal Handbook;
*Construction Disputes: Liability and the
Expert Witness* ; Odgers: *Pleadings and
Practice*; *Consumer Credit Law and Prac-
tice*; *Medical Negligence: Case law*; *Archi-
tect's Legal Handbook*; *Butterworths
Personal Injury Litigation Service*;
*Commercial Litigation: Pre-emptive Reme-
dies*; *Personal Injury Litigation Law*;
Cordery on Solicitors; *Butterworths Profes-
sional Negligence Service*.

Chambers' brochure is available on
request.

13 KING'S BENCH WALK

1st Floor, Temple, London, EC4Y 7EN
0171 353 7204
Fax: 0171 583 0252; DX 359 London
Other comms: Lix: Lon 066
E-mail: clerks@13kbw.law.co.uk

Chambers of Roger Ellis QC
*Clerks: Stephen Buckingham, Kevin Kelly;
Administrator: Penny McFall; Chambers
Director: Claire Makin*

Annexe: King's Bench Chambers, 32
Beaumont Street, Oxford, OX1 2NP
Tel: 01865 311066
Fax: 01865 311077

Ellis, Roger QC *1962*	**Grant**, David *1975‡*
Williams, Graeme QC *1959†*	**Reid**, Paul *1975*
Baughan, Julian QC *1967†*	**Tracy Forster**, Jane *1975*
Ashton, David *1962*	**Bright**, David *1976†*
Dawson, Alexander *1969†*	**Draycott**, Simon *1977‡*
McGeorge, Anthony *1969*	**Brough**, Alasdair *1979*
Lamb, Robert *1973*	**Daly**, Nigel *1979*
Richardson, David *1973†*	**Syfret**, Nicholas *1979*
Goodwin, Deirdre *1974*	**Glennie**, Andrew *1982*
	Williams, A *1983*

Coode, Jonathan *1984*	**Walters**, Edmund *1991*
Vickery, Neil *1985*	**Wenlock**, Heather *1991*
Moore, Neil *1986*	**Walters**, Vivian *1991*
Gibbons, Sarah *1987*	**Panesar**, Deshpal *1993*
Blake, Arthur *1988*	**Chan**, Susan *1994*
Cramsie, Sinclair *1988*	**Mitchell**, Paul *1994*
Hay, Fiona *1989*	**Cox**, James *1997*
Pote, Andrew *1983*	**White**, Matthew *1997*
Higgins, Adrian *1990*	**Owens**, Lucy *1997*

**Types of work (and number of counsel practising in
that area if supplied)**
Arbitration · Banking · Bankruptcy · Care
proceedings · Chancery (general) ·
Chancery land law · Club law · Commercial
· Commercial litigation · Commercial
property · Common law (general) ·
Company and commercial · Construction ·
Consumer law · Conveyancing · Crime ·
Crime – corporate fraud · Discrimination ·
Employment · Environment · Family ·
Family provision · Immigration ·
Insolvency · Insurance · Landlord and
tenant · Licensing · Local government ·
Medical negligence · Mental health ·
Partnerships · Personal injury · Professional
negligence · Sale and carriage of goods

Chambers established: 1971
Opening times: 8.30 am-6.30 pm

Chambers' facilities
Disks accepted, Conference rooms in
London and Oxford

Languages spoken
Cantonese, French, Italian, Portuguese

Fees policy
Fees are charged on an hourly basis, by
reference to the complexity and value of
the matter and the seniority of counsel. The
senior clerks will be pleased to discuss the
level of fees in advance of work
commencing on any matter.

2 KING'S BENCH WALK CHAMBERS

2
*Kings Bench Walk Chambers
(Lord Campbell of Alloway)
Temple
London EC4Y 7DE*

*1st Floor, 2 King's Bench Walk, Temple,
London, EC4Y 7DE*
020 7353 9276

Fax: 020 7353 9949; DX 477 London
E-mail: chambers@2kbw.co.uk
Out of hours telephone: 0790 1553396

Chambers of Rene Wong
Clerks: Alex Mark, Carla Owen;
Administrator: Brenda Anderson

Campbell of Alloway, Lord QC *1939*	Kapur, Deepak *1984*
Thomas, David Owen QC *1952*	Livesey, Simon *1987*
	Perian, Steven *1987*
Wong, Rene *1973*	Alban-Lloyd, Nan *1988*
Rueff, Philip *1969†*	Gokhool, Vishnu *1978*
Dalgleish, Anthony *1971*	Meadowcroft, Gregory *1990*
Evans, Alun *1971*	Lorenzo, Claudia *1991*
Colegate-Stone, Jefferson *1975*	Kennedy, Brian *1992*
Slack, Ian *1974*	Callman, Tanya *1993*
Hudson Davies, Ednyfed *1975*	Katyar, Arun *1993*
	Sandeman, David *1993*
Mendes Da Costa, David *1976*	Freeman, Lee *1994*
Gifford, Robert *1977*	Johnson, Janice *1994*
Mason, Ian *1978*	Kirby, James *1994*
Lloyd, Patricia *1979*	Dean, Abigail *1995*
Papageorgis, George *1981*	Donelon, Anne *1995*
Shrimpton, R James *1981*	Wilson, Lachlan *1996*
Gaylord, Sheila *1983*	Walsh, Mark *1996*
Levy, Anthony *1983*	Livesey, Julia *1974**
Lynn, Jeremy *1983*	Baker, Robert *1977**
Davies, Sarah *1984*	Lam, Osmond *1988**
	Yaqub, Zahd *1991**
	Watters, Simon *1992**

KING'S CHAMBERS

49a Broadway, Stratford, London,
E15 4BW
Fax: 0181 368 8130; DX 5400 Stratford

Chambers of Mr V C S Gokhool

KINGSWAY CHAMBERS

88 Kingsway, Holborn, London,
WC2B 6AA
07000 653529
Fax: 07000 781115; DX 205 Chancery Lane

Chambers of Mr Lanre Oke

Types of Work
Use the types of work listings in Parts A and B to locate chambers and individual barristers who specialise in particular areas of work.

LAMB BUILDING

Ground Floor, Temple, London, EC4Y 7AS
020 7797 7788
Fax: 020 7353 0535/797 7453; DX 1038 London
E-mail: lamb.building@link.org
Out of hours telephone: 0421 339232

Chambers of Ami Feder
Clerks: Gary Goodger, David Corne, Paul Hammond, Simon Bewsey, Lisa Thomas

Also at: 3 Temple Gardens

Feder, Ami *1965*	Sawhney, Debbie *1987*
Wheeler, Kenneth *1956*	Cotterill, Susan *1988*
Krolick, Ivan *1966*	Richmond, Bernard *1988*
Edlin, David *1971*	Terry, Jane *1988*
Fox, John *1973*	Brounger, David *1990*
Edie, Anthony *1974*	Hindle, Frances *1990*
Gordon, Jeremy *1974*	Crampin, Paul *1992*
Waters, John *1974*	Geser, Anita *1992*
Barton, Alan *1975*	Kearney, Seamus *1992*
Hilliard, Spenser *1975*	Weinstein, Lindsay *1992*
Perry, Jacqueline *1975*	Cole, Martin *1994*
Hartman, Michael *1975*	Dykers, Joy *1995*
Hodes, Angela *1979*	Bitmead, Paul *1996*
Phillips, Michael *1980*	Faul, Anne *1996*
Cook, David *1982*	Peterson, Geri *1997*
Roberts, Richard *1983*	

Types of work (and number of counsel practising in that area if supplied)
Arbitration · Banking · Bankruptcy · Care proceedings · Chancery (general) · Chancery land law · Common law (general) · Company and commercial · Construction · Courts martial · Crime · Crime – corporate fraud · Employment · Equity, wills and trusts · Family · Family provision · Foreign law · Housing · Immigration · Insolvency · Landlord and tenant · Licensing · Local government · Medical negligence · Mental health · Partnerships · Probate and administration · Professional negligence · Sale and carriage of goods · Town and country planning

C

Opening times: 8.30 am-6.30 pm

Chambers' facilities
Conference rooms, Video conferences, Disks accepted, Disabled access, E-mail

Languages spoken
Dutch, French, German, Hebrew, Italian, Spanish

Fees policy
Upon request, fees will be negotiated with the clerk depending on the case.

LAMB CHAMBERS

• L A M B   C H A M B E R S •

Lamb Building, Temple, London, EC4Y 7AS
020 7797 8300
Fax: 020 7797 8308; DX 418 London
E-mail: lambchambers@link.org

Chambers of Christopher Gardner QC
Clerk: John Kelly; Administrator: Linda Spanner

Gardner, Christopher QC 1968†
Priest, Julian QC 1954
Burke-Gaffney, Michael QC 1959
Leeming, Ian QC 1970†
Sharp, Alastair 1968†
Sterling, John 1953
McNeile, Anthony 1970
West, Mark 1973†
di Mambro, David 1973
Carey, Jeremy 1974‡
Connerty, Anthony 1974
Allston, Anthony 1975
Shaw, Stephen 1975
Brilliant, Simon 1976
Caun, Lawrence 1977
Silvester, Bruce 1983
Mendoza, Colin 1983
Emerson, Paul 1984
Williams, Simon 1984
Samuel, Gerwyn 1986
Wood, Simon 1987
Stuart, James 1990
Gough, Katherine 1990
Majumdar, Shantanu 1992
Haggerty, Elizabeth 1994
Happe, Dominic 1993
Jones, Rhiannon 1993
Hayes, Richard 1995
Frith, Timothy 1996
Prand, Annette 1995
Stagi, Alexandra 1997

8 LAMBERT JONES MEWS

Barbican, London, EC2Y 8DP
0171 638 8804

Chambers of Mr M C B West QC

29A LAMBS CONDUIT STREET

Holborn, London, WC1N 3NG
0171 831 9907
Fax: 0171 831 9907

Chambers of Mr J M Taylor

21 LAUDERDALE TOWER

Barbican, London, EC2Y 8BY
0171 920 9308
Fax: 0171 628 8124

Chambers of Mr E J Wollner

LEONE CHAMBERS

72 Evelyn Avenue, Kingsbury, London, NW9 OJH
0181 200 4020
Fax: 0181 905 8881
E-mail: festus4@leonechambers.co.uk
Out of hours telephone: 0181 931 1712

Chambers of Mr D E J George
Practice Manager: Danny Currie; Administrator: Vincent de Weld Nicholas

George, Donald 1973
Harding, Christine 1966
Tucker, Peter Louis 1970
Bash-Taqi, Shahineh 1972
Harding, Gladys Modwyn Cicely 1979
Minhas, Rafhat 1994

LION COURT

Chancery House, 53-64 Chancery Lane, London, WC2A 1SJ
0171 404 6565
Fax: 0171 404 6659; DX 98 LDE Chancery Lane

† Recorder ‡ Assistant Recorder *Door Tenant

Chambers of David Wolchover
Clerk: Kevin Tarrant

Wolchover, David *1971*	**Bailey**, Stephen *1991*
Boyd, Gerard *1967*	**McCullough**, Louise *1991*
Kaye, Laraine *1971*	**Mendel**, Philippa *1992*
Cooksley, Subhashini *1975*	**Kaffel**, Paul *1993*
Nicholas, Georgina *1983*	**Myerson**, Victoria *1994*
Hosking, Steve *1988*	**Krikler**, Alex *1995*
Brinkworth, Paul *1990*	**Kennedy**, Brian *1996*
Newberry, David *1990*	**Grimshaw**, Gary *1998*
Honey, John *1990*	

LITTLETON CHAMBERS

3 King's Bench Walk North, Temple,
London, EC4Y 7HR
0171 797 8600
Fax: 0171 797 8699/97; DX 1047 London,
Chancery Lane
E-mail: clerks@littletonchambers.co.uk
Out of hours telephone: Answerphone or
David Douglas: 01525 876495, Deborah
Anderson: 0171 701 0576

Chambers of M L Kallipetis QC
Clerks: David Douglas (Chief Executive),
Deborah Anderson, Alistair Coyne, Tim
Tarring, Tony Shaddock (Fees Clerk), Nita
Johnston (Accounts Receivable Manager)

Kallipetis, Michel QC *1968†*	**Davies**, John *1981*
Serota, Daniel QC *1969†*	**Bothroyd**, Shirley *1982*
Mayes, Ian QC *1974*	**Bloch**, Selwyn *1982*
Price, Richard QC OBE *1969*	**Sendall**, Antony *1984*
	Gatt, Ian *1985*
Freedman, Clive QC *1978‡*	**Duggan**, Michael *1984*
Clarke, Andrew QC *1980*	**Trepte**, Peter *1987*
Bowers, John QC *1979*	**Lowenstein**, Paul *1988*
Manning, Colin *1970*	**Downey**, Raoul *1988*
Perkoff, Richard *1971*	**Barklem**, Martyn *1989*
Bartle, Philip *1976*	**Samek**, Charles *1989*
Lomas, Mark *1977*	**Bacon**, Jeffrey *1989*
Higginson, Timothy *1977*	**Lewis**, Jeremy *1992*
Stafford, Andrew *1980*	**Ellenbogen**, Naomi *1992*
Harry Thomas, Caroline *1981*	**Tatton-Brown**, Daniel *1994*
	Bather, Victoria *1995*

Ritchie, Stuart *1995*	**Harris**, Donald *1958**
Davis, Carol *1996*	**MacCormick**, Prof Neil QC *1971**
Martin, Dale *1997*	
De Silva, Niran *1997*	

Types of work (and number of counsel practising in that area if supplied)
ADR 11 · Arbitration 8 · Banking 7 · Bankruptcy 10 · Care proceedings 2 · Chancery (general) 11 · Commercial litigation 31 · Common law (general) 31 · Company and commercial 10 · Competition 8 · Construction 12 · Copyright 12 · Crime – corporate fraud 6 · Defamation 8 · Discrimination 25 · EC and competition law 6 · Education 20 · Employment 25 · Entertainment 30 · Family 2 · Film, cable, TV 10 · Financial services 10 · Information technology 7 · Insolvency 10 · Insurance 7 · Intellectual property 15 · International trade 5 · Landlord and tenant 3 · Medical negligence 5 · Parliamentary 2 · Partnerships 6 · Personal injury 5 · Professional negligence 27 · Sale and carriage of goods 8 · Share options 2 · Sports 8 · Trademarks 10

Chambers established: 1954
Opening times: 8.30 am-8.30 pm Monday-Thursday 8.30 am-6.30 pm Friday

Chambers' facilities
Conference rooms, Disks accepted, Disabled access, E-mail, Pre-meeting room, Out of hours contacts, Access to video conferences, Arbitration rooms, Lectures

Languages spoken
French, German, Greek, Hebrew, Italian, Mandarin Chinese

Fees policy
We have a flexible approach to fees and a dedicated fees negotiator who will be happy to provide quotations and discuss fees for individual cases.

Additional information
Littleton Chambers is a broad commercial set, able and determined to solve problems speedily and to offer a complete service in the commercial field. We aim to respond quickly and efficiently to instructions and in particular to the need for injunctive or other interlocutory relief.

As barristers we feel our special role and expertise is in advocacy, litigation strategy and aiming for the resolution of disputes by the most effective means possible.

C

---

† Recorder ‡ Assistant Recorder *Door Tenant

Specialities of individual members of chambers include: Employment and Industrial Relations law, Intellectual Property and Entertainment, Banking and Insolvency, Commercial Crime and Tax Fraud, Professional Negligence, Defamation, Building and Construction law and Official Referees' Business and Public law and ADR (numerous members CEDR accredited).

Chambers has recently formed Littleton Dispute Resolution Services Ltd to provide a comprehensive and competitive mediation service.

Chambers recognises the requirement to provide a comprehensive and efficient service to both solicitors and lay clients. Barristers are organised into teams, covering all ranges of experience, in the main areas of specialism. Members have embraced new technology, in addition to word processing ability, extensive use is made of electronic mail, disk exchange is operated and video conferencing arranged.

Clerical support is provided through experienced staff structured into specialist functional units. Members of the team are happy to provide guidance and assistance and welcome all inquiries.

Professor Jean-Yves de Cara is an Associate Tenant in Chambers.

LITTMAN CHAMBERS

LITTMAN CHAMBERS
B A R R I S T E R S

12
GRAY'S INN SQUARE

12 Gray's Inn Square, London, WC1R 5JP
020 7404 4866
Fax: 020 7404 4812; DX 0055 Chancery Lane
E-mail: admin@littmanchambers.com
URL: http://www.littmanchambers.com.
Out of hours telephone: 07798 787186 - 01992 421630

Chambers of Mark Littman QC

Clerks: Lee Cutler (Senior Clerk), Stephen Lawrence; Administrator: Karen Raymond

Littman, Mark QC *1947*	**Hewson,** Barbara *1985*
Tackaberry, John QC *1967*†	**Allan,** Monique *1986*
	Naidoo, Seán *1990*
Lewis, Philip *1958**	**Gibson,** Martin *1990*
Stimpson, Michael *1969*	**Higgins,** Rupert *1991*
Finnis, John *1970**	**McCarthy,** Niamh *1991*
Kirk, Robert *1972*	**Anderson,** Julie *1993*
McClure, Brian *1976*	**Falkowski,** Damian *1994*
Planterose, Rowan *1978*	**Hickey,** Alexander *1995*
Kolodziej, Andrzej *1978*	**Roberts,** James *1996*
Tecks, Jonathan *1978*	**Holden,** Richard *1996*

Types of work (and number of counsel practising in that area if supplied)
Administrative · Arbitration · Banking · Bankruptcy · Chancery (general) · Chancery land law · Commercial litigation · Commercial property · Company and commercial · Competition · Construction · Conveyancing · Discrimination · EC and competition law · Employment · Energy · Environment · Equity, wills and trusts · Immigration · Information technology · Insolvency · Insurance · International trade · Landlord and tenant · Partnerships · Private international · Probate and administration · Professional negligence · Sale and carriage of goods · Shipping, admiralty · Telecommunications · Town and country planning

Chambers established: 1980
Opening times: 8.30 am-6.30 pm

Chambers' facilities
Conference rooms, Disks accepted, E-mail

Languages spoken
Afrikaans, Dutch, French, German, Polish, Russian, Spanish

Fees policy
The clerks will be pleased to provide information on the fees by reference to hourly rates. In many cases all–inclusive fees may be fixed in advance. A fee scale showing hourly rates is available upon request.

114 LIVERPOOL ROAD

Islington, London, N1 0RE
0171 226 9863
Fax: 0171 704 1111

Chambers of Mr M Eldridge

235 LONDON ROAD

Twickenham, London, TW1 1ES
0181 892 5947
Fax: 0181 892 5947

Chambers of Mr L S Munasinghe

LUTON BEDFORD CHAMBERS

C/O Mr Alex Reid, 92 Holly Park Road,
Friern Barnet, London, N11 3HB
0181 361 9024/0181 444 6337

Chambers of Miss M A Gee

5 MARNEY ROAD

Battersea, London, SW11 1ES
0171 978 4492
Fax: 0181 679 5037

22 MELCOMBE REGIS COURT

Weymouth Street, London, W1N 3LG
0171 487 5589
Fax: 0171 224 1152
E-mail: fbresler@aol.com

Chambers of Mr Fenton Bresler
Clerk: Frederic Constant

Bresler, Fenton *1951*

1 MIDDLE TEMPLE LANE

Middle Temple Lane

Temple, London, EC4Y 1LT
0171 583 0659 (12 Lines)
Fax: 0171 353 0652; DX 464 London
Other comms: Mobile: 0976 281902
E-mail: chambers@1mtl.co.uk
Out of hours telephone: 01708 641671

**Chambers of Colin Edward Dines, Andrew H
Trollope QC**
*Clerks: John Pyne (Senior Clerk), Clifford
Strong, Richard Vile, Richard Willicombe,*

*Peter Sutherland; Administrator: Stanley
Mott*

Dines, Colin *1970*†	**Kaul**, Kaly *1983*
Trollope, Andrew QC *1971*†	**Amor**, Christopher *1984*
Purnell, Paul QC *1962*†	**Gluckstein**, Emma *1985*
Backhouse, Roger QC *1965***	**Mayo**, Simon *1985*
	Rainsford, Mark *1985*
Ashby, David *1963*	**Marshall**, Andrew *1986*
Gardiner, Nicholas *1967*	**Butcher**, Richard *1985*
Docking, Tony *1969*	**Strachan**, Barbara *1986*
Arran, Graham *1969*†	**Lachkovic**, James *1987*
Browne, Godfree *1971*	**Bowyer**, Harry *1989*
Davies, Jonathan *1971*†	**Korda**, Anthony *1988*
Argyle, Brian *1972*†	**Newton**, Andrew *1989*
Campbell, Andrew *1972*‡	**Chaudhuri**, Avirup *1990*
Hooper, Gopal *1973*†	**Bright**, Rachel *1991*
King, Philip *1974*	**Beynon**, Richard *1990*
Reece, Brian *1974*	**Graffius**, Mark *1990*
Plumstead, John *1975*	**Murphy**, Philomena *1992*
Borrelli, Michael *1977*	**Wong**, Natasha *1993*
Copeman, Ian *1977*	**Jones**, Robert *1993*
Eaton, Bernard *1978*	**Clarke**, Sarah *1994*
Lucas, Noel *1979*‡	**Cammerman**, Gideon *1996*

**Types of work (and number of counsel practising in
that area if supplied)**
Crime 41 · Crime – corporate fraud 25 ·
Immigration 3 · Licensing 3 · Medical
negligence 2 · Personal injury 2

Chambers established: 1976
Opening times: 8.30 am-6.30 pm

Languages spoken
Bengali, French, German

1A MIDDLE TEMPLE LANE

Ground Floor, Temple, London, EC4Y 9AA
0171 353 8815
Fax: 0171 353 8815; DX 200650 Cheam

Chambers of Mrs J S Wallace

2 MIDDLE TEMPLE LANE

3rd Floor, Temple, London, EC4Y 9AA
0171 583 4540
Fax: 0171 583 9178

Chambers of Mr S M Khan

10 MILLFIELDS ROAD

London, E5 OSB
0181 986 8059
Fax: 0181 986 8059

Chambers of Mr M A Syed

1 MITRE COURT BUILDINGS

Temple, London, EC4Y 7BS
0171 797 7070
Fax: 0171 797 7435; DX Chancery Lane 342
E-mail: clerks@1mcb.com
URL: http://www.1mcb.com
Out of hours telephone: 0797 7070 707

Chambers of Bruce Blair QC
Clerks: Richard Beams, Steven McCrone

Blair, Bruce QC 1969†
Horowitz, Michael QC 1968†
Posnansky, Jeremy QC 1972‡
Hughes, Judith QC 1974†
Everall, Mark QC 1975†
Pointer, Martin QC 1976
Mostyn, Nicholas QC 1980‡
Elvidge, John 1968†
Nicholls, Michael 1975
Spon-Smith, Robin 1976†
Le Grice, Valentine 1977
Pope, Heather 1977
Carden, Nicholas 1981
Murfitt, Catriona 1981‡
Smith, Gavin 1981
Dyer, Nigel 1982
Moor, Philip 1982
Todd, Charles 1983
Wood, Christopher 1986
Cusworth, Nicholas 1986
Davidson, Katharine 1987

Todd, Richard 1988
Platts, Rachel 1989
Bishop, Timothy 1991
Kingscote, Geoffrey 1993
Potter, Louise 1993
Trowell, Stephen 1995
Warshaw, Justin 1995
Yates, Nicholas 1996
Webster, Simon 1997
Tyzack, David QC 1970*
Swift, Jonathan 1977*
Bradley, Sally QC 1978*
Hershman, David 1981*
Leong, Jacqueline QC (Hong Kong) 1970*
Ryder, Ernest QC 1981*
Dodds, Stephen 1976*
Kefford, Anthony 1980*
Hodgkin, Harry 1983*
Irving, Gillian 1984*
Bickerdike, Roger 1986*
Smithburn, Prof Eric 1989*

2 MITRE COURT BUILDINGS

2 MITRE COURT BUILDINGS
Barristers' Chambers

1st Floor, Temple, London, EC4Y 7BX
0171 353 1353
Fax: 0171 353 8188; DX 0023 London
Out of hours telephone: 0181 954 9656

Chambers of Roger Gray
Clerks: John H Markham (Senior Clerk), Miss Julie Kempston

O'Donoghue, Florence 1959
Parker, John 1975
Forward, Barry 1981
Gray, Roger 1984
O'Toole, Simon 1984
Holmes-Milner, James 1989
Evans, Delyth 1991
Mehendale, Neelima 1993

McCormack, Philip 1994
Shaw, Michael 1994
Roberts, Matthew John Piers 1994
Parker, Timothy 1995
Latimer-Sayer, William Laurence 1995
Goodwin, Michael 1996
Cooper, Mark 1997

2 MITRE COURT BUILDINGS

2MCB

2nd Floor, Temple, London, EC4Y 7BX
0171 583 1380
Fax: 0171 353 7772; DX 0032 London
E-mail: clerks@2mcb.co.uk
Out of hours telephone: 01372 466348

Chambers of Michael Fitzgerald QC
Clerks: Robert Woods, Frances Kaliszewska, Kirstie Conway, Errol McKenzie; Administrator: Joan Matthewson

Fitzgerald, Michael QC 1961
Widdicombe, David QC 1950
Silsoe, Lord QC 1955

Moriarty, Gerald QC 1951
Anderson, Anthony QC 1964†
Taylor, John QC 1958
Horton, Matthew QC 1969

Roots, Guy QC *1969‡*
Alesbury, Alun *1974*
Fookes, Robert *1975*
Burton, Nicholas *1979*
King, Neil *1980*
Humphries, Michael *1982*
Glover, Richard *1984*

Macpherson, Mary *1984*
Druce, Michael *1988*
Taylor, Reuben *1990*
Moore, Victor *1992*
Boyle, Christopher *1994*
Warren, Rupert *1994*
Wald, Richard Daniel *1997*

MITRE COURT CHAMBERS

3rd Floor, Temple, London, EC4Y 7BP
0171 353 9394
Fax: 0171 353 1488; DX 449 London
E-mail: mitrecourt.com
Out of hours telephone: 0171 353 9394

Chambers of John M Burton
*Clerk: William Ingleton; Practice
Manager: Alistair Adams*

Burton, John *1979*
Shier, Peter *1952*
Ford, Graeme *1972*
Frost, Gillian *1979*
Hofford, Peter *1979*
O'Toole, Bartholomew *1980*
Laban, Alexander *1981*
Wise, Leslie *1985*
Briegel, Pieter *1986*
Bridge, Ian *1988*
Mercer, Neil *1988*
Forsyth, Andrew *1989*

Blake, Christopher *1990*
Hackman, Carl *1990*
Brown, Philip *1991*
Goring, Julia *1991*
Otwal, Mukhtiar *1991*
Espley, Andrew *1993*
Bolton, Lucy *1994*
Glass, Adam *1994*
Newell, Charlotte *1994*
Thorowgood, Max *1995*
Mileham, Felicity *1996*
Williams, Zillah *1997*

Types of work (and number of counsel practising in that area if supplied)
Bankruptcy · Care proceedings · Chancery (general) · Chancery land law · Clinical negligence · Commercial property · Commodities · Common land · Common law (general) · Company and commercial · Construction · Copyright · Crime · Crime – corporate fraud · Discrimination · Ecclesiastical · Employment · Equity, wills and trusts · Family · Family provision · Financial services · Housing · Immigration · Information technology · Insolvency · Insurance · Insurance/reinsurance ·

Landlord and tenant · Licensing · Local government · Mental health · Partnerships · Personal injury · Probate and administration · Professional negligence · Sale and carriage of goods · Sports · Telecommunications · Town and country planning

Opening times: 7.30 am-6.30 pm

Chambers' facilities
Conference rooms, Disks accepted, Conferences out of Chambers

Languages spoken
French, German, Serbo-Croat, Spanish

Fees policy
Up to five years call £50–90, Up to ten years call £90–130, Over ten years call £130–200. Fees within those rates depend upon time engaged, urgency of instructions and complexity. We also accept conditional fees.

MITRE HOUSE CHAMBERS

MITRE
m
HOUSE
CHAMBERS

15-19 Devereux Court, London, WC2R 3JJ
0171 583 8233
Fax: 0171 583 2692; DX 0005 London, Chancery Lane
Out of hours telephone: 0956 316 404

Chambers of F P Gilbert
*Clerk: Osman Avdji; Administrator:
Frances Shaw*

Barry, Joseph *1987*
Bond, Jackie *1994*
Chadwick, Charles *1992*
Cooray, Upali *1974*
Dent, Sally *1989*
Fripp, Eric *1994*
Gilbert, Francis *1980*
Gilling, Denise *1992*
Glanville, Susan *1991*
Henry, Jennifer *1990*
Holloway, Sharon *1994*

Illingworth, Stephen *1993*
Kirby, Ruth *1994*
Lawrenson, Mary *1994*
Lygo, Carl *1991*
McCarthy, Damian *1994*
McCrindell, James *1993*
McVay, Bridget *1990*
Osman, Osman *1995*
Osman, Sona *1986*
Pontac, Sandra *1981*
Raffell, Andrew *1983*

C

Rashid, Jamilla *1996*
Rogers, Donald *1991*
Rohard, Adrian *1993*
Samimi, Maryam *1994*
Steadman, Russell *1995*
Teggin, Victoria *1990*

Toms, Nicholas *1996*
Urquhart, Doris *1967*
Gingell, Melanie *1988**
Thomas, Christine *1991**
Walker, Stuart *1990**

Types of work (and number of counsel practising in that area if supplied)
Administrative 6 · Care proceedings 11 · Chancery (general) 1 · Chancery land law 1 · Charities 1 · Civil liberties 12 · Common law (general) 7 · Construction 1 · Courts martial 2 · Crime 18 · Crime – corporate fraud 6 · Discrimination 4 · EC and competition law 1 · Education 1 · Employment 12 · Environment 2 · Equity, wills and trusts 1 · Family 12 · Family provision 7 · Foreign law 1 · Housing 7 · Immigration 7 · Landlord and tenant 6 · Licensing 3 · Local government 2 · Medical negligence 2 · Mental health 3 · Pensions 2 · Personal injury 10 · Professional disciplinary matters (sols) – CICB · Professional negligence 1

Chambers established: 1984
Opening times: 8.45 am-6.30 pm

Chambers' facilities
Conference rooms, Video facilities

Languages spoken
Farsi, French, German, Hindi, Italian, Sinhala, Spanish, Turkish

Fees policy
Please refer to the clerks.

Additional information
Mitre House is well established as a busy, progressive set with efficient clerking. The main areas of work are criminal defence, family law and civil litigation, which is continuing to expand with a particular emphasis on civil liberties, civil actions against the police, immigration, personal injury, employment, housing and judicial review. A full prospectus of work undertaken by individual tenants is available on request. From the beginning Mitre House has undertaken work free of charge or at a reduced rate in appropriate cases, particularly before tribunals for which legal aid is not available. Chambers provides an informed and reliable service to our professional clients.

MONCKTON CHAMBERS

4 Raymond Buildings, Gray's Inn, London, WC1R 5BP
0171 405 7211
Fax: 0171 405 2084; DX 257 London
E-mail: chambers@monckton.co.uk
URL: http://www.monckton.co.uk
Out of hours telephone: 0973 757979

Chambers of John Swift QC
Clerk: Graham Lister; Chambers Director: Alexandrina le Clezio

Swift, John Anthony QC *1965*
Lever, Jeremy Frederick QC *1957*
Fowler, Richard QC *1969*
Seymour, Richard QC *1972†*
Parker, Kenneth QC *1975*
Lasok, Paul QC *1977*
Roth, Peter QC *1976*
Paines, Nicholas QC *1978*
Vajda, Christopher QC *1979*
Bailey, Edward *1970†*
Pelling, Mark *1979*
Anderson, Rupert *1981*
Patchett-Joyce, Michael *1981*

Hall, Melanie *1982*
Macnab, Andrew *1986*
Turner, Jonathan *1988*
Mantle, Peter *1989*
Thompson, Rhodri *1989*
Skilbeck, Jennifer *1991*
Hill, Raymond *1992*
Simor, Jessica *1992*
Harris, Paul *1994*
Haynes, Rebecca *1994*
Ward, Tim *1994*
Smith, Kassie *1995*
Beard, Daniel *1996*
Peretz, George *1990*
Kemp, David QC *1948**
Forde, Michael SC *1987**

Types of work (and number of counsel practising in that area if supplied)
Administrative 19 · Agriculture 12 · Arbitration 5 · Aviation 1 · Banking 3 · Civil liberties 4 · Commercial 7 · Commercial litigation 17 · Company and commercial 3 · Competition 20 · Construction 8 · Consumer law 5 · Copyright 3 · Crime – corporate fraud 2 · EC and competition law 19 · Employment 10 · Environment 6 · Film, cable, TV 4 · Immigration 2 · Insolvency 3 · Insurance/reinsurance 1 · Intellectual property 1 · International trade 2 · Pensions 2 · Private international 6 · Professional negligence 9 · Public international 6 · Sale and carriage of goods 4 · Sports 11 · Telecommunications 3 · Trademarks 2 · VAT and Customs & Excise 13

Chambers established: 1940
Opening times: 8.30 am-6.30 pm

       † Recorder   ‡ Assistant Recorder   *Door Tenant

Chambers' facilities
Conference rooms, Disks accepted, E-mail

Languages spoken
Dutch, French, German, Japanese

Fees policy
As a general guide Chambers' fees are charged on an hourly rate basis agreed in advance. Hourly rates for each member of Chambers are available upon request. The clerks are happy to discuss other bases for calculating fees and will always try and accommodate the clients' requirements.

MOTTINGHAM BARRISTER'S CHAMBERS

43 West Park, London, SE9 4RZ
0181 857 5565
Fax: 0181 857 5565

Chambers of Mr C A Deve

CHAMBERS OF JANAKI MYLVAGANAM

8B Aristole Road, London, SW4 2HZ
0171 627 4006
Fax: 0171 627 4741

Chambers of Ms J I Mylvaganam

CHAMBERS OF DR JAMAL NASIR

1st Floor, Lincoln's Inn, London, WC2A 3RH
0171 405 3818/9
Fax: 0171 831 1971

Chambers of J J Nasir
Clerk: Mrs A Bianchet

Nasir, Jamal *1948*

NEW COURT

NEW COURT

Temple, London, EC4Y 9BE
0171 583 5123/0510

Fax: 0171 353 3383; DX 0018 London
Out of hours telephone: 0421 830320

Chambers of John Gilmartin
Clerks: Paul Bloomfield, Paul Leahy, James Stammers

Also at: 175 Via Degli Scipioni, 00192 Rome, Italy Tel: 00 3906 322 3893

Gilmartin, John *1972*	**Charlton**, Judith *1991*
Gordon, John *1970*	**Todman**, Deborah *1991*
Randolph, Paul *1971*	**Levy**, Juliette *1992*
Cala, Guiseppe *1971*	**Hasslacher**, James *1993*
Arnold, Robert *1974*	**Taylor**, Nigel *1993*
Kumalo, Dabi *1974*	**Bain**, Giles *1993*
Kingsley, Richard *1977*	**Webb**, Kelly *1993*
Harrison, Michael *1979*	**Powell**, Robin *1993*
Jenkins, Alun *1981*	**Bullock**, Sally *1995*
Whitehouse, Stuart *1987*	**Lewis**, Danielle *1995*
Courtney, Ann *1987*	**Ferris**, Caitlin *1996*
Maynard, Christopher *1988*	**Garrood**, Jeremy *1996*
Livingstone, Douglas *1989*	**Poole**, Christopher *1996*
Lamb, John *1990*	**Hodgkinson**, Stephen *1997*
Laming, Norma *1990*	**Dudley-Jones**, Elizabeth *1997*
Soffa, Helen *1990*	
Rivers, Andrea *1990*	**Sullivan**, Lisa *1997*

Types of work (and number of counsel practising in that area if supplied)
Banking 1 · Bankruptcy 1 · Care proceedings 9 · Chancery (general) 5 · Common law (general) 10 · Crime 13 · Crime – corporate fraud 13 · Employment 5 · Family 12 · Family provision 10 · Foreign law 1 · Housing 5 · Insolvency 1 · Landlord and tenant 6 · Licensing 2 · Medical negligence 6 · Mental health 2 · Personal injury 8 · Probate and administration 2 · Professional negligence 8

Chambers established: 1981
Opening times: 8.30 am-6.30 pm

Chambers' facilities
Conference rooms, Video conferences

Languages spoken
French, German, Italian, Russian

Fees policy
Fees will be negotiated with clerk depending on the case, seniority of counsel and nature of work involved.

C

NEW COURT CHAMBERS

5 Verulam Buildings, Gray's Inn, London, WC1R 5LY
0171 831 9500
Fax: 0171 269 5700; DX 363 London
E-mail: mail@newcourtchambers.com
URL: http://www.newcourtchambers.com

Chambers of George Carman QC
Clerks: Bill Conner (Senior Clerk), Paul Read, Kathryn Jolly, Andrew Burrows, David Poyser

Carman, George QC 1953	Steinert, Jonathan 1986
Reynold, Frederic QC 1960	Davies, Andrew 1988
Susman, Peter QC 1966†	Mangat, Dr Tejina 1990
Howard, Charles QC 1975	Gatty, Daniel 1990
Sarony, Neville QC (Hong Kong) 1964	Donovan, Joel 1991
Knott, Malcolm 1968†	Wagstaffe, Christopher 1992
Clover, Anthony 1971†	Korn, Adam 1992
Pratt, Duncan 1971	Shukla, Vina 1992
Brompton, Michael 1973	Grant, Tom 1993
Stewart, Paul 1975	Overs, Estelle 1994
Carrodus, Gail 1978	Pelling, Alexander 1995
McParland, Michael 1983	Warrender, Nichola 1995
Tomlinson, Hugh 1983	Pliener, David 1996
Bergin, Terence 1985	

Types of work (and number of counsel practising in that area if supplied)
Care proceedings · Civil liberties · Commercial · Commercial property · Common law (general) · Defamation · Discrimination · Employment · Family · Family provision · Information technology · Landlord and tenant · Medical negligence · Personal injury · Probate and administration · Professional negligence · Sports · Travel and holiday law

Chambers established: 1981
Opening times: 8.30 am-6.30 pm (Monday to Friday)

Chambers' facilities
Conference rooms, Video conferences, Disks accepted, Disabled access, E-mail, Accredited by the Law Society as an authorised external course provider

Languages spoken
French, German, Hebrew, Hindi, Nepali

1 NEW SQUARE

Ground Floor, Lincoln's Inn, London, WC2A 3SA
0171 405 0884/5/6/7
Fax: 0171 831 6109 Group 2; DX 295 London
E-mail: clerks@1newsquare.law.co.uk
URL: http://www.1newsquare.law.co.uk

Chambers of Eben W Hamilton QC
Clerks: Warren Lee (0193 2828546), Haydn Powell (0181 301 6546), Justin Brown (0181 347 9690)

Hamilton, Eben QC 1962	Lampard, Kathryn 1984
McDonnell, John QC 1968‡	Eaton Turner, David 1984
Munby, James QC 1971	Graham, Thomas 1985
Hollington, Robin QC 1979	Corbett, Sandra 1988
Stewart-Smith, Rodney 1964†	Wilkins, Colette 1989
	Van Tonder, Gerard 1990
Kennedy, Michael 1967	Hubbard, Mark 1991
Chapple, Malcolm 1975	Eidinow, John 1992
Semken, Christopher 1977	Prentis, Sebastian 1996
Roberts, Michael 1978	Warner, David 1996
Jones, Clive 1981	

Types of work (and number of counsel practising in that area if supplied)
Arbitration 10 · Banking 10 · Bankruptcy 15 · Chancery (general) 19 · Chancery land law 19 · Charities 3 · Commercial property 15 · Common land 10 · Common law (general) 10 · Company and commercial 15 · Competition 2 · Conveyancing 15 · Corporate finance 8 · Employment 2 · Entertainment 5 · Equity, wills and trusts 15 · Family 1 · Housing 1 · Insolvency 15 · Insurance/reinsurance 5 · Intellectual property 2 · Landlord and tenant 19 · Local government 2 · Partnerships 19 · Pensions 2 · Personal injury 1 · Probate and administration 19 · Professional negligence 19 · Share options 15 · Sports 5

The Chambers of
Lord Goodhart Q.C.

3 New Square, Lincoln's Inn, London, WC2A 3RS
Tel: 0171 405 5577 Fax: 0171 404 5032 Dx: 384 London/Chancery Lane
E. Mail: law@threenewsquare.demon.co.uk

3 New Square is a modern commercial chancery set committed to a vigorous tradition of excellence. Advocacy, advice and drafting are available in all areas, with efficient administration.

Members of Chambers

Lord Goodhart Q.C.	Andrew Walker	Adam Deacock
Hubert Picarda Q.C.	Michael Heywood	Justin Holmes
Hedley Marten	Josephine Hayes	Mary Hughes
David Rowell	Thomas Jefferies	Dov Ohrenstein
David Parry	Roger Mullis	Camilla Lamont
Bernard Weatherill Q.C.	Charles Marquand	

Work Undertaken

Commercial: banking, credit and security, competition, contracts, consumer credit, economic torts, finance, franchising, fraud, forgery and misrepresentation, guarantees, partnerships, title retention, restitution and tracing.

Company: companies Court, capital charges, directors' disqualification, directors' duties, liquidation, receiverships, securities, shareholder disputes.

European law: all aspects relating to other work undertaken.

Financial Services: city regulation; tribunals; derivative instruments, prospetuses, investment advertisements.

Insolvency: corporate and personal, including international. Judicial Review

Professional negligence: legal, financial, surveyors and valuers.

Pension Schemes: all aspects of occupational and personal pension schemes; fraud and insolvency.

Property: commercial, agricultural and residential: constructive trusts, conveyancing, easements, highways, landlord and tenant, Lands Tribunal, leasehold valuation tribunals, licences, mortgages and securities, property related torts, restrictive covenants.

Traditional Chancery: Charities, Court of Protection, equitable remedies, fiduciary duties, probate, tax and tax planning (including VAT), trusts & settlements, wills.

Publications

Specific Performance (2nd Ed 1996) by Lord Goodhart QC (with Prof Gareth Jones QC); The Law & Practice Relating to Charities (2nd Ed 1995) by Hubert Picarda QC; The Law Relating to Receivers, Managers & Administrators by Hubert Picarda QC;

Halsbury's Laws of England (4th Ed): Titles on Corporations by Lord Goodhart QC and Charles Marquand; on Money by Charles Marquand and Dov Ohrenstein; Mortgages by Thomas Jefferies, assisted by Camilla Lamont; Specific Perfomance by Lord Goodhart QC; and Receivers by Hubert Picarda QC.

Clerks: Richard Bayliss   Alister Williams   David Bingham

Opening times: 8.30 am-6.30 pm

Chambers' facilities
Conference rooms, Disks accepted, E-mail

Languages spoken
French

CHAMBERS OF LORD GOODHART QC

Ground Floor, 3 New Square, Lincoln's Inn, London, WC2A 3RS
0171 405 5577
Fax: 0171 404 5032; DX 384 London
E-mail: law@threenewsquare.demon.co.uk
Out of hours telephone: 04325 106926

Chambers of Lord Goodhart QC
Clerks: Richard A Bayliss, Alister Williams, David Bingham

Goodhart, Lord QC *1957*	**Jefferies,** Thomas *1981*
Picarda, Hubert QC *1962*	**Mullis,** Roger *1987*
Marten, Hedley *1966*	**Marquand,** Charles *1987*
Rowell, David *1972*	**Deacock,** Adam *1991*
Parry, David *1972†*	**Holmes,** Justin *1994*
Weatherill, Bernard QC *1974‡*	**Hughes,** Mary *1995*
Walker, Andrew *1975*	**Ohrenstein,** Dov *1995*
Heywood, Michael *1975*	**Lamont,** Camilla *1995*
Hayes, Josephine *1980*	**Dowse,** John *1973**

Types of work (and number of counsel practising in that area if supplied)
Agriculture · Banking · Bankruptcy · Chancery (general) · Chancery land law · Charities · Commercial property · Common land · Company and commercial · Conveyancing · Equity, wills and trusts · Family provision · Financial services · Insolvency · Landlord and tenant · Partnerships · Pensions · Probate and administration · Professional negligence · Tax – capital and income

Chambers established: Before 1890
Opening times: 8.30 am-6.30 pm Mon-Fri

Chambers' facilities
Conference rooms, Disks accepted, E-mail

Fees policy
Fees by negotiation, fixed or hourly basis.

3 NEW SQUARE

THREE NEW SQUARE
INTELLECTUAL PROPERTY

Lincoln's Inn, London, WC2A 3RS
0171 405 1111
Fax: 0171 405 7800/404 7802; DX 454 London
E-mail: 3newsquareip@lineone.net
URL: http://website.lineone.net/~3newsquareip
Out of hours telephone: 01582 765502

Chambers of D E M Young QC
Clerk: Ian Bowie

Young, David QC *1966†*	**Birss,** Colin *1990*
Watson, Antony QC *1968*	**Turner,** Justin *1992*
Thorley, Simon QC *1972*	**Campbell,** Douglas *1993*
Miller, Richard QC *1976*	**Mitcheson,** Thomas *1996*
Burkill, Guy *1981*	**Hinchliffe,** Tom *1997*
Waugh, Andrew QC *1982*	**Pritchard,** Geoffrey *1998*
McFarland, Denise *1987*	

Types of work (and number of counsel practising in that area if supplied)
Arbitration 10 · Copyright 13 · EC and competition law 5 · Entertainment 10 · Environment 1 · Film, cable, TV 7 · Franchising 5 · Information technology 4 · Intellectual property 13 · Licensing 4 · Patents 13 · Professional negligence 3 · Sale and carriage of goods 7 · Telecommunications 10 · Trademarks 13

Chambers established: 1940
Opening times: 8.45 am-7.30 pm

Chambers' facilities
Conference rooms, Disks accepted, E-mail

Languages spoken
Japanese

CHAMBERS OF JOHN L POWELL QC

FOUR NEW SQUARE

LINCOLN'S INN

Four New Square, Lincoln's Inn, London, WC2A 3RJ
0171 797 8000

Fax: 0171 797 8001; DX 1041 London
E-mail: barristers@4newsquare.com
URL: http://www.4newsquare.com
Out of hours telephone: 0171 223 7593,
Mobile: 07775 707300

Chambers of J L Powell QC
Clerk: Lizzy Wiseman (Senior Clerk)

Powell, John QC 1974‡	Carr, Sue 1987
Livesey, Bernard QC 1969†	Evans, Hugh 1987
Fenwick, Justin QC 1980‡	Asif, Jalil 1988
Brooke, Michael QC 1968‡	Tettenborn, Prof Andrew
Gibson, Christopher QC 1976	1988
Hughes, Iain QC 1974‡	Sinclair, Fiona 1989
Critchlow, Christopher 1972†	Brown, Nicholas 1989
Lomnicka, Prof Eva 1974	Nicol, Andrew 1991
Russen, Simon 1976	Hubble, Benedict 1992
Douthwaite, Charles 1977	Phipps, Charles 1992
Tyrell, Glen 1977	Sutherland, Paul 1992
Soole, Michael 1977‡	Mulcahy, Leigh-Ann 1993
Hamilton, Gavin 1979	McPherson, Graeme 1993
Kaplan, Barbara 1980	Bijlani, Dr Aisha 1993
Monty, Simon 1982	Shaldon, Nicola 1994
Fodder, Martin 1983	Goldberg, Charlotte 1995
Cannon, Mark 1985	Smith, Jamie 1995
Holtum, Ian 1985	Day, Anneliese 1996
Parker, Paul 1986	Elkington, Ben 1996
Stewart, Roger 1986	Gilmore, Seánin 1996
	Mirchandani, Siân 1997

Types of work (and number of counsel practising in that area if supplied)
Administrative 10 · Arbitration 10 · Banking 1 · Chancery (general) 5 · Commercial litigation 25 · Common law (general) 36 · Company and commercial 4 · Construction 28 · Discrimination 5 · Education 3 · Employment 10 · Environment 10 · Financial services 3 · Insolvency 3 · Insurance 11 · Insurance/reinsurance 11 · Landlord and tenant 6 · Medical negligence 15 · Partnerships 5 · Personal injury 15 · Private international 3 · Professional negligence 36 · Sale and carriage of goods 5 · Town and country planning 3 · Unit trusts 2

Chambers established: 1940
Opening times: 8.30 am-7 pm

Chambers' facilities
Disks accepted, Disabled access, E-mail

Languages spoken
French, German, Hindi, Italian, Spanish

Additional information
The Set: Based for over fifty years in the Temple, chambers will be moving in September 1999 to a larger single site in Lincoln's Inn. This new accommodation will enable chambers to continue to provide a friendly and efficient service at reasonable rates for commercial and other clients.

Types of work undertaken: Chambers has particular expertise in the field of professional liability and covers the full range of claims against professionals, not just negligence, but fraud, breach of fiduciary duty and trust and disciplinary and regulatory proceedings. The main professions covered are accountants and auditors, architects and engineers, solicitors and barristers, financial intermediaries and institutions (including banks, insurance intermediaries, Lloyd's agents, surveyors and valuers and medical practioners). Other major areas of practice include construction and engineering, banking and financial services (including UK, EU and international securities regulation), insurance and reinsurance, employment, commercial litigation, product liability and clinical negligence. Chambers has considerable experience in multi-party litigation in the context of product liability, professional negligence, fraud recovery and disaster claims. In all these areas members of chambers appear as advocates in the courts, arbitrations and overseas.

5 NEW SQUARE

Ground Floor, Lincoln's Inn, London, WC2A 3RJ
020 7404 0404
Fax: 020 7831 6016; DX 272 London
Other comms: Pager: 01426 109206
E-mail: chambers@fivenewsquare.demon.co.uk
URL: http://www.five-new-square.demon.co.uk

Chambers of Jonathan Rayner James QC
Clerks: Ian Duggan, Clive Nicholls, Ian Kitchen

Rayner James, Jonathan QC 1971†	Bragiel, Edward 1977
Garnett, Kevin QC 1975‡	Dickens, Paul ARCO 1978
Sunnucks, James 1950	Michaels, Amanda 1981
Scamell, Ernest 1949	Clark, Julia 1984
Sinclair, Sir Patrick 1961	Caddick, Nicholas 1986
Ross Martyn, John FCIArb 1969†	Harbottle, Gwilym 1987
Stewart, Alexander 1975	Sugar, Simon 1990
	Norris, Andrew 1995
	Abbott, Alistair 1996

7 NEW SQUARE

Lincoln's Inn, London, WC2A 3QS
0171 430 1660
Fax: 0171 430 1531; DX 106 Chancery Lane

Chambers of Mr B Pearl

7 NEW SQUARE

7 NEW SQUARE
Intellectual Property

*1st Floor, Lincoln's Inn, London,
WC2A 3QS*
020 7404 5484
Fax: 020 7404 5369; DX 420 London,
Chancery Lane
E-mail: clerks@7newsquare.com
URL: http://www.7newsquare.com
Out of hours telephone: 020 8856 1077

Chambers of John V Fitzgerald
Clerk: Simon Coomber

Fitzgerald, John *1971*	Fern, Gary *1992*
Firth, Alison *1980*	Davis, Richard *1992*
Kime, Matthew *1988*	Ludbrook, Timothy *1996*
Engelman, Mark *1987*	

8 NEW SQUARE

8
NEW SQUARE
LINCOLN'S INN

Lincoln's Inn, London, WC2A 3QP
0171 405 4321
Fax: 0171 405 9955; DX 379 London,
Chancery Lane
Other comms: Mobile: 07887 763 993
E-mail: clerks@8newsquare.co.uk
URL: http://www.8newsquare.co.uk
Out of hours telephone: 07887 763993

Chambers of M Fysh QC SC
*Clerks: John F Call (Senior Clerk), Tony
Liddon (Deputy Senior Clerk), Nick Wise,*

*Martin Williams, Martin Kilbey, Andrew
Clayton; Administrator: Celia Bond*

Fysh, Michael QC SC *1965*	Onslow, Robert *1991*
Prescott, Peter QC *1970*	Meade, Richard *1991*
Baldwin, John QC *1977*	Speck, Adrian *1993*
Kitchin, David QC *1977*	St Ville, James *1995*
Platts-Mills, Mark QC *1974*	May, Charlotte *1995*
Howe, Martin QC *1978*	Moody-Stuart, Thomas
Vitoria, Mary QC *1975*	*1995*
Hamer, George *1974*	Lane, Lindsay *1996*
Clark, Fiona *1982*	Abrahams, James *1997*
Mellor, James *1986*	Cornish, William Rudolph
Alexander, Daniel *1988*	QC *1965**
Tappin, Michael *1991*	

**Types of work (and number of counsel practising in
that area if supplied)**
Breach of confidence 20 · Competition 20 ·
Copyright 20 · EC and competition law 20 ·
Entertainment 20 · Film, cable, TV 20 ·
Information technology 20 · Intellectual
property 20 · Patents 20 ·
Telecommunications 20 · Trademarks 20

Chambers established: Over 80 years
Opening times: 8.30 am-7 pm

Languages spoken
French, German, Italian, Spanish

Additional information
8 New Square is one of the largest sets in
the UK specialising in intellectual property
and related fields of law. Members of chambers have a very wide range of legal, technical and strategic expertise covering every
aspect of intellectual property and a wide
variety of other cases, especially those
where technical knowledge is of importance. Cases undertaken by members cover
four principal areas:

Intellectual property
Work includes patents, trade and service
marks, copyright (industrial and artistic),
registered and unregistered designs,
passing-off, counterfeiting and trade libel,
confidential information and trade secrets,
technology transfer and licensing, plant
breeders' rights, merchandising, and franchising.

High technology and information technology
This covers biotechnology, data protection
and privacy, technical commercial disputes,
pharmaceutical regulation and licensing,
computers and electronic engineering,
environmental regulation, and public
inquiries.

Media and entertainment

Work undertaken includes performers' rights, television (including cable and satellite), broadcasting, film, literary, musical and artistic copyright litigation, publishing and entertainment contracts and disputes, advertising and marketing.

Competition and EC law

This includes restraint of trade, restrictive trade practices, trade descriptions, competition aspects of intellectual property, EC competition law, and free movement of goods and services.

Several members of chambers are editors of, or contributors to, the leading books and encyclopedias on intellectual property, EC law, and related subjects. All members belong to the Patent Bar Association, Chancery Bar Association, and the Intellectual Property Lawyers Organisation.

Chambers is open from 8.30 am to 7pm Mondays to Fridays but arrangements can be made for conferences and other services outside these hours.

Our senior clerks, John Call and Tony Liddon have each been with chambers over 20 years. They have considerable experience and excellent links with the court administration. They will be happy to assist you in choice of counsel.

Former members of chambers include Mr Justice Jacob and Mr Justice Laddie. Professor William Cornish (Cambridge University) is among the door tenants.

All members of chambers and the clerks have e-mail. Clients are invited to visit our web site for more information on chambers services, and a bulletin board.

CHAMBERS OF JOHN GARDINER QC

1st Floor, 11 New Square, Lincoln's Inn, London, WC2A 3QB
0171 242 4017
Fax: 0171 831 2391; DX 315 London
E-mail: taxlaw@11newsquare.com
URL: http://www.11newsquare.com

Chambers of J R Gardiner QC

Clerks: John Moore (Senior Clerk), John Casey

Gardiner, John QC *1968*	Trevett, Peter QC *1971*

Peacock, Jonathan *1987*	Maugham, Jolyon *1997*
Fitzpatrick, Francis *1990*	

12 NEW SQUARE

Lincoln's Inn, London, WC2A 3SW
0171 419 1212
Fax: 0171 419 1313; DX 366 London
E-mail: chambers@12newsquare.co.uk
Out of hours telephone: 01621 816904

Chambers of W John Mowbray QC

Clerk: Clive Petchey

Also at: Sovereign Chambers, 25 Park Square, Leeds, LS1 2PW Tel: 0113 245 8141 Fax: 0113 242 0194

Mowbray, John QC *1953*	Staddon, Claire *1985*
Macdonald, John QC *1955*	Crail, Ross *1986*
Purle, Charles QC *1970*	Schaw Miller, Stephen
Laurence, George QC *1972‡*	*1988*
	Peacock, Ian *1990*
Mathew, Robin QC *1974*	Adamyk, Simon *1991*
Tucker, Lynton *1971*	Evans-Gordon, Jane *1992*
Braham, Colin *1971*	Terras, Nicholas *1993*
Russell, Christopher *1971*	Davies, Louise *1995*
Munro, Kenneth *1973*	Simpson, Edwin *1990*
Bennett, Gordon *1974*	Buckley, Richard *1969*
Le Poidevin, Nicholas *1975*	Elleray, Anthony QC *1977**
Barber, Stuart *1979*	Sterling, Robert *1970**
Hargreaves, Sara *1979*	Birch, Roger *1979**
Smith, Stephen *1983*	Cawson, Mark *1982**
Sagar, Leigh *1983*	

Types of work (and number of counsel practising in that area if supplied)

Administrative 4 · Arbitration 24 · Banking 8 · Bankruptcy 6 · Chancery (general) 24 · Chancery land law 24 · Charities 5 · Civil liberties 3 · Commercial litigation 19 · Commercial property 20 · Common land 5 · Company and commercial 24 · Conveyancing 10 · Corporate finance 4 · Crime – corporate fraud 8 · Entertainment 6 · Environment 7 · Equity, wills and trusts 13 · Family provision 10 · Financial services 7 · Foreign law 10 · Information technology 3 · Insolvency 18 · Insurance 6 · Insurance/reinsurance 6 · Intellectual property 2 · International trade 9 · Landlord and tenant 24 · Local government 8 · Medical negligence 4 · Mental health 2 · Parliamentary 3 · Partnerships 24 · Pensions 6 · Private international 7 · Probate and administration 8 · Professional negligence 24 · Public international 3 · Sale and carriage of goods 6 · Sports 4 · Tax – capital

C

and income 4 · Tax – corporate 4 · Town and country planning 9 · Unit trusts 2

Opening times: 8.30 am-7 pm

Chambers' facilities
Conference rooms, Disks accepted, E-mail

Languages spoken
French, German

Fees policy
Before any work is undertaken, the clerks will if requested give an estimate of the fee for a particular set of papers and of how long the work is likely to take.

Additional information
12 New Square undertakes litigation and advisory work; both in the UK and internationally, including direct professional access and legal aid work. The set acts for corporate clients, local authorities and individuals.

The work of chambers centres on company, commercial and property litigation and includes arbitration, personal and corporate insolvency, civil aspects of commercial fraud, intellectual property, landlord and tenant, building societies and mortgages, construction, freezing injunctions and search orders, partnership disputes, trusts, equity, pension schemes, capital taxation and professional negligence, including public/administrative law aspects of these areas. Such work covers judicial review of actions by central and local government, constitutional law, human rights, environmental law, highways, Public Inquiries and the promotion of, or petitioning against, private bills in Parliament.

The practice is international, with members having advised, conferred or negotiated in New York, Washington, Detroit, Toronto, Santo Domingo, Berlin and Geneva. In human rights cases, members have represented Soviet dissidents, the people of Ocean Island, Canadian Indians and the Illois who were removed from Diego Garcia to make way for a US base. Members have appeared in courts in the Bahamas, Antigua, Zurich, the Cayman Islands, Hong Kong, British Virgin Islands, and before the European Court of Human Rights at Strasbourg. John Mowbray QC is a member of the Bahamian Bar and he has also been called to the Eastern Caribbean Bar as have John Macdonald QC, Charles Purle QC,

Stephen Smith and Nicholas Terras. Nicholas Le Poidevin is a member of the Isle of Man Bar. In London the set has worked with lawyers from all parts of the world.

John Mowbray QC, Lynton Tucker, Nicholas Le Poidevin and Edwin Simpson are currently preparing the 17th edition of *Lewin on Trusts*. George Laurence QC and Ross Crail are on the editorial board of *Rights of Way Law Review*. Jane Evans-Gordon wrote the Property chapter of *Cohabitation – Law and Precedents*. She also co-wrote the Wills and Intestacy chapter.

12 New Square chambers aims to provide a speedy and efficient service. A brochure, which includes a variety of reported cases in many different fields, is available on request or via our web site: www.12newsquare.co.uk. For further information please contact the Senior Clerk.

NORTH LONDON CHAMBERS

14 Keyes Road, London, NW2 3XA
0181 208 4651
Fax: 0181 208 2075

Chambers of Mr T D Putnam

ODOGOR CHAMBERS

14 Cairns Road, Battersea, London, SW11 1ES

Chambers of Mr N D A Ezechie

CHAMBERS OF JOY OKOYE

Suite 1, 2nd Floor Gray's Inn Chambers, Gray's Inn, London, WC1R 5JA
0171 405 7011
Fax: 0171 405 7012; DX 442 LDE

Chambers of Joy Okoye

Types of Work
Use the types of work listings in Parts A and B to locate chambers and individual barristers who specialise in particular areas of work.

19 OLD BUILDINGS

Lincoln's Inn, London, WC2A 3UP
0171 405 2001
Fax: 0171 405 0001; DX 397 London
E-mail: clerks@oldbuildingsip.com
URL: http://www.oldbuildingsip.com

Chambers of A J D Wilson QC
Clerk: Barbara Harris

Reed, Jeremy Nigel *1997*
Holman, Tamsin *1995*
Sullivan, Rory *1992*
Puckrin, Cedric *1990*
Colley, Peter *1989*

Wilson, Alastair QC *1968†*
Shipley, Graham *1973*
Reid, Brian *1971*
Hicks, Michael *1976*

22 OLD BUILDINGS

Lincoln's Inn, London, WC2A 3UJ
0171 831 0222
Fax: 0171 831 2239; DX 201 Chancery Lane
Out of hours telephone: 0181 658 6869
(mobile: 0374 757701) (Alan Brewer)

Chambers of Mr B A Hytner QC
*Clerks: Alan Brewer (London), Peter
Collison (Manchester)*

Also at: All the silks are based at 25 Byrom
Street, Manchester and all the juniors at 22
Old Buildings, Lincoln's Inn

Hytner, Benet QC *1952*
Price, John QC *1961*
Wingate-Saul, Giles QC *1967*
Leveson, Brian QC *1970*
Scholes, Rodney QC *1968*
King, Timothy QC *1973*
Tattersall, Geoffrey QC *1970*
Swift, Caroline QC *1977*
Moran, Andrew QC *1976*

Allan, David QC *1974*
Black, Michael QC *1978*
Stewart, Stephen QC *1975*
Hamlin, Patrick *1970†*
Batchelor, Mark *1971*
Cooper, Susan *1976*
Daiches, Michael *1977*
Ralphs, Anne *1977‡*
Utley, Charles *1979*
Hill, Jane *1980*
Lederman, Howard *1982*

19 Old Buildings

One of the few dedicated intellectual property sets, all tenants are members of the Intellectual Property Bar Association and most have degrees or higher level qualifications in scientific, computing or mathematical disciplines. The work of Chambers covers every aspect of advice and litigation relating to the following:

Intellectual Property – patents, copyright, designs, moral rights, trade marks, passing off, confidential information;

Science and Technology – cases with scientific or technical issues, including contractual disputes, inquiries, applications for licences or registrations, and other litigation;

Computers and Information Technology – including data protection and internet disputes;

Entertainment and Media – publishing, public performance, film and recording rights, broadcasting, cable and satellite distribution, rights of performers, and merchandising;

EU Competition and Free Trade – particularly relating to intellectual property, research and development, employment contracts, franchising and distribution and restraint of trade.

Members of Chambers appear before a wide variety of Courts, the Patent Office and Trade Mark Registry, and other tribunals in London and elsewhere in the UK. Some tenants also have experience in the European Patent Office and the European Court of Justice.

Publications include *European Patent Office Reports, Melville on Forms and Licensing* and *A Practical Guide to Patent Law* amongst many others.

---

† Recorder ‡ Assistant Recorder *Door Tenant

Azim, Rehna *1984*	**Oudkerk,** Daniel *1992*
Bennett, Jonathan *1985*	**Uduje,** Benjamin *1992*
Sahonte, Rajinder *1986*	**Horan,** John *1993*
Cook, Tina *1988*	**McCourt,** Christopher *1993*
Chapman, Simon *1988*	**Hutchings,** Matthew *1993*
Feehan, Frank *1988*	**Hawkes,** Naomi *1994*
Taylor, Gemma *1988*	**Nuvoloni,** Stefano *1994*
Berry, Nicholas *1988*	**Woodward-Carlton,**
Coster, Ronald *1989*	Damian *1995*
Jerman, Anthony *1989*	**Thomas,** Anna *1995*
Arnot, Lee *1990*	**Withington,** Angus *1995*
Furniss, Richard *1991*	**Pitchers,** Henry *1996*
Lazarus, Mary *1991*	**Compton,** Gareth *1997*
Lonergan, Paul *1991*	**Watkin,** Toby Paul *1996*
Hyde, Marcia *1992*	**Gardner,** Eilidh *1997*

Types of work (and number of counsel practising in that area if supplied)
Administrative 10 · Bankruptcy 8 · Care proceedings 25 · Chancery (general) 10 · Chancery land law 5 · Common law (general) 23 · Company and commercial 8 · Construction 5 · Conveyancing 4 · Education 6 · Employment 10 · Environment 8 · Family 20 · Family provision 20 · Housing 10 · Insolvency 8 · Insurance 5 · Landlord and tenant 15 · Licensing 8 · Local government 10 · Medical negligence 7 · Mental health 4 · Partnerships 6 · Personal injury 24 · Professional negligence 22 · Sale and carriage of goods 15 · Town and country planning 6

Opening times: 8.30 am-6.30 pm

Chambers' facilities
Conference rooms, Disks accepted, Disabled access

Languages spoken
French, Italian

TWENTY-FOUR OLD BUILDINGS

XXIV
Twenty Four
Old Buildings

Ground Floor, Lincoln's Inn, London, WC2A 3UP
0171 404 0946
Fax: 0171 405 1360; DX 307 London

Other comms: Lix: Lon 073; Link: Jeremy Hopkins
E-mail: clerks@24oldbuildings.law.co.uk
URL: http://www.24oldbuildings.law.co.uk
Out of hours telephone: 0374 240 112

Chambers of Martin Mann QC, Alan Steinfield QC
Clerks: Nicholas Luckman (Senior Clerk), Jeremy Hopkins (First Junior); Administrator: Marshall Thomson; Listing: Christopher Lane; Fees Administration: Tony Steeden

Mann, Martin QC *1968*†	**Moverley Smith,** Stephen *1985*
Steinfeld, Alan QC *1968*	
Kaye, Roger QC *1970*†	**Galley,** Helen *1987*
Cohen, Lawrence QC *1974*†	**Francis,** Adrian *1988*
Baxendale, Thomas *1962*	**Harington,** Amanda *1989*
King, Michael *1971*	**Talbot Rice,** Elspeth *1990*
Shepherd, Philip *1975*‡	**Cherryman,** Nicholas *1991*
Teverson, Paul *1976*	**Young,** Christopher *1988*
Davies, John *1977*	**Stanley,** Clare *1994*
Ritchie, Richard *1978*	**Adair,** Stuart *1995*
Tregear, Francis *1980*	**Shah,** Bajul *1996*
Gadd, Michael *1981*	**Thompson,** Steven *1996*
Gerrans, Daniel *1981*	**Chappell,** Jessica *1997*
Weaver, Elizabeth *1982*	**Staff,** Marcus *1994**
	Virgo, Graham *1989**

Types of work (and number of counsel practising in that area if supplied)
Aviation 2 · Banking 3 · Bankruptcy 26 · Chancery (general) 26 · Chancery land law 26 · Commercial litigation 24 · Commercial property 26 · Common land 3 · Company and commercial 26 · Conveyancing 3 · Ecclesiastical 1 · Entertainment 5 · Equity, wills and trusts 12 · Family 5 · Family provision 5 · Financial services 7 · Insolvency 24 · Landlord and tenant 26 · Partnerships 25 · Pensions 5 · Probate and administration 10 · Professional negligence 23 · Share options 1 · Town and country planning 1

Chambers established: 1968
Opening times: 8 am-7 pm

Chambers' facilities
Conference rooms, Disks accepted, E-mail, Link, Lix

Languages spoken
French, Italian, Spanish

Fees policy
Under three years call £35–100, three to five years call £100–125, five to ten years call £125–175. Chambers adopts a flexible and open approach to fees and all areas of

† Recorder ‡ Assistant Recorder *Door Tenant

administration. Fees are charged either on a time–costed or inclusive 'global' basis. Estimates can be provided or limits agreed prior to work being undertaken.

Additional information
24 Old Buildings is an established chambers, specialising in advising on and conducting litigation across a broad range of commercial and Chancery work. Members of chambers are instructed by large and small firms both in London and the provinces, acting for a wide range of clients from major financial institutions to legally-aided individuals.

Members include Martin Mann QC, Alan Steinfeld QC and Roger Kaye QC, who sit as Deputy Judges in the Chancery Division of the High Court. Richard Ritchie is Standing Counsel to the Department of Trade and Industry (Insolvency) and Junior Counsel to the Crown (Chancery). Stephen Moverley Smith is Junior Counsel to the Crown (Chancery).

Members appear in the civil courts (particularly the High Court Chancery and Queen's Bench Divisions – including Commercial Court and Official Referees – and county courts throughout the UK), tribunals (including Insolvency Practitioners and the Institute of Chartered Accountants) and overseas courts (including the Cayman Islands, the British Virgin Islands, Bermuda, Hong Kong, Singapore, Malaysia and the Turks and Caicos). Chambers has connections in New York, Geneva, Rome and Milan.

24 OLD BUILDINGS

First Floor, Lincoln's Inn, London, WC2A 3UP
020 7242 2744
Fax: 020 7831 8095; DX 386 London
E-mail: taxchambers@compuserve.com

Chambers of G R Bretten QC
Clerk: Anthony Hall

Bretten, George QC *1965*	**Lyons**, Timothy *1980*
Venables, Robert QC *1973*	**Kessler**, James *1984*
Brandon, Stephen QC *1978*	**Ghosh**, Julian *1993*
Argles, Guy *1965*	**Hardy**, Amanda *1993*
Sokol, Christopher *1975*	

9 OLD SQUARE

Ground Floor, Lincoln's Inn, London, WC2A 3SR
0171 405 4682
Fax: 0171 831 7107; DX 305 London
Other comms: Lix: Lon 069
E-mail: chambers@9oldsquare.co.uk
Out of hours telephone: 0777 553 1524/ 01474 333 719

Chambers of Michael Driscoll QC
Clerk: Christopher McSweeney (Senior Clerk)

Driscoll, Michael QC *1970*	**Leech**, Thomas *1988*
Patten, Nicholas QC *1974*	**Holland**, Katharine *1989*
Jackson, Judith QC *1975*	**Stoner**, Christopher *1991*
Berry, Simon QC *1977*	**Walker**, Andrew P D *1991*
Hodge, David QC *1979*	**Burrell**, Simon *1988*
Hochberg, Daniel *1982*	**Pryor**, Michael *1992*
Dagnall, John *1983*	**Johns**, Alan *1994*
McGhee, John *1984*	**Tozer**, Stephanie *1996*
Harry, Timothy *1983*	**Norris**, William V W *1997*
Johnson, Edwin *1987*	**Clarke**, Paul Sebastian *1997*

Types of work (and number of counsel practising in that area if supplied)
Administrative · Agriculture · Arbitration · Banking · Bankruptcy · Chancery (general) · Chancery land law · Charities · Commercial property · Common land · Common law (general) · Company and commercial · Conveyancing · Energy · Environment · Equity, wills and trusts · Family provision · Financial services · Insolvency · Landlord and tenant · Local government · Partnerships · Probate and administration · Professional negligence · Sports · Tax – capital and income

Opening times: 8.30 am-6.30 pm

Languages spoken
French, German, Spanish

Additional information
9 Old Square is a modern set of Chancery chambers specialising in a wide range of

commercial and property litigation. All members of chambers have expertise in real property, professional negligence, landlord and tenant and securities. Other areas of expertise include banking, insolvency, company and partnership disputes, trusts, judicial review and local government, sports law, minerals and mining.

Members of chambers accept direct instructions from recognised professional clients and carry out Legal Aid work, and they appear in courts, tribunals and arbitrations in the UK and overseas.

Further details and a brochure can be obtained from the Senior Clerk.

THE CHAMBERS OF LEOLIN PRICE CBE, QC

10 OLD SQUARE

10 Old Square, Lincoln's Inn, London, WC2A 3SU
0171 405 0758
Fax: 0171 831 8237; DX 306 London

Chambers of Leolin Price CBE QC
Clerk: Keith Plowman

Price, Leolin QC CBE 1949
Bonney, James QC 1975
Mello, Michael J QC (Bermuda) 1972
Rossdale, Philip 1948
Ainger, David 1961
Barlow, Francis 1965
Ritchie, David 1970
Burton, Frances 1970*
Hill, Gregory 1972
Wallington, Richard 1972
Newsom, George 1973*
Price, Jeffrey 1975*
Schmitz, David 1976
Rhys, Owen 1976
Thomas, Geraint 1976*
Taube, Simon 1980
De La Rosa, Andrew 1981
Michell, Michael 1984
Stafford, Dr Paul 1987
Partington, David 1987*
Roberts, Julian (Rechtsanwelt) 1987
Meadway, Susannah 1988
Rajah, Eason 1989
D'Cruz, Rupert 1989
Callman, Jeremy 1991
Gavaghan, Jonathan 1992
Laughton, Samuel 1993
Farrelly, Kevin 1993
Waterworth, Michael 1994
Norbury, Luke 1995
Harries, Nicholas 1995
Arnfield, Robert 1996
Price, Evan David Lewis 1997

11 OLD SQUARE

Ground Floor, Lincoln's Inn, London, WC2A 3TS
0171 242 5022/405 1074
Fax: 0171 404 0445; DX 164 London
Out of hours telephone: 0181 462 1917

Chambers of Simeon Thrower
Clerk: Christopher Watts

Thrower, Simeon 1973
Quint, Francesca 1970
Cutting, Christopher 1973
Mydeen, Kalandar 1973
Wellesley-Cole, Patrice 1975
Apsion, Robert 1977
Sinclair, Malcolm 1978
Macleod-James, Nicholas 1986
Maitland, Marc 1988
Lloyd, John 1988
Gray, Jennifer 1992
Buttimore, Gabriel 1993
Ball, Steven 1995
MacLennan, Alison 1996

11 OLD SQUARE

⑪ OLD SQUARE

Ground Floor, Lincoln's Inn, London, WC2A 3TS
020 7430 0341
Fax: 020 7831 2469; DX 1031 London
E-mail: clerks@11oldsquare.co.uk
URL: http://www.11oldsquare.co.uk

Chambers of Grant Crawford & Jonathan Simpkiss
Clerks: K Nagle, A Downey; Administrator: Isobel Gurrie

Ellis, Carol QC 1951
Davidson, Edward QC 1966
Nurse, Gordon 1973
Crawford, Grant 1974
Simpkiss, Jonathan 1975
Smith, Peter QC 1975*†
Harrison, Reziya 1975
Waters, Malcolm QC 1977
Acton, Stephen 1977
Ovey, Elizabeth 1978
Rowley, Keith 1979
Thomas, Siân 1981
Campbell, Glenn 1985
West, Mark 1987
McQuail, Katherine 1989
Burroughs, Nigel 1991
Dodge, Peter 1992
Oakley, Tony 1994
Davey, Benjamin 1994
Sandells, Nicole 1994
Selway, Kate 1995
Hall Taylor, Alex 1996
Bowmer, Michael 1997

Types of work (and number of counsel practising in that area if supplied)
Agriculture 1 · American law 1 · Arbitration 2 · Bahamas law 1 · Banking 7 · Bankruptcy 7 · Chancery (general) 22 · Chancery land law 22 · Charities 9 · Commercial property 11 · Common law (general) 6 · Company

and commercial 8 · Conveyancing 11 · Copyright 1 · Ecclesiastical 1 · Equity, wills and trusts 13 · Family provision 10 · Financial services 1 · Housing 2 · Insolvency 8 · Intellectual property 1 · Landlord and tenant 13 · Mines and minerals 1 · Partnerships 10 · Pensions 6 · Probate and administration 11 · Professional negligence 12 · Tax – capital and income 2 · Trademarks 1

Opening times: 9 am-6.30 pm

Chambers' facilities
Disks accepted

Languages spoken
French, Spanish

Additional information
Chambers covers a wide range of Chancery, company and commercial work, with an emphasis towards advice and litigation in both the Chancery and Queen's Bench Divisions. Junior members of chambers also appear frequently in the county court. Chambers' work includes:

Real property and the sale of land
Mortgages; landlord and tenant (including rent reviews, agricultural tenancies and leasehold enfranchisement); easements; nuisance and other property-related torts; covenants and licences affecting land.

Commercial work
Contracts (including sale of goods); economic torts; restraint of trade; abuse of confidence; copyright; passing-off; equitable doctrines and remedies including tracing, resulting and constructive trusts, Mareva and Anton Piller orders and other injunctions; banking; securities and guarantees; insurance; mortgage and other financial or security-related frauds.

Company law and insolvency
Shareholder and other company disputes; corporate insolvency including administration, receivership, and liquidation; partnership; and bankruptcy.

Professional negligence
Involving solicitors, barristers, accountants, surveyors, financial advisers and intermediaries, and others.

Trusts, charities and administration of estates
Creation, administration, and variation of trusts; wills and probate; family provision.

Members of chambers also undertake work involving building societies including their constitution and powers, relations with members and third parties, mergers, takeovers, and conversion and standard form documentation; financial services; capital taxation; pension schemes; judicial review; and interest rate swaps.

Jonathan Simpkiss and Reziya Harrison are Fellows of the Chartered Institute of Arbitrators. All members of chambers accept instructions under the direct professional access arrangements.

Malcolm Waters, Elizabeth Ovey and Kate Selway are the editors of *Wurtzburg & Mills on Building Society Law*. Malcolm Waters and Elizabeth Ovey wrote the commentary to the Building Societies Act 1986 in *Current Law Statutes*.

Publications:

Mark West
Chapter 4, *Swaps and Local Authorities: A Mistake?* Mark West and Catherine Newman QC in: *Swaps and Off-Exchange Derivatives Trading: Law and Regulation*, Editors: Eric Bettelheim, Helen Parry and William Rees, FT Law & Tax (1996).

Reziya Harrison FCI (Arb)
Good Faith in Sales, Sweet & Maxwell (1997).

Tony Oakley
Constructive Trusts, Sweet & Maxwell (3rd edn 1997) *Parker & Mellows The Modern Law of Trusts*, Sweet & Maxwell (7th edn 1998).

Nicole Sandells
Pending – Lifetime Gifts, Jordans (1999) Co-Author.

12 OLD SQUARE

1st Floor, Lincoln's Inn, London,
WC2A 3TX
0171 404 0875
Fax: 0171 404 3877; DX 130 London

Chambers of Miss C Boaitey

13 OLD SQUARE

Ground Floor, Lincoln's Inn, London,
WC2A 3UA
0171 404 4800
Fax: 0171 405 4267; DX 326 London
E-mail: clerks@13oldsquare.law.co.uk
URL: http://www.13oldsquare.co.uk
Out of hours telephone: 01992 441374/
445142

Chambers of Michael Lyndon-Stanford QC
Clerk: John C Moore

Lyndon-Stanford, Michael QC *1962*	**Trace,** Anthony QC *1981*
McCall, Christopher QC *1966*	**Girolami,** Paul *1983*
Oliver, David QC *1972*	**Collings,** Matthew *1985*
Williamson, Hazel QC *1972†*	**Nicholls,** John *1986*
McCombe, Richard QC *1975†*	**Walton,** Carolyn *1980*
Thomas, Nigel *1976*	**Russen,** Jonathan *1986*
Pymont, Christopher QC *1979*	**Morgan,** Richard *1988*
Newman, Catherine QC *1979‡*	**Peacock,** Nicholas *1989*
Evans, Timothy *1979*	**Banner,** Gregory *1989*
Barker, Simon *1979‡*	**Tipples,** Amanda *1991*
Cunningham, Mark *1980*	**Gibbon,** Michael *1993*
	Stubbs, Rebecca *1994*
	Aldridge, James *1994*
	Ayres, Andrew *1996*
	Swerling, Robert *1996*
	Lipstein, Kurt QC *1950**
	Shankardass, Vijay *1972**

OLD SQUARE CHAMBERS

OLD SQUARE CHAMBERS

1 Verulam Buildings, Gray's Inn, London,
WC1R 5LQ
0171 269 0300
Fax: 0171 405 1387; DX 1046 London

E-mail: clerks@oldsquarechambers.co.uk
URL: http://www.oldsquarechambers.co.uk
Out of hours telephone: 0973 330793

Chambers of The Hon J M Williams QC, (John Hendy QC from Jan 2000)
Clerks: John Taylor, William Meade,
Andrew York, Robert Bocock, Oliver
Parkhouse, David Portch

Also at: Old Square Chambers, Hanover House, 47 Corn Street, Bristol Tel: 0117 9277111 Fax: 0117 9273478

Williams, The Hon John QC *1955†*	**Cotter,** Barry *1985*
Hendy, John QC *1972*	**Chudleigh,** Louise *1987*
Hand, John QC *1972†*	**Omambala,** Ijeoma *1989*
Wedderburn of Charlton, Lord QC *1953*	**Eady,** Jennifer *1989*
McMullen, Jeremy QC *1971†*	**Mead,** Philip *1989*
Truscott, Ian QC (Scot) *1995*	**Brown,** Damian *1989*
Kelly, Matthias QC *1979*	**Clarke,** Jonathan *1990*
Lewis, Charles *1963*	**Gill,** Tess *1990*
Carling, Christopher *1969*	**Walker,** Christopher *1990*
Birtles, William *1970†*	**Booth,** Nicholas *1991*
Brahams, Diana *1972*	**Moor,** Sarah *1991*
Bates, John *1973*	**Scott,** Ian *1991*
Cooksley, Nigel *1975*	**Segal,** Oliver *1992*
Makey, Christopher *1975*	**Gower,** Helen *1992*
Pugh, Charles *1975*	**Lewis,** Prof Roy *1992*
Kempster, Toby *1980*	**Whitcombe,** Mark *1994*
Rose, Paul *1981*	**Melville,** Elizabeth *1994*
McNeill, Jane *1982*	**Tether,** Melanie *1995*
	Smith, Emma *1995*
	Pirani, Rohan *1995*
	Birkett, Peter QC *1972**

Types of work (and number of counsel practising in that area if supplied)
Administrative · Arbitration · Chancery (general) · Civil liberties · Clinical negligence 12 · Commercial litigation · Construction · Discrimination · EC and competition law · Education · Employment 29 · Environment 12 · Personal injury 25 · Product liability 10 · Professional negligence · Sports

Chambers established: 1986
Opening times: 8.30 am-7 pm

Chambers' facilities
Conference rooms, Computer/phone link to Bristol/London

Languages spoken
Dutch, French, Ibo, Italian, Spanish

Fees policy
Fees are calculated by a variety of methods.

Hourly rates, size and complexity of the case and counsels' seniority are all taken into consideration as are the clients' means. We aim to be flexible and practical in our approach to fees and offer a range of counsel experienced in our specialisms. Members of chambers undertake pro bono work mainly through the DDARAP and ELAAS and Bar Pro Bono Unit schemes. In relation to personal injury and CFAs we currently adopt the latest APIL/PIBA III agreement. This extends to clinical negligence work. We continue to accept Legal Aid work wherever it is available. For work in Bristol and the South West, fees are calculated on the basis of travel time and cost from Bristol and not London whether counsel are based in Bristol or London.

Types of work undertaken
Employment Law Chambers boasts several of the UK's leading specialists in this field. Cases involve all aspects of individual and collective employment law including interpretation of EU directives.

All forms of **Personal Injury** work are covered and we have specialists in all areas of the work. We have particular expertise in disaster litigation and complex multi-party actions. Recent matters handled have included the VWF litigation and the Guards and Shunters Deafness litigation. Members of chambers have acted as consultants to the EC on the implementation of European health and safety directives in the UK.

Environmental work includes statutory appeals, scientifically complex nuisance and personal injury claims, prosecution and defence work, as well as judicial review. Other areas of expertise include water law, contaminated land, and the application of European law.

The **Product Liability** special interest group has advised a large number of companies, local authorities, individuals and specialist associations with regard to virtually all aspects of civil and criminal liability in respect of defective and unsafe products.

Sports Law is another area in which members of chambers have represented various clubs and other sporting bodies as well as individual sports people.

Seminars are provided in both London and Bristol, (Law Society accredited for CPD). Members regularly feature at professionally organised conferences and many are respected authors in their area of specialisation. Brochure available on request.

THE OUTER TEMPLE

Room 26, 222/225 Strand, London, WC2R 1BQ
0171 353 4647
Fax: 0171 353 4655

Chambers of Mr P M Hayward

90 OVERSTRAND MANSIONS

Prince of Wales Drive, London, SW11 4EU
0171 622 7415
Fax: 0171 622 6929

Chambers of Mr D Hood

ONE PAPER BUILDINGS

ONE PAPER BUILDINGS

Ground Floor, Temple, London, EC4Y 7EP
0171 583 7355
Fax: 0171 353 2144; DX 80 London
Other comms: Voice Mail: 0171 583 1004;
Lix: Lon 070
E-mail: clerks@1pb.co.uk
Out of hours telephone: 01689 816767
Julian Campbell Home No or Mobile 0797 197 5613

Chambers of Michael Spencer QC
Clerks: Julian Campbell, Mark Walter, Kevin McCourt, Paul Greatorey, David Edwards; Administrator: Lea Hudson

Spencer, Michael QC *1970†*	**Bickford-Smith,** Margaret *1973†*
Slater, John QC *1969†*	
Bartlett, Andrew QC *1974*	**Nixon,** Colin *1973*
Brown, Simon QC *1976*	**Davies,** Nicholas *1975*
Powers, Michael QC *1979*	**Powles,** John *1975*
Stevenson, William QC *1968†*	**Waite,** Jonathan *1978*
	Catford, Gordon *1980*
Hone, Richard QC *1970†*	**Field,** Julian *1980*
Berkin, Martyn *1966*	**Davies,** Jane *1981*

Coles, Steven *1983*
Franklin, Kim *1984*
Medd, James *1985*
Ferris, Shaun *1985*
Platt, David *1987*
Egan, Marion *1988*
Vandyck, William *1988*
Power, Erica *1990*
Newman, Benedict *1991*

Gee, Toby *1992*
Antelme, Alexander *1993*
Branthwaite, Margaret *1993*
Toogood, Claire *1995*
Haque, Mohammed *1997*
Lindsey, Susan *1997*
Quiney, Ben *1998*

1 PAPER BUILDINGS

1st Floor, Temple, London, EC4Y 7EP
0171 353 3728/4953
Fax: 0171 353 2911; DX 332 London

Chambers of R N Titheridge QC

2 PAPER BUILDINGS

1st Floor, Temple, London, EC4Y 7ET
020 7556 5500
Fax: 020 7583 3423; DX LDE 494
E-mail: clerks@2pbbarristers.co.uk
URL: http://www.2pbbarristers.co.uk
Out of hours telephone: 0860 416061

Chambers of Desmond de Silva QC
Clerks: Robin Driscoll (Senior Clerk), Stephen Ball, Lynn Pilkington, Marc Jennings (Fees Clerk), Joel Mason; Administrator: Marc Jennings

de Silva, Desmond QC *1964*
Richard, Lord QC *1955*
Salts, Nigel QC *1961*
de Silva, Harendra QC *1970†*
Massih, Michel QC *1979*
Kothari, Vasant *1960*
Zorbas, Panaylotis Christophorou *1964*
Martin, Peter *1969*
Lewis, Raymond *1971*

Pearse Wheatley, Robin *1971†*
Corrigan, Peter *1972*
Hoon, Notu *1975*
Johnson, Roderick *1975*
O'Donovan, Paul *1975*
Sutton-Mattocks, Chris *1975*
Strachan, Chris *1975*
Hayes, Jerry *1977*
Cahill, Patrick *1979*
Hollis, Kim *1979*

Campbell, Colin *1979*
Brock, David *1984*
Ward, Simon *1984*
Karu, Lee *1985*
Femi-Ola, John *1985*
McCoy, Gerard QC (Hong Kong) *1986*
Berrick, Steven *1986*
Baxter, Sharon *1987*
Folkes, Sandra *1989*
Benson, Charles *1990*
Martin, Zoe *1990*
Samat, Daren *1992*
Henderson, Fiona *1993*
Mylvaganam, Paul *1993*

D'Souza, Dominic *1993*
Brassington, Stephen *1994*
Kearney, John *1994*
Panayi, Pavlos *1995*
Tilbury, James *1996*
Summers, Mark *1996*
Durose, David William *1996*
Williams, Mark *1996*
Meek, Susan *1997*
Hinchcliffe, Doreen *1953**
Read, James *1954**
Beardsmore, Valerie *1990**
James, Delyth *1990**
Al-Qasim, Anis *1950**

Types of work (and number of counsel practising in that area if supplied)
Civil liberties · Common law (general) · Courts martial · Crime · Crime – corporate fraud · Family · Foreign law · Housing · Immigration · Landlord and tenant · Licensing · Sports

Opening times: 8.30 am-6.30 pm

Chambers' facilities
Disks accepted, Large conference rooms, E-mail

Languages spoken
Arabic, Cantonese, French, German, Greek, Hindi, Italian, Marathi, Polish, Spanish

Fees policy
Please contact the clerks who will be happy to discuss fees.

Additional information
The Chambers: "2 Paper Buildings, Chambers of Desmond de Silva QC", is one of the largest and longest-established sets in the Temple, specialising in criminal work and providing a complete service from the Magistrates' Court upwards. This service includes the provision of counsel for overnight cases and cases at weekends and Bank Holidays. This service can be arranged by ringing an out-of-hours number (0860 416061 24-hours).

Work Undertaken: Chambers is a specialist Criminal Defence set practising principally in white-collar fraud, terrorist cases, major drugs and sexual abuse cases. This set has a very long-standing Commonwealth connection acting in appeals to the Privy Council. The international flavour of Chambers is reflected in its diverse membership. Members practice primarily within the criminal field, at all levels. Several members of Chambers also practice in the civil, family and immigration courts. This is a set that has always had a strong civil liberties tradition. In particular, several members of Chambers specialise in civil actions against the police some of which have arisen out of criminal matters conducted by Chambers. The set is one of the very few chambers in which the same barrister who conducted the criminal trial will deal with any subsequent civil action against the police.

"2 Paper Buildings, Chambers of Desmond de Silva QC", also present seminars on specialist areas of criminal law and these are open to all solicitors. Chambers are an accredited Law Society Course Provider. Recent topics have included: Human Rights Legislation, Disclosure and Civil Actions Against the Police. Seminars are provided on suggested topics to individual firms of solicitors.

"2 Paper Buildings, Chambers of Desmond de Silva QC", aim to continue to improve the efficiency of their service for both lay and professional clients. Though a traditional set, Chambers are approachable and at the forefront of the modernisation and technological changes that the Bar has experienced in recent times.

2 PAPER BUILDINGS, BASEMENT NORTH

Temple, London, EC4Y 7ET
0171 936 2613
Fax: 0171 353 9439; DX 210 Chancery
E-mail: post@2paper.co.uk
URL: http://www.2paper.co.uk
Out of hours telephone: 0802 482912

Chambers of M Love
Clerks: Stephen Lavell, Marc Newson, Jamie Thornton

Love, Mark *1979*	**Briggs-Watson,** Sandra *1985*
Griffiths, Robin *1970*	
Hayden, Richard *1964*	**Sapsard,** Jamal *1987*
Ogden, Eric *1983*	**Robins,** Alison *1987*
Fisher Gordon, Wendy *1983*	**Comfort,** Polly-Anne *1988*
	Talbot-Bagnall, John *1988*
Purdy, Quentin *1983*	**Dent,** Kevin *1991*
Petersen, Neil *1983*	**Tolkien,** Simon *1994*
Evans, Andrew *1984*	**Pathak,** Pankaj *1992*
Dennison, James *1986*	**Keysell,** Tania Jane *1992*
Stern, Mark *1988*	**Dempster,** Jennifer *1993*

Syed, Maryam *1993*	**Dahlsen,** Peter *1996*
Whysall, Caroline *1993*	**Hancox,** Sally *1996*
Baker, Fay *1994*	**Gee,** Peta *1973**
Reid, Silas *1995*	

3 PAPER BUILDINGS

Ground Floor, Temple, London, EC4Y 7EU
0171 797 7000
Fax: 0171 797 7100; DX 0071 London

Chambers of I E Jacob

3 PAPER BUILDINGS

THE CHAMBERS OF MICHAEL PARROY Q.C.

Temple, London, EC4Y 7EU
020 7583 8055
Fax: 020 7353 6271; DX 1024 London
E-mail: London@3paper.com
Out of hours telephone: 0777 1603929 (Alan - mobile)

Chambers of M P Parroy QC
Clerks: J C Charlick (Chief Clerk), Alan Odiam (Senior Clerk), David Phillips, Danny Carroll, William Parmenter, Paul Queenan (Fees/Admin), Helen Binks (Bursar)

Annexe: 3 Paper Buildings (Oxford), 1 Alfred Street, High Street, Oxford, OX1 4EH
Tel: 01865 793736
Fax: 01865 790760

Annexe: 3 Paper Buildings (Bournemouth), 20 Lorne Park Road, Bournemouth, Dorset BH1 1JN
Tel: 01202 292102
Fax: 01202 298498

Annexe: 3 Paper Buildings (Winchester), 4 St Peter Street, Winchester, SO23 8BW
Tel: 01962 868884
Fax: 01962 868644

Parroy, Michael QC *1969*	**Aspinall,** John QC *1971*
Harris, David QC *1969†*	**Parrish,** Samuel *1962*
Hughes, Peter QC *1971*	**Solomon,** Susan *1967*
Jones, Stewart QC *1972†*	**Trevethan,** Susan *1967*

Haynes, John 1968
Swinstead, David 1970
Aylwin, Christopher 1970
Hope, Derwin 1970†
Norman, Michael 1971†
Curran, Leo 1972
Jennings, Peter 1972
Coleman, Anthony 1973
Stephenson, Ben 1973
Litchfield, Linda 1974
Bartlett, David 1975†
Richardson, Garth 1975
Tyson, Richard 1975‡
Henry, Peter 1977
Mitchell, Nigel 1978
Seed, Nigel 1978‡
Kent, Peter 1978
Partridge, Ian 1979
Grey, Robert 1979
Leviseur, Nicholas 1979
Coombes, Timothy 1980
Cairnes, Paul 1980
Marshall, David 1981
Edge, Ian 1981
Strutt, Martin 1981
Lickley, Nigel 1983
Lomas, Mark 1983
Maccabe, Irvine 1983
Branigan, Kate 1984
O'Hara, Sarah 1984
Chamberlain, Francis 1985
Sanderson, David 1985
Bailey, Russell 1985
Parker, Christopher 1986

Hudson, Elisabeth 1987
Letman, Paul 1987
Rowland, Nicholas 1988
Kelly, Patricia 1988
Woolgar, Dermot 1988
Hester, Paul 1989
Opperman, Guy 1989
Bradbury, Timothy 1989
Killen, Geoffrey 1990
Kilpatrick, Jean 1990
Buckley-Clarke, Amanda 1991
Ross, Iain 1991
Steenson, David 1991
Sweeney, Christian 1992
Bingham, Tony 1992
Kirkpatrick, Krystyna 1965
Fitzharris, Ginnette 1993
Clargo, John 1994
Earle, Judy 1994
Walter, Francesca 1994
Reid, David 1994
Williams, Ben 1994
Sutherland Williams, Mark 1995
Hughes, Melanie 1995
McIlroy, David 1995
Strachan, Elaine 1995
Case, Richard 1996
Kay, Dominic 1997
Leech, Ben 1997
Purdy, Catherine 1997
Sullivan, Mark 1997

Types of work (and number of counsel practising in that area if supplied)

Arbitration · Bankruptcy · Care proceedings · Chancery (general) · Chancery land law · Commercial · Commercial litigation · Commercial property · Common law (general) · Company and commercial · Construction · Courts martial · Crime · Crime – corporate fraud · Ecclesiastical · Employment · Family · Family provision · Foreign law · Information technology · Insolvency · Intellectual property · Landlord and tenant · Licensing · Medical negligence · Personal injury · Planning · Professional negligence · Sale and carriage of goods · Town and country planning

Chambers established: 1892
Opening times: 8.30 am-6.15 pm

Chambers' facilities

Conference rooms, Video conferences, Disks accepted, E-mail

Languages spoken

Arabic, French, German, Greek, Spanish, Welsh

Fees policy

We do not have a formal band of fees. We aim to be as flexible as possible and are happy to supply estimates and fix fees in advance. Fees will be negotiated on the basis of the weight and financial implications of the case, the expertise of counsel and the importance of the issues.

4 PAPER BUILDINGS

4 Paper Buildings

Ground Floor, Temple, London, EC4Y 7EX
0171 353 3366/583 7155
Fax: 0171 353 5778; DX 1036 London Chancery Lane
E-mail: clerks@4paperbuildings.com
URL: http://www.4paperbuildings.com
Out of hours telephone: 01277 264828

Chambers of Harvey McGregor QC
Clerks: Stephen Smith (Senior Clerk), Michael Kilbey

McGregor, Harvey QC 1955
Wadsworth, James QC 1963†
Burnett, Harold QC 1962†
Ritchie, Jean QC 1970†
Davidson, Nicholas QC 1974
Pooles, Michael QC 1978
Sharpston, Eleanor QC 1980
Goddard, Keith QC 1959*†
Gorna, Christina 1960
Keane, Michael 1963†
De Freitas, Anthony 1971‡
West-Knights, Laurence 1977†
Mishcon, Jane 1979
Spencer, Martin 1979

Holwill, Derek 1982
Lawrence, Patrick 1985
Jackson, Matthew 1986
Bacon, Francis 1988
Flenley, William 1988
Picton, Julian 1988
Price, Clare 1988
Gulliver, Alison 1989
Simpson, Mark 1992
Moser, Philip 1992
Reid, Graham 1993
Wilton, Simon 1993
Christie-Brown, Sarah 1994
Charlwood, Spike 1994
Beal, Kieron 1995
Ewins, Catherine 1995
Sawyer, Katrine 1996

Types of work (and number of counsel practising in that area if supplied)

Administrative · Agriculture · Arbitration · Civil liberties · Commercial · Commodities · Competition · Construction · Consumer law · Damages · Defamation · EC and competition law · Foreign law · Housing · Information technology · Insurance · Landlord and tenant · Licensing · Medical negligence · Mental health · Parliamentary · Partnerships · Personal injury · Private international · Professional negligence · Sale and carriage of goods · Sports

Opening times: 8 am-6 pm

Chambers' facilities
Conference rooms, Video conferences, Disks accepted, E-mail

Languages spoken
Danish, Dutch, French, German, Italian, Portuguese, Russian, Spanish

Fees policy
Please refer to the Senior Clerk. The Senior Clerk is alive to the need to agree competitive fees, and is pleased to discuss fees in advance of barristers being instructed. Work is accepted by direct professional access and pursuant to conditional fees, by agreement.

Work undertaken
Main Areas of Work: The set specialises in professional and clinical negligence, commercial contract work, European law and personal injury. Members of Chambers act for both Claimants and Defendants. In the field of professional negligence they act in cases concerning all of the professions, particularly solicitors, barristers, accountants, surveyors and insurance brokers, and in the area of clinical negligence represent patients, NHS Trusts, and doctors. Chambers has a long tradition in personal injury and commercial contract work, Harvey McGregor QC being the author of *McGregor on Damages*. The Brussels Convention and Human Rights are expanding areas of practice in chambers. Eleanor Sharpston QC heads a team of specialist juniors in EC law who undertake both judicial review and civil actions.

Additional Specialisations: Chambers also has considerable expertise in information technology law, landlord and tenant and professional disciplinary work.

Services to Clients: Chambers aims to provide a service of excellence, adopting a flexible, practical and commercial approach to litigation which is driven by the needs and convenience of our clients. Members of chambers are happy to give lectures and seminars in their specialist areas.

4 PAPER BUILDINGS

1st Floor, Temple, London, EC4Y 7EX
0171 583 0816/353 1131
Fax: 0171 353 4979; DX 1035 London
E-mail: clerks@4paperbuildings.co.uk
Out of hours telephone: 01708 379332

Chambers of Lionel Swift QC
Clerks: Michael Reeves, Mike Lay;
Chambers Manager: Kay May

Swift, Lionel QC *1959*	**Johnstone**, Mark *1984*
Murdoch, Gordon QC *1970†*	**Coleman**, Elizabeth *1985*
	Wood, Catherine *1985*
Pauffley, Anna QC *1979†*	**Rosenblatt**, Jeremy *1985*
Cohen, Jonathan QC *1974†*	**Neaman**, Sam *1988*
Turcan, Henry *1965†*	**Morgan**, Adrienne *1988*
Smith, Roger *1968*	**Mills**, Barbara *1990*
Barrington-Smyth, Amanda *1972*	**Cope**, Christopher *1990*
	Brereton, Joy *1990*
Ridd, Ian *1975*	**Mansfield**, Gavin *1992*
Barda, Robin *1975*	**Larizadeh**, Cyrus *1992*
Sternberg, Michael *1975*	**Hansen**, William *1992*
Jackson, Peter *1978‡*	**Ageros**, Justin *1993*
Coney, Christopher *1979*	**Murray**, Judith *1994*
Scott-Manderson, Marcus *1980*	**Lowe**, Sarah *1995*
	Schofield, Alexander *1997*
Joseph, Charles *1980*	**Johnston**, Justine *1997*
Stern, Michael *1983*	**Copley**, James *1997*
Reade, David *1983*	

Types of work (and number of counsel practising in that area if supplied)
Arbitration 2 · Banking 3 · Bankruptcy 1 · Chancery (general) 2 · Chancery land law 1 · Commercial property 3 · Company and commercial 7 · Construction 4 · Crime – corporate fraud 1 · Discrimination 9 · Employment 9 · Family 25 · Family provision 25 · Foreign law 4 · Insolvency 1 · Landlord and tenant 11 · Medical negligence 5 · Partnerships 11 · Personal injury 5 · Professional negligence 5 · Sale and carriage of goods 5

Chambers established: 1946
Opening times: 8.30 am-6.30 pm

---

† Recorder   ‡ Assistant Recorder   *Door Tenant

Chambers' facilities
Disks accepted, E-mail

Languages spoken
French, German, Hebrew, Spanish

Fees policy
Quotation available from clerks upon request.

5 PAPER BUILDINGS

Ground Floor, Temple, London, EC4Y 7HB
0171 583 9275/583 4555
Fax: 0171 583 1926/2031; DX 415 London
E-mail: 5paper@link.org

Chambers of A D P J M Bueno QC
Clerk: Alan Stammers

Bueno, Antonio QC *1964†*	Devonshire, Simon *1988*
Nicol, Angus *1963†*	Rich, Jonathan *1989*
Walsh, Steven *1965*	Hyams, Oliver *1989*
Denman, Robert *1970*	Nichols, Stuart *1989*
Platford, Graham *1970*	Gill, Satinder *1991*
Wood, Nicholas *1970†*	Evans, Richard *1993*
Broatch, Donald *1971*	Rushton, Nicola *1993*
Percival, Robert *1971*	Adjei, Cyril *1995*
King, Richard *1978*	Reichert, Klaus *1996*
Iles, Adrian *1980*	Harrap, Robert Philip *1997*
Infield, Paul *1980*	Davies, Jake Sebastian
Wright, Ian *1983*	Hunter *1997*
Jacobson, Lawrence *1985*	McCafferty, Lynne *1997*

Types of work (and number of counsel practising in that area if supplied)
Administrative 4 · Banking 7 · Bankruptcy 4 · Commercial litigation 20 · Company and commercial 3 · Competition 4 · Construction 4 · Copyright 1 · EC and competition law 4 · Education 1 · Employment 8 · Equity, wills and trusts 2 · Family 7 · Family provision 7 · Financial services 2 · Foreign law 2 · Immigration 4 · Insolvency 4 · International trade 4 · Landlord and tenant 14 · Medical negligence 2 · Personal injury 18 · Private international 5 · Probate and

administration 1 · Professional negligence 18 · Sale and carriage of goods 15 · Tax – capital and income 1

Opening times: 8 am-6.30 pm

Chambers' facilities
Video conferences, Disks accepted

Languages spoken
French, Gaelic, German, Italian, Punjabi, Spanish

Fees policy
On application to the senior clerk.

FIVE PAPER BUILDINGS

1st Floor, Five Paper Bldgs, Temple, London, EC4Y 7HB
0171 583 6117
Fax: 0171 353 0075; DX 365 London
E-mail: clerks@5-paperbuildings.law.co.uk

Chambers of Jonathan Caplan QC, Godfrey Carey QC
Clerk: Stuart Bryant (Senior Clerk)

Mathew, John QC *1949*	Wyeth, Mark *1983*
Corkery, Michael QC *1949*	Pinto, Amanda *1983*
Cassel, Timothy QC *1965*	Bennett, Miles *1986*
Stokes, David QC *1968†*	Groome, David *1987*
Carey, Godfrey QC *1969†*	O'Sullivan, Robert *1988*
Caplan, Jonathan QC *1973†*	Christopher, Julian *1988*
Singh, Kuldip QC *1975*	Evans, Martin *1989*
Tabor, James QC *1974**	Dhir, Anuja *1989*
Sells, Oliver QC *1972†*	Cole, Justin *1992*
Hughes, Stanley *1971*	Griffin, Nicholas *1992*
Jenkins, Edward *1977*	Deacon, Emma *1993*
Wade, Ian *1977*	Allen, Tom *1994*
Trembath, Graham *1978*	Hick, Michael *1995*
Fooks, Nicholas *1978*	Bailin, Alex *1995*
Mehigan, Simon QC *1980*	Barry, Denis *1996*
Rector, Penny *1980*	Barton, Charles QC *1969**
Judge, Charles *1981*	Hawkesworth, Gareth *1972**
Aston, Maurice *1982*	
Moore, Miranda *1983*	Franklin, Stephen *1974**

PEPYS' CHAMBERS

17 Fleet Street, London, EC4Y 1AA
0171 936 2710
Fax: 0171 936 2501; DX 463 London, Chancery Lane
Out of hours telephone: 0171 936 2710

Chambers of Terence de Lury
Clerk: Wanda Bogucka

de Lury, Terence *1985*	Skinner, Conor *1979**
Joseph, Clifford *1975*	Brown, James *1989*
Pawlowski, Mark *1978**	Morton, Gary *1993*
De Speville, Patrice *1978**	Ng, Alex Ching-Wong *1991*
Ferguson, Christopher *1979**	Veloso, Linda *1996*

PHOENIX CHAMBERS

First Floor, Gray's Inn Chambers, Gray's Inn, London, WC1R 5JA
0171 404 7888
Fax: 0171 404 7897; DX 78 Chancery Lane
E-mail: clerks@phoenix-chambers.co.uk
URL: http://www.phoenix-chambers.co.uk

Chambers of The Hon B M D Pitt
Practice Manager: Laurie Galloghy; Administrator: Sean Phelan; Other Admin: Mark Jordan

Pitt, Bruce *1970**	Roberts, Adrian *1993*
Bradley, Denis *1965*	Kendal, Mark *1993*
Lane, David QC *1968*	Smith, Lisa *1994*
Campbell, Donald *1976*	McAteer, Shanda *1994*
Fama, Gudrun *1991*	Reed, Jason *1994*
Boumphrey, John *1992*	Bustani, Navaz *1995*
Cavender, Simon *1992*	Chipperfield, Jeremy *1995*
Cole, Vanessa *1992*	Momtaz, Sam *1995*
Reiff-Musgrove, Kaja *1992*	Allen, Frances *1995*
Zahed, Yasreeb *1993*	Choudhury, Fareha *1995*
Blackmore, Sarah *1993*	Alakija, Ayodele Hugh *1996*
Coy, Michael *1993*	Griffiths, Dafydd *1997*
Hussein, Tim *1993*	Jones, Daniel *1997*
Payne, Brian *1993*	Mutch, Alison *1995**

PLOWDEN BUILDINGS

2nd Floor, 2 Plowden Buildings, Middle Temple Lane, London, EC4Y 9BU
0171 583 0808
Fax: 0171 583 5106; DX 0020 Chancery Lane
E-mail: bar@plowdenbuildings.co.uk

Chambers of William Lowe QC
Clerk: Paul Hurst; Administrator: Sylvia Donaghey

Also at: Newcastle-upon-Tyne

Lowe, William QC *1972†*	Dines, Sarah *1988*
McIntyre, Bruce *1969†*	Cooper, Roger *1989*
MacKenzie Smith, Catherine *1960*	James, Michael *1989*
Cooper, Arnold *1969*	Haukeland, Martin *1989*
Buckhaven, Charlotte *1969*	De Rohan, Jonathan *1989*
Hindmarsh, Elizabeth *1974*	Cox, Kerry *1990*
Trotter, David *1975*	Watson-Gandy, Mark *1990*
Azam, Javaid *1981*	Henderson, Sophie *1990*
Williams, Christopher *1981*	Anthony, Christina *1990*
Wood, Simon *1981*	Lindsay, Claire *1991*
Freedman, Jeremy *1982*	Freeman, Peter *1992*
Kramer, Philip *1982*	Farbey, Judith *1992*
Dacey, Mark *1985*	Cox, Simon *1992*
Holmes, Jonathan *1985*	Walsh, John *1993*
McNulty, Lawrence *1985*	Bajwa, Ali *1993*
Foster, Catherine *1986*	Zammit, Frances *1993*
Bailey, Michael *1986*	MacKenzie, Anna *1994*
Lyons, David *1987*	Clarke, Jamie *1995*
Dyer, Simon *1987*	Broome, Edward *1996*
Morton, Peter *1988*	Vullo, Stephen *1996*
Jones, Lawrence *1988*	Bayne, Dominic *1997*
Brook, David *1988*	Quigley, Camilla *1988**
Gordon, Kate *1988*	Lowe, John *1976**

PRINCE HENRY'S CHAMBER

109 Grosvenor Road, Westminster, London, SW1V 3LG
0171 834 2572
Fax: 0171 931 7483

Chambers of Mr A J Pickford

PRINCE HENRY'S CHAMBERS

2 Tamar House, 12 Tavistock Place,
London, WC1H 9RA
0171 713 0376
Fax: 0171 713 0377

Chambers of David R Harris

Harris, David *1973*

1 PUMP COURT

Lower Ground Floor, Temple, London,
EC4Y 7AB
0171 583 2012/353 4341
Fax: 0171 353 4944; DX 109 London
Other comms: Lix: Lon 217
E-mail: [name]@1pumpcourt.co.uk
URL: http://www.1pumpcourt.co.uk
Out of hours telephone: 0374 238444

Chambers of Jane Hoyal
Clerks: Ian Burrow (Senior Clerk), Mycal
Thomas, Sonia Philp, Gary Carney,
Joanna Day, Martin Cornwell (Fees
Clerk); Receptionist: Deborah Coles

Adams, Lindsay *1987*	Hilken, Alice *1994*
Atreya, Navita *1994*	Hoyal, Jane *1976*
Barry, Simon Mark *1997*	Hussein, Tim *1993*
Bevan, Stephen *1986*	Isles, Mary *1984*
Boswell, Jenny *1982*	Johnson, Melanie Jane
Bradley, Sally *1989*	*1996*
Bruce, Gaenor *1997*	Kaler, Manjeet *1993*
Bryan, Deborah *1987*	Keegan, Leslie *1989*
Campbell, David *1992*	Khanzada, Najma *1992*
Carne, Rosalind *1986*	Killeen, Robert *1995*
Chesters, Colette *1996*	Knapp, Sophie *1990*
Farnon, Patricia *1986*	McCabe, Margaret *1981*
Frances, Jill *1992*	Montague, Susan *1981*
Friedman, Charlotte *1982*	More O'Ferrall, Geraldine
Garwood, Joshua *1992*	*1983*
Gordon, Christina Jayne	Nabi, Zia *1991*
1997	Nicol, Nicholas *1986*
Higham, Paul *1982*	Polson, Alistair *1989*

Rogers, Nicola Helen *1997*	Connolly, James *1985**
Russell, Alison *1983*	Sprack, John *1984**
Teji, Usha *1981*	Wallace, Ann *1979**
Vine, Sarah Jane *1997*	Bradley, Phillip *1993**
Willers, Marc *1987*	

Types of work (and number of counsel practising in that area if supplied)
Administrative · Care proceedings · Chancery (general) · Chancery land law · Civil liberties · Common law (general) · Crime · Crime – corporate fraud · Discrimination · Education · Employment · Environment · Equity, wills and trusts · Family · Family provision · Housing · Immigration · Landlord and tenant · Licensing · Local government · Medical negligence · Mental health · Personal injury · Professional negligence

Chambers established: 1978
Opening times: 8.45 am-6.30 pm

Chambers' facilities
Conference rooms, Disks accepted, E-mail

Languages spoken
Bulgarian, Dutch, French, German, Gujarati, Hindi, Punjabi, Spanish, Urdu

Fees policy
We adopt a flexible fee policy to enable all clients access to members of chambers. Please contact our clerks for further information.

Additional information
1 PUMP COURT is a radical and progressive set of chambers providing a specialist service to legally-aided and private clients, and which seeks to secure equality of access to justice. Chambers undertakes work at all levels, and members practise in the following specialist groups: crime, family, housing and civil.

Criminal practitioners practise in criminal defence and civil actions against the police. Family practitioners provide a progressive, multi-disciplinary and socially-responsible approach to family legal services in all areas of national and international law. Housing work concentrates on problems faced by tenants and the homeless. The civil group specialises in social security, employment, immigration, mental health, personal injury and medical negligence. Judicial review is an important and expanding area of work within chambers.

Chambers works closely with Law Centres and other agencies addressing unmet legal needs. Members are prominent in legal pressure groups and voluntary organisations, seeking to reform and improve the provision of legal services and access to justice. 1 PUMP COURT seeks to ensure equality of opportunity both in the work we undertake and in the structures within chambers. Chambers has a strong commitment to its equal opportunities policy, ensuring we reflect the community we serve. 1 Pump Court is the only legal organisation to have been awarded the Times/Annual Woman Lawyer Conference Award for its achievements in equal opportunities.

1 Pump Court also offers Family Mediation in all issues, children, divorce, finance and property.

Chambers is acredited by the Law Society to hold continuing professional education courses for solicitors.

2 PUMP COURT

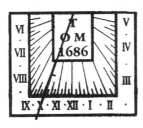

1st Floor, Temple, London, EC4Y 7AH
0171 353 5597
Fax: 0171 583 2122; DX 290 London
Out of hours telephone: 01708 732138

Chambers of P F Singer QC
Clerk: John Arter

Singer, Philip QC *1964*†
Grenfell, Gibson QC *1969*†
Giovene, Laurence *1962*†
Lyons, Graham *1972*
Russell, Jeremy *1973*
Mallender, Paul *1974*
Renouf, Gerard *1977*
Barrett, Robert *1978*
Fleischmann, Laureen *1978*
Pigot, Diana *1978*
Dooley, Christine *1980*
Waddington, James *1983*
Davey, Helen *1984*
O'Brien, Haylee *1984*
Christie, Richard *1986*
Lickert, Martin *1986*
Agbamu, Alexander *1988*
Thompson, Polly *1990*
Aliker, Philip *1990*
Paxton, Christopher *1991*
Dugdale, Jeremy *1992*
Cronshaw, Michael *1993*
Garrido, Damian *1993*
Sugarman, Jason *1995*
Tarr, Beverly *1995*
Vout, Andrew Paul *1995*

Bainbridge, Laura Alexandra *1997*
Barber, Abigail *1997*
Grime, Stephen QC *1970**
Machell, Raymond QC *1973**
McDermott, Gerard QC *1978**

PUMP COURT CHAMBERS

Upper Ground Floor, 3 Pump Court, Temple, London, EC4Y 7AJ
0171 353 0711
Fax: 0171 353 3319; DX 362 London
E-mail: clerks@3pumpcourt.com
URL: http://www.3pumpcourt.com
Out of hours telephone: 0860 336 448

Chambers of Guy Boney QC
Clerks: David Barber, Danny Fantham; Administrator: Sally Woolley

Also at: 31 Southgate Street, Winchester SO23 9EE Tel: 01962 868161 Fax: 01962 867645; 5 Temple Chambers, Swindon SN1 1SQ Tel: 01793 539899 Fax: 01793 539866

Boney, Guy QC *1968*†
Pascoe, Nigel QC *1966*†
Clark, Christopher QC *1969*†
Garlick, Paul QC *1974*†
Still, Geoffrey *1966*†
Patterson, Stewart *1967*‡
Pearson, Adam *1969*
Moat, Frank *1970*†
Harrap, Giles *1971*†
Abbott, Frank *1972*†
Parry, Charles *1973*
Butt, Michael *1974*
Ker-Reid, John *1974*
Gabb, Charles *1975*
Gillibrand, Phillip *1975*
Barnett, Andrew *1977*†
Dineen, Michael *1977*
Mackenzie, Julie *1978*
Miller, Jane *1979*‡
O'Flynn, Timothy *1979*
Hill, Robert *1980*
Allardice, Miranda *1982*
Lochrane, Damien *1983*
Nsugbe, Oba *1985*‡
Scott, Matthew *1985*
Bloom-Davis, Desmond *1986*
Hill, Mark *1987*
Howard, Graham *1987*
Travers, Hugh *1988*
Waddington, Anne *1988*
Warren, Philip *1988*
Akiwumi, Anthony *1989*
Boydell, Edward *1989*
Gau, Justin *1989*
Samuels, Leslie *1989*
Brunton, Sean *1990*
Khan, Helen *1990*
Howe, Penny *1991*
Kelly, Geoffrey *1992*
Newton-Price, James *1992*
Poyer-Sleeman, Patricia *1992*

† Recorder ‡ Assistant Recorder *Door Tenant

Gunther, Elizabeth *1993*
Peirson, Oliver *1993*
Fields, Helen *1993*
Tregilgas-Davey, Mark *1993*
Blackburn, Luke *1993*
Ashley, Mark *1993*

Pawson, Robert *1994*
Dubbery, Mark *1996*
Ward, Anne *1997*
Arlow, Ruth *1997*
Grime, Andrew *1997*
Beaumont, Marc *1985**

Types of work (and number of counsel practising in that area if supplied)
Banking 2 · Care proceedings 19 · Commercial 13 · Commercial litigation 13 · Common land 1 · Construction 6 · Courts martial 6 · Crime 34 · Crime – corporate fraud 17 · Defamation 2 · Ecclesiastical 2 · Employment 7 · Environment 1 · Equity, wills and trusts 5 · Family 28 · Family provision 5 · Foreign law 2 · Insolvency 2 · Landlord and tenant 8 · Licensing 3 · Medical negligence 18 · Personal injury 27 · Planning 2 · Professional negligence 15 · Sports 2

Opening times: 8.30 am-6.15 pm

Chambers' facilities
Conference rooms

Languages spoken
French, German

The Chambers We are a long-established and forward looking set whose main areas of practice are Family, Crime and General Common Law.

Work undertaken Members of Chambers practise in specialist teams and their areas of particular specialisation include Professional and Medical Negligence; Personal Injury; Matrimonial; Inheritance Act; Criminal Law (including Customs and Excise, Serious Fraud, Courts Martial, Animal Litigation); Construction Law; Ecclesiastical law; Environment law; Extradition and Judicial Review; Nigerian law.

Additional areas of work Boundary disputes; Contracts; Discipline Tribunals; Employment law; Immigration law; Insolvency; Planning; Road Traffic.

Publications Mr Mark Hill is the author of *Hill on Ecclesiastical Law*.

Mr Oba Nsugbe is a barrister and solicitor of the Supreme Court of Nigeria with direct access to chambers in Lagos.
Dr Gerhard Dannemann, a door tenant, is a member of the German Bar.

4 PUMP COURT

Temple, London, EC4Y 7AN
020 7842 5555
Fax: 020 7583 2036; DX 303 London, Chancery Lane
E-mail: chambers@4pumpcourt.law.co.uk
Out of hours telephone: available on answerphone

Chambers of Bruce Mauleverer QC
Clerks: Carolyn McCombe, Simon Slattery, Carl Wall, Stewart Gibbs

Mauleverer, Bruce QC *1969†*	Hughes, Adrian *1984*
Temple, Anthony QC *1968†*	Cross, James *1985*
Friedman, David QC *1968†*	McCall, Duncan *1988*
Blunt, David QC *1967†*	Christie, Aidan *1988*
Moger, Christopher QC *1972†*	Neish, Andrew *1988*
Storey, Jeremy QC *1974†*	Vineall, Nicholas *1988*
Marks, Jonathan QC *1975*	Houghton, Kirsten *1989*
Acton Davis, Jonathan QC *1977‡*	Rowlands, Marc *1990*
Rowland, John QC *1979*	Davie, Michael *1993*
Douglas, Michael QC *1974*	Gunning, Alexander *1994*
Boswell, Lindsay QC *1982*	Brannigan, Sean *1994*
Marsh, Laurence *1975*	Vaughan-Neil, Kate *1994*
Dyer, Allen *1976*	Ansell, Rachel *1995*
Nicholson, Jeremy *1977*	Packman, Claire *1996*
Ticciati, Oliver *1979*	O'Sullivan, Sean *1997*
Tozzi, Nigel *1980*	Pilling, Ben *1997*
Fletcher, Andrew *1980*	Aird, Richard *1976**
Hamilton, Peter *1968*	Ackner, The Hon Claudia *1977**
Charlton, Alexander *1983*	Coleman, Russell *1986**
Sears, David *1984*	McCahill, Dominic *1991**
	Cheyne, Phyllida *1992**

Types of work (and number of counsel practising in that area if supplied)
Arbitration 25 · Aviation 6 · Banking 10 · Common law (general) 37 · Construction 21 · Employment 12 · Entertainment 2 · Environment 12 · Family provision 2 · Financial services 3 · Information technology 10 · Insurance 33 · Insurance/reinsurance 10 · Licensing 8 · Medical negligence 10 · Personal injury 18 · Professional negligence 37 · Sale and carriage of goods 14 · Sports 2

Chambers established: 1954
Opening times: 8.30 am-7 pm

† Recorder ‡ Assistant Recorder *Door Tenant

Chambers' facilities
Conference rooms, Disks accepted, E-mail

Languages spoken
French, German, Italian, Spanish

Fees policy
The clerks are happy to discuss hourly rates or provide estimates for brief fees. Realistic rates are charged at all levels. We are anxious that our clients understand the rationale behind fees charged and are satisfied with the value of work done.

Commercial Work
Insurance and reinsurance, including litigation and arbitration, disciplinary hearings and regulatory control; contracts, including sale of goods; restraint of trade; passing off; banking; financial services; Mareva and Anton Piller orders and other injunctive relief.

Construction and Civil Engineering
National and international arbitration and litigation, acting for employers, contractors and sub-contractors and professional advisors.

Professional Negligence
Representing plaintiffs and insurers and involving doctors and other medical professionals, solicitors and barristers, accountants, valuers and surveyors, insurance brokers and other professional advisors.

Information Technology and Telecommunications
Expertise primarily concerns disputes of a contractual nature, involving a detailed understanding of the technical aspects of computer systems, their implementation and application.

Licensing, Gaming and Lotteries
All aspects of gaming law, especially casino gaming and lotteries acting both for the regulator of the gaming industry and many of its major operators.

Other Fields
General common law including personal injury, landlord and tenant, and matrimonial finance.

Arbitration
Lord Ackner, Lord Jauncey and James Fox-Andrews QC are full-time arbitrators while other members of chambers, at different levels of seniority, also sit as arbitrators.

Direct Professional Access
DPA is welcomed by all members of chambers.

5 PUMP COURT

Ground Floor, Temple, London, EC4Y 7AP
020 7353 2532
Fax: 020 7353 5321; DX 497 London
E-mail: FivePump@netcomuk.co.uk
Out of hours telephone: 0976 368031

Chambers of R V Bryan
Clerks: Tim Markham (Senior Clerk), Jayne Goodrham

Bryan, Rex 1971†	**James,** Mark 1987
Primost, Norman 1954	**Hasan,** Tazeen 1988
Hunter, Anthony 1962	**Gooch,** Sebastian 1989
Hopkins, Simeon 1968	**Schiffer,** Corinna 1989
Dow, Kenneth 1970	**O'Sullivan,** Derek 1990
Christodoulou, Helen 1972	**Walker,** Allister 1990
Evison, John 1974	**Campbell,** Jane 1990
Keith, Alistair 1974	**Nicholls,** Jack 1991
Cartwright, Crispian 1976‡	**Ross,** Anthony 1991
Chaize, Tristan 1977	**Ellis-Jones,** Stephen 1992
Charlton, Hugo 1978	**Say,** Bradley 1993
Campbell, Graham 1979	**Smith,** Emma 1994
Ratcliffe, Anne 1981	**Marley,** Sarah 1995
Hodgkinson, Tristram 1982	**Elfield,** Laura 1996
Morris, Christina 1983	**King,** Peter 1970*
Collard, Michael 1986	**Spencer,** Hannah 1993*

Types of work (and number of counsel practising in that area if supplied)
Administrative 3 · Arbitration 3 · Bankruptcy 2 · Care proceedings 8 · Chancery (general) 3 · Chancery land law 2 · Commercial 3 · Commercial property 2 · Common law (general) 10 · Company and commercial 2 · Construction 5 · Crime 13 · EC and competition law 1 · Employment 4 · Environment 2 · Family 9 · Family provision 7 · Housing 4 · Insolvency 3 · Insurance 2 · Landlord and tenant 5 · Licensing 5 · Medical negligence 2 · Personal injury 9 · Probate and administration 1 · Professional negligence 4 · Sale and carriage of goods 2 · Town and country planning 1

Chambers established: 1870
Opening times: 8.30 am-7 pm

---

† Recorder ‡ Assistant Recorder *Door Tenant

Chambers' facilities
Conference rooms, Disks accepted, E-mail, Free parking by arrangement, Video playback facilities

Languages spoken
French, German, Greek, Hindi, Italian, Urdu

Fees policy
No set rates for paperwork, although fees can be agreed in advance on sight of the papers, or guidance given as to appropriate hourly rates.

Types of work undertaken
Five Pump Court Chambers is a long-established common law set with three specialist practice groups focusing on civil, criminal and family law. Conditional fee and DPA work is undertaken. Chambers has dedicated conference rooms with video facilities, and free parking is available. Conferences can be arranged out of London.

Principal areas of practice
Civil: Landlord and tenant, building, contract/commercial, professional negligence, personal injury, partnership, trusts, judical review, employment, arbitration, consumer credit and licensing.
Criminal: Fraud, sexual offences, DTI, serious violence, car ringing and importation of drugs.
Family: Financial provision and children.

CHAMBERS OF KIERAN COONAN QC

Ground Floor, 6 Pump Court, Temple, London, EC4Y 7AR
0171 583 6013/2510
Fax: 0171 353 0464; DX 409 London
E-mail: clerks@6-pumpcourt.law.co.uk

Chambers of K B Coonan QC
Clerks: Adrian Barrow, Stephen Somerville

Coonan, Kieran QC *1971*†	Foster, Charles *1988*
Curwen, Michael *1966*†	Post, Andrew *1988*
Williams, Jon *1970*	Gordon, John *1989*
Craven, Richard *1976*	Kennedy, Andrew *1989*
Morris, David *1976*	Garrett, Annalissa *1991*
Goodrich, Siobhan *1980*	Lacey, Roisin *1991*
Power, Richard *1983*	Hutton, Alexander *1992*
Hockton, Andrew *1984*	Peacock, Nicholas *1992*
Jenkins, Alan *1984*	Gollop, Katharine *1993*
Burden, Susan *1985*	Jenkins, Janet *1994*
Lambert, Christina *1988*	McCowan, Hester *1995*

Brown, Emma *1995*	Jeremiah, Natalia *1997*
Robertson, Alice *1996*	Davidson, Laura Anne *1996*
Friston, Mark *1997*	Davies, John *1955*

Types of work (and number of counsel practising in that area if supplied)
Care proceedings 4 · Common law (general) 20 · Crime – corporate fraud 10 · Employment 4 · Family 4 · Family provision 3 · Housing 5 · Landlord and tenant 4 · Medical negligence 24 · Mental health 10 · Personal injury 20 · Professional negligence 10

Opening times: 8.45 am-6.30 pm

Chambers' facilities
Conference rooms, Disabled access, Video conferences by arrangement

Fees policy
Fees are negotiated with the clerks who adopt a realistic charging policy.

Additional information
These Chambers have enjoyed a reputation over the past 25 years for providing specialist advice and advocacy on behalf of Plaintiffs and Defendants in the field of Healthcare Law.

Most members of Chambers specialise in the major areas of medical and dental negligence, mental health law and the professional conduct regulation of care professionals.

The work of Chambers is undertaken before Inquests, Inquiries (both public and private) and before various Judicial/Administrative Tribunals. Individual members of Chambers also undertake criminal cases which frequently incorporate medico-legal issues.

Personal injury and professional negligence work (particularly affecting solicitors), housing, family, and employment law, are strongly represented. A small group practises in the specialist area of the law relating to Costs.

Many of the leading cases in these fields have featured members of this set.

Some members of Chambers have practised formerly in the professions of medical practitioner and veterinary surgeon.

6 PUMP COURT

SIX PUMP COURT
6 Pump Court, Temple, London EC4Y 7AR

1st Floor, Temple, London, EC4Y 7AR
0171 797 8400
Fax: 0171 797 8401; DX 293 Chancery Lane, London
E-mail: clerks@6pumpcourt.co.uk
URL: http://www.6pumpcourt.co.uk

Chambers of Mr Stephen Hockman QC
Clerk: Richard Constable (Senior Clerk); Administrator: Arlene Sturgeon

Also at: 6-8 Mill Street, Maidstone, Kent ME15 6XH

Hockman, Stephen QC 1970†	**Saxby,** Oliver 1992
Goymer, Andrew 1970†	**Chamberlayne,** Patrick 1992
Williams, Adèle 1972†	**Butler,** Judith 1993
Mitchell, David 1972	**Mee,** Paul 1992
Harington, Michael 1974†	**Watson,** Mark 1994
Willard, Neville 1976	**Grant,** Edward 1994
Barraclough, Richard 1980	**Ellin,** Nina 1994
Baldock, Nicholas 1983	**Wright,** Clare 1995
Walden-Smith, David 1985	**Alcock,** Peter 1995
Gower, Peter 1985	**Nardell,** Gordon 1995
Leigh, Kevin 1986	**Beard,** Mark 1996
Harrison, Peter 1987	**Charles,** Deborah 1996
Forbes, Peter 1990	**Robinson,** Tanya 1997

PUMP COURT TAX CHAMBERS

16 Bedford Row, London, WC1R 4EB
0171 414 8080
Fax: 0171 414 8099; DX 312 London

Chambers of A R Thornhill QC
Clerks: Graham Kettle, Geraldine O'Sullivan

Thornhill, Andrew QC 1969	**Ewart,** David 1987
Milne, David QC 1970	**Woolf,** Jeremy 1986
Allcock, Stephen QC 1975	**Hitchmough,** Andrew 1991
Richards, Ian 1971	**Shipwright,** Adrian 1993
Matthews, Janek 1972	**Baldry,** Rupert 1987
Tallon, John 1975	**Wilson,** Elizabeth 1995
Massey, William QC 1977	**Henderson,** James Thomas 1997
Thomas, Roger 1979	**Vallat,** Richard Justin 1997
Prosser, Kevin QC 1982	
Goodfellow, Giles 1983	

QUEEN ELIZABETH BUILDING

Ground Floor

Ground Floor, Temple, London, EC4Y 9BS
0171 353 7181 (12 Lines)
Fax: 0171 353 3929 (2 Lines); DX 340 London

Chambers of Lindsay Burn
Clerk: Michael A Price; Administrator: Brian Warmington

Burn, Lindsay 1972†	**Bhatia,** Divya 1986
Guy, Richard 1970	**Munro,** Fiona 1986
Farror, Shelagh 1970	**Price,** Debora 1987
Miskin, Claire 1970†	**Holt,** Karen 1987
Stage, Peter 1971	**Probyn,** Jane 1988
Mandel, Richard 1972	**Philcox,** Barbara 1988
Lowen, Jonathan 1972†	**Purkiss,** Kate 1988
Prideaux-Brune, Peter 1972	**Driscoll,** Jennifer 1989
Pavry, James 1974	**Adebayo,** Ibitayo 1989
Salvesen, Keith 1974	**Scutt,** David 1989
Wild, Simon 1977	**Henderson,** Lawrence 1990
Jeremy, David 1977	**Umezuruike,** Chima 1991
Harris, Laura 1977	**Fry,** Neil 1992
Walsh, Peter 1978	**Field,** Amanda-Jane 1994
Hornsby, Walton 1980	**Sawyerr,** Sharon 1992
Blower, Graham 1980	**Weeks,** Janet 1993
Simpson, Nicola 1982	**Gore,** Susan 1993
Digby, Charles 1982	**McKenna,** Anna 1994
Haycroft, Anthony 1982	**Cartwright,** Richard 1994
Gibb, Fiona 1983	**Browne,** Gerald 1995
Atkinson, Carol 1985	**Easton,** Alison 1994
St John-Stevens, Philip 1985	**Gardiner,** Emma 1995
Devlin, Tim 1985	**Aiolfi,** Laurence 1996
	Thompson, Marcus 1996

Types of work (and number of counsel practising in that area if supplied)
Common law (general) 8 · Crime 23 · Crime – corporate fraud 8 · Education 4 · Family 15 · Licensing 5

Chambers established: 1976
Opening times: 8.15 am-7 pm

Chambers' facilities
Conference rooms, Video conferences, Disks accepted, Disabled access

Languages spoken
French, Hindi, Spanish

HOLLIS WHITEMAN CHAMBERS

Queen Elizabeth Building

Hollis Whiteman Chambers

3rd Floor, Queen Elizabeth Bldg, Temple,
London, EC4Y 9BS
020 7583 5766
Fax: 020 7353 0339; DX 482 London
E-mail: barristers@holliswhiteman.co.uk
Out of hours telephone: Duty Clerk 24
hour 07970 439915

Chambers of Julian Bevan QC, Peter Whiteman QC
Clerk: Michael J Greenaway;
Administrator: Sarah Finlayson

Bevan, Julian QC *1962*	**Ellison**, Mark *1979†*
Whiteman, Peter QC *1967†*	**Finnigan**, Peter *1979*
Carlisle of Bucklow, Lord QC *1954†*	**Wood**, Nick *1980‡*
	Rees, Gareth *1981*
Grey, Robin QC *1957†*	**Kark**, Thomas *1982‡*
Jeffreys, David QC *1958†*	**Stern**, Ian *1983‡*
Suckling, Alan QC *1963†*	**Brown**, Edward *1983*
Glass, Anthony QC *1965†*	**Sullivan**, Jane *1984‡*
Robinson, Vivian QC *1967†*	**Bennetts**, Philip *1986*
Hilton, John QC *1964†*	**Larkin**, Sean *1987*
Barker, Brian QC *1969†*	**Plaschkes**, Sarah *1988*
Evans, David QC *1972†*	**Henry**, Edward *1988*
Langdale, Timothy QC *1966†*	**Winter**, Ian *1988*
	Johnson, Zoe *1990*
Bate, David QC *1969†*	**Lowry**, Emma *1991*
Poulet, Rebecca QC *1975†*	**Barnfather**, Lydia *1992*
Kyte, Peter QC *1970†*	**Coward**, Victoria *1992*
Clarke, Peter QC *1973†*	**Wastie**, William *1993*
Wilcken, Anthony *1966†*	**Warne**, Peter *1993*
Longden, Anthony *1967*	**Ramasamy**, Selva *1992*
Mitchell, Christopher *1968†*	**Darbishire**, Adrian *1993*
Stewart, Neill *1973†*	**Summers**, Benjamin *1994*
Strudwick, Linda *1973*	**Aldred**, Mark *1996*
Paton, Ian *1975‡*	**Barnard**, Jonathan *1997*
Boyce, William *1976†*	**Evans**, Julian *1997*
Horwell, Richard *1976*	**Harris**, Rebecca *1997*
Donne, Jeremy *1978‡*	**Sibson**, Clare *1997*
Kelsey-Fry, John *1978*	

Types of work (and number of counsel practising in that area if supplied)
Courts martial 52 · Crime 52 · Crime –
corporate fraud 52 · Financial services 52 ·
Judicial review 52 · Licensing 52 · Tax –
capital and income 1 · Tax – corporate 1

Opening times: 8.30 am-7 pm

Chambers' facilities
Conference rooms, Disks accepted,
Disabled access

Languages spoken
French, German, Greek, Italian, Russian,
Spanish

Fees policy
Fees will be negotiated with the clerk.

Additional information
Hollis Whiteman Chambers (QEB) is a
long-established specialist criminal set. We
provide advocacy and advice of the highest
quality. We are dedicated to giving an effective service whenever needed, and at short
notice.

Our 53 members have expertise at all levels
of seniority: 16 QCs and four Treasury
Counsel are matched with a strong middle
order and 19 tenants of less than 15 years'
call. Eighteen tenants sit as Recorders in the
Crown Court.

We defend and prosecute from the Magistrates' Court to the House of Lords.
Members of chambers are regularly
involved in complex, high profile and grave
cases. There is also daily representation in
courts of all levels, at every stage of
proceedings.

In addition to 'pure crime', we specialise in
Confiscation Proceedings, Judicial Review,
Food Law, Health and Safety Act and
Trading Standards cases, Licensing and
Extradition. Members of chambers also
appear in other tribunals including: Public
Inquiries, the General Medical Council, the
General Optical Council, Courts Martial
and Police Disciplinary Proceedings.

Peter Whiteman QC, a Deputy High Court
Judge, provides specialist revenue advice,
particularly on corporate and international
tax law, and representation at both national
and international levels.

QUEEN ELIZABETH BUILDING

2nd Floor, Temple, London, EC4Y 9BS
0171 797 7837
Fax: 0171 353 5422; DX 339 London,
Chancery Lane

Chambers of Mr Paul Coleridge QC
Clerks: Ivor Treherne, Stephen Morley

Coleridge, Paul QC 1970†	Roberts, Jennifer 1988	Blair-Gould, John 1970†	Malcolm, Helen 1986
Baron, Florence QC 1976†	Edwards, Sarah 1990	Gouriet, Gerald 1974	Lewis, James 1987
Phillimore, Francis 1972	Firth, Matthew 1991	Muir, Andrew 1975	Hardy, John 1988
Wright, Peter 1974‡	Clarke, Elizabeth 1991	De Haan, Kevin 1976	Keith, Hugo 1989
Hosford-Tanner, Michael 1974	Henderson, Camilla 1992	Atchley, Richard 1977	Davies, Hugh 1990
	Leech, Stewart 1992	Bromley-Martin, Michael 1979	Lloyd-Jacob, Campaspe 1990
Tidbury, Andrew 1976	Thorpe, Alexander 1995	Harris, Mark 1980	Bromley-Martin, Tania 1983
Brudenell, Thomas 1977	Cowton, Catherine 1995	Hines, James 1982	
Moylan, Andrew 1978	Ewins, David James 1996	Rankin, James 1983	Wormald, Richard 1993
Blyth, Roderick 1981	Lyon, Antonia Heidi Jane 1997	Humphryes, Jane 1983‡	Williamson, Alisdair 1994
Wise, Oliver 1981		Saunders, Neil 1983	Knowles, Julian 1994
Stone, Lucy 1983	Phipps, Sarah Elizabeth 1997	Walsh, Stephen 1983	Naqshbandi, Saba 1996
Marks, Lewis 1984		Aylett, Crispin 1985	Gritt, Edmund 1997
Amos, Tim 1987	Young, Rachael 1997	Cameron, Alexander 1986	

189 RANDOLPH AVENUE

London, W9 1DJ
0171 624 9139
Fax: 0171 624 9139

Chambers of Mr J D Seal

ONE RAYMOND BUILDINGS

Gray's Inn, London, WC1R 5BH
0171 430 1234
Fax: 0171 430 1004; DX 16 Chancery Lane

Chambers of Christopher Morcom QC

3 RAYMOND BUILDINGS

RAYMOND BUILDINGS

Gray's Inn, London, WC1R 5BH
020 7831 3833
Fax: 020 7242 4221; DX 237 London
E-mail:
chambers@threeraymond.demon.co.uk

Chambers of Clive Nicholls QC
Clerk: Ian Collins; Administrator: Alison Marshall

Nicholls, Clive QC 1957	Whitehouse, David QC 1969†
Nicholls, Colin QC 1957†	
Gray, Gilbert QC 1953†	Price, Nicholas QC 1968†
Beckett, Richard QC 1965	Sherborne, Montague QC 1960
Nutting, John QC 1968†	
Batten, Stephen QC 1968†	Evans, Francis QC 1977†
Jones, Alun QC 1972†	Montgomery, Clare QC 1980‡

Types of work (and number of counsel practising in that area if supplied)
Administrative 10 · Civil liberties 4 ·
Common law (general) · Courts martial ·
Crime 34 · Crime – corporate fraud 23 ·
Environment 5 · Licensing 20

Chambers established: 1926
Opening times: 8.30 am-6.45 pm Mon-Fri

Chambers' facilities
Conference rooms, Disks accepted,
Disabled access, E-mail

Languages spoken
Arabic, Dutch, French, German, Italian,
Spanish

5 RAYMOND BUILDINGS

1st Floor, Gray's Inn, London, WC1R 5BP
0171 242 2902
Fax: 0171 831 2686; DX 1054 London
E-mail: clerks@media-ent-law.co.uk
URL: http://www.media-ent-law.co.uk

Chambers of P H Milmo QC
Clerks: Kim Janes (Senior Clerk), Jacqueline Garnham, John Sizer; Administrator: Elizabeth Szukics

Milmo, Patrick QC 1962	Rogers, Heather 1983
Bishop, Gordon 1968	Marzec, Alexandra 1990
Tugendhat, Michael QC 1969†	Sherborne, David 1992
	Rushbrooke, Justin 1992
Browne, Desmond QC 1969†	Nicklin, Matthew 1993
	Busuttil, Godwin 1994
Page, Adrienne QC 1974†	Wolanski, Adam 1995
Price, James QC 1974	Bennett, William 1994
Parkes, Richard 1977	Dean, Jacob 1995
Warby, Mark 1981	Coppola, Anna 1996
Bate, Stephen 1981	Mansoori, Sara 1997
Monson, Andrew 1983	

C

Types of work (and number of counsel practising in that area if supplied)
Commercial litigation 3 · Copyright 8 · Defamation 16 · Entertainment 5 · Film, cable, TV 1 · Information technology 1 · Insurance/reinsurance 3 · Intellectual property 8 · International trade 3 · Professional negligence 2 · Sale and carriage of goods 3 · Sports 5 · Telecommunications 1

Chambers established: 1932
Opening times: 8.30 am-6.30 pm

Languages spoken
French, German, Italian, Polish

Fees policy
Please refer to clerks.

---

18 RED LION COURT

(Off Fleet Street), London, EC4A 3EB
0171 520 6000
Fax: 0171 520 6248/49; DX 478 Chancery Lane
E-mail: chambers@18rlc.co.uk

Chambers of Anthony Arlidge QC
Clerks: Ken Darvill, Mark Bennett

Also at: Thornwood House, 102 New London Road, Chelmsford, Essex CM2 0RG Tel: 01245 280880 Fax: 01245 280882 DX: 89706 Chelmsford 2

Spencer, Sir Derek QC 1961†	**Ball,** Christopher QC 1972†
Arlidge, Anthony QC 1962†	**Carter,** Peter QC 1974
Cocks, David QC 1961†	**Horwood-Smart,** Rosamund QC 1974†
Stewart, James QC 1966†	**Peters,** Nigel QC 1976†
Green, Henry QC 1962†	**Black,** John QC 1975
Lederman, David QC 1966†	**Lynch,** Patricia QC 1979‡
Parkins, Graham QC 1972†	**Etherington,** David QC 1979‡
Stern, Linda QC 1971†	
Rook, Peter QC 1973†	**Dobbs,** Linda QC 1981
Sutton, Richard QC 1969†	**Radcliffe,** David 1966†

Johnston, Carey 1977	**Williams,** David Huw 1988
Green, David 1979‡	**Anderson,** John 1989
Harvey, Stephen 1979	**Hill,** Candida 1990
Fenn, Peter 1979	**Lawson,** Sara 1990
Fisher, Jonathan 1980	**Holborn,** David 1991
Milne, Alexander 1981	**Hammond,** Sean 1991
Sheff, Janine 1983	**Clare,** Allison 1992
Kovalevsky, Richard 1983	**Gowen,** Matthew 1992
Lucraft, Mark 1984	**Hardy,** Paul 1992
Morris, Angela 1984	**Forster,** Tom 1993
Overbury, Rupert 1984	**Jameson,** Barnaby 1993
Marshall, David 1985	**Mortimore,** Claudia 1994
Morris, Brendan 1985	**Nelson,** Michelle 1994
Spence, Simon 1985	**Hall,** Jacqueline 1994
Boyle, Robert 1985	**Wiseman,** Adam 1994
du Preez, Robin 1985	**Webster,** Elizabeth 1995
Bewsey, Jane 1986	**Jones,** Gillian 1996
Hill, Max 1987	**Requena,** Stephen 1997
Collery, Shane 1988	**Hood,** Gavin William 1997*

Types of work (and number of counsel practising in that area if supplied)
Crime · Crime – corporate fraud

Chambers established: 1946
Opening times: 8.30 am-6.30 pm

Chambers' facilities
Conference rooms

Additional information
The set has always specialised in criminal work, both prosecuting and defending. There is particular expertise in commercial fraud, Customs and Inland Revenue work and in money laundering. A number of members of chambers act frequently in sex, child abuse and pornography cases. Others have considerable expertise in domestic disciplinary tribunals particularly those connected with financial services and medicine. There is also expertise in judicial review and Human Rights cases. Individual members practise in general common law work (particularly personal injury, family work and aviation and also in licensing and environmental law). Pro Bono work is done in the Privy Council and the FRU unit.

---

20 RICHMOND WAY

1st Floor, London, W12 8LY
0181 749 2004
Fax: 0181 740 1192

Chambers of Dr J A Roberts QC DCL, FCIArb

RIDGEWAY CHAMBERS

6 The Ridgeway, Golders Green, London, NW11 8TB
0181 455 2939
Fax: 0181 905 5104

Chambers of C D H Wolchover

ROEHAMPTON CHAMBERS

30 Stoughton Close, Roehampton, London, SW15 4LS
0181 788 1238
Fax: 0181 788 1238

Chambers of Mr P G Proghoulis

ROSEMONT CHAMBERS

26 Rosemont Court, Rosemont Road, London, W3 9LS
0181 992 1100

Chambers of Mr M Byrd

NO. 1 SERJEANTS' INN

5th Floor Fleet Street, Temple, London, EC4Y 1LH
0171 415 6666
Fax: 0171 583 2033; DX 364 London
E-mail: no1serjeantsinn@btinternet.com
URL: http://www.no1serjeantsinn.co.uk
Out of hours telephone: 0171 415 6666

Chambers of Edward Faulks QC
Clerks: Clark Chessis, Ann Winders; Practice Manager: Rosemary Thorpe; Administrator: Jenny Fensham

Faulks, Edward QC 1973‡	**Yell**, Nicholas 1979
Redgrave, Adrian QC 1968†	**Norman**, John 1979
Andreae-Jones, William QC 1965*†	**Hammerton**, Alastair 1983
Foster, Jonathan QC 1970*†	**Bishop**, Edward 1985
	Paneth, Sarah 1985‡
Leech, Brian 1967†	**Waters**, Julian 1986
Ross, John 1971†	**Rivalland**, Marc 1987
Hunter, William 1972	**Althaus**, Justin 1988
Baldry, Antony MP 1975	**Pinder**, Mary 1989
Hammerton, Veronica 1977‡	**Piper**, Angus 1991
	Boyle, Gerard 1992
Pittaway, David 1977‡	**Warnock**, Andrew 1993
Readhead, Simon 1979‡	**Clarke**, Alison 1994
	Stagg, Paul 1994

Collett, Ivor 1995	**Bridgman**, David 1997
Mortimer, Sophie 1996	

1 SERJEANTS' INN

4th Floor, Temple, London, EC4Y 1NH
0171 583 1355
Fax: 0171 583 1672; DX 440 London
E-mail: clerks@serjants-inn.co.uk
Out of hours telephone: 01622 735837

Chambers of Lionel Read QC
Clerks: William King, Geoffrey Carr, Kevin Squires

Read, Lionel QC 1954†	**Morgan**, Stephen 1983
Woolley, David QC 1962	**Langham**, Richard 1986
Rumbelow, Anthony QC 1967†	**Harris**, Russell 1986
	Thomas, Megan 1987
Clarkson, Patrick QC 1972‡	**Martin**, Roy QC (Scot) 1990
Whybrow, Christopher QC 1965	**Upton**, William 1990
	White, Sasha 1991
Hicks, William QC 1975	**Douglas White**, Robert 1993
Wood, Martin 1972	
Price Lewis, Rhodri 1975†	**Harwood**, Richard 1993
Pugh-Smith, John 1977	**Edwards**, Martin 1995
Pickles, Simon 1978	**Reed**, Matthew 1995
Dagg, John 1980	**Lyness**, Scott 1996
Cameron, Neil 1982	**Zwart**, Christiaan 1997

3 SERJEANTS' INN

THREE
SERJEANTS'
INN

London, EC4Y 1BQ
0171 353 5537
Fax: 0171 353 0425; DX 421 London, Chancery Lane
E-mail: clerks@3serjeantsinn.com
Out of hours telephone: 0385 736844

Chambers of P A Naughton QC
Clerks: Nick Salt, Lee Johnson, Tracy Barker; Administrator: Helen Ensor

Naughton, Philip QC 1970	**Francis**, Robert QC 1973‡
Whitfield, Adrian QC 1964†	**Davies**, Nicola QC 1976‡

Grace, John QC *1973*	Beggs, John *1989*
Gaisford, Philip *1969*	Holl-Allen, Jonathan *1990*
Fortune, Malcolm *1972†*	Johnston, Christopher *1990*
Conlin, Geoffrey *1973†*	Horne, Michael *1992*
Lloyd, Huw *1975*	McCredie, Fionnuala *1992*
Cottle, Tony *1978*	Partridge, Richard *1994*
Watson, James *1979*	Ley-Morgan, Mark *1994*
Burns, Sue *1979*	Jackson, Anthony *1995*
Grubb, Andrew *1980*	Powell, Debra *1995*
Neale, Fiona *1981*	Thomas, George *1995*
O'Rourke, Mary *1981*	Bradley, Clodagh *1996*
Hugh-Jones, George *1983*	Davidson, Ranald *1996*
Hopkins, Adrian *1984*	Dolan, Bridget *1997*
Moon, Angus *1986*	Flockhart, Sharon *1997*
Wright, Ian *1989*	Lim, Malcolm *1989*

Types of work (and number of counsel practising in that area if supplied)
Arbitration 6 · Civil actions against the police 10 · Commercial litigation 9 · Common law (general) 24 · Construction 10 · Crime 6 · Defamation 2 · Employment 15 · Environment 10 · Medical negligence 21 · Mental health 17 · Personal injury 20 · Professional negligence 24 · Sale and carriage of goods 10

Chambers established: 1973
Opening times: 8.30 am-6.30 pm

Chambers' facilities
Conference rooms, Disks accepted, Disabled access by arrangement, Limited car parking may be available by arrangement

Languages spoken
French, German

Additional information
Medical Law and professional discipline
The largest field of specialisation in Chambers. Tenants have appeared for plaintiffs and defendants in many of the most important medical negligence, mental health and medical ethics cases. Tenants regularly appear in disciplinary tribunals including the GMC, GDC and in major public inquiries. Tenants also appear in major criminal trials concerning medical practice and inquests.
Construction and Engineering Law
Tenants act in national and international arbitration and litigation concerning standard form and special contracts relating to building, and engineering works for employers, including governments, contractors, subcontractors and professionals.
Commercial Contracts

Particularly disputes concerning contracts for the design manufacture and leasing of plant and equipment.
Professional Negligence
All medical, architects, surveyors, engineers, lawyers, accountants, valuers, etc.
Employment Law
Tenants act in unfair and wrongful dismissal cases and race and sex discrimination claims.
Civil actions involving the police
Tenants act for the majority of constabularies, principally in malicious prosecution cases.
Crime
Prosecution and defence work is undertaken. Tenants have recognised experience in environmental and medical cases.
ADR
Chambers is a member of CEDR; tenants include accredited mediators.
Other Fields
General common law, personal injury, landlord and tenant, defamation and environmental law.

SERLE COURT CHAMBERS

6 New Square, Lincoln's Inn, London, WC2A 3QS
0171 242 6105
Fax: 0171 405 4004; DX 1025 London
E-mail: clerks@serlecourt.co.uk
URL: http://www.serlecourt.co.uk

Chambers of Charles Sparrow QC DL
Clerks: Terry Buck, Steven Whitaker; Chief Executive: Helena Miles

Sparrow, Charles QC *1950*	Hoser, Philip *1982*
Talbot, Patrick QC *1969‡*	Jones, Elizabeth *1984*
Boyle, Alan QC *1972*	Walford, Richard *1984*
Briggs, Michael QC *1978*	Jones, Philip *1985*
Browne-Wilkinson, Simon QC *1981*	Marshall, Philip *1987*
	Harrison, Nicholas *1988*
Farrow, Kenneth *1966†*	Hoffmann, Clare *1990*
Asprey, Nicholas *1969*	Close, Douglas *1991*
Whittaker, John *1969*	Purkis, Kathryn *1991*
Hinks, Frank *1973*	Blayney, David *1992*
Joffe, Victor *1975*	Bruce, Andrew *1992*
Rogers, Beverly-Ann *1978*	Machell, John *1993*
Henderson, William *1978*	Drake, David *1994*
Behrens, James *1979*	Higgo, Justin *1995*
McMaster, Peter *1981*	Lightman, Daniel *1995*

† Recorder ‡ Assistant Recorder *Door Tenant

Norbury, Hugh *1995*   **Richardson,** Giles *1997*
Collingwood, Timothy *1996* **Agnew,** Sinéad *1998*

Types of work (and number of counsel practising in that area if supplied)

Chancery (commercial) · Chancery (general) · Civil fraud · Commercial litigation · Company and commercial · Insolvency · Partnerships · Professional negligence · Property

Opening times: 8.30 am-7 pm

Chambers' facilities
Disks accepted, E-mail

Languages spoken
French, German, Hebrew

Specialisms
Commercial Chancery litigation forms the core of Serle Court's work. In 1997-8 and again in 1998-9 Chambers & Partners recommended more barristers from Serle Court for commercial chancery work than any other set of chambers. Our principal practice areas are:
Chancery – Commercial . Chancery – Traditional . Civil Fraud . Commercial Litigation . Company . Insolvency . Partnership . Professional Negligence . Property.
We can provide a first-class team of barristers at all levels of call in each of these areas.

Additional Areas
Individual members of Chambers have particular expertise in the following additional areas: Charities, Commons Registration, Employment, Environmental law, Entertainment law, Financial Services, Intellectual Property, Parliamentary work, Sports law.

In the independent rankings of the *Chambers and Partners Guide* and *The Legal 500*, Serle Court Chambers is consistently recommended in every one of its principal areas of practice (listed above).

This reputation is based upon the excellence of our barristers, most of whom are individually recommended as leading practitioners in their specialist fields. This year we have recruited five new members, bringing our total to 33:

- Simon Browne-Wilkinson QC (formerly of Fountain Court) – a commercial litigator who is especially welcome for the added depth he brings to our thriving civil fraud team.
- Peter McMaster – (formerly of 3 Paper Buildings) a commercial litigator, with special experience in energy and other cases with heavy technical content.
- Andrew Bruce – (formerly of 3 Paper Buildings) an up-and-coming property and commercial lawyer.
- Giles Richardson and Sinead Agnew, on successfull completion of their pupillages.

Serle Court's particular strength, however, is in blending proven calibre with a determination to give the best possible service. We are a long-established set, thoroughly approachable, innovative and at all times responsive to the needs and interests of our clients; our very experienced clerking and administrative team sets itself the same high standards.

In February 1999 *The Lawyer* wrote: 'Serle Court is at the top of its game, providing an excellent all-round service'. We aim to keep this reputation and welcome feedback in all areas.

International
Members of Chambers appear in proceedings in the British Virgin Islands, Cayman Islands, Bermuda and the United States of America.

Administration
Office opening hours are 8.30 am to 7 pm weekdays. Out of office hours, voicemail messages may be left for individual members of Chambers on 0171 242 6105. In cases of urgency, contact Terry Buck (01268) 743324 or Steven Whitaker (01708) 478338.

Fees are based on a number of considerations, including time commitment, degree of responsibility and complexity. They may be charged on an hourly or inclusive basis, and the Senior Clerks, who each have over 25 years' clerking experience, will be glad to discuss a fee and provide information as to its composition before work is undertaken.

20 SEWARDSTONE GARDENS

Chingford, London, E4 7QE
0181 524 3054

Chambers of Mr A Amihere

SOMERSETT CHAMBERS

Somersett
Chambers
25 Bedford Row

25 Bedford Row, London, WC1R 4HE
0171 404 6701
Fax: 0171 404 6702; DX 44 LDE
E-mail: somelaw@aol.com
Out of hours telephone: 0468 814 659

Chambers of Mr E K Cofie
*Clerks: Miss Trace Grant (Senior Clerk),
Miss Tania Robinson (Junior Clerk)*

Cofie, Edmund *1980*	**Miller,** Hayley *1995*
Mobedji, Philip *1977*	**Craven,** Richard *1995*
Allen, Sylvia *1983*	**English,** Robert *1996*
Thompson, Cedric *1984*	**Enright,** Johanne *1996*
Webster, Justin *1985*	**Pidcock,** Steven *1996*
Fletcher, Stephen *1987*	**Rahman,** Luthfur *1996*
Stanislas, Paul *1989*	**Nixon,** Diane *1997*
Thomas, Janet *1994*	**Odili,** Christopher *1992**

3/4 SOUTH SQUARE

3/4 SOUTH SQUARE

Gray's Inn, London, WC1R 5HP
0171 696 9900
Fax: 0171 696 9911; DX 338 London
E-mail: clerks@southsquare.com
URL: http://www.southsquare.com

Chamber of: Please use reference point as 3/4 South Square
Administrator: Lesley Mortimer; Practice Managers: Jason Pithers (Senior Practice Manager), Mike Killick, Jim Costa, Dylan Playfoot

Crystal, Michael QC *1970*	**Brougham,** Christopher QC *1969*

Moss, Gabriel QC *1974*	**Atherton,** Stephen *1989*
Mortimore, Simon QC *1972*	**Bristoll,** Sandra *1989*
Simmons, Marion QC *1970‡*	**Goodison,** Adam *1990*
	Stonefrost, Hilary *1991*
Adkins, Richard QC *1982*	**Tamlyn,** Lloyd *1991*
Sheldon, Richard QC *1979*	**Davis,** Glen *1992*
Hacker, Richard QC *1977*	**Gledhill,** Andreas *1992*
Knowles, Robin QC *1982*	**Oditah,** Fidelis *1992*
Phillips, Mark QC *1984*	**Ismail,** Roxanne *1993*
Briggs, John *1973*	**Isaacs,** Barry *1994*
Marks, David *1974*	**Valentin,** Ben *1995*
Pascoe, Martin *1977*	**Toube,** Felicity *1995*
Trower, William *1983*	**Goldring,** Jeremy *1996*
Dicker, Robin *1986*	**Knights,** Samantha *1996*
Alexander, David *1987*	**Frazer,** Lucy *1996*
Arnold, Mark *1988*	**Allison,** David *1998*
Zacaroli, Antony James *1987*	**Cohen,** Clive *1989*
Hilliard, Lexa *1987*	**Hunter,** Prof Muir QC *1938*

Types of work (and number of counsel practising in that area if supplied)
Arbitration · Asset finance · Banking 30 · Bankruptcy 35 · Chancery (general) · Commercial litigation · Commercial property · Commodities · Common law (general) · Company and commercial · Corporate finance · Financial services 25 · Insolvency 35 · Insurance · Insurance/reinsurance · International trade · Partnerships · Pensions · Professional negligence 30 · Sale and carriage of goods · Share options · Tax – corporate

Opening times: 8 am-7 pm. Evening reception manned until 8.15 pm

Languages spoken
French, German, Italian, Mandarin Chinese, Spanish

Fees policy
Details will be provided on request.

Additional information
3-4 South Square practise primarily in business, financial and commercial law and have a well-known expertise in insolvency law. Chambers' practice regularly covers the following subjects: corporate, international and personal insolvency, including receivership, administration, liquidation, arrangements with creditors and bankruptcy; banking and finance; company law, including mergers and acquisitions, shareholders' and directors' disputes and partnership disputes; financial services.

Within chambers individual members also practise in a variety of other areas, including civil aspects of commercial fraud;

         † Recorder ‡ Assistant Recorder *Door Tenant

insurance and reinsurance; international trade; sale of goods, commercial and business agreements; professional negligence and disciplinary proceedings; tracing remedies; pre-trial remedies; enforcement of domestic and foreign judgments; obtaining evidence for foreign proceedings.

Members of chambers adopt a commercial and businesslike approach to their practices and are capable of reacting swiftly (individually or as members of a team) to urgent problems as the need may arise and are accustomed to dealing with matters at all levels of complexity, often at very short notice. Members are ready to appear as advocates and to advise outside London and are in a position to accept instructions direct from overseas lawyers and from other professional bodies such as accountants and architects. The overall aim of chambers is to provide an effective professional service to clients as promptly and efficiently as possible.

11 SOUTH SQUARE

11 SOUTH SQUARE

2nd Floor, Gray's Inn, London, WC1R 5EU
0171 405 1222 (24hr messaging service)
Fax: 0171 242 4282; DX 433 London
E-mail: clerks@11southsquare.com
Out of hours telephone: 07775 941 350 (weekdays)

Chambers of C D Floyd QC
Clerks: Rochelle Haring (Senior Clerk), Martyn Nicholls (Senior Clerk), Ashley Carr (Junior Clerk)

Floyd, Christopher QC *1975‡*	**Arnold**, Richard *1985*
	Lawrence, Heather *1990*
Whittle, Henry *1975*	**Vanhegan**, Mark *1990*
Silverleaf, Michael QC *1980*	**Reid**, Jacqueline *1992*
Carr, Henry QC *1982*	**Acland**, Piers *1993*
Hacon, Richard *1979*	**Cuddigan**, Hugo *1995*
Purvis, Iain *1986*	**Fernando**, Giles *1998*

Types of work (and number of counsel practising in that area if supplied)
Copyright 13 · Information technology 13 · Intellectual property 13 · Patents 13 · Trademarks 13

Chambers established: 1925
Opening times: 9 am-6 pm

Chambers' facilities
Conference rooms, Disks accepted, E-mail

Languages spoken
French, German

STANBROOK & HENDERSON

STANBROOK & HENDERSON
BARRISTERS

Ground Floor, 2 Harcourt Bldgs, Temple, London, EC4Y 9DB
0171 353 0101
Fax: 0171 583 2686; DX 1039 London, Chancery Lane
E-mail: clerks@harcourt.co.uk

Chambers of C St G Stanbrook QC OBE and R A Henderson QC
Clerks: John White (Chief Clerk), Simon Boutwood; Chambers Development Manager: Martin Dyke

Also at: 42 Rue du Taciturne, B-1000 Brussels

Stanbrook, Clive QC *1972*	**Holland**, Debra *1996*
Bentley, Philip QC *1970*	**Cacciotti**, Melissa *1997*

Types of work (and number of counsel practising in that area if supplied)
Administrative 7 · Arbitration 4 · Asset finance 8 · Banking 4 · Care proceedings 11 · Chancery (general) 6 · Commercial litigation 25 · Common law (general) 34 · Company and commercial 5 · Competition 8 · Construction 17 · Copyright 3 · Courts martial 3 · Crime 7 · Crime – corporate fraud 7 · Ecclesiastical 1 · Employment 20 · Environment 7 · Equity, wills and trusts 5 · Family 11 · Family provision 11 · Financial services 8 · Franchising 2 · Housing 14 · Information technology 5 · Insurance 25 · Insurance/reinsurance 25 · Intellectual property 3 · International trade 4 · Landlord and tenant 14 · Local

government 10 · Medical negligence 20 · Parliamentary 3 · Partnerships 8 · Patents 3 · Personal injury 34 · Probate and administration 3 · Professional negligence 34 · Sale and carriage of goods 20 · Sports 5 · Tax – capital and income 1 · Tax – corporate 1 · Telecommunications 4

Chambers established: 1991

Chambers' facilities
Conference rooms, Disks accepted, E-mail

Languages spoken
French, Italian, Japanese, Portuguese, Spanish

Fees policy
Fees will be negotiated with the chief clerk. Our aim is that fees will be reasonable and competitive, depending on the importance and nature of the work and the expertise and seniority of Counsel.

Additional information
Stanbrook and Henderson is an association between the chambers of Roger Henderson QC at 2 Harcourt Buildings (for a full list of members of chambers see the entry for 2 Harcourt Buildings) and the members of the European law firm of Stanbrook and Hooper in Brussels who are also members of the English bar.

The work undertaken reflects chambers' wide knowledge of EU institutions and the way in which they work – knowledge which is essential for anyone affected by EU actions or legislation. The Brussels-based barristers of Stanbrook & Henderson have a close link with daily developments in the European Commission, the Council and the Parliament Secretariat, as a result of which chambers can offer a complete legal monitoring and information service.

In business law, chambers undertakes advisory, drafting and litigation work in a wide range of areas, including environmental law; financial services; insurance, including drafting and interpreting policies and advice on the structure of the market; offshore investment funds; credit, including consumer credit and leasing; product liability; food law; sports law; and general EU regulatory policy, including the making of representations to the EU institutions in Brussels.

In the corporate sphere, chambers provides specialist advisory and drafting

expertise as well as advocacy at administrative level from UK industrial tribunals to the Competition Directorate of the European Commission in Brussels, as well as at judicial level both in the UK and in the European courts in Luxembourg.

The specialist areas covered include company law (including EU developments and freedom of establishment); joint ventures (including EU competition aspects); merger control (UK and EU); competition law (UK and EU); employment law (including EU rules on the free movement of workers and health and safety at work); distribution agreements (including the EU competition aspects); EU rules on freedom to provide services, free movement of goods and non-discrimination in fiscal and other matters; and intellectual property.

In public sector law, chambers advises local authorities in particular on local government finance, fiduciary duties and compulsory competitive tendering, combining such advice with an EU point of view. In private law, chambers provides a similarly comprehensive service, for example, in immigration and rights of free movement.

STAPLE INN CHAMBERS

1st Floor, 9 Staple Inn, Holborn Bars, London, WC1V 7QH
0171 242 5240
Fax: 0171 405 9495; DX 132 London
E-mail: clerks@staple-inn.org

Clerks: Yvonne Simmons, Brian Monument, Stuart Davis

Ramsden, Veronica *1979*	**Falk,** Charles *1994*
Sheikh, Raana *1977*	**Panagiotopoulou,** Tania *1994*
Llewellyn, Charles *1978*	
Tresman, Lewis *1980*	**McManus,** Rebecca *1994*
Limbrey, Bernard *1980*	**Brissett,** Nicola *1995*
Corry, Carol *1981*	**Panagiotopoulou,** Sophie *1995*
Jones, Paul *1981*	
Masniuk, Peter *1983*	**Feldman,** Matthew *1995*
Aslam, Qazi *1983*	**Tyler,** Tom *1996*
Trumpington, John *1985*	**Mullee,** Brendan *1996*
Brooks, Alison *1989*	**Perhar,** Simon *1997*
McCormack, Alan *1990*	**Codner,** Peter *1983**
Fordham, Allison *1990*	**Briand,** Pauline *1996**
Brown, Andrea *1991*	**Mercer,** Nicholas *1994**
Vakil, Jimmy *1993*	

CHAMBERS OF MICHAEL STEPHEN

118 Kennington Road, London, SE11 6RE
07071 780690
Fax: 0171 642 8358

Chambers of Mr M Stephen

3 STONE BUILDINGS

Lincoln's Inn, London, WC2A 3XL
0171 242 4937
Fax: 0171 405 3896; DX 317 London
E-mail: clerks@3sb.law.co.uk

Chambers of G C Vos QC
Clerk: Andrew Palmer

Vos, Geoffrey QC *1977*	**Asplin,** Sarah *1984*
Bannister, Edward QC *1974*	**Girling,** Sarah *1986*
Stanford, David *1951*	**Lord,** David *1987*
Topham, Geoffrey *1964*	**Pimentel,** Carlos *1990*
Cosedge, Andrew *1972*	**Kayani,** Asaf *1991*
Gibbons, James *1974*	**Lacey,** Sarah *1991*
Tunkel, Alan *1976*	**Conroy,** Marian *1991*
da Silva, David *1978*	**Twigger,** Andrew *1994*
Mason, Alexandra *1981*	**Moeran,** Fenner *1996*
Hantusch, Robert *1982*	

Types of work (and number of counsel practising in that area if supplied)
Banking · Bankruptcy · Chancery (general) · Chancery land law · Charities · Commercial litigation · Commercial property · Company and commercial · Conveyancing · Copyright · Entertainment · Equity, wills and trusts · Family provision · Film, cable, TV · Financial services · Insolvency · Insurance · Insurance/reinsurance · Landlord and tenant · Partnerships · Pensions · Private international · Probate and administration · Professional negligence · Sports · Tax – capital and income · Tax – corporate

Chambers established: 1938
Opening times: 8.30 am-6.30 pm

Languages spoken
French, Portuguese, Spanish

Types of work undertaken: 3 Stone Buildings is a long-established and expanding Chancery set with a considerable breadth of experience. Individual attention is combined with professional efficiency. The chambers has experienced practitioners in most areas of financial litigation and advisory work.

Litigation: The chambers has experienced practitioners in financial and property litigation and advice with particular emphasis being placed on company and commercial litigation.

Advisory: Chambers has particular expertise in revenue law and tax planning, pensions, trusts and property, insolvency, and partnership matters. As a result all aspects of families' financial and property affairs (including their trusts, companies and partnerships, the succession thereto and the tax thereon) can be dealt with in a unified manner.

Drafting: The drafting of conveyancing and commercial documentation and settlements is extensively undertaken by members of chambers.

Additional specialisations: In addition to the above, chambers has expertise in the following fields of practice: administration of estates, agricultural holdings, arbitration, banking, bankruptcy, building disputes, charities, commercial contracts, companies, conveyancing, copyright and intellectual property, corporate insolvency, Court of Protection, financial services, insurance, landlord and tenant, mortgages and securities, pensions and share schemes, professional negligence, real property, sale of goods, shipping, Stock Exchange work, taxation and tax planning, trusts, and wills and probate.

Instructions may be taken in writing, by fax, or in conference. The Senior Clerk is always willing to discuss any queries concerning choice of, and instructions to, counsel, including particular expertise, availability, and level of fees.

Direct access instructions are accepted from members of all recognised professional bodies in accordance with the guidance notes issued by the General Council of the Bar. Direct instructions are also accepted from overseas lawyers.

The chambers has founder membership of CEDR (alternative dispute resolution).

4 STONE BUILDINGS

*Ground Floor, Lincoln's Inn, London,
WC2A 3XT*
0171 242 5524
Fax: 0171 831 7907; DX 385 London
E-mail: clerks@4stonebuildings.law.co.uk
URL: http://www.4stonebuildings.com
Out of hours telephone: 01277 229180 or
0860 452552 (Senior Clerk)

Chambers of Philip Heslop QC
Clerk: David Goddard

Heslop, Philip QC *1970*	**Brettler**, Jonathan *1988*
Curry, Peter QC *1953*	**Greenwood**, Paul *1991*
Bompas, A G QC *1975*	**Clutterbuck**, Andrew *1992*
Hildyard, Robert QC *1977*	**Cox**, Nicholas *1992*
Brisby, John QC *1978*	**Hill**, Richard *1993*
Hunt, Stephen *1968*	**Fraser**, Orlando *1994*
Griffiths, Peter *1977*	**Markham**, Anna *1996*
Crow, Jonathan *1981*	**Boeddinghaus**, Hermann
Scott, John *1982*	*1996*
Davis-White, Malcolm	**De Mestre**, Andrew Etienne
1984	*1998*
Miles, Robert *1987*	**Prichard**, Michael John
Nicholson, Rosalind *1987*	*1951**
Harman, Sarah *1987*	**Seligman**, Ralph David QC
Harrison, Christopher *1988*	(Bahamas) *1996**

5 STONE BUILDINGS

Lincoln's Inn, London, WC2A 3XT
0171 242 6201
Fax: 0171 831 8102; DX 304 London,
Chancery Lane
E-mail: clerks@5-stonebuildings.law.co.uk
URL:
http://www.5-stonebuildings.law.co.uk
Out of hours telephone: 01474 709034

Chambers of Henry M Harrod
Clerk: Paul Jennings

Harrod, Henry *1963†*	**Farber**, Martin *1976*
Warnock-Smith, Shan *1971*	**Henderson**, Launcelot QC
Norris, Alastair QC *1973‡*	*1977*
Fawls, Richard *1973*	**Simmonds**, Andrew QC
Herbert, Mark QC *1974*	*1980*
Blackett-Ord, Mark *1974*	

Tidmarsh, Christopher	**Templeman**, Michael
1985	*1973**
O'Sullivan, Michael *1986*	**Hayton**, David *1968**
Rolfe, Patrick *1987*	**Orr**, Nicholas *1970**
Rich, Barbara *1990*	**Dennis**, David *1979**
Walden-Smith, Karen *1990*	**Johnson**, Ian *1982**
Angus, Tracey *1991*	**Cadwallader**, Neil *1984**
Legge, Henry *1993*	**Morris**, Paul *1986**
Rees, David *1994*	**Lund**, Celia *1988**
Clarke, Anna *1994*	**Pritchett**, Stephen *1989**
Sartin, Leon *1997*	

Types of work (and number of counsel practising in that area if supplied)
Arbitration 1 · Banking 12 · Bankruptcy 8 ·
Chancery (general) 19 · Chancery land law
19 · Charities 6 · Commercial litigation 10 ·
Commercial property 15 · Common land 8
· Conveyancing 19 · Equity, wills and trusts
19 · Family provision 18 · Financial services
6 · Insolvency 8 · Landlord and tenant 15 ·
Mental health 7 · Partnerships 12 ·
Pensions 6 · Probate and administration 18
· Professional negligence 12 · Tax – capital
and income 5

Opening times: 8.45 am-6.15 pm

Chambers' facilities
Conference rooms, Disks accepted, Disks
provided, E-mail

Languages spoken
French, Italian, Spanish

Fees policy
Fees will be negotiated with the clerk. We
are happy to give estimates. Our aim is to
be competitive.

Additional information
We are a Chancery set offering specialist
expertise in the fields of property litigation,
professional negligence and occupational
pensions. Two former members are now in
the Court of Appeal and a third has recently
been appointed to the Chancery bench.
Members have been involved in the Polly
Peck and Maxwell litigation and a number
of the leading cases on tax avoidance,
undue influence, right to buy, ethical
investment, pension surplus, duties of
pension trustees. All members are well
versed in trusts, wills, administration of
estates, land law and conveyancing. A
number of members specialise in private
client and estate planning and partnership.
Commercial litigation and insolvency work
is also undertaken. Our aim is to provide an
efficient modern service of the highest
standard.

7 STONE BUILDINGS

7 STONE BUILDINGS

Ground Floor, Lincoln's Inn, London,
WC2A 3SZ
0171 405 3886/242 3546
Fax: 0171 242 8502; DX 335 London
E-mail: chaldous@vossnet.co.uk
Out of hours telephone: 0831 816102

Chambers of C Aldous QC
Clerks: T Marsh, M Newton; Practice
Manager: Shona Kelly

Aldous, Charles QC *1967*	**Clifford,** James *1984*
Nield, Michael *1969*	**Stewart,** Lindsey *1983*
Unwin, David QC *1971*	**Cullen,** Edmund *1990*
Davis, Nigel QC *1975*†	**Carswell,** Patricia *1993*
Walton, Alastair *1977*	**Bannister,** Thomas *1993*
Randall, John QC *1978*	**Westwood,** Andrew *1994*
Newey, Guy *1982*	**Atkins,** Siward *1995*
Parker, Christopher *1984*	

Types of work (and number of counsel practising in that area if supplied)
Arbitration · Banking · Bankruptcy · Chancery (general) · Chancery land law · Charities · Commercial litigation · Commercial property · Common land · Company and commercial · Corporate finance · Energy · Entertainment · Equity, wills and trusts · Financial services · Insolvency · Intellectual property · Landlord and tenant · Partnerships · Pensions · Private international · Professional negligence

Chambers established: 1870
Opening times: 8.30 am-6.45 pm

Chambers' facilities
Disks accepted, E-mail

Languages spoken
Spanish

Fees policy
Fees will be negotiated with the clerk depending on the case.

Additional information
The work undertaken by members covers all aspects of Chancery and commercial practice other than shipping.

Principal specialisations include commercial law and contracts; company law and partnership; corporate and personal insolvency; credit and security; entertainment law; equitable remedies; financial services and regulation; fraud; insurance; landlord and tenant; passing-off, confidential information, and copyright; pensions; pre-trial remedies; professional negligence; real property; trusts, settlements, and capital taxation; and wills, probate, and the administration of estates.

Other specialist areas, such as European Community law, administrative law, and private international law, are undertaken in the context of these areas of practice.

7 STONE BUILDINGS (ALSO AT 11 BOLT COURT)

1st Floor, Lincoln's Inn, London,
WC2A 3SZ
0171 242 0961
Fax: 0171 405 7028; DX 1007 London
E-mail: larthur@7stonebuildings.law.co.uk

Clerks: John Lister (Director of Chambers),
Miss Rita Vella, Miss Sophie Butcher, Miss
Louisa Arthur

Also at: Redhill Chambers, Seloduct House, 30 Station Road, Redhill RH1 1NF
Tel: 01737 780781, Fax: 01737 761760

Alexander, Ian QC *1964*†	**Tod,** Jonathan *1990*
Ashmore, Terence *1961*	**Murch,** Stephen *1991*
Bishop, John *1970*	**Benner,** Lucinda *1992*
Martin, Gay *1970*	**Carron,** Richard *1992*
Wood, Penelope (formerly a	**Burrington,** Richard *1993*
solicitor) *1999*	**Gerrish,** Simon *1993*
Conway, Robert *1974*	**Le Quesne,** Catherine *1993*
Lynch, Julian *1976*	**Linstead,** Peter *1994*
Lewis, Robert (formerly a	**Mathias,** Anna *1994*
solicitor) *1996*	**Papazian,** Cliona *1994*
Temple-Bone, Gillian *1978*	**Rudd,** Matthew *1994*
Birks, Simon *1981*	**Casey,** Noel *1995*
Randle, Simon *1982*	**Ellis,** Jonathan *1995*
Jenkala, Adrian *1984*	**Simkin,** Iain *1995*
Manson, Juliann *1985*	**Badenoch,** Tony *1996*
Pyle, Susan *1985*	**Islam-Choudhury,** Mugni
Owens, Matthew *1988*	*1996*
Porter, Geoffrey *1988*	**McGregor,** Alexander *1996*
Airey, Simon *1989*	**Porter,** Sarah *1996*
Cave, Patricia *1989*	**Harris,** Richard *1997*
Lakha, Shabbir *1989*	**Husain,** Laureen *1997*
Swirsky, Adam *1989*	**Langton,** Steven *1998*
Gordon, Mark *1990*	**Moys,** Clive *1998*
Livingstone, Simon *1990*	

---

† Recorder ‡ Assistant Recorder *Door Tenant

8 STONE BUILDINGS

Lincoln's Inn, London, WC2A 3TA
0171 831 9881
Fax: 0171 831 9392; DX 216 Chancery Lane
E-mail: alanl@8stonebuildings.law.uk
Out of hours telephone: 0181 894 1416,
Mobile 0802 411348

Chambers of John Cherry QC, Timothy Briden
*Clerks: Alan Luff (Senior Clerk), Paul Eeles
(Junior Clerk)*

Cherry, John QC *1961†*	**Menzies,** Richard *1993*
Briden, Timothy *1976*	**Stemmer-Baldwin,** Marcus
May, Kieran *1971*	*1994*
Seaward, Martin *1978*	**Howard-Jones,** Sarah *1994*
Room, Stewart *1991*	**Hill,** Peregrine *1995*
Waddington, Nigel *1992*	**McLeish,** Martyn *1997*

9 STONE BUILDINGS

9 STONE BUILDINGS

Lincoln's Inn, London, WC2A 3NN
0171 404 5055
Fax: 0171 405 1551; DX 314 London,
Chancery Lane
E-mail: clerks@9stoneb.law.co.uk
Out of hours telephone: 0181 594 4877
Mobile 0374 989964

Chambers of Michael Ashe QC
Clerk: Alan Austin

Ashe, Michael QC QC (N Ireland) *1971‡*	**Sisley,** Timothy *1989*
Iwi, David *1961*	**Smart,** John *1989*
Jacob, Isaac *1963†*	**Flower,** Philip *1979*
Howells, Cenydd *1964†*	**Pines-Richman,** Helene *1992*
Chapman, Vivian *1970†*	**Wood,** Lana *1993*
Cant, Christopher *1973*	**Shaw,** Peter *1995*
Denehan, Edward *1981*	**Lewis,** Jonathan *1996*
Reed, Penelope *1983*	**Hanham,** James *1996*
Young, Martin *1984*	**Bromilow,** Daniel *1996*
Taylor, Araba *1985*	**Wilson,** Richard *1996*
Counsell, Lynne *1986*	**Critelli,** Nicholas *1991**
Levy, Robert *1988*	**Wood,** Graeme *1968**
Foley, Sheila *1988*	

Types of work (and number of counsel practising in that area if supplied)
Agriculture 6 · Arbitration 7 · Banking 5 ·
Bankruptcy 15 · Chancery (general) 23 ·
Chancery land law 22 · Charities 6 ·
Commercial litigation 15 · Commercial

property 20 · Commodities 3 · Common
land 4 · Company and commercial 20 ·
Conveyancing 20 · Copyright 4 · Corporate
finance 6 · Crime – corporate fraud 5 ·
Discrimination 2 · EC and competition law
3 · Employment 5 · Entertainment 4 ·
Equity, wills and trusts 23 · Family
provision 17 · Film, cable, TV 3 · Financial
services 6 · Foreign law 5 · Housing 9 ·
Information technology 3 · Insolvency 17 ·
Insurance 3 · Insurance/reinsurance 3 ·
Intellectual property 4 · International trade
3 · Landlord and tenant 22 · Medical
negligence 3 · Partnerships 18 · Pensions 2
· Personal injury 2 · Private international 5 ·
Probate and administration 18 ·
Professional negligence 18 · Share options
4 · Tax – capital and income 6 · Tax –
corporate 6 · Town and country planning 3

Chambers established: 1900
Opening times: 8.30 am-6.30 pm

Chambers' facilities
Conference rooms, Disks accepted, E-mail

Languages spoken
French

Fees policy
There is no fixed fee policy to enable all
clients access to members of chambers irre-
spective of the financial worth of the lay
client. The senior clerk would be delighted
to discuss fee levels as and when required.

11 STONE BUILDINGS

Lincoln's Inn, London, WC2A 3TG
+44 (0)207 831 6381
Fax: +44 (0)207 831 2575; DX 1022
London
E-mail: clerks@11StoneBuildings.law.co.uk
URL:
http://www.11StoneBuildings.law.co.uk
Out of hours telephone: Chris Berry: +44
(0) 208 946 9139 (Mobile: 0836 566251)
Gareth Davies: +44 (0) 208 542
1211(Mobile: 0467 443519)

Chambers of M D Beckman QC
*Clerks: Christopher Berry (Senior Clerk),
Gareth Davies, Caron Levy, Will Sheldon
(Listing), Sarah Longden (Marketing and
Client Care)*

Beckman, Michael QC *1954*	**Cousins,** Edward *1971*
Sheridan, Peter QC *1955*	**Cohen,** Edward *1972*
Rosen, Murray QC *1976*	**Bishop,** Alan *1973*

† Recorder ‡ Assistant Recorder *Door Tenant

Salter, Adrian *1973*
McCue, Donald *1974*
Phillips, John *1975**
Meares, Nigel *1975*
Deacon, Robert *1976*
Arkush, Jonathan *1977*
Giret, Jane *1981*
Ross, Sidney *1983*
Higgs, Roland *1984*
Dight, Marc *1984*
Gourgey, Alan *1984*
Kyriakides, Tina *1984*
Agnello, Raquel *1986*
Shekerdemian, Marcia *1987*
Holbech, Charles *1988*
Penny, Tim *1988*
Barber, Sally *1988*

Kennedy-McGregor, Marilyn *1989*
Middleburgh, Jonathan *1990*
Meyer, Birgitta *1992*
Macdonald, Shelia *1993*
Wilkins, Christopher *1993*
Mallin, Max *1993*
Barnard, James *1993*
Parfitt, Nicholas *1993*
Lopian, Jonathan *1994*
Daly, Denis *1995*
Boardman, Christopher *1995*
Weekes, Tom *1995*
Riley, Jamie *1995*
Watson, Alaric *1997*
Keel, Douglas *1997**

Thomson, Louise *1996*
Sefton, Mark *1996*
Ford, Jeremy Michael *1996*
Oakeshott, Roger Nicholas *1997*

Stembridge, David QC *1955**
Guest, Prof Sephen *1980**
Melton, Christopher *1982**
Coleman, Clive *1986**

Types of work (and number of counsel practising in that area if supplied)
Chancery land law · Commercial litigation · Commercial property · Common land · Common law (general) · Consumer law · Crime – corporate fraud · Discrimination · Education · Employment · Environment · Franchising · Housing · Information technology · Insolvency · Insurance · Landlord and tenant · Medical negligence · Partnerships · Personal injury · Professional negligence · Sale and carriage of goods · Sports · Utilities

199 STRAND

London, WC2R 1DR
0171 379 9779
Fax: 0171 379 9481; DX 322 London, Chancery Lane
Other comms: Link: Martin Griffiths
E-mail: chambers@199strand.co.uk
URL: http://www.199strand.co.uk
Out of hours telephone: 01233 756691

Chambers of Peter Andrews QC
Clerk: Martin Griffiths

Andrews, Peter QC *1970*†
de Wilde, Robin QC *1971*‡
Phillips, David QC *1976*‡
Wilby, David QC *1974*‡
Gumbel, Elizabeth-Anne QC *1974*
Stitcher, Malcolm *1971*
Green, Alan *1973*
Walmsley, Keith *1973*
Whitaker, Stephen *1973*
Levene, Simon *1977*‡
Tudor-Evans, Quintin *1977*
Goodman, Andrew *1978*
Treasure, Francis *1980*
Beech, Jacqueline *1981*
Hough, Christopher *1981*

Kurrein, Martin *1981*
Sadd, Patrick *1984*
Hutchings, Martin *1986*
Harrison, Philomena *1985*
Harrison, Michael *1986*
Aldridge, James *1987*
Charles, Henry *1987*
Serlin, Richard *1987*
Witcomb, Henry *1989*
Wonnacott, Mark *1989*
Garner, Sophie *1990*
Nesbitt, Timothy *1991*
Vickers, Rachel *1992*
Cheshire, Anthony *1992*
Woolf, Eliot *1993*
Isaac, Nicholas *1993*

Opening times: 8.30 am-6.30 pm

Chambers' facilities
Conference rooms, Disks accepted, Disabled access, Conditional fee work and Direct Professional Access accepted

Languages spoken
French, German, Hebrew, Japanese, Mandarin Chinese

Areas of work
Personal Injury
Employers', public and occupiers' liability, road traffic accidents, occupational diseases, health and safety, product liability, disaster litigation.

Medical Negligence
Negligence of doctors, dentists and nurses. Inquests. Hospital inquiries. Criminal cases in respect of medical malpractice. Disciplinary proceedings.

Property
Conveyancing, boundary disputes, commercial development of land and mortgages.

Landlord and Tenant
Housing, residential and commercial leases, rent reviews, dilapidation, agricultural tenancies.

Professional Indemnity
Negligence claims for and against lawyers, architects, engineers, surveyors, valuers, accountants, financial intermediaries and insurance brokers. Proceedings before professional and other regulatory bodies.

† Recorder ‡ Assistant Recorder *Door Tenant

Commercial

Contract, sale of goods, carriage of goods, insolvency, partnership, insurance, consumer credit, company law, competition law, computers and information technology, passing-off, restraint of trade, copyright, utilities, financial services, fraud, franchising, building disputes.

Employment

Wrongful and unfair dismissal, protection of confidential information, restrictive covenants, sex and race discrimination, transfer of undertakings. Disciplinary proceedings before professional and regulatory bodies.

Transport

Operators' licensing and construction and use, in the road haulage and coach industries.

SWAN HOUSE

PO Box 8749, London, W13 8ZX
0181 998 3035
Fax: 0181 998 3055; DX 5132 Ealing

Chambers of Mr G B Purves

TEMPLE CHAMBER

Suite 241, 4th Floor 3-7 Temple Avenue, London, EC4Y 0HP
0171 353 4461
Fax: 0171 353 4469

Chambers of Mr L A Adenekan

Bar Directory on the Internet
The Bar Directory is also available on the Internet at the following address:
http://www.smlawpub.co.uk/bar

TEMPLE CHAMBERS

Rooms 111/112, 3/7 Temple Avenue, London, EC4Y 0HP
0171 583 1001 (2 lines)
Fax: 0171 583 2112

Chambers of Mrs H E Adejumo

55 TEMPLE CHAMBERS

Temple Avenue, London, EC4Y 0HP
0171 353 7400
Fax: 0171 353 7100; DX 260 Chancery Lane
Out of hours telephone: 07788 746 217

Chambers of Mr C E Moll
Clerks: Donna Parham (First Junior Clerk), Fay Harris (Junior Clerk)

Moll, Christiaan *1986*	**Savla**, Sandeep *1992*
Haines, Geoffrey *1949*	**Cameron**, Viveca *1987*
Hamilton, Douglas *1990*	**Lovegrove**, Sandra *1995*
Khan, Frans *1991*	**Chanteau**, Diane *1997*
Khan, Cornelius *1993*	**Wilson**, Paola *1995*
Thompson, Samantha *1996*	**Goddard**, Paul *1996*

169 TEMPLE CHAMBERS

Temple Avenue, London, EC4Y 0DA
0171 583 7644
Fax: 0171 353 8554; DX 348 London

Chambers of E M Ashfield

TEMPLE FIELDS

Hamilton House, 1 Temple Avenue, London, EC4Y 0HA
0171 353 4212
Fax: 0171 353 6556; DX 129 London, Chancery Lane

Chambers of Mrs C L Churchill

Languages
See the Index of Languages Spoken in Part G to locate a chambers where a particular language is spoken, or find an individual who speaks a particular language.

---

† Recorder ‡ Assistant Recorder *Door Tenant

1 TEMPLE GARDENS

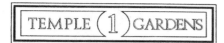

1st Floor, Temple, London, EC4Y 9BB
0171 583 1315/353 0407
Fax: 0171 353 3969; DX 382 London
E-mail: clerks@1templegardens.co.uk
Out of hours telephone: 0181 943 2507

Chambers of Hugh Carlisle QC
Clerks: Dean Norton (Senior Clerk), Nancy Fernée (First Junior Clerk); Administrator: Gaye Spencer-King

Carlisle, Hugh QC *1961*†	**Astor**, Philip *1989*
Mayhew of Twysden, Lord QC *1955*	**Morton**, Keith *1990*
	Laughland, James *1991*
Miscampbell, Norman QC *1952*†	**Ciumei**, Charles *1991*
	Curtis, Charles *1992*
Sankey, Guy QC *1966*†	**Wilkinson**, Richard *1992*
Bate-Williams, John *1976*	**Bacon**, Nicholas *1992*
Ashford-Thom, Ian *1977*	**Grant**, Marcus *1993*
Macpherson, Angus *1977*	**Barr**, David *1993*
Burnett, Ian QC *1980*‡	**Issa**, Alexandra *1993*
Hoskins, William *1980*	**Glassbrook**, Alexander *1995*
Grieve, Dominic *1980*	
Bishop, Mark *1981*	**Moss**, Nicholas *1995*
Hewitt, Alison *1984*	**Kevan**, Timothy *1996*
Tam, Robin *1986*	**Smyth**, Julia *1996*
Kilcoyne, Paul *1985*	**Hobbs**, Emma-Jane *1996*
Bell, James *1987*	**Hough**, Jonathan *1997*
Brown, Simon *1988*	**McGrath**, Paul *1997*
Llewelyn, Jane *1989*	**Adamson**, Dominic *1997*

Types of work (and number of counsel practising in that area if supplied)
Administrative · Common law (general) · Costs · Crime · Employment · Health & safety · Immigration · Insurance · Landlord and tenant · Medical negligence · Mental health · Personal injury · Professional negligence · Sale and carriage of goods

Chambers established: 1954
Opening times: 8.30 am-6.30 pm

Chambers' facilities
Conference rooms, E-mail

Languages spoken
French, German, Spanish

Fees policy
Refer to the Senior Clerk. Estimate of fees and conditional fees available.

Additional information
1 Temple Gardens is a long-established common law set committed to providing a professional, efficient and friendly service to all our clients.

The work of chambers covers most aspects of civil common law particularly personal injury, professional and medical negligence, employment law, public and administrative law and judicial review, general commercial work, public and judicial inquiries and inquests.

Individual members provide specialist services in health and safety litigation, immigration, costs and taxation reviews, landlord and tenant, and criminal law including VAT and corporate fraud.

The clerking team is happy to provide guidance on any matter and prides itself on its open and friendly approach. A brochure is available on request.

2 TEMPLE GARDENS

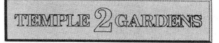

Temple, London, EC4Y 9AY
0171 583 6041
Fax: 0171 583 2094; DX 134 London, Chancery Lane
E-mail: clerks@2templegardens.co.uk
URL: http://www.2templegardens.co.uk

Chambers of Dermod O'Brien QC
Clerks: Christopher Willans, Tom Grove, Lee Tyler; Practice Manager: Chambers Director: Elizabeth Rantzen; Administrator: Louise Taghi

Phillips, Patrick QC *1964*	**Browne**, Benjamin QC *1976*‡
Preston, Timothy QC *1964*†	
O'Brien, Dermod QC *1962*†	**de Lotbiniere**, Henry *1968*
Twigg, Patrick QC *1967*†	**Foster**, Rosalind *1969*†
de Navarro, Michael QC *1968*†	**Hetherington**, Roger *1973*‡
	Pearce-Higgins, Daniel QC *1973*‡
Moxon Browne, Robert QC *1969*†	
	Palmer, Howard QC *1977*
Collender, Andrew QC *1969*†	**Stuart-Smith**, Jeremy QC *1978*‡
Lamb, Timothy QC *1974*‡	**Archer**, Stephen *1979*
Layton, Alexander QC *1976*‡	**Anyadike-Danes**, Monya *1980*
	McDonald, John *1981*

Russell, Christopher *1982*
Thomas, David *1982*
Vaughan-Jones, Sarah *1983*
Eklund, Graham *1984*
Porter, Martin *1986*
Rabey, Catherine *1987*
Miller, Andrew *1989*
Moody, Neil *1989*
Crowley, Daniel *1990*
Martin, Bradley *1990*
Otty, Timothy *1990*
Downes, Paul *1991*
Snell, John *1991*
Lord, Timothy *1992*

Kinsler, Marie *1992*
Reece, Rupert *1992*
Turner, David *1992*
Brown, Clare *1993*
Gardiner, Bruce *1994*
Green, Dore *1994*
Mort, Justin *1994*
Wyles, Lucy *1994*
Goolamali, Nina *1995*
Constable, Adam *1995*
Hext, Neil *1995*
Harris, Roger *1996*
Dougherty, Charles *1997*
Lee, Krista *1996*

Types of work (and number of counsel practising in that area if supplied)

Arbitration 10 · Aviation 4 · Banking 4 · Bankruptcy 3 · Chancery (general) 6 · Civil liberties 3 · Commercial litigation 27 · Commercial property 6 · Common law (general) 47 · Company and commercial 10 · Construction 15 · EC and competition law 4 · Employment 4 · Environment · Financial services 4 · Information technology 3 · Insolvency 4 · Insurance 15 · Insurance/reinsurance 15 · Landlord and tenant 5 · Medical negligence 3 · Personal injury 39 · Professional negligence 36 · Sale and carriage of goods 7

Chambers established: 1945
Opening times: 7.30 am-7.30 pm

Chambers' facilities
Conference rooms, Video conferences, Disks accepted, Disabled access, E-mail

Languages spoken
French, German, Italian, Spanish

Fees policy
Refer to clerks.

Languages
See the Index of Languages Spoken in Part G to locate a chambers where a particular language is spoken, or find an individual who speaks a particular language.

3 TEMPLE GARDENS

Lower Ground Floor, Temple, London, EC4Y 9AU
0171 353 3102/5/9297
Fax: 0171 353 0960; DX 485 Chancery Lane
E-mail: clerks@3tg.co.uk

Chambers of John J Coffey QC
Clerks: Kevin Aldridge (Senior Clerk), Hadyn Robson (First Junior Clerk)

Coffey, John QC *1970*†
Pegden, Jeffrey QC *1973*†
Birch, William *1972*
Ader, Peter *1973*†
Scholz, Karl *1973*
Crabtree, Richard *1974*
Reed, Piers *1974*
Gilbert, Jayne *1976*
Whittaker, Robert *1977*
Cotcher, Ann *1979*
Saunders, William *1980*
Connolly, Simon *1981*
Smith, Simon *1981*
Smith, Alisdair *1981*
Stork, Brian *1981*
Barnes, David *1981*
Halsall, Louise *1982*
Connolly, Deirdre *1982*

Reynolds, Stella *1983*
Lahiffe, Martin *1984*
Cleaver, Wayne *1986*
Ross, Gordon *1986*
Popert, Catherine *1987*
Aina, Benjamin *1987*
Krikler, Susan *1988*
Bleaney, Nicholas *1988*
Rutherford, Martin *1990*
Pearson, Carolyn *1990*
Firth, Clemency *1992*
Emir, Astra *1992*
Nuttall, Evan *1993*
Corsellis, Nicholas *1993*
Williams, Alexander *1995*
Patterson, Gareth *1995*
Hamilton, Amanda *1995*

Types of work (and number of counsel practising in that area if supplied)
Care proceedings 6 · Chancery (general) 2 · Common law (general) 7 · Courts martial 2 · Crime 28 · Crime – corporate fraud 10 · Education 1 · Employment 2 · Environment 3 · Family 10 · Family provision 10 · Housing 2 · Licensing 6 · Local government 6 · Mental health 5 · Personal injury 5 · Town and country planning 1

Chambers established: 1969
Opening times: 8.30 am-6.30 pm

Chambers' facilities
Conference rooms, Video conferences, Disks accepted

Languages spoken
French, German

The Chambers:

A well-established set of Chambers specialising in all areas of criminal law, family law and areas of common law. Members appear as advocates in the Magistrates Court, Crown Court, High Court, Queens Bench divisional court, the Court of Appeal and the House of Lords. Other tribunals include Professional Tribunals, Mental Health Tribunals, Industrial Tribunals, Inquests and other Judicial Inquiries.

Work Undertaken:

Crime: Chambers specialise in all areas of criminal law and have an extensive group of practitioners available at all levels of call. Commercial and corporate fraud is an important specialisation of a number of members and the field of sexual abuse is also a speciality.

Family Law: The matrimonial work of Chambers extends to all aspects of this field. Matrimonial property disputes and all sections of the law relating to children are the province of a number of members. Advice is given to both Local Authorities and to individual clients.

Common Law: A broad range of common law work is handled including actions for false imprisonment and malicious prosecution, personal injury matters, employment law, professional negligence claims and contractual disputes.

3 TEMPLE GARDENS

2nd Floor, Temple, London, EC4Y 9AU
0171 583 1155
Fax: 0171 353 5446; DX 0064 London

Chambers of Mr J J Goldberg QC

3 TEMPLE GARDENS

3rd Floor, Temple, London, EC4Y 9AU
0171 353 0832
Fax: 0171 353 4929; DX 427 London

Chambers of Mr D C Gordon

3 TEMPLE GARDENS

3rd Floor, Temple, London, EC4Y 9AU
0171 583 0010
Fax: 0171 353 3361; DX 0073 London

Chambers of Mr D J F Wright

TEMPLE GARDENS TAX CHAMBERS

1st Floor, 3 Temple Gardens, Temple, London, EC4Y 9AU
0171 353 7884/5 8982/3
Fax: 0171 583 2044
E-mail: clerks@taxcounsel.co.uk.

Chambers of Richard Bramwell QC
Clerks: Anne de Rose, Claire Murray

Bramwell, Richard QC *1967*	**McNicholas,** Eamon *1994*
Braham, David QC *1957*	**Southern,** David *1982*
Dick, John *1974*	**Schwarz,** Jonathan *1998*
Sherry, Michael *1978*	**Harris,** Rodger Peter *1980*
James, Alun *1986*	

THE THAMES CHAMBERS

Wickham House, 10 Cleveland Way, London, E1 4TR
0171 366 6655/790 2424 X390
Fax: 0171 366 6655

Chambers of Mr E A Oteng

THOMAS MORE CHAMBERS

52 Carey Street, Lincoln's Inn, London, WC2A 2JB
0171 404 7000
Fax: 0171 831 4606; DX 90 London

C

E-mail: clerks@thomasmore.law.co.uk

Clerks: Christopher Hallett (Senior Clerk), Stuart Sellen

Noble, Philip *1978*	**Aylott**, Colin *1989*
Garnett, Susan *1973*	**Farmer**, Sarah *1991*
Ray, Jonathan *1980*	**Egan**, Manus *1991*
Cox, Geoffrey *1982*	**Harding**, Christopher *1992*
Davison, Richard *1982*	**Cross**, Richard *1993*
Dias, Sappho *1982*	**Sherratt**, Matthew *1994*
Snelson, Anthony *1982*	**Cooper**, Sarah Lucy *1993*
Egan, Fiona *1987*	**Howells**, Katherine *1994*
Gottlieb, David *1988*	**MacLaren**, Alexander *1997*

Types of work (and number of counsel practising in that area if supplied)
Bankruptcy · Care proceedings · Civil liberties · Commercial · Common law (general) · Company and commercial · Consumer law · Contract · Courts martial · Crime · Crime – corporate fraud · Defamation · Discrimination · EC law · Employment · Family · Family provision · Financial services · Fraud · Housing · Human rights · Immigration · Insolvency · Judicial review · Landlord and tenant · Licensing · Medical negligence · Partnerships · Personal injury · Planning · Privy Council Appeals · Professional negligence · Sale and carriage of goods · Town and country planning · Trading standards

Chambers established: 1992
Opening times: 9 am-6 pm (24-hour answering service available)

Chambers' facilities
Conference rooms, Video conferences, Disks accepted

Languages spoken
French, Spanish, Urdu

CHAMBERS OF ROBERT THORESBY

37 Redbridge Lane West, Wanstead, London, E11 2JX
0181 530 5267
Fax: 0181 989 4168

Chambers of Mr R M Thoresby

> **Bar Directory on the Internet**
> *The Bar Directory* is also available on the Internet at the following address:
> http://www.smlawpub.co.uk/bar

TOLLGATE MEWS CHAMBERS

113 Tollgate Road, Tollgate Mews, North Beckton, London, E6 5JY
0171 511 1838
Fax: 0171 511 1838
E-mail:
Jonathan.dowokpor@freeserve.co.uk
Out of hours telephone: 0958 519059

Chambers of Mr J K Dowokpor

Dowokpor, Jonathan *1972*

14 TOOKS COURT

Cursitor St, London, EC4A 1LB
0171 405 8828
Fax: 0171 405 6680; DX 68 Chancery Lane
Other comms: Mobile: 0850 823676/Pager: 0941 119610
E-mail: clerks@tooks.law.co.uk

Chambers of M Mansfield QC
Clerks: C Thomas, M Parker, K Jackson, L Wakeling (Fees Clerk), Simon Gardner, Richard Caton; Administrator: Sandra Watson

Mansfield, Michael QC *1967*	**Bowen**, Stephen *1990**
Fulford, Adrian QC *1978‡*	**Chapman**, Rebecca *1990*
Reilly, John *1972*	**Wade**, Clare *1990*
Baird, Vera *1975*	**Hawley**, Carol *1990*
Belford, Dora *1977*	**Maguire**, Sarah *1990*
Roche, Patrick *1977*	**Soorjoo**, Martin *1990*
Yeboah, Yaa *1977**	**Munroe**, Allison *1992*
Kamlish, Stephen *1979*	**Drew**, Sandhya *1993*
Plange, Janet *1981*	**Moloney**, Timothy *1993*
Thornberry, Emily *1983*	**Woodcraft**, Elizabeth *1980*
Bennathan, Joel *1985*	**Guthrie**, Mark *1984*
Delahunty, Johanne *1986*	**Herbert**, Peter *1982*
Shamash, Anne *1986*	**Jordash**, Wayne *1995*
Topolski, Michael *1986*	**Heraghty**, David *1995*
Dick, Julia *1988*	**Southey**, David Hugh *1996*
Huseyin, Martin *1988*	**Kang**, Birinder *1996*
Wilcock, Peter *1988*	**Halloran**, Catherine Mary *1996*
Boye-Anawoma, Margo *1989*	**Graham**, Sandra *1982**

Types of work (and number of counsel practising in that area if supplied)
Administrative 16 · Care proceedings 12 · Civil liberties 23 · Common law (general) 5 · Crime 23 · Defamation 3 · Discrimination 9 · Education 3 · Employment 6 · Family 12 · Housing 4 · Immigration 9 · Inquests 23 · Landlord and tenant 5 · Medical

negligence 8 · Mental health 9 · Personal injury 12 · Prison law 23 · Professional negligence 7 · Public inquiries 23

Chambers established: 1984
Opening times: 8.30 am-6.30 pm

Chambers' facilities
Video conferences, Disks accepted, Disabled access

Languages spoken
French, German, Italian, Spanish, Turkish, Urdu

Additional information
Tooks Court was founded in 1984. Since then the set has demonstrated a strong and consistent commitment to providing the highest professional standards for both solicitors and lay clients. Chambers offers a broad range of civil and criminal work.

Chambers has a reputation for high-profile criminal defence work and has particular expertise in dealing with public order offences and Irish cases. However, the range of practice encompasses the full spectrum of criminal offences from murder to gross indecency, and fraud to shoplifting.

14 Tooks Court offers specialists in civil matters including family, employment, and discrimination cases, and has particular expertise in dealing with actions involving the police.

Individual members also specialise in various areas of law including family, employment, discrimination, immigration, landlord and tenant, personal injury, civil actions against the police, mental health, and administrative law and judicial review.

58 TOPHAM SQUARE

Tottenham, London, N17 7HL
0181 365 1918
Fax: 0171 365 1918

Chambers of Mr R Minhas

Bar Directory on the Internet
The Bar Directory is also available on the Internet at the following address:
http://www.smlawpub.co.uk/bar

TOWER HAMLETS BARRISTERS CHAMBERS

First Floor, 45 Brick Lane, London, E1 6PU
0171 247 9825
Fax: 0171 247 9825

TOWER HAMLETS BARRISTERS CHAMBERS

37B Princelet Street, London, E1 5LP
0171 377 8090
Fax: 0171 377 6322
E-mail: shikderka@aol.com
Out of hours telephone: 0956 182545

Clerk: Delwar Ahmed

Robinson, Michael *1976*	**Islam,** Aminul *1997*
Shikder, Kutub *1990*	**Halligan,** Brendan *1998*

TRAFALGAR CHAMBERS

53 Fleet Street, London, EC4Y 1BE
0171 583 5858
Fax: 0171 353 5302; DX 89 London

Chambers of Christopher Cleverly

2-4 TUDOR STREET

London, EC4Y 0AA
0171 797 7111
Fax: 0171 797 7120; DX 226 Chancery Lane
E-mail: clerks@rfqc.co.uk
URL: http://www.rfqc.co.uk

Chambers of Richard Ferguson QC
Clerk: John Phipps

Ferguson, Richard QC *1956* **Marshall-Andrews,** Robert QC MP *1967*

Henriques, Richard QC 1967†
Feinberg, Peter QC 1972†
Leslie, Stephen QC 1971
O'Connor, Patrick QC 1970
Goldstone, Clement QC 1971†
Farley, Roger QC 1974†
Grunwald, Henry QC 1972
Lambert, Nigel QC 1974†
Lassman, Lionel 1955
Greenwood, Alan 1970†
Martin-Sperry, David 1971
Cousens, Michael 1973
Winberg, Stephen 1974
McGrail, Peter 1977
Shields, Sonja 1977
Turton, Andrew 1977
Hunter, Robert 1979
Gillard, Isabelle 1980
Grundy, Philip 1980
Dass, Preston 1983
Ward-Jackson, Charles 1985

Canavan, Sandy 1987
Clark, Peter 1988
Beck, James 1989
Henley, Christopher 1989
Montgomery, James 1989
Sharpe, Martin 1989
Squirrell, Benjamin 1990
Modgil, Sangita 1990
Sherry, Eamonn 1990
Binder, Peter 1991
Ventham, Anthony 1991
Orchard, Anthony 1991
Tayo, Ann 1991
England, William 1991
Kincade, Julie-Anne 1991
Gruchy, Simon 1993
Doran, Gerard 1993
McGrath, David 1993
Sweet, Louise 1994
Bell, Alphege 1995
Watts, Martin 1995
Slee, Jacqueline 1995
Wootton, Victoria 1995
Haeems, David 1996

Types of work (and number of counsel practising in that area if supplied)
Civil liberties 6 · Courts martial 25 · Crime 43 · Crime – corporate fraud 38 · Defamation 1 · Licensing 30 · Sports 6

Chambers established: 1984
Opening times: 8.30 am-6.30 pm

Chambers' facilities
Conference rooms, Disks accepted, Disabled access

Languages spoken
Dutch, French, German, Hebrew, Italian, Portuguese, Spanish

CHAMBERS OF MOHAMMED HASMOT ULLAH

1st Floor, 72 Brick Lane, London, E1 6RL
0171 377 0119
Fax: 0171 247 6648

Chambers of Mohammed Hashmot Ullah

45 ULLSWATER CRESCENT

Kingston Vale, London, SW15 3RG
0181 546 9284

Chambers of Mr M N Islam

3 VERULAM BUILDINGS

 3 VERULAM BUILDINGS

London, WC1R 5NT
0171 831 8441
Fax: 0171 831 8479; DX 331 London
E-mail: clerks@3verulam.co.uk
URL: http://www.3verulam.co.uk

Chambers of Christopher Symons QC, John Jarvis QC
Clerks: Richard Ansell, Raj Lamba, Khurshid Khosla; Administrator: Christine McSweeney; Senior Practice Managers: Roger Merry-Price, Paul Cooklin

Symons, Christopher QC 1972†
Jarvis, John QC 1970†
Thomas, Neville QC 1962
Merriman, Nicholas QC 1969†
Geering, Ian QC 1974†
Blair, William QC 1972‡
Elliott, Nicholas QC 1972
Salter, Richard QC 1975‡
Turner, Janet QC 1979
Malek, Ali QC 1980‡
Mitchell, Gregory QC 1979‡
Cranston, Ross QC MP 1976†
Crawford, James SC 1999
Freedman, Clive 1975
de Lacy, Richard 1976
Birch, Elizabeth 1978
Kay, Michael 1981‡
Onslow, Andrew 1982
Cranfield, Peter 1982
Sutcliffe, Andrew 1983
Phillips, Stephen 1984
Phillips, Rory 1984
Weitzman, Thomas 1984
McQuater, Ewan 1985
Sands, Philippe 1985
Nash, Jonathan 1986

Cameron, James 1987
May, Juliet 1988
Sheridan, Maurice 1984
Start, Angharad Taelor 1988
Beltrami, Adrian 1989
Green, Amanda 1990
Hockaday, Annie 1990
Odgers, John 1990
Phillips, Jonathan Mark 1991
Evans, James 1991
Marks, Jonathan 1992
Quest, David 1993
Edwards, Richard 1993
Davies-Jones, Jonathan 1994
Pope, David 1995
Brent, Richard 1995
Tolaney, Sonia 1995
Wilson, Ian 1995
Baylis, Natalie 1996
Gibaud, Catherine 1996
Parker, Matthew Richard 1997
Head, David Ian 1997
McKendrick, Ewan Gordon 1998
Hare, Christopher 1998
Ratcliffe, Peter 1998

VERULAM CHAMBERS

Peer House, 8-14 Verulam Street, Gray's Inn, London, WC1X 8LZ
0171 813 2400
Fax: 0171 405 3870; DX 436 London
Out of hours telephone: 0467 762515

† Recorder ‡ Assistant Recorder *Door Tenant

Chambers of J M Edwards QC CBE

*Clerk: Trevor Austin (01268 711007
Mobile: 0467 762515)*

Edwards, John QC *1949*	**Williamson**, Tessa *1990**
Payton, Clifford *1972*	**Jago**, Ann *1991*
Dethridge, David *1975*	**Siddle**, Trevor *1991*
Sofaer, Moira *1975*	**Passmore**, John *1992*
Mullen, Peter *1977*	**Goodwin**, Katherine *1993*
D'Aigremont, Gilles *1978*	**O'Connor**, Gerard *1993*
Ernstzen, Olav *1981**	**Smart**, Julia *1993*
Lawe, Susan *1982*	**Smith**, Leonorah *1993*
Webber, Dominic *1985*	**Fowler**, Tracey *1994*
Mehta, Sailesh *1986*	**Quinn**, Victoria *1995*
Moore, Joan *1986*	**Welch**, Brett *1996*
Humberstone, Pearl *1987*	**Leckie**, James *1964**
McIntosh, Jacqueline *1987*	**Lewis**, Cherry *1973**
White, Joanne *1987*	**Forsey**, Stephen Michael
Sowerby, Matthew *1987*	*1995*
Giles, David *1988*	**Smaller**, Elizabeth *1995*
Gifford, Cynthia *1988*	**Monaghan**, Karon *1989*
Rifat, Maurice *1990*	

VIRTUAL CHAMBERS

*Virtual
Chambers*

online dispute solutions into the global village

www.briefstop.com

(accepting briefs soon), London,
07071 244 944
Fax: 0171 359 8203; DX 122238 Upper
Islington
Other comms: Brochure autoresponder:
brochure@virtualchambers.org.uk
E-mail: enquiries@virtualchambers.org.uk
URL: http://www.virtualchambers.org.uk
Out of hours telephone: 07071 244944

Chambers of Jason Neil Featherstone

*Clerk: clerks@virtualchambers.org.uk;
Administrator:
admin@virtualchambers.org.uk;
recruitment@virtualchambers.org.uk*

Wolchover, David *1971*	**Moses**, Rebecca *1996*
Featherstone, Jason *1995*	**Pomeroy**, Toby *1997*

WARWICK HOUSE CHAMBERS

*8 Warwick Court, Gray's Inn, London,
WC1R 5DJ*
0171 430 2323
Fax: 0171 430 9171; DX 1001 Chancery
Lane
E-mail: cdrewlaw@aol.com

Chambers of Mrs C Drew, Mr C T Drew

Practice Manager: Tracey Lord

Drew, Christopher *1969*	**Haidemenos**, Stavros *1992*
Drew, Cheryl *1972*	**Moore**, Jennifer *1992*
Wickremeratne, Upali *1962*	**Mansfield**, Eleanor *1995*
Spire, Chrystalla Anasta	**Bagral**, Ravinder *1996*
Theodora *1978*	**Latto**, Paul Stuart *1996*
Armour, Alison *1979*	**Griffiths**, James Brian *1996*
John-Jules, Charles *1983*	**Smiler**, Andrew James
Patel, Jayaben *1990*	*1996*
Rowe, Deborah *1990*	**Kennedy**, Paul *1991**

WARWICK SQUARE

London, SW1V 2AJ
0171 630 6237

Chambers of Ms V J M Asher

CHAMBERS OF PASCHAL J WELSH

*11 Carlisle House, 105 Old Church Street,
London, SW3 6DS*
Fax: DX 27 Chancery Lane

Chambers of Mr P J R Welsh

243 WESTBOURNE GROVE

London, W11 2SE
0171 229 3819
Fax: 0171 229 3819

Chambers of Miss C A Holder

1C WESTBOURNE TERRACE ROAD

London, W2 6NG

Chambers of Mr J Webster

C

CHAMBERS OF PAUL WETTON

16 Pont Street, London, SW1X 9EN
0171 235 8485
Fax: 0171 235 8485; DX 267 Chancery Lane

Chambers of Mr P N Wetton

WILBERFORCE CHAMBERS

8 New Square, Lincoln's Inn, London,
WC2A 3QP
020 7306 0102
Fax: 020 7306 0095; DX 311 London
E-mail: chambers@wilberforce.co.uk
URL: http://www.wilberforce.co.uk

Chambers of Edward Nugee QC
Clerks: Declan Redmond (Senior Clerk),
Danny Smillie, Tanya Tong;
Administrator: Louise Seaton; Chambers
Director: Suzanne Cosgrave

Nugee, Edward QC *1955*	**Wardell,** John *1979*
Sher, Jules QC *1968*	**Furness,** Michael *1982*
Barnes, Michael QC *1965*	**Tennet,** Michael *1985*
Lowe, David QC *1965*	**Seitler,** Jonathan *1985*
Etherton, Terence QC *1974*	**Lowe,** Thomas *1985*
Martin, John QC *1972*	**Karas,** Jonathan *1986*
Warren, Nicholas QC *1972†*	**Ayliffe,** James *1987*
Croxford, Ian QC *1976*	**Bryant,** Judith *1987*
Ham, Robert QC *1973*	**Smith,** Joanna *1990*
Furber, John QC *1973*	**Wicks,** Joanne *1990*
Green, Brian QC *1980*	**Newman,** Paul *1991*
Nugee, Christopher QC *1983*	**Fadipe,** Gabriel *1991*
	Furze, Caroline *1992*
Taussig, Anthony *1966*	**Evans,** Jonathan *1994*
Child, John *1966*	**Campbell,** Emily *1995*
Turnbull, Charles *1975*	**Reed,** Rupert *1996*
Seymour, Thomas *1975*	**Greenhill,** Julian *1997*
Hughes, Gabriel *1978*	**Scott,** Tiffany *1998*

Types of work (and number of counsel practising in that area if supplied)
Chancery (general) · Chancery land law · Charities · Commercial · Commercial litigation · Commercial property · Company and commercial · Ecclesiastical · Energy · Equity, wills and trusts · Financial services · Insolvency · Landlord and tenant · Pensions · Probate and administration · Professional negligence · Tax – capital and income

Opening times: 8.45 am-6.30 pm

Chambers' facilities
Conference rooms, Disks accepted, E-mail

Languages spoken
French, German

Fees policy
The clerks aim to charge realistic and reasonable fees having regard to the barrister's experience, time expended and the value of the work to the client. They aim to structure the fees accurately and appropriately for each case. Hence, hourly rates, fixed fees, brief fees, refreshers and stage payments or any combination can be considered for each piece of work or for groups of cases. Declan will be happy to discuss fees and fee structures with you.

Additional information
Wilberforce Chambers is a commercial/chancery set based in Lincoln's Inn. We have grown significantly in recent years and now comprise 35 barristers, including 12 QCs. The growth has been focused and carefully planned to ensure that with the increase in size of the set we have achieved both depth and breadth in the expertise we can offer.

Members frequently appear in jurisdictions outside the UK including Bermuda, the Cayman Islands, Hong Kong and Singapore.

We make extensive use of the latest technology, to aid legal research and to enable fast communication with all our clients. For details of each member's practice please contact Declan Redmond, Senior Clerk.

Types of work undertaken
The work of Chambers includes litigation, advice and drafting in the following areas:
– **Commercial and other contracts** (both domestic and international), banking, insurance loans and security, guarantees, financial services, Lloyds drafting and litigation, economic torts, breach of confidence, oil and gas law
– **Occupational and personal pension schemes**
– **Property** including all matters relating to land, commercial property transactions, landlord and tenant, property finance, negligence and fraud, mortgages and other securities
– **Tax** including personal tax and estate planning (including offshore tax planning)

† Recorder ‡ Assistant Recorder *Door Tenant

and a wide range of tax litigation
- **Trusts** drafting, advice on administration and construction and contentious and non-contentious litigation
- **Professional negligence** of accountants, actuaries, auditors, barristers, solicitors, surveyors and trustees and construction-related professional negligence
- **Equitable remedies** such as injunctions, tracing, constructive trusts, proprietary estoppel
- **Company law** shareholder disputes, directors' disqualification proceedings, mergers and acquisitions, partnerships and joint ventures
- **Wills, probate** (both contentious and non-contenious) administration of estates, intestacy and family provision
- **Insolvency** both corporate and individual
- **Charities, Housing Associations** partnerships, clubs, societies and the law as it relates to other associations
- **Sports and Media law**

Additional specialisms: Individual members have particular expertise in the following: local government and administrative law, employment law, heritage property, school sites, commons registration, highways, town and country planning and compulsory purchase, white collar crime eg breaches of health and safety legislation.

WYNNE CHAMBERS

1 Wynne Road, London, SW9 0BB
0181 961 6144
Fax: 0181 961 6144
E-mail: m_h_a.thomson_esq@which.net
Out of hours telephone: 0181 965 4871

Chambers of Ahmad Thomson

Thomson, Ahmad *1979*

2 GOLDINGHAM AVENUE

Loughton, Essex IG10 2JF
0181 502 4247

Chambers of Mrs F L Bolton

BERESFORD CHAMBERS

21 King Street, Luton, Bedfordshire LU1 2DW
01582 429111
Fax: 01582 612299; DX 5966 Luton 1
Other comms: Video conferencing: 01582 612299
E-mail: info@it-law.com
URL: http://www.it-law.com
Out of hours telephone: 0181 909 1800

Chambers of Mr D R Abbott
Clerk: Ms M T Fitt

Abbott, David *1987*   **Singh,** Raj *1992*

LAW CHAMBERS

2nd Floor, 5 Cardiff Road, Luton, Bedfordshire LU1 1PP
01582 431352 or 0958 674785

Chambers of Mr S H Mahmood

103 WEXHAM CLOSE

Luton, Bedfordshire LU3 3TX
01582 598394
Fax: 01582 598394

Chambers of Mr S Khan

EARL STREET CHAMBERS

47 Earl Street, Maidstone, Kent ME14 1PD
01622 671222
Fax: 01622 671776; DX 4844 Maidstone 1
E-mail: gunner-sparks@msn.com
Out of hours telephone: 0831 325122

Chambers of Kevin Sparks
Clerks: Mary Gunner (Senior Clerk), Clare Cheeseman (Junior Clerk)

Sparks, Kevin *1983*   **Scott-Phillips,** Alexander
Clarke, Michelle *1988*   *1995*

Wyatt, Guy *1981*
Halpin, Thomas *1994*
Greene, Paul *1994*

Nathan, Philip *1996*
Clarke, Simon Andrew *1997*
Burge, Edmund *1997*

MAIDSTONE CHAMBERS

MAIDSTONE CHAMBERS

33 Earl Street, Maidstone, Kent ME14 1PF
01622 688592
Fax: 01622 683305; DX 51982 Maidstone 2
E-mail: maidstonechambers@compuserve.com
Out of hours telephone: 0467 351682

Chambers of Alison Ginn and Richard Travers
Clerks: Robert Davis (Senior Clerk), James Shaw (1st Junior)

Ginn, Alison *1980*
Travers, Richard *1985*
Le Prevost, Aviva *1990*
Pottinger, Gavin *1991*
Jacobson, Mary *1992*
Dubarry, Adele *1993*
Fawcett, Michelle *1993*
Clarke, Malcolm *1994*

Burns, Rosemary *1978*
Stern, Thomas *1995*
Sinclair, Philip *1995*
Bowers, Rupert *1995*
Samuel, Richard *1996*
Williams, Caroline *1997*
Wickens, Simon *1998*

Types of work (and number of counsel practising in that area if supplied)
Care proceedings 4 · Clinical negligence · Common law (general) 13 · Courts martial 4 · Crime 13 · Employment 6 · Environment 2 · Family 6 · Family provision 4 · Immigration 3 · Landlord and tenant 4 · Licensing 4 · Personal injury 5 · Professional negligence 5 · Town and country planning 2

Chambers established: 1994 (previously the Annexe to a London set)

Chambers' facilities
Conference rooms, Disks accepted

Languages spoken
French, Italian

Bar Directory on the Internet
The Bar Directory is also available on the Internet at the following address:
http://www.smlawpub.co.uk/bar

6-8 MILL STREET

SIX PUMP COURT
6 Pump Court, Temple, London EC4Y 7AR

Maidstone, Kent ME15 6XH
01622 688094
Fax: 01622 688096; DX 51967 Maidstone 2
E-mail: annexe@6pumpcourt.co.uk
URL: http://www.6pumpcourt.co.uk

Chambers of Mr S A Hockman QC
Clerk: Richard Constable (Senior Clerk);
Administrator: Arlene Sturgeon

Also at: 6 Pump Court, Temple, London EC4Y 7AR

Hockman, Stephen QC *1970*
Goymer, Andrew *1970*
Williams, Adèle *1972*
Mitchell, David *1972*
Harington, Michael *1974*
Willard, Neville *1976*
Barraclough, Richard *1980*
Baldock, Nicholas *1983*
Walden-Smith, David *1985*
Gower, Peter *1985*
Leigh, Kevin *1986*
Harrison, Peter *1987*
Forbes, Peter *1990*

Saxby, Oliver *1992*
Chamberlayne, Patrick *1992*
Butler, Judith *1993*
Mee, Paul *1992*
Watson, Mark *1994*
Grant, Edward *1994*
Ellin, Nina *1994*
Wright, Clare *1995*
Alcock, Peter *1995*
Nardell, Gordon *1995*
Beard, Mark *1996*
Charles, Deborah *1996*
Robinson, Tanya *1997*

RESOLUTION CHAMBERS

Oak Lodge, 55 Poolbrook Road, Malvern, Worcestershire WR14 3JN
01684 561279
Fax: 01684 561279; DX 17617 Malvern 1
Other comms: Mobile: 07899 070111
E-mail: mmilne@arbitration.demon.co.uk
URL: http://www.arbitration.demon.co.uk
Out of hours telephone: 01684 561279

Chambers of Michael Milne
Clerk: Penny Milne

Milne, Michael *1987*

† Recorder ‡ Assistant Recorder *Door Tenant

BYROM STREET CHAMBERS

Byrom Street, Manchester, M3 4PF
0161 829 2100
Fax: 0161 829 2101; DX 718156
Manchester 3
E-mail: Byromst25@aol.com

Chambers of B A Hytner QC
Clerk: Peter Collison

Also at: 22 Old Buildings, Lincoln's Inn,
London WC2A 3UJ

Hytner, Benet QC *1952*	**Tattersall,** Geoffrey QC
Price, John QC *1961†*	*1970†*
Wingate-Saul, Giles QC	**Swift,** Caroline QC *1977†*
1967†	**Moran,** Andrew QC *1976†*
Leveson, Brian QC *1970†*	**Allan,** David QC *1974†*
Scholes, Rodney QC *1968†*	**Black,** Michael QC *1978‡*
King, Timothy QC *1973†*	**Stewart,** Stephen QC *1975‡*

Types of work (and number of counsel practising in that area if supplied)
Arbitration · Banking · Commercial · Common law (general) · Construction · Crime · Insurance · Intellectual property · International trade · Medical negligence · Personal injury · Professional negligence · Shipping

Opening times: 8.30 am-7 pm

Chambers' facilities
Conference rooms, Disks accepted, Disabled access

Additional information
Byrom Street Chambers consists of twelve Queen's Counsel who practise in Manchester at 25 Byrom Street and from Chambers at 22 Old Buildings, Lincoln's Inn. Manchester Chambers are exclusively dedicated to the work of Leading Counsel. The set was founded in the early 1950s. Each member offers advice and advocacy in the fields of law in which he or she practises. These include:

• Administrative Law and Judicial Review, Local Government and Public Inquiries;
• Commercial Law and in particular Banking, Financial Services, Intellectual Property and Sale of Goods;
• Company Law;
• Crime, with an emphasis on Homicide, Sexual Offences, Commercial Fraud and Conspiracy;
• Computers and Information Technology;
• Construction, Building and Engineering and associated matters of Procurement, Insurance, Funding and Professional Liabilities;
• Domestic and International Commercial Arbitration and ADR;
• Environmental Law;
• General Common Law;
• Insurance and Reinsurance;
• Personal Injury Claims, especially Disaster Litigation, Severe and Permanent Disablement, Industrial Diseases and Class Actions;
• Product Liability;
• Professional Negligence including that of Doctors, Lawyers, Architects, Engineers, Surveyors, Accountants and Financial Intermediaries;
• Shipping and International Trade;
• Sports Law;
• Tribunals and Inquiries.

Members of Chambers accept references as Arbitrators, Mediators, Adjudicators and Legal Assessors.

All Silks hold, or have held, part-time judicial office. Mr Wingate-Saul and Mr Leveson sit as Deputy High Court Judges, Mr Tattersall sits as Judge of Appeal in the Isle of Man, having succeeded Mr Hytner who was Judge of Appeal from 1980 to 1997, and who sat as a Deputy High Court Judge from 1974 to 1997 and as a Recorder from 1971 to 1996.

Former members of Chambers include the Right Honourable Sir Patrick Russell (formerly Lord Justice, who is now available through Chambers for arbitration cases), Lord Justice Rose, Mrs Justice Smith, the Senior Mercantile Judge of the Northern Circuit, Judge Michael Kershaw QC, and the Recorder of Liverpool His Honour Judge David Clarke QC. Mr Hytner was the elected Leader of the Northern Circuit from 1984 to 1988, as was Sir Patrick Russell from 1979 to 1980.

Further information regarding individual expertise and fee structure can be obtained from the senior clerk, Peter Collison.

Languages
See the Index of Languages Spoken in Part G to locate a chambers where a particular language is spoken, or find an individual who speaks a particular language.

C

CENTRAL CHAMBERS

CENTRAL CHAMBERS

89 Princess Street, Manchester, M1 4HT
0161 236 1133
Fax: 0161 236 1177; DX 14467 Manchester 2

Other comms: Emergency Number: 0973 744906 (24 hours)

Clerks: Jayne Lever, Neil Vickers

Massey, Stella *1990*	**Sastry**, Bob *1996*
Khan, Fauz *1988*	**Collins**, James *1997*
Grace, Tonia *1992*	**Evans**, Simeon *1997*
Ismail, Nazmun Nisha *1992*	**Krause**, Florence *1998*
Mansfield, Gillian *1994*	

Types of work (and number of counsel practising in that area if supplied)
Administrative · Care proceedings · Civil liberties · Crime · Crime – corporate fraud · Discrimination · Education · Employment · Family · Family provision · Housing · Immigration · Judicial review · Landlord and tenant · Medical negligence · Mental health · Personal injury · Prisoners' rights · Professional negligence

Chambers established: 1996 (formerly known as Garden Court North)
Opening times: 8.45 am-6.15 pm

Chambers' facilities
Conference rooms, Disks accepted

Languages spoken
French, German, Hebrew, Hindi, Urdu

COBDEN HOUSE CHAMBERS

19 Quay Street, Manchester, M3 3HN
0161 833 6000
Fax: 0161 833 6001; DX 14327 Manchester 3

E-mail: clerks@cobden.co.uk
URL: http://www.cobden.co.uk

Chambers of Howard Baisden
Clerks: Mr Trevor Doyle (Senior Clerk/ Practice Manager), David Hewitt (Junior Clerk), Stuart Howard-Cofield (Assistant Clerk), Daniel Monaghan (Assistant Clerk); Administrator: Mrs Jackie Morton

Baisden, Howard *1972*	**Kelly**, Sean *1990*
Keenan, Peter *1962*	**Cheetham**, Julia *1990*
Narayan, Harry *1970†*	**Willems**, Marc *1990*
Duncan, John *1971*	**Dalal**, Rajen *1991*
Broadley, John *1973*	**Smith**, Jonathan *1991*
Machin, Charles *1973*	**Woodward**, Alison *1992*
Fieldhouse, Nigel *1976*	**Riddell**, David *1993*
Neale, Stuart *1976*	**Gee**, Richard *1993*
Goldwater, Michael *1977*	**Hilsdon**, James *1993*
Oughton, Richard *1978*	**Nichol**, Simon *1994*
Fallows, Paula *1981*	**Gilmour**, Susan *1994*
Uff, David *1981*	**Littler**, Richard *1994*
Green, Colin *1982*	**Orr**, Julian *1995*
Webster, Leonard *1984*	**Maddison**, David *1994*
Blackwell, Louise *1985*	**Oakes**, Christopher *1996*
Metcalfe, Ian *1985*	**Manley**, Hilary *1996*
Hartley, Richard *1985*	**Callery**, Martin *1997*
Monaghan, Mark *1987*	**Farrow**, Adrian *1997*
Woodward, Joanne *1989*	**Jones**, Michael *1998*
Kitching, Robin *1989*	**Goddard**, Richard *1999*
Willitts, Timothy *1989*	**Heywood**, Michael *1975**
Littler, Martin *1989*	**Hymanson**, Deanna *1988**
Harrison, Sarah *1989*	**Kime**, Matthew *1988**
Gregg, William *1990*	

Types of work (and number of counsel practising in that area if supplied)
Administrative 1 · Agriculture 1 · Arbitration 1 · Banking 2 · Bankruptcy 2 · Care proceedings 5 · Chancery (general) 11 · Chancery land law 6 · Charities 2 · Commercial litigation 2 · Commercial property 5 · Common land 1 · Common law (general) 9 · Company and commercial 6 · Competition 1 · Conveyancing 7 · Copyright 1 · Courts martial 1 · Crime 18 · Crime – corporate fraud 4 · Defamation 3 · Employment 3 · Environment 2 · Equity, wills and trusts 7 · Family 8 · Family provision 12 · Housing 4 · Information technology 2 · Insolvency 5 · Intellectual property 2 · Landlord and tenant 7 · Licensing 3 · Medical negligence 5 · Partnerships 5 · Patents 1 · Pensions 1 · Personal injury 11 · Probate and administration 6 · Professional negligence 9 · Sale and carriage of goods 2 · Tax – capital and income 1 · Trademarks 1

Chambers' facilities
Conference rooms, Disks accepted, Disabled access, Facilities for seminars and arbitrations

Languages spoken
French

Additional information
Cobden House Chambers is able to offer a wide range of expertise by means of specialist departments in the areas of chancery, commercial law, crime, employment law, family, housing and personal injury. Individual members are able to offer additional specialisms and full details can be obtained from the Clerk.

Chambers provides a fast and efficient service and a timetable for the completion of instructions can be given on delivery.

In addition, Chambers provides services for Alternative Dispute Resolution and Mediation.

The Senior Clerk will be happy to discuss fee levels and tailor quotations to meet most budgets.

Further details can be found on our web site and in Chambers' brochure which can be obtained on request.

Annexe of: Deans Court Chambers, 41-43 Market Place, Preston, PR1 1AH
Tel: 01772 555163
Fax: 01772 555941

Goddard, Keith QC *1959†*	**Davies**, Russell *1983*
Henriques, Richard QC *1967†*	**Bancroft**, Louise *1985*
	Heaton, Frances *1985*
Grime, Stephen QC *1970†*	**Humphries**, Paul *1986*
Machell, Raymond QC *1973†*	**Brody**, Karen *1986*
	Hudson, Christopher *1987*
Stockdale, David QC *1975†*	**Grace**, Jonathan *1989*
Fish, David QC *1973†*	**Grimshaw**, Nicholas *1988*
Ryder, Ernest QC *1981‡*	**Morgan**, Edward *1989*
Turner, Mark QC *1981‡*	**Grantham**, Andrew *1991*
Talbot, Kevin *1970†*	**Andrew**, Seamus *1991*
Bromley-Davenport, John *1972†*	**Ironfield**, Janet *1992*
	Alty, Andrew *1992*
Gregory, John *1972*	**Edge**, Timothy *1992*
Atherton, Peter *1975†*	**Burns**, Peter *1993*
Booth, Alan *1978‡*	**Savill**, Mark *1993*
Trippier, Ruth *1978*	**Hayton**, Michael *1993*
Butler, Philip *1979‡*	**Judge**, Lisa *1993*
Sephton, Craig *1981*	**Clegg**, Sebastian *1994*
Field, Patrick *1981*	**Boyle**, David *1996*
Main, Peter *1981‡*	**McCann**, Simon *1996*
Denney, Stuart *1982*	**Whitehall**, Richard *1998*
Smith, Timothy *1982*	**Cartwright**, Sophie *1998*
Trotman, Timothy *1983*	

334 DEANSGATE

Manchester, M3 4LY
0161 834 3767
Fax: 0161 839 6868

Chambers of Mr I W McIvor

CHAMBERS OF JOHN HAND QC

9 St John Street, Manchester, M3 4DN
0161 955 9000
Fax: 0161 955 9001/9004; DX 14326 Manchester

Chambers of J L Hand QC

C

DEANS COURT CHAMBERS

24 St John Street, Manchester, M3 4DF
0161 214 6000
Fax: 0161 214 6001; DX 718155 Manchester 3
E-mail: clerks@deanscourt.co.uk
URL: http://www.deanscourt.co.uk

Chambers of H K Goddard QC
Clerk: Mrs Terry Creathorn

Languages
See the Index of Languages Spoken in Part G to locate a chambers where a particular language is spoken, or find an individual who speaks a particular language.

KENWORTHY'S CHAMBERS

83 Bridge Street, Manchester, M3 2RF
0161 832 4036/834 6954
Fax: 0161 832 0370; DX 718200
Manchester 3
E-mail: clerks@kenworthys.co.uk

Chambers of Francis Burns

Clerks: Joan Walter (Senior Clerk), Sarah Wright (First Junior), Paul Mander (Second Junior); Administrator: David Wright

Burns, Francis *1971*	**Frith**, Heather *1989*
Heap, Richard *1963*	**Korol**, Kathryn *1996*
Lambert, Deborah *1977*	**Marrs**, Andrew *1995*
Grennan, Barry *1977*	**Smith**, Mark *1997*
Cassidy, Patrick *1982*	**Ruscoe**, Janet *1995*
Pasiuk, Janina *1983*	**Shafi**, Imran *1996*
Patel, Gita *1988*	**Whelan**, Geoff *1996*

40 KING STREET

Manchester, M2 6BA
0161 832 9082
Fax: 0161 835 2139; DX 718188
Manchester
E-mail: clerks@40kingstreet.co.uk

Chambers of Philip Raynor QC
Clerks: William Brown, Colin Griffin, Michael Stubbs, Lisa Rogers (assistant),
Paul Clarke (assistant); Administrator: Gina Pinkerton

Also at: 5 Park Place, Leeds

Raynor, Philip QC *1973†*	**Dunn**, Katherine *1987*
Macleod, Nigel QC *1961†*	**Hilton**, Simon *1987*
Hoggett, John QC *1969†*	**Ashworth**, Fiona *1988*
Tackaberry, John QC *1967†*	**Stockley**, Ruth *1988*
Gilbart, Andrew QC *1972†*	**Pritchett**, Stephen *1989*
Smith, Peter QC *1975†*	**Anderson**, Lesley *1989*
Farley, Roger QC *1974†*	**Campbell**, John QC QC (Scot) *1990*
Sauvain, Stephen QC *1977*	**Singer**, Andrew *1990*
Patterson, Frances QC *1977‡*	**Tucker**, Paul *1990*
Booth, Michael QC *1981*	**Smith**, Matthew *1991*
Braslavsky, Nicholas QC *1983*	**Carter**, Martin *1992*
Owen, Eric *1969*	**Horne**, Wilson *1992*
Jackson, John *1970*	**Powis**, Lucy *1992*
Halliday, Harold *1972*	**Ghosh**, Julian *1993*
Pass, Geoffrey *1975*	**Harper**, Mark *1993*
Evans, Alan *1978*	**Lander**, Richard *1993*
Khan, Shokat *1979*	**Pritchard**, Sarah *1993*
Fraser, Vincent *1981*	**Latimer**, Andrew *1995*
Manley, David *1981*	**Doyle**, Louis *1996*
Barrett, John *1982*	**Berridge**, Elizabeth *1996*
Chaisty, Paul *1982*	**Nowell**, Katie *1996*
Halliwell, Mark *1985*	**Crawford**, Colin *1997*
	Siddall, Nicholas *1997*

Types of work (and number of counsel practising in that area if supplied)
Administrative · Arbitration · Banking · Bankruptcy · Care proceedings · Chancery (general) · Chancery land law · Charities · Commercial litigation · Common law (general) · Company and commercial · Construction · Conveyancing · Copyright · Corporate finance · Crime · Crime – corporate fraud · Defamation · Discrimination · EC and competition law · Education · Employment · Environment · Equity, wills and trusts · Family · Family provision · Financial services · Housing · Immigration · Information technology · Insolvency · Insurance · Intellectual property · Landlord and tenant · Licensing · Local government · Medical negligence · Parliamentary · Partnerships · Pensions · Personal injury · Probate and administration · Professional negligence · Sale and carriage of goods · Tax – capital and income · Tax – corporate · Town and country planning

Chambers established: 1946
Opening times: 8.30 am-7 pm

Chambers' facilities
Conference rooms, Disks accepted, E-mail, Link

Languages spoken
French, German, Norwegian, Urdu

Additional information
A wide range of specialist advisory and advocacy services, mainly: town and country planning, local government law and finance, administrative law, compulsory purchase and comprehension, highways law, environmental protection, and public health; commercial Chancery litigation, law of landlord and tenant, law of trusts, partnerships, intellectual property, and insolvency (corporate and individual); banking, wills and intestacy, civil liability, personal injury, professional liability, employment law, industrial law, and building disputes; consumer credit, sale of goods, family and matrimonial law, hire and purchase, licensing, and criminal law.

Members appear not only before the established courts, including Crown Office work, but also in front of a wide range of specialist tribunals which include the Lands Tribunal, planning, highway, compulsory purchase and other departmental inquiries, professional and disciplinary hearings, industrial tribunals and the data protection tribunal.

Additional specialisations: It is well recognised by chambers that clients often need advice on matters where specialist disciplines overlap and it is therefore able to provide a multi-disciplinary approach where this is necessary. Chambers has a heavy emphasis on planning and local government work. There is also a thriving Chancery and commercial section.

In addition, the following areas are also undertaken: judicial review, Parliamentary work, market law, crime, rating, immigration, data protection, trading standards, housing, and markets and fairs. All members accept instructions under the direct professional access arrangements.

Publications: Members have contributed to numerous publications relating to their specialist fields.

Arbitrator: Sir Iain Glidewell.

8 KING STREET CHAMBERS

8 King Street, Manchester, M2 6AQ
0161 834 9560
Fax: 0161 834 2733 Gps 2&3; DX 14354 Manchester 1
E-mail: eightking@aol.com

Chambers of Keith Armitage QC
Clerks: Peter Whitman, David Lea;
Practice Manager: Peter Whitman; Other
Admin: Rhonda Hardy

Armitage, K QC *1970†*	**Scorah,** Christopher *1991*
Rowe, John QC *1960†*	**Connolly,** Joanne *1992*
McDermott, Gerard QC *1978†*	**Naylor,** Kevin *1992*
	Sabry, Karim *1992*
Rylands, Elizabeth *1973‡*	**Barry,** Kirsten *1993*
Eccles, David *1976*	**Parr,** John *1989*
Terry, Jeffrey *1976*	**Bailey,** Graham *1993*
Jess, Digby *1978*	**Hamilton-Hague,** Rachael *1993*
Holmes, Philip *1980*	
Foudy, Kim *1982*	**Clark,** Andrew *1994*
Ahmed, Farooq *1983*	**Boyd,** James *1994*
Davies, Stephen *1985*	**Hoffman,** David Alexander *1997*
Worrall, Shirley *1987*	
Smith, Michael *1989*	**Collins,** Martin QC *1952**
Forte, Mark *1989*	**Forwood,** Nicholas QC *1970**
Vaughan, Simon *1989*	
Wood, Ian *1990*	**Worrall,** Anna QC *1959*†*
Thompson, Jonathan *1990*	**Barling,** Gerald QC *1972*†*
Hodgson, Timothy *1991*	**Prosser,** Kevin QC *1982**

Types of work (and number of counsel practising in that area if supplied)
Administrative 3 · Arbitration 4 · Banking 4 · Care proceedings 5 · Chancery (general) 2 · Chancery land law 4 · Common law (general) 20 · Company and commercial 8 · Competition 2 · Construction 4 · Courts martial 1 · Crime 5 · Crime – corporate fraud 2 · Discrimination 4 · EC and competition law 1 · Education 2 · Employment 4 · Environment 1 · Family 8 · Family provision 5 · Financial services 2 · Franchising 2 · Housing 5 · Insolvency 2 · Insurance 4 · Insurance/reinsurance 4 · Intellectual property 2 · Landlord and

tenant 4 · Licensing 3 · Local government 4 · Medical negligence 9 · Mental health 1 · Partnerships 4 · Pensions 4 · Personal injury 17 · Probate and administration 1 · Professional negligence 9 · Sale and carriage of goods 2 · Share options 3

Chambers established: 1936
Opening times: 8.30 am-6.30 pm

Chambers' facilities
Conference rooms, Video conferences, Disks accepted, Disabled access, E-mail, Website at http://www.8kingstreet.co.uk

Additional information
Established over 50 years ago we are one of the leading Civil and Commercial Chambers outside London. Our strong generalist tradition is complemented by the experience of many of our members in specialist areas of work.

Areas of particular expertise:

• Commercial contract and building contact work
• Personal injury
• Professional negligence, building and medical negligence
• Insurance law
• All aspects of family and children law
• Employment law
• General commercial litigation

In addition, some members have considerable experience in company and related work, together with insolvency litigation. Two members are Fellows of the Institute of Arbitrators (one also being a Registered Arbitrator) and another is admitted to the New York State Bar.

These chambers have the benefit of a video conferencing link, which gives direct access to other such facilities throughout the UK and abroad (including the Bar Council Offices in London).

58 KING STREET CHAMBERS

1st Floor, Kingsgate House, 51-53 South King Street, Manchester, M2 6DE
0161 831 7477
Fax: 0161 832 5645; DX 710297 Manchester 3

Chambers of Miss B A Lunt
Clerk: Fredric Greene

Lunt, Beverly *1977*	Holloran, Fiona *1989*
O'Shea, John *1983*	Matuk, Helen *1990*
Dickinson, Jonathan *1986*	Carter, Richard *1990*
Staunton, William *1986*	Brady, Michael *1992*
McMeekin, Ian *1987*	Preston, Darren *1991*
Dodd, Sara *1987*	Treble, Paul *1994*
Rankin, Ciaran *1988*	Houghton, Lisa *1994*
Singh-Hayer, Bansa *1988*	Acton, Jayne *1996*
Fitzpatrick, Thomas *1988*	Lodge, Adam Robert *1996*

LANCASTER BUILDING

77 Deansgate, Manchester, M3 2BW
0161 661 4444/0171 649 9872
Fax: 0161 661 4445; DX 14488 Manchester 2

Chambers of Mr J Lambert

LINCOLN HOUSE CHAMBERS

5th Floor, Lincoln House, 1 Brazennose Street, Manchester, M2 5EL
0161 832 5701
Fax: 0161 832 0839; DX 14338 Manchester 1
E-mail: info@lincolnhse.co.uk
URL: http://www.lincolnhse.co.uk
Out of hours telephone: 0793 0523051

Chambers of M Hussain QC
Clerks: Andrew Weaver (Senior Clerk, Direct Line: 0161 819 2506), Nick Buckley, Gary Douglas, Pauline Holden, Mandy Hyde, Andy McGuinness; Administrator: Katherine Keenan

Hussain, Mukhtar QC 1971†	Wright, Peter QC *1981*
	Davies, Hugh *1982*
Webster, Alistair QC *1976†*	Nicholls, Elizabeth *1984*
Gozem, Gaias QC *1972†*	Bloomer, Charles *1985*
Sumner, David *1963†*	Watson, Denis *1985*
Gregory, James *1970*	Goddard, Suzanne *1986*
Platts, Robert *1973†*	Baxter, Bernadette *1987*
Reid, Paul *1973†*	Lawton, Paul *1987*
Conrad, Alan QC *1976†*	Wolstenholme, Alan *1989*
Pickup, James *1976†*	Bowley, Ivan *1990*
Lasker, Jeremy *1976*	Donnelly, Kevin *1991*
Nuttall, Andrew *1978*	Simons, Richard *1991*
Curran, Philip *1979‡*	Boyd, Joe *1993*
Elias, Robert *1979*	Blackwell, Katherine *1992*
Tait, Campbell *1979‡*	Roberts, Lisa *1993*

Usher, Neil *1993**	**Nawaz,** Mohammed *1995*
Holland, Ricky *1994*	**Priestley,** Roderick *1996*

LLOYDS HOUSE CHAMBERS

3rd Floor, 18 Lloyds House, Lloyd Street,
Manchester, M2 5WA
0161 839 3371
Fax: 0161 832 3371

Chambers of P R Marshall

CHAMBERS OF IAN MACDONALD QC (IN ASSOCIATION WITH TWO GARDEN COURT, TEMPLE, LONDON)

Chambers of Ian Macdonald QC
(in association with Two Garden Court, Temple, London)

Waldorf House, 5 Cooper Street,
Manchester, M2 2FW
0161 236 1840
Fax: 0161 236 0929; DX 715637
Manchester 2
Out of hours telephone: 07970 721337

Chambers of Ian Macdonald QC
Clerks: David Skinner (Senior Clerk),
Mark Makin (Junior Clerk)

Macdonald, Ian QC *1963*	**Plimmer,** Melanie *1996*
Barlow, Mark *1992*	**Robinson,** Simon *1991*
Edusei, Francis *1989*	**Stanage,** Nick Sean *1997*
Firth, Georgina *1995*	**Stark,** James Hayden
Fullwood, Adam *1996*	Alexander *1998*
Hodson, Peter *1994*	**Weatherby,** Pete *1992*
Kaur, Rani *1993*	**Weston,** Amanda *1995*
Martin, John *1977*	

Types of work (and number of counsel practising in that area if supplied)
Administrative 12 · Care proceedings 3 · Civil liberties 14 · Common law (general) 14 · Consumer law 1 · Courts martial 2 · Crime 8 · Crime – corporate fraud 6 · Discrimination 4 · Education 4 · Employment 5 · Family 3 · Family provision 3 · Housing 4 · Immigration 3 · Landlord and tenant 4 · Licensing 6 · Local government 1 · Medical negligence 2 · Mental health 4 · Personal injury 6 · Prison law · Professional negligence 2

Chambers established: 1996
Opening times: 9 am-6 pm

Chambers' facilities
Conference rooms, Disks accepted, Disabled access

Languages spoken
British Sign Language, Danish, French, German, Hebrew, Hindi, Italian, Portuguese, Punjabi, Spanish, Urdu, Welsh

Fees policy
Details of fees and/or hourly rates will be provided upon inquiry and will vary depending upon the seniority of counsel. Conditional fee work is undertaken. Pro–bono work is also undertaken in appropriate cases where funding is unavailable, especially when legal aid has been refused and miscarriage cases.

MANCHESTER HOUSE CHAMBERS

18-22 Bridge Street, Manchester, M3 3BZ
0161 834 7007
Fax: 0161 834 3462; DX 718153 Manchester 3

Chambers of J D S Wishart

MERCHANT CHAMBERS

MERCHANT CHAMBERS

1 North Parade, Parsonage Gardens,
Manchester, M3 2NH
0161 839 7070
Fax: 0161 839 7111; DX 14319 Manchester 1
E-mail: merchant.chambers@virgin.net

Chambers of David Berkley QC
Clerk: Alastair Campbell

Berkley, David QC *1979*	**Rule,** Jonathan *1993*
Berragan, Neil *1982*	**Feetham,** Daniel *1994*
Cogley, Stephen *1984*	**Brochwicz-Lewinski,** Stefan
Fisher, Catherine *1990*	*1995*
Noble, Andrew *1992*	

Types of work (and number of counsel practising in that area if supplied)
Banking · Bankruptcy · Chancery (general) · Chancery land law · Commercial · Commercial property · Company and commercial · Construction · Copyright · Corporate finance · Employment · Equity,

wills and trusts · Financial services ·
Franchising · Housing · Insolvency ·
Insurance · Insurance/reinsurance ·
Intellectual property · Landlord and tenant
· Medical negligence · Partnerships ·
Professional negligence · Sale and carriage
of goods · Share options

Chambers established: 1996

Chambers' facilities
Conference rooms, Disks accepted, E-mail

Languages spoken
French, Hebrew, Polish, Spanish

Long, Andrew *1981*	**Baker**, William *1991*
Melton, Christopher *1982*	**Ainsworth**, Mark *1992*
Pickup, David *1984*	**Blackshaw**, Henry *1993*
Johnson, Steven *1984*	**Orme**, Richard *1993*
Sheridan, Paul *1984*	**Evans**, Claire *1994*
Pearce, Richard *1985*	**Lloyd-Smith**, Rebecca
Grout-Smith, Jeremy *1986*	*1994*
Taylor, Julian *1986*	**Morris**, June *1995*
Fryman, Neil *1989*	**Ruck**, Mary *1993*
Walsh, Martin *1990*	**McBride**, Gavin *1996*
Knowles, Graham *1990*	**Mazzag**, Anthony *1996*
Smith, Rachel *1990*	**Green**, Alan *1973**
Burrows, Simon *1990*	**Sherry**, Michael *1978**

OLD COLONY HOUSE

6 South King Street, Manchester, M2 6DQ
0161 834 4364
Fax: 0161 832 9149; DX 718160
Manchester

Chambers of P McDonald

PARSONAGE CHAMBERS

5th Floor, 3 The Parsonage, Manchester,
M3 2HW
0161 833 1996
Fax: 0161 832 5027; DX 718183
Manchester 3

Chambers of Mr M J Holt

PEEL COURT CHAMBERS

45 Hardman Street, Manchester, M3 3PL
0161 832 3791
Fax: 0161 835 3054; DX 14320 Manchester
E-mail: clerks@peelct.co.uk
Out of hours telephone: 0961 998689

Chambers of J M Shorrock QC
Clerks: Mr Shell Edmonds, Mr David
Haley, Mrs Gail McDermott;
Administrator: Miss Anna Ewbank

Shorrock, Michael QC *1966*†	**Meadowcroft**, Stephen *1973*
Morris, Anthony QC *1970*†	**Russell**, Anthony QC *1974*
Bentham, Howard QC *1970*†	**Marks**, Richard QC *1975*†
	Lever, Bernard *1975*†
Simmonds, Nicholas *1969*	**O'Byrne**, Andrew *1978*
Richardson, Paul *1972*	**Brereton**, Fiorella *1979*
	Wallace, Adrian *1979*

QUEEN'S CHAMBERS

5 John Dalton Street, Manchester, M2 6ET
0161 834 6875/4738
Fax: 0161 834 8557 Grp 2&3; DX 718182
Manchester

Chambers of Timothy Ryder
Clerk: Terence Mylchreest (Senior Clerk)

Annexe: Queens Chambers, 4 Camden
Place, Preston, PR1 3JL
Tel: 01772 828300
Fax: 01772 825380

Ryder, Timothy *1977*‡	**Grocott**, Susan *1986*
Bailey, John *1966*	**Hobson**, Heather *1987*
Stuttard, Arthur *1967*	**Thompson**, Patrick *1990*
Lamberty, Mark *1970*	**Courtney**, Nicholas *1990*
Green, Roger *1972*	**McCullough**, Judith *1991*
Buckley, Peter *1972*	**Jones**, Brian *1992*
Shannon, Eric *1974*	**Godfrey**, Christopher *1993*
Osman, Robert *1974*	**Horgan**, Peter *1993*
Bradshaw, Howard *1977*	**Rothery**, Peter *1994*
Mercer, David *1980*	**Prudhoe**, Timothy *1994*
Hennell, Gordon *1982*	**Akerman**, Kate *1994*
Brown, Charles *1982*	**Potts**, Warren *1995*
Barker, Steven *1983*	

**Types of work (and number of counsel practising in
that area if supplied)**
Care proceedings 9 · Chancery (general) 2
· Chancery land law 2 · Civil actions against
the police · Civil actions involving the
police 7 · Commercial 4 · Commercial
litigation 4 · Commercial property 2 ·
Company and commercial 4 · Construction
1 · Consumer law 2 · Crime 14 ·
Defamation 2 · Discrimination 3 ·
Employment 7 · Environment 1 · Family 13
· Family provision 8 · Housing 1 ·
Insolvency 4 · Intellectual property 1 ·
Landlord and tenant 6 · Local government
2 · Medical negligence 7 · Personal injury
19 · Probate and administration 11 · Sale

† Recorder ‡ Assistant Recorder *Door Tenant

and carriage of goods 2 · Town and country planning 3

Chambers established: 1879
Opening times: 8.30 am-6.30 pm

Languages spoken
French

ST JAMES'S CHAMBERS

68 Quay Street, Manchester, M3 3EJ
0161 834 7000
Fax: 0161 834 2341; DX 14350 Manchester 1

E-mail: clerks@stjameschambers.co.uk
Out of hours telephone: 0161 643 2630

Chambers of R A Sterling
Clerk: Stephen Diggles

Sterling, Robert *1970*
Elleray, Anthony QC *1977†*
Wood, Percy *1961*
Mundy, Robert *1966*
Searle, Barrie *1975*
Porter, David *1980*
Lyons, Timothy *1980*
Cawson, Mark *1982‡*
Mulholland, Michael *1976*
Binns, David *1983*
Foster, Ian *1988*
Wilson-Barnes, Lucy *1989*
Cannan, Jonathan *1989*
Wheeldon, Sarah *1990*
Tankel, Ruth *1990*

Cook, Christopher *1990*
Maynard-Connor, Giles *1992*
Wills, Janice *1991*
Hurd, James *1994*
Calvert, David *1995*
Fryer-Spedding, James *1994*
Taft, Christopher Heiton *1997*
Price, Collette *1997*
Dooher, Nancy *1997*
Rubin, Anthony *1960**
Jaconelli, Joseph *1972**

Types of work (and number of counsel practising in that area if supplied)
Administrative 2 · Agriculture 5 · Arbitration 3 · Aviation 1 · Banking 6 · Bankruptcy 10 · Care proceedings 8 · Chancery (general) 12 · Chancery land law 10 · Charities 10 · Civil liberties 1 · Commercial property 8 · Common land 5 · Common law (general) 13 · Company and commercial 15 · Construction 2 · Conveyancing 3 · Copyright 5 · Crime 7 · Crime – corporate fraud 2 · Defamation 2 · Discrimination 3 · Education 2 · Employment 6 · Environment 1 · Equity, wills and trusts 12 · Family 11 · Family provision 11 · Financial services 5 · Franchising 1 · Housing 1 · Information technology 1 · Insolvency 10 · Insurance 4 · Intellectual property 4 · Landlord and tenant 10 · Licensing 2 · Medical negligence 6 · Mental health 1 · Partnerships 13 · Patents 1 · Pensions 2 ·

Personal injury 9 · Probate and administration 7 · Professional negligence 15 · Sale and carriage of goods 7 · Share options 2 · Tax – capital and income 2 · Tax – corporate 2 · Telecommunications 1 · Trademarks 2

Chambers established: 1800
Opening times: 7.30 am-6.30 pm

Chambers' facilities
Conference rooms, Disks accepted, E-mail

Languages spoken
French, German, Russian, Spanish

18 ST JOHN STREET

Manchester, M3 4EA
0161 278 1800
Fax: 0161 835 2051; DX 728854 Manchester 4
E-mail: 18stjohn@lineone.net

Chambers of Jonathan Foster QC
Clerks: Dominic Longhurst, John Hammond; Administrator: Jo Kelly

Carlisle of Bucklow, Lord QC *1954*†*
Grindrod, Helen QC *1966**
Brennan, Daniel QC *1967*†*
Foster, Jonathan QC *1970†*
Birkett, Peter QC *1972†*
Steiger, Martin QC *1969†*
Blake, Andrew *1971†*
Forrest, Alastair *1972†*
Hedgeland, Roger *1972‡*
Caldwell, Jennifer *1973*
Dockery, Paul *1973*
O'Brien, Paul *1974‡*
Wigglesworth, Raymond QC *1974†*
Diamond, Christopher *1975*
Stout, Roger *1976*
McEwan, Malcolm *1976*
Fewtrell, Nicholas *1977*
Laprell, Mark *1979‡*

Heaton, David *1983*
Vardon, Richard *1985*
Williams, Brian *1986*
Healing, Yvonne *1987*
Sasse, Toby *1988*
Birtles, Samantha *1989*
Poole, Nigel *1989*
Tythcott, Elisabeth *1989*
Simpson, Raquel *1990*
Benson, Mark *1992*
Booth, Joy *1992*
Harrison, Susan *1993*
Broadhurst, Simon *1994*
Garvin, Michael *1994*
Williams, Sarah *1995*
Kilvington, Simon *1995*
Brody, Saul *1996*
Moore, Andrew *1996*
Faux, Rachel *1997*

24A ST JOHN STREET

Manchester, M3 4DF
0161 833 9628
Fax: 0161 834 0243; DX 710301 Manchester 3

Chambers of P V Chambers, J McNeill
Clerks: Lynn Wallwork, Mark Latham

Chambers, Paul 1973	Crabtree, Simon 1988
McNeill, John 1974	Wilson, John 1988
Coppel, Yvonne 1976‡	Partington, Lisa 1989
McClure, John 1975	Lavery, Michael 1990
Dennett, Angelina 1980	Simpson, Alexandra 1989
Bruce, David 1982	Rhind, Mark 1989
Campbell, Graham 1982	Holt, Abigail 1993
Harrison, Peter 1983	Barr, Finola 1994
McKee, Hugh 1983	Sutton, Ruth 1994
McKenna, Brian 1983	Eyers, Anthony 1994
Khawar, Aftab 1983	Douglas, Stephen 1994
Harrison, J Keith 1983	Lawson, Andrew 1995
Chaplin, John 1986	Reynolds, Gary 1994
Gray, Richard 1986	Frieze, Daniel 1994
Fireman, Mark 1986	Smith, Andrew 1996
Brennand, Timothy 1987	Zentar, Remy 1997
Davitt, Paula 1988	Roxborough, Adam 1998
Smith, Peter 1988	Kearney, Robert 1996

28 ST JOHN STREET

28.

St. John
Street

Manchester, M3 4DJ
0161 834 8418
Fax: 0161 835 3929; DX 728861
Manchester 4
E-mail: clerk@28stjohnst.co.uk

Chambers of Clement Goldstone QC
Clerks: Jack Pickles, Christopher Ronan;
Practice Manager: Bridget Knight

Goldstone, Clement QC 1971†	Wallwork, Bernard 1976‡
Rumbelow, Anthony QC 1967†	Rothwell, Stephen 1977
	Platts, Graham 1978‡
Gee, Anthony QC 1972†	Grundy, Philip 1980‡
Chruszcz, Charles QC 1973†	Jones, John 1981‡
	Gal, Sonia 1982‡
Kushner, Lindsey QC 1974†	Greene, Maurice 1982
Redfern, Michael QC 1970†	Singleton, Sarah 1983‡
Freedman, Clive QC 1978	Hunter, Winston 1985‡
Cattan, Philip 1970†	Vickers, Guy 1986
Humphry, Richard 1972	Rowley, James 1987
Lowcock, Andrew 1973†	Clayton, Nigel 1987
Goode, Rowena 1974†	Hayden, Anthony 1987
	Walker, Jane 1987

Humphries, David 1988	Case, Magdalen 1992
Eastwood, Charles 1988	Harrison, Sally 1992
Samuels, Jeffrey 1988	Tyrrell, Richard 1993
Batra, Bunty 1988	Mathieson, Guy 1993
Grundy, Clare 1989	Kloss, Alexander 1993
Ross, Sally-Ann 1990	Gumbs, Annette 1994
Taylor, Paul 1985	Crilley, Darrel 1996
Rawlinson, Michael 1991	Spear, Sarah 1997
Wright, Alastair 1991	Roussak, Jeremy 1996
Kloss, Diana 1986	McHugh, Pauline 1995
Norton, Richard 1992	

Types of work (and number of counsel practising in that area if supplied)
Care proceedings 17 · Chancery (general) 2 · Common law (general) 25 · Company and commercial 15 · Conveyancing 1 · Crime 26 · Crime – corporate fraud 10 · EC and competition law 1 · Employment 9 · Environment 4 · Family 17 · Family provision 17 · Landlord and tenant 7 · Licensing 4 · Medical negligence 21 · Pensions 1 · Personal injury 25 · Private international 1 · Professional negligence 21 · Tax – capital and income 1 · Town and country planning 2

Chambers established: 1930
Opening times: 8 am-6 pm

Chambers' facilities
Conference rooms, Video conferences, Disks accepted, Disabled access

Languages spoken
French, Spanish

Fees policy
Details of fees and/or hourly rates will be provided upon inquiry and will vary depending upon the seniority of counsel.

ST JOHN'S CHAMBERS

2 St John's Street, Manchester, M3 4DT
0161 832 1633
Fax: 0161 834 3048

Chambers of Ms L M Cox QC

YOUNG STREET CHAMBERS

38 Young Street, Manchester, M3 3FT
0161 833 0489
Fax: 0161 835 3938; DX 25583
Manchester 5
E-mail: clerks@young-st-chambers.com

URL:
http://www.clerks@young-st-chambers.com
Out of hours telephone: 0161 834 6588

Chambers of Miss Lesley Newton
Clerks: Mr Peter Wright (Senior Clerk), Mr
Nicholas Geary (Criminal Clerk), Miss
Fiona McKay (Civil and Family Clerk),
Krissy Juttla (Junior Clerk), Denise Nield
(Fees Clerk)

Newton, Lesley 1977‡	Blakey, Michael 1989
Limb, Christopher 1975	Mawdsley, Matthew 1991
Elliott, Christopher 1974	McIvor, Helen 1992
Jay, Grenville 1975	Johnson, Amanda 1992
Andrews, Philip 1977	Rouse, Philip 1993
Hernandez, David 1976‡	Warnock, Ceri 1993
Huffer, Ian 1979	Myers, Benjamin 1994
Nadim, Ahmed 1982	Rowley, Karl 1994
Jackson, Wayne 1984	Manasse, Paul 1995
Stansby, Alexandra 1985	Bland, Carolyn 1995
Hickland, Margaret 1988	Delaney, Rory 1996
Fox, Andrew 1990	Morwood, J T 1996
Ford, Mark 1991	Tyler, Paula 1997

WEST LODGE FARM

Wrotham Road, Meopham, Kent
DA13 0QG
01474 812280
Fax: 01474 814759; DX 51254 Longfield
E-mail: karen.gough@virgin.net
Out of hours telephone: 01474 812280

Chambers of Karen Gough
Administrator: K J Douglas

Also at: Arbitration Chambers, 22 Willes
Road, London, NW5 3DS

Gough, Karen 1983

NUMBER TEN BAKER STREET

10 Baker Street, Middlesbrough, TS1 2LH
01642 220332
Fax: 01642 220377; DX 60506
Middlesbrough

Clerk: Mrs Monica Parker

Galley, Robert 1993	Maitra, Adrian Dilip 1997
Mitchell, Anne 1994	Gregory, Ann Marie 1994
Wells, David 1995	Mawdsley, David John
McKie, Jackie 1995	1995

BAKER STREET CHAMBERS

BAKER STREET
C   H   A   M   B   E   R   S

9 Baker Street, Middlesbrough, TS1 2LF
01642 873873
Fax: 01642 873877; DX 60591
Middlesbrough

Chambers of Mr Gerard Ford
Clerks: Pam Haw, Barbara Hudson

Ford, Gerard 1986	Bradshaw, Ian 1992
Constable, John 1972	Robson, Nicholas 1994
Dodds, Shaun 1990	Dryden, Shaun 1994
Newcombe, Paul 1991	Fagan, Catherine 1993
Sabiston, Peter 1992	Soppitt, Nigel 1996
Gillette, John 1990	Baker, Christopher 1994
Constantine, Stephen 1992	Hall, Derek 1994
McMinn, Valerie 1990	Richards, Janine 1995

FOUNTAIN CHAMBERS

Cleveland Business Centre, 1 Watson
Street, Middlesbrough, TS1 2RQ
01642 804040
Fax: 01642 804060; DX 711700
Middlesbrough1

Chambers of Peter J B Armstrong

CHAMBERS OF STUART LIGHTWING

Tudor Court, Church Lane, Nunthorpe,
Middlesbrough, TS7 0PD
01642 315000
Fax: 01642 315500; DX 60524
Middlesbrough

Chambers of Mr S Lightwing

MILTON KEYNES CHAMBERS

61 London Road, Loughton, Milton
Keynes, Buckinghamshire MK5 8AF
01908 664 128
Fax: 0171 353 8554
Other comms: E-Dx: neil_rl_cawley@
link.org
E-mail: neil_cawley@compuserve.com

C

URL: http://ourworld.compuserve.com/
homepages/Neil_Cawley

Chambers of Mr Neil Cawley

Also at: 169 Temple Chambers, Temple
Avenue, London EC4Y 0DA Tel: 0171 583
7644 Fax: 0171 353 8554

Cawley, Neil *1992*

HIGHER COMBE

*Hawkcombe, Porlock, Minehead, Somerset
TA24 8LP*
01643 862722
Fax: 01643 862871; DX 117405 Minehead

Chambers of Miss S E Cotter

CHAMBERS OF HERBERT FRANCOIS

*62 St James Road, Mitcham, Surrey
CR4 2DB*
0181 640 4529

Chambers of Mr H D Francois

---

39 PARK AVENUE

Mitcham, Surrey CR4 2ER
0181 648 1684
Fax: 0181 715 6615

Chambers of Mr M A Syed

LAVENHAM CHAMBERS

*Rookery Farm, Near Lavenham, Suffolk
CO10 0BJ*
01787 248247
Fax: 01787 247846; DX 86750 Sudbury2

Chambers of Miss S A Gratwicke

BROAD CHARE

*33 Broad Chare, Newcastle upon Tyne,
NE1 3DQ*
0191 232 0541
Fax: 0191 261 0043; DX 61001 Newcastle
E-mail: clerks@broadcharechambers.law.
co.uk

URL: http://www.broadcharechambers.law.
co.uk

Chambers of E A Elliot
Clerk: Brian Bell

Elliott, Eric *1974†*	**Armstrong**, Kester *1982*
Chadwin, James QC *1958†*	**Kennerley**, Ian *1983*
Cosgrove, Patrick QC *1976†*	**McKenzie**, Lesley *1983*
	Moulder, Pauline *1983*
Batty, Paul QC *1975†*	**O'Sullivan**, John *1984*
Bradley, Sally QC *1978*	**Richardson**, Anne *1986*
Harper, James *1957*	**Rowlands**, David *1988*
Such, Frederick *1960†*	**Styles**, Mark *1988*
Harte, David *1967*	**Gumsley**, Carl *1989*
Duff, Euan *1973‡*	**Brown**, James *1990*
Harmer, Christine *1973*	**Temple**, Michelle *1992*
Hewitt, Timothy *1973†*	**Anderson**, Stanley *1993*
Mitchell, Ronald *1973†*	**Lugg**, Elizabeth *1994*
Bolton, Beatrice *1975†*	**Elsey**, Roger *1977*
Hawks, Anthony *1975*	**Clemitson**, Julie *1991*
Horner, Robin *1975*	**Smith**, Rachel *1992*
Moir, Judith *1978†*	**Robinson**, Sara *1994*
Dorman-O'Gowan, Christopher *1979*	**Faulks**, Samuel James *1997*

**Types of work (and number of counsel practising in
that area if supplied)**
Arbitration 1 · Bankruptcy 5 · Care
proceedings 12 · Chancery (general) 5 ·
Chancery land law 5 · Common law
(general) 13 · Copyright 1 · Courts martial
1 · Crime 17 · Defamation 1 · Ecclesiastical
1 · Employment 4 · Environment 1 · Equity,
wills and trusts 5 · Family 12 · Family
provision 12 · Insolvency 5 · Landlord and
tenant 5 · Licensing 7 · Medical negligence
5 · Personal injury 7 · Sale and carriage of
goods 2

Opening times: 9 am-5.30 pm

Chambers' facilities
Conference rooms

CATHEDRAL CHAMBERS

*Milburn House, Dean Street, Newcastle
upon Tyne, NE1 1LE*
0191 232 1311
Fax: 0191 232 1422; DX 61277 Newcastle
Out of hours telephone: 0191 232 1311

Clerk: Elaine Black

Manasse, Anne *1994*	**Price**, John *1990*
Martin, David *1994*	**Weatherall**, Julia *1985*
Dixon, Ian *1982*	**Addison**, Neil *1976*
Brown, David *1993*	

       † Recorder ‡ Assistant Recorder *Door Tenant

ENTERPRISE CHAMBERS

65 Quayside, Newcastle upon Tyne, NE1 3DS
0191 222 3344
Fax: 0191 222 3340; DX 61134 Newcastle upon Tyne
E-mail: enterprise.newcastle@dial.pipex.com
URL: http://www.enterprisechambers.com

Chambers of Mr G A Mann QC
Clerks: Barry Clayton, Tony Armstrong, Dylan Wendleken; Chambers Director: Elspeth Mills Rendall; Accounts Administrator: Hannah Steininger-Nath; Newcastle Receptionist: Elaine Brown

Mann, Anthony QC *1974*	**Barker**, James *1984*
Levy, Benjamin *1956*	**Jack**, Adrian *1986*
Jennings, Timothy *1962*	**Groves**, Hugo *1980*
Halpern, David *1978*	**Atherton**, Ian *1988*
Morgan, Charles *1978*	**Garcia-Miller**, Laura *1989*
Hutton, Caroline *1979*	**Bhaloo**, Zia *1990*
James, Michael *1976*	**Pickering**, James *1991*
Peacocke, Teresa *1982*	**McKinnell**, Soraya *1991*
Ife, Linden *1982*	**Jory**, Hugh *1992*
McAllister, Ann *1982*	**Williamson**, Bridget *1993*
Arden, Peter *1983*	**Richardson**, Sarah *1993*
Zelin, Geoffrey *1984*	**Hardwick**, Matthew *1994*
Baker, Jacqueline *1985*	**Francis**, Edward *1995*
Gerald, Nigel *1985*	**Mauger**, Shanti *1996*

GOSFORTH CHAMBERS

2 Lansdowne Place, Gosforth, Newcastle upon Tyne, NE3 1HR
0191 285 4664
Fax: 0191 285 6377; DX 60362 Gosforth

Chambers of Mr R W Bloomfield

MILBURN HOUSE CHAMBERS

'A' Floor, Milburn House, Dean Street, Newcastle upon Tyne, NE1 1LE
0191 230 5511
Fax: 0191 230 5544; DX 716640 Newcastle 20
E-mail: milburnhousechambers@btinternet.com
URL: btinternet.com/~milburnhousechambers/mhc.htm

Chambers of Paul Cape
Clerk: Dorothy Toase

Cape, Paul *1990*	**Falkenstein**, John *1996*
Woodwark, Jane *1995*	**Sweeney**, Seamus *1989*

NEW COURT CHAMBERS

3 Broad Chare, Newcastle upon Tyne, NE1 3DQ
0191 232 1980
Fax: 0191 232 3730; DX 61012 Newcastle

Chambers of D E H Robson QC

PLOWDEN BUILDINGS

1 Jesmond Dene Terrace, Newcastle upon Tyne, NE2 2ET
0191 281 2096

Chambers of Mr G W Lowe QC

C

Languages
See the Index of Languages Spoken in Part G to locate a chambers where a particular language is spoken, or find an individual who speaks a particular language.

TRINITY CHAMBERS

9-12 Trinity Chare, Quayside, Newcastle upon Tyne, NE1 3DF
0191 232 1927
Fax: 0191 232 7975; DX 61185 Newcastle
Other comms: Video Conference 0191 233 1004
E-mail: info@trinitychambers.co.uk
Out of hours telephone: 07798 625988

Chambers of A T Hedworth QC
Clerks: C Hands (Silks' Clerk), Sharon Robson (Criminal Clerk), Ailsa Charlton (Criminal Clerk), Christopher Swann (Family and Civil Clerk), Clare Thomas (Family and Civil Clerk); Practice Director: Simon Stewart OBE

Hedworth, Alan QC 1975†	**Hudson**, Rachel 1985
Milford, John QC 1969†	**McCrae**, Fiona 1986
Forster, Brian QC 1977†	**Goodwin**, Caroline 1988
Kelly, Charles 1965	**Routledge**, Shaun 1988
Duffield, Stephen 1969†	**Gittins**, Timothy 1990
Hargrove, Jeremy 1970	**Oliver**, Crispin 1990
Knox, Christopher 1974†	**Adams**, Robert 1993
Duff, Graham 1976	**Ditchfield**, Anthony 1993
Vane, Christopher 1976	**Scott Bell**, Rosalind 1993
Lowe, John 1976	**Stonor**, Nicholas 1993
Wilkinson, Michael 1979	**Gilbert**, Julia 1994
Smith, Duncan 1979†	**Pryke**, Stuart 1994
Smart, Jacqueline 1981	**Holland**, Charles 1994
Sloan, Paul 1981	**Woolrich**, Sarah 1994
Richardson, James 1982	**Caulfield**, Paul 1996
Spain, Timothy 1983	

Types of work (and number of counsel practising in that area if supplied)
Arbitration 5 · Banking 2 · Bankruptcy 4 · Care proceedings 7 · Chancery (general) 4 · Chancery land law 4 · Charities 2 · Commercial litigation 7 · Common land 2 · Common law (general) 9 · Company and commercial 3 · Construction 3 · Conveyancing 2 · Crime 19 · Employment 3 · Equity, wills and trusts 4 · Family provision 10 · Housing 4 · Insolvency 4 · Insurance 4 · Landlord and tenant 6 · Licensing 4 · Local government 1 · Medical negligence 4 · Partnerships 4 · Personal injury 8 · Probate and administration 3 ·

Professional negligence 8 · Sale and carriage of goods 3 · Town and country planning 1

Chambers established: 1952
Opening times: 8.30 am-6 pm

Fees policy
Up to five years call £75, Up to ten years call £85, Over ten years call £85. QC £250–300.

WESTGATE CHAMBERS

67a Westgate Road, Newcastle upon Tyne, NE1 1SG
0191 261 4407/2329785
Fax: 0191 222 1845; DX 61044 Newcastle
E-mail: pracman@westgatechambers.law.co.uk

Chambers of I J Dawson
Clerks: Shaun Murtagh, Lynn Davis; Practice Manager: Stan Zych

Dawson, Ian 1971	**Mallett**, Sarah 1988
Braithwaite, Antony 1971	**O'Brien**, Joseph 1989
Rich, Charles 1972	**Boothroyd**, Susan 1990
Hunter, Geoffrey 1979	**Jarron**, Stephanie 1990
Finch, Thomas 1981	**Middleton**, Claire 1991
Mark, Brian 1981	**Hare**, William 1994
Mason, David 1984	**Peacock**, Nicholas 1996
Selwyn Sharpe, Richard 1985	**James-Stadden**, Jodie Cara 1996
Davis, Anthony 1986	

NEWPORT CHAMBERS

12 Clytha Park Road, Newport, Gwent NP9 47L
01633 267403/255855
Fax: 01633 253441; DX 33208 Newport

Chambers of Mr H L A Roberts

CHARTLANDS CHAMBERS

3 St Giles Terrace, Northampton, NN1 2BN
01604 603322
Fax: 01604 603388; DX 12408 Northampton 1

Out of hours telephone: 01536 521859

Chambers of J E Page
Clerk: Andrew Davies

Page, Jane *1982*
Van Besouw, Eufron *1988*
Tapper, Paul *1991*
Pinkham, Joy *1993*
Slade Jones, Robin *1993*

Knight, Christopher *1994*
Robinson, Matthew *1994*
MacKillop, Norman *1994*
Maycock, Elizabeth *1996*

ERIMUS CHAMBERS

P.O.Box 458, Brixworth, Northampton, NN6 9ZT
01604 882942
Fax: 01604 882942; DX 16052 Kingsthorpe North

Chambers of Mrs K R Boyes

CHAMBERS OF MICHAEL PERT QC

24 Albion Place, Northampton, NN1 1UD
01604 602333
Fax: 01604 601600; MDX 18544 Northampton 2

Chambers of Michael Pert QC
Clerks: Martin Poulter (Senior Clerk), Graeme Logan (Silks Clerk), Joanne Pickersgill (Senior Criminal Clerk), Harri Bennetts (Criminal Clerk), Richard Cade (Civil and Family Clerk), Everton Wedderburn (Civil and Family Clerk), Lynne Edmond (Senior Fees Clerk); Practice Manager: Peter Bennett FCCA MCIM; Administrator: Louise West

Also at: 36 Bedford Row, London WC1R 4JH Tel: 0171 421 8000 Fax: 0171 421 8080; 104 New Walk, Leicester LE1 7EA Tel: 0116 249 2020 Fax: 0116 255 0885

Pert, Michael QC *1970†*
Escott-Cox, Brian QC *1954*
Bowley, Martin QC *1962*
Hunt, James QC *1968†*
Raggatt, Timothy QC *1972†*
Stokes, Michael QC *1971†*
Oldham, Frances QC *1977†*
Browne, Nicholas QC *1971†*
Benson, Richard QC *1974†*
Swindells, Heather QC *1974†*
Walker, Annabel QC *1976†*
Weekes, Anesta QC *1981‡*

Urquhart, Andrew *1963*
Waine, Stephen *1969†*
Altaras, David *1969†*
Metcalf, Christopher *1972†*
Lee, David *1973*
de Burgos, Jamie *1973*
Fowler, Michael *1974‡*
Solomons, Geoffrey *1974*
Greaves, Michael *1976*
Mainds, Allan *1977†*
Lewis, Charles *1977*
Neaves, Andrew *1977*
Morrison, Howard OBE *1977†*

Farrell, David *1978‡*
Gargan, Catherine *1978*
Beddoe, Martin *1979*
Kushner, Martine *1980*
Donnellan, Christopher *1981*
Tayton, Lynn *1981*
Farrell, Edmund *1981*
Wilson, Richard *1981*
Akman, Mercy *1982*
Plunkett, Christopher *1983*
Harbage, William *1983*
Bull, Simon *1984*
Ecob, Joanne *1985*
Underwood, Robert *1986*
Gumpert, Benjamin *1987*
Malik, Amjad *1987*
Pryce, Gregory *1988*
Aspden, Gordon *1988*
Howarth, Andrew *1988*

Johnson, Amanda *1990*
Gibson, John *1991*
Lowe, Matthew *1991*
Alford, Stuart *1992*
Gaunt, Sarah *1992*
Dean, Rosa *1993*
Lloyd-Jones, John *1993*
Johnston, Karen *1994*
Jupp, Jeffrey *1994*
Bojarski, Andrzej *1995*
Kirk, Jonathan *1995*
Ferguson, Niall *1996*
Skilbeck, Rupert *1996*
Connolly, Oliver *1997*
Brunner, Kate *1997*
Barry, Kevin *1997*
Joyce, Peter QC *1968*†
Treacy, Colman QC *1971*†
Ingham, Elizabeth *1989**
Payne, Richard *1964**

NORTHAMPTON CHAMBERS

22 Albion Place, Northampton, NN1 1UD
01604 636271
Fax: 01604 232931; DX 12464 Northampton
Other comms: Business hours: 8.30 am-6.30 pm
Out of hours telephone: 07971 285796

Chambers of Peter Hollingworth
Clerk: Russell Burton

Hollingworth, Peter *1993*
Anthony, Robert *1979*
Crouch, Stephen *1982*
Willis, Pearl *1986*
Savvides, Maria *1986*
Sutton, Clive *1987*
Deegan, Jeffrey *1989*
Lynch, Terry *1989*
Yeung, Stuart *1989*
Burns, Terry *1990*

Ellis, Michael *1993*
Holloway, Richard *1993*
Abbott, Mary *1994*
Smith, Nicola *1994*
Gow, Ben *1994*
Williams, Barbara *1995*
Willans, David *1995*
Aslett, Pepin *1996*
Evans, Steven David *1997*
Tedd, Rex QC *1970**

WESTGATE CHAMBERS

4 Copse Close, Northwood, Middlesex HA6 2XG
01923 823671
Fax: 01923 821890

Chambers of Mr H B Hargrave

C

EAST ANGLIAN CHAMBERS

57 London Street, Norwich, NR2 1HL
01603 617351
Fax: 01603 633589; DX 5213 Norwich
E-mail: norwich@ealaw.co.uk
Out of hours telephone: 0585 100461

Chambers of Roderick Newton
*Clerk: Stephen Collis (Senior Clerk);
Administrator: Carol Bull*

Also at: 52 North Hill, Essex, CO1 1PY and
5 Museum Street, Ipswich IP1 1HQ

Newton, Roderick 1982‡	Richards, David 1989
Akast, John 1968†	Greaves, Ann 1989
Wardlow, John 1971†	Greenwood, John 1990
Pearce, Marcus 1972	Jackson, Andrew 1990
Wain, Peter 1972	Bell, Marika 1991
Marsden, Andrew 1975‡	Bundell, Katharine 1991
Bryant, Caroline 1976	Smith, Raymond 1991
Levett, Martyn 1978	Barratt, Dominic 1992
McLoughlin, Timothy 1978	Parry-Jones, Carole 1992
Miller, Celia 1978	Rippon, Amanda 1993
Pugh, David 1978	Walsh, Patricia 1993
Hamey, John 1979	Gilbertson, Helen 1993
Sinclair, Graham 1979	Hanlon, Jacqueline 1994
Kefford, Anthony 1980	Phelps, Mark 1994
Brooke-Smith, John 1981‡	Preston, Hugh 1994
Parnell, Graham 1982	Kelly, Richard 1994
Redmayne, Simon 1982	Wheetman, Alan 1995
Davies, Jane 1983	Freeman, Sally 1995
Lane, Michael 1983	Leigh, Samantha 1995
Vass, Hugh 1983	Durr, Jude 1995
Shadarevian, Paul 1984	Wilson, David 1996
Cox, Lindsay 1984	Baruah, Fiona 1996
Bettle, Janet 1985	Thain, Ashley 1996
Dyble, Steven 1986	Morgans, John 1996
Bate, Anthony 1987	Ivory, Martin 1996
Degel, Rebecca 1987	Rauf, Saqib 1996
Elcombe, Nicholas 1987	McArdle, Martin 1996
Mandil-Wade, Rosalyne 1988	Cannatella, Marc 1997
	Pugh-Smith, John 1977*

OCTAGON HOUSE

19 Colegate, Norwich, NR3 1AT
01603 623186
Fax: 01603 760519; DX 5249 Norwich 1
E-mail: admin@octagon-chambers.co.uk

Chambers of A N G Lindqvist, G R Ayers
*Clerk: Corinne Ashton; Practice Manager:
Stephen Unsworth*

Lindqvist, Andrew 1968	James, Ian 1981
Ayers, Guy 1979	Richards, Jeremy 1981‡
Townshend, Timothy 1972	Butterworth, Paul 1982

Fletcher, Christopher 1984	Oliver, Andrew 1993
Aldous, Robert 1985	Prinn, Helen 1993
Clare, Michael 1986	Jones, Susannah Lucy 1997
Potts, Richard 1991	

SACKVILLE CHAMBERS

*Sackville Place, 44-48 Magdalen Street,
Norwich, NR3 1JU*
01603 613516/616221
Fax: 01603 620799; DX 5225 Norwich
Out of hours telephone: 07880 553879

Chambers of S Ridley
Clerk: Richard Nunn

Ridley, Stephen 1977	Wood, Richard 1995
Mantell-Sayer, Peter 1992	Gregory, Ann Marie 1994

70 CHARLECOTE DRIVE

Wollaton, Nottingham, NG8 2SB
0115 928 8901
Fax: 0115 928 8901

Chambers of Mrs U R Sood

HIGH PAVEMENT CHAMBERS

1 High Pavement, Nottingham, NG1 1HF
0115 9418218
Fax: 0115 9418240; DX 10168 Nottingham

Chambers of J B Milmo QC
Clerks: David Duric, Nigel Wragg

Milmo, John QC 1966*	Bhatia, Balraj 1982
Joyce, Peter QC 1968†	Palmer, Timothy 1982
Warren, John QC 1968†	Ballentyne, Errol 1983
Walmsley, Peter 1964	Napthine, Godfrey 1983
Pearce, Frederick 1975‡	Shant, Nirmal 1984
Rafferty, Stuart 1975	Campbell-Moffat, Audrey 1987
Wigoder, Lewis 1977	
Burgess, John 1978‡	Eley, Jonathan 1987
Napthine, Guy 1979	Evans, Michael 1988
Brown, Robert 1979	Stockwell, Clive 1988
Mann, Paul 1980	Egbuna, Robert 1988
Dickinson, Gregory 1981‡	Geeson, Christopher 1989
Elwick, Bryan 1981	Thatcher, Richard 1989
Smith, Shaun 1981	Auty, Michael 1990

Easteal, Andrew *1990*	Manning, Robert Michael
McNamara, James *1990*	Jonathan *1992*
Mukherjee, Avik *1990*	Coupland, Steven *1993*
Munro, Sarah *1990*	Gosnell, Steven *1995*
Hargreaves, Katie *1991*	Ahya, Sonal *1995*
King, Paul *1992*	Achurch, Timothy Mark
Pritchard, Dawn *1992*	*1996*

Clark, Bryony *1985*	Cox, Jason *1992*
Prestwich, Andrew *1986*	Davies, Deborah *1993*
Limb, Patrick *1987*	Hodgson, Elizabeth *1993*
Seabrook, Richard *1987*	Mulvein, Helen *1994*
Turton, Philip *1989*	Gregory, Richard *1993*
Stewart, Toby *1989*	Diggle, Mark *1996*
Boora, Jinder *1990*	Hogan, Andrew *1996*
Mitchell, Jonathan *1992*	

KING CHARLES HOUSE

Standard Hill, Nottingham, NG1 6FX
0115 9418851
Fax: 0115 9414169; DX 10042 Nottingham
E-mail: clerks@kch.co.uk

Chambers of W Everard
Clerks: Geoff Rotherham, Russell Hobbs

Everard, William *1973*‡	Dee, Jonathon *1989*
O'Connell, Michael *1966*	Munt, Alastair *1989*
Stobart, John *1974*	Jackson, Adrian *1990*
Bridge, Rowena *1975*	McNeilis, Sharron *1990*
Howlett, James *1980*	Jones, Richard *1991*
Buchanan, Vivien *1981*	Morris, Jane *1991*
Lowne, Stephen *1981*	Janes, Jeremy *1992*
Toombs, Richard *1983*	Leonard, Edna *1992*
Dhadli, Perminder *1984*	Straw, Jonathan *1992*
Cranny, Amanda *1984*	Grimshaw, Elizabeth *1993*
Gallagher, Patrick *1984*	Warburton, Julie *1993*
Salmon, Kevin *1984*	Kirwin, Tracey *1995*
Bradley, Caroline *1985*	Wylie, Neil *1996*
Cranmer-Brown, Michael *1986*	Hale, Grace *1998*
Van Der Zwart, Mark *1988*	Ewing, Harald Richard Wolf *1997*
Way, Ian *1988*	

ROPEWALK CHAMBERS

24 The Ropewalk, Nottingham, NG1 5EF
0115 9472581
Fax: 0115 9476532; DX 10060 Nottingham
E-mail: administration@ropewalk.co.uk
URL: http://www.ropewalk.co.uk

Chambers of R Maxwell QC
Clerk: David Austin

Maxwell, Richard QC *1968*†	Berrisford, Anthony *1972*
Woodward, William QC *1964*†	Herbert, Douglas *1973*‡
Goldstaub, Anthony QC *1972*†	Bridge, Prof Michael *1975**
	Beresford, Stephen *1976*
McLaren, Ian QC *1962*†	Gash, Simon *1977*
Owen, Robert QC *1977*‡	Hampton, Alison *1977*‡
Jarand, Godfrey *1965*	Beard, Simon *1980*
Machin, Graham *1965*	Adams, Jayne *1982*
Burns, Richard *1967*†	Coe, Rosalind *1983*
Swain, Richard *1969*‡	Din, Soofi *1984*
	Nolan, Dominic *1985*

ST MARY'S CHAMBERS

50 High Pavement, Lace Market, Nottingham, NG1 1HW
0115 9503503
Fax: 0115 9583060; DX 10036 Nottingham
E-mail: clerks@smc.law.co.uk

Chambers of Colin Anderson
Clerk: D J Wilson

Anderson, Colin *1973*	Hale, Sean *1988*
Hamilton, Andrew *1970*‡	Gilead, Beryl *1989*
Jose, Calder *1971*‡	Casey, Mairin *1989*
Butler, Christopher *1972*‡	Mulrennan, Maria *1990*
Philo, Noel *1975*	Hett, James *1991*
Rhys, Owen *1976*	Lody, Stuart *1991*
Page, Nigel *1976*	Claxton, Judith *1991*
Smart, David *1977*	McNamara, Andrew *1992*
Lea, Jeremy *1978*	Wainwright, Patrick *1994*
Watson, Hilary *1979*	Soubry, Anna *1995*
Rogers, Mark *1980*	Eckersley, Simon *1996*
Hodges, Victoria *1980*	Knight, Sarah *1996*
Reynolds, Adrian *1982*	Rowley, Rachel *1997*
Hedley, Richard *1983*	Spicer, Jonathan *1995*
Michell, Michael *1984*	Walters, Terence Charles *1993*
Farquhar, Stuart *1985*	

EASTERN CHAMBERS

Badgers Bottom, Dysons Wood Lane, Tokers Green, Oxford, RG4 9EY
0118 972 3722
Fax: 0118 972 1190

Chambers of Miss H M McGregor

HARCOURT CHAMBERS

Churchill House, 3 St Aldate's Courtyard, St Aldate's, Oxford, OX1 1BN
01865 791559

Fax: 01865 791585; DX 96453 Oxford 4
E-mail:
clerks@harcourtchambers.law.co.uk
URL:
http://www.harcourtchambers.law.co.uk

Chambers of Mr H W P Eccles QC
Clerks: Brian Wheeler, Timothy Wheeler,
Judith Partington

Annexe of: Harcourt Chambers, 1st Floor,
2 Harcourt Buildings, Temple, London,
EC4Y 9DB
Tel: 0171 353 6961
Fax: 0171 353 6968

Eccles, Patrick QC *1968†*	**Brett**, Matthew *1987*
Evans, Roger *1970‡*	**Miles**, Edward *1989*
Rodgers, June *1971†*	**Clarke**, Peter *1970**
Sefi, Benedict *1972*	**Pressdee**, Piers *1991*
Arthur, Gavyn *1975*	**Granshaw**, Sara *1991*
Dixon, John *1975‡*	**Max**, Sally *1991*
Barstow, Stephen *1976*	**Auld**, Rohan *1992*
Baker, Jonathan *1978‡*	**Vater**, John *1995*
Collinson, Alicia *1982*	**Goodwin**, Nicholas *1995*
Frazer, Christopher *1983*	**Vine**, Aidan *1995*
Judd, Frances *1984*	**Sampson**, Jonathan *1997*
Hess, Edward *1985*	**Daley**, Howard *1997*
Blackwood, Clive *1986*	

KING'S BENCH CHAMBERS

32 Beaumont Street, Oxford, OX1 2NP
01865 311066
Fax: 01865 311077; DX 4318 Oxford
Other comms: Lix: Oxf 003
E-mail: clerks@kbc-oxford.law.co.uk

Chambers of Roger Ellis QC
Clerks: Stephen Buckingham, Kevin Kelly;
Administrator: Penny McFall; Chambers
Director: Claire Makin

Annexe of: 13 King's Bench Walk, 1st
Floor, Temple, London, EC4Y 7EN
Tel: 0171 353 7204
Fax: 0171 583 0252

Ellis, Roger QC *1962*	**Coode**, Jonathan *1984*
Williams, Graeme QC *1959†*	**Vickery**, Neil *1985*
	Moore, Neil *1986*
Baughan, Julian QC *1967†*	**Gibbons**, Sarah *1987*
Ashton, David *1962*	**Blake**, Arthur *1988*
Dawson, Alexander *1969†*	**Cramsie**, Sinclair *1988*
McGeorge, Anthony *1969*	**Hay**, Fiona *1989*
Lamb, Robert *1973*	**Pote**, Andrew *1983*
Richardson, David *1973†*	**Higgins**, Adrian *1990*
Goodwin, Deirdre *1974*	**Walters**, Edmund *1991*
Grant, David *1975‡*	**Wenlock**, Heather *1991*
Reid, Paul *1975*	**Walters**, Vivian *1991*
Tracy Forster, Jane *1975*	**Panesar**, Deshpal *1993*
Bright, David *1976†*	**Chan**, Susan *1994*
Brough, Alasdair *1979*	**Mitchell**, Paul *1994*
Daly, Nigel *1979*	**Cox**, James *1997*
Syfret, Nicholas *1979*	**White**, Matthew *1997*
Glennie, Andrew *1982*	**Owens**, Lucy *1997*
Williams, A *1983*	

3 PAPER BUILDINGS (OXFORD)

THE CHAMBERS OF MICHAEL PARROY Q.C.

1 Alfred Street, High Street, Oxford,
OX1 4EH
01865 793736
Fax: 01865 790760; DX 4302 Oxford
E-mail: oxford@3paper.com

Chambers of M P Parroy QC
Clerks: Russell Porter (Senior Clerk),
David Snook

Annexe of: 3 Paper Buildings, Temple,
London, EC4Y 7EU
Tel: 020 7583 8055
Fax: 020 7353 6271

Parroy, Michael QC *1969*	**Coleman**, Anthony *1973*
Harris, David QC *1969†*	**Stephenson**, Ben *1973*
Hughes, Peter QC *1971*	**Litchfield**, Linda *1974*
Jones, Stewart QC *1972†*	**Bartlett**, David *1975†*
Aspinall, John QC *1971*	**Richardson**, Garth *1975*
Parrish, Samuel *1962*	**Tyson**, Richard *1975‡*
Solomon, Susan *1967*	**Henry**, Peter *1977*
Trevethan, Susan *1967*	**Mitchell**, Nigel *1978*
Haynes, John *1968*	**Seed**, Nigel *1978‡*
Swinstead, David *1970*	**Kent**, Peter *1978*
Aylwin, Christopher *1970*	**Partridge**, Ian *1979*
Hope, Derwin *1970†*	**Grey**, Robert *1979*
Norman, Michael *1971†*	**Leviseur**, Nicholas *1979*
Curran, Leo *1972*	**Coombes**, Timothy *1980*
Jennings, Peter *1972*	**Cairnes**, Paul *1980*

† Recorder ‡ Assistant Recorder *Door Tenant

Marshall, David *1981*
Edge, Ian *1981*
Strutt, Martin *1981*
Lickley, Nigel *1983*
Lomas, Mark *1983*
Maccabe, Irvine *1983*
Branigan, Kate *1984*
O'Hara, Sarah *1984*
Chamberlain, Francis *1985*
Sanderson, David *1985*
Bailey, Russell *1985*
Parker, Christopher *1986*
Hudson, Elisabeth *1987*
Letman, Paul *1987*
Rowland, Nicholas *1988*
Kelly, Patricia *1988*
Woolgar, Dermot *1988*
Hester, Paul *1989*
Opperman, Guy *1989*
Bradbury, Timothy *1989*
Killen, Geoffrey *1990*
Kilpatrick, Jean *1990*

Buckley-Clarke, Amanda *1991*
Ross, Iain *1991*
Steenson, David *1991*
Sweeney, Christian *1992*
Bingham, Tony *1992*
Kirkpatrick, Krystyna *1965*
Fitzharris, Ginnette *1993*
Clargo, John *1994*
Earle, Judy *1994*
Walter, Francesca *1994*
Reid, David *1994*
Williams, Ben *1994*
Sutherland Williams, Mark *1995*
Hughes, Melanie *1995*
McIlroy, David *1995*
Strachan, Elaine *1995*
Case, Richard *1996*
Kay, Dominic *1997*
Leech, Ben *1997*
Purdy, Catherine *1997*
Sullivan, Mark *1997*

28 WESTERN ROAD

Oxford, OX1 4LG
01865 204911
Fax: 01865 721692
E-mail: lawyers@28wr.freeserve.co.uk
URL: http://www.28wr.freeserve.co.uk
Out of hours telephone: 01865 204911

Chambers of R A J Purdie
Practice Manager: Jayne Richards

Purdie, Robert *1979*

PERIVALE CHAMBERS

15 Colwyn Avenue, Perivale, Middlesex UB6 8JY
0181 998 1935/081 248 0246
Fax: 0181 902 9223

Chambers of Mr S Ahmed

2 SALVIA GARDENS

Perivale, Middlesex UB6 7PG
0181 997 9905
Fax: 0181 997 9905

Chambers of Mr Y U R K Suri

FENNERS CHAMBERS

8-12 Priestgate, Peterborough, PE1 1JA
01733 562030
Fax: 01733 343660; DX 12314
Peterborough 1
E-mail: clerks@fennerschambers.co.uk
URL: http://www.fennerschambers.co.uk

Chambers of Lindsay Davies
Clerks: Mark Springham, Louis Rankin, Ian Spencer, Joanna Gray; Administrator: Jane Longhurst

Also at: Fenners Chambers, 3 Madingley Road, Cambridge, CB3 0EE Tel: 01223 368761

Davies, Lindsay *1975*‡
King, Peter *1970*
Hawkesworth, Gareth *1972*†
Jones, Geraint *1972*
Gore, Andrew *1973*
Franklin, Stephen *1974*
Espley, Susan *1976*
Pointon, Caroline *1976*
Heald, Oliver *1977*
Tattersall, Simon *1977*
Leigh-Morgan, Paul *1978*
Brown, T C E *1980*
Crimp, Michael *1980*
Hollow, Paul *1981*
Gordon-Saker, Andrew *1981*
Bridge, Stuart *1981*

Collier, Martin *1982*
Gordon-Saker, Liza *1982*
Hughes, Meryl *1987*
Foxwell, George *1987*
Wilson, Alasdair *1988*
Beasley-Murray, Caroline *1988*
Pithers, Clive *1989*
Meakin, Timothy *1989*
Taylor, Andrew *1989*
Hobson, Sally *1991*
Horton, Caroline *1993*
Myatt, Charles *1993*
Ferguson, Katharine *1995*
Josling, William *1995*
Magee, Mike *1997*
Spinks, Roderick *1997*

REGENCY CHAMBERS

Cathedral Square, Peterborough, PE1 1XW
01733 315215
Fax: 01733 315851; DX 12349
Peterborough 1

Chambers of Raymond Croxon QC

19 CHESTNUT DRIVE

Pinner, Middlesex HA5 1LX
0181 866 7603/933 2382
Fax: 0181 866 7603

Chambers of Mr K A Quddus

DEVON CHAMBERS

3 St Andrew Street, Plymouth, PL1 2AH
01752 661659
Fax: 01752 601346; DX 8290 Plymouth 2
E-mail: devonchambers.co.uk.
Out of hours telephone: 01752 794648

Chambers of R A Hough
Clerks: Peter Kerslake (Senior Clerk), Peter Dadge (Assistant Clerk)

Hough, Richard *1979*	**Taylor,** Rupert *1990*
Bush, John *1964*	**Knight,** Judith *1991*
Down, Susan *1984*	**Welsh,** James *1994*
Telford, Peter *1985*	**Bailey,** Elizabeth *1995*
Taylor, Ian *1986*	**Mann,** Daya *1995*
Linford, Robert *1987*	**Leesing,** Sarah *1997*

KING'S BENCH CHAMBERS

115 North Hill, Plymouth, PL4 8JY
01752 221551
Fax: 01752 664379; DX 8237 Plymouth

Chambers of Mr A M Donne QC

EVEREST

Twin Firs, PO Box 32, Talygarn, Pontyclun, Cardiff CF72 9BY
01443 229850
Fax: 01443 222252

Chambers of Mr R N J Everest

Everest, Roger *1968*

WINDSOR CHAMBERS

2 Penuel Lane, Pontypridd, South Wales CF37 4UF
01443 402067
Fax: 01443 400407; DX 44354 Pontypridd
E-mail: law@windsorchambers.co.uk
URL: http://www.windsorchambers.co.uk

Chambers of Miss M J M Withers
Practice Director: Iain Marsh

Withers, Michelle *1991*	**Cope,** John *1997*
Leathley, David *1980*	

Types of work (and number of counsel practising in that area if supplied)
Administrative · Arbitration · Asset finance · Bankruptcy · Care proceedings · Charities · Civil liberties · Commercial · Commercial litigation · Common law (general) · Company and commercial · Competition · Construction · Consumer law · Copyright · Corporate finance · Crime · Crime – corporate fraud · Defamation · Discrimination · EC and competition law · Employment · Environment · Equity, wills and trusts · Family · Family provision · Financial services · Franchising · Housing · Immigration · Information technology · Insolvency · Insurance · International trade · Landlord and tenant · Licensing · Local government · Medical negligence · Mental health · Patents · Pensions · Personal injury · Planning · Private international · Professional negligence · Sale and carriage of goods · Telecommunications · Town and country planning

Chambers established: 1998
Opening times: 8 am–7 pm

Chambers' facilities
Conference rooms, Video conferences, Disks accepted, Disabled access

Languages spoken
French, Italian, Welsh

Fees policy
Up to five years call £25–100 per hour, Up to ten years call £100–175 per hour, Over ten years call £175+ per hour. Chambers operates a flexible approach to fees. Fee packages can be tailored to suit the needs of particular cases or clients. Block fee arrangements are available. Hourly rates can be provided prior to work being undertaken. Please call the clerks.

EATON HOUSE

1st Floor, 4 Eaton Road, Branksome Park, Poole, Dorset BH13 6DG
01202 766301/768068

Chambers of Mr R J Massey

3 WELLINGTON ROAD

Poole, Dorset BH14 9LF
07771 905671 (Mobile)

Chambers of Mr K R Kelleher

GUILDHALL CHAMBERS PORTSMOUTH

Prudential Buildings, 16 Guildhall Walk, Portsmouth, Hampshire PO1 2DE
01705 752400
Fax: 01705 753100; DX 2225 Portsmouth 1

Chambers of Mr L T Young

HAMPSHIRE CHAMBERS

Malton House, 24 Hampshire Terrace, Portsmouth, Hampshire PO1 2QF
01705 826636/826426
Fax: 01705 291262; DX 2270 Portsmouth

Chambers of Dr P M McCormick

PORTSMOUTH BARRISTERS' CHAMBERS

Victory House, 7 Bellevue Terrace, Portsmouth, Hampshire PO5 3AT
023 92 831292/811811
Fax: 023 92 291 262; DX 2239 Portsmouth
E-mail: clerks@portsmouthbar.com
URL: http://www.portsmouthbar.com
Out of hours telephone: 023 92 553 783

Chambers of A J Parsons
Clerk: Jackie Morrison

Annexe: Portsmouth Barristers' Chambers, Winchester Annexe, First Floor, 28 St Stephens Road, Winchester, SO22 6DE
Tel: 01962 863222
Fax: 01962 855856

Annexe: Portsmouth Barristers' Chambers, Isle of Wight Annexe, 35 Alpine Road, Ventnor, Isle of Wight PO38 1BU
Tel: 01983 855 666
Fax: 01983 854 666

Parsons, Andrew *1985*	**Brookes,** Lincoln *1992*
Sabine, John *1979*	**Concannon,** Timothy *1993*
Dalby, Joseph (Irish Bar 1993) *1988*	**Booth,** Martyn *1996*
	Atwill, John *1997*

Types of work (and number of counsel practising in that area if supplied)
Arbitration · Bankruptcy · Chancery (general) · Chancery land law · Commercial litigation · Common law (general) · Company and commercial · Construction · EC and competition law · Employment · Equity, wills and trusts · Family · Family provision · Financial services · FSA related work · Insolvency · Landlord and tenant · Medical negligence · Partnerships · Pensions · Personal injury · Professional negligence · Sale and carriage of goods · Shipping, admiralty

Chambers established: 1990

Chambers' facilities
Conference rooms, Disks accepted, Conferences regularly undertaken in the late evening and at weekends, Regular use of e-mail to send draft documents

Languages spoken
French, German

Fees policy
Fees will be negotiated with the clerk depending on the case, but as a general guide: under three years call up to £90 per hour, three to five years call up to £150 per hour, five to ten years up to £200 per hour. All fees are negotiable with the clerk to chambers. By prior arrangement work may be sent to us without obligation to be considered by a member of chambers and if no fee can be agreed returned without charge.

SOLENT CHAMBERS

2nd Floor, Coronation House, 1 King's Terrace, Portsmouth, Hampshire PO5 3AR
01705 821818
Fax: 01705 821815; DX 2280 Portsmouth 1

Chambers of Mr P R Collins

SOUTHSEA CHAMBERS

PO Box 148, Southsea, Portsmouth,
Hampshire PO5 2TU
01705 291261
Fax: 01705 753152; DX 2266 Portsmouth

Chambers of Mr G H Garner

DEANS COURT CHAMBERS

41-43 Market Place, Preston, PR1 1AH
01772 555163
Fax: 01772 555941
E-mail: clerks@deanscourt.co.uk
URL: http://www.deanscourt.co.uk

Chambers of H K Goddard QC
Clerk: Mrs Terry Creathorn

Annexe: Deans Court Chambers, 24 St
John Street, Manchester, M3 4DF
Tel: 0161 214 6000
Fax: 0161 214 6001

Goddard, Keith QC *1959*†	**Denney**, Stuart *1982*
Henriques, Richard QC *1967*†	**Smith**, Timothy *1982*
Grime, Stephen QC *1970*†	**Trotman**, Timothy *1983*
Machell, Raymond QC *1973*†	**Davies**, Russell *1983*
Stockdale, David QC *1975*†	**Bancroft**, Louise *1985*
Fish, David QC *1973*†	**Heaton**, Frances *1985*
Ryder, Ernest QC *1981*‡	**Humphries**, Paul *1986*
Turner, Mark QC *1981*‡	**Brody**, Karen *1986*
Talbot, Kevin *1970*†	**Hudson**, Christopher *1987*
Bromley-Davenport, John *1972*†	**Grace**, Jonathan *1989*
Gregory, John *1972*	**Grimshaw**, Nicholas *1988*
Atherton, Peter *1975*†	**Morgan**, Edward *1989*
Booth, Alan *1978*‡	**Grantham**, Andrew *1991*
Trippier, Ruth *1978*	**Andrew**, Seamus *1991*
Butler, Philip *1979*‡	**Ironfield**, Janet *1992*
Sephton, Craig *1981*	**Alty**, Andrew *1992*
Field, Patrick *1981*	**Edge**, Timothy *1992*
Main, Peter *1981*‡	**Burns**, Peter *1993*
	Savill, Mark *1993*
	Hayton, Michael *1993*
	Judge, Lisa *1993*

Clegg, Sebastian *1994*	**Whitehall**, Richard *1998*
Boyle, David *1996*	**Cartwright**, Sophie *1998*
McCann, Simon *1996*	

NEW BAILEY CHAMBERS

NEW BAILEY CHAMBERS

TELEPHONE: (01772) 258087   10 LAWSON STREET,
FAX: (01772) 880100   PRESTON,
DX: 710050 PRESTON 10   LANCASHIRE,
   PR1 2QT

10 Lawson Street, Preston, PR1 2QT
01772 258087
Fax: 01772 880100; DX 710050 Preston 10

Chambers of Miss Patricia Bailey
Clerks: Savannah Biswas, John Stewart

Bailey, Patricia *1969*	**McGinty**, Robert *1994*
Thomas, Keith *1969*	**Watson**, Sharon *1994*
Wood, Graeme *1968**	**Lowson**, Norman *1989*
Robertson, James *1991**	**McCarthy**, William *1996*
Wright, Yasmin *1990*	**Johnson**, Carolyn Ann *1974*
Musaheb, Kevin *1990*	**Thomas**, Clare R *1998*
Dacre, Ian *1991*	**Shepherd**, Joanne *1993*
Dable, Jeremy *1987*	

QUEENS CHAMBERS

4 Camden Place, Preston, PR1 3JL
01772 828300
Fax: 01772 825380; DX 17156 Preston 1

Chambers of Timothy Ryder
Clerk: Terence Mylchreest

Annexe of: Queen's Chambers, 5 John
Dalton Street, Manchester, M2 6ET
Tel: 0161 834 6875/4738
Fax: 0161 834 8557 Grp 2&3

Ryder, Timothy *1977*‡	**Grocott**, Susan *1986*
Bailey, John *1966*	**Hobson**, Heather *1987*
Stuttard, Arthur *1967*	**Thompson**, Patrick *1990*
Lamberty, Mark *1970*	**Courtney**, Nicholas *1990*
Green, Roger *1972*	**McCullough**, Judith *1991*
Buckley, Peter *1972*	**Cohen**, Joseph *1991*
Shannon, Eric *1974*	**Jones**, Brian *1992*
Osman, Robert *1974*	**Godfrey**, Christopher *1993*
Bradshaw, Howard *1977*	**Horgan**, Peter *1993*
Mercer, David *1980*	**Rothery**, Peter *1994*
Hennell, Gordon *1982*	**Prudhoe**, Timothy *1994*
Brown, Charles *1982*	**Akerman**, Kate *1994*
Barker, Steven *1983*	**Potts**, Warren *1995*

15 WINCKLEY SQUARE

Preston, PR1 3IJ
01772 252828
Fax: 01772 258520; DX 17110 Preston 1
E-mail: clerks@winckleysq.demon.co.uk
URL: http://www.winckleysq.demon.co.uk

Chambers of R S Dodds
Clerks: Michael Jones, Nicholas Haley;
Practice Manager: John Schofield

Dodds, Stephen *1976*	**Anderson,** Peter *1988*
Bonney, James QC *1975**	**Henry,** Bruce *1988*
Baldwin, Roger *1969*	**Johnson,** Kathryn *1989*
Newell, Simon *1973*	**Bowcock,** Samantha *1990*
Watson, Barbara *1973*	**Creaner,** Paul *1990*
Crawford, Robert *1976*	**Harvey,** Louise *1991*
Kennedy, Nicholas *1977*	**Mitchell,** Marie *1991*
Haworth, Richard *1978*	**Cornah,** Emma *1992*
White, Timothy *1978*	**Livesey,** Fraser *1992*
Williams, Glyn *1981*	**Taylor,** Julie *1992*
Cross, Jane *1982*	**Whyatt,** Michael *1992*
Cross, Anthony *1982*	**Buchan,** Jonathan *1994*
Hart, Paul *1982*	**Hackett,** Martin *1995*
Kenny, David *1982*	**Blakey,** Lee *1995*
Hague, Paul *1983*	**Davis,** Paul *1996*
Woodward, John *1984*	**Dyer,** Jacob *1995*
Hunt, Richard *1985*	**Gillott,** Paul *1996*
Stuart, Mark *1985*	**Maqsood,** Zabeda *1996*
Bennett, Richard *1986*	

140 CHOLMELEY ROAD

Reading, Berkshire RG1 3LR
01189 665174
Fax: 01189 676318; DX 4078 Reading 1

Chambers of Miss C A Gordon

Bar Directory on the Internet
The Bar Directory is also available on
the Internet at the following address:
http://www.smlawpub.co.uk/bar

DR JOHNSON'S CHAMBERS

The Atrium Court, Apex Plaza, Reading,
Berkshire RG1 1AX
01734 254221
Fax: 01734 560380; DX 117880 Reading
Apex Plaza

Chambers of Lord Thomas of Gresford OBE QC

10 LAUNCESTON AVENUE

Caversham Park Village, Reading,
Berkshire RG4 6SW
01189 479548
Fax: 01189 479548

Chambers of Mr J S Price

CHAMBERS OF PAVAN SHARMA

286 Overdown Road, Tilehurst, Reading,
Berkshire RG31 6PP
0118 9625 832
Fax: 0118 9625 832

Chambers of Mr P Sharma

WESSEX CHAMBERS

Wessex

48 Queens Road, Reading, Berkshire
RG1 4BD
0118 956 8856
Fax: 0118 956 8857; DX 4012 Reading
E-mail: wessexchambers@compuserve.com
Out of hours telephone: as above or 04325
616735 (clerk's pager)

Clerk: Martin Davies

Khan, William *1971*	**McDevitt,** Colin *1995*
Smithers, Dr Roger *1990*	**Drake,** Rachel *1995*
Omar, Robina *1991*	**Ireland,** Penny *1996*
Joshi, Pramod *1992*	**Brunning,** Matthew *1997*
Duncan, Nikki *1994*	**Turtle,** Alister *1994**

REDHILL CHAMBERS

Seloduct House, 30 Station Road, Redhill,
Surrey RH1 1NF
01737 780781
Fax: 01737 761760; DX 100203 Redhill
Out of hours telephone: 0181 668 1234

Clerks: John Lister (Director of Chambers),
John Bowker; Practice Manager: Jan
Rogers

Also at: 11 Bolt Court, London, EC4A 3DQ
Tel: 0171 353 2300, Fax: 0171 353 1878

Also at: 7 Stone Buildings, 1st Floor,
Lincoln's Inn, London WC2A 3SZ Tel: 0171
242 0961, Fax: 0171 405 7028

Alexander, Ian QC *1964*†	**Tod,** Jonathan *1990*
Ashmore, Terence *1961*	**Murch,** Stephen *1991*
Bishop, John *1970*	**Benner,** Lucinda *1992*
Martin, Gay *1970*	**Carron,** Richard *1992*
Wood, Penelope (formerly a	**Burrington,** Richard *1993*
solicitor) *1999*	**Gerrish,** Simon *1993*
Conway, Robert *1974*	**Le Quesne,** Catherine *1993*
Lynch, Julian *1976*	**Linstead,** Peter *1994*
Lewis, Robert (formerly a	**Mathias,** Anna *1994*
solicitor) *1996*	**Papazian,** Cliona *1994*
Temple-Bone, Gillian *1978*	**Rudd,** Matthew *1994*
Birks, Simon *1981*	**Casey,** Noel *1995*
Randle, Simon *1982*	**Ellis,** Jonathan *1995*
Jenkala, Adrian *1984*	**Simkin,** Iain *1995*
Manson, Juliann *1985*	**Badenoch,** Tony *1996*
Pyle, Susan *1985*	**Islam-Choudhury,** Mugni
Owens, Matthew *1988*	*1996*
Porter, Geoffrey *1988*	**McGregor,** Alexander *1996*
Airey, Simon *1989*	**Porter,** Sarah *1996*
Cave, Patricia *1989*	**Harris,** Richard *1997*
Lakha, Shabbir *1989*	**Husain,** Laureen *1997*
Swirsky, Adam *1989*	**Langton,** Steven *1998*
Gordon, Mark *1990*	**Moys,** Clive *1998*
Livingstone, Simon *1990*	

7 WILTON ROAD

Redhill, Surrey RH1 6QR
01737 760264
Fax: 01737 778769

Chambers of Mr W E P McIlroy

Bar Directory on the Internet
The Bar Directory is also available on
the Internet at the following address:
http://www.smlawpub.co.uk/bar

---

12 PAXTON CLOSE

Kew Gardens, Richmond-upon-Thames,
Surrey TW9 2AW
0181 940 5895
Fax: 0181 255 4170; DX 200117 Richmond

Chambers of Mr R H Bruce

RICHMOND GREEN CHAMBERS

Greyhound House, 23-24 George Street,
Richmond-upon-Thames, Surrey TW9 1HY
0181 940 1841
Fax: 0181 948 5885; DX 100263 Richmond
2

Chambers of P B Taylor MBE

CHAMBERS OF DEREK WILLMOTT

8 Links Crescent, St Marys Bay, Romney
Marsh, Kent TN29 0RS
01303 87 3899
Fax: 01303 87 3899

Chambers of Mr W D I Willmott

MERRIEMORE COTTAGE

Sawbridge, Nr Rugby, Warwickshire
CV23 8BB
01788 891832
Fax: 01788 891832; DX 29403 Rugby
E-mail: kathleen@sawbridge.demon.co.uk

Chambers of Mrs K Hayter

Hayter, Kathleen *1982*

NEW CHAMBERS

3 Sadleir Road, St Albans, Herts AL1 2BL
0966 212126
Fax: 01727 841755; DX 6183 St Albans 1
Out of hours telephone: 0966 212126

Chambers of Mr K G Aylett
Clerk: Richard Samson

Aylett, Kenneth *1972*	**Gupta,** Usha *1984*‡

† Recorder ‡ Assistant Recorder *Door Tenant

ST ALBANS CHAMBERS

Dolphin Lodge, Dolphin Yard, Holywell Hill, St Albans, Herts AL1 1EX
01727 843383
Fax: 01727 842820; DX 6116 St Albans 1

Chambers of Mr G J Nixon-Moss
Clerk: Richard Gilbert (Senior Clerk)

Also at: Tindal Chambers, 50b Duke Street, Chelmsford, Essex Tel: 01245 267742 Fax: 01245 359766

Nixon-Moss, Gareth *1994*	**Beecroft**, Kirstie *1994*
Tyrrell, Alan QC *1956**	**Hignett**, Richard *1995*
Webb, Lorraine *1980*	**Smith**, Sean David *1995*
Moore, David *1983*	**Carvalho Gomes**, Ana
Conlon, Michael *1984*	Alexandra *1996*
Carter, Lesley *1986*	**Harris**, David Robert *1997*
Bassa, Yousef *1989*	**Rasul**, Lubna *1997*
Hayne, Jan *1991*	**Jones**, Huw *1997*
Berry, Martin *1992*	**Nall-Cain**, Richard *1997*
Shepherd, Joanne *1993*	

CHAMBERS OF MR G B STEWART

Ridge Hall, Ridge Lane, Staithes, Saltburn-by-the-Sea, Cleveland TS13 5DX
01947 840511
Fax: 01947 840222

Chambers of Mr G B Stewart

CHAMBERS OF GEOFFREY WHITE

9 The Finches, Sandy, Bedfordshire SG19 2UL
01767 692782
Fax: 01767 692782

Chambers of Mr G G N White

3 & 4 FARNHAM HALL

Farnham, Saxmundham, Suffolk IP17 1LB
01728 602758
Fax: 01728 602758

Chambers of Mr M C B West QC

23 WARHAM ROAD

Otford, Sevenoaks, Kent TN14 5PF
01959 522325
Fax: 01959 522325

Chambers of Mr D G Cracknell

BANK HOUSE CHAMBERS

Old Bank House, Hartshead, Sheffield, S1 2EL
0114 2751223
Fax: 0114 2768439; DX 10522 Sheffield

Chambers of J D D Hall QC
Clerks: Mrs Deborah Chilton, Mr W Digby

Hall, Jonathan D QC *1975†*	**Goddard**, Katherine *1987*
Battersby, Graham *1964*	**Hawkins**, David *1991*
Nimmo, Adrian *1971*	**Pimm**, Peter *1991**
England, George *1972*	**Smith**, Andrew *1991*
Smith, Robert *1974*	**Walker**, Fiona *1992*
Cranfield, Tony *1975*	**Upson**, Michael *1993*
Baird, James *1977*	**Cole**, Justine *1994*
Mason, David *1979*	**Hill**, Jason *1995*
Kelson, Peter *1981‡*	**West**, Ian *1996*
Hillis, John *1982*	**Sapsford**, Philip QC *1974**
Cook, Lesley *1984*	**Cane-Soothill**, Michael
Sheldon, Richard *1984*	*1997*

62 CORTWORTH ROAD

Ecclesall, Sheffield, S11 9LP
0114 236 0988
Fax: 0114 236 0988

Chambers of Mr J G Stevenson

15 NORTH CHURCH STREET CHAMBERS

15 North Church Street, Sheffield, S1 2DH
0114 2759708/2738380
Fax: 0114 2724915; DX 10629 Sheffield 1

Chambers of Mr D Gothorp

Bar Directory on the Internet
The Bar Directory is also available on the Internet at the following address:
http://www.smlawpub.co.uk/bar

---

† Recorder ‡ Assistant Recorder *Door Tenant

PARADISE CHAMBERS

26 Paradise Square, Sheffield, S1 2DE
0114 2738951
Fax: 0114 2760848; DX 10565 Sheffield
Other comms: Emergency Number: 0850
755440
E-mail: timbooth@paradise-sq.co.uk
URL: http://www.paradise-sq.co.uk

Chambers of Roger Keen QC
Clerk: Timothy Booth

Keen, Roger QC *1976*†	**Rosario**, Desmond *1990*
Murphy, Michael QC *1973*†	**Edwards**, Mererid *1991*
Burrell, Gary QC *1977*†	**Savage**, Timothy *1991*
Walker, Annabel QC *1976*†	**McLauchlan**, Ian *1992*
Baker, Jeremy QC *1979*‡	**Syed**, Gulzar *1983*
Phillips, Bernard *1970*†	**Hughes**, Dermot *1993*
Hargan, Martin *1964*	**Harrison**, Rachael *1993*
Bingham, Philip *1975*	**Nijabat**, Sharma *1993*
Neale, Nicholas *1972*	**Walker-Kane**, Jonathan
Robinson, Graham *1981*‡	*1994*
Watson, Paul *1978*‡	**Rhys**, Megan *1994*
Slater, Michael *1983*	**Stables**, Gordon *1995*
Wright, Sarah *1984*	**Kelly**, Siobhan *1995*
Coles, Michael *1986*	**Goldsack**, Ian *1997*
Hatton, Andrew *1987*	**Bailey**, Andrew *1997*
Crosbie, Susan *1988*	**Powell**, James *1998*
O'Reilly, Michael *1988*	**Terris**, Sally *1997*
Groom, Ian *1990*	

ABBEY CHAMBERS

*PO Box 47, 47 Ashurst Drive, Shepperton,
Middlesex TW17 0LD*
01932 560913
Fax: 01932 567764

Chambers of Arthur R A James

SLOUGH CHAMBER

*11 St Bernards Road, Slough, Berkshire
SL3 7NT*
01753 553806/817989
Fax: 01753 553806
Other comms: 07803 089 893 (mobile)
E-mail: arden@freeuk.com
Out of hours telephone: 07803 089893

Chambers of A Bhattacharyya
Clerk: S P Chadha

Also at: 1 Gray's Inn Square, London WC1
(Door Tenant)

Bhattacharyya, Ardhendu
 1974

GREENWAY

*Sonning Lane, Sonning-on-Thames,
Berkshire RG4 6ST*
0118 969 2484
Fax: 0118 969 2484

Chambers of Jack A Denbin

17 CARLTON CRESCENT

Southampton, SO15 2XR
023 8032 0320/0823 2003
Fax: 023 8032 0321; DX 96875
Southampton 10
E-mail: greg@jg17cc.co.uk
URL: http://www.jeremygibbonsqc.co.uk

Chambers of J S Gibbons QC
*Clerks: Gregory Townsend, Mark
Harrison; Administrator: Sue Benoke*

Gibbons, Jeremy QC *1973*†	**Morgan**, Dylan *1986*
Sullivan, Linda QC *1973*†	**Moores**, Timothy *1987*
Fulthorpe, Jonathan *1970*	**Doughty**, Peter *1988*
Towler, Peter *1974*†	**Holland**, Roberta *1989*
Kolanko, Michael *1975*	**Smith**, Abigail *1989*
Webster, William *1975*	**Griffiths**, Hayley *1990*
Haggan, Nicholas *1977*‡	**Hiddleston**, Adam *1990*
Merry, Hugh *1979*	**Ward**, Trevor *1991*
Spink, Peter *1979*	**Burrett**, Catherine *1992*
Gibney, Malcolm *1981*	**Tucker**, Nicholas *1993*
Howard, Timothy *1981*	**Ferrari**, Sarah *1993*
Pine-Coffin, Margaret *1981*	**Hussain**, Frida *1995*
Glen, Philip *1983*	**Savill**, Peter *1995*
Forster, Michael *1984*	**Burns**, Jeremy *1996*
Grant, Gary *1985*	**McDermott**, Caoimhe *1997*

Types of work (and number of counsel practising in that area if supplied)

Arbitration 1 · Care proceedings 8 · Chancery (general) 1 · Chancery land law 3 · Common land 3 · Common law (general) 10 · Conveyancing 1 · Crime 10 · Crime – corporate fraud 3 · Education 1 · Employment 6 · Environment 2 · Family 9 · Family provision 9 · Housing 2 · Landlord and tenant 4 · Local government 8 · Medical negligence 2 · Partnerships 1 · Personal injury 7 · Probate and administration 1 · Professional negligence 2 · Town and country planning 6

Chambers established: 1976
Opening times: 9 am-6 pm

Chambers' facilities

Conference rooms, Disks accepted, E-mail

Languages spoken

French, Italian

Fees policy

Up to five years call £30–60, Up to ten years call £45–75, Over ten years call £65–125. Our policy is to set our fee levels to reflect the work necessarily done, whilst acknowledging the requirements and abilities of our clients to pay. Therefore please approach the clerks to discuss fixed fees tailored to your case.

COLLEGE CHAMBERS

19 Carlton Cresent, Southampton, SO15 2ET
01703 230338
Fax: 01703 230376; DX 38533 Southampton 3

Chambers of R W Belben
Clerk: Wayne Effeny

Belben, Robin *1969†*	**Hand**, Anthony *1989*
Pain, Kenneth *1969*	**Habel**, Jessica *1991*
Swift, Jonathan *1977‡*	**Breslin**, Catherine *1990*
Marshall, Derek *1980*	**Self**, Gary *1991*
Taylor, Douglas *1981*	**Kinghorn**, Andrew *1991*
Stewart, Mark *1989*	**Nother**, Daniel *1994*

Grundy, Arabella *1995*	**Harrison**, Graeme *1997*
Lorie, Andrew *1996*	**Compton**, Timothy *1984**
Uppal, Baljinder *1996*	

Types of work (and number of counsel practising in that area if supplied)

Care proceedings 8 · Chancery (general) 2 · Common law (general) 13 · Company and commercial 2 · Crime 3 · Employment 3 · Environment 1 · Family 11 · Insolvency 3 · Landlord and tenant 7 · Licensing 1 · Medical negligence 4 · Mental health 1 · Personal injury 13 · Professional negligence 4 · Town and country planning 1

Chambers established: 20 November 1989
Opening times: 8.45 am-6 pm

Chambers' facilities

Conference rooms

Languages spoken

French

Fees policy

Up to five years call £30–50, Up to ten years call £50–85, Over ten years call £75–125. Solicitors are always welcome to discuss fees on any specialisms with the clerk.

EIGHTEEN CARLTON CRESCENT

Southampton, SO15 2XR
01703 639001
Fax: 01703 339625; DX 96877 Southampton 10
Out of hours telephone: 01703 639001

Chambers of J A H Haig-Haddow
Clerks: Paul Cooke, Lynda Knight

Haig-Haddow, Alastair *1972*	**Wylie**, Keith *1976*
Massey, Andrew *1969*	**Cochand**, Charles *1978*
Ailes, Ashley *1975*	**Robertson**, Angus *1978*
Fawcett, Gary *1975*	**Egleton**, Richard *1981*
	Blount, Martin *1982*

Wing, Christopher *1985*
Manuel, Elizabeth *1987*
Houston, Andrew *1989*
Malik, Omar *1990*
Munks, Christine *1991*
Robins, Imogen *1991*
Glenser, Peter *1993*
Carter, Sally *1994*
Thom, Michael *1994*
Hall, Richard *1995*

Case, Toby *1996*
Asteris, Peter *1996*
Boney, Guy QC *1968**
Ollerenshaw, Michael *1969**
Lillington, Simon *1980**
Speck, Jonathan *1990**
Pines-Richman, Helene *1992**

Types of work (and number of counsel practising in that area if supplied)
Arbitration 4 · Bankruptcy 4 · Care proceedings 12 · Chancery (general) 3 · Common law (general) 14 · Company and commercial 4 · Courts martial 4 · Crime 15 · Employment 4 · Family 17 · Family provision 10 · Information technology 2 · Insolvency 2 · Intellectual property 2 · Landlord and tenant 4 · Licensing 2 · Medical negligence 4 · Partnerships 2 · Pensions 4 · Personal injury 10 · Probate and administration 2 · Professional negligence 2 · Sale and carriage of goods 2 · Town and country planning 1

Chambers established: 1948
Opening times: 9 am-6 pm (24-hour service)

Chambers' facilities
Conference rooms, Video conferences, Law Society accredited seminars plus use of large seminar room

Languages spoken
French, German

Fees policy
Fees will be negotiated with the clerks who openly encourage any discussions in this regard on a flexible, professional basis.

FYFIELD CHAMBERS

Field Cottage, Fyfield, Southrop, Gloucestershire GL7 3NT
01367 850304
Fax: 01367 850304

Chambers of Mr B Sinclair

REGENT CHAMBERS

8 Pall Mall, Hanley, Stoke On Trent, ST1 1ER
01782 286666
Fax: 01782 201866; DX 20720 Hanley
E-mail: regent@ftech.co.uk
Out of hours telephone: 0973 906743

Chambers of Barry Cliff
Clerk: Nicola Dobson

Brown, Frederick *1983*
Cliff, Barry *1988*
Swaffield, Helen *1988*
Robinson, David *1992*
Johnson, John *1993*

Cliff, Paul *1992*
Moore, Kirstie *1994*
O'Hagan, Sophia *1996*
Ali Anis *1997*
O'Reilly, Catherine *1998*

61 ELM GROVE

Sutton, Surrey SM1 4EX
0181 643 9714
Fax: 0181 643 9714

Chambers of Miss V T Dsane

ANGEL CHAMBERS

94 Walter Road, Swansea, West Glamorgan SA1 5QA
01792 464623/464648
Fax: 01792 648501; DX 39566 Swansea
E-mail: lynne@angelchambers.co.uk
Out of hours telephone: 0410 180974

Chambers of Thomas Glanville-Jones
Clerks: Crispin Cormack, Steven Welsh, Elizabeth Bennett

Jones, Thomas *1956*†
Cronin, William *1971*
McKay, Christopher *1976*
Vosper, Christopher *1977*†
Walters, Geraint *1981*
Davis, Jim *1997*
Clee, Christopher *1983*
Clemes, Andrew *1988*
McCann, Colleen *1988*
Davies, Emily *1989*
Donovan, Alison *1987*

Wood, Joanna *1989*
Harris-Jenkins, Philip *1990*
Davies, Andrew *1992*
Harris, Elizabeth *1992*
Thomas, Dyfed *1992*
Blake, David *1992*
James, Sharon *1995*
James, Christopher *1997*
Douglas-Jones, Benjamin *1998*

> **Bar Directory on the Internet**
> *The Bar Directory* is also available on the Internet at the following address:
> http://www.smlawpub.co.uk/bar

CHAMBERS OF DAVINA GAMMON

Ground Floor, 103 Walter Road, Swansea,
West Glamorgan SA1 5QF
01792 480770
Fax: 01792 480547; DX 52982 Swansea 1
Out of hours telephone: 01792 480547

Chambers of Mrs Davina Gammon
Clerk: David Houston; Administrator:
Margaret Williams

Gammon, Davina Anne *1979*	Boothroyd, Dominic *1991*
	Powell, Nicola *1996*

ISCOED CHAMBERS

86 St Helen's Road, Swansea, West
Glamorgan SA1 4BQ
01792 652988/9/330
Fax: 01792 458089; DX 39554 Swansea

Chambers of Trefor Davies
Clerks: W J Rainbird, Jeff Evans, Kris
Thorne; Practice Manager: Sheila Budge

Davies, Trefor *1972*	Spackman, Mark *1986*
Thomas, Kenneth *1966*	Henke, Ruth *1987*
Rouch, Peter QC *1972**	Hipkin, John *1989*
Griffiths, Patrick *1972*	Harris, David *1990*
Phillips, Frank *1972*	Heyworth, Catherine *1991*
Riordan, Kevin *1972*	Hughes, Kate *1992*
Jenkins, James *1974*‡	Peters, William *1992*
Marshall, Philip *1975*‡	Pulling, Dean *1993*
Thomas, Paul *1979*	Wright, Ian *1994*
Craven, Robert *1979*	Maddox, Peter *1994*
Rees, Stephen *1979*	Davies, Iwan *1995*
Evans, Elwen *1980*	Gow, Elizabeth *1995*
Jones, Francis *1980*	Hayes, Timothy *1996*
Sandbrook-Hughes,	Rees, Matthew *1996*
Stewert *1980*	Hoffman, Simon Paul *1997*
Rees, Huw *1983*	

PENDRAGON CHAMBERS

124 Walter Road, Swansea, West
Glamorgan SA1 5RG
01792 411188
Fax: 01792 411189; DX 39572 Swansea 1

Chambers of N Wayne Beard

ST DAVID'S CHAMBERS

10 Calvert Terrace, Swansea, West
Glamorgan SA1 5AR

NESTON HOME CHAMBERS

42 Greenhill, Neston, Corsham, Wiltshire
SN13 9SQ
01225 811909
Fax: 01225 811909

Chambers of Mrs Jetta Doig

PUMP COURT CHAMBERS

5 Temple Chambers, Temple Street,
Swindon, SN1 1SQ
01793 539899
Fax: 01793 539866; DX 38639 Swindon 2
E-mail: clerks@3pumpcourt.com
URL: http://www.3pumpcourt.com

Chambers of Guy Boney QC
Clerk: Dorothy Hewitt; Administrator:
Sally Woolley

Also at: 3 Pump Court, Upper Ground
Floor, London EC4Y 7AJ Tel: 0171 353
0711 Fax: 0171 353 3319 and at 31
Southgate Street, Winchester SO23 9EE
Tel: 01962 868161 Fax: 01962 867645

Boney, Guy QC *1968*†	Butt, Michael *1974*
Pascoe, Nigel QC *1966*†	Ker-Reid, John *1974*
Clark, Christopher QC *1969*†	Gabb, Charles *1975*
Garlick, Paul QC *1974*†	Gillibrand, Phillip *1975*
Still, Geoffrey *1966*†	Barnett, Andrew *1977*†
Patterson, Stewart *1967*‡	Dineen, Michael *1977*
Pearson, Adam *1969*	Mackenzie, Julie *1978*
Moat, Frank *1970*†	Miller, Jane *1979*‡
Harrap, Giles *1971*†	O'Flynn, Timothy *1979*
Abbott, Frank *1972*†	Hill, Robert *1980*
Parry, Charles *1973*	Allardice, Miranda *1982*
	Lochrane, Damien *1983*

---

† Recorder ‡ Assistant Recorder *Door Tenant

Nsugbe, Oba 1985‡
Scott, Matthew 1985
Bloom-Davis, Desmond 1986
Hill, Mark 1987
Howard, Graham 1987
Travers, Hugh 1988
Waddington, Anne 1988
Warren, Philip 1988
Akiwumi, Anthony 1989
Samuels, Leslie 1989
Boydell, Edward 1989
Gau, Justin 1989
Brunton, Sean 1990
Khan, Helen 1990
Howe, Penny 1991

Kelly, Geoffrey 1992
Newton-Price, James 1992
Poyer-Sleeman, Patricia 1992
Tregilgas-Davey, Mark 1993
Gunther, Elizabeth 1993
Peirson, Oliver 1993
Fields, Helen 1993
Blackburn, Luke 1993
Ashley, Mark 1993
Pawson, Robert 1994
Dubbery, Mark 1996
Grime, Andrew 1997
Arlow, Ruth 1997
Ward, Anne 1997

COLLETON CHAMBERS

Powlett House, 34 High Street, Taunton, Somerset TA1 3PN
01823 324252
Fax: 01823 327489; DX 96100 Taunton 1

Chambers of R M J Meeke

SOUTH WESTERN CHAMBERS

Melville House, 12 Middle Street, Taunton, Somerset TA1 1SH
01823 331919 (24 hrs)
Fax: 01823 330553; DX 32146 Taunton
E-mail: barclerk@clara.net
URL:
http://www.southwesternchambers.co.uk

Chambers of Mr H B G Lett
Clerks: Stephen Ward, Gregory Speller

Lett, Hugh 1971†
Askham, Nigel 1973
Hickmet, Richard 1974
Osborne, David 1974
Hodgkin, Harry 1983
Dingle, Jonathan 1986
Large, Alan 1988
Counsell, Edward 1990

Galloway, Malcolm 1992
Jones, Steven 1994
Mason, Patrick David Anthony 1997
Bradberry, Rebecca 1996
Posta, Adrian Mark 1996
Wilcox, Lawrence Gaywood 1996

GODOLPHIN CHAMBERS

50 Castle Street, Truro, Cornwall TR1 3AF
01872 276312
Fax: 01872 271920; DX 81233 Truro
E-mail: theclerks@godolphin.force9.co.uk
Out of hours telephone: 01209 718354
(Senior Clerk)

Chambers of B P van den Berg
Clerks: Andrea Hellings (Senior Clerk), Beverley Ashford (1st Junior)

van den Berg, Barrie 1978
Guy, Richard 1970
Wallace, Ann 1979
Perry, Christopher 1980
Elliott, Colin 1987
Beechey, Hilary 1987

Smith, Abigail 1989
Taurah, Sheila 1991
Holland, Annie 1994
Richards, Dr Jonathan 1995
Puttick, Anthony 1971*
Mendoza, Colin 1983*

PORTSMOUTH BARRISTERS' CHAMBERS

Isle of Wight Annexe, 35 Alpine Road, Ventnor, Isle of Wight PO38 1BU
01983 855 666
Fax: 01983 854 666; DX 99229 Ventnor (Isle of Wight)

Chambers of Andrew Parsons

9 FOUNTAINS WAY

Pinders Heath, Wakefield, West Yorkshire WF1 4TQ
01924 378631
Fax: 01924 378631

Chambers of Mr P Martin

WATFORD CHAMBERS

74 Mildred Avenue, Watford, Hertfordshire WD1 7DX
01923 220553
Fax: 01923 222618; DX 42551 Bushey

Chambers of Mrs A Henthorn

Bar Directory on the Internet
The Bar Directory is also available on the Internet at the following address:
http://www.smlawpub.co.uk/bar

† Recorder ‡ Assistant Recorder *Door Tenant

GOODWIN CHAMBERS

Goodwin Cottage, 14 Doddington Road,
Wellingborough, Northamptonshire
NN8 2JG
01933 222790
Fax: 01933 222790; DX 13793 Raunds

Chambers of Miss H E Jackson

MIDDLESEX CHAMBERS

Suite 3 & 4 Stanley House, Stanley Avenue,
Wembley, Middlesex HA0 4SB
0181 902 1499
Fax: 0181 902 1509

52 WEMBLEY PARK DRIVE

Wembley, Middlesex HA9 8HB
0181 902 5629
Fax: 0181 902 5629

Chambers of Mr I S Kulatilake

CRAYSHOTT HOUSE

Woodlands Road, West Byfleet, Surrey
KT14 6JW
01932 342951
Fax: 01932 336176

Chambers of Mr R T F Turrall-Clarke

10 WINTERBOURNE GROVE

Weybridge, Surrey KT13 0PP
0181 941 3939
Fax: 0181 941 3939

Chambers of Mr M C Wyatt

3 PAPER BUILDINGS (WINCHESTER)

THE CHAMBERS OF MICHAEL PARROY Q.C.

4 St Peter Street, Winchester, SO23 8BW
01962 868884

Fax: 01962 868644; DX 2507 Winchester
E-mail: winchester@3paper.com

Chambers of M P Parroy QC
Clerks: Stuart Pringle (Senior Clerk), Lee
Giles, James Bright, Helen Chalk

Annexe of: 3 Paper Buildings, Temple,
London, EC4Y 7EU
Tel: 020 7583 8055
Fax: 020 7353 6271

Parroy, Michael QC *1969*	Chamberlain, Francis *1985*
Harris, David QC *1969†*	Sanderson, David *1985*
Hughes, Peter QC *1971*	Bailey, Russell *1985*
Jones, Stewart QC *1972†*	Parker, Christopher *1986*
Aspinall, John QC *1971*	Hudson, Elisabeth *1987*
Parrish, Samuel *1962*	Letman, Paul *1987*
Solomon, Susan *1967*	Rowland, Nicholas *1988*
Trevethan, Susan *1967*	Kelly, Patricia *1988*
Haynes, John *1968*	Woolgar, Dermot *1988*
Swinstead, David *1970*	Hester, Paul *1989*
Aylwin, Christopher *1970*	Opperman, Guy *1989*
Hope, Derwin *1970†*	Bradbury, Timothy *1989*
Norman, Michael *1971†*	Killen, Geoffrey *1990*
Curran, Leo *1972*	Kilpatrick, Jean *1990*
Jennings, Peter *1972*	Buckley-Clarke, Amanda *1991*
Coleman, Anthony *1973*	
Stephenson, Ben *1973*	Ross, Iain *1991*
Litchfield, Linda *1974*	Steenson, David *1991*
Bartlett, David *1975†*	Sweeney, Christian *1992*
Richardson, Garth *1975*	Bingham, Tony *1992*
Tyson, Richard *1975‡*	Kirkpatrick, Krystyna *1965*
Henry, Peter *1977*	Fitzharris, Ginnette *1993*
Mitchell, Nigel *1978*	Clargo, John *1994*
Seed, Nigel *1978‡*	Earle, Judy *1994*
Kent, Peter *1978*	Walter, Francesca *1994*
Partridge, Ian *1979*	Reid, David *1994*
Grey, Robert *1979*	Williams, Ben *1994*
Leviseur, Nicholas *1979*	Sutherland Williams, Mark *1995*
Coombes, Timothy *1980*	
Cairnes, Paul *1980*	Hughes, Melanie *1995*
Marshall, David *1981*	McIlroy, David *1995*
Edge, Ian *1981*	Strachan, Elaine *1995*
Strutt, Martin *1981*	Case, Richard *1996*
Lickley, Nigel *1983*	Kay, Dominic *1997*
Lomas, Mark *1983*	Leech, Ben *1997*
Maccabe, Irvine *1983*	Purdy, Catherine *1997*
Branigan, Kate *1984*	Sullivan, Mark *1997*
O'Hara, Sarah *1984*	

PORTSMOUTH BARRISTERS' CHAMBERS

Winchester Annexe, First Floor, 28 St
Stephens Road, Winchester, SO22 6DE
01962 863222
Fax: 01962 855856; DX 2555 Winchester

Chambers of Mr J F Dalby

PUMP COURT CHAMBERS

31 Southgate Street, Winchester, SO23 9EE
01962 868161
Fax: 01962 867645; DX 2514 Winchester
E-mail: clerks@3pumpcourt.com
URL: http://www.3pumpcourt.com
Out of hours telephone: 07808 933435

Chambers of Guy Boney QC
Clerks: D Barber, Tony George;
Administrator: Sally Woolley

Also at: 3 Pump Court, Upper Ground
Floor, London EC4Y 7AJ Tel: 0171 353
0711 Fax: 0171 353 3319; 5 Temple
Chambers, Swindon SN1 1SQ Tel: 01793
539899 Fax: 01793 539866

Boney, Guy QC *1968†*
Pascoe, Nigel QC *1966†*
Clark, Christopher QC *1969†*
Garlick, Paul QC *1974†*
Still, Geoffrey *1966†*
Patterson, Stewart *1967‡*
Pearson, Adam *1969*
Moat, Frank *1970†*
Harrap, Giles *1971†*
Abbott, Frank *1972†*
Parry, Charles *1973*
Butt, Michael *1974*
Ker-Reid, John *1974*
Gabb, Charles *1975*
Gillibrand, Phillip *1975*
Barnett, Andrew *1977†*
Dineen, Michael *1977*
Mackenzie, Julie *1978*
Miller, Jane *1979‡*
O'Flynn, Timothy *1979*
Hill, Robert *1980*
Allardice, Miranda *1982*
Lochrane, Damien *1983*
Nsugbe, Oba *1985‡*
Scott, Matthew *1985*
Bloom-Davis, Desmond *1986*
Hill, Mark *1987*
Howard, Graham *1987*
Travers, Hugh *1988*
Waddington, Anne *1988*
Warren, Philip *1988*
Akiwumi, Anthony *1989*
Samuels, Leslie *1989*
Boydell, Edward *1989*
Gau, Justin *1989*
Brunton, Sean *1990*
Khan, Helen *1990*
Howe, Penny *1991*
Kelly, Geoffrey *1992*
Newton-Price, James *1992*
Poyer-Sleeman, Patricia *1992*
Tregilgas-Davey, Mark *1993*
Gunther, Elizabeth *1993*
Peirson, Oliver *1993*
Fields, Helen *1993*
Blackburn, Luke *1993*
Ashley, Mark *1993*
Pawson, Robert *1994*
Dubbery, Mark *1996*
Grime, Andrew *1997*
Arlow, Ruth *1997*
Ward, Anne *1997*

WINDSOR BARRISTERS' CHAMBERS

Windsor,
01753 648899
Fax: DX 130112 Slough 6

Chambers of Mr M C Beaumont

MENDHIR CHAMBERS

38 Priest Avenue, Wokingham, Berkshire RG40 2LX
0118 9771274
Fax: 0118 9627132

Chambers of Mrs M Mendhir

CLAREMONT CHAMBERS

26 Waterloo Road, Wolverhampton, WV1 4BL
01902 426222
Fax: 01902 426333; DX 722200 Wolverhampton 15
Out of hours telephone: 0976 805643

Chambers of Ian McCulloch
Clerk: Meriel Acton

McCulloch, Ian *1951*
Edwards, Jonathan *1981*
Khan, Asif *1983*
Gidney, Jonathan *1991*
Hobbs, Naomi *1993*
Tonge, Ruth *1993*
Maxwell, David *1994*
Brown, Jain *1994*
Thorndike, Tony *1994*
Fairburn, George *1995*
Mondair, Rashpal *1995*
Harding, Fiona *1993**

CLOCK CHAMBERS

78 Darlington Street, Wolverhampton, WV1 4LY
01902 313444
Fax: 01902 421110; DX 10423 Wolverhampton 1

1 WENSLEY AVENUE

Woodford Green, Essex IG8 9HE
0181 505 9259
Fax: 0181 262 3808

Chambers of Mr Shamsul Huda
Clerk: T Tuheen; Administrator: Helen Salima

Also at: 9 King's Bench Walk, Temple (2nd Chambers)

Languages spoken
French, German

Huda, Shamsul *1976*

POINT HOUSE

Spooner Row, Wymondham, Norfolk
NR18 9LQ
01953 606965
Fax: 01953 600957

Chambers of Mr O R Daniel

YORK CHAMBERS

14 Toft Green, York, YO1 6JT
01904 620048
Fax: 01904 610056; DX 65517 York 7
E-mail: [name]@yorkchambers.co.uk

Chambers of Aidan Marron QC
Clerk: Kevin Beaumont

Marron, Aidan QC *1973*†	**Lamb**, David *1987*
Gripton, David *1969*	**Makepeace**, Peter *1988*
Grenyer, Mark *1969*	**Elvidge**, John *1988*
Bowerman, Michael *1970*‡	**Norman**, Charity *1988*
Priest, Raymond *1973*	**Cordey**, Daniel *1990*
Twist, Stephen *1979*	**Todd**, Martin *1991*
Matthews, Gillian *1985*	**Robinson**, James *1992*
Crayton, Philip *1985*	**Scott**, Richard *1992*
Proops, Helen *1986*	**Edwards**, Daniel *1993*
Johnson, Peter *1986*	**Campbell**, Diane *1995*
Terry, Robert *1986*	**Randhawa**, Ravinder *1995*
Morris, Paul *1986*	**Legard**, Edward *1996*
Lee, Rosslyn *1987*	**Bourne**, Colin *1997*
Price, Nicholas *1987*	

Types of work (and number of counsel practising in that area if supplied)
Care proceedings 9 · Commercial litigation 3 · Common land 1 · Common law (general) 1 · Company and commercial 2 · Courts martial 3 · Crime 17 · Education 2 · Employment 5 · Environment 1 · Equity, wills and trusts 2 · Family 1 · Family provision 10 · Immigration 1 · Landlord and tenant 5 · Licensing 3 · Medical negligence 8 · Mental health 3 · Personal injury 15 · Professional negligence 9 · Sale and carriage of goods 4

Opening times: 8 am-6 pm

Chambers' facilities
Conference rooms, Video conferences, Disks accepted, Disabled access, E-mail

C

---

† Recorder ‡ Assistant Recorder *Door Tenant

STUART SMALLEY & CO
Solicitors

WRIGHT & CO
Advocates

Stuart Smalley & Co practise in association with Wright & Co

CATEGORIES OF WORK

- Banking, Securities & Finance
- Company/Commercial
- Insolvency
- Insurance
- Intellectual Property
- Fiduciary & Administration Services
- Litigation
- Media & Entertainment
- Mergers/Acquisitions
- Property
- Taxation
- Trust
- UK Commercial Property
- Wills

Languages Spoken: French, German

Contacts: Jonathon Smalley*, George Stuart*, John Wright**

14 &18 St Georges Street, Douglas,
Isle of Man, IM1 1PL
Telephone: (01624) 626557/620204
Fax: (01624) 672502/616446
E-mail: mail@law-man.com

Also at
Parade Chambers, The Parade, Castletown,
Isle of Man, IM99 5UY
Telephone: (01624) 822922
Fax: (01624) 823308
E-mail: castletown@law-man.com

*Solicitors in England and Ireland   **Manx Advocate and Solicitor in England

Individual Barristers in Private Practice

This section lists Barristers in private practice. Individuals are listed alphabetically by surname and details include the chambers at which they practice, year of call to the Bar, Inn of Court and academic qualifications.

Some individuals have opted to include additional information about themselves in this part of the Directory, such as other qualifications, membership of foreign bars, other professional experience, languages spoken, publications, reported cases and a list of the types of work undertaken. Please note that details of the types of work undertaken by individual barristers who have chosen not to include this information in Part D may be found in *Part B Types of Work by Individual Barristers*.

Note: For those barristers listed in this section, information has been supplied by the Bar Council in the first instance and supplemented with information provided by individual barristers.

D

AARON SAMUEL

4-5 Gray's Inn Square
Ground Floor, Gray's Inn, London
WC1R 5JP, Telephone: 0171 404 5252
E-mail:chambers@4-5graysinnsquare.co.uk
Call Date: 1986, Gray's Inn
Qualifications: [BA, LLB (Cape Town), BA
(Hons)(S.Africa), FCI Arb.]

AARONBERG DAVID JEFFREY

Hardwicke Building
New Square, Lincoln's Inn, London
WC2A 3SB, Telephone: 020 7242 2523
E-mail: clerks@hardwicke.co.uk
Call Date: July 1981, Inner Temple
Pupil Master
Qualifications: [BA]

AARONSON GRAHAM RAPHAEL QC (1982)

One Essex Court
Ground Floor, Temple, London
EC4Y 9AR, Telephone: 020 7583 2000
E-mail: clerks@oneessexcourt.co.uk
Call Date: Nov 1966, Middle Temple
Qualifications: [MA (Cantab)]

ABBERTON DAVID EDWARD

Nicholas Street Chambers
22 Nicholas Street, Chester CH1 2NX,
Telephone: 01244 323886
E-mail: clerks@40king.co.uk
Call Date: Nov 1994, Middle Temple
Qualifications: [BA (Hons)]

ABBOTT ALISTAIR JAMES HUGH

5 New Square
Ground Floor, Lincoln's Inn, London
WC2A 3RJ, Telephone: 020 7404 0404
E-mail:chambers@fivenewsquare.demon.co.
uk
Call Date: Nov 1996, Middle Temple
Qualifications: [BA (Hons) (Cantab)]

ABBOTT DAVID ROBERT

Beresford Chambers
21 King Street, Luton, Bedfordshire,
LU1 2DW, Telephone: 01582 429111
E-mail: info@it-law.com
Call Date: July 1987, Lincoln's Inn
Qualifications: [LLB MSc DPA DMS Dip, Ed.]

ABBOTT FRANCIS ARTHUR

Pump Court Chambers
31 Southgate Street, Winchester
SO23 9EE, Telephone: 01962 868161
E-mail: clerks@3pumpcourt.com
Pump Court Chambers
Upper Ground Floor, 3 Pump Court,
Temple, London EC4Y 7AJ,
Telephone: 0171 353 0711
E-mail: clerks@3pumpcourt.com
Pump Court Chambers
5 Temple Chambers, Temple Street,
Swindon SN1 1SQ,
Telephone: 01793 539899
E-mail: clerks@3pumpcourt.com
Call Date: Nov 1972, Lincoln's Inn
Pupil Master, Recorder
Qualifications: [BA (Nott'm)]

ABBOTT MRS MARY MACCONNACHIE

Northampton Chambers
22 Albion Place, Northampton NN1 1UD,
Telephone: 01604 636271
Call Date: Oct 1994, Gray's Inn
Qualifications: [BA]

ABEBRESE OWUSU EMANUEL

12 Old Square
1st Floor, Lincoln's Inn, London
WC2A 3TX, Telephone: 0171 404 0875
Call Date: Sept 1985, Inner Temple
Qualifications: [BA (Hons), LLM]

ABEL MISS ANN PETRINA

3 Temple Gardens
3rd Floor, Temple, London EC4Y 9AU,
Telephone: 0171 353 0832
Call Date: Mar 1998, Lincoln's Inn
Qualifications: [LLB (Hons)(B'ham), BA
(Hons)(Warw)]

ABELL ANTHONY ROGER

3 Hare Court
1 Little Essex Street, London WC2R 3LD,
Telephone: 0171 395 2000
Call Date: July 1977, Gray's Inn
Pupil Master
Qualifications: [LLB (Lond)]

D

ABEY MAHIE

3 Dr Johnson's Buildings
Ground Floor, Temple, London
EC4Y 7BA, Telephone: 0171 353 4854
E-mail: clerks@3djb.co.uk
Call Date: Oct 1993, Gray's Inn
Qualifications: [BA (Cantab)]

ABRAHAMS JAMES

8 New Square
Lincoln's Inn, London WC2A 3QP,
Telephone: 0171 405 4321
E-mail: clerks@8newsquare.co.uk
Call Date: 1997, Gray's Inn
Qualifications: [BA, BCL]

ABRAHAMS JONATHAN DAVID

Barristers' Common Law Chambers
57 Whitechapel Road, Aldgate East,
London E1 1DU,
Telephone: 0171 375 3012
E-mail: barristers@hotmail.com and
barristers@lawchambers.freeserve.co.uk
Call Date: 1976, Gray's Inn
Qualifications: [LLB (Hons)]

ABRAMS NEILL

One Essex Court
Ground Floor, Temple, London
EC4Y 9AR, Telephone: 020 7583 2000
E-mail: clerks@oneessexcourt.co.uk
Call Date: Oct 1998, Inner Temple
Qualifications: [LLB (Johannesburg), LLM
(Cantab)]

ACE RICHARD WILLIAM

4 Fountain Court
Steelhouse Lane, Birmingham B4 6DR,
Telephone: 0121 236 3476
Call Date: Oct 1993, Lincoln's Inn
Qualifications: [BSc (Hons)(Reading), Dip in
Law (Lond)]

ACHESON ROBERT IAN

23 Essex Street
London WC2R 3AS,
Telephone: 0171 413 0353/836 8366
E-mail:clerks@essexstreet23.demon.co.uk
Call Date: Feb 1992, Gray's Inn
Qualifications: [BA (Oxon)]

ACHURCH TIMOTHY MARK

High Pavement Chambers
1 High Pavement, Nottingham NG1 1HF,
Telephone: 0115 9418218
Call Date: Oct 1996, Middle Temple
Qualifications: [LLB (Hons)(Manc)]

ACKERLEY DAVID ALBERT

19 Castle Street Chambers
Liverpool L2 4SX,
Telephone: 0151 236 9402
E-mail: DBrei16454@aol.com
Call Date: Nov 1992, Inner Temple
Qualifications: [LLB]

ACKNER THE HON CLAUDIA MADELEINE

4 Pump Court
Temple, London EC4Y 7AN,
Telephone: 020 7842 5555
E-mail:chambers@4pumpcourt.law.co.uk
Call Date: July 1977, Middle Temple
Qualifications: [BA (Cantab)]

ACLAND DR PIERS DYKE

11 South Square
2nd Floor, Gray's Inn, London
WC1R 5EU,
Telephone: 0171 405 1222 (24hr messagin
g service)
E-mail: clerks@11southsquare.com
Call Date: Nov 1993, Lincoln's Inn
Qualifications: [BSc (Hons), PhD (Lond)]

ACTON MISS JAYNE

58 King Street Chambers
1st Floor, Kingsgate House, 51-53 South
King Street, Manchester M2 6DE,
Telephone: 0161 831 7477
Call Date: Mar 1996, Lincoln's Inn
Qualifications: [LLB (Hons) (Sheff)]

ACTON STEPHEN NEIL

11 Old Square
Ground Floor, Lincoln's Inn, London
WC2A 3TS, Telephone: 020 7430 0341
E-mail: clerks@11oldsquare.co.uk
Call Date: July 1977, Inner Temple
Pupil Master
Qualifications: [MA (Cantab)]

ACTON DAVIS JONATHAN JAMES QC (1996)

4 Pump Court
Temple, London EC4Y 7AN,
Telephone: 020 7842 5555
E-mail:chambers@4pumpcourt.law.co.uk
Call Date: July 1977, Inner Temple
Assistant Recorder
Qualifications: [LLB (Lond)]

ADAIR STUART ANTHONY

Twenty-Four Old Buildings
Ground Floor, Lincoln's Inn, London
WC2A 3UP, Telephone: 0171 404 0946
E-mail:clerks@24oldbuildings.law.co.uk
Call Date: Oct 1995, Inner Temple
Qualifications: [LLB (Exon)]

ADAM THOMAS NOBLE

Brick Court Chambers
7-8 Essex Street, London WC2R 3LD,
Telephone: 0171 379 3550
E-mail: [surname]@brickcourt.co.uk
Call Date: Nov 1991, Inner Temple
Qualifications: [MA (Cantab)]

ADAMS CHRISTOPHER ALAN

St Philip's Chambers
Fountain Court, Steelhouse Lane,
Birmingham B4 6DR,
Telephone: 0121 246 7000
E-mail: clerks@st-philips.co.uk
Call Date: July 1986, Lincoln's Inn
Qualifications: [LLB (Lond)]

ADAMS DEREK ADAMA

2 Middle Temple Lane
3rd Floor, Temple, London EC4Y 9AA,
Telephone: 0171 583 4540
Call Date: Nov 1988, Middle Temple
Qualifications: [BA, Dip Law, LLM (LSE)]

ADAMS GUY LAIRD

St John's Chambers
Small Street, Bristol BS1 1DW,
Telephone: 0117 9213456/298514
E-mail: @stjohnschambers.co.uk
Call Date: July 1989, Middle Temple
Qualifications: [MA (Cantab)]

ADAMS JAMES ROBERT

New Court Chambers
3 Broad Chare, Newcastle upon Tyne
NE1 3DQ, Telephone: 0191 232 1980
11 King's Bench Walk
1st Floor, Temple, London EC4Y 7EQ,
Telephone: 0171 353 3337
E-mail: fmuller11@aol.com
Call Date: July 1978, Gray's Inn
Pupil Master
Qualifications: [LLB (Newc)]

ADAMS MISS JAYNE MARGARET

Ropewalk Chambers
24 The Ropewalk, Nottingham NG1 5EF,
Telephone: 0115 9472581
E-mail: administration@ropewalk co.uk
Call Date: July 1982, Gray's Inn
Pupil Master
Qualifications: [LLB]

ADAMS JOHN NORMAN

One Raymond Buildings
Gray's Inn, London WC1R 5BH,
Telephone: 0171 430 1234
E-mail: chambers@ipbar1rb.com;
clerks@ipbar1rb.com
Call Date: Nov 1984, Inner Temple
Qualifications: [LLB (Dunelm) MIEX, ACIPA]

ADAMS MS LINDSAY EVELINE

1 Pump Court
Lower Ground Floor, Temple, London
EC4Y 7AB, Telephone: 0171 583 2012/
353 4341
E-mail: [name]@1pumpcourt.co.uk
Call Date: Nov 1987, Middle Temple
Pupil Master
Qualifications: [LLB(Hons)]

ADAMS MISS LORRAINE JOAN

Pulteney Chambers
14 Johnstone Street, Bath BA2 4DH,
Telephone: 01225 723987
Call Date: Oct 1992, Inner Temple
Qualifications: [LLB]

D

ADAMS ROBERT GEORGE SETON

Trinity Chambers
9-12 Trinity Chare, Quayside, Newcastle
upon Tyne NE1 3DF,
Telephone: 0191 232 1927
E-mail: info@trinitychambers.co.uk
Call Date: Oct 1993, Inner Temple
Qualifications: [MA (Cantab)]

ADAMSON ALAN

Britton Street Chambers
1st Floor, 20 Britton Street, London
EC1M 5NQ, Telephone: 0171 608 3765
Abbey Chambers
PO Box 47, 47 Ashurst Drive, Shepperton,
Middlesex, TW17 0LD,
Telephone: 01932 560913
Call Date: Oct 1997, Inner Temple
Qualifications: [BA (Leicester), CPE
(Nottingham)]

ADAMSON DOMINIC JAMES

1 Temple Gardens
1st Floor, Temple, London EC4Y 9BB,
Telephone: 0171 583 1315/353 0407
E-mail: clerks@1templegardens.co.uk
Call Date: 1997, Lincoln's Inn
Qualifications: [LLB (Newc)]

ADAMSON MISS LILIAS LOUISA

Becket Chambers
17 New Dover Road, Canterbury, Kent,
CT1 3AS, Telephone: 01227 786331
Call Date: 1994, Gray's Inn
Qualifications: [BA (Hons) (Keele)]

ADAMYK SIMON CHARLES

12 New Square
Lincoln's Inn, London WC2A 3SW,
Telephone: 0171 419 1212
E-mail: chambers@12newsquare.co.uk
Call Date: Nov 1991, Lincoln's Inn
Qualifications: [BA (Hons) (Camb), LLM
(Harvard)]

ADDEZIO MARIO

6 Gray's Inn Square
Ground Floor, Gray's Inn, London
WC1R 5AZ, Telephone: 0171 242 1052
E-mail: 6graysinn@clara.co.uk
*Call Date: July 1971, Lincoln's Inn
Pupil Master*
Qualifications: [LLB (Lond)]

ADDISON KENNETH PAUL

3 Temple Gardens
2nd Floor, Temple, London EC4Y 9AU,
Telephone: 0171 583 1155
Call Date: July 1988, Middle Temple
Qualifications: [LLB (Hons)]

ADDISON NEIL PATRICK

Cathedral Chambers
Milburn House, Dean Street, Newcastle
upon Tyne NE1 1LE,
Telephone: 0191 232 1311
Call Date: Nov 1976, Gray's Inn
Qualifications: [BA]

ADDLEMAN MISS ANDREA MICHELE

Park Court Chambers
16 Park Place, Leeds LS1 2SJ,
Telephone: 0113 2433277
*Call Date: July 1977, Middle Temple
Pupil Master*

ADDY MISS CAROLINE KORDAI

1 Brick Court
1st Floor, Temple, London EC4Y 9BY,
Telephone: 0171 353 8845
E-mail: clerks@1brickcourt.co.uk
Call Date: Nov 1991, Inner Temple
Qualifications: [LLB (Euro)(Exon)]

ADEBAYO IBITAYO ALADE

Queen Elizabeth Building
Ground Floor, Temple, London
EC4Y 9BS,
Telephone: 0171 353 7181 (12 Lines)
Call Date: Nov 1989, Inner Temple
Qualifications: [BA (Hons)(Bris), DP in Law
(Bris)]

ADEDEJI MISS ADEYINKA OYINDAMOLA

6 King's Bench Walk
Ground, Third & Fourth Floors, Temple,
London EC4Y 7DR,
Telephone: 0171 353 4931/583 0695
Call Date: 1997, Lincoln's Inn
Qualifications: [MA (Hons)(Edinb), LLB
(Lond)]

ADEJUMO MRS HILDA EKPO

Temple Chambers
Rooms 111/112, 3/7 Temple Avenue,
London EC4Y 0HP,
Telephone: 0171 583 1001 (2 lines)
E-mail:chambers.adejumo@btinternet.com
Call Date: Nov 1989, Lincoln's Inn
Qualifications: [BSc (Nigeria), LLB (Hons)
(Lond), LLM, BL (Lond), LLM (Lond)]

ADENEKAN LATIFF AREMU

Temple Chamber
Suite 241, 4th Floor 3-7 Temple Avenue,
London EC4Y 0HP,
Telephone: 0171 353 4461
Call Date: Nov 1970, Inner Temple
Qualifications: [LLB (Lond)]

ADER PETER CHARLES

3 Temple Gardens
Lower Ground Floor, Temple, London
EC4Y 9AU, Telephone: 0171 353 3102/5/
9297 E-mail: clerks@3tg.co.uk
Call Date: July 1973, Middle Temple
Pupil Master, Recorder
Qualifications: [LLB (Hons)(So'ton)]

ADEREMI ADEDAMOLA OLASUPO

Chambers of Wilfred Forster-Jones
New Court, 1st Floor South, Temple,
London EC4Y 9BE,
Telephone: 0171 353 0853/4/7222
E-mail: chambers@newcourt.net
Call Date: Feb 1992, Inner Temple
Qualifications: [LLB (Nigeria), LLM (Nigeria)]

ADEWALE REMI ADETOKUNBO SANNI

The Chambers of Mr Ali Mohammed Azhar
Basement, 9 King's Bench Walk, Temple,
London EC4Y 7DX,
Telephone: 0171 353 9564
E-mail: jvlee@btinternet.com
Call Date: Oct 1995, Middle Temple
Qualifications: [LLB(Hons), LLM (Lond)]

ADJEI CYRIL JOHN

5 Paper Buildings
Ground Floor, Temple, London
EC4Y 7HB, Telephone: 0171 583 9275/
583 4555 E-mail: 5paper@link.org
Call Date: Oct 1995, Inner Temple
Qualifications: [LLB (Lond), LLM (Cantab),
LLD (EUI,Florence)]

ADKIN JAMES SIMON

New Court Chambers
3 Broad Chare, Newcastle upon Tyne
NE1 3DQ, Telephone: 0191 232 1980
Call Date: Oct 1992, Lincoln's Inn
Qualifications: [LLB(Hons)(Newc)]

ADKIN JONATHAN WILLIAM

One Hare Court
1st Floor, Temple, London EC4Y 7BE,
Telephone: 020 7353 3171
E-mail:admin-oneharecourt@btinternet.com
Call Date: Oct 1997, Gray's Inn
Qualifications: [MA (Oxon)]

ADKIN MS TANA MARIE THERESE

Chambers of Helen Grindrod QC
4th Floor, 15-19 Devereux Court, London
WC2R 3JJ, Telephone: 0171 583 2792
Call Date: Nov 1992, Inner Temple
Qualifications: [BA (Hons)(Leic), Dip in Law
(City)]

ADKINS RICHARD DAVID QC (1995)

3/4 South Square
Gray's Inn, London WC1R 5HP,
Telephone: 0171 696 9900
E-mail: clerks@southsquare.com
Call Date: July 1982, Middle Temple
Qualifications: [MA (Oxon)]

ADLARD WILLIAM BRICE

2 Harcourt Buildings
1st Floor, Temple, London EC4Y 9DB,
Telephone: 020 7353 2112
Call Date: July 1978, Middle Temple
Pupil Master

ADONIS GEORGIOS

1 Inner Temple Lane
Temple, London EC4Y 1AF,
Telephone: 020 7353 0933
Call Date: July 1973, Lincoln's Inn

AEBERLI PETER DOLPH

Chambers of Geoffrey Hawker
46/48 Essex Street, London WC2R 3GH,
Telephone: 0171 583 8899
Call Date: Nov 1990, Middle Temple
Recorder
Qualifications: [MA (Edin) BA (Oxon), Dip
Arch, R.I.B.A., A.R.I.A.S FCIArb]

AFEEVA MARK KUDZO DZITOSI

Cardinal Chambers
4 Old Mitre Court, 4th Floor, Temple,
London EC4Y 7BP,
Telephone: 020 7353 2622
E-mail:admin@cardinal-chambers.co.uk
Call Date: 1997, Inner Temple
Qualifications: [LLB (London), LLM
(London)]

AGBAJE EDWARD PAUL ABAYOMI

1 Gray's Inn Square
Ground Floor, London WC1R 5AA,
Telephone: 0171 405 8946/7/8
Call Date: Nov 1984, Middle Temple
Pupil Master
Qualifications: [BA(Exon)]

AGBAMU ALEXANDER ONAKOMEME

2 Pump Court
1st Floor, Temple, London EC4Y 7AH,
Telephone: 0171 353 5597
Call Date: Nov 1988, Lincoln's Inn
Qualifications: [LLB Hons (B'ham)]

AGEROS DAVID KEITH JUSTIN

4 Paper Buildings
1st Floor, Temple, London EC4Y 7EX,
Telephone: 0171 583 0816/353 1131
E-mail: clerks@4paperbuildings.co.uk
Call Date: Nov 1993, Inner Temple
Qualifications: [BA (Hons)(Cantab), Dip Law
(City)]

AGEROS JAMES HUGH PAUL

3 Hare Court
1 Little Essex Street, London WC2R 3LD,
Telephone: 0171 395 2000
Call Date: May 1990, Inner Temple
Qualifications: [B.A. (So'ton), Dip Law]

AGHA SIZA

10 King's Bench Walk
1st Floor, Temple, London EC4Y 7EB,
Telephone: 0171 353 2501
Call Date: Feb 1994, Lincoln's Inn
Qualifications: [LLB (Hons, Wales)]

AGNELLO MISS RAQUEL

11 Stone Buildings
Lincoln's Inn, London WC2A 3TG,
Telephone: +44 (0)207 831 6381
E-mail:clerks@11StoneBuildings.law.co.uk
Call Date: Nov 1986, Inner Temple
Pupil Master
Qualifications: [BA (Sussex) Dip, D'Etudes
Juridiques, Francaises, ACI Arb,
Strasbourg, ACI Arb]

AGNEW MISS CHRISTINE

3 Hare Court
1 Little Essex Street, London WC2R 3LD,
Telephone: 0171 395 2000
Call Date: Nov 1992, Inner Temple
Qualifications: [LLB]

AGNEW MS SINEAD CECILIA

Serle Court Chambers
6 New Square, Lincoln's Inn, London
WC2A 3QS, Telephone: 0171 242 6105
E-mail: clerks@serlecourt.co.uk
Call Date: Nov 1998, Gray's Inn
Qualifications: [LLB (Dublin), LLM (Oxon)]

AHERNE MISS CATHERINE HELEN

Francis Taylor Building
3rd Floor, Temple, London EC4Y 7BY,
Telephone: 0171 797 7250
Call Date: Mar 1997, Lincoln's Inn
Qualifications: [LLB (Hons)]

AHMAD NADEEM

5 Essex Court
1st Floor, Temple, London EC4Y 9AH,
Telephone: 0171 410 2000
E-mail: barristers@5essexcourt.co.uk
Call Date: Oct 1996, Gray's Inn
Qualifications: [BA (Hons)(Lond), Dip Law]

AHMAD MISS SIRAT

Chancery Chambers
1st Floor Offices, 70/72 Chancery Lane,
London WC2A 1AB,
Telephone: 0171 405 6879/6870
Call Date: Feb 1988, Lincoln's Inn
Qualifications: [LLB (Hons)]

AHMAD ZUBAIR

1 Paper Buildings
1st Floor, Temple, London EC4Y 7EP,
Telephone: 0171 353 3728/4953
Call Date: Oct 1995, Lincoln's Inn
Qualifications: [LLB (Hons)(Lond)]

AHMED MISS AMINA

Gray's Inn Chambers
5th Floor, Gray's Inn, London WC1R 5JA,
Telephone: 0171 404 1111
Call Date: Feb 1995, Middle Temple
Qualifications: [BSc (Hons)(Lond), CPE
(Lond)]

AHMED FAROOQ TAHIR

8 King Street Chambers
8 King Street, Manchester M2 6AQ,
Telephone: 0161 834 9560
E-mail: eightking@aol.com
3 Dr Johnson's Buildings
Ground Floor, Temple, London
EC4Y 7BA, Telephone: 0171 353 4854
E-mail: clerks@3djb.co.uk
Call Date: Nov 1983, Inner Temple
Qualifications: [LLB (Hons) (Lond)]

AHMED MISS JACQUELINE MICHELLE

Southernhay Chambers
33 Southernhay East, Exeter, Devon,
EX1 1NX, Telephone: 01392 255777
E-mail:southernhay.chambers@lineone.net
Call Date: July 1988, Inner Temple
Qualifications: [LLB (City)]

AHMED MOBIN UDDIN

Tower Hamlets Barristers Chambers
First Floor, 45 Brick Lane, London
E1 6PU, Telephone: 0171 247 9825
Call Date: Nov 1969, Lincoln's Inn
Qualifications: [B.Com (Dhaka)]

AHMED SALEEM

Perivale Chambers
15 Colwyn Avenue, Perivale, Middlesex,
UB6 8JY, Telephone: 0181 998 1935/
081 248 0246
Call Date: Feb 1971, Inner Temple
Pupil Master
Qualifications: [BA]

AHYA MISS SONAL

High Pavement Chambers
1 High Pavement, Nottingham NG1 1HF,
Telephone: 0115 9418218
Call Date: Nov 1995, Lincoln's Inn
Qualifications: [LLB (Hons)(Leic)]

AIKEN MRS GILLIAN MARJORIE

Clapham Chambers
21-25 Bedford Road, Clapham North,
London SW4 7SH,
Telephone: 0171 978 8482/642 5777
E-mail:claphamchambers@compuserve.co
m
Call Date: July 1993, Inner Temple
Qualifications: [BPharm, LLB (Lond), M R
Pharms, LLM (Lond)]

AIKEN MISS KIMBERLEY

4 King's Bench Walk
Ground/First Floor/Basement, Temple,
London EC4Y 7DL,
Telephone: 0171 822 8822
E-mail: 4kbw@barristersatlaw.com
Call Date: Nov 1995, Lincoln's Inn
Qualifications: [LLB (Hons)]

AILES JOHN ASHLEY

Eighteen Carlton Crescent
Southampton SO15 2XR,
Telephone: 01703 639001
Call Date: July 1975, Middle Temple
Pupil Master
Qualifications: [BA M.Phil]

AINA BENJAMIN ADEJOWON OLUFEMI

3 Temple Gardens
Lower Ground Floor, Temple, London
EC4Y 9AU, Telephone: 0171 353 3102/5/
9297 E-mail: clerks@3tg.co.uk
Call Date: July 1987, Lincoln's Inn
Pupil Master
Qualifications: [LLB LLM (London)]

AINGER WILLIAM DAWSON

The Chambers of Leolin Price CBE, QC
10 Old Square, Lincoln's Inn, London
WC2A 3SU, Telephone: 0171 405 0758
Call Date: June 1961, Lincoln's Inn
Pupil Master
Qualifications: [MA (Oxon)]

AINLEY NICHOLAS JOHN

5 Essex Court
1st Floor, Temple, London EC4Y 9AH,
Telephone: 0171 410 2000
E-mail: barristers@5essexcourt.co.uk
Call Date: July 1973, Lincoln's Inn
Pupil Master, Assistant Recorder

AINSWORTH MARK JUSTIN SIMON

Peel Court Chambers
45 Hardman Street, Manchester M3 3PL,
Telephone: 0161 832 3791
E-mail: clerks@peelct.co.uk
Call Date: Oct 1992, Lincoln's Inn
Qualifications: [BA(Hons)(L'pool), Dip Law]

AIOLFI LAURENCE

Queen Elizabeth Building
Ground Floor, Temple, London
EC4Y 9BS,
Telephone: 0171 353 7181 (12 Lines)
Call Date: Oct 1996, Inner Temple
Qualifications: [LLB (Bris)]

AIRD RICHARD ERSKINE

4 Pump Court
Temple, London EC4Y 7AN,
Telephone: 020 7842 5555
E-mail:chambers@4pumpcourt.law.co.uk
Lancaster Building
77 Deansgate, Manchester M3 2BW,
Telephone: 0161 661 4444/0171 649 9872
E-mail: sandra@lbnipc.com
Call Date: Nov 1976, Inner Temple
Qualifications: [LLB]

AIREY SIMON ANDREW

11 Bolt Court (also at 7 Stone Buildings – 1st Floor)
London EC4A 3DQ,
Telephone: 0171 353 2300
E-mail: boltct11@aol.com
Redhill Chambers
Seloduct House, 30 Station Road, Redhill,
Surrey, RH1 1NF,
Telephone: 01737 780781
7 Stone Buildings (also at 11 Bolt Court)
1st Floor, Lincoln's Inn, London
WC2A 3SZ, Telephone: 0171 242 0961
E-mail:larthur@7stonebuildings.law.co.uk
Call Date: Nov 1989, Inner Temple
Qualifications: [LLB (Sheff)]

AITKEN JOHN RUSSELL

New Court Chambers
3 Broad Chare, Newcastle upon Tyne
NE1 3DQ, Telephone: 0191 232 1980
Call Date: July 1984, Gray's Inn
Pupil Master
Qualifications: [BA]

AKAST JOHN FRANCIS

East Anglian Chambers
Gresham House, 5 Museum Street,
Ipswich, Suffolk, IP1 1HQ,
Telephone: 01473 214481
E-mail: ipswich@ealaw.co.uk
East Anglian Chambers
52 North Hill, Colchester, Essex, CO1 1PY,
Telephone: 01206 572756
E-mail: colchester@ealaw.co.uk
East Anglian Chambers
57 London Street, Norwich NR2 1HL,
Telephone: 01603 617351
E-mail: norwich@ealaw.co.uk
Call Date: Nov 1968, Inner Temple
Pupil Master, Recorder
Qualifications: [LLB]

AKENHEAD ROBERT QC (1989)

Atkin Chambers
1 Atkin Building, Gray's Inn, London
WC1R 5AT, Telephone: 020 7404 0102
E-mail: clerks@atkin-chambers.co.uk
Call Date: July 1972, Inner Temple
Recorder
Qualifications: [LLB]

AKERMAN MISS KATE LOUISE

Queen's Chambers
5 John Dalton Street, Manchester M2 6ET,
Telephone: 0161 834 6875/4738
Queens Chambers
4 Camden Place, Preston PR1 3JL,
Telephone: 01772 828300
Call Date: Oct 1994, Middle Temple
Qualifications: [LLB (Hons)(Lond)]

AKIN BARRIE SIMON

Gray's Inn Tax Chambers
3rd Floor, Gray's Inn Chambers, Gray's
Inn, London WC1R 5JA,
Telephone: 0171 242 2642
E-mail: clerks@taxbar.com
Call Date: July 1976, Middle Temple
Qualifications: [LLB, FCA]

AKINJIDE RICHARD

10 King's Bench Walk
1st Floor, Temple, London EC4Y 7EB,
Telephone: 0171 353 2501
Call Date: Feb 1956, Inner Temple
Qualifications: [LLB (London), FCIArb]

AKINSANYA JONATHAN

4 Brick Court, Chambers of Anne Rafferty QC
1st Floor, Temple, London EC4Y 9AD,
Telephone: 0171 583 8455
Call Date: Nov 1993, Inner Temple
Qualifications: [LLB (South Bank)]

AKINSANYA STEPHEN OLUBUNMI

Gray's Inn Chambers, The Chambers of Norman Patterson
First Floor, Gray's Inn Chambers, Gray's
Inn, London WC1R 5JA,
Telephone: 0171 831 5344
E-mail: s.mcblain@btinternet.com

5 Essex Court
1st Floor, Temple, London EC4Y 9AH,
Telephone: 0171 410 2000
E-mail: barristers@5essexcourt.co.uk
Call Date: Nov 1993, Inner Temple
Qualifications: [LLB (Bucks)]

AKIWUMI ANTHONY SEBASTIAN AKITAYO

Pump Court Chambers
Upper Ground Floor, 3 Pump Court,
Temple, London EC4Y 7AJ,
Telephone: 0171 353 0711
E-mail: clerks@3pumpcourt.com
Pump Court Chambers
31 Southgate Street, Winchester
SO23 9EE, Telephone: 01962 868161
E-mail: clerks@3pumpcourt.com
Pump Court Chambers
5 Temple Chambers, Temple Street,
Swindon SN1 1SQ,
Telephone: 01793 539899
E-mail: clerks@3pumpcourt.com
Call Date: July 1989, Inner Temple
Qualifications: [BA (Kent)]

AKKA LAWRENCE MARK

20 Essex Street
London WC2R 3AL,
Telephone: 0171 583 9294
E-mail: clerks@20essexst.com
Call Date: Oct 1991, Lincoln's Inn
Qualifications: [BA (Hons) (Oxon)]

AKMAN MISS MERCY LOUISE

Chambers of Michael Pert QC
36 Bedford Row, London WC1R 4JH,
Telephone: 0171 421 8000
E-mail: 36bedfordrow@link.org
Chambers of Michael Pert QC
24 Albion Place, Northampton NN1 1UD,
Telephone: 01604 602333
Chambers of Michael Pert QC
104 New Walk, Leicester LE1 7EA,
Telephone: 0116 249 2020
Call Date: Nov 1982, Gray's Inn
Qualifications: [LLB (Hons) (Wales)]

AKRAM UMER

Perivale Chambers
15 Colwyn Avenue, Perivale, Middlesex,
UB6 8JY, Telephone: 0181 998 1935/
081 248 0246
Call Date: Mar 1997, Lincoln's Inn
Qualifications: [LLB (Hons)]

AKUWUDIKE MISS EMMA CHIAWUOTU

3 Gray's Inn Square
Ground Floor, London WC1R 5AH,
Telephone: 0171 520 5600
E-mail: clerks@3gis.co.uk
Call Date: Nov 1992, Inner Temple
Qualifications: [LLB (Hons)]

AKWAGYIRAM SAMUEL MANTEAW

12 Old Square
1st Floor, Lincoln's Inn, London
WC2A 3TX, Telephone: 0171 404 0875
Call Date: Nov 1985, Inner Temple
Qualifications: [BA (Hons)]

AL'HASSAN KHADIM

Equity Chambers
3rd Floor, 153a Corporation Street,
Birmingham B4 6PH,
Telephone: 0121 233 2100
E-mail: equityatusa.com
Call Date: Nov 1993, Inner Temple
Qualifications: [LLB (Leic)]

AL-ANI DR ABDUL-HAQ

Britton Street Chambers
1st Floor, 20 Britton Street, London
EC1M 5NQ, Telephone: 0171 608 3765
Call Date: Oct 1996, Inner Temple
Qualifications: [BSc (Baghdad), MSc, PhD
(Lond), MSc (Middx), CPE (Lond)]

AL-QASIM DR ANIS

2 Paper Buildings
1st Floor, Temple, London EC4Y 7ET,
Telephone: 020 7556 5500
E-mail: clerks@2pbbarristers.co.uk
Call Date: 1950, Lincoln's Inn
Qualifications: [LLB, LLM, PhD (Lond), Dip
Oil & Gas Law , (Dallas)]

AL-RASHID MAHMUD

The Chambers of Mr Ali Mohammed Azhar
Basement, 9 King's Bench Walk, Temple,
London EC4Y 7DX,
Telephone: 0171 353 9564
E-mail: jvlee@btinternet.com
Call Date: Oct 1991, Gray's Inn
Qualifications: [LLB (Leics)]

ALAKIJA AYODELE HUGH

Phoenix Chambers
First Floor, Gray's Inn Chambers, Gray's
Inn, London WC1R 5JA,
Telephone: 0171 404 7888
E-mail:clerks@phoenix-chambers.co.uk
Call Date: Oct 1996, Gray's Inn
Qualifications: [LLB (Lond)]

ALBAN-LLOYD MRS NAN

2 King's Bench Walk Chambers
1st Floor, 2 King's Bench Walk, Temple,
London EC4Y 7DE,
Telephone: 020 7353 9276
E-mail: chambers@2kbw.co.uk
Call Date: Nov 1988, Inner Temple
Qualifications: [BFA (Boston) , LLB (Hons)]

ALBUTT IAN LESLIE

2-3 Gray's Inn Square
Gray's Inn, London WC1R 5JH,
Telephone: 0171 242 4986
E-mail:chambers@2-3graysinnsquare.co.uk
Call Date: July 1981, Gray's Inn
Pupil Master

ALCOCK PETER MICHAEL

6 Pump Court
1st Floor, Temple, London EC4Y 7AR,
Telephone: 0171 797 8400
E-mail: clerks@6pumpcourt.co.uk
6-8 Mill Street
Maidstone, Kent, ME15 6XH,
Telephone: 01622 688094
E-mail: annexe@6pumpcourt.co.uk
Call Date: 1995, Gray's Inn
Qualifications: [BA (Hons), Dip Law]

ALDER MRS CLAIRE

1 Gray's Inn Square
Ground Floor, London WC1R 5AA,
Telephone: 0171 405 8946/7/8
Call Date: July 1988, Inner Temple
Qualifications: [LLB (LSE)]

ALDERSON MISS PHILIPPA ELIZABETH LOVEDAY

6 Gray's Inn Square
Ground Floor, Gray's Inn, London
WC1R 5AZ, Telephone: 0171 242 1052
E-mail: 6graysinn@clara.co.uk
Call Date: Nov 1993, Middle Temple
Qualifications: [BA (Hons)(Dunelm)]

ALDOUS CHARLES QC (1985)

7 Stone Buildings
Ground Floor, Lincoln's Inn, London
WC2A 3SZ, Telephone: 0171 405 3886/
242 3546 E-mail: chaldous@vossnet.co.uk
Call Date: Feb 1967, Inner Temple
Qualifications: [LLB (Lond)]

ALDOUS GRAHAME LINLEY

9 Gough Square
London EC4A 3DE,
Telephone: 020 7832 0500
E-mail: clerks@9goughsq.co.uk
Call Date: July 1979, Inner Temple
Pupil Master, Assistant Recorder
Qualifications: [LLB (Exon)]

ALDOUS ROBERT JOHN

Octagon House
19 Colegate, Norwich NR3 1AT,
Telephone: 01603 623186
E-mail: admin@octagon-chambers.co.uk
Call Date: July 1985, Inner Temple
Qualifications: [BA (Cantab)]

ALDRED BRIAN PETER

Westgate Chambers
144 High Street, Lewes, East Sussex,
BN7 1XT, Telephone: 01273 480510
Call Date: Nov 1994, Inner Temple
Qualifications: [LLB (Kent)]

ALDRED MARK STEVEN

Hollis Whiteman Chambers
3rd Floor, Queen Elizabeth Bldg, Temple,
London EC4Y 9BS,
Telephone: 020 7583 5766
E-mail:barristers@holliswhiteman.co.uk
Call Date: Mar 1996, Middle Temple
Qualifications: [LLB (Hons)]

ALDRIDGE JAMES HUGH

13 Old Square
Ground Floor, Lincoln's Inn, London
WC2A 3UA, Telephone: 0171 404 4800
E-mail: clerks@13oldsquare.law.co.uk
Call Date: Oct 1994, Lincoln's Inn
Qualifications: [BA (Hons)]

ALDRIDGE JAMES WILLIAM

199 Strand
London WC2R 1DR,
Telephone: 0171 379 9779
E-mail: chambers@199strand.co.uk
Call Date: July 1987, Inner Temple
Qualifications: [BA (Lond),Dip Law]

ALEESON WARWICK LAN GRIEG

2nd Floor, Francis Taylor Building
Temple, London EC4Y 7BY,
Telephone: 0171 353 9942/3157
Call Date: Nov 1994, Gray's Inn
Qualifications: [LLB (Hons)(Wales)]

ALESBURY ALUN

2 Mitre Court Buildings
2nd Floor, Temple, London EC4Y 7BX,
Telephone: 0171 583 1380
E-mail: clerks@2mcb.co.uk
Call Date: July 1974, Inner Temple
Pupil Master
Qualifications: [MA (Cantab)]

ALEXANDER DANIEL SAKYI

8 New Square
Lincoln's Inn, London WC2A 3QP,
Telephone: 0171 405 4321
E-mail: clerks@8newsquare.co.uk
Call Date: July 1988, Middle Temple
Pupil Master
Qualifications: [BA (Hons) (Oxon), LLM
(Harvard), Dip Law]

D

ALEXANDER DAVID ROBERT JAMES

3/4 South Square
Gray's Inn, London WC1R 5HP,
Telephone: 0171 696 9900
E-mail: clerks@southsquare.com
Call Date: Nov 1987, Middle Temple
Pupil Master
Qualifications: [MA (Cantab)]

ALEXANDER IAN DOUGLAS GAVIN QC (1989)

11 Bolt Court (also at 7 Stone Buildings – 1st Floor)
London EC4A 3DQ,
Telephone: 0171 353 2300
E-mail: boltct11@aol.com
Redhill Chambers
Seloduct House, 30 Station Road, Redhill,
Surrey, RH1 1NF,
Telephone: 01737 780781
7 Stone Buildings (also at 11 Bolt Court)
1st Floor, Lincoln's Inn, London
WC2A 3SZ, Telephone: 0171 242 0961
E-mail:larthur@7stonebuildings.law.co.uk
Call Date: June 1964, Lincoln's Inn
Recorder
Qualifications: [LLB (Lond)]

ALEXANDER ROBERT DOMINIC

1 Gray's Inn Square, Chambers of the Baroness Scotland of Asthal QC
1st Floor, London WC1R 5AG,
Telephone: 0171 405 3000
E-mail: clerks@onegrays.demon.co.uk
Call Date: Nov 1995, Middle Temple
Qualifications: [BA (Hons)(Bris)]

ALFORD ROBERT JOHN

Southernhay Chambers
33 Southernhay East, Exeter, Devon,
EX1 1NX, Telephone: 01392 255777
E-mail:southernhay.chambers@lineone.net
Call Date: Nov 1970, Gray's Inn
Qualifications: [LLB (Sheff)]

ALFORD STUART ROBERT

Chambers of Michael Pert QC
36 Bedford Row, London WC1R 4JH,
Telephone: 0171 421 8000
E-mail: 36bedfordrow@link.org

Chambers of Michael Pert QC
24 Albion Place, Northampton NN1 1UD,
Telephone: 01604 602333
Chambers of Michael Pert QC
104 New Walk, Leicester LE1 7EA,
Telephone: 0116 249 2020
Call Date: Oct 1992, Middle Temple
Qualifications: [B.Sc (Hons, Reading)]

ALFRED STEPHAN HONNORAT

Holborn Chambers
6 Gate Street, Lincoln's Inn Fields, London
WC2A 3HP, Telephone: 0171 242 6060
Call Date: Oct 1996, Inner Temple
Qualifications: [LLB (Wales)]

ALGAR CLAUDIUS JOHN

10 King's Bench Walk
Ground Floor, Temple, London
EC4Y 7EB, Telephone: 0171 353 7742
E-mail: 10kbw@lineone.net
Call Date: Nov 1972, Inner Temple
Pupil Master

ALGAZY JACQUES MAX

Cloisters
1 Pump Court, Temple, London
EC4Y 7AA, Telephone: 0171 827 4000
E-mail: clerks@cloisters.com
Call Date: Nov 1980, Gray's Inn
Pupil Master
Qualifications: [LLB (Reading), D.E.S.Eu]

ALI MISS HUMA

Eastbourne Chambers
15 Hyde Gardens, Eastbourne, East
Sussex, BN21 4PR,
Telephone: 01323 642102
Call Date: Mar 1997, Gray's Inn
Qualifications: [LLB (L'pool)]

ALI MOHAMMED AZEEM

Chancery Chambers
1st Floor Offices, 70/72 Chancery Lane,
London WC2A 1AB,
Telephone: 0171 405 6879/6870
Call Date: May 1997, Lincoln's Inn
Qualifications: [LLB (Hons)(L'pool)]

ALI RAYMOND AZEEZ

Middlesex Chambers
Suite 3 & 4 Stanley House, Stanley
Avenue, Wembley, Middlesex, HA0 4SB,
Telephone: 0181 902 1499
Call Date: May 1995, Gray's Inn
Qualifications: [LLB, LLM (Lond), LEC
(Trinidad)]

ALI ZAFAR

1 Gray's Inn Square
Ground Floor, London WC1R 5AA,
Telephone: 0171 405 8946/7/8
Cardinal Chambers
4 Old Mitre Court, 4th Floor, Temple,
London EC4Y 7BP,
Telephone: 020 7353 2622
E-mail:admin@cardinal-chambers.co.uk
Call Date: Nov 1994, Middle Temple
Qualifications: [BA (Hons, Warw)]

Fax: 0171 405 1617; DX: 1013 Chancery
Lane

Other professional qualifications: BA (Hons); Dip
Law

Types of work: Crime

Circuit: South Eastern

Awards and memberships: Diplock Scholarship

Other professional experience: Ex-Army Officer
in Airborne Infantry four years

Languages spoken:

ALIKER PHILIP BLISS

2 Pump Court
1st Floor, Temple, London EC4Y 7AH,
Telephone: 0171 353 5597
Call Date: Oct 1990, Inner Temple
Qualifications: [BA (Vanderbilt), LLB
(Leeds)]

ALLAN CHRISTOPHER DAVID QC (1995)

22 Old Buildings
Lincoln's Inn, London WC2A 3UJ,
Telephone: 0171 831 0222

Byrom Street Chambers
Byrom Street, Manchester M3 4PF,
Telephone: 0161 829 2100
E-mail: Byromst25@aol.com
Call Date: July 1974, Gray's Inn
Recorder
Qualifications: [LLB]

ALLAN COLIN STEWART

3 Gray's Inn Square
Ground Floor, London WC1R 5AH,
Telephone: 0171 520 5600
E-mail: clerks@3gis.co.uk
Call Date: July 1971, Middle Temple

ALLAN DAVID ALEXANDER

9 Bedford Row
London WC1R 4AZ,
Telephone: 0171 242 3555
E-mail: clerks@9br.co.uk
Call Date: 1998, Lincoln's Inn
Qualifications: [BA (Hons)]

ALLAN MISS MONIQUE ANNE FORTUNE

Littman Chambers
12 Gray's Inn Square, London WC1R 5JP,
Telephone: 020 7404 4866
E-mail: admin@littmanchambers.com
Call Date: Nov 1986, Inner Temple
Pupil Master
Qualifications: [BA (Bristol) Dip Law,
FCIArb]

ALLARDICE MISS MIRANDA JANE

Pump Court Chambers
Upper Ground Floor, 3 Pump Court,
Temple, London EC4Y 7AJ,
Telephone: 0171 353 0711
E-mail: clerks@3pumpcourt.com
Pump Court Chambers
31 Southgate Street, Winchester
SO23 9EE, Telephone: 01962 868161
E-mail: clerks@3pumpcourt.com
Pump Court Chambers
5 Temple Chambers, Temple Street,
Swindon SN1 1SQ,
Telephone: 01793 539899
E-mail: clerks@3pumpcourt.com
Call Date: July 1982, Lincoln's Inn
Pupil Master
Qualifications: [BA (Oxon)]

ALLCOCK STEPHEN JAMES QC (1993)

Pump Court Tax Chambers
16 Bedford Row, London WC1R 4EB,
Telephone: 0171 414 8080
Call Date: July 1975, Gray's Inn
Qualifications: [BA (Cantab)]

ALLDIS CHRISTOPHER JOHN

Oriel Chambers
14 Water Street, Liverpool L2 8TD,
Telephone: 0151 236 7191/236 4321
E-mail: clerks@oriel-chambers.co.uk
Call Date: Nov 1970, Gray's Inn
Pupil Master, Recorder
Qualifications: [MA, LLB (Cantab)]

ALLEN DARRYL JOHN

Farrar's Building
Temple, London EC4Y 7BD,
Telephone: 0171 583 9241
E-mail:chambers@farrarsbuilding.co.uk
Call Date: Oct 1995, Lincoln's Inn
Qualifications: [LLB (Hons)(Leeds)]

ALLEN DAVID KENNETH

2 New Street
Leicester LE1 5NA,
Telephone: 0116 2625906
E-mail: clerks@2newstreet.co.uk
Call Date: July 1975, Middle Temple
Qualifications: [MA, BA (Hons),LLM]

ALLEN DOUGLAS STEPHEN

Goldsmith Chambers
Ground Floor, Goldsmith Building,
Temple, London EC4Y 7BL,
Telephone: 0171 353 6802/3/4/5
E-mail:clerks@goldsmithchambers.law.co.uk
Call Date: Oct 1995, Lincoln's Inn
Qualifications: [BA (Hons)(B'ham)]

ALLEN MS FRANCES

Phoenix Chambers
First Floor, Gray's Inn Chambers, Gray's
Inn, London WC1R 5JA,
Telephone: 0171 404 7888
E-mail:clerks@phoenix-chambers.co.uk
Call Date: Oct 1995, Inner Temple
Qualifications: [BSc (Lond), CPE (City)]

ALLEN JAMES HENDRICUSS QC (1995)

Chancery House Chambers
7 Lisbon Square, Leeds LS1 4LY,
Telephone: 0113 244 6691
E-mail: chanceryhouse@btinternet.com
Call Date: Nov 1973, Gray's Inn
Recorder
Qualifications: [BA Law]

ALLEN MARK GRAHAM

30 Park Place
Cardiff CF1 3BA,
Telephone: 01222 398421
E-mail: 100757.1456@compuserve.com
Call Date: July 1981, Middle Temple
Pupil Master
Qualifications: [LLB (Cardiff)]

ALLEN MICHAEL DAVID PRIOR

S Tomlinson QC
7 King's Bench Walk, Temple, London
EC4Y 7DS, Telephone: 0171 583 0404
E-mail: clerks@7kbw.law.co.uk
Call Date: Oct 1990, Gray's Inn
Pupil Master
Qualifications: [BSc, LLB, FRICS, ACIArb]

ALLEN NICHOLAS PAUL

29 Bedford Row Chambers
London WC1R 4HE,
Telephone: 0171 831 2626
Call Date: Oct 1995, Middle Temple
Qualifications: [BA (Hons), LLM]

ALLEN ROBIN GEOFFREY BRUERE QC (1995)

Cloisters
1 Pump Court, Temple, London
EC4Y 7AA, Telephone: 0171 827 4000
E-mail: clerks@cloisters.com
Call Date: Nov 1974, Middle Temple
Qualifications: [BA (Oxon)]

ALLEN MISS SYLVIA DELORES

Somersett Chambers
25 Bedford Row, London WC1R 4HE,
Telephone: 0171 404 6701
E-mail: somelaw@aol.com
Call Date: July 1983, Gray's Inn
Qualifications: [LLB (Lond)]

ALLEN THOMAS MICHAEL CHARD

Five Paper Buildings
1st Floor, Five Paper Bldgs, Temple,
London EC4Y 7HB,
Telephone: 0171 583 6117
E-mail:clerks@5-paperbuildings.law.co.uk
Call Date: Feb 1994, Middle Temple
Qualifications: [BA (Hons)(Durham), Dip in
Law (City)]

ALLEN WILLIAM ANDREW

4 Brick Court
Ground Floor, Temple, London
EC4Y 9AD, Telephone: 0171 797 7766
E-mail: chambers@4brick.co.uk
Call Date: Oct 1995, Inner Temple
Qualifications: [BA (Cantab), LLM (Lond)]

ALLFREY RICHARD FORBES

Doughty Street Chambers
11 Doughty Street, London WC1N 2PG,
Telephone: 0171 404 1313
E-mail:enquiries@doughtystreet.co.uk
Call Date: July 1974, Middle Temple
Pupil Master
Qualifications: [LLB (Lond)]

ALLINGHAM-NICHOLSON MRS ELIZABETH SARAH

2 New Street
Leicester LE1 5NA,
Telephone: 0116 2625906
E-mail: clerks@2newstreet.co.uk
Call Date: Oct 1995, Lincoln's Inn
Qualifications: [LLB (Hons)(Lond), BA
(Hons) (Toronto)]

ALLIOTT GEORGE BECKLES

2 Harcourt Buildings
Ground Floor/Left, Temple, London
EC4Y 9DB, Telephone: 0171 583 9020
E-mail: clerks@harcourt.co.uk
Call Date: July 1981, Inner Temple
Pupil Master
Qualifications: [LLB Warwick]

ALLOTT PHILIP JAMES

20 Essex Street
London WC2R 3AL,
Telephone: 0171 583 9294
E-mail: clerks@20essexst.com
Call Date: Feb 1960, Gray's Inn
Qualifications: [BA, LLB (Cantab)]

ALLOWAY TOR HUGH

3 Temple Gardens
3rd Floor, Temple, London EC4Y 9AU,
Telephone: 0171 583 0010
Call Date: July 1985, Lincoln's Inn
Pupil Master
Qualifications: [BSc BA ACII]

ALLSOP ALEXANDER NIGEL MARK

3 Temple Gardens
3rd Floor, Temple, London EC4Y 9AU,
Telephone: 0171 353 0832
Call Date: Oct 1997, Middle Temple
Qualifications: [LLB (Reading)]

ALLSTON ANTHONY STANLEY

Lamb Chambers
Lamb Building, Temple, London
EC4Y 7AS, Telephone: 020 7797 8300
E-mail: lambchambers@link.org
Call Date: July 1975, Gray's Inn
Pupil Master
Qualifications: [BA]

ALLUM DESMOND ERIC QUINTIN

8 King's Bench Walk
2nd Floor, Temple, London EC4Y 7DU,
Telephone: 0171 797 8888
8 King's Bench Walk North
1 Park Square East, Leeds LS1 2NE,
Telephone: 0113 2439797
Call Date: July 1962, Middle Temple

ALMEYDA MISS GENEVIEVE MARGARET MARY

Call Date: Nov 1994, Inner Temple
Qualifications: [LLB (Hons)(Lon), LLM]

ALOMO RICHARD OLUSOJI

14 Gray's Inn Square
Gray's Inn, London WC1R 5JP,
Telephone: 0171 242 0858
E-mail: 100712.2134@compuserve.com
Call Date: Nov 1990, Inner Temple
Qualifications: [LLB (Lond)]

ALSOLAIMANI NASIRUDDIN

10 Kingsfield Avenue
Harrow, Middlesex, HA2 6AH,
Telephone: 0181 427 8709/081 248 4943
Call Date: Nov 1971, Lincoln's Inn
Qualifications: [BA]

ALT MRS ELIZABETH JANE

4 King's Bench Walk
2nd Floor, Temple, London EC4Y 7DL,
Telephone: 020 7353 3581
E-mail: clerks@4kbw.co.uk
Call Date: July 1984, Lincoln's Inn
Qualifications: [LLB (Hull)]

ALTARAS DAVID MAURICE

Chambers of Michael Pert QC
36 Bedford Row, London WC1R 4JH,
Telephone: 0171 421 8000
E-mail: 36bedfordrow@link.org
Chambers of Michael Pert QC
24 Albion Place, Northampton NN1 1UD,
Telephone: 01604 602333
Chambers of Michael Pert QC
104 New Walk, Leicester LE1 7EA,
Telephone: 0116 249 2020
Call Date: Nov 1969, Lincoln's Inn
Pupil Master, Recorder
Qualifications: [BA MA TCD , Dip Crim
(Cantab), ACIArb]

ALTHAM JOHN ROBERT CARR

Corn Exchange Chambers
5th Floor, Fenwick Street, Liverpool
L2 7QS, Telephone: 0151 227 1081/5009
Call Date: Nov 1993, Gray's Inn
Qualifications: [BA]

ALTHAUS ANTONY JUSTIN

No. 1 Serjeants' Inn
5th Floor Fleet Street, Temple, London
EC4Y 1LH, Telephone: 0171 415 6666
E-mail:no1serjeantsinn@btinternet.com
Call Date: July 1988, Inner Temple
Qualifications: [BA (Oxon), Dip Law (City)]

ALTMAN BRIAN

3 Hare Court
1 Little Essex Street, London WC2R 3LD,
Telephone: 0171 395 2000
Call Date: July 1981, Middle Temple
Pupil Master
Qualifications: [LLB (Lond) Dip Eur, Int
(Amsterdam)]

Fax: 0171 240 8711;
Out of hours telephone: 0171 395 2032;
DX: 17 London, Chancery Lane

Other professional qualifications: Treasury
Counsel at CCC 1997-

Types of work: Crime, Crime – corporate
fraud

Circuit: South Eastern

Awards and memberships: Member CBA

ALTY ANDREW STEPHEN JOHN

Deans Court Chambers
24 St John Street, Manchester M3 4DF,
Telephone: 0161 214 6000
E-mail: clerks@deanscourt.co.uk
Deans Court Chambers
41-43 Market Place, Preston PR1 1AH,
Telephone: 01772 555163
E-mail: clerks@deanscourt.co.uk
Call Date: Feb 1992, Inner Temple
Qualifications: [LLB (Hons)]

AMAKYE MISS GRACE TINA

3 Temple Gardens
2nd Floor, Temple, London EC4Y 9AU,
Telephone: 0171 583 1155
Call Date: Nov 1983, Gray's Inn
Qualifications: [LLB (Lond)]

AMAOUCHE MISS SASSA-ANN

One Garden Court Family Law Chambers
Ground Floor, Temple, London
EC4Y 9BJ, Telephone: 0171 797 7900
E-mail: clerks@onegardencourt.co.uk
Call Date: Oct 1996, Inner Temple
Qualifications: [LLB (Lond)]

AMBROSE MISS CLARE MARY GENESTE

20 Essex Street
London WC2R 3AL,
Telephone: 0171 583 9294
E-mail: clerks@20essexst.com
Call Date: Nov 1992, Gray's Inn
Qualifications: [BA (Oxon), LLM (Cantab)]

AMBROSE EUAN JAMES

Guildhall Chambers
22-26 Broad Street, Bristol BS1 2HG,
Telephone: 0117 9273366
E-mail:civil.clerks@guildhallchambers.co.uk
and criminal.clerks@guildhallchambers.co.uk
Call Date: Nov 1992, Middle Temple
Qualifications: [BA (Hons), MA (Hons)]

AMES GEOFFREY ALAN

29 Bedford Row Chambers
London WC1R 4HE,
Telephone: 0171 831 2626
Call Date: July 1976, Lincoln's Inn
Pupil Master
Qualifications: [BSc]

AMIHERE ANWOBO

20 Sewardstone Gardens
Chingford, London E4 7QE,
Telephone: 0181 524 3054
Call Date: Nov 1970, Middle Temple
Qualifications: [LLB (Lond), ACCS]

AMIN MISS FARAH

Goldsworth Chambers
1st Floor, 11 Gray's Inn Square, London
WC1R 5JD, Telephone: 0171 405 7117

Counsels' Chambers
2nd Floor, 10-11 Gray's Inn Square,
London WC1R 5JD,
Telephone: 0171 405 2576
E-mail:clerks@10-11graysinnsquare.co.uk
Call Date: 1991, Lincoln's Inn
Qualifications: [LLB (Hons) (Lond)]

AMIRAFTABI MISS ROSHANAK

Hardwicke Building
New Square, Lincoln's Inn, London
WC2A 3SB, Telephone: 020 7242 2523
E-mail: clerks@hardwicke.co.uk
Call Date: Feb 1993, Gray's Inn
Qualifications: [BA]

AMIS CHRISTOPHER JOCELYN

2 King's Bench Walk
Ground Floor, Temple, London
EC4Y 7DE, Telephone: 0171 353 1746
E-mail: 2kbw@atlas.co.uk
King's Bench Chambers
115 North Hill, Plymouth PL4 8JY,
Telephone: 01752 221551
Call Date: Nov 1991, Gray's Inn
Qualifications: [LLB (Lond)]

AMLOT ROY DOUGLAS QC (1989)

6 King's Bench Walk
Ground Floor, Temple, London
EC4Y 7DR, Telephone: 0171 583 0410
E-mail: worsley@6kbw.freeserve.co.uk
Call Date: Nov 1963, Lincoln's Inn

AMOR CHRISTOPHER LEWIS

1 Middle Temple Lane
Temple, London EC4Y 1LT,
Telephone: 0171 583 0659 (12 Lines)
E-mail: chambers@1mtl.co.uk
Call Date: May 1984, Gray's Inn
Qualifications: [MA (Oxon)]

AMOS TIMOTHY ROBERT

Queen Elizabeth Building
2nd Floor, Temple, London EC4Y 9BS,
Telephone: 0171 797 7837
Call Date: July 1987, Lincoln's Inn
Pupil Master
Qualifications: [MA (Oxon) Dip Law]

D

ANCLIFFE MRS SHIVA EDWINA

Francis Taylor Building
Ground Floor, Temple, London
EC4Y 7BY, Telephone: 0171 353 7768/
7769/2711
E-mail:clerks@francistaylorbuilding.law.co.uk
Call Date: Nov 1991, Lincoln's Inn
Qualifications: [LLB (Hons)]

ANDENAS DR MADS

Brick Court Chambers
7-8 Essex Street, London WC2R 3LD,
Telephone: 0171 379 3550
E-mail: [surname]@brickcourt.co.uk
Call Date: July 1997, Middle Temple
Qualifications: [PhD (Cantab)]

ANDERS JONATHAN JAMES

Chambers of Helen Grindrod QC
4th Floor, 15-19 Devereux Court, London
WC2R 3JJ, Telephone: 0171 583 2792
Call Date: Feb 1990, Inner Temple
Qualifications: [LLB]

ANDERSON ANTHONY JOHN QC (1982)

2 Mitre Court Buildings
2nd Floor, Temple, London EC4Y 7BX,
Telephone: 0171 583 1380
E-mail: clerks@2mcb.co.uk
Call Date: Feb 1964, Inner Temple
Recorder
Qualifications: [MA (Oxon)]

ANDERSON BRENDAN JOSEPH

1 Dr Johnson's Buildings
Ground Floor, Temple, London
EC4Y 7AX, Telephone: 0171 353 9328
E-mail:OneDr.Johnsons@btinternet.com
Nicholas Street Chambers
22 Nicholas Street, Chester CH1 2NX,
Telephone: 01244 323886
E-mail: clerks@40king.co.uk
Call Date: July 1985, Gray's Inn
Qualifications: [LLB (Leeds)]

ANDERSON CLIVE STUART

4 King's Bench Walk
Ground/First Floor/Basement, Temple,
London EC4Y 7DL,
Telephone: 0171 822 8822
E-mail: 4kbw@barristersatlaw.com
Call Date: Nov 1976, Middle Temple
Pupil Master
Qualifications: [BA (Cantab)]

ANDERSON COLIN JAMES DOUGLAS

St Mary's Chambers
50 High Pavement, Lace Market,
Nottingham NG1 1HW,
Telephone: 0115 9503503
E-mail: clerks@smc.law.co.uk
Call Date: Nov 1973, Gray's Inn
Pupil Master
Qualifications: [MA (Cantab)]

ANDERSON DAVID WILLIAM KINLOCH QC (1999)

Brick Court Chambers
7-8 Essex Street, London WC2R 3LD,
Telephone: 0171 379 3550
E-mail: [surname]@brickcourt.co.uk
Call Date: 1985, Middle Temple
Pupil Master
Qualifications: [MA (Oxon), BA (Cantab)]

ANDERSON DONALD

Pendragon Chambers
124 Walter Road, Swansea, West
Glamorgan, SA1 5RG,
Telephone: 01792 411188
Call Date: July 1969, Inner Temple
Qualifications: [BA (Wales)]

ANDERSON JOHN ADRIAN

18 Red Lion Court
(Off Fleet Street), London EC4A 3EB,
Telephone: 0171 520 6000
E-mail: chambers@18rlc.co.uk
Thornwood House
102 New London Road, Chelmsford,
Essex, CM2 0RG,
Telephone: 01245 280880
E-mail: chambers@18rlc.co.uk
Call Date: July 1989, Middle Temple
Pupil Master

ANDERSON MISS JULIE

Littman Chambers
12 Gray's Inn Square, London WC1R 5JP,
Telephone: 020 7404 4866
E-mail: admin@littmanchambers.com
Call Date: Nov 1993, Gray's Inn
Qualifications: [BA (Hons) (Oxon), Dip Law]

Fax: 0171 404 4812;
Out of hours telephone: 0171 831 0861;
DX: 0055 London, Chancery Lane;
Other comms: E-mail
ja@littmanchambers.com

Other professional qualifications: Appointment to the Treasury Panel of Standing Counsel to the Crown

Types of work: Administrative, Chancery (general), Civil liberties, Commercial, Commercial litigation, Competition, Discrimination, EC and competition law, ECHR, Employment, Environment, Equity, wills and trusts, Insurance, Probate and administration, Tax – capital and income

Awards and memberships: Karmel Scholarship (Gray's Inn), Pegasus Scholarship (Joint Inns), Bar Council Stage Scholarship, Honorary Secretary of the Bar European Group (elected 1994)

Other professional experience: Associate lecturer in Economics at University of Surrey (1991-4); Training with the Legal Service of the EC Commission (February to July 1996)

Languages spoken: French

Publications: *Mellows: Taxation for Executors and Trustees* (Editor), 1994; *Practitioners Handbook on EC Law* (Contributor), 1998; *The Use of Offshore Jurisdictions* (Contributor), 1998; *De Voil: Indirect Tax Intelligence* (Contributor), Monthly Publication; *European Advocate* (Contributor), Quarterly Publication

Reported Cases: *BRS Automotive Ltd v Customs & Excise*, (1998) *The Times*, 4 December; [1998] STC 1210, 1998. A VAT case concerning the application of the Ramsay doctrine and the EC principle of proportionality and specialist UK VAT legislation.
Custom & Excise v Civil Service Motoring Association, [1998] STC 111, CA, 1998. A VAT case concerning taxability of credit card services.

Case C-317/94 Elida Gibbs Ltd v Customs & Excise, [1996] STC 1387, 1996. A VAT case undertaken whilst working with the Legal Service of the EC Commission.
Custom & Excise v British Telecommunications PLC, [1996] STC 818, CA, 1996. A VAT case concerning the taxability of payments made to BT by mistake of its customers.
British Olympic v Winter, [1995] SSCD (Sp C 28), 1995. This concerned the taxability of funds raised by the British Olympic Association.

ANDERSON MS LESLEY JANE

40 King Street
Manchester M2 6BA,
Telephone: 0161 832 9082
E-mail: clerks@40kingstreet.co.uk
The Chambers of Philip Raynor QC
5 Park Place, Leeds LS1 2RU,
Telephone: 0113 242 1123
Call Date: Nov 1989, Middle Temple
Pupil Master
Qualifications: [LLB (Manc)]

ANDERSON MARK ROGER

3 Fountain Court
Steelhouse Lane, Birmingham B4 6DR,
Telephone: 0121 236 5854
Call Date: July 1983, Middle Temple
Pupil Master
Qualifications: [BA (Oxon)]

ANDERSON PETER JOHN

15 Winckley Square
Preston PR1 3JJ,
Telephone: 01772 252828
E-mail:clerks@winckleysq.demon.co.uk
Call Date: July 1988, Inner Temple
Qualifications: [LLB]

ANDERSON ROBERT EDWARD

Blackstone Chambers
Blackstone House, Temple, London
EC4Y 9BW, Telephone: 0171 583 1770
E-mail:clerks@blackstonechambers.com
Call Date: Nov 1986, Middle Temple
Pupil Master
Qualifications: [BA(Cantab)]

ANDERSON RUPERT JOHN

Monckton Chambers
4 Raymond Buildings, Gray's Inn, London
WC1R 5BP, Telephone: 0171 405 7211
E-mail: chambers@monckton.co.uk
Call Date: July 1981, Inner Temple
Qualifications: [MA (Cantab)]

ANDERSON SIMON PETER BEDE

Broadway House Chambers
Broadway House, 9 Bank Street, Bradford,
West Yorkshire, BD1 1TW,
Telephone: 01274 722560
E-mail: clerks@broadwayhouse.co.uk
Broadway House Chambers
31 Park Square West, Leeds LS1 2PF,
Telephone: 0113 246 2600
Call Date: Nov 1997, Lincoln's Inn
Qualifications: [LLB (Hons)(Leeds)]

ANDERSON STANLEY

Broad Chare
33 Broad Chare, Newcastle upon Tyne
NE1 3DQ, Telephone: 0191 232 0541
E-mail:clerks@broadcharechambers.law.co.uk
Call Date: Oct 1993, Lincoln's Inn
Qualifications: [LLB (Hons)(Newc)]

ANDREAE-JONES WILLIAM PEARCE QC (1984)

Coleridge Chambers
Citadel, 190 Corporation Street,
Birmingham B4 6QD,
Telephone: 0121 233 8500
No. 1 Serjeants' Inn
5th Floor Fleet Street, Temple, London
EC4Y 1LH, Telephone: 0171 415 6666
E-mail:no1serjeantsinn@btinternet.com
King's Bench Chambers
Wellington House, 175 Holdenhurst Road,
Bournemouth, Dorset, BH8 8DQ,
Telephone: 01202 250025
E-mail: chambers@kingsbench.co.uk
Call Date: Nov 1965, Inner Temple
Recorder
Qualifications: [BA (Cantab)]

ANDREW MISS ELIZABETH HONORA

Devereux Chambers
Devereux Court, London WC2R 3JJ,
Telephone: 0171 353 7534
E-mail: mailbox@devchambers.co.uk
Call Date: Nov 1974, Middle Temple
Pupil Master, Recorder
Qualifications: [LLB (Lond)]

ANDREW SEAMUS RONALD

Deans Court Chambers
24 St John Street, Manchester M3 4DF,
Telephone: 0161 214 6000
E-mail: clerks@deanscourt.co.uk
Deans Court Chambers
41-43 Market Place, Preston PR1 1AH,
Telephone: 01772 555163
E-mail: clerks@deanscourt.co.uk
Call Date: Feb 1991, Gray's Inn
Qualifications: [LLB (Lond), LLM (Lond)]

ANDREWS MISS CLAIRE MARGUERITE

Gough Square Chambers
6-7 Gough Square, London EC4A 3DE,
Telephone: 0171 353 0924
E-mail: gsc@goughsq.co.uk
Call Date: Nov 1979, Gray's Inn
Pupil Master
Qualifications: [LLB (Manch)]

ANDREWS MISS GERALDINE MARY

Essex Court Chambers
24 Lincoln's Inn Fields, London
WC2A 3ED, Telephone: 0171 813 8000
E-mail:clerksroom@essexcourt-chambers.co.uk
Call Date: Nov 1981, Gray's Inn
Pupil Master
Qualifications: [LLB, LLM, AKC (Lond)]

ANDREWS PETER JOHN QC (1991)

199 Strand
London WC2R 1DR,
Telephone: 0171 379 9779
E-mail: chambers@199strand.co.uk
3 Fountain Court
Steelhouse Lane, Birmingham B4 6DR,
Telephone: 0121 236 5854
Call Date: 1970, Lincoln's Inn
Recorder
Qualifications: [LLB (Bris), D Crim (Cantab)]

Fax: 0171 379 9481;
Out of hours telephone: 01233 756691;
DX: 322 London, Chancery Lane;
Other comms: E-mail
pjandrews@199strand.co.uk

Types of work: Medical negligence, Personal injury

Circuit: Midland & Oxford

Awards and memberships: Professional Negligence Bar Association; Personal Injury Bar Association

Publications: *Catastrophic Injuries: A Practical Guide to Compensation*, 1997; *Quantum of Damages: Kemp & Kemp* (contributor to 'Structured Settlements'), 1998; *Personal Injury Handbook* (contributor), 1997

Reported Cases: *Smoldon v Nolan*, [1997] PIQR P133, 1996. Personal injury – spinally injured rugby player – referee's liability. *Mansfield v Weetabix*, [1997] PIQR P526, 1997. Negligence – hypoglycaemia as defence to negligent driving. *Hill v West Lancashire Health Authority*, [1997] MLR 196, 1997. Medical negligence – cerebral palsy – partial prolonged hypoxia. *Chaplain v Scout Association*, [1997] JPIL 207, 1996. Climbing accident – negligence – new cause of action. *Oksvzoglv v Kay*, [1998] TLR 26 February, 1998. Medical negligence – service of medical report – costs.

ANDREWS PHILIP BRYAN

Young Street Chambers
38 Young Street, Manchester M3 3FT,
Telephone: 0161 833 0489
E-mail: clerks@young-st-chambers.com
Call Date: Feb 1977, Inner Temple
Pupil Master
Qualifications: [LLB (Hons)]

ANDREWS SAMUEL JAMES

15 North Church Street Chambers
15 North Church Street, Sheffield
S1 2DH, Telephone: 0114 2759708/
2738380
Call Date: Nov 1991, Gray's Inn
Qualifications: [LLB (Sheff)]

ANELAY RICHARD ALFRED QC (1993)

One King's Bench Walk
1st Floor, Temple, London EC4Y 7DB,
Telephone: 0171 936 1500
E-mail: ddear@1kbw.co.uk
Call Date: July 1970, Middle Temple
Recorder
Qualifications: [BA (Bristol)]

ANGAMMANA GAMINI BERTRAM

Chambers of Gamini Angammana
'Woodcroft', 13 Woodend, Upper
Norwood, London SE19 3NU,
Telephone: 0181 240 7476
Call Date: Nov 1983, Lincoln's Inn
Qualifications: [LLB (Lond), LLM (Lond)]

ANGUS MISS TRACEY ANNE

5 Stone Buildings
Lincoln's Inn, London WC2A 3XT,
Telephone: 0171 242 6201
E-mail:clerks@5-stonebuildings.law.co.uk
Call Date: Nov 1991, Inner Temple
Pupil Master
Qualifications: [MA (Edin), Dip Law]

ANIM-ADDO PATRICK KWESI

Horizon Chambers
95a Chancery Lane, London WC2A 1DT,
Telephone: 0171 242 2440
Call Date: Nov 1974, Lincoln's Inn
Qualifications: [BA]

ANNING MICHAEL

5 Fountain Court
Steelhouse Lane, Birmingham B4 6DR,
Telephone: 0121 606 0500
E-mail:clerks@5fountaincourt.law.co.uk
Call Date: Nov 1990, Inner Temple
Qualifications: [BA (Dunelm), LLB (Lond)]

ANNING MISS SARA ELIZABETH

Park Lane Chambers
19 Westgate, Leeds LS1 2RD,
Telephone: 0113 2285000
E-mail:clerks@parklanechambers.co.uk
Call Date: Oct 1995, Inner Temple
Qualifications: [BA (Newc), CPE (Huddersfield)]

ANSELL MISS RACHEL LOUISE

4 Pump Court
Temple, London EC4Y 7AN,
Telephone: 020 7842 5555
E-mail:chambers@4pumpcourt.law.co.uk
Call Date: Oct 1995, Middle Temple
Qualifications: [BA (Hons)]

ANTELME ALEXANDER JOHN

One Paper Buildings
Ground Floor, Temple, London
EC4Y 7EP, Telephone: 0171 583 7355
E-mail: clerks@1pb.co.uk
Call Date: Oct 1993, Gray's Inn
Qualifications: [MA (Hons)(Oxon)]

ANTHONY MISS CHRISTINA

Plowden Buildings
2nd Floor, 2 Plowden Buildings, Middle
Temple Lane, London EC4Y 9BU,
Telephone: 0171 583 0808
E-mail: bar@plowdenbuildings.co.uk
Call Date: Nov 1990, Lincoln's Inn
Qualifications: [LLB (Hons)]

ANTHONY PETER FRANCIS

St Ive's Chambers
Whittall Street, Birmingham B4 6DH,
Telephone: 0121 236 0863/5720
E-mail:stives.headofchambers@btinternet.com
Call Date: July 1981, Gray's Inn
Qualifications: [LLB (Hons) (Warw)]

ANTHONY ROBERT JEFFREY BONNELL

Northampton Chambers
22 Albion Place, Northampton NN1 1UD,
Telephone: 01604 636271
Call Date: Nov 1979, Gray's Inn
Qualifications: [LLB (Hons)(Lond)]

ANTROBUS SIMON JAMES

11 King's Bench Walk
1st Floor, Temple, London EC4Y 7EQ,
Telephone: 0171 353 3337
E-mail: fmuller11@aol.com
11 King's Bench Walk
3 Park Court, Park Cross Street, Leeds
LS1 2QH, Telephone: 0113 297 1200
Call Date: Oct 1995, Inner Temple
Qualifications: [LLB (Sheff)]

ANYADIKE-DANES MRS MONYA NNENNA MARY

2 Temple Gardens
Temple, London EC4Y 9AY,
Telephone: 0171 583 6041
E-mail: clerks@2templegardens.co.uk
Call Date: July 1980, Gray's Inn
Qualifications: [BA (Bris) M.Phil, (Cantab)]

APEA JAMES BENJAMIN

Chambers of James Apea
11 Helix Road, London SW2 2JR,
Telephone: 0181 244 5545
Call Date: Nov 1971, Lincoln's Inn
Qualifications: [BA (Hons) (Lond)]

APFEL FREDDY

37 Park Square Chambers
37 Park Square, Leeds LS1 2NY,
Telephone: 0113 2439422
E-mail: chambers@no37.co.uk
Call Date: July 1986, Middle Temple
Pupil Master
Qualifications: [LLB, LLM]

APLIN HOWARD WESTON

The Clove Hitch
High Street, Iron Acton, Bristol
BS37 9UG, Telephone: 01454 228243
Call Date: Nov 1955, Inner Temple
Qualifications: [MA]

APPLEBY MISS ELIZABETH QC (1979)

4-5 Gray's Inn Square
Ground Floor, Gray's Inn, London
WC1R 5JP, Telephone: 0171 404 5252
E-mail:chambers@4-5graysinnsquare.co.uk
Call Date: July 1965, Gray's Inn
Recorder
Qualifications: [LLB (Hons)]

APSION ROBERT GORDON LENNOX O'REILLY

11 Old Square
Ground Floor, Lincoln's Inn, London
WC2A 3TS, Telephone: 0171 242 5022/
405 1074
Call Date: July 1977, Lincoln's Inn
Qualifications: [MBA (Penn)]

APTED STEPHEN PHILIP

Holborn Chambers
6 Gate Street, Lincoln's Inn Fields, London
WC2A 3HP, Telephone: 0171 242 6060
Call Date: Oct 1995, Gray's Inn
Qualifications: [LLB]

APTHORP GEORGE CHARLES

5 Essex Court
1st Floor, Temple, London EC4Y 9AH,
Telephone: 0171 410 2000
E-mail: barristers@5essexcourt.co.uk
Call Date: Feb 1983, Inner Temple
Pupil Master
Qualifications: [BA]

ARCHER MISS DEBORAH ELIZABETH

Colleton Chambers
Colleton Crescent, Exeter, Devon,
EX2 4DG, Telephone: 01392 274898/9
Call Date: Nov 1989, Inner Temple
Qualifications: [LLB]

ARCHER JAMES CHRISTOPHER

**1 Gray's Inn Square, Chambers of the
Baroness Scotland of Asthal QC**
1st Floor, London WC1R 5AG,
Telephone: 0171 405 3000
E-mail: clerks@onegrays.demon.co.uk
Call Date: Nov 1996, Gray's Inn
Qualifications: [LLB (Leeds)]

ARCHER JOHN FRANCIS ASHWEEK QC (1975)

Two Crown Office Row
Ground Floor, Temple, London
EC4Y 7HJ, Telephone: 020 7797 8100
E-mail: mail@2cor.co.uk, or to individual
barristers at: [barrister's
surname]@2cor.co.uk
Call Date: June 1950, Inner Temple
Qualifications: [BA (Oxon)]

ARCHER STEPHEN KENDRAY

2 Temple Gardens
Temple, London EC4Y 9AY,
Telephone: 0171 583 6041
E-mail: clerks@2templegardens.co.uk
Call Date: Nov 1979, Inner Temple
Pupil Master
Qualifications: [MA (Oxon)]

ARCHER OF SANDWELL THE RT HON QC (1971)

29 Bedford Row Chambers
London WC1R 4HE,
Telephone: 0171 831 2626
8 Fountain Court
Steelhouse Lane, Birmingham B4 6DR,
Telephone: 0121 236 5514/5
E-mail: clerks@no8chambers.co.uk
Call Date: Feb 1952, Gray's Inn
Qualifications: [BA, LLM]

ARDEN ANDREW PAUL RUSSEL QC (1991)

Arden Chambers
27 John Street, London WC1N 2BL,
Telephone: 020 7242 4244
E-mail:clerks@arden-chambers.law.co.uk
Call Date: Feb 1974, Gray's Inn
Qualifications: [LLB (Lond)]

ARDEN PETER LEONARD

Enterprise Chambers
9 Old Square, Lincoln's Inn, London
WC2A 3SR, Telephone: 0171 405 9471
E-mail:enterprise.london@dial.pipex.com
Enterprise Chambers
38 Park Square, Leeds LS1 2PA,
Telephone: 0113 246 0391
E-mail:enterprise.leeds@dial.pipex.com
Enterprise Chambers
65 Quayside, Newcastle upon Tyne
NE1 3DS, Telephone: 0191 222 3344
E-mail:enterprise.newcastle@dial.pipex.com
Call Date: July 1983, Gray's Inn
Pupil Master
Qualifications: [LLB (Lond), LLB, (Cantab)]

ARENTSEN ANDREW NICHOLAS

33 Park Place
Cardiff CF1 3BA,
Telephone: 02920 233313
Call Date: Oct 1995, Gray's Inn
Qualifications: [BA (Cantab)]

ARGLES (GUY) ROBERT AINSWORTH

24 Old Buildings
First Floor, Lincoln's Inn, London
WC2A 3UP, Telephone: 020 7242 2744
E-mail: taxchambers@compuserve.com
Call Date: Nov 1965, Middle Temple
Pupil Master
Qualifications: [BA (Oxon)]

D

D

ARGYLE BRIAN JOHN

1 Middle Temple Lane
Temple, London EC4Y 1LT,
Telephone: 0171 583 0659 (12 Lines)
E-mail: chambers@1mtl.co.uk
Call Date: 1972, Gray's Inn
Pupil Master, Recorder

ARGYROPOULOS KYRIAKOS

Hardwicke Building
New Square, Lincoln's Inn, London
WC2A 3SB, Telephone: 020 7242 2523
E-mail: clerks@hardwicke.co.uk
Call Date: Nov 1991, Inner Temple
Qualifications: [BA (York), Dip Law]

ARKHURST REGINALD LEON

4 King's Bench Walk
2nd Floor, Temple, London EC4Y 7DL,
Telephone: 020 7353 3581
E-mail: clerks@4kbw.co.uk
Call Date: July 1984, Middle Temple
Qualifications: [BA (Hons)(Newcastle)]

ARKUSH JONATHAN HARRY SAMUEL

11 Stone Buildings
Lincoln's Inn, London WC2A 3TG,
Telephone: +44 (0)207 831 6381
E-mail:clerks@11StoneBuildings.law.co.uk
Corn Exchange Chambers
5th Floor, Fenwick Street, Liverpool
L2 7QS, Telephone: 0151 227 1081/5009
Call Date: Nov 1977, Middle Temple
Pupil Master
Qualifications: [MA (Oxon)]

ARLIDGE ANTHONY JOHN QC (1981)

18 Red Lion Court
(Off Fleet Street), London EC4A 3EB,
Telephone: 0171 520 6000
E-mail: chambers@18rlc.co.uk
Thornwood House
102 New London Road, Chelmsford,
Essex, CM2 0RG,
Telephone: 01245 280880
E-mail: chambers@18rlc.co.uk
Call Date: Feb 1962, Middle Temple
Recorder
Qualifications: [MA (Cantab)]

ARLOW MS RUTH MARIAN

Pump Court Chambers
Upper Ground Floor, 3 Pump Court,
Temple, London EC4Y 7AJ,
Telephone: 0171 353 0711
E-mail: clerks@3pumpcourt.com
Pump Court Chambers
5 Temple Chambers, Temple Street,
Swindon SN1 1SQ,
Telephone: 01793 539899
E-mail: clerks@3pumpcourt.com
Pump Court Chambers
31 Southgate Street, Winchester
SO23 9EE, Telephone: 01962 868161
E-mail: clerks@3pumpcourt.com
Call Date: 1997, Inner Temple
Qualifications: [BA (Oxon)]

ARMITAGE ERNEST KEITH QC (1994)

8 King Street Chambers
8 King Street, Manchester M2 6AQ,
Telephone: 0161 834 9560
E-mail: eightking@aol.com
Call Date: Nov 1970, Middle Temple
Recorder
Qualifications: [LLB (Hons) (L'pool)]

ARMITAGE MRS LINDY ELIZABETH

Park Lane Chambers
19 Westgate, Leeds LS1 2RD,
Telephone: 0113 2285000
E-mail:clerks@parklanechambers.co.uk
Call Date: July 1985, Lincoln's Inn
Pupil Master, Assistant Recorder
Qualifications: [LLB (Hons)(Leeds)]

ARMOUR MISS ALISON JANE

Warwick House Chambers
8 Warwick Court, Gray's Inn, London
WC1R 5DJ, Telephone: 0171 430 2323
E-mail: cdrewlaw@aol.com
Call Date: July 1979, Lincoln's Inn
Qualifications: [MA (Business Law), BA
(Hons)(Newc)]

ARMSTRONG DEAN PAUL

6 King's Bench Walk
Ground Floor, Temple, London
EC4Y 7DR, Telephone: 0171 583 0410
E-mail: worsley@6kbw.freeserve.co.uk
Call Date: July 1985, Gray's Inn
Pupil Master
Qualifications: [MA (Cantab)]

ARMSTRONG GRANT BRUCE

Dr Johnson's Chambers
Two Dr Johnson's Buildings, Temple,
London EC4Y 7AY,
Telephone: 0171 353 4716
E-mail: clerks@2djb.freeserve.co.uk
Call Date: July 1978, Lincoln's Inn
Qualifications: [LLB (Lond)]

ARMSTRONG KESTER IDRIS SCOBELL

Broad Chare
33 Broad Chare, Newcastle upon Tyne
NE1 3DQ, Telephone: 0191 232 0541
E-mail:clerks@broadcharechambers.law.co.uk
Call Date: Nov 1982, Inner Temple
Pupil Master
Qualifications: [BA (York)]

ARMSTRONG PETER JOHN BOWDEN

Fountain Chambers
Cleveland Business Centre, 1 Watson
Street, Middlesbrough TS1 2RQ,
Telephone: 01642 804040
E-mail:fountainchambers@onyxnet.co.uk
Call Date: Nov 1974, Middle Temple
Pupil Master, Recorder
Qualifications: [MA (Cantab)]

ARMSTRONG STUART DAVID

33 Bedford Row
London WC1R 4JH,
Telephone: 0171 242 6476
E-mail:clerks@bedfordrow33.demon.co.uk
Call Date: Oct 1995, Gray's Inn
Qualifications: [LLM, LLB]

ARNEY JAMES EDWARD

2 Gray's Inn Square Chambers
2nd Floor, Gray's Inn, London WC1R 5AA,
Telephone: 020 7242 0328
E-mail: clerks@2gis.co.uk
Call Date: Oct 1992, Lincoln's Inn
Qualifications: [LLB(Hons)]

ARNFIELD ROBERT JOHN

The Chambers of Leolin Price CBE, QC
10 Old Square, Lincoln's Inn, London
WC2A 3SU, Telephone: 0171 405 0758
Call Date: Oct 1996, Inner Temple
Qualifications: [BA (Oxon), CPE]

ARNHEIM DR MICHAEL THOMAS WALTER

Chambers of Dr Michael Arnheim
101 Queen Alexandra Mansions, Judd
Street, London WC1H 9DP,
Telephone: 0171 833 5093
Call Date: July 1988, Lincoln's Inn
Qualifications: [MA,BA(Witwatersrand), LLB
(Hons) (Lond), PhD (Cantab)]

ARNOLD MARK GRAHAM

3/4 South Square
Gray's Inn, London WC1R 5HP,
Telephone: 0171 696 9900
E-mail: clerks@southsquare.com
Call Date: July 1988, Middle Temple
Qualifications: [MA (Hons) (Cantab)]

ARNOLD PETER MATTHEW MILLER

3 Fountain Court
Steelhouse Lane, Birmingham B4 6DR,
Telephone: 0121 236 5854
Call Date: July 1972, Lincoln's Inn
Pupil Master
Qualifications: [LLB]

ARNOLD RICHARD DAVID

11 South Square
2nd Floor, Gray's Inn, London
WC1R 5EU,
Telephone: 0171 405 1222 (24hr messagin
g service)
E-mail: clerks@11southsquare.com
Call Date: July 1985, Middle Temple
Pupil Master
Qualifications: [MA (Oxon) Dip Law, (PCL)]

D

ARNOLD ROBERT CHARLES

New Court
Temple, London EC4Y 9BE,
Telephone: 0171 583 5123/0510
Call Date: Nov 1974, Middle Temple
Pupil Master
Qualifications: [LLB (Edin) , LLM
(UCL,London), (IMM.PRd.SpR Urrin,
Bonn)]

ARNOT LEE ALEXANDER

22 Old Buildings
Lincoln's Inn, London WC2A 3UJ,
Telephone: 0171 831 0222
Call Date: Oct 1990, Lincoln's Inn
Qualifications: [BA (Cantab)]

ARORA MISS ANITA

**4 Brick Court, Chambers of Anne
Rafferty QC**
1st Floor, Temple, London EC4Y 9AD,
Telephone: 0171 583 8455
Call Date: Oct 1994, Lincoln's Inn
Qualifications: [LLB (Hons)(Coventry)]

ARRAN GRAHAM KENT

1 Middle Temple Lane
Temple, London EC4Y 1LT,
Telephone: 0171 583 0659 (12 Lines)
E-mail: chambers@1mtl.co.uk
Call Date: Nov 1969, Lincoln's Inn
Pupil Master, Recorder
Qualifications: [LLB]

ARTHUR GAVYN FARR

Harcourt Chambers
1st Floor, 2 Harcourt Buildings, Temple,
London EC4Y 9DB,
Telephone: 0171 353 6961
E-mail:clerks@harcourtchambers.law.co.uk
Harcourt Chambers
Churchill House, 3 St Aldate's Courtyard,
St Aldate's, Oxford OX1 1BN,
Telephone: 01865 791559
E-mail:clerks@harcourtchambers.law.co.uk
Call Date: Nov 1975, Middle Temple
Pupil Master
Qualifications: [MA (Oxon), Jurisprudence]

ASCHERSON MISS ISOBEL RUTH

23 Essex Street
London WC2R 3AS,
Telephone: 0171 413 0353/836 8366
E-mail:clerks@essexstreet23.demon.co.uk
Call Date: Feb 1991, Gray's Inn
Qualifications: [LLB (Lond)]

ASCROFT RICHARD GEOFFREY

Queens Square Chambers
56 Queens Square, Bristol BS1 4PR,
Telephone: 0117 921 1966
Call Date: Nov 1995, Lincoln's Inn
Qualifications: [LLB (Hons)(New, Zealand),
BCL (Oxon)]

ASH BRIAN MAXWELL QC (1990)

4-5 Gray's Inn Square
Ground Floor, Gray's Inn, London
WC1R 5JP, Telephone: 0171 404 5252
E-mail:chambers@4-5graysinnsquare.co.uk
Call Date: Nov 1975, Gray's Inn
Qualifications: [BA (Oxon)]

ASH EDWARD WILLIAM

3 Temple Gardens
3rd Floor, Temple, London EC4Y 9AU,
Telephone: 0171 353 0832
Call Date: Oct 1993, Middle Temple
Qualifications: [BA (Hons, B'ham), MA
(Cantab)]

ASHBY DAVID GLYNN

1 Middle Temple Lane
Temple, London EC4Y 1LT,
Telephone: 0171 583 0659 (12 Lines)
E-mail: chambers@1mtl.co.uk
Call Date: July 1963, Gray's Inn
Pupil Master
Qualifications: [LLB]

ASHCROFT MICHAEL JAMES

20 Essex Street
London WC2R 3AL,
Telephone: 0171 583 9294
E-mail: clerks@20essexst.com
Call Date: Mar 1997, Gray's Inn
Qualifications: [BA, BCL (Ocon)]

ASHE THOMAS MICHAEL QC (1994)

9 Stone Buildings
Lincoln's Inn, London WC2A 3NN,
Telephone: 0171 404 5055
E-mail: clerks@9stoneb.law.co.uk
Westgate Chambers
144 High Street, Lewes, East Sussex,
BN7 1XT, Telephone: 01273 480510
Call Date: July 1971, Middle Temple
Assistant Recorder

ASHER MS VICTORIA JUDITH MYERS

Warwick Square
London SW1V 2AJ,
Telephone: 0171 630 6237
Call Date: June 1958, Gray's Inn
Qualifications: [BA (Cantab)]

ASHFIELD EVAN MORGAN

169 Temple Chambers
Temple Avenue, London EC4Y 0DA,
Telephone: 0171 583 7644
Call Date: July 1980, Lincoln's Inn
Pupil Master
Qualifications: [LLB (Lond)]

ASHFORD-THOM IAN

1 Temple Gardens
1st Floor, Temple, London EC4Y 9BB,
Telephone: 0171 583 1315/353 0407
E-mail: clerks@1templegardens.co.uk
Call Date: July 1977, Gray's Inn
Pupil Master
Qualifications: [LL.B (Exeter)]

ASHLEY MARK ROBERT

Pump Court Chambers
5 Temple Chambers, Temple Street,
Swindon SN1 1SQ,
Telephone: 01793 539899
E-mail: clerks@3pumpcourt.com
Pump Court Chambers
Upper Ground Floor, 3 Pump Court,
Temple, London EC4Y 7AJ,
Telephone: 0171 353 0711
E-mail: clerks@3pumpcourt.com
Pump Court Chambers
31 Southgate Street, Winchester
SO23 9EE, Telephone: 01962 868161
E-mail: clerks@3pumpcourt.com
Call Date: Nov 1993, Lincoln's Inn
Qualifications: [LLB (Hons)]

ASHLEY-NORMAN JONATHAN CHARLES

3 Hare Court
1 Little Essex Street, London WC2R 3LD,
Telephone: 0171 395 2000
Call Date: July 1989, Middle Temple
Qualifications: [LLB (Exon)]

ASHMAN PETER MICHAEL

Colleton Chambers
Colleton Crescent, Exeter, Devon,
EX2 4DG, Telephone: 01392 274898/9
Call Date: July 1985, Inner Temple
Qualifications: [LLB (Exon), LLM (Inter
Business, Legal Studies),]

ASHMOLE TIMOTHY MICHAEL

4 King's Bench Walk
2nd Floor, Temple, London EC4Y 7DL,
Telephone: 020 7353 3581
E-mail: clerks@4kbw.co.uk
Call Date: Oct 1992, Inner Temple
Qualifications: [LLB (E.Ang)]

ASHMORE (TERENCE) GODFREY

**7 Stone Buildings (also at 11 Bolt
Court)**
1st Floor, Lincoln's Inn, London
WC2A 3SZ, Telephone: 0171 242 0961
E-mail:larthur@7stonebuildings.law.co.uk
**11 Bolt Court (also at 7 Stone Buildings
– 1st Floor)**
London EC4A 3DQ,
Telephone: 0171 353 2300
E-mail: boltct11@aol.com
Redhill Chambers
Seloduct House, 30 Station Road, Redhill,
Surrey, RH1 1NF,
Telephone: 01737 780781
Call Date: Nov 1961, Gray's Inn

ASHTON ARTHUR HENRY

One Raymond Buildings
Gray's Inn, London WC1R 5BH,
Telephone: 0171 430 1234
E-mail: chambers@ipbar1rb.com;
clerks@ipbar1rb.com
Call Date: July 1988, Inner Temple
Qualifications: [BA, LLB (Rhodes)]

D

ASHTON DAVID SAMBROOK

13 King's Bench Walk
1st Floor, Temple, London EC4Y 7EN,
Telephone: 0171 353 7204
E-mail: clerks@13kbw.law.co.uk
King's Bench Chambers
32 Beaumont Street, Oxford OX1 2NP,
Telephone: 01865 311066
E-mail: clerks@kbc-oxford.law.co.uk
Call Date: July 1962, Gray's Inn
Pupil Master
Qualifications: [MA (Oxon)]

ASHTON RAGLAN HALLEY

New Court Chambers
Gazette Building, 168 Corporation Street,
Birmingham B4 6TZ,
Telephone: 0121 693 6656
Call Date: Oct 1994, Lincoln's Inn
Qualifications: [LLB (Hons)(Lond)]

ASHURST STEPHEN JOHN

Fountain Chambers
Cleveland Business Centre, 1 Watson
Street, Middlesbrough TS1 2RQ,
Telephone: 01642 804040
E-mail:fountainchambers@onyxnet.co.uk
Call Date: July 1979, Inner Temple
Pupil Master, Assistant Recorder
Qualifications: [LLB (Newc)]

ASHWELL PAUL MARTYN

Sussex Chambers
9 Old Steine, Brighton, Sussex, BN1 1FJ,
Telephone: 01273 607953
Call Date: July 1977, Inner Temple
Pupil Master
Qualifications: [BA]

ASHWORTH MISS FIONA KATHERINE ANNE

40 King Street
Manchester M2 6BA,
Telephone: 0161 832 9082
E-mail: clerks@40kingstreet.co.uk
The Chambers of Philip Raynor QC
5 Park Place, Leeds LS1 2RU,
Telephone: 0113 242 1123
Call Date: July 1988, Lincoln's Inn
Pupil Master
Qualifications: [LLB (Hons)(Leeds)]

ASHWORTH LANCE DOMINIC PIERS

St Philip's Chambers
Fountain Court, Steelhouse Lane,
Birmingham B4 6DR,
Telephone: 0121 246 7000
E-mail: clerks@st-philips.co.uk
2 Harcourt Buildings
Ground Floor/Left, Temple, London
EC4Y 9DB, Telephone: 0171 583 9020
E-mail: clerks@harcourt.co.uk
Call Date: Nov 1987, Middle Temple
Pupil Master
Qualifications: [MA (Cantab)]

ASHWORTH PIERS QC (1973)

2 Harcourt Buildings
Ground Floor/Left, Temple, London
EC4Y 9DB, Telephone: 0171 583 9020
E-mail: clerks@harcourt.co.uk
Call Date: Feb 1956, Middle Temple
Recorder
Qualifications: [MA (Cantab)]

ASHWORTH WILLIAM RUPERT EVERARD

1 Paper Buildings
1st Floor, Temple, London EC4Y 7EP,
Telephone: 0171 353 3728/4953
Call Date: Nov 1996, Inner Temple
Qualifications: [BA (Cantab)]

ASIF MOHAMMED JALIL AHKTER

Chambers of John L Powell QC
Four New Square, Lincoln's Inn, London
WC2A 3RJ, Telephone: 0171 797 8000
E-mail: barristers@4newsquare.com
Call Date: Nov 1988, Lincoln's Inn
Pupil Master
Qualifications: [MA (Cantab)]

ASKEY ROBERT JOHN

19 Castle Street Chambers
Liverpool L2 4SX,
Telephone: 0151 236 9402
E-mail: DBrei16454@aol.com
Call Date: 1998, Lincoln's Inn
Qualifications: [LLB (Hons)(Wales)]

ASKHAM NIGEL HEAL

South Western Chambers
Melville House, 12 Middle Street,
Taunton, Somerset, TA1 1SH,
Telephone: 01823 331919 (24 hrs)
E-mail: barclerk@clara.net
Call Date: Feb 1973, Inner Temple
Pupil Master
Qualifications: [LLB]

ASKINS NICHOLAS PETER

Broadway House Chambers
Broadway House, 9 Bank Street, Bradford,
West Yorkshire, BD1 1TW,
Telephone: 01274 722560
E-mail: clerks@broadwayhouse.co.uk
Broadway House Chambers
31 Park Square West, Leeds LS1 2PF,
Telephone: 0113 246 2600
Call Date: Nov 1989, Gray's Inn
Qualifications: [LLB [Lond]]

ASLAM MS FARZANA ANN

1 Crown Office Row
3rd Floor, Temple, London EC4Y 7HH,
Telephone: 0171 583 9292
E-mail: onecor@link.org
Call Date: Oct 1993, Middle Temple
Qualifications: [LLB (Hons), BCL]

ASLAM QAZI MAHMUD

Staple Inn Chambers
1st Floor, 9 Staple Inn, Holborn Bars,
London WC1V 7QH,
Telephone: 0171 242 5240
E-mail: clerks@staple-inn.org
Call Date: Nov 1983, Gray's Inn
Pupil Master
Qualifications: [BA (Hons) (Leics)]

ASLANGUL MICHEL JOSEPH LEON

Britton Street Chambers
1st Floor, 20 Britton Street, London
EC1M 5NQ, Telephone: 0171 608 3765
Abbey Chambers
PO Box 47, 47 Ashurst Drive, Shepperton,
Middlesex, TW17 0LD,
Telephone: 01932 560913
Call Date: Nov 1978, Middle Temple
Qualifications: [MA (Business Law) , BA
(Hons)]

ASLETT PEPIN CHARLES MAGUIRE

Northampton Chambers
22 Albion Place, Northampton NN1 1UD,
Telephone: 01604 636271
Call Date: Nov 1996, Lincoln's Inn
Qualifications: [LLB (Hons)(Bucks)]

ASPDEN GORDON JAMES

Chambers of Michael Pert QC
36 Bedford Row, London WC1R 4JH,
Telephone: 0171 421 8000
E-mail: 36bedfordrow@link.org
Chambers of Michael Pert QC
24 Albion Place, Northampton NN1 1UD,
Telephone: 01604 602333
Chambers of Michael Pert QC
104 New Walk, Leicester LE1 7EA,
Telephone: 0116 249 2020
Call Date: Nov 1988, Gray's Inn
Qualifications: [LLB (Hull)]

ASPINALL JOHN MICHAEL
QC (1995)

3 Paper Buildings
Temple, London EC4Y 7EU,
Telephone: 020 7583 8055
E-mail: London@3paper.com
3 Paper Buildings (Bournemouth)
20 Lorne Park Road, Bournemouth,
Dorset, BH1 1JN,
Telephone: 01202 292102
E-mail: Bournemouth@3paper.com
3 Paper Buildings (Oxford)
1 Alfred Street, High Street, Oxford
OX1 4EH, Telephone: 01865 793736
E-mail: oxford@3paper.com
3 Paper Buildings (Winchester)
4 St Peter Street, Winchester SO23 8BW,
Telephone: 01962 868884
E-mail: winchester@3paper.com
Call Date: Nov 1971, Inner Temple
Qualifications: [LLB]

ASPLIN PATRICK CHRISTOPHER

St John's Chambers
Small Street, Bristol BS1 1DW,
Telephone: 0117 9213456/298514
E-mail: @stjohnschambers.co.uk
Call Date: Mar 1997, Lincoln's Inn
Qualifications: [BA (Hons)(Keele), LLM
(Cantab)]

D

ASPLIN MISS SARAH JANE

3 Stone Buildings
Lincoln's Inn, London WC2A 3XL,
Telephone: 0171 242 4937
E-mail: clerks@3sb.law.co.uk
Call Date: July 1984, Gray's Inn
Pupil Master
Qualifications: [MA(Cantab),BCL(Oxon)]

Fax: 0171 405 3896;
Out of hours telephone: 0171 242 4937;
DX: 317 London

Types of work: Chancery (general), Chancery land law, Charities, Equity, wills and trusts, Partnerships, Pensions, Probate and administration, Professional negligence

Awards and memberships: Association Pension Lawyers; Chancery Bar Association; Revenue Bar Association; Association of Women Barristers

Reported Cases: *Imperial Group Pension Trust Ltd v Imperial Tobacco Ltd*, [1991] 1 WLR 589, 1990. Major pensions case concerning duties of principal employer.
British Coal Corp v British Coal Staff Superannuation Scheme Ltd, [1994] OPLR 51, 1993. Major pensions case concerning use of surplus and return of monies to company.
Hillsdown Holdings Plc v Pensions Ombudsman, [1996] PLR 427, 1996. Major pensions case concerning merger of schemes and return of surplus to company.

Principal Areas of Practice
Pensions litigation, advice and drafting, acts for principal employers, trustees, liquidators and receivers and beneficiaries on questions arising in relation to surplus, construction of rules, winding up, merger, general administration and misappropriation of assets from pension schemes. Also advises actuaries and pensions administrators in relation to professional negligence claims and in relation to all aspects of complaints to and appeals from the Pensions Ombudsman.

ASPREY NICHOLAS

Serle Court Chambers
6 New Square, Lincoln's Inn, London
WC2A 3QS, Telephone: 0171 242 6105
E-mail: clerks@serlecourt.co.uk
Call Date: July 1969, Inner Temple
Pupil Master
Qualifications: [LLB (Edin)]

ASTANIOTIS MISS KATERINE MARGARET

2-3 Gray's Inn Square
Gray's Inn, London WC1R 5JH,
Telephone: 0171 242 4986
E-mail:chambers@2-3graysinnsquare.co.uk
Call Date: July 1985, Gray's Inn
Qualifications: [LLB (Bristol)]

ASTBURY MRS JOANNE

Park Lane Chambers
19 Westgate, Leeds LS1 2RD,
Telephone: 0113 2285000
E-mail:clerks@parklanechambers.co.uk
Call Date: July 1989, Lincoln's Inn
Qualifications: [LLB (Nott'm)]

ASTERIS PETER DAVID

Eighteen Carlton Crescent
Southampton SO15 2XR,
Telephone: 01703 639001
Call Date: Oct 1996, Lincoln's Inn
Qualifications: [LLB (Hons)(Leic)]

ASTILL MISS KATHERINE MARY

Falcon Chambers
Falcon Court, London EC4Y 1AA,
Telephone: 0171 353 2484
E-mail: clerks@falcon-chambers.com
Call Date: 1998, Middle Temple
Qualifications: [BA (Hons)(Oxon), M.Phil (Cantab), CPE (City)]

ASTON MAURICE CHARLES

Five Paper Buildings
1st Floor, Five Paper Bldgs, Temple,
London EC4Y 7HB,
Telephone: 0171 583 6117
E-mail:clerks@5-paperbuildings.law.co.uk
Call Date: July 1982, Inner Temple
Pupil Master
Qualifications: [LLB (Soton)]

ASTOR PHILIP DOUGLAS PAUL

1 Temple Gardens
1st Floor, Temple, London EC4Y 9BB,
Telephone: 0171 583 1315/353 0407
E-mail: clerks@1templegardens.co.uk
Call Date: Nov 1989, Inner Temple
Qualifications: [MA (Oxon), Dip Law (City)]

ATCHLEY RICHARD WALDEGRAVE

3 Raymond Buildings
Gray's Inn, London WC1R 5BH,
Telephone: 020 7831 3833
E-mail:chambers@threeraymond.demon.co.uk
Call Date: Nov 1977, Middle Temple
Pupil Master

ATHERTON IAN DAVID

Enterprise Chambers
9 Old Square, Lincoln's Inn, London
WC2A 3SR, Telephone: 0171 405 9471
E-mail:enterprise.london@dial.pipex.com
Enterprise Chambers
65 Quayside, Newcastle upon Tyne
NE1 3DS, Telephone: 0191 222 3344
E-mail:enterprise.newcastle@dial.pipex.com
Enterprise Chambers
38 Park Square, Leeds LS1 2PA,
Telephone: 0113 246 0391
E-mail:enterprise.leeds@dial.pipex.com
Call Date: July 1988, Inner Temple
Pupil Master
Qualifications: [BSc LLB , ARICS, ACIArb]

ATHERTON PETER

Deans Court Chambers
24 St John Street, Manchester M3 4DF,
Telephone: 0161 214 6000
E-mail: clerks@deanscourt.co.uk
Deans Court Chambers
41-43 Market Place, Preston PR1 1AH,
Telephone: 01772 555163
E-mail: clerks@deanscourt.co.uk
Call Date: July 1975, Gray's Inn
Recorder
Qualifications: [LLB (Hons) (B'ham)]

ATHERTON ROBERT KENNETH

India Buildings Chambers
Water Street, Liverpool L2 0XG,
Telephone: 0151 243 6000
E-mail: clerks@chambers.u-net.com
Call Date: July 1970, Gray's Inn
Pupil Master, Recorder
Qualifications: [LLB]

ATHERTON MISS SALLY

Bridewell Chambers
2 Bridewell Place, London EC4V 6AP,
Telephone: 020 7797 8800
E-mail:HughesGage@bridewell.law.co.uk
Call Date: July 1987, Middle Temple
Pupil Master
Qualifications: [LLB (Man)]

ATHERTON STEPHEN NICHOLAS

3/4 South Square
Gray's Inn, London WC1R 5HP,
Telephone: 0171 696 9900
E-mail: clerks@southsquare.com
Call Date: July 1989, Middle Temple
Qualifications: [LLB (Lancs), LLM (Cantab)]

ATHERTON-HAM JAMES WEST

Newport Chambers
12 Clytha Park Road, Newport, Gwent,
NP9 47L, Telephone: 01633 267403/
255855
Call Date: Oct 1994, Lincoln's Inn
Qualifications: [LLB (Hons)(Glamorg)]

ATKINS CHARLES EDWARD SPENCER

29 Bedford Row Chambers
London WC1R 4HE,
Telephone: 0171 831 2626
Call Date: July 1975, Inner Temple
Qualifications: [MA (Cantab)]

ATKINS RICHARD PAUL

1 Fountain Court
Steelhouse Lane, Birmingham B4 6DR,
Telephone: 0121 236 5721
Call Date: July 1989, Gray's Inn
Qualifications: [MA (Oxon)]

ATKINS WILLIAM SIWARD

7 Stone Buildings
Ground Floor, Lincoln's Inn, London
WC2A 3SZ, Telephone: 0171 405 3886/
242 3546 E-mail: chaldous@vossnet.co.uk
Call Date: Oct 1995, Inner Temple
Qualifications: [MA (Edinburgh), CPE (City)]

ATKINSON MISS CAROL LESLEY

Queen Elizabeth Building
Ground Floor, Temple, London
EC4Y 9BS,
Telephone: 0171 353 7181 (12 Lines)
Call Date: July 1985, Gray's Inn
Pupil Master
Qualifications: [LLB (Lancaster)]

ATKINSON MISS ELIZABETH JAYNE

New Court Chambers
3 Broad Chare, Newcastle upon Tyne
NE1 3DQ, Telephone: 0191 232 1980
Call Date: Oct 1994, Lincoln's Inn
Qualifications: [LLB (Hons)(Leeds), BCL]

ATKINSON MISS JODIE SIAN

Assize Court Chambers
14 Small Street, Bristol BS1 1DE,
Telephone: 0117 9264587
E-mail:chambers@assize-court-chambers.co.uk
Call Date: 1996, Inner Temple
Qualifications: [LLB (Lond), LLM (Lond)]

ATKINSON NICHOLAS JEREMY QC (1991)

2 Harcourt Buildings
1st Floor, Temple, London EC4Y 9DB,
Telephone: 020 7353 2112
Call Date: Nov 1971, Inner Temple
Recorder

ATKINSON PAUL CHRISTOPHER

New Walk Chambers
27 New Walk, Leicester LE1 6TE,
Telephone: 0116 2559144
Call Date: July 1978, Lincoln's Inn
Pupil Master
Qualifications: [MA (Oxon)]

ATKINSON RICHARD DUNCAN

6 King's Bench Walk
Ground Floor, Temple, London
EC4Y 7DR, Telephone: 0171 583 0410
E-mail: worsley@6kbw.freeserve.co.uk
Call Date: Oct 1995, Gray's Inn
Qualifications: [LLB (Bris)]

ATKINSON TIMOTHY GEORGE BRYANT

1 Brick Court
1st Floor, Temple, London EC4Y 9BY,
Telephone: 0171 353 8845
E-mail: clerks@1brickcourt.co.uk
Call Date: July 1988, Inner Temple
Qualifications: [BA (Oxon), Dip Law (City)]

ATREYA MS NAVITA

1 Pump Court
Lower Ground Floor, Temple, London
EC4Y 7AB, Telephone: 0171 583 2012/
353 4341
E-mail: [name]@1pumpcourt.co.uk
Call Date: Oct 1994, Lincoln's Inn
Qualifications: [BSc (Hons)(Lond)]

ATTRIDGE STEVEN JEFFREY

1 Gray's Inn Square
Ground Floor, London WC1R 5AA,
Telephone: 0171 405 8946/7/8
Call Date: Nov 1991, Inner Temple
Qualifications: [LLB]

ATTWOOD JOHN JULIAN

6 Fountain Court
Steelhouse Lane, Birmingham B4 6DR,
Telephone: 0121 233 3282
E-mail: clerks@sixfountain.co.uk
Call Date: Nov 1989, Gray's Inn
Pupil Master
Qualifications: [LLB (B'ham)]

ATTWOOLL CHRISTOPHER BENJAMIN

11 King's Bench Walk
1st Floor, Temple, London EC4Y 7EQ,
Telephone: 0171 353 3337
E-mail: fmuller11@aol.com

11 King's Bench Walk
3 Park Court, Park Cross Street, Leeds
LS1 2QH, Telephone: 0113 297 1200
Call Date: July 1980, Middle Temple
Pupil Master
Qualifications: [BA (Keele)]

ATUNWA RAZAK OLATUNDE

Britton Street Chambers
1st Floor, 20 Britton Street, London
EC1M 5NQ, Telephone: 0171 608 3765
Call Date: Oct 1994, Inner Temple
Qualifications: [LLB (Lond), LLM (Lond)]

ATWILL JOHN WILLIAM OWEN

Portsmouth Barristers' Chambers
Victory House, 7 Bellevue Terrace,
Portsmouth, Hampshire, PO5 3AT,
Telephone: 023 92 831292/811811
E-mail: clerks@portsmouthbar.com
Call Date: 1997, Inner Temple
Qualifications: [LLB (Herts)]

AUBREY DAVID JOHN MORGAN QC (1996)

32 Park Place
Cardiff CF1 3BA,
Telephone: 01222 397364
Goldsmith Building
1st Floor, Temple, London EC4Y 7BL,
Telephone: 0171 353 7881
E-mail:clerks@goldsmith-building.law.co.uk
Call Date: July 1976, Middle Temple
Recorder
Qualifications: [LLB (Hons) (Wales)]

AUBREY DAVID STUART QC (1998)

Corn Exchange Chambers
5th Floor, Fenwick Street, Liverpool
L2 7QS, Telephone: 0151 227 1081/5009
Call Date: July 1974, Gray's Inn
Recorder
Qualifications: [LLB (Hons)]

AUCKLAND MISS ELIZABETH RACHEL

30 Park Square
Leeds LS1 2PF, Telephone: 0113 2436388
E-mail: clerks@30parksquare.co.uk
Call Date: Oct 1995, Lincoln's Inn
Qualifications: [MA (Cantab)]

AUDLAND WILLIAM GRANT

12 King's Bench Walk
Temple, London EC4Y 7EL,
Telephone: 0171 583 0811
E-mail: chambers@12kbw.co.uk
Call Date: Nov 1992, Gray's Inn
Qualifications: [BA (Hons)(Oxon), Dip Law]

AULD MISS CATHERINE ROHAN

Harcourt Chambers
1st Floor, 2 Harcourt Buildings, Temple,
London EC4Y 9DB,
Telephone: 0171 353 6961
E-mail:clerks@harcourtchambers.law.co.uk
Harcourt Chambers
Churchill House, 3 St Aldate's Courtyard,
St Aldate's, Oxford OX1 1BN,
Telephone: 01865 791559
E-mail:clerks@harcourtchambers.law.co.uk
Call Date: 1992, Gray's Inn
Qualifications: [MA (Hons)(Cantab)]

AULD CHARLES JOHN DENHAM

St John's Chambers
Small Street, Bristol BS1 1DW,
Telephone: 0117 9213456/298514
E-mail: @stjohnschambers.co.uk
Call Date: July 1980, Middle Temple
Pupil Master
Qualifications: [BA (Dunelm)]

AULD STEPHEN ROBERT QC (1999)

One Essex Court
Ground Floor, Temple, London
EC4Y 9AR, Telephone: 020 7583 2000
E-mail: clerks@oneessexcourt.co.uk
Call Date: 1979, Gray's Inn
Pupil Master
Qualifications: [BA (Cantab)]

AUSTIN JONATHAN EDWARD NEWNS

30 Park Place
Cardiff CF1 3BA,
Telephone: 01222 398421
E-mail: 100757.1456@compuserve.com
Call Date: Oct 1991, Middle Temple
Qualifications: [BA (Hons), LLB (Hons)]

AUSTIN-SMITH MICHAEL GERARD QC (1990)

23 Essex Street
London WC2R 3AS,
Telephone: 0171 413 0353/836 8366
E-mail:clerks@essexstreet23.demon.co.uk
Call Date: July 1969, Inner Temple
Recorder
Qualifications: [LLB (Exeter)]

AUSTINS CHRISTOPHER JOHN

Assize Court Chambers
14 Small Street, Bristol BS1 1DE,
Telephone: 0117 9264587
E-mail:chambers@assize-court-chambers.co.uk
Call Date: July 1988, Gray's Inn
Qualifications: [LLB (Hons)]

AUTY MICHAEL ROY

High Pavement Chambers
1 High Pavement, Nottingham NG1 1HF,
Telephone: 0115 9418218
Call Date: Nov 1990, Inner Temple
Qualifications: [BA]

AXON ANDREW ELIOT

Park Lane Chambers
19 Westgate, Leeds LS1 2RD,
Telephone: 0113 2285000
E-mail:clerks@parklanechambers.co.uk
Call Date: Oct 1992, Middle Temple
Qualifications: [BA (Hons)]

AYERS GUY RUSSELL

Octagon House
19 Colegate, Norwich NR3 1AT,
Telephone: 01603 623186
E-mail: admin@octagon-chambers.co.uk
1 Paper Buildings
1st Floor, Temple, London EC4Y 7EP,
Telephone: 0171 353 3728/4953
Call Date: July 1979, Inner Temple
Pupil Master
Qualifications: [LLB (Soton)]

AYLEN WALTER STAFFORD QC (1983)

Hardwicke Building
New Square, Lincoln's Inn, London
WC2A 3SB, Telephone: 020 7242 2523
E-mail: clerks@hardwicke.co.uk
Call Date: Feb 1962, Middle Temple
Recorder
Qualifications: [MA, BCL, ACIArb]

AYLETT CRISPIN DAVID WILLIAM

3 Raymond Buildings
Gray's Inn, London WC1R 5BH,
Telephone: 020 7831 3833
E-mail:chambers@threeraymond.demon.co.uk
Call Date: July 1985, Inner Temple
Pupil Master
Qualifications: [BA (Hons)(Bris), Dip Law]

AYLETT KENNETH GEORGE

New Chambers
3 Sadleir Road, St Albans, Herts, AL1 2BL,
Telephone: 0966 212126
Call Date: July 1972, Inner Temple
Qualifications: [BA,BL]

AYLIFFE JAMES JUSTIN BARNETT

Wilberforce Chambers
8 New Square, Lincoln's Inn, London
WC2A 3QP, Telephone: 0171 306 0102
E-mail: chambers@wilberforce.co.uk
Call Date: Nov 1987, Lincoln's Inn
Pupil Master
Qualifications: [BA (Oxon), Dip Law (City)]

Types of work: Asset finance, Banking, Chancery (general), Chancery land law, Commercial litigation, Commercial property, Company and commercial, Financial services, Insolvency, Landlord and tenant, Professional negligence

AYLING MISS TRACY JANE

Farrar's Building
Temple, London EC4Y 7BD,
Telephone: 0171 583 9241
E-mail:chambers@farrarsbuilding.co.uk
Call Date: July 1983, Inner Temple
Pupil Master
Qualifications: [BA (Hons) (Dunelm)]

AYLOTT COLIN CHRISTOPHER

Thomas More Chambers
52 Carey Street, Lincoln's Inn, London
WC2A 2JB, Telephone: 0171 404 7000
E-mail: clerks@thomasmore.law.co.uk
Call Date: Nov 1989, Inner Temple
Qualifications: [LLB (B'ham)]

AYLWIN CHRISTOPHER GRANVILLE ANGUS

3 Paper Buildings
Ground Floor, Temple, London
EC4Y 7EU, Telephone: 0171 797 7000
E-mail: clerks@3pb.co.uk
3 Paper Buildings
Temple, London EC4Y 7EU,
Telephone: 020 7583 8055
E-mail: London@3paper.com
3 Paper Buildings (Winchester)
4 St Peter Street, Winchester SO23 8BW,
Telephone: 01962 868884
E-mail: winchester@3paper.com
3 Paper Buildings (Oxford)
1 Alfred Street, High Street, Oxford
OX1 4EH, Telephone: 01865 793736
E-mail: oxford@3paper.com
3 Paper Buildings (Bournemouth)
20 Lorne Park Road, Bournemouth,
Dorset, BH1 1JN,
Telephone: 01202 292102
E-mail: Bournemouth@3paper.com
Call Date: Nov 1970, Inner Temple
Pupil Master
Qualifications: [MA (Cantab)]

AYRES ANDREW JOHN WILLIAM

13 Old Square
Ground Floor, Lincoln's Inn, London
WC2A 3UA, Telephone: 0171 404 4800
E-mail: clerks@13oldsquare.law.co.uk
Call Date: Oct 1996, Gray's Inn
Qualifications: [MA (Oxon)]

AYUB MISS SALIHA

Holborn Chambers
6 Gate Street, Lincoln's Inn Fields, London
WC2A 3HP, Telephone: 0171 242 6060
Call Date: Nov 1992, Lincoln's Inn

AZAM JAVAID

Plowden Buildings
2nd Floor, 2 Plowden Buildings, Middle
Temple Lane, London EC4Y 9BU,
Telephone: 0171 583 0808
E-mail: bar@plowdenbuildings.co.uk
Call Date: 1981, Gray's Inn
Pupil Master
Qualifications: [BA (Hons)]

AZHAR ALI MOHAMMAD

The Chambers of Mr Ali Mohammed Azhar
Basement, 9 King's Bench Walk, Temple,
London EC4Y 7DX,
Telephone: 0171 353 9564
E-mail: jvlee@btinternet.com
Call Date: July 1962, Gray's Inn
Pupil Master
Qualifications: [MA]

AZHAR MISS SHABEENA

The Chambers of Mr Ali Mohammed Azhar
Basement, 9 King's Bench Walk, Temple,
London EC4Y 7DX,
Telephone: 0171 353 9564
E-mail: jvlee@btinternet.com
Call Date: Nov 1995, Inner Temple
Qualifications: [BA, CPE (Sussex)]

AZIM MISS TABSUM REHNA

22 Old Buildings
Lincoln's Inn, London WC2A 3UJ,
Telephone: 0171 831 0222
Call Date: July 1984, Middle Temple
Qualifications: [LLB]

BAATZ NICHOLAS STEPHEN QC (1998)

Atkin Chambers
1 Atkin Building, Gray's Inn, London
WC1R 5AT, Telephone: 020 7404 0102
E-mail: clerks@atkin-chambers.co.uk
Call Date: Nov 1978, Gray's Inn
Qualifications: [MA, BCL (Oxon)]

BABAJIDE IBUKUNOLU ALAO OLATOKUNBO O

Albany Chambers
91 Kentish Town Road, London
NW1 8NY, Telephone: 0171 485 5736/
5758 E-mail: albany91.freeserve.co.uk
Call Date: July 1990, Lincoln's Inn
Qualifications: [LLB (Ife), LLM (Ife)]

BACH WILLIAM STEPHEN

65-67 King Street
Leicester LE1 6RP,
Telephone: 0116 2547710
9 Bedford Row
London WC1R 4AZ,
Telephone: 0171 242 3555
E-mail: clerks@9br.co.uk
Call Date: 1972, Middle Temple
Pupil Master
Qualifications: [BA (Oxon)]

BACK PATRICK QC (1970)

10 King's Bench Walk
Ground Floor, Temple, London
EC4Y 7EB, Telephone: 0171 353 7742
E-mail: 10kbw@lineone.net
Call Date: Jan 1940, Gray's Inn
Recorder
Qualifications: [BA (Cantab)]

BACKHOUSE ROGER BAINBRIDGE QC (1984)

1 Middle Temple Lane
Temple, London EC4Y 1LT,
Telephone: 0171 583 0659 (12 Lines)
E-mail: chambers@1mtl.co.uk
Lloyds House Chambers
3rd Floor, 18 Lloyds House, Lloyd Street,
Manchester M2 5WA,
Telephone: 0161 839 3371
Call Date: July 1965, Middle Temple
Qualifications: [MA (Cantab)]

BACON FRANCIS MICHAEL

4 Paper Buildings
Ground Floor, Temple, London
EC4Y 7EX, Telephone: 0171 353 3366/
583 7155
E-mail: clerks@4paperbuildings.com
Call Date: July 1988, Gray's Inn
Pupil Master
Qualifications: [BA (Keele), MSc
(Loughborough)]

BACON JEFFREY DAVID

Littleton Chambers
3 King's Bench Walk North, Temple,
London EC4Y 7HR,
Telephone: 0171 797 8600
E-mail:clerks@littletonchambers.co.uk
Call Date: Nov 1989, Middle Temple
Qualifications: [BA Hons (Sussex), Dip EEC
(Brussels)]

BACON JONATHAN FRANCIS

Call Date: July 1989, Inner Temple
Qualifications: [LLB,BCL (Oxon)]

BACON NICHOLAS MICHAEL

1 Temple Gardens
1st Floor, Temple, London EC4Y 9BB,
Telephone: 0171 583 1315/353 0407
E-mail: clerks@1templegardens.co.uk
Call Date: Oct 1992, Inner Temple
Qualifications: [LLB (Essex)(Hons)]

BADENOCH (IAN) JAMES FORSTER QC (1989)

1 Crown Office Row
Ground Floor, Temple, London
EC4Y 7HH, Telephone: 0171 797 7500
E-mail: mail@onecrownofficerow.com
Crown Office Row Chambers
Blenheim House, 120 Church Street,
Brighton, Sussex, BN1 1WH,
Telephone: 01273 625625
E-mail: crownofficerow@clara.net
Call Date: Nov 1968, Lincoln's Inn
Recorder
Qualifications: [MA (Oxon)]

BADENOCH TONY DAVID

**7 Stone Buildings (also at 11 Bolt
Court)**
1st Floor, Lincoln's Inn, London
WC2A 3SZ, Telephone: 0171 242 0961
E-mail:larthur@7stonebuildings.law.co.uk
**11 Bolt Court (also at 7 Stone Buildings
– 1st Floor)**
London EC4A 3DQ,
Telephone: 0171 353 2300
E-mail: boltct11@aol.com

Redhill Chambers
Seloduct House, 30 Station Road, Redhill,
Surrey, RH1 1NF,
Telephone: 01737 780781
Call Date: Nov 1996, Middle Temple
Qualifications: [BSc (Hons), Dip Law]

BADLEY MISS PAMELA HILARY

25-27 Castle Street
1st Floor, Liverpool L2 4TA,
Telephone: 0151 227 5661/051 236 5072
Call Date: Nov 1974, Lincoln's Inn
Pupil Master, Recorder
Qualifications: [LLB (Warw), LLM]

BAGCHI ANDREW KUMAR

One Garden Court Family Law Chambers
Ground Floor, Temple, London
EC4Y 9BJ, Telephone: 0171 797 7900
E-mail: clerks@onegardencourt.co.uk
Call Date: July 1989, Middle Temple
Qualifications: [LLB (Lond)]

BAGLEY MICHAEL WALLACE WELSBY

Chavasse Court Chambers
2nd Floor, Chavasse Court, 24 Lord Street,
Liverpool L2 1TA,
Telephone: 0151 707 1191
Call Date: Nov 1984, Gray's Inn
Qualifications: [BSc (Bristol)]

BAGNALL MATTHEW PHILIP COOPER

Chambers of Geoffrey Hawker
46/48 Essex Street, London WC2R 3GH,
Telephone: 0171 583 8899
Call Date: Oct 1993, Middle Temple
Qualifications: [LLB (Hons)]

BAGOT CHARLES RICHARD MILO

Hardwicke Building
New Square, Lincoln's Inn, London
WC2A 3SB, Telephone: 020 7242 2523
E-mail: clerks@hardwicke.co.uk
Call Date: 1997, Inner Temple
Qualifications: [LLB (Leicester)]

BAGRAL MISS RAVINDER

Warwick House Chambers
8 Warwick Court, Gray's Inn, London
WC1R 5DJ, Telephone: 0171 430 2323
E-mail: cdrewlaw@aol.com
Call Date: Oct 1996, Inner Temple
Qualifications: [BA (Keele)]

BAILEY ANDREW

Paradise Chambers
26 Paradise Square, Sheffield S1 2DE,
Telephone: 0114 2738951
E-mail: timbooth@paradise-sq.co.uk
Call Date: Oct 1997, Lincoln's Inn
Qualifications: [LLB (Hons)]

BAILEY ANTHONY REGINALD

2 King's Bench Walk
Ground Floor, Temple, London
EC4Y 7DE, Telephone: 0171 353 1746
E-mail: 2kbw@atlas.co.uk
King's Bench Chambers
115 North Hill, Plymouth PL4 8JY,
Telephone: 01752 221551
Call Date: Nov 1972, Inner Temple
Pupil Master

BAILEY CHARLES ANDREW STUART

Trinity Chambers
140 New London Road, Chelmsford,
Essex, CM2 0AW,
Telephone: 01245 605040
E-mail:clerks@trinitychambers.law.co.uk
Call Date: Oct 1993, Lincoln's Inn
Qualifications: [BA (Hons), LLB (Lond)]

BAILEY DAVID JOHN

S Tomlinson QC
7 King's Bench Walk, Temple, London
EC4Y 7DS, Telephone: 0171 583 0404
E-mail: clerks@7kbw.law.co.uk
Call Date: July 1989, Gray's Inn
Pupil Master
Qualifications: [BA (Oxon), LLM (UCLA)]

BAILEY EDWARD GRENFELL

2 King's Bench Walk
Ground Floor, Temple, London
EC4Y 7DE, Telephone: 0171 353 1746
E-mail: 2kbw@atlas.co.uk

King's Bench Chambers
115 North Hill, Plymouth PL4 8JY,
Telephone: 01752 221551
Call Date: July 1990, Gray's Inn
Qualifications: [MA (Edin) , Dip Law (City)]

BAILEY EDWARD HENRY

Monckton Chambers
4 Raymond Buildings, Gray's Inn, London
WC1R 5BP, Telephone: 0171 405 7211
E-mail: chambers@monckton.co.uk
Call Date: Nov 1970, Middle Temple
Pupil Master, Recorder
Qualifications: [MA, LLB (Cantab)]

BAILEY MRS ELIZABETH

Devon Chambers
3 St Andrew Street, Plymouth PL1 2AH,
Telephone: 01752 661659
E-mail: devonchambers.co.uk.
Call Date: Oct 1995, Middle Temple
Qualifications: [LLB (Hons)]

BAILEY GRAHAM ROBERT

Manchester House Chambers
18-22 Bridge Street, Manchester M3 3BZ,
Telephone: 0161 834 7007
8 King Street Chambers
8 King Street, Manchester M2 6AQ,
Telephone: 0161 834 9560
E-mail: eightking@aol.com
Call Date: Feb 1993, Inner Temple
Qualifications: [LLB (Brunel) (Hons)]

BAILEY JOHN CHARLES WILLIAMS

Queen's Chambers
5 John Dalton Street, Manchester M2 6ET,
Telephone: 0161 834 6875/4738
Queens Chambers
4 Camden Place, Preston PR1 3JL,
Telephone: 01772 828300
Call Date: Nov 1966, Gray's Inn
Pupil Master
Qualifications: [MA (Oxon)]

BAILEY MICHAEL ROBERT

Plowden Buildings
2nd Floor, 2 Plowden Buildings, Middle
Temple Lane, London EC4Y 9BU,
Telephone: 0171 583 0808
E-mail: bar@plowdenbuildings.co.uk
Call Date: Nov 1986, Gray's Inn
Pupil Master
Qualifications: [BA (Essex), LLM]

BAILEY MISS PATRICIA LUCY

New Bailey Chambers
10 Lawson Street, Preston PR1 2QT,
Telephone: 01772 258087
Call Date: Nov 1969, Middle Temple
Pupil Master
Qualifications: [LLB, Dip Adv Stud Econ]

BAILEY ROBIN HOWARD STOLLERY

Clock Chambers
78 Darlington Street, Wolverhampton
WV1 4LY, Telephone: 01902 313444
Call Date: July 1984, Gray's Inn
Qualifications: [LLB (Hons)(Leics)]

BAILEY MISS ROSANA HENRIETTA

10 King's Bench Walk
Ground Floor, Temple, London
EC4Y 7EB, Telephone: 0171 353 7742
E-mail: 10kbw@lineone.net
Chambers of Martin Burr
Fourth Floor, Eldon Chambers, 30/32
Fleet Street, London EC4Y 1AA,
Telephone: 0171 353 4636
Call Date: Oct 1994, Gray's Inn
Qualifications: [LLB]

BAILEY RUSSELL STUART

3 Paper Buildings
Temple, London EC4Y 7EU,
Telephone: 020 7583 8055
E-mail: London@3paper.com
3 Paper Buildings (Bournemouth)
20 Lorne Park Road, Bournemouth,
Dorset, BH1 1JN,
Telephone: 01202 292102
E-mail: Bournemouth@3paper.com
3 Paper Buildings (Winchester)
4 St Peter Street, Winchester SO23 8BW,
Telephone: 01962 868884
E-mail: winchester@3paper.com

3 Paper Buildings (Oxford)
1 Alfred Street, High Street, Oxford
OX1 4EH, Telephone: 01865 793736
E-mail: oxford@3paper.com
Call Date: Nov 1985, Inner Temple
Pupil Master
Qualifications: [LLB (Lond)]

BAILEY STEPHEN JOHN

Lion Court
Chancery House, 53-64 Chancery Lane,
London WC2A 1SJ,
Telephone: 0171 404 6565
Call Date: July 1991, Gray's Inn
Qualifications: [LLB]

BAILEY STEVEN WILLIAM

3 Fountain Court
Steelhouse Lane, Birmingham B4 6DR,
Telephone: 0121 236 5854
Call Date: Oct 1992, Middle Temple
Qualifications: [BA (Hons Oxford), M.Phil
(Cambridge)]

BAILEY THOMAS IAIN

Bracton Chambers
95a Chancery Lane, London WC2A 1DT,
Telephone: 0171 242 4248
Call Date: July 1984, Gray's Inn
Qualifications: [BA (Oxon)]

BAILEY-KING ROBERT WYNTER

4 Breams Buildings
London EC4A 1AQ,
Telephone: 0171 353 5835/430 1221
E-mail:breams@4breamsbuildings.law.co.uk
Call Date: July 1975, Inner Temple
Pupil Master
Qualifications: [MA (Cantab)]

BAILIN ALEXANDER

Five Paper Buildings
1st Floor, Five Paper Bldgs, Temple,
London EC4Y 7HB,
Telephone: 0171 583 6117
E-mail:clerks@5-paperbuildings.law.co.uk
Call Date: Nov 1995, Lincoln's Inn
Qualifications: [MA (Hons)]

BAILLIE ANDREW BRUCE

9 Gough Square
London EC4A 3DE,
Telephone: 020 7832 0500
E-mail: clerks@9goughsq.co.uk
Call Date: Nov 1970, Inner Temple
Recorder
Qualifications: [BA]

BAIN GILES DAVID

New Court
Temple, London EC4Y 9BE,
Telephone: 0171 583 5123/0510
Call Date: Nov 1993, Lincoln's Inn
Qualifications: [LLB (Hons, Hull)]

BAINBRIDGE MISS LAURA ALEXANDRA

2 Pump Court
1st Floor, Temple, London EC4Y 7AH,
Telephone: 0171 353 5597
Call Date: Nov 1997, Middle Temple
Qualifications: [BA (Hons)]

BAIRD JAMES STEVENSON

Bank House Chambers
Old Bank House, Hartshead, Sheffield
S1 2EL, Telephone: 0114 2751223
Call Date: Nov 1977, Middle Temple
Pupil Master
Qualifications: [LLB]

BAIRD MRS VERA

14 Tooks Court
Cursitor St, London EC4A 1LB,
Telephone: 0171 405 8828
E-mail: clerks@tooks.law.co.uk
Call Date: Nov 1975, Gray's Inn
Pupil Master
Qualifications: [BA, LLB, LARTPI]

BAISDEN HOWARD RALPH

Cobden House Chambers
19 Quay Street, Manchester M3 3HN,
Telephone: 0161 833 6000
E-mail: clerks@cobden.co.uk
Call Date: July 1972, Middle Temple
Pupil Master
Qualifications: [LLM]

BAJWA ALI NASEEM

Plowden Buildings
2nd Floor, 2 Plowden Buildings, Middle
Temple Lane, London EC4Y 9BU,
Telephone: 0171 583 0808
E-mail: bar@plowdenbuildings.co.uk
Call Date: Nov 1993, Gray's Inn
Qualifications: [LLB]

BAKER ANDREW JAMES

7 New Square
Lincoln's Inn, London WC2A 3QS,
Telephone: 0171 430 1660
Richmond Green Chambers
Greyhound House, 23-24 George Street,
Richmond-upon-Thames, Surrey,
TW9 1HY, Telephone: 0181 940 1841
E-mail: ptaylor256@aol.com
5 Fountain Court
Steelhouse Lane, Birmingham B4 6DR,
Telephone: 0121 606 0500
E-mail:clerks@5fountaincourt.law.co.uk
Call Date: Oct 1990, Middle Temple
Qualifications: [BSc, Dip Law (City),
MRPharmS]

BAKER ANDREW WILLIAM

20 Essex Street
London WC2R 3AL,
Telephone: 0171 583 9294
E-mail: clerks@20essexst.com
Call Date: July 1988, Lincoln's Inn
Pupil Master
Qualifications: [BA (Hons) (Oxon), Dip Law
(City)]

BAKER MISS ANNE JACQUELINE

Enterprise Chambers
9 Old Square, Lincoln's Inn, London
WC2A 3SR, Telephone: 0171 405 9471
E-mail:enterprise.london@dial.pipex.com
Enterprise Chambers
38 Park Square, Leeds LS1 2PA,
Telephone: 0113 246 0391
E-mail:enterprise.leeds@dial.pipex.com
Enterprise Chambers
65 Quayside, Newcastle upon Tyne
NE1 3DS, Telephone: 0191 222 3344
E-mail:enterprise.newcastle@dial.pipex.com
Call Date: Nov 1985, Gray's Inn
Pupil Master
Qualifications: [BA (Oxon)]

BAKER MRS CAROLINE FRANCES

5 Fountain Court
Steelhouse Lane, Birmingham B4 6DR,
Telephone: 0121 606 0500
E-mail:clerks@5fountaincourt.law.co.uk
Call Date: July 1988, Gray's Inn
Qualifications: [BSc (Lancaster), MA
(Bristol)]

BAKER CHRISTOPHER FRANCIS JOHN

Arden Chambers
27 John Street, London WC1N 2BL,
Telephone: 020 7242 4244
E-mail:clerks@arden-chambers.law.co.uk
Call Date: July 1984, Middle Temple
Pupil Master
Qualifications: [MA (Cantab), LLM (Lond)]

BAKER CHRISTOPHER MICHAEL

Baker Street Chambers
9 Baker Street, Middlesbrough TS1 2LF,
Telephone: 01642 873873
Call Date: Oct 1994, Middle Temple
Qualifications: [LLB (Hons)(Manc)]

BAKER CLIVE ADRIAN

Corn Exchange Chambers
5th Floor, Fenwick Street, Liverpool
L2 7QS, Telephone: 0151 227 1081/5009
Call Date: Oct 1995, Gray's Inn
Qualifications: [LLB]

BAKER MS FAY ELIZABETH

2 Paper Buildings, Basement North
Temple, London EC4Y 7ET,
Telephone: 0171 936 2613
E-mail: post@2paper.co.uk
Call Date: Nov 1994, Gray's Inn
Qualifications: [BSc.Econ]

BAKER HAROLD WILLIAM

30 Park Place
Cardiff CF1 3BA,
Telephone: 01222 398421
E-mail: 100757.1456@compuserve.com
Call Date: Nov 1992, Middle Temple
Qualifications: [LLB (Hons)]

D

BAKER JEREMY RUSSELL QC (1999)

Paradise Chambers
26 Paradise Square, Sheffield S1 2DE,
Telephone: 0114 2738951
E-mail: timbooth@paradise-sq.co.uk
Call Date: 1979, Middle Temple
Pupil Master, Assistant Recorder
Qualifications: [LLB (Hull)]

BAKER JONATHAN LESLIE

Harcourt Chambers
1st Floor, 2 Harcourt Buildings, Temple,
London EC4Y 9DB,
Telephone: 0171 353 6961
E-mail:clerks@harcourtchambers.law.co.uk
Harcourt Chambers
Churchill House, 3 St Aldate's Courtyard,
St Aldate's, Oxford OX1 1BN,
Telephone: 01865 791559
E-mail:clerks@harcourtchambers.law.co.uk
Call Date: July 1978, Middle Temple
Pupil Master, Assistant Recorder
Qualifications: [MA (Cantab)]

BAKER MISS MAUREEN ANNE

9 Bedford Row
London WC1R 4AZ,
Telephone: 0171 242 3555
E-mail: clerks@9br.co.uk
Call Date: July 1984, Gray's Inn
Pupil Master
Qualifications: [BA]

BAKER MICHAEL JAMES BARRINGTON

4 Brick Court
Ground Floor, Temple, London
EC4Y 9AD, Telephone: 0171 797 7766
E-mail: chambers@4brick.co.uk
Call Date: Nov 1990, Gray's Inn
Qualifications: [BA (Cantab)]

BAKER NICHOLAS MICHAEL BRIDGMAN

Hardwicke Building
New Square, Lincoln's Inn, London
WC2A 3SB, Telephone: 020 7242 2523
E-mail: clerks@hardwicke.co.uk
Call Date: July 1980, Gray's Inn
Pupil Master
Qualifications: [BA (Oxon)]

BAKER NIGEL ROBERT JAMES QC (1988)

9 Bedford Row
London WC1R 4AZ,
Telephone: 0171 242 3555
E-mail: clerks@9br.co.uk
Call Date: Nov 1969, Middle Temple
Recorder
Qualifications: [BA (Soton), LLM, (Cantab)]

BAKER PHILIP WOOLF

Gray's Inn Tax Chambers
3rd Floor, Gray's Inn Chambers, Gray's
Inn, London WC1R 5JA,
Telephone: 0171 242 2642
E-mail: clerks@taxbar.com
Call Date: July 1979, Gray's Inn
Pupil Master
Qualifications: [MA (Cantab), BCL (Oxon),
LLM (Lond) PhD, MBA]

BAKER MS RACHEL MARY THERESA

Hardwicke Building
New Square, Lincoln's Inn, London
WC2A 3SB, Telephone: 020 7242 2523
E-mail: clerks@hardwicke.co.uk
Call Date: Nov 1990, Gray's Inn
Qualifications: [BSc (Lond)]

BAKER ROBERT EDWARD NICOLAS

2 King's Bench Walk Chambers
1st Floor, 2 King's Bench Walk, Temple,
London EC4Y 7DE,
Telephone: 020 7353 9276
E-mail: chambers@2kbw.co.uk
Call Date: Nov 1977, Middle Temple
Pupil Master

BAKER MR STEPHEN MARK

9 Bedford Row
London WC1R 4AZ,
Telephone: 0171 242 3555
E-mail: clerks@9br.co.uk
Call Date: July 1989, Middle Temple
Qualifications: [LLB (Manch), LLM (Cantab)]

BAKER STUART CHRISTOPHER

1 Fountain Court
Steelhouse Lane, Birmingham B4 6DR,
Telephone: 0121 236 5721
Call Date: Oct 1995, Middle Temple
Qualifications: [LLB (Hons) (Manch)]

BAKER WILLIAM ARTHUR

Peel Court Chambers
45 Hardman Street, Manchester M3 3PL,
Telephone: 0161 832 3791
E-mail: clerks@peelct.co.uk
Call Date: Oct 1991, Middle Temple
Qualifications: [LLB Hons (Lancaster)]

BAKER WILLIAM DAVID

1 Inner Temple Lane
Temple, London EC4Y 1AF,
Telephone: 020 7353 0933
Call Date: Oct 1992, Inner Temple
Qualifications: [LLB]

BALANCY JACQUES ALEX VIVIAN

John Street Chambers
2 John Street, London WC1N 2HJ,
Telephone: 0171 242 1911
E-mail:john.street_chambers@virgin.net
Call Date: 1992, Inner Temple
Qualifications: [LLB (Lond), MBA]

BALCHIN RICHARD ALEXANDER

Crown Office Row Chambers
Blenheim House, 120 Church Street,
Brighton, Sussex, BN1 1WH,
Telephone: 01273 625625
E-mail: crownofficerow@clara.net
Call Date: 1997, Inner Temple
Qualifications: [BA (Sussex), CPE]

BALCOMBE DAVID JULIAN

1 Crown Office Row
Ground Floor, Temple, London
EC4Y 7HH, Telephone: 0171 797 7500
E-mail: mail@onecrownofficerow.com
Crown Office Row Chambers
Blenheim House, 120 Church Street,
Brighton, Sussex, BN1 1WH,
Telephone: 01273 625625
E-mail: crownofficerow@clara.net
Call Date: Nov 1980, Lincoln's Inn
Qualifications: [BA (Kent)]

BALDOCK NICHOLAS JOHN

6 Pump Court
1st Floor, Temple, London EC4Y 7AR,
Telephone: 0171 797 8400
E-mail: clerks@6pumpcourt.co.uk

6-8 Mill Street
Maidstone, Kent, ME15 6XH,
Telephone: 01622 688094
E-mail: annexe@6pumpcourt.co.uk
Call Date: Nov 1983, Lincoln's Inn
Pupil Master
Qualifications: [MA (Cantab)]

BALDOCK MISS SUSAN ANNE

2 Gray's Inn Square Chambers
2nd Floor, Gray's Inn, London WC1R 5AA,
Telephone: 020 7242 0328
E-mail: clerks@2gis.co.uk
Call Date: July 1988, Lincoln's Inn
Qualifications: [BA (Hons) (Sussex), Dip Law (city)]

BALDRY ANTONY BRIAN

No. 1 Serjeants' Inn
5th Floor Fleet Street, Temple, London
EC4Y 1LH, Telephone: 0171 415 6666
E-mail:no1serjeantsinn@btinternet.com
Call Date: Nov 1975, Middle Temple
Qualifications: [BA, LLB (Sussex)]

BALDRY RUPERT PATRICK CRAIG

Pump Court Tax Chambers
16 Bedford Row, London WC1R 4EB,
Telephone: 0171 414 8080
Call Date: Feb 1987, Middle Temple
Qualifications: [BA (Lond) Dip Law, (City)]

BALDWIN JOHN GRANT

Oriel Chambers
14 Water Street, Liverpool L2 8TD,
Telephone: 0151 236 7191/236 4321
E-mail: clerks@oriel-chambers.co.uk
Call Date: Oct 1990, Gray's Inn
Qualifications: [MA (Cantab)]

BALDWIN JOHN PAUL QC (1991)

8 New Square
Lincoln's Inn, London WC2A 3QP,
Telephone: 0171 405 4321
E-mail: clerks@8newsquare.co.uk
Call Date: July 1977, Gray's Inn
Qualifications: [BSc, DPhil (Oxon)]

BALDWIN ROGER MILES

15 Winckley Square
Preston PR1 3JJ,
Telephone: 01772 252828
E-mail:clerks@winckleysq.demon.co.uk
Call Date: July 1969, Gray's Inn
Qualifications: [LLB]

BALL MISS ALISON QC (1995)

One Garden Court Family Law Chambers
Ground Floor, Temple, London
EC4Y 9BJ, Telephone: 0171 797 7900
E-mail: clerks@onegardencourt.co.uk
*Call Date: Nov 1972, Middle Temple
Recorder*
Qualifications: [LLB (Lond)]

BALL CHRISTOPHER GEOFFREY QC (1993)

18 Red Lion Court
(Off Fleet Street), London EC4A 3EB,
Telephone: 0171 520 6000
E-mail: chambers@18rlc.co.uk
Thornwood House
102 New London Road, Chelmsford,
Essex, CM2 0RG,
Telephone: 01245 280880
E-mail: chambers@18rlc.co.uk
*Call Date: July 1972, Middle Temple
Recorder*
Qualifications: [LLB]

BALL STEVEN

11 Old Square
Ground Floor, Lincoln's Inn, London
WC2A 3TS, Telephone: 0171 242 5022/
405 1074
Call Date: Oct 1995, Inner Temple
Qualifications: [BSc (Reading), LLB (Herts)]

BALL STEVEN JAMES

Call Date: Oct 1996, Inner Temple
Qualifications: [LLB (Hull)]

BALLANTINE DYKES THOMAS LAMPLUGH

Solent Chambers
2nd Floor, Coronation House, 1 King's
Terrace, Portsmouth, Hampshire,
PO5 3AR, Telephone: 01705 821818
Call Date: Oct 1991, Middle Temple
Qualifications: [BSc (Elect Eng), Dip Law,
Cert Ed]

BALLANTYNE PROFESSOR WILLIAM MORRIS

One Hare Court
1st Floor, Temple, London EC4Y 7BE,
Telephone: 020 7353 3171
E-mail:admin-oneharecourt@btinternet.com
Call Date: Nov 1977, Inner Temple
Qualifications: [MA (Cantab)]

BALLENTYNE ERROL STANLEY

High Pavement Chambers
1 High Pavement, Nottingham NG1 1HF,
Telephone: 0115 9418218
Call Date: Nov 1983, Gray's Inn
Qualifications: [BA]

BALOGH CHRISTOPHER THOMAS

Arden Chambers
27 John Street, London WC1N 2BL,
Telephone: 020 7242 4244
E-mail:clerks@arden-chambers.law.co.uk
Call Date: Nov 1984, Middle Temple
Qualifications: [MA (Cantab), MSc (Econ),
Dip in, Law]

BALTAIAN MISS ANNA ALICE

Mercury Chambers
Mercury House, 33-35 Clarendon Road,
Leeds LS2 9NZ,
Telephone: 0113 234 2265
E-mail:cdexter@mercurychambers.co.uk
Call Date: Feb 1995, Gray's Inn
Qualifications: [BA (Newcastle)]

BALYSZ MARK ALEXANDER

Holborn Chambers
6 Gate Street, Lincoln's Inn Fields, London
WC2A 3HP, Telephone: 0171 242 6060
Call Date: Nov 1995, Gray's Inn
Qualifications: [LLB]

BAMFORD CHRISTOPHER DAVID

Francis Taylor Building
3rd Floor, Temple, London EC4Y 7BY,
Telephone: 0171 797 7250
Call Date: Nov 1987, Inner Temple
Pupil Master
Qualifications: [LLB (Hons)(Hull)]

BAMFORD JEREMY RICHARD

Guildhall Chambers
22-26 Broad Street, Bristol BS1 2HG,
Telephone: 0117 9273366
E-mail:civil.clerks@guildhallchambers.co.uk and
criminal.clerks@guildhallchambers.co.uk
Call Date: Nov 1989, Lincoln's Inn
Qualifications: [BA (Oxon)]

BAMFORD RONALD GLEN

Guildford Chambers
Stoke House, Leapale Lane, Guildford,
Surrey, GU1 4LY,
Telephone: 01483 539131
E-mail:guildford.barristers@btinternet.com
Call Date: Nov 1972, Lincoln's Inn

BANCROFT MISS ANNA LOUISE

Deans Court Chambers
24 St John Street, Manchester M3 4DF,
Telephone: 0161 214 6000
E-mail: clerks@deanscourt.co.uk
Deans Court Chambers
41-43 Market Place, Preston PR1 1AH,
Telephone: 01772 555163
E-mail: clerks@deanscourt.co.uk
Call Date: July 1985, Inner Temple
Qualifications: [MA (Oxon)]

BANERJEE BALADEB

Chancery Chambers
1st Floor Offices, 70/72 Chancery Lane,
London WC2A 1AB,
Telephone: 0171 405 6879/6870
Call Date: July 1970, Middle Temple
Pupil Master
Qualifications: [MA, LLB]

BANGAY MISS DEBORAH JOANNA JANET

29 Bedford Row Chambers
London WC1R 4HE,
Telephone: 0171 831 2626
Call Date: Feb 1981, Gray's Inn
Pupil Master
Qualifications: [LLB (Exon)]

BANKOLE-JONES MISS GWENDOLINE NASIA

9 King's Bench Walk
Ground Floor, Temple, London
EC4Y 7DX, Telephone: 0171 353 7202/
3909 E-mail: 9kbw@compuserve.com
Call Date: Nov 1991, Middle Temple
Qualifications: [LLB Hons (Essex)]

BANKS FRANCIS ANDREW

Adrian Lyon's Chambers
14 Castle Street, Liverpool L2 0NE,
Telephone: 0151 236 4421/8240
E-mail: chambers14@aol.com
Call Date: July 1995, Gray's Inn
Qualifications: [BA]

BANKS MISS RACHAEL EDA

Adrian Lyon's Chambers
14 Castle Street, Liverpool L2 0NE,
Telephone: 0151 236 4421/8240
E-mail: chambers14@aol.com
Call Date: Nov 1993, Inner Temple
Qualifications: [LLB (Manch)]

BANKS ROBERT JAMES

100e Great Portland Street
London W1N 5PD,
Telephone: 0171 636 6323
Call Date: July 1978, Inner Temple
Pupil Master
Qualifications: [BSc (Econ) Hons]

BANKS RODERICK CHARLES I'ANSON

48 Bedford Row
London WC1R 4LR,
Telephone: 0171 430 2005
Call Date: July 1974, Lincoln's Inn
Qualifications: [LLB]

Fax: 0171 831 4885;
Out of hours telephone: 0181 857 5418;
DX: 284 London

Types of work: Limited partnerships, Partnerships

Publications: *Lindley on Partnership*, 14th edn (Co-editor), 1979; *Lindley on Partnership*, 15th edn (Co-editor), 1984; *Lindley and Banks on Partnership*, 16th edn, 1990; *Lindley & Banks on Partnership*, 17th edn, 1995; *Encyclopedia of Professional Partnerships*, 1987

Practice
Specialises exclusively in partnership law, dealing primarily with problems affecting solicitors' partnerships and other professional firms (including doctors practising within the NHS). He has extensive experience in cases involving expulsions and compulsory retirements, 'lock-ins' and 'extractions', dissolutions, garden leave provisions and restrictive covenants. He has drafted numerous partnership agreements and related documentation and is frequently asked to devise novel solutions to specific problems. He also has a particular expertise in the field of limited partnerships and in the structuring of business ventures so as to avoid partnership status. He was closely involved in the development of the new form of limited liability partnership recently introduced into Jersey law. He is known for his 'hands on' approach to partnership disputes, yet advocates a subtle and, where possible, preventative approach in the embryonic stages. He has spoken at numerous seminars and conferences and written widely on partnership-related subjects, as well as appearing in training videos for Legal Network TV. He is a founder member of the Association of Partnership Practitioners, an Hon Associate of the British Veterinary Association and a Fellow of the Institute of Continuing Professional Development. He is also acting as a consultant to the Law Commission on its review of partnership law.

BANKS TIMOTHY JAMES

Hardwicke Building
New Square, Lincoln's Inn, London WC2A 3SB, Telephone: 020 7242 2523
E-mail: clerks@hardwicke.co.uk
Call Date: Nov 1983, Inner Temple
Pupil Master
Qualifications: [BA]

BANNER GREGORY STUART

13 Old Square
Ground Floor, Lincoln's Inn, London WC2A 3UA, Telephone: 0171 404 4800
E-mail: clerks@13oldsquare.law.co.uk
Call Date: July 1989, Gray's Inn
Pupil Master
Qualifications: [MA (Cantab)]

BANNISTER EDWARD ALEXANDER QC (1991)

3 Stone Buildings
Lincoln's Inn, London WC2A 3XL, Telephone: 0171 242 4937
E-mail: clerks@3sb.law.co.uk
Call Date: July 1974, Lincoln's Inn
Qualifications: [BA (Oxon)]

BANNISTER THOMAS EDWARD JOHN

7 Stone Buildings
Ground Floor, Lincoln's Inn, London WC2A 3SZ, Telephone: 0171 405 3886/ 242 3546 E-mail: chaldous@vossnet.co.uk
Call Date: Nov 1993, Middle Temple
Qualifications: [BA (Hons)(Oxon), CPE]

BARAV DR AMIHUD

4-5 Gray's Inn Square
Ground Floor, Gray's Inn, London WC1R 5JP, Telephone: 0171 404 5252
E-mail:chambers@4-5graysinnsquare.co.uk
Call Date: Oct 1993, Gray's Inn
Qualifications: [MSc (Econ), LLM (Lond)]

BARBER MISS ABIGALE CATHERINE

2 Pump Court
1st Floor, Temple, London EC4Y 7AH, Telephone: 0171 353 5597
Call Date: 1997, Gray's Inn
Qualifications: [LLB (Bris), LLM (LSE)]

D

BARBER MISS SALLY

11 Stone Buildings
Lincoln's Inn, London WC2A 3TG,
Telephone: +44 (0)207 831 6381
E-mail:clerks@11StoneBuildings.law.co.uk
Call Date: July 1988, Lincoln's Inn
Qualifications: [BA (Hons) (Cantab)]

BARBER STUART CECIL

12 New Square
Lincoln's Inn, London WC2A 3SW,
Telephone: 0171 419 1212
E-mail: chambers@12newsquare.co.uk
Sovereign Chambers
25 Park Square, Leeds LS1 2PW,
Telephone: 0113 2451841/2/3
E-mail:sovereignchambers@btinternet.com
Call Date: July 1979, Middle Temple
Qualifications: [FCIS]

BARCA MANUEL DAVID

1 Brick Court
1st Floor, Temple, London EC4Y 9BY,
Telephone: 0171 353 8845
E-mail: clerks@1brickcourt.co.uk
Call Date: Nov 1986, Lincoln's Inn
Qualifications: [MA (Cantab)]

BARD NICHOLAS JAMES

Devereux Chambers
Devereux Court, London WC2R 3JJ,
Telephone: 0171 353 7534
E-mail: mailbox@devchambers.co.uk
Call Date: July 1979, Gray's Inn
Pupil Master
Qualifications: [MA (Oxon)]

BARDA ROBIN JOHN BLACKMORE

4 Paper Buildings
1st Floor, Temple, London EC4Y 7EX,
Telephone: 0171 583 0816/353 1131
E-mail: clerks@4paperbuildings.co.uk
Call Date: July 1975, Gray's Inn
Pupil Master
Qualifications: [BA (Hons)(Oxon)]

BARKER MISS ALISON

9-12 Bell Yard
London WC2A 2LF,
Telephone: 0171 400 1800
E-mail: clerks@bellyard.co.uk
Call Date: July 1973, Middle Temple
Qualifications: [LLB (Hons)]

BARKER ANTHONY QC (1985)

5 Fountain Court
Steelhouse Lane, Birmingham B4 6DR,
Telephone: 0121 606 0500
E-mail:clerks@5fountaincourt.law.co.uk
Call Date: Nov 1966, Middle Temple
Recorder
Qualifications: [BA (Cantab)]

BARKER BRIAN JOHN QC (1990)

Hollis Whiteman Chambers
3rd Floor, Queen Elizabeth Bldg, Temple,
London EC4Y 9BS,
Telephone: 020 7583 5766
E-mail:barristers@holliswhiteman.co.uk
Call Date: July 1969, Gray's Inn
Recorder
Qualifications: [LLB, MA]

BARKER CHARLES ASHLEY

Chichester Chambers
12 North Pallant, Chichester, West Sussex,
PO19 1TQ, Telephone: 01243 784538
E-mail:clerks@chichesterchambers.law.co.uk
Call Date: 1997, Middle Temple
Qualifications: [BA (Hons)(Dunelm), CPE
(Sussex)]

BARKER DAVID QC (1976)

65-67 King Street
Leicester LE1 6RP,
Telephone: 0116 2547710
Call Date: July 1954, Inner Temple
Recorder
Qualifications: [LLB (Lond), LLM (Michigan)]

BARKER JAMES SEBASTIAN

Enterprise Chambers
9 Old Square, Lincoln's Inn, London
WC2A 3SR, Telephone: 0171 405 9471
E-mail:enterprise.london@dial.pipex.com

Enterprise Chambers
38 Park Square, Leeds LS1 2PA,
Telephone: 0113 246 0391
E-mail:enterprise.leeds@dial.pipex.com
Enterprise Chambers
65 Quayside, Newcastle upon Tyne
NE1 3DS, Telephone: 0191 222 3344
E-mail:enterprise.newcastle@dial.pipex.com
Call Date: July 1984, Gray's Inn
Pupil Master
Qualifications: [LLB (B'Ham)]

BARKER JOHN CHARLES

6 Gray's Inn Square
Ground Floor, Gray's Inn, London
WC1R 5AZ, Telephone: 0171 242 1052
E-mail: 6graysinn@clara.co.uk
Call Date: July 1982, Middle Temple
Pupil Master
Qualifications: [BA LLM (Lond)]

BARKER JOHN STEVEN ROY

Queen's Chambers
5 John Dalton Street, Manchester M2 6ET,
Telephone: 0161 834 6875/4738
Queens Chambers
4 Camden Place, Preston PR1 3JL,
Telephone: 01772 828300
Call Date: July 1983, Lincoln's Inn
Qualifications: [MA (Cantab) , MA (Cornell)]

BARKER KERRY

Guildhall Chambers
22-26 Broad Street, Bristol BS1 2HG,
Telephone: 0117 9273366
E-mail:civil.clerks@guildhallchambers.co.uk and
criminal.clerks@guildhallchambers.co.uk
Call Date: July 1972, Gray's Inn
Qualifications: [LLB (Lond)]

BARKER NICHOLAS

30 Park Square
Leeds LS1 2PF, Telephone: 0113 2436388
E-mail: clerks@30parksquare.co.uk
Call Date: Oct 1994, Gray's Inn
Qualifications: [BA]

BARKER SIMON GEORGE HARRY

13 Old Square
Ground Floor, Lincoln's Inn, London
WC2A 3UA, Telephone: 0171 404 4800
E-mail: clerks@13oldsquare.law.co.uk
Call Date: July 1979, Lincoln's Inn
Pupil Master, Assistant Recorder
Qualifications: [BA]

Fax: 0171 405 4267;
Out of hours telephone: 0171 405 6460;
DX: LDE 326

Types of work: Accountancy, Arbitration, Banking, Bankruptcy, Commercial litigation, Company and commercial, Construction, Copyright, Copyright tribunal, Corporate finance, Entertainment, Family provision, Media, Music, film and tv, Partnerships, Professional negligence, Warranty claims

Circuit: South Eastern

Other professional experience: Assistant Recorder since 1995

Reported Cases: *AIRC v Phonographic Performance Ltd*, [1994] RPC 181. Copyright Tribunal reference concerning licences and fees for broadcasting recorded music.
Re A Debtor No 87 of 1993 (No 1 and No 2), [1996] BCC 74 and 80. Individual voluntary arrangement, debtor's duty of disclosure and challenge for material irregularity.
Neville v Wilson, [1997] Ch 144; (1997) *The Times*, 28 July. Implied and constructive trusts of shares and effect of solicitors' agreement as to costs on courts' discretion.
Coulthard v Neville Russell, [1998] BCLC 359. Potential scope of auditors' and accountants' duty of care to directors.
Candy Rock Recording v Phonographic Performance Limited, [1999] EMLR 155. Reference of terms of proposed licence to Copyright Tribunal.

BARKLEM MARTYN STEPHEN

Littleton Chambers
3 King's Bench Walk North, Temple,
London EC4Y 7HR,
Telephone: 0171 797 8600
E-mail:clerks@littletonchambers.co.uk
Call Date: July 1989, Middle Temple
Qualifications: [LLB (Lond)]

BARLING GERALD EDWARD QC (1991)

Brick Court Chambers
7-8 Essex Street, London WC2R 3LD,
Telephone: 0171 379 3550
E-mail: [surname]@brickcourt.co.uk
8 King Street Chambers
8 King Street, Manchester M2 6AQ,
Telephone: 0161 834 9560
E-mail: eightking@aol.com
Call Date: Nov 1972, Middle Temple
Recorder
Qualifications: [MA (Oxon)]

BARLOW CRAIG MARTIN

29 Bedford Row Chambers
London WC1R 4HE,
Telephone: 0171 831 2626
Call Date: Oct 1992, Gray's Inn
Qualifications: [LL.B]

BARLOW MARK DAVID

Chambers of Ian Macdonald QC (In Association with Two Garden Court, Temple, London)
Waldorf House, 5 Cooper Street,
Manchester M2 2FW,
Telephone: 0161 236 1840
Call Date: Oct 1992, Middle Temple
Qualifications: [LL.B (Hons)]

BARLOW MISS MELISSA EMMA BENSON

Colleton Chambers
Colleton Crescent, Exeter, Devon,
EX2 4DG, Telephone: 01392 274898/9
Call Date: Oct 1991, Middle Temple
Qualifications: [BA (Hons) (Exon)]

BARLOW RICHARD FRANCIS DUDLEY

The Chambers of Leolin Price CBE, QC
10 Old Square, Lincoln's Inn, London
WC2A 3SU, Telephone: 0171 405 0758
Call Date: Feb 1965, Inner Temple
Pupil Master
Qualifications: [MA (Oxon)]

BARLOW RICHARD LEONARD

11 King's Bench Walk
1st Floor, Temple, London EC4Y 7EQ,
Telephone: 0171 353 3337
E-mail: fmuller11@aol.com
11 King's Bench Walk
3 Park Court, Park Cross Street, Leeds
LS1 2QH, Telephone: 0113 297 1200
Call Date: July 1970, Middle Temple
Pupil Master
Qualifications: [LLB (Lond)]

BARLOW MISS SARAH HELEN

St Paul's House
5th Floor, St Paul's House, 23 Park Square
South, Leeds LS1 2ND,
Telephone: 0113 2455866
E-mail: catherinegrimshaw@stpauls-chambers.demon.co.uk
Call Date: Oct 1993, Gray's Inn
Qualifications: [LLB (Hons)]

BARNARD DAVID NOWELL

33 Bedford Row
London WC1R 4JH,
Telephone: 0171 242 6476
E-mail:clerks@bedfordrow33.demon.co.uk
Call Date: July 1967, Gray's Inn
Pupil Master, Recorder
Qualifications: [BA (Cantab)]

BARNARD JAMES PHILIP

11 Stone Buildings
Lincoln's Inn, London WC2A 3TG,
Telephone: +44 (0)207 831 6381
E-mail:clerks@11StoneBuildings.law.co.uk
Call Date: Oct 1993, Middle Temple
Qualifications: [BA (Hons)(Bris), CPE (City)]

BARNARD JONATHAN JAMES

Hollis Whiteman Chambers
3rd Floor, Queen Elizabeth Bldg, Temple,
London EC4Y 9BS,
Telephone: 020 7583 5766
E-mail:barristers@holliswhiteman.co.uk
Call Date: 1997, Middle Temple
Qualifications: [MA (Edinburgh), MA (Sussex), CPE (City)]

BARNES ASHLEY JAMES

First National Chambers
2nd Floor, First National Building, 24
Fenwick Street, Liverpool L2 7NE,
Telephone: 0151 236 2098
Call Date: Oct 1990, Inner Temple
Qualifications: [LLB]

BARNES DAVID JONATHAN

3 Temple Gardens
Lower Ground Floor, Temple, London
EC4Y 9AU, Telephone: 0171 353 3102/5/
9297 E-mail: clerks@3tg.co.uk
Call Date: Nov 1981, Gray's Inn
Pupil Master
Qualifications: [BSc (Econ)]

BARNES (DAVID) MICHAEL (WILLIAM) QC (1981)

Wilberforce Chambers
8 New Square, Lincoln's Inn, London
WC2A 3QP, Telephone: 0171 306 0102
E-mail: chambers@wilberforce.co.uk
Call Date: July 1965, Middle Temple
Qualifications: [BA (Oxon)]

Types of work: Commercial property, Landlord and tenant, Local government, Town
and country planning

BARNES HENRY JONATHAN

Walnut House
63 St David's Hill, Exeter, Devon,
EX4 4DW, Telephone: 01392 279751
E-mail: 106627.2451@compuserve.com
Call Date: July 1970, Gray's Inn
Pupil Master, Recorder
Qualifications: [LLB (So'ton)]

BARNES LUKE CLIVE

3 Dr Johnson's Buildings
Ground Floor, Temple, London
EC4Y 7BA, Telephone: 0171 353 4854
E-mail: clerks@3djb.co.uk
Call Date: Nov 1996, Gray's Inn
Qualifications: [BA (Oxon), MA (City), Dip
Law]

BARNES MISS MARGARET SUSANNE

3 Hare Court
1 Little Essex Street, London WC2R 3LD,
Telephone: 0171 395 2000
Call Date: July 1976, Gray's Inn
Pupil Master
Qualifications: [B of Jurisprudence]

BARNES MARK RICHARD PURCELL QC (1992)

One Essex Court
Ground Floor, Temple, London
EC4Y 9AR, Telephone: 020 7583 2000
E-mail: clerks@oneessexcourt.co.uk
Call Date: July 1974, Lincoln's Inn
Qualifications: [MA (Oxon)]

BARNES MATTHEW JOHN CAMPBELL

3 Fountain Court
Steelhouse Lane, Birmingham B4 6DR,
Telephone: 0121 236 5854
Call Date: July 1992, Middle Temple
Qualifications: [MA (Cantab)]

BARNES MISS SHANI ESTELLE

1 Hare Court
Ground Floor, Temple, London
EC4Y 7BE, Telephone: 0171 353 3982/
5324
Call Date: 1986, Middle Temple
Pupil Master, Assistant Recorder
Qualifications: [BA, Dip Law (City)]

BARNES TIMOTHY PAUL QC (1986)

9 Bedford Row
London WC1R 4AZ,
Telephone: 0171 242 3555
E-mail: clerks@9br.co.uk
Call Date: July 1968, Gray's Inn
Recorder
Qualifications: [MA (Cantab)]

BARNETT MISS ADRIENNE ELISE

8 King's Bench Walk
2nd Floor, Temple, London EC4Y 7DU,
Telephone: 0171 797 8888
8 King's Bench Walk North
1 Park Square East, Leeds LS1 2NE,
Telephone: 0113 2439797
Call Date: July 1981, Middle Temple
Qualifications: [BA Cape Town]

D

BARNETT ANDREW JOHN

Pump Court Chambers
31 Southgate Street, Winchester
SO23 9EE, Telephone: 01962 868161
E-mail: clerks@3pumpcourt.com
Pump Court Chambers
Upper Ground Floor, 3 Pump Court,
Temple, London EC4Y 7AJ,
Telephone: 0171 353 0711
E-mail: clerks@3pumpcourt.com
Pump Court Chambers
5 Temple Chambers, Temple Street,
Swindon SN1 1SQ,
Telephone: 01793 539899
E-mail: clerks@3pumpcourt.com
Call Date: Nov 1977, Gray's Inn
Pupil Master, Recorder
Qualifications: [BA (Lond)]

BARNETT DANIEL ALEXANDER

2 Gray's Inn Square Chambers
2nd Floor, Gray's Inn, London WC1R 5AA,
Telephone: 020 7242 0328
E-mail: clerks@2gis.co.uk
Call Date: Oct 1993, Lincoln's Inn
Qualifications: [LLB (Hons)(Leeds)]

BARNETT MRS DIANE JUNE

Goldsmith Chambers
Ground Floor, Goldsmith Building,
Temple, London EC4Y 7BL,
Telephone: 0171 353 6802/3/4/5
E-mail:clerks@goldsmithchambers.law.co.uk
Call Date: Nov 1978, Gray's Inn
Pupil Master
Qualifications: [BA]

BARNETT JEREMY VICTOR

St Paul's House
5th Floor, St Paul's House, 23 Park Square
South, Leeds LS1 2ND,
Telephone: 0113 2455866
E-mail: catherinegrimshaw@stpauls-
chambers.demon.co.uk
Farrar's Building
Temple, London EC4Y 7BD,
Telephone: 0171 583 9241
E-mail:chambers@farrarsbuilding.co.uk
Call Date: July 1980, Gray's Inn
Qualifications: [LLB (L'pool)]

BARNETT MISS JOANNE KAREN

32 Park Place
Cardiff CF1 3BA,
Telephone: 01222 397364
Call Date: Nov 1989, Middle Temple
Pupil Master
Qualifications: [LLB [Wales]]

BARNETT JOHN HASKINS

Thetford Lodge Farm
Santon Downham, Brandon, Suffolk,
IP27 OTU, Telephone: 01842 813132
Call Date: July 1981, Gray's Inn

BARNETT MISS SALLY LOUISE

2 New Street
Leicester LE1 5NA,
Telephone: 0116 2625906
E-mail: clerks@2newstreet.co.uk
Call Date: Nov 1987, Middle Temple
Qualifications: [LLB]

BARNFATHER MISS LYDIA HELEN

Hollis Whiteman Chambers
3rd Floor, Queen Elizabeth Bldg, Temple,
London EC4Y 9BS,
Telephone: 020 7583 5766
E-mail:barristers@holliswhiteman.co.uk
Call Date: Oct 1992, Middle Temple
Qualifications: [BA (Hons)]

BARON MISS FLORENCE JACQUELINE QC (1995)

Queen Elizabeth Building
2nd Floor, Temple, London EC4Y 9BS,
Telephone: 0171 797 7837
Call Date: Nov 1976, Middle Temple
Recorder
Qualifications: [BA (Oxon)]

BARR CHARLES DAVID

1 Temple Gardens
1st Floor, Temple, London EC4Y 9BB,
Telephone: 0171 583 1315/353 0407
E-mail: clerks@1templegardens.co.uk
Call Date: Nov 1993, Gray's Inn
Qualifications: [MA (Cantab)]

BARR EDWARD ROBERT

2 New Street
Leicester LE1 5NA,
Telephone: 0116 2625906
E-mail: clerks@2newstreet.co.uk
Call Date: Nov 1983, Inner Temple
Qualifications: [LLB]

BARR MISS FINOLA KATHERINE FRANKLAND

24a St John Street
Manchester M3 4DF,
Telephone: 0161 833 9628
Call Date: Nov 1994, Gray's Inn
Qualifications: [LLB]

BARRACLOUGH ANTHONY ROGER

25-27 Castle Street
1st Floor, Liverpool L2 4TA,
Telephone: 0151 227 5661/051 236 5072
Call Date: Nov 1978, Inner Temple
Pupil Master
Qualifications: [BA (Dunelm)]

BARRACLOUGH NICHOLAS MAYLIN

2nd Floor, Francis Taylor Building
Temple, London EC4Y 7BY,
Telephone: 0171 353 9942/3157
Call Date: Nov 1990, Inner Temple
Qualifications: [LLB (Hons)]

BARRACLOUGH RICHARD MICHAEL

6 Pump Court
1st Floor, Temple, London EC4Y 7AR,
Telephone: 0171 797 8400
E-mail: clerks@6pumpcourt.co.uk
6-8 Mill Street
Maidstone, Kent, ME15 6XH,
Telephone: 01622 688094
E-mail: annexe@6pumpcourt.co.uk
Call Date: Nov 1980, Inner Temple
Pupil Master
Qualifications: [MA (Oxon)]

BARRADELL RICHARD MARK

15 North Church Street Chambers
15 North Church Street, Sheffield
S1 2DH, Telephone: 0114 2759708/
2738380
Call Date: Oct 1990, Inner Temple
Qualifications: [LLB]

BARRATT DOMINIC ANTHONY

East Anglian Chambers
Gresham House, 5 Museum Street,
Ipswich, Suffolk, IP1 1HQ,
Telephone: 01473 214481
E-mail: ipswich@ealaw.co.uk
East Anglian Chambers
52 North Hill, Colchester, Essex, CO1 1PY,
Telephone: 01206 572756
E-mail: colchester@ealaw.co.uk
East Anglian Chambers
57 London Street, Norwich NR2 1HL,
Telephone: 01603 617351
E-mail: norwich@ealaw.co.uk
Call Date: Nov 1992, Gray's Inn
Qualifications: [BA (Hons)(Leeds)]

BARRETT JOHN MICHAEL PAUL GOWRAN

40 King Street
Manchester M2 6BA,
Telephone: 0161 832 9082
E-mail: clerks@40kingstreet.co.uk
4 Breams Buildings
London EC4A 1AQ,
Telephone: 0171 353 5835/430 1221
E-mail:breams@4breamsbuildings.law.co.uk
The Chambers of Philip Raynor QC
5 Park Place, Leeds LS1 2RU,
Telephone: 0113 242 1123
Call Date: May 1982, Gray's Inn
Pupil Master
Qualifications: [BA]

BARRETT MS PENELOPE JANE

3 Gray's Inn Square
Ground Floor, London WC1R 5AH,
Telephone: 0171 520 5600
E-mail: clerks@3gis.co.uk
Call Date: July 1982, Middle Temple
Pupil Master
Qualifications: [MA (Cantab)]

BARRETT ROBERT SCOTT

2 Pump Court
1st Floor, Temple, London EC4Y 7AH,
Telephone: 0171 353 5597
Call Date: July 1978, Gray's Inn
Pupil Master
Qualifications: [MA (Cantab)]

D

BARRIE PETER ANTHONY STANFIELD

Guildhall Chambers
22-26 Broad Street, Bristol BS1 2HG,
Telephone: 0117 9273366
E-mail:civil.clerks@guildhallchambers.co.uk
and criminal.clerks@guildhallchambers.co.uk
Call Date: Nov 1976, Middle Temple
Pupil Master, Assistant Recorder
Qualifications: [MA (Oxon)]

BARRINGTON-SMYTH MISS AMANDA ROWENA

4 Paper Buildings
1st Floor, Temple, London EC4Y 7EX,
Telephone: 0171 583 0816/353 1131
E-mail: clerks@4paperbuildings.co.uk
Call Date: Nov 1972, Middle Temple
Pupil Master
Qualifications: [LLB (Lond)]

BARRON-EAVES MRS EMMA LORRAINE

India Buildings Chambers
Water Street, Liverpool L2 0XG,
Telephone: 0151 243 6000
E-mail: clerks@chambers.u-net.com
Call Date: July 1998, Lincoln's Inn
Qualifications: [LLB (Hons)]

BARRY DENIS FINTAN PATRICK

Five Paper Buildings
1st Floor, Five Paper Bldgs, Temple,
London EC4Y 7HB,
Telephone: 0171 583 6117
E-mail:clerks@5-paperbuildings.law.co.uk
Call Date: 1996, Inner Temple
Qualifications: [LLB (B'ham), LLM (Warw)]

BARRY JOSEPH MICHAEL

Mitre House Chambers
15-19 Devereux Court, London WC2R 3JJ,
Telephone: 0171 583 8233
Call Date: Nov 1987, Lincoln's Inn
Qualifications: [BA (Hons)]

BARRY KEVIN JAMES

Chambers of Michael Pert QC
36 Bedford Row, London WC1R 4JH,
Telephone: 0171 421 8000
E-mail: 36bedfordrow@link.org

Chambers of Michael Pert QC
24 Albion Place, Northampton NN1 1UD,
Telephone: 01604 602333
Chambers of Michael Pert QC
104 New Walk, Leicester LE1 7EA,
Telephone: 0116 249 2020
Call Date: 1997, Lincoln's Inn
Qualifications: [LLB (Hons)(B'ham)]

BARRY MISS KIRSTEN LESLEY

8 King Street Chambers
8 King Street, Manchester M2 6AQ,
Telephone: 0161 834 9560
E-mail: eightking@aol.com
Call Date: Nov 1993, Lincoln's Inn
Qualifications: [LLB (Hons, Sheff)]

BARRY SIMON MARK

1 Pump Court
Lower Ground Floor, Temple, London
EC4Y 7AB, Telephone: 0171 583 2012/
353 4341
E-mail: [name]@1pumpcourt.co.uk
Call Date: Mar 1997, Middle Temple
Qualifications: [BA (Hons)]

BARSTOW STEPHEN ROYDEN

Harcourt Chambers
1st Floor, 2 Harcourt Buildings, Temple,
London EC4Y 9DB,
Telephone: 0171 353 6961
E-mail:clerks@harcourtchambers.law.co.uk
Harcourt Chambers
Churchill House, 3 St Aldate's Courtyard,
St Aldate's, Oxford OX1 1BN,
Telephone: 01865 791559
E-mail:clerks@harcourtchambers.law.co.uk
Call Date: July 1976, Gray's Inn
Qualifications: [MA (Cantab)]

BART DELANO FRANK

8 King's Bench Walk
2nd Floor, Temple, London EC4Y 7DU,
Telephone: 0171 797 8888
8 King's Bench Walk North
1 Park Square East, Leeds LS1 2NE,
Telephone: 0113 2439797
Call Date: July 1977, Lincoln's Inn
Pupil Master
Qualifications: [LLB (Lond)]

BARTLE PHILIP MARTYN

Littleton Chambers
3 King's Bench Walk North, Temple,
London EC4Y 7HR,
Telephone: 0171 797 8600
E-mail:clerks@littletonchambers.co.uk
Call Date: July 1976, Middle Temple
Pupil Master
Qualifications: [MA, BCL (Oxon)]

BARTLETT ANDREW VINCENT BRAMWELL QC (1993)

One Paper Buildings
Ground Floor, Temple, London
EC4Y 7EP, Telephone: 0171 583 7355
E-mail: clerks@1pb.co.uk
Call Date: July 1974, Middle Temple
Qualifications: [BA (Oxon), FCIArb]

BARTLETT DAVID ALAN

3 Paper Buildings
Temple, London EC4Y 7EU,
Telephone: 020 7583 8055
E-mail: London@3paper.com
3 Paper Buildings (Bournemouth)
20 Lorne Park Road, Bournemouth,
Dorset, BH1 1JN,
Telephone: 01202 292102
E-mail: Bournemouth@3paper.com
3 Paper Buildings (Winchester)
4 St Peter Street, Winchester SO23 8BW,
Telephone: 01962 868884
E-mail: winchester@3paper.com
3 Paper Buildings (Oxford)
1 Alfred Street, High Street, Oxford
OX1 4EH, Telephone: 01865 793736
E-mail: oxford@3paper.com
Call Date: July 1975, Gray's Inn
Pupil Master, Recorder
Qualifications: [BA (Oxon)]

BARTLETT ROGER JAMES LAWRENCE

1 Harcourt Buildings
2nd Floor, Temple, London EC4Y 9DA,
Telephone: 0171 353 9421/0375
E-mail:clerks@1harcourtbuildings.law.co.uk
Call Date: July 1968, Middle Temple
Pupil Master
Qualifications: [BA]

BARTLEY JONES EDWARD QC (1997)

Exchange Chambers
Pearl Assurance House, Derby Square,
Liverpool L2 9XX,
Telephone: 0151 236 7747
E-mail:exchangechambers@btinternet.com
Call Date: July 1975, Lincoln's Inn
Assistant Recorder
Qualifications: [BA (Hons)(Oxon)]

BARTON ALAN JOHN

Lamb Building
Ground Floor, Temple, London
EC4Y 7AS, Telephone: 020 7797 7788
E-mail: lamb.building@link.org
Call Date: Nov 1975, Middle Temple
Pupil Master
Qualifications: [LLB, LLM]

BARTON MISS FIONA

5 Essex Court
1st Floor, Temple, London EC4Y 9AH,
Telephone: 0171 410 2000
E-mail: barristers@5essexcourt.co.uk
Call Date: Nov 1986, Middle Temple
Pupil Master
Qualifications: [LLB(Lond)]

BARTON HUGH GEOFFREY

Doughty Street Chambers
11 Doughty Street, London WC1N 2PG,
Telephone: 0171 404 1313
E-mail:enquiries@doughtystreet.co.uk
Call Date: Nov 1989, Middle Temple
Qualifications: [BA (Hons), Dip in, Law]

BARTON JOHN CHARLES TOMLIN QC (1989)

Albion Chambers
Broad Street, Bristol BS1 1DR,
Telephone: 0117 9272144
Five Paper Buildings
1st Floor, Five Paper Bldgs, Temple,
London EC4Y 7HB,
Telephone: 0171 583 6117
E-mail:clerks@5-paperbuildings.law.co.uk
Call Date: Nov 1969, Middle Temple
Qualifications: [LLB]

BARTON RICHARD JAMES

One King's Bench Walk
1st Floor, Temple, London EC4Y 7DB,
Telephone: 0171 936 1500
E-mail: ddear@1kbw.co.uk
Call Date: Oct 1990, Lincoln's Inn
Pupil Master
Qualifications: [BA, BCL (Oxon)]

BARUAH MISS FIONA CAROLINE

East Anglian Chambers
57 London Street, Norwich NR2 1HL,
Telephone: 01603 617351
E-mail: norwich@ealaw.co.uk
East Anglian Chambers
Gresham House, 5 Museum Street,
Ipswich, Suffolk, IP1 1HQ,
Telephone: 01473 214481
E-mail: ipswich@ealaw.co.uk
East Anglian Chambers
52 North Hill, Colchester, Essex, CO1 1PY,
Telephone: 01206 572756
E-mail: colchester@ealaw.co.uk
Call Date: Oct 1996, Inner Temple
Qualifications: [LLB (L'pool)]

BARUAH MISS RIMA

Counsels' Chambers
2nd Floor, 10-11 Gray's Inn Square,
London WC1R 5JD,
Telephone: 0171 405 2576
E-mail:clerks@10-11graysinnsquare.co.uk
Call Date: Feb 1994, Inner Temple

BARWISE MISS STEPHANIE NICOLA

Atkin Chambers
1 Atkin Building, Gray's Inn, London
WC1R 5AT, Telephone: 020 7404 0102
E-mail: clerks@atkin-chambers.co.uk
Call Date: July 1988, Middle Temple
Pupil Master
Qualifications: [MA, LLM (Cantab)]

BASH-TAQI MRS SHAHINEH

Leone Chambers
72 Evelyn Avenue, Kingsbury, London
NW9 0JH, Telephone: 0181 200 4020
E-mail: festus4@leonechambers.co.uk
Call Date: 1972, Middle Temple
Qualifications: [BA (Durham)]

BASHIR NADIM

Park Court Chambers
16 Park Place, Leeds LS1 2SJ,
Telephone: 0113 2433277
Call Date: Nov 1988, Middle Temple
Qualifications: [Pg Dip (PIL), LLB (Hons)]

BASSA YOUSEF

St Albans Chambers
Dolphin Lodge, Dolphin Yard, Holywell
Hill, St Albans, Herts, AL1 1EX,
Telephone: 01727 843383
Tindal Chambers
3/5 New Street, Chelmsford, Essex,
CM1 1NT, Telephone: 01245 267742
Call Date: Nov 1989, Lincoln's Inn
Qualifications: [LLB (Essex)]

BASSANO ALARIC JULIAN

Chambers of John Hand QC
9 St John Street, Manchester M3 4DN,
Telephone: 0161 955 9000
E-mail: ninesjs@gconnect.com
Call Date: Nov 1993, Gray's Inn
Qualifications: [BA (Oxon)]

BASSETT JOHN STEWART BRITTEN

5 Essex Court
1st Floor, Temple, London EC4Y 9AH,
Telephone: 0171 410 2000
E-mail: barristers@5essexcourt.co.uk
Call Date: July 1975, Inner Temple
Pupil Master
Qualifications: [LLB (Leeds)]

BASSIRI-DEZFOULI MISS SOROUR

Horizon Chambers
95a Chancery Lane, London WC2A 1DT,
Telephone: 0171 242 2440
Call Date: Oct 1996, Lincoln's Inn
Qualifications: [LLB (Hons)(B'ham)]

BASSRA SUKHBIR SINGH

St Paul's House
5th Floor, St Paul's House, 23 Park Square
South, Leeds LS1 2ND,
Telephone: 0113 2455866
E-mail: catherinegrimshaw@stpauls-
chambers.demon.co.uk
Call Date: May 1993, Middle Temple

BASTIN ALEXANDER CHARLES

2nd Floor, Francis Taylor Building
Temple, London EC4Y 7BY,
Telephone: 0171 353 9942/3157
Call Date: Oct 1995, Middle Temple
Qualifications: [BA (Hons) (Reading), LLB (Hons)]

BASU DR DIJENDRA BHUSHAN

Devereux Chambers
Devereux Court, London WC2R 3JJ,
Telephone: 0171 353 7534
E-mail: mailbox@devchambers.co.uk
Call Date: Oct 1994, Lincoln's Inn
Qualifications: [MB, BS]

BATCHELOR MARK ALFRED LOWE

22 Old Buildings
Lincoln's Inn, London WC2A 3UJ,
Telephone: 0171 831 0222
Call Date: Nov 1971, Inner Temple
Pupil Master

BATCUP DAVID JOHN

Dr Johnson's Chambers
Two Dr Johnson's Buildings, Temple,
London EC4Y 7AY,
Telephone: 0171 353 4716
E-mail: clerks@2djb.freeserve.co.uk
Call Date: July 1974, Gray's Inn
Pupil Master, Assistant Recorder
Qualifications: [LLB (Lond)]

BATE ANTHONY JOHN

East Anglian Chambers
57 London Street, Norwich NR2 1HL,
Telephone: 01603 617351
E-mail: norwich@ealaw.co.uk
East Anglian Chambers
52 North Hill, Colchester, Essex, CO1 1PY,
Telephone: 01206 572756
E-mail: colchester@ealaw.co.uk
East Anglian Chambers
Gresham House, 5 Museum Street,
Ipswich, Suffolk, IP1 1HQ,
Telephone: 01473 214481
E-mail: ipswich@ealaw.co.uk
Call Date: July 1987, Lincoln's Inn
Pupil Master
Qualifications: [MA, Vet.MB (Cantab)]

BATE DAVID CHRISTOPHER QC (1994)

Hollis Whiteman Chambers
3rd Floor, Queen Elizabeth Bldg, Temple,
London EC4Y 9BS,
Telephone: 020 7583 5766
E-mail:barristers@holliswhiteman.co.uk
Call Date: Feb 1969, Gray's Inn
Recorder
Qualifications: [LLB]

BATE STEPHEN ROBERT DE BRETEUIL

5 Raymond Buildings
1st Floor, Gray's Inn, London WC1R 5BP,
Telephone: 0171 242 2902
E-mail: clerks@media-ent-law.co.uk
Call Date: July 1981, Middle Temple
Pupil Master
Qualifications: [MA (Cantab), Dip Law (City)]

BATE-WILLIAMS JOHN ROBERT ALEXANDER

1 Temple Gardens
1st Floor, Temple, London EC4Y 9BB,
Telephone: 0171 583 1315/353 0407
E-mail: clerks@1templegardens.co.uk
Call Date: Nov 1976, Inner Temple
Pupil Master
Qualifications: [LLB (Wales)]

BATEMAN MISS CHRISTINE JUNE

St John's Chambers
Small Street, Bristol BS1 1DW,
Telephone: 0117 9213456/298514
E-mail: @stjohnschambers.co.uk
Call Date: Nov 1992, Lincoln's Inn
Qualifications: [LLB (Hons)(Nott'm)]

BATES ALEXANDER ANDREW

St Paul's House
5th Floor, St Paul's House, 23 Park Square
South, Leeds LS1 2ND,
Telephone: 0113 2455866
E-mail: catherinegrimshaw@stpauls-
chambers.demon.co.uk
Call Date: Oct 1994, Gray's Inn
Qualifications: [BA (Hons) (Cantab)]

BATES JOHN HAYWARD

Old Square Chambers
1 Verulam Buildings, Gray's Inn, London
WC1R 5LQ, Telephone: 0171 269 0300
E-mail:clerks@oldsquarechambers.co.uk
Old Square Chambers
Hanover House, 47 Corn Street, Bristol
BS1 1HT, Telephone: 0117 9277111
E-mail: oldsqbri@globalnet.co.uk
Call Date: July 1973, Middle Temple
Pupil Master

BATES (JONATHAN) PASCAL

3 Temple Gardens
2nd Floor, Temple, London EC4Y 9AU,
Telephone: 0171 583 1155
Call Date: Nov 1994, Middle Temple
Qualifications: [BA (Hons)]

BATES RICHARD GRAHAM

Hardwicke Building
New Square, Lincoln's Inn, London
WC2A 3SB, Telephone: 020 7242 2523
E-mail: clerks@hardwicke.co.uk
Call Date: Oct 1992, Middle Temple
Qualifications: [BA (Hons, Dunelm),
Common Profesional, Examination]

BATEY DAVID MICHAEL

Stour Chambers
Barton Mill House, Barton Mill Road,
Canterbury, Kent, CT1 1BP,
Telephone: 01227 764899
E-mail: clerks@stourchambers.co.uk
Call Date: July 1989, Gray's Inn
Qualifications: [BA (Keele)]

BATHER MISS VICTORIA MACLEAN

Littleton Chambers
3 King's Bench Walk North, Temple,
London EC4Y 7HR,
Telephone: 0171 797 8600
E-mail:clerks@littletonchambers.co.uk
Call Date: Oct 1995, Middle Temple
Qualifications: [BA (Hons)]

BATHURST THE HON CHRISTOPHER HILEY LUDLOW QC (1978)

Fountain Court
Temple, London EC4Y 9DH,
Telephone: 0171 583 3335
E-mail: chambers@fountaincourt.co.uk
Call Date: Feb 1959, Gray's Inn

BATISTE SIMON ANTHONY

No. 6
6 Park Square, Leeds LS1 2LW,
Telephone: 0113 2459763
E-mail: chambers@no6.co.uk
Call Date: Oct 1995, Lincoln's Inn
Qualifications: [LLB (Hons)(Newc)]

BATRA BUNTY LALIT

28 St John Street
Manchester M3 4DJ,
Telephone: 0161 834 8418
E-mail: clerk@28stjohnst.co.uk
Call Date: Feb 1988, Gray's Inn
Qualifications: [LLB]

BATTCOCK BENJAMIN GEORGE

2 Harcourt Buildings
Ground Floor/Left, Temple, London
EC4Y 9DB, Telephone: 0171 583 9020
E-mail: clerks@harcourt.co.uk
Call Date: July 1987, Middle Temple
Qualifications: [MA (Cantab)]

BATTEN STEPHEN DUVAL QC (1989)

3 Raymond Buildings
Gray's Inn, London WC1R 5BH,
Telephone: 020 7831 3833
E-mail:chambers@threeraymond.demon.co.uk
Call Date: Nov 1968, Middle Temple
Recorder
Qualifications: [BA (Oxon)]

BATTERSBY PROF GRAHAM

Bank House Chambers
Old Bank House, Hartshead, Sheffield
S1 2EL, Telephone: 0114 2751223
Call Date: June 1964, Lincoln's Inn
Qualifications: [BA]

BATTY CHRISTOPHER MICHAEL

St Paul's House
5th Floor, St Paul's House, 23 Park Square
South, Leeds LS1 2ND,
Telephone: 0113 2455866
E-mail: catherinegrimshaw@stpauls-chambers.demon.co.uk
Call Date: July 1989, Gray's Inn
Qualifications: [LLB (L'pool)]

BATTY PAUL DANIEL QC (1995)

Broad Chare
33 Broad Chare, Newcastle upon Tyne
NE1 3DQ, Telephone: 0191 232 0541
E-mail:clerks@broadcharechambers.law.co.uk
11 King's Bench Walk
1st Floor, Temple, London EC4Y 7EQ,
Telephone: 0171 353 3337
E-mail: fmuller11@aol.com
*Call Date: July 1975, Lincoln's Inn
Recorder*
Qualifications: [LLB]

BAUGHAN ANDREW ROBERT

1 Inner Temple Lane
Temple, London EC4Y 1AF,
Telephone: 020 7353 0933
Call Date: Nov 1994, Middle Temple
Qualifications: [BA (Hons)(Lond), Dip Law]

BAUGHAN JULIAN JAMES QC (1990)

13 King's Bench Walk
1st Floor, Temple, London EC4Y 7EN,
Telephone: 0171 353 7204
E-mail: clerks@13kbw.law.co.uk
King's Bench Chambers
32 Beaumont Street, Oxford OX1 2NP,
Telephone: 01865 311066
E-mail: clerks@kbc-oxford.law.co.uk
*Call Date: Nov 1967, Inner Temple
Recorder*
Qualifications: [BA (Oxon)]

BAUM MISS VICTORIA EMMA

1 Harcourt Buildings
2nd Floor, Temple, London EC4Y 9DA,
Telephone: 0171 353 9421/0375
E-mail:clerks@1harcourtbuildings.law.co.uk
Call Date: Oct 1993, Middle Temple
Qualifications: [BA (Hons) (Oxon)]

BAUR CHRISTOPHER THOMAS

Furnival Chambers
32 Furnival Street, London EC4A 1JQ,
Telephone: 0171 405 3232
E-mail: clerks@furnivallaw.co.uk
*Call Date: July 1972, Middle Temple
Pupil Master*

BAXENDALE MISS PRESILEY LAMORNA QC (1992)

Blackstone Chambers
Blackstone House, Temple, London
EC4Y 9BW, Telephone: 0171 583 1770
E-mail:clerks@blackstonechambers.com
Call Date: July 1974, Lincoln's Inn
Qualifications: [MA (Oxon)]

BAXENDALE THOMAS DAWTREY

Twenty-Four Old Buildings
Ground Floor, Lincoln's Inn, London
WC2A 3UP, Telephone: 0171 404 0946
E-mail:clerks@24oldbuildings.law.co.uk
*Call Date: July 1962, Inner Temple
Pupil Master*

BAXTER MISS BERNADETTE

Lincoln House Chambers
5th Floor, Lincoln House, 1 Brazennose
Street, Manchester M2 5EL,
Telephone: 0161 832 5701
E-mail: info@lincolnhse.co.uk
Call Date: July 1987, Middle Temple
Qualifications: [LLB (LSE)]

BAXTER GERALD PEARSON

25-27 Castle Street
1st Floor, Liverpool L2 4TA,
Telephone: 0151 227 5661/051 236 5072
*Call Date: July 1971, Lincoln's Inn
Pupil Master*
Qualifications: [LLB (Sheff), LLM]

BAXTER MRS SHARON YVONNE VERGETTE

2 Paper Buildings
1st Floor, Temple, London EC4Y 7ET,
Telephone: 020 7556 5500
E-mail: clerks@2pbbarristers.co.uk
Call Date: July 1987, Inner Temple
Qualifications: [LLB (Oxon)]

BAXTER-PHILLIPS MISS FELICITY DAWN

Becket Chambers
17 New Dover Road, Canterbury, Kent,
CT1 3AS, Telephone: 01227 786331
Call Date: Feb 1964, Gray's Inn
Qualifications: [Diploma in Field,
Archaeology (Lond)]

BAYATI MS CHARLOTTE ELIZABETH

Gray's Inn Chambers
5th Floor, Gray's Inn, London WC1R 5JA,
Telephone: 0171 404 1111
Call Date: Nov 1995, Gray's Inn
Qualifications: [LLB]

BAYLIS MS NATALIE JAYNE

3 Verulam Buildings
London WC1R 5NT,
Telephone: 0171 831 8441
E-mail: clerks@3verulam.co.uk
Call Date: Oct 1996, Lincoln's Inn
Qualifications: [MA (Hons)(Edinburgh), Dip
in Law (City)]

BAYLISS RODERIC ALAN

Dr Johnson's Chambers
Two Dr Johnson's Buildings, Temple,
London EC4Y 7AY,
Telephone: 0171 353 4716
E-mail: clerks@2djb.freeserve.co.uk
Call Date: July 1966, Inner Temple
Pupil Master, Recorder

BAYLISS THOMAS WILLIAM MAXWELL

Park Court Chambers
16 Park Place, Leeds LS1 2SJ,
Telephone: 0113 2433277
Call Date: July 1977, Inner Temple
Pupil Master, Assistant Recorder
Qualifications: [LLB (Hons)]

BAYNE DOMINIC RICHARD NOEL

Plowden Buildings
2nd Floor, 2 Plowden Buildings, Middle
Temple Lane, London EC4Y 9BU,
Telephone: 0171 583 0808
E-mail: bar@plowdenbuildings.co.uk
Call Date: 1997, Middle Temple
Qualifications: [BSc (Hons)(Dunelm)]

BAZINI DANIEL

8 King's Bench Walk
2nd Floor, Temple, London EC4Y 7DU,
Telephone: 0171 797 8888
8 King's Bench Walk North
1 Park Square East, Leeds LS1 2NE,
Telephone: 0113 2439797
Call Date: Nov 1992, Gray's Inn
Qualifications: [BA (Econ), BA (Law)]

BAZLEY MISS JANET CLARE

One Garden Court Family Law Chambers
Ground Floor, Temple, London
EC4Y 9BJ, Telephone: 0171 797 7900
E-mail: clerks@onegardencourt.co.uk
Call Date: July 1980, Lincoln's Inn
Pupil Master
Qualifications: [LLB (Lond)]

BEAL JASON PHILIP MARCUS

2 King's Bench Walk
Ground Floor, Temple, London
EC4Y 7DE, Telephone: 0171 353 1746
E-mail: 2kbw@atlas.co.uk
King's Bench Chambers
115 North Hill, Plymouth PL4 8JY,
Telephone: 01752 221551
Call Date: Oct 1993, Gray's Inn
Qualifications: [BA]

BEAL KIERON CONRAD

4 Paper Buildings
Ground Floor, Temple, London
EC4Y 7EX, Telephone: 0171 353 3366/
583 7155
E-mail: clerks@4paperbuildings.com
Call Date: Nov 1995, Inner Temple
Qualifications: [MA (Cantab), LLM (Harvard),
BA (Cantab)]

BEALBY WALTER

5 Fountain Court
Steelhouse Lane, Birmingham B4 6DR,
Telephone: 0121 606 0500
E-mail:clerks@5fountaincourt.law.co.uk
Call Date: July 1976, Middle Temple
Pupil Master
Qualifications: [BA (Bristol)]

BEALE MISS JUDITH HELEN

Blackstone Chambers
Blackstone House, Temple, London
EC4Y 9BW, Telephone: 0171 583 1770
E-mail:clerks@blackstonechambers.com
Call Date: July 1978, Inner Temple
Qualifications: [BA, M Phil(Lond)]

BEAN ALAN SIGMUND JOCELYN

85 Springfield Road
King's Heath, Birmingham B14 7DU,
Telephone: 0121 444 2818
E-mail: alan@beanlaw.demon.co.uk
Call Date: July 1990, Lincoln's Inn
Qualifications: [BA (Oxon), MA (Lond)]

BEAN DAVID MICHAEL QC (1997)

4-5 Gray's Inn Square
Ground Floor, Gray's Inn, London
WC1R 5JP, Telephone: 0171 404 5252
E-mail:chambers@4-5graysinnsquare.co.uk
Call Date: July 1976, Middle Temple
Assistant Recorder
Qualifications: [MA (Cantab) FCI Arb]

BEAN MATTHEW ALLEN

11 King's Bench Walk
3 Park Court, Park Cross Street, Leeds
LS1 2QH, Telephone: 0113 297 1200
11 King's Bench Walk
1st Floor, Temple, London EC4Y 7EQ,
Telephone: 0171 353 3337
E-mail: fmuller11@aol.com
Call Date: 1997, Middle Temple
Qualifications: [BA (Hons)(Dunelm), CPE
(City)]

BEAR CHARLES

11 King's Bench Walk
Temple, London EC4Y 7EQ,
Telephone: 0171 632 8500/583 0610
E-mail: clerksroom@11kbw.com
Call Date: Nov 1986, Lincoln's Inn
Pupil Master
Qualifications: [BA(Oxon)]

BEARD DANIEL MATTHEW

Monckton Chambers
4 Raymond Buildings, Gray's Inn, London
WC1R 5BP, Telephone: 0171 405 7211
E-mail: chambers@monckton.co.uk
Call Date: Nov 1996, Middle Temple
Qualifications: [BA (Hons)(Cantab)]

BEARD DAVID JOHN

Bell Yard Chambers
116/118 Chancery Lane, London
WC2A 1PP, Telephone: 0171 306 9292
Call Date: Oct 1990, Lincoln's Inn
Qualifications: [LLB]

BEARD MARK CHRISTOPHER

6 Pump Court
1st Floor, Temple, London EC4Y 7AR,
Telephone: 0171 797 8400
E-mail: clerks@6pumpcourt.co.uk
6-8 Mill Street
Maidstone, Kent, ME15 6XH,
Telephone: 01622 688094
E-mail: annexe@6pumpcourt.co.uk
Call Date: Oct 1996, Gray's Inn

BEARD NEVILLE WAYNE

Pendragon Chambers
124 Walter Road, Swansea, West
Glamorgan, SA1 5RG,
Telephone: 01792 411188
Call Date: Oct 1991, Gray's Inn
Qualifications: [MA (Oxon)]

BEARD SIMON

Ropewalk Chambers
24 The Ropewalk, Nottingham NG1 5EF,
Telephone: 0115 9472581
E-mail: administration@ropewalk co.uk
Call Date: Nov 1980, Gray's Inn
Pupil Master
Qualifications: [BA (Oxon)]

BEARDSMORE DR VALERIE

2 Paper Buildings
1st Floor, Temple, London EC4Y 7ET,
Telephone: 020 7556 5500
E-mail: clerks@2pbbarristers.co.uk
Call Date: May 1990, Middle Temple
Qualifications: [B.A. (Wales), Ph.D. (Kent)]

BEARMAN JUSTIN IAN

Harrow on the Hill Chambers
60 High Street, Harrow-on-the-Hill,
Middlesex, HA1 3LL,
Telephone: 0181 423 7444
Windsor Barristers' Chambers
Windsor Telephone: 01753 648899
E-mail: law@windsorchambers.co.uk
Call Date: Nov 1992, Inner Temple
Qualifications: [LLB (Hull) (Hons)]

BEASLEY-MURRAY MRS CAROLINE WYNNE

Fenners Chambers
3 Madingley Road, Cambridge CB3 0EE,
Telephone: 01223 368761
E-mail: clerks@fennerschambers.co.uk
Fenners Chambers
8-12 Priestgate, Peterborough PE1 1JA,
Telephone: 01733 562030
E-mail: clerks@fennerschambers.co.uk
Call Date: July 1988, Inner Temple
Pupil Master
Qualifications: [MA (Cantab), CPE]

BEATSON PROFESSOR JACK QC (1998)

Essex Court Chambers
24 Lincoln's Inn Fields, London
WC2A 3ED, Telephone: 0171 813 8000
E-mail:clerksroom@essexcourt-chambers.co.uk
Call Date: Feb 1972, Inner Temple
Recorder
Qualifications: [BA, BCL (Oxon), MA]

BEATTIE MISS ANN LOUISE

Derby Square Chambers
Merchants Court, Derby Square, Liverpool
L2 1TS, Telephone: 0151 709 4222
E-mail:mail.derbysquare@pop3.hiway.co.uk
Call Date: July 1989, Middle Temple
Qualifications: [BSc (Hons)(Dunelm), Dip Law (Hons)]

BEATTIE MISS SHARON MICHELLE

Park Court Chambers
16 Park Place, Leeds LS1 2SJ,
Telephone: 0113 2433277
Call Date: Nov 1986, Inner Temple
Pupil Master
Qualifications: [LLB (Hons)(Leeds)]

BEAUMONT MARC CLIFFORD

Harrow on the Hill Chambers
60 High Street, Harrow-on-the-Hill,
Middlesex, HA1 3LL,
Telephone: 0181 423 7444
Windsor Barristers' Chambers
Windsor Telephone: 01753 648899
E-mail: law@windsorchambers.co.uk
Pump Court Chambers
Upper Ground Floor, 3 Pump Court,
Temple, London EC4Y 7AJ,
Telephone: 0171 353 0711
E-mail: clerks@3pumpcourt.com
Call Date: 1985, Gray's Inn
Pupil Master
Qualifications: [LLB (Manch)]

Fax: 0181 423 7368;
Out of hours telephone: 01753 648899;
DX: 130112 Slough 6

Types of work: Administrative, Chancery land law, Commercial litigation, Commercial property, Common law (general), Competition, Consumer law, Conveyancing, Education, Employment, Family provision, Franchising, Insurance, Landlord and tenant, Local government, Partnerships, Professional negligence

Circuit: South Eastern

Awards and memberships: Head of Chambers; Elected Member General Council of the Bar; Committee Member South Eastern Circuit Bar Mess; Committee Member London Common Law and Commercial Bar Association; Committee North London Bar Mess

Languages spoken: French

Publications: *Effective Mortgage Enforcement* (New Law Publishing), May 1998; Various articles in legal journals and periodicals; Lectures on Mortgage Law

Reported Cases
Doble v Haymills (1988) *The Times*, 5 July; (1988) SJ 1063
Writ extension.

Abbey National BS v Cann [1991] 1 AC 56, HL
A leading case on overriding interests, LRA s 70(1)(g); equitable subordination.

Jones v Jones [1993] 2 FLR 377
Committal.

S v W [1995] 1 FLR 862; (1994) *The Times*, 26 December
A leading case on s 11 of the Limitation Act 1980; action for damages for childhood sexual abuse/limitation.

Re Jayham Ltd [1995] 2 BCLC 455
Restoration to Companies Register – s 653 Companies Act 1985.

First National Bank v Ann[1998] CCLR 1; [1997] 1 CLY 963 February; [1997] Hals, March; Encyc of Consumer Credit
Limitation period for extortionate credit bargain claim.

Popat v Shonchhatra [1997] 3 All ER 799; [1997] 1 WLR 1367
Division of post-dissolution partnership profits.

Hurstanger Ltd v Ricketts [1998] CCLR 5; [1997] 1 CLY 962
Following *FNB v Ann* above, strike out – limitation period for extortionate credit bargain claim – issue estoppel – abuse of process.

R v Rotherham MBC ex parte Clark and others [1998] 2 ELR 152, CA
Education – a leading case on school admissions – judicial review of school admissions policy based on catchment areas rather than parental preference – s 411 Education Act 1996.

Hill Samuel Personal Finance v Grundy 19 November 1997, CA: [1997] All ER (D) 81
Unless orders.

Barclays Bank v Clifton [1998] BPIR 566
Personal insolvency – mortgage fraud – agency – setting aside statutory demand – nature of appeal to single judge of the Chancery Division.

R v London Borough of Redbridge ex parte Benning & Ors [1999] ELR
School admissions, s 411 Education Act 1996, catchment areas and ECHR.

Abbey National plc v Tufts [1999] FLR, CA
Mortgage fraud LPA s 199, reasonable enquiries, application of *Quennell v Maltby* test.

Hurstanger Ltd v Wood & Wood [1999] CL May
Following *FNB v Ann* and *Hurtstanger Ltd v Ricketts* above, strike out/ limitation

period for extortionate credit bargain claim.

R v Sheffield CC ex parte Ashmore and others [1999] ELR 242
School admissions, s 411 Education Act 1996, conduct of appeals.

Practice Details
In 1990, I established Harrow-on-the-Hill Barristers' Chambers. Whilst at the time, this was a novel and unorthodox idea, the set is now firmly established, both within the London area and across the country.

My practice is partly property and litigation orientated (embracing mortgages, banking, conveyancing, professional negligence and business and commercial litigation) and partly public law based. I have appeared in leading cases in the property and education fields. I try to bring to my work a fighting will to win and a streak of originality.

BEAZLEY THOMAS ALAN GEORGE

Blackstone Chambers
Blackstone House, Temple, London EC4Y 9BW, Telephone: 0171 583 1770
E-mail:clerks@blackstonechambers.com
Call Date: July 1979, Middle Temple
Pupil Master
Qualifications: [BA (Cantab), LLB]

BEBB GORDON MONTFORT

2 King's Bench Walk
Ground Floor, Temple, London EC4Y 7DE, Telephone: 0171 353 1746
E-mail: 2kbw@atlas.co.uk
King's Bench Chambers
115 North Hill, Plymouth PL4 8JY, Telephone: 01752 221551
Call Date: Nov 1975, Middle Temple
Pupil Master
Qualifications: [BA (Oxon)]

BECK JAMES HARRISON

2-4 Tudor Street
London EC4Y 0AA,
Telephone: 0171 797 7111
E-mail: clerks@rfqc.co.uk
Call Date: July 1989, Lincoln's Inn
Qualifications: [BSc, MSc (LSE)]

BECKER PAUL ANTONY

Chavasse Court Chambers
2nd Floor, Chavasse Court, 24 Lord Street,
Liverpool L2 1TA,
Telephone: 0151 707 1191
Call Date: Nov 1990, Gray's Inn
Qualifications: [LLB (Hons)(Leeds)]

BECKER TIMOTHY GEORGE CHRISTIE

King's Bench Chambers
Wellington House, 175 Holdenhurst Road,
Bournemouth, Dorset, BH8 8DQ,
Telephone: 01202 250025
E-mail: chambers@kingsbench.co.uk
Call Date: July 1992, Middle Temple
Qualifications: [BA (Hons) (Lond), Dip Law,
A.K.C.]

BECKETT RICHARD GERVASE QC (1988)

3 Raymond Buildings
Gray's Inn, London WC1R 5BH,
Telephone: 020 7831 3833
E-mail:chambers@threeraymond.demon.co.uk
Call Date: Nov 1965, Middle Temple

BECKHOUGH MISS JENNIFER ANNE LINDSAY

Call Date: July 1973, Inner Temple
Qualifications: [LLB (Lond)]

BECKHOUGH NIGEL CHARLES LINDSAY

1 Gray's Inn Square, Chambers of the Baroness Scotland of Asthal QC
1st Floor, London WC1R 5AG,
Telephone: 0171 405 3000
E-mail: clerks@onegrays.demon.co.uk
Call Date: Nov 1976, Middle Temple
Pupil Master

BECKMAN MICHAEL DAVID QC (1976)

11 Stone Buildings
Lincoln's Inn, London WC2A 3TG,
Telephone: +44 (0)207 831 6381
E-mail:clerks@11StoneBuildings.law.co.uk

Chichester Chambers
12 North Pallant, Chichester, West Sussex,
PO19 1TQ, Telephone: 01243 784538
E-mail:clerks@chichesterchambers.law.co.uk
Call Date: May 1954, Lincoln's Inn
Qualifications: [LLB (Lond)]

BEDDOE MARTIN WILLIAM DENTON

Chambers of Michael Pert QC
36 Bedford Row, London WC1R 4JH,
Telephone: 0171 421 8000
E-mail: 36bedfordrow@link.org
Chambers of Michael Pert QC
24 Albion Place, Northampton NN1 1UD,
Telephone: 01604 602333
Chambers of Michael Pert QC
104 New Walk, Leicester LE1 7EA,
Telephone: 0116 249 2020
Call Date: Nov 1979, Gray's Inn
Pupil Master
Qualifications: [MA (Cantab)]

BEDEAU STEPHEN

Sovereign Chambers
25 Park Square, Leeds LS1 2PW,
Telephone: 0113 2451841/2/3
E-mail:sovereignchambers@btinternet.com
Lancaster Building
77 Deansgate, Manchester M3 2BW,
Telephone: 0161 661 4444/0171 649 9872
E-mail: sandra@lbnipc.com
Call Date: July 1980, Lincoln's Inn
Pupil Master
Qualifications: [LLB (Hull)]

BEDELL-PEARCE MISS SHERON IRENE

Brentwood Chambers
Denton, North Yorkshire, LS29 OHE,
Telephone: 01943 817230
One Garden Court Family Law Chambers
Ground Floor, Temple, London
EC4Y 9BJ, Telephone: 0171 797 7900
E-mail: clerks@onegardencourt.co.uk
Call Date: July 1978, Inner Temple
Qualifications: [LLB (Bris)]

BEDFORD BECKET NATHANIEL

5 Fountain Court
Steelhouse Lane, Birmingham B4 6DR,
Telephone: 0121 606 0500
E-mail:clerks@5fountaincourt.law.co.uk

Francis Taylor Building
3rd Floor, Temple, London EC4Y 7BY,
Telephone: 0171 797 7250
Call Date: Nov 1989, Middle Temple
Qualifications: [LLB (Hons)(Cardiff), Deug 1
(Nantes)]

BEDFORD MICHAEL CHARLES ANTHONY

2-3 Gray's Inn Square
Gray's Inn, London WC1R 5JH,
Telephone: 0171 242 4986
E-mail:chambers@2-3graysinnsquare.co.uk
Call Date: July 1985, Gray's Inn
Pupil Master
Qualifications: [LLB (Lond)]

BEDFORD STEPHEN JOHN

India Buildings Chambers
Water Street, Liverpool L2 0XG,
Telephone: 0151 243 6000
E-mail: clerks@chambers.u-net.com
Call Date: July 1974, Gray's Inn
Assistant Recorder
Qualifications: [BA (Oxon)]

BEDINGFIELD DAVID HERBERT

14 Gray's Inn Square
Gray's Inn, London WC1R 5JP,
Telephone: 0171 242 0858
E-mail: 100712.2134@compuserve.com
Call Date: Nov 1991, Gray's Inn
Qualifications: [BA (Florida State), Juris
Doctor (Emory)]

Fax: 0171 771 1401;
Out of hours telephone: 0171 733 2604

Types of work: Care proceedings, Education,
Employment, Equity, wills and trusts,
Family, Family provision, Local government

Membership of foreign bars: State Bar of
Georgia; American Bar Association

Circuit: South Eastern

Publications: *The Child in Need : Children,*
the State and the Law (Jordan's Publishing,
Inc), March 1998; 'Drugs, Money and the
Law', in *Criminal Law Review*, March 1992;
'Privacy or Publicity?', in *Modern Law*
Review, May 1991

Reported Cases: *Re L (Sexual Abuse; Disclo-*
sure), [1999] 1 WLR 299, CA, 1998.
Whether a Local Authority might disclose
civil findings of sexual abuse to another
Local Authority where the abuser now lives.
Re H (Application to remove from jurisdic-
tion), [1998] 1 FLR 848, CA, 1998. The
appropriate test to apply when a parent
seeks to remove a child from the jurisdiction against the wishes of the other parent.
L v London Borough of Bexley, [1996] 2
FLR 595, FD, 1996. Proper conduct of
proceedings when care order designating
Local Authority other than the applicant.
Re S (Minors; Inherent Jurisdiction;
Ouster), [1994] 1 FLR 623, FD, 1994.
Whether Local Authority might use
inherent jurisdiction of High Court to
achieve ouster of sex abuser.

BEECH MS JACQUELINE ELAINE

199 Strand
London WC2R 1DR,
Telephone: 0171 379 9779
E-mail: chambers@199strand.co.uk
Call Date: Nov 1981, Middle Temple
Pupil Master
Qualifications: [BA]

BEECHEY MISS HILARY JANE

Godolphin Chambers
50 Castle Street, Truro, Cornwall,
TR1 3AF, Telephone: 01872 276312
E-mail:theclerks@godolphin.force9.co.uk
Call Date: Nov 1987, Middle Temple
Qualifications: [BA (Hons), Dip Law (City)]

BEECROFT MISS KIRSTIE

Tindal Chambers
3/5 New Street, Chelmsford, Essex,
CM1 1NT, Telephone: 01245 267742
St Albans Chambers
Dolphin Lodge, Dolphin Yard, Holywell
Hill, St Albans, Herts, AL1 1EX,
Telephone: 01727 843383
Call Date: Feb 1994, Inner Temple
Qualifications: [LLB (Leic)]

BEECROFT ROBERT GEORGE

1 Harcourt Buildings
2nd Floor, Temple, London EC4Y 9DA,
Telephone: 0171 353 9421/0375
E-mail:clerks@1harcourtbuildings.law.co.uk
Call Date: Nov 1977, Gray's Inn
Pupil Master
Qualifications: [LLB]

BEER JASON BARRINGTON

5 Essex Court
1st Floor, Temple, London EC4Y 9AH,
Telephone: 0171 410 2000
E-mail: barristers@5essexcourt.co.uk
Call Date: Oct 1992, Inner Temple
Qualifications: [LLB (Warw)]

BEESE MISS NICOLA HELEN

Victoria Chambers
3rd Floor, 177 Corporation Street,
Birmingham B4 6RG,
Telephone: 0121 236 9900
E-mail: viccham@aol.com
Call Date: 1998, Lincoln's Inn
Qualifications: [LLB (Hons)(Sheff)]

BEESON NIGEL ADRIAN LAURENCE

First National Chambers
2nd Floor, First National Building, 24
Fenwick Street, Liverpool L2 7NE,
Telephone: 0151 236 2098
Call Date: July 1983, Lincoln's Inn
Pupil Master
Qualifications: [LLB (Hons)]

BEEVER EDMUND DAMIAN

St Philip's Chambers
Fountain Court, Steelhouse Lane,
Birmingham B4 6DR,
Telephone: 0121 246 7000
E-mail: clerks@st-philips.co.uk
Call Date: Oct 1990, Lincoln's Inn
Qualifications: [BA (Oxon)]

BEGGS JOHN PETER

3 Serjeants' Inn
London EC4Y 1BQ,
Telephone: 0171 353 5537
E-mail: clerks@3serjeantsinn.com
Call Date: Nov 1989, Gray's Inn
Pupil Master
Qualifications: [LLB (Brunel)]

BEGLAN WAYNE STUART

2-3 Gray's Inn Square
Gray's Inn, London WC1R 5JH,
Telephone: 0171 242 4986
E-mail:chambers@2-3graysinnsquare.co.uk
Call Date: Oct 1996, Lincoln's Inn
Qualifications: [BA (Hons)(Keele)]

BEGLEY MISS LAURA ANNE

9 Gough Square
London EC4A 3DE,
Telephone: 020 7832 0500
E-mail: clerks@9goughsq.co.uk
Call Date: Nov 1993, Lincoln's Inn
Qualifications: [LLB (Hons, Leeds)]

BEHAR RICHARD VICTOR MONTAGUE EDWARD

One Essex Court
Ground Floor, Temple, London
EC4Y 9AR, Telephone: 020 7583 2000
E-mail: clerks@oneessexcourt.co.uk
Call Date: Nov 1965, Middle Temple
Pupil Master, Recorder
Qualifications: [MA(Oxon)]

BEHRENS JAMES NICHOLAS EDWARD

Serle Court Chambers
6 New Square, Lincoln's Inn, London
WC2A 3QS, Telephone: 0171 242 6105
E-mail: clerks@serlecourt.co.uk
Call Date: July 1979, Middle Temple
Pupil Master
Qualifications: [MA (Cantab)]

BEKOE SAMUEL YAW

Chancery Chambers
1st Floor Offices, 70/72 Chancery Lane,
London WC2A 1AB,
Telephone: 0171 405 6879/6870
Call Date: Nov 1980, Lincoln's Inn
Qualifications: [BA (Manch)]

BELBEN ROBIN WILLIAM

College Chambers
19 Carlton Cresent, Southampton
SO15 2ET, Telephone: 01703 230338
Call Date: Nov 1969, Lincoln's Inn
Pupil Master, Recorder
Qualifications: [LLB (Hons)(Lond)]

BELBIN MISS HEATHER PATRICIA

Oriel Chambers
14 Water Street, Liverpool L2 8TD,
Telephone: 0151 236 7191/236 4321
E-mail: clerks@oriel-chambers.co.uk
Call Date: Oct 1992, Lincoln's Inn
Qualifications: [LLB(Hons)(Shef)]

BELFORD MISS DORA JOY

14 Tooks Court
Cursitor St, London EC4A 1LB,
Telephone: 0171 405 8828
E-mail: clerks@tooks.law.co.uk
Call Date: July 1977, Middle Temple
Pupil Master

BELGER TYRONE

Dr Johnson's Chambers
Two Dr Johnson's Buildings, Temple,
London EC4Y 7AY,
Telephone: 0171 353 4716
E-mail: clerks@2djb.freeserve.co.uk
Call Date: July 1984, Inner Temple
Qualifications: [LLB (Lond)]

BELGRAVE MISS SUSAN LORRAINE

4 Brick Court
Ground Floor, Temple, London
EC4Y 9AD, Telephone: 0171 797 7766
E-mail: chambers@4brick.co.uk
Call Date: July 1989, Inner Temple
Qualifications: [BA, LLB, MSc (Econ),
Lic.Spec.En Droit, European (LLM)]

BELL ALPHEGE

2-4 Tudor Street
London EC4Y 0AA,
Telephone: 0171 797 7111
E-mail: clerks@rfqc.co.uk
Call Date: Oct 1995, Inner Temple
Qualifications: [BA (Oxon)]

BELL MISS ANNE MARGARET

Holborn Chambers
6 Gate Street, Lincoln's Inn Fields, London
WC2A 3HP, Telephone: 0171 242 6060
Middlesex Chambers
Suite 3 & 4 Stanley House, Stanley
Avenue, Wembley, Middlesex, HA0 4SB,
Telephone: 0181 902 1499
Call Date: Nov 1975, Gray's Inn
Pupil Master
Qualifications: [BA (Hons)]

BELL ANTHONY JOHN

4 Brick Court
Temple, London EC4Y 9AD,
Telephone: 0171 797 8910
E-mail: medhurst@dial.pipex.com
Call Date: Nov 1985, Inner Temple
Pupil Master
Qualifications: [BA (Hons)]

BELL DOMINIC MICHAEL ST. JOHN

2 Dyers Buildings
London EC1N 2JT,
Telephone: 0171 404 1881
Call Date: Nov 1992, Inner Temple
Qualifications: [LLB (Lond)]

BELL GARY TERENCE

Equity Chambers
3rd Floor, 153a Corporation Street,
Birmingham B4 6PH,
Telephone: 0121 233 2100
E-mail: equityatusa.com
Call Date: Feb 1989, Inner Temple
Qualifications: [LLB (Bris)]

BELL JAMES

1 Temple Gardens
1st Floor, Temple, London EC4Y 9BB,
Telephone: 0171 583 1315/353 0407
E-mail: clerks@1templegardens.co.uk
Call Date: Nov 1987, Middle Temple
Pupil Master
Qualifications: [LLB(Hons) Wales]

BELL MISS MARIKA PAMELA TRACEY

East Anglian Chambers
57 London Street, Norwich NR2 1HL,
Telephone: 01603 617351
E-mail: norwich@ealaw.co.uk
East Anglian Chambers
52 North Hill, Colchester, Essex, CO1 1PY,
Telephone: 01206 572756
E-mail: colchester@ealaw.co.uk
East Anglian Chambers
Gresham House, 5 Museum Street,
Ipswich, Suffolk, IP1 1HQ,
Telephone: 01473 214481
E-mail: ipswich@ealaw.co.uk
Call Date: Nov 1991, Gray's Inn
Qualifications: [LLB (B'ham)]

BELLAMY JONATHAN MARK

39 Essex Street
London WC2R 3AT,
Telephone: 0171 832 1111
E-mail: clerks@39essex.co.uk
Call Date: Nov 1986, Lincoln's Inn
Pupil Master
Qualifications: [MA(Oxon)]

BELLAMY STEPHEN HOWARD QC (1996)

One King's Bench Walk
1st Floor, Temple, London EC4Y 7DB,
Telephone: 0171 936 1500
E-mail: ddear@1kbw.co.uk
Call Date: Nov 1974, Lincoln's Inn
Recorder
Qualifications: [MA (Cantab), ACIArb]

BELLIS WILLIAM GORDON

Corn Exchange Chambers
5th Floor, Fenwick Street, Liverpool
L2 7QS, Telephone: 0151 227 1081/5009
Call Date: July 1972, Inner Temple
Qualifications: [MA (Cantab)]

BELOFF THE HON MICHAEL JACOB QC (1981)

4-5 Gray's Inn Square
Ground Floor, Gray's Inn, London
WC1R 5JP, Telephone: 0171 404 5252
E-mail:chambers@4-5graysinnsquare.co.uk
Call Date: Nov 1967, Gray's Inn
Recorder
Qualifications: [MA (Oxon)]

BELSON MISS EMILY ELIZABETH

23 Essex Street
London WC2R 3AS,
Telephone: 0171 413 0353/836 8366
E-mail:clerks@essexstreet23.demon.co.uk
Call Date: Oct 1997, Middle Temple
Qualifications: [BA (Hons)(Cantab)]

BELSON MISS JANE ELIZABETH

17 Bedford Row
London WC1R 4EB,
Telephone: 0171 831 7314
E-mail: iboard7314@aol.com
Call Date: July 1978, Inner Temple
Pupil Master
Qualifications: [BA (Oxon)]

BELTRAMI ADRIAN JOSEPH

3 Verulam Buildings
London WC1R 5NT,
Telephone: 0171 831 8441
E-mail: clerks@3verulam.co.uk
Call Date: July 1989, Lincoln's Inn
Pupil Master
Qualifications: [BA (Cantab), LLM (Harvard)]

BENBOW MISS SARA ELIZABETH

Hardwicke Building
New Square, Lincoln's Inn, London
WC2A 3SB, Telephone: 020 7242 2523
E-mail: clerks@hardwicke.co.uk
Call Date: Nov 1990, Middle Temple
Pupil Master
Qualifications: [LLB (Exon)]

BENDALL RICHARD GILES

33 Bedford Row
London WC1R 4JH,
Telephone: 0171 242 6476
E-mail:clerks@bedfordrow33.demon.co.uk
Call Date: July 1979, Lincoln's Inn
Pupil Master
Qualifications: [LLB]

BENEDICT JOHN IDOWU

One Essex Court
1st Floor, Temple, London EC4Y 9AR,
Telephone: 0171 936 3030
E-mail: one.essex_court@virgin.net
Call Date: July 1963, Middle Temple

BENNATHAN JOEL NATHAN

14 Tooks Court
Cursitor St, London EC4A 1LB,
Telephone: 0171 405 8828
E-mail: clerks@tooks.law.co.uk
Call Date: Nov 1985, Middle Temple
Pupil Master
Qualifications: [LLB(Lond)]

BENNER MISS LUCINDA DIANA KATE

11 Bolt Court (also at 7 Stone Buildings – 1st Floor)
London EC4A 3DQ,
Telephone: 0171 353 2300
E-mail: boltct11@aol.com
Redhill Chambers
Seloduct House, 30 Station Road, Redhill,
Surrey, RH1 1NF,
Telephone: 01737 780781
7 Stone Buildings (also at 11 Bolt Court)
1st Floor, Lincoln's Inn, London
WC2A 3SZ, Telephone: 0171 242 0961
E-mail:larthur@7stonebuildings.law.co.uk
Call Date: Oct 1992, Middle Temple
Qualifications: [LL.B (Hons, Leeds)]

BENNET MS PAULINE AGNES

Regency Chambers
Cathedral Square, Peterborough
PE1 1XW, Telephone: 01733 315215
Regency Chambers
Sheraton House, Castle Park, Cambridge
CB3 0AX, Telephone: 01223 301517
Call Date: Oct 1991, Lincoln's Inn
Qualifications: [BSc (Hons, Lond), BA (Lond)]

BENNETT CHARLES HENRY

1 Harcourt Buildings
2nd Floor, Temple, London EC4Y 9DA,
Telephone: 0171 353 9421/0375
E-mail:clerks@1harcourtbuildings.law.co.uk
Call Date: July 1972, Inner Temple
Qualifications: [BA (Oxon)]

BENNETT DAVID LAURENCE

Castle Street Chambers
2nd Floor, 42 Castle Street, Liverpool
L2 7LD, Telephone: 0151 242 0500
Call Date: Nov 1977, Middle Temple
Pupil Master
Qualifications: [BA (Hons)]

BENNETT GORDON IRVINE

12 New Square
Lincoln's Inn, London WC2A 3SW,
Telephone: 0171 419 1212
E-mail: chambers@12newsquare.co.uk
Call Date: Feb 1974, Gray's Inn
Qualifications: [LLB, LLM (Calif), Dip Int Law (Cantab)]

BENNETT IEUAN GEREINT

33 Park Place
Cardiff CF1 3BA,
Telephone: 02920 233313
Call Date: July 1989, Middle Temple
Qualifications: [LLB (Wales), MA (Hull)]

BENNETT JOHN MARTYN

Oriel Chambers
14 Water Street, Liverpool L2 8TD,
Telephone: 0151 236 7191/236 4321
E-mail: clerks@oriel-chambers.co.uk
Call Date: July 1969, Gray's Inn
Pupil Master
Qualifications: [LLB]

Fax: 01829 781524;
Out of hours telephone: 01829 781524

Types of work: Care proceedings, Employment, Family, Family provision, Medical negligence, Professional negligence

Circuit: Northern

Awards and memberships: FLBA; Associate Member of BALM

Other professional experience: Non-executive Director of family manufacturing company

Publications: 'The Cost of the Clean Break' in *Family Law*, 1989; 'The Mechanics of the Offer: The Art of Settlement' in *Family Law*, 1990; 'Challenging Ancillary Relief Orders' in *Family Law*, 1993

Reported Cases: *F v Wirral MBC*, [1991] 2 All ER 648, 1990. Whether right of action in tort for interference with parental rights. *Vicary v Vicary*, [1992] 2 FLR, 1991. Substantial assets – weight to be given to 'Duxbury' calculation – correct approach as to costs as a need. *Halford v Sharples*, [1992] 3 All ER 624, 1992. Whether police complaints and disciplinary files protected from disclosure by reason of public interest immunity. *Welsh v Chief Constable of Merseyside Police*, [1993] 1 All ER 692, 1993. Duty of care in tort owed by CPS to accused in criminal case. *Re Y (mental incapacity: bone marrow transplant)*, [1996] 2 FLR 787, 1996. Test for giving consent to transplant operation involving adult sibling with mental incapacity.

BENNETT JONATHAN CHARLES LYDDON

22 Old Buildings
Lincoln's Inn, London WC2A 3UJ,
Telephone: 0171 831 0222
Call Date: July 1985, Gray's Inn
Pupil Master
Qualifications: [MA (Cantab)]

BENNETT MISS MARY

5 Fountain Court
Steelhouse Lane, Birmingham B4 6DR,
Telephone: 0121 606 0500
E-mail:clerks@5fountaincourt.law.co.uk
Call Date: Oct 1990, Gray's Inn
Qualifications: [LLB]

BENNETT MILES ALEXANDER FORDHAM

Five Paper Buildings
1st Floor, Five Paper Bldgs, Temple,
London EC4Y 7HB,
Telephone: 0171 583 6117
E-mail:clerks@5-paperbuildings.law.co.uk
Call Date: Nov 1986, Inner Temple
Pupil Master
Qualifications: [LLB(Hull)]

BENNETT RICHARD ANTHONY

Fountain Chambers
Cleveland Business Centre, 1 Watson
Street, Middlesbrough TS1 2RQ,
Telephone: 01642 804040
E-mail:fountainchambers@onyxnet.co.uk
Call Date: Oct 1996, Inner Temple
Qualifications: [BSc (Hons) (Newc), CPE]

BENNETT RICHARD JOHN

15 Winckley Square
Preston PR1 3JJ,
Telephone: 01772 252828
E-mail:clerks@winckleysq.demon.co.uk
Call Date: July 1986, Middle Temple
Qualifications: [LLB]

BENNETT WILLIAM

5 Raymond Buildings
1st Floor, Gray's Inn, London WC1R 5BP,
Telephone: 0171 242 2902
E-mail: clerks@media-ent-law.co.uk
Call Date: Oct 1994, Inner Temple
Qualifications: [BA (L'pool), CPE]

BENNETT JENKINS MISS SALLIE ANN

1 Hare Court
Ground Floor, Temple, London
EC4Y 7BE, Telephone: 0171 353 3982/
5324
Call Date: 1984, Gray's Inn
Pupil Master, Assistant Recorder
Qualifications: [LLB (Lond)]

BENNETTS PHILIP JAMES

Hollis Whiteman Chambers
3rd Floor, Queen Elizabeth Bldg, Temple,
London EC4Y 9BS,
Telephone: 020 7583 5766
E-mail:barristers@holliswhiteman.co.uk
Call Date: July 1986, Lincoln's Inn
Qualifications: [LLB (Brunel)]

BENNINGTON MS JANE SUSAN

Chambers of Norman Palmer
2 Field Court, Gray's Inn, London
WC1R 5BB, Telephone: 0171 405 6114
E-mail: fieldct2@netcomuk.co.uk
Call Date: July 1981, Gray's Inn
Qualifications: [BA Hons]

BENSON CHARLES JEFFERIUS WOODBURN

2 Paper Buildings
1st Floor, Temple, London EC4Y 7ET,
Telephone: 020 7556 5500
E-mail: clerks@2pbbarristers.co.uk
Call Date: Feb 1990, Middle Temple
Qualifications: [MA LLM (Cantab), B.Admin
(Hons)]

BENSON JAMES D'ARCY

Derby Square Chambers
Merchants Court, Derby Square, Liverpool
L2 1TS, Telephone: 0151 709 4222
E-mail:mail.derbysquare@pop3.hiway.co.uk
Call Date: Nov 1995, Gray's Inn
Qualifications: [BA]

BENSON JEREMY KEITH

1 Hare Court
Ground Floor, Temple, London
EC4Y 7BE, Telephone: 0171 353 3982/
5324
Call Date: July 1978, Middle Temple
Pupil Master, Recorder
Qualifications: [BA]

BENSON JOHN TREVOR

Adrian Lyon's Chambers
14 Castle Street, Liverpool L2 0NE,
Telephone: 0151 236 4421/8240
E-mail: chambers14@aol.com
Call Date: July 1978, Middle Temple
Pupil Master
Qualifications: [LLB (Hons) (L'pool)]

BENSON JULIAN CHRISTOPHER WOODBURN

One Essex Court
1st Floor, Temple, London EC4Y 9AR,
Telephone: 0171 936 3030
E-mail: one.essex_court@virgin.net
Call Date: Nov 1991, Middle Temple
Qualifications: [BA Hons (Dunelm), BA
Hons,LLM (Cantab)]

BENSON MARK GILPIN

18 St John Street
Manchester M3 4EA,
Telephone: 0161 278 1800
E-mail: 18stjohn@lineone.net
Call Date: Oct 1992, Middle Temple
Qualifications: [BA (Hons, B'ham)]

BENSON PETER CHARLES

St Paul's House
5th Floor, St Paul's House, 23 Park Square
South, Leeds LS1 2ND,
Telephone: 0113 2455866
E-mail: catherinegrimshaw@stpauls-
chambers.demon.co.uk
Call Date: July 1975, Middle Temple
Pupil Master, Recorder
Qualifications: [BSc]

BENSON RICHARD ANTHONY QC (1995)

Chambers of Michael Pert QC
36 Bedford Row, London WC1R 4JH,
Telephone: 0171 421 8000
E-mail: 36bedfordrow@link.org
Chambers of Michael Pert QC
24 Albion Place, Northampton NN1 1UD,
Telephone: 01604 602333
Chambers of Michael Pert QC
104 New Walk, Leicester LE1 7EA,
Telephone: 0116 249 2020
Call Date: July 1974, Inner Temple
Recorder

BENSTED MISS REBECCA CLAIRE

Bracton Chambers
95a Chancery Lane, London WC2A 1DT,
Telephone: 0171 242 4248
Call Date: Nov 1993, Gray's Inn
Qualifications: [MA (Cantab)]

BENTHAM HOWARD LOWNDS QC (1996)

Peel Court Chambers
45 Hardman Street, Manchester M3 3PL,
Telephone: 0161 832 3791
E-mail: clerks@peelct.co.uk
Call Date: Nov 1970, Gray's Inn
Recorder
Qualifications: [LLB]

BENTLEY ANTHONY PHILIP QC (1991)

Stanbrook & Henderson
Ground Floor, 2 Harcourt Bldgs, Temple,
London EC4Y 9DB,
Telephone: 0171 353 0101
E-mail: clerks@harcourt.co.uk
Call Date: Nov 1970, Lincoln's Inn

BENTLEY DAVID NEIL

Doughty Street Chambers
11 Doughty Street, London WC1N 2PG,
Telephone: 0171 404 1313
E-mail:enquiries@doughtystreet.co.uk
Call Date: Feb 1984, Gray's Inn
Pupil Master
Qualifications: [LLB (Lond)]

BENTLEY STEPHEN

1 Gray's Inn Square
Ground Floor, London WC1R 5AA,
Telephone: 0171 405 8946/7/8
Call Date: Nov 1997, Middle Temple
Qualifications: [LLB (Hons)]

BENTWOOD RICHARD

Chambers of Geoffrey Hawker
46/48 Essex Street, London WC2R 3GH,
Telephone: 0171 583 8899
Call Date: Nov 1994, Inner Temple
Qualifications: [LLB (Notts)]

BENZYNIE ROBERT JOSEPH

Dr Johnson's Chambers
Two Dr Johnson's Buildings, Temple,
London EC4Y 7AY,
Telephone: 0171 353 4716
E-mail: clerks@2djb.freeserve.co.uk
Call Date: Nov 1992, Gray's Inn
Qualifications: [LLB (Buckingham)]

BERESFORD COLIN THOMAS

4 Brick Court
Ground Floor, Temple, London
EC4Y 9AD, Telephone: 0171 797 7766
E-mail: chambers@4brick.co.uk
Call Date: Feb 1979, Gray's Inn
Qualifications: [BA]

BERESFORD STEPHEN ROGER

Ropewalk Chambers
24 The Ropewalk, Nottingham NG1 5EF,
Telephone: 0115 9472581
E-mail: administration@ropewalk co.uk
Call Date: July 1976, Gray's Inn
Pupil Master
Qualifications: [LLB (B'ham)]

BERESFORD-EVANS MISS CERYS

St David's Chambers
10 Calvert Terrace, Swansea, West
Glamorgan, SA1 5AR,
Call Date: Nov 1995, Middle Temple
Qualifications: [LLB (Hons)]

BERGENTHAL RONNIE MARK

**Gray's Inn Chambers, The Chambers of
Norman Patterson**
First Floor, Gray's Inn Chambers, Gray's
Inn, London WC1R 5JA,
Telephone: 0171 831 5344
E-mail: s.mcblain@btinternet.com
Call Date: Oct 1993, Middle Temple
Qualifications: [BA (Hons), LLB (Hons)]

BERGIN TERENCE EDWARD

New Court Chambers
5 Verulam Buildings, Gray's Inn, London
WC1R 5LY, Telephone: 0171 831 9500
E-mail: mail@newcourtchambers.com
Harrow on the Hill Chambers
60 High Street, Harrow-on-the-Hill,
Middlesex, HA1 3LL,
Telephone: 0181 423 7444
Call Date: 1985, Inner Temple
Pupil Master
Qualifications: [BA(Cantab)]

BERGIN TIMOTHY WILLIAM

Crown Office Row Chambers
Blenheim House, 120 Church Street,
Brighton, Sussex, BN1 1WH,
Telephone: 01273 625625
E-mail: crownofficerow@clara.net
Call Date: July 1987, Middle Temple
Pupil Master
Qualifications: [LLB, M.Phil (Exon)]

BERKIN MARTYN DAVID MAURICE

One Paper Buildings
Ground Floor, Temple, London
EC4Y 7EP, Telephone: 0171 583 7355
E-mail: clerks@1pb.co.uk
Call Date: July 1966, Inner Temple
Pupil Master
Qualifications: [MA (Cantab)]

BERKLEY DAVID NAHUM QC (1999)

Merchant Chambers
1 North Parade, Parsonage Gardens,
Manchester M3 2NH,
Telephone: 0161 839 7070
E-mail: merchant.chambers@virgin.net
Call Date: 1979, Middle Temple
Pupil Master
Qualifications: [LLB (Manch)]

BERKLEY MICHAEL STUART

Rougemont Chambers
8 Colleton Crescent, Exeter, Devon,
EX1 1RR, Telephone: 01392 208484
E-mail:rougemont.chambers@eclipse.co.uk
Call Date: July 1989, Middle Temple
Pupil Master
Qualifications: [LLB (Hons)(Bus. Law)]

BERKSON SIMON NATHANIEL

Exchange Chambers
Pearl Assurance House, Derby Square,
Liverpool L2 9XX,
Telephone: 0151 236 7747
E-mail:exchangechambers@btinternet.com
Call Date: July 1986, Gray's Inn
Pupil Master
Qualifications: [LLB]

BERLIN BARRY ADRIAN

St Ive's Chambers
Whittall Street, Birmingham B4 6DH,
Telephone: 0121 236 0863/5720
E-mail:stives.headofchambers@btinternet.com
Call Date: July 1981, Gray's Inn
Pupil Master
Qualifications: [BSc (Hons) (Brunel), MSc
Environmental, Health]

BERMINGHAM GERALD EDWARD

Francis Taylor Building
Ground Floor, Temple, London
EC4Y 7BY, Telephone: 0171 353 7768/
7769/2711
E-mail:clerks@francistaylorbuilding.law.co.uk
Westgate Chambers
144 High Street, Lewes, East Sussex,
BN7 1XT, Telephone: 01273 480510
Call Date: Feb 1985, Gray's Inn
Pupil Master
Qualifications: [LLB (Hons)(Sheff)]

BERRAGAN (HOWARD) NEIL

Merchant Chambers
1 North Parade, Parsonage Gardens,
Manchester M3 2NH,
Telephone: 0161 839 7070
E-mail: merchant.chambers@virgin.net
Call Date: July 1982, Gray's Inn
Pupil Master
Qualifications: [BA (Oxon)]

BERRICK STEVEN ISAAC

2 Paper Buildings
1st Floor, Temple, London EC4Y 7ET,
Telephone: 020 7556 5500
E-mail: clerks@2pbbarristers.co.uk
Call Date: July 1986, Middle Temple
Qualifications: [BA London]

BERRIDGE MISS ELIZABETH ROSE

40 King Street
Manchester M2 6BA,
Telephone: 0161 832 9082
E-mail: clerks@40kingstreet.co.uk
The Chambers of Philip Raynor QC
5 Park Place, Leeds LS1 2RU,
Telephone: 0113 242 1123
Call Date: Nov 1996, Inner Temple
Qualifications: [BA (Cantab)]

BERRIMAN TREVOR ST JOHN

10 King's Bench Walk
1st Floor, Temple, London EC4Y 7EB,
Telephone: 0171 353 2501
Call Date: Nov 1988, Inner Temple
Qualifications: [LLB (Hons)]

BERRISFORD ANTHONY EDWARD

Ropewalk Chambers
24 The Ropewalk, Nottingham NG1 5EF,
Telephone: 0115 9472581
E-mail: administration@ropewalk co.uk
Call Date: July 1972, Inner Temple

BERRY ANTHONY CHARLES QC (1994)

**4 Brick Court, Chambers of Anne
Rafferty QC**
1st Floor, Temple, London EC4Y 9AD,
Telephone: 0171 583 8455
Call Date: July 1976, Gray's Inn
Assistant Recorder
Qualifications: [BA (Oxon)]

BERRY MARTIN DAMIAN JOSEPH

Tindal Chambers
3/5 New Street, Chelmsford, Essex,
CM1 1NT, Telephone: 01245 267742
St Albans Chambers
Dolphin Lodge, Dolphin Yard, Holywell
Hill, St Albans, Herts, AL1 1EX,
Telephone: 01727 843383
Call Date: Nov 1992, Lincoln's Inn
Qualifications: [BA (Hons)]

BERRY NICHOLAS MICHAEL

Southernhay Chambers
33 Southernhay East, Exeter, Devon,
EX1 1NX, Telephone: 01392 255777
E-mail:southernhay.chambers@lineone.net
1 Gray's Inn Square
Ground Floor, London WC1R 5AA,
Telephone: 0171 405 8946/7/8
22 Old Buildings
Lincoln's Inn, London WC2A 3UJ,
Telephone: 0171 831 0222
Call Date: Nov 1988, Inner Temple
Qualifications: [BA (Hons)]

BERRY SIMON QC (1990)

9 Old Square
Ground Floor, Lincoln's Inn, London
WC2A 3SR, Telephone: 0171 405 4682
E-mail: chambers@9oldsquare.co.uk
Call Date: July 1977, Middle Temple
Qualifications: [LLB]

BERRY STEVEN JOHN

Essex Court Chambers
24 Lincoln's Inn Fields, London
WC2A 3ED, Telephone: 0171 813 8000
E-mail:clerksroom@essexcourt-chambers.co.u
k
Call Date: Nov 1984, Middle Temple
Pupil Master
Qualifications: [BA,BCL (Oxon)]

BEST STANLEY PHILIP

Veritas Chambers
33 Corn Street, Bristol BS1 1HT,
Telephone: 0117 930 8802
Call Date: July 1989, Middle Temple

BETHEL MARTIN QC (1983)

Park Lane Chambers
19 Westgate, Leeds LS1 2RD,
Telephone: 0113 2285000
E-mail:clerks@parklanechambers.co.uk
Call Date: Nov 1965, Inner Temple
Recorder
Qualifications: [MA, LLM (Cantab)]

BETHLEHEM DANIEL LINCOLN

20 Essex Street
London WC2R 3AL,
Telephone: 0171 583 9294
E-mail: clerks@20essexst.com
Call Date: Nov 1988, Middle Temple
Qualifications: [BA (Witwatersrand), LLB
(Bris), LLM (Cantab)]

BETTLE MRS JANET ROSEMARY

East Anglian Chambers
52 North Hill, Colchester, Essex, CO1 1PY,
Telephone: 01206 572756
E-mail: colchester@ealaw.co.uk
East Anglian Chambers
57 London Street, Norwich NR2 1HL,
Telephone: 01603 617351
E-mail: norwich@ealaw.co.uk
East Anglian Chambers
Gresham House, 5 Museum Street,
Ipswich, Suffolk, IP1 1HQ,
Telephone: 01473 214481
E-mail: ipswich@ealaw.co.uk
Call Date: July 1985, Inner Temple
Pupil Master
Qualifications: [LLB (London)]

BEVAN EDWARD JULIAN QC (1991)

Hollis Whiteman Chambers
3rd Floor, Queen Elizabeth Bldg, Temple,
London EC4Y 9BS,
Telephone: 020 7583 5766
E-mail:barristers@holliswhiteman.co.uk
Call Date: Nov 1962, Gray's Inn

BEVAN HUGH KEITH

Wilberforce Chambers
7 Bishop Lane, Hull, East Yorkshire,
HU1 1PA, Telephone: 01482 323264
E-mail: clerks@hullbar.demon.co.uk

17 Bedford Row
London WC1R 4EB,
Telephone: 0171 831 7314
E-mail: iboard7314@aol.com
Call Date: June 1959, Middle Temple
Qualifications: [LLM]

BEVAN JOHN PENRY VAUGHAN QC (1997)

2 Harcourt Buildings
1st Floor, Temple, London EC4Y 9DB,
Telephone: 020 7353 2112
Call Date: July 1970, Middle Temple
Recorder
Qualifications: [MA (Cantab)]

BEVAN STEPHEN THOMAS ROWLAND

1 Pump Court
Lower Ground Floor, Temple, London
EC4Y 7AB, Telephone: 0171 583 2012/
353 4341
E-mail: [name]@1pumpcourt.co.uk
Call Date: Nov 1986, Inner Temple
Pupil Master
Qualifications: [BA]

BEVIS DOMINIC JOSEPH

10 King's Bench Walk
Ground Floor, Temple, London
EC4Y 7EB, Telephone: 0171 353 7742
E-mail: 10kbw@lineone.net
Call Date: Nov 1996, Middle Temple
Qualifications: [BSc (Hons) (Wales)]

BEVITT MISS ANN

Francis Taylor Building
3rd Floor, Temple, London EC4Y 7BY,
Telephone: 0171 797 7250
Call Date: Oct 1992, Gray's Inn
Qualifications: [BA (Hons)(Oxon)]

BEWSEY MISS JANE

18 Red Lion Court
(Off Fleet Street), London EC4A 3EB,
Telephone: 0171 520 6000
E-mail: chambers@18rlc.co.uk

Thornwood House
102 New London Road, Chelmsford,
Essex, CM2 0RG,
Telephone: 01245 280880
E-mail: chambers@18rlc.co.uk
Call Date: July 1986, Inner Temple
Pupil Master
Qualifications: [MA (Cantab)]

BEX MISS KATHARINE

1 Hare Court
Ground Floor, Temple, London
EC4Y 7BE, Telephone: 0171 353 3982/
5324
Call Date: Nov 1992, Inner Temple
Qualifications: [BA]

BEXLEY SIMON MARK

3 Temple Gardens
3rd Floor, Temple, London EC4Y 9AU,
Telephone: 0171 353 0832
Call Date: Oct 1993, Inner Temple
Qualifications: [LLB (Hull)]

BEYNON RICHARD JOHN LLEWELLYN

1 Middle Temple Lane
Temple, London EC4Y 1LT,
Telephone: 0171 583 0659 (12 Lines)
E-mail: chambers@1mtl.co.uk
Call Date: Oct 1990, Inner Temple
Qualifications: [LLB]

BEYTS CHESTER ANDOE MICHAEL

3 Gray's Inn Square
Ground Floor, London WC1R 5AH,
Telephone: 0171 520 5600
E-mail: clerks@3gis.co.uk
Call Date: Nov 1978, Inner Temple
Pupil Master
Qualifications: [BA (Hons) (Lond)]

BEZZAM MISS JAYASHREE

2 Middle Temple Lane
3rd Floor, Temple, London EC4Y 9AA,
Telephone: 0171 583 4540
Call Date: 1997, Lincoln's Inn
Qualifications: [BSc (Andhra), BL, ML
(Madras)]

BHAKAR SURINDER SINGH

2 Gray's Inn Square Chambers
2nd Floor, Gray's Inn, London WC1R 5AA,
Telephone: 020 7242 0328
E-mail: clerks@2gis.co.uk
Call Date: Nov 1986, Gray's Inn
Qualifications: [LLB(Lon) LLM(Cantab)]

BHALLA BITU

One Essex Court
1st Floor, Temple, London EC4Y 9AR,
Telephone: 0171 936 3030
E-mail: one.essex_court@virgin.net
Call Date: Nov 1978, Gray's Inn
Qualifications: [LLB, LLM, AKC (Lond), LLM
(USA)]

BHALOO MISS ZIA KURBAN

Enterprise Chambers
9 Old Square, Lincoln's Inn, London
WC2A 3SR, Telephone: 0171 405 9471
E-mail:enterprise.london@dial.pipex.com
Enterprise Chambers
38 Park Square, Leeds LS1 2PA,
Telephone: 0113 246 0391
E-mail:enterprise.leeds@dial.pipex.com
Enterprise Chambers
65 Quayside, Newcastle upon Tyne
NE1 3DS, Telephone: 0191 222 3344
E-mail:enterprise.newcastle@dial.pipex.com
Call Date: Nov 1990, Middle Temple
Pupil Master
Qualifications: [LLB (UCL), LLM (Lond)]

BHANJI SHIRAZ MUSA

4 Bingham Place
London W1M 3FF,
Telephone: 0171 486 5347/071 487 5910
Call Date: July 1979, Gray's Inn
Qualifications: [BSc (Wales)]

BHARDWAJ MISS UMA

12 Old Square
1st Floor, Lincoln's Inn, London
WC2A 3TX, Telephone: 0171 404 0875
Call Date: Nov 1984, Middle Temple
Qualifications: [LLB (Lond)]

BHATIA BALRAJ SINGH

High Pavement Chambers
1 High Pavement, Nottingham NG1 1HF,
Telephone: 0115 9418218
Call Date: Nov 1982, Inner Temple
Pupil Master
Qualifications: [LLB]

BHATIA MISS DIVYA

Queen Elizabeth Building
Ground Floor, Temple, London
EC4Y 9BS,
Telephone: 0171 353 7181 (12 Lines)
Call Date: July 1986, Middle Temple
Qualifications: [MA (Oxon)]

BHATTACHARYYA ARDHENDU

Slough Chamber
11 St Bernards Road, Slough, Berkshire,
SL3 7NT, Telephone: 01753 553806/
817989
1 Gray's Inn Square
Ground Floor, London WC1R 5AA,
Telephone: 0171 405 8946/7/8
Call Date: Nov 1974, Inner Temple
Qualifications: [BA, FBIM, FCIS, ACIArb, Dip
CL]

BHOSE RANJIT

2-3 Gray's Inn Square
Gray's Inn, London WC1R 5JH,
Telephone: 0171 242 4986
E-mail:chambers@2-3graysinnsquare.co.uk
Call Date: Nov 1989, Gray's Inn
Qualifications: [BA [Oxon]]

BIBI MISS SAMIYYA

Britton Street Chambers
1st Floor, 20 Britton Street, London
EC1M 5NQ, Telephone: 0171 608 3765
Call Date: Nov 1996, Inner Temple
Qualifications: [BSc (Portsmouth)]

BICKERDIKE ROGER JOHN

9 Woodhouse Square
Leeds LS3 1AD,
Telephone: 0113 2451986
E-mail: clerks@9woodhouse.co.uk

1 Mitre Court Buildings
Temple, London EC4Y 7BS,
Telephone: 0171 797 7070
E-mail: clerks@1mcb.com
Call Date: Nov 1986, Lincoln's Inn
Qualifications: [LLB (Notts)]

BICKERSTAFF MISS DEBORAH JANE

6 Gray's Inn Square
Ground Floor, Gray's Inn, London
WC1R 5AZ, Telephone: 0171 242 1052
E-mail: 6graysinn@clara.co.uk
Call Date: Nov 1989, Inner Temple
Qualifications: [LLB]

BICKFORD-SMITH MRS MARGARET OSBORNE

One Paper Buildings
Ground Floor, Temple, London
EC4Y 7EP, Telephone: 0171 583 7355
E-mail: clerks@1pb.co.uk
Call Date: July 1973, Inner Temple
Pupil Master, Recorder
Qualifications: [BA (Oxon)]

BICKFORD-SMITH STEPHEN WILLIAM

4 Breams Buildings
London EC4A 1AQ,
Telephone: 0171 353 5835/430 1221
E-mail:breams@4breamsbuildings.law.co.uk
Call Date: July 1972, Inner Temple
Pupil Master
Qualifications: [BA (Oxon), FCIArb]

BICKLER SIMON LLOYD

St Paul's House
5th Floor, St Paul's House, 23 Park Square
South, Leeds LS1 2ND,
Telephone: 0113 2455866
E-mail: catherinegrimshaw@stpauls-
chambers.demon.co.uk
Call Date: Nov 1988, Inner Temple
Qualifications: [BA (Hons)(Sheffield)]

BIDDER NEIL QC (1998)

33 Park Place
Cardiff CF1 3BA,
Telephone: 02920 233313

Goldsmith Building
1st Floor, Temple, London EC4Y 7BL,
Telephone: 0171 353 7881
E-mail:clerks@goldsmith-building.law.co.uk
Call Date: July 1976, Lincoln's Inn
Assistant Recorder
Qualifications: [MA (Cantab), LLM]

BIDDLE NEVILLE LESLIE

25-27 Castle Street
1st Floor, Liverpool L2 4TA,
Telephone: 0151 227 5661/051 236 5072
Call Date: Nov 1974, Gray's Inn
Pupil Master, Assistant Recorder
Qualifications: [BSc Econ , (Aberystwyth)]

BIGNALL JOHN FRANCIS

S Tomlinson QC
7 King's Bench Walk, Temple, London
EC4Y 7DS, Telephone: 0171 583 0404
E-mail: clerks@7kbw.law.co.uk
Call Date: Nov 1996, Lincoln's Inn
Qualifications: [MA (Hons)]

BIGNALL MISS PAULA-ANN

John Street Chambers
2 John Street, London WC1N 2HJ,
Telephone: 0171 242 1911
E-mail:john.street_chambers@virgin.net
Call Date: Nov 1988, Middle Temple
Qualifications: [LLB (Hons)(Manc)]

BIGNELL MISS JANET SUSAN

Falcon Chambers
Falcon Court, London EC4Y 1AA,
Telephone: 0171 353 2484
E-mail: clerks@falcon-chambers.com
Call Date: Oct 1992, Lincoln's Inn
Qualifications: [MA (Hons) (Cantab), BCL
(Hons) (Oxon)]

BIJLANI DR AISHA

Chambers of John L Powell QC
Four New Square, Lincoln's Inn, London
WC2A 3RJ, Telephone: 0171 797 8000
E-mail: barristers@4newsquare.com
Call Date: 1993, Middle Temple
Qualifications: [MB, BS (Lond), CPE (City),
Dip Law]

BILLINGHAM REX RICHARD

New Court Chambers
Gazette Building, 168 Corporation Street,
Birmingham B4 6TZ,
Telephone: 0121 693 6656
Call Date: Oct 1990, Inner Temple
Pupil Master
Qualifications: [BA (E Anglia), Dip Law]

BILLINGTON MISS MOIRA ANN

Nicholas Street Chambers
22 Nicholas Street, Chester CH1 2NX,
Telephone: 01244 323886
E-mail: clerks@40king.co.uk
Call Date: May 1988, Middle Temple
Qualifications: [LLB(Hons) Manchester]

BINDER PETER HARDWICKE MALCOLM

2-4 Tudor Street
London EC4Y 0AA,
Telephone: 0171 797 7111
E-mail: clerks@rfqc.co.uk
Call Date: Apr 1991, Middle Temple
Pupil Master
Qualifications: [BA (Durham)]

BINDLOSS EDWARD CHRISTOPHER JAMES

Chambers of Andrew Campbell QC
10 Park Square, Leeds LS1 2LH,
Telephone: 0113 2455438
E-mail: clerks@10pksq.co.uk
Call Date: Nov 1993, Gray's Inn
Qualifications: [BA (York), Dip Law (City)]

BINGHAM ANTHONY WILLIAM

3 Paper Buildings
Ground Floor, Temple, London
EC4Y 7EU, Telephone: 0171 797 7000
E-mail: clerks@3pb.co.uk
3 Paper Buildings
Temple, London EC4Y 7EU,
Telephone: 020 7583 8055
E-mail: London@3paper.com
3 Paper Buildings (Bournemouth)
20 Lorne Park Road, Bournemouth,
Dorset, BH1 1JN,
Telephone: 01202 292102
E-mail: Bournemouth@3paper.com

3 Paper Buildings (Oxford)
1 Alfred Street, High Street, Oxford
OX1 4EH, Telephone: 01865 793736
E-mail: oxford@3paper.com
3 Paper Buildings (Winchester)
4 St Peter Street, Winchester SO23 8BW,
Telephone: 01962 868884
E-mail: winchester@3paper.com
Call Date: 1992, Lincoln's Inn
Qualifications: [LLB (Hons) (Lond), FCIArb]

BINGHAM MISS CAMILLA

One Essex Court
Ground Floor, Temple, London
EC4Y 9AR, Telephone: 020 7583 2000
E-mail: clerks@oneessexcourt.co.uk
Call Date: Oct 1996, Inner Temple
Qualifications: [BA (Oxon), CPE (Lond)]

BINGHAM PHILIP JOHN

Paradise Chambers
26 Paradise Square, Sheffield S1 2DE,
Telephone: 0114 2738951
E-mail: timbooth@paradise-sq.co.uk
Call Date: July 1975, Middle Temple
Pupil Master
Qualifications: [LLB]

BINNS DAVID ANDREW

St James's Chambers
68 Quay Street, Manchester M3 3EJ,
Telephone: 0161 834 7000
E-mail: clerks@stjameschambers.co.uk
Call Date: July 1983, Middle Temple
Qualifications: [LLB (Hons)(L'pool)]

BIRCH MISS ELIZABETH BLANCHE

3 Verulam Buildings
London WC1R 5NT,
Telephone: 0171 831 8441
E-mail: clerks@3verulam.co.uk
Call Date: July 1978, Gray's Inn
Pupil Master
Qualifications: [LLB (Lond)]

BIRCH ROGER ALLEN

Sovereign Chambers
25 Park Square, Leeds LS1 2PW,
Telephone: 0113 2451841/2/3
E-mail:sovereignchambers@btinternet.com

12 New Square
Lincoln's Inn, London WC2A 3SW,
Telephone: 0171 419 1212
E-mail: chambers@12newsquare.co.uk
Call Date: Nov 1979, Gray's Inn
Qualifications: [BA (Cantab)]

BIRCH WILLIAM CHARLES JOSEPH G

3 Temple Gardens
Lower Ground Floor, Temple, London
EC4Y 9AU, Telephone: 0171 353 3102/5/
9297 E-mail: clerks@3tg.co.uk
Call Date: Feb 1972, Lincoln's Inn
Pupil Master
Qualifications: [MA (Lond)]

BIRD ANDREW JAMES

1 Harcourt Buildings
2nd Floor, Temple, London EC4Y 9DA,
Telephone: 0171 353 9421/0375
E-mail:clerks@1harcourtbuildings.law.co.uk
Call Date: July 1987, Inner Temple
Pupil Master
Qualifications: [MA (Cantab)]

BIRD NIGEL DAVID

Chambers of John Hand QC
9 St John Street, Manchester M3 4DN,
Telephone: 0161 955 9000
E-mail: ninesjs@gconnect.com
Call Date: Nov 1991, Inner Temple
Qualifications: [BA (Cambs)]

BIRD SIMON CHRISTOPHER

2-3 Gray's Inn Square
Gray's Inn, London WC1R 5JH,
Telephone: 0171 242 4986
E-mail:chambers@2-3graysinnsquare.co.uk
Call Date: July 1987, Middle Temple
Qualifications: [LLB (Reading)]

BIRK MISS DEWINDER

2 New Street
Leicester LE1 5NA,
Telephone: 0116 2625906
E-mail: clerks@2newstreet.co.uk
Call Date: July 1988, Lincoln's Inn
Qualifications: [LLB (Hons) (Essex)]

BIRKBY PETER DAVID

Broadway House Chambers
Broadway House, 9 Bank Street, Bradford,
West Yorkshire, BD1 1TW,
Telephone: 01274 722560
E-mail: clerks@broadwayhouse.co.uk
Broadway House Chambers
31 Park Square West, Leeds LS1 2PF,
Telephone: 0113 246 2600
Call Date: July 1987, Lincoln's Inn
Qualifications: [BA (Manc) Dip Law, City
Univ, Dip in Education, (Sheff)]

BIRKETT PETER VIDLER QC (1989)

18 St John Street
Manchester M3 4EA,
Telephone: 0161 278 1800
E-mail: 18stjohn@lineone.net
Old Square Chambers
1 Verulam Buildings, Gray's Inn, London
WC1R 5LQ, Telephone: 0171 269 0300
E-mail:clerks@oldsquarechambers.co.uk
Call Date: July 1972, Inner Temple
Recorder
Qualifications: [LLB]

BIRKS SIMON ALEXANDER

7 Stone Buildings (also at 11 Bolt Court)
1st Floor, Lincoln's Inn, London
WC2A 3SZ, Telephone: 0171 242 0961
E-mail:larthur@7stonebuildings.law.co.uk
11 Bolt Court (also at 7 Stone Buildings – 1st Floor)
London EC4A 3DQ,
Telephone: 0171 353 2300
E-mail: boltct11@aol.com
Redhill Chambers
Seloduct House, 30 Station Road, Redhill,
Surrey, RH1 1NF,
Telephone: 01737 780781
Call Date: May 1981, Middle Temple
Qualifications: [BA]

BIRNBAUM MICHAEL IAN QC (1992)

9-12 Bell Yard
London WC2A 2LF,
Telephone: 0171 400 1800
E-mail: clerks@bellyard.co.uk
New Court Chambers
Gazette Building, 168 Corporation Street,
Birmingham B4 6TZ,
Telephone: 0121 693 6656
Call Date: Nov 1969, Middle Temple

D

Recorder
Qualifications: [BA (Oxon)]

BIRSS COLIN IAN

3 New Square
Lincoln's Inn, London WC2A 3RS,
Telephone: 0171 405 1111
E-mail: 3newsquareip@lineone.net
Call Date: Oct 1990, Middle Temple
Pupil Master
Qualifications: [MA (Cantab)]

BIRTLES MISS SAMANTHA JANE

18 St John Street
Manchester M3 4EA,
Telephone: 0161 278 1800
E-mail: 18stjohn@lineone.net
Call Date: July 1989, Lincoln's Inn
Qualifications: [LLB (B'ham)]

BIRTLES WILLIAM

Old Square Chambers
1 Verulam Buildings, Gray's Inn, London
WC1R 5LQ, Telephone: 0171 269 0300
E-mail:clerks@oldsquarechambers.co.uk
Old Square Chambers
Hanover House, 47 Corn Street, Bristol
BS1 1HT, Telephone: 0117 9277111
E-mail: oldsqbri@globalnet.co.uk
Call Date: Nov 1970, Gray's Inn
Recorder
Qualifications: [LLM (Lond & Harv), AKC]

BIRTS PETER WILLIAM QC (1990)

Farrar's Building
Temple, London EC4Y 7BD,
Telephone: 0171 583 9241
E-mail:chambers@farrarsbuilding.co.uk
St Philip's Chambers
Fountain Court, Steelhouse Lane,
Birmingham B4 6DR,
Telephone: 0121 246 7000
E-mail: clerks@st-philips.co.uk
Call Date: July 1968, Gray's Inn
Recorder
Qualifications: [MA (Cantab)]

BISARYA NEIL

25-27 Castle Street
1st Floor, Liverpool L2 4TA,
Telephone: 0151 227 5661/051 236 5072
Call Date: Nov 1998, Lincoln's Inn
Qualifications: [BA (Hons)]

BISHOP ALAN RICHARD

11 Stone Buildings
Lincoln's Inn, London WC2A 3TG,
Telephone: +44 (0)207 831 6381
E-mail:clerks@11StoneBuildings.law.co.uk
Call Date: July 1973, Middle Temple
Pupil Master
Qualifications: [LLB (Lond), ACII]

BISHOP EDWARD JAMES

No. 1 Serjeants' Inn
5th Floor Fleet Street, Temple, London
EC4Y 1LH, Telephone: 0171 415 6666
E-mail:no1serjeantsinn@btinternet.com
Call Date: Nov 1985, Middle Temple
Pupil Master
Qualifications: [MA (Cantab), , Dip Law]

BISHOP GORDON WILLIAM

5 Raymond Buildings
1st Floor, Gray's Inn, London WC1R 5BP,
Telephone: 0171 242 2902
E-mail: clerks@media-ent-law.co.uk
Call Date: Nov 1968, Middle Temple
Pupil Master
Qualifications: [MA (Cantab)]

BISHOP JOHN MICHAEL

**7 Stone Buildings (also at 11 Bolt
Court)**
1st Floor, Lincoln's Inn, London
WC2A 3SZ, Telephone: 0171 242 0961
E-mail:larthur@7stonebuildings.law.co.uk
**11 Bolt Court (also at 7 Stone Buildings
– 1st Floor)**
London EC4A 3DQ,
Telephone: 0171 353 2300
E-mail: boltct11@aol.com
Redhill Chambers
Seloduct House, 30 Station Road, Redhill,
Surrey, RH1 1NF,
Telephone: 01737 780781
Call Date: Nov 1970, Middle Temple
Pupil Master
Qualifications: [LLB (Lond)]

BISHOP MISS KEELEY SUSAN

1 Crown Office Row
Ground Floor, Temple, London
EC4Y 7HH, Telephone: 0171 797 7500
E-mail: mail@onecrownofficerow.com

Crown Office Row Chambers
Blenheim House, 120 Church Street,
Brighton, Sussex, BN1 1WH,
Telephone: 01273 625625
E-mail: crownofficerow@clara.net
Call Date: Oct 1990, Gray's Inn
Qualifications: [BSc, GIBIOL]

BISHOP MALCOLM LESLIE QC (1993)

Dr Johnson's Chambers
Two Dr Johnson's Buildings, Temple,
London EC4Y 7AY,
Telephone: 0171 353 4716
E-mail: clerks@2djb.freeserve.co.uk
30 Park Place
Cardiff CF1 3BA,
Telephone: 01222 398421
E-mail: 100757.1456@compuserve.com
Equity Chambers
3rd Floor, 153a Corporation Street,
Birmingham B4 6PH,
Telephone: 0121 233 2100
E-mail: equityatusa.com
Call Date: 1968, Inner Temple
Assistant Recorder
Qualifications: [MA (Oxon)]

BISHOP MARK ANDREW

1 Temple Gardens
1st Floor, Temple, London EC4Y 9BB,
Telephone: 0171 583 1315/353 0407
E-mail: clerks@1templegardens.co.uk
Call Date: July 1981, Middle Temple
Pupil Master
Qualifications: [MA (Cantab)]

BISHOP TIMOTHY HARPER PAUL

1 Mitre Court Buildings
Temple, London EC4Y 7BS,
Telephone: 0171 797 7070
E-mail: clerks@1mcb.com
Call Date: Nov 1991, Inner Temple
Pupil Master
Qualifications: [MA (Hons)(Cantab)]

BISPHAM MISS CHRISTINE

Corn Exchange Chambers
5th Floor, Fenwick Street, Liverpool
L2 7QS, Telephone: 0151 227 1081/5009
Call Date: Oct 1991, Lincoln's Inn
Qualifications: [LLB (Hons) (Leics)]

BISWAS MISS NISHA SUJATA

Chavasse Court Chambers
2nd Floor, Chavasse Court, 24 Lord Street,
Liverpool L2 1TA,
Telephone: 0151 707 1191
Call Date: Oct 1996, Lincoln's Inn
Qualifications: [LLB (Hons)(L'pool)]

BITMEAD PAUL GRAHAM

Lamb Building
Ground Floor, Temple, London
EC4Y 7AS, Telephone: 020 7797 7788
E-mail: lamb.building@link.org
Call Date: Oct 1996, Middle Temple
Qualifications: [BA (Hons) (Essex)]

BLACK MISS HARRIETTE

2 Dyers Buildings
London EC1N 2JT,
Telephone: 0171 404 1881
Call Date: Nov 1986, Lincoln's Inn
Qualifications: [LLB]

BLACK MRS JILL MARGARET QC (1994)

30 Park Square
Leeds LS1 2PF, Telephone: 0113 2436388
E-mail: clerks@30parksquare.co.uk
Call Date: July 1976, Inner Temple
Recorder
Qualifications: [BA (Dunelm)]

BLACK JOHN ALEXANDER QC (1998)

18 Red Lion Court
(Off Fleet Street), London EC4A 3EB,
Telephone: 0171 520 6000
E-mail: chambers@18rlc.co.uk
Thornwood House
102 New London Road, Chelmsford,
Essex, CM2 0RG,
Telephone: 01245 280880
E-mail: chambers@18rlc.co.uk
Call Date: July 1975, Inner Temple
Qualifications: [LLB Hons]

BLACK MICHAEL JONATHAN QC (1995)

22 Old Buildings
Lincoln's Inn, London WC2A 3UJ,
Telephone: 0171 831 0222

D

Byrom Street Chambers
Byrom Street, Manchester M3 4PF,
Telephone: 0161 829 2100
E-mail: Byromst25@aol.com
Call Date: Feb 1978, Middle Temple
Assistant Recorder
Qualifications: [LLB (Lond), FCIArb]

BLACKBURN MRS ELIZABETH QC (1998)

4 Field Court
Gray's Inn, London WC1R 5EA,
Telephone: 0171 440 6900
E-mail: chambers@4fieldcourt.co.uk
Call Date: July 1978, Middle Temple
Qualifications: [BA]

BLACKBURN JOHN QC (1984)

Atkin Chambers
1 Atkin Building, Gray's Inn, London
WC1R 5AT, Telephone: 020 7404 0102
E-mail: clerks@atkin-chambers.co.uk
Call Date: July 1969, Middle Temple
Qualifications: [BA (Oxon)]

BLACKBURN LUKE SEBASTIAN

Pump Court Chambers
Upper Ground Floor, 3 Pump Court,
Temple, London EC4Y 7AJ,
Telephone: 0171 353 0711
E-mail: clerks@3pumpcourt.com
Pump Court Chambers
31 Southgate Street, Winchester
SO23 9EE, Telephone: 01962 868161
E-mail: clerks@3pumpcourt.com
Pump Court Chambers
5 Temple Chambers, Temple Street,
Swindon SN1 1SQ,
Telephone: 01793 539899
E-mail: clerks@3pumpcourt.com
Call Date: Nov 1993, Middle Temple
Qualifications: [MA (Cantab)]

BLACKETT-ORD MARK

5 Stone Buildings
Lincoln's Inn, London WC2A 3XT,
Telephone: 0171 242 6201
E-mail:clerks@5-stonebuildings.law.co.uk
Call Date: July 1974, Lincoln's Inn
Pupil Master
Qualifications: [MA (Oxon)]

Fax: 0171 831 8102; DX: 304 London,
Chancery Lane

Types of work: Chancery land law,
Conveyancing, Equity, wills and trusts,
Family provision, Landlord and tenant,
Partnerships, Probate and administration,
Professional negligence

Awards and memberships: Member of STEP,
ACTAPS and APP

Publications: *Partnership*, 1997; *Partnership*
(4th edn title, *Halsbury's Laws of
England*), 1981

Reported Cases: *Webb v Webb*, [1994] QB
696, ECJ and [1997] CA 8 July 1997, 1994
and 1997. Whether English courts may
resolve the issue of a disputed gift of French
land between English domiciliaries.
Re A Company No 007816 of 1994, [1996]
2 BCLC 685, CA, 1996. What is the
meaning of the statutory prohibition of
unauthorised 'carrying on insurance business'.
Re Murphy's Settlement, [1998] 3 All ER 1.
Extent of duty of a settler to disclose information to a beneficiary.

BLACKFORD ROBERT

**The Chambers of Mr Ali Mohammed
Azhar**
Basement, 9 King's Bench Walk, Temple,
London EC4Y 7DX,
Telephone: 0171 353 9564
E-mail: jvlee@btinternet.com
Call Date: Nov 1988, Inner Temple
Pupil Master
Qualifications: [LLB (Hons) (Lond), FCIArb]

BLACKFORD SIMON JOHN

Barnard's Inn Chambers
6th Floor, Halton House, 20-23 Holborn,
London EC1N 2JD,
Telephone: 0171 369 6969
E-mail: clerks@biclaw.co.uk
Call Date: July 1979, Middle Temple
Qualifications: [MA]

BLACKMORE JOHN HUGH

St John's Chambers
Small Street, Bristol BS1 1DW,
Telephone: 0117 9213456/298514
E-mail: @stjohnschambers.co.uk
Call Date: May 1983, Inner Temple
Pupil Master
Qualifications: [LLB (Lond)]

BLACKMORE MISS SARAH ELIZABETH

Phoenix Chambers
First Floor, Gray's Inn Chambers, Gray's
Inn, London WC1R 5JA,
Telephone: 0171 404 7888
E-mail:clerks@phoenix-chambers.co.uk
Call Date: Oct 1993, Inner Temple
Qualifications: [LLB]

BLACKSHAW HENRY WILLIAM RANDLE

Peel Court Chambers
45 Hardman Street, Manchester M3 3PL,
Telephone: 0161 832 3791
E-mail: clerks@peelct.co.uk
Call Date: Oct 1993, Middle Temple
Qualifications: [BA (Hons)(Dunelm), CPE,
Dip Law]

BLACKWELL MISS KATHERINE ELIZABETH

Lincoln House Chambers
5th Floor, Lincoln House, 1 Brazennose
Street, Manchester M2 5EL,
Telephone: 0161 832 5701
E-mail: info@lincolnhse.co.uk
Call Date: Oct 1992, Lincoln's Inn
Qualifications: [LLB(Hons)(B'ham)]

BLACKWELL MISS LOUISE MARY

Cobden House Chambers
19 Quay Street, Manchester M3 3HN,
Telephone: 0161 833 6000
E-mail: clerks@cobden.co.uk
Call Date: July 1985, Lincoln's Inn
Qualifications: [LLB (Hons) (Leeds)]

BLACKWOOD ANDREW GUY

4 Field Court
Gray's Inn, London WC1R 5EA,
Telephone: 0171 440 6900
E-mail: chambers@4fieldcourt.co.uk
Call Date: Oct 1997, Inner Temple
Qualifications: [MB (London), LLB
(London)]

BLACKWOOD CLIVE DAVID

Harcourt Chambers
1st Floor, 2 Harcourt Buildings, Temple,
London EC4Y 9DB,
Telephone: 0171 353 6961
E-mail:clerks@harcourtchambers.law.co.uk
Harcourt Chambers
Churchill House, 3 St Aldate's Courtyard,
St Aldate's, Oxford OX1 1BN,
Telephone: 01865 791559
E-mail:clerks@harcourtchambers.law.co.uk
Call Date: Nov 1986, Inner Temple
Pupil Master
Qualifications: [BA(Cantab)]

BLACKWOOD MISS FRANCESCA MARY

3 Dr Johnson's Buildings
Ground Floor, Temple, London
EC4Y 7BA, Telephone: 0171 353 4854
E-mail: clerks@3djb.co.uk
Call Date: 1997, Lincoln's Inn
Qualifications: [BA (Lond), MA]

BLADON KENNETH NORMAN

St Ive's Chambers
Whittall Street, Birmingham B4 6DH,
Telephone: 0121 236 0863/5720
E-mail:stives.headofchambers@btinternet.com
Call Date: July 1980, Gray's Inn
Qualifications: [LLB (Hons) (Exon)]

BLAIR BRUCE GRAEME DONALD QC (1989)

1 Mitre Court Buildings
Temple, London EC4Y 7BS,
Telephone: 0171 797 7070
E-mail: clerks@1mcb.com
Call Date: July 1969, Middle Temple
Recorder
Qualifications: [MA (Cantab)]

BLAIR PETER MICHAEL

Guildhall Chambers
22-26 Broad Street, Bristol BS1 2HG,
Telephone: 0117 9273366
E-mail:civil.clerks@guildhallchambers.co.uk and
criminal.clerks@guildhallchambers.co.uk
Call Date: July 1983, Inner Temple
Pupil Master, Assistant Recorder
Qualifications: [MA (Oxon)]

BLAIR MISS RUTH MARY

2 King's Bench Walk
Ground Floor, Temple, London
EC4Y 7DE, Telephone: 0171 353 1746
E-mail: 2kbw@atlas.co.uk
King's Bench Chambers
115 North Hill, Plymouth PL4 8JY,
Telephone: 01752 221551
Call Date: July 1987, Middle Temple
Pupil Master
Qualifications: [LLB (Dunelm)]

BLAIR WILLIAM JAMES LYNTON QC (1994)

3 Verulam Buildings
London WC1R 5NT,
Telephone: 0171 831 8441
E-mail: clerks@3verulam.co.uk
Call Date: July 1972, Lincoln's Inn
Assistant Recorder
Qualifications: [BA (Oxon)]

BLAIR-GOULD JOHN ANTHONY

3 Raymond Buildings
Gray's Inn, London WC1R 5BH,
Telephone: 020 7831 3833
E-mail:chambers@threeraymond.demon.co.uk
Call Date: Apr 1970, Inner Temple
Recorder

BLAKE ALAN GEOFFREY

4 King's Bench Walk
2nd Floor, Temple, London EC4Y 7DL,
Telephone: 020 7353 3581
E-mail: clerks@4kbw.co.uk
Call Date: 1997, Gray's Inn
Qualifications: [BA]

BLAKE ANDREW NICHOLAS HUBERT

18 St John Street
Manchester M3 4EA,
Telephone: 0161 278 1800
E-mail: 18stjohn@lineone.net
Call Date: Nov 1971, Inner Temple
Recorder
Qualifications: [MA (Oxon)]

BLAKE ARTHUR JOSEPH

13 King's Bench Walk
1st Floor, Temple, London EC4Y 7EN,
Telephone: 0171 353 7204
E-mail: clerks@13kbw.law.co.uk
King's Bench Chambers
32 Beaumont Street, Oxford OX1 2NP,
Telephone: 01865 311066
E-mail: clerks@kbc-oxford.law.co.uk
Call Date: Feb 1988, Inner Temple
Qualifications: [LLB]

BLAKE CHRISTOPHER IAN

Mitre Court Chambers
3rd Floor, Temple, London EC4Y 7BP,
Telephone: 0171 353 9394
E-mail: mitrecourt.com
Call Date: Nov 1990, Inner Temple
Qualifications: [LLB (Hons)]

BLAKE DAVID ANTHONY

Angel Chambers
94 Walter Road, Swansea, West
Glamorgan, SA1 5QA,
Telephone: 01792 464623/464648
E-mail: lynne@angelchambers.co.uk
Call Date: Feb 1992, Lincoln's Inn
Qualifications: [BA (Hons) (Cantab)]

BLAKE NICHOLAS JOHN GORROD QC (1994)

Two Garden Court
1st Floor, Middle Temple, London
EC4Y 9BL, Telephone: 0171 353 1633
E-mail:barristers@2gardenct.law.co.uk
Call Date: 1974, Middle Temple
Assistant Recorder
Qualifications: [BA (Cantab)]

BLAKE RICHARD ANDREW

Chambers of Helen Grindrod QC
4th Floor, 15-19 Devereux Court, London
WC2R 3JJ, Telephone: 0171 583 2792
Call Date: Nov 1982, Gray's Inn
Pupil Master

BLAKEMORE MISS JESSICA MARY CASSANDRA

1 Harcourt Buildings
2nd Floor, Temple, London EC4Y 9DA,
Telephone: 0171 353 9421/0375
E-mail:clerks@1harcourtbuildings.law.co.uk
Call Date: Oct 1995, Inner Temple
Qualifications: [BA (Soton), CPE]

BLAKER GARY MARK

Francis Taylor Building
3rd Floor, Temple, London EC4Y 7BY,
Telephone: 0171 797 7250
Call Date: Oct 1993, Middle Temple
Qualifications: [MA (Cantab)]

BLAKESLEY PATRICK JAMES

Two Crown Office Row
Ground Floor, Temple, London
EC4Y 7HJ, Telephone: 020 7797 8100
E-mail: mail@2cor.co.uk, or to individual
barristers at: [barrister's
surname]@2cor.co.uk
Call Date: Nov 1993, Inner Temple
Qualifications: [MA (Oxon), CPE (City)]

BLAKEY LEE

15 Winckley Square
Preston PR1 3JJ,
Telephone: 01772 252828
E-mail:clerks@winckleysq.demon.co.uk
Call Date: Oct 1995, Lincoln's Inn
Qualifications: [LLB (Hons)(Lanc)]

BLAKEY MICHAEL CHARLES

Young Street Chambers
38 Young Street, Manchester M3 3FT,
Telephone: 0161 833 0489
E-mail: clerks@young-st-chambers.com
Call Date: Nov 1989, Middle Temple
Qualifications: [LLB (Hons)]

BLANCHARD MISS CLAIRE

Essex Court Chambers
24 Lincoln's Inn Fields, London
WC2A 3ED, Telephone: 0171 813 8000
E-mail:clerksroom@essexcourt-chambers.co.uk
Call Date: Oct 1992, Gray's Inn
Qualifications: [LLB (Hons) (L'pool)]

BLAND MISS CAROLYN

Young Street Chambers
38 Young Street, Manchester M3 3FT,
Telephone: 0161 833 0489
E-mail: clerks@young-st-chambers.com
Call Date: July 1995, Inner Temple
Qualifications: [LLB (Reading)]

BLANTERN ROBERT IAN

Broadway House Chambers
Broadway House, 9 Bank Street, Bradford,
West Yorkshire, BD1 1TW,
Telephone: 01274 722560
E-mail: clerks@broadwayhouse.co.uk
Call Date: Oct 1996, Middle Temple
Qualifications: [LLB (Hons)(Northum)]

BLATCH MISS FRANCESCA JANE

Guildford Chambers
Stoke House, Leapale Lane, Guildford,
Surrey, GU1 4LY,
Telephone: 01483 539131
E-mail:guildford.barristers@btinternet.com
Call Date: Nov 1987, Lincoln's Inn
Pupil Master
Qualifications: [BA(Hons)]

BLAXLAND CHRISTOPHER HENRY

Two Garden Court
1st Floor, Middle Temple, London
EC4Y 9BL, Telephone: 0171 353 1633
E-mail:barristers@2gardenct.law.co.uk
Call Date: Nov 1978, Middle Temple
Pupil Master
Qualifications: [BA (York)]

BLAYNEY DAVID JAMES

Serle Court Chambers
6 New Square, Lincoln's Inn, London
WC2A 3QS, Telephone: 0171 242 6105
E-mail: clerks@serlecourt.co.uk
Call Date: Oct 1992, Lincoln's Inn
Qualifications: [BA(Hons)]

BLEANEY NICHOLAS SIMON

3 Temple Gardens
Lower Ground Floor, Temple, London
EC4Y 9AU, Telephone: 0171 353 3102/5/
9297 E-mail: clerks@3tg.co.uk
Call Date: Nov 1988, Lincoln's Inn
Pupil Master
Qualifications: [LLB Hons (Nott'm)]

BLEASDALE MISS MARIE-CLAIRE

Chambers of Mr Peter Crampin QC
Ground Floor, 11 New Square, Lincoln's
Inn, London WC2A 3QB,
Telephone: 020 7831 0081
E-mail: 11newsquare.co.uk
Call Date: Oct 1993, Lincoln's Inn
Qualifications: [MA (Cantab), Dip in, Law
(Westminster)]

BLEASDALE PAUL EDWARD

5 Fountain Court
Steelhouse Lane, Birmingham B4 6DR,
Telephone: 0121 606 0500
E-mail:clerks@5fountaincourt.law.co.uk
*Call Date: July 1978, Inner Temple
Pupil Master, Recorder*
Qualifications: [LLB (Lond)]

BLOCH MICHAEL GORDON QC (1998)

One Essex Court
Ground Floor, Temple, London
EC4Y 9AR, Telephone: 020 7583 2000
E-mail: clerks@oneessexcourt.co.uk
Call Date: July 1979, Lincoln's Inn
Qualifications: [MA (Cantab), M.Phil (UEA)]

BLOCH SELWYN IRVING

Littleton Chambers
3 King's Bench Walk North, Temple,
London EC4Y 7HR,
Telephone: 0171 797 8600
E-mail:clerks@littletonchambers.co.uk
*Call Date: July 1982, Middle Temple
Pupil Master*
Qualifications: [BA, LLB]

BLOCK NEIL SELWYN

39 Essex Street
London WC2R 3AT,
Telephone: 0171 832 1111
E-mail: clerks@39essex.co.uk
*Call Date: July 1980, Gray's Inn
Pupil Master*
Qualifications: [BA (Hons), LLM (Exon)]

BLOHM LESLIE ADRIAN

St John's Chambers
Small Street, Bristol BS1 1DW,
Telephone: 0117 9213456/298514
E-mail: @stjohnschambers.co.uk
*Call Date: July 1982, Lincoln's Inn
Pupil Master*
Qualifications: [MA (Oxon)]

BLOM-COOPER SIR LOUIS JACQUES QC (1970)

Doughty Street Chambers
11 Doughty Street, London WC1N 2PG,
Telephone: 0171 404 1313
E-mail:enquiries@doughtystreet.co.uk
Call Date: July 1952, Middle Temple
Qualifications: [LLB (Lond), Dr Jur
(Amsterdam)]

BLOOM DR MARGARET

Goldsmith Building
1st Floor, Temple, London EC4Y 7BL,
Telephone: 0171 353 7881
E-mail:clerks@goldsmith-building.law.co.uk
Call Date: Oct 1994, Lincoln's Inn
Qualifications: [B.Med.Sci, BM, BS, MRCGP
(Notts), CPE (Notts)]

BLOOM MS TRACEY DORA

Doughty Street Chambers
11 Doughty Street, London WC1N 2PG,
Telephone: 0171 404 1313
E-mail:enquiries@doughtystreet.co.uk
*Call Date: July 1984, Gray's Inn
Pupil Master*
Qualifications: [MA (Cantab)]

BLOOM-DAVIS DESMOND NIALL LAURENCE

Pump Court Chambers
31 Southgate Street, Winchester
SO23 9EE, Telephone: 01962 868161
E-mail: clerks@3pumpcourt.com
Pump Court Chambers
Upper Ground Floor, 3 Pump Court,
Temple, London EC4Y 7AJ,
Telephone: 0171 353 0711
E-mail: clerks@3pumpcourt.com

Pump Court Chambers
5 Temple Chambers, Temple Street,
Swindon SN1 1SQ,
Telephone: 01793 539899
E-mail: clerks@3pumpcourt.com
Call Date: July 1986, Inner Temple
Pupil Master
Qualifications: [BA (Lond)]

BLOOMER CHARLES HOWARD

Lincoln House Chambers
5th Floor, Lincoln House, 1 Brazennose
Street, Manchester M2 5EL,
Telephone: 0161 832 5701
E-mail: info@lincolnhse.co.uk
Call Date: July 1985, Lincoln's Inn
Qualifications: [LLB (Nott'n)]

BLOOMFIELD RICHARD WILLIAM

Gosforth Chambers
2 Lansdowne Place, Gosforth, Newcastle
upon Tyne NE3 1HR,
Telephone: 0191 285 4664
Durham Barristers' Chambers
27 Old Elvet, Durham DH1 3HN,
Telephone: 0191 386 9199
Call Date: July 1984, Gray's Inn
Pupil Master
Qualifications: [BA (Hons)]

BLORE MISS CAROLYN ANNE

Furnival Chambers
32 Furnival Street, London EC4A 1JQ,
Telephone: 0171 405 3232
E-mail: clerks@furnivallaw.co.uk
Call Date: July 1985, Gray's Inn
Qualifications: [LLB(Cardiff)]

BLOUNT MARTIN JOHN

Eighteen Carlton Crescent
Southampton SO15 2XR,
Telephone: 01703 639001
Call Date: July 1982, Gray's Inn
Pupil Master
Qualifications: [LL.B (Soton)]

BLOWER GRAHAM ROBERT

Queen Elizabeth Building
Ground Floor, Temple, London
EC4Y 9BS,
Telephone: 0171 353 7181 (12 Lines)
Call Date: Nov 1980, Gray's Inn
Pupil Master
Qualifications: [BA (Leeds)]

BLOWER MATTHEW JOHN

3 Temple Gardens
3rd Floor, Temple, London EC4Y 9AU,
Telephone: 0171 353 0832
Call Date: Oct 1997, Inner Temple
Qualifications: [BA (Oxon)]

BLUNT DAVID JOHN QC (1991)

4 Pump Court
Temple, London EC4Y 7AN,
Telephone: 020 7842 5555
E-mail:chambers@4pumpcourt.law.co.uk
Call Date: Nov 1967, Middle Temple
Recorder
Qualifications: [MA (Cantab)]

BLUNT OLIVER SIMON PETER QC (1994)

Furnival Chambers
32 Furnival Street, London EC4A 1JQ,
Telephone: 0171 405 3232
E-mail: clerks@furnivallaw.co.uk
Call Date: Nov 1974, Middle Temple
Recorder
Qualifications: [LLB]

BLYTH JOHN RODERICK MORRISON

Queen Elizabeth Building
2nd Floor, Temple, London EC4Y 9BS,
Telephone: 0171 797 7837
Call Date: July 1981, Lincoln's Inn
Pupil Master
Qualifications: [BA (Oxon)]

BOAITEY MISS CHARLOTTE

12 Old Square
1st Floor, Lincoln's Inn, London
WC2A 3TX, Telephone: 0171 404 0875
Call Date: Nov 1976, Middle Temple
Pupil Master
Qualifications: [LLB (Lond), Dip Soc
Anthrop, (Oxon)]

D

D

BOARDMAN CHRISTOPHER LEIGH WILSON

11 Stone Buildings
Lincoln's Inn, London WC2A 3TG,
Telephone: +44 (0)207 831 6381
E-mail:clerks@11StoneBuildings.law.co.uk
Call Date: Oct 1995, Lincoln's Inn
Qualifications: [LLB (Hons), LLM (Lond)]

BOARDMAN MICHAEL LEOPOLD

6 Gray's Inn Square
Ground Floor, Gray's Inn, London
WC1R 5AZ, Telephone: 0171 242 1052
E-mail: 6graysinn@clara.co.uk
Call Date: July 1979, Middle Temple
Pupil Master
Qualifications: [BA (Manch), LLB (Lond)]

BOATENG PAUL YAW

8 King's Bench Walk
2nd Floor, Temple, London EC4Y 7DU,
Telephone: 0171 797 8888
8 King's Bench Walk North
1 Park Square East, Leeds LS1 2NE,
Telephone: 0113 2439797
Call Date: Nov 1989, Gray's Inn
Qualifications: [LLB (Bris)]

BOEDDINGHAUS HERMANN

4 Stone Buildings
Ground Floor, Lincoln's Inn, London
WC2A 3XT, Telephone: 0171 242 5524
E-mail:clerks@4stonebuildings.law.co.uk
Call Date: Nov 1996, Lincoln's Inn
Qualifications: [BSc(Hons)(Cape Town),
BCL, MA (Oxon)]

BOGAN PAUL SIMON

Doughty Street Chambers
11 Doughty Street, London WC1N 2PG,
Telephone: 0171 404 1313
E-mail:enquiries@doughtystreet.co.uk
Call Date: July 1983, Gray's Inn
Pupil Master
Qualifications: [BA (Hons)]

BOGGIS-ROLFE HARRY MARK

1 Brick Court
1st Floor, Temple, London EC4Y 9BY,
Telephone: 0171 353 8845
E-mail: clerks@1brickcourt.co.uk
Call Date: Nov 1969, Middle Temple
Pupil Master
Qualifications: [MA (Cantab)]

BOGLE JAMES STEWART LOCKHART

10 King's Bench Walk
Ground Floor, Temple, London
EC4Y 7EB, Telephone: 0171 353 7742
E-mail: 10kbw@lineone.net
Call Date: Oct 1991, Middle Temple
Qualifications: [BA, Dip Law, ACIArb]

BOJARSKI ANDRZEJ LEONARD

Chambers of Michael Pert QC
36 Bedford Row, London WC1R 4JH,
Telephone: 0171 421 8000
E-mail: 36bedfordrow@link.org
Chambers of Michael Pert QC
24 Albion Place, Northampton NN1 1UD,
Telephone: 01604 602333
Chambers of Michael Pert QC
104 New Walk, Leicester LE1 7EA,
Telephone: 0116 249 2020
Call Date: Oct 1995, Gray's Inn
Qualifications: [LLB]

BOJCZUK WILLIAM JOHN

Hardwicke Building
New Square, Lincoln's Inn, London
WC2A 3SB, Telephone: 020 7242 2523
E-mail: clerks@hardwicke.co.uk
Call Date: July 1983, Inner Temple
Pupil Master
Qualifications: [LLB (Lond), MA]

BOLTON MISS BEATRICE MAUD

Broad Chare
33 Broad Chare, Newcastle upon Tyne
NE1 3DQ, Telephone: 0191 232 0541
E-mail:clerks@broadcharechambers.law.co.uk
Call Date: July 1975, Gray's Inn
Recorder
Qualifications: [LLB]

BOLTON MRS FRANCES LAWJUA

2 Goldingham Avenue
Loughton, Essex, IG10 2JF,
Telephone: 0181 502 4247
Call Date: July 1981, Middle Temple
Qualifications: [LLB (Hons)]

BOLTON MISS LUCY CAROLINE

Mitre Court Chambers
3rd Floor, Temple, London EC4Y 7BP,
Telephone: 0171 353 9394
E-mail: mitrecourt.com
Call Date: Oct 1994, Lincoln's Inn
Qualifications: [BA (Hons)(Notts), Dip in
Law (City)]

BOLTON ROBERT JOHN

2 King's Bench Walk
Ground Floor, Temple, London
EC4Y 7DE, Telephone: 0171 353 1746
E-mail: 2kbw@atlas.co.uk
King's Bench Chambers
115 North Hill, Plymouth PL4 8JY,
Telephone: 01752 221551
Call Date: July 1987, Gray's Inn
Qualifications: [B.A. (Manch)]

BOLTON MRS SALLY ANN

Nicholas Street Chambers
22 Nicholas Street, Chester CH1 2NX,
Telephone: 01244 323886
E-mail: clerks@40king.co.uk
Call Date: May 1997, Gray's Inn
Qualifications: [BA (Kent)]

BOMPAS ANTHONY GEORGE QC (1994)

4 Stone Buildings
Ground Floor, Lincoln's Inn, London
WC2A 3XT, Telephone: 0171 242 5524
E-mail:clerks@4stonebuildings.law.co.uk
Call Date: July 1975, Middle Temple
Qualifications: [MA (Oxon)]

BOND MISS JACQUELINE KATHRYN

Mitre House Chambers
15-19 Devereux Court, London WC2R 3JJ,
Telephone: 0171 583 8233
Call Date: Oct 1994, Middle Temple
Qualifications: [LLB (Hons)]

BOND RICHARD IAN WINSOR

Coleridge Chambers
Citadel, 190 Corporation Street,
Birmingham B4 6QD,
Telephone: 0121 233 8500
Call Date: July 1988, Middle Temple
Qualifications: [LLB (Hons) (Manch)]

BONEY GUY THOMAS KNOWLES QC (1990)

Pump Court Chambers
31 Southgate Street, Winchester
SO23 9EE, Telephone: 01962 868161
E-mail: clerks@3pumpcourt.com
Pump Court Chambers
Upper Ground Floor, 3 Pump Court,
Temple, London EC4Y 7AJ,
Telephone: 0171 353 0711
E-mail: clerks@3pumpcourt.com
Harrow on the Hill Chambers
60 High Street, Harrow-on-the-Hill,
Middlesex, HA1 3LL,
Telephone: 0181 423 7444
Pump Court Chambers
5 Temple Chambers, Temple Street,
Swindon SN1 1SQ,
Telephone: 01793 539899
E-mail: clerks@3pumpcourt.com
Eighteen Carlton Crescent
Southampton SO15 2XR,
Telephone: 01703 639001
Call Date: 1968, Middle Temple
Recorder
Qualifications: [BA]

BONNEY JAMES WILLIAM QC (1995)

The Chambers of Leolin Price CBE, QC
10 Old Square, Lincoln's Inn, London
WC2A 3SU, Telephone: 0171 405 0758
15 Winckley Square
Preston PR1 3JJ,
Telephone: 01772 252828
E-mail:clerks@winckleysq.demon.co.uk
Call Date: Nov 1975, Lincoln's Inn
Qualifications: [BCL,MA (Oxon)]

BOOKER MRS CHRISTINE MARGARET

Doughty Street Chambers
11 Doughty Street, London WC1N 2PG,
Telephone: 0171 404 1313
E-mail:enquiries@doughtystreet.co.uk
Call Date: Feb 1978, Middle Temple
Qualifications: [BA (Lond)]

D

BOOLS DR MICHAEL DAVID

Brick Court Chambers
7-8 Essex Street, London WC2R 3LD,
Telephone: 0171 379 3550
E-mail: [surname]@brickcourt.co.uk
Call Date: Oct 1991, Middle Temple
Qualifications: [LLB Hons (E.Anglia), D.Phil
(Oxon)]

BOORA JINDER SINGH

Ropewalk Chambers
24 The Ropewalk, Nottingham NG1 5EF,
Telephone: 0115 9472581
E-mail: administration@ropewalk co.uk
Call Date: Oct 1990, Gray's Inn
Qualifications: [LLB , LLM (Warw)]

BOOTH ALAN JAMES

Deans Court Chambers
24 St John Street, Manchester M3 4DF,
Telephone: 0161 214 6000
E-mail: clerks@deanscourt.co.uk
Deans Court Chambers
41-43 Market Place, Preston PR1 1AH,
Telephone: 01772 555163
E-mail: clerks@deanscourt.co.uk
Call Date: July 1978, Gray's Inn
Assistant Recorder
Qualifications: [MA (Cantab)]

BOOTH MISS CHERIE QC (1995)

4-5 Gray's Inn Square
Ground Floor, Gray's Inn, London
WC1R 5JP, Telephone: 0171 404 5252
E-mail:chambers@4-5graysinnsquare.co.uk
Call Date: July 1976, Lincoln's Inn
Recorder
Qualifications: [LLB (Lond)]

BOOTH MARTYN PARKINSON

Portsmouth Barristers' Chambers
Victory House, 7 Bellevue Terrace,
Portsmouth, Hampshire, PO5 3AT,
Telephone: 023 92 831292/811811
E-mail: clerks@portsmouthbar.com
Call Date: Oct 1996, Lincoln's Inn
Qualifications: [LLB (Hons)(Soton)]

BOOTH MICHAEL JOHN QC (1999)

40 King Street
Manchester M2 6BA,
Telephone: 0161 832 9082
E-mail: clerks@40kingstreet.co.uk
The Chambers of Philip Raynor QC
5 Park Place, Leeds LS1 2RU,
Telephone: 0113 242 1123
Call Date: 1981, Lincoln's Inn
Pupil Master
Qualifications: [MA (Cantab)]

BOOTH NICHOLAS JOHN

Old Square Chambers
1 Verulam Buildings, Gray's Inn, London
WC1R 5LQ, Telephone: 0171 269 0300
E-mail:clerks@oldsquarechambers.co.uk
Old Square Chambers
Hanover House, 47 Corn Street, Bristol
BS1 1HT, Telephone: 0117 9277111
E-mail: oldsqbri@globalnet.co.uk
Call Date: July 1991, Middle Temple
Qualifications: [MA , BCL]

BOOTH RICHARD JOHN

1 Crown Office Row
Ground Floor, Temple, London
EC4Y 7HH, Telephone: 0171 797 7500
E-mail: mail@onecrownofficerow.com
Call Date: Oct 1993, Middle Temple
Qualifications: [MA (Hons)(Cantab), Lic Spec
Dr Eur, (Brussels)]

BOOTH ROGER GEORGE

Old Colony House
6 South King Street, Manchester M2 6DQ,
Telephone: 0161 834 4364
Bell Yard Chambers
116/118 Chancery Lane, London
WC2A 1PP, Telephone: 0171 306 9292
Call Date: Nov 1966, Gray's Inn
Pupil Master
Qualifications: [LLB]

BOOTH SIMON MARK

Adrian Lyon's Chambers
14 Castle Street, Liverpool L2 0NE,
Telephone: 0151 236 4421/8240
E-mail: chambers14@aol.com
Call Date: Nov 1985, Lincoln's Inn
Qualifications: [LLB (L'pool)]

BOOTH MISS SYLVIA JOY

18 St John Street
Manchester M3 4EA,
Telephone: 0161 278 1800
E-mail: 18stjohn@lineone.net
Call Date: Oct 1992, Gray's Inn
Qualifications: [LLB (Sheff)]

BOOTHBY JOSEPH JOHN

Bridewell Chambers
2 Bridewell Place, London EC4V 6AP,
Telephone: 020 7797 8800
E-mail:HughesGage@bridewell.law.co.uk
Call Date: July 1972, Middle Temple
Pupil Master, Recorder
Qualifications: [BA (Lond)]

BOOTHROYD ALEC DOMINIC

Chambers of Davina Gammon
Ground Floor, 103 Walter Road, Swansea,
West Glamorgan, SA1 5QF,
Telephone: 01792 480770
Call Date: 1991, Inner Temple
Qualifications: [LLB]

BOOTHROYD MISS SUSAN ELIZABETH

Westgate Chambers
67a Westgate Road, Newcastle upon Tyne
NE1 1SG, Telephone: 0191 261 4407/
2329785
E-mail:pracman@westgatechambers.law.co.uk
Call Date: Oct 1990, Lincoln's Inn
Qualifications: [LLB (Newc)]

BORRELLI MICHAEL FRANCIS ANTONY

1 Middle Temple Lane
Temple, London EC4Y 1LT,
Telephone: 0171 583 0659 (12 Lines)
E-mail: chambers@1mtl.co.uk
Call Date: Nov 1977, Middle Temple
Pupil Master

BORTHWICK MISS LORNA

6 Fountain Court
Steelhouse Lane, Birmingham B4 6DR,
Telephone: 0121 233 3282
E-mail: clerks@sixfountain.co.uk
Call Date: 1997, Lincoln's Inn
Qualifications: [LLB (Hons)(Birm'ham)]

BOSOMWORTH MICHAEL JOHN

39 Park Square
Leeds LS1 2NU,
Telephone: 0113 2456633
Call Date: July 1979, Middle Temple
Qualifications: [BA (Nottm)]

BOSTON MISS JANET SUSAN

10 King's Bench Walk
Ground Floor, Temple, London
EC4Y 7EB, Telephone: 0171 353 7742
E-mail: 10kbw@lineone.net
Call Date: Nov 1976, Middle Temple
Qualifications: [LLB (Lond)]

BOSWELL MISS JENNIFER MARY

1 Pump Court
Lower Ground Floor, Temple, London
EC4Y 7AB, Telephone: 0171 583 2012/
353 4341
E-mail: [name]@1pumpcourt.co.uk
Call Date: July 1982, Middle Temple
Qualifications: [BA Sussex]

BOSWELL MISS LINDSAY ALICE QC (1997)

4 Pump Court
Temple, London EC4Y 7AN,
Telephone: 020 7842 5555
E-mail:chambers@4pumpcourt.law.co.uk
Call Date: July 1982, Gray's Inn
Qualifications: [BSc(London), Dip Law (City)]

BOSWOOD ANTHONY RICHARD QC (1986)

Fountain Court
Temple, London EC4Y 9DH,
Telephone: 0171 583 3335
E-mail: chambers@fountaincourt.co.uk
Call Date: Nov 1970, Middle Temple
Qualifications: [MA, BCL]

BOTHROYD MISS SHIRLEY ANN

Littleton Chambers
3 King's Bench Walk North, Temple,
London EC4Y 7HR,
Telephone: 0171 797 8600
E-mail:clerks@littletonchambers.co.uk
Call Date: July 1982, Middle Temple
Pupil Master
Qualifications: [BA]

BOTT CHARLES ADRIAN

3 Gray's Inn Square
Ground Floor, London WC1R 5AH,
Telephone: 0171 520 5600
E-mail: clerks@3gis.co.uk
Call Date: Nov 1979, Gray's Inn
Pupil Master
Qualifications: [MA (Cantab)]

BOULD DUNCAN JOHN

Nicholas Street Chambers
22 Nicholas Street, Chester CH1 2NX,
Telephone: 01244 323886
E-mail: clerks@40king.co.uk
Call Date: July 1984, Gray's Inn
Pupil Master
Qualifications: [BSc, LLB (Lond)]

BOULDING PHILIP VINCENT QC (1996)

Keating Chambers
10 Essex Street, Outer Temple, London
WC2R 3AA, Telephone: 0171 544 2600
Call Date: Nov 1979, Gray's Inn
Qualifications: [BA,M, LLB (Cantab)]

BOULTER TERENCE

2 Dyers Buildings
London EC1N 2JT,
Telephone: 0171 404 1881
Call Date: July 1986, Lincoln's Inn
Pupil Master
Qualifications: [BA(Hons)]

BOULTON DAVID JOHN

Martins Building
2nd Floor, No 4 Water Street, Liverpool
L2 3SP, Telephone: 0151 236 5818/4919
Call Date: July 1970, Middle Temple
Pupil Master, Recorder
Qualifications: [LLB]

BOUMPHREY JOHN ROSS STAVELEY

Phoenix Chambers
First Floor, Gray's Inn Chambers, Gray's
Inn, London WC1R 5JA,
Telephone: 0171 404 7888
E-mail:clerks@phoenix-chambers.co.uk
Call Date: Nov 1992, Inner Temple
Qualifications: [BA (Hons)(Warw), Dip in
Law]

BOURN COLIN JAMES

65-67 King Street
Leicester LE1 6RP,
Telephone: 0116 2547710
Call Date: Nov 1974, Middle Temple
Qualifications: [B.Sc. London]

BOURNE CHARLES GREGORY

2 Harcourt Buildings
Ground Floor/Left, Temple, London
EC4Y 9DB, Telephone: 0171 583 9020
E-mail: clerks@harcourt.co.uk
Call Date: Oct 1991, Middle Temple
Qualifications: [MA Hons (Cantab), Dip Law
(PCL), , Maitrise en Lettres, Modernes
(Sorbonne)]

BOURNE COLIN PETER

York Chambers
14 Toft Green, York YO1 6JT,
Telephone: 01904 620048
E-mail: [name]@yorkchambers.co.uk
Call Date: 1997, Gray's Inn
Qualifications: [LLB (Manc)]

BOURNE GEOFFREY ROBERT

4 Field Court
Gray's Inn, London WC1R 5EA,
Telephone: 0171 440 6900
E-mail: chambers@4fieldcourt.co.uk
Call Date: Nov 1978, Gray's Inn
Pupil Master
Qualifications: [MA (Oxon)]

BOURNE IAN MACLEAN

3 Temple Gardens
2nd Floor, Temple, London EC4Y 9AU,
Telephone: 0171 583 1155
Call Date: July 1977, Inner Temple
Pupil Master
Qualifications: [LLB Hons (Exon)]

BOURNE-ARTON SIMON NICHOLAS QC (1994)

Park Court Chambers
16 Park Place, Leeds LS1 2SJ,
Telephone: 0113 2433277
Call Date: Nov 1975, Inner Temple
Recorder
Qualifications: [LLB (Hons),]

BOWCOCK MISS SAMANTHA JANE

15 Winckley Square
Preston PR1 3JJ,
Telephone: 01772 252828
E-mail:clerks@winckleysq.demon.co.uk
Call Date: Oct 1990, Middle Temple
Qualifications: [LLB (Manch)]

BOWDERY MARTIN

Atkin Chambers
1 Atkin Building, Gray's Inn, London
WC1R 5AT, Telephone: 020 7404 0102
E-mail: clerks@atkin-chambers.co.uk
Call Date: July 1980, Inner Temple
Pupil Master
Qualifications: [BA (Oxon)]

BOWEN DOMINIC

Holborn Chambers
6 Gate Street, Lincoln's Inn Fields, London
WC2A 3HP, Telephone: 0171 242 6060
Call Date: Nov 1995, Lincoln's Inn
Qualifications: [BA (Hons)]

BOWEN JAMES FRANCIS

6 King's Bench Walk
Ground, Third & Fourth Floors, Temple,
London EC4Y 7DR,
Telephone: 0171 353 4931/583 0695
Call Date: Nov 1979, Gray's Inn
Pupil Master
Qualifications: [LLB (Exon)]

BOWEN NICHOLAS JAMES HUGH

29 Bedford Row Chambers
London WC1R 4HE,
Telephone: 0171 831 2626
Call Date: Nov 1984, Gray's Inn
Pupil Master
Qualifications: [BA (Sussex)]

BOWEN PAUL EDWARD

4 King's Bench Walk
Ground/First Floor/Basement, Temple,
London EC4Y 7DL,
Telephone: 0171 822 8822
E-mail: 4kbw@barristersatlaw.com
Call Date: Nov 1993, Inner Temple
Qualifications: [LLB (Exon)]

BOWEN STEPHEN

14 Tooks Court
Cursitor St, London EC4A 1LB,
Telephone: 0171 405 8828
E-mail: clerks@tooks.law.co.uk
Call Date: Nov 1990, Middle Temple
Qualifications: [MA, LLM]

BOWERMAN MICHAEL JOHN

York Chambers
14 Toft Green, York YO1 6JT,
Telephone: 01904 620048
E-mail: [name]@yorkchambers.co.uk
Call Date: July 1970, Inner Temple
Pupil Master, Assistant Recorder
Qualifications: [MA (Oxon)]

BOWERS JOHN SIMON QC (1998)

Littleton Chambers
3 King's Bench Walk North, Temple,
London EC4Y 7HR,
Telephone: 0171 797 8600
E-mail:clerks@littletonchambers.co.uk
Call Date: Nov 1979, Middle Temple
Qualifications: [MA, BCL (Oxon)]

Fax: 0171 797 8699;
Out of hours telephone: 0181 458 1031;
DX: 1047 London, Chancery Lane;
Other comms: E-mail
franksbower@compuserve.com

Circuit: Midland & Oxford

Awards and memberships: Employment Law
Bar Association; Administrative Law Bar
Association; Employment Lawyers Associa-
tion; Bar Council Race Relations
Committee; Home Office Human Rights
Task Force

Publications: *Transfer of Undertakings*
Encyclopaedia, 1998; *Bowers on Employ-*
ment Law (4th edn), 1997; *Textbook on*
Employment Law (5th edn), 1998; *Employ-*

D

ment *Tribunal Practice* (2nd edn), 1997;
Modern Law of Strikes, 1988

Reported Cases: *Chessington World of Adventures v Reed*, [1997] IRLR 550, 1997. Coverage of transsexuals by the Sex Discrimination Act.
Tracey v Crosville (Wales) Ltd, [1997] ICR 862, 1997. Whether deductions for contributory fault may be made from unfair dismissal compensation in the event of strikes.
Marley Tiles v Anderson, [1996] ICR 728, 1996. The test of reasonable practicability in late presentation of unfair dismissal applications.
BBC v Kelly Phillips, [1998] ICR 489. The proper construction of fixed term contracts.
University College Hospital v Various, [1999] IRLR 173, CA. Whether a strike about transfer of undertaking has immunity from suit in tort.

BOWERS RUPERT JOHN

Maidstone Chambers
33 Earl Street, Maidstone, Kent, ME14 1PF,
Telephone: 01622 688592
E-mail:maidstonechambers@compuserve.com
Call Date: Oct 1995, Gray's Inn
Qualifications: [BA (Hons)(Newcastle), Dip Law]

BOWES MICHAEL ANTHONY

2 King's Bench Walk
Ground Floor, Temple, London
EC4Y 7DE, Telephone: 0171 353 1746
E-mail: 2kbw@atlas.co.uk
King's Bench Chambers
115 North Hill, Plymouth PL4 8JY,
Telephone: 01752 221551
Call Date: July 1980, Middle Temple
Pupil Master
Qualifications: [LLB (Manch)]

BOWKER ROBERT JAMES

2nd Floor, Francis Taylor Building
Temple, London EC4Y 7BY,
Telephone: 0171 353 9942/3157
Call Date: Nov 1995, Lincoln's Inn
Qualifications: [BA (Hons)(So'ton)]

BOWLEY IVAN RICHARD

Lincoln House Chambers
5th Floor, Lincoln House, 1 Brazennose Street, Manchester M2 5EL,
Telephone: 0161 832 5701
E-mail: info@lincolnhse.co.uk
Call Date: Nov 1990, Middle Temple
Qualifications: [Bsc (Newc), Dip Law (PCL)]

BOWLEY MARTIN RICHARD QC (1981)

Chambers of Michael Pert QC
36 Bedford Row, London WC1R 4JH,
Telephone: 0171 421 8000
E-mail: 36bedfordrow@link.org
Chambers of Michael Pert QC
104 New Walk, Leicester LE1 7EA,
Telephone: 0116 249 2020
Chambers of Michael Pert QC
24 Albion Place, Northampton NN1 1UD,
Telephone: 01604 602333
Call Date: Feb 1962, Inner Temple
Qualifications: [MA, BCL (Oxon)]

BOWMER MICHAEL PAUL

11 Old Square
Ground Floor, Lincoln's Inn, London
WC2A 3TS, Telephone: 020 7430 0341
E-mail: clerks@11oldsquare.co.uk
Call Date: 1997, Middle Temple
Qualifications: [LLB (Hons)(Lond)]

BOWN PHILIP CLIVE

6 Fountain Court
Steelhouse Lane, Birmingham B4 6DR,
Telephone: 0121 233 3282
E-mail: clerks@sixfountain.co.uk
Call Date: Nov 1974, Middle Temple
Pupil Master
Qualifications: [LLB, FCIArb]

BOWRING WILLIAM SCHUYLER BEAKBANE

Chambers of Norman Palmer
2 Field Court, Gray's Inn, London
WC1R 5BB, Telephone: 0171 405 6114
E-mail: fieldct2@netcomuk.co.uk
Call Date: Nov 1974, Middle Temple
Qualifications: [BA (Kent)]

BOWRON MISS MARGARET RUTH

1 Crown Office Row
Ground Floor, Temple, London
EC4Y 7HH, Telephone: 0171 797 7500
E-mail: mail@onecrownofficerow.com
Crown Office Row Chambers
Blenheim House, 120 Church Street,
Brighton, Sussex, BN1 1WH,
Telephone: 01273 625625
E-mail: crownofficerow@clara.net
Call Date: Nov 1978, Inner Temple
Recorder
Qualifications: [LLB (Lond)]

BOWSHER MICHAEL FREDERICK THOMAS

Keating Chambers
10 Essex Street, Outer Temple, London
WC2R 3AA, Telephone: 0171 544 2600
Call Date: Nov 1985, Middle Temple
Pupil Master
Qualifications: [BA (Oxon), ACIArb]

BOWYER HENRY MARTIN MITFORD

1 Middle Temple Lane
Temple, London EC4Y 1LT,
Telephone: 0171 583 0659 (12 Lines)
E-mail: chambers@1mtl.co.uk
Call Date: Nov 1989, Inner Temple
Qualifications: [LLB (Buck)]

BOWYER MISS JULIET ELIZBETH CATHERINE

Dr Johnson's Chambers
Two Dr Johnson's Buildings, Temple,
London EC4Y 7AY,
Telephone: 0171 353 4716
E-mail: clerks@2djb.freeserve.co.uk
Call Date: 1997, Lincoln's Inn
Qualifications: [BA (Hons)(Reading)]

BOWYER MARTIN JOHN

6 King's Bench Walk
Ground Floor, Temple, London
EC4Y 7DR, Telephone: 0171 583 0410
E-mail: worsley@6kbw.freeserve.co.uk
Call Date: Nov 1984, Inner Temple
Pupil Master
Qualifications: [BA Hons (Cantab)]

BOYCE WILLIAM

Hollis Whiteman Chambers
3rd Floor, Queen Elizabeth Bldg, Temple,
London EC4Y 9BS,
Telephone: 020 7583 5766
E-mail:barristers@holliswhiteman.co.uk
Call Date: July 1976, Gray's Inn
Pupil Master, Recorder
Qualifications: [BA]

BOYD DAVID MARTIN

4 Brick Court
Ground Floor, Temple, London
EC4Y 9AD, Telephone: 0171 797 7766
E-mail: chambers@4brick.co.uk
Call Date: Feb 1977, Middle Temple
Pupil Master
Qualifications: [LLB (B'ham)]

BOYD GERARD DESMOND DWYER

Lion Court
Chancery House, 53-64 Chancery Lane,
London WC2A 1SJ,
Telephone: 0171 404 6565
Call Date: July 1967, Middle Temple
Pupil Master

BOYD JAMES ANDREW DONALDSON

8 King Street Chambers
8 King Street, Manchester M2 6AQ,
Telephone: 0161 834 9560
E-mail: eightking@aol.com
Call Date: Nov 1994, Inner Temple
Qualifications: [LLB (Manc), LLM (U.S.A.)]

BOYD MISS KERSTIN MARGARET

2nd Floor, Francis Taylor Building
Temple, London EC4Y 7BY,
Telephone: 0171 353 9942/3157
Call Date: July 1979, Gray's Inn
Pupil Master
Qualifications: [BA (Cantab)]

BOYD PHILLIP JOSEPH GEORGE

Lincoln House Chambers
5th Floor, Lincoln House, 1 Brazennose
Street, Manchester M2 5EL,
Telephone: 0161 832 5701
E-mail: info@lincolnhse.co.uk
Call Date: Nov 1993, Gray's Inn
Qualifications: [MA (Cantab)]

D

BOYD ROLAND PHILIP

Veritas Chambers
33 Corn Street, Bristol BS1 1HT,
Telephone: 0117 930 8802
Call Date: Oct 1997, Gray's Inn
Qualifications: [AKC, M.Soc.Sc (B'ham), Msc (Aston)]

BOYD STEPHEN JAMES HARVEY

29 Bedford Row Chambers
London WC1R 4HE,
Telephone: 0171 831 2626
Call Date: July 1977, Gray's Inn
Pupil Master
Qualifications: [BSc]

BOYD STEWART CRAUFURD QC (1981)

Essex Court Chambers
24 Lincoln's Inn Fields, London
WC2A 3ED, Telephone: 0171 813 8000
E-mail:clerksroom@essexcourt-chambers.co.uk
Call Date: July 1967, Middle Temple
Recorder
Qualifications: [MA (Cantab)]

BOYD THOMAS DIXON

33 Bedford Row
London WC1R 4JH,
Telephone: 0171 242 6476
E-mail:clerks@bedfordrow33.demon.co.uk
Call Date: Nov 1995, Inner Temple
Qualifications: [BA (Oxon), CPE]

BOYDELL EDWARD PATRICK STIRRUP

Pump Court Chambers
Upper Ground Floor, 3 Pump Court,
Temple, London EC4Y 7AJ,
Telephone: 0171 353 0711
E-mail: clerks@3pumpcourt.com
Pump Court Chambers
31 Southgate Street, Winchester
SO23 9EE, Telephone: 01962 868161
E-mail: clerks@3pumpcourt.com

Pump Court Chambers
5 Temple Chambers, Temple Street,
Swindon SN1 1SQ,
Telephone: 01793 539899
E-mail: clerks@3pumpcourt.com
Call Date: Nov 1989, Middle Temple
Pupil Master
Qualifications: [B.Ed Hons (Cantab)]

BOYE-ANAWOMA MISS MARGO CIARA

14 Tooks Court
Cursitor St, London EC4A 1LB,
Telephone: 0171 405 8828
E-mail: clerks@tooks.law.co.uk
Call Date: Nov 1989, Inner Temple
Qualifications: [LLB]

BOYES MRS KAREN ROSALIE

Erimus Chambers
P.O.Box 458, Brixworth, Northampton
NN6 9ZT, Telephone: 01604 882942
E-mail: karenrboyes@acklam.clara.net
Call Date: Oct 1991, Middle Temple
Qualifications: [LLB Hons (Newc)]

BOYLE ALAN GORDON QC (1991)

Serle Court Chambers
6 New Square, Lincoln's Inn, London
WC2A 3QS, Telephone: 0171 242 6105
E-mail: clerks@serlecourt.co.uk
Call Date: Nov 1972, Lincoln's Inn
Qualifications: [BA (Oxon)]

BOYLE CHRISTOPHER ALEXANDER DAVID

2 Mitre Court Buildings
2nd Floor, Temple, London EC4Y 7BX,
Telephone: 0171 583 1380
E-mail: clerks@2mcb.co.uk
Call Date: Nov 1994, Lincoln's Inn
Qualifications: [BA (Hons)]

BOYLE DAVID STUART

Deans Court Chambers
24 St John Street, Manchester M3 4DF,
Telephone: 0161 214 6000
E-mail: clerks@deanscourt.co.uk

Deans Court Chambers
41-43 Market Place, Preston PR1 1AH,
Telephone: 01772 555163
E-mail: clerks@deanscourt.co.uk
Call Date: Mar 1996, Gray's Inn
Qualifications: [BA]

BOYLE GERARD JAMES

No. 1 Serjeants' Inn
5th Floor Fleet Street, Temple, London
EC4Y 1LH, Telephone: 0171 415 6666
E-mail:no1serjeantsinn@btinternet.com
Call Date: Nov 1992, Gray's Inn
Qualifications: [BA (Cantab)]

BOYLE ROBERT ALEXANDER

18 Red Lion Court
(Off Fleet Street), London EC4A 3EB,
Telephone: 0171 520 6000
E-mail: chambers@18rlc.co.uk
Thornwood House
102 New London Road, Chelmsford,
Essex, CM2 0RG,
Telephone: 01245 280880
E-mail: chambers@18rlc.co.uk
Call Date: Nov 1985, Middle Temple
Qualifications: [BSc (Surrey)]

BRABIN MICHAEL EDWARD

Colleton Chambers
Colleton Crescent, Exeter, Devon,
EX2 4DG, Telephone: 01392 274898/9
Farrar's Building
Temple, London EC4Y 7BD,
Telephone: 0171 583 9241
E-mail:chambers@farrarsbuilding.co.uk
Call Date: May 1976, Inner Temple
Pupil Master

BRACE MICHAEL WESLEY

33 Park Place
Cardiff CF1 3BA,
Telephone: 02920 233313
Call Date: Apr 1991, Lincoln's Inn
Qualifications: [LLB (Hons)(Lond)]

BRADBERRY MISS REBECCA

South Western Chambers
Melville House, 12 Middle Street,
Taunton, Somerset, TA1 1SH,
Telephone: 01823 331919 (24 hrs)
E-mail: barclerk@clara.net
Call Date: Oct 1996, Lincoln's Inn
Qualifications: [BA (Hons)(Warw), Dip in
Law (Exon)]

BRADBURY TIMOTHY BLACKBURN

3 Paper Buildings
Temple, London EC4Y 7EU,
Telephone: 020 7583 8055
E-mail: London@3paper.com
3 Paper Buildings (Bournemouth)
20 Lorne Park Road, Bournemouth,
Dorset, BH1 1JN,
Telephone: 01202 292102
E-mail: Bournemouth@3paper.com
3 Paper Buildings (Winchester)
4 St Peter Street, Winchester SO23 8BW,
Telephone: 01962 868884
E-mail: winchester@3paper.com
3 Paper Buildings (Oxford)
1 Alfred Street, High Street, Oxford
OX1 4EH, Telephone: 01865 793736
E-mail: oxford@3paper.com
Call Date: July 1989, Inner Temple
Qualifications: [LLB (So'ton)]

BRADLEY ANTHONY WILFRED

Cloisters
1 Pump Court, Temple, London
EC4Y 7AA, Telephone: 0171 827 4000
E-mail: clerks@cloisters.com
Call Date: Apr 1989, Inner Temple
Qualifications: [BA,MA,LLM (Cantab)]

BRADLEY MISS CAROLINE

King Charles House
Standard Hill, Nottingham NG1 6FX,
Telephone: 0115 9418851
E-mail: clerks@kch.co.uk
Call Date: Nov 1985, Middle Temple
Pupil Master
Qualifications: [BA (Hons)]

BRADLEY MISS CLODAGH MARIA

3 Serjeants' Inn
London EC4Y 1BQ,
Telephone: 0171 353 5537
E-mail: clerks@3serjeantsinn.com
Call Date: Oct 1996, Middle Temple
Qualifications: [BA (Hons)(Cantab)]

BRADLEY DENIS ARTHUR ROBERT

Phoenix Chambers
First Floor, Gray's Inn Chambers, Gray's
Inn, London WC1R 5JA,
Telephone: 0171 404 7888
E-mail:clerks@phoenix-chambers.co.uk
Call Date: Feb 1965, Gray's Inn

BRADLEY PHILLIP JAMES

Equity Chambers
3rd Floor, 153a Corporation Street,
Birmingham B4 6PH,
Telephone: 0121 233 2100
E-mail: equityatusa.com
1 Pump Court
Lower Ground Floor, Temple, London
EC4Y 7AB, Telephone: 0171 583 2012/
353 4341
E-mail: [name]@1pumpcourt.co.uk
Call Date: Nov 1993, Lincoln's Inn
Qualifications: [BA (Hons)]

BRADLEY RICHARD

Oriel Chambers
14 Water Street, Liverpool L2 8TD,
Telephone: 0151 236 7191/236 4321
E-mail: clerks@oriel-chambers.co.uk
Call Date: July 1978, Middle Temple
Pupil Master
Qualifications: [LLB]

BRADLEY MS SALLY CHRISTINA

1 Pump Court
Lower Ground Floor, Temple, London
EC4Y 7AB, Telephone: 0171 583 2012/
353 4341
E-mail: [name]@1pumpcourt.co.uk
Call Date: Nov 1989, Inner Temple
Qualifications: [BA]

BRADLEY MS SALLY FRANCES QC (1999)

Broad Chare
33 Broad Chare, Newcastle upon Tyne
NE1 3DQ, Telephone: 0191 232 0541
E-mail:clerks@broadcharechambers.law.co.uk
1 Mitre Court Buildings
Temple, London EC4Y 7BS,
Telephone: 0171 797 7070
E-mail: clerks@1mcb.com
Call Date: 1978, Lincoln's Inn
Pupil Master
Qualifications: [LLB]

BRADLY DAVID LAWRENCE

39 Essex Street
London WC2R 3AT,
Telephone: 0171 832 1111
E-mail: clerks@39essex.co.uk
Call Date: July 1987, Middle Temple
Pupil Master
Qualifications: [LLB (Lond)]

BRADSHAW DAVID LAWRENCE

Chambers of Andrew Campbell QC
10 Park Square, Leeds LS1 2LH,
Telephone: 0113 2455438
E-mail: clerks@10pksq.co.uk
Call Date: July 1975, Inner Temple
Pupil Master, Recorder
Qualifications: [LLB]

BRADSHAW HOWARD SYDNEY

Queen's Chambers
5 John Dalton Street, Manchester M2 6ET,
Telephone: 0161 834 6875/4738
Queens Chambers
4 Camden Place, Preston PR1 3JL,
Telephone: 01772 828300
Call Date: July 1977, Middle Temple
Pupil Master
Qualifications: [MA (Cantab)]

BRADSHAW IAN CHARLES

Baker Street Chambers
9 Baker Street, Middlesbrough TS1 2LF,
Telephone: 01642 873873
Call Date: Oct 1992, Middle Temple
Qualifications: [LLB(Nott'm), LLM(Wales),
MA(Hull)]

BRADY MICHAEL ANTONY

58 King Street Chambers
1st Floor, Kingsgate House, 51-53 South
King Street, Manchester M2 6DE,
Telephone: 0161 831 7477
Call Date: Oct 1992, Gray's Inn
Qualifications: [LL.B (Hons)]

BRAGANZA MISS NICOLA JANICE

6 King's Bench Walk
Ground, Third & Fourth Floors, Temple,
London EC4Y 7DR,
Telephone: 0171 353 4931/583 0695
Call Date: Oct 1992, Middle Temple
Qualifications: [LL.B (Hons, Reading)]

BRAGIEL EDWARD BRONISLAW HENRYK

5 New Square
Ground Floor, Lincoln's Inn, London
WC2A 3RJ, Telephone: 020 7404 0404
E-mail:chambers@fivenewsquare.demon.co.
uk
Call Date: July 1977, Middle Temple
Pupil Master
Qualifications: [MA (Cantab)]

BRAHAM COLIN PHILIP LESLIE

12 New Square
Lincoln's Inn, London WC2A 3SW,
Telephone: 0171 419 1212
E-mail: chambers@12newsquare.co.uk
Sovereign Chambers
25 Park Square, Leeds LS1 2PW,
Telephone: 0113 2451841/2/3
E-mail:sovereignchambers@btinternet.com
Call Date: Nov 1971, Middle Temple
Pupil Master
Qualifications: [MA (Cantab), MSc (Lond)]

BRAHAM DAVID GERALD HENRY QC (1979)

Temple Gardens Tax Chambers
1st Floor, 3 Temple Gardens, Temple,
London EC4Y 9AU,
Telephone: 0171 353 7884/5 8982/3
E-mail: clerks@taxcounsel.co.uk.
Call Date: Feb 1957, Middle Temple
Qualifications: [BA (Cantab)]

BRAHAMS MRS DIANA JOYCE

Old Square Chambers
1 Verulam Buildings, Gray's Inn, London
WC1R 5LQ, Telephone: 0171 269 0300
E-mail:clerks@oldsquarechambers.co.uk
Old Square Chambers
Hanover House, 47 Corn Street, Bristol
BS1 1HT, Telephone: 0117 9277111
E-mail: oldsqbri@globalnet.co.uk
Call Date: July 1972, Middle Temple

BRAIN MISS PAMELA FRANCIS

Chambers of Helen Grindrod QC
4th Floor, 15-19 Devereux Court, London
WC2R 3JJ, Telephone: 0171 583 2792
Call Date: Nov 1985, Inner Temple
Pupil Master
Qualifications: [LLB (Lond)]

BRAITHWAITE CHARLES ANTONY ELLIOTT

Westgate Chambers
67a Westgate Road, Newcastle upon Tyne
NE1 1SG, Telephone: 0191 261 4407/
2329785
E-mail:pracman@westgatechambers.law.co.u
k
Call Date: July 1971, Gray's Inn
Qualifications: [MA (Cantab)]

BRAITHWAITE GARFIELD ZIBEAN

Francis Taylor Building
Ground Floor, Temple, London
EC4Y 7BY, Telephone: 0171 353 7768/
7769/2711
E-mail:clerks@francistaylorbuilding.law.co.uk
Call Date: Feb 1987, Gray's Inn
Pupil Master
Qualifications: [LLB (Lanc)]

BRAITHWAITE THOMAS JAMES

One Hare Court
1st Floor, Temple, London EC4Y 7BE,
Telephone: 020 7353 3171
E-mail:admin-oneharecourt@btinternet.com
Call Date: Oct 1998, Lincoln's Inn
Qualifications: [BA (Hons)(Cantab)]

BRAITHWAITE WILLIAM THOMAS SCATCHARD QC (1992)

Exchange Chambers
Pearl Assurance House, Derby Square,
Liverpool L2 9XX,
Telephone: 0151 236 7747
E-mail:exchangechambers@btinternet.com
Call Date: 1970, Gray's Inn
Recorder
Qualifications: [LLB (L'pool)]

BRAMWELL RICHARD MERVYN QC (1989)

Temple Gardens Tax Chambers
1st Floor, 3 Temple Gardens, Temple,
London EC4Y 9AU,
Telephone: 0171 353 7884/5 8982/3
E-mail: clerks@taxcounsel.co.uk.
Call Date: July 1967, Middle Temple
Qualifications: [LLM]

BRANCH MISS ELIZABETH JAYNE

4 Fountain Court
Steelhouse Lane, Birmingham B4 6DR,
Telephone: 0121 236 3476
Call Date: Oct 1992, Lincoln's Inn
Qualifications: [LLB(Hons)(Manch)]

BRANCHFLOWER GEORGE

Chambers of Andrew Campbell QC
10 Park Square, Leeds LS1 2LH,
Telephone: 0113 2455438
E-mail: clerks@10pksq.co.uk
Call Date: 1997, Lincoln's Inn
Qualifications: [LLB (Hons)(Leeds)]

BRAND MISS RACHEL RENNIE VIRGINIA ANN

Coleridge Chambers
Citadel, 190 Corporation Street,
Birmingham B4 6QD,
Telephone: 0121 233 8500
Call Date: July 1981, Gray's Inn
Qualifications: [BA]

BRAND SIMON DAVID

Coleridge Chambers
Citadel, 190 Corporation Street,
Birmingham B4 6QD,
Telephone: 0121 233 8500
Call Date: Nov 1973, Gray's Inn
Pupil Master
Qualifications: [LLB (Lond)]

BRANDON DAVID STEPHEN QC (1996)

24 Old Buildings
First Floor, Lincoln's Inn, London
WC2A 3UP, Telephone: 020 7242 2744
E-mail: taxchambers@compuserve.com
Call Date: July 1978, Gray's Inn
Qualifications: [BA (Nottm) LLM, (Keele)]

BRANDON MISS HELEN ELIZABETH

Oriel Chambers
14 Water Street, Liverpool L2 8TD,
Telephone: 0151 236 7191/236 4321
E-mail: clerks@oriel-chambers.co.uk
Call Date: Oct 1993, Middle Temple
Qualifications: [LLB (Hons)(Lanc)]

BRANIGAN MISS KATE VICTORIA

3 Paper Buildings
Temple, London EC4Y 7EU,
Telephone: 020 7583 8055
E-mail: London@3paper.com
3 Paper Buildings (Winchester)
4 St Peter Street, Winchester SO23 8BW,
Telephone: 01962 868884
E-mail: winchester@3paper.com
3 Paper Buildings (Bournemouth)
20 Lorne Park Road, Bournemouth,
Dorset, BH1 1JN,
Telephone: 01202 292102
E-mail: Bournemouth@3paper.com
3 Paper Buildings (Oxford)
1 Alfred Street, High Street, Oxford
OX1 4EH, Telephone: 01865 793736
E-mail: oxford@3paper.com
Call Date: July 1984, Inner Temple
Pupil Master
Qualifications: [LLB (Soton)]

BRANN MISS ELIZABETH NINA

Gray's Inn Chambers
5th Floor, Gray's Inn, London WC1R 5JA,
Telephone: 0171 404 1111
Call Date: July 1970, Middle Temple
Pupil Master

BRANNIGAN PETER JOHN SEAN

4 Pump Court
Temple, London EC4Y 7AN,
Telephone: 020 7842 5555
E-mail:chambers@4pumpcourt.law.co.uk
Call Date: Oct 1994, Gray's Inn
Qualifications: [BA]

BRANT PAUL DAVID

Oriel Chambers
14 Water Street, Liverpool L2 8TD,
Telephone: 0151 236 7191/236 4321
E-mail: clerks@oriel-chambers.co.uk
Call Date: Oct 1993, Lincoln's Inn
Qualifications: [LLB (Hons)(L'pool)]

BRANTHWAITE DR MARGARET ANNIE

One Paper Buildings
Ground Floor, Temple, London
EC4Y 7EP, Telephone: 0171 583 7355
E-mail: clerks@1pb.co.uk
Call Date: Oct 1993, Lincoln's Inn
Qualifications: [BA, MB Bchir, MD, FRCP, FFARCS]

BRASLAVSKY NICHOLAS JUSTIN QC (1999)

40 King Street
Manchester M2 6BA,
Telephone: 0161 832 9082
E-mail: clerks@40kingstreet.co.uk
The Chambers of Philip Raynor QC
5 Park Place, Leeds LS1 2RU,
Telephone: 0113 242 1123
Call Date: 1983, Inner Temple
Pupil Master
Qualifications: [LLB, M jur, PhD(B'ha]

BRASSE MISS GILLIAN DENISE

14 Gray's Inn Square
Gray's Inn, London WC1R 5JP,
Telephone: 0171 242 0858
E-mail: 100712.2134@compuserve.com
Call Date: July 1977, Gray's Inn
Pupil Master
Qualifications: [BA(L'pool)]

BRASSINGTON STEPHEN DAVID

2 Paper Buildings
1st Floor, Temple, London EC4Y 7ET,
Telephone: 020 7556 5500
E-mail: clerks@2pbbarristers.co.uk
Call Date: Nov 1994, Inner Temple
Qualifications: [BSc (Lond), CPE]

BRAZIL DOMINIC THOMAS GEORGE

14 Gray's Inn Square
Gray's Inn, London WC1R 5JP,
Telephone: 0171 242 0858
E-mail: 100712.2134@compuserve.com
Call Date: Nov 1995, Middle Temple
Qualifications: [BA (Hons)]

BREALEY MARK PHILIP

Brick Court Chambers
7-8 Essex Street, London WC2R 3LD,
Telephone: 0171 379 3550
E-mail: [surname]@brickcourt.co.uk
Call Date: July 1984, Middle Temple
Pupil Master
Qualifications: [LLB, LLM, DEA]

BREDEMEAR ZACHARY CHARLES

Barnard's Inn Chambers
6th Floor, Halton House, 20-23 Holborn,
London EC1N 2JD,
Telephone: 0171 369 6969
E-mail: clerks@biclaw.co.uk
Call Date: Oct 1996, Inner Temple
Qualifications: [LLB (Reading), LLM (Lond)]

BREEN CARLO ENRICO

Chambers of John Hand QC
9 St John Street, Manchester M3 4DN,
Telephone: 0161 955 9000
E-mail: ninesjs@gconnect.com
Call Date: Nov 1987, Middle Temple
Qualifications: [LLB (Essex)]

D

BREESE-LAUGHRAN MS ELEANORE DELPHINE

8 King's Bench Walk
2nd Floor, Temple, London EC4Y 7DU,
Telephone: 0171 797 8888
8 King's Bench Walk North
1 Park Square East, Leeds LS1 2NE,
Telephone: 0113 2439797
Call Date: Oct 1991, Lincoln's Inn
Qualifications: [MA (Hons) (Camb)]

BREHENY MARK PATRICK

Oriel Chambers
14 Water Street, Liverpool L2 8TD,
Telephone: 0151 236 7191/236 4321
E-mail: clerks@oriel-chambers.co.uk
Call Date: Nov 1986, Lincoln's Inn
Qualifications: [BA Law (Kent)]

BRENNAN CHRISTOPHER PATRICK

Goldsmith Chambers
Ground Floor, Goldsmith Building,
Temple, London EC4Y 7BL,
Telephone: 0171 353 6802/3/4/5
E-mail:clerks@goldsmithchambers.law.co.uk
Call Date: Feb 1995, Gray's Inn
Qualifications: [LLB (Cardiff)]

BRENNAN DANIEL JOSEPH QC (1985)

39 Essex Street
London WC2R 3AT,
Telephone: 0171 832 1111
E-mail: clerks@39essex.co.uk
18 St John Street
Manchester M3 4EA,
Telephone: 0161 278 1800
E-mail: 18stjohn@lineone.net
Call Date: July 1967, Gray's Inn
Recorder
Qualifications: [LLB (Manch)]

BRENNAN MISS JANICE LESLEY

2 King's Bench Walk
Ground Floor, Temple, London
EC4Y 7DE, Telephone: 0171 353 1746
E-mail: 2kbw@atlas.co.uk
King's Bench Chambers
115 North Hill, Plymouth PL4 8JY,
Telephone: 01752 221551
Call Date: July 1980, Middle Temple
Qualifications: [LLB (Lond)]

BRENNAN JOHN DAVID

4 Fountain Court
Steelhouse Lane, Birmingham B4 6DR,
Telephone: 0121 236 3476
Call Date: Mar 1996, Lincoln's Inn
Qualifications: [BA (Hons)]

BRENNAN TIMOTHY ROGER

Devereux Chambers
Devereux Court, London WC2R 3JJ,
Telephone: 0171 353 7534
E-mail: mailbox@devchambers.co.uk
Call Date: Nov 1981, Gray's Inn
Pupil Master, Assistant Recorder
Qualifications: [BCL,MA (Oxon)]

BRENNAND TIMOTHY WILLIAM

24a St John Street
Manchester M3 4DF,
Telephone: 0161 833 9628
Call Date: Nov 1987, Gray's Inn
Qualifications: [LLB (Hons)]

BRENT MICHAEL LEON QC (1983)

9 Gough Square
London EC4A 3DE,
Telephone: 020 7832 0500
E-mail: clerks@9goughsq.co.uk
Call Date: May 1961, Gray's Inn
Recorder
Qualifications: [LLB (Manch)]

BRENT RICHARD

3 Verulam Buildings
London WC1R 5NT,
Telephone: 0171 831 8441
E-mail: clerks@3verulam.co.uk
Call Date: July 1995, Middle Temple
Qualifications: [BA (Hons) (Cantab), D.Phil
(Oxon)]

BRENTON TIMOTHY DEANE QC (1998)

4 Essex Court
Temple, London EC4Y 9AJ,
Telephone: 020 7797 7970
E-mail: clerks@4essexcourt.law.co.uk
Call Date: July 1981, Middle Temple
Qualifications: [LLB]

BRERETON MRS FIORELLA

Peel Court Chambers
45 Hardman Street, Manchester M3 3PL,
Telephone: 0161 832 3791
E-mail: clerks@peelct.co.uk
Call Date: Nov 1979, Gray's Inn
Pupil Master
Qualifications: [BA (Hons)]

BRERETON MISS JOY

4 Paper Buildings
1st Floor, Temple, London EC4Y 7EX,
Telephone: 0171 583 0816/353 1131
E-mail: clerks@4paperbuildings.co.uk
Call Date: Nov 1990, Gray's Inn
Pupil Master
Qualifications: [LLB (Cardiff), LLM (Bristol)]

BRESLER FENTON SHEA

22 Melcombe Regis Court
Weymouth Street, London W1N 3LG,
Telephone: 0171 487 5589
E-mail: fbresler@aol.com
Call Date: June 1951, Middle Temple
Qualifications: [LLB (Lond)(Hons)]

BRESLIN MISS CATHERINE ELIZABETH

College Chambers
19 Carlton Cresent, Southampton
SO15 2ET, Telephone: 01703 230338
Call Date: Nov 1990, Inner Temple
Pupil Master
Qualifications: [LLB (Hons)(Lond)]

BRETHERTON MS KERRY LOUISE

Arden Chambers
27 John Street, London WC1N 2BL,
Telephone: 020 7242 4244
E-mail:clerks@arden-chambers.law.co.uk
Call Date: Oct 1992, Lincoln's Inn
Qualifications: [BA(Hons)(B'ham),
CPE(B'ham)]

BRETT MATTHEW CHRISTOPHER ANTHONY

Harcourt Chambers
1st Floor, 2 Harcourt Buildings, Temple,
London EC4Y 9DB,
Telephone: 0171 353 6961
E-mail:clerks@harcourtchambers.law.co.uk

Harcourt Chambers
Churchill House, 3 St Aldate's Courtyard,
St Aldate's, Oxford OX1 1BN,
Telephone: 01865 791559
E-mail:clerks@harcourtchambers.law.co.uk
Call Date: Nov 1987, Middle Temple
Qualifications: [BA (Oxon)]

BRETTEN (GEORGE) REX QC (1980)

24 Old Buildings
First Floor, Lincoln's Inn, London
WC2A 3UP, Telephone: 020 7242 2744
E-mail: taxchambers@compuserve.com
Call Date: May 1965, Lincoln's Inn
Qualifications: [MA, LLM (Cantab)]

BRETTLER JONATHAN SAMUEL

4 Stone Buildings
Ground Floor, Lincoln's Inn, London
WC2A 3XT, Telephone: 0171 242 5524
E-mail:clerks@4stonebuildings.law.co.uk
Call Date: July 1988, Middle Temple
Qualifications: [LLB (Hons) (LSE), BCL
(Oxon)]

BRIAND MISS PAULINE MARY

Staple Inn Chambers
1st Floor, 9 Staple Inn, Holborn Bars,
London WC1V 7QH,
Telephone: 0171 242 5240
E-mail: clerks@staple-inn.org
Call Date: July 1996, Middle Temple
Qualifications: [LLB (Hons)(Staffs)]

BRICE GEOFFREY JAMES BARRINGTON QC (1979)

4 Field Court
Gray's Inn, London WC1R 5EA,
Telephone: 0171 440 6900
E-mail: chambers@4fieldcourt.co.uk
Call Date: July 1960, Middle Temple
Recorder
Qualifications: [LLB]

BRICKMAN MISS LAURA GILLIAN

10 King's Bench Walk
1st Floor, Temple, London EC4Y 7EB,
Telephone: 0171 353 2501
Call Date: July 1976, Inner Temple
Pupil Master

BRIDEN RICHARD JOHN

96 Gray's Inn Road
London WC1X 8AL,
Telephone: 0171 405 0585
Call Date: Nov 1982, Gray's Inn
Pupil Master
Qualifications: [LLB (Hons) (E.Ang), FCIArb]

BRIDEN TIMOTHY JOHN

8 Stone Buildings
Lincoln's Inn, London WC2A 3TA,
Telephone: 0171 831 9881
E-mail: alanl@8stonebuildings.law.uk
Call Date: July 1976, Inner Temple
Pupil Master
Qualifications: [MA, LLB (Cantab)]

Fax: 0171 831 9342; DX: 216 London,
Chancery Lane

Types of work: Ecclesiastical, Insurance,
Medical negligence, Personal injury, Professional negligence

Circuit: South Eastern

Publications: *Macmorran's Handbook for
Churchwardens and Parochial Church
Councillors*, 1997 edn; *Moore's Introduc-
tion to English Canon Law* (3rd edn), 1992

Reported Cases: *Re West Norwood Cemetery*,
[1994] Fam 210, 1994. Municipal cemetery
– consecrated part – unauthorised distur-
bance of graves – powers of Consistory
Court.
Re St Luke the Evangelist, Maidstone,
[1995] Fam 1, 1994. Reordering of interior
of church – whether adversely affecting
character of building – necessity for
change.
Lightfoot v National Westminster Bank,
[1996] I WLR 583, 1995. County Court –
practice – automatic directions – striking
out.
R v Board of Trustees of Science Museum,
[1993] I WLR 1171, 1993. Health and
Safety – bacteria in air conditioning system
– whether exposure of public a risk to
health.

BRIDGE IAN CHARLES

Mitre Court Chambers
3rd Floor, Temple, London EC4Y 7BP,
Telephone: 0171 353 9394
E-mail: mitrecourt.com
Call Date: Nov 1988, Inner Temple
Pupil Master
Qualifications: [LLB (Hons) (Sheff)]

BRIDGE PROFESSOR MICHAEL GREENHALGH

Ropewalk Chambers
24 The Ropewalk, Nottingham NG1 5EF,
Telephone: 0115 9472581
E-mail: administration@ropewalk co.uk
Call Date: Nov 1975, Middle Temple
Qualifications: [LLM]

BRIDGE MRS ROWENA

King Charles House
Standard Hill, Nottingham NG1 6FX,
Telephone: 0115 9418851
E-mail: clerks@kch.co.uk
Call Date: Nov 1975, Middle Temple
Pupil Master
Qualifications: [LLB (Lond), LLB,BCL
(McGill)]

BRIDGE STUART NIGEL

Fenners Chambers
3 Madingley Road, Cambridge CB3 0EE,
Telephone: 01223 368761
E-mail: clerks@fennerschambers.co.uk
Fenners Chambers
8-12 Priestgate, Peterborough PE1 1JA,
Telephone: 01733 562030
E-mail: clerks@fennerschambers.co.uk
Call Date: July 1981, Middle Temple
Qualifications: [MA (Cantab)]

BRIDGMAN DAVID MARTIN

No. 1 Serjeants' Inn
5th Floor Fleet Street, Temple, London
EC4Y 1LH, Telephone: 0171 415 6666
E-mail:no1serjeantsinn@btinternet.com
Call Date: 1997, Gray's Inn
Qualifications: [BA]

BRIEFEL CHARLES JONATHAN

Hardwicke Building
New Square, Lincoln's Inn, London
WC2A 3SB, Telephone: 020 7242 2523
E-mail: clerks@hardwicke.co.uk
Call Date: July 1984, Gray's Inn
Qualifications: [LLB (Manch)]

BRIEGEL PIETER DAVID ROY

Mitre Court Chambers
3rd Floor, Temple, London EC4Y 7BP,
Telephone: 0171 353 9394
E-mail: mitrecourt.com
Call Date: Nov 1986, Middle Temple
Pupil Master
Qualifications: [LLB (Lond) (Hons)]

BRIERLEY ANDREW DUNCAN

6 King's Bench Walk
Ground Floor, Temple, London
EC4Y 7DR, Telephone: 0171 583 0410
E-mail: worsley@6kbw.freeserve.co.uk
Call Date: July 1984, Middle Temple
Pupil Master
Qualifications: [BA]

BRIGDEN ANTHONY JOHN

Bell Yard Chambers
116/118 Chancery Lane, London
WC2A 1PP, Telephone: 0171 306 9292
Call Date: July 1967, Inner Temple
Pupil Master, Recorder
Qualifications: [LLB]

BRIGGS ADRIAN

Blackstone Chambers
Blackstone House, Temple, London
EC4Y 9BW, Telephone: 0171 583 1770
E-mail:clerks@blackstonechambers.com
Call Date: Apr 1989, Middle Temple
Qualifications: [BCL, MA (Oxon)]

BRIGGS MISS JOANNE MARY ROBSON

Sussex Chambers
9 Old Steine, Brighton, Sussex, BN1 1FJ,
Telephone: 01273 607953

Cardinal Chambers
4 Old Mitre Court, 4th Floor, Temple,
London EC4Y 7BP,
Telephone: 020 7353 2622
E-mail:admin@cardinal-chambers.co.uk
Call Date: Oct 1993, Middle Temple
Qualifications: [M.Phil, CPE (Lond)]

BRIGGS JOHN

India Buildings Chambers
Water Street, Liverpool L2 0XG,
Telephone: 0151 243 6000
E-mail: clerks@chambers.u-net.com
Call Date: June 1953, Inner Temple
Qualifications: [BCL, MA]

BRIGGS JOHN BONAR

3/4 South Square
Gray's Inn, London WC1R 5HP,
Telephone: 0171 696 9900
E-mail: clerks@southsquare.com
Call Date: July 1973, Gray's Inn
Pupil Master
Qualifications: [LLB (Lond), Ex Du D d'u
(NANCY)]

BRIGGS MICHAEL TOWNLEY FEATHERSTONE QC (1994)

Serle Court Chambers
6 New Square, Lincoln's Inn, London
WC2A 3QS, Telephone: 0171 242 6105
E-mail: clerks@serlecourt.co.uk
Call Date: Nov 1978, Lincoln's Inn
Qualifications: [BA (Oxon)]

BRIGGS NICHOLAS NORMAN

Queens Square Chambers
56 Queens Square, Bristol BS1 4PR,
Telephone: 0117 921 1966
Call Date: Oct 1994, Lincoln's Inn
Qualifications: [Dip in Valuation &, Estate
Management, CPE (Bris)]

BRIGGS-WATSON MISS SANDRA MICHELLE

2 Paper Buildings, Basement North
Temple, London EC4Y 7ET,
Telephone: 0171 936 2613
E-mail: post@2paper.co.uk
Call Date: Nov 1985, Middle Temple
Pupil Master
Qualifications: [LLB (London)]

BRIGHT ANDREW JOHN

4 Brick Court, Chambers of Anne Rafferty QC
1st Floor, Temple, London EC4Y 9AD,
Telephone: 0171 583 8455
Call Date: July 1973, Middle Temple
Pupil Master, Assistant Recorder
Qualifications: [LLB (Lond)]

BRIGHT CHRISTOPHER JOHN

3 Fountain Court
Steelhouse Lane, Birmingham B4 6DR,
Telephone: 0121 236 5854
Call Date: Nov 1985, Gray's Inn
Pupil Master
Qualifications: [BA (Dunelm)]

BRIGHT DAVID REGINALD

13 King's Bench Walk
1st Floor, Temple, London EC4Y 7EN,
Telephone: 0171 353 7204
E-mail: clerks@13kbw.law.co.uk
King's Bench Chambers
32 Beaumont Street, Oxford OX1 2NP,
Telephone: 01865 311066
E-mail: clerks@kbc-oxford.law.co.uk
Call Date: July 1976, Lincoln's Inn
Pupil Master, Recorder

BRIGHT MISS RACHEL ZELDA

1 Middle Temple Lane
Temple, London EC4Y 1LT,
Telephone: 0171 583 0659 (12 Lines)
E-mail: chambers@1mtl.co.uk
Call Date: Oct 1991, Lincoln's Inn
Qualifications: [LLB (Hons) (Manch)]

BRIGHT ROBERT GRAHAM

S Tomlinson QC
7 King's Bench Walk, Temple, London
EC4Y 7DS, Telephone: 0171 583 0404
E-mail: clerks@7kbw.law.co.uk
Call Date: Nov 1987, Gray's Inn
Pupil Master
Qualifications: [BA, BCL (Oxon)]

BRILLIANT SIMON HOWARD

Lamb Chambers
Lamb Building, Temple, London
EC4Y 7AS, Telephone: 020 7797 8300
E-mail: lambchambers@link.org
Call Date: July 1976, Middle Temple
Pupil Master
Qualifications: [LLB (Manch), BCL (Ox)]

BRIMELOW MISS JANINE KIRSTY

2nd Floor, Francis Taylor Building
Temple, London EC4Y 7BY,
Telephone: 0171 353 9942/3157
Call Date: Oct 1991, Gray's Inn
Qualifications: [LLB (Hons)]

BRINDLE MICHAEL JOHN QC (1992)

Fountain Court
Temple, London EC4Y 9DH,
Telephone: 0171 583 3335
E-mail: chambers@fountaincourt.co.uk
Call Date: Nov 1975, Lincoln's Inn
Qualifications: [MA (Oxon)]

BRINKWORTH PAUL GREGORY

Lion Court
Chancery House, 53-64 Chancery Lane,
London WC2A 1SJ,
Telephone: 0171 404 6565
Call Date: Oct 1990, Lincoln's Inn
Qualifications: [BA]

BRISBY JOHN CONSTANT SHANNON MCBURNEY QC (1996)

4 Stone Buildings
Ground Floor, Lincoln's Inn, London
WC2A 3XT, Telephone: 0171 242 5524
E-mail:clerks@4stonebuildings.law.co.uk
Call Date: July 1978, Lincoln's Inn
Qualifications: [MA (Oxon)]

BRISCOE MISS CONSTANCE

4 Brick Court
Ground Floor, Temple, London
EC4Y 9AD, Telephone: 0171 797 7766
E-mail: chambers@4brick.co.uk
Call Date: Nov 1983, Inner Temple
Qualifications: [LLB (Newcastle)]

BRISSETT MISS NICOLA LUANA

Staple Inn Chambers
1st Floor, 9 Staple Inn, Holborn Bars,
London WC1V 7QH,
Telephone: 0171 242 5240
E-mail: clerks@staple-inn.org
Call Date: Feb 1995, Lincoln's Inn
Qualifications: [BA (Hons)(Lond)]

BRISTOLL MISS SANDRA JAYNE

3/4 South Square
Gray's Inn, London WC1R 5HP,
Telephone: 0171 696 9900
E-mail: clerks@southsquare.com
Call Date: July 1989, Middle Temple
Qualifications: [MA (Cantab)]

BRITCLIFFE MISS ANNE ELIZABETH

White Friars Chambers
21 White Friars, Chester CH1 1NZ,
Telephone: 01244 323070
E-mail:whitefriarschambers@btinternet.com
Call Date: Apr 1989, Gray's Inn
Qualifications: [LLB (Bristol)]

BRITTAIN MARC JOHN

10 King's Bench Walk
1st Floor, Temple, London EC4Y 7EB,
Telephone: 0171 353 2501
Call Date: July 1983, Gray's Inn
Pupil Master
Qualifications: [BA (Business Law)]

BRITTAIN RICHARD PAUL

India Buildings Chambers
Water Street, Liverpool L2 0XG,
Telephone: 0151 243 6000
E-mail: clerks@chambers.u-net.com
Call Date: Nov 1971, Inner Temple
Pupil Master, Recorder
Qualifications: [MA, LLB]

BRITTON ROBERT ALEXANDER

1 Dr Johnson's Buildings
Ground Floor, Temple, London
EC4Y 7AX, Telephone: 0171 353 9328
E-mail:OneDr.Johnsons@btinternet.com

Dr Johnson's Chambers
The Atrium Court, Apex Plaza, Reading,
Berkshire, RG1 1AX,
Telephone: 01734 254221
Call Date: July 1973, Inner Temple
Pupil Master, Recorder
Qualifications: [BA]

BROADBENT EDMUND JOHN

20 Essex Street
London WC2R 3AL,
Telephone: 0171 583 9294
E-mail: clerks@20essexst.com
Call Date: July 1980, Gray's Inn
Pupil Master
Qualifications: [MA, LLB (Cantab)]

BROADBENT MISS EMMA LOUISE

6 King's Bench Walk
Ground Floor, Temple, London
EC4Y 7DR, Telephone: 0171 583 0410
E-mail: worsley@6kbw.freeserve.co.uk
Call Date: Nov 1986, Inner Temple
Pupil Master
Qualifications: [BA (Lond), Dip Law (City)]

BROADHURST SIMON THOMAS

18 St John Street
Manchester M3 4EA,
Telephone: 0161 278 1800
E-mail: 18stjohn@lineone.net
Call Date: Nov 1994, Inner Temple
Qualifications: [BA (Oxon), CPE]

BROADLEY JOHN

Cobden House Chambers
19 Quay Street, Manchester M3 3HN,
Telephone: 0161 833 6000
E-mail: clerks@cobden.co.uk
Call Date: July 1973, Middle Temple
Pupil Master
Qualifications: [LLB (Hons)]

BROATCH MICHAEL DONALD

5 Paper Buildings
Ground Floor, Temple, London
EC4Y 7HB, Telephone: 0171 583 9275/
583 4555 E-mail: 5paper@link.org
Call Date: May 1971, Middle Temple
Pupil Master
Qualifications: [LLB, LLM (Lond)]

D

BROBBEY DR BENJAMIN ASARE

26 Shaftesbury Road
Earlsdon, Coventry, Warwickshire,
CV5 6FN, Telephone: 01203 677337
Call Date: Nov 1968, Inner Temple
Qualifications: [LLB, LLM, PhD (Lond)]

BROCHWICZ-LEWINSKI STEFAN ANDREW

Merchant Chambers
1 North Parade, Parsonage Gardens,
Manchester M3 2NH,
Telephone: 0161 839 7070
E-mail: merchant.chambers@virgin.net
Call Date: Nov 1995, Gray's Inn
Qualifications: [LLB (Bris), LLB (Euro)]

BROCK DAVID JAMES

2 Paper Buildings
1st Floor, Temple, London EC4Y 7ET,
Telephone: 020 7556 5500
E-mail: clerks@2pbbarristers.co.uk
Call Date: Nov 1984, Middle Temple
Pupil Master
Qualifications: [BHum (Lond)]

BROCK JONATHAN SIMON QC (1997)

Falcon Chambers
Falcon Court, London EC4Y 1AA,
Telephone: 0171 353 2484
E-mail: clerks@falcon-chambers.com
Call Date: July 1977, Lincoln's Inn
Recorder
Qualifications: [MA (Cantab), FCIArb]

BROCKLEY NIGEL SIMON

Bracton Chambers
95a Chancery Lane, London WC2A 1DT,
Telephone: 0171 242 4248
Call Date: Nov 1992, Lincoln's Inn
Qualifications: [BA (Hons), CPE]

BRODIE GRAHAM PAUL

1 Dr Johnson's Buildings
Ground Floor, Temple, London
EC4Y 7AX, Telephone: 0171 353 9328
E-mail:OneDr.Johnsons@btinternet.com

Dr Johnson's Chambers
The Atrium Court, Apex Plaza, Reading,
Berkshire, RG1 1AX,
Telephone: 01734 254221
Call Date: July 1989, Middle Temple
Qualifications: [LLB (Lond)]

BRODIE (JAMES) BRUCE

39 Essex Street
London WC2R 3AT,
Telephone: 0171 832 1111
E-mail: clerks@39essex.co.uk
Call Date: May 1993, Inner Temple
Qualifications: [BA (S.Africa), MA (Cantab)]

BRODIE STANLEY ERIC QC (1975)

Blackstone Chambers
Blackstone House, Temple, London
EC4Y 9BW, Telephone: 0171 583 1770
E-mail:clerks@blackstonechambers.com
Call Date: Feb 1954, Inner Temple
Qualifications: [MA (Oxon)]

BRODRICK WILLIAM HENRY

New Court Chambers
3 Broad Chare, Newcastle upon Tyne
NE1 3DQ, Telephone: 0191 232 1980
Call Date: Oct 1991, Gray's Inn
Qualifications: [BA, M Th]

BRODWELL JOHN SHENTON

9 Woodhouse Square
Leeds LS3 1AD,
Telephone: 0113 2451986
E-mail: clerks@9woodhouse.co.uk
Call Date: Oct 1998, Inner Temple
Qualifications: [LLB (Soton)]

BRODY MISS KAREN RACHEL

Deans Court Chambers
24 St John Street, Manchester M3 4DF,
Telephone: 0161 214 6000
E-mail: clerks@deanscourt.co.uk
Deans Court Chambers
41-43 Market Place, Preston PR1 1AH,
Telephone: 01772 555163
E-mail: clerks@deanscourt.co.uk
Call Date: Nov 1986, Gray's Inn
Qualifications: [LLB (Notts)]

BRODY SAUL AMOS

18 St John Street
Manchester M3 4EA,
Telephone: 0161 278 1800
E-mail: 18stjohn@lineone.net
Call Date: Oct 1996, Inner Temple
Qualifications: [LLB (Leeds)]

BROGAN MICHAEL SHAUN

Manchester House Chambers
18-22 Bridge Street, Manchester M3 3BZ,
Telephone: 0161 834 7007
Call Date: Oct 1990, Inner Temple
Qualifications: [LLB (Hons)]

BROMFIELD COLIN HUGH

6 Gray's Inn Square
Ground Floor, Gray's Inn, London
WC1R 5AZ, Telephone: 0171 242 1052
E-mail: 6graysinn@clara.co.uk
Call Date: Nov 1988, Gray's Inn
Qualifications: [LLB (Hons)]

BROMILOW DANIEL JOHN

9 Stone Buildings
Lincoln's Inn, London WC2A 3NN,
Telephone: 0171 404 5055
E-mail: clerks@9stoneb.law.co.uk
Call Date: Nov 1996, Gray's Inn
Qualifications: [BA (Cantab)]

BROMILOW RICHARD BRUCE DAVIES

St John's Chambers
Small Street, Bristol BS1 1DW,
Telephone: 0117 9213456/298514
E-mail: @stjohnschambers.co.uk
Call Date: July 1977, Gray's Inn
Pupil Master, Assistant Recorder
Qualifications: [LLB]

BROMLEY-DAVENPORT JOHN

Deans Court Chambers
24 St John Street, Manchester M3 4DF,
Telephone: 0161 214 6000
E-mail: clerks@deanscourt.co.uk
Deans Court Chambers
41-43 Market Place, Preston PR1 1AH,
Telephone: 01772 555163
E-mail: clerks@deanscourt.co.uk
Call Date: Feb 1972, Gray's Inn
Pupil Master, Recorder

BROMLEY-MARTIN MICHAEL GRANVILLE

3 Raymond Buildings
Gray's Inn, London WC1R 5BH,
Telephone: 020 7831 3833
E-mail:chambers@threeraymond.demon.co.uk
Call Date: Nov 1979, Gray's Inn
Pupil Master
Qualifications: [BSc (Soton)]

BROMLEY-MARTIN MISS TANIA CATHERINE

3 Raymond Buildings
Gray's Inn, London WC1R 5BH,
Telephone: 020 7831 3833
E-mail:chambers@threeraymond.demon.co.uk
Call Date: July 1983, Gray's Inn
Qualifications: [BA]

BROMPTON MICHAEL JOHN

New Court Chambers
5 Verulam Buildings, Gray's Inn, London
WC1R 5LY, Telephone: 0171 831 9500
E-mail: mail@newcourtchambers.com
Call Date: Nov 1973, Middle Temple
Qualifications: [BA (Sussex)]

BROOK DAVID LESLIE

Plowden Buildings
2nd Floor, 2 Plowden Buildings, Middle
Temple Lane, London EC4Y 9BU,
Telephone: 0171 583 0808
E-mail: bar@plowdenbuildings.co.uk
Call Date: July 1988, Inner Temple
Pupil Master
Qualifications: [BA (Lond), Dip Law (City)]

BROOK IAN STUART

Hardwicke Building
New Square, Lincoln's Inn, London
WC2A 3SB, Telephone: 020 7242 2523
E-mail: clerks@hardwicke.co.uk
Call Date: July 1983, Lincoln's Inn
Qualifications: [BA (Law)(Hons)]

D

BROOK PAUL ANTONY

Chambers of Andrew Campbell QC
10 Park Square, Leeds LS1 2LH,
Telephone: 0113 2455438
E-mail: clerks@10pksq.co.uk
Call Date: Nov 1986, Inner Temple
Qualifications: [LLB (Leeds)]

BROOK SMITH PHILIP ANDREW

Fountain Court
Temple, London EC4Y 9DH,
Telephone: 0171 583 3335
E-mail: chambers@fountaincourt.co.uk
Call Date: July 1982, Middle Temple
Pupil Master
Qualifications: [BSc, MSc]

BROOKE DAVID MICHAEL GRAHAM

11 King's Bench Walk
1st Floor, Temple, London EC4Y 7EQ,
Telephone: 0171 353 3337
E-mail: fmuller11@aol.com
11 King's Bench Walk
3 Park Court, Park Cross Street, Leeds
LS1 2QH, Telephone: 0113 297 1200
Call Date: Nov 1990, Inner Temple
Qualifications: [BA (Dunelm), Dip Law
(City)]

BROOKE JOHAN ERIC

Frederick Place Chambers
9 Frederick Place, Clifton, Bristol
BS8 1AS, Telephone: 0117 9738667
Call Date: Oct 1997, Lincoln's Inn
Qualifications: [LLB (Hons)(Bris)]

BROOKE MICHAEL ECCLES MACKLIN QC (1994)

Chambers of John L Powell QC
Four New Square, Lincoln's Inn, London
WC2A 3RJ, Telephone: 0171 797 8000
E-mail: barristers@4newsquare.com
Call Date: Nov 1968, Gray's Inn
Assistant Recorder
Qualifications: [LLB (Edin)]

BROOKE-SMITH JOHN

East Anglian Chambers
52 North Hill, Colchester, Essex, CO1 1PY,
Telephone: 01206 572756
E-mail: colchester@ealaw.co.uk

East Anglian Chambers
Gresham House, 5 Museum Street,
Ipswich, Suffolk, IP1 1HQ,
Telephone: 01473 214481
E-mail: ipswich@ealaw.co.uk
East Anglian Chambers
57 London Street, Norwich NR2 1HL,
Telephone: 01603 617351
E-mail: norwich@ealaw.co.uk
Call Date: July 1981, Gray's Inn
Pupil Master, Assistant Recorder
Qualifications: [LLB (Exon)]

BROOKES LINCOLN PAUL

Portsmouth Barristers' Chambers
Victory House, 7 Bellevue Terrace,
Portsmouth, Hampshire, PO5 3AT,
Telephone: 023 92 831292/811811
E-mail: clerks@portsmouthbar.com
Call Date: Nov 1992, Inner Temple
Qualifications: [LLB (Hons)(Lond)]

BROOKS MISS ALISON LOUISE

Staple Inn Chambers
1st Floor, 9 Staple Inn, Holborn Bars,
London WC1V 7QH,
Telephone: 0171 242 5240
E-mail: clerks@staple-inn.org
Call Date: July 1989, Inner Temple
Qualifications: [LLB (Hons)]

BROOKS JOHN DYLAN

Pendragon Chambers
124 Walter Road, Swansea, West
Glamorgan, SA1 5RG,
Telephone: 01792 411188
Call Date: Feb 1990, Gray's Inn
Qualifications: [LLB (Wales)]

BROOKS MS LOUISE MARIA DIANA

Cloisters
1 Pump Court, Temple, London
EC4Y 7AA, Telephone: 0171 827 4000
E-mail: clerks@cloisters.com
Call Date: Nov 1994, Middle Temple
Qualifications: [BA (Hons)]

BROOKS MR PAUL ANTHONY

Doughty Street Chambers
11 Doughty Street, London WC1N 2PG,
Telephone: 0171 404 1313
E-mail:enquiries@doughtystreet.co.uk
Call Date: July 1989, Middle Temple
Qualifications: [LLB]

BROOKS PETER ANTHONY CHRISTOPHER

9 Park Place
Cardiff CF1 3DP,
Telephone: 01222 382731
Call Date: July 1986, Gray's Inn
Pupil Master
Qualifications: [LLB (L'pool)]

BROOME CHARLES EDWARD

Plowden Buildings
2nd Floor, 2 Plowden Buildings, Middle
Temple Lane, London EC4Y 9BU,
Telephone: 0171 583 0808
E-mail: bar@plowdenbuildings.co.uk
Call Date: Nov 1996, Inner Temple
Qualifications: [BA (Oxon)]

BROTHERTON JOHN PAUL

New Court Chambers
Gazette Building, 168 Corporation Street,
Birmingham B4 6TZ,
Telephone: 0121 693 6656
Call Date: Nov 1994, Lincoln's Inn
Qualifications: [BA (Hons)(Leeds)]

BROUGH ALASDAIR MATHESON

13 King's Bench Walk
1st Floor, Temple, London EC4Y 7EN,
Telephone: 0171 353 7204
E-mail: clerks@13kbw.law.co.uk
King's Bench Chambers
32 Beaumont Street, Oxford OX1 2NP,
Telephone: 01865 311066
E-mail: clerks@kbc-oxford.law.co.uk
Call Date: July 1979, Gray's Inn
Pupil Master
Qualifications: [MA (Cantab)]

BROUGHAM CHRISTOPHER JOHN QC (1988)

3/4 South Square
Gray's Inn, London WC1R 5HP,
Telephone: 0171 696 9900
E-mail: clerks@southsquare.com
Call Date: Nov 1969, Inner Temple
Qualifications: [BA (Oxon)]

BROUNGER DAVID WILLIAM JOHN

Lamb Building
Ground Floor, Temple, London
EC4Y 7AS, Telephone: 020 7797 7788
E-mail: lamb.building@link.org
Call Date: Nov 1990, Inner Temple
Pupil Master
Qualifications: [LLB]

BROWN MISS ALTHEA SONIA

Doughty Street Chambers
11 Doughty Street, London WC1N 2PG,
Telephone: 0171 404 1313
E-mail:enquiries@doughtystreet.co.uk
Call Date: Feb 1995, Lincoln's Inn
Qualifications: [LLB (Hons)(Leic)]

BROWN MISS ANDREA MARIE

Staple Inn Chambers
1st Floor, 9 Staple Inn, Holborn Bars,
London WC1V 7QH,
Telephone: 0171 242 5240
E-mail: clerks@staple-inn.org
Call Date: Nov 1991, Lincoln's Inn
Qualifications: [LLB (Hons)]

BROWN ANDREW CHARLES

Queen's Chambers
5 John Dalton Street, Manchester M2 6ET,
Telephone: 0161 834 6875/4738
Queens Chambers
4 Camden Place, Preston PR1 3JL,
Telephone: 01772 828300
Call Date: Nov 1982, Gray's Inn
Qualifications: [BSc (Lond) DipL.]

BROWN ANTHONY JAMES

Broad Chare
33 Broad Chare, Newcastle upon Tyne
NE1 3DQ, Telephone: 0191 232 0541
E-mail:clerks@broadcharechambers.law.co.uk
Call Date: Nov 1990, Lincoln's Inn
Qualifications: [LLB (Hons)]

BROWN MISS CATHERINE ROBERTA

12 King's Bench Walk
Temple, London EC4Y 7EL,
Telephone: 0171 583 0811
E-mail: chambers@12kbw.co.uk
Call Date: Oct 1990, Middle Temple
Qualifications: [BCom (B'ham), Dip Law]

BROWN MISS CLARE VICTORIA

2 Temple Gardens
Temple, London EC4Y 9AY,
Telephone: 0171 583 6041
E-mail: clerks@2templegardens.co.uk
Call Date: Oct 1993, Middle Temple
Qualifications: [BA (Hons)]

BROWN DAMIAN ROBERT

Old Square Chambers
1 Verulam Buildings, Gray's Inn, London
WC1R 5LQ, Telephone: 0171 269 0300
E-mail:clerks@oldsquarechambers.co.uk
Old Square Chambers
Hanover House, 47 Corn Street, Bristol
BS1 1HT, Telephone: 0117 9277111
E-mail: oldsqbri@globalnet.co.uk
Call Date: Feb 1989, Inner Temple
Pupil Master
Qualifications: [BA (Lond)]

Fax: 0171 405 1387; DX: 1046 London

Types of work: Discrimination, Employment

Awards and memberships: Industrial Law
Society; Employment Law Bar Association;
Employment Lawyers Association

Other professional experience: Lecturer in International Labour Law, King's College,
London (current)

Publications: *Tolley's Employment Law*
(contributor) Looseleaf 1994 (1st edn)
1997 (14th update); *Employment Tribunal
Practice and Procedure* (co-author), 1987,
1994, 1995; *Employment Precedents and
Company Policy Documents* (contributor),
1996

Reported Cases: *Port of London Authority v
Payne*, [1994] ICR 555, 1994. Trade Union
activities, dismissal, international law,
human rights.
Kwik Save v Greaves, The Times, 1998.
Pregnancy, European law.
Burrell v Safeways, [1997] ICR 523, 1997.
Redundancy, meaning of.

RJB Mining v NUM, [1997] IRLR 621, 1997.
Industrial action, balloting, injunctions.
*University College London Hospital NHS
Trust v UNISON*, [1999] IRLR 31, 1999.
Industrial action.

BROWN DAVID CHARLES

Cathedral Chambers
Milburn House, Dean Street, Newcastle
upon Tyne NE1 1LE,
Telephone: 0191 232 1311
Southsea Chambers
PO Box 148, Southsea, Portsmouth,
Hampshire, PO5 2TU,
Telephone: 01705 291261
Call Date: Feb 1993, Middle Temple
Qualifications: [B.Sc (Hons)]

BROWN EDWARD FRANCIS TREVENEN

Hollis Whiteman Chambers
3rd Floor, Queen Elizabeth Bldg, Temple,
London EC4Y 9BS,
Telephone: 020 7583 5766
E-mail:barristers@holliswhiteman.co.uk
Call Date: July 1983, Gray's Inn
Pupil Master
Qualifications: [LLB (Bucks)]

BROWN MISS EMMA KATE

Chambers of Kieran Coonan QC
Ground Floor, 6 Pump Court, Temple,
London EC4Y 7AR,
Telephone: 0171 583 6013/2510
E-mail: clerks@6-pumpcourt.law.co.uk
Call Date: Oct 1995, Middle Temple
Qualifications: [BA (Hons)]

BROWN FREDERICK HUGH

Regent Chambers
8 Pall Mall, Hanley, Stoke On Trent
ST1 1ER, Telephone: 01782 286666
E-mail: regent@ftech.co.uk
Call Date: Nov 1983, Middle Temple
Pupil Master
Qualifications: [BSc (Eng), BA, AMIMechE]

BROWN GEOFFREY BARLOW

39 Essex Street
London WC2R 3AT,
Telephone: 0171 832 1111
E-mail: clerks@39essex.co.uk
Call Date: July 1981, Inner Temple
Pupil Master
Qualifications: [MA (Cantab)]

BROWN (GEOFFREY) CHARLES

39 Essex Street
London WC2R 3AT,
Telephone: 0171 832 1111
E-mail: clerks@39essex.co.uk
Call Date: July 1976, Middle Temple
Qualifications: [MA (Oxon)]

BROWN MS GRACE

1 Gray's Inn Square
Ground Floor, London WC1R 5AA,
Telephone: 0171 405 8946/7/8
Call Date: Oct 1995, Inner Temple
Qualifications: [BA (Hons)(Lond), CPE
(City)]

BROWN MISS HANNAH BEATRICE

One Essex Court
Ground Floor, Temple, London
EC4Y 9AR, Telephone: 020 7583 2000
E-mail: clerks@oneessexcourt.co.uk
Call Date: Oct 1992, Inner Temple
Qualifications: [BA (Cambs)]

BROWN IAN KEITH RAE

Broadway House Chambers
Broadway House, 9 Bank Street, Bradford,
West Yorkshire, BD1 1TW,
Telephone: 01274 722560
E-mail: clerks@broadwayhouse.co.uk
Broadway House Chambers
31 Park Square West, Leeds LS1 2PF,
Telephone: 0113 246 2600
Call Date: Nov 1971, Middle Temple

BROWN MISS JAIN RUSKIN

Claremont Chambers
26 Waterloo Road, Wolverhampton
WV1 4BL, Telephone: 01902 426222
Call Date: Oct 1994, Lincoln's Inn
Qualifications: [BSc (Hons)]

BROWN JAMES PATRICK

Pepys' Chambers
17 Fleet Street, London EC4Y 1AA,
Telephone: 0171 936 2710
Call Date: Nov 1989, Gray's Inn
Qualifications: [LLB]

BROWN MISS JILLIAN CLARE

4 Brick Court
Ground Floor, Temple, London
EC4Y 9AD, Telephone: 0171 797 7766
E-mail: chambers@4brick.co.uk
Call Date: Nov 1991, Middle Temple
Qualifications: [BA Hons (Oxon)]

BROWN MISS JOANNE

2 Gray's Inn Square Chambers
2nd Floor, Gray's Inn, London WC1R 5AA,
Telephone: 020 7242 0328
E-mail: clerks@2gis.co.uk
Call Date: Nov 1990, Inner Temple
Pupil Master
Qualifications: [LLB (Brunel)]

BROWN LAURENCE FREDERICK MARK

Corn Exchange Chambers
5th Floor, Fenwick Street, Liverpool
L2 7QS, Telephone: 0151 227 1081/5009
Call Date: 1975, Inner Temple
Pupil Master, Recorder
Qualifications: [BA (Dunelm)]

BROWN MISS LINDA

Westminster Chambers
3 Crosshall Street, Liverpool L1 6DQ,
Telephone: 0151 236 4774
Call Date: Nov 1983, Middle Temple
Qualifications: [LLB (Lond), A.C.I.Arb]

BROWN NICHOLAS ROBERT DELANO

Chambers of John L Powell QC
Four New Square, Lincoln's Inn, London
WC2A 3RJ, Telephone: 0171 797 8000
E-mail: barristers@4newsquare.com
Call Date: Nov 1989, Lincoln's Inn
Qualifications: [BA (Cantab)]

BROWN PAUL MARTIN

4-5 Gray's Inn Square
Ground Floor, Gray's Inn, London
WC1R 5JP, Telephone: 0171 404 5252
E-mail:chambers@4-5graysinnsquare.co.uk
Call Date: Nov 1991, Inner Temple
Qualifications: [LLB (Cant), PhD (Cambs)]

BROWN PHILIP STEPHEN

Mitre Court Chambers
3rd Floor, Temple, London EC4Y 7BP,
Telephone: 0171 353 9394
E-mail: mitrecourt.com
Call Date: Oct 1991, Lincoln's Inn
Qualifications: [LLB (Hons) (Leeds)]

BROWN MISS REBECCA JANE

14 Gray's Inn Square
Gray's Inn, London WC1R 5JP,
Telephone: 0171 242 0858
E-mail: 100712.2134@compuserve.com
Call Date: July 1989, Inner Temple
Qualifications: [BA (York), Dip Law (City)]

BROWN RICHARD GORDON

2 King's Bench Walk
Ground Floor, Temple, London
EC4Y 7DE, Telephone: 0171 353 1746
E-mail: 2kbw@atlas.co.uk
King's Bench Chambers
115 North Hill, Plymouth PL4 8JY,
Telephone: 01752 221551
Call Date: Oct 1997, Inner Temple
Qualifications: [BA (Cantab), CPE]

BROWN ROBERT ALAN

2 New Street
Leicester LE1 5NA,
Telephone: 0116 2625906
E-mail: clerks@2newstreet.co.uk
High Pavement Chambers
1 High Pavement, Nottingham NG1 1HF,
Telephone: 0115 9418218
Call Date: Nov 1979, Inner Temple
Pupil Master
Qualifications: [LLB (Lond)]

BROWN ROBERT CHARLES WARREN

3 Temple Gardens
3rd Floor, Temple, London EC4Y 9AU,
Telephone: 0171 353 0832
Call Date: Nov 1992, Lincoln's Inn
Qualifications: [BSc (Lond), Dip in Law]

BROWN ROBERT LORIMER

Francis Taylor Building
Ground Floor, Temple, London
EC4Y 7BY, Telephone: 0171 353 7768/
7769/2711
E-mail:clerks@francistaylorbuilding.law.co.uk
Call Date: July 1983, Gray's Inn
Pupil Master
Qualifications: [LLB (Leic)]

BROWN ROGER CHARLES ARTHUR

Old Colony House
6 South King Street, Manchester M2 6DQ,
Telephone: 0161 834 4364
Call Date: Nov 1976, Inner Temple
Pupil Master
Qualifications: [LLB]

BROWN SIMON GIDEON JONATHAN

1 Temple Gardens
1st Floor, Temple, London EC4Y 9BB,
Telephone: 0171 583 1315/353 0407
E-mail: clerks@1templegardens.co.uk
Call Date: July 1988, Gray's Inn
Pupil Master
Qualifications: [LLB (Lond)]

BROWN SIMON STALEY QC (1995)

One Paper Buildings
Ground Floor, Temple, London
EC4Y 7EP, Telephone: 0171 583 7355
E-mail: clerks@1pb.co.uk
Call Date: July 1976, Inner Temple
Qualifications: [MA (Cantab)]

BROWN MISS STEPHANIE AMANDA

5 Fountain Court
Steelhouse Lane, Birmingham B4 6DR,
Telephone: 0121 606 0500
E-mail:clerks@5fountaincourt.law.co.uk
Call Date: July 1982, Lincoln's Inn
Pupil Master
Qualifications: [LLB (Exon)]

BROWN STUART CHRISTOPHER QC (1991)

Park Lane Chambers
19 Westgate, Leeds LS1 2RD,
Telephone: 0113 2285000
E-mail:clerks@parklanechambers.co.uk
Call Date: July 1974, Inner Temple
Recorder
Qualifications: [BA, BCL (Oxon)]

BROWN MISS SUSAN MARGARET

9 King's Bench Walk
Ground Floor, Temple, London
EC4Y 7DX, Telephone: 0171 353 7202/
3909 E-mail: 9kbw@compuserve.com
Call Date: July 1989, Lincoln's Inn
Qualifications: [BSc, LLB (Lond)]

BROWN THOMAS CHRISTOPHER ELLIS

Fenners Chambers
3 Madingley Road, Cambridge CB3 0EE,
Telephone: 01223 368761
E-mail: clerks@fennerschambers.co.uk
Fenners Chambers
8-12 Priestgate, Peterborough PE1 1JA,
Telephone: 01733 562030
E-mail: clerks@fennerschambers.co.uk
Call Date: Nov 1980, Gray's Inn
Qualifications: [MA (Cantab)]

BROWNBILL DAVID JOHN

8 Gray's Inn Square
Gray's Inn, London WC1R 5AZ,
Telephone: 0171 242 3529
Call Date: July 1989, Gray's Inn
Qualifications: [LLB [Nott'm]]

BROWNE BENJAMIN JAMES QC (1996)

2 Temple Gardens
Temple, London EC4Y 9AY,
Telephone: 0171 583 6041
E-mail: clerks@2templegardens.co.uk
Call Date: July 1976, Inner Temple
Assistant Recorder
Qualifications: [MA (Oxon)]

BROWNE DESMOND JOHN MICHAEL QC (1990)

5 Raymond Buildings
1st Floor, Gray's Inn, London WC1R 5BP,
Telephone: 0171 242 2902
E-mail: clerks@media-ent-law.co.uk
Call Date: Nov 1969, Gray's Inn
Recorder
Qualifications: [BA (Oxon)]

BROWNE DR GERALD ROBERT

Queen Elizabeth Building
Ground Floor, Temple, London
EC4Y 9BS,
Telephone: 0171 353 7181 (12 Lines)
Call Date: Nov 1995, Inner Temple
Qualifications: [MBChB (B'ham)]

BROWNE HAROLD GODFREE RODAN

1 Middle Temple Lane
Temple, London EC4Y 1LT,
Telephone: 0171 583 0659 (12 Lines)
E-mail: chambers@1mtl.co.uk
Call Date: Nov 1971, Gray's Inn
Pupil Master
Qualifications: [LLB (Lond)]

BROWNE JAMES NICHOLAS QC (1995)

Chambers of Michael Pert QC
36 Bedford Row, London WC1R 4JH,
Telephone: 0171 421 8000
E-mail: 36bedfordrow@link.org
Chambers of Michael Pert QC
24 Albion Place, Northampton NN1 1UD,
Telephone: 01604 602333
Chambers of Michael Pert QC
104 New Walk, Leicester LE1 7EA,
Telephone: 0116 249 2020
Call Date: July 1971, Inner Temple
Recorder
Qualifications: [LLB (L'pool)]

BROWNE JAMES WILLIAM

96 Gray's Inn Road
London WC1X 8AL,
Telephone: 0171 405 0585
Call Date: Oct 1994, Middle Temple
Qualifications: [BA (Hons)(B'ham), M.Litt
(Oxon), Dip in Law (City)]

BROWNE MISS JULIE REBECCA

Goldsmith Building
1st Floor, Temple, London EC4Y 7BL,
Telephone: 0171 353 7881
E-mail:clerks@goldsmith-building.law.co.uk
Call Date: Nov 1989, Middle Temple
Qualifications: [LLB (Leic)]

BROWNE LOUIS BARTHOLOMEW ANTHONY

India Buildings Chambers
Water Street, Liverpool L2 0XG,
Telephone: 0151 243 6000
E-mail: clerks@chambers.u-net.com
Call Date: Nov 1988, Lincoln's Inn
Qualifications: [LLB (Hons), BCL (Oxon)]

BROWNE MISS SHEREENER DONNA

6 King's Bench Walk
Ground, Third & Fourth Floors, Temple,
London EC4Y 7DR,
Telephone: 0171 353 4931/583 0695
Call Date: 1996, Inner Temple
Qualifications: [LLB]

BROWNE SIMON PETER BUCHANAN

Farrar's Building
Temple, London EC4Y 7BD,
Telephone: 0171 583 9241
E-mail:chambers@farrarsbuilding.co.uk
Call Date: Nov 1982, Middle Temple
Pupil Master
Qualifications: [LLB (Hons)]

BROWNE-WILKINSON SIMON QC (1998)

Serle Court Chambers
6 New Square, Lincoln's Inn, London
WC2A 3QS, Telephone: 0171 242 6105
E-mail: clerks@serlecourt.co.uk
Call Date: 1981, Lincoln's Inn
Qualifications: [BA (Oxon)]

BROWNHILL MISS JOANNA FRANCESA

One Essex Court
1st Floor, Temple, London EC4Y 9AR,
Telephone: 0171 936 3030
E-mail: one.essex_court@virgin.net
Call Date: 1997, Gray's Inn
Qualifications: [BA (Oxon)]

BROWNLIE IAN QC (1979)

Blackstone Chambers
Blackstone House, Temple, London
EC4Y 9BW, Telephone: 0171 583 1770
E-mail:clerks@blackstonechambers.com
Call Date: Feb 1958, Gray's Inn
Qualifications: [BA, DPhil, DCL (Oxon), FBA]

BRUCE ANDREW JONATHAN

Serle Court Chambers
6 New Square, Lincoln's Inn, London
WC2A 3QS, Telephone: 0171 242 6105
E-mail: clerks@serlecourt.co.uk
Call Date: Oct 1992, Middle Temple
Qualifications: [MA (Oxon)]

BRUCE DAVID LIVINGSTONE

24a St John Street
Manchester M3 4DF,
Telephone: 0161 833 9628
Call Date: July 1982, Middle Temple
Qualifications: [LLB (Lond)]

BRUCE MISS GAENOR

1 Pump Court
Lower Ground Floor, Temple, London
EC4Y 7AB, Telephone: 0171 583 2012/
353 4341
E-mail: [name]@1pumpcourt.co.uk
Call Date: Oct 1997, Middle Temple
Qualifications: [BA (Hons)(Exon), CPE]

BRUCE RICHARD HENDERSON

Dr Johnson's Chambers
Two Dr Johnson's Buildings, Temple,
London EC4Y 7AY,
Telephone: 0171 353 4716
E-mail: clerks@2djb.freeserve.co.uk
12 Paxton Close
Kew Gardens, Richmond-upon-Thames,
Surrey, TW9 2AW,
Telephone: 0181 940 5895
Call Date: July 1974, Gray's Inn
Qualifications: [LLB (Bris), FCIArb]

BRUDENELL THOMAS MERVYN

Queen Elizabeth Building
2nd Floor, Temple, London EC4Y 9BS,
Telephone: 0171 797 7837
Call Date: Nov 1977, Inner Temple
Pupil Master

BRUNNEN DAVID MARK

Derby Square Chambers
Merchants Court, Derby Square, Liverpool
L2 1TS, Telephone: 0151 709 4222
E-mail:mail.derbysquare@pop3.hiway.co.uk
Goldsmith Building
1st Floor, Temple, London EC4Y 7BL,
Telephone: 0171 353 7881
E-mail:clerks@goldsmith-building.law.co.uk
Call Date: July 1976, Middle Temple
Pupil Master, Assistant Recorder
Qualifications: [MA (Oxon)]

BRUNNER ADRIAN JOHN NELSON QC (1994)

2 Harcourt Buildings
Ground Floor/Left, Temple, London
EC4Y 9DB, Telephone: 0171 583 9020
E-mail: clerks@harcourt.co.uk
Call Date: July 1968, Inner Temple
Recorder

BRUNNER MS CATHERINE JANE

Chambers of Michael Pert QC
36 Bedford Row, London WC1R 4JH,
Telephone: 0171 421 8000
E-mail: 36bedfordrow@link.org
Chambers of Michael Pert QC
24 Albion Place, Northampton NN1 1UD,
Telephone: 01604 602333
Chambers of Michael Pert QC
104 New Walk, Leicester LE1 7EA,
Telephone: 0116 249 2020
Call Date: 1997, Inner Temple
Qualifications: [MA (Edinburgh), CPE (City)]

BRUNNER PETER ROLAND

Brick Court Chambers
7-8 Essex Street, London WC2R 3LD,
Telephone: 0171 379 3550
E-mail: [surname]@brickcourt.co.uk
Call Date: July 1971, Middle Temple
Pupil Master
Qualifications: [BA, LLB (Cantab)]

BRUNNING MATTHEW DAVID GEORGE

Wessex Chambers
48 Queens Road, Reading, Berkshire,
RG1 4BD, Telephone: 0118 956 8856
E-mail:wessexchambers@compuserve.com
Call Date: 1997, Middle Temple
Qualifications: [BA (Hons)]

BRUNT PHILIP EDWIN

Rowchester Chambers
4 Rowchester Court, Whittall Street,
Birmingham B4 6DH,
Telephone: 0121 233 2327/2361951
Call Date: Nov 1991, Lincoln's Inn
Qualifications: [BSc (Econ) (Hons), Dip Law]

BRUNTON SEAN ALEXANDER MCKAY

Pump Court Chambers
31 Southgate Street, Winchester
SO23 9EE, Telephone: 01962 868161
E-mail: clerks@3pumpcourt.com
Pump Court Chambers
Upper Ground Floor, 3 Pump Court,
Temple, London EC4Y 7AJ,
Telephone: 0171 353 0711
E-mail: clerks@3pumpcourt.com
Pump Court Chambers
5 Temple Chambers, Temple Street,
Swindon SN1 1SQ,
Telephone: 01793 539899
E-mail: clerks@3pumpcourt.com
Call Date: Oct 1990, Middle Temple
Qualifications: [BA (Cantab)]

BRYAN MISS CARMEL MARY

Holborn Chambers
6 Gate Street, Lincoln's Inn Fields, London
WC2A 3HP, Telephone: 0171 242 6060
Call Date: Nov 1993, Middle Temple
Qualifications: [LLB (Hons)(Lond)]

BRYAN MS DEBORAH

1 Pump Court
Lower Ground Floor, Temple, London
EC4Y 7AB, Telephone: 0171 583 2012/
353 4341
E-mail: [name]@1pumpcourt.co.uk
Call Date: July 1987, Lincoln's Inn
Qualifications: [LLB]

BRYAN MISS HELEN WEBSTER

Call Date: July 1985, Inner Temple
Qualifications: [BA (Columbia)]

BRYAN MRS JAYNE MARIE

Wilberforce Chambers
7 Bishop Lane, Hull, East Yorkshire,
HU1 1PA, Telephone: 01482 323264
E-mail: clerks@hullbar.demon.co.uk
Call Date: Feb 1994, Gray's Inn
Qualifications: [LLB]

BRYAN REX VICTOR

5 Pump Court
Ground Floor, Temple, London
EC4Y 7AP, Telephone: 020 7353 2532
E-mail: FivePump@netcomuk.co.uk
Call Date: Nov 1971, Lincoln's Inn
Pupil Master, Recorder
Qualifications: [MA (Oxon)]

BRYAN ROBERT JOHN

1 Paper Buildings
1st Floor, Temple, London EC4Y 7EP,
Telephone: 0171 353 3728/4953
Call Date: Oct 1992, Middle Temple
Qualifications: [LL.B (Hons)]

BRYAN SIMON JAMES

Essex Court Chambers
24 Lincoln's Inn Fields, London
WC2A 3ED, Telephone: 0171 813 8000
E-mail:clerksroom@essexcourt-chambers.co.u
k
Call Date: July 1988, Lincoln's Inn
Pupil Master
Qualifications: [MA (Hons) (Cantab)]

BRYANT MISS CAROLINE

East Anglian Chambers
Gresham House, 5 Museum Street,
Ipswich, Suffolk, IP1 1HQ,
Telephone: 01473 214481
E-mail: ipswich@ealaw.co.uk
East Anglian Chambers
57 London Street, Norwich NR2 1HL,
Telephone: 01603 617351
E-mail: norwich@ealaw.co.uk
East Anglian Chambers
52 North Hill, Colchester, Essex, CO1 1PY,
Telephone: 01206 572756
E-mail: colchester@ealaw.co.uk
Call Date: July 1976, Middle Temple
Qualifications: [LLB]

BRYANT MISS CERI JANE

Erskine Chambers
30 Lincoln's Inn Fields, Lincoln's Inn,
London WC2A 3PF,
Telephone: 0171 242 5532
E-mail:clerks@erskine-chambers.co.uk
Call Date: July 1984, Lincoln's Inn
Pupil Master
Qualifications: [MA, LLM (Cantab)]

BRYANT JOHN MALCOLM CORNELIUS

Barnard's Inn Chambers
6th Floor, Halton House, 20-23 Holborn,
London EC1N 2JD,
Telephone: 0171 369 6969
E-mail: clerks@biclaw.co.uk
Call Date: Nov 1976, Inner Temple
Pupil Master
Qualifications: [MA (Cantab)]

BRYANT MISS JUDITH ANNE

Wilberforce Chambers
8 New Square, Lincoln's Inn, London
WC2A 3QP, Telephone: 0171 306 0102
E-mail: chambers@wilberforce.co.uk
Call Date: July 1987, Lincoln's Inn
Pupil Master
Qualifications: [BA, LLM (Cantab)]

Types of work: Chancery (general), Charities,
Equity, wills and trusts, Family provision,
Pensions, Probate and administration,
Professional negligence, Tax – capital and
income

BRYANT KEITH

Devereux Chambers
Devereux Court, London WC2R 3JJ,
Telephone: 0171 353 7534
E-mail: mailbox@devchambers.co.uk
Call Date: Oct 1991, Middle Temple
Qualifications: [BA Hons (Cantab), CPE, MA
(Cantab), Dip.Com Sci (Cantab)]

BRYANT-HERON MARK NICHOLAS

9-12 Bell Yard
London WC2A 2LF,
Telephone: 0171 400 1800
E-mail: clerks@bellyard.co.uk
Call Date: Nov 1986, Middle Temple
Pupil Master
Qualifications: [MA(Cantab)]

BSIS MISS IBTIHAL ISMAIL

2 Dyers Buildings
London EC1N 2JT,
Telephone: 0171 404 1881
Call Date: Feb 1995, Gray's Inn
Qualifications: [LLB]

BUBB TIMOTHY MICHAEL ANTHONY

39 Park Square
Leeds LS1 2NU,
Telephone: 0113 2456633
Call Date: July 1970, Gray's Inn
Pupil Master, Assistant Recorder
Qualifications: [LLB]

BUCHAN ANDREW

Cloisters
1 Pump Court, Temple, London
EC4Y 7AA, Telephone: 0171 827 4000
E-mail: clerks@cloisters.com
Call Date: July 1981, Gray's Inn
Pupil Master
Qualifications: [LLB (Leeds)]

BUCHAN JONATHAN MAXFIELD

15 Winckley Square
Preston PR1 3JJ,
Telephone: 01772 252828
E-mail:clerks@winckleysq.demon.co.uk
Call Date: Oct 1994, Middle Temple
Qualifications: [MA (Cantab), CPE]

BUCHANAN GRAHAM JAMES

De Montfort Chambers
95 Princess Road East, Leicester LE1 7DQ,
Telephone: 0116 254 8686
E-mail: dmcbar@aol.com
Call Date: July 1971, Inner Temple
Pupil Master
Qualifications: [LLB]

BUCHANAN JAMES IAN CHARLES

3 Temple Gardens
2nd Floor, Temple, London EC4Y 9AU,
Telephone: 0171 583 1155
Call Date: Nov 1993, Gray's Inn
Qualifications: [BA (Nott'm)]

BUCHANAN MISS VIVIEN JEAN

King Charles House
Standard Hill, Nottingham NG1 6FX,
Telephone: 0115 9418851
E-mail: clerks@kch.co.uk
Call Date: July 1981, Inner Temple
Qualifications: [LLB (Hons) (Soton)]

BUCK DR ANDREW THEODORE

Chambers of Martin Burr
Fourth Floor, Eldon Chambers, 30/32
Fleet Street, London EC4Y 1AA,
Telephone: 0171 353 4636
Call Date: Nov 1992, Inner Temple
Qualifications: [Bsc, PhD (Lond), Msc
(Aston), LLB]

BUCK JOHN

Dr Johnson's Chambers
Two Dr Johnson's Buildings, Temple,
London EC4Y 7AY,
Telephone: 0171 353 4716
E-mail: clerks@2djb.freeserve.co.uk
Call Date: Nov 1987, Gray's Inn
Pupil Master
Qualifications: [BA, MA (Hons) (Oxon), Dip
Law]

BUCKETT EDWIN GORDON

9 Gough Square
London EC4A 3DE,
Telephone: 020 7832 0500
E-mail: clerks@9goughsq.co.uk
Call Date: July 1988, Inner Temple
Pupil Master
Qualifications: [LLB (Hull)]

BUCKHAVEN MRS CHARLOTTE VANDERLIP

Plowden Buildings
2nd Floor, 2 Plowden Buildings, Middle
Temple Lane, London EC4Y 9BU,
Telephone: 0171 583 0808
E-mail: bar@plowdenbuildings.co.uk
Call Date: July 1969, Middle Temple
Qualifications: [MA (St Andrews)]

D

BUCKHAVEN SIMON

1 Harcourt Buildings
2nd Floor, Temple, London EC4Y 9DA,
Telephone: 0171 353 9421/0375
E-mail:clerks@1harcourtbuildings.law.co.uk
Call Date: July 1970, Gray's Inn
Pupil Master

BUCKINGHAM MRS KATHLEEN ROSEMARY BERNADETTE

30 Park Square
Leeds LS1 2PF, Telephone: 0113 2436388
E-mail: clerks@30parksquare.co.uk
Call Date: July 1986, Middle Temple
Pupil Master
Qualifications: [BA (Hons) (Leeds) , Dip Law
(City), PhD]

BUCKINGHAM MISS SARAH-JAYNE

5 Essex Court
1st Floor, Temple, London EC4Y 9AH,
Telephone: 0171 410 2000
E-mail: barristers@5essexcourt.co.uk
Call Date: Oct 1991, Inner Temple
Qualifications: [LLB (Hons)]

BUCKINGHAM STEWART JOHN

4 Essex Court
Temple, London EC4Y 9AJ,
Telephone: 020 7797 7970
E-mail: clerks@4essexcourt.law.co.uk
Call Date: Nov 1996, Middle Temple
Qualifications: [BA (Hons), BCL]

BUCKLAND MATTHEW STEPHEN

1 Paper Buildings
1st Floor, Temple, London EC4Y 7EP,
Telephone: 0171 353 3728/4953
Call Date: Mar 1998, Lincoln's Inn
Qualifications: [BA (Hons)]

BUCKLAND ROBERT JAMES

30 Park Place
Cardiff CF1 3BA,
Telephone: 01222 398421
E-mail: 100757.1456@compuserve.com
Call Date: Oct 1991, Inner Temple
Pupil Master
Qualifications: [BA (Dunelm)]

BUCKLE JONATHAN

Regency Chambers
Cathedral Square, Peterborough
PE1 1XW, Telephone: 01733 315215
Regency Chambers
Sheraton House, Castle Park, Cambridge
CB3 0AX, Telephone: 01223 301517
Call Date: Nov 1990, Lincoln's Inn
Qualifications: [BA (Hons), Dip Law]

BUCKLEY BERNARD CHRISTOPHER

1 Paper Buildings
1st Floor, Temple, London EC4Y 7EP,
Telephone: 0171 353 3728/4953
Call Date: Feb 1970, Gray's Inn
Pupil Master
Qualifications: [LLB (Lond), LLM (Cantab)]

BUCKLEY CHRISTOPHER JOHN

Call Date: Mar 1997, Gray's Inn
Qualifications: [BA (L'pool)]

BUCKLEY MISS GERARDINE MARIA

Stour Chambers
Barton Mill House, Barton Mill Road,
Canterbury, Kent, CT1 1BP,
Telephone: 01227 764899
E-mail: clerks@stourchambers.co.uk
Call Date: Nov 1991, Gray's Inn
Qualifications: [BA (Kent)]

BUCKLEY PETER EVERED

Queen's Chambers
5 John Dalton Street, Manchester M2 6ET,
Telephone: 0161 834 6875/4738
Queens Chambers
4 Camden Place, Preston PR1 3JL,
Telephone: 01772 828300
Call Date: July 1972, Gray's Inn
Pupil Master
Qualifications: [BA (Oxon)]

BUCKLEY PROFESSOR RICHARD ANTHONY

12 New Square
Lincoln's Inn, London WC2A 3SW,
Telephone: 0171 419 1212
E-mail: chambers@12newsquare.co.uk
Call Date: Nov 1969, Lincoln's Inn
Qualifications: [MA, DPhil (Oxon)]

BUCKLEY-CLARKE MRS AMANDA VICTORIA

3 Paper Buildings
Temple, London EC4Y 7EU,
Telephone: 020 7583 8055
E-mail: London@3paper.com
3 Paper Buildings (Bournemouth)
20 Lorne Park Road, Bournemouth,
Dorset, BH1 1JN,
Telephone: 01202 292102
E-mail: Bournemouth@3paper.com
3 Paper Buildings (Winchester)
4 St Peter Street, Winchester SO23 8BW,
Telephone: 01962 868884
E-mail: winchester@3paper.com
3 Paper Buildings (Oxford)
1 Alfred Street, High Street, Oxford
OX1 4EH, Telephone: 01865 793736
E-mail: oxford@3paper.com
Call Date: Oct 1991, Lincoln's Inn
Qualifications: [BA (Oxon)]

BUCKNALL MISS BELINDA QC (1988)

4 Essex Court
Temple, London EC4Y 9AJ,
Telephone: 020 7797 7970
E-mail: clerks@4essexcourt.law.co.uk
Call Date: Nov 1974, Middle Temple
Recorder
Qualifications: [MA (Oxon)]

BUCKPITT MICHAEL DAVID

2nd Floor, Francis Taylor Building
Temple, London EC4Y 7BY,
Telephone: 0171 353 9942/3157
Call Date: Feb 1988, Gray's Inn
Pupil Master
Qualifications: [LLB]

BUDALY MISS SUSAN

One Garden Court Family Law Chambers
Ground Floor, Temple, London
EC4Y 9BJ, Telephone: 0171 797 7900
E-mail: clerks@onegardencourt.co.uk
Call Date: Oct 1994, Middle Temple
Qualifications: [LLB (Hons)]

BUDDEN MISS CAROLINE RACHEL

One King's Bench Walk
1st Floor, Temple, London EC4Y 7DB,
Telephone: 0171 936 1500
E-mail: ddear@1kbw.co.uk
Call Date: Nov 1977, Inner Temple
Pupil Master, Assistant Recorder
Qualifications: [LLB (Bris)]

BUDWORTH ADAM JOHN DUTTON

3 Hare Court
1 Little Essex Street, London WC2R 3LD,
Telephone: 0171 395 2000
Call Date: Nov 1992, Inner Temple
Qualifications: [BA (Lond), Dip in Law]

BUEHRLEN MISS VERONIQUE EIRA

Fountain Court
Temple, London EC4Y 9DH,
Telephone: 0171 583 3335
E-mail: chambers@fountaincourt.co.uk
Call Date: Oct 1991, Middle Temple
Qualifications: [MA Hons , Dip Law]

BUENO ANTONIO DE PADUA JOSE MARIA QC (1989)

5 Paper Buildings
Ground Floor, Temple, London
EC4Y 7HB, Telephone: 0171 583 9275/
583 4555 E-mail: 5paper@link.org
Call Date: June 1964, Middle Temple
Recorder

BUGEJA MISS EVELYN

8 Fountain Court
Steelhouse Lane, Birmingham B4 6DR,
Telephone: 0121 236 5514/5
E-mail: clerks@no8chambers.co.uk
Call Date: Oct 1997, Middle Temple
Qualifications: [LLB (Hons)(L'pool)]

BUGG IAN STEPHEN

Crown Office Row Chambers
Blenheim House, 120 Church Street,
Brighton, Sussex, BN1 1WH,
Telephone: 01273 625625
E-mail: crownofficerow@clara.net
Call Date: Oct 1992, Middle Temple
Qualifications: [LL.B (Hons)]

D

BUI MISS VICTORIA

10 King's Bench Walk
Ground Floor, Temple, London
EC4Y 7EB, Telephone: 0171 353 7742
E-mail: 10kbw@lineone.net
Call Date: Nov 1996, Gray's Inn
Qualifications: [LLB (Essex)]

BULL (DONALD) ROGER

One Essex Court
1st Floor, Temple, London EC4Y 9AR,
Telephone: 0171 936 3030
E-mail: one.essex_court@virgin.net
Call Date: July 1974, Middle Temple
Pupil Master
Qualifications: [LLB (Lond)]

BULL GREGORY

33 Park Place
Cardiff CF1 3BA,
Telephone: 02920 233313
Call Date: July 1976, Inner Temple
Pupil Master, Assistant Recorder
Qualifications: [LLB (B'ham)]

BULL SIMON KEITH

Chambers of Michael Pert QC
36 Bedford Row, London WC1R 4JH,
Telephone: 0171 421 8000
E-mail: 36bedfordrow@link.org
Chambers of Michael Pert QC
24 Albion Place, Northampton NN1 1UD,
Telephone: 01604 602333
Chambers of Michael Pert QC
104 New Walk, Leicester LE1 7EA,
Telephone: 0116 249 2020
Call Date: Feb 1984, Gray's Inn
Pupil Master
Qualifications: [BA (Cantab), LLM (Cantab)]

BULLEN JAMES EDWARD

1 Paper Buildings
1st Floor, Temple, London EC4Y 7EP,
Telephone: 0171 353 3728/4953
Call Date: July 1966, Gray's Inn
Pupil Master, Recorder
Qualifications: [LLB (Lond)]

BULLOCH MS ANNE

Chambers of Harjit Singh
Ground Floor, 2 Middle Temple Lane,
Temple, London EC4Y 9AA,
Telephone: 0171 353 1356 (4 Lines)
Call Date: Nov 1989, Gray's Inn
Qualifications: [MA (Hons) (Cantab)]

BULLOCK ANDREW JOHN

169 Temple Chambers
Temple Avenue, London EC4Y 0DA,
Telephone: 0171 583 7644
Call Date: May 1992, Lincoln's Inn
Qualifications: [LLB (Hons) (Manch)]

BULLOCK DAVID NEIL

4 Brick Court
Ground Floor, Temple, London
EC4Y 9AD, Telephone: 0171 797 7766
E-mail: chambers@4brick.co.uk
Call Date: Nov 1989, Middle Temple
Qualifications: [BA]

BULLOCK IAN DAVID

St John's Chambers
Small Street, Bristol BS1 1DW,
Telephone: 0117 9213456/298514
E-mail: @stjohnschambers.co.uk
Call Date: Nov 1975, Inner Temple
Pupil Master
Qualifications: [LLB]

BULLOCK MRS SALLY

New Court
Temple, London EC4Y 9BE,
Telephone: 0171 583 5123/0510
Call Date: 1995, Middle Temple
Qualifications: [CPE]

BUNDELL MISS KATHARINE MICHELLE

East Anglian Chambers
Gresham House, 5 Museum Street,
Ipswich, Suffolk, IP1 1HQ,
Telephone: 01473 214481
E-nail: ipswich@ealaw.co.uk
East Anglian Chambers
57 London Street, Norwich NR2 1HL,
Telephone: 01603 617351
E-mail: norwich@ealaw.co.uk

East Anglian Chambers
52 North Hill, Colchester, Essex, CO1 1PY,
Telephone: 01206 572756
E-mail: colchester@ealaw.co.uk
Call Date: Oct 1991, Middle Temple
Qualifications: [MA (Hons)(Cantab)]

BUNDRED MISS GILLIAN SARAH

Oriel Chambers
14 Water Street, Liverpool L2 8TD,
Telephone: 0151 236 7191/236 4321
E-mail: clerks@oriel-chambers.co.uk
Call Date: July 1982, Gray's Inn
Qualifications: [LLB (Lond)]

BURBIDGE JAMES MICHAEL

St Philip's Chambers
Fountain Court, Steelhouse Lane,
Birmingham B4 6DR,
Telephone: 0121 246 7000
E-mail: clerks@st-philips.co.uk
Call Date: 1979, Lincoln's Inn
Pupil Master, Assistant Recorder
Qualifications: [LLB (Leic)]

BURDEN EDWARD ANGUS

St Philip's Chambers
Fountain Court, Steelhouse Lane,
Birmingham B4 6DR,
Telephone: 0121 246 7000
E-mail: clerks@st-philips.co.uk
Call Date: Nov 1994, Lincoln's Inn
Qualifications: [BA (Hons)(Exon)]

BURDEN MISS EMMA LOUISE VERENA

2 New Street
Leicester LE1 5NA,
Telephone: 0116 2625906
E-mail: clerks@2newstreet.co.uk
Sovereign Chambers
25 Park Square, Leeds LS1 2PW,
Telephone: 0113 2451841/2/3
E-mail:sovereignchambers@btinternet.com
Call Date: Oct 1994, Lincoln's Inn
Qualifications: [LLB (Hons)(Newc)]

BURDEN MISS SUSAN JANE

Chambers of Kieran Coonan QC
Ground Floor, 6 Pump Court, Temple,
London EC4Y 7AR,
Telephone: 0171 583 6013/2510
E-mail: clerks@6-pumpcourt.law.co.uk
Call Date: July 1985, Inner Temple
Pupil Master
Qualifications: [BA (Oxon)]

BURDON MICHAEL STEWART

37 Park Square Chambers
37 Park Square, Leeds LS1 2NY,
Telephone: 0113 2439422
E-mail: chambers@no37.co.uk
Call Date: Nov 1993, Lincoln's Inn
Qualifications: [LLB (Hons)(Leeds)]

BURGE EDMUND JOHN

Earl Street Chambers
47 Earl Street, Maidstone, Kent,
ME14 1PD, Telephone: 01622 671222
E-mail: gunner-sparks@msn.com
Call Date: 1997, Lincoln's Inn
Qualifications: [BA (Hons)(York), Dip in
Law]

BURGESS DAVID CLIFFORD

4 Brick Court
Temple, London EC4Y 9AD,
Telephone: 0171 797 8910
E-mail: medhurst@dial.pipex.com
Call Date: July 1975, Lincoln's Inn
Pupil Master
Qualifications: [LLB (Hons)]

BURGESS EDWARD NORMAN

St John's Chambers
Small Street, Bristol BS1 1DW,
Telephone: 0117 9213456/298514
E-mail: @stjohnschambers.co.uk
Call Date: Nov 1993, Inner Temple
Qualifications: [BA (Hons)(Oxon) , MA
(Bris), CPE (Bris)]

BURGESS MISS EMMA VICTORIA

Chichester Chambers
12 North Pallant, Chichester, West Sussex,
PO19 1TQ, Telephone: 01243 784538
E-mail:clerks@chichesterchambers.law.co.uk
Call Date: Feb 1995, Middle Temple
Qualifications: [LLB (Hons)(Bris)]

D

BURGESS JOHN

1 Gray's Inn Square
Ground Floor, London WC1R 5AA,
Telephone: 0171 405 8946/7/8
Call Date: Oct 1997, Inner Temple
Qualifications: [LLB (Lond)]

BURGESS JOHN EDWARD RAMSEY

High Pavement Chambers
1 High Pavement, Nottingham NG1 1HF,
Telephone: 0115 9418218
Call Date: July 1978, Middle Temple
Pupil Master, Assistant Recorder
Qualifications: [LLB (Exon)]

BURGESS ROY ANTHONY

2 South Avenue
Cleverley, Lancashire,
Call Date: Nov 1970, Lincoln's Inn
Qualifications: [LLB (Bris) M Phil, (Lond)]

BURGHER BENJIMIN GEORGE

Francis Taylor Building
3rd Floor, Temple, London EC4Y 7BY,
Telephone: 0171 797 7250
Call Date: Nov 1995, Gray's Inn
Qualifications: [LLB (Hons) (Manc)]

BURKE BRENDAN EDWARD

19 Castle Street Chambers
Liverpool L2 4SX,
Telephone: 0151 236 9402
E-mail: DBrei16454@aol.com
Call Date: Oct 1995, Inner Temple
Qualifications: [MA (Cantab), CPE
(Northumbria)]

BURKE JEFFREY PETER QC (1984)

Devereux Chambers
Devereux Court, London WC2R 3JJ,
Telephone: 0171 353 7534
E-mail: mailbox@devchambers.co.uk
Call Date: June 1964, Inner Temple
Recorder
Qualifications: [MA (Oxon)]

BURKE MICHAEL JOHN

33 Bedford Row
London WC1R 4JH,
Telephone: 0171 242 6476
E-mail:clerks@bedfordrow33.demon.co.uk
Call Date: Nov 1985, Gray's Inn
Pupil Master
Qualifications: [LLB (L'pool)]

BURKE MISS PATRICIA ANN

Fountain Chambers
Cleveland Business Centre, 1 Watson
Street, Middlesbrough TS1 2RQ,
Telephone: 01642 804040
E-mail:fountainchambers@onyxnet.co.uk
Call Date: Oct 1990, Gray's Inn
Qualifications: [LLB (Newc)]

BURKE TREVOR MICHAEL

10 King's Bench Walk
1st Floor, Temple, London EC4Y 7EB,
Telephone: 0171 353 2501
Call Date: July 1981, Middle Temple
Pupil Master
Qualifications: [BA]

BURKE-GAFFNEY MICHAEL ANTHONY BOWES QC (1977)

Lamb Chambers
Lamb Building, Temple, London
EC4Y 7AS, Telephone: 020 7797 8300
E-mail: lambchambers@link.org
Call Date: June 1959, Gray's Inn

BURKE-GAFFNEY RUPERT DAVID CHARLES JOHN

1 Paper Buildings
1st Floor, Temple, London EC4Y 7EP,
Telephone: 0171 353 3728/4953
Call Date: Nov 1988, Gray's Inn
Qualifications: [BSc (Lond)]

BURKETT FRANCIS MARTIN THOMAS

Walnut House
63 St David's Hill, Exeter, Devon,
EX4 4DW, Telephone: 01392 279751
E-mail: 106627.2451@compuserve.com
Call Date: Nov 1969, Inner Temple
Pupil Master
Qualifications: [LLB (Exon)]

BURKILL GUY ALEXANDER

3 New Square
Lincoln's Inn, London WC2A 3RS,
Telephone: 0171 405 1111
E-mail: 3newsquareip@lineone.net
Call Date: Feb 1981, Middle Temple
Pupil Master
Qualifications: [MA (Cantab)]

BURLES DAVID JOHN

Goldsmith Building
1st Floor, Temple, London EC4Y 7BL,
Telephone: 0171 353 7881
E-mail:clerks@goldsmith-building.law.co.uk
Call Date: Nov 1984, Middle Temple
Qualifications: [LLB (Bris)]

BURN COLIN RICHARD

30 Park Square
Leeds LS1 2PF, Telephone: 0113 2436388
E-mail: clerks@30parksquare.co.uk
Call Date: Nov 1985, Middle Temple
Pupil Master
Qualifications: [LLB (Hons)]

BURN LINDSAY STUART

Queen Elizabeth Building
Ground Floor, Temple, London
EC4Y 9BS,
Telephone: 0171 353 7181 (12 Lines)
Call Date: July 1972, Middle Temple
Pupil Master, Recorder
Qualifications: [LLB]

BURNETT HAROLD WALLACE QC (1982)

4 Paper Buildings
Ground Floor, Temple, London
EC4Y 7EX, Telephone: 0171 353 3366/
583 7155
E-mail: clerks@4paperbuildings.com
Call Date: Feb 1962, Gray's Inn
Recorder
Qualifications: [BA (Oxon)]

BURNETT IAIN

Gray's Inn Chambers, The Chambers of Norman Patterson
First Floor, Gray's Inn Chambers, Gray's
Inn, London WC1R 5JA,
Telephone: 0171 831 5344
E-mail: s.mcblain@btinternet.com
Call Date: Oct 1993, Lincoln's Inn
Qualifications: [LLB (Hons)(Wales)]

BURNETT IAN DUNCAN QC (1998)

1 Temple Gardens
1st Floor, Temple, London EC4Y 9BB,
Telephone: 0171 583 1315/353 0407
E-mail: clerks@1templegardens.co.uk
Call Date: 1980, Middle Temple
Assistant Recorder
Qualifications: [MA (Oxon)]

BURNHAM MISS ULELE IMOINDA

Cloisters
1 Pump Court, Temple, London
EC4Y 7AA, Telephone: 0171 827 4000
E-mail: clerks@cloisters.com
Call Date: Mar 1997, Inner Temple
Qualifications: [BA (Sussex), MPhil (Cantab),
CPE (Sussex)]

BURNS ALEXANDER LAURENCE

New Court Chambers
3 Broad Chare, Newcastle upon Tyne
NE1 3DQ, Telephone: 0191 232 1980
Call Date: July 1988, Inner Temple
Qualifications: [LLB (Sheffield)]

BURNS ANDREW PHILIP

Devereux Chambers
Devereux Court, London WC2R 3JJ,
Telephone: 0171 353 7534
E-mail: mailbox@devchambers.co.uk
Call Date: Oct 1993, Middle Temple
Qualifications: [BA (Hons)(Cantab)]

BURNS FRANCIS JOSEPH

Kenworthy's Chambers
83 Bridge Street, Manchester M3 2RF,
Telephone: 0161 832 4036/834 6954
E-mail: clerks@kenworthys.co.uk
Call Date: May 1971, Gray's Inn
Pupil Master
Qualifications: [LLB]

D

BURNS JEREMY STUART

17 Carlton Crescent
Southampton SO15 2XR,
Telephone: 023 8032 0320/0823 2003
E-mail: greg@jg17cc.co.uk
Call Date: Nov 1996, Lincoln's Inn
Qualifications: [BA (Cape Town), LLB
(Natal), LLM (Cantab)]

BURNS PETER RICHARD

Deans Court Chambers
24 St John Street, Manchester M3 4DF,
Telephone: 0161 214 6000
E-mail: clerks@deanscourt.co.uk
Deans Court Chambers
41-43 Market Place, Preston PR1 1AH,
Telephone: 01772 555163
E-mail: clerks@deanscourt.co.uk
Call Date: Oct 1993, Gray's Inn
Qualifications: [BA]

BURNS RICHARD HARCOURT

Ropewalk Chambers
24 The Ropewalk, Nottingham NG1 5EF,
Telephone: 0115 9472581
E-mail: administration@ropewalk co.uk
*Call Date: Nov 1967, Middle Temple
Recorder*
Qualifications: [LLB]

BURNS MRS ROSEMARY ANNE MACMAHON

Maidstone Chambers
33 Earl Street, Maidstone, Kent, ME14 1PF,
Telephone: 01622 688592
E-mail:maidstonechambers@compuserve.co
m
Call Date: Nov 1978, Inner Temple

BURNS SIMON HAMER

Albion Chambers
Broad Street, Bristol BS1 1DR,
Telephone: 0117 9272144
Call Date: Oct 1992, Middle Temple
Qualifications: [LL.B (Hons)]

BURNS MISS SUSAN LINDA

3 Serjeants' Inn
London EC4Y 1BQ,
Telephone: 0171 353 5537
E-mail: clerks@3serjeantsinn.com
Call Date: July 1979, Gray's Inn
Qualifications: [LLB (L'pool)]

BURNS TERENCE

Northampton Chambers
22 Albion Place, Northampton NN1 1UD,
Telephone: 01604 636271
Call Date: 1990, Middle Temple
Qualifications: [BA (Hons)]

BURNTON STANLEY JEFFREY QC (1982)

One Essex Court
Ground Floor, Temple, London
EC4Y 9AR, Telephone: 020 7583 2000
E-mail: clerks@oneessexcourt.co.uk
*Call Date: Feb 1965, Middle Temple
Assistant Recorder*
Qualifications: [MA (Oxon)]

BURR ANDREW CHARLES

Atkin Chambers
1 Atkin Building, Gray's Inn, London
WC1R 5AT, Telephone: 020 7404 0102
E-mail: clerks@atkin-chambers.co.uk
*Call Date: Nov 1981, Inner Temple
Pupil Master*
Qualifications: [MA (Cantab), ACIArb]

BURR MARTIN JOHN

Chambers of Martin Burr
Fourth Floor, Eldon Chambers, 30/32
Fleet Street, London EC4Y 1AA,
Telephone: 0171 353 4636
7 New Square
Lincoln's Inn, London WC2A 3QS,
Telephone: 0171 430 1660
*Call Date: July 1978, Middle Temple
Pupil Master*
Qualifications: [MA (Oxon), Dip Comp, Phil,
ACIArb, TEP]

BURRELL FRANCIS GARY QC (1996)

Paradise Chambers
26 Paradise Square, Sheffield S1 2DE,
Telephone: 0114 2738951
E-mail: timbooth@paradise-sq.co.uk

9 Gough Square
London EC4A 3DE,
Telephone: 020 7832 0500
E-mail: clerks@9goughsq.co.uk
Call Date: July 1977, Inner Temple
Recorder
Qualifications: [LLB]

BURRELL SIMON WILLIAM

9 Old Square
Ground Floor, Lincoln's Inn, London
WC2A 3SR, Telephone: 0171 405 4682
E-mail: chambers@9oldsquare.co.uk
Call Date: July 1988, Inner Temple
Pupil Master
Qualifications: [MA (Oxon)]

BURRETT MRS CATHERINE

17 Carlton Crescent
Southampton SO15 2XR,
Telephone: 023 8032 0320/0823 2003
E-mail: greg@jg17cc.co.uk
Call Date: Oct 1992, Middle Temple
Qualifications: [LL.B (Hons, Lond)]

BURRINGTON RICHARD JAMES HENRY

7 Stone Buildings (also at 11 Bolt Court)
1st Floor, Lincoln's Inn, London
WC2A 3SZ, Telephone: 0171 242 0961
E-mail:larthur@7stonebuildings.law.co.uk
11 Bolt Court (also at 7 Stone Buildings – 1st Floor)
London EC4A 3DQ,
Telephone: 0171 353 2300
E-mail: boltct11@aol.com
Redhill Chambers
Seloduct House, 30 Station Road, Redhill,
Surrey, RH1 1NF,
Telephone: 01737 780781
Call Date: Nov 1993, Inner Temple
Qualifications: [BA ((Hons)(So'ton)]

BURROUGHS NIGEL ALFRED

11 Old Square
Ground Floor, Lincoln's Inn, London
WC2A 3TS, Telephone: 020 7430 0341
E-mail: clerks@11oldsquare.co.uk
Call Date: Apr 1991, Middle Temple
Qualifications: [BA (Hons)]

BURROW JOHN RICHARD

Goldsmith Chambers
Ground Floor, Goldsmith Building,
Temple, London EC4Y 7BL,
Telephone: 0171 353 6802/3/4/5
E-mail:clerks@goldsmithchambers.law.co.uk
Call Date: July 1980, Middle Temple
Pupil Master
Qualifications: [BA (Essex)]

BURROWS EUAN MACLEAN

2 Harcourt Buildings
2nd Floor, Temple, London EC4Y 9DB,
Telephone: 020 7353 8415
E-mail: clerks@2hb.law.co.uk
Call Date: Nov 1995, Middle Temple
Qualifications: [MA (Hons) (Cantab)]

BURROWS MICHAEL PETER

3 Fountain Court
Steelhouse Lane, Birmingham B4 6DR,
Telephone: 0121 236 5854
Call Date: Nov 1979, Inner Temple
Pupil Master
Qualifications: [BA (Cantab)]

BURROWS SIMON PAUL

Peel Court Chambers
45 Hardman Street, Manchester M3 3PL,
Telephone: 0161 832 3791
E-mail: clerks@peelct.co.uk
Call Date: Nov 1990, Inner Temple
Qualifications: [BA (Dunelm), Dip Law (City)]

BURTON CHARLES DOMINIC PAUL

2 Dyers Buildings
London EC1N 2JT,
Telephone: 0171 404 1881
Call Date: Nov 1983, Inner Temple
Qualifications: [BA (Lond)]

BURTON MRS FRANCES ROSEMARY

The Chambers of Leolin Price CBE, QC
10 Old Square, Lincoln's Inn, London
WC2A 3SU, Telephone: 0171 405 0758
Call Date: Nov 1970, Middle Temple
Qualifications: [LLB (Lond), LLM (Leic)]

BURTON FRANK QC (1998)

12 King's Bench Walk
Temple, London EC4Y 7EL,
Telephone: 0171 583 0811
E-mail: chambers@12kbw.co.uk
Call Date: 1982, Gray's Inn
Assistant Recorder
Qualifications: [BA (Kent), PhD (Lond)]

BURTON JOHN MALCOLM

Mitre Court Chambers
3rd Floor, Temple, London EC4Y 7BP,
Telephone: 0171 353 9394
E-mail: mitrecourt.com
Call Date: July 1979, Inner Temple
Pupil Master
Qualifications: [LLB (Lond) (Hons)]

BURTON NICHOLAS ANTHONY

2 Mitre Court Buildings
2nd Floor, Temple, London EC4Y 7BX,
Telephone: 0171 583 1380
E-mail: clerks@2mcb.co.uk
Call Date: Nov 1979, Gray's Inn
Pupil Master
Qualifications: [BA (Cantab)]

BURWIN MRS HEATHER REES

2 King's Bench Walk
Ground Floor, Temple, London
EC4Y 7DE, Telephone: 0171 353 1746
E-mail: 2kbw@atlas.co.uk
King's Bench Chambers
115 North Hill, Plymouth PL4 8JY,
Telephone: 01752 221551
Call Date: July 1983, Inner Temple
Pupil Master
Qualifications: [LLB Exon]

BURY MARK

Wilberforce Chambers
7 Bishop Lane, Hull, East Yorkshire,
HU1 1PA, Telephone: 01482 323264
E-mail: clerks@hullbar.demon.co.uk
Call Date: July 1986, Inner Temple
Pupil Master
Qualifications: [LLB (Hull)]

BUSBY THOMAS ANDREW

1 Fountain Court
Steelhouse Lane, Birmingham B4 6DR,
Telephone: 0121 236 5721
Call Date: July 1975, Lincoln's Inn
Qualifications: [LLB (Lond)]

BUSH JOHN ANTHONY

Devon Chambers
3 St Andrew Street, Plymouth PL1 2AH,
Telephone: 01752 661659
E-mail: devonchambers.co.uk.
Call Date: Feb 1964, Gray's Inn
Pupil Master
Qualifications: [BA (Oxon)]

BUSH KEITH

30 Park Place
Cardiff CF1 3BA,
Telephone: 01222 398421
E-mail: 100757.1456@compuserve.com
Call Date: July 1977, Gray's Inn
Pupil Master, Recorder
Qualifications: [BSc, LLM(Lond) MICE,]

BUSH MISS ROSALIND HILARY

5 Fountain Court
Steelhouse Lane, Birmingham B4 6DR,
Telephone: 0121 606 0500
E-mail:clerks@5fountaincourt.law.co.uk
Call Date: Nov 1978, Gray's Inn
Pupil Master
Qualifications: [LLB(B'ham)]

BUSHELL TERENCE JOHN

6 Fountain Court
Steelhouse Lane, Birmingham B4 6DR,
Telephone: 0121 233 3282
E-mail: clerks@sixfountain.co.uk
Call Date: July 1982, Middle Temple
Qualifications: [BA]

BUSTANI MISS NAVAZ

Phoenix Chambers
First Floor, Gray's Inn Chambers, Gray's
Inn, London WC1R 5JA,
Telephone: 0171 404 7888
E-mail:clerks@phoenix-chambers.co.uk
Call Date: Nov 1995, Lincoln's Inn
Qualifications: [BA (Hons), LLB (Hons)]

BUSUTTIL GODWIN JOHN ANTOINE

5 Raymond Buildings
1st Floor, Gray's Inn, London WC1R 5BP,
Telephone: 0171 242 2902
E-mail: clerks@media-ent-law.co.uk
Call Date: Oct 1994, Lincoln's Inn
Qualifications: [MA; MPhil (Cantab), Dip in
Law (City)]

BUSWELL RICHARD THOMAS

Goldsmith Chambers
Ground Floor, Goldsmith Building,
Temple, London EC4Y 7BL,
Telephone: 0171 353 6802/3/4/5
E-mail:clerks@goldsmithchambers.law.co.uk
14 Gray's Inn Square
Gray's Inn, London WC1R 5JP,
Telephone: 0171 242 0858
E-mail: 100712.2134@compuserve.com
Call Date: July 1985, Middle Temple
Pupil Master
Qualifications: [LLB Lond]

BUTCHER CHRISTOPHER JOHN

S Tomlinson QC
7 King's Bench Walk, Temple, London
EC4Y 7DS, Telephone: 0171 583 0404
E-mail: clerks@7kbw.law.co.uk
Call Date: July 1986, Gray's Inn
Pupil Master
Qualifications: [MA(Oxon) Dip Law,
Dip.Eur.Law]

BUTCHER JOHN MARCUS

5 Essex Court
1st Floor, Temple, London EC4Y 9AH,
Telephone: 0171 410 2000
E-mail: barristers@5essexcourt.co.uk
Trinity Chambers
140 New London Road, Chelmsford,
Essex, CM2 0AW,
Telephone: 01245 605040
E-mail:clerks@trinitychambers.law.co.uk
Call Date: July 1984, Inner Temple
Pupil Master
Qualifications: [Dip Law]

BUTCHER RICHARD

1 Middle Temple Lane
Temple, London EC4Y 1LT,
Telephone: 0171 583 0659 (12 Lines)
E-mail: chambers@1mtl.co.uk
Call Date: Nov 1985, Gray's Inn
Pupil Master
Qualifications: [LLB (Cardiff)]

BUTLER ANDREW

2nd Floor, Francis Taylor Building
Temple, London EC4Y 7BY,
Telephone: 0171 353 9942/3157
Call Date: Nov 1993, Middle Temple
Qualifications: [BA, MA]

BUTLER MISS AZEB MAGUEDA

Chancery Chambers
1st Floor Offices, 70/72 Chancery Lane,
London WC2A 1AB,
Telephone: 0171 405 6879/6870
Call Date: July 1966, Lincoln's Inn
Qualifications: [MA, LLB (Hons)]

BUTLER CHRISTOPHER MICHAEL

St Mary's Chambers
50 High Pavement, Lace Market,
Nottingham NG1 1HW,
Telephone: 0115 9503503
E-mail: clerks@smc.law.co.uk
Devereux Chambers
Devereux Court, London WC2R 3JJ,
Telephone: 0171 353 7534
E-mail: mailbox@devchambers.co.uk
Call Date: 1972, Inner Temple
Pupil Master, Assistant Recorder
Qualifications: [LLB (Lond)]

BUTLER GERALD QC (1975)

One Essex Court
Ground Floor, Temple, London
EC4Y 9AR, Telephone: 020 7583 2000
E-mail: clerks@oneessexcourt.co.uk
Call Date: Oct 1955, Middle Temple

BUTLER MISS JOAN QC (1998)

9 Bedford Row
London WC1R 4AZ,
Telephone: 0171 242 3555
E-mail: clerks@9br.co.uk
Call Date: July 1977, Inner Temple

Recorder
Qualifications: [BA (Hons)]

BUTLER JONATHAN CHARLES

India Buildings Chambers
Water Street, Liverpool L2 0XG,
Telephone: 0151 243 6000
E-mail: clerks@chambers.u-net.com
Call Date: Oct 1992, Gray's Inn
Qualifications: [BA (Hons)(Lond), MA, MED]

BUTLER MISS JUDITH JANE SCOTT

6 Pump Court
1st Floor, Temple, London EC4Y 7AR,
Telephone: 0171 797 8400
E-mail: clerks@6pumpcourt.co.uk
6-8 Mill Street
Maidstone, Kent, ME15 6XH,
Telephone: 01622 688094
E-mail: annexe@6pumpcourt.co.uk
Call Date: Oct 1993, Middle Temple
Qualifications: [BA (Hons)(Lond)]

BUTLER PHILIP ANDREW

Deans Court Chambers
24 St John Street, Manchester M3 4DF,
Telephone: 0161 214 6000
E-mail: clerks@deanscourt.co.uk
Deans Court Chambers
41-43 Market Place, Preston PR1 1AH,
Telephone: 01772 555163
E-mail: clerks@deanscourt.co.uk
Call Date: July 1979, Middle Temple
Assistant Recorder
Qualifications: [LLB, LLM (Manch)]

BUTLER RUPERT JAMES

29 Bedford Row Chambers
London WC1R 4HE,
Telephone: 0171 831 2626
Call Date: July 1988, Middle Temple
Qualifications: [LLB (Hons) (Manch)]

BUTLER SIMON DAVID

10 King's Bench Walk
Ground Floor, Temple, London
EC4Y 7EB, Telephone: 0171 353 7742
E-mail: 10kbw@lineone.net
Call Date: Oct 1996, Inner Temple
Qualifications: [LLB (Hons)]

BUTT MICHAEL ROBERT

Pump Court Chambers
5 Temple Chambers, Temple Street,
Swindon SN1 1SQ,
Telephone: 01793 539899
E-mail: clerks@3pumpcourt.com
Pump Court Chambers
Upper Ground Floor, 3 Pump Court,
Temple, London EC4Y 7AJ,
Telephone: 0171 353 0711
E-mail: clerks@3pumpcourt.com
Pump Court Chambers
31 Southgate Street, Winchester
SO23 9EE, Telephone: 01962 868161
E-mail: clerks@3pumpcourt.com
Call Date: Nov 1974, Middle Temple
Pupil Master
Qualifications: [LLB (Lond)]

BUTT MISS ROMASA

Goldsworth Chambers
1st Floor, 11 Gray's Inn Square, London
WC1R 5JD, Telephone: 0171 405 7117
Call Date: Nov 1985, Lincoln's Inn
Qualifications: [BA (Hons)]

BUTTERFIELD JOHN ARTHUR

3 Fountain Court
Steelhouse Lane, Birmingham B4 6DR,
Telephone: 0121 236 5854
Call Date: Oct 1995, Lincoln's Inn
Qualifications: [LLB (Hons)(L'pool)]

BUTTERS JAMES SEBASTIAN

Call Date: July 1994, Lincoln's Inn
Qualifications: [BA (Oxon), LLM (Florence),
LLM (Cantab)]

BUTTERWORTH MARTIN FRANK

Coleridge Chambers
Citadel, 190 Corporation Street,
Birmingham B4 6QD,
Telephone: 0121 233 8500
Call Date: July 1985, Lincoln's Inn
Pupil Master
Qualifications: [BA (Business Law)]

BUTTERWORTH PAUL ANTHONY

Octagon House
19 Colegate, Norwich NR3 1AT,
Telephone: 01603 623186
E-mail: admin@octagon-chambers.co.uk
Call Date: July 1982, Middle Temple
Pupil Master
Qualifications: [BA (Lond)]

BUTTIMORE GABRIEL

11 Old Square
Ground Floor, Lincoln's Inn, London
WC2A 3TS, Telephone: 0171 242 5022/
405 1074
Call Date: Feb 1993, Gray's Inn
Qualifications: [LLB (Anglia)]

BUTTON RICHARD JAMES

High Street Chambers
102 High Street, Godalming, Surrey,
GU7 1DS, Telephone: 01483 861170
Call Date: Oct 1993, Gray's Inn
Qualifications: [LLB]

BUXTON MISS SARAH RUTH

1 Fountain Court
Steelhouse Lane, Birmingham B4 6DR,
Telephone: 0121 236 5721
Call Date: July 1988, Inner Temple
Qualifications: [LLB (Sheffield)]

BUXTON THOMAS JUSTIN

Dr Johnson's Chambers
Two Dr Johnson's Buildings, Temple,
London EC4Y 7AY,
Telephone: 0171 353 4716
E-mail: clerks@2djb.freeserve.co.uk
Call Date: July 1983, Gray's Inn
Qualifications: [LLB (Nottm)]

BYRD MICHAEL

Rosemont Chambers
26 Rosemont Court, Rosemont Road,
London W3 9LS,
Telephone: 0181 992 1100
Call Date: July 1952, Middle Temple
Qualifications: [MA (Oxon), LLB Hons
(Lond)]

BYRNE GARRETT THOMAS

23 Essex Street
London WC2R 3AS,
Telephone: 0171 413 0353/836 8366
E-mail:clerks@essexstreet23.demon.co.uk
Call Date: Nov 1986, Gray's Inn
Pupil Master
Qualifications: [LLB]

BYRNE JAMES PATRICK

Derby Square Chambers
Merchants Court, Derby Square, Liverpool
L2 1TS, Telephone: 0151 709 4222
E-mail:mail.derbysquare@pop3.hiway.co.uk
Call Date: July 1983, Gray's Inn
Pupil Master
Qualifications: [LLB (Hons L'Pool)]

BYRNE MICHAEL DAVID

India Buildings Chambers
Water Street, Liverpool L2 0XG,
Telephone: 0151 243 6000
E-mail: clerks@chambers.u-net.com
Call Date: July 1971, Gray's Inn
Pupil Master, Recorder
Qualifications: [BA, LLB]

BYRNES MISS AISLING ALICE ELIZABETH

3 Gray's Inn Square
Ground Floor, London WC1R 5AH,
Telephone: 0171 520 5600
E-mail: clerks@3gis.co.uk
Call Date: Oct 1994, Gray's Inn
Qualifications: [LLB]

CACCIOTTI MISS MELISSA ERSILIA DOREEN

Stanbrook & Henderson
Ground Floor, 2 Harcourt Bldgs, Temple,
London EC4Y 9DB,
Telephone: 0171 353 0101
E-mail: clerks@harcourt.co.uk
Call Date: 1997, Gray's Inn
Qualifications: [LLB (Lancs)]

CADDICK NICHOLAS DAVID

5 New Square
Ground Floor, Lincoln's Inn, London
WC2A 3RJ, Telephone: 020 7404 0404
E-mail:chambers@fivenewsquare.demon.co.
uk
Call Date: Nov 1986, Middle Temple
Pupil Master
Qualifications: [MA, BCL (Oxon)]

CADDLE MISS SHERRIE LORETTA

Furnival Chambers
32 Furnival Street, London EC4A 1JQ,
Telephone: 0171 405 3232
E-mail: clerks@furnivallaw.co.uk
Call Date: Nov 1983, Lincoln's Inn
Qualifications: [BSc, Soc (Brunel)]

CADE MRS DIANA

Trinity Chambers
140 New London Road, Chelmsford,
Essex, CM2 0AW,
Telephone: 01245 605040
E-mail:clerks@trinitychambers.law.co.uk
Call Date: Nov 1994, Inner Temple
Qualifications: [LLB (Anglia), LLM (Essex)]

CADIN DAVID MICHAEL

King's Bench Chambers
115 North Hill, Plymouth PL4 8JY,
Telephone: 01752 221551
2 King's Bench Walk
Ground Floor, Temple, London
EC4Y 7DE, Telephone: 0171 353 1746
E-mail: 2kbw@atlas.co.uk
Call Date: Oct 1990, Middle Temple
Qualifications: [LLB (Exon)]

CADMAN DAVID JAMES

Goldsmith Chambers
Ground Floor, Goldsmith Building,
Temple, London EC4Y 7BL,
Telephone: 0171 353 6802/3/4/5
E-mail:clerks@goldsmithchambers.law.co.uk
Call Date: Nov 1996, Lincoln's Inn
Qualifications: [BA (Hons) (Dunelm)]

CADNEY PAUL DAVID

Queens Square Chambers
56 Queens Square, Bristol BS1 4PR,
Telephone: 0117 921 1966
Call Date: July 1984, Inner Temple
Pupil Master
Qualifications: [BA (Bristol), Dip La]

CADWALADR STEPHEN KENNETH

6 Fountain Court
Steelhouse Lane, Birmingham B4 6DR,
Telephone: 0121 233 3282
E-mail: clerks@sixfountain.co.uk
Call Date: July 1992, Middle Temple

CADWALLADER NEIL ANTHONY

Exchange Chambers
Pearl Assurance House, Derby Square,
Liverpool L2 9XX,
Telephone: 0151 236 7747
E-mail:exchangechambers@btinternet.com
5 Stone Buildings
Lincoln's Inn, London WC2A 3XT,
Telephone: 0171 242 6201
E-mail:clerks@5-stonebuildings.law.co.uk
Call Date: July 1984, Inner Temple
Pupil Master
Qualifications: [MA (Cantab)]

CADWALLADER PETER

Chambers of John Hand QC
9 St John Street, Manchester M3 4DN,
Telephone: 0161 955 9000
E-mail: ninesjs@gconnect.com
Call Date: July 1973, Gray's Inn
Pupil Master
Qualifications: [LLB (Lond)]

CAFFERKEY MISS ANNETTE MARIE

Enfield Chambers
First Floor, Refuge House, 9-10 River
Front, Enfield, Middlesex, EN1 3SZ,
Telephone: 0181 364 5627
E-mail:enfieldchambers@compuserve.com
Call Date: Nov 1994, Inner Temple
Qualifications: [LLB (Hons)]

CAHILL PATRICK JOHN

2 Paper Buildings
1st Floor, Temple, London EC4Y 7ET,
Telephone: 020 7556 5500
E-mail: clerks@2pbbarristers.co.uk
Call Date: July 1979, Lincoln's Inn
Pupil Master
Qualifications: [BL (Dublin)]

CAHILL PAUL JEREMY

5 Fountain Court
Steelhouse Lane, Birmingham B4 6DR,
Telephone: 0121 606 0500
E-mail:clerks@5fountaincourt.law.co.uk
Call Date: July 1975, Middle Temple
Pupil Master
Qualifications: [LLB (L'pool)]

CAHILL MRS SALLY ELIZABETH MARY

Park Lane Chambers
19 Westgate, Leeds LS1 2RD,
Telephone: 0113 2285000
E-mail:clerks@parklanechambers.co.uk
Call Date: July 1978, Gray's Inn
Pupil Master, Assistant Recorder
Qualifications: [LLB (Leeds)]

CAINS MS LINDA HILARY

37 Park Square Chambers
37 Park Square, Leeds LS1 2NY,
Telephone: 0113 2439422
E-mail: chambers@no37.co.uk
Call Date: Oct 1990, Middle Temple
Qualifications: [BA (Leeds)]

CAIRNES SIMON PAUL STEVEN

3 Paper Buildings
Temple, London EC4Y 7EU,
Telephone: 020 7583 8055
E-mail: London@3paper.com
3 Paper Buildings (Bournemouth)
20 Lorne Park Road, Bournemouth,
Dorset, BH1 1JN,
Telephone: 01202 292102
E-mail: Bournemouth@3paper.com
3 Paper Buildings (Winchester)
4 St Peter Street, Winchester SO23 8BW,
Telephone: 01962 868884
E-mail: winchester@3paper.com

3 Paper Buildings (Oxford)
1 Alfred Street, High Street, Oxford
OX1 4EH, Telephone: 01865 793736
E-mail: oxford@3paper.com
Call Date: Nov 1980, Gray's Inn
Pupil Master
Qualifications: [LLB (Wales)]

CAKEBREAD STUART ALAN CHARLES

2nd Floor, Francis Taylor Building
Temple, London EC4Y 7BY,
Telephone: 0171 353 9942/3157
Call Date: Nov 1978, Middle Temple
Pupil Master
Qualifications: [BA (Exon)]

Fax: 0171 353 9924; DX: LDE 211 London;
Other comms: E-mail
cakebread@btinternet.com

Types of work: Administrative, Commercial
litigation, Defamation, Landlord and
tenant, Local government, Sports

Circuit: South Eastern

Awards and memberships: ALBA

Other professional experience: 4 years as
London borough councillor

Languages spoken: French

Reported Cases: *Edwards v British Athletics
Federation*, (1997) *The Times*, June 30,
1997. Applicability of Article 59 of Treaty of
Rome to drugs ban.
Porter v Magill, Week v Magill, (1999) *The
Times*, May 6, 1999, 1999. Westminster
'homes for votes' case.

CALA DR GUISEPPE

New Court
Temple, London EC4Y 9BE,
Telephone: 0171 583 5123/0510
Call Date: Jan 1971, Inner Temple
Qualifications: [Doctor at Law]

CALCUTT SIR DAVID CHARLES QC (1972)

35 Essex Street
Temple, London WC2R 3AR,
Telephone: 0171 353 6381
E-mail: derek_jenkins@link.org
Call Date: June 1955, Middle Temple
Qualifications: [MA, LLB, MusB (Canta]

CALDECOTT ANDREW HILARY QC (1994)

1 Brick Court
1st Floor, Temple, London EC4Y 9BY,
Telephone: 0171 353 8845
E-mail: clerks@1brickcourt.co.uk
Call Date: July 1975, Inner Temple
Qualifications: [BA (Oxon)]

CALDER MISS RENEE JOYCE

Chambers of Harjit Singh
Ground Floor, 2 Middle Temple Lane,
Temple, London EC4Y 9AA,
Telephone: 0171 353 1356 (4 Lines)
Call Date: Nov 1978, Lincoln's Inn
Qualifications: [BA Hons (Leeds)]

CALDERWOOD MISS PATRICIA JAYNE

3 Fountain Court
Steelhouse Lane, Birmingham B4 6DR,
Telephone: 0121 236 5854
Call Date: Apr 1964, Gray's Inn
Qualifications: [BA (Oxon)]

CALDIN PETER GILES

4 Essex Court
Temple, London EC4Y 9AJ,
Telephone: 020 7797 7970
E-mail: clerks@4essexcourt.law.co.uk
Call Date: Nov 1974, Middle Temple
Pupil Master
Qualifications: [LLB]

CALDWELL MRS JENNIFER JOAN

18 St John Street
Manchester M3 4EA,
Telephone: 0161 278 1800
E-mail: 18stjohn@lineone.net
Call Date: Nov 1973, Middle Temple
Qualifications: [LLB (Manch)]

CALDWELL PETER HUGH COYLES

2 Dyers Buildings
London EC1N 2JT,
Telephone: 0171 404 1881
Call Date: Oct 1995, Gray's Inn
Qualifications: [BA (York), MA]

CALLAN DAVID ST CLAIR

New Court Chambers
3 Broad Chare, Newcastle upon Tyne
NE1 3DQ, Telephone: 0191 232 1980
Call Date: July 1979, Middle Temple
Pupil Master
Qualifications: [MA]

CALLAWAY ANTHONY LEONARD

17 Bedford Row
London WC1R 4EB,
Telephone: 0171 831 7314
E-mail: iboard7314@aol.com
Call Date: Nov 1978, Middle Temple
Pupil Master
Qualifications: [BA (Hons), MA]

CALLERY MARTIN

Cobden House Chambers
19 Quay Street, Manchester M3 3HN,
Telephone: 0161 833 6000
E-mail: clerks@cobden.co.uk
Call Date: Mar 1997, Middle Temple
Qualifications: [LLB (Hons)(Wales)]

CALLMAN JEREMY DAVID

The Chambers of Leolin Price CBE, QC
10 Old Square, Lincoln's Inn, London
WC2A 3SU, Telephone: 0171 405 0758
Call Date: Oct 1991, Middle Temple
Pupil Master
Qualifications: [MA (Hons) (Cantab)]

CALLMAN MISS TANYA SARA

2 King's Bench Walk Chambers
1st Floor, 2 King's Bench Walk, Temple,
London EC4Y 7DE,
Telephone: 020 7353 9276
E-mail: chambers@2kbw.co.uk
Call Date: Oct 1993, Middle Temple
Qualifications: [MA (Hons) (Cantab)]

CALVER NEIL RICHARD

Brick Court Chambers
7-8 Essex Street, London WC2R 3LD,
Telephone: 0171 379 3550
E-mail: [surname]@brickcourt.co.uk
Call Date: Nov 1987, Gray's Inn
Pupil Master
Qualifications: [MA (Cantab)]

CALVERT DAVID EDWARD

St James's Chambers
68 Quay Street, Manchester M3 3EJ,
Telephone: 0161 834 7000
E-mail: clerks@stjameschambers.co.uk
Call Date: Nov 1995, Inner Temple
Qualifications: [BA (Oxon)]

CALVERT PETER CHARLES

Goldsmith Building
1st Floor, Temple, London EC4Y 7BL,
Telephone: 0171 353 7881
E-mail:clerks@goldsmith-building.law.co.uk
Call Date: July 1975, Middle Temple
Pupil Master
Qualifications: [BA]

CALWAY MARK EDWARD

Goldsmith Chambers
Ground Floor, Goldsmith Building,
Temple, London EC4Y 7BL,
Telephone: 0171 353 6802/3/4/5
E-mail:clerks@goldsmithchambers.law.co.uk
Call Date: Feb 1989, Inner Temple
Qualifications: [BA (Kent)]

CAMERON ALLAN ALEXANDER

3 Raymond Buildings
Gray's Inn, London WC1R 5BH,
Telephone: 020 7831 3833
E-mail:chambers@threeraymond.demon.co.uk
Call Date: Nov 1986, Inner Temple
Pupil Master
Qualifications: [LLB (Bris)]

CAMERON MISS BARBARA ALEXANDER

2 Harcourt Buildings
Ground Floor/Left, Temple, London
EC4Y 9DB, Telephone: 0171 583 9020
E-mail: clerks@harcourt.co.uk
Call Date: Nov 1979, Lincoln's Inn
Pupil Master
Qualifications: [MA (Cantab)]

Fax: 0171 583 2686;
Out of hours telephone: 0181 650 5759;
DX: LDE 1039

Types of work: Clinical negligence, Common law (general), Equity, wills and trusts, Family, Family provision, Personal injury, Professional negligence

Circuit: South Eastern

Awards and memberships: Member London Legal Aid Committee; Legal Assessor to Royal College of Nursing UK Conduct & Health Committees; Member of Inner Temple Disciplinary Tribunal Panel; Former executive committee member of Professional Negligence Bar Association; Member Family Law Bar Association and Personal Injury Bar Association

Other professional experience: 10 years as Practice Manager/Nurse in NHS and Harley Street oral surgery practices

Reported Cases: *Northampton Health Authority v OS & Governors of St Andrews Hospital*, [1994] 2 FCR 206 (CA), 1994. Governors of secure hospital re legality of enforced medical treatment on disturbed adolescents – *Gillick* issues explored and costs implications.

CAMERON JONATHAN JAMES O'GRADY

3 Verulam Buildings
London WC1R 5NT,
Telephone: 0171 831 8441
E-mail: clerks@3verulam.co.uk
Call Date: Nov 1987, Inner Temple
Qualifications: [LLB (Lond) LLM, (Cantab)]

CAMERON KENNETH ANGUS

King's Bench Chambers
Wellington House, 175 Holdenhurst Road,
Bournemouth, Dorset, BH8 8DQ,
Telephone: 01202 250025
E-mail: chambers@kingsbench.co.uk
Call Date: Nov 1969, Middle Temple
Pupil Master
Qualifications: [BA (Cantab)]

CAMERON NEIL ALEXANDER

Wilberforce Chambers
7 Bishop Lane, Hull, East Yorkshire,
HU1 1PA, Telephone: 01482 323264
E-mail: clerks@hullbar.demon.co.uk
Call Date: July 1984, Gray's Inn
Pupil Master
Qualifications: [LLB (Leics)]

CAMERON NEIL ST CLAIR

1 Serjeants' Inn
4th Floor, Temple, London EC4Y 1NH,
Telephone: 0171 583 1355
E-mail: clerks@serjeants-inn.co.uk
Call Date: July 1982, Gray's Inn
Pupil Master
Qualifications: [BA (Dunelm)]

CAMERON MISS SHEILA MORAG CLARK QC (1983)

2 Harcourt Buildings
2nd Floor, Temple, London EC4Y 9DB,
Telephone: 020 7353 8415
E-mail: clerks@2hb.law.co.uk
Call Date: 1957, Middle Temple
Recorder
Qualifications: [MA (Oxon)]

CAMERON MISS VIVECA CECILE

Belmarsh Chambers
20 Warland Road, London SE18 2EU,
Telephone: 0181 316 7322
55 Temple Chambers
Temple Avenue, London EC4Y 0HP,
Telephone: 0171 353 7400
Call Date: Feb 1987, Middle Temple
Qualifications: [LLB]

CAMMEGH JOHN STEPHEN

4 Brick Court, Chambers of Anne Rafferty QC
1st Floor, Temple, London EC4Y 9AD,
Telephone: 0171 583 8455
Call Date: Nov 1987, Inner Temple
Qualifications: [LLB (London)]

CAMMERMAN GIDEON SAUL

1 Middle Temple Lane
Temple, London EC4Y 1LT,
Telephone: 0171 583 0659 (12 Lines)
E-mail: chambers@1mtl.co.uk
Call Date: 1996, Middle Temple
Qualifications: [BA (Hons) (Cantab), Dip Law]

CAMPBELL MISS ALEXIS ANNE

Hardwicke Building
New Square, Lincoln's Inn, London
WC2A 3SB, Telephone: 020 7242 2523
E-mail: clerks@hardwicke.co.uk
Call Date: Nov 1990, Inner Temple
Qualifications: [LLB (Leeds)]

CAMPBELL ANDREW BRUCE

1 Middle Temple Lane
Temple, London EC4Y 1LT,
Telephone: 0171 583 0659 (12 Lines)
E-mail: chambers@1mtl.co.uk
Call Date: July 1972, Inner Temple
Pupil Master, Assistant Recorder
Qualifications: [MA (Oxon)]

CAMPBELL ANDREW NEVILLE QC (1994)

Chambers of Andrew Campbell QC
10 Park Square, Leeds LS1 2LH,
Telephone: 0113 2455438
E-mail: clerks@10pksq.co.uk
Call Date: Nov 1972, Middle Temple
Recorder
Qualifications: [BA]

CAMPBELL COLIN WILLIAM

2 Paper Buildings
1st Floor, Temple, London EC4Y 7ET,
Telephone: 020 7556 5500
E-mail: clerks@2pbbarristers.co.uk
Call Date: July 1979, Gray's Inn
Pupil Master
Qualifications: [BA(Hons) (Kent)]

CAMPBELL DAVID

1 Pump Court
Lower Ground Floor, Temple, London
EC4Y 7AB, Telephone: 0171 583 2012/
353 4341
E-mail: [name]@1pumpcourt.co.uk
Call Date: Nov 1992, Inner Temple
Qualifications: [LLB (Sheff)]

CAMPBELL MISS DIANE EVA

York Chambers
14 Toft Green, York YO1 6JT,
Telephone: 01904 620048
E-mail: [name]@yorkchambers.co.uk
Call Date: Oct 1995, Gray's Inn
Qualifications: [LLB]

CAMPBELL DONALD

Phoenix Chambers
First Floor, Gray's Inn Chambers, Gray's
Inn, London WC1R 5JA,
Telephone: 0171 404 7888
E-mail:clerks@phoenix-chambers.co.uk
Call Date: Nov 1976, Inner Temple
Pupil Master

CAMPBELL DOUGLAS JAMES

3 New Square
Lincoln's Inn, London WC2A 3RS,
Telephone: 0171 405 1111
E-mail: 3newsquareip@lineone.net
Call Date: Oct 1993, Inner Temple
Qualifications: [MA (Oxon), Dip Law (City)]

CAMPBELL MISS EMILY CHARLOTTE

Wilberforce Chambers
8 New Square, Lincoln's Inn, London
WC2A 3QP, Telephone: 0171 306 0102
E-mail: chambers@wilberforce.co.uk
Call Date: Nov 1995, Lincoln's Inn
Qualifications: [MA (Oxon), BCL]

Types of work: Chancery (general), Chancery
land law, Charities, Ecclesiastical, Equity,
wills and trusts, Mental health, Pensions,
Private international, Professional negligence, Tax – capital and income, Tax –
corporate

CAMPBELL MISS GAYLE ELIZABETH

Nicholas Street Chambers
22 Nicholas Street, Chester CH1 2NX,
Telephone: 01244 323886
E-mail: clerks@40king.co.uk
Call Date: Oct 1997, Middle Temple
Qualifications: [LLB (Hons)(Lond)]

CAMPBELL GLENN

11 Old Square
Ground Floor, Lincoln's Inn, London
WC2A 3TS, Telephone: 020 7430 0341
E-mail: clerks@11oldsquare.co.uk
Call Date: July 1985, Lincoln's Inn
Pupil Master
Qualifications: [LLB (Manchester), LLM,
QMWC]

CAMPBELL GRAHAM JOHN

24a St John Street
Manchester M3 4DF,
Telephone: 0161 833 9628
Call Date: Nov 1982, Middle Temple
Pupil Master
Qualifications: [BA (Hons)]

CAMPBELL MISS JANE CHARLOTTE

5 Pump Court
Ground Floor, Temple, London
EC4Y 7AP, Telephone: 020 7353 2532
E-mail: FivePump@netcomuk.co.uk
Call Date: 1990, Inner Temple
Qualifications: [BA (Newc), Dip Law]

CAMPBELL MISS JOAN CAROLYN

33 Park Place
Cardiff CF1 3BA,
Telephone: 02920 233313
Call Date: Nov 1996, Lincoln's Inn
Qualifications: [LLB(Jnt Hons)(Wales)]

CAMPBELL JOHN DAVID QC (1981)

40 King Street
Manchester M2 6BA,
Telephone: 0161 832 9082
E-mail: clerks@40kingstreet.co.uk
The Chambers of Philip Raynor QC
5 Park Place, Leeds LS1 2RU,
Telephone: 0113 242 1123
Call Date: 1990, Lincoln's Inn
Qualifications: [LLB (Edin)]

D

CAMPBELL NICHOLAS CHARLES WILSON

11 King's Bench Walk
1st Floor, Temple, London EC4Y 7EQ,
Telephone: 0171 353 3337
E-mail: fmuller11@aol.com
11 King's Bench Walk
3 Park Court, Park Cross Street, Leeds
LS1 2QH, Telephone: 0113 297 1200
Call Date: July 1978, Inner Temple
Pupil Master
Qualifications: [BA (Cantab)]

CAMPBELL OLIVER EDWARD WILHELM

2 Harcourt Buildings
Ground Floor/Left, Temple, London
EC4Y 9DB, Telephone: 0171 583 9020
E-mail: clerks@harcourt.co.uk
Call Date: Oct 1992, Middle Temple
Qualifications: [MA (Hons)]

CAMPBELL MS RHONA LYNN

4 Fountain Court
Steelhouse Lane, Birmingham B4 6DR,
Telephone: 0121 236 3476
Call Date: Oct 1993, Inner Temple
Qualifications: [BA (Dunelm)]

CAMPBELL ROBIN ALEXANDER

4-5 Gray's Inn Square
Ground Floor, Gray's Inn, London
WC1R 5JP, Telephone: 0171 404 5252
E-mail:chambers@4-5graysinnsquare.co.uk
Call Date: Apr 1967, Middle Temple
Qualifications: [MA (Oxon)]

CAMPBELL MS SARAH JANE

23 Essex Street
London WC2R 3AS,
Telephone: 0171 413 0353/836 8366
E-mail:clerks@essexstreet23.demon.co.uk
Call Date: Oct 1997, Inner Temple
Qualifications: [BA (Cantab)]

CAMPBELL STAFFORD GRAHAM

5 Pump Court
Ground Floor, Temple, London
EC4Y 7AP, Telephone: 020 7353 2532
E-mail: FivePump@netcomuk.co.uk
Call Date: July 1979, Gray's Inn
Pupil Master
Qualifications: [LLB (Lond)]

CAMPBELL STEPHEN GORDON

St Philip's Chambers
Fountain Court, Steelhouse Lane,
Birmingham B4 6DR,
Telephone: 0121 246 7000
E-mail: clerks@st-philips.co.uk
Call Date: July 1982, Middle Temple
Qualifications: [LLB (L'pool)]

CAMPBELL MISS SUSAN CLAIRE

Southernhay Chambers
33 Southernhay East, Exeter, Devon,
EX1 1NX, Telephone: 01392 255777
E-mail:southernhay.chambers@lineone.net
Call Date: Nov 1986, Middle Temple
Qualifications: [MA (Cantab)]

CAMPBELL OF ALLOWAY LORD QC (1965)

2 King's Bench Walk Chambers
1st Floor, 2 King's Bench Walk, Temple,
London EC4Y 7DE,
Telephone: 020 7353 9276
E-mail: chambers@2kbw.co.uk
Call Date: May 1939, Inner Temple
Qualifications: [MA (Cantab)]

CAMPBELL-BROWN MISS ANNE LOUISE

Bracton Chambers
95a Chancery Lane, London WC2A 1DT,
Telephone: 0171 242 4248
Call Date: Nov 1993, Middle Temple
Qualifications: [BA (Hons)(York), MA
(Lond), Dip in Law (City)]

D

CAMPBELL-CLYNE CHRISTOPHER FRANCIS GEORGE

3 Hare Court
1 Little Essex Street, London WC2R 3LD,
Telephone: 0171 395 2000
Call Date: Nov 1988, Middle Temple
Pupil Master
Qualifications: [LLB Hons]

CAMPBELL-MOFFAT MRS AUDREY PATRICIA

High Pavement Chambers
1 High Pavement, Nottingham NG1 1HF,
Telephone: 0115 9418218
Call Date: July 1987, Middle Temple
Qualifications: [LLM (London), LLB (Reading)]

CAMPBELL-TIECH ANDREW

2 Dyers Buildings
London EC1N 2JT,
Telephone: 0171 404 1881
Call Date: July 1978, Inner Temple
Pupil Master

CANAVAN MISS SHEELAGH MARY

2-4 Tudor Street
London EC4Y 0AA,
Telephone: 0171 797 7111
E-mail: clerks@rfqc.co.uk
Call Date: July 1987, Lincoln's Inn
Pupil Master
Qualifications: [LLB (Hons) (Lond)]

CANDLER MISS LINDA JEAN

Furnival Chambers
32 Furnival Street, London EC4A 1JQ,
Telephone: 0171 405 3232
E-mail: clerks@furnivallaw.co.uk
Call Date: 1997, Middle Temple
Qualifications: [Juris Doctor, (George Washington)]

CANDLIN JAMES RICHARD

Chambers of Geoffrey Hawker
46/48 Essex Street, London WC2R 3GH,
Telephone: 0171 583 8899
Call Date: Oct 1991, Lincoln's Inn
Qualifications: [BSc (Hons) , Dip Law]

CANE-SOOTHILL MICHAEL STEPHEN

Bank House Chambers
Old Bank House, Hartshead, Sheffield
S1 2EL, Telephone: 0114 2751223
Call Date: 1997, Lincoln's Inn
Qualifications: [LLB (Hons)(Sheff)]

CANNAN JONATHAN MICHAEL

St James's Chambers
68 Quay Street, Manchester M3 3EJ,
Telephone: 0161 834 7000
E-mail: clerks@stjameschambers.co.uk
Broadway House Chambers
Broadway House, 9 Bank Street, Bradford,
West Yorkshire, BD1 1TW,
Telephone: 01274 722560
E-mail: clerks@broadwayhouse.co.uk
Broadway House Chambers
31 Park Square West, Leeds LS1 2PF,
Telephone: 0113 246 2600
Call Date: 1989, Gray's Inn
Qualifications: [LLB (Lond), FCA, ATII]

CANNATELLA MARC

East Anglian Chambers
Gresham House, 5 Museum Street,
Ipswich, Suffolk, IP1 1HQ,
Telephone: 01473 214481
E-mail: ipswich@ealaw.co.uk
East Anglian Chambers
52 North Hill, Colchester, Essex, CO1 1PY,
Telephone: 01206 572756
E-mail: colchester@ealaw.co.uk
East Anglian Chambers
57 London Street, Norwich NR2 1HL,
Telephone: 01603 617351
E-mail: norwich@ealaw.co.uk
Call Date: 1997, Lincoln's Inn
Qualifications: [LLB (Hons)(Middx)]

CANNON ADAM RICHARD

96 Gray's Inn Road
London WC1X 8AL,
Telephone: 0171 405 0585
Call Date: 1997, Middle Temple
Qualifications: [BA (Hons)(Cantab)]

D

CANNON MARK RENNISON NORRIS

Chambers of John L Powell QC
Four New Square, Lincoln's Inn, London
WC2A 3RJ, Telephone: 0171 797 8000
E-mail: barristers@4newsquare.com
Call Date: July 1985, Middle Temple
Pupil Master
Qualifications: [BA(Oxon)]

CANT CHRISTOPHER IAN

9 Stone Buildings
Lincoln's Inn, London WC2A 3NN,
Telephone: 0171 404 5055
E-mail: clerks@9stoneb.law.co.uk
Call Date: July 1973, Lincoln's Inn
Pupil Master
Qualifications: [MA (Cantab)]

CAPE ROBERT PAUL

Milburn House Chambers
'A' Floor, Milburn House, Dean Street,
Newcastle upon Tyne NE1 1LE,
Telephone: 0191 230 5511
E-mail:milburnhousechambers@btinternet.co
m
Call Date: Oct 1990, Middle Temple
Pupil Master
Qualifications: [LLB]

CAPLAN JONATHAN MICHAEL QC (1991)

Five Paper Buildings
1st Floor, Five Paper Bldgs, Temple,
London EC4Y 7HB,
Telephone: 0171 583 6117
E-mail:clerks@5-paperbuildings.law.co.uk
Call Date: July 1973, Gray's Inn
Recorder
Qualifications: [MA (Cantab)]

CAPON PHILIP CHRISTOPHER WILLIAM

St Philip's Chambers
Fountain Court, Steelhouse Lane,
Birmingham B4 6DR,
Telephone: 0121 246 7000
E-mail: clerks@st-philips.co.uk
Call Date: Oct 1990, Inner Temple
Qualifications: [LLB (B'ham)]

CAPSTICK TIMOTHY

No. 6
6 Park Square, Leeds LS1 2LW,
Telephone: 0113 2459763
E-mail: chambers@no6.co.uk
Call Date: July 1986, Gray's Inn
Qualifications: [BA]

CARAMAZZA (FRANCO) LILLO

Amhurst Chambers
76 Amhurst Park, London N16 5AR,
Telephone: 0181 800 5817
Call Date: Nov 1987, Middle Temple
Qualifications: [LLB(Hons) Essex]

CARDEN NICHOLAS

1 Mitre Court Buildings
Temple, London EC4Y 7BS,
Telephone: 0171 797 7070
E-mail: clerks@1mcb.com
Call Date: July 1981, Gray's Inn
Pupil Master
Qualifications: [LLB (Lond)]

CAREY GODFREY MOHUN CECIL QC (1991)

Five Paper Buildings
1st Floor, Five Paper Bldgs, Temple,
London EC4Y 7HB,
Telephone: 0171 583 6117
E-mail:clerks@5-paperbuildings.law.co.uk
Call Date: July 1969, Inner Temple
Recorder

CAREY JEREMY REYNOLDS PATRICK

Lamb Chambers
Lamb Building, Temple, London
EC4Y 7AS, Telephone: 020 7797 8300
E-mail: lambchambers@link.org
Call Date: July 1974, Inner Temple
Pupil Master, Assistant Recorder
Qualifications: [MA (Cantab)]

CAREY-HUGHES RICHARD JOHN

4 Brick Court, Chambers of Anne Rafferty QC
1st Floor, Temple, London EC4Y 9AD,
Telephone: 0171 583 8455
Call Date: July 1977, Gray's Inn
Pupil Master, Assistant Recorder

CARGILL-THOMPSON MISS PERDITA

Essex Court Chambers
24 Lincoln's Inn Fields, London
WC2A 3ED, Telephone: 0171 813 8000
E-mail:clerksroom@essexcourt-chambers.co.uk
Call Date: Feb 1993, Middle Temple
Qualifications: [BA (Hons)(Oxon), LLM (Lond)]

CARLILE ALEXANDER CHARLES QC (1984)

9-12 Bell Yard
London WC2A 2LF,
Telephone: 0171 400 1800
E-mail: clerks@bellyard.co.uk
Sedan House
Stanley Place, Chester CH1 2LU,
Telephone: 01244 320480/348282
Call Date: July 1970, Gray's Inn
Recorder
Qualifications: [LLB (AKC)]

CARLING CHRISTOPHER JAMES

Old Square Chambers
1 Verulam Buildings, Gray's Inn, London
WC1R 5LQ, Telephone: 0171 269 0300
E-mail:clerks@oldsquarechambers.co.uk
Old Square Chambers
Hanover House, 47 Corn Street, Bristol
BS1 1HT, Telephone: 0117 9277111
E-mail: oldsqbri@globalnet.co.uk
Call Date: Nov 1969, Lincoln's Inn
Qualifications: [MA (Cantab)]

CARLISLE HUGH BERNARD HARWOOD QC (1978)

1 Temple Gardens
1st Floor, Temple, London EC4Y 9BB,
Telephone: 0171 583 1315/353 0407
E-mail: clerks@1templegardens.co.uk
Call Date: Feb 1961, Middle Temple
Recorder
Qualifications: [MA (Cantab)]

CARLISLE TIMOTHY ST JOHN OGILVIE

Chambers of Norman Palmer
2 Field Court, Gray's Inn, London
WC1R 5BB, Telephone: 0171 405 6114
E-mail: fieldct2@netcomuk.co.uk
Call Date: Nov 1984, Gray's Inn
Pupil Master

CARLISLE OF BUCKLOW THE RT HON LORD QC (1971)

Hollis Whiteman Chambers
3rd Floor, Queen Elizabeth Bldg, Temple,
London EC4Y 9BS,
Telephone: 020 7583 5766
E-mail:barristers@holliswhiteman.co.uk
18 St John Street
Manchester M3 4EA,
Telephone: 0161 278 1800
E-mail: 18stjohn@lineone.net
Call Date: Feb 1954, Gray's Inn
Recorder
Qualifications: [LLB, MA (Cantab)]

CARMAN GEORGE ALFRED QC (1971)

New Court Chambers
5 Verulam Buildings, Gray's Inn, London
WC1R 5LY, Telephone: 0171 831 9500
E-mail: mail@newcourtchambers.com
Call Date: June 1953, Lincoln's Inn
Qualifications: [BA (Oxon)]

CARMICHAEL JOHN

Furnival Chambers
32 Furnival Street, London EC4A 1JQ,
Telephone: 0171 405 3232
E-mail: clerks@furnivallaw.co.uk
Call Date: July 1984, Inner Temple
Pupil Master
Qualifications: [BA (Leeds) Dip Law, (City)]

CARNE ROGER ENYS

4 Brick Court, Chambers of Anne Rafferty QC
1st Floor, Temple, London EC4Y 9AD,
Telephone: 0171 583 8455
Queens Square Chambers
56 Queens Square, Bristol BS1 4PR,
Telephone: 0117 921 1966
Call Date: Nov 1969, Inner Temple
Pupil Master
Qualifications: [LLB (Lond)]

CARNE MS ROSALIND PATRICIA

1 Pump Court
Lower Ground Floor, Temple, London
EC4Y 7AB, Telephone: 0171 583 2012/353 4341
E-mail: [name]@1pumpcourt.co.uk
Call Date: Nov 1986, Inner Temple
Qualifications: [BA (Oxon)]

D

CARNES ANDREW JAMES

23 Essex Street
London WC2R 3AS,
Telephone: 0171 413 0353/836 8366
E-mail:clerks@essexstreet23.demon.co.uk
Call Date: July 1984, Lincoln's Inn
Pupil Master
Qualifications: [LLB (Leics)]

CARNEY ANDREW PATRICK

Martins Building
2nd Floor, No 4 Water Street, Liverpool
L2 3SP, Telephone: 0151 236 5818/4919
Call Date: Oct 1995, Inner Temple
Qualifications: [BA (Durham), MSc (Lond)]

CARNEY MISS CAROLINE MARY

The Law Library, Four Courts, Dublin 7
Telephone: 01001 720622
Call Date: Nov 1980, Middle Temple
Qualifications: [BA (Belfast)]

CARPENTER MISS JANE PATRICIA ANNE

2nd Floor, Francis Taylor Building
Temple, London EC4Y 7BY,
Telephone: 0171 353 9942/3157
Call Date: Nov 1984, Inner Temple
Pupil Master
Qualifications: [BSc Hons]

CARPENTER RICHARD JOHN

Chancery House Chambers
7 Lisbon Square, Leeds LS1 4LY,
Telephone: 0113 244 6691
E-mail: chanceryhouse@btinternet.com
Call Date: July 1981, Gray's Inn
Qualifications: [BSc]

CARR BRUCE CONRAD

Devereux Chambers
Devereux Court, London WC2R 3JJ,
Telephone: 0171 353 7534
E-mail: mailbox@devchambers.co.uk
Call Date: Nov 1986, Inner Temple
Assistant Recorder
Qualifications: [BSc(Econ)(Lond)]

CARR CHRISTOPHER QC (1983)

One Essex Court
Ground Floor, Temple, London
EC4Y 9AR, Telephone: 020 7583 2000
E-mail: clerks@oneessexcourt.co.uk
Call Date: Nov 1968, Lincoln's Inn
Qualifications: [LLB]

CARR HENRY JAMES QC (1998)

11 South Square
2nd Floor, Gray's Inn, London
WC1R 5EU,
Telephone: 0171 405 1222 (24hr messagin
g service)
E-mail: clerks@11southsquare.com
Call Date: May 1982, Gray's Inn
Qualifications: [BA (Oxon) LLM, (British
Columbia)]

CARR JONATHAN OLSON

New Court Chambers
3 Broad Chare, Newcastle upon Tyne
NE1 3DQ, Telephone: 0191 232 1980
Call Date: Nov 1990, Middle Temple
Qualifications: [LLB (Newc)]

CARR PETER

St Ive's Chambers
Whittall Street, Birmingham B4 6DH,
Telephone: 0121 236 0863/5720
E-mail:stives.headofchambers@btinternet.com
Call Date: Nov 1976, Inner Temple
Pupil Master
Qualifications: [LLB (Hons) (Birm)]

CARR SIMON ANDREW

9 Gough Square
London EC4A 3DE,
Telephone: 020 7832 0500
E-mail: clerks@9goughsq.co.uk
Call Date: July 1984, Inner Temple
Pupil Master
Qualifications: [LLB (Soton)]

CARR MISS SUE LASCELLES

Chambers of John L Powell QC
Four New Square, Lincoln's Inn, London
WC2A 3RJ, Telephone: 0171 797 8000
E-mail: barristers@4newsquare.com
Call Date: July 1987, Inner Temple
Pupil Master
Qualifications: [MA (Cantab)]

CARRASCO GLENN LAWRENCE

3 Temple Gardens
3rd Floor, Temple, London EC4Y 9AU,
Telephone: 0171 353 0832
Call Date: Oct 1997, Inner Temple
Qualifications: [BA (London), MSc (LSE),
CPE]

CARRINGTON DOMINIC

Britton Street Chambers
1st Floor, 20 Britton Street, London
EC1M 5NQ, Telephone: 0171 608 3765
Call Date: Nov 1996, Middle Temple
Qualifications: [LLB (Hons)]

CARRINGTON MISS GILLIAN ELIZABETH

2-3 Gray's Inn Square
Gray's Inn, London WC1R 5JH,
Telephone: 0171 242 4986
E-mail:chambers@2-3graysinnsquare.co.uk
Call Date: Nov 1990, Inner Temple
Qualifications: [BA (Oxon), Dip Law (City)]

CARRODUS MISS GAIL CAROLINE

New Court Chambers
5 Verulam Buildings, Gray's Inn, London
WC1R 5LY, Telephone: 0171 831 9500
E-mail: mail@newcourtchambers.com
Call Date: Nov 1978, Gray's Inn
Pupil Master
Qualifications: [BSc (L'pool)]

CARROLL JONATHAN NEIL

9 Woodhouse Square
Leeds LS3 1AD,
Telephone: 0113 2451986
E-mail: clerks@9woodhouse.co.uk
Call Date: Oct 1994, Gray's Inn
Qualifications: [BA, AKC]

CARRON RICHARD BYRON

**11 Bolt Court (also at 7 Stone Buildings
– 1st Floor)**
London EC4A 3DQ,
Telephone: 0171 353 2300
E-mail: boltct11@aol.com
Redhill Chambers
Seloduct House, 30 Station Road, Redhill,
Surrey, RH1 1NF,
Telephone: 01737 780781

**7 Stone Buildings (also at 11 Bolt
Court)**
1st Floor, Lincoln's Inn, London
WC2A 3SZ, Telephone: 0171 242 0961
E-mail:larthur@7stonebuildings.law.co.uk
Call Date: Oct 1992, Middle Temple
Qualifications: [BA (Hons, Cantab)]

CARROTT SYLVESTER EMANUEL

6 King's Bench Walk
Ground, Third & Fourth Floors, Temple,
London EC4Y 7DR,
Telephone: 0171 353 4931/583 0695
Call Date: July 1980, Gray's Inn
Pupil Master
Qualifications: [LLB (Lond)]

CARSS-FRISK MISS MONICA GUNNEL CONSTANCE

Blackstone Chambers
Blackstone House, Temple, London
EC4Y 9BW, Telephone: 0171 583 1770
E-mail:clerks@blackstonechambers.com
Call Date: July 1985, Gray's Inn
Pupil Master
Qualifications: [LLB (Lond) , BCL (Oxon)]

CARSWELL MISS PATRICIA LOUISE

7 Stone Buildings
Ground Floor, Lincoln's Inn, London
WC2A 3SZ, Telephone: 0171 405 3886/
242 3546 E-mail: chaldous@vossnet.co.uk
Call Date: Feb 1993, Middle Temple
Qualifications: [BA (Hons)(Oxon)]

CARTER DAVID JOHN

Arden Chambers
27 John Street, London WC1N 2BL,
Telephone: 020 7242 4244
E-mail:clerks@arden-chambers.law.co.uk
Call Date: Nov 1971, Gray's Inn
Pupil Master
Qualifications: [LLB]

CARTER MISS HOLLY EUGENIE SOPHIA

3 Dr Johnson's Buildings
Ground Floor, Temple, London
EC4Y 7BA, Telephone: 0171 353 4854
E-mail: clerks@3djb.co.uk
Call Date: Oct 1993, Inner Temple
Qualifications: [BA (Manch), CPE]

D

CARTER MISS LESLEY ANN

25-27 Castle Street
1st Floor, Liverpool L2 4TA,
Telephone: 0151 227 5661/051 236 5072
Call Date: Oct 1990, Gray's Inn
Qualifications: [BA (Sheff)]

CARTER MISS LESLEY ANNE

Tindal Chambers
3/5 New Street, Chelmsford, Essex,
CM1 1NT, Telephone: 01245 267742
St Albans Chambers
Dolphin Lodge, Dolphin Yard, Holywell
Hill, St Albans, Herts, AL1 1EX,
Telephone: 01727 843383
Call Date: Nov 1986, Inner Temple
Qualifications: [BA]

CARTER MARTIN RICHARD

40 King Street
Manchester M2 6BA,
Telephone: 0161 832 9082
E-mail: clerks@40kingstreet.co.uk
The Chambers of Philip Raynor QC
5 Park Place, Leeds LS1 2RU,
Telephone: 0113 242 1123
Call Date: Nov 1992, Middle Temple
Qualifications: [BA (Hons)]

CARTER PETER QC (1995)

18 Red Lion Court
(Off Fleet Street), London EC4A 3EB,
Telephone: 0171 520 6000
E-mail: chambers@18rlc.co.uk
Thornwood House
102 New London Road, Chelmsford,
Essex, CM2 0RG,
Telephone: 01245 280880
E-mail: chambers@18rlc.co.uk
Call Date: July 1974, Gray's Inn
Qualifications: [LLB (Lond)]

Fax: 0171 520 6248/9;
Out of hours telephone: chambers
answerphone; DX: 478 Chancery Lane

Types of work: Civil liberties, Crime, Crime –
corporate fraud, Environment

Publications: *Offences of Violence* (Sweet &
Maxwell), 1997

Reported Cases: *DPR Futures*, 1990. One of
first fraud cases to employ moving graphics
to present evidence.

AKBAR, 1993. First of the BCCI cases.
Hancock v Warner, [1996] Cr App R P554,
1996. Whether jury has to agree on partic-
ulars pleaded in conspiracy to defraud.

CARTER PETER BASIL QC (1990)

Fountain Court
Temple, London EC4Y 9DH,
Telephone: 0171 583 3335
E-mail: chambers@fountaincourt.co.uk
Call Date: June 1947, Middle Temple
Qualifications: [BCL; MA (Oxon)]

CARTER RICHARD CHARLES

58 King Street Chambers
1st Floor, Kingsgate House, 51-53 South
King Street, Manchester M2 6DE,
Telephone: 0161 831 7477
Call Date: Nov 1990, Inner Temple
Qualifications: [LLB (Hons)(Manc)]

CARTER MISS ROSALYN FRANCES

St Philip's Chambers
Fountain Court, Steelhouse Lane,
Birmingham B4 6DR,
Telephone: 0121 246 7000
E-mail: clerks@st-philips.co.uk
Call Date: Nov 1994, Lincoln's Inn
Qualifications: [LLB (Hons)(Leeds)]

CARTER MISS SALLY CLAIRE

Eighteen Carlton Crescent
Southampton SO15 2XR,
Telephone: 01703 639001
Call Date: Nov 1994, Inner Temple
Qualifications: [LLB (Soton)]

CARTER WILLIAM ANDREW

23 Essex Street
London WC2R 3AS,
Telephone: 0171 413 0353/836 8366
E-mail:clerks@essexstreet23.demon.co.uk
Call Date: July 1989, Gray's Inn
Pupil Master
Qualifications: [BA (Oxon)]

CARTER-MANNING JEREMY JAMES QC (1993)

9-12 Bell Yard
London WC2A 2LF,
Telephone: 0171 400 1800
E-mail: clerks@bellyard.co.uk
Call Date: Apr 1975, Middle Temple
Recorder

CARTER-STEPHENSON GEORGE ANTHONY QC (1998)

3 Gray's Inn Square
Ground Floor, London WC1R 5AH,
Telephone: 0171 520 5600
E-mail: clerks@3gis.co.uk
Call Date: July 1975, Inner Temple
Qualifications: [LLB (Leeds)]

CARTMELL NICHOLAS JAMES

New Court Chambers
3 Broad Chare, Newcastle upon Tyne
NE1 3DQ, Telephone: 0191 232 1980
Call Date: Oct 1990, Inner Temple
Qualifications: [LLB (Hons)]

CARTWRIGHT DAVID CRISPIAN HIMLEY

5 Pump Court
Ground Floor, Temple, London
EC4Y 7AP, Telephone: 020 7353 2532
E-mail: FivePump@netcomuk.co.uk
Call Date: Nov 1976, Middle Temple
Pupil Master, Assistant Recorder
Qualifications: [MA (Oxon)]

CARTWRIGHT IVAN MATTHEW

Derby Square Chambers
Merchants Court, Derby Square, Liverpool
L2 1TS, Telephone: 0151 709 4222
E-mail:mail.derbysquare@pop3.hiway.co.uk
Call Date: Nov 1993, Gray's Inn
Qualifications: [LLB (Hons)]

CARTWRIGHT JAMES D'ARCY CAYLEY

Fleet Chambers
Mitre House, 44-46 Fleet Street, London
EC4Y 1BN, Telephone: 0171 936 3707
E-mail: rr@fleetchambers.demon.co.uk

Southsea Chambers
PO Box 148, Southsea, Portsmouth,
Hampshire, PO5 2TU,
Telephone: 01705 291261
Call Date: Feb 1968, Gray's Inn
Pupil Master

CARTWRIGHT JOHN MARTIN

Francis Taylor Building
Ground Floor, Temple, London
EC4Y 7BY, Telephone: 0171 353 7768/
7769/2711
E-mail:clerks@francistaylorbuilding.law.co.uk
Call Date: June 1964, Gray's Inn
Pupil Master

CARTWRIGHT NICHOLAS FREDERICK

St Philip's Chambers
Fountain Court, Steelhouse Lane,
Birmingham B4 6DR,
Telephone: 0121 246 7000
E-mail: clerks@st-philips.co.uk
Call Date: July 1986, Middle Temple
Qualifications: [LLB (L'Pool)]

CARTWRIGHT RICHARD JOHN

Queen Elizabeth Building
Ground Floor, Temple, London
EC4Y 9BS,
Telephone: 0171 353 7181 (12 Lines)
Call Date: Nov 1994, Inner Temple
Qualifications: [BA (Hons)(Manch), FCA]

CARTWRIGHT MISS SOPHIE PAMELA

Deans Court Chambers
41-43 Market Place, Preston PR1 1AH,
Telephone: 01772 555163
E-mail: clerks@deanscourt.co.uk
Deans Court Chambers
24 St John Street, Manchester M3 4DF,
Telephone: 0161 214 6000
E-mail: clerks@deanscourt.co.uk
Call Date: 1998, Inner Temple
Qualifications: [LLB (Warw)]

CARTWRIGHT MISS SUZANNE JANE

Holborn Chambers
6 Gate Street, Lincoln's Inn Fields, London
WC2A 3HP, Telephone: 0171 242 6060
Call Date: Oct 1994, Lincoln's Inn
Qualifications: [BA (Hons)(Warw)]

CARUS RODERICK QC (1990)

Chambers of John Hand QC
9 St John Street, Manchester M3 4DN,
Telephone: 0161 955 9000
E-mail: ninesjs@gconnect.com
Call Date: Nov 1971, Gray's Inn
Recorder
Qualifications: [BA (Oxon)]

CARVALHO GOMES MISS ANA ALEXANDRA

St Albans Chambers
Dolphin Lodge, Dolphin Yard, Holywell
Hill, St Albans, Herts, AL1 1EX,
Telephone: 01727 843383
Call Date: Oct 1996, Middle Temple
Qualifications: [LLB (Hons)(Wales)]

CARVILLE OWEN BRENDAN NEVILLE

25-27 Castle Street
1st Floor, Liverpool L2 4TA,
Telephone: 0151 227 5661/051 236 5072
Call Date: July 1980, Inner Temple
Qualifications: [BA]

CASE MRS JANET RUTH

Nicholas Street Chambers
22 Nicholas Street, Chester CH1 2NX,
Telephone: 01244 323886
E-mail: clerks@40king.co.uk
Call Date: July 1975, Inner Temple
Pupil Master, Recorder
Qualifications: [LLB]

CASE MISS JULIE

Exchange Chambers
Pearl Assurance House, Derby Square,
Liverpool L2 9XX,
Telephone: 0151 236 7747
E-mail:exchangechambers@btinternet.com
Call Date: Oct 1990, Middle Temple
Qualifications: [LLB (Leic)]

CASE MISS MAGDALEN MARY CLAIRE

28 St John Street
Manchester M3 4DJ,
Telephone: 0161 834 8418
E-mail: clerk@28stjohnst.co.uk
Call Date: Oct 1992, Middle Temple
Qualifications: [MA (Oxon), Dip Law]

CASE RICHARD JOHN

3 Paper Buildings
Temple, London EC4Y 7EU,
Telephone: 020 7583 8055
E-mail: London@3paper.com
3 Paper Buildings (Winchester)
4 St Peter Street, Winchester SO23 8BW,
Telephone: 01962 868884
E-mail: winchester@3paper.com
3 Paper Buildings (Bournemouth)
20 Lorne Park Road, Bournemouth,
Dorset, BH1 1JN,
Telephone: 01202 292102
E-mail: Bournemouth@3paper.com
3 Paper Buildings (Oxford)
1 Alfred Street, High Street, Oxford
OX1 4EH, Telephone: 01865 793736
E-mail: oxford@3paper.com
Call Date: Oct 1996, Middle Temple
Qualifications: [BA (Hons)(Cantab)]

CASE TOBY EDWARD JAMES

Eighteen Carlton Crescent
Southampton SO15 2XR,
Telephone: 01703 639001
Call Date: Oct 1996, Inner Temple
Qualifications: [LLB (So'ton)]

CASEMENT DAVID JOHN

Exchange Chambers
Pearl Assurance House, Derby Square,
Liverpool L2 9XX,
Telephone: 0151 236 7747
E-mail:exchangechambers@btinternet.com
Call Date: Oct 1992, Middle Temple
Qualifications: [BA (Hons, Oxon)]

CASEY AIDAN PATRICK

1 Crown Office Row
3rd Floor, Temple, London EC4Y 7HH,
Telephone: 0171 583 9292
E-mail: onecor@link.org
Call Date: Nov 1992, Gray's Inn
Qualifications: [LLB]

CASEY DERMOT FINTAN

4 Brick Court
Ground Floor, Temple, London
EC4Y 9AD, Telephone: 0171 797 7766
E-mail: chambers@4brick.co.uk
Call Date: Nov 1994, Middle Temple
Qualifications: [BA (Hons), M.Sc, C.Q.S.W,
Dip Law (City)]

CASEY MISS MAIRIN

St Mary's Chambers
50 High Pavement, Lace Market,
Nottingham NG1 1HW,
Telephone: 0115 9503503
E-mail: clerks@smc.law.co.uk
Call Date: Nov 1989, Inner Temple
Qualifications: [BA, LLB (Galway)]

CASEY NOEL

7 Stone Buildings (also at 11 Bolt Court)
1st Floor, Lincoln's Inn, London
WC2A 3SZ, Telephone: 0171 242 0961
E-mail:larthur@7stonebuildings.law.co.uk
11 Bolt Court (also at 7 Stone Buildings – 1st Floor)
London EC4A 3DQ,
Telephone: 0171 353 2300
E-mail: boltct11@aol.com
Redhill Chambers
Seloduct House, 30 Station Road, Redhill,
Surrey, RH1 1NF,
Telephone: 01737 780781
Call Date: Nov 1995, Lincoln's Inn
Qualifications: [BA (Hons)]

CASH MISS JOANNE CATHERINE

Farrar's Building
Temple, London EC4Y 7BD,
Telephone: 0171 583 9241
E-mail:chambers@farrarsbuilding.co.uk
Call Date: Oct 1994, Gray's Inn
Qualifications: [BA (Hons) (Oxon)]

CASSEL TIMOTHY FELIX HAROLD QC (1988)

Five Paper Buildings
1st Floor, Five Paper Bldgs, Temple,
London EC4Y 7HB,
Telephone: 0171 583 6117
E-mail:clerks@5-paperbuildings.law.co.uk
Call Date: July 1965, Lincoln's Inn

CASSIDY PATRICK STEPHEN

Kenworthy's Chambers
83 Bridge Street, Manchester M3 2RF,
Telephone: 0161 832 4036/834 6954
E-mail: clerks@kenworthys.co.uk
Call Date: July 1982, Lincoln's Inn
Pupil Master
Qualifications: [BA]

CASTLE PETER BOLTON

Chambers of Mr Peter Crampin QC
Ground Floor, 11 New Square, Lincoln's
Inn, London WC2A 3QB,
Telephone: 020 7831 0081
E-mail: 11newsquare.co.uk
Call Date: July 1970, Middle Temple
Pupil Master
Qualifications: [LLB (Lond)]

CASTLE MISS SUSAN ELIZABETH

33 Bedford Row
London WC1R 4JH,
Telephone: 0171 242 6476
E-mail:clerks@bedfordrow33.demon.co.uk
Call Date: July 1986, Middle Temple
Pupil Master
Qualifications: [MA]

CASWELL BENJAMIN CECIL

No. 6
6 Park Square, Leeds LS1 2LW,
Telephone: 0113 2459763
E-mail: chambers@no6.co.uk
Call Date: Oct 1993, Middle Temple
Qualifications: [BA (Hons)(Oxon), MA (Lond)]

CASWELL MATTHEW

11 King's Bench Walk
1st Floor, Temple, London EC4Y 7EQ,
Telephone: 0171 353 3337
E-mail: fmuller11@aol.com
11 King's Bench Walk
3 Park Court, Park Cross Street, Leeds
LS1 2QH, Telephone: 0113 297 1200
Call Date: May 1968, Middle Temple
Pupil Master
Qualifications: [MA]

CASWELL MISS REBECCA MARY

11 King's Bench Walk
1st Floor, Temple, London EC4Y 7EQ,
Telephone: 0171 353 3337
E-mail: fmuller11@aol.com
11 King's Bench Walk
3 Park Court, Park Cross Street, Leeds
LS1 2QH, Telephone: 0113 297 1200
Call Date: July 1983, Middle Temple
Pupil Master
Qualifications: [MA (Oxon)]

CASWELL TIMOTHY CHARLES

8 King's Bench Walk North
1 Park Square East, Leeds LS1 2NE,
Telephone: 0113 2439797
8 King's Bench Walk
2nd Floor, Temple, London EC4Y 7DU,
Telephone: 0171 797 8888
Call Date: 1994, Inner Temple
Qualifications: [BA (Bradford), CPE
(Huddersfield)]

CATCHPOLE STUART PAUL

39 Essex Street
London WC2R 3AT,
Telephone: 0171 832 1111
E-mail: clerks@39essex.co.uk
Call Date: July 1987, Inner Temple
Pupil Master
Qualifications: [BA (Dunelm)]

Fax: 0171 353 3978;
Out of hours telephone: 0171 832 1159;
DX: 298 Chancery Lane;
Other comms: E-mail sc@39essex.co.uk

Types of work: Administrative, Arbitration,
Commercial litigation, Common law
(general), Construction, Immigration,
Insurance, Professional negligence

Languages spoken: French, French

Publications: *Halsbury's Laws* (4th edition),
Crown Proceedings, 1998 reissue;
Halsbury's Laws (4th edition), Crown
Proceedings, 1988 reissue; *Halsbury's
Laws* (4th edition), Administrative Law
(research assistant only), 1989 reissue

Reported Cases: *M v Home Office*, [1994] AC
377 (HL), 1993. Leading authority on
whether injunctive relief is available against
the Crown in judicial review proceedings.
*R v Secretary of State for the Home Department
ex parte Fayed*, [1997] I All ER 228,
1997. Acting for the Respondent in judicial
review proceedings in connection with an
application for British citizenship.
*Davy Offshore Ltd v Emerald Field
Contracting Ltd*, [1992] 2 Lloyd's Rep 142,
1992. Dispute as to when property passed
under a contract for the construction and
supply of an offshore oil platform.
*R v Secretary of State for the Home Department
ex parte Hill*, [1997] 2 All ER 638,
1997. Acting for Respondent on application for judicial review of a decision to
issue a certificate under s 671 of the Extradition Act 1989.
Giles v Thompson, [1994] 1 AC 142, 1993.
Consideration of whether certain agreements were champertous and thus
contrary to public policy.

I have a First Class Honours Degree in Law
from Durham University (1986).

I have a very broad range of experience
both as an advocate and in an advisory
capacity. My practice covers both public law
and private law disputes. On the private law
side, I have considerable experience of
large commercial, construction industry,
insurance and professional negligence
claims. On the public law side, I was
appointed to the Supplemental Treasury
Panel of Counsel (Common Law) in May
1992 (transferred to the Treasury 'B' Panel
in November 1998). In July 1999 I was
appointed to be Junior Counsel to the
Crown ('A' Panel). I have considerable
experience of acting for central Government and other public authorities
including numerous appearances in applications for judicial review.

In addition, I have been involved in two
large Public Inquiries, appearing as Junior
Counsel for Sheffield Wednesday FC at the
Inquiry into the disaster at the
Hillsborough Stadium in the summer of
1989 (and, subsequently, at the inquests
into the deaths at the stadium). I am
currently Counsel for the Ministry of Agriculture Fisheries and Food at the BSE
Inquiry (appointed February 1998).

CATFORD GORDON BAXTER

One Paper Buildings
Ground Floor, Temple, London
EC4Y 7EP, Telephone: 0171 583 7355
E-mail: clerks@1pb.co.uk
Call Date: July 1980, Lincoln's Inn
Pupil Master
Qualifications: [LLB (Lond)]

CATON PETER CHARLES DAVID

9-12 Bell Yard
London WC2A 2LF,
Telephone: 0171 400 1800
E-mail: clerks@bellyard.co.uk
Call Date: May 1963, Gray's Inn
Pupil Master
Qualifications: [MA (Oxon)]

CATTAN PHILIP DAVID

28 St John Street
Manchester M3 4DJ,
Telephone: 0161 834 8418
E-mail: clerk@28stjohnst.co.uk
Call Date: Nov 1970, Gray's Inn
Pupil Master, Recorder
Qualifications: [LLB (Manch)]

CATTERSON MISS MARIE THERESE

5 Essex Court
1st Floor, Temple, London EC4Y 9AH,
Telephone: 0171 410 2000
E-mail: barristers@5essexcourt.co.uk
Call Date: Nov 1972, Gray's Inn
Pupil Master, Recorder
Qualifications: [LLB (Lond)]

CATTLE DAVID JAMES

4 King's Bench Walk
Ground/First Floor/Basement, Temple,
London EC4Y 7DL,
Telephone: 0171 822 8822
E-mail: 4kbw@barristersatlaw.com
Call Date: July 1975, Middle Temple
Qualifications: [BA (Cantab)]

CAUDLE JOHN ARTHUR

3 Hare Court
1 Little Essex Street, London WC2R 3LD,
Telephone: 0171 395 2000
Call Date: Nov 1976, Middle Temple
Pupil Master
Qualifications: [LLB (Lond)]

CAULFIELD PAUL ANTHONY

Trinity Chambers
9-12 Trinity Chare, Quayside, Newcastle
upon Tyne NE1 3DF,
Telephone: 0191 232 1927
E-mail: info@trinitychambers.co.uk
Call Date: May 1996, Middle Temple
Qualifications: [LLB (Hons)]

CAUN LAWRENCE

Lamb Chambers
Lamb Building, Temple, London
EC4Y 7AS, Telephone: 020 7797 8300
E-mail: lambchambers@link.org
Call Date: Nov 1977, Lincoln's Inn
Pupil Master
Qualifications: [MA (Oxon)]

CAUSER JOHN CHARLES

23 Essex Street
London WC2R 3AS,
Telephone: 0171 413 0353/836 8366
E-mail:clerks@essexstreet23.demon.co.uk
Call Date: July 1979, Inner Temple
Qualifications: [BA (Lond)]

CAVANAGH JOHN PATRICK

11 King's Bench Walk
Temple, London EC4Y 7EQ,
Telephone: 0171 632 8500/583 0610
E-mail: clerksroom@11kbw.com
Call Date: Nov 1985, Middle Temple
Pupil Master
Qualifications: [MA (Oxon), LLM, (Cantab)]

CAVE JEREMY STEPHEN

1 Crown Office Row
Ground Floor, Temple, London
EC4Y 7HH, Telephone: 0171 797 7500
E-mail: mail@onecrownofficerow.com
Crown Office Row Chambers
Blenheim House, 120 Church Street,
Brighton, Sussex, BN1 1WH,
Telephone: 01273 625625
E-mail: crownofficerow@clara.net
Call Date: Nov 1992, Middle Temple
Qualifications: [LLB (Hons, Manch)]

CAVE MISS PATRICIA ANN

7 Stone Buildings (also at 11 Bolt Court)
1st Floor, Lincoln's Inn, London
WC2A 3SZ, Telephone: 0171 242 0961
E-mail:larthur@7stonebuildings.law.co.uk
11 Bolt Court (also at 7 Stone Buildings – 1st Floor)
London EC4A 3DQ,
Telephone: 0171 353 2300
E-mail: boltct11@aol.com
Redhill Chambers
Seloduct House, 30 Station Road, Redhill,
Surrey, RH1 1NF,
Telephone: 01737 780781
Call Date: Nov 1989, Middle Temple
Qualifications: [BA Hons [Manc], Dip in Law]

CAVENDER DAVID JOHN

One Essex Court
Ground Floor, Temple, London
EC4Y 9AR, Telephone: 020 7583 2000
E-mail: clerks@oneessexcourt.co.uk
Call Date: July 1993, Middle Temple
Qualifications: [LLB (Lond)]

CAVENDER SIMON JUSTIN

Phoenix Chambers
First Floor, Gray's Inn Chambers, Gray's
Inn, London WC1R 5JA,
Telephone: 0171 404 7888
E-mail:clerks@phoenix-chambers.co.uk
Call Date: Oct 1992, Middle Temple
Qualifications: [LL.B (Hons)(Exon)]

CAWLEY NEIL ROBERT LOUDOUN

169 Temple Chambers
Temple Avenue, London EC4Y 0DA,
Telephone: 0171 583 7644
Milton Keynes Chambers
61 London Road, Loughton, Milton
Keynes, Buckinghamshire, MK5 8AF,
Telephone: 01908 664 128
E-mail: neil_cawley@compuserve.com
Call Date: Nov 1992, Inner Temple
Qualifications: [LLB (Buckingham)]

CAWS EIAN RICHARD EDWIN

4 Breams Buildings
London EC4A 1AQ,
Telephone: 0171 353 5835/430 1221
E-mail:breams@4breamsbuildings.law.co.uk
Call Date: Nov 1974, Inner Temple
Pupil Master
Qualifications: [BA (Oxon)]

CAWSON PETER MARK

St James's Chambers
68 Quay Street, Manchester M3 3EJ,
Telephone: 0161 834 7000
E-mail: clerks@stjameschambers.co.uk
12 New Square
Lincoln's Inn, London WC2A 3SW,
Telephone: 0171 419 1212
E-mail: chambers@12newsquare.co.uk

Park Lane Chambers
19 Westgate, Leeds LS1 2RD,
Telephone: 0113 2285000
E-mail:clerks@parklanechambers.co.uk
Call Date: 1982, Lincoln's Inn
Pupil Master, Assistant Recorder
Qualifications: [LLB]

CAYFORD PHILIP JOHN BERKELEY

29 Bedford Row Chambers
London WC1R 4HE,
Telephone: 0171 831 2626
Call Date: July 1975, Middle Temple
Pupil Master
Qualifications: [BA]

CELLAN-JONES DEINIOL JAMES

One King's Bench Walk
1st Floor, Temple, London EC4Y 7DB,
Telephone: 0171 936 1500
E-mail: ddear@1kbw.co.uk
Call Date: Nov 1988, Middle Temple
Qualifications: [BA (Oxon)]

CHADD PAUL QC (1972)

Theatre House
Percival Road, Clifton, Bristol BS8 3LE,
Telephone: 0117 974 1553
Colleton Chambers
Colleton Crescent, Exeter, Devon,
EX2 4DG, Telephone: 01392 274898/9
Call Date: July 1952, Lincoln's Inn
Qualifications: [LLB]

CHADWICK CHARLES

Mitre House Chambers
15-19 Devereux Court, London WC2R 3JJ,
Telephone: 0171 583 8233
Call Date: Nov 1992, Lincoln's Inn
Qualifications: [BSc (Pittsburgh), MBA, LLB
(Hons)(Lond)]

CHADWICK MISS EMMA JANE

King's Chambers
5a Gildredge Road, Eastbourne, East
Sussex, BN21 4RB,
Telephone: 01323 416053
Call Date: Oct 1996, Inner Temple
Qualifications: [LLB (Sheff) (Hons)]

CHADWICK MISS JOANNA CERIDWEN

5 Fountain Court
Steelhouse Lane, Birmingham B4 6DR,
Telephone: 0121 606 0500
E-mail:clerks@5fountaincourt.law.co.uk
Call Date: Nov 1988, Middle Temple
Qualifications: [LLB (Leeds)]

CHADWIN JAMES ARMSTRONG QC (1976)

Park Court Chambers
16 Park Place, Leeds LS1 2SJ,
Telephone: 0113 2433277
6 Gray's Inn Square
Ground Floor, Gray's Inn, London
WC1R 5AZ, Telephone: 0171 242 1052
E-mail: 6graysinn@clara.co.uk
Broad Chare
33 Broad Chare, Newcastle upon Tyne
NE1 3DQ, Telephone: 0191 232 0541
E-mail:clerks@broadcharechambers.law.co.uk
Call Date: Feb 1958, Gray's Inn
Recorder
Qualifications: [MA, LLB]

CHAHALL MISS JASBINDER PAL

Two Garden Court
1st Floor, Middle Temple, London
EC4Y 9BL, Telephone: 0171 353 1633
E-mail:barristers@2gardenct.law.co.uk
Call Date: Nov 1991, Middle Temple
Qualifications: [BA Hons (Econ), LLM
(Nott'm), Dip Law]

CHAISTY PAUL

40 King Street
Manchester M2 6BA,
Telephone: 0161 832 9082
E-mail: clerks@40kingstreet.co.uk
The Chambers of Philip Raynor QC
5 Park Place, Leeds LS1 2RU,
Telephone: 0113 242 1123
Call Date: July 1982, Lincoln's Inn
Pupil Master
Qualifications: [LLB (Notts), BCL (Oxon)]

CHAIZE TRISTAN PAUL

5 Pump Court
Ground Floor, Temple, London
EC4Y 7AP, Telephone: 020 7353 2532
E-mail: FivePump@netcomuk.co.uk
Call Date: Nov 1977, Inner Temple
Pupil Master

CHALLEN MISS LYDIA ANN

Arden Chambers
27 John Street, London WC1N 2BL,
Telephone: 020 7242 4244
E-mail:clerks@arden-chambers.law.co.uk
Call Date: Oct 1995, Gray's Inn
Qualifications: [MA (Cantab), M.Jur (Oxon)]

CHALLENGER COLIN WESTCOTT

Bridewell Chambers
2 Bridewell Place, London EC4V 6AP,
Telephone: 020 7797 8800
E-mail:HughesGage@bridewell.law.co.uk
Call Date: Nov 1970, Inner Temple
Pupil Master
Qualifications: [LLB (Lond), MBA,
(Berkeley)]

CHALLINOR ROBERT MICHAEL

3 Fountain Court
Steelhouse Lane, Birmingham B4 6DR,
Telephone: 0121 236 5854
Call Date: July 1974, Gray's Inn
Pupil Master, Recorder
Qualifications: [LLB]

CHALMERS GAVIN JAMES

Albion Chambers
Broad Street, Bristol BS1 1DR,
Telephone: 0117 9272144
Call Date: July 1978, Inner Temple
Pupil Master
Qualifications: [BA (Dunelm)]

CHALMERS MISS SUZANNE FRANCES

Two Crown Office Row
Ground Floor, Temple, London
EC4Y 7HJ, Telephone: 020 7797 8100
E-mail: mail@2cor.co.uk, or to individual
barristers at: [barrister's
surname]@2cor.co.uk
Call Date: Oct 1995, Gray's Inn
Qualifications: [BA]

D

CHAMBERLAIN MS EMMA JANE MARY

8 Gray's Inn Square
Gray's Inn, London WC1R 5AZ,
Telephone: 0171 242 3529
Call Date: 1998, Lincoln's Inn
Qualifications: [BA (Hons)(Oxon)]

CHAMBERLAIN FRANCIS GEORGE NEVILLE

3 Paper Buildings
Temple, London EC4Y 7EU,
Telephone: 020 7583 8055
E-mail: London@3paper.com
3 Paper Buildings (Winchester)
4 St Peter Street, Winchester SO23 8BW,
Telephone: 01962 868884
E-mail: winchester@3paper.com
3 Paper Buildings (Bournemouth)
20 Lorne Park Road, Bournemouth,
Dorset, BH1 1JN,
Telephone: 01202 292102
E-mail: Bournemouth@3paper.com
3 Paper Buildings (Oxford)
1 Alfred Street, High Street, Oxford
OX1 4EH, Telephone: 01865 793736
E-mail: oxford@3paper.com
Call Date: July 1985, Lincoln's Inn
Pupil Master
Qualifications: [LLB (Leeds)]

CHAMBERLAIN MARTIN DANIEL

4-5 Gray's Inn Square
Ground Floor, Gray's Inn, London
WC1R 5JP, Telephone: 0171 404 5252
E-mail:chambers@4-5graysinnsquare.co.uk
Call Date: 1997, Middle Temple
Qualifications: [BA (Hons)(Oxon), CPE
(Lond)]

CHAMBERLAYNE PATRICK ALLIN GERRARD TANKERVI

6 Pump Court
1st Floor, Temple, London EC4Y 7AR,
Telephone: 0171 797 8400
E-mail: clerks@6pumpcourt.co.uk
6-8 Mill Street
Maidstone, Kent, ME15 6XH,
Telephone: 01622 688094
Call Date: Nov 1992, Inner Temple
Qualifications: [BA (Hons)(Cantab), MA
(Cantab)]

CHAMBERS ADAM RUSHBY

12 King's Bench Walk
Temple, London EC4Y 7EL,
Telephone: 0171 583 0811
E-mail: chambers@12kbw.co.uk
Call Date: July 1989, Middle Temple
Pupil Master
Qualifications: [BA (Leeds), Dip Law]

CHAMBERS DOMINIC KERN

Brick Court Chambers
7-8 Essex Street, London WC2R 3LD,
Telephone: 0171 379 3550
E-mail: [surname]@brickcourt.co.uk
Call Date: Nov 1987, Gray's Inn
Pupil Master
Qualifications: [LLB (Lond)]

CHAMBERS GREGORY JOHN ELLIS

1 Crown Office Row
Ground Floor, Temple, London
EC4Y 7HH, Telephone: 0171 797 7500
E-mail: mail@onecrownofficerow.com
Crown Office Row Chambers
Blenheim House, 120 Church Street,
Brighton, Sussex, BN1 1WH,
Telephone: 01273 625625
E-mail: crownofficerow@clara.net
Call Date: July 1973, Middle Temple
Qualifications: [MA (Dublin)]

CHAMBERS JONATHAN

4 Essex Court
Temple, London EC4Y 9AJ,
Telephone: 020 7797 7970
E-mail: clerks@4essexcourt.law.co.uk
Call Date: Oct 1996, Inner Temple
Qualifications: [BA(Oxon), C.P.L.S., BCL
(Oxon)]

CHAMBERS MICHAEL LAURENCE

Sedan House
Stanley Place, Chester CH1 2LU,
Telephone: 01244 320480/348282
Call Date: July 1980, Lincoln's Inn
Pupil Master, Assistant Recorder
Qualifications: [MA (Oxon)]

CHAMBERS NICHOLAS MORDAUNT QC (1985)

Brick Court Chambers
7-8 Essex Street, London WC2R 3LD,
Telephone: 0171 379 3550
E-mail: [surname]@brickcourt.co.uk
Call Date: July 1966, Gray's Inn
Recorder
Qualifications: [MA (Oxon)]

CHAMBERS PAUL VICTOR

24a St John Street
Manchester M3 4DF,
Telephone: 0161 833 9628
Call Date: Nov 1973, Gray's Inn
Pupil Master
Qualifications: [BA Hons]

CHAMPION MISS DEBORAH CURTIS

3 Hare Court
1 Little Essex Street, London WC2R 3LD,
Telephone: 0171 395 2000
Call Date: July 1970, Gray's Inn
Recorder

CHAMPION MS ROWENA ELIZABETH

Chambers of Norman Palmer
2 Field Court, Gray's Inn, London
WC1R 5BB, Telephone: 0171 405 6114
E-mail: fieldct2@netcomuk.co.uk
Call Date: Feb 1990, Middle Temple
Qualifications: [BSc]

CHAN MISS ABBERLAINE DIANNE PAO CHE

9-12 Bell Yard
London WC2A 2LF,
Telephone: 0171 400 1800
E-mail: clerks@bellyard.co.uk
Call Date: July 1979, Gray's Inn
Qualifications: [LLB (Bris)]

CHAN MISS SUSAN

13 King's Bench Walk
1st Floor, Temple, London EC4Y 7EN,
Telephone: 0171 353 7204
E-mail: clerks@13kbw.law.co.uk

King's Bench Chambers
32 Beaumont Street, Oxford OX1 2NP,
Telephone: 01865 311066
E-mail: clerks@kbc-oxford.law.co.uk
Call Date: Oct 1994, Gray's Inn
Qualifications: [BA]

CHANDLER ALEXANDER CHARLES ROSS

One Garden Court Family Law Chambers
Ground Floor, Temple, London
EC4Y 9BJ, Telephone: 0171 797 7900
E-mail: clerks@onegardencourt.co.uk
Call Date: Oct 1995, Middle Temple
Qualifications: [MA (Oxon), Dip Law (City)]

CHANDLER MISS KATE

12 King's Bench Walk
Temple, London EC4Y 7EL,
Telephone: 0171 583 0811
E-mail: chambers@12kbw.co.uk
Call Date: Oct 1990, Inner Temple
Qualifications: [LLB (Lond)]

CHANDRAN MISS PAROSHA

Bridewell Chambers
2 Bridewell Place, London EC4V 6AP,
Telephone: 020 7797 8800
E-mail:HughesGage@bridewell.law.co.uk
Call Date: Oct 1997, Lincoln's Inn
Qualifications: [LLB (Hons), LLM (Lond),
Dip. Human Rights, (Strasborg)]

CHANTEAU MISS DIANE HELENE GENEVIEVE MARJORIE

55 Temple Chambers
Temple Avenue, London EC4Y 0HP,
Telephone: 0171 353 7400
Call Date: 1997, Middle Temple
Qualifications: [LLB (Hons)(Westmin)]

CHAPLAIN MISS JAYNE LOUISE

Broadway House Chambers
Broadway House, 9 Bank Street, Bradford,
West Yorkshire, BD1 1TW,
Telephone: 01274 722560
E-mail: clerks@broadwayhouse.co.uk

Broadway House Chambers
31 Park Square West, Leeds LS1 2PF,
Telephone: 0113 246 2600
Call Date: Nov 1995, Middle Temple
Qualifications: [MA (Hons)(Cantab)]

CHAPLIN ADRIAN ROLAND

9-12 Bell Yard
London WC2A 2LF,
Telephone: 0171 400 1800
E-mail: clerks@bellyard.co.uk
Call Date: Oct 1990, Gray's Inn
Qualifications: [B.A (CANTAB)]

CHAPLIN JOHN LAWTON

24a St John Street
Manchester M3 4DF,
Telephone: 0161 833 9628
Call Date: Nov 1986, Inner Temple
Qualifications: [BA (Exon)]

CHAPMAN JEFFREY PAUL

Fountain Court
Temple, London EC4Y 9DH,
Telephone: 0171 583 3335
E-mail: chambers@fountaincourt.co.uk
Call Date: Nov 1989, Middle Temple
Qualifications: [BA Hons (Sussex), LLM
(Cantab)]

CHAPMAN MATTHEW JAMES

Barnard's Inn Chambers
6th Floor, Halton House, 20-23 Holborn,
London EC1N 2JD,
Telephone: 0171 369 6969
E-mail: clerks@biclaw.co.uk
Call Date: Oct 1994, Gray's Inn
Qualifications: [LLB, LLM]

CHAPMAN MICHAEL ANDREW

Barnard's Inn Chambers
6th Floor, Halton House, 20-23 Holborn,
London EC1N 2JD,
Telephone: 0171 369 6969
E-mail: clerks@biclaw.co.uk
Call Date: Nov 1994, Middle Temple
Qualifications: [MA]

CHAPMAN NICHOLAS JOHN

29 Bedford Row Chambers
London WC1R 4HE,
Telephone: 0171 831 2626
Call Date: Oct 1990, Inner Temple
Qualifications: [BSc (UCL), Dip Law (City)]

CHAPMAN MS REBECCA KATE

14 Tooks Court
Cursitor St, London EC4A 1LB,
Telephone: 0171 405 8828
E-mail: clerks@tooks.law.co.uk
Call Date: Nov 1990, Inner Temple
Qualifications: [BA (York), Dip Law (PCL)]

CHAPMAN RENNICK ANDREW

Lloyds House Chambers
3rd Floor, 18 Lloyds House, Lloyd Street,
Manchester M2 5WA,
Telephone: 0161 839 3371
Call Date: Mar 1997, Middle Temple
Qualifications: [LLB (Hons)]

CHAPMAN SIMON CHARLES

22 Old Buildings
Lincoln's Inn, London WC2A 3UJ,
Telephone: 0171 831 0222
Call Date: July 1988, Inner Temple
Qualifications: [LLB (Bristol)]

CHAPMAN VIVIAN ROBERT

9 Stone Buildings
Lincoln's Inn, London WC2A 3NN,
Telephone: 0171 404 5055
E-mail: clerks@9stoneb.law.co.uk
2 New Street
Leicester LE1 5NA,
Telephone: 0116 2625906
E-mail: clerks@2newstreet.co.uk
Call Date: July 1970, Middle Temple
Pupil Master, Recorder
Qualifications: [MA LLM (Cantab)]

CHAPPELL MISS JESSICA KATHARINE

Twenty-Four Old Buildings
Ground Floor, Lincoln's Inn, London
WC2A 3UP, Telephone: 0171 404 0946
E-mail:clerks@24oldbuildings.law.co.uk
Call Date: 1997, Lincoln's Inn
Qualifications: [BA (Hons)]

CHAPPLE JAMES MALCOLM DUNDAS

1 New Square
Ground Floor, Lincoln's Inn, London
WC2A 3SA, Telephone: 0171 405 0884/5/6/
7 E-mail: clerks@1newsquare.law.co.uk
Call Date: Nov 1975, Gray's Inn
Pupil Master
Qualifications: [BSc (Hons), FCIArb]

CHARALAMBOUS CONSTANDINO

1 Gray's Inn Square
Ground Floor, London WC1R 5AA,
Telephone: 0171 405 8946/7/8
Call Date: Oct 1990, Middle Temple
Qualifications: [LLB]

CHARBIT MISS VALERIE JUDITH

3 Hare Court
1 Little Essex Street, London WC2R 3LD,
Telephone: 0171 395 2000
Call Date: Oct 1992, Middle Temple
Qualifications: [LL.B (Hons, Sheff)]

CHARKHAM GRAHAM HAROLD

20 Essex Street
London WC2R 3AL,
Telephone: 0171 583 9294
E-mail: clerks@20essexst.com
Call Date: May 1993, Inner Temple
Qualifications: [BSc (Bristol)]

CHARLES MS DEBORAH ANN

6 Pump Court
1st Floor, Temple, London EC4Y 7AR,
Telephone: 0171 797 8400
E-mail: clerks@6pumpcourt.co.uk
6-8 Mill Street
Maidstone, Kent, ME15 6XH,
Telephone: 01622 688094
E-mail: annexe@6pumpcourt.co.uk
Call Date: Oct 1996, Lincoln's Inn
Qualifications: [BA (Hons)(Warw), CPE
(Middx)]

CHARLES HENRY FREDERICK

199 Strand
London WC2R 1DR,
Telephone: 0171 379 9779
E-mail: chambers@199strand.co.uk
Call Date: Nov 1987, Inner Temple
Pupil Master
Qualifications: [LLB, LLM (Lond)]

CHARLTON ALEXANDER MURRAY

4 Pump Court
Temple, London EC4Y 7AN,
Telephone: 020 7842 5555
E-mail:chambers@4pumpcourt.law.co.uk
Call Date: July 1983, Middle Temple
Pupil Master
Qualifications: [MA (St Andrews), Dip Law
(City)]

CHARLTON MISS JUDITH ANNE DOROTHY

New Court
Temple, London EC4Y 9BE,
Telephone: 0171 583 5123/0510
Call Date: Nov 1991, Inner Temple
Pupil Master
Qualifications: [LLB (Lond)]

CHARLTON TIMOTHY ROGER QC (1993)

Brick Court Chambers
7-8 Essex Street, London WC2R 3LD,
Telephone: 0171 379 3550
E-mail: [surname]@brickcourt.co.uk
Call Date: Nov 1974, Inner Temple
Qualifications: [BA (Oxon)]

CHARLTON WILLIAM WINGATE HUGO

5 Pump Court
Ground Floor, Temple, London
EC4Y 7AP, Telephone: 020 7353 2532
E-mail: FivePump@netcomuk.co.uk
Call Date: July 1978, Gray's Inn
Qualifications: [BA (York)]

CHARLWOOD SPIKE LLEWELLYN

4 Paper Buildings
Ground Floor, Temple, London
EC4Y 7EX, Telephone: 0171 353 3366/
583 7155
E-mail: clerks@4paperbuildings.com
Call Date: Nov 1994, Inner Temple
Qualifications: [BA (Law), MA (Cantab)]

CHARMAN ANDREW JULIAN

St Philip's Chambers
Fountain Court, Steelhouse Lane,
Birmingham B4 6DR,
Telephone: 0121 246 7000
E-mail: clerks@st-philips.co.uk
Call Date: 1994, Lincoln's Inn
Qualifications: [MA (Cantab), A.C.I.Arb]

CHATTERJEE MISS ADREEJA JULIA

3 Fountain Court
Steelhouse Lane, Birmingham B4 6DR,
Telephone: 0121 236 5854
Call Date: Nov 1997, Gray's Inn
Qualifications: [BA (Cantab)]

CHATTERJEE DR CHARLES

**1 Gray's Inn Square, Chambers of the
Baroness Scotland of Asthal QC**
1st Floor, London WC1R 5AG,
Telephone: 0171 405 3000
E-mail: clerks@onegrays.demon.co.uk
Call Date: Nov 1992, Inner Temple
Qualifications: [LLB, LLM, LLM, PhD]

CHATTERJEE MISS MIRA

4 Brick Court
Temple, London EC4Y 9AD,
Telephone: 0171 797 8910
E-mail: medhurst@dial.pipex.com
Call Date: Nov 1973, Middle Temple
Pupil Master

CHATTERTON MARK

Martins Building
2nd Floor, No 4 Water Street, Liverpool
L2 3SP, Telephone: 0151 236 5818/4919
Call Date: July 1983, Gray's Inn
Qualifications: [LLB (L'Pool)]

CHAUDHRY FAROOQ AHMAD

27 Rose Grove
Bury, Greater Manchester, BL8 2UJ,
Telephone: 0161 763 4739
Call Date: July 1970, Lincoln's Inn

CHAUDHRY MISS SABUHI ASHFAQ

Hardwicke Building
New Square, Lincoln's Inn, London
WC2A 3SB, Telephone: 020 7242 2523
E-mail: clerks@hardwicke.co.uk
Call Date: Oct 1993, Lincoln's Inn
Qualifications: [LLB (Hons)(Lond)]

CHAUDHRY ZIA UDDIN

India Buildings Chambers
Water Street, Liverpool L2 0XG,
Telephone: 0151 243 6000
E-mail: clerks@chambers.u-net.com
Call Date: Nov 1991, Inner Temple
Qualifications: [LLB (Hons)(Manch)]

CHAUDHURI AVIRUP

1 Middle Temple Lane
Temple, London EC4Y 1LT,
Telephone: 0171 583 0659 (12 Lines)
E-mail: chambers@1mtl.co.uk
Call Date: Feb 1990, Middle Temple
Qualifications: [LLB Hons [Lond]]

CHAUDHURI ROBIN GORA

New Walk Chambers
27 New Walk, Leicester LE1 6TE,
Telephone: 0116 2559144
Call Date: Nov 1988, Lincoln's Inn
Qualifications: [BA Hons (Leics), Dip Law
(City)]

CHAVASSE MISS HILARY ANN

3 Fountain Court
Steelhouse Lane, Birmingham B4 6DR,
Telephone: 0121 236 5854
Call Date: May 1971, Gray's Inn
Pupil Master
Qualifications: [LLB (Bristol)]

CHAWATAMA SYDNEY

1 Crown Office Row
Ground Floor, Temple, London
EC4Y 7HH, Telephone: 0171 797 7500
E-mail: mail@onecrownofficerow.com
Call Date: Oct 1994, Middle Temple
Qualifications: [LLB (Hons)(Essex)]

CHAWLA MUKUL

9-12 Bell Yard
London WC2A 2LF,
Telephone: 0171 400 1800
E-mail: clerks@bellyard.co.uk
Call Date: July 1983, Gray's Inn
Pupil Master
Qualifications: [LLB (Lond)]

CHEAH ALBERT SENG HEE

Chambers of Geoffrey Hawker
46/48 Essex Street, London WC2R 3GH,
Telephone: 0171 583 8899
Call Date: Nov 1989, Inner Temple
Qualifications: [LLB (Hons) (UCL), LLM
(LSE)]

CHEEMA MISS PARMJIT KAUR

1 Hare Court
Ground Floor, Temple, London
EC4Y 7BE, Telephone: 0171 353 3982/
5324
Call Date: July 1989, Gray's Inn
Pupil Master
Qualifications: [LLB [Lond]]

CHEETHAM JAMES SIMON

10 King's Bench Walk
1st Floor, Temple, London EC4Y 7EB,
Telephone: 0171 353 2501
Call Date: Oct 1991, Middle Temple
Qualifications: [MA]

CHEETHAM MISS JULIA ANN

Cobden House Chambers
19 Quay Street, Manchester M3 3HN,
Telephone: 0161 833 6000
E-mail: clerks@cobden.co.uk
Call Date: Oct 1990, Lincoln's Inn
Qualifications: [LLB (Nott'm)]

CHELTENHAM MS JACQUELINE MIRANDA

John Street Chambers
2 John Street, London WC1N 2HJ,
Telephone: 0171 242 1911
E-mail:john.street_chambers@virgin.net
Call Date: Nov 1992, Middle Temple
Qualifications: [BA (Hons, Dunelm)]

CHERRILL MRS BEVERLEY SUSAN

Chichester Chambers
12 North Pallant, Chichester, West Sussex,
PO19 1TQ, Telephone: 01243 784538
E-mail:clerks@chichesterchambers.law.co.uk
Call Date: Oct 1996, Middle Temple
Qualifications: [BA (Hons)(Sussex)]

CHERRILL RICHARD

9-12 Bell Yard
London WC2A 2LF,
Telephone: 0171 400 1800
E-mail: clerks@bellyard.co.uk
Call Date: July 1965, Middle Temple
Qualifications: [MA (Cantab), LLB]

CHERRY JOHN MITCHELL QC (1988)

8 Stone Buildings
Lincoln's Inn, London WC2A 3TA,
Telephone: 0171 831 9881
E-mail: alanl@8stonebuildings.law.uk
Call Date: Nov 1961, Gray's Inn
Recorder

CHERRYMAN JOHN RICHARD QC (1982)

4 Breams Buildings
London EC4A 1AQ,
Telephone: 0171 353 5835/430 1221
E-mail:breams@4breamsbuildings.law.co.uk
Call Date: June 1955, Gray's Inn
Recorder
Qualifications: [LLB]

CHERRYMAN NICHOLAS CHARLES

Twenty-Four Old Buildings
Ground Floor, Lincoln's Inn, London
WC2A 3UP, Telephone: 0171 404 0946
E-mail:clerks@24oldbuildings.law.co.uk
Call Date: Nov 1991, Lincoln's Inn
Qualifications: [Ba (Hons)]

CHESHIRE ANTHONY PETER

199 Strand
London WC2R 1DR,
Telephone: 0171 379 9779
E-mail: chambers@199strand.co.uk
Call Date: Oct 1992, Middle Temple
Qualifications: [BA (Oxon)]

CHESNER HOWARD MICHAEL

Bracton Chambers
95a Chancery Lane, London WC2A 1DT,
Telephone: 0171 242 4248
Call Date: July 1995, Gray's Inn
Qualifications: [LLB (Lond), MBA]

CHESTERS MS COLETTE LOUISE

1 Pump Court
Lower Ground Floor, Temple, London
EC4Y 7AB, Telephone: 0171 583 2012/
353 4341
E-mail: [name]@1pumpcourt.co.uk
Call Date: Mar 1996, Middle Temple
Qualifications: [LLB (Hons)]

CHEVES SIMON THOMSON

Francis Taylor Building
Ground Floor, Temple, London
EC4Y 7BY, Telephone: 0171 353 7768/
7769/2711
E-mail:clerks@francistaylorbuilding.law.co.uk
Call Date: July 1980, Inner Temple
Qualifications: [BA(Dunelm)]

CHHOTU JASVANT

189 Randolph Avenue
London W9 1DJ,
Telephone: 0171 624 9139
Call Date: July 1979, Gray's Inn
Qualifications: [BA (Hons)]

CHICHESTER JULIAN EDWARD MICHAEL

4-5 Gray's Inn Square
Ground Floor, Gray's Inn, London
WC1R 5JP, Telephone: 0171 404 5252
E-mail:chambers@4-5graysinnsquare.co.uk
Call Date: Nov 1977, Inner Temple

CHILD JOHN FREDERICK

Wilberforce Chambers
8 New Square, Lincoln's Inn, London
WC2A 3QP, Telephone: 0171 306 0102
E-mail: chambers@wilberforce.co.uk
Call Date: Nov 1966, Lincoln's Inn
Pupil Master
Qualifications: [BA, LLM, Dip American Law]

Types of work: Charities, Equity, wills and
trusts, Private international, Probate and
administration, Society of Lloyd's, Tax –
capital and income

CHINEGWUNDOH HAROLD EJIKE

Chancery Chambers
1st Floor Offices, 70/72 Chancery Lane,
London WC2A 1AB,
Telephone: 0171 405 6879/6870
Call Date: Oct 1994, Gray's Inn
Qualifications: [LLB]

CHINN ANTONY NIGEL CATON

**4 Brick Court, Chambers of Anne
Rafferty QC**
1st Floor, Temple, London EC4Y 9AD,
Telephone: 0171 583 8455
Call Date: Nov 1972, Middle Temple
Pupil Master, Assistant Recorder

CHIPPECK STEPHEN

5 King's Bench Walk
Temple, London EC4Y 7DN,
Telephone: 0171 353 5638
Call Date: July 1988, Lincoln's Inn
Qualifications: [LLB (Hons) (Leeds)]

CHIPPERFIELD JEREMY STEVEN

Phoenix Chambers
First Floor, Gray's Inn Chambers, Gray's
Inn, London WC1R 5JA,
Telephone: 0171 404 7888
E-mail:clerks@phoenix-chambers.co.uk
Call Date: Oct 1995, Inner Temple
Qualifications: [BA (Warw), CPE]

CHIPPINDALL ADAM COURTENAY

Guildhall Chambers
22-26 Broad Street, Bristol BS1 2HG,
Telephone: 0117 9273366
E-mail:civil.clerks@guildhallchambers.co.uk and
criminal.clerks@guildhallchambers.co.uk
Call Date: Nov 1975, Gray's Inn
Pupil Master, Recorder
Qualifications: [LLB (Soton)]

CHIRIMUUTA GILBERT MUSHORE

2nd Floor, Francis Taylor Building
Temple, London EC4Y 7BY,
Telephone: 0171 353 9942/3157
Call Date: Nov 1990, Lincoln's Inn
Qualifications: [BL (Rhodesia), LLM (Lond)]

CHISHOLM MALCOLM DAVID

3 Dr Johnson's Buildings
Ground Floor, Temple, London
EC4Y 7BA, Telephone: 0171 353 4854
E-mail: clerks@3djb.co.uk
Call Date: Nov 1989, Inner Temple
Qualifications: [MA(Cantab)]

CHIVERS (TOM) DAVID

Erskine Chambers
30 Lincoln's Inn Fields, Lincoln's Inn,
London WC2A 3PF,
Telephone: 0171 242 5532
E-mail:clerks@erskine-chambers.co.uk
Call Date: July 1983, Lincoln's Inn
Pupil Master
Qualifications: [BA (Cantab)]

CHOO CHOY ALAIN

One Essex Court
Ground Floor, Temple, London
EC4Y 9AR, Telephone: 020 7583 2000
E-mail: clerks@oneessexcourt.co.uk
Call Date: Nov 1991, Inner Temple
Qualifications: [LLB (London)]

CHOONGH SATNAM SINGH

Call Date: Oct 1994, Lincoln's Inn
Qualifications: [LLB (Hons)(Warw), D.Phil]

CHOUDHURY AKHLAQ

11 King's Bench Walk
Temple, London EC4Y 7EQ,
Telephone: 0171 632 8500/583 0610
E-mail: clerksroom@11kbw.com
Call Date: Oct 1992, Inner Temple
Qualifications: [BSc (Glasgow), LLB (Lond)]

CHOUDHURY MRS FAREHA ISLAM

Phoenix Chambers
First Floor, Gray's Inn Chambers, Gray's
Inn, London WC1R 5JA,
Telephone: 0171 404 7888
E-mail:clerks@phoenix-chambers.co.uk
Call Date: Nov 1995, Gray's Inn
Qualifications: [LLB (Sussex)]

CHOUDHURY MISS NAFEESA

New Court Chambers
3 Broad Chare, Newcastle upon Tyne
NE1 3DQ, Telephone: 0191 232 1980
Call Date: Nov 1990, Inner Temple
Qualifications: [LLB]

CHOWDHARY ISLAMUDDIN

The Chambers of Mr Ali Mohammed Azhar
Basement, 9 King's Bench Walk, Temple,
London EC4Y 7DX,
Telephone: 0171 353 9564
E-mail: jvlee@btinternet.com
Call Date: July 1982, Lincoln's Inn
Pupil Master
Qualifications: [BA, LLB (Punjab), LLM
(Lond)]

CHRISTENSEN CARLTON

10 King's Bench Walk
Ground Floor, Temple, London
EC4Y 7EB, Telephone: 0171 353 7742
E-mail: 10kbw@lineone.net
Call Date: July 1977, Middle Temple
Pupil Master
Qualifications: [BSc, MSc, PhD (Manch]

CHRISTIE AIDAN PATRICK

4 Pump Court
Temple, London EC4Y 7AN,
Telephone: 020 7842 5555
E-mail:chambers@4pumpcourt.law.co.uk
Call Date: July 1988, Middle Temple
Pupil Master
Qualifications: [BA (Hons) (Oxon), MA
(Hons) (Cantab)]

CHRISTIE DAVID HENDERSON

9 Bedford Row
London WC1R 4AZ,
Telephone: 0171 242 3555
E-mail: clerks@9br.co.uk
Call Date: July 1973, Inner Temple
Pupil Master
Qualifications: [BCom]

CHRISTIE RICHARD HAMISH

2 Pump Court
1st Floor, Temple, London EC4Y 7AH,
Telephone: 0171 353 5597
Call Date: July 1986, Inner Temple
Pupil Master
Qualifications: [LLB (Manch), ACA (Part)]

CHRISTIE RONALD DANIEL

32 Park Place
Cardiff CF1 3BA,
Telephone: 01222 397364
Call Date: July 1974, Lincoln's Inn
Pupil Master
Qualifications: [LLB]

CHRISTIE SIMON PAUL WILLIAM

Chavasse Court Chambers
2nd Floor, Chavasse Court, 24 Lord Street,
Liverpool L2 1TA,
Telephone: 0151 707 1191
Call Date: Feb 1988, Middle Temple
Pupil Master
Qualifications: [LLB (L'pool)]

CHRISTIE-BROWN MISS SARAH LOUISE

4 Paper Buildings
Ground Floor, Temple, London
EC4Y 7EX, Telephone: 0171 353 3366/
583 7155
E-mail: clerks@4paperbuildings.com
Call Date: Oct 1994, Middle Temple
Qualifications: [BA (Hons)(Oxon), Dip Law
(City)]

CHRISTODOULOU MISS HELEN JOAN

5 Pump Court
Ground Floor, Temple, London
EC4Y 7AP, Telephone: 020 7353 2532
E-mail: FivePump@netcomuk.co.uk
Call Date: July 1972, Middle Temple
Pupil Master
Qualifications: [LLB (Lond)]

CHRISTOPHER JULIAN MARK CARMICHAEL

Five Paper Buildings
1st Floor, Five Paper Bldgs, Temple,
London EC4Y 7HB,
Telephone: 0171 583 6117
E-mail:clerks@5-paperbuildings.law.co.uk
Call Date: Nov 1988, Gray's Inn
Pupil Master
Qualifications: [BA (Hons)(Cantab)]

CHRUSZCZ CHARLES FRANCIS QC (1992)

28 St John Street
Manchester M3 4DJ,
Telephone: 0161 834 8418
E-mail: clerk@28stjohnst.co.uk
Call Date: July 1973, Middle Temple
Recorder
Qualifications: [LLB]

CHUDLEIGH MISS LOUISE KATRINA

Old Square Chambers
1 Verulam Buildings, Gray's Inn, London
WC1R 5LQ, Telephone: 0171 269 0300
E-mail:clerks@oldsquarechambers.co.uk
Old Square Chambers
Hanover House, 47 Corn Street, Bristol
BS1 1HT, Telephone: 0117 9277111
E-mail: oldsqbri@globalnet.co.uk
Call Date: July 1987, Lincoln's Inn
Pupil Master
Qualifications: [BA Law (Kent)]

CHUKWUEMEKA JOHN OKECHUKWU

India Buildings Chambers
Water Street, Liverpool L2 0XG,
Telephone: 0151 243 6000
E-mail: clerks@chambers.u-net.com
Call Date: Nov 1994, Lincoln's Inn
Qualifications: [BSc (Hons)(Lond)]

CHURCH JOHN STEPHEN

2 Gray's Inn Square Chambers
2nd Floor, Gray's Inn, London WC1R 5AA,
Telephone: 020 7242 0328
E-mail: clerks@2gis.co.uk
Call Date: Nov 1984, Lincoln's Inn
Qualifications: [BA]

CHURCHILL MRS CAROL LENA

Temple Fields
Hamilton House, 1 Temple Avenue,
London EC4Y 0HA,
Telephone: 0171 353 4212
Call Date: Nov 1979, Middle Temple
Qualifications: [BA (Hons)Kent), Maitre Du
Droit]

CHURCHILL MISS MARINA SPENCER

Call Date: July 1989, Inner Temple
Qualifications: [LLB (Bucks)]

CHUTE MS ANDREA ALEXANDRA

Chambers of Joy Okoye
Suite 1, 2nd Floor Gray's Inn Chambers,
Gray's Inn, London WC1R 5JA,
Telephone: 0171 405 7011
Call Date: Oct 1995, Middle Temple
Qualifications: [LLB (Hons), LLM (Hons)]

CIUMEI CHARLES GREGG

1 Temple Gardens
1st Floor, Temple, London EC4Y 9BB,
Telephone: 0171 583 1315/353 0407
E-mail: clerks@1templegardens.co.uk
Call Date: Oct 1991, Middle Temple
Qualifications: [BA Hons (Oxon), Dip Law]

CLAPPISON WILLIAM JAMES

Chambers of Andrew Campbell QC
10 Park Square, Leeds LS1 2LH,
Telephone: 0113 2455438
E-mail: clerks@10pksq.co.uk
Call Date: Nov 1981, Gray's Inn
Qualifications: [BA (Oxon)]

CLARE MISS ALLISON JEAN

18 Red Lion Court
(Off Fleet Street), London EC4A 3EB,
Telephone: 0171 520 6000
E-mail: chambers@18rlc.co.uk
Thornwood House
102 New London Road, Chelmsford,
Essex, CM2 0RG,
Telephone: 01245 280880
E-mail: chambers@18rlc.co.uk
Call Date: Oct 1992, Gray's Inn
Qualifications: [BA , BCL (Oxon)]

CLARE MICHAEL CHRISTOPHER

Octagon House
19 Colegate, Norwich NR3 1AT,
Telephone: 01603 623186
E-mail: admin@octagon-chambers.co.uk
1 Paper Buildings
1st Floor, Temple, London EC4Y 7EP,
Telephone: 0171 353 3728/4953
Call Date: Nov 1986, Gray's Inn
Qualifications: [LLB (E Anglia)]

CLARE REGINALD STUART

Corn Exchange Chambers
5th Floor, Fenwick Street, Liverpool
L2 7QS, Telephone: 0151 227 1081/5009
Call Date: May 1997, Middle Temple

CLARGO JOHN PAUL

3 Paper Buildings (Bournemouth)
20 Lorne Park Road, Bournemouth,
Dorset, BH1 1JN,
Telephone: 01202 292102
E-mail: Bournemouth@3paper.com
3 Paper Buildings (Oxford)
1 Alfred Street, High Street, Oxford
OX1 4EH, Telephone: 01865 793736
E-mail: oxford@3paper.com
3 Paper Buildings
Temple, London EC4Y 7EU,
Telephone: 020 7583 8055
E-mail: London@3paper.com

3 Paper Buildings (Winchester)
4 St Peter Street, Winchester SO23 8BW,
Telephone: 01962 868884
E-mail: winchester@3paper.com
Call Date: Oct 1994, Middle Temple
Qualifications: [BA (Hons)(Oxon), CPE]

CLARIDGE MISS RACHAEL SARAH

King's Chambers
5a Gildredge Road, Eastbourne, East
Sussex, BN21 4RB,
Telephone: 01323 416053
Call Date: Oct 1996, Inner Temple
Qualifications: [LLB (Buck'ham)(Hons)]

CLARK ANDREW RICHARD

Manchester House Chambers
18-22 Bridge Street, Manchester M3 3BZ,
Telephone: 0161 834 7007
8 King Street Chambers
8 King Street, Manchester M2 6AQ,
Telephone: 0161 834 9560
E-mail: eightking@aol.com
Call Date: July 1994, Inner Temple
Qualifications: [MA (Oxon)]

CLARK MISS BRYONY JANE

Ropewalk Chambers
24 The Ropewalk, Nottingham NG1 5EF,
Telephone: 0115 9472581
E-mail: administration@ropewalk co.uk
Call Date: July 1985, Middle Temple
Qualifications: [LLB (Leeds)]

CLARK CHRISTOPHER HARVEY QC (1989)

Pump Court Chambers
31 Southgate Street, Winchester
SO23 9EE, Telephone: 01962 868161
E-mail: clerks@3pumpcourt.com
Pump Court Chambers
Upper Ground Floor, 3 Pump Court,
Temple, London EC4Y 7AJ,
Telephone: 0171 353 0711
E-mail: clerks@3pumpcourt.com
Westgate Chambers
144 High Street, Lewes, East Sussex,
BN7 1XT, Telephone: 01273 480510
Pump Court Chambers
5 Temple Chambers, Temple Street,
Swindon SN1 1SQ,
Telephone: 01793 539899
E-mail: clerks@3pumpcourt.com

Harrow on the Hill Chambers
60 High Street, Harrow-on-the-Hill,
Middlesex, HA1 3LL,
Telephone: 0181 423 7444
Call Date: 1969, Gray's Inn
Recorder
Qualifications: [MA (Cantab), Member of
Institute, of Arbitrators]

CLARK DINGLE

1 Dr Johnson's Buildings
Ground Floor, Temple, London
EC4Y 7AX, Telephone: 0171 353 9328
E-mail:OneDr.Johnsons@btinternet.com
Dr Johnson's Chambers
The Atrium Court, Apex Plaza, Reading,
Berkshire, RG1 1AX,
Telephone: 01734 254221
Call Date: July 1981, Middle Temple
Pupil Master
Qualifications: [BSc (Soton)]

CLARK MISS FIONA JANE STEWART

8 New Square
Lincoln's Inn, London WC2A 3QP,
Telephone: 0171 405 4321
E-mail: clerks@8newsquare.co.uk
Call Date: July 1982, Middle Temple
Pupil Master
Qualifications: [MA (Cantab)]

CLARK MISS GERALDINE

4-5 Gray's Inn Square
Ground Floor, Gray's Inn, London
WC1R 5JP, Telephone: 0171 404 5252
E-mail:chambers@4-5graysinnsquare.co.uk
Call Date: July 1988, Gray's Inn
Pupil Master
Qualifications: [LLB (Hons), Dip Law]

CLARK MS JULIA ELISABETH

5 New Square
Ground Floor, Lincoln's Inn, London
WC2A 3RJ, Telephone: 020 7404 0404
E-mail:chambers@fivenewsquare.demon.co.
uk
Call Date: July 1984, Gray's Inn
Pupil Master
Qualifications: [MA (Oxon),MA (Lond)]

CLARK NEIL ANDREW

No. 6
6 Park Square, Leeds LS1 2LW,
Telephone: 0113 2459763
E-mail: chambers@no6.co.uk
Call Date: July 1987, Inner Temple
Qualifications: [LLB (Leeds)]

CLARK PAUL ROBERT

Exchange Chambers
Pearl Assurance House, Derby Square,
Liverpool L2 9XX,
Telephone: 0151 236 7747
E-mail:exchangechambers@btinternet.com
Call Date: May 1994, Middle Temple
Qualifications: [LLB (Hons)]

CLARK PETER LESTOR

2-4 Tudor Street
London EC4Y 0AA,
Telephone: 0171 797 7111
E-mail: clerks@rfqc.co.uk
Call Date: Nov 1988, Middle Temple
Pupil Master
Qualifications: [BA (Oxon), Dip Law]

CLARK MISS REBECCA JANE

Exchange Chambers
Pearl Assurance House, Derby Square,
Liverpool L2 9XX,
Telephone: 0151 236 7747
E-mail:exchangechambers@btinternet.com
Call Date: July 1989, Inner Temple
Qualifications: [LLB [Sheff]]

CLARK TIMOTHY ELWYN

1 Inner Temple Lane
Temple, London EC4Y 1AF,
Telephone: 020 7353 0933
Call Date: Feb 1993, Inner Temple
Qualifications: [LLB (Hons, Bris)]

CLARK TIMOTHY NOEL

2 New Street
Leicester LE1 5NA,
Telephone: 0116 2625906
E-mail: clerks@2newstreet.co.uk
Call Date: July 1974, Middle Temple
Pupil Master, Assistant Recorder
Qualifications: [BA (Hons)]

CLARK WAYNE VINCENT

Falcon Chambers
Falcon Court, London EC4Y 1AA,
Telephone: 0171 353 2484
E-mail: clerks@falcon-chambers.com
Call Date: July 1982, Middle Temple
Pupil Master
Qualifications: [LLB (Lond), BCL, (Oxon)]

CLARKE MISS ALISON LEE

No. 1 Serjeants' Inn
5th Floor Fleet Street, Temple, London
EC4Y 1LH, Telephone: 0171 415 6666
E-mail:no1serjeantsinn@btinternet.com
Call Date: Oct 1994, Lincoln's Inn
Qualifications: [LLB (Hons)(Leic)]

CLARKE ANDREW BERTRAM QC (1997)

Littleton Chambers
3 King's Bench Walk North, Temple,
London EC4Y 7HR,
Telephone: 0171 797 8600
E-mail:clerks@littletonchambers.co.uk
Call Date: July 1980, Middle Temple
Qualifications: [LLB, AKC (Lond), BCL]

CLARKE ANDREW STANLEY ROBERT

Sedan House
Stanley Place, Chester CH1 2LU,
Telephone: 01244 320480/348282
Call Date: July 1996, Gray's Inn

CLARKE MISS ANNA VICTORIA

5 Stone Buildings
Lincoln's Inn, London WC2A 3XT,
Telephone: 0171 242 6201
E-mail:clerks@5-stonebuildings.law.co.uk
Call Date: Nov 1994, Inner Temple
Qualifications: [BA (Lond), CPE (Notts)]

CLARKE CHRISTOPHER SIMON COURTENAY S QC (1984)

Brick Court Chambers
7-8 Essex Street, London WC2R 3LD,
Telephone: 0171 379 3550
E-mail: [surname]@brickcourt.co.uk
Call Date: Nov 1969, Middle Temple
Recorder
Qualifications: [MA (Cantab)]

CLARKE MISS ELIZABETH ANNE

Queen Elizabeth Building
2nd Floor, Temple, London EC4Y 9BS,
Telephone: 0171 797 7837
Call Date: Nov 1991, Gray's Inn
Qualifications: [LLB (Oxon), BA
(Hons)(Oxon), Jurisprudence]

CLARKE MISS FRANCESCA LOUISE

Forest House Chambers
15 Granville Road, Walthamstow, London
E17 9BS, Telephone: 0181 925 2240
Call Date: Nov 1981, Inner Temple
Qualifications: [BA]

CLARKE GEORGE ROBERT IVAN

Chambers of Geoffrey Hawker
46/48 Essex Street, London WC2R 3GH,
Telephone: 0171 583 8899
Call Date: Nov 1973, Gray's Inn
Pupil Master
Qualifications: [LLB (Hons)]

CLARKE GERARD JOSEPH PATRICK

Blackstone Chambers
Blackstone House, Temple, London
EC4Y 9BW, Telephone: 0171 583 1770
E-mail:clerks@blackstonechambers.com
Call Date: July 1986, Middle Temple
Pupil Master
Qualifications: [MA (Oxon), Dip Law]

CLARKE MS HELEN

6 King's Bench Walk
Ground, Third & Fourth Floors, Temple,
London EC4Y 7DR,
Telephone: 0171 353 4931/583 0695
Call Date: Nov 1988, Middle Temple
Pupil Master
Qualifications: [BA (Hons) (Oxon), Dip Law]

CLARKE IAN JAMES

Hardwicke Building
New Square, Lincoln's Inn, London
WC2A 3SB, Telephone: 020 7242 2523
E-mail: clerks@hardwicke.co.uk
Call Date: Oct 1990, Lincoln's Inn
Pupil Master
Qualifications: [LLB (Hons)(Newc)]

CLARKE JAMIE ROY

Plowden Buildings
2nd Floor, 2 Plowden Buildings, Middle
Temple Lane, London EC4Y 9BU,
Telephone: 0171 583 0808
E-mail: bar@plowdenbuildings.co.uk
Call Date: Nov 1995, Gray's Inn
Qualifications: [BA (Oxon)]

CLARKE JEFFREY JOHN

Nicholas Street Chambers
22 Nicholas Street, Chester CH1 2NX,
Telephone: 01244 323886
E-mail: clerks@40king.co.uk
Call Date: Nov 1985, Middle Temple
Qualifications: [B.Soc.Sc (Keele)]

CLARKE MS JOANNA M

Gray's Inn Chambers
5th Floor, Gray's Inn, London WC1R 5JA,
Telephone: 0171 404 1111
Call Date: Oct 1993, Gray's Inn
Qualifications: [MA (Oxon)]

CLARKE MS JOANNE ELIZABETH

33 Bedford Row
London WC1R 4JH,
Telephone: 0171 242 6476
E-mail:clerks@bedfordrow33.demon.co.uk
Call Date: Nov 1993, Inner Temple
Qualifications: [LLB]

CLARKE JONATHAN CHRISTOPHER ST JOHN

Old Square Chambers
Hanover House, 47 Corn Street, Bristol
BS1 1HT, Telephone: 0117 9277111
E-mail: oldsqbri@globalnet.co.uk
Old Square Chambers
1 Verulam Buildings, Gray's Inn, London
WC1R 5LQ, Telephone: 0171 269 0300
E-mail:clerks@oldsquarechambers.co.uk
Call Date: Oct 1990, Middle Temple
Qualifications: [BA (Hons)(Ulster), Dip Law]

CLARKE KEVIN GORDON CHARLES

2nd Floor, Francis Taylor Building
Temple, London EC4Y 7BY,
Telephone: 0171 353 9942/3157
Call Date: Feb 1983, Inner Temple
Pupil Master
Qualifications: [LLB (Lond)(Hons)]

CLARKE MISS LISA TARIN

Clapham Chambers
21-25 Bedford Road, Clapham North,
London SW4 7SH,
Telephone: 0171 978 8482/642 5777
E-mail:claphamchambers@compuserve.com
Call Date: Oct 1995, Gray's Inn
Qualifications: [BA (Cantab)]

CLARKE MALCOLM JOHN

Maidstone Chambers
33 Earl Street, Maidstone, Kent, ME14 1PF,
Telephone: 01622 688592
E-mail:maidstonechambers@compuserve.com
Call Date: Oct 1994, Gray's Inn
Qualifications: [LLB]

CLARKE MISS MICHELLE NICOLA

Earl Street Chambers
47 Earl Street, Maidstone, Kent,
ME14 1PD, Telephone: 01622 671222
E-mail: gunner-sparks@msn.com
Bell Yard Chambers
116/118 Chancery Lane, London
WC2A 1PP, Telephone: 0171 306 9292
Call Date: July 1988, Inner Temple
Qualifications: [LLB (Soton)]

CLARKE NICHOLAS STEPHEN

Chambers of John Hand QC
9 St John Street, Manchester M3 4DN,
Telephone: 0161 955 9000
E-mail: ninesjs@gconnect.com
Call Date: July 1981, Middle Temple
Pupil Master
Qualifications: [LLB (Hons)]

CLARKE PAUL SEBASTIAN

9 Old Square
Ground Floor, Lincoln's Inn, London
WC2A 3SR, Telephone: 0171 405 4682
E-mail: chambers@9oldsquare.co.uk
Call Date: Nov 1997, Gray's Inn
Qualifications: [MA (St Andrews)]

CLARKE PETER JOHN

St Philip's Chambers
Fountain Court, Steelhouse Lane,
Birmingham B4 6DR,
Telephone: 0121 246 7000
E-mail: clerks@st-philips.co.uk
Harcourt Chambers
1st Floor, 2 Harcourt Buildings, Temple,
London EC4Y 9DB,
Telephone: 0171 353 6961
E-mail:clerks@harcourtchambers.law.co.uk
Harcourt Chambers
Churchill House, 3 St Aldate's Courtyard,
St Aldate's, Oxford OX1 1BN,
Telephone: 01865 791559
E-mail:clerks@harcourtchambers.law.co.uk
Call Date: Nov 1970, Lincoln's Inn
Qualifications: [MA (Oxon), BCL (Oxon)]

CLARKE PETER WILLIAM QC (1997)

Hollis Whiteman Chambers
3rd Floor, Queen Elizabeth Bldg, Temple,
London EC4Y 9BS,
Telephone: 020 7583 5766
E-mail:barristers@holliswhiteman.co.uk
Call Date: July 1973, Lincoln's Inn
Recorder

CLARKE RORY JAMES

2-3 Gray's Inn Square
Gray's Inn, London WC1R 5JH,
Telephone: 0171 242 4986
E-mail:chambers@2-3graysinnsquare.co.uk
Call Date: Nov 1996, Inner Temple
Qualifications: [BA (Cantab)]

CLARKE MISS SARAH ANNE

1 Middle Temple Lane
Temple, London EC4Y 1LT,
Telephone: 0171 583 0659 (12 Lines)
E-mail: chambers@1mtl.co.uk
Chambers of Andrew Campbell QC
10 Park Square, Leeds LS1 2LH,
Telephone: 0113 2455438
E-mail: clerks@10pksq.co.uk
Call Date: Oct 1994, Inner Temple
Qualifications: [BA (Durham)]

CLARKE SIMON ANDREW

Earl Street Chambers
47 Earl Street, Maidstone, Kent,
ME14 1PD, Telephone: 01622 671222
E-mail: gunner-sparks@msn.com
Call Date: 1997, Lincoln's Inn
Qualifications: [LLB (Hons)]

CLARKE MISS SUSAN LESLEY

Oriel Chambers
14 Water Street, Liverpool L2 8TD,
Telephone: 0151 236 7191/236 4321
E-mail: clerks@oriel-chambers.co.uk
Call Date: Oct 1996, Middle Temple
Qualifications: [LLB (Hons), LLM (L'pool)]

CLARKE TIMOTHY JOHN

8 Fountain Court
Steelhouse Lane, Birmingham B4 6DR,
Telephone: 0121 236 5514/5
E-mail: clerks@no8chambers.co.uk
Call Date: Oct 1992, Middle Temple
Qualifications: [MA (Cantab)]

CLARKSON PATRICK ROBERT JAMES QC (1991)

1 Serjeants' Inn
4th Floor, Temple, London EC4Y 1NH,
Telephone: 0171 583 1355
E-mail: clerks@serjeants-inn.co.uk
Call Date: July 1972, Lincoln's Inn
Assistant Recorder

Types of work: Local government, Parliamentary, Planning, Town and country planning

CLARKSON STUART JAMES MACGREGOR

St Ive's Chambers
Whittall Street, Birmingham B4 6DH,
Telephone: 0121 236 0863/5720
E-mail:stives.headofchambers@btinternet.com
Call Date: Nov 1987, Gray's Inn
Qualifications: [BA (Hons) (L'pool)]

CLAXTON ELROY GERALDO

23 Essex Street
London WC2R 3AS,
Telephone: 0171 413 0353/836 8366
E-mail:clerks@essexstreet23.demon.co.uk
Call Date: July 1983, Inner Temple
Pupil Master, Assistant Recorder
Qualifications: [LLB (Lond)]

CLAXTON MISS JUDITH MARY

St Mary's Chambers
50 High Pavement, Lace Market,
Nottingham NG1 1HW,
Telephone: 0115 9503503
E-mail: clerks@smc.law.co.uk
Call Date: Oct 1991, Middle Temple
Qualifications: [LLB Hons]

CLAY JONATHAN ROGER

2-3 Gray's Inn Square
Gray's Inn, London WC1R 5JH,
Telephone: 0171 242 4986
E-mail:chambers@2-3graysinnsquare.co.uk
Call Date: Oct 1990, Lincoln's Inn
Pupil Master
Qualifications: [BSc, LLB]

CLAY ROBERT CHARLES

Atkin Chambers
1 Atkin Building, Gray's Inn, London
WC1R 5AT, Telephone: 020 7404 0102
E-mail: clerks@atkin-chambers.co.uk
Call Date: July 1989, Inner Temple
Pupil Master
Qualifications: [D Phil (Oxon), BA (Oxon),
Dip Law]

CLAYSON TIMOTHY

No. 6
6 Park Square, Leeds LS1 2LW,
Telephone: 0113 2459763
E-mail: chambers@no6.co.uk
Call Date: July 1974, Gray's Inn
Pupil Master, Recorder
Qualifications: [LLB (Lond)]

CLAYTON MISS JOANNA DENISE

2 Harcourt Buildings
2nd Floor, Temple, London EC4Y 9DB,
Telephone: 020 7353 8415
E-mail: clerks@2hb.law.co.uk
Call Date: Nov 1995, Lincoln's Inn
Qualifications: [LLB (Euro)(Hons), (Bris)]

CLAYTON NIGEL GARVIN

28 St John Street
Manchester M3 4DJ,
Telephone: 0161 834 8418
E-mail: clerk@28stjohnst.co.uk
Call Date: July 1987, Inner Temple
Pupil Master
Qualifications: [LLB]

CLAYTON RICHARD ANTHONY

Devereux Chambers
Devereux Court, London WC2R 3JJ,
Telephone: 0171 353 7534
E-mail: mailbox@devchambers.co.uk
Call Date: Nov 1977, Middle Temple
Pupil Master
Qualifications: [MA (Oxon)]

CLAYTON MISS ROSALIND

95A Chancery Lane
London WC2A 1DT,
Telephone: 0171 405 3101
Call Date: Nov 1988, Middle Temple
Qualifications: [LLB (Shef), BA (Open U), MA
(Brunel), Dip Law]

CLAYTON STEPHEN CHARLES RAYNOR

2 Harcourt Buildings
1st Floor, Temple, London EC4Y 9DB,
Telephone: 020 7353 2112
Call Date: May 1973, Inner Temple

CLEASBY JOHN PAUL

39 Park Square
Leeds LS1 2NU,
Telephone: 0113 2456633
Call Date: Oct 1994, Lincoln's Inn
Qualifications: [LLB (Hons)(Leic)]

CLEAVE MRS BARBARA LESTER

1 Gray's Inn Square, Chambers of the Baroness Scotland of Asthal QC
1st Floor, London WC1R 5AG,
Telephone: 0171 405 3000
E-mail: clerks@onegrays.demon.co.uk
Call Date: July 1989, Inner Temple
Qualifications: [LLB]

CLEAVE MISS GILLIAN MARGARET

One Garden Court Family Law Chambers
Ground Floor, Temple, London
EC4Y 9BJ, Telephone: 0171 797 7900
E-mail: clerks@onegardencourt.co.uk
Call Date: Nov 1988, Inner Temple
Qualifications: [BA (Oxon), Dip Law (City)]

CLEAVER HENRY WILLIAM MANSEL

3 Temple Gardens
3rd Floor, Temple, London EC4Y 9AU,
Telephone: 0171 583 0010
Call Date: July 1985, Inner Temple
Pupil Master
Qualifications: [BA, Dip Law]

CLEAVER WAYNE DAVID

3 Temple Gardens
Lower Ground Floor, Temple, London
EC4Y 9AU, Telephone: 0171 353 3102/5/
9297 E-mail: clerks@3tg.co.uk
Call Date: July 1986, Inner Temple
Pupil Master
Qualifications: [LLB Wales]

CLEE CHRISTOPHER

Angel Chambers
94 Walter Road, Swansea, West
Glamorgan, SA1 5QA,
Telephone: 01792 464623/464648
E-mail: lynne@angelchambers.co.uk
Call Date: July 1983, Gray's Inn
Pupil Master
Qualifications: [LLB Hons (Cardiff)]

CLEEVE THOMAS D'AUVERGNE

33 Bedford Row
London WC1R 4JH,
Telephone: 0171 242 6476
E-mail:clerks@bedfordrow33.demon.co.uk
Call Date: Feb 1993, Lincoln's Inn
Qualifications: [B.Sc, Diploma of Law]

CLEGG ADAM GORDON

Stour Chambers
Barton Mill House, Barton Mill Road,
Canterbury, Kent, CT1 1BP,
Telephone: 01227 764899
E-mail: clerks@stourchambers.co.uk
Call Date: Nov 1994, Gray's Inn
Qualifications: [BA (Kent)]

CLEGG SEBASTIAN JAMES BARWICK

Deans Court Chambers
24 St John Street, Manchester M3 4DF,
Telephone: 0161 214 6000
E-mail: clerks@deanscourt.co.uk
Deans Court Chambers
41-43 Market Place, Preston PR1 1AH,
Telephone: 01772 555163
E-mail: clerks@deanscourt.co.uk
Call Date: May 1994, Inner Temple
Qualifications: [BA (Bris), CPE]

CLEGG SIMON ROBERT JONATHAN

4 Fountain Court
Steelhouse Lane, Birmingham B4 6DR,
Telephone: 0121 236 3476
Call Date: July 1980, Lincoln's Inn
Pupil Master
Qualifications: [LLB (Lond)]

CLEGG WILLIAM QC (1991)

3 Hare Court
1 Little Essex Street, London WC2R 3LD,
Telephone: 0171 395 2000
Call Date: July 1972, Gray's Inn
Recorder
Qualifications: [LLB]

CLEMENS ADAM

Bridewell Chambers
2 Bridewell Place, London EC4V 6AP,
Telephone: 020 7797 8800
E-mail: HughesGage@bridewell.law.co.uk
Call Date: July 1985, Lincoln's Inn
Pupil Master
Qualifications: [LLB (Newc)]

CLEMENT PETER GUY

2 Harcourt Buildings
1st Floor, Temple, London EC4Y 9DB,
Telephone: 020 7353 2112
Call Date: Nov 1988, Inner Temple
Qualifications: [LLB,LLM(Lond)]

CLEMENTS MISS PAULA KATE

Guildford Chambers
Stoke House, Leapale Lane, Guildford,
Surrey, GU1 4LY,
Telephone: 01483 539131
E-mail:guildford.barristers@btinternet.com
Call Date: July 1985, Inner Temple
Qualifications: [LLB (So'ton)]

CLEMES ANDREW JOHN

Angel Chambers
94 Walter Road, Swansea, West
Glamorgan, SA1 5QA,
Telephone: 01792 464623/464648
E-mail: lynne@angelchambers.co.uk
Call Date: Nov 1984, Gray's Inn
Pupil Master
Qualifications: [MA (Oxon)]

CLEMITSON MISS JULIE

Broad Chare
33 Broad Chare, Newcastle upon Tyne
NE1 3DQ, Telephone: 0191 232 0541
E-mail:clerks@broadcharechambers.law.co.uk
Call Date: Nov 1991, Inner Temple
Qualifications: [LLB (New)]

CLEVERLY CHRISTOPHER JOHN

Trafalgar Chambers
53 Fleet Street, London EC4Y 1BE,
Telephone: 0171 583 5858
E-mail:trafalgarchambers@easynet.co.uk
Call Date: Nov 1990, Middle Temple
Pupil Master
Qualifications: [LLB (Lond)]

CLEWS RICHARD ANTHONY

No. 6
6 Park Square, Leeds LS1 2LW,
Telephone: 0113 2459763
E-mail: chambers@no6.co.uk
Call Date: July 1986, Gray's Inn
Qualifications: [LLB]

CLIFF BARRY GEORGE

Regent Chambers
8 Pall Mall, Hanley, Stoke On Trent
ST1 1ER, Telephone: 01782 286666
E-mail: regent@ftech.co.uk
Call Date: July 1988, Lincoln's Inn
Pupil Master
Qualifications: [LLB (Hons) , IMEMME]

D

CLIFF MISS ELIZABETH DUNBAR

Chavasse Court Chambers
2nd Floor, Chavasse Court, 24 Lord Street,
Liverpool L2 1TA,
Telephone: 0151 707 1191
Call Date: July 1975, Middle Temple

CLIFF GRAHAM HILTON

St Philip's Chambers
Fountain Court, Steelhouse Lane,
Birmingham B4 6DR,
Telephone: 0121 246 7000
E-mail: clerks@st-philips.co.uk
Call Date: July 1973, Middle Temple
Pupil Master
Qualifications: [LLB(Hons)(Lond)]

CLIFF PAUL RICHARD

Regent Chambers
8 Pall Mall, Hanley, Stoke On Trent
ST1 1ER, Telephone: 01782 286666
E-mail: regent@ftech.co.uk
Call Date: Nov 1992, Gray's Inn
Qualifications: [LLB]

CLIFFORD (NIGEL) JAMES

7 Stone Buildings
Ground Floor, Lincoln's Inn, London
WC2A 3SZ, Telephone: 0171 405 3886/
242 3546 E-mail: chaldous@vossnet.co.uk
Call Date: July 1984, Lincoln's Inn
Pupil Master
Qualifications: [BA (Oxon)]

CLIMIE ROGER STEPHEN

35 Essex Street
Temple, London WC2R 3AR,
Telephone: 0171 353 6381
E-mail: derek_jenkins@link.org
Call Date: July 1982, Lincoln's Inn
Pupil Master, Assistant Recorder
Qualifications: [BA]

CLOMPUS JOEL

Furnival Chambers
32 Furnival Street, London EC4A 1JQ,
Telephone: 0171 405 3232
E-mail: clerks@furnivallaw.co.uk
Call Date: July 1976, Inner Temple
Pupil Master
Qualifications: [BA, PhD (Cantab)]

CLOSE DOUGLAS JONATHAN

Serle Court Chambers
6 New Square, Lincoln's Inn, London
WC2A 3QS, Telephone: 0171 242 6105
E-mail: clerks@serlecourt.co.uk
Call Date: Nov 1991, Lincoln's Inn
Pupil Master
Qualifications: [BA (Hons) (Oxon), BCL
(Oxon)]

CLOSE JON RICHARD

Oriel Chambers
14 Water Street, Liverpool L2 8TD,
Telephone: 0151 236 7191/236 4321
E-mail: clerks@oriel-chambers.co.uk
Call Date: 1997, Lincoln's Inn
Qualifications: [LLB (Hons)(Warks)]

CLOUGH GEOFFREY DUNCOMBE

Coleridge Chambers
Citadel, 190 Corporation Street,
Birmingham B4 6QD,
Telephone: 0121 233 8500
Call Date: Nov 1961, Gray's Inn
Pupil Master
Qualifications: [BA]

CLOUGH RICHARD WILLIAM BUTLER

Gray's Inn Chambers
5th Floor, Gray's Inn, London WC1R 5JA,
Telephone: 0171 404 1111
Call Date: Nov 1971, Inner Temple
Pupil Master

CLOUT MISS EMMA MARGARET

Sussex Chambers
9 Old Steine, Brighton, Sussex, BN1 1FJ,
Telephone: 01273 607953
Call Date: Nov 1989, Middle Temple
Qualifications: [BA Hons (Lond)]

CLOVER MISS SARAH

5 Fountain Court
Steelhouse Lane, Birmingham B4 6DR,
Telephone: 0121 606 0500
E-mail:clerks@5fountaincourt.law.co.uk
Call Date: Nov 1993, Lincoln's Inn
Qualifications: [BA (Oxon)(Hons), LLM
(UPenn)]

D

CLOVER (THOMAS) ANTHONY

New Court Chambers
5 Verulam Buildings, Gray's Inn, London
WC1R 5LY, Telephone: 0171 831 9500
E-mail: mail@newcourtchambers.com
Call Date: July 1971, Middle Temple
Pupil Master, Recorder
Qualifications: [BA (Oxon)]

CLUTTERBUCK ANDREW MAURICE GRAY

4 Stone Buildings
Ground Floor, Lincoln's Inn, London
WC2A 3XT, Telephone: 0171 242 5524
E-mail:clerks@4stonebuildings.law.co.uk
Call Date: Oct 1992, Middle Temple
Qualifications: [BA (Hons)]

COATES GEORGE ALEXANDER NIGEL

Guildford Chambers
Stoke House, Leapale Lane, Guildford,
Surrey, GU1 4LY,
Telephone: 01483 539131
E-mail:guildford.barristers@btinternet.com
Call Date: Nov 1990, Middle Temple
Qualifications: [BA (Cantab)]

COATES JOHN PAUL

1 Gray's Inn Square
Ground Floor, London WC1R 5AA,
Telephone: 0171 405 8946/7/8
Call Date: Nov 1988, Middle Temple
Qualifications: [LLB (Warwick)]

COBB STEPHEN WILLIAM SCOTT

One Garden Court Family Law Chambers
Ground Floor, Temple, London
EC4Y 9BJ, Telephone: 0171 797 7900
E-mail: clerks@onegardencourt.co.uk
Call Date: July 1985, Inner Temple
Pupil Master
Qualifications: [LLB (L'pool)]

COBBS MISS LAURA SUSAN

2 Harcourt Buildings
1st Floor, Temple, London EC4Y 9DB,
Telephone: 020 7353 2112
Call Date: Nov 1989, Middle Temple
Pupil Master
Qualifications: [LLB (Hons)(Bucks)]

COBURN MICHAEL JEREMY PATRICK

20 Essex Street
London WC2R 3AL,
Telephone: 0171 583 9294
E-mail: clerks@20essexst.com
Call Date: Nov 1990, Inner Temple
Qualifications: [BA (Oxon), Dip Law (City)]

COCHAND CHARLES MACLEAN

Eighteen Carlton Crescent
Southampton SO15 2XR,
Telephone: 01703 639001
Call Date: Feb 1978, Middle Temple
Pupil Master
Qualifications: [BA (Hons)]

COCHRANE CHRISTOPHER DUNCAN QC (1988)

2-3 Gray's Inn Square
Gray's Inn, London WC1R 5JH,
Telephone: 0171 242 4986
E-mail:chambers@2-3graysinnsquare.co.uk
Call Date: Feb 1965, Middle Temple
Recorder
Qualifications: [BA (Oxon)]

COCKERILL MISS SARA ELIZABETH

Essex Court Chambers
24 Lincoln's Inn Fields, London
WC2A 3ED, Telephone: 0171 813 8000
E-mail:clerksroom@essexcourt-chambers.co.uk
Call Date: Oct 1990, Lincoln's Inn
Pupil Master
Qualifications: [MA (Oxon)]

COCKINGS GILES FRANCIS SACHEVERAL

Furnival Chambers
32 Furnival Street, London EC4A 1JQ,
Telephone: 0171 405 3232
E-mail: clerks@furnivallaw.co.uk
Call Date: Oct 1996, Middle Temple
Qualifications: [BSc (Hons)(Reading), LLB (Hons)(City)]

COCKRILL TIMOTHY ROBERT

New Walk Chambers
27 New Walk, Leicester LE1 6TE,
Telephone: 0116 2559144
Call Date: July 1991, Gray's Inn
Qualifications: [MA (Cantab)]

COCKS DAVID JOHN QC (1982)

18 Red Lion Court
(Off Fleet Street), London EC4A 3EB,
Telephone: 0171 520 6000
E-mail: chambers@18rlc.co.uk
Thornwood House
102 New London Road, Chelmsford,
Essex, CM2 0RG,
Telephone: 01245 280880
E-mail: chambers@18rlc.co.uk
Call Date: June 1961, Lincoln's Inn
Recorder
Qualifications: [MA (Juris Oxon)]

CODNER PETER FYNES TIMOTHY LEIGH

Devizes Chambers
11 High Street, Potterne, Devizes,
Wiltshire, SN10 5PY,
Telephone: 01380 724896
Staple Inn Chambers
1st Floor, 9 Staple Inn, Holborn Bars,
London WC1V 7QH,
Telephone: 0171 242 5240
E-mail: clerks@staple-inn.org
Call Date: July 1983, Inner Temple
Qualifications: [BA]

COE MRS ROSALIND

Ropewalk Chambers
24 The Ropewalk, Nottingham NG1 5EF,
Telephone: 0115 9472581
E-mail: administration@ropewalk co.uk
Call Date: July 1983, Middle Temple
Pupil Master
Qualifications: [LLB (Nott'm)]

COEN MISS YVONNE ANNE

9 Bedford Row
London WC1R 4AZ,
Telephone: 0171 242 3555
E-mail: clerks@9br.co.uk
Call Date: Nov 1982, Lincoln's Inn
Pupil Master, Assistant Recorder
Qualifications: [MA (Oxon)]

COFFEY JOHN JOSEPH QC (1996)

3 Temple Gardens
Lower Ground Floor, Temple, London
EC4Y 9AU, Telephone: 0171 353 3102/5/
9297 E-mail: clerks@3tg.co.uk
Call Date: Nov 1970, Middle Temple
Recorder
Qualifications: [LLB (Lond)(Hons)]

COFIE EDMUND KPAKPO

Somersett Chambers
25 Bedford Row, London WC1R 4HE,
Telephone: 0171 404 6701
E-mail: somelaw@aol.com
Call Date: July 1980, Middle Temple
Pupil Master
Qualifications: [LLB Hons (Lond)]

COGAN MICHAEL JAMES

6 King's Bench Walk
Ground, Third & Fourth Floors, Temple,
London EC4Y 7DR,
Telephone: 0171 353 4931/583 0695
Call Date: Feb 1986, Middle Temple
Qualifications: [BA (Hons)]

COGGINS JONATHAN

1 Harcourt Buildings
2nd Floor, Temple, London EC4Y 9DA,
Telephone: 0171 353 9421/0375
E-mail:clerks@1harcourtbuildings.law.co.uk
Call Date: July 1980, Middle Temple
Pupil Master
Qualifications: [BA]

COGHLAN TERENCE QC (1993)

1 Crown Office Row
Ground Floor, Temple, London
EC4Y 7HH, Telephone: 0171 797 7500
E-mail: mail@onecrownofficerow.com
Crown Office Row Chambers
Blenheim House, 120 Church Street,
Brighton, Sussex, BN1 1WH,
Telephone: 01273 625625
E-mail: crownofficerow@clara.net
Call Date: Nov 1968, Inner Temple
Recorder
Qualifications: [MA (Oxon)]

D

D

COGHLIN THOMAS ASHLEY

Cloisters
1 Pump Court, Temple, London
EC4Y 7AA, Telephone: 0171 827 4000
E-mail: clerks@cloisters.com
Call Date: 1998, Inner Temple
Qualifications: [BA, BCL (Oxon)]

COGLEY STEPHEN WILLIAM

Merchant Chambers
1 North Parade, Parsonage Gardens,
Manchester M3 2NH,
Telephone: 0161 839 7070
E-mail: merchant.chambers@virgin.net
Call Date: Nov 1984, Gray's Inn
Pupil Master
Qualifications: [LLB (Hons) (Newc)]

COGSWELL MISS FREDERICA NATASHA

Gough Square Chambers
6-7 Gough Square, London EC4A 3DE,
Telephone: 0171 353 0924
E-mail: gsc@goughsq.co.uk
Call Date: Nov 1995, Lincoln's Inn
Qualifications: [BSc (Hons)(Maths), BSc
(Hons)(Chem), MSc (Lond)]

COHEN ANDREW RONALD

4 Brick Court
Ground Floor, Temple, London
EC4Y 9AD, Telephone: 0171 797 7766
E-mail: chambers@4brick.co.uk
Call Date: Nov 1982, Gray's Inn
Pupil Master
Qualifications: [BA (Hons) (Keele)]

COHEN EDWARD MERVYN

11 Stone Buildings
Lincoln's Inn, London WC2A 3TG,
Telephone: +44 (0)207 831 6381
E-mail:clerks@11StoneBuildings.law.co.uk
Call Date: July 1972, Middle Temple
Qualifications: [MA (Cantab)]

COHEN JONATHAN LIONEL QC (1997)

4 Paper Buildings
1st Floor, Temple, London EC4Y 7EX,
Telephone: 0171 583 0816/353 1131
E-mail: clerks@4paperbuildings.co.uk
Call Date: July 1974, Lincoln's Inn
Recorder
Qualifications: [BA]

COHEN JOSEPH MICHAEL

Old Colony House
6 South King Street, Manchester M2 6DQ,
Telephone: 0161 834 4364
Queens Chambers
4 Camden Place, Preston PR1 3JL,
Telephone: 01772 828300
Call Date: 1991, Gray's Inn
Qualifications: [BA (Hons)(Lancs)]

COHEN LAWRENCE FRANCIS RICHARD QC (1993)

Twenty-Four Old Buildings
Ground Floor, Lincoln's Inn, London
WC2A 3UP, Telephone: 0171 404 0946
E-mail:clerks@24oldbuildings.law.co.uk
Call Date: July 1974, Gray's Inn
Recorder
Qualifications: [LLB]

COHEN MISS LINDA

39 Windsor Road
London N3 3SN,
Telephone: 0181 349 9194
E-mail: lindacohen@cobeck.clara.net
Call Date: July 1985, Middle Temple
Qualifications: [MA (Wark)]

COHEN RAPHAEL GIDEON

Mercury Chambers
Mercury House, 33-35 Clarendon Road,
Leeds LS2 9NZ,
Telephone: 0113 234 2265
E-mail:cdexter@mercurychambers.co.uk
Call Date: July 1981, Lincoln's Inn
Pupil Master
Qualifications: [LLB]

COHEN MISS SAMANTHA LOUISE

4 Brick Court, Chambers of Anne Rafferty QC
1st Floor, Temple, London EC4Y 9AD,
Telephone: 0171 583 8455
Call Date: Nov 1995, Inner Temple
Qualifications: [BA (Soton), CPE (City)]

COKE EDWARD PETER

St Ive's Chambers
Whittall Street, Birmingham B4 6DH,
Telephone: 0121 236 0863/5720
E-mail:stives.headofchambers@btinternet.com
Call Date: July 1976, Inner Temple
Pupil Master
Qualifications: [LLB (Hons) (Warwick)]

COKER WILLIAM JOHN QC (1994)

9 Bedford Row
London WC1R 4AZ,
Telephone: 0171 242 3555
E-mail: clerks@9br.co.uk
Call Date: Nov 1973, Gray's Inn
Recorder
Qualifications: [LLB]

COLBEY RICHARD (ALAN)

Francis Taylor Building
3rd Floor, Temple, London EC4Y 7BY,
Telephone: 0171 797 7250
Guildhall Chambers Portsmouth
Prudential Buildings, 16 Guildhall Walk,
Portsmouth, Hampshire, PO1 2DE,
Telephone: 01705 752400
Call Date: July 1984, Inner Temple
Qualifications: [LLB (Exon)]

Types of work: Common law (general), Consumer law, Employment, Food poisoning, Insurance, Landlord and tenant, Personal injury, Professional negligence

Other professional experience: Editor of *Litigation Journal* for five years, regular writer for the *Guardian* and contributor to the *New Statesman* and *New Law Journal*

Publications: *Residential Tenancies*, 1988, 1990, 1996; *Resident Landlords and Owner Occupancies*, 1985

Reported Cases: *Sargent v GRE*, (1997) *The Times*, 25 April, 1997. Interpretation of a personal accident insurance policy.

ESS v Johnson, [1998] IRLR 382, 1997. Validity of covenant preventing employee working for competitor.
D v R, (1997) SJ 764, 1996. Claim by food poisoning victim under personal accident policy.
Singh & Co v Hay, C9100096 Civil Appeals Transcript, 1998. Extent to which solicitors' negligence deprives him of entire fee.
Beardcard Properties v Day, [1984] ICR 837, 1984. Whether tribunal entitled to strike out for procedural default.

COLBORNE MISS MICHELLE DIANE

Broadway House Chambers
Broadway House, 9 Bank Street, Bradford, West Yorkshire, BD1 1TW,
Telephone: 01274 722560
E-mail: clerks@broadwayhouse.co.uk
Broadway House Chambers
31 Park Square West, Leeds LS1 2PF,
Telephone: 0113 246 2600
Call Date: May 1993, Gray's Inn
Qualifications: [LLB (Mid Glamorgan)]

COLE EDWARD ARTHUR

Falcon Chambers
Falcon Court, London EC4Y 1AA,
Telephone: 0171 353 2484
E-mail: clerks@falcon-chambers.com
Call Date: July 1980, Gray's Inn
Pupil Master
Qualifications: [MA (Oxon)]

COLE GORDON STEWART

Exchange Chambers
Pearl Assurance House, Derby Square, Liverpool L2 9XX,
Telephone: 0151 236 7747
E-mail:exchangechambers@btinternet.com
Call Date: July 1979, Inner Temple
Pupil Master
Qualifications: [BA (L'Pool)]

COLE JUSTIN MARK

Five Paper Buildings
1st Floor, Five Paper Bldgs, Temple, London EC4Y 7HB,
Telephone: 0171 583 6117
E-mail:clerks@5-paperbuildings.law.co.uk
Call Date: May 1992, Inner Temple
Qualifications: [LLB (Notts)]

D

COLE MISS JUSTINE AMANDA

Bank House Chambers
Old Bank House, Hartshead, Sheffield
S1 2EL, Telephone: 0114 2751223
Call Date: Nov 1994, Inner Temple
Qualifications: [LLB (Sheff) (Hons)]

COLE MISS LORNA

Wilberforce Chambers
7 Bishop Lane, Hull, East Yorkshire,
HU1 1PA, Telephone: 01482 323264
E-mail: clerks@hullbar.demon.co.uk
Call Date: Nov 1950, Lincoln's Inn
Pupil Master
Qualifications: [LLB]

COLE MARTIN DAVID

Lamb Building
Ground Floor, Temple, London
EC4Y 7AS, Telephone: 020 7797 7788
E-mail: lamb.building@link.org
Call Date: Nov 1994, Inner Temple
Qualifications: [LLB (Hons)]

COLE NICHOLAS ARTHUR

St Ive's Chambers
Whittall Street, Birmingham B4 6DH,
Telephone: 0121 236 0863/5720
E-mail:stives.headofchambers@btinternet.com
Call Date: Oct 1993, Lincoln's Inn
Qualifications: [BSc (Hons)(B'ham), CPE]

COLE RICHARD JOHN

Lancaster Building
77 Deansgate, Manchester M3 2BW,
Telephone: 0161 661 4444/0171 649 9872
E-mail: sandra@lbnipc.com
Call Date: July 1988, Gray's Inn
Qualifications: [BSc (Eng), ACGI , LLB ,
C.Eng, MIEE, MBCS]

COLE ROBERT IAN GAWAIN

30 Park Square
Leeds LS1 2PF, Telephone: 0113 2436388
E-mail: clerks@30parksquare.co.uk
Call Date: Oct 1991, Middle Temple
Qualifications: [LLM]

COLE MISS VANESSA ANNE

Phoenix Chambers
First Floor, Gray's Inn Chambers, Gray's
Inn, London WC1R 5JA,
Telephone: 0171 404 7888
E-mail:clerks@phoenix-chambers.co.uk
Call Date: Oct 1992, Lincoln's Inn
Qualifications: [LLB(Hons)(Manch)]

COLE-WILSON MS LOIS EKUNDAYO

1 Gray's Inn Square
Ground Floor, London WC1R 5AA,
Telephone: 0171 405 8946/7/8
Call Date: Nov 1995, Inner Temple
Qualifications: [BA (Warwick), MA (Lond),
CPE (Lond), LLB (Hons)]

COLE-WILSON MISS YATONI IYAMIDE ELIZABETH

Lancaster Building
77 Deansgate, Manchester M3 2BW,
Telephone: 0161 661 4444/0171 649 9872
E-mail: sandra@lbnipc.com
Call Date: Nov 1980, Lincoln's Inn
Qualifications: [BA (Hons)]

COLEGATE-STONE JEFFERSON MARK

2 King's Bench Walk Chambers
1st Floor, 2 King's Bench Walk, Temple,
London EC4Y 7DE,
Telephone: 020 7353 9276
E-mail: chambers@2kbw.co.uk
Call Date: Nov 1975, Inner Temple

COLEMAN ANTHONY JOHN SCOTT

3 Paper Buildings
Temple, London EC4Y 7EU,
Telephone: 020 7583 8055
E-mail: London@3paper.com
3 Paper Buildings (Bournemouth)
20 Lorne Park Road, Bournemouth,
Dorset, BH1 1JN,
Telephone: 01202 292102
E-mail: Bournemouth@3paper.com
3 Paper Buildings (Oxford)
1 Alfred Street, High Street, Oxford
OX1 4EH, Telephone: 01865 793736
E-mail: oxford@3paper.com

3 Paper Buildings (Winchester)
4 St Peter Street, Winchester SO23 8BW,
Telephone: 01962 868884
E-mail: winchester@3paper.com
Call Date: July 1973, Middle Temple
Pupil Master
Qualifications: [MA (Oxon)]

COLEMAN BRUCE ROBERT

One Garden Court Family Law Chambers
Ground Floor, Temple, London
EC4Y 9BJ, Telephone: 0171 797 7900
E-mail: clerks@onegardencourt.co.uk
Call Date: July 1972, Inner Temple
Pupil Master, Assistant Recorder
Qualifications: [LLB]

COLEMAN CLIVE RUSSELL

199 Strand
London WC2R 1DR,
Telephone: 0171 379 9779
E-mail: chambers@199strand.co.uk
Call Date: July 1986, Lincoln's Inn
Qualifications: [BA (York) Dip Law]

COLEMAN DANIEL GERALD MAYOW

Essex House Chambers
Unit 6 (Part 2nd Floor South), Stratford
Office Village, 14-30 Romford Road,
London E15 4BZ,
Telephone: 0181 536 1077
Call Date: Nov 1994, Gray's Inn
Qualifications: [BA (Lond)]

COLEMAN MISS ELIZABETH JOANNE

4 Paper Buildings
1st Floor, Temple, London EC4Y 7EX,
Telephone: 0171 583 0816/353 1131
E-mail: clerks@4paperbuildings.co.uk
Call Date: July 1985, Inner Temple
Qualifications: [MA (Cantab)]

COLEMAN RICHARD JAMES LEE

Fountain Court
Temple, London EC4Y 9DH,
Telephone: 0171 583 3335
E-mail: chambers@fountaincourt.co.uk
Call Date: Feb 1994, Lincoln's Inn
Qualifications: [MA (Cantab), LLM ((Yale)]

COLEMAN RUSSELL ADAM

4 Pump Court
Temple, London EC4Y 7AN,
Telephone: 020 7842 5555
E-mail:chambers@4pumpcourt.law.co.uk
Call Date: July 1986, Inner Temple
Qualifications: [LLB (Wales)]

COLERIDGE PAUL JAMES DUKE QC (1993)

Queen Elizabeth Building
2nd Floor, Temple, London EC4Y 9BS,
Telephone: 0171 797 7837
Call Date: July 1970, Middle Temple
Recorder

COLES MICHAEL EDEN

Paradise Chambers
26 Paradise Square, Sheffield S1 2DE,
Telephone: 0114 2738951
E-mail: timbooth@paradise-sq.co.uk
Call Date: July 1986, Inner Temple
Qualifications: [LLB (Bristol)]

COLES STEVEN FREDERICK

One Paper Buildings
Ground Floor, Temple, London
EC4Y 7EP, Telephone: 0171 583 7355
E-mail: clerks@1pb.co.uk
Call Date: July 1983, Middle Temple
Pupil Master
Qualifications: [MA (Cantab)]

COLEY MISS CLARE LOUISE

Clock Chambers
78 Darlington Street, Wolverhampton
WV1 4LY, Telephone: 01902 313444
Call Date: Nov 1978, Middle Temple

COLEY WILLIAM LYNDALL

35 Essex Street
Temple, London WC2R 3AR,
Telephone: 0171 353 6381
E-mail: derek_jenkins@link.org
Call Date: July 1980, Middle Temple
Pupil Master
Qualifications: [BA (Cantab)]

COLIN GILES DAVID

Crown Office Row Chambers
Blenheim House, 120 Church Street,
Brighton, Sussex, BN1 1WH,
Telephone: 01273 625625
E-mail: crownofficerow@clara.net
Call Date: Feb 1994, Inner Temple
Qualifications: [BA (Dunelm), Dip Law]

COLLACO MORAES FRANCIS THOMAS

2 Gray's Inn Square Chambers
2nd Floor, Gray's Inn, London WC1R 5AA,
Telephone: 020 7242 0328
E-mail: clerks@2gis.co.uk
Call Date: Nov 1985, Lincoln's Inn
Qualifications: [BA (Hons)]

COLLARD MICHAEL DAVID

5 Pump Court
Ground Floor, Temple, London
EC4Y 7AP, Telephone: 020 7353 2532
E-mail: FivePump@netcomuk.co.uk
Call Date: July 1986, Middle Temple
Pupil Master
Qualifications: [LLB (Bristol)]

COLLENDER ANDREW ROBERT QC (1991)

2 Temple Gardens
Temple, London EC4Y 9AY,
Telephone: 0171 583 6041
E-mail: clerks@2templegardens.co.uk
Call Date: July 1969, Lincoln's Inn
Recorder
Qualifications: [LLB (Bris)]

COLLERY SHANE EDWARD

18 Red Lion Court
(Off Fleet Street), London EC4A 3EB,
Telephone: 0171 520 6000
E-mail: chambers@18rlc.co.uk
Thornwood House
102 New London Road, Chelmsford,
Essex, CM2 0RG,
Telephone: 01245 280880
E-mail: chambers@18rlc.co.uk
Call Date: July 1988, Lincoln's Inn
Pupil Master
Qualifications: [LLB (Hons) (Notts)]

COLLETT GAVIN CHARLES

Rougemont Chambers
8 Colleton Crescent, Exeter, Devon,
EX1 1RR, Telephone: 01392 208484
E-mail:rougemont.chambers@eclipse.co.uk
Call Date: Oct 1993, Inner Temple
Qualifications: [LLB]

COLLETT IVOR WILLIAM

No. 1 Serjeants' Inn
5th Floor Fleet Street, Temple, London
EC4Y 1LH, Telephone: 0171 415 6666
E-mail:no1serjeantsinn@btinternet.com
Call Date: Oct 1995, Middle Temple
Qualifications: [BA (Hons)]

COLLETT MICHAEL JOHN

20 Essex Street
London WC2R 3AL,
Telephone: 0171 583 9294
E-mail: clerks@20essexst.com
Call Date: Oct 1995, Gray's Inn
Qualifications: [BA]

COLLEY MISS CHRISTINE ELIZABETH

39 Park Square
Leeds LS1 2NU,
Telephone: 0113 2456633
Call Date: Oct 1992, Middle Temple
Qualifications: [LL.B (Hons)]

COLLEY DR PETER MCLEAN

19 Old Buildings
Lincoln's Inn, London WC2A 3UP,
Telephone: 0171 405 2001
E-mail: clerks@oldbuildingsip.com
Call Date: July 1989, Gray's Inn
Pupil Master
Qualifications: [BSc (Lond), PhD (Lond), LLB
(Lond)]

Fax: 0171 405 0001; DX: 397 Chancery
Lane;
Other comms: E-mail
clerks@oldbuildingsip.com; URL: http://
www.oldbuildingsip.com

Types of work: Copyright, EC and competition law, Intellectual property, Patents, Scientific and technical disputes, Trademarks

Awards and memberships: MRI; Intellectual Property Bar Association

Publications: *Forms and Agreements on Intellectual Property and International Licensing*

Reported Cases: *A Ltd v B Bank and Bank of X*, [1997] FSR 165, 1996. Do foreign bank notes alleged to infringe a British patent give rise to an act justiciable before the English courts?

COLLIER MS JANE SARAH

Blackstone Chambers
Blackstone House, Temple, London EC4Y 9BW, Telephone: 0171 583 1770
E-mail:clerks@blackstonechambers.com
Call Date: Nov 1994, Middle Temple
Qualifications: [BA (Hons)]

COLLIER JOHN GREENWOOD

20 Essex Street
London WC2R 3AL,
Telephone: 0171 583 9294
E-mail: clerks@20essexst.com
Call Date: Nov 1961, Gray's Inn
Qualifications: [MA,LLB (Cantab)]

COLLIER MARTIN MELTON

Fenners Chambers
3 Madingley Road, Cambridge CB3 0EE,
Telephone: 01223 368761
E-mail: clerks@fennerschambers.co.uk
Fenners Chambers
8-12 Priestgate, Peterborough PE1 1JA,
Telephone: 01733 562030
E-mail: clerks@fennerschambers.co.uk
Call Date: July 1982, Gray's Inn
Pupil Master
Qualifications: [MA(Oxon)]

COLLIER MS PATRICIA

Call Date: July 1983, Gray's Inn
Pupil Master
Qualifications: [LLB]

COLLIER PETER NEVILLE QC (1992)

30 Park Square
Leeds LS1 2PF, Telephone: 0113 2436388
E-mail: clerks@30parksquare.co.uk
Call Date: July 1970, Inner Temple

Recorder
Qualifications: [MA (Cantab)]

COLLINGS ANDREW SIMON JOHN

5 King's Bench Walk
Temple, London EC4Y 7DN,
Telephone: 0171 353 5638
Call Date: Nov 1987, Gray's Inn
Qualifications: [LLB]

COLLINGS MATTHEW GLYNN BURKINSHAW

13 Old Square
Ground Floor, Lincoln's Inn, London WC2A 3UA, Telephone: 0171 404 4800
E-mail: clerks@13oldsquare.law.co.uk
Call Date: July 1985, Lincoln's Inn
Pupil Master
Qualifications: [LLB (Hons) (Lond)]

COLLINGS NICHOLAS STEWART

Atkin Chambers
1 Atkin Building, Gray's Inn, London WC1R 5AT, Telephone: 020 7404 0102
E-mail: clerks@atkin-chambers.co.uk
Call Date: Nov 1997, Gray's Inn
Qualifications: [LLB (Bris)]

COLLINGWOOD TIMOTHY DONALD

Serle Court Chambers
6 New Square, Lincoln's Inn, London WC2A 3QS, Telephone: 0171 242 6105
E-mail: clerks@serlecourt.co.uk
Call Date: Oct 1996, Gray's Inn
Qualifications: [BA, BCL (Oxon)]

COLLINS BENJAMIN ROGER

1 Crown Office Row
Ground Floor, Temple, London EC4Y 7HH, Telephone: 0171 797 7500
E-mail: mail@onecrownofficerow.com
Call Date: Nov 1996, Middle Temple
Qualifications: [MA (Hons)(Cantab)]

COLLINS JAMES

Central Chambers
89 Princess Street, Manchester M1 4HT,
Telephone: 0161 236 1133
Call Date: Mar 1997, Gray's Inn
Qualifications: [BA (Lond)]

COLLINS JAMES DOUGLAS

Essex Court Chambers
24 Lincoln's Inn Fields, London
WC2A 3ED, Telephone: 0171 813 8000
E-mail:clerksroom@essexcourt-chambers.co.uk
Call Date: Feb 1995, Gray's Inn
Qualifications: [BA (Cantab)]

COLLINS MISS JENNIFER CLAIR

Eastbourne Chambers
15 Hyde Gardens, Eastbourne, East
Sussex, BN21 4PR,
Telephone: 01323 642102
Call Date: Oct 1994, Gray's Inn
Qualifications: [BSc]

COLLINS JOHN JOSEPH

Westgate Chambers
144 High Street, Lewes, East Sussex,
BN7 1XT, Telephone: 01273 480510
Westgate Chambers
16-17 Wellington Square, Hastings, East
Sussex, TN34 1PB,
Telephone: 01424 432105
Call Date: July 1971, Middle Temple
Pupil Master

COLLINS JOHN MARTIN QC (1972)

Keating Chambers
10 Essex Street, Outer Temple, London
WC2R 3AA, Telephone: 0171 544 2600
8 King Street Chambers
8 King Street, Manchester M2 6AQ,
Telephone: 0161 834 9560
E-mail: eightking@aol.com
Call Date: July 1952, Gray's Inn
Qualifications: [LLB (Manch)]

COLLINS JOHN MORRIS

9 Woodhouse Square
Leeds LS3 1AD,
Telephone: 0113 2451986
E-mail: clerks@9woodhouse.co.uk
11 King's Bench Walk
1st Floor, Temple, London EC4Y 7EQ,
Telephone: 0171 353 3337
E-mail: fmuller11@aol.com
Call Date: Feb 1956, Middle Temple
Pupil Master, Recorder
Qualifications: [MA (Oxon)]

COLLINS KENNETH GUY WYNDHAM

3 Dr Johnson's Buildings
Ground Floor, Temple, London
EC4Y 7BA, Telephone: 0171 353 4854
E-mail: clerks@3djb.co.uk
Call Date: Oct 1996, Inner Temple
Qualifications: [LLB, LLM (Sussex)]

COLLINS MICHAEL ANTONY

37 Park Square Chambers
37 Park Square, Leeds LS1 2NY,
Telephone: 0113 2439422
E-mail: chambers@no37.co.uk
Call Date: 1998, Middle Temple
Qualifications: [LLB (Hons)]

COLLINS MICHAEL GEOFFREY QC (1988)

Essex Court Chambers
24 Lincoln's Inn Fields, London
WC2A 3ED, Telephone: 0171 813 8000
E-mail:clerksroom@essexcourt-chambers.co.uk
Call Date: Nov 1971, Gray's Inn
Recorder
Qualifications: [LLB (Exon)]

COLLINS PETER RICHARD

Solent Chambers
2nd Floor, Coronation House, 1 King's
Terrace, Portsmouth, Hampshire,
PO5 3AR, Telephone: 01705 821818
Call Date: Oct 1993, Gray's Inn
Qualifications: [LLB]

COLLINS ROBERT URQUHART

8 King's Bench Walk North
1 Park Square East, Leeds LS1 2NE,
Telephone: 0113 2439797
8 King's Bench Walk
2nd Floor, Temple, London EC4Y 7DU,
Telephone: 0171 797 8888
Call Date: July 1978, Gray's Inn

COLLINS MISS ROSALEEN

Guildhall Chambers
22-26 Broad Street, Bristol BS1 2HG,
Telephone: 0117 9273366
E-mail:civil.clerks@guildhallchambers.co.uk and
criminal.clerks@guildhallchambers.co.uk
Call Date: 1996, Inner Temple
Qualifications: [LLB (Kent), BA]

COLLINS SCOTT LEONARD

Arden Chambers
27 John Street, London WC1N 2BL,
Telephone: 020 7242 4244
E-mail:clerks@arden-chambers.law.co.uk
Call Date: Nov 1994, Gray's Inn
Qualifications: [BA (Queensland), LLB
(Sydney), LLM (Lond)]

COLLINSON MISS ALICIA HESTER

Harcourt Chambers
1st Floor, 2 Harcourt Buildings, Temple,
London EC4Y 9DB,
Telephone: 0171 353 6961
E-mail:clerks@harcourtchambers.law.co.uk
Harcourt Chambers
Churchill House, 3 St Aldate's Courtyard,
St Aldate's, Oxford OX1 1BN,
Telephone: 01865 791559
E-mail:clerks@harcourtchambers.law.co.uk
*Call Date: July 1982, Middle Temple
Pupil Master*
Qualifications: [MA (Oxon), M Phil (Oxon)]

COLMAN ANDREW

1 Hare Court
Ground Floor, Temple, London
EC4Y 7BE, Telephone: 0171 353 3982/
5324
*Call Date: July 1980, Lincoln's Inn
Pupil Master*
Qualifications: [LLB (Lond)]

COLOVER ROBERT MARK

4 Brick Court
Temple, London EC4Y 9AD,
Telephone: 0171 797 8910
E-mail: medhurst@dial.pipex.com
*Call Date: Nov 1975, Middle Temple
Pupil Master*
Qualifications: [Cert of Criminology]

COLQUHOUN MISS CELINA DAPHNE MARION

2-3 Gray's Inn Square
Gray's Inn, London WC1R 5JH,
Telephone: 0171 242 4986
E-mail:chambers@2-3graysinnsquare.co.uk
Call Date: Oct 1990, Gray's Inn
Qualifications: [LLB (Buck'm)]

COLTON MISS MARY WINIFRED

4 Brick Court, Chambers of Anne Rafferty QC
1st Floor, Temple, London EC4Y 9AD,
Telephone: 0171 583 8455
*Call Date: Feb 1955, Middle Temple
Pupil Master, Recorder*
Qualifications: [LLB (Lond)]

COLVILLE IAIN DAVID

Arden Chambers
27 John Street, London WC1N 2BL,
Telephone: 020 7242 4244
E-mail:clerks@arden-chambers.law.co.uk
Call Date: July 1989, Inner Temple
Qualifications: [LLB]

COLVIN ANDREW DUNCAN ROBSON

1 Dr Johnson's Buildings
Ground Floor, Temple, London
EC4Y 7AX, Telephone: 0171 353 9328
E-mail:OneDr.Johnsons@btinternet.com
Call Date: July 1972, Middle Temple
Qualifications: [BA (Hons), Dott.Giuris
(Siena)]

COMAISH ANDREW JAMES CHRISTIAN

Wilberforce Chambers
7 Bishop Lane, Hull, East Yorkshire,
HU1 1PA, Telephone: 01482 323264
E-mail: clerks@hullbar.demon.co.uk
Call Date: Nov 1989, Middle Temple
Qualifications: [MA Hons (Cantab)]

COMFORT MISS POLLY-ANNE

2 Paper Buildings, Basement North
Temple, London EC4Y 7ET,
Telephone: 0171 936 2613
E-mail: post@2paper.co.uk
Call Date: Feb 1988, Lincoln's Inn
Qualifications: [LLB (Hons) (Lond)]

COMPTON ALLAN SPENCER

Trinity Chambers
140 New London Road, Chelmsford,
Essex, CM2 0AW,
Telephone: 01245 605040
E-mail:clerks@trinitychambers.law.co.uk
Call Date: Nov 1994, Inner Temple
Qualifications: [LLB (Soton)]

COMPTON GARETH FRANCIS THOMAS

22 Old Buildings
Lincoln's Inn, London WC2A 3UJ,
Telephone: 0171 831 0222
Call Date: Mar 1997, Middle Temple
Qualifications: [MA (Hons)(Cantab)]

COMPTON TIMOTHY MARK

Gray's Inn Chambers
5th Floor, Gray's Inn, London WC1R 5JA,
Telephone: 0171 404 1111
College Chambers
19 Carlton Cresent, Southampton
SO15 2ET, Telephone: 01703 230338
Call Date: July 1984, Inner Temple
Pupil Master
Qualifications: [BA (Bristol), Dip Law]

COMPTON-RICKETT MISS MARY ANNE

Martins Building
2nd Floor, No 4 Water Street, Liverpool
L2 3SP, Telephone: 0151 236 5818/4919
Call Date: July 1972, Gray's Inn
Qualifications: [LLB]

COMPTON-WELSTEAD BENJAMIN EDWARD

2 King's Bench Walk
Ground Floor, Temple, London
EC4Y 7DE, Telephone: 0171 353 1746
E-mail: 2kbw@atlas.co.uk
King's Bench Chambers
115 North Hill, Plymouth PL4 8JY,
Telephone: 01752 221551
Call Date: Nov 1979, Lincoln's Inn
Pupil Master

COMYN TIMOTHY JOHN

2 Harcourt Buildings
2nd Floor, Temple, London EC4Y 9DB,
Telephone: 020 7353 8415
E-mail: clerks@2hb.law.co.uk
Call Date: July 1980, Inner Temple
Pupil Master
Qualifications: [LLB (Hull)]

CONCANNON TIMOTHY THOMAS PAUL

Portsmouth Barristers' Chambers
Victory House, 7 Bellevue Terrace,
Portsmouth, Hampshire, PO5 3AT,
Telephone: 023 92 831292/811811
E-mail: clerks@portsmouthbar.com
Call Date: May 1993, Inner Temple

CONE JOHN CRAWFORD

Erskine Chambers
30 Lincoln's Inn Fields, Lincoln's Inn,
London WC2A 3PF,
Telephone: 0171 242 5532
E-mail:clerks@erskine-chambers.co.uk
Call Date: July 1975, Middle Temple
Pupil Master
Qualifications: [LLB (L'pool)]

CONEY CHRISTOPHER RONALD RAMSDEN

4 Paper Buildings
1st Floor, Temple, London EC4Y 7EX,
Telephone: 0171 583 0816/353 1131
E-mail: clerks@4paperbuildings.co.uk
Call Date: July 1979, Inner Temple
Pupil Master
Qualifications: [LLB (Soton)]

CONLIN GEOFFREY DAVID

3 Serjeants' Inn
London EC4Y 1BQ,
Telephone: 0171 353 5537
E-mail: clerks@3serjeantsinn.com
Call Date: July 1973, Inner Temple
Pupil Master, Recorder

CONLON MICHAEL ANTHONY

One Essex Court
Ground Floor, Temple, London
EC4Y 9AR, Telephone: 020 7583 2000
E-mail: clerks@oneessexcourt.co.uk
Call Date: July 1974, Inner Temple
Qualifications: [MA (Cantab), FT11, AIIT, FRSA]

Fax: 0171 583 0118;
Out of hours telephone: 0171 583 2000;
DX: 430 London;
Other comms: E-mail
clerks@oneessexcourt.uk.com

Other professional qualifications: Fellow of the Chartered Institute of Taxation

Types of work: Commercial litigation, EC and competition law, Tax – corporate, VAT and Customs & Excise

Awards and memberships: FTII, FSALS, FRSA, FICPD, AIIT, National President VAT Practitioners Group; President of the Institute of Indirect Taxation; member of Tax Law Review Committee; Court Assistant to the Guild of Tax Advisers; Revenue Bar Association; Chancery Bar Association; COMBAR; Bar European Group

Other professional experience: Formerly a Senior Legal Adviser with HM Customs & Excise (1976-86); Tax Partner Coopers & Lybrand (1989-91); Solicitor (1992-7); Tax Partner Allen & Overy (1993-7); Director Watchfield Publishing Limited (from 1997)

Languages spoken: Afrikaans

Practice
Specialises in all aspects of indirect taxation advice, investigations and litigation before courts and tribunals (including related administrative, commercial and criminal law matters). Clients include major banks and financial institutions (particularly in partial exemption and property matters), developers and property investors, manufacturers and retailers and charitable and educational bodies. Several current cases involve novel and complex issues of European Community law. Instructions come from solicitors and other professionals under Direct Professional Access arrangements.

CONLON MICHAEL JOHN PATRICK

4 Overdale Road
Knighton, Leicester LE2 3YH,
Telephone: 0116 2883930
St Albans Chambers
Dolphin Lodge, Dolphin Yard, Holywell Hill, St Albans, Herts, AL1 1EX,
Telephone: 01727 843383
Tindal Chambers
3/5 New Street, Chelmsford, Essex, CM1 1NT, Telephone: 01245 267742
Call Date: Nov 1984, Inner Temple
Qualifications: [LLB (Hull)]

CONNELL EDWARD SAMUEL

1 Inner Temple Lane
Temple, London EC4Y 1AF,
Telephone: 020 7353 0933
Call Date: Oct 1996, Middle Temple
Qualifications: [BA (Hons)(Keele), CPE]

CONNERTY ANTHONY ROBIN

Lamb Chambers
Lamb Building, Temple, London
EC4Y 7AS, Telephone: 020 7797 8300
E-mail: lambchambers@link.org
Call Date: July 1974, Inner Temple
Pupil Master
Qualifications: [FCIArb]

CONNING MICHAEL CHRISTOPHER

4 Brick Court
Ground Floor, Temple, London
EC4Y 9AD, Telephone: 0171 797 7766
E-mail: chambers@4brick.co.uk
Call Date: Nov 1990, Middle Temple
Qualifications: [BSc (Cardiff)]

CONNOLLY MRS BARBARA WINIFRED

9 Bedford Row
London WC1R 4AZ,
Telephone: 0171 242 3555
E-mail: clerks@9br.co.uk
Call Date: July 1986, Inner Temple
Qualifications: [LLB (Hons)]

CONNOLLY MS DEIRDRE JOAN

3 Temple Gardens
Lower Ground Floor, Temple, London
EC4Y 9AU, Telephone: 0171 353 3102/5/
9297 E-mail: clerks@3tg.co.uk
Call Date: Nov 1982, Gray's Inn
Qualifications: [LLB (L'pool)]

CONNOLLY DOMINIC REGAN

1 Harcourt Buildings
2nd Floor, Temple, London EC4Y 9DA,
Telephone: 0171 353 9421/0375
E-mail:clerks@1harcourtbuildings.law.co.uk
Call Date: Feb 1989, Middle Temple
Qualifications: [LLB (LSE)]

CONNOLLY JAMES MARTIN PHILIP

1 Pump Court
Lower Ground Floor, Temple, London
EC4Y 7AB, Telephone: 0171 583 2012/
353 4341
E-mail: [name]@1pumpcourt.co.uk
Call Date: May 1985, Middle Temple
Qualifications: [MA (Dublin), LLB (Dublin)]

CONNOLLY MISS JOANNE MARIE

8 King Street Chambers
8 King Street, Manchester M2 6AQ,
Telephone: 0161 834 9560
E-mail: eightking@aol.com
Call Date: Oct 1992, Middle Temple
Qualifications: [LL.B (Hons)(Nott'm)]

CONNOLLY MICHAEL

Chavasse Court Chambers
2nd Floor, Chavasse Court, 24 Lord Street,
Liverpool L2 1TA,
Telephone: 0151 707 1191
Call Date: July 1985, Gray's Inn
Qualifications: [BA]

CONNOLLY SIMON JAMES

3 Temple Gardens
Lower Ground Floor, Temple, London
EC4Y 9AU, Telephone: 0171 353 3102/5/
9297 E-mail: clerks@3tg.co.uk
Call Date: July 1981, Middle Temple
Pupil Master
Qualifications: [BA]

CONNOR GINO PHILIP

Furnival Chambers
32 Furnival Street, London EC4A 1JQ,
Telephone: 0171 405 3232
E-mail: clerks@furnivallaw.co.uk
Call Date: Nov 1974, Gray's Inn
Pupil Master

CONNOR MARK JONATHAN DOMINIC

White Friars Chambers
21 White Friars, Chester CH1 1NZ,
Telephone: 01244 323070
E-mail:whitefriarschambers@btinternet.com
Call Date: May 1994, Inner Temple
Qualifications: [LLB (Hons)]

CONRAD ALAN DAVID QC (1999)

Lincoln House Chambers
5th Floor, Lincoln House, 1 Brazennose
Street, Manchester M2 5EL,
Telephone: 0161 832 5701
E-mail: info@lincolnhse.co.uk
Call Date: 1976, Middle Temple
Pupil Master, Recorder
Qualifications: [BA (Oxon)]

CONRATH PHILIP BERNARD

2nd Floor, Francis Taylor Building
Temple, London EC4Y 7BY,
Telephone: 0171 353 9942/3157
Call Date: July 1972, Gray's Inn
Pupil Master

CONROY MISS MARIAN

3 Stone Buildings
Lincoln's Inn, London WC2A 3XL,
Telephone: 0171 242 4937
E-mail: clerks@3sb.law.co.uk
Call Date: Nov 1991, Inner Temple
Qualifications: [LLB (Hull)]

CONRY MICHAEL HARVEY

1 Fountain Court
Steelhouse Lane, Birmingham B4 6DR,
Telephone: 0121 236 5721
Call Date: July 1979, Gray's Inn
Qualifications: [LLB (Reading)]

CONSIDINE PAUL CHRISTOPHER

1 Fountain Court
Steelhouse Lane, Birmingham B4 6DR,
Telephone: 0121 236 5721
Call Date: Oct 1992, Middle Temple
Qualifications: [MA (Oxon), Diploma in
Law(City)]

CONSTABLE ADAM MICHAEL

2 Temple Gardens
Temple, London EC4Y 9AY,
Telephone: 0171 583 6041
E-mail: clerks@2templegardens.co.uk
Call Date: Oct 1995, Inner Temple
Qualifications: [BA (Oxon)]

CONSTABLE JOHN MARTYN CHESTER

Baker Street Chambers
9 Baker Street, Middlesbrough TS1 2LF,
Telephone: 01642 873873
Call Date: Feb 1972, Gray's Inn
Qualifications: [LLB (Hull), LLM (Leics), MA (York)]

CONSTANTINE STEPHEN ALLAN

Baker Street Chambers
9 Baker Street, Middlesbrough TS1 2LF,
Telephone: 01642 873873
Call Date: Oct 1992, Middle Temple
Qualifications: [B.Sc. (Hons)]

CONVEY CHRISTOPHER MICHAEL

Furnival Chambers
32 Furnival Street, London EC4A 1JQ,
Telephone: 0171 405 3232
E-mail: clerks@furnivallaw.co.uk
Call Date: 1994, Lincoln's Inn
Qualifications: [LLB (Hons)(Lond)]

CONWAY CHARLES

3 Hare Court
1 Little Essex Street, London WC2R 3LD,
Telephone: 0171 395 2000
Call Date: July 1969, Middle Temple
Qualifications: [MA, LLB (Cantab)]

CONWAY ROBERT DAVID

7 Stone Buildings (also at 11 Bolt Court)
1st Floor, Lincoln's Inn, London
WC2A 3SZ, Telephone: 0171 242 0961
E-mail:larthur@7stonebuildings.law.co.uk
11 Bolt Court (also at 7 Stone Buildings – 1st Floor)
London EC4A 3DQ,
Telephone: 0171 353 2300
E-mail: boltct11@aol.com
Redhill Chambers
Seloduct House, 30 Station Road, Redhill,
Surrey, RH1 1NF,
Telephone: 01737 780781
Call Date: Nov 1974, Inner Temple
Pupil Master
Qualifications: [LLB (Lond)]

COODE JONATHAN GRAHAM

13 King's Bench Walk
1st Floor, Temple, London EC4Y 7EN,
Telephone: 0171 353 7204
E-mail: clerks@13kbw.law.co.uk
King's Bench Chambers
32 Beaumont Street, Oxford OX1 2NP,
Telephone: 01865 311066
E-mail: clerks@kbc-oxford.law.co.uk
Call Date: July 1984, Middle Temple
Qualifications: [BA (East Anglia), Dip Law]

COOK MISS ALISON NOELE

St Philip's Chambers
Fountain Court, Steelhouse Lane,
Birmingham B4 6DR,
Telephone: 0121 246 7000
E-mail: clerks@st-philips.co.uk
Call Date: Feb 1989, Gray's Inn
Qualifications: [LLB (Manch) (Hons)]

COOK CHARLES STUART

33 Park Place
Cardiff CF1 3BA,
Telephone: 02920 233313
Call Date: Nov 1966, Lincoln's Inn
Pupil Master, Recorder
Qualifications: [MA (Oxon)]

COOK CHRISTOPHER GRAHAM

St James's Chambers
68 Quay Street, Manchester M3 3EJ,
Telephone: 0161 834 7000
E-mail: clerks@stjameschambers.co.uk
Call Date: Oct 1990, Inner Temple
Qualifications: [BSc, BCom (B'ham), Dip Law (City)]

COOK GARY WILLIAM

Victoria Chambers
3rd Floor, 177 Corporation Street,
Birmingham B4 6RG,
Telephone: 0121 236 9900
E-mail: viccham@aol.com
Call Date: Nov 1989, Middle Temple
Qualifications: [B.Ed Hons]

COOK IAN REGINALD BLACKLIN

One King's Bench Walk
1st Floor, Temple, London EC4Y 7DB,
Telephone: 0171 936 1500
E-mail: ddear@1kbw.co.uk
Call Date: Nov 1994, Inner Temple
Qualifications: [BA (Hons)(Lond), CPE
(City)]

COOK JEREMY DAVID

Lamb Building
Ground Floor, Temple, London
EC4Y 7AS, Telephone: 020 7797 7788
E-mail: lamb.building@link.org
Call Date: July 1982, Gray's Inn
Pupil Master
Qualifications: [BA (Keele)]

COOK MISS LESLEY ANN

Bank House Chambers
Old Bank House, Hartshead, Sheffield
S1 2EL, Telephone: 0114 2751223
Call Date: Nov 1984, Middle Temple
Qualifications: [BA (Oxon)]

COOK MISS MARY JANE

2-3 Gray's Inn Square
Gray's Inn, London WC1R 5JH,
Telephone: 0171 242 4986
E-mail:chambers@2-3graysinnsquare.co.uk
Call Date: July 1982, Inner Temple
Pupil Master
Qualifications: [LLB (Cardiff)]

COOK PAUL GRAHAM WHALLEY

Albion Chambers
Broad Street, Bristol BS1 1DR,
Telephone: 0117 9272144
Call Date: Nov 1992, Middle Temple
Qualifications: [BA (Hons)(Kent), Dip in
Law]

COOK MISS TINA GAIL

22 Old Buildings
Lincoln's Inn, London WC2A 3UJ,
Telephone: 0171 831 0222
Call Date: July 1988, Middle Temple
Pupil Master
Qualifications: [BA (Hons) (Oxon)]

COOK MISS WENDY ANNE

2nd Floor, Francis Taylor Building
Temple, London EC4Y 7BY,
Telephone: 0171 353 9942/3157
Call Date: 1997, Middle Temple
Qualifications: [BA (Hons)]

COOKE GRAHAM OWEN JOHN

23 Essex Street
London WC2R 3AS,
Telephone: 0171 413 0353/836 8366
E-mail:clerks@essexstreet23.demon.co.uk
Call Date: July 1983, Lincoln's Inn
Pupil Master

COOKE JEREMY LIONEL QC (1990)

S Tomlinson QC
7 King's Bench Walk, Temple, London
EC4Y 7DS, Telephone: 0171 583 0404
E-mail: clerks@7kbw.law.co.uk
Call Date: July 1976, Lincoln's Inn
Assistant Recorder
Qualifications: [MA (Oxon)]

COOKE JULIAN HUMPHREY SPENCER

20 Essex Street
London WC2R 3AL,
Telephone: 0171 583 9294
E-mail: clerks@20essexst.com
Call Date: July 1965, Lincoln's Inn
Pupil Master
Qualifications: [MA, LLB (Cantab)]

COOKE NICHOLAS ORTON QC (1998)

9 Park Place
Cardiff CF1 3DP,
Telephone: 01222 382731
Farrar's Building
Temple, London EC4Y 7BD,
Telephone: 0171 583 9241
E-mail:chambers@farrarsbuilding.co.uk
Call Date: 1977, Middle Temple
Assistant Recorder
Qualifications: [LLB]

COOKE PETER RAYMOND

6 Fountain Court
Steelhouse Lane, Birmingham B4 6DR,
Telephone: 0121 233 3282
E-mail: clerks@sixfountain.co.uk
Call Date: July 1985, Lincoln's Inn
Pupil Master
Qualifications: [LLB(Manchester)]

COOKSLEY NIGEL JAMES

Old Square Chambers
1 Verulam Buildings, Gray's Inn, London
WC1R 5LQ, Telephone: 0171 269 0300
E-mail:clerks@oldsquarechambers.co.uk
Old Square Chambers
Hanover House, 47 Corn Street, Bristol
BS1 1HT, Telephone: 0117 9277111
E-mail: oldsqbri@globalnet.co.uk
Call Date: July 1975, Inner Temple
Pupil Master
Qualifications: [BA (Cantab)]

COOKSLEY MRS SUBHASHINI ANN

Lion Court
Chancery House, 53-64 Chancery Lane,
London WC2A 1SJ,
Telephone: 0171 404 6565
Call Date: Nov 1975, Gray's Inn

COOMBE PETER MICHAEL AENEAS

2 Harcourt Buildings
1st Floor, Temple, London EC4Y 9DB,
Telephone: 020 7353 2112
Call Date: Nov 1993, Middle Temple
Qualifications: [BA (Hons)(Oxon)]

COOMBES TIMOTHY JAMES

3 Paper Buildings
Temple, London EC4Y 7EU,
Telephone: 020 7583 8055
E-mail: London@3paper.com
3 Paper Buildings (Bournemouth)
20 Lorne Park Road, Bournemouth,
Dorset, BH1 1JN,
Telephone: 01202 292102
E-mail: Bournemouth@3paper.com
3 Paper Buildings (Winchester)
4 St Peter Street, Winchester SO23 8BW,
Telephone: 01962 868884
E-mail: winchester@3paper.com

3 Paper Buildings (Oxford)
1 Alfred Street, High Street, Oxford
OX1 4EH, Telephone: 01865 793736
E-mail: oxford@3paper.com
Call Date: July 1980, Inner Temple
Pupil Master
Qualifications: [BA (Dunelm)]

COOMBES DAVIES DR MAIR

30 Park Place
Cardiff CF1 3BA,
Telephone: 01222 398421
E-mail: 100757.1456@compuserve.com
Call Date: July 1988, Lincoln's Inn
Qualifications: [BSc(Hons), BArch, , PhD
(Wales), CPE]

COONAN KIERAN BENET QC (1990)

Chambers of Kieran Coonan QC
Ground Floor, 6 Pump Court, Temple,
London EC4Y 7AR,
Telephone: 0171 583 6013/2510
E-mail: clerks@6-pumpcourt.law.co.uk
Call Date: July 1971, Gray's Inn
Recorder
Qualifications: [Dip Eur Law]

COOPER ADRIAN EDGAR MARK

2 Harcourt Buildings
Ground Floor/Left, Temple, London
EC4Y 9DB, Telephone: 0171 583 9020
E-mail: clerks@harcourt.co.uk
Call Date: July 1970, Inner Temple
Assistant Recorder
Qualifications: [MA (Oxon)]

COOPER ALAN GEORGE

39 Essex Street
London WC2R 3AT,
Telephone: 0171 832 1111
E-mail: clerks@39essex.co.uk
Call Date: July 1969, Gray's Inn
Pupil Master

COOPER ARNOLD JAMES

Plowden Buildings
2nd Floor, 2 Plowden Buildings, Middle
Temple Lane, London EC4Y 9BU,
Telephone: 0171 583 0808
E-mail: bar@plowdenbuildings.co.uk
Call Date: July 1969, Lincoln's Inn
Pupil Master
Qualifications: [LLB]

COOPER GILEAD PATRICK

Chambers of Mr Peter Crampin QC
Ground Floor, 11 New Square, Lincoln's
Inn, London WC2A 3QB,
Telephone: 020 7831 0081
E-mail: 11newsquare.co.uk
Call Date: Nov 1983, Middle Temple
Qualifications: [MA (Oxon), Dip Law]

COOPER JOHN GORDON

3 Gray's Inn Square
Ground Floor, London WC1R 5AH,
Telephone: 0171 520 5600
E-mail: clerks@3gis.co.uk
Call Date: July 1983, Middle Temple
Pupil Master
Qualifications: [LLB (Hons)(Newc),
Butterworths Law, Prizeman]

COOPER JOHN MICHAEL

11 King's Bench Walk
1st Floor, Temple, London EC4Y 7EQ,
Telephone: 0171 353 3337
E-mail: fmuller11@aol.com
11 King's Bench Walk
3 Park Court, Park Cross Street, Leeds
LS1 2QH, Telephone: 0113 297 1200
Call Date: July 1985, Inner Temple
Qualifications: [LLB(Reading)]

COOPER MARK ANTHONY JOHN

2 Mitre Court Buildings
1st Floor, Temple, London EC4Y 7BX,
Telephone: 0171 353 1353
Call Date: 1997, Middle Temple
Qualifications: [LLB (Hons)(Kent)]

COOPER MORRIS

St Philip's Chambers
Fountain Court, Steelhouse Lane,
Birmingham B4 6DR,
Telephone: 0121 246 7000
E-mail: clerks@st-philips.co.uk
Call Date: July 1979, Gray's Inn

COOPER NICHOLAS JEROME

Acre Lane Neighbourhood Chambers
30A Acre Lane, London SW2 5SG,
Telephone: 0171 274 4400
E-mail:barristerschambers@acrelane.demon.co.u
k
Call Date: 1997, Middle Temple
Qualifications: [BA (Hons)]

COOPER NIGEL STUART

4 Essex Court
Temple, London EC4Y 9AJ,
Telephone: 020 7797 7970
E-mail: clerks@4essexcourt.law.co.uk
Call Date: July 1987, Lincoln's Inn
Pupil Master
Qualifications: [LLB (Leeds),
DIPE.1(Amsterdam), LLM (Lond)]

COOPER MS PENELOPE ELISABETH

4 Brick Court
Temple, London EC4Y 9AD,
Telephone: 0171 797 8910
E-mail: medhurst@dial.pipex.com
Call Date: 1990, Inner Temple
Qualifications: [BSc (Hons)]

COOPER PETER JAMES QC (1993)

2 Harcourt Buildings
1st Floor, Temple, London EC4Y 9DB,
Telephone: 020 7353 2112
Call Date: Nov 1974, Gray's Inn
Recorder

COOPER PETER JOHN

St Ive's Chambers
Whittall Street, Birmingham B4 6DH,
Telephone: 0121 236 0863/5720
E-mail:stives.headofchambers@btinternet.com
Call Date: 1996, Gray's Inn
Qualifications: [BA (Hons) (Oxon)]

COOPER ROGER BERNARD

Plowden Buildings
2nd Floor, 2 Plowden Buildings, Middle
Temple Lane, London EC4Y 9BU,
Telephone: 0171 583 0808
E-mail: bar@plowdenbuildings.co.uk
Call Date: July 1989, Inner Temple
Qualifications: [BSc (L'pool), Dip Law]

COOPER MISS SARAH LUCY

Thomas More Chambers
52 Carey Street, Lincoln's Inn, London
WC2A 2JB, Telephone: 0171 404 7000
E-mail: clerks@thomasmore.law.co.uk
Call Date: Nov 1993, Inner Temple
Qualifications: [BA (Dunelm), Dip in Law]

COOPER MISS SUSAN JOY

22 Old Buildings
Lincoln's Inn, London WC2A 3UJ,
Telephone: 0171 831 0222
Call Date: Nov 1976, Gray's Inn
Pupil Master
Qualifications: [LLB]

COORAY TARAKNATH UPALI

Mitre House Chambers
15-19 Devereux Court, London WC2R 3JJ,
Telephone: 0171 583 8233
Call Date: July 1974, Middle Temple
Qualifications: [BSc (Econ), LLB (London),
MA]

COPE CHRISTOPHER DOUGLAS BAILYE

4 Paper Buildings
1st Floor, Temple, London EC4Y 7EX,
Telephone: 0171 583 0816/353 1131
E-mail: clerks@4paperbuildings.co.uk
Call Date: Oct 1990, Inner Temple
Qualifications: [MA (Cantab)]

COPE JOHN THOMAS

Windsor Chambers
2 Penuel Lane, Pontypridd, South Wales,
CF37 4UF, Telephone: 01443 402067
E-mail: law@windsorchambers.co.uk
Call Date: 1997, Middle Temple
Qualifications: [BA (Hons)(Leeds)]

COPELAND ANDREW JOHN

Chambers of Geoffrey Hawker
46/48 Essex Street, London WC2R 3GH,
Telephone: 0171 583 8899
Call Date: Nov 1992, Gray's Inn
Qualifications: [LLB]

COPEMAN IAN DAVID

1 Middle Temple Lane
Temple, London EC4Y 1LT,
Telephone: 0171 583 0659 (12 Lines)
E-mail: chambers@1mtl.co.uk
Call Date: Nov 1977, Inner Temple
Pupil Master

COPLEY JAMES EDWARD

4 Paper Buildings
1st Floor, Temple, London EC4Y 7EX,
Telephone: 0171 583 0816/353 1131
E-mail: clerks@4paperbuildings.co.uk
Call Date: 1997, Inner Temple
Qualifications: [LLB (Manchester)]

COPLIN RICHARD JAMES

Keating Chambers
10 Essex Street, Outer Temple, London
WC2R 3AA, Telephone: 0171 544 2600
Call Date: Oct 1997, Middle Temple
Qualifications: [BA (Hons)(Exon), CPE
(City)]

COPNALL RICHARD ANTHONY

Park Lane Chambers
19 Westgate, Leeds LS1 2RD,
Telephone: 0113 2285000
E-mail:clerks@parklanechambers.co.uk
Call Date: Oct 1990, Inner Temple
Qualifications: [BSc, CPE (Nott'm)]

COPPEL JASON ALASTAIR

11 King's Bench Walk
Temple, London EC4Y 7EQ,
Telephone: 0171 632 8500/583 0610
E-mail: clerksroom@11kbw.com
Call Date: Nov 1994, Inner Temple
Qualifications: [BA (Oxon), LLM
(EUI,Florence)]

COPPEL PHILIP ANTONY

2-3 Gray's Inn Square
Gray's Inn, London WC1R 5JH,
Telephone: 0171 242 4986
E-mail:chambers@2-3graysinnsquare.co.uk
Call Date: Nov 1994, Lincoln's Inn
Pupil Master
Qualifications: [BA, LLB (Australia)]

COPPEL MISS YVONNE RUTH

24a St John Street
Manchester M3 4DF,
Telephone: 0161 833 9628
Call Date: July 1976, Inner Temple
Pupil Master, Assistant Recorder
Qualifications: [LLB (Hons)]

COPPOLA MISS ANNA FRANCESCA

5 Raymond Buildings
1st Floor, Gray's Inn, London WC1R 5BP,
Telephone: 0171 242 2902
E-mail: clerks@media-ent-law.co.uk
Call Date: Nov 1996, Lincoln's Inn
Qualifications: [BA (Hons)(Lond), Dip Law]

CORBEN PAUL ANTHONY

169 Temple Chambers
Temple Avenue, London EC4Y 0DA,
Telephone: 0171 583 7644
Call Date: July 1979, Gray's Inn
Pupil Master
Qualifications: [MA (Cantab), FCIArb]

CORBETT JAMES PATRICK QC (1999)

St Philip's Chambers
Fountain Court, Steelhouse Lane,
Birmingham B4 6DR,
Telephone: 0121 246 7000
E-mail: clerks@st-philips.co.uk
Chambers of Andrew Campbell QC
10 Park Square, Leeds LS1 2LH,
Telephone: 0113 2455438
E-mail: clerks@10pksq.co.uk
Call Date: 1975, Inner Temple
Pupil Master, Assistant Recorder
Qualifications: [LLB, LLM (Exon), ACIArb]

CORBETT MISS MICHELLE JANE

14 Gray's Inn Square
Gray's Inn, London WC1R 5JP,
Telephone: 0171 242 0858
E-mail: 100712.2134@compuserve.com
Call Date: July 1987, Inner Temple
Pupil Master
Qualifications: [LLB (Leeds)]

CORBETT MRS SANDRA MARGARET

1 New Square
Ground Floor, Lincoln's Inn, London
WC2A 3SA, Telephone: 0171 405 0884/5/6/
7 E-mail: clerks@1newsquare.law.co.uk
Call Date: July 1988, Middle Temple
Pupil Master
Qualifications: [LLB (Hons) (Lond)]

CORDARA RODERICK CHARLES QC (1994)

Essex Court Chambers
24 Lincoln's Inn Fields, London
WC2A 3ED, Telephone: 0171 813 8000
E-mail:clerksroom@essexcourt-chambers.co.u
k
Call Date: July 1975, Middle Temple
Qualifications: [MA (Cantab)]

CORDEY DANIEL ROE

York Chambers
14 Toft Green, York YO1 6JT,
Telephone: 01904 620048
E-mail: [name]@yorkchambers.co.uk
Call Date: Nov 1990, Gray's Inn
Qualifications: [LLB (Lond)]

CORFIELD MISS SHEELAGH MARJORIE

Guildhall Chambers
22-26 Broad Street, Bristol BS1 2HG,
Telephone: 0117 9273366
E-mail:civil.clerks@guildhallchambers.co.uk and
criminal.clerks@guildhallchambers.co.uk
Call Date: July 1975, Middle Temple
Pupil Master
Qualifications: [LLB (Bristol)]

CORKERY MICHAEL QC (1981)

Five Paper Buildings
1st Floor, Five Paper Bldgs, Temple,
London EC4Y 7HB,
Telephone: 0171 583 6117
E-mail:clerks@5-paperbuildings.law.co.uk
Call Date: Nov 1949, Lincoln's Inn

CORLESS JOHN VINCENT

Adrian Lyon's Chambers
14 Castle Street, Liverpool L2 0NE,
Telephone: 0151 236 4421/8240
E-mail: chambers14@aol.com
Call Date: Nov 1984, Middle Temple
Pupil Master
Qualifications: [MA (St Andrews)]

CORNAH MS EMMA LOUISE

15 Winckley Square
Preston PR1 3JJ,
Telephone: 01772 252828
E-mail:clerks@winckleysq.demon.co.uk
Call Date: Nov 1992, Inner Temple
Qualifications: [LLB (Hons)]

CORNER TIMOTHY FRANK

4-5 Gray's Inn Square
Ground Floor, Gray's Inn, London
WC1R 5JP, Telephone: 0171 404 5252
E-mail:chambers@4-5graysinnsquare.co.uk
Call Date: Nov 1981, Gray's Inn
Pupil Master
Qualifications: [MA, BCL (Oxon)]

CORNFORD HUGH CHARLES THOMAS

Fleet Chambers
Mitre House, 44-46 Fleet Street, London
EC4Y 1BN, Telephone: 0171 936 3707
E-mail: rr@fleetchambers.demon.co.uk
Call Date: Nov 1994, Middle Temple
Qualifications: [BA (Hons) (Exon)]

CORNISH WILLIAM RUDOLPH QC (1997)

8 New Square
Lincoln's Inn, London WC2A 3QP,
Telephone: 0171 405 4321
E-mail: clerks@8newsquare.co.uk
Call Date: 1965, Gray's Inn
Qualifications: [LLB(Adelaide), BCL(Oxon)]

CORNWALL CHRISTOPHER JOHN

Exchange Chambers
Pearl Assurance House, Derby Square,
Liverpool L2 9XX,
Telephone: 0151 236 7747
E-mail:exchangechambers@btinternet.com
Call Date: July 1975, Lincoln's Inn
Pupil Master, Recorder
Qualifications: [BA (Oxon)]

CORNWALL MISS VIRGINIA MARGARET

1 Inner Temple Lane
Temple, London EC4Y 1AF,
Telephone: 020 7353 0933
Call Date: Oct 1990, Middle Temple
Qualifications: [LLB (Hons)]

CORRELLA-DAVID ANDREW GEORGE EDWARD

St David's Chambers
10 Calvert Terrace, Swansea, West
Glamorgan, SA1 5AR,
Call Date: Nov 1986, Gray's Inn
Qualifications: [LLB (Wales)]

CORRIGAN PETER ANTHONY

2 Paper Buildings
1st Floor, Temple, London EC4Y 7ET,
Telephone: 020 7556 5500
E-mail: clerks@2pbbarristers.co.uk
Call Date: July 1972, Middle Temple
Pupil Master
Qualifications: [MA (Oxon)]

CORRY MISS CAROL ELIZABETH

Staple Inn Chambers
1st Floor, 9 Staple Inn, Holborn Bars,
London WC1V 7QH,
Telephone: 0171 242 5240
E-mail: clerks@staple-inn.org
Call Date: July 1981, Lincoln's Inn
Qualifications: [BA (Hons)]

CORSELLIS NICHOLAS ROBERT ALEXANDER

3 Temple Gardens
Lower Ground Floor, Temple, London
EC4Y 9AU, Telephone: 0171 353 3102/5/
9297 E-mail: clerks@3tg.co.uk
Call Date: Nov 1993, Lincoln's Inn
Qualifications: [LLB (Hons)]

CORY-WRIGHT CHARLES ALEXANDER

39 Essex Street
London WC2R 3AT,
Telephone: 0171 832 1111
E-mail: clerks@39essex.co.uk
Call Date: Feb 1984, Middle Temple
Pupil Master
Qualifications: [BA (Oxon), Dip Law (City)]

COSEDGE ANDREW JOHN

3 Stone Buildings
Lincoln's Inn, London WC2A 3XL,
Telephone: 0171 242 4937
E-mail: clerks@3sb.law.co.uk
Call Date: July 1972, Inner Temple
Pupil Master
Qualifications: [LLB]

COSGROVE PATRICK JOSEPH QC (1994)

Broad Chare
33 Broad Chare, Newcastle upon Tyne
NE1 3DQ, Telephone: 0191 232 0541
E-mail:clerks@broadcharechambers.law.co.uk
Call Date: July 1976, Gray's Inn
Recorder

COSGROVE MR. THOMAS JAMES

2-3 Gray's Inn Square
Gray's Inn, London WC1R 5JH,
Telephone: 0171 242 4986
E-mail:chambers@2-3graysinnsquare.co.uk
Call Date: Oct 1994, Inner Temple
Qualifications: [MA (Cantab)]

COSTER RONALD DAVID

22 Old Buildings
Lincoln's Inn, London WC2A 3UJ,
Telephone: 0171 831 0222
Call Date: July 1989, Lincoln's Inn
Qualifications: [BSC (Lanc), Dip Law]

COTCHER MISS ANN LOUISE

3 Temple Gardens
Lower Ground Floor, Temple, London
EC4Y 9AU, Telephone: 0171 353 3102/5/
9297 E-mail: clerks@3tg.co.uk
Call Date: July 1979, Middle Temple
Pupil Master
Qualifications: [LLB (Soton)]

COTTAGE MISS ROSINA

9 Gough Square
London EC4A 3DE,
Telephone: 020 7832 0500
E-mail: clerks@9goughsq.co.uk
Call Date: Nov 1988, Inner Temple
Pupil Master
Qualifications: [LLB (Bris)]

COTTER BARRY PAUL

Old Square Chambers
Hanover House, 47 Corn Street, Bristol
BS1 1HT, Telephone: 0117 9277111
E-mail: oldsqbri@globalnet.co.uk
Old Square Chambers
1 Verulam Buildings, Gray's Inn, London
WC1R 5LQ, Telephone: 0171 269 0300
E-mail:clerks@oldsquarechambers.co.uk
Call Date: July 1985, Lincoln's Inn
Pupil Master
Qualifications: [LLB (Lond)]

COTTER MARK JAMES

Holborn Chambers
6 Gate Street, Lincoln's Inn Fields, London
WC2A 3HP, Telephone: 0171 242 6060
Call Date: Nov 1994, Middle Temple
Qualifications: [LLB (Hons), LLM, (Wales)]

COTTER MISS RACHEL JOSLIN ANN

5 Fountain Court
Steelhouse Lane, Birmingham B4 6DR,
Telephone: 0121 606 0500
E-mail:clerks@5fountaincourt.law.co.uk
Call Date: Nov 1994, Middle Temple
Qualifications: [BA (Hons)]

D

COTTER MISS SARA ELIZABETH

Higher Combe
Hawkcombe, Porlock, Minehead,
Somerset, TA24 8LP,
Telephone: 01643 862722
Call Date: Oct 1990, Middle Temple
Qualifications: [BA, Dip Law]

COTTERILL MISS IMOGEN KATE

Call Date: Nov 1995, Gray's Inn
Qualifications: [LLB (Reading)]

COTTERILL MISS SUSAN AMANDA

Lamb Building
Ground Floor, Temple, London
EC4Y 7AS, Telephone: 020 7797 7788
E-mail: lamb.building@link.org
*Call Date: July 1988, Lincoln's Inn
Pupil Master*
Qualifications: [LLB (Hons) (Essex)]

COTTLE MAURICE ANTHONY HAYDEN

3 Serjeants' Inn
London EC4Y 1BQ,
Telephone: 0171 353 5537
E-mail: clerks@3serjeantsinn.com
Call Date: July 1978, Gray's Inn
Qualifications: [LLB (Lond), M.Phil (Lond)]

COTTLE STEPHEN CHARLES

Two Garden Court
1st Floor, Middle Temple, London
EC4Y 9BL, Telephone: 0171 353 1633
E-mail:barristers@2gardenct.law.co.uk
*Call Date: Nov 1984, Inner Temple
Pupil Master*
Qualifications: [BA, Dip Law]

COTTON MISS DIANA ROSEMARY QC (1983)

Devereux Chambers
Devereux Court, London WC2R 3JJ,
Telephone: 0171 353 7534
E-mail: mailbox@devchambers.co.uk
*Call Date: 1964, Middle Temple
Recorder*
Qualifications: [MA (Oxon)]

COTTRELL MATTHEW ROBERT

Oriel Chambers
14 Water Street, Liverpool L2 8TD,
Telephone: 0151 236 7191/236 4321
E-mail: clerks@oriel-chambers.co.uk
Call Date: Oct 1996, Gray's Inn
Qualifications: [LLB (Sheff)]

COUGHLIN VINCENT WILLIAM

Furnival Chambers
32 Furnival Street, London EC4A 1JQ,
Telephone: 0171 405 3232
E-mail: clerks@furnivallaw.co.uk
*Call Date: July 1980, Middle Temple
Pupil Master*
Qualifications: [LLB (Lond)]

COULSON PETER DAVID WILLIAM

Keating Chambers
10 Essex Street, Outer Temple, London
WC2R 3AA, Telephone: 0171 544 2600
*Call Date: Nov 1982, Gray's Inn
Pupil Master*
Qualifications: [BA (Keele), ACIArb]

COULTER BARRY JOHN

One Essex Court
1st Floor, Temple, London EC4Y 9AR,
Telephone: 0171 936 3030
E-mail: one.essex_court@virgin.net
Call Date: Nov 1985, Inner Temple
Qualifications: [LLB]

COULTHARD ALAN TERENCE

33 Park Place
Cardiff CF1 3BA,
Telephone: 02920 233313
Call Date: July 1987, Middle Temple
Qualifications: [LLB (Lond), BCL, (Oxon)]

COUNSELL EDWARD FREDERICK

South Western Chambers
Melville House, 12 Middle Street,
Taunton, Somerset, TA1 1SH,
Telephone: 01823 331919 (24 hrs)
E-mail: barclerk@clara.net
Call Date: Nov 1990, Inner Temple
Qualifications: [BA, BCL (Oxon)]

COUNSELL JAMES HENRY

2 King's Bench Walk
Ground Floor, Temple, London
EC4Y 7DE, Telephone: 0171 353 1746
E-mail: 2kbw@atlas.co.uk
King's Bench Chambers
115 North Hill, Plymouth PL4 8JY,
Telephone: 01752 221551
Call Date: July 1984, Inner Temple
Pupil Master
Qualifications: [MA (Cantab)]

COUNSELL MISS LYNNE MARGARET

9 Stone Buildings
Lincoln's Inn, London WC2A 3NN,
Telephone: 0171 404 5055
E-mail: clerks@9stoneb.law.co.uk
Call Date: Nov 1986, Inner Temple
Pupil Master
Qualifications: [BA (Lond) Dip Law, (City)]

COUPLAND STEVEN MICHAEL EDWARD

High Pavement Chambers
1 High Pavement, Nottingham NG1 1HF,
Telephone: 0115 9418218
Call Date: May 1993, Lincoln's Inn
Qualifications: [LLB (Hons) (Wales)]

COURTNEY MS ANN

New Court
Temple, London EC4Y 9BE,
Telephone: 0171 583 5123/0510
Call Date: Nov 1987, Inner Temple
Qualifications: [LLB (Hons)]

COURTNEY NICHOLAS PIERS

Queen's Chambers
5 John Dalton Street, Manchester M2 6ET,
Telephone: 0161 834 6875/4738
Queens Chambers
4 Camden Place, Preston PR1 3JL,
Telephone: 01772 828300
Call Date: Nov 1990, Middle Temple
Qualifications: [LLB (Manch)]

COUSENS MICHAEL PATRICK

2-4 Tudor Street
London EC4Y 0AA,
Telephone: 0171 797 7111
E-mail: clerks@rfqc.co.uk
Call Date: Feb 1973, Lincoln's Inn
Pupil Master

COUSINS CHRISTOPHER HUGH JAMES

4 King's Bench Walk
2nd Floor, Temple, London EC4Y 7DL,
Telephone: 020 7353 3581
E-mail: clerks@4kbw.co.uk
Call Date: July 1969, Middle Temple
Pupil Master

COUSINS EDWARD FRANCIS

11 Stone Buildings
Lincoln's Inn, London WC2A 3TG,
Telephone: +44 (0)207 831 6381
E-mail:clerks@11StoneBuildings.law.co.uk
Chichester Chambers
12 North Pallant, Chichester, West Sussex,
PO19 1TQ, Telephone: 01243 784538
E-mail:clerks@chichesterchambers.law.co.uk
Call Date: July 1971, Gray's Inn
Qualifications: [BA (L'pool), LLM (Lo]

COUSINS JEREMY VINCENT QC (1999)

4 Fountain Court
Steelhouse Lane, Birmingham B4 6DR,
Telephone: 0121 236 3476
Call Date: 1977, Middle Temple
Pupil Master, Assistant Recorder
Qualifications: [LLB (Warks)]

COVER MISS MARTHA JUNE

4 Brick Court
Ground Floor, Temple, London
EC4Y 9AD, Telephone: 0171 797 7766
E-mail: chambers@4brick.co.uk
Call Date: Nov 1979, Gray's Inn
Pupil Master
Qualifications: [BA (W. Ontario), BA , LLM (Lond), LLB (Lond)]

COWAN JACK

Martins Building
2nd Floor, No 4 Water Street, Liverpool
L2 3SP, Telephone: 0151 236 5818/4919
Call Date: Nov 1971, Inner Temple
Pupil Master
Qualifications: [LLB]

COWAN PETER SHERWOOD MCCREA

Oriel Chambers
14 Water Street, Liverpool L2 8TD,
Telephone: 0151 236 7191/236 4321
E-mail: clerks@oriel-chambers.co.uk
Call Date: July 1980, Middle Temple
Pupil Master, Assistant Recorder
Qualifications: [MA (Oxon)]

COWARD JOHN STEPHEN QC (1984)

9 Bedford Row
London WC1R 4AZ,
Telephone: 0171 242 3555
E-mail: clerks@9br.co.uk
Call Date: Apr 1964, Inner Temple
Recorder
Qualifications: [LLB]

COWARD MISS VICTORIA JANE

Hollis Whiteman Chambers
3rd Floor, Queen Elizabeth Bldg, Temple,
London EC4Y 9BS,
Telephone: 020 7583 5766
E-mail:barristers@holliswhiteman.co.uk
Call Date: Oct 1992, Middle Temple
Qualifications: [B.Sc (Hons, Manch),
Diploma In Law(City)]

COWEN GARY ADAM

Falcon Chambers
Falcon Court, London EC4Y 1AA,
Telephone: 0171 353 2484
E-mail: clerks@falcon-chambers.com
Call Date: Oct 1990, Inner Temple
Pupil Master
Qualifications: [LLB (Bris)]

COWEN JONATHAN MICHAEL

Gray's Inn Chambers
5th Floor, Gray's Inn, London WC1R 5JA,
Telephone: 0171 404 1111
Call Date: Nov 1983, Middle Temple
Pupil Master
Qualifications: [BA (Oxon) , Dip Law]

COWEN MISS SALLY EMMA

Chambers of Geoffrey Hawker
46/48 Essex Street, London WC2R 3GH,
Telephone: 0171 583 8899
Call Date: Oct 1995, Inner Temple
Qualifications: [LLB (Leeds)]

COWEN TIMOTHY ARIEH

Barnard's Inn Chambers
6th Floor, Halton House, 20-23 Holborn,
London EC1N 2JD,
Telephone: 0171 369 6969
E-mail: clerks@biclaw.co.uk
Call Date: Oct 1993, Inner Temple
Qualifications: [BA]

COWLEY ROBERT

8 Fountain Court
Steelhouse Lane, Birmingham B4 6DR,
Telephone: 0121 236 5514/5
E-mail: clerks@no8chambers.co.uk
Call Date: Oct 1992, Lincoln's Inn
Qualifications: [LLB(Hons)(Leic)]

COWTON MISS CATHERINE JUDITH

Queen Elizabeth Building
2nd Floor, Temple, London EC4Y 9BS,
Telephone: 0171 797 7837
Call Date: Nov 1995, Middle Temple
Qualifications: [BA (Hons)]

COX MISS ANTONIA SARAH

Holborn Chambers
6 Gate Street, Lincoln's Inn Fields, London
WC2A 3HP, Telephone: 0171 242 6060
Call Date: Oct 1996, Middle Temple
Qualifications: [LLB (Hons)(Manc)]

COX BRYAN RICHARD

9 Woodhouse Square
Leeds LS3 1AD,
Telephone: 0113 2451986
E-mail: clerks@9woodhouse.co.uk
Call Date: July 1979, Middle Temple
Pupil Master
Qualifications: [LLB (Leeds)]

COX BUSTER

Gray's Inn Chambers
5th Floor, Gray's Inn, London WC1R 5JA,
Telephone: 0171 404 1111
Call Date: Nov 1993, Gray's Inn
Qualifications: [B.Sc (Manch), LLB]

COX MISS CATHERINE AILSA

St Philip's Chambers
Fountain Court, Steelhouse Lane,
Birmingham B4 6DR,
Telephone: 0121 246 7000
E-mail: clerks@st-philips.co.uk
Call Date: July 1989, Middle Temple
Qualifications: [LLB (Manch)]

COX CHARLES GEOFFREY

Thomas More Chambers
52 Carey Street, Lincoln's Inn, London
WC2A 2JB, Telephone: 0171 404 7000
E-mail: clerks@thomasmore.law.co.uk
Call Date: July 1982, Middle Temple
Pupil Master
Qualifications: [BA (Cantab)]

COX DOMINIC

3 Temple Gardens
3rd Floor, Temple, London EC4Y 9AU,
Telephone: 0171 583 0010
Call Date: Nov 1994, Lincoln's Inn
Qualifications: [BA (Hons)(Kent)]

COX JAMES DUNCAN MALCOM

13 King's Bench Walk
1st Floor, Temple, London EC4Y 7EN,
Telephone: 0171 353 7204
E-mail: clerks@13kbw.law.co.uk
King's Bench Chambers
32 Beaumont Street, Oxford OX1 2NP,
Telephone: 01865 311066
E-mail: clerks@kbc-oxford.law.co.uk
Call Date: 1997, Gray's Inn
Qualifications: [LLB (Wales)]

COX JASON DAVID

Ropewalk Chambers
24 The Ropewalk, Nottingham NG1 5EF,
Telephone: 0115 9472581
E-mail: administration@ropewalk co.uk
Call Date: Oct 1992, Gray's Inn
Qualifications: [LLB (Nott'm)]

COX MISS KERRY AMANDA

Plowden Buildings
2nd Floor, 2 Plowden Buildings, Middle
Temple Lane, London EC4Y 9BU,
Telephone: 0171 583 0808
E-mail: bar@plowdenbuildings.co.uk
Call Date: Oct 1990, Inner Temple
Qualifications: [MA (Hons)(St Andrew), Dip
Law]

COX MISS KHARIN PAULINE

**1 Gray's Inn Square, Chambers of the
Baroness Scotland of Asthal QC**
1st Floor, London WC1R 5AG,
Telephone: 0171 405 3000
E-mail: clerks@onegrays.demon.co.uk
Call Date: July 1982, Middle Temple
Pupil Master
Qualifications: [BA (Cantab)]

COX MS LAURA MARY QC (1994)

Cloisters
1 Pump Court, Temple, London
EC4Y 7AA, Telephone: 0171 827 4000
E-mail: clerks@cloisters.com
Call Date: Nov 1975, Inner Temple
Recorder
Qualifications: [LLB, LLM]

COX LINDSAY RANDALL

East Anglian Chambers
Gresham House, 5 Museum Street,
Ipswich, Suffolk, IP1 1HQ,
Telephone: 01473 214481
E-mail: ipswich@ealaw.co.uk
East Anglian Chambers
52 North Hill, Colchester, Essex, CO1 1PY,
Telephone: 01206 572756
E-mail: colchester@ealaw.co.uk
East Anglian Chambers
57 London Street, Norwich NR2 1HL,
Telephone: 01603 617351
E-mail: norwich@ealaw.co.uk
Call Date: July 1984, Middle Temple
Pupil Master
Qualifications: [LLB (East Anglia)]

COX NICHOLAS IVAN

4 Stone Buildings
Ground Floor, Lincoln's Inn, London
WC2A 3XT, Telephone: 0171 242 5524
E-mail:clerks@4stonebuildings.law.co.uk
Call Date: Oct 1992, Middle Temple
Qualifications: [BA (Hons)(Oxon), MBA
(Warw)]

COX NIGEL JOHN

Gray's Inn Chambers
5th Floor, Gray's Inn, London WC1R 5JA,
Telephone: 0171 404 1111
Call Date: Nov 1986, Inner Temple
Qualifications: [MA(E.Illinois), BA (Hons),
Dip Law]

COX RAYMOND EDWIN

Fountain Court
Temple, London EC4Y 9DH,
Telephone: 0171 583 3335
E-mail: chambers@fountaincourt.co.uk
Call Date: July 1982, Gray's Inn
Pupil Master
Qualifications: [BA (Oxon)]

COX SIMON FRANCIS

Plowden Buildings
2nd Floor, 2 Plowden Buildings, Middle
Temple Lane, London EC4Y 9BU,
Telephone: 0171 583 0808
E-mail: bar@plowdenbuildings.co.uk
Call Date: Nov 1992, Inner Temple
Qualifications: [LLB (Wales)]

COX MS SITA

Stour Chambers
Barton Mill House, Barton Mill Road,
Canterbury, Kent, CT1 1BP,
Telephone: 01227 764899
E-mail: clerks@stourchambers.co.uk
Call Date: Nov 1987, Middle Temple
Qualifications: [BA (Hons)]

COY MICHAEL KEVIN

Phoenix Chambers
First Floor, Gray's Inn Chambers, Gray's
Inn, London WC1R 5JA,
Telephone: 0171 404 7888
E-mail:clerks@phoenix-chambers.co.uk
Call Date: Oct 1993, Middle Temple
Qualifications: [BA (Hons)(Lancs), CPE
(Lond)]

CRABB RICHARD BLECHYNDEN

Colleton Chambers
Colleton Crescent, Exeter, Devon,
EX2 4DG, Telephone: 01392 274898/9
Call Date: Nov 1975, Middle Temple

CRABB MISS SAMANTHA JILL

4 Fountain Court
Steelhouse Lane, Birmingham B4 6DR,
Telephone: 0121 236 3476
Call Date: Nov 1996, Inner Temple
Qualifications: [LLB (L'pool)]

CRABTREE RICHARD JOHN

3 Temple Gardens
Lower Ground Floor, Temple, London
EC4Y 9AU, Telephone: 0171 353 3102/5/
9297 E-mail: clerks@3tg.co.uk
Call Date: July 1974, Gray's Inn
Pupil Master
Qualifications: [LLB]

CRABTREE SIMON JEREMY GERHARD

24a St John Street
Manchester M3 4DF,
Telephone: 0161 833 9628
Call Date: Nov 1988, Lincoln's Inn
Qualifications: [LLB Hons (Leeds)]

CRACKNELL DOUGLAS GEORGE

23 Warham Road
Otford, Sevenoaks, Kent, TN14 5PF,
Telephone: 01959 522325
Call Date: May 1957, Middle Temple
Qualifications: [LLB]

CRAGG STEPHEN JAMES

Two Garden Court
1st Floor, Middle Temple, London
EC4Y 9BL, Telephone: 0171 353 1633
E-mail:barristers@2gardenct.law.co.uk
Call Date: Nov 1996, Middle Temple
Qualifications: [LLB (Hons)(Lond), MA
(Brunel)]

CRAIG ALISTAIR TREVOR

Chambers of Mr Peter Crampin QC
Ground Floor, 11 New Square, Lincoln's
Inn, London WC2A 3QB,
Telephone: 020 7831 0081
E-mail: 11newsquare.co.uk
Call Date: July 1983, Lincoln's Inn
Qualifications: [MA, (TCD)]

CRAIG AUBREY JOHN

5 Fountain Court
Steelhouse Lane, Birmingham B4 6DR,
Telephone: 0121 606 0500
E-mail:clerks@5fountaincourt.law.co.uk
Call Date: Nov 1987, Inner Temple
Qualifications: [LLB]

CRAIG DAVID MARK

Devereux Chambers
Devereux Court, London WC2R 3JJ,
Telephone: 0171 353 7534
E-mail: mailbox@devchambers.co.uk
Call Date: 1997, Inner Temple
Qualifications: [BSc (Manch), MPhil
(Cantab), CPE (City)]

CRAIG KENNETH ALLEN

Hardwicke Building
New Square, Lincoln's Inn, London
WC2A 3SB, Telephone: 020 7242 2523
E-mail: clerks@hardwicke.co.uk
Call Date: July 1975, Lincoln's Inn
Pupil Master
Qualifications: [BA]

CRAIL MISS (ELSPETH) ROSS

12 New Square
Lincoln's Inn, London WC2A 3SW,
Telephone: 0171 419 1212
E-mail: chambers@12newsquare.co.uk

Sovereign Chambers
25 Park Square, Leeds LS1 2PW,
Telephone: 0113 2451841/2/3
E-mail:sovereignchambers@btinternet.com
Call Date: July 1986, Lincoln's Inn
Qualifications: [MA (Oxon), Dip Law (City)]

CRALLAN RICHARD WHARTON

Chavasse Court Chambers
2nd Floor, Chavasse Court, 24 Lord Street,
Liverpool L2 1TA,
Telephone: 0151 707 1191
10 King's Bench Walk
Ground Floor, Temple, London
EC4Y 7EB, Telephone: 0171 353 7742
E-mail: 10kbw@lineone.net
Call Date: 1991, Inner Temple
Qualifications: [LLB (L'pool)]

CRAMPIN PAUL

Lamb Building
Ground Floor, Temple, London
EC4Y 7AS, Telephone: 020 7797 7788
E-mail: lamb.building@link.org
Call Date: Oct 1992, Middle Temple
Qualifications: [LL.B (Hons)]

CRAMPIN PETER QC (1993)

Chambers of Mr Peter Crampin QC
Ground Floor, 11 New Square, Lincoln's
Inn, London WC2A 3QB,
Telephone: 020 7831 0081
E-mail: 11newsquare.co.uk
Call Date: Nov 1976, Middle Temple
Recorder
Qualifications: [MA (Oxon)]

CRAMSIE JAMES SINCLAIR BERESFORD

13 King's Bench Walk
1st Floor, Temple, London EC4Y 7EN,
Telephone: 0171 353 7204
E-mail: clerks@13kbw.law.co.uk
King's Bench Chambers
32 Beaumont Street, Oxford OX1 2NP,
Telephone: 01865 311066
E-mail: clerks@kbc-oxford.law.co.uk
Call Date: Nov 1988, Inner Temple
Pupil Master
Qualifications: [LLB (Leeds)]

CRAN MARK DYSON GORDON QC (1988)

Brick Court Chambers
7-8 Essex Street, London WC2R 3LD,
Telephone: 0171 379 3550
E-mail: [surname]@brickcourt.co.uk
Call Date: July 1973, Gray's Inn
Qualifications: [LLB (Bris)]

CRANBROOK ALEXANDER DOUGLAS JOHN

9-12 Bell Yard
London WC2A 2LF,
Telephone: 0171 400 1800
E-mail: clerks@bellyard.co.uk
Call Date: July 1975, Gray's Inn
Pupil Master
Qualifications: [BA (Hons)]

CRANE MICHAEL JOHN QC (1994)

Fountain Court
Temple, London EC4Y 9DH,
Telephone: 0171 583 3335
E-mail: chambers@fountaincourt.co.uk
Call Date: Nov 1975, Middle Temple
Qualifications: [BA (Oxon)]

CRANE MISS SUZANNE DENISE

New Court Chambers
Gazette Building, 168 Corporation Street,
Birmingham B4 6TZ,
Telephone: 0121 693 6656
Call Date: Nov 1995, Lincoln's Inn
Qualifications: [LLB (Hons)]

CRANFIELD PETER ANTHONY

3 Verulam Buildings
London WC1R 5NT,
Telephone: 0171 831 8441
E-mail: clerks@3verulam.co.uk
Call Date: July 1982, Gray's Inn
Pupil Master
Qualifications: [BA, BCL (Oxon)]

CRANFIELD MRS ROSEMARY SHIRLEY ANNE

Sussex Chambers
9 Old Steine, Brighton, Sussex, BN1 1FJ,
Telephone: 01273 607953
Call Date: Feb 1992, Inner Temple
Qualifications: [BA (Hons)(Oxon)]

CRANFIELD TONY

Bank House Chambers
Old Bank House, Hartshead, Sheffield
S1 2EL, Telephone: 0114 2751223
Call Date: Nov 1975, Middle Temple
Pupil Master
Qualifications: [LLB]

CRANGLE MISS CHARLOTTE MARY

Parsonage Chambers
5th Floor, 3 The Parsonage, Manchester
M3 2HW, Telephone: 0161 833 1996
Call Date: Oct 1995, Gray's Inn
Qualifications: [LLB (Sheff)]

CRANMER-BROWN MICHAEL TIMOTHY

King Charles House
Standard Hill, Nottingham NG1 6FX,
Telephone: 0115 9418851
E-mail: clerks@kch.co.uk
Call Date: Nov 1986, Middle Temple
Qualifications: [BA (Hons)(Oxon), Dip Law
(City)]

CRANNY MISS AMANDA LOUISE

King Charles House
Standard Hill, Nottingham NG1 6FX,
Telephone: 0115 9418851
E-mail: clerks@kch.co.uk
Call Date: Nov 1984, Lincoln's Inn
Pupil Master
Qualifications: [LLB (Bristol)]

CRANSTON-MORRIS WAYNE

23 Essex Street
London WC2R 3AS,
Telephone: 0171 413 0353/836 8366
E-mail:clerks@essexstreet23.demon.co.uk
Call Date: July 1986, Lincoln's Inn
Qualifications: [LLB (Brunel)]

CRASNOW MS RACHEL

Cloisters
1 Pump Court, Temple, London
EC4Y 7AA, Telephone: 0171 827 4000
E-mail: clerks@cloisters.com
Call Date: Nov 1994, Middle Temple
Qualifications: [BA (Hons) (Oxon)]

CRAVEN RICHARD GEOFFREY

Chambers of Kieran Coonan QC
Ground Floor, 6 Pump Court, Temple,
London EC4Y 7AR,
Telephone: 0171 583 6013/2510
E-mail: clerks@6-pumpcourt.law.co.uk
Call Date: July 1976, Inner Temple
Qualifications: [MA (Cantab)]

CRAVEN RICHARD JOHN

Somersett Chambers
25 Bedford Row, London WC1R 4HE,
Telephone: 0171 404 6701
E-mail: somelaw@aol.com
Call Date: Oct 1995, Gray's Inn
Qualifications: [LLB]

CRAVEN ROBERT MICHAEL

Iscoed Chambers
86 St Helen's Road, Swansea, West
Glamorgan, SA1 4BQ,
Telephone: 01792 652988/9/330
Call Date: Nov 1979, Gray's Inn
Pupil Master
Qualifications: [MA, BCL (Oxon)]

CRAWFORD COLIN

40 King Street
Manchester M2 6BA,
Telephone: 0161 832 9082
E-mail: clerks@40kingstreet.co.uk
The Chambers of Philip Raynor QC
5 Park Place, Leeds LS1 2RU,
Telephone: 0113 242 1123
Call Date: July 1997, Middle Temple
Qualifications: [LLB (Hons), LLM,
(Edinburgh)]

CRAWFORD GRANT

11 Old Square
Ground Floor, Lincoln's Inn, London
WC2A 3TS, Telephone: 020 7430 0341
E-mail: clerks@11oldsquare.co.uk
Call Date: July 1974, Middle Temple
Pupil Master
Qualifications: [MA (Cantab)]

CRAWFORD LINCOLN SANTO

12 King's Bench Walk
Temple, London EC4Y 7EL,
Telephone: 0171 583 0811
E-mail: chambers@12kbw.co.uk
Call Date: Nov 1977, Gray's Inn
Pupil Master, Recorder

CRAWFORD MISS MARIE-BERNADETTE CLAIRE

Eastbourne Chambers
15 Hyde Gardens, Eastbourne, East
Sussex, BN21 4PR,
Telephone: 01323 642102
Call Date: Oct 1992, Lincoln's Inn
Qualifications: [LLB(Hons)(Leeds)]

CRAWFORD ROBERT DAVID

15 Winckley Square
Preston PR1 3JJ,
Telephone: 01772 252828
E-mail:clerks@winckleysq.demon.co.uk
Call Date: July 1976, Lincoln's Inn
Pupil Master
Qualifications: [MA (Cantab)]

CRAWFORTH MISS EMMA

Southernhay Chambers
33 Southernhay East, Exeter, Devon,
EX1 1NX, Telephone: 01392 255777
E-mail:southernhay.chambers@lineone.net
Call Date: Nov 1992, Middle Temple
Qualifications: [LL.B (Hons)]

CRAWLEY GARY THOMAS BERNARD

One Garden Court Family Law Chambers
Ground Floor, Temple, London
EC4Y 9BJ, Telephone: 0171 797 7900
E-mail: clerks@onegardencourt.co.uk
Call Date: Feb 1988, Middle Temple
Pupil Master
Qualifications: [LLB, LLM (Lond)]

CRAY TIMOTHY JAMES

6 King's Bench Walk
Ground Floor, Temple, London
EC4Y 7DR, Telephone: 0171 583 0410
E-mail: worsley@6kbw.freeserve.co.uk
Call Date: Nov 1989, Inner Temple
Qualifications: [BA (Dunelm)]

CRAYTON PHILIP PATRICK

York Chambers
14 Toft Green, York YO1 6JT,
Telephone: 01904 620048
E-mail: [name]@yorkchambers.co.uk
Call Date: July 1985, Gray's Inn
Pupil Master
Qualifications: [LLB (Cardiff)]

CREAN ANTHONY

5 Fountain Court
Steelhouse Lane, Birmingham B4 6DR,
Telephone: 0121 606 0500
E-mail:clerks@5fountaincourt.law.co.uk
Call Date: July 1987, Gray's Inn
Qualifications: [MPhil (Manchester)]

CREAN MISS MARY ANGELA

First National Chambers
2nd Floor, First National Building, 24
Fenwick Street, Liverpool L2 7NE,
Telephone: 0151 236 2098
Call Date: Oct 1996, Gray's Inn
Qualifications: [LLB (L'pool)]

CREANER PAUL ANTHONY

15 Winckley Square
Preston PR1 3JJ,
Telephone: 01772 252828
E-mail:clerks@winckleysq.demon.co.uk
Call Date: Oct 1990, Lincoln's Inn
Qualifications: [BSc, LLB, ARICS]

CREGAN JOHN-PAUL FITZJAMES

Westgate Chambers
144 High Street, Lewes, East Sussex,
BN7 1XT, Telephone: 01273 480510
Call Date: Nov 1990, Middle Temple
Qualifications: [BCL (Ireland)]

CRIGMAN DAVID IAN QC (1989)

1 Fountain Court
Steelhouse Lane, Birmingham B4 6DR,
Telephone: 0121 236 5721
Call Date: July 1969, Gray's Inn
Recorder
Qualifications: [LLB]

CRILLEY DR DARREL

28 St John Street
Manchester M3 4DJ,
Telephone: 0161 834 8418
E-mail: clerk@28stjohnst.co.uk
Call Date: Mar 1996, Inner Temple
Qualifications: [BA (Oxon), LLB (London),
PhD (London)]

CRIMP MICHAEL WILLIAM JASON

Fenners Chambers
3 Madingley Road, Cambridge CB3 0EE,
Telephone: 01223 368761
E-mail: clerks@fennerschambers.co.uk
Fenners Chambers
8-12 Priestgate, Peterborough PE1 1JA,
Telephone: 01733 562030
E-mail: clerks@fennerschambers.co.uk
Call Date: 1980, Gray's Inn
Qualifications: [BA, MA]

CRIPPS MISS BEVERLY MARY

Newport Chambers
12 Clytha Park Road, Newport, Gwent,
NP9 47L, Telephone: 01633 267403/
255855
Call Date: Nov 1988, Gray's Inn
Qualifications: [BA]

CRIPPS DR YVONNE MARIA

Director of Studies in Law, Emmanuel
College, Cambridge CB2 3AP,
Telephone: 01223 334283/334200
Call Date: Nov 1991, Inner Temple
Qualifications: [LLM (Cantab), Ph.D
(Cantab)]

CRITCHLEY JOHN STEPHEN

17 Bedford Row
London WC1R 4EB,
Telephone: 0171 831 7314
E-mail: iboard7314@aol.com
Call Date: July 1985, Gray's Inn
Pupil Master
Qualifications: [LLB (Bristol)]

D

D

CRITCHLOW CHRISTOPHER ALLAN

Chambers of John L Powell QC
Four New Square, Lincoln's Inn, London
WC2A 3RJ, Telephone: 0171 797 8000
E-mail: barristers@4newsquare.com
Call Date: 1972, Inner Temple
Pupil Master, *Recorder*
Qualifications: [LLB (Exeter), FICArb]

CRITELLI NICHOLAS

9 Stone Buildings
Lincoln's Inn, London WC2A 3NN,
Telephone: 0171 404 5055
E-mail: clerks@9stoneb.law.co.uk
Call Date: July 1991, Middle Temple
Qualifications: [Juris of Drake Uni]

CROALL SIMON MARTIN

4 Essex Court
Temple, London EC4Y 9AJ,
Telephone: 020 7797 7970
E-mail: clerks@4essexcourt.law.co.uk
Call Date: Nov 1986, Middle Temple
Pupil Master
Qualifications: [MA (Cantab)]

CROALLY MILES JAMES

17 Bedford Row
London WC1R 4EB,
Telephone: 0171 831 7314
E-mail: iboard7314@aol.com
Call Date: Nov 1987, Middle Temple
Pupil Master
Qualifications: [BA, Dip Law]

CRONIN MISS TACEY MARGUERITE

Albion Chambers
Broad Street, Bristol BS1 1DR,
Telephone: 0117 9272144
Call Date: July 1982, Middle Temple
Qualifications: [LLB (Hons) (Bris)]

CRONIN WILLIAM DAVID

Angel Chambers
94 Walter Road, Swansea, West
Glamorgan, SA1 5QA,
Telephone: 01792 464623/464648
E-mail: lynne@angelchambers.co.uk
Call Date: July 1971, Inner Temple
Pupil Master
Qualifications: [LLB]

CRONSHAW MICHAEL JOHN

2 Pump Court
1st Floor, Temple, London EC4Y 7AH,
Telephone: 0171 353 5597
Call Date: Oct 1993, Middle Temple
Qualifications: [MA (Hons)(Oxon), MSc , Dip
in Law (City)]

CROOK ADAM JAMES

6 Gray's Inn Square
Ground Floor, Gray's Inn, London
WC1R 5AZ, Telephone: 0171 242 1052
E-mail: 6graysinn@clara.co.uk
Call Date: Nov 1994, Inner Temple
Qualifications: [BA (Keele)]

CROOKENDEN SIMON ROBERT
QC (1996)

Essex Court Chambers
24 Lincoln's Inn Fields, London
WC2A 3ED, Telephone: 0171 813 8000
E-mail:clerksroom@essexcourt-chambers.co.u
k
Call Date: Nov 1975, Gray's Inn
Assistant Recorder
Qualifications: [MA (Cantab)]

CROOKES MISS ALISON NAOMI

Rougemont Chambers
8 Colleton Crescent, Exeter, Devon,
EX1 1RR, Telephone: 01392 208484
E-mail:rougemont.chambers@eclipse.co.uk
Call Date: Oct 1996, Middle Temple
Qualifications: [LLB (Hons) (Wales)]

CROSBIE MISS SUSAN MAUREEN

Paradise Chambers
26 Paradise Square, Sheffield S1 2DE,
Telephone: 0114 2738951
E-mail: timbooth@paradise-sq.co.uk
Call Date: Nov 1988, Inner Temple
Pupil Master
Qualifications: [LLB (Shef)]

CROSFILL JOHN

17 Bedford Row
London WC1R 4EB,
Telephone: 0171 831 7314
E-mail: iboard7314@aol.com
Call Date: Nov 1995, Middle Temple
Qualifications: [LLB (Hons), BSc]

CROSLAND JAMES BENJAMIN

Broadway House Chambers
Broadway House, 9 Bank Street, Bradford,
West Yorkshire, BD1 1TW,
Telephone: 01274 722560
E-mail: clerks@broadwayhouse.co.uk
Broadway House Chambers
31 Park Square West, Leeds LS1 2PF,
Telephone: 0113 246 2600
Call Date: Feb 1993, Gray's Inn
Qualifications: [MA (Cantab)]

CROSLAND TIMOTHY JOHN EDWARD

5 King's Bench Walk
Temple, London EC4Y 7DN,
Telephone: 0171 353 5638
Call Date: Nov 1994, Inner Temple
Qualifications: [BA (Oxon), CPE (Lond)]

CROSS ANTHONY MAURICE

15 Winckley Square
Preston PR1 3JJ,
Telephone: 01772 252828
E-mail:clerks@winckleysq.demon.co.uk
Call Date: Nov 1982, Middle Temple
Pupil Master
Qualifications: [LLB (Manc)]

CROSS GEOFFREY PAUL

New Court Chambers
3 Broad Chare, Newcastle upon Tyne
NE1 3DQ, Telephone: 0191 232 1980
Call Date: July 1981, Gray's Inn
Pupil Master
Qualifications: [BA (Cantab)]

CROSS JAMES EDWARD MICHAEL

4 Pump Court
Temple, London EC4Y 7AN,
Telephone: 020 7842 5555
E-mail:chambers@4pumpcourt.law.co.uk
Call Date: July 1985, Gray's Inn
Pupil Master
Qualifications: [MA (Oxon)]

CROSS MISS JANE ELIZABETH

15 Winckley Square
Preston PR1 3JJ,
Telephone: 01772 252828
E-mail:clerks@winckleysq.demon.co.uk
Call Date: July 1982, Middle Temple
Qualifications: [LLB (L'pool)]

CROSS MRS JOANNA

9 Woodhouse Square
Leeds LS3 1AD,
Telephone: 0113 2451986
E-mail: clerks@9woodhouse.co.uk
Call Date: Oct 1992, Lincoln's Inn
Qualifications: [BSc(St Andrew), MB ChB
(Manc), Dip Law]

CROSS (JOSEPH) EDWARD

2 Gray's Inn Square Chambers
2nd Floor, Gray's Inn, London WC1R 5AA,
Telephone: 020 7242 0328
E-mail: clerks@2gis.co.uk
Call Date: July 1975, Inner Temple
Pupil Master
Qualifications: [LLB (Bris)]

CROSS RICHARD NOEL

Thomas More Chambers
52 Carey Street, Lincoln's Inn, London
WC2A 2JB, Telephone: 0171 404 7000
E-mail: clerks@thomasmore.law.co.uk
Call Date: Oct 1993, Lincoln's Inn
Qualifications: [BA(Hons)(Bris)]

CROSSFIELD MISS ANNE

4 King's Bench Walk
Ground/First Floor/Basement, Temple,
London EC4Y 7DL,
Telephone: 0171 822 8822
E-mail: 4kbw@barristersatlaw.com
Call Date: July 1993, Lincoln's Inn
Qualifications: [LLB (B'ham), MBA (Nott'm)]

CROSSLEY SIMON JUSTIN

9 Woodhouse Square
Leeds LS3 1AD,
Telephone: 0113 2451986
E-mail: clerks@9woodhouse.co.uk
Call Date: Nov 1993, Inner Temple
Qualifications: [LLB]

CROSSLEY STEVEN RICHARD

37 Park Square Chambers
37 Park Square, Leeds LS1 2NY,
Telephone: 0113 2439422
E-mail: chambers@no37.co.uk
Call Date: Nov 1992, Inner Temple
Qualifications: [LLB (Exon)]

CROSTHWAITE GRAHAM ANDREW

One King's Bench Walk
1st Floor, Temple, London EC4Y 7DB,
Telephone: 0171 936 1500
E-mail: ddear@1kbw.co.uk
Call Date: Nov 1995, Inner Temple
Qualifications: [BA (Oxon)]

CROUCH ANDREW CHARLES MACKESAY

Fountain Chambers
Cleveland Business Centre, 1 Watson
Street, Middlesbrough TS1 2RQ,
Telephone: 01642 804040
E-mail:fountainchambers@onyxnet.co.uk
Call Date: Nov 1990, Inner Temple
Qualifications: [LLB (Lancaster)]

CROUCH STEPHEN WILLIAM MICHAEL

Northampton Chambers
22 Albion Place, Northampton NN1 1UD,
Telephone: 01604 636271
Call Date: July 1982, Inner Temple
Pupil Master
Qualifications: [BSc (Hons), Dip Law]

CROW JONATHAN RUPERT

4 Stone Buildings
Ground Floor, Lincoln's Inn, London
WC2A 3XT, Telephone: 0171 242 5524
E-mail:clerks@4stonebuildings.law.co.uk
Call Date: July 1981, Lincoln's Inn
Pupil Master
Qualifications: [BA (Oxon)]

CROWLEY DANIEL JOHN

2 Temple Gardens
Temple, London EC4Y 9AY,
Telephone: 0171 583 6041
E-mail: clerks@2templegardens.co.uk
Call Date: Oct 1990, Gray's Inn
Qualifications: [BA,LLB, BCL (Oxon)]

CROWLEY MRS JANE ELIZABETH QC (1998)

30 Park Place
Cardiff CF1 3BA,
Telephone: 01222 398421
E-mail: 100757.1456@compuserve.com

One Garden Court Family Law Chambers

Ground Floor, Temple, London
EC4Y 9BJ, Telephone: 0171 797 7900
E-mail: clerks@onegardencourt.co.uk
Call Date: July 1976, Gray's Inn
Recorder
Qualifications: [LLB (Lond)]

CROWLEY JOHN DESMOND QC (1982)

Two Crown Office Row
Ground Floor, Temple, London
EC4Y 7HJ, Telephone: 020 7797 8100
E-mail: mail@2cor.co.uk, or to individual
barristers at: [barrister's
surname]@2cor.co.uk
Call Date: May 1962, Inner Temple
Recorder
Qualifications: [BA, LLB (Cantab)]

CROWN GILES HUMPHRY

1 Brick Court
1st Floor, Temple, London EC4Y 9BY,
Telephone: 0171 353 8845
E-mail: clerks@1brickcourt.co.uk
Call Date: Oct 1993, Middle Temple
Qualifications: [MA, LLM (London)]

CROWSON HOWARD KEITH

St Paul's House
5th Floor, St Paul's House, 23 Park Square
South, Leeds LS1 2ND,
Telephone: 0113 2455866
E-mail: catherinegrimshaw@stpauls-
chambers.demon.co.uk
Call Date: July 1987, Inner Temple
Qualifications: [LLB (Hons) (Leeds)]

CROWTHER JEREMY GAGE

9 Gough Square
London EC4A 3DE,
Telephone: 020 7832 0500
E-mail: clerks@9goughsq.co.uk
Call Date: Oct 1991, Middle Temple
Qualifications: [LLB Hons (Reading)]

CROWTHER THOMAS EDWARD

30 Park Place
Cardiff CF1 3BA,
Telephone: 01222 398421
E-mail: 100757.1456@compuserve.com
Call Date: Nov 1993, Inner Temple
Qualifications: [BSc, BA (Exon)]

CROXFORD IAN LIONEL QC (1993)

Wilberforce Chambers
8 New Square, Lincoln's Inn, London
WC2A 3QP, Telephone: 0171 306 0102
E-mail: chambers@wilberforce.co.uk
Call Date: July 1976, Gray's Inn
Qualifications: [LLB]

Types of work: Chancery (general), Common
law (general), Construction, Professional
negligence

CROXFORD THOMAS HENRY

Blackstone Chambers
Blackstone House, Temple, London
EC4Y 9BW, Telephone: 0171 583 1770
E-mail:clerks@blackstonechambers.com
Call Date: Oct 1992, Middle Temple
Qualifications: [BA (Hons)]

CROXON RAYMOND PATRICK QC (1983)

8 King's Bench Walk
2nd Floor, Temple, London EC4Y 7DU,
Telephone: 0171 797 8888
Regency Chambers
Cathedral Square, Peterborough
PE1 1XW, Telephone: 01733 315215
Regency Chambers
Sheraton House, Castle Park, Cambridge
CB3 0AX, Telephone: 01223 301517
Call Date: Feb 1960, Gray's Inn
Qualifications: [LLB, MSR]

CROZIER RAWDON ROWLAND CRAIG

King's Bench Chambers
115 North Hill, Plymouth PL4 8JY,
Telephone: 01752 221551
2 King's Bench Walk
Ground Floor, Temple, London
EC4Y 7DE, Telephone: 0171 353 1746
E-mail: 2kbw@atlas.co.uk
Call Date: Nov 1984, Middle Temple
Pupil Master
Qualifications: [LLB (Lond)]

CRUICKSHANK MISS CYNTHIA MARILYN BENTON

1 Gray's Inn Square
Ground Floor, London WC1R 5AA,
Telephone: 0171 405 8946/7/8
Call Date: Nov 1968, Lincoln's Inn

CRYSTAL JONATHAN

Cloisters
1 Pump Court, Temple, London
EC4Y 7AA, Telephone: 0171 827 4000
E-mail: clerks@cloisters.com
Call Date: July 1972, Middle Temple
Pupil Master
Qualifications: [LLB (Hons)(Lond)]

CRYSTAL MICHAEL QC (1984)

3/4 South Square
Gray's Inn, London WC1R 5HP,
Telephone: 0171 696 9900
E-mail: clerks@southsquare.com
Call Date: Nov 1970, Middle Temple
Qualifications: [LLB (Lond), BCL (Oxon)]

CSOKA SIMON

Lloyds House Chambers
3rd Floor, 18 Lloyds House, Lloyd Street,
Manchester M2 5WA,
Telephone: 0161 839 3371
Call Date: Nov 1991, Gray's Inn
Qualifications: [MA (Cantab)]

CUDBY MS MARKANZA NICOLA

Two Garden Court
1st Floor, Middle Temple, London
EC4Y 9BL, Telephone: 0171 353 1633
E-mail:barristers@2gardenct.law.co.uk
Call Date: July 1983, Middle Temple
Pupil Master
Qualifications: [BA]

CUDDIGAN HUGO JONATHAN PATRICK

11 South Square
2nd Floor, Gray's Inn, London
WC1R 5EU,
Telephone: 0171 405 1222 (24hr messagin
g service)
E-mail: clerks@11southsquare.com
Call Date: Nov 1995, Middle Temple
Qualifications: [BA (Hons)]

D

CULL MS LESLEY-ANNE SUSAN

4 Brick Court
Ground Floor, Temple, London
EC4Y 9AD, Telephone: 0171 797 7766
E-mail: chambers@4brick.co.uk
Call Date: Oct 1995, Inner Temple
Qualifications: [BA (Cardiff), CPE]

CULLEN EDMUND WILLIAM HECTOR

7 Stone Buildings
Ground Floor, Lincoln's Inn, London
WC2A 3SZ, Telephone: 0171 405 3886/
242 3546 E-mail: chaldous@vossnet.co.uk
Call Date: Oct 1990, Lincoln's Inn
Pupil Master
Qualifications: [BA (Bris)]

CULLEN MRS FELICITY ANN

Gray's Inn Tax Chambers
3rd Floor, Gray's Inn Chambers, Gray's
Inn, London WC1R 5JA,
Telephone: 0171 242 2642
E-mail: clerks@taxbar.com
Call Date: July 1985, Lincoln's Inn
Qualifications: [LLB (B'ham) LLM, (Cantab)]

CULLUM MICHAEL

Albion Chambers
Broad Street, Bristol BS1 1DR,
Telephone: 0117 9272144
Call Date: Apr 1991, Gray's Inn
Qualifications: [LLB (Warwick)]

CULVER THOMAS STATEN

Cloisters
1 Pump Court, Temple, London
EC4Y 7AA, Telephone: 0171 827 4000
E-mail: clerks@cloisters.com
Call Date: Nov 1976, Middle Temple
Pupil Master, Recorder
Qualifications: [LLB (Cantab)]

CUMMING GEORGE AUGUSTUS GERARD

Inns of Court, School of Law, 4 Gray's Inn
Place, London WC1R 5DX,
Telephone: 0171 404 5787
Call Date: Feb 1988, Inner Temple
Qualifications: [LLB (Lond), BA, MA, PhD]

CUMMINGS BRIAN

Exchange Chambers
Pearl Assurance House, Derby Square,
Liverpool L2 9XX,
Telephone: 0151 236 7747
E-mail:exchangechambers@btinternet.com
Call Date: Nov 1988, Lincoln's Inn
Qualifications: [MA Hons (Cantab)]

CUMMINS BRIAN DOMINIC

Bridewell Chambers
2 Bridewell Place, London EC4V 6AP,
Telephone: 020 7797 8800
E-mail:HughesGage@bridewell.law.co.uk
Call Date: Oct 1992, Middle Temple
Qualifications: [LL.B (Hons) & LL.M]

CUNNINGHAM MISS CLAIRE LOUISE

St Philip's Chambers
Fountain Court, Steelhouse Lane,
Birmingham B4 6DR,
Telephone: 0121 246 7000
E-mail: clerks@st-philips.co.uk
Call Date: Nov 1996, Middle Temple
Qualifications: [BA (Hons)(Cantab)]

CUNNINGHAM MISS ELIZABETH ALICE

Albion Chambers
Broad Street, Bristol BS1 1DR,
Telephone: 0117 9272144
Call Date: Oct 1995, Middle Temple
Qualifications: [BA (Hons)(Bris)]

CUNNINGHAM GRAHAM TAYLOR

Francis Taylor Building
Ground Floor, Temple, London
EC4Y 7BY, Telephone: 0171 353 7768/
7769/2711
E-mail:clerks@francistaylorbuilding.law.co.uk
Call Date: July 1976, Gray's Inn
Qualifications: [LLB (Hons)]

CUNNINGHAM MARK JAMES

13 Old Square
Ground Floor, Lincoln's Inn, London
WC2A 3UA, Telephone: 0171 404 4800
E-mail: clerks@13oldsquare.law.co.uk
Call Date: Nov 1980, Inner Temple
Pupil Master
Qualifications: [BA (Oxon)]

CURLEY MRS MAUREEN

Clock Chambers
78 Darlington Street, Wolverhampton
WV1 4LY, Telephone: 01902 313444
Call Date: Oct 1996, Gray's Inn
Qualifications: [BA (Anglia)]

CURNOW MISS (ELIZABETH) ANN (MARGUERITE) QC (1985)

6 King's Bench Walk
Ground Floor, Temple, London
EC4Y 7DR, Telephone: 0171 583 0410
E-mail: worsley@6kbw.freeserve.co.uk
Call Date: Feb 1957, Gray's Inn
Recorder

CURRAN LEO

3 Paper Buildings
Temple, London EC4Y 7EU,
Telephone: 020 7583 8055
E-mail: London@3paper.com
3 Paper Buildings (Oxford)
1 Alfred Street, High Street, Oxford
OX1 4EH, Telephone: 01865 793736
E-mail: oxford@3paper.com
3 Paper Buildings (Bournemouth)
20 Lorne Park Road, Bournemouth,
Dorset, BH1 1JN,
Telephone: 01202 292102
E-mail: Bournemouth@3paper.com
3 Paper Buildings (Winchester)
4 St Peter Street, Winchester SO23 8BW,
Telephone: 01962 868884
E-mail: winchester@3paper.com
Call Date: July 1972, Gray's Inn
Pupil Master
Qualifications: [MA (Oxon)]

CURRAN PATRICK DAVID QC (1995)

9-12 Bell Yard
London WC2A 2LF,
Telephone: 0171 400 1800
E-mail: clerks@bellyard.co.uk
30 Park Place
Cardiff CF1 3BA,
Telephone: 01222 398421
E-mail: 100757.1456@compuserve.com
Call Date: July 1972, Gray's Inn
Recorder
Qualifications: [MA (Oxon)]

CURRAN PHILIP PETER

Lincoln House Chambers
5th Floor, Lincoln House, 1 Brazennose
Street, Manchester M2 5EL,
Telephone: 0161 832 5701
E-mail: info@lincolnhse.co.uk
Call Date: 1979, Lincoln's Inn
Pupil Master, Assistant Recorder
Qualifications: [BA (Hons)]

CURRIE FERGUS HUGH

Assize Court Chambers
14 Small Street, Bristol BS1 1DE,
Telephone: 0117 9264587
E-mail:chambers@assize-court-chambers.co.uk
Call Date: Mar 1997, Gray's Inn
Qualifications: [BA (Oxon)]

CURRY THOMAS PETER ELLISON QC (1973)

4 Stone Buildings
Ground Floor, Lincoln's Inn, London
WC2A 3XT, Telephone: 0171 242 5524
E-mail:clerks@4stonebuildings.law.co.uk
Call Date: June 1953, Middle Temple
Qualifications: [MA (Oxon)]

CURSHAM GEOFFREY MARK

De Montfort Chambers
95 Princess Road East, Leicester LE1 7DQ,
Telephone: 0116 254 8686
E-mail: dmcbar@aol.com
Call Date: June 1964, Gray's Inn
Pupil Master
Qualifications: [BA, LLB (Cantab)]

CURTIS CHARLES JOHN

1 Temple Gardens
1st Floor, Temple, London EC4Y 9BB,
Telephone: 0171 583 1315/353 0407
E-mail: clerks@1templegardens.co.uk
Call Date: Oct 1992, Lincoln's Inn
Qualifications: [BA(Hons)(Dunelm)]

CURTIS MS HELEN JANE

4 Brick Court
Ground Floor, Temple, London
EC4Y 9AD, Telephone: 0171 797 7766
E-mail: chambers@4brick.co.uk
Call Date: Nov 1992, Middle Temple
Qualifications: [LLB (Hons, Leic)]

D

D

CURTIS JAMES WILLIAM OCKFORD QC (1993)

6 King's Bench Walk
Ground Floor, Temple, London
EC4Y 7DR, Telephone: 0171 583 0410
E-mail: worsley@6kbw.freeserve.co.uk
Call Date: July 1970, Inner Temple
Recorder
Qualifications: [MA (Oxon)]

CURTIS MICHAEL ALEXANDER

Two Crown Office Row
Ground Floor, Temple, London
EC4Y 7HJ, Telephone: 020 7797 8100
E-mail: mail@2cor.co.uk, or to individual
barristers at: [barrister's
surname]@2cor.co.uk
Call Date: Nov 1982, Middle Temple
Pupil Master
Qualifications: [MA (Oxon), MSc, ACIArb]

CURTIS MISS NICOLE DIANE

1 Paper Buildings
1st Floor, Temple, London EC4Y 7EP,
Telephone: 0171 353 3728/4953
Call Date: Oct 1992, Gray's Inn
Qualifications: [MA (Cantab)]

CURTIS MISS REBECCA LOUISE

Albion Chambers
Broad Street, Bristol BS1 1DR,
Telephone: 0117 9272144
Call Date: Oct 1993, Inner Temple
Qualifications: [BSc, CPE]

CURTIS-RALEIGH GILES

23 Essex Street
London WC2R 3AS,
Telephone: 0171 413 0353/836 8366
E-mail:clerks@essexstreet23.demon.co.uk
Call Date: 1992, Middle Temple
Qualifications: [BA (Hons), MA , Dip in Law]

CURWEN DAVID CHRISTIAN

Assize Court Chambers
14 Small Street, Bristol BS1 1DE,
Telephone: 0117 9264587
E-mail:chambers@assize-court-chambers.co.uk

1 Gray's Inn Square
Ground Floor, London WC1R 5AA,
Telephone: 0171 405 8946/7/8
Call Date: July 1982, Gray's Inn
Qualifications: [BA (Warw), Dip Law]

CURWEN MICHAEL JONATHAN

Chambers of Kieran Coonan QC
Ground Floor, 6 Pump Court, Temple,
London EC4Y 7AR,
Telephone: 0171 583 6013/2510
E-mail: clerks@6-pumpcourt.law.co.uk
Call Date: July 1966, Inner Temple
Recorder
Qualifications: [BA (Oxon)]

CUSWORTH NICHOLAS NEVILLE GRYLLS

1 Mitre Court Buildings
Temple, London EC4Y 7BS,
Telephone: 0171 797 7070
E-mail: clerks@1mcb.com
Call Date: Nov 1986, Lincoln's Inn
Pupil Master
Qualifications: [MA (Oxon)]

CUTTING CHRISTOPHER HUGH

11 Old Square
Ground Floor, Lincoln's Inn, London
WC2A 3TS, Telephone: 0171 242 5022/
405 1074
Call Date: Nov 1973, Middle Temple
Pupil Master
Qualifications: [LLM]

CUTTS MISS JOHANNAH

23 Essex Street
London WC2R 3AS,
Telephone: 0171 413 0353/836 8366
E-mail:clerks@essexstreet23.demon.co.uk
Call Date: Nov 1986, Inner Temple
Pupil Master
Qualifications: [LLB]

D'AIGREMONT GILLES LOUIS

Verulam Chambers
Peer House, 8-14 Verulam Street, Gray's
Inn, London WC1X 8LZ,
Telephone: 0171 813 2400
Call Date: July 1978, Lincoln's Inn
Pupil Master
Qualifications: [Maitrise En Droit, Dip de
L'Institut, d'Etudes Politiques, (Paris),
Avocat a la Cour De, Paris]

D'ARCY MISS KATHARINE LOUISE

**4 Brick Court, Chambers of Anne
Rafferty QC**
1st Floor, Temple, London EC4Y 9AD,
Telephone: 0171 583 8455
Call Date: Nov 1988, Inner Temple
Qualifications: [LLB (Leic)]

D'ARCY LEO EUGENE MARY PETER CHANEL

**1 Gray's Inn Square, Chambers of the
Baroness Scotland of Asthal QC**
1st Floor, London WC1R 5AG,
Telephone: 0171 405 3000
E-mail: clerks@onegrays.demon.co.uk
Call Date: May 1983, Gray's Inn
Qualifications: [BA (Dublin)]

D'CRUZ VINOD RUPERT

The Chambers of Leolin Price CBE, QC
10 Old Square, Lincoln's Inn, London
WC2A 3SU, Telephone: 0171 405 0758
Call Date: Nov 1989, Lincoln's Inn
Qualifications: [BA (Nott'm)]

D'CRUZ VIVEK RUFUS

Cloisters
1 Pump Court, Temple, London
EC4Y 7AA, Telephone: 0171 827 4000
E-mail: clerks@cloisters.com
Call Date: Oct 1993, Lincoln's Inn
Qualifications: [BA (Hons)(B'ham), CPE
(Lond)]

D'SOUZA MISS CAROLYN AMANDA

12 King's Bench Walk
Temple, London EC4Y 7EL,
Telephone: 0171 583 0811
E-mail: chambers@12kbw.co.uk
Call Date: Oct 1994, Middle Temple
Qualifications: [LLB (Hons)(Lond), LLM
(Hons)(Harvard)]

D'SOUZA DOMINIC CHARLES

2 Paper Buildings
1st Floor, Temple, London EC4Y 7ET,
Telephone: 020 7556 5500
E-mail: clerks@2pbbarristers.co.uk
Call Date: Nov 1993, Inner Temple
Qualifications: [BA (Lond), CPE (City)]

DA COSTA MISS ELISSA JOSEPHINE

Arlington Chambers
5 Park Crescent Mews East, Great Portland
Street, London W1N 5HB,
Telephone: 0171 580 9188
E-mail: ejdc1@aol.com
Call Date: Oct 1990, Middle Temple
Qualifications: [BA , Dip Law, LLM]

Fax: 0171 580 9189;
Out of hours telephone: 0831 777 477;
Other comms: E-mail ejdc1@aol.com

Other professional qualifications: LLM in
advanced civil litigation (1997)

Types of work: Care proceedings, Common
law (general), Employment, Family, Family
provision

Circuit: South Eastern

Awards and memberships: Member: Association
of Law Teachers

Other professional experience: 10 years as a law
lecturer

Publications: *The Family and Matrimonial
Practitioner*, Autumn 1999; *Blackstone's
Civil Practice* (Contributor) 2nd edition,
Autumn 1999

While maintaining a busy practice, also
creates, designs and delivers training
courses for solicitors and other professionals on Family Law and, most recently,
the new Civil Procedure Rules. Courses are
tailor-made to meet the needs of individual

D

firms and often take the form of interactive workshops.

NITA (National Institute of Trial Advocacy) trained, teaches practical advocacy to trainee solicitors.

DA SILVA DAVID VERE AUSTIN CLEMENT PETER

3 Stone Buildings
Lincoln's Inn, London WC2A 3XL,
Telephone: 0171 242 4937
E-mail: clerks@3sb.law.co.uk
Call Date: Nov 1978, Middle Temple
Pupil Master
Qualifications: [MA (Oxon)]

DABBS DAVID LESLIE

Goldsmith Chambers
Ground Floor, Goldsmith Building,
Temple, London EC4Y 7BL,
Telephone: 0171 353 6802/3/4/5
E-mail:clerks@goldsmithchambers.law.co.uk
Call Date: July 1984, Lincoln's Inn
Pupil Master
Qualifications: [LLB (Manchester)]

DABLE JEREMY RICHARD

New Bailey Chambers
10 Lawson Street, Preston PR1 2QT,
Telephone: 01772 258087
Call Date: Nov 1987, Gray's Inn
Qualifications: [LLB (Leeds)]

DACEY MARK

Plowden Buildings
2nd Floor, 2 Plowden Buildings, Middle
Temple Lane, London EC4Y 9BU,
Telephone: 0171 583 0808
E-mail: bar@plowdenbuildings.co.uk
Call Date: Nov 1985, Middle Temple
Pupil Master
Qualifications: [BA]

DACRE IAN THOMAS

New Bailey Chambers
10 Lawson Street, Preston PR1 2QT,
Telephone: 01772 258087
Call Date: Nov 1991, Middle Temple
Qualifications: [BA;MA (Lond)]

DAGG JOHN DOUGLAS

1 Serjeants' Inn
4th Floor, Temple, London EC4Y 1NH,
Telephone: 0171 583 1355
E-mail: clerks@serjeants-inn.co.uk
Trinity Chambers
140 New London Road, Chelmsford,
Essex, CM2 0AW,
Telephone: 01245 605040
E-mail:clerks@trinitychambers.law.co.uk
Call Date: July 1980, Middle Temple
Pupil Master
Qualifications: [BSc (Dunelm), LLB (Lond),
M.C.D (L'pool), MRTPI]

DAGNALL JOHN MARSHALL ANTHONY

9 Old Square
Ground Floor, Lincoln's Inn, London
WC2A 3SR, Telephone: 0171 405 4682
E-mail: chambers@9oldsquare.co.uk
Call Date: Nov 1983, Lincoln's Inn
Pupil Master
Qualifications: [BA, BCL(Oxon)]

DAHLSEN PETER JOHN MORGAN

2 Paper Buildings, Basement North
Temple, London EC4Y 7ET,
Telephone: 0171 936 2613
E-mail: post@2paper.co.uk
Call Date: Oct 1996, Gray's Inn
Qualifications: [LLB (Lond)]

DAICHES MICHAEL SALIS

22 Old Buildings
Lincoln's Inn, London WC2A 3UJ,
Telephone: 0171 831 0222
Call Date: July 1977, Middle Temple
Pupil Master

DAJANI MISS RAFEEF ISMAIL

Chambers of Wilfred Forster-Jones
New Court, 1st Floor South, Temple,
London EC4Y 9BE,
Telephone: 0171 353 0853/4/7222
E-mail: chambers@newcourt.net
Call Date: 1996, Lincoln's Inn
Qualifications: [BA (Hons)(Lond)]

DAKYNS MS ISABEL ANNE FRANCES

9 Bedford Row
London WC1R 4AZ,
Telephone: 0171 242 3555
E-mail: clerks@9br.co.uk
Call Date: Nov 1992, Lincoln's Inn
Qualifications: [BA (Hons)]

DALAL RAJEN CHARLES JAMES

Cobden House Chambers
19 Quay Street, Manchester M3 3HN,
Telephone: 0161 833 6000
E-mail: clerks@cobden.co.uk
Call Date: Oct 1991, Lincoln's Inn
Qualifications: [LLB (Hons) (Manc)]

DALBY JOSEPH FRANCIS

Portsmouth Barristers' Chambers
Winchester Annexe, First Floor, 28 St
Stephens Road, Winchester SO22 6DE,
Telephone: 01962 863222
E-mail: dalby@zetnet.co.uk
Portsmouth Barristers' Chambers
Victory House, 7 Bellevue Terrace,
Portsmouth, Hampshire, PO5 3AT,
Telephone: 023 92 831292/811811
E-mail: clerks@portsmouthbar.com
Call Date: 1988, Middle Temple
Qualifications: [LLB (Hons), LIC.SP.DR.EUR]

DALE DERRICK RALPH

Fountain Court
Temple, London EC4Y 9DH,
Telephone: 0171 583 3335
E-mail: chambers@fountaincourt.co.uk
Call Date: Oct 1990, Middle Temple
Qualifications: [BA (Cantab), LLM (Harvard)]

DALE JONATHAN PAUL

Martins Building
2nd Floor, No 4 Water Street, Liverpool
L2 3SP, Telephone: 0151 236 5818/4919
Call Date: Oct 1991, Gray's Inn
Qualifications: [BA (Oxon)]

DALE JULIAN CHARLES RIGBY

Eastbourne Chambers
15 Hyde Gardens, Eastbourne, East
Sussex, BN21 4PR,
Telephone: 01323 642102
Call Date: Nov 1991, Middle Temple
Qualifications: [LLB (Hons)]

DALEY HOWARD MARTIN

Harcourt Chambers
1st Floor, 2 Harcourt Buildings, Temple,
London EC4Y 9DB,
Telephone: 0171 353 6961
E-mail:clerks@harcourtchambers.law.co.uk
Harcourt Chambers
Churchill House, 3 St Aldate's Courtyard,
St Aldate's, Oxford OX1 1BN,
Telephone: 01865 791559
E-mail:clerks@harcourtchambers.law.co.uk
Call Date: 1997, Gray's Inn
Qualifications: [BA]

DALGLEISH ANTHONY JAMES

2 King's Bench Walk Chambers
1st Floor, 2 King's Bench Walk, Temple,
London EC4Y 7DE,
Telephone: 020 7353 9276
E-mail: chambers@2kbw.co.uk
Call Date: Nov 1971, Inner Temple
Pupil Master
Qualifications: [LLB]

DALLAS ANDREW THOMAS ALASTAIR

Chambers of Andrew Campbell QC
10 Park Square, Leeds LS1 2LH,
Telephone: 0113 2455438
E-mail: clerks@10pksq.co.uk
Call Date: Nov 1978, Gray's Inn
Pupil Master, Assistant Recorder
Qualifications: [MA (Cantab)]

DALY DAVID

Francis Taylor Building
3rd Floor, Temple, London EC4Y 7BY,
Telephone: 0171 797 7250
Call Date: July 1979, Middle Temple
Qualifications: [BA, LLB (Lond), AKC]

DALY DENIS MICHAEL PATRICK SHEPSTON

11 Stone Buildings
Lincoln's Inn, London WC2A 3TG,
Telephone: +44 (0)207 831 6381
E-mail:clerks@11StoneBuildings.law.co.uk
Call Date: Feb 1995, Lincoln's Inn
Qualifications: [BA , LLB (Natal,S.Africa),
LLM (Cantab)]

D

DALY NIGEL JONATHAN

13 King's Bench Walk
1st Floor, Temple, London EC4Y 7EN,
Telephone: 0171 353 7204
E-mail: clerks@13kbw.law.co.uk
King's Bench Chambers
32 Beaumont Street, Oxford OX1 2NP,
Telephone: 01865 311066
E-mail: clerks@kbc-oxford.law.co.uk
Call Date: July 1979, Gray's Inn
Pupil Master
Qualifications: [LLB (Lond)]

DALZIEL ALARIC JAMES GENGE

Park Lane Chambers
19 Westgate, Leeds LS1 2RD,
Telephone: 0113 2285000
E-mail:clerks@parklanechambers.co.uk
Call Date: July 1967, Inner Temple
Recorder

DANESHYAR OSAMA

Chambers of Wilfred Forster-Jones
New Court, 1st Floor South, Temple,
London EC4Y 9BE,
Telephone: 0171 353 0853/4/7222
E-mail: chambers@newcourt.net
Call Date: 1996, Inner Temple
Qualifications: [BA (Notts)]

DANGOR MRS PATRICIA MADREE TRENTON

14 Gray's Inn Square
Gray's Inn, London WC1R 5JP,
Telephone: 0171 242 0858
E-mail: 100712.2134@compuserve.com
Call Date: July 1970, Middle Temple
Pupil Master, Recorder

DANIEL LEON ROGER

6 King's Bench Walk
Ground, Third & Fourth Floors, Temple,
London EC4Y 7DR,
Telephone: 0171 353 4931/583 0695
Call Date: July 1992, Gray's Inn
Qualifications: [LLB]

DANIEL NIGEL

10 King's Bench Walk
1st Floor, Temple, London EC4Y 7EB,
Telephone: 0171 353 2501
Call Date: Nov 1988, Inner Temple
Qualifications: [LLB (Exon)]

DANIEL (OWEN) RICHARD

Point House
Spooner Row, Wymondham, Norfolk,
NR18 9LQ, Telephone: 01953 606965
Call Date: Feb 1977, Inner Temple
Pupil Master

DANIELLS-SMITH ROGER CHARLES

8 King's Bench Walk
2nd Floor, Temple, London EC4Y 7DU,
Telephone: 0171 797 8888
8 King's Bench Walk North
1 Park Square East, Leeds LS1 2NE,
Telephone: 0113 2439797
Call Date: Nov 1974, Middle Temple
Pupil Master
Qualifications: [AKC, LLB]

DANIELS DAVID WILLIAM

Clock Chambers
78 Darlington Street, Wolverhampton
WV1 4LY, Telephone: 01902 313444
Southsea Chambers
PO Box 148, Southsea, Portsmouth,
Hampshire, PO5 2TU,
Telephone: 01705 291261
Call Date: Oct 1995, Lincoln's Inn
Qualifications: [LLB (Hons)(Lond), B.Com]

DANIELS IAIN JAMES

10 King's Bench Walk
1st Floor, Temple, London EC4Y 7EB,
Telephone: 0171 353 2501
Call Date: Oct 1992, Lincoln's Inn
Qualifications: [LLB(Hons)(Sheff)]

DANIELS NICHOLAS ANDREW

3 Dr Johnson's Buildings
Ground Floor, Temple, London
EC4Y 7BA, Telephone: 0171 353 4854
E-mail: clerks@3djb.co.uk
Call Date: Feb 1988, Inner Temple
Qualifications: [LLB (Bristol)]

DANIELS MISS PHILIPPA CATHERINE

Fleet Chambers
Mitre House, 44-46 Fleet Street, London
EC4Y 1BN, Telephone: 0171 936 3707
E-mail: rr@fleetchambers.demon.co.uk
Call Date: Oct 1995, Inner Temple
Qualifications: [BA (Hons)(S.Africa)]

DARBISHIRE ADRIAN MUNRO

Hollis Whiteman Chambers
3rd Floor, Queen Elizabeth Bldg, Temple,
London EC4Y 9BS,
Telephone: 020 7583 5766
E-mail:barristers@holliswhiteman.co.uk
Call Date: Oct 1993, Lincoln's Inn
Qualifications: [BA (Hons), Dip in Law
(City), LLM (Lond)]

DARBY PATRICK MICHAEL

3 Fountain Court
Steelhouse Lane, Birmingham B4 6DR,
Telephone: 0121 236 5854
Call Date: July 1978, Middle Temple
Pupil Master
Qualifications: [MA (Cantab)]

DARBYSHIRE WILLIAM ROBERT

Chambers of John Hand QC
9 St John Street, Manchester M3 4DN,
Telephone: 0161 955 9000
E-mail: ninesjs@gconnect.com
Call Date: Nov 1995, Lincoln's Inn
Qualifications: [BA (Hons), LLM]

DARIAN MISS ANN

Queens Square Chambers
56 Queens Square, Bristol BS1 4PR,
Telephone: 0117 921 1966
Call Date: July 1974, Middle Temple
Qualifications: [LLB (Lond)]

DARLING IAN GALEN

2 Harcourt Buildings
1st Floor, Temple, London EC4Y 9DB,
Telephone: 020 7353 2112
Call Date: July 1985, Middle Temple
Pupil Master
Qualifications: [LLB (Lond)]

DARLING PAUL ANTHONY QC (1999)

Keating Chambers
10 Essex Street, Outer Temple, London
WC2R 3AA, Telephone: 0171 544 2600
Call Date: 1983, Middle Temple
Pupil Master
Qualifications: [BA, BCL(Oxon)]

DARLOW MISS ANNABEL CHARLOTTE

6 King's Bench Walk
Ground Floor, Temple, London
EC4Y 7DR, Telephone: 0171 583 0410
E-mail: worsley@6kbw.freeserve.co.uk
Call Date: Oct 1993, Middle Temple
Qualifications: [BA (Hons)(Cantab), Dip in
Law (City)]

DARROCH MISS FIONA CULVERWELL

Counsels' Chambers
2nd Floor, 10-11 Gray's Inn Square,
London WC1R 5JD,
Telephone: 0171 405 2576
E-mail:clerks@10-11graysinnsquare.co.uk
Call Date: 1994, Inner Temple
Qualifications: [BA (Lond), Diploma in
Music, CPE]

DARTON CLIFFORD JOHN

Chichester Chambers
12 North Pallant, Chichester, West Sussex,
PO19 1TQ, Telephone: 01243 784538
E-mail:clerks@chichesterchambers.law.co.uk
Call Date: July 1988, Middle Temple
Pupil Master
Qualifications: [BA (Hons) (Oxon)]

DARUWALLA MISS NAVAZ SOLI

3 Hare Court
1 Little Essex Street, London WC2R 3LD,
Telephone: 0171 395 2000
Call Date: 1997, Middle Temple
Qualifications: [LLB (Hons)(Lond)]

D

D

DARWALL-SMITH MISS BELINDA CLAIRE

2 King's Bench Walk
Ground Floor, Temple, London
EC4Y 7DE, Telephone: 0171 353 1746
E-mail: 2kbw@atlas.co.uk
Call Date: Nov 1997, Gray's Inn
Qualifications: [BA (Hull)]

DAS MISS KAMALA

St John's Chambers
Small Street, Bristol BS1 1DW,
Telephone: 0117 9213456/298514
E-mail: @stjohnschambers.co.uk
Call Date: Nov 1975, Middle Temple
Qualifications: [BA]

DASHWOOD PROFESSOR ARTHUR ALAN

2 Harcourt Buildings
Ground Floor/Left, Temple, London
EC4Y 9DB, Telephone: 0171 583 9020
E-mail: clerks@harcourt.co.uk
Call Date: Nov 1969, Inner Temple
Qualifications: [MA (Oxon)]

DASHWOOD ROBERT THOMAS

Gray's Inn Chambers
5th Floor, Gray's Inn, London WC1R 5JA,
Telephone: 0171 404 1111
Call Date: Nov 1984, Inner Temple
Qualifications: [BA (Bristol), Dip Law]

DASS PRESTON

2-4 Tudor Street
London EC4Y 0AA,
Telephone: 0171 797 7111
E-mail: clerks@rfqc.co.uk
Call Date: Nov 1983, Inner Temple
Qualifications: [BA Kent]

DATE JULIAN RICHARD

17 Bedford Row
London WC1R 4EB,
Telephone: 0171 831 7314
E-mail: iboard7314@aol.com
Call Date: Nov 1988, Middle Temple
Pupil Master
Qualifications: [BA (Oxon)]

DATTA MRS WENDY PATRICIA MIZAL

Alban Chambers
27 Old Gloucester Street, London
WC1N 3XX, Telephone: 0171 419 5051
E-mail: wpmd@clara.net
Call Date: Oct 1990, Middle Temple
Qualifications: [Dip Ed (Lond), LLB (Hons)]

DAVENPORT SIMON NICHOLAS

5 Essex Court
1st Floor, Temple, London EC4Y 9AH,
Telephone: 0171 410 2000
E-mail: barristers@5essexcourt.co.uk
Call Date: Nov 1987, Inner Temple
Pupil Master
Qualifications: [LLB (Leeds), ACIArb]

DAVEY (ASTLEY) CHARLES

India Buildings Chambers
Water Street, Liverpool L2 0XG,
Telephone: 0151 243 6000
E-mail: clerks@chambers.u-net.com
Call Date: Feb 1989, Middle Temple
Qualifications: [MA (Oxon)]

DAVEY BENJAMIN NICHOLAS

11 Old Square
Ground Floor, Lincoln's Inn, London
WC2A 3TS, Telephone: 020 7430 0341
E-mail: clerks@11oldsquare.co.uk
Call Date: Oct 1994, Middle Temple
Qualifications: [BA (Hons)(Oxon)]

DAVEY MISS HELEN MARGARET

2 Pump Court
1st Floor, Temple, London EC4Y 7AH,
Telephone: 0171 353 5597
Call Date: July 1984, Inner Temple
Pupil Master
Qualifications: [BSc (Cardiff)]

DAVEY MISS KATHERINE ANNE TERESA

1 Gray's Inn Square, Chambers of the Baroness Scotland of Asthal QC
1st Floor, London WC1R 5AG,
Telephone: 0171 405 3000
E-mail: clerks@onegrays.demon.co.uk
Call Date: May 1988, Inner Temple
Qualifications: [MA (Cantab)]

DAVEY MICHAEL PHILIP

4 Field Court
Gray's Inn, London WC1R 5EA,
Telephone: 0171 440 6900
E-mail: chambers@4fieldcourt.co.uk
Call Date: Nov 1990, Gray's Inn
Qualifications: [LLB (Lond), BCL (Oxon)]

DAVEY MISS MICHELLE MARIA

Adrian Lyon's Chambers
14 Castle Street, Liverpool L2 0NE,
Telephone: 0151 236 4421/8240
E-mail: chambers14@aol.com
Call Date: Nov 1993, Lincoln's Inn
Qualifications: [LLB (Hons, L'pool)]

DAVEY NEIL MARTIN

39 Park Square
Leeds LS1 2NU,
Telephone: 0113 2456633
Call Date: July 1978, Middle Temple
Pupil Master
Qualifications: [MA (Oxon)]

DAVEY ROGER LAWRENCE

Dr Johnson's Chambers
Two Dr Johnson's Buildings, Temple,
London EC4Y 7AY,
Telephone: 0171 353 4716
E-mail: clerks@2djb.freeserve.co.uk
Call Date: Feb 1978, Inner Temple

DAVEY MISS TINA ELAINE

9-12 Bell Yard
London WC2A 2LF,
Telephone: 0171 400 1800
E-mail: clerks@bellyard.co.uk
Call Date: Nov 1993, Middle Temple
Qualifications: [LLB (Hons)(Cardiff)]

DAVEY TOBIAS BENJAMIN

2-3 Gray's Inn Square
Gray's Inn, London WC1R 5JH,
Telephone: 0171 242 4986
E-mail:chambers@2-3graysinnsquare.co.uk
Call Date: Feb 1977, Gray's Inn
Pupil Master
Qualifications: [LLB (Lond)]

DAVIDSON ARTHUR QC (1978)

Cloisters
1 Pump Court, Temple, London
EC4Y 7AA, Telephone: 0171 827 4000
E-mail: clerks@cloisters.com
Call Date: Feb 1953, Middle Temple

DAVIDSON EDWARD ALAN QC (1994)

11 Old Square
Ground Floor, Lincoln's Inn, London
WC2A 3TS, Telephone: 020 7430 0341
E-mail: clerks@11oldsquare.co.uk
Call Date: Nov 1966, Gray's Inn
Qualifications: [MA LLB (Cantab)]

DAVIDSON MISS KATHARINE MARY

1 Mitre Court Buildings
Temple, London EC4Y 7BS,
Telephone: 0171 797 7070
E-mail: clerks@1mcb.com
Call Date: Nov 1987, Lincoln's Inn
Pupil Master
Qualifications: [MA (Oxon)]

DAVIDSON MISS LAURA ANNE

Chambers of Kieran Coonan QC
Ground Floor, 6 Pump Court, Temple,
London EC4Y 7AR,
Telephone: 0171 583 6013/2510
E-mail: clerks@6-pumpcourt.law.co.uk
Call Date: 1996, Lincoln's Inn
Qualifications: [MA (Hons)(Edinburgh),
PGCE (Oxon), Dip in Law, LLM (Cantab)]

DAVIDSON NICHOLAS RANKING QC (1993)

4 Paper Buildings
Ground Floor, Temple, London
EC4Y 7EX, Telephone: 0171 353 3366/
583 7155
E-mail: clerks@4paperbuildings.com
Call Date: July 1974, Inner Temple
Qualifications: [BA (Cantab)]

DAVIDSON DR RANALD DUNBAR

3 Serjeants' Inn
London EC4Y 1BQ,
Telephone: 0171 353 5537
E-mail: clerks@3serjeantsinn.com
Call Date: Nov 1996, Inner Temple
Qualifications: [MB, ChB (Edinburgh), LLB (Lond)]

DAVIE MICHAEL JAMES

4 Pump Court
Temple, London EC4Y 7AN,
Telephone: 020 7842 5555
E-mail:chambers@4pumpcourt.law.co.uk
Call Date: Nov 1993, Middle Temple
Qualifications: [LLB (Hons)(Strathcl), D.Phil (Oxon)]

DAVIES ANDREW

Angel Chambers
94 Walter Road, Swansea, West Glamorgan, SA1 5QA,
Telephone: 01792 464623/464648
E-mail: lynne@angelchambers.co.uk
Call Date: Oct 1992, Lincoln's Inn
Qualifications: [LLB(Hons)(Lancaster), LLM(Hull)]

DAVIES ANDREW CHRISTOPHER

New Court Chambers
5 Verulam Buildings, Gray's Inn, London WC1R 5LY, Telephone: 0171 831 9500
E-mail: mail@newcourtchambers.com
Call Date: July 1988, Inner Temple
Pupil Master
Qualifications: [BA (Oxon)]

DAVIES ANTHONY MARTIN QC (1999)

1 Paper Buildings
1st Floor, Temple, London EC4Y 7EP,
Telephone: 0171 353 3728/4953
Call Date: 1971, Gray's Inn
Pupil Master, Recorder

DAVIES MISS CAROL ELIZABETH

2 New Street
Leicester LE1 5NA,
Telephone: 0116 2625906
E-mail: clerks@2newstreet.co.uk
Call Date: Oct 1995, Middle Temple
Qualifications: [LLB (Hons)]

DAVIES DR CHARLES EDWARD

4 Field Court
Gray's Inn, London WC1R 5EA,
Telephone: 0171 440 6900
E-mail: chambers@4fieldcourt.co.uk
Call Date: Nov 1995, Middle Temple
Qualifications: [BA (Hons), D.Phil]

DAVIES MISS CHARLOTTE ANNE

3 Temple Gardens
3rd Floor, Temple, London EC4Y 9AU,
Telephone: 0171 353 0832
Call Date: Nov 1996, Middle Temple
Qualifications: [LLB (Hons)(Manch)]

DAVIES DAVID COLIN

33 Park Place
Cardiff CF1 3BA,
Telephone: 02920 233313
Call Date: Nov 1973, Gray's Inn
Pupil Master
Qualifications: [MA (Oxon)]

DAVIES THE RT HON DAVID JOHN DENZIL

96 Gray's Inn Road
London WC1X 8AL,
Telephone: 0171 405 0585
8 Gray's Inn Square
Gray's Inn, London WC1R 5AZ,
Telephone: 0171 242 3529
Call Date: 1965, Gray's Inn
Pupil Master
Qualifications: [MA]

DAVIES DAVID PETER

33 Park Place
Cardiff CF1 3BA,
Telephone: 02920 233313
Call Date: May 1996, Lincoln's Inn
Qualifications: [LLB (Hons) (Hull)]

DAVIES MISS DEBORAH SUSAN

Ropewalk Chambers
24 The Ropewalk, Nottingham NG1 5EF,
Telephone: 0115 9472581
E-mail: administration@ropewalk co.uk
Call Date: Oct 1993, Inner Temple
Qualifications: [LLB]

DAVIES MISS ELIZABETH JANE

One Paper Buildings
Ground Floor, Temple, London
EC4Y 7EP, Telephone: 0171 583 7355
E-mail: clerks@1pb.co.uk
Call Date: Nov 1981, Middle Temple
Pupil Master
Qualifications: [MA (Oxon)]

DAVIES MS ELIZABETH MARY

Two Garden Court
1st Floor, Middle Temple, London
EC4Y 9BL, Telephone: 0171 353 1633
E-mail:barristers@2gardenct.law.co.uk
Call Date: Feb 1994, Inner Temple
Qualifications: [LLB (Hons)(Lond)]

DAVIES MISS EMILY JANE

Angel Chambers
94 Walter Road, Swansea, West
Glamorgan, SA1 5QA,
Telephone: 01792 464623/464648
E-mail: lynne@angelchambers.co.uk
Call Date: Nov 1989, Gray's Inn
Qualifications: [LLB (Wales)]

DAVIES EVAN HUW

Essex Court Chambers
24 Lincoln's Inn Fields, London
WC2A 3ED, Telephone: 0171 813 8000
E-mail:clerksroom@essexcourt-chambers.co.uk
Call Date: Nov 1985, Gray's Inn
Pupil Master
Qualifications: [LLB (Cardiff)]

DAVIES MISS FELICITY ANNE

Chambers of Andrew Campbell QC
10 Park Square, Leeds LS1 2LH,
Telephone: 0113 2455438
E-mail: clerks@10pksq.co.uk
Call Date: July 1980, Middle Temple
Pupil Master, Assistant Recorder
Qualifications: [BA (York)]

DAVIES FRANCIS PETER

Corn Exchange Chambers
5th Floor, Fenwick Street, Liverpool
L2 7QS, Telephone: 0151 227 1081/5009
Call Date: July 1986, Gray's Inn
Qualifications: [BA]

DAVIES GRAHAM BRUCE

Dr Johnson's Chambers
Two Dr Johnson's Buildings, Temple,
London EC4Y 7AY,
Telephone: 0171 353 4716
E-mail: clerks@2djb.freeserve.co.uk
Call Date: 1986, Middle Temple
Qualifications: [MA, LLM Cantab]

DAVIES GRAHAM JOHN

Dr Johnson's Chambers
Two Dr Johnson's Buildings, Temple,
London EC4Y 7AY,
Telephone: 0171 353 4716
E-mail: clerks@2djb.freeserve.co.uk
Call Date: 1971, Inner Temple
Pupil Master
Qualifications: [LLM (Lond)]

DAVIES MISS HELEN LOUISE

Brick Court Chambers
7-8 Essex Street, London WC2R 3LD,
Telephone: 0171 379 3550
E-mail: [surname]@brickcourt.co.uk
Call Date: Nov 1991, Inner Temple
Pupil Master
Qualifications: [BA (Cambs)]

DAVIES HUGH CURRY

3 Raymond Buildings
Gray's Inn, London WC1R 5BH,
Telephone: 020 7831 3833
E-mail:chambers@threeraymond.demon.co.uk
Call Date: Oct 1990, Lincoln's Inn
Qualifications: [BA (Oxon)]

DAVIES HUGH MICHAEL

Lincoln House Chambers
5th Floor, Lincoln House, 1 Brazennose
Street, Manchester M2 5EL,
Telephone: 0161 832 5701
E-mail: info@lincolnhse.co.uk
Call Date: July 1982, Middle Temple
Pupil Master
Qualifications: [MA (Oxon)]

DAVIES HUW

30 Park Place
Cardiff CF1 3BA,
Telephone: 01222 398421
E-mail: 100757.1456@compuserve.com

Farrar's Building
Temple, London EC4Y 7BD,
Telephone: 0171 583 9241
E-mail:chambers@farrarsbuilding.co.uk
Call Date: Nov 1978, Gray's Inn
Pupil Master, Assistant Recorder
Qualifications: [LLB (Wales), MPhil (Cantab)]

DAVIES HUW REES

Pendragon Chambers
124 Walter Road, Swansea, West
Glamorgan, SA1 5RG,
Telephone: 01792 411188
Call Date: Nov 1982, Gray's Inn
Qualifications: [LLB (Wales)]

DAVIES IWAN RHUN

Iscoed Chambers
86 St Helen's Road, Swansea, West
Glamorgan, SA1 4BQ,
Telephone: 01792 652988/9/330
Call Date: Feb 1995, Gray's Inn
Qualifications: [LLB (Wales & Cantab), LLM,
PhD (Wales)]

DAVIES JAKE SEBASTIAN HUNTER

5 Paper Buildings
Ground Floor, Temple, London
EC4Y 7HB, Telephone: 0171 583 9275/
583 4555 E-mail: 5paper@link.org
Call Date: Oct 1997, Inner Temple
Qualifications: [BA (Cantab), CPE (City)]

DAVIES DR JANE ELIZABETH

East Anglian Chambers
57 London Street, Norwich NR2 1HL,
Telephone: 01603 617351
E-mail: norwich@ealaw.co.uk
East Anglian Chambers
52 North Hill, Colchester, Essex, CO1 1PY,
Telephone: 01206 572756
E-mail: colchester@ealaw.co.uk
East Anglian Chambers
Gresham House, 5 Museum Street,
Ipswich, Suffolk, IP1 1HQ,
Telephone: 01473 214481
E-mail: ipswich@ealaw.co.uk
Call Date: July 1983, Middle Temple
Pupil Master
Qualifications: [LLB, PhD(B'ham)]

DAVIES JOHN LLEWELLYN

Twenty-Four Old Buildings
Ground Floor, Lincoln's Inn, London
WC2A 3UP, Telephone: 0171 404 0946
E-mail:clerks@24oldbuildings.law.co.uk
Call Date: Nov 1977, Gray's Inn
Pupil Master
Qualifications: [BA]

DAVIES JOHN MEIRION

32 Park Place
Cardiff CF1 3BA,
Telephone: 01222 397364
Call Date: 1975, Gray's Inn
Pupil Master
Qualifications: [LLB (Wales)]

DAVIES JOHN RICHARD

Littleton Chambers
3 King's Bench Walk North, Temple,
London EC4Y 7HR,
Telephone: 0171 797 8600
E-mail:clerks@littletonchambers.co.uk
Call Date: July 1981, Middle Temple
Pupil Master
Qualifications: [MA (Cantab)]

DAVIES JOHN VERDIN

Chambers of Kieran Coonan QC
Ground Floor, 6 Pump Court, Temple,
London EC4Y 7AR,
Telephone: 0171 583 6013/2510
E-mail: clerks@6-pumpcourt.law.co.uk
Call Date: Feb 1955, Gray's Inn
Qualifications: [LLB (Manch), FCIA]

DAVIES JONATHAN NORVAL

9-12 Bell Yard
London WC2A 2LF,
Telephone: 0171 400 1800
E-mail: clerks@bellyard.co.uk
Call Date: July 1981, Inner Temple
Pupil Master
Qualifications: [LLB (Lond)]

DAVIES JONATHAN TREFOR LLEWELYN

1 Middle Temple Lane
Temple, London EC4Y 1LT,
Telephone: 0171 583 0659 (12 Lines)
E-mail: chambers@1mtl.co.uk
Call Date: Nov 1971, Middle Temple
Pupil Master, Recorder
Qualifications: [MA (Cantab)]

DAVIES MISS LINDSAY JANE

Fenners Chambers
3 Madingley Road, Cambridge CB3 0EE,
Telephone: 01223 368761
E-mail: clerks@fennerschambers.co.uk
Fenners Chambers
8-12 Priestgate, Peterborough PE1 1JA,
Telephone: 01733 562030
E-mail: clerks@fennerschambers.co.uk
Call Date: July 1975, Gray's Inn
Pupil Master, Assistant Recorder
Qualifications: [LLB (Wales)]

DAVIES MS MANON WYNNE

9 Park Place
Cardiff CF1 3DP,
Telephone: 01222 382731
Call Date: 1997, Inner Temple
Qualifications: [BA (Oxon), CPE
(Glamorgan)]

DAVIES MS MARIA CHRISTINE

Park Court Chambers
16 Park Place, Leeds LS1 2SJ,
Telephone: 0113 2433277
Call Date: Nov 1988, Middle Temple
Qualifications: [LLB (Leeds)]

DAVIES MICHAEL IWAN

Martins Building
2nd Floor, No 4 Water Street, Liverpool
L2 3SP, Telephone: 0151 236 5818/4919
Call Date: July 1979, Middle Temple
Pupil Master
Qualifications: [LLB (L'pool)]

DAVIES NICHOLAS JEREMY

One Paper Buildings
Ground Floor, Temple, London
EC4Y 7EP, Telephone: 0171 583 7355
E-mail: clerks@1pb.co.uk
Call Date: July 1975, Inner Temple
Pupil Master
Qualifications: [BA]

DAVIES MISS NICOLA VELFOR QC (1992)

3 Serjeants' Inn
London EC4Y 1BQ,
Telephone: 0171 353 5537
E-mail: clerks@3serjeantsinn.com
Call Date: July 1976, Gray's Inn
Assistant Recorder
Qualifications: [LLB]

DAVIES OWEN HANDEL QC (1999)

Two Garden Court
1st Floor, Middle Temple, London
EC4Y 9BL, Telephone: 0171 353 1633
E-mail:barristers@2gardenct.law.co.uk
Call Date: 1973, Inner Temple
Pupil Master
Qualifications: [BA (Cantab)]

DAVIES MISS PENNY MAY

Chambers of Harjit Singh
Ground Floor, 2 Middle Temple Lane,
Temple, London EC4Y 9AA,
Telephone: 0171 353 1356 (4 Lines)
Call Date: Oct 1995, Inner Temple
Qualifications: [LLB]

DAVIES PHILIP

9 Park Place
Cardiff CF1 3DP,
Telephone: 01222 382731
Call Date: Apr 1978, Middle Temple
Pupil Master
Qualifications: [MA (Cantab)]

DAVIES MISS REBECCA LUCINDA

3 Temple Gardens
3rd Floor, Temple, London EC4Y 9AU,
Telephone: 0171 583 0010
Call Date: Nov 1996, Lincoln's Inn
Qualifications: [LLB (Hons)(Lond)]

DAVIES RICHARD LLEWELLYN QC (1994)

39 Essex Street
London WC2R 3AT,
Telephone: 0171 832 1111
E-mail: clerks@39essex.co.uk
Call Date: July 1973, Inner Temple
Qualifications: [LLB (L'pool)]

DAVIES ROBERT HOWARD

Guildhall Chambers
22-26 Broad Street, Bristol BS1 2HG,
Telephone: 0117 9273366
E-mail:civil.clerks@guildhallchambers.co.uk and
criminal.clerks@guildhallchambers.co.uk
Call Date: Oct 1990, Lincoln's Inn
Qualifications: [LLB (B'ham)]

DAVIES ROBERT LEIGHTON QC (1994)

Farrar's Building
Temple, London EC4Y 7BD,
Telephone: 0171 583 9241
E-mail:chambers@farrarsbuilding.co.uk
9 Park Place
Cardiff CF1 3DP,
Telephone: 01222 382731
Call Date: Feb 1975, Gray's Inn
Recorder
Qualifications: [BA, BCL (Oxon)]

DAVIES RUSSELL DEWI THOMAS

Deans Court Chambers
24 St John Street, Manchester M3 4DF,
Telephone: 0161 214 6000
E-mail: clerks@deanscourt.co.uk
Deans Court Chambers
41-43 Market Place, Preston PR1 1AH,
Telephone: 01772 555163
E-mail: clerks@deanscourt.co.uk
Call Date: Nov 1983, Middle Temple
Qualifications: [LLB (L'pool)]

DAVIES MISS SARAH JEANNETTE

2 King's Bench Walk Chambers
1st Floor, 2 King's Bench Walk, Temple,
London EC4Y 7DE,
Telephone: 020 7353 9276
E-mail: chambers@2kbw.co.uk
Call Date: Feb 1984, Gray's Inn
Pupil Master
Qualifications: [BA Hons (Kent)]

DAVIES MISS SARAH-JANE

4-5 Gray's Inn Square
Ground Floor, Gray's Inn, London
WC1R 5JP, Telephone: 0171 404 5252
E-mail:chambers@4-5graysinnsquare.co.uk
Call Date: Oct 1996, Inner Temple
Qualifications: [BA (Cantab)]

DAVIES MISS SHEILAGH ELIZABETH

10 King's Bench Walk
1st Floor, Temple, London EC4Y 7EB,
Telephone: 0171 353 2501
Call Date: Nov 1974, Middle Temple
Pupil Master
Qualifications: [LLB (Lond)]

DAVIES STEPHEN REES

Guildhall Chambers
22-26 Broad Street, Bristol BS1 2HG,
Telephone: 0117 9273366
E-mail:civil.clerks@guildhallchambers.co.uk and
criminal.clerks@guildhallchambers.co.uk
Call Date: July 1983, Gray's Inn
Pupil Master
Qualifications: [LLB (Lond) LLB, (Cantab)]

DAVIES STEPHEN RICHARD

8 King Street Chambers
8 King Street, Manchester M2 6AQ,
Telephone: 0161 834 9560
E-mail: eightking@aol.com
Call Date: July 1985, Middle Temple
Pupil Master
Qualifications: [MA (Cantab)]

DAVIES MISS (SUSAN) LOUISE

12 New Square
Lincoln's Inn, London WC2A 3SW,
Telephone: 0171 419 1212
E-mail: chambers@12newsquare.co.uk
Sovereign Chambers
25 Park Square, Leeds LS1 2PW,
Telephone: 0113 2451841/2/3
E-mail:sovereignchambers@btinternet.com
Call Date: Oct 1995, Inner Temple
Qualifications: [BA, BCL (Oxon)]

DAVIES TREFOR

Iscoed Chambers
86 St Helen's Road, Swansea, West
Glamorgan, SA1 4BQ,
Telephone: 01792 652988/9/330
Call Date: July 1972, Inner Temple
Pupil Master

DAVIES TREVOR GLYN

9 Gough Square
London EC4A 3DE,
Telephone: 020 7832 0500
E-mail: clerks@9goughsq.co.uk
Call Date: July 1978, Gray's Inn
Pupil Master
Qualifications: [BA (Nott'm)]

DAVIES WILLIAM RHODRI QC (1999)

One Essex Court
Ground Floor, Temple, London
EC4Y 9AR, Telephone: 020 7583 2000
E-mail: clerks@oneessexcourt.co.uk
Call Date: 1979, Middle Temple
Pupil Master
Qualifications: [BA (Cantab)]

DAVIES-JONES JONATHAN

3 Verulam Buildings
London WC1R 5NT,
Telephone: 0171 831 8441
E-mail: clerks@3verulam.co.uk
Call Date: Nov 1994, Middle Temple
Qualifications: [MA]

DAVIS ADAM DAVID

2 Dyers Buildings
London EC1N 2JT,
Telephone: 0171 404 1881
Call Date: Nov 1985, Inner Temple
Pupil Master
Qualifications: [LLB (Lond)]

DAVIS ADRIAN MARTIN

Chambers of Norman Palmer
2 Field Court, Gray's Inn, London
WC1R 5BB, Telephone: 0171 405 6114
E-mail: fieldct2@netcomuk.co.uk
Call Date: Oct 1996, Gray's Inn
Qualifications: [B.Sc (Dunelm), LLB (Notts)]

DAVIS ANDREW PAUL

Two Crown Office Row
Ground Floor, Temple, London
EC4Y 7HJ, Telephone: 020 7797 8100
E-mail: mail@2cor.co.uk, or to individual
barristers at: [barrister's
surname]@2cor.co.uk
Call Date: Oct 1996, Gray's Inn
Qualifications: [LLB (Hons)]

DAVIS ANTHONY JOHN

Westgate Chambers
67a Westgate Road, Newcastle upon Tyne
NE1 1SG, Telephone: 0191 261 4407/
2329785
E-mail:pracman@westgatechambers.law.co.uk
Call Date: Nov 1986, Gray's Inn
Qualifications: [BA (Hons)]

DAVIS BRENDAN JOHN

4 King's Bench Walk
2nd Floor, Temple, London EC4Y 7DL,
Telephone: 020 7353 3581
E-mail: clerks@4kbw.co.uk
Call Date: Oct 1994, Gray's Inn
Qualifications: [MA (Oxon)]

DAVIS MISS CAROL JANE

Littleton Chambers
3 King's Bench Walk North, Temple,
London EC4Y 7HR,
Telephone: 0171 797 8600
E-mail:clerks@littletonchambers.co.uk
Call Date: Oct 1996, Middle Temple
Qualifications: [BA (Hons)(Sussex), CPE]

DAVIS GLEN MILTON

3/4 South Square
Gray's Inn, London WC1R 5HP,
Telephone: 0171 696 9900
E-mail: clerks@southsquare.com
Call Date: Oct 1992, Middle Temple
Qualifications: [MA (Hons)(Oxon), Dip Law
(City), MA]

DAVIS GREVILLE LEIGH BLAKEMAN

4 King's Bench Walk
Ground/First Floor/Basement, Temple,
London EC4Y 7DL,
Telephone: 0171 822 8822
E-mail: 4kbw@barristersatlaw.com
Call Date: July 1976, Lincoln's Inn
Pupil Master
Qualifications: [LLB (Lond)]

DAVIS JAMES BURNHAM

Angel Chambers
94 Walter Road, Swansea, West
Glamorgan, SA1 5QA,
Telephone: 01792 464623/464648
E-mail: lynne@angelchambers.co.uk
Call Date: July 1997, Gray's Inn

DAVIS JOHN ANTHONY

Trinity Chambers
140 New London Road, Chelmsford,
Essex, CM2 0AW,
Telephone: 01245 605040
E-mail:clerks@trinitychambers.law.co.uk
Call Date: July 1983, Gray's Inn
Pupil Master
Qualifications: [LLB (Hull)]

DAVIS JONATHAN MURRAY

6 Fountain Court
Steelhouse Lane, Birmingham B4 6DR,
Telephone: 0121 233 3282
E-mail: clerks@sixfountain.co.uk
Call Date: July 1983, Middle Temple
Qualifications: [MA (Oxon)]

DAVIS MISS LUCINDA JANE

Chichester Chambers
12 North Pallant, Chichester, West Sussex,
PO19 1TQ, Telephone: 01243 784538
E-mail:clerks@chichesterchambers.law.co.uk
Call Date: Nov 1981, Gray's Inn
Pupil Master
Qualifications: [LLB (Lond)]

DAVIS LYNDELL GEORGE MONTAGUE

Chancery Chambers
1st Floor Offices, 70/72 Chancery Lane,
London WC2A 1AB,
Telephone: 0171 405 6879/6870
Call Date: Nov 1963, Lincoln's Inn

DAVIS NIGEL ANTHONY LAMERT QC (1992)

7 Stone Buildings
Ground Floor, Lincoln's Inn, London
WC2A 3SZ, Telephone: 0171 405 3886/
242 3546 E-mail: chaldous@vossnet.co.uk
Call Date: 1975, Lincoln's Inn
Recorder
Qualifications: [MA (Oxon)]

DAVIS PAUL JOHN

15 Winckley Square
Preston PR1 3JJ,
Telephone: 01772 252828
E-mail:clerks@winckleysq.demon.co.uk
Call Date: Nov 1996, Inner Temple
Qualifications: [BA (Trent)]

DAVIS RICHARD JOLYON HAROLD

7 New Square
1st Floor, Lincoln's Inn, London
WC2A 3QS, Telephone: 020 7404 5484
E-mail: clerks@7newsquare.com
Call Date: 1992, Gray's Inn
Qualifications: [MA (Cantab), Dip Law,
AMI.E.E.]

DAVIS RICHARD SIMON

23 Essex Street
London WC2R 3AS,
Telephone: 0171 413 0353/836 8366
E-mail:clerks@essexstreet23.demon.co.uk
Call Date: Nov 1978, Inner Temple
Pupil Master, Assistant Recorder
Qualifications: [LLB (Leics)]

DAVIS SIMON JOHN

6 Fountain Court
Steelhouse Lane, Birmingham B4 6DR,
Telephone: 0121 233 3282
E-mail: clerks@sixfountain.co.uk
Call Date: Oct 1990, Middle Temple
Qualifications: [BA (Cantab), Dip Law]

DAVIS WILLIAM EASTHOPE QC (1998)

St Philip's Chambers
Fountain Court, Steelhouse Lane,
Birmingham B4 6DR,
Telephone: 0121 246 7000
E-mail: clerks@st-philips.co.uk
Call Date: July 1975, Inner Temple
Recorder
Qualifications: [LLB]

DAVIS-WHITE MALCOLM

4 Stone Buildings
Ground Floor, Lincoln's Inn, London
WC2A 3XT, Telephone: 0171 242 5524
E-mail:clerks@4stonebuildings.law.co.uk
Call Date: July 1984, Middle Temple
Pupil Master
Qualifications: [MA, BCL (Oxon)]

DAVISON RICHARD HAROLD

Thomas More Chambers
52 Carey Street, Lincoln's Inn, London
WC2A 2JB, Telephone: 0171 404 7000
E-mail: clerks@thomasmore.law.co.uk
Call Date: July 1982, Gray's Inn
Pupil Master
Qualifications: [BA (Oxon)]

DAVITT MISS PAULA AINE

24a St John Street
Manchester M3 4DF,
Telephone: 0161 833 9628
Call Date: Nov 1988, Gray's Inn
Qualifications: [LLB Hons]

DAW CHRISTOPHER

Parsonage Chambers
5th Floor, 3 The Parsonage, Manchester
M3 2HW, Telephone: 0161 833 1996
Call Date: Nov 1993, Gray's Inn
Qualifications: [LLB (Manch)]

DAWAR MISS ARCHNA

Assize Court Chambers
14 Small Street, Bristol BS1 1DE,
Telephone: 0117 9264587
E-mail:chambers@assize-court-chambers.co.uk
Call Date: Oct 1996, Lincoln's Inn
Qualifications: [LLB (Hons)(L'pool)]

DAWES JAMES CHRISTOPHER

2 Harcourt Buildings
1st Floor, Temple, London EC4Y 9DB,
Telephone: 020 7353 2112
Call Date: Nov 1993, Inner Temple
Qualifications: [BA (Dunelm), CPE]

DAWES SIMON ROBERT

Derby Square Chambers
Merchants Court, Derby Square, Liverpool
L2 1TS, Telephone: 0151 709 4222
E-mail:mail.derbysquare@pop3.hiway.co.uk
Call Date: Oct 1990, Inner Temple
Qualifications: [LLB (Hons L'pool)]

DAWSON ALEXANDER WILLIAM

13 King's Bench Walk
1st Floor, Temple, London EC4Y 7EN,
Telephone: 0171 353 7204
E-mail: clerks@13kbw.law.co.uk
King's Bench Chambers
32 Beaumont Street, Oxford OX1 2NP,
Telephone: 01865 311066
E-mail: clerks@kbc-oxford.law.co.uk
Call Date: July 1969, Middle Temple
Recorder
Qualifications: [MA (Oxon)]

DAWSON IAN JEFFERIES

Westgate Chambers
67a Westgate Road, Newcastle upon Tyne
NE1 1SG, Telephone: 0191 261 4407/
2329785
E-mail:pracman@westgatechambers.law.co.u
k
Call Date: July 1971, Lincoln's Inn
Pupil Master
Qualifications: [LLB]

DAWSON JAMES

1 Hare Court
Ground Floor, Temple, London
EC4Y 7BE, Telephone: 0171 353 3982/
5324
Call Date: Nov 1984, Middle Temple
Pupil Master
Qualifications: [BA (Hons)]

DAWSON JAMES ROBERT

Oriel Chambers
14 Water Street, Liverpool L2 8TD,
Telephone: 0151 236 7191/236 4321
E-mail: clerks@oriel-chambers.co.uk
Call Date: Nov 1994, Inner Temple
Qualifications: [LLB (Soton)]

DAWSON MISS JUDY ELIZABETH

Assize Court Chambers
14 Small Street, Bristol BS1 1DE,
Telephone: 0117 9264587
E-mail:chambers@assize-court-chambers.co.uk
Call Date: Oct 1993, Gray's Inn
Qualifications: [BA]

DAY MISS ANNELIESE MARY

Chambers of John L Powell QC
Four New Square, Lincoln's Inn, London
WC2A 3RJ, Telephone: 0171 797 8000
E-mail: barristers@4newsquare.com
Call Date: Oct 1996, Inner Temple
Qualifications: [MA (Cantab)]

DAY DORIAN STEPHEN

Goldsmith Chambers
Ground Floor, Goldsmith Building,
Temple, London EC4Y 7BL,
Telephone: 0171 353 6802/3/4/5
E-mail:clerks@goldsmithchambers.law.co.uk
Call Date: July 1987, Middle Temple
Pupil Master
Qualifications: [BA (Hons)]

DAY DOUGLAS HENRY QC (1989)

Farrar's Building
Temple, London EC4Y 7BD,
Telephone: 0171 583 9241
E-mail:chambers@farrarsbuilding.co.uk
Call Date: July 1967, Lincoln's Inn
Recorder
Qualifications: [MA (Cantab)]

DE BERTODANO MISS SYLVIA PHILIPPA THERESA

3 Gray's Inn Square
Ground Floor, London WC1R 5AH,
Telephone: 0171 520 5600
E-mail: clerks@3gis.co.uk
Call Date: Nov 1993, Middle Temple
Qualifications: [BA (Hons)(Oxon)]

DE BONO JOHN HUGH

Derby Square Chambers
Merchants Court, Derby Square, Liverpool
L2 1TS, Telephone: 0151 709 4222
E-mail:mail.derbysquare@pop3.hiway.co.uk
Call Date: Oct 1995, Gray's Inn
Qualifications: [BA (Hons) (Oxon)]

DE BURGOS JAMIE MICHAEL ABULAFIA

Chambers of Michael Pert QC
36 Bedford Row, London WC1R 4JH,
Telephone: 0171 421 8000
E-mail: 36bedfordrow@link.org
Chambers of Michael Pert QC
24 Albion Place, Northampton NN1 1UD,
Telephone: 01604 602333
Chambers of Michael Pert QC
104 New Walk, Leicester LE1 7EA,
Telephone: 0116 249 2020
Call Date: July 1973, Inner Temple
Pupil Master
Qualifications: [MA (Cantab)]

DE COSTA LEONEL LUIS

Furnival Chambers
32 Furnival Street, London EC4A 1JQ,
Telephone: 0171 405 3232
E-mail: clerks@furnivallaw.co.uk
Call Date: 1992, Gray's Inn
Qualifications: [BA (Hons)]

DE COTTA JOHN MILNES

4 Essex Court
Temple, London EC4Y 9AJ,
Telephone: 020 7797 7970
E-mail: clerks@4essexcourt.law.co.uk
Call Date: Nov 1955, Middle Temple
Qualifications: [MA (Oxon), Licensiado de,
Derecho (Madrid)]

DE FREITAS ANTHONY PETER STANLEY

4 Paper Buildings
Ground Floor, Temple, London
EC4Y 7EX, Telephone: 0171 353 3366/
583 7155
E-mail: clerks@4paperbuildings.com
Call Date: July 1971, Inner Temple
Pupil Master, Assistant Recorder
Qualifications: [MA (Oxon)]

DE GARR ROBINSON ANTHONY JOHN

One Essex Court
Ground Floor, Temple, London
EC4Y 9AR, Telephone: 020 7583 2000
E-mail: clerks@oneessexcourt.co.uk
Call Date: July 1987, Lincoln's Inn
Pupil Master
Qualifications: [BA (Oxon)]

DE HAAN KEVIN CHARLES

3 Raymond Buildings
Gray's Inn, London WC1R 5BH,
Telephone: 020 7831 3833
E-mail: chambers@threeraymond.demon.co.uk
Call Date: July 1976, Inner Temple
Pupil Master
Qualifications: [LLB (Lond), LLM (Bru)]

DE HAAS MISS MARGARET RUTH QC (1998)

Corn Exchange Chambers
5th Floor, Fenwick Street, Liverpool
L2 7QS, Telephone: 0151 227 1081/5009
12 King's Bench Walk
Temple, London EC4Y 7EL,
Telephone: 0171 583 0811
E-mail: chambers@12kbw.co.uk
Call Date: 1977, Middle Temple
Recorder
Qualifications: [LLB]

DE HAVAS CHRISTOPHER FREDERIC ERIC

Westgate Chambers
144 High Street, Lewes, East Sussex,
BN7 1XT, Telephone: 01273 480510
Call Date: Feb 1984, Gray's Inn
Pupil Master
Qualifications: [BA (Kent)]

DE JEHAN DAVID

St Paul's House
5th Floor, St Paul's House, 23 Park Square
South, Leeds LS1 2ND,
Telephone: 0113 2455866
E-mail: catherinegrimshaw@stpauls-chambers.demon.co.uk
Call Date: Feb 1988, Inner Temple
Pupil Master
Qualifications: [LLB (Hons), LLM (Bristol)]

DE KAUWE LALITH CHRISTOPHER

Two Garden Court
1st Floor, Middle Temple, London
EC4Y 9BL, Telephone: 0171 353 1633
E-mail: barristers@2gardenct.law.co.uk
Call Date: Nov 1978, Gray's Inn
Pupil Master
Qualifications: [BA (Hons)]

DE LA MARE THOMAS ORLANDO

Blackstone Chambers
Blackstone House, Temple, London
EC4Y 9BW, Telephone: 0171 583 1770
E-mail: clerks@blackstonechambers.com
Call Date: Oct 1995, Middle Temple
Qualifications: [BA (Hons), LLM]

DE LA PIQUERIE PAUL ANDRE LEO ALPHONSE

Falcon Chambers
Falcon Court, London EC4Y 1AA,
Telephone: 0171 353 2484
E-mail: clerks@falcon-chambers.com
Call Date: July 1966, Gray's Inn
Recorder
Qualifications: [LLB (B'ham)(Hons)]

DE LA ROSA ANDREW JAMES

The Chambers of Leolin Price CBE, QC
10 Old Square, Lincoln's Inn, London
WC2A 3SU, Telephone: 0171 405 0758
Call Date: July 1981, Inner Temple
Pupil Master
Qualifications: [BA, Dip LL, JD]

DE LACY RICHARD MICHAEL

3 Verulam Buildings
London WC1R 5NT,
Telephone: 0171 831 8441
E-mail: clerks@3verulam.co.uk
Call Date: July 1976, Middle Temple
Pupil Master
Qualifications: [MA (Cantab), FCIArb]

DE LOTBINIERE HENRY JOLY

2 Temple Gardens
Temple, London EC4Y 9AY,
Telephone: 0171 583 6041
E-mail: clerks@2templegardens.co.uk
Call Date: July 1968, Inner Temple
Pupil Master
Qualifications: [MA (Cantab)]

DE LURY TERENCE WILLIAM

Pepys' Chambers
17 Fleet Street, London EC4Y 1AA,
Telephone: 0171 936 2710
Call Date: July 1985, Gray's Inn
Qualifications: [F.I.Plant.E, F.C.I.Arb,
F.M.E.W.I., Forensic Eng.]

DE MELLO REMBERT JOSEPH JULIUS

6 King's Bench Walk
Ground, Third & Fourth Floors, Temple,
London EC4Y 7DR,
Telephone: 0171 353 4931/583 0695
New Court Chambers
Gazette Building, 168 Corporation Street,
Birmingham B4 6TZ,
Telephone: 0121 693 6656
Call Date: 1983, Lincoln's Inn
Pupil Master
Qualifications: [BA, MA (Madras), LLM, LLB
(Lond)]

DE MESTRE ANDREW ETIENNE

4 Stone Buildings
Ground Floor, Lincoln's Inn, London
WC2A 3XT, Telephone: 0171 242 5524
E-mail:clerks@4stonebuildings.law.co.uk
Call Date: Mar 1998, Middle Temple
Qualifications: [BA (Hons)(Cantab)]

DE MOLLER ANDRE LECH

38 Eldon Chambers
30 Fleet Street, London EC4Y 1AA,
Telephone: 0171 353 8822
Call Date: Nov 1965, Middle Temple
Pupil Master

DE NAVARRO MICHAEL ANTONY QC (1990)

2 Temple Gardens
Temple, London EC4Y 9AY,
Telephone: 0171 583 6041
E-mail: clerks@2templegardens.co.uk
Call Date: July 1968, Inner Temple
Recorder
Qualifications: [BA (Cantab)]

DE ROHAN JONATHAN STEWART

Plowden Buildings
2nd Floor, 2 Plowden Buildings, Middle
Temple Lane, London EC4Y 9BU,
Telephone: 0171 583 0808
E-mail: bar@plowdenbuildings.co.uk
Call Date: July 1989, Middle Temple
Qualifications: [BA (Read), Dip Law]

DE SILVA GEORGE DESMOND LORENZ QC (1984)

2 Paper Buildings
1st Floor, Temple, London EC4Y 7ET,
Telephone: 020 7556 5500
E-mail: clerks@2pbbarristers.co.uk
Call Date: June 1964, Middle Temple

DE SILVA HARENDRA ANEURIN DOMINGO QC (1995)

2 Paper Buildings
1st Floor, Temple, London EC4Y 7ET,
Telephone: 020 7556 5500
E-mail: clerks@2pbbarristers.co.uk
Call Date: July 1970, Middle Temple
Recorder
Qualifications: [MA, LLM (Cantab)]

DE SILVA NIRAN SIMON LIYANAGE

Littleton Chambers
3 King's Bench Walk North, Temple,
London EC4Y 7HR,
Telephone: 0171 797 8600
E-mail:clerks@littletonchambers.co.uk
Call Date: 1997, Lincoln's Inn
Qualifications: [BA (Hons)(Oxon)]

DE WAAL JOHN HENRY LOWNDES

St Philip's Chambers
Fountain Court, Steelhouse Lane,
Birmingham B4 6DR,
Telephone: 0121 246 7000
E-mail: clerks@st-philips.co.uk
Call Date: Oct 1992, Middle Temple
Qualifications: [MA (Cantab)]

DE WILDE (ALAN) ROBIN QC (1993)

199 Strand
London WC2R 1DR,
Telephone: 0171 379 9779
E-mail: chambers@199strand.co.uk
Call Date: Nov 1971, Inner Temple

Assistant Recorder

DE ZONIE MISS JANE

14 Gray's Inn Square
Gray's Inn, London WC1R 5JP,
Telephone: 0171 242 0858
E-mail: 100712.2134@compuserve.com
Call Date: Nov 1993, Middle Temple
Qualifications: [BA (Hons)(Lond), Dip in
Law (Westmin)]

DEACOCK ADAM JASON

Chambers of Lord Goodhart QC
Ground Floor, 3 New Square, Lincoln's
Inn, London WC2A 3RS,
Telephone: 0171 405 5577
E-mail:law@threenewsquare.demon.co.uk
Call Date: Nov 1991, Middle Temple
Qualifications: [BA (Oxon), Dip Law]

DEACON MS EMMA REBECCA

Five Paper Buildings
1st Floor, Five Paper Bldgs, Temple,
London EC4Y 7HB,
Telephone: 0171 583 6117
E-mail:clerks@5-paperbuildings.law.co.uk
Call Date: Nov 1993, Inner Temple
Qualifications: [LLB (Lond)]

DEACON ROBERT MURRAY

11 Stone Buildings
Lincoln's Inn, London WC2A 3TG,
Telephone: +44 (0)207 831 6381
E-mail:clerks@11StoneBuildings.law.co.uk
Chichester Chambers
12 North Pallant, Chichester, West Sussex,
PO19 1TQ, Telephone: 01243 784538
E-mail:clerks@chichesterchambers.law.co.uk
Call Date: July 1976, Gray's Inn
Pupil Master
Qualifications: [LL.B (Manchester)]

DEAL MISS KATHERINE ALISON FRANCES

1 Crown Office Row
3rd Floor, Temple, London EC4Y 7HH,
Telephone: 0171 583 9292
E-mail: onecor@link.org
Call Date: Oct 1997, Middle Temple
Qualifications: [BA (Hons)(Oxon), CPE
(Lond)]

DEAL TIMOTHY JOHN

Deal Chambers
60 Moordown, Shooters Hill, London
SE18 3NG, Telephone: 0181 856 8738
E-mail: timothy.deal@btinternet.com
**Gray's Inn Chambers, The Chambers of
Norman Patterson**
First Floor, Gray's Inn Chambers, Gray's
Inn, London WC1R 5JA,
Telephone: 0171 831 5344
E-mail: s.mcblain@btinternet.com
Call Date: July 1988, Gray's Inn
Qualifications: [LLB (Warwick)]

DEAN MISS ABIGAIL ELIZABETH

2 King's Bench Walk Chambers
1st Floor, 2 King's Bench Walk, Temple,
London EC4Y 7DE,
Telephone: 020 7353 9276
E-mail: chambers@2kbw.co.uk
Call Date: Oct 1995, Gray's Inn
Qualifications: [BA]

DEAN BRIAN JOHN ANTHONY

St Philip's Chambers
Fountain Court, Steelhouse Lane,
Birmingham B4 6DR,
Telephone: 0121 246 7000
E-mail: clerks@st-philips.co.uk
Call Date: Nov 1994, Gray's Inn
Qualifications: [LLB (Manch)]

DEAN JACOB

5 Raymond Buildings
1st Floor, Gray's Inn, London WC1R 5BP,
Telephone: 0171 242 2902
E-mail: clerks@media-ent-law.co.uk
Call Date: Oct 1995, Inner Temple
Qualifications: [BA (Oxon), CPE (City)]

DEAN JAMES PATRICK

1 Dr Johnson's Buildings
Ground Floor, Temple, London
EC4Y 7AX, Telephone: 0171 353 9328
E-mail:OneDr.Johnsons@btinternet.com
Dr Johnson's Chambers
The Atrium Court, Apex Plaza, Reading,
Berkshire, RG1 1AX,
Telephone: 01734 254221
Call Date: Nov 1977, Lincoln's Inn
Pupil Master

DEAN NICHOLAS

9 Bedford Row
London WC1R 4AZ,
Telephone: 0171 242 3555
E-mail: clerks@9br.co.uk
Call Date: Nov 1982, Lincoln's Inn
Pupil Master
Qualifications: [LLB (Leeds)]

DEAN PAUL BENJAMIN

Two Crown Office Row
Ground Floor, Temple, London
EC4Y 7HJ, Telephone: 020 7797 8100
E-mail: mail@2cor.co.uk, or to individual
barristers at: [barrister's
surname]@2cor.co.uk
Call Date: July 1982, Inner Temple
Pupil Master
Qualifications: [BA (Oxon)Dip Law]

DEAN PETER THOMAS

1 Crown Office Row
3rd Floor, Temple, London EC4Y 7HH,
Telephone: 0171 583 9292
E-mail: onecor@link.org
Call Date: Nov 1987, Middle Temple
Pupil Master
Qualifications: [BA (Oxon), Dip Law, (City)]

DEAN MS ROSA MARY

Chambers of Michael Pert QC
36 Bedford Row, London WC1R 4JH,
Telephone: 0171 421 8000
E-mail: 36bedfordrow@link.org
Chambers of Michael Pert QC
24 Albion Place, Northampton NN1 1UD,
Telephone: 01604 602333
Chambers of Michael Pert QC
104 New Walk, Leicester LE1 7EA,
Telephone: 0116 249 2020
Call Date: Oct 1993, Gray's Inn
Qualifications: [BA (Oxon)]

DEANE VINCENT

19 Castle Street Chambers
Liverpool L2 4SX,
Telephone: 0151 236 9402
E-mail: DBrei16454@aol.com
Call Date: July 1976, Lincoln's Inn
Pupil Master
Qualifications: [LLB]

DECAMP MISS JANE LOUISE

Two Crown Office Row
Ground Floor, Temple, London
EC4Y 7HJ, Telephone: 020 7797 8100
E-mail: mail@2cor.co.uk, or to individual
barristers at: [barrister's
surname]@2cor.co.uk
Call Date: Nov 1987, Gray's Inn
Pupil Master
Qualifications: [BA (Oxon)]

DEDEZADE TANER

Tindal Chambers
3/5 New Street, Chelmsford, Essex,
CM1 1NT, Telephone: 01245 267742
Call Date: Nov 1996, Gray's Inn
Qualifications: [LLB (Lond)]

DEDMAN PETER GEORGE

12 King's Bench Walk
Temple, London EC4Y 7EL,
Telephone: 0171 583 0811
E-mail: chambers@12kbw.co.uk
Call Date: July 1968, Gray's Inn
Pupil Master, Recorder

DEE JONATHON ANTHONY

King Charles House
Standard Hill, Nottingham NG1 6FX,
Telephone: 0115 9418851
E-mail: clerks@kch.co.uk
Call Date: Nov 1989, Inner Temple
Qualifications: [LLB (Bris)]

DEEGAN LAWRENCE JEFFREY

Northampton Chambers
22 Albion Place, Northampton NN1 1UD,
Telephone: 01604 636271
Call Date: 1989, Inner Temple
Pupil Master
Qualifications: [LLB]

DEGEL MISS REBECCA EMMELINE HYDE

East Anglian Chambers
52 North Hill, Colchester, Essex, CO1 1PY,
Telephone: 01206 572756
E-mail: colchester@ealaw.co.uk
East Anglian Chambers
57 London Street, Norwich NR2 1HL,
Telephone: 01603 617351
E-mail: norwich@ealaw.co.uk

East Anglian Chambers
Gresham House, 5 Museum Street,
Ipswich, Suffolk, IP1 1HQ,
Telephone: 01473 214481
E-mail: ipswich@ealaw.co.uk
Call Date: Nov 1987, Middle Temple
Qualifications: [LLB Hons]

DEHN CONRAD FRANCIS QC (1968)

Fountain Court
Temple, London EC4Y 9DH,
Telephone: 0171 583 3335
E-mail: chambers@fountaincourt.co.uk
Call Date: July 1952, Gray's Inn
Recorder
Qualifications: [MA (Oxon)]

DEIGHTON RICHARD ANDREW GRAHAM

Chambers of Norman Palmer
2 Field Court, Gray's Inn, London
WC1R 5BB, Telephone: 0171 405 6114
E-mail: fieldct2@netcomuk.co.uk
Call Date: July 1990, Middle Temple

DEIGNAN DR MARY TERESA

Dr Johnson's Chambers
Two Dr Johnson's Buildings, Temple,
London EC4Y 7AY,
Telephone: 0171 353 4716
E-mail: clerks@2djb.freeserve.co.uk
Call Date: 1991, Middle Temple
Qualifications: [BSc (Aston), PhD (Belfast)]

DEIN JEREMY SYDNEY

3 Gray's Inn Square
Ground Floor, London WC1R 5AH,
Telephone: 0171 520 5600
E-mail: clerks@3gis.co.uk
Call Date: Nov 1982, Middle Temple
Pupil Master
Qualifications: [LLB (Lond)]

DEL FABBRO OSCAR

23 Essex Street
London WC2R 3AS,
Telephone: 0171 413 0353/836 8366
E-mail:clerks@essexstreet23.demon.co.uk
Call Date: July 1982, Gray's Inn
Pupil Master
Qualifications: [B Com(Witwatersrand)]

DELAHUNTY MISS JOHANNE ERICA

14 Tooks Court
Cursitor St, London EC4A 1LB,
Telephone: 0171 405 8828
E-mail: clerks@tooks.law.co.uk
Call Date: Nov 1986, Middle Temple
Qualifications: [BA , MA (Oxon)]

DELAMERE MISS ISABEL SARAH

9 King's Bench Walk
Ground Floor, Temple, London
EC4Y 7DX, Telephone: 0171 353 7202/
3909 E-mail: 9kbw@compuserve.com
Call Date: Nov 1985, Middle Temple
Qualifications: [BA(Hull)]

DELANEY KENNETH JOSEPH

Derby Square Chambers
Merchants Court, Derby Square, Liverpool
L2 1TS, Telephone: 0151 709 4222
E-mail:mail.derbysquare@pop3.hiway.co.uk
Call Date: Oct 1996, Inner Temple
Qualifications: [LLB (Hons), M.Phil (Cantab)]

DELANEY ROYSTON HARLOW

Young Street Chambers
38 Young Street, Manchester M3 3FT,
Telephone: 0161 833 0489
E-mail: clerks@young-st-chambers.com
Call Date: Nov 1996, Lincoln's Inn
Qualifications: [MA (Cantab)]

DEMETRIOU MS MARIE-ELENI

4-5 Gray's Inn Square
Ground Floor, Gray's Inn, London
WC1R 5JP, Telephone: 0171 404 5252
E-mail:chambers@4-5graysinnsquare.co.uk
Call Date: Nov 1995, Middle Temple
Qualifications: [BA (Hons) , BCL]

DEMPSEY BRIAN PAUL

Lancaster Building
77 Deansgate, Manchester M3 2BW,
Telephone: 0161 661 4444/0171 649 9872
E-mail: sandra@lbnipc.com
Call Date: May 1972, Lincoln's Inn
Qualifications: [BCL, LLB(Dub)]

DEMPSTER MISS JENNIFER MARGARET PERT

2 Paper Buildings, Basement North
Temple, London EC4Y 7ET,
Telephone: 0171 936 2613
E-mail: post@2paper.co.uk
Call Date: May 1993, Lincoln's Inn
Qualifications: [LLB (Hons)]

DEMPSTER DR TINA DOREEN ANNE

11 King's Bench Walk
1st Floor, Temple, London EC4Y 7EQ,
Telephone: 0171 353 3337
E-mail: fmuller11@aol.com
11 King's Bench Walk
3 Park Court, Park Cross Street, Leeds
LS1 2QH, Telephone: 0113 297 1200
Call Date: Nov 1997, Middle Temple
Qualifications: [LLB (Hons), PhD, (B'ham)]

DENBIN JACK ARNOLD

Greenway
Sonning Lane, Sonning-on-Thames,
Berkshire, RG4 6ST,
Telephone: 0118 969 2484
Call Date: July 1973, Inner Temple
Qualifications: [BSc (Reading), , C Biol, MI
Biol, FCIArb]

DENCER MARK RICHARD

2nd Floor, Francis Taylor Building
Temple, London EC4Y 7BY,
Telephone: 0171 353 9942/3157
Call Date: Apr 1978, Lincoln's Inn
Pupil Master
Qualifications: [LLB (Lond)]

DENEHAN EDWARD

9 Stone Buildings
Lincoln's Inn, London WC2A 3NN,
Telephone: 0171 404 5055
E-mail: clerks@9stoneb.law.co.uk
Call Date: July 1981, Lincoln's Inn
Pupil Master
Qualifications: [LLB (Warw)]

DENISON SIMON NEIL

6 King's Bench Walk
Ground Floor, Temple, London
EC4Y 7DR, Telephone: 0171 583 0410
E-mail: worsley@6kbw.freeserve.co.uk
Call Date: Nov 1984, Lincoln's Inn
Pupil Master
Qualifications: [MA (Cantab)]

DENMAN ROBERT ELLISON

5 Paper Buildings
Ground Floor, Temple, London
EC4Y 7HB, Telephone: 0171 583 9275/
583 4555 E-mail: 5paper@link.org
Call Date: July 1970, Gray's Inn
Pupil Master
Qualifications: [MA (Cantab)]

DENNETT MISS ANGELINA BRUNHILDE

24a St John Street
Manchester M3 4DF,
Telephone: 0161 833 9628
Call Date: Nov 1980, Middle Temple
Pupil Master
Qualifications: [BA (Hons), LLM (Lond)]

DENNEY STUART HENRY MACDONALD

Deans Court Chambers
24 St John Street, Manchester M3 4DF,
Telephone: 0161 214 6000
E-mail: clerks@deanscourt.co.uk
Deans Court Chambers
41-43 Market Place, Preston PR1 1AH,
Telephone: 01772 555163
E-mail: clerks@deanscourt.co.uk
Call Date: July 1982, Inner Temple
Pupil Master
Qualifications: [MA (Cantab)]

DENNIS DAVID EDWARD

Adrian Lyon's Chambers
14 Castle Street, Liverpool L2 0NE,
Telephone: 0151 236 4421/8240
E-mail: chambers14@aol.com
5 Stone Buildings
Lincoln's Inn, London WC2A 3XT,
Telephone: 0171 242 6201
E-mail:clerks@5-stonebuildings.law.co.uk
Call Date: July 1979, Inner Temple
Qualifications: [LLB (Hull)]

DENNIS MARK JONATHAN

6 King's Bench Walk
Ground Floor, Temple, London
EC4Y 7DR, Telephone: 0171 583 0410
E-mail: worsley@6kbw.freeserve.co.uk
Call Date: July 1977, Middle Temple
Pupil Master, Assistant Recorder
Qualifications: [MA (Cantab)]

DENNIS MISS REBECCA LOUISE

Queens Square Chambers
56 Queens Square, Bristol BS1 4PR,
Telephone: 0117 921 1966
Call Date: July 1994, Gray's Inn
Qualifications: [LLB , LLM (Bris)]

DENNISON JAMES ANGUS

2 Paper Buildings, Basement North
Temple, London EC4Y 7ET,
Telephone: 0171 936 2613
E-mail: post@2paper.co.uk
Call Date: July 1986, Inner Temple
Qualifications: [BA (Dunelm)]

DENNISON STEPHEN RANDELL

Atkin Chambers
1 Atkin Building, Gray's Inn, London
WC1R 5AT, Telephone: 020 7404 0102
E-mail: clerks@atkin-chambers.co.uk
Call Date: Nov 1985, Middle Temple
Pupil Master
Qualifications: [LLB (Manch)]

DENNISS JOHN ANNEAR

4 King's Bench Walk
2nd Floor, Temple, London EC4Y 7DL,
Telephone: 020 7353 3581
E-mail: clerks@4kbw.co.uk
Call Date: July 1974, Inner Temple
Pupil Master
Qualifications: [LLB (Hons)]

DENNY ROBIN HENRY ALISDAIR

39 Park Square
Leeds LS1 2NU,
Telephone: 0113 2456633
Call Date: May 1969, Inner Temple
Pupil Master
Qualifications: [BA (Oxon)]

DENNYS NICHOLAS CHARLES JONATHAN QC (1991)

Atkin Chambers
1 Atkin Building, Gray's Inn, London
WC1R 5AT, Telephone: 020 7404 0102
E-mail: clerks@atkin-chambers.co.uk
Call Date: Nov 1975, Middle Temple
Assistant Recorder
Qualifications: [BA (Oxon)]

DENT ADRIAN RONALD

Chancery House Chambers
7 Lisbon Square, Leeds LS1 4LY,
Telephone: 0113 244 6691
E-mail: chanceryhouse@btinternet.com
Call Date: July 1974, Lincoln's Inn
Pupil Master
Qualifications: [LLB]

DENT KEVIN JOSEPH

2 Paper Buildings, Basement North
Temple, London EC4Y 7ET,
Telephone: 0171 936 2613
E-mail: post@2paper.co.uk
Call Date: Nov 1991, Inner Temple
Qualifications: [BA (Hons)(Sussex)]

DENT MS SALLY CLAIRE LEIGH

Mitre House Chambers
15-19 Devereux Court, London WC2R 3JJ,
Telephone: 0171 583 8233
Call Date: July 1989, Lincoln's Inn
Qualifications: [BA (Reading), Dip Law]

DENT STEPHEN ROBERT CHARLES

Guildhall Chambers
22-26 Broad Street, Bristol BS1 2HG,
Telephone: 0117 9273366
E-mail:civil.clerks@guildhallchambers.co.uk and
criminal.clerks@guildhallchambers.co.uk
Call Date: Feb 1991, Gray's Inn
Qualifications: [LLB (Manch)]

DENTON MISS AMANDA

15 North Church Street Chambers
15 North Church Street, Sheffield
S1 2DH, Telephone: 0114 2759708/
2738380
Call Date: Nov 1993, Lincoln's Inn
Qualifications: [LLB (Hons)]

DENTON MISS MICHELLE JAYNE

9-12 Bell Yard
London WC2A 2LF,
Telephone: 0171 400 1800
E-mail: clerks@bellyard.co.uk
Call Date: Oct 1996, Inner Temple
Qualifications: [LLB (So'ton)]

DENYER RODERICK LAWRENCE QC (1990)

St John's Chambers
Small Street, Bristol BS1 1DW,
Telephone: 0117 9213456/298514
E-mail: @stjohnschambers.co.uk
Call Date: July 1970, Inner Temple
Recorder
Qualifications: [LLM]

DENYER-GREEN BARRY PETER DOUGLAS

Falcon Chambers
Falcon Court, London EC4Y 1AA,
Telephone: 0171 353 2484
E-mail: clerks@falcon-chambers.com
Call Date: Nov 1972, Middle Temple
Pupil Master
Qualifications: [LLM, PhD, FRICS]

DERBYSHIRE THOMAS WILLIAM

3 Hare Court
1 Little Essex Street, London WC2R 3LD,
Telephone: 0171 395 2000
Call Date: 1989, Inner Temple
Qualifications: [LLB]

DESCHAMPSNEUFS MISS ALICE NORA

9 King's Bench Walk
Ground Floor, Temple, London
EC4Y 7DX, Telephone: 0171 353 7202/
3909 E-mail: 9kbw@compuserve.com
Call Date: July 1976, Inner Temple
Pupil Master
Qualifications: [BA (Lond)]

DESMOND DENIS JOHN

6 Fountain Court
Steelhouse Lane, Birmingham B4 6DR,
Telephone: 0121 233 3282
E-mail: clerks@sixfountain.co.uk
Call Date: Nov 1974, Middle Temple
Pupil Master
Qualifications: [BA]

DESOUZA MS ESPERANZA LOUISA MARIA ANGELA

Britton Street Chambers
1st Floor, 20 Britton Street, London
EC1M 5NQ, Telephone: 0171 608 3765
Call Date: Nov 1994, Gray's Inn
Qualifications: [BSc (Lond), PGCE, Dip in
Law]

DESOUZA MRS JOSEPHINE CLAUDIA

Chancery Chambers
1st Floor Offices, 70/72 Chancery Lane,
London WC2A 1AB,
Telephone: 0171 405 6879/6870
Call Date: Nov 1992, Lincoln's Inn
Qualifications: [LLB (Hons)]

DETHRIDGE DAVID JOHN

Verulam Chambers
Peer House, 8-14 Verulam Street, Gray's
Inn, London WC1X 8LZ,
Telephone: 0171 813 2400
Call Date: July 1975, Lincoln's Inn
Pupil Master
Qualifications: [MA (Oxon)]

DETTER DE LUPIS FRANKOPAN COUNTESS (THYRA) INGRID HILDEGARD DOIMI

One Hare Court
1st Floor, Temple, London EC4Y 7BE,
Telephone: 020 7353 3171
E-mail:admin-oneharecourt@btinternet.com
Call Date: July 1977, Middle Temple
Qualifications: [DPhil (Oxon), Lic en droit
(Paris), CESE (Turin), Jur Kand, Jur Lic,
Jur Dr (Stockholm)]

DEVE CHRISTOPHER AGAMA

Mottingham Barrister's Chambers
43 West Park, London SE9 4RZ,
Telephone: 0181 857 5565
Call Date: Nov 1990, Inner Temple
Qualifications: [LLB]

DEVINE MICHAEL BUXTON

95A Chancery Lane
London WC2A 1DT,
Telephone: 0171 405 3101
Call Date: July 1995, Gray's Inn
Qualifications: [BA, JD, MPA, Diploma
Advanced Int, Legal Studies, LLM]

DEVLIN BERNARD JOSEPH

1 Harcourt Buildings
2nd Floor, Temple, London EC4Y 9DA,
Telephone: 0171 353 9421/0375
E-mail:clerks@1harcourtbuildings.law.co.uk
Call Date: Nov 1980, Gray's Inn
Pupil Master
Qualifications: [LLB (Reading) LLM, (Lond)]

DEVLIN JONATHAN NICHOLAS PONTON

Park Court Chambers
16 Park Place, Leeds LS1 2SJ,
Telephone: 0113 2433277
Call Date: Nov 1978, Inner Temple
Pupil Master
Qualifications: [LLB (Leeds)]

DEVLIN TIMOTHY ROBERT

Queen Elizabeth Building
Ground Floor, Temple, London
EC4Y 9BS,
Telephone: 0171 353 7181 (12 Lines)
Call Date: July 1985, Lincoln's Inn
Qualifications: [BA, (Lond), Dip Law]

DEVONSHIRE SIMON PETER

5 Paper Buildings
Ground Floor, Temple, London
EC4Y 7HB, Telephone: 0171 583 9275/
583 4555 E-mail: 5paper@link.org
Call Date: Feb 1988, Gray's Inn
Pupil Master
Qualifications: [BA(Oxon)]

DEWSBERY RICHARD MARK

St Ive's Chambers
Whittall Street, Birmingham B4 6DH,
Telephone: 0121 236 0863/5720
E-mail:stives.headofchambers@btinternet.com
Call Date: Oct 1992, Inner Temple
Qualifications: [LLB (Hons) (Essex)]

DHADLI MRS PERMINDER

King Charles House
Standard Hill, Nottingham NG1 6FX,
Telephone: 0115 9418851
E-mail: clerks@kch.co.uk
Call Date: Nov 1984, Middle Temple
Pupil Master
Qualifications: [BA (Hons)]

DHALIWAL MISS DAVINDER KAUR

New Court Chambers
Gazette Building, 168 Corporation Street,
Birmingham B4 6TZ,
Telephone: 0121 693 6656
Call Date: Nov 1990, Middle Temple
Qualifications: [LLB (Hons)(B'ham)]

DHILLON JASBIR SINGH

Brick Court Chambers
7-8 Essex Street, London WC2R 3LD,
Telephone: 0171 379 3550
E-mail: [surname]@brickcourt.co.uk
Call Date: 1996, Gray's Inn
Qualifications: [BA (Oxon), LLM (Harvard)]

DHIR MISS ANUJA RAVINDRA

Five Paper Buildings
1st Floor, Five Paper Bldgs, Temple,
London EC4Y 7HB,
Telephone: 0171 583 6117
E-mail:clerks@5-paperbuildings.law.co.uk
Call Date: Nov 1989, Gray's Inn
Qualifications: [LLB (Dundee)]

DI MAMBRO DAVID JESSE ANDREW

Lamb Chambers
Lamb Building, Temple, London
EC4Y 7AS, Telephone: 020 7797 8300
E-mail: lambchambers@link.org
Call Date: Nov 1973, Middle Temple
Pupil Master
Qualifications: [LLB (Lond),ACIArb]

D

D

DIAMOND MISS ANNA CATRIONA

5 Fountain Court
Steelhouse Lane, Birmingham B4 6DR,
Telephone: 0121 606 0500
E-mail:clerks@5fountaincourt.law.co.uk
Call Date: Oct 1995, Gray's Inn
Qualifications: [BA]

DIAMOND CHRISTOPHER LESLIE WILLIAM

18 St John Street
Manchester M3 4EA,
Telephone: 0161 278 1800
E-mail: 18stjohn@lineone.net
Call Date: Nov 1975, Gray's Inn
Pupil Master
Qualifications: [LLB]

DIAMOND IAN PAUL HUGH

Call Date: July 1985, Middle Temple
Qualifications: [BA (Exon), LLM (Cantab)]

DIAS CHANDRAJITH ASOKA WILLIAM

6 King's Bench Walk
Ground, Third & Fourth Floors, Temple,
London EC4Y 7DR,
Telephone: 0171 353 4931/583 0695
Call Date: July 1989, Lincoln's Inn
Qualifications: [LLB (Warw)]

DIAS JUDE DEXTER

Two Garden Court
1st Floor, Middle Temple, London
EC4Y 9BL, Telephone: 0171 353 1633
E-mail:barristers@2gardenct.law.co.uk
Call Date: Feb 1988, Inner Temple
Qualifications: [BA (Durham)]

DIAS MISS SAPPHO

Thomas More Chambers
52 Carey Street, Lincoln's Inn, London
WC2A 2JB, Telephone: 0171 404 7000
E-mail: clerks@thomasmore.law.co.uk
Call Date: Nov 1982, Gray's Inn
Pupil Master
Qualifications: [BA (Cantab)]

DICK JOHN OSWALD

Temple Gardens Tax Chambers
1st Floor, 3 Temple Gardens, Temple,
London EC4Y 9AU,
Telephone: 0171 353 7884/5 8982/3
E-mail: clerks@taxcounsel.co.uk.
Call Date: July 1974, Gray's Inn
Pupil Master
Qualifications: [MA (Oxon)]

DICK MISS JULIA MARGARET

14 Tooks Court
Cursitor St, London EC4A 1LB,
Telephone: 0171 405 8828
E-mail: clerks@tooks.law.co.uk
Call Date: Nov 1988, Middle Temple
Qualifications: [B.Tech (Bradford), Dip Law (City)]

DICKENS ANDREW WILLIAM

Gray's Inn Chambers, The Chambers of Norman Patterson
First Floor, Gray's Inn Chambers, Gray's
Inn, London WC1R 5JA,
Telephone: 0171 831 5344
E-mail: s.mcblain@btinternet.com
Call Date: Nov 1983, Gray's Inn
Pupil Master
Qualifications: [Dip Law]

DICKENS PAUL MICHAEL JOHN

5 New Square
Ground Floor, Lincoln's Inn, London
WC2A 3RJ, Telephone: 020 7404 0404
E-mail:chambers@fivenewsquare.demon.co.uk
Call Date: 1978, Lincoln's Inn
Pupil Master
Qualifications: [MA (Cantab),ARCO]

DICKER ROBIN MARK

3/4 South Square
Gray's Inn, London WC1R 5HP,
Telephone: 0171 696 9900
E-mail: clerks@southsquare.com
Call Date: Apr 1986, Middle Temple
Pupil Master
Qualifications: [BA, BCL (Oxon)]

DICKINSON GREGORY DAVID MARK

High Pavement Chambers
1 High Pavement, Nottingham NG1 1HF,
Telephone: 0115 9418218
Call Date: July 1981, Gray's Inn
Pupil Master, Assistant Recorder
Qualifications: [LLB]

DICKINSON JOHN FINCH HENEAGE

St John's Chambers
Small Street, Bristol BS1 1DW,
Telephone: 0117 9213456/298514
E-mail: @stjohnschambers.co.uk
Call Date: Oct 1995, Middle Temple
Qualifications: [BA (Hons)]

DICKINSON JONATHAN DAVID

58 King Street Chambers
1st Floor, Kingsgate House, 51-53 South
King Street, Manchester M2 6DE,
Telephone: 0161 831 7477
Call Date: Nov 1986, Inner Temple
Qualifications: [LLB (Hons) (Bristol)]

DICKS ANTHONY RICHARD

Essex Court Chambers
24 Lincoln's Inn Fields, London
WC2A 3ED, Telephone: 0171 813 8000
E-mail:clerksroom@essexcourt-chambers.co.u
k
Call Date: May 1961, Inner Temple
Qualifications: [MA, LLB (Cantab)]

DIGBY CHARLES SPENCER

Queen Elizabeth Building
Ground Floor, Temple, London
EC4Y 9BS,
Telephone: 0171 353 7181 (12 Lines)
Call Date: July 1982, Middle Temple
Pupil Master
Qualifications: [BA]

DIGGLE MARK JAMES

Ropewalk Chambers
24 The Ropewalk, Nottingham NG1 5EF,
Telephone: 0115 9472581
E-mail: administration@ropewalk co.uk
Call Date: 1996, Inner Temple
Qualifications: [LLM (Nott'm), LLB
(Glamorgan)]

DIGHT MARC DAVID

11 Stone Buildings
Lincoln's Inn, London WC2A 3TG,
Telephone: +44 (0)207 831 6381
E-mail:clerks@11StoneBuildings.law.co.uk
Chichester Chambers
12 North Pallant, Chichester, West Sussex,
PO19 1TQ, Telephone: 01243 784538
E-mail:clerks@chichesterchambers.law.co.uk
Call Date: July 1984, Inner Temple
Pupil Master
Qualifications: [LLB (Bristol)]

DIGNEY PETER NEIL

1 Dr Johnson's Buildings
Ground Floor, Temple, London
EC4Y 7AX, Telephone: 0171 353 9328
E-mail:OneDr.Johnsons@btinternet.com
Dr Johnson's Chambers
The Atrium Court, Apex Plaza, Reading,
Berkshire, RG1 1AX,
Telephone: 01734 254221
Call Date: July 1968, Middle Temple
Pupil Master, Recorder
Qualifications: [BA (Cantab)]

DIGNUM MARCUS BENEDICT

1 Crown Office Row
3rd Floor, Temple, London EC4Y 7HH,
Telephone: 0171 583 9292
E-mail: onecor@link.org
Call Date: Oct 1994, Middle Temple
Qualifications: [BA (Hons)(Lond)]

DILHORNE THE RT HON VISCOUNT

4 Breams Buildings
London EC4A 1AQ,
Telephone: 0171 353 5835/430 1221
E-mail:breams@4breamsbuildings.law.co.uk
Call Date: Nov 1979, Inner Temple
Pupil Master
Qualifications: [FTII]

DILLON THOMAS WILLIAM MATTHEW

1 Fountain Court
Steelhouse Lane, Birmingham B4 6DR,
Telephone: 0121 236 5721
Call Date: July 1983, Middle Temple
Qualifications: [MA (Cantab), Dip IPL]

DIN SOOFI PERVAZE IQBAL

Ropewalk Chambers
24 The Ropewalk, Nottingham NG1 5EF,
Telephone: 0115 9472581
E-mail: administration@ropewalk co.uk
Call Date: Nov 1984, Lincoln's Inn
Qualifications: [BA (Manch)]

DINAN-HAYWARD MISS DEBORAH LOUISE

Albion Chambers
Broad Street, Bristol BS1 1DR,
Telephone: 0117 9272144
Call Date: Nov 1988, Inner Temple
Pupil Master
Qualifications: [LLB (Shef)]

DINEEN MS MARIA THERESE

3 Hare Court
1 Little Essex Street, London WC2R 3LD,
Telephone: 0171 395 2000
Call Date: 1997, Inner Temple
Qualifications: [LLB (Nottingham)]

DINEEN MICHAEL LAURENCE

Pump Court Chambers
31 Southgate Street, Winchester
SO23 9EE, Telephone: 01962 868161
E-mail: clerks@3pumpcourt.com
Pump Court Chambers
Upper Ground Floor, 3 Pump Court,
Temple, London EC4Y 7AJ,
Telephone: 0171 353 0711
E-mail: clerks@3pumpcourt.com
Queens Square Chambers
56 Queens Square, Bristol BS1 4PR,
Telephone: 0117 921 1966
Pump Court Chambers
5 Temple Chambers, Temple Street,
Swindon SN1 1SQ,
Telephone: 01793 539899
E-mail: clerks@3pumpcourt.com
Call Date: Nov 1977, Inner Temple
Pupil Master
Qualifications: [BA (Oxon) LLB, (Cantab)]

DINES COLIN EDWARD

1 Middle Temple Lane
Temple, London EC4Y 1LT,
Telephone: 0171 583 0659 (12 Lines)
E-mail: chambers@1mtl.co.uk

Westgate Chambers
144 High Street, Lewes, East Sussex,
BN7 1XT, Telephone: 01273 480510
Call Date: Nov 1970, Middle Temple
Pupil Master, Recorder

DINES MISS SARAH ELIZABETH

Plowden Buildings
2nd Floor, 2 Plowden Buildings, Middle
Temple Lane, London EC4Y 9BU,
Telephone: 0171 583 0808
E-mail: bar@plowdenbuildings.co.uk
Call Date: July 1988, Lincoln's Inn
Qualifications: [LLB (Hons) (Brunel)]

DINGEMANS JAMES MICHAEL

1 Crown Office Row
3rd Floor, Temple, London EC4Y 7HH,
Telephone: 0171 583 9292
E-mail: onecor@link.org
Call Date: July 1987, Inner Temple
Pupil Master
Qualifications: [BA (Oxon)]

DINGLE JONATHAN CRISPIN

South Western Chambers
Melville House, 12 Middle Street,
Taunton, Somerset, TA1 1SH,
Telephone: 01823 331919 (24 hrs)
E-mail: barclerk@clara.net
Call Date: July 1986, Middle Temple
Pupil Master
Qualifications: [LLB (Lond)]

DINKIN ANTHONY DAVID QC (1991)

2-3 Gray's Inn Square
Gray's Inn, London WC1R 5JH,
Telephone: 0171 242 4986
E-mail:chambers@2-3graysinnsquare.co.uk
Call Date: Nov 1968, Lincoln's Inn
Recorder
Qualifications: [BSc (Lond), BSc (Lond)]

DISMORR EDWARD SEEL

St Ive's Chambers
Whittall Street, Birmingham B4 6DH,
Telephone: 0121 236 0863/5720
E-mail:stives.headofchambers@btinternet.com
Call Date: July 1983, Inner Temple
Qualifications: [MA (Oxon) Dip Law Ci]

DITCHFIELD ANTHONY MICHAEL

Trinity Chambers
9-12 Trinity Chare, Quayside, Newcastle
upon Tyne NE1 3DF,
Telephone: 0191 232 1927
E-mail: info@trinitychambers.co.uk
Call Date: Oct 1993, Middle Temple
Qualifications: [BA (Hons, Kent), LLM
(Sheff)]

DIWAN RICKY

Essex Court Chambers
24 Lincoln's Inn Fields, London
WC2A 3ED, Telephone: 0171 813 8000
E-mail:clerksroom@essexcourt-chambers.co.uk
Call Date: Oct 1998, Lincoln's Inn
Qualifications: [BA (Hons)(Cantab), LLM
(Harvard)]

DIX-DYER MISS FIONA JANE

St Paul's House
5th Floor, St Paul's House, 23 Park Square
South, Leeds LS1 2ND,
Telephone: 0113 2455866
E-mail: catherinegrimshaw@stpauls-
chambers.demon.co.uk
Call Date: July 1986, Lincoln's Inn
Qualifications: [LLB (Hons)(Leeds)]

DIXEY IAN ROGER

St John's Chambers
Small Street, Bristol BS1 1DW,
Telephone: 0117 9213456/298514
E-mail: @stjohnschambers.co.uk
Call Date: Nov 1984, Inner Temple
Pupil Master

DIXON MISS ANNE

Counsels' Chambers
2nd Floor, 10-11 Gray's Inn Square,
London WC1R 5JD,
Telephone: 0171 405 2576
E-mail:clerks@10-11graysinnsquare.co.uk
Call Date: Nov 1991, Middle Temple
Qualifications: [LLB (Hons), RGN]

DIXON DAVID STEVEN

Sovereign Chambers
25 Park Square, Leeds LS1 2PW,
Telephone: 0113 2451841/2/3
E-mail:sovereignchambers@btinternet.com
Call Date: Oct 1992, Lincoln's Inn
Qualifications: [LLB(Hons)(Newc)]

DIXON MS EMMA LOUISE

Blackstone Chambers
Blackstone House, Temple, London
EC4Y 9BW, Telephone: 0171 583 1770
E-mail:clerks@blackstonechambers.com
Call Date: Oct 1994, Gray's Inn
Qualifications: [BA]

DIXON IAN FREDERICK

Cathedral Chambers
Milburn House, Dean Street, Newcastle
upon Tyne NE1 1LE,
Telephone: 0191 232 1311
Call Date: Nov 1982, Gray's Inn

DIXON JOHN

India Buildings Chambers
Water Street, Liverpool L2 0XG,
Telephone: 0151 243 6000
E-mail: clerks@chambers.u-net.com
Call Date: Nov 1995, Gray's Inn
Qualifications: [LLB (Essex)]

DIXON JOHN WATTS

Harcourt Chambers
1st Floor, 2 Harcourt Buildings, Temple,
London EC4Y 9DB,
Telephone: 0171 353 6961
E-mail:clerks@harcourtchambers.law.co.uk
Harcourt Chambers
Churchill House, 3 St Aldate's Courtyard,
St Aldate's, Oxford OX1 1BN,
Telephone: 01865 791559
E-mail:clerks@harcourtchambers.law.co.uk
Call Date: Feb 1975, Middle Temple
Pupil Master, Assistant Recorder
Qualifications: [MA (Oxon)]

DIXON PHILIP JOHN

2nd Floor, Francis Taylor Building
Temple, London EC4Y 7BY,
Telephone: 0171 353 9942/3157
Call Date: July 1986, Middle Temple
Qualifications: [MA(Cantab)]

DIXON RALPH JOHN PETER

St John's Chambers
Small Street, Bristol BS1 1DW,
Telephone: 0117 9213456/298514
E-mail: @stjohnschambers.co.uk
Call Date: Nov 1980, Middle Temple
Pupil Master
Qualifications: [BA (York)]

DIXON MISS SORREL HELEN

2 Gray's Inn Square Chambers
2nd Floor, Gray's Inn, London WC1R 5AA,
Telephone: 020 7242 0328
E-mail: clerks@2gis.co.uk
Call Date: July 1987, Middle Temple
Qualifications: [LLB (Bristol)]

DOBBS MISS LINDA PENELOPE QC (1998)

18 Red Lion Court
(Off Fleet Street), London EC4A 3EB,
Telephone: 0171 520 6000
E-mail: chambers@18rlc.co.uk
Thornwood House
102 New London Road, Chelmsford,
Essex, CM2 0RG,
Telephone: 01245 280880
E-mail: chambers@18rlc.co.uk
Call Date: July 1981, Gray's Inn
Qualifications: [BSc, LLM, PhD (Lond)]

DOCKERY PAUL

18 St John Street
Manchester M3 4EA,
Telephone: 0161 278 1800
E-mail: 18stjohn@lineone.net
Call Date: July 1973, Gray's Inn
Pupil Master
Qualifications: [LLB (London)]

DOCKING TONY WILFRED JAMES

1 Middle Temple Lane
Temple, London EC4Y 1LT,
Telephone: 0171 583 0659 (12 Lines)
E-mail: chambers@1mtl.co.uk
Call Date: Nov 1969, Gray's Inn
Pupil Master

DOCTOR BRIAN ERNEST QC (1999)

Fountain Court
Temple, London EC4Y 9DH,
Telephone: 0171 583 3335
E-mail: chambers@fountaincourt.co.uk
Call Date: 1991, Lincoln's Inn
Pupil Master
Qualifications: [BA (S Africa), LLB
(Witwatersand), BCL]

DODD CHRISTOPHER JOHN NICHOLAS

9 Woodhouse Square
Leeds LS3 1AD,
Telephone: 0113 2451986
E-mail: clerks@9woodhouse.co.uk
Call Date: Nov 1984, Lincoln's Inn
Pupil Master
Qualifications: [LLB (Leics)]

DODD JOHN STANISLAUS

3 Hare Court
1 Little Essex Street, London WC2R 3LD,
Telephone: 0171 395 2000
Call Date: Nov 1979, Gray's Inn
Pupil Master
Qualifications: [LLB (Leics)]

DODD MRS MARGARET ANN

3 Hare Court
1 Little Essex Street, London WC2R 3LD,
Telephone: 0171 395 2000
Call Date: 1979, Middle Temple
Qualifications: [LLB [So'ton]]

DODD MISS SARA

58 King Street Chambers
1st Floor, Kingsgate House, 51-53 South
King Street, Manchester M2 6DE,
Telephone: 0161 831 7477
Call Date: July 1987, Lincoln's Inn
Qualifications: [LLB]

DODDS ROBERT STEPHEN

15 Winckley Square
Preston PR1 3JJ,
Telephone: 01772 252828
E-mail:clerks@winckleysq.demon.co.uk

1 Mitre Court Buildings
Temple, London EC4Y 7BS,
Telephone: 0171 797 7070
E-mail: clerks@1mcb.com
Call Date: July 1976, Gray's Inn
Pupil Master
Qualifications: [LLB (Lond)]

DODDS SHAUN

Baker Street Chambers
9 Baker Street, Middlesbrough TS1 2LF,
Telephone: 01642 873873
Call Date: July 1990, Gray's Inn
Qualifications: [LLB (Lond)]

DODGE PETER CLIVE

11 Old Square
Ground Floor, Lincoln's Inn, London
WC2A 3TS, Telephone: 020 7430 0341
E-mail: clerks@11oldsquare.co.uk
Call Date: Oct 1992, Lincoln's Inn
Qualifications: [BA(Hons), MA, Dip Law]

DODGSON PAUL

1 Hare Court
Ground Floor, Temple, London
EC4Y 7BE, Telephone: 0171 353 3982/
5324
Call Date: July 1975, Inner Temple
Pupil Master, Recorder
Qualifications: [LLB]

DODSON MISS JOANNA QC (1993)

14 Gray's Inn Square
Gray's Inn, London WC1R 5JP,
Telephone: 0171 242 0858
E-mail: 100712.2134@compuserve.com
Park Court Chambers
16 Park Place, Leeds LS1 2SJ,
Telephone: 0113 2433277
Call Date: Nov 1970, Middle Temple
Qualifications: [MA (Cantab)]

DOERRIES MISS CHANTAL-AIMEE RENEE AEMELIA ANNEMARIE

Atkin Chambers
1 Atkin Building, Gray's Inn, London
WC1R 5AT, Telephone: 020 7404 0102
E-mail: clerks@atkin-chambers.co.uk
Call Date: 1992, Middle Temple
Qualifications: [MA (Hons, Cantab)]

DOGGART PIERS GRAHAM

King's Chambers
5a Gildredge Road, Eastbourne, East
Sussex, BN21 4RB,
Telephone: 01323 416053
Call Date: Oct 1991, Lincoln's Inn
Pupil Master
Qualifications: [LLB (Hons) (Leeds)]

DOHERTY BERNARD JAMES

39 Essex Street
London WC2R 3AT,
Telephone: 0171 832 1111
E-mail: clerks@39essex.co.uk
Call Date: Nov 1990, Middle Temple
Pupil Master
Qualifications: [MA (Cantab), Dip Law (City)]

DOHERTY NICHOLAS BRUDENELL

10 King's Bench Walk
1st Floor, Temple, London EC4Y 7EB,
Telephone: 0171 353 2501
Call Date: July 1983, Lincoln's Inn
Pupil Master
Qualifications: [LLB]

DOHMANN MISS BARBARA QC (1987)

Blackstone Chambers
Blackstone House, Temple, London
EC4Y 9BW, Telephone: 0171 583 1770
E-mail:clerks@blackstonechambers.com
Call Date: Nov 1971, Gray's Inn
Recorder
Qualifications: [Graduate of Mainz &, Paris
Universities]

DOIG GAVIN ANDREW

St John's Chambers
Small Street, Bristol BS1 1DW,
Telephone: 0117 9213456/298514
E-mail: @stjohnschambers.co.uk
Call Date: Oct 1995, Lincoln's Inn
Qualifications: [LLB (Hons)(Bris)]

DOIG MRS JEANETTA ROSE

Neston Home Chambers
42 Greenhill, Neston, Corsham, Wiltshire,
SN13 9SQ, Telephone: 01225 811909
Call Date: July 1988, Lincoln's Inn
Qualifications: [CPE, PhC, FETC, M R Pharm
S]

DOLAN DR BRIDGET MAURA

3 Serjeants' Inn
London EC4Y 1BQ,
Telephone: 0171 353 5537
E-mail: clerks@3serjeantsinn.com
Call Date: 1997, Middle Temple
Qualifications: [BSc (Hons), PhD (Bradford),
CPE (Brighton)]

DOMENGE MRS VICTORIA JANE

29 Bedford Row Chambers
London WC1R 4HE,
Telephone: 0171 831 2626
Call Date: Nov 1993, Middle Temple
Qualifications: [BA (Hons)(Exon), Dip in
Law]

DONALDSON DAVID TORRANCE QC (1984)

Blackstone Chambers
Blackstone House, Temple, London
EC4Y 9BW, Telephone: 0171 583 1770
E-mail:clerks@blackstonechambers.com
Call Date: Nov 1968, Gray's Inn
Recorder
Qualifications: [MA (Cantab), DrJur]

DONNE ANTHONY MAURICE QC (1988)

2 King's Bench Walk
Ground Floor, Temple, London
EC4Y 7DE, Telephone: 0171 353 1746
E-mail: 2kbw@atlas.co.uk
King's Bench Chambers
115 North Hill, Plymouth PL4 8JY,
Telephone: 01752 221551
Queens Square Chambers
56 Queens Square, Bristol BS1 4PR,
Telephone: 0117 921 1966
Call Date: Nov 1973, Middle Temple
Recorder
Qualifications: [BA (Oxon)]

DONNE JEREMY NIGEL

Hollis Whiteman Chambers
3rd Floor, Queen Elizabeth Bldg, Temple,
London EC4Y 9BS,
Telephone: 020 7583 5766
E-mail:barristers@holliswhiteman.co.uk
Call Date: Nov 1978, Middle Temple
Pupil Master, Assistant Recorder

DONNELLAN CHRISTOPHER JOHN

Chambers of Michael Pert QC
36 Bedford Row, London WC1R 4JH,
Telephone: 0171 421 8000
E-mail: 36bedfordrow@link.org
Chambers of Michael Pert QC
24 Albion Place, Northampton NN1 1UD,
Telephone: 01604 602333
Chambers of Michael Pert QC
104 New Walk, Leicester LE1 7EA,
Telephone: 0116 249 2020
Call Date: July 1981, Inner Temple
Pupil Master
Qualifications: [BA (Oxon)]

DONNELLY MISS CATHERINE MARY

5 King's Bench Walk
Temple, London EC4Y 7DN,
Telephone: 0171 353 5638
Call Date: Mar 1997, Middle Temple
Qualifications: [BA (Hons)(Lond)]

DONNELLY JOHN PATRICK

Counsels' Chambers
2nd Floor, 10-11 Gray's Inn Square,
London WC1R 5JD,
Telephone: 0171 405 2576
E-mail:clerks@10-11graysinnsquare.co.uk
Call Date: Nov 1983, Inner Temple
Pupil Master
Qualifications: [LLB (Hull)]

DONNELLY KEVIN GERARD EASTWOOD

Lincoln House Chambers
5th Floor, Lincoln House, 1 Brazennose
Street, Manchester M2 5EL,
Telephone: 0161 832 5701
E-mail: info@lincolnhse.co.uk
Call Date: Oct 1991, Lincoln's Inn
Qualifications: [BA (Hons) (Cambs)]

DONOGHUE STEVEN MICHAEL

9 Park Place
Cardiff CF1 3DP,
Telephone: 01222 382731
Call Date: Oct 1992, Middle Temple
Qualifications: [LL.B (Hons, Wales)]

DONOVAN MISS ALISON MARY

Angel Chambers
94 Walter Road, Swansea, West
Glamorgan, SA1 5QA,
Telephone: 01792 464623/464648
E-mail: lynne@angelchambers.co.uk
Call Date: 1987, Middle Temple
Qualifications: [BA (Oxon)]

DONOVAN ANTHONY FRANCIS SCOTT

Derby Square Chambers
Merchants Court, Derby Square, Liverpool
L2 1TS, Telephone: 0151 709 4222
E-mail:mail.derbysquare@pop3.hiway.co.uk
Call Date: July 1975, Gray's Inn
Pupil Master, Recorder
Qualifications: [BA (Oxon) MA (USA)]

DONOVAN JOEL

New Court Chambers
5 Verulam Buildings, Gray's Inn, London
WC1R 5LY, Telephone: 0171 831 9500
E-mail: mail@newcourtchambers.com
Call Date: July 1991, Lincoln's Inn
Qualifications: [BA (Hons) (Durham)]

DOOHER MISS NANCY HELEN

St James's Chambers
68 Quay Street, Manchester M3 3EJ,
Telephone: 0161 834 7000
E-mail: clerks@stjameschambers.co.uk
Call Date: 1997, Lincoln's Inn
Qualifications: [LLB (Hons)(Lond)]

DOOKHY RIYAD ABDOOL CADER

The Thames Chambers
Wickham House, 10 Cleveland Way,
London E1 4TR,
Telephone: 0171 366 6655/790 2424 X390
E-mail: thames-chambers@usa.net
Call Date: Nov 1992, Gray's Inn
Qualifications: [LLB (Sheff)]

DOOLEY ALLAN KEITH

5 Fountain Court
Steelhouse Lane, Birmingham B4 6DR,
Telephone: 0121 606 0500
E-mail:clerks@5fountaincourt.law.co.uk
Call Date: Apr 1991, Lincoln's Inn
Pupil Master, Recorder
Qualifications: [LLB (Hons) (Liver)]

DOOLEY MS CHRISTINE

2 Pump Court
1st Floor, Temple, London EC4Y 7AH,
Telephone: 0171 353 5597
Call Date: July 1980, Gray's Inn
Pupil Master
Qualifications: [BA (Hons)]

DORAN GERARD PATRICK

2-4 Tudor Street
London EC4Y 0AA,
Telephone: 0171 797 7111
E-mail: clerks@rfqc.co.uk
Call Date: Nov 1993, Gray's Inn
Qualifications: [LLB (Hons)]

DORMAN-O'GOWAN CHRISTOPHER PATRICK DESMOND

Broad Chare
33 Broad Chare, Newcastle upon Tyne
NE1 3DQ, Telephone: 0191 232 0541
E-mail:clerks@broadcharechambers.law.co.uk
Call Date: Nov 1979, Lincoln's Inn
Pupil Master
Qualifications: [BA (Newc)]

DORRELL MS ALISON GLENDA

15 North Church Street Chambers
15 North Church Street, Sheffield
S1 2DH, Telephone: 0114 2759708/
2738380
Call Date: Feb 1992, Gray's Inn
Qualifications: [LLB (Sheff)]

DORRINGTON MILES HAMILTON

Call Date: 1996, Lincoln's Inn
Qualifications: [BA(Jnt Hons)(Dunelm)]

DOSWELL RUPERT JOHN

Clock Chambers
78 Darlington Street, Wolverhampton
WV1 4LY, Telephone: 01902 313444
Call Date: Oct 1996, Inner Temple
Qualifications: [LLB (Cardiff)]

DOUGHERTY CHARLES EGMONT

2 Temple Gardens
Temple, London EC4Y 9AY,
Telephone: 0171 583 6041
E-mail: clerks@2templegardens.co.uk
Call Date: 1997, Middle Temple
Qualifications: [BA (Hons)(Oxon)]

DOUGHERTY NIGEL PETER

Erskine Chambers
30 Lincoln's Inn Fields, Lincoln's Inn,
London WC2A 3PF,
Telephone: 0171 242 5532
E-mail:clerks@erskine-chambers.co.uk
Call Date: Oct 1993, Gray's Inn
Qualifications: [BA, LLM (Cantab)]

DOUGHTY PETER

17 Carlton Crescent
Southampton SO15 2XR,
Telephone: 023 8032 0320/0823 2003
E-mail: greg@jg17cc.co.uk
Call Date: July 1988, Lincoln's Inn
Qualifications: [LLB (Hons) (Cardiff)]

DOUGLAS MICHAEL JOHN QC (1997)

4 Pump Court
Temple, London EC4Y 7AN,
Telephone: 020 7842 5555
E-mail:chambers@4pumpcourt.law.co.uk
Call Date: Nov 1974, Gray's Inn
Qualifications: [BA (Oxon)]

DOUGLAS STEPHEN JOHN

24a St John Street
Manchester M3 4DF,
Telephone: 0161 833 9628
Call Date: Nov 1994, Inner Temple
Qualifications: [LLB (Manc), CPE
(Staffordshire)]

DOUGLAS WHITE ROBERT

1 Serjeants' Inn
4th Floor, Temple, London EC4Y 1NH,
Telephone: 0171 583 1355
E-mail: clerks@serjeants-inn.co.uk
Call Date: Nov 1993, Inner Temple
Qualifications: [LLB (LSE)]

DOUGLAS-JONES BENJAMIN TIMOTHY

Angel Chambers
94 Walter Road, Swansea, West
Glamorgan, SA1 5QA,
Telephone: 01792 464623/464648
E-mail: lynne@angelchambers.co.uk
Call Date: 1998, Gray's Inn
Qualifications: [LLB (Reading)]

DOUGLASS MISS GERALDINE MAISIE

Carmarthen Chambers
30 Spilman Street, Carmarthen, Dyfed,
SA31 1LQ, Telephone: 01267 234410
E-mail: law@in-wales.com
Lancaster Building
77 Deansgate, Manchester M3 2BW,
Telephone: 0161 661 4444/0171 649 9872
E-mail: sandra@lbnipc.com
Call Date: Nov 1976, Middle Temple

DOUTHWAITE CHARLES PHILIP

Chambers of John L Powell QC
Four New Square, Lincoln's Inn, London
WC2A 3RJ, Telephone: 0171 797 8000
E-mail: barristers@4newsquare.com
Call Date: July 1977, Gray's Inn
Pupil Master
Qualifications: [MA (Cantab)]

DOVE IAN WILLIAM

5 Fountain Court
Steelhouse Lane, Birmingham B4 6DR,
Telephone: 0121 606 0500
E-mail:clerks@5fountaincourt.law.co.uk
Call Date: July 1986, Inner Temple
Pupil Master
Qualifications: [BA (Oxon)]

DOW KENNETH

5 Pump Court
Ground Floor, Temple, London
EC4Y 7AP, Telephone: 020 7353 2532
E-mail: FivePump@netcomuk.co.uk
Call Date: Nov 1970, Lincoln's Inn
Pupil Master
Qualifications: [BA]

DOWDEN ANDREW PHILIP

Harrow on the Hill Chambers
60 High Street, Harrow-on-the-Hill,
Middlesex, HA1 3LL,
Telephone: 0181 423 7444
Windsor Barristers' Chambers
Windsor Telephone: 01753 648899
E-mail: law@windsorchambers.co.uk
Southsea Chambers
PO Box 148, Southsea, Portsmouth,
Hampshire, PO5 2TU,
Telephone: 01705 291261
Call Date: Oct 1991, Lincoln's Inn
Qualifications: [BA (Hons) (Manch), M Phil
(Cambs)]

DOWDING NICHOLAS ALAN TATHAM QC (1997)

Falcon Chambers
Falcon Court, London EC4Y 1AA,
Telephone: 0171 353 2484
E-mail: clerks@falcon-chambers.com
Call Date: July 1979, Inner Temple
Qualifications: [MA (Cantab)]

DOWELL GREGORY HAMILTON

**Gray's Inn Chambers, The Chambers of
Norman Patterson**
First Floor, Gray's Inn Chambers, Gray's
Inn, London WC1R 5JA,
Telephone: 0171 831 5344
E-mail: s.mcblain@btinternet.com
Call Date: Oct 1990, Middle Temple
Qualifications: [LLB]

DOWLEY DOMINIC MYLES

One Hare Court
1st Floor, Temple, London EC4Y 7BE,
Telephone: 020 7353 3171
E-mail:admin-oneharecourt@btinternet.com
Call Date: July 1983, Gray's Inn
Pupil Master
Qualifications: [MA Oxon]

DOWN JONATHAN CHARLES

5 Fountain Court
Steelhouse Lane, Birmingham B4 6DR,
Telephone: 0121 606 0500
E-mail:clerks@5fountaincourt.law.co.uk
Call Date: Nov 1993, Gray's Inn
Qualifications: [BA (Kent)]

DOWN MISS SUSAN

Devon Chambers
3 St Andrew Street, Plymouth PL1 2AH,
Telephone: 01752 661659
E-mail: devonchambers.co.uk.
Call Date: Nov 1984, Middle Temple
Qualifications: [LLB (Hons)(E Anglia)]

DOWNES GARRY KEITH

Australia,
Call Date: Feb 1995, Inner Temple
Qualifications: [BA, LLB (Sydney)]

DOWNES PAUL SIMON

2 Temple Gardens
Temple, London EC4Y 9AY,
Telephone: 0171 583 6041
E-mail: clerks@2templegardens.co.uk
Call Date: Oct 1991, Gray's Inn
Qualifications: [BA (Oxon)]

DOWNEY MISS AILEEN PATRICIA

9 Gough Square
London EC4A 3DE,
Telephone: 020 7832 0500
E-mail: clerks@9goughsq.co.uk
Call Date: Nov 1991, Lincoln's Inn
Qualifications: [LLB (Hons) (Lond)]

DOWNEY CHARLES BERNARD RAOUL DESCHAMPS

Littleton Chambers
3 King's Bench Walk North, Temple,
London EC4Y 7HR,
Telephone: 0171 797 8600
E-mail:clerks@littletonchambers.co.uk
Call Date: July 1988, Lincoln's Inn
Qualifications: [BSc (Hons) (LSE), Dip Law]

DOWNEY NEIL JAMES

Adrian Lyon's Chambers
14 Castle Street, Liverpool L2 0NE,
Telephone: 0151 236 4421/8240
E-mail: chambers14@aol.com
Call Date: Mar 1997, Middle Temple
Qualifications: [BA (Hons)(Oxon)]

DOWNHAM MISS GILLIAN CELIA

Rougemont Chambers
8 Colleton Crescent, Exeter, Devon,
EX1 1RR, Telephone: 01392 208484
E-mail:rougemont.chambers@eclipse.co.uk
Call Date: Nov 1993, Middle Temple
Qualifications: [BSc Soc.Sci (Hons), (So'ton),
MA Econ, (Manc)]

DOWNIE ANDREW JAMES

Martins Building
2nd Floor, No 4 Water Street, Liverpool
L2 3SP, Telephone: 0151 236 5818/4919
Call Date: Nov 1990, Gray's Inn
Qualifications: [BA, MA]

DOWNING JOHN

**1 Gray's Inn Square, Chambers of the
Baroness Scotland of Asthal QC**
1st Floor, London WC1R 5AG,
Telephone: 0171 405 3000
E-mail: clerks@onegrays.demon.co.uk
Call Date: June 1958, Gray's Inn
Qualifications: [LLB (Lond)]

DOWNING MISS RUTH ELIZABETH

Devereux Chambers
Devereux Court, London WC2R 3JJ,
Telephone: 0171 353 7534
E-mail: mailbox@devchambers.co.uk
Call Date: July 1978, Gray's Inn
Pupil Master, Assistant Recorder
Qualifications: [BA (Cantab)]

DOWNS MARTIN JOHN

1 Crown Office Row
Ground Floor, Temple, London
EC4Y 7HH, Telephone: 0171 797 7500
E-mail: mail@onecrownofficerow.com
Crown Office Row Chambers
Blenheim House, 120 Church Street,
Brighton, Sussex, BN1 1WH,
Telephone: 01273 625625
E-mail: crownofficerow@clara.net
Call Date: Nov 1990, Inner Temple
Qualifications: [BA (Oxon), Dip Law (City)]

DOWOKPOR JONATHAN KUKASI

Tollgate Mews Chambers
113 Tollgate Road, Tollgate Mews, North
Beckton, London E6 5JY,
Telephone: 0171 511 1838
E-mail:Jonathon.dowokpor@freeserve.co.uk
Call Date: July 1972, Lincoln's Inn
Qualifications: [MA, LLB (Lond)]

DOWSE JOHN

Chambers of John Hand QC
9 St John Street, Manchester M3 4DN,
Telephone: 0161 955 9000
E-mail: ninesjs@gconnect.com
Chambers of Lord Goodhart QC
Ground Floor, 3 New Square, Lincoln's
Inn, London WC2A 3RS,
Telephone: 0171 405 5577
E-mail:law@threenewsquare.demon.co.uk
Call Date: July 1973, Lincoln's Inn
Pupil Master, Recorder
Qualifications: [LLB]

DOYLE JAMES GAVIN CHARLES

Bridewell Chambers
2 Bridewell Place, London EC4V 6AP,
Telephone: 020 7797 8800
E-mail:HughesGage@bridewell.law.co.uk
Call Date: July 1985, Middle Temple
Pupil Master
Qualifications: [LLB]

DOYLE LOUIS GEORGE

40 King Street
Manchester M2 6BA,
Telephone: 0161 832 9082
E-mail: clerks@40kingstreet.co.uk
The Chambers of Philip Raynor QC
5 Park Place, Leeds LS1 2RU,
Telephone: 0113 242 1123
Call Date: Nov 1996, Lincoln's Inn
Qualifications: [LLB (Hons)(Leeds), LLM
(B'ham)]

DOYLE PETER JOHN

9-12 Bell Yard
London WC2A 2LF,
Telephone: 0171 400 1800
E-mail: clerks@bellyard.co.uk
Call Date: July 1975, Middle Temple
Pupil Master
Qualifications: [LLB]

DRABBLE RICHARD JOHN BLOOR QC (1995)

4 Breams Buildings
London EC4A 1AQ,
Telephone: 0171 353 5835/430 1221
E-mail:breams@4breamsbuildings.law.co.uk
Call Date: Nov 1975, Inner Temple
Qualifications: [BA (Cantab)]

DRAKE DAVID CHRISTOPHER

Serle Court Chambers
6 New Square, Lincoln's Inn, London
WC2A 3QS, Telephone: 0171 242 6105
E-mail: clerks@serlecourt.co.uk
Call Date: Nov 1994, Inner Temple
Qualifications: [BA (Oxon), BCL (Oxon)]

DRAKE JAMES FREDERICK

S Tomlinson QC
7 King's Bench Walk, Temple, London
EC4Y 7DS, Telephone: 0171 583 0404
E-mail: clerks@7kbw.law.co.uk
Call Date: 1998, Lincoln's Inn
Qualifications: [BA (Acc)(S.Australia,
(S.Australia), , LLB (Hons)(Adelaide), LLM
(Columbia)]

DRAKE MISS RACHEL ALEXIA

Wessex Chambers
48 Queens Road, Reading, Berkshire,
RG1 4BD, Telephone: 0118 956 8856
E-mail:wessexchambers@compuserve.com
Call Date: Nov 1995, Middle Temple
Qualifications: [LLB (Hons)(Brunel)]

DRAKE MISS SOPHIE HELENA

Broadway House Chambers
Broadway House, 9 Bank Street, Bradford,
West Yorkshire, BD1 1TW,
Telephone: 01274 722560
E-mail: clerks@broadwayhouse.co.uk
Broadway House Chambers
31 Park Square West, Leeds LS1 2PF,
Telephone: 0113 246 2600
Call Date: Oct 1990, Gray's Inn
Qualifications: [LLB (Leic)]

DRANE MISS AMANDA TERESA LOVE

4 King's Bench Walk
2nd Floor, Temple, London EC4Y 7DL,
Telephone: 020 7353 3581
E-mail: clerks@4kbw.co.uk
Call Date: Oct 1996, Lincoln's Inn
Qualifications: [BA (Hons)(Cantab)]

DRAY MARTIN BENEDICT ANTONY

Falcon Chambers
Falcon Court, London EC4Y 1AA,
Telephone: 0171 353 2484
E-mail: clerks@falcon-chambers.com
Call Date: Oct 1992, Gray's Inn
Qualifications: [LL.B (Bris)]

DRAYCOTT MRS MARGARET JEAN BRUNTON

5 Fountain Court
Steelhouse Lane, Birmingham B4 6DR,
Telephone: 0121 606 0500
E-mail:clerks@5fountaincourt.law.co.uk
Call Date: July 1980, Middle Temple
Qualifications: [LLB (B'ham)]

DRAYCOTT SIMON DOUGLAS

13 King's Bench Walk
1st Floor, Temple, London EC4Y 7EN,
Telephone: 0171 353 7204
E-mail: clerks@13kbw.law.co.uk
Call Date: July 1977, Middle Temple
Pupil Master, Assistant Recorder

DRAYTON HENRY ALEXANDER

2 Gray's Inn Square Chambers
2nd Floor, Gray's Inn, London WC1R 5AA,
Telephone: 020 7242 0328
E-mail: clerks@2gis.co.uk
Call Date: Feb 1993, Inner Temple
Qualifications: [BA]

DREW MRS CHERYL

Warwick House Chambers
8 Warwick Court, Gray's Inn, London
WC1R 5DJ, Telephone: 0171 430 2323
E-mail: cdrewlaw@aol.com
Call Date: Nov 1972, Gray's Inn
Pupil Master

DREW CHRISTOPHER THOMAS

Warwick House Chambers
8 Warwick Court, Gray's Inn, London
WC1R 5DJ, Telephone: 0171 430 2323
E-mail: cdrewlaw@aol.com
Call Date: Nov 1969, Gray's Inn
Pupil Master
Qualifications: [LLB (Lond)]

DREW MISS JANE MARIAN

4 Brick Court
Ground Floor, Temple, London
EC4Y 9AD, Telephone: 0171 797 7766
E-mail: chambers@4brick.co.uk
Call Date: July 1976, Middle Temple
Pupil Master
Qualifications: [BA (Dunelm)]

DREW MS SANDHYA

14 Tooks Court
Cursitor St, London EC4A 1LB,
Telephone: 0171 405 8828
E-mail: clerks@tooks.law.co.uk
Call Date: Oct 1993, Gray's Inn
Qualifications: [MA (Oxon), Dip Law (City)]

DREW SIMON PATRICK

5 Fountain Court
Steelhouse Lane, Birmingham B4 6DR,
Telephone: 0121 606 0500
E-mail:clerks@5fountaincourt.law.co.uk
Call Date: Nov 1987, Lincoln's Inn
Pupil Master
Qualifications: [LLB (Leeds)]

DRINKWATER PHILIP MURRAY

Colleton Chambers
Colleton Crescent, Exeter, Devon,
EX2 4DG, Telephone: 01392 274898/9
Call Date: Nov 1995, Inner Temple
Qualifications: [LLB (Exon)]

DRISCOLL MRS JENNIFER JANE

Queen Elizabeth Building
Ground Floor, Temple, London
EC4Y 9BS,
Telephone: 0171 353 7181 (12 Lines)
Call Date: July 1989, Lincoln's Inn
Qualifications: [BA (Cantab), Dip Law (City)]

DRISCOLL MISS LYNN

Sovereign Chambers
25 Park Square, Leeds LS1 2PW,
Telephone: 0113 2451841/2/3
E-mail:sovereignchambers@btinternet.com
Call Date: July 1981, Middle Temple
Qualifications: [BA, LLM (Lond), Dip Law]

DRISCOLL MICHAEL JOHN QC (1992)

9 Old Square
Ground Floor, Lincoln's Inn, London
WC2A 3SR, Telephone: 0171 405 4682
E-mail: chambers@9oldsquare.co.uk
Call Date: July 1970, Middle Temple
Qualifications: [BA, LLB (Cantab)]

DRIVER MS EMILY ROSE

6 King's Bench Walk
Ground, Third & Fourth Floors, Temple,
London EC4Y 7DR,
Telephone: 0171 353 4931/583 0695
Call Date: Nov 1988, Inner Temple
Qualifications: [BA (Oxon), Dip Law (City)]

DRIVER SIMON GREGORY

25-27 Castle Street
1st Floor, Liverpool L2 4TA,
Telephone: 0151 227 5661/051 236 5072
Call Date: Nov 1991, Inner Temple
Qualifications: [BA (Reading)]

DRIVER STUART FRANK

Adrian Lyon's Chambers
14 Castle Street, Liverpool L2 0NE,
Telephone: 0151 236 4421/8240
E-mail: chambers14@aol.com
Call Date: Nov 1988, Gray's Inn
Qualifications: [BA (Oxon)]

DRUCE MICHAEL JAMES

2 Mitre Court Buildings
2nd Floor, Temple, London EC4Y 7BX,
Telephone: 0171 583 1380
E-mail: clerks@2mcb.co.uk
Call Date: July 1988, Inner Temple
Pupil Master
Qualifications: [MA (Cantab)]

DRUMMOND BRUCE JONATHON HUTCHEON

Nicholas Street Chambers
22 Nicholas Street, Chester CH1 2NX,
Telephone: 01244 323886
E-mail: clerks@40king.co.uk
Call Date: Oct 1992, Gray's Inn
Qualifications: [B.Sc (Wales)]

DRY NICHOLAS DAVID

St Paul's House
5th Floor, St Paul's House, 23 Park Square
South, Leeds LS1 2ND,
Telephone: 0113 2455866
E-mail: catherinegrimshaw@stpauls-
chambers.demon.co.uk
Call Date: Nov 1996, Lincoln's Inn
Qualifications: [BA (Hons)(Cantab)]

DRYDEN SHAUN

Baker Street Chambers
9 Baker Street, Middlesbrough TS1 2LF,
Telephone: 01642 873873
Call Date: Nov 1994, Lincoln's Inn
Qualifications: [LLB (Hons)(Lond)]

DSANE MISS VICTORIA TSOTSOO

61 Elm Grove
Sutton, Surrey, SM1 4EX,
Telephone: 0181 643 9714
Call Date: Nov 1971, Middle Temple
Pupil Master
Qualifications: [BA, LLB, MA]

DU CANN CHRISTIAN DILLON LOTT

39 Essex Street
London WC2R 3AT,
Telephone: 0171 832 1111
E-mail: clerks@39essex.co.uk
Call Date: July 1982, Gray's Inn
Pupil Master
Qualifications: [BA Cantab]

DU PREEZ HENRY ROBERT

18 Red Lion Court
(Off Fleet Street), London EC4A 3EB,
Telephone: 0171 520 6000
E-mail: chambers@18rlc.co.uk
Call Date: Nov 1985, Inner Temple
Pupil Master
Qualifications: [BA (Law)]

DUBARRY MS ADELE KATHERINE

Maidstone Chambers
33 Earl Street, Maidstone, Kent, ME14 1PF,
Telephone: 01622 688592
E-mail:maidstonechambers@compuserve.com
Call Date: Nov 1993, Middle Temple
Qualifications: [LLB (Hons), LLM (E.Anglia)]

DUBB TARLOWCHAN

Victoria Chambers
3rd Floor, 177 Corporation Street,
Birmingham B4 6RG,
Telephone: 0121 236 9900
E-mail: viccham@aol.com
Call Date: 1997, Lincoln's Inn
Qualifications: [LLB (Hons)]

DUBBERY MARK EDWARD

Pump Court Chambers
Upper Ground Floor, 3 Pump Court,
Temple, London EC4Y 7AJ,
Telephone: 0171 353 0711
E-mail: clerks@3pumpcourt.com
Pump Court Chambers
31 Southgate Street, Winchester
SO23 9EE, Telephone: 01962 868161
E-mail: clerks@3pumpcourt.com
Pump Court Chambers
5 Temple Chambers, Temple Street,
Swindon SN1 1SQ,
Telephone: 01793 539899
E-mail: clerks@3pumpcourt.com
Call Date: Oct 1996, Middle Temple
Qualifications: [BSc (Hons)(Lond), LLB
(Hons)(City)]

DUCK MICHAEL CHARLES

3 Fountain Court
Steelhouse Lane, Birmingham B4 6DR,
Telephone: 0121 236 5854
Call Date: Nov 1988, Gray's Inn
Qualifications: [LLB]

DUCKWORTH (ARTHUR) PETER

29 Bedford Row Chambers
London WC1R 4HE,
Telephone: 0171 831 2626
Call Date: July 1971, Middle Temple
Pupil Master
Qualifications: [LLB]

DUDDRIDGE ROBERT JAMES

2 Gray's Inn Square Chambers
2nd Floor, Gray's Inn, London WC1R 5AA,
Telephone: 020 7242 0328
E-mail: clerks@2gis.co.uk
Call Date: Feb 1992, Lincoln's Inn
Qualifications: [BA (Hons) (Oxon)]

DUDKOWSKI DOMINIC CHRISTIAN

Chambers of Dominic Dudkowski
7 White Street, Brighton, Sussex, BN2 2JH,
Telephone: 0973 314252
E-mail: barrister@pobox.com
Call Date: Nov 1986, Inner Temple
Qualifications: [BA(Sussex)]

DUDLEY MICHAEL JOHN

1 Fountain Court
Steelhouse Lane, Birmingham B4 6DR,
Telephone: 0121 236 5721
Call Date: July 1972, Lincoln's Inn
Pupil Master, Recorder
Qualifications: [LLB; G.Cert.Ed]

DUDLEY ROBERT MICHAEL

Exchange Chambers
Pearl Assurance House, Derby Square,
Liverpool L2 9XX,
Telephone: 0151 236 7747
E-mail:exchangechambers@btinternet.com
Call Date: Oct 1993, Gray's Inn
Qualifications: [MA (Cantab)]

DUDLEY-JONES MS ELIZABETH SARAH

New Court
Temple, London EC4Y 9BE,
Telephone: 0171 583 5123/0510
Call Date: 1997, Inner Temple
Qualifications: [LLB (Hull)]

DUFF EUAN CAMERON

Broad Chare
33 Broad Chare, Newcastle upon Tyne
NE1 3DQ, Telephone: 0191 232 0541
E-mail:clerks@broadcharechambers.law.co.uk
Call Date: July 1973, Inner Temple
Pupil Master, Assistant Recorder
Qualifications: [MA (Cantab)]

DUFF GRAHAM

Trinity Chambers
9-12 Trinity Chare, Quayside, Newcastle
upon Tyne NE1 3DF,
Telephone: 0191 232 1927
E-mail: info@trinitychambers.co.uk
Call Date: 1976, Lincoln's Inn
Qualifications: [BA, PGCE]

DUFF MISS MORAG AILEEN

Call Date: Nov 1991, Middle Temple
Qualifications: [LLB (Hons) (Lond)]

DUFFIELD STEPHEN MICHAEL

Trinity Chambers
9-12 Trinity Chare, Quayside, Newcastle
upon Tyne NE1 3DF,
Telephone: 0191 232 1927
E-mail: info@trinitychambers.co.uk
Call Date: July 1969, Gray's Inn
Pupil Master, Recorder
Qualifications: [BA (Oxon)]

DUFFY DEREK JAMES

St Paul's House
5th Floor, St Paul's House, 23 Park Square
South, Leeds LS1 2ND,
Telephone: 0113 2455866
E-mail: catherinegrimshaw@stpauls-
chambers.demon.co.uk
Call Date: Mar 1997, Gray's Inn
Qualifications: [BA (Hons)(Sheffield)]

DUFFY MISS JOANNE

5 Fountain Court
Steelhouse Lane, Birmingham B4 6DR,
Telephone: 0121 606 0500
E-mail:clerks@5fountaincourt.law.co.uk
Call Date: Oct 1994, Lincoln's Inn
Qualifications: [LLB (Hons)(Leic)]

DUFFY MICHAEL

Cathedral Chambers, Ely
P O Box 24, Ely, Cambridgeshire, CB6 1SL,
Telephone: 01353 666775
Call Date: July 1992, Lincoln's Inn

DUGDALE JEREMY KEITH

2 Pump Court
1st Floor, Temple, London EC4Y 7AH,
Telephone: 0171 353 5597
Call Date: Oct 1992, Inner Temple
Qualifications: [MA (Oxon)]

DUGDALE NICHOLAS

4 Field Court
Gray's Inn, London WC1R 5EA,
Telephone: 0171 440 6900
E-mail: chambers@4fieldcourt.co.uk
Call Date: Feb 1992, Middle Temple
Qualifications: [BA (Auckland), LLB
(Auckland)]

DUGDALE PAUL DAMIAN NORWOOD

2 King's Bench Walk
Ground Floor, Temple, London
EC4Y 7DE, Telephone: 0171 353 1746
E-mail: 2kbw@atlas.co.uk
King's Bench Chambers
115 North Hill, Plymouth PL4 8JY,
Telephone: 01752 221551
Call Date: Oct 1990, Gray's Inn
Qualifications: [LLB (Lond)]

DUGGAN JAMES ROSS

India Buildings Chambers
Water Street, Liverpool L2 0XG,
Telephone: 0151 243 6000
E-mail: clerks@chambers.u-net.com
Call Date: July 1978, Middle Temple
Pupil Master, Recorder
Qualifications: [LLB (L'pool)]

DUGGAN MICHAEL

Littleton Chambers
3 King's Bench Walk North, Temple,
London EC4Y 7HR,
Telephone: 0171 797 8600
E-mail:clerks@littletonchambers.co.uk
Call Date: July 1984, Gray's Inn
Pupil Master
Qualifications: [BA,BCL , LLM (Cantab)]

DUKE PAUL STUART

Old Colony House
6 South King Street, Manchester M2 6DQ,
Telephone: 0161 834 4364
Call Date: Nov 1989, Gray's Inn
Qualifications: [LLB (Hons)]

DULOVIC MILAN

2 Gray's Inn Square Chambers
2nd Floor, Gray's Inn, London WC1R 5AA,
Telephone: 020 7242 0328
E-mail: clerks@2gis.co.uk
Call Date: July 1982, Gray's Inn
Pupil Master
Qualifications: [LLB (Lond)]

DUMARESQ MS DELIA JANE

Atkin Chambers
1 Atkin Building, Gray's Inn, London
WC1R 5AT, Telephone: 020 7404 0102
E-mail: clerks@atkin-chambers.co.uk
Call Date: July 1984, Inner Temple
Pupil Master
Qualifications: [MA, Dip Law]

DUMBILL ERIC ALEXANDER

65-67 King Street
Leicester LE1 6RP,
Telephone: 0116 2547710
Call Date: Nov 1971, Gray's Inn
Qualifications: [LLB (Nott'm)]

DUMONT THOMAS JULIAN BRADLEY

Chambers of Mr Peter Crampin QC
Ground Floor, 11 New Square, Lincoln's
Inn, London WC2A 3QB,
Telephone: 020 7831 0081
E-mail: 11newsquare.co.uk
Call Date: Nov 1979, Gray's Inn
Pupil Master
Qualifications: [MA (Cantab)]

DUNCAN JOHN CHRISTOPHER

Cobden House Chambers
19 Quay Street, Manchester M3 3HN,
Telephone: 0161 833 6000
E-mail: clerks@cobden.co.uk
Call Date: July 1971, Inner Temple
Qualifications: [BSc,BA]

DUNCAN MS NICOLA EMILY

Wessex Chambers
48 Queens Road, Reading, Berkshire,
RG1 4BD, Telephone: 0118 956 8856
E-mail:wessexchambers@compuserve.com
Call Date: 1994, Gray's Inn
Qualifications: [LLB (Exon)]

DUNFORD MATTHEW SIMON

Nicholas Street Chambers
22 Nicholas Street, Chester CH1 2NX,
Telephone: 01244 323886
E-mail: clerks@40king.co.uk
Call Date: Oct 1992, Lincoln's Inn
Qualifications: [LLB(Hons)(Newc)]

DUNFORD ROBERT CHARLES

65-67 King Street
Leicester LE1 6RP,
Telephone: 0116 2547710
Call Date: Nov 1995, Middle Temple
Qualifications: [BA (Hons)(Toronto)]

DUNKELS PAUL RENTON QC (1993)

Walnut House
63 St David's Hill, Exeter, Devon,
EX4 4DW, Telephone: 01392 279751
E-mail: 106627.2451@compuserve.com
Albion Chambers
Broad Street, Bristol BS1 1DR,
Telephone: 0117 9272144
Call Date: May 1972, Inner Temple
Recorder

DUNLOP HAMISH MICHAEL

1 Harcourt Buildings
2nd Floor, Temple, London EC4Y 9DA,
Telephone: 0171 353 9421/0375
E-mail:clerks@1harcourtbuildings.law.co.uk
Call Date: Nov 1991, Middle Temple
Qualifications: [LLB Hons (Warw)]

DUNN ALEXANDER

8 King's Bench Walk
2nd Floor, Temple, London EC4Y 7DU,
Telephone: 0171 797 8888
8 King's Bench Walk North
1 Park Square East, Leeds LS1 2NE,
Telephone: 0113 2439797
Call Date: Feb 1985, Middle Temple
Pupil Master
Qualifications: [BA]

DUNN CHRISTOPHER

Sovereign Chambers
25 Park Square, Leeds LS1 2PW,
Telephone: 0113 2451841/2/3
E-mail:sovereignchambers@btinternet.com
Call Date: Oct 1996, Gray's Inn
Qualifications: [B.Sc , MA, LLM (Newc)]

DUNN MISS KATHERINE ELSPETH

40 King Street
Manchester M2 6BA,
Telephone: 0161 832 9082
E-mail: clerks@40kingstreet.co.uk
The Chambers of Philip Raynor QC
5 Park Place, Leeds LS1 2RU,
Telephone: 0113 242 1123
Call Date: Nov 1987, Middle Temple
Pupil Master
Qualifications: [BA (Cantab)]

DUNN MISS KATHERINE LOUISE

4 King's Bench Walk
Ground/First Floor/Basement, Temple,
London EC4Y 7DL,
Telephone: 0171 822 8822
E-mail: 4kbw@barristersatlaw.com
Call Date: Oct 1993, Lincoln's Inn
Qualifications: [LLB (Hons)(Lond)]

DUNN-SHAW JASON DAVID

6 King's Bench Walk
Ground Floor, Temple, London
EC4Y 7DR, Telephone: 0171 583 0410
E-mail: worsley@6kbw.freeserve.co.uk
Call Date: Oct 1992, Lincoln's Inn
Qualifications: [BA(Hons)(Manch)]

DUNNE JONATHAN ANTHONY

3 Temple Gardens
2nd Floor, Temple, London EC4Y 9AU,
Telephone: 0171 583 1155
Call Date: July 1986, Inner Temple
Pupil Master
Qualifications: [LLB (Leics)]

DUNNING FRANCIS JOHN GROVE

37 Park Square Chambers
37 Park Square, Leeds LS1 2NY,
Telephone: 0113 2439422
E-mail: chambers@no37.co.uk
Call Date: July 1973, Inner Temple
Pupil Master
Qualifications: [BSc]

DUNNING GRAHAM

Essex Court Chambers
24 Lincoln's Inn Fields, London
WC2A 3ED, Telephone: 0171 813 8000
E-mail:clerksroom@essexcourt-chambers.co.uk
Call Date: July 1982, Lincoln's Inn
Pupil Master
Qualifications: [MA (Cantab), LLM (Harvard)]

DUNSTAN JAMES PETER

6 Fountain Court
Steelhouse Lane, Birmingham B4 6DR,
Telephone: 0121 233 3282
E-mail: clerks@sixfountain.co.uk
Call Date: Feb 1995, Gray's Inn
Qualifications: [BA (Oxon)]

DUROSE DAVID WILLIAM

2 Paper Buildings
1st Floor, Temple, London EC4Y 7ET,
Telephone: 020 7556 5500
E-mail: clerks@2pbbarristers.co.uk
Call Date: Oct 1996, Lincoln's Inn
Qualifications: [BA (Hons)(Oxon)]

DURR JUDE PATRICK

East Anglian Chambers
Gresham House, 5 Museum Street,
Ipswich, Suffolk, IP1 1HQ,
Telephone: 01473 214481
E-mail: ipswich@ealaw.co.uk
East Anglian Chambers
57 London Street, Norwich NR2 1HL,
Telephone: 01603 617351
E-mail: norwich@ealaw.co.uk
East Anglian Chambers
52 North Hill, Colchester, Essex, CO1 1PY,
Telephone: 01206 572756
E-mail: colchester@ealaw.co.uk
Call Date: Oct 1995, Inner Temple
Qualifications: [MA, CPE]

DURRAN MISS ALEXIA GRAINNE

23 Essex Street
London WC2R 3AS,
Telephone: 0171 413 0353/836 8366
E-mail:clerks@essexstreet23.demon.co.uk
Call Date: Oct 1995, Middle Temple
Qualifications: [BA (Hons)]

DUTCHMAN-SMITH MALCOLM CHARLES

Martins Building
2nd Floor, No 4 Water Street, Liverpool
L2 3SP, Telephone: 0151 236 5818/4919
Call Date: Feb 1995, Gray's Inn
Qualifications: [LLB (Hull)]

DUTHIE MISS CATRIONA ANN MACPHERSON

Guildhall Chambers
22-26 Broad Street, Bristol BS1 2HG,
Telephone: 0117 9273366
E-mail:civil.clerks@guildhallchambers.co.uk and
criminal.clerks@guildhallchambers.co.uk
Call Date: July 1981, Inner Temple
Qualifications: [LLB (Nottm) MSc, (Edin)]

DUTHIE MALCOLM JAMES

5 Fountain Court
Steelhouse Lane, Birmingham B4 6DR,
Telephone: 0121 606 0500
E-mail:clerks@5fountaincourt.law.co.uk
Call Date: July 1989, Inner Temple
Qualifications: [LLB [Buck], LLM [Lond]]

DUTTA MISS NANDINI

8 Fountain Court
Steelhouse Lane, Birmingham B4 6DR,
Telephone: 0121 236 5514/5
E-mail: clerks@no8chambers.co.uk
Call Date: Feb 1993, Middle Temple
Qualifications: [LLB (Hons)]

DUTTON TIMOTHY CHRISTOPHER

Barnard's Inn Chambers
6th Floor, Halton House, 20-23 Holborn,
London EC1N 2JD,
Telephone: 0171 369 6969
E-mail: clerks@biclaw.co.uk
Call Date: July 1985, Inner Temple
Qualifications: [BA(Durham)]

DUTTON TIMOTHY JAMES QC (1998)

Farrar's Building
Temple, London EC4Y 7BD,
Telephone: 0171 583 9241
E-mail:chambers@farrarsbuilding.co.uk
Call Date: Nov 1979, Middle Temple
Assistant Recorder
Qualifications: [BA (Oxon)]

DUVAL ROBERT MICHAEL LOUIS

St John's Chambers
Small Street, Bristol BS1 1DW,
Telephone: 0117 9213456/298514
E-mail: @stjohnschambers.co.uk
Call Date: Nov 1979, Gray's Inn
Pupil Master
Qualifications: [LLB (Wales)]

DYBLE STEVEN JOHN

East Anglian Chambers
52 North Hill, Colchester, Essex, CO1 1PY,
Telephone: 01206 572756
E-mail: colchester@ealaw.co.uk
East Anglian Chambers
57 London Street, Norwich NR2 1HL,
Telephone: 01603 617351
E-mail: norwich@ealaw.co.uk
East Anglian Chambers
Gresham House, 5 Museum Street,
Ipswich, Suffolk, IP1 1HQ,
Telephone: 01473 214481
E-mail: ipswich@ealaw.co.uk
Call Date: Nov 1986, Lincoln's Inn
Qualifications: [LLB (West England)]

DYE BRIAN WILLIAM

Essex Court Chambers
24 Lincoln's Inn Fields, London
WC2A 3ED, Telephone: 0171 813 8000
E-mail: clerksroom@essexcourt-chambers.co.uk
Call Date: Oct 1991, Middle Temple
Qualifications: [MA (Hons) (Oxon)]

DYER ALLEN GORDON

4 Pump Court
Temple, London EC4Y 7AN,
Telephone: 020 7842 5555
E-mail: chambers@4pumpcourt.law.co.uk
Call Date: July 1976, Inner Temple
Pupil Master
Qualifications: [BA (Bristol)]

DYER DAVID ROGER

St Philip's Chambers
Fountain Court, Steelhouse Lane,
Birmingham B4 6DR,
Telephone: 0121 246 7000
E-mail: clerks@st-philips.co.uk
Call Date: Nov 1980, Middle Temple
Qualifications: [BA, Dip Arch., RIBA, FCIArb,
FFAS]

DYER JACOB JACKSON

15 Winckley Square
Preston PR1 3JJ,
Telephone: 01772 252828
E-mail: clerks@winckleysq.demon.co.uk
Call Date: Nov 1995, Lincoln's Inn
Qualifications: [MA (Cantab)]

DYER NIGEL INGRAM JOHN

1 Mitre Court Buildings
Temple, London EC4Y 7BS,
Telephone: 0171 797 7070
E-mail: clerks@1mcb.com
Call Date: Feb 1982, Inner Temple
Pupil Master
Qualifications: [BA Hons (Dunelm)]

DYER SIMON CHRISTOPHER

Plowden Buildings
2nd Floor, 2 Plowden Buildings, Middle
Temple Lane, London EC4Y 9BU,
Telephone: 0171 583 0808
E-mail: bar@plowdenbuildings.co.uk
Call Date: July 1987, Middle Temple
Pupil Master
Qualifications: [BA (Kent)]

DYKERS MISS CORNELIA JOY

Lamb Building
Ground Floor, Temple, London
EC4Y 7AS, Telephone: 020 7797 7788
E-mail: lamb.building@link.org
Call Date: Oct 1995, Gray's Inn
Qualifications: [BA]

DYMOND ANDREW MARK

Arden Chambers
27 John Street, London WC1N 2BL,
Telephone: 020 7242 4244
E-mail: clerks@arden-chambers.law.co.uk
Call Date: Nov 1991, Middle Temple
Qualifications: [MA (Oxon)]

EADE MS PHILLIPA SARAH

New Walk Chambers
27 New Walk, Leicester LE1 6TE,
Telephone: 0116 2559144
Call Date: Oct 1992, Inner Temple
Qualifications: [LLB (Leics)]

EADES ROBERT MARK

5 Fountain Court
Steelhouse Lane, Birmingham B4 6DR,
Telephone: 0121 606 0500
E-mail:clerks@5fountaincourt.law.co.uk
Call Date: 1974, Middle Temple
Pupil Master, Assistant Recorder
Qualifications: [LLB]

EADIE JAMES RAYMOND

One Hare Court
1st Floor, Temple, London EC4Y 7BE,
Telephone: 020 7353 3171
E-mail:admin-oneharecourt@btinternet.com
Call Date: July 1984, Middle Temple
Pupil Master
Qualifications: [MA (Cantab)]

EADY MISS JENNIFER JANE

Old Square Chambers
1 Verulam Buildings, Gray's Inn, London
WC1R 5LQ, Telephone: 0171 269 0300
E-mail:clerks@oldsquarechambers.co.uk
Old Square Chambers
Hanover House, 47 Corn Street, Bristol
BS1 1HT, Telephone: 0117 9277111
E-mail: oldsqbri@globalnet.co.uk
Call Date: July 1989, Inner Temple
Pupil Master
Qualifications: [BA [Oxon], Dip Law]

EARLAM SIMON LAWRENCE

Exchange Chambers
Pearl Assurance House, Derby Square,
Liverpool L2 9XX,
Telephone: 0151 236 7747
E-mail:exchangechambers@btinternet.com
Call Date: Feb 1975, Gray's Inn
Pupil Master, Assistant Recorder
Qualifications: [MA (Oxon) BCL]

EARLE JAMES CHRISTOPHER REGINALD ST JOHN

Tindal Chambers
3/5 New Street, Chelmsford, Essex,
CM1 1NT, Telephone: 01245 267742
Call Date: Oct 1996, Gray's Inn
Qualifications: [BA (Kent), MA (Lond)]

EARLE MISS JUDY ESTELLE

3 Paper Buildings
Temple, London EC4Y 7EU,
Telephone: 020 7583 8055
E-mail: London@3paper.com
3 Paper Buildings (Bournemouth)
20 Lorne Park Road, Bournemouth,
Dorset, BH1 1JN,
Telephone: 01202 292102
E-mail: Bournemouth@3paper.com
3 Paper Buildings (Winchester)
4 St Peter Street, Winchester SO23 8BW,
Telephone: 01962 868884
E-mail: winchester@3paper.com
3 Paper Buildings (Oxford)
1 Alfred Street, High Street, Oxford
OX1 4EH, Telephone: 01865 793736
E-mail: oxford@3paper.com
Call Date: Oct 1994, Middle Temple
Qualifications: [LLB (Hons)(Lond)]

EARNSHAW STEPHEN

Furnival Chambers
32 Furnival Street, London EC4A 1JQ,
Telephone: 0171 405 3232
E-mail: clerks@furnivallaw.co.uk
Call Date: May 1990, Middle Temple
Qualifications: [LL.B. (Brunel)]

EASTEAL ANDREW FRANCIS MARTIN

High Pavement Chambers
1 High Pavement, Nottingham NG1 1HF,
Telephone: 0115 9418218
Call Date: Feb 1990, Inner Temple
Qualifications: [BA (Oxon)]

EASTERMAN NICHOLAS BARRIE

Goldsmith Chambers
Ground Floor, Goldsmith Building,
Temple, London EC4Y 7BL,
Telephone: 0171 353 6802/3/4/5
E-mail:clerks@goldsmithchambers.law.co.uk
Call Date: July 1975, Lincoln's Inn
Pupil Master
Qualifications: [LLB (Lond)]

D

EASTMAN ROGER

2 Harcourt Buildings
Ground Floor/Left, Temple, London
EC4Y 9DB, Telephone: 0171 583 9020
E-mail: clerks@harcourt.co.uk
Call Date: Nov 1978, Gray's Inn
Pupil Master
Qualifications: [BA (Dunelm)]

EASTON MISS ALISON JANE

Queen Elizabeth Building
Ground Floor, Temple, London
EC4Y 9BS,
Telephone: 0171 353 7181 (12 Lines)
Call Date: Nov 1994, Inner Temple
Qualifications: [LLB (B'ham)]

EASTON JONATHAN MARK

2-3 Gray's Inn Square
Gray's Inn, London WC1R 5JH,
Telephone: 0171 242 4986
E-mail:chambers@2-3graysinnsquare.co.uk
Call Date: Nov 1996, Gray's Inn
Qualifications: [LLB (Warw), LLM (Florence)]

EASTWOOD CHARLES PETER

28 St John Street
Manchester M3 4DJ,
Telephone: 0161 834 8418
E-mail: clerk@28stjohnst.co.uk
Call Date: July 1988, Lincoln's Inn
Qualifications: [BA (Hons) (Oxon)]

EASTY MISS VALERIE STEPHANIE

Two Garden Court
1st Floor, Middle Temple, London
EC4Y 9BL, Telephone: 0171 353 1633
E-mail:barristers@2gardenct.law.co.uk
Call Date: Oct 1992, Middle Temple
Qualifications: [B.Sc (Hons), Diploma in
Law]

EATON MISS DEBORAH ANN

One King's Bench Walk
1st Floor, Temple, London EC4Y 7DB,
Telephone: 0171 936 1500
E-mail: ddear@1kbw.co.uk
Call Date: July 1985, Inner Temple
Pupil Master
Qualifications: [B Soc Sc (Keele),Dip]

EATON JAMES BERNARD

1 Middle Temple Lane
Temple, London EC4Y 1LT,
Telephone: 0171 583 0659 (12 Lines)
E-mail: chambers@1mtl.co.uk
Call Date: Nov 1978, Middle Temple
Pupil Master
Qualifications: [LLB (Hons) (Liv)]

EATON NIGEL TREVOR

Essex Court Chambers
24 Lincoln's Inn Fields, London
WC2A 3ED, Telephone: 0171 813 8000
E-mail:clerksroom@essexcourt-chambers.co.u
k
Call Date: Nov 1991, Gray's Inn
Qualifications: [BA, BCL (Oxon)]

EATON RICHARD MARK COOPER

Westgate Chambers
144 High Street, Lewes, East Sussex,
BN7 1XT, Telephone: 01273 480510
Call Date: May 1982, Lincoln's Inn
Qualifications: [LLB (Hons), A.C.I.Arb]

EATON THOMAS EDWARD DAVID

Adrian Lyon's Chambers
14 Castle Street, Liverpool L2 0NE,
Telephone: 0151 236 4421/8240
E-mail: chambers14@aol.com
Call Date: Nov 1976, Middle Temple
Pupil Master
Qualifications: [LLB (Hons) (Lond)]

EATON HART ANDREW MICHAEL

Walnut House
63 St David's Hill, Exeter, Devon,
EX4 4DW, Telephone: 01392 279751
E-mail: 106627.2451@compuserve.com
Call Date: July 1989, Gray's Inn
Qualifications: [LLB [Exon]]

EATON TURNER DAVID MURRAY

1 New Square
Ground Floor, Lincoln's Inn, London
WC2A 3SA, Telephone: 0171 405 0884/5/6/
7 E-mail: clerks@1newsquare.law.co.uk
Call Date: July 1984, Lincoln's Inn
Pupil Master
Qualifications: [LLB (Lond)]

EBOO ISMAIL PIRBHAI

2 Middle Temple Lane
3rd Floor, Temple, London EC4Y 9AA,
Telephone: 0171 583 4540
Call Date: Nov 1970, Inner Temple

ECCLES DAVID THOMAS

8 King Street Chambers
8 King Street, Manchester M2 6AQ,
Telephone: 0161 834 9560
E-mail: eightking@aol.com
Call Date: July 1976, Middle Temple
Pupil Master
Qualifications: [MA (Cantab)]

ECCLES HUGH WILLIAM PATRICK QC (1990)

Harcourt Chambers
1st Floor, 2 Harcourt Buildings, Temple,
London EC4Y 9DB,
Telephone: 0171 353 6961
E-mail:clerks@harcourtchambers.law.co.uk
Harcourt Chambers
Churchill House, 3 St Aldate's Courtyard,
St Aldate's, Oxford OX1 1BN,
Telephone: 01865 791559
E-mail:clerks@harcourtchambers.law.co.uk
Call Date: July 1968, Middle Temple
Recorder
Qualifications: [MA (Oxon)]

ECKERSLEY SIMON RICHARD

St Mary's Chambers
50 High Pavement, Lace Market,
Nottingham NG1 1HW,
Telephone: 0115 9503503
E-mail: clerks@smc.law.co.uk
Call Date: Mar 1996, Lincoln's Inn
Qualifications: [BA (Hons) (Oxon)]

ECOB MISS JOANNE ANITA

Chambers of Michael Pert QC
36 Bedford Row, London WC1R 4JH,
Telephone: 0171 421 8000
E-mail: 36bedfordrow@link.org
Chambers of Michael Pert QC
24 Albion Place, Northampton NN1 1UD,
Telephone: 01604 602333

Chambers of Michael Pert QC
104 New Walk, Leicester LE1 7EA,
Telephone: 0116 249 2020
Call Date: July 1985, Inner Temple
Pupil Master
Qualifications: [LLB (Newc)]

ECONOMOU GEORGE COSTAS

4 Essex Court
Temple, London EC4Y 9AJ,
Telephone: 020 7797 7970
E-mail: clerks@4essexcourt.law.co.uk
Call Date: Nov 1965, Lincoln's Inn
Qualifications: [FCIArb]

EDELMAN COLIN NEIL QC (1995)

Devereux Chambers
Devereux Court, London WC2R 3JJ,
Telephone: 0171 353 7534
E-mail: mailbox@devchambers.co.uk
Call Date: July 1977, Middle Temple
Recorder
Qualifications: [MA (Cantab)]

EDENBOROUGH MICHAEL SIMON

One Raymond Buildings
Gray's Inn, London WC1R 5BH,
Telephone: 0171 430 1234
E-mail: chambers@ipbar1rb.com;
clerks@ipbar1rb.com
Call Date: Oct 1992, Middle Temple
Pupil Master
Qualifications: [BA (Hons), MA, M.Sc, D.Phil, MRSC]

EDER (HENRY) BERNARD QC (1990)

Essex Court Chambers
24 Lincoln's Inn Fields, London
WC2A 3ED, Telephone: 0171 813 8000
E-mail:clerksroom@essexcourt-chambers.co.uk
Call Date: July 1975, Inner Temple
Assistant Recorder
Qualifications: [BA (Cantab)]

EDEY PHILIP DAVID

20 Essex Street
London WC2R 3AL,
Telephone: 0171 583 9294
E-mail: clerks@20essexst.com
Call Date: Nov 1994, Gray's Inn
Qualifications: [BA]

EDGE IAN DAVID

3 Paper Buildings
Temple, London EC4Y 7EU,
Telephone: 020 7583 8055
E-mail: London@3paper.com
3 Paper Buildings (Bournemouth)
20 Lorne Park Road, Bournemouth,
Dorset, BH1 1JN,
Telephone: 01202 292102
E-mail: Bournemouth@3paper.com
3 Paper Buildings (Winchester)
4 St Peter Street, Winchester SO23 8BW,
Telephone: 01962 868884
E-mail: winchester@3paper.com
3 Paper Buildings (Oxford)
1 Alfred Street, High Street, Oxford
OX1 4EH, Telephone: 01865 793736
E-mail: oxford@3paper.com
Call Date: Feb 1981, Middle Temple
Qualifications: [BA,LLM (Cantab)]

EDGE TIMOTHY RICHARD

Deans Court Chambers
41-43 Market Place, Preston PR1 1AH,
Telephone: 01772 555163
E-mail: clerks@deanscourt.co.uk
Deans Court Chambers
24 St John Street, Manchester M3 4DF,
Telephone: 0161 214 6000
E-mail: clerks@deanscourt.co.uk
Call Date: Oct 1992, Gray's Inn
Qualifications: [MA]

EDGINTON HORACE RONALD

Becket Chambers
17 New Dover Road, Canterbury, Kent,
CT1 3AS, Telephone: 01227 786331
Westgate Chambers
144 High Street, Lewes, East Sussex,
BN7 1XT, Telephone: 01273 480510
Call Date: 1984, Gray's Inn
Qualifications: [RGN, BA(Hons)(Law), LLM
(Exon)]

EDHEM MISS EMMA

4 King's Bench Walk
Ground/First Floor/Basement, Temple,
London EC4Y 7DL,
Telephone: 0171 822 8822
E-mail: 4kbw@barristersatlaw.com
Call Date: Oct 1993, Gray's Inn
Qualifications: [BSc]

EDIE ALASTAIR SCOTT KER

Two Garden Court
1st Floor, Middle Temple, London
EC4Y 9BL, Telephone: 0171 353 1633
E-mail:barristers@2gardenct.law.co.uk
Call Date: Oct 1992, Middle Temple
Qualifications: [BA(Hons)(Kent)]

EDIE ANTHONY THOMAS KER

Lamb Building
Ground Floor, Temple, London
EC4Y 7AS, Telephone: 020 7797 7788
E-mail: lamb.building@link.org
Call Date: Feb 1974, Gray's Inn
Pupil Master
Qualifications: [LLB]

EDIS ANDREW JEREMY COULTER QC (1997)

Adrian Lyon's Chambers
14 Castle Street, Liverpool L2 0NE,
Telephone: 0151 236 4421/8240
E-mail: chambers14@aol.com
Call Date: July 1980, Middle Temple
Recorder
Qualifications: [MA (Oxon)]

Types of work: Crime, Crime – corporate
fraud, Medical negligence, Personal injury,
Professional negligence

Circuit: Northern

Awards and memberships: Personal Injury Bar
Association, Bar Sports Law Group,
Northern Circuit Commercial Bar Associa-
tion

Reported Cases: *Arthur 35 Hall & Co v Simons
CA,* (1998) *The Times,*18 December (to be
reported soon), 1998. Forensic immunity
for solicitors acting in cases which compromised.
Barrand v British Cellophane Plc, (1995)
The Times, 16 February (CA), 1995. Limitation periods in industrial deafness claims.
Stringman v McArdle, [1994] 1 WLR 1653
(CA), 1994. Interim payments in personal
injury actions.
Oldham v Chief Constable of Merseyside,
[1997] PIQR Q82 (CA), 1997. Costs in
personal injury actions.

EDIS ANGUS WILLIAM BUTLER

1 Crown Office Row
Ground Floor, Temple, London
EC4Y 7HH, Telephone: 0171 797 7500
E-mail: mail@onecrownofficerow.com
Call Date: July 1985, Lincoln's Inn
Pupil Master
Qualifications: [BA(Oxon)]

EDLIN DAVID MILES TIMOTHY

Lamb Building
Ground Floor, Temple, London
EC4Y 7AS, Telephone: 020 7797 7788
E-mail: lamb.building@link.org
Call Date: July 1971, Middle Temple
Pupil Master
Qualifications: [MA (Oxon)]

EDMONDSON MISS HARRIET JANE

30 Park Place
Cardiff CF1 3BA,
Telephone: 01222 398421
E-mail: 100757.1456@compuserve.com
Call Date: Nov 1997, Gray's Inn
Qualifications: [LLB (Wales)]

EDMUNDS MARTIN JAMES SIMPSON

Walnut House
63 St David's Hill, Exeter, Devon,
EX4 4DW, Telephone: 01392 279751
E-mail: 106627.2451@compuserve.com
Call Date: July 1983, Middle Temple
Pupil Master, Assistant Recorder
Qualifications: [MA (Cantab)]

EDUSEI FRANCIS VICTOR BURG

**Chambers of Ian Macdonald QC (In
Association with Two Garden Court,
Temple, London)**
Waldorf House, 5 Cooper Street,
Manchester M2 2FW,
Telephone: 0161 236 1840
Call Date: July 1989, Inner Temple
Qualifications: [LLB]

EDWARDS MS ANN MERERID

Paradise Chambers
26 Paradise Square, Sheffield S1 2DE,
Telephone: 0114 2738951
E-mail: timbooth@paradise-sq.co.uk
Call Date: Oct 1991, Gray's Inn
Qualifications: [LLB (Wales)]

EDWARDS ANTHONY HOWARD

Oriel Chambers
14 Water Street, Liverpool L2 8TD,
Telephone: 0151 236 7191/236 4321
E-mail: clerks@oriel-chambers.co.uk
Call Date: Nov 1972, Inner Temple
Pupil Master, Recorder
Qualifications: [LLB (L'pool)]

EDWARDS MISS CLAIRE FRANCES

Carmarthen Chambers
30 Spilman Street, Carmarthen, Dyfed,
SA31 1LQ, Telephone: 01267 234410
E-mail: law@in-wales.com
Call Date: Nov 1990, Inner Temple
Qualifications: [LLB]

EDWARDS DANIEL HUGH

York Chambers
14 Toft Green, York YO1 6JT,
Telephone: 01904 620048
E-mail: [name]@yorkchambers.co.uk
Call Date: Oct 1993, Lincoln's Inn
Qualifications: [BA (Hons)(York), Dip in Law
(Lond)]

EDWARDS DAVID GARETH

Martins Building
2nd Floor, No 4 Water Street, Liverpool
L2 3SP, Telephone: 0151 236 5818/4919
Call Date: Oct 1994, Gray's Inn
Qualifications: [LLB (Warw)]

EDWARDS DAVID LESLIE

S Tomlinson QC
7 King's Bench Walk, Temple, London
EC4Y 7DS, Telephone: 0171 583 0404
E-mail: clerks@7kbw.law.co.uk
Call Date: July 1989, Lincoln's Inn
Qualifications: [MA (Cantab)]

EDWARDS GLYN TUDOR

St John's Chambers
Small Street, Bristol BS1 1DW,
Telephone: 0117 9213456/298514
E-mail: @stjohnschambers.co.uk
Call Date: July 1987, Lincoln's Inn
Qualifications: [MA (Cantab), LLM (Cantab)]

EDWARDS HEATH IAN

9 Park Place
Cardiff CF1 3DP,
Telephone: 01222 382731
Call Date: 1996, Gray's Inn
Qualifications: [LLB (Warks)]

EDWARDS MISS HELEN JANE

33 Park Place
Cardiff CF1 3BA,
Telephone: 02920 233313
Call Date: July 1995, Inner Temple
Qualifications: [LLB (Middx)]

EDWARDS MISS JACQUELINE ELIZABETH ANNE

Parsonage Chambers
5th Floor, 3 The Parsonage, Manchester
M3 2HW, Telephone: 0161 833 1996
Call Date: Mar 1997, Lincoln's Inn
Qualifications: [BA (Jnt Hons)(Keele)]

EDWARDS MISS JENNIFER MARY

Dr Johnson's Chambers
Two Dr Johnson's Buildings, Temple,
London EC4Y 7AY,
Telephone: 0171 353 4716
E-mail: clerks@2djb.freeserve.co.uk
Call Date: Oct 1992, Gray's Inn
Qualifications: [BA (Nott'm)]

EDWARDS JOHN DAVID

St Philip's Chambers
Fountain Court, Steelhouse Lane,
Birmingham B4 6DR,
Telephone: 0121 246 7000
E-mail: clerks@st-philips.co.uk
Call Date: July 1983, Inner Temple
Pupil Master
Qualifications: [BA]

EDWARDS (JOHN) MICHAEL QC (1981)

Verulam Chambers
Peer House, 8-14 Verulam Street, Gray's
Inn, London WC1X 8LZ,
Telephone: 0171 813 2400
Call Date: Nov 1949, Middle Temple
Qualifications: [BCL,MA,FCIArb]

EDWARDS JONATHAN GWYN MENDUS

Claremont Chambers
26 Waterloo Road, Wolverhampton
WV1 4BL, Telephone: 01902 426222
Call Date: July 1981, Lincoln's Inn

EDWARDS JONATHAN WILLIAM

Westgate Chambers
144 High Street, Lewes, East Sussex,
BN7 1XT, Telephone: 01273 480510
Call Date: Nov 1994, Lincoln's Inn
Qualifications: [LLB (Hons)]

EDWARDS MARTIN RICHARD

1 Serjeants' Inn
4th Floor, Temple, London EC4Y 1NH,
Telephone: 0171 583 1355
E-mail: clerks@serjeants-inn.co.uk
Call Date: Nov 1995, Inner Temple
Qualifications: [BA (Kent), MA]

EDWARDS MS NICOLA MADELAINE

12 Old Square
1st Floor, Lincoln's Inn, London
WC2A 3TX, Telephone: 0171 404 0875
Call Date: Oct 1991, Lincoln's Inn
Qualifications: [LLB (Hons), RGN]

EDWARDS NIGEL ROYSTON

St Paul's House
5th Floor, St Paul's House, 23 Park Square
South, Leeds LS1 2ND,
Telephone: 0113 2455866
E-mail: catherinegrimshaw@stpauls-
chambers.demon.co.uk
Call Date: Nov 1995, Lincoln's Inn
Qualifications: [LLB (Hons)(Sheff)]

EDWARDS OWEN MEIRION

Sedan House
Stanley Place, Chester CH1 2LU,
Telephone: 01244 320480/348282
Call Date: Oct 1992, Lincoln's Inn
Qualifications: [LLB(Hons)(Wales)]

EDWARDS PERCY JOHN OSBORNE

15 North Church Street Chambers
15 North Church Street, Sheffield
S1 2DH, Telephone: 0114 2759708/
2738380
Call Date: Nov 1994, Gray's Inn
Qualifications: [LLB (Hull), MA (Leeds)]

EDWARDS PETER ALAN

Devereux Chambers
Devereux Court, London WC2R 3JJ,
Telephone: 0171 353 7534
E-mail: mailbox@devchambers.co.uk
Call Date: Oct 1992, Inner Temple
Qualifications: [BA (Kent)]

EDWARDS PHILIP DOUGLAS

2 Harcourt Buildings
2nd Floor, Temple, London EC4Y 9DB,
Telephone: 020 7353 8415
E-mail: clerks@2hb.law.co.uk
Call Date: Nov 1992, Lincoln's Inn
Qualifications: [LLB (Hons)(B'ham)]

EDWARDS RICHARD HUW WYN

9 Park Place
Cardiff CF1 3DP,
Telephone: 01222 382731
Call Date: 1997, Lincoln's Inn
Qualifications: [B.Eng (Hons)(City), LLB
(Hons)(Wales)]

EDWARDS RICHARD JOHN

Counsels' Chambers
2nd Floor, 10-11 Gray's Inn Square,
London WC1R 5JD,
Telephone: 0171 405 2576
E-mail:clerks@10-11graysinnsquare.co.uk
Call Date: 1994, Middle Temple
Qualifications: [BA (Hons), MA]

EDWARDS RICHARD JULIAN HENSHAW

3 Verulam Buildings
London WC1R 5NT,
Telephone: 0171 831 8441
E-mail: clerks@3verulam.co.uk
Call Date: Oct 1993, Middle Temple
Qualifications: [MA (Cantab), M.Phil
(Cantab)]

EDWARDS MISS SARAH LOUISE ELIZABETH

Queen Elizabeth Building
2nd Floor, Temple, London EC4Y 9BS,
Telephone: 0171 797 7837
Call Date: Nov 1990, Inner Temple
Qualifications: [BA (Cantab)]

EDWARDS SIMON DAVID

1 Paper Buildings
1st Floor, Temple, London EC4Y 7EP,
Telephone: 0171 353 3728/4953
Call Date: Nov 1987, Gray's Inn
Qualifications: [LLB (Leics)]

EDWARDS SIMON JOHN MAY

29 Bedford Row Chambers
London WC1R 4HE,
Telephone: 0171 831 2626
Call Date: Nov 1978, Middle Temple
Qualifications: [MA (Cantab)]

EDWARDS MISS SUSAN MAY QC (1993)

23 Essex Street
London WC2R 3AS,
Telephone: 0171 413 0353/836 8366
E-mail:clerks@essexstreet23.demon.co.uk
*Call Date: Nov 1972, Middle Temple
Recorder*
Qualifications: [LLB (Soton)]

EDWARDS-STUART ANTONY JAMES COBHAM QC (1991)

Two Crown Office Row
Ground Floor, Temple, London
EC4Y 7HJ, Telephone: 020 7797 8100
E-mail: mail@2cor.co.uk, or to individual
barristers at: [barrister's
surname]@2cor.co.uk
*Call Date: May 1976, Gray's Inn
Assistant Recorder*
Qualifications: [MA (Cantab)]

EGAN MISS CAROLINE ANN

6 Fountain Court
Steelhouse Lane, Birmingham B4 6DR,
Telephone: 0121 233 3282
E-mail: clerks@sixfountain.co.uk
Call Date: Nov 1993, Gray's Inn
Qualifications: [BA]

EGAN EUGENE CHRISTOPHER

30 Park Place
Cardiff CF1 3BA,
Telephone: 01222 398421
E-mail: 100757.1456@compuserve.com
Call Date: Oct 1993, Lincoln's Inn
Qualifications: [MA (Oxon)]

EGAN MISS FIONA JUNE CECILE

Thomas More Chambers
52 Carey Street, Lincoln's Inn, London
WC2A 2JB, Telephone: 0171 404 7000
E-mail: clerks@thomasmore.law.co.uk
Call Date: Nov 1987, Middle Temple
Qualifications: [LLB]

EGAN MISS FRANCES TWINKLE

Lancaster Building
77 Deansgate, Manchester M3 2BW,
Telephone: 0161 661 4444/0171 649 9872
E-mail: sandra@lbnipc.com
Call Date: Nov 1986, Middle Temple
Qualifications: [BCL (Dublin)]

EGAN MISS MARION TERESA

One Paper Buildings
Ground Floor, Temple, London
EC4Y 7EP, Telephone: 0171 583 7355
E-mail: clerks@1pb.co.uk
Call Date: July 1988, Middle Temple
Pupil Master
Qualifications: [MA (Hons) (Cantab)]

EGAN MICHAEL FLYNN JOHN

9-12 Bell Yard
London WC2A 2LF,
Telephone: 0171 400 1800
E-mail: clerks@bellyard.co.uk
Call Date: Nov 1981, Gray's Inn
Pupil Master

EGAN PATRICK MANUS DERMOT

Thomas More Chambers
52 Carey Street, Lincoln's Inn, London
WC2A 2JB, Telephone: 0171 404 7000
E-mail: clerks@thomasmore.law.co.uk
Call Date: Nov 1991, Middle Temple
Qualifications: [LLB (Hons)]

EGBUNA ROBERT OBIORA

High Pavement Chambers
1 High Pavement, Nottingham NG1 1HF,
Telephone: 0115 9418218
Call Date: Nov 1988, Gray's Inn
Pupil Master
Qualifications: [LLB]

EGERTON MISS CHRISTINE ANNE

39 Park Square
Leeds LS1 2NU,
Telephone: 0113 2456633
Call Date: Oct 1992, Inner Temple
Qualifications: [LLB (Lond), LLM (Lond)]

EGLETON RICHARD WILDMAN

Eighteen Carlton Crescent
Southampton SO15 2XR,
Telephone: 01703 639001
Call Date: July 1981, Gray's Inn
Pupil Master
Qualifications: [MA (Oxon)]

EICKE TIM

Francis Taylor Building
3rd Floor, Temple, London EC4Y 7BY,
Telephone: 0171 797 7250
Essex Court Chambers
24 Lincoln's Inn Fields, London
WC2A 3ED, Telephone: 0171 813 8000
E-mail:clerksroom@essexcourt-chambers.co.uk
Call Date: Oct 1993, Middle Temple
Qualifications: [LLB (Hons)(Dundee)]

EIDINOW JOHN SAMUEL CHRISTOPHER

1 New Square
Ground Floor, Lincoln's Inn, London
WC2A 3SA, Telephone: 0171 405 0884/5/6/7 E-mail: clerks@1newsquare.law.co.uk
Call Date: Nov 1992, Middle Temple
Qualifications: [BA (Hons), Dip in Law]

EILLEDGE MISS AMANDA GAIL CAROLINE

1 Harcourt Buildings
2nd Floor, Temple, London EC4Y 9DA,
Telephone: 0171 353 9421/0375
E-mail:clerks@1harcourtbuildings.law.co.uk
Call Date: Oct 1991, Lincoln's Inn
Qualifications: [BA (Hons), BCL (Oxon)]

EISSA ADRIAN NADIR

Two Garden Court
1st Floor, Middle Temple, London
EC4Y 9BL, Telephone: 0171 353 1633
E-mail:barristers@2gardenct.law.co.uk
Call Date: Nov 1988, Inner Temple
Qualifications: [LLB (Warwick)]

EKANEY NKUMBE

Albion Chambers
Broad Street, Bristol BS1 1DR,
Telephone: 0117 9272144
Call Date: Oct 1990, Gray's Inn
Qualifications: [LLB (Bris)]

EKLUND GRAHAM NICHOLAS

2 Temple Gardens
Temple, London EC4Y 9AY,
Telephone: 0171 583 6041
E-mail: clerks@2templegardens.co.uk
Call Date: May 1984, Inner Temple
Pupil Master
Qualifications: [BA, LLB (Hons)(Auckland)]

EL-FALAHI SAMI DAVID

International Law Chambers
ILC House, 77/79 Chepstow Road,
Bayswater, London W2 5QR,
Telephone: 0171 221 5684/5/4840
E-mail: ilcuk@aol.com
Call Date: July 1972, Inner Temple
Qualifications: [MA (Oxon), MSc Econ, FCI
ARB.]

ELCOMBE NICHOLAS JOHN

East Anglian Chambers
52 North Hill, Colchester, Essex, CO1 1PY,
Telephone: 01206 572756
E-mail: colchester@ealaw.co.uk
East Anglian Chambers
57 London Street, Norwich NR2 1HL,
Telephone: 01603 617351
E-mail: norwich@ealaw.co.uk

East Anglian Chambers
Gresham House, 5 Museum Street,
Ipswich, Suffolk, IP1 1HQ,
Telephone: 01473 214481
E-mail: ipswich@ealaw.co.uk
Call Date: July 1987, Inner Temple
Pupil Master
Qualifications: [LLB]

ELDER MISS FIONA ANN MORAG

Queens Square Chambers
56 Queens Square, Bristol BS1 4PR,
Telephone: 0117 921 1966
Call Date: July 1988, Gray's Inn
Qualifications: [LLB (Sheffield)]

ELDERGILL EDMUND MALCOLM

Counsels' Chambers
2nd Floor, 10-11 Gray's Inn Square,
London WC1R 5JD,
Telephone: 0171 405 2576
E-mail:clerks@10-11graysinnsquare.co.uk
Call Date: Nov 1991, Inner Temple
Qualifications: [BA (East Ang), Dip Law,
PCGE]

ELDRED ANDREW COLIN

College of Law, 14 Store Street, London
WC1E 7DE, Telephone: 0171 291 1200
Call Date: Nov 1994, Middle Temple
Qualifications: [MA (Oxon), Dip Law (City)]

ELDRIDGE MARK

3 Temple Gardens
3rd Floor, Temple, London EC4Y 9AU,
Telephone: 0171 353 0832
114 Liverpool Road
Islington, London N1 0RE,
Telephone: 0171 226 9863
Call Date: July 1982, Gray's Inn
Pupil Master
Qualifications: [BA (Hons)(Lancaster), Dip in
Law]

ELEY MISS JOANNE MARY

Trinity Chambers
140 New London Road, Chelmsford,
Essex, CM2 0AW,
Telephone: 01245 605040
E-mail:clerks@trinitychambers.law.co.uk
Call Date: Oct 1997, Middle Temple
Qualifications: [BA (Hull), CPE]

ELEY JOHNATHAN DESMOND HUGH

High Pavement Chambers
1 High Pavement, Nottingham NG1 1HF,
Telephone: 0115 9418218
Call Date: July 1987, Middle Temple
Qualifications: [BA]

ELFIELD MISS LAURA ELAINE

5 Pump Court
Ground Floor, Temple, London
EC4Y 7AP, Telephone: 020 7353 2532
E-mail: FivePump@netcomuk.co.uk
Call Date: Mar 1996, Gray's Inn
Qualifications: [BA]

ELGOT HOWARD CHARLES

Park Lane Chambers
19 Westgate, Leeds LS1 2RD,
Telephone: 0113 2285000
E-mail:clerks@parklanechambers.co.uk
Call Date: July 1974, Gray's Inn
Pupil Master
Qualifications: [BA, BCL (Oxon)]

ELIAS DAVID

9 Park Place
Cardiff CF1 3DP,
Telephone: 01222 382731
Call Date: May 1994, Inner Temple
Qualifications: [MA (Cantab)]

ELIAS GERARD QC (1984)

Farrar's Building
Temple, London EC4Y 7BD,
Telephone: 0171 583 9241
E-mail:chambers@farrarsbuilding.co.uk
9 Park Place
Cardiff CF1 3DP,
Telephone: 01222 382731
Call Date: July 1968, Inner Temple
Recorder
Qualifications: [LLB]

ELIAS ROBERT WILLOUGHBY

Lincoln House Chambers
5th Floor, Lincoln House, 1 Brazennose
Street, Manchester M2 5EL,
Telephone: 0161 832 5701
E-mail: info@lincolnhse.co.uk
Call Date: July 1979, Middle Temple
Pupil Master
Qualifications: [LLB (Hons) (Sheff)]

ELKINGTON BENJAMIN MICHAEL GORDON

Chambers of John L Powell QC
Four New Square, Lincoln's Inn, London
WC2A 3RJ, Telephone: 0171 797 8000
E-mail: barristers@4newsquare.com
Call Date: Oct 1996, Gray's Inn
Qualifications: [MA (Cantab), LLM (Virginia)]

ELLACOTT STUART IAN

Guildhall Chambers Portsmouth
Prudential Buildings, 16 Guildhall Walk,
Portsmouth, Hampshire, PO1 2DE,
Telephone: 01705 752400
Call Date: Nov 1989, Inner Temple
Qualifications: [BA]

ELLENBOGEN MISS NAOMI LISA

Littleton Chambers
3 King's Bench Walk North, Temple,
London EC4Y 7HR,
Telephone: 0171 797 8600
E-mail:clerks@littletonchambers.co.uk
Call Date: Oct 1992, Gray's Inn
Qualifications: [MA (Oxon)]

ELLERAY ANTHONY JOHN QC (1993)

St James's Chambers
68 Quay Street, Manchester M3 3EJ,
Telephone: 0161 834 7000
E-mail: clerks@stjameschambers.co.uk
12 New Square
Lincoln's Inn, London WC2A 3SW,
Telephone: 0171 419 1212
E-mail: chambers@12newsquare.co.uk
Park Lane Chambers
19 Westgate, Leeds LS1 2RD,
Telephone: 0113 2285000
E-mail:clerks@parklanechambers.co.uk
Call Date: 1977, Inner Temple
Recorder
Qualifications: [MA (Cantab)]

Fax: 0161 834 2341; DX: 14350 Manchester 1

Other professional qualifications: MA (Cantab)

Types of work: Bankruptcy, Chancery (general), Chancery land law, Charities, Commercial litigation, Commercial property, Company and commercial, Copyright, Equity, wills and trusts, Family provision, Insolvency, Intellectual property, Landlord and tenant, Partnerships, Professional negligence

Circuit: Northern

Awards and memberships: Inner Temple Major Award; CBA; PNBA; NCBA (chairman)

Other professional experience: Recorder

Languages spoken: French

Reported Cases: *Walker v Turpin*, CA, 1993. Payments in.
Jervis v Harris, CA, 1995. Landlord and tenant.
Salford Van Hire v Bolcholt, CA, 1995. Landlord and tenant.
Bass v Latham Crossley Davis, CA, 1996. Partnership.
Shah v Bolton MBC, CA, 1996. Compulsory purchase.

Additional Reported Cases
Pearce Deceased, CA, 1998. Inheritance Act.

Conroy v Kenny, CA, 1998. Money lender 'in the course of...'

Wibbeley v Insley, HL, 1999. Boundaries.

ELLIN MISS NINA CAROLINE

6 Pump Court
1st Floor, Temple, London EC4Y 7AR,
Telephone: 0171 797 8400
E-mail: clerks@6pumpcourt.co.uk
6-8 Mill Street
Maidstone, Kent, ME15 6XH,
Telephone: 01622 688094
E-mail: annexe@6pumpcourt.co.uk
Call Date: Nov 1994, Inner Temple
Qualifications: [LLB (Lond), Maitrise, en Droit Francais, (Paris I, Sorg)]

ELLINS DR JULIA ELISABETH

Blackstone Chambers
Blackstone House, Temple, London
EC4Y 9BW, Telephone: 0171 583 1770
E-mail:clerks@blackstonechambers.com
Call Date: Oct 1994, Gray's Inn
Qualifications: [LLB (Lond),LLM, Dr.Jur (Munich)]

ELLIOTT CHRISTOPHER DAVID

Young Street Chambers
38 Young Street, Manchester M3 3FT,
Telephone: 0161 833 0489
E-mail: clerks@young-st-chambers.com
Call Date: July 1974, Gray's Inn
Pupil Master
Qualifications: [BA (Hons)]

ELLIOTT DR CHRISTOPHER JAMES

95A Chancery Lane
London WC2A 1DT,
Telephone: 0171 405 3101
Call Date: Oct 1997, Gray's Inn
Qualifications: [BA, MA, PLD]

ELLIOTT COLIN DOUGLAS

Godolphin Chambers
50 Castle Street, Truro, Cornwall,
TR1 3AF, Telephone: 01872 276312
E-mail:theclerks@godolphin.force9.co.uk
Call Date: July 1987, Gray's Inn
Qualifications: [BSc (Lond), Dip Law]

ELLIOTT ERIC ALAN

Broad Chare
33 Broad Chare, Newcastle upon Tyne
NE1 3DQ, Telephone: 0191 232 0541
E-mail:clerks@broadcharechambers.law.co.uk
Call Date: July 1974, Gray's Inn
Recorder
Qualifications: [LLB]

ELLIOTT JASON

Barnard's Inn Chambers
6th Floor, Halton House, 20-23 Holborn,
London EC1N 2JD,
Telephone: 0171 369 6969
E-mail: clerks@biclaw.co.uk
Call Date: Oct 1993, Inner Temple
Qualifications: [BA]

ELLIOTT MISS MARGOT MARY

Regency Chambers
Cathedral Square, Peterborough
PE1 1XW, Telephone: 01733 315215
Regency Chambers
Sheraton House, Castle Park, Cambridge
CB3 0AX, Telephone: 01223 301517
Call Date: Nov 1989, Gray's Inn
Pupil Master
Qualifications: [LLB (Newc)]

D

ELLIOTT NICHOLAS BLETHYN QC (1995)

3 Verulam Buildings
London WC1R 5NT,
Telephone: 0171 831 8441
E-mail: clerks@3verulam.co.uk
Call Date: July 1972, Gray's Inn
Qualifications: [LLB]

ELLIOTT RUPERT EDMUND IVO

1 Brick Court
1st Floor, Temple, London EC4Y 9BY,
Telephone: 0171 353 8845
E-mail: clerks@1brickcourt.co.uk
Call Date: July 1988, Inner Temple
Pupil Master
Qualifications: [MA (Cantab)]

ELLIOTT MS SARAH JULIA

4 Brick Court
Ground Floor, Temple, London
EC4Y 9AD, Telephone: 0171 797 7766
E-mail: chambers@4brick.co.uk
Call Date: Oct 1996, Gray's Inn
Qualifications: [BA (Sussex)]

ELLIOTT TIMOTHY STANLEY QC (1992)

Keating Chambers
10 Essex Street, Outer Temple, London
WC2R 3AA, Telephone: 0171 544 2600
Call Date: July 1975, Middle Temple
Qualifications: [MA (Oxon)]

ELLIS MISS CAROL JACQUELINE QC (1980)

11 Old Square
Ground Floor, Lincoln's Inn, London
WC2A 3TS, Telephone: 020 7430 0341
E-mail: clerks@11oldsquare.co.uk
Call Date: Nov 1951, Gray's Inn
Qualifications: [LLB]

ELLIS MISS CATHERINE ANNE

Derby Square Chambers
Merchants Court, Derby Square, Liverpool
L2 1TS, Telephone: 0151 709 4222
E-mail:mail.derbysquare@pop3.hiway.co.uk
Call Date: July 1987, Lincoln's Inn
Qualifications: [LLB (Lanc)]

ELLIS CHRISTOPHER ANDREW

Regency Chambers
Cathedral Square, Peterborough
PE1 1XW, Telephone: 01733 315215
Regency Chambers
Sheraton House, Castle Park, Cambridge
CB3 0AX, Telephone: 01223 301517
Call Date: Oct 1991, Gray's Inn
Qualifications: [LLB (Hons, Cantab), LLM
(Hons, Cantab)]

ELLIS MISS DIANA

3 Gray's Inn Square
Ground Floor, London WC1R 5AH,
Telephone: 0171 520 5600
E-mail: clerks@3gis.co.uk
Call Date: July 1978, Inner Temple
Pupil Master, Assistant Recorder
Qualifications: [LLB (Lond)]

ELLIS MICHAEL TYRONE

Northampton Chambers
22 Albion Place, Northampton NN1 1UD,
Telephone: 01604 636271
Call Date: Oct 1993, Middle Temple
Qualifications: [LLB (Hons)(Bucks)]

ELLIS DR PETER SIMON

7 New Square
Lincoln's Inn, London WC2A 3QS,
Telephone: 0171 430 1660
Call Date: Nov 1997, Middle Temple
Qualifications: [MB.BS (Lond), MRCP (St
Marys Hosp)]

ELLIS ROGER JOHN QC (1996)

13 King's Bench Walk
1st Floor, Temple, London EC4Y 7EN,
Telephone: 0171 353 7204
E-mail: clerks@13kbw.law.co.uk
King's Bench Chambers
32 Beaumont Street, Oxford OX1 2NP,
Telephone: 01865 311066
E-mail: clerks@kbc-oxford.law.co.uk
Call Date: July 1962, Gray's Inn
Qualifications: [LLB (Lond), BSc]

ELLIS MISS ROSALIND MORAG

2-3 Gray's Inn Square
Gray's Inn, London WC1R 5JH,
Telephone: 0171 242 4986
E-mail:chambers@2-3graysinnsquare.co.uk
Call Date: July 1984, Gray's Inn
Pupil Master
Qualifications: [MA (Cantab)]

ELLIS MISS SARAH LOUISE

9-12 Bell Yard
London WC2A 2LF,
Telephone: 0171 400 1800
E-mail: clerks@bellyard.co.uk
Call Date: Nov 1989, Gray's Inn
Qualifications: [LLB [Wales]]

ELLIS WESLEY JONATHAN

7 Stone Buildings (also at 11 Bolt Court)
1st Floor, Lincoln's Inn, London
WC2A 3SZ, Telephone: 0171 242 0961
E-mail:larthur@7stonebuildings.law.co.uk
11 Bolt Court (also at 7 Stone Buildings – 1st Floor)
London EC4A 3DQ,
Telephone: 0171 353 2300
E-mail: boltct11@aol.com
Redhill Chambers
Seloduct House, 30 Station Road, Redhill,
Surrey, RH1 1NF,
Telephone: 01737 780781
Call Date: Feb 1995, Gray's Inn
Qualifications: [MA (Cantab)]

ELLIS-JONES STEPHEN

5 Pump Court
Ground Floor, Temple, London
EC4Y 7AP, Telephone: 020 7353 2532
E-mail: FivePump@netcomuk.co.uk
Call Date: Nov 1992, Middle Temple
Qualifications: [B.Eng (L'pool)]

ELLISON MARK CHRISTOPHER

Hollis Whiteman Chambers
3rd Floor, Queen Elizabeth Bldg, Temple,
London EC4Y 9BS,
Telephone: 020 7583 5766
E-mail:barristers@holliswhiteman.co.uk
Call Date: Nov 1979, Gray's Inn
Pupil Master, Recorder
Qualifications: [LLB (Wales)]

ELSEY ROGER WILLIAM

Broad Chare
33 Broad Chare, Newcastle upon Tyne
NE1 3DQ, Telephone: 0191 232 0541
E-mail:clerks@broadcharechambers.law.co.uk
Call Date: May 1977, Gray's Inn
Qualifications: [LLB]

ELSOM MICHAEL ROBERT

5 Fountain Court
Steelhouse Lane, Birmingham B4 6DR,
Telephone: 0121 606 0500
E-mail:clerks@5fountaincourt.law.co.uk
Call Date: July 1972, Inner Temple
Pupil Master, Assistant Recorder
Qualifications: [BA (Dunelm)]

ELVIDGE JOHN ALLAN

1 Mitre Court Buildings
Temple, London EC4Y 7BS,
Telephone: 0171 797 7070
E-mail: clerks@1mcb.com
Call Date: Nov 1968, Lincoln's Inn
Recorder
Qualifications: [MA, LLB (Cantab)]

ELVIDGE JOHN COWIE

York Chambers
14 Toft Green, York YO1 6JT,
Telephone: 01904 620048
E-mail: [name]@yorkchambers.co.uk
Call Date: Nov 1988, Gray's Inn
Qualifications: [LLB (Newc)]

ELVIN DAVID JOHN

4 Breams Buildings
London EC4A 1AQ,
Telephone: 0171 353 5835/430 1221
E-mail:breams@4breamsbuildings.law.co.uk
Call Date: Nov 1983, Middle Temple
Pupil Master
Qualifications: [BA (Oxon), BCL (Oxon)]

ELWICK BRYAN MARTIN

High Pavement Chambers
1 High Pavement, Nottingham NG1 1HF,
Telephone: 0115 9418218
Call Date: July 1981, Middle Temple
Qualifications: [LLB (Nott'm)]

EMANUEL MARK PERING WOLFF

14 Gray's Inn Square
Gray's Inn, London WC1R 5JP,
Telephone: 0171 242 0858
E-mail: 100712.2134@compuserve.com
Call Date: Nov 1985, Inner Temple
Pupil Master
Qualifications: [BA (Hons)]

EMERSON PAUL MICHAEL

Lamb Chambers
Lamb Building, Temple, London
EC4Y 7AS, Telephone: 020 7797 8300
E-mail: lambchambers@link.org
Call Date: July 1984, Middle Temple
Pupil Master
Qualifications: [LLB]

EMERSON WILLIAM BRADLEY

Chichester Chambers
12 North Pallant, Chichester, West Sussex,
PO19 1TQ, Telephone: 01243 784538
E-mail:clerks@chichesterchambers.law.co.uk
Call Date: Nov 1992, Middle Temple
Qualifications: [LLB (Hons)]

EMIR MISS ASTRA

3 Temple Gardens
Lower Ground Floor, Temple, London
EC4Y 9AU, Telephone: 0171 353 3102/5/
9297 E-mail: clerks@3tg.co.uk
Call Date: Oct 1992, Gray's Inn
Qualifications: [BA (Oxon)]

EMLYN JONES WILLIAM NICHOLAS

2 Harcourt Buildings
1st Floor, Temple, London EC4Y 9DB,
Telephone: 020 7353 2112
Call Date: Oct 1996, Inner Temple
Qualifications: [LLB (So'ton)]

EMM ROGER GARETH

Chancery House Chambers
7 Lisbon Square, Leeds LS1 4LY,
Telephone: 0113 244 6691
E-mail: chanceryhouse@btinternet.com
Call Date: July 1977, Middle Temple
Pupil Master
Qualifications: [BA, MPhil]

EMMERSON (MICHAEL) BENEDICT

Doughty Street Chambers
11 Doughty Street, London WC1N 2PG,
Telephone: 0171 404 1313
E-mail:enquiries@doughtystreet.co.uk
Call Date: Nov 1986, Middle Temple
Qualifications: [LLB (Bristol)]

ENGEL ANTHONY JOHN

3 Fountain Court
Steelhouse Lane, Birmingham B4 6DR,
Telephone: 0121 236 5854
Call Date: Nov 1965, Inner Temple
Qualifications: [MA (Cantab)]

ENGELMAN MARK TREVOR

7 New Square
1st Floor, Lincoln's Inn, London
WC2A 3QS, Telephone: 020 7404 5484
E-mail: clerks@7newsquare.com
Call Date: 1987, Gray's Inn
Qualifications: [BSc, Dip Law]

ENGELMAN PHILIP

Cardinal Chambers
4 Old Mitre Court, 4th Floor, Temple,
London EC4Y 7BP,
Telephone: 020 7353 2622
E-mail:admin@cardinal-chambers.co.uk
Call Date: July 1979, Gray's Inn
Pupil Master
Qualifications: [LLB (Lond)]

ENGLAND GEORGE

Bank House Chambers
Old Bank House, Hartshead, Sheffield
S1 2EL, Telephone: 0114 2751223
Call Date: Feb 1972, Middle Temple
Pupil Master
Qualifications: [LLB]

ENGLAND MRS LISA JOHANNA LOUISE

Guildhall Chambers Portsmouth
Prudential Buildings, 16 Guildhall Walk,
Portsmouth, Hampshire, PO1 2DE,
Telephone: 01705 752400
Call Date: Nov 1992, Gray's Inn
Qualifications: [LLB (Hons)(Lond)]

ENGLAND WILLIAM EDWARD CHARLES

2-4 Tudor Street
London EC4Y 0AA,
Telephone: 0171 797 7111
E-mail: clerks@rfqc.co.uk
Call Date: Nov 1991, Inner Temple
Qualifications: [LLB, LLM (Lond)]

ENGLEHART ROBERT MICHAEL QC (1986)

Blackstone Chambers
Blackstone House, Temple, London
EC4Y 9BW, Telephone: 0171 583 1770
E-mail:clerks@blackstonechambers.com
Call Date: Nov 1969, Middle Temple
Recorder
Qualifications: [MA (Oxon),LLM (Harv)]

ENGLISH MISS CAROLINE FRANCES

Francis Taylor Building
Ground Floor, Temple, London
EC4Y 7BY, Telephone: 0171 353 7768/
7769/2711
E-mail:clerks@francistaylorbuilding.law.co.uk
Call Date: Nov 1989, Inner Temple
Qualifications: [LLB]

ENGLISH RICHARD WARREN

Queens Square Chambers
56 Queens Square, Bristol BS1 4PR,
Telephone: 0117 921 1966
Call Date: Nov 1995, Middle Temple
Qualifications: [LLB (Hons)(Wales)]

ENGLISH ROBERT ANTHONY

Somersett Chambers
25 Bedford Row, London WC1R 4HE,
Telephone: 0171 404 6701
E-mail: somelaw@aol.com
Call Date: 1996, Inner Temple
Qualifications: [BA (Sussex), LLM (Lond)]

ENOCH DAFYDD HUW

Bridewell Chambers
2 Bridewell Place, London EC4V 6AP,
Telephone: 020 7797 8800
E-mail:HughesGage@bridewell.law.co.uk
Call Date: Nov 1985, Gray's Inn
Pupil Master
Qualifications: [BA Buckingham]

ENRIGHT MS JOHANNE

Somersett Chambers
25 Bedford Row, London WC1R 4HE,
Telephone: 0171 404 6701
E-mail: somelaw@aol.com
Call Date: 1996, Lincoln's Inn
Qualifications: [LLB (Hons), C.A.A.W.]

ENRIGHT SEAN

9-12 Bell Yard
London WC2A 2LF,
Telephone: 0171 400 1800
E-mail: clerks@bellyard.co.uk
Call Date: July 1982, Middle Temple
Pupil Master
Qualifications: [LL.B(Nottingham)]

EPHGRAVE MISS AMY JOANNA

Queens Square Chambers
56 Queens Square, Bristol BS1 4PR,
Telephone: 0117 921 1966
Call Date: Nov 1997, Gray's Inn
Qualifications: [BA (Exon)]

EPSTEIN MICHAEL PAUL

3 Hare Court
1 Little Essex Street, London WC2R 3LD,
Telephone: 0171 395 2000
Call Date: Nov 1992, Middle Temple
Qualifications: [LLB (Hons, Manch)]

EPSTEIN PAUL JEREMY

Cloisters
1 Pump Court, Temple, London
EC4Y 7AA, Telephone: 0171 827 4000
E-mail: clerks@cloisters.com
Call Date: Nov 1988, Middle Temple
Pupil Master
Qualifications: [BA (Oxon)]

ERNSTZEN OLAV GUSTAV

Eurolawyer Chambers
PO Box 3621, London N7 0BQ,
Telephone: 0171 607 0075
Verulam Chambers
Peer House, 8-14 Verulam Street, Gray's
Inn, London WC1X 8LZ,
Telephone: 0171 813 2400
Call Date: July 1981, Middle Temple
Pupil Master

D

ERWOOD MISS HEATHER MARY ELLISTON

3 Dr Johnson's Buildings
Ground Floor, Temple, London
EC4Y 7BA, Telephone: 0171 353 4854
E-mail: clerks@3djb.co.uk
Call Date: Oct 1993, Middle Temple
Qualifications: [LLB (Hons), LLM (Lond)]

ESCOTT-COX BRIAN ROBERT QC (1974)

Chambers of Michael Pert QC
36 Bedford Row, London WC1R 4JH,
Telephone: 0171 421 8000
E-mail: 36bedfordrow@link.org
3 Fountain Court
Steelhouse Lane, Birmingham B4 6DR,
Telephone: 0121 236 5854
Chambers of Michael Pert QC
104 New Walk, Leicester LE1 7EA,
Telephone: 0116 249 2020
Chambers of Michael Pert QC
24 Albion Place, Northampton NN1 1UD,
Telephone: 01604 602333
Call Date: July 1954, Lincoln's Inn
Qualifications: [MA (Oxon)]

ESHAGHIAN MISS YASMINE

12 Old Square
1st Floor, Lincoln's Inn, London
WC2A 3TX, Telephone: 0171 404 0875
Call Date: Feb 1995, Lincoln's Inn
Qualifications: [BA (Hons)(Lond)]

ESPLEY ANDREW ROBERT

Mitre Court Chambers
3rd Floor, Temple, London EC4Y 7BP,
Telephone: 0171 353 9394
E-mail: mitrecourt.com
Call Date: 1993, Gray's Inn
Qualifications: [LLB]

ESPLEY MISS SUSAN

Fenners Chambers
3 Madingley Road, Cambridge CB3 0EE,
Telephone: 01223 368761
E-mail: clerks@fennerschambers.co.uk
Fenners Chambers
8-12 Priestgate, Peterborough PE1 1JA,
Telephone: 01733 562030
E-mail: clerks@fennerschambers.co.uk
Call Date: July 1976, Gray's Inn
Qualifications: [LLB (Leeds)]

ESPRIT BENOIT

23 Harries Road
Hayes, Middlesex, UB4 9DD,
Telephone: 0181 841 8236
Call Date: Nov 1982, Inner Temple
Qualifications: [BA, BSc (Brunel), MA, LLM
(London), ADV.Dip.EDU (London)]

ESPRIT SHAUN ANDREW

One King's Bench Walk
1st Floor, Temple, London EC4Y 7DB,
Telephone: 0171 936 1500
E-mail: ddear@1kbw.co.uk
Call Date: Nov 1996, Lincoln's Inn
Qualifications: [BA (Hons), CPE]

ETHERINGTON DAVID CHARLES LYNCH QC (1998)

18 Red Lion Court
(Off Fleet Street), London EC4A 3EB,
Telephone: 0171 520 6000
E-mail: chambers@18rlc.co.uk
Thornwood House
102 New London Road, Chelmsford,
Essex, CM2 0RG,
Telephone: 01245 280880
E-mail: chambers@18rlc.co.uk
*Call Date: Nov 1979, Middle Temple
Assistant Recorder*
Qualifications: [BA, Dip Soc & Pub, Admin
(Oxon)]

ETHERTON MISS GILLIAN

1 Inner Temple Lane
Temple, London EC4Y 1AF,
Telephone: 020 7353 0933
*Call Date: July 1988, Middle Temple
Pupil Master*
Qualifications: [LLB (Hons)]

ETHERTON TERENCE MICHAEL ELKAN BARNET QC (1990)

Wilberforce Chambers
8 New Square, Lincoln's Inn, London
WC2A 3QP, Telephone: 0171 306 0102
E-mail: chambers@wilberforce.co.uk
Call Date: July 1974, Gray's Inn
Qualifications: [MA, LLM (Cantab), FCIArb]

Types of work: Banking, Commercial litigation, Commercial property, Equity, wills
and trusts, Financial services, Pensions,
Professional negligence

ETIENNE CLANCY ANTHONY

Chancery Chambers
1st Floor Offices, 70/72 Chancery Lane,
London WC2A 1AB,
Telephone: 0171 405 6879/6870
Call Date: Oct 1995, Middle Temple
Qualifications: [MA (Lond)]

EVANS ALAN

40 King Street
Manchester M2 6BA,
Telephone: 0161 832 9082
E-mail: clerks@40kingstreet.co.uk
The Chambers of Philip Raynor QC
5 Park Place, Leeds LS1 2RU,
Telephone: 0113 242 1123
*Call Date: July 1978, Lincoln's Inn
Pupil Master*
Qualifications: [MA, LLB (Cantab)]

EVANS ALUN HOWARD

2 King's Bench Walk Chambers
1st Floor, 2 King's Bench Walk, Temple,
London EC4Y 7DE,
Telephone: 020 7353 9276
E-mail: chambers@2kbw.co.uk
Westgate Chambers
144 High Street, Lewes, East Sussex,
BN7 1XT, Telephone: 01273 480510
*Call Date: Nov 1971, Gray's Inn
Pupil Master*
Qualifications: [BSc (Lond)]

EVANS ANDREW SUTHERLAND

10 King's Bench Walk
Ground Floor, Temple, London
EC4Y 7EB, Telephone: 0171 353 7742
E-mail: 10kbw@lineone.net
2 Paper Buildings, Basement North
Temple, London EC4Y 7ET,
Telephone: 0171 936 2613
E-mail: post@2paper.co.uk
Call Date: July 1984, Gray's Inn
Qualifications: [LLB (Manchester)]

EVANS MRS ANN

6 Gray's Inn Square
Ground Floor, Gray's Inn, London
WC1R 5AZ, Telephone: 0171 242 1052
E-mail: 6graysinn@clara.co.uk
Call Date: July 1983, Gray's Inn

EVANS BARNABY ST JOHN

4 King's Bench Walk
2nd Floor, Temple, London EC4Y 7DL,
Telephone: 020 7353 3581
E-mail: clerks@4kbw.co.uk
Call Date: July 1978, Inner Temple
Qualifications: [MA (Cantab)]

EVANS MISS CAROLINE MAY

12 King's Bench Walk
Temple, London EC4Y 7EL,
Telephone: 0171 583 0811
E-mail: chambers@12kbw.co.uk
Call Date: Oct 1991, Inner Temple
Qualifications: [MA (Cantab)]

EVANS MS CATRIN MIRANDA

1 Brick Court
1st Floor, Temple, London EC4Y 9BY,
Telephone: 0171 353 8845
E-mail: clerks@1brickcourt.co.uk
Call Date: Nov 1994, Inner Temple
Qualifications: [BA (Essex), CPE]

EVANS CHARLES HENRY FREDERICK

Goldsmith Chambers
Ground Floor, Goldsmith Building,
Temple, London EC4Y 7BL,
Telephone: 0171 353 6802/3/4/5
E-mail:clerks@goldsmithchambers.law.co.uk
*Call Date: Nov 1988, Middle Temple
Pupil Master*
Qualifications: [LLB]

EVANS MISS CLAIRE LOUISE

Peel Court Chambers
45 Hardman Street, Manchester M3 3PL,
Telephone: 0161 832 3791
E-mail: clerks@peelct.co.uk
Call Date: Oct 1994, Middle Temple
Qualifications: [BSc (Hons)(Manc), CPE
(Manc)]

EVANS MISS CLARE MARSHALL

**1 Gray's Inn Square, Chambers of the
Baroness Scotland of Asthal QC**
1st Floor, London WC1R 5AG,
Telephone: 0171 405 3000
E-mail: clerks@onegrays.demon.co.uk
Call Date: Oct 1995, Inner Temple
Qualifications: [BA (Lond), CPE]

EVANS DAVID ALEXANDER

Walnut House
63 St David's Hill, Exeter, Devon,
EX4 4DW, Telephone: 01392 279751
E-mail: 106627.2451@compuserve.com
Call Date: Mar 1996, Gray's Inn
Qualifications: [BA]

EVANS DAVID ANTHONY QC (1983)

9-12 Bell Yard
London WC2A 2LF,
Telephone: 0171 400 1800
E-mail: clerks@bellyard.co.uk
Call Date: July 1965, Gray's Inn
Recorder
Qualifications: [BA (Cantab)]

EVANS DAVID HOWARD QC (1991)

Hollis Whiteman Chambers
3rd Floor, Queen Elizabeth Bldg, Temple,
London EC4Y 9BS,
Telephone: 020 7583 5766
E-mail:barristers@holliswhiteman.co.uk
Call Date: Nov 1972, Middle Temple
Recorder
Qualifications: [MSc (Lond), BA (Oxon]

EVANS DAVID HUW

32 Park Place
Cardiff CF1 3BA,
Telephone: 01222 397364
Call Date: July 1985, Lincoln's Inn
Pupil Master
Qualifications: [BA (Hons)]

EVANS DAVID LEWIS

1 Crown Office Row
Ground Floor, Temple, London
EC4Y 7HH, Telephone: 0171 797 7500
E-mail: mail@onecrownofficerow.com
Call Date: July 1988, Middle Temple
Pupil Master
Qualifications: [MA (Hons)(Cantab)]

EVANS MISS DELYTH MARY

2 Mitre Court Buildings
1st Floor, Temple, London EC4Y 7BX,
Telephone: 0171 353 1353
Call Date: Oct 1991, Middle Temple
Pupil Master
Qualifications: [LLB (Hons, Lond)]

EVANS DYLAN

3 Temple Gardens
3rd Floor, Temple, London EC4Y 9AU,
Telephone: 0171 583 0010
Call Date: Apr 1989, Gray's Inn
Qualifications: [LLB (E Anglia), BA
(Hons)(Lond)]

EVANS MISS ELWEN MAIR

Iscoed Chambers
86 St Helen's Road, Swansea, West
Glamorgan, SA1 4BQ,
Telephone: 01792 652988/9/330
Call Date: July 1980, Gray's Inn
Pupil Master
Qualifications: [MA (Cantab)]

EVANS FRANCIS WALTON HERMIT QC (1994)

3 Raymond Buildings
Gray's Inn, London WC1R 5BH,
Telephone: 020 7831 3833
E-mail:chambers@threeraymond.demon.co.u
k
Call Date: July 1977, Middle Temple
Recorder
Qualifications: [BA]

EVANS FRANKLIN ST CLAIR MELVILLE

Chambers of Norman Palmer
2 Field Court, Gray's Inn, London
WC1R 5BB, Telephone: 0171 405 6114
E-mail: fieldct2@netcomuk.co.uk
Call Date: Nov 1981, Gray's Inn
Pupil Master
Qualifications: [BA Hons (Lancaster),]

EVANS GARETH ROBERT WILLIAM QC (1994)

5 Fountain Court
Steelhouse Lane, Birmingham B4 6DR,
Telephone: 0121 606 0500
E-mail:clerks@5fountaincourt.law.co.uk
Call Date: Nov 1973, Gray's Inn
Recorder
Qualifications: [LLB (Lond)]

EVANS HUGH LEWIS

Chambers of John L Powell QC
Four New Square, Lincoln's Inn, London
WC2A 3RJ, Telephone: 0171 797 8000
E-mail: barristers@4newsquare.com
Call Date: Nov 1987, Middle Temple
Pupil Master
Qualifications: [MA (Cantab), BCL (Oxon)]

EVANS JAMES FREDERICK MEURIG

3 Verulam Buildings
London WC1R 5NT,
Telephone: 0171 831 8441
E-mail: clerks@3verulam.co.uk
Call Date: Nov 1991, Gray's Inn
Qualifications: [BA (Cantab), LLM (Lond)]

EVANS MISS JANE LOIS

32 Park Place
Cardiff CF1 3BA,
Telephone: 01222 397364
Call Date: July 1971, Gray's Inn

EVANS MS JILL ANNALIESE

Doughty Street Chambers
11 Doughty Street, London WC1N 2PG,
Telephone: 0171 404 1313
E-mail:enquiries@doughtystreet.co.uk
Call Date: July 1986, Gray's Inn
Pupil Master
Qualifications: [BA (Hons) (Kent)]

EVANS JOHN

New Court Chambers
3 Broad Chare, Newcastle upon Tyne
NE1 3DQ, Telephone: 0191 232 1980
Call Date: Nov 1973, Gray's Inn
Pupil Master, Assistant Recorder
Qualifications: [BA]

EVANS JOHN WAINWRIGHT

1 Fountain Court
Steelhouse Lane, Birmingham B4 6DR,
Telephone: 0121 236 5721
Call Date: July 1983, Inner Temple
Qualifications: [LLB (Leic)]

EVANS JONATHAN EDWARD

Wilberforce Chambers
8 New Square, Lincoln's Inn, London
WC2A 3QP, Telephone: 0171 306 0102
E-mail: chambers@wilberforce.co.uk
Call Date: Nov 1994, Middle Temple
Qualifications: [BA (Hons)]

Types of work: Chancery (general), Commercial litigation, Commercial property, Landlord and tenant, Pensions, Professional negligence

EVANS MISS JUDI

St John's Chambers
Small Street, Bristol BS1 1DW,
Telephone: 0117 9213456/298514
E-mail: @stjohnschambers.co.uk
Call Date: Nov 1996, Middle Temple
Qualifications: [LLB (Hons)(Bucks), M.Phil (Cantab)]

EVANS JULIAN JACOB

Hollis Whiteman Chambers
3rd Floor, Queen Elizabeth Bldg, Temple,
London EC4Y 9BS,
Telephone: 020 7583 5766
E-mail:barristers@holliswhiteman.co.uk
Call Date: 1997, Middle Temple
Qualifications: [BA (Hons)(Cantab)]

EVANS KEITH ERIC

4 King's Bench Walk
Ground/First Floor/Basement, Temple,
London EC4Y 7DL,
Telephone: 0171 822 8822
E-mail: 4kbw@barristersatlaw.com
Call Date: Nov 1962, Middle Temple
Pupil Master
Qualifications: [MA (Cantab)]

EVANS LEE JOHN

Farrar's Building
Temple, London EC4Y 7BD,
Telephone: 0171 583 9241
E-mail:chambers@farrarsbuilding.co.uk
Call Date: Nov 1996, Gray's Inn
Qualifications: [MA (Cantab)]

EVANS MISS LISA CLAIRE

St Philip's Chambers
Fountain Court, Steelhouse Lane,
Birmingham B4 6DR,
Telephone: 0121 246 7000
E-mail: clerks@st-philips.co.uk
Call Date: Oct 1991, Inner Temple
Qualifications: [LLB (Hons)]

EVANS MARK QC (1995)

Queens Square Chambers
56 Queens Square, Bristol BS1 4PR,
Telephone: 0117 921 1966
Call Date: Nov 1971, Gray's Inn
Recorder
Qualifications: [LLB]

EVANS MARTIN ALAN LANGHAM

Five Paper Buildings
1st Floor, Five Paper Bldgs, Temple,
London EC4Y 7HB,
Telephone: 0171 583 6117
E-mail:clerks@5-paperbuildings.law.co.uk
Call Date: Nov 1989, Middle Temple
Qualifications: [BA Hons (Sussex), Dip Law]

EVANS MICHAEL RITHO

High Pavement Chambers
1 High Pavement, Nottingham NG1 1HF,
Telephone: 0115 9418218
Call Date: Nov 1988, Middle Temple
Qualifications: [LLB]

EVANS PAUL TIMOTHY

Exchange Chambers
Pearl Assurance House, Derby Square,
Liverpool L2 9XX,
Telephone: 0151 236 7747
E-mail:exchangechambers@btinternet.com
Call Date: Nov 1992, Gray's Inn
Qualifications: [MA (Oxon), LLM (Lond),
LLM (East Anglia)]

EVANS PHILIP

6 Gray's Inn Square
Ground Floor, Gray's Inn, London
WC1R 5AZ, Telephone: 0171 242 1052
E-mail: 6graysinn@clara.co.uk
Call Date: Oct 1995, Lincoln's Inn
Qualifications: [LLB (Hons)(Wales), MA
(Soton)]

EVANS RICHARD GARETH

5 Paper Buildings
Ground Floor, Temple, London
EC4Y 7HB, Telephone: 0171 583 9275/
583 4555 E-mail: 5paper@link.org
Call Date: Nov 1993, Lincoln's Inn
Qualifications: [LLB (Hons, Leeds)]

EVANS ROBERT JONATHAN

Keating Chambers
10 Essex Street, Outer Temple, London
WC2R 3AA, Telephone: 0171 544 2600
Call Date: July 1989, Gray's Inn
Pupil Master
Qualifications: [MA [Cantab], LLB [Lond],
C.Eng, M.I.C.E, FCIArb, MHKIE]

EVANS ROGER KENNETH

Harcourt Chambers
1st Floor, 2 Harcourt Buildings, Temple,
London EC4Y 9DB,
Telephone: 0171 353 6961
E-mail:clerks@harcourtchambers.law.co.uk
Harcourt Chambers
Churchill House, 3 St Aldate's Courtyard,
St Aldate's, Oxford OX1 1BN,
Telephone: 01865 791559
E-mail:clerks@harcourtchambers.law.co.uk
Call Date: Nov 1970, Middle Temple
Pupil Master, Assistant Recorder
Qualifications: [MA (Cantab)]

EVANS SIMEON VAUGHAN

Central Chambers
89 Princess Street, Manchester M1 4HT,
Telephone: 0161 236 1133
Call Date: Nov 1997, Lincoln's Inn
Qualifications: [BA (Hons)(Manch)]

EVANS STEPHEN JAMES

8 King's Bench Walk
2nd Floor, Temple, London EC4Y 7DU,
Telephone: 0171 797 8888
8 King's Bench Walk North
1 Park Square East, Leeds LS1 2NE,
Telephone: 0113 2439797
Call Date: Oct 1992, Middle Temple
Qualifications: [BA (Hons)]

EVANS STEVEN DAVID

Northampton Chambers
22 Albion Place, Northampton NN1 1UD,
Telephone: 01604 636271
Call Date: Oct 1997, Middle Temple
Qualifications: [LLB (Hons))(De Mont),
CQSW (Sheff)]

EVANS MISS SUSAN LOUISE CARR

St John's Chambers
Small Street, Bristol BS1 1DW,
Telephone: 0117 9213456/298514
E-mail: @stjohnschambers.co.uk
Call Date: Nov 1989, Gray's Inn
Qualifications: [LLB]

EVANS MISS SUZANNE MARIE

Oriel Chambers
14 Water Street, Liverpool L2 8TD,
Telephone: 0151 236 7191/236 4321
E-mail: clerks@oriel-chambers.co.uk
Call Date: Nov 1985, Middle Temple
Qualifications: [MA (Oxon)]

EVANS THOMAS GARETH

Rougemont Chambers
8 Colleton Crescent, Exeter, Devon,
EX1 1RR, Telephone: 01392 208484
E-mail:rougemont.chambers@eclipse.co.uk
Call Date: Oct 1996, Middle Temple
Qualifications: [LLB (Hons)(Exon)]

EVANS TIMOTHY AYLMER

Assize Court Chambers
14 Small Street, Bristol BS1 1DE,
Telephone: 0117 9264587
E-mail:chambers@assize-court-chambers.co.uk
Call Date: July 1982, Gray's Inn
Pupil Master
Qualifications: [LLB (Lond)]

EVANS TIMOTHY JOHN

33 Park Place
Cardiff CF1 3BA,
Telephone: 02920 233313
Call Date: July 1984, Gray's Inn
Pupil Master
Qualifications: [LLB (Nottm)]

EVANS TIMOTHY WENTWORTH EYRE

13 Old Square
Ground Floor, Lincoln's Inn, London
WC2A 3UA, Telephone: 0171 404 4800
E-mail: clerks@13oldsquare.law.co.uk
Call Date: July 1979, Lincoln's Inn
Pupil Master
Qualifications: [BA (Oxon)]

EVANS-GORDON MRS JANE-ANNE MARY

12 New Square
Lincoln's Inn, London WC2A 3SW,
Telephone: 0171 419 1212
E-mail: chambers@12newsquare.co.uk
Sovereign Chambers
25 Park Square, Leeds LS1 2PW,
Telephone: 0113 2451841/2/3
E-mail:sovereignchambers@btinternet.com
Call Date: Nov 1992, Inner Temple
Qualifications: [LLB (Reading)]

EVANS-TOVEY JASON ROBERT

Two Crown Office Row
Ground Floor, Temple, London
EC4Y 7HJ, Telephone: 020 7797 8100
E-mail: mail@2cor.co.uk, or to individual
barristers at: [barrister's
surname]@2cor.co.uk
Call Date: Oct 1990, Gray's Inn
Qualifications: [MA (Cantab), LLM]

EVERALL MARK ANDREW QC (1994)

1 Mitre Court Buildings
Temple, London EC4Y 7BS,
Telephone: 0171 797 7070
E-mail: clerks@1mcb.com
Call Date: Nov 1975, Inner Temple
Recorder
Qualifications: [MA (Oxon)]

EVERARD WILLIAM FIELDING

King Charles House
Standard Hill, Nottingham NG1 6FX,
Telephone: 0115 9418851
E-mail: clerks@kch.co.uk
Call Date: Nov 1973, Middle Temple
Pupil Master, Assistant Recorder
Qualifications: [LLB (Belfast)]

EVERED MRS JACLINE LANDIS

Inns of Court School of Law, 39 Eagle
Street, London WC1R 4AJ,
Telephone: 0171 404 5787 x 422
Call Date: Oct 1991, Middle Temple
Qualifications: [BA, Juris Doctorate]

EVEREST ROGER NORMAN JOSEPH

Everest
Twin Firs, PO Box 32, Talygarn, Pontyclun,
Cardiff, CF72 9BY,
Telephone: 01443 229850
Call Date: Nov 1968, Gray's Inn
Qualifications: [BA]

EVERETT STEVEN GEORGE

Sedan House
Stanley Place, Chester CH1 2LU,
Telephone: 01244 320480/348282
Call Date: Apr 1989, Gray's Inn
Pupil Master, Assistant Recorder
Qualifications: [BA]

EVISON JOHN

5 Pump Court
Ground Floor, Temple, London
EC4Y 7AP, Telephone: 020 7353 2532
E-mail: FivePump@netcomuk.co.uk
Call Date: July 1974, Lincoln's Inn
Pupil Master
Qualifications: [LLB (Lond)]

EWART DAVID SCOTT

Pump Court Tax Chambers
16 Bedford Row, London WC1R 4EB,
Telephone: 0171 414 8080
Call Date: Nov 1987, Gray's Inn
Pupil Master
Qualifications: [BA (Oxon)]

EWING HARALD RICHARD WOLF

King Charles House
Standard Hill, Nottingham NG1 6FX,
Telephone: 0115 9418851
E-mail: clerks@kch.co.uk
Call Date: Nov 1997, Gray's Inn
Qualifications: [BA (Cantab)]

EWINS MISS CATHERINE JANE

4 Paper Buildings
Ground Floor, Temple, London
EC4Y 7EX, Telephone: 0171 353 3366/
583 7155
E-mail: clerks@4paperbuildings.com
Call Date: Nov 1995, Gray's Inn
Qualifications: [BA , Licence Speciale En,
Droit European, U.L.B. (Brussels), MA
(Cantab)]

EWINS DAVID JAMES

Queen Elizabeth Building
2nd Floor, Temple, London EC4Y 9BS,
Telephone: 0171 797 7837
Call Date: 1996, Middle Temple
Qualifications: [BA (Hons)]

EXALL GORDON DAVID

Chambers of Andrew Campbell QC
10 Park Square, Leeds LS1 2LH,
Telephone: 0113 2455438
E-mail: clerks@10pksq.co.uk
Call Date: Apr 1991, Lincoln's Inn
Qualifications: [BA (Warwick)]

EYERS ANTHONY

24a St John Street
Manchester M3 4DF,
Telephone: 0161 833 9628
Call Date: Nov 1994, Inner Temple
Qualifications: [BA (Oxon), CPE (Lond)]

EYRE GILES STEPHEN

2 Gray's Inn Square Chambers
2nd Floor, Gray's Inn, London WC1R 5AA,
Telephone: 020 7242 0328
E-mail: clerks@2gis.co.uk
Call Date: July 1974, Gray's Inn
Pupil Master
Qualifications: [LLB]

EYRE SIR GRAHAM NEWMAN QC (1970)

2-3 Gray's Inn Square
Gray's Inn, London WC1R 5JH,
Telephone: 0171 242 4986
E-mail:chambers@2-3graysinnsquare.co.uk
Call Date: Nov 1954, Middle Temple
Recorder
Qualifications: [MA, LLB (Cantab)]

EYRE STEPHEN JOHN ARTHUR

1 Fountain Court
Steelhouse Lane, Birmingham B4 6DR,
Telephone: 0121 236 5721
Call Date: July 1981, Inner Temple
Pupil Master
Qualifications: [MA, BCL (Oxon)]

EZECHIE NICHOLAS DIDEKI ASIAELUE

Odogor Chambers
14 Cairns Road, Battersea, London
SW11 1ES,
Call Date: July 1967, Gray's Inn
Qualifications: [LLB (Lond)]

EZECHIE MISS NICHOLINA NKEMDILIM

5 Marney Road
Battersea, London SW11 1ES,
Telephone: 0171 978 4492
Call Date: July 1990, Gray's Inn
Qualifications: [LLB]

EZEKIEL MS ADINA SEJI

6 King's Bench Walk
Ground Floor, Temple, London
EC4Y 7DR, Telephone: 0171 583 0410
E-mail: worsley@6kbw.freeserve.co.uk
Call Date: 1997, Inner Temple
Qualifications: [LLB (London)]

FABER TREVOR MARTYN

3 Fountain Court
Steelhouse Lane, Birmingham B4 6DR,
Telephone: 0121 236 5854
Call Date: July 1970, Gray's Inn
Pupil Master, Recorder
Qualifications: [MA (Oxon)]

FADIPE GABRIEL CHARLES

Wilberforce Chambers
8 New Square, Lincoln's Inn, London
WC2A 3QP, Telephone: 0171 306 0102
E-mail: chambers@wilberforce.co.uk
Call Date: Nov 1991, Inner Temple
Qualifications: [BA (Kent), M.EN.D.
(Bordeaux)]

Types of work: Bankruptcy, Chancery
(general), Commercial litigation, Equity,
wills and trusts, Insolvency, Insurance,
Landlord and tenant, Partnerships,
Pensions, Professional negligence

FAGAN MISS CATHERINE JOSEPHINE

Baker Street Chambers
9 Baker Street, Middlesbrough TS1 2LF,
Telephone: 01642 873873
Call Date: Oct 1993, Gray's Inn
Qualifications: [BA (Hons)]

FAIRBANK NICHOLAS JAMES

Becket Chambers
17 New Dover Road, Canterbury, Kent,
CT1 3AS, Telephone: 01227 786331
Call Date: 1996, Lincoln's Inn
Qualifications: [MA (Hons)(Cantab), CPE]

FAIRBURN GEORGE EDWARD HENRY

Claremont Chambers
26 Waterloo Road, Wolverhampton
WV1 4BL, Telephone: 01902 426222
Call Date: Oct 1995, Lincoln's Inn
Qualifications: [BSc (Hons)]

FAIRHEAD ALLEN JOHN HUBERT

5 King's Bench Walk
Temple, London EC4Y 7DN,
Telephone: 0171 353 5638
Call Date: Nov 1978, Middle Temple
Pupil Master
Qualifications: [BA (Dunelm)]

FALK CHARLES MORTON JAMES

Staple Inn Chambers
1st Floor, 9 Staple Inn, Holborn Bars,
London WC1V 7QH,
Telephone: 0171 242 5240
E-mail: clerks@staple-inn.org
Call Date: Oct 1994, Middle Temple
Qualifications: [BA (Hons)(Keele), CPE
(Middx)]

FALK MISS JOSEPHINE RUTH ANN

12 Old Square
1st Floor, Lincoln's Inn, London
WC2A 3TX, Telephone: 0171 404 0875
Call Date: Nov 1994, Lincoln's Inn
Qualifications: [MA (Cantab), Dip in Law]

FALKENSTEIN JOHN ROY

Milburn House Chambers
'A' Floor, Milburn House, Dean Street,
Newcastle upon Tyne NE1 1LE,
Telephone: 0191 230 5511
E-mail:milburnhousechambers@btinternet.com
Call Date: Oct 1996, Lincoln's Inn
Qualifications: [BA (Hons)]

FALKOWSKI DAMIAN

Littman Chambers
12 Gray's Inn Square, London WC1R 5JP,
Telephone: 020 7404 4866
E-mail: admin@littmanchambers.com
Call Date: Oct 1994, Gray's Inn
Qualifications: [ARCM, B.Mus, M.Mus,
LLDip]

FALLOWS MISS MARY PAULA

Cobden House Chambers
19 Quay Street, Manchester M3 3HN,
Telephone: 0161 833 6000
E-mail: clerks@cobden.co.uk
Call Date: 1981, Lincoln's Inn
Qualifications: [BA (Hons)]

FALUYI ALBERT OSAMUDIAMEN

Chambers of Martin Burr
Fourth Floor, Eldon Chambers, 30/32
Fleet Street, London EC4Y 1AA,
Telephone: 0171 353 4636
Call Date: Nov 1995, Inner Temple
Qualifications: [BA (Nigeria), MA (Nigeria),
LLB (Lond)]

FAMA MRS GUDRUN HILDEGARD

Phoenix Chambers
First Floor, Gray's Inn Chambers, Gray's
Inn, London WC1R 5JA,
Telephone: 0171 404 7888
E-mail:clerks@phoenix-chambers.co.uk
Call Date: Oct 1991, Gray's Inn
Pupil Master
Qualifications: [BA, MA, LLB]

FANCOURT TIMOTHY MILES

Falcon Chambers
Falcon Court, London EC4Y 1AA,
Telephone: 0171 353 2484
E-mail: clerks@falcon-chambers.com
Call Date: Nov 1987, Lincoln's Inn
Pupil Master
Qualifications: [MA (Cantab)]

FANE MISS ANGELA ELIZABETH

Goldsmith Building
1st Floor, Temple, London EC4Y 7BL,
Telephone: 0171 353 7881
E-mail:clerks@goldsmith-building.law.co.uk
Call Date: Nov 1992, Middle Temple
Qualifications: [BA]

FARBER JAMES HENRY MARTIN

5 Stone Buildings
Lincoln's Inn, London WC2A 3XT,
Telephone: 0171 242 6201
E-mail:clerks@5-stonebuildings.law.co.uk
Call Date: July 1976, Gray's Inn
Pupil Master

FARBEY MISS JUDITH SARAH

Plowden Buildings
2nd Floor, 2 Plowden Buildings, Middle
Temple Lane, London EC4Y 9BU,
Telephone: 0171 583 0808
E-mail: bar@plowdenbuildings.co.uk
Call Date: Oct 1992, Middle Temple
Qualifications: [BA (Hons)(Oxon), Dip Law
(City)]

FARLEY ROGER BOYD QC (1993)

40 King Street
Manchester M2 6BA,
Telephone: 0161 832 9082
E-mail: clerks@40kingstreet.co.uk
The Chambers of Philip Raynor QC
5 Park Place, Leeds LS1 2RU,
Telephone: 0113 242 1123
2-4 Tudor Street
London EC4Y 0AA,
Telephone: 0171 797 7111
E-mail: clerks@rfqc.co.uk
Call Date: May 1974, Middle Temple
Recorder
Qualifications: [LLB (L'pool)]

FARMER GABRIEL JOHN-HENRY

Guildhall Chambers
22-26 Broad Street, Bristol BS1 2HG,
Telephone: 0117 9273366
E-mail:civil.clerks@guildhallchambers.co.uk and
criminal.clerks@guildhallchambers.co.uk
Call Date: Nov 1994, Gray's Inn
Qualifications: [BSc (Reading)]

FARMER JOHN MICHAEL HEREWARD

1 Paper Buildings
1st Floor, Temple, London EC4Y 7EP,
Telephone: 0171 353 3728/4953
Call Date: Nov 1970, Gray's Inn
Pupil Master
Qualifications: [MA (Cantab)]

FARMER DR KIMBERLY

4 King's Bench Walk
Ground/First Floor/Basement, Temple,
London EC4Y 7DL,
Telephone: 0171 822 8822
E-mail: 4kbw@barristersatlaw.com
Call Date: Mar 1997, Inner Temple
Qualifications: [BA (Louisiana), MPhil, MA
(Boston), CPE (Lond)]

FARMER MATTHEW JONATHAN

2 Harcourt Buildings
1st Floor, Temple, London EC4Y 9DB,
Telephone: 020 7353 2112
Call Date: July 1987, Inner Temple
Pupil Master
Qualifications: [BA (Lond), Dip Law]

FARMER PRYCE MICHAEL QC (1995)

Goldsmith Building
1st Floor, Temple, London EC4Y 7BL,
Telephone: 0171 353 7881
E-mail:clerks@goldsmith-building.law.co.uk
Sedan House
Stanley Place, Chester CH1 2LU,
Telephone: 01244 320480/348282
Call Date: July 1972, Gray's Inn
Recorder
Qualifications: [BA (Lond)]

FARMER MS SARAH LOUISE

Thomas More Chambers
52 Carey Street, Lincoln's Inn, London
WC2A 2JB, Telephone: 0171 404 7000
E-mail: clerks@thomasmore.law.co.uk
Call Date: Nov 1991, Lincoln's Inn
Pupil Master
Qualifications: [BA (Hons) (Oxon)]

FARNON MS PATRICIA RONA GABRIELLE

1 Pump Court
Lower Ground Floor, Temple, London
EC4Y 7AB, Telephone: 0171 583 2012/
353 4341
E-mail: [name]@1pumpcourt.co.uk
Call Date: Nov 1986, Inner Temple
Qualifications: [LLB (Lond)]

FARQUHAR STUART ALASTAIR

St Mary's Chambers
50 High Pavement, Lace Market,
Nottingham NG1 1HW,
Telephone: 0115 9503503
E-mail: clerks@smc.law.co.uk
Call Date: July 1985, Inner Temple
Pupil Master
Qualifications: [LLB (Manchester)]

FARQUHARSON MISS JANE CAROLINE

One Essex Court
1st Floor, Temple, London EC4Y 9AR,
Telephone: 0171 936 3030
E-mail: one.essex_court@virgin.net
Call Date: Oct 1993, Inner Temple
Qualifications: [LLB]

FARQUHARSON JONATHAN

Colleton Chambers
Colleton Crescent, Exeter, Devon,
EX2 4DG, Telephone: 01392 274898/9
Call Date: July 1988, Inner Temple
Qualifications: [BA (Hons) (Dunelm)]

FARR MISS SUSANNAH MARGARET

5 King's Bench Walk
Temple, London EC4Y 7DN,
Telephone: 0171 353 5638
Call Date: July 1990, Inner Temple
Qualifications: [BA (E Anglia), Dip Law]

FARRELL DAVID ANTHONY

Chambers of Michael Pert QC
36 Bedford Row, London WC1R 4JH,
Telephone: 0171 421 8000
E-mail: 36bedfordrow@link.org
Chambers of Michael Pert QC
24 Albion Place, Northampton NN1 1UD,
Telephone: 01604 602333
Chambers of Michael Pert QC
104 New Walk, Leicester LE1 7EA,
Telephone: 0116 249 2020
Call Date: July 1978, Inner Temple
Pupil Master, Assistant Recorder
Qualifications: [LLB (Manch)]

FARRELL EDMUND GILBERT

Chambers of Michael Pert QC
36 Bedford Row, London WC1R 4JH,
Telephone: 0171 421 8000
E-mail: 36bedfordrow@link.org
Chambers of Michael Pert QC
24 Albion Place, Northampton NN1 1UD,
Telephone: 01604 602333
Chambers of Michael Pert QC
104 New Walk, Leicester LE1 7EA,
Telephone: 0116 249 2020
Call Date: July 1981, Gray's Inn
Pupil Master
Qualifications: [LLM (Cantab), LLB Hons]

FARRELL SIMON HENRY

Two Garden Court
1st Floor, Middle Temple, London
EC4Y 9BL, Telephone: 0171 353 1633
E-mail:barristers@2gardenct.law.co.uk
Call Date: Nov 1983, Lincoln's Inn
Pupil Master
Qualifications: [MA(Cantab) Dip Law C]

FARRELLY KEVIN JAMES

The Chambers of Leolin Price CBE, QC
10 Old Square, Lincoln's Inn, London
WC2A 3SU, Telephone: 0171 405 0758
Call Date: May 1993, Middle Temple
Qualifications: [BA (Hons)]

FARRER ADAM MICHAEL

4 Fountain Court
Steelhouse Lane, Birmingham B4 6DR,
Telephone: 0121 236 3476
Call Date: Oct 1992, Gray's Inn
Qualifications: [LL.B (Nott'n)]

FARRER DAVID JOHN QC (1986)

9 Bedford Row
London WC1R 4AZ,
Telephone: 0171 242 3555
E-mail: clerks@9br.co.uk
Call Date: Apr 1967, Middle Temple
Recorder
Qualifications: [MA (Cantab), LLB]

FARRER PAUL AINSWORTH

1 Fountain Court
Steelhouse Lane, Birmingham B4 6DR,
Telephone: 0121 236 5721
Call Date: Feb 1988, Gray's Inn
Qualifications: [LLB (Nottm)]

FARRIMOND MISS STEPHANIE ANNE

5 Essex Court
1st Floor, Temple, London EC4Y 9AH,
Telephone: 0171 410 2000
E-mail: barristers@5essexcourt.co.uk
Call Date: July 1987, Middle Temple
Pupil Master
Qualifications: [LLB (Essex)]

FARRINGTON DAVID

3 Gray's Inn Square
Ground Floor, London WC1R 5AH,
Telephone: 0171 520 5600
E-mail: clerks@3gis.co.uk
Call Date: July 1972, Middle Temple
Pupil Master
Qualifications: [LLB]

FARROR MISS SHELAGH ANN

Queen Elizabeth Building
Ground Floor, Temple, London
EC4Y 9BS,
Telephone: 0171 353 7181 (12 Lines)
Call Date: Nov 1970, Middle Temple
Pupil Master
Qualifications: [MA (Oxon)]

FARROW ADRIAN JOHN

Cobden House Chambers
19 Quay Street, Manchester M3 3HN,
Telephone: 0161 833 6000
E-mail: clerks@cobden.co.uk
Call Date: July 1997, Middle Temple
Qualifications: [LLB (Hons)(Leics)]

FARROW KENNETH JOHN

Serle Court Chambers
6 New Square, Lincoln's Inn, London
WC2A 3QS, Telephone: 0171 242 6105
E-mail: clerks@serlecourt.co.uk
Call Date: July 1966, Gray's Inn
Recorder
Qualifications: [MA, BCL (Oxon)]

FAUL MISS ANNE FRANCES LOUISE

Lamb Building
Ground Floor, Temple, London
EC4Y 7AS, Telephone: 020 7797 7788
E-mail: lamb.building@link.org
Call Date: 1996, Middle Temple
Qualifications: [LLB (Hons)(Greenwi)]

FAULKS EDWARD PETER LAWLESS QC (1996)

No. 1 Serjeants' Inn
5th Floor Fleet Street, Temple, London
EC4Y 1LH, Telephone: 0171 415 6666
E-mail:no1serjeantsinn@btinternet.com
Call Date: Nov 1973, Middle Temple
Assistant Recorder
Qualifications: [MA (Oxon)]

FAULKS SAMUEL JAMES

Broad Chare
33 Broad Chare, Newcastle upon Tyne
NE1 3DQ, Telephone: 0191 232 0541
E-mail:clerks@broadcharechambers.law.co.uk
Call Date: Oct 1997, Inner Temple
Qualifications: [LLB (Northumbria)]

FAUX ANDREW JOHN

Rowchester Chambers
4 Rowchester Court, Whittall Street,
Birmingham B4 6DH,
Telephone: 0121 233 2327/2361951
Call Date: Nov 1995, Inner Temple
Qualifications: [BA (Sheff), CPE (Manc)]

FAUX MISS RACHEL ELIZABETH

18 St John Street
Manchester M3 4EA,
Telephone: 0161 278 1800
E-mail: 18stjohn@lineone.net
Call Date: 1997, Lincoln's Inn
Qualifications: [LLB (Hons)(Notts)]

FAWCETT GARY

Eighteen Carlton Crescent
Southampton SO15 2XR,
Telephone: 01703 639001
Call Date: Nov 1975, Lincoln's Inn
Pupil Master
Qualifications: [LLB (Soton)]

FAWCETT MISS MICHELLE EVELYN

Maidstone Chambers
33 Earl Street, Maidstone, Kent, ME14 1PF,
Telephone: 01622 688592
E-mail:maidstonechambers@compuserve.com
Call Date: Nov 1993, Inner Temple
Qualifications: [LLB (Kent)]

FAWLS RICHARD GRANVILLE

5 Stone Buildings
Lincoln's Inn, London WC2A 3XT,
Telephone: 0171 242 6201
E-mail:clerks@5-stonebuildings.law.co.uk
Call Date: July 1973, Inner Temple
Qualifications: [LLB (Lond)]

FAY MICHAEL JOHN

Call Date: July 1989, Lincoln's Inn
Qualifications: [LLB]

FEALY MICHAEL

One Essex Court
Ground Floor, Temple, London
EC4Y 9AR, Telephone: 020 7583 2000
E-mail: clerks@oneessexcourt.co.uk
Call Date: May 1997, Middle Temple
Qualifications: [BCL (Dublin)]

FEATHERBY WILLIAM ALAN

12 King's Bench Walk
Temple, London EC4Y 7EL,
Telephone: 0171 583 0811
E-mail: chambers@12kbw.co.uk
Call Date: Nov 1978, Middle Temple
Pupil Master
Qualifications: [MA (Oxon)]

FEATHERSTONE JASON NEIL

Virtual Chambers
(accepting briefs soon), London
Telephone: 07071 244 944
E-mail:enquiries@virtualchambers.org.uk
Barristers' Common Law Chambers
57 Whitechapel Road, Aldgate East,
London E1 1DU,
Telephone: 0171 375 3012
E-mail: barristers@hotmail.com and
barristers@lawchambers.freeserve.co.uk
Call Date: Nov 1995, Inner Temple
Qualifications: [LLB (Newc)]

FEDER AMI

Lamb Building
Ground Floor, Temple, London
EC4Y 7AS, Telephone: 020 7797 7788
E-mail: lamb.building@link.org
Call Date: July 1965, Inner Temple
Qualifications: [LLB]

FEEHAN FRANCIS THOMAS

22 Old Buildings
Lincoln's Inn, London WC2A 3UJ,
Telephone: 0171 831 0222
Call Date: July 1988, Lincoln's Inn
Pupil Master
Qualifications: [BA (Hons) (Cantab)]

FEENY CHARLES SHERIDAN

Castle Street Chambers
2nd Floor, 42 Castle Street, Liverpool
L2 7LD, Telephone: 0151 242 0500
Call Date: Nov 1977, Inner Temple
Pupil Master
Qualifications: [BA (Cantab)]

FEEST ADAM SEBASTIAN

2 King's Bench Walk
Ground Floor, Temple, London
EC4Y 7DE, Telephone: 0171 353 1746
E-mail: 2kbw@atlas.co.uk
King's Bench Chambers
115 North Hill, Plymouth PL4 8JY,
Telephone: 01752 221551
Call Date: Feb 1994, Inner Temple
Qualifications: [BA (Oxon)]

FEETHAM DANIEL ANTHONY

Merchant Chambers
1 North Parade, Parsonage Gardens,
Manchester M3 2NH,
Telephone: 0161 839 7070
E-mail: merchant.chambers@virgin.net
Call Date: Feb 1994, Gray's Inn
Qualifications: [BA (Reading), LLB (Manc)]

FEINBERG PETER ERIC QC (1992)

2-4 Tudor Street
London EC4Y 0AA,
Telephone: 0171 797 7111
E-mail: clerks@rfqc.co.uk
Park Court Chambers
16 Park Place, Leeds LS1 2SJ,
Telephone: 0113 2433277
Call Date: July 1972, Inner Temple
Recorder
Qualifications: [LLB (Lond)]

FELDMAN MATTHEW RICHARD BANKES

Staple Inn Chambers
1st Floor, 9 Staple Inn, Holborn Bars,
London WC1V 7QH,
Telephone: 0171 242 5240
E-mail: clerks@staple-inn.org
Call Date: Oct 1995, Inner Temple
Qualifications: [BA Joint(Hons)(Manc), CPE]

FELL ALISTAIR ALEXANDER

Chambers of Wilfred Forster-Jones
New Court, 1st Floor South, Temple,
London EC4Y 9BE,
Telephone: 0171 353 0853/4/7222
E-mail: chambers@newcourt.net
Call Date: Nov 1994, Middle Temple
Qualifications: [LLB (Hons), LLM]

FELTHAM PIERS JONATHAN

Chambers of Mr Peter Crampin QC
Ground Floor, 11 New Square, Lincoln's
Inn, London WC2A 3QB,
Telephone: 020 7831 0081
E-mail: 11newsquare.co.uk
Call Date: July 1985, Gray's Inn
Pupil Master
Qualifications: [BA (Cantab)]

FEMI-OLA ABIODUN JOHN

2 Paper Buildings
1st Floor, Temple, London EC4Y 7ET,
Telephone: 020 7556 5500
E-mail: clerks@2pbbarristers.co.uk
Call Date: Nov 1985, Gray's Inn
Pupil Master
Qualifications: [BA]

FENDER CARL DAVID

Regency Chambers
Cathedral Square, Peterborough
PE1 1XW, Telephone: 01733 315215
Regency Chambers
Sheraton House, Castle Park, Cambridge
CB3 0AX, Telephone: 01223 301517
Call Date: Feb 1994, Middle Temple
Qualifications: [BA (Hons)(Kent)]

FENHALLS MARK ROYDON ALLEN

23 Essex Street
London WC2R 3AS,
Telephone: 0171 413 0353/836 8366
E-mail:clerks@essexstreet23.demon.co.uk
Call Date: Oct 1992, Gray's Inn
Qualifications: [BA, M.Sc]

FENN PETER JOHN

18 Red Lion Court
(Off Fleet Street), London EC4A 3EB,
Telephone: 0171 520 6000
E-mail: chambers@18rlc.co.uk
Call Date: July 1979, Middle Temple
Pupil Master
Qualifications: [MA (Oxon)]

FENNY IAN CHARLES

Guildhall Chambers
22-26 Broad Street, Bristol BS1 2HG,
Telephone: 0117 9273366
E-mail:civil.clerks@guildhallchambers.co.uk and
criminal.clerks@guildhallchambers.co.uk
Call Date: July 1978, Gray's Inn
Pupil Master
Qualifications: [LLB]

FENSTON MISS FELICIA DONOVAN

2 Harcourt Buildings
Ground Floor/Left, Temple, London
EC4Y 9DB, Telephone: 0171 583 9020
E-mail: clerks@harcourt.co.uk
Call Date: Nov 1994, Inner Temple
Qualifications: [BA (Oxon)]

FENTON ADAM TIMOTHY DOWNS

S Tomlinson QC
7 King's Bench Walk, Temple, London
EC4Y 7DS, Telephone: 0171 583 0404
E-mail: clerks@7kbw.law.co.uk
Call Date: Nov 1984, Inner Temple
Pupil Master
Qualifications: [BA (Oxon)]

FENWICK JUSTIN FRANCIS QUINTUS QC (1993)

Chambers of John L Powell QC
Four New Square, Lincoln's Inn, London
WC2A 3RJ, Telephone: 0171 797 8000
E-mail: barristers@4newsquare.com
Call Date: Nov 1980, Inner Temple
Assistant Recorder
Qualifications: [MA (Cantab)]

FERGUSON CHRISTOPHER MARK

Assize Court Chambers
14 Small Street, Bristol BS1 1DE,
Telephone: 0117 9264587
E-mail:chambers@assize-court-chambers.co.uk
Pepys' Chambers
17 Fleet Street, London EC4Y 1AA,
Telephone: 0171 936 2710
Call Date: May 1979, Middle Temple
Pupil Master

FERGUSON CRAIG CHARLES

1 Hare Court
Ground Floor, Temple, London
EC4Y 7BE, Telephone: 0171 353 3982/5324
Call Date: Feb 1992, Middle Temple
Qualifications: [LLB (Hons)]

FERGUSON FREDERICK MORRIS GIFFORD

9 Gough Square
London EC4A 3DE,
Telephone: 020 7832 0500
E-mail: clerks@9goughsq.co.uk
Call Date: July 1978, Middle Temple
Pupil Master
Qualifications: [BA (Oxon)]

FERGUSON MRS KATHARINE ANN

Fenners Chambers
3 Madingley Road, Cambridge CB3 0EE,
Telephone: 01223 368761
E-mail: clerks@fennerschambers.co.uk
Fenners Chambers
8-12 Priestgate, Peterborough PE1 1JA,
Telephone: 01733 562030
E-mail: clerks@fennerschambers.co.uk
Call Date: Feb 1995, Inner Temple
Qualifications: [BA (Oxon)]

FERGUSON NIALL

Chambers of Michael Pert QC
36 Bedford Row, London WC1R 4JH,
Telephone: 0171 421 8000
E-mail: 36bedfordrow@link.org
Chambers of Michael Pert QC
24 Albion Place, Northampton NN1 1UD,
Telephone: 01604 602333
Chambers of Michael Pert QC
104 New Walk, Leicester LE1 7EA,
Telephone: 0116 249 2020
Call Date: July 1996, Middle Temple
Qualifications: [BA (Hons)(Dunelm)]

FERGUSON RICHARD QC (1986)

2-4 Tudor Street
London EC4Y 0AA,
Telephone: 0171 797 7111
E-mail: clerks@rfqc.co.uk
Call Date: 1956, Gray's Inn
Qualifications: [LLB, BA]

FERGUSON STEPHEN MICHAEL

1 Paper Buildings
1st Floor, Temple, London EC4Y 7EP,
Telephone: 0171 353 3728/4953
Call Date: Nov 1991, Inner Temple
Qualifications: [BA (Oxon)]

FERM RODNEY ERIC

37 Park Square Chambers
37 Park Square, Leeds LS1 2NY,
Telephone: 0113 2439422
E-mail: chambers@no37.co.uk
Call Date: July 1972, Middle Temple
Pupil Master
Qualifications: [BA (Oxon)]

FERN GARY

7 New Square
1st Floor, Lincoln's Inn, London
WC2A 3QS, Telephone: 020 7404 5484
E-mail: clerks@7newsquare.com
Call Date: Oct 1992, Lincoln's Inn
Qualifications: [B.Eng (Hons), CPE, LLM]

FERNANDO GILES RUDYARD

11 South Square
2nd Floor, Gray's Inn, London
WC1R 5EU,
Telephone: 0171 405 1222 (24hr messaging service)
E-mail: clerks@11southsquare.com
Call Date: 1998, Gray's Inn
Qualifications: [BA (Oxon)]

FERNYHOUGH RICHARD QC (1986)

Keating Chambers
10 Essex Street, Outer Temple, London
WC2R 3AA, Telephone: 0171 544 2600
Call Date: Nov 1970, Middle Temple
Recorder
Qualifications: [LLB, FCIArb]

FERRARI MS SARAH JANE

17 Carlton Crescent
Southampton SO15 2XR,
Telephone: 023 8032 0320/0823 2003
E-mail: greg@jg17cc.co.uk
Call Date: Nov 1993, Gray's Inn
Qualifications: [LLB]

FERRIER IAN GILBERT STRATON

8 Gray's Inn Square
Gray's Inn, London WC1R 5AZ,
Telephone: 0171 242 3529
Call Date: July 1976, Middle Temple
Pupil Master
Qualifications: [MA (Oxon)]

FERRIER MRS SUSAN

9 Park Place
Cardiff CF1 3DP,
Telephone: 01222 382731
Call Date: Nov 1985, Gray's Inn
Qualifications: [BSc (Hons)(Cardiff)]

FERRIS MS CAITLIN TARA

New Court
Temple, London EC4Y 9BE,
Telephone: 0171 583 5123/0510
Call Date: Mar 1996, Inner Temple
Qualifications: [BA (Leeds)]

FERRIS JONATHAN MORETON

29 Bedford Row Chambers
London WC1R 4HE,
Telephone: 0171 831 2626
Call Date: Nov 1979, Middle Temple
Pupil Master, Assistant Recorder
Qualifications: [BA (Dunelm)]

FERRIS SHAUN

One Paper Buildings
Ground Floor, Temple, London
EC4Y 7EP, Telephone: 0171 583 7355
E-mail: clerks@1pb.co.uk
Call Date: Nov 1985, Gray's Inn
Pupil Master
Qualifications: [BA (Oxon)]

FESSAL IGNATIUS

8 King's Bench Walk
2nd Floor, Temple, London EC4Y 7DU,
Telephone: 0171 797 8888
8 King's Bench Walk North
1 Park Square East, Leeds LS1 2NE,
Telephone: 0113 2439797
Call Date: Nov 1981, Inner Temple
Qualifications: [LLB]

FETHERSTONHAUGH GUY CUTHBERT CHARLES

Falcon Chambers
Falcon Court, London EC4Y 1AA,
Telephone: 0171 353 2484
E-mail: clerks@falcon-chambers.com
Call Date: July 1983, Inner Temple
Pupil Master
Qualifications: [BSc (Bris)]

FEWTRELL NICHOLAS AUSTIN

18 St John Street
Manchester M3 4EA,
Telephone: 0161 278 1800
E-mail: 18stjohn@lineone.net
Call Date: Nov 1977, Inner Temple
Pupil Master
Qualifications: [LLB (Lond)]

FFITCH NIGEL ANTHONY

Trafalgar Chambers
53 Fleet Street, London EC4Y 1BE,
Telephone: 0171 583 5858
E-mail:trafalgarchambers@easynet.co.uk
Call Date: Oct 1996, Gray's Inn
Qualifications: [LLB (Hons) (Lond)]

FIELD MISS AMANDA JANE

Queen Elizabeth Building
Ground Floor, Temple, London
EC4Y 9BS,
Telephone: 0171 353 7181 (12 Lines)
Call Date: Feb 1994, Middle Temple
Qualifications: [MA (Dublin)]

FIELD JULIAN NIGEL

One Paper Buildings
Ground Floor, Temple, London
EC4Y 7EP, Telephone: 0171 583 7355
E-mail: clerks@1pb.co.uk
Call Date: Nov 1980, Gray's Inn
Pupil Master
Qualifications: [LLB (Lond)]

FIELD MARTIN CHARLES

9-12 Bell Yard
London WC2A 2LF,
Telephone: 0171 400 1800
E-mail: clerks@bellyard.co.uk
Call Date: Nov 1966, Inner Temple
Pupil Master, Recorder

FIELD PATRICK JOHN

Deans Court Chambers
24 St John Street, Manchester M3 4DF,
Telephone: 0161 214 6000
E-mail: clerks@deanscourt.co.uk

Deans Court Chambers
41-43 Market Place, Preston PR1 1AH,
Telephone: 01772 555163
E-mail: clerks@deanscourt.co.uk
Call Date: Nov 1981, Gray's Inn
Pupil Master
Qualifications: [LLB (Lond)]

FIELD RICHARD ALAN QC (1987)

11 King's Bench Walk
Temple, London EC4Y 7EQ,
Telephone: 0171 632 8500/583 0610
E-mail: clerksroom@11kbw.com
Call Date: July 1977, Inner Temple
Recorder
Qualifications: [LLB (Bristol) LLM, (Lond)]

FIELD RORY DOMINIC

Hardwicke Building
New Square, Lincoln's Inn, London
WC2A 3SB, Telephone: 020 7242 2523
E-mail: clerks@hardwicke.co.uk
Call Date: July 1980, Middle Temple
Qualifications: [BA (Hons) (Cantab)]

FIELD STEPHEN ANTHONY

Counsels' Chambers
2nd Floor, 10-11 Gray's Inn Square,
London WC1R 5JD,
Telephone: 0171 405 2576
E-mail:clerks@10-11graysinnsquare.co.uk
Call Date: Nov 1993, Gray's Inn
Qualifications: [LLB (Lond)]

FIELDEN DR CHRISTA MARIA

6 King's Bench Walk
Ground, Third & Fourth Floors, Temple,
London EC4Y 7DR,
Telephone: 0171 353 4931/583 0695
Call Date: Nov 1982, Lincoln's Inn
Pupil Master
Qualifications: [BSc, MSc, PhD]

FIELDHOUSE NIGEL RICHARD ARNOLD

Cobden House Chambers
19 Quay Street, Manchester M3 3HN,
Telephone: 0161 833 6000
E-mail: clerks@cobden.co.uk
Call Date: July 1976, Gray's Inn
Pupil Master
Qualifications: [LLB (Hons)]

FIELDS MISS HELEN SARAH

Pump Court Chambers
31 Southgate Street, Winchester
SO23 9EE, Telephone: 01962 868161
E-mail: clerks@3pumpcourt.com
Pump Court Chambers
Upper Ground Floor, 3 Pump Court,
Temple, London EC4Y 7AJ,
Telephone: 0171 353 0711
E-mail: clerks@3pumpcourt.com
Pump Court Chambers
5 Temple Chambers, Temple Street,
Swindon SN1 1SQ,
Telephone: 01793 539899
E-mail: clerks@3pumpcourt.com
Call Date: Oct 1993, Middle Temple
Qualifications: [LLB (Hons)(E.Ang)]

FIELDSEND JAMES WILLIAM

2nd Floor, Francis Taylor Building
Temple, London EC4Y 7BY,
Telephone: 0171 353 9942/3157
Call Date: Oct 1997, Lincoln's Inn
Qualifications: [LLB (Hons)(Newc)]

FINCH MRS NADINE ELIZABETH

Doughty Street Chambers
11 Doughty Street, London WC1N 2PG,
Telephone: 0171 404 1313
E-mail:enquiries@doughtystreet.co.uk
Call Date: 1991, Middle Temple
Pupil Master
Qualifications: [BA Hons (E Anglia), Dip
Law]

FINCH THOMAS MICHAEL

Westgate Chambers
67a Westgate Road, Newcastle upon Tyne
NE1 1SG, Telephone: 0191 261 4407/
2329785
E-mail:pracman@westgatechambers.law.co.u
k
Call Date: Nov 1981, Lincoln's Inn
Pupil Master
Qualifications: [BA Hons]

FINDLAY JAMES DE CARDONNEL

2-3 Gray's Inn Square
Gray's Inn, London WC1R 5JH,
Telephone: 0171 242 4986
E-mail:chambers@2-3graysinnsquare.co.uk
Call Date: Nov 1984, Middle Temple
Pupil Master
Qualifications: [MA (Cantab)]

FINLAY ANDREW STEVEN

Fountain Chambers
Cleveland Business Centre, 1 Watson
Street, Middlesbrough TS1 2RQ,
Telephone: 01642 804040
E-mail:fountainchambers@onyxnet.co.uk
Call Date: Oct 1993, Gray's Inn
Qualifications: [LLB (Hons)(Manc)]

FINLAY DARREN

Sovereign Chambers
25 Park Square, Leeds LS1 2PW,
Telephone: 0113 2451841/2/3
E-mail:sovereignchambers@btinternet.com
Call Date: Oct 1994, Gray's Inn
Qualifications: [BA (Keele)]

FINN TERENCE

Chambers of Martin Burr
Fourth Floor, Eldon Chambers, 30/32
Fleet Street, London EC4Y 1AA,
Telephone: 0171 353 4636
Call Date: Oct 1995, Lincoln's Inn
Qualifications: [LLB (Hons)(Bournem)]

FINNERTY MISS ANGELA CATHERINE

Park Lane Chambers
19 Westgate, Leeds LS1 2RD,
Telephone: 0113 2285000
E-mail:clerks@parklanechambers.co.uk
Call Date: July 1976, Middle Temple
Pupil Master, Recorder
Qualifications: [LLB (Leeds)]

FINNIGAN PETER ANTHONY

Hollis Whiteman Chambers
3rd Floor, Queen Elizabeth Bldg, Temple,
London EC4Y 9BS,
Telephone: 020 7583 5766
E-mail:barristers@holliswhiteman.co.uk
Call Date: 1979, Lincoln's Inn
Pupil Master
Qualifications: [LLB (Newc)]

FINNIS JOHN MITCHELL

Littman Chambers
12 Gray's Inn Square, London WC1R 5JP,
Telephone: 020 7404 4866
E-mail: admin@littmanchambers.com
Call Date: Nov 1970, Gray's Inn
Qualifications: [LLB (Adelaide), MA,]

FINUCANE BRENDAN GODFREY EAMONN

23 Essex Street
London WC2R 3AS,
Telephone: 0171 413 0353/836 8366
E-mail:clerks@essexstreet23.demon.co.uk
Call Date: July 1976, Middle Temple
Qualifications: [BSc (Lond)]

FIREMAN MARK PHILLIP

24a St John Street
Manchester M3 4DF,
Telephone: 0161 833 9628
Call Date: Feb 1986, Gray's Inn
Qualifications: [LLB (Lond)(Hons)]

FIRTH MISS ALISON MARY LESTER

7 New Square
1st Floor, Lincoln's Inn, London
WC2A 3QS, Telephone: 020 7404 5484
E-mail: clerks@7newsquare.com
Call Date: Nov 1980, Middle Temple
Qualifications: [MA (Oxon), MSc]

FIRTH MISS CLEMENCY MARY LEE

3 Temple Gardens
Lower Ground Floor, Temple, London
EC4Y 9AU, Telephone: 0171 353 3102/5/
9297 E-mail: clerks@3tg.co.uk
Call Date: Nov 1992, Inner Temple
Qualifications: [LLB (Newc)]

D

FIRTH MISS GEORGINA ELIZABETH

Chambers of Ian Macdonald QC (In Association with Two Garden Court, Temple, London)
Waldorf House, 5 Cooper Street,
Manchester M2 2FW,
Telephone: 0161 236 1840
Call Date: Oct 1995, Middle Temple
Qualifications: [LLB (Hons)]

FIRTH MATTHEW ALEXANDER

Queen Elizabeth Building
2nd Floor, Temple, London EC4Y 9BS,
Telephone: 0171 797 7837
Call Date: Oct 1991, Gray's Inn
Qualifications: [MA (Oxon)]

FIRTH-BUTTERFIELD MISS KAY

1 Gray's Inn Square, Chambers of the Baroness Scotland of Asthal QC
1st Floor, London WC1R 5AG,
Telephone: 0171 405 3000
E-mail: clerks@onegrays.demon.co.uk
Call Date: July 1980, Inner Temple
Qualifications: [BA (Sussex)]

FISCHEL ROBERT GUSTAV QC (1998)

5 King's Bench Walk
Temple, London EC4Y 7DN,
Telephone: 0171 353 5638
Call Date: July 1975, Middle Temple
Qualifications: [LLB (Lond)]

FISH DAVID THOMAS QC (1997)

Deans Court Chambers
24 St John Street, Manchester M3 4DF,
Telephone: 0161 214 6000
E-mail: clerks@deanscourt.co.uk
Deans Court Chambers
41-43 Market Place, Preston PR1 1AH,
Telephone: 01772 555163
E-mail: clerks@deanscourt.co.uk
Goldsmith Chambers
Ground Floor, Goldsmith Building,
Temple, London EC4Y 7BL,
Telephone: 0171 353 6802/3/4/5
E-mail:clerks@goldsmithchambers.law.co.uk
Call Date: July 1973, Inner Temple
Recorder
Qualifications: [LLB]

FISHER MISS CATHERINE JANE

Merchant Chambers
1 North Parade, Parsonage Gardens,
Manchester M3 2NH,
Telephone: 0161 839 7070
E-mail: merchant.chambers@virgin.net
Call Date: Oct 1990, Gray's Inn
Qualifications: [LLB (Lond), BCL (Oxon)]

FISHER DAVID

9 Gough Square
London EC4A 3DE,
Telephone: 020 7832 0500
E-mail: clerks@9goughsq.co.uk
Call Date: Nov 1985, Lincoln's Inn
Pupil Master
Qualifications: [BA (Cantab)]

FISHER DAVID PAUL QC (1996)

6 King's Bench Walk
Ground Floor, Temple, London
EC4Y 7DR, Telephone: 0171 583 0410
E-mail: worsley@6kbw.freeserve.co.uk
Call Date: July 1973, Gray's Inn
Recorder

FISHER JERVIS ANDREW

Coleridge Chambers
Citadel, 190 Corporation Street,
Birmingham B4 6QD,
Telephone: 0121 233 8500
Call Date: July 1980, Gray's Inn
Qualifications: [LLB (Lond)]

FISHER JONATHAN SIMON

18 Red Lion Court
(Off Fleet Street), London EC4A 3EB,
Telephone: 0171 520 6000
E-mail: chambers@18rlc.co.uk
Thornwood House
102 New London Road, Chelmsford,
Essex, CM2 0RG,
Telephone: 01245 280880
E-mail: chambers@18rlc.co.uk
Call Date: July 1980, Gray's Inn
Pupil Master
Qualifications: [BA, LLB (Cantab)]

Fax: 0171 520 6248/9; DX: 478 LDE;
Other comms: E-mail
Jonathan.Fisher@BTInternet.com; URL:
http://www.jonathan-fisher.co.uk
(reported cases details listed on web site).

Other professional qualifications: Standing Counsel (criminal) to the Inland Revenue, Central Criminal Court and London Crown Courts

Types of work: Administrative, Common law (general), Crime, Crime – corporate fraud, Financial services, Pharmacy

Circuit: South Eastern

Awards and memberships: Criminal Bar Association; Administrative Law Bar Association; International Bar Association

Other professional experience: Senior Visiting Fellow, City University Business School (PVM)

Publications: *The Law of Investor Protection* (Sweet & Maxwell), 1997; *Pharmacy Law & Practice* (Blackwell Science), 1997 (2nd edn); Sweet & Maxwell Practical Research Paper: *Incoming Requests for Mutual Assistance*, 1998; Sweet & Maxwell Practical Research Paper: *Out-going Letters of Request for International Assistance*, 1998

FISHER MISS JUSTINE STACEY

1 Gray's Inn Square
Ground Floor, London WC1R 5AA,
Telephone: 0171 405 8946/7/8
Call Date: Nov 1994, Inner Temple
Qualifications: [LLB, LLM (Notts)]

FISHER RICHARD ALAN

Francis Taylor Building
Ground Floor, Temple, London
EC4Y 7BY, Telephone: 0171 353 7768/
7769/2711
E-mail:clerks@francistaylorbuilding.law.co.uk
Call Date: 1994, Lincoln's Inn
Qualifications: [LLB (Bris)]

FISHER MS SANDRA

1 Gray's Inn Square, Chambers of the Baroness Scotland of Asthal QC
1st Floor, London WC1R 5AG,
Telephone: 0171 405 3000
E-mail: clerks@onegrays.demon.co.uk
Call Date: Nov 1993, Inner Temple
Qualifications: [LLB]

FISHER GORDON MRS WENDY VIVIENNE

2 Paper Buildings, Basement North
Temple, London EC4Y 7ET,
Telephone: 0171 936 2613
E-mail: post@2paper.co.uk
Call Date: July 1983, Gray's Inn
Pupil Master
Qualifications: [BA (Hons), Dip Law]

FISHWICK GREGORY DAVID PHILIP KYLE

2 Dyers Buildings
London EC1N 2JT,
Telephone: 0171 404 1881
Call Date: Oct 1996, Gray's Inn
Qualifications: [LLB, LLM (Exon)]

FITCH-HOLLAND ANDREW ROBERT

Trinity Chambers
140 New London Road, Chelmsford,
Essex, CM2 0AW,
Telephone: 01245 605040
E-mail:clerks@trinitychambers.law.co.uk
Call Date: Nov 1990, Inner Temple
Qualifications: [LLB (Buck'ham)]

FITTON MICHAEL DAVID GUY

Albion Chambers
Broad Street, Bristol BS1 1DR,
Telephone: 0117 9272144
Call Date: Nov 1991, Gray's Inn
Pupil Master
Qualifications: [MA (Oxon)]

FITTON-BROWN MISS REBECCA MARY

New Walk Chambers
27 New Walk, Leicester LE1 6TE,
Telephone: 0116 2559144
Call Date: July 1981, Inner Temple
Qualifications: [LLB]

FITZGERALD EDWARD HAMILTON QC (1995)

Doughty Street Chambers
11 Doughty Street, London WC1N 2PG,
Telephone: 0171 404 1313
E-mail:enquiries@doughtystreet.co.uk
Call Date: Nov 1978, Inner Temple
Qualifications: [BA (Oxon), MPhil (Ca]

FITZGERALD JOHN VINCENT

7 New Square
1st Floor, Lincoln's Inn, London
WC2A 3QS, Telephone: 020 7404 5484
E-mail: clerks@7newsquare.com
Call Date: July 1971, Middle Temple
Pupil Master
Qualifications: [BSc]

FITZGERALD MICHAEL FREDERICK CLIVE QC (1980)

2 Mitre Court Buildings
2nd Floor, Temple, London EC4Y 7BX,
Telephone: 0171 583 1380
E-mail: clerks@2mcb.co.uk
Call Date: Feb 1961, Middle Temple
Pupil Master
Qualifications: [MA (Cantab)]

FITZGERALD MISS SUSANNA QC (1999)

One Essex Court
Ground Floor, Temple, London
EC4Y 9AR, Telephone: 020 7583 2000
E-mail: clerks@oneessexcourt.co.uk
Call Date: 1973, Inner Temple
Pupil Master
Qualifications: [LLB (Hons)]

FITZGERALD TOBY JONATHAN

2 Harcourt Buildings
1st Floor, Temple, London EC4Y 9DB,
Telephone: 020 7353 2112
Call Date: Oct 1993, Lincoln's Inn
Qualifications: [BSc (Hons)(Bris)]

FITZGIBBON FRANCIS GEORGE HERBERT DILLON

33 Bedford Row
London WC1R 4JH,
Telephone: 0171 242 6476
E-mail: clerks@bedfordrow33.demon.co.uk
Call Date: Feb 1986, Middle Temple
Pupil Master
Qualifications: [BA (Oxon)]

FITZGIBBON NEIL KEVIN

Goldsmith Chambers
Ground Floor, Goldsmith Building,
Temple, London EC4Y 7BL,
Telephone: 0171 353 6802/3/4/5
E-mail: clerks@goldsmithchambers.law.co.uk
Call Date: Nov 1989, Lincoln's Inn
Qualifications: [LLB (Hons) (Lond)]

FITZHARRIS MISS GINNETTE

3 Paper Buildings
Temple, London EC4Y 7EU,
Telephone: 020 7583 8055
E-mail: London@3paper.com
3 Paper Buildings (Oxford)
1 Alfred Street, High Street, Oxford
OX1 4EH, Telephone: 01865 793736
E-mail: oxford@3paper.com
3 Paper Buildings (Winchester)
4 St Peter Street, Winchester SO23 8BW,
Telephone: 01962 868884
E-mail: winchester@3paper.com
3 Paper Buildings (Bournemouth)
20 Lorne Park Road, Bournemouth,
Dorset, BH1 1JN,
Telephone: 01202 292102
E-mail: Bournemouth@3paper.com
Call Date: Nov 1993, Lincoln's Inn
Qualifications: [LLB (Hons, Leeds)]

FITZMAURICE MAURICE EVELYN FORBES

Blackstone Chambers
Blackstone House, Temple, London
EC4Y 9BW, Telephone: 0171 583 1770
E-mail: clerks@blackstonechambers.com
Call Date: Nov 1969, Middle Temple
Qualifications: [BA (Cantab)]

FITZPATRICK EDWARD JAMES

8 King's Bench Walk
2nd Floor, Temple, London EC4Y 7DU,
Telephone: 0171 797 8888
Call Date: Nov 1990, Gray's Inn
Pupil Master
Qualifications: [LLB (L'pool)]

FITZPATRICK EDWARD PETER

Furnival Chambers
32 Furnival Street, London EC4A 1JQ,
Telephone: 0171 405 3232
E-mail: clerks@furnivallaw.co.uk
Call Date: 1985, Gray's Inn
Qualifications: [BA]

FITZPATRICK FRANCIS PAUL

Chambers of John Gardiner QC
1st Floor, 11 New Square, Lincoln's Inn,
London WC2A 3QB,
Telephone: 0171 242 4017
E-mail: taxlaw@11newsquare.com
Call Date: Nov 1990, Inner Temple
Pupil Master
Qualifications: [BA (Hons)(Oxon), BCL
(Oxon)]

FITZPATRICK JEREMY PAUL

4 Brick Court
Ground Floor, Temple, London
EC4Y 9AD, Telephone: 0171 797 7766
E-mail: chambers@4brick.co.uk
Call Date: Mar 1996, Middle Temple
Qualifications: [BA (Hons)]

FITZPATRICK THOMAS ANDREW MICHAEL

58 King Street Chambers
1st Floor, Kingsgate House, 51-53 South
King Street, Manchester M2 6DE,
Telephone: 0161 831 7477
Call Date: Nov 1988, Lincoln's Inn
Qualifications: [LLB]

FLACH ROBERT THOMAS FRANCIS

3 Hare Court
1 Little Essex Street, London WC2R 3LD,
Telephone: 0171 395 2000
Call Date: Jan 1950, Middle Temple
Qualifications: [LLB (Tas)]

FLAHIVE DANIEL MICHAEL

Hardwicke Building
New Square, Lincoln's Inn, London
WC2A 3SB, Telephone: 020 7242 2523
E-mail: clerks@hardwicke.co.uk
Call Date: July 1982, Gray's Inn
Pupil Master
Qualifications: [LLB (Lond)]

FLANAGAN MISS JULIA MARY ALICE

Dr Johnson's Chambers
Two Dr Johnson's Buildings, Temple,
London EC4Y 7AY,
Telephone: 0171 353 4716
E-mail: clerks@2djb.freeserve.co.uk
Call Date: Oct 1993, Lincoln's Inn
Qualifications: [BA (Hons), Dip in Law
(Lond), CPE]

FLATHER GARY QC (1984)

4-5 Gray's Inn Square
Ground Floor, Gray's Inn, London
WC1R 5JP, Telephone: 0171 404 5252
E-mail:chambers@4-5graysinnsquare.co.uk
Call Date: May 1962, Inner Temple
Recorder
Qualifications: [MA (Oxon)]

FLAUX JULIAN MARTIN QC (1994)

S Tomlinson QC
7 King's Bench Walk, Temple, London
EC4Y 7DS, Telephone: 0171 583 0404
E-mail: clerks@7kbw.law.co.uk
Call Date: July 1978, Inner Temple
Qualifications: [MA, BCL (Oxon)]

FLEISCHMANN MRS LAUREEN ANN

2 Pump Court
1st Floor, Temple, London EC4Y 7AH,
Telephone: 0171 353 5597
Call Date: July 1978, Inner Temple
Pupil Master
Qualifications: [LLB (Hons) (Lond)]

FLEMING ADRIAN

2 King's Bench Walk
Ground Floor, Temple, London
EC4Y 7DE, Telephone: 0171 353 1746
E-mail: 2kbw@atlas.co.uk
King's Bench Chambers
115 North Hill, Plymouth PL4 8JY,
Telephone: 01752 221551
Call Date: Nov 1991, Middle Temple
Qualifications: [BA Hons (Cantab), Dip Law]

D

D

FLEMING PAUL STEPHEN

37 Park Square Chambers
37 Park Square, Leeds LS1 2NY,
Telephone: 0113 2439422
E-mail: chambers@no37.co.uk
Call Date: Nov 1983, Gray's Inn
Pupil Master

FLENLEY WILLIAM DAVID WINGATE

4 Paper Buildings
Ground Floor, Temple, London
EC4Y 7EX, Telephone: 0171 353 3366/
583 7155
E-mail: clerks@4paperbuildings.com
Call Date: Nov 1988, Middle Temple
Pupil Master
Qualifications: [BA, BCL (Oxon), LLM
(Cornell)]

FLESCH MICHAEL CHARLES QC (1983)

Gray's Inn Tax Chambers
3rd Floor, Gray's Inn Chambers, Gray's
Inn, London WC1R 5JA,
Telephone: 0171 242 2642
E-mail: clerks@taxbar.com
Call Date: May 1963, Gray's Inn
Qualifications: [LLB]

FLETCHER ANDREW FITZROY STEPHEN

4 Pump Court
Temple, London EC4Y 7AN,
Telephone: 020 7842 5555
E-mail:chambers@4pumpcourt.law.co.uk
Call Date: Nov 1980, Inner Temple
Pupil Master
Qualifications: [MA (Cantab)]

FLETCHER CHRISTOPHER MICHAEL

Octagon House
19 Colegate, Norwich NR3 1AT,
Telephone: 01603 623186
E-mail: admin@octagon-chambers.co.uk
Call Date: Nov 1984, Inner Temple
Pupil Master
Qualifications: [LLB (Exeter)]

FLETCHER DAVID HAMILTON

Albion Chambers
Broad Street, Bristol BS1 1DR,
Telephone: 0117 9272144
Call Date: July 1971, Gray's Inn
Pupil Master
Qualifications: [MA (Cantab)]

FLETCHER MARCUS ALEXANDER

One King's Bench Walk
1st Floor, Temple, London EC4Y 7DB,
Telephone: 0171 936 1500
E-mail: ddear@1kbw.co.uk
Call Date: Oct 1990, Lincoln's Inn
Pupil Master
Qualifications: [BA (Hons)]

FLETCHER STEPHEN JEFFERY

Somersett Chambers
25 Bedford Row, London WC1R 4HE,
Telephone: 0171 404 6701
E-mail: somelaw@aol.com
Call Date: Nov 1987, Middle Temple
Qualifications: [LLB Hons (Lond)]

FLETTON MARK JOHN

Broadway House Chambers
Broadway House, 9 Bank Street, Bradford,
West Yorkshire, BD1 1TW,
Telephone: 01274 722560
E-mail: clerks@broadwayhouse.co.uk
Broadway House Chambers
31 Park Square West, Leeds LS1 2PF,
Telephone: 0113 246 2600
Call Date: Feb 1991, Lincoln's Inn
Qualifications: [LLB , LLM (Cantab)]

FLEWITT NEIL

Corn Exchange Chambers
5th Floor, Fenwick Street, Liverpool
L2 7QS, Telephone: 0151 227 1081/5009
Call Date: 1981, Middle Temple
Pupil Master, Assistant Recorder
Qualifications: [LLB (Hons, L'pool)]

FLINT CHARLES JOHN RAFFLES QC (1995)

Blackstone Chambers
Blackstone House, Temple, London
EC4Y 9BW, Telephone: 0171 583 1770
E-mail:clerks@blackstonechambers.com
Call Date: July 1975, Middle Temple
Qualifications: [MA (Cantab)]

FLOCKHART MISS SHARON LINDA

3 Serjeants' Inn
London EC4Y 1BQ,
Telephone: 0171 353 5537
E-mail: clerks@3serjeantsinn.com
Call Date: 1997, Middle Temple
Qualifications: [LLB (Hons)(Lond)]

FLOOD DAVID EDWARD

India Buildings Chambers
Water Street, Liverpool L2 0XG,
Telephone: 0151 243 6000
E-mail: clerks@chambers.u-net.com
Call Date: Feb 1993, Middle Temple
Qualifications: [LLB (Hons)]

FLOOD DIARMUID BRENDAN MARTIN

19 Castle Street Chambers
Liverpool L2 4SX,
Telephone: 0151 236 9402
E-mail: DBrei16454@aol.com
Guildford Chambers
Stoke House, Leapale Lane, Guildford,
Surrey, GU1 4LY,
Telephone: 01483 539131
E-mail:guildford.barristers@btinternet.com
Call Date: Apr 1989, Lincoln's Inn
Qualifications: [LLB (Lond), Maitrise (Paris)]

FLORIDA-JAMES MARK

King's Bench Chambers
Wellington House, 175 Holdenhurst Road,
Bournemouth, Dorset, BH8 8DQ,
Telephone: 01202 250025
E-mail: chambers@kingsbench.co.uk
Call Date: Oct 1995, Inner Temple
Qualifications: [BA (Sussex), MPhil
(Aberystwyth), Dip German Law,Bonn]

FLOWER PHILIP RONALD

9 Stone Buildings
Lincoln's Inn, London WC2A 3NN,
Telephone: 0171 404 5055
E-mail: clerks@9stoneb.law.co.uk
Call Date: Nov 1979, Inner Temple
Qualifications: [MA]

FLOYD CHRISTOPHER DAVID QC (1992)

11 South Square
2nd Floor, Gray's Inn, London
WC1R 5EU,
Telephone: 0171 405 1222 (24hr messagin
g service)
E-mail: clerks@11southsquare.com
Call Date: July 1975, Inner Temple
Assistant Recorder
Qualifications: [MA (Cantab)]

FLYNN JAMES EDWARD

Brick Court Chambers
7-8 Essex Street, London WC2R 3LD,
Telephone: 0171 379 3550
E-mail: [surname]@brickcourt.co.uk
Call Date: July 1978, Middle Temple
Qualifications: [BA (Oxon)]

FLYNN VERNON JAMES HENNESSY

Essex Court Chambers
24 Lincoln's Inn Fields, London
WC2A 3ED, Telephone: 0171 813 8000
E-mail:clerksroom@essexcourt-chambers.co.u
k
Call Date: Oct 1991, Lincoln's Inn
Qualifications: [BA (Cantab)]

FODDER MARTIN JOHN

Chambers of John L Powell QC
Four New Square, Lincoln's Inn, London
WC2A 3RJ, Telephone: 0171 797 8000
E-mail: barristers@4newsquare.com
Call Date: July 1983, Inner Temple
Pupil Master
Qualifications: [BA (Lond) LLM, (Cantab)
Dip Law, (City)]

FOGARTY PETER DOMINIC

Oriel Chambers
14 Water Street, Liverpool L2 8TD,
Telephone: 0151 236 7191/236 4321
E-mail: clerks@oriel-chambers.co.uk
Call Date: July 1982, Lincoln's Inn
Qualifications: [MA (Cantab)]

FOGG ANTHONY GEORGE

Dr Johnson's Chambers
Two Dr Johnson's Buildings, Temple,
London EC4Y 7AY,
Telephone: 0171 353 4716
E-mail: clerks@2djb.freeserve.co.uk
Call Date: Nov 1970, Gray's Inn
Pupil Master
Qualifications: [MSc]

FOINETTE IAN

1 Harcourt Buildings
2nd Floor, Temple, London EC4Y 9DA,
Telephone: 0171 353 9421/0375
E-mail:clerks@1harcourtbuildings.law.co.uk
Call Date: Nov 1986, Middle Temple
Pupil Master
Qualifications: [BA (Kent)]

FOLEY MISS SHEILA MARIE

9 Stone Buildings
Lincoln's Inn, London WC2A 3NN,
Telephone: 0171 404 5055
E-mail: clerks@9stoneb.law.co.uk
Call Date: Nov 1988, Inner Temple
Pupil Master
Qualifications: [BA]

FOLKES MISS SANDRA GILLIAN

2 Paper Buildings
1st Floor, Temple, London EC4Y 7ET,
Telephone: 020 7556 5500
E-mail: clerks@2pbbarristers.co.uk
Call Date: Nov 1989, Lincoln's Inn
Qualifications: [LLB]

FOOKES ROBERT LAWRENCE

2 Mitre Court Buildings
2nd Floor, Temple, London EC4Y 7BX,
Telephone: 0171 583 1380
E-mail: clerks@2mcb.co.uk
Call Date: July 1975, Lincoln's Inn
Pupil Master
Qualifications: [MA (Cantab)]

FOOKS NICHOLAS DAVID

Five Paper Buildings
1st Floor, Five Paper Bldgs, Temple,
London EC4Y 7HB,
Telephone: 0171 583 6117
E-mail:clerks@5-paperbuildings.law.co.uk
Thornwood House
102 New London Road, Chelmsford,
Essex, CM2 0RG,
Telephone: 01245 280880
E-mail: chambers@18rlc.co.uk
Call Date: Nov 1978, Inner Temple
Pupil Master
Qualifications: [MA (L'pool)]

FORBES PETER GEORGE

6 Pump Court
1st Floor, Temple, London EC4Y 7AR,
Telephone: 0171 797 8400
E-mail: clerks@6pumpcourt.co.uk
6-8 Mill Street
Maidstone, Kent, ME15 6XH,
Telephone: 01622 688094
E-mail: annexe@6pumpcourt.co.uk
Call Date: Oct 1990, Inner Temple
Qualifications: [LLB (Lond)]

FORD ANDREW JAMES

Goldsmith Chambers
Ground Floor, Goldsmith Building,
Temple, London EC4Y 7BL,
Telephone: 0171 353 6802/3/4/5
E-mail:clerks@goldsmithchambers.law.co.uk
Call Date: 1997, Middle Temple
Qualifications: [BA (Hons)(Sheff), CPE]

FORD MISS CAROLINE EMMA

37 Park Square Chambers
37 Park Square, Leeds LS1 2NY,
Telephone: 0113 2439422
E-mail: chambers@no37.co.uk
Call Date: Oct 1993, Gray's Inn
Qualifications: [LLM (Buck'ham)]

FORD DAVID GRAEME

Mitre Court Chambers
3rd Floor, Temple, London EC4Y 7BP,
Telephone: 0171 353 9394
E-mail: mitrecourt.com
Call Date: 1972, Inner Temple
Qualifications: [LLB (Lond)]

FORD GERARD JAMES

Baker Street Chambers
9 Baker Street, Middlesbrough TS1 2LF,
Telephone: 01642 873873
Call Date: July 1986, Inner Temple
Pupil Master
Qualifications: [BSc, MA (Wark), CQSW]

FORD JEREMY MICHAEL

199 Strand
London WC2R 1DR,
Telephone: 0171 379 9779
E-mail: chambers@199strand.co.uk
Call Date: Oct 1996, Lincoln's Inn
Qualifications: [LLB (Hons)(Leeds)]

FORD MARK STEVEN

Young Street Chambers
38 Young Street, Manchester M3 3FT,
Telephone: 0161 833 0489
E-mail: clerks@young-st-chambers.com
Call Date: Nov 1991, Gray's Inn
Qualifications: [LLB (Hons((B'ham)]

FORD MICHAEL DAVID

Doughty Street Chambers
11 Doughty Street, London WC1N 2PG,
Telephone: 0171 404 1313
E-mail:enquiries@doughtystreet.co.uk
Call Date: July 1992, Middle Temple
Qualifications: [LLB (Hons) (Brist), MA
(Sheff)]

FORD MISS MONICA DOROTHY PATIENCE

14 Gray's Inn Square
Gray's Inn, London WC1R 5JP,
Telephone: 0171 242 0858
E-mail: 100712.2134@compuserve.com
Call Date: July 1984, Middle Temple
Pupil Master
Qualifications: [LLB (Hons)(L'pool)]

FORD NEIL MURRAY QC (1997)

Albion Chambers
Broad Street, Bristol BS1 1DR,
Telephone: 0117 9272144
Call Date: Nov 1976, Inner Temple
Qualifications: [BA]

FORD STEVEN CHARLES

9 Bedford Row
London WC1R 4AZ,
Telephone: 0171 242 3555
E-mail: clerks@9br.co.uk
Call Date: Oct 1992, Middle Temple
Qualifications: [LLB (Hons), L.R.A.M.]

FORDE MARTIN ANDREW

1 Crown Office Row
Ground Floor, Temple, London
EC4Y 7HH, Telephone: 0171 797 7500
E-mail: mail@onecrownofficerow.com
Call Date: Feb 1984, Middle Temple
Pupil Master
Qualifications: [BA (Oxon)]

FORDHAM MRS JUDITH

Exchange Chambers
Pearl Assurance House, Derby Square,
Liverpool L2 9XX,
Telephone: 0151 236 7747
E-mail:exchangechambers@btinternet.com
Call Date: July 1991, Inner Temple

FORDHAM MRS MARGARET ALLISON

Staple Inn Chambers
1st Floor, 9 Staple Inn, Holborn Bars,
London WC1V 7QH,
Telephone: 0171 242 5240
E-mail: clerks@staple-inn.org
Call Date: Oct 1990, Gray's Inn
Qualifications: [BA (U.W.I.), LLB
(Hons)(Buck'm)]

FORDHAM MICHAEL JOHN

Blackstone Chambers
Blackstone House, Temple, London
EC4Y 9BW, Telephone: 0171 583 1770
E-mail:clerks@blackstonechambers.com
Call Date: Feb 1990, Gray's Inn
Pupil Master
Qualifications: [BA (Oxon), BCL (Oxon),
LLM (Virginia)]

FORDHAM ROBERT ALLAN QC (1993)

Martins Building
2nd Floor, No 4 Water Street, Liverpool
L2 3SP, Telephone: 0151 236 5818/4919
Call Date: Nov 1967, Inner Temple

Recorder
Qualifications: [LLB]

FORGAN HUGH MALCOLM

5 King's Bench Walk
Temple, London EC4Y 7DN,
Telephone: 0171 353 5638
Call Date: Nov 1989, Lincoln's Inn
Qualifications: [BA (Cantab)]

FORLIN GERARD EMLYN

Hardwicke Building
New Square, Lincoln's Inn, London
WC2A 3SB, Telephone: 020 7242 2523
E-mail: clerks@hardwicke.co.uk
Call Date: Feb 1984, Lincoln's Inn
Qualifications: [LLB (Hons) (Lond), LLM
(Lond), M.Phil (Cantab), Diploma in Air &
, Space Law]

FORMBY MS EMILY JANE

Hardwicke Building
New Square, Lincoln's Inn, London
WC2A 3SB, Telephone: 020 7242 2523
E-mail: clerks@hardwicke.co.uk
Call Date: Oct 1993, Middle Temple
Qualifications: [BA (Hons)(Oxon), CPE
(City)]

FORREST ALASTAIR JOHN

18 St John Street
Manchester M3 4EA,
Telephone: 0161 278 1800
E-mail: 18stjohn@lineone.net
Call Date: July 1972, Gray's Inn
Pupil Master, Recorder
Qualifications: [MA (Oxon)]

FORRESTER IAN STEWART

Blackstone Chambers
Blackstone House, Temple, London
EC4Y 9BW, Telephone: 0171 583 1770
E-mail: clerks@blackstonechambers.com
Call Date: Oct 1996, Middle Temple
Qualifications: [MA, LLB (Glasgow), MCL
(Tulane)]

FORSDICK DAVID JOHN

4 Breams Buildings
London EC4A 1AQ,
Telephone: 0171 353 5835/430 1221
E-mail:breams@4breamsbuildings.law.co.uk
Call Date: Oct 1993, Gray's Inn
Qualifications: [BA (Warw)]

FORSEY STEPHEN MICHAEL

Verulam Chambers
Peer House, 8-14 Verulam Street, Gray's
Inn, London WC1X 8LZ,
Telephone: 0171 813 2400
Call Date: Nov 1995, Lincoln's Inn
Qualifications: [LLB (Hons)(Exon)]

FORSHALL MS ISABELLA LOUISE

Doughty Street Chambers
11 Doughty Street, London WC1N 2PG,
Telephone: 0171 404 1313
E-mail:enquiries@doughtystreet.co.uk
Call Date: Feb 1982, Gray's Inn
Pupil Master
Qualifications: [BA (Cantab)]

FORSHAW MISS SARAH ANNE

5 King's Bench Walk
Temple, London EC4Y 7DN,
Telephone: 0171 353 5638
Call Date: Nov 1987, Middle Temple
Pupil Master
Qualifications: [LLB (Lond)]

FORSTER BRIAN CLIVE QC (1999)

Trinity Chambers
9-12 Trinity Chare, Quayside, Newcastle
upon Tyne NE1 3DF,
Telephone: 0191 232 1927
E-mail: info@trinitychambers.co.uk
Call Date: 1977, Lincoln's Inn
Pupil Master, Recorder
Qualifications: [LLB (Newcastle)]

FORSTER MICHAEL WILLIAMS

17 Carlton Crescent
Southampton SO15 2XR,
Telephone: 023 8032 0320/0823 2003
E-mail: greg@jg17cc.co.uk
Call Date: Feb 1984, Gray's Inn
Qualifications: [LLB (Lond)]

FORSTER MS SARAH JUDITH

14 Gray's Inn Square
Gray's Inn, London WC1R 5JP,
Telephone: 0171 242 0858
E-mail: 100712.2134@compuserve.com
Westgate Chambers
144 High Street, Lewes, East Sussex,
BN7 1XT, Telephone: 01273 480510
Call Date: Nov 1976, Middle Temple
Pupil Master
Qualifications: [LLB, Dip Law, Medical
Ethics]

FORSTER THOMAS BERNARD

18 Red Lion Court
(Off Fleet Street), London EC4A 3EB,
Telephone: 0171 520 6000
E-mail: chambers@18rlc.co.uk
Thornwood House
102 New London Road, Chelmsford,
Essex, CM2 0RG,
Telephone: 01245 280880
E-mail: chambers@18rlc.co.uk
Call Date: 1993, Inner Temple
Qualifications: [LLB (Lond)]

FORSTER TIMOTHY SHANE CAVANAGH

Furnival Chambers
32 Furnival Street, London EC4A 1JQ,
Telephone: 0171 405 3232
E-mail: clerks@furnivallaw.co.uk
Call Date: Oct 1990, Middle Temple
Qualifications: [LLB (Hons Cardiff)]

FORSTER-JONES WILFRED JENNER EMANUEL

Chambers of Wilfred Forster-Jones
New Court, 1st Floor South, Temple,
London EC4Y 9BE,
Telephone: 0171 353 0853/4/7222
E-mail: chambers@newcourt.net
Call Date: Nov 1976, Middle Temple
Pupil Master
Qualifications: [BA (Lond)]

FORSYTH ANDREW ALLAN

Mitre Court Chambers
3rd Floor, Temple, London EC4Y 7BP,
Telephone: 0171 353 9394
E-mail: mitrecourt.com
Call Date: Nov 1989, Inner Temple
Qualifications: [LLB (Hons) (Wales)]

FORSYTH MISS JULIE PATRICIA

Chavasse Court Chambers
2nd Floor, Chavasse Court, 24 Lord Street,
Liverpool L2 1TA,
Telephone: 0151 707 1191
Call Date: July 1983, Gray's Inn
Pupil Master
Qualifications: [LLB (L'pool)]

FORSYTH MISS SAMANTHA

Coleridge Chambers
Citadel, 190 Corporation Street,
Birmingham B4 6QD,
Telephone: 0121 233 8500
Call Date: July 1988, Inner Temple
Qualifications: [LLB (Wales)]

FORTE MARK JULIAN CARMINO

8 King Street Chambers
8 King Street, Manchester M2 6AQ,
Telephone: 0161 834 9560
E-mail: eightking@aol.com
Call Date: Nov 1989, Inner Temple
Qualifications: [LLB]

FORTE TIMOTHY AXEL

2 Dyers Buildings
London EC1N 2JT,
Telephone: 0171 404 1881
Call Date: Oct 1994, Gray's Inn
Qualifications: [BA]

FORTSON RUDI FLETCHER

3 Gray's Inn Square
Ground Floor, London WC1R 5AH,
Telephone: 0171 520 5600
E-mail: clerks@3gis.co.uk
Call Date: Nov 1976, Middle Temple
Pupil Master
Qualifications: [LLB (Lond)]

FORTUNE MALCOLM DONALD PORTER

3 Serjeants' Inn
London EC4Y 1BQ,
Telephone: 0171 353 5537
E-mail: clerks@3serjeantsinn.com
Call Date: July 1972, Middle Temple
Pupil Master, Recorder

FORTUNE PETER CARL MICHAEL

2 Gray's Inn Square Chambers
2nd Floor, Gray's Inn, London WC1R 5AA,
Telephone: 020 7242 0328
E-mail: clerks@2gis.co.uk
Guildhall Chambers Portsmouth
Prudential Buildings, 16 Guildhall Walk,
Portsmouth, Hampshire, PO1 2DE,
Telephone: 01705 752400
Call Date: July 1978, Inner Temple
Pupil Master
Qualifications: [BA (Leeds)]

FORTUNE ROBERT ANDREW

4 Brick Court, Chambers of Anne Rafferty QC
1st Floor, Temple, London EC4Y 9AD,
Telephone: 0171 583 8455
Call Date: Feb 1976, Middle Temple
Pupil Master
Qualifications: [LLB (Lond)]

FORWARD BARRY MILES

2 Mitre Court Buildings
1st Floor, Temple, London EC4Y 7BX,
Telephone: 0171 353 1353
Call Date: July 1981, Gray's Inn
Pupil Master
Qualifications: [BSc (Econ), Dip Law]

FORWOOD NICHOLAS JAMES QC (1987)

Brick Court Chambers
7-8 Essex Street, London WC2R 3LD,
Telephone: 0171 379 3550
E-mail: [surname]@brickcourt.co.uk
8 King Street Chambers
8 King Street, Manchester M2 6AQ,
Telephone: 0161 834 9560
E-mail: eightking@aol.com
Call Date: 1970, Middle Temple
Qualifications: [MA (Cantab)]

FOSKETT DAVID ROBERT QC (1991)

1 Crown Office Row
Ground Floor, Temple, London
EC4Y 7HH, Telephone: 0171 797 7500
E-mail: mail@onecrownofficerow.com
Call Date: July 1972, Gray's Inn
Recorder
Qualifications: [LLB (Lond)]

FOSTER MISS ALISON LEE CAROLINE

39 Essex Street
London WC2R 3AT,
Telephone: 0171 832 1111
E-mail: clerks@39essex.co.uk
Call Date: July 1984, Inner Temple
Pupil Master
Qualifications: [BA (Oxon), M.Phil, Dip.Law]

FOSTER BRIAN IAN

St James's Chambers
68 Quay Street, Manchester M3 3EJ,
Telephone: 0161 834 7000
E-mail: clerks@stjameschambers.co.uk
Park Lane Chambers
19 Westgate, Leeds LS1 2RD,
Telephone: 0113 2285000
E-mail:clerks@parklanechambers.co.uk
Call Date: July 1988, Lincoln's Inn
Qualifications: [LLB (Hons) Newcastle]

FOSTER MISS CATHERINE MARY

Plowden Buildings
2nd Floor, 2 Plowden Buildings, Middle
Temple Lane, London EC4Y 9BU,
Telephone: 0171 583 0808
E-mail: bar@plowdenbuildings.co.uk
Call Date: July 1986, Inner Temple
Pupil Master
Qualifications: [LLB (Nott'm)]

FOSTER CHARLES ANDREW

Chambers of Kieran Coonan QC
Ground Floor, 6 Pump Court, Temple,
London EC4Y 7AR,
Telephone: 0171 583 6013/2510
E-mail: clerks@6-pumpcourt.law.co.uk
Call Date: July 1988, Inner Temple
Pupil Master
Qualifications: [MA, Vet MB (Cantab),
MRCVS]

Fax: 0171 353 0464; DX: 409 London,
Chancery Lane;
Other comms: E-mail
charles_foster@link.org

Types of work: Common law (general), Defamation, Medical negligence, Personal injury, Professional negligence

Membership of foreign bars: Member of the Irish Bar

D

Circuit: North Eastern

Awards and memberships: Professional Negligence Bar Association; Medico-Legal Society

Other professional experience: Qualified Veterinary Surgeon

Languages spoken:

Publications: *Personal Injury Toolkit* (Sweet & Maxwell), 1997 2nd Ed. 1998; *Disclosure and Confidentiality* (Sweet & Maxwell), 1996; *Tripping and Slipping Cases*, 2nd edn (Sweet & Maxwell), 1996; Numerous legal articles in *Solicitors' Journal, NLJ* and specialist medico-legal publications, and non-legal articles in other publications

Reported Cases: *Briggs v Pitt-Payne & Lias*, [1999] Lloyd's LR: Medical 1, 1999. Definition of 'significant injury' and 'attributable' in issues of limitation where negligent misprescription of drugs is alleged.
Drake v Pontefract HA, [1998] Lloyd's LR: Medical 425. Psychiatric team's liability for failure to control depression and prevent suicide attempt.
Reed v Sunderland HA, (1998) *The Times*, 16 October. Discounting for future contingencies. The status of the Judicial Studies Board Guidelines.
Fallows v Randle, [1997] 8 Med LR 160. Laparoscopic sterilisation. Fallope ring found later to be in incorrect position. Application for maxim *res ipsa loquitur*.
Bancroft v Harrogate Health Authority, [1997] 8 Med LR 398. Whether failure to perform a total (cp sub-total) hysterectomy after finding certain histological changes in service was negligent.

Additional Reported Cases
Hind v York Health Authority [1997] 8 Med LR 377; [1998] PIQR P235
Damage to anal sphincter. Immediate knowledge of faecal incontinence. When the Plaintiff acquired date of knowledge for purposes of limitation.

Ogden v Airedale Health Authority [1996] 7 Med LR 153
Liability of health authority to radiographer for occupational asthma caused by inhalation of x-ray developing chemicals.

Kahl v Freistaat Bayern [1995] PIQR P401
Abuse of process. Two actions arising from the same cause of action. Recoverability by a foreign state of sums paid under its own domestic legislation in respect of the financial consequences of a tort in England.

Reed v Doncaster MBC [1995] 11 CL 560
Liability of local authorities for the acts of third parties.

Giles v Pontefract Health Authority (1993) Kemp H2-014
Assessment of future loss of earnings when the Plaintiff is a young child. *Smith v Manchester* or multiplier-multiplicand basis?

Additional Information
St John's College, Cambridge: Medical Sciences Tripos, Law Tripos and Clinical Veterinary Medicine. Research in wild animal anaesthesia and tranquilisation in Saudi Arabia and comparative anatomy at the Royal College of Surgeons. Research Fellow, Hebrew University, Jerusalem, and research assistant to Aharon Barak of the Supreme Court of Israel.

FOSTER FRANCIS ALEXANDER

St Paul's House
5th Floor, St Paul's House, 23 Park Square South, Leeds LS1 2ND,
Telephone: 0113 2455866
E-mail: catherinegrimshaw@stpauls-chambers.demon.co.uk
Call Date: Oct 1990, Inner Temple
Qualifications: [LLB (Huddersfield)]

FOSTER MISS ILAINE VIVIENNE JULIA

University of Hertfordshire, 7 Hatfield Road, St Albans, Herts AL1 3LS,
Telephone: 01727 286200
Call Date: July 1982, Lincoln's Inn
Qualifications: [BA, LLM (Cantab)]

FOSTER JONATHAN ROWE QC (1989)

18 St John Street
Manchester M3 4EA,
Telephone: 0161 278 1800
E-mail: 18stjohn@lineone.net
No. 1 Serjeants' Inn
5th Floor Fleet Street, Temple, London EC4Y 1LH, Telephone: 0171 415 6666
E-mail:no1serjeantsinn@btinternet.com
Call Date: July 1970, Gray's Inn

Recorder
Qualifications: [MA (Oxon)]

FOSTER JULIEN ANDREW STEWART

Goldsmith Chambers
Ground Floor, Goldsmith Building,
Temple, London EC4Y 7BL,
Telephone: 0171 353 6802/3/4/5
E-mail:clerks@goldsmithchambers.law.co.uk
Call Date: Oct 1995, Middle Temple
Qualifications: [BA (Hons) (York)]

FOSTER MISS JULIET KATE

Southernhay Chambers
33 Southernhay East, Exeter, Devon,
EX1 1NX, Telephone: 01392 255777
E-mail:southernhay.chambers@lineone.net
Call Date: Nov 1989, Middle Temple
Qualifications: [LLB]

FOSTER MS MARGARET MARY

John Street Chambers
2 John Street, London WC1N 2HJ,
Telephone: 0171 242 1911
E-mail:john.street_chambers@virgin.net
Call Date: Feb 1993, Lincoln's Inn
Qualifications: [LLB]

FOSTER PETER

Oriel Chambers
14 Water Street, Liverpool L2 8TD,
Telephone: 0151 236 7191/236 4321
E-mail: clerks@oriel-chambers.co.uk
Call Date: Nov 1992, Middle Temple
Qualifications: [LLB (Hons, Manch)]

FOSTER MISS ROSALIND MARY

2 Temple Gardens
Temple, London EC4Y 9AY,
Telephone: 0171 583 6041
E-mail: clerks@2templegardens.co.uk
Call Date: Nov 1969, Middle Temple
Pupil Master, Recorder
Qualifications: [BA (Oxon)]

FOSTER SIMON HARVEY STENNETT

2 King's Bench Walk
Ground Floor, Temple, London
EC4Y 7DE, Telephone: 0171 353 1746
E-mail: 2kbw@atlas.co.uk

King's Bench Chambers
115 North Hill, Plymouth PL4 8JY,
Telephone: 01752 221551
Call Date: July 1982, Middle Temple
Pupil Master
Qualifications: [LLB (Exon)]

FOUDY MISS KIM FRANCES

8 King Street Chambers
8 King Street, Manchester M2 6AQ,
Telephone: 0161 834 9560
E-mail: eightking@aol.com
Call Date: July 1982, Gray's Inn
Pupil Master
Qualifications: [LLB]

FOULKES MISS ALISON-MARIE

6 King's Bench Walk
Ground Floor, Temple, London
EC4Y 7DR, Telephone: 0171 583 0410
E-mail: worsley@6kbw.freeserve.co.uk
Call Date: 1997, Middle Temple
Qualifications: [BA (Hons)(Cantab)]

FOULKES CHRISTOPHER DAVID

1 Hare Court
Ground Floor, Temple, London
EC4Y 7BE, Telephone: 0171 353 3982/
5324
Call Date: Oct 1994, Lincoln's Inn
Qualifications: [BA (Hons), LLB
(Hons)(Leeds)]

FOULSER MISS JANE HELENA SUSAN

32 Park Place
Cardiff CF1 3BA,
Telephone: 01222 397364
Call Date: Feb 1994, Gray's Inn
Qualifications: [LLB (Wales), LLM (Wales)]

FOWLER EDMUND IAN CARLOSS

5 King's Bench Walk
Temple, London EC4Y 7DN,
Telephone: 0171 353 5638
Call Date: Oct 1992, Gray's Inn
Qualifications: [LL.B]

FOWLER MICHAEL GLYN

Chambers of Michael Pert QC
36 Bedford Row, London WC1R 4JH,
Telephone: 0171 421 8000
E-mail: 36bedfordrow@link.org
Chambers of Michael Pert QC
24 Albion Place, Northampton NN1 1UD,
Telephone: 01604 602333
Chambers of Michael Pert QC
104 New Walk, Leicester LE1 7EA,
Telephone: 0116 249 2020
Call Date: July 1974, Middle Temple
Pupil Master, Assistant Recorder
Qualifications: [LLB Lond]

FOWLER RICHARD NICHOLAS QC (1989)

Monckton Chambers
4 Raymond Buildings, Gray's Inn, London
WC1R 5BP, Telephone: 0171 405 7211
E-mail: chambers@monckton.co.uk
Call Date: Nov 1969, Middle Temple
Qualifications: [BA (Oxon)]

FOWLER MISS TRACEY

Verulam Chambers
Peer House, 8-14 Verulam Street, Gray's
Inn, London WC1X 8LZ,
Telephone: 0171 813 2400
Call Date: Feb 1994, Inner Temple
Qualifications: [LLB (Lond)]

FOX ANDREW PATRICK

Young Street Chambers
38 Young Street, Manchester M3 3FT,
Telephone: 0161 833 0489
E-mail: clerks@young-st-chambers.com
Call Date: Oct 1990, Lincoln's Inn
Qualifications: [LLB (Buck'm)]

FOX MISS ANNA KATHERINE HELEN

Oriel Chambers
14 Water Street, Liverpool L2 8TD,
Telephone: 0151 236 7191/236 4321
E-mail: clerks@oriel-chambers.co.uk
Call Date: July 1986, Middle Temple
Qualifications: [LLB (L'pool)]

FOX LADY HAZEL MARY QC (1993)

4-5 Gray's Inn Square
Ground Floor, Gray's Inn, London
WC1R 5JP, Telephone: 0171 404 5252
E-mail:chambers@4-5graysinnsquare.co.uk
Call Date: June 1950, Lincoln's Inn
Qualifications: [MA (Oxon)]

FOX IAN ANTONY

Chambers of Norman Palmer
2 Field Court, Gray's Inn, London
WC1R 5BB, Telephone: 0171 405 6114
E-mail: fieldct2@netcomuk.co.uk
Call Date: Oct 1990, Middle Temple
Qualifications: [LLB]

FOX JOHN HARVEY

Lamb Building
Ground Floor, Temple, London
EC4Y 7AS, Telephone: 020 7797 7788
E-mail: lamb.building@link.org
Call Date: July 1973, Inner Temple
Qualifications: [LLB (Lond), BDS, LDS]

FOX MISS NICOLA SUSAN

One Garden Court Family Law Chambers
Ground Floor, Temple, London
EC4Y 9BJ, Telephone: 0171 797 7900
E-mail: clerks@onegardencourt.co.uk
Call Date: Oct 1996, Middle Temple
Qualifications: [BSc (Hons)(Lond), MSc ,
CPE (City)]

FOX DR SIMON JAMES

Exchange Chambers
Pearl Assurance House, Derby Square,
Liverpool L2 9XX,
Telephone: 0151 236 7747
E-mail:exchangechambers@btinternet.com
St Philip's Chambers
Fountain Court, Steelhouse Lane,
Birmingham B4 6DR,
Telephone: 0121 246 7000
E-mail: clerks@st-philips.co.uk
Call Date: Nov 1994, Inner Temple
Qualifications: [MB, BS, CPE (City)]

FOXTON DAVID ANDREW

Essex Court Chambers
24 Lincoln's Inn Fields, London
WC2A 3ED, Telephone: 0171 813 8000
E-mail:clerksroom@essexcourt-chambers.co.uk
Call Date: Feb 1989, Gray's Inn
Pupil Master
Qualifications: [BA, BCL (Oxon)]

FOXWELL GEORGE (AUGUSTUS)

Fenners Chambers
3 Madingley Road, Cambridge CB3 0EE,
Telephone: 01223 368761
E-mail: clerks@fennerschambers.co.uk
Fenners Chambers
8-12 Priestgate, Peterborough PE1 1JA,
Telephone: 01733 562030
E-mail: clerks@fennerschambers.co.uk
Call Date: Nov 1987, Middle Temple
Qualifications: [LLB (Leeds)]

FOY JOHN LEONARD QC (1998)

9 Gough Square
London EC4A 3DE,
Telephone: 020 7832 0500
E-mail: clerks@9goughsq.co.uk
Call Date: July 1969, Gray's Inn
Assistant Recorder
Qualifications: [LLB]

FRANCE-HAYHURST MRS JEAN GAYNOR

India Buildings Chambers
Water Street, Liverpool L2 0XG,
Telephone: 0151 243 6000
E-mail: clerks@chambers.u-net.com
Call Date: Nov 1972, Gray's Inn
Qualifications: [LLB (Hons, Wales)]

FRANCES MISS JILL

1 Pump Court
Lower Ground Floor, Temple, London
EC4Y 7AB, Telephone: 0171 583 2012/
353 4341
E-mail: [name]@1pumpcourt.co.uk
Call Date: Nov 1992, Inner Temple
Qualifications: [LLB (So'ton)]

FRANCIS ADRIAN

Twenty-Four Old Buildings
Ground Floor, Lincoln's Inn, London
WC2A 3UP, Telephone: 0171 404 0946
E-mail:clerks@24oldbuildings.law.co.uk
Call Date: Nov 1988, Lincoln's Inn
Pupil Master
Qualifications: [LLB Hons (Wales), BCL (Oxon)]

FRANCIS ANDREW JAMES

Chambers of Mr Peter Crampin QC
Ground Floor, 11 New Square, Lincoln's
Inn, London WC2A 3QB,
Telephone: 020 7831 0081
E-mail: 11newsquare.co.uk
Call Date: Nov 1977, Lincoln's Inn
Pupil Master
Qualifications: [BA (Oxon)]

FRANCIS EDWARD GERALD FRANCIS

Enterprise Chambers
9 Old Square, Lincoln's Inn, London
WC2A 3SR, Telephone: 0171 405 9471
E-mail:enterprise.london@dial.pipex.com
Enterprise Chambers
38 Park Square, Leeds LS1 2PA,
Telephone: 0113 246 0391
E-mail:enterprise.leeds@dial.pipex.com
Enterprise Chambers
65 Quayside, Newcastle upon Tyne
NE1 3DS, Telephone: 0191 222 3344
E-mail:enterprise.newcastle@dial.pipex.com
Call Date: Nov 1995, Inner Temple
Qualifications: [BA (Oxon), CPE (Lond)]

FRANCIS NICHOLAS

29 Bedford Row Chambers
London WC1R 4HE,
Telephone: 0171 831 2626
Call Date: July 1981, Middle Temple
Pupil Master
Qualifications: [MA (Cantab)]

FRANCIS RICHARD MAURICE

9 Park Place
Cardiff CF1 3DP,
Telephone: 01222 382731
Call Date: Nov 1974, Gray's Inn
Pupil Master
Qualifications: [BA (Dunelm)]

FRANCIS ROBERT ANTHONY QC (1992)

3 Serjeants' Inn
London EC4Y 1BQ,
Telephone: 0171 353 5537
E-mail: clerks@3serjeantsinn.com
Call Date: July 1973, Inner Temple
Assistant Recorder
Qualifications: [LLB (Exon)]

FRANCK RICHARD DAVID WILLIAM

Equity Chambers
3rd Floor, 153a Corporation Street,
Birmingham B4 6PH,
Telephone: 0121 233 2100
E-mail: equityatusa.com
Call Date: Oct 1993, Middle Temple
Qualifications: [BA (Hons)(Bris), CPE]

FRANCO GIANPIERO

2 Middle Temple Lane
3rd Floor, Temple, London EC4Y 9AA,
Telephone: 0171 583 4540
Call Date: Nov 1988, Inner Temple
Qualifications: [MA (Cantab), LLB (Lond)]

FRANCOIS HERBERT DOLTON

Chambers of Herbert Francois
62 St James Road, Mitcham, Surrey,
CR4 2DB, Telephone: 0181 640 4529
Call Date: July 1972, Inner Temple
Qualifications: [BA (Hons)]

FRANK IVOR RICHARD BAINTON

1 Gray's Inn Square, Chambers of the Baroness Scotland of Asthal QC
1st Floor, London WC1R 5AG,
Telephone: 0171 405 3000
E-mail: clerks@onegrays.demon.co.uk
Call Date: July 1979, Gray's Inn
Pupil Master
Qualifications: [LLB (Lond) LLM, (Georgetown USA)]

FRANKLIN MISS KIM

One Paper Buildings
Ground Floor, Temple, London
EC4Y 7EP, Telephone: 0171 583 7355
E-mail: clerks@1pb.co.uk
Call Date: Nov 1984, Middle Temple
Pupil Master
Qualifications: [LLB (Warwick)]

Fax: 0171 353 2144; DX: 80 Chancery Lane

Types of work: Adjudication, Arbitration, Construction, Professional negligence

Awards and memberships: TecBA; SCL; Arbitration Club; Forum for Construction Law Reform; Council Member Chartered Institute of Arbitrators

Other professional experience: Fellow Chartered Institute Arbitrators; Approved for appointment as Arbitrator by the President of the RICS

Publications: Co-Editor, *Construction Law Journal*, Bi-monthly; *Legal Obligations of the Architect*, 1996; *Architect's Journal* (columnist), Weekly; *Architect's Journal Legal Handbook*, New Edition; *'Damages for Heartache' The award of general damages in building cases*, 1988 and 1992

Reported Cases: *Surrey Heath BC v Lovell Construction*, [1989] 4 Const LJ 226, 1989. Fire insurance provisions of JCT 180.
West Faulkner Associates v LB Newham, 61 BLR 81, 71 BLR, CA, 1994. Architect's duties and determination provisions of JCT 63.
Bernhard's Rugby Lansayres v Stockley Park Consortium, [1989] 14 Const LJ, 1998. Certifier's functions – breakdown of contract machinery – jurisdiction.

FRANKLIN STEPHEN HALL

Fenners Chambers
3 Madingley Road, Cambridge CB3 0EE,
Telephone: 01223 368761
E-mail: clerks@fennerschambers.co.uk
Fenners Chambers
8-12 Priestgate, Peterborough PE1 1JA,
Telephone: 01733 562030
E-mail: clerks@fennerschambers.co.uk
Five Paper Buildings
1st Floor, Five Paper Bldgs, Temple,
London EC4Y 7HB,
Telephone: 0171 583 6117
E-mail:clerks@5-paperbuildings.law.co.uk
Call Date: Nov 1974, Gray's Inn
Qualifications: [BA (Dunelm)]

D

FRANSMAN LAURENS FRANCOIS

Two Garden Court
1st Floor, Middle Temple, London
EC4Y 9BL, Telephone: 0171 353 1633
E-mail:barristers@2gardenct.law.co.uk
Call Date: July 1979, Middle Temple
Pupil Master
Qualifications: [LLB]

FRASER ALAN RODERICK

Dr Johnson's Chambers
Two Dr Johnson's Buildings, Temple,
London EC4Y 7AY,
Telephone: 0171 353 4716
E-mail: clerks@2djb.freeserve.co.uk
Call Date: Oct 1990, Gray's Inn
Qualifications: [BSc, MSc (London), Dip
Law]

FRASER NIGEL HUGH

8 King's Bench Walk
2nd Floor, Temple, London EC4Y 7DU,
Telephone: 0171 797 8888
8 King's Bench Walk North
1 Park Square East, Leeds LS1 2NE,
Telephone: 0113 2439797
Call Date: Feb 1986, Inner Temple
Qualifications: [LL.B., C.N.A.A.]

FRASER ORLANDO GREGORY

4 Stone Buildings
Ground Floor, Lincoln's Inn, London
WC2A 3XT, Telephone: 0171 242 5524
E-mail:clerks@4stonebuildings.law.co.uk
Call Date: Nov 1994, Inner Temple
Qualifications: [BA (Cantab), CPE (Lond)]

FRASER PETER DONALD

Atkin Chambers
1 Atkin Building, Gray's Inn, London
WC1R 5AT, Telephone: 020 7404 0102
E-mail: clerks@atkin-chambers.co.uk
Call Date: 1989, Middle Temple
Pupil Master
Qualifications: [MA Hons, LLM (Cantab)]

FRASER VINCENT

40 King Street
Manchester M2 6BA,
Telephone: 0161 832 9082
E-mail: clerks@40kingstreet.co.uk

The Chambers of Philip Raynor QC
5 Park Place, Leeds LS1 2RU,
Telephone: 0113 242 1123
Call Date: July 1981, Gray's Inn
Pupil Master
Qualifications: [MA (Oxon)]

FRASER-URQUHART ANDREW

4-5 Gray's Inn Square
Ground Floor, Gray's Inn, London
WC1R 5JP, Telephone: 0171 404 5252
E-mail:chambers@4-5graysinnsquare.co.uk
Call Date: Oct 1993, Middle Temple
Qualifications: [MA (Hons)(Cantab)]

FRAZER CHRISTOPHER MARK

Harcourt Chambers
1st Floor, 2 Harcourt Buildings, Temple,
London EC4Y 9DB,
Telephone: 0171 353 6961
E-mail:clerks@harcourtchambers.law.co.uk
Harcourt Chambers
Churchill House, 3 St Aldate's Courtyard,
St Aldate's, Oxford OX1 1BN,
Telephone: 01865 791559
E-mail:clerks@harcourtchambers.law.co.uk
Call Date: July 1983, Middle Temple
Pupil Master
Qualifications: [MA, LLM (Cantab)]

FRAZER MISS LUCY CLAIRE

3/4 South Square
Gray's Inn, London WC1R 5HP,
Telephone: 0171 696 9900
E-mail: clerks@southsquare.com
Call Date: Oct 1996, Middle Temple
Qualifications: [BA (Hons)(Cantab)]

FREEBORN MS SUSAN CHRISTINE

35 Essex Street
Temple, London WC2R 3AR,
Telephone: 0171 353 6381
E-mail: derek_jenkins@link.org
Call Date: July 1989, Gray's Inn
Qualifications: [BA [Cantab]]

FREEDLAND PROFESSOR MARK ROBERT

St John's College, Oxford OX1 3JP,
Telephone: 01865 277387
Call Date: Nov 1971, Gray's Inn
Qualifications: [LLB (Lond), MA,DPhil (Oxon)]

FREEDMAN BENJAMIN CLIVE QC (1997)

Littleton Chambers
3 King's Bench Walk North, Temple,
London EC4Y 7HR,
Telephone: 0171 797 8600
E-mail:clerks@littletonchambers.co.uk
28 St John Street
Manchester M3 4DJ,
Telephone: 0161 834 8418
E-mail: clerk@28stjohnst.co.uk
Call Date: July 1978, Middle Temple Assistant Recorder
Qualifications: [MA (Cantab)]

FREEDMAN JEREMY STUART

New Court Chambers
3 Broad Chare, Newcastle upon Tyne
NE1 3DQ, Telephone: 0191 232 1980
Plowden Buildings
2nd Floor, 2 Plowden Buildings, Middle
Temple Lane, London EC4Y 9BU,
Telephone: 0171 583 0808
E-mail: bar@plowdenbuildings.co.uk
Call Date: July 1982, Middle Temple Pupil Master
Qualifications: [BA (Hons), Dip Law (City)]

FREEDMAN SAMPSON CLIVE

3 Verulam Buildings
London WC1R 5NT,
Telephone: 0171 831 8441
E-mail: clerks@3verulam.co.uk
Call Date: July 1975, Gray's Inn Pupil Master
Qualifications: [MA (Cantab)]

FREELAND SIMON DENNIS MARSDEN

5 Essex Court
1st Floor, Temple, London EC4Y 9AH,
Telephone: 0171 410 2000
E-mail: barristers@5essexcourt.co.uk
Call Date: July 1978, Gray's Inn Pupil Master, Assistant Recorder
Qualifications: [LLB (Manc)]

FREEMAN KEITH NICHOLAS

1 Crown Office Row
Ground Floor, Temple, London
EC4Y 7HH, Telephone: 0171 797 7500
E-mail: mail@onecrownofficerow.com
Call Date: July 1985, Lincoln's Inn Pupil Master
Qualifications: [MA (City), BA (Reading) Dip Law]

FREEMAN LEE ACRES

2 King's Bench Walk Chambers
1st Floor, 2 King's Bench Walk, Temple,
London EC4Y 7DE,
Telephone: 020 7353 9276
E-mail: chambers@2kbw.co.uk
Call Date: Oct 1994, Lincoln's Inn
Qualifications: [LLB (Hons)(Lond), LLM (Lond)]

FREEMAN MRS MARILYN ANNE

Gray's Inn Chambers
5th Floor, Gray's Inn, London WC1R 5JA,
Telephone: 0171 404 1111
Call Date: Feb 1986, Middle Temple
Qualifications: [BA (Hons), LLM Lond]

FREEMAN PETER MARK

Plowden Buildings
2nd Floor, 2 Plowden Buildings, Middle
Temple Lane, London EC4Y 9BU,
Telephone: 0171 583 0808
E-mail: bar@plowdenbuildings.co.uk
Call Date: Oct 1992, Middle Temple
Qualifications: [LL.B (Hons)]

FREEMAN MRS SALLY JANE

East Anglian Chambers
Gresham House, 5 Museum Street,
Ipswich, Suffolk, IP1 1HQ,
Telephone: 01473 214481
E-mail: ipswich@ealaw.co.uk

East Anglian Chambers
52 North Hill, Colchester, Essex, CO1 1PY,
Telephone: 01206 572756
E-mail: colchester@ealaw.co.uk
East Anglian Chambers
57 London Street, Norwich NR2 1HL,
Telephone: 01603 617351
E-mail: norwich@ealaw.co.uk
Call Date: Nov 1995, Lincoln's Inn
Qualifications: [LLB (Hons)]

FREESTON MISS LYNN ROBERTA

Hardwicke Building
New Square, Lincoln's Inn, London
WC2A 3SB, Telephone: 020 7242 2523
E-mail: clerks@hardwicke.co.uk
Call Date: Oct 1996, Gray's Inn
Qualifications: [BA (Canada), LLB (Lond)]

FRENCH JONATHAN GABRIEL

Chancery House Chambers
7 Lisbon Square, Leeds LS1 4LY,
Telephone: 0113 244 6691
E-mail: chanceryhouse@btinternet.com
Call Date: Nov 1997, Lincoln's Inn
Qualifications: [LLB (Hons)(Manch)]

FRENCH LOUIS CHARLES

**4 Brick Court, Chambers of Anne
Rafferty QC**
1st Floor, Temple, London EC4Y 9AD,
Telephone: 0171 583 8455
Call Date: Nov 1979, Inner Temple
Pupil Master
Qualifications: [MA (Oxon)]

FRENCH PAUL BECKINTON

Guildhall Chambers
22-26 Broad Street, Bristol BS1 2HG,
Telephone: 0117 9273366
E-mail:civil.clerks@guildhallchambers.co.uk and
criminal.clerks@guildhallchambers.co.uk
Call Date: July 1989, Inner Temple
Qualifications: [LLB (Hons)]

FRICKER MRS MARILYN ANN

Sovereign Chambers
25 Park Square, Leeds LS1 2PW,
Telephone: 0113 2451841/2/3
E-mail:sovereignchambers@btinternet.com

Farrar's Building
Temple, London EC4Y 7BD,
Telephone: 0171 583 9241
E-mail:chambers@farrarsbuilding.co.uk
Call Date: Nov 1969, Gray's Inn
Pupil Master

FRIDAY STEPHEN JOHN

Park Lane Chambers
19 Westgate, Leeds LS1 2RD,
Telephone: 0113 2285000
E-mail:clerks@parklanechambers.co.uk
Call Date: Oct 1996, Lincoln's Inn
Qualifications: [LLB (Hons)(E.Ang)]

FRIDD NICHOLAS TIMOTHY

Queens Square Chambers
56 Queens Square, Bristol BS1 4PR,
Telephone: 0117 921 1966
Bell Yard Chambers
116/118 Chancery Lane, London
WC2A 1PP, Telephone: 0171 306 9292
Call Date: Nov 1975, Inner Temple
Pupil Master
Qualifications: [MA (Oxon)]

FRIEDMAN MS CHARLOTTE EVE

1 Pump Court
Lower Ground Floor, Temple, London
EC4Y 7AB, Telephone: 0171 583 2012/
353 4341
E-mail: [name]@1pumpcourt.co.uk
Call Date: July 1982, Gray's Inn
Qualifications: [BA, Msc]

FRIEDMAN DANIEL SIMON

Two Garden Court
1st Floor, Middle Temple, London
EC4Y 9BL, Telephone: 0171 353 1633
E-mail:barristers@2gardenct.law.co.uk
Call Date: Oct 1996, Middle Temple
Qualifications: [BA (Hons) (Oxon), LLM
(Lond)]

FRIEDMAN DAVID PETER QC (1990)

4 Pump Court
Temple, London EC4Y 7AN,
Telephone: 020 7842 5555
E-mail:chambers@4pumpcourt.law.co.uk
Call Date: 1968, Inner Temple
Recorder
Qualifications: [MA, (Oxon), BCL]

FRIEL JOHN ANTHONY

Goldsmith Building
1st Floor, Temple, London EC4Y 7BL,
Telephone: 0171 353 7881
E-mail:clerks@goldsmith-building.law.co.uk
Southsea Chambers
PO Box 148, Southsea, Portsmouth,
Hampshire, PO5 2TU,
Telephone: 01705 291261
Call Date: July 1974, Gray's Inn
Pupil Master
Qualifications: [LLB (Lond)]

FRIEL MISS MICHELE

5 Fountain Court
Steelhouse Lane, Birmingham B4 6DR,
Telephone: 0121 606 0500
E-mail:clerks@5fountaincourt.law.co.uk
Call Date: Oct 1991, Lincoln's Inn
Qualifications: [LLB (Hons)]

FRIESNER DAVID JONATHAN

Chambers of John Hand QC
9 St John Street, Manchester M3 4DN,
Telephone: 0161 955 9000
E-mail: ninesjs@gconnect.com
Call Date: Nov 1988, Gray's Inn
Pupil Master
Qualifications: [LLB (Hons)(Manch)]

FRIEZE DANIEL ISAAC

24a St John Street
Manchester M3 4DF,
Telephone: 0161 833 9628
Call Date: Oct 1994, Gray's Inn
Qualifications: [BA (Manch)]

FRIEZE ROBIN BENNETT

No. 6
6 Park Square, Leeds LS1 2LW,
Telephone: 0113 2459763
E-mail: chambers@no6.co.uk
Call Date: July 1985, Lincoln's Inn
Qualifications: [LLB (Leeds)]

FRIPP ERIC WILLIAM BURTIN

Mitre House Chambers
15-19 Devereux Court, London WC2R 3JJ,
Telephone: 0171 583 8233
Call Date: Oct 1994, Gray's Inn
Qualifications: [MA, LLM]

FRISTON DR MARK HARPHAM

Chambers of Kieran Coonan QC
Ground Floor, 6 Pump Court, Temple,
London EC4Y 7AR,
Telephone: 0171 583 6013/2510
E-mail: clerks@6-pumpcourt.law.co.uk
Call Date: 1997, Middle Temple
Qualifications: [MA, BS, BM (Cantab),
B.Chir., MRCP (UK), Dip Law]

FRITH MS ALEXANDRA HELEN

Westgate Chambers
144 High Street, Lewes, East Sussex,
BN7 1XT, Telephone: 01273 480510
Call Date: Feb 1993, Lincoln's Inn
Qualifications: [LLB (Hons)]

FRITH MISS HEATHER VIVIEN

Kenworthy's Chambers
83 Bridge Street, Manchester M3 2RF,
Telephone: 0161 832 4036/834 6954
E-mail: clerks@kenworthys.co.uk
Call Date: July 1989, Middle Temple
Qualifications: [LLB (Hons) (Bristol)]

FRITH NICHOLAS JOHN

30 Park Square
Leeds LS1 2PF, Telephone: 0113 2436388
E-mail: clerks@30parksquare.co.uk
Call Date: Oct 1992, Gray's Inn
Qualifications: [LLB, LLM (Bucks)]

FRITH TIMOTHY GEORGE

Lamb Chambers
Lamb Building, Temple, London
EC4Y 7AS, Telephone: 020 7797 8300
E-mail: lambchambers@link.org
Call Date: Nov 1996, Middle Temple
Qualifications: [MA (Hons), Dip Law]

FRODSHAM ALEXANDER MILES

Oriel Chambers
14 Water Street, Liverpool L2 8TD,
Telephone: 0151 236 7191/236 4321
E-mail: clerks@oriel-chambers.co.uk
Call Date: Oct 1996, Lincoln's Inn
Qualifications: [LLB (Hons)(L'pool)]

FROST MISS GILLIAN

Mitre Court Chambers
3rd Floor, Temple, London EC4Y 7BP,
Telephone: 0171 353 9394
E-mail: mitrecourt.com
Call Date: Nov 1979, Lincoln's Inn
Pupil Master
Qualifications: [BA (Lond) (Hons)]

FRY NEIL JOHN

Queen Elizabeth Building
Ground Floor, Temple, London
EC4Y 9BS,
Telephone: 0171 353 7181 (12 Lines)
Call Date: Feb 1992, Inner Temple
Qualifications: [LLB (Exeter)]

FRYER ANTHONY JAMES

St Philip's Chambers
Fountain Court, Steelhouse Lane,
Birmingham B4 6DR,
Telephone: 0121 246 7000
E-mail: clerks@st-philips.co.uk
Call Date: July 1995, Gray's Inn
Qualifications: [LLB (Manc)]

FRYER-SPEDDING JAMES WALTER

St James's Chambers
68 Quay Street, Manchester M3 3EJ,
Telephone: 0161 834 7000
E-mail: clerks@stjameschambers.co.uk
Call Date: Feb 1994, Gray's Inn
Qualifications: [LLB (Lond), BCL (Oxon)]

FRYMAN NEIL

Peel Court Chambers
45 Hardman Street, Manchester M3 3PL,
Telephone: 0161 832 3791
E-mail: clerks@peelct.co.uk
Call Date: July 1989, Middle Temple
Qualifications: [LLB [Leic]]

FRYMANN ANDREW PHILIP

Fleet Chambers
Mitre House, 44-46 Fleet Street, London
EC4Y 1BN, Telephone: 0171 936 3707
E-mail: rr@fleetchambers.demon.co.uk
Call Date: Nov 1995, Inner Temple
Qualifications: [LLB (Dunelm)]

FUAD KERIM

Chambers of Helen Grindrod QC
4th Floor, 15-19 Devereux Court, London
WC2R 3JJ, Telephone: 0171 583 2792
Call Date: Nov 1992, Inner Temple
Qualifications: [LLB (Hons)(Lond)]

FULFORD ADRIAN BRUCE QC (1994)

14 Tooks Court
Cursitor St, London EC4A 1LB,
Telephone: 0171 405 8828
E-mail: clerks@tooks.law.co.uk
Call Date: July 1978, Middle Temple
Assistant Recorder
Qualifications: [BA (Soton)]

FULLER ALAN PETER

Albion Chambers
Broad Street, Bristol BS1 1DR,
Telephone: 0117 9272144
Call Date: Oct 1993, Gray's Inn
Qualifications: [LLB (Warw)]

FULLER JONATHAN PAUL

2 King's Bench Walk
Ground Floor, Temple, London
EC4Y 7DE, Telephone: 0171 353 1746
E-mail: 2kbw@atlas.co.uk
King's Bench Chambers
115 North Hill, Plymouth PL4 8JY,
Telephone: 01752 221551
Call Date: July 1977, Lincoln's Inn
Qualifications: [LLB (Lond)]

FULLERTON MICHAEL ANDREW

Sussex Chambers
9 Old Steine, Brighton, Sussex, BN1 1FJ,
Telephone: 01273 607953
Call Date: Feb 1990, Inner Temple
Qualifications: [BA, LLB]

FULLWOOD ADAM GARRETT

Chambers of Ian Macdonald QC (In Association with Two Garden Court, Temple, London)
Waldorf House, 5 Cooper Street,
Manchester M2 2FW,
Telephone: 0161 236 1840
Call Date: Mar 1996, Gray's Inn
Qualifications: [BA, MA (Bris)]

FULTHORPE JONATHAN MARK

17 Carlton Crescent
Southampton SO15 2XR,
Telephone: 023 8032 0320/0823 2003
E-mail: greg@jg17cc.co.uk
Call Date: Nov 1970, Inner Temple
Qualifications: [LLB (Hons), LLM (Lond),
FRGS]

FURBER (ROBERT) JOHN QC (1995)

Wilberforce Chambers
8 New Square, Lincoln's Inn, London
WC2A 3QP, Telephone: 0171 306 0102
E-mail: chambers@wilberforce.co.uk
Call Date: July 1973, Inner Temple
Qualifications: [MA (Cantab)]

Types of work: Chancery land law, Commercial property, Landlord and tenant, Town and country planning

FURLONG RICHARD CRAVEN

3 Gray's Inn Square
Ground Floor, London WC1R 5AH,
Telephone: 0171 520 5600
E-mail: clerks@3gis.co.uk
Call Date: Oct 1994, Lincoln's Inn
Qualifications: [MA , CPE (Lond)]

FURMINGER MICHAEL ASHLEY

Herons Rest
Parkham Lane, Brixham, Devon, TQ5 9JR,
Telephone: 01803 882293
Call Date: Oct 1991, Gray's Inn
Qualifications: [LLB (Lond)]

FURNESS CORIN JOHN

Park Lane Chambers
19 Westgate, Leeds LS1 2RD,
Telephone: 0113 2285000
E-mail:clerks@parklanechambers.co.uk
Call Date: Oct 1994, Lincoln's Inn
Qualifications: [LLB (Hons)(Hull)]

FURNESS (HUGH) JONATHAN

30 Park Place
Cardiff CF1 3BA,
Telephone: 01222 398421
E-mail: 100757.1456@compuserve.com
Call Date: 1979, Gray's Inn
Pupil Master, Assistant Recorder
Qualifications: [MA (Cantab)]

FURNESS MICHAEL JAMES

Wilberforce Chambers
8 New Square, Lincoln's Inn, London
WC2A 3QP, Telephone: 0171 306 0102
E-mail: chambers@wilberforce.co.uk
Call Date: July 1982, Lincoln's Inn
Pupil Master
Qualifications: [MA (Cantab) BCL, (Oxon)]

Types of work: Chancery (general), Charities, Equity, wills and trusts, Pensions, Professional negligence

FURNISS RICHARD ALEXANDER

22 Old Buildings
Lincoln's Inn, London WC2A 3UJ,
Telephone: 0171 831 0222
Call Date: Oct 1991, Middle Temple
Qualifications: [MA (Cantab)]

FURST STEPHEN ANDREW QC (1991)

Keating Chambers
10 Essex Street, Outer Temple, London
WC2R 3AA, Telephone: 0171 544 2600
Call Date: July 1975, Middle Temple
Recorder
Qualifications: [BA (Oxon), LLB
(Hons)(Leeds)]

FURZE MISS CAROLINE MARY

Wilberforce Chambers
8 New Square, Lincoln's Inn, London
WC2A 3QP, Telephone: 0171 306 0102
E-mail: chambers@wilberforce.co.uk
Call Date: Oct 1992, Lincoln's Inn
Qualifications: [BA (Cantab)]

Types of work: Chancery (general), Chancery land law, Charities, Commercial litigation, Equity, wills and trusts, Family provision, Pensions, Probate and administration, Professional negligence

FYSH MICHAEL QC (1989)

8 New Square
Lincoln's Inn, London WC2A 3QP,
Telephone: 0171 405 4321
E-mail: clerks@8newsquare.co.uk
Call Date: May 1965, Inner Temple
Qualifications: [MA (Oxon)]

GABB CHARLES HENRY ESCOTT

Pump Court Chambers
31 Southgate Street, Winchester
SO23 9EE, Telephone: 01962 868161
E-mail: clerks@3pumpcourt.com
Pump Court Chambers
Upper Ground Floor, 3 Pump Court,
Temple, London EC4Y 7AJ,
Telephone: 0171 353 0711
E-mail: clerks@3pumpcourt.com
Pump Court Chambers
5 Temple Chambers, Temple Street,
Swindon SN1 1SQ,
Telephone: 01793 539899
E-mail: clerks@3pumpcourt.com
Call Date: Feb 1975, Middle Temple
Qualifications: [LLB]

GABBAY EDMOND

2 Middle Temple Lane
3rd Floor, Temple, London EC4Y 9AA,
Telephone: 0171 583 4540
Call Date: June 1958, Lincoln's Inn

GADD MICHAEL JOHN

Twenty-Four Old Buildings
Ground Floor, Lincoln's Inn, London
WC2A 3UP, Telephone: 0171 404 0946
E-mail:clerks@24oldbuildings.law.co.uk
Call Date: July 1981, Lincoln's Inn
Pupil Master
Qualifications: [BA (Dunelm)]

GADD RONALD PATRICK

Newport Chambers
12 Clytha Park Road, Newport, Gwent,
NP9 47L, Telephone: 01633 267403/
255855
Call Date: Feb 1971, Gray's Inn
Qualifications: [LL.M]

GADNEY GEORGE MUNRO

Two Crown Office Row
Ground Floor, Temple, London
EC4Y 7HJ, Telephone: 020 7797 8100
E-mail: mail@2cor.co.uk, or to individual
barristers at: [barrister's
surname]@2cor.co.uk
Call Date: Nov 1974, Gray's Inn
Pupil Master
Qualifications: [BA (Cantab)]

GADSDEN MARK JEREMY

2 Harcourt Buildings
1st Floor, Temple, London EC4Y 9DB,
Telephone: 020 7353 2112
Call Date: July 1980, Middle Temple
Pupil Master
Qualifications: [BA (Oxon)]

GAISFORD PHILIP DAVID

3 Serjeants' Inn
London EC4Y 1BQ,
Telephone: 0171 353 5537
E-mail: clerks@3serjeantsinn.com
Call Date: Nov 1969, Gray's Inn
Qualifications: [LLB (Soton)]

GAISMAN JONATHAN NICHOLAS CRISPIN QC (1995)

S Tomlinson QC
7 King's Bench Walk, Temple, London
EC4Y 7DS, Telephone: 0171 583 0404
E-mail: clerks@7kbw.law.co.uk
Call Date: Nov 1979, Inner Temple
Qualifications: [MA, BCL (Oxon)]

GAITSKELL ROBERT QC (1994)

Keating Chambers
10 Essex Street, Outer Temple, London
WC2R 3AA, Telephone: 0171 544 2600
Call Date: July 1978, Gray's Inn
Assistant Recorder
Qualifications: [BSc (Eng), F.I.E.E., FCIArb,
C.Eng]

GAL MS SONIA

28 St John Street
Manchester M3 4DJ,
Telephone: 0161 834 8418
E-mail: clerk@28stjohnst.co.uk
Call Date: Nov 1982, Inner Temple
Assistant Recorder
Qualifications: [BA]

GALBERG MARC KAY

33 Bedford Row
London WC1R 4JH,
Telephone: 0171 242 6476
E-mail:clerks@bedfordrow33.demon.co.uk
Call Date: July 1982, Middle Temple
Pupil Master
Qualifications: [MA (Oxon)]

GALBRAITH-MARTEN JASON NICHOLAS

Cloisters
1 Pump Court, Temple, London
EC4Y 7AA, Telephone: 0171 827 4000
E-mail: clerks@cloisters.com
Call Date: Oct 1991, Middle Temple
Qualifications: [BA Hons (Cantab)]

GALE MICHAEL QC (1979)

One King's Bench Walk
1st Floor, Temple, London EC4Y 7DB,
Telephone: 0171 936 1500
E-mail: ddear@1kbw.co.uk
Call Date: Feb 1957, Middle Temple
Qualifications: [MA (Cantab)]

GALLAFENT MS KATE SELINA

Blackstone Chambers
Blackstone House, Temple, London
EC4Y 9BW, Telephone: 0171 583 1770
E-mail:clerks@blackstonechambers.com
Call Date: 1997, Gray's Inn
Qualifications: [BA]

GALLAGHER BRIAN JOSEPH

12 King's Bench Walk
Temple, London EC4Y 7EL,
Telephone: 0171 583 0811
E-mail: chambers@12kbw.co.uk
Call Date: July 1975, Inner Temple
Pupil Master
Qualifications: [LLB, BL (Kings Inn)]

GALLAGHER JOHN DAVID EDMUND

Goldsmith Building
1st Floor, Temple, London EC4Y 7BL,
Telephone: 0171 353 7881
E-mail:clerks@goldsmith-building.law.co.uk
Call Date: Nov 1974, Gray's Inn
Pupil Master, Assistant Recorder
Qualifications: [BA, AKC (Lond)]

GALLAGHER PATRICK

King Charles House
Standard Hill, Nottingham NG1 6FX,
Telephone: 0115 9418851
E-mail: clerks@kch.co.uk
Call Date: July 1984, Gray's Inn
Qualifications: [BSc (Econ), LLB (Lond)]

GALLAGHER STANLEY HAROLD

Arden Chambers
27 John Street, London WC1N 2BL,
Telephone: 020 7242 4244
E-mail:clerks@arden-chambers.law.co.uk
Call Date: Feb 1994, Lincoln's Inn
Qualifications: [B.Ec,LLB (Austraila)]

GALLEY MRS HELEN MARGARET

Twenty-Four Old Buildings
Ground Floor, Lincoln's Inn, London
WC2A 3UP, Telephone: 0171 404 0946
E-mail:clerks@24oldbuildings.law.co.uk
Call Date: July 1987, Gray's Inn
Pupil Master
Qualifications: [LLB (Lond)]

GALLEY ROBERT EDWARD

Number Ten Baker Street
10 Baker Street, Middlesbrough TS1 2LH,
Telephone: 01642 220332
Call Date: Oct 1993, Lincoln's Inn
Qualifications: [BSc (Econ)(Hons), CPE]

GALLIVAN TERENCE JOHN

6 King's Bench Walk
Ground, Third & Fourth Floors, Temple,
London EC4Y 7DR,
Telephone: 0171 353 4931/583 0695
Call Date: July 1981, Inner Temple
Qualifications: [BA (Dunelm) , LLB (Cantab)]

GALLOWAY MALCOLM KENNITH WILLIAM

South Western Chambers
Melville House, 12 Middle Street,
Taunton, Somerset, TA1 1SH,
Telephone: 01823 331919 (24 hrs)
E-mail: barclerk@clara.net
Call Date: Oct 1992, Inner Temple
Qualifications: [BA (Hons)]

GALPIN MISS DIANA FELICITY

10 King's Bench Walk
Ground Floor, Temple, London
EC4Y 7EB, Telephone: 0171 353 7742
E-mail: 10kbw@lineone.net
Call Date: Nov 1995, Middle Temple
Qualifications: [BA (Hons)]

D

GALVIN KIERAN JOHN MICHAEL CHRISTOPHER

3 Hare Court
1 Little Essex Street, London WC2R 3LD,
Telephone: 0171 395 2000
Call Date: 1996, Middle Temple
Qualifications: [LLB (Hons)(Lond)]

GAMBLE SAMIYYA

John Street Chambers
2 John Street, London WC1N 2HJ,
Telephone: 0171 242 1911
E-mail:john.street_chambers@virgin.net
Call Date: 1998, Lincoln's Inn
Qualifications: [LLB (Hons)(L'pool)]

GAMMIE MALCOLM JAMES

One Essex Court
Ground Floor, Temple, London
EC4Y 9AR, Telephone: 020 7583 2000
E-mail: clerks@oneessexcourt.co.uk
Call Date: Oct 1997, Middle Temple
Qualifications: [MA (Hons)(Cantab)]

GAMMON MRS DAVINA ANNE

Chambers of Davina Gammon
Ground Floor, 103 Walter Road, Swansea,
West Glamorgan, SA1 5QF,
Telephone: 01792 480770
Carmarthen Chambers
30 Spilman Street, Carmarthen, Dyfed,
SA31 1LQ, Telephone: 01267 234410
E-mail: law@in-wales.com
Call Date: July 1979, Middle Temple
Pupil Master
Qualifications: [BA (Hons)]

GANDHI MS PAULENE

Goldsworth Chambers
1st Floor, 11 Gray's Inn Square, London
WC1R 5JD, Telephone: 0171 405 7117
Call Date: Oct 1995, Inner Temple
Qualifications: [BSc (Aberdeen), BA]

GANNER JOSEPH MICHAEL

Nicholas Street Chambers
22 Nicholas Street, Chester CH1 2NX,
Telephone: 01244 323886
E-mail: clerks@40king.co.uk
Call Date: July 1983, Inner Temple
Qualifications: [LLB]

GANNON KEVIN FRANCIS

8 King's Bench Walk
2nd Floor, Temple, London EC4Y 7DU,
Telephone: 0171 797 8888
8 King's Bench Walk North
1 Park Square East, Leeds LS1 2NE,
Telephone: 0113 2439797
Call Date: Nov 1993, Inner Temple
Qualifications: [BSc (Loughborough), CPE]

GARCIA-MILLER MISS LAURA

Enterprise Chambers
9 Old Square, Lincoln's Inn, London
WC2A 3SR, Telephone: 0171 405 9471
E-mail:enterprise.london@dial.pipex.com
Enterprise Chambers
38 Park Square, Leeds LS1 2PA,
Telephone: 0113 246 0391
E-mail:enterprise.leeds@dial.pipex.com
Enterprise Chambers
65 Quayside, Newcastle upon Tyne
NE1 3DS, Telephone: 0191 222 3344
E-mail:enterprise.newcastle@dial.pipex.com
Call Date: July 1989, Middle Temple
Pupil Master
Qualifications: [LLB Hons, Dip in French]

GARDEN IAN HARRISON

Derby Square Chambers
Merchants Court, Derby Square, Liverpool
L2 1TS, Telephone: 0151 709 4222
E-mail:mail.derbysquare@pop3.hiway.co.uk
Call Date: July 1989, Lincoln's Inn
Qualifications: [LLB (Hons Wales)]

GARDINER BRUCE DOUGLAS

2 Temple Gardens
Temple, London EC4Y 9AY,
Telephone: 0171 583 6041
E-mail: clerks@2templegardens.co.uk
Call Date: Oct 1994, Middle Temple
Qualifications: [BA (Hons)(Oxon)]

GARDINER CHARLES NICHOLAS

1 Middle Temple Lane
Temple, London EC4Y 1LT,
Telephone: 0171 583 0659 (12 Lines)
E-mail: chambers@1mtl.co.uk
Call Date: Apr 1967, Middle Temple
Pupil Master

GARDINER MISS EMMA

Queen Elizabeth Building
Ground Floor, Temple, London
EC4Y 9BS,
Telephone: 0171 353 7181 (12 Lines)
Call Date: Nov 1995, Inner Temple
Qualifications: [BA (Oxon)]

GARDINER JOHN RALPH QC (1982)

Chambers of John Gardiner QC
1st Floor, 11 New Square, Lincoln's Inn,
London WC2A 3QB,
Telephone: 0171 242 4017
E-mail: taxlaw@11newsquare.com
Call Date: Nov 1968, Middle Temple
Qualifications: [MA, LLM (Cantab)]

GARDINER RICHARD KINGSWELL

4 Essex Court
Temple, London EC4Y 9AJ,
Telephone: 020 7797 7970
E-mail: clerks@4essexcourt.law.co.uk
Call Date: July 1969, Lincoln's Inn
Qualifications: [MA (Oxon), LL.M. (London)]

GARDINER SEBASTIAN

3 Gray's Inn Square
Ground Floor, London WC1R 5AH,
Telephone: 0171 520 5600
E-mail: clerks@3gis.co.uk
Call Date: Oct 1997, Inner Temple
Qualifications: [BA (Manchester), CPE]

GARDINER WILLIAM DAVID HUGH

95A Chancery Lane
London WC2A 1DT,
Telephone: 0171 405 3101
Call Date: Nov 1976, Middle Temple
Qualifications: [BSc (Chemistry)]

GARDNER ALAN JAMES

One King's Bench Walk
1st Floor, Temple, London EC4Y 7DB,
Telephone: 0171 936 1500
E-mail: ddear@1kbw.co.uk
Call Date: 1997, Middle Temple
Qualifications: [BA (Hons)(Leeds), CPE
(Leeds)]

GARDNER CHRISTOPHER JAMES ELLIS QC (1994)

Lamb Chambers
Lamb Building, Temple, London
EC4Y 7AS, Telephone: 020 7797 8300
E-mail: lambchambers@link.org
Call Date: July 1968, Gray's Inn
Recorder
Qualifications: [MA (Cantab)]

GARDNER MISS EILIDH ANNE MAIRI

22 Old Buildings
Lincoln's Inn, London WC2A 3UJ,
Telephone: 0171 831 0222
Call Date: 1997, Middle Temple
Qualifications: [LLB (Hons)(Newc)]

GARFIELD ROGER GLYN

33 Park Place
Cardiff CF1 3BA,
Telephone: 02920 233313
Farrar's Building
Temple, London EC4Y 7BD,
Telephone: 0171 583 9241
E-mail:chambers@farrarsbuilding.co.uk
Call Date: July 1965, Gray's Inn
Qualifications: [MA, LLB (Cantab)]

GARGAN MISS CATHERINE JANE

Chambers of Michael Pert QC
36 Bedford Row, London WC1R 4JH,
Telephone: 0171 421 8000
E-mail: 36bedfordrow@link.org
Chambers of Michael Pert QC
24 Albion Place, Northampton NN1 1UD,
Telephone: 01604 602333
Chambers of Michael Pert QC
104 New Walk, Leicester LE1 7EA,
Telephone: 0116 249 2020
Call Date: July 1978, Middle Temple
Pupil Master
Qualifications: [LLB (L'pool)]

GARGAN MARK PATRICK

No. 6
6 Park Square, Leeds LS1 2LW,
Telephone: 0113 2459763
E-mail: chambers@no6.co.uk
Call Date: July 1983, Middle Temple
Pupil Master
Qualifications: [MA (Oxon)]

GARLAND MS ANNA ELIZABETH MCCLENNON

4 Fountain Court
Steelhouse Lane, Birmingham B4 6DR,
Telephone: 0121 236 3476
Call Date: Feb 1994, Inner Temple
Qualifications: [BA (Cantab)]

GARLAND DAVID ROBERTSON

Brick Court Chambers
7-8 Essex Street, London WC2R 3LD,
Telephone: 0171 379 3550
E-mail: [surname]@brickcourt.co.uk
Call Date: Nov 1986, Middle Temple
Pupil Master
Qualifications: [LLB, LLM, AKC (Lond)]

GARLICK PAUL RICHARD QC (1996)

Pump Court Chambers
Upper Ground Floor, 3 Pump Court,
Temple, London EC4Y 7AJ,
Telephone: 0171 353 0711
E-mail: clerks@3pumpcourt.com
Pump Court Chambers
31 Southgate Street, Winchester
SO23 9EE, Telephone: 01962 868161
E-mail: clerks@3pumpcourt.com
Pump Court Chambers
5 Temple Chambers, Temple Street,
Swindon SN1 1SQ,
Telephone: 01793 539899
E-mail: clerks@3pumpcourt.com
Call Date: July 1974, Middle Temple
Recorder

GARNER ADRIAN JOHN ROBINSON

2 Harcourt Buildings
Ground Floor/Left, Temple, London
EC4Y 9DB, Telephone: 0171 583 9020
E-mail: clerks@harcourt.co.uk
Call Date: Nov 1985, Middle Temple
Qualifications: [LLB (Buck)]

GARNER GRAHAM HOWARD

Southsea Chambers
PO Box 148, Southsea, Portsmouth,
Hampshire, PO5 2TU,
Telephone: 01705 291261
Call Date: Feb 1966, Gray's Inn
Pupil Master

GARNER MISS SOPHIE JANE

199 Strand
London WC2R 1DR,
Telephone: 0171 379 9779
E-mail: chambers@199strand.co.uk
Call Date: Nov 1990, Middle Temple
Pupil Master
Qualifications: [LLB]

GARNETT KEVIN MITCHELL QC (1991)

5 New Square
Ground Floor, Lincoln's Inn, London
WC2A 3RJ, Telephone: 020 7404 0404
E-mail:chambers@fivenewsquare.demon.co.uk
Call Date: Nov 1975, Middle Temple
Assistant Recorder
Qualifications: [MA (Oxon)]

GARNETT MRS SUSAN JANE LOUISA

Thomas More Chambers
52 Carey Street, Lincoln's Inn, London
WC2A 2JB, Telephone: 0171 404 7000
E-mail: clerks@thomasmore.law.co.uk
Call Date: July 1973, Lincoln's Inn
Pupil Master
Qualifications: [BA]

GARNHAM NEIL STEPHEN

1 Crown Office Row
Ground Floor, Temple, London
EC4Y 7HH, Telephone: 0171 797 7500
E-mail: mail@onecrownofficerow.com
Crown Office Row Chambers
Blenheim House, 120 Church Street,
Brighton, Sussex, BN1 1WH,
Telephone: 01273 625625
E-mail: crownofficerow@clara.net
Call Date: July 1982, Middle Temple
Pupil Master
Qualifications: [MA (Cantab)]

GARNHAM TOM EDWARD KARL

Guildhall Chambers Portsmouth
Prudential Buildings, 16 Guildhall Walk,
Portsmouth, Hampshire, PO1 2DE,
Telephone: 01705 752400
Call Date: Nov 1995, Middle Temple
Qualifications: [BA (Hons)]

GARNIER EDWARD HENRY QC (1995)

1 Brick Court
1st Floor, Temple, London EC4Y 9BY,
Telephone: 0171 353 8845
E-mail: clerks@1brickcourt.co.uk
Call Date: July 1976, Middle Temple
Assistant Recorder
Qualifications: [MA (Oxon)]

GARRETT MISS ANNALISSA

Chambers of Kieran Coonan QC
Ground Floor, 6 Pump Court, Temple,
London EC4Y 7AR,
Telephone: 0171 583 6013/2510
E-mail: clerks@6-pumpcourt.law.co.uk
Call Date: Nov 1991, Inner Temple
Qualifications: [BA (Hons)(Dunelm)]

GARRETT MICHAEL OWEN

St Philip's Chambers
Fountain Court, Steelhouse Lane,
Birmingham B4 6DR,
Telephone: 0121 246 7000
E-mail: clerks@st-philips.co.uk
Call Date: July 1967, Gray's Inn
Pupil Master

GARRIDO DAMIAN ROBIN LEON

2 Pump Court
1st Floor, Temple, London EC4Y 7AH,
Telephone: 0171 353 5597
Call Date: Nov 1993, Middle Temple
Qualifications: [BA (Hons)(Kent), Dip Law
(City)]

GARROOD JEREMY DAVID

New Court
Temple, London EC4Y 9BE,
Telephone: 0171 583 5123/0510
Call Date: May 1996, Lincoln's Inn
Qualifications: [BA (Hons)]

GARSIDE CHARLES ROGER QC (1993)

Chambers of John Hand QC
9 St John Street, Manchester M3 4DN,
Telephone: 0161 955 9000
E-mail: ninesjs@gconnect.com

**4 Brick Court, Chambers of Anne
Rafferty QC**
1st Floor, Temple, London EC4Y 9AD,
Telephone: 0171 583 8455
Call Date: Nov 1971, Gray's Inn
Recorder

GARSIDE DAVID VERNON

White Friars Chambers
21 White Friars, Chester CH1 1NZ,
Telephone: 01244 323070
E-mail:whitefriarschambers@btinternet.com
Call Date: Nov 1982, Gray's Inn
Pupil Master
Qualifications: [LLB (Hons)]

GARSIDE MR MARK KIRKLAND

Victoria Chambers
3rd Floor, 177 Corporation Street,
Birmingham B4 6RG,
Telephone: 0121 236 9900
E-mail: viccham@aol.com
Call Date: Feb 1993, Inner Temple
Qualifications: [BA]

GARTH STEVEN DAVID

Sovereign Chambers
25 Park Square, Leeds LS1 2PW,
Telephone: 0113 2451841/2/3
E-mail:sovereignchambers@btinternet.com
Call Date: Nov 1983, Gray's Inn
Pupil Master
Qualifications: [LLB (Hons) (Leeds)]

GARVIN MICHAEL

18 St John Street
Manchester M3 4EA,
Telephone: 0161 278 1800
E-mail: 18stjohn@lineone.net
Call Date: Nov 1994, Inner Temple
Qualifications: [BA (Oxon)]

GARWOOD JOSHUA DAHREN

1 Pump Court
Lower Ground Floor, Temple, London
EC4Y 7AB, Telephone: 0171 583 2012/
353 4341
E-mail: [name]@1pumpcourt.co.uk
Call Date: Nov 1992, Middle Temple
Qualifications: [BA (Hons)(Lancs)]

GASH WILLIAM SIMON WALKER

Ropewalk Chambers
24 The Ropewalk, Nottingham NG1 5EF,
Telephone: 0115 9472581
E-mail: administration@ropewalk co.uk
Call Date: July 1977, Gray's Inn
Pupil Master

GASKELL NICHOLAS JOSEPH JAMES

4 Essex Court
Temple, London EC4Y 9AJ,
Telephone: 020 7797 7970
E-mail: clerks@4essexcourt.law.co.uk
Call Date: July 1976, Inner Temple

GASKELL RICHARD CARL

65-67 King Street
Leicester LE1 6RP,
Telephone: 0116 2547710
Call Date: July 1971, Lincoln's Inn
Pupil Master, Recorder
Qualifications: [LLB]

GASSMAN MISS CAROLINE DORA

8 King's Bench Walk
2nd Floor, Temple, London EC4Y 7DU,
Telephone: 0171 797 8888
8 King's Bench Walk North
1 Park Square East, Leeds LS1 2NE,
Telephone: 0113 2439797
Call Date: July 1974, Inner Temple
Qualifications: [LLB (Leeds)(Hons)]

GASTON GRAEME

39 Park Square
Leeds LS1 2NU,
Telephone: 0113 2456633
Call Date: Oct 1991, Lincoln's Inn
Qualifications: [LLB (Hons) (Leeds)]

GASZTOWICZ STEVEN

2-3 Gray's Inn Square
Gray's Inn, London WC1R 5JH,
Telephone: 0171 242 4986
E-mail:chambers@2-3graysinnsquare.co.uk
2 New Street
Leicester LE1 5NA,
Telephone: 0116 2625906
E-mail: clerks@2newstreet.co.uk
Call Date: July 1981, Gray's Inn
Pupil Master
Qualifications: [LLB]

GATENBY JAMES MICHAEL

First National Chambers
2nd Floor, First National Building, 24
Fenwick Street, Liverpool L2 7NE,
Telephone: 0151 236 2098
Call Date: Oct 1994, Middle Temple
Qualifications: [LLB (Hons)(L'pool)]

GATESHILL JOSEPH BERNARD

Wilberforce Chambers
7 Bishop Lane, Hull, East Yorkshire,
HU1 1PA, Telephone: 01482 323264
E-mail: clerks@hullbar.demon.co.uk
Call Date: July 1972, Lincoln's Inn
Pupil Master, Assistant Recorder
Qualifications: [MA (Cantab)]

GATLAND GLENN DALE

New Court Chambers
3 Broad Chare, Newcastle upon Tyne
NE1 3DQ, Telephone: 0191 232 1980
Call Date: Nov 1972, Gray's Inn
Pupil Master
Qualifications: [LLB (Hons) Fellow of,
Caribbean Law , Institute]

GATLEY MARK DOUGLAS

Chambers of Helen Grindrod QC
4th Floor, 15-19 Devereux Court, London
WC2R 3JJ, Telephone: 0171 583 2792
Call Date: Oct 1993, Gray's Inn
Qualifications: [BA]

GATT IAN ANDREW

Littleton Chambers
3 King's Bench Walk North, Temple,
London EC4Y 7HR,
Telephone: 0171 797 8600
E-mail:clerks@littletonchambers.co.uk
Call Date: July 1985, Lincoln's Inn
Pupil Master
Qualifications: [BA (Oxon)]

GATTO MISS NICOLA ESTERINA

8 King's Bench Walk
2nd Floor, Temple, London EC4Y 7DU,
Telephone: 0171 797 8888
8 King's Bench Walk North
1 Park Square East, Leeds LS1 2NE,
Telephone: 0113 2439797
Call Date: Nov 1987, Middle Temple
Qualifications: [LLB (B'ham)]

GATTY DANIEL SIMON

New Court Chambers
5 Verulam Buildings, Gray's Inn, London
WC1R 5LY, Telephone: 0171 831 9500
E-mail: mail@newcourtchambers.com
Call Date: Oct 1990, Middle Temple
Pupil Master
Qualifications: [BA (Manch), Dip Law]

GAU JUSTIN CHARLES

Pump Court Chambers
Upper Ground Floor, 3 Pump Court,
Temple, London EC4Y 7AJ,
Telephone: 0171 353 0711
E-mail: clerks@3pumpcourt.com
Pump Court Chambers
31 Southgate Street, Winchester
SO23 9EE, Telephone: 01962 868161
E-mail: clerks@3pumpcourt.com
Pump Court Chambers
5 Temple Chambers, Temple Street,
Swindon SN1 1SQ,
Telephone: 01793 539899
E-mail: clerks@3pumpcourt.com
Call Date: July 1989, Middle Temple
Pupil Master
Qualifications: [LLB (Lond)]

GAULT SIMON ANGUS GRAHAM LESLIE

4 Essex Court
Temple, London EC4Y 9AJ,
Telephone: 020 7797 7970
E-mail: clerks@4essexcourt.law.co.uk
Call Date: Nov 1970, Gray's Inn
Recorder
Qualifications: [LLB]

GAUNT JONATHAN ROBERT QC (1991)

Falcon Chambers
Falcon Court, London EC4Y 1AA,
Telephone: 0171 353 2484
E-mail: clerks@falcon-chambers.com
Call Date: July 1972, Lincoln's Inn
Qualifications: [BA (Oxon)]

GAUNT MISS SARAH LEVINA

Chambers of Michael Pert QC
36 Bedford Row, London WC1R 4JH,
Telephone: 0171 421 8000
E-mail: 36bedfordrow@link.org

Chambers of Michael Pert QC
24 Albion Place, Northampton NN1 1UD,
Telephone: 01604 602333
Chambers of Michael Pert QC
104 New Walk, Leicester LE1 7EA,
Telephone: 0116 249 2020
Call Date: Oct 1992, Lincoln's Inn
Qualifications: [LLB(Hons)(Wales), MPhil
(Cantab)]

GAVAGHAN JONATHAN DAVID

The Chambers of Leolin Price CBE, QC
10 Old Square, Lincoln's Inn, London
WC2A 3SU, Telephone: 0171 405 0758
Call Date: Oct 1992, Lincoln's Inn
Qualifications: [MA(Hons), BCL (Oxon)]

GAVRON MS JESSICA LEAH

9-12 Bell Yard
London WC2A 2LF,
Telephone: 0171 400 1800
E-mail: clerks@bellyard.co.uk
Call Date: Oct 1995, Inner Temple
Qualifications: [BA (Cantab), CPE (City)]

GAYLORD MRS SHEILA

2 King's Bench Walk Chambers
1st Floor, 2 King's Bench Walk, Temple,
London EC4Y 7DE,
Telephone: 020 7353 9276
E-mail: chambers@2kbw.co.uk
Call Date: Nov 1983, Gray's Inn
Pupil Master
Qualifications: [LLM LLB (Lond)]

GBESAN JAMES YOMI

Chambers of Martin Burr
Fourth Floor, Eldon Chambers, 30/32
Fleet Street, London EC4Y 1AA,
Telephone: 0171 353 4636
Call Date: Feb 1992, Lincoln's Inn
Qualifications: [LLB (Hon)]

D

GEARTY PROFESSOR CONOR ANTHONY

Essex Court Chambers
24 Lincoln's Inn Fields, London
WC2A 3ED, Telephone: 0171 813 8000
E-mail:clerksroom@essexcourt-chambers.co.u
k
Call Date: 1995, Middle Temple
Qualifications: [BCL , LLB (Hons), PhD
(Cantab)]

GEARY GAVIN JOHN

S Tomlinson QC
7 King's Bench Walk, Temple, London
EC4Y 7DS, Telephone: 0171 583 0404
E-mail: clerks@7kbw.law.co.uk
Call Date: Feb 1989, Gray's Inn
Qualifications: [BA (Oxon)]

GEDDES MS JOANNA FAY

One Garden Court Family Law Chambers
Ground Floor, Temple, London
EC4Y 9BJ, Telephone: 0171 797 7900
E-mail: clerks@onegardencourt.co.uk
Call Date: Nov 1992, Gray's Inn
Qualifications: [BA (Lond)]

GEDERON MARVIN THEOPHILUS

Britton Street Chambers
1st Floor, 20 Britton Street, London
EC1M 5NQ, Telephone: 0171 608 3765
Call Date: Nov 1979, Lincoln's Inn
Pupil Master
Qualifications: [BA]

GEDGE SIMON JOHN FRANCIS

Chambers of Helen Grindrod QC
4th Floor, 15-19 Devereux Court, London
WC2R 3JJ, Telephone: 0171 583 2792
Call Date: Nov 1984, Inner Temple
Pupil Master
Qualifications: [MA (Oxon)]

GEE ANTHONY HALL QC (1990)

28 St John Street
Manchester M3 4DJ,
Telephone: 0161 834 8418
E-mail: clerk@28stjohnst.co.uk
Call Date: July 1972, Gray's Inn
Recorder

GEE MISS MARGARET ANN

Luton Bedford Chambers
C/O Mr Alex Reid, 92 Holly Park Road,
Friern Barnet, London N11 3HB,
Telephone: 0181 361 9024/0181 444 6637
Call Date: July 1979, Gray's Inn
Qualifications: [BA (Lond)]

GEE RICHARD SIMON

Cobden House Chambers
19 Quay Street, Manchester M3 3HN,
Telephone: 0161 833 6000
E-mail: clerks@cobden.co.uk
Call Date: Oct 1993, Lincoln's Inn
Qualifications: [MA (Oxon), Dip Law (Lond)]

GEE STEVEN MARK QC (1993)

4 Field Court
Gray's Inn, London WC1R 5EA,
Telephone: 0171 440 6900
E-mail: chambers@4fieldcourt.co.uk
Call Date: July 1975, Middle Temple
Qualifications: [MA (Oxon)]

GEE TOBY DAVID

One Paper Buildings
Ground Floor, Temple, London
EC4Y 7EP, Telephone: 0171 583 7355
E-mail: clerks@1pb.co.uk
Call Date: Oct 1992, Inner Temple
Qualifications: [MA (Cantab), CPE]

GEEKIE CHARLES NAIRN

One Garden Court Family Law Chambers
Ground Floor, Temple, London
EC4Y 9BJ, Telephone: 0171 797 7900
E-mail: clerks@onegardencourt.co.uk
Call Date: July 1985, Inner Temple
Pupil Master
Qualifications: [LLB(Bristol)]

GEERING IAN WALTER QC (1991)

3 Verulam Buildings
London WC1R 5NT,
Telephone: 0171 831 8441
E-mail: clerks@3verulam.co.uk
Call Date: Nov 1974, Inner Temple
Recorder
Qualifications: [BVMS]

GEESON CHRISTOPHER PAUL

High Pavement Chambers
1 High Pavement, Nottingham NG1 1HF,
Telephone: 0115 9418218
Call Date: Nov 1989, Gray's Inn
Qualifications: [BA]

GEEY DAVID SIMON

Martins Building
2nd Floor, No 4 Water Street, Liverpool
L2 3SP, Telephone: 0151 236 5818/4919
Call Date: July 1970, Inner Temple
Pupil Master, Recorder
Qualifications: [LLB]

GELBART GEOFFREY ALAN

1 Gray's Inn Square
Ground Floor, London WC1R 5AA,
Telephone: 0171 405 8946/7/8
Call Date: Nov 1982, Lincoln's Inn
Pupil Master
Qualifications: [BA (Hons), LLM, (Lond)]

GELDART WILLIAM RALPH

6 King's Bench Walk
Ground, Third & Fourth Floors, Temple,
London EC4Y 7DR,
Telephone: 0171 353 4931/583 0695
Call Date: July 1975, Inner Temple
Pupil Master
Qualifications: [BA (Open)]

GENN MS YVETTE NAOMI

Two Garden Court
1st Floor, Middle Temple, London
EC4Y 9BL, Telephone: 0171 353 1633
E-mail:barristers@2gardenct.law.co.uk
Call Date: Oct 1991, Inner Temple
Qualifications: [BA (Warw), Dip Law]

GENNEY PAUL WALTON

Wilberforce Chambers
7 Bishop Lane, Hull, East Yorkshire,
HU1 1PA, Telephone: 01482 323264
E-mail: clerks@hullbar.demon.co.uk
Call Date: May 1976, Middle Temple
Qualifications: [BDS]

GEORGE ANDREW JAMES

Blackstone Chambers
Blackstone House, Temple, London
EC4Y 9BW, Telephone: 0171 583 1770
E-mail:clerks@blackstonechambers.com
Call Date: Oct 1997, Gray's Inn
Qualifications: [BA]

GEORGE CHARLES RICHARD QC (1992)

2 Harcourt Buildings
2nd Floor, Temple, London EC4Y 9DB,
Telephone: 020 7353 8415
E-mail: clerks@2hb.law.co.uk
Call Date: July 1974, Inner Temple
Recorder
Qualifications: [MA (Oxon)]

GEORGE DONALD ERIC JOSEPH

Leone Chambers
72 Evelyn Avenue, Kingsbury, London
NW9 OJH, Telephone: 0181 200 4020
E-mail: festus4@leonechambers.co.uk
Call Date: July 1973, Gray's Inn
Pupil Master
Qualifications: [BA (Durham)]

GEORGE MISS JUDITH SARAH

St Philip's Chambers
Fountain Court, Steelhouse Lane,
Birmingham B4 6DR,
Telephone: 0121 246 7000
E-mail: clerks@st-philips.co.uk
Call Date: Oct 1991, Middle Temple
Qualifications: [BA Hons (Cantab)]

GEORGE MARK MCHALLAM

Two Garden Court
1st Floor, Middle Temple, London
EC4Y 9BL, Telephone: 0171 353 1633
E-mail:barristers@2gardenct.law.co.uk
Call Date: Nov 1976, Inner Temple
Pupil Master
Qualifications: [BA (Cantab)]

D

GEORGE MICHAEL DAVID ROBERTS

Goldsmith Chambers
Ground Floor, Goldsmith Building,
Temple, London EC4Y 7BL,
Telephone: 0171 353 6802/3/4/5
E-mail:clerks@goldsmithchambers.law.co.uk
Call Date: Nov 1990, Gray's Inn
Pupil Master
Qualifications: [LLB]

GEORGE NICHOLAS FRANK RAYMOND

New Walk Chambers
27 New Walk, Leicester LE1 6TE,
Telephone: 0116 2559144
Call Date: July 1983, Inner Temple
Qualifications: [LLB (Manch)]

GEORGE MISS SUSAN DEBORAH

8 King's Bench Walk
2nd Floor, Temple, London EC4Y 7DU,
Telephone: 0171 797 8888
8 King's Bench Walk North
1 Park Square East, Leeds LS1 2NE,
Telephone: 0113 2439797
Call Date: Nov 1990, Gray's Inn
Qualifications: [LLB Hons (Lond)]

GEORGES ANTONIS

Martins Building
2nd Floor, No 4 Water Street, Liverpool
L2 3SP, Telephone: 0151 236 5818/4919
Call Date: July 1972, Inner Temple
Qualifications: [LLB]

GEORGHIADES ELIKKOS

Bromley Chambers
39 Durham Road, Bromley, Kent,
BR2 0SN, Telephone: 0181 325 0863
Call Date: July 1975, Middle Temple
Qualifications: [LLB (Lond)]

GERALD NIGEL MORTIMER

Enterprise Chambers
9 Old Square, Lincoln's Inn, London
WC2A 3SR, Telephone: 0171 405 9471
E-mail:enterprise.london@dial.pipex.com
Enterprise Chambers
38 Park Square, Leeds LS1 2PA,
Telephone: 0113 246 0391
E-mail:enterprise.leeds@dial.pipex.com

Enterprise Chambers
65 Quayside, Newcastle upon Tyne
NE1 3DS, Telephone: 0191 222 3344
E-mail:enterprise.newcastle@dial.pipex.com
Call Date: July 1985, Gray's Inn
Pupil Master
Qualifications: [LLB (Lond)]

GERASIMIDIS NICOLAS

Furnival Chambers
32 Furnival Street, London EC4A 1JQ,
Telephone: 0171 405 3232
E-mail: clerks@furnivallaw.co.uk
Call Date: Nov 1988, Inner Temple
Qualifications: [LLB (So'ton)]

GERMAIN RICHARD

4 Brick Court, Chambers of Anne Rafferty QC
1st Floor, Temple, London EC4Y 9AD,
Telephone: 0171 583 8455
Call Date: July 1968, Inner Temple
Pupil Master

GERRANS DANIEL

Twenty-Four Old Buildings
Ground Floor, Lincoln's Inn, London
WC2A 3UP, Telephone: 0171 404 0946
E-mail:clerks@24oldbuildings.law.co.uk
Call Date: Nov 1981, Middle Temple
Pupil Master
Qualifications: [LLB (Cantab)]

GERRARD LEE JOHN

The Chambers of Mr Ali Mohammed Azhar
Basement, 9 King's Bench Walk, Temple,
London EC4Y 7DX,
Telephone: 0171 353 9564
E-mail: jvlee@btinternet.com
Call Date: Mar 1996, Gray's Inn
Qualifications: [BA (Hons)(Newc), CPE]

GERREY DAVID CLIFF

9 Gough Square
London EC4A 3DE,
Telephone: 020 7832 0500
E-mail: clerks@9goughsq.co.uk
Call Date: Feb 1975, Gray's Inn
Recorder
Qualifications: [LLB]

GERRISH SIMON DAVID PETER

7 Stone Buildings (also at 11 Bolt Court)
1st Floor, Lincoln's Inn, London
WC2A 3SZ, Telephone: 0171 242 0961
E-mail:larthur@7stonebuildings.law.co.uk
11 Bolt Court (also at 7 Stone Buildings – 1st Floor)
London EC4A 3DQ,
Telephone: 0171 353 2300
E-mail: boltct11@aol.com
Redhill Chambers
Seloduct House, 30 Station Road, Redhill, Surrey, RH1 1NF,
Telephone: 01737 780781
Call Date: Oct 1993, Gray's Inn
Qualifications: [MA (Hons)(Oxon)]

GERRY MISS FELICITY RUTH

2 New Street
Leicester LE1 5NA,
Telephone: 0116 2625906
E-mail: clerks@2newstreet.co.uk
Call Date: Oct 1994, Middle Temple
Qualifications: [LLB (Hons)]

GERSCH ADAM NISSEN

Trafalgar Chambers
53 Fleet Street, London EC4Y 1BE,
Telephone: 0171 583 5858
E-mail:trafalgarchambers@easynet.co.uk
Call Date: Oct 1993, Lincoln's Inn
Qualifications: [LLB (Hons)]

GESER MS ANITA

Lamb Building
Ground Floor, Temple, London
EC4Y 7AS, Telephone: 020 7797 7788
E-mail: lamb.building@link.org
Call Date: Feb 1992, Middle Temple
Qualifications: [BA (Econ) (Lond)]

GHAFFAR ARSHAD

4 Field Court
Gray's Inn, London WC1R 5EA,
Telephone: 0171 440 6900
E-mail: chambers@4fieldcourt.co.uk
Call Date: Oct 1991, Middle Temple
Qualifications: [LLB Hons (Exon), LLM (Cantab)]

GHAFFAR RASIB

12 Old Square
1st Floor, Lincoln's Inn, London
WC2A 3TX, Telephone: 0171 404 0875
Call Date: July 1995, Lincoln's Inn
Qualifications: [LLB (Hons), LLM]

GHORPADE BHASKER YESHWANT

Call Date: Nov 1973, Lincoln's Inn
Qualifications: [BA (Lond)]

GHOSE MISS KATIE

Call Date: Oct 1996, Middle Temple
Qualifications: [BA (Hons)(Oxon)]

GHOSH INDRANIL JULIAN

24 Old Buildings
First Floor, Lincoln's Inn, London
WC2A 3UP, Telephone: 020 7242 2744
E-mail: taxchambers@compuserve.com
40 King Street
Manchester M2 6BA,
Telephone: 0161 832 9082
E-mail: clerks@40kingstreet.co.uk
The Chambers of Philip Raynor QC
5 Park Place, Leeds LS1 2RU,
Telephone: 0113 242 1123
Call Date: July 1993, Lincoln's Inn
Qualifications: [LLB (Edinburgh), LLM (Lond), Fellow of Queen Mary, & Westfield College, University of London]

GIBAUD MISS CATHERINE ALISON ANNETTA

3 Verulam Buildings
London WC1R 5NT,
Telephone: 0171 831 8441
E-mail: clerks@3verulam.co.uk
Call Date: Oct 1996, Gray's Inn
Qualifications: [B.Bus.Sc (Hons), (Cape Town)]

GIBB MISS FIONA MARGARET

Queen Elizabeth Building
Ground Floor, Temple, London
EC4Y 9BS,
Telephone: 0171 353 7181 (12 Lines)
Call Date: July 1983, Middle Temple
Qualifications: [LLB (B'ham)]

D

GIBBERD MISS ANNE HEATHER

4 Brick Court
Ground Floor, Temple, London
EC4Y 9AD, Telephone: 0171 797 7766
E-mail: chambers@4brick.co.uk
Call Date: Nov 1985, Gray's Inn
Qualifications: [LLB (Sheffield)]

GIBBON MISS JULIET REBECCA

32 Park Place
Cardiff CF1 3BA,
Telephone: 01222 397364
Call Date: Oct 1994, Lincoln's Inn
Qualifications: [LLB (Hons)(Glamorg)]

GIBBON MICHAEL NEIL

13 Old Square
Ground Floor, Lincoln's Inn, London
WC2A 3UA, Telephone: 0171 404 4800
E-mail: clerks@13oldsquare.law.co.uk
Call Date: Nov 1993, Gray's Inn
Qualifications: [BA, M.Phil]

GIBBONS CHRISTOPHER CHARLES

Rowchester Chambers
4 Rowchester Court, Whittall Street,
Birmingham B4 6DH,
Telephone: 0121 233 2327/2361951
Call Date: July 1977, Gray's Inn
Pupil Master
Qualifications: [BSc (B'ham)]

GIBBONS JAMES FRANCIS

3 Stone Buildings
Lincoln's Inn, London WC2A 3XL,
Telephone: 0171 242 4937
E-mail: clerks@3sb.law.co.uk
Call Date: July 1974, Gray's Inn
Pupil Master

GIBBONS JEREMY STEWART QC (1995)

17 Carlton Crescent
Southampton SO15 2XR,
Telephone: 023 8032 0320/0823 2003
E-mail: greg@jg17cc.co.uk
35 Essex Street
Temple, London WC2R 3AR,
Telephone: 0171 353 6381
E-mail: derek_jenkins@link.org
Call Date: July 1973, Gray's Inn
Recorder

GIBBONS ORLANDO ADZIMA

10 King's Bench Walk
Ground Floor, Temple, London
EC4Y 7EB, Telephone: 0171 353 7742
E-mail: 10kbw@lineone.net
Call Date: Nov 1982, Gray's Inn
Pupil Master
Qualifications: [LLB (Lond)]

GIBBONS MRS SARAH ISOBEL

13 King's Bench Walk
1st Floor, Temple, London EC4Y 7EN,
Telephone: 0171 353 7204
E-mail: clerks@13kbw.law.co.uk
King's Bench Chambers
32 Beaumont Street, Oxford OX1 2NP,
Telephone: 01865 311066
E-mail: clerks@kbc-oxford.law.co.uk
Call Date: Nov 1987, Middle Temple
Qualifications: [BA(Hons) B'ham, Dip Law
(City)]

GIBBS MRS JOCELYN IDA

8 King's Bench Walk
2nd Floor, Temple, London EC4Y 7DU,
Telephone: 0171 797 8888
Call Date: Nov 1972, Lincoln's Inn
Pupil Master
Qualifications: [LLB (Hons) (Lond)]

GIBBS MS LISA KLAIRE

Enfield Chambers
First Floor, Refuge House, 9-10 River
Front, Enfield, Middlesex, EN1 3SZ,
Telephone: 0181 364 5627
E-mail:enfieldchambers@compuserve.com
Call Date: Oct 1995, Inner Temple
Qualifications: [BA (Lond), CPE (City)]

GIBBS PATRICK MICHAEL EVAN

2 Harcourt Buildings
1st Floor, Temple, London EC4Y 9DB,
Telephone: 020 7353 2112
Call Date: Nov 1986, Middle Temple
Pupil Master
Qualifications: [BA(Oxon) Dip Law Cit]

GIBBS PHILIP MARK

De Montfort Chambers
95 Princess Road East, Leicester LE1 7DQ,
Telephone: 0116 254 8686
E-mail: dmcbar@aol.com
Call Date: Oct 1991, Inner Temple
Qualifications: [BA (E Anglia), Dip Law]

GIBNEY MALCOLM THOMAS PATRICK

17 Carlton Crescent
Southampton SO15 2XR,
Telephone: 023 8032 0320/0823 2003
E-mail: greg@jg17cc.co.uk
Call Date: July 1981, Inner Temple
Pupil Master
Qualifications: [LLB (Cardiff)]

GIBSON ARTHUR GEORGE ADRIAN

Adrian Lyon's Chambers
14 Castle Street, Liverpool L2 0NE,
Telephone: 0151 236 4421/8240
E-mail: chambers14@aol.com
Call Date: July 1980, Lincoln's Inn
Qualifications: [LLB Hons (Lond)]

GIBSON MISS CAROLINE CATHERINE ROSE

One King's Bench Walk
1st Floor, Temple, London EC4Y 7DB,
Telephone: 0171 936 1500
E-mail: ddear@1kbw.co.uk
Call Date: Nov 1990, Inner Temple
Qualifications: [BA (Oxon), Dip Law (City)]

GIBSON CHARLES ANTHONY WARNEFORD

2 Harcourt Buildings
Ground Floor/Left, Temple, London
EC4Y 9DB, Telephone: 0171 583 9020
E-mail: clerks@harcourt.co.uk
Call Date: July 1984, Inner Temple
Pupil Master
Qualifications: [BA (Dunelm) Dip Law]

GIBSON CHRISTOPHER ALLEN WOOD QC (1995)

Chambers of John L Powell QC
Four New Square, Lincoln's Inn, London
WC2A 3RJ, Telephone: 0171 797 8000
E-mail: barristers@4newsquare.com
Call Date: July 1976, Middle Temple
Qualifications: [BA (Oxon)]

GIBSON MISS JILL MAUREEN

Chambers of Mr Peter Crampin QC
Ground Floor, 11 New Square, Lincoln's
Inn, London WC2A 3QB,
Telephone: 020 7831 0081
E-mail: 11newsquare.co.uk
Call Date: July 1972, Middle Temple
Qualifications: [BA (Hons) (Bristol)]

GIBSON JOHN ARTHUR

India Buildings Chambers
Water Street, Liverpool L2 0XG,
Telephone: 0151 243 6000
E-mail: clerks@chambers.u-net.com
Call Date: Nov 1993, Lincoln's Inn
Qualifications: [LLB (Hons, B'ham)]

GIBSON JOHN WILLIAM

Chambers of Michael Pert QC
36 Bedford Row, London WC1R 4JH,
Telephone: 0171 421 8000
E-mail: 36bedfordrow@link.org
Chambers of Michael Pert QC
24 Albion Place, Northampton NN1 1UD,
Telephone: 01604 602333
Chambers of Michael Pert QC
104 New Walk, Leicester LE1 7EA,
Telephone: 0116 249 2020
Call Date: Nov 1991, Inner Temple
Qualifications: [LLB (Dunelm)]

GIBSON JONATHAN HEDLEY

Broadway House Chambers
Broadway House, 9 Bank Street, Bradford,
West Yorkshire, BD1 1TW,
Telephone: 01274 722560
E-mail: clerks@broadwayhouse.co.uk
Broadway House Chambers
31 Park Square West, Leeds LS1 2PF,
Telephone: 0113 246 2600
Call Date: 1982, Gray's Inn
Pupil Master, Assistant Recorder
Qualifications: [LLB (Nottm)]

GIBSON MARTIN JOHN

Littman Chambers
12 Gray's Inn Square, London WC1R 5JP,
Telephone: 020 7404 4866
E-mail: admin@littmanchambers.com
Call Date: Oct 1990, Lincoln's Inn
Pupil Master
Qualifications: [BA (Oxon)]

GIBSON ROBERT MARK TIMOTHY

Oriel Chambers
14 Water Street, Liverpool L2 8TD,
Telephone: 0151 236 7191/236 4321
E-mail: clerks@oriel-chambers.co.uk
Call Date: Nov 1981, Middle Temple
Qualifications: [MA (Oxon)]

GIBSON-LEE DAVID MICHAEL

Bell Yard Chambers
116/118 Chancery Lane, London
WC2A 1PP, Telephone: 0171 306 9292
Call Date: July 1970, Lincoln's Inn
Pupil Master
Qualifications: [LLB]

GIDNEY JONATHAN ALFRED

Claremont Chambers
26 Waterloo Road, Wolverhampton
WV1 4BL, Telephone: 01902 426222
Call Date: Oct 1991, Inner Temple
Qualifications: [BA (Hons)]

GIFFIN NIGEL DYSON

11 King's Bench Walk
Temple, London EC4Y 7EQ,
Telephone: 0171 632 8500/583 0610
E-mail: clerksroom@11kbw.com
Call Date: Nov 1986, Inner Temple
Pupil Master
Qualifications: [MA (Oxon)]

GIFFORD ANDREW JAMES MORRIS

7 New Square
Lincoln's Inn, London WC2A 3QS,
Telephone: 0171 430 1660
Call Date: July 1988, Lincoln's Inn
Qualifications: [BA (Hons) (Oxon), Dip Law
(City)]

GIFFORD LORD ANTHONY MAURICE QC (1982)

8 King's Bench Walk
2nd Floor, Temple, London EC4Y 7DU,
Telephone: 0171 797 8888
8 King's Bench Walk North
1 Park Square East, Leeds LS1 2NE,
Telephone: 0113 2439797
Call Date: July 1962, Middle Temple
Qualifications: [MA (Cantab)]

GIFFORD MISS CYNTHIA ALICE SOPHIE

Verulam Chambers
Peer House, 8-14 Verulam Street, Gray's
Inn, London WC1X 8LZ,
Telephone: 0171 813 2400
Call Date: July 1988, Gray's Inn
Qualifications: [BA (Hons)(Manc), MSc
(LSE), Dip Law]

GIFFORD ROBERT GUTHRIE

2 King's Bench Walk Chambers
1st Floor, 2 King's Bench Walk, Temple,
London EC4Y 7DE,
Telephone: 020 7353 9276
E-mail: chambers@2kbw.co.uk
Call Date: Nov 1977, Inner Temple
Pupil Master

GILBART ANDREW JAMES QC (1991)

40 King Street
Manchester M2 6BA,
Telephone: 0161 832 9082
E-mail: clerks@40kingstreet.co.uk
4 Breams Buildings
London EC4A 1AQ,
Telephone: 0171 353 5835/430 1221
E-mail:breams@4breamsbuildings.law.co.uk
The Chambers of Philip Raynor QC
5 Park Place, Leeds LS1 2RU,
Telephone: 0113 242 1123
Call Date: Nov 1972, Middle Temple
Recorder
Qualifications: [MA (Cantab)]

GILBERT BARRY DAVID

10 King's Bench Walk
1st Floor, Temple, London EC4Y 7EB,
Telephone: 0171 353 2501
Call Date: July 1978, Gray's Inn
Pupil Master
Qualifications: [LLB (So'ton), Dip Ara
(Lond)]

GILBERT FRANCIS HUMPHREY SHUBRICK QC (1992)

Walnut House
63 St David's Hill, Exeter, Devon,
EX4 4DW, Telephone: 01392 279751
E-mail: 106627.2451@compuserve.com
Call Date: July 1970, Lincoln's Inn
Recorder
Qualifications: [MA (Dublin)]

GILBERT FRANCIS PETER

Mitre House Chambers
15-19 Devereux Court, London WC2R 3JJ,
Telephone: 0171 583 8233
Call Date: July 1980, Lincoln's Inn
Pupil Master
Qualifications: [BD, AKC, MA]

GILBERT MRS JAYNE EILEEN

3 Temple Gardens
Lower Ground Floor, Temple, London
EC4Y 9AU, Telephone: 0171 353 3102/5/
9297 E-mail: clerks@3tg.co.uk
Call Date: July 1976, Middle Temple
Pupil Master

GILBERT MS JULIA JANE

Trinity Chambers
9-12 Trinity Chare, Quayside, Newcastle
upon Tyne NE1 3DF,
Telephone: 0191 232 1927
E-mail: info@trinitychambers.co.uk
Call Date: Nov 1994, Middle Temple
Qualifications: [LLB (Hons)]

GILBERT ROBERT JOHN

Fountain Chambers
Cleveland Business Centre, 1 Watson
Street, Middlesbrough TS1 2RQ,
Telephone: 01642 804040
E-mail:fountainchambers@onyxnet.co.uk
Call Date: Apr 1986, Middle Temple
Qualifications: [LLB (L'pool), P.G.C.E.]

GILBERTSON MRS HELEN ALISON

East Anglian Chambers
52 North Hill, Colchester, Essex, CO1 1PY,
Telephone: 01206 572756
E-mail: colchester@ealaw.co.uk
East Anglian Chambers
57 London Street, Norwich NR2 1HL,
Telephone: 01603 617351
E-mail: norwich@ealaw.co.uk
East Anglian Chambers
Gresham House, 5 Museum Street,
Ipswich, Suffolk, IP1 1HQ,
Telephone: 01473 214481
E-mail: ipswich@ealaw.co.uk
Call Date: Nov 1993, Middle Temple
Qualifications: [LLB (Hons)(E.Anglia)]

GILCHRIST DAVID SOMERLED

Chambers of John Hand QC
9 St John Street, Manchester M3 4DN,
Telephone: 0161 955 9000
E-mail: ninesjs@gconnect.com
Call Date: Nov 1987, Inner Temple
Qualifications: [BA (Dunelm)]

GILCHRIST MISS NAOMI ROBERTA

5 Fountain Court
Steelhouse Lane, Birmingham B4 6DR,
Telephone: 0121 606 0500
E-mail:clerks@5fountaincourt.law.co.uk
Call Date: July 1996, Inner Temple
Qualifications: [LLB (Reading)]

GILCHRIST NICHOLAS JOHN

Corn Exchange Chambers
5th Floor, Fenwick Street, Liverpool
L2 7QS, Telephone: 0151 227 1081/5009
Call Date: July 1975, Gray's Inn
Recorder
Qualifications: [LLB (Aberystwyth)]

GILEAD MISS BERYL LOUISE

St Mary's Chambers
50 High Pavement, Lace Market,
Nottingham NG1 1HW,
Telephone: 0115 9503503
E-mail: clerks@smc.law.co.uk
Call Date: Feb 1989, Inner Temple
Pupil Master
Qualifications: [BA (Keele)]

D

GILES DAVID WILLIAM

Verulam Chambers
Peer House, 8-14 Verulam Street, Gray's
Inn, London WC1X 8LZ,
Telephone: 0171 813 2400
Call Date: Nov 1988, Lincoln's Inn
Pupil Master
Qualifications: [LLB Hons]

GILES ROGER STEPHEN

5 Fountain Court
Steelhouse Lane, Birmingham B4 6DR,
Telephone: 0121 606 0500
E-mail:clerks@5fountaincourt.law.co.uk
Call Date: July 1976, Gray's Inn
Qualifications: [BA]

GILL MISS BALJINDER

Watford Chambers
74 Mildred Avenue, Watford,
Hertfordshire, WD1 7DX,
Telephone: 01923 220553
Call Date: Oct 1996, Inner Temple
Qualifications: [BA (Wolves)]

GILL CLIFFORD WILLIAM

Call Date: July 1989, Inner Temple
Qualifications: [MA [Oxon], ACA]

GILL GURNAM SINGH

Rowchester Chambers
4 Rowchester Court, Whittall Street,
Birmingham B4 6DH,
Telephone: 0121 233 2327/2361951
Call Date: Nov 1978, Middle Temple
Qualifications: [BSc (Lond)]

GILL MISS JANE ELIZABETH

17 Bedford Row
London WC1R 4EB,
Telephone: 0171 831 7314
E-mail: iboard7314@aol.com
Call Date: July 1973, Gray's Inn
Qualifications: [MA]

GILL MANJIT SINGH

6 King's Bench Walk
Ground, Third & Fourth Floors, Temple,
London EC4Y 7DR,
Telephone: 0171 353 4931/583 0695
Call Date: July 1982, Gray's Inn
Pupil Master
Qualifications: [LLB (Lond)]

GILL MISS MEENA

4 Brick Court
Ground Floor, Temple, London
EC4Y 9AD, Telephone: 0171 797 7766
E-mail: chambers@4brick.co.uk
Call Date: July 1982, Middle Temple
Pupil Master

GILL MISS PAMILLA

1 Dr Johnson's Buildings
Ground Floor, Temple, London
EC4Y 7AX, Telephone: 0171 353 9328
E-mail:OneDr.Johnsons@btinternet.com
Call Date: Apr 1989, Lincoln's Inn
Qualifications: [LLB(Hons)]

GILL MS SARAH TERESA

Old Square Chambers
1 Verulam Buildings, Gray's Inn, London
WC1R 5LQ, Telephone: 0171 269 0300
E-mail:clerks@oldsquarechambers.co.uk
Old Square Chambers
Hanover House, 47 Corn Street, Bristol
BS1 1HT, Telephone: 0117 9277111
E-mail: oldsqbri@globalnet.co.uk
Call Date: Feb 1990, Lincoln's Inn
Pupil Master
Qualifications: [BA Hons (Manc)]

Fax: 0171 405 1387;
Out of hours telephone: 07971 269 492;
DX: 1046 Chancery Lane

Types of work: Civil liberties, Discrimination,
Employment, Environment, Pensions,
Personal injury

Awards and memberships: Public Law project;
Industrial Law Society; ELBA; ELA

Other professional experience: Solicitor; Editorial Board Equal Opportunity Report;
Part-time Employment Tribunal Chairman
1995 to date

Publications: *Health and Safety Liability and Litigation*, 1996

Reported Cases: *Halpenny v IGE Medical Systems*, [1999] IRLR 177 (CA), 1999. Maternity/dismissal/sex discrimination. *Strathclyde Regional Council v Wallace*, [1998] ICR 205 (HL), 1998. Equal pay/ material factor; defence and requirement on employer to objectively justify pay difference. *Carmichael v National Power Plc*, [1998] IRLR 301 (CA), 1998. Ruling on when casual workers are employees. *Grant v South West Trains*, [1998] IRLR 188 (HL), 1998. Contract of employment and non-incorporation of equal opportunities policy. *Scullard v Knowles*, [1996] ICR 1007 (EAT), 1996. Equal Pay Act, Article 119 and requirement for comparator to be in the same employment.

GILL SATINDER SINGH

5 Paper Buildings
Ground Floor, Temple, London
EC4Y 7HB, Telephone: 0171 583 9275/
583 4555 E-mail: 5paper@link.org
Call Date: Feb 1991, Middle Temple
Qualifications: [LLB (Manch)]

GILL SIMON MURRAY

29 Bedford Row Chambers
London WC1R 4HE,
Telephone: 0171 831 2626
Call Date: July 1977, Middle Temple
Pupil Master
Qualifications: [LLB]

GILLAN MRS DOMINIQUE LYE-PING

Guildford Chambers
Stoke House, Leapale Lane, Guildford,
Surrey, GU1 4LY,
Telephone: 01483 539131
E-mail:guildford.barristers@btinternet.com
Call Date: Oct 1998, Gray's Inn
Qualifications: [LLB (Belfast)]

GILLANCE KENNETH

39 Park Square
Leeds LS1 2NU,
Telephone: 0113 2456633
Call Date: Nov 1977, Gray's Inn
Pupil Master, Recorder
Qualifications: [MA (Keele) LLB, (Lond)]

GILLARD MISS ISABELLE

2-4 Tudor Street
London EC4Y 0AA,
Telephone: 0171 797 7111
E-mail: clerks@rfqc.co.uk
Call Date: July 1980, Middle Temple
Pupil Master
Qualifications: [LLB (B'Ham)]

GILLESPIE CHRISTOPHER MICHAEL

3 Temple Gardens
2nd Floor, Temple, London EC4Y 9AU,
Telephone: 0171 583 1155
Call Date: Nov 1991, Gray's Inn
Qualifications: [BA (Cantab)]

GILLESPIE JAMES EDWARD

Enfield Chambers
First Floor, Refuge House, 9-10 River
Front, Enfield, Middlesex, EN1 3SZ,
Telephone: 0181 364 5627
E-mail:enfieldchambers@compuserve.com
Call Date: Nov 1991, Middle Temple
Qualifications: [BA Hons (Dunelm)]

GILLETTE JOHN CHARLES

Baker Street Chambers
9 Baker Street, Middlesbrough TS1 2LF,
Telephone: 01642 873873
Call Date: Oct 1990, Middle Temple
Qualifications: [LLB (Manc)]

GILLIATT MS JACQUELINE

Francis Taylor Building
3rd Floor, Temple, London EC4Y 7BY,
Telephone: 0171 797 7250
Call Date: Feb 1992, Middle Temple
Qualifications: [BA (Hon) (Oxon), Dip Law]

GILLIBRAND PHILIP MARTIN MANGNALL

Pump Court Chambers
31 Southgate Street, Winchester
SO23 9EE, Telephone: 01962 868161
E-mail: clerks@3pumpcourt.com
Pump Court Chambers
Upper Ground Floor, 3 Pump Court,
Temple, London EC4Y 7AJ,
Telephone: 0171 353 0711
E-mail: clerks@3pumpcourt.com
Pump Court Chambers
5 Temple Chambers, Temple Street,
Swindon SN1 1SQ,
Telephone: 01793 539899
E-mail: clerks@3pumpcourt.com
Call Date: July 1975, Gray's Inn
Pupil Master
Qualifications: [LLB (Lond)]

GILLING MISS DENISE ANN

Mitre House Chambers
15-19 Devereux Court, London WC2R 3JJ,
Telephone: 0171 583 8233
Call Date: Oct 1992, Lincoln's Inn
Qualifications: [LLB(Hons)]

GILLIS RICHARD LESLIE IRVINE

One Essex Court
Ground Floor, Temple, London
EC4Y 9AR, Telephone: 020 7583 2000
E-mail: clerks@oneessexcourt.co.uk
Call Date: Nov 1982, Lincoln's Inn
Pupil Master
Qualifications: [BA, BCL (Oxon)]

GILLMAN MISS RACHEL MARY

3 Dr Johnson's Buildings
Ground Floor, Temple, London
EC4Y 7BA, Telephone: 0171 353 4854
E-mail: clerks@3djb.co.uk
Call Date: July 1988, Gray's Inn
Pupil Master
Qualifications: [LLB (Lond)]

GILLOTT PAUL ALAN ASHLEY

15 Winckley Square
Preston PR1 3JJ,
Telephone: 01772 252828
E-mail:clerks@winckleysq.demon.co.uk
Call Date: Oct 1996, Middle Temple
Qualifications: [BA (Hons)(Oxon), CPE (City)]

GILLYON PHILIP JEFFREY

Erskine Chambers
30 Lincoln's Inn Fields, Lincoln's Inn,
London WC2A 3PF,
Telephone: 0171 242 5532
E-mail:clerks@erskine-chambers.co.uk
Call Date: July 1988, Middle Temple
Pupil Master
Qualifications: [MA (Hons) (Cantab)]

GILMAN JONATHAN CHARLES BAGOT QC (1990)

Essex Court Chambers
24 Lincoln's Inn Fields, London
WC2A 3ED, Telephone: 0171 813 8000
E-mail:clerksroom@essexcourt-chambers.co.uk
Call Date: Feb 1965, Middle Temple
Qualifications: [MA (Oxon)]

GILMARTIN JOHN

New Court
Temple, London EC4Y 9BE,
Telephone: 0171 583 5123/0510
Call Date: Nov 1972, Lincoln's Inn
Pupil Master
Qualifications: [BA, BCom]

GILMORE IAN MARTIN

30 Park Square
Leeds LS1 2PF, Telephone: 0113 2436388
E-mail: clerks@30parksquare.co.uk
Call Date: Oct 1996, Middle Temple
Qualifications: [BA (Hons)(Oxon), CPE (Leeds)]

GILMORE MISS MARY SEANIN

Chambers of John L Powell QC
Four New Square, Lincoln's Inn, London
WC2A 3RJ, Telephone: 0171 797 8000
E-mail: barristers@4newsquare.com
Call Date: Nov 1996, Gray's Inn
Qualifications: [BA (Cantab)]

GILMOUR NIGEL BENJAMIN DOUGLAS QC (1990)

Oriel Chambers
14 Water Street, Liverpool L2 8TD,
Telephone: 0151 236 7191/236 4321
E-mail: clerks@oriel-chambers.co.uk
Call Date: July 1970, Inner Temple

Recorder
Qualifications: [LLB (L'pool)]

GILMOUR MS SUSAN EVELYN MARY

Cobden House Chambers
19 Quay Street, Manchester M3 3HN,
Telephone: 0161 833 6000
E-mail: clerks@cobden.co.uk
Call Date: Nov 1994, Inner Temple
Qualifications: [LLB (Sussex)]

GILROY PAUL

Chambers of John Hand QC
9 St John Street, Manchester M3 4DN,
Telephone: 0161 955 9000
E-mail: ninesjs@gconnect.com
Farrar's Building
Temple, London EC4Y 7BD,
Telephone: 0171 583 9241
E-mail:chambers@farrarsbuilding.co.uk
Call Date: Nov 1985, Gray's Inn
Qualifications: [LLB (Dundee)]

GIMLETTE JOHN ELIOT

1 Crown Office Row
Ground Floor, Temple, London
EC4Y 7HH, Telephone: 0171 797 7500
E-mail: mail@onecrownofficerow.com
Call Date: July 1986, Inner Temple
Pupil Master
Qualifications: [BA Cantab]

GINN MISS ALISON IRENE

Maidstone Chambers
33 Earl Street, Maidstone, Kent, ME14 1PF,
Telephone: 01622 688592
E-mail:maidstonechambers@compuserve.co
m
Call Date: July 1980, Gray's Inn
Pupil Master
Qualifications: [BA, LL.M (Lond)]

GINNIFF NIGEL THOMAS

Adrian Lyon's Chambers
14 Castle Street, Liverpool L2 0NE,
Telephone: 0151 236 4421/8240
E-mail: chambers14@aol.com
Call Date: July 1978, Inner Temple
Qualifications: [LLB]

GINNS JOHN ALFRED BERNARD

New Walk Chambers
27 New Walk, Leicester LE1 6TE,
Telephone: 0116 2559144
Call Date: Nov 1977, Inner Temple
Qualifications: [LLB (Lond), ACIS]

GINSBURG MRS AMANDA

37 Park Square Chambers
37 Park Square, Leeds LS1 2NY,
Telephone: 0113 2439422
E-mail: chambers@no37.co.uk
Call Date: July 1986, Lincoln's Inn
Qualifications: [LLB (London)]

GIOSERANO RICHARD STEPHEN

No. 6
6 Park Square, Leeds LS1 2LW,
Telephone: 0113 2459763
E-mail: chambers@no6.co.uk
Call Date: Nov 1992, Gray's Inn
Qualifications: [LLB (Newc)]

GIOVANNETTI MISS LISA CATERINA

Chambers of Norman Palmer
2 Field Court, Gray's Inn, London
WC1R 5BB, Telephone: 0171 405 6114
E-mail: fieldct2@netcomuk.co.uk
Call Date: Nov 1990, Gray's Inn
Qualifications: [LLB]

GIOVENE LAURENCE

2 Pump Court
1st Floor, Temple, London EC4Y 7AH,
Telephone: 0171 353 5597
Call Date: July 1962, Lincoln's Inn
Pupil Master, Recorder
Qualifications: [MA (Cantab)]

GIRET JOSEPH JOHN BELA LESLIE

Francis Taylor Building
Ground Floor, Temple, London
EC4Y 7BY, Telephone: 0171 353 7768/
7769/2711
E-mail:clerks@francistaylorbuilding.law.co.uk
Call Date: Feb 1985, Gray's Inn
Qualifications: [LLB Hons (Warwick)]

D

GIRET MRS JOSEPHINE JANE

11 Stone Buildings
Lincoln's Inn, London WC2A 3TG,
Telephone: +44 (0)207 831 6381
E-mail:clerks@11StoneBuildings.law.co.uk
Chichester Chambers
12 North Pallant, Chichester, West Sussex,
PO19 1TQ, Telephone: 01243 784538
E-mail:clerks@chichesterchambers.law.co.uk
Call Date: July 1981, Inner Temple
Pupil Master
Qualifications: [Diploma in Law]

GIRLING MISS SARAH ELIZABETH

3 Stone Buildings
Lincoln's Inn, London WC2A 3XL,
Telephone: 0171 242 4937
E-mail: clerks@3sb.law.co.uk
Call Date: July 1986, Gray's Inn
Pupil Master
Qualifications: [BA (Cantab)]

GIROLAMI PAUL JULIAN

13 Old Square
Ground Floor, Lincoln's Inn, London
WC2A 3UA, Telephone: 0171 404 4800
E-mail: clerks@13oldsquare.law.co.uk
Call Date: Nov 1983, Middle Temple
Pupil Master
Qualifications: [BA (Cantab)]

GITTINS TIMOTHY JAMES

Trinity Chambers
9-12 Trinity Chare, Quayside, Newcastle
upon Tyne NE1 3DF,
Telephone: 0191 232 1927
E-mail: info@trinitychambers.co.uk
Call Date: Oct 1990, Middle Temple
Qualifications: [LLB (Manch)]

GIULIANI MARK PAUL ROBINSON

Furnival Chambers
32 Furnival Street, London EC4A 1JQ,
Telephone: 0171 405 3232
E-mail:clerks@furnivallaw.co.uk
Call Date: Oct 1993, Gray's Inn
Qualifications: [BSc (Warw)]

GIZ MISS ALEV AYSE

6 King's Bench Walk
Ground, Third & Fourth Floors, Temple,
London EC4Y 7DR,
Telephone: 0171 353 4931/583 0695
Call Date: Nov 1988, Gray's Inn
Qualifications: [LLB (Hons) (Lond)]

GLADWELL SIMON MARK

John Street Chambers
2 John Street, London WC1N 2HJ,
Telephone: 0171 242 1911
E-mail:john.street_chambers@virgin.net
Call Date: Oct 1996, Inner Temple
Qualifications: [BA (Lond)]

GLAH ROBERT KWAO

Equity Barristers' Chambers
Temple Chambers, Second Floor rooms
152-153, 3-7 Temple Avenue, London
EC4Y 0NP, Telephone: 0181 558 8336
E-mail: equitylawyer@equitybar.co.uk
Call Date: 1971, Inner Temple
Qualifications: [LLM, PhD (Lond)]

GLANCY ROBERT PETER QC (1997)

Devereux Chambers
Devereux Court, London WC2R 3JJ,
Telephone: 0171 353 7534
E-mail: mailbox@devchambers.co.uk
Call Date: July 1972, Middle Temple
Recorder
Qualifications: [MA (Cantab)]

GLANVILLE MISS SUSAN ELIZABETH

Mitre House Chambers
15-19 Devereux Court, London WC2R 3JJ,
Telephone: 0171 583 8233
Call Date: Oct 1991, Inner Temple
Qualifications: [BA (Lond), CPE]

GLASGOW EDWIN JOHN QC (1987)

39 Essex Street
London WC2R 3AT,
Telephone: 0171 832 1111
E-mail: clerks@39essex.co.uk
Call Date: Nov 1969, Gray's Inn
Qualifications: [LLB (Lond)]

GLASGOW OLIVER EDWIN JAMES

1 Hare Court
Ground Floor, Temple, London
EC4Y 7BE, Telephone: 0171 353 3982/
5324
Call Date: Nov 1995, Middle Temple
Qualifications: [BA (Hons)]

GLASS ADAM SOLOMON

Mitre Court Chambers
3rd Floor, Temple, London EC4Y 7BP,
Telephone: 0171 353 9394
E-mail: mitrecourt.com
Call Date: Oct 1994, Lincoln's Inn
Qualifications: [BA (Hons)(L'pool)]

GLASS ANTHONY TREVOR QC (1986)

Hollis Whiteman Chambers
3rd Floor, Queen Elizabeth Bldg, Temple,
London EC4Y 9BS,
Telephone: 020 7583 5766
E-mail:barristers@holliswhiteman.co.uk
Call Date: July 1965, Inner Temple
Recorder
Qualifications: [BA (Oxon)]

GLASSBROOK ALEXANDER JAMES

1 Temple Gardens
1st Floor, Temple, London EC4Y 9BB,
Telephone: 0171 583 1315/353 0407
E-mail: clerks@1templegardens.co.uk
Call Date: Oct 1995, Middle Temple
Qualifications: [BA (Bris)]

GLASSON JONATHAN JOSEPH

Doughty Street Chambers
11 Doughty Street, London WC1N 2PG,
Telephone: 0171 404 1313
E-mail:enquiries@doughtystreet.co.uk
Call Date: Mar 1996, Middle Temple
Qualifications: [MA]

GLAZE ANTHONY JOHN

Clock Chambers
78 Darlington Street, Wolverhampton
WV1 4LY, Telephone: 01902 313444
Call Date: Feb 1992, Inner Temple
Qualifications: [BA, CPE (Lond)]

GLEDHILL ANDREAS NIKOLAUS

3/4 South Square
Gray's Inn, London WC1R 5HP,
Telephone: 0171 696 9900
E-mail: clerks@southsquare.com
Call Date: Nov 1992, Middle Temple
Qualifications: [MA (Hons) (Cantab), CPE]

GLEDHILL KRIS

Camberwell Chambers
66 Grove Park, Camberwell, London
SE5 8LF, Telephone: 0171 274 0830
E-mail: 100622.3604@compuserve.com
Call Date: July 1989, Inner Temple
Qualifications: [BA (Oxon), LLM (Virginia)]

GLEDHILL MICHAEL GEOFFREY JAMES

2 Dyers Buildings
London EC1N 2JT,
Telephone: 0171 404 1881
Call Date: July 1976, Middle Temple
Pupil Master, Recorder
Qualifications: [MA (Oxon)]

GLEN IAN DOUGLAS QC (1996)

Guildhall Chambers
22-26 Broad Street, Bristol BS1 2HG,
Telephone: 0117 9273366
E-mail:civil.clerks@guildhallchambers.co.uk and
criminal.clerks@guildhallchambers.co.uk
Call Date: Nov 1973, Gray's Inn
Assistant Recorder
Qualifications: [LLB (Lond)]

GLEN PHILIP ALEXANDER

17 Carlton Crescent
Southampton SO15 2XR,
Telephone: 023 8032 0320/0823 2003
E-mail: greg@jg17cc.co.uk
Call Date: July 1983, Middle Temple
Qualifications: [LLB(Lond)]

GLENN PAUL ANTHONY

4 Fountain Court
Steelhouse Lane, Birmingham B4 6DR,
Telephone: 0121 236 3476
Call Date: Nov 1983, Gray's Inn
Qualifications: [LLB (L'pool)]

GLENNIE ANDREW DAVID

13 King's Bench Walk
1st Floor, Temple, London EC4Y 7EN,
Telephone: 0171 353 7204
E-mail: clerks@13kbw.law.co.uk
King's Bench Chambers
32 Beaumont Street, Oxford OX1 2NP,
Telephone: 01865 311066
E-mail: clerks@kbc-oxford.law.co.uk
Call Date: July 1982, Middle Temple
Pupil Master
Qualifications: [MA (Oxon)]

GLENNIE ANGUS JAMES SCOTT QC (1991)

20 Essex Street
London WC2R 3AL,
Telephone: 0171 583 9294
E-mail: clerks@20essexst.com
Call Date: July 1974, Lincoln's Inn
Qualifications: [MA (Cantab)]

GLENSER PETER HEATH

Eighteen Carlton Crescent
Southampton SO15 2XR,
Telephone: 01703 639001
Call Date: Oct 1993, Inner Temple
Qualifications: [LLB (S'ton)]

GLICK IAN BERNARD QC (1987)

One Essex Court
Ground Floor, Temple, London
EC4Y 9AR, Telephone: 020 7583 2000
E-mail: clerks@oneessexcourt.co.uk
Call Date: Nov 1970, Inner Temple
Qualifications: [MA, BCL (Oxon)]

GLOAG ANGUS ROBIN

1 Gray's Inn Square
Ground Floor, London WC1R 5AA,
Telephone: 0171 405 8946/7/8
Call Date: Oct 1992, Inner Temple
Qualifications: [LLB (Hons)]

GLOBE HENRY BRIAN QC (1994)

Exchange Chambers
Pearl Assurance House, Derby Square,
Liverpool L2 9XX,
Telephone: 0151 236 7747
E-mail:exchangechambers@btinternet.com
Call Date: July 1972, Middle Temple

Recorder
Qualifications: [LLB]

GLOSSOP GEORGE WILLIAM

1 Harcourt Buildings
2nd Floor, Temple, London EC4Y 9DA,
Telephone: 0171 353 9421/0375
E-mail:clerks@1harcourtbuildings.law.co.uk
Call Date: Nov 1969, Lincoln's Inn
Pupil Master
Qualifications: [BA (Keele)]

GLOSTER MISS ELIZABETH QC (1989)

One Essex Court
Ground Floor, Temple, London
EC4Y 9AR, Telephone: 020 7583 2000
E-mail: clerks@oneessexcourt.co.uk
Call Date: Feb 1971, Inner Temple
Recorder
Qualifications: [BA (Cantab)]

GLOVER RICHARD MICHAEL

2 Mitre Court Buildings
2nd Floor, Temple, London EC4Y 7BX,
Telephone: 0171 583 1380
E-mail: clerks@2mcb.co.uk
Call Date: July 1984, Inner Temple
Pupil Master
Qualifications: [BA (Cantab)]

GLOVER STEPHEN JULIAN

37 Park Square Chambers
37 Park Square, Leeds LS1 2NY,
Telephone: 0113 2439422
E-mail: chambers@no37.co.uk
Call Date: July 1978, Middle Temple
Pupil Master
Qualifications: [LLB]

GLUCKSTEIN MISS EMMA CLARE

1 Middle Temple Lane
Temple, London EC4Y 1LT,
Telephone: 0171 583 0659 (12 Lines)
E-mail: chambers@1mtl.co.uk
Call Date: Nov 1985, Lincoln's Inn
Qualifications: [BA]

GLYN CASPAR HILARY GORDON

Cloisters
1 Pump Court, Temple, London
EC4Y 7AA, Telephone: 0171 827 4000
E-mail: clerks@cloisters.com
Call Date: Nov 1992, Inner Temple
Qualifications: [LLB (Manch)]

GLYNN MISS JOANNA ELIZABETH

23 Essex Street
London WC2R 3AS,
Telephone: 0171 413 0353/836 8366
E-mail:clerks@essexstreet23.demon.co.uk
Call Date: Nov 1983, Middle Temple
Pupil Master, Assistant Recorder
Qualifications: [BA (Lond)]

GLYNN STEPHEN PETER

9 Gough Square
London EC4A 3DE,
Telephone: 020 7832 0500
E-mail: clerks@9goughsq.co.uk
Call Date: Oct 1990, Middle Temple
Qualifications: [LLB (Bris)]

GOATLEY PETER SEAMUS PATRICK

5 Fountain Court
Steelhouse Lane, Birmingham B4 6DR,
Telephone: 0121 606 0500
E-mail:clerks@5fountaincourt.law.co.uk
Call Date: May 1992, Inner Temple
Qualifications: [MA (Oxon)]

GODDARD ANDREW STEPHEN

Atkin Chambers
1 Atkin Building, Gray's Inn, London
WC1R 5AT, Telephone: 020 7404 0102
E-mail: clerks@atkin-chambers.co.uk
Call Date: Nov 1985, Inner Temple
Pupil Master
Qualifications: [BA Law]

GODDARD CHRISTOPHER JOHN FRANCIS

Devereux Chambers
Devereux Court, London WC2R 3JJ,
Telephone: 0171 353 7534
E-mail: mailbox@devchambers.co.uk
Call Date: July 1973, Middle Temple
Pupil Master
Qualifications: [LLB]

GODDARD HAROLD KEITH QC (1979)

Deans Court Chambers
24 St John Street, Manchester M3 4DF,
Telephone: 0161 214 6000
E-mail: clerks@deanscourt.co.uk
Deans Court Chambers
41-43 Market Place, Preston PR1 1AH,
Telephone: 01772 555163
E-mail: clerks@deanscourt.co.uk
4 Paper Buildings
Ground Floor, Temple, London
EC4Y 7EX, Telephone: 0171 353 3366/
583 7155
E-mail: clerks@4paperbuildings.com
Call Date: June 1959, Gray's Inn
Recorder
Qualifications: [MA,LLM (Cantab)]

GODDARD MISS KATHERINE LESLEY

Bank House Chambers
Old Bank House, Hartshead, Sheffield
S1 2EL, Telephone: 0114 2751223
Call Date: Nov 1987, Inner Temple
Qualifications: [BA (Keele)]

GODDARD PAUL GERARD

55 Temple Chambers
Temple Avenue, London EC4Y 0HP,
Telephone: 0171 353 7400
Call Date: 1996, Gray's Inn
Qualifications: [LLB (Leeds)]

GODDARD PHILIP DAMIAN

4 King's Bench Walk
2nd Floor, Temple, London EC4Y 7DL,
Telephone: 020 7353 3581
E-mail: clerks@4kbw.co.uk
Call Date: Nov 1985, Inner Temple
Qualifications: [BA (Kent)]

GODDARD RICHARD ANDREW KEITH

Cobden House Chambers
19 Quay Street, Manchester M3 3HN,
Telephone: 0161 833 6000
E-mail: clerks@cobden.co.uk
Call Date: 1999, Gray's Inn
Qualifications: [BA]

GODDARD MISS SUZANNE HAZEL

Lincoln House Chambers
5th Floor, Lincoln House, 1 Brazennose
Street, Manchester M2 5EL,
Telephone: 0161 832 5701
E-mail: info@lincolnhse.co.uk
Call Date: Nov 1986, Gray's Inn
Qualifications: [LLB (Hons) (Manch)]

GODFREY CHRISTOPHER NICHOLAS

Queen's Chambers
5 John Dalton Street, Manchester M2 6ET,
Telephone: 0161 834 6875/4738
Queens Chambers
4 Camden Place, Preston PR1 3JL,
Telephone: 01772 828300
Call Date: Feb 1993, Lincoln's Inn
Qualifications: [BA (Hons)]

GODFREY MISS EMMA CHARLOTTE

Chambers of Norman Palmer
2 Field Court, Gray's Inn, London
WC1R 5BB, Telephone: 0171 405 6114
E-mail: fieldct2@netcomuk.co.uk
Call Date: Nov 1995, Lincoln's Inn
Qualifications: [BA (Hons)]

GODFREY HOWARD ANTHONY QC (1991)

3 Hare Court
1 Little Essex Street, London WC2R 3LD,
Telephone: 0171 395 2000
*Call Date: Nov 1970, Middle Temple
Recorder*
Qualifications: [LLB (Lond)]

GODFREY JOHN PAUL

Wilberforce Chambers
7 Bishop Lane, Hull, East Yorkshire,
HU1 1PA, Telephone: 01482 323264
E-mail: clerks@hullbar.demon.co.uk
Call Date: May 1985, Gray's Inn
Qualifications: [BSc(Econ) (Lond)]

GODFREY JONATHAN SAUL

St Paul's House
5th Floor, St Paul's House, 23 Park Square
South, Leeds LS1 2ND,
Telephone: 0113 2455866
E-mail: catherinegrimshaw@stpauls-
chambers.demon.co.uk
Call Date: Nov 1990, Inner Temple
Qualifications: [LLB (Essex)]

GODFREY MISS LOUISE SARAH QC (1991)

Park Court Chambers
16 Park Place, Leeds LS1 2SJ,
Telephone: 0113 2433277
14 Gray's Inn Square
Gray's Inn, London WC1R 5JP,
Telephone: 0171 242 0858
E-mail: 100712.2134@compuserve.com
*Call Date: July 1972, Middle Temple
Recorder*
Qualifications: [MA (Oxon)]

GODSMARK NIGEL GRAHAM

9 Bedford Row
London WC1R 4AZ,
Telephone: 0171 242 3555
E-mail: clerks@9br.co.uk
*Call Date: Nov 1979, Gray's Inn
Pupil Master*
Qualifications: [LLB (Nottm)]

GODWIN WILLIAM GEORGE HENRY

Atkin Chambers
1 Atkin Building, Gray's Inn, London
WC1R 5AT, Telephone: 020 7404 0102
E-mail: clerks@atkin-chambers.co.uk
*Call Date: Nov 1986, Middle Temple
Pupil Master*
Qualifications: [BA (Lond), B.Phil (Oxon),
D.Phil (Oxon)]

GOFF ANTHONY THOMAS

25-27 Castle Street
1st Floor, Liverpool L2 4TA,
Telephone: 0151 227 5661/051 236 5072
Call Date: July 1978, Middle Temple
Qualifications: [BA (Oxon)]

GOH ALLAN LEE GUAN

Chambers of Geoffrey Hawker
46/48 Essex Street, London WC2R 3GH,
Telephone: 0171 583 8899
Call Date: July 1984, Gray's Inn
Pupil Master
Qualifications: [LLB]

GOKHOOL VISHNU (CHANDRIKA) (SING)

King's Chambers
49a Broadway, Stratford, London
E15 4BW,
2 King's Bench Walk Chambers
1st Floor, 2 King's Bench Walk, Temple,
London EC4Y 7DE,
Telephone: 020 7353 9276
E-mail: chambers@2kbw.co.uk
Call Date: Nov 1978, Inner Temple
Pupil Master

GOLD MISS DEBRA ANNE

Two Garden Court
1st Floor, Middle Temple, London
EC4Y 9BL, Telephone: 0171 353 1633
E-mail:barristers@2gardenct.law.co.uk
Call Date: July 1985, Middle Temple
Qualifications: [BA (Oxon), Dip Law]

GOLD JEREMY SPENCER

Westgate Chambers
144 High Street, Lewes, East Sussex,
BN7 1XT, Telephone: 01273 480510
**1 Gray's Inn Square, Chambers of the
Baroness Scotland of Asthal QC**
1st Floor, London WC1R 5AG,
Telephone: 0171 405 3000
E-mail: clerks@onegrays.demon.co.uk
Call Date: July 1977, Middle Temple
Pupil Master
Qualifications: [BA]

GOLDBERG DAVID GERARD QC (1987)

Gray's Inn Tax Chambers
3rd Floor, Gray's Inn Chambers, Gray's
Inn, London WC1R 5JA,
Telephone: 0171 242 2642
E-mail: clerks@taxbar.com
Call Date: July 1971, Lincoln's Inn
Qualifications: [LLM]

GOLDBERG MS ILFRA HILARY CHARLOTTE

Chambers of John L Powell QC
Four New Square, Lincoln's Inn, London
WC2A 3RJ, Telephone: 0171 797 8000
E-mail: barristers@4newsquare.com
Call Date: Oct 1995, Gray's Inn
Qualifications: [BA (Hons), MA, LLM]

GOLDBERG JONATHAN JACOB QC (1989)

3 Temple Gardens
2nd Floor, Temple, London EC4Y 9AU,
Telephone: 0171 583 1155
Westgate Chambers
144 High Street, Lewes, East Sussex,
BN7 1XT, Telephone: 01273 480510
Call Date: Feb 1971, Middle Temple
Qualifications: [MA, LLB (Cantab)]

GOLDBLATT SIMON QC (1972)

39 Essex Street
London WC2R 3AT,
Telephone: 0171 832 1111
E-mail: clerks@39essex.co.uk
Call Date: June 1953, Gray's Inn
Qualifications: [MA (Cantab)]

GOLDER-WELBY ANDREW DOMINIC

Wilberforce Chambers
7 Bishop Lane, Hull, East Yorkshire,
HU1 1PA, Telephone: 01482 323264
E-mail: clerks@hullbar.demon.co.uk
Call Date: Nov 1992, Inner Temple
Qualifications: [LLB (Leic)]

GOLDMAN MRS LINDA

7 New Square
Lincoln's Inn, London WC2A 3QS,
Telephone: 0171 430 1660
Call Date: Oct 1990, Middle Temple
Qualifications: [BDS (Lond), LLB (Lond), Dip
Crim (Lond), Dip Psych (Lond)]

GOLDREIN ERIC GODFREY

Adrian Lyon's Chambers
14 Castle Street, Liverpool L2 0NE,
Telephone: 0151 236 4421/8240
E-mail: chambers14@aol.com
Call Date: June 1961, Middle Temple
Qualifications: [MA (Cantab)]

GOLDREIN IAIN SAVILLE QC (1997)

Corn Exchange Chambers
5th Floor, Fenwick Street, Liverpool
L2 7QS, Telephone: 0151 227 1081/5009
12 King's Bench Walk
Temple, London EC4Y 7EL,
Telephone: 0171 583 0811
E-mail: chambers@12kbw.co.uk
Call Date: July 1975, Inner Temple
Assistant Recorder
Qualifications: [MA (Cantab)]

GOLDRING MISS JENNIFER LEONIE

1 Harcourt Buildings
2nd Floor, Temple, London EC4Y 9DA,
Telephone: 0171 353 9421/0375
E-mail:clerks@1harcourtbuildings.law.co.uk
Call Date: Nov 1993, Middle Temple
Qualifications: [BA (Hons)(Oxon)]

GOLDRING JEREMY EDWARD

3/4 South Square
Gray's Inn, London WC1R 5HP,
Telephone: 0171 696 9900
E-mail: clerks@southsquare.com
Call Date: Oct 1996, Lincoln's Inn
Qualifications: [BA (Hons)(Oxon), MA (Yale),
Dip in Law (City)]

GOLDRING JOHN BERNARD QC (1987)

9 Bedford Row
London WC1R 4AZ,
Telephone: 0171 242 3555
E-mail: clerks@9br.co.uk
Call Date: May 1969, Lincoln's Inn
Recorder
Qualifications: [LLB]

GOLDSACK IAN

Paradise Chambers
26 Paradise Square, Sheffield S1 2DE,
Telephone: 0114 2738951
E-mail: timbooth@paradise-sq.co.uk
Call Date: May 1997, Gray's Inn
Qualifications: [BA (Oxon)]

GOLDSMITH PETER HENRY QC (1987)

Fountain Court
Temple, London EC4Y 9DH,
Telephone: 0171 583 3335
E-mail: chambers@fountaincourt.co.uk
Call Date: 1972, Gray's Inn
Recorder
Qualifications: [MA (Cantab), LLM (Lond)]

GOLDSTAUB ANTHONY JAMES QC (1992)

Ropewalk Chambers
24 The Ropewalk, Nottingham NG1 5EF,
Telephone: 0115 9472581
E-mail: administration@ropewalk co.uk
12 King's Bench Walk
Temple, London EC4Y 7EL,
Telephone: 0171 583 0811
E-mail: chambers@12kbw.co.uk
Call Date: July 1972, Middle Temple
Recorder

GOLDSTONE DAVID JULIAN

4 Field Court
Gray's Inn, London WC1R 5EA,
Telephone: 0171 440 6900
E-mail: chambers@4fieldcourt.co.uk
Call Date: Apr 1986, Middle Temple
Pupil Master
Qualifications: [MA (Cantab), BCL (Oxon)]

GOLDSTONE LEONARD CLEMENT QC (1993)

28 St John Street
Manchester M3 4DJ,
Telephone: 0161 834 8418
E-mail: clerk@28stjohnst.co.uk
2-4 Tudor Street
London EC4Y 0AA,
Telephone: 0171 797 7111
E-mail: clerks@rfqc.co.uk
Call Date: July 1971, Middle Temple
Recorder
Qualifications: [BA (Cantab)]

GOLDWATER MICHAEL PHILIP

Cobden House Chambers
19 Quay Street, Manchester M3 3HN,
Telephone: 0161 833 6000
E-mail: clerks@cobden.co.uk
Call Date: July 1977, Middle Temple
Pupil Master
Qualifications: [MA (Oxon)]

GOLINSKI ROBERT FELIX

Adrian Lyon's Chambers
14 Castle Street, Liverpool L2 0NE,
Telephone: 0151 236 4421/8240
E-mail: chambers14@aol.com
Call Date: Oct 1990, Middle Temple
Qualifications: [BA]

GOLLOP MS KATHARINE SUSANNAH

Chambers of Kieran Coonan QC
Ground Floor, 6 Pump Court, Temple,
London EC4Y 7AR,
Telephone: 0171 583 6013/2510
E-mail: clerks@6-pumpcourt.law.co.uk
Call Date: Nov 1993, Gray's Inn
Qualifications: [BA (Hons), CPE, ICSL]

GOMPERTZ JEREMY QC (1988)

5 Essex Court
1st Floor, Temple, London EC4Y 9AH,
Telephone: 0171 410 2000
E-mail: barristers@5essexcourt.co.uk
Call Date: July 1962, Gray's Inn
Recorder
Qualifications: [MA (Cantab)]

GOOCH SEBASTIAN DAVID

5 Pump Court
Ground Floor, Temple, London
EC4Y 7AP, Telephone: 020 7353 2532
E-mail: FivePump@netcomuk.co.uk
Call Date: July 1989, Lincoln's Inn
Qualifications: [LLB (Leic)]

GOODALL CHARLES VERNON

Queens Square Chambers
56 Queens Square, Bristol BS1 4PR,
Telephone: 0117 921 1966
Call Date: July 1986, Inner Temple
Qualifications: [BA, Dip Law]

GOODALL MISS EMMA

1 Inner Temple Lane
Temple, London EC4Y 1AF,
Telephone: 020 7353 0933
Call Date: 1996, Gray's Inn
Qualifications: [LLB (L'pool)]

GOODALL PATRICK JOHN

Fountain Court
Temple, London EC4Y 9DH,
Telephone: 0171 583 3335
E-mail: chambers@fountaincourt.co.uk
Call Date: Mar 1998, Inner Temple
Qualifications: [LLB (So'ton), BCL (Oxon)]

GOODBODY PETER JAMES

Oriel Chambers
14 Water Street, Liverpool L2 8TD,
Telephone: 0151 236 7191/236 4321
E-mail: clerks@oriel-chambers.co.uk
Call Date: July 1986, Lincoln's Inn
Pupil Master
Qualifications: [LLB (Manchester)]

GOODCHILD MRS ELIZABETH ANN

Watford Chambers
74 Mildred Avenue, Watford,
Hertfordshire, WD1 7DX,
Telephone: 01923 220553
Call Date: July 1981, Middle Temple
Pupil Master
Qualifications: [LLB (Lond), ACIArb]

GOODE MISS ROWENA MARGARET

28 St John Street
Manchester M3 4DJ,
Telephone: 0161 834 8418
E-mail: clerk@28stjohnst.co.uk
Dr Johnson's Chambers
The Atrium Court, Apex Plaza, Reading,
Berkshire, RG1 1AX,
Telephone: 01734 254221
Call Date: July 1974, Gray's Inn
Pupil Master, Recorder
Qualifications: [LLB]

D

D

GOODE ROYSTON MILES QC (1990)

Blackstone Chambers
Blackstone House, Temple, London
EC4Y 9BW, Telephone: 0171 583 1770
E-mail:clerks@blackstonechambers.com
Call Date: Feb 1988, Inner Temple
Qualifications: [LLB (Lond), LLD (Lond),
FBA]

GOODFELLOW GILES WILLIAM JEREMY

Pump Court Tax Chambers
16 Bedford Row, London WC1R 4EB,
Telephone: 0171 414 8080
Call Date: July 1983, Middle Temple
Pupil Master
Qualifications: [MA (Cantab), LLM (UVa)]

GOODHART LORD QC (1979)

Chambers of Lord Goodhart QC
Ground Floor, 3 New Square, Lincoln's
Inn, London WC2A 3RS,
Telephone: 0171 405 5577
E-mail:law@threenewsquare.demon.co.uk
Call Date: Feb 1957, Lincoln's Inn
Qualifications: [MA (Cantab), LLM (Harvard)]

GOODISON ADAM HENRY

3/4 South Square
Gray's Inn, London WC1R 5HP,
Telephone: 0171 696 9900
E-mail: clerks@southsquare.com
Call Date: Oct 1990, Middle Temple
Qualifications: [BA (Dunelm)]

GOODMAN ANDREW DAVID

199 Strand
London WC2R 1DR,
Telephone: 0171 379 9779
E-mail: chambers@199strand.co.uk
Call Date: July 1978, Inner Temple
Pupil Master
Qualifications: [LLB (Soton), ACIArb]

GOODMAN MISS BERNADETTE TRACY

Derby Square Chambers
Merchants Court, Derby Square, Liverpool
L2 1TS, Telephone: 0151 709 4222
E-mail:mail.derbysquare@pop3.hiway.co.uk
Call Date: Nov 1983, Inner Temple
Pupil Master
Qualifications: [BA (Keele, Joint, Hons Law &
Music)]

GOODMAN SIMON CHARLES

St John's Chambers
Small Street, Bristol BS1 1DW,
Telephone: 0117 9213456/298514
E-mail: @stjohnschambers.co.uk
Call Date: Nov 1996, Gray's Inn
Qualifications: [BA (Bris)]

GOODRICH MISS SIOBHAN CATHERINE

Chambers of Kieran Coonan QC
Ground Floor, 6 Pump Court, Temple,
London EC4Y 7AR,
Telephone: 0171 583 6013/2510
E-mail: clerks@6-pumpcourt.law.co.uk
Call Date: Nov 1980, Gray's Inn
Pupil Master
Qualifications: [LLB (Lond)]

GOODWILL GRAHAM

12 Page Court
Ely, Cambridgeshire, CB7 4SD,
Telephone: 01353 669213
Call Date: July 1983, Inner Temple
Qualifications: [MA, LLB(Cantab)]

GOODWIN MISS CAROLINE TRACY

Trinity Chambers
9-12 Trinity Chare, Quayside, Newcastle
upon Tyne NE1 3DF,
Telephone: 0191 232 1927
E-mail: info@trinitychambers.co.uk
Call Date: Nov 1988, Inner Temple
Qualifications: [BA (Hons) (Newc), Dip Law]

GOODWIN MISS DEIRDRE EVELYN

13 King's Bench Walk
1st Floor, Temple, London EC4Y 7EN,
Telephone: 0171 353 7204
E-mail: clerks@13kbw.law.co.uk

King's Bench Chambers
32 Beaumont Street, Oxford OX1 2NP,
Telephone: 01865 311066
E-mail: clerks@kbc-oxford.law.co.uk
Call Date: July 1974, Gray's Inn
Pupil Master
Qualifications: [LLB]

GOODWIN MISS KATHERINE LOUISE

Verulam Chambers
Peer House, 8-14 Verulam Street, Gray's
Inn, London WC1X 8LZ,
Telephone: 0171 813 2400
Call Date: Nov 1993, Lincoln's Inn
Qualifications: [BA (Hons)(Oxon)]

GOODWIN MICHAEL GARY

2 Mitre Court Buildings
1st Floor, Temple, London EC4Y 7BX,
Telephone: 0171 353 1353
Call Date: 1996, Inner Temple
Qualifications: [BSc (Leeds), CPE (Lond)]

GOODWIN NICHOLAS ALEXANDER JOHN

Harcourt Chambers
1st Floor, 2 Harcourt Buildings, Temple,
London EC4Y 9DB,
Telephone: 0171 353 6961
E-mail:clerks@harcourtchambers.law.co.uk
Harcourt Chambers
Churchill House, 3 St Aldate's Courtyard,
St Aldate's, Oxford OX1 1BN,
Telephone: 01865 791559
E-mail:clerks@harcourtchambers.law.co.uk
Call Date: Oct 1995, Inner Temple
Qualifications: [BA (Oxon), CPE]

GOOLAMALI MISS NINA SORAYA

2 Temple Gardens
Temple, London EC4Y 9AY,
Telephone: 0171 583 6041
E-mail: clerks@2templegardens.co.uk
Call Date: Oct 1995, Middle Temple
Qualifications: [BA (Hons)]

GOOLD ALEXANDER MICHAEL

Hardwicke Building
New Square, Lincoln's Inn, London
WC2A 3SB, Telephone: 020 7242 2523
E-mail: clerks@hardwicke.co.uk
Call Date: Nov 1994, Lincoln's Inn
Qualifications: [MA (Cantab)]

GOOSE JULIAN NICHOLAS

Chambers of Andrew Campbell QC
10 Park Square, Leeds LS1 2LH,
Telephone: 0113 2455438
E-mail: clerks@10pksq.co.uk
Call Date: July 1984, Lincoln's Inn
Pupil Master, Assistant Recorder
Qualifications: [LLB (Leeds)]

GOPINATHAN MISS ANUPAMA

Harrow on the Hill Chambers
60 High Street, Harrow-on-the-Hill,
Middlesex, HA1 3LL,
Telephone: 0181 423 7444
Windsor Barristers' Chambers
Windsor Telephone: 01753 648899
E-mail: law@windsorchambers.co.uk
Call Date: Nov 1994, Inner Temple
Qualifications: [LLB (Hons) (Essex)]

GORDON ASHLEY LOUIS

6 Gray's Inn Square
Ground Floor, Gray's Inn, London
WC1R 5AZ, Telephone: 0171 242 1052
E-mail: 6graysinn@clara.co.uk
Call Date: Nov 1973, Inner Temple
Pupil Master
Qualifications: [MA (Cantab)]

GORDON MISS CATHERINE ANNE

140 Cholmeley Road
Reading, Berkshire, RG1 3LR,
Telephone: 01189 665174
Call Date: July 1989, Middle Temple
Qualifications: [LLB]

GORDON MISS CHRISTINA JAYNE

1 Pump Court
Lower Ground Floor, Temple, London
EC4Y 7AB, Telephone: 0171 583 2012/
353 4341
E-mail: [name]@1pumpcourt.co.uk
Call Date: Oct 1997, Middle Temple
Qualifications: [LLB (Hons)(B'ham)]

D

GORDON MS CLARE

8 King's Bench Walk
2nd Floor, Temple, London EC4Y 7DU,
Telephone: 0171 797 8888
Call Date: Oct 1995, Middle Temple
Qualifications: [LLB (Hons)]

GORDON DAVID MYER

Sovereign Chambers
25 Park Square, Leeds LS1 2PW,
Telephone: 0113 2451841/2/3
E-mail:sovereignchambers@btinternet.com
Call Date: July 1984, Inner Temple
Pupil Master, Assistant Recorder
Qualifications: [MA (Oxon), Dip Law (City)]

GORDON DONALD CAMERON

3 Temple Gardens
3rd Floor, Temple, London EC4Y 9AU,
Telephone: 0171 353 0832
Call Date: June 1956, Middle Temple
Pupil Master
Qualifications: [MA (Oxon)]

GORDON JEREMY

Lamb Building
Ground Floor, Temple, London
EC4Y 7AS, Telephone: 020 7797 7788
E-mail: lamb.building@link.org
Call Date: July 1974, Inner Temple
Pupil Master
Qualifications: [LLB]

GORDON JOHN SANDFORD

New Court
Temple, London EC4Y 9BE,
Telephone: 0171 583 5123/0510
Call Date: Nov 1970, Gray's Inn
Pupil Master
Qualifications: [LLB (Hons) (Lond)]

GORDON JOHN STUART

Chambers of Kieran Coonan QC
Ground Floor, 6 Pump Court, Temple,
London EC4Y 7AR,
Telephone: 0171 583 6013/2510
E-mail: clerks@6-pumpcourt.law.co.uk
Call Date: Feb 1989, Inner Temple
Qualifications: [LLB (B'ham)]

GORDON MRS KATHERINE ELIZABETH

Plowden Buildings
2nd Floor, 2 Plowden Buildings, Middle
Temple Lane, London EC4Y 9BU,
Telephone: 0171 583 0808
E-mail: bar@plowdenbuildings.co.uk
Call Date: Feb 1988, Lincoln's Inn
Qualifications: [BA (Hons), BCL(Hons)
Oxon]

GORDON MARK JOHN

**11 Bolt Court (also at 7 Stone Buildings
– 1st Floor)**
London EC4A 3DQ,
Telephone: 0171 353 2300
E-mail: boltct11@aol.com
Redhill Chambers
Seloduct House, 30 Station Road, Redhill,
Surrey, RH1 1NF,
Telephone: 01737 780781
**7 Stone Buildings (also at 11 Bolt
Court)**
1st Floor, Lincoln's Inn, London
WC2A 3SZ, Telephone: 0171 242 0961
E-mail:larthur@7stonebuildings.law.co.uk
Call Date: Feb 1990, Lincoln's Inn
Qualifications: [LLB Hons (B'Ham)]

GORDON RICHARD JOHN FRANCIS QC (1994)

Brick Court Chambers
7-8 Essex Street, London WC2R 3LD,
Telephone: 0171 379 3550
E-mail: [surname]@brickcourt.co.uk
Call Date: July 1972, Middle Temple
Qualifications: [MA (Oxon), LLM (Lond)]

GORDON-SAKER ANDREW STEPHEN

Fenners Chambers
3 Madingley Road, Cambridge CB3 0EE,
Telephone: 01223 368761
E-mail: clerks@fennerschambers.co.uk
Fenners Chambers
8-12 Priestgate, Peterborough PE1 1JA,
Telephone: 01733 562030
E-mail: clerks@fennerschambers.co.uk
Call Date: July 1981, Middle Temple
Pupil Master
Qualifications: [LLB, UEA]

GORDON-SAKER MRS LIZA HELEN

Fenners Chambers
3 Madingley Road, Cambridge CB3 0EE,
Telephone: 01223 368761
E-mail: clerks@fennerschambers.co.uk
Fenners Chambers
8-12 Priestgate, Peterborough PE1 1JA,
Telephone: 01733 562030
E-mail: clerks@fennerschambers.co.uk
Call Date: July 1982, Gray's Inn
Qualifications: [LLB (East Anglia)]

GORE ALLAN PETER

12 King's Bench Walk
Temple, London EC4Y 7EL,
Telephone: 0171 583 0811
E-mail: chambers@12kbw.co.uk
Call Date: 1977, Middle Temple
Pupil Master, Assistant Recorder
Qualifications: [MA, LLB (Cantab)]

GORE ANDREW JULIAN MARK

37 Park Square Chambers
37 Park Square, Leeds LS1 2NY,
Telephone: 0113 2439422
E-mail: chambers@no37.co.uk
Call Date: Nov 1994, Middle Temple

GORE ANDREW ROGER

Fenners Chambers
3 Madingley Road, Cambridge CB3 0EE,
Telephone: 01223 368761
E-mail: clerks@fennerschambers.co.uk
Fenners Chambers
8-12 Priestgate, Peterborough PE1 1JA,
Telephone: 01733 562030
E-mail: clerks@fennerschambers.co.uk
Call Date: Nov 1973, Middle Temple
Pupil Master
Qualifications: [MA (Cantab), FCIArb]

GORE MRS HARRIET NKECHI ADIMORA

Chancery Chambers
1st Floor Offices, 70/72 Chancery Lane,
London WC2A 1AB,
Telephone: 0171 405 6879/6870
Call Date: Mar 1997, Middle Temple
Qualifications: [LLB (Hons)]

GORE MRS SUSAN DIANA

Queen Elizabeth Building
Ground Floor, Temple, London
EC4Y 9BS,
Telephone: 0171 353 7181 (12 Lines)
Call Date: Nov 1993, Middle Temple
Qualifications: [LLB (Hons)(E.Anglia)]

GORE-ANDREWS GAVIN ANGUS RUSSELL

2 Harcourt Buildings
Ground Floor/Left, Temple, London
EC4Y 9DB, Telephone: 0171 583 9020
E-mail: clerks@harcourt.co.uk
Call Date: July 1972, Lincoln's Inn
Pupil Master
Qualifications: [LLB (Lond)]

GORING MISS JULIA MICHELE

Mitre Court Chambers
3rd Floor, Temple, London EC4Y 7BP,
Telephone: 0171 353 9394
E-mail: mitrecourt.com
Call Date: Oct 1991, Lincoln's Inn
Qualifications: [LLB (Hons) (Birm)]

GORNA MISS ANNE CHRISTINA

Cathedral Chambers (Jan Wood Independent Barristers' Clerk)
1 Maple Road, Exeter, Devon, EX4 1BN,
Telephone: 01392 210900
E-mail:cathedral.chambers@eclipse.co.uk
4 Paper Buildings
Ground Floor, Temple, London
EC4Y 7EX, Telephone: 0171 353 3366/
583 7155
E-mail: clerks@4paperbuildings.com
Call Date: July 1960, Middle Temple
Pupil Master
Qualifications: [LLB Hons]

GORTON SIMON ANTHONY

Adrian Lyon's Chambers
14 Castle Street, Liverpool L2 0NE,
Telephone: 0151 236 4421/8240
E-mail: chambers14@aol.com
Call Date: July 1988, Inner Temple
Qualifications: [LLB (Lond)]

GOSLAND CHRISTOPHER ANDREW JAMES

Guildhall Chambers
22-26 Broad Street, Bristol BS1 2HG,
Telephone: 0117 9273366
E-mail:civil.clerks@guildhallchambers.co.uk and
criminal.clerks@guildhallchambers.co.uk
Call Date: July 1966, Middle Temple
Qualifications: [MA (Oxon)]

GOSLING JONATHAN VINCENT RONALD

4 Fountain Court
Steelhouse Lane, Birmingham B4 6DR,
Telephone: 0121 236 3476
Call Date: Nov 1980, Middle Temple
Qualifications: [BA]

GOSNELL STEVEN JAMES

High Pavement Chambers
1 High Pavement, Nottingham NG1 1HF,
Telephone: 0115 9418218
Call Date: Nov 1995, Gray's Inn
Qualifications: [BSc (Wales)]

GOSS JAMES RICHARD WILLIAM QC (1997)

No. 6
6 Park Square, Leeds LS1 2LW,
Telephone: 0113 2459763
E-mail: chambers@no6.co.uk
Call Date: July 1975, Inner Temple
Recorder
Qualifications: [BA]

GOTHORP DAVID

15 North Church Street Chambers
15 North Church Street, Sheffield
S1 2DH, Telephone: 0114 2759708/
2738380
Call Date: Nov 1970, Gray's Inn
Pupil Master
Qualifications: [Gray's Inn , Prizewinner]

GOTT PAUL ANDREW

Fountain Court
Temple, London EC4Y 9DH,
Telephone: 0171 583 3335
E-mail: chambers@fountaincourt.co.uk
Call Date: Oct 1991, Lincoln's Inn
Qualifications: [BA (Hons) (Cambs), BCL]

GOTTLIEB DAVID ANTHONY

Thomas More Chambers
52 Carey Street, Lincoln's Inn, London
WC2A 2JB, Telephone: 0171 404 7000
E-mail: clerks@thomasmore.law.co.uk
Call Date: Nov 1988, Inner Temple
Qualifications: [LLB (Bris)]

GOUDIE JAMES QC (1984)

11 King's Bench Walk
Temple, London EC4Y 7EQ,
Telephone: 0171 632 8500/583 0610
E-mail: clerksroom@11kbw.com
Call Date: July 1970, Inner Temple
Recorder
Qualifications: [LLB (Lond)]

Fax: 0171 583 3690/9123;
Out of hours telephone: 0171 583 0610;
DX: LDE 368;
Other comms: E-mail
clerksroom@11kbw.com

Other professional qualifications: Fellow of the
Chartered Institute of Arbitrators

Types of work: Administrative, Commercial
litigation, Discrimination, Education,
Employment, Entertainment, Environment, Local government, Sports

Membership of foreign bars: Antigua

Circuit: South Eastern

Awards and memberships: Past Chairman,
Administrative Law Bar Association

Other professional experience: Deputy High
Court Judge, Queen's Bench and Chancery
Divisions; Recorder

Publications: *Judicial Review* (Co-editor),
1997 (2nd edn); *Butterworths Local
Government Law* (Co-Editor), 1998;
Butterworths Local Government Reports
(Consultant Editor); 'Audit Commission Act
1998', *Current Law Statutes*

Reported Cases: *Ahmed v United Kingdom*,
[1999] IRLR 188. Freedom of expression
under ECHR and political restrictions on
public employees.
Baxter v Camden LBC (No 2), [1999] 2
WLR 566. Noise nuisance following
conversion of building into flats.
R v Rotherham MBC, ex parte Clark,
[1998] 96 LGR 214. Duty of education

authority to comply with parental preferences for school.
Betts v Brintel, [1998] 2 CMLR 22. Leading Court of Appeal decision on TUPE.
R v Bolton MBC, ex parte Kirkman, [1998] Env LR 560. Waste incineration plant as best practicable environmental option.

GOUDIE WILLIAM MARTIN PHILLIP

Dr Johnson's Chambers
Two Dr Johnson's Buildings, Temple, London EC4Y 7AY,
Telephone: 0171 353 4716
E-mail: clerks@2djb.freeserve.co.uk
Call Date: Oct 1996, Inner Temple
Qualifications: [LLB (Exon)]

GOUGH MISS KAREN LOUISE

West Lodge Farm
Wrotham Road, Meopham, Kent,
DA13 0QG, Telephone: 01474 812280
E-mail: karen.gough@virgin.net
Arbitration Chambers
22 Willes Road, London NW5 3DS,
Telephone: 020 7267 2137
E-mail: jatqc@atack.demon.co.uk
Call Date: July 1983, Inner Temple
Qualifications: [LLB (So'ton), FCIArb]

GOUGH MISS KATHERINE MARY

Lamb Chambers
Lamb Building, Temple, London
EC4Y 7AS, Telephone: 020 7797 8300
E-mail: lambchambers@link.org
Call Date: Nov 1990, Inner Temple
Qualifications: [BA (Oxon)]

GOULD MISS DEBORAH SAMANTHA

India Buildings Chambers
Water Street, Liverpool L2 0XG,
Telephone: 0151 243 6000
E-mail: clerks@chambers.u-net.com
Call Date: Feb 1990, Inner Temple
Qualifications: [LLB (Hons) (Warw)]

GOULD DENNIS

Call Date: Nov 1969, Middle Temple
Qualifications: [MA (Cantab)]

GOULD JAMES ANDREW

15 North Church Street Chambers
15 North Church Street, Sheffield
S1 2DH, Telephone: 0114 2759708/ 2738380
Call Date: Nov 1997, Gray's Inn
Qualifications: [LLB (Leeds)]

GOULDING JONATHAN STEVEN

Gough Square Chambers
6-7 Gough Square, London EC4A 3DE,
Telephone: 0171 353 0924
E-mail: gsc@goughsq.co.uk
Call Date: July 1984, Inner Temple
Pupil Master
Qualifications: [LLB (Manch)]

GOULDING PAUL ANTHONY

Blackstone Chambers
Blackstone House, Temple, London
EC4Y 9BW, Telephone: 0171 583 1770
E-mail:clerks@blackstonechambers.com
Call Date: Nov 1984, Middle Temple
Pupil Master
Qualifications: [MA, BCL (Oxon)]

GOURGEY ALAN

11 Stone Buildings
Lincoln's Inn, London WC2A 3TG,
Telephone: +44 (0)207 831 6381
E-mail:clerks@11StoneBuildings.law.co.uk
Call Date: July 1984, Lincoln's Inn
Pupil Master
Qualifications: [LL.B (Bristol)]

GOURIET GERALD WILLIAM

3 Raymond Buildings
Gray's Inn, London WC1R 5BH,
Telephone: 020 7831 3833
E-mail:chambers@threeraymond.demon.co.uk
Call Date: July 1974, Inner Temple
Qualifications: [BMus (Lond)]

GOURLEY MISS CLAIRE ROBERTA JEAN

Exchange Chambers
Pearl Assurance House, Derby Square,
Liverpool L2 9XX,
Telephone: 0151 236 7747
E-mail:exchangechambers@btinternet.com
Call Date: Oct 1996, Middle Temple
Qualifications: [BA (Hons)(Cantab)]

GOW MISS ELIZABETH SUZANNE

Iscoed Chambers
86 St Helen's Road, Swansea, West
Glamorgan, SA1 4BQ,
Telephone: 01792 652988/9/330
Call Date: Oct 1995, Inner Temple
Qualifications: [MA (Oxon), LLM (Lond)]

GOW FERGUS BENJAMIN HARPER

Northampton Chambers
22 Albion Place, Northampton NN1 1UD,
Telephone: 01604 636271
Call Date: Nov 1994, Inner Temple
Qualifications: [BA (Newc), CPE (Lond)]

GOW HENRY

19 Castle Street Chambers
Liverpool L2 4SX,
Telephone: 0151 236 9402
E-mail: DBrei16454@aol.com
Call Date: Oct 1995, Gray's Inn
Qualifications: [LLB]

GOWEN MATTHEW ROBERT

18 Red Lion Court
(Off Fleet Street), London EC4A 3EB,
Telephone: 0171 520 6000
E-mail: chambers@18rlc.co.uk
Call Date: Oct 1992, Lincoln's Inn
Qualifications: [LLB(Hons)]

GOWER MISS HELEN CLARE

Old Square Chambers
Hanover House, 47 Corn Street, Bristol
BS1 1HT, Telephone: 0117 9277111
E-mail: oldsqbri@globalnet.co.uk
Old Square Chambers
1 Verulam Buildings, Gray's Inn, London
WC1R 5LQ, Telephone: 0171 269 0300
E-mail:clerks@oldsquarechambers.co.uk
Call Date: Oct 1992, Middle Temple
Qualifications: [BA (Hons), LL.M]

GOWER PETER JOHN DE PEAULY

6 Pump Court
1st Floor, Temple, London EC4Y 7AR,
Telephone: 0171 797 8400
E-mail: clerks@6pumpcourt.co.uk
6-8 Mill Street
Maidstone, Kent, ME15 6XH,
Telephone: 01622 688094
E-mail: annexe@6pumpcourt.co.uk
Call Date: July 1985, Lincoln's Inn
Qualifications: [MA (Oxon)]

GOY DAVID JOHN LISTER QC (1991)

Gray's Inn Tax Chambers
3rd Floor, Gray's Inn Chambers, Gray's
Inn, London WC1R 5JA,
Telephone: 0171 242 2642
E-mail: clerks@taxbar.com
Call Date: May 1973, Middle Temple
Qualifications: [LLM]

GOYMER ANDREW ALFRED

6 Pump Court
1st Floor, Temple, London EC4Y 7AR,
Telephone: 0171 797 8400
E-mail: clerks@6pumpcourt.co.uk
6-8 Mill Street
Maidstone, Kent, ME15 6XH,
Telephone: 01622 688094
E-mail: annexe@6pumpcourt.co.uk
Call Date: July 1970, Gray's Inn
Pupil Master, Recorder
Qualifications: [MA (Oxon)]

GOZEM GAIAS QC (1997)

Lincoln House Chambers
5th Floor, Lincoln House, 1 Brazennose
Street, Manchester M2 5EL,
Telephone: 0161 832 5701
E-mail: info@lincolnhse.co.uk
Call Date: Nov 1972, Middle Temple
Recorder
Qualifications: [LLB (Lond)]

GRABINER ANTHONY STEPHEN QC (1981)

One Essex Court
Ground Floor, Temple, London
EC4Y 9AR, Telephone: 020 7583 2000
E-mail: clerks@oneessexcourt.co.uk
Call Date: 1968, Lincoln's Inn
Recorder
Qualifications: [LLB, LLM (Lond)]

GRACE JOHN OLIVER BOWMAN QC (1994)

3 Serjeants' Inn
London EC4Y 1BQ,
Telephone: 0171 353 5537
E-mail: clerks@3serjeantsinn.com
Call Date: July 1973, Middle Temple
Qualifications: [LLB (Soton)]

GRACE JONATHAN ROBERT

Deans Court Chambers
24 St John Street, Manchester M3 4DF,
Telephone: 0161 214 6000
E-mail: clerks@deanscourt.co.uk
Deans Court Chambers
41-43 Market Place, Preston PR1 1AH,
Telephone: 01772 555163
E-mail: clerks@deanscourt.co.uk
Call Date: Feb 1989, Middle Temple
Qualifications: [BA (Oxon), Dip Law]

GRACE TIMOTHY MICHAEL

Adrian Lyon's Chambers
14 Castle Street, Liverpool L2 0NE,
Telephone: 0151 236 4421/8240
E-mail: chambers14@aol.com
Call Date: Nov 1993, Middle Temple
Qualifications: [BA (Hons)(Oxon)]

GRACE MISS TONIA LINDSEY

Central Chambers
89 Princess Street,
Manchester M1 4HT,
Telephone: 0161 236 1133
Call Date: Oct 1992, Middle Temple
Qualifications: [LL.B (Hons)]

GRAFFIUS MARK NARAYAN

1 Middle Temple Lane
Temple, London EC4Y 1LT,
Telephone: 0171 583 0659 (12 Lines)
E-mail: chambers@1mtl.co.uk
Call Date: Oct 1990, Middle Temple
Qualifications: [LLB (Leic)]

GRAHAM MRS ALANA NICOLE

Clock Chambers
78 Darlington Street, Wolverhampton
WV1 4LY, Telephone: 01902 313444
Call Date: Nov 1993, Lincoln's Inn
Qualifications: [BA (Hons) , LLB (Hons, Brunel)]

GRAHAM CHARLES ROBERT STEPHEN

One Essex Court
Ground Floor, Temple, London
EC4Y 9AR, Telephone: 020 7583 2000
E-mail: clerks@oneessexcourt.co.uk
Call Date: Nov 1986, Middle Temple
Pupil Master
Qualifications: [MA (Oxon), Dip Law (City)]

GRAHAM IAN DAVID

New Court Chambers
3 Broad Chare, Newcastle upon Tyne
NE1 3DQ, Telephone: 0191 232 1980
Call Date: July 1978, Middle Temple
Pupil Master
Qualifications: [MA (Oxon)]

GRAHAM JAMES HENRY FERGUS

One Raymond Buildings
Gray's Inn, London WC1R 5BH,
Telephone: 0171 430 1234
E-mail: chambers@ipbar1rb.com;
clerks@ipbar1rb.com
Call Date: Nov 1994, Inner Temple
Qualifications: [B.Eng, M.Sc (Bris), CPE]

GRAHAM JOHN MALCOLM

37 Park Square Chambers
37 Park Square, Leeds LS1 2NY,
Telephone: 0113 2439422
E-mail: chambers@no37.co.uk
11 King's Bench Walk
1st Floor, Temple, London EC4Y 7EQ,
Telephone: 0171 353 3337
E-mail: fmuller11@aol.com
Call Date: Nov 1955, Middle Temple
Pupil Master
Qualifications: [LLB]

GRAHAM MISS SANDRA CLARA

14 Tooks Court
Cursitor St, London EC4A 1LB,
Telephone: 0171 405 8828
E-mail: clerks@tooks.law.co.uk
Call Date: July 1982, Inner Temple
Pupil Master
Qualifications: [BA]

GRAHAM STUART CHARLES

Gosforth Chambers
2 Lansdowne Place, Gosforth, Newcastle
upon Tyne NE3 1HR,
Telephone: 0191 285 4664
Call Date: July 1996, Lincoln's Inn
Qualifications: [LLB (Hons)]

GRAHAM THOMAS PATRICK HENRY

1 New Square
Ground Floor, Lincoln's Inn, London
WC2A 3SA, Telephone: 0171 405 0884/5/6/
7 E-mail: clerks@1newsquare.law.co.uk
Call Date: Nov 1985, Middle Temple
Pupil Master
Qualifications: [MA (Cantab)]

GRAHAME MISS NINA STEPHANIE

1 Hare Court
Ground Floor, Temple, London
EC4Y 7BE, Telephone: 0171 353 3982/
5324
Call Date: Nov 1993, Middle Temple
Qualifications: [BA (Hons)(Warwick), CPE
(City)]

GRAINGER IAN DAVID

One Essex Court
Ground Floor, Temple, London
EC4Y 9AR, Telephone: 020 7583 2000
E-mail: clerks@oneessexcourt.co.uk
Call Date: July 1978, Inner Temple
Qualifications: [MA (Oxon)]

GRAINGER NORMAN REVELL

2 Middle Temple Lane
3rd Floor, Temple, London EC4Y 9AA,
Telephone: 0171 583 4540
26 Morley Avenue
Ashgate, Chesterfield S40 4DA,
Telephone: 01246 234790/01298 871350
Call Date: July 1973, Gray's Inn
Qualifications: [M Phil (York), BA, MA
(York), DMS]

GRANSHAW MISS SARA ELIZABETH

Harcourt Chambers
1st Floor, 2 Harcourt Buildings, Temple,
London EC4Y 9DB,
Telephone: 0171 353 6961
E-mail:clerks@harcourtchambers.law.co.uk

Harcourt Chambers
Churchill House, 3 St Aldate's Courtyard,
St Aldate's, Oxford OX1 1BN,
Telephone: 01865 791559
E-mail:clerks@harcourtchambers.law.co.uk
Call Date: Oct 1991, Lincoln's Inn
Qualifications: [BA (Hons) (Oxon)]

GRANT DAVID EUAN BARRON

13 King's Bench Walk
1st Floor, Temple, London EC4Y 7EN,
Telephone: 0171 353 7204
E-mail: clerks@13kbw.law.co.uk
King's Bench Chambers
32 Beaumont Street, Oxford OX1 2NP,
Telephone: 01865 311066
E-mail: clerks@kbc-oxford.law.co.uk
Call Date: July 1975, Middle Temple
Pupil Master, Assistant Recorder
Qualifications: [MA, LLB (Cantab)]

GRANT EDWARD WILLIAM

6 Pump Court
1st Floor, Temple, London EC4Y 7AR,
Telephone: 0171 797 8400
E-mail: clerks@6pumpcourt.co.uk
6-8 Mill Street
Maidstone, Kent, ME15 6XH,
Telephone: 01622 688094
E-mail: annexe@6pumpcourt.co.uk
Call Date: Nov 1994, Inner Temple
Qualifications: [BA (Oxon), CPE]

GRANT GARY ANDREW

17 Carlton Crescent
Southampton SO15 2XR,
Telephone: 023 8032 0320/0823 2003
E-mail: greg@jg17cc.co.uk
Call Date: Nov 1985, Middle Temple
Qualifications: [MA (Oxon)]

GRANT GARY STEVEN

3 Temple Gardens
2nd Floor, Temple, London EC4Y 9AU,
Telephone: 0171 583 1155
Call Date: Oct 1994, Gray's Inn
Qualifications: [BA]

GRANT KENNETH JOHN

25-27 Castle Street
1st Floor, Liverpool L2 4TA,
Telephone: 0151 227 5661/051 236 5072
Call Date: Mar 1998, Inner Temple
Qualifications: [BA (York)]

GRANT MISS KIM AMANDA

1 Crown Office Row
Ground Floor, Temple, London
EC4Y 7HH, Telephone: 0171 797 7500
E-mail: mail@onecrownofficerow.com
Call Date: Nov 1988, Gray's Inn
Qualifications: [LLB (Cardiff)]

GRANT MARCUS H JAMES

1 Temple Gardens
1st Floor, Temple, London EC4Y 9BB,
Telephone: 0171 583 1315/353 0407
E-mail: clerks@1templegardens.co.uk
Call Date: Oct 1993, Lincoln's Inn
Qualifications: [BA (Hons)(Reading)]

GRANT THOMAS PAUL WENTWORTH

New Court Chambers
5 Verulam Buildings, Gray's Inn, London
WC1R 5LY, Telephone: 0171 831 9500
E-mail: mail@newcourtchambers.com
Call Date: 1993, Middle Temple
Qualifications: [BA (Hons)(Bris), Dip Law
(City)]

GRANTHAM ANDREW TIMOTHY

Deans Court Chambers
24 St John Street, Manchester M3 4DF,
Telephone: 0161 214 6000
E-mail: clerks@deanscourt.co.uk
Deans Court Chambers
41-43 Market Place, Preston PR1 1AH,
Telephone: 01772 555163
E-mail: clerks@deanscourt.co.uk
Call Date: Oct 1991, Middle Temple
Qualifications: [MA, BCL (Oxon)]

Fax: 0161 214 6001;
Out of hours telephone: 0161 428 5835;
DX: 718155 Manchester 3;
Other comms: E-mail
grantham@deanscourt.co.uk

Types of work: Arbitration, Banking, Bankruptcy, Chancery (general), Commercial, Commercial litigation, Company and commercial, Construction, Consumer law, Equity, wills and trusts, Financial services, Franchising, Insolvency, Insurance, Insurance/reinsurance, International trade, Partnerships, Private international, Professional negligence, Sale and carriage of goods

Circuit: Northern

Awards and memberships: Member Northern Circuit Commercial Bar Association, Chancery Bar Association, Northern Chancery Bar Association

Other professional experience: Lecturer in Law, Wadham College, Oxford, 1989-90; Part-time lecturer in Law, King's College, London 1990-1

Reported Cases: *Partington v Turners Bakery and Tomkins v Griffiths*, [1998] 2 All ER 513. A defence admitting negligence and some damage was not an admission to enable an action to be struck out under CCR Ord 9 r 10.

GRANVILLE ALEXANDER MACGREGOR

1 Dr Johnson's Buildings
Ground Floor, Temple, London
EC4Y 7AX, Telephone: 0171 353 9328
E-mail:OneDr.Johnsons@btinternet.com
Dr Johnson's Chambers
The Atrium Court, Apex Plaza, Reading,
Berkshire, RG1 1AX,
Telephone: 01734 254221
Call Date: July 1978, Lincoln's Inn
Qualifications: [LLB (Lond)]

GRANVILLE STAFFORD ANDREW

4 King's Bench Walk
2nd Floor, Temple, London EC4Y 7DL,
Telephone: 020 7353 3581
E-mail: clerks@4kbw.co.uk
Call Date: July 1987, Gray's Inn
Pupil Master
Qualifications: [MA (Cantab)]

GRANVILLE-FALL ANTHONY

30 Park Square
Leeds LS1 2PF, Telephone: 0113 2436388
E-mail: clerks@30parksquare.co.uk
Call Date: Nov 1990, Lincoln's Inn
Qualifications: [LLB]

GRATWICKE CHARLES JAMES PHILLIP

1 Harcourt Buildings
2nd Floor, Temple, London EC4Y 9DA,
Telephone: 0171 353 9421/0375
E-mail:clerks@1harcourtbuildings.law.co.uk
Call Date: July 1974, Middle Temple
Pupil Master, Assistant Recorder
Qualifications: [LLB (Leeds)]

GRATWICKE MISS SUSAN AILEEN

Lavenham Chambers
Rookery Farm, Near Lavenham, Suffolk,
CO10 0BJ, Telephone: 01787 248247
Call Date: Nov 1976, Gray's Inn
Qualifications: [LLB]

GRAVES MISS CELIA TERESE ROSANNA

Two Garden Court
1st Floor, Middle Temple, London
EC4Y 9BL, Telephone: 0171 353 1633
E-mail:barristers@2gardenct.law.co.uk
Call Date: July 1981, Gray's Inn
Qualifications: [BA]

GRAY GILBERT QC (1971)

3 Raymond Buildings
Gray's Inn, London WC1R 5BH,
Telephone: 020 7831 3833
E-mail:chambers@threeraymond.demon.co.uk
Park Court Chambers
16 Park Place, Leeds LS1 2SJ,
Telephone: 0113 2433277
Call Date: Nov 1953, Gray's Inn
Recorder
Qualifications: [LLB]

GRAY HOWARD ROGER

Chambers of Joy Okoye
Suite 1, 2nd Floor Gray's Inn Chambers,
Gray's Inn, London WC1R 5JA,
Telephone: 0171 405 7011
Call Date: Nov 1980, Lincoln's Inn
Qualifications: [BSc ARICS ACI Arb]

GRAY MISS JENNIFER

11 Old Square
Ground Floor, Lincoln's Inn, London
WC2A 3TS, Telephone: 0171 242 5022/
405 1074
Call Date: Oct 1992, Middle Temple
Qualifications: [LL.B (Hons)]

GRAY JUSTIN HENRY WALFORD

Gray's Inn Chambers
5th Floor, Gray's Inn, London WC1R 5JA,
Telephone: 0171 404 1111
Call Date: Nov 1993, Inner Temple
Qualifications: [BA, CPE]

GRAY MRS KAREN LOUISE

96 Gray's Inn Road
London WC1X 8AL,
Telephone: 0171 405 0585
Call Date: Nov 1995, Lincoln's Inn
Qualifications: [LLB (Hons)]

GRAY MARK JULIAN

First National Chambers
2nd Floor, First National Building, 24
Fenwick Street, Liverpool L2 7NE,
Telephone: 0151 236 2098
Call Date: Nov 1996, Gray's Inn
Qualifications: [B.Eng (L'pool), B.Eng
(L'pool)]

GRAY MISS NICHOLA JAYNE

29 Bedford Row Chambers
London WC1R 4HE,
Telephone: 0171 831 2626
Call Date: Oct 1991, Lincoln's Inn
Qualifications: [BA (Hons) (Oxon)]

GRAY PETER HENRY ST JOHN

Bridewell Chambers
2 Bridewell Place, London EC4V 6AP,
Telephone: 020 7797 8800
E-mail:HughesGage@bridewell.law.co.uk
Call Date: Nov 1984, Inner Temple
Qualifications: [BA,Dip Law PCL]

GRAY RICHARD

24a St John Street
Manchester M3 4DF,
Telephone: 0161 833 9628
Call Date: Nov 1986, Middle Temple
Qualifications: [LLB (Liverpool)]

GRAY RICHARD PAUL QC (1993)

39 Essex Street
London WC2R 3AT,
Telephone: 0171 832 1111
E-mail: clerks@39essex.co.uk
Call Date: July 1970, Inner Temple
Qualifications: [LLB]

GRAY ROBERT

Cathedral Chambers (Jan Wood Independent Barristers' Clerk)
1 Maple Road, Exeter, Devon, EX4 1BN,
Telephone: 01392 210900
E-mail:cathedral.chambers@eclipse.co.uk
Call Date: 1993, Gray's Inn
Qualifications: [BA (Hons), LLM (Exon),
DipICArb, ACIArb]

GRAY ROGER ANDERSON

2 Mitre Court Buildings
1st Floor, Temple, London EC4Y 7BX,
Telephone: 0171 353 1353
Call Date: July 1984, Lincoln's Inn
Pupil Master
Qualifications: [MA, Dip Law]

GRAYSON EDWARD

9-12 Bell Yard
London WC2A 2LF,
Telephone: 0171 400 1800
E-mail: clerks@bellyard.co.uk
Call Date: Nov 1948, Middle Temple
Pupil Master
Qualifications: [MA (Oxon)]

Fax: 0171 404 1405;
Out of hours telephone: 0171 583 6207;
DX: LDE 390

Types of work: Administrative, Chancery (general), Common law (general), Copyright, Crime, EC and competition law, Intellectual property, Medical negligence, Personal injury, Sports, Sports medicine

Circuit: South Eastern

Awards and memberships: Founding President British Association for Sport and Law; Bar Sports Law Group; Australian and New Zealand Sports Law Association; Pan-European Organisation of Personal Injury Lawyers; Association of Personal Injury Lawyers; Action for Victims of Medical Accidents; Administrative Bar Association; Criminal Bar Association; British Association of Sport and Medicine; Fellow Royal Society of Medicine

Other professional experience: Consultant, Central Council of Physical Recreation; National Playing Fields Association; Sports Council; Former Counsel Professional Footballers' and Trainers' Association (now PFA)

Publications: *Sport and the Law*, 1978, 1988, 1994, 1999; *Ethics, Injuries and the Law in Sports Medicine*, 1999; *Medicine, Sport and the Law* (Co-editor, Co-author), 1990; *Medico-Legal Hazards of Rugby Union* (Co-editor, Co-author), 1991; *Sponsorship of Sport, Arts and Leisure* (Co-author), 1984

Reported Cases: *Elliott v Saunders and Liverpool Football Club*, (1994) NLJ, 5 August, 1994. Liability for personal injury/negligence between Premier League professional footballers requires no higher duty than traditional duty of care with foreseeable risk of injury
Morell v Owen and others, (1993) *The Times*, 14 December, 1993. Higher duty of care owed to disabled adult athlete than to able-bodied adult consistent with all persons under disability
Worthing Rugby Football Club Trustees v IRC; Frampton v IRC, [1985] 1 WLR; [1987] STC 273, 1985. Unincorporated association liable for tax as distinct from individual members notwithstanding association known to law only through membership with no separate legal identity
Alder v Moore, [1961] 1 All ER 1 [1961] 2 WLR 426 [1961] 2 QB 57, 1961. Monies paid under insurance policy described as penalty to disabled professional footballer recoverable as pre-existing determination of damages, notwithstanding description as penalty
Serville v Constance, [1954] 1 WLR 487; [1954] 1 All ER 622; 71 RPC 146, 1954. 'Welter Weight Champion of Trinidad' failed to restrain competitor from using title under passing off because boxer and title unknown in United Kingdom

Background
'. . . acknowledged as the "founding father" of British sports law' (per *Sports Law*, Cavendish Publishing Limited, 1998, page 35). Accused publicly by Chief Executive of Football Association at 1988 Central Council Physical Recreation Conference of having invented it. Addressed conferences internationally and domestically: International Athletic Federation (Monaco); South African Sports Medicine Congress (Cape Town); Potsdam University (Germany); Pan-European Organisation of Personal Injury Lawyers (Barcelona). Contributor to legal, sporting and national media sources on radio, television on all aspects of sporting legal issues. Co-author with late Lord Havers of *Royal Baccarat Scandal –* cheating at cards Tranby Croft trial (1997; 1988). Also author of *Corinthians and Cricketers* (4 editions: 1955, 1957, 1983, 1996) and inaugural professional lecture, Anglia Law School: *Sport and the Law: A Return to Corinthian Values?* (*British Association for Sport and Law Journal*, Summer 1998): Without the Rule of Law in Society anarchy reigns. Without the Rule of Law in Sport chaos exists.

GREANEY PAUL RICHARD

Park Court Chambers
16 Park Place, Leeds LS1 2SJ,
Telephone: 0113 2433277
Call Date: Oct 1993, Inner Temple
Qualifications: [BA (Hons) (Dunelm)]

GREATOREX MS HELEN LOUISE

9 Woodhouse Square
Leeds LS3 1AD,
Telephone: 0113 2451986
E-mail: clerks@9woodhouse.co.uk
Call Date: Nov 1997, Inner Temple
Qualifications: [BSc (Edin)]

GREAVES MISS ANN

East Anglian Chambers
Gresham House, 5 Museum Street,
Ipswich, Suffolk, IP1 1HQ,
Telephone: 01473 214481
E-mail: ipswich@ealaw.co.uk
East Anglian Chambers
52 North Hill, Colchester, Essex, CO1 1PY,
Telephone: 01206 572756
E-mail: colchester@ealaw.co.uk

East Anglian Chambers
57 London Street, Norwich NR2 1HL,
Telephone: 01603 617351
E-mail: norwich@ealaw.co.uk
Call Date: Nov 1989, Inner Temple
Pupil Master
Qualifications: [LLB (Hons)]

GREAVES JOHN

9-12 Bell Yard
London WC2A 2LF,
Telephone: 0171 400 1800
E-mail: clerks@bellyard.co.uk
Call Date: July 1973, Middle Temple
Pupil Master
Qualifications: [LLB (Lond)]

GREAVES MICHAEL

Chambers of Michael Pert QC
36 Bedford Row, London WC1R 4JH,
Telephone: 0171 421 8000
E-mail: 36bedfordrow@link.org
Chambers of Michael Pert QC
24 Albion Place, Northampton NN1 1UD,
Telephone: 01604 602333
Chambers of Michael Pert QC
104 New Walk, Leicester LE1 7EA,
Telephone: 0116 249 2020
Call Date: Nov 1976, Middle Temple
Qualifications: [LLB (B'ham)]

GREEN ALAN LAURENCE

199 Strand
London WC2R 1DR,
Telephone: 0171 379 9779
E-mail: chambers@199strand.co.uk
Peel Court Chambers
45 Hardman Street, Manchester M3 3PL,
Telephone: 0161 832 3791
E-mail: clerks@peelct.co.uk
Call Date: Feb 1973, Gray's Inn
Pupil Master
Qualifications: [BA]

GREEN MISS ALISON ANNE

4 Field Court
Gray's Inn, London WC1R 5EA,
Telephone: 0171 440 6900
E-mail: chambers@4fieldcourt.co.uk
Call Date: July 1974, Middle Temple
Pupil Master
Qualifications: [LLM (Lond)]

GREEN SIR ALLAN DAVID QC (1987)

1 Hare Court
Ground Floor, Temple, London
EC4Y 7BE, Telephone: 0171 353 3982/
5324
Call Date: June 1959, Inner Temple
Qualifications: [MA (Cantab)]

GREEN MISS AMANDA JANE

3 Verulam Buildings
London WC1R 5NT,
Telephone: 0171 831 8441
E-mail: clerks@3verulam.co.uk
Call Date: Oct 1990, Middle Temple
Qualifications: [BA (Cantab)]

GREEN ANDREW

30 Park Place
Cardiff CF1 3BA,
Telephone: 01222 398421
E-mail: 100757.1456@compuserve.com
Call Date: July 1974, Gray's Inn
Pupil Master
Qualifications: [BA (Oxon) (Hons)]

GREEN ANDREW JAMES

White Friars Chambers
21 White Friars, Chester CH1 1NZ,
Telephone: 01244 323070
E-mail:whitefriarschambers@btinternet.com
Call Date: Oct 1992, Gray's Inn
Qualifications: [LL.B (Sheff)]

GREEN ANDREW JAMES DOMINIC

Blackstone Chambers
Blackstone House, Temple, London
EC4Y 9BW, Telephone: 0171 583 1770
E-mail:clerks@blackstonechambers.com
Call Date: Nov 1988, Inner Temple
Pupil Master
Qualifications: [LLB (LSE)]

GREEN BRIAN RUSSELL QC (1997)

Wilberforce Chambers
8 New Square, Lincoln's Inn, London
WC2A 3QP, Telephone: 0171 306 0102
E-mail: chambers@wilberforce.co.uk
Call Date: Nov 1980, Middle Temple
Qualifications: [BA, BCL (Oxon)]

GREEN COLIN RICHARD

Cobden House Chambers
19 Quay Street, Manchester M3 3HN,
Telephone: 0161 833 6000
E-mail: clerks@cobden.co.uk
Call Date: July 1982, Lincoln's Inn
Qualifications: [BA (Leeds), Diplaw]

GREEN DAVID CAMERON

Adrian Lyon's Chambers
14 Castle Street, Liverpool L2 0NE,
Telephone: 0151 236 4421/8240
E-mail: chambers14@aol.com
Call Date: Oct 1993, Lincoln's Inn
Qualifications: [LLB (Hons)(Lanc)]

GREEN DAVID JOHN MARK

18 Red Lion Court
(Off Fleet Street), London EC4A 3EB,
Telephone: 0171 520 6000
E-mail: chambers@18rlc.co.uk
Thornwood House
102 New London Road, Chelmsford,
Essex, CM2 0RG,
Telephone: 01245 280880
E-mail: chambers@18rlc.co.uk
Call Date: July 1979, Inner Temple
Pupil Master, Assistant Recorder
Qualifications: [MA (Cantab)]

GREEN DORE JOHN

2 Temple Gardens
Temple, London EC4Y 9AY,
Telephone: 0171 583 6041
E-mail: clerks@2templegardens.co.uk
Call Date: Feb 1994, Lincoln's Inn
Qualifications: [BSc (Hons)]

GREEN HENRY QC (1988)

18 Red Lion Court
(Off Fleet Street), London EC4A 3EB,
Telephone: 0171 520 6000
E-mail: chambers@18rlc.co.uk
Thornwood House
102 New London Road, Chelmsford,
Essex, CM2 0RG,
Telephone: 01245 280880
E-mail: chambers@18rlc.co.uk
Call Date: July 1962, Gray's Inn
Recorder
Qualifications: [LLB (Lond) , MA (Cantab)]

D

GREEN MISS JANE ELIZABETH

Design Chambers
30 Fleet Street, London EC4Y 1AA,
Telephone: 0171 353 0747
E-mail: manager@designchambers.co.uk
Chambers of Martin Burr
Fourth Floor, Eldon Chambers, 30/32
Fleet Street, London EC4Y 1AA,
Telephone: 0171 353 4636
Call Date: Feb 1993, Inner Temple
Qualifications: [Designer of the , Royal
College of Art]

GREEN JONATHAN PAUL

2nd Floor, Francis Taylor Building
Temple, London EC4Y 7BY,
Telephone: 0171 353 9942/3157
Call Date: Oct 1993, Gray's Inn
Qualifications: [B.Sc (L'pool)]

GREEN MICHAEL ANTHONY

Fountain Court
Temple, London EC4Y 9DH,
Telephone: 0171 583 3335
E-mail: chambers@fountaincourt.co.uk
Call Date: July 1987, Lincoln's Inn
Pupil Master
Qualifications: [MA (Cantab)]

GREEN NICHOLAS NIGEL QC (1998)

Brick Court Chambers
7-8 Essex Street, London WC2R 3LD,
Telephone: 0171 379 3550
E-mail: [surname]@brickcourt.co.uk
Call Date: July 1986, Inner Temple
Qualifications: [LLB, LLM, Ph.d]

GREEN PATRICK CURTIS

2 Harcourt Buildings
Ground Floor/Left, Temple, London
EC4Y 9DB, Telephone: 0171 583 9020
E-mail: clerks@harcourt.co.uk
Call Date: Oct 1990, Middle Temple
Qualifications: [BA (Cantab), ACI.Arb]

GREEN ROBIN CHARLES DAVID MAGNUS

2-3 Gray's Inn Square
Gray's Inn, London WC1R 5JH,
Telephone: 0171 242 4986
E-mail:chambers@2-3graysinnsquare.co.uk
Call Date: Oct 1992, Inner Temple
Qualifications: [LLB (Lond)]

GREEN ROGER JOHN BAILEY

Queen's Chambers
5 John Dalton Street, Manchester M2 6ET,
Telephone: 0161 834 6875/4738
Queens Chambers
4 Camden Place, Preston PR1 3JL,
Telephone: 01772 828300
Call Date: July 1972, Lincoln's Inn
Pupil Master
Qualifications: [LLB (Lond)]

GREEN TIMOTHY SINCLAIR

3 Fountain Court
Steelhouse Lane, Birmingham B4 6DR,
Telephone: 0121 236 5854
Call Date: Oct 1996, Gray's Inn
Qualifications: [BA (Oxon)]

GREEN MISS VICTORIA LOUISE

Harrow on the Hill Chambers
60 High Street, Harrow-on-the-Hill,
Middlesex, HA1 3LL,
Telephone: 0181 423 7444
Call Date: Oct 1994, Gray's Inn
Qualifications: [LLB (Hons)]

GREENAN JOHN JOSEPH GILCHRIST

Hardwicke Building
New Square, Lincoln's Inn, London
WC2A 3SB, Telephone: 020 7242 2523
E-mail: clerks@hardwicke.co.uk
Call Date: July 1984, Gray's Inn
Qualifications: [LLB (B'ham)]

GREENAN MISS SARAH OCTAVIA

9 Woodhouse Square
Leeds LS3 1AD,
Telephone: 0113 2451986
E-mail: clerks@9woodhouse.co.uk
Call Date: July 1987, Gray's Inn
Pupil Master
Qualifications: [BA (Oxon)]

GREENBERG MISS JOANNA ELISHEVER GABRIELLE QC (1994)

3 Temple Gardens
2nd Floor, Temple, London EC4Y 9AU,
Telephone: 0171 583 1155
Call Date: July 1972, Gray's Inn
Recorder
Qualifications: [LLB Hons (Lond)]

GREENBOURNE JOHN HUGO

Two Crown Office Row
Ground Floor, Temple, London
EC4Y 7HJ, Telephone: 020 7797 8100
E-mail: mail@2cor.co.uk, or to individual
barristers at: [barrister's
surname]@2cor.co.uk
Call Date: July 1978, Gray's Inn
Pupil Master
Qualifications: [MA (Cantab)]

GREENE MAURICE ALAN

28 St John Street
Manchester M3 4DJ,
Telephone: 0161 834 8418
E-mail: clerk@28stjohnst.co.uk
Call Date: Nov 1982, Inner Temple
Pupil Master
Qualifications: [BA (Hons)]

GREENE PAUL MARTIN

Earl Street Chambers
47 Earl Street, Maidstone, Kent,
ME14 1PD, Telephone: 01622 671222
E-mail: gunner-sparks@msn.com
Call Date: Oct 1994, Middle Temple
Qualifications: [LLB (Hons)(Bris)]

GREENFIELD ALEX JEREMY

Martins Building
2nd Floor, No 4 Water Street, Liverpool
L2 3SP, Telephone: 0151 236 5818/4919
Call Date: Oct 1995, Inner Temple
Qualifications: [B.Com (L'pool), CPE
(Wolves)]

GREENFIELD PETER CHARLES

King's Bench Chambers
Wellington House, 175 Holdenhurst Road,
Bournemouth, Dorset, BH8 8DQ,
Telephone: 01202 250025
E-mail: chambers@kingsbench.co.uk
Call Date: Nov 1989, Middle Temple
Qualifications: [BA (Lond)]

GREENHILL JULIAN RUTHERFORD

Wilberforce Chambers
8 New Square, Lincoln's Inn, London
WC2A 3QP, Telephone: 0171 306 0102
E-mail: chambers@wilberforce.co.uk
Call Date: 1997, Inner Temple
Qualifications: [BA (Cantab)]

Types of work: Chancery (general), Commercial litigation

GREENING RICHARD JONATHAN

Devereux Chambers
Devereux Court, London WC2R 3JJ,
Telephone: 0171 353 7534
E-mail: mailbox@devchambers.co.uk
Call Date: Nov 1975, Middle Temple
Pupil Master
Qualifications: [MA (Cantab)]

GREENSLADE HENRY MICHAEL

9 King's Bench Walk
Ground Floor, Temple, London
EC4Y 7DX, Telephone: 0171 353 7202/
3909 E-mail: 9kbw@compuserve.com
Call Date: Nov 1982, Gray's Inn
Qualifications: [BA (Hons)(Law), BL
(Ireland)]

GREENWOOD ALAN ELIEZER

2-4 Tudor Street
London EC4Y 0AA,
Telephone: 0171 797 7111
E-mail: clerks@rfqc.co.uk
Call Date: July 1970, Middle Temple
Pupil Master, Recorder
Qualifications: [LLB (Hons)]

D

GREENWOOD MISS CELESTINE LESLEY

Chavasse Court Chambers
2nd Floor, Chavasse Court, 24 Lord Street,
Liverpool L2 1TA,
Telephone: 0151 707 1191
Call Date: Oct 1991, Lincoln's Inn
Qualifications: [LLB (Hons)(L'pool)]

GREENWOOD PROFESSOR CHRISTOPHER JOHN QC (1999)

Essex Court Chambers
24 Lincoln's Inn Fields, London
WC2A 3ED, Telephone: 0171 813 8000
E-mail:clerksroom@essexcourt-chambers.co.u
k
Call Date: 1978, Middle Temple
Qualifications: [MA, LLB (Cantab)]

GREENWOOD JOHN

East Anglian Chambers
Gresham House, 5 Museum Street,
Ipswich, Suffolk, IP1 1HQ,
Telephone: 01473 214481
E-mail: ipswich@ealaw.co.uk
East Anglian Chambers
52 North Hill, Colchester, Essex, CO1 1PY,
Telephone: 01206 572756
E-mail: colchester@ealaw.co.uk
East Anglian Chambers
57 London Street, Norwich NR2 1HL,
Telephone: 01603 617351
E-mail: norwich@ealaw.co.uk
Call Date: Oct 1990, Lincoln's Inn
Qualifications: [MA (Oxon)]

GREENWOOD PAUL JEROME

4 Stone Buildings
Ground Floor, Lincoln's Inn, London
WC2A 3XT, Telephone: 0171 242 5524
E-mail:clerks@4stonebuildings.law.co.uk
Call Date: Nov 1991, Lincoln's Inn
Qualifications: [BA (Hons) , BCL (Oxon)]

GREGG WILLIAM JONATHAN

Cobden House Chambers
19 Quay Street, Manchester M3 3HN,
Telephone: 0161 833 6000
E-mail: clerks@cobden.co.uk
Call Date: Oct 1990, Gray's Inn
Qualifications: [LLB (Hons)(Newc)]

GREGORY MS ANN MARIE

Sackville Chambers
Sackville Place, 44-48 Magdalen Street,
Norwich NR3 1JU,
Telephone: 01603 613516/616221
Number Ten Baker Street
10 Baker Street, Middlesbrough TS1 2LH,
Telephone: 01642 220332
Call Date: 1994, Middle Temple
Qualifications: [LLB (Hons)]

GREGORY BARRY GEORGE

Furnival Chambers
32 Furnival Street, London EC4A 1JQ,
Telephone: 0171 405 3232
E-mail: clerks@furnivallaw.co.uk
Call Date: Nov 1987, Gray's Inn
Pupil Master

GREGORY JAMES HANS

Lincoln House Chambers
5th Floor, Lincoln House, 1 Brazennose
Street, Manchester M2 5EL,
Telephone: 0161 832 5701
E-mail: info@lincolnhse.co.uk
Call Date: Feb 1970, Gray's Inn
Pupil Master
Qualifications: [BA (Lond)]

GREGORY JOHN RAYMOND

Deans Court Chambers
24 St John Street, Manchester M3 4DF,
Telephone: 0161 214 6000
E-mail: clerks@deanscourt.co.uk
Deans Court Chambers
41-43 Market Place, Preston PR1 1AH,
Telephone: 01772 555163
E-mail: clerks@deanscourt.co.uk
Call Date: July 1972, Middle Temple
Pupil Master
Qualifications: [LLB]

GREGORY MISS KAREN ANN

Exchange Chambers
Pearl Assurance House, Derby Square,
Liverpool L2 9XX,
Telephone: 0151 236 7747
E-mail:exchangechambers@btinternet.com
Call Date: July 1985, Middle Temple
Pupil Master
Qualifications: [BA (L'pool), Dip Law]

GREGORY PETER JOSEPH

Martins Building
2nd Floor, No 4 Water Street, Liverpool
L2 3SP, Telephone: 0151 236 5818/4919
Call Date: July 1982, Gray's Inn
Pupil Master
Qualifications: [LLB(Manch)]

GREGORY PHILIP JOHN

6 Fountain Court
Steelhouse Lane, Birmingham B4 6DR,
Telephone: 0121 233 3282
E-mail: clerks@sixfountain.co.uk
Call Date: July 1975, Middle Temple
Pupil Master, Assistant Recorder
Qualifications: [MA (Oxon)]

GREGORY RICHARD HAMILTON

Ropewalk Chambers
24 The Ropewalk, Nottingham NG1 5EF,
Telephone: 0115 9472581
E-mail: administration@ropewalk co.uk
Call Date: Oct 1993, Middle Temple
Qualifications: [BA (Hons)(Cantab), CPE
(Notts)]

GRENFELL GIBSON QC (1994)

2 Pump Court
1st Floor, Temple, London EC4Y 7AH,
Telephone: 0171 353 5597
Call Date: Nov 1969, Middle Temple
Recorder
Qualifications: [MA (Cantab)]

GRENNAN BARRY EDWARD

Kenworthy's Chambers
83 Bridge Street, Manchester M3 2RF,
Telephone: 0161 832 4036/834 6954
E-mail: clerks@kenworthys.co.uk
Call Date: July 1977, Lincoln's Inn
Pupil Master
Qualifications: [BA (Hons)]

GRENYER MARK

York Chambers
14 Toft Green, York YO1 6JT,
Telephone: 01904 620048
E-mail: [name]@yorkchambers.co.uk
Call Date: Nov 1969, Gray's Inn
Pupil Master

GRESTY MISS DENISE LYNN

Sovereign Chambers
25 Park Square, Leeds LS1 2PW,
Telephone: 0113 2451841/2/3
E-mail:sovereignchambers@btinternet.com
Call Date: Nov 1990, Inner Temple
Qualifications: [LLB (Sheff)]

GREWAL MISS HARJIT

6 King's Bench Walk
Ground, Third & Fourth Floors, Temple,
London EC4Y 7DR,
Telephone: 0171 353 4931/583 0695
Call Date: July 1980, Gray's Inn
Qualifications: [MA (Cantab)]

GREY MISS ELEANOR MARY GRACE

39 Essex Street
London WC2R 3AT,
Telephone: 0171 832 1111
E-mail: clerks@39essex.co.uk
Call Date: Oct 1990, Gray's Inn
Qualifications: [BA (Oxon), Dip Law]

GREY MICHAEL HENRY JOHN

Coleridge Chambers
Citadel, 190 Corporation Street,
Birmingham B4 6QD,
Telephone: 0121 233 8500
Call Date: Nov 1975, Middle Temple
Pupil Master
Qualifications: [LLB]

GREY PHILIP JOHN

Hardwicke Building
New Square, Lincoln's Inn, London
WC2A 3SB, Telephone: 020 7242 2523
E-mail: clerks@hardwicke.co.uk
Call Date: 1996, Gray's Inn
Qualifications: [BA (Hons)(Cantab)]

GREY ROBERT WILLIAM

3 Paper Buildings
Temple, London EC4Y 7EU,
Telephone: 020 7583 8055
E-mail: London@3paper.com
3 Paper Buildings (Bournemouth)
20 Lorne Park Road, Bournemouth,
Dorset, BH1 1JN,
Telephone: 01202 292102
E-mail: Bournemouth@3paper.com

D

3 Paper Buildings (Winchester)
4 St Peter Street, Winchester SO23 8BW,
Telephone: 01962 868884
E-mail: winchester@3paper.com
3 Paper Buildings (Oxford)
1 Alfred Street, High Street, Oxford
OX1 4EH, Telephone: 01865 793736
E-mail: oxford@3paper.com
Call Date: July 1979, Gray's Inn
Pupil Master
Qualifications: [BA (Lancaster)]

GREY ROBIN DOUGLAS QC (1979)

Hollis Whiteman Chambers
3rd Floor, Queen Elizabeth Bldg, Temple,
London EC4Y 9BS,
Telephone: 020 7583 5766
E-mail:barristers@holliswhiteman.co.uk
Call Date: Feb 1957, Gray's Inn
Recorder
Qualifications: [LLB (Lond)]

GREY MISS SIOBHAN

Dr Johnson's Chambers
Two Dr Johnson's Buildings, Temple,
London EC4Y 7AY,
Telephone: 0171 353 4716
E-mail: clerks@2djb.freeserve.co.uk
Call Date: Oct 1994, Gray's Inn
Qualifications: [BA]

GRIBBLE PETER JOHN

9 King's Bench Walk
Ground Floor, Temple, London
EC4Y 7DX, Telephone: 0171 353 7202/
3909 E-mail: 9kbw@compuserve.com
Call Date: July 1972, Gray's Inn
Pupil Master

GRICE ALAN KEVIN

Corn Exchange Chambers
5th Floor, Fenwick Street, Liverpool
L2 7QS, Telephone: 0151 227 1081/5009
Call Date: July 1977, Gray's Inn
Pupil Master, Assistant Recorder
Qualifications: [LLB]

GRICE MISS JOANNA HARRISON

One King's Bench Walk
1st Floor, Temple, London EC4Y 7DB,
Telephone: 0171 936 1500
E-mail: ddear@1kbw.co.uk
Call Date: Oct 1991, Middle Temple
Qualifications: [MA Hons (Cantab)]

GRICE PETER ROBERT

St Ive's Chambers
Whittall Street, Birmingham B4 6DH,
Telephone: 0121 236 0863/5720
E-mail:stives.headofchambers@btinternet.com
Call Date: July 1984, Gray's Inn
Qualifications: [LLB (Hons)]

GRICE TIMOTHY JAMES

St John's Chambers
Small Street, Bristol BS1 1DW,
Telephone: 0117 9213456/298514
E-mail: @stjohnschambers.co.uk
Call Date: July 1975, Middle Temple
Pupil Master
Qualifications: [MA (Oxon)]

GRIEF MISS ALISON SARAH

Two Garden Court
1st Floor, Middle Temple, London
EC4Y 9BL, Telephone: 0171 353 1633
E-mail:barristers@2gardenct.law.co.uk
Call Date: Oct 1990, Inner Temple
Qualifications: [LLB]

GRIERSON JACOB

One Essex Court
Ground Floor, Temple, London
EC4Y 9AR, Telephone: 020 7583 2000
E-mail: clerks@oneessexcourt.co.uk
Call Date: Oct 1993, Lincoln's Inn
Qualifications: [BA (Hons) (Oxon), Dip in
Law (City)]

GRIEVE DOMINIC CHARLES ROBERTS

1 Temple Gardens
1st Floor, Temple, London EC4Y 9BB,
Telephone: 0171 583 1315/353 0407
E-mail: clerks@1templegardens.co.uk
Call Date: Nov 1980, Middle Temple
Pupil Master
Qualifications: [BA (Oxon)]

GRIEVE MICHAEL ROBERTSON CRICHTON QC (1998)

Doughty Street Chambers
11 Doughty Street, London WC1N 2PG,
Telephone: 0171 404 1313
E-mail:enquiries@doughtystreet.co.uk
Call Date: Nov 1975, Middle Temple
Assistant Recorder
Qualifications: [BA (Oxon)]

GRIEVES EDWARD JAMES

Counsels' Chambers
2nd Floor, 10-11 Gray's Inn Square,
London WC1R 5JD,
Telephone: 0171 405 2576
E-mail:clerks@10-11graysinnsquare.co.uk
Call Date: 1996, Middle Temple
Qualifications: [BSc (Hons), CPE (Notts)]

GRIEVES-SMITH PETER MICHAEL

6 King's Bench Walk
Ground Floor, Temple, London
EC4Y 7DR, Telephone: 0171 583 0410
E-mail: worsley@6kbw.freeserve.co.uk
Call Date: Nov 1989, Middle Temple
Qualifications: [LLB (Hons)(Leic)]

GRIFFIN IAN ROSS

4 Brick Court
Temple, London EC4Y 9AD,
Telephone: 0171 797 8910
E-mail: medhurst@dial.pipex.com
Call Date: 1997, Middle Temple
Qualifications: [LLB (Hons), MA, (Lond)]

GRIFFIN MISS LYNN MYFANWY

23 Essex Street
London WC2R 3AS,
Telephone: 0171 413 0353/836 8366
E-mail:clerks@essexstreet23.demon.co.uk
Call Date: Oct 1991, Gray's Inn
Pupil Master
Qualifications: [LLB (Brunel)]

GRIFFIN NEIL PATRICK LUKE

9-12 Bell Yard
London WC2A 2LF,
Telephone: 0171 400 1800
E-mail: clerks@bellyard.co.uk
Call Date: Oct 1996, Gray's Inn
Qualifications: [LLB (Hons) (Lond)]

GRIFFIN NICHOLAS JOHN

Five Paper Buildings
1st Floor, Five Paper Bldgs, Temple,
London EC4Y 7HB,
Telephone: 0171 583 6117
E-mail:clerks@5-paperbuildings.law.co.uk
Call Date: Oct 1992, Inner Temple
Qualifications: [LLB (Hons) (Bristol)]

GRIFFIN PAUL

4 Essex Court
Temple, London EC4Y 9AJ,
Telephone: 020 7797 7970
E-mail: clerks@4essexcourt.law.co.uk
Call Date: Nov 1979, Gray's Inn
Qualifications: [MA, BCL (Oxon)]

GRIFFITH MARTIN LEONARD

1 Harcourt Buildings
2nd Floor, Temple, London EC4Y 9DA,
Telephone: 0171 353 9421/0375
E-mail:clerks@1harcourtbuildings.law.co.uk
Call Date: July 1977, Inner Temple
Pupil Master
Qualifications: [LLB (Lond)]

GRIFFITH PETER MALCOLM

3 Temple Gardens
3rd Floor, Temple, London EC4Y 9AU,
Telephone: 0171 583 0010
Guildhall Chambers Portsmouth
Prudential Buildings, 16 Guildhall Walk,
Portsmouth, Hampshire, PO1 2DE,
Telephone: 01705 752400
Call Date: Feb 1964, Inner Temple
Qualifications: [MA (Cantab),MIPD]

GRIFFITH WILLIAMS JOHN QC (1985)

Goldsmith Building
1st Floor, Temple, London EC4Y 7BL,
Telephone: 0171 353 7881
E-mail:clerks@goldsmith-building.law.co.uk
33 Park Place
Cardiff CF1 3BA,
Telephone: 02920 233313
Call Date: Nov 1968, Gray's Inn
Recorder
Qualifications: [BA (Oxon)]

D

GRIFFITH-JONES DAVID ERIC

Devereux Chambers
Devereux Court, London WC2R 3JJ,
Telephone: 0171 353 7534
E-mail: mailbox@devchambers.co.uk
Call Date: Nov 1975, Middle Temple
Pupil Master, Recorder
Qualifications: [LLB (Bristol), FCI Arb]

GRIFFITH-JONES RICHARD HAYDN

1 Fountain Court
Steelhouse Lane, Birmingham B4 6DR,
Telephone: 0121 236 5721
Call Date: July 1974, Middle Temple
Pupil Master, Recorder
Qualifications: [LLB (Leeds)]

GRIFFITHS ALAN PAUL

One Essex Court
Ground Floor, Temple, London
EC4Y 9AR, Telephone: 020 7583 2000
E-mail: clerks@oneessexcourt.co.uk
Call Date: Feb 1981, Gray's Inn
Pupil Master
Qualifications: [MA, BCL (Oxon)]

GRIFFITHS CONRAD PAUL RADCLIFFE

2 Harcourt Buildings
Ground Floor/Left, Temple, London
EC4Y 9DB, Telephone: 0171 583 9020
E-mail: clerks@harcourt.co.uk
Call Date: Nov 1986, Gray's Inn
Qualifications: [LLB(E.Anglia)]

GRIFFITHS COURTENAY QC (1998)

Two Garden Court
1st Floor, Middle Temple, London
EC4Y 9BL, Telephone: 0171 353 1633
E-mail: barristers@2gardenct.law.co.uk
Call Date: July 1980, Gray's Inn
Assistant Recorder
Qualifications: [LLB (Hons)(Lond)]

GRIFFITHS DAFYDD

Phoenix Chambers
First Floor, Gray's Inn Chambers, Gray's
Inn, London WC1R 5JA,
Telephone: 0171 404 7888
E-mail: clerks@phoenix-chambers.co.uk
Call Date: Mar 1997, Gray's Inn
Qualifications: [LLB (Lond)]

GRIFFITHS HUGH ROBERT JAMES

Furnival Chambers
32 Furnival Street, London EC4A 1JQ,
Telephone: 0171 405 3232
E-mail: clerks@furnivallaw.co.uk
Call Date: Nov 1972, Inner Temple

GRIFFITHS JAMES BRIAN

Warwick House Chambers
8 Warwick Court, Gray's Inn, London
WC1R 5DJ, Telephone: 0171 430 2323
E-mail: cdrewlaw@aol.com
Call Date: 1996, Middle Temple
Qualifications: [B.Soc.Sci (Manch)]

GRIFFITHS JOHN ALFRED

2 King's Bench Walk
Ground Floor, Temple, London
EC4Y 7DE, Telephone: 0171 353 1746
E-mail: 2kbw@atlas.co.uk
Call Date: Nov 1948, Lincoln's Inn
Qualifications: [MA (Oxon)]

GRIFFITHS (JOHN) PETER (GWYNNE) QC (1995)

30 Park Place
Cardiff CF1 3BA,
Telephone: 01222 398421
E-mail: 100757.1456@compuserve.com
3 Hare Court
1 Little Essex Street, London WC2R 3LD,
Telephone: 0171 395 2000
Call Date: Nov 1970, Gray's Inn
Recorder
Qualifications: [LLB (Lond)]

GRIFFITHS MARTIN ALEXANDER

Essex Court Chambers
24 Lincoln's Inn Fields, London
WC2A 3ED, Telephone: 0171 813 8000
E-mail: clerksroom@essexcourt-chambers.co.uk
Call Date: Nov 1986, Inner Temple
Pupil Master
Qualifications: [MA (Oxon), Dip Law (City)]

GRIFFITHS PATRICK THOMAS JOHN

Iscoed Chambers
86 St Helen's Road, Swansea, West
Glamorgan, SA1 4BQ,
Telephone: 01792 652988/9/330
Call Date: Nov 1972, Gray's Inn
Pupil Master
Qualifications: [MA (Oxon)]

GRIFFITHS PETER ROBERT

4 Stone Buildings
Ground Floor, Lincoln's Inn, London
WC2A 3XT, Telephone: 0171 242 5524
E-mail:clerks@4stonebuildings.law.co.uk
Call Date: July 1977, Inner Temple
Pupil Master
Qualifications: [MA (Cantab)]

GRIFFITHS RICHARD STEPHEN

Carmarthen Chambers
30 Spilman Street, Carmarthen, Dyfed,
SA31 1LQ, Telephone: 01267 234410
E-mail: law@in-wales.com
Call Date: Nov 1983, Gray's Inn
Pupil Master
Qualifications: [BA]

GRIFFITHS ROBIN CLIVE

2 Paper Buildings, Basement North
Temple, London EC4Y 7ET,
Telephone: 0171 936 2613
E-mail: post@2paper.co.uk
Call Date: Nov 1970, Middle Temple
Pupil Master
Qualifications: [BA (Hons)(Oxon) , Dip Crim
(Cantab)]

GRIFFITHS ROGER VAUGHAN

32 Park Place
Cardiff CF1 3BA,
Telephone: 01222 397364
Call Date: July 1983, Gray's Inn
Pupil Master
Qualifications: [LLB (Wales)]

GRIFFITHS MISS SIAN HAYLEY

17 Carlton Crescent
Southampton SO15 2XR,
Telephone: 023 8032 0320/0823 2003
E-mail: greg@jg17cc.co.uk
Call Date: Oct 1990, Inner Temple
Qualifications: [LLB (Cardiff)]

GRIFFITHS MISS TANIA VERONICA

Exchange Chambers
Pearl Assurance House, Derby Square,
Liverpool L2 9XX,
Telephone: 0151 236 7747
E-mail:exchangechambers@btinternet.com
Call Date: July 1982, Gray's Inn
Qualifications: [BA]

GRIFFITHS (WILLIAM) ROBERT QC (1993)

4-5 Gray's Inn Square
Ground Floor, Gray's Inn, London
WC1R 5JP, Telephone: 0171 404 5252
E-mail:chambers@4-5graysinnsquare.co.uk
Call Date: Nov 1974, Middle Temple
Qualifications: [MA, BCL (Oxon)]

GRIME JOHN ANDREW

Pump Court Chambers
5 Temple Chambers, Temple Street,
Swindon SN1 1SQ,
Telephone: 01793 539899
E-mail: clerks@3pumpcourt.com
Pump Court Chambers
Upper Ground Floor, 3 Pump Court,
Temple, London EC4Y 7AJ,
Telephone: 0171 353 0711
E-mail: clerks@3pumpcourt.com
Pump Court Chambers
31 Southgate Street, Winchester
SO23 9EE, Telephone: 01962 868161
E-mail: clerks@3pumpcourt.com
Call Date: 1997, Lincoln's Inn
Qualifications: [LLB (Hons)(B'ham)]

GRIME MARK STEPHEN EASTBURN QC (1987)

Deans Court Chambers
24 St John Street, Manchester M3 4DF,
Telephone: 0161 214 6000
E-mail: clerks@deanscourt.co.uk
2 Pump Court
1st Floor, Temple, London EC4Y 7AH,
Telephone: 0171 353 5597
Deans Court Chambers
41-43 Market Place, Preston PR1 1AH,
Telephone: 01772 555163
E-mail: clerks@deanscourt.co.uk
Call Date: Feb 1970, Middle Temple
Recorder
Qualifications: [MA (Oxon)]

GRIMSHAW MISS ELIZABETH ANNE

King Charles House
Standard Hill, Nottingham NG1 6FX,
Telephone: 0115 9418851
E-mail: clerks@kch.co.uk
Call Date: Oct 1993, Gray's Inn
Qualifications: [LLB (Buck'ham)]

GRIMSHAW GARY LEO

Lion Court
Chancery House, 53-64 Chancery Lane,
London WC2A 1SJ,
Telephone: 0171 404 6565
Call Date: 1998, Inner Temple
Qualifications: [LLB (Hons)(Leeds)]

GRIMSHAW NICHOLAS EDWARD

Deans Court Chambers
24 St John Street, Manchester M3 4DF,
Telephone: 0161 214 6000
E-mail: clerks@deanscourt.co.uk
Deans Court Chambers
41-43 Market Place, Preston PR1 1AH,
Telephone: 01772 555163
E-mail: clerks@deanscourt.co.uk
Call Date: Nov 1988, Inner Temple
Qualifications: [BA (Oxon)]

GRINDROD MRS HELEN M QC (1982)

Chambers of Helen Grindrod QC
4th Floor, 15-19 Devereux Court, London
WC2R 3JJ, Telephone: 0171 583 2792
18 St John Street
Manchester M3 4EA,
Telephone: 0161 278 1800
E-mail: 18stjohn@lineone.net
Call Date: July 1966, Lincoln's Inn
Qualifications: [MA (Oxon)]

GRIPTON DAVID JOHN

York Chambers
14 Toft Green, York YO1 6JT,
Telephone: 01904 620048
E-mail: [name]@yorkchambers.co.uk
Call Date: July 1969, Middle Temple
Pupil Master
Qualifications: [LLB]

GRITT EDMUND MATTHEW WILLIAM

3 Raymond Buildings
Gray's Inn, London WC1R 5BH,
Telephone: 020 7831 3833
E-mail:chambers@threeraymond.demon.co.uk
Call Date: 1997, Gray's Inn
Qualifications: [BA]

GROBEL PETER

12 King's Bench Walk
Temple, London EC4Y 7EL,
Telephone: 0171 583 0811
E-mail: chambers@12kbw.co.uk
Call Date: July 1967, Lincoln's Inn
Pupil Master, Recorder
Qualifications: [LLB (Lond)]

GROCOTT MISS SUSAN

Queen's Chambers
5 John Dalton Street, Manchester M2 6ET,
Telephone: 0161 834 6875/4738
Queens Chambers
4 Camden Place, Preston PR1 3JL,
Telephone: 01772 828300
Call Date: Nov 1986, Middle Temple
Pupil Master
Qualifications: [BA (Oxon)]

GRODZINSKI SAMUEL MARC

39 Essex Street
London WC2R 3AT,
Telephone: 0171 832 1111
E-mail: clerks@39essex.co.uk
Call Date: Mar 1996, Middle Temple
Qualifications: [BA (Hons)]

GROOM IAN JOHN

Paradise Chambers
26 Paradise Square, Sheffield S1 2DE,
Telephone: 0114 2738951
E-mail: timbooth@paradise-sq.co.uk
Call Date: Nov 1990, Middle Temple
Qualifications: [LLB (Wales)]

GROOME DAVID

Five Paper Buildings
1st Floor, Five Paper Bldgs, Temple,
London EC4Y 7HB,
Telephone: 0171 583 6117
E-mail:clerks@5-paperbuildings.law.co.uk
Call Date: Nov 1987, Middle Temple
Pupil Master
Qualifications: [LLB (London)]

GROSS PETER HENRY QC (1992)

20 Essex Street
London WC2R 3AL,
Telephone: 0171 583 9294
E-mail: clerks@20essexst.com
Call Date: July 1977, Gray's Inn
Recorder
Qualifications: [MA, BCL (Oxon)]

GROUND REGINALD PATRICK QC (1981)

2-3 Gray's Inn Square
Gray's Inn, London WC1R 5JH,
Telephone: 0171 242 4986
E-mail:chambers@2-3graysinnsquare.co.uk
Call Date: Feb 1960, Inner Temple
Qualifications: [MA (Cantab), M.Litt (Oxon)]

GROUND RICHARD WILLIAM SCOTT

2-3 Gray's Inn Square
Gray's Inn, London WC1R 5JH,
Telephone: 0171 242 4986
E-mail:chambers@2-3graysinnsquare.co.uk
Call Date: Oct 1994, Inner Temple
Qualifications: [BA (Cantab), CPE]

GROUT-SMITH JEREMY GAYWOOD

Peel Court Chambers
45 Hardman Street, Manchester M3 3PL,
Telephone: 0161 832 3791
E-mail: clerks@peelct.co.uk
Call Date: July 1986, Inner Temple
Qualifications: [LLB, LLM (Bristol)]

GROVER TIM RUSSELL

Martins Building
2nd Floor, No 4 Water Street, Liverpool
L2 3SP, Telephone: 0151 236 5818/4919
Call Date: Nov 1991, Inner Temple
Qualifications: [LLB (Essex)]

GROVES HUGO GERARD

Enterprise Chambers
9 Old Square, Lincoln's Inn, London
WC2A 3SR, Telephone: 0171 405 9471
E-mail:enterprise.london@dial.pipex.com
Enterprise Chambers
38 Park Square, Leeds LS1 2PA,
Telephone: 0113 246 0391
E-mail:enterprise.leeds@dial.pipex.com
Enterprise Chambers
65 Quayside, Newcastle upon Tyne
NE1 3DS, Telephone: 0191 222 3344
E-mail:enterprise.newcastle@dial.pipex.com
Call Date: July 1980, Gray's Inn
Qualifications: [LLB (Leic), LLM (Lond)]

GRUBB PROFESSOR ANDREW

3 Serjeants' Inn
London EC4Y 1BQ,
Telephone: 0171 353 5537
E-mail: clerks@3serjeantsinn.com
Call Date: July 1980, Inner Temple
Qualifications: [MA (Cantab)]

GRUCHY SIMON GEOFFREY

2-4 Tudor Street
London EC4Y 0AA,
Telephone: 0171 797 7111
E-mail: clerks@rfqc.co.uk
Call Date: May 1993, Middle Temple
Qualifications: [BSc(Nautical Studies,),
Diploma in Law]

GRUDER JEFFREY NIGEL QC (1997)

One Essex Court
Ground Floor, Temple, London
EC4Y 9AR, Telephone: 020 7583 2000
E-mail: clerks@oneessexcourt.co.uk
Call Date: July 1977, Middle Temple
Qualifications: [MA (Cantab)]

GRUFFYDD JOHN

Oriel Chambers
14 Water Street, Liverpool L2 8TD,
Telephone: 0151 236 7191/236 4321
E-mail: clerks@oriel-chambers.co.uk
Call Date: Feb 1992, Gray's Inn
Qualifications: [LLB (Lond)]

GRUMBAR PAUL HARRY JULIAN

St John's Chambers
Small Street, Bristol BS1 1DW,
Telephone: 0117 9213456/298514
E-mail: @stjohnschambers.co.uk
Call Date: Nov 1974, Middle Temple
Pupil Master
Qualifications: [BA]

GRUNDY MISS ARABELLA ELIZABETH LOUISE

College Chambers
19 Carlton Cresent, Southampton
SO15 2ET, Telephone: 01703 230338
Call Date: Oct 1995, Inner Temple
Qualifications: [MA , CPE (City)]

GRUNDY MS CLARE

28 St John Street
Manchester M3 4DJ,
Telephone: 0161 834 8418
E-mail: clerk@28stjohnst.co.uk
Call Date: July 1989, Gray's Inn
Qualifications: [LLB (B'ham)]

GRUNDY JAMES MILTON

Gray's Inn Tax Chambers
3rd Floor, Gray's Inn Chambers, Gray's
Inn, London WC1R 5JA,
Telephone: 0171 242 2642
E-mail: clerks@taxbar.com
Call Date: Nov 1954, Inner Temple
Qualifications: [MA (Cantab)]

GRUNDY LIAM

Adrian Lyon's Chambers
14 Castle Street, Liverpool L2 0NE,
Telephone: 0151 236 4421/8240
E-mail: chambers14@aol.com
Call Date: July 1995, Inner Temple
Qualifications: [LLB (Hull), LLM (Cantab)]

GRUNDY NICHOLAS JOHN

One Essex Court
1st Floor, Temple, London EC4Y 9AR,
Telephone: 0171 936 3030
E-mail: one.essex_court@virgin.net
Call Date: Oct 1993, Gray's Inn
Qualifications: [MA (Cantab), MSc, Dip Law]

GRUNDY NIGEL LAWRENCE JOHN

Chambers of John Hand QC
9 St John Street, Manchester M3 4DN,
Telephone: 0161 955 9000
E-mail: ninesjs@gconnect.com
Call Date: July 1983, Middle Temple
Qualifications: [MA (Oxon)]

GRUNDY PHILIP MICHAEL DAVID

28 St John Street
Manchester M3 4DJ,
Telephone: 0161 834 8418
E-mail: clerk@28stjohnst.co.uk
2-4 Tudor Street
London EC4Y 0AA,
Telephone: 0171 797 7111
E-mail: clerks@rfqc.co.uk
Call Date: July 1980, Middle Temple
Pupil Master, Assistant Recorder
Qualifications: [LLB (Wales)]

GRUNWALD HENRY CYRIL QC (1999)

2-4 Tudor Street
London EC4Y 0AA,
Telephone: 0171 797 7111
E-mail: clerks@rfqc.co.uk
Call Date: 1972, Gray's Inn
Pupil Master
Qualifications: [LLB (Lond)]

GUBBAY JEFFREY

3 Temple Gardens
3rd Floor, Temple, London EC4Y 9AU,
Telephone: 0171 353 0832
Call Date: Oct 1992, Inner Temple
Qualifications: [LLB (Bucks)]

GUEST MS HELEN

3 Temple Gardens
2nd Floor, Temple, London EC4Y 9AU,
Telephone: 0171 583 1155
Call Date: Oct 1996, Lincoln's Inn
Qualifications: [BA (Hons)(Lond)]

GUEST NEIL

3 Temple Gardens
2nd Floor, Temple, London EC4Y 9AU,
Telephone: 0171 583 1155
Call Date: July 1989, Lincoln's Inn
Pupil Master
Qualifications: [LLB (Hons)]

GUEST PETER LIAM

Cloisters
1 Pump Court, Temple, London
EC4Y 7AA, Telephone: 0171 827 4000
E-mail: clerks@cloisters.com
Call Date: July 1975, Inner Temple
Pupil Master
Qualifications: [BA (Hons) (Dunelm)]

GUEST PROFESSOR STEPHEN FRANCIS DEXTER

199 Strand
London WC2R 1DR,
Telephone: 0171 379 9779
E-mail: chambers@199strand.co.uk
Call Date: 1980, Inner Temple
Qualifications: [BA, LLB, B Litt, PhD]

GUGGENHEIM MISS ANNA MAEVE

Two Crown Office Row
Ground Floor, Temple, London
EC4Y 7HJ, Telephone: 020 7797 8100
E-mail: mail@2cor.co.uk, or to individual
barristers at: [barrister's
surname]@2cor.co.uk
Call Date: July 1982, Gray's Inn
Pupil Master
Qualifications: [BA (Oxon)]

GUIRGUIS MISS SHEREN

White Friars Chambers
21 White Friars, Chester CH1 1NZ,
Telephone: 01244 323070
E-mail:whitefriarschambers@btinternet.com
Call Date: Oct 1996, Inner Temple
Qualifications: [LLB (B'ham)]

GUISHARD DAVID ELSWORTH KELLY

Rowchester Chambers
4 Rowchester Court, Whittall Street,
Birmingham B4 6DH,
Telephone: 0121 233 2327/2361951
Call Date: Feb 1978, Middle Temple
Pupil Master
Qualifications: [LLB]

GULLIFER MRS LOUISE JOAN

Call Date: July 1984, Gray's Inn
Qualifications: [MA (Oxon), BCL]

GULLIVER MISS ALISON LOUISE

4 Paper Buildings
Ground Floor, Temple, London
EC4Y 7EX, Telephone: 0171 353 3366/
583 7155
E-mail: clerks@4paperbuildings.com
Call Date: Nov 1989, Middle Temple
Pupil Master
Qualifications: [MA (Oxon)]

GUMBEL MISS ELIZABETH ANNE QC (1999)

199 Strand
London WC2R 1DR,
Telephone: 0171 379 9779
E-mail: chambers@199strand.co.uk
Call Date: 1974, Inner Temple
Pupil Master
Qualifications: [MA (Oxon)]

GUMBITI-ZIMUTO ANDREW

6 King's Bench Walk
Ground, Third & Fourth Floors, Temple,
London EC4Y 7DR,
Telephone: 0171 353 4931/583 0695
Call Date: Nov 1983, Inner Temple
Pupil Master
Qualifications: [BA (Hons)(Sussex)]

GUMBS MISS ANNETTE PATRICIA

28 St John Street
Manchester M3 4DJ,
Telephone: 0161 834 8418
E-mail: clerk@28stjohnst.co.uk
Call Date: Oct 1994, Gray's Inn
Qualifications: [LLB]

GUMPERT RUSSELL BENJAMIN WALLACE

Chambers of Michael Pert QC
36 Bedford Row, London WC1R 4JH,
Telephone: 0171 421 8000
E-mail: 36bedfordrow@link.org
Chambers of Michael Pert QC
24 Albion Place, Northampton NN1 1UD,
Telephone: 01604 602333
Chambers of Michael Pert QC
104 New Walk, Leicester LE1 7EA,
Telephone: 0116 249 2020
Call Date: Feb 1987, Inner Temple
Qualifications: [MA (Cantab)]

D

GUMSLEY CARL JOHN

Broad Chare
33 Broad Chare, Newcastle upon Tyne
NE1 3DQ, Telephone: 0191 232 0541
E-mail:clerks@broadcharechambers.law.co.uk
Call Date: Nov 1989, Inner Temple
Qualifications: [LLB (Sheff)]

GUN CUNINGHAME JULIAN ARTHUR

Gough Square Chambers
6-7 Gough Square, London EC4A 3DE,
Telephone: 0171 353 0924
E-mail: gsc@goughsq.co.uk
Call Date: Nov 1989, Lincoln's Inn
Qualifications: [MA (Edin)]

GUNASEKARA PRINS

12 Old Square
1st Floor, Lincoln's Inn, London
WC2A 3TX, Telephone: 0171 404 0875
Call Date: Nov 1993, Middle Temple
Qualifications: [BA (Hons) (Lond)]

GUNNING ALEXANDER RUPERT

4 Pump Court
Temple, London EC4Y 7AN,
Telephone: 020 7842 5555
E-mail:chambers@4pumpcourt.law.co.uk
Call Date: Nov 1994, Inner Temple
Qualifications: [LLB, LLM (Lond)]

GUNTHER MISS ELIZABETH ANN

Pump Court Chambers
31 Southgate Street, Winchester
SO23 9EE, Telephone: 01962 868161
E-mail: clerks@3pumpcourt.com
Pump Court Chambers
Upper Ground Floor, 3 Pump Court,
Temple, London EC4Y 7AJ,
Telephone: 0171 353 0711
E-mail: clerks@3pumpcourt.com
Pump Court Chambers
5 Temple Chambers, Temple Street,
Swindon SN1 1SQ,
Telephone: 01793 539899
E-mail: clerks@3pumpcourt.com
Call Date: Oct 1993, Lincoln's Inn
Qualifications: [LLB (Hons)(B'ham)]

GUPTA TEERTHA

**1 Gray's Inn Square, Chambers of the
Baroness Scotland of Asthal QC**
1st Floor, London WC1R 5AG,
Telephone: 0171 405 3000
E-mail: clerks@onegrays.demon.co.uk
Call Date: Nov 1990, Inner Temple
Qualifications: [LLB (Leeds)]

GUPTA MISS USHA

New Chambers
3 Sadleir Road, St Albans, Herts, AL1 2BL,
Telephone: 0966 212126
Call Date: July 1984, Middle Temple
Assistant Recorder
Qualifications: [BA (Modern Studies, Dip
Law), BA (Hons)]

GURSOY RAMIZ ALI

One Essex Court
1st Floor, Temple, London EC4Y 9AR,
Telephone: 0171 936 3030
E-mail: one.essex_court@virgin.net
Call Date: Nov 1991, Middle Temple
Qualifications: [BA Hons (Essex), Dip Law
(City)]

GUTHRIE JAMES DALGLISH QC (1993)

1 Crown Office Row
3rd Floor, Temple, London EC4Y 7HH,
Telephone: 0171 583 9292
E-mail: onecor@link.org
Call Date: 1975, Inner Temple
Recorder
Qualifications: [BA (Oxon)]

GUTHRIE MARK JONATHAN

14 Tooks Court
Cursitor St, London EC4A 1LB,
Telephone: 0171 405 8828
E-mail: clerks@tooks.law.co.uk
Call Date: July 1984, Middle Temple
Pupil Master
Qualifications: [LLB (Manch)]

GUTTERIDGE MISS BEVERLEY JANE

Chambers of Beverley Gutteridge
36 Dunmore Road, Wimbledon, London
SW20 8TN, Telephone: 0181 947 0717
Call Date: July 1987, Middle Temple
Qualifications: [BA (Keele)]

GUY JOHN DAVID COLIN

Francis Taylor Building
3rd Floor, Temple, London EC4Y 7BY,
Telephone: 0171 797 7250
Call Date: July 1972, Gray's Inn
Pupil Master
Qualifications: [BA, FCIArb]

GUY RICHARD PERRAN

Queen Elizabeth Building
Ground Floor, Temple, London
EC4Y 9BS,
Telephone: 0171 353 7181 (12 Lines)
Godolphin Chambers
50 Castle Street, Truro, Cornwall,
TR1 3AF, Telephone: 01872 276312
E-mail:theclerks@godolphin.force9.co.uk
Call Date: Nov 1970, Inner Temple
Qualifications: [MA (Oxon)]

GUY-DAVIES MRS JUDITH MARY

Bell Yard Chambers
116/118 Chancery Lane, London
WC2A 1PP, Telephone: 0171 306 9292
Call Date: Nov 1976, Gray's Inn
Qualifications: [LLB]

HABBOO MISS CAMILLE FRANCES

1 Dr Johnson's Buildings
Ground Floor, Temple, London
EC4Y 7AX, Telephone: 0171 353 9328
E-mail:OneDr.Johnsons@btinternet.com
Dr Johnson's Chambers
The Atrium Court, Apex Plaza, Reading,
Berkshire, RG1 1AX,
Telephone: 01734 254221
Call Date: July 1987, Gray's Inn
Pupil Master
Qualifications: [LLB (L'pool)]

HABEL MRS JESSICA JENNET

College Chambers
19 Carlton Cresent, Southampton
SO15 2ET, Telephone: 01703 230338
Call Date: July 1991, Middle Temple
Qualifications: [MA (Oxon)]

HABIB DR MUSTAFA SALMAN

10 King's Bench Walk
Ground Floor, Temple, London
EC4Y 7EB, Telephone: 0171 353 7742
E-mail: 10kbw@lineone.net
Call Date: 1980, Lincoln's Inn
Qualifications: [BPharm (Lond), PhD]

HACKER RICHARD DANIEL QC (1998)

3/4 South Square
Gray's Inn, London WC1R 5HP,
Telephone: 0171 696 9900
E-mail: clerks@southsquare.com
Call Date: July 1977, Lincoln's Inn
Qualifications: [MA (Cantab)]

HACKETT MARTIN JOHN

15 Winckley Square
Preston PR1 3JJ,
Telephone: 01772 252828
E-mail:clerks@winckleysq.demon.co.uk
Call Date: Feb 1995, Middle Temple
Qualifications: [LLB (Hons)(Wales)]

HACKETT PHILIP GEORGE QC (1999)

3 Hare Court
1 Little Essex Street, London WC2R 3LD,
Telephone: 0171 395 2000
Call Date: 1978, Middle Temple
Pupil Master
Qualifications: [BA]

HACKING ANTHONY STEPHEN QC (1983)

One King's Bench Walk
1st Floor, Temple, London EC4Y 7DB,
Telephone: 0171 936 1500
E-mail: ddear@1kbw.co.uk
Call Date: Nov 1965, Inner Temple
Recorder
Qualifications: [MA (Oxon)]

HACKMAN CARL

Mitre Court Chambers
3rd Floor, Temple, London EC4Y 7BP,
Telephone: 0171 353 9394
E-mail: mitrecourt.com
Call Date: Nov 1990, Gray's Inn
Qualifications: [LLB]

HACON RICHARD DAVID

11 South Square
2nd Floor, Gray's Inn, London
WC1R 5EU,
Telephone: 0171 405 1222 (24hr messaging service)
E-mail: clerks@11southsquare.com
Call Date: Nov 1979, Gray's Inn
Pupil Master
Qualifications: [BSc (Leeds)]

HADDON-CAVE CHARLES ANTHONY QC (1999)

4 Essex Court
Temple, London EC4Y 9AJ,
Telephone: 020 7797 7970
E-mail: clerks@4essexcourt.law.co.uk
Call Date: 1978, Gray's Inn
Pupil Master, Assistant Recorder
Qualifications: [MA (Cantab)]

HADLEY STEVEN FRANK

1 Inner Temple Lane
Temple, London EC4Y 1AF,
Telephone: 020 7353 0933
Call Date: July 1987, Inner Temple
Pupil Master
Qualifications: [BA (Hons)(Wales), BIB Studies/Phil, BD (Hons)(Wales), Dip Law]

HADRILL KEITH PAUL

9-12 Bell Yard
London WC2A 2LF,
Telephone: 0171 400 1800
E-mail: clerks@bellyard.co.uk
Call Date: July 1977, Lincoln's Inn
Pupil Master

HAEEMS DAVID RALPH

2-4 Tudor Street
London EC4Y 0AA,
Telephone: 0171 797 7111
E-mail: clerks@rfqc.co.uk
Call Date: Oct 1996, Inner Temple
Qualifications: [LLB]

HAGGAN NICHOLAS SOMERSET

17 Carlton Crescent
Southampton SO15 2XR,
Telephone: 023 8032 0320/0823 2003
E-mail: greg@jg17cc.co.uk
Call Date: July 1977, Middle Temple
Pupil Master, Assistant Recorder

HAGGERTY MISS ELIZABETH FRANCES

Lamb Chambers
Lamb Building, Temple, London
EC4Y 7AS, Telephone: 020 7797 8300
E-mail: lambchambers@link.org
Call Date: Feb 1994, Lincoln's Inn
Qualifications: [LLB (Hons)]

HAGGIS ROBERT ARTHUR

65-67 King Street
Leicester LE1 6RP,
Telephone: 0116 2547710
Call Date: Nov 1980, Gray's Inn
Qualifications: [BA Hons]

HAGUE PAUL FRANCIS

15 Winckley Square
Preston PR1 3JJ,
Telephone: 01772 252828
E-mail:clerks@winckleysq.demon.co.uk
Call Date: July 1983, Lincoln's Inn
Qualifications: [BA]

HAIDEMENOS STAVROS

Warwick House Chambers
8 Warwick Court, Gray's Inn, London
WC1R 5DJ, Telephone: 0171 430 2323
E-mail: cdrewlaw@aol.com
Call Date: Oct 1992, Lincoln's Inn
Qualifications: [LLB(Hons)(Lond),
LLM(Lond), Maitrise (Paris II), ACIArb]

HAIG-HADDOW JOHN ALASTAIR HAIG

Eighteen Carlton Crescent
Southampton SO15 2XR,
Telephone: 01703 639001
Call Date: July 1972, Middle Temple
Pupil Master
Qualifications: [BA]

HAIGH MARTIN JAMES

30 Park Square
Leeds LS1 2PF, Telephone: 0113 2436388
E-mail: clerks@30parksquare.co.uk
Call Date: Nov 1970, Gray's Inn
Qualifications: [LLB]

HAILSTONE MISS CATHARINE ELIZABETH

Albion Chambers
Broad Street, Bristol BS1 1DR,
Telephone: 0117 9272144
Call Date: July 1962, Middle Temple
Pupil Master
Qualifications: [LLB (Lond)]

HAINES GEOFFREY RALPH

55 Temple Chambers
Temple Avenue, London EC4Y 0HP,
Telephone: 0171 353 7400
Call Date: June 1949, Lincoln's Inn

HAINES JOHN WILLIAM

2-3 Gray's Inn Square
Gray's Inn, London WC1R 5JH,
Telephone: 0171 242 4986
E-mail:chambers@2-3graysinnsquare.co.uk
Call Date: Nov 1967, Middle Temple
Pupil Master, Recorder
Qualifications: [BA (Oxon)]

HAJI MISS SHAHEEN

Bell Yard Chambers
116/118 Chancery Lane, London
WC2A 1PP, Telephone: 0171 306 9292
Call Date: 1997, Middle Temple
Qualifications: [BA , LLB (Hons)]

HAJIMITSIS ANTHONY PAUL

Chambers of Andrew Campbell QC
10 Park Square, Leeds LS1 2LH,
Telephone: 0113 2455438
E-mail: clerks@10pksq.co.uk
Call Date: Nov 1984, Inner Temple
Pupil Master
Qualifications: [BA (Oxon)]

HALE CHARLES STANLEY

Dr Johnson's Chambers
Two Dr Johnson's Buildings, Temple,
London EC4Y 7AY,
Telephone: 0171 353 4716
E-mail: clerks@2djb.freeserve.co.uk
Call Date: Oct 1992, Middle Temple
Qualifications: [LLB (Hons)]

HALE MRS GRACE WAI YI

King Charles House
Standard Hill, Nottingham NG1 6FX,
Telephone: 0115 9418851
E-mail: clerks@kch.co.uk
Call Date: Mar 1998, Gray's Inn
Qualifications: [LLB, LLM (Lond)]

HALE SEAN MARTIN PHILIP

St Mary's Chambers
50 High Pavement, Lace Market,
Nottingham NG1 1HW,
Telephone: 0115 9503503
E-mail: clerks@smc.law.co.uk
Call Date: Nov 1988, Inner Temple
Qualifications: [BA (Dunelm)]

HALEEMA MISS SAFINA

Trafalgar Chambers
53 Fleet Street, London EC4Y 1BE,
Telephone: 0171 583 5858
E-mail:trafalgarchambers@easynet.co.uk
Call Date: Oct 1993, Lincoln's Inn
Qualifications: [LLB (Hons)(L'pool), MA (Leic)]

HALES MISS SALLY ANN

9 Gough Square
London EC4A 3DE,
Telephone: 020 7832 0500
E-mail: clerks@9goughsq.co.uk
Call Date: July 1988, Gray's Inn
Pupil Master
Qualifications: [LLB (Hons)]

HALKERSTON GRAEME ALEXANDER

One Essex Court
Ground Floor, Temple, London
EC4Y 9AR, Telephone: 020 7583 2000
E-mail: clerks@oneessexcourt.co.uk
Call Date: Nov 1994, Middle Temple
Qualifications: [BA (Hons), LLM (Pennsylvania)]

HALKERSTON MISS SALLY

2 Harcourt Buildings
1st Floor, Temple, London EC4Y 9DB,
Telephone: 020 7353 2112
Call Date: Oct 1994, Middle Temple
Qualifications: [LLB (Hons)]

HALKYARD MISS (ALYSON) KAY

One Garden Court Family Law Chambers
Ground Floor, Temple, London
EC4Y 9BJ, Telephone: 0171 797 7900
E-mail: clerks@onegardencourt.co.uk
Call Date: July 1980, Gray's Inn
Pupil Master
Qualifications: [LLB (Lond)]

HALL ADRIAN

Enfield Chambers
First Floor, Refuge House, 9-10 River
Front, Enfield, Middlesex, EN1 3SZ,
Telephone: 0181 364 5627
E-mail:enfieldchambers@compuserve.com
Southsea Chambers
PO Box 148, Southsea, Portsmouth,
Hampshire, PO5 2TU,
Telephone: 01705 291261
Call Date: July 1989, Inner Temple
Pupil Master
Qualifications: [LLB (Hull), B.Ed (Hull)]

HALL ANDREW JOSEPH

Doughty Street Chambers
11 Doughty Street, London WC1N 2PG,
Telephone: 0171 404 1313
E-mail:enquiries@doughtystreet.co.uk
Call Date: Feb 1991, Gray's Inn
Pupil Master
Qualifications: [LLB (B'ham), MA (Sheff)]

HALL DAVID PERCY

9 Woodhouse Square
Leeds LS3 1AD,
Telephone: 0113 2451986
E-mail: clerks@9woodhouse.co.uk
Call Date: July 1980, Gray's Inn
Pupil Master
Qualifications: [BA]

HALL DEREK

Baker Street Chambers
9 Baker Street, Middlesbrough TS1 2LF,
Telephone: 01642 873873
Call Date: Nov 1994, Middle Temple
Qualifications: [LLB (Hons)]

HALL MISS JACQUELINE ANN

18 Red Lion Court
(Off Fleet Street), London EC4A 3EB,
Telephone: 0171 520 6000
E-mail: chambers@18rlc.co.uk
Thornwood House
102 New London Road, Chelmsford,
Essex, CM2 0RG,
Telephone: 01245 280880
E-mail: chambers@18rlc.co.uk
Call Date: Nov 1994, Lincoln's Inn
Qualifications: [BA (Hons)(Warw)]

HALL JEREMY JOHN

Becket Chambers
17 New Dover Road, Canterbury, Kent,
CT1 3AS, Telephone: 01227 786331
Call Date: 1988, Gray's Inn
Qualifications: [LLB (Hons) (East, Anglia)]

HALL MISS JOANNA MARY

14 Gray's Inn Square
Gray's Inn, London WC1R 5JP,
Telephone: 0171 242 0858
E-mail: 100712.2134@compuserve.com
Call Date: Nov 1973, Inner Temple
Pupil Master
Qualifications: [LLB (Lond)]

HALL JOHN ANTHONY SANDERSON QC (1967)

Francis Taylor Building
3rd Floor, Temple, London EC4Y 7BY,
Telephone: 0171 797 7250
Call Date: Nov 1948, Inner Temple
Qualifications: [MA (Cantab), FCI Arb]

HALL JONATHAN DAVID DURHAM QC (1995)

Bank House Chambers
Old Bank House, Hartshead, Sheffield
S1 2EL, Telephone: 0114 2751223

D

New Walk Chambers
27 New Walk, Leicester LE1 6TE,
Telephone: 0116 2559144
Goldsmith Chambers
Ground Floor, Goldsmith Building,
Temple, London EC4Y 7BL,
Telephone: 0171 353 6802/3/4/5
E-mail:clerks@goldsmithchambers.law.co.uk
Call Date: July 1975, Gray's Inn
Recorder
Qualifications: [LLB (Hons)]

HALL JONATHAN RUPERT

5 King's Bench Walk
Temple, London EC4Y 7DN,
Telephone: 0171 353 5638
Call Date: Nov 1994, Inner Temple
Qualifications: [BA (Oxon), CPE (City)]

HALL MRS MELANIE RUTH

Monckton Chambers
4 Raymond Buildings, Gray's Inn, London
WC1R 5BP, Telephone: 0171 405 7211
E-mail: chambers@monckton.co.uk
Call Date: Nov 1982, Inner Temple
Pupil Master
Qualifications: [BA Law (Dunelm)]

HALL MICHAEL LEBERT

Two Garden Court
1st Floor, Middle Temple, London
EC4Y 9BL, Telephone: 0171 353 1633
E-mail:barristers@2gardenct.law.co.uk
Call Date: July 1983, Middle Temple
Qualifications: [BA]

HALL MICHAEL RICHARD

Fleet Chambers
Mitre House, 44-46 Fleet Street, London
EC4Y 1BN, Telephone: 0171 936 3707
E-mail: rr@fleetchambers.demon.co.uk
Call Date: 1996, Inner Temple
Qualifications: [LLB (Reading)]

HALL NICHOLAS

Sussex Chambers
9 Old Steine, Brighton, Sussex, BN1 1FJ,
Telephone: 01273 607953
Call Date: July 1973, Gray's Inn
Pupil Master
Qualifications: [MA (Oxon)]

HALL PHILIP JOHN

Chavasse Court Chambers
2nd Floor, Chavasse Court, 24 Lord Street,
Liverpool L2 1TA,
Telephone: 0151 707 1191
Call Date: Nov 1973, Gray's Inn
Pupil Master
Qualifications: [LLB (Lond)]

HALL RICHARD ANDREW

Eighteen Carlton Crescent
Southampton SO15 2XR,
Telephone: 01703 639001
Call Date: Nov 1995, Inner Temple
Qualifications: [LLB (Soton)]

HALL RICHARD ARTHUR

Adrian Lyon's Chambers
14 Castle Street, Liverpool L2 0NE,
Telephone: 0151 236 4421/8240
E-mail: chambers14@aol.com
Call Date: Nov 1991, Lincoln's Inn
Qualifications: [MA (Oxon)]

HALL MRS YASMIN MUNIR

Guildhall Chambers Portsmouth
Prudential Buildings, 16 Guildhall Walk,
Portsmouth, Hampshire, PO1 2DE,
Telephone: 01705 752400
Call Date: Nov 1993, Lincoln's Inn
Qualifications: [LLB (Hons)]

HALL TAYLOR ALEXANDER EDWARD

11 Old Square
Ground Floor, Lincoln's Inn, London
WC2A 3TS, Telephone: 020 7430 0341
E-mail: clerks@11oldsquare.co.uk
Call Date: Oct 1996, Inner Temple
Qualifications: [BA (Hons)(Bris), CPE
(Lond)]

HALL-SMITH MARTIN CLIVE WILLIAM

Goldsmith Building
1st Floor, Temple, London EC4Y 7BL,
Telephone: 0171 353 7881
E-mail:clerks@goldsmith-building.law.co.uk
Call Date: July 1972, Inner Temple
Pupil Master
Qualifications: [LLB (Edin) , MA (Cantab)]

D

HALLAM JACOB WILLIAM

6 King's Bench Walk
Ground Floor, Temple, London
EC4Y 7DR, Telephone: 0171 583 0410
E-mail: worsley@6kbw.freeserve.co.uk
Call Date: 1996, Gray's Inn
Qualifications: [MA (Cantab)]

HALLAM MISS RONA MARY LOUISE

30 Park Square
Leeds LS1 2PF, Telephone: 0113 2436388
E-mail: clerks@30parksquare.co.uk
Call Date: July 1984, Inner Temple
Pupil Master, Assistant Recorder
Qualifications: [MA (Edinburgh), LLB]

HALLIDAY HAROLD DAVID

40 King Street
Manchester M2 6BA,
Telephone: 0161 832 9082
E-mail: clerks@40kingstreet.co.uk
The Chambers of Philip Raynor QC
5 Park Place, Leeds LS1 2RU,
Telephone: 0113 242 1123
Call Date: July 1972, Gray's Inn
Pupil Master
Qualifications: [MA (Oxon)]

HALLIDAY IAN NICOLAS

Assize Court Chambers
14 Small Street, Bristol BS1 1DE,
Telephone: 0117 9264587
E-mail:chambers@assize-court-chambers.co.uk
Call Date: 1989, Lincoln's Inn
Qualifications: [LLB (Leeds)]

HALLIGAN BRENDAN

Tower Hamlets Barristers Chambers
37B Princelet Street, London E1 5LP,
Telephone: 0171 377 8090
E-mail: shikderka@aol.com
Call Date: 1998, Middle Temple
Qualifications: [LLB (Hons)(E.Lond)]

HALLIGAN RODNEY LEWTON

Martins Building
2nd Floor, No 4 Water Street, Liverpool
L2 3SP, Telephone: 0151 236 5818/4919
Call Date: July 1972, Gray's Inn
Qualifications: [LLB]

HALLISSEY MISS CAROLINE MARIA

Hardwicke Building
New Square, Lincoln's Inn, London
WC2A 3SB, Telephone: 020 7242 2523
E-mail: clerks@hardwicke.co.uk
Call Date: Feb 1990, Inner Temple
Qualifications: [BA (E Anglia), Dip Law]

HALLIWELL MARK GARETH

40 King Street
Manchester M2 6BA,
Telephone: 0161 832 9082
E-mail: clerks@40kingstreet.co.uk
The Chambers of Philip Raynor QC
5 Park Place, Leeds LS1 2RU,
Telephone: 0113 242 1123
Call Date: July 1985, Lincoln's Inn
Pupil Master
Qualifications: [B.Sc(Econ), Diploma]

HALLIWELL TOBY GEORGE

Assize Court Chambers
14 Small Street, Bristol BS1 1DE,
Telephone: 0117 9264587
E-mail:chambers@assize-court-chambers.co.uk
Call Date: Nov 1992, Middle Temple
Qualifications: [LLB (Hons, Manch)]

HALLORAN MS CATHERINE MARY

14 Tooks Court
Cursitor St, London EC4A 1LB,
Telephone: 0171 405 8828
E-mail: clerks@tooks.law.co.uk
Call Date: Nov 1996, Lincoln's Inn
Qualifications: [LLB (Hons)(Lancs)]

HALLORAN MS CEILIDH ANN

Arden Chambers
27 John Street, London WC1N 2BL,
Telephone: 020 7242 4244
E-mail:clerks@arden-chambers.law.co.uk
Call Date: Nov 1992, Lincoln's Inn
Qualifications: [MA (Psych), MEd (Psych),
Dip.TEFL (Psych)]

HALLOWES RUPERT JOHN MICHAEL

Britton Street Chambers
1st Floor, 20 Britton Street, London
EC1M 5NQ, Telephone: 0171 608 3765
Call Date: Oct 1995, Inner Temple
Qualifications: [BA (Bris), CPE]

HALPERN DAVID ANTHONY

Enterprise Chambers
9 Old Square, Lincoln's Inn, London
WC2A 3SR, Telephone: 0171 405 9471
E-mail:enterprise.london@dial.pipex.com
Enterprise Chambers
38 Park Square, Leeds LS1 2PA,
Telephone: 0113 246 0391
E-mail:enterprise.leeds@dial.pipex.com
Enterprise Chambers
65 Quayside, Newcastle upon Tyne
NE1 3DS, Telephone: 0191 222 3344
E-mail:enterprise.newcastle@dial.pipex.com
Call Date: July 1978, Gray's Inn
Pupil Master
Qualifications: [MA (Oxon)]

HALPIN THOMAS GAVIN

Earl Street Chambers
47 Earl Street, Maidstone, Kent,
ME14 1PD, Telephone: 01622 671222
E-mail: gunner-sparks@msn.com
Call Date: Nov 1994, Inner Temple
Qualifications: [LLB (Lond)]

HALSALL MISS LOUISE KIM

3 Temple Gardens
Lower Ground Floor, Temple, London
EC4Y 9AU, Telephone: 0171 353 3102/5/
9297 E-mail: clerks@3tg.co.uk
Call Date: July 1982, Middle Temple
Pupil Master

HALSALL STEPHEN JAMES

Enfield Chambers
First Floor, Refuge House, 9-10 River
Front, Enfield, Middlesex, EN1 3SZ,
Telephone: 0181 364 5627
E-mail:enfieldchambers@compuserve.com
Barristers' Common Law Chambers
57 Whitechapel Road, Aldgate East,
London E1 1DU,
Telephone: 0171 375 3012
E-mail: barristers@hotmail.com and
barristers@lawchambers.freeserve.co.uk
Call Date: 1997, Inner Temple
Qualifications: [BA (Cantab), Dip Law, CPE
(City)]

HALSEY MARK STEPHEN

3 Hare Court
1 Little Essex Street, London WC2R 3LD,
Telephone: 0171 395 2000
Call Date: Feb 1974, Inner Temple
Qualifications: [LLB (Bris)]

HALSTEAD ROBIN BERNARD

Fleet Chambers
Mitre House, 44-46 Fleet Street, London
EC4Y 1BN, Telephone: 0171 936 3707
E-mail: rr@fleetchambers.demon.co.uk
Call Date: Oct 1996, Inner Temple
Qualifications: [BA (Oxon)]

HAM NICHOLAS TREHARNE

Counsels' Chambers
2nd Floor, 10-11 Gray's Inn Square,
London WC1R 5JD,
Telephone: 0171 405 2576
E-mail:clerks@10-11graysinnsquare.co.uk
Call Date: 1997, Middle Temple
Qualifications: [BA (Hons)(Bris)]

HAM ROBERT WALLACE QC (1994)

Wilberforce Chambers
8 New Square, Lincoln's Inn, London
WC2A 3QP, Telephone: 0171 306 0102
E-mail: chambers@wilberforce.co.uk
Call Date: Nov 1973, Middle Temple
Qualifications: [BCL, BA (Oxon)]

Types of work: Chancery (general), Charities,
Equity, wills and trusts, Pensions, Probate
and administration

HAMBLEN NICHOLAS ARCHIBALD QC (1997)

20 Essex Street
London WC2R 3AL,
Telephone: 0171 583 9294
E-mail: clerks@20essexst.com
Call Date: July 1981, Lincoln's Inn
Qualifications: [MA (Oxon),LLM (Harv)]

HAMBLIN NICHOLAS HOWARD

Westgate Chambers
144 High Street, Lewes, East Sussex,
BN7 1XT, Telephone: 01273 480510

1 Dr Johnson's Buildings
Ground Floor, Temple, London
EC4Y 7AX, Telephone: 0171 353 9328
E-mail:OneDr.Johnsons@btinternet.com
Call Date: Nov 1981, Lincoln's Inn
Pupil Master
Qualifications: [LLB (Hons)]

HAMBLIN STEWART WAYNE

2 Harcourt Buildings
1st Floor, Temple, London EC4Y 9DB,
Telephone: 020 7353 2112
Call Date: Oct 1990, Middle Temple
Qualifications: [BA (Leic), Dip Law]

HAMER GEORGE CLEMENS

8 New Square
Lincoln's Inn, London WC2A 3QP,
Telephone: 0171 405 4321
E-mail: clerks@8newsquare.co.uk
Call Date: Nov 1974, Gray's Inn
Pupil Master
Qualifications: [BSc, ARCS (Lond)]

HAMER MICHAEL HOWARD KENNETH

2 Harcourt Buildings
Ground Floor/Left, Temple, London
EC4Y 9DB, Telephone: 0171 583 9020
E-mail: clerks@harcourt.co.uk
Westgate Chambers
144 High Street, Lewes, East Sussex,
BN7 1XT, Telephone: 01273 480510
Call Date: Apr 1975, Inner Temple
Pupil Master, Assistant Recorder

HAMES CHRISTOPHER WILLIAM

3 Dr Johnson's Buildings
Ground Floor, Temple, London
EC4Y 7BA, Telephone: 0171 353 4854
E-mail: clerks@3djb.co.uk
Call Date: July 1987, Inner Temple
Pupil Master
Qualifications: [LLB (Sheffield)]

HAMEY JOHN ANTHONY

East Anglian Chambers
57 London Street, Norwich NR2 1HL,
Telephone: 01603 617351
E-mail: norwich@ealaw.co.uk

East Anglian Chambers
52 North Hill, Colchester, Essex, CO1 1PY,
Telephone: 01206 572756
E-mail: colchester@ealaw.co.uk
East Anglian Chambers
Gresham House, 5 Museum Street,
Ipswich, Suffolk, IP1 1HQ,
Telephone: 01473 214481
E-mail: ipswich@ealaw.co.uk
Call Date: July 1979, Inner Temple
Pupil Master
Qualifications: [MA (Cantab)]

HAMID MRS BEEBEE NAZMOON

Clapham Chambers
21-25 Bedford Road, Clapham North,
London SW4 7SH,
Telephone: 0171 978 8482/642 5777
E-mail:claphamchambers@compuserve.com
Call Date: July 1980, Lincoln's Inn
Pupil Master
Qualifications: [BA (Hons) (Lond)]

HAMILL HUGH ANTHONY

12 King's Bench Walk
Temple, London EC4Y 7EL,
Telephone: 0171 583 0811
E-mail: chambers@12kbw.co.uk
Call Date: July 1988, Inner Temple
Qualifications: [BA (Dublin), Dip Law (City)]

HAMILTON ADRIAN WALTER QC (1973)

S Tomlinson QC
7 King's Bench Walk, Temple, London
EC4Y 7DS, Telephone: 0171 583 0404
E-mail: clerks@7kbw.law.co.uk
Call Date: June 1949, Lincoln's Inn
Qualifications: [MA (Oxon)]

HAMILTON MISS AMANDA JEAN

3 Temple Gardens
Lower Ground Floor, Temple, London
EC4Y 9AU, Telephone: 0171 353 3102/5/
9297 E-mail: clerks@3tg.co.uk
Call Date: Oct 1995, Lincoln's Inn
Qualifications: [BA (Hons)(Lond)]

HAMILTON ANDREW NINIAN ROBERTS

St Mary's Chambers
50 High Pavement, Lace Market,
Nottingham NG1 1HW,
Telephone: 0115 9503503
E-mail: clerks@smc.law.co.uk
Call Date: Nov 1970, Gray's Inn
Pupil Master, Assistant Recorder
Qualifications: [LLB (B'ham)]

HAMILTON MS CAROLYN PAULA

17 Bedford Row
London WC1R 4EB,
Telephone: 0171 831 7314
E-mail: iboard7314@aol.com
Call Date: 1996, Gray's Inn
Qualifications: [LLB (Bristol)]

HAMILTON DOUGLAS WILLIAM SETH

55 Temple Chambers
Temple Avenue, London EC4Y 0HP,
Telephone: 0171 353 7400
Call Date: Oct 1990, Inner Temple
Qualifications: [BA (Sussex), Dip, Law, Dip
Management, Studies]

HAMILTON EBEN WILLIAM QC (1981)

1 New Square
Ground Floor, Lincoln's Inn, London
WC2A 3SA, Telephone: 0171 405 0884/5/6/
7 E-mail: clerks@1newsquare.law.co.uk
Call Date: May 1962, Inner Temple
Qualifications: [MA (Cantab)]

HAMILTON MISS ELEANOR WARWICK QC (1999)

No. 6
6 Park Square, Leeds LS1 2LW,
Telephone: 0113 2459763
E-mail: chambers@no6.co.uk
Call Date: 1979, Inner Temple
Pupil Master, Assistant Recorder
Qualifications: [LLB (Hull)]

HAMILTON GAVIN

Chambers of John L Powell QC
Four New Square, Lincoln's Inn, London
WC2A 3RJ, Telephone: 0171 797 8000
E-mail: barristers@4newsquare.com
Call Date: July 1979, Gray's Inn
Pupil Master
Qualifications: [BA (Oxon)]

HAMILTON MISS GEORGINA CAROLINE

3 Temple Gardens
3rd Floor, Temple, London EC4Y 9AU,
Telephone: 0171 583 0010
Call Date: 1989, Middle Temple
Qualifications: [LLB]

HAMILTON GRAEME MONTAGU QC (1978)

Two Crown Office Row
Ground Floor, Temple, London
EC4Y 7HJ, Telephone: 020 7797 8100
E-mail: mail@2cor.co.uk, or to individual
barristers at: [barrister's
surname]@2cor.co.uk
Call Date: Feb 1959, Gray's Inn
Qualifications: [MA (Cantab)]

HAMILTON JAIME RICHARD

Chambers of John Hand QC
9 St John Street, Manchester M3 4DN,
Telephone: 0161 955 9000
E-mail: ninesjs@gconnect.com
Call Date: Oct 1993, Gray's Inn
Qualifications: [LLB (Wales)]

HAMILTON JOHN CONRAD

Chambers of Norman Palmer
2 Field Court, Gray's Inn, London
WC1R 5BB, Telephone: 0171 405 6114
E-mail: fieldct2@netcomuk.co.uk
Call Date: Nov 1988, Gray's Inn
Pupil Master
Qualifications: [BSc (City),Dip Law]

D

HAMILTON NIGEL JOHN MAWDESLEY QC (1981)

St John's Chambers
Small Street, Bristol BS1 1DW,
Telephone: 0117 9213456/298514
E-mail: @stjohnschambers.co.uk
Call Date: Nov 1965, Inner Temple
Qualifications: [MA (Cantab)]

HAMILTON PETER BERNARD

4 Pump Court
Temple, London EC4Y 7AN,
Telephone: 020 7842 5555
E-mail:chambers@4pumpcourt.law.co.uk
Call Date: Feb 1968, Inner Temple
Pupil Master
Qualifications: [BA (Rhodes), MA (Cantab)]

HAMILTON MISS PHILIPPA ANNE

Fountain Court
Temple, London EC4Y 9DH,
Telephone: 0171 583 3335
E-mail: chambers@fountaincourt.co.uk
Call Date: Oct 1996, Lincoln's Inn
Qualifications: [MA (Hons)(Oxon), Dip in
Law (City)]

HAMILTON-HAGUE MISS RACHAEL ELIZABETH

8 King Street Chambers
8 King Street, Manchester M2 6AQ,
Telephone: 0161 834 9560
E-mail: eightking@aol.com
Call Date: Oct 1993, Gray's Inn
Qualifications: [BA (Hons)(Keele)]

HAMILTON-SHIELD MISS ANNA-MARIA

Dr Johnson's Chambers
Two Dr Johnson's Buildings, Temple,
London EC4Y 7AY,
Telephone: 0171 353 4716
E-mail: clerks@2djb.freeserve.co.uk
Call Date: Nov 1989, Middle Temple
Qualifications: [LLb Hons]

HAMLIN PATRICK LINDOP

22 Old Buildings
Lincoln's Inn, London WC2A 3UJ,
Telephone: 0171 831 0222
Call Date: Nov 1970, Gray's Inn
Pupil Master, Recorder

HAMMERTON ALASTAIR ROLF

No. 1 Serjeants' Inn
5th Floor Fleet Street, Temple, London
EC4Y 1LH, Telephone: 0171 415 6666
E-mail:no1serjeantsinn@btinternet.com
Call Date: July 1983, Inner Temple
Pupil Master
Qualifications: [MA (Cantab), LLM (Virginia)]

HAMMERTON MISS VERONICA LESLEY

No. 1 Serjeants' Inn
5th Floor Fleet Street, Temple, London
EC4Y 1LH, Telephone: 0171 415 6666
E-mail:no1serjeantsinn@btinternet.com
Call Date: July 1977, Inner Temple
Assistant Recorder
Qualifications: [MA (Cantab)]

HAMMOND KOBINA TAHIR

Chancery Chambers
1st Floor Offices, 70/72 Chancery Lane,
London WC2A 1AB,
Telephone: 0171 405 6879/6870
Call Date: Nov 1991, Gray's Inn
Qualifications: [BA (Ghana)]

HAMMOND SEAN FRANCIS

18 Red Lion Court
(Off Fleet Street), London EC4A 3EB,
Telephone: 0171 520 6000
E-mail: chambers@18rlc.co.uk
Thornwood House
102 New London Road, Chelmsford,
Essex, CM2 0RG,
Telephone: 01245 280880
E-mail: chambers@18rlc.co.uk
Call Date: Oct 1991, Lincoln's Inn
Qualifications: [LLB (Hons)]

HAMPTON MISS ALISON WENDY

Ropewalk Chambers
24 The Ropewalk, Nottingham NG1 5EF,
Telephone: 0115 9472581
E-mail: administration@ropewalk co.uk
Call Date: July 1977, Gray's Inn
Pupil Master, Assistant Recorder
Qualifications: [LLB]

HANBURY WILLIAM EDMUND

Park Lane Chambers
19 Westgate, Leeds LS1 2RD,
Telephone: 0113 2285000
E-mail:clerks@parklanechambers.co.uk
Call Date: Nov 1985, Inner Temple
Pupil Master
Qualifications: [LLB (Manch)]

HANCOCK CHRISTOPHER PATRICK

20 Essex Street
London WC2R 3AL,
Telephone: 0171 583 9294
E-mail: clerks@20essexst.com
Call Date: July 1983, Middle Temple
Pupil Master
Qualifications: [MA (Cantab) , LLM
(Harvard)]

HANCOCK MS MARIA

Westgate Chambers
144 High Street, Lewes, East Sussex,
BN7 1XT, Telephone: 01273 480510
Westgate Chambers
16-17 Wellington Square, Hastings, East
Sussex, TN34 1PB,
Telephone: 01424 432105
Call Date: Oct 1995, Gray's Inn
Qualifications: [BA (Hons)]

HANCOX MISS SALLY ELIZABETH

2 Paper Buildings, Basement North
Temple, London EC4Y 7ET,
Telephone: 0171 936 2613
E-mail: post@2paper.co.uk
Call Date: Oct 1996, Lincoln's Inn
Qualifications: [BSc (Hons)(Bath)]

HANCOX STEPHEN HARRY

Newport Chambers
12 Clytha Park Road, Newport, Gwent,
NP9 47L, Telephone: 01633 267403/
255855

Francis Taylor Building
3rd Floor, Temple, London EC4Y 7BY,
Telephone: 0171 797 7250
Call Date: Nov 1986, Inner Temple
Pupil Master
Qualifications: [BD (Lond), Dip Law]

HAND ANTHONY RICHARD

College Chambers
19 Carlton Cresent, Southampton
SO15 2ET, Telephone: 01703 230338
Call Date: July 1989, Lincoln's Inn
Pupil Master
Qualifications: [LLB (Lond)]

HAND JOHN LESTER QC (1988)

Chambers of John Hand QC
9 St John Street, Manchester M3 4DN,
Telephone: 0161 955 9000
E-mail: ninesjs@gconnect.com
Old Square Chambers
1 Verulam Buildings, Gray's Inn, London
WC1R 5LQ, Telephone: 0171 269 0300
E-mail:clerks@oldsquarechambers.co.uk
Old Square Chambers
Hanover House, 47 Corn Street, Bristol
BS1 1HT, Telephone: 0117 9277111
E-mail: oldsqbri@globalnet.co.uk
Call Date: July 1972, Gray's Inn
Recorder
Qualifications: [LLB (Nott'm)]

HAND JONATHAN ELLIOTT SHEERMAN

35 Essex Street
Temple, London WC2R 3AR,
Telephone: 0171 353 6381
E-mail: derek_jenkins@link.org
Call Date: Nov 1990, Inner Temple
Qualifications: [BA (Oxon)]

HANDS DAVID RICHARD GRANVILLE QC (1988)

4 Breams Buildings
London EC4A 1AQ,
Telephone: 0171 353 5835/430 1221
E-mail:breams@4breamsbuildings.law.co.uk
Call Date: July 1965, Inner Temple

HANDS MISS JANE ELIZABETH

Wilberforce Chambers
7 Bishop Lane, Hull, East Yorkshire,
HU1 1PA, Telephone: 01482 323264
E-mail: clerks@hullbar.demon.co.uk
Call Date: July 1978, Inner Temple
Qualifications: [BA (Lond)]

HANDYSIDE RICHARD NEIL

Fountain Court
Temple, London EC4Y 9DH,
Telephone: 0171 583 3335
E-mail: chambers@fountaincourt.co.uk
Call Date: Oct 1993, Lincoln's Inn
Qualifications: [LLB (Hons)(Bris), BCL
(Oxon)]

HANHAM JAMES CHARLES FERGUSON

9 Stone Buildings
Lincoln's Inn, London WC2A 3NN,
Telephone: 0171 404 5055
E-mail: clerks@9stoneb.law.co.uk
Call Date: Oct 1996, Middle Temple
Qualifications: [BA (Hons)(Oxon), CPE
(City)]

HANKIN JONAS KEITH

Coleridge Chambers
Citadel, 190 Corporation Street,
Birmingham B4 6QD,
Telephone: 0121 233 8500
Call Date: Nov 1994, Middle Temple
Qualifications: [BA (Hons)]

HANLON MISS JACQUELINE PATRICIA

East Anglian Chambers
57 London Street, Norwich NR2 1HL,
Telephone: 01603 617351
E-mail: norwich@ealaw.co.uk
East Anglian Chambers
Gresham House, 5 Museum Street,
Ipswich, Suffolk, IP1 1HQ,
Telephone: 01473 214481
E-mail: ipswich@ealaw.co.uk
East Anglian Chambers
52 North Hill, Colchester, Essex, CO1 1PY,
Telephone: 01206 572756
E-mail: colchester@ealaw.co.uk
Call Date: Nov 1994, Gray's Inn
Qualifications: [LLB]

HANNAFORD MISS SARAH JANE

Keating Chambers
10 Essex Street, Outer Temple, London
WC2R 3AA, Telephone: 0171 544 2600
Call Date: July 1989, Middle Temple
Pupil Master
Qualifications: [BA [Oxon]]

HANNAM TIMOTHY JAMES

4 Fountain Court
Steelhouse Lane, Birmingham B4 6DR,
Telephone: 0121 236 3476
Call Date: Oct 1995, Gray's Inn
Qualifications: [BA (Hons)]

HANSEN WILLIAM JOSEPH

4 Paper Buildings
1st Floor, Temple, London EC4Y 7EX,
Telephone: 0171 583 0816/353 1131
E-mail: clerks@4paperbuildings.co.uk
Call Date: Nov 1992, Lincoln's Inn
Qualifications: [BSc (Econ)(Hons), M.Phil
(Cantab)]

HANSON TIMOTHY VINCENT RICHARD

St Philip's Chambers
Fountain Court, Steelhouse Lane,
Birmingham B4 6DR,
Telephone: 0121 246 7000
E-mail: clerks@st-philips.co.uk
Call Date: July 1989, Inner Temple
Qualifications: [LLB Hons]

HANTUSCH ROBERT ANTHONY

3 Stone Buildings
Lincoln's Inn, London WC2A 3XL,
Telephone: 0171 242 4937
E-mail: clerks@3sb.law.co.uk
Call Date: July 1982, Inner Temple
Pupil Master
Qualifications: [MA (Cantab)]

Fax: 0171 405 3896/01302 752 662;
Out of hours telephone: 01302 743 261;
DX: 317 London;
Other comms: Mobile 0860 302460;
E-mail RAHantusch@link.org;
RAHantusch@compuserve.com and
RHantusch@3sb.law.co.uk

Types of work: Banking, Bankruptcy, Chancery (general), Chancery land law,

Commercial, Commercial litigation, Company and commercial, Construction, Conveyancing, Equity, wills and trusts, Financial services, Insolvency, Landlord and tenant, Partnerships, Probate and administration, Professional negligence, Sale and carriage of goods

Awards and memberships: Chancery Bar Association

Reported Cases: *John Dee Group v WMH (21) Ltd (formerly Magnet Ltd)*, [1998] BCC 972; [1997] BCC 518, 1998. The application of non-insolvency set off in the context of administrative receivership.
Wake and Eastgate Motor Company v Renault UK Ltd, (1996) *The Times*, 1 August, 1996. Mandatory injunctive relief granted to enforce a collateral contract preventing the termination of a motor dealer's franchise.
Moon v Franklin, [1996] BPIL 196, 1990. Consideration of the form of relief to be granted on an application under s 423 of the Insolvency Act 1986.
Ebert v Venvil & Others, (1999) *The Times*, 28 April, 1999. Consideration of the extent of the inherent jurisdiction of the High Court to restrain vexatious legal proceedings.
Re Barrow Borough Transport, [1990] Ch 227, 1989. Whether a debenture can be registered out of time after the grantor is subject to an administration order.

HAPGOOD MARK BERNARD QC (1994)

Brick Court Chambers
7-8 Essex Street, London WC2R 3LD,
Telephone: 0171 379 3550
E-mail: [surname]@brickcourt.co.uk
Call Date: Feb 1979, Gray's Inn
Qualifications: [LLB (Nott'm)]

HAQUE GAZI MOSTA GAWSAL

197 Ellesmere Road
London NW10 1LG,
Telephone: 0181 208 1663
Call Date: July 1970, Inner Temple
Qualifications: [MA]

HARBAGE WILLIAM JOHN HIRONS

Chambers of Michael Pert QC
36 Bedford Row, London WC1R 4JH,
Telephone: 0171 421 8000
E-mail: 36bedfordrow@link.org
Chambers of Michael Pert QC
24 Albion Place, Northampton NN1 1UD,
Telephone: 01604 602333
Chambers of Michael Pert QC
104 New Walk, Leicester LE1 7EA,
Telephone: 0116 249 2020
Call Date: July 1983, Middle Temple
Pupil Master
Qualifications: [MA (Cantab)]

HARBOTTLE GWILYM THOMAS

5 New Square
Ground Floor, Lincoln's Inn, London
WC2A 3RJ, Telephone: 020 7404 0404
E-mail:chambers@fivenewsquare.demon.co.uk
Call Date: Nov 1987, Lincoln's Inn
Pupil Master
Qualifications: [BA (Oxon), Dip Law, (City)]

HARDIMAN ADRIAN PATRICK

Doughty Street Chambers
11 Doughty Street, London WC1N 2PG,
Telephone: 0171 404 1313
E-mail:enquiries@doughtystreet.co.uk
Call Date: May 1988, Middle Temple
Qualifications: [BA(Hons) Dublin]

HARDING MISS CHERRY JACINTA

Gray's Inn Chambers
5th Floor, Gray's Inn, London WC1R 5JA,
Telephone: 0171 404 1111
Call Date: Nov 1978, Gray's Inn
Pupil Master
Qualifications: [LLB (Lond)]

HARDING MRS CHRISTINE LAURETTA AYODELE

Leone Chambers
72 Evelyn Avenue, Kingsbury, London
NW9 0JH, Telephone: 0181 200 4020
E-mail: festus4@leonechambers.co.uk
Call Date: Feb 1966, Lincoln's Inn

D

HARDING CHRISTOPHER JAMES

Thomas More Chambers
52 Carey Street, Lincoln's Inn, London
WC2A 2JB, Telephone: 0171 404 7000
E-mail: clerks@thomasmore.law.co.uk
Call Date: Nov 1992, Inner Temple
Qualifications: [LLB (Lond)]

HARDING MISS FIONA SUZANNE

Claremont Chambers
26 Waterloo Road, Wolverhampton
WV1 4BL, Telephone: 01902 426222
Call Date: Feb 1993, Gray's Inn
Qualifications: [BA]

HARDING DR GLADYS MODWYN CICELY

Leone Chambers
72 Evelyn Avenue, Kingsbury, London
NW9 OJH, Telephone: 0181 200 4020
E-mail: festus4@leonechambers.co.uk
Call Date: 1979, Gray's Inn
Qualifications: [MA, M.Ed (Dunelm), PhD
(Illinois)]

HARDING MISS PATRICIA JANE

10 King's Bench Walk
Ground Floor, Temple, London
EC4Y 7EB, Telephone: 0171 353 7742
E-mail: 10kbw@lineone.net
Call Date: Nov 1994, Lincoln's Inn
Qualifications: [BSc (Hons)(Bris)]

HARDING RICHARD ANTHONY

Keating Chambers
10 Essex Street, Outer Temple, London
WC2R 3AA, Telephone: 0171 544 2600
Call Date: Oct 1992, Middle Temple
Qualifications: [MA (Hons), Common
Profesional, Examination]

HARDWICK MATTHEW RICHARD

Enterprise Chambers
9 Old Square, Lincoln's Inn, London
WC2A 3SR, Telephone: 0171 405 9471
E-mail: enterprise.london@dial.pipex.com
Enterprise Chambers
38 Park Square, Leeds LS1 2PA,
Telephone: 0113 246 0391
E-mail: enterprise.leeds@dial.pipex.com

Enterprise Chambers
65 Quayside, Newcastle upon Tyne
NE1 3DS, Telephone: 0191 222 3344
E-mail: enterprise.newcastle@dial.pipex.com
Call Date: Oct 1994, Gray's Inn
Qualifications: [MA, Licence Speciale, En
Droit Europeen]

HARDY MRS AMANDA JANE

24 Old Buildings
First Floor, Lincoln's Inn, London
WC2A 3UP, Telephone: 020 7242 2744
E-mail: taxchambers@compuserve.com
Call Date: Nov 1993, Middle Temple
Qualifications: [LLB (Hons), LLM (Lond),
AKC]

HARDY DAVID ROBERT

9 Park Place
Cardiff CF1 3DP,
Telephone: 01222 382731
Call Date: Oct 1993, Lincoln's Inn
Qualifications: [LLB (Hons)(Bris), BCL
(Oxon)]

HARDY JOHN SYDNEY

3 Raymond Buildings
Gray's Inn, London WC1R 5BH,
Telephone: 020 7831 3833
E-mail: chambers@threeraymond.demon.co.u
k
Call Date: Nov 1988, Gray's Inn
Pupil Master
Qualifications: [BA (Hons) (Oxon), Dip Law]

HARDY PAUL CHRISTIAN KINNEAR

18 Red Lion Court
(Off Fleet Street), London EC4A 3EB,
Telephone: 0171 520 6000
E-mail: chambers@18rlc.co.uk
Thornwood House
102 New London Road, Chelmsford,
Essex, CM2 0RG,
Telephone: 01245 280880
E-mail: chambers@18rlc.co.uk
Call Date: Nov 1992, Inner Temple
Qualifications: [MA (St.Andrews), Dip in
Law]

HARE CHRISTOPHER VINCENT MARK

3 Verulam Buildings
London WC1R 5NT,
Telephone: 0171 831 8441
E-mail: clerks@3verulam.co.uk
Call Date: 1998, Lincoln's Inn
Qualifications: [BA (Hons)(Cantab), LLM
(Harvard), BCL (Oxon)]

HARE MISS ROSINA SELINA ALICE QC (1976)

10 King's Bench Walk
Ground Floor, Temple, London
EC4Y 7EB, Telephone: 0171 353 7742
E-mail: 10kbw@lineone.net
*Call Date: Feb 1956, Middle Temple
Recorder*

HARE WILLIAM RICHARD

Westgate Chambers
67a Westgate Road, Newcastle upon Tyne
NE1 1SG, Telephone: 0191 261 4407/
2329785
E-mail:pracman@westgatechambers.law.co.u
k
Call Date: Nov 1994, Inner Temple
Qualifications: [BA (Newc)]

HARFORD-BELL MISS NERIDA

Two Garden Court
1st Floor, Middle Temple, London
EC4Y 9BL, Telephone: 0171 353 1633
E-mail:barristers@2gardenct.law.co.uk
*Call Date: Nov 1984, Middle Temple
Pupil Master*
Qualifications: [MA (Sussex), BA (Hons)]

HARGAN JAMES JOHN

30 Park Square
Leeds LS1 2PF, Telephone: 0113 2436388
E-mail: clerks@30parksquare.co.uk
Call Date: Feb 1990, Middle Temple
Qualifications: [LLB (Hons)]

HARGAN JOHN CARL

1 Gray's Inn Square
Ground Floor, London WC1R 5AA,
Telephone: 0171 405 8946/7/8
Call Date: Nov 1995, Lincoln's Inn
Qualifications: [LLB (Hons)]

HARGAN MARTIN CAMPBELL MCLAREN

Paradise Chambers
26 Paradise Square, Sheffield S1 2DE,
Telephone: 0114 2738951
E-mail: timbooth@paradise-sq.co.uk
Call Date: Nov 1964, Gray's Inn
Qualifications: [LLB (Lond)]

HARGRAVE HENRY BRIAN

Westgate Chambers
4 Copse Close, Northwood, Middlesex,
HA6 2XG, Telephone: 01923 823671
Call Date: May 1988, Inner Temple
Qualifications: [LLB (Lond)]

HARGREAVES BENJAMIN THOMAS

Goldsmith Chambers
Ground Floor, Goldsmith Building,
Temple, London EC4Y 7BL,
Telephone: 0171 353 6802/3/4/5
E-mail:clerks@goldsmithchambers.law.co.uk
Call Date: Nov 1989, Lincoln's Inn
Qualifications: [LLB (Hons) (Wales)]

HARGREAVES MISS KATIE JANE

High Pavement Chambers
1 High Pavement, Nottingham NG1 1HF,
Telephone: 0115 9418218
Call Date: Nov 1991, Gray's Inn
Qualifications: [LLB (L'pool)]

HARGREAVES MISS SARA JANE

12 New Square
Lincoln's Inn, London WC2A 3SW,
Telephone: 0171 419 1212
E-mail: chambers@12newsquare.co.uk
Sovereign Chambers
25 Park Square, Leeds LS1 2PW,
Telephone: 0113 2451841/2/3
E-mail:sovereignchambers@btinternet.com
*Call Date: July 1979, Middle Temple
Pupil Master*
Qualifications: [LLB (Lond)]

HARGREAVES SIMON JOHN ROBERT

Keating Chambers
10 Essex Street, Outer Temple, London
WC2R 3AA, Telephone: 0171 544 2600
Call Date: Oct 1991, Inner Temple
Qualifications: [BA (Oxon)]

HARGROVE JEREMY JOHN LOVEDAY

Trinity Chambers
9-12 Trinity Chare, Quayside, Newcastle
upon Tyne NE1 3DF,
Telephone: 0191 232 1927
E-mail: info@trinitychambers.co.uk
Call Date: Nov 1970, Inner Temple
Pupil Master
Qualifications: [LLB]

HARING SIMON NICHOLAS

30 Park Square
Leeds LS1 2PF, Telephone: 0113 2436388
E-mail: clerks@30parksquare.co.uk
Call Date: July 1982, Lincoln's Inn
Qualifications: [LLB (Leeds)]

HARINGTON MISS AMANDA

Twenty-Four Old Buildings
Ground Floor, Lincoln's Inn, London
WC2A 3UP, Telephone: 0171 404 0946
E-mail:clerks@24oldbuildings.law.co.uk
Call Date: July 1989, Inner Temple
Pupil Master
Qualifications: [BA (Cantab)]

HARINGTON MICHAEL KENNETH

6 Pump Court
1st Floor, Temple, London EC4Y 7AR,
Telephone: 0171 797 8400
E-mail: clerks@6pumpcourt.co.uk
6-8 Mill Street
Maidstone, Kent, ME15 6XH,
Telephone: 01622 688094
E-mail: annexe@6pumpcourt.co.uk
Call Date: July 1974, Inner Temple
Pupil Master, Recorder
Qualifications: [MA (Oxon)]

HARKUS GEORGE EVERARD

Goldsmith Chambers
Ground Floor, Goldsmith Building,
Temple, London EC4Y 7BL,
Telephone: 0171 353 6802/3/4/5
E-mail:clerks@goldsmithchambers.law.co.uk
Call Date: Nov 1975, Inner Temple
Pupil Master
Qualifications: [LLB (Leeds), DPA, MA]

HARLE ALAN

Chambers of Alan Harle
19 Summerhouse Farm, East Rainton,
Houghton-le-Spring, Tyne & Wear,
DH5 9QQ, Telephone: 0191 5844604
Call Date: July 1982, Middle Temple
Pupil Master
Qualifications: [BA Hons]

HARMAN MISS SARAH JANE

4 Stone Buildings
Ground Floor, Lincoln's Inn, London
WC2A 3XT, Telephone: 0171 242 5524
E-mail:clerks@4stonebuildings.law.co.uk
Call Date: Nov 1987, Lincoln's Inn
Qualifications: [BA (Oxon)]

HARMER MISS CHRISTINE

Broad Chare
33 Broad Chare, Newcastle upon Tyne
NE1 3DQ, Telephone: 0191 232 0541
E-mail:clerks@broadcharechambers.law.co.uk
Call Date: July 1973, Middle Temple
Pupil Master
Qualifications: [BA]

HAROUNOFF DAVID

4 King's Bench Walk
Ground/First Floor/Basement, Temple,
London EC4Y 7DL,
Telephone: 0171 822 8822
E-mail: 4kbw@barristersatlaw.com
Call Date: Nov 1984, Middle Temple
Pupil Master
Qualifications: [BA (Sussex)]

HARPER ANDREW GRAHAM

De Montfort Chambers
95 Princess Road East, Leicester LE1 7DQ,
Telephone: 0116 254 8686
E-mail: dmcbar@aol.com
Call Date: Feb 1989, Middle Temple
Qualifications: [LLB (Leic)]

HARPER JAMES NORMAN

Broad Chare
33 Broad Chare, Newcastle upon Tyne
NE1 3DQ, Telephone: 0191 232 0541
E-mail:clerks@broadcharechambers.law.co.uk
Call Date: July 1957, Gray's Inn
Qualifications: [BA (Oxon)]

HARPER JOSEPH CHARLES QC (1992)

4 Breams Buildings
London EC4A 1AQ,
Telephone: 0171 353 5835/430 1221
E-mail:breams@4breamsbuildings.law.co.uk
Call Date: July 1970, Gray's Inn
Qualifications: [BA, LLM (Lond)]

HARPER MARK ELIOT GEORGE

40 King Street
Manchester M2 6BA,
Telephone: 0161 832 9082
E-mail: clerks@40kingstreet.co.uk
The Chambers of Philip Raynor QC
5 Park Place, Leeds LS1 2RU,
Telephone: 0113 242 1123
Call Date: Oct 1993, Lincoln's Inn
Qualifications: [BA (Hons)]

HARPER ROGER ALAN

Queens Square Chambers
56 Queens Square, Bristol BS1 4PR,
Telephone: 0117 921 1966
Call Date: May 1994, Lincoln's Inn
Qualifications: [LLB (Hons, B'ham)]

HARPER MISS VICTORIA JANE TRYPHOSA

3 Temple Gardens
3rd Floor, Temple, London EC4Y 9AU,
Telephone: 0171 353 0832
Call Date: Oct 1996, Middle Temple
Qualifications: [BA (Hons)(Cantab), CPE (City)]

HARPWOOD MRS VIVIENNE MARGARET

30 Park Place
Cardiff CF1 3BA,
Telephone: 01222 398421
E-mail: 100757.1456@compuserve.com
Call Date: July 1969, Gray's Inn
Qualifications: [LLB]

HARRAP GILES THRESHER

Pump Court Chambers
31 Southgate Street, Winchester
SO23 9EE, Telephone: 01962 868161
E-mail: clerks@3pumpcourt.com

Pump Court Chambers
Upper Ground Floor, 3 Pump Court,
Temple, London EC4Y 7AJ,
Telephone: 0171 353 0711
E-mail: clerks@3pumpcourt.com
Pump Court Chambers
5 Temple Chambers, Temple Street,
Swindon SN1 1SQ,
Telephone: 01793 539899
E-mail: clerks@3pumpcourt.com
Call Date: Nov 1971, Inner Temple
Pupil Master, Recorder
Qualifications: [LLB (Lond)]

Fax: 01962 867645;
Out of hours telephone: 01420 22359

Types of work: Family provision, Medical negligence, Personal injury, Professional negligence

Circuit: Western

Awards and memberships: Professional Negligence Bar Association; Family Law Bar Association; Personal Injury Bar Association

Publications: 'Update: Inheritance (Provision for Family and Dependants) Act 1975', *Solicitors Journal*, 23 January 1993; 'Provision for Co-habitants on Death', *Family Law*, June 1997

Reported Cases: *Re Coventry, deceased*, [1980] Ch 461, 1979. Application for provision on death by adult son in work.
Re Callaghan, deceased, [1985] Fam 1, 1984. Application for provision on death by man treated as a child of the deceased.
Re Dawkins, deceased, [1986] 2 FLR 360, 1986. Application to set aside disposition intended to defeat family provision claim.
Jessop v Jessop, [1992] 1 FLR 591, 1991. Exercise of court's power in family provision cases to treat deceased's share of jointly-held property as part of estate.
Peach Grey & Co v Sommers, [1995] 2 All ER 513, 1995. Power of Divisional Court to commit for contempt following interference with witnesses before industrial tribunal.

HARRAP ROBERT PHILIP

5 Paper Buildings
Ground Floor, Temple, London
EC4Y 7HB, Telephone: 0171 583 9275/583 4555 E-mail: 5paper@link.org
Call Date: Oct 1997, Inner Temple
Qualifications: [BA (London), CPE]

D

HARRIES MARK ROBERT

6 Gray's Inn Square
Ground Floor, Gray's Inn, London
WC1R 5AZ, Telephone: 0171 242 1052
E-mail: 6graysinn@clara.co.uk
Call Date: Oct 1995, Lincoln's Inn
Qualifications: [LLB (Hons)(Lond)]

HARRIES NICHOLAS JOHN SAMUEL

The Chambers of Leolin Price CBE, QC
10 Old Square, Lincoln's Inn, London
WC2A 3SU, Telephone: 0171 405 0758
Call Date: Nov 1995, Lincoln's Inn
Qualifications: [BA (Hons)]

HARRIES RAYMOND ELWYN

Bracton Chambers
95a Chancery Lane, London WC2A 1DT,
Telephone: 0171 242 4248
Call Date: July 1988, Lincoln's Inn
Qualifications: [BA (Hons) (Cardiff), Dip Law
(City), FCA, ATII, ACIArb, ATII, ACIArb]

HARRILL MISS JAYNE ANNE

8 King's Bench Walk
2nd Floor, Temple, London EC4Y 7DU,
Telephone: 0171 797 8888
8 King's Bench Walk North
1 Park Square East, Leeds LS1 2NE,
Telephone: 0113 2439797
Call Date: Oct 1990, Middle Temple
Qualifications: [BA]

HARRINGTON PATRICK JOHN QC (1993)

Farrar's Building
Temple, London EC4Y 7BD,
Telephone: 0171 583 9241
E-mail:chambers@farrarsbuilding.co.uk
30 Park Place
Cardiff CF1 3BA,
Telephone: 01222 398421
E-mail: 100757.1456@compuserve.com
Call Date: July 1973, Gray's Inn
Recorder
Qualifications: [LLB (Lond)]

HARRINGTON TIMOTHY MARK

Coleridge Chambers
Citadel, 190 Corporation Street,
Birmingham B4 6QD,
Telephone: 0121 233 8500
Call Date: Mar 1997, Gray's Inn
Qualifications: [LLB (Glamorgan)]

HARRINGTON MISS TINA AMANDA

Trinity Chambers
140 New London Road, Chelmsford,
Essex, CM2 0AW,
Telephone: 01245 605040
E-mail:clerks@trinitychambers.law.co.uk
9 Gough Square
London EC4A 3DE,
Telephone: 020 7832 0500
E-mail: clerks@9goughsq.co.uk
Call Date: 1985, Middle Temple
Pupil Master
Qualifications: [BA]

HARRIS MISS ANNMARIE

3 Dr Johnson's Buildings
Ground Floor, Temple, London
EC4Y 7BA, Telephone: 0171 353 4854
E-mail: clerks@3djb.co.uk
Call Date: July 1975, Middle Temple
Qualifications: [BA]

HARRIS MS BETHAN ELEANOR

Two Garden Court
1st Floor, Middle Temple, London
EC4Y 9BL, Telephone: 0171 353 1633
E-mail:barristers@2gardenct.law.co.uk
Call Date: May 1990, Middle Temple
Qualifications: [B.A. (Oxon)]

HARRIS BRIAN THOMAS QC (1982)

4-5 Gray's Inn Square
Ground Floor, Gray's Inn, London
WC1R 5JP, Telephone: 0171 404 5252
E-mail:chambers@4-5graysinnsquare.co.uk
Call Date: Nov 1960, Gray's Inn
Qualifications: [LLB (Lond)]

HARRIS DAVID ANDREW WALLACE

Iscoed Chambers
86 St Helen's Road, Swansea, West
Glamorgan, SA1 4BQ,
Telephone: 01792 652988/9/330
Call Date: Oct 1990, Gray's Inn
Qualifications: [BA (Sussex)]

HARRIS REV DAVID JAMES

32 Park Place
Cardiff CF1 3BA,
Telephone: 01222 397364
Call Date: Nov 1979, Gray's Inn
Pupil Master
Qualifications: [BA (Wales)]

HARRIS DAVID MICHAEL QC (1989)

India Buildings Chambers
Water Street, Liverpool L2 0XG,
Telephone: 0151 243 6000
E-mail: clerks@chambers.u-net.com
3 Paper Buildings
Temple, London EC4Y 7EU,
Telephone: 020 7583 8055
E-mail: London@3paper.com
3 Paper Buildings (Winchester)
4 St Peter Street, Winchester SO23 8BW,
Telephone: 01962 868884
E-mail: winchester@3paper.com
3 Paper Buildings (Oxford)
1 Alfred Street, High Street, Oxford
OX1 4EH, Telephone: 01865 793736
E-mail: oxford@3paper.com
3 Paper Buildings (Bournemouth)
20 Lorne Park Road, Bournemouth,
Dorset, BH1 1JN,
Telephone: 01202 292102
E-mail: Bournemouth@3paper.com
Call Date: Nov 1969, Middle Temple
Recorder
Qualifications: [MA (Oxon), PhD , (Cantab)]

HARRIS DAVID RAYMOND

Prince Henry's Chambers
2 Tamar House, 12 Tavistock Place,
London WC1H 9RA,
Telephone: 0171 713 0376
Call Date: Nov 1973, Lincoln's Inn
Qualifications: [LLM (Lond)]

HARRIS DAVID ROBERT

St Albans Chambers
Dolphin Lodge, Dolphin Yard, Holywell
Hill, St Albans, Herts, AL1 1EX,
Telephone: 01727 843383
Call Date: Oct 1997, Lincoln's Inn
Qualifications: [LLB (Hons)(Luton)]

HARRIS DONALD RENSHAW

Littleton Chambers
3 King's Bench Walk North, Temple,
London EC4Y 7HR,
Telephone: 0171 797 8600
E-mail:clerks@littletonchambers.co.uk
Call Date: June 1958, Inner Temple
Qualifications: [BCL, MA (Oxon)]

HARRIS MISS ELIZABETH MARY

Angel Chambers
94 Walter Road, Swansea, West
Glamorgan, SA1 5QA,
Telephone: 01792 464623/464648
E-mail: lynne@angelchambers.co.uk
Call Date: Nov 1992, Inner Temple
Qualifications: [LLB (Hull)]

HARRIS FRANCIS RICHARD

**11 Bolt Court (also at 7 Stone Buildings
– 1st Floor)**
London EC4A 3DQ,
Telephone: 0171 353 2300
E-mail: boltct11@aol.com
**7 Stone Buildings (also at 11 Bolt
Court)**
1st Floor, Lincoln's Inn, London
WC2A 3SZ, Telephone: 0171 242 0961
E-mail:larthur@7stonebuildings.law.co.uk
Redhill Chambers
Seloduct House, 30 Station Road, Redhill,
Surrey, RH1 1NF,
Telephone: 01737 780781
Call Date: 1997, Inner Temple
Qualifications: [BA, LLB (Victoria, Australia)]

HARRIS GLENN PETER

Trafalgar Chambers
53 Fleet Street, London EC4Y 1BE,
Telephone: 0171 583 5858
E-mail:trafalgarchambers@easynet.co.uk
Call Date: Oct 1994, Lincoln's Inn
Qualifications: [LLB (Hons)(Hull)]

HARRIS IAN ROBERT

25-27 Castle Street
1st Floor, Liverpool L2 4TA,
Telephone: 0151 227 5661/051 236 5072
Call Date: Nov 1990, Inner Temple

HARRIS JAMES

1 Harcourt Buildings
2nd Floor, Temple, London EC4Y 9DA,
Telephone: 0171 353 9421/0375
E-mail:clerks@1harcourtbuildings.law.co.uk
Call Date: Nov 1975, Gray's Inn
Pupil Master
Qualifications: [MA (Oxon)]

HARRIS MISS JOANNE OLGA CHARLOTTE

Two Garden Court
1st Floor, Middle Temple, London
EC4Y 9BL, Telephone: 0171 353 1633
E-mail:barristers@2gardenct.law.co.uk
Call Date: Oct 1991, Gray's Inn
Pupil Master
Qualifications: [BA (L'pool), MSc (London),
Diploma in Law]

HARRIS JOHN HENRY EDGAR

Forest House Chambers
15 Granville Road, Walthamstow, London
E17 9BS, Telephone: 0181 925 2240
Call Date: Oct 1993, Lincoln's Inn
Qualifications: [MSc , LLB (Hons)(Sheff)]

HARRIS MISS LAURA

Queen Elizabeth Building
Ground Floor, Temple, London
EC4Y 9BS,
Telephone: 0171 353 7181 (12 Lines)
Call Date: Nov 1977, Middle Temple
Pupil Master
Qualifications: [BA (Oxon)]

HARRIS MARK GEOFFREY CHARLES

3 Raymond Buildings
Gray's Inn, London WC1R 5BH,
Telephone: 020 7831 3833
E-mail:chambers@threeraymond.demon.co.uk
Call Date: July 1980, Gray's Inn
Qualifications: [BA (Oxon)]

HARRIS MELVYN

7 New Square
Lincoln's Inn, London WC2A 3QS,
Telephone: 0171 430 1660
Call Date: Oct 1997, Lincoln's Inn
Qualifications: [LLB (Hons)(Middx)]

HARRIS MICHAEL PETER

10 King's Bench Walk
Ground Floor, Temple, London
EC4Y 7EB, Telephone: 0171 353 7742
E-mail: 10kbw@lineone.net
Call Date: Oct 1993, Gray's Inn
Qualifications: [BA (Hons)(Cantab)]

HARRIS MISS NICOLA JANE

33 Park Place
Cardiff CF1 3BA,
Telephone: 02920 233313
Call Date: Oct 1992, Middle Temple
Qualifications: [MA (Hons, Cantab), MA
(Toronto)]

HARRIS PAUL BEST

Monckton Chambers
4 Raymond Buildings, Gray's Inn, London
WC1R 5BP, Telephone: 0171 405 7211
E-mail: chambers@monckton.co.uk
Call Date: Oct 1994, Gray's Inn
Qualifications: [LLB, LLM]

HARRIS MS REBECCA ELIZABETH

Hollis Whiteman Chambers
3rd Floor, Queen Elizabeth Bldg, Temple,
London EC4Y 9BS,
Telephone: 020 7583 5766
E-mail:barristers@holliswhiteman.co.uk
Call Date: 1997, Inner Temple
Qualifications: [LLB (London)]

HARRIS RODGER PETER

Temple Gardens Tax Chambers
1st Floor, 3 Temple Gardens, Temple,
London EC4Y 9AU,
Telephone: 0171 353 7884/5 8982/3
E-mail: clerks@taxcounsel.co.uk.
Call Date: July 1980, Middle Temple
Qualifications: [LLB (Hons)(Manc), Dip ICEI
(Amsterdam)]

HARRIS ROGER CHARLES JAMES

2 Temple Gardens
Temple, London EC4Y 9AY,
Telephone: 0171 583 6041
E-mail: clerks@2templegardens.co.uk
Call Date: Oct 1996, Inner Temple
Qualifications: [BA (Exeter)]

HARRIS RUSSELL JAMES

1 Serjeants' Inn
4th Floor, Temple, London EC4Y 1NH,
Telephone: 0171 583 1355
E-mail: clerks@serjeants-inn.co.uk
33 Park Place
Cardiff CF1 3BA,
Telephone: 02920 233313
Call Date: Nov 1986, Gray's Inn
Pupil Master
Qualifications: [MA (Cantab)]

HARRIS WILBERT ARTHURLYN

Rowchester Chambers
4 Rowchester Court, Whittall Street,
Birmingham B4 6DH,
Telephone: 0121 233 2327/2361951
Call Date: Nov 1973, Inner Temple
Pupil Master
Qualifications: [BA, FCIArb]

HARRIS-JENKINS PHILIP LEIGH

Angel Chambers
94 Walter Road, Swansea, West
Glamorgan, SA1 5QA,
Telephone: 01792 464623/464648
E-mail: lynne@angelchambers.co.uk
Call Date: Nov 1990, Gray's Inn
Qualifications: [LLB (Hons)(Wales)]

HARRISON MS AVERIL

Chambers of Averil Harrison
7 King George Street, Greenwich, London
SE10 8QJ, Telephone: 0181 692 4949
Call Date: Oct 1990, Gray's Inn
Pupil Master
Qualifications: [BA (Lond)]

HARRISON CHRISTOPHER JOHN

4 Stone Buildings
Ground Floor, Lincoln's Inn, London
WC2A 3XT, Telephone: 0171 242 5524
E-mail:clerks@4stonebuildings.law.co.uk
Call Date: Nov 1988, Gray's Inn
Pupil Master
Qualifications: [MA (Cantab)]

HARRISON GORDON WILLIAM

3 Temple Gardens
3rd Floor, Temple, London EC4Y 9AU,
Telephone: 0171 353 0832
Call Date: Oct 1996, Inner Temple
Qualifications: [LLB (Reading)]

HARRISON DR GRAEME

College Chambers
19 Carlton Cresent, Southampton
SO15 2ET, Telephone: 01703 230338
Call Date: Mar 1997, Inner Temple
Qualifications: [MA (Oxon), DPhil (Oxon)]

HARRISON JOHN FOSTER

St Paul's House
5th Floor, St Paul's House, 23 Park Square
South, Leeds LS1 2ND,
Telephone: 0113 2455866
E-mail: catherinegrimshaw@stpauls-
chambers.demon.co.uk
Call Date: Oct 1994, Lincoln's Inn
Qualifications: [BA (Hons)(Notts), LLB
(Hons)(Leeds), M.Soc.Sc.(B'ham)]

HARRISON (JOHN) KEITH

24a St John Street
Manchester M3 4DF,
Telephone: 0161 833 9628
Call Date: Nov 1983, Lincoln's Inn
Qualifications: [LLB (Hons) (Newc)]

HARRISON MISS LEONA MELANIE

India Buildings Chambers
Water Street, Liverpool L2 0XG,
Telephone: 0151 243 6000
E-mail: clerks@chambers.u-net.com
Call Date: Oct 1993, Middle Temple
Qualifications: [LLB (Hons)(Manc)]

D

HARRISON MICHAEL LEE

New Court
Temple, London EC4Y 9BE,
Telephone: 0171 583 5123/0510
Call Date: Nov 1979, Inner Temple
Pupil Master
Qualifications: [LLB (Hons) (Sheff)]

HARRISON MICHAEL THOMAS

199 Strand
London WC2R 1DR,
Telephone: 0171 379 9779
E-mail: chambers@199strand.co.uk
Call Date: July 1986, Lincoln's Inn
Pupil Master
Qualifications: [MA (Oxon), Dip Law (City)]

HARRISON NICHOLAS FRANCIS

Serle Court Chambers
6 New Square, Lincoln's Inn, London
WC2A 3QS, Telephone: 0171 242 6105
E-mail: clerks@serlecourt.co.uk
Call Date: July 1988, Lincoln's Inn
Pupil Master
Qualifications: [BA (Hons) (Oxon)]

HARRISON PETER JOHN

24a St John Street
Manchester M3 4DF,
Telephone: 0161 833 9628
Call Date: July 1983, Middle Temple
Pupil Master
Qualifications: [LLB Hons (L'pool)]

HARRISON PETER JOHN

6 Pump Court
1st Floor, Temple, London EC4Y 7AR,
Telephone: 0171 797 8400
E-mail: clerks@6pumpcourt.co.uk
6-8 Mill Street
Maidstone, Kent, ME15 6XH,
Telephone: 01622 688094
E-mail: annexe@6pumpcourt.co.uk
Call Date: July 1987, Inner Temple
Pupil Master
Qualifications: [BA (Hons) (Dunelm)]

HARRISON MISS PHILOMENA MARY

199 Strand
London WC2R 1DR,
Telephone: 0171 379 9779
E-mail: chambers@199strand.co.uk
Call Date: Nov 1985, Middle Temple
Pupil Master
Qualifications: [BA (Lond), Dip Law (City)]

HARRISON PIERS WILLIAM BENEDICT

33 Bedford Row
London WC1R 4JH,
Telephone: 0171 242 6476
E-mail:clerks@bedfordrow33.demon.co.uk
Call Date: 1997, Lincoln's Inn
Qualifications: [BA (Hons) (Manch)]

HARRISON MISS RACHAEL

Paradise Chambers
26 Paradise Square, Sheffield S1 2DE,
Telephone: 0114 2738951
E-mail: timbooth@paradise-sq.co.uk
Call Date: Nov 1993, Inner Temple
Qualifications: [LLB (Hons)]

HARRISON MRS REZIYA

11 Old Square
Ground Floor, Lincoln's Inn, London
WC2A 3TS, Telephone: 020 7430 0341
E-mail: clerks@11oldsquare.co.uk
Call Date: July 1975, Lincoln's Inn
Qualifications: [MA (Oxon), FCI Arb]

HARRISON RICHARD ANDREW

Devereux Chambers
Devereux Court, London WC2R 3JJ,
Telephone: 0171 353 7534
E-mail: mailbox@devchambers.co.uk
Call Date: Nov 1991, Lincoln's Inn
Qualifications: [BA (Hons)(Cantab)]

HARRISON RICHARD TRISTAN

One King's Bench Walk
1st Floor, Temple, London EC4Y 7DB,
Telephone: 0171 936 1500
E-mail: ddear@1kbw.co.uk
Call Date: Nov 1993, Inner Temple
Qualifications: [MA (Hons)(Cantab), Dip law
(City)]

HARRISON ROBERT JOHN MACKINTOSH

30 Park Place
Cardiff CF1 3BA,
Telephone: 01222 398421
E-mail: 100757.1456@compuserve.com
Call Date: Feb 1988, Lincoln's Inn
Pupil Master
Qualifications: [LLB (Cardiff)]

HARRISON ROBERT MICHAEL QC (1987)

Park Court Chambers
16 Park Place, Leeds LS1 2SJ,
Telephone: 0113 2433277
Call Date: Nov 1969, Gray's Inn
Recorder
Qualifications: [LLB]

HARRISON ROBIN JAMES

Holborn Chambers
6 Gate Street, Lincoln's Inn Fields, London
WC2A 3HP, Telephone: 0171 242 6060
Call Date: Oct 1995, Gray's Inn
Qualifications: [B.Sc]

HARRISON ROGER DONALD

1 Paper Buildings
1st Floor, Temple, London EC4Y 7EP,
Telephone: 0171 353 3728/4953
Call Date: Feb 1970, Gray's Inn
Pupil Master, Assistant Recorder
Qualifications: [LLB]

HARRISON MISS SALLY

28 St John Street
Manchester M3 4DJ,
Telephone: 0161 834 8418
E-mail: clerk@28stjohnst.co.uk
Call Date: Oct 1992, Gray's Inn
Qualifications: [B.Sc (Reading), Dip Law
(City)]

HARRISON MS SARAH LOUISE

Cobden House Chambers
19 Quay Street, Manchester M3 3HN,
Telephone: 0161 833 6000
E-mail: clerks@cobden.co.uk
Call Date: Nov 1989, Lincoln's Inn
Qualifications: [LLB (Leic)]

HARRISON MS STEPHANIE JAYNE

Two Garden Court
1st Floor, Middle Temple, London
EC4Y 9BL, Telephone: 0171 353 1633
E-mail:barristers@2gardenct.law.co.uk
Call Date: Nov 1991, Middle Temple
Qualifications: [BSc Hons (Bris), MSc
(Lond), Dip Law]

HARRISON MISS SUSAN KATHRYN

18 St John Street
Manchester M3 4EA,
Telephone: 0161 278 1800
E-mail: 18stjohn@lineone.net
Call Date: Oct 1993, Middle Temple
Qualifications: [BA (Hons)(Bris)]

HARRISON-HALL GILES ARTHUR

1 Fountain Court
Steelhouse Lane, Birmingham B4 6DR,
Telephone: 0121 236 5721
Call Date: July 1977, Gray's Inn
Pupil Master
Qualifications: [MA (Oxon)]

HARROD HENRY MARK

5 Stone Buildings
Lincoln's Inn, London WC2A 3XT,
Telephone: 0171 242 6201
E-mail:clerks@5-stonebuildings.law.co.uk
Call Date: July 1963, Lincoln's Inn
Pupil Master, Recorder
Qualifications: [MA (Oxon)]

HARROP-GRIFFITHS HILTON

Chambers of Norman Palmer
2 Field Court, Gray's Inn, London
WC1R 5BB, Telephone: 0171 405 6114
E-mail: fieldct2@netcomuk.co.uk
Call Date: July 1978, Inner Temple
Pupil Master
Qualifications: [BA Hons (Manchester)]

HARRY TIMOTHY HAWKINS

9 Old Square
Ground Floor, Lincoln's Inn, London
WC2A 3SR, Telephone: 0171 405 4682
E-mail: chambers@9oldsquare.co.uk
Call Date: July 1983, Lincoln's Inn
Pupil Master
Qualifications: [MA, BCL (Oxon)]

D

D

HARRY THOMAS MISS CAROLINE JANE

Littleton Chambers
3 King's Bench Walk North, Temple,
London EC4Y 7HR,
Telephone: 0171 797 8600
E-mail:clerks@littletonchambers.co.uk
Call Date: Feb 1981, Middle Temple
Pupil Master
Qualifications: [LLB (Hons) (Exon)]

HART COLIN JOHN JEFFREY DINE

10 King's Bench Walk
Ground Floor, Temple, London
EC4Y 7EB, Telephone: 0171 353 7742
E-mail: 10kbw@lineone.net
Call Date: Nov 1966, Middle Temple
Pupil Master
Qualifications: [MA (Oxon), Dip Ecom]

HART DAVID TIMOTHY NELSON

1 Crown Office Row
Ground Floor, Temple, London
EC4Y 7HH, Telephone: 0171 797 7500
E-mail: mail@onecrownofficerow.com
Crown Office Row Chambers
Blenheim House, 120 Church Street,
Brighton, Sussex, BN1 1WH,
Telephone: 01273 625625
E-mail: crownofficerow@clara.net
Call Date: July 1982, Middle Temple
Pupil Master
Qualifications: [BA (Cantab)]

HART MS JENNIFER ANN

1 Inner Temple Lane
Temple, London EC4Y 1AF,
Telephone: 020 7353 0933
Call Date: Oct 1993, Middle Temple
Qualifications: [BA (Hons)(Lond), LLB
(Reading)]

HART NEIL HUGH THOMAS

Essex Court Chambers
24 Lincoln's Inn Fields, London
WC2A 3ED, Telephone: 0171 813 8000
E-mail:clerksroom@essexcourt-chambers.co.uk
Call Date: 1998, Gray's Inn
Qualifications: [BA (Oxon)]

HART PAUL

15 Winckley Square
Preston PR1 3JJ,
Telephone: 01772 252828
E-mail:clerks@winckleysq.demon.co.uk
Call Date: July 1982, Gray's Inn
Pupil Master
Qualifications: [LLB (Newc)]

HART WILLIAM STEPHEN

Albion Chambers
Broad Street, Bristol BS1 1DR,
Telephone: 0117 9272144
Call Date: July 1979, Middle Temple
Pupil Master
Qualifications: [LLB (Exon)]

HART-LEVERTON COLIN ALLEN QC (1979)

8 King's Bench Walk
2nd Floor, Temple, London EC4Y 7DU,
Telephone: 0171 797 8888
8 King's Bench Walk North
1 Park Square East, Leeds LS1 2NE,
Telephone: 0113 2439797
Call Date: May 1957, Middle Temple

HARTE JOHN DAVID CHESTERS

Broad Chare
33 Broad Chare, Newcastle upon Tyne
NE1 3DQ, Telephone: 0191 232 0541
E-mail:clerks@broadcharechambers.law.co.uk
Call Date: July 1967, Gray's Inn
Qualifications: [MA (Cantab), Dip Crim
(Cantab)]

HARTLEY ANTONY ARNOLD

8 Fountain Court
Steelhouse Lane, Birmingham B4 6DR,
Telephone: 0121 236 5514/5
E-mail: clerks@no8chambers.co.uk
Call Date: Feb 1991, Gray's Inn
Qualifications: [LLB (Bris)]

HARTLEY RICHARD ANTHONY

Cobden House Chambers
19 Quay Street, Manchester M3 3HN,
Telephone: 0161 833 6000
E-mail: clerks@cobden.co.uk
Call Date: July 1985, Middle Temple
Pupil Master
Qualifications: [LLB (Hons)]

HARTLEY RICHARD LESLIE CLIFFORD QC (1976)

1 Brick Court
1st Floor, Temple, London EC4Y 9BY,
Telephone: 0171 353 8845
E-mail: clerks@1brickcourt.co.uk
Call Date: June 1956, Gray's Inn
Qualifications: [MA (Cantab)]

HARTLEY ROBERT EDWARD

3 Temple Gardens
3rd Floor, Temple, London EC4Y 9AU,
Telephone: 0171 353 0832
Call Date: Oct 1995, Middle Temple
Qualifications: [BA (Hon), LLM]

HARTLEY TIMOTHY GUY

Park Court Chambers
16 Park Place, Leeds LS1 2SJ,
Telephone: 0113 2433277
Call Date: July 1970, Gray's Inn
Qualifications: [LLB]

HARTLEY-DAVIES PAUL KEVIL

30 Park Place
Cardiff CF1 3BA,
Telephone: 01222 398421
E-mail: 100757.1456@compuserve.com
Call Date: July 1977, Gray's Inn
Pupil Master
Qualifications: [LLB (Hons) (Wales)]

HARTMAN MICHAEL

Lamb Building
Ground Floor, Temple, London
EC4Y 7AS, Telephone: 020 7797 7788
E-mail: lamb.building@link.org
Call Date: Nov 1975, Lincoln's Inn
Pupil Master

HARVEY COLIN TREVOR

St Paul's House
5th Floor, St Paul's House, 23 Park Square
South, Leeds LS1 2ND,
Telephone: 0113 2455866
E-mail: catherinegrimshaw@stpauls-
chambers.demon.co.uk
Call Date: July 1975, Middle Temple
Qualifications: [LLB (Lond)]

HARVEY JOHN GILBERT

5 Fountain Court
Steelhouse Lane, Birmingham B4 6DR,
Telephone: 0121 606 0500
E-mail:clerks@5fountaincourt.law.co.uk
Call Date: 1973, Gray's Inn
Qualifications: [LLB (Hons), FCIArb]

HARVEY JONATHAN ROBERT WILLIAM

2 Harcourt Buildings
Ground Floor/Left, Temple, London
EC4Y 9DB, Telephone: 0171 583 9020
E-mail: clerks@harcourt.co.uk
Call Date: July 1974, Inner Temple
Pupil Master
Qualifications: [BA (Cantab)]

HARVEY MISS LOUISE BARBARA

15 Winckley Square
Preston PR1 3JJ,
Telephone: 01772 252828
E-mail:clerks@winckleysq.demon.co.uk
Call Date: Oct 1991, Lincoln's Inn
Qualifications: [LLB (Hons)]

HARVEY MICHAEL LLEWELLYN TUCKER QC (1982)

Two Crown Office Row
Ground Floor, Temple, London
EC4Y 7HJ, Telephone: 020 7797 8100
E-mail: mail@2cor.co.uk, or to individual
barristers at: [barrister's
surname]@2cor.co.uk
Call Date: July 1966, Gray's Inn
Recorder
Qualifications: [MA, LLB (Cantab)]

HARVEY SIMON GRANT

3 Fountain Court
Steelhouse Lane, Birmingham B4 6DR,
Telephone: 0121 236 5854
Call Date: Oct 1994, Lincoln's Inn
Qualifications: [LLB (Hons)(Leeds)]

HARVEY STEPHEN FRANK

18 Red Lion Court
(Off Fleet Street), London EC4A 3EB,
Telephone: 0171 520 6000
E-mail: chambers@18rlc.co.uk

Thornwood House
102 New London Road, Chelmsford,
Essex, CM2 0RG,
Telephone: 01245 280880
E-mail: chambers@18rlc.co.uk
Call Date: July 1979, Gray's Inn
Pupil Master
Qualifications: [LLB (Lond)]

HARVIE JONATHAN ALEXANDER QC (1992)

Blackstone Chambers
Blackstone House, Temple, London
EC4Y 9BW, Telephone: 0171 583 1770
E-mail:clerks@blackstonechambers.com
Call Date: July 1973, Middle Temple
Assistant Recorder
Qualifications: [MA (Oxon)]

HARWOOD RICHARD JOHN

1 Serjeants' Inn
4th Floor, Temple, London EC4Y 1NH,
Telephone: 0171 583 1355
E-mail: clerks@serjeants-inn.co.uk
Call Date: Nov 1993, Middle Temple
Qualifications: [MA, LLM (Cantab)]

HARWOOD-STEVENSON JOHN FRANCIS RICHARD

9-12 Bell Yard
London WC2A 2LF,
Telephone: 0171 400 1800
E-mail: clerks@bellyard.co.uk
Call Date: Nov 1975, Inner Temple
Pupil Master
Qualifications: [MA (Oxon)]

HASAN MISS AYESHA

3 Dr Johnson's Buildings
Ground Floor, Temple, London
EC4Y 7BA, Telephone: 0171 353 4854
E-mail: clerks@3djb.co.uk
Call Date: July 1987, Gray's Inn
Pupil Master
Qualifications: [LLB (Nigeria) LLM, (Cantab)]

HASAN MISS TAZEEN

5 Pump Court
Ground Floor, Temple, London
EC4Y 7AP, Telephone: 020 7353 2532
E-mail: FivePump@netcomuk.co.uk
Call Date: Nov 1988, Lincoln's Inn
Qualifications: [BA Hons (Oxon), LLM (LSE)]

HASELHURST IAN SHAND

Adrian Lyon's Chambers
14 Castle Street, Liverpool L2 0NE,
Telephone: 0151 236 4421/8240
E-mail: chambers14@aol.com
Call Date: July 1976, Gray's Inn
Pupil Master
Qualifications: [LLB (L'pool)]

HASLAM ANDREW PETER

Sovereign Chambers
25 Park Square, Leeds LS1 2PW,
Telephone: 0113 2451841/2/3
E-mail:sovereignchambers@btinternet.com
Call Date: Oct 1991, Gray's Inn
Qualifications: [LLB (Hons((Leics)]

HASSALL JAMES CHRISTOPHER

Southernhay Chambers
33 Southernhay East, Exeter, Devon,
EX1 1NX, Telephone: 01392 255777
E-mail:southernhay.chambers@lineone.net
Call Date: Nov 1995, Lincoln's Inn
Qualifications: [LLB (Hons)]

HASSLACHER JAMES MICHAEL ROCHE

New Court
Temple, London EC4Y 9BE,
Telephone: 0171 583 5123/0510
Call Date: Nov 1993, Middle Temple
Qualifications: [LLB (Hons)(Keele)]

HASTINGS MISS FRANCES MARIA

Call Date: Oct 1990, Inner Temple
Qualifications: [BA (L'pool), Dip Law]

HATCH MISS LISA SHARMILA

4 King's Bench Walk
Ground/First Floor/Basement, Temple,
London EC4Y 7DL,
Telephone: 0171 822 8822
E-mail: 4kbw@barristersatlaw.com
Call Date: 1995, Middle Temple
Qualifications: [LLB (Hons)]

HATCHER MS NICHOLA JANE

High Street Chambers
102 High Street, Godalming, Surrey,
GU7 1DS, Telephone: 01483 861170
Call Date: Oct 1995, Inner Temple
Qualifications: [LLB (B'ham)]

HATFIELD MS SALLY ANNE

Doughty Street Chambers
11 Doughty Street, London WC1N 2PG,
Telephone: 0171 404 1313
E-mail:enquiries@doughtystreet.co.uk
Call Date: Nov 1988, Inner Temple
Qualifications: [BA (Oxon)]

HATTON ANDREW JOHN

Paradise Chambers
26 Paradise Square, Sheffield S1 2DE,
Telephone: 0114 2738951
E-mail: timbooth@paradise-sq.co.uk
Call Date: July 1987, Gray's Inn
Pupil Master
Qualifications: [LLB]

HATTON DAVID WILLIAM QC (1996)

Park Court Chambers
16 Park Place, Leeds LS1 2SJ,
Telephone: 0113 2433277
Call Date: July 1976, Gray's Inn
Recorder
Qualifications: [LLB (Hons)]

HAUGHTY JEREMY NICHOLAS

Rougemont Chambers
8 Colleton Crescent, Exeter, Devon,
EX1 1RR, Telephone: 01392 208484
E-mail:rougemont.chambers@eclipse.co.uk
Call Date: Nov 1989, Lincoln's Inn
Qualifications: [LLB, LLM (Exon)]

HAUKELAND MARTIN JONATHAN

Plowden Buildings
2nd Floor, 2 Plowden Buildings, Middle
Temple Lane, London EC4Y 9BU,
Telephone: 0171 583 0808
E-mail: bar@plowdenbuildings.co.uk
Call Date: Feb 1989, Middle Temple
Qualifications: [Dip Law,BA]

HAVELOCK-ALLAN ANTHONY MARK DAVID QC (1993)

20 Essex Street
London WC2R 3AL,
Telephone: 0171 583 9294
E-mail: clerks@20essexst.com
Call Date: July 1974, Inner Temple
Assistant Recorder
Qualifications: [BA (Dunelm), LLB (Cantab)]

HAVEN KEVIN

2 Gray's Inn Square Chambers
2nd Floor, Gray's Inn, London WC1R 5AA,
Telephone: 020 7242 0328
E-mail: clerks@2gis.co.uk
Call Date: July 1982, Gray's Inn
Qualifications: [BA (Kent)]

HAVERS THE HON PHILIP NIGEL QC (1995)

1 Crown Office Row
Ground Floor, Temple, London
EC4Y 7HH, Telephone: 0171 797 7500
E-mail: mail@onecrownofficerow.com
Crown Office Row Chambers
Blenheim House, 120 Church Street,
Brighton, Sussex, BN1 1WH,
Telephone: 01273 625625
E-mail: crownofficerow@clara.net
Call Date: July 1974, Inner Temple
Recorder
Qualifications: [BA (Cantab)]

HAVEY PETER SUNIL

4-5 Gray's Inn Square
Ground Floor, Gray's Inn, London
WC1R 5JP, Telephone: 0171 404 5252
E-mail:chambers@4-5graysinnsquare.co.uk
Call Date: July 1984, Gray's Inn
Pupil Master
Qualifications: [MA (Oxon)]

HAWES NEIL ASHLEY

Dr Johnson's Chambers
Two Dr Johnson's Buildings, Temple,
London EC4Y 7AY,
Telephone: 0171 353 4716
E-mail: clerks@2djb.freeserve.co.uk
Call Date: Nov 1989, Inner Temple
Qualifications: [LLB]

HAWKER GEOFFREY FORT

Chambers of Geoffrey Hawker
46/48 Essex Street, London WC2R 3GH,
Telephone: 0171 583 8899
Call Date: Apr 1970, Gray's Inn
Pupil Master
Qualifications: [BSc(Eng) FEng FICE, C Eng
FIEI, FIStructE, MSoclS(France), MConsE
FCIArb]

HAWKES MISS NAOMI NANTEZA ASTRID WALLUSIMBI

22 Old Buildings
Lincoln's Inn, London WC2A 3UJ,
Telephone: 0171 831 0222
Call Date: Oct 1994, Middle Temple
Qualifications: [BA (Hons)(Cantab)]

HAWKESWORTH (WALTER) GARETH

Fenners Chambers
3 Madingley Road, Cambridge CB3 0EE,
Telephone: 01223 368761
E-mail: clerks@fennerschambers.co.uk
Fenners Chambers
8-12 Priestgate, Peterborough PE1 1JA,
Telephone: 01733 562030
E-mail: clerks@fennerschambers.co.uk
Five Paper Buildings
1st Floor, Five Paper Bldgs, Temple,
London EC4Y 7HB,
Telephone: 0171 583 6117
E-mail: clerks@5-paperbuildings.law.co.uk
Call Date: Nov 1972, Gray's Inn
Pupil Master, Recorder
Qualifications: [MA (Cantab)]

HAWKINS DAVID JAMES

Bank House Chambers
Old Bank House, Hartshead, Sheffield
S1 2EL, Telephone: 0114 2751223
Call Date: Oct 1991, Gray's Inn
Qualifications: [B Ed (Exeter), LLB (Sheff)]

HAWKINS MISS LUCY ELIZABETH

St Ive's Chambers
Whittall Street, Birmingham B4 6DH,
Telephone: 0121 236 0863/5720
E-mail:stives.headofchambers@btinternet.com
Call Date: Nov 1994, Lincoln's Inn
Qualifications: [BA (Hons)(Durham), CPE]

HAWKS ANTHONY JOSEPH VINCENT

Broad Chare
33 Broad Chare, Newcastle upon Tyne
NE1 3DQ, Telephone: 0191 232 0541
E-mail:clerks@broadcharechambers.law.co.uk
Call Date: Nov 1975, Middle Temple
Pupil Master
Qualifications: [LLB]

HAWLEY MS CAROL ANNE

14 Tooks Court
Cursitor St, London EC4A 1LB,
Telephone: 0171 405 8828
E-mail: clerks@tooks.law.co.uk
Call Date: Oct 1990, Gray's Inn
Qualifications: [LLB (Hons, Lond)]

HAWORTH RICHARD ANTHONY

15 Winckley Square
Preston PR1 3JJ,
Telephone: 01772 252828
E-mail:clerks@winckleysq.demon.co.uk
Call Date: Nov 1978, Inner Temple
Pupil Master
Qualifications: [LLB (Leeds)]

HAWTHORNE MRS PATRICIA VERONICA

Victoria Chambers
3rd Floor, 177 Corporation Street,
Birmingham B4 6RG,
Telephone: 0121 236 9900
E-mail: viccham@aol.com
Call Date: 1995, Middle Temple
Qualifications: [BA (Hons)]

HAY MS DEBORAH JANE

Goldsmith Building
1st Floor, Temple, London EC4Y 7BL,
Telephone: 0171 353 7881
E-mail:clerks@goldsmith-building.law.co.uk
Call Date: Apr 1991, Middle Temple
Qualifications: [BA]

HAY MISS FIONA RUTH

13 King's Bench Walk
1st Floor, Temple, London EC4Y 7EN,
Telephone: 0171 353 7204
E-mail: clerks@13kbw.law.co.uk
King's Bench Chambers
32 Beaumont Street, Oxford OX1 2NP,
Telephone: 01865 311066
E-mail: clerks@kbc-oxford.law.co.uk
Call Date: Nov 1989, Inner Temple
Pupil Master
Qualifications: [BSc, BA (Exon)]

HAY MALCOLM JOHN MARSHALL

3 Dr Johnson's Buildings
Ground Floor, Temple, London
EC4Y 7BA, Telephone: 0171 353 4854
E-mail: clerks@3djb.co.uk
Call Date: Nov 1972, Gray's Inn
Pupil Master
Qualifications: [BA (Oxon)]

HAY ROBIN WILLIAM PATRICK HAMILTON

Goldsmith Building
1st Floor, Temple, London EC4Y 7BL,
Telephone: 0171 353 7881
E-mail:clerks@goldsmith-building.law.co.uk
Call Date: Nov 1964, Inner Temple
Pupil Master, Recorder
Qualifications: [MA, LLB (Cantab)]

HAYATALLY TARIK RUMI

Call Date: Feb 1990, Gray's Inn
Qualifications: [BA, LLB (Lond)]

HAYCROFT ANTHONY MARK

Queen Elizabeth Building
Ground Floor, Temple, London
EC4Y 9BS,
Telephone: 0171 353 7181 (12 Lines)
Call Date: Nov 1982, Middle Temple
Pupil Master
Qualifications: [LLB (Reading), BCL (Oxon)]

HAYDEN ANTHONY PAUL

28 St John Street
Manchester M3 4DJ,
Telephone: 0161 834 8418
E-mail: clerk@28stjohnst.co.uk
Call Date: Nov 1987, Middle Temple
Qualifications: [BA (Manch) Dip Law, (City)]

HAYDEN RICHARD

2 Paper Buildings, Basement North
Temple, London EC4Y 7ET,
Telephone: 0171 936 2613
E-mail: post@2paper.co.uk
Call Date: June 1964, Gray's Inn
Pupil Master
Qualifications: [LLB (Lond)]

HAYDON ALEC GUY

Brick Court Chambers
7-8 Essex Street, London WC2R 3LD,
Telephone: 0171 379 3550
E-mail: [surname]@brickcourt.co.uk
Call Date: Oct 1993, Gray's Inn
Qualifications: [BA (Cantab), LLM (Harvard)]

HAYES JEREMY JOSEPH JAMES

2 Paper Buildings
1st Floor, Temple, London EC4Y 7ET,
Telephone: 020 7556 5500
E-mail: clerks@2pbbarristers.co.uk
Call Date: Nov 1977, Middle Temple
Qualifications: [LLB]

HAYES JOHN ALLAN

Chambers of Andrew Campbell QC
10 Park Square, Leeds LS1 2LH,
Telephone: 0113 2455438
E-mail: clerks@10pksq.co.uk
Call Date: Nov 1992, Lincoln's Inn
Qualifications: [BA (Hons)]

HAYES MISS JOSEPHINE MARY

Chambers of Lord Goodhart QC
Ground Floor, 3 New Square, Lincoln's
Inn, London WC2A 3RS,
Telephone: 0171 405 5577
E-mail:law@threenewsquare.demon.co.uk
Call Date: July 1980, Lincoln's Inn
Pupil Master
Qualifications: [MA (Oxon), LLM (Yale)]

D

HAYES RICHARD JAMES

Lamb Chambers
Lamb Building, Temple, London
EC4Y 7AS, Telephone: 020 7797 8300
E-mail: lambchambers@link.org
Call Date: Oct 1995, Lincoln's Inn
Qualifications: [LLB (Hons)(Durham)]

HAYES TIMOTHY BARRINGTON

Iscoed Chambers
86 St Helen's Road, Swansea, West
Glamorgan, SA1 4BQ,
Telephone: 01792 652988/9/330
Call Date: Oct 1996, Gray's Inn
Qualifications: [LLB (Lond)]

HAYGARTH EDMUND BRUCE

25-27 Castle Street
1st Floor, Liverpool L2 4TA,
Telephone: 0151 227 5661/051 236 5072
Call Date: Nov 1988, Gray's Inn
Qualifications: [LLB (Lond)]

HAYHOE JUSTIN OLIVER

Parsonage Chambers
5th Floor, 3 The Parsonage, Manchester
M3 2HW, Telephone: 0161 833 1996
Call Date: Oct 1994, Gray's Inn
Qualifications: [BA]

HAYHOW MRS LYNDSAY JILL

5 Essex Court
1st Floor, Temple, London EC4Y 9AH,
Telephone: 0171 410 2000
E-mail: barristers@5essexcourt.co.uk
Call Date: Nov 1990, Inner Temple
Qualifications: [LLB (Hons)]

HAYNE MISS JANETTE ELIZABETH

Tindal Chambers
3/5 New Street, Chelmsford, Essex,
CM1 1NT, Telephone: 01245 267742
St Albans Chambers
Dolphin Lodge, Dolphin Yard, Holywell
Hill, St Albans, Herts, AL1 1EX,
Telephone: 01727 843383
Call Date: 1991, Inner Temple
Qualifications: [BA (Lond)]

HAYNES JOHN CHARLES

3 Paper Buildings
Temple, London EC4Y 7EU,
Telephone: 020 7583 8055
E-mail: London@3paper.com
3 Paper Buildings (Bournemouth)
20 Lorne Park Road, Bournemouth,
Dorset, BH1 1JN,
Telephone: 01202 292102
E-mail: Bournemouth@3paper.com
3 Paper Buildings (Winchester)
4 St Peter Street, Winchester SO23 8BW,
Telephone: 01962 868884
E-mail: winchester@3paper.com
3 Paper Buildings (Oxford)
1 Alfred Street, High Street, Oxford
OX1 4EH, Telephone: 01865 793736
E-mail: oxford@3paper.com
Call Date: Nov 1968, Middle Temple

HAYNES MATTHEW THOMAS BONIFACE

St Ive's Chambers
Whittall Street, Birmingham B4 6DH,
Telephone: 0121 236 0863/5720
E-mail:stives.headofchambers@btinternet.com
Call Date: Nov 1991, Lincoln's Inn
Qualifications: [MA (Hons) (Oxon)]

HAYNES MICHAEL JOHN

4 Brick Court
Temple, London EC4Y 9AD,
Telephone: 0171 797 8910
E-mail: medhurst@dial.pipex.com
Call Date: July 1979, Gray's Inn
Qualifications: [LLB (Leic)]

HAYNES PETER

St Philip's Chambers
Fountain Court, Steelhouse Lane,
Birmingham B4 6DR,
Telephone: 0121 246 7000
E-mail: clerks@st-philips.co.uk
Call Date: July 1983, Gray's Inn
Pupil Master
Qualifications: [LLB (B'ham)]

HAYNES MISS REBECCA

Monckton Chambers
4 Raymond Buildings, Gray's Inn, London
WC1R 5BP, Telephone: 0171 405 7211
E-mail: chambers@monckton.co.uk
Call Date: Nov 1994, Inner Temple
Qualifications: [LLB (Lond), LLM (Lond)]

HAYTER MRS KATHLEEN

Merriemore Cottage
Sawbridge, Nr Rugby, Warwickshire,
CV23 8BB, Telephone: 01788 891832
E-mail:kathleen@sawbridge.demon.co.uk
Call Date: July 1982, Middle Temple
Qualifications: [LLB (leics)]

HAYTON PROFESSOR DAVID JOHN

5 Stone Buildings
Lincoln's Inn, London WC2A 3XT,
Telephone: 0171 242 6201
E-mail:clerks@5-stonebuildings.law.co.uk
Call Date: Nov 1968, Inner Temple
Qualifications: [LLD (Newc)]

HAYTON MRS LINDA PATRICIA

Arden Chambers
27 John Street, London WC1N 2BL,
Telephone: 020 7242 4244
E-mail:clerks@arden-chambers.law.co.uk
Call Date: Nov 1975, Lincoln's Inn
Qualifications: [LLB]

HAYTON MICHAEL PEARSON

Deans Court Chambers
24 St John Street, Manchester M3 4DF,
Telephone: 0161 214 6000
E-mail: clerks@deanscourt.co.uk
Deans Court Chambers
41-43 Market Place, Preston PR1 1AH,
Telephone: 01772 555163
E-mail: clerks@deanscourt.co.uk
Call Date: Oct 1993, Lincoln's Inn
Qualifications: [BA (Hons)]

HAYWARD JAMES GERALD STEPHEN

Cathedral Chambers (Jan Wood Independent Barristers' Clerk)
1 Maple Road, Exeter, Devon, EX4 1BN,
Telephone: 01392 210900
E-mail:cathedral.chambers@eclipse.co.uk
Call Date: July 1985, Middle Temple
Pupil Master
Qualifications: [MA (Cantab)]

HAYWARD PETER MICHAEL

The Outer Temple
Room 26, 222/225 Strand, London
WC2R 1BQ, Telephone: 0171 353 4647
E-mail: njj606@mcmail.com
Call Date: July 1974, Gray's Inn
Qualifications: [BA, BCL (Oxon)]

HAYWARD-SMITH RODGER QC (1988)

One King's Bench Walk
1st Floor, Temple, London EC4Y 7DB,
Telephone: 0171 936 1500
E-mail: ddear@1kbw.co.uk
Call Date: July 1967, Gray's Inn
Recorder
Qualifications: [MA (Oxon)]

HAYWOOD MISS JANET

Guildford Chambers
Stoke House, Leapale Lane, Guildford,
Surrey, GU1 4LY,
Telephone: 01483 539131
E-mail:guildford.barristers@btinternet.com
Call Date: July 1985, Inner Temple
Qualifications: [BA, Dip Law City]

HAYWOOD MISS JANETTE

Gray's Inn Chambers
5th Floor, Gray's Inn, London WC1R 5JA,
Telephone: 0171 404 1111
Call Date: Nov 1977, Middle Temple
Qualifications: [LLM (Lond) LLB, (Cardiff)]

HEAD DAVID IAN

3 Verulam Buildings
London WC1R 5NT,
Telephone: 0171 831 8441
E-mail: clerks@3verulam.co.uk
Call Date: Nov 1997, Middle Temple
Qualifications: [BA (Hons)(Oxon)]

HEAD JOHN PHILIP TREVELYAN

9 Bedford Row
London WC1R 4AZ,
Telephone: 0171 242 3555
E-mail: clerks@9br.co.uk
Call Date: July 1976, Middle Temple
Pupil Master, Assistant Recorder
Qualifications: [MA (Oxon), LLM, (Virginia)]

HEADLAM ROY WASHINGTON

Furnival Chambers
32 Furnival Street, London EC4A 1JQ,
Telephone: 0171 405 3232
E-mail: clerks@furnivallaw.co.uk
Call Date: Nov 1983, Gray's Inn
Qualifications: [BA]

HEAL MISS JOANNA MARY

Devereux Chambers
Devereux Court, London WC2R 3JJ,
Telephone: 0171 353 7534
E-mail: mailbox@devchambers.co.uk
Call Date: July 1988, Inner Temple
Qualifications: [MA (Cantab)]

HEAL MRS MADELEINE

4 Field Court
Gray's Inn, London WC1R 5EA,
Telephone: 0171 440 6900
E-mail: chambers@4fieldcourt.co.uk
Call Date: May 1996, Lincoln's Inn
Qualifications: [BA & LLB, (New Zealand)]

HEALD OLIVER

Fenners Chambers
3 Madingley Road, Cambridge CB3 0EE,
Telephone: 01223 368761
E-mail: clerks@fennerschambers.co.uk
Fenners Chambers
8-12 Priestgate, Peterborough PE1 1JA,
Telephone: 01733 562030
E-mail: clerks@fennerschambers.co.uk
Call Date: July 1977, Middle Temple
Qualifications: [MA (Cantab)]

HEALEY MS SUSAN HILARY

Trafalgar Chambers
53 Fleet Street, London EC4Y 1BE,
Telephone: 0171 583 5858
E-mail:trafalgarchambers@easynet.co.uk
Call Date: Nov 1995, Middle Temple
Qualifications: [BA (Hons)]

HEALING MISS YVONNE MARY

18 St John Street
Manchester M3 4EA,
Telephone: 0161 278 1800
E-mail: 18stjohn@lineone.net
Call Date: May 1987, Inner Temple
Qualifications: [LLB (L'pool)]

HEALY MISS ALEXANDRA

9-12 Bell Yard
London WC2A 2LF,
Telephone: 0171 400 1800
E-mail: clerks@bellyard.co.uk
Call Date: Oct 1992, Gray's Inn
Qualifications: [MA (Cantab)]

HEALY BRIAN PATRICK JAMES

St Philip's Chambers
Fountain Court, Steelhouse Lane,
Birmingham B4 6DR,
Telephone: 0121 246 7000
E-mail: clerks@st-philips.co.uk
Call Date: Nov 1967, Gray's Inn
Pupil Master
Qualifications: [LLB (Lond) , LLM (Lond)]

HEALY MISS SIOBAN

S Tomlinson QC
7 King's Bench Walk, Temple, London
EC4Y 7DS, Telephone: 0171 583 0404
E-mail: clerks@7kbw.law.co.uk
Call Date: July 1993, Inner Temple
Qualifications: [BA, LLM]

HEAP GERARD MILES

Mercury Chambers
Mercury House, 33-35 Clarendon Road,
Leeds LS2 9NZ,
Telephone: 0113 234 2265
E-mail:cdexter@mercurychambers.co.uk
Call Date: July 1985, Gray's Inn
Qualifications: [MA (Cantab)]

HEAP WALTER RICHARD CARTWRIGHT

Kenworthy's Chambers
83 Bridge Street, Manchester M3 2RF,
Telephone: 0161 832 4036/834 6954
E-mail: clerks@kenworthys.co.uk
Call Date: 1963, Inner Temple
Pupil Master
Qualifications: [LLB]

HEATH STEPHEN DAVID

2nd Floor, Francis Taylor Building
Temple, London EC4Y 7BY,
Telephone: 0171 353 9942/3157
Call Date: Feb 1992, Lincoln's Inn
Qualifications: [BA (Hons) (Cambs), Dip Law]

HEATHER CHRISTOPHER MARK

2nd Floor, Francis Taylor Building
Temple, London EC4Y 7BY,
Telephone: 0171 353 9942/3157
Call Date: Oct 1995, Middle Temple
Qualifications: [MA (Cantab)]

Fax: 0171 353 9924; DX: 211 London

Types of work: Commercial litigation, Commercial property, Common law (general), Housing, Insolvency, Landlord and tenant, Local government, Professional negligence

Reported Cases: *Agecrest Ltd v Gwynedd County Council*, [1998] JPL 325; [1996] EGCS 115, 1996. Validity of outline planning permission granted in 1964 – whether works in 1967 were performed with intention to develop site.

HEATON CLIVE WILLIAM

Chambers of Andrew Campbell QC
10 Park Square, Leeds LS1 2LH,
Telephone: 0113 2455438
E-mail: clerks@10pksq.co.uk
Call Date: July 1992, Gray's Inn
Qualifications: [MA (Oxon)]

HEATON DAVID MICHAEL

18 St John Street
Manchester M3 4EA,
Telephone: 0161 278 1800
E-mail: 18stjohn@lineone.net
Call Date: July 1983, Middle Temple
Pupil Master
Qualifications: [MA (Cantab)]

HEATON MISS FRANCES MARGARET

Deans Court Chambers
24 St John Street, Manchester M3 4DF,
Telephone: 0161 214 6000
E-mail: clerks@deanscourt.co.uk

Deans Court Chambers
41-43 Market Place, Preston PR1 1AH,
Telephone: 01772 555163
E-mail: clerks@deanscourt.co.uk
4 Brick Court
Ground Floor, Temple, London
EC4Y 9AD, Telephone: 0171 797 7766
E-mail: chambers@4brick.co.uk
Call Date: Nov 1985, Gray's Inn
Qualifications: [LLB (Hons)]

HEATON-ARMSTRONG ANTHONY EUSTACE JOHN

9-12 Bell Yard
London WC2A 2LF,
Telephone: 0171 400 1800
E-mail: clerks@bellyard.co.uk
Call Date: July 1973, Gray's Inn
Pupil Master
Qualifications: [LLB]

HEAVEY MISS CIARA

1 Gray's Inn Square
Ground Floor, London WC1R 5AA,
Telephone: 0171 405 8946/7/8
Call Date: Nov 1992, Middle Temple
Qualifications: [BA (Hons)(Lond), Dip in Law]

HEBRON HAROLD

1 Alfred Street, High Street, Oxford OX1 4EH, Telephone: 01865 793736
Call Date: Feb 1960, Middle Temple

HEDGECOE JOHN PHILIP

White Friars Chambers
21 White Friars, Chester CH1 1NZ,
Telephone: 01244 323070
E-mail:whitefriarschambers@btinternet.com
Call Date: Nov 1972, Inner Temple
Pupil Master
Qualifications: [LLB (Hull)]

HEDGELAND ROGER

18 St John Street
Manchester M3 4EA,
Telephone: 0161 278 1800
E-mail: 18stjohn@lineone.net
Call Date: Nov 1972, Gray's Inn
Assistant Recorder
Qualifications: [MA (Cantab)]

D

HEDLEY RICHARD PHILIP

St Mary's Chambers
50 High Pavement, Lace Market,
Nottingham NG1 1HW,
Telephone: 0115 9503503
E-mail: clerks@smc.law.co.uk
Call Date: Nov 1983, Middle Temple
Pupil Master
Qualifications: [LLB (Leic)]

HEDWORTH ALAN TOBY QC (1996)

Trinity Chambers
9-12 Trinity Chare, Quayside, Newcastle
upon Tyne NE1 3DF,
Telephone: 0191 232 1927
E-mail: info@trinitychambers.co.uk
11 King's Bench Walk
1st Floor, Temple, London EC4Y 7EQ,
Telephone: 0171 353 3337
E-mail: fmuller11@aol.com
Call Date: July 1975, Inner Temple
Recorder
Qualifications: [MA (Cantab)]

HEDWORTH LEONARD

10 King's Bench Walk
Ground Floor, Temple, London
EC4Y 7EB, Telephone: 0171 353 7742
E-mail: 10kbw@lineone.net
Call Date: July 1979, Lincoln's Inn
Qualifications: [BSc (Lond)]

HEER MISS DEANNA MARY

Hardwicke Building
New Square, Lincoln's Inn, London
WC2A 3SB, Telephone: 020 7242 2523
E-mail: clerks@hardwicke.co.uk
Call Date: Oct 1994, Gray's Inn
Qualifications: [LLB]

HEGARTY KEVIN JOHN

St Philip's Chambers
Fountain Court, Steelhouse Lane,
Birmingham B4 6DR,
Telephone: 0121 246 7000
E-mail: clerks@st-philips.co.uk
Call Date: Nov 1982, Middle Temple
Pupil Master
Qualifications: [LLB (Hons) (Newc)]

HEHIR CHRISTOPHER JOSEPH

1 Hare Court
Ground Floor, Temple, London
EC4Y 7BE, Telephone: 0171 353 3982/
5324
Call Date: Oct 1990, Inner Temple
Pupil Master
Qualifications: [BA (Oxon)]

HEILBRON MISS HILARY NORA QC (1987)

Brick Court Chambers
7-8 Essex Street, London WC2R 3LD,
Telephone: 0171 379 3550
E-mail: [surname]@brickcourt.co.uk
Call Date: July 1971, Gray's Inn
Qualifications: [MA (Oxon)]

HEIM PAUL EMIL

Wearne Wych, Picts Hill, Langport,
Somerset TA10 9AA,
Telephone: 01458 252097
Call Date: June 1956, Lincoln's Inn
Qualifications: [LLB Dunelm]

HEIMLER GEORGE ERNEST

6 Gray's Inn Square
Ground Floor, Gray's Inn, London
WC1R 5AZ, Telephone: 0171 242 1052
E-mail: 6graysinn@clara.co.uk
Call Date: July 1978, Inner Temple
Pupil Master
Qualifications: [LLB]

HELLER MRS ANNE

John Street Chambers
2 John Street, London WC1N 2HJ,
Telephone: 0171 242 1911
E-mail:john.street_chambers@virgin.net
Call Date: Nov 1995, Gray's Inn
Qualifications: [BA (Kent), LLB]

HELY MICHAEL HAMILTON MCMATH

Helions Chambers
Pilgrims' Way, Camps Road, Helions
Bumpstead, Haverhill, Suffolk, CB9 7AS,
Telephone: 01440 730523
E-mail: helionslaw@aol.com
Call Date: July 1975, Middle Temple
Qualifications: [MA (Cantab), C Eng, MIEE]

HELY HUTCHINSON MRS CAROLINE DEBORAH

One Garden Court Family Law Chambers
Ground Floor, Temple, London
EC4Y 9BJ, Telephone: 0171 797 7900
E-mail: clerks@onegardencourt.co.uk
Call Date: July 1983, Gray's Inn
Qualifications: [LLB (Bristol)]

HENDERSON (ANTHONY) MARK

Doughty Street Chambers
11 Doughty Street, London WC1N 2PG,
Telephone: 0171 404 1313
E-mail:enquiries@doughtystreet.co.uk
Call Date: Oct 1994, Gray's Inn
Qualifications: [BA (Oxon)]

HENDERSON MISS CAMILLA SOPHIE

Queen Elizabeth Building
2nd Floor, Temple, London EC4Y 9BS,
Telephone: 0171 797 7837
Call Date: Oct 1992, Inner Temple
Qualifications: [BA (Hons)(Cantab)]

HENDERSON MISS FIONA ELIZABETH

2 Paper Buildings
1st Floor, Temple, London EC4Y 7ET,
Telephone: 020 7556 5500
E-mail: clerks@2pbbarristers.co.uk
Call Date: Oct 1993, Lincoln's Inn
Qualifications: [BA (Hons) (Bris)]

HENDERSON IAN FRANCIS

8 King's Bench Walk
2nd Floor, Temple, London EC4Y 7DU,
Telephone: 0171 797 8888
8 King's Bench Walk North
1 Park Square East, Leeds LS1 2NE,
Telephone: 0113 2439797
Call Date: Nov 1990, Inner Temple
Qualifications: [LLB]

HENDERSON JAMES FROWYKE

4 Brick Court, Chambers of Anne Rafferty QC
1st Floor, Temple, London EC4Y 9AD,
Telephone: 0171 583 8455
Call Date: July 1984, Middle Temple
Pupil Master
Qualifications: [LLB]

HENDERSON JAMES THOMAS

Pump Court Tax Chambers
16 Bedford Row, London WC1R 4EB,
Telephone: 0171 414 8080
Call Date: Nov 1997, Gray's Inn
Qualifications: [BA]

HENDERSON MISS JOSEPHINE

Arden Chambers
27 John Street, London WC1N 2BL,
Telephone: 020 7242 4244
E-mail:clerks@arden-chambers.law.co.uk
Call Date: Nov 1990, Inner Temple
Qualifications: [BSc (Bris), Dip Law (PCL)]

HENDERSON LAUNCELOT DINADAN JAMES QC (1995)

5 Stone Buildings
Lincoln's Inn, London WC2A 3XT,
Telephone: 0171 242 6201
E-mail:clerks@5-stonebuildings.law.co.uk
Call Date: Nov 1977, Lincoln's Inn
Qualifications: [MA (Oxon)]

HENDERSON LAWRENCE MARK

Queen Elizabeth Building
Ground Floor, Temple, London
EC4Y 9BS,
Telephone: 0171 353 7181 (12 Lines)
Call Date: Nov 1990, Middle Temple
Qualifications: [LLB]

HENDERSON MISS LYNNE MCLEOD

Queens Square Chambers
56 Queens Square, Bristol BS1 4PR,
Telephone: 0117 921 1966
Call Date: Nov 1993, Inner Temple
Qualifications: [LLB (So'ton)]

HENDERSON RODERICK ST CLAIR MAWSON

St Ive's Chambers
Whittall Street, Birmingham B4 6DH,
Telephone: 0121 236 0863/5720
E-mail:stives.headofchambers@btinternet.com
Call Date: Nov 1978, Middle Temple
Pupil Master
Qualifications: [BA (Hons) (Oxon)]

D

HENDERSON ROGER ANTHONY QC (1980)

2 Harcourt Buildings
Ground Floor/Left, Temple, London
EC4Y 9DB, Telephone: 0171 583 9020
E-mail: clerks@harcourt.co.uk
Call Date: Nov 1964, Inner Temple
Recorder
Qualifications: [MA (Cantab)]

HENDERSON SIMON ALEXANDER

4 Pump Court
Temple, London EC4Y 7AN,
Telephone: 020 7842 5555
E-mail:chambers@4pumpcourt.law.co.uk
Call Date: Oct 1993, Inner Temple
Qualifications: [BA (Dunelm), Dip Law
(City)]

HENDERSON MISS SOPHIE

Plowden Buildings
2nd Floor, 2 Plowden Buildings, Middle
Temple Lane, London EC4Y 9BU,
Telephone: 0171 583 0808
E-mail: bar@plowdenbuildings.co.uk
Call Date: Oct 1990, Middle Temple
Qualifications: [BA (Hons) , Dip Law]

HENDERSON WILLIAM HUGO

Serle Court Chambers
6 New Square, Lincoln's Inn, London
WC2A 3QS, Telephone: 0171 242 6105
E-mail: clerks@serlecourt.co.uk
Call Date: July 1978, Inner Temple
Pupil Master
Qualifications: [BA (Cantab)]

HENDRON GERALD JAMES

Broadway House Chambers
Broadway House, 9 Bank Street, Bradford,
West Yorkshire, BD1 1TW,
Telephone: 01274 722560
E-mail: clerks@broadwayhouse.co.uk
Broadway House Chambers
31 Park Square West, Leeds LS1 2PF,
Telephone: 0113 246 2600
Call Date: Oct 1992, Lincoln's Inn
Qualifications: [LLB(Hons)(Leeds)]

HENDRY MISS HELEN MARY LOW

9 Woodhouse Square
Leeds LS3 1AD,
Telephone: 0113 2451986
E-mail: clerks@9woodhouse.co.uk
Call Date: Nov 1983, Middle Temple
Qualifications: [BSc (Lond), Dip Law]

HENDY JOHN GILES QC (1987)

Old Square Chambers
1 Verulam Buildings, Gray's Inn, London
WC1R 5LQ, Telephone: 0171 269 0300
E-mail:clerks@oldsquarechambers.co.uk
Old Square Chambers
Hanover House, 47 Corn Street, Bristol
BS1 1HT, Telephone: 0117 9277111
E-mail: oldsqbri@globalnet.co.uk
Call Date: July 1972, Gray's Inn
Qualifications: [LLB, LLM]

Fax: 0171 405 1387;
Out of hours telephone: 0171 269 0331;
DX: LDE 1046; URL: http://
www.oldsquarechambers.co.uk

Types of work: Employment, Medical negligence, Personal injury

Membership of foreign bars: Australia; New South Wales

Circuit: South Eastern; Western

Awards and memberships: Employment Law Bar Association – member of EC; PIBA; ALBA; CL & CBA; Fellow Royal Society of Medicine; Fellow Institute of Advanced Legal Studies; Fellow University of Kent School of Law

Other professional experience: Three years as full-time director of a Law Centre

Languages spoken: French

Publications: *Redgrave's Health and Safety at Work* 3rd edn, 1998; *Monkman on Employers' Liability* 12th edn, 1995; *Personal Injury Practice* 3rd edn, 1999; *The Human Rights Act, Article 11 and the Right to Strike*, 1998; *Every Worker Shall Have the Right to be Represented at Work by a Trade Union*, 1998

Reported Cases: *University College London Hospital NHS Trust v UNISON*, [1999] IRLR 31 (CA), 1999. Trade dispute – subject matter immunity.

BBC v Kelly Phillips, [1998] IRLR 294 (CA), 1998. Fixed term contracts of employment.
Armstrong v British Coal Corporation, [1998] JPIL 320 (CA), 1998. Personal injury – mineworkers VWF group action.
Binks v Maken and Avon Health Authority, [1998] PIQR P1 (CA), 1998. Medical negligence – amendment of pleading.
Associated Newspapers Ltd v Wilson, [1995] AC 454 (HL), 1995. Trade union activities – action short of dismissal.

HENDY MRS PAULINE FRANCES

Cloisters
1 Pump Court, Temple, London
EC4Y 7AA, Telephone: 0171 827 4000
E-mail: clerks@cloisters.com
Call Date: Nov 1985, Lincoln's Inn
Pupil Master
Qualifications: [BA(Lond)]

HENKE MISS RUTH SARA MARGARET

Iscoed Chambers
86 St Helen's Road, Swansea, West Glamorgan, SA1 4BQ,
Telephone: 01792 652988/9/330
Call Date: Nov 1987, Inner Temple
Pupil Master
Qualifications: [MA (Oxon)]

HENLEY ANDREW MICHAEL

Furnival Chambers
32 Furnival Street, London EC4A 1JQ,
Telephone: 0171 405 3232
E-mail: clerks@furnivallaw.co.uk
Call Date: Oct 1992, Middle Temple
Qualifications: [LLB(Hons)(Lond)]

HENLEY MR CHRISTOPHER MICHAEL

2-4 Tudor Street
London EC4Y 0AA,
Telephone: 0171 797 7111
E-mail: clerks@rfqc.co.uk
Call Date: July 1989, Gray's Inn
Qualifications: [LLB [Bris]]

HENLEY MARK ROBERT DANIEL

9 Woodhouse Square
Leeds LS3 1AD,
Telephone: 0113 2451986
E-mail: clerks@9woodhouse.co.uk
Call Date: Oct 1994, Lincoln's Inn
Qualifications: [MA (Cantab)]

HENLEY RAYMOND FRANCIS ST LUKE

Lancaster Building
77 Deansgate, Manchester M3 2BW,
Telephone: 0161 661 4444/0171 649 9872
E-mail: sandra@lbnipc.com
Call Date: July 1998, Lincoln's Inn
Qualifications: [BSc (Hons)(L'pool)]

HENNELL PETER GORDON

Queen's Chambers
5 John Dalton Street, Manchester M2 6ET,
Telephone: 0161 834 6875/4738
Queens Chambers
4 Camden Place, Preston PR1 3JL,
Telephone: 01772 828300
Call Date: July 1982, Middle Temple
Qualifications: [MA (Cantab)]

HENNESSY MISS SHIRLEY JANE

Derby Square Chambers
Merchants Court, Derby Square, Liverpool L2 1TS, Telephone: 0151 709 4222
E-mail:mail.derbysquare@pop3.hiway.co.uk
Call Date: Oct 1997, Lincoln's Inn
Qualifications: [BA (Hons)(Oxon)]

HENRIQUES RICHARD HENRY QUIXANO QC (1986)

Deans Court Chambers
24 St John Street, Manchester M3 4DF,
Telephone: 0161 214 6000
E-mail: clerks@deanscourt.co.uk
2-4 Tudor Street
London EC4Y 0AA,
Telephone: 0171 797 7111
E-mail: clerks@rfqc.co.uk
Deans Court Chambers
41-43 Market Place, Preston PR1 1AH,
Telephone: 01772 555163
E-mail: clerks@deanscourt.co.uk
Call Date: Nov 1967, Inner Temple
Recorder
Qualifications: [MA (Oxon)]

HENRY ALISTAIR ROBERT

38 Eldon Chambers
30 Fleet Street, London EC4Y 1AA,
Telephone: 0171 353 8822
Call Date: Mar 1998, Inner Temple
Qualifications: [BA (Dunelm)]

HENRY MISS ANNETTE PHYLLIS

10 King's Bench Walk
1st Floor, Temple, London EC4Y 7EB,
Telephone: 0171 353 2501
Call Date: July 1984, Gray's Inn
Qualifications: [LLB (Hons), (Manchester)]

HENRY EDWARD JOSEPH ALOYSIUS

Hollis Whiteman Chambers
3rd Floor, Queen Elizabeth Bldg, Temple,
London EC4Y 9BS,
Telephone: 020 7583 5766
E-mail:barristers@holliswhiteman.co.uk
Call Date: Nov 1988, Lincoln's Inn
Pupil Master
Qualifications: [BA Hons (Cantab), Dip Law
(City)]

HENRY MISS JENNIFER LORRAINE

Mitre House Chambers
15-19 Devereux Court, London WC2R 3JJ,
Telephone: 0171 583 8233
Call Date: Oct 1990, Middle Temple
Qualifications: [BA (Kent)]

HENRY PETER CLIFFORD

3 Paper Buildings
Temple, London EC4Y 7EU,
Telephone: 020 7583 8055
E-mail: London@3paper.com
3 Paper Buildings (Winchester)
4 St Peter Street, Winchester SO23 8BW,
Telephone: 01962 868884
E-mail: winchester@3paper.com
3 Paper Buildings (Bournemouth)
20 Lorne Park Road, Bournemouth,
Dorset, BH1 1JN,
Telephone: 01202 292102
E-mail: Bournemouth@3paper.com
3 Paper Buildings (Oxford)
1 Alfred Street, High Street, Oxford
OX1 4EH, Telephone: 01865 793736
E-mail: oxford@3paper.com
Call Date: Nov 1977, Inner Temple
Qualifications: [LLB (Exon)]

HENRY PHILIP BRUCE

15 Winckley Square
Preston PR1 3JJ,
Telephone: 01772 252828
E-mail:clerks@winckleysq.demon.co.uk
Call Date: Nov 1988, Middle Temple
Qualifications: [LLB (Lond), AKC]

HENSON MISS CHRISTINE RUTH

3 Hare Court
1 Little Essex Street, London WC2R 3LD,
Telephone: 0171 395 2000
Call Date: Oct 1994, Middle Temple
Qualifications: [BA (Warw)]

HENSON GRAHAM STANLEY

Furnival Chambers
32 Furnival Street, London EC4A 1JQ,
Telephone: 0171 405 3232
E-mail: clerks@furnivallaw.co.uk
Call Date: July 1976, Gray's Inn
Pupil Master
Qualifications: [BA (Cantab)]

HENTHORN MRS AISHA

Watford Chambers
74 Mildred Avenue, Watford,
Hertfordshire, WD1 7DX,
Telephone: 01923 220553
Call Date: July 1981, Middle Temple
Pupil Master
Qualifications: [BA (Hons) Law]

HEPHER PAUL ARTHUR RICHARD

2 Gray's Inn Square Chambers
2nd Floor, Gray's Inn, London WC1R 5AA,
Telephone: 020 7242 0328
E-mail: clerks@2gis.co.uk
Call Date: Oct 1994, Gray's Inn
Qualifications: [MA (Oxon)]

HEPPENSTALL MISS CLAIRE NORAH

3 Dr Johnson's Buildings
Ground Floor, Temple, London
EC4Y 7BA, Telephone: 0171 353 4854
E-mail: clerks@3djb.co.uk
Call Date: Nov 1990, Inner Temple
Qualifications: [LLM (Lond)]

HEPPENSTALL MISS RACHAEL ELIZABETH

Sovereign Chambers
25 Park Square, Leeds LS1 2PW,
Telephone: 0113 2451841/2/3
E-mail:sovereignchambers@btinternet.com
Call Date: 1997, Middle Temple
Qualifications: [BSc (Hons)(Surrey)]

HEPPLE PROFESSOR BOB ALEXANDER QC (1996)

Blackstone Chambers
Blackstone House, Temple, London
EC4Y 9BW, Telephone: 0171 583 1770
E-mail:clerks@blackstonechambers.com
Call Date: July 1966, Gray's Inn
Qualifications: [MA, LLD (Camb)]

HERAGHTY DAVID ANDREW PAUL

14 Tooks Court
Cursitor St, London EC4A 1LB,
Telephone: 0171 405 8828
E-mail: clerks@tooks.law.co.uk
Call Date: Oct 1995, Inner Temple
Qualifications: [BSc (Hons), CPE]

HERBERG JAVAN WILLIAM

Blackstone Chambers
Blackstone House, Temple, London
EC4Y 9BW, Telephone: 0171 583 1770
E-mail:clerks@blackstonechambers.com
Call Date: Oct 1992, Lincoln's Inn
Qualifications: [LLB(Hons)(Lond), BCL]

HERBERT DAVID RICHARD

2 New Street
Leicester LE1 5NA,
Telephone: 0116 2625906
E-mail: clerks@2newstreet.co.uk
Call Date: Nov 1992, Gray's Inn
Qualifications: [BA (So'ton)]

HERBERT (DONALD) PETER

14 Tooks Court
Cursitor St, London EC4A 1LB,
Telephone: 0171 405 8828
E-mail: clerks@tooks.law.co.uk
Call Date: Nov 1982, Gray's Inn
Pupil Master
Qualifications: [LLB (Lond)]

HERBERT DOUGLAS CHURCHILL

Ropewalk Chambers
24 The Ropewalk, Nottingham NG1 5EF,
Telephone: 0115 9472581
E-mail: administration@ropewalk co.uk
Devereux Chambers
Devereux Court, London WC2R 3JJ,
Telephone: 0171 353 7534
E-mail: mailbox@devchambers.co.uk
Call Date: 1973, Middle Temple
Pupil Master, Assistant Recorder
Qualifications: [LLB]

HERBERT GARRY GERARD PAUL

10 King's Bench Walk
1st Floor, Temple, London EC4Y 7EB,
Telephone: 0171 353 2501
Call Date: Nov 1995, Lincoln's Inn
Qualifications: [MBE, BA (Hons), Dip in Law]

HERBERT MARK JEREMY QC (1995)

5 Stone Buildings
Lincoln's Inn, London WC2A 3XT,
Telephone: 0171 242 6201
E-mail:clerks@5-stonebuildings.law.co.uk
Call Date: July 1974, Lincoln's Inn
Qualifications: [BA (Lond)]

Fax: 0171 831 8102; DX: 304 London;
Other comms: E-Mail
mherbert@5-stonebuildings.law.co.uk;
URL: http://
www.5-stonebuildings.law.co.uk

Types of work: Chancery (general), Equity, wills and trusts, Pensions, Probate and administration, Tax – capital and income

Awards and memberships: Member: Chancery Bar Association; Revenue Bar Association; Association of Pension Lawyers; Society of Trust and Estate Practitioners

Publications: *Whiteman on Capital Gains Tax* (Co-editor), 1988; *Drafting and Variation of Wills*, 1989

Reported Cases: *IRC v Fitzwilliam*, [1993] 1 WLR 1189, 1993. Application of the *Ramsay* principle to capital transfer tax.
Mettoy Pension Trustees v Evans, [1990] 1 WLR 1587, 1989. Exercise of fiduciary powers conferred by pension scheme.
R v OPRA ex parte Littlewoods, [1998] PLR 63, 1997. Entitlement to cash equivalent from occupational pension scheme.

HERBERT MRS REBECCA MARY

2 New Street
Leicester LE1 5NA,
Telephone: 0116 2625906
E-mail: clerks@2newstreet.co.uk
Call Date: Oct 1993, Gray's Inn
Qualifications: [LLB (Manch)]

HERMAN RAYMOND CHARLES

India Buildings Chambers
Water Street, Liverpool L2 0XG,
Telephone: 0151 243 6000
E-mail: clerks@chambers.u-net.com
Call Date: Feb 1972, Inner Temple
Pupil Master, Recorder
Qualifications: [LLB]

HERMER RICHARD SIMON

Doughty Street Chambers
11 Doughty Street, London WC1N 2PG,
Telephone: 0171 404 1313
E-mail:enquiries@doughtystreet.co.uk
30 Park Place
Cardiff CF1 3BA,
Telephone: 01222 398421
E-mail: 100757.1456@compuserve.com
Call Date: Oct 1993, Middle Temple
Qualifications: [BA (Hons)(Manc)]

HERNANDEZ DAVID ANTHONY

Young Street Chambers
38 Young Street, Manchester M3 3FT,
Telephone: 0161 833 0489
E-mail: clerks@young-st-chambers.com
Call Date: Nov 1976, Lincoln's Inn
Pupil Master, Assistant Recorder
Qualifications: [MA (Oxon)]

HERSHMAN DAVID ALLAN

St Philip's Chambers
Fountain Court, Steelhouse Lane,
Birmingham B4 6DR,
Telephone: 0121 246 7000
E-mail: clerks@st-philips.co.uk
1 Mitre Court Buildings
Temple, London EC4Y 7BS,
Telephone: 0171 797 7070
E-mail: clerks@1mcb.com
Call Date: July 1981, Gray's Inn
Pupil Master
Qualifications: [LLB (Lond)]

HESLOP MARTIN SYDNEY QC (1995)

1 Hare Court
Ground Floor, Temple, London
EC4Y 7BE, Telephone: 0171 353 3982/
5324
Call Date: July 1972, Lincoln's Inn
Recorder
Qualifications: [LLB (Hons)]

HESLOP PHILIP LINNELL QC (1985)

4 Stone Buildings
Ground Floor, Lincoln's Inn, London
WC2A 3XT, Telephone: 0171 242 5524
E-mail:clerks@4stonebuildings.law.co.uk
Call Date: Nov 1970, Lincoln's Inn
Qualifications: [BA, LLM (Cantab)]

HESS EDWARD JOHN WATKIN

Harcourt Chambers
1st Floor, 2 Harcourt Buildings, Temple,
London EC4Y 9DB,
Telephone: 0171 353 6961
E-mail:clerks@harcourtchambers.law.co.uk
Harcourt Chambers
Churchill House, 3 St Aldate's Courtyard,
St Aldate's, Oxford OX1 1BN,
Telephone: 01865 791559
E-mail:clerks@harcourtchambers.law.co.uk
Call Date: Nov 1985, Middle Temple
Pupil Master
Qualifications: [MA (Cantab)]

HESTER PAUL STEPHEN

3 Paper Buildings
Temple, London EC4Y 7EU,
Telephone: 020 7583 8055
E-mail: London@3paper.com
3 Paper Buildings (Bournemouth)
20 Lorne Park Road, Bournemouth,
Dorset, BH1 1JN,
Telephone: 01202 292102
E-mail: Bournemouth@3paper.com
3 Paper Buildings (Winchester)
4 St Peter Street, Winchester SO23 8BW,
Telephone: 01962 868884
E-mail: winchester@3paper.com
3 Paper Buildings (Oxford)
1 Alfred Street, High Street, Oxford
OX1 4EH, Telephone: 01865 793736
E-mail: oxford@3paper.com
Call Date: July 1989, Middle Temple
Qualifications: [BA (Warw), Dip Law]

HETHERINGTON ROGER ROOKE

2 Temple Gardens
Temple, London EC4Y 9AY,
Telephone: 0171 583 6041
E-mail: clerks@2templegardens.co.uk
Call Date: July 1973, Middle Temple
Pupil Master, Assistant Recorder
Qualifications: [BA (Cantab)]

HETT JAMES

St Mary's Chambers
50 High Pavement, Lace Market,
Nottingham NG1 1HW,
Telephone: 0115 9503503
E-mail: clerks@smc.law.co.uk
Call Date: Nov 1991, Middle Temple
Qualifications: [LLB (Hons) (Birm)]

HEWITSON WILLIAM ANDREW

1 Crown Office Row
3rd Floor, Temple, London EC4Y 7HH,
Telephone: 0171 583 9292
E-mail: onecor@link.org
Call Date: July 1975, Gray's Inn
Pupil Master
Qualifications: [MB, BS, FRCS]

HEWITT MISS ALEXANDRA HELEN

Nicholas Street Chambers
22 Nicholas Street, Chester CH1 2NX,
Telephone: 01244 323886
E-mail: clerks@40king.co.uk
Call Date: Oct 1995, Middle Temple
Qualifications: [BA (Hons)]

HEWITT MISS ALISON BRYDIE

1 Temple Gardens
1st Floor, Temple, London EC4Y 9BB,
Telephone: 0171 583 1315/353 0407
E-mail: clerks@1templegardens.co.uk
Call Date: July 1984, Middle Temple
Pupil Master
Qualifications: [LLB (lond)]

HEWITT DAVID EDWARD MILES

1 Harcourt Buildings
2nd Floor, Temple, London EC4Y 9DA,
Telephone: 0171 353 9421/0375
E-mail:clerks@1harcourtbuildings.law.co.uk
Call Date: Feb 1991, Middle Temple
Qualifications: [BSc (Cardiff)]

HEWITT MISS SUSAN ELIZABETH

Chambers of Wilfred Forster-Jones
New Court, 1st Floor South, Temple,
London EC4Y 9BE,
Telephone: 0171 353 0853/4/7222
E-mail: chambers@newcourt.net
Call Date: 1997, Lincoln's Inn
Qualifications: [BSc (Hons), Dip in Law
(City)]

HEWITT TIMOTHY

Broad Chare
33 Broad Chare, Newcastle upon Tyne
NE1 3DQ, Telephone: 0191 232 0541
E-mail:clerks@broadcharechambers.law.co.uk
Call Date: July 1973, Middle Temple
Pupil Master, Recorder
Qualifications: [LLB]

HEWSON MISS BARBARA MARY

Littman Chambers
12 Gray's Inn Square, London WC1R 5JP,
Telephone: 020 7404 4866
E-mail: admin@littmanchambers.com
Call Date: Nov 1985, Middle Temple
Pupil Master
Qualifications: [MA (Cantab)]

HEXT NEIL FRASER

2 Temple Gardens
Temple, London EC4Y 9AY,
Telephone: 0171 583 6041
E-mail: clerks@2templegardens.co.uk
Call Date: Oct 1995, Gray's Inn
Qualifications: [LLB (Bris)]

HEYWOOD MARK ADRIAN

5 King's Bench Walk
Temple, London EC4Y 7DN,
Telephone: 0171 353 5638
Call Date: July 1985, Gray's Inn
Pupil Master
Qualifications: [BA(Cantab)]

HEYWOOD MARK STEPHEN

5 Fountain Court
Steelhouse Lane, Birmingham B4 6DR,
Telephone: 0121 606 0500
E-mail:clerks@5fountaincourt.law.co.uk
Call Date: July 1986, Gray's Inn
Qualifications: [LLB (Newcastle)]

HEYWOOD MICHAEL EDMUNDSON

Chambers of Lord Goodhart QC
Ground Floor, 3 New Square, Lincoln's
Inn, London WC2A 3RS,
Telephone: 0171 405 5577
E-mail:law@threenewsquare.demon.co.uk
Cobden House Chambers
19 Quay Street, Manchester M3 3HN,
Telephone: 0161 833 6000
E-mail: clerks@cobden.co.uk
Call Date: July 1975, Inner Temple
Pupil Master
Qualifications: [BSc Soc(Lond)]

HEYWOOD PETER LESLIE

Queens Square Chambers
56 Queens Square, Bristol BS1 4PR,
Telephone: 0117 921 1966
Call Date: Nov 1988, Gray's Inn
Pupil Master
Qualifications: [LLB (Wales), MA (City)]

HEYWORTH MISS CATHERINE LOUISE

Iscoed Chambers
86 St Helen's Road, Swansea, West
Glamorgan, SA1 4BQ,
Telephone: 01792 652988/9/330
Call Date: Nov 1991, Inner Temple
Qualifications: [LLB (Hons)]

HIBBERT WILLIAM JOHN

Gough Square Chambers
6-7 Gough Square, London EC4A 3DE,
Telephone: 0171 353 0924
E-mail: gsc@goughsq.co.uk
Call Date: July 1979, Inner Temple
Pupil Master
Qualifications: [BA (Oxon)]

HIBBERTS JONATHAN JAMES

Holborn Chambers
6 Gate Street, Lincoln's Inn Fields, London
WC2A 3HP, Telephone: 0171 242 6060
Call Date: Oct 1996, Lincoln's Inn
Qualifications: [BA (Hons)(Keele)]

HICK MICHAEL ANDREW

Five Paper Buildings
1st Floor, Five Paper Bldgs, Temple,
London EC4Y 7HB,
Telephone: 0171 583 6117
E-mail:clerks@5-paperbuildings.law.co.uk
Call Date: Oct 1995, Gray's Inn
Qualifications: [BA, ACA]

HICKEY ALEXANDER FREDERICK

Littman Chambers
12 Gray's Inn Square, London WC1R 5JP,
Telephone: 020 7404 4866
E-mail: admin@littmanchambers.com
Call Date: Nov 1995, Lincoln's Inn
Qualifications: [BA (Oxon)]

HICKEY EUGENE JAMES

5 Fountain Court
Steelhouse Lane, Birmingham B4 6DR,
Telephone: 0121 606 0500
E-mail:clerks@5fountaincourt.law.co.uk
Call Date: July 1988, Lincoln's Inn
Qualifications: [LLB (Hons) (Leeds)]

HICKEY SIMON ROGER GREENWOOD

Chambers of Andrew Campbell QC
10 Park Square, Leeds LS1 2LH,
Telephone: 0113 2455438
E-mail: clerks@10pksq.co.uk
Call Date: Nov 1985, Gray's Inn
Pupil Master
Qualifications: [LLB]

HICKLAND MISS MARGARET

Young Street Chambers
38 Young Street, Manchester M3 3FT,
Telephone: 0161 833 0489
E-mail: clerks@young-st-chambers.com
Call Date: July 1988, Gray's Inn
Qualifications: [LLB (Wales)]

HICKLING MISS SALLY BARBARA

1 Paper Buildings
1st Floor, Temple, London EC4Y 7EP,
Telephone: 0171 353 3728/4953
Call Date: Oct 1993, Gray's Inn
Qualifications: [M.Soc.Sci (B'ham)]

HICKMAN MISS CLAIRE LOUISE

1 Dr Johnson's Buildings
Ground Floor, Temple, London
EC4Y 7AX, Telephone: 0171 353 9328
E-mail:OneDr.Johnsons@btinternet.com
Call Date: Nov 1994, Inner Temple
Qualifications: [LLB (Hons) (Lond)]

HICKMAN DEREK JOHN

Call Date: July 1982, Middle Temple
Pupil Master
Qualifications: [MA (Oxon)]

HICKMAN MRS SALLY LOUISE

8 Fountain Court
Steelhouse Lane, Birmingham B4 6DR,
Telephone: 0121 236 5514/5
E-mail: clerks@no8chambers.co.uk
Call Date: Nov 1987, Middle Temple
Qualifications: [LLB (Hons)]

HICKMET RICHARD SALADIN

South Western Chambers
Melville House, 12 Middle Street,
Taunton, Somerset, TA1 1SH,
Telephone: 01823 331919 (24 hrs)
E-mail: barclerk@clara.net
Call Date: July 1974, Inner Temple
Pupil Master
Qualifications: [BA]

HICKS MARTIN LESLIE ARTHUR

1 Hare Court
Ground Floor, Temple, London
EC4Y 7BE, Telephone: 0171 353 3982/
5324
Call Date: May 1977, Inner Temple
Pupil Master
Qualifications: [LLB (Lond)]

HICKS MICHAEL CHARLES

19 Old Buildings
Lincoln's Inn, London WC2A 3UP,
Telephone: 0171 405 2001
E-mail: clerks@oldbuildingsip.com
Call Date: Nov 1976, Inner Temple
Pupil Master
Qualifications: [BA (Cantab)]

Fax: 0171 405 0001; DX: 397 London,
Chancery Lane;
Other comms: E-mail
clerks@oldbuildingsip.com; URL: http://
www.oldbuildingsip.com

Types of work: Competition, Copyright, EC
and competition law, Entertainment, Film,
cable, TV, Franchising, Intellectual property, Patents, Trademarks

Awards and memberships: Intellectual Property
Bar Association; Chancery Bar Association

Reported Cases: *PCR Ltd v Dow Jones*, [1998]
FSR 170, 1997. Confidential information,
copyright and fair dealing.
Designers Guild v Russell Williams, [1998]
FSR 275, 1997. Textile copyright infringe-
ment.
Roger Bance's Application, [1996] RPC
667, 1996. Copyright licence of right case.
BL v Armstrong, [1986] AC 577, 1986.
Spare parts monopoly case.
BT v One in a Million, [1999] FSR 1, 1998.
Internet trademarks case.

HICKS WILLIAM DAVID ANTHONY QC (1995)

1 Serjeants' Inn
4th Floor, Temple, London EC4Y 1NH,
Telephone: 0171 583 1355
E-mail: clerks@serjeants-inn.co.uk
Call Date: July 1975, Inner Temple
Qualifications: [MA (Cantab)]

HIDDLESTON ADAM WALLACE

17 Carlton Crescent
Southampton SO15 2XR,
Telephone: 023 8032 0320/0823 2003
E-mail: greg@jg17cc.co.uk
Call Date: Oct 1990, Inner Temple
Qualifications: [LLB (Newc)]

HIGGINS ADRIAN JOHN

13 King's Bench Walk
1st Floor, Temple, London EC4Y 7EN,
Telephone: 0171 353 7204
E-mail: clerks@13kbw.law.co.uk
King's Bench Chambers
32 Beaumont Street, Oxford OX1 2NP,
Telephone: 01865 311066
E-mail: clerks@kbc-oxford.law.co.uk
Call Date: Oct 1990, Lincoln's Inn
Qualifications: [BA (Oxon)]

HIGGINS ANTHONY PAUL

Goldsmith Building
1st Floor, Temple, London EC4Y 7BL,
Telephone: 0171 353 7881
E-mail:clerks@goldsmith-building.law.co.uk
Call Date: Nov 1978, Gray's Inn
Qualifications: [BA (Oxon), LLM]

HIGGINS PAUL ANDREW

Old Colony House
6 South King Street, Manchester M2 6DQ,
Telephone: 0161 834 4364
Call Date: Mar 1996, Lincoln's Inn
Qualifications: [BA (Hons) , BA
(Hons)(Oxon)]

HIGGINS RUPERT JAMES HALE

Littman Chambers
12 Gray's Inn Square, London WC1R 5JP,
Telephone: 020 7404 4866
E-mail: admin@littmanchambers.com
Call Date: Oct 1991, Inner Temple
Pupil Master
Qualifications: [BA (Cantab)]

HIGGINSON MISS LUCY VERNON MARIE

33 Park Place
Cardiff CF1 3BA,
Telephone: 02920 233313
Call Date: Oct 1992, Gray's Inn
Qualifications: [LLB (Hons)(Cardiff)]

HIGGINSON PETER ST GEORGE

Dr Johnson's Chambers
Two Dr Johnson's Buildings, Temple,
London EC4Y 7AY,
Telephone: 0171 353 4716
E-mail: clerks@2djb.freeserve.co.uk
Call Date: July 1975, Lincoln's Inn
Pupil Master
Qualifications: [BA (Queens Canada)]

HIGGINSON TIMOTHY NICHOLAS BENNETT

Littleton Chambers
3 King's Bench Walk North, Temple,
London EC4Y 7HR,
Telephone: 0171 797 8600
E-mail:clerks@littletonchambers.co.uk
Call Date: Nov 1977, Inner Temple
Qualifications: [LLB]

HIGGO JUSTIN BERESFORD

Serle Court Chambers
6 New Square, Lincoln's Inn, London
WC2A 3QS, Telephone: 0171 242 6105
E-mail: clerks@serlecourt.co.uk
Call Date: Feb 1995, Gray's Inn
Qualifications: [BA (Oxon)]

HIGGS BRIAN JAMES QC (1974)

5 King's Bench Walk
Temple, London EC4Y 7DN,
Telephone: 0171 353 5638
Call Date: Nov 1955, Gray's Inn
Recorder

HIGGS JONATHAN ALEXANDER CAMERON

5 King's Bench Walk
Temple, London EC4Y 7DN,
Telephone: 0171 353 5638
Call Date: Nov 1987, Middle Temple
Recorder
Qualifications: [BA]

HIGGS ROLAND FRANCIS

11 Stone Buildings
Lincoln's Inn, London WC2A 3TG,
Telephone: +44 (0)207 831 6381
E-mail:clerks@11StoneBuildings.law.co.uk
Call Date: Feb 1984, Gray's Inn
Pupil Master
Qualifications: [MA (Oxon)]

HIGHAM JOHN ARTHUR QC (1992)

Call Date: July 1976, Lincoln's Inn
Qualifications: [MA, LLM (Cantab)]

HIGHAM PAUL JOSEPH FRANCIS

1 Pump Court
Lower Ground Floor, Temple, London
EC4Y 7AB, Telephone: 0171 583 2012/
353 4341
E-mail: [name]@1pumpcourt.co.uk
Call Date: Feb 1982, Gray's Inn
Pupil Master
Qualifications: [MA (Cantab)]

HIGNETT RICHARD JAMES

St Albans Chambers
Dolphin Lodge, Dolphin Yard, Holywell
Hill, St Albans, Herts, AL1 1EX,
Telephone: 01727 843383
Call Date: Nov 1995, Inner Temple
Qualifications: [BA (Keele)]

HIGSON-SMITH MISS GILLIAN MARY

Gray's Inn Chambers
5th Floor, Gray's Inn, London WC1R 5JA,
Telephone: 0171 404 1111
Call Date: Nov 1973, Inner Temple
Pupil Master

HILDER MISS CAROLYN HAYLEY-JANE

3 Fountain Court
Steelhouse Lane, Birmingham B4 6DR,
Telephone: 0121 236 5854
Call Date: Oct 1991, Lincoln's Inn
Qualifications: [BA (Cambs)]

HILDYARD MISS MARIANNA CATHERINE THOROTON

4 Brick Court
Temple, London EC4Y 9AD,
Telephone: 0171 797 8910
E-mail: medhurst@dial.pipex.com
Call Date: Nov 1977, Inner Temple
Pupil Master

HILDYARD ROBERT HENRY THOROTON QC (1994)

4 Stone Buildings
Ground Floor, Lincoln's Inn, London
WC2A 3XT, Telephone: 0171 242 5524
E-mail:clerks@4stonebuildings.law.co.uk
Call Date: Nov 1977, Inner Temple
Qualifications: [BA (Oxon)]

HILKEN MS ALICE MARY

1 Pump Court
Lower Ground Floor, Temple, London
EC4Y 7AB, Telephone: 0171 583 2012/
353 4341
E-mail: [name]@1pumpcourt.co.uk
Call Date: Nov 1994, Middle Temple
Qualifications: [BA (Hons)]

HILL ANDREW CHARLES ROWLAND

8 King's Bench Walk
2nd Floor, Temple, London EC4Y 7DU,
Telephone: 0171 797 8888
Harrow on the Hill Chambers
60 High Street, Harrow-on-the-Hill,
Middlesex, HA1 3LL,
Telephone: 0181 423 7444
8 King's Bench Walk North
1 Park Square East, Leeds LS1 2NE,
Telephone: 0113 2439797
Call Date: 1982, Gray's Inn
Qualifications: [LLB]

HILL CAMERON ANGUS

Lancaster Building
77 Deansgate, Manchester M3 2BW,
Telephone: 0161 661 4444/0171 649 9872
E-mail: sandra@lbnipc.com
Call Date: Oct 1997, Middle Temple
Qualifications: [LLM, LLB, Maitrise
(Sorbonne)]

HILL MISS CANDIDA TAMARA LOUISE

18 Red Lion Court
(Off Fleet Street), London EC4A 3EB,
Telephone: 0171 520 6000
E-mail: chambers@18rlc.co.uk
Call Date: Oct 1990, Middle Temple
Qualifications: [LLB (Hons)]

HILL MISS CAROL JANE

22 Old Buildings
Lincoln's Inn, London WC2A 3UJ,
Telephone: 0171 831 0222
Call Date: Nov 1980, Gray's Inn
Pupil Master
Qualifications: [LLB B'ham]

Fax: +44(0)171 831 2239; DX: 201
London;
Other comms: E-mail janehill2@aol.com.;
URL: http://www.janehill.com

Types of work: Information technology

Circuit: South Eastern

Awards and memberships: American Bar Association; International Bar Association

HILL MISS CATHERINE LOUISE

30 Park Square
Leeds LS1 2PF, Telephone: 0113 2436388
E-mail: clerks@30parksquare.co.uk
Call Date: July 1988, Gray's Inn
Qualifications: [BA (Hons)(Dunelm)]

HILL MS ELEANOR MARY HENRIETTA

Cloisters
1 Pump Court, Temple, London
EC4Y 7AA, Telephone: 0171 827 4000
E-mail: clerks@cloisters.com
Call Date: 1997, Inner Temple
Qualifications: [BA (Cantab)]

HILL (ELIOT) MICHAEL QC (1979)

23 Essex Street
London WC2R 3AS,
Telephone: 0171 413 0353/836 8366
E-mail:clerks@essexstreet23.demon.co.uk
Call Date: June 1958, Gray's Inn
Qualifications: [MA (Oxon)]

HILL GREGORY JOHN SUMMERS

The Chambers of Leolin Price CBE, QC
10 Old Square, Lincoln's Inn, London
WC2A 3SU, Telephone: 0171 405 0758
Call Date: July 1972, Lincoln's Inn
Pupil Master
Qualifications: [MA, BCL (Oxon)]

HILL JAMES MICHAEL

Fountain Chambers
Cleveland Business Centre, 1 Watson
Street, Middlesbrough TS1 2RQ,
Telephone: 01642 804040
E-mail:fountainchambers@onyxnet.co.uk
Call Date: July 1984, Inner Temple
Pupil Master
Qualifications: [LLB (Manch)]

HILL JASON

Bank House Chambers
Old Bank House, Hartshead, Sheffield
S1 2EL, Telephone: 0114 2751223
Call Date: Oct 1995, Lincoln's Inn
Qualifications: [BSc (Hons)(Sheff)]

HILL MAX BENJAMIN ROWLAND

18 Red Lion Court
(Off Fleet Street), London EC4A 3EB,
Telephone: 0171 520 6000
E-mail: chambers@18rlc.co.uk
Call Date: Nov 1987, Middle Temple
Pupil Master
Qualifications: [BA (Oxon)]

HILL NICHOLAS IAN

No. 6
6 Park Square, Leeds LS1 2LW,
Telephone: 0113 2459763
E-mail: chambers@no6.co.uk
Call Date: Oct 1993, Lincoln's Inn
Qualifications: [BA (Hons)]

HILL NICHOLAS MARK

Pump Court Chambers
Upper Ground Floor, 3 Pump Court,
Temple, London EC4Y 7AJ,
Telephone: 0171 353 0711
E-mail: clerks@3pumpcourt.com
Pump Court Chambers
31 Southgate Street, Winchester
SO23 9EE, Telephone: 01962 868161
E-mail: clerks@3pumpcourt.com
Pump Court Chambers
5 Temple Chambers, Temple Street,
Swindon SN1 1SQ,
Telephone: 01793 539899
E-mail: clerks@3pumpcourt.com
Call Date: July 1987, Middle Temple
Pupil Master
Qualifications: [LLB (Lond), AKC, LLM]

Fax: 0171 353 3319; DX: 362 Chancery
Lane;
Other comms: E-mail
mark.hill8@virgin.net

Other professional qualifications: LLM (Common
Law) AKC

Types of work: Administrative, Ecclesiastical,
Medical negligence, Personal injury,
Planning, Professional negligence, Town
and country planning

Circuit: Western

Awards and memberships: Research Fellow, Centre for Law and Religion, Cardiff Law School; Formerly visiting fellow of Emmanuel College Cambridge; Member of Professional Negligence Bar Association and Personal Injury Bar Association

Other professional experience: Chancellor of the Diocese of Chichester; Deputy Chancellor of the Diocese of Winchester; Case Notes editor, *Ecclesiastical Law Journal*; Member of Legal Aid Commission of the General Synod of the Church of England

Publications: *Ecclesiastical Law*, 1995; *English Canon Law* (editor), 1998; *Professional Duties in the Instruction of Experts*, 1998

Reported Cases: *Tribe v Tribe*, [1996] Ch 107 (CA), 1995. Illegality in contracts. Doctrine of *ex turpi causa*.
National Employers Mutual Insurance Co v Jones, [1990] 1 AC 24 (HL), 1989. Successive ownership of stolen goods. Application of *nemo dat* principle.
Pacific Associates v Baxter, [1990] 1 QB 993, 1989. Duty of care of surveyor in building cases.
Re St Peter, Oundle, [1997] 4 Ecc LJ 163, 1996. Erection of human likenesses in parish church.

HILL PEREGRINE EDWARD

8 Stone Buildings
Lincoln's Inn, London WC2A 3TA,
Telephone: 0171 831 9881
E-mail: alanl@8stonebuildings.law.uk
Call Date: Nov 1995, Inner Temple
Qualifications: [BA (Manc)]

HILL PIERS NICHOLAS

37 Park Square Chambers
37 Park Square, Leeds LS1 2NY,
Telephone: 0113 2439422
E-mail: chambers@no37.co.uk
Call Date: July 1987, Inner Temple
Qualifications: [LLB (Hull)]

HILL RAYMOND

Monckton Chambers
4 Raymond Buildings, Gray's Inn, London WC1R 5BP, Telephone: 0171 405 7211
E-mail: chambers@monckton.co.uk
Call Date: Oct 1992, Lincoln's Inn
Qualifications: [BA(Hons)]

HILL RICHARD GEOFFREY

4 Stone Buildings
Ground Floor, Lincoln's Inn, London WC2A 3XT, Telephone: 0171 242 5524
E-mail:clerks@4stonebuildings.law.co.uk
Call Date: Oct 1993, Gray's Inn
Qualifications: [BA (Cantab)]

HILL ROBERT DOUGLAS

Pump Court Chambers
31 Southgate Street, Winchester
SO23 9EE, Telephone: 01962 868161
E-mail: clerks@3pumpcourt.com
Pump Court Chambers
Upper Ground Floor, 3 Pump Court,
Temple, London EC4Y 7AJ,
Telephone: 0171 353 0711
E-mail: clerks@3pumpcourt.com
Pump Court Chambers
5 Temple Chambers, Temple Street,
Swindon SN1 1SQ,
Telephone: 01793 539899
E-mail: clerks@3pumpcourt.com
Call Date: July 1980, Gray's Inn
Pupil Master
Qualifications: [LLB (Wales)]

HILL THOMAS PATRICK JAMES

4-5 Gray's Inn Square
Ground Floor, Gray's Inn, London
WC1R 5JP, Telephone: 0171 404 5252
E-mail:chambers@4-5graysinnsquare.co.uk
Call Date: July 1988, Lincoln's Inn
Qualifications: [MA (Hons) (Cantab)]

HILL TIMOTHY JOHN

4 Field Court
Gray's Inn, London WC1R 5EA,
Telephone: 0171 440 6900
E-mail: chambers@4fieldcourt.co.uk
Call Date: Oct 1990, Middle Temple
Pupil Master
Qualifications: [LLB (Lond), DLS (Cantab), BCL (Oxon)]

D

HILL-BAKER JEREMY ROBERT

No. 6
6 Park Square, Leeds LS1 2LW,
Telephone: 0113 2459763
E-mail: chambers@no6.co.uk
Call Date: July 1983, Inner Temple
Qualifications: [LLB Leeds]

HILL-SMITH ALEXANDER GEORGE LEVANDER

12 King's Bench Walk
Temple, London EC4Y 7EL,
Telephone: 0171 583 0811
E-mail: chambers@12kbw.co.uk
Call Date: July 1978, Gray's Inn
Pupil Master
Qualifications: [LLB, MA (Cantab)]

HILLEN JOHN MALCOLM

5 King's Bench Walk
Temple, London EC4Y 7DN,
Telephone: 0171 353 5638
Call Date: Nov 1976, Middle Temple
Pupil Master
Qualifications: [MA (Oxon)]

HILLIARD NICHOLAS RICHARD MAYBURY

6 King's Bench Walk
Ground Floor, Temple, London
EC4Y 7DR, Telephone: 0171 583 0410
E-mail: worsley@6kbw.freeserve.co.uk
Call Date: July 1981, Middle Temple
Pupil Master
Qualifications: [MA (Oxon)]

HILLIARD MISS (PIERS) ALEXANDRA

3/4 South Square
Gray's Inn, London WC1R 5HP,
Telephone: 0171 696 9900
E-mail: clerks@southsquare.com
Call Date: Nov 1987, Middle Temple
Qualifications: [LLB (Lond)]

HILLIARD SPENSER RODNEY

Lamb Building
Ground Floor, Temple, London
EC4Y 7AS, Telephone: 020 7797 7788
E-mail: lamb.building@link.org
Call Date: Nov 1975, Middle Temple
Pupil Master
Qualifications: [LLB]

HILLIER ANDREW CHARLES

11 King's Bench Walk
Temple, London EC4Y 7EQ,
Telephone: 0171 632 8500/583 0610
E-mail: clerksroom@11kbw.com
Call Date: July 1972, Gray's Inn
Pupil Master
Qualifications: [BA]

HILLIER MRS NANCY ROSE

65-67 King Street
Leicester LE1 6RP,
Telephone: 0116 2547710
Call Date: July 1984, Inner Temple
Qualifications: [LEU (LLB)]

HILLIER NICOLAS PETER

9 Gough Square
London EC4A 3DE,
Telephone: 020 7832 0500
E-mail: clerks@9goughsq.co.uk
Call Date: July 1982, Inner Temple
Pupil Master
Qualifications: [LLB (So'ton)]

HILLIS JOHN

Bank House Chambers
Old Bank House, Hartshead, Sheffield
S1 2EL, Telephone: 0114 2751223
Call Date: July 1982, Gray's Inn
Pupil Master
Qualifications: [LLB (Sheff)]

HILLMAN BASIL

4 King's Bench Walk
2nd Floor, Temple, London EC4Y 7DL,
Telephone: 020 7353 3581
E-mail: clerks@4kbw.co.uk
Call Date: Nov 1968, Gray's Inn
Qualifications: [MA (MOD)]

HILLMAN ROGER JOHN

Exchange Chambers
Pearl Assurance House, Derby Square,
Liverpool L2 9XX,
Telephone: 0151 236 7747
E-mail:exchangechambers@btinternet.com
Call Date: July 1983, Gray's Inn
Qualifications: [LLB (L'Pool)]

HILLS TIMOTHY JAMES

Albion Chambers
Broad Street, Bristol BS1 1DR,
Telephone: 0117 9272144
Call Date: July 1968, Lincoln's Inn
Pupil Master

HILSDON JAMES SPENCER

Cobden House Chambers
19 Quay Street, Manchester M3 3HN,
Telephone: 0161 833 6000
E-mail: clerks@cobden.co.uk
Call Date: Nov 1993, Lincoln's Inn
Qualifications: [MA (Hons)]

HILTON ALAN JOHN HOWARD QC (1990)

Hollis Whiteman Chambers
3rd Floor, Queen Elizabeth Bldg, Temple,
London EC4Y 9BS,
Telephone: 020 7583 5766
E-mail:barristers@holliswhiteman.co.uk
Call Date: Nov 1964, Middle Temple
Recorder
Qualifications: [LLB (Manch)]

HILTON MS SAISAMPAN

95A Chancery Lane
London WC2A 1DT,
Telephone: 0171 405 3101
Call Date: Oct 1994, Gray's Inn
Qualifications: [BA, MA]

HILTON SIMON JONATHAN

40 King Street
Manchester M2 6BA,
Telephone: 0161 832 9082
E-mail: clerks@40kingstreet.co.uk

The Chambers of Philip Raynor QC
5 Park Place, Leeds LS1 2RU,
Telephone: 0113 242 1123
Call Date: Nov 1987, Gray's Inn
Pupil Master
Qualifications: [BA (Oxon)]

HIMSWORTH MISS EMMA KATHERINE

One Essex Court
Ground Floor, Temple, London
EC4Y 9AR, Telephone: 020 7583 2000
E-mail: clerks@oneessexcourt.co.uk
Call Date: Oct 1993, Gray's Inn
Qualifications: [BSc (Edin), Dip Law, (City),
Dip EC Law, (Kings)]

HINCHCLIFFE DR DOREEN

2 Paper Buildings
1st Floor, Temple, London EC4Y 7ET,
Telephone: 020 7556 5500
E-mail: clerks@2pbbarristers.co.uk
Gray's Inn Chambers
5th Floor, Gray's Inn, London WC1R 5JA,
Telephone: 0171 404 1111
Call Date: Nov 1953, Gray's Inn
Qualifications: [LLB, PhD]

HINCHLIFF BENJAMIN JOHN

1 Brick Court
1st Floor, Temple, London EC4Y 9BY,
Telephone: 0171 353 8845
E-mail: clerks@1brickcourt.co.uk
Call Date: Nov 1992, Gray's Inn
Qualifications: [MA (Oxon)]

HINCHLIFFE PHILIP NICHOLAS QC (1999)

Chambers of John Hand QC
9 St John Street, Manchester M3 4DN,
Telephone: 0161 955 9000
E-mail: ninesjs@gconnect.com
Call Date: 1980, Middle Temple
Qualifications: [LLB (Manch)]

D

HINCHLIFFE THOMAS RICHARD

3 New Square
Lincoln's Inn, London WC2A 3RS,
Telephone: 0171 405 1111
E-mail: 3newsquareip@lineone.net
Call Date: 1997, Middle Temple
Qualifications: [BA (Hons)(Oxon), CPE
(Lond)]

HIND KENNETH HARVARD

3 Temple Gardens
2nd Floor, Temple, London EC4Y 9AU,
Telephone: 0171 583 1155
Call Date: July 1973, Gray's Inn
Pupil Master
Qualifications: [LLB (Hons)]

HINDLE MISS RACHEL FRANCES

Lamb Building
Ground Floor, Temple, London
EC4Y 7AS, Telephone: 020 7797 7788
E-mail: lamb.building@link.org
Call Date: Oct 1990, Inner Temple
Qualifications: [LLB]

HINDMARSH MISS ELIZABETH

Plowden Buildings
2nd Floor, 2 Plowden Buildings, Middle
Temple Lane, London EC4Y 9BU,
Telephone: 0171 583 0808
E-mail: bar@plowdenbuildings.co.uk
Call Date: July 1974, Inner Temple
Qualifications: [BA (Dunelm)]

HINDS ORIEL GLENVERE

66 Worthington Road
Surbiton, Kingston-Upon-Thames, Surrey,
KT6,
Call Date: July 1988, Inner Temple
Qualifications: [LLB]

HINE CHARLES RODERICK JOHN

King's Bench Chambers
Wellington House, 175 Holdenhurst Road,
Bournemouth, Dorset, BH8 8DQ,
Telephone: 01202 250025
E-mail: chambers@kingsbench.co.uk
Call Date: Nov 1985, Gray's Inn
Qualifications: [B.Com (B'ham), Dip in Law,
Cert Ed]

HINES JAMES PHILIP

3 Raymond Buildings
Gray's Inn, London WC1R 5BH,
Telephone: 020 7831 3833
E-mail:chambers@threeraymond.demon.co.u
k
Call Date: July 1982, Gray's Inn
Pupil Master
Qualifications: [BA]

HINGSTON MS THERESA CLOTHILDE

**1 Gray's Inn Square, Chambers of the
Baroness Scotland of Asthal QC**
1st Floor, London WC1R 5AG,
Telephone: 0171 405 3000
E-mail: clerks@onegrays.demon.co.uk
Call Date: July 1978, Inner Temple

HINKS FRANK PETER

Serle Court Chambers
6 New Square, Lincoln's Inn, London
WC2A 3QS, Telephone: 0171 242 6105
E-mail: clerks@serlecourt.co.uk
Call Date: July 1973, Lincoln's Inn
Pupil Master
Qualifications: [MA, BCL (Oxon)]

HINTON NEIL PEARSE

King's Bench Chambers
Wellington House, 175 Holdenhurst Road,
Bournemouth, Dorset, BH8 8DQ,
Telephone: 01202 250025
E-mail: chambers@kingsbench.co.uk
Call Date: Nov 1997, Lincoln's Inn
Qualifications: [BA (Hons)(Nott'm)]

HIORNS ROGER MARTIN FAIRCHILD

9 Gough Square
London EC4A 3DE,
Telephone: 020 7832 0500
E-mail: clerks@9goughsq.co.uk
Call Date: July 1983, Middle Temple
Pupil Master
Qualifications: [LLB (B'ham)]

HIPKIN JOHN LESLIE

Iscoed Chambers
86 St Helen's Road, Swansea, West
Glamorgan, SA1 4BQ,
Telephone: 01792 652988/9/330
Call Date: Nov 1989, Gray's Inn
Pupil Master
Qualifications: [LLB [Manch]]

HIRST JONATHAN WILLIAM QC (1990)

Brick Court Chambers
7-8 Essex Street, London WC2R 3LD,
Telephone: 0171 379 3550
E-mail: [surname]@brickcourt.co.uk
Call Date: July 1975, Inner Temple
Qualifications: [MA (Cantab)]

HIRST SIMON DAVID

Wilberforce Chambers
7 Bishop Lane, Hull, East Yorkshire,
HU1 1PA, Telephone: 01482 323264
E-mail: clerks@hullbar.demon.co.uk
Call Date: Oct 1993, Lincoln's Inn
Qualifications: [LLB (Hons)(Hull)]

HIRST WILLIAM TIMOTHY JOHN

Park Court Chambers
16 Park Place, Leeds LS1 2SJ,
Telephone: 0113 2433277
Call Date: Nov 1970, Inner Temple
Recorder
Qualifications: [BA (Oxon), IDIL (German)]

HISLOP DAVID SEYMOUR

Doughty Street Chambers
11 Doughty Street, London WC1N 2PG,
Telephone: 0171 404 1313
E-mail:enquiries@doughtystreet.co.uk
Call Date: Feb 1989, Gray's Inn
Pupil Master
Qualifications: [LLB (Auckland)]

HITCHCOCK MS PATRICIA ANN

Cloisters
1 Pump Court, Temple, London
EC4Y 7AA, Telephone: 0171 827 4000
E-mail: clerks@cloisters.com
Call Date: Nov 1988, Inner Temple
Pupil Master
Qualifications: [BA (Oxon)]

HITCHCOCK RICHARD GUY

35 Essex Street
Temple, London WC2R 3AR,
Telephone: 0171 353 6381
E-mail: derek_jenkins@link.org
Call Date: Nov 1989, Gray's Inn
Pupil Master
Qualifications: [BA [Oxon]]

HITCHCOCK TIMOTHY JOHN

5 King's Bench Walk
Temple, London EC4Y 7DN,
Telephone: 0171 353 5638
Call Date: Nov 1986, Inner Temple
Pupil Master
Qualifications: [BA(Durham)]

HITCHEN JOHN DAVID

No. 6
6 Park Square, Leeds LS1 2LW,
Telephone: 0113 2459763
E-mail: chambers@no6.co.uk
Call Date: June 1961, Lincoln's Inn
Pupil Master, Recorder
Qualifications: [BA (Oxon)]

HITCHING MISS ISABEL JOY

5 Fountain Court
Steelhouse Lane, Birmingham B4 6DR,
Telephone: 0121 606 0500
E-mail:clerks@5fountaincourt.law.co.uk
Call Date: Oct 1992, Middle Temple
Qualifications: [BA(Hons)(Oxon),
BCL(Oxon)]

HITCHMOUGH ANDREW JOHN

Pump Court Tax Chambers
16 Bedford Row, London WC1R 4EB,
Telephone: 0171 414 8080
Call Date: Oct 1991, Inner Temple
Pupil Master
Qualifications: [LLB (So'ton)]

HOARE GREGORY BLAKE

Martins Building
2nd Floor, No 4 Water Street, Liverpool
L2 3SP, Telephone: 0151 236 5818/4919
Call Date: Nov 1992, Gray's Inn
Qualifications: [LLB]

HOBBS MISS EMMA-JANE

1 Temple Gardens
1st Floor, Temple, London EC4Y 9BB,
Telephone: 0171 583 1315/353 0407
E-mail: clerks@1templegardens.co.uk
Call Date: Oct 1996, Gray's Inn
Qualifications: [BA (Bris)]

HOBBS GEOFFREY WILLIAM QC (1991)

One Essex Court
Ground Floor, Temple, London
EC4Y 9AR, Telephone: 020 7583 2000
E-mail: clerks@oneessexcourt.co.uk
Call Date: July 1977, Inner Temple
Qualifications: [LLB (So'ton)]

HOBBS MS NAOMI JOSEPHINE

Claremont Chambers
26 Waterloo Road, Wolverhampton
WV1 4BL, Telephone: 01902 426222
Call Date: Oct 1993, Gray's Inn
Qualifications: [LLB]

HOBHOUSE MS HELEN ROSAMUND

Farrar's Building
Temple, London EC4Y 7BD,
Telephone: 0171 583 9241
E-mail:chambers@farrarsbuilding.co.uk
Call Date: Oct 1990, Inner Temple
Qualifications: [B.Soc Sci, Dip Law]

HOBSON MISS HEATHER FIONA

Queen's Chambers
5 John Dalton Street, Manchester M2 6ET,
Telephone: 0161 834 6875/4738
Queens Chambers
4 Camden Place, Preston PR1 3JL,
Telephone: 01772 828300
Call Date: Nov 1987, Lincoln's Inn
Qualifications: [LLB (Hons) (Lond)]

HOBSON JOHN GRAHAM

4-5 Gray's Inn Square
Ground Floor, Gray's Inn, London
WC1R 5JP, Telephone: 0171 404 5252
E-mail:chambers@4-5graysinnsquare.co.uk
Call Date: July 1980, Inner Temple
Pupil Master, Assistant Recorder
Qualifications: [LLM (Cantab)]

HOBSON MISS SALLY ANNE

Fenners Chambers
8-12 Priestgate, Peterborough PE1 1JA,
Telephone: 01733 562030
E-mail: clerks@fennerschambers.co.uk
Fenners Chambers
3 Madingley Road, Cambridge CB3 0EE,
Telephone: 01223 368761
E-mail: clerks@fennerschambers.co.uk
Call Date: 1991, Inner Temple
Qualifications: [LLB, LLM]

HOCHBERG DANIEL ALAN

9 Old Square
Ground Floor, Lincoln's Inn, London
WC2A 3SR, Telephone: 0171 405 4682
E-mail: chambers@9oldsquare.co.uk
Call Date: July 1982, Lincoln's Inn
Pupil Master
Qualifications: [MA (Oxon)]

HOCHHAUSER ANDREW ROMAIN QC (1997)

Essex Court Chambers
24 Lincoln's Inn Fields, London
WC2A 3ED, Telephone: 0171 813 8000
E-mail:clerksroom@essexcourt-chambers.co.uk
Call Date: July 1977, Middle Temple
Qualifications: [LLB (Bris), LLM (Lond)]

HOCKADAY MISS ANNIE

3 Verulam Buildings
London WC1R 5NT,
Telephone: 0171 831 8441
E-mail: clerks@3verulam.co.uk
Call Date: Oct 1990, Gray's Inn
Pupil Master
Qualifications: [MA (Cantab), LLM Commercial, (Lond)]

HOCKMAN STEPHEN ALEXANDER QC (1990)

6 Pump Court
1st Floor, Temple, London EC4Y 7AR,
Telephone: 0171 797 8400
E-mail: clerks@6pumpcourt.co.uk
6-8 Mill Street
Maidstone, Kent, ME15 6XH,
Telephone: 01622 688094
E-mail: annexe@6pumpcourt.co.uk
Call Date: July 1970, Middle Temple

Recorder
Qualifications: [MA (Cantab)]

Fax: 0171 797 8401;
Out of hours telephone: 07775 894862;
DX: 293 LDE;
Other comms: E-mail
StephenHockman@6PumpCourt.co.uk;
URL: http://www.qc@shed31.demon.co.uk

Other professional qualifications: MA (Cantab)

Types of work: Administrative, Common law (general), Crime, Crime – corporate fraud, Environment, Local government, Medical negligence, Parliamentary, Personal injury, Planning, Professional negligence, Town and country planning

Circuit: South Eastern

Languages spoken: French

Publications: *Blackstone's Planning Practice*, May 1999

Reported Cases: *Lowsley v Forbes*, [1998] 3 WLR 501, 1998. Major House of Lords decision on limitation period for enforcement of judgments.
Waddell & Ors v Royal Borough of Kensington & Chelsea, (1999) *The Times*, 30 April, 1999. First legal challange to designation of 'red routes' in London.
R v London Borough of Camden ex parte Cran & Ors, [1995] RTR 346, 1995. Challange to parking scheme under road traffic regulations.
R v Rook, [1993] 97 Cr App R 327, 1992. Leading decision on *mens rea* in homicide.

HOCKTON ANDREW IAN CALLINAN

Chambers of Kieran Coonan QC
Ground Floor, 6 Pump Court, Temple, London EC4Y 7AR,
Telephone: 0171 583 6013/2510
E-mail: clerks@6-pumpcourt.law.co.uk
Call Date: Nov 1984, Middle Temple
Pupil Master
Qualifications: [BA (Oxon), Dip Law]

HODES MISS ANGELA EVE

Lamb Building
Ground Floor, Temple, London
EC4Y 7AS, Telephone: 020 7797 7788
E-mail: lamb.building@link.org
Call Date: Nov 1979, Middle Temple
Pupil Master
Qualifications: [BA]

HODGE DAVID RALPH QC (1997)

9 Old Square
Ground Floor, Lincoln's Inn, London
WC2A 3SR, Telephone: 0171 405 4682
E-mail: chambers@9oldsquare.co.uk
Call Date: July 1979, Inner Temple
Qualifications: [BA, BCL (Oxon)]

HODGES MISS VICTORIA LESLEY

St Mary's Chambers
50 High Pavement, Lace Market,
Nottingham NG1 1HW,
Telephone: 0115 9503503
E-mail: clerks@smc.law.co.uk
Call Date: July 1980, Gray's Inn
Qualifications: [LLB (B'ham)]

HODGKIN HARRY JOHN

South Western Chambers
Melville House, 12 Middle Street,
Taunton, Somerset, TA1 1SH,
Telephone: 01823 331919 (24 hrs)
E-mail: barclerk@clara.net
1 Mitre Court Buildings
Temple, London EC4Y 7BS,
Telephone: 0171 797 7070
E-mail: clerks@1mcb.com
Call Date: July 1983, Middle Temple
Pupil Master
Qualifications: [LLB]

HODGKINSON JOHN ROBERT

1 Fountain Court
Steelhouse Lane, Birmingham B4 6DR,
Telephone: 0121 236 5721
Call Date: Nov 1968, Inner Temple
Pupil Master
Qualifications: [MA (Cantab)]

D

HODGKINSON STEPHEN PETER GEORGE

New Court
Temple, London EC4Y 9BE,
Telephone: 0171 583 5123/0510
Call Date: 1997, Inner Temple
Qualifications: [LLB (London)]

HODGKINSON TRISTRAM PATRICK

5 Pump Court
Ground Floor, Temple, London
EC4Y 7AP, Telephone: 020 7353 2532
E-mail: FivePump@netcomuk.co.uk
Call Date: July 1982, Middle Temple
Qualifications: [LLB,LLM]

Fax: 0171 353 5321;
Out of hours telephone: 0171 622 4680;
DX: LDE 497 Chancery Lane;
Other comms: E-mail
hodglaw@globalnet.co.uk

Types of work: Asset finance, Banking,
Commercial litigation, Consumer credit,
Consumer law, Financial services, Mortgages and borrowers, Professional negligence, Sale and carriage of goods

Circuit: South Eastern

Awards and memberships: Middle Temple
Winston Churchill Prize

Other professional experience: Speaker at legal
conferences and seminars

Languages spoken: French

Publications: *Expert Evidence: Law and Practice* (Sweet & Maxwell), 1990; Various articles in newspapers and legal journals

Reported Cases: *City Mortgage Corporation v
Baptiste*, [1997] CCLR 64, 1997. Consumer
credit – extortionate credit bargain – mortgage possession.
Sparks v Harland, [1997] 1 WLR 143,
1997. Damages for sexual abuse – European Human Rights Convention – limitation – stay of proceedings.
*Swain & Co v Woodchester Lease Finance
(CA)*, [1999] 1 WLR 263, 1998. Consumer
credit – validity of default notice
containing incorrect details – contractual
penalty.
*Carlyle Finance Ltd v Pallas Industrial
Finance (CA)*, [1999] 1 All ER (Comm)
659, 1999. Consumer credit – agency of

dealer – communication of acceptance by
conduct – preliminary bailment. (Recent
cases)

HODGSON MISS ELIZABETH JANE

Ropewalk Chambers
24 The Ropewalk, Nottingham NG1 5EF,
Telephone: 0115 9472581
E-mail: administration@ropewalk co.uk
Call Date: Oct 1993, Gray's Inn
Qualifications: [LLB (L'Pool)]

HODGSON MS JANE

9 Woodhouse Square
Leeds LS3 1AD,
Telephone: 0113 2451986
E-mail: clerks@9woodhouse.co.uk
Call Date: July 1989, Gray's Inn
Qualifications: [BA [Oxon]]

HODGSON JOHN ARNOLD

3 Dr Johnson's Buildings
Ground Floor, Temple, London
EC4Y 7BA, Telephone: 0171 353 4854
E-mail: clerks@3djb.co.uk
Call Date: Feb 1963, Gray's Inn
Qualifications: [LLB (Lond)]

HODGSON MRS MARGARET ANN

Horizon Chambers
95a Chancery Lane, London WC2A 1DT,
Telephone: 0171 242 2440
Call Date: Oct 1996, Lincoln's Inn
Qualifications: [BA (Hons)]

HODGSON MISS MARGARET JULIA

St Ive's Chambers
Whittall Street, Birmingham B4 6DH,
Telephone: 0121 236 0863/5720
E-mail:stives.headofchambers@btinternet.com
Call Date: 1975, Lincoln's Inn
Pupil Master
Qualifications: [LLB (Hons)(Warw)]

HODGSON MARTIN DERRICK

8 King's Bench Walk
2nd Floor, Temple, London EC4Y 7DU,
Telephone: 0171 797 8888

8 King's Bench Walk North
1 Park Square East, Leeds LS1 2NE,
Telephone: 0113 2439797
Call Date: July 1980, Middle Temple
Pupil Master
Qualifications: [BA]

HODGSON RICHARD ANDREW

Design Chambers
30 Fleet Street, London EC4Y 1AA,
Telephone: 0171 353 0747
E-mail: manager@designchambers.co.uk
Call Date: Nov 1980, Inner Temple
Qualifications: [BSc (Eng) (Lond)]

HODGSON TIMOTHY PAUL

8 King Street Chambers
8 King Street, Manchester M2 6AQ,
Telephone: 0161 834 9560
E-mail: eightking@aol.com
Call Date: Nov 1991, Inner Temple
Qualifications: [BA (Victoria, New, Zealand),
BA (Hons) , D.Phil (Oxon), Dip Law
(City)]

HODSON MICHAEL JOHN

New Court Chambers
3 Broad Chare, Newcastle upon Tyne
NE1 3DQ, Telephone: 0191 232 1980
Call Date: Feb 1977, Middle Temple
Pupil Master

HODSON PETER DAVID

**Chambers of Ian Macdonald QC (In
Association with Two Garden Court,
Temple, London)**
Waldorf House, 5 Cooper Street,
Manchester M2 2FW,
Telephone: 0161 236 1840
Call Date: Nov 1994, Inner Temple
Qualifications: [LLB (Hons), Dip CE]

HOFFMAN DAVID ALEXANDER

8 King Street Chambers
8 King Street, Manchester M2 6AQ,
Telephone: 0161 834 9560
E-mail: eightking@aol.com
Call Date: Oct 1997, Lincoln's Inn
Qualifications: [BA (Hons), BCL (Oxon)]

HOFFMAN SIMON PAUL

Iscoed Chambers
86 St Helen's Road, Swansea, West
Glamorgan, SA1 4BQ,
Telephone: 01792 652988/9/330
Call Date: Oct 1997, Lincoln's Inn
Qualifications: [LLB (Hons)(Wales)]

HOFFMANN MISS JOCELYN CLARE

Serle Court Chambers
6 New Square, Lincoln's Inn, London
WC2A 3QS, Telephone: 0171 242 6105
E-mail: clerks@serlecourt.co.uk
Call Date: Oct 1990, Gray's Inn
Qualifications: [BA]

HOFFORD PETER JOHN

Mitre Court Chambers
3rd Floor, Temple, London EC4Y 7BP,
Telephone: 0171 353 9394
E-mail: mitrecourt.com
Call Date: Nov 1979, Gray's Inn
Pupil Master
Qualifications: [BA (Hons) (Wales), Dip Law
(City)]

HOFMEYR STEPHEN MURRAY

S Tomlinson QC
7 King's Bench Walk, Temple, London
EC4Y 7DS, Telephone: 0171 583 0404
E-mail: clerks@7kbw.law.co.uk
Call Date: July 1982, Gray's Inn
Pupil Master
Qualifications: [MA (Oxon), LLB, (Cape
Town), B.Com]

HOGAN ANDREW PETER JOSEPH EDWARD

Ropewalk Chambers
24 The Ropewalk, Nottingham NG1 5EF,
Telephone: 0115 9472581
E-mail: administration@ropewalk co.uk
Call Date: 1996, Inner Temple
Qualifications: [LLB (Bris), LLM (Sussex)]

D

HOGAN MISS EMMA JANE

5 Fountain Court
Steelhouse Lane, Birmingham B4 6DR,
Telephone: 0121 606 0500
E-mail:clerks@5fountaincourt.law.co.uk
Call Date: Oct 1996, Middle Temple
Qualifications: [BA (Hons)(Oxon), CPE
(City)]

HOGARTH ANDREW ALLAN

12 King's Bench Walk
Temple, London EC4Y 7EL,
Telephone: 0171 583 0811
E-mail: chambers@12kbw.co.uk
Call Date: July 1974, Lincoln's Inn
Pupil Master
Qualifications: [MA (Cantab)]

HOGBEN PAUL RAYMOND

Chambers of Paul Hogben
199 Kingsworth Road, Ashford, Kent,
TN23 6NB, Telephone: 01233 645805
Call Date: Feb 1993, Gray's Inn
Qualifications: [LLB]

HOGG THE HON DOUGLAS MARTIN QC (1990)

37 Park Square Chambers
37 Park Square, Leeds LS1 2NY,
Telephone: 0113 2439422
E-mail: chambers@no37.co.uk
Cathedral Chambers (Jan Wood Independent Barristers' Clerk)
1 Maple Road, Exeter, Devon, EX4 1BN,
Telephone: 01392 210900
E-mail:cathedral.chambers@eclipse.co.uk
Call Date: July 1968, Lincoln's Inn
Qualifications: [MA (Oxon)]

HOGG MISS KATHARINE ELIZABETH

1 Crown Office Row
Ground Floor, Temple, London
EC4Y 7HH, Telephone: 0171 797 7500
E-mail: mail@onecrownofficerow.com
Call Date: Oct 1996, Middle Temple
Qualifications: [MA (Hons)(Cantab), CPE
(Westminster)]

HOGGETT ANTHONY JOHN CHRISTOPHER QC (1986)

40 King Street
Manchester M2 6BA,
Telephone: 0161 832 9082
E-mail: clerks@40kingstreet.co.uk
The Chambers of Philip Raynor QC
5 Park Place, Leeds LS1 2RU,
Telephone: 0113 242 1123
Call Date: July 1969, Gray's Inn
Recorder
Qualifications: [MA, LLB, PhD]

HOLBECH CHARLES EDWARD

11 Stone Buildings
Lincoln's Inn, London WC2A 3TG,
Telephone: +44 (0)207 831 6381
E-mail:clerks@11StoneBuildings.law.co.uk
Call Date: July 1988, Lincoln's Inn
Qualifications: [BA (Hons) (Oxon)]

HOLBORN DAVID REGINALD

18 Red Lion Court
(Off Fleet Street), London EC4A 3EB,
Telephone: 0171 520 6000
E-mail: chambers@18rlc.co.uk
Thornwood House
102 New London Road, Chelmsford,
Essex, CM2 0RG,
Telephone: 01245 280880
E-mail: chambers@18rlc.co.uk
Call Date: Oct 1991, Inner Temple
Pupil Master
Qualifications: [LLB (Essex)]

HOLBROOK JON

Two Garden Court
1st Floor, Middle Temple, London
EC4Y 9BL, Telephone: 0171 353 1633
E-mail:barristers@2gardenct.law.co.uk
Call Date: Nov 1991, Inner Temple
Qualifications: [BA (Sheff)]

HOLDEN RICHARD DERRICK JAMES

Littman Chambers
12 Gray's Inn Square, London WC1R 5JP,
Telephone: 020 7404 4866
E-mail: admin@littmanchambers.com
Call Date: 1996, Lincoln's Inn
Qualifications: [BA (Hons)(Oxon)]

HOLDER MISS CLAIRE ALISON

243 Westbourne Grove
London W11 2SE,
Telephone: 0171 229 3819
Call Date: July 1978, Lincoln's Inn
Qualifications: [MA]

HOLDER SIMON MICHAEL

India Buildings Chambers
Water Street, Liverpool L2 0XG,
Telephone: 0151 243 6000
E-mail: clerks@chambers.u-net.com
Call Date: July 1989, Inner Temple
Qualifications: [LLB [Lond]]

HOLDER TERENCE

Colleton Chambers
Powlett House, 34 High Street, Taunton,
Somerset, TA1 3PN,
Telephone: 01823 324252
Colleton Chambers
Colleton Crescent, Exeter, Devon,
EX2 4DG, Telephone: 01392 274898/9
Call Date: Nov 1984, Gray's Inn

HOLDSWORTH JAMES ARTHUR

Two Crown Office Row
Ground Floor, Temple, London
EC4Y 7HJ, Telephone: 020 7797 8100
E-mail: mail@2cor.co.uk, or to individual
barristers at: [barrister's
surname]@2cor.co.uk
Call Date: Feb 1977, Middle Temple
Pupil Master
Qualifications: [MA (Oxon)]

HOLGATE DAVID JOHN QC (1997)

4 Breams Buildings
London EC4A 1AQ,
Telephone: 0171 353 5835/430 1221
E-mail:breams@4breamsbuildings.law.co.uk
Call Date: July 1978, Middle Temple
Qualifications: [BA (Oxon)]

HOLL-ALLEN JONATHAN GUY

3 Serjeants' Inn
London EC4Y 1BQ,
Telephone: 0171 353 5537
E-mail: clerks@3serjeantsinn.com
Call Date: Nov 1990, Inner Temple
Pupil Master
Qualifications: [MA, LLM (Cantab)]

HOLLAND MRS ANNE ROSEMARY

Godolphin Chambers
50 Castle Street, Truro, Cornwall,
TR1 3AF, Telephone: 01872 276312
E-mail:theclerks@godolphin.force9.co.uk
Call Date: 1994, Middle Temple
Qualifications: [LLB (Hons), RGN]

HOLLAND CHARLES CHRISTOPHER

Trinity Chambers
9-12 Trinity Chare, Quayside, Newcastle
upon Tyne NE1 3DF,
Telephone: 0191 232 1927
E-mail: info@trinitychambers.co.uk
Call Date: Nov 1994, Inner Temple
Qualifications: [LLB (Notts)]

HOLLAND MISS CHARLOTTE KATE

Old Colony House
6 South King Street, Manchester M2 6DQ,
Telephone: 0161 834 4364
Call Date: Oct 1996, Lincoln's Inn
Qualifications: [BA (Hons)(B'ham), CPE
(Manc)]

HOLLAND DAVID MOORE

29 Bedford Row Chambers
London WC1R 4HE,
Telephone: 0171 831 2626
Call Date: July 1986, Inner Temple
Pupil Master
Qualifications: [MA (Cantab) LLM,
(Toronto)]

HOLLAND MISS DEBRA JOANNE

Stanbrook & Henderson
Ground Floor, 2 Harcourt Bldgs, Temple,
London EC4Y 9DB,
Telephone: 0171 353 0101
E-mail: clerks@harcourt.co.uk
Call Date: Oct 1996, Lincoln's Inn
Qualifications: [LLB (Hons)(Leic)]

HOLLAND DR JAMES ANTONY

University of the West of, England, Bristol,
Frenchay Campus, Bristol BS16 1QY,
Telephone: 0117 965 6261
Call Date: July 1996, Middle Temple
Qualifications: [LLB (Hons)(Bris), PhD
(Soton)]

HOLLAND MISS KATHARINE JANE

9 Old Square
Ground Floor, Lincoln's Inn, London
WC2A 3SR, Telephone: 0171 405 4682
E-mail: chambers@9oldsquare.co.uk
Call Date: July 1989, Middle Temple
Qualifications: [BA [Oxon], BCL [Oxon]]

HOLLAND MICHAEL FREDERICK RICHARD

1 Hare Court
Ground Floor, Temple, London
EC4Y 7BE, Telephone: 0171 353 3982/
5324
*Call Date: Nov 1984, Inner Temple
Pupil Master*
Qualifications: [BA (Dunelm)]

HOLLAND RICKY JOHN

Lincoln House Chambers
5th Floor, Lincoln House, 1 Brazennose
Street, Manchester M2 5EL,
Telephone: 0161 832 5701
E-mail: info@lincolnhse.co.uk
Call Date: Nov 1994, Gray's Inn
Qualifications: [LLB]

HOLLAND MRS ROBERTA

17 Carlton Crescent
Southampton SO15 2XR,
Telephone: 023 8032 0320/0823 2003
E-mail: greg@jg17cc.co.uk
*Call Date: Nov 1989, Lincoln's Inn
Pupil Master*
Qualifications: [BSc (Bath), LLB]

HOLLAND WILLIAM

2nd Floor, Francis Taylor Building
Temple, London EC4Y 7BY,
Telephone: 0171 353 9942/3157
*Call Date: July 1982, Gray's Inn
Pupil Master*
Qualifications: [LLB (Lond)]

HOLLANDER CHARLES SIMON QC (1999)

Brick Court Chambers
7-8 Essex Street, London WC2R 3LD,
Telephone: 0171 379 3550
E-mail: [surname]@brickcourt.co.uk
*Call Date: 1978, Gray's Inn
Pupil Master*
Qualifications: [MA (Cantab)]

HOLLIER MARK ANTHONY

Queens Square Chambers
56 Queens Square, Bristol BS1 4PR,
Telephone: 0117 921 1966
Call Date: May 1994, Inner Temple
Qualifications: [LLB]

HOLLINGTON ROBIN FRANK QC (1999)

1 New Square
Ground Floor, Lincoln's Inn, London
WC2A 3SA, Telephone: 0171 405 0884/5/6/
7 E-mail: clerks@1newsquare.law.co.uk
*Call Date: 1979, Lincoln's Inn
Pupil Master*
Qualifications: [MA (Oxon), LLM (Penn]

HOLLINGWORTH PETER JAMES MICHAEL

Northampton Chambers
22 Albion Place, Northampton NN1 1UD,
Telephone: 01604 636271
Call Date: May 1993, Lincoln's Inn
Qualifications: [MA (Oxon)]

HOLLIS MRS KIM

2 Paper Buildings
1st Floor, Temple, London EC4Y 7ET,
Telephone: 020 7556 5500
E-mail: clerks@2pbbarristers.co.uk
*Call Date: July 1979, Gray's Inn
Pupil Master*
Qualifications: [LLB (Lond)]

HOLLORAN MS FIONA ANNE

58 King Street Chambers
1st Floor, Kingsgate House, 51-53 South
King Street, Manchester M2 6DE,
Telephone: 0161 831 7477
Call Date: Nov 1989, Gray's Inn
Qualifications: [LLB (Warw)]

HOLLOW PAUL JOHN

Fenners Chambers
3 Madingley Road, Cambridge CB3 0EE,
Telephone: 01223 368761
E-mail: clerks@fennerschambers.co.uk
Fenners Chambers
8-12 Priestgate, Peterborough PE1 1JA,
Telephone: 01733 562030
E-mail: clerks@fennerschambers.co.uk
Call Date: Nov 1981, Gray's Inn
Pupil Master
Qualifications: [LLB (E.Ang)]

HOLLOWAY RICHARD MARK

Northampton Chambers
22 Albion Place, Northampton NN1 1UD,
Telephone: 01604 636271
Call Date: Nov 1993, Gray's Inn
Qualifications: [B.Phil , Dip Law]

HOLLOWAY MS SHARON LOUISE

Mitre House Chambers
15-19 Devereux Court, London WC2R 3JJ,
Telephone: 0171 583 8233
Call Date: Oct 1994, Inner Temple
Qualifications: [BA (York), CPE
(Staffordshire)]

HOLLOWAY TIMOTHY RICHARD

Derby Square Chambers
Merchants Court, Derby Square, Liverpool
L2 1TS, Telephone: 0151 709 4222
E-mail:mail.derbysquare@pop3.hiway.co.uk
Call Date: Nov 1991, Inner Temple
Qualifications: [MA (Cantab)]

HOLLYOAK MISS KATE ELAINE

Chambers of John Hand QC
9 St John Street, Manchester M3 4DN,
Telephone: 0161 955 9000
E-mail: ninesjs@gconnect.com
Call Date: Nov 1997, Gray's Inn
Qualifications: [LLB (Manch)]

HOLMAN MISS TAMSIN PERDITA

19 Old Buildings
Lincoln's Inn, London WC2A 3UP,
Telephone: 0171 405 2001
E-mail: clerks@oldbuildingsip.com
Call Date: Oct 1995, Middle Temple
Qualifications: [MA (Oxon)]

HOLMES JONATHAN MAURICE

Plowden Buildings
2nd Floor, 2 Plowden Buildings, Middle
Temple Lane, London EC4Y 9BU,
Telephone: 0171 583 0808
E-mail: bar@plowdenbuildings.co.uk
Call Date: July 1985, Inner Temple
Qualifications: [LLB (Newcastle), ACIARB]

HOLMES JUSTIN FRANCIS

Chambers of Lord Goodhart QC
Ground Floor, 3 New Square, Lincoln's
Inn, London WC2A 3RS,
Telephone: 0171 405 5577
E-mail:law@threenewsquare.demon.co.uk
Call Date: Feb 1994, Inner Temple
Qualifications: [MA (Cantab)]

HOLMES PHILIP JOHN

8 King Street Chambers
8 King Street, Manchester M2 6AQ,
Telephone: 0161 834 9560
E-mail: eightking@aol.com
Call Date: July 1980, Lincoln's Inn
Pupil Master
Qualifications: [MA (Cantab)]

HOLMES MISS SUSAN ELIZABETH MICHAELA

2 King's Bench Walk
Ground Floor, Temple, London
EC4Y 7DE, Telephone: 0171 353 1746
E-mail: 2kbw@atlas.co.uk
King's Bench Chambers
115 North Hill, Plymouth PL4 8JY,
Telephone: 01752 221551
Call Date: July 1989, Middle Temple
Qualifications: [LLB Hons (Bris)]

HOLMES-MILNER JAMES NEIL

2 Mitre Court Buildings
1st Floor, Temple, London EC4Y 7BX,
Telephone: 0171 353 1353
Call Date: July 1989, Middle Temple
Pupil Master
Qualifications: [MA (Cantab), Dip Law]

HOLROYD CHARLES WILFRID

S Tomlinson QC
7 King's Bench Walk, Temple, London
EC4Y 7DS, Telephone: 0171 583 0404
E-mail: clerks@7kbw.law.co.uk
Call Date: Oct 1997, Gray's Inn
Qualifications: [BA, Diplome d'etudes,
superieurs (Geneva)]

HOLROYD MS JOANNE

37 Park Square Chambers
37 Park Square, Leeds LS1 2NY,
Telephone: 0113 2439422
E-mail: chambers@no37.co.uk
Call Date: Nov 1994, Middle Temple
Qualifications: [BA (Hons)]

HOLROYD JOHN JAMES

9 Woodhouse Square
Leeds LS3 1AD,
Telephone: 0113 2451986
E-mail: clerks@9woodhouse.co.uk
Call Date: Nov 1989, Gray's Inn
Qualifications: [BSc (Nott'm), LLB, MICE, C
Eng, ACI Arb]

HOLROYDE TIMOTHY VICTOR QC (1996)

Exchange Chambers
Pearl Assurance House, Derby Square,
Liverpool L2 9XX,
Telephone: 0151 236 7747
E-mail:exchangechambers@btinternet.com
Call Date: Nov 1977, Middle Temple
Assistant Recorder
Qualifications: [BA (Oxon)]

HOLT MISS ABIGAIL CLAIRE

24a St John Street
Manchester M3 4DF,
Telephone: 0161 833 9628
Call Date: Oct 1993, Lincoln's Inn
Qualifications: [BA (Hons)(Oxon)]

HOLT MISS KAREN JANE

Queen Elizabeth Building
Ground Floor, Temple, London
EC4Y 9BS,
Telephone: 0171 353 7181 (12 Lines)
Call Date: Nov 1987, Lincoln's Inn
Pupil Master
Qualifications: [LLB (Leeds)]

HOLT MISS MARGARET EVELYN

First National Chambers
2nd Floor, First National Building, 24
Fenwick Street, Liverpool L2 7NE,
Telephone: 0151 236 2098
Call Date: Feb 1978, Lincoln's Inn
Qualifications: [BA, LLB]

HOLT MICHAEL JULIAN

Parsonage Chambers
5th Floor, 3 The Parsonage, Manchester
M3 2HW, Telephone: 0161 833 1996
Call Date: Feb 1982, Middle Temple
Pupil Master
Qualifications: [BA]

HOLT ROBERT CHARLES STEPHEN

Furnival Chambers
32 Furnival Street, London EC4A 1JQ,
Telephone: 0171 405 3232
E-mail: clerks@furnivallaw.co.uk
Call Date: Nov 1978, Gray's Inn
Pupil Master
Qualifications: [BSc]

HOLTUM IAN ROBERT

Chambers of John L Powell QC
Four New Square, Lincoln's Inn, London
WC2A 3RJ, Telephone: 0171 797 8000
E-mail: barristers@4newsquare.com
Call Date: July 1985, Gray's Inn
Pupil Master
Qualifications: [BA (Oxon), Dip Law, (City)]

HOLWILL DEREK PAUL WINSOR

4 Paper Buildings
Ground Floor, Temple, London
EC4Y 7EX, Telephone: 0171 353 3366/
583 7155
E-mail: clerks@4paperbuildings.com
Call Date: July 1982, Gray's Inn
Pupil Master
Qualifications: [MA (Cantab)]

HOMER MISS MADELINE JANE

Mendhir Chambers
38 Priest Avenue, Wokingham, Berkshire,
RG40 2LX, Telephone: 0118 9771274
Call Date: Oct 1994, Gray's Inn
Qualifications: [LLB]

HONE RICHARD MICHAEL QC (1997)

One Paper Buildings
Ground Floor, Temple, London
EC4Y 7EP, Telephone: 0171 583 7355
E-mail: clerks@1pb.co.uk
Call Date: July 1970, Middle Temple
Recorder
Qualifications: [MA (Oxon)]

HONEY JOHN FRANCIS

Lion Court
Chancery House, 53-64 Chancery Lane,
London WC2A 1SJ,
Telephone: 0171 404 6565
Call Date: Nov 1990, Inner Temple
Qualifications: [BA (Cantab), Dip Law (PCL)]

HOOD DAVID

90 Overstrand Mansions
Prince of Wales Drive, London SW11 4EU,
Telephone: 0171 622 7415
Call Date: Nov 1980, Inner Temple
Qualifications: [LLB (Lond)]

HOOD GAVIN WILLIAM

18 Red Lion Court
(Off Fleet Street), London EC4A 3EB,
Telephone: 0171 520 6000
E-mail: chambers@18rlc.co.uk
Call Date: Nov 1997, Middle Temple
Qualifications: [BA (Hons), LLB (Durham)]

HOOD NIGEL ANTHONY

4 King's Bench Walk
Ground/First Floor/Basement, Temple,
London EC4Y 7DL,
Telephone: 0171 822 8822
E-mail: 4kbw@barristersatlaw.com
Call Date: Oct 1993, Inner Temple
Qualifications: [BA (Bournemouth), MBA
(Missouri), CPE]

HOOKWAY RICHARD AELRED

Chambers of Andrew Campbell QC
10 Park Square, Leeds LS1 2LH,
Telephone: 0113 2455438
E-mail: clerks@10pksq.co.uk
Call Date: Nov 1990, Gray's Inn
Qualifications: [LLB (B'ham)]

HOOLEY RICHARD JOHN ALEXANDER

Fountain Court
Temple, London EC4Y 9DH,
Telephone: 0171 583 3335
E-mail: chambers@fountaincourt.co.uk
Call Date: July 1984, Middle Temple
Qualifications: [MA (Cantab)]

HOON PRITHVIJIT NOTU SINGH

2 Paper Buildings
1st Floor, Temple, London EC4Y 7ET,
Telephone: 020 7556 5500
E-mail: clerks@2pbbarristers.co.uk
Call Date: Nov 1975, Inner Temple
Pupil Master

HOOPER DAVID JOHN

3 Gray's Inn Square
Ground Floor, London WC1R 5AH,
Telephone: 0171 520 5600
E-mail: clerks@3gis.co.uk
Call Date: Feb 1971, Middle Temple
Pupil Master

HOOPER GOPAL ARTHUR JOHN

1 Middle Temple Lane
Temple, London EC4Y 1LT,
Telephone: 0171 583 0659 (12 Lines)
E-mail: chambers@1mtl.co.uk
Call Date: 1973, Middle Temple
Pupil Master, Recorder
Qualifications: [LLB]

HOOPER MARTIN CHARLES

3 Temple Gardens
3rd Floor, Temple, London EC4Y 9AU,
Telephone: 0171 583 0010
Call Date: July 1988, Middle Temple
Pupil Master
Qualifications: [LLB (Hons)]

HOOPER TOBY JULIEN ANDERSON

12 King's Bench Walk
Temple, London EC4Y 7EL,
Telephone: 0171 583 0811
E-mail: chambers@12kbw.co.uk
Call Date: July 1973, Inner Temple
Pupil Master, Assistant Recorder
Qualifications: [BA]

HOPE ANTONY DERWIN

3 Paper Buildings
Temple, London EC4Y 7EU,
Telephone: 020 7583 8055
E-mail: London@3paper.com
3 Paper Buildings (Winchester)
4 St Peter Street, Winchester SO23 8BW,
Telephone: 01962 868884
E-mail: winchester@3paper.com
3 Paper Buildings (Bournemouth)
20 Lorne Park Road, Bournemouth,
Dorset, BH1 1JN,
Telephone: 01202 292102
E-mail: Bournemouth@3paper.com
3 Paper Buildings (Oxford)
1 Alfred Street, High Street, Oxford
OX1 4EH, Telephone: 01865 793736
E-mail: oxford@3paper.com
Call Date: Nov 1970, Middle Temple
Recorder
Qualifications: [BSc (Lond) Est Man, (Lond)]

HOPE MISS HEATHER ROSALIND

Trafalgar Chambers
53 Fleet Street, London EC4Y 1BE,
Telephone: 0171 583 5858
E-mail:trafalgarchambers@easynet.co.uk
Call Date: Oct 1993, Gray's Inn
Qualifications: [LLB (Hons)]

HOPE MISS NADINE SAMANTHA

19 Castle Street Chambers
Liverpool L2 4SX,
Telephone: 0151 236 9402
E-mail: DBrei16454@aol.com
Call Date: Feb 1988, Lincoln's Inn
Pupil Master
Qualifications: [LLB (Hons) , MA]

HOPEWELL GREGORY TURTLE

John Street Chambers
2 John Street, London WC1N 2HJ,
Telephone: 0171 242 1911
E-mail:john.street_chambers@virgin.net
Call Date: Feb 1992, Inner Temple
Qualifications: [BA, LLB (Hons)]

HOPKINS ADRIAN MARK

3 Serjeants' Inn
London EC4Y 1BQ,
Telephone: 0171 353 5537
E-mail: clerks@3serjeantsinn.com
Call Date: Nov 1984, Lincoln's Inn
Pupil Master
Qualifications: [BA (Oxon)]

HOPKINS MISS ANDREA LOUISE

St John's Chambers
Small Street, Bristol BS1 1DW,
Telephone: 0117 9213456/298514
E-mail: @stjohnschambers.co.uk
Call Date: Nov 1992, Gray's Inn
Qualifications: [LLB (Exeter)]

HOPKINS PAUL ANDREW

9 Park Place
Cardiff CF1 3DP,
Telephone: 01222 382731
Call Date: July 1989, Gray's Inn
Pupil Master
Qualifications: [LLB (B'ham)]

HOPKINS MISS PHILIPPA MARY

Essex Court Chambers
24 Lincoln's Inn Fields, London
WC2A 3ED, Telephone: 0171 813 8000
E-mail:clerksroom@essexcourt-chambers.co.uk
Call Date: Oct 1994, Middle Temple
Qualifications: [BA (Hons), BCL (Oxon)]

HOPKINS ROWLAND RHYS

Rowchester Chambers
4 Rowchester Court, Whittall Street,
Birmingham B4 6DH,
Telephone: 0121 233 2327/2361951
Call Date: Nov 1970, Inner Temple
Pupil Master
Qualifications: [LLB (Lond)]

HOPKINS SIMEON FRANCIS MCKAY

5 Pump Court
Ground Floor, Temple, London
EC4Y 7AP, Telephone: 020 7353 2532
E-mail: FivePump@netcomuk.co.uk
Call Date: Nov 1968, Inner Temple
Pupil Master

HOPKINS STEPHEN JOHN

30 Park Place
Cardiff CF1 3BA,
Telephone: 01222 398421
E-mail: 100757.1456@compuserve.com
Call Date: Nov 1973, Gray's Inn
Recorder
Qualifications: [LLB (Wales)]

HOPMEIER MICHAEL ANDREW PHILIP

Hardwicke Building
New Square, Lincoln's Inn, London
WC2A 3SB, Telephone: 020 7242 2523
E-mail: clerks@hardwicke.co.uk
King's Bench Chambers
Wellington House, 175 Holdenhurst Road,
Bournemouth, Dorset, BH8 8DQ,
Telephone: 01202 250025
E-mail: chambers@kingsbench.co.uk
Call Date: July 1974, Middle Temple
Pupil Master, Recorder
Qualifications: [MA (Oxon), LLM (Lond]

HORAN JOHN PATRICK

22 Old Buildings
Lincoln's Inn, London WC2A 3UJ,
Telephone: 0171 831 0222
Call Date: Feb 1993, Inner Temple
Qualifications: [BA, Diploma in Law]

HORGAN PETER THOMAS

Queen's Chambers
5 John Dalton Street, Manchester M2 6ET,
Telephone: 0161 834 6875/4738
Queens Chambers
4 Camden Place, Preston PR1 3JL,
Telephone: 01772 828300
Call Date: Oct 1993, Middle Temple
Qualifications: [BA (Hons)(Manc), Dip in
Law (City)]

HORGAN TIMOTHY GEORGE

Cardinal Chambers
4 Old Mitre Court, 4th Floor, Temple,
London EC4Y 7BP,
Telephone: 020 7353 2622
E-mail:admin@cardinal-chambers.co.uk
Call Date: July 1982, Inner Temple
Pupil Master
Qualifications: [LLB (Leeds)]

HORLICK LADY FIONA

23 Essex Street
London WC2R 3AS,
Telephone: 0171 413 0353/836 8366
E-mail:clerks@essexstreet23.demon.co.uk
Call Date: May 1992, Middle Temple
Qualifications: [LLB (Hons) (Lond)]

HORLOCK TIMOTHY JOHN QC (1997)

Chambers of John Hand QC
9 St John Street, Manchester M3 4DN,
Telephone: 0161 955 9000
E-mail: ninesjs@gconnect.com
Call Date: July 1981, Middle Temple
Assistant Recorder
Qualifications: [BA (Cantab), MA]

HORNBY ROBERT CHRISTOPHER

Sedan House
Stanley Place, Chester CH1 2LU,
Telephone: 01244 320480/348282
Call Date: Oct 1990, Lincoln's Inn
Pupil Master
Qualifications: [LLB]

HORNE CHARLES HUGH WILSON

40 King Street
Manchester M2 6BA,
Telephone: 0161 832 9082
E-mail: clerks@40kingstreet.co.uk
The Chambers of Philip Raynor QC
5 Park Place, Leeds LS1 2RU,
Telephone: 0113 242 1123
Call Date: Oct 1992, Lincoln's Inn
Qualifications: [LLB(Hons)(Leeds)]

HORNE KENDERIK THOMAS CLARKE

Adrian Lyon's Chambers
14 Castle Street, Liverpool L2 0NE,
Telephone: 0151 236 4421/8240
E-mail: chambers14@aol.com
Call Date: Mar 1996, Lincoln's Inn
Qualifications: [BA (Hons)]

HORNE MICHAEL ANDREW

3 Serjeants' Inn
London EC4Y 1BQ,
Telephone: 0171 353 5537
E-mail: clerks@3serjeantsinn.com
Call Date: Oct 1992, Gray's Inn
Qualifications: [BA]

HORNE ROGER COZENS-HARDY

Chambers of Mr Peter Crampin QC
Ground Floor, 11 New Square, Lincoln's
Inn, London WC2A 3QB,
Telephone: 020 7831 0081
E-mail: 11newsquare.co.uk
Call Date: July 1967, Lincoln's Inn
Pupil Master
Qualifications: [LLB (St Andrews)]

HORNE-ROBERTS MRS JENNIFER

Westgate Chambers
144 High Street, Lewes, East Sussex,
BN7 1XT, Telephone: 01273 480510
Westgate Chambers
16-17 Wellington Square, Hastings, East
Sussex, TN34 1PB,
Telephone: 01424 432105
Call Date: Nov 1976, Middle Temple
Pupil Master
Qualifications: [BA (Hons)(Lond)]

HORNER ROBIN MICHAEL

Broad Chare
33 Broad Chare, Newcastle upon Tyne
NE1 3DQ, Telephone: 0191 232 0541
E-mail: clerks@broadcharechambers.law.co.uk
Call Date: July 1975, Lincoln's Inn
Pupil Master
Qualifications: [LLB]

HORNETT STUART IAN

29 Bedford Row Chambers
London WC1R 4HE,
Telephone: 0171 831 2626
Call Date: Oct 1992, Middle Temple
Qualifications: [LL.B (Hons) & M.Phil, (Leic)]

HORNSBY WALTON FRANCIS PETRE

Queen Elizabeth Building
Ground Floor, Temple, London
EC4Y 9BS,
Telephone: 0171 353 7181 (12 Lines)
Call Date: July 1980, Lincoln's Inn
Pupil Master
Qualifications: [BA (Oxon)]

HOROWITZ MICHAEL QC (1990)

1 Mitre Court Buildings
Temple, London EC4Y 7BS,
Telephone: 0171 797 7070
E-mail: clerks@1mcb.com

Mercury Chambers
Mercury House, 33-35 Clarendon Road,
Leeds LS2 9NZ,
Telephone: 0113 234 2265
E-mail: cdexter@mercurychambers.co.uk
Call Date: July 1968, Lincoln's Inn
Recorder
Qualifications: [MA, LLB (Cantab)]

HORROCKS PETER LESLIE

One Garden Court Family Law Chambers
Ground Floor, Temple, London
EC4Y 9BJ, Telephone: 0171 797 7900
E-mail: clerks@onegardencourt.co.uk
Call Date: Nov 1977, Middle Temple
Pupil Master
Qualifications: [MA (Cantab)]

HORSTEAD SEAN KEVAN

Acre Lane Neighbourhood Chambers
30A Acre Lane, London SW2 5SG,
Telephone: 0171 274 4400
E-mail: barristerschambers@acrelane.demon.co.uk
Call Date: Oct 1996, Middle Temple
Qualifications: [BA (Hons)(Sussex), MA,
CPE]

HORTON MISS CAROLINE ANN

Fenners Chambers
3 Madingley Road, Cambridge CB3 0EE,
Telephone: 01223 368761
E-mail: clerks@fennerschambers.co.uk
Fenners Chambers
8-12 Priestgate, Peterborough PE1 1JA,
Telephone: 01733 562030
E-mail: clerks@fennerschambers.co.uk
Call Date: Oct 1993, Middle Temple
Qualifications: [LLB (Hons, Nott)]

HORTON MARK ANTHONY

St John's Chambers
Small Street, Bristol BS1 1DW,
Telephone: 0117 9213456/298514
E-mail: @stjohnschambers.co.uk
Call Date: July 1976, Middle Temple
Pupil Master, Assistant Recorder
Qualifications: [LLB]

HORTON MARK VARNEY

Colleton Chambers
Colleton Crescent, Exeter, Devon,
EX2 4DG, Telephone: 01392 274898/9
Call Date: July 1981, Middle Temple
Qualifications: [LLB (Lond)]

HORTON MATTHEW BETHELL QC (1989)

2 Mitre Court Buildings
2nd Floor, Temple, London EC4Y 7BX,
Telephone: 0171 583 1380
E-mail: clerks@2mcb.co.uk
Call Date: July 1969, Middle Temple
Qualifications: [MA, LLB (Cantab)]

HORTON MICHAEL JOHN EDWARD

4 Brick Court
Ground Floor, Temple, London
EC4Y 9AD, Telephone: 0171 797 7766
E-mail: chambers@4brick.co.uk
Call Date: Nov 1993, Gray's Inn
Qualifications: [BA]

HORWELL RICHARD ERIC

Hollis Whiteman Chambers
3rd Floor, Queen Elizabeth Bldg, Temple,
London EC4Y 9BS,
Telephone: 020 7583 5766
E-mail:barristers@holliswhiteman.co.uk
Call Date: Nov 1976, Gray's Inn
Pupil Master

HORWOOD MISS ANYA LOUISE

25-27 Castle Street
1st Floor, Liverpool L2 4TA,
Telephone: 0151 227 5661/051 236 5072
Call Date: Nov 1991, Inner Temple
Qualifications: [LLB (Lancs)]

HORWOOD-SMART MISS ROSAMUND QC (1996)

18 Red Lion Court
(Off Fleet Street), London EC4A 3EB,
Telephone: 0171 520 6000
E-mail: chambers@18rlc.co.uk

Thornwood House
102 New London Road, Chelmsford,
Essex, CM2 0RG,
Telephone: 01245 280880
E-mail: chambers@18rlc.co.uk
Call Date: July 1974, Inner Temple
Recorder

HOSER PHILIP JACOB

Serle Court Chambers
6 New Square, Lincoln's Inn, London
WC2A 3QS, Telephone: 0171 242 6105
E-mail: clerks@serlecourt.co.uk
Call Date: Nov 1982, Lincoln's Inn
Pupil Master
Qualifications: [BA (Cantab)]

HOSFORD-TANNER (JOSEPH) MICHAEL

Queen Elizabeth Building
2nd Floor, Temple, London EC4Y 9BS,
Telephone: 0171 797 7837
Call Date: Nov 1974, Inner Temple
Pupil Master
Qualifications: [BA, LLB]

HOSKING STEVE

Lion Court
Chancery House, 53-64 Chancery Lane,
London WC2A 1SJ,
Telephone: 0171 404 6565
Call Date: Nov 1988, Inner Temple
Qualifications: [BA (Nott'm)]

HOSKINS MARK GEORGE

Brick Court Chambers
7-8 Essex Street, London WC2R 3LD,
Telephone: 0171 379 3550
E-mail: [surname]@brickcourt.co.uk
Call Date: Nov 1991, Gray's Inn
Qualifications: [MA (Oxon),BCL (Oxon),
Lic.Spec Dr Eur, (Brussels)]

HOSKINS WILLIAM GUERIN

1 Temple Gardens
1st Floor, Temple, London EC4Y 9BB,
Telephone: 0171 583 1315/353 0407
E-mail: clerks@1templegardens.co.uk
Call Date: Nov 1980, Middle Temple
Pupil Master
Qualifications: [MA (Oxon)]

HOSSAIN AJMALUL QC (1998)

29 Bedford Row Chambers
London WC1R 4HE,
Telephone: 0171 831 2626
Call Date: Nov 1976, Lincoln's Inn
Qualifications: [LLB (Hons)LLM (Lond),
FCIArb]

Fax: 0171 831 0626;
Out of hours telephone: 0370 966 505;
DX: 1044 LDE

Other professional qualifications: Fellow of the
Chartered Institute of Arbitrators

Types of work: Arbitration, Banking, Commercial, Commercial litigation, Company and commercial, Employment, Foreign law, Insolvency, International trade, Private international

Membership of foreign bars: Senior Advocate
Bangladesh Supreme Court

Circuit: South Eastern

Awards and memberships: Buchanan Prizewinner, Lincoln's Inn 1976 Member City Disputes Panel

Other professional experience: Arbitrator in commercial/financial disputes

Languages spoken: Arabic, Bengali, Hindi, Urdu

Reported Cases
Janata Bank v Ahmed [1981] ICR 791 (CA)
Employment.
Sonali Bank v Rahman & anor [1989] ICR
314 (EAT)
Employment.
Justfern v D'Ingerthorpe [1994] ICR 286
(EAT)
Employment.
Harvey v Institute of Motor Industry
[1995] IRLR 416 (EAT)
Employment.
*Kydon Compania Naviera v National
Westminster Bank & others (The Lena)*
[1981] 1 Lloyd's Rep 68 (QB, Com Ct)
Banking.
Ban Hin Lee Bank Berhad v Sonali Bank
(1988) *The Independent*, 29 November
(CA)
Banking, civil procedure.
BCCI HK v Sonali [1995] 1 Lloyd's Rep
227 (QB, Com Ct)
Banking, private international law.

BCCI v Malik (1995) *The Independent*, 13
March (Ch D) [1996] BCC 15
Banking, commercial contract.
BEI v SKI [1995] 2 Lloyd's Rep 1 (CA)
International trade.
Cargill International SA v BSFIC (QB, Com
Ct) Morison J [1996] 2 Lloyd's Rep 526
Banking, commercial contract, international trade.
Pentagen Technologies Ltd v Express Secretaries Ltd (1995) *The Times*, 7 April (CA)
Company.
Re BCCI (No 10) [1995] BCLC 362
(Companies Court)
Corporate insolvency.
Re BCCI SA (in liquidation) (No 9) (1996)
The Times, 8 October (Companies Court)
Corporate insolvency.
*Bengal Liner Ltd and anor v Shadharan
Bima Corporation* (Bangladesh Supreme
Court) [1996] BLC (AD) 127
Bangladeshi law.
Alam & ors v BCCI SA & ors (Breach of
trust action, claim for US$400 million,
settled for US$136 million – reported in
the national press from time to time)
Corporate insolvency, equity & trusts,
private international law.

Ajmalul Hossain QC was born in Dhaka and
received his schooling and college education in Dhaka. He came to England in 1971
and read law for his first degree at King's
College, University of London. He obtained
his Bachelor of Laws Honours Degree (LLB
Hons) in June 1976 and in the same year
took his Bar Finals. He stood third in order
of merit from all candidates in England and
first from the Lincoln's Inn candidates. He
was awarded the 1976 Buchanan Prize by
Lincoln's Inn for his academic results. He
obtained his Master of Laws (LLM) degree
in the year 1977 also from King's College,
University of London.

He was enrolled to practise in the High
Court and Appellate Divisions of the
Supreme Court of Bangladesh in 1977 and
1980 respectively. He has been regularly
practising in the superior courts of Bangladesh and England from his chambers in
Dhaka and London specialising in Banking,
Financial, Company, Commercial and
Employment law. Many of the cases in
which Mr Hossain has appeared have been
reported in the law reports in England and
in Bangladesh.

Ajmalul Hossain was elected a Fellow of the
Chartered Institute of Arbitrators of
England and Wales in September 1994 and

has chaired domestic and international commercial arbitrations. He also holds a part-time judicial appointment as a Chairman of Employment Tribunals in the London North region.

In 1998, Mr Hossain was appointed both Queen's Counsel in England and also a Senior Advocate of the Supreme Court of Bangladesh.

HOSSAIN SYED MOHAMMAD SA'AD ANSARUL

One Essex Court
Ground Floor, Temple, London
EC4Y 9AR, Telephone: 020 7583 2000
E-mail: clerks@oneessexcourt.co.uk
Call Date: Nov 1995, Gray's Inn
Qualifications: [BA]

HOTTEN CHRISTOPHER PETER QC (1994)

9 Bedford Row
London WC1R 4AZ,
Telephone: 0171 242 3555
E-mail: clerks@9br.co.uk
St Philip's Chambers
Fountain Court, Steelhouse Lane,
Birmingham B4 6DR,
Telephone: 0121 246 7000
E-mail: clerks@st-philips.co.uk
Call Date: 1972, Inner Temple
Recorder
Qualifications: [LLB (Leics)]

HOTTEN KEITH ROBERT

23 Essex Street
London WC2R 3AS,
Telephone: 0171 413 0353/836 8366
E-mail:clerks@essexstreet23.demon.co.uk
Call Date: Nov 1990, Middle Temple
Qualifications: [MA PhD (Lond)]

HOUGH CHRISTOPHER SIMON

199 Strand
London WC2R 1DR,
Telephone: 0171 379 9779
E-mail: chambers@199strand.co.uk

Doughty Street Chambers
11 Doughty Street, London WC1N 2PG,
Telephone: 0171 404 1313
E-mail:enquiries@doughtystreet.co.uk
Call Date: July 1981, Middle Temple
Pupil Master
Qualifications: [LLB]

HOUGH JONATHAN ANTHONY

1 Temple Gardens
1st Floor, Temple, London EC4Y 9BB,
Telephone: 0171 583 1315/353 0407
E-mail: clerks@1templegardens.co.uk
Call Date: 1997, Middle Temple
Qualifications: [MA (Hons)(Oxon), CPE (Lond)]

HOUGH RICHARD ANTHONY

Devon Chambers
3 St Andrew Street, Plymouth PL1 2AH,
Telephone: 01752 661659
E-mail: devonchambers.co.uk.
Call Date: Nov 1979, Gray's Inn
Pupil Master

HOUGHTON MISS KIRSTEN ANNETTE

4 Pump Court
Temple, London EC4Y 7AN,
Telephone: 020 7842 5555
E-mail:chambers@4pumpcourt.law.co.uk
Call Date: July 1989, Inner Temple
Qualifications: [BA (Cantab)]

HOUGHTON MISS LISA JAYNE

58 King Street Chambers
1st Floor, Kingsgate House, 51-53 South
King Street, Manchester M2 6DE,
Telephone: 0161 831 7477
Call Date: Oct 1994, Gray's Inn
Qualifications: [BA (Lancs)]

HOUGHTON MARK

33 Bedford Row
London WC1R 4JH,
Telephone: 0171 242 6476
E-mail:clerks@bedfordrow33.demon.co.uk
Call Date: Nov 1980, Middle Temple
Qualifications: [BA]

HOULDER BRUCE QC (1994)

6 King's Bench Walk
Ground Floor, Temple, London
EC4Y 7DR, Telephone: 0171 583 0410
E-mail: worsley@6kbw.freeserve.co.uk
Call Date: July 1969, Gray's Inn
Recorder

HOUSE JAMES MICHAEL

De Montfort Chambers
95 Princess Road East, Leicester LE1 7DQ,
Telephone: 0116 254 8686
E-mail: dmcbar@aol.com
Call Date: Oct 1995, Inner Temple
Qualifications: [BA (Lanc), CPE]

HOUSE MICHAEL JOHN

Two Garden Court
1st Floor, Middle Temple, London
EC4Y 9BL, Telephone: 0171 353 1633
E-mail:barristers@2gardenct.law.co.uk
Call Date: July 1972, Inner Temple
Qualifications: [MA (Oxon)]

HOUSEMAN STEPHEN TERENCE

Essex Court Chambers
24 Lincoln's Inn Fields, London
WC2A 3ED, Telephone: 0171 813 8000
E-mail:clerksroom@essexcourt-chambers.co.uk
Call Date: Nov 1995, Inner Temple
Qualifications: [BA, BCL (Oxon)]

HOUSTON ANDREW

Eighteen Carlton Crescent
Southampton SO15 2XR,
Telephone: 01703 639001
Call Date: July 1989, Inner Temple
Qualifications: [LLB (So'ton)]

HOUSTON DAVID JOHN

Gray's Inn Chambers
5th Floor, Gray's Inn, London WC1R 5JA,
Telephone: 0171 404 1111
Call Date: Nov 1976, Gray's Inn
Pupil Master
Qualifications: [BA (Dunelm)]

HOUSTON DAVID MARTIN RUSSELL

3 Dr Johnson's Buildings
Ground Floor, Temple, London
EC4Y 7BA, Telephone: 0171 353 4854
E-mail: clerks@3djb.co.uk
Call Date: Nov 1973, Gray's Inn
Pupil Master
Qualifications: [LLB (Lond)]

HOWARD MISS AMANDA JAYNE

Derby Square Chambers
Merchants Court, Derby Square, Liverpool
L2 1TS, Telephone: 0151 709 4222
E-mail:mail.derbysquare@pop3.hiway.co.uk
Call Date: Nov 1994, Inner Temple
Qualifications: [LLB (Hons)]

HOWARD ANTHONY JOHN

Chambers of John Hand QC
9 St John Street, Manchester M3 4DN,
Telephone: 0161 955 9000
E-mail: ninesjs@gconnect.com
Call Date: Oct 1992, Inner Temple
Qualifications: [LLB (Lancs)]

HOWARD CHARLES ANTHONY FREDERICK QC (1999)

New Court Chambers
5 Verulam Buildings, Gray's Inn, London
WC1R 5LY, Telephone: 0171 831 9500
E-mail: mail@newcourtchambers.com
Call Date: 1975, Inner Temple
Pupil Master
Qualifications: [MA (Cantab)]

HOWARD GRAHAM JOHN

Pump Court Chambers
31 Southgate Street, Winchester
SO23 9EE, Telephone: 01962 868161
E-mail: clerks@3pumpcourt.com
Pump Court Chambers
Upper Ground Floor, 3 Pump Court,
Temple, London EC4Y 7AJ,
Telephone: 0171 353 0711
E-mail: clerks@3pumpcourt.com
Pump Court Chambers
5 Temple Chambers, Temple Street,
Swindon SN1 1SQ,
Telephone: 01793 539899
E-mail: clerks@3pumpcourt.com
Call Date: Nov 1987, Lincoln's Inn
Pupil Master
Qualifications: [LLB (Hons)]

HOWARD IAN

Broadway House Chambers
Broadway House, 9 Bank Street, Bradford,
West Yorkshire, BD1 1TW,
Telephone: 01274 722560
E-mail: clerks@broadwayhouse.co.uk
Broadway House Chambers
31 Park Square West, Leeds LS1 2PF,
Telephone: 0113 246 2600
Call Date: Nov 1987, Lincoln's Inn
Qualifications: [LLB(Hons) Newcastle]

HOWARD JONATHAN ROY

12 King's Bench Walk
Temple, London EC4Y 7EL,
Telephone: 0171 583 0811
E-mail: chambers@12kbw.co.uk
Call Date: Nov 1983, Middle Temple
Qualifications: [MA (Cantab)]

HOWARD MISS MARGARET JOAN

4 King's Bench Walk
Ground/First Floor/Basement, Temple,
London EC4Y 7DL,
Telephone: 0171 822 8822
E-mail: 4kbw@barristersatlaw.com
Call Date: July 1977, Middle Temple
Qualifications: [LLB(B'ham)]

HOWARD MARK STEVEN QC (1996)

Brick Court Chambers
7-8 Essex Street, London WC2R 3LD,
Telephone: 0171 379 3550
E-mail: [surname]@brickcourt.co.uk
Call Date: July 1980, Gray's Inn
Qualifications: [LLB, LLM (Lond)]

HOWARD MICHAEL NEWMAN QC (1986)

4 Essex Court
Temple, London EC4Y 9AJ,
Telephone: 020 7797 7970
E-mail: clerks@4essexcourt.law.co.uk
Call Date: May 1971, Gray's Inn
Recorder
Qualifications: [MA, BCL]

HOWARD MISS NICOLA

3 Gray's Inn Square
Ground Floor, London WC1R 5AH,
Telephone: 0171 520 5600
E-mail: clerks@3gis.co.uk
Call Date: Oct 1995, Middle Temple
Qualifications: [B.Sc (Hons)]

HOWARD ROBIN WILLIAM JOHN

Trinity Chambers
140 New London Road, Chelmsford,
Essex, CM2 0AW,
Telephone: 01245 605040
E-mail:clerks@trinitychambers.law.co.uk
Call Date: Feb 1986, Middle Temple
Pupil Master
Qualifications: [BA (Oxon)]

HOWARD TIMOTHY DOUGLAS

17 Carlton Crescent
Southampton SO15 2XR,
Telephone: 023 8032 0320/0823 2003
E-mail: greg@jg17cc.co.uk
Call Date: July 1981, Lincoln's Inn
Pupil Master
Qualifications: [LLB (Manch)]

HOWARD-JONES MISS SARAH RACHEL

8 Stone Buildings
Lincoln's Inn, London WC2A 3TA,
Telephone: 0171 831 9881
E-mail: alanl@8stonebuildings.law.uk
Call Date: Nov 1994, Middle Temple
Qualifications: [BA (Hons)(Cantab)]

HOWARTH ANDREW

Chambers of Michael Pert QC
36 Bedford Row, London WC1R 4JH,
Telephone: 0171 421 8000
E-mail: 36bedfordrow@link.org
Chambers of Michael Pert QC
24 Albion Place, Northampton NN1 1UD,
Telephone: 01604 602333
Chambers of Michael Pert QC
104 New Walk, Leicester LE1 7EA,
Telephone: 0116 249 2020
Call Date: Nov 1988, Lincoln's Inn
Qualifications: [BA (Oxon)]

HOWARTH SIMON STUART

Two Crown Office Row
Ground Floor, Temple, London
EC4Y 7HJ, Telephone: 020 7797 8100
E-mail: mail@2cor.co.uk, or to individual
barristers at: [barrister's
surname]@2cor.co.uk
Call Date: Oct 1991, Gray's Inn
Qualifications: [BA (Oxon)]

HOWAT ROBIN DAVID CHALMERS

6 King's Bench Walk
Ground, Third & Fourth Floors, Temple,
London EC4Y 7DR,
Telephone: 0171 353 4931/583 0695
Call Date: Nov 1986, Inner Temple
Pupil Master
Qualifications: [BA(Dunelm)]

HOWD STEPHEN EDMUND JEFFERSON

Chancery House Chambers
7 Lisbon Square, Leeds LS1 4LY,
Telephone: 0113 244 6691
E-mail: chanceryhouse@btinternet.com
Call Date: July 1989, Middle Temple
Qualifications: [BA (Oxon), Dip Law]

HOWE MISS CAROLE ANNE

8 King's Bench Walk North
1 Park Square East, Leeds LS1 2NE,
Telephone: 0113 2439797
8 King's Bench Walk
2nd Floor, Temple, London EC4Y 7DU,
Telephone: 0171 797 8888
Call Date: Nov 1984, Gray's Inn
Qualifications: [DMS]

HOWE DARREN FRANCIS

Sussex Chambers
9 Old Steine, Brighton, Sussex, BN1 1FJ,
Telephone: 01273 607953
Call Date: Oct 1992, Gray's Inn
Qualifications: [LL.B (Hull)]

HOWE MARTIN RUSSELL THOMSON QC (1996)

8 New Square
Lincoln's Inn, London WC2A 3QP,
Telephone: 0171 405 4321
E-mail: clerks@8newsquare.co.uk
Call Date: July 1978, Middle Temple
Qualifications: [BA (Cantab)]

HOWE MISS PENELOPE ANNE MACGREGOR

Pump Court Chambers
Upper Ground Floor, 3 Pump Court,
Temple, London EC4Y 7AJ,
Telephone: 0171 353 0711
E-mail: clerks@3pumpcourt.com
Pump Court Chambers
31 Southgate Street, Winchester
SO23 9EE, Telephone: 01962 868161
E-mail: clerks@3pumpcourt.com
Pump Court Chambers
5 Temple Chambers, Temple Street,
Swindon SN1 1SQ,
Telephone: 01793 539899
E-mail: clerks@3pumpcourt.com
Call Date: Nov 1991, Inner Temple
Qualifications: [BA (Cambs)]

HOWE PETER ST JOHN

9 King's Bench Walk
Ground Floor, Temple, London
EC4Y 7DX, Telephone: 0171 353 7202/
3909 E-mail: 9kbw@compuserve.com
Call Date: July 1992, Middle Temple

HOWE ROBERT PAUL THOMPSON

Blackstone Chambers
Blackstone House, Temple, London
EC4Y 9BW, Telephone: 0171 583 1770
E-mail:clerks@blackstonechambers.com
Call Date: Nov 1988, Middle Temple
Pupil Master
Qualifications: [MA (Cantab), BCL (Oxon)]

HOWE MISS RUTH ALYSON

Derby Square Chambers
Merchants Court, Derby Square, Liverpool
L2 1TS, Telephone: 0151 709 4222
E-mail:mail.derbysquare@pop3.hiway.co.uk
Call Date: July 1983, Lincoln's Inn
Pupil Master
Qualifications: [BA (Hons)]

HOWE MISS SARA-LISE ANGELIQUE

Westgate Chambers
16-17 Wellington Square, Hastings, East
Sussex, TN34 1PB,
Telephone: 01424 432105
Westgate Chambers
144 High Street, Lewes, East Sussex,
BN7 1XT, Telephone: 01273 480510
Call Date: Oct 1993, Lincoln's Inn
Qualifications: [BA (Hons)(Leic)]

HOWE TIMOTHY JEAN-PAUL

Fountain Court
Temple, London EC4Y 9DH,
Telephone: 0171 583 3335
E-mail: chambers@fountaincourt.co.uk
Call Date: Nov 1987, Middle Temple
Pupil Master
Qualifications: [MA (Oxon)]

HOWELL JOHN QC (1993)

4 Breams Buildings
London EC4A 1AQ,
Telephone: 0171 353 5835/430 1221
E-mail:breams@4breamsbuildings.law.co.uk
Call Date: Feb 1979, Middle Temple
Qualifications: [BA (Oxon)]

HOWELL WILLIAMS CRAIG

2 Harcourt Buildings
2nd Floor, Temple, London EC4Y 9DB,
Telephone: 020 7353 8415
E-mail: clerks@2hb.law.co.uk
Call Date: July 1983, Gray's Inn
Pupil Master
Qualifications: [BA (Leeds)]

HOWELLS MISS CATHERINE JANE

Exchange Chambers
Pearl Assurance House, Derby Square,
Liverpool L2 9XX,
Telephone: 0151 236 7747
E-mail:exchangechambers@btinternet.com
Call Date: July 1989, Gray's Inn
Qualifications: [LLB [L'pool]]

HOWELLS CENYDD IORWERTH

9 Stone Buildings
Lincoln's Inn, London WC2A 3NN,
Telephone: 0171 404 5055
E-mail: clerks@9stoneb.law.co.uk

33 Park Place
Cardiff CF1 3BA,
Telephone: 02920 233313
Call Date: June 1964, Lincoln's Inn
Recorder
Qualifications: [MA LLM (Cantab) , FCIArb]

HOWELLS JAMES RICHARD

Atkin Chambers
1 Atkin Building, Gray's Inn, London
WC1R 5AT, Telephone: 020 7404 0102
E-mail: clerks@atkin-chambers.co.uk
Call Date: Nov 1995, Middle Temple
Qualifications: [BA (Hons), MA, BCL]

HOWELLS JOHN JULIAN

Assize Court Chambers
14 Small Street, Bristol BS1 1DE,
Telephone: 0117 9264587
E-mail:chambers@assize-court-chambers.co.uk
Call Date: Nov 1985, Gray's Inn
Pupil Master
Qualifications: [LLB (Lond)]

HOWELLS MISS KATHERINE JANE

7 New Square
Lincoln's Inn, London WC2A 3QS,
Telephone: 0171 430 1660
Thomas More Chambers
52 Carey Street, Lincoln's Inn, London
WC2A 2JB, Telephone: 0171 404 7000
E-mail: clerks@thomasmore.law.co.uk
Call Date: 1994, Gray's Inn
Qualifications: [BA (Oxon)]

HOWES MISS SALLY MARGARET

1 Hare Court
Ground Floor, Temple, London
EC4Y 7BE, Telephone: 0171 353 3982/
5324
Call Date: Nov 1983, Middle Temple
Pupil Master
Qualifications: [BA (Newc), Dip Law]

HOWKER DAVID THOMAS

1 Hare Court
Ground Floor, Temple, London
EC4Y 7BE, Telephone: 0171 353 3982/
5324
Call Date: July 1982, Inner Temple
Assistant Recorder
Qualifications: [LLB (B'ham)]

HOWLETT JAMES ANTHONY

King Charles House
Standard Hill, Nottingham NG1 6FX,
Telephone: 0115 9418851
E-mail: clerks@kch.co.uk
Call Date: July 1980, Middle Temple
Pupil Master
Qualifications: [LLB (Bris)]

HOWLING REX ANDREW

Chambers of Norman Palmer
2 Field Court, Gray's Inn, London
WC1R 5BB, Telephone: 0171 405 6114
E-mail: fieldct2@netcomuk.co.uk
Call Date: Oct 1991, Middle Temple
Qualifications: [BSc (Hons) (Sussex), Dip
Law]

HOYAL MS JANE

1 Pump Court
Lower Ground Floor, Temple, London
EC4Y 7AB, Telephone: 0171 583 2012/
353 4341
E-mail: [name]@1pumpcourt.co.uk
Call Date: Nov 1976, Middle Temple
Pupil Master
Qualifications: [LLB MA]

Fax: 0171 353 4944

Other professional qualifications: Associate of the
College of Family Mediators (ACFM)

Types of work: Care proceedings, Civil liberties, ECHR, Family, Private international

Circuit: South Eastern

Awards and memberships: Management
Committee Grandparents' Federation;
Ex-Chair of PAIN (Parents against injustice);
in 1999, she was re-elected to the legal
committee of BAAF; *Member:* FLBA; Family
Rights Group; Association of Lawyers for
Children; The Haldane Society; Rights of
Women; Liberty; Association of Women
Barristers; The Howard League for Penal
Reform; BASPCAN; Commonwealth
Lawyers' Association; International Bar
Association; Amnesty International; Justice;
Fawcett Society; Society of Labour Lawyers;
National Council for Family Proceedings;
Friend: Mothers apart from their children

Other professional experience: Member of Social
Security Appeals Tribunals for 14 years to
1991

Publications: List available from Chambers

Reported Cases
Rv Woodgreen Crown Court ex parte P
[1983] 1 FLR 206,
Re J (a minor) (Care Order: Wardship)
[1984] FLR 43,
Re BA (Wardship and Adoption) [1985]
FLR 1008,
M v Westminster CC [1985] FLR 325,
*R v Salisbury and Tisbury and Mere
Combined JC ex parte B* [1986] FLR 1,
R v the United Kingdom Government
[1988] 2 FLR 445,
Re F (minors) (denial of contact) [1993] 2
FLR 667,
*Re P (minors) (contact with children in
care)* [1993] 2 FLR 156,
*Re D (a minor) (Care or Supervision
order)* [1993] 2 FLR 423,
R v LB Brent ex parte S [1994] 1 FLR 203,
R v LB Barnet ex parte B [1994] 1 FLR 592,

*Re W (minors) (Removal from Jurisdic-
tion)* [1994] 1 FLR 842,
Re H (a minor) (Adoption Proceedings)
[1994] 2 FLR 437,
Re W (Wardship: discharge: publicity)
[1995] 2 FLR 466,
Re E (Parental responsibility: blood tests)
[1995] 1 FLR 392,
*Re M (Care: Contact: Grandmother's
Application)* [1995] 2 FLR 81,
*Re C (a minor) (Grandfather's applica-
tion)* [1997] Fam Law 456,
Re D (abduction: aquiescence) [1998] 1
FLR 686.

JANE HOYAL is a founder member of Chambers, and Head of the 20-strong family law
team. She writes articles and reviews for
various publications including *Family Law*,
Legal Action, *Childright*, *Representing
Children*, and the *Association of Lawyers
for Children*. She has advised the media
and appeared in some TV and radio docu-
mentaries. She writes legal submissions in
respect of family law-related issues and
proof-reads some legal publications and
DoH sponsored research. She is committed
to the implementation of equality
throughout the legal system. She chaired
the National Conference on domestic
violence and children in 1998 which lead to
the report *A cry in the dark – children and
domestic violence*, which was launched in
1999 to support the making and implementation of a comprehensive, interdepart-
mental Government strategy in respect of
the eradication of violence in the home.

Jane lives in Kent with her husband and their three sons.

HOYLE MARK STANLEY WADIH

1 Gray's Inn Square, Chambers of the Baroness Scotland of Asthal QC
1st Floor, London WC1R 5AG,
Telephone: 0171 405 3000
E-mail: clerks@onegrays.demon.co.uk
Call Date: July 1978, Inner Temple
Pupil Master
Qualifications: [BA, PhD, FCIArb]

HUBBARD MARK IAIN

1 New Square
Ground Floor, Lincoln's Inn, London
WC2A 3SA, Telephone: 0171 405 0884/5/6/
7 E-mail: clerks@1newsquare.law.co.uk
Call Date: Nov 1991, Middle Temple
Pupil Master

HUBBARD MICHAEL JOSEPH QC (1985)

1 Paper Buildings
1st Floor, Temple, London EC4Y 7EP,
Telephone: 0171 353 3728/4953
Call Date: May 1972, Gray's Inn
Recorder

HUBBLE BENEDICT JOHN WAKELIN

Chambers of John L Powell QC
Four New Square, Lincoln's Inn, London
WC2A 3RJ, Telephone: 0171 797 8000
E-mail: barristers@4newsquare.com
Call Date: Nov 1992, Middle Temple
Qualifications: [BA (Hons), Dip in Law]

HUCKLE THEODORE DAVID

33 Park Place
Cardiff CF1 3BA,
Telephone: 02920 233313
Call Date: July 1985, Lincoln's Inn
Pupil Master
Qualifications: [BA, LLM (Cantab)]

HUDA MISS ABIDA ALIA JEHAN

8 King's Bench Walk
2nd Floor, Temple, London EC4Y 7DU,
Telephone: 0171 797 8888

8 King's Bench Walk North
1 Park Square East, Leeds LS1 2NE,
Telephone: 0113 2439797
Call Date: Nov 1989, Middle Temple
Qualifications: [LLB Hons]

HUDA SHAMSUL

1 Wensley Avenue
Woodford Green, Essex, IG8 9HE,
Telephone: 0181 505 9259
The Chambers of Mr Ali Mohammed Azhar
Basement, 9 King's Bench Walk, Temple,
London EC4Y 7DX,
Telephone: 0171 353 9564
E-mail: jvlee@btinternet.com
Call Date: July 1976, Lincoln's Inn
Qualifications: [MA]

HUDSON ANTHONY SEAN

Doughty Street Chambers
11 Doughty Street, London WC1N 2PG,
Telephone: 0171 404 1313
E-mail:enquiries@doughtystreet.co.uk
Call Date: Nov 1996, Middle Temple
Qualifications: [LLB (Hons)(Exon)]

HUDSON CHRISTOPHER JOHN

Deans Court Chambers
24 St John Street, Manchester M3 4DF,
Telephone: 0161 214 6000
E-mail: clerks@deanscourt.co.uk
Deans Court Chambers
41-43 Market Place, Preston PR1 1AH,
Telephone: 01772 555163
E-mail: clerks@deanscourt.co.uk
Call Date: May 1987, Lincoln's Inn
Qualifications: [MA (Oxon)]

HUDSON MISS ELISABETH HELEN

3 Paper Buildings
Temple, London EC4Y 7EU,
Telephone: 020 7583 8055
E-mail: London@3paper.com
3 Paper Buildings (Bournemouth)
20 Lorne Park Road, Bournemouth,
Dorset, BH1 1JN,
Telephone: 01202 292102
E-mail: Bournemouth@3paper.com
3 Paper Buildings (Winchester)
4 St Peter Street, Winchester SO23 8BW,
Telephone: 01962 868884
E-mail: winchester@3paper.com

3 Paper Buildings (Oxford)
1 Alfred Street, High Street, Oxford
OX1 4EH, Telephone: 01865 793736
E-mail: oxford@3paper.com
Call Date: Nov 1987, Gray's Inn
Pupil Master
Qualifications: [LLB (Bucks)]

HUDSON MS EMMA CAROLYN VAUGHAN

One Garden Court Family Law Chambers
Ground Floor, Temple, London
EC4Y 9BJ, Telephone: 0171 797 7900
E-mail: clerks@onegardencourt.co.uk
Call Date: Feb 1995, Inner Temple
Qualifications: [MA (Edinburgh), CPE (Lond)]

HUDSON MISS KATHRYN JANE

14 Gray's Inn Square
Gray's Inn, London WC1R 5JP,
Telephone: 0171 242 0858
E-mail: 100712.2134@compuserve.com
Call Date: July 1981, Middle Temple
Pupil Master
Qualifications: [LLB (Bris)]

HUDSON MISS RACHEL SOPHIA MARGARET

Trinity Chambers
9-12 Trinity Chare, Quayside, Newcastle
upon Tyne NE1 3DF,
Telephone: 0191 232 1927
E-mail: info@trinitychambers.co.uk
Call Date: July 1985, Middle Temple
Pupil Master
Qualifications: [LLB (Lond)]

HUFFER THOMAS IAN

Young Street Chambers
38 Young Street, Manchester M3 3FT,
Telephone: 0161 833 0489
E-mail: clerks@young-st-chambers.com
Call Date: Nov 1979, Gray's Inn
Qualifications: [MA (Oxon)]

HUFFORD MISS VICTORIA RACHEL

Assize Court Chambers
14 Small Street, Bristol BS1 1DE,
Telephone: 0117 9264587
E-mail:chambers@assize-court-chambers.co.uk
Call Date: Oct 1994, Gray's Inn
Qualifications: [BA]

HUGH-JONES GEORGE

3 Serjeants' Inn
London EC4Y 1BQ,
Telephone: 0171 353 5537
E-mail: clerks@3serjeantsinn.com
Call Date: Nov 1983, Middle Temple
Pupil Master
Qualifications: [MA (Cantab), Dip Law]

HUGHES ADRIAN WARWICK

4 Pump Court
Temple, London EC4Y 7AN,
Telephone: 020 7842 5555
E-mail:chambers@4pumpcourt.law.co.uk
Call Date: July 1984, Middle Temple
Pupil Master
Qualifications: [MA (Oxon)]

HUGHES MISS ANNA GABRIEL

Wilberforce Chambers
8 New Square, Lincoln's Inn, London
WC2A 3QP, Telephone: 0171 306 0102
E-mail: chambers@wilberforce.co.uk
Call Date: Apr 1978, Lincoln's Inn
Qualifications: [BA (Cantab)]

Types of work: Chancery (general), Commercial property, Equity, wills and trusts, Pensions

HUGHES DR CONSTANCE MARY

Counsels' Chambers
2nd Floor, 10-11 Gray's Inn Square,
London WC1R 5JD,
Telephone: 0171 405 2576
E-mail:clerks@10-11graysinnsquare.co.uk
Call Date: Oct 1994, Inner Temple
Qualifications: [BA (Hull), MPhil (Notts), PhD, CPE (Middx)]

HUGHES DAVID LLOYD

2 Gray's Inn Square Chambers
2nd Floor, Gray's Inn, London WC1R 5AA,
Telephone: 020 7242 0328
E-mail: clerks@2gis.co.uk
Call Date: July 1980, Inner Temple
Pupil Master
Qualifications: [LLB (Hull)]

HUGHES DERMOT FRANCIS

Paradise Chambers
26 Paradise Square, Sheffield S1 2DE,
Telephone: 0114 2738951
E-mail: timbooth@paradise-sq.co.uk
Call Date: Nov 1993, Gray's Inn
Qualifications: [LLB, LLM]

HUGHES GARETH DUNCAN

**1 Gray's Inn Square, Chambers of the
Baroness Scotland of Asthal QC**
1st Floor, London WC1R 5AG,
Telephone: 0171 405 3000
E-mail: clerks@onegrays.demon.co.uk
Call Date: Nov 1985, Gray's Inn
Pupil Master
Qualifications: [LLB (Lond)]

HUGHES HYWEL TUDOR

30 Park Place
Cardiff CF1 3BA,
Telephone: 01222 398421
E-mail: 100757.1456@compuserve.com
Call Date: Oct 1995, Gray's Inn
Qualifications: [LLB (Wales)]

HUGHES IAIN HAMILTON-DOUGLAS QC (1996)

Chambers of John L Powell QC
Four New Square, Lincoln's Inn, London
WC2A 3RJ, Telephone: 0171 797 8000
E-mail: barristers@4newsquare.com
Call Date: July 1974, Inner Temple
Assistant Recorder
Qualifications: [LLB]

HUGHES IGNATIUS LOYOLA

Albion Chambers
Broad Street, Bristol BS1 1DR,
Telephone: 0117 9272144
Call Date: Apr 1986, Middle Temple
Pupil Master
Qualifications: [LLB (N'Castle)]

HUGHES MISS JUDITH CAROLINE ANNE QC (1994)

1 Mitre Court Buildings
Temple, London EC4Y 7BS,
Telephone: 0171 797 7070
E-mail: clerks@1mcb.com
Call Date: July 1974, Inner Temple
Recorder
Qualifications: [LLB]

HUGHES MISS KATHRYN ANN

Iscoed Chambers
86 St Helen's Road, Swansea, West
Glamorgan, SA1 4BQ,
Telephone: 01792 652988/9/330
Call Date: Nov 1992, Inner Temple
Qualifications: [LLB (Bris)]

HUGHES LEIGHTON ALEXANDER

Newport Chambers
12 Clytha Park Road, Newport, Gwent,
NP9 47L, Telephone: 01633 267403/
255855
Call Date: July 1989, Inner Temple
Qualifications: [LLB Hons]

HUGHES MISS MARY JOSEPHINE

Chambers of Lord Goodhart QC
Ground Floor, 3 New Square, Lincoln's
Inn, London WC2A 3RS,
Telephone: 0171 405 5577
E-mail:law@threenewsquare.demon.co.uk
Call Date: Feb 1995, Gray's Inn
Qualifications: [BA, Dip Law]

HUGHES MRS MELANIE CATHERINE

3 Paper Buildings
Temple, London EC4Y 7EU,
Telephone: 020 7583 8055
E-mail: London@3paper.com
3 Paper Buildings (Bournemouth)
20 Lorne Park Road, Bournemouth,
Dorset, BH1 1JN,
Telephone: 01202 292102
E-mail: Bournemouth@3paper.com
3 Paper Buildings (Oxford)
1 Alfred Street, High Street, Oxford
OX1 4EH, Telephone: 01865 793736
E-mail: oxford@3paper.com

D

3 Paper Buildings (Winchester)
4 St Peter Street, Winchester SO23 8BW,
Telephone: 01962 868884
E-mail: winchester@3paper.com
Call Date: Nov 1995, Middle Temple
Qualifications: [BA (Hons)(W.Indies)]

HUGHES MISS MERYL ELIZABETH

Fenners Chambers
3 Madingley Road, Cambridge CB3 0EE,
Telephone: 01223 368761
E-mail: clerks@fennerschambers.co.uk
Fenners Chambers
8-12 Priestgate, Peterborough PE1 1JA,
Telephone: 01733 562030
E-mail: clerks@fennerschambers.co.uk
Call Date: Nov 1987, Gray's Inn
Qualifications: [LLB (Leeds)]

HUGHES PETER THOMAS QC (1993)

3 Paper Buildings
Temple, London EC4Y 7EU,
Telephone: 020 7583 8055
E-mail: London@3paper.com
Nicholas Street Chambers
22 Nicholas Street, Chester CH1 2NX,
Telephone: 01244 323886
E-mail: clerks@40king.co.uk
3 Paper Buildings (Bournemouth)
20 Lorne Park Road, Bournemouth,
Dorset, BH1 1JN,
Telephone: 01202 292102
E-mail: Bournemouth@3paper.com
3 Paper Buildings (Winchester)
4 St Peter Street, Winchester SO23 8BW,
Telephone: 01962 868884
E-mail: winchester@3paper.com
3 Paper Buildings (Oxford)
1 Alfred Street, High Street, Oxford
OX1 4EH, Telephone: 01865 793736
E-mail: oxford@3paper.com
*Call Date: July 1971, Gray's Inn
Recorder*
Qualifications: [LLB (Hons)(Bris), Tribunals]

HUGHES MISS RACHEL

Oriel Chambers
14 Water Street, Liverpool L2 8TD,
Telephone: 0151 236 7191/236 4321
E-mail: clerks@oriel-chambers.co.uk
Call Date: Nov 1995, Gray's Inn
Qualifications: [BA]

HUGHES SIMON DAVID

Keating Chambers
10 Essex Street, Outer Temple, London
WC2R 3AA, Telephone: 0171 544 2600
Call Date: Nov 1995, Gray's Inn
Qualifications: [BA]

HUGHES STANLEY GEORGE

Five Paper Buildings
1st Floor, Five Paper Bldgs, Temple,
London EC4Y 7HB,
Telephone: 0171 583 6117
E-mail:clerks@5-paperbuildings.law.co.uk
*Call Date: July 1971, Lincoln's Inn
Pupil Master*

HUGHES THOMAS MERFYN QC (1994)

Goldsmith Building
1st Floor, Temple, London EC4Y 7BL,
Telephone: 0171 353 7881
E-mail:clerks@goldsmith-building.law.co.uk
Nicholas Street Chambers
22 Nicholas Street, Chester CH1 2NX,
Telephone: 01244 323886
E-mail: clerks@40king.co.uk
*Call Date: Nov 1971, Inner Temple
Recorder*
Qualifications: [LLB (L'pool)]

HUGHES WILLIAM LLOYD

9-12 Bell Yard
London WC2A 2LF,
Telephone: 0171 400 1800
E-mail: clerks@bellyard.co.uk
*Call Date: Nov 1989, Gray's Inn
Pupil Master*
Qualifications: [BSc (Leic)]

HUGHES YWAIN GWYDION

9 Park Place
Cardiff CF1 3DP,
Telephone: 01222 382731
Call Date: Nov 1994, Gray's Inn
Qualifications: [LLB (Wales)]

HULL LESLIE DAVID

Chambers of John Hand QC
9 St John Street, Manchester M3 4DN,
Telephone: 0161 955 9000
E-mail: ninesjs@gconnect.com
Call Date: Nov 1972, Middle Temple
Pupil Master, Recorder
Qualifications: [MA (Oxon)]

HULME MISS AMANDA CLAIRE

Gough Square Chambers
6-7 Gough Square, London EC4A 3DE,
Telephone: 0171 353 0924
E-mail: gsc@goughsq.co.uk
Call Date: 1997, Middle Temple
Qualifications: [LLB (Hons)(Kent)]

HULME GRAHAM ERNEST

4 King's Bench Walk
Ground/First Floor/Basement, Temple,
London EC4Y 7DL,
Telephone: 0171 822 8822
E-mail: 4kbw@barristersatlaw.com
Call Date: Nov 1977, Lincoln's Inn
Pupil Master
Qualifications: [LLB (Leeds)]

HULME JOHN TRELAWNEY STEWART

Goldsmith Chambers
Ground Floor, Goldsmith Building,
Temple, London EC4Y 7BL,
Telephone: 0171 353 6802/3/4/5
E-mail:clerks@goldsmithchambers.law.co.uk
Call Date: Nov 1983, Middle Temple
Pupil Master
Qualifications: [BSC, Dip Law]

HUMBERSTONE MRS PEARL EDITH

Verulam Chambers
Peer House, 8-14 Verulam Street, Gray's
Inn, London WC1X 8LZ,
Telephone: 0171 813 2400
Call Date: Nov 1987, Middle Temple
Pupil Master
Qualifications: [LLB]

HUMPAGE MISS HEATHER JUNE

9 Woodhouse Square
Leeds LS3 1AD,
Telephone: 0113 2451986
E-mail: clerks@9woodhouse.co.uk
Call Date: Oct 1996, Middle Temple
Qualifications: [LLB (Hons)(B'Ham)]

HUMPHREYS MS JACQUELINE LOUISE

St John's Chambers
Small Street, Bristol BS1 1DW,
Telephone: 0117 9213456/298514
E-mail: @stjohnschambers.co.uk
Call Date: Oct 1994, Lincoln's Inn
Qualifications: [BA (Hons)]

HUMPHREYS RICHARD WILLIAM

4-5 Gray's Inn Square
Ground Floor, Gray's Inn, London
WC1R 5JP, Telephone: 0171 404 5252
E-mail:chambers@4-5graysinnsquare.co.uk
Call Date: July 1986, Inner Temple
Qualifications: [LLB (Notts), LLM (Cantab)]

HUMPHRIES DAVID JOHN

28 St John Street
Manchester M3 4DJ,
Telephone: 0161 834 8418
E-mail: clerk@28stjohnst.co.uk
Call Date: July 1988, Middle Temple
Qualifications: [LLB (Hons)]

HUMPHRIES MICHAEL JOHN

2 Mitre Court Buildings
2nd Floor, Temple, London EC4Y 7BX,
Telephone: 0171 583 1380
E-mail: clerks@2mcb.co.uk
Call Date: July 1982, Inner Temple
Pupil Master
Qualifications: [LLB (Leic)]

HUMPHRIES PAUL BENEDICT

Deans Court Chambers
24 St John Street, Manchester M3 4DF,
Telephone: 0161 214 6000
E-mail: clerks@deanscourt.co.uk

Deans Court Chambers
41-43 Market Place, Preston PR1 1AH,
Telephone: 01772 555163
E-mail: clerks@deanscourt.co.uk
Call Date: Nov 1986, Middle Temple
Qualifications: [BA (Oxon)]

HUMPHRY RICHARD MICHAEL

28 St John Street
Manchester M3 4DJ,
Telephone: 0161 834 8418
E-mail: clerk@28stjohnst.co.uk
Call Date: July 1972, Gray's Inn
Qualifications: [MA (Cantab), LLB]

HUMPHRYES MISS JANE CAROLE

3 Raymond Buildings
Gray's Inn, London WC1R 5BH,
Telephone: 020 7831 3833
E-mail:chambers@threeraymond.demon.co.uk
Call Date: July 1983, Middle Temple
Pupil Master, Assistant Recorder
Qualifications: [BA (Kent)]

HUNGERFORD WALTER GUY BECHER

1 Harcourt Buildings
2nd Floor, Temple, London EC4Y 9DA,
Telephone: 0171 353 9421/0375
E-mail:clerks@1harcourtbuildings.law.co.uk
Call Date: Nov 1971, Middle Temple

HUNJAN SATINDER PAL SINGH

5 Fountain Court
Steelhouse Lane, Birmingham B4 6DR,
Telephone: 0121 606 0500
E-mail:clerks@5fountaincourt.law.co.uk
Call Date: July 1984, Gray's Inn
Qualifications: [LLB (B'ham)]

HUNT MISS ALISON JANET

St Paul's House
5th Floor, St Paul's House, 23 Park Square
South, Leeds LS1 2ND,
Telephone: 0113 2455866
E-mail: catherinegrimshaw@stpauls-
chambers.demon.co.uk
Call Date: July 1986, Gray's Inn
Qualifications: [BA (Cantab)]

HUNT DAVID RODERIC NOTLEY QC (1987)

Blackstone Chambers
Blackstone House, Temple, London
EC4Y 9BW, Telephone: 0171 583 1770
E-mail:clerks@blackstonechambers.com
Call Date: July 1969, Gray's Inn
Recorder
Qualifications: [MA (Hons) (Cantab)]

HUNT JAMES QC (1987)

Chambers of Michael Pert QC
36 Bedford Row, London WC1R 4JH,
Telephone: 0171 421 8000
E-mail: 36bedfordrow@link.org
Chambers of Michael Pert QC
104 New Walk, Leicester LE1 7EA,
Telephone: 0116 249 2020
Chambers of Michael Pert QC
24 Albion Place, Northampton NN1 1UD,
Telephone: 01604 602333
Call Date: July 1968, Gray's Inn
Recorder
Qualifications: [MA (Oxon)]

HUNT MURRAY ROBERT

4-5 Gray's Inn Square
Ground Floor, Gray's Inn, London
WC1R 5JP, Telephone: 0171 404 5252
E-mail:chambers@4-5graysinnsquare.co.uk
Call Date: Nov 1992, Middle Temple
Qualifications: [BA (Hons), BCL, LLM]

HUNT RICHARD MARK

15 Winckley Square
Preston PR1 3JJ,
Telephone: 01772 252828
E-mail:clerks@winckleysq.demon.co.uk
Call Date: July 1985, Lincoln's Inn
Qualifications: [LLB]

HUNT RODERICK IRVIN

Fountain Chambers
Cleveland Business Centre, 1 Watson
Street, Middlesbrough TS1 2RQ,
Telephone: 01642 804040
E-mail:fountainchambers@onyxnet.co.uk
Call Date: July 1981, Middle Temple
Qualifications: [MA (Cantab)]

HUNT STEPHEN

4 Stone Buildings
Ground Floor, Lincoln's Inn, London
WC2A 3XT, Telephone: 0171 242 5524
E-mail:clerks@4stonebuildings.law.co.uk
Call Date: July 1968, Lincoln's Inn
Pupil Master
Qualifications: [MA (Oxon)]

HUNTER ANDREW MICHAEL

Blackstone Chambers
Blackstone House, Temple, London
EC4Y 9BW, Telephone: 0171 583 1770
E-mail:clerks@blackstonechambers.com
Call Date: Oct 1993, Middle Temple
Qualifications: [BA (Hons)(Oxon)]

HUNTER ANTHONY CHARLES BRYAN

5 Pump Court
Ground Floor, Temple, London
EC4Y 7AP, Telephone: 020 7353 2532
E-mail: FivePump@netcomuk.co.uk
Call Date: Nov 1962, Inner Temple
Pupil Master
Qualifications: [BA (Oxon)]

HUNTER MISS CAROLINE MARGARET

Arden Chambers
27 John Street, London WC1N 2BL,
Telephone: 020 7242 4244
E-mail:clerks@arden-chambers.law.co.uk
Call Date: Nov 1985, Middle Temple
Qualifications: [BA (Oxon)]

HUNTER GEOFFREY MARTIN

Westgate Chambers
67a Westgate Road, Newcastle upon Tyne
NE1 1SG, Telephone: 0191 261 4407/
2329785
E-mail:pracman@westgatechambers.law.co.u
k
Call Date: Feb 1979, Gray's Inn
Qualifications: [LLB (Newc)]

HUNTER IAN GERALD ADAMSON QC (1980)

Essex Court Chambers
24 Lincoln's Inn Fields, London
WC2A 3ED, Telephone: 0171 813 8000
E-mail:clerksroom@essexcourt-chambers.co.u
k
Call Date: Nov 1967, Inner Temple
Recorder
Qualifications: [MA, LLB (Cantab), LLM
(Harvard)]

HUNTER (JAMES) MARTIN HUGH

Essex Court Chambers
24 Lincoln's Inn Fields, London
WC2A 3ED, Telephone: 0171 813 8000
E-mail:clerksroom@essexcourt-chambers.co.u
k
Call Date: May 1994, Lincoln's Inn
Qualifications: [BA (Cantab)]

HUNTER JOHN DAVID

Alexandra Chambers
163 Albert Road, London N22 7AQ,
Telephone: 0181 881 8523
Call Date: Feb 1991, Lincoln's Inn
Qualifications: [LLB (Buck'ham)]

HUNTER MACK ROBERT

2-4 Tudor Street
London EC4Y 0AA,
Telephone: 0171 797 7111
E-mail: clerks@rfqc.co.uk
Call Date: 1979, Gray's Inn
Pupil Master
Qualifications: [MA (Oxon)]

HUNTER PROFESSOR MUIR VANE SKERRETT QC (1965)

3/4 South Square
Gray's Inn, London WC1R 5HP,
Telephone: 0171 696 9900
E-mail: clerks@southsquare.com
Call Date: 1938, Gray's Inn
Qualifications: [MA, MRI]

HUNTER MISS SUSAN CLARE

St John's Chambers
Small Street, Bristol BS1 1DW,
Telephone: 0117 9213456/298514
E-mail: @stjohnschambers.co.uk
Call Date: July 1985, Inner Temple
Pupil Master
Qualifications: [MA (Cantab) Dip Law]

HUNTER WILLIAM EDWARD HENRY

Veritas Chambers
33 Corn Street, Bristol BS1 1HT,
Telephone: 0117 930 8802
Call Date: July 1982, Gray's Inn
Qualifications: [BA (Hons)]

HUNTER WILLIAM QUIGLEY

No. 1 Serjeants' Inn
5th Floor Fleet Street, Temple, London
EC4Y 1LH, Telephone: 0171 415 6666
E-mail:no1serjeantsinn@btinternet.com
Call Date: July 1972, Inner Temple
Pupil Master
Qualifications: [MA (Cantab)]

HUNTER MISS WINIFRED

6 Gray's Inn Square
Ground Floor, Gray's Inn, London
WC1R 5AZ, Telephone: 0171 242 1052
E-mail: 6graysinn@clara.co.uk
Call Date: Nov 1990, Middle Temple
Qualifications: [LLB (Lond)]

HUNTER WINSTON RONALD

28 St John Street
Manchester M3 4DJ,
Telephone: 0161 834 8418
E-mail: clerk@28stjohnst.co.uk
Call Date: July 1985, Lincoln's Inn
Pupil Master, Assistant Recorder
Qualifications: [LLB (Leeds)]

HURD JAMES ROBERT

St James's Chambers
68 Quay Street, Manchester M3 3EJ,
Telephone: 0161 834 7000
E-mail: clerks@stjameschambers.co.uk
Call Date: Oct 1994, Gray's Inn
Qualifications: [LLB]

HURD MARK DUNSDON

2 New Street
Leicester LE1 5NA,
Telephone: 0116 2625906
E-mail: clerks@2newstreet.co.uk
Call Date: Feb 1993, Gray's Inn
Qualifications: [LLB]

HURLOCK LUGARD JOHN

3 Hare Court
1 Little Essex Street, London WC2R 3LD,
Telephone: 0171 395 2000
Call Date: Oct 1993, Gray's Inn
Qualifications: [LLB (Coventry)]

HURST ANDREW ROBERT

23 Essex Street
London WC2R 3AS,
Telephone: 0171 413 0353/836 8366
E-mail:clerks@essexstreet23.demon.co.uk
Call Date: Nov 1992, Inner Temple
Qualifications: [MA (Oxon)]

HURST BRIAN

17 Bedford Row
London WC1R 4EB,
Telephone: 0171 831 7314
E-mail: iboard7314@aol.com
Call Date: July 1983, Middle Temple
Pupil Master
Qualifications: [MA (Oxon)]

HURST MARTIN RICHARD JOHN

4 King's Bench Walk
Ground/First Floor/Basement, Temple,
London EC4Y 7DL,
Telephone: 0171 822 8822
E-mail: 4kbw@barristersatlaw.com
Call Date: July 1985, Middle Temple
Pupil Master
Qualifications: [LLB (L'pool)]

HURTLEY MISS DIANE ELAINE

Furnival Chambers
32 Furnival Street, London EC4A 1JQ,
Telephone: 0171 405 3232
E-mail: clerks@furnivallaw.co.uk
Call Date: Oct 1990, Gray's Inn
Qualifications: [LLB]

HURWORTH MISS JILLIAN MARY

10 King's Bench Walk
Ground Floor, Temple, London
EC4Y 7EB, Telephone: 0171 353 7742
E-mail: 10kbw@lineone.net
4 King's Bench Walk
2nd Floor, Temple, London EC4Y 7DL,
Telephone: 020 7353 3581
E-mail: clerks@4kbw.co.uk
Call Date: Oct 1993, Inner Temple
Qualifications: [BA (Cantab)]

HUSAIN MISS LAUREEN ANWAR

**11 Bolt Court (also at 7 Stone Buildings
– 1st Floor)**
London EC4A 3DQ,
Telephone: 0171 353 2300
E-mail: boltct11@aol.com
**7 Stone Buildings (also at 11 Bolt
Court)**
1st Floor, Lincoln's Inn, London
WC2A 3SZ, Telephone: 0171 242 0961
E-mail:larthur@7stonebuildings.law.co.uk
Redhill Chambers
Seloduct House, 30 Station Road, Redhill,
Surrey, RH1 1NF,
Telephone: 01737 780781
Call Date: 1997, Lincoln's Inn
Qualifications: [LLB (Warw)]

HUSAIN SYED RAZA

Two Garden Court
1st Floor, Middle Temple, London
EC4Y 9BL, Telephone: 0171 353 1633
E-mail:barristers@2gardenct.law.co.uk
Call Date: Nov 1993, Middle Temple
Qualifications: [BA (Hons)(Oxon), CPE
(London)]

HUSCROFT RICHARD MICHAEL

Dr Johnson's Chambers
The Atrium Court, Apex Plaza, Reading,
Berkshire, RG1 1AX,
Telephone: 01734 254221
Call Date: Nov 1990, Middle Temple
Qualifications: [BA (Oxon), Dip Law (PCL)]

HUSEYIN MARTIN TREVOR

14 Tooks Court
Cursitor St, London EC4A 1LB,
Telephone: 0171 405 8828
E-mail: clerks@tooks.law.co.uk
Call Date: Nov 1988, Inner Temple
Qualifications: [BA (Sussex),Dip Law]

HUSKINSON GEORGE NICHOLAS NEVIL

4-5 Gray's Inn Square
Ground Floor, Gray's Inn, London
WC1R 5JP, Telephone: 0171 404 5252
E-mail:chambers@4-5graysinnsquare.co.uk
Call Date: July 1971, Gray's Inn
Recorder
Qualifications: [MA (Cantab)]

HUSSAIN BASHARAT

Goldsworth Chambers
1st Floor, 11 Gray's Inn Square, London
WC1R 5JD, Telephone: 0171 405 7117
Call Date: Nov 1997, Gray's Inn
Qualifications: [LLB (Manch)]

HUSSAIN MISS FRIDA KHANAM

17 Carlton Crescent
Southampton SO15 2XR,
Telephone: 023 8032 0320/0823 2003
E-mail: greg@jg17cc.co.uk
Call Date: Oct 1995, Inner Temple
Qualifications: [LLB (Hons) , (Huddersfield)]

HUSSAIN MUKHTAR QC (1992)

Lincoln House Chambers
5th Floor, Lincoln House, 1 Brazennose
Street, Manchester M2 5EL,
Telephone: 0161 832 5701
E-mail: info@lincolnhse.co.uk
Call Date: July 1971, Middle Temple
Recorder

HUSSAIN RAFAQUAT MAHMOOD

2 Middle Temple Lane
3rd Floor, Temple, London EC4Y 9AA,
Telephone: 0171 583 4540
Call Date: Oct 1996, Middle Temple
Qualifications: [BA (Hons), CPE (Lancs)]

D

HUSSEIN TIMUR

Phoenix Chambers
First Floor, Gray's Inn Chambers, Gray's
Inn, London WC1R 5JA,
Telephone: 0171 404 7888
E-mail:clerks@phoenix-chambers.co.uk
1 Pump Court
Lower Ground Floor, Temple, London
EC4Y 7AB, Telephone: 0171 583 2012/
353 4341
E-mail: [name]@1pumpcourt.co.uk
Call Date: 1993, Inner Temple
Qualifications: [LLB]

HUSSEY MISS ANN ELIZABETH

29 Bedford Row Chambers
London WC1R 4HE,
Telephone: 0171 831 2626
Call Date: July 1981, Middle Temple
Qualifications: [BA (Hons)]

HUSTON GRAHAM MARTIN

4 King's Bench Walk
Ground/First Floor/Basement, Temple,
London EC4Y 7DL,
Telephone: 0171 822 8822
E-mail: 4kbw@barristersatlaw.com
Call Date: Feb 1991, Inner Temple
Pupil Master
Qualifications: [LLB (PCL)]

HUTCHIN EDWARD ALISTER DAVID

Bracton Chambers
95a Chancery Lane, London WC2A 1DT,
Telephone: 0171 242 4248
Call Date: 1996, Middle Temple
Qualifications: [LLB (Hons)(Notts)]

HUTCHINGS MARTIN ANTHONY

199 Strand
London WC2R 1DR,
Telephone: 0171 379 9779
E-mail: chambers@199strand.co.uk
Call Date: Feb 1986, Middle Temple
Pupil Master
Qualifications: [MA (Oxon)]

HUTCHINGS MATTHEW HOWARD OLSEN

22 Old Buildings
Lincoln's Inn, London WC2A 3UJ,
Telephone: 0171 831 0222
Call Date: Nov 1993, Inner Temple
Qualifications: [BA (Oxon), LLB (City)]

HUTCHINSON COLIN THOMAS

Two Garden Court
1st Floor, Middle Temple, London
EC4Y 9BL, Telephone: 0171 353 1633
E-mail:barristers@2gardenct.law.co.uk
Call Date: Oct 1990, Middle Temple
Pupil Master
Qualifications: [LLB (Hons)]

HUTT MICHAEL ARTHUR

6 Fountain Court
Steelhouse Lane, Birmingham B4 6DR,
Telephone: 0121 233 3282
E-mail: clerks@sixfountain.co.uk
Call Date: Nov 1968, Middle Temple
Qualifications: [BA, LLB (Cantab)]

HUTTON ALEXANDER FORBES

Chambers of Kieran Coonan QC
Ground Floor, 6 Pump Court, Temple,
London EC4Y 7AR,
Telephone: 0171 583 6013/2510
E-mail: clerks@6-pumpcourt.law.co.uk
Call Date: Oct 1992, Gray's Inn
Qualifications: [B.Sc (Bris)]

HUTTON MISS CAROLINE

Enterprise Chambers
9 Old Square, Lincoln's Inn, London
WC2A 3SR, Telephone: 0171 405 9471
E-mail:enterprise.london@dial.pipex.com
Enterprise Chambers
38 Park Square, Leeds LS1 2PA,
Telephone: 0113 246 0391
E-mail:enterprise.leeds@dial.pipex.com
Enterprise Chambers
65 Quayside, Newcastle upon Tyne
NE1 3DS, Telephone: 0191 222 3344
E-mail:enterprise.newcastle@dial.pipex.com
Call Date: Nov 1979, Middle Temple
Pupil Master
Qualifications: [MA (Cantab)]

HUYTON BRIAN JAMES

17 Bedford Row
London WC1R 4EB,
Telephone: 0171 831 7314
E-mail: iboard7314@aol.com
Call Date: July 1977, Inner Temple
Pupil Master
Qualifications: [BA, LLB (Lond)]

HYAM JEREMY RUPERT DANIEL

1 Crown Office Row
Ground Floor, Temple, London
EC4Y 7HH, Telephone: 0171 797 7500
E-mail: mail@onecrownofficerow.com
Call Date: Nov 1995, Gray's Inn
Qualifications: [BA (Hons)]

HYAMS OLIVER MARKS

5 Paper Buildings
Ground Floor, Temple, London
EC4Y 7HB, Telephone: 0171 583 9275/
583 4555 E-mail: 5paper@link.org
Call Date: July 1989, Middle Temple
Qualifications: [LLB]

HYAMS-PARISH ANTONY ROBERT

Acre Lane Neighbourhood Chambers
30A Acre Lane, London SW2 5SG,
Telephone: 0171 274 4400
E-mail:barristerschambers@acrelane.demon.co.uk
Call Date: May 1995, Gray's Inn
Qualifications: [B.ED (Hons)]

HYDE CHARLES GORDON

Albion Chambers
Broad Street, Bristol BS1 1DR,
Telephone: 0117 9272144
Call Date: July 1988, Middle Temple
Pupil Master
Qualifications: [LLB (Hons) (Manch)]

HYDE MS MARCIA

22 Old Buildings
Lincoln's Inn, London WC2A 3UJ,
Telephone: 0171 831 0222
Call Date: Oct 1992, Inner Temple
Qualifications: [BA (Leeds), MA, Dip Law]

HYLAND JAMES GRAHAM KEITH QC (1998)

Broadway House Chambers
Broadway House, 9 Bank Street, Bradford,
West Yorkshire, BD1 1TW,
Telephone: 01274 722560
E-mail: clerks@broadwayhouse.co.uk
Broadway House Chambers
31 Park Square West, Leeds LS1 2PF,
Telephone: 0113 246 2600
Call Date: July 1978, Inner Temple
Recorder
Qualifications: [BA (Newc)]

HYMANSON MISS DEANNA SUSAN

Cobden House Chambers
19 Quay Street, Manchester M3 3HN,
Telephone: 0161 833 6000
E-mail: clerks@cobden.co.uk
Call Date: Feb 1988, Middle Temple
Qualifications: [LLB (Hons) (Lond)]

HYNES PAUL RICHARD

3 Gray's Inn Square
Ground Floor, London WC1R 5AH,
Telephone: 0171 520 5600
E-mail: clerks@3gis.co.uk
Call Date: Nov 1987, Lincoln's Inn
Pupil Master
Qualifications: [BA (Hons)]

HYTNER BENET ALAN QC (1970)

22 Old Buildings
Lincoln's Inn, London WC2A 3UJ,
Telephone: 0171 831 0222
Byrom Street Chambers
Byrom Street, Manchester M3 4PF,
Telephone: 0161 829 2100
E-mail: Byromst25@aol.com
Call Date: Feb 1952, Middle Temple
Qualifications: [MA (Cantab)]

IFE MISS LINDEN ELIZABETH

Enterprise Chambers
9 Old Square, Lincoln's Inn, London
WC2A 3SR, Telephone: 0171 405 9471
E-mail:enterprise.london@dial.pipex.com
Enterprise Chambers
38 Park Square, Leeds LS1 2PA,
Telephone: 0113 246 0391
E-mail:enterprise.leeds@dial.pipex.com

Enterprise Chambers
65 Quayside, Newcastle upon Tyne
NE1 3DS, Telephone: 0191 222 3344
E-mail:enterprise.newcastle@dial.pipex.com
Call Date: Nov 1982, Middle Temple
Pupil Master
Qualifications: [MA (Oxon)]

IGORI KINGSLEY IZEHIUWA

8 King's Bench Walk
2nd Floor, Temple, London EC4Y 7DU,
Telephone: 0171 797 8888
Call Date: Feb 1993, Inner Temple
Qualifications: [LLB]

IHUOMAH MISS BIBIANA CHIWUBA

10 King's Bench Walk
1st Floor, Temple, London EC4Y 7EB,
Telephone: 0171 353 2501
Call Date: Nov 1986, Lincoln's Inn
Qualifications: [LLB(Hons)]

ILES ADRIAN

5 Paper Buildings
Ground Floor, Temple, London
EC4Y 7HB, Telephone: 0171 583 9275/
583 4555 E-mail: 5paper@link.org
Call Date: July 1980, Inner Temple
Pupil Master
Qualifications: [MA (Cantab)]

ILES DAVID

5 Fountain Court
Steelhouse Lane, Birmingham B4 6DR,
Telephone: 0121 606 0500
E-mail:clerks@5fountaincourt.law.co.uk
Call Date: July 1977, Inner Temple
Qualifications: [LLB (Lond)]

ILLINGWORTH STEPHEN JOHN

Mitre House Chambers
15-19 Devereux Court, London WC2R 3JJ,
Telephone: 0171 583 8233
Call Date: Feb 1993, Gray's Inn
Qualifications: [LLB (Hons)]

IMONA-RUSSEL ALFRED OMOAFENA

Essex House Chambers
Unit 6 (Part 2nd Floor South), Stratford
Office Village, 14-30 Romford Road,
London E15 4BZ,
Telephone: 0181 536 1077
Call Date: Nov 1992, Inner Temple
Qualifications: [LLB (Lond)]

INFIELD PAUL LOUIS

5 Paper Buildings
Ground Floor, Temple, London
EC4Y 7HB, Telephone: 0171 583 9275/
583 4555 E-mail: 5paper@link.org
Call Date: July 1980, Inner Temple
Pupil Master
Qualifications: [LLB (Sheff)]

INGHAM MISS ELIZABETH CLAIRE

Walnut House
63 St David's Hill, Exeter, Devon,
EX4 4DW, Telephone: 01392 279751
E-mail: 106627.2451@compuserve.com
Chambers of Michael Pert QC
36 Bedford Row, London WC1R 4JH,
Telephone: 0171 421 8000
E-mail: 36bedfordrow@link.org
Chambers of Michael Pert QC
24 Albion Place, Northampton NN1 1UD,
Telephone: 01604 602333
Chambers of Michael Pert QC
104 New Walk, Leicester LE1 7EA,
Telephone: 0116 249 2020
Call Date: Nov 1989, Middle Temple
Qualifications: [BA (Hons) (Oxon)]

INGHAM RICHARD LEE

32 Park Place
Cardiff CF1 3BA,
Telephone: 01222 397364
Call Date: Nov 1994, Lincoln's Inn
Qualifications: [LLB (Hons)(B'ham)]

INGLIS ALAN

One Garden Court Family Law Chambers
Ground Floor, Temple, London
EC4Y 9BJ, Telephone: 0171 797 7900
E-mail: clerks@onegardencourt.co.uk
Call Date: July 1989, Middle Temple
Pupil Master
Qualifications: [BA (Essex), MA (Warw), Dip
Law, C.Q.S.W]

PART D INDIVIDUAL BARRISTERS IN PRIVATE PRACTICE

INGLIS-JONES NIGEL JOHN QC (1982)

35 Essex Street
Temple, London WC2R 3AR,
Telephone: 0171 353 6381
E-mail: derek_jenkins@link.org
Call Date: June 1959, Inner Temple
Qualifications: [BA (Oxon)]

INGRAM JONATHAN ANTONY

Francis Taylor Building
Ground Floor, Temple, London
EC4Y 7BY, Telephone: 0171 353 7768/
7769/2711
E-mail:clerks@francistaylorbuilding.law.co.uk
Call Date: July 1984, Inner Temple
Pupil Master
Qualifications: [BA (Lond)]

INGRAM NIGEL COLQUHOUN

3 Hare Court
1 Little Essex Street, London WC2R 3LD,
Telephone: 0171 395 2000
Call Date: 1974, Inner Temple
Pupil Master

INMAN MELBOURNE DONALD QC (1998)

1 Fountain Court
Steelhouse Lane, Birmingham B4 6DR,
Telephone: 0121 236 5721
Call Date: July 1979, Inner Temple
Recorder
Qualifications: [MA (Oxon)]

INSALL RICHARD STUART

65-67 King Street
Leicester LE1 6RP,
Telephone: 0116 2547710
Call Date: Nov 1952, Gray's Inn
Pupil Master

INWARD MS LOUISE JANE

Sussex Chambers
9 Old Steine, Brighton, Sussex, BN1 1FJ,
Telephone: 01273 607953
Call Date: Nov 1995, Middle Temple
Qualifications: [LLB (Hons)]

INYUNDO RICHARD KWAME SWAKA

Chambers of Helen Grindrod QC
4th Floor, 15-19 Devereux Court, London
WC2R 3JJ, Telephone: 0171 583 2792
Call Date: 1997, Gray's Inn
Qualifications: [BA (L'pool)]

IQBAL ABDUL SHAFFAQ

Chambers of Andrew Campbell QC
10 Park Square, Leeds LS1 2LH,
Telephone: 0113 2455438
E-mail: clerks@10pksq.co.uk
Call Date: Oct 1994, Gray's Inn
Qualifications: [B.Pharm (Brad), Dip Law]

IRELAND MISS PENELOPE JANE

Wessex Chambers
48 Queens Road, Reading, Berkshire,
RG1 4BD, Telephone: 0118 956 8856
E-mail:wessexchambers@compuserve.com
Call Date: Oct 1996, Gray's Inn
Qualifications: [LLB (Bris)]

IRO AUGUSTINE OKEVURUMBA

First National Chambers
2nd Floor, First National Building, 24
Fenwick Street, Liverpool L2 7NE,
Telephone: 0151 236 2098
Call Date: May 1995, Gray's Inn
Qualifications: [LLB]

IRONFIELD MISS JANET RUTH

Deans Court Chambers
24 St John Street, Manchester M3 4DF,
Telephone: 0161 214 6000
E-mail: clerks@deanscourt.co.uk
Deans Court Chambers
41-43 Market Place, Preston PR1 1AH,
Telephone: 01772 555163
E-mail: clerks@deanscourt.co.uk
Call Date: Oct 1992, Gray's Inn
Qualifications: [BA]

IRVIN PETER

Brick Court Chambers
7-8 Essex Street, London WC2R 3LD,
Telephone: 0171 379 3550
E-mail: [surname]@brickcourt.co.uk
Call Date: July 1972, Gray's Inn
Pupil Master
Qualifications: [BA (Oxon)]

D

IRVINE MICHAEL FRASER

1 Crown Office Row
3rd Floor, Temple, London EC4Y 7HH,
Telephone: 0171 583 9292
E-mail: onecor@link.org
Call Date: Feb 1964, Inner Temple
Pupil Master
Qualifications: [BA (Oxon)]

IRVING MISS GILLIAN

Chambers of John Hand QC
9 St John Street, Manchester M3 4DN,
Telephone: 0161 955 9000
E-mail: ninesjs@gconnect.com
1 Mitre Court Buildings
Temple, London EC4Y 7BS,
Telephone: 0171 797 7070
E-mail: clerks@1mcb.com
Call Date: July 1984, Inner Temple
Qualifications: [BA (Hons)]

IRWIN GAVIN DAVID

2 Dyers Buildings
London EC1N 2JT,
Telephone: 0171 404 1881
Call Date: Nov 1996, Gray's Inn
Qualifications: [LLB (Newcastle)]

IRWIN STEPHEN JOHN QC (1997)

Doughty Street Chambers
11 Doughty Street, London WC1N 2PG,
Telephone: 0171 404 1313
E-mail:enquiries@doughtystreet.co.uk
Call Date: Nov 1976, Gray's Inn
Assistant Recorder
Qualifications: [BA (Hons) (Cantab)]

ISAAC NICHOLAS DUDLEY

199 Strand
London WC2R 1DR,
Telephone: 0171 379 9779
E-mail: chambers@199strand.co.uk
Call Date: Oct 1993, Gray's Inn
Qualifications: [BA (Leeds)]

ISAACS BARRY RUSSELL

3/4 South Square
Gray's Inn, London WC1R 5HP,
Telephone: 0171 696 9900
E-mail: clerks@southsquare.com
Call Date: Nov 1994, Inner Temple
Qualifications: [MA (Oxon), MA (Harvard),
ASA]

ISAACS MISS ELIZABETH

3 Fountain Court
Steelhouse Lane, Birmingham B4 6DR,
Telephone: 0121 236 5854
Call Date: 1998, Lincoln's Inn
Qualifications: [BA (Hons)(Dunelm), MA
(Leic), LLB (Hons)(Coventry)]

ISAACS PAUL RICHARD

Mercury Chambers
Mercury House, 33-35 Clarendon Road,
Leeds LS2 9NZ,
Telephone: 0113 234 2265
E-mail:cdexter@mercurychambers.co.uk
Call Date: Feb 1974, Middle Temple
Pupil Master, Recorder
Qualifications: [MA (Cantab)]

ISAACS STUART LINDSAY QC (1991)

4-5 Gray's Inn Square
Ground Floor, Gray's Inn, London
WC1R 5JP, Telephone: 0171 404 5252
E-mail:chambers@4-5graysinnsquare.co.uk
Call Date: July 1975, Lincoln's Inn
Assistant Recorder
Qualifications: [MA (Cantab), Licencie
special en , droit eur (Brussels)]

ISHERWOOD JOHN STANLEY

Assize Court Chambers
14 Small Street, Bristol BS1 1DE,
Telephone: 0117 9264587
E-mail:chambers@assize-court-chambers.co.uk
Call Date: July 1978, Gray's Inn
Pupil Master
Qualifications: [MA (Cantab)]

ISHMAEL COLIN

4 Brick Court
Temple, London EC4Y 9AD,
Telephone: 0171 797 8910
E-mail: medhurst@dial.pipex.com
Call Date: Feb 1989, Lincoln's Inn
Pupil Master
Qualifications: [BA]

ISLAM AMINUL RUHUL

Tower Hamlets Barristers Chambers
37B Princelet Street, London E1 5LP,
Telephone: 0171 377 8090
E-mail: shikderka@aol.com
Call Date: 1997, Lincoln's Inn
Qualifications: [LLB (E.London)]

ISLAM MOHAMMED NURAL

45 Ullswater Crescent
Kingston Vale, London SW15 3RG,
Telephone: 0181 546 9284
Call Date: June 1959, Lincoln's Inn
Qualifications: [MA]

ISLAM-CHOUDHURY MUGNI

**11 Bolt Court (also at 7 Stone Buildings
– 1st Floor)**
London EC4A 3DQ,
Telephone: 0171 353 2300
E-mail: boltct11@aol.com
Redhill Chambers
Seloduct House, 30 Station Road, Redhill,
Surrey, RH1 1NF,
Telephone: 01737 780781
**7 Stone Buildings (also at 11 Bolt
Court)**
1st Floor, Lincoln's Inn, London
WC2A 3SZ, Telephone: 0171 242 0961
E-mail:larthur@7stonebuildings.law.co.uk
Call Date: Oct 1996, Lincoln's Inn
Qualifications: [LLB (Hons)(Lond)]

ISLES MS MARY PATRICIA THERESA

1 Pump Court
Lower Ground Floor, Temple, London
EC4Y 7AB, Telephone: 0171 583 2012/
353 4341
E-mail: [name]@1pumpcourt.co.uk
Call Date: Nov 1984, Inner Temple
Pupil Master
Qualifications: [BSc, BA]

ISMAIL MISS NAZMUN NISHA

Central Chambers
89 Princess Street,
Manchester M1 4HT,
Telephone: 0161 236 1133
Call Date: Oct 1992, Lincoln's Inn
Qualifications: [BA(Hons)]

ISMAIL MISS ROXANNE

3/4 South Square
Gray's Inn, London WC1R 5HP,
Telephone: 0171 696 9900
E-mail: clerks@southsquare.com
Call Date: Oct 1993, Lincoln's Inn
Qualifications: [LLB (Hons)(Lond)]

ISSA MISS ALEXANDRA HANNAH

1 Temple Gardens
1st Floor, Temple, London EC4Y 9BB,
Telephone: 0171 583 1315/353 0407
E-mail: clerks@1templegardens.co.uk
Call Date: Nov 1993, Lincoln's Inn
Qualifications: [MA (Hons)(Oxon)]

IVENS MS JEMIMA

8 King's Bench Walk
2nd Floor, Temple, London EC4Y 7DU,
Telephone: 0171 797 8888
8 King's Bench Walk North
1 Park Square East, Leeds LS1 2NE,
Telephone: 0113 2439797
Call Date: Feb 1994, Lincoln's Inn
Qualifications: [LLB (Hons)]

IVERS MICHAEL JOSEPH

Counsels' Chambers
2nd Floor, 10-11 Gray's Inn Square,
London WC1R 5JD,
Telephone: 0171 405 2576
E-mail:clerks@10-11graysinnsquare.co.uk
Call Date: Nov 1991, Middle Temple
Qualifications: [LLB Hons (Lond)]

IVES MRS ANNE ELIZABETH

1 Gray's Inn Square
Ground Floor, London WC1R 5AA,
Telephone: 0171 405 8946/7/8
Call Date: Feb 1994, Gray's Inn
Qualifications: [BSc (Econ)(Wales)]

D

IVILL SCOTT ASHLEY

Holborn Chambers
6 Gate Street, Lincoln's Inn Fields, London
WC2A 3HP, Telephone: 0171 242 6060
Call Date: Nov 1997, Gray's Inn
Qualifications: [LLB (De Montfort)]

IVIMY MS CECILIA RACHEL

11 King's Bench Walk
Temple, London EC4Y 7EQ,
Telephone: 0171 632 8500/583 0610
E-mail: clerksroom@11kbw.com
Call Date: Nov 1995, Middle Temple
Qualifications: [BA (Hons) (Oxon)]

IVORY MARTIN

Tindal Chambers
3/5 New Street, Chelmsford, Essex,
CM1 1NT, Telephone: 01245 267742
East Anglian Chambers
Gresham House, 5 Museum Street,
Ipswich, Suffolk, IP1 1HQ,
Telephone: 01473 214481
E-mail: ipswich@ealaw.co.uk
East Anglian Chambers
52 North Hill, Colchester, Essex, CO1 1PY,
Telephone: 01206 572756
E-mail: colchester@ealaw.co.uk
East Anglian Chambers
57 London Street, Norwich NR2 1HL,
Telephone: 01603 617351
E-mail: norwich@ealaw.co.uk
Call Date: 1996, Gray's Inn
Qualifications: [LLB (Lond)]

IVORY THOMAS PETER GERARD QC (1998)

One Essex Court
Ground Floor, Temple, London
EC4Y 9AR, Telephone: 020 7583 2000
E-mail: clerks@oneessexcourt.co.uk
Call Date: July 1978, Lincoln's Inn
Qualifications: [MA (Cantab)]

IWI IAN DAVID

9 Stone Buildings
Lincoln's Inn, London WC2A 3NN,
Telephone: 0171 404 5055
E-mail: clerks@9stoneb.law.co.uk
Call Date: Feb 1961, Gray's Inn
Qualifications: [MA (Cantab)]

IWI QUINTIN JOSEPH

2 Harcourt Buildings
Ground Floor/Left, Temple, London
EC4Y 9DB, Telephone: 0171 583 9020
E-mail: clerks@harcourt.co.uk
Call Date: Feb 1956, Gray's Inn
Pupil Master
Qualifications: [MA (Oxon)]

IYER SUNIL KRISHNA

Bracton Chambers
95a Chancery Lane, London WC2A 1DT,
Telephone: 0171 242 4248
Call Date: July 1988, Gray's Inn
Qualifications: [LLB (Dundee)]

JABATI MISS MARIA HANNAH

2 Middle Temple Lane
3rd Floor, Temple, London EC4Y 9AA,
Telephone: 0171 583 4540
Call Date: Nov 1986, Lincoln's Inn
Qualifications: [BA, LLM (Lond)]

JACK ADRIAN LAURENCE ROBERT

Enterprise Chambers
9 Old Square, Lincoln's Inn, London
WC2A 3SR, Telephone: 0171 405 9471
E-mail:enterprise.london@dial.pipex.com
Enterprise Chambers
65 Quayside, Newcastle upon Tyne
NE1 3DS, Telephone: 0191 222 3344
E-mail:enterprise.newcastle@dial.pipex.com
Enterprise Chambers
38 Park Square, Leeds LS1 2PA,
Telephone: 0113 246 0391
E-mail:enterprise.leeds@dial.pipex.com
Call Date: Nov 1986, Middle Temple
Pupil Master
Qualifications: [MA(Oxon)]

JACK DR ANDREW MICHAEL

Counsels' Chambers
2nd Floor, 10-11 Gray's Inn Square,
London WC1R 5JD,
Telephone: 0171 405 2576
E-mail:clerks@10-11graysinnsquare.co.uk
Call Date: 1997, Middle Temple
Qualifications: [BA (Hons)(Lond), B.Phil,
D.Phil (Oxon), CPE (Lond)]

JACK MISS KATRINA MABEL

Prince Henry's Chamber
109 Grosvenor Road, Westminster,
London SW1V 3LG,
Telephone: 0171 834 2572
Call Date: July 1978, Lincoln's Inn

JACK SIMON MICHAEL

9 Woodhouse Square
Leeds LS3 1AD,
Telephone: 0113 2451986
E-mail: clerks@9woodhouse.co.uk
Call Date: July 1974, Middle Temple
Recorder
Qualifications: [BA (Cantab)]

JACKLIN MISS SUSAN ELIZABETH

St John's Chambers
Small Street, Bristol BS1 1DW,
Telephone: 0117 9213456/298514
E-mail: @stjohnschambers.co.uk
Call Date: Nov 1980, Inner Temple
Pupil Master, Assistant Recorder
Qualifications: [BA (Dunelm)]

JACKSON ADRIAN PHILIP

King Charles House
Standard Hill, Nottingham NG1 6FX,
Telephone: 0115 9418851
E-mail: clerks@kch.co.uk
Call Date: Oct 1990, Lincoln's Inn
Qualifications: [MA (Hons)(Cantab)]

JACKSON ANDREW FRASER

East Anglian Chambers
52 North Hill, Colchester, Essex, CO1 1PY,
Telephone: 01206 572756
E-mail: colchester@ealaw.co.uk
East Anglian Chambers
57 London Street, Norwich NR2 1HL,
Telephone: 01603 617351
E-mail: norwich@ealaw.co.uk
East Anglian Chambers
Gresham House, 5 Museum Street,
Ipswich, Suffolk, IP1 1HQ,
Telephone: 01473 214481
E-mail: ipswich@ealaw.co.uk
Call Date: Oct 1990, Inner Temple
Qualifications: [BA (Hons)]

JACKSON ANDREW JOHN

3 Fountain Court
Steelhouse Lane, Birmingham B4 6DR,
Telephone: 0121 236 5854
Call Date: July 1986, Lincoln's Inn
Qualifications: [BA (Manch), Dip Law]

JACKSON ANTHONY WARREN

3 Serjeants' Inn
London EC4Y 1BQ,
Telephone: 0171 353 5537
E-mail: clerks@3serjeantsinn.com
Call Date: Oct 1995, Inner Temple
Qualifications: [MA, M.Phil (Cantab), LLM
(Illinois)]

JACKSON DAVID

St Ive's Chambers
Whittall Street, Birmingham B4 6DH,
Telephone: 0121 236 0863/5720
E-mail:stives.headofchambers@btinternet.com
Call Date: July 1986, Gray's Inn
Qualifications: [Dip of Magisterial, Law]

JACKSON DIRIK GEORGE ALLAN

Chambers of Mr Peter Crampin QC
Ground Floor, 11 New Square, Lincoln's
Inn, London WC2A 3QB,
Telephone: 020 7831 0081
E-mail: 11newsquare.co.uk
Call Date: Nov 1969, Lincoln's Inn
Pupil Master, Recorder
Qualifications: [BA, LLB (Cantab)]

JACKSON MISS HELEN ELIZABETH

Goodwin Chambers
Goodwin Cottage, 14 Doddington Road,
Wellingborough, Northamptonshire,
NN8 2JG, Telephone: 01933 222790
Call Date: Nov 1975, Middle Temple
Qualifications: [MA (Hons), LLB]

JACKSON HUGH WOODWARD

Hardwicke Building
New Square, Lincoln's Inn, London
WC2A 3SB, Telephone: 020 7242 2523
E-mail: clerks@hardwicke.co.uk
Call Date: July 1981, Middle Temple
Pupil Master
Qualifications: [LLB Sheff]

JACKSON JOHN EDGAR

40 King Street
Manchester M2 6BA,
Telephone: 0161 832 9082
E-mail: clerks@40kingstreet.co.uk
The Chambers of Philip Raynor QC
5 Park Place, Leeds LS1 2RU,
Telephone: 0113 242 1123
Call Date: July 1970, Middle Temple
Pupil Master

JACKSON MISS JUDITH QC (1994)

9 Old Square
Ground Floor, Lincoln's Inn, London
WC2A 3SR, Telephone: 0171 405 4682
E-mail: chambers@9oldsquare.co.uk
Call Date: Nov 1975, Inner Temple
Qualifications: [LLB (Hons), LLM (Lond)]

JACKSON KEVIN ROY

Becket Chambers
17 New Dover Road, Canterbury, Kent,
CT1 3AS, Telephone: 01227 786331
Call Date: 1984, Middle Temple
Qualifications: [BA (Hons)(Law)]

JACKSON MATTHEW DAVID EVERARD

4 Paper Buildings
Ground Floor, Temple, London
EC4Y 7EX, Telephone: 0171 353 3366/
583 7155
E-mail: clerks@4paperbuildings.com
Call Date: July 1986, Middle Temple
Qualifications: [MA(Cantab)]

JACKSON MYLES GERALD

9 King's Bench Walk
Ground Floor, Temple, London
EC4Y 7DX, Telephone: 0171 353 7202/
3909 E-mail: 9kbw@compuserve.com
Call Date: Oct 1995, Lincoln's Inn
Qualifications: [LLB (Hons) (Lond); MA
(York)]

JACKSON NICHOLAS DAVID KINGSLEY

Adrian Lyon's Chambers
14 Castle Street, Liverpool L2 0NE,
Telephone: 0151 236 4421/8240
E-mail: chambers14@aol.com
Call Date: Nov 1992, Lincoln's Inn
Qualifications: [LLB (Hons)(Newc)]

JACKSON PETER ARTHUR BRIAN

4 Paper Buildings
1st Floor, Temple, London EC4Y 7EX,
Telephone: 0171 583 0816/353 1131
E-mail: clerks@4paperbuildings.co.uk
Call Date: 1978, Inner Temple
Pupil Master, Assistant Recorder
Qualifications: [BA (Oxon)]

JACKSON MISS ROSEMARY ELIZABETH

Keating Chambers
10 Essex Street, Outer Temple, London
WC2R 3AA, Telephone: 0171 544 2600
Call Date: July 1981, Middle Temple
Pupil Master
Qualifications: [LLB (Lond), AKC]

JACKSON SIMON MALCOLM DERMOT

Park Court Chambers
16 Park Place, Leeds LS1 2SJ,
Telephone: 0113 2433277
Call Date: Nov 1982, Gray's Inn
Pupil Master
Qualifications: [LLB (Leeds)]

JACKSON MISS STEPHANIE

12 King's Bench Walk
Temple, London EC4Y 7EL,
Telephone: 0171 583 0811
E-mail: chambers@12kbw.co.uk
Call Date: Oct 1992, Inner Temple
Qualifications: [LLB (Reading)]

JACKSON WAYNE THOMAS

Young Street Chambers
38 Young Street, Manchester M3 3FT,
Telephone: 0161 833 0489
E-mail: clerks@young-st-chambers.com
Call Date: Nov 1984, Middle Temple
Qualifications: [LLB (Sheff)]

JACKSON WILLIAM GORDON

One King's Bench Walk
1st Floor, Temple, London EC4Y 7DB,
Telephone: 0171 936 1500
E-mail: ddear@1kbw.co.uk
Call Date: 1989, Lincoln's Inn
Qualifications: [LLB (St Andrew's)]

JACKSON DR WILLIAM THOMAS

Westgate Chambers
144 High Street, Lewes, East Sussex,
BN7 1XT, Telephone: 01273 480510
Call Date: Nov 1975, Lincoln's Inn
Qualifications: [MRCVS, DVSM, FCIARb]

JACOB ISAAC ELLIS

9 Stone Buildings
Lincoln's Inn, London WC2A 3NN,
Telephone: 0171 404 5055
E-mail: clerks@9stoneb.law.co.uk
Call Date: July 1963, Lincoln's Inn
Pupil Master, Recorder
Qualifications: [LLB (Manchester), FCIArb]

JACOBS CHRISTOPHER PETER

9 King's Bench Walk
Ground Floor, Temple, London
EC4Y 7DX, Telephone: 0171 353 7202/
3909 E-mail: 9kbw@compuserve.com
Call Date: Oct 1994, Lincoln's Inn
Qualifications: [LLB (Hons)(Hull)]

JACOBS MS CLAIRE VANESSA

4 King's Bench Walk
2nd Floor, Temple, London EC4Y 7DL,
Telephone: 020 7353 3581
E-mail: clerks@4kbw.co.uk
Call Date: July 1989, Gray's Inn
Qualifications: [LLB (Hons)]

JACOBS NIGEL ROBERT

4 Essex Court
Temple, London EC4Y 9AJ,
Telephone: 020 7797 7970
E-mail: clerks@4essexcourt.law.co.uk
Call Date: Nov 1983, Middle Temple
Pupil Master
Qualifications: [BA, LLM (Cantab)]

JACOBS RICHARD DAVID QC (1998)

Essex Court Chambers
24 Lincoln's Inn Fields, London
WC2A 3ED, Telephone: 0171 813 8000
E-mail:clerksroom@essexcourt-chambers.co.uk
Call Date: Nov 1979, Middle Temple
Qualifications: [BA (Cantab)]

JACOBSON LAWRENCE

5 Paper Buildings
Ground Floor, Temple, London
EC4Y 7HB, Telephone: 0171 583 9275/
583 4555 E-mail: 5paper@link.org
Call Date: Nov 1985, Gray's Inn
Qualifications: [BA, LLB (UCT), Dip Law
(PCL)]

JACOBSON MS MARY INGE

Maidstone Chambers
33 Earl Street, Maidstone, Kent, ME14 1PF,
Telephone: 01622 688592
E-mail:maidstonechambers@compuserve.com
Call Date: Oct 1992, Middle Temple
Qualifications: [MA (Cantab), LLB (Hons)]

JACONELLI JOSEPH

St James's Chambers
68 Quay Street, Manchester M3 3EJ,
Telephone: 0161 834 7000
E-mail: clerks@stjameschambers.co.uk
Call Date: Feb 1972, Lincoln's Inn
Qualifications: [MA, LLB (Cantab), Ph.D
(Manchester)]

JAFFA RONALD MERVYN

3 Gray's Inn Square
Ground Floor, London WC1R 5AH,
Telephone: 0171 520 5600
E-mail: clerks@3gis.co.uk
Call Date: July 1974, Gray's Inn
Pupil Master
Qualifications: [LLB]

JAFFERJEE AFTAB ASGER

2 Harcourt Buildings
1st Floor, Temple, London EC4Y 9DB,
Telephone: 020 7353 2112
Call Date: Nov 1980, Inner Temple
Pupil Master
Qualifications: [BA (Dunelm)]

JAFFERJI ZAINULABEDIN HATIM

Chambers of Harjit Singh
Ground Floor, 2 Middle Temple Lane,
Temple, London EC4Y 9AA,
Telephone: 0171 353 1356 (4 Lines)
Call Date: 1999, Lincoln's Inn
Qualifications: [BSc (Econ)(Hons), (LSE)]

JAGO MISS ANN LOUISE

Verulam Chambers
Peer House, 8-14 Verulam Street, Gray's
Inn, London WC1X 8LZ,
Telephone: 0171 813 2400
Call Date: Nov 1991, Middle Temple
Qualifications: [LLB (Hons)]

JAISRI SHASHI SATYENDRA

Chancery Chambers
1st Floor Offices, 70/72 Chancery Lane,
London WC2A 1AB,
Telephone: 0171 405 6879/6870
Call Date: Nov 1995, Lincoln's Inn
Qualifications: [LLB (Hons)]

JAKENS MISS CLAIRE

Westgate Chambers
144 High Street, Lewes, East Sussex,
BN7 1XT, Telephone: 01273 480510
Goldsmith Chambers
Ground Floor, Goldsmith Building,
Temple, London EC4Y 7BL,
Telephone: 0171 353 6802/3/4/5
E-mail:clerks@goldsmithchambers.law.co.uk
Call Date: July 1988, Middle Temple
Pupil Master
Qualifications: [BA (Hons) (Reading), MPhil
(Lond), Dip Law]

JAMES ALUN EDWARD

Temple Gardens Tax Chambers
1st Floor, 3 Temple Gardens, Temple,
London EC4Y 9AU,
Telephone: 0171 353 7884/5 8982/3
E-mail: clerks@taxcounsel.co.uk.
Exchange Chambers
Pearl Assurance House, Derby Square,
Liverpool L2 9XX,
Telephone: 0151 236 7747
E-mail:exchangechambers@btinternet.com
Call Date: Nov 1986, Middle Temple
Pupil Master
Qualifications: [MA (Oxon), BCL]

JAMES ARTHUR RONALD ALFRED

Abbey Chambers
PO Box 47, 47 Ashurst Drive, Shepperton,
Middlesex, TW17 0LD,
Telephone: 01932 560913
Richmond Green Chambers
Greyhound House, 23-24 George Street,
Richmond-upon-Thames, Surrey,
TW9 1HY, Telephone: 0181 940 1841
E-mail: ptaylor256@aol.com
Call Date: Nov 1975, Middle Temple
Pupil Master
Qualifications: [LLB]

JAMES CHRISTOPHER GLYNNE LAWRENCE

Angel Chambers
94 Walter Road, Swansea, West
Glamorgan, SA1 5QA,
Telephone: 01792 464623/464648
E-mail: lynne@angelchambers.co.uk
Call Date: 1997, Gray's Inn
Qualifications: [LLB (B'ham)]

JAMES MISS DELYTH ANGHARAD

2 Paper Buildings
1st Floor, Temple, London EC4Y 7ET,
Telephone: 020 7556 5500
E-mail: clerks@2pbbarristers.co.uk
Call Date: July 1990, Lincoln's Inn
Qualifications: [LLB, MA(Keele)]

JAMES ERNEST PARKER

Bridewell Chambers
2 Bridewell Place, London EC4V 6AP,
Telephone: 020 7797 8800
E-mail:HughesGage@bridewell.law.co.uk
Call Date: Nov 1977, Gray's Inn
Pupil Master

JAMES GEORGE CHRISTOPHER MOHUN

5 Fountain Court
Steelhouse Lane, Birmingham B4 6DR,
Telephone: 0121 606 0500
E-mail:clerks@5fountaincourt.law.co.uk
Call Date: July 1977, Middle Temple
Qualifications: [LLB]

JAMES GRAHAME HOWARD

Goldsmith Chambers
Ground Floor, Goldsmith Building,
Temple, London EC4Y 7BL,
Telephone: 0171 353 6802/3/4/5
E-mail:clerks@goldsmithchambers.law.co.uk
Call Date: Apr 1989, Gray's Inn
Qualifications: [LLB]

JAMES IAN FREDERICK

Octagon House
19 Colegate, Norwich NR3 1AT,
Telephone: 01603 623186
E-mail: admin@octagon-chambers.co.uk
1 Paper Buildings
1st Floor, Temple, London EC4Y 7EP,
Telephone: 0171 353 3728/4953
Call Date: July 1981, Gray's Inn
Pupil Master
Qualifications: [LLB Lond]

JAMES MARK DAVID BARTON

5 Pump Court
Ground Floor, Temple, London
EC4Y 7AP, Telephone: 020 7353 2532
E-mail: FivePump@netcomuk.co.uk
Call Date: Nov 1987, Middle Temple
Pupil Master
Qualifications: [BA (Oxon)]

JAMES MICHAEL FRANK

Enterprise Chambers
9 Old Square, Lincoln's Inn, London
WC2A 3SR, Telephone: 0171 405 9471
E-mail:enterprise.london@dial.pipex.com
Enterprise Chambers
38 Park Square, Leeds LS1 2PA,
Telephone: 0113 246 0391
E-mail:enterprise.leeds@dial.pipex.com
Enterprise Chambers
65 Quayside, Newcastle upon Tyne
NE1 3DS, Telephone: 0191 222 3344
E-mail:enterprise.newcastle@dial.pipex.com
Call Date: Feb 1976, Lincoln's Inn

JAMES MICHAEL PETER

Plowden Buildings
2nd Floor, 2 Plowden Buildings, Middle
Temple Lane, London EC4Y 9BU,
Telephone: 0171 583 0808
E-mail: bar@plowdenbuildings.co.uk
Call Date: Nov 1989, Gray's Inn
Qualifications: [LLB]

JAMES MISS RACHAEL ELIZABETH

33 Bedford Row
London WC1R 4JH,
Telephone: 0171 242 6476
E-mail:clerks@bedfordrow33.demon.co.uk
Call Date: Oct 1992, Middle Temple
Qualifications: [BA (Hons, Leic), Diploma in
Law(City)]

JAMES MISS REBECCA ELIZABETH ANGELA

Call Date: Oct 1992, Gray's Inn
Qualifications: [BA (Hons) Dip in Law]

JAMES RODERICK MORRICE

23 Essex Street
London WC2R 3AS,
Telephone: 0171 413 0353/836 8366
E-mail:clerks@essexstreet23.demon.co.uk
Call Date: July 1979, Gray's Inn
Pupil Master
Qualifications: [BA (Cantab)]

JAMES MISS SHARON ANN SARAH

Angel Chambers
94 Walter Road, Swansea, West
Glamorgan, SA1 5QA,
Telephone: 01792 464623/464648
E-mail: lynne@angelchambers.co.uk
Call Date: Oct 1995, Gray's Inn
Qualifications: [LLB (Wales), LLM (Bris)]

JAMES SIMON JOHN

Chambers of John Hand QC
9 St John Street, Manchester M3 4DN,
Telephone: 0161 955 9000
E-mail: ninesjs@gconnect.com
Call Date: Nov 1988, Lincoln's Inn
Qualifications: [LLB Hons (Leeds)]

JAMES MRS VENICE IMOGEN

Rowchester Chambers
4 Rowchester Court, Whittall Street,
Birmingham B4 6DH,
Telephone: 0121 233 2327/2361951
Call Date: July 1983, Lincoln's Inn
Qualifications: [BA (Warw) Dip Law, (City)]

D

JAMES-STADDEN MISS JODIE CARA

Westgate Chambers
67a Westgate Road, Newcastle upon Tyne
NE1 1SG, Telephone: 0191 261 4407/
2329785
E-mail:pracman@westgatechambers.law.co.uk
Call Date: Oct 1996, Gray's Inn
Qualifications: [LLB (Bris)]

JAMESON BARNABY LUKE CONRAD

18 Red Lion Court
(Off Fleet Street), London EC4A 3EB,
Telephone: 0171 520 6000
E-mail: chambers@18rlc.co.uk
Thornwood House
102 New London Road, Chelmsford,
Essex, CM2 0RG,
Telephone: 01245 280880
E-mail: chambers@18rlc.co.uk
Call Date: Nov 1993, Middle Temple
Qualifications: [BA (Hons)(Lond), CPE
(City)]

JAMESON RODNEY MELLOR MAPLES

No. 6
6 Park Square, Leeds LS1 2LW,
Telephone: 0113 2459763
E-mail: chambers@no6.co.uk
Call Date: July 1976, Middle Temple
Pupil Master, Assistant Recorder
Qualifications: [BA (Hons) (York)]

JAMIESON ANTHONY GEORGE

White Friars Chambers
21 White Friars, Chester CH1 1NZ,
Telephone: 01244 323070
E-mail:whitefriarschambers@btinternet.com
Call Date: July 1974, Gray's Inn
Pupil Master
Qualifications: [BA, LLB (Wales)]

JAMIL MISS AISHA

Broadway House Chambers
Broadway House, 9 Bank Street, Bradford,
West Yorkshire, BD1 1TW,
Telephone: 01274 722560
E-mail: clerks@broadwayhouse.co.uk
Broadway House Chambers
31 Park Square West, Leeds LS1 2PF,
Telephone: 0113 246 2600
Call Date: Nov 1995, Lincoln's Inn
Qualifications: [LLB (Hons)]

JANES JEREMY NICHOLAS

King Charles House
Standard Hill, Nottingham NG1 6FX,
Telephone: 0115 9418851
E-mail: clerks@kch.co.uk
Call Date: Oct 1992, Lincoln's Inn
Qualifications: [BA(Hons)(Bris), Dip Law]

JANNER DANIEL JOSEPH MITCHELL

23 Essex Street
London WC2R 3AS,
Telephone: 0171 413 0353/836 8366
E-mail:clerks@essexstreet23.demon.co.uk
Call Date: July 1980, Middle Temple
Pupil Master
Qualifications: [MA (Cantab)]

JANNEY MS DIANA KEZIA

38 Eldon Chambers
30 Fleet Street, London EC4Y 1AA,
Telephone: 0171 353 8822
Call Date: Nov 1997, Inner Temple
Qualifications: [BA, MA (Lond)]

JANUSZ PIERRE PHILIP

1 Crown Office Row
3rd Floor, Temple, London EC4Y 7HH,
Telephone: 0171 583 9292
E-mail: onecor@link.org
Call Date: July 1979, Middle Temple
Pupil Master
Qualifications: [BA (Lond)]

JAPHETH MISS BETHAN

Sedan House
Stanley Place, Chester CH1 2LU,
Telephone: 01244 320480/348282
Call Date: Oct 1997, Gray's Inn
Qualifications: [LLB (Wales)]

JARAND GODFREY WILLIAM MACKENZIE

Ropewalk Chambers
24 The Ropewalk, Nottingham NG1 5EF,
Telephone: 0115 9472581
E-mail: administration@ropewalk co.uk
Call Date: Nov 1965, Inner Temple
Pupil Master
Qualifications: [BA, LLB (Dub)]

JARMAN JOHN MILWYN

9 Park Place
Cardiff CF1 3DP,
Telephone: 01222 382731
Call Date: July 1980, Gray's Inn
Pupil Master
Qualifications: [LLM (Cantab), LLB, (Wales)]

JARMAN MARK CHRISTOPHER

14 Gray's Inn Square
Gray's Inn, London WC1R 5JP,
Telephone: 0171 242 0858
E-mail: 100712.2134@compuserve.com
Call Date: Nov 1989, Inner Temple
Qualifications: [LLB (Hons)]

JARMAN NICHOLAS FRANCIS BARNABY QC (1985)

4 King's Bench Walk
2nd Floor, Temple, London EC4Y 7DL,
Telephone: 020 7353 3581
E-mail: clerks@4kbw.co.uk
Call Date: Feb 1965, Inner Temple
Recorder
Qualifications: [MA (Oxon)]

JARMAN SAMUEL JAMES GUTHRIE

4 King's Bench Walk
Ground/First Floor/Basement, Temple,
London EC4Y 7DL,
Telephone: 0171 822 8822
E-mail: 4kbw@barristersatlaw.com
Call Date: July 1989, Inner Temple
Pupil Master
Qualifications: [LLB (Lond)]

JARRON MISS STEPHANIE ALLAN

Westgate Chambers
67a Westgate Road, Newcastle upon Tyne
NE1 1SG, Telephone: 0191 261 4407/
2329785
E-mail:pracman@westgatechambers.law.co.u
k
Call Date: Oct 1990, Lincoln's Inn
Qualifications: [BA , ACIArb]

JARVIS JOHN MANNERS QC (1989)

3 Verulam Buildings
London WC1R 5NT,
Telephone: 0171 831 8441
E-mail: clerks@3verulam.co.uk
Call Date: July 1970, Lincoln's Inn

Recorder
Qualifications: [MA (Cantab)]

JARVIS OLIVER MARTIN

Nicholas Street Chambers
22 Nicholas Street, Chester CH1 2NX,
Telephone: 01244 323886
E-mail: clerks@40king.co.uk
Call Date: Nov 1992, Inner Temple
Qualifications: [LLB]

JARZABKOWSKI MISS JULIA MARIE ANTIONETTE

Hardwicke Building
New Square, Lincoln's Inn, London
WC2A 3SB, Telephone: 020 7242 2523
E-mail: clerks@hardwicke.co.uk
Call Date: Oct 1993, Middle Temple
Qualifications: [BA (Hons)(Cantab), MA
(Cantab)]

JAY ADAM MARC

One King's Bench Walk
1st Floor, Temple, London EC4Y 7DB,
Telephone: 0171 936 1500
E-mail: ddear@1kbw.co.uk
Call Date: Nov 1995, Gray's Inn
Qualifications: [LLB (Hons)(Bris)]

JAY MISS ELIZABETH RACHEL

1 Dr Johnson's Buildings
Ground Floor, Temple, London
EC4Y 7AX, Telephone: 0171 353 9328
E-mail:OneDr.Johnsons@btinternet.com
Call Date: Oct 1996, Middle Temple
Qualifications: [BA (Hons)(Lond), MSc
(Econs) (Lond), CPE]

JAY GRENVILLE RICHARD

Young Street Chambers
38 Young Street, Manchester M3 3FT,
Telephone: 0161 833 0489
E-mail: clerks@young-st-chambers.com
Call Date: Nov 1975, Inner Temple
Qualifications: [MA (Cantab)]

D

JAY ROBERT MAURICE QC (1998)

39 Essex Street
London WC2R 3AT,
Telephone: 0171 832 1111
E-mail: clerks@39essex.co.uk
Call Date: July 1981, Middle Temple
Qualifications: [BA (Oxon)]

JAYANATHAN MISS SHAMINI

30 Park Place
Cardiff CF1 3BA,
Telephone: 01222 398421
E-mail: 100757.1456@compuserve.com
Call Date: Nov 1996, Lincoln's Inn
Qualifications: [LLB (Hons)(Wales)]

JEANS CHRISTOPHER JAMES MARWOOD QC (1997)

11 King's Bench Walk
Temple, London EC4Y 7EQ,
Telephone: 0171 632 8500/583 0610
E-mail: clerksroom@11kbw.com
Call Date: July 1980, Gray's Inn
Qualifications: [LLB (Lond), BCL, (Oxon)]

JEARY STEPHEN JOHN

32 Park Place
Cardiff CF1 3BA,
Telephone: 01222 397364
Call Date: July 1987, Inner Temple
Qualifications: [LLB, APMI]

JEBB ANDREW JOHN

Nicholas Street Chambers
22 Nicholas Street, Chester CH1 2NX,
Telephone: 01244 323886
E-mail: clerks@40king.co.uk
Call Date: Oct 1993, Gray's Inn
Qualifications: [LLB (Hons, Exon)]

JEFFERIES ANDREW

2 Dyers Buildings
London EC1N 2JT,
Telephone: 0171 404 1881
Call Date: Oct 1990, Middle Temple
Pupil Master
Qualifications: [LLB (E Anglia)]

JEFFERIES THOMAS ROBERT

Chambers of Lord Goodhart QC
Ground Floor, 3 New Square, Lincoln's
Inn, London WC2A 3RS,
Telephone: 0171 405 5577
E-mail:law@threenewsquare.demon.co.uk
Call Date: Nov 1981, Middle Temple
Pupil Master
Qualifications: [BA, Dip Law]

JEFFERIS ARTHUR MICHAEL QUENTIN

Chambers of Mr Peter Crampin QC
Ground Floor, 11 New Square, Lincoln's
Inn, London WC2A 3QB,
Telephone: 020 7831 0081
E-mail: 11newsquare.co.uk
Call Date: July 1976, Middle Temple
Pupil Master
Qualifications: [LLB (Hons) (Lond), AKC]

JEFFORD MISS NERYS ANGHARAD

Keating Chambers
10 Essex Street, Outer Temple, London
WC2R 3AA, Telephone: 0171 544 2600
Call Date: Nov 1986, Gray's Inn
Pupil Master
Qualifications: [MA (Oxon), LLM (UVA)]

JEFFREYS ALAN HOWARD QC (1996)

Farrar's Building
Temple, London EC4Y 7BD,
Telephone: 0171 583 9241
E-mail:chambers@farrarsbuilding.co.uk
Call Date: July 1970, Gray's Inn
Recorder
Qualifications: [LLB]

JEFFREYS DAVID ALFRED QC (1981)

Hollis Whiteman Chambers
3rd Floor, Queen Elizabeth Bldg, Temple,
London EC4Y 9BS,
Telephone: 020 7583 5766
E-mail:barristers@holliswhiteman.co.uk
Call Date: Nov 1958, Gray's Inn
Recorder
Qualifications: [BA (Cantab)]

JEGARAJAH MISS SHIVANI

Gray's Inn Chambers
5th Floor, Gray's Inn, London WC1R 5JA,
Telephone: 0171 404 1111
Call Date: July 1993, Middle Temple
Qualifications: [BA (Hons)(Lond)]

JENKALA ADRIAN ALEKSANDER

**11 Bolt Court (also at 7 Stone Buildings
– 1st Floor)**
London EC4A 3DQ,
Telephone: 0171 353 2300
E-mail: boltct11@aol.com
Redhill Chambers
Seloduct House, 30 Station Road, Redhill,
Surrey, RH1 1NF,
Telephone: 01737 780781
**7 Stone Buildings (also at 11 Bolt
Court)**
1st Floor, Lincoln's Inn, London
WC2A 3SZ, Telephone: 0171 242 0961
E-mail:larthur@7stonebuildings.law.co.uk
Call Date: July 1984, Middle Temple
Pupil Master
Qualifications: [BSc LLB ACIArb]

JENKINS ALAN MICHAEL

Chambers of Kieran Coonan QC
Ground Floor, 6 Pump Court, Temple,
London EC4Y 7AR,
Telephone: 0171 583 6013/2510
E-mail: clerks@6-pumpcourt.law.co.uk
Call Date: Feb 1984, Middle Temple
Pupil Master
Qualifications: [BA Warw, DipLaw City]

JENKINS ALUN AUSTEN

New Court
Temple, London EC4Y 9BE,
Telephone: 0171 583 5123/0510
Call Date: May 1981, Gray's Inn
Pupil Master
Qualifications: [LLB (Warw)]

JENKINS MISS CATHERINE PHILLIDA

One Garden Court Family Law Chambers
Ground Floor, Temple, London
EC4Y 9BJ, Telephone: 0171 797 7900
E-mail: clerks@onegardencourt.co.uk
Call Date: Nov 1990, Middle Temple
Qualifications: [BA (Keele)]

JENKINS DAVID CROFTON

2 King's Bench Walk
Ground Floor, Temple, London
EC4Y 7DE, Telephone: 0171 353 1746
E-mail: 2kbw@atlas.co.uk
King's Bench Chambers
115 North Hill, Plymouth PL4 8JY,
Telephone: 01752 221551
Call Date: Nov 1967, Inner Temple
Pupil Master
Qualifications: [LLB]

JENKINS DAVID MORGAN

32 Park Place
Cardiff CF1 3BA,
Telephone: 01222 397364
Call Date: Oct 1990, Gray's Inn
Qualifications: [LLB (Cardiff)]

JENKINS EDWARD NICHOLAS

Five Paper Buildings
1st Floor, Five Paper Bldgs, Temple,
London EC4Y 7HB,
Telephone: 0171 583 6117
E-mail:clerks@5-paperbuildings.law.co.uk
Call Date: July 1977, Middle Temple
Pupil Master
Qualifications: [BA (Cantab)]

JENKINS MISS ELIZABETH

12 Old Square
1st Floor, Lincoln's Inn, London
WC2A 3TX, Telephone: 0171 404 0875
Call Date: Oct 1995, Lincoln's Inn
Qualifications: [LLB (Hons)(Newc)]

JENKINS HYWEL IESTYN

35 Essex Street
Temple, London WC2R 3AR,
Telephone: 0171 353 6381
E-mail: derek_jenkins@link.org
Call Date: July 1974, Inner Temple
Pupil Master
Qualifications: [LLB]

JENKINS JAMES JOHN

Iscoed Chambers
86 St Helen's Road, Swansea, West
Glamorgan, SA1 4BQ,
Telephone: 01792 652988/9/330

Farrar's Building
Temple, London EC4Y 7BD,
Telephone: 0171 583 9241
E-mail:chambers@farrarsbuilding.co.uk
Call Date: Nov 1974, Gray's Inn
Pupil Master, Assistant Recorder
Qualifications: [LLB]

JENKINS DR JANET CAROLINE

Chambers of Kieran Coonan QC
Ground Floor, 6 Pump Court, Temple,
London EC4Y 7AR,
Telephone: 0171 583 6013/2510
E-mail: clerks@6-pumpcourt.law.co.uk
Call Date: Nov 1994, Middle Temple
Qualifications: [MB, BS]

JENKINS JEREMY DAVID

33 Park Place
Cardiff CF1 3BA,
Telephone: 02920 233313
Call Date: July 1984, Inner Temple
Pupil Master
Qualifications: [BA]

JENKINS JOHN DAVID QC (1990)

30 Park Place
Cardiff CF1 3BA,
Telephone: 01222 398421
E-mail: 100757.1456@compuserve.com
Call Date: July 1970, Gray's Inn
Recorder
Qualifications: [LLB (Lond) (Hons)]

JENKINS MARTIN STEPHEN

Coleridge Chambers
Citadel, 190 Corporation Street,
Birmingham B4 6QD,
Telephone: 0121 233 8500
Call Date: Nov 1994, Gray's Inn
Qualifications: [BA (Keele)]

JENKINS MISS MELANIE KIM

**1 Gray's Inn Square, Chambers of the
Baroness Scotland of Asthal QC**
1st Floor, London WC1R 5AG,
Telephone: 0171 405 3000
E-mail: clerks@onegrays.demon.co.uk
Call Date: July 1982, Gray's Inn
Pupil Master
Qualifications: [BA (Keele)]

JENKINS ROWAN MATTHEW

King's Bench Chambers
Wellington House, 175 Holdenhurst Road,
Bournemouth, Dorset, BH8 8DQ,
Telephone: 01202 250025
E-mail: chambers@kingsbench.co.uk
Call Date: Nov 1994, Lincoln's Inn
Qualifications: [MA (Botany), D.Phil
(Botany), CPE]

JENKINS THOMAS ALUN QC (1996)

Queens Square Chambers
56 Queens Square, Bristol BS1 4PR,
Telephone: 0117 921 1966
3 Hare Court
1 Little Essex Street, London WC2R 3LD,
Telephone: 0171 395 2000
Call Date: July 1972, Lincoln's Inn
Assistant Recorder
Qualifications: [LLB]

JENNINGS ANTHONY FRANCIS

Two Garden Court
1st Floor, Middle Temple, London
EC4Y 9BL, Telephone: 0171 353 1633
E-mail:barristers@2gardenct.law.co.uk
Call Date: July 1983, Gray's Inn
Pupil Master
Qualifications: [LLB (Warw)]

JENNINGS NIGEL CALVERLEY

17 Bedford Row
London WC1R 4EB,
Telephone: 0171 831 7314
E-mail: iboard7314@aol.com
Call Date: Nov 1967, Gray's Inn

JENNINGS PETER NIGEL

3 Paper Buildings
Temple, London EC4Y 7EU,
Telephone: 020 7583 8055
E-mail: London@3paper.com
3 Paper Buildings (Bournemouth)
20 Lorne Park Road, Bournemouth,
Dorset, BH1 1JN,
Telephone: 01202 292102
E-mail: Bournemouth@3paper.com
3 Paper Buildings (Winchester)
4 St Peter Street, Winchester SO23 8BW,
Telephone: 01962 868884
E-mail: winchester@3paper.com

3 Paper Buildings (Oxford)
1 Alfred Street, High Street, Oxford
OX1 4EH, Telephone: 01865 793736
E-mail: oxford@3paper.com
Call Date: July 1972, Middle Temple
Pupil Master
Qualifications: [MA (Cantab), LLM (Lond)]

JENNINGS TIMOTHY ROBIN
FINNEGAN

Enterprise Chambers
9 Old Square, Lincoln's Inn, London
WC2A 3SR, Telephone: 0171 405 9471
E-mail:enterprise.london@dial.pipex.com
Enterprise Chambers
38 Park Square, Leeds LS1 2PA,
Telephone: 0113 246 0391
E-mail:enterprise.leeds@dial.pipex.com
Enterprise Chambers
65 Quayside, Newcastle upon Tyne
NE1 3DS, Telephone: 0191 222 3344
E-mail:enterprise.newcastle@dial.pipex.com
Call Date: Nov 1962, Gray's Inn
Qualifications: [LLM (Lond)]

JENRICK MISS KATE HENRIETTA

Arden Chambers
27 John Street, London WC1N 2BL,
Telephone: 020 7242 4244
E-mail:clerks@arden-chambers.law.co.uk
Call Date: Nov 1990, Inner Temple
Qualifications: [LLB (So'ton)]

JEREMIAH MS NATALIA LISSA

Chambers of Kieran Coonan QC
Ground Floor, 6 Pump Court, Temple,
London EC4Y 7AR,
Telephone: 0171 583 6013/2510
E-mail: clerks@6-pumpcourt.law.co.uk
Call Date: 1997, Inner Temple
Qualifications: [BA (Cantab), CPE (City)]

JEREMY DAVID HUGH THOMAS

Queen Elizabeth Building
Ground Floor, Temple, London
EC4Y 9BS,
Telephone: 0171 353 7181 (12 Lines)
Call Date: July 1977, Middle Temple
Pupil Master
Qualifications: [LLB]

JERMAN ANTHONY IVAN

22 Old Buildings
Lincoln's Inn, London WC2A 3UJ,
Telephone: 0171 831 0222
Call Date: Nov 1989, Middle Temple
Pupil Master
Qualifications: [BA Hons [Lond], Dip in Law]

JERRAM MISS HARRIET ANNE

35 Essex Street
Temple, London WC2R 3AR,
Telephone: 0171 353 6381
E-mail: derek_jenkins@link.org
Call Date: 1998, Gray's Inn
Qualifications: [BA (Cantab)]

JERVIS CHRISTOPHER ROBERT

Albion Chambers
Broad Street, Bristol BS1 1DR,
Telephone: 0117 9272144
Call Date: July 1966, Inner Temple
Pupil Master
Qualifications: [MA (Oxon)]

JESS DIGBY CHARLES

8 King Street Chambers
8 King Street, Manchester M2 6AQ,
Telephone: 0161 834 9560
E-mail: eightking@aol.com
Call Date: July 1978, Gray's Inn
Pupil Master
Qualifications: [BSc.Hons, (Aston) , LLM
(Manchester), FCIArb]

JESSEL MRS PHILIPPA BRIGID

6 King's Bench Walk
Ground Floor, Temple, London
EC4Y 7DR, Telephone: 0171 583 0410
E-mail: worsley@6kbw.freeserve.co.uk
Call Date: July 1978, Inner Temple
Pupil Master
Qualifications: [BSc (Hons)(Lond)]

JESSUP MISS ANNE ELIZABETH

Two Garden Court
1st Floor, Middle Temple, London
EC4Y 9BL, Telephone: 0171 353 1633
E-mail:barristers@2gardenct.law.co.uk
Call Date: Nov 1981, Gray's Inn
Pupil Master
Qualifications: [BA (Lond)]

JESUDASON MISS CHRISTINE PREMILA

Nicholas Street Chambers
22 Nicholas Street, Chester CH1 2NX,
Telephone: 01244 323886
E-mail: clerks@40king.co.uk
Call Date: Oct 1993, Middle Temple
Qualifications: [BA (Juris, Oxon)]

JEWELL MATTHEW

1 Paper Buildings
1st Floor, Temple, London EC4Y 7EP,
Telephone: 0171 353 3728/4953
Call Date: Nov 1989, Lincoln's Inn
Pupil Master
Qualifications: [BA (Oxon), Dip Law (City)]

JIBOWU OLUMUYIWA OLUBUKUNOLA A.O.

Chancery Chambers
1st Floor Offices, 70/72 Chancery Lane,
London WC2A 1AB,
Telephone: 0171 405 6879/6870
Call Date: Oct 1993, Middle Temple
Qualifications: [LLB (Hons)(Lond)]

JINADU ABDUL-LATEEF ABODURIN OLAYINKA

Keating Chambers
10 Essex Street, Outer Temple, London
WC2R 3AA, Telephone: 0171 544 2600
Call Date: Nov 1995, Middle Temple
Qualifications: [BA (Hons), LLM (Hons)
(Cantab)]

JOBLING IAN MICHAEL THOMAS

2 Dyers Buildings
London EC1N 2JT,
Telephone: 0171 404 1881
Call Date: Nov 1982, Gray's Inn
Pupil Master
Qualifications: [LLB (Lond)]

JOFFE MISS NATASHA JULIET LOUISE

Devereux Chambers
Devereux Court, London WC2R 3JJ,
Telephone: 0171 353 7534
E-mail: mailbox@devchambers.co.uk
Call Date: Oct 1992, Gray's Inn
Qualifications: [BA (Hons)]

JOFFE VICTOR HOWARD

Serle Court Chambers
6 New Square, Lincoln's Inn, London
WC2A 3QS, Telephone: 0171 242 6105
E-mail: clerks@serlecourt.co.uk
Call Date: Nov 1975, Middle Temple
Pupil Master
Qualifications: [MA (Cantab) LLB]

JOHAL MISS DEVINDER KAUR

Holborn Chambers
6 Gate Street, Lincoln's Inn Fields, London
WC2A 3HP, Telephone: 0171 242 6060
Call Date: Oct 1995, Gray's Inn
Qualifications: [LLB]

JOHAL MISS SUKHJINDER KAUR

10 King's Bench Walk
Ground Floor, Temple, London
EC4Y 7EB, Telephone: 0171 353 7742
E-mail: 10kbw@lineone.net
Call Date: 1991, Middle Temple
Qualifications: [LLB Hons (Wales)]

JOHN MISS (EMMA) CATRIN

30 Park Place
Cardiff CF1 3BA,
Telephone: 01222 398421
E-mail: 100757.1456@compuserve.com
Call Date: Oct 1992, Gray's Inn
Qualifications: [LL.B (Wales)]

JOHN PETER CHARLES

One Essex Court
1st Floor, Temple, London EC4Y 9AR,
Telephone: 0171 936 3030
E-mail: one.essex_court@virgin.net
Call Date: Nov 1989, Inner Temple
Qualifications: [LLB (Lond)]

JOHN STEPHEN ALUN

9-12 Bell Yard
London WC2A 2LF,
Telephone: 0171 400 1800
E-mail: clerks@bellyard.co.uk
Call Date: July 1975, Middle Temple
Qualifications: [MA (Oxon)]

JOHN-JULES CHARLES

Warwick House Chambers
8 Warwick Court, Gray's Inn, London
WC1R 5DJ, Telephone: 0171 430 2323
E-mail: cdrewlaw@aol.com
Call Date: July 1983, Gray's Inn
Qualifications: [LLB Hons (Soton)]

JOHNS ALAN GRANT

9 Old Square
Ground Floor, Lincoln's Inn, London
WC2A 3SR, Telephone: 0171 405 4682
E-mail: chambers@9oldsquare.co.uk
Call Date: Oct 1994, Gray's Inn
Qualifications: [BA]

JOHNSON ALAN MICHAEL BORTHWICK

1 Gray's Inn Square
Ground Floor, London WC1R 5AA,
Telephone: 0171 405 8946/7/8
Call Date: July 1971, Middle Temple
Pupil Master
Qualifications: [MA (Oxon)]

JOHNSON MISS AMANDA

Young Street Chambers
38 Young Street, Manchester M3 3FT,
Telephone: 0161 833 0489
E-mail: clerks@young-st-chambers.com
Call Date: Oct 1992, Gray's Inn
Qualifications: [LL.B (Wales)]

JOHNSON MISS AMANDA JANE

Chambers of Michael Pert QC
36 Bedford Row, London WC1R 4JH,
Telephone: 0171 421 8000
E-mail: 36bedfordrow@link.org
Chambers of Michael Pert QC
24 Albion Place, Northampton NN1 1UD,
Telephone: 01604 602333
Chambers of Michael Pert QC
104 New Walk, Leicester LE1 7EA,
Telephone: 0116 249 2020
Call Date: Nov 1990, Middle Temple
Qualifications: [LLB (Lond)]

JOHNSON MRS CAROLYN ANN

New Bailey Chambers
10 Lawson Street, Preston PR1 2QT,
Telephone: 01772 258087
Call Date: Nov 1974, Gray's Inn

JOHNSON MISS CHRISTINE MARGARET

Adrian Lyon's Chambers
14 Castle Street, Liverpool L2 0NE,
Telephone: 0151 236 4421/8240
E-mail: chambers14@aol.com
Call Date: Nov 1991, Middle Temple
Qualifications: [LLB (Hons)]

JOHNSON DAVID BURNHAM QC (1978)

20 Essex Street
London WC2R 3AL,
Telephone: 0171 583 9294
E-mail: clerks@20essexst.com
Call Date: July 1967, Inner Temple
Recorder

JOHNSON EDWIN GEOFFREY

9 Old Square
Ground Floor, Lincoln's Inn, London
WC2A 3SR, Telephone: 0171 405 4682
E-mail: chambers@9oldsquare.co.uk
Call Date: Nov 1987, Lincoln's Inn
Pupil Master
Qualifications: [BA (Oxon)]

JOHNSON IAN FREDERICK

Adrian Lyon's Chambers
14 Castle Street, Liverpool L2 0NE,
Telephone: 0151 236 4421/8240
E-mail: chambers14@aol.com
5 Stone Buildings
Lincoln's Inn, London WC2A 3XT,
Telephone: 0171 242 6201
E-mail:clerks@5-stonebuildings.law.co.uk
Call Date: July 1982, Gray's Inn
Qualifications: [LLB (Reading)]

JOHNSON MRS JANICE COSIE

2 King's Bench Walk Chambers
1st Floor, 2 King's Bench Walk, Temple,
London EC4Y 7DE,
Telephone: 020 7353 9276
E-mail: chambers@2kbw.co.uk
Call Date: Nov 1994, Inner Temple
Qualifications: [LLB (Anglia)]

JOHNSON JEREMY CHARLES

5 Essex Court
1st Floor, Temple, London EC4Y 9AH,
Telephone: 0171 410 2000
E-mail: barristers@5essexcourt.co.uk
Call Date: Oct 1994, Middle Temple
Qualifications: [BA (Hons)(Oxon)]

JOHNSON JOHN RICHARD HENESEY

Regent Chambers
8 Pall Mall, Hanley, Stoke On Trent
ST1 1ER, Telephone: 01782 286666
E-mail: regent@ftech.co.uk
Call Date: Oct 1993, Middle Temple
Qualifications: [MA (Hons)(Oxon),
Dip.B.Admin, CPE]

JOHNSON MS KATHYRN MARGARET

15 Winckley Square
Preston PR1 3JJ,
Telephone: 01772 252828
E-mail:clerks@winckleysq.demon.co.uk
Call Date: July 1989, Gray's Inn
Qualifications: [LLB (Sheff)]

JOHNSON MISS MELANIE JANE

1 Pump Court
Lower Ground Floor, Temple, London
EC4Y 7AB, Telephone: 0171 583 2012/
353 4341
E-mail: [name]@1pumpcourt.co.uk
Call Date: Oct 1996, Middle Temple
Qualifications: [B.Sc (Hons) (Bucks)]

JOHNSON MICHAEL SLOAN

Chambers of John Hand QC
9 St John Street, Manchester M3 4DN,
Telephone: 0161 955 9000
E-mail: ninesjs@gconnect.com
*Call Date: Nov 1971, Lincoln's Inn
Pupil Master, Assistant Recorder*
Qualifications: [MA, LLM (Cantab)]

JOHNSON NICHOLAS JAMES

Park Court Chambers
16 Park Place, Leeds LS1 2SJ,
Telephone: 0113 2433277
Call Date: Nov 1994, Inner Temple
Qualifications: [BA (York), CPE]

JOHNSON NICHOLAS ROBERT

25-27 Castle Street
1st Floor, Liverpool L2 4TA,
Telephone: 0151 227 5661/051 236 5072
Call Date: July 1987, Inner Temple
Qualifications: [BA (Leeds)]

JOHNSON PETER TIMOTHY

York Chambers
14 Toft Green, York YO1 6JT,
Telephone: 01904 620048
E-mail: [name]@yorkchambers.co.uk
*Call Date: July 1986, Inner Temple
Pupil Master*
Qualifications: [BA (Durham)]

JOHNSON ROBIN PETER

5 King's Bench Walk
Temple, London EC4Y 7DN,
Telephone: 0171 353 5638
*Call Date: Nov 1979, Gray's Inn
Pupil Master*
Qualifications: [BA (Exon)]

JOHNSON RODERICK STOWERS

2 Paper Buildings
1st Floor, Temple, London EC4Y 7ET,
Telephone: 020 7556 5500
E-mail: clerks@2pbbarristers.co.uk
*Call Date: Nov 1975, Lincoln's Inn
Pupil Master*
Qualifications: [MA (Oxon)]

JOHNSON MISS RUTH

*Call Date: July 1984, Lincoln's Inn
Pupil Master*
Qualifications: [LLB (Lond)]

JOHNSON SIMON NICHOLAS

Stour Chambers
Barton Mill House, Barton Mill Road,
Canterbury, Kent, CT1 1BP,
Telephone: 01227 764899
E-mail: clerks@stourchambers.co.uk
*Call Date: July 1987, Gray's Inn
Pupil Master*
Qualifications: [LLB (Hons) (Wales)]

JOHNSON STEVEN

Chambers of John Hand QC
9 St John Street, Manchester M3 4DN,
Telephone: 0161 955 9000
E-mail: ninesjs@gconnect.com
Peel Court Chambers
45 Hardman Street, Manchester M3 3PL,
Telephone: 0161 832 3791
E-mail: clerks@peelct.co.uk
Call Date: July 1984, Middle Temple
Pupil Master
Qualifications: [LLB (Hons) (Lond)]

JOHNSON MISS SUSANNAH MALEHLOHONOLO

9 Bedford Row
London WC1R 4AZ,
Telephone: 0171 242 3555
E-mail: clerks@9br.co.uk
Call Date: Nov 1996, Middle Temple
Qualifications: [LLB (Hons)(Kent)]

JOHNSON MISS ZOE ELISABETH

Hollis Whiteman Chambers
3rd Floor, Queen Elizabeth Bldg, Temple,
London EC4Y 9BS,
Telephone: 020 7583 5766
E-mail:barristers@holliswhiteman.co.uk
Call Date: Nov 1990, Inner Temple
Qualifications: [BA (Oxon), Dip Law (City)]

JOHNSTON MISS ANNE-MARIE

1 Paper Buildings
1st Floor, Temple, London EC4Y 7EP,
Telephone: 0171 353 3728/4953
Call Date: Oct 1990, Inner Temple
Qualifications: [LLB]

JOHNSTON ANTHONY PAUL

1 Fountain Court
Steelhouse Lane, Birmingham B4 6DR,
Telephone: 0121 236 5721
Call Date: Nov 1993, Middle Temple
Qualifications: [BA (Hons)(Cantab)]

JOHNSTON MISS CAREY ANN

18 Red Lion Court
(Off Fleet Street), London EC4A 3EB,
Telephone: 0171 520 6000
E-mail: chambers@18rlc.co.uk

Thornwood House
102 New London Road, Chelmsford,
Essex, CM2 0RG,
Telephone: 01245 280880
E-mail: chambers@18rlc.co.uk
Call Date: July 1977, Middle Temple
Pupil Master
Qualifications: [LLM (Warwick)]

JOHNSTON CHRISTOPHER GEORGE

3 Serjeants' Inn
London EC4Y 1BQ,
Telephone: 0171 353 5537
E-mail: clerks@3serjeantsinn.com
Call Date: Nov 1990, Gray's Inn
Pupil Master
Qualifications: [MA (Cantab) (Hons)]

JOHNSTON CHRISTOPHER MARK

Chambers of Helen Grindrod QC
4th Floor, 15-19 Devereux Court, London
WC2R 3JJ, Telephone: 0171 583 2792
Call Date: Nov 1983, Gray's Inn
Pupil Master
Qualifications: [BA, LLB]

JOHNSTON MISS JILL

Call Date: Oct 1990, Lincoln's Inn
Qualifications: [MA (Cantab)]

JOHNSTON MISS JUSTINE JANE

4 Paper Buildings
1st Floor, Temple, London EC4Y 7EX,
Telephone: 0171 583 0816/353 1131
E-mail: clerks@4paperbuildings.co.uk
Call Date: 1997, Middle Temple
Qualifications: [BA (Australia), LLB
(Hons)(Lond)]

JOHNSTON MS KAREN ANN

Chambers of Michael Pert QC
36 Bedford Row, London WC1R 4JH,
Telephone: 0171 421 8000
E-mail: 36bedfordrow@link.org
Chambers of Michael Pert QC
24 Albion Place, Northampton NN1 1UD,
Telephone: 01604 602333
Chambers of Michael Pert QC
104 New Walk, Leicester LE1 7EA,
Telephone: 0116 249 2020
Call Date: Nov 1994, Inner Temple
Qualifications: [MA (Oxon), CPE (City)]

D

JOHNSTONE MARK ANTHONY

4 Paper Buildings
1st Floor, Temple, London EC4Y 7EX,
Telephone: 0171 583 0816/353 1131
E-mail: clerks@4paperbuildings.co.uk
Call Date: July 1984, Inner Temple
Pupil Master
Qualifications: [MSc (Lond), LLB (Lond)]

JOLOWICZ JOHN ANTHONY
QC (1990)

Brick Court Chambers
7-8 Essex Street, London WC2R 3LD,
Telephone: 0171 379 3550
E-mail: [surname]@brickcourt.co.uk
Call Date: Nov 1952, Inner Temple

JONATHAN-JONES GARETH

32 Park Place
Cardiff CF1 3BA,
Telephone: 01222 397364
Call Date: Oct 1991, Inner Temple

JONES MISS ALISON

23 Essex Street
London WC2R 3AS,
Telephone: 0171 413 0353/836 8366
E-mail:clerks@essexstreet23.demon.co.uk
Call Date: Nov 1988, Inner Temple
Qualifications: [BA (Manchester)]

JONES ANDREW CRAIG

30 Park Place
Cardiff CF1 3BA,
Telephone: 01222 398421
E-mail: 100757.1456@compuserve.com
Call Date: Oct 1996, Inner Temple
Qualifications: [LLB (Bris)]

JONES BENJAMIN WILLIAM

India Buildings Chambers
Water Street, Liverpool L2 0XG,
Telephone: 0151 243 6000
E-mail: clerks@chambers.u-net.com
Call Date: Feb 1993, Middle Temple
Qualifications: [LLB (Hons)(L'pool)]

JONES BRIAN EDWARD

Manchester House Chambers
18-22 Bridge Street, Manchester M3 3BZ,
Telephone: 0161 834 7007
Call Date: Oct 1994, Middle Temple
Qualifications: [LLB (Hons)]

JONES BRIAN LLOYD

9 Park Place
Cardiff CF1 3DP,
Telephone: 01222 382731
Queen's Chambers
5 John Dalton Street, Manchester M2 6ET,
Telephone: 0161 834 6875/4738
Queens Chambers
4 Camden Place, Preston PR1 3JL,
Telephone: 01772 828300
Call Date: July 1992, Gray's Inn
Qualifications: [BA (Wales)]

JONES MISS CAROLYN NERYS

1 Fountain Court
Steelhouse Lane, Birmingham B4 6DR,
Telephone: 0121 236 5721
Clock Chambers
78 Darlington Street, Wolverhampton
WV1 4LY, Telephone: 01902 313444
Call Date: 1995, Lincoln's Inn
Qualifications: [LLB (Hons)(Lond)]

JONES CARWYN HOWELL

32 Park Place
Cardiff CF1 3BA,
Telephone: 01222 397364
Call Date: Nov 1989, Gray's Inn
Qualifications: [LLB [Wales]]

JONES MISS CATHERINE ANNE

Pendragon Chambers
124 Walter Road, Swansea, West
Glamorgan, SA1 5RG,
Telephone: 01792 411188
Call Date: Oct 1992, Gray's Inn
Qualifications: [BA (Hons)(Swansea), Dip in
Law]

JONES MISS (CATHERINE) CHARLOTTE

Two Crown Office Row
Ground Floor, Temple, London
EC4Y 7HJ, Telephone: 020 7797 8100
E-mail: mail@2cor.co.uk, or to individual
barristers at: [barrister's
surname]@2cor.co.uk
Call Date: July 1982, Middle Temple
Pupil Master
Qualifications: [MA (Cantab)]

JONES MS CHERYL STEPHANIE

Fleet Chambers
Mitre House, 44-46 Fleet Street, London
EC4Y 1BN, Telephone: 0171 936 3707
E-mail: rr@fleetchambers.demon.co.uk
Call Date: Oct 1996, Gray's Inn
Qualifications: [LLB (Lancs)]

JONES CLIVE HUGH

1 New Square
Ground Floor, Lincoln's Inn, London
WC2A 3SA, Telephone: 0171 405 0884/5/6/
7 E-mail: clerks@1newsquare.law.co.uk
Call Date: July 1981, Middle Temple
Pupil Master
Qualifications: [BA (Oxon),ACIA]

JONES DANIEL

Phoenix Chambers
First Floor, Gray's Inn Chambers, Gray's
Inn, London WC1R 5JA,
Telephone: 0171 404 7888
E-mail:clerks@phoenix-chambers.co.uk
Call Date: 1997, Lincoln's Inn

JONES DANIEL OSKAR

Dr Johnson's Chambers
Two Dr Johnson's Buildings, Temple,
London EC4Y 7AY,
Telephone: 0171 353 4716
E-mail: clerks@2djb.freeserve.co.uk
Call Date: Oct 1994, Gray's Inn
Qualifications: [BA (Hons), CPE]

JONES DAVID ALAN FREEBORN

3 Fountain Court
Steelhouse Lane, Birmingham B4 6DR,
Telephone: 0121 236 5854
Call Date: July 1967, Gray's Inn
Pupil Master, Recorder
Qualifications: [LLB(Nottm)]

JONES DAVID JAMES

8 King's Bench Walk
2nd Floor, Temple, London EC4Y 7DU,
Telephone: 0171 797 8888
8 King's Bench Walk North
1 Park Square East, Leeds LS1 2NE,
Telephone: 0113 2439797
Call Date: Nov 1994, Lincoln's Inn
Qualifications: [LLB (Hons), LLM (Lond)]

JONES DAVID LLOYD QC (1999)

Brick Court Chambers
7-8 Essex Street, London WC2R 3LD,
Telephone: 0171 379 3550
E-mail: [surname]@brickcourt.co.uk
Call Date: 1975, Middle Temple
Pupil Master, Recorder
Qualifications: [MA, LLB (Cantab)]

JONES DAVID NICHOLAS

Broadway House Chambers
Broadway House, 9 Bank Street, Bradford,
West Yorkshire, BD1 1TW,
Telephone: 01274 722560
E-mail: clerks@broadwayhouse.co.uk
Broadway House Chambers
31 Park Square West, Leeds LS1 2PF,
Telephone: 0113 246 2600
Call Date: July 1985, Gray's Inn
Pupil Master
Qualifications: [LLB (Hons, Lond)]

JONES DOUGLAS PETER RICHARD

King Charles House
Standard Hill, Nottingham NG1 6FX,
Telephone: 0115 9418851
E-mail: clerks@kch.co.uk
Call Date: Oct 1991, Lincoln's Inn
Qualifications: [BSc (Hons) (Notts), Dip
Law]

JONES MISS ELAINE THOMSON

Corn Exchange Chambers
5th Floor, Fenwick Street, Liverpool
L2 7QS, Telephone: 0151 227 1081/5009
Call Date: July 1984, Lincoln's Inn
Qualifications: [BA (Hons)]

JONES MISS ELISABETH BARBARA

2 King's Bench Walk
Ground Floor, Temple, London
EC4Y 7DE, Telephone: 0171 353 1746
E-mail: 2kbw@atlas.co.uk
Call Date: Nov 1997, Inner Temple
Qualifications: [LLB (Western, Australia)]

JONES MISS ELIZABETH SIAN

Serle Court Chambers
6 New Square, Lincoln's Inn, London
WC2A 3QS, Telephone: 0171 242 6105
E-mail: clerks@serlecourt.co.uk
Call Date: Nov 1984, Middle Temple
Pupil Master
Qualifications: [BA (Cantab)]

JONES FRANCIS HUMPHREY

Iscoed Chambers
86 St Helen's Road, Swansea, West
Glamorgan, SA1 4BQ,
Telephone: 01792 652988/9/330
Call Date: July 1980, Inner Temple
Pupil Master
Qualifications: [MA (Oxon)]

JONES GARETH DARYL

India Buildings Chambers
Water Street, Liverpool L2 0XG,
Telephone: 0151 243 6000
E-mail: clerks@chambers.u-net.com
Call Date: Nov 1984, Gray's Inn
Pupil Master
Qualifications: [LLB (Wales)]

JONES GARETH JOHN

33 Park Place
Cardiff CF1 3BA,
Telephone: 02920 233313
Call Date: Feb 1992, Inner Temple
Qualifications: [MA (Camb)]

JONES GERAINT ANTHONY

9 Park Place
Cardiff CF1 3DP,
Telephone: 01222 382731
Farrar's Building
Temple, London EC4Y 7BD,
Telephone: 0171 583 9241
E-mail:chambers@farrarsbuilding.co.uk
Call Date: July 1976, Middle Temple
Pupil Master
Qualifications: [MA (Cantab)]

JONES GERAINT MARTYN

Fenners Chambers
3 Madingley Road, Cambridge CB3 0EE,
Telephone: 01223 368761
E-mail: clerks@fennerschambers.co.uk
Fenners Chambers
8-12 Priestgate, Peterborough PE1 1JA,
Telephone: 01733 562030
E-mail: clerks@fennerschambers.co.uk
Call Date: Nov 1972, Gray's Inn
Pupil Master
Qualifications: [MA, LLM (Cantab)]

JONES GERALD WILLIAM

Exchange Chambers
Pearl Assurance House, Derby Square,
Liverpool L2 9XX,
Telephone: 0151 236 7747
E-mail:exchangechambers@btinternet.com
Call Date: July 1995, Gray's Inn
Qualifications: [LLB (Sheff)]

JONES MISS GILLIAN HUNTER

18 Red Lion Court
(Off Fleet Street), London EC4A 3EB,
Telephone: 0171 520 6000
E-mail: chambers@18rlc.co.uk
Thornwood House
102 New London Road, Chelmsford,
Essex, CM2 0RG,
Telephone: 01245 280880
E-mail: chambers@18rlc.co.uk
Call Date: Oct 1996, Lincoln's Inn
Qualifications: [LLB (Hons)(Leic)]

JONES GREGORY PERCY

2 Harcourt Buildings
2nd Floor, Temple, London EC4Y 9DB,
Telephone: 020 7353 8415
E-mail: clerks@2hb.law.co.uk
Call Date: Nov 1991, Lincoln's Inn
Pupil Master
Qualifications: [MA (Hons) (Oxon)]

JONES GUY TREHARN HOWEL

32 Park Place
Cardiff CF1 3BA,
Telephone: 01222 397364
Call Date: July 1975, Gray's Inn
Qualifications: [LLB]

JONES HOWARD PETER

2nd Floor, Francis Taylor Building
Temple, London EC4Y 7BY,
Telephone: 0171 353 9942/3157
Call Date: Oct 1992, Gray's Inn
Qualifications: [MA (Hons)(Cantab)]

JONES HUW MICHAEL REES

St Albans Chambers
Dolphin Lodge, Dolphin Yard, Holywell
Hill, St Albans, Herts, AL1 1EX,
Telephone: 01727 843383
Call Date: 1997, Lincoln's Inn
Qualifications: [LLB (Hons)(Essex)]

JONES IFAN WYN LLOYD

Sedan House
Stanley Place, Chester CH1 2LU,
Telephone: 01244 320480/348282
Call Date: Nov 1979, Lincoln's Inn
Pupil Master
Qualifications: [LLB (Wales), BCL, (Oxon)]

JONES MISS JENNIFER CLAIRE

5 Fountain Court
Steelhouse Lane, Birmingham B4 6DR,
Telephone: 0121 606 0500
E-mail:clerks@5fountaincourt.law.co.uk
Call Date: Oct 1991, Lincoln's Inn
Qualifications: [LLB (Hons) (Birm)]

JONES MISS JESSICA FAY

One Raymond Buildings
Gray's Inn, London WC1R 5BH,
Telephone: 0171 430 1234
E-mail: chambers@ipbar1rb.com;
clerks@ipbar1rb.com
Call Date: Nov 1991, Inner Temple
Pupil Master
Qualifications: [BSc (So'ton), Dip Law]

JONES JOHN EVAN

4 King's Bench Walk
Ground/First Floor/Basement, Temple,
London EC4Y 7DL,
Telephone: 0171 822 8822
E-mail: 4kbw@barristersatlaw.com
Call Date: 1982, Inner Temple
Pupil Master
Qualifications: [BA (Hons) (Dunelm)]

JONES JOHN RICHARD

28 St John Street
Manchester M3 4DJ,
Telephone: 0161 834 8418
E-mail: clerk@28stjohnst.co.uk
Call Date: July 1981, Middle Temple
Pupil Master, Assistant Recorder
Qualifications: [LLB]

JONES JONATHAN ARTHUR DAVID

3 Fountain Court
Steelhouse Lane, Birmingham B4 6DR,
Telephone: 0121 236 5854
Call Date: Oct 1994, Gray's Inn
Qualifications: [MA]

JONES MISS KAY MARY

Chambers of Norman Palmer
2 Field Court, Gray's Inn, London
WC1R 5BB, Telephone: 0171 405 6114
E-mail: fieldct2@netcomuk.co.uk
Call Date: July 1974, Gray's Inn
Pupil Master
Qualifications: [BA (Hons) (Sussex), Cert
Universit, d'Aix/Marseille]

D

JONES LAURENCE ANDREW

Newport Chambers
12 Clytha Park Road, Newport, Gwent,
NP9 47L, Telephone: 01633 267403/
255855
Call Date: Oct 1997, Gray's Inn
Qualifications: [BA (Wales), MSc]

JONES LAWRENCE VICTOR

Plowden Buildings
2nd Floor, 2 Plowden Buildings, Middle
Temple Lane, London EC4Y 9BU,
Telephone: 0171 583 0808
E-mail: bar@plowdenbuildings.co.uk
Call Date: July 1988, Lincoln's Inn
Pupil Master
Qualifications: [LLB (Hons)]

JONES MISS LESLEY ANN

Trafalgar Chambers
53 Fleet Street, London EC4Y 1BE,
Telephone: 0171 583 5858
E-mail:trafalgarchambers@easynet.co.uk
Call Date: Oct 1995, Inner Temple
Qualifications: [LLB (Lond) (Hons)]

JONES MISS MARGARET EMMA

Two Garden Court
1st Floor, Middle Temple, London
EC4Y 9BL, Telephone: 0171 353 1633
E-mail:barristers@2gardenct.law.co.uk
Call Date: Nov 1990, Middle Temple
Qualifications: [BA (Dunelm)]

JONES MARK SIMEON

Goldsmith Chambers
Ground Floor, Goldsmith Building,
Temple, London EC4Y 7BL,
Telephone: 0171 353 6802/3/4/5
E-mail:clerks@goldsmithchambers.law.co.uk
Call Date: 1997, Middle Temple
Qualifications: [BA (Hons)(Cantab)]

JONES MARTIN WYNNE

8 King's Bench Walk
2nd Floor, Temple, London EC4Y 7DU,
Telephone: 0171 797 8888

8 King's Bench Walk North
1 Park Square East, Leeds LS1 2NE,
Telephone: 0113 2439797
Call Date: Nov 1977, Inner Temple
Pupil Master
Qualifications: [MA (Warwick), LLB (Lond)]

JONES MICHAEL

Cobden House Chambers
19 Quay Street, Manchester M3 3HN,
Telephone: 0161 833 6000
E-mail: clerks@cobden.co.uk
Call Date: Oct 1998, Lincoln's Inn
Qualifications: [LLB (Hons)(B'ham)]

JONES MICHAEL ADRIAN LYSTER

Sussex Chambers
9 Old Steine, Brighton, Sussex, BN1 1FJ,
Telephone: 01273 607953
Call Date: July 1972, Inner Temple
Pupil Master
Qualifications: [BA]

JONES MICHAEL SELWYN TUDOR

Pendragon Chambers
124 Walter Road, Swansea, West
Glamorgan, SA1 5RG,
Telephone: 01792 411188
Call Date: July 1995, Middle Temple
Qualifications: [BA (Hons)]

JONES MICHAEL WYN

25-27 Castle Street
1st Floor, Liverpool L2 4TA,
Telephone: 0151 227 5661/051 236 5072
Call Date: 1999, Gray's Inn

JONES NICHOLAS DAVID JULIAN

33 Park Place
Cardiff CF1 3BA,
Telephone: 02920 233313
Call Date: Nov 1987, Gray's Inn
Pupil Master
Qualifications: [BSc Econ (Wales), LLM
(Cantab)]

JONES NICHOLAS GARETH

33 Park Place
Cardiff CF1 3BA,
Telephone: 02920 233313

Goldsmith Building
1st Floor, Temple, London EC4Y 7BL,
Telephone: 0171 353 7881
E-mail:clerks@goldsmith-building.law.co.uk
Call Date: 1970, Gray's Inn
Pupil Master, Assistant Recorder

JONES NICHOLAS GRAHAM

4 Brick Court, Chambers of Anne Rafferty QC
1st Floor, Temple, London EC4Y 9AD,
Telephone: 0171 583 8455
Call Date: July 1975, Inner Temple
Pupil Master, Recorder
Qualifications: [MA (Oxon)]

JONES MS NICOLA JANE

Coleridge Chambers
Citadel, 190 Corporation Street,
Birmingham B4 6QD,
Telephone: 0121 233 8500
Call Date: Oct 1996, Gray's Inn
Qualifications: [BA (Oxon), MA (Sussex)]

JONES NIGEL DOUGLAS QC (1999)

Hardwicke Building
New Square, Lincoln's Inn, London
WC2A 3SB, Telephone: 020 7242 2523
E-mail: clerks@hardwicke.co.uk
Call Date: 1976, Gray's Inn
Pupil Master
Qualifications: [LLB (Lond)]

JONES PAUL ALAN

Staple Inn Chambers
1st Floor, 9 Staple Inn, Holborn Bars,
London WC1V 7QH,
Telephone: 0171 242 5240
E-mail: clerks@staple-inn.org
Call Date: July 1981, Inner Temple
Qualifications: [BA (Hons)]

JONES PETER WILLIAM WARBURTON

4 Brick Court
Ground Floor, Temple, London
EC4Y 9AD, Telephone: 0171 797 7766
E-mail: chambers@4brick.co.uk
Call Date: July 1969, Gray's Inn
Pupil Master
Qualifications: [BA (Cantab)]

JONES PHILIP ALUN

9 Gough Square
London EC4A 3DE,
Telephone: 020 7832 0500
E-mail: clerks@9goughsq.co.uk
Call Date: Nov 1990, Middle Temple
Qualifications: [BA (Cantab), LLM (Lond)]

JONES PHILIP JOHN

Serle Court Chambers
6 New Square, Lincoln's Inn, London
WC2A 3QS, Telephone: 0171 242 6105
E-mail: clerks@serlecourt.co.uk
Call Date: July 1985, Lincoln's Inn
Pupil Master
Qualifications: [MA,BCL (Oxon) LLM, (Dalhousie Canada)]

JONES MISS RHIANNON

Lamb Chambers
Lamb Building, Temple, London
EC4Y 7AS, Telephone: 020 7797 8300
E-mail: lambchambers@link.org
Call Date: Nov 1993, Inner Temple
Qualifications: [B Mus AKC Dip Law, MA]

JONES RHYS CHARLES MANSEL

33 Bedford Row
London WC1R 4JH,
Telephone: 0171 242 6476
E-mail:clerks@bedfordrow33.demon.co.uk
Call Date: May 1990, Middle Temple
Qualifications: [MA (Cantab)]

JONES RICHARD ALAN

33 Park Place
Cardiff CF1 3BA,
Telephone: 02920 233313
Farrar's Building
Temple, London EC4Y 7BD,
Telephone: 0171 583 9241
E-mail:chambers@farrarsbuilding.co.uk
Call Date: Nov 1969, Gray's Inn
Qualifications: [MA (Oxon), LLB (Cantab)]

JONES RICHARD FREDERICK THOMAS

Queens Square Chambers
56 Queens Square, Bristol BS1 4PR,
Telephone: 0117 921 1966

8 Fountain Court
Steelhouse Lane, Birmingham B4 6DR,
Telephone: 0121 236 5514/5
E-mail: clerks@no8chambers.co.uk
Call Date: July 1979, Gray's Inn
Pupil Master
Qualifications: [LLB (Bris) MICE, FCIArb]

JONES RICHARD HENRY QC (1996)

1 Crown Office Row
3rd Floor, Temple, London EC4Y 7HH,
Telephone: 0171 583 9292
E-mail: onecor@link.org
Call Date: 1972, Inner Temple
Assistant Recorder
Qualifications: [MA (Oxon)]

JONES RICHARD HUW FRANKLYN

Francis Taylor Building
Ground Floor, Temple, London
EC4Y 7BY, Telephone: 0171 353 7768/
7769/2711
E-mail:clerks@francistaylorbuilding.law.co.uk
Call Date: July 1984, Gray's Inn
Pupil Master
Qualifications: [LLB (Wales)]

JONES ROBERT ALUN QC (1989)

3 Raymond Buildings
Gray's Inn, London WC1R 5BH,
Telephone: 020 7831 3833
E-mail:chambers@threeraymond.demon.co.uk
Call Date: Nov 1972, Gray's Inn
Recorder
Qualifications: [BSc]

JONES ROBERT FFRANCON WYN

1 Middle Temple Lane
Temple, London EC4Y 1LT,
Telephone: 0171 583 0659 (12 Lines)
E-mail: chambers@1mtl.co.uk
Call Date: Nov 1993, Lincoln's Inn
Qualifications: [BA (Hons)]

JONES RODERICK JAMES WATSON

4 Brick Court
Ground Floor, Temple, London
EC4Y 9AD, Telephone: 0171 797 7766
E-mail: chambers@4brick.co.uk

Guildhall Chambers Portsmouth
Prudential Buildings, 16 Guildhall Walk,
Portsmouth, Hampshire, PO1 2DE,
Telephone: 01705 752400
Call Date: July 1983, Gray's Inn
Pupil Master
Qualifications: [BA]

JONES MISS SARAH FRANCES

2 King's Bench Walk
Ground Floor, Temple, London
EC4Y 7DE, Telephone: 0171 353 1746
E-mail: 2kbw@atlas.co.uk
Call Date: Nov 1996, Lincoln's Inn
Qualifications: [BA (Hons)]

JONES SEAN WILLIAM PAUL

11 King's Bench Walk
Temple, London EC4Y 7EQ,
Telephone: 0171 632 8500/583 0610
E-mail: clerksroom@11kbw.com
Call Date: Oct 1991, Inner Temple
Qualifications: [BA,BCL (Oxon)]

JONES STEPHEN HUGH

Farrar's Building
Temple, London EC4Y 7BD,
Telephone: 0171 583 9241
E-mail:chambers@farrarsbuilding.co.uk
Call Date: Nov 1978, Inner Temple
Pupil Master
Qualifications: [MA (Oxon)]

JONES STEVEN CHARLES

South Western Chambers
Melville House, 12 Middle Street,
Taunton, Somerset, TA1 1SH,
Telephone: 01823 331919 (24 hrs)
E-mail: barclerk@clara.net
Call Date: Oct 1994, Middle Temple
Qualifications: [LLB (Hons)(Exeter)]

JONES STEWART ELGAN QC (1994)

3 Paper Buildings
Temple, London EC4Y 7EU,
Telephone: 020 7583 8055
E-mail: London@3paper.com
3 Paper Buildings (Bournemouth)
20 Lorne Park Road, Bournemouth,
Dorset, BH1 1JN,
Telephone: 01202 292102
E-mail: Bournemouth@3paper.com

3 Paper Buildings (Winchester)
4 St Peter Street, Winchester SO23 8BW,
Telephone: 01962 868884
E-mail: winchester@3paper.com
3 Paper Buildings (Oxford)
1 Alfred Street, High Street, Oxford
OX1 4EH, Telephone: 01865 793736
E-mail: oxford@3paper.com
*Call Date: Nov 1972, Gray's Inn
Recorder*
Qualifications: [MA (Oxon)]

JONES MISS SUSANNAH LUCY

Octagon House
19 Colegate, Norwich NR3 1AT,
Telephone: 01603 623186
E-mail: admin@octagon-chambers.co.uk
Call Date: Oct 1997, Middle Temple
Qualifications: [B.Ed (Hons)(Cantab), CPE
(Lond)]

JONES THOMAS GLANVILLE

Angel Chambers
94 Walter Road, Swansea, West
Glamorgan, SA1 5QA,
Telephone: 01792 464623/464648
E-mail: lynne@angelchambers.co.uk
*Call Date: Nov 1956, Gray's Inn
Pupil Master, Recorder*
Qualifications: [LLB (Lond)]

JONES TIMOTHY ARTHUR

St Philip's Chambers
Fountain Court, Steelhouse Lane,
Birmingham B4 6DR,
Telephone: 0121 246 7000
E-mail: clerks@st-philips.co.uk
Arden Chambers
27 John Street, London WC1N 2BL,
Telephone: 020 7242 4244
E-mail:clerks@arden-chambers.law.co.uk
*Call Date: July 1975, Inner Temple
Pupil Master*
Qualifications: [LLB (Lond), ACIArb, F.R.G.S,
F.R.S.A]

Fax: 0121 246 7001; 020 7242 3224;
Out of hours telephone: 0966 195228;
DX: 16073 Birmingham 4/29 Chancery
Lane;
Other comms: E-mail timjones@link.org;
Link: Timothy Jones; URL: http://
www.st-philips.co.uk; http://
www.arden-chambers.co.uk/
arden-chambers

Other professional qualifications: Fellow Chartered Institute of Arbitrators

Types of work: Administrative, ECHR, Environment, Local government, Town and country planning

Membership of foreign bars: Ireland, Northern Ireland

Circuit: Midland & Oxford

Awards and memberships: Member: Planning and Environment Bar Association; Administrative Law Bar Association; UK Environmental Law Association; Fellow Royal Geographical Society

Languages spoken: French, Italian

Publications: 'Property Rights, Planning Law and the European Convention', *European Human Rights Law Review* 233, 1996; *A Practitioner's Guide to the Impact of the Human Rights Act 1998* (Hart Publishing): Chapter on Planning and Environment Law, 1999; 'Judicial Interpretation of the Arbitration Act 1996' *Arbitration Journal*, 1999; 'Human Rights Act – what you need to know as a property lawyer' – *Commercial Property*, 1998

Cases
Buckley v United Kingdom 23 EHRR 101
[1996] JPL 1018 [1995] JPL 633 (ECtHR)
Burton v United Kingdom 22 EHRR CD134
(ECommHR)
McDonalds Restaurants v Greenwich LBC
9 PAD 473
Hughes v Environment Secretary 71 P&CR
168
NHBC v Sandwell MBC [1991] COD 17
(DC)
R v Bexley LBC ex parte B [1995] CLY 3225
R v Bristol CC ex parte McDonough [1993]
CLY 3891
R v Duckworth 16 CrAppR(S) 529 (CA)
*R v Hereford & Worcester CC ex parte
Smith* [1994] COD 129 (CA)
*R v Housing Benefit Review Board ex
parte Smith* 19 HLR 217
R v Oldbury Justices ex parte Smith [1995]
7AdminLR 315
R v Sandwell MBC ex parte Lyn 34 RVR 126
R v Sandwell MBC ex parte Wilkinson 31
HLR 22
R v Environment Secretary ex parte Davies
61 P&CR 487 (CA)
R v Environment Secretary ex parte Smith
[1988] COD 3

D

R v South Herefordshire DC ex parte Miles
17 HLR 82
R v Warley Justices ex parte Callis [1994]
COD 240
Safeways v Greenwich LBC [1995] JPL 865
Sainsbury v Greenwich LBC [1997] JPL
774
South Northamptonshire DC v Power
[1987] 1 WLR 1433 (CA)
Stirk v Bridgnorth DC 73 P&CR 439 (CA)
Stirrup v Environment Secretary LA Law 1/
94
Turner v United Kingdom 23 EHRR CD
181
Webb v Environment Secretary 71 P&CR
411
Woodhouse v Walsall MBC [1994] EnvLR
30
Woolhead v Environment Secretary 71
P&CR 419
Wychavon DC v Environment Secretary
[1994] 2 EnvLR 239
Wyre Forest DC v Bostock [1993] 1 EnvLR
235 (CA)
Wyre Forest DC v Environment Secretary
[1990] 2 AC 357 (HL)

JONES WILLIAM JOHN

1 Hare Court
Ground Floor, Temple, London
EC4Y 7BE, Telephone: 0171 353 3982/
5324
Call Date: Nov 1972, Inner Temple
Pupil Master, Recorder

JOPLING ADRIAN ROLAND

Phydeaux Chambers
Dunelm, Mount Pleasant Road, Camborne,
Cornwall, TR14 7RJ,
Telephone: 01209 715285
Call Date: Nov 1985, Middle Temple
Qualifications: [BA]

JORDAN ANDREW

2 Harcourt Buildings
Ground Floor/Left, Temple, London
EC4Y 9DB, Telephone: 0171 583 9020
E-mail: clerks@harcourt.co.uk
Call Date: July 1973, Lincoln's Inn
Qualifications: [LLB (Warwick)]

JORDASH WAYNE DARREN

14 Tooks Court
Cursitor St, London EC4A 1LB,
Telephone: 0171 405 8828
E-mail: clerks@tooks.law.co.uk
Call Date: Nov 1995, Middle Temple
Qualifications: [BSc (Hons)]

JORY RICHARD NORMAN

9-12 Bell Yard
London WC2A 2LF,
Telephone: 0171 400 1800
E-mail: clerks@bellyard.co.uk
Call Date: Oct 1993, Middle Temple
Qualifications: [BA (Hons)(Reading), CPE
(Middx)]

JORY ROBERT JOHN HUGH

Enterprise Chambers
9 Old Square, Lincoln's Inn, London
WC2A 3SR, Telephone: 0171 405 9471
E-mail:enterprise.london@dial.pipex.com
Enterprise Chambers
38 Park Square, Leeds LS1 2PA,
Telephone: 0113 246 0391
E-mail:enterprise.leeds@dial.pipex.com
Enterprise Chambers
65 Quayside, Newcastle upon Tyne
NE1 3DS, Telephone: 0191 222 3344
E-mail:enterprise.newcastle@dial.pipex.com
Call Date: Oct 1992, Lincoln's Inn
Qualifications: [MA, Dip Law]

JOSE RICHARD CALDER

St Mary's Chambers
50 High Pavement, Lace Market,
Nottingham NG1 1HW,
Telephone: 0115 9503503
E-mail: clerks@smc.law.co.uk
Call Date: Nov 1971, Gray's Inn
Assistant Recorder
Qualifications: [BA (Hons)]

JOSEPH CHARLES HENRY

4 Paper Buildings
1st Floor, Temple, London EC4Y 7EX,
Telephone: 0171 583 0816/353 1131
E-mail: clerks@4paperbuildings.co.uk
Call Date: July 1980, Lincoln's Inn
Pupil Master
Qualifications: [BA (Hons), FCIArb]

JOSEPH CLIFFORD DEREK

Pepys' Chambers
17 Fleet Street, London EC4Y 1AA,
Telephone: 0171 936 2710
Call Date: Apr 1975, Gray's Inn
Pupil Master
Qualifications: [MA (Oxon), LMRTPI]

JOSEPH DAVID PHILIP

Essex Court Chambers
24 Lincoln's Inn Fields, London
WC2A 3ED, Telephone: 0171 813 8000
E-mail:clerksroom@essexcourt-chambers.co.u
k
Call Date: Nov 1984, Middle Temple
Pupil Master
Qualifications: [MA (Cantab)]

JOSEPH MRS ELIZABETH ANN AYODELE

Emmanuel Chambers
259 Gray's Inn Road, London WC1X 8QT,
Telephone: 0171 713 7772
6 King's Bench Walk
Ground, Third & Fourth Floors, Temple,
London EC4Y 7DR,
Telephone: 0171 353 4931/583 0695
Call Date: July 1983, Gray's Inn
Qualifications: [BA, LLM]

JOSEPH SELLAPPH JOB

2 Middle Temple Lane
3rd Floor, Temple, London EC4Y 9AA,
Telephone: 0171 583 4540
Call Date: Nov 1983, Middle Temple
Qualifications: [LLB (Lond), LLB (Sri Lanka)]

JOSEPH MS WENDY ROSE QC (1998)

6 King's Bench Walk
Ground Floor, Temple, London
EC4Y 7DR, Telephone: 0171 583 0410
E-mail: worsley@6kbw.freeserve.co.uk
Call Date: Nov 1975, Gray's Inn
Recorder
Qualifications: [MA (Cantab)]

JOSHI PRAMOD KUMAR

Wessex Chambers
48 Queens Road, Reading, Berkshire,
RG1 4BD, Telephone: 0118 956 8856
E-mail:wessexchambers@compuserve.com
Call Date: Nov 1992, Inner Temple
Qualifications: [LLB (Hons), MBA]

JOSLING WILLIAM HENRY CHARLES

Fenners Chambers
3 Madingley Road, Cambridge CB3 0EE,
Telephone: 01223 368761
E-mail: clerks@fennerschambers.co.uk
Fenners Chambers
8-12 Priestgate, Peterborough PE1 1JA,
Telephone: 01733 562030
E-mail: clerks@fennerschambers.co.uk
Call Date: Nov 1995, Lincoln's Inn
Qualifications: [MA (Cantab), Dip.Law]

JOSS NORMAN JAMES

One Essex Court
1st Floor, Temple, London EC4Y 9AR,
Telephone: 0171 936 3030
E-mail: one.essex_court@virgin.net
Call Date: July 1982, Lincoln's Inn
Pupil Master
Qualifications: [BA (Hons)]

JOSSE DAVID BENJAMIN

Bridewell Chambers
2 Bridewell Place, London EC4V 6AP,
Telephone: 020 7797 8800
E-mail:HughesGage@bridewell.law.co.uk
Call Date: July 1985, Middle Temple
Pupil Master
Qualifications: [BA (Lond)]

JOURDAN STEPHEN ERIC

Falcon Chambers
Falcon Court, London EC4Y 1AA,
Telephone: 0171 353 2484
E-mail: clerks@falcon-chambers.com
Call Date: Nov 1989, Gray's Inn
Pupil Master
Qualifications: [MA (Cantab)]

JOWELL DANIEL SIMON SUZMAN

One Essex Court
Ground Floor, Temple, London
EC4Y 9AR, Telephone: 020 7583 2000
E-mail: clerks@oneessexcourt.co.uk
Call Date: Nov 1995, Middle Temple
Qualifications: [BA (Hons), LLM]

JOWELL PROFESSOR JEFFREY LIONEL QC (1993)

Blackstone Chambers
Blackstone House, Temple, London
EC4Y 9BW, Telephone: 0171 583 1770
E-mail:clerks@blackstonechambers.com
Call Date: Feb 1965, Middle Temple
Qualifications: [BA, LLB (C.Town), MA
(Oxon), LLM, SJD (Harvard), LLD]

JOWITT MATTHEW THOMAS

9 Bedford Row
London WC1R 4AZ,
Telephone: 0171 242 3555
E-mail: clerks@9br.co.uk
Call Date: Nov 1994, Middle Temple
Qualifications: [MA (Oxons)]

JOY HENRY MARTIN

5 King's Bench Walk
Temple, London EC4Y 7DN,
Telephone: 0171 353 5638
Call Date: July 1971, Lincoln's Inn
Qualifications: [LLB (Soton)]

JOY MICHAEL TENNENT

17 Bedford Row
London WC1R 4EB,
Telephone: 0171 831 7314
E-mail: iboard7314@aol.com
Call Date: 1997, Middle Temple
Qualifications: [M.Chem (Oxon)]

JOYCE MICHAEL JOHN

9 Gough Square
London EC4A 3DE,
Telephone: 020 7832 0500
E-mail: clerks@9goughsq.co.uk
Call Date: Nov 1976, Gray's Inn
Pupil Master
Qualifications: [LLB (Lond)]

JOYCE PETER STUART LANGFORD QC (1991)

High Pavement Chambers
1 High Pavement, Nottingham NG1 1HF,
Telephone: 0115 9418218
Chambers of Michael Pert QC
36 Bedford Row, London WC1R 4JH,
Telephone: 0171 421 8000
E-mail: 36bedfordrow@link.org
Chambers of Michael Pert QC
24 Albion Place, Northampton NN1 1UD,
Telephone: 01604 602333
Chambers of Michael Pert QC
104 New Walk, Leicester LE1 7EA,
Telephone: 0116 249 2020
Call Date: July 1968, Inner Temple
Recorder

JUBB BRIAN PATRICK

Gray's Inn Chambers
5th Floor, Gray's Inn, London WC1R 5JA,
Telephone: 0171 404 1111
Call Date: Nov 1971, Gray's Inn
Pupil Master

JUCKES ROBERT WILLIAM SOMERVILLE QC (1999)

3 Fountain Court
Steelhouse Lane, Birmingham B4 6DR,
Telephone: 0121 236 5854
Call Date: 1974, Inner Temple
Pupil Master, Recorder
Qualifications: [BA (Exon)]

JUDD MISS FRANCES JEAN

Harcourt Chambers
1st Floor, 2 Harcourt Buildings, Temple,
London EC4Y 9DB,
Telephone: 0171 353 6961
E-mail:clerks@harcourtchambers.law.co.uk
Harcourt Chambers
Churchill House, 3 St Aldate's Courtyard,
St Aldate's, Oxford OX1 1BN,
Telephone: 01865 791559
E-mail:clerks@harcourtchambers.law.co.uk
Call Date: Nov 1984, Middle Temple
Pupil Master
Qualifications: [BA(Cantab)]

JUDGE ANDREW JOHN

Westgate Chambers
144 High Street, Lewes, East Sussex,
BN7 1XT, Telephone: 01273 480510
Call Date: July 1986, Middle Temple
Pupil Master
Qualifications: [BA (Hons)]

JUDGE CHARLES JOSEPH

Five Paper Buildings
1st Floor, Five Paper Bldgs, Temple,
London EC4Y 7HB,
Telephone: 0171 583 6117
E-mail:clerks@5-paperbuildings.law.co.uk
Call Date: July 1981, Inner Temple
Pupil Master
Qualifications: [BA (Hons)]

JUDGE MISS LISA JANE

Deans Court Chambers
24 St John Street, Manchester M3 4DF,
Telephone: 0161 214 6000
E-mail: clerks@deanscourt.co.uk
Deans Court Chambers
41-43 Market Place, Preston PR1 1AH,
Telephone: 01772 555163
E-mail: clerks@deanscourt.co.uk
Call Date: Oct 1993, Gray's Inn
Qualifications: [LLB (Hons)]

JULIEN MISS CHRISTINE HELEN

3 Temple Gardens
3rd Floor, Temple, London EC4Y 9AU,
Telephone: 0171 583 0010
Call Date: Nov 1991, Inner Temple
Qualifications: [LLB (Hons)(L'pool)]

JUNAID-ADAMSON MISS SHEKINAH ADEBISI

Chancery Chambers
1st Floor Offices, 70/72 Chancery Lane,
London WC2A 1AB,
Telephone: 0171 405 6879/6870
Call Date: Nov 1994, Lincoln's Inn
Qualifications: [LLB (Hons)]

JUPP JEFFREY ERNEST

Chambers of Michael Pert QC
36 Bedford Row, London WC1R 4JH,
Telephone: 0171 421 8000
E-mail: 36bedfordrow@link.org
Chambers of Michael Pert QC
24 Albion Place, Northampton NN1 1UD,
Telephone: 01604 602333
Chambers of Michael Pert QC
104 New Walk, Leicester LE1 7EA,
Telephone: 0116 249 2020
Call Date: Nov 1994, Inner Temple
Qualifications: [BA , CPE]

JURENKO MISS RENATA ANNA

95A Chancery Lane
London WC2A 1DT,
Telephone: 0171 405 3101
Call Date: Oct 1993, Middle Temple
Qualifications: [B.Ed (Hons)]

JUSS DR SATVINDER SINGH

6 King's Bench Walk
Ground, Third & Fourth Floors, Temple,
London EC4Y 7DR,
Telephone: 0171 353 4931/583 0695
Call Date: Nov 1989, Gray's Inn
Qualifications: [BA, Ph.D (Cantab)]

KADRI SADAKAT

Doughty Street Chambers
11 Doughty Street, London WC1N 2PG,
Telephone: 0171 404 1313
E-mail:enquiries@doughtystreet.co.uk
Call Date: Nov 1989, Inner Temple
Qualifications: [BA (Cantab), LLM (Harvard)]

KADRI SIBGHATULLAH QC (1989)

6 King's Bench Walk
Ground, Third & Fourth Floors, Temple,
London EC4Y 7DR,
Telephone: 0171 353 4931/583 0695
Call Date: Nov 1969, Inner Temple
Qualifications: [FRSA]

KAFFEL PAUL ELLIOTT

Lion Court
Chancery House, 53-64 Chancery Lane,
London WC2A 1SJ,
Telephone: 0171 404 6565
Call Date: Nov 1993, Inner Temple
Qualifications: [BSc (Manc), CPE]

KAIHIVA ABIUD KARATE

Chambers of Martin Burr
Fourth Floor, Eldon Chambers, 30/32
Fleet Street, London EC4Y 1AA,
Telephone: 0171 353 4636
Call Date: Feb 1993, Inner Temple
Qualifications: [BCOM, LLB,]

KALER MISS MANJEET KAUR

1 Pump Court
Lower Ground Floor, Temple, London
EC4Y 7AB, Telephone: 0171 583 2012/
353 4341
E-mail: [name]@1pumpcourt.co.uk
Call Date: Feb 1993, Middle Temple
Qualifications: [LLB (Hons)(Middx)]

KALLIPETIS MICHEL LOUIS QC (1989)

Littleton Chambers
3 King's Bench Walk North, Temple,
London EC4Y 7HR,
Telephone: 0171 797 8600
E-mail:clerks@littletonchambers.co.uk
Call Date: July 1968, Gray's Inn
Recorder
Qualifications: [LLB (Lond)]

KALSI MRS MANINDER

New Court Chambers
Gazette Building, 168 Corporation Street,
Birmingham B4 6TZ,
Telephone: 0121 693 6656
Call Date: Nov 1992, Inner Temple
Qualifications: [LLB]

KAMILL MISS LOUISE NAIMA RACHEL

1 Hare Court
Ground Floor, Temple, London
EC4Y 7BE, Telephone: 0171 353 3982/
5324
Call Date: July 1974, Inner Temple
Pupil Master, Recorder

KAMLISH STEPHEN MICHAEL ADRIAN

14 Tooks Court
Cursitor St, London EC4A 1LB,
Telephone: 0171 405 8828
E-mail: clerks@tooks.law.co.uk
Call Date: July 1979, Gray's Inn
Qualifications: [BA (Hons)]

KANE ADAM VINCENT SIMON

1 Dr Johnson's Buildings
Ground Floor, Temple, London
EC4Y 7AX, Telephone: 0171 353 9328
E-mail:OneDr.Johnsons@btinternet.com
Call Date: Nov 1993, Gray's Inn
Qualifications: [BA (Oxon), CPE]

KANG MISS BIRINDER KAUR

14 Tooks Court
Cursitor St, London EC4A 1LB,
Telephone: 0171 405 8828
E-mail: clerks@tooks.law.co.uk
Call Date: 1996, Inner Temple
Qualifications: [LLB (Lond), M.Phil (Cantab)]

KAPLAN MRS BARBARA JANE

Chambers of John L Powell QC
Four New Square, Lincoln's Inn, London
WC2A 3RJ, Telephone: 0171 797 8000
E-mail: barristers@4newsquare.com
Call Date: Nov 1980, Inner Temple
Qualifications: [MA (Cantab) ACIArb]

KAPUR DEEPAK KUMAR

2 King's Bench Walk Chambers
1st Floor, 2 King's Bench Walk, Temple,
London EC4Y 7DE,
Telephone: 020 7353 9276
E-mail: chambers@2kbw.co.uk
Call Date: July 1984, Lincoln's Inn
Pupil Master
Qualifications: [BA (Hons)]

KARALLIS MISS CONSTANTINA DINA

10 King's Bench Walk
1st Floor, Temple, London EC4Y 7EB,
Telephone: 0171 353 2501
Call Date: Nov 1989, Gray's Inn
Qualifications: [LLB (Kingston), LLM]

KARAS JONATHAN MARCUS

Wilberforce Chambers
8 New Square, Lincoln's Inn, London
WC2A 3QP, Telephone: 0171 306 0102
E-mail: chambers@wilberforce.co.uk
Call Date: July 1986, Middle Temple
Pupil Master
Qualifications: [MA (Oxon), Dip Law]

Types of work: Chancery land law, Commercial property, Common law (general), Conveyancing, Landlord and tenant, Local government, Town and country planning

KARK THOMAS VICTOR WILLIAM

Hollis Whiteman Chambers
3rd Floor, Queen Elizabeth Bldg, Temple,
London EC4Y 9BS,
Telephone: 020 7583 5766
E-mail:barristers@holliswhiteman.co.uk
Call Date: July 1982, Inner Temple
Pupil Master, Assistant Recorder

KARMY-JONES MISS RIEL MEREDITH

1 Hare Court
Ground Floor, Temple, London
EC4Y 7BE, Telephone: 0171 353 3982/
5324
Call Date: Nov 1995, Lincoln's Inn
Qualifications: [BA (Alberta), LLB (Hons)]

KARU LEE N

2 Paper Buildings
1st Floor, Temple, London EC4Y 7ET,
Telephone: 020 7556 5500
E-mail: clerks@2pbbarristers.co.uk
Call Date: July 1985, Lincoln's Inn
Pupil Master
Qualifications: [BA (Hons)]

KASHMIRI MISS SOPHIA

Gray's Inn Chambers, The Chambers of Norman Patterson
First Floor, Gray's Inn Chambers, Gray's
Inn, London WC1R 5JA,
Telephone: 0171 831 5344
E-mail: s.mcblain@btinternet.com
Call Date: Oct 1994, Gray's Inn
Qualifications: [LLB]

KATAN JONATHAN MAX

Goldsmith Chambers
Ground Floor, Goldsmith Building,
Temple, London EC4Y 7BL,
Telephone: 0171 353 6802/3/4/5
E-mail:clerks@goldsmithchambers.law.co.uk
Call Date: Oct 1990, Gray's Inn
Qualifications: [LLB]

KATKOWSKI CHRISTOPHER ANDREW MARK QC (1999)

4 Breams Buildings
London EC4A 1AQ,
Telephone: 0171 353 5835/430 1221
E-mail:breams@4breamsbuildings.law.co.uk
Call Date: 1982, Gray's Inn
Pupil Master
Qualifications: [MA, LLB (Cantab)]

KATRAK CYRUS PESI

Gough Square Chambers
6-7 Gough Square, London EC4A 3DE,
Telephone: 0171 353 0924
E-mail: gsc@goughsq.co.uk
Call Date: Oct 1991, Gray's Inn
Qualifications: [LLB]

KATYAR ARUN KUMAR

2 King's Bench Walk Chambers
1st Floor, 2 King's Bench Walk, Temple,
London EC4Y 7DE,
Telephone: 020 7353 9276
E-mail: chambers@2kbw.co.uk
Call Date: Nov 1993, Lincoln's Inn
Qualifications: [LLB (Hons)]

KATZ PHILIP ALEC JACKSON

9-12 Bell Yard
London WC2A 2LF,
Telephone: 0171 400 1800
E-mail: clerks@bellyard.co.uk
Call Date: Nov 1976, Middle Temple
Pupil Master
Qualifications: [MA (Oxon)]

KAUFMANN MS PHILLIPPA JANE

Doughty Street Chambers
11 Doughty Street, London WC1N 2PG,
Telephone: 0171 404 1313
E-mail:enquiries@doughtystreet.co.uk
Call Date: Oct 1991, Gray's Inn
Qualifications: [MA (Sheffield), LLB (Bris)]

KAUL MISS KALYANI

1 Middle Temple Lane
Temple, London EC4Y 1LT,
Telephone: 0171 583 0659 (12 Lines)
E-mail: chambers@1mtl.co.uk
Call Date: July 1983, Middle Temple
Qualifications: [LLB]

KAUR MISS HARINDER

New Walk Chambers
27 New Walk, Leicester LE1 6TE,
Telephone: 0116 2559144
Call Date: May 1995, Inner Temple
Qualifications: [LLB (Hons), LLM]

KAUR MISS RANI

Chambers of Ian Macdonald QC (In Association with Two Garden Court, Temple, London)
Waldorf House, 5 Cooper Street,
Manchester M2 2FW,
Telephone: 0161 236 1840
Acre Lane Neighbourhood Chambers
30A Acre Lane, London SW2 5SG,
Telephone: 0171 274 4400
E-mail:barristerschambers@acrelane.demon.co.uk
Call Date: Nov 1993, Gray's Inn
Qualifications: [LLB (Hull)]

KAVANAGH MRS JENNIFER

Albany Chambers
91 Kentish Town Road, London
NW1 8NY, Telephone: 0171 485 5736/
5758 E-mail: albany91.freeserve.co.uk
Call Date: Nov 1993, Lincoln's Inn
Qualifications: [LLB (Hons, L'pool)]

KAY DOMINIC MATTHEW

3 Paper Buildings
Temple, London EC4Y 7EU,
Telephone: 020 7583 8055
E-mail: London@3paper.com
3 Paper Buildings (Bournemouth)
20 Lorne Park Road, Bournemouth,
Dorset, BH1 1JN,
Telephone: 01202 292102
E-mail: Bournemouth@3paper.com
3 Paper Buildings (Winchester)
4 St Peter Street, Winchester SO23 8BW,
Telephone: 01962 868884
E-mail: winchester@3paper.com

3 Paper Buildings (Oxford)
1 Alfred Street, High Street, Oxford
OX1 4EH, Telephone: 01865 793736
E-mail: oxford@3paper.com
Call Date: 1997, Gray's Inn
Qualifications: [BSc (Brighton)]

KAY MICHAEL JACK DAVID

3 Verulam Buildings
London WC1R 5NT,
Telephone: 0171 831 8441
E-mail: clerks@3verulam.co.uk
Park Lane Chambers
19 Westgate, Leeds LS1 2RD,
Telephone: 0113 2285000
E-mail:clerks@parklanechambers.co.uk
Call Date: July 1981, Lincoln's Inn
Pupil Master, Assistant Recorder
Qualifications: [MA (Cantab)]

KAY MISS NICOLA JUDITH

1 Gray's Inn Square
Ground Floor, London WC1R 5AA,
Telephone: 0171 405 8946/7/8
Call Date: Oct 1996, Inner Temple
Qualifications: [BA (Hull), LLB (Wolves)]

KAY ROBERT JERVIS QC (1996)

4 Field Court
Gray's Inn, London WC1R 5EA,
Telephone: 0171 440 6900
E-mail: chambers@4fieldcourt.co.uk
Call Date: Nov 1972, Lincoln's Inn
Qualifications: [LLB]

KAY STEVEN WALTON QC (1997)

3 Gray's Inn Square
Ground Floor, London WC1R 5AH,
Telephone: 0171 520 5600
E-mail: clerks@3gis.co.uk
Call Date: Nov 1977, Inner Temple
Assistant Recorder
Qualifications: [LLB (Leeds)]

KAYANI (MOHAMMED) ASAF (REHMAT)

3 Stone Buildings
Lincoln's Inn, London WC2A 3XL,
Telephone: 0171 242 4937
E-mail: clerks@3sb.law.co.uk
Call Date: Nov 1991, Lincoln's Inn
Qualifications: [LLB (Hons) (Leeds), BCL
(Oxon)]

KAYE MISS LARAINE

Lion Court
Chancery House, 53-64 Chancery Lane,
London WC2A 1SJ,
Telephone: 0171 404 6565
Call Date: July 1971, Middle Temple
Pupil Master
Qualifications: [LLB (Lond), LLM (Lon]

KAYE ROGER GODFREY QC (1989)

Twenty-Four Old Buildings
Ground Floor, Lincoln's Inn, London
WC2A 3UP, Telephone: 0171 404 0946
E-mail:clerks@24oldbuildings.law.co.uk
St John's Chambers
Small Street, Bristol BS1 1DW,
Telephone: 0117 9213456/298514
E-mail: @stjohnschambers.co.uk
Call Date: Nov 1970, Lincoln's Inn
Recorder
Qualifications: [LLB]

KAYMAN MRS ESTHER LEBE

10 King's Bench Walk
1st Floor, Temple, London EC4Y 7EB,
Telephone: 0171 353 2501
Call Date: July 1974, Gray's Inn
Pupil Master

KAYNE CHARLES ADRIAN

3 Gray's Inn Square
Ground Floor, London WC1R 5AH,
Telephone: 0171 520 5600
E-mail: clerks@3gis.co.uk
Call Date: Nov 1989, Inner Temple
Qualifications: [LLB (Hons)]

KEALEY GAVIN SEAN JAMES QC (1994)

S Tomlinson QC
7 King's Bench Walk, Temple, London
EC4Y 7DS, Telephone: 0171 583 0404
E-mail: clerks@7kbw.law.co.uk
Call Date: Feb 1977, Inner Temple
Qualifications: [BA (Oxon)]

KEALEY SIMON THOMAS

Chambers of Andrew Campbell QC
10 Park Square, Leeds LS1 2LH,
Telephone: 0113 2455438
E-mail: clerks@10pksq.co.uk
Call Date: Apr 1991, Inner Temple
Qualifications: [LLB (Liverpool)]

KEALY CHARLES BRIAN

Chambers of Andrew Campbell QC
10 Park Square, Leeds LS1 2LH,
Telephone: 0113 2455438
E-mail: clerks@10pksq.co.uk
Call Date: Nov 1965, Middle Temple
Recorder

KEANE DESMOND ST JOHN QC (1981)

Pendragon Chambers
124 Walter Road, Swansea, West
Glamorgan, SA1 5RG,
Telephone: 01792 411188
Call Date: June 1964, Middle Temple
Qualifications: [MA (Oxon)]

KEANE MICHAEL LEO

4 Paper Buildings
Ground Floor, Temple, London
EC4Y 7EX, Telephone: 0171 353 3366/
583 7155
E-mail: clerks@4paperbuildings.com
Call Date: Nov 1963, Middle Temple
Recorder
Qualifications: [MA (Cantab)]

KEANE MICHAEL PETER

29 Bedford Row Chambers
London WC1R 4HE,
Telephone: 0171 831 2626
Call Date: July 1979, Gray's Inn
Pupil Master
Qualifications: [MA (Cantab)]

D

KEANE OWEN ASHLEY

Design Chambers
30 Fleet Street, London EC4Y 1AA,
Telephone: 0171 353 0747
E-mail: manager@designchambers.co.uk
Call Date: Nov 1988, Inner Temple
Qualifications: [LLB]

KEANY BRENDAN JOSEPH

3 Gray's Inn Square
Ground Floor, London WC1R 5AH,
Telephone: 0171 520 5600
E-mail: clerks@3gis.co.uk
Call Date: July 1974, Middle Temple
Qualifications: [BA (Lond)]

KEARL GUY ALEXANDER

St Paul's House
5th Floor, St Paul's House, 23 Park Square
South, Leeds LS1 2ND,
Telephone: 0113 2455866
E-mail: catherinegrimshaw@stpauls-
chambers.demon.co.uk
Call Date: July 1982, Middle Temple
Qualifications: [BA]

KEARNEY JAMES MARTIN

Lamb Building
Ground Floor, Temple, London
EC4Y 7AS, Telephone: 020 7797 7788
E-mail: lamb.building@link.org
Call Date: Feb 1992, Gray's Inn
Qualifications: [LLB (Dublin)]

KEARNEY JOHN

2 Paper Buildings
1st Floor, Temple, London EC4Y 7ET,
Telephone: 020 7556 5500
E-mail: clerks@2pbbarristers.co.uk
Call Date: Nov 1994, Middle Temple
Qualifications: [LLB (Hons)]

KEARNEY ROBERT MICHAEL

24a St John Street
Manchester M3 4DF,
Telephone: 0161 833 9628
Call Date: Nov 1996, Inner Temple
Qualifications: [LLB]

KEATING DERMOT JOHN

8 King's Bench Walk
2nd Floor, Temple, London EC4Y 7DU,
Telephone: 0171 797 8888
Call Date: 1997, Inner Temple
Qualifications: [LLB (Brunel)]

KEEGAN LESLIE FRANCIS

1 Pump Court
Lower Ground Floor, Temple, London
EC4Y 7AB, Telephone: 0171 583 2012/
353 4341
E-mail: [name]@1pumpcourt.co.uk
Call Date: Nov 1989, Middle Temple
Qualifications: [BA [Dub], B.Sc [Dun], Dip in
Law]

KEEHAN MICHAEL JOSEPH

St Ive's Chambers
Whittall Street, Birmingham B4 6DH,
Telephone: 0121 236 0863/5720
E-mail:stives.headofchambers@btinternet.com
Call Date: July 1982, Middle Temple
Pupil Master
Qualifications: [LLB (Hons) (B'ham)]

KEEL DOUGLAS VINCENT

11 Stone Buildings
Lincoln's Inn, London WC2A 3TG,
Telephone: +44 (0)207 831 6381
E-mail:clerks@11StoneBuildings.law.co.uk
Call Date: 1997, Lincoln's Inn
Qualifications: [MA (Oxon), DIP in Law
(Westmin)]

KEELEY JAMES FRANCIS

Sovereign Chambers
25 Park Square, Leeds LS1 2PW,
Telephone: 0113 2451841/2/3
E-mail:sovereignchambers@btinternet.com
Call Date: Oct 1993, Middle Temple
Qualifications: [LLB (Hons)(Kingston)]

KEELING ADRIAN FRANCIS

3 Fountain Court
Steelhouse Lane, Birmingham B4 6DR,
Telephone: 0121 236 5854
Call Date: Oct 1990, Inner Temple
Qualifications: [BA (Cantab)]

KEEN GRAEME

4 Breams Buildings
London EC4A 1AQ,
Telephone: 0171 353 5835/430 1221
E-mail:breams@4breamsbuildings.law.co.uk
Call Date: Oct 1995, Middle Temple
Qualifications: [LLB (Hons)]

KEEN KENNETH ROGER QC (1991)

Paradise Chambers
26 Paradise Square, Sheffield S1 2DE,
Telephone: 0114 2738951
E-mail: timbooth@paradise-sq.co.uk
Call Date: Feb 1976, Gray's Inn
Recorder

KEENAN PETER BERNARD

Cobden House Chambers
19 Quay Street, Manchester M3 3HN,
Telephone: 0161 833 6000
E-mail: clerks@cobden.co.uk
Call Date: Nov 1962, Gray's Inn
Pupil Master
Qualifications: [LLB, B (Litt)]

KEENE MRS GILLIAN MARGARET

Fountain Court
Temple, London EC4Y 9DH,
Telephone: 0171 583 3335
E-mail: chambers@fountaincourt.co.uk
Call Date: Nov 1980, Gray's Inn
Pupil Master
Qualifications: [MA (Oxon)]

KEFFORD ANTHONY JOHN ROLAND

East Anglian Chambers
57 London Street, Norwich NR2 1HL,
Telephone: 01603 617351
E-mail: norwich@ealaw.co.uk
East Anglian Chambers
52 North Hill, Colchester, Essex, CO1 1PY,
Telephone: 01206 572756
E-mail: colchester@ealaw.co.uk
East Anglian Chambers
Gresham House, 5 Museum Street,
Ipswich, Suffolk, IP1 1HQ,
Telephone: 01473 214481
E-mail: ipswich@ealaw.co.uk

1 Mitre Court Buildings
Temple, London EC4Y 7BS,
Telephone: 0171 797 7070
E-mail: clerks@1mcb.com
Call Date: Nov 1980, Middle Temple
Qualifications: [BSc]

KEIGAN MISS LINDA DIONE

Chambers of Helen Grindrod QC
4th Floor, 15-19 Devereux Court, London
WC2R 3JJ, Telephone: 0171 583 2792
Call Date: Nov 1992, Inner Temple
Qualifications: [LLB]

KEITH ALISTAIR JOHN

5 Pump Court
Ground Floor, Temple, London
EC4Y 7AP, Telephone: 020 7353 2532
E-mail: FivePump@netcomuk.co.uk
Call Date: Nov 1974, Middle Temple
Qualifications: [BD (Lond)]

KEITH HUGO GEORGE

3 Raymond Buildings
Gray's Inn, London WC1R 5BH,
Telephone: 020 7831 3833
E-mail:chambers@threeraymond.demon.co.u
k
Call Date: Nov 1989, Gray's Inn
Pupil Master
Qualifications: [MA (Oxon)]

KEITH THOMAS HAMILTON

Fountain Court
Temple, London EC4Y 9DH,
Telephone: 0171 583 3335
E-mail: chambers@fountaincourt.co.uk
Call Date: July 1983, Gray's Inn
Pupil Master
Qualifications: [BA (Oxon)]

KELBRICK ANTHONY MICHAEL

37 Park Square Chambers
37 Park Square, Leeds LS1 2NY,
Telephone: 0113 2439422
E-mail: chambers@no37.co.uk
Call Date: Feb 1992, Gray's Inn
Qualifications: [BA]

KELEHER PAUL ROBERT

3 Gray's Inn Square
Ground Floor, London WC1R 5AH,
Telephone: 0171 520 5600
E-mail: clerks@3gis.co.uk
Call Date: July 1980, Gray's Inn
Pupil Master
Qualifications: [BA (Cantab)]

KELLEHER BENEDICT PETER JOHN

2 Harcourt Buildings
1st Floor, Temple, London EC4Y 9DB,
Telephone: 020 7353 2112
Call Date: Nov 1994, Inner Temple
Qualifications: [LLB, MSc (Bris)]

KELLEHER KEITH ROY

3 Wellington Road
Poole, Dorset, BH14 9LF,
Telephone: 07771 905671 (Mobile)
Bell Yard Chambers
116/118 Chancery Lane, London
WC2A 1PP, Telephone: 0171 306 9292
Call Date: Nov 1987, Gray's Inn
Qualifications: [LLB (Hons)]

KELLETT JOHN CHARLES

1 Paper Buildings
1st Floor, Temple, London EC4Y 7EP,
Telephone: 0171 353 3728/4953
Call Date: Nov 1971, Middle Temple
Pupil Master
Qualifications: [BA (Cantab)]

KELLY BRENDAN DAMIEN

1 Hare Court
Ground Floor, Temple, London
EC4Y 7BE, Telephone: 0171 353 3982/
5324
Call Date: July 1988, Gray's Inn
Qualifications: [LLB]

KELLY CHARLES LAYTON

Trinity Chambers
9-12 Trinity Chare, Quayside, Newcastle
upon Tyne NE1 3DF,
Telephone: 0191 232 1927
E-mail: info@trinitychambers.co.uk
Call Date: Feb 1965, Inner Temple
Qualifications: [MA (Cantab)]

KELLY DAVID

Broadway House Chambers
Broadway House, 9 Bank Street, Bradford,
West Yorkshire, BD1 1TW,
Telephone: 01274 722560
E-mail: clerks@broadwayhouse.co.uk
Broadway House Chambers
31 Park Square West, Leeds LS1 2PF,
Telephone: 0113 246 2600
Call Date: July 1980, Gray's Inn
Pupil Master
Qualifications: [LLB (L'pool)]

KELLY MISS EMMA LOUISE

New Court Chambers
Gazette Building, 168 Corporation Street,
Birmingham B4 6TZ,
Telephone: 0121 693 6656
Call Date: 1997, Lincoln's Inn
Qualifications: [LLB (Hons)(Sheff)]

KELLY GEOFFREY ROBERT

Pump Court Chambers
Upper Ground Floor, 3 Pump Court,
Temple, London EC4Y 7AJ,
Telephone: 0171 353 0711
E-mail: clerks@3pumpcourt.com
Pump Court Chambers
31 Southgate Street, Winchester
SO23 9EE, Telephone: 01962 868161
E-mail: clerks@3pumpcourt.com
Pump Court Chambers
5 Temple Chambers, Temple Street,
Swindon SN1 1SQ,
Telephone: 01793 539899
E-mail: clerks@3pumpcourt.com
Call Date: Feb 1992, Middle Temple
Qualifications: [LLB (Hons) (Lond), LLM
(Lond)]

KELLY MISS GERALDINE THERESE

Chambers of Andrew Campbell QC
10 Park Square, Leeds LS1 2LH,
Telephone: 0113 2455438
E-mail: clerks@10pksq.co.uk
Call Date: Oct 1996, Gray's Inn
Qualifications: [LLB]

KELLY MARK

Francis Taylor Building
3rd Floor, Temple, London EC4Y 7BY,
Telephone: 0171 797 7250
Call Date: Nov 1985, Gray's Inn
Pupil Master
Qualifications: [LLB (Bristol), Dip in Law
(Belgium)]

KELLY MARTYN ALEXANDER

9 Park Place
Cardiff CF1 3DP,
Telephone: 01222 382731
Call Date: Nov 1972, Inner Temple
Pupil Master
Qualifications: [MA (Oxon)]

KELLY MATTHIAS JOHN QC (1999)

Old Square Chambers
1 Verulam Buildings, Gray's Inn, London
WC1R 5LQ, Telephone: 0171 269 0300
E-mail:clerks@oldsquarechambers.co.uk
Old Square Chambers
Hanover House, 47 Corn Street, Bristol
BS1 1HT, Telephone: 0117 9277111
E-mail: oldsqbri@globalnet.co.uk
Call Date: 1979, Gray's Inn
Pupil Master
Qualifications: [BA (Hons), LLB (Dub)]

KELLY MRS PATRICIA ANN

3 Paper Buildings
Temple, London EC4Y 7EU,
Telephone: 020 7583 8055
E-mail: London@3paper.com
3 Paper Buildings (Winchester)
4 St Peter Street, Winchester SO23 8BW,
Telephone: 01962 868884
E-mail: winchester@3paper.com
3 Paper Buildings (Bournemouth)
20 Lorne Park Road, Bournemouth,
Dorset, BH1 1JN,
Telephone: 01202 292102
E-mail: Bournemouth@3paper.com
3 Paper Buildings (Oxford)
1 Alfred Street, High Street, Oxford
OX1 4EH, Telephone: 01865 793736
E-mail: oxford@3paper.com
Call Date: July 1988, Inner Temple
Qualifications: [LLB (Soton)]

KELLY RICHARD BERNARD

East Anglian Chambers
52 North Hill, Colchester, Essex, CO1 1PY,
Telephone: 01206 572756
E-mail: colchester@ealaw.co.uk
East Anglian Chambers
57 London Street, Norwich NR2 1HL,
Telephone: 01603 617351
E-mail: norwich@ealaw.co.uk
East Anglian Chambers
Gresham House, 5 Museum Street,
Ipswich, Suffolk, IP1 1HQ,
Telephone: 01473 214481
E-mail: ipswich@ealaw.co.uk
Call Date: Oct 1994, Gray's Inn
Qualifications: [BA]

KELLY SEAN

Cobden House Chambers
19 Quay Street, Manchester M3 3HN,
Telephone: 0161 833 6000
E-mail: clerks@cobden.co.uk
Call Date: Oct 1990, Gray's Inn
Qualifications: [MA (Cantab)]

KELLY MS SIOBHAN FRANCES

Trafalgar Chambers
53 Fleet Street, London EC4Y 1BE,
Telephone: 0171 583 5858
E-mail:trafalgarchambers@easynet.co.uk
Call Date: Oct 1995, Middle Temple
Qualifications: [BA (Hons)]

KELLY MISS SIOBHAN MARIE

Paradise Chambers
26 Paradise Square, Sheffield S1 2DE,
Telephone: 0114 2738951
E-mail: timbooth@paradise-sq.co.uk
Call Date: 1995, Gray's Inn
Qualifications: [BA]

KELLY THOMAS ANDREW

2 Harcourt Buildings
2nd Floor, Temple, London EC4Y 9DB,
Telephone: 020 7353 8415
E-mail: clerks@2hb.law.co.uk
Call Date: July 1978, Lincoln's Inn
Pupil Master
Qualifications: [MA (Oxon)]

KELMAN ALISTAIR BRUCE

Lancaster Building
77 Deansgate, Manchester M3 2BW,
Telephone: 0161 661 4444/0171 649 9872
E-mail: sandra@lbnipc.com
Call Date: July 1977, Middle Temple
Pupil Master
Qualifications: [BSc (Eng), ACIArb, AMBCS]

KELSEY-FRY JOHN

Hollis Whiteman Chambers
3rd Floor, Queen Elizabeth Bldg, Temple,
London EC4Y 9BS,
Telephone: 020 7583 5766
E-mail:barristers@holliswhiteman.co.uk
Call Date: Nov 1978, Gray's Inn
Pupil Master

KELSON PETER JOHN

Bank House Chambers
Old Bank House, Hartshead, Sheffield
S1 2EL, Telephone: 0114 2751223
Call Date: July 1981, Middle Temple
Pupil Master, Assistant Recorder
Qualifications: [LLB]

KEMBER RICHARD

32 Park Place
Cardiff CF1 3BA,
Telephone: 01222 397364
Call Date: Oct 1993, Middle Temple
Qualifications: [MA (Oxon)]

KEMP CHRISTOPHER MARK

35 Essex Street
Temple, London WC2R 3AR,
Telephone: 0171 353 6381
E-mail: derek_jenkins@link.org
Call Date: Nov 1984, Middle Temple
Pupil Master
Qualifications: [BA (Oxon) Dip Law]

KEMP STEPHEN RICHARD

Oriel Chambers
14 Water Street, Liverpool L2 8TD,
Telephone: 0151 236 7191/236 4321
E-mail: clerks@oriel-chambers.co.uk
Call Date: Oct 1995, Lincoln's Inn
Qualifications: [BA (Hons)(York), Dip in
Law]

KEMPSTER IVOR TOBY CHALMERS

Old Square Chambers
Hanover House, 47 Corn Street, Bristol
BS1 1HT, Telephone: 0117 9277111
E-mail: oldsqbri@globalnet.co.uk
Old Square Chambers
1 Verulam Buildings, Gray's Inn, London
WC1R 5LQ, Telephone: 0171 269 0300
E-mail:clerks@oldsquarechambers.co.uk
Call Date: July 1980, Inner Temple
Pupil Master
Qualifications: [LLB (Leic)]

KENDAL MARK GILES

Phoenix Chambers
First Floor, Gray's Inn Chambers, Gray's
Inn, London WC1R 5JA,
Telephone: 0171 404 7888
E-mail:clerks@phoenix-chambers.co.uk
Call Date: Feb 1993, Inner Temple
Qualifications: [LLB]

KENDALL JOEL CAMILO TEPLITZ

12 King's Bench Walk
Temple, London EC4Y 7EL,
Telephone: 0171 583 0811
E-mail: chambers@12kbw.co.uk
Call Date: Oct 1993, Middle Temple
Qualifications: [BA (Hons)(Oxon)]

KENDALL TIMOTHY JAMES

3 Hare Court
1 Little Essex Street, London WC2R 3LD,
Telephone: 0171 395 2000
Call Date: Nov 1985, Gray's Inn
Pupil Master
Qualifications: [LLB]

KENDRICK DOMINIC JOHN QC (1997)

S Tomlinson QC
7 King's Bench Walk, Temple, London
EC4Y 7DS, Telephone: 0171 583 0404
E-mail: clerks@7kbw.law.co.uk
Call Date: July 1981, Middle Temple
Qualifications: [MA (Cantab)]

KENEFICK TIMOTHY

S Tomlinson QC
7 King's Bench Walk, Temple, London
EC4Y 7DS, Telephone: 0171 583 0404
E-mail: clerks@7kbw.law.co.uk
Call Date: Oct 1996, Gray's Inn
Qualifications: [BA (Cantab)]

KENNEDY ANDREW IAN

Chambers of Kieran Coonan QC
Ground Floor, 6 Pump Court, Temple,
London EC4Y 7AR,
Telephone: 0171 583 6013/2510
E-mail: clerks@6-pumpcourt.law.co.uk
Call Date: Nov 1989, Middle Temple
Qualifications: [BA Hons (Newc), Dip Law]

KENNEDY BERESFORD ROLAND GEORGE

King's Bench Chambers
Wellington House, 175 Holdenhurst Road,
Bournemouth, Dorset, BH8 8DQ,
Telephone: 01202 250025
E-mail: chambers@kingsbench.co.uk
Call Date: Oct 1995, Middle Temple
Qualifications: [LLB (Hons)]

KENNEDY BRIAN JAMES

Lion Court
Chancery House, 53-64 Chancery Lane,
London WC2A 1SJ,
Telephone: 0171 404 6565
Call Date: 1996, Inner Temple
Qualifications: [BA]

KENNEDY BRIAN JOSEPH

2 King's Bench Walk Chambers
1st Floor, 2 King's Bench Walk, Temple,
London EC4Y 7DE,
Telephone: 020 7353 9276
E-mail: chambers@2kbw.co.uk
Call Date: Oct 1992, Middle Temple
Qualifications: [LL.B (Hons)]

KENNEDY CHRISTOPHER LAURENCE PAUL

Chambers of John Hand QC
9 St John Street, Manchester M3 4DN,
Telephone: 0161 955 9000
E-mail: ninesjs@gconnect.com
Call Date: July 1989, Gray's Inn
Qualifications: [BA [Cantab]]

KENNEDY MATTHEW ANTHONY

4 Brick Court, Chambers of Anne Rafferty QC
1st Floor, Temple, London EC4Y 9AD,
Telephone: 0171 583 8455
Call Date: Nov 1981, Gray's Inn
Pupil Master
Qualifications: [BSc]

KENNEDY MICHAEL JOHN

India Buildings Chambers
Water Street, Liverpool L2 0XG,
Telephone: 0151 243 6000
E-mail: clerks@chambers.u-net.com
Call Date: May 1985, Middle Temple
Pupil Master
Qualifications: [LLB (Bristol)]

KENNEDY MICHAEL KIRK INCHES

1 New Square
Ground Floor, Lincoln's Inn, London
WC2A 3SA, Telephone: 0171 405 0884/5/6/
7 E-mail: clerks@1newsquare.law.co.uk
Call Date: July 1967, Middle Temple
Qualifications: [BA (Cantab)]

KENNEDY PETER NICHOLAS DODGSON

15 Winckley Square
Preston PR1 3JJ,
Telephone: 01772 252828
E-mail:clerks@winckleysq.demon.co.uk
Call Date: July 1977, Lincoln's Inn
Pupil Master
Qualifications: [LLB (Lond)]

D

KENNEDY OF THE SHAWS
BARONESS QC (1991)

Doughty Street Chambers
11 Doughty Street, London WC1N 2PG,
Telephone: 0171 404 1313
E-mail:enquiries@doughtystreet.co.uk
Call Date: July 1972, Gray's Inn

KENNEDY-MCGREGOR MS MARILYN

11 Stone Buildings
Lincoln's Inn, London WC2A 3TG,
Telephone: +44 (0)207 831 6381
E-mail:clerks@11StoneBuildings.law.co.uk
Call Date: July 1989, Gray's Inn
Pupil Master
Qualifications: [BA (Newc), Dip in Law]

KENNEDY-MORRISON MISS CAROLINE LOUISE

3 Temple Gardens
2nd Floor, Temple, London EC4Y 9AU,
Telephone: 0171 583 1155
Call Date: Feb 1990, Middle Temple
Qualifications: [BA Hons]

KENNERLEY IAN LESLIE

Broad Chare
33 Broad Chare, Newcastle upon Tyne
NE1 3DQ, Telephone: 0191 232 0541
E-mail:clerks@broadcharechambers.law.co.uk
Call Date: July 1983, Gray's Inn
Pupil Master
Qualifications: [BA]

KENNING THOMAS PATRICK

New Court Chambers
Gazette Building, 168 Corporation Street,
Birmingham B4 6TZ,
Telephone: 0121 693 6656
Call Date: Feb 1989, Lincoln's Inn
Pupil Master
Qualifications: [BSc (Cardiff)]

KENNY MISS CHARLOTTE

Exchange Chambers
Pearl Assurance House, Derby Square,
Liverpool L2 9XX,
Telephone: 0151 236 7747
E-mail:exchangechambers@btinternet.com
Call Date: Nov 1993, Gray's Inn
Qualifications: [BA (Hull), Dip in Law (City)]

KENNY DAVID JOSEPH

15 Winckley Square
Preston PR1 3JJ,
Telephone: 01772 252828
E-mail:clerks@winckleysq.demon.co.uk
Call Date: Nov 1982, Middle Temple
Pupil Master
Qualifications: [BA, MPhil (Nott'm)]

KENNY JULIAN HECTOR MARRIOTT

20 Essex Street
London WC2R 3AL,
Telephone: 0171 583 9294
E-mail: clerks@20essexst.com
Call Date: Nov 1997, Gray's Inn
Qualifications: [BA (Oxon)]

KENNY STEPHEN CHARLES WILFRID

S Tomlinson QC
7 King's Bench Walk, Temple, London
EC4Y 7DS, Telephone: 0171 583 0404
E-mail: clerks@7kbw.law.co.uk
Call Date: July 1987, Inner Temple
Pupil Master
Qualifications: [MA, BCL (Oxon)]

KENT ALAN PETER

23 Essex Street
London WC2R 3AS,
Telephone: 0171 413 0353/836 8366
E-mail:clerks@essexstreet23.demon.co.uk
Call Date: Nov 1986, Inner Temple
Pupil Master
Qualifications: [LLB]

KENT MISS GEORGINA

5 Essex Court
1st Floor, Temple, London EC4Y 9AH,
Telephone: 0171 410 2000
E-mail: barristers@5essexcourt.co.uk
Call Date: Nov 1989, Gray's Inn
Pupil Master
Qualifications: [LLB (Lond)]

KENT MISS JENNY MARY

Park Court Chambers
16 Park Place, Leeds LS1 2SJ,
Telephone: 0113 2433277
Call Date: Oct 1993, Lincoln's Inn
Qualifications: [BA (Hons) (Oxon), Dip in
Law (Lond)]

KENT MICHAEL HARCOURT QC (1996)

Two Crown Office Row
Ground Floor, Temple, London
EC4Y 7HJ, Telephone: 020 7797 8100
E-mail: mail@2cor.co.uk, or to individual
barristers at: [barrister's
surname]@2cor.co.uk
Call Date: July 1975, Middle Temple
Qualifications: [BA (Sussex)]

KENT PETER BRYAN CARLYLE

3 Paper Buildings
Temple, London EC4Y 7EU,
Telephone: 020 7583 8055
E-mail: London@3paper.com
3 Paper Buildings (Oxford)
1 Alfred Street, High Street, Oxford
OX1 4EH, Telephone: 01865 793736
E-mail: oxford@3paper.com
3 Paper Buildings (Bournemouth)
20 Lorne Park Road, Bournemouth,
Dorset, BH1 1JN,
Telephone: 01202 292102
E-mail: Bournemouth@3paper.com
3 Paper Buildings (Winchester)
4 St Peter Street, Winchester SO23 8BW,
Telephone: 01962 868884
E-mail: winchester@3paper.com
Call Date: Nov 1978, Gray's Inn
Pupil Master
Qualifications: [LLB, FCI (Arb)]

KENTRIDGE SYDNEY QC (1984)

Brick Court Chambers
7-8 Essex Street, London WC2R 3LD,
Telephone: 0171 379 3550
E-mail: [surname]@brickcourt.co.uk
Call Date: 1977, Lincoln's Inn
Qualifications: [BA (Witw), MA (Oxon)]

KENWARD RICHARD FRANCIS

Watford Chambers
74 Mildred Avenue, Watford,
Hertfordshire, WD1 7DX,
Telephone: 01923 220553
Call Date: Oct 1990, Inner Temple
Qualifications: [LLB]

KENWARD TIMOTHY DAVID NELSON

25-27 Castle Street
1st Floor, Liverpool L2 4TA,
Telephone: 0151 227 5661/051 236 5072
Call Date: Nov 1987, Gray's Inn
Qualifications: [MA (Oxon)]

KEOGH ANDREW JOHN

8 King's Bench Walk
2nd Floor, Temple, London EC4Y 7DU,
Telephone: 0171 797 8888
8 King's Bench Walk North
1 Park Square East, Leeds LS1 2NE,
Telephone: 0113 2439797
Call Date: Nov 1978, Inner Temple
Pupil Master
Qualifications: [BSc (Econ)]

KEOGH RICHARD THOMAS

Chambers of Geoffrey Hawker
46/48 Essex Street, London WC2R 3GH,
Telephone: 0171 583 8899
Call Date: Nov 1991, Middle Temple
Qualifications: [LLB (Hons) (Essex)]

KER-REID JOHN

Pump Court Chambers
Upper Ground Floor, 3 Pump Court,
Temple, London EC4Y 7AJ,
Telephone: 0171 353 0711
E-mail: clerks@3pumpcourt.com
Pump Court Chambers
31 Southgate Street, Winchester
SO23 9EE, Telephone: 01962 868161
E-mail: clerks@3pumpcourt.com
Pump Court Chambers
5 Temple Chambers, Temple Street,
Swindon SN1 1SQ,
Telephone: 01793 539899
E-mail: clerks@3pumpcourt.com
Call Date: Nov 1974, Inner Temple
Qualifications: [MA (Cantab)]

KERNER MRS ANGELA

Bell Yard Chambers
116/118 Chancery Lane, London
WC2A 1PP, Telephone: 0171 306 9292
Call Date: July 1965, Inner Temple
Qualifications: [LLB (Lond)]

KERR CHRISTOPHER RICHARD

5 Essex Court
1st Floor, Temple, London EC4Y 9AH,
Telephone: 0171 410 2000
E-mail: barristers@5essexcourt.co.uk
Call Date: Nov 1988, Middle Temple
Pupil Master
Qualifications: [MA (Oxon)]

KERR DAVID MILNE

Martins Building
2nd Floor, No 4 Water Street, Liverpool
L2 3SP, Telephone: 0151 236 5818/4919
Call Date: Nov 1971, Inner Temple
Pupil Master, Recorder
Qualifications: [LLB (Lond)]

KERR DEREK WILLIAM

Francis Taylor Building
Ground Floor, Temple, London
EC4Y 7BY, Telephone: 0171 353 7768/
7769/2711
E-mail:clerks@francistaylorbuilding.law.co.uk
Call Date: Oct 1994, Middle Temple
Qualifications: [LLB (Hons)(Reading)]

KERR JOHN STUART

Trafalgar Chambers
53 Fleet Street, London EC4Y 1BE,
Telephone: 0171 583 5858
E-mail:trafalgarchambers@easynet.co.uk
Call Date: Nov 1995, Inner Temple
Qualifications: [MA (Edin), CPE]

KERR SIMON ALEXANDER

S Tomlinson QC
7 King's Bench Walk, Temple, London
EC4Y 7DS, Telephone: 0171 583 0404
E-mail: clerks@7kbw.law.co.uk
Call Date: 1997, Lincoln's Inn
Qualifications: [MA (Hons), Dip Law (City)]

KERR TIM JULIAN

4-5 Gray's Inn Square
Ground Floor, Gray's Inn, London
WC1R 5JP, Telephone: 0171 404 5252
E-mail:chambers@4-5graysinnsquare.co.uk
Call Date: Nov 1983, Gray's Inn
Pupil Master
Qualifications: [BA (Oxon)]

KERRIGAN HERBERT AIRD

9-12 Bell Yard
London WC2A 2LF,
Telephone: 0171 400 1800
E-mail: clerks@bellyard.co.uk
Call Date: July 1990, Middle Temple
Qualifications: [LLB (Hons), MA (Keele)]

KERSHAW ANDREW

30 Park Square
Leeds LS1 2PF, Telephone: 0113 2436388
E-mail: clerks@30parksquare.co.uk
Call Date: July 1975, Middle Temple
Pupil Master
Qualifications: [LLB (Lond)]

KERSHAW DEAN

Rowchester Chambers
4 Rowchester Court, Whittall Street,
Birmingham B4 6DH,
Telephone: 0121 233 2327/2361951
Call Date: Nov 1995, Lincoln's Inn
Qualifications: [LLB]

KERSHAW MRS JENNIFER CHRISTINE QC (1998)

No. 6
6 Park Square, Leeds LS1 2LW,
Telephone: 0113 2459763
E-mail: chambers@no6.co.uk
Call Date: Nov 1974, Lincoln's Inn
Assistant Recorder
Qualifications: [LLB]

KERSHEN LAWRENCE DAVID QC (1992)

Cloisters
1 Pump Court, Temple, London
EC4Y 7AA, Telephone: 0171 827 4000
E-mail: clerks@cloisters.com
Call Date: July 1967, Middle Temple

KESSLER JAMES RICHARD

24 Old Buildings
First Floor, Lincoln's Inn, London
WC2A 3UP, Telephone: 020 7242 2744
E-mail: taxchambers@compuserve.com
Call Date: July 1984, Gray's Inn
Pupil Master
Qualifications: [MA (Oxon)]

KESSLER MARK

King's Bench Chambers
Wellington House, 175 Holdenhurst Road,
Bournemouth, Dorset, BH8 8DQ,
Telephone: 01202 250025
E-mail: chambers@kingsbench.co.uk
Call Date: Nov 1988, Inner Temple
Qualifications: [LLB]

KESSLING CHRISTOPHER DAVID

65-67 King Street
Leicester LE1 6RP,
Telephone: 0116 2547710
Call Date: Oct 1992, Middle Temple
Qualifications: [LL.B (Hons)]

KEVAN TIMOTHY LOWIS

1 Temple Gardens
1st Floor, Temple, London EC4Y 9BB,
Telephone: 0171 583 1315/353 0407
E-mail: clerks@1templegardens.co.uk
Call Date: Oct 1996, Middle Temple
Qualifications: [BA (Cantab)]

KEY DR PAUL ANTHONY

Essex Court Chambers
24 Lincoln's Inn Fields, London
WC2A 3ED, Telephone: 0171 813 8000
E-mail:clerksroom@essexcourt-chambers.co.uk
Call Date: July 1997, Inner Temple
Qualifications: [PhD (Cantab), LLB
(Auckland)]

KEYSELL MISS TANIA JANE

2 Paper Buildings, Basement North
Temple, London EC4Y 7ET,
Telephone: 0171 936 2613
E-mail: post@2paper.co.uk
Call Date: Oct 1992, Lincoln's Inn
Qualifications: [BA(Hons)(Wales)]

KEYSER ANDREW JOHN

9 Park Place
Cardiff CF1 3DP,
Telephone: 01222 382731
Call Date: Nov 1986, Middle Temple
Pupil Master
Qualifications: [MA (Oxon)]

KHALIL KARIM SHAKIR

1 Paper Buildings
1st Floor, Temple, London EC4Y 7EP,
Telephone: 0171 353 3728/4953
Call Date: July 1984, Lincoln's Inn
Pupil Master
Qualifications: [MA (Cantab)]

KHALIQUE MISS NAGEENA

5 Fountain Court
Steelhouse Lane, Birmingham B4 6DR,
Telephone: 0121 606 0500
E-mail:clerks@5fountaincourt.law.co.uk
Call Date: Oct 1994, Gray's Inn
Qualifications: [BDS, LDSRCS]

KHAMISA MOHAMMED JAFFER

9-12 Bell Yard
London WC2A 2LF,
Telephone: 0171 400 1800
E-mail: clerks@bellyard.co.uk
Call Date: Nov 1985, Middle Temple
Pupil Master
Qualifications: [BA (Hons) (Lond)]

KHAN ANWAR WILLIAM

Eastbourne Chambers
15 Hyde Gardens, Eastbourne, East
Sussex, BN21 4PR,
Telephone: 01323 642102
Wessex Chambers
48 Queens Road, Reading, Berkshire,
RG1 4BD, Telephone: 0118 956 8856
E-mail:wessexchambers@compuserve.com
Call Date: Nov 1971, Gray's Inn
Pupil Master
Qualifications: [LLB (Lond)]

KHAN ASHRAF

A K Chambers
19 Headlands Drive, Hessle, Hull
HU13 0JP, Telephone: 01482 641180
Call Date: July 1960, Middle Temple
Qualifications: [LLM]

KHAN AVICENNA ALKINDI CORNELIUS

55 Temple Chambers
Temple Avenue, London EC4Y 0HP,
Telephone: 0171 353 7400
Call Date: July 1993, Lincoln's Inn
Qualifications: [BA (Hons)]

KHAN BASHARAT JAMIL

Corn Exchange Chambers
5th Floor, Fenwick Street, Liverpool
L2 7QS, Telephone: 0151 227 1081/5009
Call Date: July 1986, Lincoln's Inn
Qualifications: [LLB (Hons)]

KHAN FAUZ MOHAMMAD

Central Chambers
89 Princess Street, Manchester M1 4HT,
Telephone: 0161 236 1133
Call Date: July 1988, Middle Temple
Pupil Master
Qualifications: [LLB (Hons)(Lond)]

KHAN MISS HELEN MARY GRACE

Pump Court Chambers
Upper Ground Floor, 3 Pump Court,
Temple, London EC4Y 7AJ,
Telephone: 0171 353 0711
E-mail: clerks@3pumpcourt.com
Pump Court Chambers
31 Southgate Street, Winchester
SO23 9EE, Telephone: 01962 868161
E-mail: clerks@3pumpcourt.com
Pump Court Chambers
5 Temple Chambers, Temple Street,
Swindon SN1 1SQ,
Telephone: 01793 539899
E-mail: clerks@3pumpcourt.com
Call Date: Nov 1990, Middle Temple
Pupil Master
Qualifications: [LLB (Hons)(Leic)]

KHAN MS JUDITH

Two Garden Court
1st Floor, Middle Temple, London
EC4Y 9BL, Telephone: 0171 353 1633
E-mail:barristers@2gardenct.law.co.uk
Call Date: Nov 1989, Middle Temple
Qualifications: [LLB (Hons)]

KHAN MOHAMED WAHID

**The Chambers of Mr Ali Mohammed
Azhar**
Basement, 9 King's Bench Walk, Temple,
London EC4Y 7DX,
Telephone: 0171 353 9564
E-mail: jvlee@btinternet.com
Call Date: Nov 1969, Lincoln's Inn
Pupil Master
Qualifications: [MA Econ agra]

KHAN MOHAMMAD TAYYAB

Melbury House
55 Manor Road, Oadby, Leicester LE2 2LL,
Telephone: 0116 2711848
Call Date: Feb 1972, Lincoln's Inn

KHAN MOHAMMED ASIF

Claremont Chambers
26 Waterloo Road, Wolverhampton
WV1 4BL, Telephone: 01902 426222
Call Date: Nov 1983, Lincoln's Inn
Qualifications: [LLB, DPL]

KHAN SAADALLAH FRANS HASSAN

55 Temple Chambers
Temple Avenue, London EC4Y 0HP,
Telephone: 0171 353 7400
Call Date: 1991, Lincoln's Inn
Qualifications: [BSc , LLB (Hons)]

KHAN SHAFI

103 Wexham Close
Luton, Bedfordshire, LU3 3TX,
Telephone: 01582 598394
Perivale Chambers
15 Colwyn Avenue, Perivale, Middlesex,
UB6 8JY, Telephone: 0181 998 1935/
081 248 0246
Call Date: Feb 1994, Lincoln's Inn
Qualifications: [BA (Punjab), MA (Brunel) ,
LLB (Hons, Karachi)]

KHAN SHAUKAT ALI

2 Middle Temple Lane
3rd Floor, Temple, London EC4Y 9AA,
Telephone: 0171 583 4540
Call Date: July 1971, Lincoln's Inn
Pupil Master
Qualifications: [BA, LLB]

KHAN SHOKAT

40 King Street
Manchester M2 6BA,
Telephone: 0161 832 9082
E-mail: clerks@40kingstreet.co.uk
The Chambers of Philip Raynor QC
5 Park Place, Leeds LS1 2RU,
Telephone: 0113 242 1123
Call Date: Nov 1979, Middle Temple
Qualifications: [LLB (Warw) LLM (Lond]

KHAN TAHIR

Broadway House Chambers
Broadway House, 9 Bank Street, Bradford,
West Yorkshire, BD1 1TW,
Telephone: 01274 722560
E-mail: clerks@broadwayhouse.co.uk
Broadway House Chambers
31 Park Square West, Leeds LS1 2PF,
Telephone: 0113 246 2600
Call Date: July 1986, Lincoln's Inn
Qualifications: [LLB (Hons)]

KHANGURE AVTAR AMARJIT SINGH

6 Fountain Court
Steelhouse Lane, Birmingham B4 6DR,
Telephone: 0121 233 3282
E-mail: clerks@sixfountain.co.uk
Call Date: 1985, Gray's Inn
Assistant Recorder
Qualifications: [BA, LLM (Cantab)]

KHANZADA MS NAJMA SABRA RAHMAN

1 Pump Court
Lower Ground Floor, Temple, London
EC4Y 7AB, Telephone: 0171 583 2012/
353 4341
E-mail: [name]@1pumpcourt.co.uk
Call Date: Oct 1992, Inner Temple
Qualifications: [BA, LLB]

KHAWAR AFTAB

24a St John Street
Manchester M3 4DF,
Telephone: 0161 833 9628
Call Date: July 1983, Gray's Inn
Qualifications: [LLB Hons (Lancaster)]

KHAYAT GEORGES MARIO QC (1992)

10 King's Bench Walk
1st Floor, Temple, London EC4Y 7EB,
Telephone: 0171 353 2501
Call Date: Nov 1967, Lincoln's Inn
Recorder

KHOKHAR MUSHTAQ AHMED

Sovereign Chambers
25 Park Square, Leeds LS1 2PW,
Telephone: 0113 2451841/2/3
E-mail:sovereignchambers@btinternet.com
Call Date: July 1982, Lincoln's Inn
Pupil Master, Assistant Recorder
Qualifications: [LLB, LLM (Lond)]

KHUBBER RANJIV

3 Temple Gardens
3rd Floor, Temple, London EC4Y 9AU,
Telephone: 0171 353 0832
Call Date: Nov 1994, Middle Temple
Qualifications: [BA (Hons) (Kent), MA
(Sussex)]

KHUBLALL NATURAM

Chancery Chambers
1st Floor Offices, 70/72 Chancery Lane,
London WC2A 1AB,
Telephone: 0171 405 6879/6870
Call Date: July 1981, Lincoln's Inn

KHURSHID JAWDAT

S Tomlinson QC
7 King's Bench Walk, Temple, London
EC4Y 7DS, Telephone: 0171 583 0404
E-mail: clerks@7kbw.law.co.uk
Call Date: Oct 1994, Lincoln's Inn
Qualifications: [BA (Hons)(Oxon)]

KIBLING THOMAS

Cloisters
1 Pump Court, Temple, London
EC4Y 7AA, Telephone: 0171 827 4000
E-mail: clerks@cloisters.com
Call Date: Nov 1990, Middle Temple
Pupil Master
Qualifications: [LLB]

KIDD MISS JOANNE TERESA

39 Park Square
Leeds LS1 2NU,
Telephone: 0113 2456633
Call Date: Oct 1995, Lincoln's Inn
Qualifications: [BA (Hons)(Cantab)]

KIDD PETER WILLIAM

Martins Building
2nd Floor, No 4 Water Street, Liverpool
L2 3SP, Telephone: 0151 236 5818/4919
Call Date: July 1987, Lincoln's Inn
Qualifications: [LLB (L'pool)]

KILCOYNE PATRICK DESMOND OLIVER

Arden Chambers
27 John Street, London WC1N 2BL,
Telephone: 020 7242 4244
E-mail:clerks@arden-chambers.law.co.uk
Call Date: May 1990, Inner Temple
Qualifications: [LL.B. (So'ton), LL.M. (Lond)]

KILCOYNE PAUL ANTHONY JAMES

1 Temple Gardens
1st Floor, Temple, London EC4Y 9BB,
Telephone: 0171 583 1315/353 0407
E-mail: clerks@1templegardens.co.uk
Call Date: Nov 1985, Lincoln's Inn
Pupil Master
Qualifications: [LLB (B'ham)]

KILGOUR PETER JAMES

Durham Barristers' Chambers
27 Old Elvet, Durham DH1 3HN,
Telephone: 0191 386 9199
Call Date: July 1984, Lincoln's Inn
Qualifications: [STB Comillas, (Madrid) Dip
Law]

KILLALEA STEPHEN JOSEPH

Devereux Chambers
Devereux Court, London WC2R 3JJ,
Telephone: 0171 353 7534
E-mail: mailbox@devchambers.co.uk
Call Date: July 1981, Middle Temple
Pupil Master
Qualifications: [LLB]

KILLEEN ROBERT WILLIAM

1 Pump Court
Lower Ground Floor, Temple, London
EC4Y 7AB, Telephone: 0171 583 2012/
353 4341
E-mail: [name]@1pumpcourt.co.uk
Call Date: Oct 1995, Middle Temple
Qualifications: [LLB (Hons)]

KILLEEN SIMON JOHN

Corn Exchange Chambers
5th Floor, Fenwick Street, Liverpool
L2 7QS, Telephone: 0151 227 1081/5009
Call Date: July 1984, Inner Temple
Qualifications: [BA]

KILLEN GEOFFREY JAMES

3 Paper Buildings
Ground Floor, Temple, London
EC4Y 7EU, Telephone: 0171 797 7000
E-mail: clerks@3pb.co.uk
3 Paper Buildings
Temple, London EC4Y 7EU,
Telephone: 020 7583 8055
E-mail: London@3paper.com
3 Paper Buildings (Bournemouth)
20 Lorne Park Road, Bournemouth,
Dorset, BH1 1JN,
Telephone: 01202 292102
E-mail: Bournemouth@3paper.com
3 Paper Buildings (Winchester)
4 St Peter Street, Winchester SO23 8BW,
Telephone: 01962 868884
E-mail: winchester@3paper.com
3 Paper Buildings (Oxford)
1 Alfred Street, High Street, Oxford
OX1 4EH, Telephone: 01865 793736
E-mail: oxford@3paper.com
Call Date: Oct 1990, Inner Temple
Qualifications: [LLB]

KILPATRICK MISS ALYSON

Arden Chambers
27 John Street, London WC1N 2BL,
Telephone: 020 7242 4244
E-mail:clerks@arden-chambers.law.co.uk
Call Date: July 1991, Middle Temple
Qualifications: [LLB (Hons) (Belfast),
Advanced Dip]

KILPATRICK MRS JEAN MARY

3 Paper Buildings
Temple, London EC4Y 7EU,
Telephone: 020 7583 8055
E-mail: London@3paper.com
3 Paper Buildings (Oxford)
1 Alfred Street, High Street, Oxford
OX1 4EH, Telephone: 01865 793736
E-mail: oxford@3paper.com
3 Paper Buildings (Winchester)
4 St Peter Street, Winchester SO23 8BW,
Telephone: 01962 868884
E-mail: winchester@3paper.com

3 Paper Buildings (Bournemouth)
20 Lorne Park Road, Bournemouth,
Dorset, BH1 1JN,
Telephone: 01202 292102
E-mail: Bournemouth@3paper.com
Call Date: Oct 1990, Middle Temple
Qualifications: [BA (Sheff)]

KILVINGTON SIMON CHARLES

18 St John Street
Manchester M3 4EA,
Telephone: 0161 278 1800
E-mail: 18stjohn@lineone.net
Call Date: Nov 1995, Lincoln's Inn
Qualifications: [BA (Hons) (Oxon)]

KIMBELL JOHN ASHLEY

4 Essex Court
Temple, London EC4Y 9AJ,
Telephone: 020 7797 7970
E-mail: clerks@4essexcourt.law.co.uk
Call Date: Nov 1995, Inner Temple
Qualifications: [BA, M.Phil (Cantab)]

KIME MATTHEW JONATHAN

7 New Square
1st Floor, Lincoln's Inn, London
WC2A 3QS, Telephone: 020 7404 5484
E-mail: clerks@7newsquare.com
Cobden House Chambers
19 Quay Street, Manchester M3 3HN,
Telephone: 0161 833 6000
E-mail: clerks@cobden.co.uk
Call Date: July 1988, Middle Temple
Qualifications: [MA, DPhil (Oxon), LLB
(Lond), Dip Law (City)]

KIMMINS CHARLES DOMINIC

20 Essex Street
London WC2R 3AL,
Telephone: 0171 583 9294
E-mail: clerks@20essexst.com
Call Date: Nov 1994, Inner Temple
Qualifications: [BA (Cantab)]

KIMSEY MARK FENTON

Harrow on the Hill Chambers
60 High Street, Harrow-on-the-Hill,
Middlesex, HA1 3LL,
Telephone: 0181 423 7444

Windsor Barristers' Chambers
Windsor Telephone: 01753 648899
E-mail: law@windsorchambers.co.uk
Call Date: Oct 1990, Inner Temple
Qualifications: [LLB (Hons)]

KINCADE MS JULIE-ANNE

2-4 Tudor Street
London EC4Y 0AA,
Telephone: 0171 797 7111
E-mail: clerks@rfqc.co.uk
Call Date: Nov 1991, Inner Temple
Qualifications: [LLB]

KINCH CHRISTOPHER ANTHONY QC (1999)

23 Essex Street
London WC2R 3AS,
Telephone: 0171 413 0353/836 8366
E-mail:clerks@essexstreet23.demon.co.uk
Call Date: 1976, Lincoln's Inn
Pupil Master, Recorder
Qualifications: [MA (Oxon)]

KING MISS ANNE FAWZIA

2 Gray's Inn Square Chambers
2nd Floor, Gray's Inn, London WC1R 5AA,
Telephone: 020 7242 0328
E-mail: clerks@2gis.co.uk
Call Date: Nov 1985, Middle Temple
Pupil Master
Qualifications: [BA.Law]

KING CHARLES GRANVILLE

96 Gray's Inn Road
London WC1X 8AL,
Telephone: 0171 405 0585
Call Date: Nov 1995, Middle Temple
Qualifications: [LLB (Hons)]

KING GELAGA PERRY

3 Hare Court
1 Little Essex Street, London WC2R 3LD,
Telephone: 0171 395 2000
Call Date: July 1985, Gray's Inn
Pupil Master
Qualifications: [LLB (Hull)]

D

KING JOHN PATRICK

1 Gray's Inn Square
Ground Floor, London WC1R 5AA,
Telephone: 0171 405 8946/7/8
Cardinal Chambers
4 Old Mitre Court, 4th Floor, Temple,
London EC4Y 7BP,
Telephone: 020 7353 2622
E-mail:admin@cardinal-chambers.co.uk
Call Date: July 1983, Gray's Inn

KING JOHN SAWREY

12 King's Bench Walk
Temple, London EC4Y 7EL,
Telephone: 0171 583 0811
E-mail: chambers@12kbw.co.uk
Call Date: Nov 1973, Inner Temple
Pupil Master
Qualifications: [LLB (Lond)]

KING KARL ERROL

Hardwicke Building
New Square, Lincoln's Inn, London
WC2A 3SB, Telephone: 020 7242 2523
E-mail: clerks@hardwicke.co.uk
Call Date: Nov 1985, Gray's Inn
Qualifications: [BA (Lond)]

KING MICHAEL RICHARD

Twenty-Four Old Buildings
Ground Floor, Lincoln's Inn, London
WC2A 3UP, Telephone: 0171 404 0946
E-mail:clerks@24oldbuildings.law.co.uk
Call Date: July 1971, Gray's Inn
Pupil Master
Qualifications: [BA (Cantab)]

KING NEIL GERALD ALEXANDER

2 Mitre Court Buildings
2nd Floor, Temple, London EC4Y 7BX,
Telephone: 0171 583 1380
E-mail: clerks@2mcb.co.uk
Call Date: July 1980, Inner Temple
Pupil Master
Qualifications: [MA (Oxon)]

KING PAUL STUART

High Pavement Chambers
1 High Pavement, Nottingham NG1 1HF,
Telephone: 0115 9418218
Call Date: July 1992, Inner Temple
Qualifications: [LLB (Leeds)]

KING PETER DUNCAN

Fenners Chambers
3 Madingley Road, Cambridge CB3 0EE,
Telephone: 01223 368761
E-mail: clerks@fennerschambers.co.uk
5 Pump Court
Ground Floor, Temple, London
EC4Y 7AP, Telephone: 020 7353 2532
E-mail: FivePump@netcomuk.co.uk
Fenners Chambers
8-12 Priestgate, Peterborough PE1 1JA,
Telephone: 01733 562030
E-mail: clerks@fennerschambers.co.uk
Call Date: Nov 1970, Gray's Inn
Pupil Master
Qualifications: [LLB MA (Cantab) AKC]

KING PHILLIP HENRY RUSSELL

1 Middle Temple Lane
Temple, London EC4Y 1LT,
Telephone: 0171 583 0659 (12 Lines)
E-mail: chambers@1mtl.co.uk
Call Date: Nov 1974, Inner Temple
Pupil Master
Qualifications: [BA]

KING RICHARD

5 Paper Buildings
Ground Floor, Temple, London
EC4Y 7HB, Telephone: 0171 583 9275/
583 4555 E-mail: 5paper@link.org
Call Date: July 1978, Inner Temple
Pupil Master
Qualifications: [BA (Dunelm)]

KING MISS SAMANTHA LEONIE

14 Gray's Inn Square
Gray's Inn, London WC1R 5JP,
Telephone: 0171 242 0858
E-mail: 100712.2134@compuserve.com
Call Date: Nov 1990, Middle Temple
Qualifications: [BA (Cantab)]

KING SIMON PAUL

9 Bedford Row
London WC1R 4AZ,
Telephone: 0171 242 3555
E-mail: clerks@9br.co.uk
Call Date: Nov 1987, Gray's Inn
Pupil Master
Qualifications: [MA (Oxon)]

KING TIMOTHY ROGER ALAN QC (1991)

22 Old Buildings
Lincoln's Inn, London WC2A 3UJ,
Telephone: 0171 831 0222
Byrom Street Chambers
Byrom Street, Manchester M3 4PF,
Telephone: 0161 829 2100
E-mail: Byromst25@aol.com
Call Date: Nov 1973, Lincoln's Inn
Recorder
Qualifications: [BCL, MA (Oxon)]

KING-SMITH JAMES

1 Crown Office Row
Ground Floor, Temple, London
EC4Y 7HH, Telephone: 0171 797 7500
E-mail: mail@onecrownofficerow.com
Crown Office Row Chambers
Blenheim House, 120 Church Street,
Brighton, Sussex, BN1 1WH,
Telephone: 01273 625625
E-mail: crownofficerow@clara.net
Call Date: Nov 1980, Middle Temple
Pupil Master
Qualifications: [BA (Oxon)]

KINGHORN ANDREW DAVID

College Chambers
19 Carlton Cresent, Southampton
SO15 2ET, Telephone: 01703 230338
Call Date: Nov 1991, Gray's Inn
Qualifications: [LLB]

KINGSCOTE GEOFFREY LLEWELYN WOODWARD

1 Mitre Court Buildings
Temple, London EC4Y 7BS,
Telephone: 0171 797 7070
E-mail: clerks@1mcb.com
Call Date: Nov 1993, Inner Temple
Qualifications: [BA (Oxon), M.Phil (Cantab)]

KINGSLAND LORD QC (1988)

4 Breams Buildings
London EC4A 1AQ,
Telephone: 0171 353 5835/430 1221
E-mail:breams@4breamsbuildings.law.co.uk
Call Date: Nov 1972, Middle Temple
Qualifications: [DPhil]

KINGSLEY DANIEL

3 Temple Gardens
3rd Floor, Temple, London EC4Y 9AU,
Telephone: 0171 583 0010
Call Date: Oct 1994, Lincoln's Inn
Qualifications: [MA (Hons)(Cantab)]

KINGSLEY RICHARD CHARLES

New Court
Temple, London EC4Y 9BE,
Telephone: 0171 583 5123/0510
Call Date: July 1977, Inner Temple
Pupil Master
Qualifications: [LLB (Hons)]

KINGSTON WILLIAM MARTIN QC (1992)

5 Fountain Court
Steelhouse Lane, Birmingham B4 6DR,
Telephone: 0121 606 0500
E-mail:clerks@5fountaincourt.law.co.uk
Call Date: July 1972, Middle Temple
Recorder
Qualifications: [LLB]

KINLEY GEOFFREY DORAN

4 Essex Court
Temple, London EC4Y 9AJ,
Telephone: 020 7797 7970
E-mail: clerks@4essexcourt.law.co.uk
Call Date: Nov 1970, Gray's Inn
Pupil Master
Qualifications: [BA (L'pool) MA, (Oxon)]

KINNEAR JONATHAN SHEA

9-12 Bell Yard
London WC2A 2LF,
Telephone: 0171 400 1800
E-mail: clerks@bellyard.co.uk
Call Date: Oct 1994, Gray's Inn
Qualifications: [LLB]

KINNIER ANDREW JOHN

2 Harcourt Buildings
Ground Floor/Left, Temple, London
EC4Y 9DB, Telephone: 0171 583 9020
E-mail: clerks@harcourt.co.uk
Call Date: Oct 1996, Middle Temple
Qualifications: [MA (Hons)(Cantab)]

KINSKY CYRIL (NORMAN)(FRANCIS)

Brick Court Chambers
7-8 Essex Street, London WC2R 3LD,
Telephone: 0171 379 3550
E-mail: [surname]@brickcourt.co.uk
Call Date: Nov 1988, Middle Temple
Pupil Master
Qualifications: [BA (Cantab), Dip Law (City)]

KINSLER MISS MARIE LOUISE

2 Temple Gardens
Temple, London EC4Y 9AY,
Telephone: 0171 583 6041
E-mail: clerks@2templegardens.co.uk
Call Date: July 1992, Inner Temple
Qualifications: [BA (Cambs), Dip Ad Eur
Studies]

KIRBY JAMES PATRICK

2 King's Bench Walk Chambers
1st Floor, 2 King's Bench Walk, Temple,
London EC4Y 7DE,
Telephone: 020 7353 9276
E-mail: chambers@2kbw.co.uk
Call Date: Oct 1994, Gray's Inn
Qualifications: [BA (Manch)]

KIRBY PETER JOHN

Hardwicke Building
New Square, Lincoln's Inn, London
WC2A 3SB, Telephone: 020 7242 2523
E-mail: clerks@hardwicke.co.uk
Call Date: July 1989, Inner Temple
Pupil Master
Qualifications: [LLB (Hull)]

KIRBY MISS RUTH MARY ANTHONY

Mitre House Chambers
15-19 Devereux Court, London WC2R 3JJ,
Telephone: 0171 583 8233
Call Date: Oct 1994, Middle Temple
Qualifications: [BCL , LLM (Lond), CPE]

KIRK ANTHONY JAMES NIGEL

One King's Bench Walk
1st Floor, Temple, London EC4Y 7DB,
Telephone: 0171 936 1500
E-mail: ddear@1kbw.co.uk
Call Date: July 1981, Gray's Inn
Pupil Master
Qualifications: [LLB (Lond), AKC]

KIRK JONATHAN

Chambers of Michael Pert QC
36 Bedford Row, London WC1R 4JH,
Telephone: 0171 421 8000
E-mail: 36bedfordrow@link.org
Chambers of Michael Pert QC
24 Albion Place, Northampton NN1 1UD,
Telephone: 01604 602333
Chambers of Michael Pert QC
104 New Walk, Leicester LE1 7EA,
Telephone: 0116 249 2020
Call Date: Nov 1995, Lincoln's Inn
Qualifications: [LLB (Hons)]

KIRK ROBERT WILSON

Littman Chambers
12 Gray's Inn Square, London WC1R 5JP,
Telephone: 020 7404 4866
E-mail: admin@littmanchambers.com
Call Date: Nov 1972, Lincoln's Inn
Pupil Master
Qualifications: [MA (Cantab), FCIArb]

KIRKPATRICK MRS KRYSTYNA MARIA

3 Paper Buildings
Temple, London EC4Y 7EU,
Telephone: 020 7583 8055
E-mail: London@3paper.com
3 Paper Buildings (Bournemouth)
20 Lorne Park Road, Bournemouth,
Dorset, BH1 1JN,
Telephone: 01202 292102
E-mail: Bournemouth@3paper.com
3 Paper Buildings (Winchester)
4 St Peter Street, Winchester SO23 8BW,
Telephone: 01962 868884
E-mail: winchester@3paper.com
3 Paper Buildings (Oxford)
1 Alfred Street, High Street, Oxford
OX1 4EH, Telephone: 01865 793736
E-mail: oxford@3paper.com
Call Date: Feb 1965, Gray's Inn

KIRSTEN ADRIAN RICHARD CALTHORPE

Manchester House Chambers
18-22 Bridge Street, Manchester M3 3BZ,
Telephone: 0161 834 7007
Call Date: Nov 1962, Gray's Inn
Qualifications: [LLM]

KIRTLEY PAUL GEORGE

37 Park Square Chambers
37 Park Square, Leeds LS1 2NY,
Telephone: 0113 2439422
E-mail: chambers@no37.co.uk
Call Date: July 1982, Middle Temple
Pupil Master
Qualifications: [MA (Cantab)]

KIRWAN MRS HELEN ANN HERMIONE

Stour Chambers
Barton Mill House, Barton Mill Road,
Canterbury, Kent, CT1 1BP,
Telephone: 01227 764899
E-mail: clerks@stourchambers.co.uk
Call Date: Nov 1983, Middle Temple
Qualifications: [BSS (Hons), LLB (Dublin)]

KIRWIN MS TRACEY

King Charles House
Standard Hill, Nottingham NG1 6FX,
Telephone: 0115 9418851
E-mail: clerks@kch.co.uk
Call Date: Oct 1995, Middle Temple
Qualifications: [LLB (Hons)]

KISHORE PAUL JEWANLALL

Chancery Chambers
1st Floor Offices, 70/72 Chancery Lane,
London WC2A 1AB,
Telephone: 0171 405 6879/6870
Call Date: Nov 1982, Lincoln's Inn
Pupil Master
Qualifications: [LLB (Lond), BA, ACP,
ACIArb]

KITCHEN SIMON DUGALD OWEN RALPH

2 Dyers Buildings
London EC1N 2JT,
Telephone: 0171 404 1881
Call Date: Nov 1988, Lincoln's Inn
Qualifications: [LLB Hons]

KITCHENER NEIL DAVID

One Essex Court
Ground Floor, Temple, London
EC4Y 9AR, Telephone: 020 7583 2000
E-mail: clerks@oneessexcourt.co.uk
Call Date: Oct 1991, Middle Temple
Qualifications: [BA (Oxon)]

KITCHIN DAVID JAMES TYSON QC (1994)

8 New Square
Lincoln's Inn, London WC2A 3QP,
Telephone: 0171 405 4321
E-mail: clerks@8newsquare.co.uk
Call Date: July 1977, Gray's Inn
Qualifications: [MA (Cantab)]

KITCHING ROBIN MILES

Cobden House Chambers
19 Quay Street, Manchester M3 3HN,
Telephone: 0161 833 6000
E-mail: clerks@cobden.co.uk
Call Date: Nov 1989, Middle Temple
Qualifications: [BA (Hons) (Manc), C.P.E]

KIVDEH SHAHROKH-SEAN

Chambers of Wilfred Forster-Jones
New Court, 1st Floor South, Temple,
London EC4Y 9BE,
Telephone: 0171 353 0853/4/7222
E-mail: chambers@newcourt.net
Call Date: Nov 1992, Middle Temple
Qualifications: [LLB (Hons, Lond), LLM
(UCL)]

KLEIN JONATHAN SIMON

Chancery House Chambers
7 Lisbon Square, Leeds LS1 4LY,
Telephone: 0113 244 6691
E-mail: chanceryhouse@btinternet.com
Call Date: Oct 1992, Lincoln's Inn
Qualifications: [LLB(Hons)(Essex), BCL]

KLEIN MS LEONORA JANE

**1 Gray's Inn Square, Chambers of the
Baroness Scotland of Asthal QC**
1st Floor, London WC1R 5AG,
Telephone: 0171 405 3000
E-mail: clerks@onegrays.demon.co.uk
Call Date: Nov 1989, Gray's Inn
Qualifications: [BA (Lond)]

KLONIN MISS SUSAN JANE

Old Colony House
6 South King Street, Manchester M2 6DQ,
Telephone: 0161 834 4364
Call Date: Nov 1970, Gray's Inn
Pupil Master
Qualifications: [LLB (Hons)]

KLOSS ALEXANDER WOLFGANG

28 St John Street
Manchester M3 4DJ,
Telephone: 0161 834 8418
E-mail: clerk@28stjohnst.co.uk
Call Date: Oct 1993, Gray's Inn
Qualifications: [BA (Bris)]

KLOSS MRS DIANA MARY

28 St John Street
Manchester M3 4DJ,
Telephone: 0161 834 8418
E-mail: clerk@28stjohnst.co.uk
Call Date: July 1986, Gray's Inn
Qualifications: [LLB Lond LLM Tulane]

KNAFLER STEPHEN

6 King's Bench Walk
Ground, Third & Fourth Floors, Temple,
London EC4Y 7DR,
Telephone: 0171 353 4931/583 0695
Call Date: May 1993, Lincoln's Inn
Qualifications: [MA (Cantab)]

KNAPP EDWARD IAN

4 Brick Court
Temple, London EC4Y 9AD,
Telephone: 0171 797 8910
E-mail: medhurst@dial.pipex.com
Call Date: Feb 1992, Lincoln's Inn
Qualifications: [LLB (Hons)]

KNAPP MISS SOPHIE JACQUELINE

1 Pump Court
Lower Ground Floor, Temple, London
EC4Y 7AB, Telephone: 0171 583 2012/
353 4341
E-mail: [name]@1pumpcourt.co.uk
Call Date: Feb 1990, Gray's Inn
Qualifications: [BA [Lond]]

KNAPP STEPHEN JOHN

Martins Building
2nd Floor, No 4 Water Street, Liverpool
L2 3SP, Telephone: 0151 236 5818/4919
Call Date: July 1986, Gray's Inn
Pupil Master
Qualifications: [LLB (Lond)]

KNIFTON DAVID ALAN

Corn Exchange Chambers
5th Floor, Fenwick Street, Liverpool
L2 7QS, Telephone: 0151 227 1081/5009
Call Date: July 1986, Inner Temple
Qualifications: [LLB (Nottingahm)]

KNIGHT MISS ADRIENNE

Bridewell Chambers
2 Bridewell Place, London EC4V 6AP,
Telephone: 020 7797 8800
E-mail:HughesGage@bridewell.law.co.uk
Call Date: July 1981, Gray's Inn
Pupil Master
Qualifications: [LLB]

KNIGHT MISS CAROLINE SARAH DARLEY

1 Harcourt Buildings
2nd Floor, Temple, London EC4Y 9DA,
Telephone: 0171 353 9421/0375
E-mail:clerks@1harcourtbuildings.law.co.uk
Call Date: July 1985, Inner Temple
Qualifications: [LLB (B'ham), Diplome
D'etudes, Juridiques , Francaises]

KNIGHT CHRISTOPHER HARRINGTON

Chartlands Chambers
3 St Giles Terrace, Northampton
NN1 2BN, Telephone: 01604 603322
Call Date: Oct 1994, Gray's Inn
Qualifications: [BA (York)]

KNIGHT CHRISTOPHER MICHAEL ST JOHN

Chambers of John Hand QC
9 St John Street, Manchester M3 4DN,
Telephone: 0161 955 9000
E-mail: ninesjs@gconnect.com
Call Date: Nov 1966, Middle Temple
Qualifications: [BA (Cantab)]

KNIGHT MISS JENNIFER CLAUDIA

2 Harcourt Buildings
1st Floor, Temple, London EC4Y 9DB,
Telephone: 020 7353 2112
Call Date: Oct 1996, Gray's Inn
Qualifications: [LLB (Exon)]

KNIGHT MS JUDITH

Devon Chambers
3 St Andrew Street, Plymouth PL1 2AH,
Telephone: 01752 661659
E-mail: devonchambers.co.uk.
Call Date: Oct 1991, Lincoln's Inn
Qualifications: [LLB (Hons) (Notts)]

KNIGHT KEITH LESLIE FRANCIS

2 Gray's Inn Square Chambers
2nd Floor, Gray's Inn, London WC1R 5AA,
Telephone: 020 7242 0328
E-mail: clerks@2gis.co.uk
Call Date: Nov 1969, Gray's Inn
Pupil Master
Qualifications: [BCL]

KNIGHT MISS SARAH LOUISE

St Mary's Chambers
50 High Pavement, Lace Market,
Nottingham NG1 1HW,
Telephone: 0115 9503503
E-mail: clerks@smc.law.co.uk
Call Date: July 1996, Middle Temple
Qualifications: [BA (Hons)(Notts), Dip Law
(Lond)]

KNIGHTON MISS CLAIRE LOUISE

65-67 King Street
Leicester LE1 6RP,
Telephone: 0116 2547710
Call Date: Oct 1996, Lincoln's Inn
Qualifications: [LLB (Hons)(Leic)]

KNIGHTS MISS SAMANTHA JANE

3/4 South Square
Gray's Inn, London WC1R 5HP,
Telephone: 0171 696 9900
E-mail: clerks@southsquare.com
Call Date: Nov 1996, Lincoln's Inn
Qualifications: [BA (Hons)(Oxon)]

KNOTT MALCOLM STEPHEN

New Court Chambers
5 Verulam Buildings, Gray's Inn, London
WC1R 5LY, Telephone: 0171 831 9500
E-mail: mail@newcourtchambers.com
Call Date: July 1968, Inner Temple
Recorder

KNOTTS MISS CAROL ELAINE

Coleridge Chambers
Citadel, 190 Corporation Street,
Birmingham B4 6QD,
Telephone: 0121 233 8500
Call Date: Nov 1996, Inner Temple
Qualifications: [LLB (B'ham)]

KNOWLES GRAHAM ROY

Peel Court Chambers
45 Hardman Street, Manchester M3 3PL,
Telephone: 0161 832 3791
E-mail: clerks@peelct.co.uk
Call Date: Oct 1990, Middle Temple
Qualifications: [MA (Cantab)]

KNOWLES MS GWYNNETH FRANCES

4 Brick Court
Temple, London EC4Y 9AD,
Telephone: 0171 797 8910
E-mail: medhurst@dial.pipex.com
Call Date: Oct 1993, Gray's Inn
Qualifications: [BA, M.Sc]

KNOWLES JULIAN BERNARD

3 Raymond Buildings
Gray's Inn, London WC1R 5BH,
Telephone: 020 7831 3833
E-mail:chambers@threeraymond.demon.co.u
k
Call Date: Nov 1994, Inner Temple
Qualifications: [BA (Oxon), CPE]

KNOWLES MISS LINDA

Goldsmith Building
1st Floor, Temple, London EC4Y 7BL,
Telephone: 0171 353 7881
E-mail:clerks@goldsmith-building.law.co.uk
Call Date: Oct 1993, Gray's Inn
Qualifications: [LLB (Hons)]

KNOWLES MARK DAVID

Equity Chambers
3rd Floor, 153a Corporation Street,
Birmingham B4 6PH,
Telephone: 0121 233 2100
E-mail: equityatusa.com
Call Date: Nov 1989, Middle Temple
Pupil Master
Qualifications: [LLB Hons [Leic]]

KNOWLES ROBIN ST JOHN QC (1999)

3/4 South Square
Gray's Inn, London WC1R 5HP,
Telephone: 0171 696 9900
E-mail: clerks@southsquare.com
Call Date: 1982, Middle Temple
Pupil Master
Qualifications: [MA (Cantab)]

KNOX CHRISTOPHER JOHN

Trinity Chambers
9-12 Trinity Chare, Quayside, Newcastle
upon Tyne NE1 3DF,
Telephone: 0191 232 1927
E-mail: info@trinitychambers.co.uk
Call Date: July 1974, Inner Temple
Pupil Master, Recorder
Qualifications: [BA (Dunelm)]

KNOX SIMON CHRISTOPHER PETER

1 Crown Office Row
3rd Floor, Temple, London EC4Y 7HH,
Telephone: 0171 583 9292
E-mail: onecor@link.org
Call Date: Nov 1983, Middle Temple
Pupil Master
Qualifications: [BA (Oxon)]

KODAGODA FRITZ ST CLAIR

The Chambers of Mr Ali Mohammed Azhar
Basement, 9 King's Bench Walk, Temple,
London EC4Y 7DX,
Telephone: 0171 353 9564
E-mail: jvlee@btinternet.com
Call Date: Nov 1993, Lincoln's Inn

KOGAN BARRY ISAAC

33 Bedford Row
London WC1R 4JH,
Telephone: 0171 242 6476
E-mail:clerks@bedfordrow33.demon.co.uk
Call Date: July 1973, Inner Temple
Pupil Master, Assistant Recorder
Qualifications: [LLB (Hull)]

KOLANKO MICHAEL PHILIP

17 Carlton Crescent
Southampton SO15 2XR,
Telephone: 023 8032 0320/0823 2003
E-mail: greg@jg17cc.co.uk
Call Date: July 1975, Middle Temple
Pupil Master
Qualifications: [LLB (Manch)]

KOLODYNSKI STEFAN RICHARD

New Court Chambers
Gazette Building, 168 Corporation Street,
Birmingham B4 6TZ,
Telephone: 0121 693 6656
Call Date: Oct 1993, Lincoln's Inn
Qualifications: [BSc (Hons)(Lond), CPE
(Huddesfield)]

KOLODZIEJ ANDRZEJ JOZEF

Littman Chambers
12 Gray's Inn Square, London WC1R 5JP,
Telephone: 020 7404 4866
E-mail: admin@littmanchambers.com
Call Date: Nov 1978, Gray's Inn
Pupil Master
Qualifications: [BA (Oxon), FCIArb, LLM
(Kings)]

Fax: 020 7404 4812;
Out of hours telephone: 07798 787186;
DX: 0055 London, Chancery Lane;
Other comms: E-mail
admin@littmanchambers.com; URL: http://
www.littmanchambers.com

Other professional qualifications: LLM (London)

Types of work: Arbitration, Banking, Chancery
(general), Commercial litigation, Common
law (general), Company and commercial,
Construction, Defamation, EC and competition law, Employment, Franchising, Insurance, International trade, Private
international, Professional negligence, Sale
and carriage of goods

Membership of foreign bars: New South Wales, Australia

Awards and memberships: Bar European Group; British Polish Legal Association; COMBAR

Other professional experience: Sits as an arbitrator, domestically and internationally; registered on the list of arbitrators of International Arbitral Centre of the Austrian Federal Economic Chamber, Vienna

Languages spoken: French, Polish

KOLVIN PHILIP ALAN

2-3 Gray's Inn Square
Gray's Inn, London WC1R 5JH,
Telephone: 0171 242 4986
E-mail:chambers@2-3graysinnsquare.co.uk
Call Date: July 1985, Inner Temple
Pupil Master
Qualifications: [BA (Oxon)]

KOPIECZEK ALOYSIUS MICHAEL

6 Gray's Inn Square
Ground Floor, Gray's Inn, London
WC1R 5AZ, Telephone: 0171 242 1052
E-mail: 6graysinn@clara.co.uk
Call Date: Nov 1983, Gray's Inn
Pupil Master
Qualifications: [LLB]

KORAH PROF VALENTINE

Guildford Chambers
Stoke House, Leapale Lane, Guildford,
Surrey, GU1 4LY,
Telephone: 01483 539131
E-mail:guildford.barristers@btinternet.com
Call Date: Nov 1952, Lincoln's Inn
Qualifications: [LL.M (Lond), PhD]

KORDA ANTHONY

1 Middle Temple Lane
Temple, London EC4Y 1LT,
Telephone: 0171 583 0659 (12 Lines)
E-mail: chambers@1mtl.co.uk
Call Date: July 1988, Inner Temple
Pupil Master
Qualifications: [LLB (Lond)]

KORN ADAM RICHARD

New Court Chambers
5 Verulam Buildings, Gray's Inn, London
WC1R 5LY, Telephone: 0171 831 9500
E-mail: mail@newcourtchambers.com
Park Lane Chambers
19 Westgate, Leeds LS1 2RD,
Telephone: 0113 2285000
E-mail:clerks@parklanechambers.co.uk
Call Date: Oct 1992, Middle Temple
Qualifications: [BA (Hons), MA, Diploma in Law, A.K.C.]

KORN ANTHONY HENRY

Barnard's Inn Chambers
6th Floor, Halton House, 20-23 Holborn,
London EC1N 2JD,
Telephone: 0171 369 6969
E-mail: clerks@biclaw.co.uk
Call Date: Nov 1978, Gray's Inn
Qualifications: [BA (Oxon)]

KORNER MISS JOANNA CHRISTIAN MARY QC (1993)

6 King's Bench Walk
Ground Floor, Temple, London
EC4Y 7DR, Telephone: 0171 583 0410
E-mail: worsley@6kbw.freeserve.co.uk
Call Date: Nov 1974, Inner Temple
Recorder

KOROL MS KATHRYN MARGARET

Kenworthy's Chambers
83 Bridge Street, Manchester M3 2RF,
Telephone: 0161 832 4036/834 6954
E-mail: clerks@kenworthys.co.uk
Call Date: Mar 1996, Middle Temple
Qualifications: [LLB (Hons)]

KOSMIN LESLIE GORDON QC (1994)

Erskine Chambers
30 Lincoln's Inn Fields, Lincoln's Inn,
London WC2A 3PF,
Telephone: 0171 242 5532
E-mail:clerks@erskine-chambers.co.uk
Call Date: July 1976, Middle Temple
Qualifications: [MA, LLM (Cantab), LLM (Harvard)]

KOTHARI MISS SIMA

4 Brick Court
Ground Floor, Temple, London
EC4Y 9AD, Telephone: 0171 797 7766
E-mail: chambers@4brick.co.uk
Call Date: Oct 1992, Gray's Inn
Qualifications: [LLB (Lond)]

KOTHARI VASANT CHUNILAL

2 Paper Buildings
1st Floor, Temple, London EC4Y 7ET,
Telephone: 020 7556 5500
E-mail: clerks@2pbbarristers.co.uk
Call Date: July 1960, Lincoln's Inn
Pupil Master
Qualifications: [BA (Hons)]

KOVALEVSKY RICHARD TARAS

18 Red Lion Court
(Off Fleet Street), London EC4A 3EB,
Telephone: 0171 520 6000
E-mail: chambers@18rlc.co.uk
Thornwood House
102 New London Road, Chelmsford,
Essex, CM2 0RG,
Telephone: 01245 280880
E-mail: chambers@18rlc.co.uk
Call Date: July 1983, Gray's Inn
Pupil Master
Qualifications: [LLB Manchester]

KOVATS STEVEN LASZLO

39 Essex Street
London WC2R 3AT,
Telephone: 0171 832 1111
E-mail: clerks@39essex.co.uk
Call Date: July 1989, Middle Temple
Pupil Master
Qualifications: [BA [Cantab]]

KRAMER PHILIP ANTHONY

New Court Chambers
3 Broad Chare, Newcastle upon Tyne
NE1 3DQ, Telephone: 0191 232 1980
Plowden Buildings
2nd Floor, 2 Plowden Buildings, Middle
Temple Lane, London EC4Y 9BU,
Telephone: 0171 583 0808
E-mail: bar@plowdenbuildings.co.uk
Call Date: July 1982, Inner Temple
Pupil Master
Qualifications: [LLB (Newc)]

KRAMER STEPHEN ERNEST QC (1995)

1 Hare Court
Ground Floor, Temple, London
EC4Y 7BE, Telephone: 0171 353 3982/
5324
Call Date: July 1970, Gray's Inn
Recorder
Qualifications: [MA (Oxon)]

Fax: 0171 353 0667; DX: LDE 444 Chancery
Lane

Types of work: Crime, Crime – corporate
fraud

Circuit: South Eastern

Awards and memberships: Vice-Chairman of the
Criminal Bar Association 1999-2000

Other professional experience: Standing
Counsel (Crime) HM Customs and Excise
(1989-95) SE Circuit

Languages spoken: French

KRAUSE MS FLORENCE

Central Chambers
89 Princess Street,
Manchester M1 4HT,
Telephone: 0161 236 1133
Call Date: July 1998, Lincoln's Inn
Qualifications: [LLB (Hons)(Sheff)]

KREMEN PHILIP MICHAEL

Hardwicke Building
New Square, Lincoln's Inn, London
WC2A 3SB, Telephone: 020 7242 2523
E-mail: clerks@hardwicke.co.uk
Call Date: Nov 1975, Gray's Inn
Pupil Master
Qualifications: [BSc (Hons)]

KRIKLER ALEXANDER RICHARD

Lion Court
Chancery House, 53-64 Chancery Lane,
London WC2A 1SJ,
Telephone: 0171 404 6565
Call Date: Nov 1995, Middle Temple
Qualifications: [BA (Hons)(Manch)]

KRIKLER MISS SUSAN

3 Temple Gardens
Lower Ground Floor, Temple, London
EC4Y 9AU, Telephone: 0171 353 3102/5/
9297 E-mail: clerks@3tg.co.uk
Call Date: Nov 1988, Middle Temple
Qualifications: [BA (Oxon), Dip Law (City)]

KRISH MISS JULIA ROSALIE

4 Brick Court
Ground Floor, Temple, London
EC4Y 9AD, Telephone: 0171 797 7766
E-mail: chambers@4brick.co.uk
Call Date: Feb 1992, Middle Temple
Qualifications: [MA (Oxon)]

KRISHNADASAN MISS DOUSHKA

One Garden Court Family Law Chambers
Ground Floor, Temple, London
EC4Y 9BJ, Telephone: 0171 797 7900
E-mail: clerks@onegardencourt.co.uk
Call Date: July 1991, Middle Temple
Qualifications: [LLB (Hons) (Lond)]

KROLICK IVAN

Lamb Building
Ground Floor, Temple, London
EC4Y 7AS, Telephone: 020 7797 7788
E-mail: lamb.building@link.org
Call Date: Nov 1966, Gray's Inn
Pupil Master
Qualifications: [LLB (Dunelm), FCIArb]

KRONE MRS MAXINE JANE

De Montfort Chambers
95 Princess Road East, Leicester LE1 7DQ,
Telephone: 0116 254 8686
E-mail: dmcbar@aol.com
Call Date: July 1980, Middle Temple
Qualifications: [BA (Leics) (Hons)]

KUBIK MISS HEIDI MARIE

3 Fountain Court
Steelhouse Lane, Birmingham B4 6DR,
Telephone: 0121 236 5854
Call Date: Oct 1993, Lincoln's Inn
Qualifications: [BA (Hons)(Notts)]

KULATILAKE INDRA SEMAGE

52 Wembley Park Drive
Wembley, Middlesex, HA9 8HB,
Telephone: 0181 902 5629
Call Date: July 1971, Inner Temple
Pupil Master

KUMALO DABI SIMON

New Court
Temple, London EC4Y 9BE,
Telephone: 0171 583 5123/0510
Call Date: Nov 1974, Inner Temple
Pupil Master
Qualifications: [MA (Oxon)]

KUMAR MISS MOUSUMI

Chambers of Joy Okoye
Suite 1, 2nd Floor Gray's Inn Chambers,
Gray's Inn, London WC1R 5JA,
Telephone: 0171 405 7011
Call Date: Oct 1992, Gray's Inn
Qualifications: [LLB (Lond)]

KUMAR UMESH

1 Crown Office Row
3rd Floor, Temple, London EC4Y 7HH,
Telephone: 0171 583 9292
E-mail: onecor@link.org
Call Date: Oct 1995, Inner Temple
Qualifications: [BA (Oxon)]

KUMI ISHMAEL JOB

Cromwell-Ayeh-Kumi Chambers
1st Floor Suite, 119 Cricklewood
Broadway, London NW2 3JG,
Telephone: 0181 450 6620
E-mail: ishmael@mcmail.com
Call Date: Nov 1977, Gray's Inn
Qualifications: [MA (Oxon) Maitrise,
(Sorbonne)]

KURREIN MARTIN GEORGE

199 Strand
London WC2R 1DR,
Telephone: 0171 379 9779
E-mail: chambers@199strand.co.uk
Call Date: July 1981, Middle Temple
Pupil Master
Qualifications: [BA (Hons)]

KUSCHKE LEON SIEGFRIED

Erskine Chambers
30 Lincoln's Inn Fields, Lincoln's Inn,
London WC2A 3PF,
Telephone: 0171 242 5532
E-mail:clerks@erskine-chambers.co.uk
Call Date: July 1993, Lincoln's Inn
Qualifications: [B.Comm, LLB]

KUSHNER MISS LINDSEY JOY QC (1992)

28 St John Street
Manchester M3 4DJ,
Telephone: 0161 834 8418
E-mail: clerk@28stjohnst.co.uk
14 Gray's Inn Square
Gray's Inn, London WC1R 5JP,
Telephone: 0171 242 0858
E-mail: 100712.2134@compuserve.com
Call Date: July 1974, Middle Temple
Recorder
Qualifications: [LLB]

KUSHNER MISS MARTINE

Chambers of Michael Pert QC
36 Bedford Row, London WC1R 4JH,
Telephone: 0171 421 8000
E-mail: 36bedfordrow@link.org
Chambers of Michael Pert QC
24 Albion Place, Northampton NN1 1UD,
Telephone: 01604 602333
Chambers of Michael Pert QC
104 New Walk, Leicester LE1 7EA,
Telephone: 0116 249 2020
Call Date: July 1980, Middle Temple
Pupil Master
Qualifications: [LLB (B'ham)]

KVERNDAL SIMON RICHARD

4 Essex Court
Temple, London EC4Y 9AJ,
Telephone: 020 7797 7970
E-mail: clerks@4essexcourt.law.co.uk
Call Date: Nov 1982, Middle Temple
Pupil Master
Qualifications: [MA (Cantab)]

KWIATKOWSKI FELIKS JERZY

Goldsworth Chambers
1st Floor, 11 Gray's Inn Square, London
WC1R 5JD, Telephone: 0171 405 7117
Call Date: July 1977, Middle Temple
Qualifications: [LLB (Hons)(Bris)]

KYNOCH DUNCAN STUART SANDERSON

29 Bedford Row Chambers
London WC1R 4HE,
Telephone: 0171 831 2626
Call Date: Nov 1994, Gray's Inn
Qualifications: [LLB (Bris)]

KYRIAKIDES MISS TINA

11 Stone Buildings
Lincoln's Inn, London WC2A 3TG,
Telephone: +44 (0)207 831 6381
E-mail:clerks@11StoneBuildings.law.co.uk
Call Date: July 1984, Lincoln's Inn
Qualifications: [MA(Cantab)]

KYTE PETER ERIC QC (1996)

Hollis Whiteman Chambers
3rd Floor, Queen Elizabeth Bldg, Temple,
London EC4Y 9BS,
Telephone: 020 7583 5766
E-mail:barristers@holliswhiteman.co.uk
Call Date: July 1970, Gray's Inn
Recorder
Qualifications: [MA (Cantab)]

LABAN ALEXANDER

Mitre Court Chambers
3rd Floor, Temple, London EC4Y 7BP,
Telephone: 0171 353 9394
E-mail: mitrecourt.com
Call Date: Nov 1981, Inner Temple
Pupil Master
Qualifications: [BA Dip Law]

LABELLE JEAN-MARIE

John Street Chambers
2 John Street, London WC1N 2HJ,
Telephone: 0171 242 1911
E-mail:john.street_chambers@virgin.net
Call Date: Nov 1992, Inner Temple
Qualifications: [MSc (Surrey), Dip in Law]

LACEY MISS ROISIN MARY

Chambers of Kieran Coonan QC
Ground Floor, 6 Pump Court, Temple,
London EC4Y 7AR,
Telephone: 0171 583 6013/2510
E-mail: clerks@6-pumpcourt.law.co.uk
Call Date: Nov 1991, Middle Temple
Qualifications: [BA (Hons) (Dublin), BL (Dublin)]

LACEY MISS SARAH HELEN

3 Stone Buildings
Lincoln's Inn, London WC2A 3XL,
Telephone: 0171 242 4937
E-mail: clerks@3sb.law.co.uk
Call Date: Nov 1991, Middle Temple
Qualifications: [LLB Hons (Cantab)]

LACHKOVIC JAMES ADRIAN GEORGE

1 Middle Temple Lane
Temple, London EC4Y 1LT,
Telephone: 0171 583 0659 (12 Lines)
E-mail: chambers@1mtl.co.uk
Call Date: Nov 1987, Gray's Inn
Pupil Master
Qualifications: [LLB (Hull)]

LACHKOVIC MISS VERONICA MARGARET MARY

One Garden Court Family Law Chambers
Ground Floor, Temple, London
EC4Y 9BJ, Telephone: 0171 797 7900
E-mail: clerks@onegardencourt.co.uk
Call Date: July 1982, Gray's Inn
Pupil Master
Qualifications: [LLB (Lond)]

LADAK MISS TAHERA

8 King's Bench Walk
2nd Floor, Temple, London EC4Y 7DU,
Telephone: 0171 797 8888
8 King's Bench Walk North
1 Park Square East, Leeds LS1 2NE,
Telephone: 0113 2439797
Call Date: Nov 1986, Gray's Inn
Pupil Master
Qualifications: [LLB (Essex)]

LADDIE JAMES MATTHEW LANG

Cloisters
1 Pump Court, Temple, London
EC4Y 7AA, Telephone: 0171 827 4000
E-mail: clerks@cloisters.com
Call Date: Nov 1995, Middle Temple
Qualifications: [BA (Hons) (Cantab)]

LADMORE RICHARD JAMES

Call Date: Feb 1995, Middle Temple
Qualifications: [BA (Hons)(Sussex)]

LAHIFFE MARTIN PATRICK JOSEPH

3 Temple Gardens
Lower Ground Floor, Temple, London
EC4Y 9AU, Telephone: 0171 353 3102/5/
9297 E-mail: clerks@3tg.co.uk
Call Date: Nov 1984, Middle Temple
Pupil Master
Qualifications: [BA (Hons)]

LAIDLAW JONATHAN JAMES

1 Hare Court
Ground Floor, Temple, London
EC4Y 7BE, Telephone: 0171 353 3982/
5324
Call Date: July 1982, Inner Temple
Pupil Master, Assistant Recorder
Qualifications: [LLB (Hull)]

LAING MISS CHRISTINE KATHERINE

9-12 Bell Yard
London WC2A 2LF,
Telephone: 0171 400 1800
E-mail: clerks@bellyard.co.uk
Call Date: July 1984, Lincoln's Inn
Qualifications: [LLB]

LAING MISS ELISABETH MARY CAROLINE

11 King's Bench Walk
Temple, London EC4Y 7EQ,
Telephone: 0171 632 8500/583 0610
E-mail: clerksroom@11kbw.com
Call Date: July 1980, Middle Temple
Pupil Master, Assistant Recorder
Qualifications: [BA (Cantab)]

LAIRD FRANCIS JOSEPH

3 Fountain Court
Steelhouse Lane, Birmingham B4 6DR,
Telephone: 0121 236 5854
Call Date: Nov 1986, Gray's Inn
Qualifications: [LLB (N'Castle)]

LAKE MRS LISA (JANE)

One Essex Court
Ground Floor, Temple, London
EC4Y 9AR, Telephone: 020 7583 2000
E-mail: clerks@oneessexcourt.co.uk
Call Date: Oct 1994, Inner Temple
Qualifications: [MA (Cantab)]

D

LAKHA ABBAS

4 Brick Court, Chambers of Anne Rafferty QC
1st Floor, Temple, London EC4Y 9AD,
Telephone: 0171 583 8455
Call Date: Nov 1984, Inner Temple
Pupil Master
Qualifications: [BA (Hons)]

LAKHA MURTAZA AHMED

Chambers of Harjit Singh
Ground Floor, 2 Middle Temple Lane,
Temple, London EC4Y 9AA,
Telephone: 0171 353 1356 (4 Lines)
Call Date: Nov 1961, Lincoln's Inn
Pupil Master

LAKHA SHABBIR

7 Stone Buildings (also at 11 Bolt Court)
1st Floor, Lincoln's Inn, London
WC2A 3SZ, Telephone: 0171 242 0961
E-mail:larthur@7stonebuildings.law.co.uk
11 Bolt Court (also at 7 Stone Buildings – 1st Floor)
London EC4A 3DQ,
Telephone: 0171 353 2300
E-mail: boltct11@aol.com
Redhill Chambers
Seloduct House, 30 Station Road, Redhill,
Surrey, RH1 1NF,
Telephone: 01737 780781
Call Date: July 1989, Lincoln's Inn
Qualifications: [LLB (Hons), M.Phil (Cantab)]

LAKIN GORDON

No. 6
6 Park Square, Leeds LS1 2LW,
Telephone: 0113 2459763
E-mail: chambers@no6.co.uk
Call Date: July 1972, Middle Temple
Qualifications: [LLB (Leeds)]

LAKIN MISS TRACY

Victoria Chambers
3rd Floor, 177 Corporation Street,
Birmingham B4 6RG,
Telephone: 0121 236 9900
E-mail: viccham@aol.com
Call Date: Oct 1993, Inner Temple
Qualifications: [LLB]

LAL SANJAY

10 King's Bench Walk
1st Floor, Temple, London EC4Y 7EB,
Telephone: 0171 353 2501
Call Date: Oct 1993, Lincoln's Inn
Qualifications: [LLB (Hons), LLM (Lond)]

LALENG PER CHRISTIAN

Castle Street Chambers
2nd Floor, 42 Castle Street, Liverpool
L2 7LD, Telephone: 0151 242 0500
Call Date: Mar 1997, Gray's Inn
Qualifications: [BA (Kent), MPhil (Cantab)]

LALLIE RANJIT SINGH

Equity Chambers
3rd Floor, 153a Corporation Street,
Birmingham B4 6PH,
Telephone: 0121 233 2100
E-mail: equityatusa.com
Call Date: Oct 1997, Lincoln's Inn
Qualifications: [LLB (Hons)]

LAM CHUEN FAT

King's Chambers
49a Broadway, Stratford, London
E15 4BW,
Call Date: Nov 1994, Lincoln's Inn
Qualifications: [BA (Hons)(Wolves)]

LAMACRAFT IAN RICHARD

Bracton Chambers
95a Chancery Lane, London WC2A 1DT,
Telephone: 0171 242 4248
Call Date: July 1989, Lincoln's Inn
Qualifications: [LLB]

LAMB DAVID STEPHEN

York Chambers
14 Toft Green, York YO1 6JT,
Telephone: 01904 620048
E-mail: [name]@yorkchambers.co.uk
Call Date: Nov 1987, Middle Temple
Qualifications: [LLB Hons (Cardiff)]

LAMB ERIC ALAN

Exchange Chambers
Pearl Assurance House, Derby Square,
Liverpool L2 9XX,
Telephone: 0151 236 7747
E-mail:exchangechambers@btinternet.com
Call Date: July 1975, Lincoln's Inn
Pupil Master
Qualifications: [LLB]

LAMB JEFFREY THOMAS

Sussex Chambers
9 Old Steine, Brighton, Sussex, BN1 1FJ,
Telephone: 01273 607953
Call Date: Oct 1992, Middle Temple
Qualifications: [BA(Hons)(Sussex),
MA(Susex), Dip Law]

LAMB JOHN RICHARD

New Court
Temple, London EC4Y 9BE,
Telephone: 0171 583 5123/0510
Call Date: May 1990, Middle Temple
Qualifications: [B.A.]

LAMB MISS MARIA-JANE CARMEL

1 Paper Buildings
1st Floor, Temple, London EC4Y 7EP,
Telephone: 0171 353 3728/4953
Call Date: Nov 1984, Gray's Inn
Qualifications: [MA (Cantab)]

LAMB ROBERT GLASSON

13 King's Bench Walk
1st Floor, Temple, London EC4Y 7EN,
Telephone: 0171 353 7204
E-mail: clerks@13kbw.law.co.uk
King's Bench Chambers
32 Beaumont Street, Oxford OX1 2NP,
Telephone: 01865 311066
E-mail: clerks@kbc-oxford.law.co.uk
Call Date: July 1973, Middle Temple
Qualifications: [MA (Cantab)]

LAMB MS SOPHIE JANE

One Essex Court
Ground Floor, Temple, London
EC4Y 9AR, Telephone: 020 7583 2000
E-mail: clerks@oneessexcourt.co.uk
Call Date: Nov 1998, Gray's Inn
Qualifications: [LLB (Manch), LLM (LSE)]

LAMB TIMOTHY ROBERT QC (1995)

2 Temple Gardens
Temple, London EC4Y 9AY,
Telephone: 0171 583 6041
E-mail: clerks@2templegardens.co.uk
Call Date: Nov 1974, Gray's Inn
Assistant Recorder
Qualifications: [MA (Oxon)]

LAMBERT MISS CHRISTINA CAROLINE

Chambers of Kieran Coonan QC
Ground Floor, 6 Pump Court, Temple,
London EC4Y 7AR,
Telephone: 0171 583 6013/2510
E-mail: clerks@6-pumpcourt.law.co.uk
Call Date: Nov 1988, Inner Temple
Qualifications: [MA (Cantab), Dip Law (City)]

LAMBERT MISS DEBORAH MARY

Kenworthy's Chambers
83 Bridge Street, Manchester M3 2RF,
Telephone: 0161 832 4036/834 6954
E-mail: clerks@kenworthys.co.uk
Call Date: May 1977, Lincoln's Inn
Pupil Master
Qualifications: [BA (Oxon)]

LAMBERT JOHN

Lancaster Building
77 Deansgate, Manchester M3 2BW,
Telephone: 0161 661 4444/0171 649 9872
E-mail: sandra@lbnipc.com
Call Date: July 1977, Lincoln's Inn
Pupil Master
Qualifications: [MA, FCIArb]

LAMBERT NIGEL ROBERT WOOLF QC (1999)

2-4 Tudor Street
London EC4Y 0AA,
Telephone: 0171 797 7111
E-mail: clerks@rfqc.co.uk
Call Date: 1974, Gray's Inn
Pupil Master, Recorder
Qualifications: [also Inn of Court I]

D

LAMBERT PAUL JULIAN LAY

Albion Chambers
Broad Street, Bristol BS1 1DR,
Telephone: 0117 9272144
Call Date: July 1983, Middle Temple
Pupil Master
Qualifications: [LLB (Lond)]

LAMBERT MISS SARAH KATRINA

1 Crown Office Row
Ground Floor, Temple, London
EC4Y 7HH, Telephone: 0171 797 7500
E-mail: mail@onecrownofficerow.com
Call Date: Oct 1994, Gray's Inn
Qualifications: [BA]

LAMBERT STUART GRAY

Sussex Chambers
9 Old Steine, Brighton, Sussex, BN1 1FJ,
Telephone: 01273 607953
Call Date: July 1965, Gray's Inn
Pupil Master, Assistant Recorder
Qualifications: [MA (Oxon)]

LAMBERTY MARK JULIAN HARKER

Queen's Chambers
5 John Dalton Street, Manchester M2 6ET,
Telephone: 0161 834 6875/4738
Queens Chambers
4 Camden Place, Preston PR1 3JL,
Telephone: 01772 828300
Call Date: Nov 1970, Gray's Inn
Qualifications: [BCL, MA (Oxon)]

LAMBIS MARIOS PAMBOS

1 Hare Court
Ground Floor, Temple, London
EC4Y 7BE, Telephone: 0171 353 3982/
5324
Call Date: Nov 1989, Middle Temple
Qualifications: [BA Hons (Sus), Dip in Law]

LAMING MS NORMA YVONNE

New Court
Temple, London EC4Y 9BE,
Telephone: 0171 583 5123/0510
Call Date: July 1990, Middle Temple

LAMMING DAVID JOHN

2-3 Gray's Inn Square
Gray's Inn, London WC1R 5JH,
Telephone: 0171 242 4986
E-mail:chambers@2-3graysinnsquare.co.uk
Call Date: Nov 1972, Gray's Inn
Pupil Master
Qualifications: [LLB (Lond), LLM (Lon]

LAMONT MISS CAMILLA ROSE

Chambers of Lord Goodhart QC
Ground Floor, 3 New Square, Lincoln's
Inn, London WC2A 3RS,
Telephone: 0171 405 5577
E-mail:law@threenewsquare.demon.co.uk
Call Date: Nov 1995, Middle Temple
Qualifications: [BA (Hons), BCL (Oxon)]

LAMS BARNABAS JEFFREY

Chambers of Wilfred Forster-Jones
New Court, 1st Floor South, Temple,
London EC4Y 9BE,
Telephone: 0171 353 0853/4/7222
E-mail: chambers@newcourt.net
Call Date: Oct 1995, Gray's Inn
Qualifications: [BA (Hons) (Bristol), MA
(UEA)]

LANCASTER PHILIP STUART

39 Park Square
Leeds LS1 2NU,
Telephone: 0113 2456633
Call Date: July 1982, Inner Temple
Qualifications: [BA (Cantab)]

LANDALE MISS TINA JEANETTE

Old Colony House
6 South King Street, Manchester M2 6DQ,
Telephone: 0161 834 4364
Call Date: July 1988, Middle Temple
Qualifications: [LLB (Hons)]

LANDAU TOBY THOMAS

Essex Court Chambers
24 Lincoln's Inn Fields, London
WC2A 3ED, Telephone: 0171 813 8000
E-mail:clerksroom@essexcourt-chambers.co.u
k
Call Date: Nov 1993, Middle Temple
Qualifications: [MA (Hons), BCL (Oxon),
LLM (Harvard)]

LANDAW JOHN NICHOLAS

Hardwicke Building
New Square, Lincoln's Inn, London
WC2A 3SB, Telephone: 020 7242 2523
E-mail: clerks@hardwicke.co.uk
Call Date: Feb 1976, Gray's Inn
Pupil Master
Qualifications: [BA (Oxon), MA]

LANDER CHARLES GIDEON

25-27 Castle Street
1st Floor, Liverpool L2 4TA,
Telephone: 0151 227 5661/051 236 5072
Call Date: Nov 1993, Lincoln's Inn
Qualifications: [LLB (Leeds)]

LANDER RICHARD MARK

40 King Street
Manchester M2 6BA,
Telephone: 0161 832 9082
E-mail: clerks@40kingstreet.co.uk
The Chambers of Philip Raynor QC
5 Park Place, Leeds LS1 2RU,
Telephone: 0113 242 1123
Call Date: Oct 1993, Lincoln's Inn
Qualifications: [BA (Hons)]

LANDES MISS ANNA-ROSE

St Philip's Chambers
Fountain Court, Steelhouse Lane,
Birmingham B4 6DR,
Telephone: 0121 246 7000
E-mail: clerks@st-philips.co.uk
Call Date: Nov 1986, Gray's Inn
Qualifications: [BA (Oxon)]

LANDSBURY ALAN PAUL

6 Gray's Inn Square
Ground Floor, Gray's Inn, London
WC1R 5AZ, Telephone: 0171 242 1052
E-mail: 6graysinn@clara.co.uk
Call Date: Nov 1975, Gray's Inn
Pupil Master

LANE DAVID GOODWIN QC (1991)

Phoenix Chambers
First Floor, Gray's Inn Chambers, Gray's
Inn, London WC1R 5JA,
Telephone: 0171 404 7888
E-mail:clerks@phoenix-chambers.co.uk

Queens Square Chambers
56 Queens Square, Bristol BS1 4PR,
Telephone: 0117 921 1966
Call Date: Nov 1968, Gray's Inn
Recorder
Qualifications: [LLB]

LANE MS LINDSAY RUTH BUSFIELD

8 New Square
Lincoln's Inn, London WC2A 3QP,
Telephone: 0171 405 4321
E-mail: clerks@8newsquare.co.uk
Call Date: Oct 1996, Middle Temple
Qualifications: [BA (Hons) (Camb), MA
(Florence)]

LANE MICHAEL JOHN

East Anglian Chambers
52 North Hill, Colchester, Essex, CO1 1PY,
Telephone: 01206 572756
E-mail: colchester@ealaw.co.uk
East Anglian Chambers
Gresham House, 5 Museum Street,
Ipswich, Suffolk, IP1 1HQ,
Telephone: 01473 214481
E-mail: ipswich@ealaw.co.uk
East Anglian Chambers
57 London Street, Norwich NR2 1HL,
Telephone: 01603 617351
E-mail: norwich@ealaw.co.uk
Call Date: July 1983, Middle Temple
Pupil Master
Qualifications: [BA (Cantab), Dip.Soc (Kent)]

LANE PATRICK MICHAEL MACE

Atkin Chambers
1 Atkin Building, Gray's Inn, London
WC1R 5AT, Telephone: 020 7404 0102
E-mail: clerks@atkin-chambers.co.uk
Call Date: July 1997, Gray's Inn
Qualifications: [BA, LLB]

LANE-SMITH MISS ZOE VICTORIA

Cardinal Chambers
4 Old Mitre Court, 4th Floor, Temple,
London EC4Y 7BP,
Telephone: 020 7353 2622
E-mail:admin@cardinal-chambers.co.uk
Call Date: 1997, Middle Temple
Qualifications: [BA (Hons)(Dunelm)]

D

LANG MISS BEVERLEY ANN MACNAUGHTON

Blackstone Chambers
Blackstone House, Temple, London
EC4Y 9BW, Telephone: 0171 583 1770
E-mail:clerks@blackstonechambers.com
Call Date: Nov 1978, Inner Temple
Pupil Master
Qualifications: [BA (Oxon)]

LANGDALE ADRIAN MARK

Enfield Chambers
First Floor, Refuge House, 9-10 River
Front, Enfield, Middlesex, EN1 3SZ,
Telephone: 0181 364 5627
E-mail:enfieldchambers@compuserve.com
Call Date: Mar 1996, Gray's Inn
Qualifications: [LLB (L'pool)]

LANGDALE MISS RACHEL

9 Bedford Row
London WC1R 4AZ,
Telephone: 0171 242 3555
E-mail: clerks@9br.co.uk
Call Date: Oct 1990, Middle Temple
Qualifications: [LLB (Hons), M Phil (Cantab)]

LANGDALE TIMOTHY JAMES QC (1992)

Hollis Whiteman Chambers
3rd Floor, Queen Elizabeth Bldg, Temple,
London EC4Y 9BS,
Telephone: 020 7583 5766
E-mail:barristers@holliswhiteman.co.uk
Call Date: July 1966, Lincoln's Inn
Recorder
Qualifications: [MA (St Andrews)]

LANGDON ANDREW DOMINIC

Guildhall Chambers
22-26 Broad Street, Bristol BS1 2HG,
Telephone: 0117 9273366
E-mail:civil.clerks@guildhallchambers.co.uk and
criminal.clerks@guildhallchambers.co.uk
Call Date: July 1986, Middle Temple
Pupil Master
Qualifications: [LLB (Bristol)]

LANGHAM RICHARD GEOFFREY

1 Serjeants' Inn
4th Floor, Temple, London EC4Y 1NH,
Telephone: 0171 583 1355
E-mail: clerks@serjeants-inn.co.uk
Call Date: Nov 1986, Lincoln's Inn
Pupil Master
Qualifications: [BA (Oxon)]

LANGLOIS PETER JOHN

Assize Court Chambers
14 Small Street, Bristol BS1 1DE,
Telephone: 0117 9264587
E-mail:chambers@assize-court-chambers.co.uk
Call Date: Oct 1991, Lincoln's Inn
Qualifications: [LLB (Hons) (E.Ang)]

LANGRIDGE MS NICOLA DAWN

Hardwicke Building
New Square, Lincoln's Inn, London
WC2A 3SB, Telephone: 020 7242 2523
E-mail: clerks@hardwicke.co.uk
Call Date: Nov 1993, Lincoln's Inn
Qualifications: [LLB (Hons, Sheff)]

LANGSTAFF BRIAN FREDERICK JAMES QC (1994)

Cloisters
1 Pump Court, Temple, London
EC4Y 7AA, Telephone: 0171 827 4000
E-mail: clerks@cloisters.com
Call Date: July 1971, Middle Temple
Recorder
Qualifications: [BA (Cantab)]

LANGTON STEVEN ROBERT

11 Bolt Court (also at 7 Stone Buildings – 1st Floor)
London EC4A 3DQ,
Telephone: 0171 353 2300
E-mail: boltct11@aol.com
7 Stone Buildings (also at 11 Bolt Court)
1st Floor, Lincoln's Inn, London
WC2A 3SZ, Telephone: 0171 242 0961
E-mail:larthur@7stonebuildings.law.co.uk
Redhill Chambers
Seloduct House, 30 Station Road, Redhill,
Surrey, RH1 1NF,
Telephone: 01737 780781
Call Date: 1998, Lincoln's Inn
Qualifications: [LLB (Hons)(Staffs)]

LANIGAN WILLIAM CHARLES

10 King's Bench Walk
Ground Floor, Temple, London
EC4Y 7EB, Telephone: 0171 353 7742
E-mail: 10kbw@lineone.net
Call Date: July 1980, Middle Temple
Pupil Master

LANLEHIN OLAJIDE ADEBOLA

Britton Street Chambers
1st Floor, 20 Britton Street, London
EC1M 5NQ, Telephone: 0171 608 3765
Call Date: Nov 1994, Inner Temple
Qualifications: [LLB (Lond)]

LAPRELL MARK DIETER

18 St John Street
Manchester M3 4EA,
Telephone: 0161 278 1800
E-mail: 18stjohn@lineone.net
Call Date: Nov 1979, Gray's Inn
Pupil Master, Assistant Recorder
Qualifications: [BA (Oxon)]

LARGE ALAN MACDONALD

South Western Chambers
Melville House, 12 Middle Street,
Taunton, Somerset, TA1 1SH,
Telephone: 01823 331919 (24 hrs)
E-mail: barclerk@clara.net
Call Date: July 1988, Middle Temple
Pupil Master
Qualifications: [LLB (Hons) (Manch)]

LARIZADEH CYRUS RAIS

4 Paper Buildings
1st Floor, Temple, London EC4Y 7EX,
Telephone: 0171 583 0816/353 1131
E-mail: clerks@4paperbuildings.co.uk
Call Date: Nov 1992, Inner Temple
Qualifications: [BA (Kent), Certificat De
Droit, Francais (Bordeaux)]

LARKIN SEAN

Hollis Whiteman Chambers
3rd Floor, Queen Elizabeth Bldg, Temple,
London EC4Y 9BS,
Telephone: 020 7583 5766
E-mail:barristers@holliswhiteman.co.uk
Call Date: July 1987, Inner Temple
Pupil Master
Qualifications: [LLB (London)]

LASKER JEREMY STEWART

Lincoln House Chambers
5th Floor, Lincoln House, 1 Brazennose
Street, Manchester M2 5EL,
Telephone: 0161 832 5701
E-mail: info@lincolnhse.co.uk
Call Date: July 1976, Inner Temple
Pupil Master
Qualifications: [LLB (B'ham)]

LASOK DOMINIK QC (1982)

Call Date: Nov 1954, Middle Temple
Qualifications: [LLM, PhD, Dr juris,]

LASOK KAROL PAUL EDWARD QC (1994)

Monckton Chambers
4 Raymond Buildings, Gray's Inn, London
WC1R 5BP, Telephone: 0171 405 7211
E-mail: chambers@monckton.co.uk
Call Date: July 1977, Middle Temple
Qualifications: [MA (Cantab), LLM,PhD
(Exon)]

LASSMAN LIONEL KING

2-4 Tudor Street
London EC4Y 0AA,
Telephone: 0171 797 7111
E-mail: clerks@rfqc.co.uk
Call Date: Feb 1955, Middle Temple
Pupil Master

LATHAM MICHAEL RAYMOND HENRI

Furnival Chambers
32 Furnival Street, London EC4A 1JQ,
Telephone: 0171 405 3232
E-mail: clerks@furnivallaw.co.uk
Call Date: Nov 1975, Gray's Inn
Pupil Master
Qualifications: [LLB]

LATHAM RICHARD BRUNTON QC (1991)

9 Bedford Row
London WC1R 4AZ,
Telephone: 0171 242 3555
E-mail: clerks@9br.co.uk
Call Date: July 1971, Gray's Inn
Recorder
Qualifications: [LLB (B'ham)]

D

LATHAM ROBERT JAMES

Doughty Street Chambers
11 Doughty Street, London WC1N 2PG,
Telephone: 0171 404 1313
E-mail:enquiries@doughtystreet.co.uk
Call Date: July 1976, Middle Temple
Pupil Master
Qualifications: [BA (Cantab)]

LATIF MOHAMMED

Equity Chambers
3rd Floor, 153a Corporation Street,
Birmingham B4 6PH,
Telephone: 0121 233 2100
E-mail: equityatusa.com
Call Date: July 1985, Lincoln's Inn
Pupil Master
Qualifications: [BA]

LATIMER ANDREW GERARD

40 King Street
Manchester M2 6BA,
Telephone: 0161 832 9082
E-mail: clerks@40kingstreet.co.uk
The Chambers of Philip Raynor QC
5 Park Place, Leeds LS1 2RU,
Telephone: 0113 242 1123
Call Date: Nov 1995, Gray's Inn
Qualifications: [BA, BCL]

LATIMER-SAYER WILLIAM LAURENCE

2 Mitre Court Buildings
1st Floor, Temple, London EC4Y 7BX,
Telephone: 0171 353 1353
Call Date: Oct 1995, Gray's Inn
Qualifications: [LLB (Leic), MA (Lond)]

LATTER MERTON EDWARD

Clapham Chambers
21-25 Bedford Road, Clapham North,
London SW4 7SH,
Telephone: 0171 978 8482/642 5777
E-mail:claphamchambers@compuserve.co
m
Call Date: Mar 1997, Gray's Inn
Qualifications: [LLB (Leeds)]

LATTIMER MISS JUSTINE ADELE

3 Fountain Court
Steelhouse Lane, Birmingham B4 6DR,
Telephone: 0121 236 5854
Call Date: May 1992, Inner Temple
Qualifications: [BA (Oxon)]

LATTO PAUL STUART

Warwick House Chambers
8 Warwick Court, Gray's Inn, London
WC1R 5DJ, Telephone: 0171 430 2323
E-mail: cdrewlaw@aol.com
Call Date: 1996, Inner Temple
Qualifications: [BA (Oxon), CPE]

LAU MARTIN WILHELM

Essex Court Chambers
24 Lincoln's Inn Fields, London
WC2A 3ED, Telephone: 0171 813 8000
E-mail:clerksroom@essexcourt-chambers.co.u
k
Call Date: Oct 1996, Middle Temple
Qualifications: [MA (Lond), CPE (Lond)]

LAUGHLAND JAMES RUSSELL

1 Temple Gardens
1st Floor, Temple, London EC4Y 9BB,
Telephone: 0171 583 1315/353 0407
E-mail: clerks@1templegardens.co.uk
Call Date: Nov 1991, Inner Temple
Qualifications: [BA (Kent)]

LAUGHTON SAMUEL DENNIS

The Chambers of Leolin Price CBE, QC
10 Old Square, Lincoln's Inn, London
WC2A 3SU, Telephone: 0171 405 0758
Call Date: Feb 1993, Middle Temple
Qualifications: [MA (Cantab), Dip in Law]

LAURENCE GEORGE FREDERICK QC (1991)

12 New Square
Lincoln's Inn, London WC2A 3SW,
Telephone: 0171 419 1212
E-mail: chambers@12newsquare.co.uk
Sovereign Chambers
25 Park Square, Leeds LS1 2PW,
Telephone: 0113 2451841/2/3
E-mail:sovereignchambers@btinternet.com
Call Date: 1972, Middle Temple

Assistant Recorder
Qualifications: [MA (Oxon), BA (Cape Town)]

LAUTERPACHT ELIHU QC (1970)

20 Essex Street
London WC2R 3AL,
Telephone: 0171 583 9294
E-mail: clerks@20essexst.com
Call Date: Nov 1950, Gray's Inn
Qualifications: [MA, LLB (Cantab)]

LAVENDER NICHOLAS

One Hare Court
1st Floor, Temple, London EC4Y 7BE,
Telephone: 020 7353 3171
E-mail:admin-oneharecourt@btinternet.com
Call Date: July 1989, Inner Temple
Pupil Master
Qualifications: [MA (Cantab), BCL (Oxon)]

LAVERS MICHAEL

Dr Johnson's Chambers
Two Dr Johnson's Buildings, Temple,
London EC4Y 7AY,
Telephone: 0171 353 4716
E-mail: clerks@2djb.freeserve.co.uk
Call Date: Oct 1990, Middle Temple
Qualifications: [BA (Sussex), Dip Law (City)]

LAVERY MICHAEL JAMES

24a St John Street
Manchester M3 4DF,
Telephone: 0161 833 9628
Call Date: Feb 1990, Gray's Inn
Qualifications: [LLB (Hons)]

LAW JOHN EDWARD

33 Bedford Row
London WC1R 4JH,
Telephone: 0171 242 6476
E-mail:clerks@bedfordrow33.demon.co.uk
Call Date: Oct 1996, Lincoln's Inn
Qualifications: [BA (Hons)(Oxon), Dip Law (City)]

LAWE MISS SUSAN PATRICIA

Verulam Chambers
Peer House, 8-14 Verulam Street, Gray's
Inn, London WC1X 8LZ,
Telephone: 0171 813 2400
Call Date: July 1982, Middle Temple
Qualifications: [BA (Hons)]

LAWLER SIMON WILLIAM QC (1993)

No. 6
6 Park Square, Leeds LS1 2LW,
Telephone: 0113 2459763
E-mail: chambers@no6.co.uk
11 King's Bench Walk
1st Floor, Temple, London EC4Y 7EQ,
Telephone: 0171 353 3337
E-mail: fmuller11@aol.com
Call Date: Nov 1971, Inner Temple
Qualifications: [LLB]

LAWRENCE DR HEATHER BUNTING ELIZABETH

11 South Square
2nd Floor, Gray's Inn, London
WC1R 5EU,
Telephone: 0171 405 1222 (24hr messaging service)
E-mail: clerks@11southsquare.com
Call Date: Oct 1990, Middle Temple
Pupil Master
Qualifications: [MA, D Phil (Oxon)]

LAWRENCE SIR IVAN JOHN QC (1981)

One Essex Court
1st Floor, Temple, London EC4Y 9AR,
Telephone: 0171 936 3030
E-mail: one.essex_court@virgin.net
Call Date: Feb 1962, Inner Temple
Recorder
Qualifications: [MA (Oxon)]

LAWRENCE NALLATHAMBY MEROLIS KARUPIAH

Call Date: May 1987, Middle Temple
Qualifications: [LLB (Hons)]

LAWRENCE NIGEL STUART

Martins Building
2nd Floor, No 4 Water Street, Liverpool
L2 3SP, Telephone: 0151 236 5818/4919
Call Date: July 1988, Lincoln's Inn
Qualifications: [LLB (Hons) (Leics)]

LAWRENCE MISS PAMELA AVRIL

Albany Chambers
91 Kentish Town Road, London
NW1 8NY, Telephone: 0171 485 5736/
5758 E-mail: albany91.freeserve.co.uk
Call Date: Nov 1975, Inner Temple
Pupil Master
Qualifications: [LLB (Lond)]

LAWRENCE THE HON PATRICK JOHN TRISTRAM

4 Paper Buildings
Ground Floor, Temple, London
EC4Y 7EX, Telephone: 0171 353 3366/
583 7155
E-mail: clerks@4paperbuildings.com
Call Date: Feb 1985, Inner Temple
Pupil Master
Qualifications: [BA (Oxon)]

LAWRENCE MISS RACHEL CAMILLA

One Essex Court
1st Floor, Temple, London EC4Y 9AR,
Telephone: 0171 936 3030
E-mail: one.essex_court@virgin.net
Call Date: Oct 1992, Inner Temple
Qualifications: [LLB (LSE)]

LAWRENSON MRS MARY CHRISTINE

Mitre House Chambers
15-19 Devereux Court, London WC2R 3JJ,
Telephone: 0171 583 8233
Call Date: Nov 1994, Lincoln's Inn
Qualifications: [B.Ed (Hons)(Lanc)_, LLB
(Hons)(Northumb)]

LAWRIE IAN DOUGLAS

Bridewell Chambers
2 Bridewell Place, London EC4V 6AP,
Telephone: 020 7797 8800
E-mail:HughesGage@bridewell.law.co.uk
Call Date: Nov 1985, Gray's Inn
Pupil Master
Qualifications: [LLB (Wark)]

LAWS MISS ELEANOR JANE

5 King's Bench Walk
Temple, London EC4Y 7DN,
Telephone: 0171 353 5638
Call Date: Oct 1990, Inner Temple
Qualifications: [BA (B'ham), Dip Law]

LAWS SIMON REGINALD

Walnut House
63 St David's Hill, Exeter, Devon,
EX4 4DW, Telephone: 01392 279751
E-mail: 106627.2451@compuserve.com
6 King's Bench Walk
Ground Floor, Temple, London
EC4Y 7DR, Telephone: 0171 583 0410
E-mail: worsley@6kbw.freeserve.co.uk
Call Date: Oct 1991, Inner Temple
Qualifications: [BA (York), Dip Law]

LAWSON ANDREW CHARLES

24a St John Street
Manchester M3 4DF,
Telephone: 0161 833 9628
Call Date: Oct 1995, Inner Temple
Qualifications: [BA (Leeds), Dip Law (Lanc)]

LAWSON DANIEL GEORGE

Goldsmith Building
1st Floor, Temple, London EC4Y 7BL,
Telephone: 0171 353 7881
E-mail:clerks@goldsmith-building.law.co.uk
Call Date: Nov 1994, Inner Temple
Qualifications: [BA (Oxon), MA (Lond), CPE]

LAWSON EDMUND JAMES QC (1988)

9-12 Bell Yard
London WC2A 2LF,
Telephone: 0171 400 1800
E-mail: clerks@bellyard.co.uk
Call Date: Feb 1971, Gray's Inn
Qualifications: [BA (Cantab)]

LAWSON MISS ELIZABETH ANN QC (1989)

Cloisters
1 Pump Court, Temple, London
EC4Y 7AA, Telephone: 0171 827 4000
E-mail: clerks@cloisters.com
Call Date: July 1969, Gray's Inn
Qualifications: [LLB]

LAWSON MATTHEW CHRISTOPHER

1 Gray's Inn Square
Ground Floor, London WC1R 5AA,
Telephone: 0171 405 8946/7/8
Call Date: Nov 1995, Gray's Inn
Qualifications: [LLB]

**LAWSON MICHAEL HENRY
QC (1991)**

23 Essex Street
London WC2R 3AS,
Telephone: 0171 413 0353/836 8366
E-mail:clerks@essexstreet23.demon.co.uk
Call Date: Nov 1969, Inner Temple
Recorder
Qualifications: [LLB (Lond)]

LAWSON ROBERT JOHN

4 Essex Court
Temple, London EC4Y 9AJ,
Telephone: 020 7797 7970
E-mail: clerks@4essexcourt.law.co.uk
Call Date: Nov 1989, Inner Temple
Pupil Master
Qualifications: [BA (Oxon), Dip Law (City)]

LAWSON MISS SARA LUCY JANE

18 Red Lion Court
(Off Fleet Street), London EC4A 3EB,
Telephone: 0171 520 6000
E-mail: chambers@18rlc.co.uk
Thornwood House
102 New London Road, Chelmsford,
Essex, CM2 0RG,
Telephone: 01245 280880
E-mail: chambers@18rlc.co.uk
Call Date: Oct 1990, Inner Temple
Qualifications: [LLB]

**LAWSON ROGERS GEORGE STUART
QC (1994)**

23 Essex Street
London WC2R 3AS,
Telephone: 0171 413 0353/836 8366
E-mail:clerks@essexstreet23.demon.co.uk
Call Date: July 1969, Gray's Inn
Recorder
Qualifications: [LLB Hons]

LAWTON PAUL ANTHONY

Lincoln House Chambers
5th Floor, Lincoln House, 1 Brazennose
Street, Manchester M2 5EL,
Telephone: 0161 832 5701
E-mail: info@lincolnhse.co.uk
Call Date: Nov 1987, Lincoln's Inn
Qualifications: [LLB(Hons) Manchester]

LAYNE RONALD BALFOUR ROBERT

12 Old Square
1st Floor, Lincoln's Inn, London
WC2A 3TX, Telephone: 0171 404 0875
Call Date: Oct 1992, Lincoln's Inn
Qualifications: [LLB (Hons)(Lond), LLM
(Comm & Corp)]

**LAYTON ALEXANDER WILLIAM
QC (1995)**

2 Temple Gardens
Temple, London EC4Y 9AY,
Telephone: 0171 583 6041
E-mail: clerks@2templegardens.co.uk
Call Date: July 1976, Middle Temple
Assistant Recorder
Qualifications: [MA (Oxon)]

LAZARUS GRANT PHILIP

Corn Exchange Chambers
5th Floor, Fenwick Street, Liverpool
L2 7QS, Telephone: 0151 227 1081/5009
Call Date: Nov 1981, Gray's Inn
Pupil Master
Qualifications: [LLB (Hons)]

LAZARUS MISS MARY HELEN

22 Old Buildings
Lincoln's Inn, London WC2A 3UJ,
Telephone: 0171 831 0222
Call Date: Oct 1991, Middle Temple
Qualifications: [MA (Cantab), CPE]

LAZARUS MICHAEL STEVEN

1 Crown Office Row
3rd Floor, Temple, London EC4Y 7HH,
Telephone: 0171 583 9292
E-mail: onecor@link.org
Call Date: Nov 1987, Middle Temple
Pupil Master
Qualifications: [MA (Cantab)]

LE BROCQ MARK WILLIAM

Nicholas Street Chambers
22 Nicholas Street, Chester CH1 2NX,
Telephone: 01244 323886
E-mail: clerks@40king.co.uk
Call Date: Nov 1982, Middle Temple
Pupil Master
Qualifications: [MA (Cantab)]

LE CORNU PHILIP JOHN

St Philip's Chambers
Fountain Court, Steelhouse Lane,
Birmingham B4 6DR,
Telephone: 0121 246 7000
E-mail: clerks@st-philips.co.uk
Call Date: Oct 1992, Middle Temple
Qualifications: [LL.B (Hons, B'ham)]

LE FOE MISS SARAH HARRIET

1 Inner Temple Lane
Temple, London EC4Y 1AF,
Telephone: 020 7353 0933
Call Date: Nov 1989, Middle Temple
Qualifications: [BA (Hons, Lond), Dip in
Law]

LE GRICE VALENTINE

1 Mitre Court Buildings
Temple, London EC4Y 7BS,
Telephone: 0171 797 7070
E-mail: clerks@1mcb.com
Southernhay Chambers
33 Southernhay East, Exeter, Devon,
EX1 1NX, Telephone: 01392 255777
E-mail:southernhay.chambers@lineone.net
Call Date: July 1977, Middle Temple
Qualifications: [BA (Dunelm)]

LE POIDEVIN NICHOLAS PETER

12 New Square
Lincoln's Inn, London WC2A 3SW,
Telephone: 0171 419 1212
E-mail: chambers@12newsquare.co.uk
Sovereign Chambers
25 Park Square, Leeds LS1 2PW,
Telephone: 0113 2451841/2/3
E-mail:sovereignchambers@btinternet.com
Call Date: Nov 1975, Middle Temple
Pupil Master
Qualifications: [MA, LLB (Cantab)]

LE PREVOST MRS AVIVA

Westgate Chambers
144 High Street, Lewes, East Sussex,
BN7 1XT, Telephone: 01273 480510
Maidstone Chambers
33 Earl Street, Maidstone, Kent, ME14 1PF,
Telephone: 01622 688592
E-mail:maidstonechambers@compuserve.com
Call Date: Nov 1990, Inner Temple
Qualifications: [BA (Manch), Dip Law (PCL)]

LE QUESNE MS CATHERINE MARY

**7 Stone Buildings (also at 11 Bolt
Court)**
1st Floor, Lincoln's Inn, London
WC2A 3SZ, Telephone: 0171 242 0961
E-mail:larthur@7stonebuildings.law.co.uk
**11 Bolt Court (also at 7 Stone Buildings
– 1st Floor)**
London EC4A 3DQ,
Telephone: 0171 353 2300
E-mail: boltct11@aol.com
Redhill Chambers
Seloduct House, 30 Station Road, Redhill,
Surrey, RH1 1NF,
Telephone: 01737 780781
Call Date: Nov 1993, Inner Temple
Qualifications: [BA (Manc), Dip in Periodical,
Journalism, CPE (City)]

LE QUESNE SIR JOHN GODFRAY QC (1962)

1 Crown Office Row
3rd Floor, Temple, London EC4Y 7HH,
Telephone: 0171 583 9292
E-mail: onecor@link.org
Call Date: Nov 1947, Inner Temple
Qualifications: [MA (Oxon)]

LEA JEREMY HUGH CHALONER

St Mary's Chambers
50 High Pavement, Lace Market,
Nottingham NG1 1HW,
Telephone: 0115 9503503
E-mail: clerks@smc.law.co.uk
Call Date: July 1978, Middle Temple
Pupil Master
Qualifications: [BA, LLB (Sussex)]

LEACH ROBIN ANTHONY LANGLEY

2 Harcourt Buildings
1st Floor, Temple, London EC4Y 9DB,
Telephone: 020 7353 2112
Call Date: July 1979, Lincoln's Inn
Pupil Master
Qualifications: [MA (St Andrews)]

LEADBETTER IAIN WILLIAM

Walnut House
63 St David's Hill, Exeter, Devon,
EX4 4DW, Telephone: 01392 279751
E-mail: 106627.2451@compuserve.com
Call Date: Nov 1975, Middle Temple
Pupil Master
Qualifications: [LLB (So'ton)]

LEADER PROFESSOR SHELDON LAWRENCE

33 Bedford Row
London WC1R 4JH,
Telephone: 0171 242 6476
E-mail:clerks@bedfordrow33.demon.co.uk
Call Date: May 1980, Gray's Inn
Qualifications: [BA (Yale), BA, DPhil, (Oxon)]

LEADER TIMOTHY JAMES

3 Fountain Court
Steelhouse Lane, Birmingham B4 6DR,
Telephone: 0121 236 5854
Call Date: Oct 1994, Middle Temple
Qualifications: [BSc (Hons)(B'ham), MA (Sheff), CPE (B'ham)]

LEAFE DANIEL JOHN

Albion Chambers
Broad Street, Bristol BS1 1DR,
Telephone: 0117 9272144
Call Date: Nov 1996, Gray's Inn
Qualifications: [LLB (Bris)]

LEASON MS KAREN DAWN

St Philip's Chambers
Fountain Court, Steelhouse Lane,
Birmingham B4 6DR,
Telephone: 0121 246 7000
E-mail: clerks@st-philips.co.uk
Call Date: 1997, Inner Temple
Qualifications: [LLB (Wolverhampton)]

LEATHLEY DAVID JONATHAN

Windsor Chambers
2 Penuel Lane, Pontypridd, South Wales,
CF37 4UF, Telephone: 01443 402067
E-mail: law@windsorchambers.co.uk
Call Date: 1980, Lincoln's Inn
Pupil Master
Qualifications: [LLB (Hons)(B'ham)]

LEAVER PETER LAWRENCE OPPENHEIM QC (1987)

One Essex Court
Ground Floor, Temple, London
EC4Y 9AR, Telephone: 020 7583 2000
E-mail: clerks@oneessexcourt.co.uk
Call Date: July 1967, Lincoln's Inn
Assistant Recorder

LEBASCI MS JETSUN RYONEN

St John's Chambers
Small Street, Bristol BS1 1DW,
Telephone: 0117 9213456/298514
E-mail: @stjohnschambers.co.uk
Call Date: July 1995, Inner Temple
Qualifications: [LLB (Wales)]

LECKIE DAVID ERIC WILLIAM

Hardwicke Building
New Square, Lincoln's Inn, London
WC2A 3SB, Telephone: 020 7242 2523
E-mail: clerks@hardwicke.co.uk
Call Date: Oct 1994, Gray's Inn
Qualifications: [LLB (Hons)]

LECKIE JAMES HARRY LAIRD

Westleigh Chambers
Westleigh Wiltown, Curry Rivel, Langport,
Somerset, TA10 OJE,
Telephone: 01458 251261
E-mail: jhlleckie@aol.com
Verulam Chambers
Peer House, 8-14 Verulam Street, Gray's
Inn, London WC1X 8LZ,
Telephone: 0171 813 2400
Cathedral Chambers (Jan Wood Independent Barristers' Clerk)
1 Maple Road, Exeter, Devon, EX4 1BN,
Telephone: 01392 210900
E-mail:cathedral.chambers@eclipse.co.uk
Call Date: June 1964, Gray's Inn
Qualifications: [MA, LLM, FCIArb]

LECOINTE MS ELPHA MARY

4 Brick Court
Ground Floor, Temple, London
EC4Y 9AD, Telephone: 0171 797 7766
E-mail: chambers@4brick.co.uk
Call Date: Nov 1988, Lincoln's Inn
Pupil Master
Qualifications: [LLB Hons]

LEDERMAN DAVID QC (1990)

18 Red Lion Court
(Off Fleet Street), London EC4A 3EB,
Telephone: 0171 520 6000
E-mail: chambers@18rlc.co.uk
Thornwood House
102 New London Road, Chelmsford,
Essex, CM2 0RG,
Telephone: 01245 280880
E-mail: chambers@18rlc.co.uk
Call Date: July 1966, Inner Temple
Recorder
Qualifications: [BA (Cantab)]

LEDERMAN HOWARD DAVID

22 Old Buildings
Lincoln's Inn, London WC2A 3UJ,
Telephone: 0171 831 0222
Call Date: July 1982, Gray's Inn
Pupil Master
Qualifications: [BA (Hons) (Oxon)]

LEE DAVID CHARLES

Chambers of Michael Pert QC
36 Bedford Row, London WC1R 4JH,
Telephone: 0171 421 8000
E-mail: 36bedfordrow@link.org
Chambers of Michael Pert QC
24 Albion Place, Northampton NN1 1UD,
Telephone: 01604 602333
Chambers of Michael Pert QC
104 New Walk, Leicester LE1 7EA,
Telephone: 0116 249 2020
Call Date: July 1973, Gray's Inn
Pupil Master
Qualifications: [BA (Cantab), BA (Har]

LEE IAN

Devereux Chambers
Devereux Court, London WC2R 3JJ,
Telephone: 0171 353 7534
E-mail: mailbox@devchambers.co.uk
Call Date: July 1973, Gray's Inn
Qualifications: [LLM]

LEE JOHN MICHAEL HUBERT

Bell Yard Chambers
116/118 Chancery Lane, London
WC2A 1PP, Telephone: 0171 306 9292
Call Date: May 1960, Middle Temple
Pupil Master

LEE JONATHAN JAMES WILTON

Keating Chambers
10 Essex Street, Outer Temple, London
WC2R 3AA, Telephone: 0171 544 2600
Call Date: Oct 1993, Gray's Inn
Qualifications: [B.Eng (Sheff)]

LEE MISS KRISTA CHUI LAN

2 Temple Gardens
Temple, London EC4Y 9AY,
Telephone: 0171 583 6041
E-mail: clerks@2templegardens.co.uk
Call Date: 1996, Lincoln's Inn
Qualifications: [BA (Hons)(Oxon)]

LEE MICHAEL HAL

10 King's Bench Walk
1st Floor, Temple, London EC4Y 7EB,
Telephone: 0171 353 2501
Call Date: July 1987, Middle Temple
Qualifications: [BA (Cal) JD (USA), LLM
(LSE)]

LEE RICHARD THOMAS

5 Fountain Court
Steelhouse Lane, Birmingham B4 6DR,
Telephone: 0121 606 0500
E-mail:clerks@5fountaincourt.law.co.uk
Call Date: May 1993, Gray's Inn
Qualifications: [LLB (Belfast)]

LEE ROSSLYN ALEXANDER

York Chambers
14 Toft Green, York YO1 6JT,
Telephone: 01904 620048
E-mail: [name]@yorkchambers.co.uk
Call Date: Nov 1987, Gray's Inn
Qualifications: [BA, MA (Oxon)]

LEE MISS SARAH JOANNE

Brick Court Chambers
7-8 Essex Street, London WC2R 3LD,
Telephone: 0171 379 3550
E-mail: [surname]@brickcourt.co.uk
Call Date: Nov 1990, Middle Temple
Qualifications: [BA, BCL (Oxon)]

LEE MISS TARYN JANE

37 Park Square Chambers
37 Park Square, Leeds LS1 2NY,
Telephone: 0113 2439422
E-mail: chambers@no37.co.uk
Call Date: July 1992, Inner Temple
Qualifications: [LLB]

LEECH BENEDICT

3 Paper Buildings
Temple, London EC4Y 7EU,
Telephone: 020 7583 8055
E-mail: London@3paper.com
3 Paper Buildings (Bournemouth)
20 Lorne Park Road, Bournemouth,
Dorset, BH1 1JN,
Telephone: 01202 292102
E-mail: Bournemouth@3paper.com
3 Paper Buildings (Winchester)
4 St Peter Street, Winchester SO23 8BW,
Telephone: 01962 868884
E-mail: winchester@3paper.com
3 Paper Buildings (Oxford)
1 Alfred Street, High Street, Oxford
OX1 4EH, Telephone: 01865 793736
E-mail: oxford@3paper.com
Call Date: 1997, Inner Temple
Qualifications: [BA (Cantab), CPE]

LEECH BRIAN WALTER THOMAS

No. 1 Serjeants' Inn
5th Floor Fleet Street, Temple, London
EC4Y 1LH, Telephone: 0171 415 6666
E-mail:no1serjeantsinn@btinternet.com
Call Date: Nov 1967, Middle Temple
Pupil Master, Recorder

LEECH GEOFFREY ANTHONY

Advolex Chambers
70 Coulsdon Road, Coulsdon, Surrey,
CR5 2LB, Telephone: 0181 763 2345
Call Date: Nov 1992, Lincoln's Inn
Qualifications: [BSc (Hons)(Lough), CPE
(City)]

LEECH STEWART

Queen Elizabeth Building
2nd Floor, Temple, London EC4Y 9BS,
Telephone: 0171 797 7837
Call Date: Oct 1992, Lincoln's Inn
Qualifications: [MA(Oxon)]

LEECH THOMAS ALEXANDER CRISPIN

9 Old Square
Ground Floor, Lincoln's Inn, London
WC2A 3SR, Telephone: 0171 405 4682
E-mail: chambers@9oldsquare.co.uk
Call Date: Nov 1988, Middle Temple
Pupil Master
Qualifications: [MA, BCL (Oxon)]

LEEK MISS SAMANTHA LOUISE

5 Essex Court
1st Floor, Temple, London EC4Y 9AH,
Telephone: 0171 410 2000
E-mail: barristers@5essexcourt.co.uk
Call Date: Oct 1993, Gray's Inn
Qualifications: [BA (Oxon)]

LEEMING IAN QC (1988)

Chambers of John Hand QC
9 St John Street, Manchester M3 4DN,
Telephone: 0161 955 9000
E-mail: ninesjs@gconnect.com
Lamb Chambers
Lamb Building, Temple, London
EC4Y 7AS, Telephone: 020 7797 8300
E-mail: lambchambers@link.org
Call Date: Nov 1970, Gray's Inn
Recorder
Qualifications: [LLB (Manch)]

LEEMING MICHAEL PETER GEORGE

Chambers of John Hand QC
9 St John Street, Manchester M3 4DN,
Telephone: 0161 955 9000
E-mail: ninesjs@gconnect.com
Call Date: July 1983, Inner Temple
Qualifications: [LLB (Hons) (Leeds)]

LEEPER THOMAS RICHARD GEOFFREY

35 Essex Street
Temple, London WC2R 3AR,
Telephone: 0171 353 6381
E-mail: derek_jenkins@link.org
Call Date: Nov 1991, Middle Temple
Qualifications: [BA Hons (Dunelm)]

LEES ANDREW JAMES

St Paul's House
5th Floor, St Paul's House, 23 Park Square
South, Leeds LS1 2ND,
Telephone: 0113 2455866
E-mail: catherinegrimshaw@stpauls-
chambers.demon.co.uk
Call Date: July 1984, Gray's Inn
Pupil Master
Qualifications: [LLB (Liverpool)]

LEES MISS PATRICIA SUSAN VIRGINIA

Furnival Chambers
32 Furnival Street, London EC4A 1JQ,
Telephone: 0171 405 3232
E-mail: clerks@furnivallaw.co.uk
Call Date: Nov 1988, Lincoln's Inn
Qualifications: [LLB Hons]

LEESING MS SARAH

Devon Chambers
3 St Andrew Street, Plymouth PL1 2AH,
Telephone: 01752 661659
E-mail: devonchambers.co.uk.
Call Date: Oct 1997, Inner Temple
Qualifications: [BA (York), CPE]

LEGARD EDWARD THOMAS

York Chambers
14 Toft Green, York YO1 6JT,
Telephone: 01904 620048
E-mail: [name]@yorkchambers.co.uk
Call Date: Oct 1996, Gray's Inn
Qualifications: [MA (St Andrews)]

LEGGATT GEORGE ANDREW MIDSOMER QC (1997)

Brick Court Chambers
7-8 Essex Street, London WC2R 3LD,
Telephone: 0171 379 3550
E-mail: [surname]@brickcourt.co.uk
Call Date: July 1983, Middle Temple
Qualifications: [MA (Cantab)]

LEGGE HENRY

5 Stone Buildings
Lincoln's Inn, London WC2A 3XT,
Telephone: 0171 242 6201
E-mail:clerks@5-stonebuildings.law.co.uk
Call Date: Nov 1993, Middle Temple
Qualifications: [MA (Hons)(Oxon), CPE
(City)]

LEGH-JONES PIERS NICHOLAS QC (1987)

20 Essex Street
London WC2R 3AL,
Telephone: 0171 583 9294
E-mail: clerks@20essexst.com
Call Date: Nov 1968, Lincoln's Inn
Qualifications: [MA (Oxon)]

LEIGH CHRISTOPHER HUMPHREY DE VERD QC (1989)

1 Paper Buildings
1st Floor, Temple, London EC4Y 7EP,
Telephone: 0171 353 3728/4953
Call Date: Nov 1967, Lincoln's Inn
Recorder

LEIGH EDWARD JULIAN EGERTON

Goldsmith Chambers
Ground Floor, Goldsmith Building,
Temple, London EC4Y 7BL,
Telephone: 0171 353 6802/3/4/5
E-mail:clerks@goldsmithchambers.law.co.uk
Call Date: Nov 1977, Inner Temple
Qualifications: [BA (Dunelm)]

LEIGH KEVIN

6 Pump Court
1st Floor, Temple, London EC4Y 7AR,
Telephone: 0171 797 8400
E-mail: clerks@6pumpcourt.co.uk

Regency Chambers
Cathedral Square, Peterborough
PE1 1XW, Telephone: 01733 315215
Westgate Chambers
144 High Street, Lewes, East Sussex,
BN7 1XT, Telephone: 01273 480510
6-8 Mill Street
Maidstone, Kent, ME15 6XH,
Telephone: 01622 688094
E-mail: annexe@6pumpcourt.co.uk
Call Date: July 1986, Lincoln's Inn
Pupil Master
Qualifications: [LLB (Leics)]

LEIGH MISS SAMANTHA CERI

East Anglian Chambers
52 North Hill, Colchester, Essex, CO1 1PY,
Telephone: 01206 572756
E-mail: colchester@ealaw.co.uk
East Anglian Chambers
57 London Street, Norwich NR2 1HL,
Telephone: 01603 617351
E-mail: norwich@ealaw.co.uk
East Anglian Chambers
Gresham House, 5 Museum Street,
Ipswich, Suffolk, IP1 1HQ,
Telephone: 01473 214481
E-mail: ipswich@ealaw.co.uk
Call Date: Nov 1995, Inner Temple
Qualifications: [BA (Essex), CPE]

LEIGH MISS SARAH SIOBHAN

Nicholas Street Chambers
22 Nicholas Street, Chester CH1 2NX,
Telephone: 01244 323886
E-mail: clerks@40king.co.uk
Call Date: July 1983, Inner Temple
Pupil Master
Qualifications: [LLB (Hull)]

LEIGH-MORGAN (DAVID) PAUL

Fenners Chambers
3 Madingley Road, Cambridge CB3 0EE,
Telephone: 01223 368761
E-mail: clerks@fennerschambers.co.uk
Fenners Chambers
8-12 Priestgate, Peterborough PE1 1JA,
Telephone: 01733 562030
E-mail: clerks@fennerschambers.co.uk
Call Date: Nov 1978, Gray's Inn
Qualifications: [LLB (Exon)]

LEIGHTON PETER LEONARD

2 Gray's Inn Square Chambers
2nd Floor, Gray's Inn, London WC1R 5AA,
Telephone: 020 7242 0328
E-mail: clerks@2gis.co.uk
Call Date: July 1966, Inner Temple
Pupil Master
Qualifications: [LLB (Lond)]

LEIPER RICHARD THOMAS

11 King's Bench Walk
Temple, London EC4Y 7EQ,
Telephone: 0171 632 8500/583 0610
E-mail: clerksroom@11kbw.com
Call Date: Oct 1996, Gray's Inn
Qualifications: [LLB (B'ham), M.Iuris
(Oxon)]

LEIST IAN DOUGLAS

1 Hare Court
Ground Floor, Temple, London
EC4Y 7BE, Telephone: 0171 353 3982/
5324
Call Date: July 1981, Inner Temple
Pupil Master
Qualifications: [BA]

LEMMY MICHAEL DAVID

Old Colony House
6 South King Street, Manchester M2 6DQ,
Telephone: 0161 834 4364
Call Date: Nov 1994, Middle Temple
Qualifications: [LLB (Hons)]

LEMON MISS JANE KATHERINE

Keating Chambers
10 Essex Street, Outer Temple, London
WC2R 3AA, Telephone: 0171 544 2600
Call Date: Nov 1993, Inner Temple
Qualifications: [BA (Hons), CPE]

LEMON ROY

Devereux Chambers
Devereux Court, London WC2R 3JJ,
Telephone: 0171 353 7534
E-mail: mailbox@devchambers.co.uk
Call Date: July 1970, Gray's Inn
Pupil Master
Qualifications: [LLB]

LENNARD STEPHEN CHARLES

Hardwicke Building
New Square, Lincoln's Inn, London
WC2A 3SB, Telephone: 020 7242 2523
E-mail: clerks@hardwicke.co.uk
Call Date: July 1976, Gray's Inn
Pupil Master, Assistant Recorder
Qualifications: [LLB (Manch), Dip Crim
(Cantab)]

LENNON DESMOND JOSEPH

25-27 Castle Street
1st Floor, Liverpool L2 4TA,
Telephone: 0151 227 5661/051 236 5072
Call Date: Nov 1986, Gray's Inn
Qualifications: [BA]

LENNON JOHN FRANCIS

1 Gray's Inn Square
Ground Floor, London WC1R 5AA,
Telephone: 0171 405 8946/7/8
Call Date: Mar 1997, Lincoln's Inn
Qualifications: [BA (Hons)]

LENON ANDREW RALPH FITZMAURICE

One Essex Court
Ground Floor, Temple, London
EC4Y 9AR, Telephone: 020 7583 2000
E-mail: clerks@oneessexcourt.co.uk
Call Date: Nov 1982, Lincoln's Inn
Pupil Master
Qualifications: [BA (Oxon), Dip Law (City)]

LEON MARC EDWARD

Lloyds House Chambers
3rd Floor, 18 Lloyds House, Lloyd Street,
Manchester M2 5WA,
Telephone: 0161 839 3371
Call Date: May 1988, Middle Temple
Qualifications: [LLB (Hons)]

LEONARD ANTHONY JAMES QC (1999)

6 King's Bench Walk
Ground Floor, Temple, London
EC4Y 7DR, Telephone: 0171 583 0410
E-mail: worsley@6kbw.freeserve.co.uk
Call Date: 1978, Inner Temple
Pupil Master, Assistant Recorder

LEONARD CHARLES ROBERT WESTON

Goldsmith Building
1st Floor, Temple, London EC4Y 7BL,
Telephone: 0171 353 7881
E-mail:clerks@goldsmith-building.law.co.uk
Call Date: July 1976, Inner Temple
Pupil Master
Qualifications: [BA (Dublin)]

LEONARD MS EDNA JEAN

King Charles House
Standard Hill, Nottingham NG1 6FX,
Telephone: 0115 9418851
E-mail: clerks@kch.co.uk
Call Date: Oct 1992, Gray's Inn
Qualifications: [BSc Hons (Oxon)]

LEONARD JAMES ALEXANDER

2 King's Bench Walk
Ground Floor, Temple, London
EC4Y 7DE, Telephone: 0171 353 1746
E-mail: 2kbw@atlas.co.uk
King's Bench Chambers
115 North Hill, Plymouth PL4 8JY,
Telephone: 01752 221551
Call Date: Nov 1989, Inner Temple
Qualifications: [BA]

LEREGO MICHAEL JOHN QC (1995)

Fountain Court
Temple, London EC4Y 9DH,
Telephone: 0171 583 3335
E-mail: chambers@fountaincourt.co.uk
Call Date: July 1972, Inner Temple
Qualifications: [MA (Oxon), BCL, FCIArb]

LESLIE NIGEL TERENCE

Chambers of Harjit Singh
Ground Floor, 2 Middle Temple Lane,
Temple, London EC4Y 9AA,
Telephone: 0171 353 1356 (4 Lines)
Call Date: Nov 1994, Gray's Inn
Qualifications: [BA (Sheff)]

D

LESLIE STEPHEN WINDSOR QC (1993)

2-4 Tudor Street
London EC4Y 0AA,
Telephone: 0171 797 7111
E-mail: clerks@rfqc.co.uk
Call Date: Feb 1971, Lincoln's Inn
Qualifications: [LLB (Lond)]

LESTER OF HERNE HILL LORD QC (1975)

Blackstone Chambers
Blackstone House, Temple, London
EC4Y 9BW, Telephone: 0171 583 1770
E-mail:clerks@blackstonechambers.com
Call Date: Feb 1963, Lincoln's Inn
Qualifications: [BA (Cantab), LLM (Harvard)]

LETHBRIDGE MISS NEMONE SUSAN

2nd Floor, Francis Taylor Building
Temple, London EC4Y 7BY,
Telephone: 0171 353 9942/3157
Call Date: June 1956, Gray's Inn
Pupil Master
Qualifications: [BA (Oxon)]

LETMAN PAUL ST JOHN

3 Paper Buildings
Temple, London EC4Y 7EU,
Telephone: 020 7583 8055
E-mail: London@3paper.com
3 Paper Buildings (Bournemouth)
20 Lorne Park Road, Bournemouth,
Dorset, BH1 1JN,
Telephone: 01202 292102
E-mail: Bournemouth@3paper.com
3 Paper Buildings (Winchester)
4 St Peter Street, Winchester SO23 8BW,
Telephone: 01962 868884
E-mail: winchester@3paper.com
3 Paper Buildings (Oxford)
1 Alfred Street, High Street, Oxford
OX1 4EH, Telephone: 01865 793736
E-mail: oxford@3paper.com
Call Date: Nov 1987, Middle Temple
Qualifications: [BSc, Dip Law]

LETT HUGH BRIAN GORDON

South Western Chambers
Melville House, 12 Middle Street,
Taunton, Somerset, TA1 1SH,
Telephone: 01823 331919 (24 hrs)
E-mail: barclerk@clara.net
Call Date: Nov 1971, Inner Temple
Pupil Master, Recorder

LEVENE MISS JACQUELINE DIANE

3 Temple Gardens
3rd Floor, Temple, London EC4Y 9AU,
Telephone: 0171 583 0010
Call Date: Nov 1970, Inner Temple
Pupil Master
Qualifications: [LLB (Lond)]

LEVENE SIMON

199 Strand
London WC2R 1DR,
Telephone: 0171 379 9779
E-mail: chambers@199strand.co.uk
Call Date: July 1977, Middle Temple
Pupil Master, Assistant Recorder
Qualifications: [MA (Cantab)]

LEVENE VICTOR

1 Gray's Inn Square
Ground Floor, London WC1R 5AA,
Telephone: 0171 405 8946/7/8
Call Date: Nov 1961, Middle Temple
Pupil Master
Qualifications: [LLB]

LEVER THE HON BERNARD LEWIS

Peel Court Chambers
45 Hardman Street, Manchester M3 3PL,
Telephone: 0161 832 3791
E-mail: clerks@peelct.co.uk
Harcourt Chambers
1st Floor, 2 Harcourt Buildings, Temple,
London EC4Y 9DB,
Telephone: 0171 353 6961
E-mail:clerks@harcourtchambers.law.co.uk
Call Date: July 1975, Middle Temple
Pupil Master, Recorder
Qualifications: [MA (Oxon)]

LEVER JEREMY FREDERICK QC (1972)

Monckton Chambers
4 Raymond Buildings, Gray's Inn, London
WC1R 5BP, Telephone: 0171 405 7211
E-mail: chambers@monckton.co.uk
Call Date: Nov 1957, Gray's Inn
Qualifications: [MA (Oxon)]

LEVER JOHN

Nicholas Street Chambers
22 Nicholas Street, Chester CH1 2NX,
Telephone: 01244 323886
E-mail: clerks@40king.co.uk
*Call Date: Nov 1978, Middle Temple
Pupil Master*
Qualifications: [LLB (L'pool)]

LEVESON BRIAN HENRY QC (1986)

22 Old Buildings
Lincoln's Inn, London WC2A 3UJ,
Telephone: 0171 831 0222
Byrom Street Chambers
Byrom Street, Manchester M3 4PF,
Telephone: 0161 829 2100
E-mail: Byromst25@aol.com
*Call Date: Nov 1970, Middle Temple
Recorder*
Qualifications: [MA (Oxon)]

LEVETT MARTYN NEALE

East Anglian Chambers
52 North Hill, Colchester, Essex, CO1 1PY,
Telephone: 01206 572756
E-mail: colchester@ealaw.co.uk
East Anglian Chambers
57 London Street, Norwich NR2 1HL,
Telephone: 01603 617351
E-mail: norwich@ealaw.co.uk
East Anglian Chambers
Gresham House, 5 Museum Street,
Ipswich, Suffolk, IP1 1HQ,
Telephone: 01473 214481
E-mail: ipswich@ealaw.co.uk
*Call Date: Nov 1978, Middle Temple
Pupil Master*
Qualifications: [BSc (Leeds)]

LEVIN CRAIG MICHAEL

Lancaster Building
77 Deansgate, Manchester M3 2BW,
Telephone: 0161 661 4444/0171 649 9872
E-mail: sandra@lbnipc.com
Call Date: July 1997, Lincoln's Inn
Qualifications: [BA, LLB, (Witwatersrand)]

LEVINE STEVEN ADRIAN

Lloyds House Chambers
3rd Floor, 18 Lloyds House, Lloyd Street,
Manchester M2 5WA,
Telephone: 0161 839 3371
Call Date: Nov 1989, Lincoln's Inn
Qualifications: [LLB (Hons), LLM (Lond)]

LEVINSON JUSTIN MAURICE

1 Dr Johnson's Buildings
Ground Floor, Temple, London
EC4Y 7AX, Telephone: 0171 353 9328
E-mail:OneDr.Johnsons@btinternet.com
Call Date: Oct 1994, Middle Temple
Qualifications: [LLB (Hons)]

LEVISEUR NICHOLAS TEMPLAR

3 Paper Buildings
Temple, London EC4Y 7EU,
Telephone: 020 7583 8055
E-mail: London@3paper.com
3 Paper Buildings (Bournemouth)
20 Lorne Park Road, Bournemouth,
Dorset, BH1 1JN,
Telephone: 01202 292102
E-mail: Bournemouth@3paper.com
3 Paper Buildings (Winchester)
4 St Peter Street, Winchester SO23 8BW,
Telephone: 01962 868884
E-mail: winchester@3paper.com
3 Paper Buildings (Oxford)
1 Alfred Street, High Street, Oxford
OX1 4EH, Telephone: 01865 793736
E-mail: oxford@3paper.com
*Call Date: Nov 1979, Gray's Inn
Pupil Master*
Qualifications: [MA(Oxon)]

LEVITT MISS ALISON FRANCES JOSEPHINE

3 Gray's Inn Square
Ground Floor, London WC1R 5AH,
Telephone: 0171 520 5600
E-mail: clerks@3gis.co.uk
Call Date: July 1988, Inner Temple
Pupil Master
Qualifications: [MA (St Andrews), Dip Law]

LEVY ALLAN EDWARD QC (1989)

17 Bedford Row
London WC1R 4EB,
Telephone: 0171 831 7314
E-mail: iboard7314@aol.com
Call Date: Nov 1969, Inner Temple
Recorder
Qualifications: [LLB]

LEVY ANTHONY JULIAN

2 King's Bench Walk Chambers
1st Floor, 2 King's Bench Walk, Temple,
London EC4Y 7DE,
Telephone: 020 7353 9276
E-mail: chambers@2kbw.co.uk
Call Date: Nov 1983, Middle Temple
Qualifications: [LLB]

LEVY BENJAMIN KEITH

Enterprise Chambers
9 Old Square, Lincoln's Inn, London
WC2A 3SR, Telephone: 0171 405 9471
E-mail:enterprise.london@dial.pipex.com
Enterprise Chambers
38 Park Square, Leeds LS1 2PA,
Telephone: 0113 246 0391
E-mail:enterprise.leeds@dial.pipex.com
Enterprise Chambers
65 Quayside, Newcastle upon Tyne
NE1 3DS, Telephone: 0191 222 3344
E-mail:enterprise.newcastle@dial.pipex.com
Call Date: Nov 1956, Lincoln's Inn
Pupil Master
Qualifications: [MA, LLB (Cantab)]

LEVY GERALD

Blackstone Chambers
Blackstone House, Temple, London
EC4Y 9BW, Telephone: 0171 583 1770
E-mail:clerks@blackstonechambers.com
Call Date: Apr 1964, Gray's Inn
Qualifications: [MA (Oxon)]

LEVY JACOB

9 Gough Square
London EC4A 3DE,
Telephone: 020 7832 0500
E-mail: clerks@9goughsq.co.uk
Call Date: July 1986, Inner Temple
Pupil Master
Qualifications: [LLB (Lond)]

LEVY MISS JULIETTE

New Court
Temple, London EC4Y 9BE,
Telephone: 0171 583 5123/0510
Call Date: Nov 1992, Middle Temple
Qualifications: [BA (Hons), MA (Lond)]

LEVY MICHAEL PETER

3 Hare Court
1 Little Essex Street, London WC2R 3LD,
Telephone: 0171 395 2000
Call Date: Nov 1979, Gray's Inn
Pupil Master
Qualifications: [LLB Hons]

LEVY NEIL HOWARD

St John's Chambers
Small Street, Bristol BS1 1DW,
Telephone: 0117 9213456/298514
E-mail: @stjohnschambers.co.uk
Call Date: July 1986, Lincoln's Inn
Pupil Master
Qualifications: [LLB (Exeter)]

LEVY PHILIP GRENVILLE

3 Temple Gardens
2nd Floor, Temple, London EC4Y 9AU,
Telephone: 0171 583 1155
Call Date: Nov 1968, Inner Temple
Pupil Master
Qualifications: [LLB (Manch)]

LEVY ROBERT STUART

9 Stone Buildings
Lincoln's Inn, London WC2A 3NN,
Telephone: 0171 404 5055
E-mail: clerks@9stoneb.law.co.uk

D

Assize Court Chambers
14 Small Street, Bristol BS1 1DE,
Telephone: 0117 9264587
E-mail:chambers@assize-court-chambers.co.uk
Call Date: Nov 1988, Middle Temple
Pupil Master
Qualifications: [LLB, LLM (Cantab)]

LEWER MICHAEL EDWARD QC (1983)

Farrar's Building
Temple, London EC4Y 7BD,
Telephone: 0171 583 9241
E-mail:chambers@farrarsbuilding.co.uk
Call Date: June 1958, Gray's Inn
Recorder
Qualifications: [MA (Oxon)]

LEWERS NIGEL CHRISTOPHER

12 King's Bench Walk
Temple, London EC4Y 7EL,
Telephone: 0171 583 0811
E-mail: chambers@12kbw.co.uk
Call Date: Nov 1986, Gray's Inn
Pupil Master
Qualifications: [BA(Oxon)]

LEWIN LT CDR NICHOLAS ANTON

2 King's Bench Walk
Ground Floor, Temple, London
EC4Y 7DE, Telephone: 0171 353 1746
E-mail: 2kbw@atlas.co.uk
King's Bench Chambers
115 North Hill, Plymouth PL4 8JY,
Telephone: 01752 221551
Call Date: July 1989, Gray's Inn
Qualifications: [BA]

LEWIS ADAM VALENTINE SHERVEY

Blackstone Chambers
Blackstone House, Temple, London
EC4Y 9BW, Telephone: 0171 583 1770
E-mail:clerks@blackstonechambers.com
Call Date: July 1985, Gray's Inn
Pupil Master
Qualifications: [MA (Cantab)]

LEWIS ANDREW SIMON

Francis Taylor Building
Ground Floor, Temple, London
EC4Y 7BY, Telephone: 0171 353 7768/
7769/2711
E-mail:clerks@francistaylorbuilding.law.co.uk
Call Date: Nov 1986, Middle Temple
Pupil Master
Qualifications: [BA(Oxon)]

LEWIS ANDREW WILLIAM

Sovereign Chambers
25 Park Square, Leeds LS1 2PW,
Telephone: 0113 2451841/2/3
E-mail:sovereignchambers@btinternet.com
Call Date: July 1985, Lincoln's Inn
Pupil Master
Qualifications: [BA]

LEWIS MS ANYA LOUISE

Two Garden Court
1st Floor, Middle Temple, London
EC4Y 9BL, Telephone: 0171 353 1633
E-mail:barristers@2gardenct.law.co.uk
Call Date: 1997, Inner Temple
Qualifications: [LLB (So'ton)]

LEWIS CHARLES JAMES

Old Square Chambers
1 Verulam Buildings, Gray's Inn, London
WC1R 5LQ, Telephone: 0171 269 0300
E-mail:clerks@oldsquarechambers.co.uk
Old Square Chambers
Hanover House, 47 Corn Street, Bristol
BS1 1HT, Telephone: 0117 9277111
E-mail: oldsqbri@globalnet.co.uk
Call Date: July 1963, Inner Temple
Qualifications: [MA (Oxon)]

LEWIS CHARLES WILLIAM

Chambers of Michael Pert QC
36 Bedford Row, London WC1R 4JH,
Telephone: 0171 421 8000
E-mail: 36bedfordrow@link.org
Chambers of Michael Pert QC
24 Albion Place, Northampton NN1 1UD,
Telephone: 01604 602333
Chambers of Michael Pert QC
104 New Walk, Leicester LE1 7EA,
Telephone: 0116 249 2020
Call Date: July 1977, Inner Temple
Pupil Master
Qualifications: [MA (Oxon)]

LEWIS MRS CHERRY ANNE

Verulam Chambers
Peer House, 8-14 Verulam Street, Gray's
Inn, London WC1X 8LZ,
Telephone: 0171 813 2400
Call Date: July 1973, Inner Temple
Qualifications: [FCIArb]

LEWIS CLIVE BUCKLAND

4-5 Gray's Inn Square
Ground Floor, Gray's Inn, London
WC1R 5JP, Telephone: 0171 404 5252
E-mail:chambers@4-5graysinnsquare.co.uk
Call Date: Nov 1987, Middle Temple
Qualifications: [MA (Cambs), LLM (Dalhousie
Uni), Fellow Selwyn Cambs]

LEWIS MISS DANIELLE SORAYA

New Court
Temple, London EC4Y 9BE,
Telephone: 0171 583 5123/0510
Call Date: 1995, Lincoln's Inn
Qualifications: [LLB (Hons)]

LEWIS DAVID NICHOLAS

Goldsmith Building
1st Floor, Temple, London EC4Y 7BL,
Telephone: 0171 353 7881
E-mail:clerks@goldsmith-building.law.co.uk
Call Date: Nov 1997, Lincoln's Inn
Qualifications: [LLB (Hons)(Sheff)]

LEWIS DAVID RALPH QC (1999)

5 Fountain Court
Steelhouse Lane, Birmingham B4 6DR,
Telephone: 0121 606 0500
E-mail:clerks@5fountaincourt.law.co.uk
Call Date: 1978, Middle Temple
Pupil Master, Assistant Recorder
Qualifications: [BA (Oxon)]

LEWIS EDWARD TREVOR GWYN

Francis Taylor Building
Ground Floor, Temple, London
EC4Y 7BY, Telephone: 0171 353 7768/
7769/2711
E-mail:clerks@francistaylorbuilding.law.co.uk
Call Date: July 1972, Gray's Inn

LEWIS MISS ELERI VODDEN

Chambers of Norman Palmer
2 Field Court, Gray's Inn, London
WC1R 5BB, Telephone: 0171 405 6114
E-mail: fieldct2@netcomuk.co.uk
Call Date: Nov 1989, Middle Temple
Qualifications: [LLB (Lond)]

LEWIS HUGH WILSON

Southernhay Chambers
33 Southernhay East, Exeter, Devon,
EX1 1NX, Telephone: 01392 255777
E-mail:southernhay.chambers@lineone.net
Call Date: July 1970, Middle Temple
Qualifications: [LLB]

LEWIS IAN ANTHONY

Gray's Inn Chambers
5th Floor, Gray's Inn, London WC1R 5JA,
Telephone: 0171 404 1111
Call Date: Feb 1989, Middle Temple
Pupil Master
Qualifications: [MA (Cantab)]

LEWIS JAMES THOMAS

3 Raymond Buildings
Gray's Inn, London WC1R 5BH,
Telephone: 020 7831 3833
E-mail:chambers@threeraymond.demon.co.u
k
Call Date: July 1987, Gray's Inn
Pupil Master
Qualifications: [BSc (Hons), Dip Law]

LEWIS MISS JANE ALEXIS

1 Hare Court
Ground Floor, Temple, London
EC4Y 7BE, Telephone: 0171 353 3982/
5324
Call Date: Nov 1990, Middle Temple
Qualifications: [BA (McGill), Dip Law (PCL)]

LEWIS JEFFREY ALLAN

9 Woodhouse Square
Leeds LS3 1AD,
Telephone: 0113 2451986
E-mail: clerks@9woodhouse.co.uk
Call Date: July 1978, Middle Temple
Pupil Master, Recorder
Qualifications: [BA, LLB]

LEWIS JEREMY STEPHEN

Littleton Chambers
3 King's Bench Walk North, Temple,
London EC4Y 7HR,
Telephone: 0171 797 8600
E-mail:clerks@littletonchambers.co.uk
Call Date: May 1992, Lincoln's Inn
Qualifications: [BA , BCL]

LEWIS JONATHAN MARK

9 Stone Buildings
Lincoln's Inn, London WC2A 3NN,
Telephone: 0171 404 5055
E-mail: clerks@9stoneb.law.co.uk
Call Date: Mar 1996, Inner Temple
Qualifications: [LLB (Manch)]

LEWIS MISS MARIAN ELENA

30 Park Place
Cardiff CF1 3BA,
Telephone: 01222 398421
E-mail: 100757.1456@compuserve.com
Farrar's Building
Temple, London EC4Y 7BD,
Telephone: 0171 583 9241
E-mail:chambers@farrarsbuilding.co.uk
Call Date: Nov 1977, Middle Temple
Pupil Master
Qualifications: [LLB (Lond) (Hons)]

LEWIS MARTIN RICHARD

1 Gray's Inn Square
Ground Floor, London WC1R 5AA,
Telephone: 0171 405 8946/7/8
Call Date: July 1998, Gray's Inn
Qualifications: [BA]

LEWIS MISS MELANIE ELIZABETH

4 Brick Court
Ground Floor, Temple, London
EC4Y 9AD, Telephone: 0171 797 7766
E-mail: chambers@4brick.co.uk
Call Date: Nov 1980, Gray's Inn
Pupil Master
Qualifications: [LLB (L'pool), LLM (Leic)]

LEWIS MEYRIC

2 Harcourt Buildings
2nd Floor, Temple, London EC4Y 9DB,
Telephone: 020 7353 8415
E-mail: clerks@2hb.law.co.uk
Call Date: Nov 1986, Gray's Inn
Pupil Master
Qualifications: [BA (Bris)]

LEWIS MICHAEL AP GWILYM QC (1975)

3 Hare Court
1 Little Essex Street, London WC2R 3LD,
Telephone: 0171 395 2000
Call Date: Nov 1956, Gray's Inn
Recorder
Qualifications: [MA (Oxon)]

LEWIS OWEN PRYS

9 Park Place
Cardiff CF1 3DP,
Telephone: 01222 382731
Call Date: July 1985, Middle Temple
Pupil Master
Qualifications: [LLM (Cantab), LLB, (Wales)]

LEWIS PATRICK JOHN

Two Garden Court
1st Floor, Middle Temple, London
EC4Y 9BL, Telephone: 0171 353 1633
E-mail:barristers@2gardenct.law.co.uk
Call Date: Nov 1997, Middle Temple
Qualifications: [BSc (Hons)(Lond)]

LEWIS PAUL KEITH

30 Park Place
Cardiff CF1 3BA,
Telephone: 01222 398421
E-mail: 100757.1456@compuserve.com
Call Date: 1981, Gray's Inn
Pupil Master, Assistant Recorder
Qualifications: [LLB (Leic) (Hons)]

LEWIS PETER REES

Francis Taylor Building
Ground Floor, Temple, London
EC4Y 7BY, Telephone: 0171 353 7768/
7769/2711
E-mail:clerks@francistaylorbuilding.law.co.uk
Call Date: June 1964, Gray's Inn
Pupil Master
Qualifications: [LLM]

LEWIS PHILIP SIMON COLEMAN

Littman Chambers
12 Gray's Inn Square, London WC1R 5JP,
Telephone: 020 7404 4866
E-mail: admin@littmanchambers.com
Call Date: Feb 1958, Lincoln's Inn
Qualifications: [MA (Oxon)]

LEWIS RAYMOND JOSEPH

2 Paper Buildings
1st Floor, Temple, London EC4Y 7ET,
Telephone: 020 7556 5500
E-mail: clerks@2pbbarristers.co.uk
Call Date: July 1971, Middle Temple
Pupil Master

LEWIS RAYMOND SPENCER

32 Park Place
Cardiff CF1 3BA,
Telephone: 01222 397364
Call Date: July 1994, Inner Temple

LEWIS ROBERT

11 Bolt Court (also at 7 Stone Buildings – 1st Floor)
London EC4A 3DQ,
Telephone: 0171 353 2300
E-mail: boltct11@aol.com
7 Stone Buildings (also at 11 Bolt Court)
1st Floor, Lincoln's Inn, London
WC2A 3SZ, Telephone: 0171 242 0961
E-mail:larthur@7stonebuildings.law.co.uk
Redhill Chambers
Seloduct House, 30 Station Road, Redhill,
Surrey, RH1 1NF,
Telephone: 01737 780781
Call Date: 1996, Gray's Inn
Qualifications: [MA, BCL (Oxon)]

LEWIS PROFESSOR ROY MALCOLM

Old Square Chambers
1 Verulam Buildings, Gray's Inn, London
WC1R 5LQ, Telephone: 0171 269 0300
E-mail:clerks@oldsquarechambers.co.uk
Old Square Chambers
Hanover House, 47 Corn Street, Bristol
BS1 1HT, Telephone: 0117 9277111
E-mail: oldsqbri@globalnet.co.uk
Call Date: May 1992, Lincoln's Inn
Qualifications: [LLB, MSc (Econ)]

LEWIS THOMAS ROBIN ARWEL

St Philip's Chambers
Fountain Court, Steelhouse Lane,
Birmingham B4 6DR,
Telephone: 0121 246 7000
E-mail: clerks@st-philips.co.uk
Call Date: Nov 1991, Inner Temple
Qualifications: [MA (Cantab)]

LEWIS-JONES MEIRION

Sedan House
Stanley Place, Chester CH1 2LU,
Telephone: 01244 320480/348282
Call Date: Nov 1971, Gray's Inn
Pupil Master
Qualifications: [LLB (Lond)]

LEWISON KIM MARTIN JORDAN QC (1991)

Falcon Chambers
Falcon Court, London EC4Y 1AA,
Telephone: 0171 353 2484
E-mail: clerks@falcon-chambers.com
Call Date: July 1975, Lincoln's Inn
Recorder
Qualifications: [MA (Cantab)]

LEWSLEY CHRISTOPHER STANTON

4 Breams Buildings
London EC4A 1AQ,
Telephone: 0171 353 5835/430 1221
E-mail:breams@4breamsbuildings.law.co.uk
Call Date: July 1976, Lincoln's Inn
Qualifications: [BSc PhD CEng, MiStructE]

LEWTHWAITE MISS JOANNE ELIZABETH

Oriel Chambers
14 Water Street, Liverpool L2 8TD,
Telephone: 0151 236 7191/236 4321
E-mail: clerks@oriel-chambers.co.uk
Call Date: Oct 1990, Inner Temple
Qualifications: [LLB (L'pool)]

LEY NIGEL JOSEPH

Gray's Inn Chambers
Chambers of Nigel Ley (2nd Floor), Gray's
Inn, London WC1R 5JA,
Telephone: 0171 831 7888 (Chambers)/
0171 831 7904 (Mr M Ullah)
Call Date: 1969, Gray's Inn
Qualifications: [LLM (Manch)]

LEY (NIGEL) SPENCER

Farrar's Building
Temple, London EC4Y 7BD,
Telephone: 0171 583 9241
E-mail:chambers@farrarsbuilding.co.uk
Call Date: July 1985, Middle Temple
Qualifications: [MA (Cantab)]

LEY-MORGAN MARK JOHN

3 Serjeants' Inn
London EC4Y 1BQ,
Telephone: 0171 353 5537
E-mail: clerks@3serjeantsinn.com
Call Date: Oct 1994, Gray's Inn
Qualifications: [BSc, LLB]

LICKERT EDWARD MARTIN

2 Pump Court
1st Floor, Temple, London EC4Y 7AH,
Telephone: 0171 353 5597
Call Date: Nov 1986, Middle Temple
Pupil Master
Qualifications: [LLB (Hons)]

LICKLEY NIGEL JAMES DOMINIC

3 Paper Buildings
Temple, London EC4Y 7EU,
Telephone: 020 7583 8055
E-mail: London@3paper.com
3 Paper Buildings (Winchester)
4 St Peter Street, Winchester SO23 8BW,
Telephone: 01962 868884
E-mail: winchester@3paper.com
3 Paper Buildings (Bournemouth)
20 Lorne Park Road, Bournemouth,
Dorset, BH1 1JN,
Telephone: 01202 292102
E-mail: Bournemouth@3paper.com

3 Paper Buildings (Oxford)
1 Alfred Street, High Street, Oxford
OX1 4EH, Telephone: 01865 793736
E-mail: oxford@3paper.com
Call Date: July 1983, Gray's Inn
Pupil Master
Qualifications: [LLB (Lond)]

LIDDIARD MARTIN THOMAS

5 Fountain Court
Steelhouse Lane, Birmingham B4 6DR,
Telephone: 0121 606 0500
E-mail:clerks@5fountaincourt.law.co.uk
Call Date: Nov 1989, Inner Temple
Qualifications: [LLB (B'ham)]

LIDDY SIMON TERENCE

New Walk Chambers
27 New Walk, Leicester LE1 6TE,
Telephone: 0116 2559144
Call Date: July 1979, Middle Temple
Qualifications: [LLM]

LIEBRECHT JOHN MICHAEL

One Garden Court Family Law Chambers
Ground Floor, Temple, London
EC4Y 9BJ, Telephone: 0171 797 7900
E-mail: clerks@onegardencourt.co.uk
Call Date: Nov 1989, Inner Temple
Qualifications: [BA (Oxon), LLM (Cantab)]

LIEVEN MS NATHALIE MARIE DANIELLA

4 Breams Buildings
London EC4A 1AQ,
Telephone: 0171 353 5835/430 1221
E-mail:breams@4breamsbuildings.law.co.uk
Call Date: July 1989, Gray's Inn
Pupil Master
Qualifications: [BA [Cantab]]

LIGHT PROFESSOR ROY ALAN

St John's Chambers
Small Street, Bristol BS1 1DW,
Telephone: 0117 9213456/298514
E-mail: @stjohnschambers.co.uk
Call Date: Feb 1992, Gray's Inn
Qualifications: [LLB (Lond), LLM (Lond),
MPhil (Cambs), PhD (Cambs)]

LIGHTMAN DANIEL

Serle Court Chambers
6 New Square, Lincoln's Inn, London
WC2A 3QS, Telephone: 0171 242 6105
E-mail: clerks@serlecourt.co.uk
Call Date: Oct 1995, Lincoln's Inn
Qualifications: [BA (Hons)(Oxon), CPE]

LIGHTWING STUART

Chambers of Stuart Lightwing
Tudor Court, Church Lane, Nunthorpe,
Middlesbrough TS7 0PD,
Telephone: 01642 315000
Call Date: July 1972, Middle Temple
Pupil Master
Qualifications: [LLB, FCIS, MIMgt, FRSA,
FCIArb]

LILLINGTON SIMON DOUGLAS

**1 Gray's Inn Square, Chambers of the
Baroness Scotland of Asthal QC**
1st Floor, London WC1R 5AG,
Telephone: 0171 405 3000
E-mail: clerks@onegrays.demon.co.uk
Eighteen Carlton Crescent
Southampton SO15 2XR,
Telephone: 01703 639001
Call Date: 1980, Middle Temple
Pupil Master
Qualifications: [BA, LLM]

LIM MALCOLM KIAN-LENG

3 Serjeants' Inn
London EC4Y 1BQ,
Telephone: 0171 353 5537
E-mail: clerks@3serjeantsinn.com
Call Date: July 1989, Inner Temple
Qualifications: [BA (Keele), LLM (Lond)]

LIMB CHRISTOPHER

Young Street Chambers
38 Young Street, Manchester M3 3FT,
Telephone: 0161 833 0489
E-mail: clerks@young-st-chambers.com
Call Date: July 1975, Gray's Inn
Pupil Master
Qualifications: [LLB]

LIMB PATRICK FRANCIS

Ropewalk Chambers
24 The Ropewalk, Nottingham NG1 5EF,
Telephone: 0115 9472581
E-mail: administration@ropewalk co.uk
Call Date: July 1987, Middle Temple
Pupil Master
Qualifications: [BA (Cantab)]

LIMBREY BERNARD MARTIN

Staple Inn Chambers
1st Floor, 9 Staple Inn, Holborn Bars,
London WC1V 7QH,
Telephone: 0171 242 5240
E-mail: clerks@staple-inn.org
Call Date: Nov 1980, Middle Temple
Qualifications: [MSc (Lond)]

LIMONT WILLIAM ANTHONY

Chavasse Court Chambers
2nd Floor, Chavasse Court, 24 Lord Street,
Liverpool L2 1TA,
Telephone: 0151 707 1191
Call Date: Nov 1964, Gray's Inn
Qualifications: [LLB (L'pool)]

LINDBLOM KEITH JOHN QC (1996)

2 Harcourt Buildings
2nd Floor, Temple, London EC4Y 9DB,
Telephone: 020 7353 8415
E-mail: clerks@2hb.law.co.uk
Call Date: July 1980, Gray's Inn
Qualifications: [MA (Oxon)]

LINDEN THOMAS DOMINIC

4-5 Gray's Inn Square
Ground Floor, Gray's Inn, London
WC1R 5JP, Telephone: 0171 404 5252
E-mail:chambers@4-5graysinnsquare.co.uk
Call Date: Nov 1989, Gray's Inn
Qualifications: [BA,(Oxon), BCL]

LINDOP MISS SARAH LOUISE

1 Inner Temple Lane
Temple, London EC4Y 1AF,
Telephone: 020 7353 0933
Call Date: Nov 1989, Gray's Inn
Pupil Master
Qualifications: [LLB (Hons)]

LINDQVIST ANDREW NILS GUNNAR

Octagon House
19 Colegate, Norwich NR3 1AT,
Telephone: 01603 623186
E-mail: admin@octagon-chambers.co.uk
Call Date: Nov 1968, Middle Temple
Pupil Master
Qualifications: [MA (Cantab)]

LINDSAY MISS CLAIRE LOUISE

Plowden Buildings
2nd Floor, 2 Plowden Buildings, Middle
Temple Lane, London EC4Y 9BU,
Telephone: 0171 583 0808
E-mail: bar@plowdenbuildings.co.uk
Call Date: Oct 1991, Middle Temple
Qualifications: [LLB (Leic)]

LINDSAY JEREMY MARK HENRY

37 Park Square Chambers
37 Park Square, Leeds LS1 2NY,
Telephone: 0113 2439422
E-mail: chambers@no37.co.uk
Call Date: July 1986, Gray's Inn
Qualifications: [LLB (Hons)(Nott'm),
Postgraduate Diploma, in Radio
Journalism]

LINDSAY MARTIN ROSS

Call Date: July 1977, Gray's Inn
Pupil Master

LINDSEY MS SUSAN

One Paper Buildings
Ground Floor, Temple, London
EC4Y 7EP, Telephone: 0171 583 7355
E-mail: clerks@1pb.co.uk
Call Date: 1997, Inner Temple
Qualifications: [BSc (Lond), MSc, (Lond),
RIBA]

LINEHAN STEPHEN JOHN QC (1993)

5 Fountain Court
Steelhouse Lane, Birmingham B4 6DR,
Telephone: 0121 606 0500
E-mail:clerks@5fountaincourt.law.co.uk
Call Date: Feb 1970, Lincoln's Inn
Recorder
Qualifications: [LLB (Lond)]

LINFORD ROBERT FRANK

Devon Chambers
3 St Andrew Street, Plymouth PL1 2AH,
Telephone: 01752 661659
E-mail: devonchambers.co.uk.
Call Date: Nov 1987, Gray's Inn
Pupil Master
Qualifications: [LLB (Hons) (Wales)]

LINKLATER MISS LISA MARGARET

Chancery House Chambers
7 Lisbon Square, Leeds LS1 4LY,
Telephone: 0113 244 6691
E-mail: chanceryhouse@btinternet.com
Call Date: Oct 1995, Inner Temple
Qualifications: [BA (Cantab)]

LINNEMANN BERNARD MARIA

3 Fountain Court
Steelhouse Lane, Birmingham B4 6DR,
Telephone: 0121 236 5854
Call Date: Nov 1980, Gray's Inn
Qualifications: [BA (Tcd)]

LINSTEAD PETER JAMES

**11 Bolt Court (also at 7 Stone Buildings
– 1st Floor)**
London EC4A 3DQ,
Telephone: 0171 353 2300
E-mail: boltct11@aol.com
**7 Stone Buildings (also at 11 Bolt
Court)**
1st Floor, Lincoln's Inn, London
WC2A 3SZ, Telephone: 0171 242 0961
E-mail:larthur@7stonebuildings.law.co.uk
Redhill Chambers
Seloduct House, 30 Station Road, Redhill,
Surrey, RH1 1NF,
Telephone: 01737 780781
Call Date: Oct 1994, Gray's Inn
Qualifications: [BA]

LINTOTT DAVID JAMES

2-3 Gray's Inn Square
Gray's Inn, London WC1R 5JH,
Telephone: 0171 242 4986
E-mail:chambers@2-3graysinnsquare.co.uk
Call Date: Oct 1996, Gray's Inn
Qualifications: [BA (Cantab)]

LIPSTEIN KURT QC (1998)

13 Old Square
Ground Floor, Lincoln's Inn, London
WC2A 3UA, Telephone: 0171 404 4800
E-mail: clerks@13oldsquare.law.co.uk
Call Date: Jan 1950, Middle Temple
Qualifications: [PhD]

LISSACK RICHARD ANTHONY QC (1994)

35 Essex Street
Temple, London WC2R 3AR,
Telephone: 0171 353 6381
E-mail: derek_jenkins@link.org
Call Date: Nov 1978, Inner Temple
Recorder

LISTER MISS CAROLINE JANE

One King's Bench Walk
1st Floor, Temple, London EC4Y 7DB,
Telephone: 0171 936 1500
E-mail: ddear@1kbw.co.uk
Call Date: Nov 1980, Middle Temple
Pupil Master
Qualifications: [BSc (Lond)]

LITCHFIELD MISS LINDA

3 Paper Buildings
Temple, London EC4Y 7EU,
Telephone: 020 7583 8055
E-mail: London@3paper.com
3 Paper Buildings (Bournemouth)
20 Lorne Park Road, Bournemouth,
Dorset, BH1 1JN,
Telephone: 01202 292102
E-mail: Bournemouth@3paper.com
3 Paper Buildings (Winchester)
4 St Peter Street, Winchester SO23 8BW,
Telephone: 01962 868884
E-mail: winchester@3paper.com
3 Paper Buildings (Oxford)
1 Alfred Street, High Street, Oxford
OX1 4EH, Telephone: 01865 793736
E-mail: oxford@3paper.com
Call Date: July 1974, Inner Temple
Pupil Master
Qualifications: [BA (Kingston), BCL (Oxon)]

LITHMAN NIGEL LLOYD QC (1997)

3 Hare Court
1 Little Essex Street, London WC2R 3LD,
Telephone: 0171 395 2000
Call Date: Nov 1976, Inner Temple

Assistant Recorder
Qualifications: [LLB (Hons)]

LITTLE GEOFFREY WILLIAM

Sedan House
Stanley Place, Chester CH1 2LU,
Telephone: 01244 320480/348282
Dr Johnson's Chambers
The Atrium Court, Apex Plaza, Reading,
Berkshire, RG1 1AX,
Telephone: 01734 254221
Call Date: July 1973, Middle Temple
Pupil Master, Assistant Recorder
Qualifications: [MA (Cantab) LLM,
(Warwick)]

LITTLE IAN

Chambers of John Hand QC
9 St John Street, Manchester M3 4DN,
Telephone: 0161 955 9000
E-mail: ninesjs@gconnect.com
Call Date: Feb 1989, Middle Temple
Qualifications: [BA (Oxon), Dip Law (City)]

LITTLE TOM CHARLES

9 Gough Square
London EC4A 3DE,
Telephone: 020 7832 0500
E-mail: clerks@9goughsq.co.uk
Call Date: Oct 1997, Middle Temple
Qualifications: [BA (Hons)(Notts), CPE]

LITTLER MARTIN GORDON

Cobden House Chambers
19 Quay Street, Manchester M3 3HN,
Telephone: 0161 833 6000
E-mail: clerks@cobden.co.uk
Call Date: Nov 1989, Gray's Inn
Qualifications: [LLB]

LITTLER RICHARD MARK

Cobden House Chambers
19 Quay Street, Manchester M3 3HN,
Telephone: 0161 833 6000
E-mail: clerks@cobden.co.uk
Call Date: Oct 1994, Gray's Inn
Qualifications: [LLB (Hons)]

D

LITTLEWOOD MISS REBECCA MAE

Trafalgar Chambers
53 Fleet Street, London EC4Y 1BE,
Telephone: 0171 583 5858
E-mail:trafalgarchambers@easynet.co.uk
Call Date: Nov 1988, Inner Temple
Pupil Master
Qualifications: [LLB (Soton)]

LITTLEWOOD ROBERT

Two Garden Court
1st Floor, Middle Temple, London
EC4Y 9BL, Telephone: 0171 353 1633
E-mail:barristers@2gardenct.law.co.uk
Call Date: Oct 1993, Inner Temple
Qualifications: [BA, CPE]

LITTMAN JEFFREY JAMES

Chambers of Norman Palmer
2 Field Court, Gray's Inn, London
WC1R 5BB, Telephone: 0171 405 6114
E-mail: fieldct2@netcomuk.co.uk
Call Date: July 1974, Middle Temple
Pupil Master
Qualifications: [MA (Cantab)]

LITTMAN MARK QC (1961)

Littman Chambers
12 Gray's Inn Square, London WC1R 5JP,
Telephone: 020 7404 4866
E-mail: admin@littmanchambers.com
Call Date: June 1947, Middle Temple
Qualifications: [MA (Oxon), BSc (Econ)]

LITTON JOHN LETABLERE

4 Breams Buildings
London EC4A 1AQ,
Telephone: 0171 353 5835/430 1221
E-mail:breams@4breamsbuildings.law.co.uk
Call Date: July 1989, Middle Temple
Pupil Master
Qualifications: [LLB (So'ton)]

LIVESEY BERNARD JOSEPH EDWARD QC (1990)

Chambers of John L Powell QC
Four New Square, Lincoln's Inn, London
WC2A 3RJ, Telephone: 0171 797 8000
E-mail: barristers@4newsquare.com
Call Date: July 1969, Lincoln's Inn
Recorder
Qualifications: [MA, LLB (Cantab)]

LIVESEY FRASER MICHAEL STANIER

15 Winckley Square
Preston PR1 3JJ,
Telephone: 01772 252828
E-mail:clerks@winckleysq.demon.co.uk
Call Date: Oct 1992, Lincoln's Inn
Qualifications: [LLB(Hons)(Newc)]

LIVESEY JOHN WILLIAM ALLAN

Albion Chambers
Broad Street, Bristol BS1 1DR,
Telephone: 0117 9272144
Call Date: Nov 1990, Lincoln's Inn
Qualifications: [LLB (Bris)]

LIVESEY SIMON PETER

2 King's Bench Walk Chambers
1st Floor, 2 King's Bench Walk, Temple,
London EC4Y 7DE,
Telephone: 020 7353 9276
E-mail: chambers@2kbw.co.uk
Call Date: July 1987, Inner Temple
Qualifications: [BSc (Leicester)]

LIVING MARC STEPHEN

Holborn Chambers
6 Gate Street, Lincoln's Inn Fields, London
WC2A 3HP, Telephone: 0171 242 6060
Call Date: July 1983, Middle Temple
Qualifications: [BA (Hons) (Kent),]

LIVINGSTON RICHARD JOHN

3 Hare Court
1 Little Essex Street, London WC2R 3LD,
Telephone: 0171 395 2000
Call Date: July 1980, Gray's Inn
Pupil Master
Qualifications: [BA (Oxon),LLM (Lond)]

LIVINGSTONE SIMON JOHN

Redhill Chambers
Seloduct House, 30 Station Road, Redhill,
Surrey, RH1 1NF,
Telephone: 01737 780781
**11 Bolt Court (also at 7 Stone Buildings
– 1st Floor)**
London EC4A 3DQ,
Telephone: 0171 353 2300
E-mail: boltct11@aol.com

7 Stone Buildings (also at 11 Bolt Court)
1st Floor, Lincoln's Inn, London
WC2A 3SZ, Telephone: 0171 242 0961
E-mail:larthur@7stonebuildings.law.co.uk
Call Date: Oct 1990, Inner Temple
Qualifications: [LLB (Bris)]

LIVINGSTONE THOMAS DOUGLAS

New Court
Temple, London EC4Y 9BE,
Telephone: 0171 583 5123/0510
Call Date: Nov 1989, Inner Temple
Qualifications: [LLB (Lond)]

LLEWELLYN CHARLES IVOR

Staple Inn Chambers
1st Floor, 9 Staple Inn, Holborn Bars,
London WC1V 7QH,
Telephone: 0171 242 5240
E-mail: clerks@staple-inn.org
Call Date: July 1978, Gray's Inn
Qualifications: [LLB (Hons) (Lond)]

LLEWELLYN-JONES CHRISTOPHER GEOFFREY QC (1990)

Goldsmith Building
1st Floor, Temple, London EC4Y 7BL,
Telephone: 0171 353 7881
E-mail:clerks@goldsmith-building.law.co.uk
9 Park Place
Cardiff CF1 3DP,
Telephone: 01222 382731
Call Date: Nov 1965, Middle Temple
Recorder
Qualifications: [MA (Cantab)]

LLEWELYN MISS JANE RHIANNON

1 Temple Gardens
1st Floor, Temple, London EC4Y 9BB,
Telephone: 0171 583 1315/353 0407
E-mail: clerks@1templegardens.co.uk
Call Date: July 1989, Middle Temple
Qualifications: [MA [Cantab]]

LLOYD (DAVID) HUW

3 Serjeants' Inn
London EC4Y 1BQ,
Telephone: 0171 353 5537
E-mail: clerks@3serjeantsinn.com
Call Date: July 1975, Middle Temple
Qualifications: [LLB (Leics)]

LLOYD FRANCIS ZACHARY

Hardwicke Building
New Square, Lincoln's Inn, London
WC2A 3SB, Telephone: 020 7242 2523
E-mail: clerks@hardwicke.co.uk
Call Date: July 1987, Inner Temple
Qualifications: [BA (Exon), Dip Law]

LLOYD MISS GAYNOR ELIZABETH

Sedan House
Stanley Place, Chester CH1 2LU,
Telephone: 01244 320480/348282
Call Date: Oct 1992, Lincoln's Inn
Qualifications: [LLB(Hons)(Nott'm)]

LLOYD MISS HEATHER CLAIRE

Chavasse Court Chambers
2nd Floor, Chavasse Court, 24 Lord Street,
Liverpool L2 1TA,
Telephone: 0151 707 1191
Call Date: July 1979, Gray's Inn
Pupil Master
Qualifications: [LLB (L'pool)]

LLOYD JAMES DAVID

5 King's Bench Walk
Temple, London EC4Y 7DN,
Telephone: 0171 353 5638
Call Date: Feb 1985, Middle Temple
Pupil Master
Qualifications: [MA (Oxon)]

LLOYD JOHN NESBITT

11 Old Square
Ground Floor, Lincoln's Inn, London
WC2A 3TS, Telephone: 0171 242 5022/
405 1074
Call Date: Nov 1988, Inner Temple
Qualifications: [BA (Natal), MA, LLB (Exon)]

LLOYD JULIAN ALASTAIR

White Friars Chambers
21 White Friars, Chester CH1 1NZ,
Telephone: 01244 323070
E-mail:whitefriarschambers@btinternet.com
Call Date: July 1985, Gray's Inn
Pupil Master
Qualifications: [MA, LLM (Cantab)]

D

LLOYD LLOYD

4 Field Court
Gray's Inn, London WC1R 5EA,
Telephone: 0171 440 6900
E-mail: chambers@4fieldcourt.co.uk
Call Date: July 1973, Gray's Inn
Qualifications: [MA (Cantab), LLM (Lond)]

LLOYD MISS PATRICIA

2 King's Bench Walk Chambers
1st Floor, 2 King's Bench Walk, Temple,
London EC4Y 7DE,
Telephone: 020 7353 9276
E-mail: chambers@2kbw.co.uk
Call Date: July 1979, Gray's Inn
Qualifications: [LLB(Hons)]

LLOYD STEPHEN JAMES GEORGE

Chambers of Mr Peter Crampin QC
Ground Floor, 11 New Square, Lincoln's
Inn, London WC2A 3QB,
Telephone: 020 7831 0081
E-mail: 11newsquare.co.uk
Call Date: July 1971, Middle Temple

LLOYD MISS WENDY-JANE

25-27 Castle Street
1st Floor, Liverpool L2 4TA,
Telephone: 0151 227 5661/051 236 5072
Call Date: July 1983, Middle Temple
Qualifications: [LLB (L'pool)]

LLOYD-ELEY ANDREW JAMES

1 Hare Court
Ground Floor, Temple, London
EC4Y 7BE, Telephone: 0171 353 3982/
5324
Call Date: Nov 1979, Middle Temple
Pupil Master
Qualifications: [LLB]

LLOYD-JACOB MISS CAMPASPE CLARE HELEN

3 Raymond Buildings
Gray's Inn, London WC1R 5BH,
Telephone: 020 7831 3833
E-mail:chambers@threeraymond.demon.co.u
k
Call Date: Nov 1990, Gray's Inn
Qualifications: [MA (Oxon)]

LLOYD-JONES JOHN BENEDICT

Chambers of Michael Pert QC
36 Bedford Row, London WC1R 4JH,
Telephone: 0171 421 8000
E-mail: 36bedfordrow@link.org
Chambers of Michael Pert QC
24 Albion Place, Northampton NN1 1UD,
Telephone: 01604 602333
Chambers of Michael Pert QC
104 New Walk, Leicester LE1 7EA,
Telephone: 0116 249 2020
Call Date: Nov 1993, Inner Temple
Qualifications: [BA (Hons) (Dunelm), CPE]

LLOYD-SMITH MISS REBECCA JANE

Peel Court Chambers
45 Hardman Street, Manchester M3 3PL,
Telephone: 0161 832 3791
E-mail: clerks@peelct.co.uk
Call Date: Oct 1994, Lincoln's Inn
Qualifications: [BA (Hons)(Leic), CPE (Leic)]

LLWYD ELFYN

Sedan House
Stanley Place, Chester CH1 2LU,
Telephone: 01244 320480/348282
Call Date: Nov 1997, Gray's Inn
Qualifications: [LLB (Wales)]

LO BERNARD NORMAN

17 Bedford Row
London WC1R 4EB,
Telephone: 0171 831 7314
E-mail: iboard7314@aol.com
Call Date: Nov 1991, Inner Temple
Qualifications: [BA (Bristol), Dip Law]

LOADES JONATHAN CHARLES

9 Gough Square
London EC4A 3DE,
Telephone: 020 7832 0500
E-mail: clerks@9goughsq.co.uk
Call Date: Nov 1986, Middle Temple
Pupil Master
Qualifications: [BSc (Bradford) Dip, Law]

D

LOBBENBERG NICHOLAS

6 Gray's Inn Square
Ground Floor, Gray's Inn, London
WC1R 5AZ, Telephone: 0171 242 1052
E-mail: 6graysinn@clara.co.uk
Call Date: Nov 1987, Gray's Inn
Pupil Master
Qualifications: [BA (Oxon)]

LOCHRANE DAMIEN HORATIO ROSS

Pump Court Chambers
Upper Ground Floor, 3 Pump Court,
Temple, London EC4Y 7AJ,
Telephone: 0171 353 0711
E-mail: clerks@3pumpcourt.com
Pump Court Chambers
31 Southgate Street, Winchester
SO23 9EE, Telephone: 01962 868161
E-mail: clerks@3pumpcourt.com
Pump Court Chambers
5 Temple Chambers, Temple Street,
Swindon SN1 1SQ,
Telephone: 01793 539899
E-mail: clerks@3pumpcourt.com
Call Date: Nov 1983, Gray's Inn
Pupil Master
Qualifications: [MA (Oxon)]

LOCKEY JOHN CHARLTON GERARD

Essex Court Chambers
24 Lincoln's Inn Fields, London
WC2A 3ED, Telephone: 0171 813 8000
E-mail: clerksroom@essexcourt-chambers.co.uk
Call Date: July 1987, Middle Temple
Pupil Master
Qualifications: [MA (Cantab) LLM, (Harvard)]

LOCKHART ANDREW WILLIAM JARDINE

St Philip's Chambers
Fountain Court, Steelhouse Lane,
Birmingham B4 6DR,
Telephone: 0121 246 7000
E-mail: clerks@st-philips.co.uk
Call Date: Oct 1991, Lincoln's Inn
Qualifications: [LLB (Hons) (Lond)]

LOCKHART-MUMMERY CHRISTOPHER JOHN QC (1986)

4 Breams Buildings
London EC4A 1AQ,
Telephone: 0171 353 5835/430 1221
E-mail: breams@4breamsbuildings.law.co.uk
Call Date: July 1971, Inner Temple
Qualifications: [BA (Cantab)]

LOCKYER MISS BARBARA JANE

4 Brick Court, Chambers of Anne Rafferty QC
1st Floor, Temple, London EC4Y 9AD,
Telephone: 0171 583 8455
Call Date: July 1970, Gray's Inn
Pupil Master
Qualifications: [LLB (Soton)]

LODDER PETER NORMAN

3 Hare Court
1 Little Essex Street, London WC2R 3LD,
Telephone: 0171 395 2000
Call Date: July 1981, Middle Temple
Pupil Master
Qualifications: [LLB (B'ham)]

LODGE ADAM ROBERT

58 King Street Chambers
1st Floor, Kingsgate House, 51-53 South
King Street, Manchester M2 6DE,
Telephone: 0161 831 7477
Call Date: Oct 1996, Gray's Inn
Qualifications: [LLB]

LODGE ANTON JAMES CORDUFF QC (1989)

Park Court Chambers
16 Park Place, Leeds LS1 2SJ,
Telephone: 0113 2433277
Call Date: Nov 1966, Gray's Inn
Recorder
Qualifications: [MA (Cantab)]

D

LODGE GRAHAM

Francis Taylor Building
Ground Floor, Temple, London
EC4Y 7BY, Telephone: 0171 353 7768/
7769/2711
E-mail:clerks@francistaylorbuilding.law.co.uk
Call Date: July 1971, Middle Temple
Pupil Master
Qualifications: [LLB (Lond)]

LODGE JOHN ROBERT

Park Court Chambers
16 Park Place, Leeds LS1 2SJ,
Telephone: 0113 2433277
Call Date: July 1980, Middle Temple
Pupil Master
Qualifications: [MA (Oxon)]

LODGE NICHOLAS CHARLES GARA

65-67 King Street
Leicester LE1 6RP,
Telephone: 0116 2547710
Call Date: July 1979, Gray's Inn
Qualifications: [BA, MT.heal, Dip Law]

LODY TUSTIAN STUART

St Mary's Chambers
50 High Pavement, Lace Market,
Nottingham NG1 1HW,
Telephone: 0115 9503503
E-mail: clerks@smc.law.co.uk
Call Date: Nov 1991, Gray's Inn
Qualifications: [BA]

LOFTHOUSE JOHN CHARLES

2 King's Bench Walk
Ground Floor, Temple, London
EC4Y 7DE, Telephone: 0171 353 1746
E-mail: 2kbw@atlas.co.uk
King's Bench Chambers
115 North Hill, Plymouth PL4 8JY,
Telephone: 01752 221551
Call Date: May 1979, Middle Temple
Qualifications: [MA (Oxon)]

LOFTHOUSE SIMON TIMOTHY

Atkin Chambers
1 Atkin Building, Gray's Inn, London
WC1R 5AT, Telephone: 020 7404 0102
E-mail: clerks@atkin-chambers.co.uk
Call Date: Nov 1988, Gray's Inn
Pupil Master
Qualifications: [LLB (Hons)(Lond)]

LOFTUS MISS TERESA ANNE MARTINE

25-27 Castle Street
1st Floor, Liverpool L2 4TA,
Telephone: 0151 227 5661/051 236 5072
Call Date: Feb 1995, Lincoln's Inn
Qualifications: [LLB (Hull)]

LOGAN MISS MAURA

St John's Chambers
One High Elm Drive, Hale Barns,
Cheshire, WA15 0JD,
Telephone: 0161 980 7379
Call Date: July 1971, Inner Temple

LOGSDON MICHAEL ANTHONY

1 Hare Court
Ground Floor, Temple, London
EC4Y 7BE, Telephone: 0171 353 3982/
5324
Call Date: Feb 1988, Inner Temple
Qualifications: [LLB (Soton)]

LOMAS MARK HENRY

Littleton Chambers
3 King's Bench Walk North, Temple,
London EC4Y 7HR,
Telephone: 0171 797 8600
E-mail:clerks@littletonchambers.co.uk
Call Date: Nov 1977, Middle Temple
Pupil Master
Qualifications: [MA (Cantab)]

LOMAS MARK STEPHEN

3 Paper Buildings
Temple, London EC4Y 7EU,
Telephone: 020 7583 8055
E-mail: London@3paper.com
3 Paper Buildings (Winchester)
4 St Peter Street, Winchester SO23 8BW,
Telephone: 01962 868884
E-mail: winchester@3paper.com

D

3 Paper Buildings (Bournemouth)
20 Lorne Park Road, Bournemouth,
Dorset, BH1 1JN,
Telephone: 01202 292102
E-mail: Bournemouth@3paper.com
3 Paper Buildings (Oxford)
1 Alfred Street, High Street, Oxford
OX1 4EH, Telephone: 01865 793736
E-mail: oxford@3paper.com
Call Date: July 1983, Middle Temple
Pupil Master
Qualifications: [BA (Keele)]

LOMNICKA MISS EVA ZOFIA

Chambers of John L Powell QC
Four New Square, Lincoln's Inn, London
WC2A 3RJ, Telephone: 0171 797 8000
E-mail: barristers@4newsquare.com
Call Date: 1974, Middle Temple
Qualifications: [MA, LLB (Cantab)]

LONERGAN PAUL HENRY

22 Old Buildings
Lincoln's Inn, London WC2A 3UJ,
Telephone: 0171 831 0222
Call Date: Oct 1991, Lincoln's Inn
Qualifications: [MA (Cantab)]

LONG ANDREW PETER

Peel Court Chambers
45 Hardman Street, Manchester M3 3PL,
Telephone: 0161 832 3791
E-mail: clerks@peelct.co.uk
Call Date: July 1981, Inner Temple
Pupil Master
Qualifications: [LLB (Sheff)]

LONG TOBIAS CHARLES

8 King's Bench Walk
2nd Floor, Temple, London EC4Y 7DU,
Telephone: 0171 797 8888
8 King's Bench Walk North
1 Park Square East, Leeds LS1 2NE,
Telephone: 0113 2439797
Call Date: Nov 1988, Inner Temple
Pupil Master
Qualifications: [BA(E.Anglia),Dip Law]

LONGDEN ANTHONY GORDON

Hollis Whiteman Chambers
3rd Floor, Queen Elizabeth Bldg, Temple,
London EC4Y 9BS,
Telephone: 020 7583 5766
E-mail:barristers@holliswhiteman.co.uk
Call Date: Nov 1967, Inner Temple
Pupil Master
Qualifications: [BA (Oxon)]

LONGHURST-WOODS MS LESLEY

47 Banbury House
Banbury Road, London E9 7EB,
Telephone: 0181 985 8716
Call Date: Nov 1992, Gray's Inn
Qualifications: [BA]

LONGMAN MICHAEL JAMES

St John's Chambers
Small Street, Bristol BS1 1DW,
Telephone: 0117 9213456/298514
E-mail: @stjohnschambers.co.uk
Call Date: July 1978, Middle Temple
Pupil Master
Qualifications: [MA (Cantab)]

LONGWORTH ANTONY STEPHEN

Old Colony House
6 South King Street, Manchester M2 6DQ,
Telephone: 0161 834 4364
Call Date: July 1978, Middle Temple
Pupil Master
Qualifications: [BA (Oxon)]

LONSDALE DAVID JAMES

33 Bedford Row
London WC1R 4JH,
Telephone: 0171 242 6476
E-mail:clerks@bedfordrow33.demon.co.uk
Call Date: Nov 1988, Inner Temple
Qualifications: [BA (Oxon)(Hons)]

LONSDALE MISS MARION MARY

Chambers of Geoffrey Hawker
46/48 Essex Street, London WC2R 3GH,
Telephone: 0171 583 8899
Call Date: July 1984, Gray's Inn
Qualifications: [BSC Hons (Nott'm), LLB
Hons (Lond), ATII]

D

LOOSEMORE MRS MARY

Chichester Chambers
12 North Pallant, Chichester, West Sussex,
PO19 1TQ, Telephone: 01243 784538
E-mail:clerks@chichesterchambers.law.co.uk
Call Date: May 1992, Inner Temple
Qualifications: [BSc (Lond)]

LOPEZ PAUL ANTHONY

St Ive's Chambers
Whittall Street, Birmingham B4 6DH,
Telephone: 0121 236 0863/5720
E-mail:stives.headofchambers@btinternet.com
Call Date: July 1982, Middle Temple
Pupil Master
Qualifications: [LLB (Hons) (B'ham)]

LOPEZ RONALD

Forest House Chambers
15 Granville Road, Walthamstow, London
E17 9BS, Telephone: 0181 925 2240
Call Date: Nov 1992, Lincoln's Inn
Qualifications: [LLB (Hons)]

LOPIAN DR JONATHAN BERNARD

11 Stone Buildings
Lincoln's Inn, London WC2A 3TG,
Telephone: +44 (0)207 831 6381
E-mail:clerks@11StoneBuildings.law.co.uk
Call Date: Nov 1994, Middle Temple
Qualifications: [MA, Ph.D (Cantab), Dip Law
(City)]

LORAINE-SMITH NICHOLAS GEORGE EDWARD

2 Harcourt Buildings
1st Floor, Temple, London EC4Y 9DB,
Telephone: 020 7353 2112
Call Date: Nov 1977, Inner Temple
Pupil Master, Assistant Recorder
Qualifications: [BA (Oxon)]

LORAM MISS MARY CAROLINE

Coleridge Chambers
Citadel, 190 Corporation Street,
Birmingham B4 6QD,
Telephone: 0121 233 8500
Call Date: Nov 1995, Inner Temple
Qualifications: [BA (Oxon), M.Phil (Cantab)]

LORD DAVID WILLIAM

3 Stone Buildings
Lincoln's Inn, London WC2A 3XL,
Telephone: 0171 242 4937
E-mail: clerks@3sb.law.co.uk
Call Date: July 1987, Middle Temple
Pupil Master
Qualifications: [LLB (Bristol)]

LORD RICHARD DENYER

Brick Court Chambers
7-8 Essex Street, London WC2R 3LD,
Telephone: 0171 379 3550
E-mail: [surname]@brickcourt.co.uk
Call Date: Nov 1981, Inner Temple
Pupil Master
Qualifications: [MA (Cantab)]

LORD TIMOTHY MICHAEL

2 Temple Gardens
Temple, London EC4Y 9AY,
Telephone: 0171 583 6041
E-mail: clerks@2templegardens.co.uk
Call Date: Nov 1992, Inner Temple
Qualifications: [MA (Cantab)]

LORENZO MS CLAUDIA

2 King's Bench Walk Chambers
1st Floor, 2 King's Bench Walk, Temple,
London EC4Y 7DE,
Telephone: 020 7353 9276
E-mail: chambers@2kbw.co.uk
Call Date: Apr 1991, Inner Temple
Qualifications: [BA (Hons) , LLB (Hons) ,
LLM]

LORIE ANDREW GIDEON

College Chambers
19 Carlton Cresent, Southampton
SO15 2ET, Telephone: 01703 230338
Call Date: Oct 1996, Middle Temple
Qualifications: [BA (Hons)(UWE Bris), CPE
(Westminster)]

LOUGHRAN PAUL VINCENT

Call Date: Feb 1988, Gray's Inn
Qualifications: [LLB (Hons) Belfast]

LOVE DUDLEY MARK

2 Paper Buildings, Basement North
Temple, London EC4Y 7ET,
Telephone: 0171 936 2613
E-mail: post@2paper.co.uk
Call Date: Nov 1979, Gray's Inn
Pupil Master
Qualifications: [BSc (Lond)]

LOVE MISS SHARON ANN

Chancery Chambers
1st Floor Offices, 70/72 Chancery Lane,
London WC2A 1AB,
Telephone: 0171 405 6879/6870
Call Date: Oct 1997, Gray's Inn
Qualifications: [BA]

LOVEDAY MARK ALAN

Francis Taylor Building
3rd Floor, Temple, London EC4Y 7BY,
Telephone: 0171 797 7250
Call Date: July 1986, Inner Temple
Pupil Master
Qualifications: [BA (Hons)(Kent)]

LOVEGROVE RICHARD QUENTIN CLOUDESLEY

Sussex Chambers
9 Old Steine, Brighton, Sussex, BN1 1FJ,
Telephone: 01273 607953
Call Date: July 1986, Middle Temple
Qualifications: [LLB (Hons)(Bris)]

LOVEGROVE MRS SANDRA LORENCA

55 Temple Chambers
Temple Avenue, London EC4Y 0HP,
Telephone: 0171 353 7400
Call Date: 1995, Inner Temple
Qualifications: [LLB]

LOVELL MISS MILDRED JEANETTE

Britton Street Chambers
1st Floor, 20 Britton Street, London
EC1M 5NQ, Telephone: 0171 608 3765
Call Date: July 1976, Middle Temple

LOVELL-PANK DORIAN CHRISTOPHER QC (1993)

6 King's Bench Walk
Ground Floor, Temple, London
EC4Y 7DR, Telephone: 0171 583 0410
E-mail: worsley@6kbw.freeserve.co.uk
Call Date: July 1971, Inner Temple
Recorder

LOVERIDGE ANDREW ROBERT

Corn Exchange Chambers
5th Floor, Fenwick Street, Liverpool
L2 7QS, Telephone: 0151 227 1081/5009
Call Date: July 1983, Lincoln's Inn
Qualifications: [LLB (Newc)]

LOWCOCK ANDREW CHARLES

28 St John Street
Manchester M3 4DJ,
Telephone: 0161 834 8418
E-mail: clerk@28stjohnst.co.uk
Call Date: July 1973, Middle Temple
Pupil Master, Recorder
Qualifications: [MA (Oxon)]

LOWE ALAN VAUGHAN

Essex Court Chambers
24 Lincoln's Inn Fields, London
WC2A 3ED, Telephone: 0171 813 8000
E-mail:clerksroom@essexcourt-chambers.co.u
k
Call Date: Feb 1993, Gray's Inn
Qualifications: [LLB, LLM, , Ph.D (Cardiff)]

LOWE ANTHONY MARSHALL

6 Fountain Court
Steelhouse Lane, Birmingham B4 6DR,
Telephone: 0121 233 3282
E-mail: clerks@sixfountain.co.uk
Call Date: July 1976, Middle Temple
Pupil Master
Qualifications: [MA (Oxon)]

LOWE CRAIG DAVID

New Walk Chambers
27 New Walk, Leicester LE1 6TE,
Telephone: 0116 2559144
Call Date: Oct 1994, Lincoln's Inn
Qualifications: [LLB (Hons)(Lond)]

D

LOWE DAVID ALEXANDER QC (1984)

Wilberforce Chambers
8 New Square, Lincoln's Inn, London
WC2A 3QP, Telephone: 0171 306 0102
E-mail: chambers@wilberforce.co.uk
Call Date: July 1965, Middle Temple
Qualifications: [MA (Cantab)]

Types of work: Chancery (general), Charities,
Commercial litigation, Commercial property, Equity, wills and trusts, Pensions

LOWE MISS EMMA MARY ELIZABETH

1 Hare Court
Ground Floor, Temple, London
EC4Y 7BE, Telephone: 0171 353 3982/
5324
Call Date: 1996, Gray's Inn
Qualifications: [BSc (Surrey)]

LOWE GEOFFREY JAMES

India Buildings Chambers
Water Street, Liverpool L2 0XG,
Telephone: 0151 243 6000
E-mail: clerks@chambers.u-net.com
Call Date: July 1975, Gray's Inn
Pupil Master
Qualifications: [LLB]

LOWE GEORGE WILLIAM QC (1997)

Plowden Buildings
2nd Floor, 2 Plowden Buildings, Middle
Temple Lane, London EC4Y 9BU,
Telephone: 0171 583 0808
E-mail: bar@plowdenbuildings.co.uk
9 Woodhouse Square
Leeds LS3 1AD,
Telephone: 0113 2451986
E-mail: clerks@9woodhouse.co.uk
Call Date: July 1972, Lincoln's Inn
Recorder
Qualifications: [LLB]

LOWE JOHN

Trinity Chambers
9-12 Trinity Chare, Quayside, Newcastle
upon Tyne NE1 3DF,
Telephone: 0191 232 1927
E-mail: info@trinitychambers.co.uk

Plowden Buildings
2nd Floor, 2 Plowden Buildings, Middle
Temple Lane, London EC4Y 9BU,
Telephone: 0171 583 0808
E-mail: bar@plowdenbuildings.co.uk
Call Date: July 1976, Gray's Inn
Qualifications: [LLB]

LOWE MATTHEW JUSTIN

Chambers of Michael Pert QC
36 Bedford Row, London WC1R 4JH,
Telephone: 0171 421 8000
E-mail: 36bedfordrow@link.org
Chambers of Michael Pert QC
24 Albion Place, Northampton NN1 1UD,
Telephone: 01604 602333
Chambers of Michael Pert QC
104 New Walk, Leicester LE1 7EA,
Telephone: 0116 249 2020
Call Date: Nov 1991, Inner Temple
Qualifications: [LLb (Exeter)]

LOWE NICHOLAS MARK QC (1996)

2-3 Gray's Inn Square
Gray's Inn, London WC1R 5JH,
Telephone: 0171 242 4986
E-mail:chambers@2-3graysinnsquare.co.uk
Call Date: July 1972, Gray's Inn
Qualifications: [LLB]

LOWE MISS SARAH LOUISE

4 Paper Buildings
1st Floor, Temple, London EC4Y 7EX,
Telephone: 0171 583 0816/353 1131
E-mail: clerks@4paperbuildings.co.uk
Call Date: Nov 1995, Middle Temple
Qualifications: [MA (Hons)]

LOWE THOMAS WILLIAM GORDON

Wilberforce Chambers
8 New Square, Lincoln's Inn, London
WC2A 3QP, Telephone: 0171 306 0102
E-mail: chambers@wilberforce.co.uk
Call Date: Nov 1985, Inner Temple
Pupil Master
Qualifications: [LLB (Lond), LLM (Cantab)]

Types of work: Chancery (general), Commercial litigation, Financial services, Insolvency, Professional negligence

LOWEN JONATHAN ANDREW MICHAEL

Queen Elizabeth Building
Ground Floor, Temple, London
EC4Y 9BS,
Telephone: 0171 353 7181 (12 Lines)
Call Date: Nov 1972, Gray's Inn
Recorder
Qualifications: [MA (Oxon), BA (Rand)]

LOWENSTEIN PAUL DAVID

Littleton Chambers
3 King's Bench Walk North, Temple,
London EC4Y 7HR,
Telephone: 0171 797 8600
E-mail:clerks@littletonchambers.co.uk
Call Date: Nov 1988, Middle Temple
Pupil Master
Qualifications: [LLB (Manch), LLM (Cantab)]

LOWNE STEPHEN MARK

King Charles House
Standard Hill, Nottingham NG1 6FX,
Telephone: 0115 9418851
E-mail: clerks@kch.co.uk
Call Date: July 1981, Inner Temple
Pupil Master
Qualifications: [BA (Hons)]

LOWRY MISS ANNE-MARIE SUZANNE

9 King's Bench Walk
Ground Floor, Temple, London
EC4Y 7DX, Telephone: 0171 353 7202/
3909 E-mail: 9kbw@compuserve.com
Call Date: Oct 1995, Middle Temple
Qualifications: [LLB (Hons) (Exon)]

LOWRY CHARLES STEPHEN

Colleton Chambers
Colleton Crescent, Exeter, Devon,
EX2 4DG, Telephone: 01392 274898/9
Call Date: Feb 1960, Inner Temple
Pupil Master
Qualifications: [MA (Oxon)]

LOWRY MISS EMMA MARGARET COLLINS

Hollis Whiteman Chambers
3rd Floor, Queen Elizabeth Bldg, Temple,
London EC4Y 9BS,
Telephone: 020 7583 5766
E-mail:barristers@holliswhiteman.co.uk
Call Date: Oct 1991, Inner Temple
Qualifications: [MA (Oxon)]

LOWSON NORMAN LAURENCE

New Bailey Chambers
10 Lawson Street, Preston PR1 2QT,
Telephone: 01772 258087
Call Date: July 1989, Lincoln's Inn
Qualifications: [Dip Law]

LUBA JAN MICHAEL ANDREW

Two Garden Court
1st Floor, Middle Temple, London
EC4Y 9BL, Telephone: 0171 353 1633
E-mail:barristers@2gardenct.law.co.uk
Call Date: July 1980, Middle Temple
Pupil Master
Qualifications: [LLB (Lond), LLM (Leics)]

LUCAS MISS BRIDGET ANN

Serle Court Chambers
6 New Square, Lincoln's Inn, London
WC2A 3QS, Telephone: 0171 242 6105
E-mail: clerks@serlecourt.co.uk
Fountain Court
Temple, London EC4Y 9DH,
Telephone: 0171 583 3335
E-mail: chambers@fountaincourt.co.uk
Call Date: Nov 1989, Inner Temple
Qualifications: [BA (Oxon)]

LUCAS EDWARD ALLAN

Queens Square Chambers
56 Queens Square, Bristol BS1 4PR,
Telephone: 0117 921 1966
Call Date: Oct 1991, Middle Temple
Qualifications: [MA, MLitt, , D.Phil (Oxon)]

LUCAS NOEL JOHN MAC

1 Middle Temple Lane
Temple, London EC4Y 1LT,
Telephone: 0171 583 0659 (12 Lines)
E-mail: chambers@1mtl.co.uk
Call Date: July 1979, Middle Temple
Pupil Master, Assistant Recorder
Qualifications: [BSc (Lond)]

LUCAS PHILLIP JOHN

1 Gray's Inn Square
Ground Floor, London WC1R 5AA,
Telephone: 0171 405 8946/7/8
Call Date: Oct 1995, Middle Temple
Qualifications: [LLB (Hons)]

LUCKING MRS ADRIENNE SIMONE

De Montfort Chambers
95 Princess Road East, Leicester LE1 7DQ,
Telephone: 0116 254 8686
E-mail: dmcbar@aol.com
Call Date: Nov 1989, Inner Temple
Pupil Master
Qualifications: [LLB (Hons)]

LUCRAFT MARK

18 Red Lion Court
(Off Fleet Street), London EC4A 3EB,
Telephone: 0171 520 6000
E-mail: chambers@18rlc.co.uk
Thornwood House
102 New London Road, Chelmsford,
Essex, CM2 0RG,
Telephone: 01245 280880
E-mail: chambers@18rlc.co.uk
Call Date: July 1984, Inner Temple
Pupil Master
Qualifications: [BA (Kent)]

LUDBROOK TIMOTHY VIVIAN

7 New Square
1st Floor, Lincoln's Inn, London
WC2A 3QS, Telephone: 020 7404 5484
E-mail: clerks@7newsquare.com
Call Date: 1996, Inner Temple
Qualifications: [LLB]

LUGG MISS ELIZABETH CLAIRE

Broad Chare
33 Broad Chare, Newcastle upon Tyne
NE1 3DQ, Telephone: 0191 232 0541
E-mail:clerks@broadcharechambers.law.co.uk
Call Date: Oct 1994, Gray's Inn
Qualifications: [BA]

LUMLEY GERALD

9 Woodhouse Square
Leeds LS3 1AD,
Telephone: 0113 2451986
E-mail: clerks@9woodhouse.co.uk
Call Date: July 1972, Inner Temple
Pupil Master
Qualifications: [LLB (Lond)]

LUMLEY NICHOLAS JAMES HENRY

Sovereign Chambers
25 Park Square, Leeds LS1 2PW,
Telephone: 0113 2451841/2/3
E-mail:sovereignchambers@btinternet.com
Call Date: Oct 1992, Lincoln's Inn
Qualifications: [LLB(Hons)(Newc)]

LUMSDON JOHN STUART

Call Date: July 1991, Inner Temple
Qualifications: [BA (Notts), MSc (Warwick),
LLB]

LUMSDON MISS KATHERINE JANE

2 King's Bench Walk
Ground Floor, Temple, London
EC4Y 7DE, Telephone: 0171 353 1746
E-mail: 2kbw@atlas.co.uk
King's Bench Chambers
115 North Hill, Plymouth PL4 8JY,
Telephone: 01752 221551
Call Date: Oct 1993, Middle Temple
Qualifications: [BA (Hons)(Manc), CPE
(Lond)]

LUND MRS CELIA

Adrian Lyon's Chambers
14 Castle Street, Liverpool L2 0NE,
Telephone: 0151 236 4421/8240
E-mail: chambers14@aol.com

D

5 Stone Buildings
Lincoln's Inn, London WC2A 3XT,
Telephone: 0171 242 6201
E-mail:clerks@5-stonebuildings.law.co.uk
Call Date: Nov 1988, Lincoln's Inn
Qualifications: [LLB Hons]

LUNDIE CHRISTOPHER CARLTON

1 Harcourt Buildings
2nd Floor, Temple, London EC4Y 9DA,
Telephone: 0171 353 9421/0375
E-mail:clerks@1harcourtbuildings.law.co.uk
Call Date: Nov 1991, Inner Temple
Qualifications: [MA (Cantab)]

LUNT MISS BEVERLY ANNE

58 King Street Chambers
1st Floor, Kingsgate House, 51-53 South
King Street, Manchester M2 6DE,
Telephone: 0161 831 7477
Call Date: July 1977, Gray's Inn
Pupil Master
Qualifications: [BA (Lond)]

LUNT STEVEN

9 Woodhouse Square
Leeds LS3 1AD,
Telephone: 0113 2451986
E-mail: clerks@9woodhouse.co.uk
Call Date: Oct 1991, Inner Temple
Qualifications: [LLB (Leeds)]

LURIE SYDNEY JONATHAN JOSEPH

10 King's Bench Walk
1st Floor, Temple, London EC4Y 7EB,
Telephone: 0171 353 2501
Call Date: Nov 1972, Middle Temple
Pupil Master

LYDIARD ANDREW JOHN

Brick Court Chambers
7-8 Essex Street, London WC2R 3LD,
Telephone: 0171 379 3550
E-mail: [surname]@brickcourt.co.uk
Call Date: July 1980, Inner Temple
Pupil Master
Qualifications: [BA (Oxon), LLM]

LYELL THE RT HON SIR NICHOLAS WALTER QC (1980)

Brick Court Chambers
7-8 Essex Street, London WC2R 3LD,
Telephone: 0171 379 3550
E-mail: [surname]@brickcourt.co.uk
Call Date: 1965, Inner Temple
Qualifications: [MA (Oxon)]

LYGO CARL RAYMOND

Mitre House Chambers
15-19 Devereux Court, London WC2R 3JJ,
Telephone: 0171 583 8233
Call Date: Oct 1991, Middle Temple
Qualifications: [LLB (Hons), LLM (E Anglia)]

LYNAGH RICHARD DUDLEY QC (1996)

Two Crown Office Row
Ground Floor, Temple, London
EC4Y 7HJ, Telephone: 020 7797 8100
E-mail: mail@2cor.co.uk, or to individual
barristers at: [barrister's
surname]@2cor.co.uk
Call Date: July 1975, Gray's Inn
Qualifications: [LLB]

LYNCH ADRIAN CHARLES EDMUND

11 King's Bench Walk
Temple, London EC4Y 7EQ,
Telephone: 0171 632 8500/583 0610
E-mail: clerksroom@11kbw.com
Call Date: Nov 1983, Gray's Inn
Pupil Master
Qualifications: [LLB (Lond)]

LYNCH JEROME

Cloisters
1 Pump Court, Temple, London
EC4Y 7AA, Telephone: 0171 827 4000
E-mail: clerks@cloisters.com
Call Date: July 1983, Lincoln's Inn
Pupil Master
Qualifications: [BA (Hons)]

LYNCH JULIAN

7 Stone Buildings (also at 11 Bolt Court)
1st Floor, Lincoln's Inn, London
WC2A 3SZ, Telephone: 0171 242 0961
E-mail:larthur@7stonebuildings.law.co.uk

11 Bolt Court (also at 7 Stone Buildings – 1st Floor)
London EC4A 3DQ,
Telephone: 0171 353 2300
E-mail: boltct11@aol.com
Redhill Chambers
Seloduct House, 30 Station Road, Redhill,
Surrey, RH1 1NF,
Telephone: 01737 780781
Call Date: Nov 1976, Inner Temple
Qualifications: [LLB (Lond)]

LYNCH MISS PATRICIA QC (1998)

18 Red Lion Court
(Off Fleet Street), London EC4A 3EB,
Telephone: 0171 520 6000
E-mail: chambers@18rlc.co.uk
Thornwood House
102 New London Road, Chelmsford,
Essex, CM2 0RG,
Telephone: 01245 280880
E-mail: chambers@18rlc.co.uk
Call Date: Nov 1979, Inner Temple
Assistant Recorder
Qualifications: [LLB (Hull)]

LYNCH PATRICK DENIS

Clock Chambers
78 Darlington Street, Wolverhampton
WV1 4LY, Telephone: 01902 313444
Call Date: July 1988, Inner Temple
Qualifications: [BEd (Lond), Dip Law]

LYNCH PETER GARETH

4 Brick Court
Temple, London EC4Y 9AD,
Telephone: 0171 797 8910
E-mail: medhurst@dial.pipex.com
Call Date: July 1985, Lincoln's Inn
Qualifications: [BSc, Dip Law]

LYNCH TERRY JOHN

Northampton Chambers
22 Albion Place, Northampton NN1 1UD,
Telephone: 01604 636271
Call Date: Nov 1989, Inner Temple
Pupil Master
Qualifications: [BA]

LYNDON-STANFORD MICHAEL ANDREW FLEMYNG QC (1979)

13 Old Square
Ground Floor, Lincoln's Inn, London
WC2A 3UA, Telephone: 0171 404 4800
E-mail: clerks@13oldsquare.law.co.uk
Call Date: Feb 1962, Inner Temple
Qualifications: [MA (Cantab)]

LYNE MARK HILARY

One Essex Court
1st Floor, Temple, London EC4Y 9AR,
Telephone: 0171 936 3030
E-mail: one.essex_court@virgin.net
Call Date: Nov 1981, Inner Temple
Pupil Master
Qualifications: [MA (Cantab)]

LYNESS SCOTT EDWARD

1 Serjeants' Inn
4th Floor, Temple, London EC4Y 1NH,
Telephone: 0171 583 1355
E-mail: clerks@serjeants-inn.co.uk
Call Date: Oct 1996, Lincoln's Inn
Qualifications: [LLB (Hons)(Hull)]

LYNN JEREMY DAVID

2 King's Bench Walk Chambers
1st Floor, 2 King's Bench Walk, Temple,
London EC4Y 7DE,
Telephone: 020 7353 9276
E-mail: chambers@2kbw.co.uk
Call Date: Nov 1983, Inner Temple
Pupil Master
Qualifications: [BSc Cardiff]

LYON ADRIAN PIRRIE

Adrian Lyon's Chambers
14 Castle Street, Liverpool L2 0NE,
Telephone: 0151 236 4421/8240
E-mail: chambers14@aol.com
Call Date: July 1975, Gray's Inn
Pupil Master, Assistant Recorder
Qualifications: [LLB (Lond)]

LYON MISS ANTONIA HEIDI JANE

Queen Elizabeth Building
2nd Floor, Temple, London EC4Y 9BS,
Telephone: 0171 797 7837
Call Date: 1997, Middle Temple
Qualifications: [BA (Hons)(Cantab)]

LYON MRS SHANE VALERIE

Walnut House
63 St David's Hill, Exeter, Devon,
EX4 4DW, Telephone: 01392 279751
E-mail: 106627.2451@compuserve.com
Call Date: Nov 1976, Middle Temple
Qualifications: [LLB (Exon)]

LYON STEPHEN JOHN

14 Gray's Inn Square
Gray's Inn, London WC1R 5JP,
Telephone: 0171 242 0858
E-mail: 100712.2134@compuserve.com
Westgate Chambers
144 High Street, Lewes, East Sussex,
BN7 1XT, Telephone: 01273 480510
Call Date: July 1987, Inner Temple
Pupil Master
Qualifications: [LLB (Notts)]

LYON VICTOR LAWRENCE

Essex Court Chambers
24 Lincoln's Inn Fields, London
WC2A 3ED, Telephone: 0171 813 8000
E-mail:clerksroom@essexcourt-chambers.co.uk
Call Date: July 1980, Gray's Inn
Pupil Master
Qualifications: [MA (Cantab)]

LYONS DAVID WAKEFIELD

Plowden Buildings
2nd Floor, 2 Plowden Buildings, Middle
Temple Lane, London EC4Y 9BU,
Telephone: 0171 583 0808
E-mail: bar@plowdenbuildings.co.uk
Call Date: July 1987, Middle Temple
Pupil Master
Qualifications: [BA (Hons)]

LYONS GRAHAM ANTHONY

2 Pump Court
1st Floor, Temple, London EC4Y 7AH,
Telephone: 0171 353 5597
Call Date: July 1972, Inner Temple
Pupil Master

LYONS JOHN ADAM

4 Brick Court
Ground Floor, Temple, London
EC4Y 9AD, Telephone: 0171 797 7766
E-mail: chambers@4brick.co.uk
Call Date: July 1986, Middle Temple
Pupil Master
Qualifications: [BA (Dunelm) Dip Law]

LYONS TIMOTHY JOHN

24 Old Buildings
First Floor, Lincoln's Inn, London
WC2A 3UP, Telephone: 020 7242 2744
E-mail: taxchambers@compuserve.com
St James's Chambers
68 Quay Street, Manchester M3 3EJ,
Telephone: 0161 834 7000
E-mail: clerks@stjameschambers.co.uk
Call Date: July 1980, Inner Temple
Pupil Master
Qualifications: [LLB (Bris), LLM Phd , (Lon)
FTII, TEP]

MABB DAVID MICHAEL

Erskine Chambers
30 Lincoln's Inn Fields, Lincoln's Inn,
London WC2A 3PF,
Telephone: 0171 242 5532
E-mail:clerks@erskine-chambers.co.uk
Call Date: July 1979, Lincoln's Inn
Pupil Master
Qualifications: [MA (Cantab)]

MABLY LOUIS ASA LUKE ALEXIS DYLAN

6 King's Bench Walk
Ground Floor, Temple, London
EC4Y 7DR, Telephone: 0171 583 0410
E-mail: worsley@6kbw.freeserve.co.uk
Call Date: 1997, Lincoln's Inn
Qualifications: [BA (Hons)(Leeds)]

MACADAM JASON ANGUS ALAISTER ROBERT L

37 Park Square Chambers
37 Park Square, Leeds LS1 2NY,
Telephone: 0113 2439422
E-mail: chambers@no37.co.uk
Call Date: Nov 1990, Lincoln's Inn
Qualifications: [LLB (Wales), B.TEC]

MACAULAY BERTHAN

1 Gray's Inn Square
Ground Floor, London WC1R 5AA,
Telephone: 0171 405 8946/7/8
Call Date: Nov 1953, Gray's Inn
Qualifications: [MA, LLB]

MACAULAY MISS DONORA MARIE

Chambers of Wilfred Forster-Jones
New Court, 1st Floor South, Temple,
London EC4Y 9BE,
Telephone: 0171 353 0853/4/7222
E-mail: chambers@newcourt.net
Call Date: Nov 1982, Middle Temple
Pupil Master
Qualifications: [LLB (Bucks)]

MACCABE IRVINE JOHN

3 Paper Buildings
Temple, London EC4Y 7EU,
Telephone: 020 7583 8055
E-mail: London@3paper.com
3 Paper Buildings (Bournemouth)
20 Lorne Park Road, Bournemouth,
Dorset, BH1 1JN,
Telephone: 01202 292102
E-mail: Bournemouth@3paper.com
3 Paper Buildings (Winchester)
4 St Peter Street, Winchester SO23 8BW,
Telephone: 01962 868884
E-mail: winchester@3paper.com
3 Paper Buildings (Oxford)
1 Alfred Street, High Street, Oxford
OX1 4EH, Telephone: 01865 793736
E-mail: oxford@3paper.com
Call Date: July 1983, Gray's Inn
Qualifications: [MA (Cantab)]

MACDONALD ALISTAIR NEIL

Park Court Chambers
16 Park Place, Leeds LS1 2SJ,
Telephone: 0113 2433277
Call Date: July 1983, Gray's Inn
Pupil Master, Assistant Recorder
Qualifications: [BSc (Bath), Dip Law (City)]

MACDONALD ALISTAIR WILLIAM ORCHARD

St Philip's Chambers
Fountain Court, Steelhouse Lane,
Birmingham B4 6DR,
Telephone: 0121 246 7000
E-mail: clerks@st-philips.co.uk
Call Date: Nov 1995, Inner Temple
Qualifications: [BA (Hons)(Notts), Dip in Law (Lond)]

MACDONALD CHARLES ADAM QC (1992)

4 Essex Court
Temple, London EC4Y 9AJ,
Telephone: 020 7797 7970
E-mail: clerks@4essexcourt.law.co.uk
Call Date: Nov 1972, Lincoln's Inn
Assistant Recorder
Qualifications: [MA (Oxon)]

MACDONALD IAIN

Gough Square Chambers
6-7 Gough Square, London EC4A 3DE,
Telephone: 0171 353 0924
E-mail: gsc@goughsq.co.uk
Call Date: July 1996, Middle Temple
Qualifications: [BA (Hons)(Oxon)]

MACDONALD IAN ALEXANDER QC (1988)

Two Garden Court
1st Floor, Middle Temple, London
EC4Y 9BL, Telephone: 0171 353 1633
E-mail:barristers@2gardenct.law.co.uk
Chambers of Ian Macdonald QC (In Association with Two Garden Court, Temple, London)
Waldorf House, 5 Cooper Street,
Manchester M2 2FW,
Telephone: 0161 236 1840
Call Date: Feb 1963, Middle Temple
Qualifications: [MA, LLB]

MACDONALD JOHN REGINALD QC (1976)

12 New Square
Lincoln's Inn, London WC2A 3SW,
Telephone: 0171 419 1212
E-mail: chambers@12newsquare.co.uk

Sovereign Chambers
25 Park Square, Leeds LS1 2PW,
Telephone: 0113 2451841/2/3
E-mail:sovereignchambers@btinternet.com
Call Date: June 1955, Lincoln's Inn
Qualifications: [MA (Cantab)]

MACDONALD KENNETH DONALD JOHN QC (1997)

Two Garden Court
1st Floor, Middle Temple, London
EC4Y 9BL, Telephone: 0171 353 1633
E-mail:barristers@2gardenct.law.co.uk
Call Date: July 1978, Inner Temple
Qualifications: [BA (Oxon)]

MACDONALD MISS LINDSEY RACHEL

Hardwicke Building
New Square, Lincoln's Inn, London
WC2A 3SB, Telephone: 020 7242 2523
E-mail: clerks@hardwicke.co.uk
Call Date: Feb 1985, Lincoln's Inn
Qualifications: [LLB (Bris)]

MACDONALD MISS SHELIA HAMILTON

11 Stone Buildings
Lincoln's Inn, London WC2A 3TG,
Telephone: +44 (0)207 831 6381
E-mail:clerks@11StoneBuildings.law.co.uk
Call Date: Feb 1993, Middle Temple
Qualifications: [MA (Hons)(Glas), LLB
(Hons)(Lond)]

MACEY-DARE THOMAS CHARLES

4 Essex Court
Temple, London EC4Y 9AJ,
Telephone: 020 7797 7970
E-mail: clerks@4essexcourt.law.co.uk
Call Date: Feb 1994, Middle Temple
Qualifications: [MA (Cantab), LLM, (Cantab),
LLM (USA)]

MACFARLANE ANDREW LENNOX

Guildhall Chambers
22-26 Broad Street, Bristol BS1 2HG,
Telephone: 0117 9273366
E-mail:civil.clerks@guildhallchambers.co.uk and
criminal.clerks@guildhallchambers.co.uk
Call Date: May 1995, Inner Temple

MACFAUL DONALD WILLIAM

Durham Barristers' Chambers
27 Old Elvet, Durham DH1 3HN,
Telephone: 0191 386 9199
Call Date: Mar 1998, Inner Temple
Qualifications: [LLB (Newcastle)]

MACGREGOR ALASTAIR RANKIN QC (1994)

One Essex Court
Ground Floor, Temple, London
EC4Y 9AR, Telephone: 020 7583 2000
E-mail: clerks@oneessexcourt.co.uk
Call Date: July 1974, Lincoln's Inn
Qualifications: [MA (Oxon)]

MACGREGOR MRS HEATHER MARGARET

Gray's Inn Chambers
5th Floor, Gray's Inn, London WC1R 5JA,
Telephone: 0171 404 1111
Call Date: July 1982, Gray's Inn
Qualifications: [BA, Dip Law (Lond)]

MACHELL JOHN WILLIAM

Serle Court Chambers
6 New Square, Lincoln's Inn, London
WC2A 3QS, Telephone: 0171 242 6105
E-mail: clerks@serlecourt.co.uk
Call Date: Oct 1993, Inner Temple
Qualifications: [LLB (So'ton)]

MACHELL RAYMOND DONATUS QC (1988)

Deans Court Chambers
24 St John Street, Manchester M3 4DF,
Telephone: 0161 214 6000
E-mail: clerks@deanscourt.co.uk
2 Pump Court
1st Floor, Temple, London EC4Y 7AH,
Telephone: 0171 353 5597
Deans Court Chambers
41-43 Market Place, Preston PR1 1AH,
Telephone: 01772 555163
E-mail: clerks@deanscourt.co.uk
Call Date: July 1973, Gray's Inn
Recorder
Qualifications: [MA, LLB (Cantab)]

D

MACHIN CHARLES KIM

Cobden House Chambers
19 Quay Street, Manchester M3 3HN,
Telephone: 0161 833 6000
E-mail: clerks@cobden.co.uk
Call Date: Nov 1973, Lincoln's Inn
Pupil Master
Qualifications: [MA (Oxon)]

MACHIN GRAHAM EDWARD

Ropewalk Chambers
24 The Ropewalk, Nottingham NG1 5EF,
Telephone: 0115 9472581
E-mail: administration@ropewalk co.uk
Call Date: July 1965, Gray's Inn

MACIEL MISS KAREENA

Britton Street Chambers
1st Floor, 20 Britton Street, London
EC1M 5NQ, Telephone: 0171 608 3765
Call Date: July 1994, Lincoln's Inn
Qualifications: [LLB (Hons)]

MACKAY COLIN CRICHTON QC (1989)

39 Essex Street
London WC2R 3AT,
Telephone: 0171 832 1111
E-mail: clerks@39essex.co.uk
Call Date: July 1967, Middle Temple
Recorder
Qualifications: [MA (Oxon)]

MACKENZIE MISS ANNA KAREEN

Plowden Buildings
2nd Floor, 2 Plowden Buildings, Middle
Temple Lane, London EC4Y 9BU,
Telephone: 0171 583 0808
E-mail: bar@plowdenbuildings.co.uk
Call Date: Nov 1994, Lincoln's Inn
Qualifications: [LLB (Hons)(L'pool)]

MACKENZIE MISS JULIE FIONA

Colleton Chambers
Colleton Crescent, Exeter, Devon,
EX2 4DG, Telephone: 01392 274898/9
Colleton Chambers
Powlett House, 34 High Street, Taunton,
Somerset, TA1 3PN,
Telephone: 01823 324252

Pump Court Chambers
5 Temple Chambers, Temple Street,
Swindon SN1 1SQ,
Telephone: 01793 539899
E-mail: clerks@3pumpcourt.com
Pump Court Chambers
Upper Ground Floor, 3 Pump Court,
Temple, London EC4Y 7AJ,
Telephone: 0171 353 0711
E-mail: clerks@3pumpcourt.com
Pump Court Chambers
31 Southgate Street, Winchester
SO23 9EE, Telephone: 01962 868161
E-mail: clerks@3pumpcourt.com
Call Date: Nov 1978, Lincoln's Inn
Pupil Master

MACKENZIE SMITH CATHERINE JOANNA

Plowden Buildings
2nd Floor, 2 Plowden Buildings, Middle
Temple Lane, London EC4Y 9BU,
Telephone: 0171 583 0808
E-mail: bar@plowdenbuildings.co.uk
Call Date: Nov 1960, Inner Temple

MACKESON-SANDBACH MISS ANTOINETTE GERALDINE

**4 Brick Court, Chambers of Anne
Rafferty QC**
1st Floor, Temple, London EC4Y 9AD,
Telephone: 0171 583 8455
Call Date: Oct 1993, Lincoln's Inn
Qualifications: [BA (Hons)(Notts), LLM
(Notts)]

MACKIE MS JEANNIE

1 Dr Johnson's Buildings
Ground Floor, Temple, London
EC4Y 7AX, Telephone: 0171 353 9328
E-mail:OneDr.Johnsons@btinternet.com
Call Date: July 1995, Inner Temple
Qualifications: [BA (Cantab)]

MACKILLOP NORMAN MALCOLM

Chartlands Chambers
3 St Giles Terrace, Northampton
NN1 2BN, Telephone: 01604 603322
Call Date: Oct 1994, Gray's Inn
Qualifications: [MA]

MACKINNON THOMAS JOSEPH

8 King's Bench Walk
2nd Floor, Temple, London EC4Y 7DU,
Telephone: 0171 797 8888
8 King's Bench Walk North
1 Park Square East, Leeds LS1 2NE,
Telephone: 0113 2439797
Call Date: July 1982, Middle Temple
Pupil Master
Qualifications: [LLB,LLM (Sheff)]

MACLAREN ALEXANDER PETER

Thomas More Chambers
52 Carey Street, Lincoln's Inn, London
WC2A 2JB, Telephone: 0171 404 7000
E-mail: clerks@thomasmore.law.co.uk
Call Date: Mar 1997, Lincoln's Inn
Qualifications: [BA (Hons)(York)]

MACLAREN MISS CATRIONA LONGUEVILLE

2nd Floor, Francis Taylor Building
Temple, London EC4Y 7BY,
Telephone: 0171 353 9942/3157
Call Date: Oct 1993, Inner Temple
Qualifications: [MA (Cantab)]

MACLEAN ALAN JOHN

39 Essex Street
London WC2R 3AT,
Telephone: 0171 832 1111
E-mail: clerks@39essex.co.uk
Call Date: Oct 1993, Gray's Inn
Qualifications: [BA (Oxon)]

MACLEAN KENNETH WALTER

One Essex Court
Ground Floor, Temple, London
EC4Y 9AR, Telephone: 020 7583 2000
E-mail: clerks@oneessexcourt.co.uk
Call Date: May 1985, Gray's Inn
Pupil Master
Qualifications: [MA (Cantab) LLM, (Harvard)]

MACLENNAN MS ALISON

11 Old Square
Ground Floor, Lincoln's Inn, London
WC2A 3TS, Telephone: 0171 242 5022/
405 1074
Call Date: 1996, Gray's Inn
Qualifications: [LLB (Reading)]

MACLEOD DUNCAN

9 Gough Square
London EC4A 3DE,
Telephone: 020 7832 0500
E-mail: clerks@9goughsq.co.uk
Call Date: July 1980, Middle Temple
Pupil Master
Qualifications: [BA (Lond), LLB (Cardiff)]

MACLEOD NIGEL RONALD BUCHANAN QC (1979)

4 Breams Buildings
London EC4A 1AQ,
Telephone: 0171 353 5835/430 1221
E-mail:breams@4breamsbuildings.law.co.uk
40 King Street
Manchester M2 6BA,
Telephone: 0161 832 9082
E-mail: clerks@40kingstreet.co.uk
The Chambers of Philip Raynor QC
5 Park Place, Leeds LS1 2RU,
Telephone: 0113 242 1123
Call Date: Feb 1961, Gray's Inn
Recorder
Qualifications: [MA, BCL (Oxon)]

MACLEOD-JAMES NICHOLAS MARK

11 Old Square
Ground Floor, Lincoln's Inn, London
WC2A 3TS, Telephone: 0171 242 5022/
405 1074
Call Date: Nov 1986, Lincoln's Inn
Qualifications: [BA, BSc (Lond)]

MACNAB ALEXANDER ANDREW

Monckton Chambers
4 Raymond Buildings, Gray's Inn, London
WC1R 5BP, Telephone: 0171 405 7211
E-mail: chambers@monckton.co.uk
Call Date: July 1986, Middle Temple
Pupil Master
Qualifications: [MA,LLM (Cantab)]

MACPHERSON ANGUS JOHN

1 Temple Gardens
1st Floor, Temple, London EC4Y 9BB,
Telephone: 0171 583 1315/353 0407
E-mail: clerks@1templegardens.co.uk
Call Date: July 1977, Inner Temple
Pupil Master
Qualifications: [MA (Cantab)]

D

MACPHERSON DUNCAN CHARLES STEWART

Bracton Chambers
95a Chancery Lane, London WC2A 1DT,
Telephone: 0171 242 4248
Call Date: May 1994, Middle Temple
Qualifications: [BA (Hons)]

MACPHERSON THE HON MARY STEWART

2 Mitre Court Buildings
2nd Floor, Temple, London EC4Y 7BX,
Telephone: 0171 583 1380
E-mail: clerks@2mcb.co.uk
Call Date: July 1984, Inner Temple
Pupil Master
Qualifications: [MA (Hons) (Edin), Dip Law]

MACRAE ROBERT JAMES

Walnut House
63 St David's Hill, Exeter, Devon,
EX4 4DW, Telephone: 01392 279751
E-mail: 106627.2451@compuserve.com
Call Date: Oct 1990, Middle Temple
Qualifications: [LLB (Exon)]

MACRORY RICHARD BRABAZON

Brick Court Chambers
7-8 Essex Street, London WC2R 3LD,
Telephone: 0171 379 3550
E-mail: [surname]@brickcourt.co.uk
Call Date: Nov 1974, Gray's Inn
Qualifications: [MA (Oxon)]

MACUR MISS JULIA QC (1998)

St Ive's Chambers
Whittall Street, Birmingham B4 6DH,
Telephone: 0121 236 0863/5720
E-mail:stives.headofchambers@btinternet.com
Call Date: July 1979, Lincoln's Inn
Qualifications: [LLB (Hons) (Sheff)]

MADAN PANKAJ

Chambers of Andrew Campbell QC
10 Park Square, Leeds LS1 2LH,
Telephone: 0113 2455438
E-mail: clerks@10pksq.co.uk
Call Date: 1997, Middle Temple
Qualifications: [BA (Hons)(Cantab)]

MADDICK FRANCIS BRUCE

2 King's Bench Walk
Ground Floor, Temple, London
EC4Y 7DE, Telephone: 0171 353 1746
E-mail: 2kbw@atlas.co.uk
King's Bench Chambers
115 North Hill, Plymouth PL4 8JY,
Telephone: 01752 221551
Call Date: July 1970, Gray's Inn
Pupil Master

MADDISON DAVID THOMAS JAMES

Cobden House Chambers
19 Quay Street, Manchester M3 3HN,
Telephone: 0161 833 6000
E-mail: clerks@cobden.co.uk
Call Date: 1994, Gray's Inn
Qualifications: [LLB]

MADDOX PETER

Iscoed Chambers
86 St Helen's Road, Swansea, West
Glamorgan, SA1 4BQ,
Telephone: 01792 652988/9/330
Call Date: Feb 1994, Gray's Inn
Qualifications: [LLB (Wales)]

MAGARIAN MICHAEL

2 Dyers Buildings
London EC1N 2JT,
Telephone: 0171 404 1881
Call Date: July 1988, Gray's Inn
Qualifications: [BA (Hons, Cantab)]

MAGEE MICHAEL JAMES

Fenners Chambers
8-12 Priestgate, Peterborough PE1 1JA,
Telephone: 01733 562030
E-mail: clerks@fennerschambers.co.uk
Fenners Chambers
3 Madingley Road, Cambridge CB3 0EE,
Telephone: 01223 368761
E-mail: clerks@fennerschambers.co.uk
Call Date: 1997, Inner Temple
Qualifications: [MA (Cantab), CPE (City)]

MAGEE MISS ROSEIN MOIRA

Chichester Chambers
12 North Pallant, Chichester, West Sussex,
PO19 1TQ, Telephone: 01243 784538
E-mail:clerks@chichesterchambers.law.co.uk
Call Date: Oct 1994, Gray's Inn
Qualifications: [BA (Hons)(Keele)]

MAGILL CIARAN SEOSA

Counsels' Chambers
2nd Floor, 10-11 Gray's Inn Square,
London WC1R 5JD,
Telephone: 0171 405 2576
E-mail:clerks@10-11graysinnsquare.co.uk
Call Date: Nov 1988, Middle Temple
Pupil Master
Qualifications: [LLB (Hons), BL]

MAGLOIRE MICHAEL

Chancery Chambers
1st Floor Offices, 70/72 Chancery Lane,
London WC2A 1AB,
Telephone: 0171 405 6879/6870
Call Date: Nov 1982, Middle Temple
Pupil Master
Qualifications: [BA, LLB]

MAGUIRE ALBERT MICHAEL QC (1967)

Goldsmith Building
1st Floor, Temple, London EC4Y 7BL,
Telephone: 0171 353 7881
E-mail:clerks@goldsmith-building.law.co.uk
Call Date: Jan 1949, Middle Temple
Qualifications: [BA (Cantab)]

MAGUIRE ANDREW JAMES

St Ive's Chambers
Whittall Street, Birmingham B4 6DH,
Telephone: 0121 236 0863/5720
E-mail:stives.headofchambers@btinternet.com
Call Date: Nov 1988, Inner Temple
Qualifications: [LLB (Hons) (Hull)]

MAGUIRE MARTIN BENN

4 King's Bench Walk
2nd Floor, Temple, London EC4Y 7DL,
Telephone: 020 7353 3581
E-mail: clerks@4kbw.co.uk
Call Date: Nov 1994, Inner Temple
Qualifications: [BA (Hons), MA]

MAGUIRE MS SARAH RUTH

14 Tooks Court
Cursitor St, London EC4A 1LB,
Telephone: 0171 405 8828
E-mail: clerks@tooks.law.co.uk
Call Date: Nov 1990, Inner Temple
Qualifications: [BA, Dip Law (PCL)]

MAHER MS MARTHA JOHANNA DOROTHY

Guildhall Chambers
22-26 Broad Street, Bristol BS1 2HG,
Telephone: 0117 9273366
E-mail:civil.clerks@guildhallchambers.co.uk and
criminal.clerks@guildhallchambers.co.uk
Call Date: Nov 1987, Inner Temple
Qualifications: [BCL,LLB (Cork), LLM
(Cantab)]

MAHER MICHAEL JAMES

**4 Brick Court, Chambers of Anne
Rafferty QC**
1st Floor, Temple, London EC4Y 9AD,
Telephone: 0171 583 8455
Call Date: Nov 1995, Gray's Inn
Qualifications: [BA (Dunelm), LLM
(Edinburgh)]

MAHMOOD ABID

8 Fountain Court
Steelhouse Lane, Birmingham B4 6DR,
Telephone: 0121 236 5514/5
E-mail: clerks@no8chambers.co.uk
Call Date: Nov 1992, Inner Temple
Qualifications: [LLB (Hons)]

MAHMOOD IMRAN WASEEM

Holborn Chambers
6 Gate Street, Lincoln's Inn Fields, London
WC2A 3HP, Telephone: 0171 242 6060
Call Date: July 1992, Middle Temple
Qualifications: [LLB (Hons)]

MAHMOOD SALIM HUSSAIN

Law Chambers
2nd Floor, 5 Cardiff Road, Luton,
Bedfordshire, LU1 1PP,
Telephone: 01582 431352 or 0958 674785
Call Date: July 1979, Lincoln's Inn
Qualifications: [BA]

MAHON BRIAN PATRICK

Equity Chambers
3rd Floor, 153a Corporation Street,
Birmingham B4 6PH,
Telephone: 0121 233 2100
E-mail: equityatusa.com
Call Date: Oct 1996, Lincoln's Inn
Qualifications: [LLB (Hons)(B'ham)]

MAIDMENT KIERAN FRANCIS

Doughty Street Chambers
11 Doughty Street, London WC1N 2PG,
Telephone: 0171 404 1313
E-mail:enquiries@doughtystreet.co.uk
Call Date: Nov 1989, Gray's Inn
Pupil Master
Qualifications: [LLB (LSE), MA (KCL)]

MAIDMENT MRS SUSAN RACHEL

One King's Bench Walk
1st Floor, Temple, London EC4Y 7DB,
Telephone: 0171 936 1500
E-mail: ddear@1kbw.co.uk
Call Date: July 1968, Lincoln's Inn
Pupil Master, Assistant Recorder
Qualifications: [LLB, LLM (Lond), LLD]

MAILER CLIFFORD ROWLAND

1 Dr Johnson's Buildings
Ground Floor, Temple, London
EC4Y 7AX, Telephone: 0171 353 9328
E-mail:OneDr.Johnsons@btinternet.com
Dr Johnson's Chambers
The Atrium Court, Apex Plaza, Reading,
Berkshire, RG1 1AX,
Telephone: 01734 254221
Call Date: July 1987, Middle Temple
Pupil Master
Qualifications: [BA, LLB (Witwater), LLB
(Cantab), LLM]

MAIN PETER RAMSAY

Deans Court Chambers
24 St John Street, Manchester M3 4DF,
Telephone: 0161 214 6000
E-mail: clerks@deanscourt.co.uk

Deans Court Chambers
41-43 Market Place, Preston PR1 1AH,
Telephone: 01772 555163
E-mail: clerks@deanscourt.co.uk
Call Date: July 1981, Inner Temple
Pupil Master, Assistant Recorder
Qualifications: [LLB (LSE), Dip Pet Law
(Dundee)]

MAINDS ALLAN GILFILLAN

Chambers of Michael Pert QC
36 Bedford Row, London WC1R 4JH,
Telephone: 0171 421 8000
E-mail: 36bedfordrow@link.org
Chambers of Michael Pert QC
24 Albion Place, Northampton NN1 1UD,
Telephone: 01604 602333
Chambers of Michael Pert QC
104 New Walk, Leicester LE1 7EA,
Telephone: 0116 249 2020
Call Date: Feb 1977, Inner Temple
Pupil Master, Recorder

MAINWARING [ROBERT] PAUL CLASON

Carmarthen Chambers
30 Spilman Street, Carmarthen, Dyfed,
SA31 1LQ, Telephone: 01267 234410
E-mail: law@in-wales.com
Call Date: Nov 1996, Gray's Inn
Qualifications: [LLM (Bris)]

MAIRS ROBIN GORDON JAMES

St Paul's House
5th Floor, St Paul's House, 23 Park Square
South, Leeds LS1 2ND,
Telephone: 0113 2455866
E-mail: catherinegrimshaw@stpauls-
chambers.demon.co.uk
Call Date: Oct 1992, Gray's Inn
Qualifications: [LLB (Hons), LLM (Cantab)]

MAITLAND ANDREW HENRY REAVELY

King's Bench Chambers
115 North Hill, Plymouth PL4 8JY,
Telephone: 01752 221551
2 King's Bench Walk
Ground Floor, Temple, London
EC4Y 7DE, Telephone: 0171 353 1746
E-mail: 2kbw@atlas.co.uk
Call Date: July 1970, Lincoln's Inn
Pupil Master, Recorder
Qualifications: [LLB (St Andrews)]

MAITLAND MARC CLAUDE

11 Old Square
Ground Floor, Lincoln's Inn, London
WC2A 3TS, Telephone: 0171 242 5022/
405 1074
Call Date: July 1988, Middle Temple
Qualifications: [LLB (Hons), LLM [Cantab]]

MAITLAND JONES MARK GRIFFITH

Goldsmith Building
1st Floor, Temple, London EC4Y 7BL,
Telephone: 0171 353 7881
E-mail:clerks@goldsmith-building.law.co.uk
Call Date: Nov 1986, Middle Temple
Qualifications: [MA (Edinburgh) Dip, Law
(City)]

MAITRA ADRIAN DILIP

Number Ten Baker Street
10 Baker Street, Middlesbrough TS1 2LH,
Telephone: 01642 220332
Call Date: May 1997, Gray's Inn
Qualifications: [LLB (Northumbria)]

MAJUMDAR SHANTANU

Lamb Chambers
Lamb Building, Temple, London
EC4Y 7AS, Telephone: 020 7797 8300
E-mail: lambchambers@link.org
Call Date: Nov 1992, Middle Temple
Qualifications: [BA (Hons)]

MAKEPEACE PETER ANTHONY

York Chambers
14 Toft Green, York YO1 6JT,
Telephone: 01904 620048
E-mail: [name]@yorkchambers.co.uk
Call Date: July 1988, Lincoln's Inn
Qualifications: [LLB (Hons) (Wales)]

MAKEY CHRISTOPHER DOUGLAS

Old Square Chambers
1 Verulam Buildings, Gray's Inn, London
WC1R 5LQ, Telephone: 0171 269 0300
E-mail:clerks@oldsquarechambers.co.uk
Old Square Chambers
Hanover House, 47 Corn Street, Bristol
BS1 1HT, Telephone: 0117 9277111
E-mail: oldsqbri@globalnet.co.uk
Call Date: July 1975, Middle Temple
Pupil Master
Qualifications: [LLB, ACIArb]

MALCOLM ALASTAIR RICHARD QC (1996)

1 Paper Buildings
1st Floor, Temple, London EC4Y 7EP,
Telephone: 0171 353 3728/4953
Call Date: Feb 1971, Inner Temple
Recorder
Qualifications: [BA (Oxon)]

MALCOLM MISS HELEN KATHARINE LUCY

3 Raymond Buildings
Gray's Inn, London WC1R 5BH,
Telephone: 020 7831 3833
E-mail:chambers@threeraymond.demon.co.uk
Call Date: Nov 1986, Gray's Inn
Pupil Master
Qualifications: [MA (Oxon)]

MALCOLM MISS ROSALIND NIVEN

Field Court Chambers
2nd Floor, 3 Field Court, Gray's Inn,
London WC1R 5EP,
Telephone: 0171 404 7474
Call Date: July 1977, Middle Temple
Qualifications: [LLB (Lond)]

MALCOLM MRS ROZANNA

Gray's Inn Chambers
5th Floor, Gray's Inn, London WC1R 5JA,
Telephone: 0171 404 1111
Call Date: Nov 1974, Gray's Inn
Pupil Master

MALDEN MISS GRACE

35 Essex Street
Temple, London WC2R 3AR,
Telephone: 0171 353 6381
E-mail: derek_jenkins@link.org
Call Date: Nov 1993, Gray's Inn
Qualifications: [BA]

MALE JOHN MARTIN

4 Breams Buildings
London EC4A 1AQ,
Telephone: 0171 353 5835/430 1221
E-mail:breams@4breamsbuildings.law.co.uk
Call Date: July 1976, Lincoln's Inn
Pupil Master
Qualifications: [BA (Cantab)]

D

MALECKA DR MARY MARGARET

3 Temple Gardens
3rd Floor, Temple, London EC4Y 9AU,
Telephone: 0171 353 0832
65-67 King Street
Leicester LE1 6RP,
Telephone: 0116 2547710
Call Date: Oct 1994, Inner Temple
Qualifications: [BA (Illinois), PGCE
(Leicester), PhD (Notts), CPE (City)]

Fax: 0171 727 5092;
Out of hours telephone: Mobile: 0973
425313; DX: 427 Chancery Lane;
Other comms: E-mail
marymm@compuserve.com

Types of work: Administrative, Chancery
(general), Children, Common law
(general), Discrimination, Education,
Employment, Entertainment, Environment, Immigration, Local government,
Personal injury, Sports

Circuit: Midland & Oxford

Awards and memberships: Administrative Law
Bar Association; Immigration Law Practitioners Association; Employment Law Bar
Association; Education Law Association;
Fellow of The Royal Society for the Encour-
agement of the Arts, Manufacture and
Commerce; Fellow of the Institute of Directors; Member of the Royal Institute of International Affairs at Chatham House; Member
of the Bar European Group

Other professional experience: Eleven years'
non-executive company director, regional
and London theatre; Bar Pro Bono Unit
panel; part-time lecturer in law, Westminster University 1994-96; seminar lecturer,
English contract and trust law for Polish
lawyers, Allen & Overy, Warsaw 1994

Languages spoken:

Publications: *The Integration of Disabled
Children into Mainstream Education*
OECD/CERI Paris; ISBN 926414071-9 in
English; ISBN 926424071-3 in French;
translated also into Japanese, 1993;
Contributor to 3rd Edition of *Sport and The
Law*, 1999

MALEK ALI QC (1996)

3 Verulam Buildings
London WC1R 5NT,
Telephone: 0171 831 8441
E-mail: clerks@3verulam.co.uk
Call Date: July 1980, Gray's Inn
Assistant Recorder
Qualifications: [MA, BCL (Oxon)]

MALEK MEHDI (HODGE) QC (1999)

4-5 Gray's Inn Square
Ground Floor, Gray's Inn, London
WC1R 5JP, Telephone: 0171 404 5252
E-mail:chambers@4-5graysinnsquare.co.uk
Call Date: 1983, Gray's Inn
Pupil Master
Qualifications: [BA, BCL (Oxon)]

MALES STEPHEN MARTIN QC (1998)

20 Essex Street
London WC2R 3AL,
Telephone: 0171 583 9294
E-mail: clerks@20essexst.com
Call Date: July 1978, Middle Temple
Qualifications: [MA (Cantab)]

MALET DURAND DAVID GRENVILLE

Holborn Chambers
6 Gate Street, Lincoln's Inn Fields, London
WC2A 3HP, Telephone: 0171 242 6060
Call Date: Oct 1992, Middle Temple
Qualifications: [BA (Hons, Denelm)]

MALEY WILLIAM RAYMOND

3 Gray's Inn Square
Ground Floor, London WC1R 5AH,
Telephone: 0171 520 5600
E-mail: clerks@3gis.co.uk
Call Date: July 1982, Gray's Inn
Qualifications: [LLB (Warw)]

MALHOTRA MISS MEHTAB ROSHAN

2 Middle Temple Lane
3rd Floor, Temple, London EC4Y 9AA,
Telephone: 0171 583 4540
Call Date: Oct 1996, Lincoln's Inn
Qualifications: [LLB (Hons)(Lond), LLM
(Lond)]

MALHOTRA RAGHUBIR SINGH

Perivale Chambers
15 Colwyn Avenue, Perivale, Middlesex,
UB6 8JY, Telephone: 0181 998 1935/
081 248 0246
Call Date: July 1994, Lincoln's Inn
Qualifications: [BA, LLB, MA (India), LLM
(Lond)]

MALIK AMJAD RAZA

Chambers of Michael Pert QC
36 Bedford Row, London WC1R 4JH,
Telephone: 0171 421 8000
E-mail: 36bedfordrow@link.org
Chambers of Michael Pert QC
24 Albion Place, Northampton NN1 1UD,
Telephone: 01604 602333
Chambers of Michael Pert QC
104 New Walk, Leicester LE1 7EA,
Telephone: 0116 249 2020
Call Date: Nov 1987, Lincoln's Inn
Pupil Master
Qualifications: [LLM (UCL)]

MALIK OMAR LATIF

Eighteen Carlton Crescent
Southampton SO15 2XR,
Telephone: 01703 639001
Call Date: Nov 1990, Inner Temple
Qualifications: [LLB (So'ton)]

MALINS JULIAN HENRY QC (1991)

One Hare Court
1st Floor, Temple, London EC4Y 7BE,
Telephone: 020 7353 3171
E-mail:admin-onecharecourt@btinternet.com
Call Date: July 1972, Middle Temple
Qualifications: [MA (Oxon)]

MALLALIEU THE BARONESS ANN QC (1988)

6 King's Bench Walk
Ground Floor, Temple, London
EC4Y 7DR, Telephone: 0171 583 0410
E-mail: worsley@6kbw.freeserve.co.uk
Call Date: July 1970, Inner Temple
Qualifications: [MA, LLM (Cantab)]

MALLENDER PAUL NIGEL

2 Pump Court
1st Floor, Temple, London EC4Y 7AH,
Telephone: 0171 353 5597
Call Date: Nov 1974, Lincoln's Inn
Pupil Master
Qualifications: [LLB (Lond)]

MALLETT MISS SARAH JANE VICTORIA

Westgate Chambers
67a Westgate Road, Newcastle upon Tyne
NE1 1SG, Telephone: 0191 261 4407/
2329785
E-mail:pracman@westgatechambers.law.co.uk
Call Date: Nov 1988, Inner Temple
Qualifications: [BA (Dunelm)]

MALLETT SIMON JEREMY

11 King's Bench Walk
1st Floor, Temple, London EC4Y 7EQ,
Telephone: 0171 353 3337
E-mail: fmuller11@aol.com
11 King's Bench Walk
3 Park Court, Park Cross Street, Leeds
LS1 2QH, Telephone: 0113 297 1200
Call Date: July 1986, Inner Temple
Qualifications: [LLB(Sheffield)]

MALLICK MISS NABILA HANI

Clapham Chambers
21-25 Bedford Road, Clapham North,
London SW4 7SH,
Telephone: 0171 978 8482/642 5777
E-mail:claphamchambers@compuserve.com
Call Date: Nov 1992, Gray's Inn
Qualifications: [LLB (Lond), LLM]

MALLIN MAXWELL JAMES

11 Stone Buildings
Lincoln's Inn, London WC2A 3TG,
Telephone: +44 (0)207 831 6381
E-mail:clerks@11StoneBuildings.law.co.uk
Call Date: Oct 1993, Inner Temple
Qualifications: [BA (Cantab), CPE
(Coventry)]

MALLISON MISS CATHERINE MARY HELEN

2nd Floor, Francis Taylor Building
Temple, London EC4Y 7BY,
Telephone: 0171 353 9942/3157
Call Date: Nov 1974, Middle Temple
Pupil Master

MALLON MISS JOANNA

Derby Square Chambers
Merchants Court, Derby Square, Liverpool
L2 1TS, Telephone: 0151 709 4222
E-mail:mail.derbysquare@pop3.hiway.co.uk
Call Date: Oct 1996, Lincoln's Inn
Qualifications: [BA (Hons)(Dunelm), Law
Dip (Chester)]

MALONE MICHAEL JULIAN

One Essex Court
Ground Floor, Temple, London
EC4Y 9AR, Telephone: 020 7583 2000
E-mail: clerks@oneessexcourt.co.uk
Call Date: Nov 1975, Gray's Inn
Pupil Master
Qualifications: [BA]

MANASSE MRS ANNE KATHERINE

Cathedral Chambers
Milburn House, Dean Street, Newcastle
upon Tyne NE1 1LE,
Telephone: 0191 232 1311
Call Date: Nov 1994, Inner Temple
Qualifications: [BA (Durham), CPE
(Northumbria)]

MANASSE DR PAUL REUBEN

Young Street Chambers
38 Young Street, Manchester M3 3FT,
Telephone: 0161 833 0489
E-mail: clerks@young-st-chambers.com
Call Date: Oct 1995, Gray's Inn
Qualifications: [B.Sc, Ph.D (L'pool)]

MANDALIA VINESH LALJI

Harrow on the Hill Chambers
60 High Street, Harrow-on-the-Hill,
Middlesex, HA1 3LL,
Telephone: 0181 423 7444
Call Date: 1997, Inner Temple
Qualifications: [LLB (Coventry)]

MANDEL RICHARD

Queen Elizabeth Building
Ground Floor, Temple, London
EC4Y 9BS,
Telephone: 0171 353 7181 (12 Lines)
Call Date: July 1972, Gray's Inn
Pupil Master
Qualifications: [MA, BCL (Oxon)]

MANDIL-WADE MISS ROSALYNE HELEN

East Anglian Chambers
52 North Hill, Colchester, Essex, CO1 1PY,
Telephone: 01206 572756
E-mail: colchester@ealaw.co.uk
East Anglian Chambers
57 London Street, Norwich NR2 1HL,
Telephone: 01603 617351
E-mail: norwich@ealaw.co.uk
East Anglian Chambers
Gresham House, 5 Museum Street,
Ipswich, Suffolk, IP1 1HQ,
Telephone: 01473 214481
E-mail: ipswich@ealaw.co.uk
Call Date: Nov 1988, Inner Temple
Qualifications: [BA (Hons)]

MANGAT DR TEJINA KIRAN

New Court Chambers
5 Verulam Buildings, Gray's Inn, London
WC1R 5LY, Telephone: 0171 831 9500
E-mail: mail@newcourtchambers.com
Call Date: Oct 1990, Middle Temple
Qualifications: [BSc,MBBS (Lond)]

MANLEY DAVID ERIC

40 King Street
Manchester M2 6BA,
Telephone: 0161 832 9082
E-mail: clerks@40kingstreet.co.uk
The Chambers of Philip Raynor QC
5 Park Place, Leeds LS1 2RU,
Telephone: 0113 242 1123
Call Date: July 1981, Inner Temple
Pupil Master
Qualifications: [BA (Hons) (Leeds)]

D

MANLEY MS HILARY

Cobden House Chambers
19 Quay Street, Manchester M3 3HN,
Telephone: 0161 833 6000
E-mail: clerks@cobden.co.uk
Call Date: Nov 1996, Gray's Inn
Qualifications: [LLB (Lond)]

MANLEY MISS LESLEY PATRICA

Chambers of Helen Grindrod QC
4th Floor, 15-19 Devereux Court, London
WC2R 3JJ, Telephone: 0171 583 2792
Call Date: Nov 1983, Middle Temple
Pupil Master
Qualifications: [BA (Liverpool)]

MANN MISS DAYA LUCIENNE CATHERINE

Devon Chambers
3 St Andrew Street, Plymouth PL1 2AH,
Telephone: 01752 661659
E-mail: devonchambers.co.uk.
Call Date: Feb 1995, Lincoln's Inn
Qualifications: [BA (Joint Hons)(Lon), Dip
Law, CPE]

MANN GEORGE ANTHONY QC (1992)

Enterprise Chambers
9 Old Square, Lincoln's Inn, London
WC2A 3SR, Telephone: 0171 405 9471
E-mail:enterprise.london@dial.pipex.com
Enterprise Chambers
38 Park Square, Leeds LS1 2PA,
Telephone: 0113 246 0391
E-mail:enterprise.leeds@dial.pipex.com
Enterprise Chambers
65 Quayside, Newcastle upon Tyne
NE1 3DS, Telephone: 0191 222 3344
E-mail:enterprise.newcastle@dial.pipex.com
Call Date: July 1974, Lincoln's Inn
Qualifications: [MA (Oxon)]

MANN JONATHAN SIMON

8 King's Bench Walk
2nd Floor, Temple, London EC4Y 7DU,
Telephone: 0171 797 8888
8 King's Bench Walk North
1 Park Square East, Leeds LS1 2NE,
Telephone: 0113 2439797
Call Date: Nov 1989, Inner Temple
Qualifications: [LLB (Essex)]

MANN MARTIN EDWARD QC (1983)

Twenty-Four Old Buildings
Ground Floor, Lincoln's Inn, London
WC2A 3UP, Telephone: 0171 404 0946
E-mail:clerks@24oldbuildings.law.co.uk
St John's Chambers
Small Street, Bristol BS1 1DW,
Telephone: 0117 9213456/298514
E-mail: @stjohnschambers.co.uk
Call Date: July 1968, Gray's Inn
Recorder

MANN PAUL

High Pavement Chambers
1 High Pavement, Nottingham NG1 1HF,
Telephone: 0115 9418218
Call Date: Nov 1980, Gray's Inn
Pupil Master
Qualifications: [BA]

MANN MISS REBECCA CLAIRE

Pendragon Chambers
124 Walter Road, Swansea, West
Glamorgan, SA1 5RG,
Telephone: 01792 411188
Call Date: Oct 1995, Lincoln's Inn
Qualifications: [LLB (Hons)(Leic)]

MANN MISS SARA ANGELA

India Buildings Chambers
Water Street, Liverpool L2 0XG,
Telephone: 0151 243 6000
E-mail: clerks@chambers.u-net.com
Call Date: Nov 1994, Middle Temple
Qualifications: [LLB (Hons)]

MANNAN CHARLES MANDANI FUAD

Clapham Chambers
21-25 Bedford Road, Clapham North,
London SW4 7SH,
Telephone: 0171 978 8482/642 5777
E-mail:claphamchambers@compuserve.co
m
Call Date: Nov 1993, Lincoln's Inn
Qualifications: [BSc (Econ, Hons)]

MANNERS MISS HENRIETTA LOUISE

2nd Floor, Francis Taylor Building
Temple, London EC4Y 7BY,
Telephone: 0171 353 9942/3157
Call Date: July 1981, Middle Temple
Qualifications: [LLB]

MANNING COLIN

Littleton Chambers
3 King's Bench Walk North, Temple,
London EC4Y 7HR,
Telephone: 0171 797 8600
E-mail:clerks@littletonchambers.co.uk
Call Date: July 1970, Gray's Inn
Pupil Master
Qualifications: [LLB]

MANNING JONATHAN DAVID GRANT

Arden Chambers
27 John Street, London WC1N 2BL,
Telephone: 020 7242 4244
E-mail:clerks@arden-chambers.law.co.uk
Call Date: July 1989, Inner Temple
Pupil Master
Qualifications: [MA (Cantab)]

MANNING ROBERT MICHAEL JONATHAN

High Pavement Chambers
1 High Pavement, Nottingham NG1 1HF,
Telephone: 0115 9418218
Call Date: Nov 1992, Inner Temple
Qualifications: [LLB]

MANNION JOHN DENNIS

Westgate Chambers
144 High Street, Lewes, East Sussex,
BN7 1XT, Telephone: 01273 480510
Frederick Place Chambers
9 Frederick Place, Clifton, Bristol
BS8 1AS, Telephone: 0117 9738667
Call Date: May 1987, Middle Temple
Pupil Master
Qualifications: [BA LLM]

MANSELL RICHARD AUSTIN

No. 6
6 Park Square, Leeds LS1 2LW,
Telephone: 0113 2459763
E-mail: chambers@no6.co.uk
Call Date: Oct 1991, Gray's Inn
Qualifications: [LLB (Hons)(Leeds)]

MANSFIELD MS ELEANOR CLARE

Warwick House Chambers
8 Warwick Court, Gray's Inn, London
WC1R 5DJ, Telephone: 0171 430 2323
E-mail: cdrewlaw@aol.com
Call Date: Oct 1995, Inner Temple
Qualifications: [LLB (Lond)]

MANSFIELD GAVIN HARRISON

4 Paper Buildings
1st Floor, Temple, London EC4Y 7EX,
Telephone: 0171 583 0816/353 1131
E-mail: clerks@4paperbuildings.co.uk
Call Date: Nov 1992, Middle Temple
Qualifications: [MA (Hons)(Cantab)]

MANSFIELD MISS GILLIAN

Central Chambers
89 Princess Street,
Manchester M1 4HT,
Telephone: 0161 236 1133
Call Date: Oct 1994, Lincoln's Inn
Qualifications: [BA (Hons)(Warw), CPE
(Leeds)]

MANSFIELD THE HON GUY RHYS JOHN QC (1994)

1 Crown Office Row
Ground Floor, Temple, London
EC4Y 7HH, Telephone: 0171 797 7500
E-mail: mail@onecrownofficerow.com
Call Date: Nov 1972, Middle Temple
Recorder
Qualifications: [MA (Oxon)]

MANSFIELD MICHAEL QC (1989)

14 Tooks Court
Cursitor St, London EC4A 1LB,
Telephone: 0171 405 8828
E-mail: clerks@tooks.law.co.uk
Call Date: Nov 1967, Gray's Inn
Qualifications: [BA, LLB]

MANSON MISS JULIE-ANN

**11 Bolt Court (also at 7 Stone Buildings
– 1st Floor)**
London EC4A 3DQ,
Telephone: 0171 353 2300
E-mail: boltct11@aol.com

Redhill Chambers
Seloduct House, 30 Station Road, Redhill,
Surrey, RH1 1NF,
Telephone: 01737 780781
7 Stone Buildings (also at 11 Bolt Court)
1st Floor, Lincoln's Inn, London
WC2A 3SZ, Telephone: 0171 242 0961
E-mail:larthur@7stonebuildings.law.co.uk
Call Date: July 1985, Middle Temple
Pupil Master
Qualifications: [BA (Bris) Dip Law]

8 King's Bench Walk
2nd Floor, Temple, London EC4Y 7DU,
Telephone: 0171 797 8888
Call Date: 1996, Inner Temple
Qualifications: [LLB (B'ham)]

MANTELL-SAYER PETER GEORGE

Sackville Chambers
Sackville Place, 44-48 Magdalen Street,
Norwich NR3 1JU,
Telephone: 01603 613516/616221
Tindal Chambers
3/5 New Street, Chelmsford, Essex,
CM1 1NT, Telephone: 01245 267742
Call Date: Oct 1992, Lincoln's Inn
Qualifications: [LLB(Hons)(Lond)]

MANTLE PETER JOHN

Monckton Chambers
4 Raymond Buildings, Gray's Inn, London
WC1R 5BP, Telephone: 0171 405 7211
E-mail: chambers@monckton.co.uk
Call Date: July 1989, Inner Temple
Qualifications: [BA (Oxon), LLM (Cantab)]

MANUEL MISS ELIZABETH

Eighteen Carlton Crescent
Southampton SO15 2XR,
Telephone: 01703 639001
Call Date: Nov 1987, Middle Temple
Pupil Master
Qualifications: [LLB (B'ham)]

MANZONI CHARLES PETER

39 Essex Street
London WC2R 3AT,
Telephone: 0171 832 1111
E-mail: clerks@39essex.co.uk
Call Date: July 1988, Middle Temple
Pupil Master
Qualifications: [B.Sc, A.M.I, Mech Eng
(Bristol)]

MAQSOOD MISS ZABEDA KHATOON

15 Winckley Square
Preston PR1 3JJ,
Telephone: 01772 252828
E-mail:clerks@winckleysq.demon.co.uk
Call Date: 1996, Gray's Inn
Qualifications: [LLB (Derby)]

MARCUS GILBERT JOHN

Doughty Street Chambers
11 Doughty Street, London WC1N 2PG,
Telephone: 0171 404 1313
E-mail:enquiries@doughtystreet.co.uk
Call Date: 1999, Gray's Inn
Qualifications: [BA, LLB, (Witwatersand),
LLB (Cantab)]

MARGOLIN DANIEL GEORGE

Chambers of Mr Peter Crampin QC
Ground Floor, 11 New Square, Lincoln's
Inn, London WC2A 3QB,
Telephone: 020 7831 0081
E-mail: 11newsquare.co.uk
Call Date: Nov 1995, Gray's Inn
Qualifications: [BA]

MARGREE MISS SARAH LOUISE

11 King's Bench Walk
1st Floor, Temple, London EC4Y 7EQ,
Telephone: 0171 353 3337
E-mail: fmuller11@aol.com
11 King's Bench Walk
3 Park Court, Park Cross Street, Leeds
LS1 2QH, Telephone: 0113 297 1200
Call Date: Oct 1996, Lincoln's Inn
Qualifications: [LLB (Hons)(Leic)]

MARK ANDREW BRIAN

Westgate Chambers
67a Westgate Road, Newcastle upon Tyne
NE1 1SG, Telephone: 0191 261 4407/
2329785
E-mail:pracman@westgatechambers.law.co.u
k
Call Date: Nov 1981, Inner Temple
Qualifications: [BA (N'castle)]

MARKESINIS DR BASIL SPYRIDONOS QC (1998)

Call Date: July 1972, Gray's Inn
Qualifications: [MA, PhD (Cantab)]

MARKHAM MISS ANNA VICTORIA

4 Stone Buildings
Ground Floor, Lincoln's Inn, London
WC2A 3XT, Telephone: 0171 242 5524
E-mail:clerks@4stonebuildings.law.co.uk
Call Date: Oct 1996, Lincoln's Inn
Qualifications: [BA (Hons), MA
(Hons)(Oxon)]

MARKHAM DAVID HAROLD

Goldsmith Chambers
Ground Floor, Goldsmith Building,
Temple, London EC4Y 7BL,
Telephone: 0171 353 6802/3/4/5
E-mail:clerks@goldsmithchambers.law.co.uk
Call Date: Nov 1983, Gray's Inn
Pupil Master
Qualifications: [BA, MA Business Law]

MARKLEW LEE JONATHON

6 Fountain Court
Steelhouse Lane, Birmingham B4 6DR,
Telephone: 0121 233 3282
E-mail: clerks@sixfountain.co.uk
Call Date: May 1993, Gray's Inn
Qualifications: [BA (Sheff)]

MARKS DAVID GEORGES MAINFROY

3/4 South Square
Gray's Inn, London WC1R 5HP,
Telephone: 0171 696 9900
E-mail: clerks@southsquare.com
Call Date: Nov 1974, Gray's Inn
Qualifications: [MA, BCL (Oxon)]

MARKS MISS GILLIAN

Gray's Inn Chambers
5th Floor, Gray's Inn, London WC1R 5JA,
Telephone: 0171 404 1111
Call Date: July 1981, Gray's Inn
Pupil Master
Qualifications: [BA(Sussex)]

MARKS MISS JACQUELINE STEPHANIE

2 Gray's Inn Square Chambers
2nd Floor, Gray's Inn, London WC1R 5AA,
Telephone: 020 7242 0328
E-mail: clerks@2gis.co.uk
Call Date: July 1984, Middle Temple
Qualifications: [BA]

MARKS JONATHAN CLIVE QC (1995)

4 Pump Court
Temple, London EC4Y 7AN,
Telephone: 020 7842 5555
E-mail:chambers@4pumpcourt.law.co.uk
Call Date: July 1975, Inner Temple
Qualifications: [BA (Oxon)]

MARKS JONATHAN HAROLD

3 Verulam Buildings
London WC1R 5NT,
Telephone: 0171 831 8441
E-mail: clerks@3verulam.co.uk
Call Date: Oct 1992, Inner Temple
Qualifications: [BA (Oxon), BCL]

MARKS LEWIS

Queen Elizabeth Building
2nd Floor, Temple, London EC4Y 9BS,
Telephone: 0171 797 7837
Call Date: 1984, Middle Temple
Pupil Master
Qualifications: [BA Hons (Oxon)]

MARKS PETER

3 Temple Gardens
3rd Floor, Temple, London EC4Y 9AU,
Telephone: 0171 353 0832
Call Date: Nov 1987, Middle Temple
Qualifications: [MB, ChB, MRCP & MSc, LLB,
MA]

MARKS RICHARD LEON QC (1999)

Peel Court Chambers
45 Hardman Street, Manchester M3 3PL,
Telephone: 0161 832 3791
E-mail: clerks@peelct.co.uk
Call Date: 1975, Gray's Inn
Pupil Master, Recorder
Qualifications: [LLB (Manch)]

MARKSON JONATHAN

4 Brick Court, Chambers of Anne Rafferty QC
1st Floor, Temple, London EC4Y 9AD,
Telephone: 0171 583 8455
Call Date: July 1980, Middle Temple
Pupil Master
Qualifications: [BA (Oxon)]

MARKUS MS KATE

Doughty Street Chambers
11 Doughty Street, London WC1N 2PG,
Telephone: 0171 404 1313
E-mail:enquiries@doughtystreet.co.uk
Call Date: Nov 1981, Gray's Inn
Pupil Master
Qualifications: [LLB (Manch)]

MARLEY MISS SARAH ANNE

5 Pump Court
Ground Floor, Temple, London
EC4Y 7AP, Telephone: 020 7353 2532
E-mail: FivePump@netcomuk.co.uk
Call Date: Oct 1995, Lincoln's Inn
Qualifications: [LLB (Hons)(Leic)]

MARLOW MS CLAIRE DEBORAH

Queens Square Chambers
56 Queens Square, Bristol BS1 4PR,
Telephone: 0117 921 1966
Call Date: July 1983, Gray's Inn
Pupil Master
Qualifications: [BA]

MARLOW MRS PATRICIA

Bell Yard Chambers
116/118 Chancery Lane, London
WC2A 1PP, Telephone: 0171 306 9292
Call Date: Nov 1988, Middle Temple
Qualifications: [BA]

MARQUAND CHARLES NICHOLAS HILARY

Chambers of Lord Goodhart QC
Ground Floor, 3 New Square, Lincoln's
Inn, London WC2A 3RS,
Telephone: 0171 405 5577
E-mail:law@threenewsquare.demon.co.uk
Call Date: Nov 1987, Inner Temple
Qualifications: [MA (Oxon), MA LAW, (City),
Dip E C Law, (Lond)]

MARRACHE ISAAC SAMUEL

5 Cannon Lane, Gibraltar
Telephone: (Gib) 79918
Call Date: July 1982, Inner Temple
Qualifications: [LLB, LLM (Lond)]

MARRIAGE MRS HENRIETTA-JANE

Call Date: Oct 1993, Inner Temple
Qualifications: [LLB (Hons)(Lond)]

MARRIN JOHN WHEELER QC (1990)

Keating Chambers
10 Essex Street, Outer Temple, London
WC2R 3AA, Telephone: 0171 544 2600
Call Date: Nov 1974, Inner Temple
Recorder
Qualifications: [MA (Cantab)]

MARRON AIDAN STEPHEN QC (1993)

York Chambers
14 Toft Green, York YO1 6JT,
Telephone: 01904 620048
E-mail: [name]@yorkchambers.co.uk
Call Date: July 1973, Lincoln's Inn
Recorder

MARRS ANDREW CHARLES

Kenworthy's Chambers
83 Bridge Street, Manchester M3 2RF,
Telephone: 0161 832 4036/834 6954
E-mail: clerks@kenworthys.co.uk
Call Date: Nov 1995, Inner Temple
Qualifications: [BA (Oxon), CPE (Manc)]

MARSDEN ANDREW CHARLES

Queens Square Chambers
56 Queens Square, Bristol BS1 4PR,
Telephone: 0117 921 1966
Call Date: May 1994, Lincoln's Inn
Qualifications: [BA, BCL Hons)]

MARSDEN ANDREW GUY

East Anglian Chambers
52 North Hill, Colchester, Essex, CO1 1PY,
Telephone: 01206 572756
E-mail: colchester@ealaw.co.uk
East Anglian Chambers
57 London Street, Norwich NR2 1HL,
Telephone: 01603 617351
E-mail: norwich@ealaw.co.uk
East Anglian Chambers
Gresham House, 5 Museum Street,
Ipswich, Suffolk, IP1 1HQ,
Telephone: 01473 214481
E-mail: ipswich@ealaw.co.uk
Call Date: July 1975, Middle Temple
Pupil Master, Assistant Recorder
Qualifications: [MA (Oxon)]

MARSDEN-LYNCH JOHN FRANCIS

Sussex Chambers
9 Old Steine, Brighton, Sussex, BN1 1FJ,
Telephone: 01273 607953
Call Date: Nov 1988, Middle Temple
Qualifications: [BA (Sydney), LLB (Lond), MA
(Lond)]

MARSH MISS CAROLYN DEBORAH

Dr Johnson's Chambers
Two Dr Johnson's Buildings, Temple,
London EC4Y 7AY,
Telephone: 0171 353 4716
E-mail: clerks@2djb.freeserve.co.uk
Call Date: July 1985, Inner Temple
Qualifications: [LLB (Bris)]

MARSH MISS ELIZABETH ANN QC (1999)

4 Brick Court, Chambers of Anne Rafferty QC
1st Floor, Temple, London EC4Y 9AD,
Telephone: 0171 583 8455
Call Date: 1979, Gray's Inn
Pupil Master
Qualifications: [BA]

MARSH JOHN

Parsonage Chambers
5th Floor, 3 The Parsonage, Manchester
M3 2HW, Telephone: 0161 833 1996
Call Date: July 1977, Gray's Inn
Pupil Master

MARSH LAURENCE JOHN

4 Pump Court
Temple, London EC4Y 7AN,
Telephone: 020 7842 5555
E-mail:chambers@4pumpcourt.law.co.uk
Call Date: July 1975, Middle Temple
Pupil Master
Qualifications: [BA (Oxon)]

MARSH PETER PAUL

9 King's Bench Walk
Ground Floor, Temple, London
EC4Y 7DX, Telephone: 0171 353 7202/
3909 E-mail: 9kbw@compuserve.com
Abbey Chambers
PO Box 47, 47 Ashurst Drive, Shepperton,
Middlesex, TW17 0LD,
Telephone: 01932 560913
Call Date: July 1975, Middle Temple
Qualifications: [MA (Cantab), DipPols
(Oxon)]

MARSHALL ANDREW

1 Middle Temple Lane
Temple, London EC4Y 1LT,
Telephone: 0171 583 0659 (12 Lines)
E-mail: chambers@1mtl.co.uk
Call Date: July 1986, Inner Temple
Pupil Master
Qualifications: [LLB (UCL)]

MARSHALL ANDREW DAVID MICHAEL CREAGH

3 Paper Buildings
Ground Floor, Temple, London
EC4Y 7EU, Telephone: 0171 797 7000
E-mail: clerks@3pb.co.uk
3 Paper Buildings
Temple, London EC4Y 7EU,
Telephone: 020 7583 8055
E-mail: London@3paper.com
3 Paper Buildings (Bournemouth)
20 Lorne Park Road, Bournemouth,
Dorset, BH1 1JN,
Telephone: 01202 292102
E-mail: Bournemouth@3paper.com

3 Paper Buildings (Winchester)
4 St Peter Street, Winchester SO23 8BW,
Telephone: 01962 868884
E-mail: winchester@3paper.com
3 Paper Buildings (Oxford)
1 Alfred Street, High Street, Oxford
OX1 4EH, Telephone: 01865 793736
E-mail: oxford@3paper.com
Call Date: July 1981, Lincoln's Inn
Pupil Master
Qualifications: [MA (Oxon)]

MARSHALL DAVID

18 Red Lion Court
(Off Fleet Street), London EC4A 3EB,
Telephone: 0171 520 6000
E-mail: chambers@18rlc.co.uk
Thornwood House
102 New London Road, Chelmsford,
Essex, CM2 0RG,
Telephone: 01245 280880
E-mail: chambers@18rlc.co.uk
Call Date: July 1985, Gray's Inn
Qualifications: [LLB (Leeds)]

MARSHALL DEREK STANLEY

College Chambers
19 Carlton Cresent, Southampton
SO15 2ET, Telephone: 01703 230338
Call Date: July 1980, Inner Temple
Pupil Master
Qualifications: [LLB (Soton)]

MARSHALL MISS ELOISE MARY KATHERINE SELINA

23 Essex Street
London WC2R 3AS,
Telephone: 0171 413 0353/836 8366
E-mail:clerks@essexstreet23.demon.co.uk
Call Date: Oct 1994, Gray's Inn
Qualifications: [BA]

MARSHALL MISS ITA DELORIS

Horizon Chambers
95a Chancery Lane, London WC2A 1DT,
Telephone: 0171 242 2440
Call Date: July 1980, Middle Temple
Pupil Master
Qualifications: [LLB (Hons), MA (Bus.Law)]

MARSHALL PAUL DAVID JOHN

1 Crown Office Row
3rd Floor, Temple, London EC4Y 7HH,
Telephone: 0171 583 9292
E-mail: onecor@link.org
Call Date: Oct 1991, Inner Temple
Qualifications: [BA (Cantab), BSc (Lond)]

MARSHALL PAUL ROBERT

Lloyds House Chambers
3rd Floor, 18 Lloyds House, Lloyd Street,
Manchester M2 5WA,
Telephone: 0161 839 3371
Call Date: Nov 1982, Middle Temple
Pupil Master
Qualifications: [B.Ed (Manch)]

MARSHALL PETER DAVID

Trafalgar Chambers
53 Fleet Street, London EC4Y 1BE,
Telephone: 0171 583 5858
E-mail:trafalgarchambers@easynet.co.uk
Call Date: Nov 1991, Lincoln's Inn
Qualifications: [LLB (Hons)(Warw)]

MARSHALL PHILIP DEREK

Iscoed Chambers
86 St Helen's Road, Swansea, West
Glamorgan, SA1 4BQ,
Telephone: 01792 652988/9/330
Farrar's Building
Temple, London EC4Y 7BD,
Telephone: 0171 583 9241
E-mail:chambers@farrarsbuilding.co.uk
Call Date: Nov 1975, Middle Temple
Pupil Master, Assistant Recorder
Qualifications: [MA (Cantab)]

MARSHALL PHILIP JOHN

One King's Bench Walk
1st Floor, Temple, London EC4Y 7DB,
Telephone: 0171 936 1500
E-mail: ddear@1kbw.co.uk
Call Date: July 1989, Gray's Inn
Pupil Master
Qualifications: [LLB [L'pool]]

MARSHALL PHILIP SCOTT

Serle Court Chambers
6 New Square, Lincoln's Inn, London
WC2A 3QS, Telephone: 0171 242 6105
E-mail: clerks@serlecourt.co.uk
Call Date: July 1987, Lincoln's Inn
Pupil Master
Qualifications: [MA (Hons) (Cantab),
LLM(Harvard)]

MARSHALL MISS VANESSA JULIETTE

9 Bedford Row
London WC1R 4AZ,
Telephone: 0171 242 3555
E-mail: clerks@9br.co.uk
Call Date: Oct 1994, Gray's Inn
Qualifications: [RGN, LLB]

MARSHALL-ANDREWS ROBERT GRAHAM QC (1987)

37 Park Square Chambers
37 Park Square, Leeds LS1 2NY,
Telephone: 0113 2439422
E-mail: chambers@no37.co.uk
2-4 Tudor Street
London EC4Y 0AA,
Telephone: 0171 797 7111
E-mail: clerks@rfqc.co.uk
Call Date: Feb 1967, Gray's Inn
Qualifications: [LLB (Bris)]

MARSON GEOFFREY CHARLES QC (1997)

Sovereign Chambers
25 Park Square, Leeds LS1 2PW,
Telephone: 0113 2451841/2/3
E-mail:sovereignchambers@btinternet.com
Call Date: Nov 1975, Gray's Inn
Recorder
Qualifications: [LLB (Lond)]

MARSTON NICHOLAS RICHARD

St John's Chambers
Small Street, Bristol BS1 1DW,
Telephone: 0117 9213456/298514
E-mail: @stjohnschambers.co.uk
Call Date: July 1975, Middle Temple
Pupil Master, Assistant Recorder
Qualifications: [LLB (Wales)]

MARTEN RICHARD HEDLEY WESTWOOD

Chambers of Lord Goodhart QC
Ground Floor, 3 New Square, Lincoln's
Inn, London WC2A 3RS,
Telephone: 0171 405 5577
E-mail:law@threenewsquare.demon.co.uk
Call Date: Nov 1966, Lincoln's Inn
Pupil Master
Qualifications: [MA (Cantab)]

MARTIGNETTI IAN R

Regency Chambers
Cathedral Square, Peterborough
PE1 1XW, Telephone: 01733 315215
Regency Chambers
Sheraton House, Castle Park, Cambridge
CB3 0AX, Telephone: 01223 301517
Call Date: Nov 1990, Inner Temple
Pupil Master
Qualifications: [LLB]

MARTIN ALEXANDER JOHN HOWARD

**Chambers of Ian Macdonald QC (In
Association with Two Garden Court,
Temple, London)**
Waldorf House, 5 Cooper Street,
Manchester M2 2FW,
Telephone: 0161 236 1840
Call Date: Nov 1977, Gray's Inn

MARTIN BRADLEY DAVID

2 Temple Gardens
Temple, London EC4Y 9AY,
Telephone: 0171 583 6041
E-mail: clerks@2templegardens.co.uk
Call Date: Oct 1990, Lincoln's Inn
Qualifications: [LLB (Leic)]

MARTIN DALE

Littleton Chambers
3 King's Bench Walk North, Temple,
London EC4Y 7HR,
Telephone: 0171 797 8600
E-mail:clerks@littletonchambers.co.uk
Call Date: Oct 1997, Inner Temple
Qualifications: [LLB (Nottingham)]

MARTIN DAVID JOHN

Cathedral Chambers
Milburn House, Dean Street, Newcastle
upon Tyne NE1 1LE,
Telephone: 0191 232 1311
Call Date: Oct 1994, Gray's Inn
Qualifications: [BSc]

MARTIN THE HON DAVID JOHN PATTISON

Queens Square Chambers
56 Queens Square, Bristol BS1 4PR,
Telephone: 0117 921 1966
Call Date: July 1969, Inner Temple
Qualifications: [BA (Cantab)]

MARTIN MRS DIANNE JOAN ABEGAIL

St John's Chambers
Small Street, Bristol BS1 1DW,
Telephone: 0117 9213456/298514
E-mail: @stjohnschambers.co.uk
Call Date: Oct 1992, Gray's Inn
Qualifications: [LL.B]

MARTIN MRS GAY MADELEINE ANNESLEY

7 Stone Buildings (also at 11 Bolt Court)
1st Floor, Lincoln's Inn, London
WC2A 3SZ, Telephone: 0171 242 0961
E-mail:larthur@7stonebuildings.law.co.uk
11 Bolt Court (also at 7 Stone Buildings – 1st Floor)
London EC4A 3DQ,
Telephone: 0171 353 2300
E-mail: boltct11@aol.com
Redhill Chambers
Seloduct House, 30 Station Road, Redhill,
Surrey, RH1 1NF,
Telephone: 01737 780781
Call Date: July 1970, Inner Temple
Pupil Master

MARTIN GERARD JAMES

Exchange Chambers
Pearl Assurance House, Derby Square,
Liverpool L2 9XX,
Telephone: 0151 236 7747
E-mail:exchangechambers@btinternet.com
Call Date: July 1978, Middle Temple
Pupil Master, Assistant Recorder
Qualifications: [MA (Cantab)]

MARTIN MRS JILL ELIZABETH

Barnard's Inn Chambers
6th Floor, Halton House, 20-23 Holborn,
London EC1N 2JD,
Telephone: 0171 369 6969
E-mail: clerks@biclaw.co.uk
Call Date: Nov 1993, Lincoln's Inn
Qualifications: [LLB(Hons) LLM (Lond)]

MARTIN JOHN VANDELEUR QC (1991)

Wilberforce Chambers
8 New Square, Lincoln's Inn, London
WC2A 3QP, Telephone: 0171 306 0102
E-mail: chambers@wilberforce.co.uk
Call Date: July 1972, Lincoln's Inn
Qualifications: [MA (Cantab)]

Types of work: Chancery (general), Chancery
land law, Commercial litigation, Commercial property, Company and commercial,
Equity, wills and trusts, Landlord and
tenant, Professional negligence

MARTIN JONATHAN DAVID

10 King's Bench Walk
Ground Floor, Temple, London
EC4Y 7EB, Telephone: 0171 353 7742
E-mail: 10kbw@lineone.net
Call Date: Nov 1994, Middle Temple
Qualifications: [BA (Hons) (Oxon)]

MARTIN PETER

9 Fountains Way
Pinders Heath, Wakefield, West Yorkshire,
WF1 4TQ, Telephone: 01924 378631
Call Date: Feb 1990, Gray's Inn
Qualifications: [LLB (Lond), MA (Sheff)]

MARTIN PETER JOHN

2 Paper Buildings
1st Floor, Temple, London EC4Y 7ET,
Telephone: 020 7556 5500
E-mail: clerks@2pbbarristers.co.uk
Call Date: July 1969, Gray's Inn
Pupil Master
Qualifications: [BSc, MSc]

MARTIN PHILIP ROGER

Albany Chambers
91 Kentish Town Road, London
NW1 8NY, Telephone: 0171 485 5736/
5758 E-mail: albany91.freeserve.co.uk
Call Date: Oct 1995, Inner Temple
Qualifications: [BA (York), CPE (Lond)]

MARTIN RICHARD HENRY BOLAM

Rowchester Chambers
4 Rowchester Court, Whittall Street,
Birmingham B4 6DH,
Telephone: 0121 233 2327/2361951
Call Date: Nov 1978, Inner Temple
Qualifications: [BSc (Econ)]

MARTIN ROY LOGAN

1 Serjeants' Inn
4th Floor, Temple, London EC4Y 1NH,
Telephone: 0171 583 1355
E-mail: clerks@serjeants-inn.co.uk
Call Date: July 1990, Lincoln's Inn
Qualifications: [LLB (Glas)]

MARTIN MISS ZOE VICTORIA

2 Paper Buildings
1st Floor, Temple, London EC4Y 7ET,
Telephone: 020 7556 5500
E-mail: clerks@2pbbarristers.co.uk
Call Date: Oct 1990, Gray's Inn
Qualifications: [LLB]

MARTIN-JENKINS JAMES TELFORD ALEXANDER

2 Harcourt Buildings
Ground Floor/Left, Temple, London
EC4Y 9DB, Telephone: 0171 583 9020
E-mail: clerks@harcourt.co.uk
Call Date: 1997, Middle Temple
Qualifications: [BA (Hons)(Oxon)]

MARTIN-SPERRY DAVID ANTHONY

2-4 Tudor Street
London EC4Y 0AA,
Telephone: 0171 797 7111
E-mail: clerks@rfqc.co.uk
Call Date: Nov 1971, Inner Temple
Pupil Master
Qualifications: [MA (Cantab)]

MARTINEAU HENRY RALPH ADEANE

Goldsmith Building
1st Floor, Temple, London EC4Y 7BL,
Telephone: 0171 353 7881
E-mail:clerks@goldsmith-building.law.co.uk
Call Date: Nov 1966, Inner Temple
Pupil Master, Recorder
Qualifications: [BA (Cantab)]

MARTINO ANTHONY R.

Fountain Court
Temple, London EC4Y 9DH,
Telephone: 0171 583 3335
E-mail: chambers@fountaincourt.co.uk
Call Date: Nov 1982, Inner Temple
Qualifications: [MA]

MARTINS MISS YETUNDE TOKUNBO

Albany Chambers
91 Kentish Town Road, London
NW1 8NY, Telephone: 0171 485 5736/
5758 E-mail: albany91.freeserve.co.uk
Call Date: July 1989, Middle Temple
Qualifications: [BA (Hons)]

MARVEN ROBERT

Assize Court Chambers
14 Small Street, Bristol BS1 1DE,
Telephone: 0117 9264587
E-mail:chambers@assize-court-chambers.co.uk
Call Date: Oct 1994, Middle Temple
Qualifications: [BA (Hons)(Cantab)]

MARYNIAK RUPERT ANDREW WARD

1 Gray's Inn Square
Ground Floor, London WC1R 5AA,
Telephone: 0171 405 8946/7/8
Call Date: Nov 1991, Inner Temple
Qualifications: [BSc, MSc (Lond), Dip Law]

MARZEC MS ALEXANDRA

5 Raymond Buildings
1st Floor, Gray's Inn, London WC1R 5BP,
Telephone: 0171 242 2902
E-mail: clerks@media-ent-law.co.uk
Call Date: Nov 1990, Middle Temple
Pupil Master
Qualifications: [LLB (Warw)]

MASEFIELD ROGER FRANCIS

Brick Court Chambers
7-8 Essex Street, London WC2R 3LD,
Telephone: 0171 379 3550
E-mail: [surname]@brickcourt.co.uk
Call Date: Nov 1994, Middle Temple
Qualifications: [MA (Cantab), BCL, (Oxon)]

MASKREY SIMEON ANDREW QC (1995)

9 Bedford Row
London WC1R 4AZ,
Telephone: 0171 242 3555
E-mail: clerks@9br.co.uk
Call Date: July 1977, Gray's Inn
Recorder
Qualifications: [LLB]

MASNIUK PETER

Staple Inn Chambers
1st Floor, 9 Staple Inn, Holborn Bars,
London WC1V 7QH,
Telephone: 0171 242 5240
E-mail: clerks@staple-inn.org
Call Date: July 1983, Inner Temple
Qualifications: [BA (Hons), BA (Econ)]

MASON MISS ALEXANDRA

3 Stone Buildings
Lincoln's Inn, London WC2A 3XL,
Telephone: 0171 242 4937
E-mail: clerks@3sb.law.co.uk
Call Date: Nov 1981, Gray's Inn
Pupil Master
Qualifications: [BA (Lond)]

MASON DAVID BUCHANAN

3 Fountain Court
Steelhouse Lane, Birmingham B4 6DR,
Telephone: 0121 236 5854
Call Date: July 1986, Middle Temple
Pupil Master
Qualifications: [LLB (Leics)]

MASON DAVID HUGH ROTHWELL

Westgate Chambers
67a Westgate Road, Newcastle upon Tyne
NE1 1SG, Telephone: 0191 261 4407/
2329785
E-mail:pracman@westgatechambers.law.co.u
k
Call Date: Feb 1984, Middle Temple
Qualifications: [LLB Notts]

MASON DAVID JOHN

Bank House Chambers
Old Bank House, Hartshead, Sheffield
S1 2EL, Telephone: 0114 2751223
Call Date: July 1979, Gray's Inn
Pupil Master
Qualifications: [LLB]

MASON IAN DOUGLAS

2 King's Bench Walk Chambers
1st Floor, 2 King's Bench Walk, Temple,
London EC4Y 7DE,
Telephone: 020 7353 9276
E-mail: chambers@2kbw.co.uk
Call Date: Nov 1978, Lincoln's Inn
Pupil Master
Qualifications: [BA]

MASON JAMES WILLIAM

Francis Taylor Building
Ground Floor, Temple, London
EC4Y 7BY, Telephone: 0171 353 7768/
7769/2711
E-mail:clerks@francistaylorbuilding.law.co.uk
Call Date: July 1969, Gray's Inn
Pupil Master

MASON JOHN JOSEPH

6 Fountain Court
Steelhouse Lane, Birmingham B4 6DR,
Telephone: 0121 233 3282
E-mail: clerks@sixfountain.co.uk
Call Date: Nov 1971, Inner Temple
Pupil Master
Qualifications: [LLB]

MASON NICHOLAS ALAN

Nicholas Street Chambers
22 Nicholas Street, Chester CH1 2NX,
Telephone: 01244 323886
E-mail: clerks@40king.co.uk
Call Date: July 1984, Gray's Inn
Qualifications: [B.A., Dip Law]

MASON PATRICK DAVID ANTHONY

South Western Chambers
Melville House, 12 Middle Street,
Taunton, Somerset, TA1 1SH,
Telephone: 01823 331919 (24 hrs)
E-mail: barclerk@clara.net
Call Date: Oct 1997, Inner Temple

MASSEY ANDREW HUGH

Eighteen Carlton Crescent
Southampton SO15 2XR,
Telephone: 01703 639001
Call Date: July 1969, Gray's Inn
Pupil Master
Qualifications: [BA (Cantab)]

MASSEY RUPERT JOHN

Eaton House
1st Floor, 4 Eaton Road, Branksome Park,
Poole, Dorset, BH13 6DG,
Telephone: 01202 766301/768068
Call Date: July 1972, Inner Temple
Qualifications: [BA (Oxon)]

MASSEY MISS STELLA MARIA

Central Chambers
89 Princess Street,
Manchester M1 4HT,
Telephone: 0161 236 1133
Call Date: Feb 1990, Middle Temple
Qualifications: [BA Hons, PGCE]

MASSEY WAYNE RICHARD

Parsonage Chambers
5th Floor, 3 The Parsonage, Manchester
M3 2HW, Telephone: 0161 833 1996
Call Date: July 1986, Inner Temple
Qualifications: [BA (Hons)]

MASSEY WILLIAM GREVILLE SALE QC (1996)

Pump Court Tax Chambers
16 Bedford Row, London WC1R 4EB,
Telephone: 0171 414 8080
Call Date: July 1977, Middle Temple
Qualifications: [BA (Oxon)]

MASSIH MICHAEL GEORGES ABDEL QC (1999)

2 Paper Buildings
1st Floor, Temple, London EC4Y 7ET,
Telephone: 020 7556 5500
E-mail: clerks@2pbbarristers.co.uk
Call Date: 1979, Middle Temple
Pupil Master
Qualifications: [LLB (Lond)]

MASTERS ALAN BRUCE RAYMOND

Counsels' Chambers
2nd Floor, 10-11 Gray's Inn Square,
London WC1R 5JD,
Telephone: 0171 405 2576
E-mail:clerks@10-11graysinnsquare.co.uk
Call Date: July 1979, Middle Temple
Pupil Master
Qualifications: [LLB (Wales), BL]

MASTERS LEE AUBREY GEORGE

Victoria Chambers
3rd Floor, 177 Corporation Street,
Birmingham B4 6RG,
Telephone: 0121 236 9900
E-mail: viccham@aol.com
Call Date: Nov 1984, Middle Temple
Pupil Master
Qualifications: [BA]

MASTERS MISS SARA ALAYNA

20 Essex Street
London WC2R 3AL,
Telephone: 0171 583 9294
E-mail: clerks@20essexst.com
Call Date: Oct 1993, Middle Temple
Qualifications: [BA (Hons)(Cantab)]

MATES THOMAS RORY

Castle Street Chambers
2nd Floor, 42 Castle Street, Liverpool
L2 7LD, Telephone: 0151 242 0500
Call Date: Oct 1993, Middle Temple
Qualifications: [BA (Hons)(Kent)]

MATHER MISS KATE

4 King's Bench Walk
2nd Floor, Temple, London EC4Y 7DL,
Telephone: 020 7353 3581
E-mail: clerks@4kbw.co.uk
Call Date: Oct 1990, Gray's Inn
Qualifications: [LLB (Lond)]

MATHER-LEES MICHAEL ANTHONY

Albion Chambers
Broad Street, Bristol BS1 1DR,
Telephone: 0117 9272144
Call Date: Feb 1981, Inner Temple
Pupil Master
Qualifications: [LLB (Lond)]

MATHESON DUNCAN QC (1989)

1 Crown Office Row
Ground Floor, Temple, London
EC4Y 7HH, Telephone: 0171 797 7500
E-mail: mail@onecrownofficerow.com
Crown Office Row Chambers
Blenheim House, 120 Church Street,
Brighton, Sussex, BN1 1WH,
Telephone: 01273 625625
E-mail: crownofficerow@clara.net
Call Date: July 1965, Inner Temple
Recorder
Qualifications: [MA, LLM (Cantab)]

MATHEW JOHN CHARLES QC (1977)

Five Paper Buildings
1st Floor, Five Paper Bldgs, Temple,
London EC4Y 7HB,
Telephone: 0171 583 6117
E-mail:clerks@5-paperbuildings.law.co.uk
Call Date: June 1949, Lincoln's Inn

MATHEW MISS NERGIS-ANNE

2 Gray's Inn Square Chambers
2nd Floor, Gray's Inn, London WC1R 5AA,
Telephone: 020 7242 0328
E-mail: clerks@2gis.co.uk

St Philip's Chambers
Fountain Court, Steelhouse Lane,
Birmingham B4 6DR,
Telephone: 0121 246 7000
E-mail: clerks@st-philips.co.uk
Call Date: Nov 1981, Inner Temple
Pupil Master
Qualifications: [BSc (Hons)]

MATHEW ROBERT KNOX QC (1992)

12 New Square
Lincoln's Inn, London WC2A 3SW,
Telephone: 0171 419 1212
E-mail: chambers@12newsquare.co.uk
Call Date: 1974, Lincoln's Inn
Qualifications: [BA (Dublin)]

MATHEWS DENI

8 Fountain Court
Steelhouse Lane, Birmingham B4 6DR,
Telephone: 0121 236 5514/5
E-mail: clerks@no8chambers.co.uk
Call Date: Oct 1996, Gray's Inn
Qualifications: [BSc (B'ham), LLB (Bucks)]

MATHIAS MISS ANNA

**11 Bolt Court (also at 7 Stone Buildings
– 1st Floor)**
London EC4A 3DQ,
Telephone: 0171 353 2300
E-mail: boltct11@aol.com
**7 Stone Buildings (also at 11 Bolt
Court)**
1st Floor, Lincoln's Inn, London
WC2A 3SZ, Telephone: 0171 242 0961
E-mail:larthur@7stonebuildings.law.co.uk
Redhill Chambers
Seloduct House, 30 Station Road, Redhill,
Surrey, RH1 1NF,
Telephone: 01737 780781
Call Date: Oct 1994, Lincoln's Inn
Qualifications: [LLB (Hons)(Warw)]

MATHIESON GUY ALASTAIR DAVID

28 St John Street
Manchester M3 4DJ,
Telephone: 0161 834 8418
E-mail: clerk@28stjohnst.co.uk
Call Date: Oct 1993, Middle Temple
Qualifications: [BA (Hons)]

MATOVU DANIEL MBUSI SAJABI

Farrar's Building
Temple, London EC4Y 7BD,
Telephone: 0171 583 9241
E-mail:chambers@farrarsbuilding.co.uk
Call Date: Nov 1985, Inner Temple
Pupil Master
Qualifications: [BA(Oxon)]

MATOVU HAROLD NSAMBA

Brick Court Chambers
7-8 Essex Street, London WC2R 3LD,
Telephone: 0171 379 3550
E-mail: [surname]@brickcourt.co.uk
Call Date: July 1988, Inner Temple
Pupil Master
Qualifications: [BA (Oxon), Dip Law]

MATSUSHIMA MISS MASUMI

1-9-2 Shakujii – Machi, Nerima – Ku,
Tokoyo 177, Tokoyo, Japan,
Call Date: Oct 1990, Lincoln's Inn
Qualifications: [BA (Cantab)]

MATTHEW ALFRED DAVID HUGH

9 Bedford Row
London WC1R 4AZ,
Telephone: 0171 242 3555
E-mail: clerks@9br.co.uk
Call Date: Nov 1987, Inner Temple
Qualifications: [MA (E'burgh),Dip Law]

MATTHEWS MISS ALISON REBECCA

Call Date: Nov 1989, Middle Temple
Qualifications: [LLB Hons (Wales)]

MATTHEWS MRS ANN MARIE

King's Bench Chambers
Wellington House, 175 Holdenhurst Road,
Bournemouth, Dorset, BH8 8DQ,
Telephone: 01202 250025
E-mail: chambers@kingsbench.co.uk
Call Date: Oct 1994, Middle Temple
Qualifications: [LLB (Hons)]

MATTHEWS DENNIS ROLAND

Two Crown Office Row
Ground Floor, Temple, London
EC4Y 7HJ, Telephone: 020 7797 8100
E-mail: mail@2cor.co.uk, or to individual
barristers at: [barrister's
surname]@2cor.co.uk
Call Date: July 1973, Middle Temple
Pupil Master
Qualifications: [LLM]

MATTHEWS DUNCAN HENRY ROWLAND

20 Essex Street
London WC2R 3AL,
Telephone: 0171 583 9294
E-mail: clerks@20essexst.com
Call Date: Nov 1986, Gray's Inn
Pupil Master
Qualifications: [MA (Oxon)]

MATTHEWS MISS GILLIAN

York Chambers
14 Toft Green, York YO1 6JT,
Telephone: 01904 620048
E-mail: [name]@yorkchambers.co.uk
Call Date: July 1985, Inner Temple
Pupil Master
Qualifications: [LLB (Hull)]

MATTHEWS JANEK PAUL

Pump Court Tax Chambers
16 Bedford Row, London WC1R 4EB,
Telephone: 0171 414 8080
Call Date: July 1972, Gray's Inn
Pupil Master
Qualifications: [MA (Cantab), FCA]

MATTHEWS JULIAN DAVID

9 Bedford Row
London WC1R 4AZ,
Telephone: 0171 242 3555
E-mail: clerks@9br.co.uk
Call Date: July 1979, Middle Temple
Pupil Master
Qualifications: [LLB (Lond)]

MATTHEWS MISS LISA

Furnival Chambers
32 Furnival Street, London EC4A 1JQ,
Telephone: 0171 405 3232
E-mail: clerks@furnivallaw.co.uk
Call Date: Nov 1974, Gray's Inn
Pupil Master

MATTHEWS PHILLIP ROWLAND

2nd Floor, Francis Taylor Building
Temple, London EC4Y 7BY,
Telephone: 0171 353 9942/3157
Call Date: 1974, Inner Temple
Recorder
Qualifications: [MA (Cantab)]

MATTHEWS RICHARD ANDREW

3 Hare Court
1 Little Essex Street, London WC2R 3LD,
Telephone: 0171 395 2000
Call Date: Feb 1989, Inner Temple
Pupil Master
Qualifications: [MA (Cantab)]

MATTHEWS MRS SUZAN PATRICIA QC (1993)

Guildford Chambers
Stoke House, Leapale Lane, Guildford,
Surrey, GU1 4LY,
Telephone: 01483 539131
E-mail:guildford.barristers@btinternet.com
Call Date: July 1974, Middle Temple
Recorder
Qualifications: [BSc]

MATTHEWS-STROUD MISS JACQUELINE

2nd Floor, Francis Taylor Building
Temple, London EC4Y 7BY,
Telephone: 0171 353 9942/3157
Call Date: Nov 1984, Gray's Inn
Qualifications: [LLB (Bris)]

MATTHEWSON SCOTT

1 Gray's Inn Square, Chambers of the Baroness Scotland of Asthal QC
1st Floor, London WC1R 5AG,
Telephone: 0171 405 3000
E-mail: clerks@onegrays.demon.co.uk
Call Date: Oct 1996, Inner Temple
Qualifications: [BA (Lond), CPE]

MATTHIAS DAVID HUW

Hardwicke Building
New Square, Lincoln's Inn, London
WC2A 3SB, Telephone: 020 7242 2523
E-mail: clerks@hardwicke.co.uk
Call Date: July 1980, Inner Temple
Pupil Master
Qualifications: [BA]

MATTISON ANDREW

Chavasse Court Chambers
2nd Floor, Chavasse Court, 24 Lord Street,
Liverpool L2 1TA,
Telephone: 0151 707 1191
Call Date: Nov 1963, Gray's Inn
Pupil Master
Qualifications: [LLB (L'pool)]

MATUK MS HELEN ANTOINETTE

58 King Street Chambers
1st Floor, Kingsgate House, 51-53 South
King Street, Manchester M2 6DE,
Telephone: 0161 831 7477
Call Date: July 1990, Gray's Inn
Qualifications: [LLB]

MAUDSLAY MISS DIANA ELIZABETH

Sovereign Chambers
25 Park Square, Leeds LS1 2PW,
Telephone: 0113 2451841/2/3
E-mail:sovereignchambers@btinternet.com
Call Date: Oct 1997, Gray's Inn
Qualifications: [LLB (Sheff)]

MAUGER MISS CLAIRE SHANTI ANDREA

Enterprise Chambers
9 Old Square, Lincoln's Inn, London
WC2A 3SR, Telephone: 0171 405 9471
E-mail:enterprise.london@dial.pipex.com
Enterprise Chambers
65 Quayside, Newcastle upon Tyne
NE1 3DS, Telephone: 0191 222 3344
E-mail:enterprise.newcastle@dial.pipex.com
Enterprise Chambers
38 Park Square, Leeds LS1 2PA,
Telephone: 0113 246 0391
E-mail:enterprise.leeds@dial.pipex.com
Call Date: Oct 1996, Inner Temple
Qualifications: [BA (Oxon)]

MAUGHAM JOLYON TOBY DENNIS

Chambers of John Gardiner QC
1st Floor, 11 New Square, Lincoln's Inn,
London WC2A 3QB,
Telephone: 0171 242 4017
E-mail: taxlaw@11newsquare.com
Call Date: Mar 1997, Middle Temple
Qualifications: [LLB (Hons)(Dunelm)]

MAULEVERER PETER BRUCE QC (1985)

4 Pump Court
Temple, London EC4Y 7AN,
Telephone: 020 7842 5555
E-mail:chambers@4pumpcourt.law.co.uk
Call Date: July 1969, Inner Temple
Recorder
Qualifications: [BA (Dunelm), FCIArb]

MAUNDER DAVID JAMES

St John's Chambers
Small Street, Bristol BS1 1DW,
Telephone: 0117 9213456/298514
E-mail: @stjohnschambers.co.uk
Call Date: Oct 1993, Middle Temple
Qualifications: [BA(Hons)(Oxon), Dip in Law
(City), ISCL]

MAURICI JAMES PATRICK

4 Breams Buildings
London EC4A 1AQ,
Telephone: 0171 353 5835/430 1221
E-mail:breams@4breamsbuildings.law.co.uk
Call Date: Oct 1996, Inner Temple
Qualifications: [BA, BCL (Oxon)]

MAWDSLEY DAVID JOHN

Number Ten Baker Street
10 Baker Street, Middlesbrough TS1 2LH,
Telephone: 01642 220332
Call Date: Nov 1995, Gray's Inn
Qualifications: [BA, LLB]

MAWDSLEY MATTHEW EDWARD

Manchester House Chambers
18-22 Bridge Street, Manchester M3 3BZ,
Telephone: 0161 834 7007

Young Street Chambers
38 Young Street, Manchester M3 3FT,
Telephone: 0161 833 0489
E-mail: clerks@young-st-chambers.com
Call Date: Nov 1991, Inner Temple
Qualifications: [LLB (Hons)]

MAWHINNEY RICHARD MARTIN

35 Essex Street
Temple, London WC2R 3AR,
Telephone: 0171 353 6381
E-mail: derek_jenkins@link.org
Call Date: Nov 1977, Middle Temple
Pupil Master, Assistant Recorder
Qualifications: [BA (Oxon)]

MAWREY RICHARD BROOKS QC (1986)

2 Harcourt Buildings
Ground Floor/Left, Temple, London
EC4Y 9DB, Telephone: 0171 583 9020
E-mail: clerks@harcourt.co.uk
Call Date: Feb 1964, Gray's Inn
Recorder
Qualifications: [MA (Oxon)]

MAWSON STEPHEN JOHN CHRISTOPHER

Guildford Chambers
Stoke House, Leapale Lane, Guildford,
Surrey, GU1 4LY,
Telephone: 01483 539131
E-mail:guildford.barristers@btinternet.com
Call Date: Oct 1994, Gray's Inn
Qualifications: [MA]

MAX MISS SALLY ANN

Harcourt Chambers
1st Floor, 2 Harcourt Buildings, Temple,
London EC4Y 9DB,
Telephone: 0171 353 6961
E-mail:clerks@harcourtchambers.law.co.uk
Harcourt Chambers
Churchill House, 3 St Aldate's Courtyard,
St Aldate's, Oxford OX1 1BN,
Telephone: 01865 791559
E-mail:clerks@harcourtchambers.law.co.uk
Call Date: Oct 1991, Lincoln's Inn
Qualifications: [BA (Hons) (Cambs)]

MAXWELL ADRIAN ROBERT JOHN

4 King's Bench Walk
Ground/First Floor/Basement, Temple,
London EC4Y 7DL,
Telephone: 0171 822 8822
E-mail: 4kbw@barristersatlaw.com
Call Date: Nov 1993, Middle Temple
Qualifications: [MA (Hons)(Oxon)]

MAXWELL DAVID

Claremont Chambers
26 Waterloo Road, Wolverhampton
WV1 4BL, Telephone: 01902 426222
Call Date: Feb 1994, Inner Temple
Qualifications: [LLB (Warw)]

MAXWELL JOHN FREDERICK MICHAEL

4 Fountain Court
Steelhouse Lane, Birmingham B4 6DR,
Telephone: 0121 236 3476
Call Date: Feb 1965, Inner Temple
Pupil Master, Recorder
Qualifications: [MA (Oxon)]

MAXWELL JOHN JOSEPH

Old Colony House
6 South King Street, Manchester M2 6DQ,
Telephone: 0161 834 4364
Call Date: July 1985, Inner Temple
Qualifications: [BA]

MAXWELL MISS JUDITH MARY ANGELA

The Garden House
14 New Square, Lincoln's Inn, London
WC2A 3SH, Telephone: 0171 404 6150
Call Date: July 1988, Lincoln's Inn
Qualifications: [LLB (Hons) (B'ham)]

MAXWELL MISS KAREN LAETITIA

20 Essex Street
London WC2R 3AL,
Telephone: 0171 583 9294
E-mail: clerks@20essexst.com
Call Date: Oct 1992, Lincoln's Inn
Qualifications: [BA(Hons), BCL]

MAXWELL RICHARD QC (1988)

Ropewalk Chambers
24 The Ropewalk, Nottingham NG1 5EF,
Telephone: 0115 9472581
E-mail: administration@ropewalk co.uk
Doughty Street Chambers
11 Doughty Street, London WC1N 2PG,
Telephone: 0171 404 1313
E-mail:enquiries@doughtystreet.co.uk
Call Date: July 1968, Inner Temple
Recorder
Qualifications: [BA (Oxon)]

MAXWELL-SCOTT JAMES HERBERT

Two Crown Office Row
Ground Floor, Temple, London
EC4Y 7HJ, Telephone: 020 7797 8100
E-mail: mail@2cor.co.uk, or to individual
barristers at: [barrister's
surname]@2cor.co.uk
Call Date: Nov 1995, Gray's Inn
Qualifications: [MA (Cantab), BCL]

MAY ALAN

23 Essex Street
London WC2R 3AS,
Telephone: 0171 413 0353/836 8366
E-mail:clerks@essexstreet23.demon.co.uk
Call Date: Oct 1995, Inner Temple
Qualifications: [LLB (Plymouth)]

MAY MISS CHARLOTTE LOUISA

8 New Square
Lincoln's Inn, London WC2A 3QP,
Telephone: 0171 405 4321
E-mail: clerks@8newsquare.co.uk
Call Date: Nov 1995, Inner Temple
Qualifications: [BA (Oxon), CPE (City)]

MAY CHRISTOPHER JOHN

1 Harcourt Buildings
2nd Floor, Temple, London EC4Y 9DA,
Telephone: 0171 353 9421/0375
E-mail:clerks@1harcourtbuildings.law.co.uk
Call Date: Nov 1983, Middle Temple
Qualifications: [MA (Cantab)]

MAY MISS JULIET MARY

3 Verulam Buildings
London WC1R 5NT,
Telephone: 0171 831 8441
E-mail: clerks@3verulam.co.uk
Call Date: July 1988, Inner Temple
Pupil Master
Qualifications: [BA (Oxon), M Phil (Lond),
Dip Law (City)]

MAY KIERAN LAURENCE

8 Stone Buildings
Lincoln's Inn, London WC2A 3TA,
Telephone: 0171 831 9881
E-mail: alanl@8stonebuildings.law.uk
Call Date: Feb 1971, Middle Temple
Pupil Master
Qualifications: [BA (Oxon)]

MAY MISS NICOLA JANE

Trinity Chambers
140 New London Road, Chelmsford,
Essex, CM2 0AW,
Telephone: 01245 605040
E-mail:clerks@trinitychambers.law.co.uk
Call Date: Nov 1993, Gray's Inn
Qualifications: [LLB]

MAY MRS PATRICIA ROSEMARY

**4 Brick Court, Chambers of Anne
Rafferty QC**
1st Floor, Temple, London EC4Y 9AD,
Telephone: 0171 583 8455
Call Date: July 1965, Gray's Inn
Pupil Master, Recorder
Qualifications: [LLB (Lond)]

MAY (WILLIAM) NIGEL

33 Bedford Row
London WC1R 4JH,
Telephone: 0171 242 6476
E-mail:clerks@bedfordrow33.demon.co.uk
Call Date: July 1974, Inner Temple
Pupil Master, Assistant Recorder
Qualifications: [BA, Dip Criminology,
(Cantab)]

MAYALL DAVID WILLIAM

Francis Taylor Building
Ground Floor, Temple, London
EC4Y 7BY, Telephone: 0171 353 7768/
7769/2711
E-mail:clerks@francistaylorbuilding.law.co.uk
Call Date: July 1979, Gray's Inn
Pupil Master
Qualifications: [MA (Cantab)]

MAYCOCK MISS ELIZABETH JANE

Chartlands Chambers
3 St Giles Terrace, Northampton
NN1 2BN, Telephone: 01604 603322
Call Date: 1996, Inner Temple
Qualifications: [BA (Warw)]

MAYER MRS VERA

4 Brick Court
Ground Floor, Temple, London
EC4Y 9AD, Telephone: 0171 797 7766
E-mail: chambers@4brick.co.uk
Call Date: July 1978, Inner Temple
Pupil Master
Qualifications: [BA (Israel), MSc (Lond)]

MAYES IAN QC (1993)

Littleton Chambers
3 King's Bench Walk North, Temple,
London EC4Y 7HR,
Telephone: 0171 797 8600
E-mail:clerks@littletonchambers.co.uk
Call Date: July 1974, Middle Temple
Qualifications: [BA (Cantab)]

MAYHEW JEROME PATRICK BURKE

Goldsmith Building
1st Floor, Temple, London EC4Y 7BL,
Telephone: 0171 353 7881
E-mail:clerks@goldsmith-building.law.co.uk
Call Date: Nov 1995, Middle Temple

MAYLIN MS KERRY FIONA

Chambers of Helen Grindrod QC
4th Floor, 15-19 Devereux Court, London
WC2R 3JJ, Telephone: 0171 583 2792
Call Date: Oct 1994, Gray's Inn
Qualifications: [LLB]

MAYNARD CHRISTOPHER HOWARD

New Court
Temple, London EC4Y 9BE,
Telephone: 0171 583 5123/0510
Call Date: July 1988, Gray's Inn
Pupil Master
Qualifications: [BA Hons (York), Dip Law]

MAYNARD-CONNOR GILES

St James's Chambers
68 Quay Street, Manchester M3 3EJ,
Telephone: 0161 834 7000
E-mail: clerks@stjameschambers.co.uk
Call Date: Nov 1992, Inner Temple
Qualifications: [LLB (Lancs)]

MAYO KHUDA BAKHSH KAHN

55 Frith Road
Leytonstone, London E11 4EX,
Call Date: Nov 1979, Lincoln's Inn

MAYO RUPERT CHARLES

9 Bedford Row
London WC1R 4AZ,
Telephone: 0171 242 3555
E-mail: clerks@9br.co.uk
Call Date: Nov 1987, Gray's Inn
Pupil Master
Qualifications: [BA (Dunelm)]

MAYO SIMON PETER

1 Middle Temple Lane
Temple, London EC4Y 1LT,
Telephone: 0171 583 0659 (12 Lines)
E-mail: chambers@1mtl.co.uk
Call Date: Nov 1985, Inner Temple
Pupil Master
Qualifications: [BA (Lond)]

MAZZAG ANTHONY JAMES

Peel Court Chambers
45 Hardman Street, Manchester M3 3PL,
Telephone: 0161 832 3791
E-mail: clerks@peelct.co.uk
Call Date: Nov 1996, Lincoln's Inn
Qualifications: [MA]

MBATHA MRS MYRTLE

54 Anne Way
Ilford, Essex, IG6 2RL,
Telephone: 0181 501 4311
Call Date: Nov 1977, Lincoln's Inn
Qualifications: [BA, LLM]

MCALINDEN BARRY O'NEILL

17 Bedford Row
London WC1R 4EB,
Telephone: 0171 831 7314
E-mail: iboard7314@aol.com
Call Date: Oct 1993, Inner Temple
Qualifications: [BA (Hons) (Cantab)]

MCALLISTER MISS EIMEAR JANE

9 Woodhouse Square
Leeds LS3 1AD,
Telephone: 0113 2451986
E-mail: clerks@9woodhouse.co.uk
Call Date: Oct 1992, Gray's Inn
Qualifications: [LLB (Hull)]

MCALLISTER MISS ELIZABETH ANN

Enterprise Chambers
9 Old Square, Lincoln's Inn, London
WC2A 3SR, Telephone: 0171 405 9471
E-mail:enterprise.london@dial.pipex.com
Enterprise Chambers
38 Park Square, Leeds LS1 2PA,
Telephone: 0113 246 0391
E-mail:enterprise.leeds@dial.pipex.com
Enterprise Chambers
65 Quayside, Newcastle upon Tyne
NE1 3DS, Telephone: 0191 222 3344
E-mail:enterprise.newcastle@dial.pipex.com
Call Date: Nov 1982, Lincoln's Inn
Pupil Master
Qualifications: [MA (Cantab), LLM (Lond)]

MCARDLE MARTIN PATRICK BRIAN

East Anglian Chambers
Gresham House, 5 Museum Street,
Ipswich, Suffolk, IP1 1HQ,
Telephone: 01473 214481
E-mail: ipswich@ealaw.co.uk
East Anglian Chambers
52 North Hill, Colchester, Essex, CO1 1PY,
Telephone: 01206 572756
E-mail: colchester@ealaw.co.uk

D

East Anglian Chambers
57 London Street, Norwich NR2 1HL,
Telephone: 01603 617351
E-mail: norwich@ealaw.co.uk
Call Date: 1996, Inner Temple
Qualifications: [BSSc (Belfast), CPE (Manch)]

MCATASNEY MISS PHILIPPA MARY

9-12 Bell Yard
London WC2A 2LF,
Telephone: 0171 400 1800
E-mail: clerks@bellyard.co.uk
Call Date: Nov 1985, Lincoln's Inn
Pupil Master
Qualifications: [LLB (Lond)]

MCATEER MISS SHANDA LOUISE

Phoenix Chambers
First Floor, Gray's Inn Chambers, Gray's
Inn, London WC1R 5JA,
Telephone: 0171 404 7888
E-mail:clerks@phoenix-chambers.co.uk
Call Date: Oct 1994, Gray's Inn
Qualifications: [BA (Hons)(Oxon)]

MCAULAY MARK JOHN

6 Gray's Inn Square
Ground Floor, Gray's Inn, London
WC1R 5AZ, Telephone: 0171 242 1052
E-mail: 6graysinn@clara.co.uk
Call Date: Oct 1993, Inner Temple
Qualifications: [LLB (Hons)]

MCBRIDE GAVIN JOHN

Peel Court Chambers
45 Hardman Street, Manchester M3 3PL,
Telephone: 0161 832 3791
E-mail: clerks@peelct.co.uk
Call Date: Oct 1996, Middle Temple
Qualifications: [BA (Cantab), CPE Dip Law]

MCCABE MISS LOUISE ANNE

St Philip's Chambers
Fountain Court, Steelhouse Lane,
Birmingham B4 6DR,
Telephone: 0121 246 7000
E-mail: clerks@st-philips.co.uk
Call Date: Oct 1996, Inner Temple
Qualifications: [BA (Hons)(Dunelm)]

MCCABE MS MARGARET ANN

1 Pump Court
Lower Ground Floor, Temple, London
EC4Y 7AB, Telephone: 0171 583 2012/
353 4341
E-mail: [name]@1pumpcourt.co.uk
Sovereign Chambers
25 Park Square, Leeds LS1 2PW,
Telephone: 0113 2451841/2/3
E-mail:sovereignchambers@btinternet.com
Call Date: July 1981, Middle Temple
Pupil Master
Qualifications: [BA, LLB Lond]

MCCAFFERTY MISS LYNNE

5 Paper Buildings
Ground Floor, Temple, London
EC4Y 7HB, Telephone: 0171 583 9275/
583 4555 E-mail: 5paper@link.org
Call Date: Oct 1997, Middle Temple
Qualifications: [BA (Hons)(Oxon), CPE
(Lond)]

MCCAHEY MISS CATHERINE ANNE MARY

St Philip's Chambers
Fountain Court, Steelhouse Lane,
Birmingham B4 6DR,
Telephone: 0121 246 7000
E-mail: clerks@st-philips.co.uk
Call Date: Oct 1996, Inner Temple
Qualifications: [LLB (Notts)]

MCCAHILL DOMINIC TERENCE JOHN

4 Pump Court
Temple, London EC4Y 7AN,
Telephone: 020 7842 5555
E-mail:chambers@4pumpcourt.law.co.uk
Call Date: Oct 1991, Lincoln's Inn
Qualifications: [BA (Hons)]

MCCAHILL PATRICK GERARD QC (1996)

St Philip's Chambers
Fountain Court, Steelhouse Lane,
Birmingham B4 6DR,
Telephone: 0121 246 7000
E-mail: clerks@st-philips.co.uk
Chambers of Andrew Campbell QC
10 Park Square, Leeds LS1 2LH,
Telephone: 0113 2455438
E-mail: clerks@10pksq.co.uk
Call Date: July 1975, Gray's Inn

Recorder
Qualifications: [MA (Cantab), FCIArb]

MCCALL CHRISTOPHER HUGH QC (1987)

13 Old Square
Ground Floor, Lincoln's Inn, London
WC2A 3UA, Telephone: 0171 404 4800
E-mail: clerks@13oldsquare.law.co.uk
Call Date: Nov 1966, Lincoln's Inn
Qualifications: [BA (Oxon)]

MCCALL DUNCAN JAMES

4 Pump Court
Temple, London EC4Y 7AN,
Telephone: 020 7842 5555
E-mail:chambers@4pumpcourt.law.co.uk
Call Date: Feb 1988, Gray's Inn
Pupil Master
Qualifications: [BA (Oxon)]

MCCALLA TARQUIN JEFFREY

Dr Johnson's Chambers
Two Dr Johnson's Buildings, Temple,
London EC4Y 7AY,
Telephone: 0171 353 4716
E-mail: clerks@2djb.freeserve.co.uk
Call Date: Oct 1994, Lincoln's Inn
Qualifications: [BA (Hons)(Hull)]

MCCANDLESS PAUL JAMES

2 New Street
Leicester LE1 5NA,
Telephone: 0116 2625906
E-mail: clerks@2newstreet.co.uk
Call Date: Nov 1991, Lincoln's Inn
Qualifications: [LLB (Hons) (Manch)]

MCCANN MISS CATRYN ANNE

1 Inner Temple Lane
Temple, London EC4Y 1AF,
Telephone: 020 7353 0933
Call Date: July 1988, Lincoln's Inn
Qualifications: [LLM, LLB (Hons) SOAS]

MCCANN MISS COLLEEN MARIA

Angel Chambers
94 Walter Road, Swansea, West
Glamorgan, SA1 5QA,
Telephone: 01792 464623/464648
E-mail: lynne@angelchambers.co.uk
Call Date: Nov 1988, Inner Temple
Qualifications: [LLB (Wales)]

MCCANN JOHN MICHAEL

65-67 King Street
Leicester LE1 6RP,
Telephone: 0116 2547710
St Ive's Chambers
Whittall Street, Birmingham B4 6DH,
Telephone: 0121 236 0863/5720
E-mail:stives.headofchambers@btinternet.com
Call Date: 1983, Gray's Inn
Qualifications: [LLB L'pool]

MCCANN SIMON HOWARD

Deans Court Chambers
24 St John Street, Manchester M3 4DF,
Telephone: 0161 214 6000
E-mail: clerks@deanscourt.co.uk
Deans Court Chambers
41-43 Market Place, Preston PR1 1AH,
Telephone: 01772 555163
E-mail: clerks@deanscourt.co.uk
Call Date: Nov 1996, Gray's Inn
Qualifications: [BA (Leeds)]

MCCARRAHER COLIN FRASER

1 Paper Buildings
1st Floor, Temple, London EC4Y 7EP,
Telephone: 0171 353 3728/4953
Call Date: Oct 1990, Lincoln's Inn
Qualifications: [MA (Cantab)]

MCCARROLL JOHN JOHNSTON

Exchange Chambers
Pearl Assurance House, Derby Square,
Liverpool L2 9XX,
Telephone: 0151 236 7747
E-mail:exchangechambers@btinternet.com
Call Date: Nov 1988, Inner Temple
Pupil Master
Qualifications: [LLB (Dub)]

MCCARTHY DAMIAN PAUL

Mitre House Chambers
15-19 Devereux Court, London WC2R 3JJ,
Telephone: 0171 583 8233
Call Date: Nov 1994, Gray's Inn
Qualifications: [LLB (Warw)]

MCCARTHY MARTIN RAYMOND

8 King's Bench Walk
2nd Floor, Temple, London EC4Y 7DU,
Telephone: 0171 797 8888
8 King's Bench Walk North
1 Park Square East, Leeds LS1 2NE,
Telephone: 0113 2439797
Call Date: Nov 1994, Gray's Inn
Qualifications: [LLB]

MCCARTHY MISS MARY ANN

Walnut House
63 St David's Hill, Exeter, Devon,
EX4 4DW, Telephone: 01392 279751
E-mail: 106627.2451@compuserve.com
Call Date: Oct 1994, Middle Temple
Qualifications: [LLB (Hons)(Exeter)]

MCCARTHY MISS NIAMH JANE

Littman Chambers
12 Gray's Inn Square, London WC1R 5JP,
Telephone: 020 7404 4866
E-mail: admin@littmanchambers.com
Call Date: Nov 1991, Gray's Inn
Qualifications: [LLB (Dublin), Dip De Hantes
Etudes, Europeenes (Bruges)]

MCCARTHY ROGER JOHN QC (1996)

Cloisters
1 Pump Court, Temple, London
EC4Y 7AA, Telephone: 0171 827 4000
E-mail: clerks@cloisters.com
Call Date: July 1975, Gray's Inn
Qualifications: [BA (Hons)]

MCCARTHY WILLIAM

New Bailey Chambers
10 Lawson Street, Preston PR1 2QT,
Telephone: 01772 258087
Call Date: Nov 1996, Middle Temple
Qualifications: [LLB (Hons)(Leeds)]

MCCARTNEY MISS JOANNE

Enfield Chambers
First Floor, Refuge House, 9-10 River
Front, Enfield, Middlesex, EN1 3SZ,
Telephone: 0181 364 5627
E-mail:enfieldchambers@compuserve.com
Call Date: Nov 1990, Inner Temple
Qualifications: [LLB (Warw), LLM]

MCCARTNEY JOHN KEVIN

Hardwicke Building
New Square, Lincoln's Inn, London
WC2A 3SB, Telephone: 020 7242 2523
E-mail: clerks@hardwicke.co.uk
Call Date: Nov 1991, Middle Temple
Qualifications: [LLB Hons (Manch)]

MCCARTNEY PETER

St Philip's Chambers
Fountain Court, Steelhouse Lane,
Birmingham B4 6DR,
Telephone: 0121 246 7000
E-mail: clerks@st-philips.co.uk
Call Date: Nov 1983, Inner Temple
Qualifications: [BA]

MCCAUGHRAN JOHN

One Essex Court
Ground Floor, Temple, London
EC4Y 9AR, Telephone: 020 7583 2000
E-mail: clerks@oneessexcourt.co.uk
Call Date: July 1982, Gray's Inn
Pupil Master
Qualifications: [MA (Cantab)]

MCCAUL COLIN BROWNLIE

39 Essex Street
London WC2R 3AT,
Telephone: 0171 832 1111
E-mail: clerks@39essex.co.uk
Call Date: July 1978, Gray's Inn
Pupil Master
Qualifications: [LLB (Lond)]

MCCLUGGAGE BRIAN THOMAS

Chambers of John Hand QC
9 St John Street, Manchester M3 4DN,
Telephone: 0161 955 9000
E-mail: ninesjs@gconnect.com
Call Date: Oct 1995, Middle Temple
Qualifications: [MA (Cantab), LLM
(Toronto)]

MCCLURE BRIAN DAVID

Littman Chambers
12 Gray's Inn Square, London WC1R 5JP,
Telephone: 020 7404 4866
E-mail: admin@littmanchambers.com
Call Date: May 1976, Gray's Inn
Pupil Master
Qualifications: [BA (Cantab)]

MCCLURE JOHN PATRICK

24a St John Street
Manchester M3 4DF,
Telephone: 0161 833 9628
Call Date: Nov 1975, Middle Temple
Qualifications: [LLB (Hons)]

MCCOMBE RICHARD GEORGE BRAMWELL QC (1989)

13 Old Square
Ground Floor, Lincoln's Inn, London
WC2A 3UA, Telephone: 0171 404 4800
E-mail: clerks@13oldsquare.law.co.uk
Call Date: July 1975, Lincoln's Inn
Recorder
Qualifications: [MA (Cantab)]

MCCONNELL CHRISTOPHER RONALD

2 Gray's Inn Square Chambers
2nd Floor, Gray's Inn, London WC1R 5AA,
Telephone: 020 7242 0328
E-mail: clerks@2gis.co.uk
Call Date: July 1979, Lincoln's Inn
Pupil Master
Qualifications: [MA (Oxon)]

MCCONNOCHIE DR KATHRYN

Pendragon Chambers
124 Walter Road, Swansea, West
Glamorgan, SA1 5RG,
Telephone: 01792 411188
Call Date: Oct 1997, Gray's Inn
Qualifications: [BSc (St Andrews), MBChB
(Manc), LLB (Wales)]

MCCONVILLE DONALD ALEXANDER

3 Fountain Court
Steelhouse Lane, Birmingham B4 6DR,
Telephone: 0121 236 5854
Call Date: Feb 1963, Lincoln's Inn
Pupil Master
Qualifications: [LLM]

MCCORMACK ALAN

Staple Inn Chambers
1st Floor, 9 Staple Inn, Holborn Bars,
London WC1V 7QH,
Telephone: 0171 242 5240
E-mail: clerks@staple-inn.org
Call Date: Oct 1990, Lincoln's Inn
Pupil Master
Qualifications: [LLB (Hons)]

MCCORMACK MISS HELEN

10 King's Bench Walk
1st Floor, Temple, London EC4Y 7EB,
Telephone: 0171 353 2501
Call Date: Feb 1986, Middle Temple
Qualifications: [LLB(L'pool)]

MCCORMACK PHILIP ALEXANDER

2 Mitre Court Buildings
1st Floor, Temple, London EC4Y 7BX,
Telephone: 0171 353 1353
Call Date: Oct 1994, Gray's Inn
Qualifications: [LLB (Wales)]

MCCORMICK MISS ALISON CLAIRE

35 Essex Street
Temple, London WC2R 3AR,
Telephone: 0171 353 6381
E-mail: derek_jenkins@link.org
Call Date: Nov 1988, Middle Temple
Pupil Master
Qualifications: [BA (Hons)]

MCCORMICK DR PAUL MARTIN

Hampshire Chambers
Malton House, 24 Hampshire Terrace,
Portsmouth, Hampshire, PO1 2QF,
Telephone: 01705 826636/826426
Call Date: July 1983, Middle Temple
Qualifications: [Dip Soc Stud, MA, MPhil,
DPhil (Oxon)]

MCCORMICK WILLIAM THOMAS

10 King's Bench Walk
1st Floor, Temple, London EC4Y 7EB,
Telephone: 0171 353 2501
Call Date: July 1985, Gray's Inn
Pupil Master
Qualifications: [LLB (Hons) (Cardiff)]

D

MCCOURT CHRISTOPHER

22 Old Buildings
Lincoln's Inn, London WC2A 3UJ,
Telephone: 0171 831 0222
Call Date: Nov 1993, Inner Temple
Qualifications: [LLB (Nott'm)]

MCCOWAN MISS HESTER XANTHE JANE

Chambers of Kieran Coonan QC
Ground Floor, 6 Pump Court, Temple,
London EC4Y 7AR,
Telephone: 0171 583 6013/2510
E-mail: clerks@6-pumpcourt.law.co.uk
Call Date: Nov 1995, Gray's Inn
Qualifications: [BA]

MCCOY GERARD JOHN XAVIER

2 Paper Buildings
1st Floor, Temple, London EC4Y 7ET,
Telephone: 020 7556 5500
E-mail: clerks@2pbbarristers.co.uk
Call Date: 1986, Middle Temple
Qualifications: [BA, LLB, MSc]

MCCRACKEN ROBERT HENRY JOY

2 Harcourt Buildings
2nd Floor, Temple, London EC4Y 9DB,
Telephone: 020 7353 8415
E-mail: clerks@2hb.law.co.uk
Call Date: July 1973, Inner Temple
Pupil Master
Qualifications: [MA (Oxon)]

MCCRAE MISS FIONA

Trinity Chambers
9-12 Trinity Chare, Quayside, Newcastle
upon Tyne NE1 3DF,
Telephone: 0191 232 1927
E-mail: info@trinitychambers.co.uk
Call Date: July 1986, Gray's Inn
Qualifications: [LLB Newcastle]

MCCREATH MS FIONA MARY

4 King's Bench Walk
2nd Floor, Temple, London EC4Y 7DL,
Telephone: 020 7353 3581
E-mail: clerks@4kbw.co.uk
Call Date: Oct 1991, Gray's Inn
Qualifications: [LLB (Lond)]

MCCREATH MISS JEAN ALEXANDER

Counsels' Chambers
2nd Floor, 10-11 Gray's Inn Square,
London WC1R 5JD,
Telephone: 0171 405 2576
E-mail:clerks@10-11graysinnsquare.co.uk
Call Date: July 1978, Gray's Inn
Pupil Master
Qualifications: [BA (Hons) (Hull), AFBPsS]

MCCREDIE MISS FIONNUALA MARY CONSTANCE

3 Serjeants' Inn
London EC4Y 1BQ,
Telephone: 0171 353 5537
E-mail: clerks@3serjeantsinn.com
Call Date: Oct 1992, Middle Temple
Qualifications: [B.Sc (Hons, Manch), MA
(Brunel), Common Profesional ,
Examination]

MCCRIMMON MISS CATHRYN JANE

Counsels' Chambers
2nd Floor, 10-11 Gray's Inn Square,
London WC1R 5JD,
Telephone: 0171 405 2576
E-mail:clerks@10-11graysinnsquare.co.uk
Call Date: Nov 1991, Middle Temple
Qualifications: [LLB (Hons)]

MCCRINDELL JAMES DERREY

Mitre House Chambers
15-19 Devereux Court, London WC2R 3JJ,
Telephone: 0171 583 8233
Call Date: Oct 1993, Middle Temple
Qualifications: [BSc (Hons)(Lond), Dip in
Law (City)]

MCCUE DONALD

11 Stone Buildings
Lincoln's Inn, London WC2A 3TG,
Telephone: +44 (0)207 831 6381
E-mail:clerks@11StoneBuildings.law.co.uk
Call Date: July 1974, Lincoln's Inn
Qualifications: [MA (Cantab)]

MCCULLOCH IAN

Bracton Chambers
95a Chancery Lane, London WC2A 1DT,
Telephone: 0171 242 4248

Lloyds House Chambers
3rd Floor, 18 Lloyds House, Lloyd Street,
Manchester M2 5WA,
Telephone: 0161 839 3371
Claremont Chambers
26 Waterloo Road, Wolverhampton
WV1 4BL, Telephone: 01902 426222
Call Date: Nov 1951, Middle Temple
Pupil Master
Qualifications: [BA, LLB (Cantab)]

MCCULLOUGH ANGUS MAXWELL THOMAS

1 Crown Office Row
Ground Floor, Temple, London
EC4Y 7HH, Telephone: 0171 797 7500
E-mail: mail@onecrownofficerow.com
Call Date: Oct 1990, Middle Temple
Qualifications: [BA (Oxon), Dip Law]

MCCULLOUGH MISS JUDITH ANN

Queen's Chambers
5 John Dalton Street, Manchester M2 6ET,
Telephone: 0161 834 6875/4738
Queens Chambers
4 Camden Place, Preston PR1 3JL,
Telephone: 01772 828300
Call Date: Apr 1991, Middle Temple
Qualifications: [LLB (Hons)]

MCCULLOUGH MISS LOUISE CLARE

Lion Court
Chancery House, 53-64 Chancery Lane,
London WC2A 1SJ,
Telephone: 0171 404 6565
Call Date: Oct 1991, Middle Temple
Qualifications: [LLB Hons (Lond)]

MCCUTCHEON BARRY DUFF

8 Gray's Inn Square
Gray's Inn, London WC1R 5AZ,
Telephone: 0171 242 3529
Call Date: Nov 1975, Inner Temple
Qualifications: [BA, LLM, FTII]

MCDERMOTT MISS CAOIMHE

17 Carlton Crescent
Southampton SO15 2XR,
Telephone: 023 8032 0320/0823 2003
E-mail: greg@jg17cc.co.uk
Call Date: 1997, Middle Temple
Qualifications: [BA (Hons)(Warks), CPE (Bournemouth)]

MCDERMOTT GERARD FRANCIS QC (1999)

8 King Street Chambers
8 King Street, Manchester M2 6AQ,
Telephone: 0161 834 9560
E-mail: eightking@aol.com
2 Pump Court
1st Floor, Temple, London EC4Y 7AH,
Telephone: 0171 353 5597
Call Date: July 1978, Middle Temple
Pupil Master, Recorder
Qualifications: [LLB (Manchester)]

MCDERMOTT JOHN RAYMUND

Chavasse Court Chambers
2nd Floor, Chavasse Court, 24 Lord Street,
Liverpool L2 1TA,
Telephone: 0151 707 1191
Call Date: Nov 1976, Gray's Inn
Pupil Master
Qualifications: [LLB]

MCDERMOTT THOMAS FRANCIS

Farrar's Building
Temple, London EC4Y 7BD,
Telephone: 0171 583 9241
E-mail:chambers@farrarsbuilding.co.uk
Call Date: July 1980, Gray's Inn
Pupil Master
Qualifications: [LLB (Lond), MPhil, (Cantab)]

MCDEVITT COLIN JOHN

Wessex Chambers
48 Queens Road, Reading, Berkshire,
RG1 4BD, Telephone: 0118 956 8856
E-mail:wessexchambers@compuserve.com
Call Date: Oct 1995, Inner Temple
Qualifications: [BSc (Reading), CPE (City)]

D

MCDONAGH MATTHEW BARTLY ANTHONY

1 Inner Temple Lane
Temple, London EC4Y 1AF,
Telephone: 020 7353 0933
Call Date: Oct 1994, Middle Temple
Qualifications: [LLB (Hons)(B'ham)]

MCDONALD ANDREW

Martins Building
2nd Floor, No 4 Water Street, Liverpool
L2 3SP, Telephone: 0151 236 5818/4919
Call Date: July 1971, Gray's Inn
Pupil Master
Qualifications: [LLB (L'pool)]

MCDONALD MISS JANET

9 Park Place
Cardiff CF1 3DP,
Telephone: 01222 382731
Call Date: July 1984, Gray's Inn
Qualifications: [LLB]

MCDONALD JOHN WILLIAM

2 Temple Gardens
Temple, London EC4Y 9AY,
Telephone: 0171 583 6041
E-mail: clerks@2templegardens.co.uk
Call Date: Nov 1981, Middle Temple
Pupil Master
Qualifications: [MA (St Andrews) FRSA]

MCDONALD MARK PAUL

Tindal Chambers
3/5 New Street, Chelmsford, Essex,
CM1 1NT, Telephone: 01245 267742
Call Date: Oct 1997, Lincoln's Inn
Qualifications: [LLB (Hons)]

MCDONALD MS MELANIE SHARON

5 Fountain Court
Steelhouse Lane, Birmingham B4 6DR,
Telephone: 0121 606 0500
E-mail:clerks@5fountaincourt.law.co.uk
Call Date: Nov 1990, Inner Temple
Qualifications: [MA (Kent), Dip Law (City)]

MCDONALD PAUL

Old Colony House
6 South King Street, Manchester M2 6DQ,
Telephone: 0161 834 4364
Call Date: July 1975, Lincoln's Inn
Pupil Master
Qualifications: [LLB (Hons)]

MCDONNELL CONRAD MORTIMER

Gray's Inn Tax Chambers
3rd Floor, Gray's Inn Chambers, Gray's
Inn, London WC1R 5JA,
Telephone: 0171 242 2642
E-mail: clerks@taxbar.com
Call Date: Oct 1994, Lincoln's Inn
Qualifications: [MA (Oxon)]

MCDONNELL JOHN BERESFORD WILLIAM QC (1984)

1 New Square
Ground Floor, Lincoln's Inn, London
WC2A 3SA, Telephone: 0171 405 0884/5/6/
7 E-mail: clerks@1newsquare.law.co.uk
Call Date: July 1968, Inner Temple
Assistant Recorder
Qualifications: [MA (Oxon), LLM (Harvard)]

MCEVILLY GERARD MARTIN

Furnival Chambers
32 Furnival Street, London EC4A 1JQ,
Telephone: 0171 405 3232
E-mail: clerks@furnivallaw.co.uk
Call Date: Oct 1994, Lincoln's Inn
Qualifications: [LLB (Hons)(Wolves)]

MCEWAN MALCOLM CHARLES

18 St John Street
Manchester M3 4EA,
Telephone: 0161 278 1800
E-mail: 18stjohn@lineone.net
Call Date: July 1976, Middle Temple
Pupil Master
Qualifications: [MA (Oxon)]

MCEWAN MISS VERA GEORGINA

30 Lombard Drive, North Lodge,
Chester-Le-Street, Co Durham DH3 4BD
Call Date: Nov 1979, Inner Temple
Qualifications: [MA, LLM, M.Sc, Dip.Ed]

MCFARLAND MISS DENISE

3 New Square
Lincoln's Inn, London WC2A 3RS,
Telephone: 0171 405 1111
E-mail: 3newsquareip@lineone.net
Call Date: July 1987, Inner Temple
Pupil Master
Qualifications: [MA (Cantab)]

MCFARLANE ALASTAIR DUNCAN JAMES

Francis Taylor Building
Ground Floor, Temple, London
EC4Y 7BY, Telephone: 0171 353 7768/
7769/2711
E-mail:clerks@francistaylorbuilding.law.co.uk
Call Date: July 1985, Middle Temple
Qualifications: [LLB]

MCFARLANE ANDREW EWART QC (1998)

One King's Bench Walk
1st Floor, Temple, London EC4Y 7DB,
Telephone: 0171 936 1500
E-mail: ddear@1kbw.co.uk
St Philip's Chambers
Fountain Court, Steelhouse Lane,
Birmingham B4 6DR,
Telephone: 0121 246 7000
E-mail: clerks@st-philips.co.uk
Call Date: July 1977, Gray's Inn
Recorder
Qualifications: [BA (Dunelm)]

MCGAHEY MISS CATHRYN MARGARET

9 Bedford Row
London WC1R 4AZ,
Telephone: 0171 242 3555
E-mail: clerks@9br.co.uk
Call Date: Nov 1990, Inner Temple
Qualifications: [MA (Cantab)]

MCGAHEY MISS ELIZABETH CLARE

30 Park Place
Cardiff CF1 3BA,
Telephone: 01222 398421
E-mail: 100757.1456@compuserve.com
Call Date: Nov 1994, Inner Temple
Qualifications: [BA (Wales), CPE
(Glamorgan)]

MCGEE MISS TAMALA LOUISE

4 King's Bench Walk
2nd Floor, Temple, London EC4Y 7DL,
Telephone: 020 7353 3581
E-mail: clerks@4kbw.co.uk
Call Date: 1995, Lincoln's Inn
Qualifications: [LLB (Hons), LLM (Notts)]

MCGEE TRISTAN PAUL

Frederick Place Chambers
9 Frederick Place, Clifton, Bristol
BS8 1AS, Telephone: 0117 9738667
Call Date: Nov 1997, Middle Temple
Qualifications: [BA (Hons)(S.Africa), MSc,
PhD (Nott'm)]

MCGEORGE ANTHONY WILLIAM

13 King's Bench Walk
1st Floor, Temple, London EC4Y 7EN,
Telephone: 0171 353 7204
E-mail: clerks@13kbw.law.co.uk
King's Bench Chambers
32 Beaumont Street, Oxford OX1 2NP,
Telephone: 01865 311066
E-mail: clerks@kbc-oxford.law.co.uk
Call Date: Nov 1969, Inner Temple
Pupil Master
Qualifications: [MA (Cantab)]

MCGHEE JOHN ALEXANDER

9 Old Square
Ground Floor, Lincoln's Inn, London
WC2A 3SR, Telephone: 0171 405 4682
E-mail: chambers@9oldsquare.co.uk
Call Date: July 1984, Lincoln's Inn
Pupil Master
Qualifications: [MA (Oxon)]

MCGINN DOMINIC STUART

3 Temple Gardens
2nd Floor, Temple, London EC4Y 9AU,
Telephone: 0171 583 1155
Call Date: Nov 1990, Gray's Inn
Qualifications: [LLB (Cardiff)]

MCGINTY ROBERT FRASER

New Bailey Chambers
10 Lawson Street, Preston PR1 2QT,
Telephone: 01772 258087
Call Date: Nov 1994, Inner Temple
Qualifications: [BA (Oxon)]

MCGIVERN WILLIAM JOSEPH

9 King's Bench Walk
Ground Floor, Temple, London
EC4Y 7DX, Telephone: 0171 353 7202/
3909 E-mail: 9kbw@compuserve.com
Call Date: Nov 1987, Inner Temple
Qualifications: [LLB (Hull)]

MCGONIGAL DAVID AMBROSE

30 Park Square
Leeds LS1 2PF, Telephone: 0113 2436388
E-mail: clerks@30parksquare.co.uk
Broadway House Chambers
Broadway House, 9 Bank Street, Bradford,
West Yorkshire, BD1 1TW,
Telephone: 01274 722560
E-mail: clerks@broadwayhouse.co.uk
Call Date: July 1982, Gray's Inn
Pupil Master
Qualifications: [BA]

MCGOVERN SEAN PATRICK

New Walk Chambers
27 New Walk, Leicester LE1 6TE,
Telephone: 0116 2559144
Call Date: Nov 1990, Inner Temple
Pupil Master
Qualifications: [LLB]

MCGOWAN MISS MAURA PATRICIA

3 Hare Court
1 Little Essex Street, London WC2R 3LD,
Telephone: 0171 395 2000
Call Date: Nov 1980, Middle Temple
Pupil Master, Assistant Recorder
Qualifications: [LLB (Manch)]

MCGRAIL PETER RONALD

2-4 Tudor Street
London EC4Y 0AA,
Telephone: 0171 797 7111
E-mail: clerks@rfqc.co.uk
Call Date: July 1977, Gray's Inn
Pupil Master
Qualifications: [LLB (Lond)]

MCGRATH ANDREW JOHN

5 Fountain Court
Steelhouse Lane, Birmingham B4 6DR,
Telephone: 0121 606 0500
E-mail:clerks@5fountaincourt.law.co.uk
Call Date: Nov 1983, Gray's Inn
Qualifications: [BA]

MCGRATH DAVID THOMAS

2-4 Tudor Street
London EC4Y 0AA,
Telephone: 0171 797 7111
E-mail: clerks@rfqc.co.uk
Call Date: Nov 1993, Inner Temple
Qualifications: [LLB (Bris)]

MCGRATH MISS ELIZABETH ANN

St Philip's Chambers
Fountain Court, Steelhouse Lane,
Birmingham B4 6DR,
Telephone: 0121 246 7000
E-mail: clerks@st-philips.co.uk
Call Date: Nov 1987, Inner Temple
Pupil Master
Qualifications: [LLB (Hull)]

MCGRATH PAUL ANTHONY

Essex Court Chambers
24 Lincoln's Inn Fields, London
WC2A 3ED, Telephone: 0171 813 8000
E-mail:clerksroom@essexcourt-chambers.co.u
k
Call Date: Nov 1994, Inner Temple
Qualifications: [BA (Hons), BCL (Oxon)]

MCGRATH PAUL FRANCIS

1 Temple Gardens
1st Floor, Temple, London EC4Y 9BB,
Telephone: 0171 583 1315/353 0407
E-mail: clerks@1templegardens.co.uk
Call Date: 1997, Gray's Inn
Qualifications: [LLB (Lond)]

MCGREGOR ALEXANDER SCOTT

**11 Bolt Court (also at 7 Stone Buildings
– 1st Floor)**
London EC4A 3DQ,
Telephone: 0171 353 2300
E-mail: boltct11@aol.com

7 Stone Buildings (also at 11 Bolt Court)
1st Floor, Lincoln's Inn, London
WC2A 3SZ, Telephone: 0171 242 0961
E-mail:larthur@7stonebuildings.law.co.uk
Redhill Chambers
Seloduct House, 30 Station Road, Redhill,
Surrey, RH1 1NF,
Telephone: 01737 780781
Call Date: 1996, Lincoln's Inn
Qualifications: [BA (Oxon)]

MCGREGOR ALISTAIR JOHN QC (1997)

11 King's Bench Walk
Temple, London EC4Y 7EQ,
Telephone: 0171 632 8500/583 0610
E-mail: clerksroom@11kbw.com
Call Date: July 1974, Middle Temple
Qualifications: [LLB (Lond)]

MCGREGOR HARVEY QC (1978)

4 Paper Buildings
Ground Floor, Temple, London
EC4Y 7EX, Telephone: 0171 353 3366/
583 7155
E-mail: clerks@4paperbuildings.com
Call Date: Feb 1955, Inner Temple
Qualifications: [MA, DCL, SJD (Harv)]

MCGREGOR MISS HELEN MARGARET

Eastern Chambers
Badgers Bottom, Dysons Wood Lane,
Tokers Green, Oxford RG4 9EY,
Telephone: 0118 972 3722
E-mail: helen@bevis.tcom.co.uk
Call Date: July 1980, Inner Temple
Qualifications: [BSc, LLB (Lond)]

MCGUINNESS JOHN FRANCIS

9-12 Bell Yard
London WC2A 2LF,
Telephone: 0171 400 1800
E-mail: clerks@bellyard.co.uk
Call Date: July 1980, Lincoln's Inn
Pupil Master
Qualifications: [BA (Lond)]

MCGUINNESS-WAY ANDREW JEFFREY SEBASTIAN B

3 Temple Gardens
3rd Floor, Temple, London EC4Y 9AU,
Telephone: 0171 353 0832
Call Date: Oct 1992, Middle Temple
Qualifications: [BA (Hons)(Cantab)]

MCGUIRE BRYAN NICHOLAS

Chambers of Norman Palmer
2 Field Court, Gray's Inn, London
WC1R 5BB, Telephone: 0171 405 6114
E-mail: fieldct2@netcomuk.co.uk
Call Date: July 1983, Middle Temple
Pupil Master
Qualifications: [LLB (Lond), M Phil,
(Cantab)]

MCGUIRE MISS DEIRDRE MARIA

Martins Building
2nd Floor, No 4 Water Street, Liverpool
L2 3SP, Telephone: 0151 236 5818/4919
Call Date: Nov 1983, Inner Temple
Qualifications: [LLB (Leeds)]

MCHUGH DENIS DAVID

Bracton Chambers
95a Chancery Lane, London WC2A 1DT,
Telephone: 0171 242 4248
Call Date: Oct 1994, Lincoln's Inn
Qualifications: [LLB (Hons)(Hull)]

MCHUGH MISS KAREN

4 Breams Buildings
London EC4A 1AQ,
Telephone: 0171 353 5835/430 1221
E-mail:breams@4breamsbuildings.law.co.uk
Call Date: Nov 1992, Middle Temple
Qualifications: [BA (Hons) (Keele), Dip in
Law]

MCHUGH MISS PAULINE MARY

28 St John Street
Manchester M3 4DJ,
Telephone: 0161 834 8418
E-mail: clerk@28stjohnst.co.uk
Call Date: 1995, Gray's Inn
Qualifications: [BA]

MCILROY MR DAVID HALLIDAY

3 Paper Buildings
Temple, London EC4Y 7EU,
Telephone: 020 7583 8055
E-mail: London@3paper.com
3 Paper Buildings (Oxford)
1 Alfred Street, High Street, Oxford
OX1 4EH, Telephone: 01865 793736
E-mail: oxford@3paper.com
3 Paper Buildings (Winchester)
4 St Peter Street, Winchester SO23 8BW,
Telephone: 01962 868884
E-mail: winchester@3paper.com
3 Paper Buildings (Bournemouth)
20 Lorne Park Road, Bournemouth,
Dorset, BH1 1JN,
Telephone: 01202 292102
E-mail: Bournemouth@3paper.com
Call Date: Nov 1995, Inner Temple
Qualifications: [BA (Cantab)]

MCILROY WILLIAM EWART PATRICK

7 Wilton Road
Redhill, Surrey, RH1 6QR,
Telephone: 01737 760264
Call Date: Nov 1952, Gray's Inn
Qualifications: [MA (Oxon)]

MCILWAIN SYLVESTER DAVID

1 Dr Johnson's Buildings
Ground Floor, Temple, London
EC4Y 7AX, Telephone: 0171 353 9328
E-mail:OneDr.Johnsons@btinternet.com
Dr Johnson's Chambers
The Atrium Court, Apex Plaza, Reading,
Berkshire, RG1 1AX,
Telephone: 01734 254221
Call Date: July 1985, Lincoln's Inn
Pupil Master
Qualifications: [LLB (Warwick)]

MCINTOSH MISS JACQUELINE LORRAINE

Verulam Chambers
Peer House, 8-14 Verulam Street, Gray's
Inn, London WC1X 8LZ,
Telephone: 0171 813 2400
Call Date: July 1987, Inner Temple
Qualifications: [LLB]

MCINTYRE BRUCE MACGILLIVRAY

Plowden Buildings
2nd Floor, 2 Plowden Buildings, Middle
Temple Lane, London EC4Y 9BU,
Telephone: 0171 583 0808
E-mail: bar@plowdenbuildings.co.uk
Plowden Buildings
1 Jesmond Dene Terrace, Newcastle upon
Tyne NE2 2ET,
Telephone: 0191 281 2096
Call Date: Nov 1969, Middle Temple
Pupil Master, Recorder
Qualifications: [LLB (Cantab), LLB (Manch)]

MCIVOR MISS (FRANCES) JANE

3 Hare Court
1 Little Essex Street, London WC2R 3LD,
Telephone: 0171 395 2000
Call Date: July 1983, Inner Temple
Pupil Master
Qualifications: [LLB (E Anglia)]

MCIVOR MISS HELEN SUSANNAH

Young Street Chambers
38 Young Street, Manchester M3 3FT,
Telephone: 0161 833 0489
E-mail: clerks@young-st-chambers.com
Call Date: Oct 1992, Gray's Inn
Qualifications: [LLB (Hons)(Leic)]

MCIVOR IAN WALKER

334 Deansgate
Manchester M3 4LY,
Telephone: 0161 834 3767
Call Date: July 1973, Inner Temple
Qualifications: [LLB (Hons)(Lond)]

MCKAY MISS ANNMARIE

6 Gray's Inn Square
Ground Floor, Gray's Inn, London
WC1R 5AZ, Telephone: 0171 242 1052
E-mail: 6graysinn@clara.co.uk
Call Date: Nov 1992, Lincoln's Inn
Qualifications: [LLB (Hons)(Lond)]

MCKAY CHRISTOPHER ALEXANDER

Angel Chambers
94 Walter Road, Swansea, West
Glamorgan, SA1 5QA,
Telephone: 01792 464623/464648
E-mail: lynne@angelchambers.co.uk
Call Date: Nov 1976, Gray's Inn
Pupil Master
Qualifications: [LLB (Lond)]

MCKAY HUGH JOSEPH PETER

Gray's Inn Tax Chambers
3rd Floor, Gray's Inn Chambers, Gray's
Inn, London WC1R 5JA,
Telephone: 0171 242 2642
E-mail: clerks@taxbar.com
Call Date: Oct 1990, Lincoln's Inn
Pupil Master
Qualifications: [LLM , MA, FTII]

MCKECHNIE STUART IAIN WILLIAM

2 Gray's Inn Square Chambers
2nd Floor, Gray's Inn, London WC1R 5AA,
Telephone: 020 7242 0328
E-mail: clerks@2gis.co.uk
Call Date: 1997, Inner Temple
Qualifications: [LLB (Nottingham)]

MCKEE HUGH ANTHONY

24a St John Street
Manchester M3 4DF,
Telephone: 0161 833 9628
Call Date: Nov 1983, Middle Temple
Pupil Master
Qualifications: [BA]

MCKENDRICK EWAN GORDON

3 Verulam Buildings
London WC1R 5NT,
Telephone: 0171 831 8441
E-mail: clerks@3verulam.co.uk
Call Date: Mar 1998, Gray's Inn
Qualifications: [LLB (Edinburgh), BCL
(Oxon)]

MCKENNA MISS ANNA LOUISE

Queen Elizabeth Building
Ground Floor, Temple, London
EC4Y 9BS,
Telephone: 0171 353 7181 (12 Lines)
Call Date: Nov 1994, Middle Temple
Qualifications: [BA (Hons) (Leeds)]

MCKENNA BRIAN MALACHY

24a St John Street
Manchester M3 4DF,
Telephone: 0161 833 9628
Call Date: July 1983, Middle Temple
Qualifications: [LLB (Liverpool)]

MCKENZIE MISS LESLEY SHARON

Broad Chare
33 Broad Chare, Newcastle upon Tyne
NE1 3DQ, Telephone: 0191 232 0541
E-mail: clerks@broadcharechambers.law.co.uk
Call Date: Feb 1983, Lincoln's Inn
Qualifications: [LLB (Newc)]

MCKEON JAMES PATRICK

Martins Building
2nd Floor, No 4 Water Street, Liverpool
L2 3SP, Telephone: 0151 236 5818/4919
Call Date: Nov 1982, Lincoln's Inn
Qualifications: [LLB (L'pool)]

MCKEONE MS MARY BRENDA

Two Garden Court
1st Floor, Middle Temple, London
EC4Y 9BL, Telephone: 0171 353 1633
E-mail:barristers@2gardenct.law.co.uk
Call Date: Feb 1986, Gray's Inn
Qualifications: [LLB]

MCKIE MISS JACQUELINE

Number Ten Baker Street
10 Baker Street, Middlesbrough TS1 2LH,
Telephone: 01642 220332
Call Date: Oct 1995, Inner Temple
Qualifications: [LLB (Northumbria)]

MCKIERNAN EDWARD JOSEPH

Holborn Chambers
6 Gate Street, Lincoln's Inn Fields, London
WC2A 3HP, Telephone: 0171 242 6060
Watford Chambers
74 Mildred Avenue, Watford,
Hertfordshire, WD1 7DX,
Telephone: 01923 220553
Middlesex Chambers
Suite 3 & 4 Stanley House, Stanley
Avenue, Wembley, Middlesex, HA0 4SB,
Telephone: 0181 902 1499
Call Date: Nov 1981, Lincoln's Inn
Pupil Master
Qualifications: [LLB(Lond)]

MCKINLEY GREGOR CHARLES

Holborn Chambers
6 Gate Street, Lincoln's Inn Fields, London
WC2A 3HP, Telephone: 0171 242 6060
Call Date: Oct 1992, Gray's Inn
Qualifications: [BA (Hons)(Belfast), Dip Law]

MCKINNELL MISS SORAYA JANE

Enterprise Chambers
9 Old Square, Lincoln's Inn, London
WC2A 3SR, Telephone: 0171 405 9471
E-mail:enterprise.london@dial.pipex.com
Enterprise Chambers
65 Quayside, Newcastle upon Tyne
NE1 3DS, Telephone: 0191 222 3344
E-mail:enterprise.newcastle@dial.pipex.com
Enterprise Chambers
38 Park Square, Leeds LS1 2PA,
Telephone: 0113 246 0391
E-mail:enterprise.leeds@dial.pipex.com
Call Date: Oct 1991, Middle Temple
Qualifications: [LLB Hons (Exon)]

MCKONE MARK DESMOND

Sovereign Chambers
25 Park Square, Leeds LS1 2PW,
Telephone: 0113 2451841/2/3
E-mail:sovereignchambers@btinternet.com
Call Date: Nov 1988, Lincoln's Inn
Qualifications: [LLB Hons (Leeds)]

MCLACHLAN DAVID ROBERT

25-27 Castle Street
1st Floor, Liverpool L2 4TA,
Telephone: 0151 227 5661/051 236 5072
Call Date: Oct 1996, Inner Temple
Qualifications: [LLB, LLM (Essex)]

MCLAREN IAN ALBAN BRYANT QC (1993)

Ropewalk Chambers
24 The Ropewalk, Nottingham NG1 5EF,
Telephone: 0115 9472581
E-mail: administration@ropewalk co.uk
Call Date: Nov 1962, Gray's Inn
Recorder
Qualifications: [LLB (Nott'm)]

MCLAREN THE HON MICHAEL DUNCAN

Fountain Court
Temple, London EC4Y 9DH,
Telephone: 0171 583 3335
E-mail: chambers@fountaincourt.co.uk
Call Date: Nov 1981, Middle Temple
Pupil Master
Qualifications: [MA (Cantab)]

MCLAREN MISS NICOLA RUTH

1 Harcourt Buildings
2nd Floor, Temple, London EC4Y 9DA,
Telephone: 0171 353 9421/0375
E-mail:clerks@1harcourtbuildings.law.co.uk
Call Date: Nov 1991, Inner Temple
Qualifications: [LLB (Hull)]

MCLAUCHLAN IAN JOHN GERALD

Paradise Chambers
26 Paradise Square, Sheffield S1 2DE,
Telephone: 0114 2738951
E-mail: timbooth@paradise-sq.co.uk
Call Date: Oct 1992, Lincoln's Inn
Qualifications: [LLB(Hons)]

MCLAUGHLIN ANDREW PETER

St John's Chambers
Small Street, Bristol BS1 1DW,
Telephone: 0117 9213456/298514
E-mail: @stjohnschambers.co.uk
Call Date: Nov 1993, Middle Temple
Qualifications: [BA (Hons)(York), CPE (Lancs)]

MCLAUGHLIN MISS ELAINE

8 King's Bench Walk
2nd Floor, Temple, London EC4Y 7DU,
Telephone: 0171 797 8888
Call Date: Nov 1993, Middle Temple
Qualifications: [LLB (Hons)]

MCLAUGHLIN MISS KAREN JANET

14 Gray's Inn Square
Gray's Inn, London WC1R 5JP,
Telephone: 0171 242 0858
E-mail: 100712.2134@compuserve.com
Call Date: July 1982, Middle Temple
Pupil Master
Qualifications: [BA (Hons)]

MCLEAN MRS MANDY RACHEL

5 Essex Court
1st Floor, Temple, London EC4Y 9AH,
Telephone: 0171 410 2000
E-mail: barristers@5essexcourt.co.uk
Call Date: Oct 1996, Middle Temple
Qualifications: [LLB (Hons)(Kent)]

MCLEISH MARTYN LEE

8 Stone Buildings
Lincoln's Inn, London WC2A 3TA,
Telephone: 0171 831 9881
E-mail: alanl@8stonebuildings.law.uk
Call Date: 1997, Inner Temple
Qualifications: [BA (Oxon) PhD (Oxon),
CPE]

MCLEOD IAIN

1 Crown Office Row
3rd Floor, Temple, London EC4Y 7HH,
Telephone: 0171 583 9292
E-mail: onecor@link.org
Call Date: July 1969, Inner Temple
Recorder
Qualifications: [LLB]

MCLEVY MS TRACEY

Goldsmith Chambers
Ground Floor, Goldsmith Building,
Temple, London EC4Y 7BL,
Telephone: 0171 353 6802/3/4/5
E-mail:clerks@goldsmithchambers.law.co.uk
Call Date: Nov 1993, Lincoln's Inn
Qualifications: [LLB (Hons)]

MCLINDEN JOHN VINCENT BARRY

17 Bedford Row
London WC1R 4EB,
Telephone: 0171 831 7314
E-mail: iboard7314@aol.com
Call Date: 1991, Inner Temple
Pupil Master
Qualifications: [LLB (Hons), LLM (New,
Zealand)]

MCLOUGHLIN IAN

Francis Taylor Building
Ground Floor, Temple, London
EC4Y 7BY, Telephone: 0171 353 7768/
7769/2711
E-mail:clerks@francistaylorbuilding.law.co.uk
Call Date: Nov 1993, Lincoln's Inn
Qualifications: [B.Soc.Sci (Hons)]

MCLOUGHLIN TIMOTHY PATRICK

East Anglian Chambers
57 London Street, Norwich NR2 1HL,
Telephone: 01603 617351
E-mail: norwich@ealaw.co.uk
East Anglian Chambers
52 North Hill, Colchester, Essex, CO1 1PY,
Telephone: 01206 572756
E-mail: colchester@ealaw.co.uk
East Anglian Chambers
Gresham House, 5 Museum Street,
Ipswich, Suffolk, IP1 1HQ,
Telephone: 01473 214481
E-mail: ipswich@ealaw.co.uk
Call Date: Nov 1978, Lincoln's Inn
Pupil Master
Qualifications: [BA]

MCMANUS JONATHAN RICHARD QC (1999)

4-5 Gray's Inn Square
Ground Floor, Gray's Inn, London
WC1R 5JP, Telephone: 0171 404 5252
E-mail:chambers@4-5graysinnsquare.co.uk
Call Date: 1982, Middle Temple
Pupil Master
Qualifications: [MA (Cantab)]

MCMANUS MISS REBECCA JANE

Staple Inn Chambers
1st Floor, 9 Staple Inn, Holborn Bars,
London WC1V 7QH,
Telephone: 0171 242 5240
E-mail: clerks@staple-inn.org
Call Date: Nov 1994, Middle Temple
Qualifications: [BA (Hons)]

MCMASTER PETER

Serle Court Chambers
6 New Square, Lincoln's Inn, London
WC2A 3QS, Telephone: 0171 242 6105
E-mail: clerks@serlecourt.co.uk
Call Date: July 1981, Middle Temple
Pupil Master
Qualifications: [LLB (Lond)]

MCMEEKIN IAN

58 King Street Chambers
1st Floor, Kingsgate House, 51-53 South
King Street, Manchester M2 6DE,
Telephone: 0161 831 7477
Call Date: July 1987, Middle Temple
Qualifications: [BA (Hons) (Leeds), Dip Law
(City)]

MCMEEL GERARD PATRICK

Guildhall Chambers
22-26 Broad Street, Bristol BS1 2HG,
Telephone: 0117 9273366
E-mail:civil.clerks@guildhallchambers.co.uk and
criminal.clerks@guildhallchambers.co.uk
Call Date: 1993, Inner Temple
Qualifications: [BCL, MA (Oxon)]

MCMILLAN MRS CAROL ANN

15 North Church Street Chambers
15 North Church Street, Sheffield
S1 2DH, Telephone: 0114 2759708/
2738380
Call Date: Nov 1996, Middle Temple
Qualifications: [BA (Hons)(So'ton), MPhil
(Lond)]

MCMINN MISS VALERIE KATHLEEN

Baker Street Chambers
9 Baker Street, Middlesbrough TS1 2LF,
Telephone: 01642 873873
Call Date: Oct 1990, Gray's Inn
Qualifications: [BA (Hons), LLB (Lond)]

MCMORROW PATRICK JOSEPH

169 Temple Chambers
Temple Avenue, London EC4Y 0DA,
Telephone: 0171 583 7644
Call Date: Oct 1996, Inner Temple
Qualifications: [LLB (LSE)]

MCMULLAN MANUS ANTHONY

Atkin Chambers
1 Atkin Building, Gray's Inn, London
WC1R 5AT, Telephone: 020 7404 0102
E-mail: clerks@atkin-chambers.co.uk
Call Date: Nov 1994, Middle Temple
Qualifications: [BA (Hons)]

MCMULLEN JEREMY JOHN
QC (1994)

Old Square Chambers
1 Verulam Buildings, Gray's Inn, London
WC1R 5LQ, Telephone: 0171 269 0300
E-mail:clerks@oldsquarechambers.co.uk
Old Square Chambers
Hanover House, 47 Corn Street, Bristol
BS1 1HT, Telephone: 0117 9277111
E-mail: oldsqbri@globalnet.co.uk
Call Date: Nov 1971, Middle Temple
Recorder
Qualifications: [MA (Oxon), MSc (Lond)]

Fax: 0171 405 1387; DX: 1046 London

Other professional qualifications: QC N Ireland

Types of work: Civil liberties, Discrimination,
Employment

Awards and memberships: Vice President:
Industrial Law Society, Employment Law
Bar Association

Other professional experience: 11 years as union
official; Employment Tribunal Chairman
1993; Assistant Recorder 1997

Languages spoken: French

Publications: *Employment Tribunal Proce-*
dure, 1996; *Employment Precedents &*
Company Policies, 1996–; *Labour Law*
Review, Annual; *Civil Liberties – NCCL*
Handbook, 1990; *Rights at Work*, 1983

Reported Cases: *Porter v Magill*, (1999) *The*
Times, 6 May, 1999. Westminster 'homes
for votes' appeal. Represented successful
applicant Porter.
Crosville Wales v Tracey, [1998] AC 167,
1998. Compensation for workers unfairly
dismissed during a strike.
British Coal v Smith, [1996] ICR 515,
1996. Successful appeal for 1,200 women
claiming equal pay.
Burgoine v LB Waltham Forest, [1996] 95
LGR 520, 1996. Indemnity for local govern-

ment officers on boards of joint venture companies.
Cornwall County Care v Brightman, [1998] ICR 529, 1998. TUPE claim for workers dismissed and re-hired on lesser terms.

MCNAB MISS MHAIRI SHUNA ELSPETH

14 Gray's Inn Square
Gray's Inn, London WC1R 5JP,
Telephone: 0171 242 0858
E-mail: 100712.2134@compuserve.com
Call Date: July 1974, Middle Temple
Pupil Master

MCNALLY JOHN JOSEPH

10 King's Bench Walk
Ground Floor, Temple, London
EC4Y 7EB, Telephone: 0171 353 7742
E-mail: 10kbw@lineone.net
Call Date: Nov 1996, Gray's Inn
Qualifications: [BSc (Surrey), LLM (Lond)]

MCNAMARA ANDREW DAVID

St Mary's Chambers
50 High Pavement, Lace Market,
Nottingham NG1 1HW,
Telephone: 0115 9503503
E-mail: clerks@smc.law.co.uk
Call Date: Nov 1992, Inner Temple
Qualifications: [BA (So'ton), LLB (Leeds)]

MCNAMARA JAMES

High Pavement Chambers
1 High Pavement, Nottingham NG1 1HF,
Telephone: 0115 9418218
Call Date: May 1990, Inner Temple
Qualifications: [B.A.]

MCNEILE ANTHONY MICHAEL

Lamb Chambers
Lamb Building, Temple, London
EC4Y 7AS, Telephone: 020 7797 8300
E-mail: lambchambers@link.org
Call Date: July 1970, Gray's Inn

MCNEILIS MISS SHARRON DAWN

King Charles House
Standard Hill, Nottingham NG1 6FX,
Telephone: 0115 9418851
E-mail: clerks@kch.co.uk
Call Date: Oct 1990, Gray's Inn
Qualifications: [LLB]

MCNEILL MISS ELIZABETH JANE

Old Square Chambers
1 Verulam Buildings, Gray's Inn, London
WC1R 5LQ, Telephone: 0171 269 0300
E-mail:clerks@oldsquarechambers.co.uk
Old Square Chambers
Hanover House, 47 Corn Street, Bristol
BS1 1HT, Telephone: 0117 9277111
E-mail: oldsqbri@globalnet.co.uk
Call Date: Nov 1982, Lincoln's Inn
Pupil Master
Qualifications: [BA (Oxon), Dip Law (City)]

Fax: 0171 405 1387;
Out of hours telephone: 0171 354 5191;
DX: 1046 London;
Other comms: E-mail
jane.mcneill@virgin.net

Types of work: Employment, Medical negligence, Personal injury

Circuit: South Eastern

Languages spoken:

Reported Cases: *Preston v Wolverhampton, Fletcher v Midland Bank PLC*, [1997] ICR 895 (CA); [1998] ICR 227 (HL), Continuing. Test cases concerning pension rights of part-time workers.
Barclays Bank PLC v Kapur, [1991] ICR 208 (HL), 1991. Leading case on continuing acts of discrimination.
Setiya v East Yorkshire Health Authority, [1995] ICR 799, 1995. Time limits for appeal to Employment Appeal Tribunal following clarification of law by HL.
R v Chief Constable of BT Police ex parte Farmer, (1998) *The Times*, 4 September, 1998. Powers of Chief Constable to terminate service of probationary constable.

D

MCNEILL MISS FIONA KIRSTY

Chavasse Court Chambers
2nd Floor, Chavasse Court, 24 Lord Street,
Liverpool L2 1TA,
Telephone: 0151 707 1191
Call Date: Oct 1992, Lincoln's Inn
Qualifications: [LLB(Hons)(Nott'm)]

MCNEILL JOHN SEDDON

24a St John Street
Manchester M3 4DF,
Telephone: 0161 833 9628
Call Date: July 1974, Gray's Inn
Pupil Master
Qualifications: [BSc (Hons)]

MCNICHOLAS EAMON JOHN

Temple Gardens Tax Chambers
1st Floor, 3 Temple Gardens, Temple,
London EC4Y 9AU,
Telephone: 0171 353 7884/5 8982/3
E-mail: clerks@taxcounsel.co.uk.
Call Date: Oct 1994, Lincoln's Inn
Qualifications: [BA (Hons)(Leic), Dip in Law
(City), ACMA]

MCNIFF MATTHEW JAMES

1 Inner Temple Lane
Temple, London EC4Y 1AF,
Telephone: 020 7353 0933
Call Date: Oct 1992, Gray's Inn
Qualifications: [LLB (Hons)]

MCNULTY LAWRENCE JAMES

Plowden Buildings
2nd Floor, 2 Plowden Buildings, Middle
Temple Lane, London EC4Y 9BU,
Telephone: 0171 583 0808
E-mail: bar@plowdenbuildings.co.uk
Call Date: Nov 1985, Middle Temple
Qualifications: [BA (Kent), BCL (Oxon)]

MCPARLAND MICHAEL JOSEPH

New Court Chambers
5 Verulam Buildings, Gray's Inn, London
WC1R 5LY, Telephone: 0171 831 9500
E-mail: mail@newcourtchambers.com
Call Date: July 1983, Inner Temple
Pupil Master
Qualifications: [BA (Oxon)]

MCPHERSON GRAEME PAUL

Chambers of John L Powell QC
Four New Square, Lincoln's Inn, London
WC2A 3RJ, Telephone: 0171 797 8000
E-mail: barristers@4newsquare.com
Call Date: Oct 1993, Gray's Inn
Qualifications: [MA (Hons)]

MCQUAIL MS KATHERINE EMMA

11 Old Square
Ground Floor, Lincoln's Inn, London
WC2A 3TS, Telephone: 020 7430 0341
E-mail: clerks@11oldsquare.co.uk
Call Date: Nov 1989, Middle Temple
Pupil Master
Qualifications: [BA (Hons) (Oxon)]

MCQUATER EWAN ALAN

3 Verulam Buildings
London WC1R 5NT,
Telephone: 0171 831 8441
E-mail: clerks@3verulam.co.uk
Call Date: July 1985, Middle Temple
Pupil Master
Qualifications: [MA (Cantab)]

MCVAY MS BRIDGET SIOBHAN

Mitre House Chambers
15-19 Devereux Court, London WC2R 3JJ,
Telephone: 0171 583 8233
Call Date: Feb 1990, Inner Temple
Qualifications: [LLB (Hons)]

MEACHIN MISS (SARAH) VANESSA VERONICA

St Philip's Chambers
Fountain Court, Steelhouse Lane,
Birmingham B4 6DR,
Telephone: 0121 246 7000
E-mail: clerks@st-philips.co.uk
Call Date: Oct 1990, Inner Temple
Qualifications: [LLB (B'ham)]

MEAD JOHN PHILIP

Old Square Chambers
1 Verulam Buildings, Gray's Inn, London
WC1R 5LQ, Telephone: 0171 269 0300
E-mail:clerks@oldsquarechambers.co.uk

Old Square Chambers
Hanover House, 47 Corn Street, Bristol
BS1 1HT, Telephone: 0117 9277111
E-mail: oldsqbri@globalnet.co.uk
Call Date: July 1989, Lincoln's Inn
Qualifications: [LLB (B'ham), LLM (EUI
Florence)]

MEADE RICHARD DAVID

8 New Square
Lincoln's Inn, London WC2A 3QP,
Telephone: 0171 405 4321
E-mail: clerks@8newsquare.co.uk
Call Date: Nov 1991, Lincoln's Inn
Pupil Master
Qualifications: [BA (Hons) (Oxon)]

MEADOWCROFT GREGORY JOHN

2 King's Bench Walk Chambers
1st Floor, 2 King's Bench Walk, Temple,
London EC4Y 7DE,
Telephone: 020 7353 9276
E-mail: chambers@2kbw.co.uk
Call Date: Nov 1990, Middle Temple
Qualifications: [LLB]

MEADOWCROFT STEPHEN CHRISTIAN

Peel Court Chambers
45 Hardman Street, Manchester M3 3PL,
Telephone: 0161 832 3791
E-mail: clerks@peelct.co.uk
Call Date: Nov 1973, Gray's Inn
Pupil Master

MEADWAY MISS SUSANNAH LAWTON

The Chambers of Leolin Price CBE, QC
10 Old Square, Lincoln's Inn, London
WC2A 3SU, Telephone: 0171 405 0758
Call Date: July 1988, Middle Temple
Qualifications: [MA (Oxon), Dip Law (City)]

MEAKIN TIMOTHY WILLIAM

Fenners Chambers
3 Madingley Road, Cambridge CB3 0EE,
Telephone: 01223 368761
E-mail: clerks@fennerschambers.co.uk

Fenners Chambers
8-12 Priestgate, Peterborough PE1 1JA,
Telephone: 01733 562030
E-mail: clerks@fennerschambers.co.uk
Call Date: July 1989, Middle Temple
Qualifications: [BA (Leeds), Dip Law, LLM
(LSE)]

MEARES NIGEL LESLIE VELLACOTT

11 Stone Buildings
Lincoln's Inn, London WC2A 3TG,
Telephone: +44 (0)207 831 6381
E-mail:clerks@11StoneBuildings.law.co.uk
Call Date: Nov 1975, Middle Temple
Qualifications: [BA (Cantab)]

MEDD JAMES POWYS

One Paper Buildings
Ground Floor, Temple, London
EC4Y 7EP, Telephone: 0171 583 7355
E-mail: clerks@1pb.co.uk
Call Date: July 1985, Middle Temple
Pupil Master
Qualifications: [MA (Cantab)]

MEDHURST DAVID CHARLES

4 Brick Court
Temple, London EC4Y 9AD,
Telephone: 0171 797 8910
E-mail: medhurst@dial.pipex.com
Call Date: Nov 1969, Gray's Inn
Pupil Master
Qualifications: [LLB (Manch)]

MEDLAND SIMON EDWARD

23 Essex Street
London WC2R 3AS,
Telephone: 0171 413 0353/836 8366
E-mail:clerks@essexstreet23.demon.co.uk
Nicholas Street Chambers
22 Nicholas Street, Chester CH1 2NX,
Telephone: 01244 323886
E-mail: clerks@40king.co.uk
Call Date: Oct 1991, Middle Temple
Qualifications: [BA (Hull), Dip Law]

MEE PAUL MICHAEL

6 Pump Court
1st Floor, Temple, London EC4Y 7AR,
Telephone: 0171 797 8400
E-mail: clerks@6pumpcourt.co.uk

6-8 Mill Street
Maidstone, Kent, ME15 6XH,
Telephone: 01622 688094
E-mail: annexe@6pumpcourt.co.uk
Call Date: Nov 1992, Middle Temple
Qualifications: [B.Sc (Hons)(Aston)]

MEECH MISS ANITA ELLEN

Queens Square Chambers
56 Queens Square, Bristol BS1 4PR,
Telephone: 0117 921 1966
Call Date: Oct 1991, Lincoln's Inn
Qualifications: [LLB (Hons), M Phil (Cantab)]

MEEK MISS SUSAN ELIZABETH

2 Paper Buildings
1st Floor, Temple, London EC4Y 7ET,
Telephone: 020 7556 5500
E-mail: clerks@2pbbarristers.co.uk
Call Date: 1997, Gray's Inn
Qualifications: [LLB (Lond)]

MEEKE ROBERT MARTIN JAMES

Colleton Chambers
Colleton Crescent, Exeter, Devon,
EX2 4DG, Telephone: 01392 274898/9
Call Date: July 1973, Gray's Inn
Pupil Master, Assistant Recorder
Qualifications: [LLB (Bristol)]

MEESON NIGEL KEITH

4 Field Court
Gray's Inn, London WC1R 5EA,
Telephone: 0171 440 6900
E-mail: chambers@4fieldcourt.co.uk
Call Date: Nov 1982, Middle Temple
Pupil Master
Qualifications: [MA (Oxon)]

MEHENDALE MS NEELIMA KRISHNA

2 Mitre Court Buildings
1st Floor, Temple, London EC4Y 7BX,
Telephone: 0171 353 1353
Call Date: Oct 1993, Inner Temple
Qualifications: [BA (Hons) (Oxon)]

MEHIGAN SIMON PETER QC (1998)

Five Paper Buildings
1st Floor, Five Paper Bldgs, Temple,
London EC4Y 7HB,
Telephone: 0171 583 6117
E-mail:clerks@5-paperbuildings.law.co.uk
Call Date: July 1980, Lincoln's Inn
Qualifications: [LLB (Lond)]

MEHTA SAILESH

Verulam Chambers
Peer House, 8-14 Verulam Street, Gray's
Inn, London WC1X 8LZ,
Telephone: 0171 813 2400
Call Date: July 1986, Lincoln's Inn
Pupil Master
Qualifications: [LLB (Manch)]

MEIKLE ROBERT WILLIAM

Goldsmith Chambers
Ground Floor, Goldsmith Building,
Temple, London EC4Y 7BL,
Telephone: 0171 353 6802/3/4/5
E-mail:clerks@goldsmithchambers.law.co.uk
Call Date: July 1970, Gray's Inn
Pupil Master
Qualifications: [LLB (B'ham)]

MEJZNER STEPHEN JOHN

Dr Johnson's Chambers
Two Dr Johnson's Buildings, Temple,
London EC4Y 7AY,
Telephone: 0171 353 4716
E-mail: clerks@2djb.freeserve.co.uk
Call Date: Nov 1978, Middle Temple
Pupil Master
Qualifications: [LLB (Sheff)]

MELLOR EDWARD JAMES WILSON

8 New Square
Lincoln's Inn, London WC2A 3QP,
Telephone: 0171 405 4321
E-mail: clerks@8newsquare.co.uk
Call Date: July 1986, Middle Temple
Pupil Master
Qualifications: [MA (Cantab)]

MELLOR JOHN WALTER

30 Park Square
Leeds LS1 2PF, Telephone: 0113 2436388
E-mail: clerks@30parksquare.co.uk
Call Date: Feb 1953, Gray's Inn
Qualifications: [LLB]

MELLY MISS KAMA LOUISE

37 Park Square Chambers
37 Park Square, Leeds LS1 2NY,
Telephone: 0113 2439422
E-mail: chambers@no37.co.uk
Call Date: 1997, Middle Temple
Qualifications: [LLB (Hons)(Leeds)]

MELTON CHRISTOPHER

Peel Court Chambers
45 Hardman Street, Manchester M3 3PL,
Telephone: 0161 832 3791
E-mail: clerks@peelct.co.uk
199 Strand
London WC2R 1DR,
Telephone: 0171 379 9779
E-mail: chambers@199strand.co.uk
Call Date: July 1982, Gray's Inn
Pupil Master
Qualifications: [LLB (Bristol)]

MELVILLE MISS ELIZABETH EMMA JANE

Old Square Chambers
1 Verulam Buildings, Gray's Inn, London
WC1R 5LQ, Telephone: 0171 269 0300
E-mail:clerks@oldsquarechambers.co.uk
Old Square Chambers
Hanover House, 47 Corn Street, Bristol
BS1 1HT, Telephone: 0117 9277111
E-mail: oldsqbri@globalnet.co.uk
Call Date: Oct 1994, Gray's Inn
Qualifications: [BA]

MELVILLE RICHARD DAVID

39 Essex Street
London WC2R 3AT,
Telephone: 0171 832 1111
E-mail: clerks@39essex.co.uk
Call Date: July 1975, Inner Temple
Pupil Master
Qualifications: [MA (Cantab)]

Types of work: Commercial, Commercial litigation, Common law (general), Employment, Foreign law, Insurance, International

trade, Medical negligence, Personal injury, Private international, Professional negligence, Sale and carriage of goods, Shipping, admiralty

Languages spoken: French

Reported Cases: *Hough v P & O Contracts Ltd,* [1998] 3 WLR 851, 1998. Conflict of laws. Jurisdiction under European Convention. Third Party Claims. Civil Jurisdiction and Judgments Act 1982, Schedule 1 Arts 62 and 17.

MELVILLE-SHREEVE MICHAEL DAVID

Walnut House
63 St David's Hill, Exeter, Devon,
EX4 4DW, Telephone: 01392 279751
E-mail: 106627.2451@compuserve.com
Call Date: July 1986, Gray's Inn
Pupil Master
Qualifications: [LLB (Exeter)]

MELWANI MISS POONAM ARJANDAS

4 Essex Court
Temple, London EC4Y 9AJ,
Telephone: 020 7797 7970
E-mail: clerks@4essexcourt.law.co.uk
Call Date: Nov 1989, Inner Temple
Pupil Master
Qualifications: [MA (Cantab)]

MENARY ANDREW GWYN

Martins Building
2nd Floor, No 4 Water Street, Liverpool
L2 3SP, Telephone: 0151 236 5818/4919
Call Date: Nov 1982, Inner Temple
Pupil Master
Qualifications: [BA]

MENDEL MS PHILIPPA

Lion Court
Chancery House, 53-64 Chancery Lane,
London WC2A 1SJ,
Telephone: 0171 404 6565
Call Date: May 1992, Inner Temple
Qualifications: [LLB (Newcastle)]

MENDELLE PAUL MICHAEL

3 Gray's Inn Square
Ground Floor, London WC1R 5AH,
Telephone: 0171 520 5600
E-mail: clerks@3gis.co.uk
Call Date: July 1981, Lincoln's Inn
Pupil Master
Qualifications: [LLB Lond]

MENDELSON PROFESSOR MAURICE HARVEY QC (1992)

Blackstone Chambers
Blackstone House, Temple, London
EC4Y 9BW, Telephone: 0171 583 1770
E-mail:clerks@blackstonechambers.com
Call Date: Nov 1965, Lincoln's Inn
Qualifications: [MA,DPhil (Oxon)]

MENDES DA COSTA DAVID

2 King's Bench Walk Chambers
1st Floor, 2 King's Bench Walk, Temple,
London EC4Y 7DE,
Telephone: 020 7353 9276
E-mail: chambers@2kbw.co.uk
Call Date: Nov 1976, Inner Temple
Pupil Master

MENDHIR MRS MANJEET

Mendhir Chambers
38 Priest Avenue, Wokingham, Berkshire,
RG40 2LX, Telephone: 0118 9771274
Call Date: Nov 1980, Lincoln's Inn
Qualifications: [BA Law]

MENDOZA COLIN JOHN

Lamb Chambers
Lamb Building, Temple, London
EC4Y 7AS, Telephone: 020 7797 8300
E-mail: lambchambers@link.org
Doughty Street Chambers
11 Doughty Street, London WC1N 2PG,
Telephone: 0171 404 1313
E-mail:enquiries@doughtystreet.co.uk
Godolphin Chambers
50 Castle Street, Truro, Cornwall,
TR1 3AF, Telephone: 01872 276312
E-mail:theclerks@godolphin.force9.co.uk
Call Date: Nov 1983, Inner Temple
Pupil Master
Qualifications: [BA (Kent), LLM (Cantab)]

MENDOZA NEIL DAVID PEREIRA

Hardwicke Building
New Square, Lincoln's Inn, London
WC2A 3SB, Telephone: 020 7242 2523
E-mail: clerks@hardwicke.co.uk
Call Date: July 1982, Inner Temple
Pupil Master
Qualifications: [MA (Cantab)]

MENON HARIGOVIND

New Court Chambers
3 Broad Chare, Newcastle upon Tyne
NE1 3DQ, Telephone: 0191 232 1980
Call Date: July 1989, Gray's Inn
Qualifications: [BSc (Aberdeen), LLB
(Newc)]

MENON RAJIV

Two Garden Court
1st Floor, Middle Temple, London
EC4Y 9BL, Telephone: 0171 353 1633
E-mail:barristers@2gardenct.law.co.uk
Call Date: Nov 1993, Middle Temple
Qualifications: [MSc (Lond), CPE]

MENSAH MISS BARBARA

1 Gray's Inn Square
Ground Floor, London WC1R 5AA,
Telephone: 0171 405 8946/7/8
Call Date: July 1984, Lincoln's Inn
Qualifications: [BSc (lond), Dip Law]

MENZIES RICHARD MARK

8 Stone Buildings
Lincoln's Inn, London WC2A 3TA,
Telephone: 0171 831 9881
E-mail: alanl@8stonebuildings.law.uk
Call Date: Nov 1993, Middle Temple
Qualifications: [BA (Hons)(Cantab), MA
(Cantab)]

MERCER DAVID PAUL

Queen's Chambers
5 John Dalton Street, Manchester M2 6ET,
Telephone: 0161 834 6875/4738
Queens Chambers
4 Camden Place, Preston PR1 3JL,
Telephone: 01772 828300
Call Date: July 1980, Lincoln's Inn
Qualifications: [BA (Oxon) Dip Law]

MERCER GEOFFREY MICHAEL

Walnut House
63 St David's Hill, Exeter, Devon,
EX4 4DW, Telephone: 01392 279751
E-mail: 106627.2451@compuserve.com
Call Date: Nov 1975, Inner Temple
Pupil Master, Recorder
Qualifications: [LLB (Soton)]

MERCER HUGH CHARLES

Essex Court Chambers
24 Lincoln's Inn Fields, London
WC2A 3ED, Telephone: 0171 813 8000
E-mail:clerksroom@essexcourt-chambers.co.uk
Call Date: July 1985, Middle Temple
Pupil Master
Qualifications: [MA (Cantab)]

Fax: 0171 813 8080; DX: 320 Chancery Lane

Types of work: Administrative, Agriculture, Arbitration, Commercial, Commercial litigation, Competition, EC and competition law, EC law, ECHR, Energy, European law, Film, cable, TV, Foreign law, Human rights, International trade, Private international, Sports

Awards and memberships: Chairman, European Union Sub-Committee of the Bar Council of England & Wales; Union Internationale des Avocats; Bar European Group; Agricultural Law Association

Other professional experience: Tutor, Commercial Law, London School of Economics (1987-8); Lecturer on King's College Summer Course for European Law (1989 to date); Frequent lecturer in UK and abroad on issues of EU law and conflict of laws.

Languages spoken: French, German, Italian, Spanish

Publications: *Commercial Debt in Europe: Recovery & Remedies*, 1991; *The European Advocate* (co-editor), Quarterly Review; *The Practitioner's Handbook of EC Law* (chapter on the Brussels Convention), 1998; *Languages as a Barrier to Trade in EU Law*, [1996] ECLR 308; *Property Law – The Human Rights Dimension* RICS Blundell Memorial Lecture, 1999

Reported Cases: *R v Department of Health ex parte Eastside Cheese*, Duckett intervening, (1998) *The Times*, 1 December, 1998. European law judicial review in context of government loan on cheese producer – whether proportionate – agricultural law/food law.
Stevenage Borough Football Club v The Football League, [1997] 9 Admin LR, 1996. Restrictive practices/competition law – imposing restrictive rules on football clubs for entry to higher league – injunctive relief.
Kitechnology v Unicor, [1994] IL Pr 560, 1994. Jurisdiction – Brussels Convention – conflict of laws – place where harmful event occurred.
L/M International v Circle Limited Partnership, [1992] 37 Con LR 72, 1992. Commercial litigation – security for costs against defendants with counter claim – jurisdiction over Danish bank.
Fox v Fontana, 1999 *White Book* 14/4/45, 1991. Discharge of Mareva injunction over assets in Spain by reason of delay in pursuing proceedings – foreign law in English courts.

MERCER NEIL STANLEY

Mitre Court Chambers
3rd Floor, Temple, London EC4Y 7BP,
Telephone: 0171 353 9394
E-mail: mitrecourt.com
Call Date: Nov 1988, Lincoln's Inn
Qualifications: [LLB Hons (Wales)]

MEREDITH CHRISTOPHER WILLIAM

1 Gray's Inn Square, Chambers of the Baroness Scotland of Asthal QC
1st Floor, London WC1R 5AG,
Telephone: 0171 405 3000
E-mail: clerks@onegrays.demon.co.uk
Call Date: Nov 1988, Inner Temple
Pupil Master
Qualifications: [LLB]

MEREDITH GEORGE HUBBARD

Southernhay Chambers
33 Southernhay East, Exeter, Devon,
EX1 1NX, Telephone: 01392 255777
E-mail:southernhay.chambers@lineone.net
Call Date: July 1969, Gray's Inn

MEREDITH PHILIP GRANVILLE

Westgate Chambers
144 High Street, Lewes, East Sussex,
BN7 1XT, Telephone: 01273 480510
Call Date: July 1979, Inner Temple
Pupil Master
Qualifications: [BA (Dunelm)]

MEREDITH-HARDY JOHN OCTAVIAN

2 King's Bench Walk
Ground Floor, Temple, London
EC4Y 7DE, Telephone: 0171 353 1746
E-mail: 2kbw@atlas.co.uk
King's Bench Chambers
115 North Hill, Plymouth PL4 8JY,
Telephone: 01752 221551
Call Date: Nov 1989, Inner Temple
Qualifications: [MA (St Andrews), Dip Law]

MERRETT MISS LOUISE ANN

Fountain Court
Temple, London EC4Y 9DH,
Telephone: 0171 583 3335
E-mail: chambers@fountaincourt.co.uk
Call Date: Oct 1995, Gray's Inn
Qualifications: [BA]

MERRETT RICHARD JAMES

Colleton Chambers
Colleton Crescent, Exeter, Devon,
EX2 4DG, Telephone: 01392 274898/9
Call Date: June 1959, Inner Temple
Qualifications: [MA (Oxon)]

MERRICK MISS NICOLA

Furnival Chambers
32 Furnival Street, London EC4A 1JQ,
Telephone: 0171 405 3232
E-mail: clerks@furnivallaw.co.uk
Call Date: Nov 1983, Gray's Inn
Qualifications: [BA, LLB]

MERRIMAN NICHOLAS FLAVELLE QC (1988)

3 Verulam Buildings
London WC1R 5NT,
Telephone: 0171 831 8441
E-mail: clerks@3verulam.co.uk
Call Date: Feb 1969, Inner Temple
Recorder

MERRITT JOHN RICHARD

Fountain Chambers
Cleveland Business Centre, 1 Watson
Street, Middlesbrough TS1 2RQ,
Telephone: 01642 804040
E-mail:fountainchambers@onyxnet.co.uk
Call Date: May 1981, Middle Temple
Pupil Master
Qualifications: [LLB (Manch)]

MERRY HUGH GAIRNS

17 Carlton Crescent
Southampton SO15 2XR,
Telephone: 023 8032 0320/0823 2003
E-mail: greg@jg17cc.co.uk
Call Date: July 1979, Inner Temple
Pupil Master
Qualifications: [LLB (Bris)]

MERRYLEES RICHARD GAVIN

2nd Floor, Francis Taylor Building
Temple, London EC4Y 7BY,
Telephone: 0171 353 9942/3157
Call Date: Nov 1964, Gray's Inn
Pupil Master
Qualifications: [LLB (Lond)]

MERZ RICHARD JAMES

9-12 Bell Yard
London WC2A 2LF,
Telephone: 0171 400 1800
E-mail: clerks@bellyard.co.uk
Call Date: July 1972, Inner Temple
Pupil Master
Qualifications: [LLB (So'ton)]

MESSLING LAWRENCE DAVID

St Philip's Chambers
Fountain Court, Steelhouse Lane,
Birmingham B4 6DR,
Telephone: 0121 246 7000
E-mail: clerks@st-philips.co.uk
Call Date: 1983, Middle Temple
Qualifications: [BA (Keele)]

METAXA WILLIAM ALEXANDER

Gray's Inn Chambers
5th Floor, Gray's Inn, London WC1R 5JA,
Telephone: 0171 404 1111
Call Date: Nov 1995, Middle Temple
Qualifications: [BA (Hons)]

METCALF CHRISTOPHER SHERWOOD JOHN

Chambers of Michael Pert QC
36 Bedford Row, London WC1R 4JH,
Telephone: 0171 421 8000
E-mail: 36bedfordrow@link.org
Chambers of Michael Pert QC
24 Albion Place, Northampton NN1 1UD,
Telephone: 01604 602333
Chambers of Michael Pert QC
104 New Walk, Leicester LE1 7EA,
Telephone: 0116 249 2020
Call Date: Feb 1972, Middle Temple
Pupil Master, Recorder

METCALF JOHN CHARLES

4 King's Bench Walk
2nd Floor, Temple, London EC4Y 7DL,
Telephone: 020 7353 3581
E-mail: clerks@4kbw.co.uk
Call Date: Feb 1990, Inner Temple
Qualifications: [BSc (Hons), MSc]

METCALF MS LOUISE KAREN

Exchange Chambers
Pearl Assurance House, Derby Square,
Liverpool L2 9XX,
Telephone: 0151 236 7747
E-mail: exchangechambers@btinternet.com
Call Date: 1997, Inner Temple
Qualifications: [BA (Oxon), CPE]

METCALFE IAN MICHAEL

Cobden House Chambers
19 Quay Street, Manchester M3 3HN,
Telephone: 0161 833 6000
E-mail: clerks@cobden.co.uk
Call Date: Nov 1985, Middle Temple
Qualifications: [LLB (Hons)]

METHUEN RICHARD ST BARBE QC (1997)

12 King's Bench Walk
Temple, London EC4Y 7EL,
Telephone: 0171 583 0811
E-mail: chambers@12kbw.co.uk
Call Date: Nov 1972, Lincoln's Inn

METZER ANTHONY DAVID ERWIN

Doughty Street Chambers
11 Doughty Street, London WC1N 2PG,
Telephone: 0171 404 1313
E-mail: enquiries@doughtystreet.co.uk
Call Date: Nov 1987, Middle Temple
Pupil Master
Qualifications: [MA (Oxon)]

METZGER KEVIN ALBERT

Chambers of Wilfred Forster-Jones
New Court, 1st Floor South, Temple,
London EC4Y 9BE,
Telephone: 0171 353 0853/4/7222
E-mail: chambers@newcourt.net
Call Date: Nov 1984, Middle Temple
Pupil Master
Qualifications: [BA (Hons)]

METZGER KEVIN RAYMOND

Horizon Chambers
95a Chancery Lane, London WC2A 1DT,
Telephone: 0171 242 2440
Call Date: Apr 1986, Gray's Inn
Qualifications: [LLB (Cardiff) (Hons)]

MEUSZ MISS AMANDA JANE

Two Garden Court
1st Floor, Middle Temple, London
EC4Y 9BL, Telephone: 0171 353 1633
E-mail: barristers@2gardenct.law.co.uk
Call Date: July 1986, Gray's Inn
Pupil Master
Qualifications: [LLB (UCL)]

MEW GRAEME STEUART

One Essex Court
1st Floor, Temple, London EC4Y 9AR,
Telephone: 0171 936 3030
E-mail: one.essex_court@virgin.net
Call Date: July 1982, Middle Temple
Qualifications: [BA, LLB(Windsor)]

MEYER MISS BIRGITTA SARAH GRACE

11 Stone Buildings
Lincoln's Inn, London WC2A 3TG,
Telephone: +44 (0)207 831 6381
E-mail: clerks@11StoneBuildings.law.co.uk
Call Date: Nov 1992, Middle Temple
Qualifications: [BA (Hons, Cantab)]

D

MEYER MISS LORNA GILLIAN

5 Fountain Court
Steelhouse Lane, Birmingham B4 6DR,
Telephone: 0121 606 0500
E-mail:clerks@5fountaincourt.law.co.uk
Call Date: July 1986, Inner Temple
Qualifications: [LLB (Sheffield)]

MIAH ZACHARIAS AZAD AFZAL

9 King's Bench Walk
Ground Floor, Temple, London
EC4Y 7DX, Telephone: 0171 353 7202/
3909 E-mail: 9kbw@compuserve.com
Call Date: Nov 1990, Inner Temple
Pupil Master
Qualifications: [LLB]

MICHAEL SIMON LAURENCE

Bedford Chambers
2 Park Hill, Ampthill, Bedford, MK45 2LW,
Telephone: 0870 7337333
E-mail:simonmichael@pilawyer.demon.co.uk
Call Date: Nov 1978, Middle Temple
Qualifications: [LLB Hons (Lond)]

Fax: 0870 733 7331;
Out of hours telephone: 070500 99557;
DX: 36901 Ampthill;
Other comms: E-mail
simonmichael@pilawyer.demon.co.uk

Types of work: Medical negligence, Personal
injury

Circuit: South Eastern

Awards and memberships: Member: Association
of Personal Injury Lawyers; Personal Injury
Bar Association; Professional Negligence
Bar Association

Other professional experience: Lecturer in Law
(Business Law and Contract)

Languages spoken: French

MICHAELS MISS AMANDA LOUISE

5 New Square
Ground Floor, Lincoln's Inn, London
WC2A 3RJ, Telephone: 020 7404 0404
E-mail:chambers@fivenewsquare.demon.co.
uk
Call Date: July 1981, Gray's Inn
Pupil Master
Qualifications: [BA (Dunelm) MA, (Bruges)]

MICHALOS MISS CHRISTINA ANTIGONE DIANA

17 Bedford Row
London WC1R 4EB,
Telephone: 0171 831 7314
E-mail: iboard7314@aol.com
Call Date: Oct 1994, Gray's Inn
Qualifications: [LLB]

MICHELL MICHAEL JOHN

The Chambers of Leolin Price CBE, QC
10 Old Square, Lincoln's Inn, London
WC2A 3SU, Telephone: 0171 405 0758
St Mary's Chambers
50 High Pavement, Lace Market,
Nottingham NG1 1HW,
Telephone: 0115 9503503
E-mail: clerks@smc.law.co.uk
Call Date: July 1984, Inner Temple
Pupil Master
Qualifications: [MA (Oxon)]

MICHELL PAUL JOSEPH

Bridewell Chambers
2 Bridewell Place, London EC4V 6AP,
Telephone: 020 7797 8800
E-mail:HughesGage@bridewell.law.co.uk
Call Date: Nov 1991, Middle Temple
Pupil Master
Qualifications: [MA (Cantab), Dip Law]

MICKLETHWAIT DAVID JOHN

One Raymond Buildings
Gray's Inn, London WC1R 5BH,
Telephone: 0171 430 1234
E-mail: chambers@ipbar1rb.com;
clerks@ipbar1rb.com
Call Date: Nov 1970, Middle Temple
Pupil Master
Qualifications: [MA (Cantab)]

MIDDLEBURGH JONATHAN SIMON

11 Stone Buildings
Lincoln's Inn, London WC2A 3TG,
Telephone: +44 (0)207 831 6381
E-mail:clerks@11StoneBuildings.law.co.uk
Call Date: Nov 1990, Inner Temple
Qualifications: [BA (Oxon)]

MIDDLETON MS CLAIRE LOUISE

Westgate Chambers
67a Westgate Road, Newcastle upon Tyne
NE1 1SG, Telephone: 0191 261 4407/
2329785
E-mail:pracman@westgatechambers.law.co.u
k
Call Date: Oct 1991, Lincoln's Inn
Qualifications: [LLB (Hons) (New)]

MIDDLETON MS DIANNE

Goldsmith Chambers
Ground Floor, Goldsmith Building,
Temple, London EC4Y 7BL,
Telephone: 0171 353 6802/3/4/5
E-mail:clerks@goldsmithchambers.law.co.uk
Call Date: 1997, Inner Temple
Qualifications: [BA (Manchester), CPE, BPP]

MIDDLETON MISS GEORGINA CLAIRE

Farrar's Building
Temple, London EC4Y 7BD,
Telephone: 0171 583 9241
E-mail:chambers@farrarsbuilding.co.uk
Call Date: Nov 1989, Middle Temple
Qualifications: [BA Hons [Bris]]

MIDDLETON JOSEPH

Doughty Street Chambers
11 Doughty Street, London WC1N 2PG,
Telephone: 0171 404 1313
E-mail:enquiries@doughtystreet.co.uk
Call Date: Nov 1997, Inner Temple
Qualifications: [BSc (Surrey), LLM (Lond)]

MIDDLETON SEAN

Goldsworth Chambers
1st Floor, 11 Gray's Inn Square, London
WC1R 5JD, Telephone: 0171 405 7117
Call Date: Nov 1991, Lincoln's Inn
Qualifications: [BA (Hons) (Keele), Dip Law,
LLM (Osnabruck)]

MIER ANDREW STANLEY

Gray's Inn Chambers, The Chambers of Norman Patterson
First Floor, Gray's Inn Chambers, Gray's
Inn, London WC1R 5JA,
Telephone: 0171 831 5344
E-mail: s.mcblain@btinternet.com
Call Date: 1973, Middle Temple
Qualifications: [LLB (Lond)]

MIFFLIN MISS HELEN

30 Park Place
Cardiff CF1 3BA,
Telephone: 01222 398421
E-mail: 100757.1456@compuserve.com
Call Date: July 1982, Lincoln's Inn
Pupil Master
Qualifications: [LLB (Hons) (Leics)]

MIGDAL STEPHEN DAVID

Victoria Chambers
3rd Floor, 177 Corporation Street,
Birmingham B4 6RG,
Telephone: 0121 236 9900
E-mail: viccham@aol.com
Call Date: July 1974, Inner Temple
Qualifications: [BA]

MILDON DAVID WALLIS

Essex Court Chambers
24 Lincoln's Inn Fields, London
WC2A 3ED, Telephone: 0171 813 8000
E-mail:clerksroom@essexcourt-chambers.co.u
k
Call Date: July 1980, Middle Temple
Pupil Master
Qualifications: [MA, LLB (Cantab)]

MILEHAM MISS FELICITY ANNE

Mitre Court Chambers
3rd Floor, Temple, London EC4Y 7BP,
Telephone: 0171 353 9394
E-mail: mitrecourt.com
Call Date: 1996, Lincoln's Inn
Qualifications: [MA (Hons)]

MILES EDWARD NAPIER TREMAYNE

Harcourt Chambers
1st Floor, 2 Harcourt Buildings, Temple,
London EC4Y 9DB,
Telephone: 0171 353 6961
E-mail:clerks@harcourtchambers.law.co.uk

D

Harcourt Chambers
Churchill House, 3 St Aldate's Courtyard,
St Aldate's, Oxford OX1 1BN,
Telephone: 01865 791559
E-mail:clerks@harcourtchambers.law.co.uk
Call Date: Feb 1989, Inner Temple
Qualifications: [BA (Oxon)]

MILES ROBERT JOHN

4 Stone Buildings
Ground Floor, Lincoln's Inn, London
WC2A 3XT, Telephone: 0171 242 5524
E-mail:clerks@4stonebuildings.law.co.uk
Call Date: Nov 1987, Lincoln's Inn
Pupil Master
Qualifications: [BA, BCL (Oxon)]

MILFORD JOHN TILLMAN QC (1989)

Trinity Chambers
9-12 Trinity Chare, Quayside, Newcastle
upon Tyne NE1 3DF,
Telephone: 0191 232 1927
E-mail: info@trinitychambers.co.uk
Call Date: Nov 1969, Inner Temple
Recorder
Qualifications: [LLB (Exon)]

MILL IAN ALEXANDER QC (1999)

Blackstone Chambers
Blackstone House, Temple, London
EC4Y 9BW, Telephone: 0171 583 1770
E-mail:clerks@blackstonechambers.com
Call Date: 1981, Middle Temple
Pupil Master
Qualifications: [MA (Cantab)]

MILLAR GAVIN JAMES

Doughty Street Chambers
11 Doughty Street, London WC1N 2PG,
Telephone: 0171 404 1313
E-mail:enquiries@doughtystreet.co.uk
Call Date: July 1981, Lincoln's Inn
Pupil Master
Qualifications: [BA (Oxon)]

MILLARD MARTIN RICHARD

Gray's Inn Chambers, The Chambers of
Norman Patterson
First Floor, Gray's Inn Chambers, Gray's
Inn, London WC1R 5JA,
Telephone: 0171 831 5344
E-mail: s.mcblain@btinternet.com
Call Date: Oct 1995, Middle Temple
Qualifications: [BA (New York), Dip in Law]

MILLER ANDREW

2 Temple Gardens
Temple, London EC4Y 9AY,
Telephone: 0171 583 6041
E-mail: clerks@2templegardens.co.uk
Call Date: July 1989, Inner Temple
Pupil Master
Qualifications: [LLB [So'ton]]

MILLER MRS CELIA FRANCES

East Anglian Chambers
Gresham House, 5 Museum Street,
Ipswich, Suffolk, IP1 1HQ,
Telephone: 01473 214481
E-mail: ipswich@ealaw.co.uk
East Anglian Chambers
52 North Hill, Colchester, Essex, CO1 1PY,
Telephone: 01206 572756
E-mail: colchester@ealaw.co.uk
East Anglian Chambers
57 London Street, Norwich NR2 1HL,
Telephone: 01603 617351
E-mail: norwich@ealaw.co.uk
Call Date: July 1978, Inner Temple
Qualifications: [BA, LLB (Lond)]

MILLER MS HAYLEY JANE

Somersett Chambers
25 Bedford Row, London WC1R 4HE,
Telephone: 0171 404 6701
E-mail: somelaw@aol.com
Call Date: Oct 1995, Inner Temple
Qualifications: [LLB (Sussex)]

MILLER MISS JANE ELIZABETH
MACKAY

Pump Court Chambers
Upper Ground Floor, 3 Pump Court,
Temple, London EC4Y 7AJ,
Telephone: 0171 353 0711
E-mail: clerks@3pumpcourt.com

Pump Court Chambers
31 Southgate Street, Winchester
SO23 9EE, Telephone: 01962 868161
E-mail: clerks@3pumpcourt.com
Pump Court Chambers
5 Temple Chambers, Temple Street,
Swindon SN1 1SQ,
Telephone: 01793 539899
E-mail: clerks@3pumpcourt.com
Call Date: Nov 1979, Inner Temple
Pupil Master, Assistant Recorder
Qualifications: [LLB (Bris)]

MILLER JOHN NICHOLAS

Guildhall Chambers
22-26 Broad Street, Bristol BS1 2HG,
Telephone: 0117 9273366
E-mail:civil.clerks@guildhallchambers.co.uk and
criminal.clerks@guildhallchambers.co.uk
Call Date: July 1994, Inner Temple
Qualifications: [LLB]

MILLER JONATHAN

One Essex Court
1st Floor, Temple, London EC4Y 9AR,
Telephone: 0171 936 3030
E-mail: one.essex_court@virgin.net
Call Date: Nov 1996, Middle Temple
Qualifications: [BA (Hons)(Oxon)]

MILLER KEITH STEWART HUNTER

Fountain Chambers
Cleveland Business Centre, 1 Watson
Street, Middlesbrough TS1 2RQ,
Telephone: 01642 804040
E-mail:fountainchambers@onyxnet.co.uk
Call Date: July 1973, Middle Temple
Pupil Master, Recorder
Qualifications: [LLB]

MILLER PAUL WAIND

Wilberforce Chambers
7 Bishop Lane, Hull, East Yorkshire,
HU1 1PA, Telephone: 01482 323264
E-mail: clerks@hullbar.demon.co.uk
Call Date: July 1974, Lincoln's Inn
Pupil Master, Assistant Recorder
Qualifications: [MA (Oxon)]

MILLER PETER OWEN MICHAEL

2-3 Gray's Inn Square
Gray's Inn, London WC1R 5JH,
Telephone: 0171 242 4986
E-mail:chambers@2-3graysinnsquare.co.uk
Call Date: Oct 1993, Lincoln's Inn
Qualifications: [LLB (Hons)(Lond)]

MILLER RICHARD HUGH QC (1995)

3 New Square
Lincoln's Inn, London WC2A 3RS,
Telephone: 0171 405 1111
E-mail: 3newsquareip@lineone.net
Call Date: July 1976, Middle Temple
Qualifications: [BSc]

MILLER RICHARD JAMES

Newport Chambers
12 Clytha Park Road, Newport, Gwent,
NP9 47L, Telephone: 01633 267403/
255855
Call Date: Oct 1991, Gray's Inn
Qualifications: [LLB (Wales)]

MILLER ROBIN ANTHONY

2 King's Bench Walk
Ground Floor, Temple, London
EC4Y 7DE, Telephone: 0171 353 1746
E-mail: 2kbw@atlas.co.uk
King's Bench Chambers
115 North Hill, Plymouth PL4 8JY,
Telephone: 01752 221551
Call Date: Nov 1960, Middle Temple
Recorder
Qualifications: [BA (Oxon)]

MILLER MISS SARAH ELIZABETH BARBARA

4 Field Court
Gray's Inn, London WC1R 5EA,
Telephone: 0171 440 6900
E-mail: chambers@4fieldcourt.co.uk
Call Date: Nov 1971, Gray's Inn

MILLER SIMON RICHARD ANDREW

Enfield Chambers
First Floor, Refuge House, 9-10 River
Front, Enfield, Middlesex, EN1 3SZ,
Telephone: 0181 364 5627
E-mail:enfieldchambers@compuserve.com
Call Date: Oct 1996, Lincoln's Inn
Qualifications: [LLB (Hons)(Leic)]

MILLER STEPHEN MACKENZIE QC (1990)

1 Crown Office Row
Ground Floor, Temple, London
EC4Y 7HH, Telephone: 0171 797 7500
E-mail: mail@onecrownofficerow.com
Crown Office Row Chambers
Blenheim House, 120 Church Street,
Brighton, Sussex, BN1 1WH,
Telephone: 01273 625625
E-mail: crownofficerow@clara.net
Call Date: July 1971, Middle Temple
Recorder
Qualifications: [BA Hons (Oxon)]

MILLETT KENNETH JAMES

1 Hare Court
Ground Floor, Temple, London
EC4Y 7BE, Telephone: 0171 353 3982/
5324
Call Date: July 1988, Inner Temple
Pupil Master
Qualifications: [LLB]

MILLETT RICHARD LESTER

Essex Court Chambers
24 Lincoln's Inn Fields, London
WC2A 3ED, Telephone: 0171 813 8000
E-mail:clerksroom@essexcourt-chambers.co.u
k
Call Date: July 1985, Lincoln's Inn
Pupil Master
Qualifications: [BA Cantab]

MILLIGAN IAIN ANSTRUTHER QC (1991)

20 Essex Street
London WC2R 3AL,
Telephone: 0171 583 9294
E-mail: clerks@20essexst.com
Call Date: July 1973, Inner Temple
Qualifications: [MA (Cantab)]

MILLIKEN-SMITH MARK GORDON

3 Hare Court
1 Little Essex Street, London WC2R 3LD,
Telephone: 0171 395 2000
Call Date: Nov 1986, Gray's Inn
Pupil Master
Qualifications: [LLB(Bristol)]

MILLINGTON CHRISTOPHER JOHN

1 Fountain Court
Steelhouse Lane, Birmingham B4 6DR,
Telephone: 0121 236 5721
Call Date: July 1976, Gray's Inn
Pupil Master, Recorder
Qualifications: [LLM(B'ham)]

MILLS MISS BARBARA

4 Paper Buildings
1st Floor, Temple, London EC4Y 7EX,
Telephone: 0171 583 0816/353 1131
E-mail: clerks@4paperbuildings.co.uk
Call Date: Oct 1990, Inner Temple
Qualifications: [LLB (Hull)]

MILLS CHRISTOPHER DAVID

15 North Church Street Chambers
15 North Church Street, Sheffield
S1 2DH, Telephone: 0114 2759708/
2738380
Call Date: July 1972, Inner Temple
Pupil Master
Qualifications: [LLB (Lond)]

MILLS COREY ARTHUR

Becket Chambers
17 New Dover Road, Canterbury, Kent,
CT1 3AS, Telephone: 01227 786331
Call Date: 1987, Middle Temple
Qualifications: [LLB]

MILLS REGINALD STUART

First National Chambers
2nd Floor, First National Building, 24
Fenwick Street, Liverpool L2 7NE,
Telephone: 0151 236 2098
Call Date: Oct 1992, Middle Temple
Qualifications: [LL.B (Hons)]

MILLS SIMON MARK

White Friars Chambers
21 White Friars, Chester CH1 1NZ,
Telephone: 01244 323070
E-mail:whitefriarschambers@btinternet.com
Call Date: Nov 1986, Inner Temple
Pupil Master
Qualifications: [LLB(Birm)]

MILLS SIMON THOMAS

One Essex Court
1st Floor, Temple, London EC4Y 9AR,
Telephone: 0171 936 3030
E-mail: one.essex_court@virgin.net
Call Date: Nov 1994, Lincoln's Inn
Qualifications: [MA (Cantab)]

MILMO JOHN BOYLE MARTIN QC (1984)

High Pavement Chambers
1 High Pavement, Nottingham NG1 1HF,
Telephone: 0115 9418218
9 Bedford Row
London WC1R 4AZ,
Telephone: 0171 242 3555
E-mail: clerks@9br.co.uk
Call Date: Nov 1966, Lincoln's Inn
Qualifications: [MA, LLB (Dub)]

MILMO PATRICK HELENUS QC (1985)

5 Raymond Buildings
1st Floor, Gray's Inn, London WC1R 5BP,
Telephone: 0171 242 2902
E-mail: clerks@media-ent-law.co.uk
Call Date: July 1962, Middle Temple
Qualifications: [MA (Cantab)]

MILNE ALEXANDER HUGH

18 Red Lion Court
(Off Fleet Street), London EC4A 3EB,
Telephone: 0171 520 6000
E-mail: chambers@18rlc.co.uk
Thornwood House
102 New London Road, Chelmsford,
Essex, CM2 0RG,
Telephone: 01245 280880
E-mail: chambers@18rlc.co.uk
Call Date: Nov 1981, Gray's Inn
Pupil Master
Qualifications: [BA]

MILNE DAVID CALDER QC (1987)

Pump Court Tax Chambers
16 Bedford Row, London WC1R 4EB,
Telephone: 0171 414 8080
Call Date: July 1970, Lincoln's Inn
Qualifications: [MA (Oxon), FCA]

MILNE MICHAEL

Resolution Chambers
Oak Lodge, 55 Poolbrook Road, Malvern,
Worcestershire, WR14 3JN,
Telephone: 01684 561279
E-mail:mmilne@arbitration.demon.co.uk
Chambers of Geoffrey Hawker
46/48 Essex Street, London WC2R 3GH,
Telephone: 0171 583 8899
Call Date: July 1987, Lincoln's Inn
Qualifications: [BA, Dip Law, FRICS, FCIArb]

MILNE RICHARD JAMES

23 Essex Street
London WC2R 3AS,
Telephone: 0171 413 0353/836 8366
E-mail:clerks@essexstreet23.demon.co.uk
Call Date: Oct 1992, Middle Temple
Qualifications: [MA (Hons)(Oxon), Diploma in Law]

MILNER JONATHAN DAVID BENJAMIN

2 Harcourt Buildings
2nd Floor, Temple, London EC4Y 9DB,
Telephone: 020 7353 8415
E-mail: clerks@2hb.law.co.uk
Call Date: July 1977, Inner Temple
Pupil Master
Qualifications: [LLB (Lond)]

MILSOM MS CATHERINE MARY

One Essex Court
1st Floor, Temple, London EC4Y 9AR,
Telephone: 0171 936 3030
E-mail: one.essex_court@virgin.net
Call Date: 1994, Inner Temple
Qualifications: [BA (Hons), LLM]

MINHAS MS RAFHAT

Leone Chambers
72 Evelyn Avenue, Kingsbury, London
NW9 OJH, Telephone: 0181 200 4020
E-mail: festus4@leonechambers.co.uk
Call Date: 1994, Gray's Inn
Qualifications: [BSc, LLB]

D

D

MINIHAN SEAN THOMAS

6 Gray's Inn Square
Ground Floor, Gray's Inn, London
WC1R 5AZ, Telephone: 0171 242 1052
E-mail: 6graysinn@clara.co.uk
Call Date: Nov 1988, Gray's Inn
Pupil Master
Qualifications: [LLB]

MINTZ SIMON HAROLD

Chavasse Court Chambers
2nd Floor, Chavasse Court, 24 Lord Street,
Liverpool L2 1TA,
Telephone: 0151 707 1191
Call Date: Nov 1996, Inner Temple
Qualifications: [BA (Newcastle)]

MIRCHANDANI MS SIAN

Chambers of John L Powell QC
Four New Square, Lincoln's Inn, London
WC2A 3RJ, Telephone: 0171 797 8000
E-mail: barristers@4newsquare.com
Call Date: 1997, Inner Temple
Qualifications: [VetMB (Cantab), MA
(Cantab), CPE (City)]

MIRIC ROBIN

10 King's Bench Walk
1st Floor, Temple, London EC4Y 7EB,
Telephone: 0171 353 2501
Call Date: July 1978, Gray's Inn
Pupil Master
Qualifications: [LLB]

MIRWITCH MISS JANE

**4 Brick Court, Chambers of Anne
Rafferty QC**
1st Floor, Temple, London EC4Y 9AD,
Telephone: 0171 583 8455
Call Date: Nov 1974, Middle Temple
Pupil Master
Qualifications: [LLM (Lond)]

MISCAMPBELL NORMAN ALEXANDER QC (1974)

1 Temple Gardens
1st Floor, Temple, London EC4Y 9BB,
Telephone: 0171 583 1315/353 0407
E-mail: clerks@1templegardens.co.uk
Call Date: May 1952, Inner Temple
Recorder
Qualifications: [MA (Oxon)]

MISCAMPBELL MISS P. BERNADETTE

10 King's Bench Walk
Ground Floor, Temple, London
EC4Y 7EB, Telephone: 0171 353 7742
E-mail: 10kbw@lineone.net
Call Date: Nov 1980, Middle Temple
Qualifications: [LLB (Lond), M.Sc (Lond)]

MISHCON MISS JANE MALCA

4 Paper Buildings
Ground Floor, Temple, London
EC4Y 7EX, Telephone: 0171 353 3366/
583 7155
E-mail: clerks@4paperbuildings.com
Call Date: July 1979, Gray's Inn
Pupil Master
Qualifications: [BA (Oxon), MA (Oxon)]

MISHCON OLIVER ZEBEDEE

4 King's Bench Walk
Ground/First Floor/Basement, Temple,
London EC4Y 7DL,
Telephone: 0171 822 8822
E-mail: 4kbw@barristersatlaw.com
Call Date: Nov 1993, Gray's Inn
Qualifications: [LLB]

MISKIN CHARLES JAMES MONCKTON QC (1998)

23 Essex Street
London WC2R 3AS,
Telephone: 0171 413 0353/836 8366
E-mail:clerks@essexstreet23.demon.co.uk
Call Date: July 1975, Gray's Inn
Recorder
Qualifications: [MA (Oxon)]

MISKIN MISS CLAIRE MARIANNE

Queen Elizabeth Building
Ground Floor, Temple, London
EC4Y 9BS,
Telephone: 0171 353 7181 (12 Lines)
Call Date: Nov 1970, Middle Temple
Pupil Master, Recorder
Qualifications: [LLM (Lond)]

D

MISNER PHILIP LAWRENCE IAN

6 Gray's Inn Square
Ground Floor, Gray's Inn, London
WC1R 5AZ, Telephone: 0171 242 1052
E-mail: 6graysinn@clara.co.uk
Call Date: July 1984, Middle Temple
Pupil Master
Qualifications: [LLB (B'ham)]

MISZKIEL MISS URSULA

Chambers of Harjit Singh
Ground Floor, 2 Middle Temple Lane,
Temple, London EC4Y 9AA,
Telephone: 0171 353 1356 (4 Lines)
Call Date: Oct 1994, Gray's Inn
Qualifications: [LLB (Leeds)]

MITCHELL ANDREW EDWARD

Fountain Court
Temple, London EC4Y 9DH,
Telephone: 0171 583 3335
E-mail: chambers@fountaincourt.co.uk
Call Date: Nov 1992, Middle Temple
Qualifications: [MA Hons (Cantab), BCL
(Oxon)]

MITCHELL ANDREW JONATHAN MILLS

No. 6
6 Park Square, Leeds LS1 2LW,
Telephone: 0113 2459763
E-mail: chambers@no6.co.uk
Call Date: Nov 1991, Lincoln's Inn
Qualifications: [LLB (Hons) (Leeds)]

MITCHELL ANDREW ROBERT QC (1998)

Furnival Chambers
32 Furnival Street, London EC4A 1JQ,
Telephone: 0171 405 3232
E-mail: clerks@furnivallaw.co.uk
Call Date: July 1976, Gray's Inn
Recorder

MITCHELL MS ANNE CUMMING

Number Ten Baker Street
10 Baker Street, Middlesbrough TS1 2LH,
Telephone: 01642 220332
Call Date: Oct 1994, Gray's Inn
Qualifications: [LLB]

MITCHELL BRENTON BALLINGTINE

Bell Yard Chambers
116/118 Chancery Lane, London
WC2A 1PP, Telephone: 0171 306 9292
Call Date: July 1973, Lincoln's Inn
Pupil Master
Qualifications: [DipCrim]

MITCHELL CHRISTOPHER RICHARD

Hollis Whiteman Chambers
3rd Floor, Queen Elizabeth Bldg, Temple,
London EC4Y 9BS,
Telephone: 020 7583 5766
E-mail:barristers@holliswhiteman.co.uk
Call Date: Nov 1968, Gray's Inn
Pupil Master, Recorder
Qualifications: [LLB, MA (Oxon)]

MITCHELL DAVID CHARLES

6 Pump Court
1st Floor, Temple, London EC4Y 7AR,
Telephone: 0171 797 8400
E-mail: clerks@6pumpcourt.co.uk
Broadway House Chambers
31 Park Square West, Leeds LS1 2PF,
Telephone: 0113 246 2600
6-8 Mill Street
Maidstone, Kent, ME15 6XH,
Telephone: 01622 688094
E-mail: annexe@6pumpcourt.co.uk
Broadway House Chambers
Broadway House, 9 Bank Street, Bradford,
West Yorkshire, BD1 1TW,
Telephone: 01274 722560
E-mail: clerks@broadwayhouse.co.uk
Call Date: 1972, Inner Temple
Recorder
Qualifications: [MA (Oxon)]

MITCHELL DAVID JOHN

5 Fountain Court
Steelhouse Lane, Birmingham B4 6DR,
Telephone: 0121 606 0500
E-mail:clerks@5fountaincourt.law.co.uk
Call Date: Oct 1995, Lincoln's Inn
Qualifications: [BSc (Hons)(Lond), LLB
(Hons)(City)]

MITCHELL GREGORY CHARLES MATHEW QC (1997)

3 Verulam Buildings
London WC1R 5NT,
Telephone: 0171 831 8441
E-mail: clerks@3verulam.co.uk
Call Date: July 1979, Gray's Inn
Assistant Recorder
Qualifications: [BA (Lond), PhD]

MITCHELL JACK

Enfield Chambers
First Floor, Refuge House, 9-10 River
Front, Enfield, Middlesex, EN1 3SZ,
Telephone: 0181 364 5627
E-mail:enfieldchambers@compuserve.com
Call Date: Oct 1994, Inner Temple
Qualifications: [LLB (Huddersfield)]

MITCHELL JAMES RONALD

Broad Chare
33 Broad Chare, Newcastle upon Tyne
NE1 3DQ, Telephone: 0191 232 0541
E-mail:clerks@broadcharechambers.law.co.uk
Call Date: July 1973, Inner Temple
Recorder

MITCHELL MISS JANET VIVIAN

4 Brick Court
Temple, London EC4Y 9AD,
Telephone: 0171 797 8910
E-mail: medhurst@dial.pipex.com
Call Date: Feb 1978, Middle Temple
Qualifications: [BA (Lond)]

MITCHELL JONATHAN HOWARD

Ropewalk Chambers
24 The Ropewalk, Nottingham NG1 5EF,
Telephone: 0115 9472581
E-mail: administration@ropewalk co.uk
Call Date: Oct 1992, Gray's Inn
Qualifications: [LL.B (Wales)]

MITCHELL JONATHAN STUART

3 Gray's Inn Square
Ground Floor, London WC1R 5AH,
Telephone: 0171 520 5600
E-mail: clerks@3gis.co.uk
Call Date: Nov 1974, Middle Temple
Qualifications: [MA]

MITCHELL MISS JULIANNA MARIE

2 Harcourt Buildings
Ground Floor/Left, Temple, London
EC4Y 9DB, Telephone: 0171 583 9020
E-mail: clerks@harcourt.co.uk
Call Date: Oct 1994, Lincoln's Inn
Qualifications: [LLB (Hons)(B'ham), BCL
(Oxon)]

MITCHELL KEITH ARNO

3 Hare Court
1 Little Essex Street, London WC2R 3LD,
Telephone: 0171 395 2000
Call Date: Nov 1981, Inner Temple
Pupil Master
Qualifications: [BA]

MITCHELL MS LESLEY

Chambers of Lesley Mitchell
Stapleton Lodge, 71 Hamilton Road,
Brentford, Middlesex, TW8 0QJ,
Telephone: 0181 568 2164
E-mail: oli.lesley@btinternet.com
Call Date: Nov 1987, Inner Temple
Qualifications: [B.Sc (Lond), Dip in Law]

MITCHELL MISS MARIE CATHLEEN

15 Winckley Square
Preston PR1 3JJ,
Telephone: 01772 252828
E-mail:clerks@winckleysq.demon.co.uk
Call Date: Oct 1991, Gray's Inn
Qualifications: [LLB]

MITCHELL NIGEL CAMPBELL

3 Paper Buildings
Temple, London EC4Y 7EU,
Telephone: 020 7583 8055
E-mail: London@3paper.com
3 Paper Buildings (Bournemouth)
20 Lorne Park Road, Bournemouth,
Dorset, BH1 1JN,
Telephone: 01202 292102
E-mail: Bournemouth@3paper.com
3 Paper Buildings (Winchester)
4 St Peter Street, Winchester SO23 8BW,
Telephone: 01962 868884
E-mail: winchester@3paper.com

3 Paper Buildings (Oxford)
1 Alfred Street, High Street, Oxford
OX1 4EH, Telephone: 01865 793736
E-mail: oxford@3paper.com
Call Date: Feb 1978, Lincoln's Inn
Pupil Master
Qualifications: [LLB (Lond)]

MITCHELL PAUL

13 King's Bench Walk
1st Floor, Temple, London EC4Y 7EN,
Telephone: 0171 353 7204
E-mail: clerks@13kbw.law.co.uk
King's Bench Chambers
32 Beaumont Street, Oxford OX1 2NP,
Telephone: 01865 311066
E-mail: clerks@kbc-oxford.law.co.uk
Call Date: Nov 1994, Inner Temple
Qualifications: [BA (York), CPE (City)]

MITCHELL PETER

29 Bedford Row Chambers
London WC1R 4HE,
Telephone: 0171 831 2626
Call Date: Oct 1996, Inner Temple
Qualifications: [LLB (Lond)]

MITCHELL THOMAS JARLETH DAVID

11 King's Bench Walk
3 Park Court, Park Cross Street, Leeds
LS1 2QH, Telephone: 0113 297 1200
11 King's Bench Walk
1st Floor, Temple, London EC4Y 7EQ,
Telephone: 0171 353 3337
E-mail: fmuller11@aol.com
Call Date: Oct 1995, Lincoln's Inn
Qualifications: [BA (Hons) MA (Oxon), CPE
(Manc)]

MITCHELL-HEGGS CHRISTOPHER KENNETH

Francis Taylor Building
3rd Floor, Temple, London EC4Y 7BY,
Telephone: 0171 797 7250
Call Date: Feb 1966, Inner Temple
Qualifications: [Diplome d'Etudes Sup,
Diplome de Droit, (Strasbourg)]

MITCHESON THOMAS GEORGE MOSELEY

3 New Square
Lincoln's Inn, London WC2A 3RS,
Telephone: 0171 405 1111
E-mail: 3newsquareip@lineone.net
Call Date: Oct 1996, Inner Temple
Qualifications: [BA (Cantab), CPE (Lond)]

MITROPOULOS CHRISTOS

Chambers of Geoffrey Hawker
46/48 Essex Street, London WC2R 3GH,
Telephone: 0171 583 8899
Call Date: 1997, Lincoln's Inn
Qualifications: [BA (Hons) (Cantab)]

MITROPOULOS MS GEORGIA

Chambers of Geoffrey Hawker
46/48 Essex Street, London WC2R 3GH,
Telephone: 0171 583 8899
Call Date: July 1989, Gray's Inn
Qualifications: [BA (Wales), DipLaw]

MITTING JOHN EDWARD QC (1987)

4 Fountain Court
Steelhouse Lane, Birmingham B4 6DR,
Telephone: 0121 236 3476
Call Date: July 1970, Gray's Inn
Recorder
Qualifications: [BA, LLB (Cantab)]

MOAT FRANK ROBERT

Pump Court Chambers
Upper Ground Floor, 3 Pump Court,
Temple, London EC4Y 7AJ,
Telephone: 0171 353 0711
E-mail: clerks@3pumpcourt.com
Pump Court Chambers
31 Southgate Street, Winchester
SO23 9EE, Telephone: 01962 868161
E-mail: clerks@3pumpcourt.com
Pump Court Chambers
5 Temple Chambers, Temple Street,
Swindon SN1 1SQ,
Telephone: 01793 539899
E-mail: clerks@3pumpcourt.com
Call Date: Nov 1970, Lincoln's Inn
Pupil Master, Recorder
Qualifications: [LLB]

MOAT RICHARD MARK

5 Fountain Court
Steelhouse Lane, Birmingham B4 6DR,
Telephone: 0121 606 0500
E-mail:clerks@5fountaincourt.law.co.uk
Call Date: July 1985, Lincoln's Inn
Pupil Master
Qualifications: [BA (Oxon)]

MOBEDJI FIRDAUS JEHANGIR

Somersett Chambers
25 Bedford Row, London WC1R 4HE,
Telephone: 0171 404 6701
E-mail: somelaw@aol.com
Call Date: 1977, Lincoln's Inn
Qualifications: [BA (Hons)]

MODGIL MISS SANGITA

2-4 Tudor Street
London EC4Y 0AA,
Telephone: 0171 797 7111
E-mail: clerks@rfqc.co.uk
Call Date: Oct 1990, Gray's Inn
Qualifications: [LLB (Leic)]

MOERAN FENNER OLANDO

3 Stone Buildings
Lincoln's Inn, London WC2A 3XL,
Telephone: 0171 242 4937
E-mail: clerks@3sb.law.co.uk
Call Date: Oct 1996, Lincoln's Inn
Qualifications: [BSc (Hons)(Bris), Dip in Law
(City)]

MOFFETT JONATHAN KEITH

4-5 Gray's Inn Square
Ground Floor, Gray's Inn, London
WC1R 5JP, Telephone: 0171 404 5252
E-mail:chambers@4-5graysinnsquare.co.uk
Call Date: Oct 1996, Inner Temple
Qualifications: [BA, LLM (Cantab)]

MOGER CHRISTOPHER RICHARD DERWENT QC (1992)

4 Pump Court
Temple, London EC4Y 7AN,
Telephone: 020 7842 5555
E-mail:chambers@4pumpcourt.law.co.uk
Call Date: July 1972, Inner Temple
Recorder
Qualifications: [LLB (Bris), FCIArb]

MOGRIDGE FRASER MCLEAN

Chichester Chambers
12 North Pallant, Chichester, West Sussex,
PO19 1TQ, Telephone: 01243 784538
E-mail:clerks@chichesterchambers.law.co.uk
Call Date: Nov 1995, Inner Temple
Qualifications: [LLB (Soton)]

MOHABIR GERALD YOGIN

3 Temple Gardens
3rd Floor, Temple, London EC4Y 9AU,
Telephone: 0171 353 0832
Call Date: Oct 1996, Middle Temple
Qualifications: [MA, LLB (Anglia)]

MOIR MRS JUDITH PATRICIA

Broad Chare
33 Broad Chare, Newcastle upon Tyne
NE1 3DQ, Telephone: 0191 232 0541
E-mail:clerks@broadcharechambers.law.co.uk
Call Date: Nov 1978, Gray's Inn
Pupil Master, Recorder
Qualifications: [BA (Oxon)]

MOLE DAVID RICHARD PENTON QC (1990)

4-5 Gray's Inn Square
Ground Floor, Gray's Inn, London
WC1R 5JP, Telephone: 0171 404 5252
E-mail:chambers@4-5graysinnsquare.co.uk
Call Date: Nov 1970, Inner Temple
Recorder
Qualifications: [MA (TCD) LLM (Lond)]

MOLL CHRISTIAAN ERIC

55 Temple Chambers
Temple Avenue, London EC4Y 0HP,
Telephone: 0171 353 7400
Call Date: July 1986, Middle Temple
Pupil Master
Qualifications: [BA (Hons) (Oxon)]

MOLLOY MISS PHILIPPA RUTH

Albany Chambers
91 Kentish Town Road, London
NW1 8NY, Telephone: 0171 485 5736/
5758 E-mail: albany91.freeserve.co.uk
Call Date: 1995, Lincoln's Inn
Qualifications: [LLB (Hons)]

D

MOLONEY PATRICK MARTIN JOSEPH QC (1998)

1 Brick Court
1st Floor, Temple, London EC4Y 9BY,
Telephone: 0171 353 8845
E-mail: clerks@1brickcourt.co.uk
Call Date: 1976, Middle Temple
Assistant Recorder
Qualifications: [BA, BCL (Oxon)]

MOLONEY TIMOTHY JOHN

14 Tooks Court
Cursitor St, London EC4A 1LB,
Telephone: 0171 405 8828
E-mail: clerks@tooks.law.co.uk
Call Date: Nov 1993, Middle Temple
Qualifications: [LLB (Hons)(B'ham), Ph.D
(B'ham)]

MOLYNEUX BRENTON JOHN

29 Bedford Row Chambers
London WC1R 4HE,
Telephone: 0171 831 2626
Call Date: Feb 1994, Lincoln's Inn
Qualifications: [BA (Hons, Oxon), Dip, in
Law]

MOLYNEUX SIMON ROWLEY

4 Brick Court
Temple, London EC4Y 9AD,
Telephone: 0171 797 8910
E-mail: medhurst@dial.pipex.com
Call Date: Apr 1986, Inner Temple
Pupil Master
Qualifications: [BSc (Econ) MA, (Wales)
M.Phil]

MOMTAZ SAM

Phoenix Chambers
First Floor, Gray's Inn Chambers, Gray's
Inn, London WC1R 5JA,
Telephone: 0171 404 7888
E-mail:clerks@phoenix-chambers.co.uk
Call Date: Nov 1995, Lincoln's Inn
Qualifications: [LLB (Hons)]

MONAGHAN MS KARON

Cloisters
1 Pump Court, Temple, London
EC4Y 7AA, Telephone: 0171 827 4000
E-mail: clerks@cloisters.com

Verulam Chambers
Peer House, 8-14 Verulam Street, Gray's
Inn, London WC1X 8LZ,
Telephone: 0171 813 2400
Call Date: July 1989, Inner Temple
Pupil Master
Qualifications: [LLB]

MONAGHAN MARK TERENCE

Cobden House Chambers
19 Quay Street, Manchester M3 3HN,
Telephone: 0161 833 6000
E-mail: clerks@cobden.co.uk
Call Date: July 1987, Lincoln's Inn
Qualifications: [LLB (Hons) (Sheff)]

MONAGHAN MS SUSAN MARY

Enfield Chambers
First Floor, Refuge House, 9-10 River
Front, Enfield, Middlesex, EN1 3SZ,
Telephone: 0181 364 5627
E-mail:enfieldchambers@compuserve.com
Call Date: Oct 1995, Inner Temple
Qualifications: [BA (Galway), LLB (Wales)]

MONDAIR RASHPAL SINGH

Claremont Chambers
26 Waterloo Road, Wolverhampton
WV1 4BL, Telephone: 01902 426222
Call Date: Nov 1995, Middle Temple
Qualifications: [Dip Law, BDS]

MONEY ERNLE DAVID DRUMMOND

1 Gray's Inn Square
Ground Floor, London WC1R 5AA,
Telephone: 0171 405 8946/7/8
Call Date: Feb 1958, Lincoln's Inn
Pupil Master
Qualifications: [MA (Oxon)]

MONK DAVID KENNETH

2 New Street
Leicester LE1 5NA,
Telephone: 0116 2625906
E-mail: clerks@2newstreet.co.uk
Call Date: July 1991, Middle Temple
Qualifications: [BA (Hons)]

MONKCOM STEPHEN PHILIP

Francis Taylor Building
3rd Floor, Temple, London EC4Y 7BY,
Telephone: 0171 797 7250
Call Date: Nov 1974, Middle Temple
Pupil Master
Qualifications: [BA (Oxon)]

MONRO DAVIES MS TIFFANY LEE

**4 Brick Court, Chambers of Anne
Rafferty QC**
1st Floor, Temple, London EC4Y 9AD,
Telephone: 0171 583 8455
Call Date: July 1984, Gray's Inn
Qualifications: [LLB Hons (Lond)]

MONSON THE HON ANDREW ANTHONY JOHN

5 Raymond Buildings
1st Floor, Gray's Inn, London WC1R 5BP,
Telephone: 0171 242 2902
E-mail: clerks@media-ent-law.co.uk
Call Date: Nov 1983, Middle Temple
Pupil Master
Qualifications: [MA (Oxon)]

MONTAGUE MS SUSAN

1 Pump Court
Lower Ground Floor, Temple, London
EC4Y 7AB, Telephone: 0171 583 2012/
353 4341
E-mail: [name]@1pumpcourt.co.uk
Call Date: Nov 1981, Inner Temple
Qualifications: [BA]

MONTEITH KEIR BARTLEY

Acre Lane Neighbourhood Chambers
30A Acre Lane, London SW2 5SG,
Telephone: 0171 274 4400
E-mail:barristerschambers@acrelane.demon.co.uk
Call Date: May 1994, Lincoln's Inn
Qualifications: [LLB (Hons, Essex)]

MONTGOMERY MISS CLARE PATRICIA QC (1996)

3 Raymond Buildings
Gray's Inn, London WC1R 5BH,
Telephone: 020 7831 3833
E-mail:chambers@threeraymond.demon.co.uk
Call Date: Nov 1980, Gray's Inn
Assistant Recorder
Qualifications: [LLB (Lond)]

MONTGOMERY JAMES ARDRAN

2-4 Tudor Street
London EC4Y 0AA,
Telephone: 0171 797 7111
E-mail: clerks@rfqc.co.uk
Call Date: Nov 1989, Lincoln's Inn
Qualifications: [LLB]

MONTGOMERY PROFESSOR JOHN WARWICK

Francis Taylor Building
3rd Floor, Temple, London EC4Y 7BY,
Telephone: 0171 797 7250
Call Date: July 1984, Middle Temple
Qualifications: [PhD Chicago, D de 1U
Strasbourg, MPhil Essex, Dip Intl Inst
Human, Rights Strasbourg, D d'U
Strasbourg]

MONTGOMERY MISS KRISTINA (AILEEN)

3 Fountain Court
Steelhouse Lane, Birmingham B4 6DR,
Telephone: 0121 236 5854
Call Date: Oct 1993, Middle Temple
Qualifications: [LLB (Hons)(Lond)]

MONTGOMERY TONY KEVIN

Fleet Chambers
Mitre House, 44-46 Fleet Street, London
EC4Y 1BN, Telephone: 0171 936 3707
E-mail: rr@fleetchambers.demon.co.uk
Call Date: Nov 1987, Inner Temple
Qualifications: [LLB (Brunel)]

MONTROSE RODNEY STUART

Cloisters
1 Pump Court, Temple, London
EC4Y 7AA, Telephone: 0171 827 4000
E-mail: clerks@cloisters.com
Call Date: May 1972, Middle Temple
Pupil Master
Qualifications: [LLB]

MONTY SIMON TREVOR

Chambers of John L Powell QC
Four New Square, Lincoln's Inn, London
WC2A 3RJ, Telephone: 0171 797 8000
E-mail: barristers@4newsquare.com
Call Date: July 1982, Middle Temple
Pupil Master
Qualifications: [LLB]

MOODY NEIL ROBERT

2 Temple Gardens
Temple, London EC4Y 9AY,
Telephone: 0171 583 6041
E-mail: clerks@2templegardens.co.uk
Call Date: Nov 1989, Gray's Inn
Pupil Master
Qualifications: [MA (Oxon)]

MOODY-STUART THOMAS

8 New Square
Lincoln's Inn, London WC2A 3QP,
Telephone: 0171 405 4321
E-mail: clerks@8newsquare.co.uk
Call Date: Nov 1995, Middle Temple
Qualifications: [BA (Hons)]

MOOLLAN SALIM ABDOOL HAMID MOOLLAN

Essex Court Chambers
24 Lincoln's Inn Fields, London
WC2A 3ED, Telephone: 0171 813 8000
E-mail:clerksroom@essexcourt-chambers.co.uk
Call Date: 1998, Middle Temple
Qualifications: [BA (Hons)(Cantab)]

MOON PHILIP CHARLES ANGUS

3 Serjeants' Inn
London EC4Y 1BQ,
Telephone: 0171 353 5537
E-mail: clerks@3serjeantsinn.com
Call Date: Nov 1986, Middle Temple
Pupil Master
Qualifications: [MA (Cantab)]

MOONCEY EBRAHAM MOHAMED

9 Bedford Row
London WC1R 4AZ,
Telephone: 0171 242 3555
E-mail: clerks@9br.co.uk
Call Date: Nov 1983, Gray's Inn
Pupil Master
Qualifications: [LLB]

MOONEY STEPHEN JOHN

Albion Chambers
Broad Street, Bristol BS1 1DR,
Telephone: 0117 9272144
Call Date: Nov 1987, Inner Temple
Qualifications: [LLB (Hull)]

MOOR PHILIP DRURY

1 Mitre Court Buildings
Temple, London EC4Y 7BS,
Telephone: 0171 797 7070
E-mail: clerks@1mcb.com
Call Date: July 1982, Inner Temple
Pupil Master
Qualifications: [MA (Oxon)]

MOOR MISS SARAH KATHRYN

Old Square Chambers
1 Verulam Buildings, Gray's Inn, London
WC1R 5LQ, Telephone: 0171 269 0300
E-mail:clerks@oldsquarechambers.co.uk
Old Square Chambers
Hanover House, 47 Corn Street, Bristol
BS1 1HT, Telephone: 0117 9277111
E-mail: oldsqbri@globalnet.co.uk
Call Date: Oct 1991, Middle Temple
Qualifications: [BA Hons (Cantab)]

D

MOORE MISS ALISON DENISE

Counsels' Chambers
2nd Floor, 10-11 Gray's Inn Square,
London WC1R 5JD,
Telephone: 0171 405 2576
E-mail:clerks@10-11graysinnsquare.co.uk
Call Date: Oct 1994, Middle Temple
Qualifications: [BA (Hons)(Oxon)]

MOORE ANDREW DAVID

18 St John Street
Manchester M3 4EA,
Telephone: 0161 278 1800
E-mail: 18stjohn@lineone.net
Call Date: Nov 1996, Inner Temple
Qualifications: [BA, PHd (Manch)]

MOORE ARTHUR JAMES

Arden Chambers
27 John Street, London WC1N 2BL,
Telephone: 020 7242 4244
E-mail:clerks@arden-chambers.law.co.uk
Call Date: Oct 1992, Gray's Inn
Qualifications: [BA (Oxon), Dip Law (City)]

MOORE MR CRAIG IAN

Barnard's Inn Chambers
6th Floor, Halton House, 20-23 Holborn,
London EC1N 2JD,
Telephone: 0171 369 6969
E-mail: clerks@biclaw.co.uk
Park Lane Chambers
19 Westgate, Leeds LS1 2RD,
Telephone: 0113 2285000
E-mail:clerks@parklanechambers.co.uk
Call Date: 1989, Middle Temple
Qualifications: [LLB [Lond]]

MOORE DANNY GEORGE

5 King's Bench Walk
Temple, London EC4Y 7DN,
Telephone: 0171 353 5638
Call Date: Nov 1994, Middle Temple
Qualifications: [LLB (Hons)]

MOORE DAVID JAMES

Tindal Chambers
3/5 New Street, Chelmsford, Essex,
CM1 1NT, Telephone: 01245 267742

St Albans Chambers
Dolphin Lodge, Dolphin Yard, Holywell
Hill, St Albans, Herts, AL1 1EX,
Telephone: 01727 843383
Call Date: July 1983, Middle Temple
Pupil Master
Qualifications: [BA, MA (Lond)]

MOORE DOUGLAS MARKS

6 King's Bench Walk
Ground Floor, Temple, London
EC4Y 7DR, Telephone: 0171 583 0410
E-mail: worsley@6kbw.freeserve.co.uk
Call Date: Nov 1979, Gray's Inn
Pupil Master, Assistant Recorder
Qualifications: [BA (Belfast), Dip.Soc.Anth]

MOORE JAMES ANTHONY

2 Gray's Inn Square Chambers
2nd Floor, Gray's Inn, London WC1R 5AA,
Telephone: 020 7242 0328
E-mail: clerks@2gis.co.uk
Call Date: July 1984, Lincoln's Inn
Qualifications: [BA]

MOORE MISS JENNIFER MARY

Warwick House Chambers
8 Warwick Court, Gray's Inn, London
WC1R 5DJ, Telephone: 0171 430 2323
E-mail: cdrewlaw@aol.com
Call Date: Oct 1992, Gray's Inn
Qualifications: [LL.B (Brunel)]

MOORE MISS JOAN YVETTE

Verulam Chambers
Peer House, 8-14 Verulam Street, Gray's
Inn, London WC1X 8LZ,
Telephone: 0171 813 2400
Call Date: Nov 1986, Lincoln's Inn
Qualifications: [LLB]

MOORE MISS KATHERINE ELIZABETH

1 Paper Buildings
1st Floor, Temple, London EC4Y 7EP,
Telephone: 0171 353 3728/4953
Call Date: Oct 1995, Middle Temple
Qualifications: [BA (Hons)]

MOORE MISS KIRSTIE ELIZABETH

Regent Chambers
8 Pall Mall, Hanley, Stoke On Trent
ST1 1ER, Telephone: 01782 286666
E-mail: regent@ftech.co.uk
Call Date: Oct 1994, Middle Temple
Qualifications: [LLB (Hons)(Lond), LLM
(Sheff)]

MOORE MARTIN LUKE

Erskine Chambers
30 Lincoln's Inn Fields, Lincoln's Inn,
London WC2A 3PF,
Telephone: 0171 242 5532
E-mail:clerks@erskine-chambers.co.uk
Call Date: July 1982, Lincoln's Inn
Pupil Master
Qualifications: [BA (Oxon)]

MOORE MISS MIRANDA JAYNE

Five Paper Buildings
1st Floor, Five Paper Bldgs, Temple,
London EC4Y 7HB,
Telephone: 0171 583 6117
E-mail:clerks@5-paperbuildings.law.co.uk
Call Date: July 1983, Lincoln's Inn
Pupil Master
Qualifications: [BSc (Aston)]

MOORE NEIL PATRICK

13 King's Bench Walk
1st Floor, Temple, London EC4Y 7EN,
Telephone: 0171 353 7204
E-mail: clerks@13kbw.law.co.uk
King's Bench Chambers
32 Beaumont Street, Oxford OX1 2NP,
Telephone: 01865 311066
E-mail: clerks@kbc-oxford.law.co.uk
Call Date: July 1986, Gray's Inn
Qualifications: [LLB (Hons) (Notts)]

MOORE RODERICK ANDREW MCGOWAN

3 Temple Gardens
3rd Floor, Temple, London EC4Y 9AU,
Telephone: 0171 353 0832
Call Date: Nov 1993, Inner Temple
Qualifications: [LLB (So'ton)]

MOORE ROGER ANSON

New Court Chambers
3 Broad Chare, Newcastle upon Tyne
NE1 3DQ, Telephone: 0191 232 1980
Call Date: July 1969, Lincoln's Inn
Pupil Master
Qualifications: [LLM]

MOORE MISS SARAH ELIZABETH

4-5 Gray's Inn Square
Ground Floor, Gray's Inn, London
WC1R 5JP, Telephone: 0171 404 5252
E-mail:chambers@4-5graysinnsquare.co.uk
Call Date: Nov 1990, Middle Temple
Qualifications: [BA, LLM (Cantab)]

MOORE MRS THERESE FINOLA

3 Dr Johnson's Buildings
Ground Floor, Temple, London
EC4Y 7BA, Telephone: 0171 353 4854
E-mail: clerks@3djb.co.uk
Call Date: July 1988, Lincoln's Inn
Pupil Master
Qualifications: [MA, BA (Hons) Soton]

MOORE PROFESSOR VICTOR WILLIAM EDWARD

2 Mitre Court Buildings
2nd Floor, Temple, London EC4Y 7BX,
Telephone: 0171 583 1380
E-mail: clerks@2mcb.co.uk
Call Date: May 1992, Gray's Inn
Qualifications: [LLB (Lond), LLM (Lond)]

MOORE-GRAHAM MISS FIONA ADELE

5 King's Bench Walk
Temple, London EC4Y 7DN,
Telephone: 0171 353 5638
Call Date: Nov 1986, Gray's Inn
Qualifications: [LLB (Hons)(Leic)]

MOORES TIMOTHY KIERON

17 Carlton Crescent
Southampton SO15 2XR,
Telephone: 023 8032 0320/0823 2003
E-mail: greg@jg17cc.co.uk
Call Date: July 1987, Lincoln's Inn
Qualifications: [LLB (Bristol)]

MOORMAN MISS LUCINDA CLAIRE

Farrar's Building
Temple, London EC4Y 7BD,
Telephone: 0171 583 9241
E-mail:chambers@farrarsbuilding.co.uk
Call Date: Nov 1992, Inner Temple
Qualifications: [LLM (Cantab)]

MORAN ANDREW GERARD QC (1994)

22 Old Buildings
Lincoln's Inn, London WC2A 3UJ,
Telephone: 0171 831 0222
Byrom Street Chambers
Byrom Street, Manchester M3 4PF,
Telephone: 0161 829 2100
E-mail: Byromst25@aol.com
*Call Date: Nov 1976, Gray's Inn
Recorder*
Qualifications: [MA (Oxon)]

MORAN ANDREW JOHN

One Hare Court
1st Floor, Temple, London EC4Y 7BE,
Telephone: 020 7353 3171
E-mail:admin-oneharecourt@btinternet.com
Call Date: Feb 1989, Middle Temple
Qualifications: [LLB (Lond), BCL (Oxon)]

MORAN THOMAS

New Court Chambers
3 Broad Chare, Newcastle upon Tyne
NE1 3DQ, Telephone: 0191 232 1980
Call Date: Nov 1996, Gray's Inn
Qualifications: [LLB (B'ham)]

MORAN VINCENT JOHN

12 King's Bench Walk
Temple, London EC4Y 7EL,
Telephone: 0171 583 0811
E-mail: chambers@12kbw.co.uk
Call Date: Oct 1991, Gray's Inn
Qualifications: [MA (Cantab), Dip Law (City)]

MORCOM CHRISTOPHER QC (1991)

One Raymond Buildings
Gray's Inn, London WC1R 5BH,
Telephone: 0171 430 1234
E-mail: chambers@ipbar1rb.com;
clerks@ipbar1rb.com
Call Date: July 1963, Middle Temple
Qualifications: [MA (Cantab)]

MORE O'FERRALL MISS GERALDINE ANN

1 Pump Court
Lower Ground Floor, Temple, London
EC4Y 7AB, Telephone: 0171 583 2012/
353 4341
E-mail: [name]@1pumpcourt.co.uk
*Call Date: July 1983, Middle Temple
Pupil Master*

MOREL PETER HOWITT EDWARD

Counsels' Chambers
2nd Floor, 10-11 Gray's Inn Square,
London WC1R 5JD,
Telephone: 0171 405 2576
E-mail:clerks@10-11graysinnsquare.co.uk
Call Date: Oct 1993, Inner Temple
Qualifications: [BA (Manch), CPE]

MORELAND MISS PENELOPE JANE

New Court Chambers
3 Broad Chare, Newcastle upon Tyne
NE1 3DQ, Telephone: 0191 232 1980
*Call Date: July 1986, Gray's Inn
Pupil Master*
Qualifications: [MA (Cantab)]

MORELLI MISS LUISA TERESA

Westgate Chambers
16-17 Wellington Square, Hastings, East
Sussex, TN34 1PB,
Telephone: 01424 432105
Call Date: Nov 1993, Middle Temple
Qualifications: [BA (Hons)(Sussex), CPE
(Brighton), Dip in Law]

MORGAN ADAM GEOFFREY

Dr Johnson's Chambers
Two Dr Johnson's Buildings, Temple,
London EC4Y 7AY,
Telephone: 0171 353 4716
E-mail: clerks@2djb.freeserve.co.uk
Call Date: Nov 1996, Gray's Inn
Qualifications: [LLB, LLM (Lond)]

MORGAN MS ADRIENNE

4 Paper Buildings
1st Floor, Temple, London EC4Y 7EX,
Telephone: 0171 583 0816/353 1131
E-mail: clerks@4paperbuildings.co.uk
Call Date: Nov 1988, Gray's Inn
Pupil Master
Qualifications: [BA (Hons) (Lond)]

MORGAN ANDREW JAMES

St Philip's Chambers
Fountain Court, Steelhouse Lane,
Birmingham B4 6DR,
Telephone: 0121 246 7000
E-mail: clerks@st-philips.co.uk
Call Date: Oct 1996, Inner Temple
Qualifications: [BA (Cantab)]

MORGAN DR AUSTEN JUDE

3 Temple Gardens
3rd Floor, Temple, London EC4Y 9AU,
Telephone: 0171 353 0832
Call Date: Oct 1995, Lincoln's Inn
Qualifications: [BSc (Hons)(Bris), PhD
(Belfast)]

MORGAN CHARLES JAMES ARTHUR

Enterprise Chambers
9 Old Square, Lincoln's Inn, London
WC2A 3SR, Telephone: 0171 405 9471
E-mail:enterprise.london@dial.pipex.com
Enterprise Chambers
65 Quayside, Newcastle upon Tyne
NE1 3DS, Telephone: 0191 222 3344
E-mail:enterprise.newcastle@dial.pipex.com
Enterprise Chambers
38 Park Square, Leeds LS1 2PA,
Telephone: 0113 246 0391
E-mail:enterprise.leeds@dial.pipex.com
Call Date: July 1978, Middle Temple
Pupil Master
Qualifications: [MA, FCIArb]

MORGAN CHRISTOPHER JOHN

1 Paper Buildings
1st Floor, Temple, London EC4Y 7EP,
Telephone: 0171 353 3728/4953
Call Date: July 1987, Middle Temple
Qualifications: [LLB (Hons)]

MORGAN COLIN THOMAS PATRICK

Chichester Chambers
12 North Pallant, Chichester, West Sussex,
PO19 1TQ, Telephone: 01243 784538
E-mail:clerks@chichesterchambers.law.co.uk
Call Date: Nov 1989, Middle Temple
Qualifications: [BA (Oxon), Dip Law]

MORGAN DAVID SIMON SELBY

St John's Chambers
Small Street, Bristol BS1 1DW,
Telephone: 0117 9213456/298514
E-mail: @stjohnschambers.co.uk
Call Date: Nov 1988, Gray's Inn
Pupil Master

MORGAN DAVID WYNN

30 Park Place
Cardiff CF1 3BA,
Telephone: 01222 398421
E-mail: 100757.1456@compuserve.com
Farrar's Building
Temple, London EC4Y 7BD,
Telephone: 0171 583 9241
E-mail:chambers@farrarsbuilding.co.uk
Call Date: Nov 1976, Gray's Inn
Pupil Master, Recorder
Qualifications: [BA (Oxon) (Hons)]

MORGAN DYLAN ROBERT

17 Carlton Crescent
Southampton SO15 2XR,
Telephone: 023 8032 0320/0823 2003
E-mail: greg@jg17cc.co.uk
Call Date: July 1986, Gray's Inn
Qualifications: [LLB (CNAA)]

MORGAN EDWARD PATRICK

Deans Court Chambers
24 St John Street, Manchester M3 4DF,
Telephone: 0161 214 6000
E-mail: clerks@deanscourt.co.uk
Deans Court Chambers
41-43 Market Place, Preston PR1 1AH,
Telephone: 01772 555163
E-mail: clerks@deanscourt.co.uk
Call Date: July 1989, Lincoln's Inn
Qualifications: [LLB, ACIArb]

D

MORGAN MISS HELEN ELIZABETH

1 Gray's Inn Square, Chambers of the Baroness Scotland of Asthal QC
1st Floor, London WC1R 5AG,
Telephone: 0171 405 3000
E-mail: clerks@onegrays.demon.co.uk
Call Date: Nov 1993, Gray's Inn
Qualifications: [BA]

MORGAN MS LYNNE MARY

32 Park Place
Cardiff CF1 3BA,
Telephone: 01222 397364
Call Date: July 1984, Middle Temple
Pupil Master
Qualifications: [LLB (Wales)]

MORGAN PAUL QC (1992)

Falcon Chambers
Falcon Court, London EC4Y 1AA,
Telephone: 0171 353 2484
E-mail: clerks@falcon-chambers.com
Call Date: July 1975, Lincoln's Inn
Qualifications: [MA (Cantab)]

MORGAN RICHARD HUGO LYNDON

13 Old Square
Ground Floor, Lincoln's Inn, London
WC2A 3UA, Telephone: 0171 404 4800
E-mail: clerks@13oldsquare.law.co.uk
Call Date: Nov 1988, Gray's Inn
Pupil Master
Qualifications: [LLB UBucks), LLM (Cantab)]

MORGAN MISS SARAH MARY

One Garden Court Family Law Chambers
Ground Floor, Temple, London
EC4Y 9BJ, Telephone: 0171 797 7900
E-mail: clerks@onegardencourt.co.uk
Call Date: Nov 1988, Gray's Inn
Qualifications: [LLB (Brunel)]

MORGAN STEPHEN FRANCIS

1 Serjeants' Inn
4th Floor, Temple, London EC4Y 1NH,
Telephone: 0171 583 1355
E-mail: clerks@serjeants-inn.co.uk
Call Date: Nov 1983, Gray's Inn
Pupil Master
Qualifications: [LLB (Warw), MA, (Nottm)]

MORGAN (THOMAS) JEREMY

39 Essex Street
London WC2R 3AT,
Telephone: 0171 832 1111
E-mail: clerks@39essex.co.uk
Call Date: Apr 1989, Middle Temple
Pupil Master
Qualifications: [BA (Oxon), BA (Kent)]

MORGANS JOHN MORGAN

East Anglian Chambers
57 London Street, Norwich NR2 1HL,
Telephone: 01603 617351
E-mail: norwich@ealaw.co.uk
East Anglian Chambers
Gresham House, 5 Museum Street,
Ipswich, Suffolk, IP1 1HQ,
Telephone: 01473 214481
E-mail: ipswich@ealaw.co.uk
East Anglian Chambers
52 North Hill, Colchester, Essex, CO1 1PY,
Telephone: 01206 572756
E-mail: colchester@ealaw.co.uk
Call Date: Nov 1996, Middle Temple
Qualifications: [LLB (Hons)(Lancs), LLM]

MORIARTY GERALD EVELYN QC (1974)

2 Mitre Court Buildings
2nd Floor, Temple, London EC4Y 7BX,
Telephone: 0171 583 1380
E-mail: clerks@2mcb.co.uk
Call Date: June 1951, Lincoln's Inn

MORIARTY STEPHEN QC (1999)

Fountain Court
Temple, London EC4Y 9DH,
Telephone: 0171 583 3335
E-mail: chambers@fountaincourt.co.uk
Call Date: 1986, Middle Temple
Pupil Master
Qualifications: [BCL, MA (Oxon)]

MORLAND MS CAMILLE

Broadway House Chambers
Broadway House, 9 Bank Street, Bradford,
West Yorkshire, BD1 1TW,
Telephone: 01274 722560
E-mail: clerks@broadwayhouse.co.uk

Broadway House Chambers
31 Park Square West, Leeds LS1 2PF,
Telephone: 0113 246 2600
Call Date: Nov 1996, Gray's Inn
Qualifications: [BA (Hons) (Bradford)]

MORLEY GARETH EDWARD

3 Temple Gardens
3rd Floor, Temple, London EC4Y 9AU,
Telephone: 0171 583 0010
Call Date: July 1982, Middle Temple
Pupil Master
Qualifications: [LLB]

MORLEY IAIN CHARLES

23 Essex Street
London WC2R 3AS,
Telephone: 0171 413 0353/836 8366
E-mail:clerks@essexstreet23.demon.co.uk
Call Date: July 1988, Inner Temple
Pupil Master
Qualifications: [BA (Oxon)]

MORLEY STEPHEN DOUGLAS

Bridewell Chambers
2 Bridewell Place, London EC4V 6AP,
Telephone: 020 7797 8800
E-mail:HughesGage@bridewell.law.co.uk
Call Date: 1996, Inner Temple
Qualifications: [LLB (Westminster)]

MORPUSS GUY

20 Essex Street
London WC2R 3AL,
Telephone: 0171 583 9294
E-mail: clerks@20essexst.com
Call Date: Oct 1991, Lincoln's Inn
Qualifications: [LLB (Hons) (Birm)]

MORRELL MISS ROXANNE TRACIE

3 Temple Gardens
3rd Floor, Temple, London EC4Y 9AU,
Telephone: 0171 583 0010
Call Date: July 1996, Middle Temple
Qualifications: [LLB (Hons)]

MORRIS MISS ANGELA JANE

18 Red Lion Court
(Off Fleet Street), London EC4A 3EB,
Telephone: 0171 520 6000
E-mail: chambers@18rlc.co.uk

Thornwood House
102 New London Road, Chelmsford,
Essex, CM2 0RG,
Telephone: 01245 280880
E-mail: chambers@18rlc.co.uk
Call Date: July 1984, Middle Temple
Pupil Master
Qualifications: [LLB]

MORRIS ANTHONY JOSEPH

Parsonage Chambers
5th Floor, 3 The Parsonage, Manchester
M3 2HW, Telephone: 0161 833 1996
Call Date: Nov 1986, Gray's Inn

MORRIS ANTHONY PAUL QC (1991)

Peel Court Chambers
45 Hardman Street, Manchester M3 3PL,
Telephone: 0161 832 3791
E-mail: clerks@peelct.co.uk
Call Date: July 1970, Gray's Inn
Recorder
Qualifications: [MA (Oxon)]

MORRIS MISS ANTONIA LOUISE

Trafalgar Chambers
53 Fleet Street, London EC4Y 1BE,
Telephone: 0171 583 5858
E-mail:trafalgarchambers@easynet.co.uk
Call Date: Nov 1993, Inner Temple
Qualifications: [LLB (Hons) (Lond)]

MORRIS BEN

19 Castle Street Chambers
Liverpool L2 4SX,
Telephone: 0151 236 9402
E-mail: DBrei16454@aol.com
25-27 Castle Street
1st Floor, Liverpool L2 4TA,
Telephone: 0151 227 5661/051 236 5072
Call Date: Oct 1996, Middle Temple
Qualifications: [LLB (Hons)(L'pool)]

MORRIS MISS BRENDA ALISON

14 Gray's Inn Square
Gray's Inn, London WC1R 5JP,
Telephone: 0171 242 0858
E-mail: 100712.2134@compuserve.com
Call Date: July 1978, Middle Temple
Pupil Master
Qualifications: [BSc (Lond), P.G.C.E.]

MORRIS BRENDAN ANTHONY

18 Red Lion Court
(Off Fleet Street), London EC4A 3EB,
Telephone: 0171 520 6000
E-mail: chambers@18rlc.co.uk
Thornwood House
102 New London Road, Chelmsford,
Essex, CM2 0RG,
Telephone: 01245 280880
E-mail: chambers@18rlc.co.uk
Call Date: July 1985, Middle Temple
Pupil Master
Qualifications: [BA, Dip Law (Lond)]

MORRIS MS CHRISTINA GAYE

5 Pump Court
Ground Floor, Temple, London
EC4Y 7AP, Telephone: 020 7353 2532
E-mail: FivePump@netcomuk.co.uk
Call Date: Nov 1983, Gray's Inn
Pupil Master
Qualifications: [BA (Warw)]

MORRIS CHRISTOPHER

Coleridge Chambers
Citadel, 190 Corporation Street,
Birmingham B4 6QD,
Telephone: 0121 233 8500
Call Date: July 1977, Lincoln's Inn
Pupil Master
Qualifications: [BA (Hons)]

MORRIS DAVID PAUL

Chambers of Kieran Coonan QC
Ground Floor, 6 Pump Court, Temple,
London EC4Y 7AR,
Telephone: 0171 583 6013/2510
E-mail: clerks@6-pumpcourt.law.co.uk
Call Date: July 1976, Inner Temple
Pupil Master
Qualifications: [LLB (Bris)]

MORRIS MISS DEBORAH ANNE

1 Gray's Inn Square
Ground Floor, London WC1R 5AA,
Telephone: 0171 405 8946/7/8
Call Date: July 1989, Gray's Inn
Pupil Master
Qualifications: [BEd (Hons), Dip Law]

MORRIS DERRICK

Arbitration Chambers
22 Willes Road, London NW5 3DS,
Telephone: 020 7267 2137
E-mail: jatqc@atack.demon.co.uk
Call Date: Nov 1983, Lincoln's Inn
Qualifications: [LLB (Cardiff), FRICS]

MORRIS MISS FENELLA

39 Essex Street
London WC2R 3AT,
Telephone: 0171 832 1111
E-mail: clerks@39essex.co.uk
Call Date: Oct 1990, Middle Temple
Qualifications: [BA (Hons) (Oxon), Dip Law
(City)]

MORRIS MS GILLIAN SUSAN

11 King's Bench Walk
Temple, London EC4Y 7EQ,
Telephone: 0171 632 8500/583 0610
E-mail: clerksroom@11kbw.com
Call Date: 1997, Inner Temple
Qualifications: [LLB (Bris), PhD (Cantab)]

MORRIS IEUAN JOHN

9 Park Place
Cardiff CF1 3DP,
Telephone: 01222 382731
Call Date: July 1979, Gray's Inn
Pupil Master
Qualifications: [LLB (Lond)]

MORRIS MISS JANE PENELOPE KATRIN

King Charles House
Standard Hill, Nottingham NG1 6FX,
Telephone: 0115 9418851
E-mail: clerks@kch.co.uk
Call Date: Oct 1991, Gray's Inn
Qualifications: [LLB]

MORRIS MISS JUNE VICTORIA

Peel Court Chambers
45 Hardman Street, Manchester M3 3PL,
Telephone: 0161 832 3791
E-mail: clerks@peelct.co.uk
Call Date: Oct 1995, Lincoln's Inn
Qualifications: [BA (Hons)(Manc), CPE
(Manc)]

MORRIS MICHAEL HARVEY

Goldsmith Chambers
Ground Floor, Goldsmith Building,
Temple, London EC4Y 7BL,
Telephone: 0171 353 6802/3/4/5
E-mail:clerks@goldsmithchambers.law.co.uk
Call Date: July 1984, Gray's Inn
Qualifications: [BSc (Eng) (Lond)]

MORRIS MICHAEL JOHN

169 Temple Chambers
Temple Avenue, London EC4Y 0DA,
Telephone: 0171 583 7644
Call Date: Nov 1996, Gray's Inn
Qualifications: [BA (Cantab)]

MORRIS PAUL HOWARD

5 Stone Buildings
Lincoln's Inn, London WC2A 3XT,
Telephone: 0171 242 6201
E-mail:clerks@5-stonebuildings.law.co.uk
York Chambers
14 Toft Green, York YO1 6JT,
Telephone: 01904 620048
E-mail: [name]@yorkchambers.co.uk
Call Date: Nov 1986, Lincoln's Inn
Pupil Master
Qualifications: [MA (Cantab)]

MORRIS MISS SARAH

4 Brick Court
Temple, London EC4Y 9AD,
Telephone: 0171 797 8910
E-mail: medhurst@dial.pipex.com
Call Date: Mar 1996, Lincoln's Inn
Qualifications: [LLB (Hons)(L'pool)]

MORRIS SEAN ROBERT

No. 6
6 Park Square, Leeds LS1 2LW,
Telephone: 0113 2459763
E-mail: chambers@no6.co.uk
Call Date: Nov 1983, Lincoln's Inn
Qualifications: [BA]

MORRIS MISS SHAN ELIZABETH

Sedan House
Stanley Place, Chester CH1 2LU,
Telephone: 01244 320480/348282
Call Date: 1991, Middle Temple
Qualifications: [LLB Hons (Hull)]

MORRIS STEPHEN NATHAN

20 Essex Street
London WC2R 3AL,
Telephone: 0171 583 9294
E-mail: clerks@20essexst.com
Call Date: 1981, Lincoln's Inn
Pupil Master, Assistant Recorder
Qualifications: [MA (Cantab)]

MORRIS-COOLE CHRISTOPHER

Goldsmith Building
1st Floor, Temple, London EC4Y 7BL,
Telephone: 0171 353 7881
E-mail:clerks@goldsmith-building.law.co.uk
Call Date: July 1974, Inner Temple
Pupil Master, Recorder

MORRISH PETER JEFFERY

Goldsmith Chambers
Ground Floor, Goldsmith Building,
Temple, London EC4Y 7BL,
Telephone: 0171 353 6802/3/4/5
E-mail:clerks@goldsmithchambers.law.co.uk
Call Date: May 1962, Gray's Inn

MORRISON CHRISTOPHER JAMES

Chambers of Christopher J Morrison
2 Brook Mead, Ewell Court, Epsom,
Surrey, KT19 0BD,
Telephone: 0181 393 8376
E-mail: gladeside@msn.com
Call Date: Nov 1990, Inner Temple
Qualifications: [BA (Hons)(Oxon), Dip Law]

MORRISON CHRISTOPHER QUINTIN

Durham Barristers' Chambers
27 Old Elvet, Durham DH1 3HN,
Telephone: 0191 386 9199
Call Date: Nov 1986, Inner Temple
Qualifications: [LLB (Leic), DBA (Dunelm)]

MORRISON HOWARD ANDREW CLIVE

Chambers of Michael Pert QC
36 Bedford Row, London WC1R 4JH,
Telephone: 0171 421 8000
E-mail: 36bedfordrow@link.org
Chambers of Michael Pert QC
24 Albion Place, Northampton NN1 1UD,
Telephone: 01604 602333

D

Chambers of Michael Pert QC
104 New Walk, Leicester LE1 7EA,
Telephone: 0116 249 2020
Call Date: July 1977, Gray's Inn
Pupil Master, Recorder
Qualifications: [LLB (Lond)]

MORROW GRAHAM ERIC QC (1996)

Exchange Chambers
Pearl Assurance House, Derby Square,
Liverpool L2 9XX,
Telephone: 0151 236 7747
E-mail:exchangechambers@btinternet.com
Call Date: July 1974, Lincoln's Inn
Assistant Recorder
Qualifications: [LLB (Hons)]

MORSE CHRISTOPHER GEORGE
JOHN

Blackstone Chambers
Blackstone House, Temple, London
EC4Y 9BW, Telephone: 0171 583 1770
E-mail:clerks@blackstonechambers.com
Call Date: July 1972, Middle Temple
Qualifications: [BA, BCL (Oxon)]

MORSE MALCOLM GEORGE MCEWAN

1 Fountain Court
Steelhouse Lane, Birmingham B4 6DR,
Telephone: 0121 236 5721
Call Date: July 1967, Inner Temple
Pupil Master, Recorder
Qualifications: [MA (Cantab)]

MORSHEAD TIMOTHY FRANCIS

4 Breams Buildings
London EC4A 1AQ,
Telephone: 0171 353 5835/430 1221
E-mail:breams@4breamsbuildings.law.co.uk
Call Date: Feb 1995, Lincoln's Inn
Qualifications: [BA (Hons), Dip in Law
(City)]

MORT JUSTIN JOHN GLASBROOK

2 Temple Gardens
Temple, London EC4Y 9AY,
Telephone: 0171 583 6041
E-mail: clerks@2templegardens.co.uk
Call Date: Oct 1994, Middle Temple
Qualifications: [BA (Hons)(Durham)]

MORTIMER MISS SOPHIE KATE

No. 1 Serjeants' Inn
5th Floor Fleet Street, Temple, London
EC4Y 1LH, Telephone: 0171 415 6666
E-mail:no1serjeantsinn@btinternet.com
Call Date: 1996, Lincoln's Inn
Qualifications: [BA (Hons)(Sussex)]

MORTIMORE MISS CLAUDIA

18 Red Lion Court
(Off Fleet Street), London EC4A 3EB,
Telephone: 0171 520 6000
E-mail: chambers@18rlc.co.uk
Thornwood House
102 New London Road, Chelmsford,
Essex, CM2 0RG,
Telephone: 01245 280880
E-mail: chambers@18rlc.co.uk
Call Date: Oct 1994, Middle Temple
Qualifications: [LLB (Hons)(Leeds), LLM
(Lond)]

MORTIMORE SIMON ANTHONY
QC (1991)

3/4 South Square
Gray's Inn, London WC1R 5HP,
Telephone: 0171 696 9900
E-mail: clerks@southsquare.com
Call Date: July 1972, Inner Temple
Qualifications: [LLB (Exon)]

MORTON GARY DAVID

Pepys' Chambers
17 Fleet Street, London EC4Y 1AA,
Telephone: 0171 936 2710
Call Date: Nov 1993, Gray's Inn
Qualifications: [B.Sc (Econ), MA (Warw)]

MORTON KEITH FARRANCE

1 Temple Gardens
1st Floor, Temple, London EC4Y 9BB,
Telephone: 0171 583 1315/353 0407
E-mail: clerks@1templegardens.co.uk
Call Date: Oct 1990, Lincoln's Inn
Qualifications: [BSc (Hull), Dip Law (City)]

MORTON PETER JOHN

Plowden Buildings
2nd Floor, 2 Plowden Buildings, Middle
Temple Lane, London EC4Y 9BU,
Telephone: 0171 583 0808
E-mail: bar@plowdenbuildings.co.uk
Call Date: Nov 1988, Middle Temple
Qualifications: [LLB (Lanc), LLM (Cantab)]

MORTON MISS RACHAEL JOANNA EADEN

4 Brick Court
Temple, London EC4Y 9AD,
Telephone: 0171 797 8910
E-mail: medhurst@dial.pipex.com
Call Date: Feb 1995, Lincoln's Inn
Qualifications: [LLB (Hons)(Warw)]

MORWOOD JONATHAN THOMAS BOYD

Young Street Chambers
38 Young Street, Manchester M3 3FT,
Telephone: 0161 833 0489
E-mail: clerks@young-st-chambers.com
Call Date: 1996, Middle Temple
Qualifications: [BA (Hons)(Keele)]

MOSELEY MISS JULIE RUTH

St Philip's Chambers
Fountain Court, Steelhouse Lane,
Birmingham B4 6DR,
Telephone: 0121 246 7000
E-mail: clerks@st-philips.co.uk
Call Date: Oct 1992, Inner Temple
Qualifications: [LLB (Leics)]

MOSER PHILIP CURT HAROLD

4 Paper Buildings
Ground Floor, Temple, London
EC4Y 7EX, Telephone: 0171 353 3366/
583 7155
E-mail: clerks@4paperbuildings.com
Call Date: Oct 1992, Inner Temple
Qualifications: [MA (Cantab)]

MOSES MISS REBECCA

Virtual Chambers
(accepting briefs soon), London
Telephone: 07071 244 944
E-mail:enquiries@virtualchambers.org.uk

Barristers' Common Law Chambers
57 Whitechapel Road, Aldgate East,
London E1 1DU,
Telephone: 0171 375 3012
E-mail: barristers@hotmail.com and
barristers@lawchambers.freeserve.co.uk
Call Date: Nov 1996, Inner Temple
Qualifications: [LLB (Hons)]

MOSS CHRISTOPHER JOHN QC (1994)

5 Essex Court
1st Floor, Temple, London EC4Y 9AH,
Telephone: 0171 410 2000
E-mail: barristers@5essexcourt.co.uk
Call Date: July 1972, Gray's Inn
Recorder
Qualifications: [LLB (Lond)]

MOSS GABRIEL STEPHEN QC (1989)

3/4 South Square
Gray's Inn, London WC1R 5HP,
Telephone: 0171 696 9900
E-mail: clerks@southsquare.com
Call Date: July 1974, Lincoln's Inn
Qualifications: [MA, BCL (Oxon)]

MOSS MS JOANNE ROSEMARY

Falcon Chambers
Falcon Court, London EC4Y 1AA,
Telephone: 0171 353 2484
E-mail: clerks@falcon-chambers.com
Call Date: 1976, Inner Temple
Qualifications: [MA (Cantab), FCI Arb, LLM
(Lond)]

MOSS NICHOLAS SIMON

1 Temple Gardens
1st Floor, Temple, London EC4Y 9BB,
Telephone: 0171 583 1315/353 0407
E-mail: clerks@1templegardens.co.uk
Call Date: Nov 1995, Middle Temple
Qualifications: [MA (Hons)(Cantab)]

MOSS NORMAN WILLIAM

Goldsmith Chambers
Ground Floor, Goldsmith Building,
Temple, London EC4Y 7BL,
Telephone: 0171 353 6802/3/4/5
E-mail:clerks@goldsmithchambers.law.co.uk
Call Date: Oct 1990, Inner Temple
Qualifications: [LLB (Hons Wales)]

MOSS PETER

Sedan House
Stanley Place, Chester CH1 2LU,
Telephone: 01244 320480/348282
Call Date: Nov 1980, Middle Temple
Pupil Master

MOSS PETER JONATHAN

9-12 Bell Yard
London WC2A 2LF,
Telephone: 0171 400 1800
E-mail: clerks@bellyard.co.uk
Call Date: Nov 1976, Lincoln's Inn
Pupil Master

MOSTESHAR SA'ID

Hardwicke Building
New Square, Lincoln's Inn, London
WC2A 3SB, Telephone: 020 7242 2523
E-mail: clerks@hardwicke.co.uk
Call Date: July 1975, Lincoln's Inn
Qualifications: [DPhil, FCA, B.SC, M.Sc
(Econ)]

MOSTYN NICHOLAS ANTHONY JOSEPH GHISLAIN QC (1997)

1 Mitre Court Buildings
Temple, London EC4Y 7BS,
Telephone: 0171 797 7070
E-mail: clerks@1mcb.com
Call Date: Nov 1980, Middle Temple
Assistant Recorder
Qualifications: [LLB]

MOSTYN PIERS NICHOLAS

4 Brick Court
Ground Floor, Temple, London
EC4Y 9AD, Telephone: 0171 797 7766
E-mail: chambers@4brick.com
Call Date: Nov 1989, Middle Temple
Qualifications: [B.Sc Hons [Bris], Dip in
Law]

MOTT GEOFFREY EDWARD

Gray's Inn Chambers
5th Floor, Gray's Inn, London WC1R 5JA,
Telephone: 0171 404 1111
Call Date: July 1982, Gray's Inn
Pupil Master
Qualifications: [Ba, Dip Law]

MOTT PHILIP CHARLES QC (1991)

35 Essex Street
Temple, London WC2R 3AR,
Telephone: 0171 353 6381
E-mail: derek_jenkins@link.org
Call Date: July 1970, Inner Temple
Recorder
Qualifications: [BA (Oxon)]

MOULD TIMOTHY JAMES

4 Breams Buildings
London EC4A 1AQ,
Telephone: 0171 353 5835/430 1221
E-mail:breams@4breamsbuildings.law.co.uk
Call Date: Nov 1987, Gray's Inn
Pupil Master
Qualifications: [BA (Oxon), Dip Law]

MOULDER PAUL JOHN

Guildford Chambers
Stoke House, Leapale Lane, Guildford,
Surrey, GU1 4LY,
Telephone: 01483 539131
E-mail:guildford.barristers@btinternet.com
Call Date: Oct 1997, Lincoln's Inn
Qualifications: [LLB (Hons)(Lond)]

MOULDER MISS PAULINE MARY

Broad Chare
33 Broad Chare, Newcastle upon Tyne
NE1 3DQ, Telephone: 0191 232 0541
E-mail:clerks@broadcharechambers.law.co.uk
Call Date: July 1983, Lincoln's Inn
Qualifications: [LLB (Newc)]

MOULSON PETER CHARLES EDWARD

Chambers of Andrew Campbell QC
10 Park Square, Leeds LS1 2LH,
Telephone: 0113 2455438
E-mail: clerks@10pksq.co.uk
Call Date: Oct 1991, Gray's Inn
Qualifications: [LLB , MBA]

MOUNTFIELD MS HELEN

4-5 Gray's Inn Square
Ground Floor, Gray's Inn, London
WC1R 5JP, Telephone: 0171 404 5252
E-mail:chambers@4-5graysinnsquare.co.uk
Call Date: Oct 1991, Gray's Inn
Qualifications: [BA (Oxon), Dip Law (City),
Dip European Law]

MOUSLEY TIMOTHY JOHN

2 King's Bench Walk
Ground Floor, Temple, London
EC4Y 7DE, Telephone: 0171 353 1746
E-mail: 2kbw@atlas.co.uk
King's Bench Chambers
115 North Hill, Plymouth PL4 8JY,
Telephone: 01752 221551
Call Date: July 1979, Middle Temple
Pupil Master
Qualifications: [BA (Keele)]

MOUSLEY WILLIAM HOWARD

2 King's Bench Walk
Ground Floor, Temple, London
EC4Y 7DE, Telephone: 0171 353 1746
E-mail: 2kbw@atlas.co.uk
King's Bench Chambers
115 North Hill, Plymouth PL4 8JY,
Telephone: 01752 221551
Call Date: July 1986, Middle Temple
Qualifications: [LLB (Warks)]

MOVERLEY SMITH STEPHEN PHILIP

Twenty-Four Old Buildings
Ground Floor, Lincoln's Inn, London
WC2A 3UP, Telephone: 0171 404 0946
E-mail:clerks@24oldbuildings.law.co.uk
Call Date: Feb 1985, Middle Temple
Pupil Master
Qualifications: [MA (Oxon)]

MOWBRAY (WILLIAM) JOHN QC (1974)

12 New Square
Lincoln's Inn, London WC2A 3SW,
Telephone: 0171 419 1212
E-mail: chambers@12newsquare.co.uk
Sovereign Chambers
25 Park Square, Leeds LS1 2PW,
Telephone: 0113 2451841/2/3
E-mail:sovereignchambers@btinternet.com
Call Date: June 1953, Lincoln's Inn
Qualifications: [BA (Oxon)]

MOWSCHENSON TERENCE RENNIE QC (1995)

One Essex Court
Ground Floor, Temple, London
EC4Y 9AR, Telephone: 020 7583 2000
E-mail: clerks@oneessexcourt.co.uk
Call Date: July 1977, Middle Temple
Qualifications: [LLB (Lond), BCL (Oxon),
FCIArb]

MOXON BROWNE ROBERT WILLIAM QC (1990)

2 Temple Gardens
Temple, London EC4Y 9AY,
Telephone: 0171 583 6041
E-mail: clerks@2templegardens.co.uk
Call Date: July 1969, Gray's Inn
Recorder
Qualifications: [BA (Oxon)]

MOYLAN ANDREW JOHN GREGORY

Queen Elizabeth Building
2nd Floor, Temple, London EC4Y 9BS,
Telephone: 0171 797 7837
Call Date: Nov 1978, Inner Temple
Pupil Master
Qualifications: [BA (Oxon)]

MOYS CLIVE JOHN

**11 Bolt Court (also at 7 Stone Buildings
– 1st Floor)**
London EC4A 3DQ,
Telephone: 0171 353 2300
E-mail: boltct11@aol.com
**7 Stone Buildings (also at 11 Bolt
Court)**
1st Floor, Lincoln's Inn, London
WC2A 3SZ, Telephone: 0171 242 0961
E-mail:larthur@7stonebuildings.law.co.uk
Redhill Chambers
Seloduct House, 30 Station Road, Redhill,
Surrey, RH1 1NF,
Telephone: 01737 780781
Call Date: 1998, Lincoln's Inn
Qualifications: [LLB (Hons)]

MUCHLINSKI PETER THOMAS

Brick Court Chambers
7-8 Essex Street, London WC2R 3LD,
Telephone: 0171 379 3550
E-mail: [surname]@brickcourt.co.uk
Call Date: July 1981, Lincoln's Inn
Qualifications: [LLB (Cantab), LLB (Lond)]

MUIR ANDREW CHARLES

3 Raymond Buildings
Gray's Inn, London WC1R 5BH,
Telephone: 020 7831 3833
E-mail:chambers@threeraymond.demon.co.u
k
Call Date: Nov 1975, Lincoln's Inn
Pupil Master
Qualifications: [BA (Hons)]

MUIR JOHN HENRY

9 Woodhouse Square
Leeds LS3 1AD,
Telephone: 0113 2451986
E-mail: clerks@9woodhouse.co.uk
Call Date: Nov 1969, Lincoln's Inn
Pupil Master
Qualifications: [BA, BSc (Econ), , FCIS,
ACIArb]

MUKHERJEE AVIK

High Pavement Chambers
1 High Pavement, Nottingham NG1 1HF,
Telephone: 0115 9418218
Call Date: Oct 1990, Gray's Inn
Qualifications: [LLB]

MUKHERJEE TUBLU KRISHNENDU

Enfield Chambers
First Floor, Refuge House, 9-10 River
Front, Enfield, Middlesex, EN1 3SZ,
Telephone: 0181 364 5627
E-mail:enfieldchambers@compuserve.com
Call Date: May 1996, Inner Temple
Qualifications: [BA (Hons), MA]

MULCAHY MS JANE SUZANNE

Blackstone Chambers
Blackstone House, Temple, London
EC4Y 9BW, Telephone: 0171 583 1770
E-mail:clerks@blackstonechambers.com
Call Date: Oct 1995, Middle Temple
Qualifications: [BA (Hons)]

MULCAHY MISS LEIGH-ANN MARIA

Chambers of John L Powell QC
Four New Square, Lincoln's Inn, London
WC2A 3RJ, Telephone: 0171 797 8000
E-mail: barristers@4newsquare.com
Call Date: Oct 1993, Inner Temple
Qualifications: [BA, MA, LLM]

MULHOLLAND JAMES MALACHI

Hardwicke Building
New Square, Lincoln's Inn, London
WC2A 3SB, Telephone: 020 7242 2523
E-mail: clerks@hardwicke.co.uk
Call Date: July 1986, Inner Temple
Qualifications: [LLB (Leeds)]

MULHOLLAND MS KATHRYN SHONA

One King's Bench Walk
1st Floor, Temple, London EC4Y 7DB,
Telephone: 0171 936 1500
E-mail: ddear@1kbw.co.uk
Call Date: Nov 1994, Inner Temple
Qualifications: [BA (Oxon)]

MULHOLLAND MICHAEL

St James's Chambers
68 Quay Street, Manchester M3 3EJ,
Telephone: 0161 834 7000
E-mail: clerks@stjameschambers.co.uk
Call Date: Nov 1976, Gray's Inn
Pupil Master
Qualifications: [MA (Oxon) Dip Crim,
(Cantab)]

MULLALLY MRS MAUREEN VINCENT

Westgate Chambers
144 High Street, Lewes, East Sussex,
BN7 1XT, Telephone: 01273 480510
Call Date: July 1957, Gray's Inn

MULLAN RICHARD FRANCIS

Sedan House
Stanley Place, Chester CH1 2LU,
Telephone: 01244 320480/348282
Call Date: Oct 1994, Gray's Inn
Qualifications: [BA (Wales)]

MULLEE BRENDAN PAUL

Staple Inn Chambers
1st Floor, 9 Staple Inn, Holborn Bars,
London WC1V 7QH,
Telephone: 0171 242 5240
E-mail: clerks@staple-inn.org
Call Date: Oct 1996, Middle Temple
Qualifications: [LLB (Hons)(Westmins)]

MULLEN MISS JAYNE ALISON

St Ive's Chambers
Whittall Street, Birmingham B4 6DH,
Telephone: 0121 236 0863/5720
E-mail:stives.headofchambers@btinternet.com
Call Date: 1989, Gray's Inn
Qualifications: [LLB (Hons) (Cardiff)]

MULLEN PATRICK ANTHONY

One Essex Court
1st Floor, Temple, London EC4Y 9AR,
Telephone: 0171 936 3030
E-mail: one.essex_court@virgin.net
Call Date: July 1967, Gray's Inn
Pupil Master
Qualifications: [MA (Cantab)]

MULLEN PETER

Verulam Chambers
Peer House, 8-14 Verulam Street, Gray's
Inn, London WC1X 8LZ,
Telephone: 0171 813 2400
Call Date: July 1977, Lincoln's Inn
Pupil Master
Qualifications: [BA (Lond)]

MULLER ANTONIE SEAN

4 Fountain Court
Steelhouse Lane, Birmingham B4 6DR,
Telephone: 0121 236 3476
Call Date: July 1990, Middle Temple
Qualifications: [MA (Cantab)]

MULLER FRANZ JOSEPH QC (1978)

11 King's Bench Walk
1st Floor, Temple, London EC4Y 7EQ,
Telephone: 0171 353 3337
E-mail: fmuller11@aol.com
11 King's Bench Walk
3 Park Court, Park Cross Street, Leeds
LS1 2QH, Telephone: 0113 297 1200
Call Date: Feb 1961, Gray's Inn
Recorder
Qualifications: [LLB Hons]

MULLER MARK OLIVER BENJAMIN

Counsels' Chambers
2nd Floor, 10-11 Gray's Inn Square,
London WC1R 5JD,
Telephone: 0171 405 2576
E-mail:clerks@10-11graysinnsquare.co.uk
Call Date: Apr 1991, Lincoln's Inn
Qualifications: [BSC(Econ) LLB(Dip)]

MULLIGAN MS ANN COLLETTE

Hardwicke Building
New Square, Lincoln's Inn, London
WC2A 3SB, Telephone: 020 7242 2523
E-mail: clerks@hardwicke.co.uk
Call Date: July 1989, Gray's Inn
Qualifications: [BA (Oxon), PPE]

MULLINS MARK

4 Brick Court
Ground Floor, Temple, London
EC4Y 9AD, Telephone: 0171 797 7766
E-mail: chambers@4brick.co.uk
Call Date: Nov 1988, Lincoln's Inn
Qualifications: [BA Hons (Oxon), Dip in Law
(City)]

MULLINS MARK LOVEL RUPERT

1 Harcourt Buildings
2nd Floor, Temple, London EC4Y 9DA,
Telephone: 0171 353 9421/0375
E-mail:clerks@1harcourtbuildings.law.co.uk
Call Date: Nov 1995, Inner Temple
Qualifications: [BA (Dunelm), CPE (Lond)]

MULLIS ANTHONY ROGER

Chambers of Lord Goodhart QC
Ground Floor, 3 New Square, Lincoln's
Inn, London WC2A 3RS,
Telephone: 0171 405 5577
E-mail:law@threenewsquare.demon.co.uk
Call Date: Nov 1987, Lincoln's Inn
Qualifications: [BA (Oxon),BCL]

MULRENNAN MISS MARIA HELEN ANNE

St Mary's Chambers
50 High Pavement, Lace Market,
Nottingham NG1 1HW,
Telephone: 0115 9503503
E-mail: clerks@smc.law.co.uk
Call Date: Nov 1990, Inner Temple
Qualifications: [BA (Sussex), LLM (Nott'm)]

MULROONEY MARK TERENCE DANIEL

Exchange Chambers
Pearl Assurance House, Derby Square,
Liverpool L2 9XX,
Telephone: 0151 236 7747
E-mail:exchangechambers@btinternet.com
Call Date: July 1988, Middle Temple
Qualifications: [BA (Hons) Kent, MPhil
(Cantab)]

MULVEIN MISS HELEN JANE

Ropewalk Chambers
24 The Ropewalk, Nottingham NG1 5EF,
Telephone: 0115 9472581
E-mail: administration@ropewalk.co.uk
Call Date: Oct 1994, Lincoln's Inn
Qualifications: [MA (Cantab), LLM]

MUNASINGHE LEELANANDA SEPALA

235 London Road
Twickenham, London TW1 1ES,
Telephone: 0181 892 5947
Call Date: Feb 1963, Lincoln's Inn

MUNBY JAMES LAWRENCE QC (1988)

1 New Square
Ground Floor, Lincoln's Inn, London
WC2A 3SA, Telephone: 0171 405 0884/5/6/
7 E-mail: clerks@1newsquare.law.co.uk
Call Date: Nov 1971, Middle Temple
Qualifications: [BA (Oxon)]

MUNDAY ANDREW HUGH QC (1996)

3 Hare Court
1 Little Essex Street, London WC2R 3LD,
Telephone: 0171 395 2000
Call Date: Nov 1973, Middle Temple
Assistant Recorder
Qualifications: [LLB]

MUNDAY MISS ANNE MARGARET

8 King's Bench Walk North
1 Park Square East, Leeds LS1 2NE,
Telephone: 0113 2439797
8 King's Bench Walk
2nd Floor, Temple, London EC4Y 7DU,
Telephone: 0171 797 8888
Call Date: Oct 1994, Lincoln's Inn
Qualifications: [LLB (Hons)(L'pool)]

MUNDY ROBERT GEOFFREY

St James's Chambers
68 Quay Street, Manchester M3 3EJ,
Telephone: 0161 834 7000
E-mail: clerks@stjameschambers.co.uk
Call Date: Nov 1966, Middle Temple
Qualifications: [LLB]

MUNIR DR ASHLEY EDWARD

1 Harcourt Buildings
2nd Floor, Temple, London EC4Y 9DA,
Telephone: 0171 353 9421/0375
E-mail:clerks@1harcourtbuildings.law.co.uk
Call Date: June 1956, Gray's Inn
Qualifications: [MA (Cantab), PhD (Lond),
M.Phil]

MUNKMAN JOHN

Chambers of Andrew Campbell QC
10 Park Square, Leeds LS1 2LH,
Telephone: 0113 2455438
E-mail: clerks@10pksq.co.uk
Call Date: Jan 1948, Middle Temple
Qualifications: [LLB]

MUNKS MRS CHRISTINE ANN

Eighteen Carlton Crescent
Southampton SO15 2XR,
Telephone: 01703 639001
Call Date: Nov 1991, Inner Temple
Qualifications: [LLB (So'ton)]

MUNONYEDI MISS IFEYINWA

Goldsmith Chambers
Ground Floor, Goldsmith Building,
Temple, London EC4Y 7BL,
Telephone: 0171 353 6802/3/4/5
E-mail:clerks@goldsmithchambers.law.co.uk
Call Date: July 1985, Gray's Inn
Pupil Master
Qualifications: [BA(Lond), Dip Law]

MUNRO KENNETH STUART

12 New Square
Lincoln's Inn, London WC2A 3SW,
Telephone: 0171 419 1212
E-mail: chambers@12newsquare.co.uk
Call Date: Nov 1973, Inner Temple
Pupil Master
Qualifications: [MA (Cantab)]

MUNRO SANDERSON WILSON

2 Dyers Buildings
London EC1N 2JT,
Telephone: 0171 404 1881
Call Date: July 1981, Gray's Inn
Pupil Master
Qualifications: [LLB (Scots)(Hons), Dip Law]

MUNRO MISS SARAH BELINDA MCLEOD

Walnut House
63 St David's Hill, Exeter, Devon,
EX4 4DW, Telephone: 01392 279751
E-mail: 106627.2451@compuserve.com
Call Date: Nov 1984, Inner Temple
Assistant Recorder
Qualifications: [BA (Exon)]

MUNRO MISS SARAH TIFFANY

High Pavement Chambers
1 High Pavement, Nottingham NG1 1HF,
Telephone: 0115 9418218
Call Date: Oct 1990, Middle Temple
Qualifications: [LLB]

MUNROE MISS VERONICA ALLISON

14 Tooks Court
Cursitor St, London EC4A 1LB,
Telephone: 0171 405 8828
E-mail: clerks@tooks.law.co.uk
Call Date: Oct 1992, Middle Temple
Qualifications: [BA (Hons)(Cantab), Diploma in Law]

MUNSI MISS AYSHEA KHATUNE

No. 6
6 Park Square, Leeds LS1 2LW,
Telephone: 0113 2459763
E-mail: chambers@no6.co.uk
Call Date: Oct 1997, Middle Temple
Qualifications: [LLB (Hons)(Leeds)]

MUNT ALASTAIR HENRY MCLAREN

King Charles House
Standard Hill, Nottingham NG1 6FX,
Telephone: 0115 9418851
E-mail: clerks@kch.co.uk
Call Date: July 1989, Gray's Inn
Qualifications: [LLB (Reading), LLM (Cantab), MPhil (Cantab)]

MUNYARD TERRY

Two Garden Court
1st Floor, Middle Temple, London
EC4Y 9BL, Telephone: 0171 353 1633
E-mail:barristers@2gardenct.law.co.uk
Call Date: July 1972, Gray's Inn
Pupil Master
Qualifications: [LLB (Lond)]

MURCH STEPHEN JAMES

11 Bolt Court (also at 7 Stone Buildings – 1st Floor)
London EC4A 3DQ,
Telephone: 0171 353 2300
E-mail: boltct11@aol.com
7 Stone Buildings (also at 11 Bolt Court)
1st Floor, Lincoln's Inn, London
WC2A 3SZ, Telephone: 0171 242 0961
E-mail:larthur@7stonebuildings.law.co.uk
Redhill Chambers
Seloduct House, 30 Station Road, Redhill,
Surrey, RH1 1NF,
Telephone: 01737 780781
Call Date: Oct 1991, Lincoln's Inn
Qualifications: [LLB (Hons) (Bucks)]

MURDOCH GORDON STUART QC (1995)

4 Paper Buildings
1st Floor, Temple, London EC4Y 7EX,
Telephone: 0171 583 0816/353 1131
E-mail: clerks@4paperbuildings.co.uk
Call Date: July 1970, Inner Temple
Recorder
Qualifications: [MA, LLB (Cantab)]

MURFITT MISS CATRIONA ANNE CAMPBELL

1 Mitre Court Buildings
Temple, London EC4Y 7BS,
Telephone: 0171 797 7070
E-mail: clerks@1mcb.com
Call Date: Nov 1981, Gray's Inn
Pupil Master, Assistant Recorder
Qualifications: [BA]

MURPHY MRS CATRIONA ANNE

1 Gray's Inn Square
Ground Floor, London WC1R 5AA,
Telephone: 0171 405 8946/7/8
Call Date: Nov 1995, Lincoln's Inn
Qualifications: [BA (Hons)]

MURPHY MISS CRESSIDA JANE

4 King's Bench Walk
2nd Floor, Temple, London EC4Y 7DL,
Telephone: 020 7353 3581
E-mail: clerks@4kbw.co.uk
Call Date: Feb 1991, Gray's Inn
Qualifications: [BA (Cantab)]

MURPHY IAN PATRICK QC (1992)

9 Park Place
Cardiff CF1 3DP,
Telephone: 01222 382731
Farrar's Building
Temple, London EC4Y 7BD,
Telephone: 0171 583 9241
E-mail:chambers@farrarsbuilding.co.uk
Call Date: July 1972, Middle Temple
Recorder
Qualifications: [LLB (Lond)]

MURPHY JAMES ST JOHN

Park Lane Chambers
19 Westgate, Leeds LS1 2RD,
Telephone: 0113 2285000
E-mail:clerks@parklanechambers.co.uk
Call Date: Nov 1993, Inner Temple
Qualifications: [BA (L'pool), CPE]

MURPHY MICHAEL JOSEPH ADRIAN QC (1993)

Paradise Chambers
26 Paradise Square, Sheffield S1 2DE,
Telephone: 0114 2738951
E-mail: timbooth@paradise-sq.co.uk
Call Date: July 1973, Inner Temple
Recorder
Qualifications: [LLB, MA]

MURPHY MICHAEL PATRICK

9 King's Bench Walk
Ground Floor, Temple, London
EC4Y 7DX, Telephone: 0171 353 7202/
3909 E-mail: 9kbw@compuserve.com
Call Date: Nov 1992, Inner Temple
Qualifications: [LLB (Essex)]

MURPHY MISS NICOLA JANE

4 King's Bench Walk
Ground/First Floor/Basement, Temple,
London EC4Y 7DL,
Telephone: 0171 822 8822
E-mail: 4kbw@barristersatlaw.com
Call Date: Oct 1995, Gray's Inn
Qualifications: [LLB (Hull)]

MURPHY PETER JOHN

30 Park Place
Cardiff CF1 3BA,
Telephone: 01222 398421
E-mail: 100757.1456@compuserve.com
Call Date: Nov 1980, Gray's Inn
Pupil Master, Assistant Recorder
Qualifications: [LLB (Leics)]

MURPHY MISS PHILOMENA CATHERINE

1 Middle Temple Lane
Temple, London EC4Y 1LT,
Telephone: 0171 583 0659 (12 Lines)
E-mail: chambers@1mtl.com
Call Date: Oct 1992, Gray's Inn
Qualifications: [BA (Hons)]

MURPHY MISS SHEILA MARY

45 Greenway
Frinton-on-Sea, Essex, CO13 9AJ,
Telephone: 01255 670699
Call Date: Oct 1992, Middle Temple
Qualifications: [LL.B (Hons)]

MURRAY ANIL PETER

Wilberforce Chambers
7 Bishop Lane, Hull, East Yorkshire,
HU1 1PA, Telephone: 01482 323264
E-mail: clerks@hullbar.demon.co.uk
Call Date: July 1989, Middle Temple
Qualifications: [LLB (Hull)]

MURRAY ASHLEY CHARLES

Oriel Chambers
14 Water Street, Liverpool L2 8TD,
Telephone: 0151 236 7191/236 4321
E-mail: clerks@oriel-chambers.co.uk
Call Date: July 1974, Middle Temple
Pupil Master, Recorder
Qualifications: [LLB (Birmingham)]

MURRAY MS CAROLE JEANNE

1 Gray's Inn Square, Chambers of the Baroness Scotland of Asthal QC
1st Floor, London WC1R 5AG,
Telephone: 0171 405 3000
E-mail: clerks@onegrays.demon.co.uk
Call Date: Nov 1989, Middle Temple
Qualifications: [MA Hons [Cantab], Dip in Law]

MURRAY MISS HARRIET CAROLINE JANE

2-3 Gray's Inn Square
Gray's Inn, London WC1R 5JH,
Telephone: 0171 242 4986
E-mail:chambers@2-3graysinnsquare.co.uk
Call Date: Nov 1992, Middle Temple
Qualifications: [B.Sc (Hons)]

MURRAY JOHN MICHAEL ANDREW

Chambers of John Hand QC
9 St John Street, Manchester M3 4DN,
Telephone: 0161 955 9000
E-mail: ninesjs@gconnect.com
Call Date: Nov 1979, Middle Temple
Pupil Master
Qualifications: [BA]

MURRAY MISS JUDITH ROWENA

4 Paper Buildings
1st Floor, Temple, London EC4Y 7EX,
Telephone: 0171 583 0816/353 1131
E-mail: clerks@4paperbuildings.co.uk
Call Date: Oct 1994, Middle Temple
Qualifications: [BA (Hons)(Oxon)]

MURRAY STEPHEN JOHN

8 Fountain Court
Steelhouse Lane, Birmingham B4 6DR,
Telephone: 0121 236 5514/5
E-mail: clerks@no8chambers.co.uk
Call Date: July 1986, Inner Temple
Pupil Master
Qualifications: [LLB (Leic)]

MURRAY-SMITH JAMES MICHAEL

8 King's Bench Walk
2nd Floor, Temple, London EC4Y 7DU,
Telephone: 0171 797 8888

8 King's Bench Walk North
1 Park Square East, Leeds LS1 2NE,
Telephone: 0113 2439797
Call Date: May 1990, Middle Temple
Qualifications: [B.A.]

MUSAALA MUKASA MISS CHRISTINE ROSE MIRANDA

Essex House Chambers
Unit 6 (Part 2nd Floor South), Stratford Office Village, 14-30 Romford Road, London E15 4BZ,
Telephone: 0181 536 1077
Call Date: Nov 1985, Gray's Inn
Qualifications: [LLB]

MUSAHEB IKBAL KEVIN

New Bailey Chambers
10 Lawson Street, Preston PR1 2QT,
Telephone: 01772 258087
Call Date: Oct 1990, Middle Temple
Qualifications: [LLB]

MUSGRAVE MISS KERRY JANE

1 Harcourt Buildings
2nd Floor, Temple, London EC4Y 9DA,
Telephone: 0171 353 9421/0375
E-mail:clerks@1harcourtbuildings.law.co.uk
Call Date: 1992, Middle Temple
Qualifications: [LLB (Hons)(Nott'm), LLM (UCL)]

MUSTAFA BIN SA'AD

146 Carshalton Park Road
Carshalton, Surrey, SM5 3SG,
Telephone: 0181 773 0531
Call Date: Nov 1981, Lincoln's Inn
Qualifications: [LLB (Hons)(LSE)]

MUSTAKIM ABDUL YUNUS AL

Call Date: May 1997, Lincoln's Inn
Qualifications: [LLB (Hons), BCL]

MUTCH MISS ALISON JANE

Phoenix Chambers
First Floor, Gray's Inn Chambers, Gray's
Inn, London WC1R 5JA,
Telephone: 0171 404 7888
E-mail:clerks@phoenix-chambers.co.uk
Call Date: Oct 1995, Middle Temple
Qualifications: [B.Sc (Hons)]

MYATT CHARLES EDWARD

Fenners Chambers
3 Madingley Road, Cambridge CB3 0EE,
Telephone: 01223 368761
E-mail: clerks@fennerschambers.co.uk
Fenners Chambers
8-12 Priestgate, Peterborough PE1 1JA,
Telephone: 01733 562030
E-mail: clerks@fennerschambers.co.uk
Call Date: Nov 1993, Gray's Inn
Qualifications: [BA (Dunelm)]

MYDEEN KALANDAR

11 Old Square
Ground Floor, Lincoln's Inn, London
WC2A 3TS, Telephone: 0171 242 5022/
405 1074
Call Date: Nov 1973, Lincoln's Inn
Pupil Master
Qualifications: [LLB]

MYERS ALLAN JAMES

4 Field Court
Gray's Inn, London WC1R 5EA,
Telephone: 0171 440 6900
E-mail: chambers@4fieldcourt.co.uk
Call Date: May 1988, Lincoln's Inn
Qualifications: [BCL (Hons) Oxon, BA, LLB
(Hons) , Melbourne]

MYERS BARRY

3 Temple Gardens
3rd Floor, Temple, London EC4Y 9AU,
Telephone: 0171 583 0010
Call Date: Nov 1988, Inner Temple
Qualifications: [BA (Hull), Dip Law]

MYERS BENJAMIN JOHN

Young Street Chambers
38 Young Street, Manchester M3 3FT,
Telephone: 0161 833 0489
E-mail: clerks@young-st-chambers.com
Call Date: Oct 1994, Inner Temple
Qualifications: [BA (Leeds), CPE (Lond)]

MYERS KEITH

**Gray's Inn Chambers, The Chambers of
Norman Patterson**
First Floor, Gray's Inn Chambers, Gray's
Inn, London WC1R 5JA,
Telephone: 0171 831 5344
E-mail: s.mcblain@btinternet.com
Call Date: Nov 1996, Inner Temple
Qualifications: [LLB (Hons)(Middx)]

MYERS SIMON MARTIN

**1 Gray's Inn Square, Chambers of the
Baroness Scotland of Asthal QC**
1st Floor, London WC1R 5AG,
Telephone: 0171 405 3000
E-mail: clerks@onegrays.demon.co.uk
Call Date: Nov 1987, Middle Temple
Pupil Master
Qualifications: [BA (Bristol) Dip, Law (City)]

MYERSON DAVID SIMON

Park Court Chambers
16 Park Place, Leeds LS1 2SJ,
Telephone: 0113 2433277
Call Date: July 1986, Middle Temple
Pupil Master
Qualifications: [MA (Cantab)]

MYERSON MISS VICTORIA

Lion Court
Chancery House, 53-64 Chancery Lane,
London WC2A 1SJ,
Telephone: 0171 404 6565
Call Date: Nov 1994, Inner Temple
Qualifications: [BA (Lond), CPE]

MYLNE NIGEL JAMES QC (1984)

2 Harcourt Buildings
1st Floor, Temple, London EC4Y 9DB,
Telephone: 020 7353 2112
Call Date: Feb 1963, Middle Temple
Recorder

MYLONAS-WIDDALL MICHAEL JOHN

4 Brick Court
Temple, London EC4Y 9AD,
Telephone: 0171 797 8910
E-mail: medhurst@dial.pipex.com
Call Date: July 1988, Gray's Inn
Pupil Master
Qualifications: [LLB (Bucks)]

MYLVAGANAM MS JANAKI INDRANI

Chambers of Janaki Mylvaganam
8B Aristole Road, London SW4 2HZ,
Telephone: 0171 627 4006
Call Date: July 1983, Gray's Inn
Qualifications: [BA (Kent)]

MYLVAGANAM PAUL JOSEPH PARAM SOTHY

2 Paper Buildings
1st Floor, Temple, London EC4Y 7ET,
Telephone: 020 7556 5500
E-mail: clerks@2pbbarristers.co.uk
Call Date: Nov 1993, Middle Temple
Qualifications: [BA (Hons)(Oxon), CPE
(Lond)]

MYNORS CHARLES BASKERVILLE

2 Harcourt Buildings
2nd Floor, Temple, London EC4Y 9DB,
Telephone: 020 7353 8415
E-mail: clerks@2hb.law.co.uk
Call Date: Nov 1988, Middle Temple
Pupil Master
Qualifications: [MA (Cantab), MA (Shef), Dip
Law, FRTPI, ARICS]

MYTTON PAUL VINCENT

Furnival Chambers
32 Furnival Street, London EC4A 1JQ,
Telephone: 0171 405 3232
E-mail: clerks@furnivallaw.co.uk
Call Date: July 1982, Lincoln's Inn
Pupil Master
Qualifications: [LLB]

NABI ZIA UL-HAQ

1 Pump Court
Lower Ground Floor, Temple, London
EC4Y 7AB, Telephone: 0171 583 2012/
353 4341
E-mail: [name]@1pumpcourt.co.uk
Call Date: Nov 1991, Middle Temple
Qualifications: [LLB Hons (Essex)]

NABIJOU DR SHARIFEH

10 King's Bench Walk
Ground Floor, Temple, London
EC4Y 7EB, Telephone: 0171 353 7742
E-mail: 10kbw@lineone.net
Call Date: 1996, Inner Temple
Qualifications: [BSc (Leeds), MSc DIC (Imp.
Coll), PhD (Lond)(Imp.Coll), CPE]

NADIM AHMED

Young Street Chambers
38 Young Street, Manchester M3 3FT,
Telephone: 0161 833 0489
E-mail: clerks@young-st-chambers.com
Call Date: July 1982, Lincoln's Inn
Pupil Master
Qualifications: [BA]

NAIDOO SEAN VAN

Littman Chambers
12 Gray's Inn Square, London WC1R 5JP,
Telephone: 020 7404 4866
E-mail: admin@littmanchambers.com
Call Date: July 1990, Lincoln's Inn
Pupil Master
Qualifications: [B.Proc,LLB (Wits) , BA,BCL
(Oxon)]

NAIK GAURANG RAMANLAL

9 Gough Square
London EC4A 3DE,
Telephone: 020 7832 0500
E-mail: clerks@9goughsq.co.uk
Call Date: July 1985, Gray's Inn
Pupil Master
Qualifications: [BSc, Dip Law]

NAIK MISS SONALI

Two Garden Court
1st Floor, Middle Temple, London
EC4Y 9BL, Telephone: 0171 353 1633
E-mail:barristers@2gardenct.law.co.uk
Call Date: Nov 1991, Middle Temple
Qualifications: [BA Hons (Oxon)]

NAIK TIMOTHY ANIL

Holborn Chambers
6 Gate Street, Lincoln's Inn Fields, London
WC2A 3HP, Telephone: 0171 242 6060
Call Date: Nov 1994, Gray's Inn
Qualifications: [LLB]

NAISH CHRISTOPHER JOHN

Southernhay Chambers
33 Southernhay East, Exeter, Devon,
EX1 1NX, Telephone: 01392 255777
E-mail:southernhay.chambers@lineone.net
Call Date: July 1980, Inner Temple
Pupil Master
Qualifications: [LLB]

NAISH RICHARD DENNIS MACAVOY

2nd Floor, Francis Taylor Building
Temple, London EC4Y 7BY,
Telephone: 0171 353 9942/3157
Call Date: Nov 1966, Middle Temple
Qualifications: [BA (Oxon)]

NAJAND MS MARYAM

6 King's Bench Walk
Ground, Third & Fourth Floors, Temple,
London EC4Y 7DR,
Telephone: 0171 353 4931/583 0695
Call Date: Nov 1993, Middle Temple
Qualifications: [BSc (Hons)(City), Dip in Law
(City)]

NALL-CAIN THE HON RICHARD CHRISTOPHER PHILIP

St Albans Chambers
Dolphin Lodge, Dolphin Yard, Holywell
Hill, St Albans, Herts, AL1 1EX,
Telephone: 01727 843383
Call Date: 1997, Inner Temple
Qualifications: [LLB (Herts)]

NANCE FRANCIS PETER

Exchange Chambers
Pearl Assurance House, Derby Square,
Liverpool L2 9XX,
Telephone: 0151 236 7747
E-mail:exchangechambers@btinternet.com
Call Date: Nov 1970, Gray's Inn
Pupil Master

NAPIER PROFESSOR BRIAN WILLIAM

Fountain Court
Temple, London EC4Y 9DH,
Telephone: 0171 583 3335
E-mail: chambers@fountaincourt.co.uk
Call Date: July 1990, Middle Temple
Qualifications: [MA, PhD (Cantab), LLB
(Edin)]

NAPTHINE DAVID ROBERT GUY

High Pavement Chambers
1 High Pavement, Nottingham NG1 1HF,
Telephone: 0115 9418218
Call Date: Nov 1979, Inner Temple
Pupil Master
Qualifications: [BA]

NAPTHINE (GODFREY) JOHN

High Pavement Chambers
1 High Pavement, Nottingham NG1 1HF,
Telephone: 0115 9418218
Call Date: July 1983, Inner Temple
Qualifications: [BA]

NAQSHBANDI MISS SABA SHAFIQUE

3 Raymond Buildings
Gray's Inn, London WC1R 5BH,
Telephone: 020 7831 3833
E-mail:chambers@threeraymond.demon.co.uk
Call Date: Oct 1996, Middle Temple
Qualifications: [LLB (Hons), LLM (Lond)]

NARAYAN HIRANYA GARBHA

Cobden House Chambers
19 Quay Street, Manchester M3 3HN,
Telephone: 0161 833 6000
E-mail: clerks@cobden.co.uk
Call Date: Nov 1970, Lincoln's Inn
Pupil Master, Recorder

NARDECCHIA NICHOLAS CHARLES

2-3 Gray's Inn Square
Gray's Inn, London WC1R 5JH,
Telephone: 0171 242 4986
E-mail:chambers@2-3graysinnsquare.co.uk
Call Date: Nov 1974, Middle Temple
Qualifications: [MA (Cantab)]

NARDELL GORDON LAWRENCE

6 Pump Court
1st Floor, Temple, London EC4Y 7AR,
Telephone: 0171 797 8400
E-mail: clerks@6pumpcourt.co.uk
6-8 Mill Street
Maidstone, Kent, ME15 6XH,
Telephone: 01622 688094
E-mail: annexe@6pumpcourt.co.uk
Call Date: 1995, Inner Temple
Qualifications: [LLB (Hons)(Leeds)]

NASH JONATHAN SCOTT

3 Verulam Buildings
London WC1R 5NT,
Telephone: 0171 831 8441
E-mail: clerks@3verulam.co.uk
Call Date: Nov 1986, Gray's Inn
Pupil Master
Qualifications: [BA(Oxon)]

NASHASHIBI ANWAR DAVID

9 Bedford Row
London WC1R 4AZ,
Telephone: 0171 242 3555
E-mail: clerks@9br.co.uk
Call Date: Nov 1995, Middle Temple
Qualifications: [BA (Hons)(Manch)]

NASIR JAMAL JAMIL

Chambers of Dr Jamal Nasir
1st Floor, Lincoln's Inn, London
WC2A 3RH, Telephone: 0171 405 3818/9
Call Date: Jan 1948, Lincoln's Inn
Qualifications: [BA, PhD (Lond)]

NASSAR MISS VICTORIA KATIE

55B Cavendish Road
Brondesbury, London NW2 3TN,
Telephone: 0181 830 1495
Call Date: Feb 1994, Gray's Inn
Qualifications: [BSc (B'ham), CPE (Manch)]

NATHAN MISS APARNA

Gray's Inn Tax Chambers
3rd Floor, Gray's Inn Chambers, Gray's
Inn, London WC1R 5JA,
Telephone: 0171 242 2642
E-mail: clerks@taxbar.com
Call Date: Nov 1994, Middle Temple
Qualifications: [LLB (Hons), LLM]

NATHAN DAVID BRIAN

10 King's Bench Walk
1st Floor, Temple, London EC4Y 7EB,
Telephone: 0171 353 2501
Call Date: Nov 1971, Middle Temple
Pupil Master
Qualifications: [LLB]

NATHAN PETER JOSEPH

One Garden Court Family Law Chambers
Ground Floor, Temple, London
EC4Y 9BJ, Telephone: 0171 797 7900
E-mail: clerks@onegardencourt.co.uk
Call Date: July 1973, Inner Temple
Pupil Master
Qualifications: [LLM (Lond)]

NATHAN PHILIP GABRIEL

Earl Street Chambers
47 Earl Street, Maidstone, Kent,
ME14 1PD, Telephone: 01622 671222
E-mail: gunner-sparks@msn.com
Call Date: Mar 1996, Lincoln's Inn
Qualifications: [LLB (Hons)]

NATHAN STEPHEN ANDREW QC (1993)

Blackstone Chambers
Blackstone House, Temple, London
EC4Y 9BW, Telephone: 0171 583 1770
E-mail:clerks@blackstonechambers.com
Call Date: Nov 1969, Middle Temple
Assistant Recorder
Qualifications: [MA (Oxon)]

NAUGHTON PHILIP ANTHONY QC (1988)

3 Serjeants' Inn
London EC4Y 1BQ,
Telephone: 0171 353 5537
E-mail: clerks@3serjeantsinn.com
Call Date: Apr 1970, Gray's Inn
Qualifications: [LLB (Nott'm)]

NAVARATNE MR FRANCIS REGINALD

The Chambers of Mr Ali Mohammed Azhar
Basement, 9 King's Bench Walk, Temple,
London EC4Y 7DX,
Telephone: 0171 353 9564
E-mail: jvlee@btinternet.com
Call Date: Nov 1990, Lincoln's Inn
Qualifications: [Bsc (Lond) , MSc
(Manchester), LLM (Leic), MA (Lond),
C.Eng, MICE, MISTRUCTE, FCIArb]

NAWAZ AMJAD

Coleridge Chambers
Citadel, 190 Corporation Street,
Birmingham B4 6QD,
Telephone: 0121 233 8500
Call Date: July 1983, Lincoln's Inn
Qualifications: [BA (Aston)]

NAWAZ MOHAMMED

Lincoln House Chambers
5th Floor, Lincoln House, 1 Brazennose
Street, Manchester M2 5EL,
Telephone: 0161 832 5701
E-mail: info@lincolnhse.co.uk
Call Date: Nov 1995, Lincoln's Inn
Qualifications: [LLB, LLM (Cantab)]

NAYLOR JONATHAN PETER

King's Chambers
5a Gildredge Road, Eastbourne, East
Sussex, BN21 4RB,
Telephone: 01323 416053
Call Date: Oct 1995, Lincoln's Inn
Qualifications: [LLB (Hons)(Lond)]

NAYLOR DR KEVIN MICHAEL THOMAS

8 King Street Chambers
8 King Street, Manchester M2 6AQ,
Telephone: 0161 834 9560
E-mail: eightking@aol.com
Call Date: Oct 1992, Lincoln's Inn
Qualifications: [MB.ChB, LLB(Hons)(Sheff),
LLM, MRCGP]

NAZARETH MISS MELANIE BERNADETTE

Gray's Inn Chambers
5th Floor, Gray's Inn, London WC1R 5JA,
Telephone: 0171 404 1111
Call Date: July 1984, Inner Temple
Qualifications: [BSc (Lond), Dip Law]

NAZIR KAISER

Park Lane Chambers
19 Westgate, Leeds LS1 2RD,
Telephone: 0113 2285000
E-mail:clerks@parklanechambers.co.uk
Call Date: Nov 1991, Lincoln's Inn
Qualifications: [LLB (Hons)]

NDLOVU LAZARUS

12 Old Square
1st Floor, Lincoln's Inn, London
WC2A 3TX, Telephone: 0171 404 0875
Call Date: July 1979, Lincoln's Inn
Qualifications: [BA,LLM (Lond)]

NDUKA-EZE CHUKWUEMEKA CECIL

New Court Chambers
Gazette Building, 168 Corporation Street,
Birmingham B4 6TZ,
Telephone: 0121 693 6656
Call Date: Oct 1990, Middle Temple
Qualifications: [LLB (Warw)]

NEAL ALAN CHRISTOPHER

2 New Street
Leicester LE1 5NA,
Telephone: 0116 2625906
E-mail: clerks@2newstreet.co.uk
Call Date: July 1975, Gray's Inn
Qualifications: [LLB (Warks), LLM (Lond),
DGLS (Stockholm)]

NEALE MISS FIONA ROSALIND

3 Serjeants' Inn
London EC4Y 1BQ,
Telephone: 0171 353 5537
E-mail: clerks@3serjeantsinn.com
Call Date: July 1981, Middle Temple
Pupil Master
Qualifications: [LLB (Lond)]

NEALE NICHOLAS LAWRENCE

Paradise Chambers
26 Paradise Square, Sheffield S1 2DE,
Telephone: 0114 2738951
E-mail: timbooth@paradise-sq.co.uk
Call Date: July 1972, Gray's Inn
Qualifications: [BA]

NEALE STUART RONALD

Cobden House Chambers
19 Quay Street, Manchester M3 3HN,
Telephone: 0161 833 6000
E-mail: clerks@cobden.co.uk
Call Date: July 1976, Middle Temple
Pupil Master
Qualifications: [MA (Cantab)]

NEAMAN SAMUEL LISTER

4 Paper Buildings
1st Floor, Temple, London EC4Y 7EX,
Telephone: 0171 583 0816/353 1131
E-mail: clerks@4paperbuildings.co.uk
Call Date: July 1988, Inner Temple
Pupil Master
Qualifications: [MA (Oxon), Dip Law (City)]

NEATHEY MISS RONA VANESSA

6 King's Bench Walk
Ground, Third & Fourth Floors, Temple,
London EC4Y 7DR,
Telephone: 0171 353 4931/583 0695
Call Date: Nov 1990, Inner Temple
Qualifications: [LLB (Hons)]

NEAVES ANDREW MICHAEL

Chambers of Michael Pert QC
36 Bedford Row, London WC1R 4JH,
Telephone: 0171 421 8000
E-mail: 36bedfordrow@link.org
Chambers of Michael Pert QC
24 Albion Place, Northampton NN1 1UD,
Telephone: 01604 602333

Chambers of Michael Pert QC
104 New Walk, Leicester LE1 7EA,
Telephone: 0116 249 2020
Call Date: July 1977, Gray's Inn
Pupil Master
Qualifications: [LLB]

NEILL ROBERT JAMES MACGILLIVRAY

3 Hare Court
1 Little Essex Street, London WC2R 3LD,
Telephone: 0171 395 2000
Call Date: July 1975, Middle Temple
Qualifications: [LLB (Lond)]

NEILL OF BLADEN LORD QC (1966)

One Hare Court
1st Floor, Temple, London EC4Y 7BE,
Telephone: 020 7353 3171
E-mail:admin-oneharecourt@btinternet.com
Call Date: Nov 1951, Gray's Inn
Qualifications: [BCL, MA, DCL (Oxon)]

NEILSON MISS LOUISE

9 Gough Square
London EC4A 3DE,
Telephone: 020 7832 0500
E-mail: clerks@9goughsq.co.uk
Call Date: Oct 1994, Middle Temple
Qualifications: [BA (Hons), LLM (Cantab)]

NEISH ANDREW GRAHAM

4 Pump Court
Temple, London EC4Y 7AN,
Telephone: 020 7842 5555
E-mail:chambers@4pumpcourt.law.co.uk
Call Date: July 1988, Lincoln's Inn
Pupil Master
Qualifications: [MA (Hons) St Andrews, Dip
Law]

NELSON CAIRNS LOUIS DAVID

5 King's Bench Walk
Temple, London EC4Y 7DN,
Telephone: 0171 353 5638
Call Date: Nov 1987, Gray's Inn
Pupil Master
Qualifications: [LLB (Lond)]

D

NELSON GILES YORICK

5 King's Bench Walk
Temple, London EC4Y 7DN,
Telephone: 0171 353 5638
Call Date: Feb 1995, Inner Temple
Qualifications: [BSc (Bris), CPE]

NELSON MS JULIA MARIA

Broadway House Chambers
Broadway House, 9 Bank Street, Bradford,
West Yorkshire, BD1 1TW,
Telephone: 01274 722560
E-mail: clerks@broadwayhouse.co.uk
Broadway House Chambers
31 Park Square West, Leeds LS1 2PF,
Telephone: 0113 246 2600
Call Date: Nov 1993, Gray's Inn
Qualifications: [BA (Manch)]

NELSON MICHAEL PAUL

4 King's Bench Walk
Ground/First Floor/Basement, Temple,
London EC4Y 7DL,
Telephone: 0171 822 8822
E-mail: 4kbw@barristersatlaw.com
Call Date: Oct 1992, Lincoln's Inn
Qualifications: [LLB(Hons)]

NELSON MISS MICHELLE

18 Red Lion Court
(Off Fleet Street), London EC4A 3EB,
Telephone: 0171 520 6000
E-mail: chambers@18rlc.co.uk
Thornwood House
102 New London Road, Chelmsford,
Essex, CM2 0RG,
Telephone: 01245 280880
E-mail: chambers@18rlc.co.uk
Call Date: Oct 1994, Middle Temple
Qualifications: [BSc (Hons)(Brunel), LLB
(Hons)(Lond)]

NELSON VINCENT LEONARD

39 Essex Street
London WC2R 3AT,
Telephone: 0171 832 1111
E-mail: clerks@39essex.co.uk
Call Date: Nov 1980, Inner Temple
Qualifications: [LLB (Birmingham)]

NESBITT TIMOTHY JOHN ROBERT

199 Strand
London WC2R 1DR,
Telephone: 0171 379 9779
E-mail: chambers@199strand.co.uk
Call Date: Feb 1991, Middle Temple
Qualifications: [BA (Dunelm), Dip Law
(PCL)]

NEUBERT JOLYON NICHOLAS

1 Gray's Inn Square
Ground Floor, London WC1R 5AA,
Telephone: 0171 405 8946/7/8
Call Date: July 1989, Middle Temple
Qualifications: [LLB (Hons)]

NEUFELD MISS MICHAELA

95A Chancery Lane
London WC2A 1DT,
Telephone: 0171 405 3101
Call Date: July 1990, Middle Temple
Qualifications: [LLB (Lond)]

NEVILLE STEPHEN JOHN

Gough Square Chambers
6-7 Gough Square, London EC4A 3DE,
Telephone: 0171 353 0924
E-mail: gsc@goughsq.co.uk
Call Date: Nov 1986, Middle Temple
Pupil Master
Qualifications: [MA(Cantab)]

NEVILLE-CLARKE SEBASTIAN ADRIAN BENNETT

1 Crown Office Row
3rd Floor, Temple, London EC4Y 7HH,
Telephone: 0171 583 9292
E-mail: onecor@link.org
Call Date: Nov 1973, Inner Temple
Pupil Master
Qualifications: [BA (Oxon)]

NEWBERRY CLIVE DOUGLAS QC (1993)

2 Harcourt Buildings
2nd Floor, Temple, London EC4Y 9DB,
Telephone: 020 7353 8415
E-mail: clerks@2hb.law.co.uk
Call Date: July 1978, Inner Temple

NEWBERRY DAVID JOHN

Lion Court
Chancery House, 53-64 Chancery Lane,
London WC2A 1SJ,
Telephone: 0171 404 6565
Call Date: Oct 1990, Middle Temple
Qualifications: [BA, Dip Law]

NEWBERY MISS FREYA PATRICIA

12 King's Bench Walk
Temple, London EC4Y 7EL,
Telephone: 0171 583 0811
E-mail: chambers@12kbw.co.uk
Call Date: Nov 1986, Middle Temple
Pupil Master
Qualifications: [MA (Cantab)]

NEWBON IAN

Broadway House Chambers
Broadway House, 9 Bank Street, Bradford,
West Yorkshire, BD1 1TW,
Telephone: 01274 722560
E-mail: clerks@broadwayhouse.co.uk
Broadway House Chambers
31 Park Square West, Leeds LS1 2PF,
Telephone: 0113 246 2600
Call Date: Feb 1977, Middle Temple
Pupil Master
Qualifications: [LLB (Leeds)]

NEWBURY RICHARD LENNOX

Sovereign Chambers
25 Park Square, Leeds LS1 2PW,
Telephone: 0113 2451841/2/3
E-mail:sovereignchambers@btinternet.com
Call Date: July 1976, Gray's Inn
Pupil Master
Qualifications: [LLB (Hons) (New)]

NEWCOMBE ANDREW BENNETT

2 Harcourt Buildings
2nd Floor, Temple, London EC4Y 9DB,
Telephone: 020 7353 8415
E-mail: clerks@2hb.law.co.uk
Call Date: July 1987, Middle Temple
Qualifications: [BA (Dunelm)]

NEWCOMBE PAUL ANTHONY

Baker Street Chambers
9 Baker Street, Middlesbrough TS1 2LF,
Telephone: 01642 873873
Call Date: Feb 1991, Inner Temple
Qualifications: [LLB (Hons)]

NEWCOMBE TIMOTHY RICHARD

St Paul's House
5th Floor, St Paul's House, 23 Park Square
South, Leeds LS1 2ND,
Telephone: 0113 2455866
E-mail: catherinegrimshaw@stpauls-
chambers.demon.co.uk
Call Date: Nov 1972, Inner Temple
Qualifications: [TD]

NEWDICK CHRISTOPHER

Call Date: Feb 1983, Gray's Inn
Qualifications: [BA, LLM (Lond)]

NEWELL MISS CHARLOTTE ANNE

Mitre Court Chambers
3rd Floor, Temple, London EC4Y 7BP,
Telephone: 0171 353 9394
E-mail: mitrecourt.com
Call Date: Oct 1994, Gray's Inn
Qualifications: [LLB]

NEWELL SIMON PETER

15 Winckley Square
Preston PR1 3JJ,
Telephone: 01772 252828
E-mail:clerks@winckleysq.demon.co.uk
Call Date: Nov 1973, Inner Temple
Pupil Master
Qualifications: [LLB]

NEWEY GUY RICHARD

7 Stone Buildings
Ground Floor, Lincoln's Inn, London
WC2A 3SZ, Telephone: 0171 405 3886/
242 3546 E-mail: chaldous@vossnet.co.uk
Call Date: July 1982, Middle Temple
Pupil Master
Qualifications: [MA, LLM (Cantab)]

NEWMAN ALAN RONALD HARVEY QC (1989)

Cloisters
1 Pump Court, Temple, London
EC4Y 7AA, Telephone: 0171 827 4000
E-mail: clerks@cloisters.com
Call Date: Nov 1968, Middle Temple
Qualifications: [MA, LLB (Cantab)]

NEWMAN AUSTIN ERIC

9 Woodhouse Square
Leeds LS3 1AD,
Telephone: 0113 2451986
E-mail: clerks@9woodhouse.co.uk
Call Date: Nov 1987, Inner Temple
Qualifications: [LLB, LLM]

NEWMAN BENEDICT GEORGE

One Paper Buildings
Ground Floor, Temple, London
EC4Y 7EP, Telephone: 0171 583 7355
E-mail: clerks@1pb.co.uk
Call Date: Nov 1991, Middle Temple
Qualifications: [LLB Hons (Bris)]

NEWMAN MISS CATHERINE MARY QC (1995)

13 Old Square
Ground Floor, Lincoln's Inn, London
WC2A 3UA, Telephone: 0171 404 4800
E-mail: clerks@13oldsquare.law.co.uk
Call Date: July 1979, Middle Temple
Assistant Recorder
Qualifications: [LLB (Hons) (Lond)]

Fax: 0171 405 4267; DX: LDE 326

Types of work: Chancery (general), Chancery land law, Commercial, Commercial litigation, Company and commercial, Crime – corporate fraud, Equity, wills and trusts, Financial services, Insolvency, Partnerships, Probate and administration, Professional negligence

Awards and memberships: Harmsworth Scholar of the Middle Temple 1979-81

Languages spoken: French

Publications: Member of Editorial Board of Sweet & Maxwell's *The Insolvency Lawyer*

Reported Cases: *Trident International v Hamlet Plc*, [1998] 2 BCLC 164, 1998. Lien or floating charge; insolvency.
Richbell Strategic Holdings Plc, [1997] 2 BCLC 429, 1997. Winding up.
Hazell v Hammersmith and Fulham LBC, [1992] 2 AC 1, 1992. Powers of local authorities to enter interest rate swap contracts.
Nemgia Ltd v AGF (UK) Ltd, [1997] LRLR 159, 1997. Net loss approach to damages.
Satnam Investments Ltd v Dunlop Heywood & Others, [1999] All ER 652 (CA), 1998. Fiduciary duty, constructive trusts.

Additional Information
Considerable experience in insolvency matters (Maxwell, BCCI) including the insolvency of insurance companies (see, for example, *Transit Casualty Co v The Policyholders' Protection Board* [1992] 2 Lloyd's Rep 358). Undertakes broad range of work including statutory construction (see for example *NRDC v The Wellcome Foundation* [1991] FSR 663), the operation of commercial contracts; professional negligence (especially lawyers, accountants and financial advisers), partnership disputes; contentious trusts work, land law. Accepts appointments to arbitrate.

NEWMAN MS INGRID

Hardwicke Building
New Square, Lincoln's Inn, London
WC2A 3SB, Telephone: 020 7242 2523
E-mail: clerks@hardwicke.co.uk
Call Date: Oct 1992, Inner Temple
Qualifications: [LLB (Lond)]

NEWMAN MISS JANET MARGARET

St Ive's Chambers
Whittall Street, Birmingham B4 6DH,
Telephone: 0121 236 0863/5720
E-mail:stives.headofchambers@btinternet.com
Call Date: 1990, Inner Temple
Qualifications: [LLB (Hons) (L'pool)]

NEWMAN PAUL LANCE

Wilberforce Chambers
8 New Square, Lincoln's Inn, London
WC2A 3QP, Telephone: 0171 306 0102
E-mail: chambers@wilberforce.co.uk
Call Date: Oct 1991, Lincoln's Inn
Qualifications: [MA (Hons) (Cantab), LLM (Harvard)]

Types of work: Chancery (general), Equity, wills and trusts, Financial services, Pensions, Professional negligence

NEWMAN PHILIP ADRIAN

1 Gray's Inn Square, Chambers of the Baroness Scotland of Asthal QC
1st Floor, London WC1R 5AG,
Telephone: 0171 405 3000
E-mail: clerks@onegrays.demon.co.uk
Call Date: Nov 1977, Gray's Inn
Pupil Master
Qualifications: [LLM (Lond), FCIArb]

NEWMAN TIMOTHY JOHN

5 Fountain Court
Steelhouse Lane, Birmingham B4 6DR,
Telephone: 0121 606 0500
E-mail:clerks@5fountaincourt.law.co.uk
Call Date: July 1981, Gray's Inn
Qualifications: [BA]

NEWSOM GEORGE LUCIEN

Guildhall Chambers
22-26 Broad Street, Bristol BS1 2HG,
Telephone: 0117 9273366
E-mail:civil.clerks@guildhallchambers.co.uk and criminal.clerks@guildhallchambers.co.uk
The Chambers of Leolin Price CBE, QC
10 Old Square, Lincoln's Inn, London
WC2A 3SU, Telephone: 0171 405 0758
Call Date: Nov 1973, Lincoln's Inn
Pupil Master
Qualifications: [MA (Oxon) FCIArb]

NEWTON ANDREW DAVID

1 Middle Temple Lane
Temple, London EC4Y 1LT,
Telephone: 0171 583 0659 (12 Lines)
E-mail: chambers@1mtl.co.uk
Call Date: Nov 1989, Inner Temple
Qualifications: [MA (Oxon), Dip Law (City), LLM]

NEWTON MISS CLAIRE ELAINE MARIA BAILEY

Goldsmith Building
1st Floor, Temple, London EC4Y 7BL,
Telephone: 0171 353 7881
E-mail:clerks@goldsmith-building.law.co.uk
Call Date: Oct 1992, Gray's Inn
Qualifications: [LL.B (Lond)]

NEWTON CLIVE RICHARD

One King's Bench Walk
1st Floor, Temple, London EC4Y 7DB,
Telephone: 0171 936 1500
E-mail: ddear@1kbw.co.uk
Call Date: Nov 1968, Middle Temple
Pupil Master
Qualifications: [MA, BCL (Oxon)]

NEWTON JOHN SIMON

Derby Square Chambers
Merchants Court, Derby Square, Liverpool
L2 1TS, Telephone: 0151 709 4222
E-mail:mail.derbysquare@pop3.hiway.co.uk
Call Date: July 1970, Middle Temple
Pupil Master
Qualifications: [LLB (Hons) (London), Diplome de l'ecole, Int'l de droit du, travail compare]

NEWTON MISS LESLEY ANNE

Young Street Chambers
38 Young Street, Manchester M3 3FT,
Telephone: 0161 833 0489
E-mail: clerks@young-st-chambers.com
Call Date: Nov 1977, Middle Temple
Pupil Master, Assistant Recorder
Qualifications: [LLB]

NEWTON PHILIP

Becket Chambers
17 New Dover Road, Canterbury, Kent,
CT1 3AS, Telephone: 01227 786331
Call Date: July 1984, Middle Temple
Pupil Master
Qualifications: [BA (Hons), LLM, Dip.Int.Human Rights, (Strasbourg)]

NEWTON RODERICK BRIAN

East Anglian Chambers
Gresham House, 5 Museum Street,
Ipswich, Suffolk, IP1 1HQ,
Telephone: 01473 214481
E-mail: ipswich@ealaw.co.uk
East Anglian Chambers
52 North Hill, Colchester, Essex, CO1 1PY,
Telephone: 01206 572756
E-mail: colchester@ealaw.co.uk

D

East Anglian Chambers
57 London Street, Norwich NR2 1HL,
Telephone: 01603 617351
E-mail: norwich@ealaw.co.uk
Call Date: July 1982, Middle Temple
Pupil Master, Assistant Recorder
Qualifications: [BA (Hons)]

NEWTON STUART RICHARD JAMES

15 North Church Street Chambers
15 North Church Street, Sheffield
S1 2DH, Telephone: 0114 2759708/
2738380
Call Date: Nov 1993, Middle Temple
Qualifications: [BA (Hons)(Lond), CPE]

NEWTON-PRICE JAMES EDWARD

Pump Court Chambers
Upper Ground Floor, 3 Pump Court,
Temple, London EC4Y 7AJ,
Telephone: 0171 353 0711
E-mail: clerks@3pumpcourt.com
Pump Court Chambers
31 Southgate Street, Winchester
SO23 9EE, Telephone: 01962 868161
E-mail: clerks@3pumpcourt.com
Pump Court Chambers
5 Temple Chambers, Temple Street,
Swindon SN1 1SQ,
Telephone: 01793 539899
E-mail: clerks@3pumpcourt.com
Call Date: Oct 1992, Middle Temple
Qualifications: [BA (Hons)]

NG ALEX CHING-WONG

Pepys' Chambers
17 Fleet Street, London EC4Y 1AA,
Telephone: 0171 936 2710
Call Date: Feb 1991, Gray's Inn
Qualifications: [BA, MA (Hong Kong), LLB
(Lond)]

NG RAY KIAN HIN

Two Crown Office Row
Ground Floor, Temple, London
EC4Y 7HJ, Telephone: 020 7797 8100
E-mail: mail@2cor.co.uk, or to individual
barristers at: [barrister's
surname]@2cor.co.uk
Call Date: July 1987, Inner Temple
Qualifications: [BA (Dunelm)]

NIBLETT ANTHONY IAN

1 Crown Office Row
Ground Floor, Temple, London
EC4Y 7HH, Telephone: 0171 797 7500
E-mail: mail@onecrownofficerow.com
Crown Office Row Chambers
Blenheim House, 120 Church Street,
Brighton, Sussex, BN1 1WH,
Telephone: 01273 625625
E-mail: crownofficerow@clara.net
Call Date: 1976, Inner Temple
Pupil Master, Recorder
Qualifications: [LLB.]

NIBLETT PROFESSOR GEORGE BRYAN FRANCIS

Lancaster Building
77 Deansgate, Manchester M3 2BW,
Telephone: 0161 661 4444/0171 649 9872
E-mail: sandra@lbnipc.com
Call Date: Nov 1966, Inner Temple
Qualifications: [MSc,PhD , FCIArb]

NICE GEOFFREY QC (1990)

Farrar's Building
Temple, London EC4Y 7BD,
Telephone: 0171 583 9241
E-mail:chambers@farrarsbuilding.co.uk
Call Date: July 1971, Inner Temple
Recorder
Qualifications: [MA (Oxon)]

NICHOL SIMON BEDE

Cobden House Chambers
19 Quay Street, Manchester M3 3HN,
Telephone: 0161 833 6000
E-mail: clerks@cobden.co.uk
Call Date: May 1994, Lincoln's Inn
Qualifications: [BSc (Hons, Manch)]

NICHOLAS MISS GEORGINA MARY

Lion Court
Chancery House, 53-64 Chancery Lane,
London WC2A 1SJ,
Telephone: 0171 404 6565
Call Date: July 1983, Gray's Inn
Pupil Master
Qualifications: [BA]

NICHOLES MS CATHERINE MARGARET ELIZABETH

4 Brick Court
Ground Floor, Temple, London
EC4Y 9AD, Telephone: 0171 797 7766
E-mail: chambers@4brick.co.uk
Call Date: May 1977, Inner Temple
Pupil Master
Qualifications: [LLB (Lond)]

NICHOLLS CHRISTOPHER BENJAMIN

1 Fountain Court
Steelhouse Lane, Birmingham B4 6DR,
Telephone: 0121 236 5721
Call Date: July 1978, Gray's Inn
Qualifications: [BA (Cantab), Dip ECL
(Lond), LLM (Wales)]

NICHOLLS CLIVE VICTOR QC (1982)

3 Raymond Buildings
Gray's Inn, London WC1R 5BH,
Telephone: 020 7831 3833
E-mail:chambers@threeraymond.demon.co.u
k
Call Date: May 1957, Gray's Inn
Qualifications: [MA, LLM]

NICHOLLS COLIN ALFRED ARTHUR QC (1981)

3 Raymond Buildings
Gray's Inn, London WC1R 5BH,
Telephone: 020 7831 3833
E-mail:chambers@threeraymond.demon.co.u
k
Call Date: July 1957, Gray's Inn
Recorder
Qualifications: [MA, LLB]

NICHOLLS MRS (DEBORAH) JANE

Oriel Chambers
14 Water Street, Liverpool L2 8TD,
Telephone: 0151 236 7191/236 4321
E-mail: clerks@oriel-chambers.co.uk
Call Date: Nov 1989, Inner Temple
Qualifications: [BA (Keele)]

NICHOLLS MISS ELIZABETH JANE

Lincoln House Chambers
5th Floor, Lincoln House, 1 Brazennose
Street, Manchester M2 5EL,
Telephone: 0161 832 5701
E-mail: info@lincolnhse.co.uk
Call Date: July 1984, Inner Temple
Qualifications: [BA (Manch), Dip Law]

NICHOLLS JOHN PETER

13 Old Square
Ground Floor, Lincoln's Inn, London
WC2A 3UA, Telephone: 0171 404 4800
E-mail: clerks@13oldsquare.law.co.uk
Call Date: July 1986, Middle Temple
Pupil Master
Qualifications: [MA (Cantab)]

NICHOLLS MICHAEL JOHN GADSBY

1 Mitre Court Buildings
Temple, London EC4Y 7BS,
Telephone: 0171 797 7070
E-mail: clerks@1mcb.com
Call Date: 1975, Middle Temple

NICHOLLS PAUL RICHARD

11 King's Bench Walk
Temple, London EC4Y 7EQ,
Telephone: 0171 632 8500/583 0610
E-mail: clerksroom@11kbw.com
Call Date: Oct 1992, Inner Temple
Qualifications: [LLB (Sheffield), BCL (Oxon)]

NICHOLLS PETER JOHN

5 Pump Court
Ground Floor, Temple, London
EC4Y 7AP, Telephone: 020 7353 2532
E-mail: FivePump@netcomuk.co.uk
Call Date: Nov 1991, Inner Temple
Qualifications: [BA(Hons)(Dunelm)]

NICHOLLS RICHARD JOHN

New Walk Chambers
27 New Walk, Leicester LE1 6TE,
Telephone: 0116 2559144
Call Date: Oct 1994, Gray's Inn
Qualifications: [LLB (Manch)]

NICHOLS STUART RICHARD

5 Paper Buildings
Ground Floor, Temple, London
EC4Y 7HB, Telephone: 0171 583 9275/
583 4555 E-mail: 5paper@link.org
Call Date: Nov 1989, Lincoln's Inn
Pupil Master
Qualifications: [LLB (Leic)]

NICHOLSON JEREMY MARK

4 Pump Court
Temple, London EC4Y 7AN,
Telephone: 020 7842 5555
E-mail:chambers@4pumpcourt.law.co.uk
Call Date: July 1977, Middle Temple
Pupil Master
Qualifications: [MA (Cantab)]

NICHOLSON MICHAEL HUGH

Chambers of Norman Palmer
2 Field Court, Gray's Inn, London
WC1R 5BB, Telephone: 0171 405 6114
E-mail: fieldct2@netcomuk.co.uk
Call Date: Oct 1993, Middle Temple
Qualifications: [LLB (Hons)(Lond)]

NICHOLSON MISS ROSALIND VERONICA

4 Stone Buildings
Ground Floor, Lincoln's Inn, London
WC2A 3XT, Telephone: 0171 242 5524
E-mail:clerks@4stonebuildings.law.co.uk
Call Date: July 1987, Gray's Inn
Pupil Master
Qualifications: [MA (Oxon)]

NICHOLSON PRATT THOMAS HYCY

Hardwicke Building
New Square, Lincoln's Inn, London
WC2A 3SB, Telephone: 020 7242 2523
E-mail: clerks@hardwicke.co.uk
Call Date: July 1986, Lincoln's Inn
Qualifications: [LLB (Lond)]

NICKLIN MATTHEW JAMES

5 Raymond Buildings
1st Floor, Gray's Inn, London WC1R 5BP,
Telephone: 0171 242 2902
E-mail: clerks@media-ent-law.co.uk
Call Date: Oct 1993, Lincoln's Inn
Qualifications: [LLB (Hons)(Newc)]

NICOL ANDREW GEORGE LINDSAY QC (1995)

Doughty Street Chambers
11 Doughty Street, London WC1N 2PG,
Telephone: 0171 404 1313
E-mail:enquiries@doughtystreet.co.uk
Call Date: July 1978, Middle Temple
Assistant Recorder
Qualifications: [BA, LLB (Cantab), LLM (Harvard)]

NICOL ANDREW ROBERT

Chambers of John L Powell QC
Four New Square, Lincoln's Inn, London
WC2A 3RJ, Telephone: 0171 797 8000
E-mail: barristers@4newsquare.com
Call Date: Nov 1991, Inner Temple
Qualifications: [MA (Cantab)]

NICOL ANGUS SEBASTIAN TORQUIL EYERS

5 Paper Buildings
Ground Floor, Temple, London
EC4Y 7HB, Telephone: 0171 583 9275/
583 4555 E-mail: 5paper@link.org
Call Date: July 1963, Middle Temple
Pupil Master, Recorder

NICOL NICHOLAS KEITH

1 Pump Court
Lower Ground Floor, Temple, London
EC4Y 7AB, Telephone: 0171 583 2012/
353 4341
E-mail: [name]@1pumpcourt.co.uk
Call Date: Nov 1986, Inner Temple
Qualifications: [LLB (Lond)]

NICOL STUART HENRY DAVID

3 Temple Gardens
3rd Floor, Temple, London EC4Y 9AU,
Telephone: 0171 353 0832
Call Date: Nov 1994, Lincoln's Inn
Qualifications: [LLB (Hons)(Lond)]

NICOL-GENT WILLIAM PHILIP TRAHAIR

King's Chambers
5a Gildredge Road, Eastbourne, East
Sussex, BN21 4RB,
Telephone: 01323 416053
Call Date: Oct 1991, Inner Temple
Pupil Master
Qualifications: [LLB (Hons) (Bucks)]

NICOLSON ARIS TONY

23 Bracken Gardens
Barnes, London SW13 9HW,
Telephone: 0181 748 4924
Call Date: July 1981, Gray's Inn
Qualifications: [LLB]

NIELD MICHAEL WILLIAM

7 Stone Buildings
Ground Floor, Lincoln's Inn, London
WC2A 3SZ, Telephone: 0171 405 3886/
242 3546 E-mail: chaldous@vossnet.co.uk
Call Date: Nov 1969, Lincoln's Inn
Pupil Master
Qualifications: [MA (Oxon)]

NIGHTINGALE MS JANE ANN

12 Old Square
1st Floor, Lincoln's Inn, London
WC2A 3TX, Telephone: 0171 404 0875
Call Date: Nov 1995, Lincoln's Inn
Qualifications: [BA (Hons)]

NIGHTINGALE PETER VINCENT JOSEPH

4 King's Bench Walk
2nd Floor, Temple, London EC4Y 7DL,
Telephone: 020 7353 3581
E-mail: clerks@4kbw.co.uk
Call Date: July 1986, Inner Temple

NIJABAT MISS SHAMA BATOOL

Paradise Chambers
26 Paradise Square, Sheffield S1 2DE,
Telephone: 0114 2738951
E-mail: timbooth@paradise-sq.co.uk
Call Date: Nov 1993, Middle Temple
Qualifications: [LLB (Hons), LLM (Lond)]

NILSEN MS WENDY MARY

Old Colony House
6 South King Street, Manchester M2 6DQ,
Telephone: 0161 834 4364
Call Date: July 1998, Gray's Inn
Qualifications: [LLB (Manch)]

NIMMO ADRIAN

Bank House Chambers
Old Bank House, Hartshead, Sheffield
S1 2EL, Telephone: 0114 2751223
Call Date: Nov 1971, Gray's Inn
Qualifications: [LLB]

NISBETT JAMES THEOPHILUS

7 Westmeath Avenue
Evington, Leicester LE5 6SS,
Telephone: 0116 2412003
Victoria Chambers
3rd Floor, 177 Corporation Street,
Birmingham B4 6RG,
Telephone: 0121 236 9900
E-mail: viccham@aol.com
Call Date: July 1973, Lincoln's Inn
Qualifications: [LLB]

NISSEN ALEXANDER DAVID

Keating Chambers
10 Essex Street, Outer Temple, London
WC2R 3AA, Telephone: 0171 544 2600
Call Date: July 1985, Middle Temple
Pupil Master
Qualifications: [LLB (Manch)]

NIXON COLIN ROSSINGTON

One Paper Buildings
Ground Floor, Temple, London
EC4Y 7EP, Telephone: 0171 583 7355
E-mail: clerks@1pb.co.uk
Call Date: July 1973, Lincoln's Inn
Pupil Master
Qualifications: [BA (Natal)]

NIXON MISS DIANE ELEANOR

Somersett Chambers
25 Bedford Row, London WC1R 4HE,
Telephone: 0171 404 6701
E-mail: somelaw@aol.com
Call Date: 1997, Middle Temple
Qualifications: [BA (Hons)(Oxon)]

D

NIXON-MOSS GARETH JAMES

Tindal Chambers
3/5 New Street, Chelmsford, Essex,
CM1 1NT, Telephone: 01245 267742
St Albans Chambers
Dolphin Lodge, Dolphin Yard, Holywell
Hill, St Albans, Herts, AL1 1EX,
Telephone: 01727 843383
Call Date: Oct 1994, Inner Temple
Qualifications: [LLB (Bucks)]

NOBLE ANDREW

Merchant Chambers
1 North Parade, Parsonage Gardens,
Manchester M3 2NH,
Telephone: 0161 839 7070
E-mail: merchant.chambers@virgin.net
10 King's Bench Walk
Ground Floor, Temple, London
EC4Y 7EB, Telephone: 0171 353 7742
E-mail: 10kbw@lineone.net
Call Date: Nov 1992, Lincoln's Inn
Qualifications: [LLB (Hons)(Manc),
FRICS,FCIArb]

NOBLE MISS ANTONIA CARTER

Chambers of Harjit Singh
Ground Floor, 2 Middle Temple Lane,
Temple, London EC4Y 9AA,
Telephone: 0171 353 1356 (4 Lines)
Call Date: Nov 1995, Middle Temple
Qualifications: [BA (Hons)]

NOBLE ARTHUR EDWIN RANDALL

Chavasse Court Chambers
2nd Floor, Chavasse Court, 24 Lord Street,
Liverpool L2 1TA,
Telephone: 0151 707 1191
Call Date: July 1965, Inner Temple
Pupil Master
Qualifications: [BA (Dub)]

NOBLE PHILIP ROBERT

Thomas More Chambers
52 Carey Street, Lincoln's Inn, London
WC2A 2JB, Telephone: 0171 404 7000
E-mail: clerks@thomasmore.law.co.uk
Call Date: July 1978, Inner Temple
Pupil Master

NOBLE RODERICK GRANT

39 Essex Street
London WC2R 3AT,
Telephone: 0171 832 1111
E-mail: clerks@39essex.co.uk
Call Date: Nov 1977, Gray's Inn
Pupil Master
Qualifications: [BSc]

NOLAN BENJAMIN QC (1992)

Mercury Chambers
Mercury House, 33-35 Clarendon Road,
Leeds LS2 9NZ,
Telephone: 0113 234 2265
E-mail:cdexter@mercurychambers.co.uk
Call Date: July 1971, Middle Temple
Recorder
Qualifications: [LLB (Lond)]

NOLAN DAMIAN FRANCIS

25-27 Castle Street
1st Floor, Liverpool L2 4TA,
Telephone: 0151 227 5661/051 236 5072
Call Date: Oct 1994, Lincoln's Inn
Qualifications: [BSc (Hons)(Cardiff)]

NOLAN DOMINIC THOMAS

Ropewalk Chambers
24 The Ropewalk, Nottingham NG1 5EF,
Telephone: 0115 9472581
E-mail: administration@ropewalk co.uk
Call Date: July 1985, Lincoln's Inn
Pupil Master
Qualifications: [LLB (Nott'm)]

NOLAN MICHAEL ALFRED ANTHONY

4 Essex Court
Temple, London EC4Y 9AJ,
Telephone: 020 7797 7970
E-mail: clerks@4essexcourt.law.co.uk
Call Date: July 1981, Middle Temple
Pupil Master
Qualifications: [MA (Oxon)]

NOORDEEN MS SAMIYA SALAMATH SAHABDEEN

169 Temple Chambers
Temple Avenue, London EC4Y 0DA,
Telephone: 0171 583 7644
Call Date: Oct 1994, Middle Temple
Qualifications: [BSc (Hons)(Lond), CPE]

NORBURY HUGH ROBERT

Serle Court Chambers
6 New Square, Lincoln's Inn, London
WC2A 3QS, Telephone: 0171 242 6105
E-mail: clerks@serlecourt.co.uk
Call Date: Nov 1995, Lincoln's Inn
Qualifications: [BA (Hons), Dip Law]

NORBURY LUKE EDWARD

The Chambers of Leolin Price CBE, QC
10 Old Square, Lincoln's Inn, London
WC2A 3SU, Telephone: 0171 405 0758
Call Date: Oct 1995, Inner Temple
Qualifications: [MA (Cantab)]

NORIE-MILLER JEFFREY REGINALD

3 Temple Gardens
3rd Floor, Temple, London EC4Y 9AU,
Telephone: 0171 353 0832
Call Date: July 1996, Inner Temple
Qualifications: [LLB (Soton)]

NORMAN MISS CHARITY JOANNA

York Chambers
14 Toft Green, York YO1 6JT,
Telephone: 01904 620048
E-mail: [name]@yorkchambers.co.uk
Call Date: July 1988, Lincoln's Inn
Qualifications: [LLB (Hons) (Exon)]

NORMAN CHRISTOPHER JOHN GEORGE

No. 1 Serjeants' Inn
5th Floor Fleet Street, Temple, London
EC4Y 1LH, Telephone: 0171 415 6666
E-mail: no1serjeantsinn@btinternet.com
Call Date: Nov 1979, Lincoln's Inn
Pupil Master
Qualifications: [LLB (Hons) (Lond)]

NORMAN MISS ELIZABETH ANNE

Rowchester Chambers
4 Rowchester Court, Whittall Street,
Birmingham B4 6DH,
Telephone: 0121 233 2327/2361951
Call Date: Nov 1977, Middle Temple
Pupil Master
Qualifications: [MA (Cantab)]

NORMAN MARK ANDREW

1 Paper Buildings
1st Floor, Temple, London EC4Y 7EP,
Telephone: 0171 353 3728/4953
Call Date: Apr 1989, Inner Temple
Pupil Master
Qualifications: [BA (Lond), Dip Law]

NORMAN MICHAEL CHARLES

3 Paper Buildings
Temple, London EC4Y 7EU,
Telephone: 020 7583 8055
E-mail: London@3paper.com
3 Paper Buildings (Bournemouth)
20 Lorne Park Road, Bournemouth,
Dorset, BH1 1JN,
Telephone: 01202 292102
E-mail: Bournemouth@3paper.com
3 Paper Buildings (Winchester)
4 St Peter Street, Winchester SO23 8BW,
Telephone: 01962 868884
E-mail: winchester@3paper.com
3 Paper Buildings (Oxford)
1 Alfred Street, High Street, Oxford
OX1 4EH, Telephone: 01865 793736
E-mail: oxford@3paper.com
Call Date: Feb 1971, Gray's Inn
Pupil Master, Recorder
Qualifications: [MA (Hons), LLB (Cantab)]

NORMAN PHILIP FRANCIS

95A Chancery Lane
London WC2A 1DT,
Telephone: 0171 405 3101
Call Date: Oct 1995, Lincoln's Inn
Qualifications: [LLB (Hons)(Bucks)]

NORRIS ALASTAIR HUBERT QC (1997)

5 Stone Buildings
Lincoln's Inn, London WC2A 3XT,
Telephone: 0171 242 6201
E-mail:clerks@5-stonebuildings.law.co.uk
Southernhay Chambers
33 Southernhay East, Exeter, Devon,
EX1 1NX, Telephone: 01392 255777
E-mail:southernhay.chambers@lineone.net
Call Date: July 1973, Lincoln's Inn
Assistant Recorder
Qualifications: [MA (Cantab), FCIArb]

NORRIS ANDREW JAMES STEEDSMAN

5 New Square
Ground Floor, Lincoln's Inn, London
WC2A 3RJ, Telephone: 020 7404 0404
E-mail:chambers@fivenewsquare.demon.co.
uk
Call Date: Nov 1995, Middle Temple
Qualifications: [BSc (Hons)]

NORRIS JAMES LESLIE

Goldsmith Chambers
Ground Floor, Goldsmith Building,
Temple, London EC4Y 7BL,
Telephone: 0171 353 6802/3/4/5
E-mail:clerks@goldsmithchambers.law.co.uk
Call Date: May 1984, Inner Temple
Qualifications: [LLB Soton]

NORRIS JOHN GERAINT

Albion Chambers
Broad Street, Bristol BS1 1DR,
Telephone: 0117 9272144
Call Date: July 1980, Lincoln's Inn
Pupil Master
Qualifications: [MA (Oxon)]

NORRIS PAUL HOWARD

One Essex Court
1st Floor, Temple, London EC4Y 9AR,
Telephone: 0171 936 3030
E-mail: one.essex_court@virgin.net
Call Date: May 1963, Middle Temple
Pupil Master, Recorder
Qualifications: [BA (Oxon)]

NORRIS WILLIAM JOHN QC (1997)

Farrar's Building
Temple, London EC4Y 7BD,
Telephone: 0171 583 9241
E-mail:chambers@farrarsbuilding.co.uk
Call Date: July 1974, Middle Temple
Qualifications: [MA (Oxon)]

NORRIS WILLIAM VERNON WESTWORTH

9 Old Square
Ground Floor, Lincoln's Inn, London
WC2A 3SR, Telephone: 0171 405 4682
E-mail: chambers@9oldsquare.co.uk
Call Date: July 1997, Lincoln's Inn

NORTHROP KEITH DOUGLAS

Call Date: Nov 1989, Inner Temple
Qualifications: [BA (Hull), Dip Law]

NORTON ANDREW DAVID

One Garden Court Family Law Chambers
Ground Floor, Temple, London
EC4Y 9BJ, Telephone: 0171 797 7900
E-mail: clerks@onegardencourt.co.uk
Call Date: Oct 1992, Inner Temple
Qualifications: [BSc (S'ton), CPE]

NORTON MISS HEATHER SOPHIA

23 Essex Street
London WC2R 3AS,
Telephone: 0171 413 0353/836 8366
E-mail:clerks@essexstreet23.demon.co.uk
Call Date: Nov 1988, Middle Temple
Qualifications: [LLB (B'ham)]

NORTON RICHARD DAMIAN

28 St John Street
Manchester M3 4DJ,
Telephone: 0161 834 8418
E-mail: clerk@28stjohnst.co.uk
Call Date: Nov 1992, Lincoln's Inn
Qualifications: [LLB (Hons)(Leeds)]

NOTHER DANIEL ROBERT

College Chambers
19 Carlton Cresent, Southampton
SO15 2ET, Telephone: 01703 230338
Call Date: Nov 1994, Inner Temple
Qualifications: [BA (Oxon)]

NOTT MISS EMMA CATHERINE

1 Dr Johnson's Buildings
Ground Floor, Temple, London
EC4Y 7AX, Telephone: 0171 353 9328
E-mail:OneDr.Johnsons@btinternet.com
Call Date: Nov 1995, Gray's Inn
Qualifications: [BA]

NOURSE EDMUND ALEXANDER MARTIN

One Essex Court
Ground Floor, Temple, London
EC4Y 9AR, Telephone: 020 7583 2000
E-mail: clerks@oneessexcourt.co.uk
Call Date: Nov 1994, Lincoln's Inn
Qualifications: [BA (Hons)(Oxon), Dip in Law (City)]

NOWELL MISS KATIE LOUISE

40 King Street
Manchester M2 6BA,
Telephone: 0161 832 9082
E-mail: clerks@40kingstreet.co.uk
The Chambers of Philip Raynor QC
5 Park Place, Leeds LS1 2RU,
Telephone: 0113 242 1123
Call Date: Oct 1996, Lincoln's Inn
Qualifications: [LLB (Hons)(Cardiff)]

NOWLAND LEE PHILIP

Old Colony House
6 South King Street, Manchester M2 6DQ,
Telephone: 0161 834 4364
Call Date: May 1997, Lincoln's Inn
Qualifications: [LLB (Hons)(Leics)]

NSUGBE OBA ERIC

Pump Court Chambers
Upper Ground Floor, 3 Pump Court,
Temple, London EC4Y 7AJ,
Telephone: 0171 353 0711
E-mail: clerks@3pumpcourt.com
Pump Court Chambers
31 Southgate Street, Winchester
SO23 9EE, Telephone: 01962 868161
E-mail: clerks@3pumpcourt.com
Pump Court Chambers
5 Temple Chambers, Temple Street,
Swindon SN1 1SQ,
Telephone: 01793 539899
E-mail: clerks@3pumpcourt.com
Call Date: July 1985, Gray's Inn
Pupil Master, Assistant Recorder
Qualifications: [LLB (Hull)]

NUGEE CHRISTOPHER GEORGE QC (1998)

Wilberforce Chambers
8 New Square, Lincoln's Inn, London
WC2A 3QP, Telephone: 0171 306 0102
E-mail: chambers@wilberforce.co.uk
Call Date: July 1983, Inner Temple
Qualifications: [BA (Oxon), Dip Law (City)]

Types of work: Chancery (general), Chancery land law, Commercial litigation, Commercial property, Landlord and tenant, Pensions, Professional negligence

NUGEE EDWARD GEORGE QC (1977)

Wilberforce Chambers
8 New Square, Lincoln's Inn, London
WC2A 3QP, Telephone: 0171 306 0102
E-mail: chambers@wilberforce.co.uk
Call Date: June 1955, Inner Temple
Qualifications: [TD, MA (Oxon)]

Types of work: Chancery (general), Chancery land law, Charities, Commercial property, Common land, Conveyancing, Ecclesiastical, Equity, wills and trusts, Financial services, Landlord and tenant, Partnerships, Pensions, Probate and administration, Share options, Tax – capital and income, Unit trusts

NUGENT COLM GERARD

Hardwicke Building
New Square, Lincoln's Inn, London
WC2A 3SB, Telephone: 020 7242 2523
E-mail: clerks@hardwicke.co.uk
Call Date: Oct 1992, Inner Temple
Qualifications: [BA (Kent)]

NUGENT PETER FRANCIS

Harrow on the Hill Chambers
60 High Street, Harrow-on-the-Hill,
Middlesex, HA1 3LL,
Telephone: 0181 423 7444
Windsor Barristers' Chambers
Windsor Telephone: 01753 648899
E-mail: law@windsorchambers.co.uk
Call Date: Feb 1994, Middle Temple
Qualifications: [BA (Hons)(Lond)]

NURSE GORDON BRAMWELL WILLIAM

11 Old Square
Ground Floor, Lincoln's Inn, London
WC2A 3TS, Telephone: 020 7430 0341
E-mail: clerks@11oldsquare.co.uk
Call Date: Nov 1973, Middle Temple
Pupil Master
Qualifications: [MA (Cantab)]

NUSRAT MAHMOOD ALI

The Chambers of Mr Ali Mohammed Azhar
Basement, 9 King's Bench Walk, Temple,
London EC4Y 7DX,
Telephone: 0171 353 9564
E-mail: jvlee@btinternet.com
Call Date: July 1977, Lincoln's Inn
Qualifications: [MA]

NUSSEY RICHARD JOHN GEORGE

Farrar's Building
Temple, London EC4Y 7BD,
Telephone: 0171 583 9241
E-mail: chambers@farrarsbuilding.co.uk
Call Date: Nov 1971, Lincoln's Inn
Pupil Master
Qualifications: [BA]

NUTTALL ANDREW PETER

Lincoln House Chambers
5th Floor, Lincoln House, 1 Brazennose
Street, Manchester M2 5EL,
Telephone: 0161 832 5701
E-mail: info@lincolnhse.co.uk
Call Date: Nov 1978, Lincoln's Inn
Qualifications: [LLB]

NUTTALL EVAN CALEB

3 Temple Gardens
Lower Ground Floor, Temple, London
EC4Y 9AU, Telephone: 0171 353 3102/5/
9297 E-mail: clerks@3tg.co.uk
Call Date: Oct 1993, Gray's Inn
Qualifications: [BA, MSc (Econ)]

NUTTER JULIAN ANDREW

3 Athol Street
Douglas, Isle of Man,
Telephone: 01624 897 420
Call Date: Nov 1979, Gray's Inn
Qualifications: [LLB (L'pool)]

NUTTING JOHN GRENFELL QC (1995)

3 Raymond Buildings
Gray's Inn, London WC1R 5BH,
Telephone: 020 7831 3833
E-mail:chambers@threeraymond.demon.co.uk
Call Date: Nov 1968, Middle Temple
Recorder
Qualifications: [BA]

NUVOLONI STEFANO VINCENZO

22 Old Buildings
Lincoln's Inn, London WC2A 3UJ,
Telephone: 0171 831 0222
Call Date: Nov 1994, Inner Temple
Qualifications: [LLB (Lond), MA (Lond)]

Types of work: Care proceedings, Family, Family provision

Languages spoken: Italian

NWOSU MISS JACINTH OGE ENYINDA

Goldsworth Chambers
1st Floor, 11 Gray's Inn Square, London
WC1R 5JD, Telephone: 0171 405 7117
Call Date: Nov 1992, Inner Temple
Qualifications: [BA]

O'BRIEN BERNARD NICHOLAS

Albion Chambers
Broad Street, Bristol BS1 1DR,
Telephone: 0117 9272144
Call Date: July 1968, Middle Temple
Pupil Master
Qualifications: [MA (Dub)]

O'BRIEN MR. DAVID

Trinity Chambers
140 New London Road, Chelmsford,
Essex, CM2 0AW,
Telephone: 01245 605040
E-mail:clerks@trinitychambers.law.co.uk
Call Date: Nov 1994, Middle Temple
Qualifications: [LLB (Hons) Dips.W,
C.Q.S.W, ASW]

O'BRIEN DERMOD PATRICK QC (1983)

2 Temple Gardens
Temple, London EC4Y 9AY,
Telephone: 0171 583 6041
E-mail: clerks@2templegardens.co.uk
Call Date: July 1962, Inner Temple
Recorder
Qualifications: [MA (Oxon)]

O'BRIEN MISS HAYLEE FIONA

2 Pump Court
1st Floor, Temple, London EC4Y 7AH,
Telephone: 0171 353 5597
Call Date: Nov 1984, Middle Temple
Qualifications: [LLB (Hons)(Lond)]

O'BRIEN JOHN

Chambers of Harjit Singh
Ground Floor, 2 Middle Temple Lane,
Temple, London EC4Y 9AA,
Telephone: 0171 353 1356 (4 Lines)
Call Date: May 1976, Middle Temple
Qualifications: [MA,LLB (Cantab),LLM]

O'BRIEN JOSEPH PATRICK ANTONY PETER

Westgate Chambers
67a Westgate Road, Newcastle upon Tyne
NE1 1SG, Telephone: 0191 261 4407/
2329785
E-mail:pracman@westgatechambers.law.co.u
k
Call Date: Nov 1989, Inner Temple
Qualifications: [LLB (Newc)]

O'BRIEN NICHOLAS JOHN

4 Brick Court
Ground Floor, Temple, London
EC4Y 9AD, Telephone: 0171 797 7766
E-mail: chambers@4brick.co.uk
Call Date: Nov 1985, Middle Temple
Pupil Master
Qualifications: [BA (Oxon), ACIArb]

O'BRIEN NICHOLAS WILLIAM WATTEBOT

Chambers of Joy Okoye
Suite 1, 2nd Floor Gray's Inn Chambers,
Gray's Inn, London WC1R 5JA,
Telephone: 0171 405 7011
Call Date: Nov 1996, Lincoln's Inn
Qualifications: [BA (Hons)(Oxon)]

O'BRIEN PAUL

18 St John Street
Manchester M3 4EA,
Telephone: 0161 278 1800
E-mail: 18stjohn@lineone.net
Call Date: Nov 1974, Gray's Inn
Assistant Recorder
Qualifications: [BA]

O'BRIEN-QUINN HUGH DAVID

5 Fountain Court
Steelhouse Lane, Birmingham B4 6DR,
Telephone: 0121 606 0500
E-mail:clerks@5fountaincourt.law.co.uk
Call Date: Feb 1992, Gray's Inn
Qualifications: [LLB (Wales)]

O'BYRNE ANDREW JOHN MARTIN

Peel Court Chambers
45 Hardman Street, Manchester M3 3PL,
Telephone: 0161 832 3791
E-mail: clerks@peelct.co.uk
Call Date: July 1978, Gray's Inn
Pupil Master
Qualifications: [LLB (L'pool)]

O'CALLAGHAN DECLAN MATHEW DENIS MARK

10 King's Bench Walk
Ground Floor, Temple, London
EC4Y 7EB, Telephone: 0171 353 7742
E-mail: 10kbw@lineone.net
Call Date: Oct 1995, Gray's Inn
Qualifications: [LLB (Exon), LLM]

O'CONNELL MICHAEL ALFRED

King Charles House
Standard Hill, Nottingham NG1 6FX,
Telephone: 0115 9418851
E-mail: clerks@kch.co.uk
Call Date: Nov 1966, Inner Temple
Qualifications: [LLB (Lond)]

O'CONNOR ANDREW MCDOUGAL

Two Crown Office Row
Ground Floor, Temple, London
EC4Y 7HJ, Telephone: 020 7797 8100
E-mail: mail@2cor.co.uk, or to individual
barristers at: [barrister's
surname]@2cor.co.uk
Call Date: Oct 1996, Gray's Inn
Qualifications: [BA (Cantab), Dip in Law]

O'CONNOR GERARD MICHAEL

Verulam Chambers
Peer House, 8-14 Verulam Street, Gray's
Inn, London WC1X 8LZ,
Telephone: 0171 813 2400
Call Date: Nov 1993, Lincoln's Inn
Qualifications: [MA (Oxon)]

O'CONNOR MARK

12 Old Square
1st Floor, Lincoln's Inn, London
WC2A 3TX, Telephone: 0171 404 0875
Counsels' Chambers
2nd Floor, 10-11 Gray's Inn Square,
London WC1R 5JD,
Telephone: 0171 405 2576
E-mail:clerks@10-11graysinnsquare.co.uk
Call Date: Oct 1994, Inner Temple
Qualifications: [LLB (Lond)]

O'CONNOR MISS MAUREEN THERESA

6 Gray's Inn Square
Ground Floor, Gray's Inn, London
WC1R 5AZ, Telephone: 0171 242 1052
E-mail: 6graysinn@clara.co.uk
Call Date: Nov 1988, Gray's Inn
Pupil Master
Qualifications: [LLB (Lond)]

O'CONNOR PATRICK MICHAEL JOSEPH QC (1993)

2-4 Tudor Street
London EC4Y 0AA,
Telephone: 0171 797 7111
E-mail: clerks@rfqc.co.uk
Call Date: Nov 1970, Inner Temple
Qualifications: [LLB (Lond)]

O'CONNOR MISS SARAH BERNADETTE ELIZABETH

One King's Bench Walk
1st Floor, Temple, London EC4Y 7DB,
Telephone: 0171 936 1500
E-mail: ddear@1kbw.co.uk
Call Date: Nov 1986, Inner Temple
Qualifications: [LLB (Hons) (Soton)]

O'DEMPSEY DECLAN JOHN

4 Brick Court
Ground Floor, Temple, London
EC4Y 9AD, Telephone: 0171 797 7766
E-mail: chambers@4brick.co.uk
Call Date: Nov 1987, Middle Temple
Pupil Master
Qualifications: [BA (Hons) (Cantab), Dip Law
(City)]

O'DONNELL DUNCAN GERARD

1 Paper Buildings
1st Floor, Temple, London EC4Y 7EP,
Telephone: 0171 353 3728/4953
Call Date: Oct 1992, Gray's Inn
Qualifications: [MA]

O'DONOGHUE FLORENCE

2 Mitre Court Buildings
1st Floor, Temple, London EC4Y 7BX,
Telephone: 0171 353 1353
Call Date: Feb 1959, Inner Temple
Qualifications: [MA (Dub),FCIArb]

O'DONOHOE ANTHONY FRANCIS

Chavasse Court Chambers
2nd Floor, Chavasse Court, 24 Lord Street,
Liverpool L2 1TA,
Telephone: 0151 707 1191
Call Date: July 1983, Middle Temple
Qualifications: [LLB (L'pool)]

O'DONOVAN JOHN MARTIN

**1 Gray's Inn Square, Chambers of the
Baroness Scotland of Asthal QC**
1st Floor, London WC1R 5AG,
Telephone: 0171 405 3000
E-mail: clerks@onegrays.demon.co.uk
Call Date: Nov 1993, Inner Temple
Qualifications: [BA, CPE]

O'DONOVAN KEVIN JOHN

5 Fountain Court
Steelhouse Lane, Birmingham B4 6DR,
Telephone: 0121 606 0500
E-mail:clerks@5fountaincourt.law.co.uk
Call Date: July 1978, Middle Temple
Pupil Master
Qualifications: [BA]

O'DONOVAN PAUL GODFREY

2 Paper Buildings
1st Floor, Temple, London EC4Y 7ET,
Telephone: 020 7556 5500
E-mail: clerks@2pbbarristers.co.uk
Call Date: Nov 1975, Inner Temple
Pupil Master

O'DONOVAN RONAN DANIEL JAMES

14 Gray's Inn Square
Gray's Inn, London WC1R 5JP,
Telephone: 0171 242 0858
E-mail: 100712.2134@compuserve.com
Call Date: Nov 1995, Lincoln's Inn
Qualifications: [BA (Hons)(Nott'm)]

O'DWYER MARTIN PATRICK

One Garden Court Family Law Chambers
Ground Floor, Temple, London
EC4Y 9BJ, Telephone: 0171 797 7900
E-mail: clerks@onegardencourt.co.uk
Call Date: Nov 1978, Middle Temple
Pupil Master, Assistant Recorder
Qualifications: [MA (Oxon)]

O'FARRELL MS FINOLA MARY

Keating Chambers
10 Essex Street, Outer Temple, London
WC2R 3AA, Telephone: 0171 544 2600
Call Date: July 1983, Inner Temple
Pupil Master
Qualifications: [BA Dunelm]

O'FLYNN TIMOTHY JAMES

Pump Court Chambers
31 Southgate Street, Winchester
SO23 9EE, Telephone: 01962 868161
E-mail: clerks@3pumpcourt.com

Pump Court Chambers
Upper Ground Floor, 3 Pump Court,
Temple, London EC4Y 7AJ,
Telephone: 0171 353 0711
E-mail: clerks@3pumpcourt.com
Pump Court Chambers
5 Temple Chambers, Temple Street,
Swindon SN1 1SQ,
Telephone: 01793 539899
E-mail: clerks@3pumpcourt.com
Call Date: July 1979, Gray's Inn
Qualifications: [LLB (Bris)]

O'GORMAN CHRISTOPHER FRANCIS

Clock Chambers
78 Darlington Street, Wolverhampton
WV1 4LY, Telephone: 01902 313444
Victoria Chambers
3rd Floor, 177 Corporation Street,
Birmingham B4 6RG,
Telephone: 0121 236 9900
E-mail: viccham@aol.com
Call Date: 1987, Gray's Inn
Qualifications: [LLB (Sheff)]

O'HAGAN MISS SOPHIA MARIA

Regent Chambers
8 Pall Mall, Hanley, Stoke On Trent
ST1 1ER, Telephone: 01782 286666
E-mail: regent@ftech.co.uk
Call Date: Oct 1996, Middle Temple
Qualifications: [LLB (Hons)(Lond), LLM
(Lond)]

O'HALLORAN MISS JILL

First National Chambers
2nd Floor, First National Building, 24
Fenwick Street, Liverpool L2 7NE,
Telephone: 0151 236 2098
Call Date: Oct 1994, Gray's Inn
Qualifications: [LLB]

O'HARA MISS SARAH LOUISE

3 Paper Buildings
Temple, London EC4Y 7EU,
Telephone: 020 7583 8055
E-mail: London@3paper.com
3 Paper Buildings (Bournemouth)
20 Lorne Park Road, Bournemouth,
Dorset, BH1 1JN,
Telephone: 01202 292102
E-mail: Bournemouth@3paper.com

3 Paper Buildings (Oxford)
1 Alfred Street, High Street, Oxford
OX1 4EH, Telephone: 01865 793736
E-mail: oxford@3paper.com
3 Paper Buildings (Winchester)
4 St Peter Street, Winchester SO23 8BW,
Telephone: 01962 868884
E-mail: winchester@3paper.com
Call Date: July 1984, Middle Temple
Qualifications: [MA (Cantab)]

O'HARE MISS ELIZABETH ANNE

Park Lane Chambers
19 Westgate, Leeds LS1 2RD,
Telephone: 0113 2285000
E-mail:clerks@parklanechambers.co.uk
Call Date: July 1980, Middle Temple
Pupil Master
Qualifications: [LLB]

O'HIGGINS JOHN GERARD

Chambers of Helen Grindrod QC
4th Floor, 15-19 Devereux Court, London
WC2R 3JJ, Telephone: 0171 583 2792
Call Date: Nov 1990, Middle Temple
Qualifications: [MA (Cantab)]

O'KEEFFE DARREN PHILIP DE VOIELS

Derby Square Chambers
Merchants Court, Derby Square, Liverpool
L2 1TS, Telephone: 0151 709 4222
E-mail:mail.derbysquare@pop3.hiway.co.uk
Call Date: July 1984, Inner Temple
Pupil Master
Qualifications: [MA (Oxon)]

O'LEARY MS MICHELE ANN

Goldsmith Chambers
Ground Floor, Goldsmith Building,
Temple, London EC4Y 7BL,
Telephone: 0171 353 6802/3/4/5
E-mail:clerks@goldsmithchambers.law.co.uk
Call Date: Nov 1983, Gray's Inn
Pupil Master
Qualifications: [LLB (Hons)(Wales)]

O'LEARY ROBERT MICHAEL

33 Park Place
Cardiff CF1 3BA,
Telephone: 02920 233313
Call Date: Oct 1990, Inner Temple
Qualifications: [LLB (Cardiff)]

O'MAHONY PATRICK JAMES MARTIN

5 King's Bench Walk
Temple, London EC4Y 7DN,
Telephone: 0171 353 5638
Call Date: July 1973, Inner Temple
Pupil Master, Assistant Recorder
Qualifications: [LLB (Lond)]

O'MALLEY MS JULIE BERNADETTE

10 King's Bench Walk
1st Floor, Temple, London EC4Y 7EB,
Telephone: 0171 353 2501
Call Date: Nov 1983, Gray's Inn
Qualifications: [LLB (Sheff)]

O'MALLEY MISS MARY HELLEN

Holborn Chambers
6 Gate Street, Lincoln's Inn Fields, London
WC2A 3HP, Telephone: 0171 242 6060
Call Date: Oct 1991, Lincoln's Inn
Qualifications: [Ba (Hons) (Kent)]

O'MAOILEOIN MICHAEL BRENDAN

3 Temple Gardens
3rd Floor, Temple, London EC4Y 9AU,
Telephone: 0171 353 0832
Call Date: Feb 1986, Inner Temple
Pupil Master
Qualifications: [BCL,LLB (Dub), ACI.Arb]

O'NEILL BRIAN PATRICK

1 Hare Court
Ground Floor, Temple, London
EC4Y 7BE, Telephone: 0171 353 3982/
5324
Call Date: Nov 1987, Gray's Inn
Pupil Master
Qualifications: [LLB Hons (Brunel)]

O'NEILL MISS LOUISE CATHERINE

St John's Chambers
Small Street, Bristol BS1 1DW,
Telephone: 0117 9213456/298514
E-mail: @stjohnschambers.co.uk
Call Date: Feb 1989, Gray's Inn
Qualifications: [BA (Dublin), LLM (Cantab)]

O'NEILL MICHAEL ALISTAIR HUGH

11 King's Bench Walk
3 Park Court, Park Cross Street, Leeds
LS1 2QH, Telephone: 0113 297 1200
11 King's Bench Walk
1st Floor, Temple, London EC4Y 7EQ,
Telephone: 0171 353 3337
E-mail: fmuller11@aol.com
*Call Date: July 1979, Inner Temple
Pupil Master*
Qualifications: [MA (Oxon)]

O'NEILL PHILIP JOHN

Corn Exchange Chambers
5th Floor, Fenwick Street, Liverpool
L2 7QS, Telephone: 0151 227 1081/5009
Call Date: Nov 1983, Gray's Inn
Qualifications: [LLB (Hons)(L'pool)]

O'NEILL MISS SALLY JANE QC (1997)

Furnival Chambers
32 Furnival Street, London EC4A 1JQ,
Telephone: 0171 405 3232
E-mail: clerks@furnivallaw.co.uk
Call Date: Nov 1976, Gray's Inn
Qualifications: [LLB (Lond)]

O'NEILL TADHG JOSEPH

1 Crown Office Row
3rd Floor, Temple, London EC4Y 7HH,
Telephone: 0171 583 9292
E-mail: onecor@link.org
*Call Date: Nov 1987, Middle Temple
Pupil Master*
Qualifications: [BA (Cantab)]

O'RAWE MISS DOLORES

Holborn Chambers
6 Gate Street, Lincoln's Inn Fields, London
WC2A 3HP, Telephone: 0171 242 6060
Call Date: Nov 1992, Middle Temple
Qualifications: [LLB (Hons) (Lond)]

O'REILLY JAMES

Essex Court Chambers
24 Lincoln's Inn Fields, London
WC2A 3ED, Telephone: 0171 813 8000
E-mail:clerksroom@essexcourt-chambers.co.uk
Call Date: July 1983, Lincoln's Inn
Qualifications: [BCL , LLB (Dublin), LLM (Yale)]

O'REILLY MISS JANE ANN ELIZABETH

Rowchester Chambers
4 Rowchester Court, Whittall Street,
Birmingham B4 6DH,
Telephone: 0121 233 2327/2361951
Call Date: Nov 1991, Lincoln's Inn
Qualifications: [LLB (Hons)]

O'REILLY MICHAEL PATRICK

Paradise Chambers
26 Paradise Square, Sheffield S1 2DE,
Telephone: 0114 2738951
E-mail: timbooth@paradise-sq.co.uk
Call Date: Nov 1988, Gray's Inn
Qualifications: [BEng (Shef), PhD (Nott'm), LLB (Lond)]

O'REILLY WALTER ANTHONY PAUL

3 Aisby Drive
Rossington, Doncaster DN11 OYY,
Telephone: 01302 866495
Call Date: Nov 1978, Lincoln's Inn
Qualifications: [BA]

O'ROURKE MISS MARY BERNADETTE

3 Serjeants' Inn
London EC4Y 1BQ,
Telephone: 0171 353 5537
E-mail: clerks@3serjeantsinn.com
*Call Date: Nov 1981, Gray's Inn
Pupil Master*
Qualifications: [Cert des Hautes , Etudes Europeenes, (Bruges), LLB (Lond)]

O'SHEA EOIN FINBARR

4 Field Court
Gray's Inn, London WC1R 5EA,
Telephone: 0171 440 6900
E-mail: chambers@4fieldcourt.co.uk
Call Date: 1996, Inner Temple
Qualifications: [BA (N.U.I), BA (Cantab)]

D

O'SHEA JOHN ANTHONY ANDREW

58 King Street Chambers
1st Floor, Kingsgate House, 51-53 South
King Street, Manchester M2 6DE,
Telephone: 0161 831 7477
Call Date: Nov 1983, Middle Temple
Pupil Master
Qualifications: [BA (Hons)]

O'SHEA PAUL ANDREW

15 North Church Street Chambers
15 North Church Street, Sheffield
S1 2DH, Telephone: 0114 2759708/
2738380
Call Date: July 1989, Inner Temple
Pupil Master
Qualifications: [LLB (L'pool)]

O'SULLIVAN BERNARD ANTHONY

2 Harcourt Buildings
Ground Floor/Left, Temple, London
EC4Y 9DB, Telephone: 0171 583 9020
E-mail: clerks@harcourt.co.uk
Call Date: July 1971, Inner Temple
Pupil Master
Qualifications: [MA (Cantab), MBA (Open
Univ)]

O'SULLIVAN DEREK ANTHONY

5 Pump Court
Ground Floor, Temple, London
EC4Y 7AP, Telephone: 020 7353 2532
E-mail: FivePump@netcomuk.co.uk
Call Date: Oct 1990, Lincoln's Inn
Qualifications: [BA (Dunelm), Dip Law]

Fax: 0171 353 5321; DX: 497 London Chancery Lane;
Other comms: E-mail
derekos@netcom.co.uk

Types of work: Personal injury

Circuit: South Eastern

Awards and memberships: Lincoln's Inn Major
Bursary

Other professional experience: Former stockbroker

O'SULLIVAN JOHN

Broad Chare
33 Broad Chare, Newcastle upon Tyne
NE1 3DQ, Telephone: 0191 232 0541
E-mail:clerks@broadcharechambers.law.co.uk
Call Date: Nov 1984, Middle Temple
Pupil Master
Qualifications: [LLB (Warwick)]

O'SULLIVAN MICHAEL KENNETH

**Gray's Inn Chambers, The Chambers of
Norman Patterson**
First Floor, Gray's Inn Chambers, Gray's
Inn, London WC1R 5JA,
Telephone: 0171 831 5344
E-mail: s.mcblain@btinternet.com
Call Date: Oct 1991, Lincoln's Inn
Qualifications: [LLB (Hons)]

O'SULLIVAN MICHAEL MORTON

5 Stone Buildings
Lincoln's Inn, London WC2A 3XT,
Telephone: 0171 242 6201
E-mail:clerks@5-stonebuildings.law.co.uk
Call Date: July 1986, Lincoln's Inn
Pupil Master
Qualifications: [MA (Cantab), BCL (Oxon)]

O'SULLIVAN MICHAEL NEIL

5 King's Bench Walk
Temple, London EC4Y 7DN,
Telephone: 0171 353 5638
Call Date: Nov 1970, Gray's Inn
Pupil Master, Recorder

O'SULLIVAN ROBERT MICHAEL

Five Paper Buildings
1st Floor, Five Paper Bldgs, Temple,
London EC4Y 7HB,
Telephone: 0171 583 6117
E-mail:clerks@5-paperbuildings.law.co.uk
Call Date: July 1988, Lincoln's Inn
Qualifications: [LLB (Hons) (Lond)]

D

O'SULLIVAN THOMAS SEAN PATRICK

4 Pump Court
Temple, London EC4Y 7AN,
Telephone: 020 7842 5555
E-mail:chambers@4pumpcourt.law.co.uk
Call Date: 1997, Middle Temple
Qualifications: [BA (Hons)(Oxon), CPE (Lond)]

O'SULLIVAN MISS ZOE SIOBHAN

One Essex Court
Ground Floor, Temple, London
EC4Y 9AR, Telephone: 020 7583 2000
E-mail: clerks@oneessexcourt.co.uk
Call Date: Oct 1993, Middle Temple
Qualifications: [BA (Hons)(Oxon), Dip Law (City)]

O'TOOLE ANTHONY JAMES

Nicholas Street Chambers
22 Nicholas Street, Chester CH1 2NX,
Telephone: 01244 323886
E-mail: clerks@40king.co.uk
Call Date: Feb 1993, Gray's Inn
Pupil Master, Assistant Recorder
Qualifications: [LLB]

O'TOOLE BARTHOLOMEW VINCENT

Mitre Court Chambers
3rd Floor, Temple, London EC4Y 7BP,
Telephone: 0171 353 9394
E-mail: mitrecourt.com
Call Date: Nov 1980, Middle Temple
Pupil Master
Qualifications: [BSc (Lond), Dip Law]

O'TOOLE SIMON GERARD

2 Mitre Court Buildings
1st Floor, Temple, London EC4Y 7BX,
Telephone: 0171 353 1353
Call Date: July 1984, Inner Temple
Qualifications: [BA (B'ham), , Dip Law (City)]

OAKES MISS ALISON DENISE

4 Breams Buildings
London EC4A 1AQ,
Telephone: 0171 353 5835/430 1221
E-mail:breams@4breamsbuildings.law.co.uk
Call Date: Oct 1996, Inner Temple
Qualifications: [BA (Dunelm), CPE (Lond)]

OAKES CHRISTOPHER NEIL

Cobden House Chambers
19 Quay Street, Manchester M3 3HN,
Telephone: 0161 833 6000
E-mail: clerks@cobden.co.uk
Call Date: Oct 1996, Lincoln's Inn
Qualifications: [B.Eng (Hons)(L'pool)]

OAKESHOTT ROGER NICHOLAS

199 Strand
London WC2R 1DR,
Telephone: 0171 379 9779
E-mail: chambers@199strand.co.uk
Call Date: Nov 1997, Middle Temple
Qualifications: [BA (Hons) (Oxon), DipLaw (City)]

OAKLEY ANTHONY JAMES

11 Old Square
Ground Floor, Lincoln's Inn, London
WC2A 3TS, Telephone: 020 7430 0341
E-mail: clerks@11oldsquare.co.uk
Call Date: Feb 1994, Lincoln's Inn
Qualifications: [BA, LLB, MA]

Fax: 0171 831 2469;
Out of hours telephone: 0860 441135;
DX: LDE 1031; LIX LON042;
Other comms: E-mail
clerks@11oldsquare.co.uk

Other professional qualifications: TEP

Types of work: Chancery (general), Chancery land law, Charities, Conveyancing, Equity, wills and trusts, Family provision, Foreign law, Pensions, Probate and administration, Professional negligence, Spanish law, Tax – capital and income

Other professional experience: 28 years as university teacher (London 1971-5, Cambridge 1975 to date)

Languages spoken:

Publications: *Constructive Trusts* (3rd edn), 1997; *Parker and Mellows: The Modern Law of Trusts* (7th edn), 1998; *Trends in Contemporary Trust Law*, 1996; *More Trends in Contemporary Trust Law*, 2001; *Megarry: Manual of the Law of Real Property* (8th edn), 2000

Reported Cases: *Nationwide Building Society v Various Solicitors (No 3)*, (1999) *The Times*, 1 March, 1998. Proceedings in

D

managed litigation against various solicitors for professional negligence and breach of fiduciary duty in residential property transactions.

OAKLEY PAUL JAMES

1 Gray's Inn Square
Ground Floor, London WC1R 5AA,
Telephone: 0171 405 8946/7/8
Call Date: Nov 1995, Gray's Inn
Qualifications: [LLB , MSc (Bris)]

OATES JOHN RICHARD

White Friars Chambers
21 White Friars, Chester CH1 1NZ,
Telephone: 01244 323070
E-mail:whitefriarschambers@btinternet.com
Call Date: July 1987, Gray's Inn

OBUKA MS OBIJUO AGWU

9 King's Bench Walk
Ground Floor, Temple, London
EC4Y 7DX, Telephone: 0171 353 7202/
3909 E-mail: 9kbw@compuserve.com
Call Date: Oct 1993, Inner Temple
Qualifications: [LLB]

ODGERS JOHN ARTHUR

3 Verulam Buildings
London WC1R 5NT,
Telephone: 0171 831 8441
E-mail: clerks@3verulam.co.uk
Call Date: Oct 1990, Gray's Inn
Pupil Master
Qualifications: [BA (Hons)(Oxon)]

ODILI CHRISTOPHER IKECHUKWU

Somersett Chambers
25 Bedford Row, London WC1R 4HE,
Telephone: 0171 404 6701
E-mail: somelaw@aol.com
Call Date: 1992, Gray's Inn
Qualifications: [BA (Sussex), LLM (Lond)]

ODITAH DR FIDELIS HILARY IZUKA

3/4 South Square
Gray's Inn, London WC1R 5HP,
Telephone: 0171 696 9900
E-mail: clerks@southsquare.com
Call Date: July 1992, Lincoln's Inn
Qualifications: [MA, BCL, D.Phil]

OFFEH JOHN KOFI

12 Old Square
1st Floor, Lincoln's Inn, London
WC2A 3TX, Telephone: 0171 404 0875
Call Date: Nov 1969, Inner Temple
Qualifications: [LLB (Lond)]

OFFENBACH ROGER LEON

3 Gray's Inn Square
Ground Floor, London WC1R 5AH,
Telephone: 0171 520 5600
E-mail: clerks@3gis.co.uk
Call Date: July 1978, Inner Temple
Pupil Master
Qualifications: [ARICS]

OFFOH JOHNSON IFEANYI

The Chambers of Mr Ali Mohammed Azhar
Basement, 9 King's Bench Walk, Temple,
London EC4Y 7DX,
Telephone: 0171 353 9564
E-mail: jvlee@btinternet.com
Call Date: Nov 1972, Inner Temple

OFORI GEORGE EDWARD

ACHMA Chambers
44 Yarnfield Square, Clayton Road,
London SE15 5JD,
Telephone: 0171 639 7817/0171 635 7904
Chancery Chambers
1st Floor Offices, 70/72 Chancery Lane,
London WC2A 1AB,
Telephone: 0171 405 6879/6870
Call Date: Nov 1982, Gray's Inn
Qualifications: [LLB Lond]

OGDEN ERIC

2 Paper Buildings, Basement North
Temple, London EC4Y 7ET,
Telephone: 0171 936 2613
E-mail: post@2paper.co.uk
Call Date: July 1983, Inner Temple
Pupil Master
Qualifications: [BA]

OGLE MISS REBECCA THEODOSIA ABIGAIL

Southernhay Chambers
33 Southernhay East, Exeter, Devon,
EX1 1NX, Telephone: 01392 255777
E-mail:southernhay.chambers@lineone.net
Call Date: July 1989, Inner Temple
Qualifications: [BA, Dip Law]

OGUNBIYI OLUWOLE AFOLABI

Horizon Chambers
95a Chancery Lane, London WC2A 1DT,
Telephone: 0171 242 2440
Call Date: July 1995, Lincoln's Inn
Qualifications: [LLB (Hons)]

OHRENSTEIN DOV

Chambers of Lord Goodhart QC
Ground Floor, 3 New Square, Lincoln's
Inn, London WC2A 3RS,
Telephone: 0171 405 5577
E-mail:law@threenewsquare.demon.co.uk
Call Date: Oct 1995, Gray's Inn
Qualifications: [MA (Cantab)]

OJI MISS ATIM ANENE IFEOMA

John Street Chambers
2 John Street, London WC1N 2HJ,
Telephone: 0171 242 1911
E-mail:john.street_chambers@virgin.net
Call Date: Nov 1992, Inner Temple
Qualifications: [BA, LLB (Lond)]

OJUTIKU MRS FADEKEMI OMOTAYO

Goldsworth Chambers
1st Floor, 11 Gray's Inn Square, London
WC1R 5JD, Telephone: 0171 405 7117
Counsels' Chambers
2nd Floor, 10-11 Gray's Inn Square,
London WC1R 5JD,
Telephone: 0171 405 2576
E-mail:clerks@10-11graysinnsquare.co.uk
Call Date: 1994, Lincoln's Inn
Qualifications: [BA (Hons)(Nigeria), LLB
(Hons)(Lond)]

OKAI ANTHONY SETH

Chancery Chambers
1st Floor Offices, 70/72 Chancery Lane,
London WC2A 1AB,
Telephone: 0171 405 6879/6870
Call Date: July 1973, Inner Temple
Pupil Master
Qualifications: [LLB (Lond)]

OKE OLANREWAJU OLADIPUPO

Kingsway Chambers
88 Kingsway, Holborn, London
WC2B 6AA, Telephone: 07000 653529
E-mail: lanreoke@cocoon.co.uk
Call Date: July 1979, Lincoln's Inn
Qualifications: [MA(Oxon)]

OKOYA WILLIAM EBIKISE

Arden Chambers
27 John Street, London WC1N 2BL,
Telephone: 020 7242 4244
E-mail:clerks@arden-chambers.law.co.uk
Call Date: Nov 1989, Gray's Inn
Qualifications: [LLM]

OKOYE MISS JOY NWAMALA

Chambers of Joy Okoye
Suite 1, 2nd Floor Gray's Inn Chambers,
Gray's Inn, London WC1R 5JA,
Telephone: 0171 405 7011
Call Date: July 1981, Inner Temple
Pupil Master
Qualifications: [BA (Hons)]

OLDHAM MS (ELIZABETH) JANE

4-5 Gray's Inn Square
Ground Floor, Gray's Inn, London
WC1R 5JP, Telephone: 0171 404 5252
E-mail:chambers@4-5graysinnsquare.co.uk
Call Date: July 1985, Middle Temple
Qualifications: [MA (Cantab)]

OLDHAM MRS FRANCES MARY THERESA QC (1994)

Chambers of Michael Pert QC
36 Bedford Row, London WC1R 4JH,
Telephone: 0171 421 8000
E-mail: 36bedfordrow@link.org
Chambers of Michael Pert QC
24 Albion Place, Northampton NN1 1UD,
Telephone: 01604 602333

Chambers of Michael Pert QC
104 New Walk, Leicester LE1 7EA,
Telephone: 0116 249 2020
Call Date: July 1977, Gray's Inn
Recorder

OLDHAM PETER ROBERT

11 King's Bench Walk
Temple, London EC4Y 7EQ,
Telephone: 0171 632 8500/583 0610
E-mail: clerksroom@11kbw.com
Call Date: Oct 1990, Gray's Inn
Pupil Master
Qualifications: [BA (Cantab), Dip Law (City)]

OLDLAND ANDREW RICHARD

Walnut House
63 St David's Hill, Exeter, Devon,
EX4 4DW, Telephone: 01392 279751
E-mail: 106627.2451@compuserve.com
6 King's Bench Walk
Ground Floor, Temple, London
EC4Y 7DR, Telephone: 0171 583 0410
E-mail: worsley@6kbw.freeserve.co.uk
Call Date: Nov 1990, Inner Temple
Qualifications: [MSc (Lond), Dip Law (City)]

OLDLAND MISS JENNIFER JANE

1 Dr Johnson's Buildings
Ground Floor, Temple, London
EC4Y 7AX, Telephone: 0171 353 9328
E-mail:OneDr.Johnsons@btinternet.com
Dr Johnson's Chambers
The Atrium Court, Apex Plaza, Reading,
Berkshire, RG1 1AX,
Telephone: 01734 254221
Call Date: Nov 1978, Inner Temple

OLIVER ANDREW JAMES

Octagon House
19 Colegate, Norwich NR3 1AT,
Telephone: 01603 623186
E-mail: admin@octagon-chambers.co.uk
Call Date: Nov 1993, Lincoln's Inn
Qualifications: [LLB (Hons)]

OLIVER PROFESSOR (ANN) DAWN (HARRISON)

Blackstone Chambers
Blackstone House, Temple, London
EC4Y 9BW, Telephone: 0171 583 1770
E-mail:clerks@blackstonechambers.com
Call Date: July 1965, Middle Temple
Qualifications: [MA (Cantab), PhD (Cantab)]

OLIVER CRISPIN ARTHUR

Trinity Chambers
9-12 Trinity Chare, Quayside, Newcastle
upon Tyne NE1 3DF,
Telephone: 0191 232 1927
E-mail: info@trinitychambers.co.uk
Call Date: Nov 1990, Middle Temple
Qualifications: [MA (St Andrews), Dip Law]

OLIVER DAVID KEIGHTLEY RIDEAL QC (1986)

13 Old Square
Ground Floor, Lincoln's Inn, London
WC2A 3UA, Telephone: 0171 404 4800
E-mail: clerks@13oldsquare.law.co.uk
Call Date: July 1972, Lincoln's Inn
Qualifications: [BA (Cantab), Licenci Spec en
, droit European , Brussels]

OLIVER MISS JULIET DIANNE

Bridewell Chambers
2 Bridewell Place, London EC4V 6AP,
Telephone: 020 7797 8800
E-mail:HughesGage@bridewell.law.co.uk
Call Date: Nov 1974, Gray's Inn
Qualifications: [LLB]

OLIVER MICHAEL RICHARD

Hardwicke Building
New Square, Lincoln's Inn, London
WC2A 3SB, Telephone: 020 7242 2523
E-mail: clerks@hardwicke.co.uk
Call Date: July 1977, Inner Temple
Pupil Master
Qualifications: [MA (Oxon)]

OLIVER SIMON JONATHAN

Guildford Chambers
Stoke House, Leapale Lane, Guildford,
Surrey, GU1 4LY,
Telephone: 01483 539131
E-mail:guildford.barristers@btinternet.com
Call Date: July 1981, Inner Temple
Pupil Master
Qualifications: [LLB (Exon)]

OLIVER-JONES STEPHEN QC (1996)

5 Fountain Court
Steelhouse Lane, Birmingham B4 6DR,
Telephone: 0121 606 0500
E-mail:clerks@5fountaincourt.law.co.uk
Call Date: Apr 1970, Inner Temple
Recorder
Qualifications: [BA (Dunelm)]

OLLENNU ASHITEY KWAME NII-AMAA

Horizon Chambers
95a Chancery Lane, London WC2A 1DT,
Telephone: 0171 242 2440
Westgate Chambers
144 High Street, Lewes, East Sussex,
BN7 1XT, Telephone: 01273 480510
Call Date: July 1981, Lincoln's Inn
Pupil Master
Qualifications: [BA (Hons)]

OLUPITAN-RUBAN MRS YETUNDE

Chancery Chambers
1st Floor Offices, 70/72 Chancery Lane,
London WC2A 1AB,
Telephone: 0171 405 6879/6870
Call Date: Nov 1996, Inner Temple
Qualifications: [BA]

OMAMBALA MISS IJEOMA CHINYELU

Old Square Chambers
1 Verulam Buildings, Gray's Inn, London
WC1R 5LQ, Telephone: 0171 269 0300
E-mail:clerks@oldsquarechambers.co.uk
Old Square Chambers
Hanover House, 47 Corn Street, Bristol
BS1 1HT, Telephone: 0117 9277111
E-mail: oldsqbri@globalnet.co.uk
Call Date: Apr 1989, Gray's Inn
Qualifications: [BA, MPhil (Cantab)]

OMAR MISS ROBINA

Wessex Chambers
48 Queens Road, Reading, Berkshire,
RG1 4BD, Telephone: 0118 956 8856
E-mail:wessexchambers@compuserve.com
Call Date: Oct 1991, Lincoln's Inn
Qualifications: [LLB (Hons)]

OMIDEYI MRS CHRISTINA AYINKE

Albany Chambers
91 Kentish Town Road, London
NW1 8NY, Telephone: 0171 485 5736/
5758 E-mail: albany91.freeserve.co.uk
Call Date: July 1987, Lincoln's Inn
Qualifications: [LLB]

ONG MISS GRACE YU MAE

One Essex Court
1st Floor, Temple, London EC4Y 9AR,
Telephone: 0171 936 3030
E-mail: one.essex_court@virgin.net
Call Date: July 1985, Lincoln's Inn
Pupil Master
Qualifications: [LLB (London)]

ONIONS JEFFERY PETER QC (1998)

One Essex Court
Ground Floor, Temple, London
EC4Y 9AR, Telephone: 020 7583 2000
E-mail: clerks@oneessexcourt.co.uk
Call Date: July 1981, Middle Temple
Qualifications: [MA, LLM (Cantab)]

ONSLOW ANDREW GEORGE

3 Verulam Buildings
London WC1R 5NT,
Telephone: 0171 831 8441
E-mail: clerks@3verulam.co.uk
Call Date: July 1982, Middle Temple
Pupil Master
Qualifications: [MA (Oxon)]

ONSLOW RICHARD ALAN DOUGLAS

2 King's Bench Walk
Ground Floor, Temple, London
EC4Y 7DE, Telephone: 0171 353 1746
E-mail: 2kbw@atlas.co.uk

King's Bench Chambers
115 North Hill, Plymouth PL4 8JY,
Telephone: 01752 221551
Call Date: July 1982, Inner Temple
Pupil Master
Qualifications: [MA (Oxon)]

ONSLOW ROBERT DENZIL

8 New Square
Lincoln's Inn, London WC2A 3QP,
Telephone: 0171 405 4321
E-mail: clerks@8newsquare.co.uk
Call Date: Oct 1991, Lincoln's Inn
Pupil Master
Qualifications: [BA (Hons) (Oxon), Dip Law]

ONUAGULUCHI JONES

Southsea Chambers
PO Box 148, Southsea, Portsmouth,
Hampshire, PO5 2TU,
Telephone: 01705 291261
Fleet Chambers
Mitre House, 44-46 Fleet Street, London
EC4Y 1BN, Telephone: 0171 936 3707
E-mail: rr@fleetchambers.demon.co.uk
Call Date: Feb 1971, Inner Temple
Qualifications: [LLM (Lond)]

OON MISS PAMELA BENG SUE

Dr Johnson's Chambers
Two Dr Johnson's Buildings, Temple,
London EC4Y 7AY,
Telephone: 0171 353 4716
E-mail: clerks@2djb.freeserve.co.uk
Call Date: July 1982, Inner Temple
Pupil Master
Qualifications: [LLL]

OPPENHEIM ROBIN FRANK

Doughty Street Chambers
11 Doughty Street, London WC1N 2PG,
Telephone: 0171 404 1313
E-mail:enquiries@doughtystreet.co.uk
Call Date: Nov 1988, Middle Temple
Pupil Master
Qualifications: [BA Hons (Manch), Dip Law]

OPPERMAN GUY THOMAS

3 Paper Buildings
Temple, London EC4Y 7EU,
Telephone: 020 7583 8055
E-mail: London@3paper.com

3 Paper Buildings (Winchester)
4 St Peter Street, Winchester SO23 8BW,
Telephone: 01962 868884
E-mail: winchester@3paper.com
3 Paper Buildings (Bournemouth)
20 Lorne Park Road, Bournemouth,
Dorset, BH1 1JN,
Telephone: 01202 292102
E-mail: Bournemouth@3paper.com
3 Paper Buildings (Oxford)
1 Alfred Street, High Street, Oxford
OX1 4EH, Telephone: 01865 793736
E-mail: oxford@3paper.com
Call Date: Nov 1989, Middle Temple
Qualifications: [LLB (Hons)(Bucks)]

ORCHARD ANTHONY EDWARD

2-4 Tudor Street
London EC4Y 0AA,
Telephone: 0171 797 7111
E-mail: clerks@rfqc.co.uk
Call Date: Oct 1991, Inner Temple
Pupil Master
Qualifications: [LLB (So'ton)]

ORCHOVER MS FRANCES RACHEL

4 Brick Court
Ground Floor, Temple, London
EC4Y 9AD, Telephone: 0171 797 7766
E-mail: chambers@4brick.co.uk
Call Date: July 1989, Middle Temple
Qualifications: [BA (Hons) (Lond), Dip Law]

ORME JOHN RICHARD

Gray's Inn Chambers
Chambers of Nigel Ley (2nd Floor), Gray's
Inn, London WC1R 5JA,
Telephone: 0171 831 7888 (Chambers)/
0171 831 7904 (Mr M Ullah)
Call Date: 1995, Lincoln's Inn
Qualifications: [BSc (Hons)(Lond), PhD, Dip
in Law (City)]

ORME RICHARD ANDREW

Peel Court Chambers
45 Hardman Street, Manchester M3 3PL,
Telephone: 0161 832 3791
E-mail: clerks@peelct.co.uk
Call Date: Oct 1993, Lincoln's Inn
Qualifications: [BA (Hons)(Leeds), CPE
(Lond)]

D

ORNSBY MISS SUZANNE DOREEN

2 Harcourt Buildings
2nd Floor, Temple, London EC4Y 9DB,
Telephone: 020 7353 8415
E-mail: clerks@2hb.law.co.uk
Call Date: Nov 1986, Middle Temple
Pupil Master
Qualifications: [LLB (UCL)]

ORR CRAIG WYNDHAM

Fountain Court
Temple, London EC4Y 9DH,
Telephone: 0171 583 3335
E-mail: chambers@fountaincourt.co.uk
Call Date: July 1986, Middle Temple
Pupil Master
Qualifications: [MA (Cantab), BCL (Oxon)]

ORR JULIAN BOYD

Cobden House Chambers
19 Quay Street, Manchester M3 3HN,
Telephone: 0161 833 6000
E-mail: clerks@cobden.co.uk
Call Date: Oct 1995, Lincoln's Inn
Qualifications: [LLB (Hons)(L'pool)]

ORR NICHOLAS GUY

Adrian Lyon's Chambers
14 Castle Street, Liverpool L2 0NE,
Telephone: 0151 236 4421/8240
E-mail: chambers14@aol.com
5 Stone Buildings
Lincoln's Inn, London WC2A 3XT,
Telephone: 0171 242 6201
E-mail:clerks@5-stonebuildings.law.co.uk
Call Date: Nov 1970, Gray's Inn
Pupil Master
Qualifications: [LLB (Bris)]

ORSULIK MICHAEL ANTHONY

9-12 Bell Yard
London WC2A 2LF,
Telephone: 0171 400 1800
E-mail: clerks@bellyard.co.uk
Call Date: Nov 1978, Middle Temple
Pupil Master
Qualifications: [BA, LLM (Lond)]

ORTON PAUL WALTER

Call Date: Nov 1988, Gray's Inn
Qualifications: [BA (Hons)]

OSBORNE DAVID THOMAS

South Western Chambers
Melville House, 12 Middle Street,
Taunton, Somerset, TA1 1SH,
Telephone: 01823 331919 (24 hrs)
E-mail: barclerk@clara.net
Call Date: July 1974, Gray's Inn
Qualifications: [BA (Hons) (McGill), CSS (Granada)]

OSBORNE MISS KATIE ANTOINETTE

Holborn Chambers
6 Gate Street, Lincoln's Inn Fields, London
WC2A 3HP, Telephone: 0171 242 6060
Call Date: Nov 1993, Middle Temple
Qualifications: [BA (Hons), CPE]

OSBORNE NIGEL JOHN

33 Park Place
Cardiff CF1 3BA,
Telephone: 02920 233313
Call Date: Nov 1993, Middle Temple
Qualifications: [LLB (Hons)(Wales)]

OSBORNE-HALSEY MRS THELMA EDWINA

Chambers of Thelma Osborne-Hadley
North Eastern Law Chambers, 19 Augustus
Drive, Alcester, Warwickshire, B49 5HH,
Telephone: 01789 766206
Call Date: July 1982, Gray's Inn
Qualifications: [BA,MA (West Indies), LLB (Hons)]

OSMAN OSMAN HASAN

Mitre House Chambers
15-19 Devereux Court, London WC2R 3JJ,
Telephone: 0171 583 8233
Call Date: Feb 1995, Inner Temple
Qualifications: [LLB (Hons) (Middx)]

OSMAN ROBERT WALTER

Queen's Chambers
5 John Dalton Street, Manchester M2 6ET,
Telephone: 0161 834 6875/4738
Queens Chambers
4 Camden Place, Preston PR1 3JL,
Telephone: 01772 828300
Call Date: July 1974, Middle Temple
Qualifications: [LLB (Lond)]

OSMAN MISS SONA KAARINA PIA

Mitre House Chambers
15-19 Devereux Court, London WC2R 3JJ,
Telephone: 0171 583 8233
Call Date: Nov 1986, Middle Temple
Qualifications: [BA(Keele) Dip Law]

OSSACK MRS TANYA RACHELLE ELISE

3 Temple Gardens
3rd Floor, Temple, London EC4Y 9AU,
Telephone: 0171 583 0010
Call Date: Oct 1993, Gray's Inn
Qualifications: [MA (Brunel)]

OTENG EMMANUEL ALDO

The Thames Chambers
Wickham House, 10 Cleveland Way,
London E1 4TR,
Telephone: 0171 366 6655/790 2424 X390
E-mail: thames-chambers@usa.net
Call Date: Feb 1963, Middle Temple
Pupil Master
Qualifications: [Diploma Legal,
Administration, (Hebrew University, of
Jerusalem 1966)]

OTTON-GOULDER MISS CATHARINE ANNE

Brick Court Chambers
7-8 Essex Street, London WC2R 3LD,
Telephone: 0171 379 3550
E-mail: [surname]@brickcourt.co.uk
Call Date: Nov 1983, Lincoln's Inn
Pupil Master
Qualifications: [MA (Oxon)]

OTTY TIMOTHY JOHN

2 Temple Gardens
Temple, London EC4Y 9AY,
Telephone: 0171 583 6041
E-mail: clerks@2templegardens.co.uk
Call Date: Oct 1990, Lincoln's Inn
Qualifications: [MA (Cantab)]

OTWAL MUKHTIAR SINGH

Mitre Court Chambers
3rd Floor, Temple, London EC4Y 7BP,
Telephone: 0171 353 9394
E-mail: mitrecourt.com
Call Date: Nov 1991, Lincoln's Inn
Qualifications: [LLB (Hons) (Leeds)]

OUAKNIN DANIEL ALAN

Goldsworth Chambers
1st Floor, 11 Gray's Inn Square, London
WC1R 5JD, Telephone: 0171 405 7117
Call Date: Nov 1998, Lincoln's Inn
Qualifications: [BSc (Hons)(Wales)]

OUDKERK DANIEL RICHARD

22 Old Buildings
Lincoln's Inn, London WC2A 3UJ,
Telephone: 0171 831 0222
Call Date: Nov 1992, Inner Temple
Qualifications: [LLB (Bris)]

OUGH DR RICHARD NORMAN

Hardwicke Building
New Square, Lincoln's Inn, London
WC2A 3SB, Telephone: 020 7242 2523
E-mail: clerks@hardwicke.co.uk
Call Date: July 1985, Inner Temple
Qualifications: [MA Law, MBBS, MSc, in
Management, FCIArb]

Fax: 0171 691 1234; DX: LDE 393;
Other comms: E-mail
richard.ough@hardwicke.co.uk; URL:
http://www.ough.com

Other professional qualifications: Deputy
Chairman NHS Tribunal

Types of work: Arbitration, Clinical negligence, Common law (general), Ecclesiastical, Mediation, Personal injury

Awards and memberships: Fellow of the Royal
Society of Medicine; Sloan Fellow, London
Business School

Other professional experience: Qualified as a
doctor in London after being Resident in
Obstetrics and Gynaecology at University of
British Columbia in Vancouver, entered
private practice in Ontario, where his
hospital experience included all major
specialities

Publications: *The Mareva Injunction and Anton Piller Order*, Butterworths 1998 (3rd edition in preparation); *MS Sufferers: can they bring a claim?*, 1997; *Automatic Strike Out [A European Court of Human Rights perspective]*, 1996

Reported Cases: *Ratcliffe v Plymouth and Torbay HA CA*, [1998] 3 PIQR 170, 1998. Leading case on *res ipsa* in medical negligence.
Appleton and Ors v Garrett, [1997] 8 Med LR 75, 1997. £2 million group action of over 100 plaintiffs: dental negligence, consent, trespass to person, aggravated damages.
Rhodes v Spokes and Farbridge, [1996] Med LR 135. Medical negligence failure to diagnose blocked cerebral shunt.
Fletcher v Sheffield HA, [1994] Med LR 156 (CA). Limitation in medical negligence actions.
Stobart v Nottingham HA, Yaffi v North Lincs HA, [1992] 3 Med LR 284, 1992. Medical negligence/discovery, whether discovery should precede inquest.

OUGHTON RICHARD DONALD

Cobden House Chambers
19 Quay Street, Manchester M3 3HN,
Telephone: 0161 833 6000
E-mail: clerks@cobden.co.uk
Call Date: July 1978, Lincoln's Inn
Qualifications: [MA (Cantab), LLM (Pennsylvania)]

OULTON RICHARD ARTHUR COURTNEY

2 King's Bench Walk
Ground Floor, Temple, London
EC4Y 7DE, Telephone: 0171 353 1746
E-mail: 2kbw@atlas.co.uk
King's Bench Chambers
115 North Hill, Plymouth PL4 8JY,
Telephone: 01752 221551
Call Date: Nov 1995, Middle Temple
Qualifications: [MA]

OUSELEY DUNCAN BRIAN WALTER QC (1992)

4-5 Gray's Inn Square
Ground Floor, Gray's Inn, London
WC1R 5JP, Telephone: 0171 404 5252
E-mail:chambers@4-5graysinnsquare.co.uk
Call Date: Feb 1973, Gray's Inn

Recorder
Qualifications: [MA (Cantab) LLM, (Lond)]

OUTHWAITE MRS WENDY-JANE TIVNAN

2 Harcourt Buildings
Ground Floor/Left, Temple, London
EC4Y 9DB, Telephone: 0171 583 9020
E-mail: clerks@harcourt.co.uk
Call Date: May 1990, Lincoln's Inn
Qualifications: [MA (Oxon), License Speciale en, Droit Europeen]

OVERBURY RUPERT SIMON

18 Red Lion Court
(Off Fleet Street), London EC4A 3EB,
Telephone: 0171 520 6000
E-mail: chambers@18rlc.co.uk
Thornwood House
102 New London Road, Chelmsford,
Essex, CM2 0RG,
Telephone: 01245 280880
E-mail: chambers@18rlc.co.uk
Call Date: July 1984, Middle Temple
Pupil Master
Qualifications: [BA (Hons)]

OVERS MS ESTELLE FAE

New Court Chambers
5 Verulam Buildings, Gray's Inn, London
WC1R 5LY, Telephone: 0171 831 9500
E-mail: mail@newcourtchambers.com
Call Date: Oct 1994, Gray's Inn
Qualifications: [BA]

OVEY MISS ELIZABETH HELEN

11 Old Square
Ground Floor, Lincoln's Inn, London
WC2A 3TS, Telephone: 020 7430 0341
E-mail: clerks@11oldsquare.co.uk
Call Date: July 1978, Middle Temple
Pupil Master
Qualifications: [BA (Oxon)]

OWEN DAVID CHRISTOPHER

20 Essex Street
London WC2R 3AL,
Telephone: 0171 583 9294
E-mail: clerks@20essexst.com
Call Date: Nov 1983, Middle Temple
Pupil Master
Qualifications: [BA (Oxon), Dip Law (City)]

OWEN DAVID MEURIG

25-27 Castle Street
1st Floor, Liverpool L2 4TA,
Telephone: 0151 227 5661/051 236 5072
Call Date: July 1981, Gray's Inn
Pupil Master
Qualifications: [BA (Keele)]

OWEN ERIC CYRIL HAMMERSLEY

40 King Street
Manchester M2 6BA,
Telephone: 0161 832 9082
E-mail: clerks@40kingstreet.co.uk
4 Breams Buildings
London EC4A 1AQ,
Telephone: 0171 353 5835/430 1221
E-mail:breams@4breamsbuildings.law.co.uk
The Chambers of Philip Raynor QC
5 Park Place, Leeds LS1 2RU,
Telephone: 0113 242 1123
Call Date: Nov 1969, Gray's Inn
Pupil Master
Qualifications: [LLB (L'pool)]

OWEN MISS GAIL ANN

India Buildings Chambers
Water Street, Liverpool L2 0XG,
Telephone: 0151 243 6000
E-mail: clerks@chambers.u-net.com
Call Date: Nov 1980, Gray's Inn
Assistant Recorder
Qualifications: [LLB (L'pool)]

OWEN MISS HELEN NNONYELUM

**Gray's Inn Chambers, The Chambers of
Norman Patterson**
First Floor, Gray's Inn Chambers, Gray's
Inn, London WC1R 5JA,
Telephone: 0171 831 5344
E-mail: s.mcblain@btinternet.com
Call Date: Nov 1994, Inner Temple
Qualifications: [BA]

OWEN PHILIP LOSCOMBE WINTRINGHAM QC (1963)

Brick Court Chambers
7-8 Essex Street, London WC2R 3LD,
Telephone: 0171 379 3550
E-mail: [surname]@brickcourt.co.uk
Call Date: Jan 1949, Middle Temple
Qualifications: [MA (Oxon)]

OWEN ROBERT FRANK QC (1996)

Ropewalk Chambers
24 The Ropewalk, Nottingham NG1 5EF,
Telephone: 0115 9472581
E-mail: administration@ropewalk co.uk
Call Date: July 1977, Inner Temple
Assistant Recorder
Qualifications: [LLB (Lond)]

OWEN ROBERT MICHAEL QC (1988)

1 Crown Office Row
Ground Floor, Temple, London
EC4Y 7HH, Telephone: 0171 797 7500
E-mail: mail@onecrownofficerow.com
Crown Office Row Chambers
Blenheim House, 120 Church Street,
Brighton, Sussex, BN1 1WH,
Telephone: 01273 625625
E-mail: crownofficerow@clara.net
Call Date: Nov 1968, Inner Temple
Recorder
Qualifications: [LLB (Exon)]

OWEN MS SARA JANE

Carmarthen Chambers
30 Spilman Street, Carmarthen, Dyfed,
SA31 1LQ, Telephone: 01267 234410
E-mail: law@in-wales.com
Call Date: Oct 1995, Inner Temple
Qualifications: [BA (Cantab)]

OWEN TIMOTHY WYNN

Doughty Street Chambers
11 Doughty Street, London WC1N 2PG,
Telephone: 0171 404 1313
E-mail:enquiries@doughtystreet.co.uk
Call Date: July 1983, Middle Temple
Pupil Master
Qualifications: [BA (Lond), Dip Law]

OWEN TUDOR WYN

9-12 Bell Yard
London WC2A 2LF,
Telephone: 0171 400 1800
E-mail: clerks@bellyard.co.uk
Call Date: July 1974, Gray's Inn
Pupil Master, Recorder
Qualifications: [LLB (Lond)]

OWEN-JONES DAVID RODERIC

3 Temple Gardens
2nd Floor, Temple, London EC4Y 9AU,
Telephone: 0171 583 1155
Call Date: July 1972, Inner Temple
Pupil Master
Qualifications: [LLM (Lond)]

OWENS MISS HILARY JANE

St Philip's Chambers
Fountain Court, Steelhouse Lane,
Birmingham B4 6DR,
Telephone: 0121 246 7000
E-mail: clerks@st-philips.co.uk
Call Date: 1994, Middle Temple
Qualifications: [BA (Hons)(Dunelm)]

OWENS MRS LUCY ISABEL

13 King's Bench Walk
1st Floor, Temple, London EC4Y 7EN,
Telephone: 0171 353 7204
E-mail: clerks@13kbw.law.co.uk
King's Bench Chambers
32 Beaumont Street, Oxford OX1 2NP,
Telephone: 01865 311066
E-mail: clerks@kbc-oxford.law.co.uk
Call Date: 1997, Middle Temple
Qualifications: [LLB (Hons)(Kingston)]

OWENS MATTHEW JOHN

7 Stone Buildings (also at 11 Bolt Court)
1st Floor, Lincoln's Inn, London
WC2A 3SZ, Telephone: 0171 242 0961
E-mail:larthur@7stonebuildings.law.co.uk
11 Bolt Court (also at 7 Stone Buildings – 1st Floor)
London EC4A 3DQ,
Telephone: 0171 353 2300
E-mail: boltct11@aol.com
Redhill Chambers
Seloduct House, 30 Station Road, Redhill,
Surrey, RH1 1NF,
Telephone: 01737 780781
Call Date: Nov 1988, Gray's Inn
Qualifications: [LLB (Lond)]

OWUSU KWABENA

Chancery Chambers
1st Floor Offices, 70/72 Chancery Lane,
London WC2A 1AB,
Telephone: 0171 405 6879/6870
Call Date: Nov 1983, Gray's Inn
Qualifications: [LLB (Warks)]

OWUSU-YIANOMA DAVID KWASI DARTEY

Chambers of Wilfred Forster-Jones
New Court, 1st Floor South, Temple,
London EC4Y 9BE,
Telephone: 0171 353 0853/4/7222
E-mail: chambers@newcourt.net
Call Date: Nov 1992, Inner Temple
Qualifications: [LLB (Hons)]

OXLADE MISS JOANNE ELIZABETH

33 Bedford Row
London WC1R 4JH,
Telephone: 0171 242 6476
E-mail:clerks@bedfordrow33.demon.co.uk
Call Date: July 1988, Middle Temple
Qualifications: [LLB (Hons)]

OYEBANJI ADAM

5 Fountain Court
Steelhouse Lane, Birmingham B4 6DR,
Telephone: 0121 606 0500
E-mail:clerks@5fountaincourt.law.co.uk
Call Date: July 1987, Inner Temple
Qualifications: [LLB (B'ham)]

OZIN PAUL DAVID

23 Essex Street
London WC2R 3AS,
Telephone: 0171 413 0353/836 8366
E-mail:clerks@essexstreet23.demon.co.uk
Call Date: Nov 1987, Middle Temple
Qualifications: [BA (Oxon)]

PACK MISS MELISSA ELIZABETH JANE

Farrar's Building
Temple, London EC4Y 7BD,
Telephone: 0171 583 9241
E-mail:chambers@farrarsbuilding.co.uk
Call Date: Nov 1995, Middle Temple
Qualifications: [MA (Hons) (Cantab)]

D

PACKMAN MISS CLAIRE GERALDINE VANCE

4 Pump Court
Temple, London EC4Y 7AN,
Telephone: 020 7842 5555
E-mail:chambers@4pumpcourt.law.co.uk
Call Date: Oct 1996, Inner Temple
Qualifications: [BA (Oxon), CPE (Lond)]

PADFIELD MS ALISON MARY

Devereux Chambers
Devereux Court, London WC2R 3JJ,
Telephone: 0171 353 7534
E-mail: mailbox@devchambers.co.uk
Call Date: Oct 1992, Lincoln's Inn
Qualifications: [BA, BCL (Oxon)]

PADFIELD NICHOLAS DAVID QC (1991)

One Hare Court
1st Floor, Temple, London EC4Y 7BE,
Telephone: 020 7353 3171
E-mail:admin-oneharecourt@btinternet.com
Call Date: 1972, Inner Temple
Recorder
Qualifications: [MA (Oxon), LLB (Cantab),
FCIArb]

PADLEY MISS CLARE MELANIE

9 Gough Square
London EC4A 3DE,
Telephone: 020 7832 0500
E-mail: clerks@9goughsq.co.uk
Call Date: Oct 1991, Inner Temple
Qualifications: [BA (Cantab)]

PADMAN ANTHONY

Crystal Chambers
25A Cintra Park, London SE19 2LH,
Telephone: 0181 402 5801
Call Date: Nov 1972, Lincoln's Inn
Qualifications: [LLB (Wales)]

PAGE MISS ADRIENNE MAY QC (1999)

5 Raymond Buildings
1st Floor, Gray's Inn, London WC1R 5BP,
Telephone: 0171 242 2902
E-mail: clerks@media-ent-law.co.uk
Call Date: 1974, Middle Temple
Pupil Master, Recorder
Qualifications: [BA (Kent)]

PAGE ARTHUR HUGO MICKLEM

Blackstone Chambers
Blackstone House, Temple, London
EC4Y 9BW, Telephone: 0171 583 1770
E-mail:clerks@blackstonechambers.com
Call Date: Nov 1977, Inner Temple
Pupil Master
Qualifications: [MA (Cantab)]

PAGE DAVID MARK

2 King's Bench Walk
Ground Floor, Temple, London
EC4Y 7DE, Telephone: 0171 353 1746
E-mail: 2kbw@atlas.co.uk
King's Bench Chambers
115 North Hill, Plymouth PL4 8JY,
Telephone: 01752 221551
Call Date: Nov 1984, Middle Temple
Qualifications: [LLB (Brunel)]

PAGE HOWARD WILLIAM BARRETT QC (1987)

One Hare Court
1st Floor, Temple, London EC4Y 7BE,
Telephone: 020 7353 3171
E-mail:admin-oneharecourt@btinternet.com
Call Date: July 1967, Lincoln's Inn
Qualifications: [MA, LLB (Cantab), FCIArb]

PAGE MRS JANE ELIZABETH

Chartlands Chambers
3 St Giles Terrace, Northampton
NN1 2BN, Telephone: 01604 603322
Call Date: July 1982, Inner Temple
Pupil Master
Qualifications: [LLB]

PAGE JONATHAN ROWLAND THOMAS

High Street Chambers
102 High Street, Godalming, Surrey,
GU7 1DS, Telephone: 01483 861170
Call Date: Oct 1996, Middle Temple
Qualifications: [B.Eng, PhD (Lond), CPE
(City)]

PAGE NIGEL BERNARD

St Mary's Chambers
50 High Pavement, Lace Market,
Nottingham NG1 1HW,
Telephone: 0115 9503503
E-mail: clerks@smc.law.co.uk
Call Date: July 1976, Gray's Inn
Pupil Master
Qualifications: [LLB (Lond)]

PAGET MICHAEL RODBOROUGH

Bracton Chambers
95a Chancery Lane, London WC2A 1DT,
Telephone: 0171 242 4248
Call Date: Oct 1995, Lincoln's Inn
Qualifications: [BSc (Hons), MA (Bris), CPE]

PAIN KENNETH WILLIAM

College Chambers
19 Carlton Cresent, Southampton
SO15 2ET, Telephone: 01703 230338
Call Date: Nov 1969, Gray's Inn

PAINES NICHOLAS PAUL BILLOT QC (1997)

Monckton Chambers
4 Raymond Buildings, Gray's Inn, London
WC1R 5BP, Telephone: 0171 405 7211
E-mail: chambers@monckton.co.uk
Call Date: Apr 1978, Gray's Inn
Qualifications: [MA , Licence Speciale en ,
droit European]

PAINTER IAN DAVID

Counsels' Chambers
2nd Floor, 10-11 Gray's Inn Square,
London WC1R 5JD,
Telephone: 0171 405 2576
E-mail:clerks@10-11graysinnsquare.co.uk
Call Date: Nov 1993, Lincoln's Inn
Qualifications: [BA (Hons)]

PALFREY MONTAGUE MARK

Hardwicke Building
New Square, Lincoln's Inn, London
WC2A 3SB, Telephone: 020 7242 2523
E-mail: clerks@hardwicke.co.uk
Call Date: Nov 1985, Middle Temple
Pupil Master
Qualifications: [LLB (Bucks)]

PALMER ADRIAN OLIVER QC (1992)

Guildhall Chambers
22-26 Broad Street, Bristol BS1 2HG,
Telephone: 0117 9273366
E-mail:civil.clerks@guildhallchambers.co.uk and
criminal.clerks@guildhallchambers.co.uk
Call Date: July 1972, Middle Temple
Recorder
Qualifications: [MA (Cantab)]

PALMER ANTHONY WHEELER QC (1979)

3 Fountain Court
Steelhouse Lane, Birmingham B4 6DR,
Telephone: 0121 236 5854
9 Gough Square
London EC4A 3DE,
Telephone: 020 7832 0500
E-mail: clerks@9goughsq.co.uk
Call Date: 1962, Gray's Inn
Recorder

PALMER MISS GILLIAN

7 New Square
Lincoln's Inn, London WC2A 3QS,
Telephone: 0171 430 1660
Call Date: Feb 1993, Gray's Inn
Qualifications: [BA]

PALMER HOWARD WILLIAM ARTHUR QC (1999)

2 Temple Gardens
Temple, London EC4Y 9AY,
Telephone: 0171 583 6041
E-mail: clerks@2templegardens.co.uk
Call Date: 1977, Inner Temple
Pupil Master
Qualifications: [MA (Oxon)]

PALMER JAMES SAVILL

2 Harcourt Buildings
Ground Floor/Left, Temple, London
EC4Y 9DB, Telephone: 0171 583 9020
E-mail: clerks@harcourt.co.uk
Call Date: Nov 1983, Middle Temple
Qualifications: [MA (Cantab)]

PALMER NATHAN EMMANUEL

Chambers of Wilfred Forster-Jones
New Court, 1st Floor South, Temple,
London EC4Y 9BE,
Telephone: 0171 353 0853/4/7222
E-mail: chambers@newcourt.net
Call Date: Oct 1994, Middle Temple
Qualifications: [LLB (Hons)(Lond)]

PALMER NORMAN ERNEST

Chambers of Norman Palmer
2 Field Court, Gray's Inn, London
WC1R 5BB, Telephone: 0171 405 6114
E-mail: fieldct2@netcomuk.co.uk
Call Date: July 1973, Gray's Inn
Pupil Master
Qualifications: [MA, BCL (Oxon)]

PALMER PATRICK JOHN STEVEN

Sovereign Chambers
25 Park Square, Leeds LS1 2PW,
Telephone: 0113 2451841/2/3
E-mail:sovereignchambers@btinternet.com
Call Date: July 1978, Inner Temple
Pupil Master, Assistant Recorder
Qualifications: [LLB (Lond)]

PALMER ROBERT HENRY

4-5 Gray's Inn Square
Ground Floor, Gray's Inn, London
WC1R 5JP, Telephone: 0171 404 5252
E-mail:chambers@4-5graysinnsquare.co.uk
Call Date: 1998, Gray's Inn

PALMER MISS SUZANNE ELIZABETH JOSEPHINE

Field Court Chambers
2nd Floor, 3 Field Court, Gray's Inn,
London WC1R 5EP,
Telephone: 0171 404 7474
Call Date: Nov 1995, Middle Temple
Qualifications: [BA (Hons)]

PALMER TIMOTHY NIGEL JOHN

High Pavement Chambers
1 High Pavement, Nottingham NG1 1HF,
Telephone: 0115 9418218
Call Date: July 1982, Middle Temple
Pupil Master
Qualifications: [LLB]

PALTENGHI MARK FRANCIS

Dr Johnson's Chambers
Two Dr Johnson's Buildings, Temple,
London EC4Y 7AY,
Telephone: 0171 353 4716
E-mail: clerks@2djb.freeserve.co.uk
Call Date: July 1979, Middle Temple
Pupil Master
Qualifications: [LLB]

PANAGIOTOPOULOU MISS SOPHIE THALIA

Staple Inn Chambers
1st Floor, 9 Staple Inn, Holborn Bars,
London WC1V 7QH,
Telephone: 0171 242 5240
E-mail: clerks@staple-inn.org
Call Date: Oct 1995, Middle Temple
Qualifications: [LLB (Hons), LLM (Hons)]

PANAGIOTOPOULOU MISS TANIA

Staple Inn Chambers
1st Floor, 9 Staple Inn, Holborn Bars,
London WC1V 7QH,
Telephone: 0171 242 5240
E-mail: clerks@staple-inn.org
Call Date: Oct 1994, Middle Temple
Qualifications: [LLB (Hons), LLM (Bucks)]

PANAYI PAVLOS PAUL

2 Paper Buildings
1st Floor, Temple, London EC4Y 7ET,
Telephone: 020 7556 5500
E-mail: clerks@2pbbarristers.co.uk
Call Date: Oct 1995, Gray's Inn
Qualifications: [LLB]

PANAYIOTOU MISS ELEFTHERIA

Furnival Chambers
32 Furnival Street, London EC4A 1JQ,
Telephone: 0171 405 3232
E-mail: clerks@furnivallaw.co.uk
Call Date: Oct 1992, Gray's Inn
Qualifications: [LL.B (Lond)]

PANESAR DESHPAL SINGH

13 King's Bench Walk
1st Floor, Temple, London EC4Y 7EN,
Telephone: 0171 353 7204
E-mail: clerks@13kbw.law.co.uk
King's Bench Chambers
32 Beaumont Street, Oxford OX1 2NP,
Telephone: 01865 311066
E-mail: clerks@kbc-oxford.law.co.uk
Call Date: Feb 1993, Inner Temple
Qualifications: [LLB (Hons)(Lond)]

PANESAR MANJIT SINGH

6 King's Bench Walk
Ground, Third & Fourth Floors, Temple,
London EC4Y 7DR,
Telephone: 0171 353 4931/583 0695
Call Date: Nov 1989, Middle Temple
Qualifications: [LLB Hons]

PANETH MISS SARAH RUTH

No. 1 Serjeants' Inn
5th Floor Fleet Street, Temple, London
EC4Y 1LH, Telephone: 0171 415 6666
E-mail:no1serjeantsinn@btinternet.com
Call Date: Nov 1985, Gray's Inn
Pupil Master, Assistant Recorder
Qualifications: [BA (York) Dip Law]

PANFORD FRANK HAIG QC (1999)

Doughty Street Chambers
11 Doughty Street, London WC1N 2PG,
Telephone: 0171 404 1313
E-mail:enquiries@doughtystreet.co.uk
Call Date: 1972, Middle Temple
Qualifications: [LLB (Lond), LLB (Cantab),
Dip Droit Prive, (Hague Academy)]

Types of work: Administrative, Civil liberties,
Common law (general), Defamation, Entertainment, Immigration, Private international

Membership of foreign bars: Gibraltar (1994
Call)

Other professional experience: 14 years as an
academic; 6 years as a senior barrister and
legal adviser at the British Board of Film
Classification

PANNICK DAVID PHILIP QC (1992)

Blackstone Chambers
Blackstone House, Temple, London
EC4Y 9BW, Telephone: 0171 583 1770
E-mail:clerks@blackstonechambers.com
Call Date: July 1979, Gray's Inn
Recorder
Qualifications: [MA, BCL (Oxon)]

PANTON ALASTAIR HOWARD

Fleet Chambers
Mitre House, 44-46 Fleet Street, London
EC4Y 1BN, Telephone: 0171 936 3707
E-mail: rr@fleetchambers.demon.co.uk
Call Date: Oct 1996, Inner Temple
Qualifications: [MA (Cantab), CPE]

PANTON WILLIAM DWIGHT

Britton Street Chambers
1st Floor, 20 Britton Street, London
EC1M 5NQ, Telephone: 0171 608 3765
Call Date: Nov 1977, Inner Temple

PAPAGEORGIS GEORGE MICHAEL

2 King's Bench Walk Chambers
1st Floor, 2 King's Bench Walk, Temple,
London EC4Y 7DE,
Telephone: 020 7353 9276
E-mail: chambers@2kbw.co.uk
Call Date: July 1981, Middle Temple
Pupil Master

PAPAZIAN MISS CLIONA CONCEPTA

**11 Bolt Court (also at 7 Stone Buildings
– 1st Floor)**
London EC4A 3DQ,
Telephone: 0171 353 2300
E-mail: boltct11@aol.com
**7 Stone Buildings (also at 11 Bolt
Court)**
1st Floor, Lincoln's Inn, London
WC2A 3SZ, Telephone: 0171 242 0961
E-mail:larthur@7stonebuildings.law.co.uk
Redhill Chambers
Seloduct House, 30 Station Road, Redhill,
Surrey, RH1 1NF,
Telephone: 01737 780781
Call Date: Nov 1994, Inner Temple
Qualifications: [BA (Wales), MA, LLB
(Ireland)]

PARDOE ALAN DOUGLAS WILLIAM
QC (1988)

Devereux Chambers
Devereux Court, London WC2R 3JJ,
Telephone: 0171 353 7534
E-mail: mailbox@devchambers.co.uk
Call Date: Nov 1971, Lincoln's Inn
Recorder
Qualifications: [MA, LLB (Cantab)]

PARDOE MATTHEW JAMES

Counsels' Chambers
2nd Floor, 10-11 Gray's Inn Square,
London WC1R 5JD,
Telephone: 0171 405 2576
E-mail:clerks@10-11graysinnsquare.co.uk
Call Date: Feb 1992, Inner Temple
Qualifications: [BA (Hons), CPE]

PARDOE RUPERT ADAM CORIN

23 Essex Street
London WC2R 3AS,
Telephone: 0171 413 0353/836 8366
E-mail:clerks@essexstreet23.demon.co.uk
Call Date: July 1984, Inner Temple
Pupil Master
Qualifications: [MA (Cantab)]

PARFITT NICHOLAS JOHN

11 Stone Buildings
Lincoln's Inn, London WC2A 3TG,
Telephone: +44 (0)207 831 6381
E-mail:clerks@11StoneBuildings.law.co.uk
Call Date: Oct 1993, Middle Temple
Qualifications: [BA (Hons)(Bris), CPE
(Lond)]

PARISH STEPHEN ADRIAN BURGIS

2 King's Bench Walk
Ground Floor, Temple, London
EC4Y 7DE, Telephone: 0171 353 1746
E-mail: 2kbw@atlas.co.uk
King's Bench Chambers
115 North Hill, Plymouth PL4 8JY,
Telephone: 01752 221551
Call Date: July 1966, Inner Temple
Recorder
Qualifications: [LLB]

PARK DAVID JOHN

5 Fountain Court
Steelhouse Lane, Birmingham B4 6DR,
Telephone: 0121 606 0500
E-mail:clerks@5fountaincourt.law.co.uk
Call Date: May 1992, Lincoln's Inn
Qualifications: [LLB (Lond)]

PARKER ALAN PHILIP

Coleridge Chambers
Citadel, 190 Corporation Street,
Birmingham B4 6QD,
Telephone: 0121 233 8500
Call Date: May 1995, Gray's Inn
Qualifications: [LLB (Manch)]

PARKER MRS ANTHEA ELIZABETH

4 Brick Court
Ground Floor, Temple, London
EC4Y 9AD, Telephone: 0171 797 7766
E-mail: chambers@4brick.co.uk
Call Date: Nov 1990, Middle Temple
Qualifications: [BA (Hons) (E Anglia), Dip
Law (PCL)]

PARKER CHRISTOPHER JAMES
FRANCIS

3 Paper Buildings
Temple, London EC4Y 7EU,
Telephone: 020 7583 8055
E-mail: London@3paper.com
3 Paper Buildings (Winchester)
4 St Peter Street, Winchester SO23 8BW,
Telephone: 01962 868884
E-mail: winchester@3paper.com
3 Paper Buildings (Bournemouth)
20 Lorne Park Road, Bournemouth,
Dorset, BH1 1JN,
Telephone: 01202 292102
E-mail: Bournemouth@3paper.com
3 Paper Buildings (Oxford)
1 Alfred Street, High Street, Oxford
OX1 4EH, Telephone: 01865 793736
E-mail: oxford@3paper.com
Call Date: July 1986, Gray's Inn
Pupil Master
Qualifications: [LLB (Hons)(Exon)]

PARKER CHRISTOPHER ROY

7 Stone Buildings
Ground Floor, Lincoln's Inn, London
WC2A 3SZ, Telephone: 0171 405 3886/
242 3546 E-mail: chaldous@vossnet.co.uk
Call Date: Nov 1984, Lincoln's Inn
Pupil Master
Qualifications: [BCL, MA (Oxon) LLM, (Ill)
LLM (Harv)]

PARKER HUGH CHRISTOPHER

King's Bench Chambers
115 North Hill, Plymouth PL4 8JY,
Telephone: 01752 221551
2 King's Bench Walk
Ground Floor, Temple, London
EC4Y 7DE, Telephone: 0171 353 1746
E-mail: 2kbw@atlas.co.uk
Call Date: Nov 1973, Gray's Inn
Qualifications: [MA (Cantab)]

PARKER JOHN

2 Mitre Court Buildings
1st Floor, Temple, London EC4Y 7BX,
Telephone: 0171 353 1353
Call Date: July 1975, Inner Temple
Qualifications: [BSc (Lond)]

PARKER MISS JUDITH MARY FRANCES QC (1991)

One King's Bench Walk
1st Floor, Temple, London EC4Y 7DB,
Telephone: 0171 936 1500
E-mail: ddear@1kbw.co.uk
Call Date: Nov 1973, Middle Temple
Assistant Recorder
Qualifications: [BA (Oxon)]

PARKER KENNETH BLADES QC (1992)

Monckton Chambers
4 Raymond Buildings, Gray's Inn, London
WC1R 5BP, Telephone: 0171 405 7211
E-mail: chambers@monckton.co.uk
Call Date: Nov 1975, Gray's Inn
Qualifications: [MA, BCL (Oxon)]

PARKER MATTHEW RICHARD

3 Verulam Buildings
London WC1R 5NT,
Telephone: 0171 831 8441
E-mail: clerks@3verulam.co.uk
Call Date: Oct 1997, Middle Temple
Qualifications: [BA (Hons)(Cantab), CPE]

PARKER PAUL ANDREW

Chambers of John L Powell QC
Four New Square, Lincoln's Inn, London
WC2A 3RJ, Telephone: 0171 797 8000
E-mail: barristers@4newsquare.com
Call Date: July 1986, Middle Temple
Pupil Master
Qualifications: [MA(Cantab)]

PARKER PHILIP LAURENCE

3 Fountain Court
Steelhouse Lane, Birmingham B4 6DR,
Telephone: 0121 236 5854
Call Date: July 1976, Middle Temple
Pupil Master, Assistant Recorder
Qualifications: [LLB (B'ham)]

PARKER STEVEN NIGEL

Corn Exchange Chambers
5th Floor, Fenwick Street, Liverpool
L2 7QS, Telephone: 0151 227 1081/5009
Call Date: Nov 1987, Gray's Inn
Qualifications: [LLB]

PARKER TIMOTHY TERENCE

2 Mitre Court Buildings
1st Floor, Temple, London EC4Y 7BX,
Telephone: 0171 353 1353
Call Date: Nov 1995, Gray's Inn
Qualifications: [BA (Lond)]

PARKER MISS WENDY (WOO)

Francis Taylor Building
Ground Floor, Temple, London
EC4Y 7BY, Telephone: 0171 353 7768/
7769/2711
E-mail:clerks@francistaylorbuilding.law.co.uk
Call Date: July 1978, Middle Temple
Pupil Master
Qualifications: [MA]

PARKES MALCOLM FRANK

4 Fountain Court
Steelhouse Lane, Birmingham B4 6DR,
Telephone: 0121 236 3476
Call Date: July 1984, Lincoln's Inn
Qualifications: [BA (Notts) LLM, (Cantab)]

PARKES RICHARD JOHN BYERLEY

5 Raymond Buildings
1st Floor, Gray's Inn, London WC1R 5BP,
Telephone: 0171 242 2902
E-mail: clerks@media-ent-law.co.uk
Call Date: Nov 1977, Gray's Inn
Pupil Master
Qualifications: [MA (Cantab)]

PARKIN MISS FIONA JANE

Atkin Chambers
1 Atkin Building, Gray's Inn, London
WC1R 5AT, Telephone: 020 7404 0102
E-mail: clerks@atkin-chambers.co.uk
Call Date: Oct 1993, Inner Temple
Qualifications: [LLB (Hons), LLB
(Hons)(Cantab)]

PARKIN JONATHAN

Chambers of John Hand QC
9 St John Street, Manchester M3 4DN,
Telephone: 0161 955 9000
E-mail: ninesjs@gconnect.com
Call Date: Nov 1978, Middle Temple
Pupil Master
Qualifications: [MA (Cantab)]

Fax: 0161 955 9001; DX: MDX 14326;
Other comms: E-mail
ninesjs@gconnect.com

Types of work: Commercial, Discrimination,
Employment, Professional negligence

Circuit: Northern

Awards and memberships: Employment Law
Bar Association; Employment Lawyers
Association; Professional Negligence Bar
Association; Bar European Group

Other professional experience: Part-time
chairman of Employment Tribunals

Languages spoken: French

PARKIN TIMOTHY CHARLES

New Court Chambers
3 Broad Chare, Newcastle upon Tyne
NE1 3DQ, Telephone: 0191 232 1980
Call Date: Nov 1971, Inner Temple
Pupil Master
Qualifications: [LLB]

PARKINS GRAHAM CHARLES QC (1990)

18 Red Lion Court
(Off Fleet Street), London EC4A 3EB,
Telephone: 0171 520 6000
E-mail: chambers@18rlc.co.uk
Thornwood House
102 New London Road, Chelmsford,
Essex, CM2 0RG,
Telephone: 01245 280880
E-mail: chambers@18rlc.co.uk
Call Date: July 1972, Inner Temple
Recorder
Qualifications: [LLB (Hons)]

PARKINSON FREDERICK BECK

Old Colony House
6 South King Street, Manchester M2 6DQ,
Telephone: 0161 834 4364
Call Date: July 1981, Middle Temple
Qualifications: [LLB]

PARKINSON MISS HELEN ESTHER

3 Temple Gardens
3rd Floor, Temple, London EC4Y 9AU,
Telephone: 0171 583 0010
Call Date: July 1986, Middle Temple
Qualifications: [LLB (Hons)]

PARKINSON WILLIAM HAROLD

Clock Chambers
78 Darlington Street, Wolverhampton
WV1 4LY, Telephone: 01902 313444
19 Castle Street Chambers
Liverpool L2 4SX,
Telephone: 0151 236 9402
E-mail: DBrei16454@aol.com
Call Date: 1997, Lincoln's Inn
Qualifications: [LLB (Hons)]

PARNELL GRAHAM

East Anglian Chambers
Gresham House, 5 Museum Street,
Ipswich, Suffolk, IP1 1HQ,
Telephone: 01473 214481
E-mail: ipswich@ealaw.co.uk
East Anglian Chambers
52 North Hill, Colchester, Essex, CO1 1PY,
Telephone: 01206 572756
E-mail: colchester@ealaw.co.uk
East Anglian Chambers
57 London Street, Norwich NR2 1HL,
Telephone: 01603 617351
E-mail: norwich@ealaw.co.uk
Call Date: Nov 1982, Middle Temple
Pupil Master
Qualifications: [MA (Oxon)]

PARR JOHN EDWARD

8 King Street Chambers
8 King Street, Manchester M2 6AQ,
Telephone: 0161 834 9560
E-mail: eightking@aol.com
Call Date: July 1989, Middle Temple
Qualifications: [LLB (Reading)]

PARR MS JUDITH MARGARET

2 Gray's Inn Square Chambers
2nd Floor, Gray's Inn, London WC1R 5AA,
Telephone: 020 7242 0328
E-mail: clerks@2gis.co.uk
Call Date: Feb 1994, Inner Temple
Qualifications: [LLB (Canterbury, New,
Zealand), Diploma Child , Protection
(ICCL &, LSE)]

PARRISH SAMUEL NEVILLE

3 Paper Buildings
Temple, London EC4Y 7EU,
Telephone: 020 7583 8055
E-mail: London@3paper.com
3 Paper Buildings (Bournemouth)
20 Lorne Park Road, Bournemouth,
Dorset, BH1 1JN,
Telephone: 01202 292102
E-mail: Bournemouth@3paper.com
3 Paper Buildings (Winchester)
4 St Peter Street, Winchester SO23 8BW,
Telephone: 01962 868884
E-mail: winchester@3paper.com

3 Paper Buildings (Oxford)
1 Alfred Street, High Street, Oxford
OX1 4EH, Telephone: 01865 793736
E-mail: oxford@3paper.com
Call Date: Feb 1962, Inner Temple
Pupil Master
Qualifications: [LLB (Hons)]

PARROY MICHAEL PICTON QC (1991)

3 Paper Buildings
Temple, London EC4Y 7EU,
Telephone: 020 7583 8055
E-mail: London@3paper.com
3 Paper Buildings (Bournemouth)
20 Lorne Park Road, Bournemouth,
Dorset, BH1 1JN,
Telephone: 01202 292102
E-mail: Bournemouth@3paper.com
3 Paper Buildings (Winchester)
4 St Peter Street, Winchester SO23 8BW,
Telephone: 01962 868884
E-mail: winchester@3paper.com
3 Paper Buildings (Oxford)
1 Alfred Street, High Street, Oxford
OX1 4EH, Telephone: 01865 793736
E-mail: oxford@3paper.com
Call Date: Nov 1969, Middle Temple
Qualifications: [BA (Oxon), MA (Oxon)]

PARRY CHARLES ROBERT

Pump Court Chambers
5 Temple Chambers, Temple Street,
Swindon SN1 1SQ,
Telephone: 01793 539899
E-mail: clerks@3pumpcourt.com
Pump Court Chambers
Upper Ground Floor, 3 Pump Court,
Temple, London EC4Y 7AJ,
Telephone: 0171 353 0711
E-mail: clerks@3pumpcourt.com
Pump Court Chambers
31 Southgate Street, Winchester
SO23 9EE, Telephone: 01962 868161
E-mail: clerks@3pumpcourt.com
Call Date: Nov 1973, Middle Temple
Pupil Master
Qualifications: [LLB (Lond)]

D

PARRY DAVID JULIAN THOMAS

Chambers of Lord Goodhart QC
Ground Floor, 3 New Square, Lincoln's
Inn, London WC2A 3RS,
Telephone: 0171 405 5577
E-mail:law@threenewsquare.demon.co.uk
Call Date: July 1972, Inner Temple
Pupil Master, Recorder

PARRY DESMOND WYNN

Nicholas Street Chambers
22 Nicholas Street, Chester CH1 2NX,
Telephone: 01244 323886
E-mail: clerks@40king.co.uk
Call Date: July 1995, Inner Temple
Qualifications: [LLB (L'pool)]

PARRY MISS ISABEL CLARE

9 Park Place
Cardiff CF1 3DP,
Telephone: 01222 382731
Call Date: July 1979, Gray's Inn
Pupil Master, Assistant Recorder
Qualifications: [MA (Cantab)]

PARRY MISS SIAN RACHEL

32 Park Place
Cardiff CF1 3BA,
Telephone: 01222 397364
Call Date: Oct 1994, Gray's Inn
Qualifications: [LLB (Hons)(Wales)]

PARRY SIMON EDWARD

White Friars Chambers
21 White Friars, Chester CH1 1NZ,
Telephone: 01244 323070
E-mail:whitefriarschambers@btinternet.com
Call Date: Nov 1997, Inner Temple
Qualifications: [LLB (Wales)]

PARRY EVANS MS MARY ALETHEA

33 Park Place
Cardiff CF1 3BA,
Telephone: 02920 233313
Call Date: June 1953, Inner Temple
Pupil Master, Recorder
Qualifications: [BCL, MA]

PARRY-JONES MRS CAROLE ANN

East Anglian Chambers
52 North Hill, Colchester, Essex, CO1 1PY,
Telephone: 01206 572756
E-mail: colchester@ealaw.co.uk
East Anglian Chambers
57 London Street, Norwich NR2 1HL,
Telephone: 01603 617351
E-mail: norwich@ealaw.co.uk
East Anglian Chambers
Gresham House, 5 Museum Street,
Ipswich, Suffolk, IP1 1HQ,
Telephone: 01473 214481
E-mail: ipswich@ealaw.co.uk
Call Date: Nov 1992, Middle Temple
Qualifications: [LLB (Hons, Westmin)]

PARRY-JONES JOHN TREVOR

Corn Exchange Chambers
5th Floor, Fenwick Street, Liverpool
L2 7QS, Telephone: 0151 227 1081/5009
Call Date: Feb 1992, Gray's Inn
Qualifications: [LLB (Hons, Wales)]

PARSLEY CHARLES RONALD

33 Park Place
Cardiff CF1 3BA,
Telephone: 02920 233313
Goldsmith Building
1st Floor, Temple, London EC4Y 7BL,
Telephone: 0171 353 7881
E-mail:clerks@goldsmith-building.law.co.uk
Call Date: 1973, Inner Temple
Qualifications: [LLB (Exon)]

PARSONS ANDREW JAMES

Portsmouth Barristers' Chambers
Victory House, 7 Bellevue Terrace,
Portsmouth, Hampshire, PO5 3AT,
Telephone: 023 92 831292/811811
E-mail: clerks@portsmouthbar.com
Call Date: July 1985, Inner Temple
Pupil Master
Qualifications: [LLB (Hons)(Lond)]

PARSONS LUKE ARTHUR

4 Essex Court
Temple, London EC4Y 9AJ,
Telephone: 020 7797 7970
E-mail: clerks@4essexcourt.law.co.uk
Call Date: July 1985, Inner Temple
Pupil Master
Qualifications: [LLB (Bris)]

PARSONS SIMON PETER

New Walk Chambers
27 New Walk, Leicester LE1 6TE,
Telephone: 0116 2559144
Call Date: Nov 1993, Inner Temple
Qualifications: [MA (Oxon)]

PARTINGTON DAVID JOHN

Chancery House Chambers
7 Lisbon Square, Leeds LS1 4LY,
Telephone: 0113 244 6691
E-mail: chanceryhouse@btinternet.com
The Chambers of Leolin Price CBE, QC
10 Old Square, Lincoln's Inn, London
WC2A 3SU, Telephone: 0171 405 0758
Call Date: July 1987, Middle Temple
Qualifications: [MA (Cantab)]

PARTINGTON MISS LISA SHIRLEY

24a St John Street
Manchester M3 4DF,
Telephone: 0161 833 9628
Call Date: July 1989, Inner Temple
Qualifications: [LLB (Hons)]

PARTINGTON PROF THOMAS MARTIN

Arden Chambers
27 John Street, London WC1N 2BL,
Telephone: 020 7242 4244
E-mail:clerks@arden-chambers.law.co.uk
Call Date: Nov 1984, Middle Temple
Qualifications: [BA, LLB (Cantab)]

PARTRIDGE IAN SIMON

3 Paper Buildings
Temple, London EC4Y 7EU,
Telephone: 020 7583 8055
E-mail: London@3paper.com
3 Paper Buildings (Bournemouth)
20 Lorne Park Road, Bournemouth,
Dorset, BH1 1JN,
Telephone: 01202 292102
E-mail: Bournemouth@3paper.com
3 Paper Buildings (Winchester)
4 St Peter Street, Winchester SO23 8BW,
Telephone: 01962 868884
E-mail: winchester@3paper.com

3 Paper Buildings (Oxford)
1 Alfred Street, High Street, Oxford
OX1 4EH, Telephone: 01865 793736
E-mail: oxford@3paper.com
Call Date: July 1979, Inner Temple
Pupil Master
Qualifications: [MA (Oxon)]

PARTRIDGE DR RICHARD CHARLES

3 Serjeants' Inn
London EC4Y 1BQ,
Telephone: 0171 353 5537
E-mail: clerks@3serjeantsinn.com
Call Date: July 1994, Lincoln's Inn
Qualifications: [MBBch, LLB (Hons),
(Cardiff)]

PASCALL MATTHEW STEPHEN

Guildford Chambers
Stoke House, Leapale Lane, Guildford,
Surrey, GU1 4LY,
Telephone: 01483 539131
E-mail:guildford.barristers@btinternet.com
Call Date: July 1984, Middle Temple
Pupil Master
Qualifications: [BA]

PASCOE MARTIN MICHAEL

3/4 South Square
Gray's Inn, London WC1R 5HP,
Telephone: 0171 696 9900
E-mail: clerks@southsquare.com
Call Date: July 1977, Lincoln's Inn
Pupil Master
Qualifications: [BA, BCL (Oxon)]

PASCOE NIGEL SPENCER KNIGHT QC (1988)

Pump Court Chambers
31 Southgate Street, Winchester
SO23 9EE, Telephone: 01962 868161
E-mail: clerks@3pumpcourt.com
Pump Court Chambers
Upper Ground Floor, 3 Pump Court,
Temple, London EC4Y 7AJ,
Telephone: 0171 353 0711
E-mail: clerks@3pumpcourt.com
Queens Square Chambers
56 Queens Square, Bristol BS1 4PR,
Telephone: 0117 921 1966

Pump Court Chambers
5 Temple Chambers, Temple Street, Swindon SN1 1SQ,
Telephone: 01793 539899
E-mail: clerks@3pumpcourt.com
Call Date: July 1966, Inner Temple
Recorder

D

PASIUK MS JANINA STEFANIA

Kenworthy's Chambers
83 Bridge Street, Manchester M3 2RF,
Telephone: 0161 832 4036/834 6954
E-mail: clerks@kenworthys.co.uk
Call Date: July 1983, Middle Temple
Qualifications: [LLB (B'ham)]

PASS GEOFFREY JAMES

40 King Street
Manchester M2 6BA,
Telephone: 0161 832 9082
E-mail: clerks@40kingstreet.co.uk
The Chambers of Philip Raynor QC
5 Park Place, Leeds LS1 2RU,
Telephone: 0113 242 1123
Call Date: July 1975, Middle Temple
Qualifications: [LLB (Lond)]

PASSMORE JOHN WILLIAM

Verulam Chambers
Peer House, 8-14 Verulam Street, Gray's Inn, London WC1X 8LZ,
Telephone: 0171 813 2400
Call Date: Oct 1992, Lincoln's Inn
Qualifications: [LLB(Hons)(Bris)]

PATCHETT-JOYCE MICHAEL THURSTON

Monckton Chambers
4 Raymond Buildings, Gray's Inn, London WC1R 5BP, Telephone: 0171 405 7211
E-mail: chambers@monckton.co.uk
Call Date: July 1981, Middle Temple
Pupil Master
Qualifications: [MA (Cantab)]

PATEL BHAVIN VINUBHAI

Chambers of Martin Burr
Fourth Floor, Eldon Chambers, 30/32 Fleet Street, London EC4Y 1AA,
Telephone: 0171 353 4636
Call Date: Nov 1991, Lincoln's Inn
Qualifications: [BA (Oxon)]

PATEL ELYAS MOHAMMED

Park Court Chambers
16 Park Place, Leeds LS1 2SJ,
Telephone: 0113 2433277
Call Date: Nov 1991, Gray's Inn
Qualifications: [LLB (Hons), LLM (Cantab)]

PATEL MISS GITA

Kenworthy's Chambers
83 Bridge Street, Manchester M3 2RF,
Telephone: 0161 832 4036/834 6954
E-mail: clerks@kenworthys.co.uk
Call Date: July 1988, Inner Temple
Qualifications: [LLB (B'ham)]

PATEL MISS JAYABEN

Warwick House Chambers
8 Warwick Court, Gray's Inn, London WC1R 5DJ, Telephone: 0171 430 2323
E-mail: cdrewlaw@aol.com
Call Date: Oct 1990, Inner Temple
Qualifications: [BA (Sussex), LLM (UCL)]

PATEL PARISHIL JAYANTILAL

39 Essex Street
London WC2R 3AT,
Telephone: 0171 832 1111
E-mail: clerks@39essex.co.uk
Call Date: Nov 1996, Middle Temple
Qualifications: [BA (Hons)(Cantab)]

PATEL SANDIP

Furnival Chambers
32 Furnival Street, London EC4A 1JQ,
Telephone: 0171 405 3232
E-mail: clerks@furnivallaw.co.uk
Call Date: July 1991, Middle Temple
Qualifications: [LLB (Hons) (Essex)]

PATERSON DAVID

2 King's Bench Walk
Ground Floor, Temple, London EC4Y 7DE, Telephone: 0171 353 1746
E-mail: 2kbw@atlas.co.uk
King's Bench Chambers
115 North Hill, Plymouth PL4 8JY,
Telephone: 01752 221551
Call Date: Nov 1961, Lincoln's Inn
Pupil Master

D

PATES RICHARD ANDREW

White Friars Chambers
21 White Friars, Chester CH1 1NZ,
Telephone: 01244 323070
E-mail:whitefriarschambers@btinternet.com
Call Date: Oct 1993, Lincoln's Inn
Qualifications: [LLB (Hons)(Wales), LLM]

PATHAK PANKAJ KUMAR

2 Paper Buildings, Basement North
Temple, London EC4Y 7ET,
Telephone: 0171 936 2613
E-mail: post@2paper.co.uk
Call Date: Oct 1992, Lincoln's Inn
Qualifications: [MA (Cantab), LLM (Lond)]

PATIENCE ANDREW QC (1990)

5 King's Bench Walk
Temple, London EC4Y 7DN,
Telephone: 0171 353 5638
Call Date: Nov 1966, Gray's Inn
Recorder
Qualifications: [MA (Oxon)]

PATON EWAN WILLIAM

Guildhall Chambers
22-26 Broad Street, Bristol BS1 2HG,
Telephone: 0117 9273366
E-mail:civil.clerks@guildhallchambers.co.uk and
criminal.clerks@guildhallchambers.co.uk
Call Date: 1996, Inner Temple
Qualifications: [MA (Oxon), BCL]

PATON IAN FRANCIS

Hollis Whiteman Chambers
3rd Floor, Queen Elizabeth Bldg, Temple,
London EC4Y 9BS,
Telephone: 020 7583 5766
E-mail:barristers@holliswhiteman.co.uk
Call Date: Apr 1975, Middle Temple
Pupil Master, Assistant Recorder

PATRICK JAMES HARRY JOHNSON

Guildhall Chambers
22-26 Broad Street, Bristol BS1 2HG,
Telephone: 0117 9273366
E-mail:civil.clerks@guildhallchambers.co.uk and
criminal.clerks@guildhallchambers.co.uk
Call Date: Nov 1989, Inner Temple
Qualifications: [LLB]

PATTEN BENEDICT JOSEPH

Two Crown Office Row
Ground Floor, Temple, London
EC4Y 7HJ, Telephone: 020 7797 8100
E-mail: mail@2cor.co.uk, or to individual
barristers at: [barrister's
surname]@2cor.co.uk
Call Date: July 1986, Middle Temple
Qualifications: [BA (Oxon)]

PATTEN NICHOLAS JOHN QC (1988)

9 Old Square
Ground Floor, Lincoln's Inn, London
WC2A 3SR, Telephone: 0171 405 4682
E-mail: chambers@9oldsquare.co.uk
Call Date: July 1974, Lincoln's Inn
Qualifications: [MA (Oxon), BCL]

PATTERSON MISS FRANCES SILVIA QC (1998)

40 King Street
Manchester M2 6BA,
Telephone: 0161 832 9082
E-mail: clerks@40kingstreet.co.uk
The Chambers of Philip Raynor QC
5 Park Place, Leeds LS1 2RU,
Telephone: 0113 242 1123
Call Date: Nov 1977, Middle Temple
Assistant Recorder
Qualifications: [BA]

PATTERSON GARETH THOMAS

3 Temple Gardens
Lower Ground Floor, Temple, London
EC4Y 9AU, Telephone: 0171 353 3102/5/
9297 E-mail: clerks@3tg.co.uk
Call Date: July 1995, Gray's Inn
Qualifications: [BA]

PATTERSON MISS JO-ANNE CLAIR

Newport Chambers
12 Clytha Park Road, Newport, Gwent,
NP9 47L, Telephone: 01633 267403/
255855
Call Date: Nov 1993, Inner Temple
Qualifications: [LLB (Bris)]

PATTERSON NORMAN WILLIAM

Gray's Inn Chambers, The Chambers of Norman Patterson
First Floor, Gray's Inn Chambers, Gray's Inn, London WC1R 5JA,
Telephone: 0171 831 5344
E-mail: s.mcblain@btinternet.com
Call Date: July 1971, Middle Temple
Pupil Master
Qualifications: [LLB (Lond)]

PATTERSON STEWART

Pump Court Chambers
31 Southgate Street, Winchester
SO23 9EE, Telephone: 01962 868161
E-mail: clerks@3pumpcourt.com
Pump Court Chambers
Upper Ground Floor, 3 Pump Court,
Temple, London EC4Y 7AJ,
Telephone: 0171 353 0711
E-mail: clerks@3pumpcourt.com
Pump Court Chambers
5 Temple Chambers, Temple Street,
Swindon SN1 1SQ,
Telephone: 01793 539899
E-mail: clerks@3pumpcourt.com
Call Date: Nov 1967, Middle Temple
Pupil Master, Assistant Recorder
Qualifications: [BA (Oxon)]

PATTON ROBIN MICHAEL

New Court Chambers
3 Broad Chare, Newcastle upon Tyne
NE1 3DQ, Telephone: 0191 232 1980
Call Date: July 1983, Inner Temple
Pupil Master
Qualifications: [BA]

PAUFFLEY MISS ANNA EVELYN HAMILTON QC (1995)

4 Paper Buildings
1st Floor, Temple, London EC4Y 7EX,
Telephone: 0171 583 0816/353 1131
E-mail: clerks@4paperbuildings.co.uk
Call Date: July 1979, Middle Temple
Recorder
Qualifications: [BA (Hons)(Lond)]

PAUL NICHOLAS MARTIN

Doughty Street Chambers
11 Doughty Street, London WC1N 2PG,
Telephone: 0171 404 1313
E-mail:enquiries@doughtystreet.co.uk

Westgate Chambers
144 High Street, Lewes, East Sussex,
BN7 1XT, Telephone: 01273 480510
Call Date: July 1980, Gray's Inn
Pupil Master
Qualifications: [BA (York)]

PAULUSZ JAN GILBERT

8 King's Bench Walk
2nd Floor, Temple, London EC4Y 7DU,
Telephone: 0171 797 8888
Call Date: July 1957, Lincoln's Inn
Recorder

PAVLOU PAVLOS KYRIACOU

9 King's Bench Walk
Ground Floor, Temple, London
EC4Y 7DX, Telephone: 0171 353 7202/
3909 E-mail: 9kbw@compuserve.com
Call Date: Nov 1993, Lincoln's Inn
Qualifications: [LLB (Hons)]

PAVRY JAMES FRANCIS

Queen Elizabeth Building
Ground Floor, Temple, London
EC4Y 9BS,
Telephone: 0171 353 7181 (12 Lines)
Call Date: July 1974, Inner Temple
Pupil Master
Qualifications: [BA (Oxon)]

PAWLAK WITOLD EXPEDYT

9 Bedford Row
London WC1R 4AZ,
Telephone: 0171 242 3555
E-mail: clerks@9br.co.uk
Call Date: Nov 1970, Inner Temple
Pupil Master, Recorder
Qualifications: [MA (Cantab)]

PAWLOWSKI MARK

Pepys' Chambers
17 Fleet Street, London EC4Y 1AA,
Telephone: 0171 936 2710
Call Date: July 1978, Middle Temple
Qualifications: [LLB (Hons), , BCL (Oxon)]

PAWSON ROBERT EDWARD CRUICKSHANK

Pump Court Chambers
31 Southgate Street, Winchester
SO23 9EE, Telephone: 01962 868161
E-mail: clerks@3pumpcourt.com
Pump Court Chambers
Upper Ground Floor, 3 Pump Court,
Temple, London EC4Y 7AJ,
Telephone: 0171 353 0711
E-mail: clerks@3pumpcourt.com
Pump Court Chambers
5 Temple Chambers, Temple Street,
Swindon SN1 1SQ,
Telephone: 01793 539899
E-mail: clerks@3pumpcourt.com
Call Date: Nov 1994, Inner Temple
Qualifications: [BA, MA (Lond), CPE]

PAXTON CHRISTOPHER

2 Pump Court
1st Floor, Temple, London EC4Y 7AH,
Telephone: 0171 353 5597
Call Date: Nov 1991, Gray's Inn
Qualifications: [LLB]

PAYNE ALAN PATRICK

1 Harcourt Buildings
2nd Floor, Temple, London EC4Y 9DA,
Telephone: 0171 353 9421/0375
E-mail:clerks@1harcourtbuildings.law.co.uk
Call Date: 1996, Middle Temple
Qualifications: [LLB (Hons)(LSE)]

PAYNE BRIAN WYNDHAM

Phoenix Chambers
First Floor, Gray's Inn Chambers, Gray's
Inn, London WC1R 5JA,
Telephone: 0171 404 7888
E-mail:clerks@phoenix-chambers.co.uk
Call Date: Nov 1993, Inner Temple
Qualifications: [BSc (Bris), Dip.L. (City)]

PAYNE RICHARD ANTHONY DOUGLAS

Chambers of Michael Pert QC
36 Bedford Row, London WC1R 4JH,
Telephone: 0171 421 8000
E-mail: 36bedfordrow@link.org
Chambers of Michael Pert QC
24 Albion Place, Northampton NN1 1UD,
Telephone: 01604 602333

Chambers of Michael Pert QC
104 New Walk, Leicester LE1 7EA,
Telephone: 0116 249 2020
Call Date: June 1964, Gray's Inn

PAYNE MISS TRACEY ELIZABETH

Call Date: Oct 1991, Inner Temple
Qualifications: [BA (Lanc), Dip Law]

PAYTON BARRY ARNOLD

95A Chancery Lane
London WC2A 1DT,
Telephone: 0171 405 3101
Call Date: Jan 1951, Middle Temple
Pupil Master
Qualifications: [LLB, LMRTPI]

PAYTON CLIFFORD CONINGSBY

Verulam Chambers
Peer House, 8-14 Verulam Street, Gray's
Inn, London WC1X 8LZ,
Telephone: 0171 813 2400
Call Date: July 1972, Inner Temple
Qualifications: [BCL,MA (Oxon)]

PEACOCK IAN CHRISTOPHER

12 New Square
Lincoln's Inn, London WC2A 3SW,
Telephone: 0171 419 1212
E-mail: chambers@12newsquare.co.uk
Sovereign Chambers
25 Park Square, Leeds LS1 2PW,
Telephone: 0113 2451841/2/3
E-mail:sovereignchambers@btinternet.com
Call Date: Oct 1990, Gray's Inn
Pupil Master
Qualifications: [BA (Cantab)]

PEACOCK JONATHAN DAVID

Chambers of John Gardiner QC
1st Floor, 11 New Square, Lincoln's Inn,
London WC2A 3QB,
Telephone: 0171 242 4017
E-mail: taxlaw@11newsquare.com
Call Date: July 1987, Middle Temple
Pupil Master
Qualifications: [MA (Oxon)]

PEACOCK MISS LISA JAYNE

3 Dr Johnson's Buildings
Ground Floor, Temple, London
EC4Y 7BA, Telephone: 0171 353 4854
E-mail: clerks@3djb.co.uk
Call Date: Oct 1992, Lincoln's Inn
Qualifications: [MA (Hons)(Cantab)]

PEACOCK NICHOLAS

Westgate Chambers
67a Westgate Road, Newcastle upon Tyne
NE1 1SG, Telephone: 0191 261 4407/
2329785
E-mail:pracman@westgatechambers.law.co.uk
Call Date: Oct 1996, Gray's Inn
Qualifications: [LLB (Coventry)]

PEACOCK NICHOLAS ALLEN

Chambers of Kieran Coonan QC
Ground Floor, 6 Pump Court, Temple,
London EC4Y 7AR,
Telephone: 0171 583 6013/2510
E-mail: clerks@6-pumpcourt.law.co.uk
Call Date: Oct 1992, Gray's Inn
Qualifications: [MA (Cantab)]

PEACOCK NICHOLAS CHRISTOPHER

13 Old Square
Ground Floor, Lincoln's Inn, London
WC2A 3UA, Telephone: 0171 404 4800
E-mail: clerks@13oldsquare.law.co.uk
Call Date: Nov 1989, Middle Temple
Pupil Master
Qualifications: [BA [Oxon]]

PEACOCKE MRS TERESA ANNE ROSEN

Enterprise Chambers
9 Old Square, Lincoln's Inn, London
WC2A 3SR, Telephone: 0171 405 9471
E-mail:enterprise.london@dial.pipex.com
Enterprise Chambers
38 Park Square, Leeds LS1 2PA,
Telephone: 0113 246 0391
E-mail:enterprise.leeds@dial.pipex.com
Enterprise Chambers
65 Quayside, Newcastle upon Tyne
NE1 3DS, Telephone: 0191 222 3344
E-mail:enterprise.newcastle@dial.pipex.com
Call Date: Nov 1982, Lincoln's Inn
Pupil Master
Qualifications: [BA, MA (Michigan)]

PEARCE FREDERICK MICHAEL

High Pavement Chambers
1 High Pavement, Nottingham NG1 1HF,
Telephone: 0115 9418218
Call Date: Feb 1975, Middle Temple
Pupil Master, Assistant Recorder

PEARCE IVAN JAMES

Furnival Chambers
32 Furnival Street, London EC4A 1JQ,
Telephone: 0171 405 3232
E-mail: clerks@furnivallaw.co.uk
Call Date: Oct 1994, Gray's Inn
Qualifications: [LLB, Ndarb]

PEARCE MISS LINDA ANN

6 King's Bench Walk
Ground, Third & Fourth Floors, Temple,
London EC4Y 7DR,
Telephone: 0171 353 4931/583 0695
Call Date: July 1982, Inner Temple
Pupil Master
Qualifications: [LLB (Soton)]

PEARCE MARCUS STEWART

East Anglian Chambers
57 London Street, Norwich NR2 1HL,
Telephone: 01603 617351
E-mail: norwich@ealaw.co.uk
East Anglian Chambers
52 North Hill, Colchester, Essex, CO1 1PY,
Telephone: 01206 572756
E-mail: colchester@ealaw.co.uk
East Anglian Chambers
Gresham House, 5 Museum Street,
Ipswich, Suffolk, IP1 1HQ,
Telephone: 01473 214481
E-mail: ipswich@ealaw.co.uk
Call Date: July 1972, Inner Temple

PEARCE RICHARD WILLIAM

Peel Court Chambers
45 Hardman Street, Manchester M3 3PL,
Telephone: 0161 832 3791
E-mail: clerks@peelct.co.uk
Call Date: July 1985, Middle Temple
Pupil Master
Qualifications: [BA (Cantab)]

PEARCE ROBERT EDGAR

Chambers of Mr Peter Crampin QC
Ground Floor, 11 New Square, Lincoln's
Inn, London WC2A 3QB,
Telephone: 020 7831 0081
E-mail: 11newsquare.co.uk
Call Date: July 1977, Middle Temple
Pupil Master
Qualifications: [MA, BCL (Oxon)]

PEARCE WALTER REID

10 King's Bench Walk
Ground Floor, Temple, London
EC4Y 7EB, Telephone: 0171 353 7742
E-mail: 10kbw@lineone.net
Call Date: Nov 1979, Middle Temple
Pupil Master
Qualifications: [BA (Toronto), LLB (Lond)]

PEARCE-HIGGINS DANIEL JOHN QC (1998)

2 Temple Gardens
Temple, London EC4Y 9AY,
Telephone: 0171 583 6041
E-mail: clerks@2templegardens.co.uk
Call Date: July 1973, Middle Temple
Assistant Recorder
Qualifications: [BSc (Bristol)]

PEARS DERRICK ALLAN

2nd Floor, Francis Taylor Building
Temple, London EC4Y 7BY,
Telephone: 0171 353 9942/3157
Call Date: July 1975, Inner Temple
Pupil Master
Qualifications: [MA (Oxon)]

PEARSE WHEATLEY ROBIN JOHN

2 Paper Buildings
1st Floor, Temple, London EC4Y 7ET,
Telephone: 020 7556 5500
E-mail: clerks@2pbbarristers.co.uk
Call Date: July 1971, Inner Temple
Pupil Master, Recorder

PEARSON MS CAROLYN JAYNE

3 Temple Gardens
Lower Ground Floor, Temple, London
EC4Y 9AU, Telephone: 0171 353 3102/5/
9297 E-mail: clerks@3tg.co.uk
Call Date: Nov 1990, Gray's Inn
Pupil Master
Qualifications: [LLB (Warw), MA (Lond)]

PEARSON CHRISTOPHER

Bridewell Chambers
2 Bridewell Place, London EC4V 6AP,
Telephone: 020 7797 8800
E-mail:HughesGage@bridewell.law.co.uk
Call Date: Oct 1995, Inner Temple
Qualifications: [BSc (Dunelm), CPE]

Fax: 0171 797 8801; DX: LDE 383

Types of work: Commercial litigation,
Common law (general), Construction,
Consumer law, Information technology,
Insolvency, Insurance, Landlord and
tenant, Medical negligence, Partnerships,
Personal injury, Professional negligence,
Sale and carriage of goods

Membership of foreign bars: Member of Bar of
Northern Ireland

Awards and memberships: Member PIBA

PEARSON DAVID EDWARD

Victoria Chambers
3rd Floor, 177 Corporation Street,
Birmingham B4 6RG,
Telephone: 0121 236 9900
E-mail: viccham@aol.com
Call Date: Feb 1983, Gray's Inn
Pupil Master

PEARSON MICHAEL

30 Park Square
Leeds LS1 2PF, Telephone: 0113 2436388
E-mail: clerks@30parksquare.co.uk
Call Date: Nov 1984, Lincoln's Inn
Qualifications: [BA Hons]

PEARSON THOMAS ADAM SPENSER

Pump Court Chambers
Upper Ground Floor, 3 Pump Court,
Temple, London EC4Y 7AJ,
Telephone: 0171 353 0711
E-mail: clerks@3pumpcourt.com
Pump Court Chambers
31 Southgate Street, Winchester
SO23 9EE, Telephone: 01962 868161
E-mail: clerks@3pumpcourt.com
Pump Court Chambers
5 Temple Chambers, Temple Street,
Swindon SN1 1SQ,
Telephone: 01793 539899
E-mail: clerks@3pumpcourt.com
Call Date: Nov 1969, Middle Temple
Pupil Master
Qualifications: [BA, LLB (Cantab)]

PEART ICAH DELANO EVERARD

Two Garden Court
1st Floor, Middle Temple, London
EC4Y 9BL, Telephone: 0171 353 1633
E-mail:barristers@2gardenct.law.co.uk
Call Date: Nov 1978, Middle Temple
Pupil Master, Assistant Recorder
Qualifications: [LLB (LSE)]

PEAY DR JILL VALERIE

Doughty Street Chambers
11 Doughty Street, London WC1N 2PG,
Telephone: 0171 404 1313
E-mail:enquiries@doughtystreet.co.uk
Call Date: Oct 1991, Gray's Inn
Qualifications: [BSc (Birm), PhD (Birm), MA
(Oxon)]

PECK MISS CATHERINE MARY ELIZABETH

12 King's Bench Walk
Temple, London EC4Y 7EL,
Telephone: 0171 583 0811
E-mail: chambers@12kbw.co.uk
Call Date: Oct 1995, Gray's Inn
Qualifications: [LLB]

PEDDIE IAN JAMES CROFTON QC (1992)

One Garden Court Family Law Chambers
Ground Floor, Temple, London
EC4Y 9BJ, Telephone: 0171 797 7900
E-mail: clerks@onegardencourt.co.uk
Call Date: July 1971, Inner Temple
Recorder
Qualifications: [LLB]

PEDRO TERRY ADEBISI

Acre Lane Neighbourhood Chambers
30A Acre Lane, London SW2 5SG,
Telephone: 0171 274 4400
E-mail:barristerschambers@acrelane.demon.co.uk
Call Date: Oct 1996, Middle Temple
Qualifications: [LLB (Hons)(Lond)]

PEEBLES ANDREW JAMES

Farrar's Building
Temple, London EC4Y 7BD,
Telephone: 0171 583 9241
E-mail:chambers@farrarsbuilding.co.uk
Call Date: Nov 1987, Inner Temple
Pupil Master
Qualifications: [MA (Cantab) Dip Law, (City)]

PEEL ROBERT ROGER

29 Bedford Row Chambers
London WC1R 4HE,
Telephone: 0171 831 2626
Call Date: Oct 1990, Middle Temple
Qualifications: [BA (Oxon), Dip Law (City)]

PEEL STUART JAMES

Bell Yard Chambers
116/118 Chancery Lane, London
WC2A 1PP, Telephone: 0171 306 9292
Call Date: Nov 1994, Inner Temple
Qualifications: [LLB (Wolverhampton)]

PEERS MS HEATHER LOUISE

Guildhall Chambers
22-26 Broad Street, Bristol BS1 2HG,
Telephone: 0117 9273366
E-mail:civil.clerks@guildhallchambers.co.uk and
criminal.clerks@guildhallchambers.co.uk
Call Date: Oct 1991, Gray's Inn
Qualifications: [BA (Durham), M Phil
(Camb)]

PEERS MISS NICOLA JANE

Broadway House Chambers
Broadway House, 9 Bank Street, Bradford,
West Yorkshire, BD1 1TW,
Telephone: 01274 722560
E-mail: clerks@broadwayhouse.co.uk
Broadway House Chambers
31 Park Square West, Leeds LS1 2PF,
Telephone: 0113 246 2600
Call Date: Oct 1996, Inner Temple
Qualifications: [BA (Hons) (Oxon)]

PEET ANDREW GERAINT

2 New Street
Leicester LE1 5NA,
Telephone: 0116 2625906
E-mail: clerks@2newstreet.co.uk
Call Date: Oct 1991, Inner Temple
Qualifications: [LLB (Manch)(Hons)]

PEGDEN JEFFREY VINCENT QC (1996)

3 Temple Gardens
Lower Ground Floor, Temple, London
EC4Y 9AU, Telephone: 0171 353 3102/5/
9297 E-mail: clerks@3tg.co.uk
Call Date: July 1973, Inner Temple
Recorder
Qualifications: [LLB]

PEGLOW DR MICHAEL ALFRED HERMAN

Chambers of Geoffrey Hawker
46/48 Essex Street, London WC2R 3GH,
Telephone: 0171 583 8899
Call Date: July 1993, Middle Temple
Qualifications: [D.Phil (Oxon), Dr.ivr.
(Saarb), M.Sc (Saarb)]

PEIRSON OLIVER JAMES

Pump Court Chambers
Upper Ground Floor, 3 Pump Court,
Temple, London EC4Y 7AJ,
Telephone: 0171 353 0711
E-mail: clerks@3pumpcourt.com
Pump Court Chambers
31 Southgate Street, Winchester
SO23 9EE, Telephone: 01962 868161
E-mail: clerks@3pumpcourt.com

Pump Court Chambers
5 Temple Chambers, Temple Street,
Swindon SN1 1SQ,
Telephone: 01793 539899
E-mail: clerks@3pumpcourt.com
Call Date: Oct 1993, Lincoln's Inn
Qualifications: [LLB (Hons)(Lond)]

PELLING (PHILIP) MARK

Monckton Chambers
4 Raymond Buildings, Gray's Inn, London
WC1R 5BP, Telephone: 0171 405 7211
E-mail: chambers@monckton.co.uk
Call Date: July 1979, Middle Temple
Pupil Master
Qualifications: [LLB, AKC (Lond)]

PELLING RICHARD ALEXANDER

New Court Chambers
5 Verulam Buildings, Gray's Inn, London
WC1R 5LY, Telephone: 0171 831 9500
E-mail: mail@newcourtchambers.com
Call Date: Oct 1995, Middle Temple
Qualifications: [MA (Hons), D.Phil]

PEMA ANES BHUMIN LALOO

9 Woodhouse Square
Leeds LS3 1AD,
Telephone: 0113 2451986
E-mail: clerks@9woodhouse.co.uk
Call Date: Nov 1994, Middle Temple
Qualifications: [BA (Hons)]

PENDLEBURY JEREMY JOHN STRINGFELLOW

9 Bedford Row
London WC1R 4AZ,
Telephone: 0171 242 3555
E-mail: clerks@9br.co.uk
Call Date: July 1980, Inner Temple
Pupil Master
Qualifications: [BA (Kent)]

PENGELLY MS SARAH KATHARINE

Arden Chambers
27 John Street, London WC1N 2BL,
Telephone: 020 7242 4244
E-mail:clerks@arden-chambers.law.co.uk
Call Date: Oct 1996, Inner Temple
Qualifications: [BA (Oxon), CPE (Lond)]

PENN JONATHAN PETER ROBERT

8 King's Bench Walk
2nd Floor, Temple, London EC4Y 7DU,
Telephone: 0171 797 8888
Call Date: 1996, Inner Temple
Qualifications: [LLB]

PENNICOTT IAN

Keating Chambers
10 Essex Street, Outer Temple, London
WC2R 3AA, Telephone: 0171 544 2600
Call Date: July 1982, Middle Temple
Pupil Master
Qualifications: [BA, LLM (Cantab)]

PENNIFER MISS KELLY

Exchange Chambers
Pearl Assurance House, Derby Square,
Liverpool L2 9XX,
Telephone: 0151 236 7747
E-mail:exchangechambers@btinternet.com
Call Date: Nov 1994, Middle Temple
Qualifications: [LLB (Hons), Maitrise en
Droit]

PENNY DUNCAN JOHN WILLIAM

6 King's Bench Walk
Ground Floor, Temple, London
EC4Y 7DR, Telephone: 0171 583 0410
E-mail: worsley@6kbw.freeserve.co.uk
Call Date: Oct 1992, Middle Temple
Qualifications: [BA (Hons)(Oxon)]

PENNY JOHN CORNELIUS

Veritas Chambers
33 Corn Street, Bristol BS1 1HT,
Telephone: 0117 930 8802
Call Date: Oct 1995, Middle Temple
Qualifications: [BA (Hons)]

PENNY TIMOTHY CHARLES

11 Stone Buildings
Lincoln's Inn, London WC2A 3TG,
Telephone: +44 (0)207 831 6381
E-mail:clerks@11StoneBuildings.law.co.uk
Call Date: July 1988, Inner Temple
Qualifications: [LLB (Hons)]

PENTOL SIMON ALEX

3 Gray's Inn Square
Ground Floor, London WC1R 5AH,
Telephone: 0171 520 5600
E-mail: clerks@3gis.co.uk
Call Date: Nov 1982, Middle Temple
Pupil Master
Qualifications: [LLB (Lond)]

PEPPER MISS THERESA

Chavasse Court Chambers
2nd Floor, Chavasse Court, 24 Lord Street,
Liverpool L2 1TA,
Telephone: 0151 707 1191
Call Date: Nov 1973, Gray's Inn
Pupil Master, Assistant Recorder

PEPPER DR WILLIAM FRANCIS

Britton Street Chambers
1st Floor, 20 Britton Street, London
EC1M 5NQ, Telephone: 0171 608 3765
Call Date: Feb 1991, Lincoln's Inn
Qualifications: [BA,MA (Columbia), EdD, JD
(Univ.Mass.), ACIArb]

PEPPERALL EDWARD BRIAN

St Philip's Chambers
Fountain Court, Steelhouse Lane,
Birmingham B4 6DR,
Telephone: 0121 246 7000
E-mail: clerks@st-philips.co.uk
Call Date: July 1989, Lincoln's Inn
Qualifications: [LLB (B'ham)]

PERCIVAL ROBERT ELDON

5 Paper Buildings
Ground Floor, Temple, London
EC4Y 7HB, Telephone: 0171 583 9275/
583 4555 E-mail: 5paper@link.org
Call Date: Nov 1971, Inner Temple
Pupil Master
Qualifications: [MA (Cantab)]

PEREIRA JAMES ALEXANDER

2 Harcourt Buildings
2nd Floor, Temple, London EC4Y 9DB,
Telephone: 020 7353 8415
E-mail: clerks@2hb.law.co.uk
Call Date: Oct 1996, Middle Temple
Qualifications: [MA (Hons)(Cantab), LLM
(Lond)]

PERETZ GEORGE MICHAEL JOHN

Monckton Chambers
4 Raymond Buildings, Gray's Inn, London
WC1R 5BP, Telephone: 0171 405 7211
E-mail: chambers@monckton.co.uk
Call Date: Nov 1990, Middle Temple
Qualifications: [BA (Oxon), Dip Law (City)]

PERHAR SIMON KANWARDEEP

Staple Inn Chambers
1st Floor, 9 Staple Inn, Holborn Bars,
London WC1V 7QH,
Telephone: 0171 242 5240
E-mail: clerks@staple-inn.org
Call Date: 1997, Gray's Inn
Qualifications: [BA (Soton)]

PERIAN STEVEN SUPPIAH

2 King's Bench Walk Chambers
1st Floor, 2 King's Bench Walk, Temple,
London EC4Y 7DE,
Telephone: 020 7353 9276
E-mail: chambers@2kbw.co.uk
Call Date: Nov 1987, Lincoln's Inn
Qualifications: [LLB (Lond)]

PERKINS ALISTAIR GEOFFREY

Gray's Inn Chambers
5th Floor, Gray's Inn, London WC1R 5JA,
Telephone: 0171 404 1111
Call Date: July 1986, Middle Temple
Pupil Master
Qualifications: [BA (Keele)]

PERKINS MISS MARIANNE YVETTE

7 New Square
Lincoln's Inn, London WC2A 3QS,
Telephone: 0171 430 1660
Call Date: Mar 1997, Gray's Inn
Qualifications: [LLB (Lond), LLM (Lond)]

PERKOFF RICHARD MICHAEL

Littleton Chambers
3 King's Bench Walk North, Temple,
London EC4Y 7HR,
Telephone: 0171 797 8600
E-mail:clerks@littletonchambers.co.uk
Call Date: July 1971, Middle Temple
Pupil Master
Qualifications: [MA (Oxon)]

PERKS JOLYON ANTHONY

4 Brick Court
Temple, London EC4Y 9AD,
Telephone: 0171 797 8910
E-mail: medhurst@dial.pipex.com
Call Date: Nov 1994, Lincoln's Inn
Qualifications: [BA (Jnt Hons)(Hull), Dip in
Law (Leeds)]

PERKS RICHARD HOWARD

3 Fountain Court
Steelhouse Lane, Birmingham B4 6DR,
Telephone: 0121 236 5854
Call Date: Nov 1977, Lincoln's Inn
Pupil Master
Qualifications: [LLB (B'ham)]

PERRINS GREGORY LLOYD

1 Paper Buildings
1st Floor, Temple, London EC4Y 7EP,
Telephone: 0171 353 3728/4953
Call Date: Oct 1997, Inner Temple
Qualifications: [LLB,LLM (Nottingham)]

PERRY MISS AMANDA

Fountain Chambers
Cleveland Business Centre, 1 Watson
Street, Middlesbrough TS1 2RQ,
Telephone: 01642 804040
E-mail:fountainchambers@onyxnet.co.uk
Call Date: Nov 1987, Lincoln's Inn
Qualifications: [LLB(B'ham)]

PERRY CHRISTOPHER ALAN

Godolphin Chambers
50 Castle Street, Truro, Cornwall,
TR1 3AF, Telephone: 01872 276312
E-mail:theclerks@godolphin.force9.co.uk
Call Date: Nov 1980, Gray's Inn
Qualifications: [BA (Hons) (Oxon)]

PERRY CHRISTOPHER DAVID WILSON

Law Office Abdul Rab A-L Malla, P.O.Box
1850, Doha Telephone: 974 424856
Call Date: Nov 1965, Middle Temple

PERRY DAVID

6 King's Bench Walk
Ground Floor, Temple, London
EC4Y 7DR, Telephone: 0171 583 0410
E-mail: worsley@6kbw.freeserve.co.uk
Call Date: July 1980, Lincoln's Inn
Pupil Master
Qualifications: [LLB, MA]

PERRY MISS JACQUELINE ANNE

Lamb Building
Ground Floor, Temple, London
EC4Y 7AS, Telephone: 020 7797 7788
E-mail: lamb.building@link.org
Call Date: Feb 1975, Gray's Inn
Pupil Master
Qualifications: [MA (Oxon)]

Fax: 0171 353 0535;
Out of hours telephone: 0171 586 4197;
DX: 1038 London

Types of work: Medical negligence, Personal injury, Professional negligence

Awards and memberships: Member: Personal Injury Bar Association; Chair of Association of Women Barristers; APIL

Other professional experience: 10 years' (extra-mural) experience in legal broadcasting/journalism

Publications: *Rights of Women, 1990; Know Your Law, 1995/6*

PERRY JOHN QC (1989)

3 Gray's Inn Square
Ground Floor, London WC1R 5AH,
Telephone: 0171 520 5600
E-mail: clerks@3gis.co.uk
Call Date: Nov 1975, Middle Temple
Recorder
Qualifications: [LLB (Lond) , MA (Warwick), LLM (Lond)]

PERRY MRS NAOMI MELANIE

3 Temple Gardens
3rd Floor, Temple, London EC4Y 9AU,
Telephone: 0171 583 0010
Call Date: July 1974, Middle Temple
Pupil Master
Qualifications: [BA (B'ham)]

PERRY NIGEL JOHN

Hickstead Cottage
Brighton Road, Hickstead, West Sussex,
RH17 5NU, Telephone: 01444 881182
Call Date: July 1984, Gray's Inn
Qualifications: [LLB (Lond)]

PERSAD SATYANAND ALAN

Clapham Chambers
21-25 Bedford Road, Clapham North,
London SW4 7SH,
Telephone: 0171 978 8482/642 5777
E-mail:claphamchambers@compuserve.com
Call Date: Feb 1968, Inner Temple

PERSEY LIONEL EDWARD QC (1997)

4 Field Court
Gray's Inn, London WC1R 5EA,
Telephone: 0171 440 6900
E-mail: chambers@4fieldcourt.co.uk
Call Date: July 1981, Gray's Inn
Qualifications: [LLB, DEJF (Limoges)]

Fax: 0171 242 0192; DX: LDE 483

Types of work: Admiralty, Arbitration, Aviation, Commercial, Commercial litigation, Commodities, Construction, EC and competition law, Insurance, Insurance/reinsurance, International trade, Private international, Sale and carriage of goods, Shipping, admiralty

Membership of foreign bars: Gibraltar

Awards and memberships: Fellow of the Institute of Advanced Legal Studies; Commercial Bar Association; London Common Law and Commercial Bar Association

Languages spoken: French

PERSHAD ROHAN

Two Crown Office Row
Ground Floor, Temple, London
EC4Y 7HJ, Telephone: 020 7797 8100
E-mail: mail@2cor.co.uk, or to individual barristers at: [barrister's surname]@2cor.co.uk
Call Date: Oct 1991, Lincoln's Inn
Qualifications: [LLB (Hons) (Lond)]

PERT MICHAEL QC (1992)

Chambers of Michael Pert QC
36 Bedford Row, London WC1R 4JH,
Telephone: 0171 421 8000
E-mail: 36bedfordrow@link.org
Chambers of Michael Pert QC
104 New Walk, Leicester LE1 7EA,
Telephone: 0116 249 2020
Chambers of Michael Pert QC
24 Albion Place, Northampton NN1 1UD,
Telephone: 01604 602333
Call Date: Apr 1970, Gray's Inn
Recorder
Qualifications: [LLB (Manchester)]

PETCHEY PHILIP NEIL

2 Harcourt Buildings
2nd Floor, Temple, London EC4Y 9DB,
Telephone: 020 7353 8415
E-mail: clerks@2hb.law.co.uk
Call Date: July 1976, Middle Temple
Pupil Master
Qualifications: [MA (Oxon)]

PETER LEVI ANDREW

4 Brick Court
Temple, London EC4Y 9AD,
Telephone: 0171 797 8910
E-mail: medhurst@dial.pipex.com
Call Date: Nov 1993, Lincoln's Inn
Qualifications: [LLB (Hons)]

PETERS EDWARD JAMES HEDLEY

Falcon Chambers
Falcon Court, London EC4Y 1AA,
Telephone: 0171 353 2484
E-mail: clerks@falcon-chambers.com
Call Date: 1998, Middle Temple
Qualifications: [BA (Hons)(Cantab)]

PETERS NIGEL MELVIN QC (1997)

18 Red Lion Court
(Off Fleet Street), London EC4A 3EB,
Telephone: 0171 520 6000
E-mail: chambers@18rlc.co.uk
Thornwood House
102 New London Road, Chelmsford,
Essex, CM2 0RG,
Telephone: 01245 280880
E-mail: chambers@18rlc.co.uk
Call Date: 1976, Lincoln's Inn
Recorder
Qualifications: [LLB]

PETERS WILLIAM JOHN STEPHEN CHARLES

Iscoed Chambers
86 St Helen's Road, Swansea, West
Glamorgan, SA1 4BQ,
Telephone: 01792 652988/9/330
Call Date: Nov 1992, Lincoln's Inn

PETERSEN LEWIS NEIL

2 Paper Buildings, Basement North
Temple, London EC4Y 7ET,
Telephone: 0171 936 2613
E-mail: post@2paper.co.uk
Call Date: July 1983, Middle Temple
Qualifications: [BA LLB (Capetown), Dip
Crim (Cantab)]

PETERSON MISS GERALDINE SHELDA

Lamb Building
Ground Floor, Temple, London
EC4Y 7AS, Telephone: 020 7797 7788
E-mail: lamb.building@link.org
Call Date: 1997, Middle Temple
Qualifications: [BA (Hons)(Cantab)]

PETO ANTHONY NICHOLAS GEORGE

Blackstone Chambers
Blackstone House, Temple, London
EC4Y 9BW, Telephone: 0171 583 1770
E-mail:clerks@blackstonechambers.com
Call Date: Feb 1985, Middle Temple
Pupil Master
Qualifications: [MA,BCL (Oxon)]

PETTS TIMOTHY DAVID

12 King's Bench Walk
Temple, London EC4Y 7EL,
Telephone: 0171 583 0811
E-mail: chambers@12kbw.co.uk
Call Date: Oct 1996, Inner Temple
Qualifications: [BA, M.Jur (Oxon)]

PEYTON DANIEL LEWIS

169 Temple Chambers
Temple Avenue, London EC4Y 0DA,
Telephone: 0171 583 7644
Call Date: Oct 1995, Inner Temple
Qualifications: [LLB (Sheff), BCL (Oxon)]

PEZZANI ROGER ROBERT NICHOLAS

Cardinal Chambers
4 Old Mitre Court, 4th Floor, Temple,
London EC4Y 7BP,
Telephone: 020 7353 2622
E-mail:admin@cardinal-chambers.co.uk
Call Date: 1997, Middle Temple
Qualifications: [BA (Hons)(Sussex)]

PHELAN MS MARGARET

Gray's Inn Chambers
5th Floor, Gray's Inn, London WC1R 5JA,
Telephone: 0171 404 1111
Call Date: Oct 1993, Inner Temple
Qualifications: [LLB (Hons)]

PHELPS MARK

East Anglian Chambers
Gresham House, 5 Museum Street,
Ipswich, Suffolk, IP1 1HQ,
Telephone: 01473 214481
E-mail: ipswich@ealaw.co.uk
East Anglian Chambers
52 North Hill, Colchester, Essex, CO1 1PY,
Telephone: 01206 572756
E-mail: colchester@ealaw.co.uk
East Anglian Chambers
57 London Street, Norwich NR2 1HL,
Telephone: 01603 617351
E-mail: norwich@ealaw.co.uk
Call Date: Nov 1994, Lincoln's Inn
Qualifications: [BA (Jnt Hons), MA (Notts),
CPE (Notts)]

PHELVIN BERNARD JOHN

9-12 Bell Yard
London WC2A 2LF,
Telephone: 0171 400 1800
E-mail: clerks@bellyard.co.uk
Call Date: July 1971, Middle Temple
Pupil Master
Qualifications: [BA (Cantab)]

PHIL-EBOSIE MISS EUNICE SHEILA NNEKA

Francis Taylor Building
3rd Floor, Temple, London EC4Y 7BY,
Telephone: 0171 797 7250
Call Date: Nov 1988, Gray's Inn
Qualifications: [LLB (Nigeria), LLM (Lond),
BL (Nigeria)]

PHILIPPS GUY WOGAN

Fountain Court
Temple, London EC4Y 9DH,
Telephone: 0171 583 3335
E-mail: chambers@fountaincourt.co.uk
Call Date: July 1986, Inner Temple
Pupil Master
Qualifications: [MA (Oxon), Dip Law]

PHILIPSON JOHN TREVOR GRAHAM QC (1989)

Fountain Court
Temple, London EC4Y 9DH,
Telephone: 0171 583 3335
E-mail: chambers@fountaincourt.co.uk
Call Date: Nov 1972, Middle Temple
Qualifications: [BA, BCL (Oxon)]

PHILLIMORE LORD FRANCIS STEPHEN

Queen Elizabeth Building
2nd Floor, Temple, London EC4Y 9BS,
Telephone: 0171 797 7837
Call Date: July 1972, Middle Temple
Pupil Master
Qualifications: [BA (Cantab)]

PHILLIMORE MISS SARAH VICTORIA

4 King's Bench Walk
2nd Floor, Temple, London EC4Y 7DL,
Telephone: 020 7353 3581
E-mail: clerks@4kbw.co.uk
Call Date: 1994, Lincoln's Inn
Qualifications: [LLB (Hons)(Lond)]

PHILLIPS ANDREW CHARLES

Two Crown Office Row
Ground Floor, Temple, London
EC4Y 7HJ, Telephone: 020 7797 8100
E-mail: mail@2cor.co.uk, or to individual
barristers at: [barrister's
surname]@2cor.co.uk
Call Date: July 1978, Middle Temple
Pupil Master
Qualifications: [BA (Oxon), MA (Cantab)]

PHILLIPS DAVID JOHN QC (1997)

199 Strand
London WC2R 1DR,
Telephone: 0171 379 9779
E-mail: chambers@199strand.co.uk

30 Park Place
Cardiff CF1 3BA,
Telephone: 01222 398421
E-mail: 100757.1456@compuserve.com
Call Date: 1976, Gray's Inn
Assistant Recorder
Qualifications: [MA (Oxon)]

PHILLIPS FRANK

Iscoed Chambers
86 St Helen's Road, Swansea, West
Glamorgan, SA1 4BQ,
Telephone: 01792 652988/9/330
Call Date: Nov 1972, Lincoln's Inn
Pupil Master
Qualifications: [LLB (Bris)]

PHILLIPS MISS JANE ROSE

1 Brick Court
1st Floor, Temple, London EC4Y 9BY,
Telephone: 0171 353 8845
E-mail: clerks@1brickcourt.co.uk
Call Date: July 1989, Inner Temple
Qualifications: [BA (Oxon)(Hons)]

PHILLIPS JEREMY PATRICK MANFRED QC (1980)

2 Temple Gardens
Temple, London EC4Y 9AY,
Telephone: 0171 583 6041
E-mail: clerks@2templegardens.co.uk
Call Date: 1964, Gray's Inn

PHILLIPS JOHN CHRISTOPHER

11 Stone Buildings
Lincoln's Inn, London WC2A 3TG,
Telephone: +44 (0)207 831 6381
E-mail:clerks@11StoneBuildings.law.co.uk
Call Date: Feb 1975, Middle Temple
Qualifications: [MA (Cantab), LLM
(Queensland), PhD (Queensland)]

PHILLIPS JONATHAN MARK

3 Verulam Buildings
London WC1R 5NT,
Telephone: 0171 831 8441
E-mail: clerks@3verulam.co.uk
Call Date: 1991, Inner Temple
Qualifications: [BA (Hons)(Cantab)]

PHILLIPS MARK PAUL QC (1999)

3/4 South Square
Gray's Inn, London WC1R 5HP,
Telephone: 0171 696 9900
E-mail: clerks@southsquare.com
Call Date: 1984, Inner Temple
Pupil Master
Qualifications: [LLB, LLM (Bris)]

PHILLIPS MATTHEW JAMES

35 Essex Street
Temple, London WC2R 3AR,
Telephone: 0171 353 6381
E-mail: derek_jenkins@link.org
Call Date: Nov 1993, Lincoln's Inn
Qualifications: [BA (Hons)]

PHILLIPS MICHAEL CHARLES

Lamb Building
Ground Floor, Temple, London
EC4Y 7AS, Telephone: 020 7797 7788
E-mail: lamb.building@link.org
Call Date: Feb 1980, Middle Temple
Pupil Master
Qualifications: [LLB (Lond)]

PHILLIPS NEVIL DAVID

4 Essex Court
Temple, London EC4Y 9AJ,
Telephone: 020 7797 7970
E-mail: clerks@4essexcourt.law.co.uk
Call Date: Oct 1992, Gray's Inn
Qualifications: [BA (So'ton), Dip Law (City),
LLM (Lond)]

PHILLIPS PAUL STUART

Dr Johnson's Chambers
Two Dr Johnson's Buildings, Temple,
London EC4Y 7AY,
Telephone: 0171 353 4716
E-mail: clerks@2djb.freeserve.co.uk
Call Date: Feb 1991, Gray's Inn
Qualifications: [LLB (Wales)]

PHILLIPS RICHARD CHARLES JONATHAN QC (1990)

2 Harcourt Buildings
2nd Floor, Temple, London EC4Y 9DB,
Telephone: 020 7353 8415
E-mail: clerks@2hb.law.co.uk
Call Date: Nov 1970, Inner Temple
Qualifications: [MA (Cantab)]

PHILLIPS RORY ANDREW LIVINGSTONE

3 Verulam Buildings
London WC1R 5NT,
Telephone: 0171 831 8441
E-mail: clerks@3verulam.co.uk
Call Date: July 1984, Inner Temple
Pupil Master
Qualifications: [MA (Cantab)]

PHILLIPS S J

S Tomlinson QC
7 King's Bench Walk, Temple, London
EC4Y 7DS, Telephone: 0171 583 0404
E-mail: clerks@7kbw.law.co.uk
Call Date: 1993, Lincoln's Inn
Qualifications: [BA (Oxon), BCL]

PHILLIPS SIMON BENJAMIN

Park Court Chambers
16 Park Place, Leeds LS1 2SJ,
Telephone: 0113 2433277
Call Date: July 1985, Inner Temple
Pupil Master
Qualifications: [BA (Sussex), LLM, (Cantab)]

PHILLIPS SIMON DAVID

1 Fountain Court
Steelhouse Lane, Birmingham B4 6DR,
Telephone: 0121 236 5721
Call Date: Oct 1996, Inner Temple
Qualifications: [BA (Cantab)]

PHILLIPS STEPHEN EDMUND

3 Verulam Buildings
London WC1R 5NT,
Telephone: 0171 831 8441
E-mail: clerks@3verulam.co.uk
Call Date: July 1984, Gray's Inn
Pupil Master
Qualifications: [BA (Oxon)]

PHILLIPS WILLIAM BERNARD

Paradise Chambers
26 Paradise Square, Sheffield S1 2DE,
Telephone: 0114 2738951
E-mail: timbooth@paradise-sq.co.uk
Call Date: July 1970, Inner Temple
Pupil Master, Recorder
Qualifications: [MA (Oxon)]

PHILLPOT HEREWARD LINDON

2 Harcourt Buildings
2nd Floor, Temple, London EC4Y 9DB,
Telephone: 020 7353 8415
E-mail: clerks@2hb.law.co.uk
Call Date: Oct 1997, Gray's Inn
Qualifications: [BA (York)]

PHILO NOEL PHILIP

St Mary's Chambers
50 High Pavement, Lace Market,
Nottingham NG1 1HW,
Telephone: 0115 9503503
E-mail: clerks@smc.law.co.uk
Call Date: Feb 1975, Gray's Inn
Pupil Master
Qualifications: [MA (Oxon)]

PHILPOTT FREDERICK ALAN

Gough Square Chambers
6-7 Gough Square, London EC4A 3DE,
Telephone: 0171 353 0924
E-mail: gsc@goughsq.co.uk
Call Date: July 1974, Gray's Inn
Pupil Master
Qualifications: [LLB (Lond)]

PHILPOTTS ROBERT JOHN

Exchange Chambers
Pearl Assurance House, Derby Square,
Liverpool L2 9XX,
Telephone: 0151 236 7747
E-mail:exchangechambers@btinternet.com
Call Date: Oct 1990, Gray's Inn
Qualifications: [BA, MPhil (L'pool)]

PHIPPS CHARLES MACKENZIE

Chambers of John L Powell QC
Four New Square, Lincoln's Inn, London
WC2A 3RJ, Telephone: 0171 797 8000
E-mail: barristers@4newsquare.com
Call Date: Nov 1992, Middle Temple
Qualifications: [BA (Oxon), Dip in Law
(City)]

PHIPPS MISS SARAH ELIZABETH

Queen Elizabeth Building
2nd Floor, Temple, London EC4Y 9BS,
Telephone: 0171 797 7837
Call Date: 1997, Lincoln's Inn
Qualifications: [BA (Hons)]

PICARDA HUBERT ALISTAIR PAUL QC (1992)

Chambers of Lord Goodhart QC
Ground Floor, 3 New Square, Lincoln's
Inn, London WC2A 3RS,
Telephone: 0171 405 5577
E-mail:law@threenewsqvare.demon.co.uk
Call Date: Feb 1962, Inner Temple
Qualifications: [MA, BCL (Oxon)]

PICKAVANCE GRAHAM MICHAEL

Chavasse Court Chambers
2nd Floor, Chavasse Court, 24 Lord Street,
Liverpool L2 1TA,
Telephone: 0151 707 1191
Call Date: Nov 1973, Gray's Inn
Pupil Master
Qualifications: [LLB]

PICKAVANCE MICHAEL JOHN

Corn Exchange Chambers
5th Floor, Fenwick Street, Liverpool
L2 7QS, Telephone: 0151 227 1081/5009
Call Date: July 1974, Middle Temple
Qualifications: [LLB (Hons)]

PICKEN SIMON DEREK

S Tomlinson QC
7 King's Bench Walk, Temple, London
EC4Y 7DS, Telephone: 0171 583 0404
E-mail: clerks@7kbw.law.co.uk
30 Park Place
Cardiff CF1 3BA,
Telephone: 01222 398421
E-mail: 100757.1456@compuserve.com
Call Date: July 1989, Middle Temple
Pupil Master
Qualifications: [LLB [Cardiff], LLM (Cantab)]

PICKERING JAMES PATRICK

Enterprise Chambers
9 Old Square, Lincoln's Inn, London
WC2A 3SR, Telephone: 0171 405 9471
E-mail:enterprise.london@dial.pipex.com
Enterprise Chambers
38 Park Square, Leeds LS1 2PA,
Telephone: 0113 246 0391
E-mail:enterprise.leeds@dial.pipex.com

Enterprise Chambers
65 Quayside, Newcastle upon Tyne
NE1 3DS, Telephone: 0191 222 3344
E-mail:enterprise.newcastle@dial.pipex.com
Call Date: Oct 1991, Middle Temple
Pupil Master
Qualifications: [BSc Hons (So'ton)]

PICKERING MURRAY ASHLEY QC (1985)

20 Essex Street
London WC2R 3AL,
Telephone: 0171 583 9294
E-mail: clerks@20essexst.com
Call Date: Nov 1963, Inner Temple
Recorder
Qualifications: [MA (NZ), LLM (Lond)]

PICKERING RICHARD ANDREW

12 King's Bench Walk
Temple, London EC4Y 7EL,
Telephone: 0171 583 0811
E-mail: chambers@12kbw.co.uk
Call Date: Nov 1987, Lincoln's Inn
Pupil Master
Qualifications: [BA(Hons) Cantab, Dip Law
(City)]

PICKERING SIMON TOBY

Wilberforce Chambers
7 Bishop Lane, Hull, East Yorkshire,
HU1 1PA, Telephone: 01482 323264
E-mail: clerks@hullbar.demon.co.uk
Call Date: 1996, Inner Temple
Qualifications: [LLB (Hull), MA (York)]

PICKERSGILL DAVID WILLIAM

Bell Yard Chambers
116/118 Chancery Lane, London
WC2A 1PP, Telephone: 0171 306 9292
Call Date: Nov 1996, Middle Temple
Qualifications: [LLB (Hons)(Kingston)]

PICKFORD ANTHONY JAMES

Prince Henry's Chamber
109 Grosvenor Road, Westminster,
London SW1V 3LG,
Telephone: 0171 834 2572
Call Date: June 1951, Lincoln's Inn
Qualifications: [LLB (Lond)]

PICKLES SIMON ROBERT

1 Serjeants' Inn
4th Floor, Temple, London EC4Y 1NH,
Telephone: 0171 583 1355
E-mail: clerks@serjeants-inn.co.uk
Call Date: July 1978, Inner Temple
Pupil Master
Qualifications: [MA (Cantab)]

PICKUP DAVID MICHAEL WALKER

Peel Court Chambers
45 Hardman Street, Manchester M3 3PL,
Telephone: 0161 832 3791
E-mail: clerks@peelct.co.uk
Call Date: July 1984, Inner Temple
Qualifications: [LLB (Leeds)]

PICKUP JAMES KENNETH

Lincoln House Chambers
5th Floor, Lincoln House, 1 Brazennose
Street, Manchester M2 5EL,
Telephone: 0161 832 5701
E-mail: info@lincolnhse.co.uk
Call Date: July 1976, Gray's Inn
Pupil Master, Recorder
Qualifications: [MA (Oxon), BCL]

PICTON JULIAN MARK

4 Paper Buildings
Ground Floor, Temple, London
EC4Y 7EX, Telephone: 0171 353 3366/
583 7155
E-mail: clerks@4paperbuildings.com
Call Date: Feb 1988, Middle Temple
Qualifications: [BA (Oxon)]

PICTON MARTIN THOMAS

Albion Chambers
Broad Street, Bristol BS1 1DR,
Telephone: 0117 9272144
Call Date: July 1981, Middle Temple
Pupil Master
Qualifications: [LLB (Lond)]

PIDCOCK STEVEN CRAWFORD

Somersett Chambers
25 Bedford Row, London WC1R 4HE,
Telephone: 0171 404 6701
E-mail: somelaw@aol.com
Call Date: Nov 1996, Lincoln's Inn
Qualifications: [LLB (Hons)(LSE)]

PIERCY MISS ARLETTE MARY

3 Gray's Inn Square
Ground Floor, London WC1R 5AH,
Telephone: 0171 520 5600
E-mail: clerks@3gis.co.uk
Call Date: Nov 1990, Lincoln's Inn
Qualifications: [LLB (Leeds)]

PIERCY HON MARK EDWARD PELHAM

Francis Taylor Building
Ground Floor, Temple, London
EC4Y 7BY, Telephone: 0171 353 7768/
7769/2711
E-mail:clerks@francistaylorbuilding.law.co.uk
Call Date: July 1976, Lincoln's Inn
Pupil Master
Qualifications: [BA (Oxon)]

PIGOT MISS DIANA MARGUERITE

2 Pump Court
1st Floor, Temple, London EC4Y 7AH,
Telephone: 0171 353 5597
Call Date: Nov 1978, Inner Temple
Qualifications: [BA (Lond)]

PILKINGTON MRS MAVIS PATRICIA

9 Woodhouse Square
Leeds LS3 1AD,
Telephone: 0113 2451986
E-mail: clerks@9woodhouse.co.uk
Call Date: Oct 1990, Lincoln's Inn
Qualifications: [LLB, LLM (B'ham)]

PILLING MISS ANNABEL LUCY

6 King's Bench Walk
Ground Floor, Temple, London
EC4Y 7DR, Telephone: 0171 583 0410
E-mail: worsley@6kbw.freeserve.co.uk
Call Date: Oct 1995, Middle Temple
Qualifications: [BA (Hons)]

PILLING BENJAMIN

4 Pump Court
Temple, London EC4Y 7AN,
Telephone: 020 7842 5555
E-mail:chambers@4pumpcourt.law.co.uk
Call Date: 1997, Inner Temple
Qualifications: [BA (Oxon) MA (City), CPE
(City)]

PILLOW NATHAN CHARLES

Essex Court Chambers
24 Lincoln's Inn Fields, London
WC2A 3ED, Telephone: 0171 813 8000
E-mail:clerksroom@essexcourt-chambers.co.u
k
Call Date: 1997, Gray's Inn
Qualifications: [BA (Oxon)]

PIMENTEL CARLOS DE SERPA ALBERTO LEGG

3 Stone Buildings
Lincoln's Inn, London WC2A 3XL,
Telephone: 0171 242 4937
E-mail: clerks@3sb.law.co.uk
Call Date: Oct 1990, Inner Temple
Qualifications: [LLB, LLM (Exon)]

PIMM PETER JULIAN

Bank House Chambers
Old Bank House, Hartshead, Sheffield
S1 2EL, Telephone: 0114 2751223
Cloisters
1 Pump Court, Temple, London
EC4Y 7AA, Telephone: 0171 827 4000
E-mail: clerks@cloisters.com
Call Date: Apr 1991, Gray's Inn
Pupil Master
Qualifications: [BSC (Bristol)]

PINDER MISS MARY ELIZABETH

No. 1 Serjeants' Inn
5th Floor Fleet Street, Temple, London
EC4Y 1LH, Telephone: 0171 415 6666
E-mail:no1serjeantsinn@btinternet.com
Call Date: July 1989, Gray's Inn
Qualifications: [LLB (Bris)]

PINE-COFFIN MISS MARGARET ANN

17 Carlton Crescent
Southampton SO15 2XR,
Telephone: 023 8032 0320/0823 2003
E-mail: greg@jg17cc.co.uk
Call Date: July 1981, Inner Temple
Qualifications: [BA (Leeds)]

PINES-RICHMAN MRS HELENE

9 Stone Buildings
Lincoln's Inn, London WC2A 3NN,
Telephone: 0171 404 5055
E-mail: clerks@9stoneb.law.co.uk

Stour Chambers
Barton Mill House, Barton Mill Road,
Canterbury, Kent, CT1 1BP,
Telephone: 01227 764899
E-mail: clerks@stourchambers.co.uk
Eighteen Carlton Crescent
Southampton SO15 2XR,
Telephone: 01703 639001
Call Date: 1992, Middle Temple
Qualifications: [BA (Hons)(University, of
Pennsylvania)]

PINI JOHN PETER JULIAN

9 Bedford Row
London WC1R 4AZ,
Telephone: 0171 242 3555
E-mail: clerks@9br.co.uk
Call Date: July 1981, Gray's Inn
Pupil Master
Qualifications: [BA]

PINKHAM MRS JOY EMMA

Chartlands Chambers
3 St Giles Terrace, Northampton
NN1 2BN, Telephone: 01604 603322
Call Date: Feb 1993, Gray's Inn
Qualifications: [LLB (Buckingham)]

PINKNEY ANDREW GILES FREDERICK

Fountain Chambers
Cleveland Business Centre, 1 Watson
Street, Middlesbrough TS1 2RQ,
Telephone: 01642 804040
E-mail:fountainchambers@onyxnet.co.uk
Call Date: Nov 1978, Gray's Inn
Pupil Master
Qualifications: [BA (Hons)]

PINTER JOSEPH PHILIP

3 Temple Gardens
3rd Floor, Temple, London EC4Y 9AU,
Telephone: 0171 353 0832
Call Date: Nov 1987, Lincoln's Inn
Qualifications: [LLB Hons]

D

PINTO MISS AMANDA EVE

Five Paper Buildings
1st Floor, Five Paper Bldgs, Temple,
London EC4Y 7HB,
Telephone: 0171 583 6117
E-mail:clerks@5-paperbuildings.law.co.uk
Call Date: Nov 1983, Middle Temple
Pupil Master
Qualifications: [MA (Cantab)]

PIPE GREGORY SIMON

Chancery House Chambers
7 Lisbon Square, Leeds LS1 4LY,
Telephone: 0113 244 6691
E-mail: chanceryhouse@btinternet.com
Call Date: Oct 1995, Lincoln's Inn
Qualifications: [BA (Hons)(Oxon), LLM
(Cantab)]

PIPER ANGUS RICHARD

No. 1 Serjeants' Inn
5th Floor Fleet Street, Temple, London
EC4Y 1LH, Telephone: 0171 415 6666
E-mail:no1serjeantsinn@btinternet.com
Call Date: Nov 1991, Lincoln's Inn
Pupil Master
Qualifications: [BA (Hons) (York), Dip Law]

PIPER SIMON WILLIAM

New Walk Chambers
27 New Walk, Leicester LE1 6TE,
Telephone: 0116 2559144
Call Date: Oct 1997, Lincoln's Inn
Qualifications: [BA (Hons)]

PIPI CHUKWUEMEKA EZEKIEL

Chambers of Martin Burr
Fourth Floor, Eldon Chambers, 30/32
Fleet Street, London EC4Y 1AA,
Telephone: 0171 353 4636
Call Date: Apr 1991, Inner Temple
Qualifications: [LLB]

PIRANI ROHAN CARL

Old Square Chambers
Hanover House, 47 Corn Street, Bristol
BS1 1HT, Telephone: 0117 9277111
E-mail: oldsqbri@globalnet.co.uk

Old Square Chambers
1 Verulam Buildings, Gray's Inn, London
WC1R 5LQ, Telephone: 0171 269 0300
E-mail:clerks@oldsquarechambers.co.uk
Call Date: Oct 1995, Middle Temple
Qualifications: [MA (Oxon), BCL (Oxon),
LLM (Toronto)]

PIROTTA MISS MONICA JOSEPHINE

8 Fountain Court
Steelhouse Lane, Birmingham B4 6DR,
Telephone: 0121 236 5514/5
E-mail: clerks@no8chambers.co.uk
Call Date: Nov 1976, Middle Temple
Qualifications: [LLB]

PITCHERS HENRY WILLIAM STODART

22 Old Buildings
Lincoln's Inn, London WC2A 3UJ,
Telephone: 0171 831 0222
Call Date: Nov 1996, Inner Temple
Qualifications: [BA (Oxon)]

PITCHFORD CHRISTOPHER JOHN QC (1987)

Farrar's Building
Temple, London EC4Y 7BD,
Telephone: 0171 583 9241
E-mail:chambers@farrarsbuilding.co.uk
30 Park Place
Cardiff CF1 3BA,
Telephone: 01222 398421
E-mail: 100757.1456@compuserve.com
Call Date: July 1969, Middle Temple
Recorder
Qualifications: [LLB]

PITHERS CLIVE ROBERT

Fenners Chambers
3 Madingley Road, Cambridge CB3 0EE,
Telephone: 01223 368761
E-mail: clerks@fennerschambers.co.uk
Fenners Chambers
8-12 Priestgate, Peterborough PE1 1JA,
Telephone: 01733 562030
E-mail: clerks@fennerschambers.co.uk
Call Date: Feb 1989, Gray's Inn
Qualifications: [LLB (Reading)]

PITT THE HON BRUCE MICHAEL DAVID

Phoenix Chambers
First Floor, Gray's Inn Chambers, Gray's Inn, London WC1R 5JA,
Telephone: 0171 404 7888
E-mail:clerks@phoenix-chambers.co.uk
Call Date: Nov 1970, Gray's Inn
Pupil Master
Qualifications: [LLB(Lond)]

PITT COLIN GEORGE

Call Date: Nov 1968, Gray's Inn
Pupil Master
Qualifications: [BA (Econ) LLB (Lond)]

PITT-LEWIS MRS JANET REBECCA

6 Fountain Court
Steelhouse Lane, Birmingham B4 6DR,
Telephone: 0121 233 3282
E-mail: clerks@sixfountain.co.uk
Call Date: July 1976, Middle Temple
Pupil Master
Qualifications: [MA (Oxon)]

PITT-PAYNE TIMOTHY SHERIDAN

11 King's Bench Walk
Temple, London EC4Y 7EQ,
Telephone: 0171 632 8500/583 0610
E-mail: clerksroom@11kbw.com
Call Date: Nov 1989, Inner Temple
Pupil Master
Qualifications: [BA, BCL (Oxon)]

Fax: 0171 583 9123/3690; DX: LDE 368

Types of work: Administrative, Commercial litigation, Discrimination, Employment, Local government

Languages spoken: French

Publications: *Judicial Review* (Eds Supperstone and Goudie), 1997

PITTAWAY MISS AMANDA MICHELLE

6 Fountain Court
Steelhouse Lane, Birmingham B4 6DR,
Telephone: 0121 233 3282
E-mail: clerks@sixfountain.co.uk
Call Date: July 1980, Gray's Inn
Qualifications: [LLB (B'ham)]

PITTAWAY DAVID MICHAEL

No. 1 Serjeants' Inn
5th Floor Fleet Street, Temple, London EC4Y 1LH, Telephone: 0171 415 6666
E-mail:no1serjeantsinn@btinternet.com
Call Date: July 1977, Inner Temple
Pupil Master, Assistant Recorder
Qualifications: [MA (Cantab)]

PITTER JASON KARL

Park Court Chambers
16 Park Place, Leeds LS1 2SJ,
Telephone: 0113 2433277
Call Date: Oct 1994, Gray's Inn
Qualifications: [LLB (Hons)]

PITTS ANTHONY BRIAN

4 Brick Court, Chambers of Anne Rafferty QC
1st Floor, Temple, London EC4Y 9AD,
Telephone: 0171 583 8455
Call Date: Nov 1975, Gray's Inn
Pupil Master, Assistant Recorder
Qualifications: [BA (Oxon)]

PIYADASA MISS SURANGANI DEVI

4 Brick Court
Temple, London EC4Y 9AD,
Telephone: 0171 797 8910
E-mail: medhurst@dial.pipex.com
Call Date: Oct 1994, Lincoln's Inn
Qualifications: [LLB (Hons)(Lond)]

PLANGE MISS JANET NYANCH

14 Tooks Court
Cursitor St, London EC4A 1LB,
Telephone: 0171 405 8828
E-mail: clerks@tooks.law.co.uk
Call Date: July 1981, Gray's Inn
Qualifications: [LLB (B'ham)]

PLANTEROSE ROWAN MICHAEL

Littman Chambers
12 Gray's Inn Square, London WC1R 5JP,
Telephone: 020 7404 4866
E-mail: admin@littmanchambers.com
Call Date: Nov 1978, Middle Temple
Pupil Master
Qualifications: [MA, LLB (Cantab), FCIARB]

PLASCHKES MS SARAH GEORGINA

Hollis Whiteman Chambers
3rd Floor, Queen Elizabeth Bldg, Temple,
London EC4Y 9BS,
Telephone: 020 7583 5766
E-mail:barristers@holliswhiteman.co.uk
Call Date: July 1988, Inner Temple
Pupil Master
Qualifications: [LLB (Soton)]

PLATFORD GRAHAM ROY

5 Paper Buildings
Ground Floor, Temple, London
EC4Y 7HB, Telephone: 0171 583 9275/
583 4555 E-mail: 5paper@link.org
Call Date: Nov 1970, Gray's Inn
Pupil Master
Qualifications: [BA]

PLATT DAVID WALLACE

One Paper Buildings
Ground Floor, Temple, London
EC4Y 7EP, Telephone: 0171 583 7355
E-mail: clerks@1pb.co.uk
Call Date: July 1987, Middle Temple
Pupil Master
Qualifications: [MA (Cantab)]

PLATT MISS ELEANOR FRANCES QC (1982)

One Garden Court Family Law Chambers
Ground Floor, Temple, London
EC4Y 9BJ, Telephone: 0171 797 7900
E-mail: clerks@onegardencourt.co.uk
Call Date: Feb 1960, Gray's Inn
Recorder
Qualifications: [LLB (Lond)]

PLATTS CHARLES GRAHAM GREGORY

28 St John Street
Manchester M3 4DJ,
Telephone: 0161 834 8418
E-mail: clerk@28stjohnst.co.uk
Call Date: July 1978, Gray's Inn
Pupil Master, Assistant Recorder
Qualifications: [MA (Cantab)]

PLATTS MISS RACHEL ELIZABETH

1 Mitre Court Buildings
Temple, London EC4Y 7BS,
Telephone: 0171 797 7070
E-mail: clerks@1mcb.com
Call Date: Nov 1989, Inner Temple
Pupil Master
Qualifications: [LLB (Hons)(Lond)]

PLATTS ROBERT

Lincoln House Chambers
5th Floor, Lincoln House, 1 Brazennose
Street, Manchester M2 5EL,
Telephone: 0161 832 5701
E-mail: info@lincolnhse.co.uk
Call Date: July 1973, Lincoln's Inn
Pupil Master, Recorder
Qualifications: [LLB (Hons) Lond, MSc (Bradford)]

PLATTS-MILLS JOHN FAITHFUL FORTESCUE QC (1964)

Cloisters
1 Pump Court, Temple, London
EC4Y 7AA, Telephone: 0171 827 4000
E-mail: clerks@cloisters.com
Call Date: Jan 1932, Inner Temple
Qualifications: [MA BCL (Oxon) LLM, (NZ)]

PLATTS-MILLS MARK FORTESCUE QC (1995)

8 New Square
Lincoln's Inn, London WC2A 3QP,
Telephone: 0171 405 4321
E-mail: clerks@8newsquare.co.uk
Call Date: July 1974, Inner Temple
Qualifications: [BA (Oxon)]

PLAUT SIMON MICHAEL

Park Lane Chambers
19 Westgate, Leeds LS1 2RD,
Telephone: 0113 2285000
E-mail:clerks@parklanechambers.co.uk
Call Date: Oct 1997, Lincoln's Inn
Qualifications: [BA (Hons)]

PLEMING NIGEL PETER QC (1992)

39 Essex Street
London WC2R 3AT,
Telephone: 0171 832 1111
E-mail: clerks@39essex.co.uk
Call Date: Feb 1971, Inner Temple
Qualifications: [LLM (Lond)]

PLENDER RICHARD OWEN QC (1989)

20 Essex Street
London WC2R 3AL,
Telephone: 0171 583 9294
E-mail: clerks@20essexst.com
Call Date: Nov 1972, Inner Temple
Recorder
Qualifications: [MA, LLB,LLD (Cantab),
JSD,LLM (Illinois)]

Fax: 0171 583 1341;
Out of hours telephone: 0181 660 2633/
642 5865; DX: 0009 London, Chancery
Lane; URL: http://www.20essexst.com.

Other professional qualifications: LLD
Cambridge (Recognition of published
work)

Types of work: Administrative, Arbitration,
Civil liberties, Commercial, EC and competition law, Immigration, Private international, Public international

Circuit: South Eastern

Awards and memberships: Senior member,
Robinson College, Cambridge since 1983.
Bencher, Inner Temple, Recorder

Other professional experience: Referendaire,
Court of Justice of the European Commu-
nities 1980-3. Legal adviser United Nations
HCR 1974-8

Languages spoken:

Publications: *European Courts Practice and
Precedents*, 1998; *The European Contracts
Convention*, 1991; *International Migra-
tion Law*, 2nd edn 1987; *Procedure in the
European Courts*, 1998; *Introduccion Al
Derecho Comunitario*, 1990

Reported Cases: *Kuwait Airways v Iraqi
Airways Company*, [1995] 3 All ER 694
(HL), 1995. Sovereign immunity of Iraq in
connection with invasion of Kuwait.

Johnston v Chief Constable, [1986] ECR
2151 (ECJ), 1986. Equal treatment for
married women: armed police in Northern
Ireland.
R v Secretary of State, ex p Sivakumaran,
[1988] AC 958 (HL), 1988. Geneva
Convention on status of refugees: meaning
of 'well-founded fear'.
British Airways v Commission, [1998]
ECR II (to be published), 1998. State aid of
FF 20 billion to Air France.
R v Minister of Agriculture ex p MAFF,
[1998] ECR I-1251, 1998. Veal calves –
Restrictions on free movement of goods in
EEC.

PLIENER DAVID JONATHAN

New Court Chambers
5 Verulam Buildings, Gray's Inn, London
WC1R 5LY, Telephone: 0171 831 9500
E-mail: mail@newcourtchambers.com
Call Date: Nov 1996, Middle Temple
Qualifications: [BSc (Hons)(Manch)]

PLIMMER MISS MELANIE ANN

**Chambers of Ian Macdonald QC (In
Association with Two Garden Court,
Temple, London)**
Waldorf House, 5 Cooper Street,
Manchester M2 2FW,
Telephone: 0161 236 1840
Call Date: Mar 1996, Gray's Inn
Qualifications: [LLB (Bris), LLM (Lond)]

PLOWDEN MRS SARAH SELENA RIXAR

Call Date: Nov 1991, Inner Temple
Qualifications: [BA (Oxon), Dip Law]

PLUMSTEAD JOHN CHARLES

1 Middle Temple Lane
Temple, London EC4Y 1LT,
Telephone: 0171 583 0659 (12 Lines)
E-mail: chambers@1mtl.co.uk
Call Date: July 1975, Middle Temple
Pupil Master
Qualifications: [LLB]

D

PLUNKETT (ANDREW) CHRISTOPHER

Chambers of Michael Pert QC
36 Bedford Row, London WC1R 4JH,
Telephone: 0171 421 8000
E-mail: 36bedfordrow@link.org
Chambers of Michael Pert QC
24 Albion Place, Northampton NN1 1UD,
Telephone: 01604 602333
Chambers of Michael Pert QC
104 New Walk, Leicester LE1 7EA,
Telephone: 0116 249 2020
Call Date: July 1983, Gray's Inn
Pupil Master
Qualifications: [LLB (Warw)]

POCOCK CHRISTOPHER JAMES

One King's Bench Walk
1st Floor, Temple, London EC4Y 7DB,
Telephone: 0171 936 1500
E-mail: ddear@1kbw.co.uk
Call Date: July 1984, Inner Temple
Pupil Master
Qualifications: [BA (Hons) Law (Oxon)]

POINTER MARTIN JOHN QC (1996)

1 Mitre Court Buildings
Temple, London EC4Y 7BS,
Telephone: 0171 797 7070
E-mail: clerks@1mcb.com
Call Date: July 1976, Gray's Inn
Qualifications: [LLB]

POINTING JOHN ERIC

Field Court Chambers
2nd Floor, 3 Field Court, Gray's Inn,
London WC1R 5EP,
Telephone: 0171 404 7474
Call Date: Oct 1992, Middle Temple
Qualifications: [BA (Hons, Keele), M.Phil,
Diploma In Law]

POINTON MISS CAROLINE JANE

Fenners Chambers
3 Madingley Road, Cambridge CB3 0EE,
Telephone: 01223 368761
E-mail: clerks@fennerschambers.co.uk
Fenners Chambers
8-12 Priestgate, Peterborough PE1 1JA,
Telephone: 01733 562030
E-mail: clerks@fennerschambers.co.uk
Call Date: July 1976, Gray's Inn
Pupil Master
Qualifications: [LLB (Hons) (Lond)]

POKU MISS MARY LAUREEN

12 Old Square
1st Floor, Lincoln's Inn, London
WC2A 3TX, Telephone: 0171 404 0875
Call Date: Nov 1993, Lincoln's Inn
Qualifications: [LLB (Hons)]

POLGLASE DAVID SUTHERLAND

19 Castle Street Chambers
Liverpool L2 4SX,
Telephone: 0151 236 9402
E-mail: DBrei16454@aol.com
Call Date: Oct 1993, Middle Temple
Qualifications: [BA (Hons)(Oxon), MA
(Oxon)]

POLLARD MISS JOANNA KATE

Blackstone Chambers
Blackstone House, Temple, London
EC4Y 9BW, Telephone: 0171 583 1770
E-mail:clerks@blackstonechambers.com
Call Date: Oct 1993, Gray's Inn
Qualifications: [BA]

POLLOCK ALAN GORDON SETON QC (1979)

Essex Court Chambers
24 Lincoln's Inn Fields, London
WC2A 3ED, Telephone: 0171 813 8000
E-mail:clerksroom@essexcourt-chambers.co.u
k
Call Date: Nov 1968, Gray's Inn
Qualifications: [MA, LLB (Cantab)]

POLLOCK DR EVELYN MARIAN MARGARET

5 Essex Court
1st Floor, Temple, London EC4Y 9AH,
Telephone: 0171 410 2000
E-mail: barristers@5essexcourt.co.uk
Call Date: Oct 1991, Inner Temple
Qualifications: [BSc, MBChB MD (Edin), Dip
Law]

POLLOCK MISS ROBERTA HILARY

1 Dr Johnson's Buildings
Ground Floor, Temple, London
EC4Y 7AX, Telephone: 0171 353 9328
E-mail:OneDr.Johnsons@btinternet.com

Dr Johnson's Chambers
The Atrium Court, Apex Plaza, Reading,
Berkshire, RG1 1AX,
Telephone: 01734 254221
Call Date: Nov 1993, Inner Temple
Qualifications: [LLB (Brunel)]

POLSON ALISTAIR JAMES

1 Pump Court
Lower Ground Floor, Temple, London
EC4Y 7AB, Telephone: 0171 583 2012/
353 4341
E-mail: [name]@1pumpcourt.co.uk
Call Date: Nov 1989, Middle Temple
Qualifications: [MA (Hons) (Glasgow), Dip in
Law]

POMEROY TOBY

Barristers' Common Law Chambers
57 Whitechapel Road, Aldgate East,
London E1 1DU,
Telephone: 0171 375 3012
E-mail: barristers@hotmail.com and
barristers@lawchambers.freeserve.co.uk
Virtual Chambers
(accepting briefs soon), London
Telephone: 07071 244 944
E-mail:enquiries@virtualchambers.org.uk
Call Date: Mar 1997, Lincoln's Inn
Qualifications: [LLB (Hons)]

PONNAMPALAM REILLY MRS LAXMI DEVI

4 Brick Court
Ground Floor, Temple, London
EC4Y 9AD, Telephone: 0171 797 7766
E-mail: chambers@4brick.co.uk
Call Date: Nov 1972, Middle Temple
Pupil Master

PONS GARY STEPHEN

Holborn Chambers
6 Gate Street, Lincoln's Inn Fields, London
WC2A 3HP, Telephone: 0171 242 6060
Call Date: Oct 1995, Gray's Inn
Qualifications: [BA (Kent)]

PONTAC MRS SANDRA GAIL

Mitre House Chambers
15-19 Devereux Court, London WC2R 3JJ,
Telephone: 0171 583 8233
Call Date: Nov 1981, Middle Temple
Pupil Master
Qualifications: [BA(Law)]

PONTER IAN MICHAEL

2-3 Gray's Inn Square
Gray's Inn, London WC1R 5JH,
Telephone: 0171 242 4986
E-mail:chambers@2-3graysinnsquare.co.uk
Call Date: Oct 1993, Middle Temple
Qualifications: [BA (Hons, Keele), LLM
(Aberdeen)]

POOLE CHRISTOPHER ROBERT

New Court
Temple, London EC4Y 9BE,
Telephone: 0171 583 5123/0510
Call Date: Nov 1996, Lincoln's Inn
Qualifications: [LLB (Hons)(Lond)]

POOLE NIGEL DAVID

18 St John Street
Manchester M3 4EA,
Telephone: 0161 278 1800
E-mail: 18stjohn@lineone.net
Call Date: Nov 1989, Middle Temple
Qualifications: [BA (Oxon), Dip in Law]

POOLES MICHAEL PHILIP HOLMES QC (1999)

4 Paper Buildings
Ground Floor, Temple, London
EC4Y 7EX, Telephone: 0171 353 3366/
583 7155
E-mail: clerks@4paperbuildings.com
Call Date: 1978, Inner Temple
Pupil Master
Qualifications: [LLB (Lond)]

POOLEY MRS MOIRA HELEN

4 King's Bench Walk
2nd Floor, Temple, London EC4Y 7DL,
Telephone: 020 7353 3581
E-mail: clerks@4kbw.co.uk
Call Date: Nov 1974, Middle Temple
Qualifications: [LLB (Hons) (Lond)]

POOTS MISS CAROLYN ELIZABETH

Queens Square Chambers
56 Queens Square, Bristol BS1 4PR,
Telephone: 0117 921 1966
Call Date: Oct 1995, Inner Temple
Qualifications: [LLB (Huddersfield)]

POPAT PRASHANT

2 Harcourt Buildings
Ground Floor/Left, Temple, London
EC4Y 9DB, Telephone: 0171 583 9020
E-mail: clerks@harcourt.co.uk
Call Date: Feb 1992, Gray's Inn
Pupil Master
Qualifications: [MA (Oxon)]

POPAT SURENDRA

9 King's Bench Walk
Ground Floor, Temple, London
EC4Y 7DX, Telephone: 0171 353 7202/
3909 E-mail: 9kbw@compuserve.com
Call Date: July 1969, Lincoln's Inn
Pupil Master, Assistant Recorder
Qualifications: [LLB (Lond),LLM (Cal)]

POPE DAVID JAMES

3 Verulam Buildings
London WC1R 5NT,
Telephone: 0171 831 8441
E-mail: clerks@3verulam.co.uk
Call Date: Feb 1995, Lincoln's Inn
Qualifications: [LLB (Hons)(Edinbur), LLM
(Harvard)]

POPE MRS HEATHER

1 Mitre Court Buildings
Temple, London EC4Y 7BS,
Telephone: 0171 797 7070
E-mail: clerks@1mcb.com
Call Date: July 1977, Inner Temple
Qualifications: [BA (Hons) (Wales) , Dip Ed
(Wales)]

POPERT MISS CATHERINE TERESA MARIE

3 Temple Gardens
Lower Ground Floor, Temple, London
EC4Y 9AU, Telephone: 0171 353 3102/5/
9297 E-mail: clerks@3tg.co.uk
Call Date: Nov 1987, Middle Temple
Pupil Master
Qualifications: [LLB (London)]

POPLAWSKI ROMAN

169 Temple Chambers
Temple Avenue, London EC4Y 0DA,
Telephone: 0171 583 7644
Call Date: Nov 1989, Lincoln's Inn
Qualifications: [LLB (B'ham)]

POPLE MISS ALISON RUTH

3 Hare Court
1 Little Essex Street, London WC2R 3LD,
Telephone: 0171 395 2000
Call Date: Nov 1993, Middle Temple
Qualifications: [LLB (Hons)]

POPPLEWELL ANDREW JOHN QC (1997)

Brick Court Chambers
7-8 Essex Street, London WC2R 3LD,
Telephone: 0171 379 3550
E-mail: [surname]@brickcourt.co.uk
Call Date: Nov 1981, Inner Temple
Qualifications: [MA (Cantab)]

PORT MS YVONNE ELIZABETH

Clock Chambers
78 Darlington Street, Wolverhampton
WV1 4LY, Telephone: 01902 313444
Call Date: Nov 1997, Inner Temple
Qualifications: [BSc (City), FBDO, MBCO]

PORTEN ANTHONY RALPH QC (1988)

2-3 Gray's Inn Square
Gray's Inn, London WC1R 5JH,
Telephone: 0171 242 4986
E-mail:chambers@2-3graysinnsquare.co.uk
Call Date: July 1969, Inner Temple
Recorder
Qualifications: [BA (Cantab)]

PORTER DAVID LEONARD

St James's Chambers
68 Quay Street, Manchester M3 3EJ,
Telephone: 0161 834 7000
E-mail: clerks@stjameschambers.co.uk
Park Lane Chambers
19 Westgate, Leeds LS1 2RD,
Telephone: 0113 2285000
E-mail:clerks@parklanechambers.co.uk
Call Date: July 1980, Lincoln's Inn
Qualifications: [LLB (Manch)]

PORTER JAMIE ROBERT

St David's Chambers
10 Calvert Terrace, Swansea, West
Glamorgan, SA1 5AR,
Call Date: 1997, Inner Temple
Qualifications: [LLB (Brunel)]

PORTER MARTIN HUGH

2 Temple Gardens
Temple, London EC4Y 9AY,
Telephone: 0171 583 6041
E-mail: clerks@2templegardens.co.uk
Call Date: July 1986, Inner Temple
Pupil Master
Qualifications: [MA (Cantab), LLM]

PORTER NIGEL JOHN

11 King's Bench Walk
Temple, London EC4Y 7EQ,
Telephone: 0171 632 8500/583 0610
E-mail: clerksroom@11kbw.com
Call Date: Nov 1994, Middle Temple
Qualifications: [MA (Cantab), LLM
(Hons)(Cantab)]

PORTER ROBERT GEOFFREY WALDEGRAVE

**11 Bolt Court (also at 7 Stone Buildings
– 1st Floor)**
London EC4A 3DQ,
Telephone: 0171 353 2300
E-mail: boltct11@aol.com
**7 Stone Buildings (also at 11 Bolt
Court)**
1st Floor, Lincoln's Inn, London
WC2A 3SZ, Telephone: 0171 242 0961
E-mail:larthur@7stonebuildings.law.co.uk
Redhill Chambers
Seloduct House, 30 Station Road, Redhill,
Surrey, RH1 1NF,
Telephone: 01737 780781
Call Date: Nov 1988, Middle Temple
Qualifications: [BA (Dunelm), Dip Law, LLM
(Pennsylvania)]

PORTER MISS SARAH RUTH

**11 Bolt Court (also at 7 Stone Buildings
– 1st Floor)**
London EC4A 3DQ,
Telephone: 0171 353 2300
E-mail: boltct11@aol.com

**7 Stone Buildings (also at 11 Bolt
Court)**
1st Floor, Lincoln's Inn, London
WC2A 3SZ, Telephone: 0171 242 0961
E-mail:larthur@7stonebuildings.law.co.uk
Redhill Chambers
Seloduct House, 30 Station Road, Redhill,
Surrey, RH1 1NF,
Telephone: 01737 780781
Call Date: Nov 1996, Gray's Inn
Qualifications: [LLB (Teeside), MA (Sheff)]

PORTNOY LESLIE REUBEN

Chambers of John Hand QC
9 St John Street, Manchester M3 4DN,
Telephone: 0161 955 9000
E-mail: ninesjs@gconnect.com
Call Date: June 1961, Gray's Inn
Pupil Master, Recorder
Qualifications: [LLB (Hons)]

POSNANSKY JEREMY ROSS LEON QC (1994)

1 Mitre Court Buildings
Temple, London EC4Y 7BS,
Telephone: 0171 797 7070
E-mail: clerks@1mcb.com
Southernhay Chambers
33 Southernhay East, Exeter, Devon,
EX1 1NX, Telephone: 01392 255777
E-mail:southernhay.chambers@lineone.net
Call Date: July 1972, Gray's Inn
Assistant Recorder

POSNER MISS GABRIELLE JAN

2 Gray's Inn Square Chambers
2nd Floor, Gray's Inn, London WC1R 5AA,
Telephone: 020 7242 0328
E-mail: clerks@2gis.co.uk
Call Date: July 1984, Inner Temple
Pupil Master
Qualifications: [LLB (Soton) LLM, (Indiana)]

POST ANDREW JOHN

Chambers of Kieran Coonan QC
Ground Floor, 6 Pump Court, Temple,
London EC4Y 7AR,
Telephone: 0171 583 6013/2510
E-mail: clerks@6-pumpcourt.law.co.uk
Call Date: July 1988, Middle Temple
Pupil Master
Qualifications: [BA (Cantab), Dip Law (City)]

POSTA ADRIAN MARK

South Western Chambers
Melville House, 12 Middle Street,
Taunton, Somerset, TA1 1SH,
Telephone: 01823 331919 (24 hrs)
E-mail: barclerk@clara.net
Call Date: Oct 1996, Middle Temple
Qualifications: [LLB (Hons)(Warw)]

POSTILL MS JULIA DALE

2 Dyers Buildings
London EC1N 2JT,
Telephone: 0171 404 1881
Call Date: Nov 1982, Inner Temple
Pupil Master
Qualifications: [BA]

POTE ANDREW THOMAS

13 King's Bench Walk
1st Floor, Temple, London EC4Y 7EN,
Telephone: 0171 353 7204
E-mail: clerks@13kbw.law.co.uk
King's Bench Chambers
32 Beaumont Street, Oxford OX1 2NP,
Telephone: 01865 311066
E-mail: clerks@kbc-oxford.law.co.uk
Call Date: Nov 1983, Gray's Inn
Qualifications: [LL.B. (E Ang)]

POTTER ANTHONY JOHN

5 Fountain Court
Steelhouse Lane, Birmingham B4 6DR,
Telephone: 0121 606 0500
E-mail:clerks@5fountaincourt.law.co.uk
Call Date: July 1994, Gray's Inn
Qualifications: [BA (Wales)]

POTTER DAVID ANDREW

White Friars Chambers
21 White Friars, Chester CH1 1NZ,
Telephone: 01244 323070
E-mail:whitefriarschambers@btinternet.com
Call Date: Oct 1990, Lincoln's Inn
Qualifications: [LLB (E.Anglia)]

POTTER REV HARRY DRUMMOND

3 Gray's Inn Square
Ground Floor, London WC1R 5AH,
Telephone: 0171 520 5600
E-mail: clerks@3gis.co.uk
Call Date: Oct 1993, Gray's Inn
Qualifications: [BA, MA, M Phil, LLB]

POTTER MISS LOUISE

1 Mitre Court Buildings
Temple, London EC4Y 7BS,
Telephone: 0171 797 7070
E-mail: clerks@1mcb.com
Call Date: Nov 1993, Inner Temple
Qualifications: [MA (Oxon), CPE]

POTTINGER GAVIN JAMES

Maidstone Chambers
33 Earl Street, Maidstone, Kent, ME14 1PF,
Telephone: 01622 688592
E-mail:maidstonechambers@compuserve.com
Call Date: Oct 1991, Inner Temple
Qualifications: [BScECON, Diploma in, Law]

POTTS JAMES RUPERT

Erskine Chambers
30 Lincoln's Inn Fields, Lincoln's Inn,
London WC2A 3PF,
Telephone: 0171 242 5532
E-mail:clerks@erskine-chambers.co.uk
Call Date: Oct 1994, Gray's Inn
Qualifications: [BA (Oxon)]

POTTS RICHARD ANDREW

Octagon House
19 Colegate, Norwich NR3 1AT,
Telephone: 01603 623186
E-mail: admin@octagon-chambers.co.uk
1 Paper Buildings
1st Floor, Temple, London EC4Y 7EP,
Telephone: 0171 353 3728/4953
Call Date: Nov 1991, Inner Temple
Qualifications: [LLB (Birm)]

POTTS ROBIN QC (1982)

Erskine Chambers
30 Lincoln's Inn Fields, Lincoln's Inn,
London WC2A 3PF,
Telephone: 0171 242 5532
E-mail:clerks@erskine-chambers.co.uk
Call Date: Nov 1968, Gray's Inn
Qualifications: [BA,BCL (Oxon)]

POTTS WARREN NIGEL

Queen's Chambers
5 John Dalton Street, Manchester M2 6ET,
Telephone: 0161 834 6875/4738

Queens Chambers
4 Camden Place, Preston PR1 3JL,
Telephone: 01772 828300
Call Date: July 1995, Middle Temple
Qualifications: [BA (Hons)]

POULET MRS REBECCA MARIA
QC (1995)

Hollis Whiteman Chambers
3rd Floor, Queen Elizabeth Bldg, Temple,
London EC4Y 9BS,
Telephone: 020 7583 5766
E-mail:barristers@holliswhiteman.co.uk
Call Date: Nov 1975, Lincoln's Inn
Recorder

POUNDER GERARD

5 Essex Court
1st Floor, Temple, London EC4Y 9AH,
Telephone: 0171 410 2000
E-mail: barristers@5essexcourt.co.uk
Call Date: July 1980, Lincoln's Inn
Pupil Master
Qualifications: [LLB (Lond), BA (Lond)]

POVOAS SIMON JOHN SPENCER

Chavasse Court Chambers
2nd Floor, Chavasse Court, 24 Lord Street,
Liverpool L2 1TA,
Telephone: 0151 707 1191
Call Date: Oct 1996, Lincoln's Inn
Qualifications: [LLB (Hons), MA]

POWELL BERNARD HILSON

Newport Chambers
12 Clytha Park Road, Newport, Gwent,
NP9 47L, Telephone: 01633 267403/
255855
Call Date: Oct 1991, Gray's Inn
Qualifications: [BSc, PhD]

POWELL DEAN

10 King's Bench Walk
Ground Floor, Temple, London
EC4Y 7EB, Telephone: 0171 353 7742
E-mail: 10kbw@lineone.net
Call Date: Nov 1982, Gray's Inn
Qualifications: [BSc (Cardiff)]

POWELL MISS DEBRA ANN

3 Serjeants' Inn
London EC4Y 1BQ,
Telephone: 0171 353 5537
E-mail: clerks@3serjeantsinn.com
Call Date: Oct 1995, Middle Temple
Qualifications: [BA (Hons)]

POWELL HENRY JAMES

Paradise Chambers
26 Paradise Square, Sheffield S1 2DE,
Telephone: 0114 2738951
E-mail: timbooth@paradise-sq.co.uk
Call Date: 1998, Middle Temple
Qualifications: [LLB (Hons)(Manch)]

POWELL JOHN LEWIS QC (1990)

Chambers of John L Powell QC
Four New Square, Lincoln's Inn, London
WC2A 3RJ, Telephone: 0171 797 8000
E-mail: barristers@4newsquare.com
Call Date: July 1974, Middle Temple
Assistant Recorder
Qualifications: [MA, LLB (Cantab)]

POWELL JONATHAN DAVID

95A Chancery Lane
London WC2A 1DT,
Telephone: 0171 405 3101
Durham Barristers' Chambers
27 Old Elvet, Durham DH1 3HN,
Telephone: 0191 386 9199
Call Date: Nov 1984, Inner Temple
Qualifications: [LLM, Legal, Assoc.RTPI]

POWELL MISS NICOLA JAYNE

Chambers of Davina Gammon
Ground Floor, 103 Walter Road, Swansea,
West Glamorgan, SA1 5QF,
Telephone: 01792 480770
Call Date: Nov 1996, Lincoln's Inn
Qualifications: [LLB (Hons)]

POWELL RICHARD FREDERIC

Victoria Chambers
3rd Floor, 177 Corporation Street,
Birmingham B4 6RG,
Telephone: 0121 236 9900
E-mail: viccham@aol.com
Call Date: Nov 1991, Inner Temple
Qualifications: [BA (Surrey), LLM (Warw)]

POWELL ROBIN EDWARD

New Court
Temple, London EC4Y 9BE,
Telephone: 0171 583 5123/0510
Call Date: Nov 1993, Inner Temple
Qualifications: [BA, CPE, LLM (Lond)]

POWELL WILLIAM GILES HUGH

5 Essex Court
1st Floor, Temple, London EC4Y 9AH,
Telephone: 0171 410 2000
E-mail: barristers@5essexcourt.co.uk
Call Date: Nov 1990, Gray's Inn
Qualifications: [LLB (Cardiff)]

POWELL WILLIAM RHYS

10 King's Bench Walk
Ground Floor, Temple, London
EC4Y 7EB, Telephone: 0171 353 7742
E-mail: 10kbw@lineone.net
Call Date: 1971, Lincoln's Inn
Qualifications: [BA (Cantab)]

POWER MISS ELIZABETH JOANNE

De Montfort Chambers
95 Princess Road East, Leicester LE1 7DQ,
Telephone: 0116 254 8686
E-mail: dmcbar@aol.com
Call Date: Oct 1996, Inner Temple
Qualifications: [LLB (Sheff)]

POWER MISS ERICA MARGARET

One Paper Buildings
Ground Floor, Temple, London
EC4Y 7EP, Telephone: 0171 583 7355
E-mail: clerks@1pb.co.uk
Call Date: Oct 1990, Lincoln's Inn
Qualifications: [MA (Cantab), LLM]

POWER LAWRENCE IMAM

4 King's Bench Walk
Ground/First Floor/Basement, Temple,
London EC4Y 7DL,
Telephone: 0171 822 8822
E-mail: 4kbw@barristersatlaw.com
Call Date: Nov 1995, Middle Temple
Qualifications: [LLB (Hons)(Notts)]

POWER LEWIS NIALL

Cardinal Chambers
4 Old Mitre Court, 4th Floor, Temple,
London EC4Y 7BP,
Telephone: 020 7353 2622
E-mail:admin@cardinal-chambers.co.uk
Call Date: Nov 1990, Gray's Inn
Qualifications: [LLB (Hons)]

POWER NIGEL JOHN

25-27 Castle Street
1st Floor, Liverpool L2 4TA,
Telephone: 0151 227 5661/051 236 5072
Call Date: Nov 1992, Inner Temple
Qualifications: [LLB (Reading)]

POWER PIERCE DECLEAN KIERAN

Westgate Chambers
144 High Street, Lewes, East Sussex,
BN7 1XT, Telephone: 01273 480510
Call Date: Apr 1989, Gray's Inn
Qualifications: [BA (Hons)]

POWER RICHARD MICHAEL ARTHUR

Chambers of Kieran Coonan QC
Ground Floor, 6 Pump Court, Temple,
London EC4Y 7AR,
Telephone: 0171 583 6013/2510
E-mail: clerks@6-pumpcourt.law.co.uk
Call Date: Nov 1983, Middle Temple
Qualifications: [BA (Oxon)]

POWERS DR MICHAEL JOHN QC (1995)

One Paper Buildings
Ground Floor, Temple, London
EC4Y 7EP, Telephone: 0171 583 7355
E-mail: clerks@1pb.co.uk
Call Date: July 1979, Lincoln's Inn
Qualifications: [BSc, MB, BS, DA]

POWIS MISS LUCY ELIZABETH

40 King Street
Manchester M2 6BA,
Telephone: 0161 832 9082
E-mail: clerks@40kingstreet.co.uk
The Chambers of Philip Raynor QC
5 Park Place, Leeds LS1 2RU,
Telephone: 0113 242 1123
Call Date: Oct 1992, Gray's Inn
Qualifications: [LLB (L'pool)]

POWIS MISS SAMANTHA INEZ

St Philip's Chambers
Fountain Court, Steelhouse Lane,
Birmingham B4 6DR,
Telephone: 0121 246 7000
E-mail: clerks@st-philips.co.uk
Call Date: Nov 1985, Lincoln's Inn
Qualifications: [LLB (UC Cardiff)]

POWLES JOHN LAMBERT

One Paper Buildings
Ground Floor, Temple, London
EC4Y 7EP, Telephone: 0171 583 7355
E-mail: clerks@1pb.co.uk
*Call Date: July 1975, Middle Temple
Pupil Master*
Qualifications: [MA (Oxon)]

POWLES STEPHEN ROBERT QC (1995)

2 Harcourt Buildings
Ground Floor/Left, Temple, London
EC4Y 9DB, Telephone: 0171 583 9020
E-mail: clerks@harcourt.co.uk
*Call Date: July 1972, Middle Temple
Recorder*
Qualifications: [MA (Oxon)]

POWNALL STEPHEN ORLANDO FLETCHER

1 Hare Court
Ground Floor, Temple, London
EC4Y 7BE, Telephone: 0171 353 3982/
5324
*Call Date: 1975, Inner Temple
Pupil Master, Recorder*

POYER-SLEEMAN MS PATRICIA

Pump Court Chambers
Upper Ground Floor, 3 Pump Court,
Temple, London EC4Y 7AJ,
Telephone: 0171 353 0711
E-mail: clerks@3pumpcourt.com
Pump Court Chambers
31 Southgate Street, Winchester
SO23 9EE, Telephone: 01962 868161
E-mail: clerks@3pumpcourt.com

Pump Court Chambers
5 Temple Chambers, Temple Street,
Swindon SN1 1SQ,
Telephone: 01793 539899
E-mail: clerks@3pumpcourt.com
Call Date: Nov 1992, Gray's Inn
Qualifications: [BA (Manc)]

PRAIS EDGAR

4 Brick Court
Ground Floor, Temple, London
EC4Y 9AD, Telephone: 0171 797 7766
E-mail: chambers@4brick.co.uk
Call Date: Nov 1990, Lincoln's Inn
Qualifications: [MA (Glas), LLB (Edin)]

PRAND MISS ANNETTE BETTINA

Lamb Chambers
Lamb Building, Temple, London
EC4Y 7AS, Telephone: 020 7797 8300
E-mail: lambchambers@link.org
Call Date: 1995, Inner Temple
Qualifications: [MA (Cantab)]

PRASAD KRISHNA

21 Craven Road
Kingston-Upon-Thames, Surrey, KT2 6LW,
Telephone: 0181 974 6799
Call Date: May 1958, Gray's Inn
Qualifications: [LLB]

PRATT ALLAN DUNCAN

New Court Chambers
5 Verulam Buildings, Gray's Inn, London
WC1R 5LY, Telephone: 0171 831 9500
E-mail: mail@newcourtchambers.com
*Call Date: Nov 1971, Middle Temple
Pupil Master*
Qualifications: [BA (Oxon)]

PRATT MRS PATRICIA MARY

India Buildings Chambers
Water Street, Liverpool L2 0XG,
Telephone: 0151 243 6000
E-mail: clerks@chambers.u-net.com
Call Date: Oct 1991, Lincoln's Inn
Qualifications: [LLB (Hons)(L'pool)]

D

PRATT RICHARD CAMDEN QC (1992)

One King's Bench Walk
1st Floor, Temple, London EC4Y 7DB,
Telephone: 0171 936 1500
E-mail: ddear@1kbw.co.uk
Call Date: July 1970, Gray's Inn
Recorder
Qualifications: [MA (Oxon)]

PRATT RICHARD JAMES

Corn Exchange Chambers
5th Floor, Fenwick Street, Liverpool
L2 7QS, Telephone: 0151 227 1081/5009
Call Date: July 1980, Gray's Inn
Pupil Master, Assistant Recorder
Qualifications: [BA]

PREEN MISS CATHERINE LOUISE

St Ive's Chambers
Whittall Street, Birmingham B4 6DH,
Telephone: 0121 236 0863/5720
E-mail:stives.headofchambers@btinternet.com
Call Date: Nov 1988, Middle Temple
Qualifications: [LLB (Hons) (Lond)]

PRENTICE PROFESSOR DANIEL DAVID

Erskine Chambers
30 Lincoln's Inn Fields, Lincoln's Inn,
London WC2A 3PF,
Telephone: 0171 242 5532
E-mail:clerks@erskine-chambers.co.uk
Call Date: Nov 1982, Lincoln's Inn
Qualifications: [LLB (Hons)(Belfast), JD
(Chicago), MA (Oxon)]

PRENTIS SEBASTIAN HUGH RUNTON

1 New Square
Ground Floor, Lincoln's Inn, London
WC2A 3SA, Telephone: 0171 405 0884/5/6/
7 E-mail: clerks@1newsquare.law.co.uk
Call Date: Oct 1996, Middle Temple
Qualifications: [BA (Hons) (Cantab)]

PRESCOTT PETER RICHARD KYLE QC (1990)

8 New Square
Lincoln's Inn, London WC2A 3QP,
Telephone: 0171 405 4321
E-mail: clerks@8newsquare.co.uk
Call Date: Nov 1970, Lincoln's Inn
Qualifications: [BSc, MSc]

PRESLAND FREDERICK JAMES ADRIAN

Chambers of Norman Palmer
2 Field Court, Gray's Inn, London
WC1R 5BB, Telephone: 0171 405 6114
E-mail: fieldct2@netcomuk.co.uk
Call Date: July 1985, Gray's Inn
Pupil Master
Qualifications: [BA Hons (E Anglia),]

PRESSDEE PIERS CHARLES WILLIAM

Harcourt Chambers
1st Floor, 2 Harcourt Buildings, Temple,
London EC4Y 9DB,
Telephone: 0171 353 6961
E-mail:clerks@harcourtchambers.law.co.uk
Harcourt Chambers
Churchill House, 3 St Aldate's Courtyard,
St Aldate's, Oxford OX1 1BN,
Telephone: 01865 791559
E-mail:clerks@harcourtchambers.law.co.uk
Call Date: Oct 1991, Middle Temple
Qualifications: [MA (Hons)(Cantab)]

PRESTON DARREN SAMUEL

58 King Street Chambers
1st Floor, Kingsgate House, 51-53 South
King Street, Manchester M2 6DE,
Telephone: 0161 831 7477
Call Date: Oct 1991, Gray's Inn
Qualifications: [LLB (Liverpool)]

PRESTON DAVID HENRY

Hardwicke Building
New Square, Lincoln's Inn, London
WC2A 3SB, Telephone: 020 7242 2523
E-mail: clerks@hardwicke.co.uk
Call Date: Nov 1993, Lincoln's Inn
Qualifications: [LLB (Auckland)]

PRESTON HUGH GEOFFREY

East Anglian Chambers
52 North Hill, Colchester, Essex, CO1 1PY,
Telephone: 01206 572756
E-mail: colchester@ealaw.co.uk
East Anglian Chambers
57 London Street, Norwich NR2 1HL,
Telephone: 01603 617351
E-mail: norwich@ealaw.co.uk
East Anglian Chambers
Gresham House, 5 Museum Street,
Ipswich, Suffolk, IP1 1HQ,
Telephone: 01473 214481
E-mail: ipswich@ealaw.co.uk
Call Date: Oct 1994, Middle Temple
Qualifications: [BA (Hons)(Durham), CPE]

PRESTON MISS KIM DEBORAH

4 King's Bench Walk
2nd Floor, Temple, London EC4Y 7DL,
Telephone: 020 7353 3581
E-mail: clerks@4kbw.co.uk
Call Date: Nov 1991, Inner Temple
Qualifications: [BSc (Hons), Dip Law]

PRESTON NICHOLAS JOHN HOLMAN

Bracton Chambers
95a Chancery Lane, London WC2A 1DT,
Telephone: 0171 242 4248
Call Date: July 1986, Gray's Inn
Qualifications: [MA]

PRESTON MRS NICOLA

5 Fountain Court
Steelhouse Lane, Birmingham B4 6DR,
Telephone: 0121 606 0500
E-mail:clerks@5fountaincourt.law.co.uk
Call Date: Nov 1992, Lincoln's Inn
Qualifications: [LLB (Hons)(Manc), LLM
(B'ham)]

PRESTON (RICHARD) DOMINIC

Arden Chambers
27 John Street, London WC1N 2BL,
Telephone: 020 7242 4244
E-mail:clerks@arden-chambers.law.co.uk
Call Date: Feb 1995, Inner Temple
Qualifications: [BA (Lond), CPE (City)]

PRESTON TIMOTHY WILLIAM QC (1982)

2 Temple Gardens
Temple, London EC4Y 9AY,
Telephone: 0171 583 6041
E-mail: clerks@2templegardens.co.uk
*Call Date: June 1964, Inner Temple
Recorder*
Qualifications: [BA (Oxon)]

PRESTWICH ANDREW

Ropewalk Chambers
24 The Ropewalk, Nottingham NG1 5EF,
Telephone: 0115 9472581
E-mail: administration@ropewalk co.uk
Call Date: Nov 1986, Gray's Inn
Qualifications: [LLB (B'ham)]

PREVATT MISS BEATRICE HILARY ROSE

Two Garden Court
1st Floor, Middle Temple, London
EC4Y 9BL, Telephone: 0171 353 1633
E-mail:barristers@2gardenct.law.co.uk
Call Date: Nov 1985, Gray's Inn
Qualifications: [BA (Oxon)]

PREVEZER MS SUSAN RACHEL

Essex Court Chambers
24 Lincoln's Inn Fields, London
WC2A 3ED, Telephone: 0171 813 8000
E-mail:clerksroom@essexcourt-chambers.co.uk
*Call Date: July 1983, Inner Temple
Pupil Master*
Qualifications: [MA (Cantab)]

PRICE ALBERT JOHN

23 Essex Street
London WC2R 3AS,
Telephone: 0171 413 0353/836 8366
E-mail:clerks@essexstreet23.demon.co.uk
*Call Date: July 1982, Inner Temple
Pupil Master*
Qualifications: [BA (Oxon)]

PRICE MISS ANNA VICTORIA

Nicholas Street Chambers
22 Nicholas Street, Chester CH1 2NX,
Telephone: 01244 323886
E-mail: clerks@40king.co.uk
Call Date: Oct 1996, Lincoln's Inn
Qualifications: [LLB (Hons)(Lond)]

PRICE (ARTHUR) LEOLIN QC (1968)

The Chambers of Leolin Price CBE, QC
10 Old Square, Lincoln's Inn, London
WC2A 3SU, Telephone: 0171 405 0758
Call Date: Nov 1949, Middle Temple
Qualifications: [MA(Oxon)]

PRICE MISS COLLETTE

St James's Chambers
68 Quay Street, Manchester M3 3EJ,
Telephone: 0161 834 7000
E-mail: clerks@stjameschambers.co.uk
Call Date: Nov 1997, Gray's Inn
Qualifications: [BA (Hons) (Cantab)]

PRICE MISS DEBORA JANET

Queen Elizabeth Building
Ground Floor, Temple, London
EC4Y 9BS,
Telephone: 0171 353 7181 (12 Lines)
Call Date: Feb 1987, Gray's Inn
Pupil Master
Qualifications: [MA (Cantab)]

PRICE EVAN DAVID LEWIS

The Chambers of Leolin Price CBE, QC
10 Old Square, Lincoln's Inn, London
WC2A 3SU, Telephone: 0171 405 0758
Call Date: Oct 1997, Middle Temple
Qualifications: [LLB (Hons)(Lond)]

PRICE GERALD ALEXANDER LEWIN QC (1992)

33 Park Place
Cardiff CF1 3BA,
Telephone: 02920 233313
Goldsmith Building
1st Floor, Temple, London EC4Y 7BL,
Telephone: 0171 353 7881
E-mail:clerks@goldsmith-building.law.co.uk
Call Date: Nov 1969, Middle Temple
Recorder

PRICE JAMES RICHARD KENRICK QC (1995)

5 Raymond Buildings
1st Floor, Gray's Inn, London WC1R 5BP,
Telephone: 0171 242 2902
E-mail: clerks@media-ent-law.co.uk
Call Date: July 1974, Inner Temple
Qualifications: [BA(Oxon)]

PRICE JEFFREY WILLIAM

The Chambers of Leolin Price CBE, QC
10 Old Square, Lincoln's Inn, London
WC2A 3SU, Telephone: 0171 405 0758
Call Date: Nov 1975, Lincoln's Inn
Qualifications: [BA (Oxon) BCL (Oxon), MA (Oxon)]

PRICE JOHN ALAN QC (1980)

22 Old Buildings
Lincoln's Inn, London WC2A 3UJ,
Telephone: 0171 831 0222
Byrom Street Chambers
Byrom Street, Manchester M3 4PF,
Telephone: 0161 829 2100
E-mail: Byromst25@aol.com
Call Date: Feb 1961, Gray's Inn
Recorder
Qualifications: [LLB]

PRICE JOHN CHARLES

St Philip's Chambers
Fountain Court, Steelhouse Lane,
Birmingham B4 6DR,
Telephone: 0121 246 7000
E-mail: clerks@st-philips.co.uk
Call Date: 1969, Gray's Inn
Pupil Master, Recorder
Qualifications: [LLB (B'ham)]

PRICE JOHN SCOTT

10 Launceston Avenue
Caversham Park Village, Reading,
Berkshire, RG4 6SW,
Telephone: 01189 479548
E-mail: jspchmbrs@aol.com
Southsea Chambers
PO Box 148, Southsea, Portsmouth,
Hampshire, PO5 2TU,
Telephone: 01705 291261

Cathedral Chambers
Milburn House, Dean Street, Newcastle
upon Tyne NE1 1LE,
Telephone: 0191 232 1311
Call Date: Oct 1990, Inner Temple
Qualifications: [LLB (Hons)(Reading)]

PRICE MISS KATHARINE CLARE HARDING

4 Paper Buildings
Ground Floor, Temple, London
EC4Y 7EX, Telephone: 0171 353 3366/
583 7155
E-mail: clerks@4paperbuildings.com
Call Date: July 1988, Middle Temple
Qualifications: [LLB (Hons) (Lond), LLM
(Cantab)]

PRICE MRS LOUISE THERESE

Guildhall Chambers
22-26 Broad Street, Bristol BS1 2HG,
Telephone: 0117 9273366
E-mail:civil.clerks@guildhallchambers.co.uk and
criminal.clerks@guildhallchambers.co.uk
Call Date: Nov 1972, Middle Temple
Qualifications: [MA (Oxon)]

PRICE NICHOLAS PETER LEES QC (1992)

3 Raymond Buildings
Gray's Inn, London WC1R 5BH,
Telephone: 020 7831 3833
E-mail:chambers@threeraymond.demon.co.u
k
Call Date: Nov 1968, Gray's Inn
Recorder
Qualifications: [LLB (Edin)]

PRICE PETER NICHOLAS

York Chambers
14 Toft Green, York YO1 6JT,
Telephone: 01904 620048
E-mail: [name]@yorkchambers.co.uk
Call Date: Nov 1987, Inner Temple
Qualifications: [LLB (Hull)]

PRICE MISS RACHAEL ELIZABETH

5 Fountain Court
Steelhouse Lane, Birmingham B4 6DR,
Telephone: 0121 606 0500
E-mail:clerks@5fountaincourt.law.co.uk
Call Date: Oct 1994, Inner Temple
Qualifications: [LLB (B'ham)]

PRICE RICHARD MERVYN QC (1996)

Littleton Chambers
3 King's Bench Walk North, Temple,
London EC4Y 7HR,
Telephone: 0171 797 8600
E-mail:clerks@littletonchambers.co.uk
Call Date: Nov 1969, Gray's Inn
Qualifications: [LLB (Lond)]

PRICE ROBERT SAMUEL

6 Fountain Court
Steelhouse Lane, Birmingham B4 6DR,
Telephone: 0121 233 3282
E-mail: clerks@sixfountain.co.uk
Call Date: Oct 1990, Middle Temple
Qualifications: [LLB (Leic)]

PRICE RODERICK MICHAEL THOMAS

Cloisters
1 Pump Court, Temple, London
EC4Y 7AA, Telephone: 0171 827 4000
E-mail: clerks@cloisters.com
Call Date: Nov 1971, Inner Temple
Pupil Master
Qualifications: [LLB]

PRICE THOMAS

6 Gray's Inn Square
Ground Floor, Gray's Inn, London
WC1R 5AZ, Telephone: 0171 242 1052
E-mail: 6graysinn@clara.co.uk
Call Date: Nov 1985, Inner Temple
Pupil Master
Qualifications: [LLB(S'ampton)]

PRICE WAYNE

32 Park Place
Cardiff CF1 3BA,
Telephone: 01222 397364
Call Date: July 1982, Gray's Inn
Qualifications: [BA]

PRICE LEWIS RHODRI

1 Serjeants' Inn
4th Floor, Temple, London EC4Y 1NH,
Telephone: 0171 583 1355
E-mail: clerks@serjeants-inn.co.uk
33 Park Place
Cardiff CF1 3BA,
Telephone: 02920 233313
Call Date: July 1975, Middle Temple
Recorder
Qualifications: [MA (Oxon), Dip.Crim
(Cantab)]

PRICE ROWLANDS GWYNN

25-27 Castle Street
1st Floor, Liverpool L2 4TA,
Telephone: 0151 227 5661/051 236 5072
Call Date: 1985, Inner Temple
Qualifications: [LLB (Liverpool); NBA;
Diploma EC Law; speaks Welsh]

PRICHARD GUY HESKETH

Frederick Place Chambers
9 Frederick Place, Clifton, Bristol
BS8 1AS, Telephone: 0117 9738667
Call Date: Nov 1986, Gray's Inn
Pupil Master
Qualifications: [BA(Oxon)]

PRICHARD MICHAEL JOHN

4 Stone Buildings
Ground Floor, Lincoln's Inn, London
WC2A 3XT, Telephone: 0171 242 5524
E-mail:clerks@4stonebuildings.law.co.uk
Call Date: June 1951, Gray's Inn

PRIDAY CHARLES NICHOLAS BRUTON

S Tomlinson QC
7 King's Bench Walk, Temple, London
EC4Y 7DS, Telephone: 0171 583 0404
E-mail: clerks@7kbw.law.co.uk
Call Date: Nov 1982, Middle Temple
Pupil Master
Qualifications: [BA (Oxon)]

PRIDEAUX-BRUNE PETER JOHN NICHOLAS

Queen Elizabeth Building
Ground Floor, Temple, London
EC4Y 9BS,
Telephone: 0171 353 7181 (12 Lines)
Call Date: Nov 1972, Inner Temple
Qualifications: [MA (Oxon)]

PRIEST JOHN RAYMOND

York Chambers
14 Toft Green, York YO1 6JT,
Telephone: 01904 620048
E-mail: [name]@yorkchambers.co.uk
Call Date: 1973, Inner Temple
Pupil Master
Qualifications: [LLB]

PRIEST JULIAN WERNET QC (1974)

Lamb Chambers
Lamb Building, Temple, London
EC4Y 7AS, Telephone: 020 7797 8300
E-mail: lambchambers@link.org
Call Date: Feb 1954, Inner Temple
Qualifications: [MA (Cantab)]

PRIESTLEY MS REBECCA JANET

2 Gray's Inn Square Chambers
2nd Floor, Gray's Inn, London WC1R 5AA,
Telephone: 020 7242 0328
E-mail: clerks@2gis.co.uk
Call Date: Nov 1989, Middle Temple
Qualifications: [BA Hons [Oxon]]

PRIESTLEY RODERICK CHARLES

Lincoln House Chambers
5th Floor, Lincoln House, 1 Brazennose
Street, Manchester M2 5EL,
Telephone: 0161 832 5701
E-mail: info@lincolnhse.co.uk
Call Date: Nov 1996, Gray's Inn
Qualifications: [BSc (Bris)]

PRIMOST NORMAN BASIL

5 Pump Court
Ground Floor, Temple, London
EC4Y 7AP, Telephone: 020 7353 2532
E-mail: FivePump@netcomuk.co.uk
Call Date: July 1954, Middle Temple
Qualifications: [LLB (Lond)]

PRINCE CHRISTOPHER JOHN

New Court Chambers
3 Broad Chare, Newcastle upon Tyne
NE1 3DQ, Telephone: 0191 232 1980
Call Date: Nov 1981, Lincoln's Inn
Pupil Master
Qualifications: [BA]

PRINCE EDWIN JACOB

Falcon Chambers
Falcon Court, London EC4Y 1AA,
Telephone: 0171 353 2484
E-mail: clerks@falcon-chambers.com
Call Date: Nov 1955, Inner Temple
Qualifications: [BA]

PRINCE DR ETHLYN AGATHA

12 Old Square
1st Floor, Lincoln's Inn, London
WC2A 3TX, Telephone: 0171 404 0875
Call Date: July 1970, Gray's Inn
Qualifications: [LLB, D.Phil]

PRINGLE GORDON ALEXANDER

Bridewell Chambers
2 Bridewell Place, London EC4V 6AP,
Telephone: 020 7797 8800
E-mail:HughesGage@bridewell.law.co.uk
Call Date: Nov 1973, Inner Temple
Pupil Master
Qualifications: [BA (Oxon)]

PRINGLE IAN DEREK

Guildhall Chambers
22-26 Broad Street, Bristol BS1 2HG,
Telephone: 0117 9273366
E-mail:civil.clerks@guildhallchambers.co.uk and
criminal.clerks@guildhallchambers.co.uk
Call Date: July 1979, Gray's Inn
Pupil Master, Assistant Recorder
Qualifications: [MA (Cantab)]

PRINN MISS HELEN ELIZABETH

Octagon House
19 Colegate, Norwich NR3 1AT,
Telephone: 01603 623186
E-mail: admin@octagon-chambers.co.uk
Call Date: Oct 1993, Middle Temple
Qualifications: [BA (Hons)(Lond), CPE
(City)]

PRIOR CHARLES ROBERT CHRISTOPHER

Adrian Lyon's Chambers
14 Castle Street, Liverpool L2 0NE,
Telephone: 0151 236 4421/8240
E-mail: chambers14@aol.com
Call Date: Oct 1995, Lincoln's Inn
Qualifications: [BA (Hons)(Oxon), Dip in
Law (City)]

PRITCHARD MISS DAWN MARIE

High Pavement Chambers
1 High Pavement, Nottingham NG1 1HF,
Telephone: 0115 9418218
Call Date: Feb 1992, Inner Temple
Qualifications: [LLB (Sheff)]

PRITCHARD GEOFFREY MICHAEL

3 New Square
Lincoln's Inn, London WC2A 3RS,
Telephone: 0171 405 1111
E-mail: 3newsquareip@lineone.net
Call Date: 1998, Middle Temple
Qualifications: [BSc (Hons)(Bris), PH.D
(Cantab), CPE (De Montfort)]

PRITCHARD RODNEY

Call Date: June 1964, Inner Temple
Qualifications: [LLB]

PRITCHARD MISS SARAH JANE

40 King Street
Manchester M2 6BA,
Telephone: 0161 832 9082
E-mail: clerks@40kingstreet.co.uk
The Chambers of Philip Raynor QC
5 Park Place, Leeds LS1 2RU,
Telephone: 0113 242 1123
Call Date: Oct 1993, Gray's Inn
Qualifications: [LLB (Manch)]

PRITCHARD MISS SARAH LOUISE

St Ive's Chambers
Whittall Street, Birmingham B4 6DH,
Telephone: 0121 236 0863/5720
E-mail:stives.headofchambers@btinternet.com
Call Date: 1997, Gray's Inn
Qualifications: [BA (Warwick)]

D

D

PRITCHARD MRS TERESA JULIA

4 Brick Court
Temple, London EC4Y 9AD,
Telephone: 0171 797 8910
E-mail: medhurst@dial.pipex.com
Call Date: Oct 1994, Lincoln's Inn
Qualifications: [MA (Hons)(St Andrew), Dip in Law (City)]

PRITCHETT STEPHEN JOHN

40 King Street
Manchester M2 6BA,
Telephone: 0161 832 9082
E-mail: clerks@40kingstreet.co.uk
5 Stone Buildings
Lincoln's Inn, London WC2A 3XT,
Telephone: 0171 242 6201
E-mail:clerks@5-stonebuildings.law.co.uk
The Chambers of Philip Raynor QC
5 Park Place, Leeds LS1 2RU,
Telephone: 0113 242 1123
Call Date: July 1989, Lincoln's Inn
Pupil Master
Qualifications: [LLB (Hons) (L'pool)]

PRIVETT FRANK SIMON KENNETH

1 Paper Buildings
1st Floor, Temple, London EC4Y 7EP,
Telephone: 0171 353 3728/4953
Call Date: July 1976, Middle Temple
Pupil Master, Assistant Recorder
Qualifications: [LLB (Edin)]

PROBERT-WOOD TIMOTHY BLAIR

2 Harcourt Buildings
1st Floor, Temple, London EC4Y 9DB,
Telephone: 020 7353 2112
Call Date: July 1983, Inner Temple
Qualifications: [LLB (Hull)]

PROBYN MISS CALISTA JANE

Queen Elizabeth Building
Ground Floor, Temple, London
EC4Y 9BS,
Telephone: 0171 353 7181 (12 Lines)
Call Date: Feb 1988, Middle Temple
Pupil Master
Qualifications: [LLB]

PROCTER MICHAEL

Fleet Chambers
Mitre House, 44-46 Fleet Street, London
EC4Y 1BN, Telephone: 0171 936 3707
E-mail: rr@fleetchambers.demon.co.uk
Call Date: Nov 1993, Gray's Inn
Qualifications: [BA]

PROGHOULIS PHILIP GEORGE

Roehampton Chambers
30 Stoughton Close, Roehampton,
London SW15 4LS,
Telephone: 0181 788 1238
Westgate Chambers
144 High Street, Lewes, East Sussex,
BN7 1XT, Telephone: 01273 480510
Call Date: Nov 1963, Inner Temple

PROOPS MISS HELEN JEANETTE

York Chambers
14 Toft Green, York YO1 6JT,
Telephone: 01904 620048
E-mail: [name]@yorkchambers.co.uk
Call Date: July 1986, Middle Temple
Qualifications: [LLB Exeter]

PROSSER ANTHONY GRIFFITH THOMAS

1 Harcourt Buildings
2nd Floor, Temple, London EC4Y 9DA,
Telephone: 0171 353 9421/0375
E-mail:clerks@1harcourtbuildings.law.co.uk
Call Date: July 1985, Inner Temple
Qualifications: [LLB (Lond)]

PROSSER HENRY WILLIAM

Park Court Chambers
16 Park Place, Leeds LS1 2SJ,
Telephone: 0113 2433277
Call Date: July 1969, Middle Temple
Recorder
Qualifications: [MA]

PROSSER KEVIN JOHN QC (1996)

Pump Court Tax Chambers
16 Bedford Row, London WC1R 4EB,
Telephone: 0171 414 8080

8 King Street Chambers
8 King Street, Manchester M2 6AQ,
Telephone: 0161 834 9560
E-mail: eightking@aol.com
Call Date: July 1982, Lincoln's Inn
Qualifications: [LLB (Lond), BCL, (Oxon)]

PROUDMAN MISS SONIA ROSEMARY SUSAN QC (1994)

Chambers of Mr Peter Crampin QC
Ground Floor, 11 New Square, Lincoln's
Inn, London WC2A 3QB,
Telephone: 020 7831 0081
E-mail: 11newsquare.co.uk
Call Date: July 1972, Lincoln's Inn
Qualifications: [MA (Oxon)]

PROWSE JAMES BARRINGTON

Derby Square Chambers
Merchants Court, Derby Square, Liverpool
L2 1TS, Telephone: 0151 709 4222
E-mail:mail.derbysquare@pop3.hiway.co.uk
Call Date: July 1986, Inner Temple
Qualifications: [LLB, MIMgt, Assoc IPD]

PRUDHOE TIMOTHY NIXON

Queen's Chambers
5 John Dalton Street, Manchester M2 6ET,
Telephone: 0161 834 6875/4738
Queens Chambers
4 Camden Place, Preston PR1 3JL,
Telephone: 01772 828300
Call Date: Oct 1994, Gray's Inn
Qualifications: [LLB (Hons)(Manc)]

PRYCE GREGORY HUGH

Chambers of Michael Pert QC
36 Bedford Row, London WC1R 4JH,
Telephone: 0171 421 8000
E-mail: 36bedfordrow@link.org
Chambers of Michael Pert QC
24 Albion Place, Northampton NN1 1UD,
Telephone: 01604 602333
Chambers of Michael Pert QC
104 New Walk, Leicester LE1 7EA,
Telephone: 0116 249 2020
Call Date: July 1988, Gray's Inn
Qualifications: [BA (Hons)]

PRYKE STUART

Trinity Chambers
9-12 Trinity Chare, Quayside, Newcastle
upon Tyne NE1 3DF,
Telephone: 0191 232 1927
E-mail: info@trinitychambers.co.uk
Call Date: Oct 1994, Lincoln's Inn
Qualifications: [BEng (Lond), MSc (Econ),
Dip in Law (City)]

PRYNNE ANDREW GEOFFREY LOCKYER QC (1995)

2 Harcourt Buildings
Ground Floor/Left, Temple, London
EC4Y 9DB, Telephone: 0171 583 9020
E-mail: clerks@harcourt.co.uk
Call Date: July 1975, Middle Temple
Qualifications: [LLB (Soton)]

PRYOR MICHAEL ROBERT

9 Old Square
Ground Floor, Lincoln's Inn, London
WC2A 3SR, Telephone: 0171 405 4682
E-mail: chambers@9oldsquare.co.uk
Call Date: Oct 1992, Inner Temple
Qualifications: [LLB (Hons)]

PUCKRIN CEDRIC ELDRED

19 Old Buildings
Lincoln's Inn, London WC2A 3UP,
Telephone: 0171 405 2001
E-mail: clerks@oldbuildingsip.com
Call Date: Nov 1990, Middle Temple
Qualifications: [BA, LLB (S Africa)]

PUGH ANDREW CARTWRIGHT QC (1988)

Blackstone Chambers
Blackstone House, Temple, London
EC4Y 9BW, Telephone: 0171 583 1770
E-mail:clerks@blackstonechambers.com
Call Date: Nov 1961, Inner Temple
Recorder
Qualifications: [MA (Oxon)]

PUGH DAVID SAMUEL

East Anglian Chambers
52 North Hill, Colchester, Essex, CO1 1PY,
Telephone: 01206 572756
E-mail: colchester@ealaw.co.uk

East Anglian Chambers
57 London Street, Norwich NR2 1HL,
Telephone: 01603 617351
E-mail: norwich@ealaw.co.uk
East Anglian Chambers
Gresham House, 5 Museum Street,
Ipswich, Suffolk, IP1 1HQ,
Telephone: 01473 214481
E-mail: ipswich@ealaw.co.uk
Call Date: July 1978, Middle Temple
Pupil Master
Qualifications: [B Sc (Salford)]

PUGH GLANVILLE VERNON QC (1986)

2-3 Gray's Inn Square
Gray's Inn, London WC1R 5JH,
Telephone: 0171 242 4986
E-mail:chambers@2-3graysinnsquare.co.uk
33 Park Place
Cardiff CF1 3BA,
Telephone: 02920 233313
Call Date: Nov 1969, Lincoln's Inn
Recorder
Qualifications: [LLB (Wales) , LLB (Cantab)]

PUGH JOHN BISHOP

John Pugh's Chambers
3rd Floor, 14 Castle Street, Liverpool
L2 0NE, Telephone: 0151 236 5415
Call Date: July 1972, Lincoln's Inn
Qualifications: [LLB (Hons)]

PUGH MICHAEL CHARLES

Old Square Chambers
1 Verulam Buildings, Gray's Inn, London
WC1R 5LQ, Telephone: 0171 269 0300
E-mail:clerks@oldsquarechambers.co.uk
Old Square Chambers
Hanover House, 47 Corn Street, Bristol
BS1 1HT, Telephone: 0117 9277111
E-mail: oldsqbri@globalnet.co.uk
Call Date: Nov 1975, Gray's Inn
Pupil Master
Qualifications: [BSc (Econ), C Dip AF]

PUGH-SMITH JOHN EDGAR

1 Serjeants' Inn
4th Floor, Temple, London EC4Y 1NH,
Telephone: 0171 583 1355
E-mail: clerks@serjeants-inn.co.uk

East Anglian Chambers
57 London Street, Norwich NR2 1HL,
Telephone: 01603 617351
E-mail: norwich@ealaw.co.uk
East Anglian Chambers
Gresham House, 5 Museum Street,
Ipswich, Suffolk, IP1 1HQ,
Telephone: 01473 214481
E-mail: ipswich@ealaw.co.uk
East Anglian Chambers
52 North Hill, Colchester, Essex, CO1 1PY,
Telephone: 01206 572756
E-mail: colchester@ealaw.co.uk
Call Date: July 1977, Gray's Inn
Pupil Master
Qualifications: [MA (Oxon)]

PULLEN TIMOTHY JOHN

33 Bedford Row
London WC1R 4JH,
Telephone: 0171 242 6476
E-mail:clerks@bedfordrow33.demon.co.uk
Call Date: Nov 1993, Middle Temple
Qualifications: [BSc (Plymouth), CPE (Lond)]

PULLING DEAN

Iscoed Chambers
86 St Helen's Road, Swansea, West
Glamorgan, SA1 4BQ,
Telephone: 01792 652988/9/330
Call Date: Nov 1993, Middle Temple
Qualifications: [LLB (Hons)(Wales)]

PULMAN GEORGE FREDERICK QC (1989)

Hardwicke Building
New Square, Lincoln's Inn, London
WC2A 3SB, Telephone: 020 7242 2523
E-mail: clerks@hardwicke.co.uk
Stour Chambers
Barton Mill House, Barton Mill Road,
Canterbury, Kent, CT1 1BP,
Telephone: 01227 764899
E-mail: clerks@stourchambers.co.uk
Call Date: July 1971, Middle Temple
Recorder
Qualifications: [MA (Cantab)]

PUNWAR PURVAISE PHILIP JAMES

Francis Taylor Building
3rd Floor, Temple, London EC4Y 7BY,
Telephone: 0171 797 7250
Call Date: Nov 1989, Inner Temple
Qualifications: [BA (B'ham), Dip Law (City)]

PURCELL GREGOR ALEXANDER MORRISON

Fountain Chambers
Cleveland Business Centre, 1 Watson Street, Middlesbrough TS1 2RQ,
Telephone: 01642 804040
E-mail:fountainchambers@onyxnet.co.uk
Call Date: Oct 1997, Lincoln's Inn
Qualifications: [LLB (Hons)(Newc)]

PURCHAS CHRISTOPHER PATRICK BROOKS QC (1990)

Two Crown Office Row
Ground Floor, Temple, London
EC4Y 7HJ, Telephone: 020 7797 8100
E-mail: mail@2cor.co.uk, or to individual barristers at: [barrister's surname]@2cor.co.uk
Call Date: July 1966, Inner Temple
Recorder
Qualifications: [MA (Cantab)]

PURCHAS ROBIN MICHAEL QC (1987)

2 Harcourt Buildings
2nd Floor, Temple, London EC4Y 9DB,
Telephone: 020 7353 8415
E-mail: clerks@2hb.law.co.uk
Call Date: 1968, Inner Temple
Recorder
Qualifications: [MA (Cantab)]

Fax: 0171 353 7622; DX: LDE 402

Types of work: Administrative, Commons, Compulsory purchase, Environment, Licensing, Local government, Parliamentary, Planning, Professional negligence, Town and country planning

Circuit: South Eastern

Awards and memberships: Senior Exhibitioner; Member of the Administrative Law Bar Association, Bar European Group, Parliamentary Bar and Planning and Environment Bar Associations, Fellow of the Society for Advanced Legal Studies

Other professional experience: Recorder (1989); sits as Deputy High Court Judge (1994); Master of Bench of Inner Temple (1996); previously on Attorney General's Supplementary Panel – Common Law

Recent Cases:

Bolton MBC v Secretary of State for the Environment (HL) [1995] 1 WLR 1176; [1995] 3 PLR 37
Reasons – approach to decisions – validity – costs.

English Property Corporation v Kingston upon Thames RBC [1999] 77 PCR 1 (CA)
Compensation – severance – re Land Compensation Act 1961.

Wards v Barclays Bank Plc [1994] 68 PCR 391 (CA)
Compensation – principle in Pointe Gourde – application of the Stokes principle.

Prudential Assurance v Waterloo Real Estate [1998] EGCS 5 (CA)
Construction/Title – adverse possession – proprietary/convention estoppel – injunctive relief.

R v Newbury DC ex parte Chieveley PC [1997] JPL 1137 (CA)
Validity of planning permission – outline and approval of details – delay – discretion.

Fletcher v SS for Transport [1998] NPC 105 (CA)
Land Compensation Act 1961 s 17 – Certificate of alternative development – date for determination – scope of scheme to be ignored.

Batchelor v Kent County Council [1990] 59 PCR 357 (CA)
Land Compensation Act 1961 – Rule 3 – Stokes principle – Pointe Gourde – reasons.

Pye (Oxford) Ltd v Kingswood BC (CA) 6 March 1998
Compensation – scheme – collateral highway benefits – ransom – reasons.

Pickering v Kettering BC [1996] EGCS 130 (CA)
Local Plan – mistake of fact – local authority duties and discretion.

Government promotions include: Channel Tunnel Rail Link and Channel Tunnel Bills.

PURDIE ROBERT ANTHONY JAMES

28 Western Road
Oxford OX1 4LG,
Telephone: 01865 204911
E-mail: lawyers@28wr.freeserve.co.uk
Call Date: July 1979, Middle Temple
Qualifications: [LLB]

PURDY MS CATHERINE LOUISE

3 Paper Buildings
Temple, London EC4Y 7EU,
Telephone: 020 7583 8055
E-mail: London@3paper.com
3 Paper Buildings (Bournemouth)
20 Lorne Park Road, Bournemouth,
Dorset, BH1 1JN,
Telephone: 01202 292102
E-mail: Bournemouth@3paper.com
3 Paper Buildings (Winchester)
4 St Peter Street, Winchester SO23 8BW,
Telephone: 01962 868884
E-mail: winchester@3paper.com
3 Paper Buildings (Oxford)
1 Alfred Street, High Street, Oxford
OX1 4EH, Telephone: 01865 793736
E-mail: oxford@3paper.com
Call Date: 1997, Inner Temple
Qualifications: [BA (Oxon)]

PURDY QUENTIN ALEXANDER

2 Paper Buildings, Basement North
Temple, London EC4Y 7ET,
Telephone: 0171 936 2613
E-mail: post@2paper.co.uk
Call Date: July 1983, Gray's Inn
Pupil Master
Qualifications: [BA (Leic), LLM, (Lond)]

PURKIS MS KATHRYN MIRANDA

Serle Court Chambers
6 New Square, Lincoln's Inn, London
WC2A 3QS, Telephone: 0171 242 6105
E-mail: clerks@serlecourt.co.uk
Call Date: Oct 1991, Lincoln's Inn
Qualifications: [BA (Hons) (Cape Twn), BA
(Hons) (Oxon)]

PURKISS MISS CATHLEEN KAREN

Queen Elizabeth Building
Ground Floor, Temple, London
EC4Y 9BS,
Telephone: 0171 353 7181 (12 Lines)
Call Date: July 1988, Lincoln's Inn
Qualifications: [BA (Hons) (Lond), Dip Law]

PURLE CHARLES LAMBERT QC (1989)

12 New Square
Lincoln's Inn, London WC2A 3SW,
Telephone: 0171 419 1212
E-mail: chambers@12newsquare.co.uk
Sovereign Chambers
25 Park Square, Leeds LS1 2PW,
Telephone: 0113 2451841/2/3
E-mail:sovereignchambers@btinternet.com
Call Date: Nov 1970, Gray's Inn
Qualifications: [LLB (Nottm), BCL (Oxon)]

PURNELL NICHOLAS ROBERT QC (1985)

23 Essex Street
London WC2R 3AS,
Telephone: 0171 413 0353/836 8366
E-mail:clerks@essexstreet23.demon.co.uk
Call Date: July 1968, Middle Temple
Recorder
Qualifications: [MA (Cantab)]

PURNELL PAUL OLIVER QC (1982)

1 Middle Temple Lane
Temple, London EC4Y 1LT,
Telephone: 0171 583 0659 (12 Lines)
E-mail: chambers@1mtl.co.uk
Call Date: Nov 1962, Inner Temple
Recorder
Qualifications: [MA (Oxon)]

PURVES GAVIN BOWMAN

Swan House
PO Box 8749, London W13 8ZX,
Telephone: 0181 998 3035
Call Date: July 1979, Gray's Inn
Qualifications: [LLB (Hons)(Brunel), DEI
(Amsterdam)]

PURVIS IAIN YOUNIE

11 South Square
2nd Floor, Gray's Inn, London
WC1R 5EU,
Telephone: 0171 405 1222 (24hr messagin
g service)
E-mail: clerks@11southsquare.com
Call Date: July 1986, Gray's Inn
Pupil Master
Qualifications: [MA (Cantab) BCL, (Oxon)]

PUSEY WILLIAM JAMES

St Philip's Chambers
Fountain Court, Steelhouse Lane,
Birmingham B4 6DR,
Telephone: 0121 246 7000
E-mail: clerks@st-philips.co.uk
Call Date: Nov 1977, Inner Temple
Pupil Master
Qualifications: [LLB (Leeds)]

PUTNAM MRS SHEELAGH

North London Chambers
14 Keyes Road, London NW2 3XA,
Telephone: 0181 208 4651
Call Date: Nov 1976, Middle Temple

PUTNAM THOMAS DREW

North London Chambers
14 Keyes Road, London NW2 3XA,
Telephone: 0181 208 4651
Call Date: July 1976, Gray's Inn
Pupil Master

PUTTICK ANTHONY DAVID

Colleton Chambers
Colleton Crescent, Exeter, Devon,
EX2 4DG, Telephone: 01392 274898/9
Godolphin Chambers
50 Castle Street, Truro, Cornwall,
TR1 3AF, Telephone: 01872 276312
E-mail:theclerks@godolphin.force9.co.uk
Call Date: May 1971, Middle Temple

PUZEY JAMES RODERICK

1 Fountain Court
Steelhouse Lane, Birmingham B4 6DR,
Telephone: 0121 236 5721
Call Date: Oct 1990, Inner Temple
Qualifications: [LLB (L'pool)]

PYE MISS MARGARET JANE

Sovereign Chambers
25 Park Square, Leeds LS1 2PW,
Telephone: 0113 2451841/2/3
E-mail:sovereignchambers@btinternet.com
Call Date: May 1995, Middle Temple
Qualifications: [BA (Hons)]

PYLE MISS SUSAN DEBORAH

7 Stone Buildings (also at 11 Bolt Court)
1st Floor, Lincoln's Inn, London
WC2A 3SZ, Telephone: 0171 242 0961
E-mail:larthur@7stonebuildings.law.co.uk
11 Bolt Court (also at 7 Stone Buildings – 1st Floor)
London EC4A 3DQ,
Telephone: 0171 353 2300
E-mail: boltct11@aol.com
Redhill Chambers
Seloduct House, 30 Station Road, Redhill,
Surrey, RH1 1NF,
Telephone: 01737 780781
Call Date: Nov 1985, Gray's Inn
Pupil Master
Qualifications: [LLB(Newcastle)]

PYMONT CHRISTOPHER HOWARD QC (1996)

13 Old Square
Ground Floor, Lincoln's Inn, London
WC2A 3UA, Telephone: 0171 404 4800
E-mail: clerks@13oldsquare.law.co.uk
Call Date: July 1979, Gray's Inn
Qualifications: [MA (Oxon)]

PYNE RUSSELL DAVID

2 King's Bench Walk
Ground Floor, Temple, London
EC4Y 7DE, Telephone: 0171 353 1746
E-mail: 2kbw@atlas.co.uk
King's Bench Chambers
115 North Hill, Plymouth PL4 8JY,
Telephone: 01752 221551
Call Date: Oct 1991, Inner Temple
Qualifications: [LLB (Bris)]

QADRI KHALID

Holborn Chambers
6 Gate Street, Lincoln's Inn Fields, London
WC2A 3HP, Telephone: 0171 242 6060
Call Date: Nov 1993, Middle Temple
Qualifications: [BA (Hons), CPE
(Wolverhampton)]

QAZI MOHAMMED AYAZ

Chambers of Harjit Singh
Ground Floor, 2 Middle Temple Lane,
Temple, London EC4Y 9AA,
Telephone: 0171 353 1356 (4 Lines)
Call Date: Feb 1993, Gray's Inn
Qualifications: [LLB]

QUADRAT SIMON VICTOR

Queens Square Chambers
56 Queens Square, Bristol BS1 4PR,
Telephone: 0117 921 1966
Call Date: Nov 1969, Inner Temple
Pupil Master
Qualifications: [LLB (Bris)]

QUDDUS KHANDAKAR ABDUL

19 Chestnut Drive
Pinner, Middlesex, HA5 1LX,
Telephone: 0181 866 7603/933 2382
Call Date: July 1968, Inner Temple
Qualifications: [MA]

QUEST DAVID CHARLES

3 Verulam Buildings
London WC1R 5NT,
Telephone: 0171 831 8441
E-mail: clerks@3verulam.co.uk
Call Date: Oct 1993, Gray's Inn
Qualifications: [BA (Cantab)]

QUIGLEY MISS CAMILLA JACINTH CALVERT

Plowden Buildings
2nd Floor, 2 Plowden Buildings, Middle
Temple Lane, London EC4Y 9BU,
Telephone: 0171 583 0808
E-mail: bar@plowdenbuildings.co.uk
Call Date: July 1988, Inner Temple
Qualifications: [BSc (Durham), Dip Law
(City)]

QUIGLEY CONOR

Brick Court Chambers
7-8 Essex Street, London WC2R 3LD,
Telephone: 0171 379 3550
E-mail: [surname]@brickcourt.co.uk
Call Date: Nov 1985, Gray's Inn
Pupil Master
Qualifications: [LLB (Lond), Dip.E.I.
(Amsterdam), MA (Oxon)]

QUINEY CHARLES BENEDICTUS ALEXANDER

One Paper Buildings
Ground Floor, Temple, London
EC4Y 7EP, Telephone: 0171 583 7355
E-mail: clerks@1pb.co.uk
Call Date: 1998, Gray's Inn
Qualifications: [BA, BCL (Oxon)]

QUINLAN CHRISTOPHER JOHN

Guildhall Chambers
22-26 Broad Street, Bristol BS1 2HG,
Telephone: 0117 9273366
E-mail:civil.clerks@guildhallchambers.co.uk and
criminal.clerks@guildhallchambers.co.uk
Call Date: Nov 1992, Inner Temple
Qualifications: [LLB (Hons)]

QUINN CHRISTOPHER JOHN

Cloisters
1 Pump Court, Temple, London
EC4Y 7AA, Telephone: 0171 827 4000
E-mail: clerks@cloisters.com
Call Date: Oct 1992, Middle Temple
Qualifications: [LL.B (Hons, Cantab), LL.M
(Queens Uni., Canada)]

QUINN JOSEPH MICHAEL

1 Gray's Inn Square
Ground Floor, London WC1R 5AA,
Telephone: 0171 405 8946/7/8
Call Date: Nov 1987, Inner Temple
Qualifications: [BA]

QUINN MS SUSAN ANN

4 Brick Court
Temple, London EC4Y 9AD,
Telephone: 0171 797 8910
E-mail: medhurst@dial.pipex.com
Call Date: Nov 1983, Gray's Inn
Pupil Master
Qualifications: [LLB (lond)]

QUINN MISS VICTORIA KATHLEEN

Verulam Chambers
Peer House, 8-14 Verulam Street, Gray's
Inn, London WC1X 8LZ,
Telephone: 0171 813 2400
Call Date: Oct 1995, Lincoln's Inn
Qualifications: [BA (Hons)(Abery)]

QUINT MRS JOAN FRANCESCA RAE

11 Old Square
Ground Floor, Lincoln's Inn, London
WC2A 3TS, Telephone: 0171 242 5022/
405 1074
Call Date: July 1970, Gray's Inn
Pupil Master
Qualifications: [LLB [Lond], A.K.C]

QUIRKE GERARD MARTIN

1 Fountain Court
Steelhouse Lane, Birmingham B4 6DR,
Telephone: 0121 236 5721
Call Date: Nov 1988, Middle Temple
Qualifications: [BA (Hull), Dip Law (City)]

QUIRKE JAMES KEIRON

6 Fountain Court
Steelhouse Lane, Birmingham B4 6DR,
Telephone: 0121 233 3282
E-mail: clerks@sixfountain.co.uk
Call Date: Nov 1974, Gray's Inn
Pupil Master
Qualifications: [BA (Oxon)]

QURESHI ABDUL SALEEM

Barclay Chambers
2a Barclay Road, Leytonstone, London
E11 3DG, Telephone: 0181 558 2289/
925 0688
Call Date: July 1972, Middle Temple
Qualifications: [BA,LLB]

QURESHI ASIF HASAN

4 Essex Court
Temple, London EC4Y 9AJ,
Telephone: 020 7797 7970
E-mail: clerks@4essexcourt.law.co.uk
Call Date: 1978, Lincoln's Inn
Qualifications: [BA, LLB punjab]

QURESHI KHAWAR MEHMOOD

One Hare Court
1st Floor, Temple, London EC4Y 7BE,
Telephone: 020 7353 3171
E-mail:admin-oneharecourt@btinternet.com
Call Date: Oct 1990, Middle Temple
Pupil Master
Qualifications: [LLB, LLM (Cantab)]

QURESHI SHAMIM AHMED

Queens Square Chambers
56 Queens Square, Bristol BS1 4PR,
Telephone: 0117 921 1966
Call Date: July 1982, Gray's Inn
Qualifications: [BA (Bris)]

RABE ROBERT MICHAEL

3 Temple Gardens
3rd Floor, Temple, London EC4Y 9AU,
Telephone: 0171 353 0832
Call Date: July 1998, Middle Temple
Qualifications: [BSc (Michigan), JD (Wayne
State)]

RABEY MISS CATHERINE MARY

2 Temple Gardens
Temple, London EC4Y 9AY,
Telephone: 0171 583 6041
E-mail: clerks@2templegardens.co.uk
Call Date: July 1987, Middle Temple
Qualifications: [BA (Oxon) Dip Law]

RABIE GERALD ALLEN

Devereux Chambers
Devereux Court, London WC2R 3JJ,
Telephone: 0171 353 7534
E-mail: mailbox@devchambers.co.uk
Call Date: Feb 1973, Inner Temple
Qualifications: [BA, LLB]

RABINOWITZ LAURENCE ANTON

One Essex Court
Ground Floor, Temple, London
EC4Y 9AR, Telephone: 020 7583 2000
E-mail: clerks@oneessexcourt.co.uk
Call Date: Nov 1987, Middle Temple
Pupil Master
Qualifications: [BA, LLB (Wits), BA, BCL
(Oxon)]

RADBURN MARK CHARLES CRISPIN

5 Fountain Court
Steelhouse Lane, Birmingham B4 6DR,
Telephone: 0121 606 0500
E-mail:clerks@5fountaincourt.law.co.uk
Call Date: Oct 1991, Lincoln's Inn
Qualifications: [LLB (Hons)]

RADCLIFFE ANDREW ALLEN

1 Hare Court
Ground Floor, Temple, London
EC4Y 7BE, Telephone: 0171 353 3982/
5324
Call Date: Nov 1975, Middle Temple
Pupil Master, Assistant Recorder
Qualifications: [BA (Oxon)]

RADCLIFFE DAVID ANDREW

18 Red Lion Court
(Off Fleet Street), London EC4A 3EB,
Telephone: 0171 520 6000
E-mail: chambers@18rlc.co.uk
Thornwood House
102 New London Road, Chelmsford,
Essex, CM2 0RG,
Telephone: 01245 280880
E-mail: chambers@18rlc.co.uk
Call Date: July 1966, Inner Temple
Pupil Master, Recorder
Qualifications: [MA (Cantab)]

RADCLIFFE FRANCIS CHARLES JOSEPH

11 King's Bench Walk
1st Floor, Temple, London EC4Y 7EQ,
Telephone: 0171 353 3337
E-mail: fmuller11@aol.com
11 King's Bench Walk
3 Park Court, Park Cross Street, Leeds
LS1 2QH, Telephone: 0113 297 1200
Call Date: Nov 1962, Gray's Inn
Qualifications: [MA (Cantab)]

RADCLIFFE MS PAMELA JOAN

Holborn Chambers
6 Gate Street, Lincoln's Inn Fields, London
WC2A 3HP, Telephone: 0171 242 6060
Call Date: July 1979, Gray's Inn
Pupil Master
Qualifications: [LLB (Warwick)]

RADEVSKY ANTHONY ERIC

Falcon Chambers
Falcon Court, London EC4Y 1AA,
Telephone: 0171 353 2484
E-mail: clerks@falcon-chambers.com
Call Date: July 1978, Inner Temple
Pupil Master
Qualifications: [LLB (Soton)]

RADFORD MRS NADINE POGGIOLI QC (1995)

2 Dyers Buildings
London EC1N 2JT,
Telephone: 0171 404 1881
Call Date: Nov 1974, Lincoln's Inn
Recorder

RAE JAMES ROBERT

Exchange Chambers
Pearl Assurance House, Derby Square,
Liverpool L2 9XX,
Telephone: 0151 236 7747
E-mail:exchangechambers@btinternet.com
Call Date: July 1976, Inner Temple

RAE JOHN WILLIAM

16a Campden Hill Court
Campden Hill Road, London W8 7HS,
Telephone: 0171 937 3492
Call Date: Nov 1961, Inner Temple
Qualifications: [MA (Oxon)]

RAESIDE MARK ANDREW

Atkin Chambers
1 Atkin Building, Gray's Inn, London
WC1R 5AT, Telephone: 020 7404 0102
E-mail: clerks@atkin-chambers.co.uk
Call Date: Nov 1982, Middle Temple
Pupil Master
Qualifications: [BA, MPhil (Cantab)]

RAFATI ALI REZA

2 King's Bench Walk
Ground Floor, Temple, London
EC4Y 7DE, Telephone: 0171 353 1746
E-mail: 2kbw@atlas.co.uk
King's Bench Chambers
115 North Hill, Plymouth PL4 8JY,
Telephone: 01752 221551
Call Date: Nov 1993, Gray's Inn
Qualifications: [LLB]

RAFFELL ANDREW JOHN

Mitre House Chambers
15-19 Devereux Court, London WC2R 3JJ,
Telephone: 0171 583 8233
Call Date: Feb 1983, Middle Temple
Qualifications: [LLB (Lond), LLM (Leic)]

RAFFERTY MISS ANGELA MARGARET MARY

1 Paper Buildings
1st Floor, Temple, London EC4Y 7EP,
Telephone: 0171 353 3728/4953
Call Date: Feb 1995, Lincoln's Inn
Qualifications: [BA (Cantab)]

RAFFERTY MISS ANNE JUDITH QC (1990)

4 Brick Court, Chambers of Anne Rafferty QC
1st Floor, Temple, London EC4Y 9AD,
Telephone: 0171 583 8455
Call Date: July 1973, Gray's Inn
Recorder
Qualifications: [LLB]

RAFFERTY STUART

High Pavement Chambers
1 High Pavement, Nottingham NG1 1HF,
Telephone: 0115 9418218
Call Date: July 1975, Gray's Inn
Pupil Master
Qualifications: [BA]

RAFFRAY FREDERIC JOSEPH

17 Bedford Row
London WC1R 4EB,
Telephone: 0171 831 7314
E-mail: iboard7314@aol.com
Call Date: Feb 1991, Middle Temple
Qualifications: [LLB (Lond), Maitrise en Droit, (Paris I)]

RAFIQUE SYED TARIQ DAUD

6 King's Bench Walk
Ground, Third & Fourth Floors, Temple,
London EC4Y 7DR,
Telephone: 0171 353 4931/583 0695

Britton Street Chambers
1st Floor, 20 Britton Street, London
EC1M 5NQ, Telephone: 0171 608 3765
Call Date: Nov 1961, Lincoln's Inn
Pupil Master
Qualifications: [BA (Cantab)]

RAGGATT TIMOTHY WALTER HAROLD QC (1993)

Chambers of Michael Pert QC
36 Bedford Row, London WC1R 4JH,
Telephone: 0171 421 8000
E-mail: 36bedfordrow@link.org
3 Fountain Court
Steelhouse Lane, Birmingham B4 6DR,
Telephone: 0121 236 5854
Chambers of Michael Pert QC
104 New Walk, Leicester LE1 7EA,
Telephone: 0116 249 2020
Chambers of Michael Pert QC
24 Albion Place, Northampton NN1 1UD,
Telephone: 01604 602333
Call Date: July 1972, Inner Temple
Recorder
Qualifications: [LLB (Lond)]

RAHAL MISS RAVINDER KAUR

Two Garden Court
1st Floor, Middle Temple, London
EC4Y 9BL, Telephone: 0171 353 1633
E-mail: barristers@2gardenct.law.co.uk
Call Date: Nov 1983, Middle Temple
Qualifications: [LLB, LLM (Cantab)]

RAHMAN LUTHFUR

Somersett Chambers
25 Bedford Row, London WC1R 4HE,
Telephone: 0171 404 6701
E-mail: somelaw@aol.com
Call Date: 1996, Middle Temple
Qualifications: [LLB (Hons)(Lond)]

RAHMAN MD ANISUR

12 Old Square
1st Floor, Lincoln's Inn, London
WC2A 3TX, Telephone: 0171 404 0875
Call Date: Nov 1990, Inner Temple
Qualifications: [MA (Bangladesh), Dip Law (PCL)]

RAHMAN MUHAMMAD ALTAFUR

Barristers' Common Law Chambers
57 Whitechapel Road, Aldgate East,
London E1 1DU,
Telephone: 0171 375 3012
E-mail: barristers@hotmail.com and
barristers@lawchambers.freeserve.co.uk
Call Date: Nov 1970, Inner Temple
Qualifications: [MA]

RAHMAN MS SADEQA SHAHEEN

1 Crown Office Row
Ground Floor, Temple, London
EC4Y 7HH, Telephone: 0171 797 7500
E-mail: mail@onecrownofficerow.com
Call Date: Nov 1996, Gray's Inn
Qualifications: [BA (B'ham)]

RAHMAN SAMI UR

**Gray's Inn Chambers, The Chambers of
Norman Patterson**
First Floor, Gray's Inn Chambers, Gray's
Inn, London WC1R 5JA,
Telephone: 0171 831 5344
E-mail: s.mcblain@btinternet.com
Call Date: Oct 1996, Lincoln's Inn
Qualifications: [LLB (Hons)(Middx)]

RAHMAN YAQUB

Oriel Chambers
14 Water Street, Liverpool L2 8TD,
Telephone: 0151 236 7191/236 4321
E-mail: clerks@oriel-chambers.co.uk
Call Date: Oct 1991, Gray's Inn
Qualifications: [BA (Hons) (Oxon), Dip Law
(PCL)]

RAI AMARJIT SINGH

St Philip's Chambers
Fountain Court, Steelhouse Lane,
Birmingham B4 6DR,
Telephone: 0121 246 7000
E-mail: clerks@st-philips.co.uk
Call Date: July 1989, Middle Temple
Qualifications: [LLB]

RAI RAJESH KUMAR

12 Old Square
1st Floor, Lincoln's Inn, London
WC2A 3TX, Telephone: 0171 404 0875

Counsels' Chambers
2nd Floor, 10-11 Gray's Inn Square,
London WC1R 5JD,
Telephone: 0171 405 2576
E-mail:clerks@10-11graysinnsquare.co.uk
Call Date: Feb 1993, Lincoln's Inn
Qualifications: [LLB (Hons)]

RAILTON DAVID QC (1996)

Fountain Court
Temple, London EC4Y 9DH,
Telephone: 0171 583 3335
E-mail: chambers@fountaincourt.co.uk
Call Date: July 1979, Gray's Inn
Qualifications: [BA (Oxon)]

RAINEY PHILIP CARSLAKE

2nd Floor, Francis Taylor Building
Temple, London EC4Y 7BY,
Telephone: 0171 353 9942/3157
Call Date: Oct 1990, Middle Temple
Qualifications: [LLB (Leic), ACIArb]

RAINEY SIMON PIERS NICHOLAS

4 Essex Court
Temple, London EC4Y 9AJ,
Telephone: 020 7797 7970
E-mail: clerks@4essexcourt.law.co.uk
Call Date: July 1982, Lincoln's Inn
Pupil Master
Qualifications: [MA (Cantab) LSDE,
(Brussels)]

RAINS RICHARD EDWIN RANDOLPH STEPHEN

Colleton Chambers
Colleton Crescent, Exeter, Devon,
EX2 4DG, Telephone: 01392 274898/9
35 Essex Street
Temple, London WC2R 3AR,
Telephone: 0171 353 6381
E-mail: derek_jenkins@link.org
Call Date: May 1963, Gray's Inn
Pupil Master
Qualifications: [LLB]

RAINSFORD MARK DAVID

1 Middle Temple Lane
Temple, London EC4Y 1LT,
Telephone: 0171 583 0659 (12 Lines)
E-mail: chambers@1mtl.co.uk
Call Date: Nov 1985, Lincoln's Inn
Pupil Master
Qualifications: [LLB (Hons) (LSE)]

RAJAH EASON THURAI

The Chambers of Leolin Price CBE, QC
10 Old Square, Lincoln's Inn, London
WC2A 3SU, Telephone: 0171 405 0758
Call Date: July 1989, Gray's Inn
Pupil Master
Qualifications: [LLB]

RAJAK HARRY HYMAN

Call Date: Nov 1968, Inner Temple
Qualifications: [LLM (Lond), BA, LLB]

RAJGOPAL MISS UTHRA DEVI

Park Court Chambers
16 Park Place, Leeds LS1 2SJ,
Telephone: 0113 2433277
Call Date: Mar 1998, Inner Temple
Qualifications: [LLB (Not'ham)]

RALLS PETER JOHN HENRY QC (1997)

29 Bedford Row Chambers
London WC1R 4HE,
Telephone: 0171 831 2626
Call Date: July 1972, Middle Temple
Qualifications: [LLB (Hons)]

RALPH MISS CAROLINE SUSAN

Assize Court Chambers
14 Small Street, Bristol BS1 1DE,
Telephone: 0117 9264587
E-mail:chambers@assize-court-chambers.co.uk
Call Date: July 1990, Inner Temple
Pupil Master
Qualifications: [BA (B'ham)]

RALPHS MISS ANNE

22 Old Buildings
Lincoln's Inn, London WC2A 3UJ,
Telephone: 0171 831 0222
Call Date: Nov 1977, Middle Temple
Assistant Recorder
Qualifications: [BSc, AcDipEd (Lond), AKC/
C'ENT.ED]

RALTON ALEXANDER JULIUS

Albion Chambers
Broad Street, Bristol BS1 1DR,
Telephone: 0117 9272144
Call Date: Oct 1990, Lincoln's Inn
Qualifications: [LLB (E. Anglia)]

RAMASAMY SELVARAJU

Hollis Whiteman Chambers
3rd Floor, Queen Elizabeth Bldg, Temple,
London EC4Y 9BS,
Telephone: 020 7583 5766
E-mail:barristers@holliswhiteman.co.uk
Call Date: 1992, Inner Temple
Qualifications: [LLB (Lond), LLM (Lond)]

RAMDEEN MISS KAMALA BERNADETTE

Britton Street Chambers
1st Floor, 20 Britton Street, London
EC1M 5NQ, Telephone: 0171 608 3765
Call Date: Nov 1978, Lincoln's Inn
Pupil Master
Qualifications: [LLB (Hons) (Brunel)]

RAMDHUN PRUSRAM JAMES

Clapham Chambers
21-25 Bedford Road, Clapham North,
London SW4 7SH,
Telephone: 0171 978 8482/642 5777
E-mail:claphamchambers@compuserve.co
m
Call Date: July 1980, Lincoln's Inn
Qualifications: [BA]

RAMPERSAD DEVAN

St Philip's Chambers
Fountain Court, Steelhouse Lane,
Birmingham B4 6DR,
Telephone: 0121 246 7000
E-mail: clerks@st-philips.co.uk
Call Date: Feb 1994, Inner Temple
Qualifications: [LLB (Lancs)]

D

RAMPTON (JOHN) RICHARD (ANTHONY) QC (1987)

1 Brick Court
1st Floor, Temple, London EC4Y 9BY,
Telephone: 0171 353 8845
E-mail: clerks@1brickcourt.co.uk
Call Date: Nov 1965, Inner Temple
Qualifications: [BA (Oxon)]

RAMSAHOYE MISS INDIRA KIM

Hardwicke Building
New Square, Lincoln's Inn, London
WC2A 3SB, Telephone: 020 7242 2523
E-mail: clerks@hardwicke.co.uk
Call Date: Nov 1980, Lincoln's Inn
Pupil Master
Qualifications: [BA]

RAMSDEN JAMES MICHAEL SCOTT

4-5 Gray's Inn Square
Ground Floor, Gray's Inn, London
WC1R 5JP, Telephone: 0171 404 5252
E-mail:chambers@4-5graysinnsquare.co.uk
Call Date: Nov 1987, Middle Temple
Pupil Master
Qualifications: [LLB (Leics)]

RAMSDEN MISS VERONICA MARY

Staple Inn Chambers
1st Floor, 9 Staple Inn, Holborn Bars,
London WC1V 7QH,
Telephone: 0171 242 5240
E-mail: clerks@staple-inn.org
Call Date: July 1979, Gray's Inn
Pupil Master
Qualifications: [LLB (Hons) (Wales)]

RAMSEY VIVIAN ARTHUR QC (1992)

Keating Chambers
10 Essex Street, Outer Temple, London
WC2R 3AA, Telephone: 0171 544 2600
Call Date: July 1979, Middle Temple
Assistant Recorder
Qualifications: [MA, C Eng, MICE]

RAMZAN MOHAMMED ANWAR

10 King's Bench Walk
Ground Floor, Temple, London
EC4Y 7EB, Telephone: 0171 353 7742
E-mail: 10kbw@lineone.net
Call Date: 1995, Lincoln's Inn
Qualifications: [LLB (Hons)(Wolves)]

RANA MOHAMMED AKRAM

Chancery Chambers
1st Floor Offices, 70/72 Chancery Lane,
London WC2A 1AB,
Telephone: 0171 405 6879/6870
Call Date: Nov 1995, Lincoln's Inn
Qualifications: [BSc (Hons), LLB (Hons)]

RANAUTA MISS MANVINDER KAUR

New Court Chambers
Gazette Building, 168 Corporation Street,
Birmingham B4 6TZ,
Telephone: 0121 693 6656
Call Date: 1997, Gray's Inn
Qualifications: [LLB (Glamorgan)]

RANDALL MS JANET

3 Temple Gardens
3rd Floor, Temple, London EC4Y 9AU,
Telephone: 0171 353 0832
Call Date: Oct 1997, Inner Temple
Qualifications: [BA (London), MPhil
(Cantab), CPE (City)]

RANDALL JOHN YEOMAN QC (1995)

St Philip's Chambers
Fountain Court, Steelhouse Lane,
Birmingham B4 6DR,
Telephone: 0121 246 7000
E-mail: clerks@st-philips.co.uk
7 Stone Buildings
Ground Floor, Lincoln's Inn, London
WC2A 3SZ, Telephone: 0171 405 3886/
242 3546 E-mail: chaldous@vossnet.co.uk
Call Date: 1978, Lincoln's Inn
Recorder
Qualifications: [MA (Cantab)]

RANDALL MISS LOUISE ELIZABETH

Keating Chambers
10 Essex Street, Outer Temple, London
WC2R 3AA, Telephone: 0171 544 2600
Call Date: July 1988, Middle Temple
Pupil Master
Qualifications: [BA (Hons) (Keele)]

RANDALL NICHOLAS CLIVE

Devereux Chambers
Devereux Court, London WC2R 3JJ,
Telephone: 0171 353 7534
E-mail: mailbox@devchambers.co.uk
Call Date: Oct 1990, Middle Temple
Qualifications: [LLB (Lond)]

RANDHAWA MISS RAVINDER KAUR

York Chambers
14 Toft Green, York YO1 6JT,
Telephone: 01904 620048
E-mail: [name]@yorkchambers.co.uk
Call Date: Oct 1995, Lincoln's Inn
Qualifications: [LLB (Hons)(Leeds)]

RANDLE SIMON PATRICK

11 Bolt Court (also at 7 Stone Buildings – 1st Floor)
London EC4A 3DQ,
Telephone: 0171 353 2300
E-mail: boltct11@aol.com
Redhill Chambers
Seloduct House, 30 Station Road, Redhill,
Surrey, RH1 1NF,
Telephone: 01737 780781
7 Stone Buildings (also at 11 Bolt Court)
1st Floor, Lincoln's Inn, London
WC2A 3SZ, Telephone: 0171 242 0961
E-mail:larthur@7stonebuildings.law.co.uk
Call Date: July 1982, Inner Temple
Qualifications: [LLB (Hull)]

RANDOLPH FERGUS MARK HARRY

Brick Court Chambers
7-8 Essex Street, London WC2R 3LD,
Telephone: 0171 379 3550
E-mail: [surname]@brickcourt.co.uk
Call Date: July 1985, Middle Temple
Pupil Master
Qualifications: [LLB, Dip French Law]

RANDOLPH PAUL LESLIE

New Court
Temple, London EC4Y 9BE,
Telephone: 0171 583 5123/0510
Call Date: Nov 1971, Inner Temple
Pupil Master
Qualifications: [LLB (Lond)]

RANK PETER MICHAEL

Call Date: July 1976, Middle Temple
Qualifications: [BCL (Oxon) LLB]

RANKIN ANDREW QC (1968)

4 Field Court
Gray's Inn, London WC1R 5EA,
Telephone: 0171 440 6900
E-mail: chambers@4fieldcourt.co.uk
Call Date: 1950, Gray's Inn
Recorder
Qualifications: [BA (Cantab), BL (Edi)]

RANKIN CIARAN EMMANUEL

58 King Street Chambers
1st Floor, Kingsgate House, 51-53 South
King Street, Manchester M2 6DE,
Telephone: 0161 831 7477
Call Date: Nov 1988, Lincoln's Inn
Qualifications: [LLB Hons]

RANKIN JAMES ROWLAND EVELYN

3 Raymond Buildings
Gray's Inn, London WC1R 5BH,
Telephone: 020 7831 3833
E-mail:chambers@threeraymond.demon.co.uk
Call Date: July 1983, Inner Temple
Pupil Master
Qualifications: [LLB (Bucks)]

RANKIN WILLIAM KERR

Oriel Chambers
14 Water Street, Liverpool L2 8TD,
Telephone: 0151 236 7191/236 4321
E-mail: clerks@oriel-chambers.co.uk
Call Date: 1994, Gray's Inn
Qualifications: [LLB]

RANKIN WILLIAM PETER

Oriel Chambers
14 Water Street, Liverpool L2 8TD,
Telephone: 0151 236 7191/236 4321
E-mail: clerks@oriel-chambers.co.uk
Call Date: Nov 1972, Gray's Inn
Pupil Master
Qualifications: [BA (Cantab)]

D

RAPPO PATRICK JAMES

4 Brick Court, Chambers of Anne Rafferty QC
1st Floor, Temple, London EC4Y 9AD,
Telephone: 0171 583 8455
Call Date: Nov 1995, Gray's Inn
Qualifications: [MA (Oxon)]

RASHID MISS JAMILLA BANO

Mitre House Chambers
15-19 Devereux Court, London WC2R 3JJ,
Telephone: 0171 583 8233
Call Date: 1996, Middle Temple
Qualifications: [LLB (Hons)(L'pool)]

RASHID MIRZA ABDUL

Commonwealth Chambers
354 Moseley Road, Birmingham B12 9AZ,
Telephone: 0121 446 5732
Call Date: Nov 1981, Lincoln's Inn
Qualifications: [BA, MA, LLB (Hons)]

RASHID OMAR

Chambers of Mr Peter Crampin QC
Ground Floor, 11 New Square, Lincoln's
Inn, London WC2A 3QB,
Telephone: 020 7831 0081
E-mail: 11newsquare.co.uk
Call Date: Oct 1997, Middle Temple
Qualifications: [BA (Hons)(Cantab)]

RASHID SHAHID

Middlesex Chambers
Suite 3 & 4 Stanley House, Stanley
Avenue, Wembley, Middlesex, HA0 4SB,
Telephone: 0181 902 1499
Call Date: Nov 1982, Middle Temple
Qualifications: [BA (Hons), LLM]

RASUL MISS LUBNA

St Albans Chambers
Dolphin Lodge, Dolphin Yard, Holywell
Hill, St Albans, Herts, AL1 1EX,
Telephone: 01727 843383
Call Date: Oct 1997, Middle Temple
Qualifications: [LLB (Hons)(Brunel)]

RATCLIFFE MISS ANNE KIRKPATRICK

5 Pump Court
Ground Floor, Temple, London
EC4Y 7AP, Telephone: 020 7353 2532
E-mail: FivePump@netcomuk.co.uk
Call Date: Feb 1981, Inner Temple
Pupil Master
Qualifications: [BSc (Soton), Dip Law]

RATCLIFFE PETER DAVID

3 Verulam Buildings
London WC1R 5NT,
Telephone: 0171 831 8441
E-mail: clerks@3verulam.co.uk
Call Date: 1998, Middle Temple
Qualifications: [BA (Hons)(Notts), CPE]

RATHBONE BRIAN BENSON

Richmond Green Chambers
Greyhound House, 23-24 George Street,
Richmond-upon-Thames, Surrey,
TW9 1HY, Telephone: 0181 940 1841
E-mail: ptaylor256@aol.com
Call Date: July 1960, Lincoln's Inn
Qualifications: [BA (Hons)]

RATTIGAN MICHAEL PAUL WILLIAM

Crawford Chambers
7 Gerrard House, 23-25 Crawford Place,
London W1H 1HY,
Telephone: 0171 724 0835
Call Date: Oct 1991, Lincoln's Inn
Qualifications: [LLB (Hons) (Lond)]

RAUDNITZ PAUL NIKOLAI

Dr Johnson's Chambers
Two Dr Johnson's Buildings, Temple,
London EC4Y 7AY,
Telephone: 0171 353 4716
E-mail: clerks@2djb.freeserve.co.uk
Call Date: Nov 1994, Inner Temple
Qualifications: [BA (Oxon), CPE]

RAUF SAQIB

East Anglian Chambers
Gresham House, 5 Museum Street,
Ipswich, Suffolk, IP1 1HQ,
Telephone: 01473 214481
E-mail: ipswich@ealaw.co.uk

East Anglian Chambers
52 North Hill, Colchester, Essex, CO1 1PY,
Telephone: 01206 572756
E-mail: colchester@ealaw.co.uk
East Anglian Chambers
57 London Street, Norwich NR2 1HL,
Telephone: 01603 617351
E-mail: norwich@ealaw.co.uk
Call Date: 1996, Gray's Inn
Qualifications: [LLB (E. Anglia), LLM (Leiden
Uni, Netherlands)]

RAW EDWARD

Francis Taylor Building
3rd Floor, Temple, London EC4Y 7BY,
Telephone: 0171 797 7250
Call Date: July 1963, Inner Temple
Pupil Master
Qualifications: [MA (Oxon)]

RAWAT BILAL MAHMAD

9 Bedford Row
London WC1R 4AZ,
Telephone: 0171 242 3555
E-mail: clerks@9br.co.uk
Call Date: Oct 1995, Middle Temple
Qualifications: [B.Sc (Hons), PhD, Dip Law]

RAWCLIFFE ANTHONY MARK WILSON

Adrian Lyon's Chambers
14 Castle Street, Liverpool L2 0NE,
Telephone: 0151 236 4421/8240
E-mail: chambers14@aol.com
Call Date: Nov 1996, Middle Temple
Qualifications: [BA (Hons)]

RAWLEY ALAN DAVID QC (1977)

35 Essex Street
Temple, London WC2R 3AR,
Telephone: 0171 353 6381
E-mail: derek_jenkins@link.org
Call Date: June 1958, Middle Temple
Recorder
Qualifications: [MA (Oxon)]

RAWLEY MISS DOMINIQUE JANE

Atkin Chambers
1 Atkin Building, Gray's Inn, London
WC1R 5AT, Telephone: 020 7404 0102
E-mail: clerks@atkin-chambers.co.uk
Call Date: Nov 1991, Middle Temple
Qualifications: [BA Hons (Cantab)]

RAWLINGS CLIVE PATRICK

Goldsmith Building
1st Floor, Temple, London EC4Y 7BL,
Telephone: 0171 353 7881
E-mail:clerks@goldsmith-building.law.co.uk
Call Date: Nov 1994, Inner Temple
Qualifications: [BA (Bradford), CPE (Middx)]

RAWLINSON MICHAEL EDWARD

28 St John Street
Manchester M3 4DJ,
Telephone: 0161 834 8418
E-mail: clerk@28stjohnst.co.uk
Call Date: Nov 1991, Inner Temple
Qualifications: [LLB (Manch)]

RAY JONATHAN RICHARD

Thomas More Chambers
52 Carey Street, Lincoln's Inn, London
WC2A 2JB, Telephone: 0171 404 7000
E-mail: clerks@thomasmore.law.co.uk
Call Date: July 1980, Gray's Inn
Pupil Master
Qualifications: [BA (Hons)]

RAY-CROSBY MISS IRENA WYVIS

6 King's Bench Walk
Ground Floor, Temple, London
EC4Y 7DR, Telephone: 0171 583 0410
E-mail: worsley@6kbw.freeserve.co.uk
Call Date: Nov 1990, Middle Temple
Qualifications: [MA (Oxon)]

RAYBAUD MRS JUNE ROSE

96 Gray's Inn Road
London WC1X 8AL,
Telephone: 0171 405 0585
Call Date: Nov 1990, Inner Temple
Qualifications: [BA (Kent)]

RAYMENT MR. BENEDICK MICHAEL

One King's Bench Walk
1st Floor, Temple, London EC4Y 7DB,
Telephone: 0171 936 1500
E-mail: ddear@1kbw.co.uk
Call Date: Oct 1996, Inner Temple
Qualifications: [MA (Hons) , BCL (Oxon)]

RAYMOND JEAN-GILLES

John Street Chambers
2 John Street, London WC1N 2HJ,
Telephone: 0171 242 1911
E-mail: john.street_chambers@virgin.net
Call Date: Nov 1982, Lincoln's Inn
Pupil Master
Qualifications: [LLB (Wales)]

RAYNER JAMES JONATHAN ELWYN QC (1988)

5 New Square
Ground Floor, Lincoln's Inn, London
WC2A 3RJ, Telephone: 020 7404 0404
E-mail: chambers@fivenewsquare.demon.co.
uk
Call Date: Nov 1971, Lincoln's Inn
Recorder
Qualifications: [MA LLM (Cantab), Lic.Sp.en
droit, Europeen]

RAYNOR PHILIP RONALD QC (1994)

40 King Street
Manchester M2 6BA,
Telephone: 0161 832 9082
E-mail: clerks@40kingstreet.co.uk
Hardwicke Building
New Square, Lincoln's Inn, London
WC2A 3SB, Telephone: 020 7242 2523
E-mail: clerks@hardwicke.co.uk
The Chambers of Philip Raynor QC
5 Park Place, Leeds LS1 2RU,
Telephone: 0113 242 1123
Call Date: July 1973, Inner Temple
Recorder
Qualifications: [MA (Cantab)]

RAYSON MISS JANE VIVIENNE

2 Gray's Inn Square Chambers
2nd Floor, Gray's Inn, London WC1R 5AA,
Telephone: 020 7242 0328
E-mail: clerks@2gis.co.uk
Call Date: July 1982, Gray's Inn
Pupil Master
Qualifications: [LLB (Hons)]

REA MISS KAREN MARIE-JEANNE

Assize Court Chambers
14 Small Street, Bristol BS1 1DE,
Telephone: 0117 9264587
E-mail: chambers@assize-court-chambers.co.uk
Call Date: July 1980, Gray's Inn
Pupil Master
Qualifications: [BA, RGN]

READ GRAHAM STEPHEN

Devereux Chambers
Devereux Court, London WC2R 3JJ,
Telephone: 0171 353 7534
E-mail: mailbox@devchambers.co.uk
Call Date: July 1981, Gray's Inn
Pupil Master
Qualifications: [MA (Cantab)]

READ PROFESSOR JAMES STRACEY

2 Paper Buildings
1st Floor, Temple, London EC4Y 7ET,
Telephone: 020 7556 5500
E-mail: clerks@2pbbarristers.co.uk
Call Date: Feb 1954, Gray's Inn

READ LIONEL FRANK QC (1973)

1 Serjeants' Inn
4th Floor, Temple, London EC4Y 1NH,
Telephone: 0171 583 1355
E-mail: clerks@serjeants-inn.co.uk
Call Date: Feb 1954, Gray's Inn
Recorder
Qualifications: [MA (Cantab)]

READ SIMON ERIC

8 King's Bench Walk
2nd Floor, Temple, London EC4Y 7DU,
Telephone: 0171 797 8888
8 King's Bench Walk North
1 Park Square East, Leeds LS1 2NE,
Telephone: 0113 2439797
Call Date: Nov 1989, Inner Temple
Qualifications: [LLB (Warc)]

READE DAVID JARRETT

4 Paper Buildings
1st Floor, Temple, London EC4Y 7EX,
Telephone: 0171 583 0816/353 1131
E-mail: clerks@4paperbuildings.co.uk
Call Date: July 1983, Middle Temple
Pupil Master
Qualifications: [LLB (B'ham)]

READE KEVIN

Martins Building
2nd Floor, No 4 Water Street, Liverpool
L2 3SP, Telephone: 0151 236 5818/4919
Call Date: July 1983, Gray's Inn
Qualifications: [LLB (L'pool)]

READHEAD SIMON JOHN HOWARD

No. 1 Serjeants' Inn
5th Floor Fleet Street, Temple, London
EC4Y 1LH, Telephone: 0171 415 6666
E-mail:no1serjeantsinn@btinternet.com
Call Date: July 1979, Middle Temple
Pupil Master, Assistant Recorder
Qualifications: [BCL, MA (Oxon)]

READINGS DOUGLAS GEORGE

St Philip's Chambers
Fountain Court, Steelhouse Lane,
Birmingham B4 6DR,
Telephone: 0121 246 7000
E-mail: clerks@st-philips.co.uk
Call Date: July 1972, Middle Temple
Assistant Recorder
Qualifications: [MA (Cantab)]

REAL MISS KIRSTY NICHOLA

Albion Chambers
Broad Street, Bristol BS1 1DR,
Telephone: 0117 9272144
Call Date: Oct 1996, Inner Temple
Qualifications: [LLB (Notts)]

REANEY MISS JANET ELIZABETH

Corn Exchange Chambers
5th Floor, Fenwick Street, Liverpool
L2 7QS, Telephone: 0151 227 1081/5009
Call Date: July 1987, Middle Temple
Qualifications: [MA (Cantab)]

RECORD MRS CELIA SAINT CLAIRE

Chambers of Harjit Singh
Ground Floor, 2 Middle Temple Lane,
Temple, London EC4Y 9AA,
Telephone: 0171 353 1356 (4 Lines)
Call Date: 1998, Middle Temple
Qualifications: [LLB (Hons)]

RECTOR MISS PENELOPE JANE

Five Paper Buildings
1st Floor, Five Paper Bldgs, Temple,
London EC4Y 7HB,
Telephone: 0171 583 6117
E-mail:clerks@5-paperbuildings.law.co.uk
Call Date: 1980, Gray's Inn
Qualifications: [LLB (Hons) (Lond)]

Fax: 0171 353 0075; DX: 365 Chancery Lane

Types of work: Common law (general),
Companies investigations, Crime, Crime –
corporate fraud, Financial services

Circuit: South Eastern

Other professional experience: Inspector
appointed by the Secretary of State for
Trade and Industry (Companies Act 1985
and Financial Services Act 1986)

REDDIFORD ANTHONY JAMES

Guildhall Chambers
22-26 Broad Street, Bristol BS1 2HG,
Telephone: 0117 9273366
E-mail:civil.clerks@guildhallchambers.co.uk and
criminal.clerks@guildhallchambers.co.uk
Call Date: Nov 1991, Inner Temple
Qualifications: [BA (Warw), Dip Law]

REDDIHOUGH JOHN HARGREAVES

9 Gough Square
London EC4A 3DE,
Telephone: 020 7832 0500
E-mail: clerks@9goughsq.co.uk
Call Date: July 1969, Gray's Inn
Recorder
Qualifications: [LLB]

REDDISH JOHN WILSON

One King's Bench Walk
1st Floor, Temple, London EC4Y 7DB,
Telephone: 0171 936 1500
E-mail: ddear@1kbw.co.uk
Call Date: July 1973, Middle Temple
Pupil Master
Qualifications: [MA (Oxon)]

REDFERN DAVID ALAN

One Essex Court
Ground Floor, Temple, London
EC4Y 9AR, Telephone: 020 7583 2000
E-mail: clerks@oneessexcourt.co.uk
Call Date: May 1995, Middle Temple
Qualifications: [MA (Cantab), FCIArb]

REDFERN MICHAEL HOWARD QC (1993)

28 St John Street
Manchester M3 4DJ,
Telephone: 0161 834 8418
E-mail: clerk@28stjohnst.co.uk
Call Date: 1970, Inner Temple
Recorder
Qualifications: [LLB (Leeds)]

REDFORD MISS JESSICA KATE

3 Dr Johnson's Buildings
Ground Floor, Temple, London
EC4Y 7BA, Telephone: 0171 353 4854
E-mail: clerks@3djb.co.uk
Call Date: Nov 1994, Inner Temple
Qualifications: [BA (Hons) (Oxon), CPE]

REDGRAVE ADRIAN ROBERT FRANK QC (1992)

No. 1 Serjeants' Inn
5th Floor Fleet Street, Temple, London
EC4Y 1LH, Telephone: 0171 415 6666
E-mail:no1serjeantsinn@btinternet.com
Call Date: Nov 1968, Inner Temple
Recorder
Qualifications: [LLB]

REDGRAVE WILLIAM ALEXANDER FRANK

9 Bedford Row
London WC1R 4AZ,
Telephone: 0171 242 3555
E-mail: clerks@9br.co.uk
Call Date: Oct 1995, Inner Temple
Qualifications: [BA (Hons), Dip Law]

REDHEAD LEROY PETER BASIL

3 Gray's Inn Square
Ground Floor, London WC1R 5AH,
Telephone: 0171 520 5600
E-mail: clerks@3gis.co.uk
Call Date: Nov 1982, Lincoln's Inn
Qualifications: [LLB (Lond); LLM]

REDMAYNE SIMON MARK

East Anglian Chambers
57 London Street, Norwich NR2 1HL,
Telephone: 01603 617351
E-mail: norwich@ealaw.co.uk
East Anglian Chambers
52 North Hill, Colchester, Essex, CO1 1PY,
Telephone: 01206 572756
E-mail: colchester@ealaw.co.uk
East Anglian Chambers
Gresham House, 5 Museum Street,
Ipswich, Suffolk, IP1 1HQ,
Telephone: 01473 214481
E-mail: ipswich@ealaw.co.uk
Call Date: July 1982, Inner Temple
Pupil Master
Qualifications: [BA (Oxon)]

REDMOND STEVEN

4 Fountain Court
Steelhouse Lane, Birmingham B4 6DR,
Telephone: 0121 236 3476
Call Date: July 1975, Gray's Inn
Pupil Master
Qualifications: [BA]

REECE BRIAN ALFRED WILLIAM

1 Middle Temple Lane
Temple, London EC4Y 1LT,
Telephone: 0171 583 0659 (12 Lines)
E-mail: chambers@1mtl.co.uk
Call Date: July 1974, Middle Temple
Pupil Master
Qualifications: [LLB (Lond)]

REECE RUPERT VAUGHAN PAYNTER

2 Temple Gardens
Temple, London EC4Y 9AY,
Telephone: 0171 583 6041
E-mail: clerks@2templegardens.co.uk
Call Date: Oct 1992, Inner Temple
Qualifications: [BA (Cambs), DESS
(Paris-Assas), Examen D'aptitude, (Paris)]

REED JASON LESLIE RICHARD

Phoenix Chambers
First Floor, Gray's Inn Chambers, Gray's
Inn, London WC1R 5JA,
Telephone: 0171 404 7888
E-mail:clerks@phoenix-chambers.co.uk
Call Date: Oct 1994, Lincoln's Inn
Qualifications: [BA (Hons)(Leeds)]

REED JEREMY NIGEL

19 Old Buildings
Lincoln's Inn, London WC2A 3UP,
Telephone: 0171 405 2001
E-mail: clerks@oldbuildingsip.com
Call Date: Oct 1997, Middle Temple
Qualifications: [BA (Hons)(Cantab), CPE
(Lond)]

REED JOHN WILLIAM RUPERT

Wilberforce Chambers
8 New Square, Lincoln's Inn, London
WC2A 3QP, Telephone: 0171 306 0102
E-mail: chambers@wilberforce.co.uk
Call Date: Oct 1996, Lincoln's Inn
Qualifications: [BA (Hons)(Oxon), BA
(Hons)(Cantab), LLM (Harvard)]

Types of work: Chancery (general), Chancery
land law, Commercial, Commercial litigation, Commercial property, Company and
commercial, Equity, wills and trusts, Family
provision, Insolvency, Landlord and tenant,
Partnerships, Pensions, Probate and administration

REED JULIAN WINN

9 Park Place
Cardiff CF1 3DP,
Telephone: 01222 382731
Call Date: Nov 1991, Inner Temple
Qualifications: [LLB]

REED MATTHEW ROBERT

1 Serjeants' Inn
4th Floor, Temple, London EC4Y 1NH,
Telephone: 0171 583 1355
E-mail: clerks@serjeants-inn.co.uk
Call Date: Nov 1995, Middle Temple
Qualifications: [MA (Hons)]

REED PAUL STUART MALCOLM

Hardwicke Building
New Square, Lincoln's Inn, London
WC2A 3SB, Telephone: 020 7242 2523
E-mail: clerks@hardwicke.co.uk
*Call Date: July 1988, Inner Temple
Pupil Master*
Qualifications: [LLB, MSc, ACIArb]

REED MISS PENELOPE JANE

9 Stone Buildings
Lincoln's Inn, London WC2A 3NN,
Telephone: 0171 404 5055
E-mail: clerks@9stoneb.law.co.uk
*Call Date: July 1983, Inner Temple
Pupil Master*
Qualifications: [LLB (Lond)]

REED PIERS KNOWLE MOORHOUSE

3 Temple Gardens
Lower Ground Floor, Temple, London
EC4Y 9AU, Telephone: 0171 353 3102/5/
9297 E-mail: clerks@3tg.co.uk
*Call Date: Nov 1974, Lincoln's Inn
Pupil Master*

REED MISS SUSAN CATHERINE

9 Bedford Row
London WC1R 4AZ,
Telephone: 0171 242 3555
E-mail: clerks@9br.co.uk
*Call Date: July 1984, Gray's Inn
Pupil Master*
Qualifications: [LLB (Manch)]

REEDER JOHN QC (1989)

4 Field Court
Gray's Inn, London WC1R 5EA,
Telephone: 0171 440 6900
E-mail: chambers@4fieldcourt.co.uk
Call Date: July 1971, Gray's Inn
Qualifications: [LLM, PhD]

REEDER STEPHEN

Doughty Street Chambers
11 Doughty Street, London WC1N 2PG,
Telephone: 0171 404 1313
E-mail:enquiries@doughtystreet.co.uk
Call Date: Nov 1991, Middle Temple
Qualifications: [LLB (Hons)]

REEDS GRAHAM JOSEPH

11 King's Bench Walk
1st Floor, Temple, London EC4Y 7EQ,
Telephone: 0171 353 3337
E-mail: fmuller11@aol.com
11 King's Bench Walk
3 Park Court, Park Cross Street, Leeds
LS1 2QH, Telephone: 0113 297 1200
Call Date: Nov 1984, Middle Temple
Pupil Master
Qualifications: [LLB (Sheff)]

REEDS MISS MADELEINE LUCIA

No. 6
6 Park Square, Leeds LS1 2LW,
Telephone: 0113 2459763
E-mail: chambers@no6.co.uk
Call Date: Nov 1988, Lincoln's Inn
Qualifications: [LLB Hons (Sheff)]

REES MISS CAROLINE ELIZABETH

33 Park Place
Cardiff CF1 3BA,
Telephone: 02920 233313
Call Date: Oct 1994, Gray's Inn
Qualifications: [LLB]

REES CHRISTOPHER LLOYD

33 Park Place
Cardiff CF1 3BA,
Telephone: 02920 233313
Call Date: Nov 1996, Lincoln's Inn
Qualifications: [BA (Cantab)]

REES DAVID BENJAMIN

5 Stone Buildings
Lincoln's Inn, London WC2A 3XT,
Telephone: 0171 242 6201
E-mail:clerks@5-stonebuildings.law.co.uk
Call Date: Oct 1994, Lincoln's Inn
Qualifications: [BA (Hons) (Oxon)]

REES EDWARD PARRY QC (1998)

Doughty Street Chambers
11 Doughty Street, London WC1N 2PG,
Telephone: 0171 404 1313
E-mail:enquiries@doughtystreet.co.uk
Call Date: Feb 1973, Gray's Inn
Qualifications: [LLB (Wales)]

REES GARETH DAVID

Hollis Whiteman Chambers
3rd Floor, Queen Elizabeth Bldg, Temple,
London EC4Y 9BS,
Telephone: 020 7583 5766
E-mail:barristers@holliswhiteman.co.uk
Call Date: July 1981, Gray's Inn
Pupil Master
Qualifications: [BA]

REES HEFIN EDNYFED

10 King's Bench Walk
1st Floor, Temple, London EC4Y 7EB,
Telephone: 0171 353 2501
Call Date: Nov 1992, Inner Temple
Qualifications: [BA (Hons)]

REES IEUAN

30 Park Place
Cardiff CF1 3BA,
Telephone: 01222 398421
E-mail: 100757.1456@compuserve.com
10 King's Bench Walk
1st Floor, Temple, London EC4Y 7EB,
Telephone: 0171 353 2501
Call Date: Nov 1982, Gray's Inn
Pupil Master
Qualifications: [BSc (Cardiff)]

REES JAMES WILLIAM STEWART

2 King's Bench Walk
Ground Floor, Temple, London
EC4Y 7DE, Telephone: 0171 353 1746
E-mail: 2kbw@atlas.co.uk
King's Bench Chambers
115 North Hill, Plymouth PL4 8JY,
Telephone: 01752 221551
Call Date: Nov 1994, Gray's Inn
Qualifications: [BA (Dumelm)]

REES JOHN CHARLES QC (1991)

33 Park Place
Cardiff CF1 3BA,
Telephone: 02920 233313
Call Date: July 1972, Lincoln's Inn
Assistant Recorder
Qualifications: [LLB (Cantab)]

REES JONATHAN DAVID

2 Harcourt Buildings
1st Floor, Temple, London EC4Y 9DB,
Telephone: 020 7353 2112
Call Date: Nov 1987, Gray's Inn
Pupil Master
Qualifications: [BA (Oxon)]

REES MATTHEW

Iscoed Chambers
86 St Helen's Road, Swansea, West
Glamorgan, SA1 4BQ,
Telephone: 01792 652988/9/330
Call Date: Oct 1996, Gray's Inn
Qualifications: [LLB (Notts)]

REES OWEN HUW

Iscoed Chambers
86 St Helen's Road, Swansea, West
Glamorgan, SA1 4BQ,
Telephone: 01792 652988/9/330
Call Date: July 1983, Gray's Inn
Pupil Master
Qualifications: [LLB (Wales)]

REES PAUL STUART

1 Crown Office Row
Ground Floor, Temple, London
EC4Y 7HH, Telephone: 0171 797 7500
E-mail: mail@onecrownofficerow.com
Call Date: Nov 1980, Gray's Inn
Qualifications: [MA, M Phil, BCL (Oxon)]

REES PHILLIP

9 Park Place
Cardiff CF1 3DP,
Telephone: 01222 382731
Farrar's Building
Temple, London EC4Y 7BD,
Telephone: 0171 583 9241
E-mail:chambers@farrarsbuilding.co.uk
Call Date: Feb 1965, Middle Temple
Pupil Master, Recorder
Qualifications: [LLB (Bris)]

REES ROBERT CHARLES DAVID

New Walk Chambers
27 New Walk, Leicester LE1 6TE,
Telephone: 0116 2559144
Call Date: Feb 1978, Middle Temple
Pupil Master
Qualifications: [BA, LLB]

REES STEPHEN ROBERT TRISTRAM

Iscoed Chambers
86 St Helen's Road, Swansea, West
Glamorgan, SA1 4BQ,
Telephone: 01792 652988/9/330
Call Date: Nov 1979, Gray's Inn
Pupil Master
Qualifications: [LLB (Wales)]

REES PROFESSOR WILLIAM MICHAEL

Barnard's Inn Chambers
6th Floor, Halton House, 20-23 Holborn,
London EC1N 2JD,
Telephone: 0171 369 6969
E-mail: clerks@biclaw.co.uk
Call Date: July 1973, Inner Temple
Qualifications: [MA (Cantab)]

REESE COLIN EDWARD QC (1987)

Atkin Chambers
1 Atkin Building, Gray's Inn, London
WC1R 5AT, Telephone: 020 7404 0102
E-mail: clerks@atkin-chambers.co.uk
Call Date: July 1973, Gray's Inn
Recorder
Qualifications: [MA (Cantab)]

REEVE MATTHEW FRANCIS

4 Essex Court
Temple, London EC4Y 9AJ,
Telephone: 020 7797 7970
E-mail: clerks@4essexcourt.law.co.uk
Call Date: Nov 1987, Inner Temple
Pupil Master
Qualifications: [MA (Cantab)]

REEVE MISS SUZANNE MARY

9-12 Bell Yard
London WC2A 2LF,
Telephone: 0171 400 1800
E-mail: clerks@bellyard.co.uk
Call Date: Nov 1993, Middle Temple
Qualifications: [BA (Hons)(Oxon)]

REEVELL SIMON JUSTIN

Chambers of Andrew Campbell QC
10 Park Square, Leeds LS1 2LH,
Telephone: 0113 2455438
E-mail: clerks@10pksq.co.uk
Call Date: Oct 1990, Lincoln's Inn
Qualifications: [BA (Econs), Dip Law]

REFFIN MISS CLARE ALYSON

One Essex Court
Ground Floor, Temple, London
EC4Y 9AR, Telephone: 020 7583 2000
E-mail: clerks@oneessexcourt.co.uk
Call Date: July 1981, Middle Temple
Pupil Master
Qualifications: [MA (Cantab)]

REGAN DAVID ROBERT

Chichester Chambers
12 North Pallant, Chichester, West Sussex,
PO19 1TQ, Telephone: 01243 784538
E-mail:clerks@chichesterchambers.law.co.uk
Call Date: Nov 1994, Inner Temple
Qualifications: [MA (Oxon), CPE (City)]

REICHERT KLAUS

5 Paper Buildings
Ground Floor, Temple, London
EC4Y 7HB, Telephone: 0171 583 9275/
583 4555 E-mail: 5paper@link.org
Call Date: Nov 1996, Middle Temple
Qualifications: [BCL (Dublin)]

REID BRIAN CHRISTOPHER

19 Old Buildings
Lincoln's Inn, London WC2A 3UP,
Telephone: 0171 405 2001
E-mail: clerks@oldbuildingsip.com
Call Date: Nov 1971, Middle Temple
Pupil Master
Qualifications: [MA (Cantab) , LLM (Lond)]

REID MISS CAROLINE OLDCORN

14 Gray's Inn Square
Gray's Inn, London WC1R 5JP,
Telephone: 0171 242 0858
E-mail: 100712.2134@compuserve.com
Call Date: Nov 1982, Middle Temple
Pupil Master
Qualifications: [BA PhD (Sheff) Dip, Law
(City)]

REID MISS CLAUDETTE PATRICIA

Chancery Chambers
1st Floor Offices, 70/72 Chancery Lane,
London WC2A 1AB,
Telephone: 0171 405 6879/6870
Call Date: Oct 1990, Gray's Inn
Qualifications: [BA, LLM]

REID DAVID DONALD WILLIAM

3 Paper Buildings
Temple, London EC4Y 7EU,
Telephone: 020 7583 8055
E-mail: London@3paper.com
3 Paper Buildings (Winchester)
4 St Peter Street, Winchester SO23 8BW,
Telephone: 01962 868884
E-mail: winchester@3paper.com
3 Paper Buildings (Bournemouth)
20 Lorne Park Road, Bournemouth,
Dorset, BH1 1JN,
Telephone: 01202 292102
E-mail: Bournemouth@3paper.com
3 Paper Buildings (Oxford)
1 Alfred Street, High Street, Oxford
OX1 4EH, Telephone: 01865 793736
E-mail: oxford@3paper.com
Call Date: Nov 1994, Gray's Inn
Qualifications: [BA (Oxon)]

REID GRAHAM MATTHEW

4 Paper Buildings
Ground Floor, Temple, London
EC4Y 7EX, Telephone: 0171 353 3366/
583 7155
E-mail: clerks@4paperbuildings.com
Call Date: Feb 1993, Middle Temple
Qualifications: [BA (Hons)(Oxon), Dip in
Law (City)]

REID HORACE DEIGHTON

12 Old Square
1st Floor, Lincoln's Inn, London
WC2A 3TX, Telephone: 0171 404 0875
Call Date: July 1975, Lincoln's Inn
Qualifications: [LLB (Lond)]

REID HOWARD BARRINGTON

5 Fountain Court
Steelhouse Lane, Birmingham B4 6DR,
Telephone: 0121 606 0500
E-mail:clerks@5fountaincourt.law.co.uk
Call Date: Feb 1991, Middle Temple
Qualifications: [BA (Hons)]

REID MISS JACQUELINE CLAIRE

11 South Square
2nd Floor, Gray's Inn, London
WC1R 5EU,
Telephone: 0171 405 1222 (24hr messagin
g service)
E-mail: clerks@11southsquare.com
Call Date: Oct 1992, Middle Temple
Qualifications: [BSc (Surrey), MPhil (Lond)]

REID PAUL CAMPBELL

Lincoln House Chambers
5th Floor, Lincoln House, 1 Brazennose
Street, Manchester M2 5EL,
Telephone: 0161 832 5701
E-mail: info@lincolnhse.co.uk
Call Date: July 1973, Gray's Inn
Pupil Master, Recorder
Qualifications: [MA (Cantab)]

REID PAUL WILLIAM

13 King's Bench Walk
1st Floor, Temple, London EC4Y 7EN,
Telephone: 0171 353 7204
E-mail: clerks@13kbw.law.co.uk
King's Bench Chambers
32 Beaumont Street, Oxford OX1 2NP,
Telephone: 01865 311066
E-mail: clerks@kbc-oxford.law.co.uk
Call Date: July 1975, Inner Temple
Pupil Master
Qualifications: [MA (Cantab)]

REID SEBASTIAN PETER SCOTT

2nd Floor, Francis Taylor Building
Temple, London EC4Y 7BY,
Telephone: 0171 353 9942/3157
Call Date: July 1982, Gray's Inn
Qualifications: [BA (Lond) AKC Dip, Law]

REID SILAS JAMES

2 Paper Buildings, Basement North
Temple, London EC4Y 7ET,
Telephone: 0171 936 2613
E-mail: post@2paper.co.uk
Acre Lane Neighbourhood Chambers
30A Acre Lane, London SW2 5SG,
Telephone: 0171 274 4400
E-mail:barristerschambers@acrelane.demon.co.uk
Call Date: 1995, Lincoln's Inn
Qualifications: [BA (Hons)(Cantab), CPE]

REID-CHALMERS MISS EMMA LOUISE

Chambers of Joy Okoye
Suite 1, 2nd Floor Gray's Inn Chambers,
Gray's Inn, London WC1R 5JA,
Telephone: 0171 405 7011
Call Date: July 1996, Lincoln's Inn
Qualifications: [LLB (Hons)]

REIFF-MUSGROVE MISS KAJA

Phoenix Chambers
First Floor, Gray's Inn Chambers, Gray's
Inn, London WC1R 5JA,
Telephone: 0171 404 7888
E-mail:clerks@phoenix-chambers.co.uk
Call Date: Nov 1992, Middle Temple
Qualifications: [BA (Hons, Sussex)]

REILLY MR. DANIEL EDWARD

King's Bench Chambers
Wellington House, 175 Holdenhurst Road,
Bournemouth, Dorset, BH8 8DQ,
Telephone: 01202 250025
E-mail: chambers@kingsbench.co.uk
Call Date: Nov 1995, Middle Temple
Qualifications: [LLB (Hons)]

REILLY JOHN JOSEPH

14 Tooks Court
Cursitor St, London EC4A 1LB,
Telephone: 0171 405 8828
E-mail: clerks@tooks.law.co.uk
Call Date: Nov 1972, Inner Temple
Pupil Master
Qualifications: [BL (Dublin)]

RENFREE PETER GERALD STANLEY

Harbour Court Chambers
11 William Price Gardens, Fareham,
Hampshire, PO16 7PD,
Telephone: 01329 827828
E-mail: peterrenfree@btinternet.com
Call Date: July 1992, Middle Temple
Qualifications: [LLB (Hons)]

RENNIE DAVID JAMES

One King's Bench Walk
1st Floor, Temple, London EC4Y 7DB,
Telephone: 0171 936 1500
E-mail: ddear@1kbw.co.uk
Call Date: July 1976, Inner Temple

Assistant Recorder
Qualifications: [BA]

RENOUF GERARD JOHN PETER

2 Pump Court
1st Floor, Temple, London EC4Y 7AH,
Telephone: 0171 353 5597
Call Date: July 1977, Inner Temple
Pupil Master

RENTON THE HON CLARE OLIVIA

29 Bedford Row Chambers
London WC1R 4HE,
Telephone: 0171 831 2626
Call Date: Nov 1972, Lincoln's Inn

REQUENA STEPHEN

18 Red Lion Court
(Off Fleet Street), London EC4A 3EB,
Telephone: 0171 520 6000
E-mail: chambers@18rlc.co.uk
Call Date: Oct 1997, Inner Temple
Qualifications: [LLB (LSE)]

RESTELL THOMAS GEORGE

Granary Chambers
4 Glenleigh Park Road, Bexhill-On-Sea,
East Sussex, TN39 4EH,
Telephone: 01424 733008
E-mail:restell@granary-law.prestel.co.uk
Call Date: Nov 1976, Middle Temple

RESTRICK ALEXANDER THOMAS

11 King's Bench Walk
Temple, London EC4Y 7EQ,
Telephone: 0171 632 8500/583 0610
E-mail: clerksroom@11kbw.com
Call Date: 1995, Middle Temple
Qualifications: [BA (Hons) (Oxon)]

REYNOLD FREDERIC QC (1982)

New Court Chambers
5 Verulam Buildings, Gray's Inn, London
WC1R 5LY, Telephone: 0171 831 9500
E-mail: mail@newcourtchambers.com
Call Date: July 1960, Gray's Inn
Qualifications: [BA (Oxon)]

REYNOLDS ADRIAN LEONARD

St Mary's Chambers
50 High Pavement, Lace Market,
Nottingham NG1 1HW,
Telephone: 0115 9503503
E-mail: clerks@smc.law.co.uk
Call Date: Nov 1982, Gray's Inn
Pupil Master
Qualifications: [MA (Oxon)]

REYNOLDS PROFESSOR FRANCIS MARTIN BAILLIE QC (ERROR)

S Tomlinson QC
7 King's Bench Walk, Temple, London
EC4Y 7DS, Telephone: 0171 583 0404
E-mail: clerks@7kbw.law.co.uk
Call Date: Feb 1961, Inner Temple
Qualifications: [DCL]

REYNOLDS GARY WILLIAM

24a St John Street
Manchester M3 4DF,
Telephone: 0161 833 9628
Call Date: Nov 1994, Lincoln's Inn
Qualifications: [BSc (Hons)(Portsm), Dip in
Law (Staff)]

REYNOLDS JONATHAN JAMES

2 Middle Temple Lane
3rd Floor, Temple, London EC4Y 9AA,
Telephone: 0171 583 4540
Call Date: Nov 1992, Inner Temple
Qualifications: [LLB (Lond)]

REYNOLDS KIRK QC (1993)

Falcon Chambers
Falcon Court, London EC4Y 1AA,
Telephone: 0171 353 2484
E-mail: clerks@falcon-chambers.com
Call Date: July 1974, Middle Temple
Qualifications: [MA (Cantab)]

REYNOLDS MISS STELLA LOUISE

3 Temple Gardens
Lower Ground Floor, Temple, London
EC4Y 9AU, Telephone: 0171 353 3102/5/
9297 E-mail: clerks@3tg.co.uk
Call Date: July 1983, Gray's Inn
Qualifications: [LLB (Liverpool)]

REYNOLDS STEPHEN ALAN

29 Bedford Row Chambers
London WC1R 4HE,
Telephone: 0171 831 2626
Call Date: Nov 1987, Inner Temple
Qualifications: [BA]

REZA HASHIM

17 Bedford Row
London WC1R 4EB,
Telephone: 0171 831 7314
E-mail: iboard7314@aol.com
Call Date: July 1981, Middle Temple
Pupil Master
Qualifications: [LLB (Leics)]

RHEE MISS DEOK-JOO

4-5 Gray's Inn Square
Ground Floor, Gray's Inn, London
WC1R 5JP, Telephone: 0171 404 5252
E-mail:chambers@4-5graysinnsquare.co.uk
Call Date: 1998, Gray's Inn
Qualifications: [BA, BCL (Oxon)]

RHIND MARK ALEXANDER

24a St John Street
Manchester M3 4DF,
Telephone: 0161 833 9628
Call Date: Nov 1989, Middle Temple
Qualifications: [LLB Hons (Manc)]

RHODES MISS AMANDA LOUISE

Holborn Chambers
6 Gate Street, Lincoln's Inn Fields, London
WC2A 3HP, Telephone: 0171 242 6060
Call Date: May 1990, Lincoln's Inn
Qualifications: [LL.B.]

RHODES COLIN HARVEY

1 Gray's Inn Square
Ground Floor, London WC1R 5AA,
Telephone: 0171 405 8946/7/8
Call Date: Nov 1994, Lincoln's Inn
Qualifications: [LLB (Hons)(Leic)]

RHODES MISS KAREN

1 Inner Temple Lane
Temple, London EC4Y 1AF,
Telephone: 020 7353 0933
Call Date: Oct 1990, Gray's Inn
Qualifications: [BH (Hons), Dip Law]

RHODES NICHOLAS PIERS

Dr Johnson's Chambers
Two Dr Johnson's Buildings, Temple,
London EC4Y 7AY,
Telephone: 0171 353 4716
E-mail: clerks@2djb.freeserve.co.uk
Call Date: July 1981, Lincoln's Inn
Pupil Master
Qualifications: [LLB (E Anglia)]

RHODES ROBERT ELLIOTT QC (1989)

4 King's Bench Walk
Ground/First Floor/Basement, Temple,
London EC4Y 7DL,
Telephone: 0171 822 8822
E-mail: 4kbw@barristersatlaw.com
Call Date: 1968, Inner Temple
Recorder
Qualifications: [MA (Oxon)]

RHYS JOHN OWEN

The Chambers of Leolin Price CBE, QC
10 Old Square, Lincoln's Inn, London
WC2A 3SU, Telephone: 0171 405 0758
St Mary's Chambers
50 High Pavement, Lace Market,
Nottingham NG1 1HW,
Telephone: 0115 9503503
E-mail: clerks@smc.law.co.uk
Call Date: July 1976, Gray's Inn
Pupil Master
Qualifications: [MA (Cantab)]

RHYS MS MEGAN JILL

Paradise Chambers
26 Paradise Square, Sheffield S1 2DE,
Telephone: 0114 2738951
E-mail: timbooth@paradise-sq.co.uk
Call Date: Nov 1994, Inner Temple
Qualifications: [LLB (Sheff)]

RICE CHRISTOPHER DOUGLAS

2 Gray's Inn Square Chambers
2nd Floor, Gray's Inn, London WC1R 5AA,
Telephone: 020 7242 0328
E-mail: clerks@2gis.co.uk
Call Date: July 1991, Middle Temple
Qualifications: [BA (Hons)]

RICH MISS ANN BARBARA

5 Stone Buildings
Lincoln's Inn, London WC2A 3XT,
Telephone: 0171 242 6201
E-mail:clerks@5-stonebuildings.law.co.uk
Call Date: Oct 1990, Gray's Inn
Pupil Master
Qualifications: [MA (Cantab), Dip Law]

RICH CHARLES STEPHEN ANTHONY

Westgate Chambers
67a Westgate Road, Newcastle upon Tyne
NE1 1SG, Telephone: 0191 261 4407/
2329785
E-mail:pracman@westgatechambers.law.co.u
k
Call Date: July 1972, Gray's Inn
Qualifications: [LLB (Hons), LLM]

RICH JONATHAN BERNARD GEORGE

5 Paper Buildings
Ground Floor, Temple, London
EC4Y 7HB, Telephone: 0171 583 9275/
583 4555 E-mail: 5paper@link.org
Call Date: July 1989, Middle Temple
Qualifications: [MA (Cantab)]

RICH SIMEON PAUL

Queens Square Chambers
56 Queens Square, Bristol BS1 4PR,
Telephone: 0117 921 1966
Call Date: Nov 1991, Lincoln's Inn
Qualifications: [LLB (Hons)]

RICHARD LORD IVOR SEWARD QC (1971)

2 Paper Buildings
1st Floor, Temple, London EC4Y 7ET,
Telephone: 020 7556 5500
E-mail: clerks@2pbbarristers.co.uk
Call Date: 1955, Inner Temple
Qualifications: [BA (Oxon)]

RICHARDS DAVID ANTHONY STEWART QC (1992)

Erskine Chambers
30 Lincoln's Inn Fields, Lincoln's Inn,
London WC2A 3PF,
Telephone: 0171 242 5532
E-mail:clerks@erskine-chambers.co.uk
Call Date: Nov 1974, Inner Temple
Qualifications: [MA (Cantab)]

RICHARDS CAPTAIN DAVID JAMES MARTIN

East Anglian Chambers
52 North Hill, Colchester, Essex, CO1 1PY,
Telephone: 01206 572756
E-mail: colchester@ealaw.co.uk
East Anglian Chambers
Gresham House, 5 Museum Street,
Ipswich, Suffolk, IP1 1HQ,
Telephone: 01473 214481
E-mail: ipswich@ealaw.co.uk
East Anglian Chambers
57 London Street, Norwich NR2 1HL,
Telephone: 01603 617351
E-mail: norwich@ealaw.co.uk
Call Date: July 1989, Middle Temple
Qualifications: [LLB (Cantab), MA (Cantab),
LLM]

RICHARDS DAVID RAWSON

1 Harcourt Buildings
2nd Floor, Temple, London EC4Y 9DA,
Telephone: 0171 353 9421/0375
E-mail:clerks@1harcourtbuildings.law.co.uk
Call Date: July 1981, Inner Temple
Qualifications: [LLB (Brunel)]

RICHARDS HUGH ALAN

5 Fountain Court
Steelhouse Lane, Birmingham B4 6DR,
Telephone: 0121 606 0500
E-mail:clerks@5fountaincourt.law.co.uk
Call Date: Nov 1992, Inner Temple
Qualifications: [BSc (Wales), Dip in Law]

RICHARDS IAN

Pump Court Tax Chambers
16 Bedford Row, London WC1R 4EB,
Telephone: 0171 414 8080
Call Date: Nov 1971, Lincoln's Inn
Pupil Master
Qualifications: [BA]

RICHARDS MISS JENNIFER

39 Essex Street
London WC2R 3AT,
Telephone: 0171 832 1111
E-mail: clerks@39essex.co.uk
Call Date: Oct 1991, Middle Temple
Pupil Master
Qualifications: [MA (Hons) (Cantab), LLM (Toronto)]

RICHARDS JEREMY SIMON

Octagon House
19 Colegate, Norwich NR3 1AT,
Telephone: 01603 623186
E-mail: admin@octagon-chambers.co.uk
Call Date: July 1981, Gray's Inn
Pupil Master, Assistant Recorder
Qualifications: [LLB (Wales)]

RICHARDS MS JOANNE

John Street Chambers
2 John Street, London WC1N 2HJ,
Telephone: 0171 242 1911
E-mail:john.street_chambers@virgin.net
Call Date: Nov 1992, Inner Temple
Qualifications: [BA, Dip in Law (City)]

RICHARDS JONATHAN GLYN

4 Fountain Court
Steelhouse Lane, Birmingham B4 6DR,
Telephone: 0121 236 3476
Call Date: 1996, Middle Temple
Qualifications: [BA (Hons)(Oxon)]

RICHARDS DR JONATHAN NICHOLAS

Godolphin Chambers
50 Castle Street, Truro, Cornwall,
TR1 3AF, Telephone: 01872 276312
E-mail:theclerks@godolphin.force9.co.uk
Call Date: 1995, Middle Temple
Qualifications: [MB, Ch.B (Bris), CPE]

RICHARDS MISS KATHY JANINE

Baker Street Chambers
9 Baker Street, Middlesbrough TS1 2LF,
Telephone: 01642 873873
Call Date: Oct 1995, Lincoln's Inn
Qualifications: [LLB (Hons)(Northumb)]

RICHARDS PHILIP BRIAN

30 Park Place
Cardiff CF1 3BA,
Telephone: 01222 398421
E-mail: 100757.1456@compuserve.com
Francis Taylor Building
3rd Floor, Temple, London EC4Y 7BY,
Telephone: 0171 797 7250
Call Date: July 1969, Inner Temple
Pupil Master, Assistant Recorder
Qualifications: [LLB (Bris) (Hons)]

RICHARDS STEPHEN THOMAS

Queens Square Chambers
56 Queens Square, Bristol BS1 4PR,
Telephone: 0117 921 1966
Call Date: Oct 1993, Middle Temple
Qualifications: [BA (Hons))L'pool), BA (Hons)(Cantab), Dip History Studies]

RICHARDSON MISS ANNE LYDIA

Broad Chare
33 Broad Chare, Newcastle upon Tyne
NE1 3DQ, Telephone: 0191 232 0541
E-mail:clerks@broadcharechambers.law.co.uk
Call Date: July 1986, Inner Temple
Pupil Master
Qualifications: [LLB (B'ham)]

RICHARDSON DAVID JOHN

13 King's Bench Walk
1st Floor, Temple, London EC4Y 7EN,
Telephone: 0171 353 7204
E-mail: clerks@13kbw.law.co.uk
King's Bench Chambers
32 Beaumont Street, Oxford OX1 2NP,
Telephone: 01865 311066
E-mail: clerks@kbc-oxford.law.co.uk
Call Date: July 1973, Middle Temple
Pupil Master, Recorder
Qualifications: [MA, LLB (Cantab)]

RICHARDSON GARTH DOUGLAS ANTHONY

3 Paper Buildings
Temple, London EC4Y 7EU,
Telephone: 020 7583 8055
E-mail: London@3paper.com
3 Paper Buildings (Bournemouth)
20 Lorne Park Road, Bournemouth,
Dorset, BH1 1JN,
Telephone: 01202 292102
E-mail: Bournemouth@3paper.com

3 Paper Buildings (Winchester)
4 St Peter Street, Winchester SO23 8BW,
Telephone: 01962 868884
E-mail: winchester@3paper.com
3 Paper Buildings (Oxford)
1 Alfred Street, High Street, Oxford
OX1 4EH, Telephone: 01865 793736
E-mail: oxford@3paper.com
Call Date: July 1975, Middle Temple
Pupil Master
Qualifications: [LLB]

RICHARDSON GILES JOHN

Serle Court Chambers
6 New Square, Lincoln's Inn, London
WC2A 3QS, Telephone: 0171 242 6105
E-mail: clerks@serlecourt.co.uk
Call Date: 1997, Inner Temple
Qualifications: [BA (Oxon) BCL (Oxon)]

RICHARDSON JAMES DAVID

Trinity Chambers
9-12 Trinity Chare, Quayside, Newcastle
upon Tyne NE1 3DF,
Telephone: 0191 232 1927
E-mail: info@trinitychambers.co.uk
Call Date: Nov 1982, Gray's Inn
Pupil Master
Qualifications: [LLB (Leic)]

RICHARDSON JEREMY WILLIAM

11 King's Bench Walk
1st Floor, Temple, London EC4Y 7EQ,
Telephone: 0171 353 3337
E-mail: fmuller11@aol.com
11 King's Bench Walk
3 Park Court, Park Cross Street, Leeds
LS1 2QH, Telephone: 0113 297 1200
Call Date: July 1980, Inner Temple
Pupil Master
Qualifications: [LLB (Lond)]

RICHARDSON PAUL

New Court Chambers
3 Broad Chare, Newcastle upon Tyne
NE1 3DQ, Telephone: 0191 232 1980
Call Date: Nov 1986, Middle Temple
Qualifications: [BA]

RICHARDSON PAUL ANDREW

Bell Yard Chambers
116/118 Chancery Lane, London
WC2A 1PP, Telephone: 0171 306 9292
Call Date: Feb 1993, Inner Temple
Qualifications: [LLB (So'ton)]

RICHARDSON PAUL BRAYSHAW

Peel Court Chambers
45 Hardman Street, Manchester M3 3PL,
Telephone: 0161 832 3791
E-mail: clerks@peelct.co.uk
Call Date: Nov 1972, Middle Temple
Pupil Master
Qualifications: [MA (Oxon)]

RICHARDSON (PETER) JAMES

23 Essex Street
London WC2R 3AS,
Telephone: 0171 413 0353/836 8366
E-mail:clerks@essexstreet23.demon.co.uk
Call Date: July 1975, Gray's Inn
Pupil Master
Qualifications: [LLM LLB (Lond) Dip, Crim
(Cantab)]

RICHARDSON MISS SARAH JANE

Enterprise Chambers
9 Old Square, Lincoln's Inn, London
WC2A 3SR, Telephone: 0171 405 9471
E-mail:enterprise.london@dial.pipex.com
Enterprise Chambers
38 Park Square, Leeds LS1 2PA,
Telephone: 0113 246 0391
E-mail:enterprise.leeds@dial.pipex.com
Enterprise Chambers
65 Quayside, Newcastle upon Tyne
NE1 3DS, Telephone: 0191 222 3344
E-mail:enterprise.newcastle@dial.pipex.com
Call Date: Oct 1993, Inner Temple
Qualifications: [BA (Nott'm)]

RICHMOND BERNARD GRANT

Lamb Building
Ground Floor, Temple, London
EC4Y 7AS, Telephone: 020 7797 7788
E-mail: lamb.building@link.org
Call Date: July 1988, Middle Temple
Pupil Master
Qualifications: [LLB (Hons)]

RICKARBY WILLIAM EDMUND

6 Fountain Court
Steelhouse Lane, Birmingham B4 6DR,
Telephone: 0121 233 3282
E-mail: clerks@sixfountain.co.uk
Call Date: July 1975, Gray's Inn
Pupil Master
Qualifications: [LLB (Hons)]

RIDD DAVID IAN MCGREGOR

4 Paper Buildings
1st Floor, Temple, London EC4Y 7EX,
Telephone: 0171 583 0816/353 1131
E-mail: clerks@4paperbuildings.co.uk
Call Date: July 1975, Middle Temple
Pupil Master
Qualifications: [BA (Hons)(Oxon), FCIArb]

RIDDELL DAVID ANDREW

Cobden House Chambers
19 Quay Street, Manchester M3 3HN,
Telephone: 0161 833 6000
E-mail: clerks@cobden.co.uk
Call Date: Oct 1993, Middle Temple
Qualifications: [MA (Hons)(Cantab)]

RIDDLE NICHOLAS FINDLAY

Adrian Lyon's Chambers
14 Castle Street, Liverpool L2 0NE,
Telephone: 0151 236 4421/8240
E-mail: chambers14@aol.com
Call Date: July 1970, Gray's Inn
Pupil Master
Qualifications: [MA (Cantab)]

RIDING HENRY

Corn Exchange Chambers
5th Floor, Fenwick Street, Liverpool
L2 7QS, Telephone: 0151 227 1081/5009
Call Date: July 1981, Middle Temple
Qualifications: [LLB (Hons)]

RIDLEY STEPHEN RONALD

Sackville Chambers
Sackville Place, 44-48 Magdalen Street,
Norwich NR3 1JU,
Telephone: 01603 613516/616221
Call Date: July 1977, Middle Temple
Qualifications: [LLB (Hons)(Lond)]

RIFAT MAURICE ALAN

Verulam Chambers
Peer House, 8-14 Verulam Street, Gray's
Inn, London WC1X 8LZ,
Telephone: 0171 813 2400
Call Date: Nov 1990, Inner Temple
Qualifications: [LLB]

RIGBY TERENCE

Chambers of John Hand QC
9 St John Street, Manchester M3 4DN,
Telephone: 0161 955 9000
E-mail: ninesjs@gconnect.com
Call Date: May 1971, Gray's Inn
Recorder
Qualifications: [LLB (Nottm), BCL (Ox]

RIGNEY ANDREW JAMES

Two Crown Office Row
Ground Floor, Temple, London
EC4Y 7HJ, Telephone: 020 7797 8100
E-mail: mail@2cor.co.uk, or to individual
barristers at: [barrister's
surname]@2cor.co.uk
Call Date: Oct 1992, Gray's Inn
Qualifications: [MA (Cantab), Dip Law (City)]

RILEY BRIAN DOUGLAS

Francis Taylor Building
3rd Floor, Temple, London EC4Y 7BY,
Telephone: 0171 797 7250
Call Date: July 1986, Gray's Inn
Pupil Master
Qualifications: [MSc, LLB]

RILEY MISS CHRISTINE ANNE

Chambers of John Hand QC
9 St John Street, Manchester M3 4DN,
Telephone: 0161 955 9000
E-mail: ninesjs@gconnect.com
Call Date: July 1974, Gray's Inn
Pupil Master
Qualifications: [LLB]

RILEY JAMIE SPENCER

11 Stone Buildings
Lincoln's Inn, London WC2A 3TG,
Telephone: +44 (0)207 831 6381
E-mail:clerks@11StoneBuildings.law.co.uk
Call Date: Nov 1995, Lincoln's Inn
Qualifications: [BA (Hons)]

RILEY MICHAEL JOHN

4 King's Bench Walk
2nd Floor, Temple, London EC4Y 7DL,
Telephone: 020 7353 3581
E-mail: clerks@4kbw.co.uk
Call Date: Nov 1983, Middle Temple
Pupil Master
Qualifications: [BA (Hons)]

RILEY-SMITH TOBIAS AUGUSTINE WILLIAM

2 Harcourt Buildings
Ground Floor/Left, Temple, London
EC4Y 9DB, Telephone: 0171 583 9020
E-mail: clerks@harcourt.co.uk
Call Date: Nov 1995, Middle Temple
Qualifications: [MA (Cantab)]

RIMMER ANTHONY MICHAEL

Francis Taylor Building
Ground Floor, Temple, London
EC4Y 7BY, Telephone: 0171 353 7768/
7769/2711
E-mail:clerks@francistaylorbuilding.law.co.uk
Call Date: July 1983, Gray's Inn
Pupil Master
Qualifications: [BA]

RIORDAN KEVIN

Iscoed Chambers
86 St Helen's Road, Swansea, West
Glamorgan, SA1 4BQ,
Telephone: 01792 652988/9/330
Call Date: Nov 1972, Gray's Inn
Pupil Master
Qualifications: [BCL (Cork)]

RIORDAN STEPHEN VAUGHAN QC (1992)

25-27 Castle Street
1st Floor, Liverpool L2 4TA,
Telephone: 0151 227 5661/051 236 5072
Call Date: July 1972, Inner Temple
Recorder
Qualifications: [LLB (L'pool)]

RIPPON MRS AMANDA JAYNE

East Anglian Chambers
52 North Hill, Colchester, Essex, CO1 1PY,
Telephone: 01206 572756
E-mail: colchester@ealaw.co.uk

East Anglian Chambers
57 London Street, Norwich NR2 1HL,
Telephone: 01603 617351
E-mail: norwich@ealaw.co.uk
East Anglian Chambers
Gresham House, 5 Museum Street,
Ipswich, Suffolk, IP1 1HQ,
Telephone: 01473 214481
E-mail: ipswich@ealaw.co.uk
Call Date: Oct 1993, Gray's Inn
Qualifications: [BA, Dip Law]

RIPPON PAUL HOWARD

One Garden Court Family Law Chambers
Ground Floor, Temple, London
EC4Y 9BJ, Telephone: 0171 797 7900
E-mail: clerks@onegardencourt.co.uk
Call Date: Nov 1985, Gray's Inn

RITCHIE ANDREW GEORGE

9 Gough Square
London EC4A 3DE,
Telephone: 020 7832 0500
E-mail: clerks@9goughsq.co.uk
Call Date: Feb 1985, Inner Temple
Pupil Master
Qualifications: [MA (Cantab)]

RITCHIE DAVID JOHN

The Chambers of Leolin Price CBE, QC
10 Old Square, Lincoln's Inn, London
WC2A 3SU, Telephone: 0171 405 0758
Call Date: Nov 1970, Middle Temple
Pupil Master
Qualifications: [MA (Oxon)]

RITCHIE MISS JEAN HARRIS QC (1992)

4 Paper Buildings
Ground Floor, Temple, London
EC4Y 7EX, Telephone: 0171 353 3366/
583 7155
E-mail: clerks@4paperbuildings.com
Call Date: July 1970, Gray's Inn
Recorder
Qualifications: [LLM (McGill) LLB, (Lond)]

RITCHIE RICHARD BULKELEY

Twenty-Four Old Buildings
Ground Floor, Lincoln's Inn, London
WC2A 3UP, Telephone: 0171 404 0946
E-mail:clerks@24oldbuildings.law.co.uk
Call Date: July 1978, Middle Temple
Pupil Master
Qualifications: [BA (Oxon)]

RITCHIE STUART MARTIN

Littleton Chambers
3 King's Bench Walk North, Temple,
London EC4Y 7HR,
Telephone: 0171 797 8600
E-mail:clerks@littletonchambers.co.uk
Call Date: Oct 1995, Middle Temple
Qualifications: [BA (Oxon)]

RITSON PROFESSOR JOHN

Clock Chambers
78 Darlington Street, Wolverhampton
WV1 4LY, Telephone: 01902 313444
Call Date: July 1967, Lincoln's Inn
Qualifications: [LLB (Hons)]

RIVALLAND MARC-EDOUARD

No. 1 Serjeants' Inn
5th Floor Fleet Street, Temple, London
EC4Y 1LH, Telephone: 0171 415 6666
E-mail:no1serjeantsinn@btinternet.com
Call Date: July 1987, Middle Temple
Pupil Master
Qualifications: [B.Com, LLB (Witwatersrand),
Dip Law, LLM]

RIVERS MRS ANDREA LOUISE

New Court
Temple, London EC4Y 9BE,
Telephone: 0171 583 5123/0510
Call Date: Nov 1990, Middle Temple
Qualifications: [MA (Cantab)]

RIZA ALPER ALI QC (1991)

10 King's Bench Walk
1st Floor, Temple, London EC4Y 7EB,
Telephone: 0171 353 2501
Lloyds House Chambers
3rd Floor, 18 Lloyds House, Lloyd Street,
Manchester M2 5WA,
Telephone: 0161 839 3371
Call Date: Nov 1973, Gray's Inn
Recorder

ROACH MISS JACQUELINE ALISON

Acre Lane Neighbourhood Chambers
30A Acre Lane, London SW2 5SG,
Telephone: 0171 274 4400
E-mail:barristerschambers@acrelane.demon.co.uk
Call Date: Nov 1996, Middle Temple
Qualifications: [LLB (Hons)(Kent)]

ROACH MISS SUSAN

169 Temple Chambers
Temple Avenue, London EC4Y 0DA,
Telephone: 0171 583 7644
Call Date: Oct 1993, Inner Temple
Qualifications: [BA (Hons)]

ROBB ADAM DUNCAN

39 Essex Street
London WC2R 3AT,
Telephone: 0171 832 1111
E-mail: clerks@39essex.co.uk
Call Date: Nov 1995, Inner Temple
Qualifications: [BA (Oxon)]

ROBBINS IAN GEOFFREY

One Garden Court Family Law Chambers
Ground Floor, Temple, London
EC4Y 9BJ, Telephone: 0171 797 7900
E-mail: clerks@onegardencourt.co.uk
Call Date: Feb 1991, Middle Temple
Qualifications: [LLB]

ROBERTS ADRIAN PAUL

2 Gray's Inn Square Chambers
2nd Floor, Gray's Inn, London WC1R 5AA,
Telephone: 020 7242 0328
E-mail: clerks@2gis.co.uk
Call Date: July 1988, Middle Temple
Qualifications: [MA (Cantab)]

ROBERTS ADRIAN PAUL

Phoenix Chambers
First Floor, Gray's Inn Chambers, Gray's
Inn, London WC1R 5JA,
Telephone: 0171 404 7888
E-mail:clerks@phoenix-chambers.co.uk
Call Date: Feb 1993, Lincoln's Inn
Qualifications: [LLB (Hons)]

ROBERTS MISS BEVERLEY JAN

1 Gray's Inn Square
Ground Floor, London WC1R 5AA,
Telephone: 0171 405 8946/7/8
Call Date: Mar 1998, Middle Temple
Qualifications: [BArch (S. Africa)]

ROBERTS MISS CATHERINE ANN

Erskine Chambers
30 Lincoln's Inn Fields, Lincoln's Inn,
London WC2A 3PF,
Telephone: 0171 242 5532
E-mail:clerks@erskine-chambers.co.uk
Call Date: Nov 1986, Lincoln's Inn
Pupil Master
Qualifications: [MA, LLM (Cantab)]

ROBERTS MISS CLARE JUSTINE

2nd Floor, Francis Taylor Building
Temple, London EC4Y 7BY,
Telephone: 0171 353 9942/3157
Call Date: Nov 1988, Middle Temple
Qualifications: [LLB (Lond)]

Fax: 0171 353 9924; DX: LDE 211

Types of work: Administrative, Housing, Local
government

Reported Cases: *R v Kensington and Chelsea
RBC ex parte Kihara*, [1997] 29 HLR 147
(CA), 1996. Homelessness, priority need of
asylum seekers.
*R v Hammersmith and Fulham ex parte
Avdic*, [1996] 30 HLR 1 (CA), 1996. Home-
lessness, local connection.
*R v Hammersmith and Fulham LBC ex
parte D*, [1999] 1 FLR 642, 1998. Duties to
children
Porter and Weeks v Magill (CA), (1999)
The Times, 6 May, 1999. Westminster
'homes for votes' case

ROBERTS DOMINIC DEOGRATIAS PERDITUS

Chambers of Wilfred Forster-Jones
New Court, 1st Floor South, Temple,
London EC4Y 9BE,
Telephone: 0171 353 0853/4/7222
E-mail: chambers@newcourt.net
Call Date: July 1977, Gray's Inn
Pupil Master
Qualifications: [LLB (Lond)]

ROBERTS HILARY LLEWELYN ARTHUR

Newport Chambers
12 Clytha Park Road, Newport, Gwent,
NP9 47L, Telephone: 01633 267403/
255855
Call Date: Nov 1978, Gray's Inn
Pupil Master
Qualifications: [LLB (Aberystwyth)]

ROBERTS HUW EIFION

Sedan House
Stanley Place, Chester CH1 2LU,
Telephone: 01244 320480/348282
Call Date: Nov 1993, Gray's Inn
Qualifications: [LLB, LLM]

ROBERTS JAMES MCCLINTOCK

One King's Bench Walk
1st Floor, Temple, London EC4Y 7DB,
Telephone: 0171 936 1500
E-mail: ddear@1kbw.co.uk
Call Date: Oct 1993, Gray's Inn
Qualifications: [BA (Hons)(Oxon)]

ROBERTS JAMES PHILIP

Littman Chambers
12 Gray's Inn Square, London WC1R 5JP,
Telephone: 020 7404 4866
E-mail: admin@littmanchambers.com
Call Date: Nov 1996, Middle Temple
Qualifications: [LLB (Hons)(Hull), MA
(Sheff)]

ROBERTS MRS JENNIFER MARY

Queen Elizabeth Building
2nd Floor, Temple, London EC4Y 9BS,
Telephone: 0171 797 7837
Call Date: July 1988, Inner Temple
Qualifications: [LLB (Soton)]

ROBERTS JEREMY MICHAEL GRAHAM QC (1982)

9 Gough Square
London EC4A 3DE,
Telephone: 020 7832 0500
E-mail: clerks@9goughsq.co.uk
Call Date: 1965, Inner Temple
Recorder
Qualifications: [BA (Oxon)]

ROBERTS DR JOHN ANTHONY QC (1988)

20 Richmond Way
1st Floor, London W12 8LY,
Telephone: 0181 749 2004
12 Old Square
1st Floor, Lincoln's Inn, London
WC2A 3TX, Telephone: 0171 404 0875
Call Date: Nov 1969, Gray's Inn
Recorder
Qualifications: [FCIArb, Doctor of Civil Law]

ROBERTS JOHN MERVYN

5 Essex Court
1st Floor, Temple, London EC4Y 9AH,
Telephone: 0171 410 2000
E-mail: barristers@5essexcourt.co.uk
Call Date: May 1963, Inner Temple
Pupil Master, Recorder
Qualifications: [LLB]

ROBERTS DR JULIAN FRANCIS

The Chambers of Leolin Price CBE, QC
10 Old Square, Lincoln's Inn, London
WC2A 3SU, Telephone: 0171 405 0758
Call Date: July 1987, Lincoln's Inn
Qualifications: [BA, MA, PhD (Cantab),
Rechtsanwalt]

ROBERTS MISS LISA

Lincoln House Chambers
5th Floor, Lincoln House, 1 Brazennose
Street, Manchester M2 5EL,
Telephone: 0161 832 5701
E-mail: info@lincolnhse.co.uk
Call Date: Oct 1993, Lincoln's Inn
Qualifications: [LLB]

ROBERTS MARC ALEXANDER

4 Brick Court
Temple, London EC4Y 9AD,
Telephone: 0171 797 8910
E-mail: medhurst@dial.pipex.com
Call Date: Nov 1984, Inner Temple
Qualifications: [BA]

ROBERTS MARK VAUGHAN

White Friars Chambers
21 White Friars, Chester CH1 1NZ,
Telephone: 01244 323070
E-mail:whitefriarschambers@btinternet.com
Call Date: Nov 1991, Inner Temple
Qualifications: [LLB (Sheff)]

ROBERTS MATTHEW JOHN PIERS

2 Mitre Court Buildings
1st Floor, Temple, London EC4Y 7BX,
Telephone: 0171 353 1353
Call Date: Nov 1994, Gray's Inn
Qualifications: [LLB (Wales) LLM (Bristol)]

ROBERTS MICHAEL CHARLES

1 New Square
Ground Floor, Lincoln's Inn, London
WC2A 3SA, Telephone: 0171 405 0884/5/6/
7 E-mail: clerks@1newsquare.law.co.uk
Call Date: July 1978, Lincoln's Inn
Pupil Master
Qualifications: [BA (Cantab)]

ROBERTS MISS PATRICIA

14 Gray's Inn Square
Gray's Inn, London WC1R 5JP,
Telephone: 0171 242 0858
E-mail: 100712.2134@compuserve.com
Call Date: Nov 1987, Gray's Inn
Pupil Master
Qualifications: [LLB (L'pool)]

ROBERTS PHILIP DUNCAN

One Essex Court
Ground Floor, Temple, London
EC4Y 9AR, Telephone: 020 7583 2000
E-mail: clerks@oneessexcourt.co.uk
Call Date: Oct 1996, Inner Temple
Qualifications: [BA (Nott'm)]

ROBERTS RICHARD JAMES LLOYD

Lamb Building
Ground Floor, Temple, London
EC4Y 7AS, Telephone: 020 7797 7788
E-mail: lamb.building@link.org
Call Date: July 1983, Middle Temple
Pupil Master
Qualifications: [BA]

ROBERTS SIR SAMUEL

Regency Chambers
Cathedral Square, Peterborough
PE1 1XW, Telephone: 01733 315215
Call Date: July 1972, Inner Temple

ROBERTS STUART ROYD

37 Park Square Chambers
37 Park Square, Leeds LS1 2NY,
Telephone: 0113 2439422
E-mail: chambers@no37.co.uk
Call Date: Nov 1994, Middle Temple
Qualifications: [BA (Hons)]

ROBERTS TIMOTHY DAVID

Fountain Chambers
Cleveland Business Centre, 1 Watson
Street, Middlesbrough TS1 2RQ,
Telephone: 01642 804040
E-mail:fountainchambers@onyxnet.co.uk
Call Date: July 1978, Gray's Inn
Pupil Master, Recorder
Qualifications: [LLB (Soton)]

ROBERTSHAW MARTIN ANDREW

39 Park Square
Leeds LS1 2NU,
Telephone: 0113 2456633
Call Date: Nov 1977, Middle Temple
Qualifications: [LLB (Sheff)]

ROBERTSHAW MISS MIRANDA-LOUISE

2 King's Bench Walk
Ground Floor, Temple, London
EC4Y 7DE, Telephone: 0171 353 1746
E-mail: 2kbw@atlas.co.uk
King's Bench Chambers
115 North Hill, Plymouth PL4 8JY,
Telephone: 01752 221551
Call Date: Nov 1985, Gray's Inn
Pupil Master
Qualifications: [BA, Dip Law]

ROBERTSON AIDAN MALCOLM DAVID

Brick Court Chambers
7-8 Essex Street, London WC2R 3LD,
Telephone: 0171 379 3550
E-mail: [surname]@brickcourt.co.uk
Call Date: July 1995, Middle Temple
Qualifications: [MA, LLM (Cantab)]

ROBERTSON MS ALICE MICHELLE

Chambers of Kieran Coonan QC
Ground Floor, 6 Pump Court, Temple,
London EC4Y 7AR,
Telephone: 0171 583 6013/2510
E-mail: clerks@6-pumpcourt.law.co.uk
Call Date: Oct 1996, Gray's Inn
Qualifications: [LLB (Sussex)]

ROBERTSON ANDREW JAMES QC (1996)

11 King's Bench Walk
1st Floor, Temple, London EC4Y 7EQ,
Telephone: 0171 353 3337
E-mail: fmuller11@aol.com
11 King's Bench Walk
3 Park Court, Park Cross Street, Leeds
LS1 2QH, Telephone: 0113 297 1200
Call Date: July 1975, Middle Temple
Recorder
Qualifications: [MA (Cantab)]

ROBERTSON ANGUS FREDERICK

Eighteen Carlton Crescent
Southampton SO15 2XR,
Telephone: 01703 639001
Call Date: July 1978, Middle Temple
Pupil Master
Qualifications: [BA]

ROBERTSON GEOFFREY RONALD QC (1988)

Doughty Street Chambers
11 Doughty Street, London WC1N 2PG,
Telephone: 0171 404 1313
E-mail:enquiries@doughtystreet.co.uk
Call Date: July 1973, Middle Temple
Recorder
Qualifications: [BA, LLB, BCL]

ROBERTSON JAMES GRAHAM

New Bailey Chambers
10 Lawson Street, Preston PR1 2QT,
Telephone: 01772 258087
Call Date: Feb 1991, Gray's Inn
Qualifications: [BSc, LLB]

ROBERTSON JAMES JOLLYON

10 King's Bench Walk
1st Floor, Temple, London EC4Y 7EB,
Telephone: 0171 353 2501
Call Date: Feb 1983, Middle Temple
Pupil Master
Qualifications: [BA]

ROBERTSON MISS PATRICIA GRACE

Fountain Court
Temple, London EC4Y 9DH,
Telephone: 0171 583 3335
E-mail: chambers@fountaincourt.co.uk
Call Date: Nov 1988, Inner Temple
Pupil Master
Qualifications: [BA (Oxon), Dip Law (City)]

ROBERTSON MS SALLY ELIZABETH

Cloisters
1 Pump Court, Temple, London
EC4Y 7AA, Telephone: 0171 827 4000
E-mail: clerks@cloisters.com
Call Date: Nov 1995, Inner Temple
Qualifications: [BA (Hons) (Reading), MSc
(LSE)]

ROBINS MISS ALISON ELIZABETH

2 Paper Buildings, Basement North
Temple, London EC4Y 7ET,
Telephone: 0171 936 2613
E-mail: post@2paper.co.uk
Call Date: Feb 1987, Gray's Inn
Qualifications: [BA Law (Dunelm)]

ROBINS MISS IMOGEN

Eighteen Carlton Crescent
Southampton SO15 2XR,
Telephone: 01703 639001
Call Date: Oct 1991, Inner Temple
Qualifications: [LLB]

ROBINSON ADRIAN CARINS

Park Court Chambers
16 Park Place, Leeds LS1 2SJ,
Telephone: 0113 2433277
Call Date: July 1981, Inner Temple
Qualifications: [MA (Oxon)]

ROBINSON MISS ALICE

4 Breams Buildings
London EC4A 1AQ,
Telephone: 0171 353 5835/430 1221
E-mail:breams@4breamsbuildings.law.co.uk
Call Date: July 1983, Gray's Inn
Pupil Master
Qualifications: [LLB (Cardiff)]

ROBINSON MISS CLAIRE MARIA

Dr Johnson's Chambers
Two Dr Johnson's Buildings, Temple,
London EC4Y 7AY,
Telephone: 0171 353 4716
E-mail: clerks@2djb.freeserve.co.uk
Call Date: Oct 1991, Gray's Inn
Qualifications: [BA (Oxon)]

ROBINSON DANIEL MICHAEL

Bell Yard Chambers
116/118 Chancery Lane, London
WC2A 1PP, Telephone: 0171 306 9292
Call Date: Nov 1993, Lincoln's Inn
Qualifications: [BSc (Hons, Wales), CPE]

ROBINSON DAVID GARIN ALEXANDER

Regent Chambers
8 Pall Mall, Hanley, Stoke On Trent
ST1 1ER, Telephone: 01782 286666
E-mail: regent@ftech.co.uk
Call Date: Oct 1992, Middle Temple
Qualifications: [BA (Hons, Wales)]

ROBINSON GRAHAM

Paradise Chambers
26 Paradise Square, Sheffield S1 2DE,
Telephone: 0114 2738951
E-mail: timbooth@paradise-sq.co.uk
Call Date: July 1981, Inner Temple
Pupil Master, Assistant Recorder
Qualifications: [LLB (Hull)]

ROBINSON JAMES EDWARD

York Chambers
14 Toft Green, York YO1 6JT,
Telephone: 01904 620048
E-mail: [name]@yorkchambers.co.uk
Call Date: Oct 1992, Middle Temple
Qualifications: [MA (St.Andrews), Diploma in Law]

ROBINSON MATTHEW JAMIE

Chartlands Chambers
3 St Giles Terrace, Northampton
NN1 2BN, Telephone: 01604 603322
Call Date: Nov 1994, Inner Temple
Qualifications: [LLB (Lond)]

ROBINSON MICHAEL JOHN

Tower Hamlets Barristers Chambers
37B Princelet Street, London E1 5LP,
Telephone: 0171 377 8090
E-mail: shikderka@aol.com
Call Date: Nov 1976, Middle Temple
Qualifications: [LLB (Lond)]

ROBINSON RICHARD JOHN

2 Gray's Inn Square Chambers
2nd Floor, Gray's Inn, London WC1R 5AA,
Telephone: 020 7242 0328
E-mail: clerks@2gis.co.uk
Call Date: July 1977, Middle Temple
Pupil Master
Qualifications: [BA (Cantab) LLM, (Lond)]

ROBINSON MISS SARA JANE

Broad Chare
33 Broad Chare, Newcastle upon Tyne
NE1 3DQ, Telephone: 0191 232 0541
E-mail:clerks@broadcharechambers.law.co.uk
Call Date: Nov 1994, Inner Temple
Qualifications: [LLB]

ROBINSON SIMON ROBERT

Chambers of Ian Macdonald QC (In Association with Two Garden Court, Temple, London)
Waldorf House, 5 Cooper Street,
Manchester M2 2FW,
Telephone: 0161 236 1840
Call Date: Oct 1991, Lincoln's Inn
Qualifications: [LLB (Hons)]

ROBINSON MS TANYA LIN

6 Pump Court
1st Floor, Temple, London EC4Y 7AR,
Telephone: 0171 797 8400
E-mail: clerks@6pumpcourt.co.uk
6-8 Mill Street
Maidstone, Kent, ME15 6XH,
Telephone: 01622 688094
E-mail: annexe@6pumpcourt.co.uk
Call Date: 1997, Inner Temple
Qualifications: [LLB (So'ton)]

ROBINSON VIVIAN QC (1986)

Hollis Whiteman Chambers
3rd Floor, Queen Elizabeth Bldg, Temple,
London EC4Y 9BS,
Telephone: 020 7583 5766
E-mail:barristers@holliswhiteman.co.uk
Call Date: July 1967, Inner Temple
Recorder
Qualifications: [BA (Cantab)]

ROBLIN MISS LARAINE ARIANWEN

Pendragon Chambers
124 Walter Road, Swansea, West
Glamorgan, SA1 5RG,
Telephone: 01792 411188
Call Date: July 1981, Lincoln's Inn
Pupil Master
Qualifications: [LLB (Wales)]

ROBOTHAM JOHN ANSEL

St Philip's Chambers
Fountain Court, Steelhouse Lane,
Birmingham B4 6DR,
Telephone: 0121 246 7000
E-mail: clerks@st-philips.co.uk
Call Date: Feb 1990, Inner Temple
Qualifications: [LLB (Manch)]

ROBSON DAVID ERNEST HENRY QC (1980)

New Court Chambers
3 Broad Chare, Newcastle upon Tyne
NE1 3DQ, Telephone: 0191 232 1980
11 King's Bench Walk
1st Floor, Temple, London EC4Y 7EQ,
Telephone: 0171 353 3337
E-mail: fmuller11@aol.com
Call Date: Feb 1965, Inner Temple
Recorder
Qualifications: [MA (Oxon)]

ROBSON JOHN MALCOLM

2 Gray's Inn Square Chambers
2nd Floor, Gray's Inn, London WC1R 5AA,
Telephone: 020 7242 0328
E-mail: clerks@2gis.co.uk
Assize Court Chambers
14 Small Street, Bristol BS1 1DE,
Telephone: 0117 9264587
E-mail:chambers@assize-court-chambers.co.uk
Call Date: July 1974, Inner Temple
Pupil Master
Qualifications: [LLB (Lond), FCIArb]

ROBSON NICHOLAS DAVID

Baker Street Chambers
9 Baker Street, Middlesbrough TS1 2LF,
Telephone: 01642 873873
Call Date: Oct 1994, Lincoln's Inn
Qualifications: [LLB (Hons)(L'pool)]

ROCHE BRENDAN KENNETH

9 Bedford Row
London WC1R 4AZ,
Telephone: 0171 242 3555
E-mail: clerks@9br.co.uk
Call Date: July 1989, Middle Temple
Qualifications: [MA (Oxon), Dip Law]

ROCHE PATRICK RICHARD REDMOND

14 Tooks Court
Cursitor St, London EC4A 1LB,
Telephone: 0171 405 8828
E-mail: clerks@tooks.law.co.uk
Call Date: July 1977, Middle Temple
Pupil Master
Qualifications: [BA (Oxon)]

ROCHFORD THOMAS NICHOLAS BEVERLEY

St Philip's Chambers
Fountain Court, Steelhouse Lane,
Birmingham B4 6DR,
Telephone: 0121 246 7000
E-mail: clerks@st-philips.co.uk
Call Date: July 1984, Inner Temple
Pupil Master
Qualifications: [MA (Cantab)]

RODDICK (GEORGE) WINSTON QC (1986)

10 King's Bench Walk
1st Floor, Temple, London EC4Y 7EB,
Telephone: 0171 353 2501
9 Park Place
Cardiff CF1 3DP,
Telephone: 01222 382731
Call Date: Nov 1968, Gray's Inn
Recorder
Qualifications: [LLM]

RODDY MISS MAUREEN BERNADETTE

India Buildings Chambers
Water Street, Liverpool L2 0XG,
Telephone: 0151 243 6000
E-mail: clerks@chambers.u-net.com
Call Date: July 1977, Middle Temple
Recorder
Qualifications: [LLB, LLM (Lond)]

RODGER ANDREW CHARLES JAMES

5 King's Bench Walk
Temple, London EC4Y 7DN,
Telephone: 0171 353 5638
Call Date: July 1993, Gray's Inn
Qualifications: [LLB]

RODGER MISS CAROLINE BANKIER

Gray's Inn Chambers
5th Floor, Gray's Inn, London WC1R 5JA,
Telephone: 0171 404 1111
Call Date: Nov 1968, Gray's Inn
Qualifications: [BA (Oxon)]

RODGER MARK STUART

30 Park Square
Leeds LS1 2PF, Telephone: 0113 2436388
E-mail: clerks@30parksquare.co.uk
Call Date: Nov 1983, Gray's Inn
Qualifications: [LLB (Hons) (Bris)]

RODGER MARTIN OWEN

Falcon Chambers
Falcon Court, London EC4Y 1AA,
Telephone: 0171 353 2484
E-mail: clerks@falcon-chambers.com
Call Date: July 1986, Middle Temple
Pupil Master
Qualifications: [BA (Oxon)]

RODGERS MISS DORIS JUNE

Harcourt Chambers
1st Floor, 2 Harcourt Buildings, Temple,
London EC4Y 9DB,
Telephone: 0171 353 6961
E-mail:clerks@harcourtchambers.law.co.uk
Harcourt Chambers
Churchill House, 3 St Aldate's Courtyard,
St Aldate's, Oxford OX1 1BN,
Telephone: 01865 791559
E-mail:clerks@harcourtchambers.law.co.uk
Call Date: Nov 1971, Middle Temple
Pupil Master, Recorder
Qualifications: [MA (Dub), MA (Oxon)]

RODHAM MISS SUSAN ANNE

**1 Gray's Inn Square, Chambers of the
Baroness Scotland of Asthal QC**
1st Floor, London WC1R 5AG,
Telephone: 0171 405 3000
E-mail: clerks@onegrays.demon.co.uk
Call Date: Nov 1989, Gray's Inn
Pupil Master
Qualifications: [LLB]

RODIKIS MISS JOANNA

Old Colony House
6 South King Street, Manchester M2 6DQ,
Telephone: 0161 834 4364
Call Date: Oct 1993, Middle Temple
Qualifications: [LLB (Hons)]

RODWAY MISS SUSAN CAROLINE

12 King's Bench Walk
Temple, London EC4Y 7EL,
Telephone: 0171 583 0811
E-mail: chambers@12kbw.co.uk
Call Date: July 1981, Middle Temple
Pupil Master
Qualifications: [BA (Hons) (Lond)]

ROE THOMAS IDRIS

Goldsmith Building
1st Floor, Temple, London EC4Y 7BL,
Telephone: 0171 353 7881
E-mail:clerks@goldsmith-building.law.co.uk
Call Date: Oct 1995, Middle Temple
Qualifications: [BA (Hons)]

ROEBUCK ROY DELVILLE

Bell Yard Chambers
116/118 Chancery Lane, London
WC2A 1PP, Telephone: 0171 306 9292
Call Date: Nov 1974, Gray's Inn
Pupil Master
Qualifications: [LLM (Leicester)]

ROGERS MISS BEVERLY-ANN

Serle Court Chambers
6 New Square, Lincoln's Inn, London
WC2A 3QS, Telephone: 0171 242 6105
E-mail: clerks@serlecourt.co.uk
Call Date: July 1978, Middle Temple
Pupil Master
Qualifications: [LLB (Lond)]

ROGERS DANIEL JAMES

Martins Building
2nd Floor, No 4 Water Street, Liverpool
L2 3SP, Telephone: 0151 236 5818/4919
Call Date: Oct 1997, Inner Temple
Qualifications: [BA (Nottingham), CPE]

ROGERS DONALD HALEY

Mitre House Chambers
15-19 Devereux Court, London WC2R 3JJ,
Telephone: 0171 583 8233
Call Date: Nov 1991, Middle Temple
Qualifications: [LLB (Hons)]

ROGERS GREGORY CHARLES

St Ive's Chambers
Whittall Street, Birmingham B4 6DH,
Telephone: 0121 236 0863/5720
E-mail:stives.headofchambers@btinternet.com
Call Date: Nov 1992, Gray's Inn
Qualifications: [BA (Hons)]

ROGERS MS HEATHER

5 Raymond Buildings
1st Floor, Gray's Inn, London WC1R 5BP,
Telephone: 0171 242 2902
E-mail: clerks@media-ent-law.co.uk
Call Date: July 1983, Middle Temple
Pupil Master
Qualifications: [LLB (LSE)]

ROGERS IAN PAUL

1 Crown Office Row
3rd Floor, Temple, London EC4Y 7HH,
Telephone: 0171 583 9292
E-mail: onecor@link.org
Call Date: Oct 1995, Gray's Inn
Qualifications: [BA]

ROGERS MARK NICHOLAS

St Mary's Chambers
50 High Pavement, Lace Market,
Nottingham NG1 1HW,
Telephone: 0115 9503503
E-mail: clerks@smc.law.co.uk
*Call Date: July 1980, Middle Temple
Pupil Master*
Qualifications: [BA (Oxon)]

ROGERS MISS NICOLA HELEN

1 Pump Court
Lower Ground Floor, Temple, London
EC4Y 7AB, Telephone: 0171 583 2012/
353 4341
E-mail: [name]@1pumpcourt.co.uk
Call Date: Nov 1997, Gray's Inn
Qualifications: [MA (Edin)]

ROGERS PAUL JOHN

1 Crown Office Row
Ground Floor, Temple, London
EC4Y 7HH, Telephone: 0171 797 7500
E-mail: mail@onecrownofficerow.com
Crown Office Row Chambers
Blenheim House, 120 Church Street,
Brighton, Sussex, BN1 1WH,
Telephone: 01273 625625
E-mail: crownofficerow@clara.net
*Call Date: July 1989, Inner Temple
Pupil Master*
Qualifications: [LLB (L'pool)]

ROHARD ADRIAN

Acre Lane Neighbourhood Chambers
30A Acre Lane, London SW2 5SG,
Telephone: 0171 274 4400
E-mail:barristerschambers@acrelane.demon.co.uk
Mitre House Chambers
15-19 Devereux Court, London WC2R 3JJ,
Telephone: 0171 583 8233
Call Date: Nov 1993, Inner Temple
Qualifications: [LLB (Hons)]

ROLFE PATRICK JOHN BENEDICT

5 Stone Buildings
Lincoln's Inn, London WC2A 3XT,
Telephone: 0171 242 6201
E-mail:clerks@5-stonebuildings.law.co.uk
*Call Date: Nov 1987, Middle Temple
Pupil Master*
Qualifications: [LLB (Lond)]

ROLLASON MICHAEL CHRISTOPHER

One Essex Court
Ground Floor, Temple, London
EC4Y 9AR, Telephone: 020 7583 2000
E-mail: clerks@oneessexcourt.co.uk
Call Date: Nov 1992, Inner Temple
Qualifications: [MA (Cantab)]

ROMAIN MISS CHARAN MARGARET HELENA

Martins Building
2nd Floor, No 4 Water Street, Liverpool
L2 3SP, Telephone: 0151 236 5818/4919
Call Date: Oct 1991, Inner Temple
Qualifications: [LLB (Hons) (Leics)]

ROMANS PHILIP RUTHERS

Furnival Chambers
32 Furnival Street, London EC4A 1JQ,
Telephone: 0171 405 3232
E-mail: clerks@furnivallaw.co.uk
Call Date: Nov 1982, Gray's Inn
Qualifications: [MA Oxon]

ROMER MISS EMMA EVELYN MARTINDALE

The College of Law, 50-52 Chancery Lane,
London WC2A 1SX,
Telephone: 0171 969 3100
Call Date: Nov 1992, Lincoln's Inn
Qualifications: [BA (Hons), CPE]

ROMILLY EDMUND HUMPHREY SAMUEL

3 Temple Gardens
3rd Floor, Temple, London EC4Y 9AU,
Telephone: 0171 583 0010
*Call Date: Nov 1983, Gray's Inn
Pupil Master*
Qualifications: [BA (Lond)]

ROMNEY MISS DAPHNE IRENE

4 Field Court
Gray's Inn, London WC1R 5EA,
Telephone: 0171 440 6900
E-mail: chambers@4fieldcourt.co.uk
Call Date: Nov 1979, Inner Temple
Pupil Master
Qualifications: [BA (Cantab)]

RONKSLEY ANDREW PETER

3 Temple Gardens
3rd Floor, Temple, London EC4Y 9AU,
Telephone: 0171 353 0832
Call Date: Oct 1995, Gray's Inn
Qualifications: [BA]

ROOCHOVE MARK NATHAN

Trinity Chambers
140 New London Road, Chelmsford,
Essex, CM2 0AW,
Telephone: 01245 605040
E-mail:clerks@trinitychambers.law.co.uk
Call Date: Oct 1994, Gray's Inn
Qualifications: [BSc (Wales)]

ROOK PETER FRANCIS GROSVENOR QC (1991)

18 Red Lion Court
(Off Fleet Street), London EC4A 3EB,
Telephone: 0171 520 6000
E-mail: chambers@18rlc.co.uk
Thornwood House
102 New London Road, Chelmsford,
Essex, CM2 0RG,
Telephone: 01245 280880
E-mail: chambers@18rlc.co.uk
Call Date: July 1973, Gray's Inn
Recorder
Qualifications: [MA (Cantab)]

ROOM STEWART

8 Stone Buildings
Lincoln's Inn, London WC2A 3TA,
Telephone: 0171 831 9881
E-mail: alanl@8stonebuildings.law.uk
Call Date: Nov 1991, Middle Temple
Pupil Master
Qualifications: [LLB Hons (B'ham)]

ROONEY ADAM CHARLES

One Essex Court
1st Floor, Temple, London EC4Y 9AR,
Telephone: 0171 936 3030
E-mail: one.essex_court@virgin.net
Call Date: Oct 1997, Inner Temple
Qualifications: [LLB (London)]

ROOTS GUY ROBERT GODFREY QC (1989)

2 Mitre Court Buildings
2nd Floor, Temple, London EC4Y 7BX,
Telephone: 0171 583 1380
E-mail: clerks@2mcb.co.uk
Call Date: July 1969, Middle Temple
Assistant Recorder
Qualifications: [MA (Oxon)]

ROSARIO DESMOND DAVID LUKE

Paradise Chambers
26 Paradise Square, Sheffield S1 2DE,
Telephone: 0114 2738951
E-mail: timbooth@paradise-sq.co.uk
Call Date: Nov 1990, Inner Temple
Qualifications: [LLB (Sheff)]

ROSE ANTHONY KENNETH

Chavasse Court Chambers
2nd Floor, Chavasse Court, 24 Lord Street,
Liverpool L2 1TA,
Telephone: 0151 707 1191
Call Date: Nov 1978, Middle Temple
Qualifications: [LLM (Lond)]

ROSE DAVID LESLIE

No. 6
6 Park Square, Leeds LS1 2LW,
Telephone: 0113 2459763
E-mail: chambers@no6.co.uk
Call Date: July 1977, Middle Temple
Pupil Master
Qualifications: [MA, LLB (Cantab)]

ROSE MISS DINAH GWEN LISON

Blackstone Chambers
Blackstone House, Temple, London
EC4Y 9BW, Telephone: 0171 583 1770
E-mail:clerks@blackstonechambers.com
Call Date: July 1989, Gray's Inn
Pupil Master
Qualifications: [BA (Oxon)]

ROSE PROFESSOR FRANCIS DENNIS

4 Essex Court
Temple, London EC4Y 9AJ,
Telephone: 020 7797 7970
E-mail: clerks@4essexcourt.law.co.uk
Call Date: Nov 1983, Gray's Inn
Qualifications: [MA BCL PhD]

ROSE JONATHAN LEE

St Paul's House
5th Floor, St Paul's House, 23 Park Square
South, Leeds LS1 2ND,
Telephone: 0113 2455866
E-mail: catherinegrimshaw@stpauls-
chambers.demon.co.uk
Call Date: July 1981, Middle Temple
Pupil Master
Qualifications: [BA (Hons)]

ROSE JONATHAN PETER

Dr Johnson's Chambers
Two Dr Johnson's Buildings, Temple,
London EC4Y 7AY,
Telephone: 0171 353 4716
E-mail: clerks@2djb.freeserve.co.uk
Call Date: Nov 1986, Middle Temple
Qualifications: [LLB (London)]

ROSE MISS PAMELA SUSAN

8 King's Bench Walk
2nd Floor, Temple, London EC4Y 7DU,
Telephone: 0171 797 8888
8 King's Bench Walk North
1 Park Square East, Leeds LS1 2NE,
Telephone: 0113 2439797
Call Date: July 1980, Inner Temple
Pupil Master
Qualifications: [BA]

ROSE PAUL TELFER

Old Square Chambers
1 Verulam Buildings, Gray's Inn, London
WC1R 5LQ, Telephone: 0171 269 0300
E-mail:clerks@oldsquarechambers.co.uk
Old Square Chambers
Hanover House, 47 Corn Street, Bristol
BS1 1HT, Telephone: 0117 9277111
E-mail: oldsqbri@globalnet.co.uk
Call Date: Nov 1981, Gray's Inn
Pupil Master
Qualifications: [LLB (Reading)]

ROSE STEPHEN PAUL

5 Essex Court
1st Floor, Temple, London EC4Y 9AH,
Telephone: 0171 410 2000
E-mail: barristers@5essexcourt.co.uk
Call Date: Nov 1995, Gray's Inn
Qualifications: [BA (Oxon)]

ROSEN MISS ANUSHKA TANYA

One Essex Court
Ground Floor, Temple, London
EC4Y 9AR, Telephone: 020 7583 2000
E-mail: clerks@oneessexcourt.co.uk
Call Date: 1997, Middle Temple
Qualifications: [BA (Hons)(Cantab)]

ROSEN MURRAY HILARY QC (1993)

11 Stone Buildings
Lincoln's Inn, London WC2A 3TG,
Telephone: +44 (0)207 831 6381
E-mail:clerks@11StoneBuildings.law.co.uk
Call Date: Nov 1976, Inner Temple
Qualifications: [BA (Cantab)]

ROSENBLATT JEREMY GEORGE

4 Paper Buildings
1st Floor, Temple, London EC4Y 7EX,
Telephone: 0171 583 0816/353 1131
E-mail: clerks@4paperbuildings.co.uk
Call Date: July 1985, Gray's Inn
Qualifications: [LLB (Hons) (LSE)]

ROSS ANTHONY JOHN

5 Pump Court
Ground Floor, Temple, London
EC4Y 7AP, Telephone: 020 7353 2532
E-mail: FivePump@netcomuk.co.uk
Call Date: Oct 1991, Lincoln's Inn
Qualifications: [LLB (Hons) (Leeds)]

ROSS DAVID JOHN

1 Harcourt Buildings
2nd Floor, Temple, London EC4Y 9DA,
Telephone: 0171 353 9421/0375
E-mail:clerks@1harcourtbuildings.law.co.uk
Call Date: Nov 1974, Middle Temple
Pupil Master
Qualifications: [LLB (Lond)]

ROSS GORDON MACRAE

3 Temple Gardens
Lower Ground Floor, Temple, London
EC4Y 9AU, Telephone: 0171 353 3102/5/
9297 E-mail: clerks@3tg.co.uk
Call Date: July 1986, Inner Temple
Qualifications: [LLB]

ROSS IAIN ALASDAIR

3 Paper Buildings
Temple, London EC4Y 7EU,
Telephone: 020 7583 8055
E-mail: London@3paper.com
3 Paper Buildings (Bournemouth)
20 Lorne Park Road, Bournemouth,
Dorset, BH1 1JN,
Telephone: 01202 292102
E-mail: Bournemouth@3paper.com
3 Paper Buildings (Winchester)
4 St Peter Street, Winchester SO23 8BW,
Telephone: 01962 868884
E-mail: winchester@3paper.com
3 Paper Buildings (Oxford)
1 Alfred Street, High Street, Oxford
OX1 4EH, Telephone: 01865 793736
E-mail: oxford@3paper.com
Call Date: Nov 1991, Inner Temple
Qualifications: [LLB (Glasgow), Dip Law]

ROSS MISS JACQUELINE GORDON

Crown Office Row Chambers
Blenheim House, 120 Church Street,
Brighton, Sussex, BN1 1WH,
Telephone: 01273 625625
E-mail: crownofficerow@clara.net
Call Date: Nov 1985, Middle Temple
Qualifications: [BA(Lond)]

ROSS JOHN GRAFFIN

No. 1 Serjeants' Inn
5th Floor Fleet Street, Temple, London
EC4Y 1LH, Telephone: 0171 415 6666
E-mail:no1serjeantsinn@btinternet.com
Call Date: July 1971, Inner Temple
Pupil Master, Recorder
Qualifications: [LLM (Lond)]

ROSS MISS SALLY-ANN

28 St John Street
Manchester M3 4DJ,
Telephone: 0161 834 8418
E-mail: clerk@28stjohnst.co.uk
Call Date: Oct 1990, Gray's Inn
Qualifications: [BA]

ROSS SIDNEY DAVID

11 Stone Buildings
Lincoln's Inn, London WC2A 3TG,
Telephone: +44 (0)207 831 6381
E-mail:clerks@11StoneBuildings.law.co.uk
Call Date: July 1983, Middle Temple
Pupil Master
Qualifications: [LLB, M.Sc, Ph.D]

ROSS MARTYN JOHN GREAVES

5 New Square
Ground Floor, Lincoln's Inn, London
WC2A 3RJ, Telephone: 020 7404 0404
E-mail:chambers@fivenewsquare.demon.co.
uk
Call Date: 1969, Middle Temple
Pupil Master, Recorder
Qualifications: [MA, LLM (Cantab), FCIArb]

Fax: 0171 831 6016;
Out of hours telephone: 0181 467 9444;
DX: 272 London, Chancery Lane;
Other comms: E-mail
chambers@fivenewsquare.cityscape.co.uk

Other professional qualifications: Fellow of the
Chartered Institute of Arbitrators

Types of work: Arbitration, Bankruptcy, Chancery (general), Chancery land law, Charities, Commercial property, Common land, Conveyancing, Equity, wills and trusts, Family provision, Insolvency, Landlord and tenant, Partnerships, Pensions, Probate and administration, Professional negligence

Circuit: South Eastern

Awards and memberships: Member, Chancery Bar Association; Professional Negligence Bar Association; Society of Trust and Estate Practitioners; Association of Contentious Trust and Probate Specialists; Ecclesiastical Law Society

Other professional experience: Recorder sitting in the County Court and the Crown Court

Publications: *Williams, Mortimer and Sunnucks on Executors, Administration and Probate* (Joint Editor), 1993; *Theobald on Wills* (Joint Editor), 1993; *Family Provision: Law and Practice*, 1985

Reported Cases: *Jones (AE) v Jones (FW)*, [1997] 1 WLR 438, 1976. Co-ownership of land; proprietary estoppel; tenants in common not liable to pay rent.
Re Beaumont, [1980] Ch 444, 1979. Inheritance (Provision for Family and Dependants) Act 1975; person maintained by deceased; assumption of responsibility.
Re Hetherington, [1990] Ch 1, 1989. Gift for Roman Catholic Masses construed as gift for public Masses and so charitable.
Re Finnemore, [1991] 1 WLR 793, 1990. Doctrine of Conditional Revocation can preserve part of earlier will to take effect with valid part of later will.
Taylor v Dickens, [1998] 1 FLR 806, 1997. Promise to leave house to gardener gave rights neither under contract nor by proprietary estoppel (an appeal was compromised).

ROSS-MUNRO COLIN WILLIAM GORDON QC (1972)

Blackstone Chambers
Blackstone House, Temple, London EC4Y 9BW, Telephone: 0171 583 1770
E-mail:clerks@blackstonechambers.com
Call Date: June 1951, Middle Temple
Qualifications: [MA (Cantab)]

ROSSDALE PHILIP SAMUEL ANTHONY

The Chambers of Leolin Price CBE, QC
10 Old Square, Lincoln's Inn, London WC2A 3SU, Telephone: 0171 405 0758
Call Date: June 1948, Inner Temple
Qualifications: [MA, LLM (Cantab)]

ROTH PETER MARCEL QC (1997)

Monckton Chambers
4 Raymond Buildings, Gray's Inn, London WC1R 5BP, Telephone: 0171 405 7211
E-mail: chambers@monckton.co.uk
Call Date: July 1976, Middle Temple
Qualifications: [LLM, MA (Oxon)]

ROTHERY PETER

Queen's Chambers
5 John Dalton Street, Manchester M2 6ET,
Telephone: 0161 834 6875/4738
Queens Chambers
4 Camden Place, Preston PR1 3JL,
Telephone: 01772 828300
Call Date: Oct 1994, Lincoln's Inn
Qualifications: [BA (Hons)(Oxon)]

ROTHWELL MISS CAROLYN ANN

Bridewell Chambers
2 Bridewell Place, London EC4V 6AP,
Telephone: 020 7797 8800
E-mail:HughesGage@bridewell.law.co.uk
Call Date: Oct 1991, Lincoln's Inn
Qualifications: [LLB (Hons)]

ROTHWELL MRS JOANNE LESLEY

6 King's Bench Walk
Ground, Third & Fourth Floors, Temple, London EC4Y 7DR,
Telephone: 0171 353 4931/583 0695
Call Date: Oct 1993, Inner Temple
Qualifications: [LLB (Hons)]

ROTHWELL STEPHEN JOHN

28 St John Street
Manchester M3 4DJ,
Telephone: 0161 834 8418
E-mail: clerk@28stjohnst.co.uk
Call Date: July 1977, Gray's Inn
Qualifications: [LLB (L'pool)]

ROUCH PETER CHRISTOPHER QC (1996)

9-12 Bell Yard
London WC2A 2LF,
Telephone: 0171 400 1800
E-mail: clerks@bellyard.co.uk
Iscoed Chambers
86 St Helen's Road, Swansea, West Glamorgan, SA1 4BQ,
Telephone: 01792 652988/9/330
Call Date: July 1972, Gray's Inn
Recorder
Qualifications: [LLB (Wales)]

ROUDETTE MISS WENDY SHIRLEY

1 Gray's Inn Square
Ground Floor, London WC1R 5AA,
Telephone: 0171 405 8946/7/8
Call Date: July 1996, Inner Temple
Qualifications: [BA (Lond), CPE]

ROUGHTON ASHLEY WENTWORTH

One Raymond Buildings
Gray's Inn, London WC1R 5BH,
Telephone: 0171 430 1234
E-mail: chambers@ipbar1rb.com;
clerks@ipbar1rb.com
Call Date: Oct 1992, Inner Temple
Pupil Master
Qualifications: [BSc (Eng)(Lond), PhD
(Cantab), Dip. Law]

ROUSE JUSTIN CLIVE DOUGLAS

**4 Brick Court, Chambers of Anne
Rafferty QC**
1st Floor, Temple, London EC4Y 9AD,
Telephone: 0171 583 8455
Call Date: July 1982, Lincoln's Inn
Pupil Master
Qualifications: [BA]

ROUSE NIGEL PHILIP

Young Street Chambers
38 Young Street, Manchester M3 3FT,
Telephone: 0161 833 0489
E-mail: clerks@young-st-chambers.com
Call Date: Feb 1993, Gray's Inn
Qualifications: [LLB (Manc)]

ROUSSAK DR JEREMY BRIAN

28 St John Street
Manchester M3 4DJ,
Telephone: 0161 834 8418
E-mail: clerk@28stjohnst.co.uk
Call Date: 1996, Middle Temple
Qualifications: [MA, MB, B.Chir (Cantab),
CPE (City)]

ROUTLEDGE SHAUN WILLIAM

Trinity Chambers
9-12 Trinity Chare, Quayside, Newcastle
upon Tyne NE1 3DF,
Telephone: 0191 232 1927
E-mail: info@trinitychambers.co.uk
Call Date: Nov 1988, Gray's Inn
Qualifications: [LLB (L'pool)]

ROUTLEY PATRICK

Goldsmith Building
1st Floor, Temple, London EC4Y 7BL,
Telephone: 0171 353 7881
E-mail:clerks@goldsmith-building.law.co.uk
Call Date: July 1979, Inner Temple
Pupil Master
Qualifications: [MA (Cantab)]

ROW CHARLES PHILIP

Queens Square Chambers
56 Queens Square, Bristol BS1 4PR,
Telephone: 0117 921 1966
Call Date: Oct 1993, Lincoln's Inn
Qualifications: [BA (Hons)(Portsmth)]

ROWE MISS DEBORAH JOY

Warwick House Chambers
8 Warwick Court, Gray's Inn, London
WC1R 5DJ, Telephone: 0171 430 2323
E-mail: cdrewlaw@aol.com
Call Date: Nov 1990, Inner Temple
Qualifications: [BSC (Hons)(Surrey), MSc
(Lond), Dip Law (City), Cert Ed]

ROWE MISS FREYA EMILY BEATRICE

Counsels' Chambers
2nd Floor, 10-11 Gray's Inn Square,
London WC1R 5JD,
Telephone: 0171 405 2576
E-mail:clerks@10-11graysinnsquare.co.uk
Call Date: 1996, Inner Temple
Qualifications: [BA (Oxon), CPE (Sussex)]

ROWE JOHN JERMYN QC (1982)

8 King Street Chambers
8 King Street, Manchester M2 6AQ,
Telephone: 0161 834 9560
E-mail: eightking@aol.com
Call Date: Feb 1960, Middle Temple
Recorder
Qualifications: [MA (Oxon)]

Fax: 0161 834 2733;
Out of hours telephone: 0161 928 7736;
DX: 14354 Manchester 1;
Other comms: E-mail jjrman@aol.com

Types of work: Crime, Crime – corporate
fraud, Medical negligence, Personal injury

Membership of foreign bars: Irish Bar, Canadian
Bar

Circuit: Northern

Awards and memberships: Criminal Bar Association, Bar European Group, Society for Computers and Law

Other professional experience: 1980-2 Prosecuting counsel Inland Revenue Northern Circuit; Parole Board 1987-90; Independent reviewer to Parliament of Prevention of Terrorism Acts 1993 to date

Languages spoken: French, Italian

Publications: *Bullen and Leake and Jacob – Pleadings and Precedents.* (Contributor), 1990; *Current Law Statutes* – annotated the Northern Ireland (Sentences) Act 1998, 1998

Reported Cases: *R v Kasim*, [1991] 3 WLR 254 (HL), 1991. Crime – execution of valuable security – meaning.
McConnell v Chief Constable/ Gtr Manchester, [1990] 1 WLR 364, 1990. Action for false imprisonment – breach of peace – arrest – private property.
Janaway v Salford Area Health Authority, [1988] 3 WLR 1350 (HL), 1988. Medical secretary – abortion – conscientious objection – Abortion Act 1967 – Judicial Review.
Taylor v Worcester Health Authority, [1991] 2 Med LR 215, 1991. Negligence – anaesthesia technique *Res ispa loquitur.*

ROWE MISS JUDITH MAY

One Garden Court Family Law Chambers
Ground Floor, Temple, London
EC4Y 9BJ, Telephone: 0171 797 7900
E-mail: clerks@onegardencourt.co.uk
Call Date: July 1979, Gray's Inn
Pupil Master, Assistant Recorder
Qualifications: [LLB (Lond)]

Fax: 0171 797 7929; DX: LDE 1034 Chancery Lane

Types of work: Care proceedings, Family, Family provision

Circuit: South Eastern

Awards and memberships: Assistant Recorder 1999

Publications: *Adoption and Contact, Sweet & Maxwell Practical Research Papers (ongoing); Care or Supervision Order,*

Sweet & Maxwell Practical Research Papers (ongoing)

Reported Cases: *Re B (agreed findings of fact)*, [1998] 2 FLR 968 (CA), 1998. Duty of Court in Care Proceedings when minimum threshold criteria agreed.
Re P (abduction: Minor's Views), [1998] 2 FLR 825 (CA), 1998. Child abduction – effect of the strongly held views of a teenager.

ROWELL DAVID STEWART

Chambers of Lord Goodhart QC
Ground Floor, 3 New Square, Lincoln's Inn, London WC2A 3RS,
Telephone: 0171 405 5577
E-mail:law@threenewsquare.demon.co.uk
Call Date: July 1972, Gray's Inn
Pupil Master
Qualifications: [BA (Oxon)]

ROWLAND MISS DERVILLE ANN

Sussex Chambers
9 Old Steine, Brighton, Sussex, BN1 1FJ,
Telephone: 01273 607953
Call Date: Oct 1996, Inner Temple
Qualifications: [LLB]

ROWLAND JOHN PETER QC (1996)

4 Pump Court
Temple, London EC4Y 7AN,
Telephone: 020 7842 5555
E-mail:chambers@4pumpcourt.law.co.uk
Call Date: Nov 1979, Middle Temple
Qualifications: [LLB (Lond) , BA (W.Aust)]

ROWLAND NICHOLAS EDWARD

3 Paper Buildings
Temple, London EC4Y 7EU,
Telephone: 020 7583 8055
E-mail: London@3paper.com
3 Paper Buildings (Bournemouth)
20 Lorne Park Road, Bournemouth, Dorset, BH1 1JN,
Telephone: 01202 292102
E-mail: Bournemouth@3paper.com
3 Paper Buildings (Winchester)
4 St Peter Street, Winchester SO23 8BW,
Telephone: 01962 868884
E-mail: winchester@3paper.com

3 Paper Buildings (Oxford)
1 Alfred Street, High Street, Oxford
OX1 4EH, Telephone: 01865 793736
E-mail: oxford@3paper.com
Call Date: July 1988, Inner Temple
Qualifications: [BA (Bristol), Dip Law (City)]

ROWLAND ROBIN FRANK

5 Fountain Court
Steelhouse Lane, Birmingham B4 6DR,
Telephone: 0121 606 0500
E-mail:clerks@5fountaincourt.law.co.uk
Call Date: Nov 1977, Middle Temple
Pupil Master
Qualifications: [LLB]

ROWLANDS MS CATHERINE JANET

Victoria Chambers
3rd Floor, 177 Corporation Street,
Birmingham B4 6RG,
Telephone: 0121 236 9900
E-mail: viccham@aol.com
Call Date: Nov 1992, Gray's Inn
Qualifications: [LLB (Lond), Maitrise en
Droit , (Paris)]

ROWLANDS DAVID PETER ANDREW

Broad Chare
33 Broad Chare, Newcastle upon Tyne
NE1 3DQ, Telephone: 0191 232 0541
E-mail:clerks@broadcharechambers.law.co.uk
Call Date: Nov 1988, Middle Temple
Qualifications: [LLB (Manch)]

ROWLANDS MARC HUMPHREYS

4 Pump Court
Temple, London EC4Y 7AN,
Telephone: 020 7842 5555
E-mail:chambers@4pumpcourt.law.co.uk
Call Date: Nov 1990, Gray's Inn
Qualifications: [BA Hons (Oxon)]

ROWLANDS PETER FRANCIS CLEVELAND

4 Brick Court
Ground Floor, Temple, London
EC4Y 9AD, Telephone: 0171 797 7766
E-mail: chambers@4brick.co.uk
Call Date: Feb 1990, Middle Temple
Pupil Master
Qualifications: [BA Hons (Oxon)]

ROWLANDS RHYS PRICE

Sedan House
Stanley Place, Chester CH1 2LU,
Telephone: 01244 320480/348282
Call Date: July 1986, Gray's Inn
Pupil Master
Qualifications: [MSc (Wales) LLB, (Lond)]

ROWLEY MRS ALISON CLAIRE

Arden Chambers
27 John Street, London WC1N 2BL,
Telephone: 020 7242 4244
E-mail:clerks@arden-chambers.law.co.uk
Call Date: Nov 1987, Middle Temple
Qualifications: [MA (Cantab)]

ROWLEY JOHN JAMES

28 St John Street
Manchester M3 4DJ,
Telephone: 0161 834 8418
E-mail: clerk@28stjohnst.co.uk
Call Date: July 1987, Lincoln's Inn
Qualifications: [MA (Cantab) Dip Law]

ROWLEY KARL JOHN

Young Street Chambers
38 Young Street, Manchester M3 3FT,
Telephone: 0161 833 0489
E-mail: clerks@young-st-chambers.com
Call Date: Nov 1994, Middle Temple
Qualifications: [BA (Hons)(Hons)]

ROWLEY KEITH NIGEL

11 Old Square
Ground Floor, Lincoln's Inn, London
WC2A 3TS, Telephone: 020 7430 0341
E-mail: clerks@11oldsquare.co.uk
Call Date: July 1979, Gray's Inn
Pupil Master
Qualifications: [LLB (Lond)]

ROWLEY MRS RACHEL ELISABETH

St Mary's Chambers
50 High Pavement, Lace Market,
Nottingham NG1 1HW,
Telephone: 0115 9503503
E-mail: clerks@smc.law.co.uk
Call Date: Nov 1997, Middle Temple
Qualifications: [BA (Hons)(Keele)]

ROWLING MISS FIONA JANE

Chambers of Helen Grindrod QC
4th Floor, 15-19 Devereux Court, London
WC2R 3JJ, Telephone: 0171 583 2792
Call Date: July 1980, Inner Temple
Qualifications: [LLB (Lond)]

ROWLINSON MISS WENDY JULIA

Chichester Chambers
12 North Pallant, Chichester, West Sussex,
PO19 1TQ, Telephone: 01243 784538
E-mail:clerks@chichesterchambers.law.co.uk
Call Date: July 1981, Gray's Inn
Qualifications: [BA]

ROWNTREE EDWARD JOHN PICKERING

Hardwicke Building
New Square, Lincoln's Inn, London
WC2A 3SB, Telephone: 020 7242 2523
E-mail: clerks@hardwicke.co.uk
Call Date: 1996, Lincoln's Inn
Qualifications: [BA (Hons)(Oxon)]

ROWSELL MISS CLAIRE LOUISE

Albion Chambers
Broad Street, Bristol BS1 1DR,
Telephone: 0117 9272144
Call Date: Feb 1991, Middle Temple
Qualifications: [LLB]

ROWSELL PAUL JOHN

2 King's Bench Walk
Ground Floor, Temple, London
EC4Y 7DE, Telephone: 0171 353 1746
E-mail: 2kbw@atlas.co.uk
King's Bench Chambers
115 North Hill, Plymouth PL4 8JY,
Telephone: 01752 221551
Call Date: July 1971, Inner Temple
Pupil Master
Qualifications: [LLB]

ROXBOROUGH ADAM BENEDICT

24a St John Street
Manchester M3 4DF,
Telephone: 0161 833 9628
Call Date: July 1998, Gray's Inn
Qualifications: [LLB (Manch)]

ROXBURGH ALAN JOHN NORTON

Brick Court Chambers
7-8 Essex Street, London WC2R 3LD,
Telephone: 0171 379 3550
E-mail: [surname]@brickcourt.co.uk
Call Date: Oct 1992, Middle Temple
Qualifications: [MA (Hons Oxon), Diploma
in Law(City)]

ROY-TOOLE CHRISTOPHER LAWRENCE

Durham Barristers' Chambers
27 Old Elvet, Durham DH1 3HN,
Telephone: 0191 386 9199
Call Date: Oct 1990, Middle Temple
Pupil Master
Qualifications: [BA (Oxon), Dip Law (City)]

ROYCE DARRYL FRASER

Atkin Chambers
1 Atkin Building, Gray's Inn, London
WC1R 5AT, Telephone: 020 7404 0102
E-mail: clerks@atkin-chambers.co.uk
Call Date: Nov 1976, Gray's Inn
Pupil Master
Qualifications: [BA]

ROYCE R JOHN QC (1987)

Guildhall Chambers
22-26 Broad Street, Bristol BS1 2HG,
Telephone: 0117 9273366
E-mail:civil.clerks@guildhallchambers.co.uk and
criminal.clerks@guildhallchambers.co.uk
Call Date: 1970, Gray's Inn
Recorder
Qualifications: [BA (Cantab)]

ROZHAN ARIFF

One Garden Court Family Law Chambers
Ground Floor, Temple, London
EC4Y 9BJ, Telephone: 0171 797 7900
E-mail: clerks@onegardencourt.co.uk
Call Date: Feb 1990, Inner Temple
Qualifications: [LLB (Read)]

D

RUBENS MISS JACQUELINE ANN

Trafalgar Chambers
53 Fleet Street, London EC4Y 1BE,
Telephone: 0171 583 5858
E-mail:trafalgarchambers@easynet.co.uk
Call Date: Nov 1989, Inner Temple
Qualifications: [BA (Florida), LLB (Hons)
(Lond)]

RUBERY PHILIP ALAN

8 King's Bench Walk
2nd Floor, Temple, London EC4Y 7DU,
Telephone: 0171 797 8888
8 King's Bench Walk North
1 Park Square East, Leeds LS1 2NE,
Telephone: 0113 2439797
Call Date: July 1973, Lincoln's Inn

RUBIN ANTHONY JOHN MEEK

St James's Chambers
68 Quay Street, Manchester M3 3EJ,
Telephone: 0161 834 7000
E-mail: clerks@stjameschambers.co.uk
Call Date: May 1960, Gray's Inn

RUBIN STEPHEN CHARLES

Farrar's Building
Temple, London EC4Y 7BD,
Telephone: 0171 583 9241
E-mail:chambers@farrarsbuilding.co.uk
Call Date: July 1977, Middle Temple
Pupil Master
Qualifications: [MA (Oxon)]

RUCK MS MARY IDA

10 King's Bench Walk
1st Floor, Temple, London EC4Y 7EB,
Telephone: 0171 353 2501
Peel Court Chambers
45 Hardman Street, Manchester M3 3PL,
Telephone: 0161 832 3791
E-mail: clerks@peelct.co.uk
Call Date: Oct 1993, Gray's Inn
Qualifications: [BA (Hons), MA]

RUDD MATTHEW ALLAN

**11 Bolt Court (also at 7 Stone Buildings
– 1st Floor)**
London EC4A 3DQ,
Telephone: 0171 353 2300
E-mail: boltct11@aol.com

Redhill Chambers
Seloduct House, 30 Station Road, Redhill,
Surrey, RH1 1NF,
Telephone: 01737 780781
**7 Stone Buildings (also at 11 Bolt
Court)**
1st Floor, Lincoln's Inn, London
WC2A 3SZ, Telephone: 0171 242 0961
E-mail:larthur@7stonebuildings.law.co.uk
Call Date: Nov 1994, Inner Temple
Qualifications: [BA (Hons)(Sheff)]

RUDLAND MARTIN WILLIAM

Chambers of Andrew Campbell QC
10 Park Square, Leeds LS1 2LH,
Telephone: 0113 2455438
E-mail: clerks@10pksq.co.uk
Call Date: July 1977, Middle Temple
Pupil Master, Recorder
Qualifications: [LLB (Hons)]

RUDMAN MISS SARA ANN

Pendragon Chambers
124 Walter Road, Swansea, West
Glamorgan, SA1 5RG,
Telephone: 01792 411188
Call Date: Nov 1992, Inner Temple
Qualifications: [LLB (Hons)]

RUEFF PHILIP EDMOND BRUNO MARCUS

2 King's Bench Walk Chambers
1st Floor, 2 King's Bench Walk, Temple,
London EC4Y 7DE,
Telephone: 020 7353 9276
E-mail: chambers@2kbw.co.uk
Call Date: Nov 1969, Gray's Inn
Pupil Master, Recorder
Qualifications: [BA (Oxon) LLM (New, York)]

RUFFELL MARK BERESFORD

4 King's Bench Walk
2nd Floor, Temple, London EC4Y 7DL,
Telephone: 020 7353 3581
E-mail: clerks@4kbw.co.uk
Call Date: Nov 1992, Middle Temple
Qualifications: [BA (Hons), Dip Law (CPE)]

RULE JONATHAN DANIEL

Merchant Chambers
1 North Parade, Parsonage Gardens,
Manchester M3 2NH,
Telephone: 0161 839 7070
E-mail: merchant.chambers@virgin.net
Call Date: Nov 1993, Gray's Inn
Qualifications: [BA (Hons, Oxon)]

RUMBELOW ARTHUR ANTHONY QC (1990)

28 St John Street
Manchester M3 4DJ,
Telephone: 0161 834 8418
E-mail: clerk@28stjohnst.co.uk
1 Serjeants' Inn
4th Floor, Temple, London EC4Y 1NH,
Telephone: 0171 583 1355
E-mail: clerks@serjeants-inn.co.uk
Call Date: July 1967, Middle Temple
Recorder
Qualifications: [BA (Cantab)]

RUMFITT NIGEL JOHN QC (1994)

9 Bedford Row
London WC1R 4AZ,
Telephone: 0171 242 3555
E-mail: clerks@9br.co.uk
Call Date: July 1974, Middle Temple
Recorder
Qualifications: [BCL (Oxon), MA (Oxon)]

RUMNEY CONRAD WILLIAM ARTHUR

St Philip's Chambers
Fountain Court, Steelhouse Lane,
Birmingham B4 6DR,
Telephone: 0121 246 7000
E-mail: clerks@st-philips.co.uk
Call Date: Feb 1988, Inner Temple
Qualifications: [MA (Oxon), Dip Law]

RUNDELL RICHARD JOHN

2-3 Gray's Inn Square
Gray's Inn, London WC1R 5JH,
Telephone: 0171 242 4986
E-mail:chambers@2-3graysinnsquare.co.uk
Call Date: Feb 1971, Gray's Inn
Pupil Master, Recorder
Qualifications: [LLB]

RUPASINHA SUNIL JAYANTHA

1 Harcourt Buildings
2nd Floor, Temple, London EC4Y 9DA,
Telephone: 0171 353 9421/0375
E-mail:clerks@1harcourtbuildings.law.co.uk
Call Date: Nov 1983, Inner Temple
Qualifications: [LLB (Cardiff)]

RUSCOE MISS JANET CAROLINE

New Walk Chambers
27 New Walk, Leicester LE1 6TE,
Telephone: 0116 2559144
Kenworthy's Chambers
83 Bridge Street, Manchester M3 2RF,
Telephone: 0161 832 4036/834 6954
E-mail: clerks@kenworthys.co.uk
Call Date: 1995, Lincoln's Inn
Qualifications: [LLB (Hons)(Northumb), LLM (Manch)]

RUSH CRAIG PETER

3 Hare Court
1 Little Essex Street, London WC2R 3LD,
Telephone: 0171 395 2000
Call Date: Nov 1989, Inner Temple
Pupil Master
Qualifications: [LLB]

RUSHBROOKE JUSTIN CHARLES NEIL

5 Raymond Buildings
1st Floor, Gray's Inn, London WC1R 5BP,
Telephone: 0171 242 2902
E-mail: clerks@media-ent-law.co.uk
Call Date: Oct 1992, Middle Temple
Qualifications: [MA (Oxon)]

RUSHTON MS NICOLA JANE

5 Paper Buildings
Ground Floor, Temple, London
EC4Y 7HB, Telephone: 0171 583 9275/
583 4555 E-mail: 5paper@link.org
Call Date: Oct 1993, Gray's Inn
Qualifications: [BA (Cantab), LLM (Canada)]

RUSSELL MS ALISON ELIZABETH

Holborn Chambers
6 Gate Street, Lincoln's Inn Fields, London
WC2A 3HP, Telephone: 0171 242 6060
Call Date: Oct 1993, Middle Temple
Qualifications: [LLB (Hons, Essex)]

RUSSELL MS ALISON HUNTER

1 Pump Court
Lower Ground Floor, Temple, London
EC4Y 7AB, Telephone: 0171 583 2012/
353 4341
E-mail: [name]@1pumpcourt.co.uk
Call Date: July 1983, Gray's Inn
Pupil Master
Qualifications: [BA (Hons)]

RUSSELL ANTHONY PATRICK QC (1999)

Peel Court Chambers
45 Hardman Street, Manchester M3 3PL,
Telephone: 0161 832 3791
E-mail: clerks@peelct.co.uk
Call Date: 1974, Middle Temple
Pupil Master
Qualifications: [MA (Oxon)]

RUSSELL MISS CHRISTINA MARTHA

9-12 Bell Yard
London WC2A 2LF,
Telephone: 0171 400 1800
E-mail: clerks@bellyard.co.uk
Call Date: Oct 1994, Gray's Inn
Qualifications: [MA (Cantab)]

RUSSELL CHRISTOPHER GARNET

12 New Square
Lincoln's Inn, London WC2A 3SW,
Telephone: 0171 419 1212
E-mail: chambers@12newsquare.co.uk
Sovereign Chambers
25 Park Square, Leeds LS1 2PW,
Telephone: 0113 2451841/2/3
E-mail:sovereignchambers@btinternet.com
Call Date: Nov 1971, Middle Temple
Pupil Master
Qualifications: [MA (Oxon)]

Out of hours telephone: 0171 383 5943

Types of work: Chancery (general), Chancery
land law, Commercial, Commercial litigation, Commercial property, Equity, wills
and trusts, Insolvency, Landlord and
tenant, Partnerships, Professional negligence

Reported Cases: *Re Islington Metal and
Plating Works*, [1984] 1 WLR 14. Company
winding up: whether unliquidated
damages claim in test provable while
company insolvent: company becoming
solvent.
Basingstoke and Deane BC v HOST Group,
[1986] 2 EGLR 107. Rent review: whether,
in general, a notional letting is to be on the
same terms, except rent, as existing lease.
Celsteel Ltd v Alton House Holdings,
[1986] 1 WLR 512 (CA). Jurisdiction to
grant *quia timet* injunction against interference with right of way.
*Alliance and Leicester Building Society v
Edgestop Ltd and Ors*, [1994] 2 All ER 38.
Contributory negligence no defence to
deceit. Vicarious liability for fraud of
employee with ostensible authority.
*R v Law Society, ex p Alliance and
Leicester Building Society*, [1997] 2 All ER
384 (CA). Judicial review of policy of Solicitors' Compensation Fund for mortgage
lenders.

RUSSELL CHRISTOPHER JOHN

2 Temple Gardens
Temple, London EC4Y 9AY,
Telephone: 0171 583 6041
E-mail: clerks@2templegardens.co.uk
Call Date: Nov 1982, Gray's Inn
Pupil Master
Qualifications: [LLB (Exon)]

RUSSELL MISS FERN

2 King's Bench Walk
Ground Floor, Temple, London
EC4Y 7DE, Telephone: 0171 353 1746
E-mail: 2kbw@atlas.co.uk
King's Bench Chambers
115 North Hill, Plymouth PL4 8JY,
Telephone: 01752 221551
Call Date: Nov 1994, Middle Temple
Qualifications: [BA (Hons)]

RUSSELL GUY JONOTHON

Westgate Chambers
144 High Street, Lewes, East Sussex,
BN7 1XT, Telephone: 01273 480510
Call Date: Nov 1985, Gray's Inn
Qualifications: [BA]

RUSSELL MISS JENNIFER ANNE

New Court Chambers
Gazette Building, 168 Corporation Street,
Birmingham B4 6TZ,
Telephone: 0121 693 6656
Call Date: 1990, Middle Temple
Qualifications: [LLB (Hons)]

RUSSELL JEREMY FRANCIS JOHN

2 Pump Court
1st Floor, Temple, London EC4Y 7AH,
Telephone: 0171 353 5597
Call Date: Nov 1973, Middle Temple
Qualifications: [MA (Cantab) LLB]

RUSSELL JEREMY JONATHAN QC (1994)

4 Essex Court
Temple, London EC4Y 9AJ,
Telephone: 020 7797 7970
E-mail: clerks@4essexcourt.law.co.uk
Call Date: Nov 1975, Middle Temple
Qualifications: [BA, LLM (Lond)]

Fax: 0171 353 0998;
Out of hours telephone: 01494 762 276;
DX: 292 London, Chancery Lane

Types of work: Admiralty, Arbitration, Aviation, Commercial, Commercial litigation, Insurance/reinsurance, International trade, Private international, Sale and carriage of goods, Shipping, admiralty

Awards and memberships: COMBAR, LCL & CBA, Fellow of Society for Advanced Legal Studies (FSALS), supporting member LMAA

Reported Cases: *Airbus Industrie GIE v Patel*, [1998] 2 All ER 257 (HL), 1998. A leading case on the extent of the English Court's jurisdiction to grant anti-suit injunctions.
The 'Herceg Novi', [1998] 2 Lloyd's 454 (CA), 1998. A leading case on the application of the principle of *forum non conveniens* in cases involving limitation of shipowners' liability.
The 'River Gurara', [1998] 1 Lloyd's 225 (CA), 1997. First consideration by English Court of the meaning of 'package or unit' under Hague Rules in a container case.
The 'Kosczerzyna', [1996] 2 Lloyd's 124 (CA), 1996. First consideration by CA of the true construction of Art 17 of the Collision Regulations.

The 'Devotion' (CA), [1995] 1 Lloyd's 589 (CA), 1995. Collision case involving consideration by Court of approach to be taken to use of computer reconstructions.

RUSSELL MISS MARGUERITE

Two Garden Court
1st Floor, Middle Temple, London
EC4Y 9BL, Telephone: 0171 353 1633
E-mail:barristers@2gardenct.law.co.uk
Call Date: July 1972, Lincoln's Inn
Pupil Master
Qualifications: [LLM]

RUSSELL MARTIN HOWARD

17 Bedford Row
London WC1R 4EB,
Telephone: 0171 831 7314
E-mail: iboard7314@aol.com
Call Date: Nov 1977, Inner Temple
Pupil Master
Qualifications: [LLB]

RUSSELL PAUL ANTHONY WELLINGTON

12 King's Bench Walk
Temple, London EC4Y 7EL,
Telephone: 0171 583 0811
E-mail: chambers@12kbw.co.uk
Call Date: July 1984, Middle Temple
Qualifications: [BA (Dunelm)]

RUSSELL ROBERT JOHN FINLAY

4 Essex Court
Temple, London EC4Y 9AJ,
Telephone: 020 7797 7970
E-mail: clerks@4essexcourt.law.co.uk
Call Date: Oct 1993, Middle Temple
Qualifications: [BA (Hons)(Oxon)]

RUSSELL FLINT SIMON COLERIDGE

23 Essex Street
London WC2R 3AS,
Telephone: 0171 413 0353/836 8366
E-mail:clerks@essexstreet23.demon.co.uk
Call Date: Nov 1980, Inner Temple
Pupil Master, Assistant Recorder
Qualifications: [BA]

D

RUSSEN JONATHAN HUW SINCLAIR

13 Old Square
Ground Floor, Lincoln's Inn, London
WC2A 3UA, Telephone: 0171 404 4800
E-mail: clerks@13oldsquare.law.co.uk
Call Date: July 1986, Lincoln's Inn
Pupil Master
Qualifications: [LLB Wales, LLM, Cantab.]

RUSSEN SIMON NICHOLAS SINCLAIR

Chambers of John L Powell QC
Four New Square, Lincoln's Inn, London
WC2A 3RJ, Telephone: 0171 797 8000
E-mail: barristers@4newsquare.com
Call Date: July 1976, Lincoln's Inn
Qualifications: [BA, FCIArb]

RUTHERFORD MARTIN

3 Temple Gardens
Lower Ground Floor, Temple, London
EC4Y 9AU, Telephone: 0171 353 3102/5/
9297 E-mail: clerks@3tg.co.uk
Call Date: Oct 1990, Lincoln's Inn
Pupil Master
Qualifications: [BA (Cardiff), Dip Law]

RUTLEDGE KELVIN ALBERT

Chambers of Norman Palmer
2 Field Court, Gray's Inn, London
WC1R 5BB, Telephone: 0171 405 6114
E-mail: fieldct2@netcomuk.co.uk
Call Date: July 1989, Middle Temple
Pupil Master
Qualifications: [LLB (Essex), LLB (Lond)]

RUTTER ANDREW MICHAEL

3 Temple Gardens
2nd Floor, Temple, London EC4Y 9AU,
Telephone: 0171 583 1155
Call Date: July 1990, Middle Temple
Qualifications: [LLB (Lond)]

RUTTLE STEPHEN QC (1997)

Brick Court Chambers
7-8 Essex Street, London WC2R 3LD,
Telephone: 0171 379 3550
E-mail: [surname]@brickcourt.co.uk
Call Date: Nov 1976, Gray's Inn
Qualifications: [BA (Cantab)]

RYAN DAVID PATRICK

Chambers of Geoffrey Hawker
46/48 Essex Street, London WC2R 3GH,
Telephone: 0171 583 8899
Call Date: Nov 1985, Inner Temple
Pupil Master
Qualifications: [LLB (Hons)]

RYAN MISS EITHNE MARY CATHERINE

Hardwicke Building
New Square, Lincoln's Inn, London
WC2A 3SB, Telephone: 020 7242 2523
E-mail: clerks@hardwicke.co.uk
Call Date: July 1990, Inner Temple
Qualifications: [LLB (Dublin)]

RYAN GERARD CHARLES QC (1981)

2 Harcourt Buildings
2nd Floor, Temple, London EC4Y 9DB,
Telephone: 020 7353 8415
E-mail: clerks@2hb.law.co.uk
Call Date: 1955, Middle Temple
Qualifications: [MA (Cantab)]

RYAN JOHN EMRYS HUGH

New Walk Chambers
27 New Walk, Leicester LE1 6TE,
Telephone: 0116 2559144
Call Date: Oct 1997, Gray's Inn
Qualifications: [LLB (Wales)]

RYAN NICHOLAS JOSEPH

Adrian Lyon's Chambers
14 Castle Street, Liverpool L2 0NE,
Telephone: 0151 236 4421/8240
E-mail: chambers14@aol.com
Call Date: July 1984, Gray's Inn
Qualifications: [BA (Lond)]

RYAN TIMOTHY JOHN

8 King's Bench Walk
2nd Floor, Temple, London EC4Y 7DU,
Telephone: 0171 797 8888
8 King's Bench Walk North
1 Park Square East, Leeds LS1 2NE,
Telephone: 0113 2439797
Call Date: Nov 1991, Inner Temple
Qualifications: [LLB (Lond)]

RYAN WILLIAM

8 King's Bench Walk
2nd Floor, Temple, London EC4Y 7DU,
Telephone: 0171 797 8888
8 King's Bench Walk North
1 Park Square East, Leeds LS1 2NE,
Telephone: 0113 2439797
Call Date: Oct 1994, Gray's Inn
Qualifications: [LLB (Hons)]

RYDER ERNEST NIGEL QC (1997)

Deans Court Chambers
24 St John Street, Manchester M3 4DF,
Telephone: 0161 214 6000
E-mail: clerks@deanscourt.co.uk
Deans Court Chambers
41-43 Market Place, Preston PR1 1AH,
Telephone: 01772 555163
E-mail: clerks@deanscourt.co.uk
1 Mitre Court Buildings
Temple, London EC4Y 7BS,
Telephone: 0171 797 7070
E-mail: clerks@1mcb.com
Call Date: July 1981, Gray's Inn
Assistant Recorder
Qualifications: [MA (Cantab)]

RYDER JOHN

6 King's Bench Walk
Ground Floor, Temple, London
EC4Y 7DR, Telephone: 0171 583 0410
E-mail: worsley@6kbw.freeserve.co.uk
Call Date: Nov 1980, Inner Temple
Pupil Master, Assistant Recorder
Qualifications: [BA Hons]

RYDER MATTHEW CONRAD

Cloisters
1 Pump Court, Temple, London
EC4Y 7AA, Telephone: 0171 827 4000
E-mail: clerks@cloisters.com
Call Date: Nov 1992, Gray's Inn
Qualifications: [BA]

RYDER TIMOTHY ROBERT

Queen's Chambers
5 John Dalton Street, Manchester M2 6ET,
Telephone: 0161 834 6875/4738

Queens Chambers
4 Camden Place, Preston PR1 3JL,
Telephone: 01772 828300
Call Date: 1977, Middle Temple
Pupil Master, Assistant Recorder
Qualifications: [MA (Cantab)]

RYLANCE JOHN RANDOLPH TREVOR

Francis Taylor Building
Ground Floor, Temple, London
EC4Y 7BY, Telephone: 0171 353 7768/
7769/2711
E-mail:clerks@francistaylorbuilding.law.co.uk
Call Date: Nov 1968, Lincoln's Inn
Pupil Master, Recorder

RYLANDS MISS MARGARET ELIZABETH

8 King Street Chambers
8 King Street, Manchester M2 6AQ,
Telephone: 0161 834 9560
E-mail: eightking@aol.com
Call Date: Nov 1973, Middle Temple
Pupil Master, Assistant Recorder
Qualifications: [LLB (Hons) (Bris)]

SABBEN-CLARE MISS REBECCA MARY

S Tomlinson QC
7 King's Bench Walk, Temple, London
EC4Y 7DS, Telephone: 0171 583 0404
E-mail: clerks@7kbw.law.co.uk
Call Date: Oct 1993, Gray's Inn
Qualifications: [MA (Oxon)]

SABIDO JOHN HARRIES

1 Dr Johnson's Buildings
Ground Floor, Temple, London
EC4Y 7AX, Telephone: 0171 353 9328
E-mail:OneDr.Johnsons@btinternet.com
Dr Johnson's Chambers
The Atrium Court, Apex Plaza, Reading,
Berkshire, RG1 1AX,
Telephone: 01734 254221
Call Date: July 1976, Lincoln's Inn
Pupil Master

SABINE JOHN ALEXANDER

Portsmouth Barristers' Chambers
Victory House, 7 Bellevue Terrace,
Portsmouth, Hampshire, PO5 3AT,
Telephone: 023 92 831292/811811
E-mail: clerks@portsmouthbar.com
Call Date: July 1979, Gray's Inn
Qualifications: [MA BCL]

SABISTON PETER JOHN

Baker Street Chambers
9 Baker Street, Middlesbrough TS1 2LF,
Telephone: 01642 873873
Call Date: Feb 1992, Gray's Inn
Qualifications: [LLB (N'Castle)]

SABRY KARIM SAMIR

Manchester House Chambers
18-22 Bridge Street, Manchester M3 3BZ,
Telephone: 0161 834 7007
8 King Street Chambers
8 King Street, Manchester M2 6AQ,
Telephone: 0161 834 9560
E-mail: eightking@aol.com
Call Date: Nov 1992, Inner Temple
Qualifications: [BA (Hons)]

SADD PATRICK JAMES THOMAS

199 Strand
London WC2R 1DR,
Telephone: 0171 379 9779
E-mail: chambers@199strand.co.uk
Call Date: Nov 1984, Middle Temple
Pupil Master
Qualifications: [BA]

SADIQ TARIQ MAHMOOD

Chambers of John Hand QC
9 St John Street, Manchester M3 4DN,
Telephone: 0161 955 9000
E-mail: ninesjs@gconnect.com
Call Date: Nov 1993, Gray's Inn
Qualifications: [BA (Hons) (Kent)]

SAGAR (EDWARD) LEIGH

12 New Square
Lincoln's Inn, London WC2A 3SW,
Telephone: 0171 419 1212
E-mail: chambers@12newsquare.co.uk

Newport Chambers
12 Clytha Park Road, Newport, Gwent,
NP9 47L, Telephone: 01633 267403/
255855
Sovereign Chambers
25 Park Square, Leeds LS1 2PW,
Telephone: 0113 2451841/2/3
E-mail:sovereignchambers@btinternet.com
Call Date: July 1983, Lincoln's Inn
Pupil Master
Qualifications: [BA (Lond)]

SAGGERSON ALAN DAVID

Barnard's Inn Chambers
6th Floor, Halton House, 20-23 Holborn,
London EC1N 2JD,
Telephone: 0171 369 6969
E-mail: clerks@biclaw.co.uk
Call Date: July 1981, Lincoln's Inn
Pupil Master
Qualifications: [MA, BCL (Oxon)]

SAHONTE RAJINDER KUMAR

22 Old Buildings
Lincoln's Inn, London WC2A 3UJ,
Telephone: 0171 831 0222
Call Date: Nov 1986, Lincoln's Inn
Pupil Master
Qualifications: [LLB (Hons)]

SAHOTA MISS SUKHJINDER

Call Date: Feb 1992, Lincoln's Inn
Qualifications: [LLB (Hons) (Bucks), LLM]

SAINI PUSHPINDER

Blackstone Chambers
Blackstone House, Temple, London
EC4Y 9BW, Telephone: 0171 583 1770
E-mail:clerks@blackstonechambers.com
Call Date: Oct 1991, Gray's Inn
Pupil Master
Qualifications: [BA (Oxon), BCL (Oxon)]

SALEEM SARWAR

Call Date: Feb 1960, Lincoln's Inn
Qualifications: [LLM (Manch), BSc]

SALES PHILIP JAMES

11 King's Bench Walk
Temple, London EC4Y 7EQ,
Telephone: 0171 632 8500/583 0610
E-mail: clerksroom@11kbw.com
Call Date: July 1985, Lincoln's Inn
Pupil Master, Assistant Recorder
Qualifications: [MA (Cantab), BCL, (Oxon)]

SALLON CHRISTOPHER ROBERT QC (1994)

Doughty Street Chambers
11 Doughty Street, London WC1N 2PG,
Telephone: 0171 404 1313
E-mail:enquiries@doughtystreet.co.uk
Westgate Chambers
144 High Street, Lewes, East Sussex,
BN7 1XT, Telephone: 01273 480510
Call Date: July 1973, Gray's Inn
Recorder

SALMON CHARLES NATHAN QC (1996)

1 Hare Court
Ground Floor, Temple, London
EC4Y 7BE, Telephone: 0171 353 3982/
5324
Call Date: Nov 1972, Inner Temple
Recorder
Qualifications: [LLB (Hons)]

SALMON JONATHAN CARL

1 Fountain Court
Steelhouse Lane, Birmingham B4 6DR,
Telephone: 0121 236 5721
Call Date: Nov 1987, Inner Temple
Qualifications: [LLB (Nottm)]

SALMON KEVIN

King Charles House
Standard Hill, Nottingham NG1 6FX,
Telephone: 0115 9418851
E-mail: clerks@kch.co.uk
Call Date: Nov 1984, Gray's Inn
Qualifications: [MA (St Andrews)]

SALMON MISS LOUISE MELISSA

Bell Yard Chambers
116/118 Chancery Lane, London
WC2A 1PP, Telephone: 0171 306 9292
Call Date: Nov 1991, Middle Temple
Qualifications: [BA Hons , LLM (Lond)]

SALOMAN TIMOTHY PETER (DAYRELL) QC (1993)

S Tomlinson QC
7 King's Bench Walk, Temple, London
EC4Y 7DS, Telephone: 0171 583 0404
E-mail: clerks@7kbw.law.co.uk
Call Date: Nov 1975, Middle Temple
Assistant Recorder
Qualifications: [BA (Oxon)]

SALTER ADRIAN NICHOLAS

11 Stone Buildings
Lincoln's Inn, London WC2A 3TG,
Telephone: +44 (0)207 831 6381
E-mail:clerks@11StoneBuildings.law.co.uk
Chichester Chambers
12 North Pallant, Chichester, West Sussex,
PO19 1TQ, Telephone: 01243 784538
E-mail:clerks@chichesterchambers.law.co.uk
Call Date: July 1973, Middle Temple
Pupil Master
Qualifications: [BA (Cantab)]

SALTER CHARLES PHILIP ARTHUR

8 King's Bench Walk
2nd Floor, Temple, London EC4Y 7DU,
Telephone: 0171 797 8888
8 King's Bench Walk North
1 Park Square East, Leeds LS1 2NE,
Telephone: 0113 2439797
Call Date: July 1981, Lincoln's Inn
Pupil Master
Qualifications: [BSc]

SALTER RICHARD STANLEY QC (1995)

3 Verulam Buildings
London WC1R 5NT,
Telephone: 0171 831 8441
E-mail: clerks@3verulam.co.uk
Call Date: July 1975, Inner Temple
Assistant Recorder
Qualifications: [MA (Oxon), ACIArb]

SALTER MISS SIBBY ANNE VICTORIA

1 Gray's Inn Square
Ground Floor, London WC1R 5AA,
Telephone: 0171 405 8946/7/8
Call Date: Oct 1991, Middle Temple
Qualifications: [BA Hons (Cantab)]

SALTS NIGEL THOMAS QC (1983)

2 Paper Buildings
1st Floor, Temple, London EC4Y 7ET,
Telephone: 020 7556 5500
E-mail: clerks@2pbbarristers.co.uk
Call Date: June 1961, Inner Temple

SALVESEN KEITH NEVILLE

Queen Elizabeth Building
Ground Floor, Temple, London
EC4Y 9BS,
Telephone: 0171 353 7181 (12 Lines)
Call Date: Nov 1974, Inner Temple
Qualifications: [MA (Cantab)]

SALZEDO SIMON LOPEZ

Brick Court Chambers
7-8 Essex Street, London WC2R 3LD,
Telephone: 0171 379 3550
E-mail: [surname]@brickcourt.co.uk
Call Date: Nov 1995, Lincoln's Inn
Qualifications: [BA (Hons)(Oxon), ACA Dip
Law (City)]

SAMAT DAREN ARMAND CAMERON

2 Paper Buildings
1st Floor, Temple, London EC4Y 7ET,
Telephone: 020 7556 5500
E-mail: clerks@2pbbarristers.co.uk
Call Date: Oct 1992, Middle Temple
Qualifications: [LL.B (Hons)]

SAMEK CHARLES STEPHEN

Littleton Chambers
3 King's Bench Walk North, Temple,
London EC4Y 7HR,
Telephone: 0171 797 8600
E-mail:clerks@littletonchambers.co.uk
Call Date: Nov 1989, Middle Temple
Pupil Master
Qualifications: [BA (Oxon), Dip Law (City)]

SAMIMI MISS MARYAM

Mitre House Chambers
15-19 Devereux Court, London WC2R 3JJ,
Telephone: 0171 583 8233
Call Date: 1994, Middle Temple
Qualifications: [BA (Hons), LLM (Lond)]

SAMPSON GRAEME WILLIAM

1 Harcourt Buildings
2nd Floor, Temple, London EC4Y 9DA,
Telephone: 0171 353 9421/0375
E-mail:clerks@1harcourtbuildings.law.co.uk
Call Date: Nov 1981, Gray's Inn
Pupil Master
Qualifications: [BA]

SAMPSON JAMES

Wilberforce Chambers
7 Bishop Lane, Hull, East Yorkshire,
HU1 1PA, Telephone: 01482 323264
E-mail: clerks@hullbar.demon.co.uk
Call Date: Nov 1985, Inner Temple
Pupil Master
Qualifications: [LLB (Nott'm)]

SAMPSON JONATHAN ROBERT

Harcourt Chambers
1st Floor, 2 Harcourt Buildings, Temple,
London EC4Y 9DB,
Telephone: 0171 353 6961
E-mail:clerks@harcourtchambers.law.co.uk
Harcourt Chambers
Churchill House, 3 St Aldate's Courtyard,
St Aldate's, Oxford OX1 1BN,
Telephone: 01865 791559
E-mail:clerks@harcourtchambers.law.co.uk
Call Date: 1997, Middle Temple
Qualifications: [BA (Hons)(Cantab)]

SAMUEL DAVID GERWYN

Lamb Chambers
Lamb Building, Temple, London
EC4Y 7AS, Telephone: 020 7797 8300
E-mail: lambchambers@link.org
Call Date: July 1986, Gray's Inn
Pupil Master
Qualifications: [MA (Oxon)]

SAMUEL GLYN ROSS

St Philip's Chambers
Fountain Court, Steelhouse Lane,
Birmingham B4 6DR,
Telephone: 0121 246 7000
E-mail: clerks@st-philips.co.uk
Call Date: 1991, Lincoln's Inn
Qualifications: [LLB (Hons)]

SAMUEL MISS JACQUELINE ELEANOR

1 Hare Court
Ground Floor, Temple, London
EC4Y 7BE, Telephone: 0171 353 3982/
5324
Call Date: July 1971, Gray's Inn
Pupil Master
Qualifications: [LLB (Hons)(Lond)]

SAMUEL RICHARD GEOFFREY GRAHAM

Maidstone Chambers
33 Earl Street, Maidstone, Kent, ME14 1PF,
Telephone: 01622 688592
E-mail:maidstonechambers@compuserve.co
m
Call Date: 1996, Middle Temple
Qualifications: [MA (Hons)(Edinburgh), LLM
(Hons) (City)]

SAMUELS JEFFREY KEITH

28 St John Street
Manchester M3 4DJ,
Telephone: 0161 834 8418
E-mail: clerk@28stjohnst.co.uk
Call Date: July 1988, Middle Temple
Qualifications: [LLB (Hons) (Leeds)]

SAMUELS LESLIE JOHN

Pump Court Chambers
Upper Ground Floor, 3 Pump Court,
Temple, London EC4Y 7AJ,
Telephone: 0171 353 0711
E-mail: clerks@3pumpcourt.com
Pump Court Chambers
31 Southgate Street, Winchester
SO23 9EE, Telephone: 01962 868161
E-mail: clerks@3pumpcourt.com

Pump Court Chambers
5 Temple Chambers, Temple Street,
Swindon SN1 1SQ,
Telephone: 01793 539899
E-mail: clerks@3pumpcourt.com
Call Date: July 1989, Gray's Inn
Pupil Master
Qualifications: [BA (Cantab), MA (Toronto)]

SANDALL MS GILLIAN DORIS

12 Old Square
1st Floor, Lincoln's Inn, London
WC2A 3TX, Telephone: 0171 404 0875
Call Date: Nov 1992, Inner Temple
Qualifications: [BA (E.Anglia), Dip in law]

SANDBROOK-HUGHES STEWERT KARL ANTHONY

Iscoed Chambers
86 St Helen's Road, Swansea, West
Glamorgan, SA1 4BQ,
Telephone: 01792 652988/9/330
Call Date: Nov 1980, Lincoln's Inn
Pupil Master
Qualifications: [BSc Econ (Wales) , Dip Law]

SANDELLS MS NICOLE

11 Old Square
Ground Floor, Lincoln's Inn, London
WC2A 3TS, Telephone: 020 7430 0341
E-mail: clerks@11oldsquare.co.uk
Call Date: Nov 1994, Inner Temple
Qualifications: [BA (Oxon)]

SANDEMAN DAVID MCEWEN

2 King's Bench Walk Chambers
1st Floor, 2 King's Bench Walk, Temple,
London EC4Y 7DE,
Telephone: 020 7353 9276
E-mail: chambers@2kbw.co.uk
Call Date: Nov 1993, Middle Temple
Qualifications: [LLB (Hons)(Kingston)]

SANDER ANDREW THOMAS

Oriel Chambers
14 Water Street, Liverpool L2 8TD,
Telephone: 0151 236 7191/236 4321
E-mail: clerks@oriel-chambers.co.uk

Goldsmith Building
1st Floor, Temple, London EC4Y 7BL,
Telephone: 0171 353 7881
E-mail:clerks@goldsmith-building.law.co.uk
Call Date: Nov 1970, Middle Temple
Pupil Master, Recorder
Qualifications: [LLB (L'pool)]

SANDERS (JAMES) DAMIAN

India Buildings Chambers
Water Street, Liverpool L2 0XG,
Telephone: 0151 243 6000
E-mail: clerks@chambers.u-net.com
Call Date: Nov 1988, Middle Temple
Qualifications: [LLB]

SANDERS NEIL JOHN TAIT

29 Bedford Row Chambers
London WC1R 4HE,
Telephone: 0171 831 2626
Call Date: July 1975, Inner Temple
Pupil Master
Qualifications: [MA (Cantab)]

SANDERSON DAVID FRANK

3 Paper Buildings
Temple, London EC4Y 7EU,
Telephone: 020 7583 8055
E-mail: London@3paper.com
3 Paper Buildings (Bournemouth)
20 Lorne Park Road, Bournemouth,
Dorset, BH1 1JN,
Telephone: 01202 292102
E-mail: Bournemouth@3paper.com
3 Paper Buildings (Winchester)
4 St Peter Street, Winchester SO23 8BW,
Telephone: 01962 868884
E-mail: winchester@3paper.com
3 Paper Buildings (Oxford)
1 Alfred Street, High Street, Oxford
OX1 4EH, Telephone: 01865 793736
E-mail: oxford@3paper.com
Call Date: Nov 1985, Inner Temple
Qualifications: [BA (Sussex)]

SANDFORD SIMON JOHN AUSTIN

5 King's Bench Walk
Temple, London EC4Y 7DN,
Telephone: 0171 353 5638
Call Date: Nov 1979, Gray's Inn
Pupil Master
Qualifications: [MA (Cantab)]

SANDHU SUNIT

Equity Chambers
3rd Floor, 153a Corporation Street,
Birmingham B4 6PH,
Telephone: 0121 233 2100
E-mail: equityatusa.com
Call Date: Feb 1990, Middle Temple
Qualifications: [LLB(Hons)(B'ham), BA]

SANDIFORD JONATHAN

St Paul's House
5th Floor, St Paul's House, 23 Park Square
South, Leeds LS1 2ND,
Telephone: 0113 2455866
E-mail: catherinegrimshaw@stpauls-
chambers.demon.co.uk
Call Date: Oct 1992, Gray's Inn
Qualifications: [LLB (Hons) (Newc)]

SANDS MR PHILIPPE JOSEPH

3 Verulam Buildings
London WC1R 5NT,
Telephone: 0171 831 8441
E-mail: clerks@3verulam.co.uk
Call Date: Nov 1985, Middle Temple
Pupil Master
Qualifications: [MA, LLM (Cantab)]

SANGSTER NIGEL QC (1998)

St Paul's House
5th Floor, St Paul's House, 23 Park Square
South, Leeds LS1 2ND,
Telephone: 0113 2455866
E-mail: catherinegrimshaw@stpauls-
chambers.demon.co.uk
23 Essex Street
London WC2R 3AS,
Telephone: 0171 413 0353/836 8366
E-mail:clerks@essexstreet23.demon.co.uk
Call Date: Nov 1976, Middle Temple
Assistant Recorder
Qualifications: [LLB (Hons)]

SANKEY GUY RICHARD QC (1991)

1 Temple Gardens
1st Floor, Temple, London EC4Y 9BB,
Telephone: 0171 583 1315/353 0407
E-mail: clerks@1templegardens.co.uk
Call Date: July 1966, Inner Temple
Recorder
Qualifications: [MA (Oxon)]

SAPIECHA DAVID JOHN

Rougemont Chambers
8 Colleton Crescent, Exeter, Devon,
EX1 1RR, Telephone: 01392 208484
E-mail:rougemont.chambers@eclipse.co.uk
Call Date: Oct 1990, Gray's Inn
Qualifications: [LLB]

SAPNARA MISS KHATUN

8 King's Bench Walk
2nd Floor, Temple, London EC4Y 7DU,
Telephone: 0171 797 8888
8 King's Bench Walk North
1 Park Square East, Leeds LS1 2NE,
Telephone: 0113 2439797
Call Date: Nov 1990, Middle Temple
Qualifications: [LLB (Lond)]

SAPSARD JAMAL PARVEZ

2 Paper Buildings, Basement North
Temple, London EC4Y 7ET,
Telephone: 0171 936 2613
E-mail: post@2paper.co.uk
Call Date: July 1987, Lincoln's Inn
Pupil Master
Qualifications: [LLB (Hons)]

SAPSFORD PHILIP ANTHONY QC (1992)

Goldsmith Chambers
Ground Floor, Goldsmith Building,
Temple, London EC4Y 7BL,
Telephone: 0171 353 6802/3/4/5
E-mail:clerks@goldsmithchambers.law.co.uk
Bank House Chambers
Old Bank House, Hartshead, Sheffield
S1 2EL, Telephone: 0114 2751223
Call Date: Nov 1974, Inner Temple
Assistant Recorder

SAPWELL TIMOTHY ROBERT

6 Fountain Court
Steelhouse Lane, Birmingham B4 6DR,
Telephone: 0121 233 3282
E-mail: clerks@sixfountain.co.uk
Call Date: 1997, Lincoln's Inn
Qualifications: [BA (Lond)]

SARONY NEVILLE LESLIE

New Court Chambers
5 Verulam Buildings, Gray's Inn, London
WC1R 5LY, Telephone: 0171 831 9500
E-mail: mail@newcourtchambers.com
Call Date: June 1964, Gray's Inn
Qualifications: [LLB (Lond), LSE]

SARTIN LEON JAMES

5 Stone Buildings
Lincoln's Inn, London WC2A 3XT,
Telephone: 0171 242 6201
E-mail:clerks@5-stonebuildings.law.co.uk
Call Date: Oct 1997, Middle Temple
Qualifications: [BSc (Hons)(Soton), LLM
(Lond)]

SASSE TOBY WILLIAM

18 St John Street
Manchester M3 4EA,
Telephone: 0161 278 1800
E-mail: 18stjohn@lineone.net
Call Date: July 1988, Middle Temple
Qualifications: [LLB (Hons) (Exon)]

SASTRY BOB AJAY DWARAKANATH

Central Chambers
89 Princess Street,
Manchester M1 4HT,
Telephone: 0161 236 1133
Call Date: Oct 1996, Inner Temple
Qualifications: [LLB (Exon)]

SAUNDERS JOHN HENRY BOULTON QC (1991)

4 Fountain Court
Steelhouse Lane, Birmingham B4 6DR,
Telephone: 0121 236 3476
Call Date: July 1972, Gray's Inn
Recorder
Qualifications: [BA (Oxon)]

SAUNDERS NEIL

3 Raymond Buildings
Gray's Inn, London WC1R 5BH,
Telephone: 020 7831 3833
E-mail:chambers@threeraymond.demon.co.u
k
Call Date: Nov 1983, Middle Temple
Pupil Master
Qualifications: [BA]

SAUNDERS NICHOLAS JOSEPH

4 Field Court
Gray's Inn, London WC1R 5EA,
Telephone: 0171 440 6900
E-mail: chambers@4fieldcourt.co.uk
Call Date: July 1989, Middle Temple
Qualifications: [LLB (Hull), LLM (Cantab)]

SAUNDERS WILLIAM ANTHONY

3 Temple Gardens
Lower Ground Floor, Temple, London
EC4Y 9AU, Telephone: 0171 353 3102/5/
9297 E-mail: clerks@3tg.co.uk
Westgate Chambers
144 High Street, Lewes, East Sussex,
BN7 1XT, Telephone: 01273 480510
Call Date: Nov 1980, Gray's Inn
Pupil Master
Qualifications: [LLB (B'ham)]

SAUNT THOMAS WILLIAM GATTY

Two Crown Office Row
Ground Floor, Temple, London
EC4Y 7HJ, Telephone: 020 7797 8100
E-mail: mail@2cor.co.uk, or to individual
barristers at: [barrister's
surname]@2cor.co.uk
Call Date: July 1974, Inner Temple
Qualifications: [LLB]

SAUVAIN STEPHEN JOHN QC (1995)

40 King Street
Manchester M2 6BA,
Telephone: 0161 832 9082
E-mail: clerks@40kingstreet.co.uk
The Chambers of Philip Raynor QC
5 Park Place, Leeds LS1 2RU,
Telephone: 0113 242 1123
Call Date: July 1977, Lincoln's Inn
Qualifications: [MA, LLB (Cantab)]

SAVAGE MISS AYISHA CAROL

**Gray's Inn Chambers, The Chambers of
Norman Patterson**
First Floor, Gray's Inn Chambers, Gray's
Inn, London WC1R 5JA,
Telephone: 0171 831 5344
E-mail: s.mcblain@btinternet.com
Call Date: July 1995, Inner Temple
Qualifications: [BA (Leic)]

SAVAGE TIMOTHY JOHN

Paradise Chambers
26 Paradise Square, Sheffield S1 2DE,
Telephone: 0114 2738951
E-mail: timbooth@paradise-sq.co.uk
Call Date: Nov 1991, Inner Temple

SAVILL MARK ASHLEY

Deans Court Chambers
24 St John Street, Manchester M3 4DF,
Telephone: 0161 214 6000
E-mail: clerks@deanscourt.co.uk
Deans Court Chambers
41-43 Market Place, Preston PR1 1AH,
Telephone: 01772 555163
E-mail: clerks@deanscourt.co.uk
Call Date: Nov 1993, Inner Temple
Qualifications: [BA (Dunelm)]

SAVILL PETER JOHN

17 Carlton Crescent
Southampton SO15 2XR,
Telephone: 023 8032 0320/0823 2003
E-mail: greg@jg17cc.co.uk
Call Date: Nov 1995, Inner Temple
Qualifications: [BA (Warw), CPE]

SAVLA SANDEEP

55 Temple Chambers
Temple Avenue, London EC4Y 0HP,
Telephone: 0171 353 7400
Call Date: Oct 1992, Middle Temple
Qualifications: [BA (Hons)]

SAVVIDES MISS MARIA

Northampton Chambers
22 Albion Place, Northampton NN1 1UD,
Telephone: 01604 636271
Call Date: July 1986, Middle Temple
Pupil Master
Qualifications: [BA (Hons)]

SAWHNEY MISS DEBBIE JANE

Lamb Building
Ground Floor, Temple, London
EC4Y 7AS, Telephone: 020 7797 7788
E-mail: lamb.building@link.org
Call Date: Nov 1987, Middle Temple
Qualifications: [BA (Keele)]

SAWYER JOHN FREDERICK

Oriel Chambers
14 Water Street, Liverpool L2 8TD,
Telephone: 0151 236 7191/236 4321
E-mail: clerks@oriel-chambers.co.uk
Call Date: Nov 1978, Inner Temple
Qualifications: [LLB (Warwick), MBIM]

SAWYERR MISS SHARON ROSE

Queen Elizabeth Building
Ground Floor, Temple, London
EC4Y 9BS,
Telephone: 0171 353 7181 (12 Lines)
Call Date: Nov 1992, Inner Temple
Qualifications: [LLB]

SAXBY OLIVER CHARLES JOHN

6 Pump Court
1st Floor, Temple, London EC4Y 7AR,
Telephone: 0171 797 8400
E-mail: clerks@6pumpcourt.co.uk
6-8 Mill Street
Maidstone, Kent, ME15 6XH,
Telephone: 01622 688094
E-mail: annexe@6pumpcourt.co.uk
Call Date: Nov 1992, Inner Temple
Qualifications: [LLB (So'ton)]

Fax: 0171 797 8401;
Out of hours telephone: 01233 820485/
0410 851045; DX: LDE 293;
Other comms: E-mail
oliver@saxby.freeserve.co.uk

Types of work: Crime

Circuit: South Eastern

Awards and memberships: Duke of Edinburgh
scholar, Inner Temple; Member of Kent Bar
Mess

SAXTON MISS NICOLA HELEN

St Paul's House
5th Floor, St Paul's House, 23 Park Square
South, Leeds LS1 2ND,
Telephone: 0113 2455866
E-mail: catherinegrimshaw@stpauls-
chambers.demon.co.uk
Call Date: Nov 1992, Inner Temple
Qualifications: [MA (Cantab)]

SAY BRADLEY JOHN

5 Pump Court
Ground Floor, Temple, London
EC4Y 7AP, Telephone: 020 7353 2532
E-mail: FivePump@netcomuk.co.uk
Call Date: Oct 1993, Inner Temple
Qualifications: [LLB]

SAYEED MUHAMMAD ABU

10 Highlever Road
North Kensington, London W10 6PS,
Telephone: 0181 969 8514
Call Date: July 1973, Inner Temple
Qualifications: [B.A.]

SAYER MR PETER EDWIN

Gough Square Chambers
6-7 Gough Square, London EC4A 3DE,
Telephone: 0171 353 0924
E-mail: gsc@goughsq.co.uk
Call Date: July 1975, Middle Temple
Qualifications: [MA (Cantab)]

SAYERS MICHAEL PATRICK QC (1988)

2 King's Bench Walk
Ground Floor, Temple, London
EC4Y 7DE, Telephone: 0171 353 1746
E-mail: 2kbw@atlas.co.uk
King's Bench Chambers
115 North Hill, Plymouth PL4 8JY,
Telephone: 01752 221551
Call Date: Nov 1970, Inner Temple
Recorder
Qualifications: [MA (Cantab)]

SCAMELL ERNEST HAROLD

5 New Square
Ground Floor, Lincoln's Inn, London
WC2A 3RJ, Telephone: 020 7404 0404
E-mail:chambers@fivenewsquare.demon.co.
uk
Call Date: Nov 1949, Lincoln's Inn
Qualifications: [LLM]

D

SCANNELL RICHARD PAUL

Two Garden Court
1st Floor, Middle Temple, London
EC4Y 9BL, Telephone: 0171 353 1633
E-mail:barristers@2gardenct.law.co.uk
Call Date: Nov 1986, Middle Temple
Pupil Master
Qualifications: [BA, LLM]

SCARRATT RICHARD JOHN

One Garden Court Family Law Chambers
Ground Floor, Temple, London
EC4Y 9BJ, Telephone: 0171 797 7900
E-mail: clerks@onegardencourt.co.uk
Call Date: July 1979, Lincoln's Inn
Pupil Master
Qualifications: [LLB (B'ham)]

SCHAFF ALISTAIR GRAHAM QC (1999)

S Tomlinson QC
7 King's Bench Walk, Temple, London
EC4Y 7DS, Telephone: 0171 583 0404
E-mail: clerks@7kbw.law.co.uk
Call Date: 1983, Inner Temple
Pupil Master
Qualifications: [MA (Cantab)]

SCHAW MILLER STEPHEN GRANT

12 New Square
Lincoln's Inn, London WC2A 3SW,
Telephone: 0171 419 1212
E-mail: chambers@12newsquare.co.uk
Call Date: 1988, Inner Temple
Qualifications: [BA (Oxon), Dip Law (City)]

SCHENKENBERG MISS BARBARA

St Ive's Chambers
Whittall Street, Birmingham B4 6DH,
Telephone: 0121 236 0863/5720
E-mail:stives.headofchambers@btinternet.com
Call Date: July 1993, Inner Temple
Qualifications: [BSc, Juris Doctorate]

SCHIFFER MISS CORINNA ANNE

5 Pump Court
Ground Floor, Temple, London
EC4Y 7AP, Telephone: 020 7353 2532
E-mail: FivePump@netcomuk.co.uk
Call Date: Nov 1989, Middle Temple
Qualifications: [BA Hons (Cantab)]

SCHMITZ DAVID REUBEN

The Chambers of Leolin Price CBE, QC
10 Old Square, Lincoln's Inn, London
WC2A 3SU, Telephone: 0171 405 0758
Call Date: Nov 1976, Lincoln's Inn
Pupil Master
Qualifications: [BA]

SCHOFIELD ALEXANDER GEORGE

4 Paper Buildings
1st Floor, Temple, London EC4Y 7EX,
Telephone: 0171 583 0816/353 1131
E-mail: clerks@4paperbuildings.co.uk
Call Date: Mar 1997, Middle Temple
Qualifications: [BA (Hons)(Oxon)]

SCHOFIELD PETER ANDREW

New Court Chambers
3 Broad Chare, Newcastle upon Tyne
NE1 3DQ, Telephone: 0191 232 1980
Call Date: Nov 1982, Gray's Inn
Pupil Master
Qualifications: [BA]

SCHOLES MICHAEL HOWARD

India Buildings Chambers
Water Street, Liverpool L2 0XG,
Telephone: 0151 243 6000
E-mail: clerks@chambers.u-net.com
Call Date: July 1996, Inner Temple
Qualifications: [LLB (Hons)(L'pool)]

SCHOLES RODNEY JAMES QC (1987)

22 Old Buildings
Lincoln's Inn, London WC2A 3UJ,
Telephone: 0171 831 0222
Byrom Street Chambers
Byrom Street, Manchester M3 4PF,
Telephone: 0161 829 2100
E-mail: Byromst25@aol.com
Call Date: July 1968, Lincoln's Inn
Recorder
Qualifications: [BA, BCL (Oxon)]

SCHOLZ KARL HUBERTUS

3 Temple Gardens
Lower Ground Floor, Temple, London
EC4Y 9AU, Telephone: 0171 353 3102/5/
9297 E-mail: clerks@3tg.co.uk
Call Date: July 1973, Gray's Inn
Pupil Master
Qualifications: [LLB (Lond)]

SCHUSMAN STEVEN PAUL

Call Date: July 1985, Middle Temple
Qualifications: [LLB (Manch)]

SCHWARZ JONATHAN SIMON

Temple Gardens Tax Chambers
1st Floor, 3 Temple Gardens, Temple,
London EC4Y 9AU,
Telephone: 0171 353 7884/5 8982/3
E-mail: clerks@taxcounsel.co.uk.
Call Date: Mar 1998, Middle Temple
Qualifications: [BA, LLB (Witwatersr-, and),
LLM, (California)]

SCOBIE JAMES TIMOTHY NORMAN

Francis Taylor Building
Ground Floor, Temple, London
EC4Y 7BY, Telephone: 0171 353 7768/
7769/2711
E-mail:clerks@francistaylorbuilding.law.co.uk
Call Date: July 1984, Gray's Inn
Pupil Master
Qualifications: [BA (Exon), Dip Law (City)]

SCOLDING MISS FIONA KATE

Goldsmith Building
1st Floor, Temple, London EC4Y 7BL,
Telephone: 0171 353 7881
E-mail:clerks@goldsmith-building.law.co.uk
Call Date: Nov 1996, Gray's Inn
Qualifications: [BA (Cantab)]

SCORAH CHRISTOPHER JAMES

8 King Street Chambers
8 King Street, Manchester M2 6AQ,
Telephone: 0161 834 9560
E-mail: eightking@aol.com
Call Date: Nov 1991, Middle Temple
Qualifications: [BA Hons (Oxon), Dip Law]

SCOREY DAVID WILLIAM JOHN

Essex Court Chambers
24 Lincoln's Inn Fields, London
WC2A 3ED, Telephone: 0171 813 8000
E-mail:clerksroom@essexcourt-chambers.co.u
k
Call Date: Oct 1997, Lincoln's Inn
Qualifications: [BA (Hons), LLM]

SCOTLAND MISS MARIA LYN

Bridewell Chambers
2 Bridewell Place, London EC4V 6AP,
Telephone: 020 7797 8800
E-mail:HughesGage@bridewell.law.co.uk
Call Date: Oct 1995, Gray's Inn
Qualifications: [B.Sc (Leeds)]

SCOTLAND OF ASTRAL BARONESS QC (1991)

**1 Gray's Inn Square, Chambers of the
Baroness Scotland of Asthal QC**
1st Floor, London WC1R 5AG,
Telephone: 0171 405 3000
E-mail: clerks@onegrays.demon.co.uk
Call Date: July 1977, Middle Temple
Recorder
Qualifications: [LLB (Lond)]

SCOTT MISS ALEXANDRA ELISABETH

2 New Street
Leicester LE1 5NA,
Telephone: 0116 2625906
E-mail: clerks@2newstreet.co.uk
Call Date: July 1983, Gray's Inn
Pupil Master
Qualifications: [LLB (Leic)]

SCOTT CHARLES EDWIN

169 Temple Chambers
Temple Avenue, London EC4Y 0DA,
Telephone: 0171 583 7644
Call Date: July 1980, Middle Temple
Pupil Master
Qualifications: [LLB (Lond), FCIArb]

SCOTT MISS CHRISTINE RUTH

Call Date: Nov 1986, Gray's Inn
Qualifications: [LLB(Reading)]

SCOTT IAN RICHARD

Old Square Chambers
1 Verulam Buildings, Gray's Inn, London
WC1R 5LQ, Telephone: 0171 269 0300
E-mail:clerks@oldsquarechambers.co.uk
Old Square Chambers
Hanover House, 47 Corn Street, Bristol
BS1 1HT, Telephone: 0117 9277111
E-mail: oldsqbri@globalnet.co.uk
Call Date: Oct 1991, Lincoln's Inn
Qualifications: [BA (Hons) (Newc), MSc
(LSE), Dip Law (City)]

SCOTT JOHN ALSTON

4 Stone Buildings
Ground Floor, Lincoln's Inn, London
WC2A 3XT, Telephone: 0171 242 5524
E-mail:clerks@4stonebuildings.law.co.uk
Call Date: July 1982, Middle Temple
Qualifications: [MA LLM (Cantab), FCIArb]

SCOTT MATTHEW JOHN

Pump Court Chambers
Upper Ground Floor, 3 Pump Court,
Temple, London EC4Y 7AJ,
Telephone: 0171 353 0711
E-mail: clerks@3pumpcourt.com
Pump Court Chambers
31 Southgate Street, Winchester
SO23 9EE, Telephone: 01962 868161
E-mail: clerks@3pumpcourt.com
Pump Court Chambers
5 Temple Chambers, Temple Street,
Swindon SN1 1SQ,
Telephone: 01793 539899
E-mail: clerks@3pumpcourt.com
Call Date: Nov 1985, Inner Temple
Qualifications: [BA (York)]

SCOTT PETER DENYS JOHN QC (1978)

Fountain Court
Temple, London EC4Y 9DH,
Telephone: 0171 583 3335
E-mail: chambers@fountaincourt.co.uk
Call Date: May 1960, Middle Temple
Qualifications: [MA (Oxon)]

SCOTT RICHARD MARK

York Chambers
14 Toft Green, York YO1 6JT,
Telephone: 01904 620048
E-mail: [name]@yorkchambers.co.uk
Call Date: Nov 1992, Middle Temple
Qualifications: [LLB (Hons)]

SCOTT TIMOTHY JOHN WHITTAKER QC (1995)

29 Bedford Row Chambers
London WC1R 4HE,
Telephone: 0171 831 2626
Call Date: Nov 1975, Gray's Inn
Assistant Recorder
Qualifications: [BA (Oxon)]

SCOTT BELL MRS ROSALIND SARA

Trinity Chambers
9-12 Trinity Chare, Quayside, Newcastle
upon Tyne NE1 3DF,
Telephone: 0191 232 1927
E-mail: info@trinitychambers.co.uk
Call Date: Oct 1993, Middle Temple
Qualifications: [LLB (Hons)(Manc)]

SCOTT-JONES MISS ALISON CLAIRE

Equity Chambers
3rd Floor, 153a Corporation Street,
Birmingham B4 6PH,
Telephone: 0121 233 2100
E-mail: equityatusa.com
Call Date: Feb 1991, Middle Temple
Qualifications: [LLB (Cardiff)]

SCOTT-MANDERSON MARCUS CHARLES WILLIAM

4 Paper Buildings
1st Floor, Temple, London EC4Y 7EX,
Telephone: 0171 583 0816/353 1131
E-mail: clerks@4paperbuildings.co.uk
Call Date: July 1980, Lincoln's Inn
Pupil Master
Qualifications: [BA, BCL (Oxon)]

SCOTT-PHILLIPS ALEXANDER JAMES

Earl Street Chambers
47 Earl Street, Maidstone, Kent,
ME14 1PD, Telephone: 01622 671222
E-mail: gunner-sparks@msn.com
Call Date: Oct 1995, Inner Temple
Qualifications: [BA (Hons)(Durham), CPE (Leic)]

SCRIVEN MISS PAMELA QC (1992)

One King's Bench Walk
1st Floor, Temple, London EC4Y 7DB,
Telephone: 0171 936 1500
E-mail: ddear@1kbw.co.uk
Call Date: Nov 1970, Inner Temple
Assistant Recorder
Qualifications: [LLB (Lond)]

SCRIVENER ANTHONY FRANK BERTRAM QC (1975)

2-3 Gray's Inn Square
Gray's Inn, London WC1R 5JH,
Telephone: 0171 242 4986
E-mail:chambers@2-3graysinnsquare.co.uk
Call Date: Nov 1958, Gray's Inn
Recorder

SCUTT DAVID ROBERT

Queen Elizabeth Building
Ground Floor, Temple, London
EC4Y 9BS,
Telephone: 0171 353 7181 (12 Lines)
Call Date: Nov 1989, Middle Temple
Pupil Master
Qualifications: [BA (Keele)]

SEABROOK RICHARD MICHAEL

Ropewalk Chambers
24 The Ropewalk, Nottingham NG1 5EF,
Telephone: 0115 9472581
E-mail: administration@ropewalk co.uk
Call Date: July 1987, Inner Temple
Pupil Master
Qualifications: [LLB]

SEABROOK ROBERT JOHN QC (1983)

1 Crown Office Row
Ground Floor, Temple, London
EC4Y 7HH, Telephone: 0171 797 7500
E-mail: mail@onecrownofficerow.com
Crown Office Row Chambers
Blenheim House, 120 Church Street,
Brighton, Sussex, BN1 1WH,
Telephone: 01273 625625
E-mail: crownofficerow@clara.net
Call Date: June 1964, Middle Temple
Recorder
Qualifications: [LLB]

SEAL JULIUS DAMIEN

189 Randolph Avenue
London W9 1DJ,
Telephone: 0171 624 9139
Call Date: Nov 1967, Lincoln's Inn
Pupil Master

SEAL KEVIN PAUL

32 Park Place
Cardiff CF1 3BA,
Telephone: 01222 397364
Call Date: 1998, Gray's Inn
Qualifications: [LLB (Manch)]

SEARLE BARRIE

St James's Chambers
68 Quay Street, Manchester M3 3EJ,
Telephone: 0161 834 7000
E-mail: clerks@stjameschambers.co.uk
Call Date: July 1975, Middle Temple
Pupil Master
Qualifications: [LLB (Hons)]

SEARLE MISS CORINNE LOUISE TEAGUE

Walnut House
63 St David's Hill, Exeter, Devon,
EX4 4DW, Telephone: 01392 279751
E-mail: 106627.2451@compuserve.com
Call Date: July 1982, Gray's Inn
Pupil Master
Qualifications: [LLB (Lond)]

SEARS ROBERT DAVID MURRAY

4 Pump Court
Temple, London EC4Y 7AN,
Telephone: 020 7842 5555
E-mail:chambers@4pumpcourt.law.co.uk
Call Date: Nov 1984, Middle Temple
Pupil Master
Qualifications: [MA (Oxon)]

SEAWARD MARTIN VINCENT

4 Brick Court
Ground Floor, Temple, London
EC4Y 9AD, Telephone: 0171 797 7766
E-mail: chambers@4brick.co.uk
8 Stone Buildings
Lincoln's Inn, London WC2A 3TA,
Telephone: 0171 831 9881
E-mail: alanl@8stonebuildings.law.uk
Call Date: Nov 1978, Gray's Inn
Pupil Master
Qualifications: [BA (Dunelm)]

SECHIARI MISS HELEN LOUISE PANDIA

Manchester House Chambers
18-22 Bridge Street, Manchester M3 3BZ,
Telephone: 0161 834 7007
Call Date: Nov 1991, Lincoln's Inn
Qualifications: [LLB (Hons)]

SECONDE DAVID GORDON

Coleridge Chambers
Citadel, 190 Corporation Street,
Birmingham B4 6QD,
Telephone: 0121 233 8500
Call Date: July 1968, Middle Temple
Qualifications: [BA (Oxon)]

SEDDON MISS DOROTHY

6 Fountain Court
Steelhouse Lane, Birmingham B4 6DR,
Telephone: 0121 233 3282
E-mail: clerks@sixfountain.co.uk
Call Date: July 1974, Middle Temple
Qualifications: [LLB (B'ham)]

SEDDON JAMES DURAN

Two Garden Court
1st Floor, Middle Temple, London
EC4Y 9BL, Telephone: 0171 353 1633
E-mail:barristers@2gardenct.law.co.uk
Call Date: Feb 1994, Middle Temple
Qualifications: [BA (Hons)(Oxon), CPE
(Manc)]

SEED NIGEL JOHN

3 Paper Buildings
Temple, London EC4Y 7EU,
Telephone: 020 7583 8055
E-mail: London@3paper.com
3 Paper Buildings (Bournemouth)
20 Lorne Park Road, Bournemouth,
Dorset, BH1 1JN,
Telephone: 01202 292102
E-mail: Bournemouth@3paper.com
3 Paper Buildings (Winchester)
4 St Peter Street, Winchester SO23 8BW,
Telephone: 01962 868884
E-mail: winchester@3paper.com
3 Paper Buildings (Oxford)
1 Alfred Street, High Street, Oxford
OX1 4EH, Telephone: 01865 793736
E-mail: oxford@3paper.com
Call Date: Nov 1978, Inner Temple
Pupil Master, Assistant Recorder
Qualifications: [BA (Dunelm)]

SEED STEPHEN NICHOLAS

Martins Building
2nd Floor, No 4 Water Street, Liverpool
L2 3SP, Telephone: 0151 236 5818/4919
Call Date: Oct 1991, Gray's Inn
Qualifications: [LLB]

SEELY JONATHAN SEBASTIAN

1 Paper Buildings
1st Floor, Temple, London EC4Y 7EP,
Telephone: 0171 353 3728/4953
Call Date: Nov 1987, Inner Temple
Qualifications: [BA,Dip Law]

SEFI BENEDICT JOHN

Harcourt Chambers
1st Floor, 2 Harcourt Buildings, Temple,
London EC4Y 9DB,
Telephone: 0171 353 6961
E-mail:clerks@harcourtchambers.law.co.uk

Harcourt Chambers
Churchill House, 3 St Aldate's Courtyard,
St Aldate's, Oxford OX1 1BN,
Telephone: 01865 791559
E-mail:clerks@harcourtchambers.law.co.uk
Call Date: July 1972, Inner Temple
Pupil Master
Qualifications: [BA (Oxon)]

SEFTON MARK THOMAS DUNBLANE

199 Strand
London WC2R 1DR,
Telephone: 0171 379 9779
E-mail: chambers@199strand.co.uk
Call Date: Nov 1996, Middle Temple
Qualifications: [MA (Hons)(Cantab)]

SEFTON-SMITH LLOYD

Bridewell Chambers
2 Bridewell Place, London EC4V 6AP,
Telephone: 020 7797 8800
E-mail:HughesGage@bridewell.law.co.uk
Call Date: Oct 1993, Lincoln's Inn
Qualifications: [BA (Hons)(Lond)]

SEGAL OLIVER LEON

Old Square Chambers
1 Verulam Buildings, Gray's Inn, London
WC1R 5LQ, Telephone: 0171 269 0300
E-mail:clerks@oldsquarechambers.co.uk
Old Square Chambers
Hanover House, 47 Corn Street, Bristol
BS1 1HT, Telephone: 0117 9277111
E-mail: oldsqbri@globalnet.co.uk
Call Date: Oct 1992, Middle Temple
Qualifications: [BA (Hons)]

SEIFERT MISS ANNE MIRIAM

4 Breams Buildings
London EC4A 1AQ,
Telephone: 0171 353 5835/430 1221
E-mail:breams@4breamsbuildings.law.co.uk
Call Date: July 1975, Inner Temple

SEITLER MS DEBORAH

**1 Gray's Inn Square, Chambers of the
Baroness Scotland of Asthal QC**
1st Floor, London WC1R 5AG,
Telephone: 0171 405 3000
E-mail: clerks@onegrays.demon.co.uk
Call Date: Nov 1991, Inner Temple
Qualifications: [BA (Leeds, Dip Law)]

SEITLER JONATHAN SIMON

Wilberforce Chambers
8 New Square, Lincoln's Inn, London
WC2A 3QP, Telephone: 0171 306 0102
E-mail: chambers@wilberforce.co.uk
Call Date: Nov 1985, Inner Temple
Pupil Master
Qualifications: [BA (Oxon)]

Types of work: Commercial property, Landlord and tenant, Professional negligence

SEKAR CHANDRA

Acre Lane Neighbourhood Chambers
30A Acre Lane, London SW2 5SG,
Telephone: 0171 274 4400
E-mail:barristerschambers@acrelane.demon.co.uk
Call Date: Mar 1996, Gray's Inn
Qualifications: [BA (Bris)]

SELBY LAWRENCE JULIAN CATELLO

**Gray's Inn Chambers, The Chambers of
Norman Patterson**
First Floor, Gray's Inn Chambers, Gray's
Inn, London WC1R 5JA,
Telephone: 0171 831 5344
E-mail: s.mcblain@btinternet.com
Call Date: Mar 1997, Gray's Inn
Qualifications: [BA (Reading)]

SELF GARY PETER

College Chambers
19 Carlton Cresent, Southampton
SO15 2ET, Telephone: 01703 230338
Call Date: Oct 1991, Lincoln's Inn
Pupil Master
Qualifications: [BA (Hons)(Manc) , Dip Law]

SELFE MICHAEL ROSS

2 King's Bench Walk
Ground Floor, Temple, London
EC4Y 7DE, Telephone: 0171 353 1746
E-mail: 2kbw@atlas.co.uk
King's Bench Chambers
115 North Hill, Plymouth PL4 8JY,
Telephone: 01752 221551
Call Date: Nov 1965, Middle Temple
Pupil Master, Recorder
Qualifications: [LLB (Soton)]

SELIGMAN MATTHEW THOMAS ARTHUR

39 Essex Street
London WC2R 3AT,
Telephone: 0171 832 1111
E-mail: clerks@39essex.co.uk
Call Date: Oct 1994, Middle Temple
Qualifications: [BA (Hons)(Oxon), CPE (Lond)]

SELIGMAN RALPH DAVID

4 Stone Buildings
Ground Floor, Lincoln's Inn, London
WC2A 3XT, Telephone: 0171 242 5524
E-mail:clerks@4stonebuildings.law.co.uk
Call Date: 1996, Gray's Inn
Qualifications: [BA, LLB, MA (Dublin)]

SELLARS MICHAEL JOHN

Adrian Lyon's Chambers
14 Castle Street, Liverpool L2 0NE,
Telephone: 0151 236 4421/8240
E-mail: chambers14@aol.com
Call Date: July 1980, Inner Temple
Qualifications: [BA (Dunelm)]

SELLERS ALAN MITCHELL

Castle Street Chambers
2nd Floor, 42 Castle Street, Liverpool
L2 7LD, Telephone: 0151 242 0500
Call Date: July 1991, Gray's Inn
Qualifications: [LLB (Lanc)]

SELLERS GRAHAM

Adrian Lyon's Chambers
14 Castle Street, Liverpool L2 0NE,
Telephone: 0151 236 4421/8240
E-mail: chambers14@aol.com
Call Date: Oct 1990, Middle Temple
Qualifications: [LLB, LLM (Cantab)]

SELLERS ROBIN ST. JOHN

Guildford Chambers
Stoke House, Leapale Lane, Guildford,
Surrey, GU1 4LY,
Telephone: 01483 539131
E-mail:guildford.barristers@btinternet.com
Call Date: Nov 1994, Inner Temple
Qualifications: [LLB (Reading)]

SELLICK WILLIAM PATRICK LLEWELLYN

King's Bench Chambers
115 North Hill, Plymouth PL4 8JY,
Telephone: 01752 221551
2 King's Bench Walk
Ground Floor, Temple, London
EC4Y 7DE, Telephone: 0171 353 1746
E-mail: 2kbw@atlas.co.uk
Call Date: July 1973, Middle Temple
Pupil Master, Recorder
Qualifications: [LLB]

SELLS OLIVER MATTHEW QC (1995)

Five Paper Buildings
1st Floor, Five Paper Bldgs, Temple,
London EC4Y 7HB,
Telephone: 0171 583 6117
E-mail:clerks@5-paperbuildings.law.co.uk
Fenners Chambers
3 Madingley Road, Cambridge CB3 0EE,
Telephone: 01223 368761
E-mail: clerks@fennerschambers.co.uk
Call Date: July 1972, Inner Temple
Recorder

SELMAN MISS ELIZABETH

One King's Bench Walk
1st Floor, Temple, London EC4Y 7DB,
Telephone: 0171 936 1500
E-mail: ddear@1kbw.co.uk
Call Date: Nov 1989, Inner Temple
Pupil Master
Qualifications: [LLB (Lond)]

SELVARATNAM MISS VASANTI EMILY INDRANI

4 Field Court
Gray's Inn, London WC1R 5EA,
Telephone: 0171 440 6900
E-mail: chambers@4fieldcourt.co.uk
Call Date: July 1983, Middle Temple
Pupil Master
Qualifications: [LLM, LLB (Lond), AKC]

SELWAY DR KATHERINE EMMA

11 Old Square
Ground Floor, Lincoln's Inn, London
WC2A 3TS, Telephone: 020 7430 0341
E-mail: clerks@11oldsquare.co.uk
Call Date: Nov 1995, Inner Temple
Qualifications: [BA (Hons)(Bris), D.Phil (Oxon), CPE (City)]

SELWOOD DR DOMINIC KIM

2 King's Bench Walk
Ground Floor, Temple, London
EC4Y 7DE, Telephone: 0171 353 1746
E-mail: 2kbw@atlas.co.uk
Call Date: Oct 1997, Lincoln's Inn
Qualifications: [LLB (Hons)(Wales), DEA
(Sorbonne,Paris), D.Phil (Oxon)]

SELWYN SHARPE RICHARD CHARLES

Westgate Chambers
67a Westgate Road, Newcastle upon Tyne
NE1 1SG, Telephone: 0191 261 4407/
2329785
E-mail:pracman@westgatechambers.law.co.u
k
2nd Floor, Francis Taylor Building
Temple, London EC4Y 7BY,
Telephone: 0171 353 9942/3157
Call Date: Nov 1985, Lincoln's Inn
Pupil Master
Qualifications: [LLB(Bristol)]

SEMKEN CHRISTOPHER RICHARD

1 New Square
Ground Floor, Lincoln's Inn, London
WC2A 3SA, Telephone: 0171 405 0884/5/6/
7 E-mail: clerks@1newsquare.law.co.uk
Call Date: July 1977, Lincoln's Inn
Qualifications: [MA (Oxon)]

SEMPLE ANDREW BLAIR

Sovereign Chambers
25 Park Square, Leeds LS1 2PW,
Telephone: 0113 2451841/2/3
E-mail:sovereignchambers@btinternet.com
Call Date: Oct 1993, Inner Temple
Qualifications: [BA (Dunelm)]

SEN ADITYA KUMAR

4 Brick Court
Ground Floor, Temple, London
EC4Y 9AD, Telephone: 0171 797 7766
E-mail: chambers@4brick.co.uk
Call Date: July 1977, Lincoln's Inn
Pupil Master
Qualifications: [MA, LLB (Cantab), BA (Hons)
(Dehli), FCA]

SENDALL ANTONY JOHN CHRISTMAS

Littleton Chambers
3 King's Bench Walk North, Temple,
London EC4Y 7HR,
Telephone: 0171 797 8600
E-mail:clerks@littletonchambers.co.uk
Call Date: July 1984, Lincoln's Inn
Pupil Master
Qualifications: [MA (Cantab)]

SEPHTON CRAIG GARDNER

Deans Court Chambers
24 St John Street, Manchester M3 4DF,
Telephone: 0161 214 6000
E-mail: clerks@deanscourt.co.uk
Deans Court Chambers
41-43 Market Place, Preston PR1 1AH,
Telephone: 01772 555163
E-mail: clerks@deanscourt.co.uk
Call Date: July 1981, Middle Temple
Pupil Master
Qualifications: [MA, BCL (Oxon)]

SERLE MS DIANA COLEMAN

10 King's Bench Walk
Ground Floor, Temple, London
EC4Y 7EB, Telephone: 0171 353 7742
E-mail: 10kbw@lineone.net
Call Date: Nov 1992, Inner Temple
Qualifications: [BA (Hons), Dip in Law]

SERLIN RICHARD ANTHONY

199 Strand
London WC2R 1DR,
Telephone: 0171 379 9779
E-mail: chambers@199strand.co.uk
Call Date: Nov 1987, Lincoln's Inn
Qualifications: [BA (Oxon) Dip Law, (City)]

SEROTA DANIEL QC (1989)

Littleton Chambers
3 King's Bench Walk North, Temple,
London EC4Y 7HR,
Telephone: 0171 797 8600
E-mail:clerks@littletonchambers.co.uk
Call Date: Nov 1969, Lincoln's Inn
Recorder
Qualifications: [MA (Oxon)]

D

SERR ASHLEY BARRIE

Mercury Chambers
Mercury House, 33-35 Clarendon Road,
Leeds LS2 9NZ,
Telephone: 0113 234 2265
E-mail:cdexter@mercurychambers.co.uk
Call Date: Nov 1996, Middle Temple
Qualifications: [LLB (Hons)(Notts), LLM
(Sydney)]

SERUGO-LUGO YOSEFALY NDAULA KIKWANGWIRA SE

Essex House Chambers
Unit 6 (Part 2nd Floor South), Stratford
Office Village, 14-30 Romford Road,
London E15 4BZ,
Telephone: 0181 536 1077
Call Date: Nov 1973, Inner Temple
Pupil Master
Qualifications: [BA]

SETHI MOHINDERPAL SINGH

Barnard's Inn Chambers
6th Floor, Halton House, 20-23 Holborn,
London EC1N 2JD,
Telephone: 0171 369 6969
E-mail: clerks@biclaw.co.uk
Call Date: 1996, Middle Temple
Qualifications: [BA (Hons)(Oxon)]

SETRIGHT HENRY JOHN

**1 Gray's Inn Square, Chambers of the
Baroness Scotland of Asthal QC**
1st Floor, London WC1R 5AG,
Telephone: 0171 405 3000
E-mail: clerks@onegrays.demon.co.uk
Call Date: Nov 1979, Middle Temple
Pupil Master
Qualifications: [MA (Oxon), DipGerms]

SETTY MISS PADMINI

Call Date: Nov 1996, Gray's Inn
Qualifications: [LLB]

SEWELL TIMOTHY WILLIAM

10 King's Bench Walk
1st Floor, Temple, London EC4Y 7EB,
Telephone: 0171 353 2501
Call Date: May 1976, Gray's Inn
Pupil Master
Qualifications: [LLB (Hons) (Leics)]

SEYMOUR MS LYDIA RUTH

Devereux Chambers
Devereux Court, London WC2R 3JJ,
Telephone: 0171 353 7534
E-mail: mailbox@devchambers.co.uk
Call Date: 1997, Inner Temple
Qualifications: [BA (Oxon), CPE (City)]

SEYMOUR MARK WILLIAM

9-12 Bell Yard
London WC2A 2LF,
Telephone: 0171 400 1800
E-mail: clerks@bellyard.co.uk
Call Date: Oct 1992, Middle Temple
Qualifications: [MA (Hons)]

SEYMOUR RICHARD WILLIAM QC (1991)

Monckton Chambers
4 Raymond Buildings, Gray's Inn, London
WC1R 5BP, Telephone: 0171 405 7211
E-mail: chambers@monckton.co.uk
Call Date: July 1972, Gray's Inn
Recorder
Qualifications: [MA (Cantab)]

SEYMOUR THOMAS OLIVER

Wilberforce Chambers
8 New Square, Lincoln's Inn, London
WC2A 3QP, Telephone: 0171 306 0102
E-mail: chambers@wilberforce.co.uk
Call Date: July 1975, Inner Temple
Pupil Master
Qualifications: [MA (Cantab)]

Types of work: Chancery (general), Commercial property, Equity, wills and trusts, Family provision, Insolvency, Landlord and tenant, Partnerships, Pensions, Professional negligence

SEYS LLEWELLYN ANTHONY JOHN

Farrar's Building
Temple, London EC4Y 7BD,
Telephone: 0171 583 9241
E-mail:chambers@farrarsbuilding.co.uk
Call Date: Nov 1972, Gray's Inn
Pupil Master, Recorder
Qualifications: [MA, BCL (Oxon)]

SHACKLEFORD MISS SUSAN ANGELA

One Garden Court Family Law Chambers
Ground Floor, Temple, London
EC4Y 9BJ, Telephone: 0171 797 7900
E-mail: clerks@onegardencourt.co.uk
Call Date: Nov 1980, Inner Temple
Pupil Master
Qualifications: [BA (Lond)]

SHADAREVIAN PAUL

East Anglian Chambers
52 North Hill, Colchester, Essex, CO1 1PY,
Telephone: 01206 572756
E-mail: colchester@ealaw.co.uk
East Anglian Chambers
Gresham House, 5 Museum Street,
Ipswich, Suffolk, IP1 1HQ,
Telephone: 01473 214481
E-mail: ipswich@ealaw.co.uk
East Anglian Chambers
57 London Street, Norwich NR2 1HL,
Telephone: 01603 617351
E-mail: norwich@ealaw.co.uk
Call Date: July 1984, Gray's Inn
Qualifications: [BA (Essex)]

SHAFI MOHAMMED IMRAN

Kenworthy's Chambers
83 Bridge Street, Manchester M3 2RF,
Telephone: 0161 832 4036/834 6954
E-mail: clerks@kenworthys.co.uk
Call Date: 1996, Lincoln's Inn
Qualifications: [LLB (Hons)(Lond)]

SHAH AKHIL

Fountain Court
Temple, London EC4Y 9DH,
Telephone: 0171 583 3335
E-mail: chambers@fountaincourt.co.uk
Call Date: Nov 1990, Inner Temple
Qualifications: [BA (Cantab)]

SHAH BAJUL AMRATLAL SOMCHAND

Twenty-Four Old Buildings
Ground Floor, Lincoln's Inn, London
WC2A 3UP, Telephone: 0171 404 0946
E-mail:clerks@24oldbuildings.law.co.uk
Call Date: Oct 1996, Lincoln's Inn
Qualifications: [BA (Hons), BCL (Oxon)]

SHAH FERDOUS

1 Garfield Road
Battersea, London SW11 5PL,
Telephone: 0171 228 1137
Call Date: July 1969, Lincoln's Inn
Qualifications: [BCom]

SHAIKH EUR.ING. (JAIKUMAR) CHRISTOPHER (SAMUEL

Avondale Chambers
2 Avondale Avenue, London N12 8EJ,
Telephone: 0181 445 9984
Equity Chambers
3rd Floor, 153a Corporation Street,
Birmingham B4 6PH,
Telephone: 0121 233 2100
E-mail: equityatusa.com
Call Date: July 1980, Gray's Inn
Qualifications: [BSc Eng (Hons)(Lond),
C.Eng, M.R.I.N.A., MI.MAR.E]

SHAIKH MOHAMMAD RASHID

The Chambers of Mr Ali Mohammed Azhar
Basement, 9 King's Bench Walk, Temple,
London EC4Y 7DX,
Telephone: 0171 353 9564
E-mail: jvlee@btinternet.com
Call Date: Nov 1968, Inner Temple
Qualifications: [BA (Hons), MA, LLB
(Karachi)]

SHAKOOR TARIQ BIN

6 Fountain Court
Steelhouse Lane, Birmingham B4 6DR,
Telephone: 0121 233 3282
E-mail: clerks@sixfountain.co.uk
Call Date: Feb 1992, Inner Temple
Qualifications: [BA (Lancs), CPE]

SHALDON MISS NICOLA

Chambers of John L Powell QC
Four New Square, Lincoln's Inn, London
WC2A 3RJ, Telephone: 0171 797 8000
E-mail: barristers@4newsquare.com
Call Date: Oct 1994, Middle Temple
Qualifications: [MA (Cantab), LLB
(Hons)(Lond)]

SHALE JUSTIN ANTON

4 King's Bench Walk
Ground/First Floor/Basement, Temple,
London EC4Y 7DL,
Telephone: 0171 822 8822
E-mail: 4kbw@barristersatlaw.com
King's Bench Chambers
Wellington House, 175 Holdenhurst Road,
Bournemouth, Dorset, BH8 8DQ,
Telephone: 01202 250025
E-mail: chambers@kingsbench.co.uk
Call Date: July 1982, Inner Temple
Pupil Master
Qualifications: [LLB (Soton)]

SHAMASH MISS ANNE MARION

14 Tooks Court
Cursitor St, London EC4A 1LB,
Telephone: 0171 405 8828
E-mail: clerks@tooks.law.co.uk
Call Date: Nov 1986, Gray's Inn
Qualifications: [BA]

SHANKARDASS VIJAY SOHAG TRILOKNATH

13 Old Square
Ground Floor, Lincoln's Inn, London
WC2A 3UA, Telephone: 0171 404 4800
E-mail: clerks@13oldsquare.law.co.uk
Call Date: Nov 1972, Lincoln's Inn
Qualifications: [B.Sc.(Delhi) , MA,LLM
(Cantab)]

SHANKS MURRAY GEORGE

Fountain Court
Temple, London EC4Y 9DH,
Telephone: 0171 583 3335
E-mail: chambers@fountaincourt.co.uk
Call Date: Nov 1984, Middle Temple
Pupil Master
Qualifications: [MA (Cantab)]

SHANNON THOMAS ERIC

Queen's Chambers
5 John Dalton Street, Manchester M2 6ET,
Telephone: 0161 834 6875/4738
Queens Chambers
4 Camden Place, Preston PR1 3JL,
Telephone: 01772 828300
Call Date: Nov 1974, Middle Temple
Pupil Master
Qualifications: [BA (Oxon)]

SHANT MISS NIRMAL KANTA

High Pavement Chambers
1 High Pavement, Nottingham NG1 1HF,
Telephone: 0115 9418218
Call Date: July 1984, Gray's Inn
Pupil Master
Qualifications: [LLB (Leics)]

SHAPIRO SELWYN

High Street Chambers
102 High Street, Godalming, Surrey,
GU7 1DS, Telephone: 01483 861170
Call Date: July 1979, Inner Temple
Pupil Master
Qualifications: [LLB (Lond)]

SHARDA ASHOK KUMAR

159 Gleneagle Road
Streatham, London SW16 6AZ,
Telephone: 0181 769 3063
Call Date: Nov 1979, Inner Temple
Qualifications: [BA]

SHARIF MS NADIA

Berkeley Chambers
1st Floor, 52 High Street, Henley-in-Arden,
Warwickshire, B95 5AN,
Telephone: 01564 795546
Call Date: Nov 1985, Lincoln's Inn
Qualifications: [BA (Hons)]

SHARLAND ANDREW JOHN

4-5 Gray's Inn Square
Ground Floor, Gray's Inn, London
WC1R 5JP, Telephone: 0171 404 5252
E-mail:chambers@4-5graysinnsquare.co.uk
Call Date: Oct 1996, Gray's Inn
Qualifications: [LLB (Lond), BCL (Oxon)]

SHARMA BHAWANI PERSAUD

Primrose Chambers
5 Primrose Way, Alperton, Middlesex,
HA0 1DS, Telephone: 0181 998 1806
Call Date: July 1975, Inner Temple
Qualifications: [FIArb]

SHARMA KISHORE

Call Date: Nov 1986, Gray's Inn
Pupil Master
Qualifications: [LLB (London)]

SHARMA PAVAN

Chambers of Pavan Sharma
286 Overdown Road, Tilehurst, Reading,
Berkshire, RG31 6PP,
Telephone: 0118 9625 832
Call Date: Oct 1993, Middle Temple
Qualifications: [LLB (Hons)(Lond)]

SHARMA MISS RAKHEE

Kingsway Chambers
88 Kingsway, Holborn, London
WC2B 6AA, Telephone: 07000 653529
E-mail: lanreoke@cocoon.co.uk
Call Date: Nov 1995, Gray's Inn
Qualifications: [LLB]

SHARMA MRS SUMAN

Chambers of Wilfred Forster-Jones
New Court, 1st Floor South, Temple,
London EC4Y 9BE,
Telephone: 0171 353 0853/4/7222
E-mail: chambers@newcourt.net
Call Date: May 1994, Middle Temple
Qualifications: [LLB (Hons)]

SHARP ALASTAIR RICHARD FRANCIS

Lamb Chambers
Lamb Building, Temple, London
EC4Y 7AS, Telephone: 020 7797 8300
E-mail: lambchambers@link.org
Call Date: 1968, Middle Temple
Pupil Master, Recorder
Qualifications: [MA (Cantab)]

SHARP CHRISTOPHER FRANCIS QC (1999)

St John's Chambers
Small Street, Bristol BS1 1DW,
Telephone: 0117 9213456/298514
E-mail: @stjohnschambers.co.uk
Call Date: 1975, Inner Temple
Pupil Master
Qualifications: [MA (Oxon)]

SHARP DAVID IAN

Francis Taylor Building
3rd Floor, Temple, London EC4Y 7BY,
Telephone: 0171 797 7250
Call Date: Nov 1986, Middle Temple
Qualifications: [BA (Oxon), MA, Dip Law]

SHARP JONATHAN JEREMY GRANVILLE

2 King's Bench Walk
Ground Floor, Temple, London
EC4Y 7DE, Telephone: 0171 353 1746
E-mail: 2kbw@atlas.co.uk
King's Bench Chambers
115 North Hill, Plymouth PL4 8JY,
Telephone: 01752 221551
Call Date: July 1987, Inner Temple
Qualifications: [BA (Oxon) Dip Law]

SHARP THE HON VICTORIA MADELEINE

1 Brick Court
1st Floor, Temple, London EC4Y 9BY,
Telephone: 0171 353 8845
E-mail: clerks@1brickcourt.co.uk
Call Date: July 1979, Inner Temple
Pupil Master, Assistant Recorder
Qualifications: [LLB (Bris)]

SHARPE ANDREW

Spon Chambers
13 Spon Street, Coventry, Warwickshire,
CV1 3BA, Telephone: 01203 632977
Call Date: Nov 1972, Gray's Inn

SHARPE DENNIS NIGEL

17 Bedford Row
London WC1R 4EB,
Telephone: 0171 831 7314
E-mail: iboard7314@aol.com
Call Date: July 1976, Inner Temple
Pupil Master
Qualifications: [LLB (Exon), BCL (Oxon)]

SHARPE MALCOLM DAVID

Adrian Lyon's Chambers
14 Castle Street, Liverpool L2 0NE,
Telephone: 0151 236 4421/8240
E-mail: chambers14@aol.com
Call Date: July 1989, Lincoln's Inn
Qualifications: [LLB (Sheff), LLM (Belfast)]

SHARPE MARTIN LAURENCE

2-4 Tudor Street
London EC4Y 0AA,
Telephone: 0171 797 7111
E-mail: clerks@rfqc.co.uk
Call Date: Nov 1989, Middle Temple
Qualifications: [BA Hons (Manc), MA
(L'pool)]

SHARPE THOMAS ANTHONY EDWARD QC (1994)

One Essex Court
Ground Floor, Temple, London
EC4Y 9AR, Telephone: 020 7583 2000
E-mail: clerks@oneessexcourt.co.uk
Call Date: May 1976, Lincoln's Inn
Qualifications: [MA(Cantab)]

SHARPLES JOHN EDMUND

St John's Chambers
Small Street, Bristol BS1 1DW,
Telephone: 0117 9213456/298514
E-mail: @stjohnschambers.co.uk
Call Date: Nov 1992, Middle Temple
Qualifications: [BA (Oxon), LLM
(Pennsylvania), LLM (Cantab)]

SHARPSTON MISS ELEANOR VERONICA ELIZABETH QC (1999)

4 Paper Buildings
Ground Floor, Temple, London
EC4Y 7EX, Telephone: 0171 353 3366/
583 7155
E-mail: clerks@4paperbuildings.com
Call Date: 1980, Middle Temple
Qualifications: [MA (Cantab)]

SHAW ANTONY MICHAEL NINIAN QC (1994)

4 Brick Court
Ground Floor, Temple, London
EC4Y 9AD, Telephone: 0171 797 7766
E-mail: chambers@4brick.co.uk
Call Date: July 1975, Middle Temple
Qualifications: [BA (Oxon)]

SHAW CHARLES NOEL

1 Gray's Inn Square
Ground Floor, London WC1R 5AA,
Telephone: 0171 405 8946/7/8
Call Date: Feb 1991, Inner Temple
Qualifications: [MA (Cantab), MSc (Lond)]

SHAW MISS ELIZABETH

Wilberforce Chambers
7 Bishop Lane, Hull, East Yorkshire,
HU1 1PA, Telephone: 01482 323264
E-mail: clerks@hullbar.demon.co.uk
Call Date: Nov 1986, Middle Temple
Qualifications: [BA]

SHAW MRS GABRIELE

3 Temple Gardens
3rd Floor, Temple, London EC4Y 9AU,
Telephone: 0171 353 0832
Call Date: Mar 1998, Inner Temple
Qualifications: [BA (Lond), LLM (Manch)]

SHAW GEOFFREY PETER QC (1991)

1 Brick Court
1st Floor, Temple, London EC4Y 9BY,
Telephone: 0171 353 8845
E-mail: clerks@1brickcourt.co.uk
Call Date: 1968, Gray's Inn
Qualifications: [BA, BCL (Oxon)]

SHAW HOWARD

29 Bedford Row Chambers
London WC1R 4HE,
Telephone: 0171 831 2626
Call Date: July 1973, Inner Temple
Pupil Master
Qualifications: [LLB (Lond)]

SHAW JAMES NICHOLAS

10 King's Bench Walk
1st Floor, Temple, London EC4Y 7EB,
Telephone: 0171 353 2501
Call Date: Nov 1988, Inner Temple
Qualifications: [LLB (Reading)]

SHAW PROF MALCOLM NATHAN

Essex Court Chambers
24 Lincoln's Inn Fields, London
WC2A 3ED, Telephone: 0171 813 8000
E-mail:clerksroom@essexcourt-chambers.co.uk
Call Date: July 1988, Gray's Inn
Qualifications: [LLB (L'pool), LLM (Israel),
PhD (Keele)]

SHAW MARK RICHARD

Blackstone Chambers
Blackstone House, Temple, London
EC4Y 9BW, Telephone: 0171 583 1770
E-mail:clerks@blackstonechambers.com
Call Date: July 1987, Inner Temple
Pupil Master
Qualifications: [BA (Durham) LLM, (Cantab)]

SHAW MICHAEL JOHN

2 Mitre Court Buildings
1st Floor, Temple, London EC4Y 7BX,
Telephone: 0171 353 1353
Call Date: Nov 1994, Middle Temple
Qualifications: [LLB (Hons)]

SHAW MISS NICOLA JANE

Gray's Inn Tax Chambers
3rd Floor, Gray's Inn Chambers, Gray's
Inn, London WC1R 5JA,
Telephone: 0171 242 2642
E-mail: clerks@taxbar.com
Call Date: Nov 1995, Inner Temple
Qualifications: [BCL, BA (Oxon)]

SHAW MS NICOLA JANE DUCKWORTH

Martins Building
2nd Floor, No 4 Water Street, Liverpool
L2 3SP, Telephone: 0151 236 5818/4919
Call Date: Oct 1992, Lincoln's Inn
Qualifications: [BA(Hons)(Leeds), CPE]

SHAW PETER FRANCIS

Cloisters
1 Pump Court, Temple, London
EC4Y 7AA, Telephone: 0171 827 4000
E-mail: clerks@cloisters.com
Call Date: Nov 1992, Inner Temple
Qualifications: [LLB (Brunel)]

SHAW PETER MAURICE

9 Stone Buildings
Lincoln's Inn, London WC2A 3NN,
Telephone: 0171 404 5055
E-mail: clerks@9stoneb.law.co.uk
Call Date: Nov 1995, Middle Temple
Qualifications: [BA (Hons)]

SHAW (RICHARD) JULIAN (FRANKLYN)

White Friars Chambers
21 White Friars, Chester CH1 1NZ,
Telephone: 01244 323070
E-mail:whitefriarschambers@btinternet.com
Call Date: Nov 1984, Gray's Inn
Pupil Master
Qualifications: [LLB (Wales)]

SHAW SAMUEL BENJAMIN BARNABY

1 Paper Buildings
1st Floor, Temple, London EC4Y 7EP,
Telephone: 0171 353 3728/4953
Call Date: Nov 1996, Middle Temple
Qualifications: [MA (Hons)(Edinburgh)]

SHAW STEPHEN

Lamb Chambers
Lamb Building, Temple, London
EC4Y 7AS, Telephone: 020 7797 8300
E-mail: lambchambers@link.org
Call Date: July 1975, Gray's Inn
Pupil Master
Qualifications: [LLB, ACIArb]

SHAY STEPHEN EVERETT

One King's Bench Walk
1st Floor, Temple, London EC4Y 7DB,
Telephone: 0171 936 1500
E-mail: ddear@1kbw.co.uk
Call Date: Nov 1984, Middle Temple
Pupil Master
Qualifications: [BA Hons (Oxon)]

SHEA MS CAROLINE MARY

Falcon Chambers
Falcon Court, London EC4Y 1AA,
Telephone: 0171 353 2484
E-mail: clerks@falcon-chambers.com
Call Date: Nov 1994, Middle Temple
Qualifications: [MA (Cantab)]

SHEARS PHILIP PETER QC (1996)

9 Bedford Row
London WC1R 4AZ,
Telephone: 0171 242 3555
E-mail: clerks@9br.co.uk
Call Date: July 1972, Middle Temple
Recorder
Qualifications: [LLB (Nottm) LLB, (Cantab)]

SHEEHAN MISS ANNE-MARIE

Bell Yard Chambers
116/118 Chancery Lane, London
WC2A 1PP, Telephone: 0171 306 9292
Call Date: July 1994, Lincoln's Inn
Qualifications: [LLB (Hons)]

SHEEHAN MALCOLM PETER

2 Harcourt Buildings
Ground Floor/Left, Temple, London
EC4Y 9DB, Telephone: 0171 583 9020
E-mail: clerks@harcourt.co.uk
Call Date: Oct 1993, Lincoln's Inn
Qualifications: [MA (Hons)(Oxon)]

SHEFF MS JANINE RACHEL

18 Red Lion Court
(Off Fleet Street), London EC4A 3EB,
Telephone: 0171 520 6000
E-mail: chambers@18rlc.co.uk
Thornwood House
102 New London Road, Chelmsford,
Essex, CM2 0RG,
Telephone: 01245 280880
E-mail: chambers@18rlc.co.uk
Call Date: July 1983, Middle Temple
Pupil Master
Qualifications: [LLB (B'ham)]

SHEFFI MISS BOSMATH

9 King's Bench Walk
Ground Floor, Temple, London
EC4Y 7DX, Telephone: 0171 353 7202/
3909 E-mail: 9kbw@compuserve.com
Call Date: Nov 1991, Middle Temple
Qualifications: [BA Hons (Kent)]

SHEIKH AMJAD IQBAL

Britton Street Chambers
1st Floor, 20 Britton Street, London
EC1M 5NQ, Telephone: 0171 608 3765
Call Date: Nov 1988, Gray's Inn
Qualifications: [BA (Hons)]

SHEIKH IRSHAD AHMED

1 Inner Temple Lane
Temple, London EC4Y 1AF,
Telephone: 020 7353 0933
Call Date: July 1983, Lincoln's Inn
Pupil Master
Qualifications: [LLB (Hons, Hull)]

SHEIKH KHALID FADHAL-RAHMAN

Harrow on the Hill Chambers
60 High Street, Harrow-on-the-Hill,
Middlesex, HA1 3LL,
Telephone: 0181 423 7444
Call Date: Feb 1993, Middle Temple
Qualifications: [LLB (Hons)(Lond), LLM
(Lond)]

SHEIKH MS RAANA

Staple Inn Chambers
1st Floor, 9 Staple Inn, Holborn Bars,
London WC1V 7QH,
Telephone: 0171 242 5240
E-mail: clerks@staple-inn.org
Call Date: Nov 1977, Middle Temple
Pupil Master
Qualifications: [LLB]

SHEKERDEMIAN MISS MARCIA ANNA-MARIA

11 Stone Buildings
Lincoln's Inn, London WC2A 3TG,
Telephone: +44 (0)207 831 6381
E-mail:clerks@11StoneBuildings.law.co.uk
Call Date: July 1987, Middle Temple
Pupil Master
Qualifications: [MA (Cantab)]

SHELDON CLIVE DAVID

11 King's Bench Walk
Temple, London EC4Y 7EQ,
Telephone: 0171 632 8500/583 0610
E-mail: clerksroom@11kbw.com
Call Date: Nov 1991, Inner Temple
Qualifications: [BA (Cantab), LLM
(Philadelphia)]

D

SHELDON RICHARD MICHAEL QC (1996)

3/4 South Square
Gray's Inn, London WC1R 5HP,
Telephone: 0171 696 9900
E-mail: clerks@southsquare.com
Call Date: July 1979, Gray's Inn
Qualifications: [MA (Cantab)]

SHELDON RICHARD NEIL

Bank House Chambers
Old Bank House, Hartshead, Sheffield
S1 2EL, Telephone: 0114 2751223
Call Date: July 1984, Lincoln's Inn
Pupil Master
Qualifications: [LLB (Leeds)]

SHELDRAKE MISS CHRISTINE ANNE

3 Dr Johnson's Buildings
Ground Floor, Temple, London
EC4Y 7BA, Telephone: 0171 353 4854
E-mail: clerks@3djb.co.uk
Call Date: July 1977, Middle Temple
Pupil Master
Qualifications: [LLB (Lond)]

SHELLARD ROBIN JAMES SPENCER

Queens Square Chambers
56 Queens Square, Bristol BS1 4PR,
Telephone: 0117 921 1966
Call Date: Nov 1992, Inner Temple
Qualifications: [BA (Wales), Dip in Law]

SHELTON GORDON EDWARD

Broadway House Chambers
Broadway House, 9 Bank Street, Bradford,
West Yorkshire, BD1 1TW,
Telephone: 01274 722560
E-mail: clerks@broadwayhouse.co.uk
Broadway House Chambers
31 Park Square West, Leeds LS1 2PF,
Telephone: 0113 246 2600
Call Date: 1981, Inner Temple
Pupil Master, Assistant Recorder
Qualifications: [LLB (Leics)]

SHENTON MISS RACHEL CLAIRE

White Friars Chambers
21 White Friars, Chester CH1 1NZ,
Telephone: 01244 323070
E-mail:whitefriarschambers@btinternet.com
Call Date: Nov 1993, Middle Temple
Qualifications: [LLB (Hons)(Lancs)]

SHENTON MISS SUZANNE HELENE

One Garden Court Family Law Chambers
Ground Floor, Temple, London
EC4Y 9BJ, Telephone: 0171 797 7900
E-mail: clerks@onegardencourt.co.uk
Call Date: July 1973, Middle Temple
Qualifications: [LLB (Manch)]

SHEPHERD MISS JOANNE ELIZABETH

St Albans Chambers
Dolphin Lodge, Dolphin Yard, Holywell
Hill, St Albans, Herts, AL1 1EX,
Telephone: 01727 843383
Tindal Chambers
3/5 New Street, Chelmsford, Essex,
CM1 1NT, Telephone: 01245 267742
New Bailey Chambers
10 Lawson Street, Preston PR1 2QT,
Telephone: 01772 258087
Call Date: 1993, Inner Temple
Qualifications: [BA]

SHEPHERD NIGEL PATRICK

8 King's Bench Walk North
1 Park Square East, Leeds LS1 2NE,
Telephone: 0113 2439797
8 King's Bench Walk
2nd Floor, Temple, London EC4Y 7DU,
Telephone: 0171 797 8888
Call Date: July 1973, Inner Temple
Pupil Master
Qualifications: [LLB]

SHEPHERD PHILIP ALEXANDER

Twenty-Four Old Buildings
Ground Floor, Lincoln's Inn, London
WC2A 3UP, Telephone: 0171 404 0946
E-mail:clerks@24oldbuildings.law.co.uk
Call Date: Nov 1975, Gray's Inn
Pupil Master, Assistant Recorder
Qualifications: [BSc (Econ)]

D

SHEPPARD MISS ABIGAIL RUTH ALICE

4 Brick Court
Temple, London EC4Y 9AD,
Telephone: 0171 797 8910
E-mail: medhurst@dial.pipex.com
Call Date: Nov 1990, Inner Temple
Qualifications: [BA , Dip Law (PCL)]

SHEPPARD TIMOTHY DERIE

Bracton Chambers
95a Chancery Lane, London WC2A 1DT,
Telephone: 0171 242 4248
Call Date: Nov 1995, Inner Temple
Qualifications: [BSc (Edinburgh), CPE
(Lond)]

SHER JULES QC (1981)

Wilberforce Chambers
8 New Square, Lincoln's Inn, London
WC2A 3QP, Telephone: 0171 306 0102
E-mail: chambers@wilberforce.co.uk
Call Date: July 1968, Inner Temple
Qualifications: [BCom, LLB (Rand) , BCL
(Oxon)]

Types of work: Chancery (general), Commercial litigation, Equity, wills and trusts, Landlord and tenant, Pensions, Professional
negligence

SHERBORNE DAVID ALEXANDER

5 Raymond Buildings
1st Floor, Gray's Inn, London WC1R 5BP,
Telephone: 0171 242 2902
E-mail: clerks@media-ent-law.co.uk
Call Date: Oct 1992, Gray's Inn
Qualifications: [BA (Oxon)]

SHERBORNE MONTAGUE QC (1993)

3 Raymond Buildings
Gray's Inn, London WC1R 5BH,
Telephone: 020 7831 3833
E-mail:chambers@threeraymond.demon.co.u
k
Call Date: Feb 1960, Middle Temple
Qualifications: [BA (Oxon)]

SHERIDAN FRANCIS ANTHONY

Furnival Chambers
32 Furnival Street, London EC4A 1JQ,
Telephone: 0171 405 3232
E-mail: clerks@furnivallaw.co.uk
Call Date: July 1980, Inner Temple
Pupil Master
Qualifications: [BA Hons]

SHERIDAN MAURICE BERNARD GERARD

3 Verulam Buildings
London WC1R 5NT,
Telephone: 0171 831 8441
E-mail: clerks@3verulam.co.uk
Call Date: July 1984, Middle Temple
Qualifications: [LLM (Cantab)]

Fax: 0171 831 8479; DX: LDE 331;
Other comms: E-mail
msheridan@mbgs.demon.co.uk

Types of work: Agriculture, Banking,
Commercial, Commercial litigation, EC
law, Environment, Private international,
Waste management

Awards and memberships: Member of Bar European Group, British-Italian Law Association, British-Bulgarian Law Association,
Associate with the Foundation for International Law and Development (FIELD)

Other professional experience: British Assistant
to the President of the Italian Constitutional Court (over two and a half years);
Assistant to the Italian Minister for European Affairs (two years)

Languages spoken: French, Italian

Publications: *EC Legal Systems: An Introductory Guide*, 1993; *EFA Legal Systems: An
Introductory Guide*, 1994; *Italian Yearbook of Civil Procedure* [1991-6] (English
Editor)

SHERIDAN NORMAN PATRICK

Call Date: Oct 1990, Middle Temple
Qualifications: [BSc (Lond), MPhil, Dip Law
(City)]

SHERIDAN PAUL ADRIAN

Manchester House Chambers
18-22 Bridge Street, Manchester M3 3BZ,
Telephone: 0161 834 7007
Peel Court Chambers
45 Hardman Street, Manchester M3 3PL,
Telephone: 0161 832 3791
E-mail: clerks@peelct.co.uk
Call Date: Nov 1984, Lincoln's Inn
Pupil Master
Qualifications: [LLB(Belfast)]

SHERIDAN PETER QC (1977)

11 Stone Buildings
Lincoln's Inn, London WC2A 3TG,
Telephone: +44 (0)207 831 6381
E-mail:clerks@11StoneBuildings.law.co.uk
Call Date: June 1955, Middle Temple
Qualifications: [BA (Oxon)]

SHERIDAN SHANE PETER BRIGHT

**4 Brick Court, Chambers of Anne
Rafferty QC**
1st Floor, Temple, London EC4Y 9AD,
Telephone: 0171 583 8455
Call Date: Feb 1973, Inner Temple
Pupil Master
Qualifications: [BSc (Hons)(Lond)]

SHERMAN ROBERT LESLIE

Dr Johnson's Chambers
Two Dr Johnson's Buildings, Temple,
London EC4Y 7AY,
Telephone: 0171 353 4716
E-mail: clerks@2djb.freeserve.co.uk
Call Date: July 1977, Gray's Inn
Pupil Master
Qualifications: [LLB (Leeds)]

SHERMAN MISS SUSAN ELIZABETH

Chavasse Court Chambers
2nd Floor, Chavasse Court, 24 Lord Street,
Liverpool L2 1TA,
Telephone: 0151 707 1191
Call Date: Nov 1993, Middle Temple
Qualifications: [LLB (Hons)(Lancs)]

SHERRARD CHARLES ISAAC

Furnival Chambers
32 Furnival Street, London EC4A 1JQ,
Telephone: 0171 405 3232
E-mail: clerks@furnivallaw.co.uk
Call Date: Nov 1986, Middle Temple
Qualifications: [LLB]

SHERRATT MATTHEW JOHN

Thomas More Chambers
52 Carey Street, Lincoln's Inn, London
WC2A 2JB, Telephone: 0171 404 7000
E-mail: clerks@thomasmore.law.co.uk
Call Date: July 1994, Inner Temple
Qualifications: [LLB (New Zealand), LLM
(Miami, USA)]

SHERRY EAMONN MARTIN

2-4 Tudor Street
London EC4Y 0AA,
Telephone: 0171 797 7111
E-mail: clerks@rfqc.co.uk
Call Date: Nov 1990, Gray's Inn
Pupil Master
Qualifications: [LLB (Hons)]

SHERRY MICHAEL GABRIEL

Temple Gardens Tax Chambers
1st Floor, 3 Temple Gardens, Temple,
London EC4Y 9AU,
Telephone: 0171 353 7884/5 8982/3
E-mail: clerks@taxcounsel.co.uk.
Peel Court Chambers
45 Hardman Street, Manchester M3 3PL,
Telephone: 0161 832 3791
E-mail: clerks@peelct.co.uk
Call Date: Nov 1978, Gray's Inn
Pupil Master
Qualifications: [MA (Oxon), FCA, ATII]

SHERWIN MISS DEBORAH ANN

Fountain Chambers
Cleveland Business Centre, 1 Watson
Street, Middlesbrough TS1 2RQ,
Telephone: 01642 804040
E-mail:fountainchambers@onyxnet.co.uk
Call Date: July 1979, Inner Temple
Pupil Master, Assistant Recorder
Qualifications: [LLB (Exon)]

D

SHETTY RAJEEV RAMA

Windsor Barristers' Chambers
Windsor Telephone: 01753 648899
E-mail: law@windsorchambers.co.uk
Call Date: Mar 1996, Inner Temple
Qualifications: [LLB (S'ton)]

SHIELD MISS DEBORAH

White Friars Chambers
21 White Friars, Chester CH1 1NZ,
Telephone: 01244 323070
E-mail:whitefriarschambers@btinternet.com
Call Date: Nov 1991, Inner Temple
Qualifications: [LLB]

SHIELDS MISS SONJA MARION

2-4 Tudor Street
London EC4Y 0AA,
Telephone: 0171 797 7111
E-mail: clerks@rfqc.co.uk
Call Date: July 1977, Inner Temple
Qualifications: [BA (Cantab)]

SHIELDS THOMAS MCGREGOR QC (1993)

1 Brick Court
1st Floor, Temple, London EC4Y 9BY,
Telephone: 0171 353 8845
E-mail: clerks@1brickcourt.co.uk
Call Date: July 1973, Inner Temple
Qualifications: [LLB]

SHIELS IAN

30 Park Square
Leeds LS1 2PF, Telephone: 0113 2436388
E-mail: clerks@30parksquare.co.uk
Call Date: Nov 1992, Inner Temple
Qualifications: [BA (Leeds), Dip in Law
(City)]

SHIER FRANCIS PETER

Mitre Court Chambers
3rd Floor, Temple, London EC4Y 7BP,
Telephone: 0171 353 9394
E-mail: mitrecourt.com
Call Date: 1952, Gray's Inn
Pupil Master

SHIKDER KUTUB UDDIN AHMED

Tower Hamlets Barristers Chambers
37B Princelet Street, London E1 5LP,
Telephone: 0171 377 8090
E-mail: shikderka@aol.com
Call Date: Nov 1990, Lincoln's Inn
Qualifications: [LLB (Hons), MA]

SHILLINGFORD GEORGE MILES

Chambers of Mr Peter Crampin QC
Ground Floor, 11 New Square, Lincoln's
Inn, London WC2A 3QB,
Telephone: 020 7831 0081
E-mail: 11newsquare.co.uk
Call Date: Apr 1964, Inner Temple
Pupil Master
Qualifications: [MA Jurisp (Oxon)]

SHILLINGFORD MS PHAEDRA CHRISTINE-ANNE O'BRIEN

95A Chancery Lane
London WC2A 1DT,
Telephone: 0171 405 3101
Call Date: Oct 1997, Lincoln's Inn
Qualifications: [LLB (Hons)(Brunel)]

SHINER BRENDAN ELIAS JOHN

Queens Square Chambers
56 Queens Square, Bristol BS1 4PR,
Telephone: 0117 921 1966
Call Date: June 1955, Middle Temple
Pupil Master
Qualifications: [MA (Oxon)]

SHIPLEY MISS JANE

No. 6
6 Park Square, Leeds LS1 2LW,
Telephone: 0113 2459763
E-mail: chambers@no6.co.uk
Call Date: July 1974, Gray's Inn
Recorder
Qualifications: [MA (Oxon)]

SHIPLEY NORMAN GRAHAM

19 Old Buildings
Lincoln's Inn, London WC2A 3UP,
Telephone: 0171 405 2001
E-mail: clerks@oldbuildingsip.com
Call Date: July 1973, Lincoln's Inn
Pupil Master
Qualifications: [MA (Cantab) Dip, Comp Sci
(Cantab)]

Fax: 0171 405 0001; DX: 397 London, Chancery Lane;
Other comms: E-mail clerks@oldbuildingsip.com; URL: http://www.oldbuildingsip.com

Types of work: Competition, Copyright, EC and competition law, Entertainment, Film, cable, TV, Information technology, Intellectual property, Patents, Trademarks

Awards and memberships: Intellectual Property Bar Association; Chancery Bar Association

Reported Cases: *British Sugar v James Robertson and Sons Ltd*, [1996] RPC 281, 1996. The 'Treat' trademark case.
Circuit Systems Ltd v Zuken Redac Ltd, [1997] 3 WLR 1177, 1997. Validity of assigning causes of action.
Roger Bance's Application, [1996] RPC 667, 1996. Copyright licence of right case.
Roger Bullivant Ltd v Ellis, [1987] FSR 172, 1987. Confidential information case and 'leap frog' injunctions.

SHIPMAN ANTHONY MICHAEL

Call Date: July 1992, Middle Temple
Qualifications: [BA (Hons) (Bristol), LLB (Hons) (Lond)]

SHIPWRIGHT ADRIAN JOHN

Pump Court Tax Chambers
16 Bedford Row, London WC1R 4EB,
Telephone: 0171 414 8080
Call Date: Feb 1993, Lincoln's Inn
Qualifications: [BCL, MA]

SHOKER MAKKAN SINGH

St Philip's Chambers
Fountain Court, Steelhouse Lane,
Birmingham B4 6DR,
Telephone: 0121 246 7000
E-mail: clerks@st-philips.co.uk
Call Date: May 1981, Inner Temple
Pupil Master
Qualifications: [LLB (Lond)]

SHORROCK JOHN MICHAEL QC (1988)

Peel Court Chambers
45 Hardman Street, Manchester M3 3PL,
Telephone: 0161 832 3791
E-mail: clerks@peelct.co.uk
Call Date: July 1966, Inner Temple
Recorder
Qualifications: [MA (Cantab)]

SHORROCK PHILIP GEOFFREY

2 Harcourt Buildings
1st Floor, Temple, London EC4Y 9DB,
Telephone: 020 7353 2112
Call Date: Nov 1978, Middle Temple
Pupil Master
Qualifications: [BA (Cantab)]

SHORT ANDREW JOHN

4 Brick Court
Ground Floor, Temple, London
EC4Y 9AD, Telephone: 0171 797 7766
E-mail: chambers@4brick.co.uk
Call Date: Nov 1990, Gray's Inn
Qualifications: [LLB (Bristol)]

SHORT MISS ANNA LOUISE

Barnard's Inn Chambers
6th Floor, Halton House, 20-23 Holborn,
London EC1N 2JD,
Telephone: 0171 369 6969
E-mail: clerks@biclaw.co.uk
Call Date: 1997, Gray's Inn
Qualifications: [BA (Cantab)]

SHORT GARY PETER

Holborn Chambers
6 Gate Street, Lincoln's Inn Fields, London
WC2A 3HP, Telephone: 0171 242 6060
Call Date: Nov 1996, Gray's Inn
Qualifications: [BA (Lond)]

SHRIMPTON MS CLAIRE ALISON

Guildford Chambers
Stoke House, Leapale Lane, Guildford,
Surrey, GU1 4LY,
Telephone: 01483 539131
E-mail:guildford.barristers@btinternet.com
Call Date: July 1983, Inner Temple
Qualifications: [LLB (Hull)]

SHRIMPTON MICHAEL

Francis Taylor Building
3rd Floor, Temple, London EC4Y 7BY,
Telephone: 0171 797 7250
Call Date: Nov 1983, Gray's Inn
Pupil Master
Qualifications: [LLB(Cardiff)]

SHRIMPTON ROBERT JAMES

2 King's Bench Walk Chambers
1st Floor, 2 King's Bench Walk, Temple,
London EC4Y 7DE,
Telephone: 020 7353 9276
E-mail: chambers@2kbw.co.uk
Call Date: July 1981, Middle Temple
Pupil Master
Qualifications: [LLB (Hons) (Hull)]

SHUKLA MS VINA

New Court Chambers
5 Verulam Buildings, Gray's Inn, London
WC1R 5LY, Telephone: 0171 831 9500
E-mail: mail@newcourtchambers.com
Call Date: 1992, Gray's Inn
Qualifications: [MA (Cantab), BCL]

SHUMAN MISS KAREN ANN ELIZABETH

Bracton Chambers
95a Chancery Lane, London WC2A 1DT,
Telephone: 0171 242 4248
Call Date: Oct 1991, Lincoln's Inn
Pupil Master
Qualifications: [LLB (Hons) (Birm)]

SHUTTLEWORTH TIMOTHY WILLIAM

Francis Taylor Building
3rd Floor, Temple, London EC4Y 7BY,
Telephone: 0171 797 7250
Call Date: July 1971, Gray's Inn
Pupil Master
Qualifications: [LLB]

SIBERRY (WILLIAM) RICHARD QC (1989)

Essex Court Chambers
24 Lincoln's Inn Fields, London
WC2A 3ED, Telephone: 0171 813 8000
E-mail:clerksroom@essexcourt-chambers.co.uk
Call Date: July 1974, Middle Temple

Assistant Recorder
Qualifications: [MA, LLB (Cantab)]

SIBSON MRS CLARE ADELE

Hollis Whiteman Chambers
3rd Floor, Queen Elizabeth Bldg, Temple,
London EC4Y 9BS,
Telephone: 020 7583 5766
E-mail:barristers@holliswhiteman.co.uk
Call Date: 1997, Middle Temple
Qualifications: [BA (Hons)(Cantab)]

SIDDALL NICHOLAS MICHAEL

40 King Street
Manchester M2 6BA,
Telephone: 0161 832 9082
E-mail: clerks@40kingstreet.co.uk
The Chambers of Philip Raynor QC
5 Park Place, Leeds LS1 2RU,
Telephone: 0113 242 1123
Call Date: 1997, Middle Temple
Qualifications: [BA (Hons)(Cantab)]

SIDDIQI FAIZUL AQTAB

Justice Court Chambers
75 Kendal Road, Willesden Green, London
NW10 1JE, Telephone: 0181 830 7786
E-mail: faiz@ndirect.co.uk
Call Date: July 1990, Lincoln's Inn
Qualifications: [LLB]

SIDDIQUE BILAL MOHAMMED

The Chambers of Mr Ali Mohammed Azhar
Basement, 9 King's Bench Walk, Temple,
London EC4Y 7DX,
Telephone: 0171 353 9564
E-mail: jvlee@btinternet.com
Call Date: Nov 1996, Gray's Inn
Qualifications: [LLB, LLM (Bucks)]

SIDDLE TREVOR BRYAN

Verulam Chambers
Peer House, 8-14 Verulam Street, Gray's
Inn, London WC1X 8LZ,
Telephone: 0171 813 2400
Call Date: Oct 1991, Gray's Inn
Qualifications: [LLB (Hons)]

SIDHU NAVJOT

Cloisters
1 Pump Court, Temple, London
EC4Y 7AA, Telephone: 0171 827 4000
E-mail: clerks@cloisters.com
Call Date: Nov 1993, Lincoln's Inn
Qualifications: [MA (Oxon), MSc (Econ)
(London)]

SIDHU SUKHWANT SINGH

Fleet Chambers
Mitre House, 44-46 Fleet Street, London
EC4Y 1BN, Telephone: 0171 936 3707
E-mail: rr@fleetchambers.demon.co.uk
Call Date: Oct 1996, Lincoln's Inn
Qualifications: [LLB (Hons)(Lond)]

SIDHU-BRAR NISHARN SINGH

New Court Chambers
Gazette Building, 168 Corporation Street,
Birmingham B4 6TZ,
Telephone: 0121 693 6656
Call Date: 1991, Gray's Inn

SIGSWORTH GEORGE PEREGRINE

Park Lane Chambers
19 Westgate, Leeds LS1 2RD,
Telephone: 0113 2285000
E-mail:clerks@parklanechambers.co.uk
Call Date: May 1977, Middle Temple
Pupil Master
Qualifications: [MA (Cantab)]

SIKAND MISS MAYA

Two Garden Court
1st Floor, Middle Temple, London
EC4Y 9BL, Telephone: 0171 353 1633
E-mail:barristers@2gardenct.law.co.uk
Call Date: Nov 1997, Middle Temple
Qualifications: [BA (Hons)(Oxon), MSc
(Lond)]

SILSOE THE LORD QC (1972)

2 Mitre Court Buildings
2nd Floor, Temple, London EC4Y 7BX,
Telephone: 0171 583 1380
E-mail: clerks@2mcb.co.uk
Call Date: Nov 1955, Inner Temple
Qualifications: [MA]

SILVERBECK MISS RACHEL NAOMI

Exchange Chambers
Pearl Assurance House, Derby Square,
Liverpool L2 9XX,
Telephone: 0151 236 7747
E-mail:exchangechambers@btinternet.com
Call Date: Oct 1996, Middle Temple
Qualifications: [BA (Hons)(Newc), CPE]

SILVERLEAF ALEXANDER MICHAEL QC (1996)

11 South Square
2nd Floor, Gray's Inn, London
WC1R 5EU,
Telephone: 0171 405 1222 (24hr messagin
g service)
E-mail: clerks@11southsquare.com
Call Date: May 1980, Gray's Inn
Qualifications: [BSc (Lond)]

SILVESTER BRUCE ROSS

Lamb Chambers
Lamb Building, Temple, London
EC4Y 7AS, Telephone: 020 7797 8300
E-mail: lambchambers@link.org
Call Date: July 1983, Inner Temple
Pupil Master
Qualifications: [LLB (Lond)]

SIMBLET STEPHEN JOHN

Two Garden Court
1st Floor, Middle Temple, London
EC4Y 9BL, Telephone: 0171 353 1633
E-mail:barristers@2gardenct.law.co.uk
Call Date: Oct 1991, Inner Temple
Qualifications: [MA (Cantab), LLM]

SIME STUART JOHN

169 Temple Chambers
Temple Avenue, London EC4Y 0DA,
Telephone: 0171 583 7644
Call Date: Nov 1983, Gray's Inn
Qualifications: [LLB]

SIMISON JEREMY CHARLES

Trinity Chambers
140 New London Road, Chelmsford,
Essex, CM2 0AW,
Telephone: 01245 605040
E-mail:clerks@trinitychambers.law.co.uk
Call Date: Oct 1993, Inner Temple
Qualifications: [BA (B'ham), CPE]

SIMKIN IAIN JAMES

7 Stone Buildings (also at 11 Bolt Court)
1st Floor, Lincoln's Inn, London
WC2A 3SZ, Telephone: 0171 242 0961
E-mail:larthur@7stonebuildings.law.co.uk
11 Bolt Court (also at 7 Stone Buildings – 1st Floor)
London EC4A 3DQ,
Telephone: 0171 353 2300
E-mail: boltct11@aol.com
Redhill Chambers
Seloduct House, 30 Station Road, Redhill,
Surrey, RH1 1NF,
Telephone: 01737 780781
Call Date: Feb 1995, Inner Temple
Qualifications: [BA, CPE (Staffs)]

SIMLER MISS INGRID ANN

Devereux Chambers
Devereux Court, London WC2R 3JJ,
Telephone: 0171 353 7534
E-mail: mailbox@devchambers.co.uk
Call Date: July 1987, Inner Temple
Pupil Master
Qualifications: [MA (Cantab), Dip EEC Law]

SIMMONDS ANDREW JOHN QC (1999)

5 Stone Buildings
Lincoln's Inn, London WC2A 3XT,
Telephone: 0171 242 6201
E-mail:clerks@5-stonebuildings.law.co.uk
Call Date: 1980, Middle Temple
Pupil Master
Qualifications: [MA (Cantab)]

SIMMONDS NICHOLAS HAROLD

Peel Court Chambers
45 Hardman Street, Manchester M3 3PL,
Telephone: 0161 832 3791
E-mail: clerks@peelct.co.uk
Call Date: July 1969, Gray's Inn
Pupil Master
Qualifications: [LLB (Manch)]

SIMMONS MISS MARION ADELE QC (1994)

3/4 South Square
Gray's Inn, London WC1R 5HP,
Telephone: 0171 696 9900
E-mail: clerks@southsquare.com
Call Date: Nov 1970, Gray's Inn

Assistant Recorder
Qualifications: [LLB (Hons) LLM(Lond)]

SIMMS ALAN JOHN GORDON

Chavasse Court Chambers
2nd Floor, Chavasse Court, 24 Lord Street,
Liverpool L2 1TA,
Telephone: 0151 707 1191
Call Date: Nov 1976, Lincoln's Inn
Pupil Master
Qualifications: [MA, LLB (Lond)]

SIMMS MISS SONIA ANGELA

Acre Lane Neighbourhood Chambers
30A Acre Lane, London SW2 5SG,
Telephone: 0171 274 4400
E-mail:barristerschambers@acrelane.demon.co.uk
Call Date: 1993, Middle Temple
Qualifications: [BSc (Hons), Dip in Law (City)]

SIMON MICHAEL HENRY

4 Brick Court
Temple, London EC4Y 9AD,
Telephone: 0171 797 8910
E-mail: medhurst@dial.pipex.com
Call Date: Nov 1992, Inner Temple
Qualifications: [LLB (L'pool)]

SIMON THE HON PEREGRINE CHARLES HUGO QC (1991)

Brick Court Chambers
7-8 Essex Street, London WC2R 3LD,
Telephone: 0171 379 3550
E-mail: [surname]@brickcourt.co.uk
Call Date: July 1973, Middle Temple
Assistant Recorder
Qualifications: [MA (Cantab)]

SIMONS MRS ANGELA MARY

1 Gray's Inn Square
Ground Floor, London WC1R 5AA,
Telephone: 0171 405 8946/7/8
Call Date: July 1985, Gray's Inn
Pupil Master
Qualifications: [BA(Oxon)]

SIMONS RICHARD GRAHAM

Lincoln House Chambers
5th Floor, Lincoln House, 1 Brazennose
Street, Manchester M2 5EL,
Telephone: 0161 832 5701
E-mail: info@lincolnhse.co.uk
Call Date: Feb 1991, Gray's Inn
Qualifications: [LLB (Hons)]

SIMOR MISS JESSICA MARGARET POPPAEA

Monckton Chambers
4 Raymond Buildings, Gray's Inn, London
WC1R 5BP, Telephone: 0171 405 7211
E-mail: chambers@monckton.co.uk
Call Date: Nov 1992, Middle Temple
Qualifications: [BA (Hons), Dip in Law]

SIMPKISS (RICHARD) JONATHAN

11 Old Square
Ground Floor, Lincoln's Inn, London
WC2A 3TS, Telephone: 020 7430 0341
E-mail: clerks@11oldsquare.co.uk
Call Date: July 1975, Middle Temple
Pupil Master
Qualifications: [MA (Cantab)]

SIMPSON MRS ALEXANDRA KATHERINE

24a St John Street
Manchester M3 4DF,
Telephone: 0161 833 9628
Call Date: Nov 1989, Lincoln's Inn
Qualifications: [LLB (Hons)]

SIMPSON DAVID JOSEPH

**The Chambers of Mr Ali Mohammed
Azhar**
Basement, 9 King's Bench Walk, Temple,
London EC4Y 7DX,
Telephone: 0171 353 9564
E-mail: jvlee@btinternet.com
Call Date: Oct 1992, Gray's Inn
Qualifications: [LLB (Hons)]

SIMPSON EDWIN JOHN FLETCHER

12 New Square
Lincoln's Inn, London WC2A 3SW,
Telephone: 0171 419 1212
E-mail: chambers@12newsquare.co.uk
Call Date: Nov 1990, Lincoln's Inn
Qualifications: [MA, BCL (Oxon)]

SIMPSON GRAEME MICHAEL

Harrow on the Hill Chambers
60 High Street, Harrow-on-the-Hill,
Middlesex, HA1 3LL,
Telephone: 0181 423 7444
Windsor Barristers' Chambers
Windsor Telephone: 01753 648899
E-mail: law@windsorchambers.co.uk
Call Date: Nov 1994, Middle Temple
Qualifications: [LLB (Hons)]

SIMPSON IAN

Bracton Chambers
95a Chancery Lane, London WC2A 1DT,
Telephone: 0171 242 4248
Call Date: Oct 1997, Lincoln's Inn
Qualifications: [LLB (Hons)(Lond)]

SIMPSON JAMES

Bell Yard Chambers
116/118 Chancery Lane, London
WC2A 1PP, Telephone: 0171 306 9292
Call Date: Feb 1990, Middle Temple
Pupil Master
Qualifications: [LLB (Lond)]

SIMPSON JONATHAN DAVID

4 King's Bench Walk
2nd Floor, Temple, London EC4Y 7DL,
Telephone: 020 7353 3581
E-mail: clerks@4kbw.co.uk
Call Date: Nov 1993, Gray's Inn
Qualifications: [LLB (Hons)]

SIMPSON KEITH

ICSL, 4 Gray's Inn Place, London WC1R
5DX
Call Date: Nov 1995, Gray's Inn
Qualifications: [BA (Sheff), MA (Sheff)]

SIMPSON MARK TAYLOR

4 Paper Buildings
Ground Floor, Temple, London
EC4Y 7EX, Telephone: 0171 353 3366/
583 7155
E-mail: clerks@4paperbuildings.com
Call Date: Oct 1992, Middle Temple
Qualifications: [MA (Hons, Oxon)]

SIMPSON MRS NICOLA JANE

Queen Elizabeth Building
Ground Floor, Temple, London
EC4Y 9BS,
Telephone: 0171 353 7181 (12 Lines)
Call Date: July 1982, Inner Temple
Qualifications: [LLB (Hons) (B'ham)]

SIMPSON PAUL RICHARD

First National Chambers
2nd Floor, First National Building, 24
Fenwick Street, Liverpool L2 7NE,
Telephone: 0151 236 2098
Call Date: Nov 1980, Lincoln's Inn
Qualifications: [LLB (L'pool)]

SIMPSON MS RAQUEL

18 St John Street
Manchester M3 4EA,
Telephone: 0161 278 1800
E-mail: 18stjohn@lineone.net
Call Date: Oct 1990, Inner Temple
Qualifications: [LLB (LSE)]

SIMS PAUL LLYSTYN

6 Gray's Inn Square
Ground Floor, Gray's Inn, London
WC1R 5AZ, Telephone: 0171 242 1052
E-mail: 6graysinn@clara.co.uk
Call Date: Nov 1990, Gray's Inn
Qualifications: [LLB]

SINAN IZZET MAHMUT

Fountain Court
Temple, London EC4Y 9DH,
Telephone: 0171 583 3335
E-mail: chambers@fountaincourt.co.uk
Call Date: July 1981, Inner Temple
Qualifications: [MA, LLM (Cantab), Licence
Speciale En, Droit European Grand,
Distinction, ULB, Brussels]

SINCLAIR BRIAN

Fyfield Chambers
Field Cottage, Fyfield, Southrop,
Gloucestershire, GL7 3NT,
Telephone: 01367 850304
Call Date: Feb 1959, Middle Temple
Qualifications: [MA (Trinity College), Dublin
University)]

SINCLAIR MISS FIONA JANE

9 Gough Square
London EC4A 3DE,
Telephone: 020 7832 0500
E-mail: clerks@9goughsq.co.uk
Call Date: Oct 1990, Gray's Inn
Qualifications: [BA (Oxon)]

SINCLAIR MISS FIONA MARY

Chambers of John L Powell QC
Four New Square, Lincoln's Inn, London
WC2A 3RJ, Telephone: 0171 797 8000
E-mail: barristers@4newsquare.com
Call Date: July 1989, Inner Temple
Pupil Master
Qualifications: [MA (Cantab), LLM (Cantab)]

SINCLAIR GRAHAM KELSO

East Anglian Chambers
57 London Street, Norwich NR2 1HL,
Telephone: 01603 617351
E-mail: norwich@ealaw.co.uk
East Anglian Chambers
52 North Hill, Colchester, Essex, CO1 1PY,
Telephone: 01206 572756
E-mail: colchester@ealaw.co.uk
East Anglian Chambers
Gresham House, 5 Museum Street,
Ipswich, Suffolk, IP1 1HQ,
Telephone: 01473 214481
E-mail: ipswich@ealaw.co.uk
Call Date: July 1979, Gray's Inn
Pupil Master
Qualifications: [LLB (Hons) (Lond)]

SINCLAIR SIR IAN MACTAGGART QC (1979)

Blackstone Chambers
Blackstone House, Temple, London
EC4Y 9BW, Telephone: 0171 583 1770
E-mail:clerks@blackstonechambers.com
Call Date: 1952, Middle Temple
Qualifications: [BA, LL B Cantab]

SINCLAIR JEAN-PAUL MEEHAN

33 Bedford Row
London WC1R 4JH,
Telephone: 0171 242 6476
E-mail:clerks@bedfordrow33.demon.co.uk
Call Date: Feb 1989, Middle Temple
Qualifications: [MA (Cantab)]

SINCLAIR MISS LISA ANNE

7 New Square
Lincoln's Inn, London WC2A 3QS,
Telephone: 0171 430 1660
Call Date: July 1993, Gray's Inn
Qualifications: [LLB (Leic), MBA]

SINCLAIR MALCOLM DAVID

11 Old Square
Ground Floor, Lincoln's Inn, London
WC2A 3TS, Telephone: 0171 242 5022/
405 1074
Call Date: July 1978, Lincoln's Inn
Pupil Master
Qualifications: [LLB (Lond), BA]

SINCLAIR SIR PATRICK ROBERT RICHARD

5 New Square
Ground Floor, Lincoln's Inn, London
WC2A 3RJ, Telephone: 020 7404 0404
E-mail:chambers@fivenewsquare.demon.co.
uk
Call Date: May 1961, Lincoln's Inn
Pupil Master
Qualifications: [MA (Oxon)]

SINCLAIR PAUL

Fountain Court
Temple, London EC4Y 9DH,
Telephone: 0171 583 3335
E-mail: chambers@fountaincourt.co.uk
Call Date: Oct 1997, Middle Temple
Qualifications: [BA (Hons)(Cantab)]

SINCLAIR MR. PHILIP JUSTYN

Maidstone Chambers
33 Earl Street, Maidstone, Kent, ME14 1PF,
Telephone: 01622 688592
E-mail:maidstonechambers@compuserve.co
m
Call Date: Oct 1995, Gray's Inn
Qualifications: [LLB (Hons)]

SINCLAIR-MORRIS CHARLES ROBERT

9 Woodhouse Square
Leeds LS3 1AD,
Telephone: 0113 2451986
E-mail: clerks@9woodhouse.co.uk
Call Date: Nov 1966, Lincoln's Inn

SINGER ANDREW MICHAEL

40 King Street
Manchester M2 6BA,
Telephone: 0161 832 9082
E-mail: clerks@40kingstreet.co.uk
The Chambers of Philip Raynor QC
5 Park Place, Leeds LS1 2RU,
Telephone: 0113 242 1123
Call Date: Nov 1990, Gray's Inn
Qualifications: [BA (Cantab)]

SINGER HARRY DAVID

Forest House Chambers
15 Granville Road, Walthamstow, London
E17 9BS, Telephone: 0181 925 2240
Call Date: Nov 1969, Middle Temple
Qualifications: [LLB (Hons)]

SINGER PHILIP FRANCIS QC (1994)

2 Pump Court
1st Floor, Temple, London EC4Y 7AH,
Telephone: 0171 353 5597
Call Date: Feb 1964, Inner Temple
Recorder
Qualifications: [MA, LLM (Cantab)]

SINGH BALBIR

Equity Chambers
3rd Floor, 153a Corporation Street,
Birmingham B4 6PH,
Telephone: 0121 233 2100
E-mail: equityatusa.com
Call Date: July 1984, Lincoln's Inn
Qualifications: [BA, LLB (Hons), Dip M.R.S]

SINGH GURDIAL

Goldsmith Chambers
Ground Floor, Goldsmith Building,
Temple, London EC4Y 7BL,
Telephone: 0171 353 6802/3/4/5
E-mail:clerks@goldsmithchambers.law.co.uk
Call Date: July 1989, Lincoln's Inn
Qualifications: [LLB (Leeds)]

SINGH HARJIT

Chambers of Harjit Singh
Ground Floor, 2 Middle Temple Lane,
Temple, London EC4Y 9AA,
Telephone: 0171 353 1356 (4 Lines)
Call Date: Nov 1956, Lincoln's Inn
Pupil Master
Qualifications: [LLB, LLM (Lond)]

SINGH KULDIP QC (1993)

Five Paper Buildings
1st Floor, Five Paper Bldgs, Temple,
London EC4Y 7HB,
Telephone: 0171 583 6117
E-mail:clerks@5-paperbuildings.law.co.uk
Call Date: July 1975, Middle Temple

SINGH RABINDER

4-5 Gray's Inn Square
Ground Floor, Gray's Inn, London
WC1R 5JP, Telephone: 0171 404 5252
E-mail:chambers@4-5graysinnsquare.co.uk
Call Date: July 1989, Lincoln's Inn
Pupil Master
Qualifications: [BA (Cantab), LLM
(California)]

SINGH MISS RANJANA

Holborn Chambers
6 Gate Street, Lincoln's Inn Fields, London
WC2A 3HP, Telephone: 0171 242 6060
Call Date: Oct 1995, Middle Temple
Qualifications: [LLB (Hons)]

SINGH TALBIR

Equity Chambers
3rd Floor, 153a Corporation Street,
Birmingham B4 6PH,
Telephone: 0121 233 2100
E-mail: equityatusa.com
Call Date: July 1997, Gray's Inn
Qualifications: [LLB (Teeside), LLM
(Warwick)]

SINGH-HAYER BANSA

58 King Street Chambers
1st Floor, Kingsgate House, 51-53 South
King Street, Manchester M2 6DE,
Telephone: 0161 831 7477
Call Date: Nov 1988, Gray's Inn
Qualifications: [LLB (Hons)]

SINGLETON BARRY NEILL QC (1989)

One King's Bench Walk
1st Floor, Temple, London EC4Y 7DB,
Telephone: 0171 936 1500
E-mail: ddear@1kbw.co.uk
Call Date: July 1968, Gray's Inn
Qualifications: [MA (Cantab)]

SINGLETON MICHAEL JOHN

St Ive's Chambers
Whittall Street, Birmingham B4 6DH,
Telephone: 0121 236 0863/5720
E-mail:stives.headofchambers@btinternet.com
Call Date: July 1987, Middle Temple
Qualifications: [LLB (Hons) (Leics)]

SINGLETON MISS SARAH LOUISE

28 St John Street
Manchester M3 4DJ,
Telephone: 0161 834 8418
E-mail: clerk@28stjohnst.co.uk
Call Date: July 1983, Middle Temple
Assistant Recorder
Qualifications: [BA (Oxon)]

SINKER ANDREW TENNANT

19 Castle Street Chambers
Liverpool L2 4SX,
Telephone: 0151 236 9402
E-mail: DBrei16454@aol.com
Call Date: Oct 1991, Lincoln's Inn
Qualifications: [LLB (Hons) (Leeds)]

SINNATT SIMON PETER RANDALL

Crown Office Row Chambers
Blenheim House, 120 Church Street,
Brighton, Sussex, BN1 1WH,
Telephone: 01273 625625
E-mail: crownofficerow@clara.net
Call Date: Oct 1993, Lincoln's Inn
Qualifications: [BA (Hons)(York), CPE]

SISLEY TIMOTHY JULIAN CRISPIN

9 Stone Buildings
Lincoln's Inn, London WC2A 3NN,
Telephone: 0171 404 5055
E-mail: clerks@9stoneb.law.co.uk

Westgate Chambers
144 High Street, Lewes, East Sussex,
BN7 1XT, Telephone: 01273 480510
Call Date: Feb 1989, Middle Temple
Pupil Master
Qualifications: [BA (Lond), BA (Lond)]

SIVA KANNAN SARAVANAPAVAANANTHAN

Bell Yard Chambers
116/118 Chancery Lane, London
WC2A 1PP, Telephone: 0171 306 9292
Call Date: Nov 1996, Gray's Inn
Qualifications: [BA]

SKELLEY MICHAEL DAVID

4 King's Bench Walk
2nd Floor, Temple, London EC4Y 7DL,
Telephone: 020 7353 3581
E-mail: clerks@4kbw.co.uk
Call Date: Oct 1991, Inner Temple
Qualifications: [BA (Oxon)]

SKELLORN MISS KATHRYN MAIR

St John's Chambers
Small Street, Bristol BS1 1DW,
Telephone: 0117 9213456/298514
E-mail: @stjohnschambers.co.uk
Call Date: Nov 1993, Gray's Inn
Qualifications: [BA (Hons)(Oxon)]

SKELLY ANDREW JON

1 Gray's Inn Square
Ground Floor, London WC1R 5AA,
Telephone: 0171 405 8946/7/8
Call Date: Oct 1994, Inner Temple
Qualifications: [LLB]

SKELT IAN STUART

11 King's Bench Walk
1st Floor, Temple, London EC4Y 7EQ,
Telephone: 0171 353 3337
E-mail: fmuller11@aol.com
11 King's Bench Walk
3 Park Court, Park Cross Street, Leeds
LS1 2QH, Telephone: 0113 297 1200
Call Date: Oct 1994, Lincoln's Inn
Qualifications: [LLB (Hons)(Newc)]

SKELTON PETER

35 Essex Street
Temple, London WC2R 3AR,
Telephone: 0171 353 6381
E-mail: derek_jenkins@link.org
Call Date: Oct 1997, Middle Temple
Qualifications: [BA (Hons)(York), CPE]

SKILBECK MRS JENNIFER SETH

Monckton Chambers
4 Raymond Buildings, Gray's Inn, London
WC1R 5BP, Telephone: 0171 405 7211
E-mail: chambers@monckton.co.uk
Call Date: Oct 1991, Lincoln's Inn
Qualifications: [BSc (Econ), MSc (Econ), Dip Law]

SKILBECK RUPERT HUGH

Chambers of Michael Pert QC
36 Bedford Row, London WC1R 4JH,
Telephone: 0171 421 8000
E-mail: 36bedfordrow@link.org
Chambers of Michael Pert QC
24 Albion Place, Northampton NN1 1UD,
Telephone: 01604 602333
Chambers of Michael Pert QC
104 New Walk, Leicester LE1 7EA,
Telephone: 0116 249 2020
Call Date: Mar 1996, Gray's Inn
Qualifications: [BA (York)]

SKINNER MISS LORNA JANE

1 Brick Court
1st Floor, Temple, London EC4Y 9BY,
Telephone: 0171 353 8845
E-mail: clerks@1brickcourt.co.uk
Call Date: Nov 1997, Middle Temple
Qualifications: [BA (Hons)]

SKINNER TOM MILNE

Francis Taylor Building
3rd Floor, Temple, London EC4Y 7BY,
Telephone: 0171 797 7250
Call Date: May 1992, Gray's Inn
Qualifications: [BA (Oxon) , LLM (Exeter)]

SLACK IAN

2 King's Bench Walk Chambers
1st Floor, 2 King's Bench Walk, Temple,
London EC4Y 7DE,
Telephone: 020 7353 9276
E-mail: chambers@2kbw.co.uk
Call Date: Nov 1974, Middle Temple
Qualifications: [BA]

SLACK KEVIN JOHN

Exchange Chambers
Pearl Assurance House, Derby Square,
Liverpool L2 9XX,
Telephone: 0151 236 7747
E-mail:exchangechambers@btinternet.com
Call Date: Oct 1997, Gray's Inn
Qualifications: [BA]

SLADE MISS ELIZABETH ANN QC (1992)

11 King's Bench Walk
Temple, London EC4Y 7EQ,
Telephone: 0171 632 8500/583 0610
E-mail: clerksroom@11kbw.com
Call Date: July 1972, Inner Temple
Recorder
Qualifications: [MA (Oxon)]

SLADE RICHARD PENKIVIL

Brick Court Chambers
7-8 Essex Street, London WC2R 3LD,
Telephone: 0171 379 3550
E-mail: [surname]@brickcourt.co.uk
Call Date: Nov 1987, Lincoln's Inn
Pupil Master
Qualifications: [BA (Hons) (Cantab)]

SLADE JONES ROBIN

Chartlands Chambers
3 St Giles Terrace, Northampton
NN1 2BN, Telephone: 01604 603322
Call Date: Oct 1993, Gray's Inn
Qualifications: [M.Eng]

SLATER IAIN JAMES

19 Castle Street Chambers
Liverpool L2 4SX,
Telephone: 0151 236 9402
E-mail: DBrei16454@aol.com
Call Date: Oct 1991, Lincoln's Inn
Qualifications: [LLB (Hons)]

SLATER JOHN CHRISTOPHER NASH QC (1987)

One Paper Buildings
Ground Floor, Temple, London
EC4Y 7EP, Telephone: 0171 583 7355
E-mail: clerks@1pb.co.uk
Call Date: Nov 1969, Middle Temple
Recorder
Qualifications: [MA (Oxon)]

SLATER MISS JULIE ANN

Victoria Chambers
3rd Floor, 177 Corporation Street,
Birmingham B4 6RG,
Telephone: 0121 236 9900
E-mail: viccham@aol.com
Call Date: July 1988, Lincoln's Inn
Qualifications: [LLB (Hons)]

SLATER MICHAEL NEAL

Paradise Chambers
26 Paradise Square, Sheffield S1 2DE,
Telephone: 0114 2738951
E-mail: timbooth@paradise-sq.co.uk
Call Date: July 1983, Inner Temple
Pupil Master
Qualifications: [LLB (Sheff)]

SLAUGHTER ANDREW FRANCIS

Bridewell Chambers
2 Bridewell Place, London EC4V 6AP,
Telephone: 020 7797 8800
E-mail:HughesGage@bridewell.law.co.uk
Call Date: Oct 1993, Middle Temple
Qualifications: [BA (Hons)]

SLEE MS JACQUELINE AMY

2-4 Tudor Street
London EC4Y 0AA,
Telephone: 0171 797 7111
E-mail: clerks@rfqc.co.uk
Call Date: Oct 1995, Gray's Inn
Qualifications: [B.Sc]

SLEEMAN MISS RACHEL SARAH ELIZABETH

One Essex Court
1st Floor, Temple, London EC4Y 9AR,
Telephone: 0171 936 3030
E-mail: one.essex_court@virgin.net
Call Date: Nov 1996, Gray's Inn
Qualifications: [LLB (Lond)]

SLEIGHTHOLME JOHN TREVOR

37 Park Square Chambers
37 Park Square, Leeds LS1 2NY,
Telephone: 0113 2439422
E-mail: chambers@no37.co.uk
Call Date: Nov 1982, Gray's Inn
Pupil Master
Qualifications: [LLB (Leeds)]

SLEVIN FRANK

The Chambers of Mr Ali Mohammed Azhar
Basement, 9 King's Bench Walk, Temple,
London EC4Y 7DX,
Telephone: 0171 353 9564
E-mail: jvlee@btinternet.com
Call Date: July 1985, Lincoln's Inn
Pupil Master
Qualifications: [BA]

SLIWINSKI ROBERT ANDREW

Chambers of Geoffrey Hawker
46/48 Essex Street, London WC2R 3GH,
Telephone: 0171 583 8899
Call Date: Oct 1990, Middle Temple
Qualifications: [BSc, LLB (Hons), ARICS, ACIArb]

SLOAN PAUL KAY

Trinity Chambers
9-12 Trinity Chare, Quayside, Newcastle
upon Tyne NE1 3DF,
Telephone: 0191 232 1927
E-mail: info@trinitychambers.co.uk
Call Date: July 1981, Inner Temple
Pupil Master
Qualifications: [LLB (Lond)]

SLOMNICKA MISS BARBARA IRENA

14 Gray's Inn Square
Gray's Inn, London WC1R 5JP,
Telephone: 0171 242 0858
E-mail: 100712.2134@compuserve.com
Call Date: Nov 1976, Middle Temple
Pupil Master
Qualifications: [LLB MJur]

SLOWE MISS EMILY JANE

Chancery Chambers
1st Floor Offices, 70/72 Chancery Lane,
London WC2A 1AB,
Telephone: 0171 405 6879/6870
Call Date: Nov 1996, Inner Temple
Qualifications: [LLB]

SMAIL ALASTAIR HAROLD KURT

St Philip's Chambers
Fountain Court, Steelhouse Lane,
Birmingham B4 6DR,
Telephone: 0121 246 7000
E-mail: clerks@st-philips.co.uk
Call Date: Nov 1987, Gray's Inn
Pupil Master
Qualifications: [BA, BCL (Oxon)]

SMALES MRS SUZANNE

No. 6
6 Park Square, Leeds LS1 2LW,
Telephone: 0113 2459763
E-mail: chambers@no6.co.uk
Call Date: Oct 1990, Inner Temple
Qualifications: [LLB (Hons) (Essex)]

SMALL MRS ARLENE ANN-MARIE

Francis Taylor Building
Ground Floor, Temple, London
EC4Y 7BY, Telephone: 0171 353 7768/
7769/2711
E-mail:clerks@francistaylorbuilding.law.co.uk
Call Date: Oct 1997, Middle Temple
Qualifications: [LLB (Hons)(Brunel)]

SMALL DEVON

2 Middle Temple Lane
3rd Floor, Temple, London EC4Y 9AA,
Telephone: 0171 583 4540
Call Date: Nov 1990, Inner Temple
Qualifications: [LLB]

D

SMALL MISS GINA LEE

King's Bench Chambers
115 North Hill, Plymouth PL4 8JY,
Telephone: 01752 221551
2 King's Bench Walk
Ground Floor, Temple, London
EC4Y 7DE, Telephone: 0171 353 1746
E-mail: 2kbw@atlas.co.uk
Call Date: Oct 1991, Lincoln's Inn
Qualifications: [BA (Hons) (Lond), Dip Law]

SMALL JONATHAN EDWIN

Falcon Chambers
Falcon Court, London EC4Y 1AA,
Telephone: 0171 353 2484
E-mail: clerks@falcon-chambers.com
Call Date: Oct 1990, Lincoln's Inn
Pupil Master
Qualifications: [BA (Nott'm), Dip Law (City)]

SMALL MISS PENELOPE SUSAN

1 Paper Buildings
1st Floor, Temple, London EC4Y 7EP,
Telephone: 0171 353 3728/4953
Call Date: Oct 1992, Inner Temple
Qualifications: [BA (Warw), Dip
Law(Westminster)]

SMALLER MISS ELIZABETH ANNE

Verulam Chambers
Peer House, 8-14 Verulam Street, Gray's
Inn, London WC1X 8LZ,
Telephone: 0171 813 2400
Call Date: 1995, Gray's Inn
Qualifications: [BA]

SMALLWOOD MISS ANNE ELIZABETH

5 Fountain Court
Steelhouse Lane, Birmingham B4 6DR,
Telephone: 0121 606 0500
E-mail:clerks@5fountaincourt.law.co.uk
Call Date: Nov 1977, Middle Temple
Pupil Master
Qualifications: [LLB]

SMALLWOOD ROBERT ANDREW

5 Fountain Court
Steelhouse Lane, Birmingham B4 6DR,
Telephone: 0121 606 0500
E-mail:clerks@5fountaincourt.law.co.uk
Call Date: Oct 1994, Lincoln's Inn
Qualifications: [LLB (Hons)(Sheff)]

SMART DAVID PETER ROSS

St Mary's Chambers
50 High Pavement, Lace Market,
Nottingham NG1 1HW,
Telephone: 0115 9503503
E-mail: clerks@smc.law.co.uk
Call Date: Nov 1977, Middle Temple
Pupil Master
Qualifications: [LLB (Bris)]

SMART MISS JACQUELINE ANNE

Trinity Chambers
9-12 Trinity Chare, Quayside, Newcastle
upon Tyne NE1 3DF,
Telephone: 0191 232 1927
E-mail: info@trinitychambers.co.uk
Call Date: Nov 1981, Middle Temple
Pupil Master
Qualifications: [LLB (Lond)]

SMART JOHN ANDREW CHARLES

9 Stone Buildings
Lincoln's Inn, London WC2A 3NN,
Telephone: 0171 404 5055
E-mail: clerks@9stoneb.law.co.uk
Call Date: Nov 1989, Middle Temple
Pupil Master
Qualifications: [B.Sc Hons (Bris), Dip Law
(City)]

SMART MISS JULIA ELIZABETH

Verulam Chambers
Peer House, 8-14 Verulam Street, Gray's
Inn, London WC1X 8LZ,
Telephone: 0171 813 2400
Call Date: Oct 1993, Gray's Inn
Qualifications: [LLB]

SMART ROGER BERNARD

**4 Brick Court, Chambers of Anne
Rafferty QC**
1st Floor, Temple, London EC4Y 9AD,
Telephone: 0171 583 8455
Call Date: July 1989, Inner Temple
Qualifications: [LLB (Hons)]

SMILER ANDREW JAMES

Warwick House Chambers
8 Warwick Court, Gray's Inn, London
WC1R 5DJ, Telephone: 0171 430 2323
E-mail: cdrewlaw@aol.com
Call Date: 1996, Gray's Inn
Qualifications: [BA (Oxon)]

SMITH MISS ABIGAIL

Godolphin Chambers
50 Castle Street, Truro, Cornwall,
TR1 3AF, Telephone: 01872 276312
E-mail:theclerks@godolphin.force9.co.uk
17 Carlton Crescent
Southampton SO15 2XR,
Telephone: 023 8032 0320/0823 2003
E-mail: greg@jg17cc.co.uk
Call Date: July 1989, Middle Temple
Qualifications: [LLB (B'ham)]

SMITH ADAM JOHN

Crown Office Row Chambers
Blenheim House, 120 Church Street,
Brighton, Sussex, BN1 1WH,
Telephone: 01273 625625
E-mail: crownofficerow@clara.net
Call Date: Nov 1987, Inner Temple
Pupil Master
Qualifications: [LLB (Hull)]

SMITH ALAN ARTHUR

Hardwicke Building
New Square, Lincoln's Inn, London
WC2A 3SB, Telephone: 020 7242 2523
E-mail: clerks@hardwicke.co.uk
Call Date: July 1981, Middle Temple
Pupil Master
Qualifications: [BA]

SMITH ALISDAIR ROBERT MACSORLEY

3 Temple Gardens
Lower Ground Floor, Temple, London
EC4Y 9AU, Telephone: 0171 353 3102/5/
9297 E-mail: clerks@3tg.co.uk
Call Date: July 1981, Gray's Inn
Pupil Master
Qualifications: [LLB (Lond)]

SMITH ANDREW CHARLES QC (1990)

Fountain Court
Temple, London EC4Y 9DH,
Telephone: 0171 583 3335
E-mail: chambers@fountaincourt.co.uk
Call Date: Nov 1974, Middle Temple
Recorder
Qualifications: [BA (Oxon)]

SMITH ANDREW DESMOND

Bank House Chambers
Old Bank House, Hartshead, Sheffield
S1 2EL, Telephone: 0114 2751223
Call Date: Oct 1991, Middle Temple
Qualifications: [LLB Hons (Sheff)]

SMITH ANDREW DUNCAN

1 Fountain Court
Steelhouse Lane, Birmingham B4 6DR,
Telephone: 0121 236 5721
Call Date: Oct 1997, Middle Temple
Qualifications: [BA (Hons)(Oxon)]

SMITH ANDREW WILLIAM

24a St John Street
Manchester M3 4DF,
Telephone: 0161 833 9628
Call Date: Oct 1996, Lincoln's Inn
Qualifications: [LLB (Hons)(Manc)]

SMITH ANTHONY THOMAS QC (1977)

Berkeley Chambers
1st Floor, 52 High Street, Henley-in-Arden,
Warwickshire, B95 5AN,
Telephone: 01564 795546
Call Date: Feb 1958, Inner Temple
Recorder
Qualifications: [MA (Cantab)]

SMITH MISS CATHERINE EMMA

5 Pump Court
Ground Floor, Temple, London
EC4Y 7AP, Telephone: 020 7353 2532
E-mail: FivePump@netcomuk.co.uk
Call Date: 1994, Middle Temple
Qualifications: [LLB (Hons) (Kent), Dip
French Law, (Grenoble)]

SMITH CHRISTOPHER DAMIAN

Francis Taylor Building
Ground Floor, Temple, London
EC4Y 7BY, Telephone: 0171 353 7768/
7769/2711
E-mail:clerks@francistaylorbuilding.law.co.uk
Call Date: 1997, Lincoln's Inn
Qualifications: [LLB (Hons)(Keele)]

SMITH CHRISTOPHER FRANK

Essex Court Chambers
24 Lincoln's Inn Fields, London
WC2A 3ED, Telephone: 0171 813 8000
E-mail:clerksroom@essexcourt-chambers.co.u
k
Call Date: July 1989, Inner Temple
Pupil Master
Qualifications: [LLB (So'ton)]

SMITH DAVID ANDREW

Goldsmith Chambers
Ground Floor, Goldsmith Building,
Temple, London EC4Y 7BL,
Telephone: 0171 353 6802/3/4/5
E-mail:clerks@goldsmithchambers.law.co.uk
Call Date: July 1988, Middle Temple
Qualifications: [LLB (Hons)]

SMITH DAVID ANTHONY

4 Breams Buildings
London EC4A 1AQ,
Telephone: 0171 353 5835/430 1221
E-mail:breams@4breamsbuildings.law.co.uk
Call Date: Nov 1980, Inner Temple
Qualifications: [LLM (Lond) LLB, (Brunel)]

SMITH DUNCAN

Trinity Chambers
9-12 Trinity Chare, Quayside, Newcastle
upon Tyne NE1 3DF,
Telephone: 0191 232 1927
E-mail: info@trinitychambers.co.uk
Call Date: July 1979, Inner Temple
Pupil Master, Recorder
Qualifications: [LLB]

SMITH MISS ELEANOR RACHEL

Broad Chare
33 Broad Chare, Newcastle upon Tyne
NE1 3DQ, Telephone: 0191 232 0541
E-mail:clerks@broadcharechambers.law.co.uk
Call Date: 1992, Middle Temple
Qualifications: [LLB (Hons) (Sheff)]

SMITH MISS EMMA LOUISE

Old Square Chambers
1 Verulam Buildings, Gray's Inn, London
WC1R 5LQ, Telephone: 0171 269 0300
E-mail:clerks@oldsquarechambers.co.uk
Old Square Chambers
Hanover House, 47 Corn Street, Bristol
BS1 1HT, Telephone: 0117 9277111
E-mail: oldsqbri@globalnet.co.uk
Call Date: Oct 1995, Lincoln's Inn
Qualifications: [LLB (Hons)(Leic)]

SMITH MISS HELEN MARY

6 Gray's Inn Square
Ground Floor, Gray's Inn, London
WC1R 5AZ, Telephone: 0171 242 1052
E-mail: 6graysinn@clara.co.uk
Call Date: Nov 1990, Inner Temple
Qualifications: [LLB]

SMITH HOWARD JAMES

Chambers of Mr Peter Crampin QC
Ground Floor, 11 New Square, Lincoln's
Inn, London WC2A 3QB,
Telephone: 020 7831 0081
E-mail: 11newsquare.co.uk
Call Date: July 1986, Inner Temple
Qualifications: [BA (Oxon), Dip Law]

SMITH IAN TRUMAN

Devereux Chambers
Devereux Court, London WC2R 3JJ,
Telephone: 0171 353 7534
E-mail: mailbox@devchambers.co.uk
Call Date: July 1972, Gray's Inn
Qualifications: [MA, LLB (Cantab)]

SMITH J STEPHEN

12 New Square
Lincoln's Inn, London WC2A 3SW,
Telephone: 0171 419 1212
E-mail: chambers@12newsquare.co.uk

Sovereign Chambers
25 Park Square, Leeds LS1 2PW,
Telephone: 0113 2451841/2/3
E-mail:sovereignchambers@btinternet.com
Call Date: July 1983, Middle Temple
Pupil Master
Qualifications: [BA (Oxon)]

SMITH JAMIE CHARLES

Chambers of John L Powell QC
Four New Square, Lincoln's Inn, London
WC2A 3RJ, Telephone: 0171 797 8000
E-mail: barristers@4newsquare.com
Call Date: Oct 1995, Lincoln's Inn
Qualifications: [BA (Hons)(Cantab)]

SMITH JASON

25-27 Castle Street
1st Floor, Liverpool L2 4TA,
Telephone: 0151 227 5661/051 236 5072
Call Date: July 1989, Middle Temple
Qualifications: [LLB [L'pool]]

SMITH MISS JOANNA ANGELA

Wilberforce Chambers
8 New Square, Lincoln's Inn, London
WC2A 3QP, Telephone: 0171 306 0102
E-mail: chambers@wilberforce.co.uk
Call Date: Nov 1990, Lincoln's Inn
Pupil Master
Qualifications: [BA (Hons)(Oxon)]

Types of work: Chancery (general), Construction, Employment, Professional negligence

SMITH JONATHAN MICHAEL

Cobden House Chambers
19 Quay Street, Manchester M3 3HN,
Telephone: 0161 833 6000
E-mail: clerks@cobden.co.uk
Call Date: Oct 1991, Gray's Inn
Qualifications: [LLB]

SMITH MISS JULIA MAIR WHELDON

Gough Square Chambers
6-7 Gough Square, London EC4A 3DE,
Telephone: 0171 353 0924
E-mail: gsc@goughsq.co.uk
Call Date: Nov 1988, Inner Temple
Qualifications: [LLB (L'pool)]

SMITH JULIAN WILLIAM

New Court Chambers
3 Broad Chare, Newcastle upon Tyne
NE1 3DQ, Telephone: 0191 232 1980
Call Date: Nov 1991, Inner Temple
Qualifications: [LLB (New)]

SMITH MS KATHERINE EMMA

Monckton Chambers
4 Raymond Buildings, Gray's Inn, London
WC1R 5BP, Telephone: 0171 405 7211
E-mail: chambers@monckton.co.uk
Call Date: Nov 1995, Inner Temple
Qualifications: [BA (Oxon), BCL (Oxon)]

SMITH MISS LEONORAH PATRICIA DOLORES

Verulam Chambers
Peer House, 8-14 Verulam Street, Gray's
Inn, London WC1X 8LZ,
Telephone: 0171 813 2400
Call Date: Nov 1993, Inner Temple
Qualifications: [BA (Surrey), CPE (Sussex)]

SMITH MISS LISA IMOGEN

Phoenix Chambers
First Floor, Gray's Inn Chambers, Gray's
Inn, London WC1R 5JA,
Telephone: 0171 404 7888
E-mail:clerks@phoenix-chambers.co.uk
Call Date: Oct 1994, Lincoln's Inn
Qualifications: [LLB (Hons)(Lond)]

SMITH MARCUS ALEXANDER

Fountain Court
Temple, London EC4Y 9DH,
Telephone: 0171 583 3335
E-mail: chambers@fountaincourt.co.uk
Call Date: Oct 1991, Lincoln's Inn
Qualifications: [MA, BCL (Oxon)]

SMITH MISS MARION HELEN

4 Essex Court
Temple, London EC4Y 9AJ,
Telephone: 020 7797 7970
E-mail: clerks@4essexcourt.law.co.uk
Call Date: July 1981, Gray's Inn
Pupil Master
Qualifications: [LLB, LLM (Lond)]

D

SMITH MARK VALENTINE

Essex Court Chambers
24 Lincoln's Inn Fields, London
WC2A 3ED, Telephone: 0171 813 8000
E-mail:clerksroom@essexcourt-chambers.co.uk
Call Date: July 1981, Lincoln's Inn
Qualifications: [MA (Cantab)]

SMITH MARK WILLIAM

Kenworthy's Chambers
83 Bridge Street, Manchester M3 2RF,
Telephone: 0161 832 4036/834 6954
E-mail: clerks@kenworthys.co.uk
Call Date: Mar 1997, Gray's Inn
Qualifications: [LLB (Nott'm)]

SMITH MATTHEW JAMES

40 King Street
Manchester M2 6BA,
Telephone: 0161 832 9082
E-mail: clerks@40kingstreet.co.uk
The Chambers of Philip Raynor QC
5 Park Place, Leeds LS1 2RU,
Telephone: 0113 242 1123
Call Date: Oct 1991, Lincoln's Inn
Qualifications: [BA (Hons)(Cantab)]

SMITH MATTHEW ROBERT

Sovereign Chambers
25 Park Square, Leeds LS1 2PW,
Telephone: 0113 2451841/2/3
E-mail:sovereignchambers@btinternet.com
Call Date: Nov 1996, Inner Temple
Qualifications: [BA (Dunelm), MPhil
(Cantab)]

SMITH MICHAEL ANTHONY

No. 6
6 Park Square, Leeds LS1 2LW,
Telephone: 0113 2459763
E-mail: chambers@no6.co.uk
Call Date: July 1980, Inner Temple
Pupil Master
Qualifications: [LLB (Newc)]

SMITH MICHAEL JOSEPH

8 King Street Chambers
8 King Street, Manchester M2 6AQ,
Telephone: 0161 834 9560
E-mail: eightking@aol.com
Call Date: July 1989, Lincoln's Inn
Pupil Master
Qualifications: [MA, BCL (Oxon)]

SMITH NICHOLAS GILBERT

Queens Square Chambers
56 Queens Square, Bristol BS1 4PR,
Telephone: 0117 921 1966
Call Date: Nov 1990, Lincoln's Inn
Qualifications: [LLB]

SMITH NICHOLAS MARTIN

1 Fountain Court
Steelhouse Lane, Birmingham B4 6DR,
Telephone: 0121 236 5721
Call Date: Oct 1994, Gray's Inn
Qualifications: [BA]

SMITH MISS NICOLA JANE

Northampton Chambers
22 Albion Place, Northampton NN1 1UD,
Telephone: 01604 636271
Call Date: Oct 1994, Gray's Inn
Qualifications: [LLB (Hons)]

SMITH PAUL ANDREW

One Hare Court
1st Floor, Temple, London EC4Y 7BE,
Telephone: 020 7353 3171
E-mail:admin-oneharecourt@btinternet.com
Call Date: July 1978, Middle Temple
Pupil Master
Qualifications: [BA (Hons) MA, FCIArb]

SMITH PETER GEOGHEGAN

Exchange Chambers
Pearl Assurance House, Derby Square,
Liverpool L2 9XX,
Telephone: 0151 236 7747
E-mail:exchangechambers@btinternet.com
Call Date: July 1954, Middle Temple
Qualifications: [MA, BCL]

SMITH PETER RICHARD

24a St John Street
Manchester M3 4DF,
Telephone: 0161 833 9628
Call Date: Nov 1988, Inner Temple
Qualifications: [LLB (Hons), (Lancaster)]

SMITH PETER WINSTON QC (1992)

40 King Street
Manchester M2 6BA,
Telephone: 0161 832 9082
E-mail: clerks@40kingstreet.co.uk
11 Old Square
Ground Floor, Lincoln's Inn, London
WC2A 3TS, Telephone: 020 7430 0341
E-mail: clerks@11oldsquare.co.uk
The Chambers of Philip Raynor QC
5 Park Place, Leeds LS1 2RU,
Telephone: 0113 242 1123
Call Date: July 1975, Lincoln's Inn
Recorder
Qualifications: [MA (Cantab)]

SMITH MS RACHEL CATHERINE

Peel Court Chambers
45 Hardman Street, Manchester M3 3PL,
Telephone: 0161 832 3791
E-mail: clerks@peelct.co.uk
Call Date: Oct 1990, Lincoln's Inn
Qualifications: [BA (Leeds), Dip Law (City)]

SMITH RAYMOND KENNETH

East Anglian Chambers
57 London Street, Norwich NR2 1HL,
Telephone: 01603 617351
E-mail: norwich@ealaw.co.uk
East Anglian Chambers
52 North Hill, Colchester, Essex, CO1 1PY,
Telephone: 01206 572756
E-mail: colchester@ealaw.co.uk
East Anglian Chambers
Gresham House, 5 Museum Street,
Ipswich, Suffolk, IP1 1HQ,
Telephone: 01473 214481
E-mail: ipswich@ealaw.co.uk
Call Date: Apr 1991, Lincoln's Inn

SMITH RICHARD LLOYD

Guildhall Chambers
22-26 Broad Street, Bristol BS1 2HG,
Telephone: 0117 9273366
E-mail:civil.clerks@guildhallchambers.co.uk and
criminal.clerks@guildhallchambers.co.uk
Call Date: July 1986, Middle Temple
Pupil Master
Qualifications: [LLB (Lond)]

SMITH ROBERT ANTHONY

Chambers of Robert Smith
16 Wilson Road, Chessington, Surrey,
KT9 2HE, Telephone: 0181 288 2594
Call Date: Nov 1980, Inner Temple
Qualifications: [BA (Hons, Kent)]

SMITH ROBERT CLIVE

Bank House Chambers
Old Bank House, Hartshead, Sheffield
S1 2EL, Telephone: 0114 2751223
Call Date: July 1974, Middle Temple
Qualifications: [MA (Cantab)]

SMITH ROBERT IAN

Mercury Chambers
Mercury House, 33-35 Clarendon Road,
Leeds LS2 9NZ,
Telephone: 0113 234 2265
E-mail:cdexter@mercurychambers.co.uk
Call Date: Oct 1995, Lincoln's Inn
Qualifications: [LLB (Hons)(Northum)]

SMITH ROBERT STEEN QC (1986)

Park Court Chambers
16 Park Place, Leeds LS1 2SJ,
Telephone: 0113 2433277
Call Date: July 1971, Inner Temple
Recorder
Qualifications: [LLB]

SMITH ROGER DENZIL HOWARD QC (1992)

6 Fountain Court
Steelhouse Lane, Birmingham B4 6DR,
Telephone: 0121 233 3282
E-mail: clerks@sixfountain.co.uk
Call Date: Feb 1972, Gray's Inn
Recorder
Qualifications: [LLM]

D

SMITH ROGER GAVIN ABBEY

1 Mitre Court Buildings
Temple, London EC4Y 7BS,
Telephone: 0171 797 7070
E-mail: clerks@1mcb.com
Call Date: Nov 1981, Middle Temple
Pupil Master
Qualifications: [BA (Oxon)]

SMITH ROGER HUGH TRAYLEN

4 Paper Buildings
1st Floor, Temple, London EC4Y 7EX,
Telephone: 0171 583 0816/353 1131
E-mail: clerks@4paperbuildings.co.uk
Call Date: 1968, Gray's Inn
Pupil Master
Qualifications: [BA (Oxon)]

SMITH MISS RUTH ELIZABETH ANNE

32 Park Place
Cardiff CF1 3BA,
Telephone: 01222 397364
Call Date: July 1987, Gray's Inn
Qualifications: [LLB (Cardiff)]

SMITH MISS SALLY ELIZABETH QC (1997)

1 Crown Office Row
Ground Floor, Temple, London
EC4Y 7HH, Telephone: 0171 797 7500
E-mail: mail@onecrownofficerow.com
Call Date: Nov 1977, Inner Temple
Qualifications: [LLB (Lond)]

SMITH MISS SALLY-ANN

Crown Office Row Chambers
Blenheim House, 120 Church Street,
Brighton, Sussex, BN1 1WH,
Telephone: 01273 625625
E-mail: crownofficerow@clara.net
Call Date: Oct 1996, Inner Temple
Qualifications: [LLB (Bris)]

SMITH SEAN DAVID

St Albans Chambers
Dolphin Lodge, Dolphin Yard, Holywell
Hill, St Albans, Herts, AL1 1EX,
Telephone: 01727 843383
Call Date: Oct 1995, Gray's Inn
Qualifications: [BA (Sheff)]

SMITH SHAUN MALDEN

High Pavement Chambers
1 High Pavement, Nottingham NG1 1HF,
Telephone: 0115 9418218
Call Date: July 1981, Gray's Inn
Pupil Master
Qualifications: [LLB (Sheff)]

SMITH SIMON NOEL

3 Temple Gardens
Lower Ground Floor, Temple, London
EC4Y 9AU, Telephone: 0171 353 3102/5/
9297 E-mail: clerks@3tg.co.uk
Call Date: July 1981, Gray's Inn
Pupil Master
Qualifications: [LLB (Lond)]

SMITH TYRONE GREGORY

3 Gray's Inn Square
Ground Floor, London WC1R 5AH,
Telephone: 0171 520 5600
E-mail: clerks@3gis.co.uk
Call Date: Oct 1994, Gray's Inn
Qualifications: [LLB]

SMITH WARWICK TIMOTHY CRESSWELL

Deans Court Chambers
24 St John Street, Manchester M3 4DF,
Telephone: 0161 214 6000
E-mail: clerks@deanscourt.co.uk
Deans Court Chambers
41-43 Market Place, Preston PR1 1AH,
Telephone: 01772 555163
E-mail: clerks@deanscourt.co.uk
Call Date: July 1982, Middle Temple
Pupil Master
Qualifications: [MA (Cantab)]

SMITH WAYNE LEONARD

De Montfort Chambers
95 Princess Road East, Leicester LE1 7DQ,
Telephone: 0116 254 8686
E-mail: dmcbar@aol.com
Call Date: July 1991, Gray's Inn
Pupil Master
Qualifications: [LLB]

SMITH MS ZOE PHILIPPA

Hardwicke Building
New Square, Lincoln's Inn, London
WC2A 3SB, Telephone: 020 7242 2523
E-mail: clerks@hardwicke.co.uk
Call Date: July 1970, Gray's Inn
Pupil Master, Recorder

SMITHERS DR ROGER HOWARD

Wessex Chambers
48 Queens Road, Reading, Berkshire,
RG1 4BD, Telephone: 0118 956 8856
E-mail:wessexchambers@compuserve.com
Call Date: Oct 1990, Inner Temple
Qualifications: [BSc,PhD (Lond), Dip Law]

SMOKER MISS KATHLEEN MARY

Queens Square Chambers
56 Queens Square, Bristol BS1 4PR,
Telephone: 0117 921 1966
Call Date: May 1974, Gray's Inn
Pupil Master
Qualifications: [LLB (B'ham)]

SMOUHA JOSEPH

Essex Court Chambers
24 Lincoln's Inn Fields, London
WC2A 3ED, Telephone: 0171 813 8000
E-mail:clerksroom@essexcourt-chambers.co.uk
Call Date: July 1986, Middle Temple
Pupil Master
Qualifications: [MA (Cantab), LLM (New York)]

SMULLEN MRS MARION

Chambers of Helen Grindrod QC
4th Floor, 15-19 Devereux Court, London
WC2R 3JJ, Telephone: 0171 583 2792
Call Date: July 1985, Gray's Inn
Pupil Master
Qualifications: [BA, LLB (Lond)]

SMYTH CHRISTOPHER JACKSON

Call Date: July 1972, Inner Temple
Pupil Master
Qualifications: [MA (Cantab)]

SMYTH MISS JULIA MADELEINE

1 Temple Gardens
1st Floor, Temple, London EC4Y 9BB,
Telephone: 0171 583 1315/353 0407
E-mail: clerks@1templegardens.co.uk
Call Date: Oct 1996, Inner Temple
Qualifications: [LLB (Lond), Dip in German Law]

SMYTH STEPHEN MARK JAMES ATHELSTAN

2 Harcourt Buildings
1st Floor, Temple, London EC4Y 9DB,
Telephone: 020 7353 2112
Call Date: July 1974, Inner Temple
Assistant Recorder

SNELL JOHN

New Walk Chambers
27 New Walk, Leicester LE1 6TE,
Telephone: 0116 2559144
Call Date: July 1973, Inner Temple
Qualifications: [LLB]

SNELL JOHN MICHAEL

2 Temple Gardens
Temple, London EC4Y 9AY,
Telephone: 0171 583 6041
E-mail: clerks@2templegardens.co.uk
Call Date: Oct 1991, Lincoln's Inn
Qualifications: [BA (Hons) (Oxon), Dip Law]

SNELLER MISS ELAINE RUTH

9 King's Bench Walk
Ground Floor, Temple, London
EC4Y 7DX, Telephone: 0171 353 7202/
3909 E-mail: 9kbw@compuserve.com
Call Date: Feb 1994, Middle Temple
Qualifications: [LLB (Hons)(Bris)]

SNELSON ANTHONY MARTIN

Thomas More Chambers
52 Carey Street, Lincoln's Inn, London
WC2A 2JB, Telephone: 0171 404 7000
E-mail: clerks@thomasmore.law.co.uk
Call Date: Nov 1982, Gray's Inn
Pupil Master
Qualifications: [LLB (L'pool)]

D

SNIDER JOHN LEOPOLD

Essex Court Chambers
24 Lincoln's Inn Fields, London
WC2A 3ED, Telephone: 0171 813 8000
E-mail:clerksroom@essexcourt-chambers.co.uk
Call Date: July 1982, Middle Temple
Qualifications: [MA (Hons) (Oxon), MBA]

SNOWDEN JOHN STEVENSON

Two Crown Office Row
Ground Floor, Temple, London
EC4Y 7HJ, Telephone: 020 7797 8100
E-mail: mail@2cor.co.uk, or to individual
barristers at: [barrister's
surname]@2cor.co.uk
Call Date: July 1989, Inner Temple
Qualifications: [BA (Nott'm)]

SNOWDEN RICHARD ANDREW

Erskine Chambers
30 Lincoln's Inn Fields, Lincoln's Inn,
London WC2A 3PF,
Telephone: 0171 242 5532
E-mail:clerks@erskine-chambers.co.uk
Call Date: July 1986, Lincoln's Inn
Pupil Master
Qualifications: [MA (Cantab), LLM (Harvard)]

SOARES PATRICK CLAUDE

8 Gray's Inn Square
Gray's Inn, London WC1R 5AZ,
Telephone: 0171 242 3529
Call Date: Nov 1983, Lincoln's Inn
Pupil Master
Qualifications: [LLB LLM (Lond) FTII]

SODEN-BIRD EDWARD MICHAEL GEORGE

16 Fairhazel Gardens
London NW6 3SJ,
Telephone: 0171 328 5486
Call Date: Nov 1986, Gray's Inn
Qualifications: [LLB (Hons)]

SOERTSZ MISS LAUREN BRIGITTE

3 Temple Gardens
2nd Floor, Temple, London EC4Y 9AU,
Telephone: 0171 583 1155
Call Date: Feb 1987, Middle Temple
Pupil Master
Qualifications: [LLB]

SOFAER MISS MOIRA

Verulam Chambers
Peer House, 8-14 Verulam Street, Gray's
Inn, London WC1X 8LZ,
Telephone: 0171 813 2400
Call Date: July 1975, Middle Temple
Qualifications: [BSc (Lond)]

SOFER JONATHAN

Chambers of Geoffrey Hawker
46/48 Essex Street, London WC2R 3GH,
Telephone: 0171 583 8899
Call Date: Apr 1942, Inner Temple
Qualifications: [BA, LLB (Cantab)]

SOFFA MISS HELEN ROSEMARY

New Court
Temple, London EC4Y 9BE,
Telephone: 0171 583 5123/0510
Call Date: Nov 1990, Inner Temple

SOKOL CHRISTOPHER JOHN FRANCIS

24 Old Buildings
First Floor, Lincoln's Inn, London
WC2A 3UP, Telephone: 020 7242 2744
E-mail: taxchambers@compuserve.com
Call Date: July 1975, Lincoln's Inn
Pupil Master
Qualifications: [MA (Cantab)]

SOLARI MISS YOLANDA ELLEN

Counsels' Chambers
2nd Floor, 10-11 Gray's Inn Square,
London WC1R 5JD,
Telephone: 0171 405 2576
E-mail:clerks@10-11graysinnsquare.co.uk
Call Date: Nov 1992, Gray's Inn
Qualifications: [LLB (Hons)]

SOLLEY STEPHEN MALCOLM QC (1989)

Cloisters
1 Pump Court, Temple, London
EC4Y 7AA, Telephone: 0171 827 4000
E-mail: clerks@cloisters.com
Call Date: Nov 1969, Inner Temple
Qualifications: [LLB (Lond)]

SOLOMON REUBEN

12 Old Square
1st Floor, Lincoln's Inn, London
WC2A 3TX, Telephone: 0171 404 0875
Call Date: Oct 1993, Lincoln's Inn
Qualifications: [LLB (Hons)]

SOLOMON MISS SUSAN ISABEL BARBARA

3 Paper Buildings
Ground Floor, Temple, London
EC4Y 7EU, Telephone: 0171 797 7000
E-mail: clerks@3pb.co.uk
3 Paper Buildings
Temple, London EC4Y 7EU,
Telephone: 020 7583 8055
E-mail: London@3paper.com
3 Paper Buildings (Winchester)
4 St Peter Street, Winchester SO23 8BW,
Telephone: 01962 868884
E-mail: winchester@3paper.com
3 Paper Buildings (Oxford)
1 Alfred Street, High Street, Oxford
OX1 4EH, Telephone: 01865 793736
E-mail: oxford@3paper.com
3 Paper Buildings (Bournemouth)
20 Lorne Park Road, Bournemouth,
Dorset, BH1 1JN,
Telephone: 01202 292102
E-mail: Bournemouth@3paper.com
Call Date: July 1967, Middle Temple
Pupil Master
Qualifications: [MA (Oxon)]

SOLOMONS MRS ELLEN BETTY

One Garden Court Family Law Chambers
Ground Floor, Temple, London
EC4Y 9BJ, Telephone: 0171 797 7900
E-mail: clerks@onegardencourt.co.uk
Call Date: Feb 1964, Inner Temple

SOLOMONS GEOFFREY

Chambers of Michael Pert QC
36 Bedford Row, London WC1R 4JH,
Telephone: 0171 421 8000
E-mail: 36bedfordrow@link.org
Chambers of Michael Pert QC
24 Albion Place, Northampton NN1 1UD,
Telephone: 01604 602333

Chambers of Michael Pert QC
104 New Walk, Leicester LE1 7EA,
Telephone: 0116 249 2020
Call Date: July 1974, Gray's Inn
Pupil Master
Qualifications: [LLB]

SOMERSET JONES ERIC QC (1978)

Goldsmith Building
1st Floor, Temple, London EC4Y 7BL,
Telephone: 0171 353 7881
E-mail:clerks@goldsmith-building.law.co.uk
Call Date: May 1952, Middle Temple
Recorder
Qualifications: [MA (Oxon)]

SOMERSET-JONES MISS FELICITY

Oriel Chambers
14 Water Street, Liverpool L2 8TD,
Telephone: 0151 236 7191/236 4321
E-mail: clerks@oriel-chambers.co.uk
Call Date: Oct 1994, Middle Temple
Qualifications: [BA (Hons)(L'pool), Dip in Law (City)]

SOMERVILLE BRYCE EDWARD

6 Fountain Court
Steelhouse Lane, Birmingham B4 6DR,
Telephone: 0121 233 3282
E-mail: clerks@sixfountain.co.uk
Call Date: July 1980, Middle Temple
Pupil Master
Qualifications: [BA (Cantab)]

SOMERVILLE THOMAS CLINTON

Oriel Chambers
14 Water Street, Liverpool L2 8TD,
Telephone: 0151 236 7191/236 4321
E-mail: clerks@oriel-chambers.co.uk
Call Date: July 1979, Middle Temple
Qualifications: [BA (Bris)]

SONES RICHARD

5 King's Bench Walk
Temple, London EC4Y 7DN,
Telephone: 0171 353 5638
Call Date: Nov 1969, Inner Temple
Pupil Master
Qualifications: [LLB (Lond)]

SOOD MRS USHA RANI

70 Charlecote Drive
Wollaton, Nottingham NG8 2SB,
Telephone: 0115 928 8901
Call Date: July 1974, Gray's Inn
Qualifications: [LLB, M.Phil]

SOOLE MICHAEL ALEXANDER

Chambers of John L Powell QC
Four New Square, Lincoln's Inn, London
WC2A 3RJ, Telephone: 0171 797 8000
E-mail: barristers@4newsquare.com
Call Date: July 1977, Inner Temple
Pupil Master, Assistant Recorder
Qualifications: [MA (Oxon)]

SOOR SMAIR SINGH

33 Bedford Row
London WC1R 4JH,
Telephone: 0171 242 6476
E-mail:clerks@bedfordrow33.demon.co.uk
Call Date: July 1988, Gray's Inn
Qualifications: [LLB]

SOORJOO MARTIN

14 Tooks Court
Cursitor St, London EC4A 1LB,
Telephone: 0171 405 8828
E-mail: clerks@tooks.law.co.uk
Call Date: Oct 1990, Lincoln's Inn
Qualifications: [LLB]

SOPPITT NIGEL

Baker Street Chambers
9 Baker Street, Middlesbrough TS1 2LF,
Telephone: 01642 873873
Call Date: Nov 1996, Gray's Inn

SOUBRY MS ANNA MARY

St Mary's Chambers
50 High Pavement, Lace Market,
Nottingham NG1 1HW,
Telephone: 0115 9503503
E-mail: clerks@smc.law.co.uk
Call Date: Nov 1995, Inner Temple
Qualifications: [LLB (B'ham)]

SOULSBY EDWARD WILLIAM

Clock Chambers
78 Darlington Street, Wolverhampton
WV1 4LY, Telephone: 01902 313444
Call Date: Oct 1996, Gray's Inn
Qualifications: [LLB (Staffs)]

SOUTHALL RICHARD ANTHONY

17 Bedford Row
London WC1R 4EB,
Telephone: 0171 831 7314
E-mail: iboard7314@aol.com
Call Date: Nov 1983, Middle Temple
Pupil Master
Qualifications: [LLB (Buckingham)]

Other comms:
E-mail richardsouthall@barrister-at-law.
freeserve.co.uk

Types of work: Banking, Bankruptcy, Chancery (general), Commercial litigation, Company and commercial, Conveyancing, Insolvency, Mortgages and borrowers, Professional negligence, Sale and carriage of goods

Circuit: South Eastern

Languages spoken: French

Reported Cases: *Zandfarid v Bank of Credit and Commerce International SA*, [1996] 1 WLR 1420, 1996. Bankruptcy – Practice – Creditor petitioning as insecured creditor – Whether proper for mortgagee to so petition in absence of other creditors.
Berkshire Capital Funding Limited v Street and Others, (1999) *The Times*, 27 May, 1999. Mortgages – order for possession in favour of second lender – order must respect rights of prior lender.

SOUTHERN DAVID BOARDMAN

Temple Gardens Tax Chambers
1st Floor, 3 Temple Gardens, Temple,
London EC4Y 9AU,
Telephone: 0171 353 7884/5 8982/3
E-mail: clerks@taxcounsel.co.uk.
Call Date: July 1982, Lincoln's Inn
Qualifications: [MA, M.Phil, D.Phil (Oxon),
FTII]

Fax: 0171 583 2044;
Out of hours telephone: 0171 488 0502;
Other comms: 0411 578612

Other professional qualifications: FTII

Types of work: Banking, Corporate finance, EC law, Tax – capital and income, Tax – corporate, VAT

Other professional experience: Senior Legal Adviser, Lloyds TSB; Inland Revenue Solicitor's Office

Languages spoken: French, German

Publications: *Tolley's Taxation of Corporate Debt and Financial Instruments* (3rd edn), 1999; *Gore-Browne on Companies* (Contributor); *Simon's Direct Tax Service* (Contributor); *De Voil's Indirect Tax Service* (Contributor)

Reported Cases: *IRC v Lloyd's Private Banking Ltd*, [1998] STC 559. *Maharani Restaurant v Customs and Exise Commissioners*, [1999] STC 295.

SOUTHERN RICHARD MICHAEL

S Tomlinson QC
7 King's Bench Walk, Temple, London EC4Y 7DS, Telephone: 0171 583 0404
E-mail: clerks@7kbw.law.co.uk
Call Date: Nov 1987, Middle Temple
Pupil Master
Qualifications: [MA (Cantab)]

SOUTHEY DAVID HUGH

14 Tooks Court
Cursitor St, London EC4A 1LB,
Telephone: 0171 405 8828
E-mail: clerks@tooks.law.co.uk
Call Date: Nov 1996, Inner Temple
Qualifications: [MEng (Lond)]

SOUTHGATE JONATHAN BLAKE

29 Bedford Row Chambers
London WC1R 4HE,
Telephone: 0171 831 2626
Call Date: Nov 1992, Middle Temple
Qualifications: [LLB]

SOUTHGATE MISS MARIE DAWN

Regency Chambers
Cathedral Square, Peterborough
PE1 1XW, Telephone: 01733 315215
Call Date: Oct 1997, Lincoln's Inn
Qualifications: [LLB (Hons)(Notts)]

SOUTHWELL RICHARD CHARLES QC (1977)

One Hare Court
1st Floor, Temple, London EC4Y 7BE,
Telephone: 020 7353 3171
E-mail:admin-oneharecourt@btinternet.com
Call Date: June 1959, Inner Temple
Recorder
Qualifications: [MA (Cantab)]

SOUTHWELL RICHARD CHARLES EDWARD

Farrar's Building
Temple, London EC4Y 7BD,
Telephone: 0171 583 9241
E-mail:chambers@farrarsbuilding.co.uk
Call Date: July 1970, Inner Temple
Recorder

SOWERBY MATTHEW GILES

Verulam Chambers
Peer House, 8-14 Verulam Street, Gray's Inn, London WC1X 8LZ,
Telephone: 0171 813 2400
Call Date: July 1987, Middle Temple
Qualifications: [BA (Sussex)]

SPACKMAN MARK ANDREW

Iscoed Chambers
86 St Helen's Road, Swansea, West Glamorgan, SA1 4BQ,
Telephone: 01792 652988/9/330
Call Date: Nov 1986, Lincoln's Inn
Pupil Master
Qualifications: [LLB (Leic)]

SPAIN TIMOTHY HARRISSON

Trinity Chambers
9-12 Trinity Chare, Quayside, Newcastle upon Tyne NE1 3DF,
Telephone: 0191 232 1927
E-mail: info@trinitychambers.co.uk
Call Date: July 1983, Gray's Inn
Pupil Master
Qualifications: [LLB (Newc)]

D

SPARKS KEVIN LAURENCE

Earl Street Chambers
47 Earl Street, Maidstone, Kent,
ME14 1PD, Telephone: 01622 671222
E-mail: gunner-sparks@msn.com
Call Date: July 1983, Gray's Inn
Pupil Master
Qualifications: [BEd (Lond), LLM]

SPARROW ALBERT CHARLES QC (1966)

Serle Court Chambers
6 New Square, Lincoln's Inn, London,
WC2A 3QS, Telephone: 0171 242 6105
E-mail: clerks@serlecourt.co.uk
Call Date: Nov 1950, Gray's Inn
Qualifications: [LLB (Lond), FSA]

SPARROW MISS CLAIRE LOUISE

Eastbourne Chambers
15 Hyde Gardens, Eastbourne, East
Sussex, BN21 4PR,
Telephone: 01323 642102
Call Date: Oct 1997, Middle Temple
Qualifications: [MA (Hons)(St Andrew), CPE
(Anglia), DIP Cred Law]

SPARROW MISS JULIE ELIZABETH

8 Fountain Court
Steelhouse Lane, Birmingham B4 6DR,
Telephone: 0121 236 5514/5
E-mail: clerks@no8chambers.co.uk
Call Date: Oct 1992, Lincoln's Inn
Qualifications: [LLB(Hons)]

SPARROW MRS MARIE-CLAIRE

95A Chancery Lane
London WC2A 1DT,
Telephone: 0171 405 3101
Call Date: Nov 1977, Lincoln's Inn
Pupil Master
Qualifications: [Maitrise en droit, (Paris),
Chevalier de L'Ordre, du Merite]

SPEAIGHT ANTHONY HUGH QC (1995)

12 King's Bench Walk
Temple, London EC4Y 7EL,
Telephone: 0171 583 0811
E-mail: chambers@12kbw.co.uk
Call Date: July 1973, Middle Temple
Qualifications: [MA (Oxon)]

SPEAK MICHAEL NORMAN

4 Brick Court, Chambers of Anne Rafferty QC
1st Floor, Temple, London EC4Y 9AD,
Telephone: 0171 583 8455
Call Date: July 1983, Lincoln's Inn
Qualifications: [BA (Hull), Dip Law]

SPEAR MS SARAH VANESSA

28 St John Street
Manchester M3 4DJ,
Telephone: 0161 834 8418
E-mail: clerk@28stjohnst.co.uk
Call Date: 1997, Inner Temple
Qualifications: [BA (Oxon), CPE]

SPEARMAN RICHARD QC (1996)

4-5 Gray's Inn Square
Ground Floor, Gray's Inn, London
WC1R 5JP, Telephone: 0171 404 5252
E-mail:chambers@4-5graysinnsquare.co.uk
Call Date: Nov 1977, Middle Temple
Qualifications: [MA (Cantab)]

SPECK ADRIAN

8 New Square
Lincoln's Inn, London WC2A 3QP,
Telephone: 0171 405 4321
E-mail: clerks@8newsquare.co.uk
Call Date: Oct 1993, Gray's Inn
Qualifications: [BA]

SPEDDING MISS CATHERINE ANN

Queens Square Chambers
56 Queens Square, Bristol BS1 4PR,
Telephone: 0117 921 1966
Call Date: Nov 1995, Inner Temple
Qualifications: [LLB (Hons)]

SPEIRS ALISTAIR CHARLES

Call Date: Oct 1995, Middle Temple
Qualifications: [LLB (Newcastle)]

SPENCE MALCOLM HUGH QC (1979)

2-3 Gray's Inn Square
Gray's Inn, London WC1R 5JH,
Telephone: 0171 242 4986
E-mail:chambers@2-3graysinnsquare.co.uk
Call Date: June 1958, Gray's Inn

Recorder
Qualifications: [MA, LLM, AciArb]

SPENCE SIMON PETER

18 Red Lion Court
(Off Fleet Street), London EC4A 3EB,
Telephone: 0171 520 6000
E-mail: chambers@18rlc.co.uk
Thornwood House
102 New London Road, Chelmsford,
Essex, CM2 0RG,
Telephone: 01245 280880
E-mail: chambers@18rlc.co.uk
Call Date: July 1985, Inner Temple
Pupil Master
Qualifications: [LLB (Leics)]

SPENCE STEPHEN NICHOLAS

1 Paper Buildings
1st Floor, Temple, London EC4Y 7EP,
Telephone: 0171 353 3728/4953
Call Date: July 1983, Gray's Inn
Qualifications: [BSc (Cardiff)]

SPENCER SIR DEREK HAROLD QC (1980)

18 Red Lion Court
(Off Fleet Street), London EC4A 3EB,
Telephone: 0171 520 6000
E-mail: chambers@18rlc.co.uk
Thornwood House
102 New London Road, Chelmsford,
Essex, CM2 0RG,
Telephone: 01245 280880
E-mail: chambers@18rlc.co.uk
Eastbourne Chambers
15 Hyde Gardens, Eastbourne, East
Sussex, BN21 4PR,
Telephone: 01323 642102
Call Date: 1961, Gray's Inn
Recorder
Qualifications: [MA, BCL (Oxon)]

SPENCER MISS HANNAH KATYA

Chambers of John Hand QC
9 St John Street, Manchester M3 4DN,
Telephone: 0161 955 9000
E-mail: ninesjs@gconnect.com
5 Pump Court
Ground Floor, Temple, London
EC4Y 7AP, Telephone: 020 7353 2532
E-mail: FivePump@netcomuk.co.uk
Call Date: Feb 1993, Inner Temple
Qualifications: [BA]

SPENCER JAMES QC (1991)

11 King's Bench Walk
1st Floor, Temple, London EC4Y 7EQ,
Telephone: 0171 353 3337
E-mail: fmuller11@aol.com
11 King's Bench Walk
3 Park Court, Park Cross Street, Leeds
LS1 2QH, Telephone: 0113 297 1200
Call Date: Nov 1975, Gray's Inn
Recorder
Qualifications: [LLB (Newc)]

SPENCER MRS MARGARET MARY

Enfield Chambers
First Floor, Refuge House, 9-10 River
Front, Enfield, Middlesex, EN1 3SZ,
Telephone: 0181 364 5627
E-mail:enfieldchambers@compuserve.com
Call Date: Nov 1992, Lincoln's Inn
Qualifications: [LLB (Hons)(Lond)]

SPENCER MARTIN BENEDICT

4 Paper Buildings
Ground Floor, Temple, London
EC4Y 7EX, Telephone: 0171 353 3366/
583 7155
E-mail: clerks@4paperbuildings.com
Call Date: July 1979, Inner Temple
Pupil Master
Qualifications: [BA, BCL (Oxon)]

SPENCER MISS MELANIE DAWN

Field Court Chambers
2nd Floor, 3 Field Court, Gray's Inn,
London WC1R 5EP,
Telephone: 0171 404 7474
Call Date: July 1986, Inner Temple
Pupil Master
Qualifications: [BA (Leeds) Dip Law]

SPENCER MICHAEL GERALD QC (1989)

One Paper Buildings
Ground Floor, Temple, London
EC4Y 7EP, Telephone: 0171 583 7355
E-mail: clerks@1pb.co.uk
Call Date: July 1970, Inner Temple
Recorder
Qualifications: [MA (Oxon)]

SPENCER PAUL ANTHONY

2 New Street
Leicester LE1 5NA,
Telephone: 0116 2625906
E-mail: clerks@2newstreet.co.uk
Call Date: Nov 1965, Inner Temple
Qualifications: [LLB]

SPENCER PAUL ANTHONY

Cloisters
1 Pump Court, Temple, London
EC4Y 7AA, Telephone: 0171 827 4000
E-mail: clerks@cloisters.com
Call Date: Nov 1988, Middle Temple
Pupil Master
Qualifications: [LLB]

SPENCER ROBIN GODFREY QC (1999)

Sedan House
Stanley Place, Chester CH1 2LU,
Telephone: 01244 320480/348282
9-12 Bell Yard
London WC2A 2LF,
Telephone: 0171 400 1800
E-mail: clerks@bellyard.co.uk
Call Date: 1978, Gray's Inn
Pupil Master, Recorder
Qualifications: [MA (Cantab)]

SPENCER SHAUN MICHAEL QC (1988)

No. 6
6 Park Square, Leeds LS1 2LW,
Telephone: 0113 2459763
E-mail: chambers@no6.co.uk
11 King's Bench Walk
1st Floor, Temple, London EC4Y 7EQ,
Telephone: 0171 353 3337
E-mail: fmuller11@aol.com
Call Date: July 1968, Lincoln's Inn
Recorder
Qualifications: [LLB]

SPENCER TIMOTHY JOHN

9 Bedford Row
London WC1R 4AZ,
Telephone: 0171 242 3555
E-mail: clerks@9br.co.uk
Call Date: July 1982, Middle Temple
Pupil Master
Qualifications: [MA (Cantab)]

SPENCER TIMOTHY ROBERT

9-12 Bell Yard
London WC2A 2LF,
Telephone: 0171 400 1800
E-mail: clerks@bellyard.co.uk
Call Date: July 1976, Lincoln's Inn
Pupil Master

SPENCER BERNARD ROBERT VERE

4 King's Bench Walk
2nd Floor, Temple, London EC4Y 7DL,
Telephone: 020 7353 3581
E-mail: clerks@4kbw.co.uk
Call Date: Nov 1969, Inner Temple
Recorder
Qualifications: [MA (Oxon)]

SPENCER-LEWIS NEVILLE JULIAN

12 King's Bench Walk
Temple, London EC4Y 7EL,
Telephone: 0171 583 0811
E-mail: chambers@12kbw.co.uk
Call Date: July 1970, Inner Temple
Pupil Master
Qualifications: [MA (Oxon)]

SPENS DAVID PATRICK QC (1995)

6 King's Bench Walk
Ground Floor, Temple, London
EC4Y 7DR, Telephone: 0171 583 0410
E-mail: worsley@6kbw.freeserve.co.uk
Call Date: Nov 1973, Inner Temple
Recorder
Qualifications: [BA]

SPENS WILLIAM DAVID RALPH

Albion Chambers
Broad Street, Bristol BS1 1DR,
Telephone: 0117 9272144
Call Date: July 1972, Inner Temple
Pupil Master
Qualifications: [MA (Cantab)]

SPICER JONATHAN RICHARD

St Mary's Chambers
50 High Pavement, Lace Market,
Nottingham NG1 1HW,
Telephone: 0115 9503503
E-mail: clerks@smc.law.co.uk
Call Date: 1995, Lincoln's Inn
Qualifications: [MA (Cantab)]

SPICER ROBERT HADEN

Frederick Place Chambers
9 Frederick Place, Clifton, Bristol
BS8 1AS, Telephone: 0117 9738667
Call Date: July 1970, Inner Temple
Qualifications: [MA (Cantab),
Dip.LegStuds(Cantab)]

SPINK ANDREW JOHN MURRAY

35 Essex Street
Temple, London WC2R 3AR,
Telephone: 0171 353 6381
E-mail: derek_jenkins@link.org
Call Date: Nov 1985, Middle Temple
Pupil Master
Qualifications: [BA (Cantab)]

SPINK PETER JOHN WILLIAM

17 Carlton Crescent
Southampton SO15 2XR,
Telephone: 023 8032 0320/0823 2003
E-mail: greg@jg17cc.co.uk
Call Date: July 1979, Gray's Inn
Pupil Master

SPINKS RODERICK CAMERON

Fenners Chambers
3 Madingley Road, Cambridge CB3 0EE,
Telephone: 01223 368761
E-mail: clerks@fennerschambers.co.uk
Fenners Chambers
8-12 Priestgate, Peterborough PE1 1JA,
Telephone: 01733 562030
E-mail: clerks@fennerschambers.co.uk
Call Date: 1997, Inner Temple
Qualifications: [LLB (Sheff)]

SPIRE MS CHRYSTALLA ANASTA THEODORA

Warwick House Chambers
8 Warwick Court, Gray's Inn, London
WC1R 5DJ, Telephone: 0171 430 2323
E-mail: cdrewlaw@aol.com
Call Date: 1978, Gray's Inn
Qualifications: [LLB (Lond)]

SPIRO MISS DAFNA MIRIAM

6 Gray's Inn Square
Ground Floor, Gray's Inn, London
WC1R 5AZ, Telephone: 0171 242 1052
E-mail: 6graysinn@clara.co.uk
Call Date: Nov 1994, Inner Temple
Qualifications: [BA (Sussex), CPE]

SPOLLON GUY MERTON

St Philip's Chambers
Fountain Court, Steelhouse Lane,
Birmingham B4 6DR,
Telephone: 0121 246 7000
E-mail: clerks@st-philips.co.uk
Call Date: Nov 1976, Gray's Inn
Pupil Master
Qualifications: [BA]

SPON-SMITH ROBIN WITTERICK

1 Mitre Court Buildings
Temple, London EC4Y 7BS,
Telephone: 0171 797 7070
E-mail: clerks@1mcb.com
Call Date: Nov 1976, Inner Temple
Pupil Master, Recorder
Qualifications: [LLM]

SPOONER HENRY NEVILLE

Westgate Chambers
144 High Street, Lewes, East Sussex,
BN7 1XT, Telephone: 01273 480510
Frederick Place Chambers
9 Frederick Place, Clifton, Bristol
BS8 1AS, Telephone: 0117 9738667
Call Date: Nov 1971, Lincoln's Inn
Pupil Master

SPOONER MISS JUDITH ANN

Hardwicke Building
New Square, Lincoln's Inn, London
WC2A 3SB, Telephone: 020 7242 2523
E-mail: clerks@hardwicke.co.uk
Call Date: July 1987, Middle Temple
Qualifications: [LLB (Hons)(Reading)]

SPRACK JOHN MAURICE

1 Pump Court
Lower Ground Floor, Temple, London
EC4Y 7AB, Telephone: 0171 583 2012/
353 4341
E-mail: [name]@1pumpcourt.co.uk
Call Date: July 1984, Gray's Inn
Qualifications: [BA, LLB (Rhodes)]

SPRATLING MRS ANNE VIRGINIA

4 Brick Court
Ground Floor, Temple, London
EC4Y 9AD, Telephone: 0171 797 7766
E-mail: chambers@4brick.co.uk
Call Date: July 1980, Lincoln's Inn
Pupil Master
Qualifications: [BA (Cantab)]

SPRATT CHRISTOPHER DAVID RICHARD DEAN

33 Bedford Row
London WC1R 4JH,
Telephone: 0171 242 6476
E-mail:clerks@bedfordrow33.demon.co.uk
Call Date: Nov 1986, Gray's Inn
Pupil Master
Qualifications: [LLB(Dundee)]

SPRATT-DAWSON MISS JOSEPHINE MARGERY

Trinity Chambers
140 New London Road, Chelmsford,
Essex, CM2 0AW,
Telephone: 01245 605040
E-mail:clerks@trinitychambers.law.co.uk
Call Date: Oct 1993, Gray's Inn
Qualifications: [LLB (Anglia)]

SPROSTON-MATTHEWS MRS LYNNE TERESA

Assize Court Chambers
14 Small Street, Bristol BS1 1DE,
Telephone: 0117 9264587
E-mail:chambers@assize-court-chambers.co.uk
Call Date: Nov 1987, Inner Temple
Qualifications: [LLB (Nottm)]

SPROULL NICHOLAS

Albion Chambers
Broad Street, Bristol BS1 1DR,
Telephone: 0117 9272144
Call Date: Nov 1992, Gray's Inn
Qualifications: [LLB (Bris)]

SPRUNKS JAMES EDWARD

32 Park Place
Cardiff CF1 3BA,
Telephone: 01222 397364
Call Date: Oct 1995, Lincoln's Inn
Qualifications: [LLB (Hons)(Notts)]

SQUIRE PHILIP DENBY

95A Chancery Lane
London WC2A 1DT,
Telephone: 0171 405 3101
Call Date: Nov 1997, Inner Temple
Qualifications: [BA (Sheff)]

SQUIRRELL BENJAMIN

2-4 Tudor Street
London EC4Y 0AA,
Telephone: 0171 797 7111
E-mail: clerks@rfqc.co.uk
Call Date: Oct 1990, Inner Temple
Qualifications: [BA (Lond), Dip Law]

ST CLAIR GAINER RICHARD

4 Brick Court
Temple, London EC4Y 9AD,
Telephone: 0171 797 8910
E-mail: medhurst@dial.pipex.com
Call Date: 1983, Middle Temple
Pupil Master
Qualifications: [BA (Kent)]

ST JOHN-STEVENS PHILIP SIMEON

Queen Elizabeth Building
Ground Floor, Temple, London
EC4Y 9BS,
Telephone: 0171 353 7181 (12 Lines)
Call Date: July 1985, Inner Temple
Pupil Master
Qualifications: [LLB (Cardiff)]

ST LOUIS BRIAN LLOYD

Hardwicke Building
New Square, Lincoln's Inn, London
WC2A 3SB, Telephone: 020 7242 2523
E-mail: clerks@hardwicke.co.uk
Call Date: Oct 1994, Middle Temple
Qualifications: [LLB (Hons), LLM (Lond)]

ST VILLE LAURENCE AUGUSTIN ISAIAH

Chancery Chambers
1st Floor Offices, 70/72 Chancery Lane,
London WC2A 1AB,
Telephone: 0171 405 6879/6870
Call Date: June 1955, Gray's Inn
Pupil Master

ST VILLE LAURENCE JAMES

8 New Square
Lincoln's Inn, London WC2A 3QP,
Telephone: 0171 405 4321
E-mail: clerks@8newsquare.co.uk
Call Date: Oct 1995, Gray's Inn
Qualifications: [MA, C.Eng, MIEE]

STABLES CHRISTOPHER HILTON

Exchange Chambers
Pearl Assurance House, Derby Square,
Liverpool L2 9XX,
Telephone: 0151 236 7747
E-mail:exchangechambers@btinternet.com
Call Date: Oct 1990, Gray's Inn
Qualifications: [LLB (L'pool)]

STABLES GORDON

Paradise Chambers
26 Paradise Square, Sheffield S1 2DE,
Telephone: 0114 2738951
E-mail: timbooth@paradise-sq.co.uk
Call Date: Oct 1995, Lincoln's Inn
Qualifications: [BA (Hons), MA, CPE
(Huddersfield)]

STADDON MISS CLAIRE ANN

12 New Square
Lincoln's Inn, London WC2A 3SW,
Telephone: 0171 419 1212
E-mail: chambers@12newsquare.co.uk

Sovereign Chambers
25 Park Square, Leeds LS1 2PW,
Telephone: 0113 2451841/2/3
E-mail:sovereignchambers@btinternet.com
Call Date: July 1985, Middle Temple
Qualifications: [LLB (Lond)]

STADDON PAUL

2nd Floor, Francis Taylor Building
Temple, London EC4Y 7BY,
Telephone: 0171 353 9942/3157
Call Date: July 1976, Inner Temple
Qualifications: [BSc (Econ) Lond.]

STADLEN NICHOLAS FELIX QC (1991)

Fountain Court
Temple, London EC4Y 9DH,
Telephone: 0171 583 3335
E-mail: chambers@fountaincourt.co.uk
Call Date: Nov 1976, Inner Temple
Assistant Recorder
Qualifications: [BA (Cantab)]

STAFFORD ANDREW BRUCE

Littleton Chambers
3 King's Bench Walk North, Temple,
London EC4Y 7HR,
Telephone: 0171 797 8600
E-mail:clerks@littletonchambers.co.uk
Call Date: July 1980, Middle Temple
Pupil Master
Qualifications: [MA (Cantab)]

STAFFORD PAUL RINALDO

The Chambers of Leolin Price CBE, QC
10 Old Square, Lincoln's Inn, London
WC2A 3SU, Telephone: 0171 405 0758
Call Date: Nov 1987, Gray's Inn
Pupil Master
Qualifications: [MA (Oxon), D Phil (Oxon),
Dip Law]

D

STAFFORD-MICHAEL SIMON ALEXANDER

4 King's Bench Walk
Ground/First Floor/Basement, Temple,
London EC4Y 7DL,
Telephone: 0171 822 8822
E-mail: 4kbw@barristersatlaw.com
Call Date: Nov 1982, Gray's Inn
Pupil Master
Qualifications: [LLB(Bristol)]

STAGE PETER JAMES

Queen Elizabeth Building
Ground Floor, Temple, London
EC4Y 9BS,
Telephone: 0171 353 7181 (12 Lines)
Call Date: July 1971, Lincoln's Inn
Pupil Master
Qualifications: [LLB]

STAGG PAUL ANDREW

No. 1 Serjeants' Inn
5th Floor Fleet Street, Temple, London
EC4Y 1LH, Telephone: 0171 415 6666
E-mail:no1serjeantsinn@btinternet.com
Call Date: Oct 1994, Gray's Inn
Qualifications: [LLB (Warw)]

STAGI MISS ALEXANDRA FRANCESCA VALERIA

Lamb Chambers
Lamb Building, Temple, London
EC4Y 7AS, Telephone: 020 7797 8300
E-mail: lambchambers@link.org
Call Date: 1997, Lincoln's Inn
Qualifications: [MA (Cantab)]

STAITE MISS SARA ELIZABETH

2 Harcourt Buildings
Ground Floor/Left, Temple, London
EC4Y 9DB, Telephone: 0171 583 9020
E-mail: clerks@harcourt.co.uk
Call Date: July 1979, Inner Temple
Pupil Master, Assistant Recorder
Qualifications: [LLB (Leeds)]

STALLWORTHY NICOLAS KYD

35 Essex Street
Temple, London WC2R 3AR,
Telephone: 0171 353 6381
E-mail: derek_jenkins@link.org
Call Date: Oct 1993, Middle Temple
Qualifications: [BA (Hons)(Oxon)]

STANAGE NICK SEAN

Chambers of Ian Macdonald QC (In Association with Two Garden Court, Temple, London)
Waldorf House, 5 Cooper Street,
Manchester M2 2FW,
Telephone: 0161 236 1840
Call Date: Oct 1997, Inner Temple
Qualifications: [MA (St Andrews), CPE (Bristol)]

STANBROOK CLIVE ST GEORGE QC (1989)

Stanbrook & Henderson
Ground Floor, 2 Harcourt Bldgs, Temple,
London EC4Y 9DB,
Telephone: 0171 353 0101
E-mail: clerks@harcourt.co.uk
Call Date: Nov 1972, Inner Temple
Qualifications: [LLB (Lond)]

STANCOMBE BARRY TERRENCE

Gough Square Chambers
6-7 Gough Square, London EC4A 3DE,
Telephone: 0171 353 0924
E-mail: gsc@goughsq.co.uk
Call Date: July 1983, Gray's Inn
Pupil Master
Qualifications: [LLB (Hons) (Lond)]

STANDFAST PHILIP ARTHUR

St Paul's House
5th Floor, St Paul's House, 23 Park Square
South, Leeds LS1 2ND,
Telephone: 0113 2455866
E-mail: catherinegrimshaw@stpauls-chambers.demon.co.uk
Call Date: July 1980, Inner Temple
Pupil Master
Qualifications: [BA (Sheff)]

STANFIELD MISS SANDRA GASCOYNE

4 King's Bench Walk
2nd Floor, Temple, London EC4Y 7DL,
Telephone: 020 7353 3581
E-mail: clerks@4kbw.co.uk
Call Date: Nov 1984, Gray's Inn
Pupil Master
Qualifications: [BA (Hons)]

STANFORD DAVID RALPH

3 Stone Buildings
Lincoln's Inn, London WC2A 3XL,
Telephone: 0171 242 4937
E-mail: clerks@3sb.law.co.uk
Call Date: Nov 1951, Middle Temple
Qualifications: [MA, LLB (Cantab)]

STANISLAS PAUL JUNIOR

Somersett Chambers
25 Bedford Row, London WC1R 4HE,
Telephone: 0171 404 6701
E-mail: somelaw@aol.com
Call Date: Feb 1989, Middle Temple
Qualifications: [LLB (PCL)]

STANISTREET MISS PENELOPE

New Walk Chambers
27 New Walk, Leicester LE1 6TE,
Telephone: 0116 2559144
Call Date: Oct 1993, Lincoln's Inn
Qualifications: [BA (Hons)(Notts), Dip in Law (Lond)]

STANLEY MISS CLARE FIONA LOUISE

Twenty-Four Old Buildings
Ground Floor, Lincoln's Inn, London
WC2A 3UP, Telephone: 0171 404 0946
E-mail:clerks@24oldbuildings.law.co.uk
Call Date: Nov 1994, Middle Temple
Qualifications: [BA (Hons) (Cantab)]

STANLEY PAUL MALLALIEU

Essex Court Chambers
24 Lincoln's Inn Fields, London
WC2A 3ED, Telephone: 0171 813 8000
E-mail:clerksroom@essexcourt-chambers.co.uk
Call Date: Nov 1993, Middle Temple
Qualifications: [BA (Hons)(Cantab), LLM (Harvard)]

STANNILAND JONATHAN PETER

Assize Court Chambers
14 Small Street, Bristol BS1 1DE,
Telephone: 0117 9264587
E-mail:chambers@assize-court-chambers.co.uk
Call Date: Nov 1993, Inner Temple
Qualifications: [LLB]

STANSBY MRS HILARY ALEXANDRA

Young Street Chambers
38 Young Street, Manchester M3 3FT,
Telephone: 0161 833 0489
E-mail: clerks@young-st-chambers.com
Call Date: Nov 1985, Middle Temple
Pupil Master
Qualifications: [MA (Cantab)]

STANSFIELD PIERS ALISTAIR

Keating Chambers
10 Essex Street, Outer Temple, London
WC2R 3AA, Telephone: 0171 544 2600
Call Date: Nov 1993, Inner Temple
Qualifications: [LLB (Bris)]

STANTON MRS CAROLYN VERITY

Sedan House
Stanley Place, Chester CH1 2LU,
Telephone: 01244 320480/348282
Call Date: Oct 1993, Middle Temple
Qualifications: [LLB (Hons)(L'pool)]

STANTON DAVID RONALD

33 Bedford Row
London WC1R 4JH,
Telephone: 0171 242 6476
E-mail:clerks@bedfordrow33.demon.co.uk
Call Date: July 1979, Gray's Inn
Pupil Master
Qualifications: [BA]

D

STANTON MISS LISA HELEN

Francis Taylor Building
3rd Floor, Temple, London EC4Y 7BY,
Telephone: 0171 797 7250
Call Date: Oct 1993, Inner Temple
Qualifications: [MA (Cantab)]

STANTON NICHOLAS PHILIP

169 Temple Chambers
Temple Avenue, London EC4Y 0DA,
Telephone: 0171 583 7644
Call Date: Feb 1991, Inner Temple
Qualifications: [BA (Oxon)]

STARCEVIC PETAR

St Philip's Chambers
Fountain Court, Steelhouse Lane,
Birmingham B4 6DR,
Telephone: 0121 246 7000
E-mail: clerks@st-philips.co.uk
Call Date: July 1983, Inner Temple
Pupil Master
Qualifications: [LLB (Bris)]

STARK JAMES HAYDEN ALEXANDER

**Chambers of Ian Macdonald QC (In
Association with Two Garden Court,
Temple, London)**
Waldorf House, 5 Cooper Street,
Manchester M2 2FW,
Telephone: 0161 236 1840
Call Date: Mar 1998, Middle Temple
Qualifications: [LLB (Hons)(Sheff)]

STARKIE MISS CLAIRE ELIZABETH

St Philip's Chambers
Fountain Court, Steelhouse Lane,
Birmingham B4 6DR,
Telephone: 0121 246 7000
E-mail: clerks@st-philips.co.uk
Call Date: Nov 1991, Lincoln's Inn
Qualifications: [MA (Hons) (Cantab)]

STARKS NICHOLAS ERNSHAW

8 Fountain Court
Steelhouse Lane, Birmingham B4 6DR,
Telephone: 0121 236 5514/5
E-mail: clerks@no8chambers.co.uk

St Ive's Chambers

Whittall Street, Birmingham B4 6DH,
Telephone: 0121 236 0863/5720
E-mail:stives.headofchambers@btinternet.com
Call Date: July 1989, Middle Temple
Qualifications: [LLB (Hons)(Manch)]

STARMER KEIR

Doughty Street Chambers
11 Doughty Street, London WC1N 2PG,
Telephone: 0171 404 1313
E-mail:enquiries@doughtystreet.co.uk
Call Date: Nov 1987, Middle Temple
Qualifications: [LLB (Leeds), BCL, (Oxon)]

START MISS ANGHARAD JOCELYN

3 Verulam Buildings
London WC1R 5NT,
Telephone: 0171 831 8441
E-mail: clerks@3verulam.co.uk
Call Date: Nov 1988, Lincoln's Inn
Qualifications: [BA (Dunelm)]

START MISS VICTORIA LOUISE

2 King's Bench Walk
Ground Floor, Temple, London
EC4Y 7DE, Telephone: 0171 353 1746
E-mail: 2kbw@atlas.co.uk
Call Date: Oct 1996, Middle Temple
Qualifications: [BA (Hons)(Oxon), LLM
(Lond)]

STARTE HARVEY NICHOLAS ADRIAN

1 Brick Court
1st Floor, Temple, London EC4Y 9BY,
Telephone: 0171 353 8845
E-mail: clerks@1brickcourt.co.uk
Call Date: Nov 1985, Gray's Inn
Pupil Master
Qualifications: [MA (Cantab)]

STATMAN PHILIP RICHARD

3 Gray's Inn Square
Ground Floor, London WC1R 5AH,
Telephone: 0171 520 5600
E-mail: clerks@3gis.co.uk
Call Date: July 1975, Middle Temple
Pupil Master, Assistant Recorder
Qualifications: [LLB (Lond)]

STAUNTON (THOMAS) ULICK (PATRICK)

Chambers of Mr Peter Crampin QC
Ground Floor, 11 New Square, Lincoln's
Inn, London WC2A 3QB,
Telephone: 020 7831 0081
E-mail: 11newsquare.co.uk
65-67 King Street
Leicester LE1 6RP,
Telephone: 0116 2547710
Call Date: July 1984, Middle Temple
Pupil Master
Qualifications: [LLB (Lond)]

STAUNTON WILLIAM JOHN PAUL

58 King Street Chambers
1st Floor, Kingsgate House, 51-53 South
King Street, Manchester M2 6DE,
Telephone: 0161 831 7477
Call Date: Feb 1986, Middle Temple
Qualifications: [MA (Cantab)]

STAVROS MS EVANTHIA

3 Temple Gardens
3rd Floor, Temple, London EC4Y 9AU,
Telephone: 0171 353 0832
Call Date: Oct 1997, Inner Temple
Qualifications: [LLB (Herts)]

STEAD MISS KATE REBECCA

Barristers' Common Law Chambers
57 Whitechapel Road, Aldgate East,
London E1 1DU,
Telephone: 0171 375 3012
E-mail: barristers@hotmail.com and
barristers@lawchambers.freeserve.co.uk
Call Date: Oct 1996, Lincoln's Inn
Qualifications: [LLB (Hons)(Middx), M.Phil
(Cantab)]

STEAD RICHARD JAMES

St John's Chambers
Small Street, Bristol BS1 1DW,
Telephone: 0117 9213456/298514
E-mail: @stjohnschambers.co.uk
Call Date: July 1979, Middle Temple
Pupil Master, Assistant Recorder
Qualifications: [MA (Cantab)]

STEAD TIMOTHY HAROLD

No. 6
6 Park Square, Leeds LS1 2LW,
Telephone: 0113 2459763
E-mail: chambers@no6.co.uk
Call Date: Nov 1979, Gray's Inn
Pupil Master
Qualifications: [BA]

STEADMAN RUSSELL CHARLES

Mitre House Chambers
15-19 Devereux Court, London WC2R 3JJ,
Telephone: 0171 583 8233
Call Date: Nov 1995, Inner Temple
Qualifications: [BA (Essex), CPE]

STEEL JOHN BRYCHAN QC (1993)

4-5 Gray's Inn Square
Ground Floor, Gray's Inn, London
WC1R 5JP, Telephone: 0171 404 5252
E-mail:chambers@4-5graysinnsquare.co.uk
Call Date: July 1978, Gray's Inn
Assistant Recorder
Qualifications: [BSc Hons]

STEELE DAVID MARK

Colleton Chambers
Colleton Crescent, Exeter, Devon,
EX2 4DG, Telephone: 01392 274898/9
Call Date: Nov 1975, Gray's Inn
Pupil Master
Qualifications: [LLB (B'ham)]

STEELE MISS LAURA CATHERINE

Harrow on the Hill Chambers
60 High Street, Harrow-on-the-Hill,
Middlesex, HA1 3LL,
Telephone: 0181 423 7444
Call Date: 1997, Inner Temple
Qualifications: [LLB (Hull)]

STEEN MARTIN GAMPER

Albion Chambers
Broad Street, Bristol BS1 1DR,
Telephone: 0117 9272144
Call Date: July 1976, Inner Temple
Pupil Master
Qualifications: [LLB (Hons)]

STEENSON DAVID SAMUEL

3 Paper Buildings
Temple, London EC4Y 7EU,
Telephone: 020 7583 8055
E-mail: London@3paper.com
3 Paper Buildings (Winchester)
4 St Peter Street, Winchester SO23 8BW,
Telephone: 01962 868884
E-mail: winchester@3paper.com
3 Paper Buildings (Bournemouth)
20 Lorne Park Road, Bournemouth,
Dorset, BH1 1JN,
Telephone: 01202 292102
E-mail: Bournemouth@3paper.com
3 Paper Buildings (Oxford)
1 Alfred Street, High Street, Oxford
OX1 4EH, Telephone: 01865 793736
E-mail: oxford@3paper.com
Call Date: Nov 1991, Lincoln's Inn
Qualifications: [LLB (Hons) (Belfast)]

STEER DAVID QC (1993)

Corn Exchange Chambers
5th Floor, Fenwick Street, Liverpool
L2 7QS, Telephone: 0151 227 1081/5009
Call Date: Nov 1974, Middle Temple
Recorder
Qualifications: [BA (Hons)]

STEER WILFRED REED QC (1972)

Park Court Chambers
16 Park Place, Leeds LS1 2SJ,
Telephone: 0113 2433277
Call Date: Nov 1950, Gray's Inn
Qualifications: [LLB (Lond)]

STEIGER MARTIN THOMAS QC (1994)

18 St John Street
Manchester M3 4EA,
Telephone: 0161 278 1800
E-mail: 18stjohn@lineone.net
Call Date: Nov 1969, Inner Temple
Recorder
Qualifications: [LLB (Nottm)]

STEIN SAMUEL

2 Dyers Buildings
London EC1N 2JT,
Telephone: 0171 404 1881
Call Date: Nov 1988, Inner Temple
Pupil Master
Qualifications: [LLB (Hons)]

STEINBERG HARRY DAVID GLYN

12 King's Bench Walk
Temple, London EC4Y 7EL,
Telephone: 0171 583 0811
E-mail: chambers@12kbw.co.uk
Call Date: 1997, Gray's Inn
Qualifications: [BA (Hons)(Cantab)]

STEINERT JONATHAN

New Court Chambers
5 Verulam Buildings, Gray's Inn, London
WC1R 5LY, Telephone: 0171 831 9500
E-mail: mail@newcourtchambers.com
Call Date: Feb 1986, Middle Temple
Pupil Master
Qualifications: [BA (Oxon) Dip Law, (PCL)]

STEINFELD ALAN GEOFFREY QC (1987)

Twenty-Four Old Buildings
Ground Floor, Lincoln's Inn, London
WC2A 3UP, Telephone: 0171 404 0946
E-mail:clerks@24oldbuildings.law.co.uk
Call Date: Nov 1968, Lincoln's Inn
Qualifications: [BA, LLB (Cantab)]

STELLING NIGEL ROY

Coleridge Chambers
Citadel, 190 Corporation Street,
Birmingham B4 6QD,
Telephone: 0121 233 8500
Call Date: July 1987, Inner Temple
Qualifications: [BA]

STEMBRIDGE DAVID HARRY QC (1990)

5 Fountain Court
Steelhouse Lane, Birmingham B4 6DR,
Telephone: 0121 606 0500
E-mail:clerks@5fountaincourt.law.co.uk
199 Strand
London WC2R 1DR,
Telephone: 0171 379 9779
E-mail: chambers@199strand.co.uk
Call Date: 1955, Gray's Inn
Recorder
Qualifications: [LLB]

STEMMER-BALDWIN MARCUS STEPHEN

8 Stone Buildings
Lincoln's Inn, London WC2A 3TA,
Telephone: 0171 831 9881
E-mail: alanl@8stonebuildings.law.uk
Call Date: Nov 1994, Inner Temple
Qualifications: [LLB (Kent)]

STENHOUSE JOHN ALEXANDER

6 Fountain Court
Steelhouse Lane, Birmingham B4 6DR,
Telephone: 0121 233 3282
E-mail: clerks@sixfountain.co.uk
Call Date: Nov 1986, Lincoln's Inn
Qualifications: [LLB]

STENT MISS CAROLINE MARGARET

Newport Chambers
12 Clytha Park Road, Newport, Gwent,
NP9 47L, Telephone: 01633 267403/
255855
Call Date: May 1993, Lincoln's Inn
Qualifications: [LLB (Hons)]

STEPHEN MICHAEL

Chambers of Michael Stephen
118 Kennington Road, London SE11 6RE,
Telephone: 07071 780690
E-mail: msllm@hotmail.com
Call Date: Nov 1966, Inner Temple
Qualifications: [JSM (Stanford)]

STEPHENS JOHN LEWIS

35 Essex Street
Temple, London WC2R 3AR,
Telephone: 0171 353 6381
E-mail: derek_jenkins@link.org
Call Date: July 1975, Middle Temple
Pupil Master
Qualifications: [BA (Oxon)]

STEPHENS MICHAEL ALLEN

5 Fountain Court
Steelhouse Lane, Birmingham B4 6DR,
Telephone: 0121 606 0500
E-mail: clerks@5fountaincourt.law.co.uk
Call Date: July 1983, Middle Temple
Pupil Master
Qualifications: [BA (Keele), A.C.I.ARB]

STEPHENSON ANTHONY MARK

First National Chambers
2nd Floor, First National Building, 24
Fenwick Street, Liverpool L2 7NE,
Telephone: 0151 236 2098
Call Date: Nov 1997, Gray's Inn
Qualifications: [LLB]

STEPHENSON CHRISTOPHER JAMES

9 Gough Square
London EC4A 3DE,
Telephone: 020 7832 0500
E-mail: clerks@9goughsq.co.uk
Call Date: Nov 1994, Lincoln's Inn
Qualifications: [MA (Hons)(Edinburgh)]

STEPHENSON GEOFFREY CHARLES

2-3 Gray's Inn Square
Gray's Inn, London WC1R 5JH,
Telephone: 0171 242 4986
E-mail:chambers@2-3graysinnsquare.co.uk
Call Date: Nov 1971, Gray's Inn
Pupil Master

STEPHENSON WILLIAM BENEDICT

3 Paper Buildings
Temple, London EC4Y 7EU,
Telephone: 020 7583 8055
E-mail: London@3paper.com
3 Paper Buildings (Bournemouth)
20 Lorne Park Road, Bournemouth,
Dorset, BH1 1JN,
Telephone: 01202 292102
E-mail: Bournemouth@3paper.com
3 Paper Buildings (Winchester)
4 St Peter Street, Winchester SO23 8BW,
Telephone: 01962 868884
E-mail: winchester@3paper.com
3 Paper Buildings (Oxford)
1 Alfred Street, High Street, Oxford
OX1 4EH, Telephone: 01865 793736
E-mail: oxford@3paper.com
Call Date: July 1973, Inner Temple
Qualifications: [MA (Oxon)]

STERLING PROFESSOR JOHN ADRIAN LAWRENCE

Lamb Chambers
Lamb Building, Temple, London
EC4Y 7AS, Telephone: 020 7797 8300
E-mail: lambchambers@link.org
Call Date: Feb 1953, Middle Temple
Qualifications: [LLB]

D

STERLING ROBERT ALAN

St James's Chambers
68 Quay Street, Manchester M3 3EJ,
Telephone: 0161 834 7000
E-mail: clerks@stjameschambers.co.uk
12 New Square
Lincoln's Inn, London WC2A 3SW,
Telephone: 0171 419 1212
E-mail: chambers@12newsquare.co.uk
Park Lane Chambers
19 Westgate, Leeds LS1 2RD,
Telephone: 0113 2285000
E-mail:clerks@parklanechambers.co.uk
Call Date: 1970, Gray's Inn
Pupil Master
Qualifications: [MA (Cantab)]

STERLING MISS VALERIE

Park Court Chambers
16 Park Place, Leeds LS1 2SJ,
Telephone: 0113 2433277
Call Date: 1981, Gray's Inn
Qualifications: [LLB]

STERN DAVID PATRICK JULIAN

4 King's Bench Walk
Ground/First Floor/Basement, Temple,
London EC4Y 7DL,
Telephone: 0171 822 8822
E-mail: 4kbw@barristersatlaw.com
Call Date: July 1989, Lincoln's Inn
Pupil Master
Qualifications: [LLB (Lond), LLM (Cantab)]

STERN IAN MICHAEL

Hollis Whiteman Chambers
3rd Floor, Queen Elizabeth Bldg, Temple,
London EC4Y 9BS,
Telephone: 020 7583 5766
E-mail:barristers@holliswhiteman.co.uk
Call Date: July 1983, Inner Temple
Pupil Master, Assistant Recorder
Qualifications: [BA (Warw) Dip Law, (City)]

STERN DR KRISTINA ANNE

39 Essex Street
London WC2R 3AT,
Telephone: 0171 832 1111
E-mail: clerks@39essex.co.uk
Call Date: Nov 1996, Inner Temple
Qualifications: [LLB (Melbourne), PhD
(Cantab)]

STERN MRS LINDA JOY QC (1991)

18 Red Lion Court
(Off Fleet Street), London EC4A 3EB,
Telephone: 0171 520 6000
E-mail: chambers@18rlc.co.uk
Thornwood House
102 New London Road, Chelmsford,
Essex, CM2 0RG,
Telephone: 01245 280880
E-mail: chambers@18rlc.co.uk
Call Date: July 1971, Gray's Inn
Recorder

STERN MARK RICHARD ALEXANDER

2 Paper Buildings, Basement North
Temple, London EC4Y 7ET,
Telephone: 0171 936 2613
E-mail: post@2paper.co.uk
Call Date: Feb 1988, Lincoln's Inn
Qualifications: [MA (Hons) (Cantab)]

STERN MICHAEL ADAM

4 Paper Buildings
1st Floor, Temple, London EC4Y 7EX,
Telephone: 0171 583 0816/353 1131
E-mail: clerks@4paperbuildings.co.uk
Call Date: July 1983, Lincoln's Inn
Pupil Master
Qualifications: [BA (Lond), Dip Law]

STERN THOMAS WILLIAM PAUL

Maidstone Chambers
33 Earl Street, Maidstone, Kent, ME14 1PF,
Telephone: 01622 688592
E-mail:maidstonechambers@compuserve.co
m
Call Date: Nov 1995, Gray's Inn
Qualifications: [LLB (Hons)]

STERNBERG MISS LESLI EDEN

John Street Chambers
2 John Street, London WC1N 2HJ,
Telephone: 0171 242 1911
E-mail:john.street_chambers@virgin.net
Call Date: Nov 1994, Gray's Inn
Qualifications: [BA]

STERNBERG MICHAEL VIVIAN

4 Paper Buildings
1st Floor, Temple, London EC4Y 7EX,
Telephone: 0171 583 0816/353 1131
E-mail: clerks@4paperbuildings.co.uk
Call Date: July 1975, Gray's Inn
Pupil Master
Qualifications: [MA (Cantab) , LLM (Cantab)]

Fax: 0171 353 4979; DX: LDE 1035;
Other comms: E-mail
clerks@4paperbuildings.co.uk

Other professional qualifications: MA, LLM
(Cantab)

Types of work: Family, Family provision,
International family law

Awards and memberships: Medaglia d'Argento
di Benemerenza of the Sacred Military
Constantinian Order of St George (1990)

Languages spoken: French

Reported Cases: *Re F (A Minor: Paternity
Test)*, [1993] 3 WLR 369 (CA), 1992.
Evidence – blood test – application for
blood test for DNA profiling by claimant for
paternity.
*H v H (Financial Provision: Capital allow-
ance)*, [1993] 2 FLR 335, 1992. Financial
provision – divorce – capital adjustment –
availability of 'Besterman Cushion' and if
court should exercise its power at all.
R v Plymouth Justices ex parte W, [1993] 2
FLR 777, 1993. Family proceedings – judicial review – rules of natural justice –
cross-examination on previous convic-
tions.
*H v H (Residence order leave to remove
from jurisdiction)*, [1995] 1 FLR 529 (CA),
1994. Applicability of Children Act 1989 to
applications to take child permanently
overseas.
Re M (Child's upbringing), [1996] 2 FLR
441 (CA), 1996. Zulu parents contesting
adoption by white woman of Zulu boy resident with her in England – importance of
cultural heritage.

Further reported cases
Re M (Petition to European Commission of
Human Rights) [1997] 1 FLR 755
Wardship – court ordering ward to be
returned to natural parents in South Africa
– woman caring for ward in England
seeking to petition ECHR on rights of ward
and herself.

S v S [1997] 1 WLR 1621
Financial relief – Inference of tax evasion
by husband – Inland Revenue receiving
copy of judgment – Confidential information – breach of confidence – public
interest.

Re S (Removal from Jurisdiction) April 1999
(Family Law)
Mother's decision to return to Chile
reasonable but notwithstanding her
proposals for it realistic – strict conditions
to be attached to permission to return
until 'mirror orders' made by Chilean
Court on contact including deposit of
£135,000 in a special account.

Unreported case
Re AMR (to be reported) February 1999
(FD) (HCJ)
Adoption – recognition of Polish orders of
Guardianship and removal of parental
authority – effect on UK adoption proceed-
ings – conflict of laws avoided.

Description of Practice
Equal division of substantial ancillary relief
cases, international adoption work and
substantial children cases, including much
work for guardians and the Official Solicitor.

STEVENS HOWARD LINTON

1 Crown Office Row
3rd Floor, Temple, London EC4Y 7HH,
Telephone: 0171 583 9292
E-mail: onecor@link.org
Call Date: Oct 1990, Middle Temple
Qualifications: [BA (Dunelm), Dip Law
(City)]

STEVENS MISS NINA PAULINE

Chambers of Wilfred Forster-Jones
New Court, 1st Floor South, Temple,
London EC4Y 9BE,
Telephone: 0171 353 0853/4/7222
E-mail: chambers@newcourt.net
Call Date: Oct 1994, Lincoln's Inn
Qualifications: [BA (Hons)]

STEVENS STUART STANDISH

Holborn Chambers
6 Gate Street, Lincoln's Inn Fields, London
WC2A 3HP, Telephone: 0171 242 6060

Middlesex Chambers
Suite 3 & 4 Stanley House, Stanley
Avenue, Wembley, Middlesex, HA0 4SB,
Telephone: 0181 902 1499
Call Date: July 1970, Gray's Inn
Pupil Master

STEVENS-HOARE MISS MICHELLE

Hardwicke Building
New Square, Lincoln's Inn, London
WC2A 3SB, Telephone: 020 7242 2523
E-mail: clerks@hardwicke.co.uk
Call Date: July 1986, Middle Temple
Pupil Master
Qualifications: [LLB (Lond), LLM
(Property)(Lond)]

STEVENSON ARTHUR WILLIAM QC (1996)

One Paper Buildings
Ground Floor, Temple, London
EC4Y 7EP, Telephone: 0171 583 7355
E-mail: clerks@1pb.co.uk
Call Date: Nov 1968, Lincoln's Inn
Recorder
Qualifications: [MA (Oxon)]

STEVENSON BRETT CARL

4 Fountain Court
Steelhouse Lane, Birmingham B4 6DR,
Telephone: 0121 236 3476
Call Date: 1998, Lincoln's Inn
Qualifications: [LLB (Hons)(Dundee)]

STEVENSON JOHN MELFORD

Two Crown Office Row
Ground Floor, Temple, London
EC4Y 7HJ, Telephone: 020 7797 8100
E-mail: mail@2cor.co.uk, or to individual
barristers at: [barrister's
surname]@2cor.co.uk
Call Date: Nov 1975, Inner Temple
Pupil Master
Qualifications: [MA (Oxon)]

STEVENSON JOSEPH GIBBS

62 Cortworth Road
Ecclesall, Sheffield S11 9LP,
Telephone: 0114 236 0988
Call Date: Feb 1960, Inner Temple

STEVENSON ROBERT ANTHONY

Wilberforce Chambers
7 Bishop Lane, Hull, East Yorkshire,
HU1 1PA, Telephone: 01482 323264
E-mail: clerks@hullbar.demon.co.uk
Call Date: July 1972, Inner Temple
Pupil Master
Qualifications: [MA (Cantab)]

STEVENSON-WATT NEVILLE WILLIAM

Chambers of Norman Palmer
2 Field Court, Gray's Inn, London
WC1R 5BB, Telephone: 0171 405 6114
E-mail: fieldct2@netcomuk.co.uk
Call Date: Nov 1985, Middle Temple
Pupil Master
Qualifications: [MA (Cantab), LLB, (Lond)]

STEVENTON MRS ELIZABETH ANNE

Chambers of Elizabeth Steventon
50 Firle Road, Brighton, Sussex, BN2 2YH,
Telephone: 01273 670394
Call Date: Oct 1991, Middle Temple
Qualifications: [LLB (Lond Ext)]

STEWART ALEXANDER JOSEPH

5 New Square
Ground Floor, Lincoln's Inn, London
WC2A 3RJ, Telephone: 020 7404 0404
E-mail:chambers@fivenewsquare.demon.co.
uk
Call Date: July 1975, Gray's Inn
Qualifications: [BA, BCL (Oxon)]

STEWART MS ALEXANDRA MARY HAMILTON

30 Park Square
Leeds LS1 2PF, Telephone: 0113 2436388
E-mail: clerks@30parksquare.co.uk
Call Date: 1997, Inner Temple
Qualifications: [LLB (Reading)]

STEWART GEORGE BARRY

Chambers of Mr G B Stewart
Ridge Hall, Ridge Lane, Staithes,
Saltburn-by-the-Sea, Cleveland, TS13 5DX,
Telephone: 01947 840511
Call Date: July 1968, Gray's Inn
Pupil Master
Qualifications: [LLB (Notts) Dip Crim, JD]

STEWART JAMES SIMEON HAMILTON QC (1982)

Park Court Chambers
16 Park Place, Leeds LS1 2SJ,
Telephone: 0113 2433277
18 Red Lion Court
(Off Fleet Street), London EC4A 3EB,
Telephone: 0171 520 6000
E-mail: chambers@18rlc.co.uk
Call Date: July 1966, Inner Temple
Recorder
Qualifications: [LLB]

STEWART MISS LINDSEY KATHLEEN

7 Stone Buildings
Ground Floor, Lincoln's Inn, London
WC2A 3SZ, Telephone: 0171 405 3886/
242 3546 E-mail: chaldous@vossnet.co.uk
Call Date: Nov 1983, Lincoln's Inn
Pupil Master
Qualifications: [MA (Oxon)]

STEWART MARK COURTNEY

College Chambers
19 Carlton Cresent, Southampton
SO15 2ET, Telephone: 01703 230338
Call Date: July 1989, Middle Temple
Qualifications: [BA (Hons), LLM [Anglia]]

STEWART NEILL ALASTAIR

Hollis Whiteman Chambers
3rd Floor, Queen Elizabeth Bldg, Temple,
London EC4Y 9BS,
Telephone: 020 7583 5766
E-mail:barristers@holliswhiteman.co.uk
Call Date: July 1973, Middle Temple
Pupil Master, Recorder
Qualifications: [BA (Cantab)]

STEWART NICHOLAS JOHN CAMERON QC (1987)

Hardwicke Building
New Square, Lincoln's Inn, London
WC2A 3SB, Telephone: 020 7242 2523
E-mail: clerks@hardwicke.co.uk
Call Date: July 1971, Inner Temple
Recorder
Qualifications: [BA (Oxon),C Dip,A.F.,
ACIArb, CEDR Accredited, Mediator]

STEWART RICHARD PAUL

New Court Chambers
5 Verulam Buildings, Gray's Inn, London
WC1R 5LY, Telephone: 0171 831 9500
E-mail: mail@newcourtchambers.com
Call Date: July 1975, Gray's Inn
Pupil Master
Qualifications: [BA (Belfast)]

STEWART ROGER PAUL DAVIDSON

Chambers of John L Powell QC
Four New Square, Lincoln's Inn, London
WC2A 3RJ, Telephone: 0171 797 8000
E-mail: barristers@4newsquare.com
Call Date: July 1986, Inner Temple
Pupil Master
Qualifications: [MA (Cantab) LLM]

STEWART SEYMOUR GEORGE

Chancery Chambers
1st Floor Offices, 70/72 Chancery Lane,
London WC2A 1AB,
Telephone: 0171 405 6879/6870
Call Date: Nov 1995, Middle Temple
Qualifications: [BA (Hons)(Kent)]

STEWART STEPHEN PAUL QC (1996)

22 Old Buildings
Lincoln's Inn, London WC2A 3UJ,
Telephone: 0171 831 0222
Byrom Street Chambers
Byrom Street, Manchester M3 4PF,
Telephone: 0161 829 2100
E-mail: Byromst25@aol.com
Call Date: July 1975, Middle Temple
Assistant Recorder
Qualifications: [MA (Oxon)]

STEWART TOBY ALASDAIR CHARLES

Ropewalk Chambers
24 The Ropewalk, Nottingham NG1 5EF,
Telephone: 0115 9472581
E-mail: administration@ropewalk co.uk
Call Date: July 1989, Middle Temple
Qualifications: [LLB (Sheff)]

D

D

STEWART-SMITH WILLIAM RODNEY

1 New Square
Ground Floor, Lincoln's Inn, London
WC2A 3SA, Telephone: 0171 405 0884/5/6/
7 E-mail: clerks@1newsquare.law.co.uk
Call Date: June 1964, Middle Temple
Pupil Master, Recorder
Qualifications: [BA, LLB]

STEYN MS KAREN MARGARET

4-5 Gray's Inn Square
Ground Floor, Gray's Inn, London
WC1R 5JP, Telephone: 0171 404 5252
E-mail:chambers@4-5graysinnsquare.co.uk
Call Date: Oct 1995, Middle Temple
Qualifications: [BA (Hons) (L'pool), Dip
Law]

STEYNOR ALAN CHARLES

Keating Chambers
10 Essex Street, Outer Temple, London
WC2R 3AA, Telephone: 0171 544 2600
Call Date: July 1975, Gray's Inn
Pupil Master, Recorder
Qualifications: [MA (Cantab), FCIArb]

STILES JOHN ERNEST

Mercury Chambers
Mercury House, 33-35 Clarendon Road,
Leeds LS2 9NZ,
Telephone: 0113 234 2265
E-mail:cdexter@mercurychambers.co.uk
Call Date: July 1986, Middle Temple
Pupil Master
Qualifications: [LLB]

STILGOE RUFUS NATHANIEL ABBOTT

23 Essex Street
London WC2R 3AS,
Telephone: 0171 413 0353/836 8366
E-mail:clerks@essexstreet23.demon.co.uk
Call Date: Oct 1994, Inner Temple
Qualifications: [BA (Durham), CPE
(Huddersfield)]

STILITZ DANIEL MALACHI

11 King's Bench Walk
Temple, London EC4Y 7EQ,
Telephone: 0171 632 8500/583 0610
E-mail: clerksroom@11kbw.com
Call Date: Oct 1992, Lincoln's Inn
Qualifications: [BA (Hons)(Oxon), MA (City)]

STILL GEOFFREY JOHN CHURCHILL

Pump Court Chambers
5 Temple Chambers, Temple Street,
Swindon SN1 1SQ,
Telephone: 01793 539899
E-mail: clerks@3pumpcourt.com
Pump Court Chambers
Upper Ground Floor, 3 Pump Court,
Temple, London EC4Y 7AJ,
Telephone: 0171 353 0711
E-mail: clerks@3pumpcourt.com
Pump Court Chambers
31 Southgate Street, Winchester
SO23 9EE, Telephone: 01962 868161
E-mail: clerks@3pumpcourt.com
Call Date: Feb 1966, Gray's Inn
Pupil Master, Recorder
Qualifications: [LLB]

STIMPSON MICHAEL EDWARD

Littman Chambers
12 Gray's Inn Square, London WC1R 5JP,
Telephone: 020 7404 4866
E-mail: admin@littmanchambers.com
Call Date: Nov 1969, Lincoln's Inn
Pupil Master

STINCHCOMBE PAUL DAVID

4-5 Gray's Inn Square
Ground Floor, Gray's Inn, London
WC1R 5JP, Telephone: 0171 404 5252
E-mail:chambers@4-5graysinnsquare.co.uk
Call Date: July 1985, Lincoln's Inn
Pupil Master
Qualifications: [MA (Cantab), LLM (Harv)]

STIRLING CHRISTOPHER WILLIAM

Bell Yard Chambers
116/118 Chancery Lane, London
WC2A 1PP, Telephone: 0171 306 9292
Call Date: Oct 1993, Inner Temple
Qualifications: [LLB]

STIRLING MR SIMON

**4 Brick Court, Chambers of Anne
Rafferty QC**
1st Floor, Temple, London EC4Y 9AD,
Telephone: 0171 583 8455
Call Date: July 1989, Gray's Inn
Qualifications: [BA (Hull)]

STITCHER MALCOLM DAVID

199 Strand
London WC2R 1DR,
Telephone: 0171 379 9779
E-mail: chambers@199strand.co.uk
Call Date: Nov 1971, Lincoln's Inn
Pupil Master
Qualifications: [LLB]

STOBART JOHN

King Charles House
Standard Hill, Nottingham NG1 6FX,
Telephone: 0115 9418851
E-mail: clerks@kch.co.uk
Call Date: July 1974, Gray's Inn
Pupil Master
Qualifications: [LLB (B'ham)]

STOCKDALE DAVID ANDREW QC (1995)

Deans Court Chambers
24 St John Street, Manchester M3 4DF,
Telephone: 0161 214 6000
E-mail: clerks@deanscourt.co.uk
Deans Court Chambers
41-43 Market Place, Preston PR1 1AH,
Telephone: 01772 555163
E-mail: clerks@deanscourt.co.uk
9 Bedford Row
London WC1R 4AZ,
Telephone: 0171 242 3555
E-mail: clerks@9br.co.uk
Call Date: July 1975, Middle Temple
Recorder
Qualifications: [MA (Oxon)]

STOCKDALE SIR THOMAS MINSHULL

Erskine Chambers
30 Lincoln's Inn Fields, Lincoln's Inn,
London WC2A 3PF,
Telephone: 0171 242 5532
E-mail:clerks@erskine-chambers.co.uk
Call Date: Nov 1966, Inner Temple
Qualifications: [MA (Oxon)]

STOCKER JOHN CRISPIN

One Garden Court Family Law Chambers
Ground Floor, Temple, London
EC4Y 9BJ, Telephone: 0171 797 7900
E-mail: clerks@onegardencourt.co.uk
Call Date: Nov 1985, Inner Temple
Pupil Master
Qualifications: [LLB (Exon), LLM (Cantab)]

STOCKILL DAVID ANDREW

5 Fountain Court
Steelhouse Lane, Birmingham B4 6DR,
Telephone: 0121 606 0500
E-mail:clerks@5fountaincourt.law.co.uk
Call Date: Nov 1985, Lincoln's Inn
Pupil Master
Qualifications: [MA (Cantab)]

STOCKLEY MISS RUTH ANGELA

40 King Street
Manchester M2 6BA,
Telephone: 0161 832 9082
E-mail: clerks@40kingstreet.co.uk
The Chambers of Philip Raynor QC
5 Park Place, Leeds LS1 2RU,
Telephone: 0113 242 1123
Call Date: July 1988, Lincoln's Inn
Qualifications: [LLB (Hons)(Notts)]

STOCKWELL GRAHAM CLIVE

High Pavement Chambers
1 High Pavement, Nottingham NG1 1HF,
Telephone: 0115 9418218
Call Date: Nov 1988, Inner Temple
Qualifications: [LLB]

STOKELL ROBERT

Two Crown Office Row
Ground Floor, Temple, London
EC4Y 7HJ, Telephone: 020 7797 8100
E-mail: mail@2cor.co.uk, or to individual
barristers at: [barrister's
surname]@2cor.co.uk
Call Date: Oct 1995, Lincoln's Inn
Qualifications: [BA (Hons)(Oxon)]

STOKER GRAHAM KENNETH ROBERT

2-3 Gray's Inn Square
Gray's Inn, London WC1R 5JH,
Telephone: 0171 242 4986
E-mail:chambers@2-3graysinnsquare.co.uk
Call Date: Nov 1977, Middle Temple
Pupil Master
Qualifications: [LLB, LLM]

STOKES DAVID MAYHEW ALLEN QC (1989)

Five Paper Buildings
1st Floor, Five Paper Bldgs, Temple,
London EC4Y 7HB,
Telephone: 0171 583 6117
E-mail:clerks@5-paperbuildings.law.co.uk
Fenners Chambers
3 Madingley Road, Cambridge CB3 0EE,
Telephone: 01223 368761
E-mail: clerks@fennerschambers.co.uk
Call Date: July 1968, Gray's Inn
Recorder
Qualifications: [MA (Cantab)]

STOKES MISS MARY ELIZABETH

Erskine Chambers
30 Lincoln's Inn Fields, Lincoln's Inn,
London WC2A 3PF,
Telephone: 0171 242 5532
E-mail:clerks@erskine-chambers.co.uk
Call Date: July 1989, Lincoln's Inn
Qualifications: [MA BCL (Oxon), LLM
(Harvard)]

STOKES MICHAEL GEORGE THOMAS QC (1994)

Chambers of Michael Pert QC
36 Bedford Row, London WC1R 4JH,
Telephone: 0171 421 8000
E-mail: 36bedfordrow@link.org
Chambers of Michael Pert QC
104 New Walk, Leicester LE1 7EA,
Telephone: 0116 249 2020
Chambers of Michael Pert QC
24 Albion Place, Northampton NN1 1UD,
Telephone: 01604 602333
St Philip's Chambers
Fountain Court, Steelhouse Lane,
Birmingham B4 6DR,
Telephone: 0121 246 7000
E-mail: clerks@st-philips.co.uk
Call Date: Nov 1971, Gray's Inn
Recorder
Qualifications: [LLB]

STONE EVAN DAVID ROBERT QC (1979)

29 Bedford Row Chambers
London WC1R 4HE,
Telephone: 0171 831 2626
Call Date: July 1954, Inner Temple
Assistant Recorder
Qualifications: [MA (Oxon)]

STONE GREGORY QC (1994)

4-5 Gray's Inn Square
Ground Floor, Gray's Inn, London
WC1R 5JP, Telephone: 0171 404 5252
E-mail:chambers@4-5graysinnsquare.co.uk
Call Date: July 1976, Inner Temple
Assistant Recorder
Qualifications: [MA (Oxon)]

Fax: 0171 242 7803; DX: 1029 London;
Other comms: E-mail
chambers@4-5graysinnsquare.co.uk

Types of work: Administrative, Environment,
Local government, Parliamentary, Town
and country planning

Circuit: South Eastern

Awards and memberships: Local Government
Planning and Environmental Bar Association; Standing Counsel to DTI for SE Circuit
1989-90

Other professional experience: Senior Econo-
mist Morgan Grenfell & Co (1973-6)

Languages spoken: French, Spanish

Publications: *Architects Journal Legal Handbook*, 1997

STONE JOSEPH

3 Gray's Inn Square
Ground Floor, London WC1R 5AH,
Telephone: 0171 520 5600
E-mail: clerks@3gis.co.uk
Call Date: July 1989, Inner Temple
Qualifications: [BA [Manch], Dip Law [City]]

STONE MISS LUCILLE MADELINE

29 Bedford Row Chambers
London WC1R 4HE,
Telephone: 0171 831 2626

Queen Elizabeth Building
2nd Floor, Temple, London EC4Y 9BS,
Telephone: 0171 797 7837
Call Date: July 1983, Middle Temple
Pupil Master
Qualifications: [MA (Cantab)]

STONE RICHARD FREDERICK QC (1968)

4 Field Court
Gray's Inn, London WC1R 5EA,
Telephone: 0171 440 6900
E-mail: chambers@4fieldcourt.co.uk
Call Date: Nov 1952, Gray's Inn
Qualifications: [MA (Cantab)]

STONE RUSSELL CLIVE ANDREW

10 King's Bench Walk
1st Floor, Temple, London EC4Y 7EB,
Telephone: 0171 353 2501
Call Date: Oct 1992, Inner Temple
Qualifications: [BA (Oxon)]

STONE MISS SALLY VICTORIA

One Garden Court Family Law Chambers
Ground Floor, Temple, London
EC4Y 9BJ, Telephone: 0171 797 7900
E-mail: clerks@onegardencourt.co.uk
Call Date: Nov 1994, Inner Temple
Qualifications: [BA (Hons) (Kent)]

STONEFROST MS HILARY

3/4 South Square
Gray's Inn, London WC1R 5HP,
Telephone: 0171 696 9900
E-mail: clerks@southsquare.com
Call Date: Nov 1991, Middle Temple
Qualifications: [MSc (Lond)]

STONER CHRISTOPHER PAUL

9 Old Square
Ground Floor, Lincoln's Inn, London
WC2A 3SR, Telephone: 0171 405 4682
E-mail: chambers@9oldsquare.co.uk
Call Date: Oct 1991, Lincoln's Inn
Qualifications: [LLB (Hons)(E.Anglia)]

STONES KEITH WILLIAM

9 King's Bench Walk
Ground Floor, Temple, London
EC4Y 7DX, Telephone: 0171 353 7202/
3909 E-mail: 9kbw@compuserve.com
Call Date: Nov 1975, Gray's Inn
Qualifications: [LLB]

STONOR NICHOLAS WILLIAM

Trinity Chambers
9-12 Trinity Chare, Quayside, Newcastle
upon Tyne NE1 3DF,
Telephone: 0191 232 1927
E-mail: info@trinitychambers.co.uk
Gray's Inn Chambers
5th Floor, Gray's Inn, London WC1R 5JA,
Telephone: 0171 404 1111
Call Date: 1993, Middle Temple
Qualifications: [LLB (Hons)]

STOPA CHRISTOPHER PAUL MICHAEL

2 King's Bench Walk
Ground Floor, Temple, London
EC4Y 7DE, Telephone: 0171 353 1746
E-mail: 2kbw@atlas.co.uk
King's Bench Chambers
115 North Hill, Plymouth PL4 8JY,
Telephone: 01752 221551
Call Date: Nov 1976, Middle Temple
Pupil Master
Qualifications: [LLB (Leeds), FCA]

STOREY CHRISTOPHER THOMAS QC (1995)

Park Lane Chambers
19 Westgate, Leeds LS1 2RD,
Telephone: 0113 2285000
E-mail:clerks@parklanechambers.co.uk
Call Date: July 1979, Lincoln's Inn
Assistant Recorder

STOREY IAN FRANCIS

15 North Church Street Chambers
15 North Church Street, Sheffield
S1 2DH, Telephone: 0114 2759708/
2738380
Call Date: Feb 1986, Gray's Inn
Qualifications: [LLB (Manch)]

STOREY JEREMY BRIAN QC (1994)

4 Pump Court
Temple, London EC4Y 7AN,
Telephone: 020 7842 5555
E-mail:chambers@4pumpcourt.law.co.uk
Call Date: July 1974, Inner Temple
Recorder
Qualifications: [MA (Cantab)]

STOREY NICHOLAS JOHN

Goldsworth Chambers
1st Floor, 11 Gray's Inn Square, London
WC1R 5JD, Telephone: 0171 405 7117
Call Date: July 1982, Gray's Inn
Pupil Master
Qualifications: [LLB London]

STOREY PAUL MARK

29 Bedford Row Chambers
London WC1R 4HE,
Telephone: 0171 831 2626
Call Date: July 1982, Lincoln's Inn
Pupil Master
Qualifications: [BA]

STOREY THOMAS SEBASTIAN

Chambers of Andrew Campbell QC
10 Park Square, Leeds LS1 2LH,
Telephone: 0113 2455438
E-mail: clerks@10pksq.co.uk
Call Date: 1993, Gray's Inn
Qualifications: [BA (Oxon)]

STOREY-REA MRS ALEXA ROSEANN

4 Brick Court
Temple, London EC4Y 9AD,
Telephone: 0171 797 8910
E-mail: medhurst@dial.pipex.com
Call Date: Feb 1990, Middle Temple
Qualifications: [LLB]

STORK BRIAN RAYMOND

3 Temple Gardens
Lower Ground Floor, Temple, London
EC4Y 9AU, Telephone: 0171 353 3102/5/
9297 E-mail: clerks@3tg.co.uk
Call Date: July 1981, Inner Temple
Pupil Master
Qualifications: [LLB (Lond)]

STORRIE TIMOTHY JAMES

Old Colony House
6 South King Street, Manchester M2 6DQ,
Telephone: 0161 834 4364
Call Date: Oct 1993, Middle Temple
Qualifications: [BA (Hons)(Oxon), CPE]

STOTESBURY DAVID CHARLES

21 Lauderdale Tower
Barbican, London EC2Y 8BY,
Telephone: 0171 920 9308
E-mail: 106712.1033@compuserve.com
Call Date: Feb 1980, Gray's Inn
Qualifications: [LLB (Lond), MA (Cantab)]

STOUT ROGER CHARLES

18 St John Street
Manchester M3 4EA,
Telephone: 0161 278 1800
E-mail: 18stjohn@lineone.net
Call Date: Nov 1976, Gray's Inn
Qualifications: [BA (Exeter)]

STOW TIMOTHY MONTAGUE FENWICK QC (1989)

12 King's Bench Walk
Temple, London EC4Y 7EL,
Telephone: 0171 583 0811
E-mail: chambers@12kbw.co.uk
Call Date: Nov 1965, Gray's Inn
Recorder

STRACHAN MISS BARBARA HELEN

1 Middle Temple Lane
Temple, London EC4Y 1LT,
Telephone: 0171 583 0659 (12 Lines)
E-mail: chambers@1mtl.co.uk
Call Date: July 1986, Inner Temple
Pupil Master
Qualifications: [LLB]

STRACHAN CHRISTOPHER WILLIAM CHARLES

2 Paper Buildings
1st Floor, Temple, London EC4Y 7ET,
Telephone: 020 7556 5500
E-mail: clerks@2pbbarristers.co.uk

Westgate Chambers
144 High Street, Lewes, East Sussex,
BN7 1XT, Telephone: 01273 480510
Call Date: July 1975, Inner Temple
Pupil Master
Qualifications: [MA (Exon)]

STRACHAN DOUGLAS MARK ARTHUR QC (1987)

1 Crown Office Row
3rd Floor, Temple, London EC4Y 7HH,
Telephone: 0171 583 9292
E-mail: onecor@link.org
Call Date: July 1969, Inner Temple
Recorder
Qualifications: [MA, BCL (Oxon)]

STRACHAN MS ELAINE JUNE

3 Paper Buildings
Temple, London EC4Y 7EU,
Telephone: 020 7583 8055
E-mail: London@3paper.com
3 Paper Buildings (Oxford)
1 Alfred Street, High Street, Oxford
OX1 4EH, Telephone: 01865 793736
E-mail: oxford@3paper.com
3 Paper Buildings (Winchester)
4 St Peter Street, Winchester SO23 8BW,
Telephone: 01962 868884
E-mail: winchester@3paper.com
3 Paper Buildings (Bournemouth)
20 Lorne Park Road, Bournemouth,
Dorset, BH1 1JN,
Telephone: 01202 292102
E-mail: Bournemouth@3paper.com
Call Date: Nov 1995, Middle Temple
Qualifications: [BA (Hons)]

STRACHAN JAMES OLIVER JOHN

4-5 Gray's Inn Square
Ground Floor, Gray's Inn, London
WC1R 5JP, Telephone: 0171 404 5252
E-mail:chambers@4-5graysinnsquare.co.uk
Call Date: Oct 1996, Middle Temple
Qualifications: [BA (Hons)]

STRAKER TIMOTHY DERRICK QC (1996)

4-5 Gray's Inn Square
Ground Floor, Gray's Inn, London
WC1R 5JP, Telephone: 0171 404 5252
E-mail:chambers@4-5graysinnsquare.co.uk
Call Date: July 1977, Gray's Inn

Assistant Recorder
Qualifications: [MA (Cantab)]

Fax: 0181 341 4158;
Out of hours telephone: 0181 341 0413;
Other comms: E-mail halsbury@msn.com

Types of work: Administrative, Civil liberties, Compulsory purchase, Discrimination, Education, Housing, Local government, Planning, Town and country planning

Circuit: South Eastern

Awards and memberships: Administrative Law Bar Association; Planning Bar Association; Downing College Prize for Law; Senior Harris Scholar; Holt Scholar of Gray's Inn; Lord Justice Holker Senior Award

Publications: *Rights of Way Law Review*, 1996; *Intelligence Services Act 1994*, 1994; *Evidence at Inquiries*, 1995; *The Registration of Political Parties Act 1998*, 1999

Reported Cases: *R v Oldham ex parte Garlick*, [1993] AC 509, 1992-3. Determined position of children under the homelessness legislation (House of Lords).
Gillenden v Surrey CC, [1997] 74 P&CR 119, 1997. Extent of reasoning to be given in adopting Local Plan (Court of Appeal).
Reckley v Minister of Public Safety, [1996] AC 527; [1995] 2 AC 491, 1995-6. Whether judicial review available to prerogative of mercy (Privy Council).
R v Cornwall ex parte Huntingdon, [1994] 1 All ER 694, 1993. Statutory provision prevents judicial review.
Hollis v Dudley MBC, [1998] 1 All ER 759, 1997. Compulsory costs in certain environmental cases.

STRANGE MS (KAREN) MICHELLE

Doughty Street Chambers
11 Doughty Street, London WC1N 2PG,
Telephone: 0171 404 1313
E-mail:enquiries@doughtystreet.co.uk
Call Date: July 1989, Lincoln's Inn
Qualifications: [BA (Oxon)]

STRATFORD MISS JEMIMA LUCY

Brick Court Chambers
7-8 Essex Street, London WC2R 3LD,
Telephone: 0171 379 3550
E-mail: [surname]@brickcourt.co.uk
Call Date: Oct 1993, Middle Temple
Qualifications: [BA (Hons)(Oxon), CPE
(City)]

STRAUSS NICHOLAS ALBERT QC (1984)

One Essex Court
Ground Floor, Temple, London
EC4Y 9AR, Telephone: 020 7583 2000
E-mail: clerks@oneessexcourt.co.uk
*Call Date: Nov 1965, Middle Temple
Assistant Recorder*
Qualifications: [MA, LLB (Cantab)]

STRAW JONATHAN JAMES

King Charles House
Standard Hill, Nottingham NG1 6FX,
Telephone: 0115 9418851
E-mail: clerks@kch.co.uk
Call Date: Oct 1992, Lincoln's Inn
Qualifications: [LLB(Hons)(Newc)]

STREATFEILD-JAMES DAVID STEWART

Atkin Chambers
1 Atkin Building, Gray's Inn, London
WC1R 5AT, Telephone: 020 7404 0102
E-mail: clerks@atkin-chambers.co.uk
*Call Date: July 1986, Inner Temple
Pupil Master*
Qualifications: [BA(Oxon)]

STRICKLAND MISS CLARE ELIZABETH

23 Essex Street
London WC2R 3AS,
Telephone: 0171 413 0353/836 8366
E-mail:clerks@essexstreet23.demon.co.uk
Call Date: Oct 1995, Lincoln's Inn
Qualifications: [LLB (Hons)(B'ham)]

STRINGER LEON

Clapham Chambers
21-25 Bedford Road, Clapham North,
London SW4 7SH,
Telephone: 0171 978 8482/642 5777
E-mail:claphamchambers@compuserve.com
Call Date: Oct 1996, Lincoln's Inn
Qualifications: [BSc (Hons)(Newc), Dip in
Computer , Studies (Aberdeen), Dip in
Law (Northum)]

STRONGMAN IAN MELVILLE

8 Fountain Court
Steelhouse Lane, Birmingham B4 6DR,
Telephone: 0121 236 5514/5
E-mail: clerks@no8chambers.co.uk
*Call Date: July 1981, Lincoln's Inn
Pupil Master*
Qualifications: [LLB (Hons)]

STRUDWICK MISS LINDA DIANE

Hollis Whiteman Chambers
3rd Floor, Queen Elizabeth Bldg, Temple,
London EC4Y 9BS,
Telephone: 020 7583 5766
E-mail:barristers@holliswhiteman.co.uk
*Call Date: July 1973, Lincoln's Inn
Pupil Master*
Qualifications: [BA]

STRUTT MARTIN ANDREW

3 Paper Buildings
Temple, London EC4Y 7EU,
Telephone: 020 7583 8055
E-mail: London@3paper.com
3 Paper Buildings (Bournemouth)
20 Lorne Park Road, Bournemouth,
Dorset, BH1 1JN,
Telephone: 01202 292102
E-mail: Bournemouth@3paper.com
3 Paper Buildings (Winchester)
4 St Peter Street, Winchester SO23 8BW,
Telephone: 01962 868884
E-mail: winchester@3paper.com
3 Paper Buildings (Oxford)
1 Alfred Street, High Street, Oxford
OX1 4EH, Telephone: 01865 793736
E-mail: oxford@3paper.com
Call Date: Nov 1981, Inner Temple
Qualifications: [BA (Cantab)]

STUART BRUCE IAN

4 King's Bench Walk
Ground/First Floor/Basement, Temple,
London EC4Y 7DL,
Telephone: 0171 822 8822
E-mail: 4kbw@barristersatlaw.com
Call Date: Nov 1977, Gray's Inn
Pupil Master

STUART DOUGLAS MARK

15 Winckley Square
Preston PR1 3JJ,
Telephone: 01772 252828
E-mail:clerks@winckleysq.demon.co.uk
Call Date: Nov 1985, Gray's Inn
Qualifications: [BA (Newc)]

STUART JAMES WILLIAM

Lamb Chambers
Lamb Building, Temple, London
EC4Y 7AS, Telephone: 020 7797 8300
E-mail: lambchambers@link.org
Call Date: Oct 1990, Gray's Inn
Qualifications: [MA (Cantab)]

STUART-SMITH JEREMY HUGH QC (1997)

2 Temple Gardens
Temple, London EC4Y 9AY,
Telephone: 0171 583 6041
E-mail: clerks@2templegardens.co.uk
Call Date: July 1978, Gray's Inn
Assistant Recorder
Qualifications: [MA (Cantab)]

STUBBS ANDREW JAMES

St Paul's House
5th Floor, St Paul's House, 23 Park Square
South, Leeds LS1 2ND,
Telephone: 0113 2455866
E-mail: catherinegrimshaw@stpauls-
chambers.demon.co.uk
Call Date: July 1988, Lincoln's Inn
Qualifications: [LLB (Hons) (Notts)]

STUBBS MISS REBECCA

13 Old Square
Ground Floor, Lincoln's Inn, London
WC2A 3UA, Telephone: 0171 404 4800
E-mail: clerks@13oldsquare.law.co.uk
Call Date: Oct 1994, Middle Temple
Qualifications: [BA (Hons)(Cantab)]

STUBBS WILLIAM FREDERICK QC (1978)

Erskine Chambers
30 Lincoln's Inn Fields, Lincoln's Inn,
London WC2A 3PF,
Telephone: 0171 242 5532
E-mail:clerks@erskine-chambers.co.uk
Call Date: July 1957, Gray's Inn
Qualifications: [MA, LLB (Cantab)]

STUDD MISS ANNE ELIZABETH

5 Essex Court
1st Floor, Temple, London EC4Y 9AH,
Telephone: 0171 410 2000
E-mail: barristers@5essexcourt.co.uk
Call Date: July 1988, Gray's Inn
Pupil Master
Qualifications: [BA (Lond)]

STUDER MARK EDGAR WALTER

Chambers of Mr Peter Crampin QC
Ground Floor, 11 New Square, Lincoln's
Inn, London WC2A 3QB,
Telephone: 020 7831 0081
E-mail: 11newsquare.co.uk
Call Date: July 1976, Lincoln's Inn
Pupil Master
Qualifications: [BA (Oxon)]

STURMAN JAMES ANTHONY

3 Hare Court
1 Little Essex Street, London WC2R 3LD,
Telephone: 0171 395 2000
Call Date: July 1982, Gray's Inn
Pupil Master
Qualifications: [LLB (Reading)]

STUTTARD ARTHUR RUPERT DAVIES

Manchester House Chambers
18-22 Bridge Street, Manchester M3 3BZ,
Telephone: 0161 834 7007
Queens Chambers
4 Camden Place, Preston PR1 3JL,
Telephone: 01772 828300
Queen's Chambers
5 John Dalton Street, Manchester M2 6ET,
Telephone: 0161 834 6875/4738
Call Date: Feb 1967, Middle Temple
Pupil Master
Qualifications: [MA (Oxon)]

D

STYLES CLIVE RICHARD

Becket Chambers
17 New Dover Road, Canterbury, Kent,
CT1 3AS, Telephone: 01227 786331
Call Date: 1990, Gray's Inn
Qualifications: [LLB (Hons)]

STYLES MARK PATRICK

Broad Chare
33 Broad Chare, Newcastle upon Tyne
NE1 3DQ, Telephone: 0191 232 0541
E-mail:clerks@broadcharechambers.law.co.uk
Call Date: July 1988, Inner Temple
Pupil Master
Qualifications: [LLB (Lancaster)]

SUCH FREDERICK RUDOLPH CHARLES

Broad Chare
33 Broad Chare, Newcastle upon Tyne
NE1 3DQ, Telephone: 0191 232 0541
E-mail:clerks@broadcharechambers.law.co.uk
Call Date: Feb 1960, Gray's Inn
Recorder
Qualifications: [MA, FCIArb]

SUCKLING ALAN BLAIR QC (1983)

Hollis Whiteman Chambers
3rd Floor, Queen Elizabeth Bldg, Temple,
London EC4Y 9BS,
Telephone: 020 7583 5766
E-mail:barristers@holliswhiteman.co.uk
Call Date: July 1963, Middle Temple
Recorder
Qualifications: [BA, LLB (Cantab)]

SUGAR SIMON GARETH

5 New Square
Ground Floor, Lincoln's Inn, London
WC2A 3RJ, Telephone: 020 7404 0404
E-mail:chambers@fivenewsquare.demon.co.uk
Call Date: Nov 1990, Middle Temple
Qualifications: [LLB (Warw)]

SUGARMAN JASON ASHLEY

2 Pump Court
1st Floor, Temple, London EC4Y 7AH,
Telephone: 0171 353 5597
Call Date: July 1995, Inner Temple
Qualifications: [BA (Dunelm), CPE (Lond)]

SUGGETT IAIN ROBERT OTTAR

Equity Chambers
3rd Floor, 153a Corporation Street,
Birmingham B4 6PH,
Telephone: 0121 233 2100
E-mail: equityatusa.com
Call Date: Nov 1989, Lincoln's Inn
Qualifications: [LLB (Hons)]

SUKUL RABI SHANKAR

Balham Chambers
82 Balham High Road, London
SW12 9AG, Telephone: 0181 675 4609
Call Date: July 1988, Lincoln's Inn
Qualifications: [LLB (Hons)]

SULLIVAN MS JANE TERESA

Hollis Whiteman Chambers
3rd Floor, Queen Elizabeth Bldg, Temple,
London EC4Y 9BS,
Telephone: 020 7583 5766
E-mail:barristers@holliswhiteman.co.uk
Call Date: July 1984, Inner Temple
Pupil Master, Assistant Recorder
Qualifications: [LLB, BA (Lond)]

SULLIVAN MISS LINDA ELIZABETH QC (1994)

35 Essex Street
Temple, London WC2R 3AR,
Telephone: 0171 353 6381
E-mail: derek_jenkins@link.org
17 Carlton Crescent
Southampton SO15 2XR,
Telephone: 023 8032 0320/0823 2003
E-mail: greg@jg17cc.co.uk
Call Date: 1973, Middle Temple
Recorder
Qualifications: [BA]

SULLIVAN MS LISA ANN

New Court
Temple, London EC4Y 9BE,
Telephone: 0171 583 5123/0510
Call Date: 1997, Inner Temple
Qualifications: [BA (Oxon)]

SULLIVAN MARK ANDREW

3 Paper Buildings
Temple, London EC4Y 7EU,
Telephone: 020 7583 8055
E-mail: London@3paper.com

3 Paper Buildings (Winchester)
4 St Peter Street, Winchester SO23 8BW,
Telephone: 01962 868884
E-mail: winchester@3paper.com
3 Paper Buildings (Bournemouth)
20 Lorne Park Road, Bournemouth,
Dorset, BH1 1JN,
Telephone: 01202 292102
E-mail: Bournemouth@3paper.com
3 Paper Buildings (Oxford)
1 Alfred Street, High Street, Oxford
OX1 4EH, Telephone: 01865 793736
E-mail: oxford@3paper.com
Call Date: 1997, Middle Temple
Qualifications: [LLB (Hons)(Bris)]

SULLIVAN MICHAEL JEROME

One Essex Court
Ground Floor, Temple, London
EC4Y 9AR, Telephone: 020 7583 2000
E-mail: clerks@oneessexcourt.co.uk
Call Date: July 1983, Middle Temple
Pupil Master
Qualifications: [LLB Hons (Manch)]

SULLIVAN RORY MYLES

19 Old Buildings
Lincoln's Inn, London WC2A 3UP,
Telephone: 0171 405 2001
E-mail: clerks@oldbuildingsip.com
Call Date: Oct 1992, Gray's Inn
Qualifications: [MA (Oxon)]

SULLIVAN SCOTT

Barnard's Inn Chambers
6th Floor, Halton House, 20-23 Holborn,
London EC1N 2JD,
Telephone: 0171 369 6969
E-mail: clerks@biclaw.co.uk
Call Date: Nov 1991, Inner Temple
Qualifications: [LLB (So'ton)]

SULTAN AMIR

Call Date: July 1983, Lincoln's Inn
Qualifications: [BA (Law)]

SULTAN MS NEELIM

Acre Lane Neighbourhood Chambers
30A Acre Lane, London SW2 5SG,
Telephone: 0171 274 4400
E-mail:barristerschambers@acrelane.demon.co.uk
Call Date: Nov 1993, Gray's Inn
Qualifications: [BA (Hull), LLM (Lond)]

SUMERAY MRS CAROLINE SARAH

4 Brick Court
Temple, London EC4Y 9AD,
Telephone: 0171 797 8910
E-mail: medhurst@dial.pipex.com
Call Date: July 1993, Middle Temple
Qualifications: [LLB (Hons)(Wolver)]

SUMMERS BENJAMIN DYLAN JAMES

Hollis Whiteman Chambers
3rd Floor, Queen Elizabeth Bldg, Temple,
London EC4Y 9BS,
Telephone: 020 7583 5766
E-mail:barristers@holliswhiteman.co.uk
Call Date: Nov 1994, Inner Temple
Qualifications: [LLB (Sussex)]

SUMMERS MARK JOHN

2 Paper Buildings
1st Floor, Temple, London EC4Y 7ET,
Telephone: 020 7556 5500
E-mail: clerks@2pbbarristers.co.uk
Call Date: Nov 1996, Inner Temple
Qualifications: [LLB (Exon)]

SUMNER DAVID MOORCROFT

Lincoln House Chambers
5th Floor, Lincoln House, 1 Brazennose
Street, Manchester M2 5EL,
Telephone: 0161 832 5701
E-mail: info@lincolnhse.co.uk
Call Date: May 1963, Lincoln's Inn
Pupil Master, Recorder

SUMPTION JONATHAN PHILIP CHADWICK QC (1986)

Brick Court Chambers
7-8 Essex Street, London WC2R 3LD,
Telephone: 0171 379 3550
E-mail: [surname]@brickcourt.co.uk
Call Date: July 1975, Inner Temple
Recorder
Qualifications: [MA (Oxon)]

SUMPTON CHRISTOPHER MARTIN WILSON

15 North Church Street Chambers
15 North Church Street, Sheffield
S1 2DH, Telephone: 0114 2759708/
2738380
Call Date: Nov 1991, Inner Temple
Qualifications: [LLB (Warw)]

SUNNUCKS JAMES HORACE GEORGE

5 New Square
Ground Floor, Lincoln's Inn, London
WC2A 3RJ, Telephone: 020 7404 0404
E-mail:chambers@fivenewsquare.demon.co.
uk
Call Date: Jan 1950, Lincoln's Inn
Pupil Master
Qualifications: [MA (Cantab)]

SUPPERSTONE MICHAEL ALAN QC (1991)

11 King's Bench Walk
Temple, London EC4Y 7EQ,
Telephone: 0171 632 8500/583 0610
E-mail: clerksroom@11kbw.com
Call Date: Nov 1973, Middle Temple
Recorder
Qualifications: [MA, BCL (Oxon)]

SURI YASIN UL RAHMAN KHAN

2 Salvia Gardens
Perivale, Middlesex, UB6 7PG,
Telephone: 0181 997 9905
Call Date: Nov 1963, Lincoln's Inn
Qualifications: [BA, LLB]

SUSMAN PETER JOSEPH QC (1997)

New Court Chambers
5 Verulam Buildings, Gray's Inn, London
WC1R 5LY, Telephone: 0171 831 9500
E-mail: mail@newcourtchambers.com
Call Date: Nov 1966, Middle Temple
Recorder
Qualifications: [MA (Oxon) JD, (Chicago)]

SUTCLIFFE ANDREW HAROLD WENTWORTH

3 Verulam Buildings
London WC1R 5NT,
Telephone: 0171 831 8441
E-mail: clerks@3verulam.co.uk
Call Date: Nov 1983, Inner Temple
Pupil Master
Qualifications: [MA (Oxon)]

SUTHERLAND PAUL JEFFREY JOHN-PAUL

Chambers of John L Powell QC
Four New Square, Lincoln's Inn, London
WC2A 3RJ, Telephone: 0171 797 8000
E-mail: barristers@4newsquare.com
Call Date: Nov 1992, Middle Temple
Qualifications: [MA (Oxon), MA (Cantab)]

SUTHERLAND WILLIAMS MARK

3 Paper Buildings
Temple, London EC4Y 7EU,
Telephone: 020 7583 8055
E-mail: London@3paper.com
3 Paper Buildings (Bournemouth)
20 Lorne Park Road, Bournemouth,
Dorset, BH1 1JN,
Telephone: 01202 292102
E-mail: Bournemouth@3paper.com
3 Paper Buildings (Winchester)
4 St Peter Street, Winchester SO23 8BW,
Telephone: 01962 868884
E-mail: winchester@3paper.com
3 Paper Buildings (Oxford)
1 Alfred Street, High Street, Oxford
OX1 4EH, Telephone: 01865 793736
E-mail: oxford@3paper.com
Call Date: Oct 1995, Inner Temple
Qualifications: [LLB (Exon)]

SUTTLE STEPHEN JOHN

1 Brick Court
1st Floor, Temple, London EC4Y 9BY,
Telephone: 0171 353 8845
E-mail: clerks@1brickcourt.co.uk
Call Date: 1980, Gray's Inn
Pupil Master
Qualifications: [MA (Oxon)]

SUTTON ALASTAIR MORRIS

Blackstone Chambers
Blackstone House, Temple, London
EC4Y 9BW, Telephone: 0171 583 1770
E-mail:clerks@blackstonechambers.com
Call Date: May 1972, Middle Temple
Qualifications: [LLB (Aberdeen), LLM (Lond),
Dip Int Air Law]

SUTTON CLIVE RAYMOND

Northampton Chambers
22 Albion Place, Northampton NN1 1UD,
Telephone: 01604 636271
Call Date: July 1987, Inner Temple
Pupil Master
Qualifications: [LLB]

SUTTON MRS KAROLINE ROSEMARIE

14 Gray's Inn Square
Gray's Inn, London WC1R 5JP,
Telephone: 0171 242 0858
E-mail: 100712.2134@compuserve.com
Call Date: Nov 1986, Middle Temple
Qualifications: [LLB (Hons)]

SUTTON KEITH ANDREW

Corn Exchange Chambers
5th Floor, Fenwick Street, Liverpool
L2 7QS, Telephone: 0151 227 1081/5009
Call Date: Nov 1988, Gray's Inn
Qualifications: [LLB]

SUTTON MARK

4 Field Court
Gray's Inn, London WC1R 5EA,
Telephone: 0171 440 6900
E-mail: chambers@4fieldcourt.co.uk
Call Date: July 1982, Middle Temple
Pupil Master
Qualifications: [BA]

SUTTON PHILIP JULIAN

Bell Yard Chambers
116/118 Chancery Lane, London
WC2A 1PP, Telephone: 0171 306 9292
Call Date: Nov 1971, Inner Temple
Pupil Master
Qualifications: [LLB (Hons)]

SUTTON RICHARD PATRICK QC (1993)

18 Red Lion Court
(Off Fleet Street), London EC4A 3EB,
Telephone: 0171 520 6000
E-mail: chambers@18rlc.co.uk
Thornwood House
102 New London Road, Chelmsford,
Essex, CM2 0RG,
Telephone: 01245 280880
E-mail: chambers@18rlc.co.uk
Call Date: July 1969, Middle Temple
Recorder
Qualifications: [BA (Oxon)]

SUTTON RICHARD WILLIAM WALLACE

Chambers of Andrew Campbell QC
10 Park Square, Leeds LS1 2LH,
Telephone: 0113 2455438
E-mail: clerks@10pksq.co.uk
Call Date: July 1968, Inner Temple
Pupil Master
Qualifications: [BA (Oxon)]

SUTTON MISS RUTH DEBORAH

24a St John Street
Manchester M3 4DF,
Telephone: 0161 833 9628
Call Date: Nov 1994, Middle Temple
Qualifications: [LLB (Hons)]

SUTTON-MATTOCKS CHRISTOPHER JOHN

2 Paper Buildings
1st Floor, Temple, London EC4Y 7ET,
Telephone: 020 7556 5500
E-mail: clerks@2pbbarristers.co.uk
Call Date: July 1975, Middle Temple
Qualifications: [MA (Oxon)]

SWAFFIELD MRS HELEN LINDA

Regent Chambers
8 Pall Mall, Hanley, Stoke On Trent
ST1 1ER, Telephone: 01782 286666
E-mail: regent@ftech.co.uk
Call Date: 1988, Lincoln's Inn
Qualifications: [LLB (Hons) (Leics), Dip D'et
Jur FR]

SWAIN MRS FIONA PATRICIA

11 King's Bench Walk
1st Floor, Temple, London EC4Y 7EQ,
Telephone: 0171 353 3337
E-mail: fmuller11@aol.com
11 King's Bench Walk
3 Park Court, Park Cross Street, Leeds
LS1 2QH, Telephone: 0113 297 1200
Call Date: July 1983, Gray's Inn
Pupil Master
Qualifications: [BA]

SWAIN MISS HANNAH

23 Essex Street
London WC2R 3AS,
Telephone: 0171 413 0353/836 8366
E-mail:clerks@essexstreet23.demon.co.uk
Call Date: Oct 1994, Gray's Inn
Qualifications: [BA]

SWAIN JON DAVID

Furnival Chambers
32 Furnival Street, London EC4A 1JQ,
Telephone: 0171 405 3232
E-mail: clerks@furnivallaw.co.uk
Call Date: Nov 1983, Lincoln's Inn
Pupil Master
Qualifications: [BSc (Hons)]

SWAIN RICHARD HENRY

Ropewalk Chambers
24 The Ropewalk, Nottingham NG1 5EF,
Telephone: 0115 9472581
E-mail: administration@ropewalk co.uk
Call Date: July 1969, Gray's Inn
Assistant Recorder
Qualifications: [LLB (B'ham)]

SWAINSON RICHARD JOSEPH

10 King's Bench Walk
Ground Floor, Temple, London
EC4Y 7EB, Telephone: 0171 353 7742
E-mail: 10kbw@lineone.net
Call Date: Oct 1994, Lincoln's Inn
Qualifications: [LLB (Hons)(Lond)]

SWAINSTON MICHAEL GEORGE

Brick Court Chambers
7-8 Essex Street, London WC2R 3LD,
Telephone: 0171 379 3550
E-mail: [surname]@brickcourt.co.uk
Call Date: Nov 1985, Lincoln's Inn
Pupil Master
Qualifications: [MA (Cantab), BCL, (Oxon)]

SWALLOW MISS JODIE

Nicholas Street Chambers
22 Nicholas Street, Chester CH1 2NX,
Telephone: 01244 323886
E-mail: clerks@40king.co.uk
Call Date: Nov 1989, Inner Temple
Qualifications: [LLB]

SWAN IAN CHRISTOPHER

Two Crown Office Row
Ground Floor, Temple, London
EC4Y 7HJ, Telephone: 020 7797 8100
E-mail: mail@2cor.co.uk, or to individual
barristers at: [barrister's
surname]@2cor.co.uk
Call Date: July 1985, Middle Temple
Pupil Master
Qualifications: [BA (Oxon)]

SWAN TIMOTHY ROBERT MUNGO

1 Paper Buildings
1st Floor, Temple, London EC4Y 7EP,
Telephone: 0171 353 3728/4953
Call Date: Nov 1983, Gray's Inn
Pupil Master
Qualifications: [BA (Oxon)]

SWAROOP SUDHANSHU

20 Essex Street
London WC2R 3AL,
Telephone: 0171 583 9294
E-mail: clerks@20essexst.com
Call Date: Oct 1997, Inner Temple
Qualifications: [MA (Cantab), BCL (Oxon)]

SWEENEY CHRISTIAN NOEL

3 Paper Buildings
Temple, London EC4Y 7EU,
Telephone: 020 7583 8055
E-mail: London@3paper.com

3 Paper Buildings (Bournemouth)
20 Lorne Park Road, Bournemouth,
Dorset, BH1 1JN,
Telephone: 01202 292102
E-mail: Bournemouth@3paper.com
3 Paper Buildings (Winchester)
4 St Peter Street, Winchester SO23 8BW,
Telephone: 01962 868884
E-mail: winchester@3paper.com
3 Paper Buildings (Oxford)
1 Alfred Street, High Street, Oxford
OX1 4EH, Telephone: 01865 793736
E-mail: oxford@3paper.com
Call Date: Oct 1992, Gray's Inn
Qualifications: [LL.B (Reading)]

SWEENEY NIGEL HAMILTON

6 King's Bench Walk
Ground Floor, Temple, London
EC4Y 7DR, Telephone: 0171 583 0410
E-mail: worsley@6kbw.freeserve.co.uk
Call Date: July 1976, Middle Temple
Pupil Master, Recorder
Qualifications: [LLB (Hons)]

SWEENEY NOEL CHRISTOPHER

Veritas Chambers
33 Corn Street, Bristol BS1 1HT,
Telephone: 0117 930 8802
Call Date: July 1975, Gray's Inn
Pupil Master
Qualifications: [LLB]

SWEET MISS LOUISE JUNE

2-4 Tudor Street
London EC4Y 0AA,
Telephone: 0171 797 7111
E-mail: clerks@rfqc.co.uk
Call Date: Oct 1994, Gray's Inn
Qualifications: [LLB (Hull)]

SWEETING DEREK ANTHONY

9 Bedford Row
London WC1R 4AZ,
Telephone: 0171 242 3555
E-mail: clerks@9br.co.uk
Call Date: July 1983, Middle Temple
Pupil Master
Qualifications: [MA (Cantab)]

SWEETING MISS MARGARET FRANCIS

New Court Chambers
3 Broad Chare, Newcastle upon Tyne
NE1 3DQ, Telephone: 0191 232 1980
Call Date: Oct 1996, Lincoln's Inn
Qualifications: [LLB (Hons)(Notts), MA
(Lond)]

SWERLING ROBERT HARRY

13 Old Square
Ground Floor, Lincoln's Inn, London
WC2A 3UA, Telephone: 0171 404 4800
E-mail: clerks@13oldsquare.law.co.uk
Call Date: Nov 1996, Lincoln's Inn
Qualifications: [BA (Hons)]

SWERSKY ABRAHAM JOWEL

Gray's Inn Tax Chambers
3rd Floor, Gray's Inn Chambers, Gray's
Inn, London WC1R 5JA,
Telephone: 0171 242 2642
E-mail: clerks@taxbar.com
Call Date: Nov 1996, Lincoln's Inn
Qualifications: [B.Comm(Witwatersrand,),
LLB (S.Africa)]

SWIFFEN GUY CHARLES

Park Lane Chambers
19 Westgate, Leeds LS1 2RD,
Telephone: 0113 2285000
E-mail:clerks@parklanechambers.co.uk
Call Date: Nov 1991, Lincoln's Inn
Qualifications: [BA (Hons), Dip Law]

SWIFT ANTONY

Harrow on the Hill Chambers
60 High Street, Harrow-on-the-Hill,
Middlesex, HA1 3LL,
Telephone: 0181 423 7444
Windsor Barristers' Chambers
Windsor Telephone: 01753 648899
E-mail: law@windsorchambers.co.uk
Call Date: 1984, Inner Temple
Qualifications: [BA (Hons) (Grad),
Inst.F.W.R.I.]

SWIFT MISS CAROLINE JANE QC (1993)

22 Old Buildings
Lincoln's Inn, London WC2A 3UJ,
Telephone: 0171 831 0222
Byrom Street Chambers
Byrom Street, Manchester M3 4PF,
Telephone: 0161 829 2100
E-mail: Byromst25@aol.com
Call Date: Nov 1977, Inner Temple
Recorder
Qualifications: [BA (Dunelm)]

SWIFT JOHN ANTHONY QC (1981)

Monckton Chambers
4 Raymond Buildings, Gray's Inn, London
WC1R 5BP, Telephone: 0171 405 7211
E-mail: chambers@monckton.co.uk
Call Date: Nov 1965, Inner Temple
Qualifications: [MA (Oxon)]

SWIFT JONATHAN MARK

11 King's Bench Walk
Temple, London EC4Y 7EQ,
Telephone: 0171 632 8500/583 0610
E-mail: clerksroom@11kbw.com
Call Date: July 1989, Inner Temple
Pupil Master
Qualifications: [BA [Oxon], LLM [Cantab]]

SWIFT JONATHAN PETER

College Chambers
19 Carlton Cresent, Southampton
SO15 2ET, Telephone: 01703 230338
1 Mitre Court Buildings
Temple, London EC4Y 7BS,
Telephone: 0171 797 7070
E-mail: clerks@1mcb.com
Call Date: Nov 1977, Inner Temple
Pupil Master, Assistant Recorder
Qualifications: [LLB (Hons)(Lond)]

SWIFT LIONEL QC (1975)

4 Paper Buildings
1st Floor, Temple, London EC4Y 7EX,
Telephone: 0171 583 0816/353 1131
E-mail: clerks@4paperbuildings.co.uk
Call Date: Feb 1959, Inner Temple
Qualifications: [LLB (lond), BCL, (Oxon), JD (Chicago)]

SWIFT MALCOLM ROBIN QC (1988)

Park Court Chambers
16 Park Place, Leeds LS1 2SJ,
Telephone: 0113 2433277
6 Gray's Inn Square
Ground Floor, Gray's Inn, London
WC1R 5AZ, Telephone: 0171 242 1052
E-mail: 6graysinn@clara.co.uk
Call Date: July 1970, Gray's Inn
Recorder
Qualifications: [LLB, AKC]

SWIFT STEVEN GEOFFREY

India Buildings Chambers
Water Street, Liverpool L2 0XG,
Telephone: 0151 243 6000
E-mail: clerks@chambers.u-net.com
Call Date: Nov 1991, Inner Temple
Qualifications: [LLB (Lan)]

SWINDELLS MISS HEATHER HUGHSON QC (1995)

Chambers of Michael Pert QC
36 Bedford Row, London WC1R 4JH,
Telephone: 0171 421 8000
E-mail: 36bedfordrow@link.org
Chambers of Michael Pert QC
104 New Walk, Leicester LE1 7EA,
Telephone: 0116 249 2020
Chambers of Michael Pert QC
24 Albion Place, Northampton NN1 1UD,
Telephone: 01604 602333
St Philip's Chambers
Fountain Court, Steelhouse Lane,
Birmingham B4 6DR,
Telephone: 0121 246 7000
E-mail: clerks@st-philips.co.uk
Call Date: Nov 1974, Middle Temple
Recorder
Qualifications: [MA (Oxon)]

SWINNERTON DAVID MICHAEL

6 Fountain Court
Steelhouse Lane, Birmingham B4 6DR,
Telephone: 0121 233 3282
E-mail: clerks@sixfountain.co.uk
Call Date: Nov 1995, Lincoln's Inn
Qualifications: [BA (Hons)]

SWINSTEAD DAVID LLOYD

3 Paper Buildings
Temple, London EC4Y 7EU,
Telephone: 020 7583 8055
E-mail: London@3paper.com
3 Paper Buildings (Winchester)
4 St Peter Street, Winchester SO23 8BW,
Telephone: 01962 868884
E-mail: winchester@3paper.com
3 Paper Buildings (Bournemouth)
20 Lorne Park Road, Bournemouth,
Dorset, BH1 1JN,
Telephone: 01202 292102
E-mail: Bournemouth@3paper.com
3 Paper Buildings (Oxford)
1 Alfred Street, High Street, Oxford
OX1 4EH, Telephone: 01865 793736
E-mail: oxford@3paper.com
Call Date: July 1970, Inner Temple
Pupil Master

SWIRSKY ADAM ABRAHAM BURL BRADBURY

7 Stone Buildings (also at 11 Bolt Court)
1st Floor, Lincoln's Inn, London
WC2A 3SZ, Telephone: 0171 242 0961
E-mail:larthur@7stonebuildings.law.co.uk
11 Bolt Court (also at 7 Stone Buildings – 1st Floor)
London EC4A 3DQ,
Telephone: 0171 353 2300
E-mail: boltct11@aol.com
Redhill Chambers
Seloduct House, 30 Station Road, Redhill,
Surrey, RH1 1NF,
Telephone: 01737 780781
Call Date: Nov 1989, Middle Temple
Pupil Master
Qualifications: [B.Sc, M.Sc [Lond]]

SWIRSKY JOSHUA MAX BRADBURY

Chambers of Norman Palmer
2 Field Court, Gray's Inn, London
WC1R 5BB, Telephone: 0171 405 6114
E-mail: fieldct2@netcomuk.co.uk
Call Date: Nov 1987, Middle Temple
Qualifications: [BA (Dunelm)]

SYDENHAM COLIN PETER

4 Breams Buildings
London EC4A 1AQ,
Telephone: 0171 353 5835/430 1221
E-mail:breams@4breamsbuildings.law.co.uk
Call Date: July 1963, Middle Temple
Pupil Master
Qualifications: [MA (Cantab)]

SYED GULZAR SHAH

Paradise Chambers
26 Paradise Square, Sheffield S1 2DE,
Telephone: 0114 2738951
E-mail: timbooth@paradise-sq.co.uk
Call Date: July 1983, Gray's Inn
Qualifications: [LLB (Lanc)]

SYED MISS MARYAM HASSAN

2 Paper Buildings, Basement North
Temple, London EC4Y 7ET,
Telephone: 0171 936 2613
E-mail: post@2paper.co.uk
Call Date: Oct 1993, Lincoln's Inn
Qualifications: [LLB (Hons)(Lond)]

SYED MOHAMMAD ALI

39 Park Avenue
Mitcham, Surrey, CR4 2ER,
Telephone: 0181 648 1684
Tower Hamlets Barristers Chambers
First Floor, 45 Brick Lane, London
E1 6PU, Telephone: 0171 247 9825
Call Date: July 1970, Lincoln's Inn
Qualifications: [BA, MA]

SYED MUZAHID ALI

10 Millfields Road
London E5 0SB,
Telephone: 0181 986 8059
Call Date: Nov 1971, Inner Temple
Qualifications: [B.Com , LLB]

SYFRET NICHOLAS

13 King's Bench Walk
1st Floor, Temple, London EC4Y 7EN,
Telephone: 0171 353 7204
E-mail: clerks@13kbw.law.co.uk

D

King's Bench Chambers
32 Beaumont Street, Oxford OX1 2NP,
Telephone: 01865 311066
E-mail: clerks@kbc-oxford.law.co.uk
Call Date: July 1979, Middle Temple
Pupil Master
Qualifications: [MA (Cantab)]

SYKES (JAMES) RICHARD QC (1981)

Erskine Chambers
30 Lincoln's Inn Fields, Lincoln's Inn,
London WC2A 3PF,
Telephone: 0171 242 5532
E-mail:clerks@erskine-chambers.co.uk
Call Date: June 1958, Lincoln's Inn
Qualifications: [MA (Cantab)]

SYKES RICHARD ROBERT

Trinity Chambers
140 New London Road, Chelmsford,
Essex, CM2 0AW,
Telephone: 01245 605040
E-mail:clerks@trinitychambers.law.co.uk
Call Date: July 1996, Inner Temple
Qualifications: [BA (Dunelm)]

SYLVESTER MIO PAUL

11 King's Bench Walk
1st Floor, Temple, London EC4Y 7EQ,
Telephone: 0171 353 3337
E-mail: fmuller11@aol.com
11 King's Bench Walk
3 Park Court, Park Cross Street, Leeds
LS1 2QH, Telephone: 0113 297 1200
Call Date: July 1980, Middle Temple
Pupil Master
Qualifications: [MA, LLB (Cantab)]

SYMMS MISS KATHRYN ANN

Martins Building
2nd Floor, No 4 Water Street, Liverpool
L2 3SP, Telephone: 0151 236 5818/4919
Call Date: Oct 1990, Gray's Inn
Qualifications: [BA (Cantab)]

SYMONS CHRISTOPHER JOHN MAURICE QC (1989)

3 Verulam Buildings
London WC1R 5NT,
Telephone: 0171 831 8441
E-mail: clerks@3verulam.co.uk
Call Date: July 1972, Middle Temple

Recorder
Qualifications: [BA (Kent)]

SYRIL GEORGE CARMEL

Law Chambers
2nd Floor, 5 Cardiff Road, Luton,
Bedfordshire, LU1 1PP,
Telephone: 01582 431352 or 0958 674785
Call Date: July 1980, Lincoln's Inn
Qualifications: [MA,LLB]

SZANTO GREGORY JOHN MICHAEL

Eastbourne Chambers
15 Hyde Gardens, Eastbourne, East
Sussex, BN21 4PR,
Telephone: 01323 642102
Call Date: July 1967, Inner Temple

SZERARD ANDREI MICHAEL

Goldsmith Chambers
Ground Floor, Goldsmith Building,
Temple, London EC4Y 7BL,
Telephone: 0171 353 6802/3/4/5
E-mail:clerks@goldsmithchambers.law.co.uk
Call Date: Apr 1986, Inner Temple
Pupil Master
Qualifications: [LLB (Hull)]

SZUMOWSKA MISS HELENA CECILIA

Westgate Chambers
144 High Street, Lewes, East Sussex,
BN7 1XT, Telephone: 01273 480510
Call Date: July 1989, Inner Temple
Qualifications: [BSc, Dip Law]

SZWED MISS ELIZABETH MARIA

One Garden Court Family Law Chambers
Ground Floor, Temple, London
EC4Y 9BJ, Telephone: 0171 797 7900
E-mail: clerks@onegardencourt.co.uk
Call Date: Nov 1974, Middle Temple
Pupil Master
Qualifications: [LLB (Leeds)]

TABACHNIK ANDREW DANIEL

4-5 Gray's Inn Square
Ground Floor, Gray's Inn, London
WC1R 5JP, Telephone: 0171 404 5252
E-mail:chambers@4-5graysinnsquare.co.uk
Call Date: Nov 1991, Inner Temple
Qualifications: [MA (Cambs), LLM
(Columbia)]

TABACHNIK ELDRED QC (1982)

11 King's Bench Walk
Temple, London EC4Y 7EQ,
Telephone: 0171 632 8500/583 0610
E-mail: clerksroom@11kbw.com
Call Date: July 1970, Inner Temple
Assistant Recorder
Qualifications: [BA, LLB (Cape, Town), LLM
(Lond)]

TABOR JAMES PATRICK QC (1995)

Albion Chambers
Broad Street, Bristol BS1 1DR,
Telephone: 0117 9272144
Five Paper Buildings
1st Floor, Five Paper Bldgs, Temple,
London EC4Y 7HB,
Telephone: 0171 583 6117
E-mail:clerks@5-paperbuildings.law.co.uk
Call Date: July 1974, Middle Temple

TACKABERRY JOHN ANTONY QC (1982)

Arbitration Chambers
22 Willes Road, London NW5 3DS,
Telephone: 020 7267 2137
E-mail: jatqc@atack.demon.co.uk
40 King Street
Manchester M2 6BA,
Telephone: 0161 832 9082
E-mail: clerks@40kingstreet.co.uk
Assize Court Chambers
14 Small Street, Bristol BS1 1DE,
Telephone: 0117 9264587
E-mail:chambers@assize-court-chambers.co.uk
Littman Chambers
12 Gray's Inn Square, London WC1R 5JP,
Telephone: 020 7404 4866
E-mail: admin@littmanchambers.com
Call Date: July 1967, Gray's Inn
Recorder
Qualifications: [MA, LLM, FCIARB, FFB]

TAFT CHRISTOPHER HEITON

St James's Chambers
68 Quay Street, Manchester M3 3EJ,
Telephone: 0161 834 7000
E-mail: clerks@stjameschambers.co.uk
Call Date: Oct 1997, Middle Temple
Qualifications: [LLB (Hons)(Manc)]

TAGER ROMIE QC (1995)

Hardwicke Building
New Square, Lincoln's Inn, London
WC2A 3SB, Telephone: 020 7242 2523
E-mail: clerks@hardwicke.co.uk
Call Date: Nov 1970, Middle Temple
Recorder
Qualifications: [LLM]

TAGGART NICHOLAS

4 Breams Buildings
London EC4A 1AQ,
Telephone: 0171 353 5835/430 1221
E-mail:breams@4breamsbuildings.law.co.uk
Call Date: Oct 1991, Middle Temple
Qualifications: [LLB (Hons)(Lond), BCL
(Oxon)]

TAGGART SAMUEL NICHOLAS

Clapham Chambers
21-25 Bedford Road, Clapham North,
London SW4 7SH,
Telephone: 0171 978 8482/642 5777
E-mail:claphamchambers@compuserve.com
Call Date: Nov 1992, Middle Temple
Qualifications: [LLB (Hons, Manch)]

TAGHAVI SHAHRAM

6 King's Bench Walk
Ground, Third & Fourth Floors, Temple,
London EC4Y 7DR,
Telephone: 0171 353 4931/583 0695
Call Date: Oct 1994, Gray's Inn
Qualifications: [LLB]

TAGLIAVINI MS LORNA MARIE

6 King's Bench Walk
Ground, Third & Fourth Floors, Temple,
London EC4Y 7DR,
Telephone: 0171 353 4931/583 0695
Call Date: Nov 1989, Inner Temple
Qualifications: [BA (Hons) (Brad), Dip Law
(City), LLM (LSE)]

TAIT ANDREW CHARLES GORDON

2 Harcourt Buildings
2nd Floor, Temple, London EC4Y 9DB,
Telephone: 020 7353 8415
E-mail: clerks@2hb.law.co.uk
Call Date: July 1981, Inner Temple
Pupil Master
Qualifications: [MA (Oxon)]

TAIT CAMPBELL

Lincoln House Chambers
5th Floor, Lincoln House, 1 Brazennose
Street, Manchester M2 5EL,
Telephone: 0161 832 5701
E-mail: info@lincolnhse.co.uk
Call Date: Nov 1979, Middle Temple
Pupil Master, Assistant Recorder
Qualifications: [LLB (Hons) (Lond)]

TAIT DONALD

Queens Square Chambers
56 Queens Square, Bristol BS1 4PR,
Telephone: 0117 921 1966
Call Date: Feb 1987, Inner Temple
Pupil Master
Qualifications: [BA (Leic)]

TALACCHI CARLO GIANCARLO

10 King's Bench Walk
Ground Floor, Temple, London
EC4Y 7EB, Telephone: 0171 353 7742
E-mail: 10kbw@lineone.net
Call Date: July 1986, Lincoln's Inn
Qualifications: [BSc (B'ham) LLM, (Cantab)]

TALBOT DENNIS

Exchange Chambers
Pearl Assurance House, Derby Square,
Liverpool L2 9XX,
Telephone: 0151 236 7747
E-mail:exchangechambers@btinternet.com
Call Date: July 1985, Gray's Inn
Qualifications: [ACMA]

TALBOT KENNEDY VERNON

Furnival Chambers
32 Furnival Street, London EC4A 1JQ,
Telephone: 0171 405 3232
E-mail: clerks@furnivallaw.co.uk
Call Date: Nov 1984, Gray's Inn
Qualifications: [BA]

TALBOT PATRICK JOHN QC (1990)

Serle Court Chambers
6 New Square, Lincoln's Inn, London
WC2A 3QS, Telephone: 0171 242 6105
E-mail: clerks@serlecourt.co.uk
Call Date: July 1969, Lincoln's Inn
Assistant Recorder
Qualifications: [MA (Oxon)]

TALBOT RICHARD KEVIN KENT

Deans Court Chambers
24 St John Street, Manchester M3 4DF,
Telephone: 0161 214 6000
E-mail: clerks@deanscourt.co.uk
Deans Court Chambers
41-43 Market Place, Preston PR1 1AH,
Telephone: 01772 555163
E-mail: clerks@deanscourt.co.uk
Call Date: July 1970, Inner Temple
Pupil Master, Recorder
Qualifications: [LLB]

TALBOT RICE MRS (ALICE) ELSPETH MIDDLETON

Twenty-Four Old Buildings
Ground Floor, Lincoln's Inn, London
WC2A 3UP, Telephone: 0171 404 0946
E-mail:clerks@24oldbuildings.law.co.uk
Call Date: Oct 1990, Lincoln's Inn
Pupil Master
Qualifications: [BA (Dunelm)]

TALBOT-BAGNALL JOHN RICHARD

2 Paper Buildings, Basement North
Temple, London EC4Y 7ET,
Telephone: 0171 936 2613
E-mail: post@2paper.co.uk
Call Date: Nov 1988, Inner Temple
Qualifications: [LLB (Shef)]

TALLON JOHN MARK

Pump Court Tax Chambers
16 Bedford Row, London WC1R 4EB,
Telephone: 0171 414 8080
4 Fountain Court
Steelhouse Lane, Birmingham B4 6DR,
Telephone: 0121 236 3476
Call Date: July 1975, Middle Temple
Pupil Master
Qualifications: [F.C.A.]

TAM ROBIN BING-KUEN

1 Temple Gardens
1st Floor, Temple, London EC4Y 9BB,
Telephone: 0171 583 1315/353 0407
E-mail: clerks@1templegardens.co.uk
Call Date: July 1986, Middle Temple
Pupil Master
Qualifications: [MA (Cantab)]

TAMLYN LLOYD JEFFREY

3/4 South Square
Gray's Inn, London WC1R 5HP,
Telephone: 0171 696 9900
E-mail: clerks@southsquare.com
Call Date: Nov 1991, Gray's Inn
Qualifications: [BA (Hons, Cantab)]

TAN MISS CHENG SIOH

1 Gray's Inn Square
Ground Floor, London WC1R 5AA,
Telephone: 0171 405 8946/7/8
Call Date: Nov 1970, Middle Temple
Pupil Master

TANKEL MRS RUTH SHOSHANA

St James's Chambers
68 Quay Street, Manchester M3 3EJ,
Telephone: 0161 834 7000
E-mail: clerks@stjameschambers.co.uk
Call Date: July 1990, Middle Temple
Qualifications: [LLB (Manch)]

TANNEY ANTHONY

Falcon Chambers
Falcon Court, London EC4Y 1AA,
Telephone: 0171 353 2484
E-mail: clerks@falcon-chambers.com
Call Date: Oct 1994, Lincoln's Inn
Qualifications: [BA (Hons), M.Jur (Durham)]

TANSEY ROCK BENEDICT QC (1990)

3 Gray's Inn Square
Ground Floor, London WC1R 5AH,
Telephone: 0171 520 5600
E-mail: clerks@3gis.co.uk
Call Date: July 1966, Lincoln's Inn
Recorder
Qualifications: [Dip Soc (Bristol) , LLB (Bristol) (Hons)]

TANZER JOHN BRIAN CAMILLE

One King's Bench Walk
1st Floor, Temple, London EC4Y 7DB,
Telephone: 0171 936 1500
E-mail: ddear@1kbw.co.uk
Call Date: Nov 1975, Gray's Inn
Pupil Master, Assistant Recorder
Qualifications: [BA]

TAPPER PAUL KENNEDY

Chartlands Chambers
3 St Giles Terrace, Northampton
NN1 2BN, Telephone: 01604 603322
Call Date: July 1991, Middle Temple
Qualifications: [LLB (Hons)]

TAPPIN MICHAEL JOHN

8 New Square
Lincoln's Inn, London WC2A 3QP,
Telephone: 0171 405 4321
E-mail: clerks@8newsquare.co.uk
Call Date: Oct 1991, Middle Temple
Pupil Master
Qualifications: [BA Hons, DPhil (Oxon, CPE]

TAPPING MISS SUSAN

10 King's Bench Walk
Ground Floor, Temple, London
EC4Y 7EB, Telephone: 0171 353 7742
E-mail: 10kbw@lineone.net
Call Date: July 1975, Middle Temple
Pupil Master, Recorder
Qualifications: [LLB (London)]

TAPSELL PAUL RICHARD

Becket Chambers
17 New Dover Road, Canterbury, Kent,
CT1 3AS, Telephone: 01227 786331
Call Date: 1991, Middle Temple
Qualifications: [LLB Hons (Lanc)]

TAPSON MISS LESLEY KATHERINE

Francis Taylor Building
Ground Floor, Temple, London
EC4Y 7BY, Telephone: 0171 353 7768/
7769/2711
E-mail:clerks@francistaylorbuilding.law.co.uk
Call Date: Nov 1982, Gray's Inn
Pupil Master
Qualifications: [LLB (Newc)]

TARBITT NICHOLAS EDWARD HENRY

6 Fountain Court
Steelhouse Lane, Birmingham B4 6DR,
Telephone: 0121 233 3282
E-mail: clerks@sixfountain.co.uk
Call Date: July 1988, Inner Temple
Qualifications: [LLB]

TARR MISS BEVERLY RUTH

2 Pump Court
1st Floor, Temple, London EC4Y 7AH,
Telephone: 0171 353 5597
Call Date: Oct 1995, Middle Temple
Qualifications: [LLB (Hons)]

TASKIS MISS CATHERINE LOUISE

Falcon Chambers
Falcon Court, London EC4Y 1AA,
Telephone: 0171 353 2484
E-mail: clerks@falcon-chambers.com
Call Date: Nov 1995, Inner Temple
Qualifications: [BA, BCL (Oxon)]

TATFORD WARWICK HENRY PATRICK

9-12 Bell Yard
London WC2A 2LF,
Telephone: 0171 400 1800
E-mail: clerks@bellyard.co.uk
Call Date: Oct 1993, Lincoln's Inn
Qualifications: [BA (Hons)(Oxon)]

TATLOW NICHOLAS MARK

4 Fountain Court
Steelhouse Lane, Birmingham B4 6DR,
Telephone: 0121 236 3476
Call Date: May 1996, Gray's Inn
Qualifications: [BA (Wales)]

TATTERSALL GEOFFREY FRANK QC (1992)

22 Old Buildings
Lincoln's Inn, London WC2A 3UJ,
Telephone: 0171 831 0222
Byrom Street Chambers
Byrom Street, Manchester M3 4PF,
Telephone: 0161 829 2100
E-mail: Byromst25@aol.com
Call Date: July 1970, Lincoln's Inn
Recorder
Qualifications: [MA (Oxon)]

TATTERSALL SIMON MARK ROGERS

Fenners Chambers
3 Madingley Road, Cambridge CB3 0EE,
Telephone: 01223 368761
E-mail: clerks@fennerschambers.co.uk
Fenners Chambers
8-12 Priestgate, Peterborough PE1 1JA,
Telephone: 01733 562030
E-mail: clerks@fennerschambers.co.uk
Call Date: Nov 1977, Middle Temple
Pupil Master
Qualifications: [LLB (Lond)]

TATTON-BROWN DANIEL NICHOLAS

Littleton Chambers
3 King's Bench Walk North, Temple,
London EC4Y 7HR,
Telephone: 0171 797 8600
E-mail:clerks@littletonchambers.co.uk
Call Date: Nov 1994, Middle Temple
Qualifications: [BA (Hons)]

TAUBE SIMON AXEL ROBIN

The Chambers of Leolin Price CBE, QC
10 Old Square, Lincoln's Inn, London
WC2A 3SU, Telephone: 0171 405 0758
Call Date: July 1980, Middle Temple
Pupil Master
Qualifications: [MA (Oxon)]

TAURAH MS SHEILA DOOLARY

Godolphin Chambers
50 Castle Street, Truro, Cornwall,
TR1 3AF, Telephone: 01872 276312
E-mail:theclerks@godolphin.force9.co.uk
Call Date: 1991, Lincoln's Inn
Qualifications: [LLB (Hons)]

TAUSSIG ANTHONY CHRISTOPHER

Wilberforce Chambers
8 New Square, Lincoln's Inn, London
WC2A 3QP, Telephone: 0171 306 0102
E-mail: chambers@wilberforce.co.uk
Call Date: Nov 1966, Gray's Inn
Qualifications: [MA (Oxon)]

Types of work: Equity, wills and trusts,
Pensions

TAVARES NATHAN WARREN

35 Essex Street
Temple, London WC2R 3AR,
Telephone: 0171 353 6381
E-mail: derek_jenkins@link.org
Call Date: Oct 1992, Middle Temple
Qualifications: [BSE (Hons), Common
Professional, Examination]

TAVENER MISS LUCINDA KAREN

Acre Lane Neighbourhood Chambers
30A Acre Lane, London SW2 5SG,
Telephone: 0171 274 4400
E-mail:barristerschambers@acrelane.demon.co.u
k
Call Date: 1997, Middle Temple
Qualifications: [BA (Hons)]

TAVERNER MARCUS LOUIS

Keating Chambers
10 Essex Street, Outer Temple, London
WC2R 3AA, Telephone: 0171 544 2600
Call Date: July 1981, Gray's Inn
Pupil Master
Qualifications: [LLB, LLM (Lond), ACIArb]

TAY ROBERT KOCUVIE

The Ralek
66 Carshalton Park Road, Carshalton,
Surrey, SM5 3SS,
Telephone: 0181 669 1777
Call Date: July 1972, Lincoln's Inn
Qualifications: [LLB]

TAYLER RICHARD JAMES

Devereux Chambers
Devereux Court, London WC2R 3JJ,
Telephone: 0171 353 7534
E-mail: mailbox@devchambers.co.uk
Call Date: Nov 1989, Middle Temple
Qualifications: [BA (Oxon), Dip in Law]

TAYLOR ALAN JEREMY

Park Court Chambers
16 Park Place, Leeds LS1 2SJ,
Telephone: 0113 2433277
Call Date: 1986, Lincoln's Inn
Qualifications: [BA(Bristol) Dip Law, MPhil
(Oxon)]

TAYLOR ANDREW PETER

Fenners Chambers
3 Madingley Road, Cambridge CB3 0EE,
Telephone: 01223 368761
E-mail: clerks@fennerschambers.co.uk
Fenners Chambers
8-12 Priestgate, Peterborough PE1 1JA,
Telephone: 01733 562030
E-mail: clerks@fennerschambers.co.uk
Call Date: Nov 1989, Gray's Inn
Qualifications: [BA (E.Anglia)]

TAYLOR ANDREW ROBERT

33 Park Place
Cardiff CF1 3BA,
Telephone: 02920 233313
Call Date: 1984, Gray's Inn
Pupil Master
Qualifications: [BSc Econ (Cardiff)]

TAYLOR MISS ARABA ARBA KURANKYIWA

9 Stone Buildings
Lincoln's Inn, London WC2A 3NN,
Telephone: 0171 404 5055
E-mail: clerks@9stoneb.law.co.uk
Call Date: July 1985, Middle Temple
Pupil Master
Qualifications: [MA (Cantab)]

TAYLOR CHARLES SPENCER

Chichester Chambers
12 North Pallant, Chichester, West Sussex,
PO19 1TQ, Telephone: 01243 784538
E-mail:clerks@chichesterchambers.law.co.uk
Call Date: July 1974, Middle Temple
Pupil Master
Qualifications: [LLB Hons]

TAYLOR CHRISTOPHER JOHN

Queens Square Chambers
56 Queens Square, Bristol BS1 4PR,
Telephone: 0117 921 1966
Call Date: Nov 1982, Gray's Inn
Pupil Master
Qualifications: [BA (Hons)]

D

TAYLOR DAVID BARTHOLOMEW

5 Fountain Court
Steelhouse Lane, Birmingham B4 6DR,
Telephone: 0121 606 0500
E-mail:clerks@5fountaincourt.law.co.uk
Call Date: Nov 1993, Lincoln's Inn
Qualifications: [BA (Hons)]

TAYLOR DAVID EDWARD

37 Park Square Chambers
37 Park Square, Leeds LS1 2NY,
Telephone: 0113 2439422
E-mail: chambers@no37.co.uk
Call Date: May 1995, Inner Temple

TAYLOR MRS DEBBIE

Hardwicke Building
New Square, Lincoln's Inn, London
WC2A 3SB, Telephone: 020 7242 2523
E-mail: clerks@hardwicke.co.uk
Call Date: July 1984, Lincoln's Inn
Pupil Master
Qualifications: [BA]

TAYLOR MISS DEBORAH FRANCES

Two Crown Office Row
Ground Floor, Temple, London
EC4Y 7HJ, Telephone: 020 7797 8100
E-mail: mail@2cor.co.uk, or to individual
barristers at: [barrister's
surname]@2cor.co.uk
Call Date: July 1983, Inner Temple
Pupil Master
Qualifications: [BA (Oxon)]

TAYLOR DOUGLAS JAMES

College Chambers
19 Carlton Cresent, Southampton
SO15 2ET, Telephone: 01703 230338
Call Date: July 1981, Middle Temple
Pupil Master
Qualifications: [BA (Hons) (Sheff)]

TAYLOR MISS GEMMA MARY

22 Old Buildings
Lincoln's Inn, London WC2A 3UJ,
Telephone: 0171 831 0222
Call Date: Feb 1988, Inner Temple
Qualifications: [LLB (London)]

TAYLOR GREGORY LYNN

9 Park Place
Cardiff CF1 3DP,
Telephone: 01222 382731
Call Date: July 1974, Middle Temple
Pupil Master
Qualifications: [BA (Keele)]

TAYLOR IAN FREDERICK

Devon Chambers
3 St Andrew Street, Plymouth PL1 2AH,
Telephone: 01752 661659
E-mail: devonchambers.co.uk.
Call Date: July 1986, Gray's Inn
Pupil Master
Qualifications: [BA (Sydney)]

TAYLOR JASON

Albion Chambers
Broad Street, Bristol BS1 1DR,
Telephone: 0117 9272144
Call Date: Nov 1995, Gray's Inn
Qualifications: [LLB (Wales)]

TAYLOR JOHN CHARLES QC (1983)

2 Mitre Court Buildings
2nd Floor, Temple, London EC4Y 7BX,
Telephone: 0171 583 1380
E-mail: clerks@2mcb.co.uk
Call Date: Feb 1958, Middle Temple
Qualifications: [MA, LLB (Cantab), LLM
Harvard]

TAYLOR JOHN CHARLES

Fountain Court
Temple, London EC4Y 9DH,
Telephone: 0171 583 3335
E-mail: chambers@fountaincourt.co.uk
Call Date: Oct 1993, Middle Temple
Qualifications: [MA (Hons)(Cantab)]

TAYLOR JOHN DAVID

Dr Johnson's Chambers
Two Dr Johnson's Buildings, Temple,
London EC4Y 7AY,
Telephone: 0171 353 4716
E-mail: clerks@2djb.freeserve.co.uk
Call Date: July 1986, Gray's Inn
Qualifications: [LLB (Cardiff)]

TAYLOR JONATHAN ANDREW

3 Temple Gardens
2nd Floor, Temple, London EC4Y 9AU,
Telephone: 0171 583 1155
Call Date: Nov 1987, Gray's Inn
Qualifications: [BA (Manch)]

TAYLOR JONATHAN FORD

India Buildings Chambers
Water Street, Liverpool L2 0XG,
Telephone: 0151 243 6000
E-mail: clerks@chambers.u-net.com
Call Date: Nov 1991, Middle Temple
Qualifications: [LLB Hons (Reading)]

TAYLOR JONATHAN MORRIS

29a Lambs Conduit Street
Holborn, London WC1N 3NG,
Telephone: 0171 831 9907
Call Date: July 1983, Gray's Inn
Qualifications: [BA (Hons)]

TAYLOR JULIAN RICHARD

Peel Court Chambers
45 Hardman Street, Manchester M3 3PL,
Telephone: 0161 832 3791
E-mail: clerks@peelct.co.uk
Call Date: July 1986, Middle Temple
Qualifications: [LLB (Bristol)]

TAYLOR MISS JULIE

15 Winckley Square
Preston PR1 3JJ,
Telephone: 01772 252828
E-mail:clerks@winckleysq.demon.co.uk
Call Date: Nov 1992, Inner Temple
Qualifications: [LLB]

TAYLOR MARTIN JOHN

6 King's Bench Walk
Ground, Third & Fourth Floors, Temple,
London EC4Y 7DR,
Telephone: 0171 353 4931/583 0695
Call Date: July 1988, Middle Temple
Pupil Master
Qualifications: [BA (Hons) (Leeds), Dip Law]

TAYLOR MISS MAUREEN JOAN

Enfield Chambers
First Floor, Refuge House, 9-10 River
Front, Enfield, Middlesex, EN1 3SZ,
Telephone: 0181 364 5627
E-mail:enfieldchambers@compuserve.com
Call Date: Oct 1993, Lincoln's Inn
Qualifications: [LLB (Hons)(Lond)]

TAYLOR MICHAEL PAUL

28 St John Street
Manchester M3 4DJ,
Telephone: 0161 834 8418
E-mail: clerk@28stjohnst.co.uk
Call Date: Nov 1985, Gray's Inn
Qualifications: [LL.B (Leeds)]

TAYLOR MICHAEL RICHARD

Park Court Chambers
16 Park Place, Leeds LS1 2SJ,
Telephone: 0113 2433277
Call Date: July 1980, Gray's Inn
Pupil Master
Qualifications: [LLB (Hons)]

TAYLOR NIGEL STUART

New Court
Temple, London EC4Y 9BE,
Telephone: 0171 583 5123/0510
Call Date: Oct 1993, Inner Temple
Qualifications: [BA , LLB (Lond)]

TAYLOR PAUL RICHARD

Doughty Street Chambers
11 Doughty Street, London WC1N 2PG,
Telephone: 0171 404 1313
E-mail:enquiries@doughtystreet.co.uk
Call Date: Nov 1989, Middle Temple
Qualifications: [LLB, LLM (Cantab), CNAA]

TAYLOR PHILLIP BRIAN

Richmond Green Chambers
Greyhound House, 23-24 George Street,
Richmond-upon-Thames, Surrey,
TW9 1HY, Telephone: 0181 940 1841
E-mail: ptaylor256@aol.com
Watford Chambers
74 Mildred Avenue, Watford,
Hertfordshire, WD1 7DX,
Telephone: 01923 220553
Call Date: Nov 1991, Lincoln's Inn
Qualifications: [LLB (Hons) (Lond)]

TAYLOR REUBEN MALLINSON

2 Mitre Court Buildings
2nd Floor, Temple, London EC4Y 7BX,
Telephone: 0171 583 1380
E-mail: clerks@2mcb.co.uk
Call Date: Oct 1990, Gray's Inn
Qualifications: [LLB (Hons) (Wales)]

TAYLOR RHYS STEADMAN

33 Park Place
Cardiff CF1 3BA,
Telephone: 02920 233313
Call Date: Nov 1996, Inner Temple
Qualifications: [LLB (Reading)]

TAYLOR RUPERT LADD

Devon Chambers
3 St Andrew Street, Plymouth PL1 2AH,
Telephone: 01752 661659
E-mail: devonchambers.co.uk.
Call Date: July 1990, Gray's Inn
Qualifications: [LLB (Hons), LLM (Lond)]

TAYLOR SIMON

Francis Taylor Building
Ground Floor, Temple, London
EC4Y 7BY, Telephone: 0171 353 7768/
7769/2711
E-mail: clerks@francistaylorbuilding.law.co.uk
Call Date: Oct 1993, Inner Temple
Qualifications: [BSc (Hons), CPE]

TAYLOR SIMON WHELDON

Cloisters
1 Pump Court, Temple, London
EC4Y 7AA, Telephone: 0171 827 4000
E-mail: clerks@cloisters.com
Call Date: July 1984, Middle Temple
Pupil Master
Qualifications: [BA (Cantab), MA (Cantab),
MB.B Chir]

TAYLOR STEVEN JAMES

8 King's Bench Walk North
1 Park Square East, Leeds LS1 2NE,
Telephone: 0113 2439797
8 King's Bench Walk
2nd Floor, Temple, London EC4Y 7DU,
Telephone: 0171 797 8888
Call Date: Oct 1992, Lincoln's Inn
Qualifications: [LLB(Hons)]

TAYLOR MS SUE

Acre Lane Neighbourhood Chambers
30A Acre Lane, London SW2 5SG,
Telephone: 0171 274 4400
E-mail:barristerschambers@acrelane.demon.co.uk
Call Date: Oct 1996, Lincoln's Inn
Qualifications: [B.Ed (Hons)(B'ham), MA
(Essex), M.Ed (Leeds)]

TAYLOR MRS SUSAN

New Court Chambers
3 Broad Chare, Newcastle upon Tyne
NE1 3DQ, Telephone: 0191 232 1980
Call Date: Nov 1987, Middle Temple
Pupil Master
Qualifications: [BA]

TAYLOR WILLIAM JAMES QC (1998)

3 Gray's Inn Square
Ground Floor, London WC1R 5AH,
Telephone: 0171 520 5600
E-mail: clerks@3gis.co.uk
Call Date: 1990, Inner Temple
Qualifications: [MA, LLB (Aberdeen)]

TAYLOR-CAMARA ALEXANDER ABDU RAHMAN

8 King's Bench Walk
2nd Floor, Temple, London EC4Y 7DU,
Telephone: 0171 797 8888
Call Date: Nov 1989, Middle Temple
Qualifications: [LLB (Hons)]

TAYO MISS ANN IBILOLA

2-4 Tudor Street
London EC4Y 0AA,
Telephone: 0171 797 7111
E-mail: clerks@rfqc.co.uk
Call Date: Oct 1991, Gray's Inn
Qualifications: [LLB]

TAYTON MISS LYNN MARGARET

Chambers of Michael Pert QC
36 Bedford Row, London WC1R 4JH,
Telephone: 0171 421 8000
E-mail: 36bedfordrow@link.org
Chambers of Michael Pert QC
24 Albion Place, Northampton NN1 1UD,
Telephone: 01604 602333

Chambers of Michael Pert QC
104 New Walk, Leicester LE1 7EA,
Telephone: 0116 249 2020
Call Date: July 1981, Gray's Inn
Pupil Master
Qualifications: [LLB (Lond)]

TEAGUE EDWARD THOMAS HENRY

Nicholas Street Chambers
22 Nicholas Street, Chester CH1 2NX,
Telephone: 01244 323886
E-mail: clerks@40king.co.uk
Call Date: July 1977, Inner Temple
Pupil Master, Recorder
Qualifications: [MA (Cantab)]

TEARE NIGEL JOHN MARTIN QC (1991)

4 Essex Court
Temple, London EC4Y 9AJ,
Telephone: 020 7797 7970
E-mail: clerks@4essexcourt.law.co.uk
Call Date: July 1974, Lincoln's Inn
Recorder
Qualifications: [MA (Oxon)]

TECKS JONATHAN HOWARD

Littman Chambers
12 Gray's Inn Square, London WC1R 5JP,
Telephone: 020 7404 4866
E-mail: admin@littmanchambers.com
Call Date: July 1978, Gray's Inn
Pupil Master
Qualifications: [MA (Cantab), FCIArb, CEDR
Accredited, Mediator]

TEDD REX HILARY QC (1993)

St Philip's Chambers
Fountain Court, Steelhouse Lane,
Birmingham B4 6DR,
Telephone: 0121 246 7000
E-mail: clerks@st-philips.co.uk
De Montfort Chambers
95 Princess Road East, Leicester LE1 7DQ,
Telephone: 0116 254 8686
E-mail: dmcbar@aol.com
Northampton Chambers
22 Albion Place, Northampton NN1 1UD,
Telephone: 01604 636271
Call Date: Feb 1970, Inner Temple
Recorder
Qualifications: [MA, BCL (Oxon)]

Fax: 0121 246 7000; DX: 16073
Birmingham

Types of work: Aviation, Banking, Chancery
(general), Commercial litigation, Common
law (general), Company and commercial,
Construction, Crime, Crime – corporate
fraud, Education, Employment, Film, cable,
TV, Insolvency, Partnerships, Personal
injury, Professional negligence, Tax –
capital and income, Tax – corporate, Town
and country planning

Circuit: Midland & Oxford

Additional Information
Leader of the Midland and Oxford Circuit.
Educated King Edwards School –
Birmingham; Yarborough-Anderson Schol-
arship – Inner Temple; Chairman of
Council of Malvern Girls' College; Former
Lecturer in Law – Nottingham University;
Former Teaching Fellow – Osgoode Hall
Law School – Toronto.

TEDORE MS AMANDA JANE

1 Inner Temple Lane
Temple, London EC4Y 1AF,
Telephone: 020 7353 0933
Call Date: Nov 1992, Middle Temple
Qualifications: [BA (Hons)(Warw), Dip in
Law]

TEEMAN MISS MIRIAM JOY

30 Park Square
Leeds LS1 2PF, Telephone: 0113 2436388
E-mail: clerks@30parksquare.co.uk
Call Date: Feb 1993, Gray's Inn
Qualifications: [LLB (L'pool)]

TEGGIN MISS VICTORIA HELEN

Mitre House Chambers
15-19 Devereux Court, London WC2R 3JJ,
Telephone: 0171 583 8233
Call Date: Nov 1990, Inner Temple
Qualifications: [BA (Hons) (UCL), Dip Law
(PCL)]

TEHRANI CHRISTOPHER

8 King's Bench Walk North
1 Park Square East, Leeds LS1 2NE,
Telephone: 0113 2439797

8 King's Bench Walk
2nd Floor, Temple, London EC4Y 7DU,
Telephone: 0171 797 8888
Call Date: Nov 1990, Inner Temple
Qualifications: [LLB]

TEJI MISS USHA DEVI

1 Pump Court
Lower Ground Floor, Temple, London
EC4Y 7AB, Telephone: 0171 583 2012/
353 4341
E-mail: [name]@1pumpcourt.co.uk
Call Date: July 1981, Lincoln's Inn
Qualifications: [LLB (Lond)]

TELFORD PETER

Devon Chambers
3 St Andrew Street, Plymouth PL1 2AH,
Telephone: 01752 661659
E-mail: devonchambers.co.uk.
Call Date: July 1985, Lincoln's Inn
Pupil Master
Qualifications: [BA (Joint Hons) , (Keele)]

TEMBLETT ROBERT HAROLD

517 Bunyan Court
Barbican, London EC2Y 8DH,
Telephone: 0171 638 5076
Call Date: Nov 1980, Middle Temple
Qualifications: [LLB]

TEMMINK ROBERT-JAN

35 Essex Street
Temple, London WC2R 3AR,
Telephone: 0171 353 6381
E-mail: derek_jenkins@link.org
Call Date: Oct 1996, Middle Temple
Qualifications: [BA (Hons)(Cantab)]

TEMPLE ANTHONY DOMINIC QC (1986)

4 Pump Court
Temple, London EC4Y 7AN,
Telephone: 020 7842 5555
E-mail:chambers@4pumpcourt.law.co.uk
Call Date: July 1968, Inner Temple
Recorder
Qualifications: [MA (Oxon)]

TEMPLE MISS MICHELLE JEAN

Broad Chare
33 Broad Chare, Newcastle upon Tyne
NE1 3DQ, Telephone: 0191 232 0541
E-mail:clerks@broadcharechambers.law.co.uk
Call Date: Oct 1992, Lincoln's Inn
Qualifications: [MA (Hons) (Oxon)]

TEMPLE SIMON ERNEST WILLIAM

Chambers of John Hand QC
9 St John Street, Manchester M3 4DN,
Telephone: 0161 955 9000
E-mail: ninesjs@gconnect.com
Call Date: July 1977, Gray's Inn
Qualifications: [BA]

TEMPLE VICTOR BEVIS AFAMADO QC (1993)

6 King's Bench Walk
Ground Floor, Temple, London
EC4Y 7DR, Telephone: 0171 583 0410
E-mail: worsley@6kbw.freeserve.co.uk
Call Date: July 1971, Inner Temple
Recorder

TEMPLE-BONE MISS GILLIAN ELIZABETH

7 Stone Buildings (also at 11 Bolt Court)
1st Floor, Lincoln's Inn, London
WC2A 3SZ, Telephone: 0171 242 0961
E-mail:larthur@7stonebuildings.law.co.uk
11 Bolt Court (also at 7 Stone Buildings – 1st Floor)
London EC4A 3DQ,
Telephone: 0171 353 2300
E-mail: boltct11@aol.com
Redhill Chambers
Seloduct House, 30 Station Road, Redhill,
Surrey, RH1 1NF,
Telephone: 01737 780781
Call Date: Nov 1978, Gray's Inn
Qualifications: [BA (Durham)]

TEMPLEMAN MARK JEREMY

Essex Court Chambers
24 Lincoln's Inn Fields, London
WC2A 3ED, Telephone: 0171 813 8000
E-mail:clerksroom@essexcourt-chambers.co.uk
Call Date: Nov 1981, Middle Temple
Pupil Master
Qualifications: [MA BCL (Oxon)]

D

TEMPLEMAN MICHAEL RICHARD

Southernhay Chambers
33 Southernhay East, Exeter, Devon,
EX1 1NX, Telephone: 01392 255777
E-mail:southernhay.chambers@lineone.net
5 Stone Buildings
Lincoln's Inn, London WC2A 3XT,
Telephone: 0171 242 6201
E-mail:clerks@5-stonebuildings.law.co.uk
Call Date: 1973, Lincoln's Inn
Qualifications: [MA (Oxon)]

TENNET MICHAEL JOHN

Wilberforce Chambers
8 New Square, Lincoln's Inn, London
WC2A 3QP, Telephone: 0171 306 0102
E-mail: chambers@wilberforce.co.uk
Call Date: July 1985, Inner Temple
Pupil Master
Qualifications: [BA (Oxon)]

Types of work: Chancery (general), Commercial litigation, Commercial property, Financial services, Pensions, Professional negligence

TEPER CARL WOLF

1 Gray's Inn Square
Ground Floor, London WC1R 5AA,
Telephone: 0171 405 8946/7/8
Call Date: July 1980, Middle Temple
Pupil Master
Qualifications: [LLB (Warw)]

TER HAAR ROGER EDUARD LOUND QC (1992)

Two Crown Office Row
Ground Floor, Temple, London
EC4Y 7HJ, Telephone: 020 7797 8100
E-mail: mail@2cor.co.uk, or to individual
barristers at: [barrister's
surname]@2cor.co.uk
Call Date: July 1974, Inner Temple
Qualifications: [BA (Oxon)]

TERRAS NICHOLAS CHARLES

12 New Square
Lincoln's Inn, London WC2A 3SW,
Telephone: 0171 419 1212
E-mail: chambers@12newsquare.co.uk

Sovereign Chambers
25 Park Square, Leeds LS1 2PW,
Telephone: 0113 2451841/2/3
E-mail:sovereignchambers@btinternet.com
Call Date: Oct 1993, Lincoln's Inn
Qualifications: [BA (Hons)(Lond), PhD
(Lond), Dip in Law (City)]

TERRIS MISS SALLY

Paradise Chambers
26 Paradise Square, Sheffield S1 2DE,
Telephone: 0114 2738951
E-mail: timbooth@paradise-sq.co.uk
Call Date: Nov 1997, Middle Temple
Qualifications: [BA (Hons)(Cantab)]

TERRY MISS MICHELLE JANE EVELYN

Lamb Building
Ground Floor, Temple, London
EC4Y 7AS, Telephone: 020 7797 7788
E-mail: lamb.building@link.org
Call Date: July 1988, Lincoln's Inn
Pupil Master
Qualifications: [LLB (Hons)]

TERRY ROBERT EDWARD LEETHAM

York Chambers
14 Toft Green, York YO1 6JT,
Telephone: 01904 620048
E-mail: [name]@yorkchambers.co.uk
Call Date: Nov 1986, Gray's Inn
Qualifications: [BA (Leeds)]

TERRY ROBERT JEFFREY

8 King Street Chambers
8 King Street, Manchester M2 6AQ,
Telephone: 0161 834 9560
E-mail: eightking@aol.com
Call Date: July 1976, Lincoln's Inn
Pupil Master
Qualifications: [FCIArb, FSALS, LLB, MA
(Lond)]

TESTAR PETER THOMAS

**4 Brick Court, Chambers of Anne
Rafferty QC**
1st Floor, Temple, London EC4Y 9AD,
Telephone: 0171 583 8455
Call Date: July 1974, Middle Temple
Pupil Master, Assistant Recorder
Qualifications: [LLB (Soton)]

D

TETHER MS MELANIE GEORGIA KIM

Old Square Chambers
1 Verulam Buildings, Gray's Inn, London
WC1R 5LQ, Telephone: 0171 269 0300
E-mail:clerks@oldsquarechambers.co.uk
Old Square Chambers
Hanover House, 47 Corn Street, Bristol
BS1 1HT, Telephone: 0117 9277111
E-mail: oldsqbri@globalnet.co.uk
Call Date: July 1995, Inner Temple
Qualifications: [MA (Oxon)]

TETLOW BERNARD GEOFFREY

Dr Johnson's Chambers
Two Dr Johnson's Buildings, Temple,
London EC4Y 7AY,
Telephone: 0171 353 4716
E-mail: clerks@2djb.freeserve.co.uk
Call Date: Nov 1984, Middle Temple
Pupil Master
Qualifications: [BA, LLM (Cantab)]

TETTENBORN ANDREW MARTIN

Regency Chambers
Cathedral Square, Peterborough
PE1 1XW, Telephone: 01733 315215
Regency Chambers
Sheraton House, Castle Park, Cambridge
CB3 0AX, Telephone: 01223 301517
Chambers of John L Powell QC
Four New Square, Lincoln's Inn, London
WC2A 3RJ, Telephone: 0171 797 8000
E-mail: barristers@4newsquare.com
Call Date: 1988, Lincoln's Inn
Qualifications: [BA Hons,LLB (Cantab), MA
(Cantab)]

TEVERSON PAUL RICHARD

Twenty-Four Old Buildings
Ground Floor, Lincoln's Inn, London
WC2A 3UP, Telephone: 0171 404 0946
E-mail:clerks@24oldbuildings.law.co.uk
Call Date: July 1976, Inner Temple
Pupil Master
Qualifications: [BA (Cantab)]

THACKER RAJEEV KUMAR

4 Brick Court
Ground Floor, Temple, London
EC4Y 9AD, Telephone: 0171 797 7766
E-mail: chambers@4brick.co.uk
Call Date: Oct 1993, Gray's Inn
Qualifications: [LLB (Wales)]

THACKRAY JOHN RICHARD DOMINIC

Wilberforce Chambers
7 Bishop Lane, Hull, East Yorkshire,
HU1 1PA, Telephone: 01482 323264
E-mail: clerks@hullbar.demon.co.uk
Call Date: Oct 1994, Lincoln's Inn
Qualifications: [LLB (Hons)(Leeds)]

THAIN MISS ASHLEY

East Anglian Chambers
52 North Hill, Colchester, Essex, CO1 1PY,
Telephone: 01206 572756
E-mail: colchester@ealaw.co.uk
East Anglian Chambers
Gresham House, 5 Museum Street,
Ipswich, Suffolk, IP1 1HQ,
Telephone: 01473 214481
E-mail: ipswich@ealaw.co.uk
East Anglian Chambers
57 London Street, Norwich NR2 1HL,
Telephone: 01603 617351
E-mail: norwich@ealaw.co.uk
Call Date: 1996, Inner Temple
Qualifications: [LLB]

THANKI BANKIM

Fountain Court
Temple, London EC4Y 9DH,
Telephone: 0171 583 3335
E-mail: chambers@fountaincourt.co.uk
Call Date: July 1988, Middle Temple
Pupil Master
Qualifications: [MA (Oxon), Dip Law (City)]

THATCHER RICHARD DAVID

High Pavement Chambers
1 High Pavement, Nottingham NG1 1HF,
Telephone: 0115 9418218
Call Date: July 1989, Inner Temple
Qualifications: [LLB]

THEIS MISS LUCY MORGAN

Chambers of Norman Palmer
2 Field Court, Gray's Inn, London
WC1R 5BB, Telephone: 0171 405 6114
E-mail: fieldct2@netcomuk.co.uk
Call Date: July 1982, Gray's Inn
Pupil Master, Assistant Recorder
Qualifications: [LLB (B'ham)]

THEMIS SAM

Call Date: Oct 1995, Inner Temple
Qualifications: [LLB (Lond)]

THIND MISS ANITA

Regency Chambers
Cathedral Square, Peterborough
PE1 1XW, Telephone: 01733 315215
Regency Chambers
Sheraton House, Castle Park, Cambridge
CB3 0AX, Telephone: 01223 301517
Call Date: Nov 1988, Inner Temple
Pupil Master
Qualifications: [LLB]

THIRLWALL MISS KATHRYN MARY QC (1999)

9 Bedford Row
London WC1R 4AZ,
Telephone: 0171 242 3555
E-mail: clerks@9br.co.uk
Call Date: 1982, Middle Temple
Pupil Master, Assistant Recorder
Qualifications: [BA (Bris)]

THOM JAMES ALEXANDER FRANCIS

4 Field Court
Gray's Inn, London WC1R 5EA,
Telephone: 0171 440 6900
E-mail: chambers@4fieldcourt.co.uk
Call Date: Nov 1974, Middle Temple
Pupil Master
Qualifications: [MA (Oxon), BCL (Oxon)]

THOM MICHAEL

Eighteen Carlton Crescent
Southampton SO15 2XR,
Telephone: 01703 639001
Call Date: Nov 1994, Inner Temple
Qualifications: [LLB (Soton)]

THOMAS ADRIAN FRANCIS TREVELYAN

2-3 Gray's Inn Square
Gray's Inn, London WC1R 5JH,
Telephone: 0171 242 4986
E-mail:chambers@2-3graysinnsquare.co.uk
Call Date: 1974, Gray's Inn
Pupil Master

THOMAS ANDREW (MARTIN)

Sedan House
Stanley Place, Chester CH1 2LU,
Telephone: 01244 320480/348282
Call Date: Nov 1989, Gray's Inn
Qualifications: [MA (Cantab)]

THOMAS ANDREW RICHARD

Brick Court Chambers
7-8 Essex Street, London WC2R 3LD,
Telephone: 0171 379 3550
E-mail: [surname]@brickcourt.co.uk
Call Date: Oct 1996, Inner Temple

THOMAS MS ANNA LOUISE

22 Old Buildings
Lincoln's Inn, London WC2A 3UJ,
Telephone: 0171 831 0222
Call Date: Nov 1995, Inner Temple
Qualifications: [MA (Oxon), CPE (City)]

THOMAS BRYAN MICHAEL

33 Park Place
Cardiff CF1 3BA,
Telephone: 02920 233313
Call Date: 1978, Gray's Inn
Pupil Master
Qualifications: [LLB Hons (Wales)]

THOMAS CHARLES AUBREY MORGAN

1 Paper Buildings
1st Floor, Temple, London EC4Y 7EP,
Telephone: 0171 353 3728/4953
Call Date: Oct 1990, Middle Temple
Qualifications: [BA (Oxon)]

THOMAS CHRISTOPHER SYDNEY QC (1989)

Keating Chambers
10 Essex Street, Outer Temple, London
WC2R 3AA, Telephone: 0171 544 2600
Call Date: July 1973, Lincoln's Inn
Assistant Recorder
Qualifications: [BA, Dip de Droit Compare, Phd]

THOMAS MISS CLARE RACHEL

New Bailey Chambers
10 Lawson Street, Preston PR1 2QT,
Telephone: 01772 258087
Call Date: 1998, Inner Temple
Qualifications: [LLB (Hull)]

THOMAS DR DAVID ARTHUR QC (1996)

Cloisters
1 Pump Court, Temple, London
EC4Y 7AA, Telephone: 0171 827 4000
E-mail: clerks@cloisters.com
Call Date: Feb 1992, Lincoln's Inn
Qualifications: [LLD (Cambs)]

THOMAS DAVID ERYL

32 Park Place
Cardiff CF1 3BA,
Telephone: 01222 397364
Call Date: July 1975, Gray's Inn
Qualifications: [MA (Oxon)]

THOMAS DAVID OWEN QC (1972)

6 Gray's Inn Square
Ground Floor, Gray's Inn, London
WC1R 5AZ, Telephone: 0171 242 1052
E-mail: 6graysinn@clara.co.uk
2 King's Bench Walk Chambers
1st Floor, 2 King's Bench Walk, Temple,
London EC4Y 7DE,
Telephone: 020 7353 9276
E-mail: chambers@2kbw.co.uk
Call Date: 1952, Middle Temple
Recorder

THOMAS MISS DOROTHY ANN

Victoria Chambers
3rd Floor, 177 Corporation Street,
Birmingham B4 6RG,
Telephone: 0121 236 9900
E-mail: viccham@aol.com
Call Date: Nov 1991, Inner Temple
Qualifications: [LLB (Hull)]

THOMAS DYFED LLION

Angel Chambers
94 Walter Road, Swansea, West
Glamorgan, SA1 5QA,
Telephone: 01792 464623/464648
E-mail: lynne@angelchambers.co.uk
Call Date: Oct 1992, Middle Temple
Qualifications: [BA (Hons)(Oxon)]

THOMAS GARETH

Arden Chambers
27 John Street, London WC1N 2BL,
Telephone: 020 7242 4244
E-mail:clerks@arden-chambers.law.co.uk
Call Date: July 1977, Gray's Inn
Qualifications: [LLB (Wales) ACII]

THOMAS GARETH DAVID

Pendragon Chambers
124 Walter Road, Swansea, West
Glamorgan, SA1 5RG,
Telephone: 01792 411188
Call Date: Nov 1993, Inner Temple
Qualifications: [LLB (Wales)]

THOMAS GEORGE LLEWELLYN

3 Serjeants' Inn
London EC4Y 1BQ,
Telephone: 0171 353 5537
E-mail: clerks@3serjeantsinn.com
Call Date: Oct 1995, Gray's Inn
Qualifications: [BA]

THOMAS GERAINT WYNN

The Chambers of Leolin Price CBE, QC
10 Old Square, Lincoln's Inn, London
WC2A 3SU, Telephone: 0171 405 0758
Call Date: July 1976, Inner Temple
Qualifications: [BA (Wales) DPhil, (Oxon)]

THOMAS IAN

St Ive's Chambers
Whittall Street, Birmingham B4 6DH,
Telephone: 0121 236 0863/5720
E-mail:stives.headofchambers@btinternet.com
Call Date: Oct 1993, Gray's Inn
Qualifications: [LLB (Hons),
(Wolverhampton)]

THOMAS MISS KATIE

Victoria Chambers
3rd Floor, 177 Corporation Street,
Birmingham B4 6RG,
Telephone: 0121 236 9900
E-mail: viccham@aol.com
Call Date: 1994, Gray's Inn
Qualifications: [LLB]

THOMAS KEITH GARFIELD

9 Park Place
Cardiff CF1 3DP,
Telephone: 01222 382731
Call Date: July 1977, Gray's Inn
Pupil Master, Assistant Recorder
Qualifications: [BA]

THOMAS KEITH SINCLAIR

New Bailey Chambers
10 Lawson Street, Preston PR1 2QT,
Telephone: 01772 258087
Call Date: July 1969, Gray's Inn
Pupil Master
Qualifications: [BA (Oxon)]

THOMAS KENNETH LLOYD

Iscoed Chambers
86 St Helen's Road, Swansea, West
Glamorgan, SA1 4BQ,
Telephone: 01792 652988/9/330
Call Date: July 1966, Lincoln's Inn
Qualifications: [MA, LLB (Cantab)]

THOMAS LESLIE

Two Garden Court
1st Floor, Middle Temple, London
EC4Y 9BL, Telephone: 0171 353 1633
E-mail:barristers@2gardenct.law.co.uk
Call Date: Nov 1988, Inner Temple
Pupil Master
Qualifications: [LLB]

THOMAS MISS MEGAN MOIRA

1 Serjeants' Inn
4th Floor, Temple, London EC4Y 1NH,
Telephone: 0171 583 1355
E-mail: clerks@serjeants-inn.co.uk
Call Date: July 1987, Gray's Inn
Pupil Master
Qualifications: [BA (Hons)(Shef)]

THOMAS MICHAEL DAVID QC (1973)

Essex Court Chambers
24 Lincoln's Inn Fields, London
WC2A 3ED, Telephone: 0171 813 8000
E-mail:clerksroom@essexcourt-chambers.co.uk
Call Date: May 1955, Middle Temple
Qualifications: [LLB (Lond), BA]

THOMAS NIGEL MATTHEW

13 Old Square
Ground Floor, Lincoln's Inn, London
WC2A 3UA, Telephone: 0171 404 4800
E-mail: clerks@13oldsquare.law.co.uk
Call Date: July 1976, Gray's Inn
Pupil Master
Qualifications: [LLB (Wales) LLB, (Cantab)]

THOMAS OWEN HUW

9 Park Place
Cardiff CF1 3DP,
Telephone: 01222 382731
Call Date: Oct 1994, Gray's Inn
Qualifications: [BA (Oxon)]

THOMAS PATRICK ANTHONY QC (1999)

4 Fountain Court
Steelhouse Lane, Birmingham B4 6DR,
Telephone: 0121 236 3476
Call Date: 1973, Gray's Inn
Pupil Master, Recorder
Qualifications: [BA (Oxon)]

THOMAS PAUL HUW

Iscoed Chambers
86 St Helen's Road, Swansea, West
Glamorgan, SA1 4BQ,
Telephone: 01792 652988/9/330
Farrar's Building
Temple, London EC4Y 7BD,
Telephone: 0171 583 9241
E-mail:chambers@farrarsbuilding.co.uk
Call Date: July 1979, Gray's Inn
Pupil Master
Qualifications: [MA (Cantab)]

THOMAS PHILIP

Pendragon Chambers
124 Walter Road, Swansea, West
Glamorgan, SA1 5RG,
Telephone: 01792 411188
Call Date: July 1982, Inner Temple
Qualifications: [LLB (Soton)]

THOMAS (ROBERT) NEVILLE QC (1975)

3 Verulam Buildings
London WC1R 5NT,
Telephone: 0171 831 8441
E-mail: clerks@3verulam.co.uk
Call Date: July 1962, Inner Temple
Qualifications: [MA (Oxon), BCL]

THOMAS ROBERT OWAIN PHILIP

4 Essex Court
Temple, London EC4Y 9AJ,
Telephone: 020 7797 7970
E-mail: clerks@4essexcourt.law.co.uk
Call Date: Nov 1992, Lincoln's Inn
Qualifications: [MA (Cantab), BCL (Oxon),
LIC.SP.Dr.Eur., (Bruxelles)]

THOMAS ROGER CHRISTOPHER

Pump Court Tax Chambers
16 Bedford Row, London WC1R 4EB,
Telephone: 0171 414 8080
Park Court Chambers
16 Park Place, Leeds LS1 2SJ,
Telephone: 0113 2433277
Call Date: July 1979, Lincoln's Inn
Pupil Master
Qualifications: [MA, BCL (Oxon)]

THOMAS ROGER LLOYD QC (1994)

9 Park Place
Cardiff CF1 3DP,
Telephone: 01222 382731
Farrar's Building
Temple, London EC4Y 7BD,
Telephone: 0171 583 9241
E-mail:chambers@farrarsbuilding.co.uk
Equity Chambers
3rd Floor, 153a Corporation Street,
Birmingham B4 6PH,
Telephone: 0121 233 2100
E-mail: equityatusa.com
Call Date: July 1969, Gray's Inn
Recorder
Qualifications: [LLB (Wales)]

THOMAS ROGER MARTIN

Broadway House Chambers
Broadway House, 9 Bank Street, Bradford,
West Yorkshire, BD1 1TW,
Telephone: 01274 722560
E-mail: clerks@broadwayhouse.co.uk
Broadway House Chambers
31 Park Square West, Leeds LS1 2PF,
Telephone: 0113 246 2600
Call Date: 1976, Inner Temple
Pupil Master, Recorder
Qualifications: [LLB (Hull)]

THOMAS ROYDON URQUHART QC (1985)

One Essex Court
Ground Floor, Temple, London
EC4Y 9AR, Telephone: 020 7583 2000
E-mail: clerks@oneessexcourt.co.uk
Call Date: July 1960, Middle Temple
Recorder
Qualifications: [BA (Cantab)]

THOMAS MISS SIAN CAROLINE MARTHA

11 Old Square
Ground Floor, Lincoln's Inn, London
WC2A 3TS, Telephone: 020 7430 0341
E-mail: clerks@11oldsquare.co.uk
Call Date: July 1981, Inner Temple
Pupil Master
Qualifications: [BA (Oxon)]

THOMAS SIMON CHRISTOPHER

9 Bedford Row
London WC1R 4AZ,
Telephone: 0171 242 3555
E-mail: clerks@9br.co.uk
Call Date: Oct 1995, Inner Temple
Qualifications: [BA (Oxon)]

THOMAS STEPHEN EDWARD OWEN

St Philip's Chambers
Fountain Court, Steelhouse Lane,
Birmingham B4 6DR,
Telephone: 0121 246 7000
E-mail: clerks@st-philips.co.uk
Call Date: July 1980, Gray's Inn
Pupil Master
Qualifications: [LLB (Exon)]

THOMAS STEPHEN JOHN

32 Park Place
Cardiff CF1 3BA,
Telephone: 01222 397364
Call Date: Feb 1993, Gray's Inn
Qualifications: [LLB (Hons)(Wales)]

THOMAS MISS SYBIL MILWYN

3 Fountain Court
Steelhouse Lane, Birmingham B4 6DR,
Telephone: 0121 236 5854
Call Date: July 1976, Gray's Inn
Pupil Master, Assistant Recorder
Qualifications: [LLB (Bris)]

THOMAS WILLIAM DAVID

2 Temple Gardens
Temple, London EC4Y 9AY,
Telephone: 0171 583 6041
E-mail: clerks@2templegardens.co.uk
Call Date: July 1982, Middle Temple
Pupil Master
Qualifications: [MA (Oxon)]

THOMAS WILLIAM OWAIN

1 Crown Office Row
Ground Floor, Temple, London
EC4Y 7HH, Telephone: 0171 797 7500
E-mail: mail@onecrownofficerow.com
Call Date: Oct 1995, Inner Temple
Qualifications: [BA (Oxon), BCL]

THOMAS MISS (YVETTE) BERNADETTE

Chancery Chambers
1st Floor Offices, 70/72 Chancery Lane,
London WC2A 1AB,
Telephone: 0171 405 6879/6870
Call Date: July 1993, Middle Temple
Qualifications: [LLB (Hons)]

THOMAS OF GRESFORD LORD QC (1979)

1 Dr Johnson's Buildings
Ground Floor, Temple, London
EC4Y 7AX, Telephone: 0171 353 9328
E-mail:OneDr.Johnsons@btinternet.com
Dr Johnson's Chambers
The Atrium Court, Apex Plaza, Reading,
Berkshire, RG1 1AX,
Telephone: 01734 254221

Sedan House
Stanley Place, Chester CH1 2LU,
Telephone: 01244 320480/348282
8 Fountain Court
Steelhouse Lane, Birmingham B4 6DR,
Telephone: 0121 236 5514/5
E-mail: clerks@no8chambers.co.uk
Call Date: Nov 1967, Gray's Inn
Recorder
Qualifications: [MA, LLB]

THOMPSON ANDREW EDWARD COURTNEY

Francis Taylor Building
3rd Floor, Temple, London EC4Y 7BY,
Telephone: 0171 797 7250
Call Date: Nov 1969, Inner Temple
Pupil Master
Qualifications: [BA (Hons), LLB (Dublin)]

THOMPSON ANDREW IAN

1 Inner Temple Lane
Temple, London EC4Y 1AF,
Telephone: 020 7353 0933
Call Date: Oct 1991, Gray's Inn
Qualifications: [MA (Oxon)]

THOMPSON ANDREW PETER

Park Court Chambers
16 Park Place, Leeds LS1 2SJ,
Telephone: 0113 2433277
Call Date: July 1989, Inner Temple
Qualifications: [LLB (Hons)]

THOMPSON ANDREW RICHARD

Erskine Chambers
30 Lincoln's Inn Fields, Lincoln's Inn,
London WC2A 3PF,
Telephone: 0171 242 5532
E-mail:clerks@erskine-chambers.co.uk
Call Date: Nov 1991, Inner Temple
Qualifications: [MA, LLM (Cantab)]

THOMPSON MISS BLONDELLE MARGUERITE

1 Fountain Court
Steelhouse Lane, Birmingham B4 6DR,
Telephone: 0121 236 5721
Call Date: July 1987, Middle Temple
Qualifications: [LLB]

THOMPSON CEDRIC AUGUSTUS

Somersett Chambers
25 Bedford Row, London WC1R 4HE,
Telephone: 0171 404 6701
E-mail: somelaw@aol.com
Call Date: Nov 1984, Gray's Inn
Qualifications: [BA Hons]

THOMPSON COLLINGWOOD FORSTER JAMES QC (1998)

9 Bedford Row
London WC1R 4AZ,
Telephone: 0171 242 3555
E-mail: clerks@9br.co.uk
Call Date: July 1975, Gray's Inn
Recorder
Qualifications: [LLB (Lond)]

THOMPSON DERMOT MICHAEL MAIN

1 Gray's Inn Square, Chambers of the Baroness Scotland of Asthal QC
1st Floor, London WC1R 5AG,
Telephone: 0171 405 3000
E-mail: clerks@onegrays.demon.co.uk
Call Date: July 1977, Gray's Inn
Pupil Master
Qualifications: [MA, LLB (Cantab)]

THOMPSON MS GLENNA

Chambers of Wilfred Forster-Jones
New Court, 1st Floor South, Temple,
London EC4Y 9BE,
Telephone: 0171 353 0853/4/7222
E-mail: chambers@newcourt.net
Call Date: Nov 1993, Inner Temple
Qualifications: [BSc (Hons)]

THOMPSON MISS (HELEN) (LOUISE) POLLY

2 Pump Court
1st Floor, Temple, London EC4Y 7AH,
Telephone: 0171 353 5597
Call Date: Nov 1990, Middle Temple
Pupil Master
Qualifications: [BA, Dip Law (Lond)]

THOMPSON HOWARD NEIL

5 Fountain Court
Steelhouse Lane, Birmingham B4 6DR,
Telephone: 0121 606 0500
E-mail:clerks@5fountaincourt.law.co.uk
Call Date: July 1982, Lincoln's Inn
Pupil Master
Qualifications: [BA]

THOMPSON JONATHAN RICHARD

8 King Street Chambers
8 King Street, Manchester M2 6AQ,
Telephone: 0161 834 9560
E-mail: eightking@aol.com
Call Date: Oct 1990, Inner Temple
Qualifications: [MA, LLM (Cantab)]

THOMPSON LYALL NORRIS

Tindal Chambers
3/5 New Street, Chelmsford, Essex,
CM1 1NT, Telephone: 01245 267742
Call Date: Oct 1995, Inner Temple
Qualifications: [LLB (Aberdeen), CPE (City)]

THOMPSON MARCUS ELLIOT GERARD

Queen Elizabeth Building
Ground Floor, Temple, London
EC4Y 9BS,
Telephone: 0171 353 7181 (12 Lines)
Call Date: Oct 1996, Inner Temple
Qualifications: [BA (Cantab), CPE]

THOMPSON PATRICK MILES

Queen's Chambers
5 John Dalton Street, Manchester M2 6ET,
Telephone: 0161 834 6875/4738
Queens Chambers
4 Camden Place, Preston PR1 3JL,
Telephone: 01772 828300
Call Date: Oct 1990, Gray's Inn
Qualifications: [LLB (Hons)(Manch)]

THOMPSON RHODRI WILLIAM RALPH

Monckton Chambers
4 Raymond Buildings, Gray's Inn, London
WC1R 5BP, Telephone: 0171 405 7211
E-mail: chambers@monckton.co.uk
Call Date: July 1989, Middle Temple
Pupil Master
Qualifications: [MA (Oxon), BPhil (Oxon)]

THOMPSON MISS SALLY

2 Harcourt Buildings
1st Floor, Temple, London EC4Y 9DB,
Telephone: 020 7353 2112
Call Date: Oct 1994, Middle Temple
Qualifications: [Dip in Music, CPE (Lond)]

THOMPSON MISS SAMANTHA

55 Temple Chambers
Temple Avenue, London EC4Y 0HP,
Telephone: 0171 353 7400
Call Date: 1996, Gray's Inn
Qualifications: [B.Sc]

THOMPSON SIMON

10 King's Bench Walk
Ground Floor, Temple, London
EC4Y 7EB, Telephone: 0171 353 7742
E-mail: 10kbw@lineone.net
Call Date: July 1988, Lincoln's Inn
Qualifications: [LLB (Hons) (Leics)]

THOMPSON STEVEN LIM

Twenty-Four Old Buildings
Ground Floor, Lincoln's Inn, London
WC2A 3UP, Telephone: 0171 404 0946
E-mail:clerks@24oldbuildings.law.co.uk
Call Date: Oct 1996, Inner Temple
Qualifications: [BA (Cantab)]

THOMSON DR DAVID JAMES RAMSAY GIBB

Barnard's Inn Chambers
6th Floor, Halton House, 20-23 Holborn,
London EC1N 2JD,
Telephone: 0171 369 6969
E-mail: clerks@biclaw.co.uk
Call Date: Nov 1994, Inner Temple
Qualifications: [MB, Ch.B (Sheff), LLB
(Lond), LLM (Cantab)]

THOMSON MRS LOUISE GILLIAN

199 Strand
London WC2R 1DR,
Telephone: 0171 379 9779
E-mail: chambers@199strand.co.uk
Call Date: Nov 1996, Lincoln's Inn
Qualifications: [BA (Hons)(E.Anglia)]

THOMSON MARTIN HALDANE AHMAD

Wynne Chambers
1 Wynne Road, London SW9 0BB,
Telephone: 0181 961 6144
E-mail: m_h_a.thomson_esq@which.net
Call Date: 1979, Gray's Inn
Qualifications: [LLB (Hons, Exeter), Dip Law
(City)]

THORESBY ROBERT MCCALL

Chambers of Robert Thoresby
37 Redbridge Lane West, Wanstead,
London E11 2JX,
Telephone: 0181 530 5267
Call Date: July 1978, Inner Temple
Qualifications: [MA (Cantab)]

THORLEY SIMON JOE QC (1989)

3 New Square
Lincoln's Inn, London WC2A 3RS,
Telephone: 0171 405 1111
E-mail: 3newsquareip@lineone.net
Call Date: July 1972, Inner Temple
Qualifications: [MA (Oxon)]

THORN ROGER ERIC QC (1990)

New Court Chambers
3 Broad Chare, Newcastle upon Tyne
NE1 3DQ, Telephone: 0191 232 1980
Call Date: Nov 1970, Middle Temple
Assistant Recorder
Qualifications: [LLB]

THORNBERRY MISS EMILY ANNE

14 Tooks Court
Cursitor St, London EC4A 1LB,
Telephone: 0171 405 8828
E-mail: clerks@tooks.law.co.uk
Call Date: Nov 1983, Gray's Inn
Pupil Master
Qualifications: [BA (Kent)]

THORNDIKE ANTHONY EDWARD

Claremont Chambers
26 Waterloo Road, Wolverhampton
WV1 4BL, Telephone: 01902 426222
Bracton Chambers
95a Chancery Lane, London WC2A 1DT,
Telephone: 0171 242 4248
Call Date: Oct 1994, Lincoln's Inn
Qualifications: [BSc (Econ), MSc, PhD]

THORNE MS KATHERINE HARRIET

Counsels' Chambers
2nd Floor, 10-11 Gray's Inn Square,
London WC1R 5JD,
Telephone: 0171 405 2576
E-mail:clerks@10-11graysinnsquare.co.uk
Call Date: Nov 1994, Inner Temple
Qualifications: [BA (Leeds), CPE]

THORNE MISS SARAH LOUISE

Westgate Chambers
144 High Street, Lewes, East Sussex,
BN7 1XT, Telephone: 01273 480510
Call Date: Feb 1995, Middle Temple
Qualifications: [LLB (Hons)(Lond)]

THORNE TIMOTHY PETER

33 Bedford Row
London WC1R 4JH,
Telephone: 0171 242 6476
E-mail:clerks@bedfordrow33.demon.co.uk
Call Date: Nov 1987, Gray's Inn
Qualifications: [MA (Oxon)]

THORNETT GARY PAUL

1 Fountain Court
Steelhouse Lane, Birmingham B4 6DR,
Telephone: 0121 236 5721
Call Date: Nov 1991, Middle Temple
Qualifications: [B Mus (Lond), ARCO, LRAM]

THORNHILL ANDREW ROBERT QC (1985)

Pump Court Tax Chambers
16 Bedford Row, London WC1R 4EB,
Telephone: 0171 414 8080
Park Court Chambers
16 Park Place, Leeds LS1 2SJ,
Telephone: 0113 2433277
Call Date: July 1969, Middle Temple
Qualifications: [BA (Oxon)]

THORNHILL MS TERESA

29 Gwilliam Street
Bristol BS3 4LT,
Telephone: 0117 966 8997
E-mail: tthornhill@freeuk.com
Call Date: July 1986, Middle Temple
Qualifications: [BA (Hons) (Oxon), Dip Law
(City), MA (Lond)]

THORNLEY DAVID

Chambers of Martin Burr
Fourth Floor, Eldon Chambers, 30/32
Fleet Street, London EC4Y 1AA,
Telephone: 0171 353 4636
Call Date: July 1988, Inner Temple
Qualifications: [BA (Hons) (Kent)]

THORNTON ANDREW JAMES

Erskine Chambers
30 Lincoln's Inn Fields, Lincoln's Inn,
London WC2A 3PF,
Telephone: 0171 242 5532
E-mail:clerks@erskine-chambers.co.uk
Call Date: Nov 1994, Lincoln's Inn
Qualifications: [LLB (Hons)(Hull)]

THORNTON MISS ANNE REBECCA

9 Woodhouse Square
Leeds LS3 1AD,
Telephone: 0113 2451986
E-mail: clerks@9woodhouse.co.uk
Call Date: July 1976, Middle Temple
Qualifications: [LLB]

THORNTON PETER RIBBLESDALE QC (1992)

Doughty Street Chambers
11 Doughty Street, London WC1N 2PG,
Telephone: 0171 404 1313
E-mail:enquiries@doughtystreet.co.uk
Call Date: July 1969, Middle Temple
Assistant Recorder
Qualifications: [BA (Cantab)]

THORNTON PHILIP CHARLES

Devereux Chambers
Devereux Court, London WC2R 3JJ,
Telephone: 0171 353 7534
E-mail: mailbox@devchambers.co.uk
Call Date: Nov 1988, Middle Temple
Qualifications: [MA (Cantab)]

THOROGOOD BERNARD

5 Fountain Court
Steelhouse Lane, Birmingham B4 6DR,
Telephone: 0121 606 0500
E-mail:clerks@5fountaincourt.law.co.uk
Call Date: July 1986, Gray's Inn
Pupil Master
Qualifications: [LLB Leeds]

THOROLD OLIVER

Doughty Street Chambers
11 Doughty Street, London WC1N 2PG,
Telephone: 0171 404 1313
E-mail:enquiries@doughtystreet.co.uk
Call Date: Nov 1971, Inner Temple
Pupil Master
Qualifications: [BA (Oxon)]

THOROWGOOD MAX CAMPBELL DE WARRENNE

Mitre Court Chambers
3rd Floor, Temple, London EC4Y 7BP,
Telephone: 0171 353 9394
E-mail: mitrecourt.com
Call Date: Nov 1995, Lincoln's Inn
Qualifications: [MA (Hons)]

THORP IAN SIMON

Park Lane Chambers
19 Westgate, Leeds LS1 2RD,
Telephone: 0113 2285000
E-mail:clerks@parklanechambers.co.uk
Call Date: July 1988, Inner Temple
Qualifications: [BA (Hull)]

THORPE ALEXANDER LAMBERT

Queen Elizabeth Building
2nd Floor, Temple, London EC4Y 9BS,
Telephone: 0171 797 7837
Call Date: Oct 1995, Inner Temple
Qualifications: [BA (Lond), CPE (Lond)]

THRELFALL RICHARD WILLIAM GEORGE

Queens Square Chambers
56 Queens Square, Bristol BS1 4PR,
Telephone: 0117 921 1966
Call Date: July 1972, Gray's Inn
Pupil Master

THROP MISS ALISON

Call Date: Oct 1992, Middle Temple
Qualifications: [BA (Hons)(York), Common
Profeional, Examination]

THROWER JAMES SIMEON

11 Old Square
Ground Floor, Lincoln's Inn, London
WC2A 3TS, Telephone: 0171 242 5022/
405 1074
Call Date: July 1973, Middle Temple
Pupil Master
Qualifications: [LLB]

THURBIN MRS DAYE BARBOT

Westgate Chambers
144 High Street, Lewes, East Sussex,
BN7 1XT, Telephone: 01273 480510
Call Date: Nov 1991, Gray's Inn
Qualifications: [BSc (Florida), Juris Doctor
(Nova)]

THWAITES RONALD QC (1987)

10 King's Bench Walk
1st Floor, Temple, London EC4Y 7EB,
Telephone: 0171 353 2501
Call Date: Nov 1970, Gray's Inn
Qualifications: [LLB (Lond)]

TICCIATI OLIVER

4 Pump Court
Temple, London EC4Y 7AN,
Telephone: 020 7842 5555
E-mail:chambers@4pumpcourt.law.co.uk
Call Date: July 1979, Inner Temple
Pupil Master
Qualifications: [MA (Cantab)]

TIDBURY ANDREW HUGH

Queen Elizabeth Building
2nd Floor, Temple, London EC4Y 9BS,
Telephone: 0171 797 7837
Call Date: July 1976, Inner Temple
Pupil Master
Qualifications: [BA (Cantab)]

D

TIDMARSH CHRISTOPHER RALPH FRANCIS

5 Stone Buildings
Lincoln's Inn, London WC2A 3XT,
Telephone: 0171 242 6201
E-mail:clerks@5-stonebuildings.law.co.uk
Call Date: Nov 1985, Lincoln's Inn
Pupil Master
Qualifications: [BA (Oxon)]

TIGHE MISS DAWN

37 Park Square Chambers
37 Park Square, Leeds LS1 2NY,
Telephone: 0113 2439422
E-mail: chambers@no37.co.uk
Call Date: Nov 1989, Lincoln's Inn
Qualifications: [LLB (Newc)]

TILBURY JAMES RICHARD

2 Paper Buildings
1st Floor, Temple, London EC4Y 7ET,
Telephone: 020 7556 5500
E-mail: clerks@2pbbarristers.co.uk
Call Date: Mar 1996, Gray's Inn
Qualifications: [LLB]

TILLETT MICHAEL BURN QC (1996)

39 Essex Street
London WC2R 3AT,
Telephone: 0171 832 1111
E-mail: clerks@39essex.co.uk
Call Date: July 1965, Inner Temple
Recorder
Qualifications: [MA (Cantab)]

TILLYARD JAMES HENRY HUGH

30 Park Place
Cardiff CF1 3BA,
Telephone: 01222 398421
E-mail: 100757.1456@compuserve.com
Farrar's Building
Temple, London EC4Y 7BD,
Telephone: 0171 583 9241
E-mail:chambers@farrarsbuilding.co.uk
Call Date: 1978, Middle Temple
Pupil Master, Assistant Recorder
Qualifications: [BSc (Leeds)]

TIPPETT GILES PETER

1 Gray's Inn Square
Ground Floor, London WC1R 5AA,
Telephone: 0171 405 8946/7/8
Call Date: Oct 1992, Middle Temple
Qualifications: [LL.B (Hons)]

TIPPLES MISS AMANDA JANE

13 Old Square
Ground Floor, Lincoln's Inn, London
WC2A 3UA, Telephone: 0171 404 4800
E-mail: clerks@13oldsquare.law.co.uk
Call Date: Oct 1991, Gray's Inn
Pupil Master
Qualifications: [MA (Cambs)]

TITHERIDGE ROGER NOEL QC (1973)

1 Paper Buildings
1st Floor, Temple, London EC4Y 7EP,
Telephone: 0171 353 3728/4953
Call Date: July 1954, Gray's Inn
Recorder
Qualifications: [MA (Oxon)]

TIWANA PARDEEP SINGH

4 Fountain Court
Steelhouse Lane, Birmingham B4 6DR,
Telephone: 0121 236 3476
Call Date: Nov 1993, Lincoln's Inn
Qualifications: [LLB (Hons)]

TIZZANO FRANCO SALVATORE

8 King's Bench Walk
2nd Floor, Temple, London EC4Y 7DU,
Telephone: 0171 797 8888
8 King's Bench Walk North
1 Park Square East, Leeds LS1 2NE,
Telephone: 0113 2439797
Call Date: Feb 1989, Middle Temple
Qualifications: [LLB]

TOAL DAVID JOHN

Old Colony House
6 South King Street, Manchester M2 6DQ,
Telephone: 0161 834 4364
Call Date: Feb 1990, Gray's Inn
Qualifications: [LLB (Hons)0]

TOBIN DANIEL ALPHONSUS JOSEPH

Chambers of Geoffrey Hawker
46/48 Essex Street, London WC2R 3GH,
Telephone: 0171 583 8899
Call Date: Oct 1994, Middle Temple
Qualifications: [LLB (Hons)(Lond)]

TOCH MISS JOANNA PATRICIA

3 Dr Johnson's Buildings
Ground Floor, Temple, London
EC4Y 7BA, Telephone: 0171 353 4854
E-mail: clerks@3djb.co.uk
Call Date: Nov 1988, Middle Temple
Qualifications: [LLB (Hons)(Lond)]

TOD JONATHAN ALAN

7 Stone Buildings (also at 11 Bolt Court)
1st Floor, Lincoln's Inn, London
WC2A 3SZ, Telephone: 0171 242 0961
E-mail:larthur@7stonebuildings.law.co.uk
11 Bolt Court (also at 7 Stone Buildings – 1st Floor)
London EC4A 3DQ,
Telephone: 0171 353 2300
E-mail: boltct11@aol.com
Redhill Chambers
Seloduct House, 30 Station Road, Redhill,
Surrey, RH1 1NF,
Telephone: 01737 780781
Call Date: Nov 1990, Inner Temple
Qualifications: [LLB (Hons)]

TODD ALAN JAMES

Farrar's Building
Temple, London EC4Y 7BD,
Telephone: 0171 583 9241
E-mail:chambers@farrarsbuilding.co.uk
Call Date: Nov 1990, Gray's Inn
Qualifications: [MA (Cantab)]

TODD CHARLES LOUIS

1 Mitre Court Buildings
Temple, London EC4Y 7BS,
Telephone: 0171 797 7070
E-mail: clerks@1mcb.com
Call Date: July 1983, Gray's Inn
Pupil Master
Qualifications: [BA,ACA]

TODD MARTIN RUSSELL

York Chambers
14 Toft Green, York YO1 6JT,
Telephone: 01904 620048
E-mail: [name]@yorkchambers.co.uk
Call Date: Nov 1991, Inner Temple
Qualifications: [LLB (Hons)]

TODD MICHAEL ALAN QC (1997)

Erskine Chambers
30 Lincoln's Inn Fields, Lincoln's Inn,
London WC2A 3PF,
Telephone: 0171 242 5532
E-mail:clerks@erskine-chambers.co.uk
Call Date: July 1977, Lincoln's Inn
Qualifications: [BA (Keele)]

TODD RICHARD FRAZER

1 Mitre Court Buildings
Temple, London EC4Y 7BS,
Telephone: 0171 797 7070
E-mail: clerks@1mcb.com
Call Date: July 1988, Middle Temple
Pupil Master
Qualifications: [MA (Hons) (Oxon)]

TODD MS SUSAN MARGARET

3 Fountain Court
Steelhouse Lane, Birmingham B4 6DR,
Telephone: 0121 236 5854
Call Date: Nov 1991, Gray's Inn
Qualifications: [BA (Cantab), MA (Sussex)]

TODMAN MRS DEBORAH

New Court
Temple, London EC4Y 9BE,
Telephone: 0171 583 5123/0510
Call Date: Oct 1991, Gray's Inn
Qualifications: [LLB (Hons)]

TOLANEY MISS SONIA

3 Verulam Buildings
London WC1R 5NT,
Telephone: 0171 831 8441
E-mail: clerks@3verulam.co.uk
Call Date: Oct 1995, Middle Temple
Qualifications: [BA (Hons)]

D

TOLEDANO DANIEL ZE'EV

One Essex Court
Ground Floor, Temple, London
EC4Y 9AR, Telephone: 020 7583 2000
E-mail: clerks@oneessexcourt.co.uk
Call Date: Oct 1993, Inner Temple
Qualifications: [MA (Hons) (Cantab)]

TOLHURST ROBERT LEIGH DOUGLAS

2 Dyers Buildings
London EC1N 2JT,
Telephone: 0171 404 1881
Call Date: Oct 1992, Middle Temple
Qualifications: [Ba (Hons)]

TOLKIEN SIMON MARIO REUEL

2 Paper Buildings, Basement North
Temple, London EC4Y 7ET,
Telephone: 0171 936 2613
E-mail: post@2paper.co.uk
Call Date: July 1994, Middle Temple
Qualifications: [BA (Hons)(Oxon)]

TOLLEY ADAM RICHARD

Fountain Court
Temple, London EC4Y 9DH,
Telephone: 0171 583 3335
E-mail: chambers@fountaincourt.co.uk
Call Date: Oct 1994, Inner Temple

TOLSON ROBIN STEWART

35 Essex Street
Temple, London WC2R 3AR,
Telephone: 0171 353 6381
E-mail: derek_jenkins@link.org
Call Date: Nov 1980, Inner Temple
Pupil Master, Assistant Recorder
Qualifications: [BA (Cantab)]

TOMASSI MARK DAVID

Dr Johnson's Chambers
Two Dr Johnson's Buildings, Temple,
London EC4Y 7AY,
Telephone: 0171 353 4716
E-mail: clerks@2djb.freeserve.co.uk
Call Date: Nov 1981, Middle Temple
Pupil Master
Qualifications: [BA (Hons)]

TOMLINSON DAVID REDVERS

5 King's Bench Walk
Temple, London EC4Y 7DN,
Telephone: 0171 353 5638
Call Date: July 1977, Inner Temple
Pupil Master, Assistant Recorder
Qualifications: [LLB (Leeds)]

TOMLINSON HUGH RICHARD EDWARD

New Court Chambers
5 Verulam Buildings, Gray's Inn, London
WC1R 5LY, Telephone: 0171 831 9500
E-mail: mail@newcourtchambers.com
Call Date: Nov 1983, Gray's Inn
Pupil Master
Qualifications: [BA (Oxon), MA(Sussex]

TOMLINSON STEPHEN MILES QC (1988)

S Tomlinson QC
7 King's Bench Walk, Temple, London
EC4Y 7DS, Telephone: 0171 583 0404
E-mail: clerks@7kbw.law.co.uk
Call Date: July 1974, Inner Temple
Recorder
Qualifications: [MA (Oxon)]

TOMS NICHOLAS ROBERT

Mitre House Chambers
15-19 Devereux Court, London WC2R 3JJ,
Telephone: 0171 583 8233
Call Date: Nov 1996, Middle Temple
Qualifications: [LLB (Hons), LLM (Cantab)]

TONGE CHRISTOPHER PAUL

15 North Church Street Chambers
15 North Church Street, Sheffield
S1 2DH, Telephone: 0114 2759708/
2738380
Call Date: July 1988, Inner Temple
Qualifications: [LLB (Sheffield)]

TONGE MISS RUTH MARGARET HAYES

Claremont Chambers
26 Waterloo Road, Wolverhampton
WV1 4BL, Telephone: 01902 426222
Call Date: Oct 1993, Gray's Inn
Qualifications: [LLB (Hons)]

TONNA JOHN PRINGLE NODWELL

29 Bedford Row Chambers
London WC1R 4HE,
Telephone: 0171 831 2626
Call Date: July 1974, Gray's Inn
Pupil Master
Qualifications: [BA (Oxon)]

TOOGOOD MISS CLAIRE VICTORIA

One Paper Buildings
Ground Floor, Temple, London
EC4Y 7EP, Telephone: 0171 583 7355
E-mail: clerks@1pb.co.uk
Call Date: Oct 1995, Middle Temple
Qualifications: [BA (Hons)]

TOOGOOD JOHN

4 King's Bench Walk
Ground/First Floor/Basement, Temple,
London EC4Y 7DL,
Telephone: 0171 822 8822
E-mail: 4kbw@barristersatlaw.com
Call Date: July 1957, Gray's Inn
Pupil Master
Qualifications: [LLM]

TOOKEY MICHAEL JOHN

95A Chancery Lane
London WC2A 1DT,
Telephone: 0171 405 3101
Call Date: Oct 1992, Lincoln's Inn
Qualifications: [LLB (Hons)]

TOOMBS RICHARD JOHN

King Charles House
Standard Hill, Nottingham NG1 6FX,
Telephone: 0115 9418851
E-mail: clerks@kch.co.uk
Call Date: July 1983, Gray's Inn
Pupil Master
Qualifications: [LLB (B'ham)]

TOONE ROBERT FRANCIS

11 King's Bench Walk
1st Floor, Temple, London EC4Y 7EQ,
Telephone: 0171 353 3337
E-mail: fmuller11@aol.com
11 King's Bench Walk
3 Park Court, Park Cross Street, Leeds
LS1 2QH, Telephone: 0113 297 1200
Call Date: Oct 1993, Inner Temple
Qualifications: [BA]

TOPHAM GEOFFREY JOHN

3 Stone Buildings
Lincoln's Inn, London WC2A 3XL,
Telephone: 0171 242 4937
E-mail: clerks@3sb.law.co.uk
Call Date: June 1964, Lincoln's Inn
Qualifications: [BA (Cantab)]

TOPHAM JOHN DAVID

Broadway House Chambers
Broadway House, 9 Bank Street, Bradford,
West Yorkshire, BD1 1TW,
Telephone: 01274 722560
E-mail: clerks@broadwayhouse.co.uk
Broadway House Chambers
31 Park Square West, Leeds LS1 2PF,
Telephone: 0113 246 2600
Call Date: July 1970, Gray's Inn
Pupil Master
Qualifications: [LLB (Lond)]

TOPLISS MISS MEGAN LOUISE

1 Paper Buildings
1st Floor, Temple, London EC4Y 7EP,
Telephone: 0171 353 3728/4953
Call Date: Oct 1994, Gray's Inn
Qualifications: [LLB (Wales)]

TOPOLSKI MICHAEL JONATHAN

14 Tooks Court
Cursitor St, London EC4A 1LB,
Telephone: 0171 405 8828
E-mail: clerks@tooks.law.co.uk
Call Date: Apr 1986, Inner Temple
Pupil Master

TORRANCE HUGH MYER BERNARD

Goldsmith Chambers
Ground Floor, Goldsmith Building,
Temple, London EC4Y 7BL,
Telephone: 0171 353 6802/3/4/5
E-mail:clerks@goldsmithchambers.law.co.uk
Call Date: May 1956, Lincoln's Inn
Pupil Master
Qualifications: [MA, LLB (Cantab)]

TOUBE MS FELICITY ROSALIND

3/4 South Square
Gray's Inn, London WC1R 5HP,
Telephone: 0171 696 9900
E-mail: clerks@southsquare.com
Call Date: Nov 1995, Inner Temple
Qualifications: [BA, BCL (Oxon)]

TOUSSAINT MISS DEBORAH

Chambers of Geoffrey Hawker
46/48 Essex Street, London WC2R 3GH,
Telephone: 0171 583 8899
Call Date: July 1988, Middle Temple
Qualifications: [LLB (Hons)]

TOWERS MARTIN PETER

Durham Barristers' Chambers
27 Old Elvet, Durham DH1 3HN,
Telephone: 0191 386 9199
Call Date: Nov 1996, Gray's Inn
Qualifications: [LLB (Bris)]

TOWLER PETER JEREMY HAMILTON

17 Carlton Crescent
Southampton SO15 2XR,
Telephone: 023 8032 0320/0823 2003
E-mail: greg@jg17cc.co.uk
Call Date: July 1974, Middle Temple
Recorder
Qualifications: [MA (Cantab), FCI Arb]

TOWNEND JAMES BARRIE STANLEY QC (1978)

One King's Bench Walk
1st Floor, Temple, London EC4Y 7DB,
Telephone: 0171 936 1500
E-mail: ddear@1kbw.co.uk
Call Date: Feb 1962, Middle Temple
Recorder
Qualifications: [MA (Oxon)]

TOWNSEND JAMES NEVILLE

Guildhall Chambers
22-26 Broad Street, Bristol BS1 2HG,
Telephone: 0117 9273366
E-mail: civil.clerks@guildhallchambers.co.uk and
criminal.clerks@guildhallchambers.co.uk
Call Date: July 1980, Inner Temple
Pupil Master
Qualifications: [MA (Oxon)]

TOWNSHEND TIMOTHY JOHN HUME

Octagon House
19 Colegate, Norwich NR3 1AT,
Telephone: 01603 623186
E-mail: admin@octagon-chambers.co.uk
Call Date: Nov 1972, Lincoln's Inn
Pupil Master
Qualifications: [MA (Cantab)]

TOZER MISS STEPHANIE

9 Old Square
Ground Floor, Lincoln's Inn, London
WC2A 3SR, Telephone: 0171 405 4682
E-mail: chambers@9oldsquare.co.uk
Call Date: Oct 1996, Lincoln's Inn
Qualifications: [BA (Hons)(Oxon)]

TOZZI NIGEL KENNETH

4 Pump Court
Temple, London EC4Y 7AN,
Telephone: 020 7842 5555
E-mail:chambers@4pumpcourt.law.co.uk
Call Date: July 1980, Gray's Inn
Pupil Master
Qualifications: [LLB (Exon)]

TRACE ANTHONY JOHN QC (1998)

13 Old Square
Ground Floor, Lincoln's Inn, London
WC2A 3UA, Telephone: 0171 404 4800
E-mail: clerks@13oldsquare.law.co.uk
Call Date: July 1981, Lincoln's Inn
Qualifications: [MA (Hons) (Cantab)]

Fax: 0171 405 4267;
Out of hours telephone: 01992 441374
(Clerk – John Moore); DX: LDE 326

Types of work: Arbitration, Banking, Bankruptcy, Chancery (general), Chancery land law, Commercial, Commercial litigation, Commercial property, Company and commercial, Equity, wills and trusts, Insolvency, Insurance/reinsurance, Landlord and tenant, Partnerships, Probate and administration, Professional negligence, Sports

Awards and memberships: Bundy Scholarship (Magdalene College, Cambridge University); Hardwick Scholar, Tancred Studentship and Droop Scholar of Lincoln's Inn; Honorary Secretary, Chancery Bar Association; Member Bar Sports Law Group, COMBAR and ACTAPS (Association of Contentious Trust and Probate Specialists)

Languages spoken: French, Swahili

Publications: *Butterworths European Law Service (Company Law)*, (Contributor), 1992; *Receivers, Administrators and Liquidators Quarterly* (RALQ), (Deputy Managing Editor), 1993 to date

Practice
After graduating from Cambridge in 1980 with First Class Honours in Law, Anthony Trace was a pupil to David Oliver (now The Hon David Oliver QC) and Colin Rimer (now The Hon Mr Justice Rimer). In 1981 he was joint winner of the Observer Mace Debating Competition and won the Crowther Advocacy Shield. He has developed a very substantial practice, both in England and in foreign jurisdictions. He has been involved in a number of cases in the Cayman Islands, The Bahamas, the Isle of Man and Hong Kong.

Reported cases in which he has appeared include:

Annangel Glory Compania Naviera SA v Golodetz Ltd 1988 PCC 37 (company charges)

Gomba Holdings UK Ltd v Homan [1986] 3 All ER 94 (receivers' duties)

Kemmis v Kemmis [1988] 1 WLR 1307 (constructive notice)

Haarhaus & Co GmbH v Law Debenture Trust Corp plc [1988] BCLC 640 (company meetings)

Ronald Preston & Partners v Markheath Securities plc [1988] 31 EG 50 (estate agents)

Re A Debtor (No 222 of 1990) [1992] BCLC 137 (voting at creditors' meetings)

Harrison v Thompson [1989] 1 WLR 1325 (equitable interest)

Re Unisoft Group Ltd (No 2) [1992] BCC 494 (security for costs against limited companies)

BBMB Finance (Hong Kong) Ltd v Eda Holdings Ltd [1991] 2 All ER 129 (conversion)

Bank of Credit and Commerce International SA v Aboody [1990] 1 QB 923 (undue influence)

Lee Panavision Ltd v Lee Lighting Ltd [1991] BCLC 575 (directors' duties)

Jelson (Estates) Ltd v Harvey [1984] 1 All ER 12 (contempt)

Re Jeffrey S Levitt Ltd [1992] BCLC 250 (privilege against self-incrimination)

Gomba Holdings (UK) Ltd v Minories Finance Ltd (No 2) [1993] BCLC 7 (mortgagee's costs)

Re Mirror Group (Holdings) Ltd [1993] BCLC 538 (liability of assignees on liquidation)

Lotteryking Ltd v AMEC Properties Ltd [1995] 28 EG 100 (set-off against assignees)

Re BCCI SA (No 10) [1996] 4 All ER 796 (insolvency set-off)

Slough Estates plc v Welwyn Hatfield District Council [1996] EGCS 132 (measure of damages for fraudulent misrepresentation)

Grand Metropolitan plc v The William Hill Group Ltd [1997] 1 BCLC 390 (rectification)

Jordan Grand Prix Ltd v Baltic Insurance Group [1998] 1 WLR 1049 (Brussels Convention)

Bogg v Raper [1998] *The Times Law Reports* 22 April (will drafting and exclusion clauses)

Plant v Plant [1998] 1 BCLC (individual voluntary arrangements)

TRACY FORSTER MISS JANE ELIZABETH

13 King's Bench Walk
1st Floor, Temple, London EC4Y 7EN,
Telephone: 0171 353 7204
E-mail: clerks@13kbw.law.co.uk

King's Bench Chambers
32 Beaumont Street, Oxford OX1 2NP,
Telephone: 01865 311066
E-mail: clerks@kbc-oxford.law.co.uk
Call Date: July 1975, Inner Temple
Pupil Master
Qualifications: [LLB (L'pool)]

TRAFFORD MARK RUSSELL

2 King's Bench Walk
Ground Floor, Temple, London
EC4Y 7DE, Telephone: 0171 353 1746
E-mail: 2kbw@atlas.co.uk
King's Bench Chambers
115 North Hill, Plymouth PL4 8JY,
Telephone: 01752 221551
Call Date: May 1992, Lincoln's Inn
Qualifications: [BSc (Hons) (Brunel), Dip
Law (City)]

TRAVERS DAVID

3 Fountain Court
Steelhouse Lane, Birmingham B4 6DR,
Telephone: 0121 236 5854
Call Date: July 1981, Middle Temple
Pupil Master
Qualifications: [LLB, LLM, AKC]

Types of work: Administrative, Consumer law,
Environment, Local government, Planning,
Waste management

Circuit: Midland & Oxford

Awards and memberships: Harmsworth
Scholar; Royal Institution Science Scholar;
Member Planning and Environment Bar
Association and Administrative Law Bar
Association; Member of the Bar Council
1995 to date and of its Law Reform and
Information Technology Committees
1996-8.

Other professional experience: Sometime occa-
sional lecturer School of Management
Sciences University of Manchester Institute
of Science and Technology; sometime libel
reader Express Newspapers; regular
lecturer at professional conferences

Publications: Editor *Kings Counsel* – The
Journal of the Faculty of Laws Kings College
London 1973; Executive Editor 1974, 1974

Reported Cases: *R v Snaresbrook Court, ex
parte Input Management Ltd*, [1999] *The
Times*, 29 April, 1999. Obligation on the
Crown Court to give reasons when sitting
in an Appellate capacity.
*Meston Technical Services Ltd v
Warwickshire CC*, [1995] Env LR 36, 1995.
Meaning of 'Waste', operation of waste
management licence.
T & S Stores v Hereford & Worcester CC,
[1995] Tr LR 337, 1995. Extent of the 'due
diligence' defence.
Janbo Trading v Dudley MBC, [1993] 157
JP 1056, 1993. Otherwise accurate trade
description rendered false by the instruc-
tions supplied with the product.
Dudley MBC v Robert Firman Ltd, (1992)
The Independent, 26 October, 1992.
Extent of the 'due diligence' defence in
relation to sufficiency of sampling.

TRAVERS HUGH

Pump Court Chambers
Upper Ground Floor, 3 Pump Court,
Temple, London EC4Y 7AJ,
Telephone: 0171 353 0711
E-mail: clerks@3pumpcourt.com
Pump Court Chambers
31 Southgate Street, Winchester
SO23 9EE, Telephone: 01962 868161
E-mail: clerks@3pumpcourt.com
Pump Court Chambers
5 Temple Chambers, Temple Street,
Swindon SN1 1SQ,
Telephone: 01793 539899
E-mail: clerks@3pumpcourt.com
Call Date: Nov 1988, Middle Temple
Qualifications: [MA (Cantab)]

TRAVERS RICHARD ETTORE NICHOLAS

Maidstone Chambers
33 Earl Street, Maidstone, Kent, ME14 1PF,
Telephone: 01622 688592
E-mail:maidstonechambers@compuserve.co
m
Call Date: Feb 1985, Lincoln's Inn
Qualifications: [BA (Lond), Dip Law]

TRAVERSI JOHN DAVID STEPHEN ANTONA

**4 Brick Court, Chambers of Anne
Rafferty QC**
1st Floor, Temple, London EC4Y 9AD,
Telephone: 0171 583 8455
Call Date: July 1977, Gray's Inn
Pupil Master
Qualifications: [MA (Oxon)]

TREACY COLMAN MAURICE QC (1990)

3 Fountain Court
Steelhouse Lane, Birmingham B4 6DR,
Telephone: 0121 236 5854
Chambers of Michael Pert QC
36 Bedford Row, London WC1R 4JH,
Telephone: 0171 421 8000
E-mail: 36bedfordrow@link.org
Chambers of Michael Pert QC
24 Albion Place, Northampton NN1 1UD,
Telephone: 01604 602333
Chambers of Michael Pert QC
104 New Walk, Leicester LE1 7EA,
Telephone: 0116 249 2020
Call Date: July 1971, Middle Temple
Recorder
Qualifications: [MA (Cantab)]

TREASURE FRANCIS SETON

199 Strand
London WC2R 1DR,
Telephone: 0171 379 9779
E-mail: chambers@199strand.co.uk
Call Date: Feb 1980, Gray's Inn
Pupil Master
Qualifications: [MA (Oxon)]

TREBLE PAUL JOSEPH

58 King Street Chambers
1st Floor, Kingsgate House, 51-53 South
King Street, Manchester M2 6DE,
Telephone: 0161 831 7477
Call Date: Nov 1994, Lincoln's Inn
Qualifications: [BSc (Hons)(Sheff), CPE
(Manc)]

TREGEAR FRANCIS BENEDICT WILLIAM

Twenty-Four Old Buildings
Ground Floor, Lincoln's Inn, London
WC2A 3UP, Telephone: 0171 404 0946
E-mail:clerks@24oldbuildings.law.co.uk
Call Date: July 1980, Middle Temple
Pupil Master
Qualifications: [BA (Cantab)]

TREGILGAS-DAVEY MARCUS IAN

Pump Court Chambers
5 Temple Chambers, Temple Street,
Swindon SN1 1SQ,
Telephone: 01793 539899
E-mail: clerks@3pumpcourt.com

Pump Court Chambers
Upper Ground Floor, 3 Pump Court,
Temple, London EC4Y 7AJ,
Telephone: 0171 353 0711
E-mail: clerks@3pumpcourt.com
Pump Court Chambers
31 Southgate Street, Winchester
SO23 9EE, Telephone: 01962 868161
E-mail: clerks@3pumpcourt.com
Call Date: 1993, Gray's Inn
Qualifications: [LLB (Southampton), LLM
(Cantab)]

TREHARNE MISS JENNET MARY LLOYD

33 Park Place
Cardiff CF1 3BA,
Telephone: 02920 233313
Hardwicke Building
New Square, Lincoln's Inn, London
WC2A 3SB, Telephone: 020 7242 2523
E-mail: clerks@hardwicke.co.uk
Call Date: July 1975, Middle Temple
Pupil Master
Qualifications: [LLB (Lond)]

TREIP MICHAEL ANTHONY JOHN

Chambers of Joy Okoye
Suite 1, 2nd Floor Gray's Inn Chambers,
Gray's Inn, London WC1R 5JA,
Telephone: 0171 405 7011
Call Date: Nov 1995, Inner Temple
Qualifications: [LLB (Lond), M.Phil (Cantab)]

TREMBATH GRAHAM ROBERT

Five Paper Buildings
1st Floor, Five Paper Bldgs, Temple,
London EC4Y 7HB,
Telephone: 0171 583 6117
E-mail:clerks@5-paperbuildings.law.co.uk
Call Date: July 1978, Middle Temple
Pupil Master
Qualifications: [LLB (Soton)]

TREMBERG DAVID

Wilberforce Chambers
7 Bishop Lane, Hull, East Yorkshire,
HU1 1PA, Telephone: 01482 323264
E-mail: clerks@hullbar.demon.co.uk
Call Date: July 1985, Lincoln's Inn
Pupil Master
Qualifications: [LLB (Hull) Dip de, Hautes
Etudes, Europeenne]

D

TRENEER EDWARD MARK

Walnut House
63 St David's Hill, Exeter, Devon,
EX4 4DW, Telephone: 01392 279751
E-mail: 106627.2451@compuserve.com
Call Date: July 1987, Inner Temple
Qualifications: [BA (Soton), Dip Law (City),
MA (City)]

TREPTE PETER ARMIN

Littleton Chambers
3 King's Bench Walk North, Temple,
London EC4Y 7HR,
Telephone: 0171 797 8600
E-mail:clerks@littletonchambers.co.uk
Call Date: July 1987, Gray's Inn
Qualifications: [BA (Hons), Licence en Droit]

TRESMAN LEWIS ROBERT SIMON

Staple Inn Chambers
1st Floor, 9 Staple Inn, Holborn Bars,
London WC1V 7QH,
Telephone: 0171 242 5240
E-mail: clerks@staple-inn.org
Call Date: Nov 1980, Gray's Inn
Pupil Master
Qualifications: [LLB (Hons) (Reading)]

TREVERTON-JONES GREGORY DENNIS

Farrar's Building
Temple, London EC4Y 7BD,
Telephone: 0171 583 9241
E-mail:chambers@farrarsbuilding.co.uk
Call Date: Nov 1977, Inner Temple
Pupil Master, Assistant Recorder
Qualifications: [MA (Oxon)]

TREVETHAN MISS SUSAN WENDY

3 Paper Buildings
Temple, London EC4Y 7EU,
Telephone: 020 7583 8055
E-mail: London@3paper.com
3 Paper Buildings (Bournemouth)
20 Lorne Park Road, Bournemouth,
Dorset, BH1 1JN,
Telephone: 01202 292102
E-mail: Bournemouth@3paper.com
3 Paper Buildings (Winchester)
4 St Peter Street, Winchester SO23 8BW,
Telephone: 01962 868884
E-mail: winchester@3paper.com

3 Paper Buildings (Oxford)
1 Alfred Street, High Street, Oxford
OX1 4EH, Telephone: 01865 793736
E-mail: oxford@3paper.com
Call Date: Nov 1967, Middle Temple

TREVETT PETER GEORGE QC (1992)

Chambers of John Gardiner QC
1st Floor, 11 New Square, Lincoln's Inn,
London WC2A 3QB,
Telephone: 0171 242 4017
E-mail: taxlaw@11newsquare.com
Call Date: July 1971, Lincoln's Inn
Qualifications: [MA, LLM (Cantab)]

TREVIS ROBERT JAMES

Counsels' Chambers
2nd Floor, 10-11 Gray's Inn Square,
London WC1R 5JD,
Telephone: 0171 405 2576
E-mail:clerks@10-11graysinnsquare.co.uk
Call Date: Feb 1990, Inner Temple
Qualifications: [LLB]

TREVOR-JONES ROBERT DAVID

Nicholas Street Chambers
22 Nicholas Street, Chester CH1 2NX,
Telephone: 01244 323886
E-mail: clerks@40king.co.uk
Call Date: July 1977, Gray's Inn
Pupil Master, Assistant Recorder
Qualifications: [LLB]

TRIGG MILES HADDON

9 King's Bench Walk
Ground Floor, Temple, London
EC4Y 7DX, Telephone: 0171 353 7202/
3909 E-mail: 9kbw@compuserve.com
Call Date: July 1987, Inner Temple
Qualifications: [LLB (Hons) (Lond)]

TRIMMER MS CAROL JANE

Wilberforce Chambers
7 Bishop Lane, Hull, East Yorkshire,
HU1 1PA, Telephone: 01482 323264
E-mail: clerks@hullbar.demon.co.uk
Call Date: Nov 1993, Gray's Inn
Qualifications: [LLB (Hull)]

TRIMMER STUART ALAN

6 Gray's Inn Square
Ground Floor, Gray's Inn, London
WC1R 5AZ, Telephone: 0171 242 1052
E-mail: 6graysinn@clara.co.uk
Call Date: July 1977, Gray's Inn
Pupil Master
Qualifications: [LLB (Lond)]

TRIPPIER LADY

Deans Court Chambers
24 St John Street, Manchester M3 4DF,
Telephone: 0161 214 6000
E-mail: clerks@deanscourt.co.uk
Deans Court Chambers
41-43 Market Place, Preston PR1 1AH,
Telephone: 01772 555163
E-mail: clerks@deanscourt.co.uk
Call Date: July 1978, Gray's Inn
Qualifications: [LLB (Manch)]

TRITTON ROBERT GUY HENTON

One Raymond Buildings
Gray's Inn, London WC1R 5BH,
Telephone: 0171 430 1234
E-mail: chambers@ipbar1rb.com;
clerks@ipbar1rb.com
Call Date: July 1987, Inner Temple
Pupil Master
Qualifications: [BSc (Dunelm), Dip Law]

TROLLOPE ANDREW DAVID HEDDERWICK QC (1991)

1 Middle Temple Lane
Temple, London EC4Y 1LT,
Telephone: 0171 583 0659 (12 Lines)
E-mail: chambers@1mtl.co.uk
Westgate Chambers
144 High Street, Lewes, East Sussex,
BN7 1XT, Telephone: 01273 480510
Call Date: Nov 1971, Inner Temple
Recorder

TROTMAN TIMOTHY OLIVER

Deans Court Chambers
24 St John Street, Manchester M3 4DF,
Telephone: 0161 214 6000
E-mail: clerks@deanscourt.co.uk

Deans Court Chambers
41-43 Market Place, Preston PR1 1AH,
Telephone: 01772 555163
E-mail: clerks@deanscourt.co.uk
Call Date: July 1983, Middle Temple
Qualifications: [MA (Cantab)]

TROTT RONALD JOHN

3 Hare Court
1 Little Essex Street, London WC2R 3LD,
Telephone: 0171 395 2000
Call Date: June 1956, Gray's Inn

TROTTER DAVID JOHN BURNELL

Plowden Buildings
2nd Floor, 2 Plowden Buildings, Middle
Temple Lane, London EC4Y 9BU,
Telephone: 0171 583 0808
E-mail: bar@plowdenbuildings.co.uk
Call Date: July 1975, Inner Temple
Pupil Master
Qualifications: [BA (Cantab), MA (Manch)]

TROUSDALE MALCOLM RAYMOND

King's Bench Chambers
Wellington House, 175 Holdenhurst Road,
Bournemouth, Dorset, BH8 8DQ,
Telephone: 01202 250025
E-mail: chambers@kingsbench.co.uk
Call Date: Oct 1993, Middle Temple
Qualifications: [BA (Hons)(Newc), MA
(Exon), CPE (Lond)]

TROWELL STEPHEN MARK

1 Mitre Court Buildings
Temple, London EC4Y 7BS,
Telephone: 0171 797 7070
E-mail: clerks@1mcb.com
Call Date: Oct 1995, Middle Temple
Qualifications: [BA (Hons) (Oxon), D.Phil]

TROWER WILLIAM SPENCER PHILIP

3/4 South Square
Gray's Inn, London WC1R 5HP,
Telephone: 0171 696 9900
E-mail: clerks@southsquare.com
Call Date: July 1983, Lincoln's Inn
Pupil Master
Qualifications: [MA (Oxon)]

TROWLER MS REBECCA

4 Brick Court
Ground Floor, Temple, London
EC4Y 9AD, Telephone: 0171 797 7766
E-mail: chambers@4brick.co.uk
Doughty Street Chambers
11 Doughty Street, London WC1N 2PG,
Telephone: 0171 404 1313
E-mail:enquiries@doughtystreet.co.uk
Call Date: Oct 1995, Gray's Inn
Qualifications: [B.Sc]

TROY ALAN LAURENCE

33 Park Place
Cardiff CF1 3BA,
Telephone: 02920 233313
Call Date: Oct 1990, Gray's Inn
Qualifications: [LLB (Aberystwyth)]

TROY MRS JILL MARY

No. 6
6 Park Square, Leeds LS1 2LW,
Telephone: 0113 2459763
E-mail: chambers@no6.co.uk
Call Date: July 1986, Middle Temple
Qualifications: [BA (Oxon)]

TROY-DAVIES MRS (CHRISTINE) KAREN

Essex Court Chambers
24 Lincoln's Inn Fields, London
WC2A 3ED, Telephone: 0171 813 8000
E-mail:clerksroom@essexcourt-chambers.co.uk
Call Date: July 1981, Lincoln's Inn
Pupil Master
Qualifications: [BA (Oxon), LLM (Virginia)]

TRUMPER MISS SARA KATHERINE

Holborn Chambers
6 Gate Street, Lincoln's Inn Fields, London
WC2A 3HP, Telephone: 0171 242 6060
Call Date: Nov 1996, Lincoln's Inn
Qualifications: [BA (Hons)(Lond)]

TRUMPINGTON JOHN HENRY

Staple Inn Chambers
1st Floor, 9 Staple Inn, Holborn Bars,
London WC1V 7QH,
Telephone: 0171 242 5240
E-mail: clerks@staple-inn.org
Call Date: Feb 1985, Middle Temple
Pupil Master
Qualifications: [BA (Hons)]

TRUSCOTT IAN DEREK

Old Square Chambers
1 Verulam Buildings, Gray's Inn, London
WC1R 5LQ, Telephone: 0171 269 0300
E-mail:clerks@oldsquarechambers.co.uk
Old Square Chambers
Hanover House, 47 Corn Street, Bristol
BS1 1HT, Telephone: 0117 9277111
E-mail: oldsqbri@globalnet.co.uk
Call Date: 1995, Gray's Inn
Qualifications: [LLB (Edinburgh), LLM (Leeds)]

TRUSSLER JONATHAN ANDREW

2 Middle Temple Lane
3rd Floor, Temple, London EC4Y 9AA,
Telephone: 0171 583 4540
Call Date: Nov 1987, Gray's Inn
Qualifications: [LLB (Hons) (Wales), F.Inst BA]

TRUSTED JAMES HARRY

35 Essex Street
Temple, London WC2R 3AR,
Telephone: 0171 353 6381
E-mail: derek_jenkins@link.org
Call Date: July 1985, Inner Temple
Pupil Master
Qualifications: [MA (Cantab)]

TRUSTMAN MRS JUDITH ANN

Watford Chambers
74 Mildred Avenue, Watford,
Hertfordshire, WD1 7DX,
Telephone: 01923 220553
Call Date: Oct 1996, Middle Temple
Qualifications: [LLB (Hons)(Notts)]

TSE NICHOLAS HON KEUNG

29 Bedford Row Chambers
London WC1R 4HE,
Telephone: 0171 831 2626
Call Date: Nov 1995, Inner Temple
Qualifications: [BA (Oxon), CPE, Maitre de
Lettres, (Sorbonne)]

TSELENTIS MICHAEL

20 Essex Street
London WC2R 3AL,
Telephone: 0171 583 9294
E-mail: clerks@20essexst.com
Call Date: Nov 1995, Gray's Inn
Qualifications: [BA, LLB (Cape Town), BCL
(Oxon)]

Fax: 0171 583 1341;
Out of hours telephone: 0171 515 6454;
DX: 0009 Chancery Lane;
Other comms: Johannesburg Chambers,
300 Innes Chambers, 84 Pritchard Street,
Johannesburg 2000 Tel: 0027 11 3372370,
Fax: 0027 11 4631609

Other professional qualifications: BA, LLB (Cape
Town); BCL (Oxford); Advocate of the
Supreme Court of South Africa; High Court
of Nambia

Types of work: Arbitration, Commercial,
Commercial litigation, Commodities,
Company and commercial, Foreign law,
Insurance/reinsurance, International trade,
Private international, Sale and carriage of
goods, Shipping, admiralty

Membership of foreign bars: Johannesburg Bar
(called 1978)

Awards and memberships: Senior Counsel
South Africa (1989); Arbitration Foundation of South Africa – appeals panel,
commercial panel and minerals panel

Other professional experience: Practice at the
Johannesburg Bar since 1978; English Bar
1996 to date

Languages spoken: Afrikaans

Reported Cases: *Seawind Tankers Corp v
Bayoil*, [1999] 1 Lloyd's Rep 211; [1998] 1
WLR 147 (CA), 1998. Status of disputed
cross-claims in winding-up petitions.
*North Sea Energy Holdings v Petroleum
Authority of Thailand*, [1999] 1 Lloyd's
Rep 483 (CA), 1998. Petroleum supply

contract; implied duties; assessment of
damages; loss of chance.
*Toepfer International GmbH v Societe
Cargill France*, [1998] 1 Lloyds Rep 379
(CA), 1997. Article 1(4) of Brussels
Convention; Anti-suit instructions; Scott &
Avery & exclusive jurisdiction clauses.
First National Bank v Lynn, 1996 (2) SA
339 (AD), 1996. Assignability of future and
contingent rights under SA law.
*Ex parte de Villiers, In Re Carbon Invest-
ments*, 1993 (1) SA 493 (AD), 1993. Subordination agreements, directors' personal
liability and schemes of arrangement in SA
law.

TUCKER ANDREW RICHARD SMETHURST

6 Fountain Court
Steelhouse Lane, Birmingham B4 6DR,
Telephone: 0121 233 3282
E-mail: clerks@sixfountain.co.uk
Call Date: July 1977, Middle Temple
Pupil Master
Qualifications: [LLB (Sheffield)]

TUCKER ASHLEY RUSSELL

Park Court Chambers
16 Park Place, Leeds LS1 2SJ,
Telephone: 0113 2433277
Call Date: Nov 1990, Middle Temple
Qualifications: [BA (Manch), Dip Law (City)]

TUCKER DAVID WILLIAM

Two Crown Office Row
Ground Floor, Temple, London
EC4Y 7HJ, Telephone: 020 7797 8100
E-mail: mail@2cor.co.uk, or to individual
barristers at: [barrister's
surname]@2cor.co.uk
Call Date: Nov 1973, Middle Temple
Pupil Master, Assistant Recorder
Qualifications: [MA (Oxon)]

TUCKER MISS KATHERINE JANE GREENING

St Philip's Chambers
Fountain Court, Steelhouse Lane,
Birmingham B4 6DR,
Telephone: 0121 246 7000
E-mail: clerks@st-philips.co.uk
Call Date: Oct 1993, Lincoln's Inn
Qualifications: [LLB (Hons)(Leic)]

TUCKER LYNTON ANTHONY

12 New Square
Lincoln's Inn, London WC2A 3SW,
Telephone: 0171 419 1212
E-mail: chambers@12newsquare.co.uk
Sovereign Chambers
25 Park Square, Leeds LS1 2PW,
Telephone: 0113 2451841/2/3
E-mail:sovereignchambers@btinternet.com
Call Date: Feb 1971, Lincoln's Inn
Pupil Master
Qualifications: [MA, BCL (Oxon)]

TUCKER NICHOLAS JAMES

17 Carlton Crescent
Southampton SO15 2XR,
Telephone: 023 8032 0320/0823 2003
E-mail: greg@jg17cc.co.uk
Call Date: Oct 1993, Inner Temple
Qualifications: [LLB]

TUCKER PAUL GEOFFREY

40 King Street
Manchester M2 6BA,
Telephone: 0161 832 9082
E-mail: clerks@40kingstreet.co.uk
The Chambers of Philip Raynor QC
5 Park Place, Leeds LS1 2RU,
Telephone: 0113 242 1123
Call Date: Nov 1990, Gray's Inn
Pupil Master
Qualifications: [MA (Cantab)]

TUCKER DR PETER LOUIS

Leone Chambers
72 Evelyn Avenue, Kingsbury, London
NW9 0JH, Telephone: 0181 200 4020
E-mail: festus4@leonechambers.co.uk
12 Old Square
1st Floor, Lincoln's Inn, London
WC2A 3TX, Telephone: 0171 404 0875
Call Date: 1970, Gray's Inn
Qualifications: [MA (Oxon), MA (Dunelm),
DCL , USL]

TUDOR-EVANS QUINTIN JOHN

199 Strand
London WC2R 1DR,
Telephone: 0171 379 9779
E-mail: chambers@199strand.co.uk
Call Date: July 1977, Lincoln's Inn
Pupil Master

TUGENDHAT MICHAEL GEORGE
QC (1986)

5 Raymond Buildings
1st Floor, Gray's Inn, London WC1R 5BP,
Telephone: 0171 242 2902
E-mail: clerks@media-ent-law.co.uk
Call Date: July 1969, Inner Temple
Recorder
Qualifications: [MA (Cantab)]

TUGHAN JOHN CHARLES RONALD

9 Gough Square
London EC4A 3DE,
Telephone: 020 7832 0500
E-mail: clerks@9goughsq.co.uk
Call Date: Nov 1991, Inner Temple
Qualifications: [LLB (L'pool)]

TULLY MS ANNE MARGARET

Eastbourne Chambers
15 Hyde Gardens, Eastbourne, East
Sussex, BN21 4PR,
Telephone: 01323 642102
Call Date: July 1989, Gray's Inn
Qualifications: [MA (Cantab), LLM (Cantab)]

TULLY RAYMOND PETER

Queens Square Chambers
56 Queens Square, Bristol BS1 4PR,
Telephone: 0117 921 1966
Call Date: Nov 1987, Inner Temple
Qualifications: [BA (Keele), Dip Law, (City)]

TUNKEL ALAN MICHAEL

3 Stone Buildings
Lincoln's Inn, London WC2A 3XL,
Telephone: 0171 242 4937
E-mail: clerks@3sb.law.co.uk
Call Date: July 1976, Middle Temple
Pupil Master
Qualifications: [BA (Oxon)]

TURAY MISS FATMATA

12 Old Square
1st Floor, Lincoln's Inn, London
WC2A 3TX, Telephone: 0171 404 0875
Call Date: July 1994, Gray's Inn
Qualifications: [LLB]

TURCAN HENRY WATSON

4 Paper Buildings
1st Floor, Temple, London EC4Y 7EX,
Telephone: 0171 583 0816/353 1131
E-mail: clerks@4paperbuildings.co.uk
Call Date: July 1965, Inner Temple
Recorder
Qualifications: [MA (Oxon)]

TURNBULL CHARLES EMERSON LOVETT

Wilberforce Chambers
8 New Square, Lincoln's Inn, London
WC2A 3QP, Telephone: 0171 306 0102
E-mail: chambers@wilberforce.co.uk
Call Date: July 1975, Inner Temple
Qualifications: [BA (Oxon)]

Types of work: Chancery (general), Charities,
Commercial property, Common land,
Conveyancing, Landlord and tenant,
Pensions, Professional negligence, School
sites

TURNER ADRIAN JOHN

Eastbourne Chambers
15 Hyde Gardens, Eastbourne, East
Sussex, BN21 4PR,
Telephone: 01323 642102
Call Date: Feb 1978, Gray's Inn

TURNER ALAN JOSEPH

Chambers of Geoffrey Hawker
46/48 Essex Street, London WC2R 3GH,
Telephone: 0171 583 8899
Call Date: Nov 1984, Gray's Inn
Qualifications: [LLB, BSc, MSc(Wales)]

TURNER AMEDEE EDWARD QC (1976)

One Raymond Buildings
Gray's Inn, London WC1R 5BH,
Telephone: 0171 430 1234
E-mail: chambers@ipbar1rb.com;
clerks@ipbar1rb.com
Call Date: Nov 1954, Inner Temple
Qualifications: [MA (Oxon)]

TURNER DAVID ANDREW QC (1991)

Exchange Chambers
Pearl Assurance House, Derby Square,
Liverpool L2 9XX,
Telephone: 0151 236 7747
E-mail:exchangechambers@btinternet.com
6 King's Bench Walk
Ground Floor, Temple, London
EC4Y 7DR, Telephone: 0171 583 0410
E-mail: worsley@6kbw.freeserve.co.uk
Call Date: Feb 1971, Gray's Inn
Recorder
Qualifications: [MA, LLM (Cantab)]

TURNER DAVID BENJAMIN

2 Temple Gardens
Temple, London EC4Y 9AY,
Telephone: 0171 583 6041
E-mail: clerks@2templegardens.co.uk
Call Date: Nov 1992, Gray's Inn
Qualifications: [BA (Cantab)]

TURNER DAVID GEORGE PATRICK

14 Gray's Inn Square
Gray's Inn, London WC1R 5JP,
Telephone: 0171 242 0858
E-mail: 100712.2134@compuserve.com
Call Date: Nov 1976, Gray's Inn
Pupil Master, Assistant Recorder
Qualifications: [LLB, (Lond), AKC]

TURNER JAMES QC (1998)

One King's Bench Walk
1st Floor, Temple, London EC4Y 7DB,
Telephone: 0171 936 1500
E-mail: ddear@1kbw.co.uk
Call Date: July 1976, Inner Temple
Qualifications: [LLB Hons (Hull)]

TURNER JAMES MICHAEL

4 Essex Court
Temple, London EC4Y 9AJ,
Telephone: 020 7797 7970
E-mail: clerks@4essexcourt.law.co.uk
Call Date: Oct 1990, Inner Temple
Pupil Master
Qualifications: [BA (Dunelm),
LLM(Tubingen), M.I.L.]

Fax: 0171 353 0998;
Other comms: E-mail jmt@link.org

Types of work: Admiralty, Arbitration, Commercial, Commercial litigation, International trade, Private international, Sale and carriage of goods, Shipping, admiralty

Awards and memberships: Member, Institute of Linguists; member of COMBAR, LCLCBA, BGJA

Languages spoken:

Reported Cases: *Red Sea Insurance v Bouygues*, [1995] 1 AC 190 (PC), 1994. Scope of exception to double-actionability rule, where law to be disapplied English.
Citi-March Ltd v Neptune Orient Lines, [1996] 1 WLR 1367; [1997] 1 Lloyd's Rep 72, 1996. Exercise of discretion to disregard contractual foreign exclusive jurisdiction clause where timebar in jurisdiction.
The 'Giuseppe Di Vittorio' (Nos 1&2), [1998] 1 Lloyd's Rep 136 (CA); [1998] 2 Lloyd's 661, 1997. Sovereign immunity and retrospective effect in ship arrest setting.
Netherlands v Yovell, [1998] 1 Lloyd's Rep 236, 1997. Scope & effect of s78(4) Marine Insurance Act 1906.
The 'MATA K', [1998] 2 Lloyd's Rep 614, 1998. Conflict between 'weight unknown' clause in bill of lading and inconsistent charterparty and Hague Rules provisions.

TURNER MISS JANET MARY QC (1996)

3 Verulam Buildings
London WC1R 5NT,
Telephone: 0171 831 8441
E-mail: clerks@3verulam.co.uk
Call Date: Nov 1979, Middle Temple
Qualifications: [LLB (Bris)]

TURNER JONATHAN CHADWICK

6 King's Bench Walk
Ground Floor, Temple, London
EC4Y 7DR, Telephone: 0171 583 0410
E-mail: worsley@6kbw.freeserve.co.uk
Call Date: July 1974, Gray's Inn
Pupil Master, Assistant Recorder

TURNER JONATHAN DAVID CHATTYN

4 Field Court
Gray's Inn, London WC1R 5EA,
Telephone: 0171 440 6900
E-mail: chambers@4fieldcourt.co.uk
Call Date: Feb 1982, Gray's Inn
Pupil Master
Qualifications: [MA (Cantab), Lic Sp, Dr Eur (Brussels)]

Fax: 0171 242 0197; DX: LDE 483;
Other comms: Mobile 07801 337157;
E-Mail Mail@JonathanTurner.com; URL:
http://www.JonathanTurner.com

Types of work: EC and competition law, Information technology, Intellectual property

Awards and memberships: Member of Intellectual Property Bar Association, Competition Law Association, Society for Computers and the Law; Associate of the Chartered Institute of Patent Agents; ICC Working Group on Domain Names

Other professional experience: Head of IP and IT Law at Coopers & Lybrand (1995-7)

Languages spoken: French

Publications: *Halsbury's Laws of England – EC Competition Law*, 1985; *Vaughan's Law of the European Communities*, 1986-97; *European Patent Office Reports*, 1986-95; *Countdown to 2000 – A Guide to the Legal Issues*, 1998; *European Patent Infringement Cases*, 1999

Reported Cases: *PLG Research v Ardon*, [1995] RPC 287, 1990-5. A major patent infringement case – scope of claims under the European Patent Convention, prior use and obviousness.
Reckitt and Colman v Borden, [1990] RPC 341, 1985-9. The Jif Lemon case – passing off in relation to visual branding.
C&H v Klucznik, [1992] FSR 421, 1991. Leading case on design right.
Potton v York Close, [1990] FSR 11, 1989. Copyright in plans of houses – account of builder's profits.
British Sky Broadcasting v Lyons, [1995] FSR 357, 1994. Rights in television signals – EC law.

TURNER JONATHAN RICHARD

Monckton Chambers
4 Raymond Buildings, Gray's Inn, London
WC1R 5BP, Telephone: 0171 405 7211
E-mail: chambers@monckton.co.uk
Call Date: Nov 1988, Middle Temple
Pupil Master
Qualifications: [BA (Cantab), LLM (Harvard)]

TURNER JUSTIN JOHN

3 New Square
Lincoln's Inn, London WC2A 3RS,
Telephone: 0171 405 1111
E-mail: 3newsquareip@lineone.net
Call Date: Nov 1992, Middle Temple
Qualifications: [Vet.Med (Lond), Ph.D
(Cantab), AFRC, Dip in Law]

TURNER MARK GEORGE QC (1998)

Deans Court Chambers
24 St John Street, Manchester M3 4DF,
Telephone: 0161 214 6000
E-mail: clerks@deanscourt.co.uk
Deans Court Chambers
41-43 Market Place, Preston PR1 1AH,
Telephone: 01772 555163
E-mail: clerks@deanscourt.co.uk
Call Date: July 1981, Gray's Inn
Assistant Recorder
Qualifications: [BA (Oxon)]

TURNER MICHAEL

Cloisters
1 Pump Court, Temple, London
EC4Y 7AA, Telephone: 0171 827 4000
E-mail: clerks@cloisters.com
Call Date: July 1981, Gray's Inn
Pupil Master
Qualifications: [BA (Hons)]

TURNER MRS RHONDA NATALIE

Clock Chambers
78 Darlington Street, Wolverhampton
WV1 4LY, Telephone: 01902 313444
Call Date: Nov 1984, Middle Temple
Qualifications: [BA(Hons)]

TURNER STEVEN MURRAY

Park Lane Chambers
19 Westgate, Leeds LS1 2RD,
Telephone: 0113 2285000
E-mail:clerks@parklanechambers.co.uk
Call Date: Nov 1993, Middle Temple
Qualifications: [BA (Hons) (Kent), CPE
(Notts)]

TURNER MRS TARYN JONES

Park Court Chambers
16 Park Place, Leeds LS1 2SJ,
Telephone: 0113 2433277
Call Date: Feb 1990, Gray's Inn
Pupil Master
Qualifications: [LLB (Hons)]

TURRALL-CLARKE ROBERT TURRALL FACER

Crayshott House
Woodlands Road, West Byfleet, Surrey,
KT14 6JW, Telephone: 01932 342951
Bond Street Chambers
Standbrook House, 2-5 Old Bond Street,
Mayfair, London W1X 3TB,
Telephone: 01932 342951
Call Date: July 1971, Middle Temple
Qualifications: [MA (Oxon), AInst Arb]

TURTLE ALISTER MARK

1 Gray's Inn Square
Ground Floor, London WC1R 5AA,
Telephone: 0171 405 8946/7/8
Wessex Chambers
48 Queens Road, Reading, Berkshire,
RG1 4BD, Telephone: 0118 956 8856
E-mail:wessexchambers@compuserve.com
Call Date: Nov 1994, Inner Temple
Qualifications: [LLB (Bris)]

TURTON ANDREW PHILIP

2-4 Tudor Street
London EC4Y 0AA,
Telephone: 0171 797 7111
E-mail: clerks@rfqc.co.uk
Call Date: July 1977, Middle Temple
Pupil Master
Qualifications: [LLB (Lond), AKC]

D

D

TURTON PHILIP JOHN

Ropewalk Chambers
24 The Ropewalk, Nottingham NG1 5EF,
Telephone: 0115 9472581
E-mail: administration@ropewalk co.uk
Call Date: Nov 1989, Gray's Inn
Qualifications: [LLB (Wales)]

TURTON ROBERT EDMUND

Fountain Chambers
Cleveland Business Centre, 1 Watson
Street, Middlesbrough TS1 2RQ,
Telephone: 01642 804040
E-mail:fountainchambers@onyxnet.co.uk
Call Date: July 1996, Inner Temple
Qualifications: [BA (Dunelm), CPE]

TWANA EKWALL SINGH

New Court Chambers
Gazette Building, 168 Corporation Street,
Birmingham B4 6TZ,
Telephone: 0121 693 6656
Call Date: Nov 1988, Middle Temple
Pupil Master
Qualifications: [LLB(Hons)]

TWIGG PATRICK ALAN QC (1986)

2 Temple Gardens
Temple, London EC4Y 9AY,
Telephone: 0171 583 6041
E-mail: clerks@2templegardens.co.uk
Call Date: July 1967, Inner Temple
Recorder
Qualifications: [LLB (Bristol) LLM, (Virginia)]

TWIGGER ANDREW MARK

3 Stone Buildings
Lincoln's Inn, London WC2A 3XL,
Telephone: 0171 242 4937
E-mail: clerks@3sb.law.co.uk
Call Date: Nov 1994, Inner Temple
Qualifications: [BA (Oxon), CPE (City)]

TWIST STEPHEN JOHN

York Chambers
14 Toft Green, York YO1 6JT,
Telephone: 01904 620048
E-mail: [name]@yorkchambers.co.uk
Call Date: July 1979, Middle Temple
Pupil Master
Qualifications: [LLB (L'pool), CACDPI]

TWOMEY MARK JAMES JOHN

Bell Yard Chambers
116/118 Chancery Lane, London
WC2A 1PP, Telephone: 0171 306 9292
Call Date: Nov 1990, Inner Temple
Qualifications: [LLB (Bris)]

TWOMLOW RICHARD WILLIAM

9 Park Place
Cardiff CF1 3DP,
Telephone: 01222 382731
Call Date: July 1976, Gray's Inn
Pupil Master, Assistant Recorder
Qualifications: [BA (Cantab)]

TYACK DAVID GUY

St Philip's Chambers
Fountain Court, Steelhouse Lane,
Birmingham B4 6DR,
Telephone: 0121 246 7000
E-mail: clerks@st-philips.co.uk
Call Date: Nov 1994, Middle Temple
Qualifications: [BA (Hons)]

TYLER MISS PAULA MARGOT

Young Street Chambers
38 Young Street, Manchester M3 3FT,
Telephone: 0161 833 0489
E-mail: clerks@young-st-chambers.com
Call Date: Nov 1997, Middle Temple
Qualifications: [BSc (Hons)(Lond)]

TYLER THOMAS GEOFFREY

Staple Inn Chambers
1st Floor, 9 Staple Inn, Holborn Bars,
London WC1V 7QH,
Telephone: 0171 242 5240
E-mail: clerks@staple-inn.org
Call Date: Oct 1996, Lincoln's Inn
Qualifications: [LLB (Hons)(Lond)]

TYLER WILLIAM JOHN

30 Park Square
Leeds LS1 2PF, Telephone: 0113 2436388
E-mail: clerks@30parksquare.co.uk
Call Date: Oct 1996, Inner Temple
Qualifications: [BA (Oxon)]

TYRELL GLEN

Chambers of John L Powell QC
Four New Square, Lincoln's Inn, London
WC2A 3RJ, Telephone: 0171 797 8000
E-mail: barristers@4newsquare.com
Call Date: July 1977, Inner Temple
Pupil Master
Qualifications: [LLB]

TYRRELL ALAN RUPERT QC (1976)

Francis Taylor Building
3rd Floor, Temple, London EC4Y 7BY,
Telephone: 0171 797 7250
St Albans Chambers
Dolphin Lodge, Dolphin Yard, Holywell
Hill, St Albans, Herts, AL1 1EX,
Telephone: 01727 843383
Tindal Chambers
3/5 New Street, Chelmsford, Essex,
CM1 1NT, Telephone: 01245 267742
Call Date: Feb 1956, Gray's Inn
Qualifications: [LLB (Lond)]

TYRRELL RICHARD MARK LAWRENCE

28 St John Street
Manchester M3 4DJ,
Telephone: 0161 834 8418
E-mail: clerk@28stjohnst.co.uk
Call Date: Nov 1993, Gray's Inn
Qualifications: [LLB (Sheff)]

TYSON RICHARD THEODORE

3 Paper Buildings
Temple, London EC4Y 7EU,
Telephone: 020 7583 8055
E-mail: London@3paper.com
3 Paper Buildings (Bournemouth)
20 Lorne Park Road, Bournemouth,
Dorset, BH1 1JN,
Telephone: 01202 292102
E-mail: Bournemouth@3paper.com
3 Paper Buildings (Winchester)
4 St Peter Street, Winchester SO23 8BW,
Telephone: 01962 868884
E-mail: winchester@3paper.com
3 Paper Buildings (Oxford)
1 Alfred Street, High Street, Oxford
OX1 4EH, Telephone: 01865 793736
E-mail: oxford@3paper.com
Call Date: Nov 1975, Inner Temple
Pupil Master, Assistant Recorder
Qualifications: [BA (Exon)]

TYSON THOMAS DAVID

Chambers of Norman Palmer
2 Field Court, Gray's Inn, London
WC1R 5BB, Telephone: 0171 405 6114
E-mail: fieldct2@netcomuk.co.uk
Call Date: Oct 1995, Gray's Inn
Qualifications: [LLB (Bris)]

TYTHCOTT MISS ELISABETH CLAIRE

18 St John Street
Manchester M3 4EA,
Telephone: 0161 278 1800
E-mail: 18stjohn@lineone.net
Call Date: Nov 1989, Inner Temple
Qualifications: [LLB]

TYZACK DAVID IAN HESLOP QC (1999)

Southernhay Chambers
33 Southernhay East, Exeter, Devon,
EX1 1NX, Telephone: 01392 255777
E-mail:southernhay.chambers@lineone.net
1 Mitre Court Buildings
Temple, London EC4Y 7BS,
Telephone: 0171 797 7070
E-mail: clerks@1mcb.com
Call Date: 1970, Inner Temple
Pupil Master, Assistant Recorder
Qualifications: [MA (Cantab)]

UDUJE BENJAMIN ELLIOTT

22 Old Buildings
Lincoln's Inn, London WC2A 3UJ,
Telephone: 0171 831 0222
Call Date: Nov 1992, Middle Temple
Qualifications: [LLB (Hons)]

UFF DAVID CHARLES

Cobden House Chambers
19 Quay Street, Manchester M3 3HN,
Telephone: 0161 833 6000
E-mail: clerks@cobden.co.uk
Call Date: July 1981, Gray's Inn
Pupil Master
Qualifications: [LLB (Hons)]

UFF JOHN FRANCIS QC (1983)

Keating Chambers
10 Essex Street, Outer Temple, London
WC2R 3AA, Telephone: 0171 544 2600
Call Date: July 1970, Gray's Inn

Assistant Recorder
Qualifications: [PhD, BScEng, F.Eng, FCIArb]

ULLAH MOHAMMED HASHMOT

Gray's Inn Chambers
Chambers of Nigel Ley (2nd Floor), Gray's
Inn, London WC1R 5JA,
Telephone: 0171 831 7888 (Chambers)/
0171 831 7904 (Mr M Ullah)
Chambers of Mohammed Hasmot Ullah
1st Floor, 72 Brick Lane, London E1 6RL,
Telephone: 0171 377 0119
Call Date: 1989, Middle Temple
Qualifications: [LLB (Bangladesh)]

ULLSTEIN AUGUSTUS RUPERT PATRICK A QC (1992)

29 Bedford Row Chambers
London WC1R 4HE,
Telephone: 0171 831 2626
Call Date: July 1970, Inner Temple
Assistant Recorder
Qualifications: [LLB (Lond)]

Fax: 0171 831 0626; DX: 1044 London

Types of work: Arbitration, Chancery
(general), Commercial litigation, Common
law (general), Family, Family provision,
Financial services, Foreign law, Insurance,
Medical negligence, Personal injury, Professional negligence, Sports

Membership of foreign bars: Gibraltar

Circuit: South Eastern

Reported Cases: *Chrzanowska v Glaxo Laboratories Ltd*, (1990) *The Times*, 16 March,
1990. Multi-party action – Directions – Case
management.
Nash v Eli Lilly, [1992] 3 Med LR 353,
1992. Limitation – multi-party action.
Relman v Department of Transport,
[1997] 2 Lloyd's Rep 648, 1997. Negligence – Duty of care of Central Government.
Wickler v Wickler, [1998] 2 FLR 326, 1998.
Decree Absolute – When court may exercise discretion to refuse.
Nurcombe v CHN Investments, [1985] 1
WLR 370, 1984. Minority shareholders
action.

UME CYRIL OBIORA

12 Old Square
1st Floor, Lincoln's Inn, London
WC2A 3TX, Telephone: 0171 404 0875
Call Date: July 1972, Gray's Inn
Pupil Master
Qualifications: [LLB (Lond), ACIArb]

UMEZURUIKE CHIMA NNADOZIE

Queen Elizabeth Building
Ground Floor, Temple, London
EC4Y 9BS,
Telephone: 0171 353 7181 (12 Lines)
Call Date: July 1991, Inner Temple
Qualifications: [LLB (Nigeria), LLM (Lond)]

UNDERHILL MISS ALISON

Tindal Chambers
3/5 New Street, Chelmsford, Essex,
CM1 1NT, Telephone: 01245 267742
Call Date: Oct 1997, Gray's Inn
Qualifications: [LLB (Wales)]

UNDERHILL NICHOLAS EDWARD QC (1992)

Fountain Court
Temple, London EC4Y 9DH,
Telephone: 0171 583 3335
E-mail: chambers@fountaincourt.co.uk
Call Date: July 1976, Gray's Inn
Recorder
Qualifications: [MA (Oxon)]

UNDERWOOD ASHLEY GRENVILLE

Chambers of Norman Palmer
2 Field Court, Gray's Inn, London
WC1R 5BB, Telephone: 0171 405 6114
E-mail: fieldct2@netcomuk.co.uk
Call Date: July 1976, Gray's Inn
Pupil Master
Qualifications: [LLB Hons (Lond)]

UNDERWOOD ROBERT ANTHONY

Chambers of Michael Pert QC
36 Bedford Row, London WC1R 4JH,
Telephone: 0171 421 8000
E-mail: 36bedfordrow@link.org
Chambers of Michael Pert QC
24 Albion Place, Northampton NN1 1UD,
Telephone: 01604 602333

Chambers of Michael Pert QC
104 New Walk, Leicester LE1 7EA,
Telephone: 0116 249 2020
Call Date: July 1986, Lincoln's Inn
Pupil Master
Qualifications: [BA]

UNSWORTH IAN STEPHEN

White Friars Chambers
21 White Friars, Chester CH1 1NZ,
Telephone: 01244 323070
E-mail:whitefriarschambers@btinternet.com
Call Date: Oct 1992, Lincoln's Inn
Qualifications: [LLB(Hons)]

UNWIN DAVID CHARLES QC (1995)

7 Stone Buildings
Ground Floor, Lincoln's Inn, London
WC2A 3SZ, Telephone: 0171 405 3886/
242 3546 E-mail: chaldous@vossnet.co.uk
Call Date: Nov 1971, Middle Temple
Qualifications: [BA (Oxon)]

UPEX PROFESSOR ROBERT VAUGHAN

29 Bedford Row Chambers
London WC1R 4HE,
Telephone: 0171 831 2626
Call Date: July 1973, Middle Temple
Qualifications: [MA, LLM (Cantab)]

UPPAL MISS BALJINDER KAUR

College Chambers
19 Carlton Cresent, Southampton
SO15 2ET, Telephone: 01703 230338
Call Date: Oct 1996, Lincoln's Inn
Qualifications: [LLB (Hons)(Warw)]

UPSON MICHAEL JAMES

Bank House Chambers
Old Bank House, Hartshead, Sheffield
S1 2EL, Telephone: 0114 2751223
Call Date: Oct 1993, Lincoln's Inn
Qualifications: [LLB (Hons)]

UPTON JAMES WILLIAM DAVID

1 Serjeants' Inn
4th Floor, Temple, London EC4Y 1NH,
Telephone: 0171 583 1355
E-mail: clerks@serjeants-inn.co.uk
Call Date: Nov 1990, Inner Temple
Qualifications: [MA (Cantab), LLM (Cantab)]

UPWARD PATRICK CHARLES QC (1996)

9 Gough Square
London EC4A 3DE,
Telephone: 020 7832 0500
E-mail: clerks@9goughsq.co.uk
Mercury Chambers
Mercury House, 33-35 Clarendon Road,
Leeds LS2 9NZ,
Telephone: 0113 234 2265
E-mail:cdexter@mercurychambers.co.uk
Call Date: July 1972, Inner Temple
Assistant Recorder
Qualifications: [LLB (Lond)]

URQUHART ANDREW ROBERT HILDYARD

Chambers of Michael Pert QC
36 Bedford Row, London WC1R 4JH,
Telephone: 0171 421 8000
E-mail: 36bedfordrow@link.org
Chambers of Michael Pert QC
24 Albion Place, Northampton NN1 1UD,
Telephone: 01604 602333
Chambers of Michael Pert QC
104 New Walk, Leicester LE1 7EA,
Telephone: 0116 249 2020
Call Date: Nov 1963, Middle Temple
Pupil Master
Qualifications: [BA (Oxon)]

URQUHART MRS DORIS

Mitre House Chambers
15-19 Devereux Court, London WC2R 3JJ,
Telephone: 0171 583 8233
Call Date: July 1967, Middle Temple
Qualifications: [BA (Michigan)]

D

D

USHER NEIL MORRIS

Lincoln House Chambers
5th Floor, Lincoln House, 1 Brazennose
Street, Manchester M2 5EL,
Telephone: 0161 832 5701
E-mail: info@lincolnhse.co.uk
Call Date: Oct 1993, Middle Temple
Qualifications: [BA (Hons)(Hull), CPE (City)]

UTLEY CHARLES EDWARD

22 Old Buildings
Lincoln's Inn, London WC2A 3UJ,
Telephone: 0171 831 0222
Call Date: Nov 1979, Middle Temple
Pupil Master

VAGG HOWARD VICTOR

6 King's Bench Walk
Ground Floor, Temple, London
EC4Y 7DR, Telephone: 0171 583 0410
E-mail: worsley@6kbw.freeserve.co.uk
Call Date: July 1974, Inner Temple
Pupil Master, Recorder
Qualifications: [LLB (Hons) (Bristol)]

VAIN RICHARD PETER

3 Dr Johnson's Buildings
Ground Floor, Temple, London
EC4Y 7BA, Telephone: 0171 353 4854
E-mail: clerks@3djb.co.uk
Call Date: Nov 1970, Middle Temple
Pupil Master
Qualifications: [MA (Cantab)]

VAITILINGAM ADAM SKANDA

Walnut House
63 St David's Hill, Exeter, Devon,
EX4 4DW, Telephone: 01392 279751
E-mail: 106627.2451@compuserve.com
Call Date: Nov 1987, Middle Temple
Qualifications: [MA (Cantab)]

VAJDA CHRISTOPHER STEPHEN QC (1997)

Monckton Chambers
4 Raymond Buildings, Gray's Inn, London
WC1R 5BP, Telephone: 0171 405 7211
E-mail: chambers@monckton.co.uk
Call Date: July 1979, Gray's Inn
Qualifications: [MA]

VAKIL JIMMY

Staple Inn Chambers
1st Floor, 9 Staple Inn, Holborn Bars,
London WC1V 7QH,
Telephone: 0171 242 5240
E-mail: clerks@staple-inn.org
Call Date: May 1993, Middle Temple
Qualifications: [LLB (Hons)(Lond)]

VALDER PAUL

1 Harcourt Buildings
2nd Floor, Temple, London EC4Y 9DA,
Telephone: 0171 353 9421/0375
E-mail:clerks@1harcourtbuildings.law.co.uk
Call Date: Nov 1994, Inner Temple
Qualifications: [BA (B'ham), CPE (City)]

VALENTIN BEN MATTHEW

3/4 South Square
Gray's Inn, London WC1R 5HP,
Telephone: 0171 696 9900
E-mail: clerks@southsquare.com
Call Date: Nov 1995, Inner Temple
Qualifications: [BA, BCL (Oxon), LLM
(Cornell)]

VALENTINE DONALD GRAHAM

Atkin Chambers
1 Atkin Building, Gray's Inn, London
WC1R 5AT, Telephone: 020 7404 0102
E-mail: clerks@atkin-chambers.co.uk
Call Date: June 1956, Lincoln's Inn
Qualifications: [MA, LLB (Cantab), Dr Jur
(Utrecht), FCIArb]

VALIOS NICHOLAS PAUL QC (1991)

Francis Taylor Building
Ground Floor, Temple, London
EC4Y 7BY, Telephone: 0171 353 7768/
7769/2711
E-mail:clerks@francistaylorbuilding.law.co.uk
Call Date: June 1964, Inner Temple
Recorder

VALKS MICHAEL

King's Chambers
5a Gildredge Road, Eastbourne, East
Sussex, BN21 4RB,
Telephone: 01323 416053
Call Date: Oct 1994, Gray's Inn
Qualifications: [LLB (Hons)(Bucks)]

VALLACK MISS JULIE ANN

St David's Chambers
10 Calvert Terrace, Swansea, West
Glamorgan, SA1 5AR,
Call Date: Oct 1993, Gray's Inn
Qualifications: [BA (Bath),LLB (Lond)]

VALLANCE PHILIP IAN FERGUS QC (1989)

1 Crown Office Row
Ground Floor, Temple, London
EC4Y 7HH, Telephone: 0171 797 7500
E-mail: mail@onecrownofficerow.com
Call Date: July 1968, Inner Temple
Qualifications: [BA (Oxon)]

VALLAT RICHARD JUSTIN

Pump Court Tax Chambers
16 Bedford Row, London WC1R 4EB,
Telephone: 0171 414 8080
Call Date: Oct 1997, Gray's Inn
Qualifications: [BA]

VALLEJO MISS JACQUELINE

**The Chambers of Mr Ali Mohammed
Azhar**
Basement, 9 King's Bench Walk, Temple,
London EC4Y 7DX,
Telephone: 0171 353 9564
E-mail: jvlee@btinternet.com
9 King's Bench Walk
Ground Floor, Temple, London
EC4Y 7DX, Telephone: 0171 353 7202/
3909 E-mail: 9kbw@compuserve.com
Call Date: 1997, Middle Temple
Qualifications: [BA (Hons)]

VALLEY MISS HELEN MARIA

3 Gray's Inn Square
Ground Floor, London WC1R 5AH,
Telephone: 0171 520 5600
E-mail: clerks@3gis.co.uk
Call Date: Oct 1990, Middle Temple
Qualifications: [BA (Hons) (Lond), Dip Law]

VALLI YUNUS

No. 6
6 Park Square, Leeds LS1 2LW,
Telephone: 0113 2459763
E-mail: chambers@no6.co.uk
Call Date: Nov 1994, Lincoln's Inn
Qualifications: [LLB (Hons)(Leeds)]

VAN BESOUW EUFRON

Chartlands Chambers
3 St Giles Terrace, Northampton
NN1 2BN, Telephone: 01604 603322
Call Date: Nov 1988, Middle Temple
Qualifications: [LLB]

VAN BUEREN MS GERALDINE LEA

Doughty Street Chambers
11 Doughty Street, London WC1N 2PG,
Telephone: 0171 404 1313
E-mail:enquiries@doughtystreet.co.uk
Call Date: Nov 1979, Middle Temple
Qualifications: [LLB (Hons) (Wales), LLM
(Lond)]

VAN DEN BERG BARRIE PATRICK

Godolphin Chambers
50 Castle Street, Truro, Cornwall,
TR1 3AF, Telephone: 01872 276312
E-mail:theclerks@godolphin.force9.co.uk
Call Date: July 1978, Middle Temple
Pupil Master
Qualifications: [BA]

VAN DER BIJL NIGEL CHARLES

1 Harcourt Buildings
2nd Floor, Temple, London EC4Y 9DA,
Telephone: 0171 353 9421/0375
E-mail:clerks@1harcourtbuildings.law.co.uk
Call Date: July 1973, Inner Temple
Pupil Master, Recorder
Qualifications: [BA, LLB]

VAN DER ZWART MARK ANDREW

King Charles House
Standard Hill, Nottingham NG1 6FX,
Telephone: 0115 9418851
E-mail: clerks@kch.co.uk
Call Date: Feb 1988, Middle Temple
Pupil Master
Qualifications: [BA (Hons) (Essex)]

VAN HAGEN CHRISTOPHER SEYMOUR NIGEL

4 King's Bench Walk
Ground/First Floor/Basement, Temple,
London EC4Y 7DL,
Telephone: 0171 822 8822
E-mail: 4kbw@barristersatlaw.com

King's Bench Chambers
Wellington House, 175 Holdenhurst Road,
Bournemouth, Dorset, BH8 8DQ,
Telephone: 01202 250025
E-mail: chambers@kingsbench.co.uk
Call Date: Nov 1980, Middle Temple
Pupil Master
Qualifications: [BA]

VAN STONE GRANT FREDERICK

6 Gray's Inn Square
Ground Floor, Gray's Inn, London
WC1R 5AZ, Telephone: 0171 242 1052
E-mail: 6graysinn@clara.co.uk
Call Date: Nov 1988, Middle Temple
Pupil Master
Qualifications: [LLB (Hons)]

VAN TONDER GERARD DIRK

1 New Square
Ground Floor, Lincoln's Inn, London
WC2A 3SA, Telephone: 0171 405 0884/5/6/
7 E-mail: clerks@1newsquare.law.co.uk
Call Date: Nov 1990, Middle Temple
Pupil Master
Qualifications: [BA, LLB (Witwatersrand)]

VANDYCK WILLIAM GEORGE

One Paper Buildings
Ground Floor, Temple, London
EC4Y 7EP, Telephone: 0171 583 7355
E-mail: clerks@1pb.co.uk
Call Date: July 1988, Lincoln's Inn
Pupil Master
Qualifications: [BA (Hons) (Cantab)]

VANE THE HON CHRISTOPHER JOHN FLETCHER

Trinity Chambers
9-12 Trinity Chare, Quayside, Newcastle
upon Tyne NE1 3DF,
Telephone: 0191 232 1927
E-mail: info@trinitychambers.co.uk
Call Date: Nov 1976, Inner Temple
Qualifications: [MA (Cantab)]

VANHEGAN MARK JAMES

11 South Square
2nd Floor, Gray's Inn, London
WC1R 5EU,
Telephone: 0171 405 1222 (24hr messagin
g service)
E-mail: clerks@11southsquare.com
Call Date: Nov 1990, Lincoln's Inn
Pupil Master
Qualifications: [MA (Cantab)]

VANHEGAN TOBY BARTHOLOMEW

Chambers of Harjit Singh
Ground Floor, 2 Middle Temple Lane,
Temple, London EC4Y 9AA,
Telephone: 0171 353 1356 (4 Lines)
Call Date: 1996, Middle Temple
Qualifications: [BA (Hons) (Oxon), LLM
(Lond)]

VARDON RICHARD STANHOPE

18 St John Street
Manchester M3 4EA,
Telephone: 0161 278 1800
E-mail: 18stjohn@lineone.net
Call Date: Nov 1985, Gray's Inn
Qualifications: [LLB (B'ham)]

VARTY MISS LOUISE JANE

9 Bedford Row
London WC1R 4AZ,
Telephone: 0171 242 3555
E-mail: clerks@9br.co.uk
Call Date: Nov 1986, Middle Temple
Pupil Master
Qualifications: [LLB (Birmingham)]

VASS HUGH PATRICK

East Anglian Chambers
Gresham House, 5 Museum Street,
Ipswich, Suffolk, IP1 1HQ,
Telephone: 01473 214481
E-mail: ipswich@ealaw.co.uk
East Anglian Chambers
57 London Street, Norwich NR2 1HL,
Telephone: 01603 617351
E-mail: norwich@ealaw.co.uk

East Anglian Chambers
52 North Hill, Colchester, Essex, CO1 1PY,
Telephone: 01206 572756
E-mail: colchester@ealaw.co.uk
Call Date: Nov 1983, Gray's Inn
Pupil Master
Qualifications: [BA]

VATER JOHN ALISTAIR PITT

Harcourt Chambers
1st Floor, 2 Harcourt Buildings, Temple,
London EC4Y 9DB,
Telephone: 0171 353 6961
E-mail:clerks@harcourtchambers.law.co.uk
Harcourt Chambers
Churchill House, 3 St Aldate's Courtyard,
St Aldate's, Oxford OX1 1BN,
Telephone: 01865 791559
E-mail:clerks@harcourtchambers.law.co.uk
Call Date: Feb 1995, Gray's Inn
Qualifications: [BA (Oxon)]

VAUDIN D'IMECOURT CHARLES

10 King's Bench Walk
Ground Floor, Temple, London
EC4Y 7EB, Telephone: 0171 353 7742
E-mail: 10kbw@lineone.net
Call Date: Nov 1971, Gray's Inn
Qualifications: [BA (Hons) (Oxon)]

VAUGHAN DAVID ARTHUR JOHN QC (1981)

Brick Court Chambers
7-8 Essex Street, London WC2R 3LD,
Telephone: 0171 379 3550
E-mail: [surname]@brickcourt.co.uk
Call Date: Nov 1963, Inner Temple
Recorder
Qualifications: [MA (Cantab)]

VAUGHAN KEITH VICTOR

8 Fountain Court
Steelhouse Lane, Birmingham B4 6DR,
Telephone: 0121 236 5514/5
E-mail: clerks@no8chambers.co.uk
Call Date: July 1968, Gray's Inn
Qualifications: [LLB (B'ham)]

VAUGHAN KIERAN PATRICK

Francis Taylor Building
Ground Floor, Temple, London
EC4Y 7BY, Telephone: 0171 353 7768/
7769/2711
E-mail:clerks@francistaylorbuilding.law.co.uk
Call Date: Nov 1993, Middle Temple
Qualifications: [LLB (Hons)]

VAUGHAN SIMON PETER

Manchester House Chambers
18-22 Bridge Street, Manchester M3 3BZ,
Telephone: 0161 834 7007
8 King Street Chambers
8 King Street, Manchester M2 6AQ,
Telephone: 0161 834 9560
E-mail: eightking@aol.com
Call Date: Nov 1989, Gray's Inn
Qualifications: [LLB,LLM (Lond)]

VAUGHAN TERENCE PAUL

Watford Chambers
74 Mildred Avenue, Watford,
Hertfordshire, WD1 7DX,
Telephone: 01923 220553
Call Date: Oct 1996, Middle Temple
Qualifications: [BSc (Salford) , Dip Law
(B'ham)]

VAUGHAN-JONES MISS SARAH JANE

2 Temple Gardens
Temple, London EC4Y 9AY,
Telephone: 0171 583 6041
E-mail: clerks@2templegardens.co.uk
Call Date: Nov 1983, Middle Temple
Pupil Master
Qualifications: [MA (Cantab)]

VAUGHAN-NEIL MISS CATHERINE MARY BERNARDINE

4 Pump Court
Temple, London EC4Y 7AN,
Telephone: 020 7842 5555
E-mail:chambers@4pumpcourt.law.co.uk
Call Date: Oct 1994, Inner Temple
Qualifications: [BA (Oxon), LLM (Cantab)]

VAUGHAN-WILLIAMS ARTHUR LAURENCE

Southsea Chambers
PO Box 148, Southsea, Portsmouth,
Hampshire, PO5 2TU,
Telephone: 01705 291261
Cathedral Chambers (Jan Wood Independent Barristers' Clerk)
1 Maple Road, Exeter, Devon, EX4 1BN,
Telephone: 01392 210900
E-mail:cathedral.chambers@eclipse.co.uk
Call Date: Nov 1988, Lincoln's Inn
Qualifications: [LLB (Bucks)]

VAVRECKA DAVID PAUL FRANK

14 Gray's Inn Square
Gray's Inn, London WC1R 5JP,
Telephone: 0171 242 0858
E-mail: 100712.2134@compuserve.com
Call Date: Oct 1992, Middle Temple
Qualifications: [LLB (Lond), LLM]

VEATS MISS ELIZABETH CLEA

Two Garden Court
1st Floor, Middle Temple, London
EC4Y 9BL, Telephone: 0171 353 1633
E-mail:barristers@2gardenct.law.co.uk
Call Date: July 1986, Middle Temple
Pupil Master
Qualifications: [LLB (B'ham), LLM]

VEEDER VAN VECHTEN QC (1986)

Essex Court Chambers
24 Lincoln's Inn Fields, London
WC2A 3ED, Telephone: 0171 813 8000
E-mail:clerksroom@essexcourt-chambers.co.uk
Call Date: Nov 1971, Inner Temple
Assistant Recorder
Qualifications: [MA (Cantab)]

VELOSO MISS LINDA

The Garden House
14 New Square, Lincoln's Inn, London
WC2A 3SH, Telephone: 0171 404 6150
Pepys' Chambers
17 Fleet Street, London EC4Y 1AA,
Telephone: 0171 936 2710
Call Date: Oct 1996, Lincoln's Inn
Qualifications: [BA (Hons)(Keele)]

VENABLES ROBERT QC (1990)

24 Old Buildings
First Floor, Lincoln's Inn, London
WC2A 3UP, Telephone: 020 7242 2744
E-mail: taxchambers@compuserve.com
Call Date: July 1973, Middle Temple
Qualifications: [MA (Oxon), LLM, FTII]

VENMORE JOHN

30 Park Place
Cardiff CF1 3BA,
Telephone: 01222 398421
E-mail: 100757.1456@compuserve.com
Call Date: Nov 1971, Lincoln's Inn
Pupil Master

VENTHAM ANTHONY MICHAEL

2-4 Tudor Street
London EC4Y 0AA,
Telephone: 0171 797 7111
E-mail: clerks@rfqc.co.uk
Call Date: Apr 1991, Middle Temple
Qualifications: [B.Sc (Hons)]

VERDAN ALEXANDER

9 Gough Square
London EC4A 3DE,
Telephone: 020 7832 0500
E-mail: clerks@9goughsq.co.uk
Call Date: Nov 1987, Inner Temple
Pupil Master
Qualifications: [BA, Dip Law]

VERDUYN DR ANTHONY JAMES

St Philip's Chambers
Fountain Court, Steelhouse Lane,
Birmingham B4 6DR,
Telephone: 0121 246 7000
E-mail: clerks@st-philips.co.uk
Call Date: Oct 1993, Lincoln's Inn
Qualifications: [BA (Hons)(Dunelm), D.Phil (Oxon), Dip Law (City)]

VERE-HODGE MICHAEL JOHN DAVY QC (1993)

2 King's Bench Walk
Ground Floor, Temple, London
EC4Y 7DE, Telephone: 0171 353 1746
E-mail: 2kbw@atlas.co.uk

Assize Court Chambers
14 Small Street, Bristol BS1 1DE,
Telephone: 0117 9264587
E-mail:chambers@assize-court-chambers.co.uk
King's Bench Chambers
115 North Hill, Plymouth PL4 8JY,
Telephone: 01752 221551
Call Date: Nov 1970, Gray's Inn
Recorder

VICKERS EDMUND BENEDICT BLYTH

3 Temple Gardens
2nd Floor, Temple, London EC4Y 9AU,
Telephone: 0171 583 1155
Call Date: Nov 1993, Middle Temple
Qualifications: [BA (Hons)(Dunelm), CPE
(City)]

VICKERS GUY JULIAN COURTNEY

28 St John Street
Manchester M3 4DJ,
Telephone: 0161 834 8418
E-mail: clerk@28stjohnst.co.uk
Call Date: Nov 1986, Middle Temple
Qualifications: [BA (Oxon)]

VICKERS MISS RACHEL CLARE

199 Strand
London WC2R 1DR,
Telephone: 0171 379 9779
E-mail: chambers@199strand.co.uk
Call Date: Oct 1992, Lincoln's Inn
Qualifications: [LLB(Hons)(Bris)]

VICKERY NEIL MICHAEL

13 King's Bench Walk
1st Floor, Temple, London EC4Y 7EN,
Telephone: 0171 353 7204
E-mail: clerks@13kbw.law.co.uk
King's Bench Chambers
32 Beaumont Street, Oxford OX1 2NP,
Telephone: 01865 311066
E-mail: clerks@kbc-oxford.law.co.uk
Call Date: July 1985, Gray's Inn
Pupil Master
Qualifications: [BA (Cantab)]

VIGARS MRS ANNA LILIAN

Guildhall Chambers
22-26 Broad Street, Bristol BS1 2HG,
Telephone: 0117 9273366
E-mail:civil.clerks@guildhallchambers.co.uk and
criminal.clerks@guildhallchambers.co.uk
Call Date: 1996, Gray's Inn
Qualifications: [BA (Oxon)]

VILLAGE PETER MALCOLM

4-5 Gray's Inn Square
Ground Floor, Gray's Inn, London
WC1R 5JP, Telephone: 0171 404 5252
E-mail:chambers@4-5graysinnsquare.co.uk
Call Date: July 1983, Inner Temple
Pupil Master
Qualifications: [LLB (Leeds)]

VILLAROSA MISS ANNUNZIATA

9 King's Bench Walk
Ground Floor, Temple, London
EC4Y 7DX, Telephone: 0171 353 7202/
3909 E-mail: 9kbw@compuserve.com
Call Date: July 1995, Middle Temple
Qualifications: [BA, PGCE (Adelaide), LLB]

VINCENT PATRICK BENJAMIN

12 King's Bench Walk
Temple, London EC4Y 7EL,
Telephone: 0171 583 0811
E-mail: chambers@12kbw.co.uk
Call Date: Oct 1992, Middle Temple
Qualifications: [BA (Hons)(Bris), Dip Law]

VINCENT MISS RUTH CAROLYN

Colleton Chambers
Colleton Crescent, Exeter, Devon,
EX2 4DG, Telephone: 01392 274898/9
Call Date: Oct 1995, Gray's Inn
Qualifications: [LLB (Manch)]

VINDIS MISS TARA

9 Gough Square
London EC4A 3DE,
Telephone: 020 7832 0500
E-mail: clerks@9goughsq.co.uk
Call Date: Nov 1996, Inner Temple
Qualifications: [LLB (Exon)]

D

VINE AIDAN JAMES WILSON

Harcourt Chambers
1st Floor, 2 Harcourt Buildings, Temple,
London EC4Y 9DB,
Telephone: 0171 353 6961
E-mail:clerks@harcourtchambers.law.co.uk
Harcourt Chambers
Churchill House, 3 St Aldate's Courtyard,
St Aldate's, Oxford OX1 1BN,
Telephone: 01865 791559
E-mail:clerks@harcourtchambers.law.co.uk
Call Date: Oct 1995, Middle Temple
Qualifications: [BA (Hons), MA]

VINE JAMES PETER STOCKMAN

Hardwicke Building
New Square, Lincoln's Inn, London
WC2A 3SB, Telephone: 020 7242 2523
E-mail: clerks@hardwicke.co.uk
Call Date: Nov 1977, Middle Temple
Pupil Master

VINE MS SARAH JANE

1 Pump Court
Lower Ground Floor, Temple, London
EC4Y 7AB, Telephone: 0171 583 2012/
353 4341
E-mail: [name]@1pumpcourt.co.uk
Call Date: Mar 1997, Inner Temple
Qualifications: [BA (B'ham), CPE]

VINEALL NICHOLAS EDWARD JOHN

4 Pump Court
Temple, London EC4Y 7AN,
Telephone: 020 7842 5555
E-mail:chambers@4pumpcourt.law.co.uk
Call Date: Nov 1988, Middle Temple
Pupil Master
Qualifications: [BA (Cantab), MA
(Pittsburgh), Dip Law (City)]

VINES ANTHONY ROBERT FRANCIS

Gough Square Chambers
6-7 Gough Square, London EC4A 3DE,
Telephone: 0171 353 0924
E-mail: gsc@goughsq.co.uk
Call Date: Nov 1993, Gray's Inn
Qualifications: [BA (Cantab)]

VINES MISS CLARE LUCY

35 Essex Street
Temple, London WC2R 3AR,
Telephone: 0171 353 6381
E-mail: derek_jenkins@link.org
Call Date: Oct 1997, Lincoln's Inn
Qualifications: [BA (Hons)]

VINEY RICHARD JOHN

12 King's Bench Walk
Temple, London EC4Y 7EL,
Telephone: 0171 583 0811
E-mail: chambers@12kbw.co.uk
Call Date: Feb 1994, Middle Temple
Qualifications: [BA (Hons)(Cantab)]

VIRDI MISS PRABHJOT KAUR

5 Essex Court
1st Floor, Temple, London EC4Y 9AH,
Telephone: 0171 410 2000
E-mail: barristers@5essexcourt.co.uk
Call Date: Oct 1995, Lincoln's Inn
Qualifications: [LLB (Hons)(Leic)]

VIRGO GRAHAM JOHN

Twenty-Four Old Buildings
Ground Floor, Lincoln's Inn, London
WC2A 3UP, Telephone: 0171 404 0946
E-mail:clerks@24oldbuildings.law.co.uk
Call Date: 1989, Lincoln's Inn
Qualifications: [MA (Cantab), BCL (Oxon)]

VIRGO JOHN ANTHONY

Guildhall Chambers
22-26 Broad Street, Bristol BS1 2HG,
Telephone: 0117 9273366
E-mail:civil.clerks@guildhallchambers.co.uk and
criminal.clerks@guildhallchambers.co.uk
Call Date: Nov 1983, Inner Temple
Pupil Master
Qualifications: [MA (Oxon)]

VITORIA MISS MARY CHRISTINE QC (1997)

8 New Square
Lincoln's Inn, London WC2A 3QP,
Telephone: 0171 405 4321
E-mail: clerks@8newsquare.co.uk
Call Date: Nov 1975, Lincoln's Inn
Qualifications: [BSc, PhD, LLB]

VOKES STEPHEN JOHN

Rowchester Chambers
4 Rowchester Court, Whittall Street,
Birmingham B4 6DH,
Telephone: 0121 233 2327/2361951
Call Date: July 1989, Lincoln's Inn
Qualifications: [BA (Wales)]

VOLZ KARL ANDREW

Chambers of Geoffrey Hawker
46/48 Essex Street, London WC2R 3GH,
Telephone: 0171 583 8899
Call Date: Nov 1993, Middle Temple
Qualifications: [BA (Hons)(Newc), CPE
(City)]

VON SANTEN-PAGAVA MAXIMILIAN KASIMIR

Forest House Chambers
15 Granville Road, Walthamstow, London
E17 9BS, Telephone: 0181 925 2240
Call Date: Nov 1993, Middle Temple
Qualifications: [LLB (Hons)(Lond)]

VOS GEOFFREY CHARLES QC (1993)

3 Stone Buildings
Lincoln's Inn, London WC2A 3XL,
Telephone: 0171 242 4937
E-mail: clerks@3sb.law.co.uk
Call Date: July 1977, Inner Temple
Qualifications: [MA (Cantab)]

VOSPER CHRISTOPHER JOHN

Angel Chambers
94 Walter Road, Swansea, West
Glamorgan, SA1 5QA,
Telephone: 01792 464623/464648
E-mail: lynne@angelchambers.co.uk
Farrar's Building
Temple, London EC4Y 7BD,
Telephone: 0171 583 9241
E-mail:chambers@farrarsbuilding.co.uk
Call Date: Nov 1977, Middle Temple
Pupil Master, Recorder
Qualifications: [MA (Oxon)]

VOUT ANDREW PAUL

2 Pump Court
1st Floor, Temple, London EC4Y 7AH,
Telephone: 0171 353 5597
Call Date: Nov 1995, Gray's Inn
Qualifications: [LLB (Warw)]

VULLO STEPHEN

Plowden Buildings
2nd Floor, 2 Plowden Buildings, Middle
Temple Lane, London EC4Y 9BU,
Telephone: 0171 583 0808
E-mail: bar@plowdenbuildings.co.uk
Call Date: Nov 1996, Middle Temple
Qualifications: [LLB (Hons)]

WADDICOR MISS JANET

1 Crown Office Row
Ground Floor, Temple, London
EC4Y 7HH, Telephone: 0171 797 7500
E-mail: mail@onecrownofficerow.com
Crown Office Row Chambers
Blenheim House, 120 Church Street,
Brighton, Sussex, BN1 1WH,
Telephone: 01273 625625
E-mail: crownofficerow@clara.net
Call Date: Nov 1985, Gray's Inn
Pupil Master
Qualifications: [MA (Oxon)]

WADDINGTON MRS ANNE LOUISE

Pump Court Chambers
Upper Ground Floor, 3 Pump Court,
Temple, London EC4Y 7AJ,
Telephone: 0171 353 0711
E-mail: clerks@3pumpcourt.com
Pump Court Chambers
31 Southgate Street, Winchester
SO23 9EE, Telephone: 01962 868161
E-mail: clerks@3pumpcourt.com
Pump Court Chambers
5 Temple Chambers, Temple Street,
Swindon SN1 1SQ,
Telephone: 01793 539899
E-mail: clerks@3pumpcourt.com
Call Date: Nov 1988, Middle Temple
Qualifications: [BA (Kent)]

WADDINGTON JAMES CHARLES

2 Pump Court
1st Floor, Temple, London EC4Y 7AH,
Telephone: 0171 353 5597
Call Date: July 1983, Gray's Inn
Pupil Master
Qualifications: [LLB (Exon)]

WADDINGTON NIGEL WILLIAM JAMES

8 Stone Buildings
Lincoln's Inn, London WC2A 3TA,
Telephone: 0171 831 9881
E-mail: alanl@8stonebuildings.law.uk
Call Date: Oct 1992, Middle Temple
Qualifications: [MSc, Dip Law]

WADE MISS CLARE CATHERINE

14 Tooks Court
Cursitor St, London EC4A 1LB,
Telephone: 0171 405 8828
E-mail: clerks@tooks.law.co.uk
Call Date: Nov 1990, Inner Temple
Qualifications: [BA (Dunelm), Dip Law
(City)]

WADE PROFESSOR SIR HENRY WILLIAM RAWSON QC (1968)

4-5 Gray's Inn Square
Ground Floor, Gray's Inn, London
WC1R 5JP, Telephone: 0171 404 5252
E-mail:chambers@4-5graysinnsquare.co.uk
Call Date: July 1946, Lincoln's Inn
Qualifications: [MA, LLD (Cantab)]

WADE IAN

Five Paper Buildings
1st Floor, Five Paper Bldgs, Temple,
London EC4Y 7HB,
Telephone: 0171 583 6117
E-mail:clerks@5-paperbuildings.law.co.uk
Call Date: Nov 1977, Gray's Inn
Pupil Master
Qualifications: [MA (Cantab)]

WADGE RICHARD

New Court Chambers
3 Broad Chare, Newcastle upon Tyne
NE1 3DQ, Telephone: 0191 232 1980
Call Date: Mar 1997, Gray's Inn
Qualifications: [BA (Dunelm)]

WADLING ANTHONY NEAL

4 Brick Court
Ground Floor, Temple, London
EC4Y 9AD, Telephone: 0171 797 7766
E-mail: chambers@4brick.co.uk
Call Date: Feb 1977, Inner Temple
Pupil Master
Qualifications: [BA (Hons), Dip EC Law]

WADOODI MISS AISHA

Fountain Chambers
Cleveland Business Centre, 1 Watson
Street, Middlesbrough TS1 2RQ,
Telephone: 01642 804040
E-mail:fountainchambers@onyxnet.co.uk
Call Date: Oct 1994, Middle Temple
Qualifications: [LLB (Hons)(Newc)]

WADSLEY PETER JOHN CAMPBELL

St John's Chambers
Small Street, Bristol BS1 1DW,
Telephone: 0117 9213456/298514
E-mail: @stjohnschambers.co.uk
Call Date: July 1984, Middle Temple
Pupil Master
Qualifications: [BA LLB (Cantab)]

WADSWORTH JAMES PATRICK QC (1981)

4 Paper Buildings
Ground Floor, Temple, London
EC4Y 7EX, Telephone: 0171 353 3366/
583 7155
E-mail: clerks@4paperbuildings.com
Call Date: Feb 1963, Inner Temple
Recorder
Qualifications: [MA (Oxon)]

WADSWORTH NICHOLAS STEPHEN

Clock Chambers
78 Darlington Street, Wolverhampton
WV1 4LY, Telephone: 01902 313444
Southsea Chambers
PO Box 148, Southsea, Portsmouth,
Hampshire, PO5 2TU,
Telephone: 01705 291261
Call Date: Feb 1993, Gray's Inn
Qualifications: [LLB]

WAGNER MRS LINDA ANN

96 Gray's Inn Road
London WC1X 8AL,
Telephone: 0171 405 0585
Call Date: Nov 1990, Middle Temple
Qualifications: [LLB (Hons)]

WAGNER MISS LYNN

Westgate Chambers
16-17 Wellington Square, Hastings, East
Sussex, TN34 1PB,
Telephone: 01424 432105
Call Date: July 1975, Lincoln's Inn
Qualifications: [BA, MA (Cantab), BA
(Australia)]

WAGSTAFFE CHRISTOPHER DAVID

New Court Chambers
5 Verulam Buildings, Gray's Inn, London
WC1R 5LY, Telephone: 0171 831 9500
E-mail: mail@newcourtchambers.com
Call Date: Nov 1992, Inner Temple
Qualifications: [LLB (Essex)]

WAHEED ERUM JUNADE

Chancery Chambers
1st Floor Offices, 70/72 Chancery Lane,
London WC2A 1AB,
Telephone: 0171 405 6879/6870
Call Date: Nov 1995, Gray's Inn
Qualifications: [LLB]

WAIN PETER

East Anglian Chambers
Gresham House, 5 Museum Street,
Ipswich, Suffolk, IP1 1HQ,
Telephone: 01473 214481
E-mail: ipswich@ealaw.co.uk
East Anglian Chambers
57 London Street, Norwich NR2 1HL,
Telephone: 01603 617351
E-mail: norwich@ealaw.co.uk
East Anglian Chambers
52 North Hill, Colchester, Essex, CO1 1PY,
Telephone: 01206 572756
E-mail: colchester@ealaw.co.uk
Call Date: July 1972, Gray's Inn
Pupil Master
Qualifications: [LLB]

WAINE STEPHEN PHILLIP

Chambers of Michael Pert QC
36 Bedford Row, London WC1R 4JH,
Telephone: 0171 421 8000
E-mail: 36bedfordrow@link.org
Chambers of Michael Pert QC
24 Albion Place, Northampton NN1 1UD,
Telephone: 01604 602333
Chambers of Michael Pert QC
104 New Walk, Leicester LE1 7EA,
Telephone: 0116 249 2020
Call Date: Nov 1969, Lincoln's Inn
Pupil Master, Recorder
Qualifications: [LLB (Soton)]

WAINWRIGHT JEREMY PATRICK

Westgate Chambers
144 High Street, Lewes, East Sussex,
BN7 1XT, Telephone: 01273 480510
Call Date: Oct 1990, Gray's Inn
Pupil Master
Qualifications: [BA (Hons), Dip Law]

WAINWRIGHT JOHN PATRICK HADEN

St Mary's Chambers
50 High Pavement, Lace Market,
Nottingham NG1 1HW,
Telephone: 0115 9503503
E-mail: clerks@smc.law.co.uk
Call Date: Oct 1994, Lincoln's Inn
Qualifications: [MA (Oxon)]

WAITE JOHN-PAUL TANGYE

Field Court Chambers
2nd Floor, 3 Field Court, Gray's Inn,
London WC1R 5EP,
Telephone: 0171 404 7474
Call Date: Nov 1995, Middle Temple
Qualifications: [BA (Hons)(Leeds)]

WAITE JONATHAN GILBERT STOKES

One Paper Buildings
Ground Floor, Temple, London
EC4Y 7EP, Telephone: 0171 583 7355
E-mail: clerks@1pb.co.uk
Call Date: July 1978, Inner Temple
Pupil Master
Qualifications: [MA (Cantab)]

WAITE KIRIL

King's Bench Chambers
Wellington House, 175 Holdenhurst Road,
Bournemouth, Dorset, BH8 8DQ,
Telephone: 01202 250025
E-mail: chambers@kingsbench.co.uk
Call Date: Nov 1997, Gray's Inn
Qualifications: [LLB (Lond)]

WAITHE JOHN ALBERT

12 Old Square
1st Floor, Lincoln's Inn, London
WC2A 3TX, Telephone: 0171 404 0875
Call Date: Nov 1972, Lincoln's Inn
Qualifications: [LLB (Lond), LLM (Lond), MA
(Business Law), (Guildhall)]

WAKEHAM PHILIP JOHN LE MESSURIER

Hardwicke Building
New Square, Lincoln's Inn, London
WC2A 3SB, Telephone: 020 7242 2523
E-mail: clerks@hardwicke.co.uk
Call Date: July 1978, Middle Temple
Pupil Master
Qualifications: [BA]

WAKERLEY PAUL CHARLES MACLENNON

4 King's Bench Walk
2nd Floor, Temple, London EC4Y 7DL,
Telephone: 020 7353 3581
E-mail: clerks@4kbw.co.uk
Call Date: Nov 1990, Gray's Inn
Qualifications: [LLB (Hons)]

WAKERLEY RICHARD MACLENNON QC (1982)

4 Fountain Court
Steelhouse Lane, Birmingham B4 6DR,
Telephone: 0121 236 3476
Call Date: Feb 1965, Gray's Inn
Recorder
Qualifications: [MA (Cantab)]

WAKSMAN DAVID MICHAEL

Fountain Court
Temple, London EC4Y 9DH,
Telephone: 0171 583 3335
E-mail: chambers@fountaincourt.co.uk
Call Date: Nov 1982, Middle Temple
Pupil Master
Qualifications: [LLB (Manch) BCL, (Oxon)]

WALBANK DAVID NICHOLAS

5 Essex Court
1st Floor, Temple, London EC4Y 9AH,
Telephone: 0171 410 2000
E-mail: barristers@5essexcourt.co.uk
Call Date: Nov 1987, Inner Temple
Qualifications: [MA (Cantab)]

WALD RICHARD DANIEL

2 Mitre Court Buildings
2nd Floor, Temple, London EC4Y 7BX,
Telephone: 0171 583 1380
E-mail: clerks@2mcb.co.uk
Call Date: Nov 1997, Gray's Inn
Qualifications: [MA (Edin)]

WALDEN-SMITH DAVID EDWARD

6 Pump Court
1st Floor, Temple, London EC4Y 7AR,
Telephone: 0171 797 8400
E-mail: clerks@6pumpcourt.co.uk
6-8 Mill Street
Maidstone, Kent, ME15 6XH,
Telephone: 01622 688094
E-mail: annexe@6pumpcourt.co.uk
Call Date: July 1985, Lincoln's Inn
Qualifications: [MA (Cantab)]

WALDEN-SMITH MISS KAREN JANE

5 Stone Buildings
Lincoln's Inn, London WC2A 3XT,
Telephone: 0171 242 6201
E-mail:clerks@5-stonebuildings.law.co.uk
Call Date: Oct 1990, Lincoln's Inn
Qualifications: [MA (Cantab)]

D

WALDRON WILLIAM FRANCIS

Exchange Chambers
Pearl Assurance House, Derby Square,
Liverpool L2 9XX,
Telephone: 0151 236 7747
E-mail:exchangechambers@btinternet.com
Call Date: Nov 1986, Gray's Inn
Pupil Master
Qualifications: [LLB]

WALDRON WILLIAM HENRY QC (1982)

Exchange Chambers
Pearl Assurance House, Derby Square,
Liverpool L2 9XX,
Telephone: 0151 236 7747
E-mail:exchangechambers@btinternet.com
Call Date: Feb 1970, Gray's Inn
Recorder

WALES ANDREW NIGEL MALCOLM

S Tomlinson QC
7 King's Bench Walk, Temple, London
EC4Y 7DS, Telephone: 0171 583 0404
E-mail: clerks@7kbw.law.co.uk
Call Date: Nov 1992, Gray's Inn
Qualifications: [MA (Cantab), LLM (Virginia
USA)]

WALES MATTHEW JAMES

Guildhall Chambers
22-26 Broad Street, Bristol BS1 2HG,
Telephone: 0117 9273366
E-mail:civil.clerks@guildhallchambers.co.uk and
criminal.clerks@guildhallchambers.co.uk
Call Date: Oct 1993, Inner Temple
Qualifications: [BA (Dunelm)]

WALEY ERIC RICHARD THOMAS

Assize Court Chambers
14 Small Street, Bristol BS1 1DE,
Telephone: 0117 9264587
E-mail:chambers@assize-court-chambers.co.uk
Call Date: Nov 1976, Inner Temple
Qualifications: [MA Hons (Cantab)]

WALEY SIMON FELIX

Chambers of Andrew Campbell QC
10 Park Square, Leeds LS1 2LH,
Telephone: 0113 2455438
E-mail: clerks@10pksq.co.uk
Call Date: Feb 1988, Middle Temple
Qualifications: [LLB (Exon)]

WALFORD RICHARD HENRY HOWARD

Serle Court Chambers
6 New Square, Lincoln's Inn, London
WC2A 3QS, Telephone: 0171 242 6105
E-mail: clerks@serlecourt.co.uk
Call Date: July 1984, Middle Temple
Pupil Master
Qualifications: [LLB (Exon)]

WALKER ALLISTER DAVID

5 Pump Court
Ground Floor, Temple, London
EC4Y 7AP, Telephone: 020 7353 2532
E-mail: FivePump@netcomuk.co.uk
Call Date: Nov 1990, Inner Temple
Qualifications: [LLB (Essex)]

WALKER ANDREW ANGUS

Chambers of Helen Grindrod QC
4th Floor, 15-19 Devereux Court, London
WC2R 3JJ, Telephone: 0171 583 2792
Call Date: Oct 1994, Middle Temple
Qualifications: [LLB (Hons)(Lond)]

WALKER ANDREW GREENFIELD

Chambers of Lord Goodhart QC
Ground Floor, 3 New Square, Lincoln's
Inn, London WC2A 3RS,
Telephone: 0171 405 5577
E-mail:law@threenewsquare.demon.co.uk
Call Date: July 1975, Lincoln's Inn
Pupil Master
Qualifications: [MA (Cantab)]

WALKER ANDREW PAUL DALTON

9 Old Square
Ground Floor, Lincoln's Inn, London
WC2A 3SR, Telephone: 0171 405 4682
E-mail: chambers@9oldsquare.co.uk
Call Date: 1991, Lincoln's Inn
Qualifications: [MA (Cantab)]

WALKER MISS ANWEN ELIZABETH

Rowchester Chambers
4 Rowchester Court, Whittall Street,
Birmingham B4 6DH,
Telephone: 0121 233 2327/2361951
Call Date: July 1992, Inner Temple
Qualifications: [LLB]

WALKER CHRISTOPHER DAVID BESTWICK

Old Square Chambers
Hanover House, 47 Corn Street, Bristol
BS1 1HT, Telephone: 0117 9277111
E-mail: oldsqbri@globalnet.co.uk
Old Square Chambers
1 Verulam Buildings, Gray's Inn, London
WC1R 5LQ, Telephone: 0171 269 0300
E-mail:clerks@oldsquarechambers.co.uk
Call Date: Oct 1990, Middle Temple
Pupil Master
Qualifications: [BA (Cantab), Licence
Speciale en, Droit Europeer]

WALKER EDWARD JEREMY BRUCE

St John's Chambers
Small Street, Bristol BS1 1DW,
Telephone: 0117 9213456/298514
E-mail: @stjohnschambers.co.uk
Call Date: Nov 1994, Gray's Inn
Qualifications: [BSc]

WALKER MRS ELIZABETH ANNABEL QC (1997)

Chambers of Michael Pert QC
36 Bedford Row, London WC1R 4JH,
Telephone: 0171 421 8000
E-mail: 36bedfordrow@link.org
Paradise Chambers
26 Paradise Square, Sheffield S1 2DE,
Telephone: 0114 2738951
E-mail: timbooth@paradise-sq.co.uk
Chambers of Michael Pert QC
24 Albion Place, Northampton NN1 1UD,
Telephone: 01604 602333
Chambers of Michael Pert QC
104 New Walk, Leicester LE1 7EA,
Telephone: 0116 249 2020
Call Date: Nov 1976, Gray's Inn
Recorder
Qualifications: [LLB]

WALKER MRS ELIZABETH MARY

St Philip's Chambers
Fountain Court, Steelhouse Lane,
Birmingham B4 6DR,
Telephone: 0121 246 7000
E-mail: clerks@st-philips.co.uk
Call Date: Oct 1994, Gray's Inn
Qualifications: [BA (Hons)(Dunelm)]

WALKER MRS FIONA

Bank House Chambers
Old Bank House, Hartshead, Sheffield
S1 2EL, Telephone: 0114 2751223
Call Date: Feb 1992, Inner Temple
Qualifications: [LLB (Manc)]

WALKER JAMES

1 Gray's Inn Square
Ground Floor, London WC1R 5AA,
Telephone: 0171 405 8946/7/8
Call Date: Oct 1994, Lincoln's Inn
Qualifications: [LLB (Hons)(Anglia)]

WALKER MISS JANE

28 St John Street
Manchester M3 4DJ,
Telephone: 0161 834 8418
E-mail: clerk@28stjohnst.co.uk
Call Date: July 1987, Middle Temple
Qualifications: [MA (Oxon)]

WALKER MISS JANE SHARMAN

43 Eglantine Road
London SW18 2DE,
Telephone: 0181 874 3469
6 Fountain Court
Steelhouse Lane, Birmingham B4 6DR,
Telephone: 0121 233 3282
E-mail: clerks@sixfountain.co.uk
Call Date: Nov 1974, Middle Temple
Qualifications: [LLB (B'ham)]

WALKER JONATHAN JOHAR

Fountain Chambers
Cleveland Business Centre, 1 Watson
Street, Middlesbrough TS1 2RQ,
Telephone: 01642 804040
E-mail:fountainchambers@onyxnet.co.uk
Call Date: Oct 1997, Lincoln's Inn
Qualifications: [BSc (Hons)(Dundee), Dip in
Law (Notts)]

WALKER MARK JONATHAN JASON

Chancery House Chambers
7 Lisbon Square, Leeds LS1 4LY,
Telephone: 0113 244 6691
E-mail: chanceryhouse@btinternet.com
Call Date: Nov 1986, Middle Temple
Qualifications: [LLB(Leeds)]

WALKER PATRICK HOWARD

Chancery House Chambers
7 Lisbon Square, Leeds LS1 4LY,
Telephone: 0113 244 6691
E-mail: chanceryhouse@btinternet.com
Call Date: July 1979, Lincoln's Inn
Pupil Master
Qualifications: [LLB (Sheff)]

WALKER PAUL CHRISTOPHER

Bridewell Chambers
2 Bridewell Place, London EC4V 6AP,
Telephone: 020 7797 8800
E-mail:HughesGage@bridewell.law.co.uk
Call Date: Oct 1993, Lincoln's Inn
Qualifications: [LLB (Hons)(Lond)]

WALKER PAUL JAMES QC (1999)

Brick Court Chambers
7-8 Essex Street, London WC2R 3LD,
Telephone: 0171 379 3550
E-mail: [surname]@brickcourt.co.uk
Call Date: 1979, Gray's Inn
Pupil Master
Qualifications: [BCL,MA (Oxon)]

WALKER PETER BRIAN

Broadway House Chambers
Broadway House, 9 Bank Street, Bradford,
West Yorkshire, BD1 1TW,
Telephone: 01274 722560
E-mail: clerks@broadwayhouse.co.uk
Broadway House Chambers
31 Park Square West, Leeds LS1 2PF,
Telephone: 0113 246 2600
Call Date: July 1985, Inner Temple

WALKER RAYMOND AUGUSTUS QC (1988)

1 Harcourt Buildings
2nd Floor, Temple, London EC4Y 9DA,
Telephone: 0171 353 9421/0375
E-mail:clerks@1harcourtbuildings.law.co.uk
Call Date: July 1966, Middle Temple

Recorder
Qualifications: [BA (Cantab)]

WALKER RONALD JACK QC (1983)

12 King's Bench Walk
Temple, London EC4Y 7EL,
Telephone: 0171 583 0811
E-mail: chambers@12kbw.co.uk
Call Date: July 1962, Gray's Inn
Recorder
Qualifications: [LLB]

WALKER STEVEN JOHN

Atkin Chambers
1 Atkin Building, Gray's Inn, London
WC1R 5AT, Telephone: 020 7404 0102
E-mail: clerks@atkin-chambers.co.uk
Call Date: Nov 1993, Lincoln's Inn
Qualifications: [LLB (Hons)]

WALKER STUART JAMES

Mitre House Chambers
15-19 Devereux Court, London WC2R 3JJ,
Telephone: 0171 583 8233
Call Date: Oct 1990, Gray's Inn
Qualifications: [BA (Oxon)]

WALKER MRS SUSANNAH MARY

One Garden Court Family Law Chambers
Ground Floor, Temple, London
EC4Y 9BJ, Telephone: 0171 797 7900
E-mail: clerks@onegardencourt.co.uk
Call Date: July 1985, Inner Temple
Pupil Master
Qualifications: [BSocSc, Dip Law (City), Dip Social Work]

WALKER MISS SUZANNE

Trinity Chambers
140 New London Road, Chelmsford,
Essex, CM2 0AW,
Telephone: 01245 605040
E-mail:clerks@trinitychambers.law.co.uk
Call Date: Oct 1995, Lincoln's Inn
Qualifications: [LLB (Hons)(Manc)]

WALKER TERENCE CARR

1 Crown Office Row
3rd Floor, Temple, London EC4Y 7HH,
Telephone: 0171 583 9292
E-mail: onecor@link.org
Call Date: July 1973, Inner Temple
Pupil Master
Qualifications: [MA (Oxon)]

WALKER TIMOTHY JOHN

29 Bedford Row Chambers
London WC1R 4HE,
Telephone: 0171 831 2626
Call Date: July 1984, Inner Temple
Pupil Master
Qualifications: [MA (Cantab)]

WALKER-KANE JONATHAN CHARLES

Paradise Chambers
26 Paradise Square, Sheffield S1 2DE,
Telephone: 0114 2738951
E-mail: timbooth@paradise-sq.co.uk
Call Date: July 1994, Gray's Inn
Qualifications: [BA]

WALKER-SMITH SIR JOHN JONAH

Doughty Street Chambers
11 Doughty Street, London WC1N 2PG,
Telephone: 0171 404 1313
E-mail:enquiries@doughtystreet.co.uk
De Montfort Chambers
95 Princess Road East, Leicester LE1 7DQ,
Telephone: 0116 254 8686
E-mail: dmcbar@aol.com
Call Date: Nov 1963, Middle Temple
Pupil Master, Assistant Recorder
Qualifications: [MA (Oxon)]

WALL MRS CARMEL MIRIAM

4 Fountain Court
Steelhouse Lane, Birmingham B4 6DR,
Telephone: 0121 236 3476
Call Date: Nov 1986, Lincoln's Inn
Qualifications: [BA (Hons)(Cantab)]

WALL CHRISTOPHER JAMES LYNTON

Becket Chambers
17 New Dover Road, Canterbury, Kent,
CT1 3AS, Telephone: 01227 786331
Call Date: Nov 1987, Lincoln's Inn
Qualifications: [LLB (Hons)]

WALL (DARYL) WILLIAM

3 Fountain Court
Steelhouse Lane, Birmingham B4 6DR,
Telephone: 0121 236 5854
Call Date: Nov 1985, Inner Temple
Qualifications: [BA (York), Dip Law (City)]

WALL MISS JACQUELINE FRANCOISE

India Buildings Chambers
Water Street, Liverpool L2 0XG,
Telephone: 0151 243 6000
E-mail: clerks@chambers.u-net.com
Call Date: July 1986, Gray's Inn
Qualifications: [LLB (Lanc)]

WALL MARK ARTHUR

4 Fountain Court
Steelhouse Lane, Birmingham B4 6DR,
Telephone: 0121 236 3476
Call Date: Nov 1985, Lincoln's Inn
Qualifications: [MA (Cantab)]

WALLACE ADRIAN ROBERT

Peel Court Chambers
45 Hardman Street, Manchester M3 3PL,
Telephone: 0161 832 3791
E-mail: clerks@peelct.co.uk
Call Date: July 1979, Middle Temple
Pupil Master
Qualifications: [BA (Cantab)]

WALLACE ANDREW DUNCAN GRAY

3 Fountain Court
Steelhouse Lane, Birmingham B4 6DR,
Telephone: 0121 236 5854
Call Date: Nov 1988, Gray's Inn
Qualifications: [LLB]

WALLACE MS ANN CHRISTINE

Godolphin Chambers
50 Castle Street, Truro, Cornwall,
TR1 3AF, Telephone: 01872 276312
E-mail:theclerks@godolphin.force9.co.uk
1 Pump Court
Lower Ground Floor, Temple, London
EC4Y 7AB, Telephone: 0171 583 2012/
353 4341
E-mail: [name]@1pumpcourt.co.uk
Call Date: July 1979, Inner Temple
Qualifications: [LLB]

WALLACE HUGH GEORGE

9 Park Place
Cardiff CF1 3DP,
Telephone: 01222 382731
Call Date: July 1993, Gray's Inn

WALLACE IAN NORMAN DUNCAN QC (1973)

Atkin Chambers
1 Atkin Building, Gray's Inn, London
WC1R 5AT, Telephone: 020 7404 0102
E-mail: clerks@atkin-chambers.co.uk
Call Date: June 1948, Middle Temple
Qualifications: [MA (Oxon)]

WALLACE MRS JANE SCOTT

1a Middle Temple Lane
Ground Floor, Temple, London
EC4Y 9AA, Telephone: 0171 353 8815
Call Date: July 1974, Inner Temple

WALLACE SHAUN ANTHONY

Call Date: Nov 1984, Inner Temple
Qualifications: [BA]

WALLBANKS MISS JOANNE

1 Fountain Court
Steelhouse Lane, Birmingham B4 6DR,
Telephone: 0121 236 5721
Rowchester Chambers
4 Rowchester Court, Whittall Street,
Birmingham B4 6DH,
Telephone: 0121 233 2327/2361951
Call Date: Oct 1997, Middle Temple
Qualifications: [LLB (Hons)(Staffs)]

WALLER MS HELEN MARGARET

Sedan House
Stanley Place, Chester CH1 2LU,
Telephone: 01244 320480/348282
Call Date: Mar 1997, Middle Temple
Qualifications: [BA (Hons)]

WALLER RICHARD BEAUMONT

S Tomlinson QC
7 King's Bench Walk, Temple, London
EC4Y 7DS, Telephone: 0171 583 0404
E-mail: clerks@7kbw.law.co.uk
Call Date: Oct 1994, Gray's Inn
Qualifications: [MA]

WALLING PHILIP THOMAS GEORGE

Mercury Chambers
Mercury House, 33-35 Clarendon Road,
Leeds LS2 9NZ,
Telephone: 0113 234 2265
E-mail:cdexter@mercurychambers.co.uk
Call Date: Nov 1986, Lincoln's Inn
Pupil Master
Qualifications: [LLB(Lanc), BL (Dublin)]

WALLINGTON PETER THOMAS

11 King's Bench Walk
Temple, London EC4Y 7EQ,
Telephone: 0171 632 8500/583 0610
E-mail: clerksroom@11kbw.com
Call Date: July 1987, Gray's Inn
Pupil Master
Qualifications: [MA, LLM (Cantab)]

WALLINGTON RICHARD ANTHONY

The Chambers of Leolin Price CBE, QC
10 Old Square, Lincoln's Inn, London
WC2A 3SU, Telephone: 0171 405 0758
Call Date: July 1972, Middle Temple
Qualifications: [MA (Cantab)]

WALLWORK BERNARD GRAHAM FRANK

28 St John Street
Manchester M3 4DJ,
Telephone: 0161 834 8418
E-mail: clerk@28stjohnst.co.uk
Call Date: Nov 1976, Middle Temple
Pupil Master, Assistant Recorder
Qualifications: [MA (Oxon)]

WALMSLEY ALAN

Bridewell Chambers
2 Bridewell Place, London EC4V 6AP,
Telephone: 020 7797 8800
E-mail:HughesGage@bridewell.law.co.uk
Call Date: Nov 1991, Inner Temple
Qualifications: [BSc]

WALMSLEY KEITH BERNARD RUPERT

199 Strand
London WC2R 1DR,
Telephone: 0171 379 9779
E-mail: chambers@199strand.co.uk
Call Date: July 1973, Inner Temple
Pupil Master
Qualifications: [LLB (Bris), DCrim (Cantab)]

WALMSLEY PETER JEREMY

High Pavement Chambers
1 High Pavement, Nottingham NG1 1HF,
Telephone: 0115 9418218
Call Date: June 1964, Inner Temple
Pupil Master

WALSH BRIAN JOSEPH

12 Old Square
1st Floor, Lincoln's Inn, London
WC2A 3TX, Telephone: 0171 404 0875
Call Date: Feb 1994, Gray's Inn
Qualifications: [BA (Dublin)]

WALSH JOHN PATRICK

Plowden Buildings
2nd Floor, 2 Plowden Buildings, Middle
Temple Lane, London EC4Y 9BU,
Telephone: 0171 583 0808
E-mail: bar@plowdenbuildings.co.uk
Call Date: Nov 1993, Inner Temple
Qualifications: [BA, MA (Ireland), LLB
(Lond)]

WALSH MARK HOWELL

2 King's Bench Walk Chambers
1st Floor, 2 King's Bench Walk, Temple,
London EC4Y 7DE,
Telephone: 020 7353 9276
E-mail: chambers@2kbw.co.uk
Call Date: 1996, Middle Temple
Qualifications: [MA (Hons)(Cantab), CPE
(City)]

WALSH MARTIN FRASER

Peel Court Chambers
45 Hardman Street, Manchester M3 3PL,
Telephone: 0161 832 3791
E-mail: clerks@peelct.co.uk
Call Date: Nov 1990, Gray's Inn
Qualifications: [LLB (Manch)]

WALSH MICHAEL STEVEN

St Ive's Chambers
Whittall Street, Birmingham B4 6DH,
Telephone: 0121 236 0863/5720
E-mail:stives.headofchambers@btinternet.com
5 Fountain Court
Steelhouse Lane, Birmingham B4 6DR,
Telephone: 0121 606 0500
E-mail:clerks@5fountaincourt.law.co.uk
Call Date: 1996, Middle Temple
Qualifications: [BA (Hons) (Lond), Dip Law
(City)]

WALSH MISS PATRICIA CLAIRE

East Anglian Chambers
52 North Hill, Colchester, Essex, CO1 1PY,
Telephone: 01206 572756
E-mail: colchester@ealaw.co.uk
East Anglian Chambers
57 London Street, Norwich NR2 1HL,
Telephone: 01603 617351
E-mail: norwich@ealaw.co.uk
East Anglian Chambers
Gresham House, 5 Museum Street,
Ipswich, Suffolk, IP1 1HQ,
Telephone: 01473 214481
E-mail: ipswich@ealaw.co.uk
Call Date: Nov 1993, Lincoln's Inn
Qualifications: [LLB (Hons)]

WALSH PETER ANTHONY JOSEPH

Queen Elizabeth Building
Ground Floor, Temple, London
EC4Y 9BS,
Telephone: 0171 353 7181 (12 Lines)
Call Date: Nov 1978, Middle Temple
Pupil Master
Qualifications: [LLB (Hons) (Lond)]

WALSH PETER PAUL

New Court Chambers
3 Broad Chare, Newcastle upon Tyne
NE1 3DQ, Telephone: 0191 232 1980
Call Date: May 1982, Gray's Inn
Pupil Master
Qualifications: [BA (Hons)]

WALSH SIMON

Bridewell Chambers
2 Bridewell Place, London EC4V 6AP,
Telephone: 020 7797 8800
E-mail:HughesGage@bridewell.law.co.uk
Call Date: Nov 1987, Middle Temple
Pupil Master
Qualifications: [MA (Oxon), Dip Law, (City),
ACIArb]

WALSH STEPHEN PAUL

3 Raymond Buildings
Gray's Inn, London WC1R 5BH,
Telephone: 020 7831 3833
E-mail:chambers@threeraymond.demon.co.u
k
Call Date: Nov 1983, Middle Temple
Pupil Master
Qualifications: [LL.B]

WALSH STEVEN JAMES FRANKLYN

5 Paper Buildings
Ground Floor, Temple, London
EC4Y 7HB, Telephone: 0171 583 9275/
583 4555 E-mail: 5paper@link.org
Call Date: Feb 1965, Lincoln's Inn
Pupil Master
Qualifications: [BA, LLB (Cantab)]

WALSHE MS ANNIE PATRICIA

Chambers of Geoffrey Hawker
46/48 Essex Street, London WC2R 3GH,
Telephone: 0171 583 8899
Call Date: Oct 1993, Inner Temple
Qualifications: [LLB]

WALTER MISS FRANCESCA ELIZABETH

3 Paper Buildings
Temple, London EC4Y 7EU,
Telephone: 020 7583 8055
E-mail: London@3paper.com
3 Paper Buildings (Bournemouth)
20 Lorne Park Road, Bournemouth,
Dorset, BH1 1JN,
Telephone: 01202 292102
E-mail: Bournemouth@3paper.com
3 Paper Buildings (Oxford)
1 Alfred Street, High Street, Oxford
OX1 4EH, Telephone: 01865 793736
E-mail: oxford@3paper.com

3 Paper Buildings (Winchester)
4 St Peter Street, Winchester SO23 8BW,
Telephone: 01962 868884
E-mail: winchester@3paper.com
Call Date: Oct 1994, Middle Temple
Qualifications: [BA (Hons)(Oxon)]

WALTERS EDMUND JOHN

13 King's Bench Walk
1st Floor, Temple, London EC4Y 7EN,
Telephone: 0171 353 7204
E-mail: clerks@13kbw.law.co.uk
King's Bench Chambers
32 Beaumont Street, Oxford OX1 2NP,
Telephone: 01865 311066
E-mail: clerks@kbc-oxford.law.co.uk
Call Date: Nov 1991, Middle Temple
Qualifications: [BA Hons (Bris), Dip Law]

WALTERS GARETH RUPEL

St Philip's Chambers
Fountain Court, Steelhouse Lane,
Birmingham B4 6DR,
Telephone: 0121 246 7000
E-mail: clerks@st-philips.co.uk
Call Date: Nov 1986, Middle Temple
Qualifications: [LLB (Wales)]

WALTERS GERAINT WYN

Angel Chambers
94 Walter Road, Swansea, West
Glamorgan, SA1 5QA,
Telephone: 01792 464623/464648
E-mail: lynne@angelchambers.co.uk
Call Date: Nov 1981, Gray's Inn
Pupil Master
Qualifications: [LLB (Wales)]

WALTERS GRAHAM ANTHONY

33 Park Place
Cardiff CF1 3BA,
Telephone: 02920 233313
Call Date: July 1986, Gray's Inn
Pupil Master
Qualifications: [MA (Oxon)]

WALTERS MISS JILL MARY

33 Park Place
Cardiff CF1 3BA,
Telephone: 02920 233313
Call Date: July 1979, Middle Temple
Pupil Master
Qualifications: [LLB (Wales)]

WALTERS JOHN LATIMER QC (1997)

Gray's Inn Tax Chambers
3rd Floor, Gray's Inn Chambers, Gray's
Inn, London WC1R 5JA,
Telephone: 0171 242 2642
E-mail: clerks@taxbar.com
Call Date: July 1977, Middle Temple
Qualifications: [MA (Oxon), FCA]

WALTERS JONATHAN GWYNNE

33 Park Place
Cardiff CF1 3BA,
Telephone: 02920 233313
Call Date: July 1984, Inner Temple
Qualifications: [LLB (Lond)]

WALTERS ROBERT GERALD

Pendragon Chambers
124 Walter Road, Swansea, West
Glamorgan, SA1 5RG,
Telephone: 01792 411188
Call Date: Nov 1974, Gray's Inn

WALTERS PROFESSOR TERENCE CHARLES

St Mary's Chambers
50 High Pavement, Lace Market,
Nottingham NG1 1HW,
Telephone: 0115 9503503
E-mail: clerks@smc.law.co.uk
Call Date: 1993, Inner Temple
Qualifications: [LLB (Wales), M.Phil (Notts),
MiMgt]

WALTERS MISS VIVIAN IRENE ELIZABETH

13 King's Bench Walk
1st Floor, Temple, London EC4Y 7EN,
Telephone: 0171 353 7204
E-mail: clerks@13kbw.law.co.uk
King's Bench Chambers
32 Beaumont Street, Oxford OX1 2NP,
Telephone: 01865 311066
E-mail: clerks@kbc-oxford.law.co.uk
Call Date: Nov 1991, Middle Temple
Qualifications: [BA Hons (Leic)]

WALTON ALASTAIR HENRY

7 Stone Buildings
Ground Floor, Lincoln's Inn, London
WC2A 3SZ, Telephone: 0171 405 3886/
242 3546 E-mail: chaldous@vossnet.co.uk
Call Date: July 1977, Lincoln's Inn
Pupil Master
Qualifications: [BA (Oxon)]

WALTON MISS CAROLYN MARGERY

13 Old Square
Ground Floor, Lincoln's Inn, London
WC2A 3UA, Telephone: 0171 404 4800
E-mail: clerks@13oldsquare.law.co.uk
Call Date: July 1980, Gray's Inn
Pupil Master
Qualifications: [LLB (Lond)]

WAN DAUD MALEK

6 King's Bench Walk
Ground, Third & Fourth Floors, Temple,
London EC4Y 7DR,
Telephone: 0171 353 4931/583 0695
Call Date: Nov 1991, Inner Temple
Qualifications: [LLB]

WARBURTON MISS JULIE

King Charles House
Standard Hill, Nottingham NG1 6FX,
Telephone: 0115 9418851
E-mail: clerks@kch.co.uk
Call Date: Oct 1993, Middle Temple
Qualifications: [LLB (Hons)(Lond)]

WARBY MARK DAVID JOHN

5 Raymond Buildings
1st Floor, Gray's Inn, London WC1R 5BP,
Telephone: 0171 242 2902
E-mail: clerks@media-ent-law.co.uk
Call Date: Nov 1981, Gray's Inn
Pupil Master
Qualifications: [MA (Oxon)]

WARD MRS ANNIE FRANCES

Pump Court Chambers
Upper Ground Floor, 3 Pump Court,
Temple, London EC4Y 7AJ,
Telephone: 0171 353 0711
E-mail: clerks@3pumpcourt.com

D

Pump Court Chambers
5 Temple Chambers, Temple Street,
Swindon SN1 1SQ,
Telephone: 01793 539899
E-mail: clerks@3pumpcourt.com
Pump Court Chambers
31 Southgate Street, Winchester
SO23 9EE, Telephone: 01962 868161
E-mail: clerks@3pumpcourt.com
Call Date: 1997, Gray's Inn
Qualifications: [BA (Oxon), MA (Essex)]

WARD ANTHONY DOUGLAS

Southernhay Chambers
33 Southernhay East, Exeter, Devon,
EX1 1NX, Telephone: 01392 255777
E-mail:southernhay.chambers@lineone.net
Call Date: July 1971, Inner Temple
Pupil Master
Qualifications: [LLB (Lond)]

WARD MARTIN

Guildford Chambers
Stoke House, Leapale Lane, Guildford,
Surrey, GU1 4LY,
Telephone: 01483 539131
E-mail:guildford.barristers@btinternet.com
Call Date: Oct 1992, Lincoln's Inn
Qualifications: [BA (Hons) (W'wick)]

WARD PETER MARK

Chambers of Harjit Singh
Ground Floor, 2 Middle Temple Lane,
Temple, London EC4Y 9AA,
Telephone: 0171 353 1356 (4 Lines)
Call Date: Oct 1996, Inner Temple
Qualifications: [LLB (Lond)]

WARD ROBERT WARWICK ROURKE

5 King's Bench Walk
Temple, London EC4Y 7DN,
Telephone: 0171 353 5638
Call Date: July 1977, Inner Temple
Qualifications: [LLB (Hons) (Lond)]

WARD SIMON JOHN

1 Fountain Court
Steelhouse Lane, Birmingham B4 6DR,
Telephone: 0121 236 5721
Call Date: July 1986, Inner Temple
Pupil Master
Qualifications: [LLB (B'ham)]

WARD SIMON KENNETH

2 Paper Buildings
1st Floor, Temple, London EC4Y 7ET,
Telephone: 020 7556 5500
E-mail: clerks@2pbbarristers.co.uk
Call Date: Nov 1984, Middle Temple
Qualifications: [BA (Durham), , MA (City)]

WARD MISS SIOBHAN MARIE LUCIA

11 King's Bench Walk
Temple, London EC4Y 7EQ,
Telephone: 0171 632 8500/583 0610
E-mail: clerksroom@11kbw.com
Call Date: Nov 1984, Inner Temple
Pupil Master
Qualifications: [MA, LLM (Cantab)]

WARD TIMOTHY JUSTIN

Monckton Chambers
4 Raymond Buildings, Gray's Inn, London
WC1R 5BP, Telephone: 0171 405 7211
E-mail: chambers@monckton.co.uk
Call Date: 1994, Gray's Inn
Qualifications: [BA, MA]

WARD TREVOR ROBERT EDWARD

17 Carlton Crescent
Southampton SO15 2XR,
Telephone: 023 8032 0320/0823 2003
E-mail: greg@jg17cc.co.uk
Call Date: Apr 1991, Middle Temple
Qualifications: [LLB (Hons), MSc]

WARD-JACKSON CHARLES

2-4 Tudor Street
London EC4Y 0AA,
Telephone: 0171 797 7111
E-mail: clerks@rfqc.co.uk
Call Date: Nov 1985, Middle Temple
Qualifications: [BA (Edin) Dip Law]

WARD-PROWSE JOHN

Guildhall Chambers Portsmouth
Prudential Buildings, 16 Guildhall Walk,
Portsmouth, Hampshire, PO1 2DE,
Telephone: 01705 752400
Call Date: Nov 1997, Lincoln's Inn
Qualifications: [Post Graduate Dip, in Legal
Practice]

WARDELL JOHN DAVID MEREDITH

Wilberforce Chambers
8 New Square, Lincoln's Inn, London
WC2A 3QP, Telephone: 0171 306 0102
E-mail: chambers@wilberforce.co.uk
Call Date: July 1979, Gray's Inn
Pupil Master
Qualifications: [LLB (Exon) MPhil, (Cantab)]

WARDLOW JAN JEFFERY

East Anglian Chambers
57 London Street, Norwich NR2 1HL,
Telephone: 01603 617351
E-mail: norwich@ealaw.co.uk
East Anglian Chambers
52 North Hill, Colchester, Essex, CO1 1PY,
Telephone: 01206 572756
E-mail: colchester@ealaw.co.uk
East Anglian Chambers
Gresham House, 5 Museum Street,
Ipswich, Suffolk, IP1 1HQ,
Telephone: 01473 214481
E-mail: ipswich@ealaw.co.uk
Call Date: July 1971, Gray's Inn
Pupil Master, Recorder

WARE MRS SUSAN PAMELA

Lancaster Building
77 Deansgate, Manchester M3 2BW,
Telephone: 0161 661 4444/0171 649 9872
E-mail: sandra@lbnipc.com
Call Date: Nov 1990, Inner Temple
Qualifications: [LLB (Sheff), LLM (Exon)]

WARITAY SAMUEL

Arden Chambers
27 John Street, London WC1N 2BL,
Telephone: 020 7242 4244
E-mail:clerks@arden-chambers.law.co.uk
Call Date: Nov 1993, Inner Temple
Qualifications: [BA (Hons)(Sussex)]

WARNE PETER LAWRENCE

Hollis Whiteman Chambers
3rd Floor, Queen Elizabeth Bldg, Temple,
London EC4Y 9BS,
Telephone: 020 7583 5766
E-mail:barristers@holliswhiteman.co.uk
Call Date: Nov 1993, Inner Temple
Qualifications: [BA (Manch), CPE]

WARNE ROY LESLIE

Stour Chambers
Barton Mill House, Barton Mill Road,
Canterbury, Kent, CT1 1BP,
Telephone: 01227 764899
E-mail: clerks@stourchambers.co.uk
Call Date: Nov 1979, Gray's Inn
Pupil Master
Qualifications: [MA (Cantab)]

WARNER ANTHONY CHARLES BROUGHTON

3 Fountain Court
Steelhouse Lane, Birmingham B4 6DR,
Telephone: 0121 236 5854
Call Date: July 1979, Gray's Inn
Pupil Master
Qualifications: [BA]

WARNER BRIAN BEN

1 Hare Court
Ground Floor, Temple, London
EC4Y 7BE, Telephone: 0171 353 3982/
5324
Call Date: 1969, Inner Temple
Pupil Master, Recorder
Qualifications: [LLB (Lond)]

WARNER DAVID ALEXANDER

1 New Square
Ground Floor, Lincoln's Inn, London
WC2A 3SA, Telephone: 0171 405 0884/5/6/
7 E-mail: clerks@1newsquare.law.co.uk
Call Date: Oct 1996, Gray's Inn
Qualifications: [LLB]

WARNER MALCOLM DIGBY

Guildhall Chambers
22-26 Broad Street, Bristol BS1 2HG,
Telephone: 0117 9273366
E-mail:civil.clerks@guildhallchambers.co.uk and
criminal.clerks@guildhallchambers.co.uk
Call Date: July 1979, Lincoln's Inn
Pupil Master
Qualifications: [BScEcon (Wales)]

WARNER MISS SHARAN PAMELA

14 Gray's Inn Square
Gray's Inn, London WC1R 5JP,
Telephone: 0171 242 0858
E-mail: 100712.2134@compuserve.com
Call Date: Feb 1985, Gray's Inn
Qualifications: [BA (Hons)]

WARNER STEPHEN CLIFFORD

Hardwicke Building
New Square, Lincoln's Inn, London
WC2A 3SB, Telephone: 020 7242 2523
E-mail: clerks@hardwicke.co.uk
Call Date: July 1976, Lincoln's Inn
Pupil Master, Assistant Recorder
Qualifications: [MA (Oxon)]

WARNOCK ALASTAIR ROBERT LYON

Adrian Lyon's Chambers
14 Castle Street, Liverpool L2 0NE,
Telephone: 0151 236 4421/8240
E-mail: chambers14@aol.com
Call Date: Nov 1977, Lincoln's Inn
Pupil Master, Assistant Recorder

WARNOCK ANDREW RONALD

No. 1 Serjeants' Inn
5th Floor Fleet Street, Temple, London
EC4Y 1LH, Telephone: 0171 415 6666
E-mail:no1serjeantsinn@btinternet.com
Call Date: Nov 1993, Inner Temple
Qualifications: [BA, Dip in French , (Cantab)]

WARNOCK MISS CERI AILSA

Young Street Chambers
38 Young Street, Manchester M3 3FT,
Telephone: 0161 833 0489
E-mail: clerks@young-st-chambers.com
Call Date: Oct 1993, Gray's Inn
Qualifications: [LLB (Hons)(Wales)]

WARNOCK-SMITH MRS SHAN

5 Stone Buildings
Lincoln's Inn, London WC2A 3XT,
Telephone: 0171 242 6201
E-mail:clerks@5-stonebuildings.law.co.uk
Call Date: July 1971, Gray's Inn
Pupil Master
Qualifications: [LLM]

WARREN JOHN QC (1994)

High Pavement Chambers
1 High Pavement, Nottingham NG1 1HF,
Telephone: 0115 9418218
Call Date: July 1968, Gray's Inn
Recorder
Qualifications: [LLB]

WARREN MS LYNNETTE KATHLEEN

Call Date: Nov 1987, Gray's Inn
Qualifications: [Dip Law]

WARREN MICHAEL JOHN DAVID

One King's Bench Walk
1st Floor, Temple, London EC4Y 7DB,
Telephone: 0171 936 1500
E-mail: ddear@1kbw.co.uk
Call Date: Nov 1971, Middle Temple
Pupil Master
Qualifications: [MA (Oxon)]

WARREN NICHOLAS ROGER QC (1993)

Wilberforce Chambers
8 New Square, Lincoln's Inn, London
WC2A 3QP, Telephone: 0171 306 0102
E-mail: chambers@wilberforce.co.uk
Call Date: Nov 1972, Middle Temple
Recorder
Qualifications: [BA (Oxon)]

Types of work: Chancery (general), Chancery
land law, Equity, wills and trusts, Pensions,
Professional negligence, Tax – capital and
income

WARREN PHILIP DAVID CHARLES

Pump Court Chambers
5 Temple Chambers, Temple Street,
Swindon SN1 1SQ,
Telephone: 01793 539899
E-mail: clerks@3pumpcourt.com
Pump Court Chambers
Upper Ground Floor, 3 Pump Court,
Temple, London EC4Y 7AJ,
Telephone: 0171 353 0711
E-mail: clerks@3pumpcourt.com

D

D

Pump Court Chambers
31 Southgate Street, Winchester
SO23 9EE, Telephone: 01962 868161
E-mail: clerks@3pumpcourt.com
Call Date: May 1988, Gray's Inn
Pupil Master
Qualifications: [LLB (Wales)]

WARREN RUPERT MILES

2 Mitre Court Buildings
2nd Floor, Temple, London EC4Y 7BX,
Telephone: 0171 583 1380
E-mail: clerks@2mcb.co.uk
Call Date: Oct 1994, Gray's Inn
Qualifications: [BA (Oxon)]

WARREN MISS SASHA

3 Temple Gardens
3rd Floor, Temple, London EC4Y 9AU,
Telephone: 0171 353 0832
Call Date: Oct 1996, Gray's Inn
Qualifications: [BA (Wales), LLB (City)]

WARRENDER MISS NICHOLA MARY

New Court Chambers
5 Verulam Buildings, Gray's Inn, London
WC1R 5LY, Telephone: 0171 831 9500
E-mail: mail@newcourtchambers.com
Call Date: Nov 1995, Inner Temple
Qualifications: [LLB (Bris)]

WARSHAW JUSTIN ALEXANDER EDWARD

1 Mitre Court Buildings
Temple, London EC4Y 7BS,
Telephone: 0171 797 7070
E-mail: clerks@1mcb.com
Call Date: Nov 1995, Gray's Inn
Qualifications: [MA (Oxon)]

WARWICK MARK GRANVILLE

29 Bedford Row Chambers
London WC1R 4HE,
Telephone: 0171 831 2626
Call Date: July 1974, Inner Temple
Pupil Master
Qualifications: [LLB (Hons)]

Fax: 0171 831 0626; DX: 1044 London

Types of work: Commercial property, Landlord and tenant

Circuit: South Eastern

Reported Cases: *Ashley Guarantee v Zacaria*,
[1993] 1 WLR 62. Mortgagee's right to
possession.
Connaught v Indoor Leisure, [1994] 1 WLR
501. Exclusion of equitable set off.
Mercantile Group v Aiyela, [1994] QB
366. Discovery – injunction against third
parties.
Romulus Trading v Comet, [1996] 2 EGLR
70. Letting adjacent premises for
competing use not a derogation from
grant.
Rainbow Estates v Tokenhold, [1998] 2 All
ER 860. Specific performance of tenant's
repairing covenant.

WASS MISS SASHA

6 King's Bench Walk
Ground Floor, Temple, London
EC4Y 7DR, Telephone: 0171 583 0410
E-mail: worsley@6kbw.freeserve.co.uk
Call Date: Nov 1981, Gray's Inn
Pupil Master, Assistant Recorder
Qualifications: [LLB (L'pool)]

WASTIE WILLIAM GRANVILLE

Hollis Whiteman Chambers
3rd Floor, Queen Elizabeth Bldg, Temple,
London EC4Y 9BS,
Telephone: 020 7583 5766
E-mail:barristers@holliswhiteman.co.uk
Call Date: Oct 1993, Middle Temple
Qualifications: [LLB (Hons)(Bris)]

WATERMAN ADRIAN MARK

11 King's Bench Walk
1st Floor, Temple, London EC4Y 7EQ,
Telephone: 0171 353 3337
E-mail: fmuller11@aol.com
11 King's Bench Walk
3 Park Court, Park Cross Street, Leeds
LS1 2QH, Telephone: 0113 297 1200
Call Date: July 1988, Inner Temple
Qualifications: [LLB (Lond)]

WATERS ANDREW JOHN

5 Essex Court
1st Floor, Temple, London EC4Y 9AH,
Telephone: 0171 410 2000
E-mail: barristers@5essexcourt.co.uk
Call Date: Nov 1987, Inner Temple
Pupil Master
Qualifications: [LLB]

WATERS DAVID EBSWORTH QC (1999)

1 Hare Court
Ground Floor, Temple, London
EC4Y 7BE, Telephone: 0171 353 3982/
5324
Call Date: 1973, Middle Temple
Pupil Master, Recorder

WATERS JOHN CLOUGH

Lamb Building
Ground Floor, Temple, London
EC4Y 7AS, Telephone: 020 7797 7788
E-mail: lamb.building@link.org
Call Date: May 1974, Lincoln's Inn
Pupil Master

WATERS JULIAN WILLIAM PENROSE

No. 1 Serjeants' Inn
5th Floor Fleet Street, Temple, London
EC4Y 1LH, Telephone: 0171 415 6666
E-mail:no1serjeantsinn@btinternet.com
Call Date: Nov 1986, Middle Temple
Pupil Master
Qualifications: [MA (Cantab)]

WATERS MALCOLM IAN QC (1997)

11 Old Square
Ground Floor, Lincoln's Inn, London
WC2A 3TS, Telephone: 020 7430 0341
E-mail: clerks@11oldsquare.co.uk
Call Date: July 1977, Lincoln's Inn
Qualifications: [MA, BCL (Oxon)]

Fax: 0171 831 2469; DX: LDE 1031

Types of work: Banking, Building societies,
Chancery (general), Chancery land law,
Charities, Conveyancing, Equity, wills and
trusts, Professional negligence

Awards and memberships: Member of the
Working Party responsible for drafting the
Standard Conditions of Sale; Member of the
Committee responsible for drafting the
Standard Commercial Property Conditions

Publications: *Wurtzburg and Mills, Building
Society Law* (Joint Author) (and annual
looseleaf releases), 1989; *The Building
Societies Act 1986* (Co-author), 1987

Reported Cases: *Peggs v Lamb*, [1994] Ch 172,
1993. Charities.
BSC v Halifax BS and Leeds PBS, [1997]
Ch 255, 1995. Conversion to Plc.
C & G v Grattidge, 25 HLR 454, 1993.
Mortgages.
Halifax v Thomas, [1996] Ch 217, 1995.
Mortgages/restitution.
C & G v Norgan, [1996] 1 WLR 343, 1995.
Mortgages.

WATERWORTH MICHAEL CHRISTOPHER

The Chambers of Leolin Price CBE, QC
10 Old Square, Lincoln's Inn, London
WC2A 3SU, Telephone: 0171 405 0758
Call Date: Oct 1994, Lincoln's Inn
Qualifications: [MA (Cantab), Dip in Law
(City)]

WATKIN TOBY PAUL

22 Old Buildings
Lincoln's Inn, London WC2A 3UJ,
Telephone: 0171 831 0222
Call Date: Oct 1996, Inner Temple
Qualifications: [BA (Cantab), MA (Cantab)]

WATKINS MYLES KENNETH GEORGE

Albion Chambers
Broad Street, Bristol BS1 1DR,
Telephone: 0117 9272144
2 Gray's Inn Square Chambers
2nd Floor, Gray's Inn, London WC1R 5AA,
Telephone: 020 7242 0328
E-mail: clerks@2gis.co.uk
Call Date: Feb 1990, Middle Temple
Pupil Master
Qualifications: [LLB]

WATKINSON DAVID ROBERT

Two Garden Court
1st Floor, Middle Temple, London
EC4Y 9BL, Telephone: 0171 353 1633
E-mail:barristers@2gardenct.law.co.uk
Call Date: July 1972, Middle Temple
Pupil Master
Qualifications: [MA, LLB (Cantab)]

WATSON ALARIC

11 Stone Buildings
Lincoln's Inn, London WC2A 3TG,
Telephone: +44 (0)207 831 6381
E-mail:clerks@11StoneBuildings.law.co.uk
Call Date: 1997, Middle Temple
Qualifications: [BA (Hons)(Bris), PhD
(Lond)]

WATSON ANTHONY DENNIS

Lincoln House Chambers
5th Floor, Lincoln House, 1 Brazennose
Street, Manchester M2 5EL,
Telephone: 0161 832 5701
E-mail: info@lincolnhse.co.uk
Call Date: July 1985, Inner Temple
Qualifications: [BA (Hons)]

WATSON ANTONY EDWARD DOUGLAS QC (1986)

3 New Square
Lincoln's Inn, London WC2A 3RS,
Telephone: 0171 405 1111
E-mail: 3newsquareip@lineone.net
Call Date: Nov 1968, Inner Temple
Qualifications: [MA (Cantab)]

WATSON MISS BARBARA JOAN

15 Winckley Square
Preston PR1 3JJ,
Telephone: 01772 252828
E-mail:clerks@winckleysq.demon.co.uk
Call Date: July 1973, Gray's Inn
Qualifications: [LLB]

WATSON BRIAN JAMES ROBB

Guildhall Chambers
22-26 Broad Street, Bristol BS1 2HG,
Telephone: 0117 9273366
E-mail:civil.clerks@guildhallchambers.co.uk and
criminal.clerks@guildhallchambers.co.uk
Call Date: July 1978, Lincoln's Inn
Pupil Master
Qualifications: [MA, LLB (Cantab)]

WATSON MS CLAIRE

3 Temple Gardens
3rd Floor, Temple, London EC4Y 9AU,
Telephone: 0171 353 0832
Call Date: Nov 1991, Lincoln's Inn
Qualifications: [LLB (Hons)]

WATSON DAVID JAMES

6 Fountain Court
Steelhouse Lane, Birmingham B4 6DR,
Telephone: 0121 233 3282
E-mail: clerks@sixfountain.co.uk
Call Date: Nov 1994, Gray's Inn
Qualifications: [BA (Bris), BA (Manch)]

WATSON DAVID WILLIAM

Adrian Lyon's Chambers
14 Castle Street, Liverpool L2 0NE,
Telephone: 0151 236 4421/8240
E-mail: chambers14@aol.com
3 Temple Gardens
3rd Floor, Temple, London EC4Y 9AU,
Telephone: 0171 583 0010
Call Date: Oct 1990, Middle Temple
Qualifications: [LLB (Brunel)]

WATSON FRANCIS PAUL

Paradise Chambers
26 Paradise Square, Sheffield S1 2DE,
Telephone: 0114 2738951
E-mail: timbooth@paradise-sq.co.uk
Call Date: Nov 1978, Gray's Inn
Pupil Master, Assistant Recorder
Qualifications: [BA (Leeds)]

WATSON MISS HILARY JANE

St Mary's Chambers
50 High Pavement, Lace Market,
Nottingham NG1 1HW,
Telephone: 0115 9503503
E-mail: clerks@smc.law.co.uk
Call Date: July 1979, Gray's Inn
Pupil Master
Qualifications: [LLB (Bris)]

WATSON MISS ISABELLE MARGARET

Francis Taylor Building
Ground Floor, Temple, London
EC4Y 7BY, Telephone: 0171 353 7768/
7769/2711
E-mail:clerks@francistaylorbuilding.law.co.uk
Call Date: Oct 1991, Middle Temple
Qualifications: [BA Hons (Cantab), Dip Law]

WATSON SIR JAMES ANDREW

4 Fountain Court
Steelhouse Lane, Birmingham B4 6DR,
Telephone: 0121 236 3476
Call Date: July 1966, Inner Temple
Pupil Master, Recorder

WATSON JAMES VERNON

3 Serjeants' Inn
London EC4Y 1BQ,
Telephone: 0171 353 5537
E-mail: clerks@3serjeantsinn.com
Call Date: July 1979, Middle Temple
Pupil Master
Qualifications: [BA (Cantab)]

WATSON MISS KIRSTIE ANN

St Paul's House
5th Floor, St Paul's House, 23 Park Square
South, Leeds LS1 2ND,
Telephone: 0113 2455866
E-mail: catherinegrimshaw@stpauls-
chambers.demon.co.uk
Call Date: Oct 1995, Middle Temple
Qualifications: [LLB (Hons)(Leeds)]

WATSON MARK

6 Pump Court
1st Floor, Temple, London EC4Y 7AR,
Telephone: 0171 797 8400
E-mail: clerks@6pumpcourt.co.uk

6-8 Mill Street
Maidstone, Kent, ME15 6XH,
Telephone: 01622 688094
E-mail: annexe@6pumpcourt.co.uk
Call Date: Oct 1994, Gray's Inn
Qualifications: [BA]

WATSON DR PHILIPPA

Essex Court Chambers
24 Lincoln's Inn Fields, London
WC2A 3ED, Telephone: 0171 813 8000
E-mail:clerksroom@essexcourt-chambers.co.u
k
Call Date: July 1988, Middle Temple
Qualifications: [MA (Dublin), LLM, PhD
(Cantab), BL (Kings Inn)]

WATSON ROBERT JEFFREY

3 Temple Gardens
2nd Floor, Temple, London EC4Y 9AU,
Telephone: 0171 583 1155
Call Date: July 1963, Inner Temple
Pupil Master

WATSON MS SHARON

New Bailey Chambers
10 Lawson Street, Preston PR1 2QT,
Telephone: 01772 258087
Call Date: Nov 1994, Middle Temple
Qualifications: [BA (Hons)]

WATSON TOM BRADLEY

Chavasse Court Chambers
2nd Floor, Chavasse Court, 24 Lord Street,
Liverpool L2 1TA,
Telephone: 0151 707 1191
Call Date: Oct 1990, Inner Temple
Qualifications: [BA (Hons) (N Wales), MA
(Keele), Dip Law]

WATSON-GANDY MARK

Plowden Buildings
2nd Floor, 2 Plowden Buildings, Middle
Temple Lane, London EC4Y 9BU,
Telephone: 0171 583 0808
E-mail: bar@plowdenbuildings.co.uk
Call Date: Oct 1990, Inner Temple
Qualifications: [LLB (Hons)]

Fax: 0171 583 5106; DX: 0020 Chancery
Lane;
Other comms: E-mail
watson-gandy.law@dial.pipex.com

Other professional qualifications: Accountant

Types of work: Banking, Commercial, Commercial litigation, Company and commercial, Corporate finance, Private international

Awards and memberships: Visiting professor to the University of Westminster; Honorary Fellow – Institute of Certified Book Keepers; past chairman – Private Equity Funding Association; member – International Bar Association (Business Section)

Publications: *Thomson Tax Guide* (Avoidance, Evasion & Tax Investigations – co-editor), 1998; *Watson-Gandy on the Law of Accounts*, 1999; *European Current Law* (Contributing editor), 1997 onwards

Reported Cases: *R v Commissioners of the Inland Revenue ex parte Hutchinson*, (1998) *The Times*, 6 July, 1998. Restraint of revenue access to banking and accounting records.
Lloyd's Names Litigation, Sundry, 1997-99.
Re 'The Hollies', Elliott v Haydock, LTL 14.8.97, 1997. Pop group share dispute.
Nedcor Bank v Bessinger, LTL 6.11.98, 1998. Conflicts of law – enforcement of bank guarantee.
Citadel v Equal, LTL 8.8.98, 1998. Banking fraud; breach of $17.6 million solicitor's undertaking.

WATSON-HOPKINSON MS GHISLAINE ELIZABETH CLARE

Guildford Chambers
Stoke House, Leapale Lane, Guildford, Surrey, GU1 4LY,
Telephone: 01483 539131
E-mail:guildford.barristers@btinternet.com
Call Date: Nov 1991, Inner Temple
Qualifications: [LLB]

WATT-PRINGLE JONATHAN HELIER

Farrar's Building
Temple, London EC4Y 7BD,
Telephone: 0171 583 9241
E-mail:chambers@farrarsbuilding.co.uk
Call Date: July 1987, Middle Temple
Pupil Master
Qualifications: [MA, BCL (Oxon), BA, LLB, (Stellenbosch)]

WATTS MISS ALISON ELFRIDA

Call Date: July 1981, Middle Temple
Qualifications: [LLB (Lond)]

WATTS SIR ARTHUR DESMOND QC (1988)

20 Essex Street
London WC2R 3AL,
Telephone: 0171 583 9294
E-mail: clerks@20essexst.com
Call Date: Nov 1957, Gray's Inn
Qualifications: [MA,LLM]

WATTS LAWRENCE PETER

St Philip's Chambers
Fountain Court, Steelhouse Lane,
Birmingham B4 6DR,
Telephone: 0121 246 7000
E-mail: clerks@st-philips.co.uk
Call Date: July 1988, Inner Temple
Qualifications: [LLB]

WATTS MR. MARTIN WILLIAM

2-4 Tudor Street
London EC4Y 0AA,
Telephone: 0171 797 7111
E-mail: clerks@rfqc.co.uk
Call Date: Oct 1995, Middle Temple
Qualifications: [MA (Oxon)]

WAUCHOPE PIERS ANDREW CHARLES

3 Temple Gardens
3rd Floor, Temple, London EC4Y 9AU,
Telephone: 0171 583 0010
Call Date: July 1985, Gray's Inn
Pupil Master
Qualifications: [BA (Manchester)]

WAUGH ANDREW PETER QC (1998)

3 New Square
Lincoln's Inn, London WC2A 3RS,
Telephone: 0171 405 1111
E-mail: 3newsquareip@lineone.net
Call Date: July 1982, Gray's Inn
Qualifications: [BSc (City), Dip Law (City)]

WAUGH MS JANE

Fountain Chambers
Cleveland Business Centre, 1 Watson
Street, Middlesbrough TS1 2RQ,
Telephone: 01642 804040
E-mail:fountainchambers@onyxnet.co.uk
Call Date: Oct 1992, Inner Temple
Qualifications: [LLB]

WAY IAN LEONARD

King Charles House
Standard Hill, Nottingham NG1 6FX,
Telephone: 0115 9418851
E-mail: clerks@kch.co.uk
Call Date: Nov 1988, Inner Temple
Pupil Master
Qualifications: [BA (Lond)]

WAY PATRICK EDWARD

8 Gray's Inn Square
Gray's Inn, London WC1R 5AZ,
Telephone: 0171 242 3529
Call Date: May 1994, Lincoln's Inn
Qualifications: [BA (Hons, Leeds)]

WAYLEN BARNABY JAMES

**1 Gray's Inn Square, Chambers of the
Baroness Scotland of Asthal QC**
1st Floor, London WC1R 5AG,
Telephone: 0171 405 3000
E-mail: clerks@onegrays.demon.co.uk
Call Date: July 1968, Inner Temple
Pupil Master, Recorder
Qualifications: [MA (Cantab)]

WAYNE NICHOLAS

1 Gray's Inn Square
Ground Floor, London WC1R 5AA,
Telephone: 0171 405 8946/7/8
Call Date: July 1994, Middle Temple
Qualifications: [BA (Hons)(Oxon)]

WEATHERALL MISS JULIA

Cathedral Chambers
Milburn House, Dean Street, Newcastle
upon Tyne NE1 1LE,
Telephone: 0191 232 1311
Call Date: July 1985, Inner Temple
Qualifications: [LLB (Brunel)]

WEATHERBY PETER FRANCIS

Two Garden Court
1st Floor, Middle Temple, London
EC4Y 9BL, Telephone: 0171 353 1633
E-mail:barristers@2gardenct.law.co.uk
**Chambers of Ian Macdonald QC (In
Association with Two Garden Court,
Temple, London)**
Waldorf House, 5 Cooper Street,
Manchester M2 2FW,
Telephone: 0161 236 1840
Call Date: Nov 1992, Gray's Inn
Qualifications: [BSc (Hons)]

WEATHERILL BERNARD RICHARD QC (1996)

Chambers of Lord Goodhart QC
Ground Floor, 3 New Square, Lincoln's
Inn, London WC2A 3RS,
Telephone: 0171 405 5577
E-mail:law@threenewsquare.demon.co.uk
Call Date: July 1974, Middle Temple
Assistant Recorder
Qualifications: [BA]

WEAVER MISS ELIZABETH ANNE

Twenty-Four Old Buildings
Ground Floor, Lincoln's Inn, London
WC2A 3UP, Telephone: 0171 404 0946
E-mail:clerks@24oldbuildings.law.co.uk
Call Date: July 1982, Lincoln's Inn
Pupil Master
Qualifications: [LLB (Bris)]

WEBB GERAINT TIMOTHY

2 Harcourt Buildings
Ground Floor/Left, Temple, London
EC4Y 9DB, Telephone: 0171 583 9020
E-mail: clerks@harcourt.co.uk
Call Date: Oct 1995, Inner Temple
Qualifications: [BA (Oxon), CPE (City)]

WEBB MISS KELLY

New Court
Temple, London EC4Y 9BE,
Telephone: 0171 583 5123/0510
Call Date: 1993, Lincoln's Inn
Qualifications: [LLB (Hons)(Lond)]

D

WEBB MISS LORRAINE ELIZABETH

Tindal Chambers
3/5 New Street, Chelmsford, Essex,
CM1 1NT, Telephone: 01245 267742
St Albans Chambers
Dolphin Lodge, Dolphin Yard, Holywell
Hill, St Albans, Herts, AL1 1EX,
Telephone: 01727 843383
Call Date: July 1980, Middle Temple
Pupil Master
Qualifications: [BA]

WEBB NICHOLAS JOHN DAVID

4 Fountain Court
Steelhouse Lane, Birmingham B4 6DR,
Telephone: 0121 236 3476
Call Date: July 1972, Middle Temple
Pupil Master, Assistant Recorder
Qualifications: [BA (Cantab)]

WEBB STANLEY GEORGE

The Chambers of Mr Ali Mohammed Azhar
Basement, 9 King's Bench Walk, Temple,
London EC4Y 7DX,
Telephone: 0171 353 9564
E-mail: jvlee@btinternet.com
Bracton Chambers
95a Chancery Lane, London WC2A 1DT,
Telephone: 0171 242 4248
Call Date: Oct 1993, Gray's Inn
Qualifications: [B.Sc (Hons)(Eng)]

WEBBER DOMINIC DENZIL FERNANDEZ

Verulam Chambers
Peer House, 8-14 Verulam Street, Gray's
Inn, London WC1X 8LZ,
Telephone: 0171 813 2400
Call Date: Nov 1985, Gray's Inn
Pupil Master
Qualifications: [BA, Dip Law]

WEBBER MISS FRANCES GAIL

Two Garden Court
1st Floor, Middle Temple, London
EC4Y 9BL, Telephone: 0171 353 1633
E-mail:barristers@2gardenct.law.co.uk
Call Date: July 1978, Gray's Inn
Pupil Master
Qualifications: [BSc]

WEBBER GARY NEIL

33 Bedford Row
London WC1R 4JH,
Telephone: 0171 242 6476
E-mail:clerks@bedfordrow33.demon.co.uk
Call Date: July 1979, Inner Temple
Pupil Master
Qualifications: [LLB (Lond)]

WEBSTER ALISTAIR STEVENSON QC (1995)

Lincoln House Chambers
5th Floor, Lincoln House, 1 Brazennose
Street, Manchester M2 5EL,
Telephone: 0161 832 5701
E-mail: info@lincolnhse.co.uk
Call Date: July 1976, Middle Temple
Recorder
Qualifications: [BA (Oxon)]

WEBSTER DAVID

15 North Church Street Chambers
15 North Church Street, Sheffield
S1 2DH, Telephone: 0114 2759708/
2738380
Call Date: Mar 1998, Middle Temple

WEBSTER DAVID FRANCIS

32 Park Place
Cardiff CF1 3BA,
Telephone: 01222 397364
Call Date: Oct 1993, Gray's Inn
Qualifications: [B.Sc (Econ, Wales)]

WEBSTER MISS ELIZABETH JANE

18 Red Lion Court
(Off Fleet Street), London EC4A 3EB,
Telephone: 0171 520 6000
E-mail: chambers@18rlc.co.uk
Thornwood House
102 New London Road, Chelmsford,
Essex, CM2 0RG,
Telephone: 01245 280880
E-mail: chambers@18rlc.co.uk
Call Date: Nov 1995, Middle Temple
Qualifications: [BA (Hons)]

WEBSTER JUSTIN

1c Westbourne Terrace Road
London W2 6NG,

Somerset Chambers
25 Bedford Row, London WC1R 4HE,
Telephone: 0171 404 6701
E-mail: somelaw@aol.com
Call Date: Feb 1985, Inner Temple
Qualifications: [BA]

WEBSTER LEONARD

Cobden House Chambers
19 Quay Street, Manchester M3 3HN,
Telephone: 0161 833 6000
E-mail: clerks@cobden.co.uk
Call Date: July 1984, Lincoln's Inn
Qualifications: [BA]

WEBSTER ROBERT MARTIN CHRISTOPHER

1 Harcourt Buildings
2nd Floor, Temple, London EC4Y 9DA,
Telephone: 0171 353 9421/0375
E-mail:clerks@1harcourtbuildings.law.co.uk
Call Date: July 1979, Inner Temple
Qualifications: [BA (Sussex)]

WEBSTER SIMON MARK

1 Mitre Court Buildings
Temple, London EC4Y 7BS,
Telephone: 0171 797 7070
E-mail: clerks@1mcb.com
Call Date: 1997, Inner Temple
Qualifications: [LLB (Lond)]

WEBSTER WILLIAM HOWARD

17 Carlton Crescent
Southampton SO15 2XR,
Telephone: 023 8032 0320/0823 2003
E-mail: greg@jg17cc.co.uk
Call Date: July 1975, Middle Temple
Pupil Master
Qualifications: [LLB (Bristol)]

WEDDELL GEOFFREY DAVID ANDREW

2 King's Bench Walk
Ground Floor, Temple, London
EC4Y 7DE, Telephone: 0171 353 1746
E-mail: 2kbw@atlas.co.uk

King's Bench Chambers
115 North Hill, Plymouth PL4 8JY,
Telephone: 01752 221551
Call Date: Nov 1989, Inner Temple
Pupil Master
Qualifications: [LLB]

WEDDERBURN OF CHARLTON LORD QC (1990)

Old Square Chambers
1 Verulam Buildings, Gray's Inn, London
WC1R 5LQ, Telephone: 0171 269 0300
E-mail:clerks@oldsquarechambers.co.uk
Old Square Chambers
Hanover House, 47 Corn Street, Bristol
BS1 1HT, Telephone: 0117 9277111
E-mail: oldsqbri@globalnet.co.uk
Call Date: Feb 1953, Middle Temple
Qualifications: [MA (Cantab), LLB, FBA, Hon
D GIUR, (Pavia)(Siena), HonD.Econ
(Siena), LLD (Stockholm)]

WEDDERSPOON MISS RACHEL LEONE

Chambers of John Hand QC
9 St John Street, Manchester M3 4DN,
Telephone: 0161 955 9000
E-mail: ninesjs@gconnect.com
Call Date: Oct 1993, Middle Temple
Qualifications: [LLB (Hons)(Manc)]

WEDDLE STEVEN EDGAR

Hardwicke Building
New Square, Lincoln's Inn, London
WC2A 3SB, Telephone: 020 7242 2523
E-mail: clerks@hardwicke.co.uk
Call Date: Nov 1977, Gray's Inn
Pupil Master
Qualifications: [BA]

WEEDEN ROSS CHARLES

Bell Yard Chambers
116/118 Chancery Lane, London
WC2A 1PP, Telephone: 0171 306 9292
Call Date: 1996, Middle Temple
Qualifications: [LLB (Hons)]

D

WEEKES MISS ANESTA GLENDORA QC (1999)

Chambers of Michael Pert QC
36 Bedford Row, London WC1R 4JH,
Telephone: 0171 421 8000
E-mail: 36bedfordrow@link.org
Chambers of Michael Pert QC
24 Albion Place, Northampton NN1 1UD,
Telephone: 01604 602333
Chambers of Michael Pert QC
104 New Walk, Leicester LE1 7EA,
Telephone: 0116 249 2020
Call Date: 1981, Gray's Inn
Pupil Master, Assistant Recorder

WEEKES THOMAS CHARLES

11 Stone Buildings
Lincoln's Inn, London WC2A 3TG,
Telephone: +44 (0)207 831 6381
E-mail:clerks@11StoneBuildings.law.co.uk
Call Date: Oct 1995, Inner Temple
Qualifications: [BA (Oxon), CPE (City)]

WEEKS MS JANET KATHLEEN

Queen Elizabeth Building
Ground Floor, Temple, London
EC4Y 9BS,
Telephone: 0171 353 7181 (12 Lines)
Call Date: Oct 1993, Inner Temple
Qualifications: [LLB (Exon)]

WEERERATNE MS RUFINA ASWINI

Doughty Street Chambers
11 Doughty Street, London WC1N 2PG,
Telephone: 0171 404 1313
E-mail:enquiries@doughtystreet.co.uk
Call Date: July 1986, Gray's Inn
Qualifications: [BSc (Sussex), Dip Law]

WEHRLE MISS JACQUELINE

Goldsmith Chambers
Ground Floor, Goldsmith Building,
Temple, London EC4Y 7BL,
Telephone: 0171 353 6802/3/4/5
E-mail:clerks@goldsmithchambers.law.co.uk
Call Date: Nov 1984, Lincoln's Inn
Pupil Master
Qualifications: [LLB (Reading)]

WEINIGER NORMAN NOAH

Gray's Inn Chambers
5th Floor, Gray's Inn, London WC1R 5JA,
Telephone: 0171 404 1111
Call Date: Nov 1984, Gray's Inn
Pupil Master
Qualifications: [LLB (Manch)]

WEINSTEIN MISS LINDSAY

Lamb Building
Ground Floor, Temple, London
EC4Y 7AS, Telephone: 020 7797 7788
E-mail: lamb.building@link.org
Call Date: Oct 1992, Middle Temple
Qualifications: [LLB (Hons)]

WEIR MISS OLIVIA

15 North Church Street Chambers
15 North Church Street, Sheffield
S1 2DH, Telephone: 0114 2759708/
2738380
Call Date: Nov 1995, Inner Temple
Qualifications: [BA]

WEIR ROBERT THOMAS MACDONALD

Devereux Chambers
Devereux Court, London WC2R 3JJ,
Telephone: 0171 353 7534
E-mail: mailbox@devchambers.co.uk
Call Date: Nov 1992, Middle Temple
Qualifications: [MA (Hons)]

WEISMAN MALCOLM

1 Gray's Inn Square
Ground Floor, London WC1R 5AA,
Telephone: 0171 405 8946/7/8
Call Date: June 1961, Middle Temple
Recorder
Qualifications: [MA (Oxon)]

WEISSELBERG TOM

Blackstone Chambers
Blackstone House, Temple, London
EC4Y 9BW, Telephone: 0171 583 1770
E-mail:clerks@blackstonechambers.com
Call Date: Oct 1995, Inner Temple
Qualifications: [BA (Oxon), CPE (City)]

WEITZMAN ADAM JOHN

9 Bedford Row
London WC1R 4AZ,
Telephone: 0171 242 3555
E-mail: clerks@9br.co.uk
Call Date: Nov 1993, Middle Temple
Qualifications: [BA (Hons)(Cantab), MA
(Manc), CPE (Lond)]

WEITZMAN THOMAS EDWARD BENJAMIN

3 Verulam Buildings
London WC1R 5NT,
Telephone: 0171 831 8441
E-mail: clerks@3verulam.co.uk
Call Date: July 1984, Gray's Inn
Pupil Master
Qualifications: [BA (Oxon)]

WELCH EDWARD BRETT

Verulam Chambers
Peer House, 8-14 Verulam Street, Gray's
Inn, London WC1X 8LZ,
Telephone: 0171 813 2400
Call Date: Oct 1996, Lincoln's Inn
Qualifications: [BA (Hons)(Manc), Dip in
Law (City), CPE]

WELLESLEY-COLE MISS PATRICE SUZANNE

11 Old Square
Ground Floor, Lincoln's Inn, London
WC2A 3TS, Telephone: 0171 242 5022/
405 1074
Call Date: Nov 1975, Inner Temple
Qualifications: [BA (Oxon)]

WELLS COLIN JOHN

3 Gray's Inn Square
Ground Floor, London WC1R 5AH,
Telephone: 0171 520 5600
E-mail: clerks@3gis.co.uk
Call Date: Nov 1987, Inner Temple
Pupil Master
Qualifications: [BSc, MA (Warwick), Dip Law]

WELLS DAVID MARLON

Number Ten Baker Street
10 Baker Street, Middlesbrough TS1 2LH,
Telephone: 01642 220332
Call Date: Nov 1995, Gray's Inn
Qualifications: [LLB]

WELLS GRAHAM HOLLAND

Derby Square Chambers
Merchants Court, Derby Square, Liverpool
L2 1TS, Telephone: 0151 709 4222
E-mail:mail.derbysquare@pop3.hiway.co.uk
Call Date: July 1982, Middle Temple
Pupil Master
Qualifications: [MA (Oxon)]

WELLS NICHOLAS THOMAS CLINTON

1 Gray's Inn Square
Ground Floor, London WC1R 5AA,
Telephone: 0171 405 8946/7/8
Call Date: Nov 1990, Lincoln's Inn
Qualifications: [BA (Cantab), Dip Law (City)]

WELSH JAMES ANTHONY KIRKMAN

Devon Chambers
3 St Andrew Street, Plymouth PL1 2AH,
Telephone: 01752 661659
E-mail: devonchambers.co.uk.
Call Date: Nov 1994, Middle Temple
Qualifications: [BA (Hons) (Dunelm), Dip
Law]

WELSH PASCHAL JUDE RICHARD

Chambers of Paschal J Welsh
11 Carlisle House, 105 Old Church Street,
London SW3 6DS,
Call Date: July 1974, Lincoln's Inn

WENLOCK MISS HEATHER

13 King's Bench Walk
1st Floor, Temple, London EC4Y 7EN,
Telephone: 0171 353 7204
E-mail: clerks@13kbw.law.co.uk
King's Bench Chambers
32 Beaumont Street, Oxford OX1 2NP,
Telephone: 01865 311066
E-mail: clerks@kbc-oxford.law.co.uk
Call Date: Oct 1991, Middle Temple
Qualifications: [BA Hons (Hull), MPhil, DPhil
(Oxon)]

WENTWORTH MISS ANNABEL HENRIETTE

4 Brick Court
Temple, London EC4Y 9AD,
Telephone: 0171 797 8910
E-mail: medhurst@dial.pipex.com
Call Date: Oct 1990, Inner Temple
Qualifications: [BA (Nott'm), Dip Law]

WERNHAM STEWART FREDERICK

1 Dr Johnson's Buildings
Ground Floor, Temple, London
EC4Y 7AX, Telephone: 0171 353 9328
E-mail:OneDr.Johnsons@btinternet.com
Call Date: July 1984, Middle Temple
Pupil Master
Qualifications: [LLB (Warwick)]

WEST IAN HERBERT

Bank House Chambers
Old Bank House, Hartshead, Sheffield
S1 2EL, Telephone: 0114 2751223
Call Date: Nov 1996, Middle Temple
Qualifications: [LLB (Hons)(Auckland)]

WEST IAN STUART

Fountain Chambers
Cleveland Business Centre, 1 Watson
Street, Middlesbrough TS1 2RQ,
Telephone: 01642 804040
E-mail:fountainchambers@onyxnet.co.uk
Call Date: Nov 1985, Inner Temple
Qualifications: [LLB (Hull)]

WEST JOHN REDVERS

5 Fountain Court
Steelhouse Lane, Birmingham B4 6DR,
Telephone: 0121 606 0500
E-mail:clerks@5fountaincourt.law.co.uk
Call Date: Feb 1965, Middle Temple
Qualifications: [BA (Cantab)]

WEST LAWRENCE JOSEPH

2 Harcourt Buildings
Ground Floor/Left, Temple, London
EC4Y 9DB, Telephone: 0171 583 9020
E-mail: clerks@harcourt.co.uk
Call Date: May 1979, Gray's Inn
Pupil Master, Assistant Recorder
Qualifications: [LLM (Lond), LLB, BA
(Toronto)]

WEST MARK

11 Old Square
Ground Floor, Lincoln's Inn, London
WC2A 3TS, Telephone: 020 7430 0341
E-mail: clerks@11oldsquare.co.uk
Call Date: July 1987, Middle Temple
Pupil Master
Qualifications: [MA, LLM (Cantab)]

Fax: 0171 831 2469; DX: LDE 1031;
Other comms: E-mail
clerks@11oldsquare.co.uk

Types of work: Bankruptcy, Chancery (general), Chancery land law, Charities, Commercial litigation, Commercial property, Common law (general), Company and commercial, Conveyancing, Equity, wills and trusts, Family provision, Insolvency, Landlord and tenant, Partnerships, Probate and administration, Professional negligence, Restitution

Awards and memberships: Chancery Bar Association; Professional Negligence Bar Association; Bar European Group

Languages spoken: French

Publications: 'Swaps & Local Authorities: A Mistake?' (with Catherine Newman QC) in *Swaps & Off-exchange Derivatives Trading: Law & Regulation* (edited by Bettelheim, Parry & Rees) (FT Law & Tax), 1996

Reported Cases: *Kleinwort Benson v Sandwell BC*, [1994] 4 All ER 890, 1993. Restitution of monies paid under *ultra vires* interest rate swap contracts.
Morgan Grenfell v Welwyn Hatfield DC; Islington LBC (third party), [1995] 1 All ER 1, 1993. Whether interest rate swap contracts are wagers within s 18 of the Gaming Act 1845/s 1 of the Gaming Act 1892.
Kleinwort Benson v Birmingham CC, [1997] QB 380, 1996. Whether passing on is a defence to restitution of monies paid under a void interest rate swap contract.
Chong Kai Tai Ringo v Lee Gee Kee, [1997] HKLRD 491, 1997. Provisional agreement for sale of flat; whether obligations of purchaser and vendor concurrent; whether liquidated damage clause a bar to specific performance.
Kleinwort Benson v Lincoln CC, [1998] 3 WLR 1095, 1998. Whether money paid under a void interest rate swap contract is

recoverable as being paid under a mistake of law.

WEST MARK ROGER

Lamb Chambers
Lamb Building, Temple, London
EC4Y 7AS, Telephone: 020 7797 8300
E-mail: lambchambers@link.org
Call Date: 1973, Inner Temple
Pupil Master, Recorder
Qualifications: [LLB]

WEST MICHAEL CHARLES BERESFORD QC (1975)

3 & 4 Farnham Hall
Farnham, Saxmundham, Suffolk, IP17 1LB,
Telephone: 01728 602758
8 Lambert Jones Mews
Barbican, London EC2Y 8DP,
Telephone: 0171 638 8804
Call Date: Nov 1952, Lincoln's Inn

WEST MISS STEPHANIE

Chambers of Helen Grindrod QC
4th Floor, 15-19 Devereux Court, London
WC2R 3JJ, Telephone: 0171 583 2792
Call Date: May 1993, Gray's Inn
Qualifications: [LLB (Huddersfield)]

WEST-KNIGHTS LAURENCE JAMES

4 Paper Buildings
Ground Floor, Temple, London
EC4Y 7EX, Telephone: 0171 353 3366/
583 7155
E-mail: clerks@4paperbuildings.com
Call Date: Nov 1977, Gray's Inn
Pupil Master, Recorder
Qualifications: [MA (Cantab)]

WESTCOTT DAVID GUY

35 Essex Street
Temple, London WC2R 3AR,
Telephone: 0171 353 6381
E-mail: derek_jenkins@link.org
Call Date: Nov 1982, Middle Temple
Pupil Master
Qualifications: [BA (Oxon)]

WESTERN ADAM JOHN BROOKS

Coleridge Chambers
Citadel, 190 Corporation Street,
Birmingham B4 6QD,
Telephone: 0121 233 8500
Call Date: Mar 1997, Gray's Inn
Qualifications: [BA (L'pool)]

WESTGATE MARTIN TREVOR

Doughty Street Chambers
11 Doughty Street, London WC1N 2PG,
Telephone: 0171 404 1313
E-mail:enquiries@doughtystreet.co.uk
Call Date: Nov 1985, Middle Temple
Pupil Master
Qualifications: [BA (Oxon)]

WESTON MS AMANDA

Chambers of Ian Macdonald QC (In Association with Two Garden Court, Temple, London)
Waldorf House, 5 Cooper Street,
Manchester M2 2FW,
Telephone: 0161 236 1840
Call Date: Oct 1995, Inner Temple
Qualifications: [LLB (Hons)]

WESTON CLIVE AUBREY RICHARD

Two Crown Office Row
Ground Floor, Temple, London
EC4Y 7HJ, Telephone: 020 7797 8100
E-mail: mail@2cor.co.uk, or to individual
barristers at: [barrister's
surname]@2cor.co.uk
Call Date: Nov 1993, Middle Temple
Qualifications: [MA (Hons)(Cantab), CPE
(City)]

WESTON JEREMY PAUL

St Ive's Chambers
Whittall Street, Birmingham B4 6DH,
Telephone: 0121 236 0863/5720
E-mail:stives.headofchambers@btinternet.com
Call Date: 1991, Inner Temple
Qualifications: [BA (Hons)]

WESTON LOUIS ROY PAUL

2 King's Bench Walk
Ground Floor, Temple, London
EC4Y 7DE, Telephone: 0171 353 1746
E-mail: 2kbw@atlas.co.uk

King's Bench Chambers
115 North Hill, Plymouth PL4 8JY,
Telephone: 01752 221551
Call Date: Nov 1994, Lincoln's Inn
Qualifications: [BA (Hons)(Bris), CPE]

WESTWOOD ANDREW DAVID

7 Stone Buildings
Ground Floor, Lincoln's Inn, London
WC2A 3SZ, Telephone: 0171 405 3886/
242 3546 E-mail: chaldous@vossnet.co.uk
Call Date: Nov 1994, Inner Temple
Qualifications: [MA (Oxon), CPE
(Huddersfield)]

WETTON PAUL NICHOLAS

Chambers of Paul Wetton
16 Pont Street, London SW1X 9EN,
Telephone: 0171 235 8485
E-mail: pwetton@hotmail.com
Call Date: Nov 1992, Middle Temple
Qualifications: [HND Business Studies, CPE]

WHAITES MISS EMMA LOUISE

1 Inner Temple Lane
Temple, London EC4Y 1AF,
Telephone: 020 7353 0933
Call Date: Nov 1994, Gray's Inn
Qualifications: [LLB (Hons)]

WHALAN MARK ANDREW

2 Gray's Inn Square Chambers
2nd Floor, Gray's Inn, London WC1R 5AA,
Telephone: 020 7242 0328
E-mail: clerks@2gis.co.uk
Call Date: Nov 1988, Middle Temple
Qualifications: [BA (Leeds), Dip Law (City)]

WHEATLEY SIMON DEREK JOHN

9 Bedford Row
London WC1R 4AZ,
Telephone: 0171 242 3555
E-mail: clerks@9br.co.uk
Call Date: July 1979, Middle Temple
Pupil Master
Qualifications: [LLB]

WHEATLY IAN NEVILL

Dr Johnson's Chambers
Two Dr Johnson's Buildings, Temple,
London EC4Y 7AY,
Telephone: 0171 353 4716
E-mail: clerks@2djb.freeserve.co.uk
Call Date: July 1977, Inner Temple
Pupil Master
Qualifications: [BA (Hons)(Kent)]

WHEELDON MISS SARAH HELEN ELIZABETH

St James's Chambers
68 Quay Street, Manchester M3 3EJ,
Telephone: 0161 834 7000
E-mail: clerks@stjameschambers.co.uk
Call Date: Oct 1990, Gray's Inn
Qualifications: [MA (Hons), Dip Law]

WHEELER ANDREW GEORGE

9 Gough Square
London EC4A 3DE,
Telephone: 020 7832 0500
E-mail: clerks@9goughsq.co.uk
Call Date: July 1988, Lincoln's Inn
Qualifications: [LLB (Hons)]

WHEELER KENNETH RICHARD

Lamb Building
Ground Floor, Temple, London
EC4Y 7AS, Telephone: 020 7797 7788
E-mail: lamb.building@link.org
Call Date: Nov 1956, Lincoln's Inn
Pupil Master

WHEELER MISS MARINA CLAIRE

2 Harcourt Buildings
Ground Floor/Left, Temple, London
EC4Y 9DB, Telephone: 0171 583 9020
E-mail: clerks@harcourt.co.uk
Call Date: Nov 1987, Gray's Inn
Qualifications: [MA (Cantab), Licence
Speciale en, Droit Enrop]

WHEELER MISS SUVI DAWN

Sussex Chambers
9 Old Steine, Brighton, Sussex, BN1 1FJ,
Telephone: 01273 607953
Call Date: Oct 1994, Lincoln's Inn
Qualifications: [BA (Hons)(Oxon)]

WHEETMAN ALAN

East Anglian Chambers
57 London Street, Norwich NR2 1HL,
Telephone: 01603 617351
E-mail: norwich@ealaw.co.uk
East Anglian Chambers
52 North Hill, Colchester, Essex, CO1 1PY,
Telephone: 01206 572756
E-mail: colchester@ealaw.co.uk
East Anglian Chambers
Gresham House, 5 Museum Street,
Ipswich, Suffolk, IP1 1HQ,
Telephone: 01473 214481
E-mail: ipswich@ealaw.co.uk
Call Date: Oct 1995, Middle Temple
Qualifications: [LLB (Hons)]

WHELAN GEOFFREY MICHAEL

Kenworthy's Chambers
83 Bridge Street, Manchester M3 2RF,
Telephone: 0161 832 4036/834 6954
E-mail: clerks@kenworthys.co.uk
Call Date: 1996, Gray's Inn
Qualifications: [LLB (Sheff)]

WHELAN MISS ROMA FELICITY

Goldsmith Chambers
Ground Floor, Goldsmith Building,
Temple, London EC4Y 7BL,
Telephone: 0171 353 6802/3/4/5
E-mail: clerks@goldsmithchambers.law.co.uk
Call Date: May 1984, Gray's Inn
Qualifications: [LLB (Belfast)]

WHIPPLE MRS PHILIPPA JANE EDWARDS

1 Crown Office Row
Ground Floor, Temple, London
EC4Y 7HH, Telephone: 0171 797 7500
E-mail: mail@onecrownofficerow.com
Call Date: Feb 1994, Middle Temple
Qualifications: [MA (Oxon)]

WHIPPMAN MRS CONSTANCE

33 Bedford Row
London WC1R 4JH,
Telephone: 0171 242 6476
E-mail: clerks@bedfordrow33.demon.co.uk
Call Date: Nov 1978, Gray's Inn
Pupil Master
Qualifications: [BA, MA]

WHITAKER JOHN STEPHEN

5 Fountain Court
Steelhouse Lane, Birmingham B4 6DR,
Telephone: 0121 606 0500
E-mail: clerks@5fountaincourt.law.co.uk
Call Date: 1970, Lincoln's Inn
Pupil Master
Qualifications: [MA, BCL (Oxon)]

WHITAKER MS QUINCY RACHEL SUZY

Doughty Street Chambers
11 Doughty Street, London WC1N 2PG,
Telephone: 0171 404 1313
E-mail: enquiries@doughtystreet.co.uk
Call Date: Nov 1991, Middle Temple
Qualifications: [BA Hons (Oxon)]

WHITAKER STEVEN DIXON

199 Strand
London WC2R 1DR,
Telephone: 0171 379 9779
E-mail: chambers@199strand.co.uk
Queens Square Chambers
56 Queens Square, Bristol BS1 4PR,
Telephone: 0117 921 1966
Call Date: July 1973, Middle Temple
Pupil Master
Qualifications: [MA (Cantab)]

WHITBY CHARLES HARLEY QC (1970)

12 King's Bench Walk
Temple, London EC4Y 7EL,
Telephone: 0171 583 0811
E-mail: chambers@12kbw.co.uk
Call Date: July 1952, Middle Temple
Recorder
Qualifications: [MA (Cantab)]

WHITCOMBE MARK DAVID

Old Square Chambers
Hanover House, 47 Corn Street, Bristol
BS1 1HT, Telephone: 0117 9277111
E-mail: oldsqbri@globalnet.co.uk
Old Square Chambers
1 Verulam Buildings, Gray's Inn, London
WC1R 5LQ, Telephone: 0171 269 0300
E-mail: clerks@oldsquarechambers.co.uk
Call Date: Nov 1994, Middle Temple
Qualifications: [BA (Hons)(Oxon), BCL
(Oxon)]

D

WHITE MISS ADELE SUSANNAH

Westgate Chambers
144 High Street, Lewes, East Sussex,
BN7 1XT, Telephone: 01273 480510
Call Date: Mar 1996, Lincoln's Inn
Qualifications: [BA (Hons)(Hull)]

WHITE MISS AMANDA JANE

8 Fountain Court
Steelhouse Lane, Birmingham B4 6DR,
Telephone: 0121 236 5514/5
E-mail: clerks@no8chambers.co.uk
Call Date: Nov 1976, Gray's Inn
Qualifications: [BA, CNAA]

WHITE ANDREW QC (1997)

Atkin Chambers
1 Atkin Building, Gray's Inn, London
WC1R 5AT, Telephone: 020 7404 0102
E-mail: clerks@atkin-chambers.co.uk
Call Date: July 1980, Lincoln's Inn
Qualifications: [LLB (Wales)]

WHITE ANTONY DENIS LOWNDES

Cloisters
1 Pump Court, Temple, London
EC4Y 7AA, Telephone: 0171 827 4000
E-mail: clerks@cloisters.com
Call Date: Nov 1983, Middle Temple
Pupil Master
Qualifications: [BA (Cantab)]

WHITE DARREN PAUL

Cathedral Chambers (Jan Wood Independent Barristers' Clerk)
1 Maple Road, Exeter, Devon, EX4 1BN,
Telephone: 01392 210900
E-mail:cathedral.chambers@eclipse.co.uk
Call Date: Oct 1996, Lincoln's Inn
Qualifications: [LLB (Hons)(Notts)]

WHITE MISS GEMMA SOPHIE GOLDER

Blackstone Chambers
Blackstone House, Temple, London
EC4Y 9BW, Telephone: 0171 583 1770
E-mail:clerks@blackstonechambers.com
Call Date: Nov 1994, Inner Temple
Qualifications: [LLB (Lond), BA (Oxon)]

WHITE GEOFFREY GEORGE NOBLE

Chambers of Geoffrey White
9 The Finches, Sandy, Bedfordshire,
SG19 2UL, Telephone: 01767 692782
Call Date: Nov 1985, Middle Temple
Qualifications: [BSc (L'pool), Dip, Law
(Westminster)]

WHITE MISS JOANNE ELIZABETH

Verulam Chambers
Peer House, 8-14 Verulam Street, Gray's
Inn, London WC1X 8LZ,
Telephone: 0171 813 2400
Call Date: July 1987, Middle Temple
Qualifications: [BA (Hons)]

WHITE MATTHEW JAMES

13 King's Bench Walk
1st Floor, Temple, London EC4Y 7EN,
Telephone: 0171 353 7204
E-mail: clerks@13kbw.law.co.uk
King's Bench Chambers
32 Beaumont Street, Oxford OX1 2NP,
Telephone: 01865 311066
E-mail: clerks@kbc-oxford.law.co.uk
Call Date: 1997, Gray's Inn
Qualifications: [BA]

WHITE PETER-JOHN SPENCER

Pembroke House
18 The Crescent, Leatherhead, Surrey,
KT22 8EE, Telephone: 01372 376160/
376493
Call Date: July 1977, Inner Temple
Pupil Master
Qualifications: [BA]

WHITE MR. ROBIN MARK

Field Court Chambers
2nd Floor, 3 Field Court, Gray's Inn,
London WC1R 5EP,
Telephone: 0171 404 7474
Call Date: Nov 1995, Gray's Inn
Qualifications: [BSc , LLB (Exon)]

WHITE SASHA NICHOLAS

1 Serjeants' Inn
4th Floor, Temple, London EC4Y 1NH,
Telephone: 0171 583 1355
E-mail: clerks@serjeants-inn.co.uk
Call Date: Oct 1991, Inner Temple
Qualifications: [BA (Cantab)]

WHITE MRS TANYA

Pembroke House
18 The Crescent, Leatherhead, Surrey,
KT22 8EE, Telephone: 01372 376160/
376493
Call Date: Feb 1983, Middle Temple
Qualifications: [BA]

WHITE TIMOTHY GORDON

15 Winckley Square
Preston PR1 3JJ,
Telephone: 01772 252828
E-mail:clerks@winckleysq.demon.co.uk
Call Date: July 1978, Middle Temple
Pupil Master
Qualifications: [BA]

WHITE TIMOTHY RICHARD

30 Park Square
Leeds LS1 2PF, Telephone: 0113 2436388
E-mail: clerks@30parksquare.co.uk
Call Date: Oct 1993, Middle Temple
Qualifications: [LLB (Hons), MA (Keele)]

WHITEHALL MARK ANTHONY

Colleton Chambers
Colleton Crescent, Exeter, Devon,
EX2 4DG, Telephone: 01392 274898/9
Call Date: July 1983, Inner Temple
Qualifications: [LLB (Exon)]

WHITEHALL RICHARD LANGDALE

Deans Court Chambers
41-43 Market Place, Preston PR1 1AH,
Telephone: 01772 555163
E-mail: clerks@deanscourt.co.uk
Deans Court Chambers
24 St John Street, Manchester M3 4DF,
Telephone: 0161 214 6000
E-mail: clerks@deanscourt.co.uk
Call Date: 1998, Lincoln's Inn
Qualifications: [LLB (Hons)(Cardiff)]

WHITEHEAD DARRON MARCUS

Chichester Chambers
12 North Pallant, Chichester, West Sussex,
PO19 1TQ, Telephone: 01243 784538
E-mail:clerks@chichesterchambers.law.co.uk
Call Date: Nov 1995, Inner Temple
Qualifications: [LLB (Sheff)]

WHITEHOUSE CHRISTOPHER JOHN

8 Gray's Inn Square
Gray's Inn, London WC1R 5AZ,
Telephone: 0171 242 3529
Call Date: 1972, Inner Temple
Qualifications: [BA, BCL (Oxon)]

WHITEHOUSE DAVID RAE BECKWITH QC (1990)

3 Raymond Buildings
Gray's Inn, London WC1R 5BH,
Telephone: 020 7831 3833
E-mail:chambers@threeraymond.demon.co.uk
Call Date: Nov 1969, Gray's Inn
Recorder
Qualifications: [MA (Cantab)]

WHITEHOUSE MRS SARAH ALICE

6 King's Bench Walk
Ground Floor, Temple, London
EC4Y 7DR, Telephone: 0171 583 0410
E-mail: worsley@6kbw.freeserve.co.uk
Call Date: Oct 1993, Lincoln's Inn
Qualifications: [MA (Hons)]

WHITEHOUSE STUART COLIN

New Court
Temple, London EC4Y 9BE,
Telephone: 0171 583 5123/0510
Call Date: July 1987, Middle Temple
Pupil Master
Qualifications: [LLB(Hons), LLM (Exon)]

WHITEHOUSE-VAUX WILLIAM EDWARD

4 Field Court
Gray's Inn, London WC1R 5EA,
Telephone: 0171 440 6900
E-mail: chambers@4fieldcourt.co.uk
Call Date: Nov 1977, Inner Temple
Qualifications: [Dr. Jur (Bologna)]

WHITEHURST IAN JOHN

Oriel Chambers
14 Water Street, Liverpool L2 8TD,
Telephone: 0151 236 7191/236 4321
E-mail: clerks@oriel-chambers.co.uk
Call Date: Nov 1994, Inner Temple
Qualifications: [LLB (Hull)]

WHITEMAN PETER GEORGE QC (1977)

Hollis Whiteman Chambers
3rd Floor, Queen Elizabeth Bldg, Temple,
London EC4Y 9BS,
Telephone: 020 7583 5766
E-mail:barristers@holliswhiteman.co.uk
Call Date: July 1967, Lincoln's Inn
Recorder
Qualifications: [LLB, LLM]

WHITFIELD ADRIAN QC (1983)

3 Serjeants' Inn
London EC4Y 1BQ,
Telephone: 0171 353 5537
E-mail: clerks@3serjeantsinn.com
Call Date: June 1964, Middle Temple
Recorder
Qualifications: [MA (Oxon)]

WHITFIELD JONATHAN

Hardwicke Building
New Square, Lincoln's Inn, London
WC2A 3SB, Telephone: 020 7242 2523
E-mail: clerks@hardwicke.co.uk
Call Date: July 1985, Middle Temple
Pupil Master
Qualifications: [BA]

WHITLEY JONATHAN DENTON

Harrow on the Hill Chambers
60 High Street, Harrow-on-the-Hill,
Middlesex, HA1 3LL,
Telephone: 0181 423 7444
Windsor Barristers' Chambers
Windsor Telephone: 01753 648899
E-mail: law@windsorchambers.co.uk
Call Date: Nov 1993, Inner Temple
Qualifications: [LLB (Hons) (Exon)]

WHITMORE JOHN

21 Portland Road
Clarendon Park, Leicester LE2 3AB,
Telephone: 0116 2706235
Cloisters
1 Pump Court, Temple, London
EC4Y 7AA, Telephone: 0171 827 4000
E-mail: clerks@cloisters.com
Call Date: May 1976, Lincoln's Inn
Qualifications: [BA, BCL (Oxon)]

WHITTAKER DAVID JOHN

4 Brick Court, Chambers of Anne Rafferty QC
1st Floor, Temple, London EC4Y 9AD,
Telephone: 0171 583 8455
Call Date: Nov 1986, Middle Temple
Qualifications: [BA (Lond) Dip Law]

WHITTAKER MISS DORNE JOANNA

Park Lane Chambers
19 Westgate, Leeds LS1 2RD,
Telephone: 0113 2285000
E-mail:clerks@parklanechambers.co.uk
Call Date: Nov 1994, Middle Temple
Qualifications: [BA (Hons), MBA]

WHITTAKER JOHN PERCIVAL

Serle Court Chambers
6 New Square, Lincoln's Inn, London
WC2A 3QS, Telephone: 0171 242 6105
E-mail: clerks@serlecourt.co.uk
Call Date: Nov 1969, Lincoln's Inn
Qualifications: [MA, BCL (Oxon)]

WHITTAKER ROBERT MICHAEL

3 Temple Gardens
Lower Ground Floor, Temple, London
EC4Y 9AU, Telephone: 0171 353 3102/5/
9297 E-mail: clerks@3tg.co.uk
Call Date: July 1977, Middle Temple
Qualifications: [LLB (Lond)]

WHITTAM MS SAMANTHA ABIGAIL

14 Gray's Inn Square
Gray's Inn, London WC1R 5JP,
Telephone: 0171 242 0858
E-mail: 100712.2134@compuserve.com
Call Date: Nov 1995, Middle Temple
Qualifications: [BA (Hons)(Bris), MA (Lond)]

WHITTAM WILLIAM RICHARD LAMONT

Furnival Chambers
32 Furnival Street, London EC4A 1JQ,
Telephone: 0171 405 3232
E-mail: clerks@furnivallaw.co.uk
Call Date: July 1983, Gray's Inn
Pupil Master
Qualifications: [LLB (Hons) (Lond)]

WHITTING JOHN JUSTIN

1 Crown Office Row
Ground Floor, Temple, London
EC4Y 7HH, Telephone: 0171 797 7500
E-mail: mail@onecrownofficerow.com
Call Date: Oct 1991, Middle Temple
Qualifications: [BA (Hons)(Oxon), LLM
(Lond)]

WHITTLE CHRISTOPHER DAVID

11 South Square
2nd Floor, Gray's Inn, London
WC1R 5EU,
Telephone: 0171 405 1222 (24hr messagin
g service)
E-mail: clerks@11southsquare.com
Call Date: 1975, Gray's Inn
Qualifications: [BSc, PhD (Lond)]

WHITTLE-MARTIN MISS LUCIA

2 Harcourt Buildings
1st Floor, Temple, London EC4Y 9DB,
Telephone: 020 7353 2112
Call Date: Nov 1985, Middle Temple
Pupil Master
Qualifications: [BSc (Lond), Dip Law]

WHITTLESTONE MISS KIM

3 Temple Gardens
2nd Floor, Temple, London EC4Y 9AU,
Telephone: 0171 583 1155
Call Date: Nov 1994, Middle Temple
Qualifications: [LLB (Hons)]

WHYATT MICHAEL GEORGE

15 Winckley Square
Preston PR1 3JJ,
Telephone: 01772 252828
E-mail:clerks@winckleysq.demon.co.uk
Call Date: Feb 1992, Gray's Inn
Qualifications: [LLB]

WHYBROW CHRISTOPHER JOHN QC (1992)

1 Serjeants' Inn
4th Floor, Temple, London EC4Y 1NH,
Telephone: 0171 583 1355
E-mail: clerks@serjeants-inn.co.uk
Call Date: July 1965, Inner Temple
Qualifications: [LLB (Lond)]

WHYSALL MISS CAROLINE SARA

2 Paper Buildings, Basement North
Temple, London EC4Y 7ET,
Telephone: 0171 936 2613
E-mail: post@2paper.co.uk
Call Date: July 1993, Inner Temple
Qualifications: [LLB (Hons)(E.Anglia)]

WHYTE MISS ANNE LYNNE

Adrian Lyon's Chambers
14 Castle Street, Liverpool L2 0NE,
Telephone: 0151 236 4421/8240
E-mail: chambers14@aol.com
Call Date: Feb 1993, Lincoln's Inn
Qualifications: [BA, Diploma in Law]

WICHEREK MISS ANN MARIE

One Garden Court Family Law Chambers
Ground Floor, Temple, London
EC4Y 9BJ, Telephone: 0171 797 7900
E-mail: clerks@onegardencourt.co.uk
Call Date: July 1978, Inner Temple
Pupil Master
Qualifications: [LLB (So'ton)]

WICKENS SIMON

Maidstone Chambers
33 Earl Street, Maidstone, Kent, ME14 1PF,
Telephone: 01622 688592
E-mail:maidstonechambers@compuserve.co
m
Call Date: 1998, Lincoln's Inn
Qualifications: [BA (Hons)]

WICKINS MISS STEFANIE LORRAINE

Trinity Chambers
140 New London Road, Chelmsford,
Essex, CM2 0AW,
Telephone: 01245 605040
E-mail:clerks@trinitychambers.law.co.uk
Call Date: Nov 1994, Lincoln's Inn
Qualifications: [LLB (Hons)(Anglia), LLM
(Bristol)]

D

D

WICKREMERATNE DR UPALI CHANDRABHAYE

Warwick House Chambers
8 Warwick Court, Gray's Inn, London
WC1R 5DJ, Telephone: 0171 430 2323
E-mail: cdrewlaw@aol.com
Call Date: July 1962, Lincoln's Inn
Qualifications: [BA (Hons)(Ceylon), BA
(Hons)(London), PhD (London)]

WICKS DAVID CHARLES

Farrar's Building
Temple, London EC4Y 7BD,
Telephone: 0171 583 9241
E-mail:chambers@farrarsbuilding.co.uk
Call Date: July 1989, Middle Temple
Qualifications: [BA]

WICKS IAIN GEORGE MACKENZIE

**4 Brick Court, Chambers of Anne
Rafferty QC**
1st Floor, Temple, London EC4Y 9AD,
Telephone: 0171 583 8455
Call Date: Nov 1990, Middle Temple
Qualifications: [LLB (Hons)]

WICKS MS JOANNE

Wilberforce Chambers
8 New Square, Lincoln's Inn, London
WC2A 3QP, Telephone: 0171 306 0102
E-mail: chambers@wilberforce.co.uk
Call Date: Nov 1990, Lincoln's Inn
Pupil Master
Qualifications: [BA (Hons)(Oxon), BCL]

Types of work: Chancery (general), Chancery
land law, Commercial litigation, Commercial property, Insurance/reinsurance, Landlord and tenant, Pensions, Probate and
administration, Professional negligence

WIDDETT MS CERI LOUISE

Park Court Chambers
16 Park Place, Leeds LS1 2SJ,
Telephone: 0113 2433277
Call Date: Oct 1994, Gray's Inn
Qualifications: [BA (Keele)]

WIDDICOMBE DAVID GRAHAM QC (1965)

2 Mitre Court Buildings
2nd Floor, Temple, London EC4Y 7BX,
Telephone: 0171 583 1380
E-mail: clerks@2mcb.co.uk
Call Date: Nov 1950, Inner Temple
Qualifications: [MA, LL.B (Cantab)]

WIDDUP STANLEY JEFFREY PONSONBY

Guildford Chambers
Stoke House, Leapale Lane, Guildford,
Surrey, GU1 4LY,
Telephone: 01483 539131
E-mail:guildford.barristers@btinternet.com
Call Date: Nov 1973, Gray's Inn
Pupil Master, Recorder

WIDE CHARLES THOMAS QC (1995)

9 Bedford Row
London WC1R 4AZ,
Telephone: 0171 242 3555
E-mail: clerks@9br.co.uk
Call Date: Feb 1974, Inner Temple
Recorder

WIGGANS MISS AMANDA JANE

Rowchester Chambers
4 Rowchester Court, Whittall Street,
Birmingham B4 6DH,
Telephone: 0121 233 2327/2361951
Call Date: Nov 1986, Middle Temple
Qualifications: [LLB (Warw)]

WIGGLESWORTH RAYMOND QC (1999)

18 St John Street
Manchester M3 4EA,
Telephone: 0161 278 1800
E-mail: 18stjohn@lineone.net
Call Date: 1974, Gray's Inn
Pupil Master, Recorder
Qualifications: [LLB (Hons) (Manch)]

WIGHTWICK (WILLIAM) IAIN

Assize Court Chambers
14 Small Street, Bristol BS1 1DE,
Telephone: 0117 9264587
E-mail:chambers@assize-court-chambers.co.uk
Call Date: Nov 1985, Inner Temple
Pupil Master
Qualifications: [BSc (Bris), Dip Law]

WIGIN MISS CAROLINE ROSEMARY

Park Court Chambers
16 Park Place, Leeds LS1 2SJ,
Telephone: 0113 2433277
Call Date: July 1984, Inner Temple
Qualifications: [BA (Exon)]

WIGLEY MISS RACHEL

Watford Chambers
74 Mildred Avenue, Watford,
Hertfordshire, WD1 7DX,
Telephone: 01923 220553
Call Date: Oct 1997, Gray's Inn
Qualifications: [LLB (Lond)]

WIGNALL EDWARD GORDON

1 Dr Johnson's Buildings
Ground Floor, Temple, London
EC4Y 7AX, Telephone: 0171 353 9328
E-mail:OneDr.Johnsons@btinternet.com
Dr Johnson's Chambers
The Atrium Court, Apex Plaza, Reading,
Berkshire, RG1 1AX,
Telephone: 01734 254221
Call Date: July 1987, Gray's Inn
Qualifications: [MA (Oxon)]

WIGODER THE HON LEWIS JUSTIN

High Pavement Chambers
1 High Pavement, Nottingham NG1 1HF,
Telephone: 0115 9418218
Call Date: July 1977, Gray's Inn
Pupil Master
Qualifications: [MA, DPhil (Oxon)]

WILBY DAVID CHRISTOPHER QC (1998)

199 Strand
London WC2R 1DR,
Telephone: 0171 379 9779
E-mail: chambers@199strand.co.uk

Park Lane Chambers
19 Westgate, Leeds LS1 2RD,
Telephone: 0113 2285000
E-mail:clerks@parklanechambers.co.uk
Call Date: July 1974, Inner Temple
Assistant Recorder
Qualifications: [MA (Cantab)]

Fax: 0171 379 9481;
Out of hours telephone: 01423 547786/
Fax: 01423 547786; DX: 322 London,
Chancery Lane/11999 Harrogate 1;
Other comms: E-mail
davidwilby@lawyer.demon.co.uk

Types of work: Commercial litigation, Crime – corporate fraud, Environment, Family provision, Medical negligence, Personal injury, Professional negligence

Membership of foreign bars: American Bar Association

Circuit: North Eastern

Awards and memberships: Member of Bar Council; Member Executive Committee Professional Negligence Bar Association; Vice Chairman Bar Conference; Personal Injury Bar Association; Family Bar Association

Publications: *Professional Negligence and Liability Law Reports* (Editor), 1996 to date; *Professional Negligence Classics*, 1999

Reported Cases: *Ramsden v Lee*, [1992] 2 All ER 205 (CA), 1992. Approach to exercise of discretion under section 33 Limitation Act 1980.
United Norwest Co-operatives Ltd v Johnson, (1994) *The Times*, 24 Feb (CA); SCP 024/5/4, 1994. Right of silence of defendant in Mareva injunction proceedings.
R v Gill & Smurthwaite, [1998] G App R 437 (CA). Effect of and guidance in respect of 578 PACE 1984 – agent provocateur, incitement
Re Port (a Bankrupt), [1994] 1 WLR 862, 1993. Basis of and grounds for striking out a claim in respect of misconduct of trustee in bankruptcy.
Re W (a Minor), [1988] 1 FLR 175 (CA), 1988. Adoption where access to child appropriate.

D

WILCKEN ANTHONY DAVID FELIX

Hollis Whiteman Chambers
3rd Floor, Queen Elizabeth Bldg, Temple,
London EC4Y 9BS,
Telephone: 020 7583 5766
E-mail:barristers@holliswhiteman.co.uk
Call Date: Nov 1966, Middle Temple
Pupil Master, Recorder

WILCOCK PETER LAZENBY

14 Tooks Court
Cursitor St, London EC4A 1LB,
Telephone: 0171 405 8828
E-mail: clerks@tooks.law.co.uk
Call Date: July 1988, Middle Temple
Qualifications: [LLB (Hons) (LSE)]

WILCOX JEROME CARL JEAN

Guildford Chambers
Stoke House, Leapale Lane, Guildford,
Surrey, GU1 4LY,
Telephone: 01483 539131
E-mail:guildford.barristers@btinternet.com
Call Date: Nov 1988, Middle Temple
Qualifications: [LLB(Bucks), Dip Law]

WILCOX LAWRENCE GAYWOOD

South Western Chambers
Melville House, 12 Middle Street,
Taunton, Somerset, TA1 1SH,
Telephone: 01823 331919 (24 hrs)
E-mail: barclerk@clara.net
Call Date: Oct 1996, Lincoln's Inn
Qualifications: [LLB (Hons)(Exon)]

WILCOX NICHOLAS HUGH

5 Essex Court
1st Floor, Temple, London EC4Y 9AH,
Telephone: 0171 410 2000
E-mail: barristers@5essexcourt.co.uk
Call Date: July 1977, Gray's Inn
Pupil Master
Qualifications: [LLB]

WILD SIMON PETER

Queen Elizabeth Building
Ground Floor, Temple, London
EC4Y 9BS,
Telephone: 0171 353 7181 (12 Lines)
Call Date: July 1977, Inner Temple
Pupil Master
Qualifications: [BA (Lond)]

WILD STEVEN

Parsonage Chambers
5th Floor, 3 The Parsonage, Manchester
M3 2HW, Telephone: 0161 833 1996
Call Date: Oct 1994, Gray's Inn
Qualifications: [LLB]

WILDBLOOD STEPHEN ROGER QC (1999)

Albion Chambers
Broad Street, Bristol BS1 1DR,
Telephone: 0117 9272144
Call Date: 1980, Inner Temple
Pupil Master
Qualifications: [LLB (Sheff)]

WILDING KEITH

65-67 King Street
Leicester LE1 6RP,
Telephone: 0116 2547710
Call Date: Oct 1990, Inner Temple
Pupil Master
Qualifications: [BA, Dip Law]

WILDING MISS LISA MARIE

2 Harcourt Buildings
1st Floor, Temple, London EC4Y 9DB,
Telephone: 020 7353 2112
Call Date: Nov 1993, Inner Temple
Qualifications: [BA Hons (Cantab)]

WILEY MISS FRANCESCA PETRA DENNING

10 King's Bench Walk
1st Floor, Temple, London EC4Y 7EB,
Telephone: 0171 353 2501
Call Date: May 1996, Gray's Inn
Qualifications: [MA]

WILKEN SEAN DAVID HENRY

39 Essex Street
London WC2R 3AT,
Telephone: 0171 832 1111
E-mail: clerks@39essex.co.uk
Call Date: Nov 1991, Middle Temple
Pupil Master
Qualifications: [BA Hons (Oxon), Dip Law]

WILKINS ANDREW LEWIS

Harrow on the Hill Chambers
60 High Street, Harrow-on-the-Hill,
Middlesex, HA1 3LL,
Telephone: 0181 423 7444
Windsor Barristers' Chambers
Windsor Telephone: 01753 648899
E-mail: law@windsorchambers.co.uk
Call Date: Oct 1995, Lincoln's Inn
Qualifications: [MA (Hons)(Oxon)]

WILKINS CHRISTOPHER JOHN

11 Stone Buildings
Lincoln's Inn, London WC2A 3TG,
Telephone: +44 (0)207 831 6381
E-mail:clerks@11StoneBuildings.law.co.uk
Call Date: May 1993, Lincoln's Inn
Qualifications: [MA (Oxon)]

WILKINS MRS COLETTE ANN

1 New Square
Ground Floor, Lincoln's Inn, London
WC2A 3SA, Telephone: 0171 405 0884/5/6/
7 E-mail: clerks@1newsquare.law.co.uk
Call Date: Nov 1989, Lincoln's Inn
Qualifications: [BA, Dip Law (City)]

WILKINS THOMAS ALEXANDER

2 Harcourt Buildings
1st Floor, Temple, London EC4Y 9DB,
Telephone: 020 7353 2112
Call Date: Oct 1993, Middle Temple
Qualifications: [BSc (Hons)(Bris), CPE
(Lond)]

WILKINSON MARC ASHLEY

5 Fountain Court
Steelhouse Lane, Birmingham B4 6DR,
Telephone: 0121 606 0500
E-mail:clerks@5fountaincourt.law.co.uk
Call Date: Nov 1992, Lincoln's Inn
Qualifications: [BA (Hons)]

WILKINSON MICHAEL JOHN

Trinity Chambers
9-12 Trinity Chare, Quayside, Newcastle
upon Tyne NE1 3DF,
Telephone: 0191 232 1927
E-mail: info@trinitychambers.co.uk
Call Date: July 1979, Gray's Inn
Qualifications: [LLB (Exon)]

WILKINSON NIGEL VIVIAN MARSHALL QC (1990)

Two Crown Office Row
Ground Floor, Temple, London
EC4Y 7HJ, Telephone: 020 7797 8100
E-mail: mail@2cor.co.uk, or to individual
barristers at: [barrister's
surname]@2cor.co.uk
*Call Date: July 1972, Middle Temple
Recorder*
Qualifications: [MA (Oxon)]

WILKINSON RICHARD JOHN

1 Temple Gardens
1st Floor, Temple, London EC4Y 9BB,
Telephone: 0171 583 1315/353 0407
E-mail: clerks@1templegardens.co.uk
Call Date: Oct 1992, Lincoln's Inn
Qualifications: [LLB(Hons)(Bris)]

WILLANS DAVID

Northampton Chambers
22 Albion Place, Northampton NN1 1UD,
Telephone: 01604 636271
Call Date: Oct 1995, Lincoln's Inn
Qualifications: [BSc (Hons)(Lond), LLB
(Hons)(City)]

WILLARD NEVILLE FREDERICK MORGAN

6 Pump Court
1st Floor, Temple, London EC4Y 7AR,
Telephone: 0171 797 8400
E-mail: clerks@6pumpcourt.co.uk
6-8 Mill Street
Maidstone, Kent, ME15 6XH,
Telephone: 01622 688094
E-mail: annexe@6pumpcourt.co.uk
*Call Date: July 1976, Gray's Inn
Pupil Master*
Qualifications: [LLB]

WILLBOURNE MISS CAROLINE CATCHPOLE

One Garden Court Family Law Chambers
Ground Floor, Temple, London
EC4Y 9BJ, Telephone: 0171 797 7900
E-mail: clerks@onegardencourt.co.uk
*Call Date: Nov 1970, Inner Temple
Pupil Master*
Qualifications: [BA]

WILLEMS MARC PAUL BERNARD ALFRED

Cobden House Chambers
19 Quay Street, Manchester M3 3HN,
Telephone: 0161 833 6000
E-mail: clerks@cobden.co.uk
Call Date: Nov 1990, Lincoln's Inn
Pupil Master
Qualifications: [BA (Nott'm)]

WILLER ROBERT MICHAEL

Hardwicke Building
New Square, Lincoln's Inn, London
WC2A 3SB, Telephone: 020 7242 2523
E-mail: clerks@hardwicke.co.uk
Call Date: July 1970, Middle Temple
Pupil Master
Qualifications: [BA (Oxon)]

WILLERS MARC LAWRENCE GEORGE

1 Pump Court
Lower Ground Floor, Temple, London
EC4Y 7AB, Telephone: 0171 583 2012/
353 4341
E-mail: [name]@1pumpcourt.co.uk
Call Date: Nov 1987, Lincoln's Inn
Pupil Master
Qualifications: [LLB, BL]

WILLIAMS A JOHN

13 King's Bench Walk
1st Floor, Temple, London EC4Y 7EN,
Telephone: 0171 353 7204
E-mail: clerks@13kbw.law.co.uk
King's Bench Chambers
32 Beaumont Street, Oxford OX1 2NP,
Telephone: 01865 311066
E-mail: clerks@kbc-oxford.law.co.uk
Call Date: July 1983, Lincoln's Inn
Pupil Master
Qualifications: [MA (Cantab)]

WILLIAMS ALAN RONALD

8 King's Bench Walk
2nd Floor, Temple, London EC4Y 7DU,
Telephone: 0171 797 8888
8 King's Bench Walk North
1 Park Square East, Leeds LS1 2NE,
Telephone: 0113 2439797
Call Date: July 1978, Middle Temple
Pupil Master
Qualifications: [BSc]

WILLIAMS ALEXANDER JAMES HYATT

3 Temple Gardens
Lower Ground Floor, Temple, London
EC4Y 9AU, Telephone: 0171 353 3102/5/
9297 E-mail: clerks@3tg.co.uk
Call Date: Nov 1995, Middle Temple
Qualifications: [BA (Hons)]

WILLIAMS ANDREW ARTHUR

Adrian Lyon's Chambers
14 Castle Street, Liverpool L2 0NE,
Telephone: 0151 236 4421/8240
E-mail: chambers14@aol.com
Call Date: Oct 1994, Gray's Inn
Qualifications: [LLB]

WILLIAMS MISS ANNA

Trinity Chambers
140 New London Road, Chelmsford,
Essex, CM2 0AW,
Telephone: 01245 605040
E-mail:clerks@trinitychambers.law.co.uk
Call Date: Nov 1990, Gray's Inn
Qualifications: [LLB]

WILLIAMS MISS ANNE MARGARET

4 Breams Buildings
London EC4A 1AQ,
Telephone: 0171 353 5835/430 1221
E-mail:breams@4breamsbuildings.law.co.uk
Call Date: Nov 1980, Gray's Inn
Pupil Master
Qualifications: [BA (Manch) MPhil, (Lond),
R.T.P.I.]

WILLIAMS MRS BARBARA ELIZABETH

Northampton Chambers
22 Albion Place, Northampton NN1 1UD,
Telephone: 01604 636271
Call Date: Oct 1995, Lincoln's Inn
Qualifications: [LLB (Hons)]

WILLIAMS BENJAMIN JAMES

3 Paper Buildings
Temple London EC4Y 7EU,
Telephone: 020 7583 8055
E-mail: London@3paper.com

3 Paper Buildings (Oxford)
1 Alfred Street, High Street, Oxford
OX1 4EH, Telephone: 01865 793736
E-mail: oxford@3paper.com
3 Paper Buildings (Winchester)
4 St Peter Street, Winchester SO23 8BW,
Telephone: 01962 868884
E-mail: winchester@3paper.com
3 Paper Buildings (Bournemouth)
20 Lorne Park Road, Bournemouth,
Dorset, BH1 1JN,
Telephone: 01202 292102
E-mail: Bournemouth@3paper.com
Call Date: Nov 1994, Lincoln's Inn
Qualifications: [BA (Hons)(Oxon), Dip in
Law (City)]

WILLIAMS BRIAN DAVID

18 St John Street
Manchester M3 4EA,
Telephone: 0161 278 1800
E-mail: 18stjohn@lineone.net
Call Date: July 1986, Inner Temple
Qualifications: [LLB (Manch)]

WILLIAMS MISS CAROLINE SARAH

Maidstone Chambers
33 Earl Street, Maidstone, Kent, ME14 1PF,
Telephone: 01622 688592
E-mail:maidstonechambers@compuserve.co
m
Call Date: 1997, Gray's Inn
Qualifications: [LLB (Hons)]

WILLIAMS MISS CHERYL ANNE

Two Garden Court
1st Floor, Middle Temple, London
EC4Y 9BL, Telephone: 0171 353 1633
E-mail:barristers@2gardenct.law.co.uk
Call Date: July 1982, Inner Temple
Pupil Master
Qualifications: [BA (Oxon), LLM (Lond)]

WILLIAMS CHRISTOPHER DAVID CURNOW

Plowden Buildings
2nd Floor, 2 Plowden Buildings, Middle
Temple Lane, London EC4Y 9BU,
Telephone: 0171 583 0808
E-mail: bar@plowdenbuildings.co.uk
Call Date: July 1981, Gray's Inn
Pupil Master

WILLIAMS CHRISTOPHER MICHAEL

32 Park Place
Cardiff CF1 3BA,
Telephone: 01222 397364
Call Date: Nov 1972, Middle Temple
Pupil Master
Qualifications: [MA (Oxon)]

WILLIAMS CHRISTOPHER PAUL

Counsels' Chambers
2nd Floor, 10-11 Gray's Inn Square,
London WC1R 5JD,
Telephone: 0171 405 2576
E-mail:clerks@10-11graysinnsquare.co.uk
Call Date: Feb 1988, Inner Temple
Pupil Master
Qualifications: [LLB]

WILLIAMS DANIEL VAUGHAN

33 Park Place
Cardiff CF1 3BA,
Telephone: 02920 233313
Call Date: May 1993, Gray's Inn
Qualifications: [LLB (B'ham)]

WILLIAMS DAVID ALAN

12 Old Square
1st Floor, Lincoln's Inn, London
WC2A 3TX, Telephone: 0171 404 0875
Call Date: Oct 1992, Middle Temple
Qualifications: [LL.B (Hons), RGN, RSCN,
RNT]

WILLIAMS DAVID BASIL

Dr Johnson's Chambers
Two Dr Johnson's Buildings, Temple,
London EC4Y 7AY,
Telephone: 0171 353 4716
E-mail: clerks@2djb.freeserve.co.uk
Call Date: Oct 1990, Inner Temple
Pupil Master
Qualifications: [LLB (Leic)]

WILLIAMS DAVID BEVERLEY

**4 Brick Court, Chambers of Anne
Rafferty QC**
1st Floor, Temple, London EC4Y 9AD,
Telephone: 0171 583 8455
Call Date: Nov 1972, Middle Temple
Pupil Master

WILLIAMS DAVID DEVOY

10 King's Bench Walk
Ground Floor, Temple, London
EC4Y 7EB, Telephone: 0171 353 7742
E-mail: 10kbw@lineone.net
Call Date: July 1989, Middle Temple
Qualifications: [BA (Oxon), MA (Cantab)]

WILLIAMS DAVID ESSEX

9 Park Place
Cardiff CF1 3DP,
Telephone: 01222 382731
Call Date: July 1975, Middle Temple
Qualifications: [LLB (Wales), ACIB]

WILLIAMS DAVID HENRY

Chavasse Court Chambers
2nd Floor, Chavasse Court, 24 Lord Street,
Liverpool L2 1TA,
Telephone: 0151 707 1191
Call Date: Feb 1990, Gray's Inn
Assistant Recorder
Qualifications: [BA (Hons)]

WILLIAMS DAVID HUW ANTHONY

18 Red Lion Court
(Off Fleet Street), London EC4A 3EB,
Telephone: 0171 520 6000
E-mail: chambers@18rlc.co.uk
Thornwood House
102 New London Road, Chelmsford,
Essex, CM2 0RG,
Telephone: 01245 280880
E-mail: chambers@18rlc.co.uk
Call Date: July 1988, Inner Temple
Pupil Master
Qualifications: [BSc (Wales), Dip Law
(Lond), GRSC]

WILLIAMS GRAEME QC (1983)

13 King's Bench Walk
1st Floor, Temple, London EC4Y 7EN,
Telephone: 0171 353 7204
E-mail: clerks@13kbw.law.co.uk
King's Bench Chambers
32 Beaumont Street, Oxford OX1 2NP,
Telephone: 01865 311066
E-mail: clerks@kbc-oxford.law.co.uk
Call Date: June 1959, Inner Temple
Recorder
Qualifications: [MA (Oxon)]

WILLIAMS MS HEATHER JEAN

Doughty Street Chambers
11 Doughty Street, London WC1N 2PG,
Telephone: 0171 404 1313
E-mail:enquiries@doughtystreet.co.uk
Call Date: July 1985, Gray's Inn
Pupil Master
Qualifications: [LLB (Lond)]

WILLIAMS HUGH DAVID HAYDN

St Philip's Chambers
Fountain Court, Steelhouse Lane,
Birmingham B4 6DR,
Telephone: 0121 246 7000
E-mail: clerks@st-philips.co.uk
Call Date: 1992, Gray's Inn
Qualifications: [BA]

WILLIAMS DR JASON SCOTT

3 Dr Johnson's Buildings
Ground Floor, Temple, London
EC4Y 7BA, Telephone: 0171 353 4854
E-mail: clerks@3djb.co.uk
Call Date: Oct 1995, Lincoln's Inn
Qualifications: [BA (Hons)(Oxon), D.Phil
(Oxon), Dip Law]

Fax: 0171 583 8784; DX: 1009 Chancery
Lane;
Other comms: E-mail
JWilliams@3DJB.co.uk

Types of work: Administrative, Chancery
(general), Common law (general),
Company and commercial, Costs, Landlord
and tenant, Personal injury, Probate and
administration

Awards and memberships: Member of Administrative Law Bar Association; Former Judicial
Assistant to the Court of Appeal

Other professional experience: Assistant editor
of the *Supreme Court Practice*. Accepts
Direct Professional Access work

Publications: *Civil and Criminal Procedure*
(Sweet & Maxwell), 1997; *The Fast Track
Practice* (Sweet & Maxwell), 1999

Reported Cases: *Thai Trading (A firm) v
Taylor*, [1998] 781; [1998] 2 WLR 839 (CA);
[1998] 2 FLR 430, 1998. The Court of
Appeal case which legitimised 'No Win No
Fee' and conditional fee agreements.
Southwark LBC v Kennedy, [1998] 10 CL
372, 1997. A case concerning estoppel in

the context of public sector tenancies and possession actions.
Tierney v Mavadia, Triedi and Regentdale Ltd, [1998] 10 CL 225 (QBD), 1998. Personal inquiry and director's personal liability qua occupier of premises.

WILLIAMS MISS JEAN ADELE

6 Pump Court
1st Floor, Temple, London EC4Y 7AR,
Telephone: 0171 797 8400
E-mail: clerks@6pumpcourt.co.uk
6-8 Mill Street
Maidstone, Kent, ME15 6XH,
Telephone: 01622 688094
E-mail: annexe@6pumpcourt.co.uk
Call Date: July 1972, Gray's Inn
Pupil Master, Recorder
Qualifications: [LLB (Lond)]

WILLIAMS MISS JEANETTE MARY

Coleridge Chambers
Citadel, 190 Corporation Street,
Birmingham B4 6QD,
Telephone: 0121 233 8500
Call Date: July 1985, Gray's Inn
Qualifications: [BA]

WILLIAMS JOHN ALBAN

9-12 Bell Yard
London WC2A 2LF,
Telephone: 0171 400 1800
E-mail: clerks@bellyard.co.uk
Call Date: Nov 1979, Middle Temple

WILLIAMS JOHN GLYN

15 Winckley Square
Preston PR1 3JJ,
Telephone: 01772 252828
E-mail:clerks@winckleysq.demon.co.uk
Call Date: Nov 1981, Inner Temple
Qualifications: [BA (Manch)]

WILLIAMS JOHN LEIGHTON QC (1986)

Farrar's Building
Temple, London EC4Y 7BD,
Telephone: 0171 583 9241
E-mail:chambers@farrarsbuilding.co.uk
Call Date: Apr 1964, Gray's Inn
Recorder
Qualifications: [MA, LLB]

WILLIAMS THE HON JOHN MELVILLE QC (1977)

Old Square Chambers
1 Verulam Buildings, Gray's Inn, London WC1R 5LQ, Telephone: 0171 269 0300
E-mail:clerks@oldsquarechambers.co.uk
Old Square Chambers
Hanover House, 47 Corn Street, Bristol BS1 1HT, Telephone: 0117 9277111
E-mail: oldsqbri@globalnet.co.uk
Call Date: June 1955, Inner Temple
Recorder
Qualifications: [BA (Cantab)]

WILLIAMS JOHN ROBERT SELWYN

2 Harcourt Buildings
1st Floor, Temple, London EC4Y 9DB,
Telephone: 020 7353 2112
Call Date: Nov 1973, Middle Temple
Pupil Master
Qualifications: [LLB]

WILLIAMS JOHN WYN

Sedan House
Stanley Place, Chester CH1 2LU,
Telephone: 01244 320480/348282
Call Date: Nov 1992, Gray's Inn
Qualifications: [LLB (Wales)]

WILLIAMS JON FREDERICK

Chambers of Kieran Coonan QC
Ground Floor, 6 Pump Court, Temple,
London EC4Y 7AR,
Telephone: 0171 583 6013/2510
E-mail: clerks@6-pumpcourt.law.co.uk
Call Date: Nov 1970, Inner Temple
Qualifications: [LLB (Lond)]

WILLIAMS KARL

9 Park Place
Cardiff CF1 3DP,
Telephone: 01222 382731
Call Date: July 1982, Middle Temple
Pupil Master
Qualifications: [LLB (Lond)]

WILLIAMS LEIGH MICHAEL

S Tomlinson QC
7 King's Bench Walk, Temple, London
EC4Y 7DS, Telephone: 0171 583 0404
E-mail: clerks@7kbw.law.co.uk
Call Date: July 1996, Inner Temple
Qualifications: [BA, BCL (Oxon)]

WILLIAMS LLOYD

30 Park Place
Cardiff CF1 3BA,
Telephone: 01222 398421
E-mail: 100757.1456@compuserve.com
Call Date: July 1981, Inner Temple
Pupil Master
Qualifications: [BA]

WILLIAMS MARK STEPHEN

2 Paper Buildings
1st Floor, Temple, London EC4Y 7ET,
Telephone: 020 7556 5500
E-mail: clerks@2pbbarristers.co.uk
Call Date: 1996, Lincoln's Inn
Qualifications: [BSC (Hons)(Surrey)]

WILLIAMS NEAL MARTIN

1 Fountain Court
Steelhouse Lane, Birmingham B4 6DR,
Telephone: 0121 236 5721
Call Date: July 1984, Lincoln's Inn
Qualifications: [LLB (Leeds)]

WILLIAMS NICHOLAS MICHAEL HEATHCOTE

12 King's Bench Walk
Temple, London EC4Y 7EL,
Telephone: 0171 583 0811
E-mail: chambers@12kbw.co.uk
Call Date: 1976, Inner Temple
Pupil Master, Assistant Recorder
Qualifications: [MA (Cantab)]

WILLIAMS MS NICOLA EGERSIS

8 King's Bench Walk
2nd Floor, Temple, London EC4Y 7DU,
Telephone: 0171 797 8888
Call Date: Nov 1985, Lincoln's Inn
Pupil Master
Qualifications: [BA (Law)]

WILLIAMS OWEN JOHN

4 Brick Court, Chambers of Anne Rafferty QC
1st Floor, Temple, London EC4Y 9AD,
Telephone: 0171 583 8455
Call Date: July 1974, Middle Temple
Pupil Master
Qualifications: [MA (Oxon)]

WILLIAMS PAUL KENNETH

3 Temple Gardens
3rd Floor, Temple, London EC4Y 9AU,
Telephone: 0171 583 0010
Call Date: July 1990, Inner Temple
Qualifications: [BA (Wales)]

WILLIAMS PAUL ROBERT

8 King's Bench Walk North
1 Park Square East, Leeds LS1 2NE,
Telephone: 0113 2439797
8 King's Bench Walk
2nd Floor, Temple, London EC4Y 7DU,
Telephone: 0171 797 8888
Call Date: Oct 1994, Inner Temple
Qualifications: [BA (Hons), CPE (Lond)]

WILLIAMS RHODRI JOHN

30 Park Place
Cardiff CF1 3BA,
Telephone: 01222 398421
E-mail: 100757.1456@compuserve.com
2 Harcourt Buildings
Ground Floor/Left, Temple, London
EC4Y 9DB, Telephone: 0171 583 9020
E-mail: clerks@harcourt.co.uk
Call Date: July 1987, Gray's Inn
Qualifications: [BA (Oxon), Dip Law]

WILLIAMS RICHARD EVAN HUW

Queens Square Chambers
56 Queens Square, Bristol BS1 4PR,
Telephone: 0117 921 1966
Call Date: Nov 1992, Lincoln's Inn
Qualifications: [LLB (Hons)(Bris)]

WILLIAMS RICHARD NOEL

Goldsmith Chambers
Ground Floor, Goldsmith Building,
Temple, London EC4Y 7BL,
Telephone: 0171 353 6802/3/4/5
E-mail:clerks@goldsmithchambers.law.co.uk
Call Date: Nov 1988, Gray's Inn
Qualifications: [LLB]

WILLIAMS MISS SARA HELEN

5 Fountain Court
Steelhouse Lane, Birmingham B4 6DR,
Telephone: 0121 606 0500
E-mail:clerks@5fountaincourt.law.co.uk
Call Date: Feb 1989, Gray's Inn
Qualifications: [LLB (Lond)]

WILLIAMS MISS SARAH VICTORIA

18 St John Street
Manchester M3 4EA,
Telephone: 0161 278 1800
E-mail: 18stjohn@lineone.net
Call Date: Nov 1995, Inner Temple
Qualifications: [BA (Bris), CPE]

WILLIAMS SIMON PAUL

Lamb Chambers
Lamb Building, Temple, London
EC4Y 7AS, Telephone: 020 7797 8300
E-mail: lambchambers@link.org
Call Date: Nov 1984, Inner Temple
Pupil Master
Qualifications: [LLB (Soton)]

WILLIAMS MISS SUSAN FRANCES

Dr Johnson's Chambers
Two Dr Johnson's Buildings, Temple,
London EC4Y 7AY,
Telephone: 0171 353 4716
E-mail: clerks@2djb.freeserve.co.uk
Call Date: Nov 1978, Middle Temple
Pupil Master
Qualifications: [LLB (Bristol)]

WILLIAMS THOMAS CHRISTOPHER CHARLES

1 Fountain Court
Steelhouse Lane, Birmingham B4 6DR,
Telephone: 0121 236 5721
Call Date: Nov 1995, Middle Temple
Qualifications: [BA (Hons)]

WILLIAMS THOMAS ELLIS

30 Park Place
Cardiff CF1 3BA,
Telephone: 01222 398421
E-mail: 100757.1456@compuserve.com
Call Date: Oct 1996, Middle Temple
Qualifications: [LLB (Hons)(Kent), Licence
En Droit , (Grenoble)]

WILLIAMS VINCENT ALLAN

9 Gough Square
London EC4A 3DE,
Telephone: 020 7832 0500
E-mail: clerks@9goughsq.co.uk
Call Date: July 1985, Middle Temple
Pupil Master
Qualifications: [BA (Cantab)]

WILLIAMS WYN LEWIS QC (1992)

39 Essex Street
London WC2R 3AT,
Telephone: 0171 832 1111
E-mail: clerks@39essex.co.uk
33 Park Place
Cardiff CF1 3BA,
Telephone: 02920 233313
Call Date: July 1974, Inner Temple
Recorder
Qualifications: [MA (Oxon)]

WILLIAMS MISS ZILLAH ELIZABETH

Mitre Court Chambers
3rd Floor, Temple, London EC4Y 7BP,
Telephone: 0171 353 9394
E-mail: mitrecourt.com
Call Date: 1997, Lincoln's Inn
Qualifications: [LLB (Hons)(L'pool)]

WILLIAMSON ADRIAN JOHN GERARD HUGHES

Keating Chambers
10 Essex Street, Outer Temple, London
WC2R 3AA, Telephone: 0171 544 2600
Call Date: Nov 1983, Middle Temple
Pupil Master
Qualifications: [MA (Cantab)]

WILLIAMSON ALISDAIR GEORGE JAMES

3 Raymond Buildings
Gray's Inn, London WC1R 5BH,
Telephone: 020 7831 3833
E-mail:chambers@threeraymond.demon.co.uk
Call Date: Nov 1994, Middle Temple
Qualifications: [MA (Oxon), DipLL, (City)]

WILLIAMSON MISS BRIDGET SUSAN

Enterprise Chambers
9 Old Square, Lincoln's Inn, London
WC2A 3SR, Telephone: 0171 405 9471
E-mail:enterprise.london@dial.pipex.com
Enterprise Chambers
38 Park Square, Leeds LS1 2PA,
Telephone: 0113 246 0391
E-mail:enterprise.leeds@dial.pipex.com
Enterprise Chambers
65 Quayside, Newcastle upon Tyne
NE1 3DS, Telephone: 0191 222 3344
E-mail:enterprise.newcastle@dial.pipex.com
Call Date: Feb 1993, Lincoln's Inn
Qualifications: [BA (Hons)]

WILLIAMSON MISS HAZEL ELEANOR QC (1988)

13 Old Square
Ground Floor, Lincoln's Inn, London
WC2A 3UA, Telephone: 0171 404 4800
E-mail: clerks@13oldsquare.law.co.uk
Call Date: July 1972, Gray's Inn
Recorder
Qualifications: [BA (Oxon)]

WILLIAMSON MISS MELANIE JANE

Chancery House Chambers
7 Lisbon Square, Leeds LS1 4LY,
Telephone: 0113 244 6691
E-mail: chanceryhouse@btinternet.com
Call Date: Oct 1990, Inner Temple
Qualifications: [LLB (Sheff)]

WILLIAMSON PATRICK LAWRENCE VICTOR

Old Colony House
6 South King Street, Manchester M2 6DQ,
Telephone: 0161 834 4364
Call Date: Nov 1989, Inner Temple
Qualifications: [BSc (Keele)]

WILLIAMSON STEPHEN WRIGHT QC (1981)

No. 6
6 Park Square, Leeds LS1 2LW,
Telephone: 0113 2459763
E-mail: chambers@no6.co.uk
2nd Floor, Francis Taylor Building
Temple, London EC4Y 7BY,
Telephone: 0171 353 9942/3157
Call Date: Feb 1964, Inner Temple
Recorder
Qualifications: [MA (Cantab)]

WILLIAMSON MISS TESSA LOUISE

Verulam Chambers
Peer House, 8-14 Verulam Street, Gray's
Inn, London WC1X 8LZ,
Telephone: 0171 813 2400
Call Date: Nov 1990, Inner Temple
Qualifications: [LLB (Hons)(Bris)]

WILLIS MISS ELIZABETH EDITH PEARL

Northampton Chambers
22 Albion Place, Northampton NN1 1UD,
Telephone: 01604 636271
Call Date: 1986, Inner Temple
Pupil Master
Qualifications: [LLB (Hull)]

WILLIS MISS RHYDDIAN ELIZABETH

2 Harcourt Buildings
1st Floor, Temple, London EC4Y 9DB,
Telephone: 020 7353 2112
Call Date: July 1984, Gray's Inn
Qualifications: [LLB (Nott'm)]

WILLITTS TIMOTHY LEONARD

Cobden House Chambers
19 Quay Street, Manchester M3 3HN,
Telephone: 0161 833 6000
E-mail: clerks@cobden.co.uk
Call Date: Nov 1989, Gray's Inn
Qualifications: [LLB (Hons) (B'Ham)]

WILLMOT MISS ELISABETH RACHEL

35 Essex Street
Temple, London WC2R 3AR,
Telephone: 0171 353 6381
E-mail: derek_jenkins@link.org
Call Date: Oct 1994, Lincoln's Inn
Qualifications: [BA (Hons), BCL]

WILLMOTT WILLIAM DEREK IAN

Chambers of Derek Willmott
8 Links Crescent, St Marys Bay, Romney
Marsh, Kent, TN29 0RS,
Telephone: 01303 87 3899
Call Date: Nov 1966, Inner Temple
Qualifications: [BA, Dip Ed]

WILLS MISS JANICE MARIE

St James's Chambers
68 Quay Street, Manchester M3 3EJ,
Telephone: 0161 834 7000
E-mail: clerks@stjameschambers.co.uk
Call Date: Oct 1991, Gray's Inn
Qualifications: [LLB]

WILLS-GOLDINGHAM MISS CLAIRE LOUISE MARGARET

Albion Chambers
Broad Street, Bristol BS1 1DR,
Telephone: 0117 9272144
Call Date: July 1988, Inner Temple
Qualifications: [LLB (B'ham)]

WILMOT-SMITH RICHARD JAMES CROSBIE QC (1994)

39 Essex Street
London WC2R 3AT,
Telephone: 0171 832 1111
E-mail: clerks@39essex.co.uk
Call Date: July 1978, Middle Temple
Qualifications: [AB (N Carolina)]

WILSHIRE SIMON VINCENT

1 Gray's Inn Square, Chambers of the Baroness Scotland of Asthal QC
1st Floor, London WC1R 5AG,
Telephone: 0171 405 3000
E-mail: clerks@onegrays.demon.co.uk
Call Date: Oct 1994, Gray's Inn
Qualifications: [BSc]

WILSON ADAM

No. 6
6 Park Square, Leeds LS1 2LW,
Telephone: 0113 2459763
E-mail: chambers@no6.co.uk
Call Date: Nov 1994, Inner Temple
Qualifications: [LLB (Lond)]

WILSON (ALAN) MARTIN QC (1982)

9 Bedford Row
London WC1R 4AZ,
Telephone: 0171 242 3555
E-mail: clerks@9br.co.uk
St Philip's Chambers
Fountain Court, Steelhouse Lane,
Birmingham B4 6DR,
Telephone: 0121 246 7000
E-mail: clerks@st-philips.co.uk
Call Date: 1963, Gray's Inn
Recorder
Qualifications: [LLB (Nottm)]

WILSON ALASDAIR JOHN

Fenners Chambers
3 Madingley Road, Cambridge CB3 0EE,
Telephone: 01223 368761
E-mail: clerks@fennerschambers.co.uk
Fenners Chambers
8-12 Priestgate, Peterborough PE1 1JA,
Telephone: 01733 562030
E-mail: clerks@fennerschambers.co.uk
Call Date: Nov 1988, Gray's Inn
Qualifications: [LLB (Wales)]

WILSON ALASTAIR JAMES DRYSDALE QC (1987)

19 Old Buildings
Lincoln's Inn, London WC2A 3UP,
Telephone: 0171 405 2001
E-mail: clerks@oldbuildingsip.com
Call Date: July 1968, Middle Temple
Recorder
Qualifications: [MA (Cantab)]

Fax: 0171 405 0001; DX: 397 London,
Chancery Lane;
Other comms: E-mail
clerks@oldbuildingsip.com; URL: http://
www.oldbuildingsip.com

Types of work: Competition, Copyright, EC
and competition law, Entertainment, Film,
cable, TV, Franchising, Information technology, Intellectual property, Patents, Telecommunications, Trademarks

Membership of foreign bars: NI, Republic of Ireland

Awards and memberships: Intellectual Property Bar Association; Chancery Bar Association; Chartered Institute of Patent Agents (Associate)

Other professional experience: Recorder

Languages spoken: French

Reported Cases: *Designers Guild v Russell Williams*, [1998] FSR 275, 1997. Textile copyright infringement.
PLG Research v Ardon International, [1995] RPC 287, 1995. Patent infringement and European law.
Lock International v Beswick, [1989] 3 All ER 373, 1989. Confidential information, ex-employees and Anton Pillers.
BT v One in a Million, [1999] FSR 1, 1998. Internet trademarks case.

WILSON ANDREW ROBERT

9 Woodhouse Square
Leeds LS3 1AD,
Telephone: 0113 2451986
E-mail: clerks@9woodhouse.co.uk
Call Date: Nov 1995, Gray's Inn
Qualifications: [BA]

WILSON CHRISTOPHER JOHN

9 Gough Square
London EC4A 3DE,
Telephone: 020 7832 0500
E-mail: clerks@9goughsq.co.uk
Call Date: July 1980, Gray's Inn
Pupil Master
Qualifications: [LLB (Hons)]

WILSON DAVID WILLIAM

East Anglian Chambers
57 London Street, Norwich NR2 1HL,
Telephone: 01603 617351
E-mail: norwich@ealaw.co.uk
East Anglian Chambers
Gresham House, 5 Museum Street,
Ipswich, Suffolk, IP1 1HQ,
Telephone: 01473 214481
E-mail: ipswich@ealaw.co.uk

East Anglian Chambers
52 North Hill, Colchester, Essex, CO1 1PY,
Telephone: 01206 572756
E-mail: colchester@ealaw.co.uk
Call Date: Oct 1996, Gray's Inn
Qualifications: [LLB (E.Anglia)]

WILSON MISS ELIZABETH HELEN

One Essex Court
1st Floor, Temple, London EC4Y 9AR,
Telephone: 0171 936 3030
E-mail: one.essex_court@virgin.net
Call Date: Nov 1989, Gray's Inn
Qualifications: [LLB (Hons)]

WILSON GEORGE RICHARD ROLAND

1 Gray's Inn Square
Ground Floor, London WC1R 5AA,
Telephone: 0171 405 8946/7/8
Call Date: Oct 1996, Middle Temple
Qualifications: [BSc (Hons)(Lond), CPE (City)]

WILSON GERALD SIMON JOHN

2nd Floor, Francis Taylor Building
Temple, London EC4Y 7BY,
Telephone: 0171 353 9942/3157
Call Date: Nov 1989, Gray's Inn
Qualifications: [BA [Oxon]]

WILSON GRAEME JOHN

3 Temple Gardens
3rd Floor, Temple, London EC4Y 9AU,
Telephone: 0171 583 0010
Call Date: Feb 1987, Inner Temple
Qualifications: [LLB (London)]

WILSON IAN ROBERT

3 Verulam Buildings
London WC1R 5NT,
Telephone: 0171 831 8441
E-mail: clerks@3verulam.co.uk
Call Date: Oct 1995, Middle Temple
Qualifications: [BA (Hons), LLM]

WILSON JAMES WILLIAM

Frederick Place Chambers
9 Frederick Place, Clifton, Bristol
BS8 1AS, Telephone: 0117 9738667
Call Date: Nov 1994, Middle Temple
Qualifications: [LLB (Hons), ACIS]

WILSON MISS JENNIFER MARY PENTREATH

Queens Square Chambers
56 Queens Square, Bristol BS1 4PR,
Telephone: 0117 921 1966
Call Date: July 1979, Gray's Inn
Pupil Master
Qualifications: [LLB (Hons)(LSE)]

WILSON JOHN ARMSTRONG

29 Bedford Row Chambers
London WC1R 4HE,
Telephone: 0171 831 2626
Call Date: July 1981, Inner Temple
Pupil Master
Qualifications: [MA (Cantab)]

WILSON JOHN BARKER

24a St John Street
Manchester M3 4DF,
Telephone: 0161 833 9628
Call Date: July 1988, Inner Temple
Qualifications: [LLB (Lancaster)]

WILSON JULIAN MARTIN

11 King's Bench Walk
Temple, London EC4Y 7EQ,
Telephone: 0171 632 8500/583 0610
E-mail: clerksroom@11kbw.com
Call Date: Oct 1997, Inner Temple
Qualifications: [BA (Oxon)]

WILSON LACHLAN BAYARD

2 King's Bench Walk Chambers
1st Floor, 2 King's Bench Walk, Temple,
London EC4Y 7DE,
Telephone: 020 7353 9276
E-mail: chambers@2kbw.co.uk
Call Date: Oct 1996, Inner Temple
Qualifications: [BA (Oxon), CPE
(Westminster)]

WILSON MS MARION JANET

5 Fountain Court
Steelhouse Lane, Birmingham B4 6DR,
Telephone: 0121 606 0500
E-mail:clerks@5fountaincourt.law.co.uk
Call Date: Oct 1991, Middle Temple
Qualifications: [LLB Hons (Lanc)]

WILSON MISS MARY ELIZABETH FRANCES

Pump Court Tax Chambers
16 Bedford Row, London WC1R 4EB,
Telephone: 0171 414 8080
Call Date: Oct 1995, Middle Temple
Qualifications: [BA (Hons)]

WILSON MYLES BRENNAND

White Friars Chambers
21 White Friars, Chester CH1 1NZ,
Telephone: 01244 323070
E-mail:whitefriarschambers@btinternet.com
Call Date: Oct 1993, Lincoln's Inn
Qualifications: [LLB (Hons)(Leeds)]

WILSON MS PAOLA ROSELLA AGATHA

55 Temple Chambers
Temple Avenue, London EC4Y 0HP,
Telephone: 0171 353 7400
Call Date: 1995, Inner Temple
Qualifications: [BA (Oxon), CPE (City)]

WILSON PAUL RICHARD

Broadway House Chambers
Broadway House, 9 Bank Street, Bradford,
West Yorkshire, BD1 1TW,
Telephone: 01274 722560
E-mail: clerks@broadwayhouse.co.uk
Broadway House Chambers
31 Park Square West, Leeds LS1 2PF,
Telephone: 0113 246 2600
Call Date: Nov 1989, Lincoln's Inn
Qualifications: [MA (Oxon)]

WILSON PETER JULIAN

Sovereign Chambers
25 Park Square, Leeds LS1 2PW,
Telephone: 0113 2451841/2/3
E-mail:sovereignchambers@btinternet.com
Call Date: Oct 1995, Middle Temple
Qualifications: [BA (Hons)]

WILSON RICHARD CARVER

Chambers of Michael Pert QC
36 Bedford Row, London WC1R 4JH,
Telephone: 0171 421 8000
E-mail: 36bedfordrow@link.org

Chambers of Michael Pert QC
24 Albion Place, Northampton NN1 1UD,
Telephone: 01604 602333
Chambers of Michael Pert QC
104 New Walk, Leicester LE1 7EA,
Telephone: 0116 249 2020
Call Date: Nov 1981, Lincoln's Inn
Pupil Master
Qualifications: [BA, LLM (Cantab)]

WILSON RICHARD COLIN

9 Stone Buildings
Lincoln's Inn, London WC2A 3NN,
Telephone: 0171 404 5055
E-mail: clerks@9stoneb.law.co.uk
Chancery House Chambers
7 Lisbon Square, Leeds LS1 4LY,
Telephone: 0113 244 6691
E-mail: chanceryhouse@btinternet.com
Call Date: 1996, Middle Temple
Qualifications: [LLB (Hons)(Sheff)]

WILSON SCOTT

St Paul's House
5th Floor, St Paul's House, 23 Park Square
South, Leeds LS1 2ND,
Telephone: 0113 2455866
E-mail: catherinegrimshaw@stpauls-
chambers.demon.co.uk
Call Date: Nov 1993, Lincoln's Inn
Qualifications: [LLB (Hons, Leic)]

WILSON STEPHEN MARK

4 Field Court
Gray's Inn, London WC1R 5EA,
Telephone: 0171 440 6900
E-mail: chambers@4fieldcourt.co.uk
Call Date: Oct 1990, Inner Temple
Qualifications: [LLB (UCL)]

WILSON-BARNES MISS LUCY EMMA

St James's Chambers
68 Quay Street, Manchester M3 3EJ,
Telephone: 0161 834 7000
E-mail: clerks@stjameschambers.co.uk
Call Date: July 1989, Inner Temple
Qualifications: [BA (Warw)]

WILSON-SMITH CHRISTOPHER QC (1986)

35 Essex Street
Temple, London WC2R 3AR,
Telephone: 0171 353 6381
E-mail: derek_jenkins@link.org
Albion Chambers
Broad Street, Bristol BS1 1DR,
Telephone: 0117 9272144
Call Date: Nov 1965, Gray's Inn
Recorder

WILTON SIMON DANIEL

4 Paper Buildings
Ground Floor, Temple, London
EC4Y 7EX, Telephone: 0171 353 3366/
583 7155
E-mail: clerks@4paperbuildings.com
Call Date: Oct 1993, Gray's Inn
Qualifications: [BA (Sussex)]

WILTSHIRE BERNARD

Horizon Chambers
95a Chancery Lane, London WC2A 1DT,
Telephone: 0171 242 2440
Call Date: Nov 1984, Gray's Inn
Pupil Master
Qualifications: [BA (York),MA (Lond), M.Phil
(Columbia)]

WINBERG STEPHEN ALEXANDER

2-4 Tudor Street
London EC4Y 0AA,
Telephone: 0171 797 7111
E-mail: clerks@rfqc.co.uk
Call Date: Nov 1974, Inner Temple
Qualifications: [BA]

WINCH JOHN

6 Ascot Road
Shotley Bridge, Consett, County Durham,
DH8 0NU, Telephone: 01207 507785
11 King's Bench Walk
1st Floor, Temple, London EC4Y 7EQ,
Telephone: 0171 353 3337
E-mail: fmuller11@aol.com
Call Date: July 1973, Gray's Inn
Qualifications: [LLM, FCIArb, FCIT,
Post.Grad Dip , (Employment Law)]

WINDSOR MISS EMILY MAY

Falcon Chambers
Falcon Court, London EC4Y 1AA,
Telephone: 0171 353 2484
E-mail: clerks@falcon-chambers.com
Call Date: Oct 1995, Gray's Inn
Qualifications: [BA, DSU (Paris)]

WING CHRISTOPHER JOHN

Eighteen Carlton Crescent
Southampton SO15 2XR,
Telephone: 01703 639001
Call Date: July 1985, Gray's Inn
Pupil Master
Qualifications: [BSc (Kent), BA]

WINGATE-SAUL GILES WINGATE QC (1983)

22 Old Buildings
Lincoln's Inn, London WC2A 3UJ,
Telephone: 0171 831 0222
Byrom Street Chambers
Byrom Street, Manchester M3 4PF,
Telephone: 0161 829 2100
E-mail: Byromst25@aol.com
Call Date: Nov 1967, Inner Temple
Recorder
Qualifications: [LLB]

WINGERT MISS RACHEL THOMAS

Gray's Inn Chambers
5th Floor, Gray's Inn, London WC1R 5JA,
Telephone: 0171 404 1111
Call Date: July 1980, Middle Temple
Pupil Master
Qualifications: [LLB (Lond), LLM (Lond)]

WINSHIP JULIAN ABDULLA

Furnival Chambers
32 Furnival Street, London EC4A 1JQ,
Telephone: 0171 405 3232
E-mail: clerks@furnivallaw.co.uk
Call Date: Oct 1995, Gray's Inn
Qualifications: [LLB]

WINTELER JOHN FRIDOLIN

No. 6
6 Park Square, Leeds LS1 2LW,
Telephone: 0113 2459763
E-mail: chambers@no6.co.uk
Call Date: July 1969, Inner Temple
Pupil Master
Qualifications: [MA (Cantab)]

WINTER IAN DAVID

Hollis Whiteman Chambers
3rd Floor, Queen Elizabeth Bldg, Temple,
London EC4Y 9BS,
Telephone: 020 7583 5766
E-mail:barristers@holliswhiteman.co.uk
Call Date: July 1988, Inner Temple
Qualifications: [LLB (Hons)]

WINTER MISS MELANIE JANE

1 Gray's Inn Square
Ground Floor, London WC1R 5AA,
Telephone: 0171 405 8946/7/8
Call Date: Oct 1996, Middle Temple
Qualifications: [LLB (Hons)(Wales)]

WINZER BENJAMIN CHARLES

Southernhay Chambers
33 Southernhay East, Exeter, Devon,
EX1 1NX, Telephone: 01392 255777
E-mail:southernhay.chambers@lineone.net
Call Date: May 1997, Middle Temple
Qualifications: [BA (Hons)(Bris)]

WISE IAN

Doughty Street Chambers
11 Doughty Street, London WC1N 2PG,
Telephone: 0171 404 1313
E-mail:enquiries@doughtystreet.co.uk
Call Date: Oct 1992, Gray's Inn
Qualifications: [BA]

WISE LESLIE MICHAEL

Mitre Court Chambers
3rd Floor, Temple, London EC4Y 7BP,
Telephone: 0171 353 9394
E-mail: mitrecourt.com
Call Date: Nov 1985, Middle Temple
Pupil Master
Qualifications: [F.C.A]

WISE OLIVER DACRES

Queen Elizabeth Building
2nd Floor, Temple, London EC4Y 9BS,
Telephone: 0171 797 7837
Call Date: July 1981, Lincoln's Inn
Pupil Master
Qualifications: [MA (Cantab)]

WISEMAN ADAM PHILIP PASTERNAK

18 Red Lion Court
(Off Fleet Street), London EC4A 3EB,
Telephone: 0171 520 6000
E-mail: chambers@18rlc.co.uk
Thornwood House
102 New London Road, Chelmsford,
Essex, CM2 0RG,
Telephone: 01245 280880
E-mail: chambers@18rlc.co.uk
Call Date: Nov 1994, Inner Temple
Qualifications: [MSc (Exon), CPE (Lond)]

WISHART JOHN DUCKWORTH SCOTT

Manchester House Chambers
18-22 Bridge Street, Manchester M3 3BZ,
Telephone: 0161 834 7007
Call Date: July 1974, Gray's Inn
Pupil Master
Qualifications: [HNC (Mechanical &,
Production Eng)]

WITCOMB HENRY JAMES

199 Strand
London WC2R 1DR,
Telephone: 0171 379 9779
E-mail: chambers@199strand.co.uk
Call Date: Apr 1989, Lincoln's Inn
Qualifications: [BA (Dunelm)]

WITHERS MISS MICHELLE JEAN MARY

Windsor Chambers
2 Penuel Lane, Pontypridd, South Wales,
CF37 4UF, Telephone: 01443 402067
E-mail: law@windsorchambers.co.uk
Call Date: Nov 1991, Inner Temple
Qualifications: [LLB (Wales)]

WITHINGTON ANGUS RICHARD

22 Old Buildings
Lincoln's Inn, London WC2A 3UJ,
Telephone: 0171 831 0222
Call Date: Nov 1995, Gray's Inn
Qualifications: [BA (Dunelm), Dip Law
(City)]

WOLANSKI ADAM MICHAEL VENANTIUS

5 Raymond Buildings
1st Floor, Gray's Inn, London WC1R 5BP,
Telephone: 0171 242 2902
E-mail: clerks@media-ent-law.co.uk
Call Date: Feb 1995, Lincoln's Inn
Qualifications: [MA Hons (Cantab)]

WOLCHOVER CHAIM DAVID HIRSCH

Ridgeway Chambers
6 The Ridgeway, Golders Green, London
NW11 8TB, Telephone: 0181 455 2939
E-mail: 101337.1722@compuserve.com
Virtual Chambers
(accepting briefs soon), London
Telephone: 07071 244 944
E-mail:enquiries@virtualchambers.org.uk
Lion Court
Chancery House, 53-64 Chancery Lane,
London WC2A 1SJ,
Telephone: 0171 404 6565
Call Date: July 1971, Gray's Inn

WOLFE DR DAVID FREDERICK HARRIS

4-5 Gray's Inn Square
Ground Floor, Gray's Inn, London
WC1R 5JP, Telephone: 0171 404 5252
E-mail:chambers@4-5graysinnsquare.co.uk
Call Date: Nov 1992, Middle Temple
Qualifications: [B.Sc M.Eng (Manch), Ph.D
(Cantab), Dip Law]

WOLFF MICHAEL EMANUEL

India Buildings Chambers
Water Street, Liverpool L2 0XG,
Telephone: 0151 243 6000
E-mail: clerks@chambers.u-net.com
Call Date: June 1964, Gray's Inn
Qualifications: [LLB]

WOLFSON DAVID

One Essex Court
Ground Floor, Temple, London
EC4Y 9AR, Telephone: 020 7583 2000
E-mail: clerks@oneessexcourt.co.uk
Call Date: Nov 1992, Inner Temple
Qualifications: [MA (Cantab)]

WOLKIND MICHAEL IAN QC (1999)

10 King's Bench Walk
1st Floor, Temple, London EC4Y 7EB,
Telephone: 0171 353 2501
Call Date: 1976, Middle Temple
Pupil Master

WOLLNER ERNEST JOHN

21 Lauderdale Tower
Barbican, London EC2Y 8BY,
Telephone: 0171 920 9308
E-mail: 106712.1033@compuserve.com
Call Date: Nov 1988, Inner Temple
Qualifications: [Dip Law]

WOLSTENHOLME ALAN JAMES

Lincoln House Chambers
5th Floor, Lincoln House, 1 Brazennose
Street, Manchester M2 5EL,
Telephone: 0161 832 5701
E-mail: info@lincolnhse.co.uk
Call Date: July 1989, Lincoln's Inn
Qualifications: [LLB (Leeds)]

WOLTON HARRY QC (1982)

2-3 Gray's Inn Square
Gray's Inn, London WC1R 5JH,
Telephone: 0171 242 4986
E-mail:chambers@2-3graysinnsquare.co.uk
Call Date: July 1969, Gray's Inn
Recorder

WONG MISS NATASHA PUI-WAI

1 Middle Temple Lane
Temple, London EC4Y 1LT,
Telephone: 0171 583 0659 (12 Lines)
E-mail: chambers@1mtl.co.uk
Call Date: Nov 1993, Middle Temple
Qualifications: [BSc (Hons)(Kingston), CPE
(Middx)]

WONG RENE YEE LOCK

2 King's Bench Walk Chambers
1st Floor, 2 King's Bench Walk, Temple,
London EC4Y 7DE,
Telephone: 020 7353 9276
E-mail: chambers@2kbw.co.uk
Call Date: Nov 1973, Inner Temple
Pupil Master

WONNACOTT MARK ANDREW

199 Strand
London WC2R 1DR,
Telephone: 0171 379 9779
E-mail: chambers@199strand.co.uk
Call Date: July 1989, Lincoln's Inn
Pupil Master
Qualifications: [LLB (Lond)]

WOOD MISS CATHERINE

4 Paper Buildings
1st Floor, Temple, London EC4Y 7EX,
Telephone: 0171 583 0816/353 1131
E-mail: clerks@4paperbuildings.co.uk
Call Date: July 1985, Middle Temple
Qualifications: [LLB (Lond)]

WOOD CHRISTOPHER MARK BRUCE

1 Mitre Court Buildings
Temple, London EC4Y 7BS,
Telephone: 0171 797 7070
E-mail: clerks@1mcb.com
Call Date: Feb 1986, Middle Temple
Pupil Master
Qualifications: [MA (Oxon), DESU
Aix-Marseille, III]

WOOD DEREK ALEXANDER QC (1978)

Falcon Chambers
Falcon Court, London EC4Y 1AA,
Telephone: 0171 353 2484
E-mail: clerks@falcon-chambers.com
Call Date: Feb 1964, Middle Temple
Recorder
Qualifications: [MA, BCL (Oxon)]

WOOD GRAEME CRESSWELL

Assize Court Chambers
14 Small Street, Bristol BS1 1DE,
Telephone: 0117 9264587
E-mail:chambers@assize-court-chambers.co.uk

New Bailey Chambers
10 Lawson Street, Preston PR1 2QT,
Telephone: 01772 258087
9 Stone Buildings
Lincoln's Inn, London WC2A 3NN,
Telephone: 0171 404 5055
E-mail: clerks@9stoneb.law.co.uk
Call Date: July 1968, Middle Temple
Pupil Master
Qualifications: [MA, LLM (Cantab)]

WOOD GRAHAM NASH

India Buildings Chambers
Water Street, Liverpool L2 0XG,
Telephone: 0151 243 6000
E-mail: clerks@chambers.u-net.com
Call Date: July 1979, Middle Temple
Pupil Master, Assistant Recorder
Qualifications: [LLB (Leeds)]

WOOD GUY NICHOLAS MARSHALL

Hollis Whiteman Chambers
3rd Floor, Queen Elizabeth Bldg, Temple,
London EC4Y 9BS,
Telephone: 020 7583 5766
E-mail:barristers@holliswhiteman.co.uk
Call Date: Nov 1980, Middle Temple
Pupil Master, Assistant Recorder
Qualifications: [MA (Oxon), LLM, (Indianna)]

WOOD IAN ROBERT

8 King Street Chambers
8 King Street, Manchester M2 6AQ,
Telephone: 0161 834 9560
E-mail: eightking@aol.com
Call Date: Oct 1990, Middle Temple
Qualifications: [BA (Manch)]

WOOD JAMES ALEXANDER DOUGLAS QC (1999)

Doughty Street Chambers
11 Doughty Street, London WC1N 2PG,
Telephone: 0171 404 1313
E-mail:enquiries@doughtystreet.co.uk
Call Date: 1975, Middle Temple
Pupil Master, Assistant Recorder
Qualifications: [LLB]

WOOD MISS JOANNA LINDA IRIS

Angel Chambers
94 Walter Road, Swansea, West
Glamorgan, SA1 5QA,
Telephone: 01792 464623/464648
E-mail: lynne@angelchambers.co.uk
Call Date: Nov 1989, Inner Temple
Pupil Master
Qualifications: [LLB]

WOOD MISS JOANNA RACHEL

9 King's Bench Walk
Ground Floor, Temple, London
EC4Y 7DX, Telephone: 0171 353 7202/
3909 E-mail: 9kbw@compuserve.com
Call Date: 1996, Inner Temple
Qualifications: [LLB (Nott'm)]

WOOD MS LANA CLAIRE

9 Stone Buildings
Lincoln's Inn, London WC2A 3NN,
Telephone: 0171 404 5055
E-mail: clerks@9stoneb.law.co.uk
Call Date: Oct 1993, Gray's Inn
Qualifications: [BA]

WOOD MARTIN

1 Serjeants' Inn
4th Floor, Temple, London EC4Y 1NH,
Telephone: 0171 583 1355
E-mail: clerks@serjeants-inn.co.uk
Call Date: July 1972, Inner Temple
Pupil Master
Qualifications: [LLB (Lond)]

WOOD MARTIN JOHN

Broadway House Chambers
Broadway House, 9 Bank Street, Bradford,
West Yorkshire, BD1 1TW,
Telephone: 01274 722560
E-mail: clerks@broadwayhouse.co.uk
Broadway House Chambers
31 Park Square West, Leeds LS1 2PF,
Telephone: 0113 246 2600
Call Date: July 1973, Inner Temple
Pupil Master
Qualifications: [MA (Cantab)]

WOOD MICHAEL JOHN

Exchange Chambers
Pearl Assurance House, Derby Square,
Liverpool L2 9XX,
Telephone: 0151 236 7747
E-mail:exchangechambers@btinternet.com
Call Date: Nov 1989, Lincoln's Inn
Qualifications: [BA (Sheff), DipIA (Bradford),
LLB (Hons I)(Sheff)]

WOOD MICHAEL MURE QC (1999)

23 Essex Street
London WC2R 3AS,
Telephone: 0171 413 0353/836 8366
E-mail:clerks@essexstreet23.demon.co.uk
Call Date: 1976, Middle Temple
Pupil Master, Recorder
Qualifications: [LLB]

WOOD MISS NATASHA

St Paul's House
5th Floor, St Paul's House, 23 Park Square
South, Leeds LS1 2ND,
Telephone: 0113 2455866
E-mail: catherinegrimshaw@stpauls-
chambers.demon.co.uk
Call Date: 1997, Lincoln's Inn
Qualifications: [BA (Hons)(Lancs), LLM
(Leeds)]

WOOD NICHOLAS ANDREW

5 Paper Buildings
Ground Floor, Temple, London
EC4Y 7HB, Telephone: 0171 583 9275/
583 4555 E-mail: 5paper@link.org
Call Date: July 1970, Inner Temple
Pupil Master, Recorder

WOOD MRS PENELOPE CAROLINE RUTH

7 Stone Buildings (also at 11 Bolt Court)
1st Floor, Lincoln's Inn, London
WC2A 3SZ, Telephone: 0171 242 0961
E-mail:larthur@7stonebuildings.law.co.uk
11 Bolt Court (also at 7 Stone Buildings – 1st Floor)
London EC4A 3DQ,
Telephone: 0171 353 2300
E-mail: boltct11@aol.com

Redhill Chambers
Seloduct House, 30 Station Road, Redhill,
Surrey, RH1 1NF,
Telephone: 01737 780781
Call Date: 1999, Lincoln's Inn
Qualifications: [LLB (Hons)(Cantab)]

WOOD PERCY

St James's Chambers
68 Quay Street, Manchester M3 3EJ,
Telephone: 0161 834 7000
E-mail: clerks@stjameschambers.co.uk
Call Date: Feb 1961, Gray's Inn
Qualifications: [MA (Cantab)]

WOOD RICHARD GILLIES

20 Essex Street
London WC2R 3AL,
Telephone: 0171 583 9294
E-mail: clerks@20essexst.com
Cathedral Chambers (Jan Wood Independent Barristers' Clerk)
1 Maple Road, Exeter, Devon, EX4 1BN,
Telephone: 01392 210900
E-mail:cathedral.chambers@eclipse.co.uk
Call Date: July 1975, Lincoln's Inn
Qualifications: [MA (Cantab), , BCL (Oxon)]

WOOD RICHARD MICHAEL

Sackville Chambers
Sackville Place, 44-48 Magdalen Street,
Norwich NR3 1JU,
Telephone: 01603 613516/616221
Call Date: Nov 1995, Gray's Inn
Qualifications: [BA]

WOOD RODERIC LIONEL JAMES QC (1993)

One King's Bench Walk
1st Floor, Temple, London EC4Y 7DB,
Telephone: 0171 936 1500
E-mail: ddear@1kbw.co.uk
Call Date: July 1974, Middle Temple
Assistant Recorder
Qualifications: [MA (Oxon)]

WOOD SIMON EDWARD

Plowden Buildings
2nd Floor, 2 Plowden Buildings, Middle
Temple Lane, London EC4Y 9BU,
Telephone: 0171 583 0808
E-mail: bar@plowdenbuildings.co.uk
Call Date: Nov 1981, Middle Temple
Pupil Master
Qualifications: [LLB]

WOOD SIMON RICHARD HENRY

Lamb Chambers
Lamb Building, Temple, London
EC4Y 7AS, Telephone: 020 7797 8300
E-mail: lambchambers@link.org
Call Date: July 1987, Middle Temple
Qualifications: [BA (Bristol), Dip Law (City)]

WOOD STEPHEN

Broadway House Chambers
Broadway House, 9 Bank Street, Bradford,
West Yorkshire, BD1 1TW,
Telephone: 01274 722560
E-mail: clerks@broadwayhouse.co.uk
Broadway House Chambers
31 Park Square West, Leeds LS1 2PF,
Telephone: 0113 246 2600
Call Date: Nov 1991, Inner Temple
Qualifications: [LLB (Hons) (Hudds)]

WOOD WILLIAM JAMES QC (1998)

Brick Court Chambers
7-8 Essex Street, London WC2R 3LD,
Telephone: 0171 379 3550
E-mail: [surname]@brickcourt.co.uk
Call Date: Nov 1980, Middle Temple
Qualifications: [BA, BCL (Oxon), LLM]

WOOD WILLIAM ROWLEY QC (1997)

5 Fountain Court
Steelhouse Lane, Birmingham B4 6DR,
Telephone: 0121 606 0500
E-mail:clerks@5fountaincourt.law.co.uk
Call Date: July 1970, Gray's Inn
Recorder
Qualifications: [BA (Oxon)]

WOODALL PETER

Goldsmith Chambers
Ground Floor, Goldsmith Building,
Temple, London EC4Y 7BL,
Telephone: 0171 353 6802/3/4/5
E-mail:clerks@goldsmithchambers.law.co.uk
Call Date: July 1983, Middle Temple
Pupil Master
Qualifications: [LLB (Leeds)]

WOODBRIDGE JULIAN GUY

One King's Bench Walk
1st Floor, Temple, London EC4Y 7DB,
Telephone: 0171 936 1500
E-mail: ddear@1kbw.co.uk
Call Date: Nov 1981, Middle Temple
Pupil Master
Qualifications: [LLB (Warwick)]

WOODCOCK JONATHAN

10 King's Bench Walk
1st Floor, Temple, London EC4Y 7EB,
Telephone: 0171 353 2501
Call Date: Nov 1981, Middle Temple
Pupil Master
Qualifications: [LLB, LLM (Lond)]

WOODCOCK ROBERT ANDREW PHILIP

New Court Chambers
3 Broad Chare, Newcastle upon Tyne
NE1 3DQ, Telephone: 0191 232 1980
Call Date: Feb 1978, Inner Temple
Pupil Master
Qualifications: [BA]

WOODCRAFT MISS ELIZABETH JANE

14 Tooks Court
Cursitor St, London EC4A 1LB,
Telephone: 0171 405 8828
E-mail: clerks@tooks.law.co.uk
Call Date: July 1980, Middle Temple
Pupil Master
Qualifications: [BA (Hons)(B'ham)]

WOODHALL GARY

Chambers of John Hand QC
9 St John Street, Manchester M3 4DN,
Telephone: 0161 955 9000
E-mail: ninesjs@gconnect.com
Call Date: Oct 1997, Gray's Inn
Qualifications: [BA]

WOODHOUSE CHARLES PHILIP

Bridewell Chambers
2 Bridewell Place, London EC4V 6AP,
Telephone: 020 7797 8800
E-mail:HughesGage@bridewell.law.co.uk
Call Date: 1997, Middle Temple
Qualifications: [LLB (Hons)(Lond)]

WOODLEY LEONARD GASTON QC (1988)

8 King's Bench Walk
2nd Floor, Temple, London EC4Y 7DU,
Telephone: 0171 797 8888
8 King's Bench Walk North
1 Park Square East, Leeds LS1 2NE,
Telephone: 0113 2439797
Call Date: July 1963, Inner Temple
Recorder
Qualifications: [Dip Int Aff (Lond)]

WOODLEY MISS SONIA QC (1996)

9-12 Bell Yard
London WC2A 2LF,
Telephone: 0171 400 1800
E-mail: clerks@bellyard.co.uk
Call Date: July 1968, Gray's Inn
Recorder

WOODRUFF MISS SARAH

Chambers of Geoffrey Hawker
46/48 Essex Street, London WC2R 3GH,
Telephone: 0171 583 8899
Call Date: Nov 1996, Middle Temple
Qualifications: [LLB (Hons)(Brunel)]

WOODS JONATHAN

Two Crown Office Row
Ground Floor, Temple, London
EC4Y 7HJ, Telephone: 020 7797 8100
E-mail: mail@2cor.co.uk, or to individual
barristers at: [barrister's
surname]@2cor.co.uk
Call Date: July 1965, Middle Temple
Recorder
Qualifications: [BA (Oxon)]

WOODS MISS RACHAEL HELEN

Manchester House Chambers
18-22 Bridge Street, Manchester M3 3BZ,
Telephone: 0161 834 7007
Call Date: Oct 1992, Gray's Inn
Qualifications: [LLB (Hons)]

WOODS TERENCE MCCARTAN

2 Gray's Inn Square Chambers
2nd Floor, Gray's Inn, London WC1R 5AA,
Telephone: 020 7242 0328
E-mail: clerks@2gis.co.uk
Call Date: Nov 1989, Middle Temple
Qualifications: [LLB Hons [Lond]]

WOODWARD MISS ALISON JANE

Cobden House Chambers
19 Quay Street, Manchester M3 3HN,
Telephone: 0161 833 6000
E-mail: clerks@cobden.co.uk
Call Date: Oct 1992, Gray's Inn
Qualifications: [LL.B (Sheff)]

WOODWARD MISS JOANNE CLAIRE

Cobden House Chambers
19 Quay Street, Manchester M3 3HN,
Telephone: 0161 833 6000
E-mail: clerks@cobden.co.uk
Call Date: Nov 1989, Gray's Inn
Qualifications: [LLB (Hons)]

WOODWARD JOHN EDWARD

15 Winckley Square
Preston PR1 3JJ,
Telephone: 01772 252828
E-mail:clerks@winckleysq.demon.co.uk
Call Date: Nov 1984, Lincoln's Inn
Qualifications: [LLB]

WOODWARD NICHOLAS FREDERICK

White Friars Chambers
21 White Friars, Chester CH1 1NZ,
Telephone: 01244 323070
E-mail:whitefriarschambers@btinternet.com
Call Date: Nov 1975, Lincoln's Inn
Pupil Master, Assistant Recorder
Qualifications: [BA]

WOODWARD WILLIAM CHARLES QC (1985)

Ropewalk Chambers
24 The Ropewalk, Nottingham NG1 5EF,
Telephone: 0115 9472581
E-mail: administration@ropewalk co.uk
Call Date: Feb 1964, Inner Temple
Recorder
Qualifications: [BA (Oxon)]

WOODWARD-CARLTON DAMIAN

22 Old Buildings
Lincoln's Inn, London WC2A 3UJ,
Telephone: 0171 831 0222
Call Date: Oct 1995, Inner Temple
Qualifications: [BSc, MA (Durham), CPE (City)]

WOODWARK MS JANE ELIZABETH

Milburn House Chambers
'A' Floor, Milburn House, Dean Street,
Newcastle upon Tyne NE1 1LE,
Telephone: 0191 230 5511
E-mail:milburnhousechambers@btinternet.com
Call Date: Nov 1995, Middle Temple
Qualifications: [BA (Hons), MSc]

WOOLF ELIOT CHARLES ANTHONY

199 Strand
London WC2R 1DR,
Telephone: 0171 379 9779
E-mail: chambers@199strand.co.uk
Call Date: Oct 1993, Inner Temple
Qualifications: [BA, CPE]

WOOLF THE HON JEREMY RICHARD GEORGE

Pump Court Tax Chambers
16 Bedford Row, London WC1R 4EB,
Telephone: 0171 414 8080
Park Court Chambers
16 Park Place, Leeds LS1 2SJ,
Telephone: 0113 2433277
Call Date: July 1986, Inner Temple
Pupil Master
Qualifications: [BA (Sussex), LLM (Cantab)]

WOOLF STEVEN JEREMY

Hardwicke Building
New Square, Lincoln's Inn, London
WC2A 3SB, Telephone: 020 7242 2523
E-mail: clerks@hardwicke.co.uk
Call Date: July 1989, Inner Temple
Pupil Master
Qualifications: [LLB]

WOOLFALL RICHARD IAN

Wilberforce Chambers
7 Bishop Lane, Hull, East Yorkshire,
HU1 1PA, Telephone: 01482 323264
E-mail: clerks@hullbar.demon.co.uk
Call Date: Nov 1992, Middle Temple
Qualifications: [LLB (Hons)]

WOOLFENDEN IVAN PETER

Adrian Lyon's Chambers
14 Castle Street, Liverpool L2 0NE,
Telephone: 0151 236 4421/8240
E-mail: chambers14@aol.com
Call Date: July 1985, Middle Temple
Qualifications: [BA(Oxon)]

WOOLGAR DERMOT GERVASE BECKET

3 Paper Buildings
Temple, London EC4Y 7EU,
Telephone: 020 7583 8055
E-mail: London@3paper.com
3 Paper Buildings (Oxford)
1 Alfred Street, High Street, Oxford
OX1 4EH, Telephone: 01865 793736
E-mail: oxford@3paper.com
3 Paper Buildings (Bournemouth)
20 Lorne Park Road, Bournemouth,
Dorset, BH1 1JN,
Telephone: 01202 292102
E-mail: Bournemouth@3paper.com
3 Paper Buildings (Winchester)
4 St Peter Street, Winchester SO23 8BW,
Telephone: 01962 868884
E-mail: winchester@3paper.com
Call Date: July 1988, Inner Temple
Pupil Master
Qualifications: [LLB (Manch)]

WOOLHOUSE OLIVER DUNCAN CAMPBELL

Victoria Chambers
3rd Floor, 177 Corporation Street,
Birmingham B4 6RG,
Telephone: 0121 236 9900
E-mail: viccham@aol.com
Call Date: 1996, Inner Temple
Qualifications: [LLB (Leics)]

D

WOOLLEY DAVID RORIE QC (1980)

1 Serjeants' Inn
4th Floor, Temple, London EC4Y 1NH,
Telephone: 0171 583 1355
E-mail: clerks@serjeants-inn.co.uk
Call Date: July 1962, Middle Temple
Qualifications: [MA (Cantab)]

WOOLLS MISS TANYA JANE

Furnival Chambers
32 Furnival Street, London EC4A 1JQ,
Telephone: 0171 405 3232
E-mail: clerks@furnivallaw.co.uk
Call Date: Feb 1991, Middle Temple
Qualifications: [LLB (Hons)]

WOOLMAN ANDREW PAUL LANDER

Chambers of Andrew Campbell QC
10 Park Square, Leeds LS1 2LH,
Telephone: 0113 2455438
E-mail: clerks@10pksq.co.uk
Call Date: Nov 1973, Inner Temple
Pupil Master, Recorder
Qualifications: [MA (Cantab)]

WOOLRICH MISS SARAH

Trinity Chambers
9-12 Trinity Chare, Quayside, Newcastle
upon Tyne NE1 3DF,
Telephone: 0191 232 1927
E-mail: info@trinitychambers.co.uk
Call Date: Nov 1994, Middle Temple
Qualifications: [LLB]

WOOSEY MISS ELIZABETH JANE

19 Castle Street Chambers
Liverpool L2 4SX,
Telephone: 0151 236 9402
E-mail: DBrei16454@aol.com
Call Date: July 1993, Lincoln's Inn
Qualifications: [LLB (Hons)]

WOOTLIFF MISS BARBARA JACQUELINE

37 Park Square Chambers
37 Park Square, Leeds LS1 2NY,
Telephone: 0113 2439422
E-mail: chambers@no37.co.uk
Call Date: May 1956, Middle Temple
Pupil Master

WOOTTON MISS VICTORIA HELEN

2-4 Tudor Street
London EC4Y 0AA,
Telephone: 0171 797 7111
E-mail: clerks@rfqc.co.uk
Call Date: Oct 1995, Gray's Inn
Qualifications: [BA (Hons)]

WORDSWORTH MRS PHILIPPA LINDSEY

Chambers of Andrew Campbell QC
10 Park Square, Leeds LS1 2LH,
Telephone: 0113 2455438
E-mail: clerks@10pksq.co.uk
Call Date: Oct 1995, Gray's Inn
Qualifications: [LLB (Manch)]

WORDSWORTH SAMUEL SHERRATT

Essex Court Chambers
24 Lincoln's Inn Fields, London
WC2A 3ED, Telephone: 0171 813 8000
E-mail:clerksroom@essexcourt-chambers.co.uk
Call Date: Nov 1997, Lincoln's Inn
Qualifications: [BA (Hons)]

WORMALD RICHARD

3 Raymond Buildings
Gray's Inn, London WC1R 5BH,
Telephone: 020 7831 3833
E-mail:chambers@threeraymond.demon.co.uk
Call Date: Oct 1993, Gray's Inn
Qualifications: [BA (York)]

WORMINGTON TIMOTHY MICHAEL

Fountain Court
Temple, London EC4Y 9DH,
Telephone: 0171 583 3335
E-mail: chambers@fountaincourt.co.uk
Call Date: Nov 1977, Middle Temple
Qualifications: [BA, BCL (Oxon)]

WORRALL MISS ANNA MAUREEN QC (1989)

Cloisters
1 Pump Court, Temple, London
EC4Y 7AA, Telephone: 0171 827 4000
E-mail: clerks@cloisters.com

8 King Street Chambers
8 King Street, Manchester M2 6AQ,
Telephone: 0161 834 9560
E-mail: eightking@aol.com
Call Date: Nov 1959, Middle Temple
Recorder
Qualifications: [LLB]

WORRALL JOHN RAYMOND GUY

Chambers of Andrew Campbell QC
10 Park Square, Leeds LS1 2LH,
Telephone: 0113 2455438
E-mail: clerks@10pksq.co.uk
Call Date: July 1984, Gray's Inn
Qualifications: [BA (Hons) LLB (Hons)]

WORRALL MISS SHIRLEY VERA FRANCES

8 King Street Chambers
8 King Street, Manchester M2 6AQ,
Telephone: 0161 834 9560
E-mail: eightking@aol.com
Call Date: Nov 1987, Gray's Inn
Qualifications: [LLB (Hons)]

WORSLEY MARK INDRA

Guildhall Chambers
22-26 Broad Street, Bristol BS1 2HG,
Telephone: 0117 9273366
E-mail:civil.clerks@guildhallchambers.co.uk and
criminal.clerks@guildhallchambers.co.uk
Call Date: 1994, Inner Temple
Qualifications: [LLB (Newc)]

WORSLEY MICHAEL DOMINIC LAURENCE QC (1985)

6 King's Bench Walk
Ground Floor, Temple, London
EC4Y 7DR, Telephone: 0171 583 0410
E-mail: worsley@6kbw.freeserve.co.uk
Call Date: June 1955, Inner Temple

WORSLEY PAUL FREDERICK QC (1990)

Park Court Chambers
16 Park Place, Leeds LS1 2SJ,
Telephone: 0113 2433277
1 Hare Court
Ground Floor, Temple, London
EC4Y 7BE, Telephone: 0171 353 3982/
5324
Call Date: July 1970, Middle Temple

Recorder
Qualifications: [MA (Oxon)]

WORSTER DAVID JAMES STEWART

St Philip's Chambers
Fountain Court, Steelhouse Lane,
Birmingham B4 6DR,
Telephone: 0121 246 7000
E-mail: clerks@st-philips.co.uk
Call Date: Nov 1980, Lincoln's Inn
Pupil Master
Qualifications: [MA (Cantab)]

WORTHINGTON STEPHEN

12 King's Bench Walk
Temple, London EC4Y 7EL,
Telephone: 0171 583 0811
E-mail: chambers@12kbw.co.uk
Call Date: Nov 1976, Gray's Inn
Pupil Master
Qualifications: [MA (Cantab)]

WRAY NIGEL DUNCAN ANDREW

12 Old Square
1st Floor, Lincoln's Inn, London
WC2A 3TX, Telephone: 0171 404 0875
Counsels' Chambers
2nd Floor, 10-11 Gray's Inn Square,
London WC1R 5JD,
Telephone: 0171 405 2576
E-mail:clerks@10-11graysinnsquare.co.uk
Call Date: 1993, Gray's Inn
Qualifications: [MA (St Andrews), Dip Law
(City)]

WRAY NIGEL HUBERT

Wilberforce Chambers
7 Bishop Lane, Hull, East Yorkshire,
HU1 1PA, Telephone: 01482 323264
E-mail: clerks@hullbar.demon.co.uk
Call Date: July 1986, Middle Temple
Qualifications: [LLB(Lond)]

WRENN MISS HELEN MARGARET

Martins Building
2nd Floor, No 4 Water Street, Liverpool
L2 3SP, Telephone: 0151 236 5818/4919
Call Date: Nov 1994, Inner Temple
Qualifications: [BA (Leeds), CPE
(Wolverhampton)]

WRIGHT ALASTAIR DAVID

28 St John Street
Manchester M3 4DJ,
Telephone: 0161 834 8418
E-mail: clerk@28stjohnst.co.uk
Call Date: Oct 1991, Lincoln's Inn
Qualifications: [MA (Oxon), Dip Law]

WRIGHT MISS CAROLINE JANE

Albion Chambers
Broad Street, Bristol BS1 1DR,
Telephone: 0117 9272144
Call Date: July 1983, Gray's Inn
Pupil Master
Qualifications: [BSc (York) Dip Law]

WRIGHT MISS CLARE ELIZABETH

6 Pump Court
1st Floor, Temple, London EC4Y 7AR,
Telephone: 0171 797 8400
E-mail: clerks@6pumpcourt.co.uk
6-8 Mill Street
Maidstone, Kent, ME15 6XH,
Telephone: 01622 688094
E-mail: annexe@6pumpcourt.co.uk
Call Date: Oct 1995, Inner Temple
Qualifications: [LLB (Bris)]

WRIGHT COLIN JOHN

4 Field Court
Gray's Inn, London WC1R 5EA,
Telephone: 0171 440 6900
E-mail: chambers@4fieldcourt.co.uk
Call Date: July 1987, Middle Temple
Qualifications: [LLB (Leics)]

WRIGHT DERMOT JOHN FETHERSTONHAUGH

3 Temple Gardens
3rd Floor, Temple, London EC4Y 9AU,
Telephone: 0171 583 0010
Call Date: July 1967, Inner Temple
Pupil Master
Qualifications: [MA (Cantab)]

WRIGHT FREDERICK GEORGE IAN

3 Serjeants' Inn
London EC4Y 1BQ,
Telephone: 0171 353 5537
E-mail: clerks@3serjeantsinn.com
Call Date: July 1989, Inner Temple
Qualifications: [BSc(Hons), MSc, DIC,
Chartered Engineer, MICE, MIStruct E,
Dip. Law]

WRIGHT IAN

5 Paper Buildings
Ground Floor, Temple, London
EC4Y 7HB, Telephone: 0171 583 9275/
583 4555 E-mail: 5paper@link.org
Call Date: Nov 1983, Middle Temple
Pupil Master
Qualifications: [BSc (Dundee) LLB, (Leic)]

WRIGHT MR. IAN BERNARD

Iscoed Chambers
86 St Helen's Road, Swansea, West
Glamorgan, SA1 4BQ,
Telephone: 01792 652988/9/330
Call Date: Nov 1994, Middle Temple
Qualifications: [LLB (Hons) (Wales)]

WRIGHT MISS JACQUELINE LESLEY

Holborn Chambers
6 Gate Street, Lincoln's Inn Fields, London
WC2A 3HP, Telephone: 0171 242 6060
Call Date: Nov 1975, Gray's Inn
Pupil Master

WRIGHT JEREMY JOHN

2 King's Bench Walk
Ground Floor, Temple, London
EC4Y 7DE, Telephone: 0171 353 1746
E-mail: 2kbw@atlas.co.uk
King's Bench Chambers
115 North Hill, Plymouth PL4 8JY,
Telephone: 01752 221551
Call Date: July 1970, Inner Temple
Pupil Master, Recorder
Qualifications: [BA (Oxon)]

WRIGHT JEREMY PAUL

5 Fountain Court
Steelhouse Lane, Birmingham B4 6DR,
Telephone: 0121 606 0500
E-mail:clerks@5fountaincourt.law.co.uk
Call Date: Oct 1996, Inner Temple
Qualifications: [LLB (Exon)]

WRIGHT NORMAN ALFRED

Oriel Chambers
14 Water Street, Liverpool L2 8TD,
Telephone: 0151 236 7191/236 4321
E-mail: clerks@oriel-chambers.co.uk
Call Date: Nov 1974, Gray's Inn
Pupil Master, Recorder
Qualifications: [LLB (L'pool)]

WRIGHT PAUL WAYNE

Brick Court Chambers
7-8 Essex Street, London WC2R 3LD,
Telephone: 0171 379 3550
E-mail: [surname]@brickcourt.co.uk
Call Date: Nov 1990, Inner Temple
Qualifications: [LLB (So'ton)]

WRIGHT PETER DUNCAN QC (1999)

Lincoln House Chambers
5th Floor, Lincoln House, 1 Brazennose
Street, Manchester M2 5EL,
Telephone: 0161 832 5701
E-mail: info@lincolnhse.co.uk
Call Date: 1981, Inner Temple
Pupil Master
Qualifications: [LLB (Hull)]

WRIGHT PETER MALCOLM

Queen Elizabeth Building
2nd Floor, Temple, London EC4Y 9BS,
Telephone: 0171 797 7837
Call Date: July 1974, Middle Temple
Pupil Master, Assistant Recorder
Qualifications: [MA (Cantab)]

WRIGHT RICHARD JAMES

No. 6
6 Park Square, Leeds LS1 2LW,
Telephone: 0113 2459763
E-mail: chambers@no6.co.uk
Call Date: 1998, Middle Temple
Qualifications: [LLB (Hons)(Leeds)]

WRIGHT MS SADIE

Goldsmith Building
1st Floor, Temple, London EC4Y 7BL,
Telephone: 0171 353 7881
E-mail:clerks@goldsmith-building.law.co.uk
Call Date: Oct 1994, Lincoln's Inn
Qualifications: [BA (Hons)]

WRIGHT MISS SARAH CAROLYN

Paradise Chambers
26 Paradise Square, Sheffield S1 2DE,
Telephone: 0114 2738951
E-mail: timbooth@paradise-sq.co.uk
Call Date: Nov 1984, Gray's Inn
Qualifications: [BA]

WRIGHT STEWART MACDONALD

Call Date: Oct 1993, Gray's Inn
Qualifications: [MA (Glasgow)]

WRIGHT TREVOR

Bell Yard Chambers
116/118 Chancery Lane, London
WC2A 1PP, Telephone: 0171 306 9292
Call Date: Nov 1992, Middle Temple
Qualifications: [LL.B (Hons, Lond)]

WRIGHT MRS YASMIN TAJDIN

New Bailey Chambers
10 Lawson Street, Preston PR1 2QT,
Telephone: 01772 258087
Call Date: Nov 1990, Inner Temple
Qualifications: [LLB]

WULWIK PETER DAVID

Devereux Chambers
Devereux Court, London WC2R 3JJ,
Telephone: 0171 353 7534
E-mail: mailbox@devchambers.co.uk
Call Date: July 1972, Gray's Inn
Pupil Master, Assistant Recorder

WURTZEL DAVID IRA

Dr Johnson's Chambers
Two Dr Johnson's Buildings, Temple,
London EC4Y 7AY,
Telephone: 0171 353 4716
E-mail: clerks@2djb.freeserve.co.uk
Call Date: Nov 1974, Middle Temple
Pupil Master
Qualifications: [MA (Cantab), MA (Lond)]

WYAND ROGER NICHOLAS LEWES QC (1997)

One Raymond Buildings
Gray's Inn, London WC1R 5BH,
Telephone: 0171 430 1234
E-mail: chambers@ipbar1rb.com;
clerks@ipbar1rb.com
Call Date: May 1973, Middle Temple
Assistant Recorder
Qualifications: [MA (Cantab)]

WYATT DERRICK ARTHUR QC (1993)

Brick Court Chambers
7-8 Essex Street, London WC2R 3LD,
Telephone: 0171 379 3550
E-mail: [surname]@brickcourt.co.uk
Call Date: July 1972, Lincoln's Inn
Qualifications: [MA, LLB (Cantab), JD
(Chicago)]

WYATT GUY PETER JAMES

Earl Street Chambers
47 Earl Street, Maidstone, Kent,
ME14 1PD, Telephone: 01622 671222
E-mail: gunner-sparks@msn.com
Call Date: July 1981, Inner Temple
Qualifications: [BA (Hons) Law]

WYATT JONATHAN MARTIN

Assize Court Chambers
14 Small Street, Bristol BS1 1DE,
Telephone: 0117 9264587
E-mail:chambers@assize-court-chambers.co.uk
Call Date: July 1973, Gray's Inn
Pupil Master
Qualifications: [LLB (Lond), FCIArb]

WYATT MARK

2 New Street
Leicester LE1 5NA,
Telephone: 0116 2625906
E-mail: clerks@2newstreet.co.uk
Call Date: July 1976, Middle Temple
Pupil Master
Qualifications: [MA (Oxon)]

WYATT MICHAEL CHRISTOPHER

10 Winterbourne Grove
Weybridge, Surrey, KT13 OPP,
Telephone: 0181 941 3939
E-mail: wyatt_taxco@compuserve.com
Call Date: July 1975, Gray's Inn
Qualifications: [LLB Hons (Bris), ATII]

WYETH MARK CHARLES

Five Paper Buildings
1st Floor, Five Paper Bldgs, Temple,
London EC4Y 7HB,
Telephone: 0171 583 6117
E-mail:clerks@5-paperbuildings.law.co.uk
Call Date: July 1983, Inner Temple
Pupil Master
Qualifications: [BA (Hons), LLM, ACI (arb)]

WYLES MISS LUCY ANNE

2 Temple Gardens
Temple, London EC4Y 9AY,
Telephone: 0171 583 6041
E-mail: clerks@2templegardens.co.uk
Call Date: Oct 1994, Lincoln's Inn
Qualifications: [BA (Hons), Licence Speciale,
Droit, (Bruxelles)]

WYLIE KEITH FRANCIS

Eighteen Carlton Crescent
Southampton SO15 2XR,
Telephone: 01703 639001
Call Date: July 1976, Gray's Inn
Pupil Master
Qualifications: [MA (Cantab)]

WYLIE NEIL RICHARD

King Charles House
Standard Hill, Nottingham NG1 6FX,
Telephone: 0115 9418851
E-mail: clerks@kch.co.uk
Call Date: Nov 1996, Gray's Inn
Qualifications: [LLB (Manch)]

WYNN TOBY

11 King's Bench Walk
1st Floor, Temple, London EC4Y 7EQ,
Telephone: 0171 353 3337
E-mail: fmuller11@aol.com
11 King's Bench Walk
3 Park Court, Park Cross Street, Leeds
LS1 2QH, Telephone: 0113 297 1200
Call Date: July 1982, Gray's Inn
Pupil Master
Qualifications: [LLB (Lond)]

WYNNE ASHLEY JOHN

5 Fountain Court
Steelhouse Lane, Birmingham B4 6DR,
Telephone: 0121 606 0500
E-mail:clerks@5fountaincourt.law.co.uk
Call Date: Nov 1990, Gray's Inn
Qualifications: [LLB (Cardiff)]

WYNNE-GRIFFITHS RALPH RICHARD DAVID

Guildhall Chambers
22-26 Broad Street, Bristol BS1 2HG,
Telephone: 0117 9273366
E-mail:civil.clerks@guildhallchambers.co.uk and
criminal.clerks@guildhallchambers.co.uk
Call Date: July 1981, Gray's Inn
Qualifications: [MA (Cantab)]

WYNTER COLIN PETER

Devereux Chambers
Devereux Court, London WC2R 3JJ,
Telephone: 0171 353 7534
E-mail: mailbox@devchambers.co.uk
Call Date: Nov 1984, Inner Temple
Pupil Master
Qualifications: [LLB MPhil]

WYVILL ALISTAIR

St Philip's Chambers
Fountain Court, Steelhouse Lane,
Birmingham B4 6DR,
Telephone: 0121 246 7000
E-mail: clerks@st-philips.co.uk
Call Date: Nov 1998, Middle Temple
Qualifications: [BA (Hons), (Queensland),
LLM (Lond)]

XYDIAS NICHOLAS

5 Fountain Court
Steelhouse Lane, Birmingham B4 6DR,
Telephone: 0121 606 0500
E-mail:clerks@5fountaincourt.law.co.uk
Call Date: Oct 1992, Lincoln's Inn
Qualifications: [LLB(Hons)(Lond),
LLM(Lond)]

YAJNIK RAM

6 Gray's Inn Square
Ground Floor, Gray's Inn, London
WC1R 5AZ, Telephone: 0171 242 1052
E-mail: 6graysinn@clara.co.uk
Call Date: Nov 1965, Inner Temple
Pupil Master
Qualifications: [BA, BCom (Bombay), LLB
(Lond)]

YAKUBU EMMANUEL MAHAMA

74 Chancery Lane
First Floor, London WC2A 1AA,
Telephone: 0171 430 0667
Call Date: July 1970, Middle Temple
Qualifications: [LLB (Lond), J.B Montague
Award, Winner]

YAQUB OMAR

One Garden Court Family Law Chambers
Ground Floor, Temple, London
EC4Y 9BJ, Telephone: 0171 797 7900
E-mail: clerks@onegardencourt.co.uk
Call Date: 1997, Inner Temple
Qualifications: [LLB (London), LLM
(London)]

YAQUB ZAHD

2 King's Bench Walk Chambers
1st Floor, 2 King's Bench Walk, Temple,
London EC4Y 7DE,
Telephone: 020 7353 9276
E-mail: chambers@2kbw.co.uk
Call Date: Feb 1991, Inner Temple
Qualifications: [BA, LLM (Lond)]

YATES NICHOLAS GILMORE

1 Mitre Court Buildings
Temple, London EC4Y 7BS,
Telephone: 0171 797 7070
E-mail: clerks@1mcb.com
Call Date: Oct 1996, Inner Temple
Qualifications: [BA (Cantab), CPE (Lond)]

YATES SEAN DAVID

Chambers of Andrew Campbell QC
10 Park Square, Leeds LS1 2LH,
Telephone: 0113 2455438
E-mail: clerks@10pksq.co.uk
Call Date: 1996, Inner Temple
Qualifications: [BA (Oxon), CPE]

YAZAWA YUTAKA

4 King's Bench Walk
Ground/First Floor/Basement, Temple,
London EC4Y 7DL,
Telephone: 0171 822 8822
E-mail: 4kbw@barristersatlaw.com
Call Date: Oct 1994, Middle Temple
Qualifications: [LLB (Hons)(Lond)]

YAZDANI GHULAM

Call Date: Feb 1963, Lincoln's Inn
Pupil Master
Qualifications: [MA, LLB (Karachi)]

YEARWOOD JEFFREY RYEBURN

8 King's Bench Walk
2nd Floor, Temple, London EC4Y 7DU,
Telephone: 0171 797 8888
8 King's Bench Walk North
1 Park Square East, Leeds LS1 2NE,
Telephone: 0113 2439797
Call Date: Nov 1975, Inner Temple
Pupil Master, Assistant Recorder
Qualifications: [BA]

YEBOAH MISS YAA FREMPOMAA

14 Tooks Court
Cursitor St, London EC4A 1LB,
Telephone: 0171 405 8828
E-mail: clerks@tooks.law.co.uk

Westgate Chambers
144 High Street, Lewes, East Sussex,
BN7 1XT, Telephone: 01273 480510
Call Date: Nov 1977, Gray's Inn
Qualifications: [LLB (Ghana) LLM,
(Harvard)]

YELL NICHOLAS ANTHONY

No. 1 Serjeants' Inn
5th Floor Fleet Street, Temple, London
EC4Y 1LH, Telephone: 0171 415 6666
E-mail:no1serjeantsinn@btinternet.com
Call Date: July 1979, Middle Temple
Pupil Master
Qualifications: [LLB (Lond)]

YEUNG STUART ROY

Northampton Chambers
22 Albion Place, Northampton NN1 1UD,
Telephone: 01604 636271
Call Date: Nov 1989, Inner Temple
Qualifications: [LLB]

YIP MRS AMANDA LOUISE

Exchange Chambers
Pearl Assurance House, Derby Square,
Liverpool L2 9XX,
Telephone: 0151 236 7747
E-mail:exchangechambers@btinternet.com
Call Date: Oct 1991, Gray's Inn
Qualifications: [MA (Cantab)]

YONG YING KEONG

Chancery Chambers
1st Floor Offices, 70/72 Chancery Lane,
London WC2A 1AB,
Telephone: 0171 405 6879/6870
Call Date: Oct 1993, Middle Temple
Qualifications: [LLB (Hons)(Notts)]

YOULL MISS JOANNA ISABEL

Chambers of Norman Palmer
2 Field Court, Gray's Inn, London
WC1R 5BB, Telephone: 0171 405 6114
E-mail: fieldct2@netcomuk.co.uk
Call Date: Nov 1989, Gray's Inn
Qualifications: [LLB (Lond)]

D

YOUNG ALASTAIR ANGUS MCLEOD

St Philip's Chambers
Fountain Court, Steelhouse Lane,
Birmingham B4 6DR,
Telephone: 0121 246 7000
E-mail: clerks@st-philips.co.uk
Call Date: 1997, Gray's Inn
Qualifications: [BSc (Manc)]

YOUNG ANDREW GEORGE

1 Crown Office Row
3rd Floor, Temple, London EC4Y 7HH,
Telephone: 0171 583 9292
E-mail: onecor@link.org
Call Date: 1977, Lincoln's Inn
Pupil Master
Qualifications: [BA (Oxon)]

YOUNG CHRISTOPHER REGINALD BOYD

Twenty-Four Old Buildings
Ground Floor, Lincoln's Inn, London
WC2A 3UP, Telephone: 0171 404 0946
E-mail:clerks@24oldbuildings.law.co.uk
Call Date: 1988, Lincoln's Inn
Qualifications: [BA (Hons) (Sussex)]

YOUNG DAVID ANTHONY

4 Brick Court, Chambers of Anne Rafferty QC
1st Floor, Temple, London EC4Y 9AD,
Telephone: 0171 583 8455
Call Date: 1986, Middle Temple
Pupil Master
Qualifications: [BA (Hons) LLM (Lond)]

YOUNG DAVID EDWARD MICHAEL QC (1980)

3 New Square
Lincoln's Inn, London WC2A 3RS,
Telephone: 0171 405 1111
E-mail: 3newsquareip@lineone.net
Call Date: 1966, Lincoln's Inn
Recorder
Qualifications: [MA (Oxon)]

YOUNG LEE TERENCE

Guildhall Chambers Portsmouth
Prudential Buildings, 16 Guildhall Walk,
Portsmouth, Hampshire, PO1 2DE,
Telephone: 01705 752400
Call Date: Oct 1991, Middle Temple
Qualifications: [LLB (Hons)]

YOUNG MARTIN FORD

9 Stone Buildings
Lincoln's Inn, London WC2A 3NN,
Telephone: 0171 404 5055
E-mail: clerks@9stoneb.law.co.uk
Call Date: 1984, Middle Temple
Pupil Master
Qualifications: [LLB, LLM (Lond)]

YOUNG MISS RACHAEL KATE

Queen Elizabeth Building
2nd Floor, Temple, London EC4Y 9BS,
Telephone: 0171 797 7837
Call Date: 1997, Lincoln's Inn
Qualifications: [BA (Hons)(Oxon)]

YOUNG MISS REBECCA LEAH

39 Park Square
Leeds LS1 2NU,
Telephone: 0113 2456633
Call Date: Nov 1993, Inner Temple
Qualifications: [LLB]

YOUNG TIMOTHY NICHOLAS QC (1996)

20 Essex Street
London WC2R 3AL,
Telephone: 0171 583 9294
E-mail: clerks@20essexst.com
Call Date: July 1977, Gray's Inn
Qualifications: [BA , BCL (Oxon)]

YOXALL BASIL JOSHUA

Francis Taylor Building
3rd Floor, Temple, London EC4Y 7BY,
Telephone: 0171 797 7250
Call Date: July 1975, Inner Temple
Pupil Master
Qualifications: [MA (Cantab), FCIArb]

ZACAROLI ANTONY JAMES

3/4 South Square
Gray's Inn, London WC1R 5HP,
Telephone: 0171 696 9900
E-mail: clerks@southsquare.com
Call Date: Nov 1987, Middle Temple
Pupil Master
Qualifications: [BA,BCL (Oxon)]

ZAHED YASREEB

Phoenix Chambers
First Floor, Gray's Inn Chambers, Gray's
Inn, London WC1R 5JA,
Telephone: 0171 404 7888
E-mail:clerks@phoenix-chambers.co.uk
Call Date: May 1993, Lincoln's Inn
Qualifications: [BSc (Hons)(City), LLM
(Lond)]

ZAMAN MOHAMMED KHALIL

St Philip's Chambers
Fountain Court, Steelhouse Lane,
Birmingham B4 6DR,
Telephone: 0121 246 7000
E-mail: clerks@st-philips.co.uk
Call Date: 1985, Gray's Inn
Pupil Master
Qualifications: [LLB (Warwick)]

ZAMAN PETER OMITAVAW

122-124 Chamber Building, Motijheel C/A,
haka 1000 Telephone: (8802) 955 2946/
889373
Call Date: Oct 1996, Lincoln's Inn
Qualifications: [LLB (Hons)(Lond)]

ZAMMIT MS FRANCES ANN

Plowden Buildings
2nd Floor, 2 Plowden Buildings, Middle
Temple Lane, London EC4Y 9BU,
Telephone: 0171 583 0808
E-mail: bar@plowdenbuildings.co.uk
Call Date: 1993, Inner Temple
Qualifications: [LLB]

ZEIDMAN MARTYN KEITH QC (1998)

33 Bedford Row
London WC1R 4JH,
Telephone: 0171 242 6476
E-mail:clerks@bedfordrow33.demon.co.uk
Call Date: 1974, Middle Temple

Recorder
Qualifications: [LLB (Lond), ACIArb]

ZEITLIN DEREK JAMES

**4 Brick Court, Chambers of Anne
Rafferty QC**
1st Floor, Temple, London EC4Y 9AD,
Telephone: 0171 583 8455
Call Date: July 1974, Lincoln's Inn
Pupil Master
Qualifications: [BSc]

ZELIN GEOFFREY ANDREW

Enterprise Chambers
9 Old Square, Lincoln's Inn, London
WC2A 3SR, Telephone: 0171 405 9471
E-mail:enterprise.london@dial.pipex.com
Enterprise Chambers
38 Park Square, Leeds LS1 2PA,
Telephone: 0113 246 0391
E-mail:enterprise.leeds@dial.pipex.com
Enterprise Chambers
65 Quayside, Newcastle upon Tyne
NE1 3DS, Telephone: 0191 222 3344
E-mail:enterprise.newcastle@dial.pipex.com
Call Date: 1984, Middle Temple
Pupil Master
Qualifications: [MA (Cantab)]

ZENTAR DR REMY PAUL

24a St John Street
Manchester M3 4DF,
Telephone: 0161 833 9628
Call Date: July 1997, Gray's Inn
Qualifications: [LLB, LLM, Ph.D (Manc)]

ZIEGER JOHN HARRY

29 Bedford Row Chambers
London WC1R 4HE,
Telephone: 0171 831 2626
Call Date: July 1962, Middle Temple

ZIMBLER MISS ALEXIA

2 King's Bench Walk
Ground Floor, Temple, London
EC4Y 7DE, Telephone: 0171 353 1746
E-mail: 2kbw@atlas.co.uk
King's Bench Chambers
115 North Hill, Plymouth PL4 8JY,
Telephone: 01752 221551
Call Date: Oct 1993, Lincoln's Inn
Qualifications: [BSc (Hons)(Lond)]

D

ZORBAS PANAYLOTIS CHRISTOPHOROU

2 Paper Buildings
1st Floor, Temple, London EC4Y 7ET,
Telephone: 020 7556 5500
E-mail: clerks@2pbbarristers.co.uk
Call Date: June 1964, Lincoln's Inn
Pupil Master

ZORNOZA MISS ISABELLE

2 Harcourt Buildings
Ground Floor/Left, Temple, London
EC4Y 9DB, Telephone: 0171 583 9020
E-mail: clerks@harcourt.co.uk
Call Date: Oct 1993, Inner Temple
Qualifications: [BA (Hons), CPE]

ZORNOZA PHILIP

One Raymond Buildings
Gray's Inn, London WC1R 5BH,
Telephone: 0171 430 1234
E-mail: chambers@ipbar1rb.com;
clerks@ipbar1rb.com
Call Date: July 1983, Middle Temple
Qualifications: [BSc (Nottm), Dip Law]

ZUCKER DAVID GRAHAM

Park Lane Chambers
19 Westgate, Leeds LS1 2RD,
Telephone: 0113 2285000
E-mail:clerks@parklanechambers.co.uk
Call Date: July 1986, Middle Temple
Pupil Master
Qualifications: [LLB]

ZWART AUBERON CHRISTIAAN CONRAD

1 Serjeants' Inn
4th Floor, Temple, London EC4Y 1NH,
Telephone: 0171 583 1355
E-mail: clerks@serjeants-inn.co.uk
Call Date: 1997, Inner Temple
Qualifications: [BA, B.Arch, (Newcastle), CPE
(City), RIBA]

Individual Barristers in Employment and Non-practising

This section lists those barristers who are in employment and those who do not practice. Barristers are listed alphabetically by surname, and details include their date of call to the Bar, their Inn of Court and academic qualifications. Barristers who are currently employed have details of their position of employment with a full address.

The symbol • indicates that a barrister is in employment.

E

Abai *Miss Joyce Ola*
Call Date: Feb 1995 (Middle Temple)
Qualifications: LLB (Hons), LLM (Lond)

Abanulo *Miss Annette Obiageli*
Call Date: Oct 1997 (Gray's Inn)
Qualifications: LLB (Essex)

Abban *Charles Kingsley*
Call Date: Oct 1996 (Gray's Inn)
Qualifications: BA (Exon)

Abbas *Nigel* •
Lawyer, Channel 4 Television Corp., 124
Horseferry Road, London SW1P 2TS,
0171 306 8731, Fax: 0171 306 9367,
Call Date: Nov 1995 (Lincoln's Inn)
Qualifications: BA (Hons)

Abbasi *Miss Sufiah Naz*
Call Date: Nov 1997 (Gray's Inn)
Qualifications: LLB (Manch)

Abbott *David Michael*
Call Date: Nov 1995 (Inner Temple)
Qualifications: LLB (Soton), LLM (Lond)

Abbott *Miss Emma-Jane Amelia*
Call Date: Nov 1996 (Gray's Inn)
Qualifications: MA (Edinburgh), LLB
(Leeds)

Abbott *Miss Helen Louise*
9 Park Place, Cardiff, CF1 3DP, Call Date:
Nov 1988 (Gray's Inn) Qualifications:
LLB (Lond)

Abbott *Stephen George*
Director of Legal Services, Birmingham
Magistrates Court, Victoria Law Courts,
Corporation Street, Birmingham B4 6QJ,
0121 212 6611, Fax: 0121 212 6766,
Call Date: July 1983 (Inner Temple)
Qualifications: LLB (Sheff), MA

Abdin *Miss Romana* •
Group Legal Advisor, Black Horse
Agencies Ltd, Salisbury Square, Hatfield,
Herts AL9 5DD, 01707 275371, Fax:
01707 274053, Call Date: July 1988
(Gray's Inn) Qualifications: LLB (Wales)

Abdul Haque *Miss Nasreen Begum*
and Member Malaysia Bar, Call Date:
Nov 1994 (Lincoln's Inn) Qualifications:
LLB (Hons)(Lond)

Abdul-Rasool *Miss Leila*
Call Date: Nov 1994 (Lincoln's Inn)
Qualifications: LLB (Hons)(Lond), Dip
in Intellectural, Property

Abdulhusein *Shamsuddin Taherali*
5 Overbury Close, Weymouth, Dorset
DT4 9UE, Call Date: Feb 1963 (Lincoln's
Inn)

Abedin *Mrs Syeda Khadizatulkubra*
Administrative Officer, Call Date: Nov
1995 (Lincoln's Inn) Qualifications: LLB
(Hons)

Abelson *Ivor Gordon*
16 Gunners Grove, London E4 9SS, 0181
529 5090, Call Date: Nov 1974 (Gray's
Inn)

Aber *Gordon*
South Africa, and Member South Africa 4
Paper Bldgs, 1st Floor, Temple, London,
EC4Y 7EX, Call Date: Mar 1996
(Lincoln's Inn) Qualifications:
BA,LLM(Johannesburg), LLM (Lond)

Abercrombie *Ian Ralph*
7 Lauder Road, Edinburgh EH9 2EW,
0131 668 2489, Fax: 0131 668 3037, QC
Scottish Bar and Member Scottish Bar,
Call Date: Apr 1991 (Lincoln's Inn)
Qualifications: LLB (Hons)

Abeysekera *Miss Samantha*
Customer Business Development
Account Manager, Procter & Gamble UK,
The Heights, Brooklands, Weybridge,
Surrey KT13 0XP, 01932 896000, Call
Date: Oct 1998 (Middle Temple)
Qualifications: LLB (Hons)(Dunelm)

Abiola *Mrs Oluremilekun Onabolu*
Part-time Chairman of Tribunal, 266
Etim Inyang Cre, Victoria Island, Lagos
Nigeria, 0171 328 0941, and Member
Nigerian Bar, Call Date: July 1990
(Middle Temple) Qualifications: LLB
(Lond), LLM (Lond)(KCL)

Abraham *Dr Chakalamannil Mathew*
Advocate of India, High Court of Kerala
and Member Indian Bar, Call Date: July
1996 (Lincoln's Inn) Qualifications: BA,
LLB, LLM,, Ph.D (Lond)

Abraham *Cheg Adrian Stephen*
Call Date: Oct 1996 (Inner Temple)
Qualifications: BSc (Dunelm), CPE

Abrahams *Anthony Claude Walter*
Partner, Top Floor, Goldsmith Building,
Temple, London EC4Y 7BL, 0171 353
7913, Fax: 0171 353 2756, Advocate and
Solicitor of Brunei Darussalam, Call
Date: Nov 1950 (Middle Temple)
Qualifications: MA (Cantab)

Abrahams *Ms Paula Anita* •
Principle Crown Prosecutor, Crown
Prosecution Service, County House, 100
New London Road, Chelmsford, Essex,
01245 252939, Fax: 01245 490476, Call
Date: Nov 1987 (Middle Temple)
Qualifications: BA.

Abrahamson *Miss Debbie*
Principal Lecturer, Inns of Court School
of Law, 39 Eagle Street, London
WC1R 4AJ, 0171 404 5787, Call Date:
July 1981 (Lincoln's Inn) Qualifications:
BA TCD

Abrahamson *Miss Judith Sharon*
Chavasse Court Chambers, 2nd Floor,
Chavasse Court, 24 Lord Street,
Liverpool, L2 1TA, Call Date: Nov 1988
(Gray's Inn) Qualifications: LLB (L'Pool)

Abrams *Daniel*
Group Finance Director, Xenova Group
PLC, 240 Bath Road, Slough SL1 4EF,
01753 706 600, Fax: 01753 706 638,
Call Date: July 1979 (Inner Temple)
Qualifications: FCA, MA (Cantab)

Acton *Ms Victoria Jane*
6 Chilcombe Heights, Quarry Road,
Winchester SO23 0HE, Call Date: Oct
1995 (Inner Temple) Qualifications: BA
(Kent), M.Phil (Leeds), Dip Law (City)

Adam *Michael William* •
Senior Legal Officer, Department of
Social Security, New Court, Carey Street,
London WC2A 2LS, Call Date: Oct 1990
(Middle Temple) Qualifications: BA
(Lond), Dip Law (City)

Adamec *Richard Vaclav* •
Senior Court Clerk, West Glam
Magistrates Ct Comm, Swansea
Magistrates' Court, Grove Place, Swansea,
West Glamorgan SA1 5DB, 01792
655171, Fax: 01792 651066, Call Date:
Nov 1988 (Gray's Inn)

Adams *Mrs Catherine Elizabeth Stella*
Court Clerk at Banbury Court, Call Date:
Feb 1994 (Gray's Inn) Qualifications:
LLB (Dundee)

Adams *Mrs Hazel Caroline*
Legal Adviser at Southampton
Magistrates' Court, Justices' Clerks
Office, 51-59 Commercial Road,
Southampton SO15 1BQ, 01703 635911,
Fax: 01703 233882, Call Date: July 1994
(Inner Temple) Qualifications: LLB
(Hons)(Lond)

Adams *Ms Hester Rose*
Call Date: July 1997 (Lincoln's Inn)
Qualifications: LLB (Hons)

Adams *Mrs Hilary* •
Specialist Lawyer & Legal Training &
Development Manager, Criminal Appeal
Office, Royal Courts of Justice, The
Strand, London WC2A 2LL, 0171 936
6631, Fax: 0171 936 6900, Call Date:
July 1976 (Gray's Inn) Qualifications:
LLB

Adams *Howard James* •
Crown Prosecution Service, C/O 50
Ludgate Hill, London EC4M 7EX, Call
Date: July 1988 (Gray's Inn)
Qualifications: LLB (Wales)

Adams *James David Seton* •
Legal Adviser, Eagle Star Holdings Plc, 60
St Mary Axe, London EC3, 0171 929
1111, Fax: 0171 626 0311, Call Date:
July 1989 (Middle Temple)
Qualifications: MA (Oxon)

Adams *John Frederick*
Special Adviser to the Secretary of State
of Wales, Welsh Office, Cathays Park,
Cardiff CF1 3NQ, Call Date: Nov 1995
(Middle Temple) Qualifications: LLB
(Hons)(L'Pool)

Adams *John McPhillamy*
c/o Lloyds Bank plc, Law Courts Branch,
222 Strand, London WC2R 1BB, and
Member New South Wales Bar, Call Date:
June 1944 (Inner Temple)
Qualifications: MA LLB(Cantab), Dip.
Trans. IoL. AIL

Adams *Miss Linda Christine*
Call Date: Nov 1987 (Gray's Inn)
Qualifications: BA (Kent)

Adams *Mrs Linda Judith* •
Head of Corporate Legal Services, The
Automobile Association, Norfolk House,
Priestley Road, Basingstoke, Hants
RG24 9NY, 01256 20123, Call Date: Nov
1994 (Inner Temple) Qualifications:
LLB (Lond)

Adamson *Benjamin Michael*
Call Date: Mar 1999 (Inner Temple)
Qualifications: BA (Cantab)

Adamson *David Iain*
Call Date: Nov 1998 (Lincoln's Inn)
Qualifications: BA (Hons), Dip Law

Adamson *Norman Joseph*
Faculty of Advocates, QC (Scotland) and
Member Scottish Bar, Call Date: Feb
1959 (Gray's Inn) Qualifications: MA,
LLB (Glas)

Adatia *Kamal*
Call Date: Nov 1995 (Gray's Inn)
Qualifications: LLB (B'ham)

Adcock *Thomas Christopher
Augustine* •
Legal Officer, The Treasury Solicitor,
Queen Anne's Chambers, 28 Broadway,
London SW1H 9JS, Call Date: Nov 1974
(Inner Temple) Qualifications: LLB

Addae *Ms Sandra Anita* •
UK General Counsel, Unisys Ltd, Bakers
Court, Bakers Road, Uxbridge,
Middlesex UB8 1RG, 01895 862517,
Fax: 01895 862010, Call Date: Nov
1988 (Middle Temple) Qualifications:
LLB (Essex)

Addison *Miss Fiona Rosalinda*
Blatchfords Solicitors, Bloomsbury,
London, Call Date: July 1993 (Inner
Temple) Qualifications: BSc (Econ),
Dip Econ, MA

Addison *Henry Yaw Larbi*
Call Date: Nov 1998 (Inner Temple)
Qualifications: BA (Keele)

Addo *Miss Cynthia Pamela (Akotaa)*
Call Date: Nov 1989 (Lincoln's Inn)
Qualifications: LLB (Lond), LLM

Addoo *Ibrahim Nee Kwamina-Ashong*
also Inn of Court L, Call Date: Nov 1980
(Middle Temple) Qualifications: RMN,
SRN Dip (Lond), Dip Nursing (Lond)

Adeane *The Hon George Edward*
B4 Albany, Piccadilly, London W1V 9RE,
Gray's Inn - Ad Eudem and Member
Gibraltar Bar, Call Date: July 1962
(Middle Temple) Qualifications: MA

Adebiyi *Samuel Durojaiye*
21-25 Broad Street, Lagos, Nigeria, and
Member Nigeria Bar, Call Date: June
1953 (Middle Temple)

Adegbola *Miss Temitope Theresa*
Call Date: Nov 1998 (Gray's Inn)
Qualifications: LLB (Kent)

Adekoya *Adedeji*
Call Date: June 1964 (Inner Temple)

Adeniji *Tajudeen Adegoke*
Awolwye Kio & Co Solicitors, 199
Stockwell Road, London SW9 9ST, Call
Date: Nov 1997 (Gray's Inn)
Qualifications: BSc (Nigeria), LLB
(Lond)

Adeoso *Miss Adeola Olujumoke*
Call Date: Mar 1999 (Lincoln's Inn)
Qualifications: LLB (Hons)(Herts)

Aderonmu *Miss Louisa*
Call Date: Mar 1998 (Gray's Inn)
Qualifications: LLB (Warw)

Adeusi *Ms Siobhan*
Call Date: Nov 1994 (Lincoln's Inn)
Qualifications: LLB (Hons)

Adie *Miss Diana Madelaine* •
Head of Intellectual Property,
Intellectual Property, British
Broadcasting Corp, White City, 201
Wood Lane, London W12 7TS, 0181
752 5252, Fax: 0181 752 5080, Call
Date: Nov 1979 (Middle Temple)
Qualifications: MA, BCL (Oxon)

Adjaye *Charles Robert*
S E Legal Advisory Services, 12 The
Crest, Knights Hill, London SE27 0EW,
0181 761 1896, Call Date: Feb 1962
(Middle Temple)

Adnan *Miss Lisa Jasmin*
Call Date: Oct 1998 (Middle Temple)
Qualifications: LLB (Hons)(Westmin)

Adutt *James Ian* •
Treasury Solicitors Dept., Queen Anne's
Chambers, 28 Broadway, London
SW1H 9JS, Call Date: Oct 1992
(Lincoln's Inn) Qualifications: MA
(Cantab)

Afariogun *Miss Remi*
Call Date: Mar 1998 (Gray's Inn)
Qualifications: LLB (Middx)

Afiari *Charles Timothy*
56 John Keats House, Commerce Road,
London N22 4EQ, 0181 881 9685, Fax:
0181 881 9685, and Member Nigeria,
Call Date: Mar 1996 (Gray's Inn)
Qualifications: LLB, LLM (Lagos)

Afzal *Miss Safira Nazli* •
Legal Counsel, Simply Contracts
Limited, Wigmore House, 22/23
Junction Mews, Sale Place, London
W21 1PN, 0171 277 7929, Call Date:
Oct 1998 (Middle Temple)
Qualifications: LLB (Hons)(Lond)

Agace *Christopher Paul*
Executive Director, Winkworth & Co
(Holdings) Ltd, 118 Kensington Church
Street, London W8, 0171 727 1117,
Call Date: Nov 1990 (Inner Temple)
Qualifications: LLB (So'ton)

Agarwala *Surendra Kumar*
Senior Legal Advisor, Norfolk Mag Crts
Committee, The Court House, College
Lane, King's Lynn, Norfolk PE30 1PQ,
01553 763341, Fax: 01553 775098,
Call Date: Nov 1975 (Gray's Inn)
Qualifications: MA (Cantab), Cert Ed

Agathangelou *Angelos Marcianos* •
Senior Principal Legal Officer, HM
Customs & Excise, New King's Beam
House, 22 Upper Ground, London
SE1 9PJ, Call Date: Nov 1983 (Middle
Temple) Qualifications: BA

Agati *Kwame Amponsah*
Legal Adviser, Newham Rights Centre,
285 Romford Road, Forest Gate,
London E7 9HJ, 0181 555 3331, Fax:
0181 519 7348, Call Date: Feb 1992
(Middle Temple) Qualifications: LLB
(Hons) Ghana, LLM (Lond), ACIS

Ager *Miss Donna Marie* •
Paralegal, Freshfields, 65 Fleet Street,
London EC4Y 1HS, 0171 427 3516, Call
Date: Nov 1998 (Lincoln's Inn)
Qualifications: LLB (Hons)(Sheff)

Aghadiuno *Charles*
Deputy Chief Clerk, Inner London
Magistrates', Courts Service, 65
Romney Street, London SW1P 3RD,
0171 799 3332, Fax: 0171 799 3072,
Call Date: Nov 1987 (Inner Temple)
Qualifications: LLB

Agutu *Solomon Ochaye* •
Assistant Borough Solicitor and Head of
Contracts, London Borough of
Southwark, The Town Hall, Peckham
Road, London SE15 8UB, 0171 525
7512, Call Date: July 1980 (Inner
Temple) Qualifications: LLB (S'ton),
LLM (Lon/LSE)

Agyeman *Bernard Osei*
Call Date: 1972 (Middle Temple)
Qualifications: BA

Agyeman *Pierre*
Call Date: Oct 1995 (Gray's Inn)
Qualifications: LLB (Leeds)

Agyeman *Miss Roselyn Michelle Serwa
Bonsu*
Call Date: Nov 1996 (Inner Temple)
Qualifications: LLB (Wales)

Agyemang *Augustus Osei*
B J Brandon & Co Solicitors, 28 Grays
Inn Road, London WC1X 8HR, 0171
242 7050, and Member Ghana,
Zimbabwe, Call Date: May 1992 (Inner
Temple) Qualifications: LLB (Ghana)

Ahluwalia *Miss Rupina*
Call Date: Nov 1994 (Lincoln's Inn)
Qualifications: LLB (Hons)(Notts)

Ahmad *Miss Aysha*
Call Date: Oct 1996 (Middle Temple)
Qualifications: BA (Hons)(Lond)

E

Ahmad *Mirza Farakh Navid* •
Assistant Director (Legal), Bolton
Metropolitan, Borough Council Town
Hall, Bolton BL1 1RU, 01204 522311
ext1111, Fax: 01204 39 2808, Elected
Member of Bar Council, Call Date: July
1984 (Gray's Inn) Qualifications: BSoc
Sci (Keele), MBA, MIMgt

Ahmed *Gulam Mortuza*
Call Date: Oct 1997 (Lincoln's Inn)
Qualifications: LLB (Hons)(B'ham)

Ahmed *Haras*
Call Date: July 1998 (Lincoln's Inn)
Qualifications: BA (Hons)(Essex)

Ahmed *Ms Rachael Amaya* •
Solicitor's Office, Inland Revenue, East
Wing, Somerset House, London
WC2R 1LB, 0171 438 6377, Call Date:
Oct 1996 (Inner Temple) Qualifications:
LLB (Lond)

Ahmed *Salahuddin*
16 Hawthorn Road, Wallington, Surrey
SM6 0SX, 0181 647 7469, Fax: 0181 286
2738, Call Date: Nov 1956 (Middle
Temple) Qualifications: LLB

Ahmed *Mrs Shahnaz*
Call Date: Feb 1994 (Gray's Inn)
Qualifications: LLB (Bucks)

Ahmed *Miss Shazia* •
Call Date: Oct 1997 (Middle Temple)
Qualifications: LLB (Hons)(Luton)

Ahuja *Raju Neil* •
Senior Crown Prosecutor, Crown
Prosecution Service, 2nd
Floor,Blackburn House,
Newcastle-Under-Lyme, Staffs ST5·1TB,
01782 611877, Fax: 01782 711026, Call
Date: Nov 1990 (Inner Temple)
Qualifications: LLB Law

Aiken *Jason Robert* •
Company Legal Advisor, Blick PLC, Blick
House, Bramble Road, Swindon, Wilts
SN2 6ER, 01793 692401, Fax: 01793
615848, Call Date: Oct 1992 (Lincoln's
Inn) Qualifications: LLB(Hons)

Ailes *Giles Matthew*
Call Date: Oct 1998 (Inner Temple)
Qualifications: BA (Warw)

Ainley *Alexander John*
Call Date: Oct 1996 (Middle Temple)
Qualifications: BA (Hons) (Oxon)

Ainslie *Mrs Rosemary Caroline Patricia*
'Glenbeigh', The Lane, Gate Helmsley,
York, North Yorkshire, 01759 372686,
Fax: 01759 373686, Inn of Court of N
Ireland and Member Northern Ireland
Bar, Call Date: Nov 1990 (Middle
Temple) Qualifications: BA (Belfast), BL
(Belfast)

Ainsworth *Noel*
Call Date: Oct 1995 (Lincoln's Inn)
Qualifications: LLB (Hons) (Lond)

Airey *Anthony Maurice*
Managing Director, Airey & Wheeler Ltd,
8 Sackville street, London W12X 1DD,
0171 734 7461, Fax: 0171 734 8616,
Call Date: July 1988 (Inner Temple)
Qualifications: LLB

Ajayi *Dr Olukonyinsola*
Consultant to United Nations Centre for
Transnational Corporations, 70 Lorne
Road, London E7 0LL, 0181 502 2944,
Fax: 0181 502 0125, and 31 Marina,
Lagos Nigeria. Tel 00234-1-2642551
Assoc Member American Bar Association
and Member Nigerian Bar, Call Date: July
1989 (Middle Temple) Qualifications:
LLB, LLM (Harvard), PhD (Cantab)

Ajoh *Anthony Afamefune*
Contract Officer, London Borough of
Ealing, Contract & Property Services,
Percival House, 1st Floor NE, 14/16
Uxbridge Road, London W5 2HL, 0181
280 1242, Call Date: Feb 1994 (Gray's
Inn) Qualifications: Btech (Hons), MSc
(Reading), LLB (Lond), ARICS, MCIOB

Ajose *Ms Oladunni Ayodele* •
Head of Corporate and Policy Office,
Forensic Science Service, 109 Lambeth
Road, London SE1 7LP, 0171 230 6621,
Fax: 0171 230 6623, Call Date: Nov 1988
(Middle Temple) Qualifications: LLB,
Dip.M, MCIM, MBA

Akbar *Anwar* •
Assistant Counsel to the, Speaker, House
of Commons, London SW1A 0AA, 0171
219 5552, Call Date: Nov 1966 (Middle
Temple) Qualifications: BCL (Oxon), MA
(Oxon)

Akeroyd *Timothy John*
Commercial/International Consultant,
21 Bunker Street, Freckleton, Nr Preston
PR4 1HA, 01772 634342, Fax: 01772
634342, Call Date: Nov 1971 (Lincoln's
Inn) Qualifications: LLB

Akhtar *Suhail Abdul Qadir* •
Crown Prosecutor, Crown Prosecution
Service, The Cooperage, Gainsford Street,
London SE1, 0171 962 2788, Call Date:
Nov 1984 (Middle Temple)
Qualifications: LLB (Lond)

Akif *Alkan*
Head of Legal Services, Tewkesbury
Magistrates' Court, Gander Lane,
Tewkesbury, Glos GL20 5DR, 01684
294632, Fax: 01684 274596, Call Date:
Nov 1975 (Middle Temple)

Akil *Munir Mehmet*
Call Date: Nov 1972 (Middle Temple)

Akin-Olugbade *Oluwajeminipe
Babarinsade*
Call Date: Oct 1998 (Lincoln's Inn)
Qualifications: LLB (Hons)(Wales)

Akonta *Victor Solomon Kudzo* •
Senior Principal Legal Officer,
Department of Social Security, New
Court, 48 Carey Street, London
WC2A 2LS, Call Date: Nov 1975 (Inner
Temple) Qualifications: MA

Akpan *Samuel Sunday*
and Member Nigeria, Call Date: Mar
1996 (Inner Temple) Qualifications:
LLB, LLM (Nigeria)

Akram *Miss Farzana*
Call Date: 1998 (Middle Temple)
Qualifications: LLB (Hons)(Middx)

Akusu-Ossai *Mrs Augusta Ovo*
Tribunal Clerk, Chancery Chambers, 1st
Floor Offices, 70/72 Chancery Lane,
London, WC2A 1AB, Call Date: Oct 1993
(Lincoln's Inn) Qualifications: LLB
(Hons)(Bucks)

Al-Harith Sinclair *Muhammad Abdullah*
Clifford Chance Limited, 200 Aldersgate
Street, London EC1A 4JJ, Call Date: Oct
1996 (Middle Temple) Qualifications: BA
(Hons)(Lond)

Al-Saleem *Ms Sally Asil*
Call Date: Oct 1997 (Inner Temple)
Qualifications: BSc (London), CPE

Al-Yunusi *Abdullah Muhammad*
Call Date: 1994 (Inner Temple)
Qualifications: BSc (Wales), CPE
(Wolverhampton)

Alabi *Babatunde Omotoso* •
Senior Crown Prosecutor, Crown
Prosecution Service, Barking & Newham
Branch, 1-9 Romford Row, Stratford,
London E15 4LJ, 0181 534 6601, Fax:
0181 519 9690, and Member Nigerian
Bar, Call Date: Oct 1992 (Lincoln's Inn)
Qualifications: LLB(Hons), LLM(Lond)

Alban-Davies *John Lewis* •
Senior Crown Prosecutor, Crown
Prosecution Service, Severn Thames,
Artillery House, Heritage Way, Droitwich,
Worcestershire WR8 8YB, 01905 779502,
Call Date: Nov 1973 (Inner Temple)
Qualifications: MA (Lond), LLB (Wales)

Albery *Oliver Peter*
Call Date: July 1972 (Lincoln's Inn)

Albon *Commander Ross* •
Legal Advisor, Royal Navy, 11 Parkhayes,
Woodbury Salterton, Devon EX5 1QS,
01395 233763, Call Date: Nov 1988
(Inner Temple) Qualifications: BSc

Alcock *Alistair Robert*
6 Bristle Hill, Buckingham MK18 1EZ,
01280 812059, Call Date: Nov 1977
(Middle Temple) Qualifications: MA
(Cantab), MSI (Dip)

Alderman *Richard John* •
Room F1, Solicitor's Office, Inland
Revenue, East Wing, Somerset House,
London WC2R 1LB, 0171 438 7262, Call
Date: June 1974 (Gray's Inn)
Qualifications: LLB [Lond]

Alderson *Christopher James*
Call Date: Oct 1993 (Lincoln's Inn)
Qualifications: LLB (Hons)(Notts)

Alexander *Miss Josephine Anne* •
Call Date: Feb 1994 (Middle Temple)
Qualifications: LLB (Hons)(Lond)

E

Alexander *Richard Charles Henry*
Research Officer, Institute of Advanced
Legal, Studies, 17 Russell Square,
London WC1B 5DR, 0171 637 1731,
Fax: 0171 580 9613, Call Date: Feb
1991 (Middle Temple) Qualifications:
MA (Cantab), Dip Law (City)

Alexander *Miss Rosemarie Simone*
Olswang, 90 Long Acre, London
WC2E 9TT, 0171 208 8888, Fax: 0171
208 8800, Call Date: Nov 1993 (Inner
Temple) Qualifications: MA (St
Andrews), CPE

Alexander *Mrs Sally Jaqueline
Ferguson*
Call Date: Nov 1997 (Gray's Inn)
Qualifications: BA (Portsmouth), LLB
(Lond)

Alexander of Weedon *Lord*
QC (NSW) Judge, Courts of Appeal
Jersey & Guernsey, House of Lords,
London SW1A 0PW, Chairman, Bar
Council 1985-86, Call Date: Nov 1961
(Middle Temple) Qualifications: MA
(Cantab)

Alexander-Wall *Michael Graeme*
Call Date: Feb 1994 (Inner Temple)
Qualifications: BA (Oxon), Dip in Law

Alfrey *Mrs Penelope Ann*
Loughborough University, School of Art
& Design, Epival Ways, Loughborough,
Leics, 01509 228911, Call Date: Oct
1995 (Middle Temple) Qualifications:
MA (Hons)

Alg *Miss Bhupinder Kaur* •
London Borough of Merton, Crown
House, London Road, Morden, Surrey
SM4 5DX, 0181 545 3341, Fax: 0181
543 7126, Call Date: Nov 1974 (Inner
Temple) Qualifications: LLB

Ali *Miss Amina Khatun*
Legal Advisor, Abbey Legal Protection
Limited, 17 Landsdowne Road,
Croydon, Surrey CR0 2BX, 0181 730
6000, Fax: 0181 730 6001, Call Date:
Nov 1996 (Gray's Inn) Qualifications:
LLB (Thames), LLM (Lond)

Ali *Ifther* •
Merrill Lynch Europe, Ropemaker
Place, 25 Ropemaker Street, London
EC2Y 9LY, 0171 867 4961, Fax: 0171
573 1998, Call Date: Nov 1994 (Inner
Temple) Qualifications: LLB (Lond)

Ali *Ishtiyaq*
Call Date: Nov 1996 (Lincoln's Inn)
Qualifications: LLB (Hons)

Ali *Miss Kaniz Fatima*
Call Date: Nov 1998 (Lincoln's Inn)
Qualifications: LLB (Hons)

Ali *Miss Rukhsana Akhtar*
Call Date: Oct 1995 (Lincoln's Inn)
Qualifications: LLB (Hons) (Lond)

Ali *Miss Shameen*
Call Date: July 1998 (Middle Temple)
Qualifications: LLB (Hons) (Teeside)

Ali *Mrs Shamim*
Call Date: July 1998 (Lincoln's Inn)
Qualifications: LLB (Hons)

Ali *Zubair* •
BTG International Ltd, 10 Fleet Place,
Limeburner Lane, London EC4M 7SB,
0171 575 1696, Fax: 0171 575 1527,
Call Date: May 1993 (Lincoln's Inn)
Qualifications: LLB (Hons), LLM
(Lond)

Ali-Selvaratnam *Mrs Rasheeda*
Housing Lawyer, South Islington Law
Centre, 131-132 Upper Street, London
N1 1QP, 0171 354 3207, Fax: 0171 354
8155, Call Date: Nov 1981 (Middle
Temple)

Alizond *Mrs Tamara Leigh*
Call Date: Nov 1995 (Lincoln's Inn)
Qualifications: BA (Hons), Dip Law, MA
(Hons) (Cantab)

Allan *Robert John*
Director of Legal Services, Haringey
Magistrates Court, Bishops Road,
Archway Road, Highgate, London
N6 4HS, 0181 340 3472, Fax: 0181 348
3343, Call Date: July 1980 (Lincoln's
Inn) Qualifications: BA

Alland *Brian David*
Call Date: July 1976 (Lincoln's Inn)
Qualifications: B.Eng,MSc

Allen *Capt Albert Eric*
Greysands, 29 Beach Road, Emsworth,
Hants PO10 7HR, 01243 372028, Call
Date: Nov 1961 (Middle Temple)

Allen *Bernard Robert*
10 Cavaye House, Cavaye Place, London
SW10 9PT, 0171 373 1471, Call Date:
Nov 1950 (Gray's Inn)

Allen *Charles Laugharne* •
SCS Lawyer (Grade 5), Ministry of
Agriculture,, Fisheries & Food, 55
Whitehall, London SW1, 0171 270
8325, Fax: 0171 270 8295, Call Date:
July 1983 (Middle Temple)
Qualifications: MA (Cantab)

Allen *Christian Darrel* •
Legal Adviser/Assistant Company
Secretary, AIG Europe (UK) Ltd, 120
Fenchurch Street, London EC3M 5BP,
0171 280 3645, Fax: 0171 280 8973,
Call Date: Nov 1992 (Inner Temple)
Qualifications: LLB (Lancs), LLM
(Nott'm)

Allen *Christopher*
Indirect Taxes Manager, Pricewater
Coopers, 1 Embankment Place,
London WC2N 6NN, 0171 213 2566,
Fax: 0171 213 4607, Call Date: Nov
1975 (Inner Temple) Qualifications:
BA (Wales)

Allen *David John*
General Business Consultant, 38 South
Hill, Catteshall Lane, Godalming,
Surrey GU2 0JX, 01483 421767, Fax:
01483 421767, Call Date: Nov 1989
(Middle Temple) Qualifications: LLB
(So'ton)

Allen *Mrs Diana*
43 Halsey Street, London SW3 2PT, Call
Date: Nov 1972 (Inner Temple)

Allen *Ms Heather Muriel*
63 Goldstone Crescent, Hove, East
Sussex BN3 6LR, 01273 553523, Fax:
01273 552550, Call Date: Nov 1977
(Inner Temple) Qualifications: BA
(Lond), FRSA, CEDR Accredited ,
Mediator

Allen *Leonard Charles*
Clerk to the Justices Somerset
Magistrates Courts County of Somerset,
Somerset Magistrates Court, The
Courthouse, Northgate, Bridgwater,
Somerset TA6 3EU, 01278 452182, Fax:
01278 453667, Call Date: July 1980
(Inner Temple) Qualifications: DML

Allen *Miss Lucianne Mary*
Call Date: Nov 1998 (Middle Temple)
Qualifications: BA (Hons) (Leeds)

Allen *Neil Edward* •
Senior Lawyer, Lewisham Legal
Services, London Borough of
Lewisham, Town Hall, Lewisham,
London, 0181 314 6912, Fax: 0181 314
3114, Call Date: Feb 1993 (Inner
Temple) Qualifications: LLB (Reading)

Allen *Miss Nicola Jayne*
Call Date: Oct 1998 (Inner Temple)
Qualifications: LLB (Wales)

Allen *William Edwin*
Call Date: Nov 1978 (Gray's Inn)
Qualifications: BA (Kent)

Allinson *Peter Anthony*
Call Date: Oct 1998 (Inner Temple)
Qualifications: BSc, MSc PhD,
(Manch), CPE (W, of England)

Allison *Clifford Howard* •
Senior Crown Prosecutor, Crown
Prosecution Service, Central Casework
(Fraud), 50 Ludgate Hill, London
EC4M 7EX, 0171 273 1349, Fax: 0171
329 8171, and Member Hong Kong
Bar, Call Date: July 1976 (Inner
Temple) Qualifications: LLB

Allison *Mrs Gillian Margaret Clarkson*
Magistrates' Courts Clerk, Inner
London Magistrates', Courts Service, 65
Romney Street, London SW1P 3DR,
0171 799 3332, Call Date: Oct 1990
(Gray's Inn)

Allison *Samuel Austin* •
Compliance and Legal Director, West
Merchant Bank, 33/36 Gracechurch
Street, London EC3V 0AX, 0171 623
8711, Fax: 0171 588 1346, Call Date:
Nov 1969 (Middle Temple)
Qualifications: BA, BCL(Oxon), FCIArb

Allnatt *Peter Brian*
30 Seymour Road, East Molesey, Surrey
KT8 0PB, 0181 979 2490, Call Date:
Feb 1953 (Gray's Inn) Qualifications:
LLB

Allott *Stephen Anthony*
Associate, Micromuse PLC, Disraeli
House, 90 Putney Bridge Road, London
SW18 1DA, 0181 875 9500, Fax: 0181
875 9995, Call Date: Nov 1981 (Gray's
Inn) Qualifications: MA (Cantab)

Allport *James Michael*
Withers Solicitors, 12 Gough Square,
London EC3A 3DE, 0171 936 1000, Fax:
0171 936 2589, Call Date: Mar 1998
(Lincoln's Inn) Qualifications: BA
(Hons)

Allsebrook *Geoffrey Pole*
The Green, Cark-in-Cartmel,
Grange-over-Sands, Cumbria LA11 7NJ,
015395 58258, Call Date: Feb 1955
(Inner Temple) Qualifications: MA
(Oxon), PPE

Allsop *David James*
Writer & Journalist, 22 Prince of Wales
Drive, London SW11 4SF, 0171 738
9965, Fax: 0171 738 9328, Call Date:
July 1981 (Middle Temple)
Qualifications: LLB (Dundee)

Alltree *Miss Eileen Mary*
23 Turnberry Grove, Leeds, West
Yorkshire LS17 7TD, Call Date: July 1972
(Middle Temple) Qualifications: LLB

Almond *Roger Buckley*
Call Date: June 1958 (Middle Temple)
Qualifications: MA, BCL, FCIS, frsa

Altman *Miss Clair Rose*
Call Date: Oct 1997 (Gray's Inn)
Qualifications: BA

Alvarez *Manuel* •
Group Legal Adviser, Marconi Electronic
Systems, The Grove, Warren Lane,
Stanmore HA7 4LY, 0181 420 3399, Fax:
0181 420 3860, Call Date: Nov 1969
(Gray's Inn) Qualifications: LLB (Hons)

Alway *Lorne Victor*
Quantity Surveyor, Alway Associates, 3
West Bar, Banbury, Oxon OX16 9SD,
01295 275975, Fax: 01295 257981, Call
Date: Nov 1990 (Middle Temple)
Qualifications: LLB (Lond), Dip QS,
FRICS

Amah *Stanley Chikanene*
Senior Legal Adviser, Ealing Magistrates
Court, Court House, Green Man Lane,
West Ealing, London W13 0SD, 0181 579
9311, Fax: 0181 579 2985, Call Date:
July 1991 (Gray's Inn) Qualifications: BA
(Nigeria), LLB (Lond)

Amaratunga *Mrs Praveen Dharshini* •
Chief Programme Officer,
Commonwealth Secretariat,
Marlborough House, Pall Mall, London
SW1Y 5HX, 0171 747 6435, Call Date:
Oct 1995 (Gray's Inn) Qualifications: BA
(Hons), LLM

Ames *Mrs Tracey Amanda* •
Stratford Office, Solar House, 1-9
Romford Road, London E15, 0181 534
6601, Call Date: Nov 1987 (Inner
Temple) Qualifications: LLB (Essex)

Amesu *Mrs Sharon Rose*
Call Date: Oct 1997 (Middle Temple)
Qualifications: LLB (Hons)(B'ham), CPE
(Manc)

Amin *Ms Neeta* •
Senior Crown Prosecutor, Crown
Prosecution Service, 1st Floor, 8
Gainsford Street, London SE1 2EN, 0171
357 7010, Fax: 0171 962 2645, Call
Date: Oct 1990 (Inner Temple)
Qualifications: LLB (Hons)

Amin *Miss Neeta Manubhai*
Call Date: July 1998 (Inner Temple)
Qualifications: LLB (Wolves)

Amin *Miss Saiqa*
Call Date: Nov 1991 (Inner Temple)
Qualifications: LLB (Hons), LLM

Amir *Miss Nasim Akhtar* •
Senior Crown Prosecutor, Crown
Prosecution Service, The Cooperage,
Gainsford Street, London SE1, 0171 357
7010, Call Date: Nov 1990 (Gray's Inn)
Qualifications: LLB

Amirfazli *Miss Farinaz* •
Crown Prosecution Service, C/O 50
Ludgate Hill, London EC4M 7EX, Call
Date: Nov 1991 (Lincoln's Inn)
Qualifications: LLB (Hons)

Amisu *Adekunle Oluwagbeminiyi*
Solicitor, Legal Services, London
Borough of Hammersmith, & Fulham,
Town Hall, Hammersmith, London
W6 9JU, 0181 576 5958, Fax: 0181 576
5176, Call Date: Nov 1992 (Lincoln's
Inn) Qualifications: LLB (Hons)(Lond)

Amoh *Miss Christine Omenaa*
Call Date: Nov 1994 (Middle Temple)
Qualifications: LLB (Hons)

Amos *William John*
Call Date: Nov 1966 (Gray's Inn)

Amstell *Anthony David* •
Senior Crown Prosecutor, Crown
Prosecution Service, River Park house,
High Road, Wood Green, London N22,
0181 888 8889, Call Date: Nov 1968
(Lincoln's Inn) Qualifications: LLB

Ancill *Miss Karen Cecile*
Call Date: Oct 1995 (Lincoln's Inn)
Qualifications: MA (Hons)(Edinburgh),
Dip in Law (Lond)

Andall *Hogarth Christopher*
Biddle & Co, 1 Gresham Street, London
EC2V 7BU, Call Date: Oct 1993
(Lincoln's Inn) Qualifications: BA
(Hons)(Oxon)

Anderson *Miss Catherine Margaret* •
Legal Assistant/Trainee Advocate,
Templar House, Don Road, St Helier,
Jersey JE4 8NU, 01534 500300, Call
Date: July 1998 (Middle Temple)
Qualifications: BSc (Hons)(Manch)

Anderson *David Heywood*
Member of the International Tribunal for
the Law of the Sea (part-time),
International Tribunal for the, Law of the
Sea, Wexstrasse 4, 20355 Hamburg,
+49 40 35 60 7261, Fax: +49 40 35 60
7245, Call Date: Feb 1963 (Gray's Inn)
Qualifications: LLM (Lond), LLB (Leeds)

Anderson *Lt Cdr Hugh Alastair*
The Ward Room, HMS Gloucester, BFPO
289, Call Date: Oct 1996 (Middle
Temple) Qualifications: LLB
(Hons)(Lond)

Anderson *Iain Massey*
Call Date: Oct 1995 (Lincoln's Inn)
Qualifications: LLB (Hons)(Newc)

Anderson *Ian George* •
Leeds City Council, Civic Hall, Leeds
LS1 1UR, Call Date: July 1984 (Gray's
Inn) Qualifications: B.Soc.Sc

Anderson *John Desmond*
Call Date: July 1998 (Lincoln's Inn)
Qualifications: LLB (Hons)

Anderson *John Victor Ronald*
Caer Rhun Hall, Conwy, Gwynedd, N
Wales LL32 8HX, 01492 650 012, Fax:
01492 650 593, Call Date: July 1972
(Gray's Inn) Qualifications: FCA, MA

Anderson *Miss Lisa Jayne*
Freshfields, 65 Fleet Street, London
EC4Y 1HS, 0171 427 3168, Fax: 0171
832 7231, Call Date: Oct 1996 (Inner
Temple) Qualifications: LLB (S'ton),
LLM (Tax)(LSE)

Anderson *Peter Robert*
Part Time Chairman of Industrial
Tribunals, Suryaloka, 9 Copp Hill Lane,
Budleigh Salterton, Devon EX9 6DT,
01395 44346, Call Date: July 1969
(Middle Temple) Qualifications: MA

Anderson *Richard Ernest*
Call Date: July 1998 (Inner Temple)
Qualifications: LLB (Dunelm)

Anderson *Richard Neil Macdiarmid*
Chairman of Social Security Tribunal, 2
Nicolson Square, Edinburgh, Scotland
EH8 9BH, 01831 830 893, Fax: 0131
668 4880, Advocate,Chartered
Accountant Attorney and Member New
York Bar Scottish Bar, Call Date: Apr
1991 (Gray's Inn) Qualifications: LLB
(Hons), CA FSA (Scot)

Anderson *Miss Sheila Drummond*
Call Date: Nov 1957 (Gray's Inn)
Qualifications: LLB

Andrew *Ms Carolyn Ruth*
Contract Manager, BBC White City, 201
Wood Lane, London W12 7TS, 0181 752
5371, Fax: 0181 752 5500, Call Date: Oct
1997 (Inner Temple) Qualifications: LLB
(London)

Andrew *Edward Alexander*
Sheffield International Ltd, 5th Floor,
Aldermary House, 10-15 Queen Street,
London EC4N 1TX, Call Date: Oct 1993
(Middle Temple) Qualifications: LLB
(Hons)

Andrew *Mrs Margaret* •
Crown Prosecutor, Crown Prosecution
Service, Prospect West, Station Road,
Croydon, Surrey CR0 2RD, Call Date:
Feb 1987 (Middle Temple)
Qualifications: Dip Law, CPE

Andrews *Edward Whybrow*
Manor House Farm, Barningham,
Richmond, North Yorkshire DL11 7DW,
Call Date: July 1972 (Lincoln's Inn)

Andrews *Miss Gillian Margaret*
Clerk to the Justices, Reading &
Newbury, Berkshire & Oxfordshire,
Magistrates Court, Easby House,
Northfield House, Henley-on-Thames,
Oxfordshire RG9 2NB, 01491 412720,
Fax: 01491 412762, Call Date: Nov
1987 (Gray's Inn)

Andrews *Miss Jane Rachel*
Call Date: Nov 1989 (Inner Temple)
Qualifications: LLB (Dub)

Andrews *Nicholas William*
0171 731 2910, Call Date: Nov 1995
(Inner Temple) Qualifications: BSc,
CPE (Sussex)

Aneke *Lloyd Chukwuma*
Court Clerk, Bromley Magistrates'
Court, The Court House, London Road,
Bromley BR1 1BY, 0181 325 4000, Fax:
0181 325 4006, and Member Nigerian
Bar, Call Date: July 1987 (Inner
Temple) Qualifications: LLB

Angelides *Ms Zorna*
Call Date: Nov 1997 (Inner Temple)
Qualifications: LLB

Angeloglou *George*
15 Oakfield Court, 252 Pampisford Rd,
South Croydon, Surrey CR2 6DD, 0181
680 0547, Fax: 0181 680 0547, Call
Date: June 1939 (Inner Temple)
Qualifications: MA (Oxon)

Angus *Matthew Richard*
Liddell Zurbrugg Solicitors, 15-17
Jockey's Fields, LondoN WC1R 4BW,
Call Date: Nov 1997 (Lincoln's Inn)
Qualifications: LLB (Hons)

Anjomshoaa *Miss Poupak*
Call Date: Oct 1996 (Middle Temple)
Qualifications: LLB (Hons)(Lond)

Anning *Miss Barbara Mary*
15 Fawley Road, West Hampstead,
London NW6 1SJ, 0171 794 4335, Fax:
0171 794 4335, Call Date: Nov 1992
(Gray's Inn) Qualifications: LLB
(Buckingham), Licence Speciale en,
Sciences de (ULB), L'Environnement

Anniss *Mrs Jane Ellen* •
Scotland, Call Date: Nov 1984 (Gray's
Inn) Qualifications: LLB (Lancaster)

Anoom *Joseph Kwesi*
Call Date: July 1998 (Middle Temple)
Qualifications: LLB (Hons)(Buck'm),
LLM

Ansari *Askar Humayun* •
Principal Legal Officer, The Inland
Revenue, Solicitor's Office, Somerset
House (East Wing), The Strand,
London WC2R 1LB, 0171 438 6248,
Call Date: July 1973 (Middle Temple)
Qualifications: BA

Ansari *Daniyal*
Call Date: Oct 1995 (Inner Temple)
Qualifications: LLB (Exon), LLM
(Cantab)

Ansari *Selman*
Call Date: Oct 1997 (Lincoln's Inn)
Qualifications: BA (Hons)(Lond)

Antell *John Jason*
Antell & Co, Ringmarsh House,
Horsington, Somerset BA8 OEL, 0973
843005, Fax: 01963 370544, Chartered
Information Systems Engineer, Call
Date: Oct 1992 (Middle Temple)
Qualifications: LL.B (Hons Lond),
MBCS, CEng

Antelme *Leopold John*
Winchcombe Lodge, Bucklebury,
Berkshire RG7 6NS, 0118 9713261,
Fax: 0118 9714696, Call Date: July
1952 (Inner Temple) Qualifications:
MA

Anthony *Farid Ray*
89 Saxon Street, Gillingham, Kent
ME7 5EG, 01634 578649, Fax: 01634
578649, and Member Sierra Leone Bar
and Gambian Bar, Call Date: Nov 1963
(Inner Temple)

Anthoson *Jason Lawrence*
Call Date: May 1985 (Lincoln's Inn)
Qualifications: BA Keele

Anucha *Dominic Uka*
Solicitor & Advocate Supreme Crt of
Nigeria and Member Nigerian Bar, Call
Date: May 1987 (Gray's Inn)
Qualifications: MA, LLB

Anyiam *Izomor Herbert*
Adviser, Plumstead Community Law
Centre, 105 Plumstead High Street,
London SE18 1SB, 0181 244 4951,
Fax: 0181 316 7903, Currently a
Solicitor and Member Nigeria Bar, Call
Date: Nov 1996 (Lincoln's Inn)
Qualifications: LLB (Hons)(Lagos)

Appiah *Kofi*
Freeman of the City of London, 57
Chambord Street, London E2 7NJ, 0171
729 4803, Fax: 0171 729 4803, and
Member Ghana Bar, Call Date: Nov
1974 (Inner Temple) Qualifications:
LLB (Lond)

Appleby *Charles Mark* •
Senior Crown Prosecutor, Crown
Prosecution Service, Heritage House,
Fisherman's Wharf, Grimsby
DN31 1SY, Kings Inn, Dublin (Dec
1970) and Member Southern Ireland
Bar, Call Date: July 1975 (Gray's Inn)

Arbel *Mrs Caroline Emma*
Call Date: July 1994 (Middle Temple)
Qualifications: LLB (Hons)(Lond)

Arbuthnot *James Norwich*
Assistant Recorder, also Lincolns Inn
1977 10 Old Square, Ground Floor,
Lincoln's Inn, London, WC2A 3SU, Call
Date: July 1975 (Inner Temple)
Qualifications: BA (Cantab)

Archer *David John* •
Principal Crown Prosecutor, Crown
Prosecution Service, 24th Floor,
Portland House, Stag Place, London
SW1E 5BH, 0171 828 9050, Call Date:
Feb 1988 (Gray's Inn) Qualifications:
BA (Oxon)

Archer *Mrs Jacqueline Ann*
Deputy Chief Clerk, Inner London
Magistrates Crt, 65 Romney Street,
London SW1P 3RD, Call Date: Feb 1988
(Gray's Inn) Qualifications: BA(Hons)

Archer *Mrs June Maureen* •
Call Date: July 1980 (Inner Temple)

Archer *Mrs Lorna Helen*
Deputy Chief Clerk, Inner London
Magistrates', Courts Service, Inner
London & City Proceeding, 59-65 Wells
Street, London W1A 3AE, 0171 323
1649, Fax: 0171 636 0617, Call Date:
Nov 1986 (Gray's Inn) Qualifications:
BA (Hons)

Archer *Mark David*
Ward Hadaway, Sandgate House, 102
Quayside, Newcastle Upon Tyne
NE1 3DX, 0191 204 4000, Fax: 0191
204 4001, Solicitor (1998), Call Date:
Oct 1995 (Inner Temple)
Qualifications: LLB (Hons)(Hudds)

Arfon-Jones *Miss Elisabeth*
Full-time Immigration Adjudicator,
Part-Time Lay Chairman NHS
Complaints Panel (vol), Member of
Lottery Charities Board (Vol), and
Member Bermuda Bar, Call Date: July
1972 (Gray's Inn) Qualifications: LLB
(Lond)

Arian *Chinsamy Chagadeven*
Legal Advisor, Call Date: Nov 1994
(Gray's Inn) Qualifications: LLB (Lon)

Aris *Jason Mark*
Call Date: Oct 1998 (Inner Temple)
Qualifications: LLB (Wolves)

Armbrister *Allan Ramsay* •
Clerk to the Justices, Teesside Law
Courts, Victoria Square, Middlesbrough,
Cleveland TS1 2AS, 01642 240301, Fax:
01642 224010, Call Date: Nov 1984
(Inner Temple) Qualifications: BA,
D.M.S., D.M.L.

Armitage *Robert*
12 Milner St, London SW3 2PU, 0171
584 0162, Call Date: June 1948 (Inner
Temple) Qualifications: MA (Cantab)

Armitage *Roderick Donald* •
Legal Director and Secretary Staveley
Industries Plc, Staveley Industries plc, 11
Dingwall Road, Croydon CR9 1BY, 0181
688 4404, Fax: 0181 760 0563, Call
Date: Feb 1979 (Middle Temple)
Qualifications: FCIS

Armstrong *Rear Admiral John Herbert
Arthur James* •
Chief Executive, The Royal Institution of,
Chartered Surveyors, 12 Great George
Street, Parliament Square SW1P 3AD,
Call Date: July 1976 (Middle Temple)
Qualifications: MA (Oxon)

Armstrong *Martin Robert* •
Legal Adviser, Philips Electronics UK, The
Philips Centre, 420-430 London Road,
Croydon CR9 3QR, 0181 781 8471, Fax:
0181 781 8888, Call Date: July 1979
(Inner Temple) Qualifications: BA
[Camb]

Arnold *Mrs Anne Mary*
Director of Legal Services Acting
Provincial Stipendiary Magistrate, P O
Box 15, Law Courts, Stafford Road,
Bournemouth BH1 1LA, 01202 745309,
Fax: 01202 711999, Call Date: Nov 1981
(Inner Temple) Qualifications: BA Hons,
MBA

Arnold *Piers John* •
Crown Prosecutor, Crown Prosecution
Service, Lombard Street, Abingdon, Oxon
OX14 5SE, 01235 555678, Fax: 01235
554144, Call Date: Nov 1992 (Inner
Temple) Qualifications: BA (Oxon), Dip
in Law

Arnold-Baker *Professor Charles*
Former Dep.Traffic Commissioner &
Licensing Authority, Editor 'Road Law'
Visiting Professor, City Uni, Top Floor, 2
Paper Bldgs, Inner Temple, London
EC4Y 7ET, 0171 353 3490, Call Date:
June 1948 (Inner Temple)
Qualifications: BA(Oxon)

Arnot *Graham Robert Erwin* •
Commercial Lawyer, 0118 947 7435,
Fax: 0118 946 1465, Call Date: July 1973
(Inner Temple) Qualifications: MA
(Oxon)

Arnot *Simon Richard Cranstoun* •
Legal Department, Allied Dunbar
Assurance plc, Allied Dunbar Centre,
Swindon SN1 1EL, 01793 514514, Call
Date: Nov 1987 (Gray's Inn)
Qualifications: BA , LLB

Arowojolu *Olutayo Olaniran*
Legal Advisor, Newham Rights Centre,
285 Romford Road, Forest Gate, London
E7 9HJ, 0181 5553331, Fax: 0181
5197348, and Member Nigerian Bar, Call
Date: Nov 1993 (Lincoln's Inn)
Qualifications: LLB (Hons, Lagos), LLM
(Lond)

Arrif *Ms Hawa Bibi Bahemia*
Call Date: July 1996 (Gray's Inn)
Qualifications: BSc. (Hertfordshire)

Arshad *Miss Farrhat*
Call Date: Nov 1998 (Inner Temple)
Qualifications: BA (Exon), LLM (LSE)

Arthur *Michael David*
Call Date: Nov 1997 (Middle Temple)
Qualifications: BA (Hons)(Lond)

Arthur *Robin Anthony* •
The Manor Hse, The Green, Hilton,
Huntingdon, Cambridgeshire PE18 9NA,
Call Date: Nov 1976 (Gray's Inn)
Qualifications: LLB (Lond)

Arthur *Mrs Susannah Jane*
Call Date: Nov 1997 (Middle Temple)
Qualifications: BSc (Hons)(Wales), LLB
(Hons)(Lond)

Asad *Miss Sabeena* •
Refugee Counsellor, Call Date: July 1989
(Middle Temple) Qualifications: LLB
(Lond)

Asante *Miss Afua Oduro*
Call Date: Oct 1998 (Gray's Inn)
Qualifications: BA, MA (Leicester)

Asare *Kwame Ohene*
Consumer/Debt Advisor, Call Date: Nov
1995 (Lincoln's Inn) Qualifications: BSc
(Hons), LLB (Hons) (Lond)

Asekun *Ms Diane Omolola*
Call Date: Mar 1998 (Middle Temple)
Qualifications: BA (Psyc)(Virginia), LLB
(Hons), LLM, (Bucks)

Ashby *Peter Marcus* •
Principal Crown Prosecutor, Crown
Prosecution Service, 2 Kimbrose Way,
Gloucester GL1 2DB, 01452 308989,
Also Inn of Court G, Call Date: Nov 1978
(Middle Temple) Qualifications: BA
(Hons)

Ashcroft *Miss Sophie Laura*
Call Date: Mar 1997 (Inner Temple)
Qualifications: BA

Ashenden *Michael Roy Edward*
25 Melrose Road, Merton Park, London
SW19, 0181 542 5019, Call Date: Jan
1949 (Middle Temple) Qualifications:
MA (Cantab)

Ashford *Stephen James* •
Director - Legal & Corporate Affairs, Veba
Oil and Gas UK Ltd, Bowater Hse, 114
Knightsbridge, London SW1X 7LD, 0171
225 7100, Fax: 0171 584 6459, Call
Date: July 1973 (Gray's Inn)
Qualifications: LLB (Lond), AKC

Ashley *Miss Gayle Beverley*
Call Date: Oct 1997 (Middle Temple)
Qualifications: LLB (Hons)(Sussex)

Ashley *Dr Graham William* •
Patent Examiner, European Patent
Office, Bayerstrasse 34, 80335 Munich,
00 49 89 2399 8420, Call Date: Oct 1996
(Lincoln's Inn) Qualifications: B.Tech
(Brunel), PhD (Cantab), MSc (Lond)

Ashley *Phillip Spencer*
Call Date: Oct 1998 (Lincoln's Inn)
Qualifications: LLB (Hons)(Greenwic)

Ashman *Peter Frank* •
Director, European Human Rights,
Foundation, 70 Ave Michel-Ange, 1000
Brussels, 32-2 734 9424, Fax: 32-2 734
6831, Call Date: Nov 1974 (Middle
Temple) Qualifications: LLB (Lond)

Ashmore *Anthony John*
Call Date: Nov 1996 (Middle Temple)
Qualifications: LLB (Hons), F.P.M.I.,
F.I.P.D., A.C.I.I.

Ashplant *Anthony John* •
Head of Legal & Compliance, M & G
Limited, 7th Floor, 3 Minster Court,
Great Tower Street, London EC3R 7HX,
0171 621 8903, Fax: 0171 283 4293,
Call Date: July 1977 (Middle Temple)
Qualifications: LLB Hons (Lond)

Ashra *Jay Kanji*
Call Date: Oct 1995 (Gray's Inn)
Qualifications: BA (Keele)

Ashton *Barry Philip* •
Senior Crown Prosecutor, Crown
Prosecution Service, East Kent Branch,
3rd Floor, Queen's House, Guildhall St,
Folkestone, Kent CT20 2DT, 01303
50533, Fax: 01303 250521, Call Date:
Nov 1985 (Gray's Inn) Qualifications:
BSc (Bradford), LLB

Ashton *Miss Bridget Lesley* •
Senior Crown Prosecutor, Crown
Prosecution Service, 3rd Floor, Black
Horse House, 8-10 Leigh Road, Eastleigh
SO50 4FH, 01703 614622, Fax: 01703
644258, Call Date: Feb 1990 (Inner
Temple) Qualifications: LLB (Hons)
Bucks

Ashton *Dr Raymond Keighley*
01494 725330, Fax: 01494 432165, and
Member Guernsey Bar, Channel Islands,
Call Date: July 1979 (Lincoln's Inn)
Qualifications: BSC (Econ, Lond) , FCA,
MSc (Econ,Lond), LLM FTII ACMA ACIS
PHD (Lond)

Ashton *Roy*
Part time Chairman Agricultural Land
Tribunal, Call Date: Feb 1954 (Lincoln's
Inn) Qualifications: LL.B

Ashton-Jones *Philip* •
Principal Legal Adviser, Associated
British Foods plc, NEM House, 3-5
Rickmansworth Road, Watford, Herts
WD1 7HG, 01923 252050, Fax: 01923
223542, Call Date: Nov 1986 (Middle
Temple) Qualifications: LLB (E Anglia)

Ashworth *John Nigel Laurence* •
Legal Adviser to the British Forces
Germany., Legal Adviser, External Affairs
Division, Joint Headquarters, British
Forces Germany, BFPO 140, Call Date:
July 1973 (Inner Temple) Qualifications:
BA (Lond)

Ashworth *Mark Heddle* •
Lombard North Central PLC, 3 Princes
Way, Redhill RH1 1NP, 0171 726 1177,
Fax: 0171 726 1035, Call Date: Nov
1987 (Lincoln's Inn) Qualifications:
MA (Oxon), Dip Law, (City)

Askew *Richard John Aldis* •
Group Legal Adviser Refined Sugar
Assoc Arbitrator ICC Arbitration
Appointments, E D & F Man Ltd, Sugar
Quay, Lower Thames Street, London
EC3R 6DU, 0171 285 3000, Fax: 0171
285 3518, Call Date: July 1978 (Inner
Temple) Qualifications: MA (Oxon),
ACIArb

Aslam *Ms Saiqa Naureen* •
Legal Advisor, Avon & Bristol Law
Centre, 2 Moon Street, Stokes Court,
Bristol BS2 8QE, 0117 924 8662, Fax:
0117 924 8020, Call Date: July 1995
(Inner Temple) Qualifications: LLB
(Wolverhampton), MA (Oxon)

Aspinall *Michael* •
Legal Adviser, Call Date: Nov 1986
(Gray's Inn) Qualifications: BSocSci,
MA (Keele)

Asquith *Anthony John* •
The Dialog Corporation plc, The
Communications BuildinG, 48
Leicester Square, London WC2H 7DB,
0171 930 6900, Fax: 0171 930 6006,
Call Date: Oct 1994 (Lincoln's Inn)
Qualifications: LLB (Hons)(Sheff)

Astbury *Malcolm John*
Chief Executive, Humberside
Magistrates Court, Court House, Station
Road, Brough, East Yorkshire
HU15 1DY, 01482 666007, Fax: 01482
666476, Call Date: Nov 1980 (Gray's
Inn) Qualifications: D.M.L

Astbury *Mrs Margaret*
Deputy Chairman of the South West
Agricultural Land Tribunal, Call Date:
Nov 1970 (Gray's Inn) Qualifications:
FCIArb

Astbury *Michael Henry Richardson*
Three Way's, Boneashe Lane, St Mary's
Platt, Sevenoaks, Kent TN15 8NW,
01732 884163, Fax: 01732 780713,
Call Date: Nov 1953 (Middle Temple)
Qualifications: MA (Cantab), ACIArb

Aston *Lee Anthony*
Call Date: Mar 1996 (Gray's Inn)
Qualifications: BA

Aston *Simon Richard*
Call Date: Mar 1996 (Middle Temple)
Qualifications: BA (Hons), M.Phil, (N.
Wales)

Astor *Richard Joseph*
also Inn of Court L, Call Date: July 1982
(Middle Temple) Qualifications: BA
(Kent), ACIArb

Atikpakpa *Ogheneovo Joshua*
Consultant, Usman & Co Solicitors, 6A
Blenheim Grove, Peckham, London
SE15 4QL, 0171 732 9101, Fax: 0171
732 9181, Call Date: Nov 1994
(Lincoln's Inn) Qualifications: LLB
(Lanc), LLM (L'pool)

Atkinson *Alexander Peter David*
3 Quick Street, Islington, London
N1 8HL, 0171 837 8001, Fax: 0171 833
3555, Call Date: July 1967 (Inner
Temple) Qualifications: MA, LLB, FCA

Atkinson *Daniel Maria Teresa Solferino*
Director - James R Knowles, James R
Knowles Limited, 53 Bedford Square,
London WC1B 3DP, 0171 580 4434,
Fax: 0171 436 4860, Call Date: July
1994 (Lincoln's Inn) Qualifications:
LLB (Hons), BSc (Hons)

Atkinson *Ms Esther Mary*
Call Date: Mar 1997 (Gray's Inn)
Qualifications: LLB (Warw)

Atkinson-Lyon *Mrs Ruth* •
Senior Crown Prosecutor, The Crown
Prosecution Service, 2nd Floor,
Windsor House, Pepper Street, Chester
CH1 1TD, 01244 348043, Call Date:
Nov 1988 (Lincoln's Inn)
Qualifications: LLB (Hons)

Attala *Jean Etienne*
Messrs Anthony Walters & Co,
Solicitors, Barrington Chambers, 23a
Victoria Avenue, Bishop Auckland, Co
Durham DL14 7NE, 01388 662222,
Fax: 01388 450603, Former Solicitor,
Call Date: May 1994 (Gray's Inn)
Qualifications: LLB

Attar *Ms Sharona*
Call Date: Oct 1997 (Inner Temple)
Qualifications: LLB (Manchester), LLM
(London)

Attenborough *Gordon Roger*
Call Date: Oct 1996 (Inner Temple)
Qualifications: LLB (Lond)

Attwood *Miss Jenifer Susan*
Call Date: Oct 1998 (Middle Temple)
Qualifications: BSc (Hons)(S.Africa),
CPE (Middx)

Aubeelack *Dhirajdass*
and Member Mauritius Bar, Call Date:
Nov 1982 (Middle Temple)
Qualifications: BA

Aubrey *Michael David*
Call Date: July 1963 (Gray's Inn)
Qualifications: LLB (Lond)

August *Mrs Rosemarie*
August Associates, 31 Walmers Avenue,
Higham, Rochester, Kent ME3 7EH,
0147482 2194, Fax: 0147482 2194,
Call Date: July 1977 (Middle Temple)

Austen-Baker *Richard Lindsay
Peregrine St Joh*
178 Hearsall Lane, Earlsdon, Coventry
CV5 6HJ, 01203 673541, Call Date: Oct
1997 (Gray's Inn) Qualifications: LLB
(Wales)

Austen-Peters *Oludotun* •
Senior Lawyer, Eastern Group plc,
Wherstead Park, Wherstead, Ipswich
IP9 2AQ, 01473 553623, Fax: 01473
533617, and Member Nigerian Bar, Call
Date: July 1983 (Inner Temple)
Qualifications: BA (Hons), LLM

Austin *Mrs Amanda Jane* •
The Treasury Solicitor's Dept, Call Date:
Nov 1993 (Gray's Inn) Qualifications:
LLB (Hons)

Austin *Miss Angela Catherine Anne*
George Corderoy & Co, 25-28
Buckingham Gate, London SW1E 6LD,
0171 834 5353, Fax: 0071 834 0373,
Fellow of Royal Institution of Chartered
Surveyors, Call Date: Mar 1998 (Gray's
Inn) Qualifications: BSc
(Hons)(Not'ham), LLB (Hons)(Lond),
ACIArb

Austin *Anthony Charles*
Call Date: Feb 1960 (Gray's Inn)

Austin *Miss Jane Margaret*
Deputy Clerk to the Justices, The Court
House, Shotfield, Wallington, Surrey
SM6 0JA, 0181 770 5950, Fax: 0181
770 5977, Call Date: Nov 1977 (Gray's
Inn) Qualifications: LLB

Austin *Miss Patricia Mary*
Call Date: Nov 1955 (Gray's Inn)

Austin *Colonel Richard Peter
Meredith* •
Officer, Army Legal Services, Army
Legal Aid (NW Europe), Calkenick
Barracks, BFPO 39, 00 49 521 9254,
Fax: 00 49 521 9254, Attorney &
Counsellor of the United States Army
Court of Military Review, Call Date: July
1976 (Inner Temple)

Avery *Miss Katrina*
Call Date: Oct 1993 (Inner Temple)
Qualifications: BA (Kent), CPE

Avgousti *Avgoustinos Andreas* •
Deputy Director, Competition and Fair
Trading, Office of Telecommunications,
Wu Chung House, 29/F 213 Queen's
Road East, Wan Chai EC4M 7JJ, and
Member Cyprus Bar, Call Date: Nov
1989 (Lincoln's Inn) Qualifications:
LLM

Awad *Anthony Joseph*
Call Date: Nov 1991 (Middle Temple)
Qualifications: Bsc (Hons); Dip Law

Awadalla *Miss Katherine Elizabeth*
Call Date: Oct 1998 (Middle Temple)
Qualifications: LLB (Hons)(Dunelm)

Awoonor-Renner *Miss Loraine Beatrice*
Call Date: Nov 1996 (Middle Temple)
Qualifications: LLB (Hons)(Sheff)

Aylett *Anthony Peter Michael* •
Grade 6 Legal Oficer, Treasury
Solicitor's Dept, Queen Anne's
Chambers, 28 Broadway, London
SW1H 9JS, 0171 210 3496, Fax: 0171
210 3410, Call Date: May 1971 (Middle
Temple) Qualifications: LLB

Ayre *Marcus Logan*
Scotland, Call Date: Oct 1997 (Middle
Temple) Qualifications: LLB
(Hons)(B'Ham)

Azhar *Miss Marina* •
Essex County Council, County Secretary's
Dept, P O Box 11, County Hall,
Chelmsford CM1 1LX, 01245 430436,
Fax: 01245 364994/352710, Call Date:
Nov 1990 (Lincoln's Inn) Qualifications:
LLB (PCL)

Azis *Osman Abdul*
Parke & Co Ltd, Mousehill Court,
Milford, Godalming GU8 5EA, 01483
860603, Fax: 01483 418348, Call Date:
July 1952 (Lincoln's Inn) Qualifications:
MA (Oxon)

Aziz *Mohammed Abdul*
Call Date: Nov 1998 (Gray's Inn)
Qualifications: LLB (Lond), LLM (Lond)

Baah *Yaw*
Call Date: Nov 1998 (Lincoln's Inn)
Qualifications: BA (Hons)(Ghana), Dip
Law

Baars *Adriaan Willem*
Assistant, Winward Fearon, 35 Bow
Street, London WC2E 7AU, 0171 420
2800, Fax: 0171 420 2801, Call Date:
Feb 1993 (Middle Temple)
Qualifications: LLB (Hons)(Bucks), LLM
(Bucks)

Babar *Jawad Altahir*
Call Date: Oct 1997 (Lincoln's Inn)
Qualifications: LLB (Hons)(Lond)

Babar *Miss Natasha*
Call Date: July 1998 (Inner Temple)
Qualifications: BSc (Leics)

Baboolal *Miss Maureen* •
Principal Legal Officer, Department of
Social Security, Office of the Solicitor,
Block 2 , Spur Govt Buildings, Honeypot
Lane, Stanmore, Middlesex HA7 1AY,
0171 972 3625, Fax: 0171 972 3671,
and Member Trinidad & Tobago Bar, Call
Date: Nov 1987 (Middle Temple)
Qualifications: BSc (Hons), LLB (Hons)

Bacarese *George Alan* •
Senior Crown Prosecutor, Crown
Prosecution Service, Princes Court, 34
York Road, Leicester LE1 5TU, Call Date:
July 1988 (Middle Temple)
Qualifications: LLB (Hons)

Backus *Duncan William Torquil* •
Senior Lawyer, Europe, Electronic Arts
Limited, Meadfield Road, Langley,
Slough, Berkshire SL3 8AL, 01753
549442, Call Date: Oct 1990 (Middle
Temple) Qualifications: LLB

Bacon *Bernard Matthew*
9 Wisley Court, West Avenue, Worthing,
W Sussex BN11 5LY, Call Date: Nov 1952
(Gray's Inn) Qualifications: MA (Cantab)

Bacon *Stephen Francis Theodore* •
Legal Adviser, Express Newspapers plc,
Ludgate House, 245 Blackfriars Road,
London SE1 9UX, 0171 922 7784, Fax:
0171 922 7967, Past Chairman of BACFI,
Call Date: July 1969 (Gray's Inn)
Qualifications: LLB (Lond), A.K.C

Badejo *Abimbola Rafiu* •
Legal Adviser/Advocate, London Borough
of Camden, Legal Services, Town Hall,
Judd Street, London WC1H 9LP, 0171
278 4444 x 5223, Fax: 0171 860 5659,
Call Date: Nov 1993 (Lincoln's Inn)
Qualifications: LLB (Hons)

Badham *Christopher Andrew* •
Mayer Brown & Platt, Bucklesbury
House, Queen Victoria Street, London
EC4N 8EL, Call Date: Oct 1994
(Lincoln's Inn) Qualifications: LLB
(Hons)(Wales)

Badom *Ms Helen*
Call Date: Oct 1997 (Inner Temple)
Qualifications: LLB

Badrudin *Nizam* •
Barry House, 20-22 Worple Road,
Wimbledon, London SW19 4DH, 0181
947 0088, Fax: 0181 947 6827, Call
Date: Nov 1969 (Middle Temple)
Qualifications: FRICS

Baggs *David John* •
Borough of Poole, Unit A, MItre Court, 16
Commercial Road, Parkstone, Poole,
Dorset BH14 0JW, 01202 253333, Fax:
01202 253345, Call Date: Nov 1975
(Lincoln's Inn) Qualifications: LLB

Baggs *John William*
Company Chairman, 10 St Margaret's
Close, Southampton SO18 5NE, 0850
40100 5, Formerly a Legal Executive, Call
Date: July 1996 (Lincoln's Inn)
Qualifications: LLB (Hons)

Bagnall *Kenneth Reginald*
Chairman, New Property Cases Ltd,
01344 84 3696, Fax: 01344 84 2934, QC
Hong Kong 1983, Call Date: Jan 1950
(Gray's Inn) Qualifications: LLB

Bagshaw *Miss Joan Ernestine*
Porte Bonheur, 87 Park Road,
Brentwood, Essex CM14 4TU, 01277
221939, Fax: 01277 221939, Call Date:
Jan 1950 (Gray's Inn)

Bahra *Miss Narita*
4 King's Bench Walk, Ground/First Floor,
Temple, London, EC4Y 7DL, Call Date:
Nov 1997 (Lincoln's Inn) Qualifications:
LLB (Hons)(Lond)

Bailey *Anthony Lee*
Call Date: Nov 1997 (Inner Temple)
Qualifications: LLB (Reading)

Bailey *Christopher Richard*
Call Date: Oct 1998 (Middle Temple)
Qualifications: BA (Hons), CPE (Wolves)

Bailey *Miss Helen Clare*
Call Date: Oct 1994 (Inner Temple)
Qualifications: LLB (Nott), LLM (Nott)

Bailey *Miss Jane Angela Tabitha* •
Legal Officer, Solicitor of Inland
Revenue, Somerset House, Strand,
London WC2R 1LB, 0171 438 7041, Fax:
0171 438 6246, Call Date: Oct 1993
(Inner Temple) Qualifications: LLB

Bailey *Jason Thomas*
Call Date: Nov 1998 (Gray's Inn)
Qualifications: BA (Staffs)

Bailey *Miss Rebecca Anne*
Solicitor of the Supreme Court, Call
Date: Oct 1994 (Lincoln's Inn)
Qualifications: LLB (Hons)(Leic)

Bailey *Sam*
45c Crouch Hill, London N4 4AJ, Call
Date: Oct 1995 (Lincoln's Inn)
Qualifications: LLB (Hons)(L'pool)

Baillie *Adrian Louis*
Call Date: Mar 1999 (Middle Temple)
Qualifications: BA (Hons)(Manch)

Baily *Christopher Hugh*
Bailys, Eden Bank, Bolton, Appleby,
Cumbria CA16 6AY, 01931 714600, Fax:
01931 714100, Member of Lord
Chancellor's Panel of Agricultural
Arbitrators, Call Date: July 1979 (Gray's
Inn) Qualifications: BA (Cantab), FRICS,,
ACIArb

Bainbridge *Dr David Ian*
Reader in Law, Aston University, Aston
Triangle, Birmingham B4 7ET, 0121 359
3611, Fax: 0121 333 4313, Call Date: Oct
1996 (Lincoln's Inn) Qualifications: BSc
(Wales), LLB (Hons), PhD (B'ham),
MICE, MBCS

Baines *Dr Arnold Herbert John*
District and Town Councillor, Finmere,
90 Eskdale Avenue, Chesham, Bucks
HP5 3AY, Call Date: June 1951 (Gray's
Inn) Qualifications: MA, PhD, FSA, FR
Hist S, FRSA , C Stat

Baines *Paul Harold*
Detective Superintendent, Merseyside
Police, PO Box 69, Liverpool L69 1JD,
0151 709 6010, Call Date: May 1988
(Lincoln's Inn) Qualifications: LLB
(L'Pool)

Bajwa *Azfar Naseem*
Call Date: July 1996 (Gray's Inn)
Qualifications: LLB (London), LLM

Baker *Miss Elisabeth Sara*
10 Park Square, Leeds, LS1 2LH, Call
Date: Nov 1970 (Middle Temple)
Qualifications: LLB (Leeds)

Baker *Mrs Elizabeth Anne* •
Senior Crown Prosecutor, Crown
Prosecution Service, Berkshire Branch
Office, Eaton Court, 112 Oxford Road,
Reading, Berkshire RG1 7LL, 0118 950
3771, Fax: 0118 950 8192, Call Date:
July 1982 (Middle Temple)
Qualifications: BA (Lond), Dip Law

Baker *Ellis David*
Call Date: Oct 1991 (Inner Temple)
Qualifications: BA (Cantab)

Baker *Mrs Helen Lesley*
The Hill, Tair Croes, Ewenny, Nr
Bridgend, Mid Glamorgan CF35 5AG,
01656 654073, Call Date: Feb 1980
(Gray's Inn) Qualifications: LLB
(Wales)

Baker *John Victor Robert*
Clerk to the Justices, Surrey
Magistrates' Court, Court House,
London Road, Dorking, Surrey
RH4 1SX, Call Date: July 1981 (Middle
Temple)

Baker *Mrs Margaret Daphne*
Call Date: Nov 1994 (Middle Temple)
Qualifications: LLB (Hons)

Baker *Matthew James*
Call Date: July 1998 (Lincoln's Inn)
Qualifications: BA (Hons)(Exon)

Baker *Michael Johnathan Charles*
Head of Regulatory Affairs, PAGB,
Vernon House, Sicilian Avenue, London
WC1A 2QH, 071 242 8331, Fax: 071
405 7719, Call Date: July 1983 (Middle
Temple) Qualifications: LLB (Newc)

Baker *Paul*
57 Kingswood Road, Shortlands,
Bromley, Kent BR2 0NL, 0181 460
0612, Hon Lt Colonel, Call Date: Nov
1949 (Middle Temple)

Baker *Peter Tustin*
Kingsclere, Groombridge, Nr Tunbridge
Wells, Kent TN3 9SH, 01892 863220,
Fax: 01892 861349, Call Date: June
1956 (Middle Temple) Qualifications:
MA

Baker *Robert John* •
Crown Prosecutor, Crown Prosecution
Service, North Staffs Branch Office,
Blackburn House, Midway, Newcastle
Under Lyme ST5 1TB, Call Date: Oct
1996 (Middle Temple) Qualifications:
LLB (Hons), LLM (Lond)

Baker *Roger* •
Grade 7 Lawyer (Nominated Officer),
Office of the Social Security, & Child
Support Commissioners, 83/86
Farringdon Street, London EC4A 4DH,
0171 353 5145, Fax: 0171 936 2171,
Call Date: Nov 1966 (Gray's Inn)

Baker *Stephen George*
Harris Fowler Solicitors, Powlett House,
High Street, Taunton, Somersett
TA1 3PN, 01823 323456, Fax: 01823
325392, Call Date: Feb 1994 (Middle
Temple) Qualifications: BA
(Hons)(York)

Baker *Stuart* •
Justices Chief Executive, West Riding,
Metropolitan, Magistrates' Crt Service,
1st Floor, Colbeck House, Bradford Rd,
Birstall, Batley WF17 9NR, 01924
424030, Fax: 01924 427910, Call Date:
Nov 1976 (Gray's Inn) Qualifications:
B.Tech (Law)

Bakhshov *Alexander Azam*
Call Date: Oct 1997 (Inner Temple)
Qualifications: LLB (London)

Bakshi *Miss Irvinder Kaur*
Head of Construction Department,
Howard Kennedy, Harcourt House, 19
Cavendish Square, London W1A 2AW,
0171 546 8821, Fax: 0171 491 2899,
Call Date: Nov 1987 (Lincoln's Inn)
Qualifications: LLB(Hons), DipICArb,
ACIArb

Baksi *Miss Catherine Jane*
Call Date: Nov 1998 (Inner Temple)
Qualifications: LLB (Brunel)

Baldry *John Charles*
Allen & Overy, One New Change,
London EC4M 9QQ, 0171 330 3000,
Fax: 0171 330 9999, Call Date: Nov
1993 (Middle Temple) Qualifications:
LLB (Hons)(Lond), LLM (Lond)

Baldwyn *Anthony Shaw* •
Senior Adviser to EC, Commission of
the European, Communities, CSM2 4/
75 Rue de la Loi 200, B-1049 Brussels,
Belgium, 00 322 2965476, Fax: 00 322
2956451, Contracted to European
Commission, Call Date: July 1977
(Middle Temple) Qualifications: LLB

Bale *Mrs Katherine Geraldine*
Call Date: Oct 1993 (Gray's Inn)
Qualifications: BA (Sheff), LLB

Balen *Miss Bernadette*
and Member Singapore, Call Date: Nov
1993 (Lincoln's Inn) Qualifications:
LLB (Hons)

Ball *Andrew Charles Manton*
VAT Partner, Deloitte & Touche, Hill
House, 1 Little New Street, London
EC4A 3TR, 0171 303 6365, Fax: 0171
303 4780, Call Date: Nov 1979 (Gray's
Inn) Qualifications: LLB (Lond)

Ball *Andrew Nicholas*
Principal Court Clerk, Stockport
Magistrates' Court, P O Box 155,
Edward Street, Stockport, Cheshire
SK1 3NF, 0161 477 2020, Fax: 0161
474 1115, Call Date: May 1993 (Middle
Temple) Qualifications: LLB
(Hons)(Aberystw)

Ball *Brian Anthony*
Call Date: July 1996 (Lincoln's Inn)
Qualifications: LLB (Hons)(Wales),
LLM (Lond)

Ball *Mrs Deborah Elizabeth*
Call Date: Nov 1992 (Middle Temple)
Qualifications: BA (Hons)

Ball *Ian David* •
Crown Prosecutor, Crown Prosecution
Service, Branch 2, 12th Floor, Colmore
Gate, 2 Colmore Row, Birmingham
B3 2QA, 0121 629 7200, Call Date: Oct
1992 (Middle Temple) Qualifications:
LLB (Hons)(B'ham)

Ball *Mrs Jane* •
Senior Crown Prosecutor, CPS, 4-12
Queen Anne'a Gate, London SW1H 9AZ,
Call Date: July 1986 (Inner Temple)
Qualifications: Dip Magisterial Law

Ball *Ms Sally Anne*
1 Alfred Street, High Street, Oxford, OX1
4EH, Call Date: Nov 1989 (Middle
Temple) Qualifications: BA Hons
(Oxon)

Ballard *David Edward*
Director, Glass and Glazing Federation,
44-48 Borough High Street, London
SE1 1XB, 0171 403 7177, Fax: 0171
357 7458, Call Date: July 1988 (Middle
Temple) Qualifications: BSc (City),MSc
(Lon), CEng., LLB, FICE , FCIArb

Ballard *Peter*
Compton Developments, 13 Compton
Avenue, Skewen, Swansea SA10 6BB,
01792 790934, Fax: 01792 702930,
Call Date: Nov 1976 (Middle Temple)
Qualifications: MA (Cantab), ACA , ATII,
MBA

Ballingal *Alexander James*
Call Date: Jan 1946 (Middle Temple)
Qualifications: MA (Oxon)

Balmforth *Graham Gregory*
Call Date: July 1998 (Lincoln's Inn)
Qualifications: BA (Hons)

Balogun *Mrs Kirsten Victoria*
James R Knowles, Wardle House, King
Street, Knutsford, Cheshire WA16 6PD,
01565 654666, Fax: 01565 755009,
Call Date: July 1997 (Lincoln's Inn)
Qualifications: LLB (Hons)(Manch),
Bsc, DipArb, ARICS, FCIArb

Balonwu *Stephen* •
Legal Advisor, ABTA, 68-71 Newman
Street, London W1P 4AH, 0171 637
2444, Fax: 0171 637 0713, Call Date:
Oct 1993 (Middle Temple)
Qualifications: BA (Hons)(Kent)

Bamforth *Miss Ruth Alexandra* •
Slaugher & May, Coleman Street,
London, Call Date: Nov 1996 (Lincoln's
Inn) Qualifications: LLB
(Hons)(Leeds), LLM (Cantab)

Bamieh *Miss Thuraya Maria* •
Senior Crown Prosecutor, Crown
Prosecution Service, 23rd Floor,
Portland House, Stag Place, London
SW1E 5BH, Call Date: Nov 1984
(Lincoln's Inn) Qualifications: BA

Banga *Balvinder Singh*
Call Date: July 1997 (Inner Temple)
Qualifications: BA (Cantab)

Banham *Mark Richard Middlecott*
Call Date: Nov 1994 (Inner Temple)
Qualifications: BA (Cantab), CPE

Bankole *Mrs Margaret*
Call Date: July 1988 (Middle Temple)
Qualifications: LLB (Hons)

Bankole-Jones *John Edward*
Call Date: Oct 1963 (Middle Temple)

Baranski *Mrs Gillian Elizabeth*
Clerk to the Cardiff Justices, Fitzalan
Place, Cardiff CF2 1RZ, 01222 463040,
Fax: 01222 456224, Call Date: July
1981 (Gray's Inn) Qualifications: LLB,
MBA

Barber *Anthony Paul*
Broomhall Manor, Norton, Nr Worcester WR5 2NU, Secretary to Lloyd's Disciplinary Committees & Appeal Tribunal, Call Date: Feb 1972 (Middle Temple) Qualifications: LLM

Barber *Keith George*
Call Date: July 1973 (Lincoln's Inn) Qualifications: MA, F.C.I.B

Barber *Nicholas William*
Call Date: Nov 1997 (Middle Temple) Qualifications: BA (Hons), BCL, (Exon)

Barber *Paul Edward Stephen* •
Legal Officer, Catholic Education Service, 39 Eccleston Square, London SW1V 1BX, 0171 828 7604, Fax: 0171 233 9802, Visiting Fellow, University of Westminster, Call Date: Oct 1992 (Middle Temple) Qualifications: MA (Cantab)

Barber *Philip James*
Call Date: Nov 1996 (Middle Temple) Qualifications: LLB(Hons)(Edinburgh)

Barber *Phillip Arthur*
Harehills & Chapeltown Law, Centre, 263 Roundhay Road, Leeds LS8 4HS, 0113 249 1100, Fax: 0113 235 1185, Call Date: Nov 1991 (Gray's Inn) Qualifications: LLB (Hull)

Barbour *David Stephen Peter*
90 Ennerdale Road, Kew Gardens, Richmond, Surrrey TW9 2DL, 0181 940 3088, Call Date: July 1984 (Lincoln's Inn) Qualifications: BA (Oxon),, LLM (Lond)

Barby *Ian Christopher Simon*
Call Date: July 1969 (Middle Temple) Qualifications: MA (Cantab)

Barclay *Rene James* •
Branch Crown Prosecutor, Crown Prosecution Service, 50 Ludgate Hill, London EC4M 7EX, 0171 273 8000, Fax: 0171 273 8028, Call Date: July 1977 (Gray's Inn) Qualifications: LLB (Lond)

Bard *Dr Basil Joseph Asher*
23 Mourne House, Maresfield Gardens, London NW3 5SL, 0171 435 5340, Call Date: June 1938 (Gray's Inn) Qualifications: PhD, BSc, M.D., N.R.D.C. (1972-5)

Bark-Jones *Antony Giles*
Also Inn of Court I, Call Date: Nov 1990 (Middle Temple) Qualifications: BA (Hons) (L'pool), Dip Law (City)

Barker *David John*
Call Date: Mar 1996 (Inner Temple) Qualifications: LLB (Leeds)

Barker *Miss Deborah Jayne*
Lecturer, College of Law, Store Street, London, Call Date: Nov 1994 (Middle Temple) Qualifications: LLB (Hons)

Barker *Miss Geraldine Mary*
17 Bedford Road, Twickenham, Middlesex, Call Date: Nov 1992 (Gray's Inn) Qualifications: LLB (Lond)

Barker *Glenn Preston*
Call Date: Nov 1994 (Inner Temple) Qualifications: BA (Manc), CPE (Wolverhampton)

Barker *Grenville Stuart* •
Principal Crown Prosecutor, Crown Prosecution Service, Pearl Assurance House, 20th Floor, Greyfriars Road, Cardiff CF1 3PL, Call Date: Nov 1984 (Middle Temple) Qualifications: LLB (Cardiff)

Barker *Jeremy*
28 High Riggs, Barnard Castle, Co Durham DL12 8HU, 01833 631299, Call Date: Nov 1996 (Gray's Inn) Qualifications: LLB (Bucks)

Barker *Miss Joanne Lesley*
Call Date: July 1998 (Lincoln's Inn) Qualifications: BA (Hons) (Leics)

Barker *John Roger*
Call Date: Oct 1992 (Inner Temple) Qualifications: BA (Hons) (B'mth)

Barker *Nicolas Michael Anthony*
Call Date: July 1986 (Lincoln's Inn) Qualifications: LLB (Hons) (Reading)

Barker *Ramsey*
Head of Legal Services, Cumbria Magistrates' Court, Carlyle's Court, 1 St Mary's Gate, Carlisle CA3 8RN, 01228 592111, Fax: 01228 598968, Call Date: Nov 1989 (Middle Temple) Qualifications: LLB (Manc), DMS

Barker *Richard John*
Legal Adviser, Hampshire Magistrates Court, Court House, Elmleigh Road, Havant PO9 2AL, 01252 366000, Fax: 01256 811447, Call Date: Feb 1986 (Middle Temple) Qualifications: BA , DMS

Barkworth *Terence Charles Cotherstone*
Room 716, Royal Courts of Justice, Strand, London WC2, 0171 242 4248, Call Date: May 1946 (Lincoln's Inn) Qualifications: BA (Oxon)

Barlay *Miss Yema*
and Member Sierra-Leone (1994), Call Date: Mar 1998 (Middle Temple) Qualifications: LLB (Hons) (Middx)

Barlow *Nigel Douglas*
Senior Court Clerk, Birmingham Magistrates Court, Victoria Law Courts, Corporation Street, Birmingham B4 6QA, 0121 212 6608, Call Date: July 1985 (Gray's Inn) Qualifications: BA, LLB

Barlow *Philip Thomas*
Legal Adviser, Hempsons Solicitors, Portland Tower, Portland street, Manchester M1 3LF, 0161 228 0011, Solicitor, Call Date: Nov 1994 (Inner Temple) Qualifications: MB, ChB (Sheff), BA (Cantab)

Barma *Aarif Tyebjee*
Hong Kong, and Member Hong Kong Bar 3 Verulam Buildings, London, WC1R 5NT, Call Date: July 1983 (Middle Temple) Qualifications: BA, BCL (Oxon)

Barma *Hussein*
Call Date: Feb 1995 (Middle Temple) Qualifications: BA (Hons), BCL (Oxon), ACA

Barnard *Anthony Christopher* •
Senior Crown Prosecutor, Crown Prosecution Service, The Cooperage, Gainsford Street, London SE1, 0171 962 2697, Call Date: Oct 1992 (Gray's Inn) Qualifications: BA (Uni E.Anglia), Dip Law (PCL)

Barnatt *Mrs Karen Elizabeth* •
Senior Crown Prosecutor, Crown Prosecution Service, King Edward Court, King Edward Street, Nottingham NG1 1EL, 0115 9480480, Call Date: July 1983 (Gray's Inn) Qualifications: BSc (Econ),Dip Law

Barnes *Adrian Francis Patrick* •
City Remembrancer, Corporation of London, PO Box 270, Guildhall, London EC2P 2EJ, 0171 332 1200, Fax: 0171 332 1895, Doyen of the Seniors in hall at Gray's Inn since 1992, Call Date: July 1973 (Gray's Inn) Qualifications: MA

Barnes *Alexander Ian*
Call Date: Nov 1996 (Lincoln's Inn) Qualifications: LLB (Hons) (L'pool)

Barnes *Miss Barbara Lucinda*
Justices' Clerk, Greenwich Magistrates Court, 9 Blackheath Road, London SE10 9PG, 0181 694 0033, Fax: 0181 692 3910, Call Date: July 1976 (Gray's Inn) Qualifications: LLB (Lond)

Barnes *Miss Kathleen Georgina*
Deputy Chief Clerk, Inner London Magistrates', Courts Service, Call Date: Nov 1969 (Middle Temple) Qualifications: LLB (Lond)

Barnes *Miss Lee Abigail* •
Competition Lawyer, OFTEL, 50 Ludgate Hill, London EC4M 7JJ, 0171 634 8700, Call Date: Feb 1990 (Lincoln's Inn) Qualifications: LLB (Hons)

Barnes *Nicholas Gerard Hugh*
Messrs Phillips, Wolverhampton Court, 15-16 London Street, Basingstoke, Hampshire RG21 7NT, 01256 460830, Fax: 01256 364333, Call Date: Oct 1996 (Inner Temple) Qualifications: LLB (Westminster)

Barnes *Miss Samantha Jane*
Call Date: Oct 1998 (Gray's Inn) Qualifications: LLB (Sheffield)

Barnett *Christopher Daniel*
Call Date: Oct 1996 (Gray's Inn) Qualifications: BSc

Barnett *Ian Simon* •
IBSA House, The Ridgeway, London NW7 1RP, 0181 906 2211, Call Date: Apr 1991 (Lincoln's Inn) Qualifications: LLB (Hons)

Barnett *Ivor David*
Call Date: July 1971 (Gray's Inn) Qualifications: BA

Barnett *Miss Nicole Ann*
Call Date: Nov 1997 (Lincoln's Inn)
Qualifications: LLB(Hons)(Keele)

Baron *Christopher John Clifford*
Call Date: Nov 1958 (Lincoln's Inn)

Baron *William Robert* •
Commercial Lawyer, Costain
Engineering &, Construction Limited,
Costain House, Nicholsons Walk,
Maidenhead, Berks SL6 1LN, 01628
842258, Fax: 01628 842271, Call Date:
Feb 1984 (Inner Temple)
Qualifications: LLB

Barraclough *David Norman Gregory*
Call Date: Nov 1976 (Inner Temple)
Qualifications: BA Hons

Barratt *Miss Julie Ann* •
Vale of Glamorgan, Civic Offices, Holton
Road, Barry, South Glamorgan, 01446
709405, Fax: 01446 745566, Call Date:
Oct 1993 (Gray's Inn) Qualifications:
B.Sc (Ulster), LLB (Lond), MCIEH

Barrett *Ms Catherine Wendy* •
Crown Prosecution Service, King's
House, Kimberley Road, Harrow,
Middlesex HA1 1YH, 0181 424 8688,
Call Date: Nov 1994 (Middle Temple)
Qualifications: BA (Hons)

Barrett *Miss Cecilia Mary*
Call Date: Oct 1998 (Inner Temple)
Qualifications: LLB (Warw)

Barrett *Miss Elizabeth Anne Mitford*
Call Date: Oct 1992 (Lincoln's Inn)
Qualifications: BA(Hons, Cantab), Dip
Law

Barrett *Ms Jill Mary* •
Assistant Legal Adviser, Legal Advisers,
Foreign & Commonwealth Office, King
Charles Street, London SW1A 2AH, Fax:
0171 270 2767, First Secretary (Legal
Adviser) to the United Kingdom Mission
to the United Nations, New York
1994-1997, Call Date: July 1989 (Gray's
Inn) Qualifications: BA [Dunelm], LLM
[Cantab]

Barrett *Marcus Morton*
Montrose House, Crewkerne, Somerset,
Call Date: Oct 1996 (Inner Temple)
Qualifications: LLB (So'ton), MA, PGCE

Barrett *Michael John* •
Counsel & Assistant Company
Secretary, Call Date: Nov 1991 (Middle
Temple) Qualifications: BA (Hons)
(Cambs), Dip Law, ACIS

Barrett *Paul James* •
Legal Assistant, Argos Plc, Avebury,
489-499 Avebury, Boulevard, Saxon
Gate West, Central Milton Keynes
MK9 2NW, 01908 600538, Fax: 01908
600721, Call Date: Feb 1993 (Lincoln's
Inn) Qualifications: LLB (Hons)

Barrett-Brown *Miss Sophia Aleka*
Call Date: Nov 1997 (Gray's Inn)
Qualifications: LLB (Wales)

Barrett-Williams *Dr Jacqueline Sally* •
Legal Manager UK Commercial
Business., National Power PLC,
Windmill Hill Business Park, Whitehill
Way, Swindon, Wiltshire SN5 6PB,
01793 892852, Fax: 01793 892851,
Call Date: July 1985 (Inner Temple)
Qualifications: BA (Lond), DPhil
(Oxon), Dip Law

Barron *Justin Simon* •
Clerk to the Justices, Swansea
Magistrates' Court, Grove Place,
Swansea SA1 5DB, 01792 655171, Fax:
01792 651066, Call Date: Nov 1985
(Lincoln's Inn) Qualifications: BA

Barrow *Charles Anthony*
Senior Lecturer, University of North
London, C/O Law School, UNL,
Ladbroke House, 62-66 Highbury
Grove, London N5 2AD, 0171 607 2789
Ext 5133, Call Date: Feb 1993
(Lincoln's Inn) Qualifications: BSc
(Econ), (Wales), LLM (LSE), Cert Ed

Barrowclough *Sir Anthony Richard*
Call Date: Nov 1949 (Inner Temple)
Qualifications: MA (Oxon)

Barry *Anthony* •
Crown Prosecutor, Crown Prosecution
Service, United House, Piccadilly, York
YO1 1PQ, Call Date: July 1986 (Gray's
Inn) Qualifications: BA

Barry *Miss Margaret Mary*
8 Rushbury Court, Station Road,
Hampton, Middlesex TW1 2DD, 0181
941 0134, Call Date: Nov 1984 (Gray's
Inn) Qualifications: BA MA (Dublin),
Dip., in European Law, (Dublin)

Barsby *Andrew Walter* •
Senior Principal Legal Adviser, The
Treasury Solicitor, Room 80/G,
H.M.Treasury, Parliment Street,
London SW1P 3AG, Call Date: July 1975
(Gray's Inn) Qualifications: LLB (Lond)

Barsby *Mrs Clare*
Law Reporter, 2 Lynwood Avenue,
Epsom, Surrey KT17 4LQ, 01372
742372, Fax: 01372 721900, Call Date:
Nov 1977 (Gray's Inn)

Bartlet *Michael James George*
Parliamentary Liason Officer, Religions
Society of Friends, (Quakers), Friends
House, 173-177 Euston Road, London
NW1 2BJ, 0171 663 1000, Fax: 0171
663 1001, Call Date: Oct 1992 (Middle
Temple) Qualifications: BA (Hons),
Diploma in Law

Bartlett *Ms Gita*
Call Date: Oct 1997 (Inner Temple)
Qualifications: BA (Western Ontario),
BA (Durham), LLB (London)

Bartlett *Robert* •
H M Customs & Excise, Solicitors
Office, New King's Beam House, 22
Upper Ground, London SE1 9PJ, Call
Date: Nov 1983 (Lincoln's Inn)
Qualifications: LLB Hons [Lond]

Barton *Charles Neville* •
Grade 6 (Legal), Her Majesty's
Treasury, Parliament Street, London
SW1P 3AG, 0171 270 1662, Fax: 0171
270 1668, Call Date: July 1986 (Inner
Temple) Qualifications: LLB (Lond)

Barton *Nigel John*
2 Stapleford Court, Sevenoaks, Kent
TN13 2LB, 0171 234 2726, Fax: 0171
234 2762, Call Date: July 1977
(Lincoln's Inn) Qualifications: BA
(Hons) Bus Law

Barton-Hanson *Mrs Renu*
Call Date: Nov 1991 (Middle Temple)
Qualifications: LLB Hons, LLM

Barwick *Glynn*
Simmons & Simmons, 21 Wilson
Street, London EC2M 2TX, 0171 825
4015, Call Date: Oct 1992 (Lincoln's
Inn) Qualifications: BA(Hons)

Basaran *Halil Attila* •
Prosecution Team Leader, Crown
Prosecution Service, The Cooperage,
Gainsford Street, London SE1 2NG,
0171 357 7010, Call Date: Nov 1978
(Gray's Inn) Qualifications: Cert Ed

Basaran *Mrs Sandra Judith* •
Company Secretary Legal Director
Compliance Officer, Consolidated
Financial Ins, Vantage West, Great West
Road, Brentford, Middlesex TW8 9AG,
0181 380 3054, Fax: 0181 380 3065,
Call Date: July 1984 (Gray's Inn)
Qualifications: LLB

Bascoe *Miss Ingrid*
Call Date: Mar 1997 (Lincoln's Inn)
Qualifications: LLB (Hons), LLM

Bashford *Keith* •
Senior Legal Adviser, J Sainsbury Plc,
Stamford House, Stamford Street,
London SE1 9LL, 0171 695 6798, Call
Date: July 1980 (Lincoln's Inn)
Qualifications: LLB

Basit-Ahmed *Kaashif*
Call Date: Nov 1994 (Lincoln's Inn)
Qualifications: LLB (Hons)(Bucks)

Baskett *Arno Romer*
13 Orchard Close, Bardsea, Ulverston,
Cumbria LA12 9QP, 01229 869681,
Call Date: June 1951 (Inner Temple)
Qualifications: LLB

Basnayake *Miss Bridget Philomena*
Messrs Sohal & Co Solicitors, 10
Church Road, London W3 8PP, 0181
896 1626, Fax: 0181 896 1628, Call
Date: Apr 1991 (Lincoln's Inn)
Qualifications: LLB (Hons)

Bassil *Jeremy Nevil Charles*
Titmuss Sainer Dechert, 2 Serjeant's
Inn, London EC4Y 1LT, Call Date: Nov
1987 (Lincoln's Inn) Qualifications:
LLB Hons

Bastin *Miss Rachel Elizabeth*
Call Date: Mar 1998 (Middle Temple)
Qualifications: LLB (Hons)(LSE)

Basu *Angelo* •
Legal & Regulatory Adviser, Telstra UK
Limited, 44-52 Paul Street, London
EC2A 4LB, 0171 858 8800, Fax: 0171
858 8801, Call Date: Nov 1994 (Inner
Temple) Qualifications: MA, BCL (Oxon)

Batchelor *Miss Alexandra Mary*
Call Date: July 1996 (Middle Temple)
Qualifications: LLB (Hons) (Lond)

Bateman *Lucas William*
Pinsent Curtis Solicitors, 41 Park Square,
Leeds LS1 2NS, 0113 244 5000, Fax:
0113 244 8000, Also Qualified as a
Solicitor in England & Wales, Call Date:
Oct 1994 (Middle Temple)
Qualifications: BA (Hons) (Oxon), CPE

Bates *Mrs Alba Heather Phyllida*
Call Date: July 1968 (Lincoln's Inn)

Bates *John Gerald Higgs*
140 Mortlake Road, Kew Gardens, Surrey
TW9 4EW, Call Date: Nov 1959 (Middle
Temple) Qualifications: MA (Cantab),
LLM (Harvard)

Bates *Peter Spensley*
Western Australia, and Member New
South Wales Bar New Walk Chambers, 27
New Walk, Leicester, LE1 6TE, Call Date:
July 1978 (Lincoln's Inn) Qualifications:
BA

Bates *Ronald Adrian*
Head of Legal Services, North West Gwent
Magistrates Courts, Gwent Magistrates'
Court Comm, 2nd Floor, Gwent House,
Gwent Square, Cwmbran, Gwent
NP44 1PL, 01633 645132, Fax: 01633
645177, Call Date: July 1978 (Gray's
Inn) Qualifications: LLB (Exon), DMS

Batstone *Rodney Karl*
Germany, Call Date: June 1961 (Inner
Temple) Qualifications: MA, LLB
(Cantab)

Batteson *Alexander*
Freshfields Solicitors, 65 Fleet Street,
London EC4Y 1HS, 0171 832 7678, Fax:
0171 832 7001, Call Date: Nov 1995
(Gray's Inn) Qualifications: BSc (L'pool)

Battle *John Gerard Stephen* •
Group Legal Adviser, Associated
Newspapers Limited, North Cliffe House,
2 Derry Street, Kensington, London
W8 5EE, 0171 938 7223, Fax: 0171 938
1092, Call Date: July 1985 (Lincoln's
Inn) Qualifications: LLB

Baty *Paul Raymond* •
Senior Crown Prosecutor, Crown
Prosecution Service, Coventry Branch,
Friars House, Manor House Drive,
Coventry CV1 2TE, 0121 629 7200
(01203) 520421, Call Date: Nov 1980
(Middle Temple) Qualifications: BA
(Hons)

Bavidge *Giles David* •
Clerk to the Justices, Sunderland
Magistrates Cts Com, Justices Clerks
Office, The Villa, Dairy Lane,
Houghton-Le-Spring, Tyne & Wear
DH4 5BL, 0191 5842392, Fax: 0191
5845809, Call Date: July 1968 (Inner
Temple) Qualifications: LLB

Bayer *Tufan*
14 Swingfield House, Templecombe
Road, London E9 7LX, 0181 533 3415,
Call Date: Oct 1997 (Lincoln's Inn)
Qualifications: LLB (Hons), LLM (Lond)

Bayfield *Daniel*
Call Date: Oct 1998 (Inner Temple)
Qualifications: BA (Cantab)

Bayley *Christopher Robert Steuart*
C/O General Council of the Bar, 3
Bedford Row, London WC1R 4DB, Call
Date: Oct 1998 (Inner Temple)
Qualifications: LLB (Bris)

Bayley *John Richard* •
Company Secretary & Group General
Counsel, Call Date: July 1962 (Middle
Temple) Qualifications: LLB

Baylis *Christopher Lloyd Gershwin*
2 Paper Buildings, Basement, Temple,
London, EC4Y 7ET, Call Date: Nov 1986
(Inner Temple) Qualifications: BA
(Hons), LLM, MTh, MBA (Cantab),
M.Phil, (Cantab)

Bayliss *Neil McKenzie* •
Call Date: July 1986 (Gray's Inn)
Qualifications: LLB (Hons)

Bayly *Mrs Julia Mary* •
Crown Prosecutor, Crown Prosecution
Service, 1st Floor Offices, Lowther
Arcade, Lowther Street, Carlisle, Call
Date: Nov 1972 (Gray's Inn)
Qualifications: LLB (Lond)

Bayman *Keith William* •
Call Date: July 1987 (Lincoln's Inn)
Qualifications: MA, LLM (Cantab)

Bayston *Mrs Ashley Robin Meredith Geist*
Call Date: Oct 1996 (Gray's Inn)
Qualifications: BA (Columbia), LLB
(City)

Baytug *Denizhan*
Hammond Suddards Solicitors, 2 Park
Lane, Leeds LS3 1ES, 0113 284 7000,
Fax: 0113 284 7001, Call Date: Oct 1992
(Lincoln's Inn) Qualifications:
LB (Hons) (Sheff)

Bazley *Stuart Richard*
45 Vicarage Road, Old Moulsham,
Chelmsford, Essex, 01245 609206, Fax:
01245 603878, Call Date: Nov 1991
(Middle Temple) Qualifications: LLB
(Hons) (Lond), LLM

Beach *Nicholas Peter* •
Treasury Solicitors Department, Queen
Anne's Chambers, 28 Broadway, London
SW1H 9JS, Call Date: Nov 1983 (Middle
Temple) Qualifications: BA
(Hons) (Oxon)

Beacham *Miss Victoria Louise*
Call Date: Oct 1997 (Middle Temple)
Qualifications: BA (Hons) (Oxon)

Beale *Professor Hugh Gurney*
School of Law, University of Warwick,
Coventry CV4 7AL, 01203 523185, Fax:
01203 524105, Call Date: Nov 1971
(Lincoln's Inn) Qualifications: BA
(Oxon)

Beamer-Downie *Ms Darcy* •
Liability Consultant, Flat 8, Thames Eyot,
Cross Deep, Twickenham TW1 4QL,
0181 892 1537, Fax: 0181 892 1537,
Call Date: Nov 1996 (Middle Temple)
Qualifications: LLB (Hons)

Beams *Miss Samantha Anne*
Call Date: Oct 1996 (Inner Temple)
Qualifications: BA (Cantab)

Bean *Miss Alison Margaret*
Scotland, Call Date: Oct 1990 (Middle
Temple) Qualifications: LLB (Lond)

Beardmore *Miss Alison Claire*
Court Clerk, The Court House, Field
Street, Leek, Staffs ST13 5ST, 01538
372858, Fax: 0538 385129, Call Date:
Oct 1991 (Gray's Inn) Qualifications:
LLB (B'ham)

Beardwell *Philip Norman*
Wace Morgan Solicitors, 2 Belmont,
Shrewsbury, Shropshire SY1 1TD, 01743
361451, Fax: 01743 231708, Call Date:
Nov 1994 (Inner Temple) Qualifications:
LLB (Hons)

Bearn *Miss Natasha Victoria*
Call Date: Nov 1995 (Middle Temple)
Qualifications: BA (Hons)

Beattie *Cameron Robert*
Legal Adviser, North Avon Magistrates,
Court House, Kennedy Way, Yate, Bristol
BS17 4PY, 01454 310505, Call Date: Feb
1991 (Lincoln's Inn) Qualifications: LLB

Beattie *Miss Naomi*
Call Date: Oct 1998 (Lincoln's Inn)
Qualifications: LLB (Hons) (L'pool)

Beaumont *Christopher Hubert*
Recorder, Call Date: June 1950 (Middle
Temple) Qualifications: MA (Oxon)

Beaumont *David Anthony* •
Lead Lawyer - Financial Services, Halifax
plc, Trinity Road, Halifax, West Yorkshire
HX1 2RG, 01422 333492, Fax: 01422
333453, Call Date: July 1987 (Lincoln's
Inn) Qualifications: BA (Durham)

Beaumont *Miss Louise Ann* •
Legal & Administation Manager Secretary
to Merseyside Passenger Transport
Executive, Mersey Travel, 24 Hatton
Garden, Liverpool L3 2AN, 0151 224
7020, Fax: 0151 224 7022, Call Date:
July 1989 (Middle Temple)
Qualifications: BA (Keele) (Hons)

Beaven *Gregory Paul* •
Crown Prosecution Service, Princes
Court, York Road, Leicester, 0116
2549333, Fax: 0116 2550855, Call
Date: Nov 1991 (Inner Temple)
Qualifications: MA (Oxon), MPHIL
(York), Pst Grd Cert Ed, LLB

Beavers *David John*
Call Date: Nov 1992 (Middle Temple)
Qualifications: LLB (Hons, L'pool)

Beazer *Dominic William Jesse*
Call Date: Feb 1994 (Inner Temple)
Qualifications: BA (Lond), Dip in Law

Beck *Miss Lauren Janet*
Call Date: Mar 1999 (Middle Temple)
Qualifications: LLB (Hons) (Leeds)

Beck *Miss Sandra Mary* •
Crown Prosecution Service, Berkshire
Branch, Eaton Court, 112 Oxford Road,
Reading RG1 7LL, 01734 503771, Call
Date: Nov 1982 (Lincoln's Inn)
Qualifications: BA

Beck *Stephen James*
Call Date: Oct 1996 (Inner Temple)
Qualifications: LLB

Beckwith *Miss Gillian*
Assistant Deputy Clerk to the Justices,
Oldham Magistrates Court, St Domingo
Place, West Street, Oldham OL1 1YY,
0161 624 2331, Fax: 0161 652 0172,
Call Date: Feb 1982 (Middle Temple)
Qualifications: DML, Dip Training &,
Development.

Beckwith *Silas Walter Lawrence*
Call Date: Oct 1993 (Lincoln's Inn)
Qualifications: LLB (Hons) (Lond)

Bedding *Paul Ashley* •
Lawyer, Office of Fair Trading, Field
House, Room 302, 15-25 Breams
Building, London EC4A 1PR, 0171 211
8000, Fax: 0171 211 8830, Call Date:
Nov 1994 (Inner Temple)
Qualifications: BA (Oxon)

Bedford *John Edgar* •
Grade 7 (Europe), Belgium, Call Date:
Nov 1993 (Middle Temple)
Qualifications: BA (Hons)(Oxon), CPE

Beer *Charles Esmond*
KPMG, One Canada Square, London
E14 5AG, 0171 311 4193, Fax: 0171
311 4088, Call Date: July 1978 (Middle
Temple) Qualifications: MA (Cantab),
ATII

Beetham *James Edward*
Call Date: Oct 1994 (Lincoln's Inn)
Qualifications: BA (Hons) (Exeter)

Beg *Miss Mosion Shazadi* •
Special Immigration Adjudicator,
Advisor to the IBA Human Rights
Institute and Chairman of Indep.Review
Panel NHS Trust, Immigration
Appellate Auth., Taylor House, 88
Roseberry Avenue, Islington, London
EC1R 4QU, 0171 862 4200, Fax: 0171
441 3636, Call Date: Nov 1984 (Inner
Temple) Qualifications: BA
(Hons)(B'ham) LLM, (So'ton)

Beggs *Miss Danielle Ann* •
Call Date: July 1983 (Inner Temple)
Qualifications: LLB (Leeds)

Begum-Baig *Miss Farah*
Call Date: Nov 1994 (Inner Temple)
Qualifications: LLB (Hons)

Beharry *Mahesh*
Call Date: Nov 1998 (Gray's Inn)
Qualifications: LLB (Wolves)

Beharrylal *Satyanand Sarju*
Call Date: Oct 1997 (Lincoln's Inn)
Qualifications: LLB (Hons) (Herts)

Behrouzi *Miss Parisa*
Call Date: Nov 1996 (Middle Temple)
Qualifications: LLB (Hons)

Behzadi Spencer *Ms Shayesteh* •
Fellow in European Community Law,
Ministry of Agriculture,, Fisheries &
Food, Legal Department, 55 Whitehall,
London SW1A 2EY, 0171 270 8541,
Fax: 0171 270 8270, Call Date: Nov
1988 (Middle Temple) Qualifications:
LLB (Hons), LLM

Bekoe-Tabiri *Christian Gottfried*
Messrs Collisons & Co, 1-3 Hildreth
Road, Balham, London SW12 9RQ, Call
Date: July 1992 (Lincoln's Inn)
Qualifications: BA (Hons), BL

Belch *Michael Andrew*
Director, Joniq (UK) Ltd, SBC House,
Restmor Way, Wallington, Surrey
SM6 7AH, 0181 288 0424, Fax: 0181
288 0425, Call Date: Nov 1993 (Middle
Temple) Qualifications: BSc
(Hons)(Wales), CPE

Beldam *Ms Alexander Gay* •
Lawyer, Criminal Appeal Office, Royal
Courts of Justice, Strand, London
WC2A 2LL, 0171 936 6314, Fax: 0171
936 6900, Call Date: Nov 1981 (Inner
Temple) Qualifications: BA (Hons)

Bell *Adrian John*
1 Serjeants' Inn, 5th Floor, Fleet Street,
Temple, London, EC4Y 1LH, Call Date:
July 1976 (Middle Temple)

Bell *Andrew John*
19 Elms Road, Clapham, London
SW4 9ER, 0171 627 1763, Fax: 0171
627 1764, Call Date: Nov 1986 (Gray's
Inn) Qualifications: MA (Cantab), MBA
(Insead)

Bell *Miss Catherine Isobel* •
Head of Business Affairs, The Chrysalis
Group Plc, The Chrysalis Building,
Bramley Road, London W10 6SP, Call
Date: Oct 1992 (Inner Temple)
Qualifications: LLB (Hons)

Bell *Miss Helen Suzanne*
Northern Ireland, 4 King's Bench Walk,
2nd Floor, Temple, London, EC4Y 7DL,
Call Date: July 1985 (Middle Temple)
Qualifications: BA (Cantab)

Bell *Miss Jane Elizabeth* •
Legal Adviser, Dept of Social Security,
New Court, 48 Carey Street, London
WC2A 2LS, Call Date: Nov 1984 (Middle
Temple) Qualifications: BA (Oxon)

Bell *Ms Kerrie Olivia* •
Principle Crown Prosecutor Team
Leader, Crown Prosecution Service, The
Cooperage, Gainsford Street, London
SE1, Call Date: July 1986 (Inner
Temple) Qualifications: LLB (Lond)

Bell *Nigel John* •
Senior Principal Legal Officer, HM
Customs & Excise, New King's Beam
House, 22 Upper Ground, London
SE1 9PJ, 0171 865 5167, Call Date: Nov
1976 (Middle Temple) Qualifications:
LLB (Lond)

Bell *Simon Richard*
Cleary Gottlieb Steen Hamilton, City
Place House, 55 Basinghall Street,
London EC2V 5EH, Call Date: Nov 1994
(Inner Temple) Qualifications: BA, BCL
(Oxon)

Bell *Mrs Susan Josephine*
96 Greenwich South Street, Greenwich,
London SE10 8UN, 0181 265 4316, Inn
of Court of Northern Ireland and
Member Northern Ireland Bar, Call
Date: Nov 1992 (Lincoln's Inn)
Qualifications: LLB (Hons)

Belle-Fortune *Roger James Alexander*
Call Date: July 1988 (Lincoln's Inn)
Qualifications: LLB (Hons)

Bellis *Neil Graham*
Call Date: July 1976 (Gray's Inn)
Qualifications: LLB

Belton *Mrs Valerie Pak Lian*
Court Clerk, Wimbledon Magistrates'
Court, Alexandra Road, Wimbledon,
London SW19 7JP, 0181 946 8622, Fax:
0181 946 7030, Call Date: July 1984
(Inner Temple) Qualifications: LLB
(buckingham)

Beltrami *Edwin Joseph* •
Crown Prosecutor, Crown Prosecution
Service, Thames/Wells Branch, 2nd
Floor, Portland House, Stag Place,
London SW1E 5BH, Call Date: July
1988 (Middle Temple) Qualifications:
LLB (Hons)

Benady *Miss Yael Horabuena Simha*
Call Date: Oct 1994 (Middle Temple)
Qualifications: LLB (Hons) (Manc)

Benjamin *Miss Gaynor*
Call Date: Feb 1994 (Lincoln's Inn)
Qualifications: LLB (Hons)

Benjamin *Ian Leroy Colin*
1 Crown Office Row, Ground Floor,
Temple, London, EC4Y 7HH, Call Date:
July 1988 (Middle Temple)
Qualifications: BA, LLM (Cantab)

Benjamin *Mark Edward*
Call Date: Nov 1992 (Gray's Inn)
Qualifications: LLB (Hons, B'ham)

Bennett *Professor Geoffrey John*
University of Notre Dame, London Law
Centre, 1 Suffolk Street, London
SW1Y 4HG, 0171 484 7822, Fax: 0171
484 7854, Francis Taylor Bldg, 3rd Floor,
Temple, London, EC4Y 7BY, Call Date:
July 1975 (Inner Temple) Qualifications:
BA (Cantab)

Bennett *Ms Helen Rachel* •
Senior Principal Lawyer, Civil Service
College, Sunningdale, Ascot, Berks,
01344 634088, Call Date: Nov 1982
(Middle Temple) Qualifications: MA
(Oxon), Dip Law

Bennett *Julian Frank Lawrence*
Call Date: Oct 1994 (Middle Temple)
Qualifications: LLB (Hons)(Lond)

Bennett *Lee*
Call Date: Nov 1998 (Middle Temple)
Qualifications: LLB (Hons)(E.Anglia),
LLM (Cantab)

Bennett *Lee Anthony*
Call Date: May 1997 (Inner Temple)
Qualifications: LLB (Lond)

Bennett *Patrick*
Recorder, Call Date: Nov 1949 (Gray's
Inn) Qualifications: MA, BCL (Oxon)

Bennett *Paul Richard*
Call Date: Nov 1995 (Inner Temple)
Qualifications: LLB (Exon)

Bennett *Thomas Christopher* •
Principal Crown Prosecutor, Crown
Prosecution Service, Hawkins House,
Rydon Lane, Pynes Hill, Exeter, Devon
EX2 5SS, 01392 422555, Fax: 01392
422111, Call Date: Nov 1980 (Middle
Temple) Qualifications: BA

Benney *Mark William* •
Legal Adviser's Office, Department of
Employment, Caxton House, Tothill
Street, London SW1H 9NF, 0171 273
6072, Call Date: July 1982 (Inner
Temple) Qualifications: BA (Dunelm)

Bennion *Francis Alan Roscoe*
5 Old Nursery View, Kennington, Oxford
OX1 5NT, 01865 735365, Fax: 01865
736807, Former Parliamentary Counsel
Member of Oxford University Law faculty,
Call Date: Jan 1951 (Middle Temple)
Qualifications: MA (Oxon)

Bennison *Craig Jeffrey*
Call Date: Oct 1997 (Lincoln's Inn)
Qualifications: LLB (Hons)(Anglia)

Benns *Miss Elizabeth Susan*
Manager, Fin & Gen Bank PLc, Age
Concern Bedfordshire, Disability
Resource Centre, Poynters House,
Poynters Road, Dunstable, Bedfordshire
LU5 4PT, 01582 470900, Fax: 01582
470977, Call Date: July 1979 (Middle
Temple) Qualifications: LLB, A.C.I.B

Bentley *Mrs Anne Louise* •
Call Date: July 1987 (Lincoln's Inn)
Qualifications: LLB (London)

Bentley *David Jeffrey*
Consultant, Home Office, 50 Queen
Annes Gate, London SW1H 9AT, 0171
273 4478, Fax: 0171 273 4075, Call
Date: Nov 1963 (Lincoln's Inn)
Qualifications: MA,BCL (Oxon)

Bentley *John Graham*
'Sundowners', Alderney, Alderney
GY9 3UP, 0148 182 2698, Fax: 0148 182
3559, and Member Malaysia Bar
Nigerian Bar Cameroon Bar, Call Date:
June 1953 (Lincoln's Inn)
Qualifications: MA (Oxon)

Bergin *Gerard Patrick*
Principal, Gerard Bergin Associates, 9
Barnacre Drive, Parkgate, South Wirral,
Cheshire L64 6RJ, 0151 336 4643, Fax:
0151 336 4643, Call Date: July 1995
(Middle Temple) Qualifications: LLB
(Hons), FRICS, FCIOB

Bergman *Mrs Sophie*
1 Sneath Avenue, London NW11 9AJ, Call
Date: Nov 1958 (Lincoln's Inn)

Berish *Joseph Michael*
15 Montagu Court, Newcastle Upon Tyne
NE3 4JL, 0191 285 4874, Call Date: Nov
1964 (Gray's Inn)

Berk *Deniz Andrew*
Call Date: Nov 1996 (Inner Temple)
Qualifications: LLB (Essex), LLM
(Germany)

Berkeley-Hill *Michael Amar Samuel*
Shearman & Sterling, 199 Bishopgate,
London EC2M 3TY, United States of
America, 0171 920 9000, Fax: 0171 920
9931, and Member New York Bar, Call
Date: Oct 1994 (Middle Temple)
Qualifications: LLB (Hons)(Lond), AKC
(Lond), LLM (Lond)

Berkowitz *Ms Nathalia Pendo* •
Senior Legal & Research Officer to the
Immigration Appellate Authority, Lord
Chancellor's Dept, IAA Taylor House, 88
Rosebury Avenue, London EC1R 4QU,
0171 862 4200, Fax: 0171 837 6648,
Call Date: Nov 1989 (Middle Temple)
Qualifications: B.Sc Hons , Dip in Law

Berkpinar *Miss Tulay*
Call Date: July 1998 (Lincoln's Inn)
Qualifications: LLB (Hons)(Dunelm),
MA (North London), BA (London)

Berman *David Michael*
Call Date: Nov 1997 (Gray's Inn)
Qualifications: BSc (Leeds), LLM, (Lond)

Berman *Sir Franklin Delow* •
Legal Adviser to the Foreign &
Commonwealth Office, Foreign &
Commonwealth Office, King Charles
Street, London SW1A 2AH, 0171 270
3000, Fax: 0171 270 3071, Call Date:
Nov 1966 (Middle Temple)
Qualifications: MA (Oxon) , BA, BSc
(Capetown)

Berman *Paul Richard* •
Assistant Legal Adviser Foreign &
Commonwealth Office, Call Date: Nov
1990 (Gray's Inn) Qualifications: BA
(Oxon), Dip Law (City), D.E.S.(Geneva)

Berman *Ms Yvonne Marie* •
Intellectual Prop Lawyer, Call Date: May
1988 (Middle Temple) Qualifications:
LLB (Hons)

Bernasko *Frank George*
Barrister and Solicitor Supreme Court of
Ghana (1970) and Member Ghana Bar,
Call Date: Nov 1988 (Gray's Inn)
Qualifications: LLB (Hons) Ghana, BSc
(Lond)

Berney *Nigel Philip*
17 Tylers Close, Kings Langley,
Hertfordshire WD4 9QA, Call Date: Feb
1990 (Inner Temple) Qualifications: LLB
(Lond)

Bernstein *Miss Elizabeth Diane Melanie*
5 Corringway, London W5 3AB, Call Date:
Nov 1986 (Lincoln's Inn) Qualifications:
BA Law

Bernstein *Ronald Harold*
Vice-President Emeritus. The Chartered
Institute of Arbitrators, Bencher 1975-,
Falcon Chambers, Fleet Street, London
EC4Y 1AA, 0171 353 2484, Fax: 0171
348 7676, Handbook of Rene Review
(1981-1997), Handbook of Arbitration
Practice 1987/1993/1997), Call Date: Jan
1948 (Middle Temple) Qualifications:
MA (Oxon), FCIArb, ARICS (Hon), F.S.V.A
(Hon)

Berrill-Cox *Adrian Leigh* •
Statutory Prosecutions Dept, Financial
Services Authority, 25 The North
Colonade, Canary Wharf, London
E14 5HS, 0171 676 1212, Fax: 0171 676
1025, Call Date: July 1986 (Inner
Temple) Qualifications: LLB (Reading)

Berry *George*
Call Date: July 1967 (Gray's Inn)
Qualifications: BSc Econ, Dip Religious
Studie

Berry *John Graham* •
Company Secretary, Iceland Group Plc,
Deeside Industrial Park, Second Avenue,
Deeside, Flintshire CH5 2NW, 01244
842329, Fax: 01244 842684, Call Date:
Nov 1976 (Lincoln's Inn) Qualifications:
BA

Berry *John Percival*
Call Date: July 1960 (Gray's Inn)

Berry *Miss Julia Mary*
Legal Adviser, Richards Butler, Beaufort House, 15 St Botolph Street, London EC3A 7EE, 0171 247 6555, Fax: 0171 247 5091, Call Date: Nov 1988 (Gray's Inn) Qualifications: LLB (Lond)

Berry *Mark Joseph*
Solicitor, Masons, 30 Aylesbury Street, London EC1R 0ER, 0171 490 4000, Fax: 0171 490 2545, Call Date: Nov 1995 (Lincoln's Inn) Qualifications: BEng(Hons), CEng

Berry *Thomas Hugh Kirk*
Call Date: July 1935 (Inner Temple) Qualifications: BA

Besomi *Michael John Guy*
Charles Russell Solicitors, 36/38 Leadenhall Street, London EC3A 1AT, 0171 458 3306, Fax: 0171 480 6640, Call Date: July 1981 (Gray's Inn) Qualifications: LLB (Warw), LLM (Lond)

Bessell *William Gregory*
Call Date: Oct 1997 (Lincoln's Inn) Qualifications: BSc (Hons)(Lond)

Best *David Mark*
Call Date: Mar 1997 (Lincoln's Inn) Qualifications: LLB (Hons)(Lond)

Best *Keith Lander*
Chief Executive, Immigration Advisory Service, County House, 190 Great Dover Street, London SE1 4YB, 0171 357 7511, Fax: 0171 403 5875, Call Date: Nov 1971 (Inner Temple) Qualifications: BA (Oxon)

Betteley *Jason Paul* •
Legal Officer, The Treasury Solicitor, Queen Anne's Chambers, 28 Broadway, LondoN, Call Date: Oct 1990 (Inner Temple) Qualifications: LLB

Bettelheim *Eric Christopher*
Mischcon De Reya, 21 Southampton Row, London WC1B 5HS, 0171 440 7127, Fax: 0171 404 3014, and Member New York, California, Call Date: Nov 1979 (Inner Temple) Qualifications: BA (Oxon), JD (Chicago)

Betts *Mrs Christine Rosemary* •
Family & Community Law Manager, Bath & NE Somerset Council, Riverside, Temple Street, Keynsham, Bristol, 01225 395223, Fax: 01225 395128, Call Date: Nov 1971 (Middle Temple) Qualifications: LLB (Hons)

Bevan *Mrs Anne* •
Consultant, Wansbroughs, Willey Hargrave, St Swithins House, 1a St Cross Road, Winchester, Hants, 01962 841444, Call Date: Nov 1979 (Middle Temple) Qualifications: BA

Bevan *Miss Sally Frances*
44 Lexington Street, London W1R 3LH, 0171 494 1100, Fax: 0171 494 2200, Media and Intellectual Property Law, Call Date: Nov 1982 (Middle Temple) Qualifications: BA(Reading) Dip Law

Bhadresa *Mrs Irene Mary* •
British Transport Police, London Underground Area, Criminal Justice Unit, 12th Floor, Telstar House, Eastbourne Terrace, London W2 6LG, 0171 918 0914, Call Date: May 1987 (Middle Temple) Qualifications: LLB (Hons)

Bhagobati *Ruben Kumar*
Call Date: Nov 1995 (Gray's Inn) Qualifications: BA (Oxon)

Bhakta *Miss Nilema* •
Principal Legal Officer, Solicitors Office, H.M.Customs & Excise, New King's Beam House, 22 Upper Ground, London SE1 9PJ, 0171 865 5211, Fax: 0171 865 5243, Call Date: Oct 1994 (Inner Temple) Qualifications: LLB (Notts) (Hons)

Bhalla *Tajinder Singh* •
Smithkline Beecham Plc, One New Horizons Court, Middlesex TW8 9EP, 0181 975 2353, Fax: 0181 975 2360, Call Date: July 1988 (Middle Temple) Qualifications: BA (Hons) (Keele), Dip Law (City), AIIT, ATII

Bhambri *Miss Sunita*
Call Date: Nov 1991 (Lincoln's Inn) Qualifications: LLB (Hons)

Bhardwaj *Mrs Sunita*
Call Date: Nov 1992 (Inner Temple) Qualifications: LLB

Bhatia *Anil*
Call Date: Nov 1994 (Middle Temple) Qualifications: LLB (Hons)

Bheeroo *Khumrajsing Sunil*
Call Date: July 1996 (Gray's Inn) Qualifications: LLB (Wolverhampton)

Bhimji *Ms Mumtaz Begum*
64 Mount Stewart Avenue, Kenton, Harrow, Middlesex HA3 0JU, 0181 907 4882, Fax: 0181 907 0787, Call Date: July 1971 (Gray's Inn) Qualifications: LLB

Biase *Mrs Claire Marie*
Call Date: Mar 1997 (Middle Temple) Qualifications: LLB (Hons)

Bibby *John Benjamin*
Kirby Mount, Warwick Drive, West Kirby, Wirral, Merseyside L48 2HT, 0151 625 8071, Fax: 0151 625 8071, Call Date: July 1981 (Gray's Inn) Qualifications: MA (Cantab)

Bibby *Peter James*
62 Oakhurst Grove, London SE22 9AQ, 0181 693 8752, Call Date: Oct 1992 (Middle Temple)

Bickerstaff *Miss Anthea Mary*
Call Date: Oct 1990 (Gray's Inn) Qualifications: BA (Keele), MA (City)

Bicknell *Mrs Louise Jean* •
Director,, Warburg Dillon Road, 100 Liverpool Street, London EC2M 2RH, 0171 568 5181, Call Date: Nov 1984 (Middle Temple) Qualifications: BA

Biddulph *Ms Jemima Jane*
Call Date: Oct 1996 (Middle Temple) Qualifications: BA (Hons) (Camb)

Bielby *Richard Mark* •
Legal Officer, London Borough of Southwark, South House, 30-32 Peckham Road, London SE5 8UB, Call Date: Oct 1994 (Gray's Inn) Qualifications: BA, Dip Law

Bignall *Mrs Gillian Meryl* •
Crown Prosecutor, CPS, 4-12 Queen Anne's Gate, London SW1H 9AZ, Call Date: Nov 1978 (Middle Temple) Qualifications: LLB

Bijlani *Rahul William*
Call Date: Mar 1998 (Gray's Inn) Qualifications: BA (Cantab)

Biker *Andrew Dunkin* •
Lawyer, HM Customs & Excise, Solicitors Office, New Kings Beam House, 22 Upper Ground, London SE1 9PJ, 0171 865 5184, Fax: 0171 865 5164, Call Date: Nov 1978 (Gray's Inn) Qualifications: MA (Cantab)

Bilewycz *Michael Domenico* •
Legal Adviser, Unilever (UK) Limited, Legal Department, Unilever House, Blackfriars, London EC4P 4BQ, 0171 822 5252 X5655, Fax: 0171 822 6539, Call Date: Nov 1988 (Middle Temple) Qualifications: BA Hons

Binder *Mrs Joanne*
Senior Court Clerk, Bucks County Council, Berkley House, Walton Street, Aylesbury, Bucks HP21 7QG, 01296 383058, Fax: 01296 383436, Call Date: July 1985 (Gray's Inn) Qualifications: BA

Binding *David Wyn* •
Group Secretary/Group Compliance Officer, Legal & General Group Plc, Temple Court, 11 Queen Victoria Street, London EC4N 4TP, 0171 528 6200, Fax: 0171 528 6221, Call Date: July 1978 (Middle Temple) Qualifications: BA

Biney *Kwamina Aubyn* •
Senior Court Clerk, Redbridge Magistrates' Court, 850 Cranbrook Road, Barkingside, Ilford, Essex IG6 1HW, 0181 551 4461, Fax: 0181 550 2101, Call Date: July 1989 (Lincoln's Inn) Qualifications: LLB (Ghana), Dip Law (City), LLM (Lond)

Biondi *Alessandro* •
Legal Adviser, Alliance & Leicester plc, Customer Services Centre, Carlton Park, Narborough, Leicester LE9 5XX, Call Date: Feb 1994 (Lincoln's Inn) Qualifications: LLB (Hons)

Birch *Miss Karen Margaret* •
European Counsel, Price Waterhouse Coopers, 1 Embankment Place, London WC2NN 6NN, 0171 939 3000, Fax: 0171 939 2673, and Member Bermuda Bar New South Wales Bar, Call Date: July 1984 (Inner Temple) Qualifications: LLB (Wales)

Birch *Keith Jeffrey*
Call Date: Nov 1994 (Lincoln's Inn) Qualifications: BA (Hons), LLM (Warw)

Birch *Paul Ronald*
Senior Court Clerk, North Sefton Magistrates, Courts Committee, Law Courts, Albert Road, Southport, Merseyside PR9 0LJ, 01704 534141, Fax: 01704 500226, Call Date: Feb 1988 (Middle Temple) Qualifications: LLB (Hons), Dip Magistrates Law

Bird *Charles Ashley Richard*
Legal Adviser Grade 6, The Treasury Solicitor, Queen Anne's Chambers, 28 Broadway, London SW1H 9JS, 0171 210 3204, Fax: 0171 210 3503, Call Date: Nov 1977 (Middle Temple) Qualifications: MA [Cantab]

Bird *Miss Elizabeth Margaret*
Senior Sub-Editor at Halsburys Statutes, Butterworths, Halsbury House, 35 Chancery Lane, London WC2A 1EL, 0171 400 2516, Fax: 0171 400 2559, Call Date: Nov 1996 (Lincoln's Inn) Qualifications: LLB (Hons)(Brunel)

Bird *Nicholas David*
Call Date: Oct 1993 (Middle Temple) Qualifications: BA (Hons)(York), CPE

Bird *Miss Penelope Hamilton*
Call Date: July 1982 (Inner Temple) Qualifications: BA

Bird *Miss Susannah Rachel Louise*
Call Date: Nov 1998 (Gray's Inn) Qualifications: LLB (Manch)

Birikorang *Charles Seth Addo* •
Principal Legal Officer, HM Customs & Excise, Solicitors Office, New King's Beam House, 22 Upper Ground, London SE1 9PJ, 0171 865 4832, Fax: 0171 865 5248, and Member Ghana Bar, Call Date: July 1987 (Lincoln's Inn) Qualifications: LLB (Ghana) LLM, (Lond)

Birkin *James Francis Richard*
Committee of Employed & Non-practising Bar Association, Call Date: Feb 1992 (Inner Temple) Qualifications: LLB, LLM

Birrell *Duncan MacCallum* •
LLB (Hons), Crown Prosecution Service, 3rd Floor, Unicentre, Lord's Walk, Preston, Lancs PR1 1DH, 01772 555015, Fax: 01772 883231, Call Date: May 1984 (Lincoln's Inn)

Bishop *Miss Angela Mary*
Call Date: July 1981 (Lincoln's Inn) Qualifications: LLB (Lond)

Bishop *Miss Helen Susan* •
Senior Crown Prosecutor, Crown Prosecution Service, 10th Floor, Grosvenor House, Basing View, Basingstoke, Hampshire, Call Date: July 1988 (Lincoln's Inn) Qualifications: LLB (Hons)

Bishop *Mrs Janice Elaine*
Deputy Chief Clerk, Call Date: July 1979 (Gray's Inn)

Bishop *Mrs Pauline* •
Senior Crown Prosecutor, Crown Prosecution Service, Eaton Court, Oxford Road, Reading, Berks, Call Date: July 1980 (Inner Temple)

Bissett *Mrs Emma Joanna* •
Lawyer - Banking Department, Rowe & Maw, Call Date: Nov 1997 (Gray's Inn) Qualifications: BA (Cantab)

Bitounis *Constantinos*
Call Date: Mar 1999 (Lincoln's Inn) Qualifications: LLB (Hons)(Coventry)

Black *Charles Michael Andrew*
Call Date: Oct 1996 (Gray's Inn) Qualifications: LLB

Black-Branch *Dr Jonathan Lee*
Call Date: Mar 1998 (Lincoln's Inn) Qualifications: BA (Canada), B.Ed (Canada), MA (Oxon), LLB (Hons)(Oxon), M.Ed, Ph.D (Toronto)

Blackburn *Barry John* •
Vice President & Chief Legal Adviser, Sun Life Assurance Company of, Canada, Basingview, Basingstoke, Hampshire RG21 2DZ, 01256 841414, Fax: 01256 460067, Call Date: Nov 1977 (Gray's Inn) Qualifications: MA (Oxon)

Blackburn *Lieut-Cdr George Richard*
Company Secretary Consultant, 26 Pearl Ct, Cornfield Terrace, Eastbourne, E Sussex BN21 4AA, 01323 411096, Call Date: Nov 1948 (Inner Temple) Qualifications: MA (Cantab), ALAM, ARAES

Blackburn *John Roger* •
Principal Legal Officer, HM Customs & Excise, New King's Beam House, 22 Upper Ground, London SE1 9PJ, 0171 865 5169, Call Date: Nov 1971 (Middle Temple) Qualifications: LLB, AKC

Blackburn-Lindley *Mrs Claire Ann* •
Principal Crown Prosecutor, CPS (Sth London & Surrey), 17th Floor, Tolworth Tower, Surbiton, Surrey KT6 7DS, Call Date: Nov 1986 (Gray's Inn) Qualifications: LLB (Nott'm), LLM (LSE)

Blacker *James*
Call Date: Nov 1986 (Gray's Inn) Qualifications: S.T.L., B.A., M.B.A.

Blackett *Captain Jeffrey*
Acting Metropolitan Stipendiary Magistrate, 10 Blount Road, Pembroke Park, Portsmouth PO1 2TD, 01705 815398, Call Date: July 1983 (Gray's Inn) Qualifications: LLB (Lond)

Blackman *Miss Sharon Annette* •
Legal Advisor, Colonial, Colonial House, Quayside, Chatham Maritime, Kent ME4 4YY, 01634 898017, Call Date: Oct 1997 (Lincoln's Inn) Qualifications: LLB (Brunel)

Blackmore *Miss Wendie Helen*
Call Date: Mar 1996 (Inner Temple) Qualifications: LLB (LSE)

Blain *Lt Cdr Roderick Graham* •
Assistant Naval Adviser OTTAWA, SLA/FOTR, Admiralty House, H M Naval Base, Portsmouth PO1 3NH, 613 237 1530 X 234, Fax: 613 232 4030, Call Date: Oct 1991 (Middle Temple) Qualifications: BA (Stirling)

Blair *Anthony Charles Lynton*
11 King's Bench Walk, Temple, London, EC4Y 7EQ, Call Date: July 1976 (Lincoln's Inn) Qualifications: BA (Oxon)

Blair *Edward George MacColl*
Call Date: Oct 1998 (Lincoln's Inn) Qualifications: BA (Hons)(Bris), CPE

Blair *Ms Linda Susan*
Housing Advisor, Central London Law Centre, 19 Whitcomb Street, London WC2H 7HA, 0181 969 2433, Fax: 0181 968 0345, Call Date: Oct 1993 (Gray's Inn) Qualifications: LLB (Hons)

Blair *Michael Campbell* •
General Counsel to the Board, Financial Services Authority, 25 The North Colonnade, Canary Wharf, London E14 5HS, 0171 676 3352, Fax: 0171 676 1071, Treasurer of the Bar Council 1995, 1996,1997,1998 Bencher, Middle Temple 3 Verulam Buildings, London, WC1R 5NT, Call Date: July 1965 (Middle Temple) Qualifications: MA, LLM (Cantab), MA (Yale)

Blake *Leslie Leonard*
Also Inn of Court G, Call Date: July 1974 (Middle Temple)

Blake *Leslie William*
Lecturer in Law, Dept of Linguistic &, International Studies, University of Surrey, Guildford, Surrey GU2 5XH, 01483 300800 Ext 2830, Fax: 01483 259527, Call Date: Nov 1972 (Lincoln's Inn) Qualifications: LLM, AKC

Blake *Ms Penelope Natasha*
Call Date: July 1996 (Gray's Inn) Qualifications: BA (Sussex)

Blake *Miss Susan Heather*
Director of Studies Bar Vocational Course, Inns of Court School of Law, 4 Gray's Inn Place, London WC1R 5PX, 0171 404 5787, Call Date: Nov 1976 (Inner Temple) Qualifications: MA, LLM (Cantab)

Blakebrough *Philip David* •
Principal Crown Prosecutor, Crown Prosecution Service, Stoke Mill, Woking Road, Guildford, Surrey GU1 1AQ, Call Date: July 1987 (Middle Temple) Qualifications: LLB (Lond)

Blakeley *John Christopher* •
Corporate Development Director,
Glynwed International plc, Headland
Hse, New Coventry Rd, Birmingham
B26 3AZ, 0121 742 2366, Fax: 0121
722 2582, Call Date: July 1967
(Lincoln's Inn) Qualifications: MA

Blakesley *Major John Cadman*
Shepherds Hill House, Pinnock,
Winchcombe, Cheltenham GL54 5AX,
01242 602620, Fax: 01242 602620,
Call Date: Nov 1966 (Middle Temple)

Blanche *Martin James*
Call Date: Nov 1997 (Middle Temple)
Qualifications: BA (Hons)(Manch)

Blanco White *Thomas Anthony*
0171 405 4321, Fax: 0171 405 9955, 8
New Square, Lincoln's Inn, London,
WC2A 3QP, Call Date: June 1937
(Lincoln's Inn) Qualifications: BA
(Cantab)

Blankson *Harry Douglas*
Call Date: Nov 1992 (Inner Temple)
Qualifications: BSc (Nigeria), LLB
(Lond)

Blatchford *Charles Robert*
Call Date: July 1997 (Inner Temple)
Qualifications: BSc (Dunelm), Dip in
Law

Blatchford *Trevor John*
Deputy Clerk to the Justices, East
Cornwall Magistrates' Crt, Launceston
Road, Bodmin, Cornwall, 01208 73873,
Fax: 01208 77198, Call Date: July 1979
(Gray's Inn) Qualifications: BA

Blin *Roger Louis*
Call Date: July 1962 (Middle Temple)
Qualifications: LLB (Lond)

Blincow *Peter Stanley Adrian*
88 Easton Street, High Wycombe,
Buckinghamshire HP11 1LT, 01494
473240, Fax: 01494 473233, Call Date:
Oct 1996 (Lincoln's Inn)
Qualifications: MSc (Reading), LLB
(Hons) (Lond), Dip in Building Econ,
(DSTN), FRICS

Blockley *Christopher John Hamilton*
Call Date: Nov 1998 (Gray's Inn)
Qualifications: LLB (W.England)

Blood *Ms Alison Jane*
Call Date: Oct 1990 (Gray's Inn)
Qualifications: BA (Lond), Dip Law

Bloom *Bryan Neville Irving*
Call Date: May 1997 (Middle Temple)
Qualifications: BPharm (Hons), MSc
(Sheff), LLB (Hons)

Blow *Detmar Hamilton Lorenz Arthur*
Call Date: Apr 1989 (Middle Temple)
Qualifications: BA (LSE), Dip Law

Blumenthal *David* •
Call Date: Feb 1993 (Middle Temple)
Qualifications: BA (Hons)(Lond), Dip
in Law (City)

Blunden *Mrs Anne-Marie* •
Crown Prosecution Service, Horsham
Branch, P.O.Box 229, Horsham, West
Sussex RH12 1YB, Fax: 01403 272 923,
Call Date: Nov 1992 (Inner Temple)
Qualifications: BA, Dip in Law (City)

Blunden *Mark Edward*
Advocate, and Member South Africa,
Call Date: Nov 1996 (Lincoln's Inn)
Qualifications: LLB (Hons)(Herts),
ACIArb

Blythe *Mark Andrew* •
Legal Adviser, HM Treasury, Treasury
Chambers, Parliament Street, London
SW1, 0171 270 1666, Lincoln's Inn (Ad
Eundem) and Member New York, Call
Date: Nov 1966 (Inner Temple)
Qualifications: BCL, MA (Oxon)

Blythin *David Andrew*
Call Date: Mar 1999 (Lincoln's Inn)
Qualifications: BA (Hons)

Boadita-Cormican *Miss Aedeen*
C/O Legal Department, Kuwait
Petroleum Corp, P O Box 26565, Sajat
13126, 1 Crown Office Row, 3rd Floor,
Temple, London, EC4Y 7HH, Call Date:
Oct 1990 (Gray's Inn) Qualifications:
LLB (Dub), LLM (Cantab)

Boase *Charles Nigel*
Vauxhall House, Monmouth NP5 4AX,
01600 715076, Call Date: Mar 1996
(Lincoln's Inn) Qualifications: BA
(Hons)

Boden *Peter Horrox*
19 Station Road, Chinley, High Peak,
Derbyshire SK23 6AR, Call Date: Feb
1965 (Gray's Inn) Qualifications: BSc
(Econ), LLB

Bogle *Paul Wakefield* •
Essex County Council, County
Secretary's Department, P O Box 11,
County Hall, Chelmsford CM1 1LX,
01245 430528, Fax: 01245 346994,
Call Date: Oct 1995 (Lincoln's Inn)
Qualifications: LLB (Hons)(Bris)

Boileau *Hugh Rufus*
Call Date: Nov 1997 (Middle Temple)
Qualifications: BA (Hons)(Oxon)

Bokszczanin *Ryszard*
34 Bradley Gardens, Ealing, London
W13, 0181 998 2874, Fax: 0181 998
2873, Call Date: Nov 1995 (Middle
Temple) Qualifications: LLB (Hons)
(Lond), BSc (Hons)

Bolt *Miss Annabelle Elizabeth* •
HM Customs & Excise, Room 3.28, New
King's Beam House, 22 Upper Ground,
London SE1 9PJ, 0171 620 1313/865
5157, Fax: 0171 865 5822, Call Date:
July 1970 (Gray's Inn)

Bolton *Miss Louise Caroline*
Call Date: Nov 1998 (Lincoln's Inn)
Qualifications: LLB (Hons)

Bondy *Rupert Mark Boden* •
SmithKline Beecham Plc, One New
Horizons Court, Brentford, Middlesex
TW8 9EP, 0181 975 2080, Fax: 0181
975 2090, and Member California, Call
Date: July 1987 (Middle Temple)
Qualifications: BA (Cantab)

Bonham-Carter *Miss Gaby*
Call Date: Nov 1997 (Lincoln's Inn)
Qualifications: BA (Hons)

Bonney *Charles John*
Call Date: Nov 1969 (Lincoln's Inn)
Qualifications: MA (Oxon)

Bontoux *Mrs Virginie Francoise
Ghislaine P*
92 Chesson Road, Baron's Court,
London W14 9QU, Call Date: Nov 1995
(Lincoln's Inn) Qualifications: LLB
(Hons), LLM

Boocock *Miss Lisa Jane*
Call Date: Oct 1998 (Gray's Inn)
Qualifications: BA (Cantab)

Boodia *Miss Anuradha Devi* •
Call Date: Oct 1994 (Gray's Inn)
Qualifications: LLB

Boone *Miss Caroline Anne* •
Legal Adviser, British Airways Plc,
Waterside (HBA3), P O Box 365,
Harmsworth UB7 0GB, Call Date: Feb
1980 (Middle Temple) Qualifications:
LLB (Soton)

Booth *Miss Amanda Jane*
0171 603 6623, Call Date: July 1979
(Gray's Inn) Qualifications: LLB
(L'pool)

Booth *Nigel Robert* •
Senior Crown Prosecutor, CPS North
West Area, Manchester South Branch,
Sunlight House, Quay Street,
Manchester M60 3PT, 0161 908 2600,
Fax: 0161 908 2617, Call Date: Oct
1994 (Gray's Inn) Qualifications: LLB,
Diploma in German , Law

Boothroyd *Paul*
Call Date: May 1995 (Lincoln's Inn)
Qualifications: BSc (Econ), FCA

Borenius *Lars Ulric*
Karelia, Stocksbridge Lane, Coombe
Bissett, Salisbury, Wiltshire SP5 4LZ,
01722 718 466, Call Date: June 1941
(Lincoln's Inn)

Borrett *Louis Albert Frank*
54 Farm Close, East Grinstead, West
Sussex RH19 3QG, 01342 312350, Call
Date: Nov 1955 (Gray's Inn)
Qualifications: LLB (Lond)

Borrie *Lord*
1 Plowden Buildings, Temple, London
EC4Y 9BU, 0171 353 4434, Call Date:
Nov 1952 (Middle Temple)
Qualifications: LLM, FCI Arb

Borrows *Miss Hayley*
Call Date: Nov 1995 (Middle Temple)
Qualifications: LLB (Hons)

Boss *Ronald William*
The Old Coach House, River Lane, Alfriston, East Sussex BN26 5SX, 01323 870813, Call Date: Nov 1958 (Middle Temple)

Boswell *Peter Douglas*
18 Market Place, Market Bosworth, Nuneaton, Warks CV13 0LE, 01455 291851, Fax: 01455 291637, Call Date: Nov 1994 (Gray's Inn) Qualifications: BA

Botros *John Michael*
Call Date: Feb 1992 (Middle Temple) Qualifications: MA (Oxon)

Bottrell *Eric Perry* •
Legal Advisor, Mid Essex Hospital Services, NHS Trust, Collingwood Road, Witham, Essex CM8 2TT, 01376 532625, Fax: 01376 532590, Call Date: Mar 1997 (Middle Temple) Qualifications: LLB (Hons)

Bough *Mrs Jennifer Christine*
Lecturer in Law, Wye College Univ. of London, Departmetn of Agriculture, Economics & Business Mngmnt., Wye College, University of London, Wye, Ashford, Kent TN25 5AH, Call Date: July 1978 (Gray's Inn) Qualifications: LLM (Lond)

Boughton *David Allan*
Deputy Chief Clerk, Inner London Magistrates', Courts Service, 65 Romney Street, London SW1P 3RD, Call Date: Nov 1970 (Gray's Inn)

Boulter *Christopher Nigel Jarvis*
Deputy Clerk to the Justices, Call Date: Nov 1975 (Middle Temple) Qualifications: LLB (Lond)

Boulton *Sir William Whytehead*
The Quarters Hse, Alresford, Colchester, Essex CO7 8AY, 01206 82 2450, Call Date: Nov 1936 (Inner Temple) Qualifications: BA

Bourke *Ms Sarah Victoria Norma*
Brent Community Law Centre, 389 High Road, Willesden, London NW10 2JR, 0181 459 7620, Call Date: Oct 1996 (Gray's Inn) Qualifications: LLB (Lond)

Bourne *Miss Judith Pullen*
Call Date: Oct 1993 (Lincoln's Inn) Qualifications: LLB (Hons) (Lond)

Bourne *Professor Nicholas*
Pendragon Chambers, 124 Walter Road, Swansea, SA1 5RG, Call Date: July 1976 (Gray's Inn) Qualifications: LLB, LLM (Wales), LLM (Cantab)

Bourne *Mrs Sharon Elsie Mary* •
Senior Crown Prosecutor, Crown Prosecution Service, 7th Floor (South), Royal Liver Building, Pier Head, Liverpool L3 1HN, 0151 2367575, Call Date: July 1985 (Gray's Inn) Qualifications: LLB (Liverpool)

Bousher *Stephen* •
Assistant Solicitor, The Inland Revenue, Solicitor's Office, Somerset House, The Strand, London WC2R 1LB, 0171 438 7085, Call Date: Nov 1975 (Gray's Inn) Qualifications: LLB

Boustred *Mrs Anne Mary* •
County Council Employed Barrister, Essex County Council, PO Box 11, County Hall, Duke Street, Chelmsford CM1 1LX, 01245 430479, Fax: 01245 346994, (nee Norman), Call Date: July 1975 (Inner Temple) Qualifications: LLB

Bowden *Benjamin James Edward*
Call Date: Oct 1996 (Gray's Inn) Qualifications: BA (Oxon)

Bowden *Gerald Francis*
Principal Lecturer in Law, 2 Paper Bldgs, 1st Floor, Temple, London, EC4Y 7ET, Call Date: July 1962 (Gray's Inn) Qualifications: MA (Oxon) FRICS

Bowden *Mrs Gwyneth Margaret*
Senior Deputy Chief Clerk, Inner London Magistrates', Courts Service, Clerkenwell Magistrates' Court, London WC1, 0171 278 6541, Fax: 0171 837 4526, Call Date: July 1968 (Gray's Inn) Qualifications: LLB

Bowen *David James Jeffreys* •
Senior Crown Prosecutor, CPS, Cumbria House, Merthyr Tydfil Industrial Est, Pentrebach, Merthyr Tydfil, Mid Glamorgan, 01443 693240, Call Date: July 1975 (Gray's Inn) Qualifications: LLB, MA

Bowen *Justin* •
GEC plc, One Briton Street, London W1X 8AQ, 0171 306 1313, Call Date: Oct 1994 (Lincoln's Inn) Qualifications: MA (Cantab)

Bower *Alastair Ross*
Forbes & Partners Solicitors, Marsden House, 28-32 Wellington Street, Blackburn, Lancashire, 01254 662831, Fax: 01254 681104, and Member New Zealand Bar, Call Date: July 1986 (Inner Temple) Qualifications: LLB (Leeds)

Bower *David Bartlett*
Obstetric & Gynaecological Surgeon Chelsea & Westminster Hospital, 17 Brook Green, London W6 7BL, Call Date: Nov 1950 (Inner Temple) Qualifications: FRCS, FRCOG

Bower *Marcus Himan*
14 Camelot Close, London SW19 7EA, Call Date: Nov 1946 (Middle Temple) Qualifications: MA, LLM (Cantab)

Bowett *Prof. Sir Derek William*
228 Hills Road, Cambridge CB2 2QE, 01223 414618, Fax: 01223 414617, Call Date: Nov 1953 (Middle Temple) Qualifications: LLD (Cantab), FBA

Bowker *Miss Cathryn Anne* •
Principal Crown Prosecutor, Crown Prosecution Service, Unit 3, Clifton Mews, Clifton Hill, Brighton, East Sussex BN1 3HR, 01273 207171, Fax: 01273 207849, Call Date: July 1983 (Gray's Inn) Qualifications: BA (Keele)

Bowler *Christopher Fairfax* •
Justices' Clerk, Justices Clerks Office, Shire Hall, Bury St Edmunds, Suffolk IP33 1HF, 01284 352300, Fax: 01284 352345, Call Date: July 1978 (Gray's Inn) Qualifications: LLB (L'pool)

Bowler-Smith *Mark*
Call Date: Nov 1997 (Middle Temple) Qualifications: LLB (Hons) (Exon)

Bowles *Edward Raymond* •
Senior Crown Prosecutor, Crown Prosecution Service, Camberwell Branch, 2nd Floor, The Cooperage, 8 Gainsford Street, London SE1 2NE, 0171 962 2706, Call Date: Oct 1993 (Middle Temple) Qualifications: LLB (Hons) (Lond)

Bowles *Philip Cranton*
Call Date: Nov 1950 (Inner Temple) Qualifications: MA

Bowman *Miss Catherine*
Call Date: Nov 1992 (Lincoln's Inn) Qualifications: BA (Hons)

Bowman *Edwin Geoffrey* •
Call Date: Nov 1968 (Lincoln's Inn) Qualifications: MA, LLM (Cantab)

Bowman *Mrs Georgina June*
Call Date: July 1973 (Gray's Inn) Qualifications: MA (Cantab)

Bowman *Timothy James Elliott*
Call Date: May 1993 (Lincoln's Inn) Qualifications: B.MUS (Hons) (Sheff), LLB (Hons) (Sheff)

Bowman-Boyles *Ms Chantal Marie Brenda*
ICO Global Commuications, 6th Floor, Commonwealth House, 2 Chalk Hill Road, London W6, 01225 752200, Fax: 01225 775527, Call Date: Oct 1994 (Middle Temple) Qualifications: BA (Hons) (Lond), CPE (City)

Boxall *Randolph Leonard*
Lamb Chambers, Lamb Building, Temple, London, EC4Y 7AS, Call Date: Nov 1951 (Inner Temple)

Boy *David Raymond*
QC (Hong Kong), Call Date: May 1954 (Gray's Inn)

Boyd *David John*
Immigration Adjudicator Chairman Axxia Systems Ltd Vice-Prersident, Council of Immigration Judges, Beeches, Upton Bishop, Ross-on-Wye, Herefordshire HR9 7UD, 01989 780214, Fax: 01989 780538, Call Date: Nov 1963 (Gray's Inn) Qualifications: MA (Cantab), FCIArb

Boyd *Duncan Rodney Lecington*
0171 723 2630, Fax: 0171 724 1460, Call Date: Nov 1994 (Lincoln's Inn) Qualifications: BA (Hons)

Boyd *Henry Marlow*
Director NYK Intl PLC, Chairman
Coalgas plc & Dominion Energy PLC,
Secretary UK Onshore Operators Group,
Director Oil Management Services
Limited Secretary General, The Gas
Forum, 63 Duke Street, London
W1M 5DH, 0171 355 3393, Fax: 0171
355 3704, Call Date: Nov 1964 (Middle
Temple) Qualifications: MA (Oxon)

Boyd *Miss Marian Elizabeth* •
Senior Crown Prosecutor, Call Date:
July 1983 (Middle Temple)
Qualifications: BA

Boydell *Peter Thomas Sherrington*
Chanc Dioc of Oxford, Call Date: Jan
1948 (Middle Temple) Qualifications:
LLB

Boyle *Professor Christopher Kevin*
University of Essex, Colchester, Essex
CO47 7SQ, (01206) 872568, Fax:
(01206) 873627, and Member
Northern Ireland Bar Southern Ireland
Bar, Call Date: May 1992 (Gray's Inn)
Qualifications: LLB (Belfast), Dip Crim
(Cantab)

Boyle *Jonathan Gavin*
Call Date: Oct 1995 (Inner Temple)
Qualifications: BA (Manc), CPE

Brabbins *Edroc Oliver*
Call Date: Nov 1998 (Inner Temple)
Qualifications: BA (Manch)

Braby-Pavitt *Mrs Lynne Louise* •
Assistant Solicitor, Essex County
Council, Chief Executive & Clerk's Dept,
PO Box 11, County Hall, Chelmsford,
Essex CM1 1LX, 01245 492211, Fax:
01245 352710, Call Date: Nov 1986
(Gray's Inn) Qualifications: LLB
(Hons)

Bracewell *Miss Julia Helen*
Partner, Brobeck Hale & Dorr,
Hasilwood House, 60 Bishopsgate,
London EC2N 4AJ, 0171 638 6688, Fax:
0171 638 5888, Call Date: July 1987
(Lincoln's Inn) Qualifications: LLB
(Bristol)

Bradbury *Christopher William*
and Member New York State Bar (USA),
Call Date: May 1997 (Inner Temple)
Qualifications: BA (Leics), LLM (Keele)

Bradbury *Ms Jeanne Brenda*
1 Old Dock Close, Kew Green, Surrey
TW9 3BL, 0181 948 8688, Fax: 0181
948 8688, Call Date: Nov 1992 (Inner
Temple) Qualifications: LLB

Bradbury *John Arthur*
Cot Hoy, Buckland, Nr Faversham, Kent
ME13 0TP, Call Date: June 1953
(Lincoln's Inn)

Bradbury *Trevor* •
Company Secretary, Tilbury Douglas
Plc, Tilbury House, Ruscombe Park,
Twyford, Reading, Berks RG10 9JU,
0118 9320123, Fax: 0118 9320206,
Call Date: Nov 1995 (Middle Temple)
Qualifications: LLB (Hons), FRICS,
ARIArb

Bradbury-Lawrence *Mrs Sara Patricia*
Call Date: Oct 1998 (Gray's Inn)
Qualifications: LLB (Manchester)

Bradford *Paul Andrew*
Call Date: Mar 1996 (Lincoln's Inn)
Qualifications: BA (Hons)

Bradley *Miss Celia Anne*
Legal Adviser, Kent Magistrates Courts
Cmmtte, The Court House, Tufton
Street, Ashford, Kent TN23 1QS, 01233
663203, Fax: 01233 663206, Call Date:
Feb 1992 (Middle Temple)
Qualifications: LLB (Hons)

Bradley *Clive*
8 Northumberland Place, Richmond,
Surrey TW10 6TS, 0181 940 7172, Fax:
0181 940 7603, Deputy Chairman,
Central London Valuation Tribunal, Call
Date: Feb 1961 (Middle Temple)
Qualifications: MA

Bradley *David Robert*
Call Date: Nov 1995 (Middle Temple)
Qualifications: LLB (Hons), BSc
(L'pool)

Bradley *John Joseph*
DETR, Zone 9/J10, Eland House,
Bressenden Place, London SW1E 5DU,
Call Date: July 1998 (Gray's Inn)
Qualifications: LLB (Warw), LLM
(Bruges)

Bradley *Nigel Frank* •
Legal Director, British Aerospace,
Systems & Services, Mill Lane, Warton
Aerodrome, Preston, Lancashire
PR4 1AX, 01772 852095, Fax: 01772
856262, Call Date: July 1981 (Lincoln's
Inn) Qualifications: LLB Hons
(Sheffield)

Bradley *Paul David*
Justices' Chief Executive, The
Courthouse, Church Hill, Easingwold,
York YO6 3JX, 01347 821776, Fax:
01347 823776, Call Date: July 1979
(Gray's Inn) Qualifications: LLB (Exon)

Bradshaw *Mrs Caron Louise*
Call Date: Oct 1994 (Lincoln's Inn)
Qualifications: LLB (Hons) (Lond)

Brady *Paul James*
Call Date: May 1995 (Inner Temple)
Qualifications: BA

Braggins *James Richard John* •
Treasury Solicitor's Department, Queen
Anne's Chambers, 28 Broadway,
London SW1, 0171 210 3000, Call
Date: July 1972 (Gray's Inn)
Qualifications: MA (Cantab)

Braich *Stephen Harmit Singh*
Bench Legal Adviser, Northampton
Magistrates' Court, Regents Pavilion,
Summerhouse Road, Moulton Park,
Northampton, 01604 497000, Fax:
01604 497010, Call Date: Nov 1987
(Gray's Inn) Qualifications: LLB, LLM
(Cantab)

Braine *Richard Michael Allix*
109 Cheyne Walk, London SW10 0DJ,
0171 352 0030, Fax: 0171 352 0030,
and Member Turks & Caicos Islands,
Call Date: July 1952 (Gray's Inn)
Qualifications: BA (Hons, Oxon)

Bramley *Steven Michael Stuart* •
Assistant Legal Adviser, THe Home
Office, 50 Queen Anne's Gate, London
SW1H 9AT, Call Date: July 1983 (Gray's
Inn) Qualifications: LLB

Bramwell *Mrs Elizabeth Anne Oxley* •
7 Penwerris Terrace, Falmouth,
Cornwall TR11 2PA, 01326 314465,
Fax: 01326 314465, Call Date: July
1971 (Lincoln's Inn) Qualifications:
LLB

Bramwell *Philip Nicholas* •
Legal Manager, Group Strategy and
Development Division, BT Group Legal
Services, BT Centre, 81 Newgate Street,
London EC1A 7AJ, 0171 356 5906, Fax:
0171 356 6638, Call Date: Nov 1983
(Lincoln's Inn) Qualifications: BA
(Hons)

Brandt *Howard Patrick* •
Legal Officer at the Financial Services
Authority, 7th Floor, One Canada
Square, London E14 5AZ, 0171 538
8860, Fax: 0171 418 9300, Call Date:
Feb 1993 (Middle Temple)
Qualifications: BA (Hons) (Oxon)

Branicki-Tolchard *Mrs Joanne Marie*
Call Date: Nov 1997 (Middle Temple)
Qualifications: LLB (Hons)

Branson *David John*
Middlesbrough College, Roman Road,
Middlesbrough TS5 5PJ, 01642 333333,
Fax: 01642 333310, Lecturer, Call
Date: July 1992 (Middle Temple)
Qualifications: BA (Hons) (Camb), LLB
(Hons) (Lond), MJUR. (Durham)

Brantingham *Leslie Andrew*
Deputy Director of Works - Palace of
Westminster, House of Commons,
London SW1A 1AA, 0171 219 6300,
Fax: 0171 219 6409, Call Date: Mar
1998 (Gray's Inn) Qualifications: BSc
(Loughborough), MSc
(Guildhall),MICE

Brassil *Michael Joseph*
Legal Adviser, Derbyshire Magistrates'
Court, Westbank House, Albion Road,
Chesterfield, Call Date: Nov 1994
(Gray's Inn) Qualifications: LLB

Braune *Mrs Janet Valerie* •
Call Date: May 1980 (Gray's Inn)

Braviner *Stephen Thomas* •
Legal Adviser, Home Office, Queen
Anne's Gate, Room 867c, London, 0171
273 2652, Call Date: Oct 1992 (Gray's
Inn) Qualifications: BA

Brawn *Daniel Hugh* •
Assistant Lawyer, Peter Kerrigan
Associates, 4 Abbots Quay, Monks Ferry,
Birkenhead, Merseyside L41 5LH, 0151
647 8862, Call Date: Oct 1996 (Gray's
Inn) Qualifications: BA (Manc), BA
(Greenwich)

Bray *Alan Hornby*
4th Floor, South Flat, 2 Garden Court,
Temple, London EC4Y 9BL, 0171 353
3437, Call Date: June 1934 (Middle
Temple) Qualifications: MA (Oxon)

Brazier *Martin*
Commercial Manager, Jarvis PLC,
Eastcroft Depot, London Road, Enderby
Road, Nottingham NG2 3AE, 0115 957
6655, Fax: 0115 957 6617, Call Date:
Nov 1997 (Middle Temple)
Qualifications: BSc (Hons), ARICS

Breckon *Miss Carolyn Constance*
Court Clerk, Call Date: Oct 1992 (Gray's
Inn) Qualifications: LL.B

Brenan *George Patrick*
Call Date: Nov 1994 (Gray's Inn)
Qualifications: BA, MSc

Brennan *Christopher John*
Call Date: Oct 1996 (Middle Temple)
Qualifications: LLB (Hons)(Lond)

Brennan *John*
6 Park Square, Leeds, LS1 2LW, Call
Date: Nov 1973 (Lincoln's Inn)
Qualifications: LLB (Lond)

Brennan *Dr John Lester*
16 Butterfield Road, Wheathampstead,
Herts AL4 8PU, 01582 832230, Call Date:
July 1971 (Middle Temple)
Qualifications: MD, MRCP, FRCPath,
LLM

Brennan *Michael Barry* •
Resident Vice President Trading Legal
Service, Citibank, N.A., 336 Strand,
London Ec2R 1HB, 0171 500 0027, Call
Date: Nov 1996 (Lincoln's Inn)
Qualifications: LLB (Hons)(Dublin)

Brereton *Miss Anita Helen*
The British Occupational, Health
Research Foundation, at Whitbread PLC,
52 Chiswell Street, London EC1Y 4SD,
0171 615 1080, Fax: 0171 615 1147,
Call Date: July 1979 (Gray's Inn)
Qualifications: BSc

Bresnahan *Miss Jane*
Call Date: July 1998 (Gray's Inn)
Qualifications: LLB (B'ham)

Bretherick *Ms Diana*
Call Date: Nov 1989 (Middle Temple)
Qualifications: BA (Hons), Dip Law

Brett-Holt *Ms Alexis Fayrer* •
Director of Legal Services, Department of
Trade & Industry, Room 309, 10 Victoria
Street, London SW1H 0NN, 0171 215
3247, Fax: 0171 215 3248, Call Date:
July 1973 (Lincoln's Inn) Qualifications:
BA Hons (Oxon)

Brew *Richard Maddock*
The Abbey, Coggeshall, Essex CO6 1RD,
01376 561246, Fax: 01376 562773, Call
Date: June 1956 (Inner Temple)
Qualifications: BA [Cantab]

Brewer *David Leonard*
Justices Clerk, Swindon Magistrates'
Court, Princes Street, Swindon, Wiltshire
SN1 2JB, 01793 527281, Fax: 01793
488525, Call Date: July 1976 (Gray's
Inn)

Brewer *Miss Imogen Melanie Fleur*
Oakwoods Farm House, Alton, Near
Selborne, Hants GU34 3BS, 01420
472470, and Member New York Bar, Call
Date: Nov 1994 (Middle Temple)
Qualifications: LLB (Hons)

Brewis *Mark*
Senior Common Room, Ranmoor
House, University of Sheffield, Shore
Lane, Sheffield, 0114 2663165, Call
Date: Oct 1993 (Lincoln's Inn)
Qualifications: LLB (Hons)(Sheff)

Brewster *David John* •
Adviser to the Board, IMRO, 25 The
North Colonnade, Canary Wharf, London
E14 5HS, 01732 741187, Fax: 01732
741182, Call Date: June 1961 (Gray's
Inn) Qualifications: MA (Cantab)

Brickman *Miss Gail Laura*
Call Date: Nov 1998 (Lincoln's Inn)
Qualifications: LLB (Hons)(Manch)

Bridge *Christian Henry Ritchie*
Call Date: July 1998 (Inner Temple)
Qualifications: BA (Essex)

Bridge *Maximilian Paul Martin*
Call Date: Nov 1997 (Middle Temple)
Qualifications: LLB (Hons)

Bridger *Henry Chris*
62 Baring Road, Hengistbury,
Bournemouth BH6 4DT, 01202 421050,
Call Date: July 1967 (Inner Temple)
Qualifications: BCom, BCL, FCIS

Bridges *Mrs Clare Jane*
Deputy Clerk to the Justices, The
Magistrate's Court, Barclay Road,
Croydon, Surrey CR9 3NG, 0181 686
8680, Fax: 0181 680 9801, Call Date: Oct
1992 (Middle Temple) Qualifications:
B.Sc (Hons, Dunelm)

Bridges *Dr Paul William* •
Dept of Health & Social, Security, New
Court, 48 Carey Street, London
WC2A 2LS, Call Date: 1984 (Gray's Inn)
Qualifications: BA, Ph.D

Briggs *Mark Edward*
Court Clerk, Stockport Magistrates Court,
PO Box 155, Court House, Edward Street,
Stockport SK1 3NF, 0161 477 2020, Fax:
0161 474 1115, Call Date: July 1982
(Inner Temple) Qualifications: BA

Briggs *Timothy Roy*
Herbert Smith, Exchange House,
Primrose Street, London EC2A 2HS,
0171 466 2506, Fax: 0171 496 0043,
Call Date: Oct 1995 (Middle Temple)
Qualifications: BA (Hons)

Brighton *Miss Pamela Dallas*
14 Tooks Court, Cursitor St, London,
EC4A 1LB, Call Date: Nov 1986 (Gray's
Inn) Qualifications: B.Sc(Econ) Dip Law

Bristow *Miss Clare* •
Commercial & Legal Adviser, HVCA, Esca
House, Palace Court, London W2 4JG,
0171 313 4918, Fax: 0171 727 9268,
Call Date: Oct 1996 (Lincoln's Inn)
Qualifications: LLB (Hons)(Leeds), MA
(Leeds)

Brittain *Mrs Maryann Catherine Corcoran*
Call Date: July 1998 (Middle Temple)
Qualifications: BA (Dublin)

Broadbent *Keith* •
Justices' Chief Executive for West
Glamorgan. Training Officer for Justices
and Staff Secretary to the Lord
Chancellor's Advisory Committee, West
Glam Magistrates Cts Comm,
Magistrates' Court, Cramic Way, Port
Talbot SA13 1RU, 01639 896718, Fax:
01639 893855, Call Date: Nov 1965
(Gray's Inn)

Broadberry *Miss Alison Lesley Caroline* •
Manager & Company Secretary, Schroder
Investment Management, Ltd, 31
Gresham Street, London EC2V, 0171 658
6000, Call Date: Oct 1991 (Lincoln's
Inn) Qualifications: BA (Hons), ATT,
TEP, ACII

Broadfoot *Miss Samantha Louise*
Call Date: Nov 1997 (Middle Temple)
Qualifications: LLB (Hons)(Kent), LLM
(Exon)

Broadway *Dennis*
87 Newdigate Road, Watnall, Nottingham
NG16 1HN, 0115 945 9097, Call Date:
Oct 1993 (Inner Temple) Qualifications:
LLB

Brock *Miss Carolyn Anne* •
Commercial Lawyer, British
Telecommunications PLC, C3004,
Westside, London Road, Hemel
Hempstead HP3 9YF, 01442 296097,
Call Date: July 1987 (Lincoln's Inn)
Qualifications: LLB

Brock *Mrs (Patricia) Ann*
Call Date: Nov 1969 (Gray's Inn)

Brock *Richard Selig Joseph*
Call Date: July 1957 (Inner Temple)
Qualifications: MA (Oxon)

Brockway *Stephen Peter* •
Legal Advisor to the Housing
Corporation, The Housing Corporation,
149 Tottenham Court Road, London
W1P 0BN, 0171 393 2107, Fax: 0171
393 2111, Call Date: July 1985
(Lincoln's Inn) Qualifications: BA
(Hons)

Broder *Milton Joseph*
Call Date: Nov 1993 (Middle Temple)
Qualifications: BA (Hons), MA, CPE

Brohi *Miss Saleema Kate*
Cameron McKenna, Sceptre Court,
Tower Hill, London EC3N 4BB, 0171
367 3000, Fax: 0171 367 2000, Call
Date: Feb 1995 (Lincoln's Inn)
Qualifications: LLB (Hons)(Lond)

Bromley-Challenor *James Roland*
170 Holland Park Avenue, London
W11 4UH, 0171 610 5416, Call Date:
May 1988 (Inner Temple)
Qualifications: LLB (Bristol)

Brooke *Miss Abigail*
Legal Advisor, Call Date: Oct 1995
(Middle Temple) Qualifications: LLB
(Hons)

Brooke *Nicholas Mark*
Call Date: Nov 1991 (Inner Temple)
Qualifications: BSc (Bristol), Dip Law

Brookes *Miss Melanie*
Call Date: Oct 1995 (Gray's Inn)
Qualifications: LLB, BA (Leeds)

Brooks *David Michael William*
Meis Limited, 34 Paradise Road,
Richmond upon Thames, Surrey
TW9 1SE, 0181 332 7171, Fax: 0181
332 7210, Call Date: Nov 1977 (Middle
Temple)

Brooks *Mrs Karen Anne* •
Senior Crown Prosecutor, Crown
Prosecution Service, 8th Floor, Sunlight
House, Quay Street, Manchester
M60 3LU, 0161 837 7402, Fax: 0161
835 2663, Call Date: July 1983 (Middle
Temple) Qualifications: LLB (Manch)

Brooks *Miss Sarah Anne* •
Crown Prosecutor, Crown Prosecution
Service, Princes Court, 34 York Road,
Leicester LE1 5TU, Call Date: Nov 1985
(Middle Temple) Qualifications: Dip
Mag Law

Brooks *Miss Shelagh* •
Legal Counsellor, Foreign &
Commonwealth Office, King Charles
Street, London SW1, and Member Hong
Kong Bar, Call Date: Nov 1978 (Inner
Temple) Qualifications: MA (Oxon),
BCL(Oxon), Licence en Droit,
European, Universite, Libre de
Bruselles

Brookwell *Paul* •
Crown Prosecutor, Crown Prosecution
Service, 1st Floor, Redrose House,
Lancaster Road, Preston, Lancashire
PO1 1DH, 01772 555015, Call Date:
Feb 1985 (Middle Temple)
Qualifications: BA

Brosnan *Mrs Teresa Sook Hian* •
Legal Adviser, The British Petroleum Co
plc, Legal Group, Britannic House, 1
Finsbury Circus, London EC2M 7BA,
0171 496 4000, Call Date: Nov 1983
(Gray's Inn) Qualifications: B.S.Sc
(Hons)

Brotherton *Matthew Sean de la Haye
Browne*
Former Solicitor, Call Date: July 1995
(Lincoln's Inn) Qualifications: MA
(Cantab), PGCE

Brough *Philip*
The Potters, Abernant, Aberdare, Mid
Glamorgan CF44 0ST, 01685 874320,
Call Date: May 1977 (Gray's Inn)

Brough *Simon*
Senior Court Clerk, Sheffield
Magistrates' Court, Castle Street,
Sheffield S3 8LU, 0114 276 0760, Fax:
0114 272 0129, Call Date: May 1987
(Gray's Inn) Qualifications: B.A.

Brown *Miss Angela Adorkor* •
First Interstate, Bank of California, 6
Agar Street, London WC2H 4HN, 0171
836 3560, Call Date: July 1984 (Middle
Temple) Qualifications: LLB, LLM

Brown *Anthony Roger Ernest* •
Company Secretary, T R Brown & Sons,
54-62 Clouds Hill Road, St George,
Bristol BS5 7LB, 0117 955 7441, Fax:
0117 941 3068, Call Date: July 1978
(Lincoln's Inn) Qualifications: BA
(Cantab), MA (Cantab), ACIS

Brown *Mrs Caroline Louise*
Call Date: May 1997 (Lincoln's Inn)
Qualifications: LLB (Hons), MSc
(Econ)

Brown *Mrs Elaine Maude* •
Lawyer (Grade 7), The Public Trust
Office, Stewart House, 24 Kingsway,
London WC2B 6JX, 0171 269 7121, Call
Date: July 1983 (Middle Temple)
Qualifications: LLM (Lond), LLB
(Lond)

Brown *Miss Elizabeth Joy*
Call Date: Oct 1998 (Lincoln's Inn)
Qualifications: BA (Wales)

Brown *George Gordon*
Call Date: Nov 1966 (Inner Temple)

Brown *Mrs Grace Kwee-Yoke*
Call Date: Nov 1993 (Middle Temple)
Qualifications: LLB (Hons)(Lond)

Brown *Graham* •
Chief Crown Prosecutor, Crown
Prosecution Service, 7th Floor South,
Royal Liver BuildinG, Liverpool L3 1HN,
0151 236 7575, Fax: 0151 255 0642,
Call Date: Nov 1982 (Gray's Inn)
Qualifications: BA

Brown *Ian Davis* •
Call Date: Nov 1987 (Middle Temple)
Qualifications: M.Phil, MA (Oxon),, Dip
Law

Brown *Mrs Jacqueline Loyola* •
Grade 7 Lawyer, The Lord Chancellor's
Dept, Selborne House, 54-60 Victoria
Street, London SW1E 6QW, Call Date:
July 1974 (Middle Temple)
Qualifications: LLB, LLM (Lond)

Brown *Miss Joanna Diana*
Call Date: Nov 1990 (Inner Temple)
Qualifications: BSc (Cardiff)

Brown *Keith William*
Justices Chief Executive, Windsor
House, Spitfire close, Ermine Business
Park, Huntingdon PE18 6XY, 01480
414455, Fax: 01480 414499, Call Date:
July 1980 (Gray's Inn) Qualifications:
D.M.L.

Brown *Kenneth*
Call Date: July 1972 (Gray's Inn)

Brown *Miss Kristina Rachel*
Call Date: Oct 1998 (Gray's Inn)
Qualifications: LLB (Durham)

Brown *Ms Mandy* •
Legal Officer, The Treasury Solicitor,
Queen Anne's Chambers, 28 Broadway,
London SW1, 0171 210 3148, Fax:
0171 210 3310, Call Date: Nov 1991
(Lincoln's Inn) Qualifications: LLB
(Hons) (Essex)

Brown *Miss Mandy Joanne*
Wansbroughs Willey Hargrave,
Solicitors, 13 Police Street, Manchester
M2 7WA, Call Date: Feb 1987 (Middle
Temple) Qualifications: LLB(Lanc)

Brown *Martin Frederick John* •
Court Clerk, Stoke-on-Trent Magistrates
Crt, Albert Square, Fenton,
Stoke-on-Trent ST4 3BX, 01782
845353, Fax: 01782 744782, Call Date:
Feb 1990 (Gray's Inn) Qualifications:
BA (Hons), LLM

Brown *Matthew James*
Call Date: Nov 1994 (Middle Temple)
Qualifications: LLB (Hons)

Brown *Miss Michelle Diane* •
Prosecutor, Crown Prosecution Service,
Level Street, Wolverhampton, West
Midlands, 01902 870900, Call Date:
Feb 1992 (Inner Temple)
Qualifications: LLB (Hons, So'ton)

Brown *Commander Neil Logan* •
Naval Prosecuting Officer, Naval
Prosecuting Authority, HMS Nelson,
Queen Street, Portsmouth PO1 3HH,
01705 727269, Fax: 01705 727189,
Call Date: Oct 1992 (Middle Temple)
Qualifications: LLB (Hons)(Queens)

Brown *Norman Francis Graham*
Henderson Investors, 3 Finsbury
Avenue, London EC2M 2PA, Call Date:
July 1981 (Middle Temple)
Qualifications: MA (Cantab)

Brown *Mrs Pauline Carol*
Call Date: Nov 1990 (Lincoln's Inn)
Qualifications: LLB (PCL)

Brown *Roger William* •
Head of Legal Services, The Law Courts,
Magistrates' Court, Bishopgate, Norwich
NR3 1UP, 01603 632421, Fax: 01603
663263, Call Date: Nov 1975 (Middle
Temple) Qualifications: LLB (Manch)

Brown *Steven David*
Call Date: Oct 1994 (Inner Temple)
Qualifications: BA (Lond), MA (Reading)

Brown *Ms Wendy Pamela*
Legal Adviser, Hambro Assistance,
Hambro House, Stephenson Road,
Colchester CO4 4QR, 0990 234500, Fax:
0990 234508, Call Date: Feb 1994
(Lincoln's Inn) Qualifications: LLB
(Hons), LLM

Brown *Winston George*
Lewisham Law Centre, 28 Deptford High
Street, London SE8 4AF, 0181 692 3217,
Call Date: Feb 1993 (Middle Temple)
Qualifications: LLB (Hons)(Anglia)

Browne *Michael Brendan*
Call Date: May 1996 (Middle Temple)
Qualifications: BA (Hons) (York)

Browning *Miss Anna Jane*
Litigator, DAS Legal Expenses Insurance,
Company Limited, DAS House, Quay
Side, Temple Back, Bristol, 0117 934
2000, Fax: 0117 943 2109, Call Date:
Nov 1997 (Lincoln's Inn) Qualifications:
LLB (Hons)

Browning *Colin Allister*
Call Date: Nov 1958 (Gray's Inn)
Qualifications: MA (Cantab)

Browning *Neil*
Call Date: Oct 1998 (Gray's Inn)
Qualifications: LLB (West of Eng)

Browning *Robert Andre* •
Legal Adviser, Sir Robert McAlpine
Limited, Yorkshire House, Grosvenor
Crescent, London SW1X 7EP, 0171 225
0064, Fax: 0171 245 9140, Call Date:
Nov 1995 (Gray's Inn) Qualifications:
LLB (Hons), FRICS,, ACIArb

Browning *Robert Mark* •
Consultant, 59 Pelham Street, South
Kensington, London SW7 2NJ, 0171 460
7489, Fax: 0171 581 8804, and Member
Turks & Caicos Islands Bar, Call Date:
Nov 1986 (Inner Temple) Qualifications:
LLB (S'hampton)

Brownlow *Miss Ann Elisabeth* •
Call Date: July 1984 (Inner Temple)
Qualifications: MA (Oxon)

Bruce *Mrs Claire Therese Helene* •
Goldman Sachs International, Legal &
Government Affairs, Peterborough Court,
133 Fleet Street, London EC4A 2BB,
0171 774 1421, Fax: 0171 774 1989,
and Member New York (1995), Call
Date: July 1992 (Inner Temple)
Qualifications: LLB (Lond), MA
(Sorbonne,Paris), LLM (Cambs), MPA
(Harvard)

Bruce *Malcolm Gray*
House of Commons, London SW1A 0AA,
0171 219 4580, Fax: 0171 219 2334,
Call Date: Nov 1995 (Gray's Inn)
Qualifications: MA, MSc

Bruce *Peter Richard* •
Legal Advisor, Call Date: Oct 1996 (Inner
Temple) Qualifications: BSc
(Greenwich), MSc (South Bank), CPE
(Lond), FRICS, ACIArb

Brudenell *Miss Kim Elaine* •
Grade 7 Lawyer, Treasury Solicitor's
Dept, 28 Broadway, London SW1H 9JS,
0171 210 3270, Call Date: Nov 1992
(Inner Temple) Qualifications: BA
(Hons), CPE

Bruggemann *Miss Emma Hamilton*
Call Date: Mar 1996 (Lincoln's Inn)
Qualifications: LLB (Hons)

Brunning *Peter David*
Deputy Chief Clerk, Inner London
Magistrates', Court Committee,
Magistrates Court, Bow Street, London
WC2E 7AS, 0171 379 4713, Fax: 0171
379 5634, Call Date: Nov 1987 (Gray's
Inn) Qualifications: BA, MA, LLB.

Brunt *Mrs Dracaena Ann*
Call Date: Nov 1989 (Middle Temple)
Qualifications: LLB (Hons)

Bruton *Thomas Howard*
Call Date: Oct 1996 (Middle Temple)
Qualifications: BSc (Hons)(Lond), CPE
(B'ham), LPC, (B'ham)

Bryan *Mrs Ethna Rose*
01283 585484, Fax: 01283 585, Call
Date: Feb 1975 (Middle Temple)

Bryan *Ms Niamh Myra*
Management Consultant, Deloitte &
Touche, Management Solutions,
Stonecutter Court, 1 Stonecutter Street,
London EC4A 4TR, 0171 303 7331, Fax:
0171 583 1198, Call Date: July 1986
(Middle Temple) Qualifications: LLB
(Hons), PGCE

Bryan-Brown *Michael John*
Call Date: July 1996 (Gray's Inn)
Qualifications: BA (Dunelm)

Bryn Davies *Mrs Mary*
Call Date: Nov 1969 (Middle Temple)

Bryson *David Thomas* •
Senior Crown Prosecutor, Crown
Prosecution Service, Coniston House,
District 4, Washington, Tyne and Wear
NE38 7RN, Call Date: Nov 1979
(Lincoln's Inn) Qualifications: MA
(Cantab)

Buchanan *Angus*
Court Clerk, Inner London Magistrates',
Courts Service, 3rd Floor, North West
Wing, Bush House, Aldwych, London
WC2, Call Date: July 1979 (Gray's Inn)

Buckenham *Giles Edward* •
Legal Adviser, D.T.I., 10 Victoria Street,
London SW1H 0NN, 0171 215 3241, Fax:
0171 215 3242, Call Date: Feb 1995
(Lincoln's Inn) Qualifications: BA
(Hons)(Warw)

Buckhurst *Brian Alfred*
Justices Chief Executive and Clerk to the
Justices, Somerset Magistrates' Cts
Comm, The Court House, Northgate,
Bridgwater, Somerset TA6 3EU, 01278
452182, Fax: 01278 453667, Call Date:
July 1975 (Gray's Inn) Qualifications: BA
(Wales)

Buckingham *Miss Lise Merie*
Court Clerk, Call Date: Feb 1992 (Gray's
Inn) Qualifications: LLB

Buckingham *Paul Richard*
Clifford Chance Solicitors, 200 Aldersgate
Street, London EC1A 4JJ, 0171 600 1000,
Fax: 0171 600 5555, Call Date: Nov 1995
(Middle Temple) Qualifications: BSc
(Hons), CEng, MIChemE

Buckland *Miss Alexandra Elizabeth Mary*
Reynolds Porter CHamberlain,
Chichester House, 278/282 High
Holborn, London WC1V 7HA, Call Date:
Oct 1996 (Inner Temple) Qualifications:
LLB (Leic)

Buckley *James Rice Kempthorne*
Flat 10, 89 Onslow Square, London
SW7 3LT, 0171 584 8436, Call Date: Feb
1952 (Middle Temple) Qualifications:
MA, LLB

Buckley *Patrick James*
Former Solicitor, Call Date: July 1998
(Gray's Inn) Qualifications: BA (Keele)

Buckman *Mrs Akosua Asaa*
Research Officer, Industrial Relations
Services, Limited, 18-20 Highbury Place,
London N5 1QP, Call Date: July 1986
(Lincoln's Inn) Qualifications: LLB
(Ghana), DipLaw

Bucknell *Patrick John*
Call Date: June 1956 (Inner Temple)
Qualifications: MA (Cantab)

Buckrell *Jonathan Mark*
Call Date: Nov 1995 (Inner Temple)
Qualifications: BA (Cantab), CPE

Bucksey *Nicholas Richard*
Call Date: July 1995 (Inner Temple)
Qualifications: LLB

Buckwell *William Dominic Heymanson*
Solicitor Advocate, Holman Fenwick &
Willan, Marlow House, Lloyds Avenue,
London EC3N 3AL, 0171 488 2300, Fax:
0171 481 0316, Call Date: Oct 1993
(Middle Temple) Qualifications: BA
(Hons)

Budd *Bernard Wilfred*
Highlands, Elham, Canterbury, Kent
CT4 6UG, (01303) 840350, Also Inn of
Court M (1968), Call Date: July 1952
(Gray's Inn) Qualifications: MA (Cantab)

Budd Dr Jeremy David
The Haven, Four Forks, Spaxton,
Bridgwater, Somerset TA5 1AD, 01278
671534, Call Date: Oct 1996 (Inner
Temple) Qualifications: MA (Cantab),
CPE (Oxon)

Budden Dr Ian
Legal and Constitution Adviser
University of London, University of
London, Senate House, Malet Street,
London WC1E 7HU, 0171 862 8231,
Fax: 0171 862 8233, Call Date: July
1993 (Middle Temple) Qualifications:
MA, Ph.D, LLB

Bueno Miss Nicola Anna Christina •
Kleinwort Benson, 10 Fenchurch
Street, London EC3M 3LB, 0171 956
6066, Call Date: Nov 1990 (Middle
Temple) Qualifications: LLB (Bris)

Bugeja Albert John •
Head of Legal Services, Rochford
District Council, Council Offices, South
St, Rochford, Essex SS4 1BW, 01702
546366, Fax: 01702 545737, Call Date:
Nov 1981 (Lincoln's Inn)
Qualifications: BA Hons

Bulbeck Miss Nicola Jane •
Grade 6, Branch Crown
Cambridgeshire, Crown Prosecution
Service, c/o 50 Ludgate Hill, LondoN
EC4M 7EX, Call Date: July 1983 (Inner
Temple) Qualifications: LLB (Leeds)

Bulgin Kenneth Arthur
Call Date: Nov 1980 (Lincoln's Inn)
Qualifications: MA (Oxon)

Bull Colin Reginald
Call Date: July 1966 (Gray's Inn)

Bullas Justin Adrian •
Crown Prosecution Service, Greenfield
House, 3 Scotland Street, Sheffield S1,
Call Date: Oct 1996 (Middle Temple)
Qualifications: LLB (Hons) (Bucks),
LLM (Sheff)

Bulleid Michael Leonard John
Also Inn of Court G and Member Hong
Kong Bar, Call Date: July 1973 (Inner
Temple) Qualifications: LLB(Lond)

Bulleyment Christopher James
Call Date: Nov 1998 (Lincoln's Inn)
Qualifications: LLB (Hons)(Reading)

Bullimore Timothy Michael Duncan
Former Solicitor, Call Date: Feb 1995
(Inner Temple) Qualifications: BA
(Cantab)

Bunker Mrs Barbara Reece
Call Date: Nov 1960 (Inner Temple)
Qualifications: LLB (Lond)

Bunting David John
Call Date: Oct 1998 (Middle Temple)
Qualifications: LLB (Hons) (Lanc)

Bunton John
3rd Floor North, 4 Stone Bldgs,
Lincoln's Inn, London WC2A 3XT, 0171
242 7971, Call Date: Nov 1952
(Lincoln's Inn) Qualifications: MA
(Cantab), C.Eng, FIEE, C.Phys,, F.inst
P.

Burchill David Jeremy Michael •
Compliance Officer Legal Adviser, M &
G Group plc, 7th Floor, 3 Minster
Court, Gt Tower Street, London
EC3R 7XH, 0171 621 8904, Fax: 0171
621 8860, Also Inn of Court N.Ireland,
Call Date: May 1983 (Gray's Inn)
Qualifications: LL.B(Belfast)

Burdess Andrew George
Call Date: Mar 1996 (Lincoln's Inn)
Qualifications: B.Ed (Hons)

Burdis-Smith Ronald Alan
Call Date: Oct 1998 (Inner Temple)
Qualifications: BSc (Open), CPE
(Lancs)

Burge Miss Natalie Heidi
Flat 2, 42 Clanricarde Gardens, London
W2 4JW, 0171 727 8938, Call Date: Nov
1994 (Inner Temple) Qualifications:
BA (Oxon), CPE (Lond)

Burgess Brian Neil •
Senior Crown Prosecutor, Crown
Prosecution Service, Sceptre House,
Luton, Bedfordshire LU1 3AJ, 015821
404808, Call Date: July 1989 (Lincoln's
Inn) Qualifications: BA (Warw)

Burgess David Brian •
Senior Crown Prosecutor, Crown
Prosecution Service, Hawkins House,
Pynes Hill, Rydon Lane, Exeter,Devon
EX2 5SS, Call Date: Nov 1989 (Inner
Temple) Qualifications: LLB

Burgess Keith John •
Group Company Secretary, Queens
Moat Houses Plc, Queens Court, 9-17
Eastern Road, Romford, Essex
RM1 3NG, 01708 730522, Fax: 01708
734848, Call Date: Nov 1977 (Inner
Temple) Qualifications: BA [Bus Law],
FCIS

Burgin Ms Catherine Ann
Call Date: Oct 1990 (Gray's Inn)
Qualifications: LLB (Lond)

Burke Miss Andrea Faith
Call Date: Oct 1994 (Lincoln's Inn)
Qualifications: LLB (Hons) (Sheff)

Burke Mrs Catherine Lucy
Call Date: Nov 1990 (Lincoln's Inn)
Qualifications: LLB (Sheff)

Burke Christopher Michael •
HM Customs & Excise, New King's
Beam House, 22 Upper Ground,
London SE1 9PJ, 0171 865 5138, Fax:
0171 865 5822, Call Date: July 1985
(Inner Temple) Qualifications: BA, Dip
Law

Burke James David
Call Date: Oct 1996 (Middle Temple)
Qualifications: BA (Hons)(Lond), CPE

Burke Malachy Columba
Call Date: Nov 1997 (Inner Temple)
Qualifications: LLB (Lond), BEng,
(South Bank)

Burke Miss Rosalie Elizabeth
Call Date: Nov 1995 (Lincoln's Inn)
Qualifications: BA (Hons)

Burke Miss Vanessa Samantha •
Principal Legal Officer, Room 515, New
Court, 48 Carey Street, London WC2,
0171 962 8000, Fax: 0171 412 1523,
Call Date: Nov 1989 (Lincoln's Inn)
Qualifications: LLB

Burke-Gaffney John Campion Anthony
94 Copse Hill, London SW20, Call Date:
Feb 1956 (Gray's Inn)

Burkill John Ernest
Senior Deputy Chief Clerk, Inner
London Magistrates', Courts Service, 65
Romney Street, London SW1P 3RD, Call
Date: July 1976 (Gray's Inn)
Qualifications: LLB

Burling Julian Michael •
Counsel to Lloyds, Corporation of
Lloyds, 51 Lime Street, London
EC3M 7HA, 0171 327 5601/327 1000,
Fax: 0171 327 5414, Also Inn of Court
G, Call Date: July 1976 (Middle
Temple) Qualifications: MA,LLB
[Cantab]

Burman Keith William
Deputy Justices' Clerk Inner London
Magistrates Court Service, Call Date:
Nov 1984 (Middle Temple)
Qualifications: Dip Mag Law

Burn Nicholas George Orwin •
Principal Crown Prosecutor, Crown
Prosecution Service, (Midlands), 11a
Princes Street, Stafford ST17 9UQ,
01785 223423, Call Date: July 1982
(Gray's Inn) Qualifications: BA (Hons)

Burnet Miss Cressida Johanna
Call Date: Nov 1989 (Middle Temple)
Qualifications: LLB

Burnett Miss Alice Margaret •
Assistant Legal Adviser to H M
Diplomatic Service., Foreign &
Commonwealth Office, London
SW1A 2AH, 0171 270 3283, Fax: 0171
270 2767, Call Date: Oct 1991 (Middle
Temple) Qualifications: BA Hons
(Cantab), MA

Burnett John Wyndham
Grafton, Albury, Nr Guildford, Surrey
GU5 9AE, Call Date: July 1962 (Middle
Temple) Qualifications: LLB

Burnett Rae Jeremy Alexander James
Fraser •
Legal Director, Fax: 0171 626 1184,
Call Date: Nov 1977 (Middle Temple)
Qualifications: MA (Oxon), MSI

• **Barrister in employment**

Burney *Miss Margaret Mitchell*
Principal Court Clerk, Victoria Law
Courts, Corporation Street, Birmingham,
0121 212 6655, Call Date: Nov 1986
(Gray's Inn) Qualifications: DML

Burnham *James Pitt* •
Prosecution Team Leader (West Berks),
Crown Prosecution Service, Eaton Court,
112 Oxford Road, Reading, Berkshire,
0118 9503771, Fax: 0118 9508192, Call
Date: July 1984 (Gray's Inn)
Qualifications: LLB (Reading)

Burns *Mrs Catherine Mary*
Call Date: Nov 1994 (Inner Temple)
Qualifications: LLB

Burns *Miss Lorna Marie* •
Prosecution Team Leader, Crown
Prosecution Service, 50 Ludgate Hill,
London SE1 2NG, Call Date: Nov 1986
(Inner Temple) Qualifications: LLB
(Leic)

Burns *Miss Rebecca Jane Katherine*
Call Date: Nov 1991 (Lincoln's Inn)
Qualifications: LLB (Hons)

Burrell *Michael John*
Also Inn of Court G, Call Date: Feb 1965
(Inner Temple) Qualifications: MA
(Cantab)

Burrell *Mrs Sarah Maureen Rose* •
Regulatory Legal Department, BBC WHite
City, London W12 7TS, 0181 752 4149,
Call Date: Oct 1990 (Lincoln's Inn)
Qualifications: LLB (Lond)

Burridge *Roger Henry Moore*
Senior Lecturer, University of Warwick,
School of Law, University of Warwick,
Coventry CV4 7AL, 01203 523094, Fax:
01203 524105, Call Date: Feb 1973
(Gray's Inn) Qualifications: LLB

Burrowes *Patrick Charles Henry*
Call Date: Nov 1988 (Inner Temple)
Qualifications: LLB (Bris)

Burrows *Mrs Carol Jane*
Senior Legal Adviser, Justices' Clerks
Office, The Court House, South Walls,
Stafford, Staffs ST16 3DW, 01785
223144, Call Date: Apr 1989 (Gray's Inn)
Qualifications: LLB

Burrows *Christon Jon* •
Legal Adviser, Call Date: July 1996
(Middle Temple) Qualifications: BA
(Hons)(Lond), Dip in Law, ACII

Burrows *Dr Fred*
Call Date: June 1950 (Gray's Inn)
Qualifications: MA (Cantab), PhD

Burt *Miss Alice Margaret*
Call Date: Oct 1997 (Middle Temple)
Qualifications: NA (Hons)(Dunelm), CPE
(Lond)

Burt *Arthur Norman*
Pen-y-Bryn Farm, Ffordd y Blaenau,
Treuddyn, Mold, Flintshire CH7 4NS,
01352 770473, Call Date: June 1953
(Lincoln's Inn) Qualifications: LLB

Burton *Miss Denise Patricia*
Call Date: Apr 1989 (Gray's Inn)
Qualifications: LLB (B'ham), FCIS

Burton *Miss Janice Elaine*
Call Date: July 1991 (Lincoln's Inn)
Qualifications: LLB (Hons)

Burton *John*
Call Date: Nov 1979 (Gray's Inn)

Burton *Dr John David Keith*
Coroner of the Queen's Household, HM
Coroner for West London, The Coroners
Court, Western District, 25 Bagleys Lane,
London SW6 2QA, 0171 371 9938, Call
Date: June 1964 (Middle Temple)
Qualifications: MB, MRCS, FFA, RCS,

Burton *Mervyn John* •
Crown Prosecution Service, C/O 50
Ludgate Hill, London EC4M 7EX, Call
Date: July 1973 (Middle Temple)
Qualifications: BA (Hons)

Burton *Paul*
Call Date: Oct 1998 (Lincoln's Inn)
Qualifications: LLB (Hons)(Staffs)

Burton *Raymond* •
Solicitor's Office, Dept Of Trade and
Industry, 10-18 Victoria Street, London
SW1H 0NN, Call Date: Nov 1968 (Gray's
Inn)

Burton *Richard*
Call Date: Nov 1996 (Middle Temple)
Qualifications: LLB (Hons)(Lond)

Burton *Dr Rosemary Ann*
Deputy Coroner - W. London, 7 Orchard
Rise, Richmond, Surrey TW10 5BX, 0181
876 5386, Call Date: July 1971 (Middle
Temple) Qualifications: MB, BS, MRCS,
LRCP,, DA

Bury *Andrew Charles*
Call Date: Mar 1999 (Lincoln's Inn)
Qualifications: LLB (Hons)

Bury *Miss Catherine Anne*
Call Date: July 1998 (Lincoln's Inn)
Qualifications: LLB (Hons)

Busfield *Miss Kathleen Nancy*
Inns Of Court Also L 1966, Call Date: Feb
1963 (Gray's Inn) Qualifications: ACIS

Bushell *Jonathan David* •
Senior Crown Prosecutor, Crown
Prosecution Service, Cambria House,
Merthyr Tydfil Industrial Prk,
Pentrebach, Metrthyr Tydfil, Mid Glam
CF48 4XA, 01443 693240, Fax: 01443
692965, Call Date: July 1990 (Lincoln's
Inn) Qualifications: MA (Oxon)

Bushnell *David Edward* •
Legal Advisor, 5 Bodenham Road,
Folkestone, Kent CT20 2NU, 01303
255803, Call Date: May 1953 (Middle
Temple)

Butcher *Anthony John*
Recorder, 1 Atkin Building, Gray's Inn,
London, WC1R 5AT, Call Date: Feb 1957
(Gray's Inn) Qualifications: MA
(Cantab), LLB

Butcher *Michael* •
General Counsel to General Utilities PLC.
Director of Central Railway PLC, Director
& General Secretary of the Franco-British
Lawyers Society Ltd. Consultant to
Reynolds Porter Chamberlain, & to
Triplet & Associes., General Utilities PLC,
37-41 Old Queen Street, Westminster,
London SW1H 9JA, 0171 393 2700, Fax:
0171 222 2376, Member of Commercial
Panel of American Arbitration Assoc.,
Call Date: July 1975 (Gray's Inn)
Qualifications: BA Hons (Keele)

Butcher *Russell Henry* •
Eastgate Assistance, Eastgate House,
Stephenson Road, The Business Park,
Colchester, EsseX CO4 4QR, Call Date:
Oct 1992 (Middle Temple)
Qualifications: BA (Hons), Diploma in
Law(City)

Butler *Miss Anne Kathleen*
Lawyer Special Casework (Retired),
Ireland, and Member Southern Ireland
Bar Nigerian Bar, Call Date: July 1972
(Gray's Inn) Qualifications: MA, LLB, B
Comm

Butler *Miss Brenda Mary* •
'PRIVATE & CONFIDENTIAL', Legal &
Contracts Adviser, c/o Talisman Energy
(UK) Ltd, Belmont House, 1 Berry Street,
Aberdeen AB1 1DL, Scotland, 01224
413200, Fax: 01224 413450, Call Date:
Nov 1992 (Gray's Inn) Qualifications:
LLB (Buckingham), LLM (Buckingham)

Butler *Miss Frances Helen*
Call Date: Nov 1975 (Lincoln's Inn)

Butler *John Spencer*
Consultant, Messrs Barlow Lyle &
Gilbert, Beaufort House, 15 St Botolph
Street, London EC3A 7NJ, 0171 247
2277, Fax: 0171 782 8500, Call Date:
Feb 1963 (Lincoln's Inn) Qualifications:
LLB (Lond)

Butler *Mark*
Martin Murray & Associates, 138 High
Street, Yiewsley, Middlesex UB7 7BD,
01895 431332, Fax: 01895 448343, Call
Date: Oct 1995 (Middle Temple)
Qualifications: LLB (Hons)

Butler *Miss Megan Veronica*
7th Floor, London Stock Exchange
Limited, Old Broad Street, London
EC2N 1HP, Call Date: July 1987 (Inner
Temple) Qualifications: LLB (Sheff)

Butt *Miss Aliya* •
Crown Prosecutor, CPS Midlands,
Birmingham Branch 2, 2 Colmore Row,
Colmore Gate, Birmingham B3 2QA, Call
Date: Oct 1994 (Gray's Inn)
Qualifications: LLB

Butt *Naeem*
32 Onslow Gardens, London SW7 3AH,
0171 581 0509, and Member Lahore
High Court Bar, Call Date: Nov 1966
(Lincoln's Inn) Qualifications: BA

Butt *Ms Saiqa Jamil*
Local Government Officer, Call Date:
Feb 1991 (Middle Temple)
Qualifications: LLB

Butt *Zahur-Ud-Din*
9a High Street, Southall, Middlesex
UB1 3HA, 0181 574 1119/571 6264,
Fax: 0181 571 6132, High Court,
Punjab, Pakistan, Call Date: Nov 1959
(Lincoln's Inn) Qualifications: BA

Butter *Timothy* •
Senior Crown Prosecutor, CPS (Inner
London), 1st Floor, The Cooperage,
Gainsford Street, London SE1 2NE,
0171 962 2609, Fax: 0171 962 0906,
Call Date: Oct 1991 (Inner Temple)
Qualifications: BA (Warw), MSc (Lond),
Dip Law

Butterfield *Charles Harris*
QC Singapore 1952, Call Date: June
1934 (Middle Temple) Qualifications:
MA

Butterfield *Cleveland Michael Geoffrey*
Call Date: Nov 1954 (Gray's Inn)
Qualifications: MA (Cantab) LLM,
(Cantab)

Butterworth *Adrian Ernest*
Financial Regulatory Group, DIBB
Lupton, Alsop Solicitors 125 London
Wall, London, EC2Y 5AE, 98 Whitley
Close, Stanwell Village, Middlesex
TW19 7EY, 0171 814 6177, Call Date:
Nov 1995 (Middle Temple)
Qualifications: BA (Hons) (Hull), ACIS

Butterworth *Mrs Barbara Susan*
Legal Adviser. Company Secretary,
Janssen Cilag Limited, P O Box 79,
Saunderton, High Wycombe, Bucks
HP14 4HJ, 01494 567567, Fax: 01494
567568, Call Date: July 1989 (Lincoln's
Inn) Qualifications: BA (York), Grad
ICSA, LLB, MBA

Buttery *Miss Alison Tracey*
Deputy Company Secretary, Jarvis plc,
Frogmore Park, Watton-at-Stone,
Hertford SG14 3RU, 01920 832800,
Fax: 01920 832832, Call Date: July
1997 (Lincoln's Inn) Qualifications: BA
(Jnt Hons) (Hull), ACIS

Buttery *Miss Louise* •
Legal Advisor, South Wales Police,
South Wales Police, Police
Headquarters, Cowbridge Road,
Bridgend, Mid Glamorgan CF31 3SU,
01656 869476, Fax: 01656 869407,
Call Date: Oct 1997 (Gray's Inn)
Qualifications: BA (Leic)

Buttler *Miss Rosalind Pamela* •
Crown Prosecutor, Crown Prosecution
Service, Dale Road, Dale End,
Birmingham, West Midlands, Call Date:
Feb 1987 (Gray's Inn) Qualifications:
LLB (B'ham)

Byatt *James Robert* •
Senior Crown Prosecutor, Crown
Prosecution Service, King William
House, 2nd Floor, Lowgate, Hull,
Humberside, Call Date: July 1983
(Gray's Inn) Qualifications: LLB (E
Anglia), LLB (Hons)

Byford *Neville Paul*
Morgan Lewis & Bockins, 4 Carlton
Gardens, Pall Mall, London SW1Y 5AA,
Call Date: July 1987 (Inner Temple)
Qualifications: LLB (Soton)

Byng *Julian Michael Edmund*
15a Chemin Rieu, 1208 Geneva, Call
Date: Feb 1954 (Inner Temple)
Qualifications: MA (Cantab)

Byrne *Dr John Patrick* •
Legal Advisor, Company Secretary,
Company Director, 2 Sloane Terrace,
London SW1X 9DQ, 0171 823 4146,
Fax: 0171 823 6764, Call Date: Feb
1995 (Lincoln's Inn) Qualifications:
BSc (Syracuse), MBA (Lond Busn.
Sch), PhD (Lond Busn. Sch), Dip in
Law

Byrne *Miss Josephine Mary*
Call Date: Nov 1981 (Lincoln's Inn)
Qualifications: BA (Hons) (Law)

Byrne *Miss Kathryn Anne* •
Company Secretary and Legal Adviser,
Call Date: July 1978 (Lincoln's Inn)
Qualifications: LLB (Lond)

Byrne *Kevin Mowbray*
Head of Legal Services, The Magistrates'
Courthouse, North Quay, Great
Yarmouth, Norfolk NR30 1PW, 01493
851127, Fax: 01493 852169, Call Date:
Nov 1983 (Middle Temple)
Qualifications: BA (Kent)

Bywater *Andre Edward*
Call Date: Oct 1993 (Middle Temple)
Qualifications: MA (Sussex), BA (Hull),
MA (Cantab)

Cabeza *Mrs Ruth Roberta Elizabeth*
Call Date: Mar 1998 (Middle Temple)
Qualifications: LLB (Hons) (Kent)

Cable *Miss Aida Anna*
0171 623 1244 (Clyde & Co), Fax: 0171
623 5427 (Clyde & Co), Call Date: Oct
1995 (Middle Temple) Qualifications:
BA (Hons), LLM (Cantab)

Cahill *Brian Francis* •
Director, Group Legal Services, Glaxo
Wellcome Plc, Glaxo Wellcome House,
Berkeley Ave, Greenford, Middlesex
UB6 ONN, 0181 966 8752, Fax: 0181
966 8330, Call Date: Nov 1977 (Gray's
Inn) Qualifications: LLB

Cain *Daniel John* •
Senior Court Clerk, Ipswich Magistrates
Court, Elm Street, Ipswich, Suffolk
IP1 2AP, 01473 217261, Fax: 01473
231249, Call Date: Feb 1990 (Inner
Temple) Qualifications: LLB (Hons)

Cain *Oliver James*
Curtis Davis Garrard, Lancaster House,
Northumberland Close, Heathrow
Airport, Staines TW19 7LN, 0181 400
2400, Fax: 0181 400 2420, Call Date:
Nov 1994 (Lincoln's Inn)
Qualifications: LLB (Hons) (Sheff)

Cairncross *Neil Francis*
Little Grange, The Green, Olveston,
Bristol BS35 4EJ, 01454 613060, Call
Date: June 1948 (Lincoln's Inn)
Qualifications: MA

Cairnduff *Steven Maximillian* •
Call Date: Oct 1997 (Lincoln's Inn)
Qualifications: LLB (Hons)

Cairns *Simon Thomas*
Call Date: Mar 1999 (Gray's Inn)
Qualifications: LLB (W'mster)

Caistor *Daniel John*
Call Date: Oct 1998 (Lincoln's Inn)
Qualifications: LLB (Hons) (Leic)

Calcroft *Christopher John*
Call Date: Oct 1996 (Middle Temple)
Qualifications: BA (Hons), B.Arch
(Manc), CPE

Caldicott *Martyn Stephen*
4 North View, Gouilon, Apergavenny,
Gwent NP7 9PW, 01873 832088, Call
Date: Nov 1994 (Inner Temple)
Qualifications: BSc

Caldwell *Andrew Frew*
Poland, Mitre House Chambers, Mitre
House, 44 Fleet Street, London, EC4Y
1BN, Call Date: July 1984 (Middle
Temple) Qualifications: MA
(Edinburgh) Dip.

Caldwell *Dr Helen Janet* •
Parliamentary Counsel, The Law
Commission, London, 0171 453 1207,
Call Date: Nov 1975 (Lincoln's Inn)
Qualifications: BA (Cantab), D.Phil
(Oxon)

Callaghan *Lee Patrick* •
General Counsel - Europe, Albright &
Wilson PLC, Corporate Headquarters,
Legal Department, 210-222 Hagley
Road West, Oldbury, Warley, West
Midlands B68 ONN, 0121 420 5361,
Fax: 0121 420 5139, Call Date: Feb
1988 (Gray's Inn) Qualifications: BA,
LLM, Dip EC, Dip COMP

Callan *Miss Joan Margaret*
Ireland, Call Date: Mar 1997 (Lincoln's
Inn) Qualifications: BCL, LLM (Dublin)

Callaway *Ian Paul* •
Senior Crown Prosecutor, Crown
Prosecution Service, Queens House,
Guildhall Street, Folkestone, Kent, Call
Date: July 1987 (Middle Temple)
Qualifications: LLB (Lond)

Callender Smith *Robin* •
Prosecution Team Leader, Crown
Prosecution Service, The Cooperage,
Gainsford Street, London SE1 2NG,
0171 357 7010, Call Date: July 1977
(Gray's Inn) Qualifications: LLB (Lond)

Caller *Mitchell Bernard* •
Senior Vice President & Legal Adviser,
The Chase Manhattan Bank, Woolgate
House, Coleman Street, London
EC2P 2HD, 0171 777 4800, Fax: 0171
777 3141, Call Date: July 1978 (Middle
Temple) Qualifications: BA (Oxon)

Callow *David Richard*
Call Date: Nov 1998 (Middle Temple)
Qualifications: LLB (Hons)(Wales)

Callow *Duncan Alexander*
House Counsel Solicitor, C/O Callow's
Law Limited, 24 Bourne Road, South
Merstham, Surrey RH1 3HF, 01737
645983, Call Date: Feb 1993 (Inner
Temple) Qualifications: LLB

Calvert *Philip Alan* •
Director Legal Services, Sea Containers
Services Ltd, Sea Containers Hse, 20
Upper Ground, London SE1, 0171 805
5202, Fax: 0171 805 5912, and Member
New York Bar, Call Date: July 1977
(Middle Temple) Qualifications: BA

Calvert-Smith *David* •
Recorder Former Senior Treasury
Counsel, Hollis Whiteman Chambers,
3rd/4th Floor, Queen Elizabeth Bldg,
Temple, London, EC4Y 9BS, Call Date:
Nov 1969 (Middle Temple)
Qualifications: MA (Cantab)

Calvert-Smith *George Richard*
9-12 Bell Yard, London, WC2A 2LF, Call
Date: Nov 1997 (Middle Temple)
Qualifications: BA (Hons) (Exon)

Cam *David Edward* •
Group Company Secretary and Director,
Blackpool Pleasure Beach Ltd, Ocean
Boulevard, Blackpool, Lancs FY4 1EZ,
01253 341013 Ext 1206, Fax: 01253
401098, Call Date: May 1981 (Middle
Temple) Qualifications: BA

Cameron *Alexander James*
Call Date: Mar 1998 (Lincoln's Inn)
Qualifications: BA (Hons)(Cantab)

Cameron *Ms Jean McKillop* •
Assistant Solicitor, Call Date: July 1989
(Inner Temple) Qualifications: BA
[Sheff], Dip Law, MA [Lond]

Cameron *Lee John Harcourt*
Call Date: Oct 1998 (Middle Temple)
Qualifications: LLB (Hons)(Westmin)

Camilletti *Peter Alfred Laurence*
Superintendent, New Scotland Yard,
0171 230 4761, Call Date: Feb 1989
(Middle Temple) Qualifications: MA
(Cantab)

Camp *Mrs Caroline Helen* •
Principal Crown Prosecutor, Crown
Prosecution Service, Greenfield House,
39 Scotland Street, Sheffield S3 7DQ,
0114 291 2000, Call Date: July 1973
(Inner Temple)

Camp *The Reverend John Edward*
1 Brick Court, 1st Floor, Temple,
London, EC4Y 9BY, Call Date: May 1969
(Inner Temple) Qualifications: MA
(Oxon) MTech, (Brunel)

Campbell *Alistair Peter*
Advocates Library, Parliment House,
Parliment Square, Edinburgh EH1 1RF,
0131 226 2881, QC, Scotland, Call Date:
Apr 1991 (Inner Temple) Qualifications:
MA (Aberdeen), LLB (Strathclyde)

Campbell *Andrew Neil*
Call Date: Nov 1988 (Middle Temple)
Qualifications: MA (Cantab)

Campbell *Colin Hugh*
Call Date: July 1987 (Lincoln's Inn)
Qualifications: MA (Oxon), D Phil, FCA

Campbell *Ms Elizabeth Cameron*
Coopers Solicitors, Clayton Court,
Downing Street, Farnham, Surrey
GU9 7PG, Call Date: Mar 1998 (Gray's
Inn) Qualifications: BA

Campbell *Mrs Kerry*
Call Date: Mar 1998 (Middle Temple)
Qualifications: BA (Hons)(Portsmouth

Campbell *Mrs Patricia Dorothy*
Deputy Clerk to the Justices,
Bedfordshire Magistrates Court, Stuart
Street, Shire Hall, Luton, Beds, 01582
402333, Fax: 01582 24852, Call Date:
Nov 1982 (Gray's Inn) Qualifications:
Dip Law

Campion *Donald John Martin*
9 Stone Buildings, 9 Stone Bldgs,
Lincoln's Inn, London, WC2A 3NN, Call
Date: June 1956 (Gray's Inn)
Qualifications: MA (Cantab)

Canavan *David Douglass*
Call Date: Nov 1978 (Gray's Inn)
Qualifications: BA (Hons)

Caney *Howard Bernard*
Call Date: May 1997 (Lincoln's Inn)
Qualifications: LLB (Hons)

Canlin *James Patrick*
2 Cheam Mansions, Station Way, Cheam,
Surrey SM3 8SA, 0181 661 9937, Fax:
0181 661 9937, Call Date: July 1967
(Middle Temple) Qualifications: LLB
(Lond)

Cannell *Alfred Edward*
Call Date: July 1968 (Gray's Inn)
Qualifications: LLB, ACIS, FIArb

Canner *Gordon Richard*
Acerhill, Berry Lane, Beer, East Devon
EX12 3JS, 01297 23118, Call Date: May
1950 (Inner Temple) Qualifications: MA
(Cantab)

Canneti *Miss Romana Francesca*
Call Date: Oct 1997 (Middle Temple)
Qualifications: BA (Hons)(Edinburgh),
CPE (Lond)

Canning *Edward* •
Senior Crown Prosecutor, Crown
Prosecution Service, Hawkins House,
Pynes Lane, Rydon Lane, Exeter, Devon
EX2 5SS, 01392 422555, Fax: 01392
422111, Call Date: July 1985 (Lincoln's
Inn) Qualifications: BA, LRAM, DSA, Dip
App Soc Studies

Cannon *Miss Claire Jacqueline* •
Crown Prosecution Service, C/O 50
Ludgate Hill, London EC4M 7EX, Call
Date: Nov 1983 (Middle Temple)
Qualifications: LLB (Lond)

Caplan *Harold*
3 The Pennards, Sunbury on Thames
TW16 5JZ, 01932 781200, Fax: 01932
779694, Associate Member: American
Bar Association, Call Date: Nov 1955
(Middle Temple) Qualifications: MSc,
CEng, ACII, FRAes, FCIArb

Caplan *Lee Richard*
Call Date: Nov 1994 (Middle Temple)
Qualifications: LLB (Hons)

Caplin *Ian*
Call Date: Oct 1995 (Lincoln's Inn)
Qualifications: BA (Hons)(Oxon)

Capon *Julius Piers* •
Crown Prosecution Service, Crown
Prosecution Service, C/O 50 Ludgate Hill,
London EC4M 7EX, Call Date: Nov 1990
(Lincoln's Inn) Qualifications: LLB
(Newc)

Capp *Jonathan Charles*
High Garth, Heathwaite, Windermere,
Cumbria LA23 2DH, 015394 46884, Fax:
015394 46884, and Member New York
Bar California BaR, Call Date: Oct 1990
(Lincoln's Inn) Qualifications: LLB
(Lond), LLM (Paris)

Capps *Deveral Carmichael*
Lecturer, University of Northumbria, at
Newcastle, Sutherland Building,
Newcastle, 0191 227 3027, Fax: 0191
227 4557, Call Date: Oct 1995 (Inner
Temple) Qualifications: LLB (Sheff),
LLM (Belfast)

Capstick *Robert Adrian* •
Call Date: Feb 1987 (Gray's Inn)
Qualifications: LLB (Lond)

Cardovillis *Ms Helen Jacqueline* •
Legal and Business Affairs Manager,
British Broadcasting Corp., Independant
Commissions, White City, 201 Wood
Lane, London W12 7TS, 0181 752 5212,
Fax: 0181 752 5237, Call Date: Nov 1995
(Inner Temple) Qualifications: BA
(Hons)

Cardwell *Paul Graham* •
Principal Crown Prosecutor, Crown
Prosecution Service, 48 Georges House,
Lever Street, Wolverhampton, Call Date:
July 1986 (Inner Temple) Qualifications:
LLB Wolverhampton

E

Carey *Charles Edward* •
Assistant Editor, Statutory Publications
Office & Secretary to the Advisory
Committee on Statute Law, Lord
Chancellor's Dept, Selborne House,
54-60 Victoria Street, London
SW1E 6QW, Also Member of Lincoln's
Inn, Call Date: Nov 1959 (Inner
Temple) Qualifications: BA, LLB

Carey *Miss Mary Frances*
Call Date: Nov 1990 (Lincoln's Inn)
Qualifications: BA (Dub), Dip Law

Carey-Yard *Gordon Michael* •
Principal Legal Officer, Solicitors
Department, Wellington House, New
Scotland Yard, London SW1H 0BG,
0171 230 7346, Call Date: Nov 1982
(Gray's Inn) Qualifications: LLB (Lond)
(Hons)

Carin-Levy *Guy*
Call Date: July 1998 (Gray's Inn)
Qualifications: LLB (Manch)

Carins *Duncan*
Call Date: Mar 1996 (Lincoln's Inn)
Qualifications: BSc, LLB (Hons)

Carle *Peter Charles* •
Senior Crown Prosecutor, CPS (Exeter
Office), Hawkins House, Pynes Hill,
Rydon Lane, Exeter, Devon EX2 5SS
DX 8363, 01392 422555, Fax: 01392
422111, Call Date: Oct 1991 (Gray's
Inn) Qualifications: BA (Hons)(Sheff)

Carlisle *David Tyrrell*
Call Date: Nov 1969 (Gray's Inn)
Qualifications: BA (Cantab)

Carne *Philip Austin*
5 Bingham Place, London W1M 3FH,
0171 486 1115, Solicitor
(1943),Notary (1944) Lincoln's Inn
(1976), Call Date: Jan 1949 (Gray's
Inn)

Carney *Mrs Julie Ann* •
Lawyer, Department of Trade &
Industry, 10 Victoria Street, London
SW1H 0NN, 0171 215 3391, Fax: 0171
215 3221, Call Date: Nov 1990 (Middle
Temple) Qualifications: LLB (Warw)

Carpenter *Michael Charles Lancaster* •
Legal Adviser Cabinet Office / Office of
Public Service & Science, Treasury
Solicitor's Dept, Queen Anne's
Chambers, 28 Broadway, London
SW1H 9JS, 0171 210 3450, Fax: 0171
210 3503, Call Date: July 1971 (Inner
Temple) Qualifications: MA (Oxon)

Carpenter *Miss Susan Caroline*
15 Edwardes Square, London W8 6HE,
0171 603 2987, and Member New York
State Bar, Call Date: Nov 1982 (Middle
Temple) Qualifications: LLB, LLM
(Lond)

Carr *Anthony Paul*
Justices' Clerk, Essex Magistrates
Courts Cmtte, Greenwood House,
P.O.Box 3010, 91-99 New London
Road, Chelmsford CM2 0SN, 01245
346989, Fax: 01245 349058, Call Date:
July 1976 (Middle Temple)
Qualifications: M.A. (Cantab)

Carr *Mrs Caroline*
Jockey Club Official, The Jockey Club,
42 Portman square, London W1H 0EN,
0171 486 4921, Call Date: July 1976
(Gray's Inn) Qualifications: LLB

Carr *Neil*
Call Date: July 1998 (Middle Temple)
Qualifications: LLB (Hons)

Carr *Richard Charles Lascelles*
Recorder, Call Date: July 1963 (Inner
Temple) Qualifications: MA (Cantab)

Carr *William Forsyth Emsley*
Call Date: June 1964 (Inner Temple)
Qualifications: BA (Hons)(Cantab)

Carrier *David James* •
Justices' Clerk, Norwich Magistrates'
Court, Bishopsgate, Norwich, Norfolk
NR3 1UP, 01603 632421, Fax: 01603
663263, Call Date: July 1980 (Gray's
Inn) Qualifications: D.M.S.

Carrington *Mrs Margaret Elaine* •
Senior Crown Prosecutor Chairman
Milk & Dairies Tribunal Eastern Region
(P/t), Crown Prosecution Service,
Justinian House, Spitfire Close, Ermine
Business Park, Huntingdon Cambs
PE17 4HJ, 01480 432333, Fax: 01482
432404, Call Date: Nov 1970 (Gray's
Inn)

Carrington *Mark Anthony* •
Senior Crown Prosecutor, Crown
Prosecution Service, Priory Gate, 29
Union Street, Maidstone, Kent
ME14 1PT, Call Date: Oct 1991 (Inner
Temple) Qualifications: BA (Kent), Dip
Soc (Kent)

Carrolan *Adam*
Call Date: Oct 1996 (Inner Temple)
Qualifications: LLB (Wales)

Carroll *Benedick James*
Call Date: Nov 1994 (Inner Temple)
Qualifications: LLB (Soton)

Carroll *Mrs Janice* •
Senior Crown Prosecutor, Crown
Prosecution Service, County House,
County Square, 100 New London Road,
Chelmsford, Essex, 01245 252939, Fax:
01245 490476, Call Date: July 1987
(Inner Temple) Qualifications: LLB
(Hons)

Carroll *Mark William John* •
Call Date: Oct 1995 (Inner Temple)
Qualifications: LLB (Hons)(Wolves)

Carroll *Professor William Alexander*
1 Paper Bldgs, Ground Floor, Temple,
London, EC4Y 7EP, Call Date: July 1980
(Middle Temple)

Carrow *Robert Duane*
Goldstein & Philips, Embarcadero
Center, Suite 880 San Francisco,
CA94111, United States of America, and
Member California Bar New York Bar
33 Bedford Row, London, WC1R 4JH,
Call Date: Nov 1981 (Middle Temple)
Qualifications: BA (Minnesota), JD,
(Stanford)

Carruthers *Stephen Robert*
32 Southborough Road, London
E9 7EF, 0181 533 5455, Fax: 0181 533
5455, Call Date: Nov 1981 (Gray's Inn)
Qualifications: MA (Cantab), Licence in
EEC Law, DSU (Paris II)

Carsley *Robert Clive* •
Boulders, Beckenham Place Park,
Beckenham, Kent BR3 5BP, 0181 658
1300, Fax: 0181 658 1300, Call Date:
Nov 1966 (Middle Temple)
Qualifications: MA (Oxon)

Carson *Stuart Crosbie* •
Corporate Counsel, Irish Life
International, Call Date: Feb 1982
(Inner Temple) Qualifications: LLB
(Wales), LLM (Lond)

Carter *Miss Charlotte Emma*
Oury Colhoun & Co Solicitors, 54
Jermyn Street, St Jame's, London
SW1Y 6LX, 0171 629 8844, Fax: 0171
629 8855, Call Date: Nov 1992 (Gray's
Inn) Qualifications: LLB (Lond)

Carter *Christopher Richard*
Call Date: Oct 1996 (Lincoln's Inn)
Qualifications: BA (Hons)(Keele)

Carter *Miss Connie*
International Consultant, 2 Mansfield
Street, London W1M 9FF, 44 (0) 171
637 0494, Fax: 44 (0) 171 637 0495,
Call Date: Oct 1997 (Lincoln's Inn)
Qualifications: LLB (Hons)(Lond)

Carter *Miss Deborah Doris Lily*
Call Date: Oct 1998 (Inner Temple)
Qualifications: LLB (Soton)

Carter *Harold Mark* •
Lawyer Grade 6, The Home Office, 50
Queen Anne's Gate, London SW1H 9AT,
Call Date: July 1984 (Gray's Inn)
Qualifications: LLB

Carter *Howard Ernest* •
Legal Director, English Heritage, 23
Savile Row, London W1X 1AB, 0171
973 3360, Call Date: Nov 1989 (Middle
Temple) Qualifications: LLB (Hons)
(Manch), LLM

Carter *Miss Jacqueline Anne* •
Senior Legal Adviser, Royal & Sun
Alliance, Insurance Group plc,
Bartholomew Lane, London EC2N 2AB,
0171 588 2345, Fax: 0171 826 1990,
Call Date: Nov 1978 (Inner Temple)
Qualifications: LLB

Carter *Mrs Janet*
Magistrates Principal Court Clerk, Leeds
Magistrate's Court, Westgate, Leeds
LS1 3JP, 0113 2459653, Call Date: Feb
1992 (Middle Temple) Qualifications:
LLB (Hons) (Lond), MIPD, DMS

Carter *Ms Melanie Catherine* •
Call Date: July 1984 (Middle Temple)
Qualifications: BA

Carter *Mrs Natalie Jane* •
Queens House, 58 Victoria Street, St
Albans, Hertfordshire AL1 3HZ, 01727
818100, Fax: 01727 851080, Call Date:
Nov 1991 (Inner Temple) Qualifications:
LLB

Carter *Patrick James*
Call Date: Feb 1994 (Gray's Inn)
Qualifications: LLB (Sheff), ACA

Cartledge *Stanley*
12 Countess Walk, Stapleton, Bristol
BS16 1EU, 0117 9658877, Call Date: July
1957 (Gray's Inn)

Carus *Anthony*
Call Date: Jan 1938 (Gray's Inn)

Casella *Bartholomew Romolo Soini*
Call Date: Oct 1995 (Lincoln's Inn)
Qualifications: LLB (Hons) (Teeside)

Casely-Hayford *Ms Margaret Henrietta
Augusta*
Denton Hall, 5 Chancery Lane, London
EC4A 1BU, 0171 242 1212/071 320
6172, Fax: 0171 404 0087/071 320
6645, Call Date: July 1983 (Gray's Inn)
Qualifications: BA (Hons) (Oxon)

Cassell *Michael*
Call Date: Nov 1998 (Lincoln's Inn)
Qualifications: BSc (Hons) (Manch), Dip
Law

Casserley *Miss Catherine*
Legal Officer at Royal National Institute
for the Blind, Royal National Institute, for
the Blind, 224 Great Portland Street,
London W1N 6AA, 0171 388 1266, Fax:
0171 388 2034, Call Date: Feb 1991
(Gray's Inn) Qualifications: LLB (Leic)

Cassidy *Hugh John Alexander*
35 Broadwater Down, Tunbridge Wells,
Kent TN2 5NU, 01892 532988, Call Date:
Nov 1961 (Inner Temple)

Cassidy *Ian*
Call Date: Nov 1990 (Gray's Inn)
Qualifications: LLB

Cassidy *Mrs Linda Jean* •
Acting Prosecution Team Leader, Crown
Prosecution Service, Fox Talbot House,
Bellinger Close, Malmesbury Road,
Chippenham SN15 1BN, 01249 443443,
Fax: 01249 440800, Call Date: Feb 1975
(Middle Temple) Qualifications: LLB
(Lond)

Castleman *Joseph Benjamin*
and Member New York Bar 1 Paper
Bldgs, Ground Floor, Temple, London,
EC4Y 7EP, Call Date: Nov 1950 (Middle
Temple)

Catliff *Geoffrey Charles*
Brook House, Berrick Salome, Nr
Wallingford, Oxfordshire OX10 6JQ,
01865 400379, Call Date: Feb 1967
(Gray's Inn) Qualifications: LLB (Lond)

Catlin *David Hamilton*
Call Date: June 1953 (Gray's Inn)
Qualifications: BA Hons [Oxon]

Catt *Miss Julie Dawn*
Call Date: Nov 1998 (Inner Temple)
Qualifications: LLB (Kent)

Catterall *Michael James*
Call Date: Oct 1995 (Lincoln's Inn)
Qualifications: BA (Hons) (Oxon)

Causton *Ms Catherine Mary* •
CPS, Gemini Centre,, 88 New London
Road, Chelmsford, Essex CM2 0BR, Call
Date: July 1990 (Gray's Inn)
Qualifications: BA

Causton *Peter Anthony Leo*
Assistant Solicitor, Pinsent Curtis
Solicitors, 3 Colmore Circus,
Birmingham B4 6BH, 0121 200 1050,
Fax: 0121 626 1040, Call Date: Oct 1995
(Middle Temple) Qualifications: MA
(Cantab), Dip Law

Cavanagh *Vincent Lawrence* •
Grinnell Manufacturing (UK), Limited,
Yew Street, Stockport SK4 2JW, 0161 477
1886, Call Date: Oct 1996 (Inner
Temple) Qualifications: BA (Oxon), CPE
(Manch)

Cave *Miss Valerie Helen*
Deputy Clerk to the Justices, Call Date:
July 1984 (Middle Temple)
Qualifications: BA (Hons)

Cavenagh *Prof Winifred Elizabeth*
Flat 20 Lingfield Court, 60 High Street,
Harborne, Birmingham, West Midlands
B17 9NE, 0121 428 2400, Call Date: Nov
1964 (Gray's Inn) Qualifications:
PhD(B'ham),BSc(Econ)

Caveney *John*
Senior Court Clerk, The Magistrates'
Court, Corporation Street, St Helens,
Merseyside WA10 1SZ, 01744 20244,
Fax: 01744 451697, Call Date: Feb 1990
(Middle Temple) Qualifications: Dip Mag

Cawley *Mrs Serene Chor Joo*
Senior Court Clerk, Buckhamshire
Magistrates' Crt, C/O Milton Keynes
Magistrates', Crt, 301 Silbury Boulevard,
Witan Gate East, Milton Keynes, Bucks
MK9 2AJ, 01908 684901, Fax: 01908
684904, Call Date: Nov 1990 (Inner
Temple) Qualifications: LLB (Lond),
MSc

Cawse *Arthur Douglas*
Woodlands, Aldwick, Wrington, Bristol
BS18 7RF, 01934 862235, Call Date:
June 1950 (Middle Temple)
Qualifications: MA (Oxon)

Cawthra *Bruce Illingworth*
Erich-Holthaus Str 1, 82211 Herrsching
Ammersee, Germany, 0 81 52 17 52, Call
Date: Feb 1962 (Middle Temple)
Qualifications: BA

Chadha *Miss Selina Kim*
Call Date: Nov 1996 (Gray's Inn)
Qualifications: LLB (Hull)

Chadwick *Stephen Paul*
Call Date: Oct 1997 (Inner Temple)
Qualifications: LLB (Sheffield)

Chahil *Ravinder*
Bird & Bird, 90 Fetter Lane, London
WC2 4JP, 0171 415 6000, Fax: 0171 415
6111, Call Date: Nov 1994 (Middle
Temple) Qualifications: B.Sc (Leeds),
Parmaology, Dip IP, Law (Bris), Dip in,
EC Competition Law, (Lond)

Chakrabarti *Miss Shami* •
Principal Legal Officer, The Home Office,
50 Queen Anne's Gate, London
SW1H 9AT, 0171 273 3000, Fax: 0171
273 4075, Call Date: Oct 1994 (Middle
Temple) Qualifications: LLB
(Hons) (Lond)

Chakrabortty *Ashis Ranjan* •
Counsellor, Immigration Advisory
Service, County House, 190 Great Dover
Street, London SE1 4YB, 0171 357 6917,
West Bengal Bar association, India, Call
Date: July 1970 (Inner Temple)
Qualifications: B.Com, LLB

Chalk *David John*
Call Date: May 1997 (Gray's Inn)
Qualifications: LLB (Wales)

Chamberlain *Kevin John* •
Deputy Legal Adviser, Foreign &
Commonwealth Office, King Charles
Street, London SW1A 2AH, Call Date: July
1965 (Inner Temple) Qualifications: LLB
(Lond)

Chamberlain *Nigel*
9 Hasted Drive, Alresford, Hampshire
SO24 9PX, Call Date: July 1975 (Middle
Temple) Qualifications: MA (Cantab)

Chamberlain *Paul* •
Senior Crown Prosecutor, Crown
Prosecution Service, The Cooperage,
Gainsford Street, London, 0171 357
7010, Fax: 0171 962 0904, Call Date:
Nov 1993 (Inner Temple) Qualifications:
BA (Reading), CPE

Chambers *Dr Douglas Robert*
HM Coroner London City, 4 Ormond
Avenue, Richmond, Surrey TW10 6TN,
0181 940 7745, Call Date: May 1965
(Lincoln's Inn) Qualifications: MB, BS,
LLB, MA, CBiol, F Inst Biol

Chambers *Mark Barrie*
Call Date: Oct 1996 (Gray's Inn)
Qualifications: LLB (Lond)

E

Chambers *Richard Morgan*
S J Berwin & Co, 222 Gray's Inn Road,
London WC1X 8HB, 0171 533 2216,
Fax: 0171 533 2000, Call Date: Nov
1993 (Gray's Inn) Qualifications: LLB
(Hons) (Wales)

Champion *Ronan Henry*
Northcrofts Management, Services
Limited, 12 Grosvenor Place, London
SW1X 7HH, 0171 839 7858, Fax: 0171
235 4401, Chartered Quantity Surveyor,
Call Date: Nov 1992 (Middle Temple)
Qualifications: B.Sc, LLB, ARICS,
MCIOB

Champness *Andrew Paul* •
Legal Adviser, Gloucestershire
Magistrates, Courts Committee, The
Court House, Gander Lane,
Tewkesbury, Gloucestershire GL20 5TR,
01684 294632, Call Date: Oct 1998
(Middle Temple) Qualifications: BSc
(Hons)(Wales), Dip in Law (Bris)

Champness *Christopher John*
Call Date: Nov 1958 (Gray's Inn)
Qualifications: MA , LLM [Cantab]

Chan *Anthony Hung-Chiu* •
Principal Crown Prosecutor, Crown
Prosecution Service, 50 Ludgate Hill,
London EC4M 7EX, 0171 273 8322,
Fax: 0171 273 1915, Call Date: Nov
1984 (Middle Temple) Qualifications:
BSc (Hons) (Dundee), Diplaw

Chan *Miss Evelyn Lillian Swee Lian*
12 Lorong Taman Pantai 6, Bukit
Pantai, 59100 Kuala Lumpur, Malaysia,
603-2821636, Call Date: July 1995
(Lincoln's Inn) Qualifications: LLB
(Hons)

Chand *Ragveer*
Call Date: Nov 1994 (Lincoln's Inn)
Qualifications: LLB (Hons)(Wolves)

Chand *Miss Shaheda*
Call Date: Mar 1999 (Middle Temple)
Qualifications: LLB (Hons)(Manch)

Chanda *Satwaki* •
Messrs Deloitte & Touche, Hill House, 1
Little New Street, London EC4A 3TR,
0171 936 3000, Call Date: Oct 1992
(Inner Temple) Qualifications: BSc,
Dip Law

Chandler *Miss Esme Katharine* •
European Vocational College, Dukes
House, 32-38 Dukes Place, London
EC3A 7CP, 0171 929 0102, Fax: 0171
929 0103, Call Date: July 1982 (Inner
Temple) Qualifications: LLB (B'ham)

Chandler *Dr William John*
FCybS, 3 Willow Grove, Welwyn Garden
City, Herts AL8 7NA, 01707 324600,
Fax: 01707 376003, Call Date: Feb
1956 (Middle Temple) Qualifications:
MA, PhD, ASCA

Chang *Miss Wai Yoong*
Call Date: Nov 1996 (Middle Temple)
Qualifications: LLB (Hons)(Lond)

Channing *Michael David*
Melrose Cottage, Mellersh Hill Road,
Wonersh Park, Wonersh, Surrey
GU5 OQJ, 01483 892032, Fax: 01483
898633, Call Date: Nov 1976 (Lincoln's
Inn) Qualifications: MA (Oxon)

Chapaneri *Mrs Dipika*
Principal Legal Adviser, Watford
Magistrates' Court, The Court House,
Clarendon Road, Watford, Herts
WD1 1ST, 01923 238111, Fax: 01923
251273, Call Date: Feb 1989 (Inner
Temple) Qualifications: LLB Hons

Chaplin *Richard James* •
Legal Manager (UK), OMV (UK)
Limited, 14 Ryder Street, London
SW1Y 6QB, 0171 333 1600, Fax: 0171
333 1610, Call Date: Feb 1992 (Middle
Temple) Qualifications: LLB (Hons),
LLM (Cantab)

Chapman *David Nathan*
Court Clerk, 4/5 Quay Street,
Carmarthen, Dyfed, 01267 221658,
Fax: 01267 221812, Call Date: Nov
1989 (Middle Temple) Qualifications:
LLB Hons (Wales)

Chapman *Keith Anthony*
Chief Executive, Padiham Group
Limited, Redbrook House, 29 Bollin
Hill, Wilmslow, Cheshire SK9 4AN,
01625 251891, Fax: 01625 251893,
Call Date: Nov 1978 (Gray's Inn)
Qualifications: MA (Oxon)

Chapman *Peter Howard John*
Arbitrator, Chartered Civil Engineer, 46/
48 Essex Street, London, WC2R 3GH,
Call Date: Apr 1991 (Gray's Inn)
Qualifications: BSc, LLB, FCI Arb, FICE,
FHKIE, FIHT, MSI Arb

Chapman *Robin Denis*
Call Date: Mar 1998 (Middle Temple)
Qualifications: LLB (Hons), BSc, ARICS,
ACIArb

Chapman *Roderick Alan Keith* •
Senior Crown Prosecutor,, CPS East
Midlands, 2 King Edward Court, King
Edward Street, Nottingham NG1 1EL,
0115 9480480, Fax: 0115 9364562,
Call Date: Nov 1983 (Middle Temple)
Qualifications: LLB Nott'm

Chapman *Stanley John*
Also Inn of Court G, Call Date: Feb
1954 (Lincoln's Inn) Qualifications:
BSc,MSc

Chapple *Darran Mark*
Call Date: Mar 1996 (Middle Temple)
Qualifications: LLB (Hons), LLM

Chapple *David Anthony*
Legal Consultant, 106 Park Avenue,
Ruislip, Middlesex HA4 7UP, 01895
635171, Call Date: July 1971 (Middle
Temple) Qualifications: BA Hons,
A.C.I.S

Charalambides *Leonidas*
Call Date: July 1998 (Inner Temple)
Qualifications: BA (Lond), MA (Lond)

Charkham *Jonathan Philip*
Director, The Great Universal Stores
PLC, Crestacare PLC, CLM Plc, Leopold
Joseph Holdings PLC Visiting Professor
City University Business School, The
Yellow House, 22 Montpelier Place,
Knightsbridge, London SW7 1HL, 0171
589 9879, Fax: 0171 581 8520, Sheriff
of the City of London 1994-95, Call
Date: June 1953 (Inner Temple)
Qualifications: MA (Cantab)

Charles *Mrs Jacqueline Fay* •
Chairman of Social Security Appeals
Tribunals and Rent Assessment
Committees, 38 Chester Close North,
London NW1 4JE, 0171 935 6968, Fax:
0171 486 3690, Call Date: June 1956
(Gray's Inn) Qualifications: LLB

Charles *Kevin Lawrence*
Call Date: Oct 1996 (Middle Temple)
Qualifications: LLB (Hons) (Essex)

Charlton *Robert Craig*
Call Date: Nov 1988 (Middle Temple)
Qualifications: Dip in Mag Law, Dip in
Law, DMG.

Charnley *Philip James* •
Crown Prosecution Service, C/O 50
Ludgate Hill, London EC4M 7EX, Call
Date: July 1983 (Gray's Inn)
Qualifications: LLB (E.Ang)

Charteris *Mrs Pamela Rogers
Townsend*
Solicitor, White Dalton Partnership, 31
High Street North, Dunstable,
Bedfordshire LU6 1HX, Call Date: July
1989 (Inner Temple) Qualifications:
Dip Law

Charters *Andrew Philip*
Call Date: Oct 1995 (Lincoln's Inn)
Qualifications: BA (Hons) (Oxon)

Chase *Miss Charlotte Elizabeth Diana* •
Senior Crown Prosecutor, Crown
Prosecution Service, St Georges House,
Lever Street, Wolverhampton WV2 1EZ,
01902 870900, Call Date: July 1976
(Lincoln's Inn) Qualifications: LLB

Chastney *Ms Carol Anne* •
Crown Prosecutor, Crown Prosecution
Service, Riding Gate House, Old Dover
Road, Canterbury, Kent, 01227 451144,
Call Date: Oct 1993 (Gray's Inn)
Qualifications: LLB (Hons)

Chataway *Benjamin Thomas Mary*
Call Date: Nov 1995 (Lincoln's Inn)
Qualifications: BA (Hons)

Chatfield *Mrs Rebecca Jane*
Call Date: Mar 1996 (Inner Temple)
Qualifications: BA (N'ham), MA (Bris)

Chaudhry *Miss Safina Habib* •
Legal Manager, Intervention Board,
Kings House, 33 Kings Road, Reading
RG1 3BU, 0118 953 1554, Fax: 0118
953 1230, Call Date: Nov 1994
(Lincoln's Inn) Qualifications: BA
(Hons)

Chaundy *Mrs Vicki Ann* ●
Senior Crown Prosecutor, Crown
Prosecution Service, Friars House,
Manor House Drive, Coventry CV1 2TE,
01203 520421, Call Date: July 1976
(Gray's Inn) Qualifications: LLB

Chauvin *Mrs Joanne Aun Leng*
Court Clerk, Kingston Magistrates Court,
19-23 High Street, Kingston, Surrey
KT1 1JW, 0181 546 5603, Call Date: July
1982 (Middle Temple) Qualifications:
LLB

Chawner *John Lovatt*
Rosecroft, Hylands Road, Epsom, Surrey
KT18 7ED, 01372 722110, Fax: 01372
812926, Call Date: Nov 1966 (Gray's
Inn) Qualifications: BSc (B'ham), BA
(Lond)

Chee *Ms Kit Wai*
Call Date: Nov 1990 (Lincoln's Inn)
Qualifications: LLB (Nott'm)(Hons)

Cheema *Miss Harminder Kaur*
Stephen Fidler & Co, 39 Doughty Street,
London WC1 2LF, Call Date: Oct 1995
(Inner Temple) Qualifications: LLB
(Lond)

Cheema *Miss Navneet Kaur*
Call Date: Nov 1997 (Middle Temple)
Qualifications: BA (Hons)(Cantab)

Cheeseman *John William*
23 Castle View Park, Mawnan Smith,
Falmouth, Cornwall TR11 5HB, 01326
250601, Call Date: June 1953 (Gray's
Inn)

Cheesman *Clive Edwin Alexander*
College of Arms, Queen Victoria Street,
London EC4V 4BT, 0171 248 2762, Call
Date: Nov 1996 (Middle Temple)
Qualifications: MA (Oxon)

Cheetham *David Alexander*
Call Date: Nov 1998 (Lincoln's Inn)
Qualifications: BSc (Hons)(Salf)

Chen *Miss Moi Kooi*
Call Date: July 1972 (Lincoln's Inn)

Chen *Mrs Moira Yang-Cher*
Deputy Chief Clerk, Inner London
Magistrates', Courts Service, 65 Romney
Street, London SW1P 3RD, 0171 799
3332, Call Date: Nov 1973 (Inner
Temple)

Chen *Simon Adam*
Call Date: Nov 1994 (Gray's Inn)
Qualifications: LLB (Bris)

Cheng *Peter Kwock Kwan*
Call Date: Mar 1996 (Lincoln's Inn)
Qualifications: LLB (Hons) (Sussex),
LLM (Lond)

Cherrington-Walker *Ms Rachel Georgina
Elizabeth*
Call Date: July 1998 (Gray's Inn)
Qualifications: LLB (Wolves)

Chesebrough-Adams *Mrs Louise Ann* ●
Senior Fiduciary Director, Barclays
Private Bank, 39/41 Broad Street, St
Helier, Jersey, Channel Islands, 01534
813009, Fax: 01534 89125, Call Date:
Nov 1982 (Lincoln's Inn) Qualifications:
BA

Cheung *Miss Susan*
Call Date: July 1996 (Lincoln's Inn)
Qualifications: LLB (Hons)

Cheung *Wen Ping*
Deloitte & Touche Corporate, Finance,
Stonecutter Court, London EC4A 4TR,
0171 303 6425, Fax: 0171 303 5949,
Call Date: Nov 1993 (Lincoln's Inn)
Qualifications: LLB (Hons), ACA

Cheyne *Miss Ilona Claire* ●
Senior Lecturer in Law, Newcastle Law
School, Newcastle University, Newcastle
upon Tyne NE1 7RU, 0191 232 8511,
Fax: 0191 212 0064, Call Date: July 1986
(Gray's Inn) Qualifications: LLB
(Edinburgh), LLM (Lond)

Cheyne *Miss Phyllida Alison*
4 Pump Court, Temple, London, EC4Y
7AN, Call Date: Nov 1992 (Inner Temple)
Qualifications: MA (Cantab), MPhil,
(Cantab)

Chhabra *Kamal*
Call Date: Oct 1998 (Lincoln's Inn)
Qualifications: BA (Hons)(Germany),
CPE (Manc)

Chia *Miss Carolyn Anne Cheow Hiang*
Wilde Sapte, 1 Fleet Place, London
EC4M 7WS, 0171 246 7000, Fax: 0171
246 7777, and Member Singapore Bar,
Call Date: July 1989 (Middle Temple)
Qualifications: (Cantab) MA(Cantab)

Chiang *Steven Joon Heng*
Call Date: Nov 1995 (Middle Temple)
Qualifications: LLB (Hons)

Chico *Jonathan Michael Raymond*
Call Date: Nov 1998 (Lincoln's Inn)
Qualifications: LLB (Hons)(Leics)

Child *Mrs Sharon Elizabeth*
Call Date: Oct 1998 (Lincoln's Inn)
Qualifications: LLB (Lanc)

Chilton *Miss Melorie Anne*
Sole Practitioner - Legal & Business
Media Consultancy, Chilton Media Law, 8
West Street, London WC2H 9NG, 0171
836 2764, Fax: 0171 836 2765, Call
Date: Nov 1980 (Gray's Inn)
Qualifications: LLB (Lond) , LLM (Lond)

Chim *Ms Sook Heng*
Messrs Royds Treadwell, 2 Crane Court,
Fleet Street, London EC4A 2BL, 0171
583 2222, Fax: 0171 583 2034, Call
Date: July 1996 (Lincoln's Inn)
Qualifications: LLB (Hons)

Chitsaka *John*
Call Date: Apr 1975 (Gray's Inn)
Qualifications: LLB(Lond)

Chittenden *Timothy Paul* ●
Call Date: Oct 1990 (Gray's Inn)
Qualifications: LLB (Lond)

Chitty *Mrs Anne Louise* ●
Principal Crown Prosecutor, Crown
Prosecution Service, 4,5,6,& 7 Prendal
Court, Aylesbury, Bucks, 01296 436441,
Call Date: July 1983 (Inner Temple)
Qualifications: LLB (Exon)

Choat *Rupert Quincey*
Call Date: Mar 1998 (Lincoln's Inn)
Qualifications: LLB (Hons)(Warw), LLM
(Cantab)

Chok *Miss Hong-Fui A*
Principal Court Clerk, Coventry
Magistrates Court, Little Park Street,
Coventry CV1 1SQ, 01203 630666/500
676, Fax: 01203 500699, Call Date: July
1987 (Middle Temple) Qualifications:
LLB (Lanc)

Choo Simons *Mrs Mei Ling*
Call Date: Oct 1994 (Middle Temple)
Qualifications: LLB (Hons)(Lond)

Chope *Christopher Robert*
House of Commons, London SW1A 0AA,
Call Date: July 1972 (Inner Temple)
Qualifications: LLB

Chopra *Gerald*
1242 519 169, and Member Alberta,
Canada Bar, Call Date: Nov 1948 (Middle
Temple) Qualifications: MA (Cantab)

Chorlton *Miss Margaret Denise*
Deans Court Chambers, Cumberland
House, Crown Square, Manchester, M3
3HA, Call Date: Nov 1935 (Inner
Temple) Qualifications: MA (Oxon)

Choudhury *Abdus Samad* ●
Somerset County Council, Legal Services,
County Hall, Taunton TA1 4DY, 01823
355965, Fax: 01823 355060, Call Date:
Mar 1996 (Gray's Inn) Qualifications:
LLB

Choudhury *Miss Amprapali* ●
Arbitration Manager, Grain & Feed Assn
(GAFTA), 6 Chapel Place, Rivington
Street, London EC2A 3DQ, 0171 814
9666, Call Date: July 1998 (Lincoln's
Inn) Qualifications: LLB
(Hons)(Sussex), LLM (LSE)

Choudhury *Bhaskar* ●
In House Barrister, Hambro Legal
Protection Ltd, Hambro House,
Stephenson Road, Business Park,
Colchester, Essex CO4 4QR, 0990
234600, Fax: 0990 234880, and Member
Calcutta, Call Date: Nov 1988 (Lincoln's
Inn) Qualifications: BSc (Calcutta), BA
(Hons), MSc, LLB, (Hons), ACMA, AICWA

Choudhury *Miss Camilla*
Call Date: Nov 1998 (Gray's Inn)
Qualifications: LLB (Herts), LLM (Lond)

Choudhury *Ms Roxana Idris*
Call Date: Mar 1996 (Inner Temple)
Qualifications: LLB

Choudhury *Tufyal Ahmed*
Call Date: Oct 1997 (Inner Temple)
Qualifications: BA (London)

Chowdhury *Atiqur Rahman*
Call Date: Mar 1999 (Lincoln's Inn)
Qualifications: LLB (Hons)(Lond), LLM
(LSE)

Chowdhury *Fazle Karim*
Call Date: Mar 1998 (Lincoln's Inn)
Qualifications: BSc (Hons)(B'ham),
CPE (Sussex)

Chowdhury *Mortoza Elahi*
Call Date: Nov 1998 (Middle Temple)
Qualifications: LLB (Hons)(Wolves)

Chrimes *David Francis William* •
Senior Crown Prosecutor, Crown
Prosecution Service, 5th Floor, St
Peter's House, Derby, 01332 621600,
Call Date: Oct 1990 (Gray's Inn)
Qualifications: LLB(Hons) (London)

Christian *John Charles*
Ferndale House, Harling Road, North
Lopham, Diss, Norfolk IP22 2NQ,
01379 687518, Fax: 01379 687704,
Call Date: July 1975 (Gray's Inn)
Qualifications: BA

Christie *Iain Robert* •
Assistant Legal Adviser, Foreign &
Commonwealth Office, (Bridgetown)
(PF 46607), King Charles Street,
London SW1A 2AH, Barbados, 001 246
430 7841, Fax: 001 246 430 7842,
Member of the High Court of Australia
and Member Australian Capital
Territory, Call Date: July 1989 (Inner
Temple) Qualifications: BA [Dunelm]

Christie *Professor Richard Hunter*
President, Association of Arbitrators
(SA) Vice-President, All Africa Council,
LCIA, 30 Harman Road, Claremont
7700, South Africa, South Africa, (27)
021 61 1928, Fax: 927) 021 61 1928,
QC Zimbabwe & Zambia, Call Date:
June 1949 (Lincoln's Inn)
Qualifications: MA LLB (Cantab),
FCIArb, FAArb

Christie *Robert Harold McLeod Hunter*
Bronderi, Llandovery Road, Llanwrtyd
Wells, Powys LD5 4TA, Call Date: July
1974 (Lincoln's Inn) Qualifications:
MA

Christie-Miller *Roderick Wallace*
Call Date: Nov 1994 (Inner Temple)
Qualifications: BA (Lond), CPE

Christofides *Miss Anna Maria*
Cyprus, Hollis Whiteman Chambers,
3rd/4th Floor, Queen Elizabeth Bldg,
Temple, London, EC4Y 9BS, Call Date:
Nov 1983 (Lincoln's Inn)
Qualifications: BA (Lond)

Christoforou *Mrs Stella Tanta*
Call Date: Nov 1991 (Middle Temple)
Qualifications: BA Hons (Kent)

Christopher *Miss Ann-Marie*
Call Date: Oct 1997 (Lincoln's Inn)
Qualifications: LLB (Hons)(Bris)

Christou *Christos*
Call Date: Mar 1999 (Middle Temple)
Qualifications: LLB (Hons)

Chronias *Nicholas John*
Legal Adviser, Beachcroft Stanleys
Solicitors, 20 Furnival Street, London
EC4A 1BN, 0171 242 1011, Fax: 0171
894 6530, Call Date: Nov 1991 (Inner
Temple) Qualifications: LLB (Lond)

Chuah *Miss Joo Ee*
No 79 Jalan Labrooy, Merdeka Garden,
30100 Ipoh, Perak, 5060192, Call Date:
July 1997 (Gray's Inn) Qualifications:
LLB (Lond)

Chubb *Francis Edward Vaudrey*
Call Date: Oct 1996 (Middle Temple)
Qualifications: BA (Hons)(L'pool), CPE

Chuhan *Maluk Singh*
and Member Punjab & Haryana Bars,
Call Date: Nov 1974 (Lincoln's Inn)
Qualifications: BA LLB

Chung *Miss Jillian*
Lawrence Graham Solicitors, 190
Strand, London WC2R 1JN, 0171 379
0000, Fax: 0171 379 6854, Solicitor,
Call Date: Nov 1989 (Gray's Inn)
Qualifications: LLB [Brunel]

Chung *Ming (Chit)*
Associate Director, Corporate Finance,
Warburg Dillon Read, 2 Finsbury
Avenue, London EC2M 2PP, and
Member Hong Kong Bar, Call Date: Nov
1993 (Inner Temple) Qualifications:
LLB

Churaman *Miss Deborah Sirojini* •
Grade 6, Dept of Trade & Industry,
Ashdown House, 123 Victoria Street,
Victoria, London, 0171 215 3130, Call
Date: Nov 1984 (Middle Temple)
Qualifications: LLB

Churaman *Miss Simone Gail* •
Senior Principal Legal Officer, DSS, 5th
Floor, Southend House, 29/37 Brighton
Road, Sutton, Surrey SM2 5AN, 0181
652 6000 X 6500, Call Date: Nov 1987
(Middle Temple) Qualifications:
BA(Hons), LLM

Church *Thomas Henry*
Call Date: Oct 1994 (Gray's Inn)
Qualifications: BA

Cladingbowl *Rodney* •
Senior Crown Prosecutor, Crown
Prosecution Service, Queens House, 58
Victoria Street, St Albans, Herts
AL1 3HZ, 01727 844753, Call Date: Nov
1970 (Gray's Inn) Qualifications: LLB
(Lond)

Claiborne *Louis Fenner*
12 Park Road, Wivenhoe, Colchester,
Essex CO7 9NB, (01206) 822430, Fax:
(01206) 824300, US Supreme Court
and Member Louisiana Bar District of
Columbia Bar, Call Date: Nov 1974
(Middle Temple) Qualifications: LLB

Claire *Rajinder Kumar*
Call Date: Oct 1997 (Inner Temple)
Qualifications: LLB (Wolverhampton)

Claisse *Victor*
11 Cambridge Drive, Bognor Regis, W
Sussex PO21 5RJ, 01243 826678, Call
Date: July 1971 (Gray's Inn)
Qualifications: LLB (Lond)

Clark *Alastair Trevor*
Electronic Data Systems Ltd, (EDS), 4
Roundwood Avenue, Stockley Park,
Uxbridge, Middlesex UB11 1BQ, 0181
848 8989, Fax: 0181 756 0130, Call
Date: Nov 1963 (Middle Temple)
Qualifications: MA (Oxon), AMA,
FSAScot, FRSSA

Clark *David Andrew* •
Inspector, CPS Inspectorate,
Directorate of Casework, Evaluation,
CPS Headquarters, 50 Ludgate Hill,
London EC4M 7EX, 0171 273 1411,
Fax: 0171 273 1950, Call Date: Nov
1987 (Middle Temple) Qualifications:
LLB

Clark *Mrs Elizabeth Anne* •
Principal Crown Prosecutor, Crown
Prosecution Service, Brighton Branch
Office, 3 Clifton Mews, Clifton Hill,
Brighton, East Sussex BN1 3HR, 01273
207171, Fax: 01273 207849, Call Date:
July 1984 (Gray's Inn) Qualifications:
BA

Clark *Miss Hazel Anne*
Call Date: Nov 1990 (Middle Temple)
Qualifications: BA (Dunelm)

Clark *Julian James*
Lawyer, Clifford Chance, 200 Aldersgate
Street, London EC1A 4JJ, 0171 600
1000, Fax: 0171 600 5555, Call Date:
Nov 1988 (Inner Temple)
Qualifications: LLB

Clark *Ms Samantha Claire*
Call Date: Mar 1996 (Lincoln's Inn)
Qualifications: LLB (Hons)

Clark *Miss Tonia Anne*
Call Date: July 1986 (Middle Temple)
Qualifications: BSc (Hons)(Aston)

Clarke *Andrew Terence*
Senior Counsel: Major Transactions.
Mobil Services Company Ltd, Mobil
Services Company Ltd, Mobil Court, 3
Clements Inn, London WC2A 2EB,
0171 412 4199, Fax: 0171 412 2666,
Call Date: July 1982 (Middle Temple)
Qualifications: MA (Cantab)

Clarke *Mrs Antonette Oluwatoyin* •
Senior Crown Prosecutor, Crown
Prosecution Service, Portland House,
Stag Place, London SW1, 0171 915
5700, Call Date: Nov 1986 (Lincoln's
Inn) Qualifications: BA

Clarke *Gerald*
The Old School House, Slaugham, near
Haywards Heath, Sussex RH17 6AG,
01444 400800/400575, and Member
Brunei, Call Date: Feb 1956 (Inner
Temple) Qualifications: MA, BCL

Clarke *Giles Nevill*
6A Norfolk Place, London W2 1QN, 0171
262 9687, Fax: 0171 402 7512, Call
Date: Nov 1976 (Middle Temple)
Qualifications: MA (Cantab) PhD,
(Lond), FTII

Clarke *Miss Gillian Marjorie* •
Legal Director, Phillips & Drew, Triton
Court, 14 Finsbury Square, London
EC2A 1PD, 0171 901 5000, Call Date:
July 1982 (Middle Temple)
Qualifications: MA (Oxon)

Clarke *Miss Gina Maria* •
Principal Lawyer, London Borough of
Islington, Town Hall, Upper Hall,
Islington, London N1 2UD, 0171 477
3213, Fax: 0171 477 3243, Call Date:
Feb 1983 (Gray's Inn) Qualifications: BA

Clarke *Mrs Jennifer* •
Senior Lawyer, HM Customs & Excise,
New King's Beam House, 22 Upper
Ground, London SE1 9PJ, 0171 865
5172, Call Date: July 1971 (Gray's Inn)
Qualifications: LLB, P.G.Cert.Ed, Dip in
Counselling

Clarke *Keith Cutts*
52 Holly Hill, Bassett, Southampton
SO16 7EW, 01703 769029, Formerly a
Solicitor, Also Inn of Court L Formerly
Clerk to City of Southampton Justices
and Clerk to Hampshire Magistrates'
Courts Committee, Call Date: May 1977
(Middle Temple) Qualifications: Hon
LLD (S'ton), FTCL, FRSA

Clarke *Keith Stanley*
Lleweni, 16 Queens Walk, Rhyl,
Denbighshire LL18 3NG, 01745 337088,
Call Date: July 1992 (Inner Temple)
Qualifications: BA (Kent)

Clarke *The Rt Hon Kenneth Harry*
Bencher of Gray's Inn 9 Gough Square,
London, EC4A 3DE, Call Date: Nov 1963
(Gray's Inn) Qualifications: BA, LLB
(Cantab)

Clarke *Malcolm Raymond*
16 Bythorne Close, Lower Earley,
Reading RG6 3BH, 0118 9667507, Fax:
0118 9261241, Call Date: July 1976
(Inner Temple)

Clarke *Mrs Mollie Marguerite*
Arbitrator, 33 The Street, Uley, Nr
Dursley, Glos GL11 5TE, 01453 860245,
Call Date: June 1950 (Middle Temple)
Qualifications: FCIArb

Clarke *Patrick James* •
Senior Principal Legal Officer, HM
Customs & Excise, New Kings Beam
House, 22 Upper Ground, London
SE1 9PJ, Call Date: July 1975 (Middle
Temple) Qualifications: LLB

Clarke *Paul*
Call Date: Feb 1995 (Inner Temple)
Qualifications: BSc (Leic)

Clarke *Paul Matthew*
IT Consultant, Greythorn Plc, 6
Southampton Place, London WC1A 2DA,
0171 576 6020, Fax: 0171 831 2233,
Call Date: Feb 1995 (Gray's Inn)
Qualifications: LLB (Warwick)

Clarke *Richard Thomas Edward*
White Dalton Partnership, Dunstable,
Call Date: Feb 1992 (Inner Temple)
Qualifications: LLB (Hons)(Hull)

Clarke *Ms Theresa Mary* •
Grade 6, Department of the
Environment, Eland House, Bressenden
Place, London SW1R 5DU, Call Date: Nov
1970 (Middle Temple) Qualifications:
LLB

Clarke-Jervoise *Miss Caroline Sarah*
Lovell White Durrant, 65 Holborn
Viaduct, London EC1A 2DY, 0171 236
0066, Fax: 0171 248 4212, Call Date:
July 1986 (Inner Temple) Qualifications:
LLB

Clarke-Melville *Dr Betty Elizabeth*
and Member Barbados Bar, Call Date:
July 1996 (Inner Temple) Qualifications:
LLB, BA

Clarke-Wills *Mrs Auriol Paulina*
Equal Opps Sub-Comm of FDA, and
Member Trinidad and Tobago, Call Date:
July 1969 (Inner Temple) Qualifications:
LLB (Hons)

Claughton-Rugg *Mrs Claire Lilian
Margaret* •
Principal Crown Prosecutor, Call Date:
Feb 1983 (Inner Temple) Qualifications:
BA Lond

Claypoole *Charles Henry*
Call Date: Nov 1997 (Inner Temple)
Qualifications: BA (Cantab), LLM
(Germany)

Clayton *Cedric*
Call Date: Nov 1960 (Middle Temple)
Qualifications: MA, LLM

Clayton *Peter David*
2302 Diamond Exchange Bldg, 8-10
Duddell Street, Central, Hong Kong, and
Member Hong Kong Bar 9 Stone
Buildings, 9 Stone Bldgs, Lincoln's Inn,
London, WC2A 3NN, Call Date: July 1977
(Middle Temple)

Clayton *Richard John* •
Assistant Legal Adviser, The Home Office,
50 Queen Anne's Gate, London
SW1H 9AT, Call Date: Nov 1969 (Middle
Temple) Qualifications: MA , BCL

Cleary *Edmund*
Deputy Clerk to the Justices, Magistrates
Court, Gillbridge Avenue, Sunderland
SR1 3AP, 0191 5141621, Call Date: Apr
1986 (Gray's Inn) Qualifications: BA

Cleave *Mrs Celia Valentine* •
Legal Officer, GMB, 205 Hook Road,
Chessington, Surrey KT9 1EA, 0181 397
8881, Call Date: Nov 1985 (Gray's Inn)
Qualifications: MA (St Andrews), Dip Law
(City)

Clegg *Richard Ninian Barwick*
Call Date: July 1960 (Inner Temple)
Qualifications: MA (Oxon)

Clemens *Ms Julie*
Call Date: Nov 1997 (Gray's Inn)
Qualifications: BA (N.E.Lond), MA
(Middx), LLB (Lond)

Clement *Ryan Wayne* •
Legal Adviser, Taylor Woodrow, Legal
Department, Taywood House, 345
Ruislip Road, Southall, Middlesex
UB1 2QX, 0181 578 2366, Fax: 0181 575
4096, Call Date: Oct 1996 (Middle
Temple) Qualifications: B.Sc (Hons),
LLM (Wolverhampton), LLDip, ACIArb

Clements *Miss Fiona Anne*
Call Date: Oct 1996 (Middle Temple)
Qualifications: MA (Oxon), M.Mus
(Sheff)

Clements *Simon Anthony* •
Legal Director, Department of Trade &
Industry, 10-18 Victoria Street, London
SW1, 0171 215 3132, Fax: 0171 215
3235, Call Date: Nov 1982 (Gray's Inn)
Qualifications: BA (Hull)

Cleminson *Craig Derrick* •
Principal Legal Adviser, Stratford
Magistrates Court, The Court House,
389/397 High Street, Stratford, London
E15 4SB, 0181 522 5000, Fax: 0181 519
9214, Call Date: Oct 1993 (Lincoln's
Inn) Qualifications: LLB (Hons)(L'pool)

Cleris *Miss Jocelyne*
Call Date: Nov 1998 (Middle Temple)
Qualifications: LLB (Hons)(Herts)

Clifford *Colin Raymond*
Justices' Chief Executive,
Buckinghamshire Magistrates, Courts
Committee, The Magistrates' Court,
Walton Street, Aylesbury, Bucks
HP21 7QZ, 01296 338959, Fax: 01296
338960, Call Date: July 1980 (Gray's
Inn) Qualifications: MBA

Clifford *John David*
Call Date: July 1998 (Inner Temple)
Qualifications: BA (Greenwich), MA
(Lond), Dip in Law (City)

Clifford *Steven Butler* •
General Legal Counsel Europe, Toshiba
Electronics (UK) Ltd, Riverside Way,
Camberley, Surrey GU15 3YA, 01276
694600, Fax: 01276 691583, Call Date:
Nov 1981 (Gray's Inn) Qualifications:
BA, LLM

Clift-Matthews *Ms Amanda Louise*
Call Date: Nov 1995 (Lincoln's Inn)
Qualifications: LLB (Lond)

Clifton *Roger Cheston*
Group Company Secretary, TBI plc, 159
New Bond Street, London W1Y 9PA, 0171
355 2345, Fax: 0171 491 2378, Call
Date: July 1996 (Gray's Inn)
Qualifications: F.C.I.S

Clifton *Russell Hugh* •
Call Date: Mar 1996 (Inner Temple)
Qualifications: LLB (Lond)

Clinch *Timothy Michael Edward*
Call Date: July 1997 (Inner Temple)
Qualifications: LLB (Lond)

Closs *Adrian Kenneth* •
Lawyer (Grade 6), MAFF, Legal
Department, 55 Whitehall, London
SW1A 2EY, 0171 270 8774, Fax: 0171
270 8755, Call Date: July 1982 (Gray's
Inn) Qualifications: BA (Lond)

Clough *Miss Pamela*
Advocates Library, Parliament House,
Edinburgh EH1 1RF, 0131 226 5071,
and Member Scottish Bar 4 Brick
Court, Ground Floor, Temple, London,
EC4Y 9AD, Call Date: July 1973 (Middle
Temple)

Clowes *Andrew Mark*
Company Secretary, 91 Southerngate
Way, London SE14 6DW, 0181 692
4545, Call Date: Oct 1996 (Inner
Temple) Qualifications: LLB (Wolves)

Clowry *Karl Joseph Konrad*
Associate, Allen & Overy, One New
Change, London EC4M 9QE, 0171 330
3000, Fax: 0171 330 9999, Solicitor,
Call Date: Nov 1994 (Inner Temple)
Qualifications: BA (Dublin), LLM
(Lond), Dip Law

Clynes *Gordon*
Call Date: July 1980 (Gray's Inn)

Coates *Reginald Ian*
61 Wharfedale, Runcorn, Cheshire
WA7 6PS, 01928 717206, Call Date:
Nov 1984 (Gray's Inn) Qualifications:
DML, MIMgt

Cocker *Daniel Richard*
104 Crosslet Vale, Greenwich, London
SE10 8DL, 0181 694 0973/0976
742779, Fax: 0181 694 0973, Call Date:
Oct 1996 (Lincoln's Inn)
Qualifications: LLB (Hons)(Leeds)

Cocker *Robert Glenville* •
Crown Prosecutor, Crown Prosecution
Service, Gemini Centre, 88 New London
Road, Chelmsford, Essex CM2 0BR,
01245 252939, Call Date: Nov 1977
(Gray's Inn) Qualifications: BA

Cockrell *Miss Teresa* •
Lawyer, Legal Secretariat to the, Law
Offices, 9 Buckingham Gate, London
SW1E 6JP, 0171 271 2417, Fax: 0171
271 2434, Call Date: Nov 1988
(Lincoln's Inn) Qualifications: BA Hons
(Lond), Dip Law, MPhil (Cantab)

Cockshutt *Ms Emma Elizabeth* •
Head of Legal & Business Affairs,
Talkback Productions Limited, 36 Percy
Street, London W1P 0LN, 0171 323
9777, Fax: 0171 637 5105, Call Date:
Nov 1983 (Inner Temple)
Qualifications: LLB Lond, LLB
(Hons)(Lond)

Codd *Michael Richard* •
Call Date: Nov 1989 (Gray's Inn)
Qualifications: BA [Oxon]

Coddington *Nicholas James*
Call Date: Oct 1997 (Middle Temple)
Qualifications: LLB (Hons)(Sheff)

Coe *Roger Graham*
Call Date: Nov 1994 (Middle Temple)
Qualifications: LLB (Hons), LLM

Coffer *Ian*
Principal Court Clerk, Justices' Clerk's
Office, Market Street (East), Newcastle
Upon Tyne NE99 1TB, 0191 232 7326,
Call Date: Nov 1985 (Inner Temple)
Qualifications: LLB (Lond)

Coffey *Nicholas Alexander*
Call Date: Nov 1994 (Inner Temple)
Qualifications: LLB, LLM (Lond)

Coford *Frederic John* •
Assistant Director, Serious Fraud Office,
Elm House, 10-16 Elm Street, London
WC1X 0BJ, Call Date: July 1971 (Middle
Temple) Qualifications: BA (Cantab)

Coggins *Matthew John*
Call Date: Oct 1998 (Gray's Inn)
Qualifications: BA (Oxon)

Cohen *Adrian Leon*
Clifford Chance, 200 Aldersgate Street,
London EC1A 4SS, 0171 600 1000, Fax:
0171 600 5555, Call Date: Nov 1988
(Middle Temple) Qualifications: LLB
(LSE), LLM (Lond)

Cohen *Clive Zev*
South Africa, and Member Member of
the Bars of Johannesburg, Swaziland
and Zimbabwe 3/4 South Square,
Gray's Inn, London, WC1R 5HP, Call
Date: Feb 1989 (Lincoln's Inn)
Qualifications: BA, LLB,
(Witwatersrand)

Cohen *Daniel James Marcus* •
Warner/Chappell Music Ltd, Griffin
House, 161 Hammersmith Road,
London W6 8BS, 0181 563 5861, Call
Date: Oct 1995 (Middle Temple)
Qualifications: LLB (Hons)(Bris)

Cohen *Dr Harvey* •
Principal Lecturer In Law, London
Guildhall University, Department of
Law, 84 Moorgate, London EC2M 6SQ,
0171 320 1455, Fax: 0171 320 1439,
Formerly a Solicitor, Call Date: Nov
1969 (Lincoln's Inn) Qualifications:
LLB, PhD (Lond)

Cohen *Howard Lawrence* •
Branch Crown Prosecutor, Crown
Prosecution Service, Highbury Branch,
Solar House, 1-9 Romford Road,
Stratford, London E15 4LJ, 0181 534
6601, Fax: 0181 522 1236, Call Date:
July 1980 (Inner Temple)
Qualifications: BA(Hons)

Cohen *Mrs Jacqueline Susan*
Call Date: Nov 1973 (Middle Temple)
Qualifications: LLB, PhD

Cohen *Mrs Lenora Annette* •
Legal Advisor Company Secretary, Call
Date: July 1977 (Middle Temple)
Qualifications: LLB (Hons)

Cohen *Michael Alan*
Chairman; The Academy of Experts, 2
South Square, Gray's Inn, London
WC1R 5HP, 0171 637 0333, Fax: 0171
637 1893, Call Date: June 1955 (Gray's
Inn) Qualifications: LLB, FCIArb, FBAE

Coldstream *Sir George Phillips*
The Gate Hse, Blatchington Hill,
Seaford, Sussex BN25 2AH, 01323
892801, American College of Trial
Lawyers American Institute of Judicial
Administration Chairman, Council of
Legal Education 1970-73 and Member
American Bar Association, Call Date:
Nov 1930 (Lincoln's Inn)
Qualifications: LLD Hon, Columbia, MA
(Oxon)

Cole *Sir Alexander Colin*
Sheriff, City of London 1976-77,
Former Garter King of Arms, Call Date:
Nov 1949 (Inner Temple)
Qualifications: BCL, MA (Oxon)

Cole *Miss Justine Mary-Louisa*
Call Date: Nov 1997 (Gray's Inn)
Qualifications: LLB (Thames V)

Cole *Mrs Sally Margaret* •
Principal Crown Prosecutor, Crown
Prosecution Service H/Q, 50 Ludgate
Hill, London EC4M 7EX, 0171 273
8000, Fax: 0171 329 8166, Call Date:
July 1982 (Gray's Inn) Qualifications:
BA Hons (Keele)

Cole *Miss Sarah Helen*
28 Kendal Court, Shoot Up Hill, London
NW2 3PD, 0181 452 2077, Call Date:
Feb 1995 (Inner Temple)
Qualifications: LLB

Coleman *Mrs Anne Elizabeth* •
Principal Court Clerk, S.E. Surrey
Magistrates Court, The Law Courts,
Hatchlands Road, Redhill, Surrey
RH1 6DH, 01737 765581, Fax: 01737
764972, Call Date: July 1982 (Inner
Temple) Qualifications: LLB (Bristol)

Coleman *Miss Sarah Catherine Mary*
Former Solicitor, Call Date: July 1996
(Gray's Inn) Qualifications: BA (Oxon)

Colenso *John Adam*
Call Date: Oct 1995 (Lincoln's Inn)
Qualifications: BA (Hons)(Newcastle),
MA (York)

Colesworthy *Peter Harry*
Flat 9, Muster Court, Muster Green,
Haywards heath, W Sussex RH16 4AW,
01444 417223, Call Date: Nov 1951
(Inner Temple) Qualifications: BA, LLB
MHCIMA

Collett *Dr Philip Michel Rene*
46 Station Way, Buckhurst Hill, Essex
IG9 6LN, Fax: 0181 504 3303, Call
Date: Oct 1991 (Inner Temple)
Qualifications: MB BS (Lond), Dip Law
(City), D.O. MRCOphth

Colley *Ms Lita Susan*
Call Date: Mar 1997 (Gray's Inn)
Qualifications: LLB (Derby)

Colley *Ms Rachel Elizabeth*
Call Date: Nov 1997 (Inner Temple)
Qualifications: LLB, LLM

Collie *Peter Andrew* •
Legal Advisor Registered Adjudicator,
Tarmac Construction Limited,
Construction House, Birch Street,
Wolverhampton WV1 4HY, 01902
316877, Fax: 01902 316687, Call Date:
July 1994 (Middle Temple)
Qualifications: LLB (Hons)(Notts),
MCIOB, ACIArb, LCGI

Collier *Leigh Howard*
46 Vallance Road, Alexandra Park,
London N22 7UB, 0181 881 9293, Call
Date: Oct 1995 (Inner Temple)
Qualifications: MA (Cantab), CPE,
M.I.Mgt, M.B.C.S.

Collier *Miss Naomi Lawson*
Call Date: July 1982 (Middle Temple)
Qualifications: LLB So'ton, ACA

Collier *Ms Shirley Diane*
Call Date: Nov 1984 (Middle Temple)
Qualifications: Dip Mag.Law

Collier *Stephen John* •
General Counsel, General Healthcare
Group Ltd, Legal Department, 210
Euston Road, London NW1 2DA, 0171
419 6021, Fax: 0171 419 6022, Call
Date: July 1980 (Lincoln's Inn)
Qualifications: LLB (Hons), Dip Ae Law,
LLM

Collier-Wright *Charles Edward Hurrell* •
Group Legal Manager, MGN Ltd, 1
Canada Square, London E14 5AD, 0171
293 3747, Fax: 0171 293 3613, Call
Date: July 1976 (Middle Temple)
Qualifications: MA (Oxon)

Collignon *Miss Laura Jacqueline*
Call Date: Oct 1998 (Lincoln's Inn)
Qualifications: BA (Hons)

Collinge *Ronald Ashton Hilton* •
The Manchester Ship Canal Co, Collier
Street, Runcorn, Cheshire WA7 1HR,
019285 67465, Fax: 019285 67469, Call
Date: June 1950 (Inner Temple)
Qualifications: MA (Oxon)

Collinge *Thomas Roden*
Call Date: Oct 1997 (Gray's Inn)
Qualifications: BA (Dunelm), MBA
(Edinburgh)

Collings *Andrew John*
Call Date: Nov 1995 (Middle Temple)
Qualifications: LLB (Hons)

Collings *Matthew Alexander*
Call Date: July 1998 (Gray's Inn)
Qualifications: LLB (L'pool), MA
(Manch)

Collins *Ms Beverley Bernice*
JP Salford Bench, 0161 707 4616, Call
Date: Nov 1995 (Inner Temple)
Qualifications: BA (York), Dip Law (City)

Collins *Mrs Jhoann Temlett*
Call Date: Nov 1991 (Gray's Inn)
Qualifications: LLB (Hons)

Collins *Michael Geoffrey* •
General Manager, Lloyds Policy Signing
Office, Chairman Broker Network
Limited, Three Oaks, 7 Manor Park
Drive, Westorning, Bedfordshire
MK45 5LS, 01525 717852, Fax: 01525
717584, Call Date: Nov 1981 (Inner
Temple) Qualifications: LLB (Lond),
FCII, MBA

Collins *Miss Nadia Anouchka*
LEASE, 8 Maddox Street, London
W1R 9PN, Call Date: Nov 1994 (Middle
Temple) Qualifications: BA (Hons), LLM

Collins *Miss Nicolette* •
Senior Crown Prosecutor, Crown
Prosecuton Service, Kings House,
Kimberley Road, Harrow, Middlesex,
0181 424 8688, Call Date: Oct 1990
(Middle Temple) Qualifications: LLB
(Bris)

Collins *Richard Alexander* •
Director - Divisional Legal Services,
U.G.C Limited, Unipart House,
Garsington Road, Cowley, Oxford
OX4 2PG, 01865 383643, Fax: 01865
384672, Call Date: Nov 1982 (Middle
Temple) Qualifications: BA (Hons)

Collis *John Charles*
Call Date: Nov 1998 (Inner Temple)
Qualifications: BA (Oxon)

Collon *Michael Hyde* •
Head of Legal Advice & Litigation
Division, Lord Chancellor's Department,
Selborne House, 54/60 Victoria Street,
London SW1E 6QW, 0171 210 0716, Fax:
0171 210 0725, Call Date: July 1970
(Middle Temple) Qualifications: MA

Colpstein *Miss Lisa Laya*
Deputy Chief Clerk, Thames Magistrates
Court, 58 Bow Road, London E3 4DJ,
Call Date: Nov 1990 (Inner Temple)
Qualifications: BA (Hons)(Kent)

Comber *John Leslie* •
Assistant Solicitor, Department of the
Environment, 2 Marsham Street, London
SW1P 3EB, Call Date: July 1970 (Gray's
Inn) Qualifications: LLB

Commaille *Douglas Henri*
Call Date: Oct 1997 (Inner Temple)
Qualifications: BA, CPE (Middlesex)

Comonte *Crispin Matthew Morton*
Call Date: Oct 1996 (Lincoln's Inn)
Qualifications: BA (Hons)(Oxon)

Compton *Jonathan Robert*
Call Date: Feb 1995 (Gray's Inn)
Qualifications: LLB (Warwick)

Conboy *Andrew* •
Crown Prosecutor, CPS, 2 King Edward
Court, King Edward Street, Nottinghham,
0115 9480480, Call Date: July 1983
(Lincoln's Inn) Qualifications: LLB
(Hons)

Conceicao *Carlos Manuel* •
Deputy Legal Adviser, Ministry of
Defence, Call Date: July 1987 (Middle
Temple) Qualifications: LLB (Hons)
(Manch)

Condon *Miss Denise Lynn* •
British Medical Association, BMA HOuse,
Tavistock Square, London, WC1H 9JP,
0171 383 6909, Fax: 0171 383 6911,
Call Date: Oct 1994 (Gray's Inn)
Qualifications: LLB, MA, AKC

Condon *Ms Elizabeth Esther Patricia*
Call Date: Feb 1994 (Inner Temple)
Qualifications: BEd, BA, MSc, MPhil,
(Lond), CPE (Nott'm)

Conlan *James Aloysius*
Call Date: Nov 1984 (Gray's Inn)
Qualifications: LLB (Lond)

Connal *Ms Sulina Larissa*
Call Date: Nov 1993 (Lincoln's Inn)
Qualifications: BA (Hons), Dip in Law

Connell *Anthony Edward* •
Branch Crown Prosecutor, Crown
Prosecution Service, Solar House,
Romford Road, London E15 4LJ, 0181
534 6601, Call Date: July 1982 (Gray's
Inn) Qualifications: LLB (B'ham)

Connell *Miss Joan Agnes*
33 Bedford Row, London, WC1R 4JH,
Call Date: July 1985 (Middle Temple)
Qualifications: BA (Hons)

Connell *Squadron Leader Paul James* •
Legal Officer, DDLS, RAF STRIKE
COMMAND, SUPPORT SERVICES
(GERMANY), 02161 474683, Fax: 02161
474505, Barrister of Northern Ireland
(Sep 1985) and Member Hong Kong, Call
Date: Apr 1991 (Middle Temple)
Qualifications: BA (Dublin)

Connell *William Howard* •
Parliamentary Drafter, Tax Law Rewrite
Project, Inland Revenue, SW Bush
House, Aldwych, London WC2, 0171 438
6504, Call Date: July 1979 (Inner
Temple) Qualifications: BA (Dunelm),
LLM (Leicester)

Connelly *Paul Michael*
Call Date: Nov 1989 (Middle Temple)
Qualifications: BSc [Exon], Dip in Law,
M Phil (Cantab)

Conner *Graham*
Call Date: Feb 1995 (Lincoln's Inn)
Qualifications: LLB (Hons)

Connick *Miss Jillian Rachael*
Call Date: Oct 1992 (Middle Temple)
Qualifications: BA (Hons), PGCE &, MA
(Leeds), Diploma in Law

Connolly *David*
Call Date: Nov 1996 (Lincoln's Inn)
Qualifications: BA (Hons)(Manch)

Connolly *Oliver Joseph*
Republic of Ireland, and Member Ireland
36 Bedford Row, London, WC1R 4JH,
Call Date: 1997 (Middle Temple)
Qualifications: LLB (Hons)(Dublin)

E

Connor *Miss Amanda Jane*
Call Date: Oct 1993 (Lincoln's Inn)
Qualifications: LLB (Hons)(Lond),
A.K.C.

Connor *Laurence Joseph*
Principal Clerk, Coventry Magistrates
Court, Court House, Little Park Street,
Coventry CV1 2SQ, 01203 630666, Fax:
01203 256513, Call Date: Dec 1973
(Middle Temple) Qualifications: LLB,
MA, Assoc IPD

Conroy *Miles Christopher*
Call Date: Feb 1995 (Middle Temple)
Qualifications: LLB (Hons)(Lond)

Conroy *Mrs Rashidah*
Call Date: July 1995 (Lincoln's Inn)
Qualifications: LLB (Hons)

Conroy Harris *Michael James*
Berwin Leighton Solicitors, Adelaide
House, London Bridge, London
EC4R 9HA, 0171 623 3144, Fax: 0171
623 4416, Call Date: Oct 1996 (Inner
Temple) Qualifications: LLB
(Kingston), ARICS, ACIArb

Cons *The Hon Sir Derek*
Call Date: June 1953 (Gray's Inn)
Qualifications: LLB, FCIArb

Constantinides *Miss Rania*
Willowdene, Maxwelton Avenue, Mill
Hill, London NW7 3SE, 0181 959 6287,
Call Date: Oct 1997 (Gray's Inn)
Qualifications: BA (Warks), LLM
(Cantab)

Contino *Mrs Marie Claire*
Call Date: Oct 1998 (Lincoln's Inn)
Qualifications: LLB (Hons)(Glamorg)

Conway *Michael David*
Legal Branch, HQNI, Honorary
member of the United States Army
Court of Military Review (1991) and
Member New South Wales Bar, Call
Date: July 1982 (Middle Temple)
Qualifications: LLB [LOND]

Conway *Nicholas Peter* •
Personal Injury Editor, Lawtel, 50
Poland Street, London W1V 4AX, 0171
970 4611, Fax: 0171 970 4693, Call
Date: July 1998 (Middle Temple)
Qualifications: LLB (Hons)(Herts)

Conyngham *John Stafford* •
Director, Control Risks Group Ltd,
Legal Advisor, Control Risks Group Ltd,
83 Victoria Street, London SW1H OHW,
0171 222 1552, Fax: 0171 222 2296,
and Member Hong Kong Bar, Call Date:
Nov 1975 (Gray's Inn) Qualifications:
LLB

Coogan *Michael Joseph* •
Director General, Council of Mortgage
Lenders, 3 Savile Row, London
W1X 1AF, 0171 440 2230, Fax: 0171
434 3791, Call Date: July 1981 (Middle
Temple) Qualifications: LLB

Cook *Andrew John*
Parkway Avenue, Sheffield S9 4UL,
0114 2700895, Fax: 0114 2724553,
Call Date: July 1972 (Gray's Inn)
Qualifications: LLB (Lond)

Cook *Jeremy Owain*
Dudley Metropolitan Council, Legal
Services Dept., 3 St. James's Road,
Dudley, West Midlands DY1 1NF, 01384
456000, Fax: 01384 453388, Call Date:
July 1982 (Middle Temple)
Qualifications: LLB (Hons), M.Soc.Sc

Cook *Ms Katherine Helen* •
Grade 6 (International & EC Division),
The Department of the, Environment,
Zone 9/H9, Eland House, London
SW1E 5DU, 0171 890 4815, Fax: 0171
890 4804, Call Date: Nov 1990 (Middle
Temple) Qualifications: BA (Oxon)

Cooke *Christopher George* •
In-House Lawyer, Warner Bros
Productions Ltd, 135 Wardour Street,
London WC1V 4AP, 0171 465 4812,
Fax: 0171 465 4810, Call Date: Oct
1993 (Inner Temple) Qualifications:
LLB (Bris)

Cooke *Peter John*
Call Date: Mar 1998 (Lincoln's Inn)
Qualifications: LLB (Hons)(Leeds)

Cooke of Thorndon *The Rt Hon. The
Lord*
QC New Zealand, PO Box 1530,
Wellington, New Zealand, President of
Court of Appeal, New Zealand Brick
Court Chambers, 7-8 Essex Street,
London, WC2R 3LD, Call Date: May
1954 (Inner Temple) Qualifications:
MA, PhD (Cantab), LLM (NZ)

Cooksammy *Miss Natalie Camille*
Call Date: Oct 1995 (Lincoln's Inn)
Qualifications: LLB (Hons)(Leeds)

Coomansingh *Miss Anamarie* •
Senior Crown Prosecutor, Crown
Prosecution Service, Branch 2,
Birmingham, 12th Floor, 2 Colmore
Gate, Birmingham, Call Date: Nov 1987
(Gray's Inn) Qualifications: LLB
(Wales)

Coomb *Ms Elizabeth Anne*
Call Date: Oct 1998 (Lincoln's Inn)
Qualifications: BSc (Hons), MA (Lond)

Coombs *Miss Geraldine Anne*
John Pickering & Partners Sols, Old
Exchange Buildings, St Ann's Panage,
29/31 King Street, Manchester M2 6BE,
0161 834 1251, Fax: 0161 834 1505,
Call Date: Oct 1995 (Gray's Inn)
Qualifications: BA (Kent)

Coombs *John Sebastian*
11th Floor, Garfield Barwick Chambers,
53 Martin Place, Sydney NSW 2000,
(02)9232 7754, Fax: (02)9221 8006,
QC (Australia) and Member New South
Wales Bar 1 Temple Gardens, 1st Floor,
Temple, London, EC4Y 9BB, Call Date:
Apr 1989 (Middle Temple)
Qualifications: LLB (Sydney)

Coonan *Miss Delia Ivory*
Inns of Court School of Law, 39 Eagle
Street, London WC1R 4AJ, 0171 404
5787, Fax: 0171 831 4188, Call Date:
July 1973 (Gray's Inn) Qualifications:
LLB, LLM, FCIArb

Cooper *Miss Beryl Phyllis*
Call Date: Feb 1960 (Gray's Inn)

Cooper *Miss Dawn* •
Treasury Solicitor Department, Queen
Anne's Chambers, 28 The Broadway,
London SW1H 9JS, 0171 210 3375, Call
Date: July 1989 (Lincoln's Inn)
Qualifications: BCL (Oxon), LLB

Cooper *Dawn Katherine*
Call Date: Oct 1998 (Inner Temple)
Qualifications: LLB (Staffs)

Cooper *Edmund Robert Roy*
Call Date: May 1997 (Lincoln's Inn)
Qualifications: BA (Hons)

Cooper *Geoffrey William* •
Legal Adviser, Vodafone Group Services
Ltd, The Courtyard, 2-4 London Road,
Newbury, Berkshire RG14 1JX, 01635
502747, Call Date: July 1967 (Lincoln's
Inn) Qualifications: LLB (Lond)

Cooper *Miss Helen Elizabeth*
Call Date: Oct 1994 (Lincoln's Inn)
Qualifications: BA (New York), CPE

Cooper *James Joseph* •
Legal Adviser, H M Treasury,
Parliament Street, London SW1P 3AG,
0171 270 1712, Fax: 0171 270 1668,
Call Date: July 1986 (Inner Temple)
Qualifications: MA, BCL (Oxon)

Cooper *John Peter* •
Assistant Legal Adviser, Off. of
Electricity Regulation, Hagley House,
Hagley Road, Edgbaston, Birmingham
B16 8QG, 0121 456 6218, Fax: 0121
456 6464, Call Date: Oct 1993
(Lincoln's Inn) Qualifications: BA
(Hons)(Oxon)

Cooper *Jonathan Paul* •
Human Rights Project Director, Justice,
59 Carter Lane, London EC4V 5AQ,
0171 329 5100, Doughty Street
Chambers, 11 Doughty Street, London,
WC1N 2PG, Call Date: Nov 1992 (Gray's
Inn) Qualifications: BA (Oxon)

Cooper *Lieutenant Kevin Simon* •
US Department of Justice, Civil Division
European Office, Embassy of the United
States of America, 24 Grosvenor
Square, London W1A 1AE, Call Date:
July 1989 (Lincoln's Inn)
Qualifications: MA (Oxon)

Cooper *Mrs Mahtab*
Call Date: July 1996 (Gray's Inn)
Qualifications: LLB (Middlesex)

Cooper *Mark*
Inner London and City Family,
Proceeding & Courts, 59-65 Wells Street,
London W1A 3AE, 0171 323 1649, Fax:
0171 636 0617, Call Date: Nov 1989
(Inner Temple) Qualifications: BA, Dip
Law

Cooper *Martin Anthony*
17 Privett Road, Fareham, Hants
PO15 6SE, 01329 847079, Call Date:
June 1959 (Lincoln's Inn)
Qualifications: MA

Cooper *Richard Vaughan* •
General Counsel, BATMark Limited,
Globe House, 4 Temple Place, London
WC2R 2PG, 0171 845 1000, Fax: 0171
845 1543, Call Date: July 1971 (Gray's
Inn) Qualifications: BSc MSc

Cooper *Commander Simon Nicholas* •
Deputy Chief Naval Judge Advocate, Call
Date: July 1982 (Middle Temple)
Qualifications: LLB (Bristol)

Cooper *William Anthony Marcus Carmody*
Call Date: Nov 1998 (Middle Temple)
Qualifications: BA (Hons)(Lond)

Coopman *Mrs Patricia Mary* •
Senior Principal Legal Officer, HM
Customs & Excise, New King's Beam
House, 22 Upper Ground, London
SE1 9PJ, Call Date: July 1970 (Middle
Temple)

Coote *Mrs Shirley Ann*
Call Date: July 1977 (Middle Temple)
Qualifications: BA (Lond), MSc

Cope *Miss Siri Alexandra Pertwee*
Call Date: Oct 1997 (Inner Temple)
Qualifications: BSc (Bristol), CPE (City)

Corbett *Anthony Ian* •
Grade 5 (Prosecutions), Ministry of
Agriculture,, Fisheries and Food, 55
Whitehall, London SW1, 0171 270 8305,
Fax: 0171 270 8755, Call Date: Nov 1973
(Lincoln's Inn) Qualifications: LLB
(Hons)

Corcos *Edward David* •
Senior Legal Adviser, Sun Life Assurance
Society PLC, Chief Office, 107 Cheapside,
London EC2V 6DU, 0171 606 7788, Fax:
0171 378 1865, Call Date: July 1980
(Gray's Inn) Qualifications: LLB (Soton)

Corcut *Andrew*
Call Date: Feb 1994 (Lincoln's Inn)
Qualifications: LLB (Hons)

Corderoy *Conor Simon Ivor Mark*
Call Date: Oct 1996 (Inner Temple)
Qualifications: LLB (Westminster)

Corfield *The Rt Hon. Sir Frederick Vernon*
Recorder, Wordings Orchard,
Sheepscombe, Stroud, Glos GL6 7RE,
Call Date: June 1945 (Middle Temple)

Corless-Smith *David*
Call Date: Oct 1993 (Inner Temple)
Qualifications: BDS (L'pool), Dip, Law,
LLM (UCL)

Corn *Matthew Adam*
Call Date: Oct 1995 (Gray's Inn)
Qualifications: BA

Cornelius *Marc*
Call Date: Oct 1997 (Inner Temple)
Qualifications: LLB (Thames Valley)

Corness *Sir Colin Ross*
Chairman, Glaxo Wellcome Pension
Trustees, Glaxo Wellcome Plc, 34
Berkeley Square, London W1X 6JT, 0171
408 8489, Fax: 0171 408 8921, Call
Date: Nov 1956 (Inner Temple)
Qualifications: MA

Corning *Miss Elizebth Ann*
Call Date: Nov 1995 (Middle Temple)
Qualifications: BA (Hons)

Cornish *Miss Emma Rachael*
Nottingham University, University Park,
Nottingham NG9 1EL, Call Date: Oct
1996 (Middle Temple) Qualifications: BA
(Hons) (Keele), LLM (Nott'm)

Corrie *Hugh Robert La Touche*
Director Legal Services, Mirror Group
Newspapers (Retired), Waterperry
House, Wineham, Nr Henfield, West
Sussex BN5 9BT, 01403 710294, Call
Date: June 1951 (Gray's Inn)
Qualifications: BA, LLB (Cantab)

Corrigan *Miss Anna Louise*
Call Date: Nov 1996 (Gray's Inn)
Qualifications: MA

Corrin *Miss Alexandra Jane*
5 Wrightons Hill, Helmdon, Northants
NN13 5UF, Call Date: July 1977 (Gray's
Inn) Qualifications: LLB (Wales)

Corsan *James David Martin*
10 Richmond Bridge Mansions,
Willoughby Road, Twickenham,
Middlesex TW1 2QJ, 0181 744 9677, Fax:
0181 744 9677, Call Date: July 1977
(Gray's Inn) Qualifications: BA

Corston *Ms Jean Ann*
St John's Chambers, Small Street,
Bristol, BS1 1DW, Call Date: Feb 1991
(Inner Temple) Qualifications: LLB

Cory *Mrs Joanna Gethin*
Penllyn Castle, Cowbridge, South
Glamorgan CF7 7RQ, Call Date: June
1956 (Inner Temple) Qualifications: MA

Cossar *Bruce James* •
Call Date: Oct 1995 (Inner Temple)
Qualifications: LLB

Costello *Paul James*
Call Date: Nov 1998 (Inner Temple)
Qualifications: LLB (Manch)

Costin *Miss Emma Rebecca*
Legal Advisor, Simpson Millar Solicitors,
20 Church Road, Lawrence Hill, Bristol
BS5 9JA, 0117 955 9800, Fax: 0117 955
7915, Call Date: Nov 1992 (Lincoln's
Inn) Qualifications: LLB (Hons) (B'ham)

Cottam *Dr David William*
Call Date: Nov 1997 (Lincoln's Inn)
Qualifications: BSc (Hons), PhD, (Sheff),
LLB (Hons), (City)

Cottam *Graeme Robin*
16 Dartmouth Street, London
SW1H 9BL, 0802 440065, Associate;
American Bar Association, Call Date: July
1978 (Middle Temple) Qualifications:
LLB Hons (Bris), FCA

Cottis *Crispus Peter*
21 Campion Road, London SW15 6NN,
0181 788 9714, Call Date: Feb 1958
(Lincoln's Inn) Qualifications: MA, B Litt

Cotton *Stephen David*
Call Date: Mar 1998 (Lincoln's Inn)
Qualifications: LLB (Hons)(So'ton)

Coughlin *Mrs Elizabeth Anne*
Furnival Chambers, 32 Furnival Street,
London, EC4A 1JQ, Call Date: 1989
(Middle Temple) Qualifications: LLB
(Hons)

Coughtrey *Keith Andrew*
Call Date: Nov 1993 (Inner Temple)
Qualifications: BSc (E.Anglia), Dip Law

Couldrey *The Hon Mr Justice John
Alexander*
Advisory Committee on the Prerogative of
Mercy in Kenya., PO Box 24984, Nairobi,
East Africa, 882 227, High Court Judge,
Kenya (Retired) Advocates Complaints
Commission, Commissioner and
Member Victoria, Australia Kenya, Call
Date: June 1948 (Middle Temple)
Qualifications: MA (Cantab)

Coulson *Francis Owen Harrison* •
Export Credits Guarantee Dept, P O Box
2200, 2 Exchange Tower, Harbour
Exchange Square, London E14 9GS,
0171 512 7849, Fax: 0171 512 7649,
Call Date: Nov 1971 (Middle Temple)
Qualifications: MA (Cantab)

Counihan *Miss Caroline Jeanne Mary*
Ireland, Gray's Inn Chambers, Gray's
Inn, London, WC1R, Call Date: Oct 1992
(Middle Temple) Qualifications: BA
French & German , BSc Psychology

Courtney *Mark St John* •
Director of European Regulatory &
Commercial Affairs., Econophone
Europe, 2 Exchange Tower, Harbour
Exchange Square, London E14 9GB,
0171 589 3333, Fax: 0171 589 6333,
Call Date: July 1981 (Middle Temple)
Qualifications: LLB

Coussey *James Romaine Henley* •
Lawyer Prosecuting Lawyer, H M
Customs & Excise, New King's Beam
House, Upper Ground, London SE1 9PJ,
0171 865 5139, Call Date: July 1971
(Middle Temple)

Coveney *Christopher James*
Call Date: July 1976 (Inner Temple)
Qualifications: LLB (Hons)

Coventry *Roger James* •
Principal Crown Prosecutor, Crown
Prosecution Service, The Courtyard,
Lombard Street, Abingdon, Oxfordshire
OX14 5SE, 01235 555678, Fax: 01235
554144, Call Date: July 1971 (Gray's
Inn) Qualifications: LLM(Lond)

Covill *Richard Vernon*
51 Elgin RoaD, Talbot Woods, Bournemouth BH3 7DJ, 01202 529301, Call Date: Feb 1963 (Inner Temple)

Cowan *Paul Joseph*
Call Date: Oct 1996 (Inner Temple) Qualifications: LLB (Dunelm)

Cowan *Mrs Veronica*
Call Date: July 1984 (Middle Temple) Qualifications: LLM (Lond), LLB, SRN, OHN

Coward *Miss Antoinette Cassandra Bernadette*
FULL NAME : Antoinette Cassandra Bernadette Coward, Call Date: Nov 1994 (Inner Temple) Qualifications: LLB (Lond)

Coward *Gerald Anthony Fenwick*
Licensed Insolvency Pract'er, 16 Croftdown Road, Harborne, Birmingham B17 8RB, 0121 427 2324, Fax: 0121 428 2599, Call Date: Feb 1959 (Gray's Inn) Qualifications: LLB, FIPA

Cowdell *James Michael*
Call Date: Feb 1994 (Inner Temple) Qualifications: BA (Oxon), CPE

Cowderoy *Miss Brenda*
Call Date: Nov 1949 (Gray's Inn) Qualifications: MA (Oxon)

Cowdroy *Dennis Antill*
Wentworth Chambers, 12/180 Phillip Street, Sydney, New South Wales 2000, 012 221 71 83, Queen's Counsel Australia and Member Australian New South Wales, Victorian, Queensland and Republic of Ireland Bars 2 Crown Office Row, Ground Floor, Temple, London, EC4Y 7HJ, Call Date: July 1991 (Lincoln's Inn) Qualifications: LLB (Sydney), LLM (Lond)

Cowen *Timothy Robert William*
Call Date: July 1985 (Inner Temple) Qualifications: BA Cantab

Cowgill *John Keith*
8 Corrie Drive, Kearsley, Bolton BL4 8RG, 0161 794 4803, Call Date: Mar 1996 (Inner Temple) Qualifications: BA (Lond), M.ED (Manch), LLB (Lond)

Cowgill *Nigel Geoffrey* •
Principal Crown Prosecutor, Crown Prosecution Service, Windsor House, Manchester Road, Bradford, 01274 742530, Call Date: Nov 1985 (Middle Temple) Qualifications: Dip Law

Cowhey *Miss Jennifer Marie*
Call Date: Nov 1996 (Lincoln's Inn) Qualifications: LLB (Hons) (Essex)

Cowley *Miss Allison Maria*
Call Date: Oct 1995 (Inner Temple) Qualifications: LLB

Cowley *Peter John*
Senior Legal Adviser, Berkshire & Oxfordshire, Magistrates Court Committee, Easby House, Northfield End, Henley-on-Thames, Oxon RG9 2NB, 01491 412720, Fax: 01491 412762, Call Date: Nov 1983 (Middle Temple) Qualifications: BA (Hons)

Cownie *Miss Fiona Caird*
Senior Lecturer in Law. Part-time Chairman Special Education Needs Tribunal., Faculty of Law, The University, University Road, Leicester LE1 7RH, 0116 252 2372, Fax: 0116 252 5023, Call Date: Nov 1985 (Lincoln's Inn) Qualifications: LLB (Leic) BA, (Bristol), LLM(Lond)

Cox *Andrew John*
Chartered Institute of Arbitrators - London Branch Committee Member & Hon Treasurer, 8 Vale Royal House, Newport Court, London WC2H 7PS, 0171 437 3179, Fax: 0171 437 3179, Chartered Surveyor - Adjudicator, Call Date: Oct 1996 (Gray's Inn) Qualifications: BSc , ARICS, FCIArb

Cox *Kerrie Ian Ernest*
Call Date: Oct 1998 (Inner Temple) Qualifications: LLB (W of England)

Cox *Oliver Ivor Zeus*
Call Date: Nov 1996 (Middle Temple) Qualifications: BA (Hons) (Manch)

Cox *Philip Joseph*
Honorary Recorder of Northampton. Chairman:Code of Practice Appeal Board of Prescription Medicine Code of Practice Auth Legal Assessor to the Disciplinary Committee of the Royal College of Veterinary Surgeons., 9 Sir Harrys Road, Edgbaston, Birmingham B15 2UY, 0121 440 0278, Call Date: Nov 1949 (Gray's Inn) Qualifications: BA (Cantab)

Cox *Miss Rosemary Jennifer*
Call Date: July 1978 (Inner Temple) Qualifications: BA (Dunelm)

Cox *Sidney Lewis*
Branch Crown Prosecutor, Whiteacre, Low Street, Elston, Nr Newark-On-Trent, Notts NG23 5PA, Call Date: July 1971 (Middle Temple) Qualifications: LLB

Cox *Stephen Gordon*
Call Date: July 1998 (Gray's Inn) Qualifications: LLB

Coy *Glyn*
1 Deacon Court, Windsor, Berkshire SL4 4LN, Call Date: July 1995 (Lincoln's Inn) Qualifications: LLB (Hons)

Coyle *Miss Susanne* •
F.A.O. Mrs S Breach, Robert Fleming & Co Ltd, 25 Copthall Avenue, London EC2R 7DR, 0171 282 4588, Fax: 0171 282 8311, Call Date: Nov 1994 (Middle Temple) Qualifications: LLB (Hons)

Coyte *Anthony Christopher* •
Director, Towry Law Trustee Company Ltd, 57 High Street, Windsor, Berks SL4 1LX, 01753 868244, Fax: 01753 621710, Call Date: Nov 1984 (Middle Temple) Qualifications: BA (Lanc), Dip Law

Crabtree *Commander Peter Dixon* •
Senior Legal Adviser, Naval Staff, Ministry of Defence, Main Building, Whitehall, London SW1A 2HB, 0171 218 3079, Call Date: July 1985 (Gray's Inn) Qualifications: BA

Craig *Mrs Muriel Margaret*
Call Date: May 1979 (Inner Temple) Qualifications: LLB

Craigen *Mrs Carolyn Ann* •
Senior Crown Prosecutor, Crown Prosecution Service, Aalbourg Square, Lancaster, Lancashire LA1 1GG, 01524 847676, Call Date: July 1985 (Gray's Inn) Qualifications: LLB (Hons)

Cramp *Laurence George Charles*
Part Time Chairman, Social Security Appeals Tribunal, Call Date: Nov 1979 (Gray's Inn) Qualifications: DML

Crampton *Nicholas Paul Deverell* •
Senior Crown Prosecutor, Crown Prosecution Service, Haldin House, Old Bank of England Court, Queen Street, Norwich NR2 4SX, 01603 666491, Fax: 01603 617989, Call Date: May 1976 (Gray's Inn) Qualifications: LLB (Soton)

Crane *Malcolm*
Winsford, Main Street, Beckley, Rye, East Sussex TN31 6RN, 01797 260 385, Call Date: Nov 1967 (Gray's Inn) Qualifications: MA

Crane *Miss Nicola Louise* •
North Somerset Council, Child Care Team, P O Box 138, Town Hall, Weston-super-Mare BS23 1AE, 01934 888888, Fax: 01934 634884, Call Date: Nov 1995 (Inner Temple) Qualifications: LLB (B'ham), LLM (Bris)

Cranfield *Mrs Freda Elizabeth*
South Wales, Call Date: Mar 1998 (Gray's Inn) Qualifications: LLB (Lond)

Cranston *Ross Frederick*
Solicitor General Recorder, Attorney General's Chambers, 9 Buckingham Gate, London SW1E 6JP, and Member New South Wales Bar Queensland Bar 3 Verulam Buildings, London, WC1R 5NT, Call Date: 1976 (Gray's Inn) Qualifications: D.Phil (Oxon)

Craven *Thomas Jock*
Call Date: Nov 1961 (Lincoln's Inn) Qualifications: MA (Oxon)

Crawford *Miss Jacqueline* •
Assistant Parliamentary Counsel, Office
of the Parliamentary, Counsel, 36
Whitehall, London SW1A 2AY, 0171 210
6627, Fax: 0171 210 6632, Call Date:
Nov 1993 (Lincoln's Inn) Qualifications:
MA (Hons)

Crawford *Professor James Richard*
Call Date: 1999 (Gray's Inn)
Qualifications: LLB, BA (Adelaide), DPhil
(Oxon)

Crawford *John Gerald* •
Senior Crown Prosecutor, CPS, 4-12
Queen Anne's Gate, London SW1H 9AZ,
Call Date: Nov 1980 (Lincoln's Inn)
Qualifications: BA, LLM

Crawford *Shane Reaney*
Call Date: Oct 1996 (Lincoln's Inn)
Qualifications: LLB (Hons), LLM
(L'pool)

Crawley *Kevin Joseph*
Call Date: July 1998 (Gray's Inn)
Qualifications: BSc (Wales), MA
(Dunelm)

Crayford *Patrick John Augustine*
Halliday Crayford Balcombe, Chambers,
21 Victoria Avenue, Harrogate HG1 5RD,
01423 523252, Fax: 01423 523838, Call
Date: July 1977 (Middle Temple)
Qualifications: LLB (Hons)

Crayford-Brown *Mrs Sarah Jane* •
Crown Prosecution Service, Grantham
Office, The Old Barracks, Sandon Road,
Grantham, Lincs NG31 9AS, 01476
401177, Fax: 01476 401188, Call Date:
Nov 1988 (Gray's Inn) Qualifications:
LLB

Creasey *Miss Barbara*
Legal Adviser, Leicestershire Magistrates'
Ct, Pocklingtons Walk, Leicester, 0116
2553666, Call Date: Oct 1994 (Inner
Temple) Qualifications: LLB

Creasy *Richard Andrew* •
Legal Advisor, Department of
Environment, Transport & The Regions,
Great Minster House, 76 Marsham
Street, London SW1, 0171 890 6460, Call
Date: Oct 1990 (Inner Temple)
Qualifications: LLB (So'ton), LLM
(Leics)

Crew *Miss Gillian Mary*
Call Date: Oct 1998 (Gray's Inn)
Qualifications: LLB (Warwick)

Crew *Michael Edwin John*
32 St Ann's Road, Chertsey, Surrey
KT16 9DQ, Call Date: July 1977 (Middle
Temple) Qualifications: BA (Lond) MA
(Dublin), BA (Mod, Dublin), BA (Hons,
O.U)

Cridge *Philip James*
Call Date: Nov 1992 (Lincoln's Inn)
Qualifications: LLB (Hons), LLM

Crisham *Ms Catherine Ann* •
Lawyer (Grade 3), Ministry of
Agriculture, Whitehall Place, London
SW1, 0171 270 8553, Fax: 0171 270
8166, Call Date: Nov 1981 (Gray's Inn)
Qualifications: BA, LLM

Crisp *Peter Charles*
Call Date: Oct 1995 (Inner Temple)
Qualifications: BA (Lond), CPE (Lond)

Crocker *Gavin Anthony*
c/o Garfield Robbins Group, 5
Wormwood Street, London EC2M 7RQ,
0171 417 1400, Call Date: July 1989
(Inner Temple) Qualifications: BSc, Dip
Law [City]

Crockford *Gary Brett* •
Head of legal Department, Chartered
Association of, Certified Accountants, 29
Lincoln's Inn Fields, London WC2A 3EE,
0171 242 6855, Fax: 0171 831 8054,
Call Date: July 1980 (Inner Temple)
Qualifications: BA

Crockford *Peter Michael*
The Garden Cottage, Boxley, Nr
Maidstone, Kent ME14 3DX, 01622
677079, Call Date: Nov 1974 (Gray's
Inn) Qualifications: LLB

Croft *Ms Caroline Charlotte Ann* •
Department of Trade & Industry, Room
207, 10 Victoria Street, London
SW1H 0NN, 0171 215 3472, Fax: 0171
215 3141, Call Date: Nov 1991 (Gray's
Inn) Qualifications: BA (Oxon), Dip. Law

Croft *Frederick Lister* •
Legal Adviser, BBC, Broadcasting House,
POrtland Place, London W1A 1AA, 0171
765 4375, Fax: 0171 765 4381, Call
Date: July 1975 (Middle Temple)
Qualifications: MA (Oxon)

Crofts *John Stanley*
Call Date: Mar 1997 (Inner Temple)
Qualifications: LLB

Crone *Thomas Gerald* •
News International, Legal Department, 1
Virginia Street, London E1 9BD, Call
Date: July 1975 (Gray's Inn)
Qualifications: LLB

Cronk *John Julian Tristam* •
Group Company Secretary, The
Hartstone Group PLC, 4 Brent Cross
Gardens, London NW4 3RJ, 0181 359
1000, Fax: 0181 359 1010, Call Date:
Nov 1972 (Inner Temple) Qualifications:
LLB

Croom *Miss Natasha Dawn*
Call Date: Nov 1997 (Gray's Inn)
Qualifications: LLB (Thames Valley)

Croot *Wayne David* •
Crown Prosecutor, Crown Prosection
Service, 21st Floor, Pearl Assurance
House, Greyfriars Road, Cardiff CF1 3PL,
Call Date: Oct 1993 (Gray's Inn)
Qualifications: BA, LLB

Cross *Charles Albert*
Call Date: June 1949 (Gray's Inn)
Qualifications: MA, LLB, DPA

Cross *Donald*
79 Albert Road West, Bolton BL1 5HW,
Call Date: Feb 1955 (Gray's Inn)
Qualifications: LLB

Cross *Ian Grenville*
Deputy Director of Public Prosecutions,
Attorney General's Chambers,
Prosecutions Division, 6/f High Block,
Queensway Government Offices, 66
Queensway, 867 2263, Fax:
852-845-1609, QC (1990) (Hong Kong)
3 Temple Gardens, 2nd Floor, Temple,
London, EC4Y 9AU, Call Date: July 1974
(Middle Temple) Qualifications: LLB
(So'ton)

Cross *Jason Lee*
Call Date: Oct 1998 (Lincoln's Inn)
Qualifications: LLB (Hons)(Herts)

Cross *Jonathan Peter* •
Sony Music Entertainment (UK),
Limited, 10 Great Marlborough Street,
London W1V 2LP, 0171 911 8200, Fax:
0171 911 8600, Call Date: Nov 1992
(Middle Temple) Qualifications: LLB
(Hons)

Cross *Kenneth*
Frondiron Uchaf, Cilgwyn, Carmel,
Caernarfon, Gwynedd LL54 7SE,
Chartered Engineer, Call Date: Nov 1989
(Inner Temple) Qualifications: BSc, LLB
(Lond), MSc (B'ham), C Eng, MIMech E,
MIEE

Cross *Miss Natalie*
Call Date: Oct 1998 (Inner Temple)
Qualifications: LLB (Teeside)

Crossley *Ashley Roger* •
Clifford Chance, 200 Aldersgate Road,
London, Call Date: Oct 1995 (Lincoln's
Inn) Qualifications: BA (Hons)(Oxon)

Crossley *Miss Vanessa Anne* •
Crown Prosecution Service, Rossmore
House, 10 Newbold Terrace,
Warwickshire CV32 4EA, 01926 450444,
Call Date: Nov 1992 (Lincoln's Inn)
Qualifications: BA (Hons)

Crosthwaite-Eyre *Oliver Nicholas* •
Eyre Holdings Ltd, The Estate Office,
Warrens House, Bramshaw, Nr
Lyndhurst, Hampshire SO43 7JH, 01703
812954, Fax: 01703 813956, Call Date:
Nov 1986 (Inner Temple) Qualifications:
LLB (Exon)

Croston *George Roy* •
Prosecution Team Leader, Crown
Prosecution Service, 4th Floor, United
House, Piccadilly, York YO1 1PQ, 01904
45 6595, Call Date: July 1987 (Middle
Temple) Qualifications: MA (Cantab)

Crouch *Miss Sonia Jane*
Deputy Chief Clerk, Inner London
Magistrates', Courts Service, 65 Romney
Street, London SW1P 3RD, Call Date: Nov
1984 (Inner Temple) Qualifications: BA

Crow *Michael Richard Stanley* •
Head of Group Taxation, Nat West
Group, 41 Lothbury, London
EC2P 2BP, 0171 726 1500, Fax: 0171
726 1599, Call Date: July 1976 (Gray's
Inn) Qualifications: BA Hons

Crown *Simon David*
Call Date: Mar 1997 (Middle Temple)
Qualifications: BA (Hons), LLM (Lond)

Crozier *Mrs Mairi*
Bench Legal Adviser, Warwickshire
Magistrates Crt, P O Box 16, 14
Hammilton Terrace, Leamington Spa,
Warwickshire CV32 4XG, 01926
883350, Fax: 01926 335051, Call Date:
Nov 1985 (Middle Temple)
Qualifications: BA

Crozier *Stuart Ross McDonald* •
Legal Advisor (Royal Navy), Naval
Prosecuting Authority, Third Floor, Jervis Block,
HMS Nelson, Portsmouth, Call Date:
Nov 1991 (Gray's Inn) Qualifications:
LLB

Cullen *Miss Deborah Elizabeth* •
CSC Computer Services Limited, 279
Farnborough Road, Farnborough,
Hants GU14 7LS, 01252 363052, Fax:
01252 372577, Call Date: Nov 1989
(Gray's Inn) Qualifications: LLB, MA
(European, Business Law)

Cullen *John Gerard*
Hamlin Slowe Solicitors Ltd, Roxburghe
House, 273-287 Regent Street, London
W1A 4SQ, 0171 629 1209, Fax: 0171
491 2259, Call Date: Nov 1992 (Inner
Temple) Qualifications: LLB (Hons
(Warw)

Cullen *Terence Lindsay Graham*
and Member Hong Kong Bar Singapore
Bar Malaysian Bar Bermuda Bar, Call
Date: Feb 1961 (Lincoln's Inn)

Culling *Miss Maria Alexia*
Call Date: Mar 1997 (Gray's Inn)
Qualifications: LLB (Lond)

Culverhouse *Miss Emily Anna Louise*
Call Date: Nov 1998 (Lincoln's Inn)
Qualifications: LLB (Hons)

Cumlajee *Mrs Angelay*
10 Shelley Gardens, Wembley, Midlesex
HA0 3QG, 0181 904 2097, Fax: 0181
908 1184, and Member Mauritius Bar,
Call Date: Nov 1985 (Gray's Inn)
Qualifications: BA, MA

Cumming *Miss Julia Helen*
Mediator, Conciliator, Health Service,
Apt 3I, 30 Gardner Road, Brookline, MA
02445, 001 617 739 2173, Call Date:
Nov 1988 (Inner Temple)
Qualifications: LLB (Cardiff), RGN

Cumming *Robert Scott*
22 Charlton Place, London N1 8AJ, Call
Date: Feb 1963 (Middle Temple)
Qualifications: MA

Cumpsty *Professor John Sutherland*
University of Cape Town, South Africa,
27 21 650 3454, Fax: 27 21 689 7575,
Call Date: Feb 1956 (Middle Temple)
Qualifications: BSc,PhD & Grad Dip,
Thel (Dunelm), MS (USA)

Cunliffe *John Alfred*
10 Garratts Lane, Banstead, Surrey
SM7 2DZ, Call Date: July 1968
(Lincoln's Inn)

Cunningham *Andrew John*
Call Date: Nov 1991 (Gray's Inn)
Qualifications: LLB (Bris)

Cunningham *Charles Joseph*
Call Date: Nov 1970 (Gray's Inn)
Qualifications: MA, MEd (Glasgow)

Cunningham *Ms Naomi Brigid*
Camden Community Law Centre, 2
Prince of Wales Road, London
NW5 3LG, 0171 485 6672, Fax: 0171
267 6218, Caseworker, Call Date: Feb
1994 (Inner Temple) Qualifications:
LLB (Reading), LLM (Bris)

Cunningham *Redvers Paul* •
Thomas Miller & Co, International
House, 26 Creechurch Lane, London
EC3A 5BA, 0171 204 2531, Fax: 0171
283 5988, Call Date: Feb 1993 (Middle
Temple) Qualifications: LLB
(Hons)(Reading)

Curphey *Miss Nicky Michelle*
Call Date: Oct 1998 (Lincoln's Inn)
Qualifications: LLB (Hons)(Coventry)

Curran *Mrs Andria Dawn*
Call Date: Oct 1991 (Gray's Inn)
Qualifications: LLB (Leics)

Curran *Sean Patrick*
Call Date: Oct 1990 (Gray's Inn)
Qualifications: LLB, MA

Currie *Heriot Whitson*
Advocates Library, Edinburgh EH1 1RF,
0131 226 5071, Fax: 0131 225 3642,
Q.C.Scotland 1992 and Member
Scottish Bar, Call Date: Apr 1991
(Gray's Inn) Qualifications: MA
(Oxford), LLb (Edin)

Currie *Sean*
Deputy Clerk to the Justices, Shropshire
Magistrates Court, The Magistrates
Court, Preston Street, Shrewsbury
SY2 5NX, 01743 458511, Fax: 01743
458502, Call Date: Nov 1982 (Middle
Temple) Qualifications: BA (Hons),
MBA

Curry *Mrs Anne Louise*
Milton Barn, 10 Lawn Farm Close,
Milton Lilbourne, Pewsey, Wiltshire
SN9 5QA, 01672 564950, Fax: 01672
564950, Call Date: Oct 1991 (Lincoln's
Inn) Qualifications: LLB (Hons Warw),
LLM (Lond)

Curtice Hillen *Mrs Monica Lilian Marie*
Deputy Chief Clerk to Inner London
Magistrates' Court Service and Parking
Adjudicator, Inner London Magistrates',
Courts Service, 65 Romney Street,
London WC2B 4PJ, 0171 233 2000, Call
Date: Nov 1975 (Gray's Inn)

Curtin *Richard John Edward*
Trade Mark Adviser, Glaxo Wellcome
PLC, Glaxo Wellcome House, Berkeley
Avenue, Greenford, Middlesex
UB6 0NN, 0171 493 4060, Fax: 0181
966 8330, Call Date: Oct 1996 (Inner
Temple) Qualifications: LLB (Hons)
(De, Montfort)

Curtis *Mrs Deborah Sarah*
Call Date: Oct 1995 (Inner Temple)
Qualifications: LLB (Hons)

Curtis *John William James*
Call Date: July 1996 (Middle Temple)
Qualifications: BA (Hons)(Warw), CPE

Curtis *Richard Anthony* •
Group Investigator, Standard Chartered
Bank, 1 Aldermanbury Square, London
EV2V 7SB, 0171 280 7343, Fax: 0171
280 7274, Call Date: July 1984 (Inner
Temple) Qualifications: LLB (Wales),
LLM (Lond)

Curtis *Stephen James*
Call Date: Oct 1998 (Inner Temple)
Qualifications: BA (Leeds)

Cush *Martin Stuart*
Senior Principal Court Clerk, Avon
Magistrates Crts Comm, Bristol
Magistrates Court, PO Box 107, Nelson
Street, Bristol BS99 7BJ, 0117 943
5100, Call Date: July 1981 (Lincoln's
Inn) Qualifications: BA

Cusworth *Paul Goodwin*
Call Date: Mar 1997 (Inner Temple)
Qualifications: LLB

Cuthbert *Mrs Gillian Lesley* •
Senior Crown Prosecutor, Crown
Prosecution Service, Tudor House,
Manchester Road, Bradford, West
Yorkshire, Call Date: Nov 1971 (Inner
Temple) Qualifications: LLB, BSc
(Econ)

Cyrus *Willan Julius* •
Reading Borough Council, Legal
Department, Civic Centre, Reading,
Berks RG1 7TD, (0118) 9390529, Fax:
(0118) 9390767, Call Date: Nov 1984
(Lincoln's Inn) Qualifications: BA
(Hons, Reading), Diploma in Law(City)

D'Alton *Edward Dermot Quan*
Woodcote Grove House, Woodcote Park,
Coulsdon CR5 2XL, 0181 660 2867,
Call Date: July 1979 (Gray's Inn)
Qualifications: FCA

D'Alton *Richard John*
Call Date: July 1979 (Lincoln's Inn)
Qualifications: BA (Hons)

D'Cruz *Miss Nalini Claris* •
Interchange Legal Advisory, Service,
Interchange Studios, Dalby Street,
London NW5 3NQ, Call Date: Oct 1993
(Lincoln's Inn) Qualifications: LLB
(Hons) (Leeds)

D'Sa *Professor Rose Maria*
Professor of European Law, European
Law Unit, Law School, University of
Glamorgan, Pontypridd, Mid Glamorgan,
Wales CF37 1DL, (01443) 480480, Fax:
(01443) 483008, Call Date: July 1981
(Middle Temple) Qualifications: LLB
PHD

D'Souza *Miss Mavis Mathilda Ursula* •
Editor in Chief Lloyd's Law Reports,
Lloyd's of London Press Ltd, 69-77 Paul
Street, London EC2A 4LQ, 0171 553
1000, Fax: 0171 553 1106, Call Date:
Nov 1975 (Middle Temple)
Qualifications: LLB (Lond)

Da Silva *Miss Rosalind*
Call Date: Oct 1994 (Lincoln's Inn)
Qualifications: BSc (Hons) (Bradford),
LLB (Hons) (Leeds)

Dabbs *Ian Peter Frank* •
Trainee Court Clerk, Leeds Magistrates'
Court, P O Box 97, Westgate, Leeds
LS1 3JP, 0113 2476870, Call Date: Oct
1993 (Gray's Inn) Qualifications: LLB

Daber *Timothy Mark*
Clerk to the Justices, The Magistrates'
Court, Bridge Street, Peterborough
PE1 1ED, 01733 63971, Fax: 01733
313749, Call Date: Nov 1981 (Gray's
Inn) Qualifications: LLB, DMS, MIMgt

Dabo *Bakary Bunja*
Call Date: July 1998 (Lincoln's Inn)
Qualifications: BA (Hons) (Ibadau)

Dachs *Miss Katherine Mary*
Call Date: Nov 1988 (Lincoln's Inn)
Qualifications: BA Hons (Cantab) , AT11

Dadial *Harpartap Singh*
Call Date: Oct 1995 (Inner Temple)
Qualifications: LLB (Lond)

Dagnall *Miss Jane Mary* •
Senior Crown Prosecutor, Crown
Prosecution Service, 8th Floor, Sunlight
House, Quay Street, Manchester
M60 3LU, 0161 837 7402, Fax: 0161 835
2663, Call Date: Nov 1987 (Inner
Temple) Qualifications: LLB (Hons)

Daines *Kristian Samuel*
Call Date: Nov 1998 (Lincoln's Inn)
Qualifications: LLB (Hons) (Lond)

Dainow-Hawkins *Mrs Deborah*
Call Date: July 1998 (Gray's Inn)
Qualifications: BA (Lond), Dip Law

Daintith *Professor Terence Charles*
Institute of Advanced Legal, Studies, 17
Russell Square, London WC1B 5DR,
0171 637 1731, Fax: 0171 580 9613,
Call Date: Nov 1966 (Lincoln's Inn)
Qualifications: MA (Oxon)

Dajani *Aziz Awni*
Call Date: Nov 1998 (Middle Temple)
Qualifications: BSc Econ (Hons) (LSE)

Dalby *Marc Charles* •
Group Legal Director & Company
Secretary, Merck Sharp & Dohme,
Hertford Road, Hoddesdon EN11 9BU,
01992 452014, Fax: 01992 470189, Call
Date: July 1986 (Inner Temple)
Qualifications: MA (Oxon)

Dalby *Thomas James*
Deloitte & Touche, 1 Woodborough
Road, Nottingham NG1 3FG, 0115 950
0511, Call Date: Oct 1995 (Lincoln's
Inn) Qualifications: LLB (Hons) (Notts)

Dale *Sir William Leonard*
20 Old Buildings, Lincoln's Inn, London
WC2A 3UP, 0171 242 9365, Also Inn of
Court L, Call Date: June 1931 (Gray's
Inn) Qualifications: LL.D

Dallow *Richard Julian*
St Mary's House, St Mary's Street,
Bridgnorth, Shropshire WV16 4DW,
01746 765061, Call Date: Nov 1991
(Inner Temple) Qualifications: MA
(Oxon)

Daly *Guy Sebastian Sawle*
Call Date: Nov 1997 (Gray's Inn)
Qualifications: LLB (Lond)

Daly *Miss Jeanette Susan*
Call Date: Oct 1995 (Middle Temple)
Qualifications: LLB (Hons)

Daly *Martin Geoffrey*
and Member Trinidad & Tobago Bar
Essex Court Chambers, 24 Lincoln's Inn
Fields, London, WC2A 3ED, Call Date:
Nov 1967 (Gray's Inn) Qualifications:
LLB (Lond)

Daly *Thomas Charles*
Construction Law Consultant, Haley
Somerset Consulting Ltd, 118 High
Street, Purley, Surrey CR8 2AD, 0181 645
9707, Fax: 0181 668 2155, Call Date:
July 1995 (Inner Temple) Qualifications:
LLB , ACIArb

Damazer *Miss Audrey Faith*
Senior Deputy Chief Clerk Training
Officer, Inner London Magistrates',
Courts Service, Romney Street, London
SW1P 3RD, Call Date: Nov 1980 (Gray's
Inn) Qualifications: BA (Hons) Law

Danbury *Richard*
Call Date: Oct 1994 (Lincoln's Inn)
Qualifications: MA (Cantab), CPE

Danby *Gerald Alwyn* •
Assistant Director (Legal), City of
Bradford Metropolitan District, Council.
Directorate of, Corporate Services, City
Hall, Bradford BD1 1HY, 01274 752236,
Fax: 01274 730337, Call Date: July 1980
(Middle Temple) Qualifications: BSc
(Hull), Dip Law, MBA, MIMgt

Dance *Mrs Iona Lorraine* •
Regional Counsel & Company Secretary,
Dow Chemical Company Limited, 2
Heathrow Boulevard, 284 Bath Road,
West Drayton, Middlesex UB7 0DQ, 0181
917 5001, Fax: 0181 917 5426, Call
Date: Nov 1982 (Middle Temple)
Qualifications: LLB (Hons) (Brunel)

Dangerfield *Phillip Edward* •
Inland Revenue, Somerset House,
London WC2R 1LB, 0171 438 6552, Fax:
0171 438 7004, Call Date: Nov 1976
(Lincoln's Inn) Qualifications: LLB
(Wales)

Daniel-Selvaratnam *Aruchunan*
Call Date: Nov 1997 (Middle Temple)
Qualifications: LLB (Hons) (Kent)

Daniels *Adrian Maurice*
Call Date: Oct 1993 (Lincoln's Inn)
Qualifications: LLB (Hons) (Leeds), MA
(Lond)

Daniels *Miss Lucy Adelaide*
Call Date: Mar 1999 (Inner Temple)
Qualifications: BA (Lond)

Daniels *Paul Dominic*
Senior Court Clerk, Sandwell Court
Committee, Lombard Street West, West
Bromwich, West Midlands, 0121 569
5805, Call Date: Nov 1990 (Gray's Inn)
Qualifications: BA

Daniels *Miss Tanya Collette* •
European Legal Advisor, Amdahl
International Group, Services,
Dogmersfield Park, Hartley Wintney,
Hampshire RG27 8TE, 01252 344400,
Fax: 01252 334211, Call Date: Nov 1985
(Lincoln's Inn) Qualifications: LLB
(Exon)

Dann *Geoffrey Leonard Keith*
Deputy Clerk to the Justices, The Court
House, Stafford Street, Walsall, West
Midlands WS2 8HA, 01922 638222, Fax:
01922 635657, Call Date: Nov 1978
(Gray's Inn) Qualifications: MA (Cantab)

Darlington *Miss Faye Louise*
Call Date: Oct 1998 (Lincoln's Inn)
Qualifications: LLB (Hons) (Manc)

Darnton *Mrs Hazel* •
Senior Crown Prosecutor, Crown
Prosecution Service, 5-7 South Parade,
Wakefield, Call Date: July 1985 (Gray's
Inn)

Darvell *Mrs Julia Frances Stockbridge*
Call Date: July 1983 (Middle Temple)
Qualifications: BA

DaSilva *Douglas Gerald St Elmo*
24 Greenway, Kenton, Harrow, Middlesex
HA3 0TT, 0181 204 3264, Call Date: Nov
1971 (Inner Temple) Qualifications: MA
(Oxon), BA (Lond), LLB (Lond)

Davda *Mrs Anjani*
Court Clerk, Secretariat Offices, The
Court House, London Road, Dorking,
Surrey RH4 1SX, 01306 885544, Call
Date: July 1969 (Lincoln's Inn)

Davey *Geoffrey Wallace*
Recorder, Call Date: July 1954
(Lincoln's Inn) Qualifications: MA
(Oxon)

David *Miss Audra Catherine*
Call Date: Nov 1997 (Middle Temple)
Qualifications: LLB (Hons)(E.Lond)

David *Derrick Huw* •
Senior Crown Prosecutor, Crown
Prosecution Service, Cambria House,
Pentrebach Ind. Est, Pentrebach,
Merthyr Tgdfil, Mid Glamorgan, 01222
378201, Call Date: July 1989 (Middle
Temple) Qualifications: LLB

Davidson *Miss Fiona Ann*
Call Date: Feb 1995 (Lincoln's Inn)
Qualifications: LLB (Hons)(Hudders),
LLM (Huddersfield)

Davidson *Guy Dixon*
Call Date: Oct 1998 (Lincoln's Inn)
Qualifications: LLB (Hons)(Newc)

Davidson *Thomas David*
10/11 Gray's Inn Square, London
WC1R 5JP, 0171 405 2576, Fax: 0171
889 0875, Call Date: July 1973 (Middle
Temple) Qualifications: LLB (Hons),
LLM

Davies *Adrian Michael*
Former Solicitor, Call Date: July 1998
(Lincoln's Inn) Qualifications: BA
(HOns), MA, (Cantab), LLM (Lond)

Davies *Miss Anne Margaret* •
Crown Prosecutor, Crown Prosecution
Service, 17th Floor, Tolworth Tower,
Surbiton, Surrey, 0181 399 5171, Fax:
0181 390 3474, Call Date: Nov 1989
(Inner Temple) Qualifications: LLB
(Hull)

Davies *Ashleigh Bevan* •
Crown Prosecutor, Call Date: July 1981
(Middle Temple) Qualifications: LLB
(Wales)

Davies *Mrs Asta Clara*
LL.B(Hons), 24 Pine Grove, Prestwich,
Manchester M25 3DR, Call Date: June
1955 (Gray's Inn)

Davies *Miss Charlotte Lisa*
Call Date: Nov 1995 (Gray's Inn)
Qualifications: LLB

Davies *Mrs Christina Elizabeth*
Call Date: Oct 1997 (Gray's Inn)
Qualifications: LLB (Wales)

Davies *Christopher Alan Robertshaw*
Call Date: Nov 1971 (Lincoln's Inn)
Qualifications: MA (Cantab)

Davies *David Ioan*
Trainee Solicitor., Ford & Warren,
Westgate Point, Westgate, Leeds
LS1 2AX, 0113 243 6601, Call Date: Oct
1992 (Lincoln's Inn) Qualifications:
LLB(Hons), MA

Davies *David Martyn*
Wray Park Lodge, 59 Alma Road,
Reigate, Surrey RH2 0DN, Call Date:
Feb 1958 (Inner Temple)

Davies *Miss Eleanor Mary*
Call Date: Oct 1998 (Inner Temple)
Qualifications: BA (Sheff), CPE
(Nott'm)

Davies *Mrs Elizabeth Caroline Sian* •
C/O CPS Headquarters, 50 Ludgate Hill,
London EC4M 7EX, 0171 273 8000,
Also Inn of Court L, Call Date: July 1980
(Gray's Inn) Qualifications: LLB
(Bristol) MA

Davies *Frederick George*
Deputy Justices' Clerk, Cambridgeshire
Mgistrates' Crt, c/o Windsor House,
Ermine Park, Spitfire Close,
Huntingdon, Cambs, 01733 63971 Ext
511, Call Date: July 1979 (Inner
Temple) Qualifications: BA (Hons) Law

Davies *Harold Rodney Olonindieh* •
London Borough of Hounslow, Civic
Centre, Lampton Road, Hounslow,
Middlesex TW3 4DN, Albany Chambers,
91 Kentish Town Road, London, NW1
8NY, Call Date: Nov 1978 (Lincoln's
Inn) Qualifications: LLB (Hons), MA
(Brunel)

Davies *Jeremy David*
Morlandes Mead, 56 Croham Manor
Road, Addington Village, South
Croydon, Surrey CR2 7BE, 0181 688
6060, Fax: 0181 667 0260, Call Date:
July 1974 (Inner Temple)
Qualifications: BSc Chem

Davies *John Llewellyn Gladstone*
Call Date: Nov 1998 (Middle Temple)
Qualifications: LLB (Hons)(Lancs)

Davies *Keith* •
Legal Adviser, British Aerospace Airbus
Ltd, New Filton House, PO Box 77,
Bristol BS99 7AR, 0117 9362224, Fax:
0117 9362680, Call Date: Nov 1976
(Inner Temple) Qualifications: MA
(Cantab) MIL

Davies *Keith Frederick* •
Case Manager, Institute of Chartered,
Accountants in England & Wales,
Professional Standards Office, 412-415
Silbury Boulevard, Milton Keynes
MK9 2AF, 01908 546322, Fax: 01908
546271, Call Date: July 1980 (Gray's
Inn)

Davies *Miss Nia Martin* •
Crown Prosecutor, Crown Prosecution
Service, Pearl Assurance House, 20th
Floor, Greyfriars Road, Cardiff CF1 3PL,
Call Date: Feb 1988 (Middle Temple)
Qualifications: MA (Hull), LLB (Wales)

Davies *Mrs Nicola Jane* •
Principal Crown Prosecutor, Mersey/
Lancashire Crown Prosecution Service,
Liverpool South Branch, 7th Floor
South, Royal Liver Building, Liverpool
L3 1HN, 0151 236 7575, Call Date: July
1978 (Middle Temple) Qualifications:
MA (Oxon)

Davies *Paul Richard*
Trainee Accountant, Ernst & Young, 1
Colmore Row, Birmingham B3 2DB,
0121 232 4018, Call Date: Oct 1994
(Lincoln's Inn) Qualifications: LLB
(Hons)(Notts)

Davies *Peter* •
Advisor, Office of Telecommunications,
50 Ludgate Hill, London EC4M 7JJ,
0171 634 8923, Fax: 0171 634 8847,
Call Date: Nov 1990 (Middle Temple)
Qualifications: LLB (Lond), FRSA

Davies *Philip Edward Hamilton*
Call Date: 1998 (Inner Temple)
Qualifications: BA (Cantab), BCL
(Oxon)

Davies *Philip John* •
Parliamentary Counsel, Office of the
Parlimentary, Counsel, 36 Whitehall,
London SW1A 2AY, 0171 210 6630,
Fax: 0171 210 6632, Call Date: Feb
1981 (Middle Temple) Qualifications:
MA (Oxon), BCL (Oxon)

Davies *Mrs Rachel Valerie* •
Legal Adviser Deputy Justices' Training
Officer, Dorset Magistrates' Courts,
Committee, The Law Courts, Park
Road, Poole, Dorset, 01202 745309,
Fax: 01202 711999, Call Date: July
1995 (Gray's Inn) Qualifications: LLB

Davies *Richard Huw*
Call Date: Oct 1998 (Middle Temple)
Qualifications: BA (Hons)(Oxon)

Davies *Robert Stephen*
Solicitor, Call Date: Nov 1994 (Gray's
Inn) Qualifications: BA, LLM (LSE),
Dip, in Law

Davies *Robin Hunkin*
19 The Common, Ealing, London W5,
Call Date: Nov 1960 (Inner Temple)
Qualifications: LLB

Davies *Miss Susan Wendy* •
The Courtyard, Lombard Street,
Abingdon, Oxon OX14 5SE, Call Date:
Nov 1984 (Gray's Inn) Qualifications:
BA

Davis *Commander Bernard James* •
Judge Advocate & Legal Advisor, SOA
Coord, Room 113, Victory Building, HM
Naval Base, Portsmouth PO1 3LS, Call
Date: July 1982 (Gray's Inn)
Qualifications: LLB (B'ham)

Davis *Mrs Emma Elizabeth*
Call Date: Nov 1995 (Inner Temple)
Qualifications: BA (Australia), M.Phil
(Cantab), CPE

Davis *Francis Patrick Reginald Peter* •
Senior Crown Prosecutor, Crown
Prosecution Service, 3rd Floor, Kings
House, Kymberley Road, Harrow,
Middlesex HA1 1YH, 0181 424 8688,
Fax: 0181 424 9134, and Member
Singapore, Call Date: Oct 1991 (Middle
Temple) Qualifications: BA Hons
(L'pool), Dip Law, DMS (Dip in,
Management Studies)

• Barrister in employment

Davis *Gerald Hugh Blakeman*
The Athenaeum, Pall Mall, London
SW1Y 5ER, 0171 930 4843, Call Date:
Feb 1959 (Lincoln's Inn)

Davis *James Charles Aylmer* •
Senior Crown Prosecutor, Call Date: Nov
1990 (Gray's Inn) Qualifications: LLB
(Hons)(Essex)

Davis *James Joseph*
Legal Adviser, The Stone House, Church
Street, West Chiltington, West Sussex
RH20 2JW, 01798 812316, Call Date: July
1952 (Lincoln's Inn) Qualifications: MA
(Cantab)

Davis *Miss Janet Elizabeth Maria*
Call Date: Nov 1994 (Lincoln's Inn)
Qualifications: LLB (Hons)(Bucks)

Davis *Julian Mark*
Call Date: July 1973 (Middle Temple)
Qualifications: LLB

Davis *Mark*
Call Date: Nov 1996 (Gray's Inn)
Qualifications: LLB (Hull)

Davis *Philip Richard* •
Group Legal Adviser, GEC Marconi
Avionics Ltd., Airport Works, Maidstone
Road, Rochester, Kent ME1 2XX, 01634
816024, Fax: 01634 816752, Call Date:
Nov 1971 (Gray's Inn) Qualifications:
BSc LiB

Davis *Mrs Sally Janine* •
Government Lawyer, Lord Chancellor's
Department, Selborne House, 54-60
Victoria Street, London SW1E 6QW, 0171
210 8920, Call Date: Nov 1987 (Inner
Temple) Qualifications: Dip Comm
Studies, Dip Law

Davis *Miss Sally-Ann*
Call Date: Nov 1998 (Middle Temple)
Qualifications: LLB (Hons)(Wales)

Davis *Miss Sarah Luise*
Contracts Oficer, Electrical Contractors
Assoc, ESCA House, 34 Palace Court,
London W2, Call Date: July 1987 (Middle
Temple) Qualifications: BA (Kent), Dip
Law (City)

Davison *Andrew Michael*
Justices' Clerk/ Chief Executive,
Rotherham Magistrates Court, P O Box
15, The Statutes, Rotherham S60 1YW,
01709 839339, Fax: 01709 370082, Call
Date: Nov 1986 (Middle Temple)
Qualifications: Dip Law

Davison *James Edward*
Call Date: Nov 1996 (Gray's Inn)
Qualifications: LLB (Wales)

Daw *Roger Keith* •
Lead Inspector, Directorate of Casework
Evaluation. Senior Civil Service., CPS
Headquarters, 50 Ludgate Hill, London
EC4M 7EX, 0171 273 8000, Call Date:
July 1982 (Middle Temple)
Qualifications: LLB (B'ham)

Dawes *Alistair Nicholas Louis*
Call Date: Feb 1995 (Inner Temple)
Qualifications: BA (Cantab)

Dawkins *James Stephen*
Call Date: Nov 1994 (Inner Temple)
Qualifications: LLB (Soton), LLM
(Soton)

Dawson *Peter*
Part Time Lecturer, 11 Rudgwick Drive,
Brandlesholme, Bury BL8 1YA, 0161 761
6180, Call Date: Feb 1971 (Gray's Inn)

Dawson *Peter Anthony Hawkins*
Fant Cottage, Garford, Nr Abingdon,
Oxfordshire OX13 5PF, 01865 391405,
Call Date: Nov 1971 (Inner Temple)

Dawson *Peter Henry* •
Legal Adviser, Friend & Falcke Limited,
293 Brompton Road, Chelsea, London
SW3 2DZ, 01604 643173, Fax: 01604
643173, Call Date: Feb 1976 (Middle
Temple) Qualifications: MA, LLB (Lond)

Dawson *Stephen Peter*
1 Reeve Gardens, Ipswich IP5 2FG,
01473 611193, Fax: 01473 631221, Call
Date: Mar 1997 (Lincoln's Inn)
Qualifications: BA (Hons)(Sheff), MA
(Leics)

Day *Nicholas John* •
Company Secretary, WT Partnership
Group, Leon House, High Street,
Croydon, Surrey CR9 1YY, 0181 686
0431, Fax: 0181 686 3195, Call Date:
July 1982 (Lincoln's Inn) Qualifications:
BA (Lond), Dip Law, FCIS

Day *Richard Christopher*
Call Date: July 1996 (Gray's Inn)
Qualifications: LLB (Middlesex)

Day *Robert* •
33 Poundfield Way, Broad Hinton,
Twyford, Berkshire RG10 0XR, 0118
9321087, Fax: 0118 9321087, Call Date:
Feb 1991 (Lincoln's Inn) Qualifications:
B Pharm, M Phil , LLB, MR Pharm S

Dayer *Mrs Penelope Andrea* •
Assistant Treasury Solicitor, Treasury
Solicitor's, Queen Anne's Chambers, 28
Broadway, London SW1, Call Date: July
1976 (Gray's Inn) Qualifications: LLB
(Lond)

De *Miss Zoe Monica* •
London Borough of Islington, Town Hall,
Upper Street, Islington N1, 0171 477
3354, Call Date: Nov 1994 (Inner
Temple) Qualifications: BA (Warw)

De Alwis *Miss Claire Louise*
Call Date: Nov 1997 (Middle Temple)
Qualifications: LLB (Hons) (Kent)

De Azevedo *Celso Luiz Cansancao* •
Clarke & Co Solicitors, 76 Shoe Lane,
London EC4A 3JB, 0171 583 5055, Fax:
0171 583 5037, Call Date: Mar 1997
(Inner Temple) Qualifications: LLB
(Lond)

De Basto *Gerald Arthur*
High Court Judge, Hong Kong,
Canterbury Lodge, 21 Canterbury Drive,
Bishopscourt 7708, (021)762 5626, Fax:
(021)762 5627, and Member New South
Wales Hong Kong Bar, Call Date: Nov
1955 (Lincoln's Inn) Qualifications: LLB
(Syd)

De Friend *Richard Henry Max*
Director College of Law, London.
Director : Public Law Project Member
Social Security Appeals Tribunal., 64
London Road, Canterbury, Kent CT2 8JZ,
0171 291 1331, Call Date: Nov 1992
(Middle Temple) Qualifications: BA
(Kent), LLM

de Graft-Johnson *Dr Edward Victor
Collins*
28a Hallswelle Road, Temple Fortune,
London NW11 0DJ, 0181 458 0421, Fax:
0181 209 1105, and Member Ghana Bar,
Call Date: June 1958 (Lincoln's Inn)
Qualifications: LLM, PhD

De Guise *Rupert James*
Call Date: Feb 1995 (Middle Temple)
Qualifications: MA (St Andrews), CPE
(Wolves)

de Havillande *Mrs Jane Elizabeth*
Senior Lecturer in Law, Kingston
University, School of Law, Kingston
University, Kingston Hill,
Kingston-Upon-Thames, Surrey KT2 7LB,
0181 547 2000 Ext 5318, Fax: 0181 547
7038, Call Date: July 1992 (Inner
Temple) Qualifications: MA (Oxon), CPE

De May *Ferdinand Leopold*
1 Edith Terrace, London SW10 0TQ,
0171 352 4465, Call Date: June 1950
(Middle Temple) Qualifications: MA

De Menezes *Raul Antonio* •
Legal Adviser, Bournemouth Magistrates
Court, The Law Courts, Stafford Road,
Bournemouth, Dorset, 01202 711905,
Call Date: Feb 1994 (Lincoln's Inn)
Qualifications: BA (Hons), LLM

De Mounteney *Jonathan Patrick*
Call Date: Nov 1994 (Gray's Inn)
Qualifications: BA (Bath)

De Rijke *Hugo Tate*
FLBA Committee, Call Date: Oct 1990
(Lincoln's Inn) Qualifications: BA
(Keele)

De Smith *Mrs Barbara*
17 Cavendish Avenue, Cambridge
CB1 4UP, Call Date: Nov 1957 (Gray's
Inn) Qualifications: LLB (Lond), MA
(Oxon)

De Speville *Andre Patrice Doger*
605 Chancery House, Lislet Geoffroy
Street, Port Louis, Mauritius, (230) 208
8618/210 3467/210 0174, Fax: (230)
210 3440, Pepys' Chambers, 17 Fleet
Street, London, EC4Y 1AA, Call Date: July
1978 (Middle Temple)

de Speville *Bertrand Edouard Doger*
Anti-Corruption Consultant, 55 The
Avenue, Richmond, Surrey TW9 2AL,
0181 940 1771, Fax: 0181 948 5176,
Formerly Solicitor General, Hong Kong
Commissioner Against Corruption,
Hong Kong, Call Date: July 1967
(Middle Temple) Qualifications: LLB
(Lond)

De Val *Peter Robert* •
Legal Adviser, The Treasury Solicitors
Dept, Central Advisory Division, Queen
Annes Chambers, 28 Broadway,
London SW1, Call Date: Nov 1988
(Inner Temple) Qualifications: LLB,
MPhil (Leic)

De Vall *David Spencer* •
78 Brackenbury Road, London
W6 0BD, 0181 932 1234, Call Date:
July 1988 (Inner Temple)
Qualifications: BSc (Bath), Dip Law
(City)

de Voghelaere Parr *Adam Stephen*
Call Date: Oct 1995 (Gray's Inn)
Qualifications: MA

de Vries *Edo Barend Philip*
France, also Inn of Court G Guildhall
Chambers Portsmouth, Prudential
Buildings, 16 Guildhall Walk,
Portsmouth, Hampshire, PO1 2DE, Call
Date: July 1969 (Inner Temple)
Qualifications: LLM (Utrecht)

De Warrene *Ms Diane Trudy*
Performer's Diploma of the Royal
College of Music, Call Date: Oct 1997
(Inner Temple) Qualifications: CPE
(Westminster)

De Winter *Miss Amanda*
Call Date: Nov 1998 (Lincoln's Inn)
Qualifications: BA (Hons) (Bradford)

De-Grey Homer *Ms Sarah Justine*
Call Date: Oct 1996 (Inner Temple)
Qualifications: LLB

Deakin *Miss Denise Lesley*
Call Date: Oct 1998 (Inner Temple)
Qualifications: LLB (Soton)

Deakin *George Anthony Hartley*
Chairman Addenbrooke's NHS Trust,
Manting Hse, Meldreth, Nr Royston,
Herts SG8 6NU, 01763 260276, Fax:
01763 260276, Call Date: Nov 1963
(Gray's Inn) Qualifications: MA
(Oxon),, MBA (INSEAD)

Deakin *Paul Kingsley*
Call Date: Nov 1972 (Middle Temple)
Qualifications: LLM (Lond)

Deal *Alexander Marc*
Call Date: Nov 1992 (Inner Temple)
Qualifications: LLB

Dealy *Nicholas John*
Call Date: Oct 1996 (Middle Temple)
Qualifications: BSc (Hons) (Hull), CPE

Dean *James Thomas*
Call Date: Nov 1997 (Middle Temple)
Qualifications: LLB (Hons) (Manch)

Deane *Michael Boyd*
Call Date: Mar 1998 (Middle Temple)
Qualifications: BSc (Hons) (LSE)

Deans *Noel Everton* •
Goodman Derrick, 90 Fetter Lane,
London EC4A 1EQ, 0171 404 0606,
Call Date: Nov 1990 (Lincoln's Inn)
Qualifications: BA (Essex), Dip Law
(City)

Dearie *Christopher William McPherson*
Call Date: Nov 1998 (Middle Temple)
Qualifications: LLB (Hons) (Bris)

Dearing *Anthony Johns*
Call Date: Nov 1998 (Middle Temple)
Qualifications: LLB (Hons) (Thames)

Dearnley *Trevor David*
Whitegate, Wetheral, Carlisle CA4 8JD,
01228 560314, Call Date: Nov 1969
(Gray's Inn)

Deason *Christopher John* •
Contracts Administrator Dip QS FRICS
FCIArb Dip EU Law, Taylor Woodrow
International, 345 Ruislip Road,
Southall, Middlesex UB1 2QP, 0181
231 1062, Fax: 0181 231 1085, Call
Date: Nov 1995 (Middle Temple)
Qualifications: LLB (Hons) (Lond)

Deave *John James*
Recorder, Call Date: July 1952 (Gray's
Inn) Qualifications: MA (Oxon)

Debono *Marius Paul Anthony*
22 Avenue De Suffren, 75015 Paris,
Call Date: May 1956 (Lincoln's Inn)
Qualifications: Licence en droit,
(Paris), AIB

Deby *John Bedford*
Recorder, Call Date: Nov 1954 (Inner
Temple) Qualifications: MA (Cantab)

Decker-Kingston *Mrs Micheline
Hildegard Franziska*
16 Alwyne Villas, London N1 2HQ, 0171
354 2046, Rechtsanwalt, Cologne,
Germany and Member Avocat a la Cour
D'appel de Paris, Call Date: July 1997
(Gray's Inn) Qualifications: Maitrise,
DEA (Paris), Dip Law

Dee *Nicholas* •
Director of Taxation, SmithKline
Beecham plc, One New Horizons Court,
Great West Road, Brentford, Middlesex
TW8 9EP, 0181 975 2350, Fax: 0181
975 2360, Call Date: July 1973
(Lincoln's Inn) Qualifications: BA,
F.C.A

Deeley *Jeremy John* •
Managing Counsel - Mobil North Sea
Limited, Mobil Court, 3 Clements Inn,
London WC2A 2EB, 0171 412 4295,
Fax: 0171 404 0035, Call Date: Nov
1980 (Gray's Inn) Qualifications: LLB
(Hons)

DeGale *David Otway*
Dernford Barn, Sweffling,
Saxmundham, Suffolk IP17 2BQ,
01728 663 402, Fax: 01728 663 402,
Call Date: Nov 1956 (Middle Temple)
Qualifications: BA (Oxon)

Degirmenci *Mrs Kyriacoulla*
Call Date: Feb 1995 (Inner Temple)
Qualifications: LLB (Sussex)

Dehn *Guy Julian*
Public Concern at Work, Lincoln's Inn
House, 42 Kingsway, London
WC2B 6EN, Call Date: July 1982
(Middle Temple) Qualifications: BA
(Bristol)

Delbourgo *Mrs Angela Marie*
Also Inn of Court I, Call Date: July 1980
(Lincoln's Inn) Qualifications: LLB

Demetriou *Miss Natasha*
Call Date: Oct 1996 (Middle Temple)
Qualifications: BA (Hons) (Dunelm),
CPE

den Brinker *Miss Melanie Jane
Margaret*
West House, Town Row, East Sussex
TN6 3QU, Call Date: July 1984 (Inner
Temple) Qualifications: LLB
(Liverpool)

Denham *Grey* •
Group Secretary, GKN Plc, P O Box 55
Ipsley Hse, Ipsley Church Lane,
Redditch, Worcs B98 0TL, 01527
517715, Fax: 01527 517700, Call Date:
Nov 1972 (Inner Temple)
Qualifications: LLB ((Lond)

Denham *Paul Victor* •
Senior Lecturer, The Law School,
University of Central England, in
Birmingham, Perry Barr, Birmingham
B42 2SU, 0121 331 5102, Call Date:
July 1996 (Inner Temple)
Qualifications: BA (Soton), LLB
(W.Eng)

Dening *Richard Dacre Lewis*
Call Date: Nov 1968 (Middle Temple)
Qualifications: BA, BCL (Oxon)

Denman *Daniel Jeremy* •
Principal Legal Officer, Office of the
Solicitor, DHSS, New Court, 48 Carey
Street, London WC2A 2LS, 0171 412
1357, Call Date: Nov 1995 (Gray's Inn)
Qualifications: MA (Cantab)

Dennis *Miss Lucy Henrietta Wesley*
6 Pump Court, Ground Floor, Temple,
London, EC4Y 7AR, Call Date: Nov 1988
(Inner Temple) Qualifications: LLB

Dennis *Philip William Coleridge*
230 Greys Road, Henley on Thames,
Oxon RG9 1QY, 01491 573554, Call
Date: June 1948 (Inner Temple)
Qualifications: MA (Oxon)

Denny *Miss Susan Louise* •
Law Reporter, Incorporated Council of
Law, Reporting for England & Wales,
Room W234, Royal Courts of Justice,
Strand, London WC2A 2LL, 0171 936
6609, Fax: 0171 405 1978, Call Date:
July 1977 (Middle Temple)
Qualifications: BA, MA, LLB

Denza *Mrs Eileen* •
Visiting Professor University College
London, Call Date: Jan 1963 (Lincoln's
Inn) Qualifications: MA (Ab & Oxon),
LLM (Harvard)

Derham *Gerald Bernard Samuel*
Clerk to the Justices, Call Date: May 1969
(Inner Temple) Qualifications: LLB

Derriman *James Parkyns*
34 Mossville Gardens, Morden, Surrey
SM4 4DG, 0181 542 4548, Call Date:
June 1947 (Lincoln's Inn)

Derrington *Jonathan McCourt*
Call Date: Oct 1998 (Inner Temple)
Qualifications: BSC (City), CPE

Derry *Ms Caroline Louise*
Call Date: Nov 1994 (Inner Temple)
Qualifications: BA (Oxon)

Desai *Jayant Nichhabhai*
Call Date: Nov 1956 (Lincoln's Inn)
Qualifications: LLB (Lond)

Desai *Sadananda Shankrappa*
46 Parkfield Road, Harrow, Middlesex
HA2 8LB, 0181 422 2855, Call Date: July
1970 (Inner Temple) Qualifications: BA,
LLB, BIM Dip

Desbruslais *Mr Anthony David*
Clerk to the Justices Justices Chief
Executive, Magistrates' Court, Carrington
Street, Nottingham NG2 1EE, 0115 955
8111, Fax: 0115 955 8131, Call Date:
July 1976 (Middle Temple)
Qualifications: LLB

Desker *Denis Shawn*
Call Date: Nov 1998 (Gray's Inn)
Qualifications: LLB

Devadasan *Miss Valentina*
Call Date: Oct 1996 (Middle Temple)
Qualifications: LLB (Hons) (Lond)

Devine *Miss Lauren*
Consultant/Lecturer, Call Date: July 1998
(Inner Temple) Qualifications: LLB
(Bris)

Devine-Baillie *Mrs Francesca Maria* •
Senior Crown Prosecutor, Crown
Prosecution Service, St Johns House,
Merton Road, Bootle, Liverpool L20,
0151 922 8711, Call Date: Feb 1984
(Gray's Inn) Qualifications: BA (Hons)

Devitt *Miss Clare Oonagh-Jane*
Legal Advisor, Squire & Co, 49 St John
Sq. London EC1V 4JL, 0171 490 3444,
Fax: 0171 250 4087, Call Date: Oct 1991
(Gray's Inn) Qualifications: BA (Lond),
Dip Law

Devitt *Stephen John*
Call Date: Nov 1994 (Lincoln's Inn)
Qualifications: BA (Hons)

Dewan *Miss Sharene*
Room 234, The Royal Courts of Justice,
Strand, London WC2A 2LL, 0171 831
6664, Fax: 0171 405 1978, Call Date: Oct
1995 (Inner Temple) Qualifications: LLB
(Lond)

Dewar *John Kinley*
Call Date: May 1995 (Gray's Inn)
Qualifications: MA, BCL

Dewar *Mrs Sarah Alison* •
Prosecution Team Leader, Crown
Prosecution Service, 8th Floor, Prospect
West, Station Road, Croydon, Surrey,
0181 251 5425, Call Date: July 1986
(Middle Temple) Qualifications: LLB

Dewhirst *Nicholas Michael* •
Legal Adviser, Unijet Group PLC,
Sandrocks, Rocky Lane, Haywards Heath,
West Sussex RH16 4RH, 01444 255600,
Fax: 01444 417799, Call Date: Nov 1990
(Lincoln's Inn) Qualifications: BA (Hull)

Dewick *Mrs Chiew Yin* •
Senior Crown Prosecutor, Crown
Prosecution Service, Harrow Branch,
2nd Floor, King's House, Kymberley
Road, Harrow, Middlesex HA1 1YH, 0181
424 8688, Fax: 0181 424 9134, Call
Date: Nov 1990 (Lincoln's Inn)
Qualifications: LLB (Reading)

Dhama *Satya Prakash*
Advocate of High Ct of Delhi, and
Member Indian Bar, Call Date: July 1972
(Lincoln's Inn) Qualifications: MA

Dhanarajan *Miss Sumithra Gayathri*
Call Date: July 1998 (Gray's Inn)
Qualifications: LLB (Dunelm)

Dhanoo *David Devanand* •
Legal Advisor, EULER Trade Indemnity, 1
Canada Square, London E14 5DX, 0171
512 9333, Fax: 0171 512 9186, and
Member Attorney of the Supreme Court
of Trinidad & Tobago, Call Date: Nov
1988 (Lincoln's Inn) Qualifications: LLB
Hons (Lond), LLM (Lond)

Dhargalkar *Mrs Jean*
Call Date: Nov 1985 (Inner Temple)
Qualifications: BA (Hull)

Dhesi *Miss Tejpal* •
North of England Protecting, and
Indemnity Association Ltd, The
Quayside, Newcastle Upon Tyne
NE1 3DU, 0191 232 5221, Fax: 0191 261
0540, Call Date: Nov 1989 (Inner
Temple) Qualifications: LLB

Dhillon *Balkar Singh*
Assistant Legal Adviser, The Retail Motor
Industry, Federation, 201 Great POrtland
Street, London NW1N 6AB, 0171 580
9122, Call Date: Feb 1992 (Lincoln's
Inn) Qualifications: LLB (Hons) (Lond),
LLM (Lond)

Dhir *Mark Christiaan*
Trident Trust Company (UK) Ltd, 7
Welbeck Street, London W1M 7PB, 0171
935 1503, Fax: 0171 935 7242, Call
Date: July 1996 (Middle Temple)
Qualifications: LLB (Hons)(Lanc)

di Mambro *Mrs Louise Jane* •
Lawyer, Civil Appeals Office, Room E320,
Royal Courts of Justice, Strand, London
WC2A 2LL, 0171 936 6738, Call Date:
July 1976 (Middle Temple)
Qualifications: LLB

Di Rienzo *Matthew James*
Call Date: Feb 1994 (Lincoln's Inn)
Qualifications: MA (Cantab)

Diaper *Miss Ruth Marguerite* •
Dept of Trade & Industry, Queen Anne's
Chambers, 28 Broadway, London
SW1H 9JS, Call Date: Feb 1991 (Gray's
Inn) Qualifications: LLB

Dias *Reginald Walter Michael*
13 Old Square, Ground Floor, Lincoln's
Inn, London, WC2A 3UA, Call Date: June
1945 (Inner Temple) Qualifications: MA
LLB (Cantab)

Dibble *Kenneth Michael* •
Manager, Legal Department London
Office, Charity Commission, St Alban's
House, 57-60 Haymarket, London
SW1Y 4QX, 0171 210 4542, Call Date:
July 1977 (Lincoln's Inn) Qualifications:
LLB, LLM, AIB, AKC

Dickens *Miss Deirdre Dawn* •
Senior Crown Prosecutor, Crown
Prosecution Service, 50 Ludgate Hill,
London EC4M 7EX, 0171 273 1178, Fax:
0171 273 8039, Call Date: July 1990
(Inner Temple) Qualifications: LLB
(Hons), LLM (Lond)

Dickerson *Miss Sara Betty*
Call Date: Nov 1998 (Inner Temple)
Qualifications: LLB

Dickie *Andrew Valentine Acworth*
Consulting Member of Trust Matters Ltd,
75 Hale drive, Mill Hill, London
NW7 3EL, 0181 906 2807, Fax: 0181 906
2807, Call Date: Oct 1994 (Lincoln's
Inn) Qualifications: MA , Dip in
Management , Studies (Middx), LLB
(Hons)

Dickie *Ms Fiona Patricia*
Plumstead Law Centre, Call Date: Oct
1993 (Inner Temple) Qualifications: BA
(Leeds), CPE

Dickinson *Ms Georgina Ann* •
Principal Crown Prosecutor, Crown
Prosecution Service, Wakefield Branch
Office, 4/5 South Parade, Wakefield, West
Yorkshire WF1 1LR, 01924 290620, Fax:
01924 369360, Call Date: July 1977
(Lincoln's Inn) Qualifications: B.A.
(Kent)

Dickman *Richard Harris*
Former Solicitor, Call Date: July 1998
(Inner Temple) Qualifications: BA
(Witwatersrand), MA (Cantab)

Dickson *Christopher William* •
Executive Counsel, Accountants Joint
Disciplinary, Scheme, First Floor, 1
White's Row, London E1 7NF, 0171 247
1511, Fax: 0171 247 9466, and
Member Northern Ireland Bar, Call
Date: July 1986 (Middle Temple)
Qualifications: BA Cantab

Dickson *Ian* •
Creative Labs (UK) Ltd, Unit 2, The
Pavilions, Ruscombe Business Park,
Ruscombe, Berks RG10 9NN, 01189
344322, Fax: 01189 344578, Call Date:
Nov 1978 (Inner Temple)
Qualifications: LLB (Lond)

Dignan *Ms Noleen Patricia* •
Legal Adviser, Sun Life Assurance
Society Plc, 107 Cheapside, London
EC2V 6DU, 0171 606 7788, Fax: 0171
378 1865, Call Date: Nov 1989 (Gray's
Inn) Qualifications: LLB

Dilks *Miss Tracy Elizabeth* •
Assistant Vice President, Credit Suisse
First Boston, One Cabot Square,
London E14 4QJ, 0171 888 8927, Fax:
0171 888 4583, Call Date: Nov 1997
(Middle Temple) Qualifications: BA
(New Brunswick), MA (Reading)

Dilworth *John* •
Senior Crown Prosecutor, Crown
Prosecution Service, 3rd Floor,
Unicentre, Lords Walk, Preston,
Lancashire PR1 1DH, 01772 555015,
Call Date: Nov 1987 (Gray's Inn)
Qualifications: LLB (Hons) DML

Dilworth *Ms Kristin*
Call Date: July 1980 (Lincoln's Inn)
Qualifications: BA

Dinan-Hayward *Miss Jacqueline Anne
Catherine*
Call Date: Mar 1998 (Middle Temple)
Qualifications: LLB (Hons)

Dindyal *Sonny*
Call Date: Nov 1998 (Lincoln's Inn)
Qualifications: BA (Hons), LLB(Hons),
(Lond)

Dingsdale *George Neville*
56 Cloncurry Street, London SW6, 0171
736 8199, Call Date: July 1966 (Inner
Temple) Qualifications: LLB (Lond),
BA

Dingwall *Howard John*
Justices' Clerk, Ealing P.S.A. Justices
Chief Executive Ealing MCC, Ealing
Magistrates' Court, The Courthouse,
Green Man Lane, London W13, 0181
579 9311, Call Date: Nov 1974
(Lincoln's Inn) Qualifications: MA LLB

Dingwall *Richard Andrew*
Call Date: Oct 1991 (Gray's Inn)
Qualifications: LLB

Diplock *Mrs Ann*
Senior Court Clerk, Wolverhampton
Magistrates Ct, The Law Courts, North
Street, Wolverhampton WV1 1RA,
01902 773151, Fax: 01902 27875, Call
Date: Nov 1985 (Lincoln's Inn)
Qualifications: BA (Hons)

Ditchburn *Mathew James*
Call Date: Mar 1996 (Lincoln's Inn)
Qualifications: LLB (Hons)

Dixon *Mrs Christine Angela* •
Court Clerk, Barnet Magistrates Court
Comm, Justice's Clerk's Office, 7C High
Street, Barnet, Herts EN5 5UE, 0181
441 9042, Call Date: Nov 1989 (Gray's
Inn) Qualifications: LLB

Dixon *Mrs Colette Yvonne* •
Senior Crown Prosecutor, Crown
Prosecution Service, Ryedale House, 60
Piccadilly, York YO1 1NS, 01904
610726, Fax: 01904 610394, Call Date:
Nov 1987 (Lincoln's Inn)
Qualifications: LLB

Dixon *Dennis Joseph* •
Legal Officer, Inland Revenue
Solicitor's, Office, Somersets House,
Strand, London WC2R 4RD, 0171 438
6107, Fax: 0171 438 62488, Call Date:
Nov 1995 (Middle Temple)
Qualifications: BA (Hons) (Cantab)

Dixon *Miss Shelley*
Call Date: Oct 1997 (Inner Temple)
Qualifications: LLB (Leeds)

Dobbin *William-Wallace* •
Director, Corporate & Strategic Affairs.,
British American Financial, Services, 22
Arlington Street, London SW1A 1RW,
0171 495 5563, Call Date: July 1982
(Gray's Inn) Qualifications: BA

Dobe *Kuljeet Singh*
Watford Chambers, 74 Mildred Avenue,
Watford, Hertfordshire, WD1 7DX, Call
Date: Nov 1993 (Lincoln's Inn)
Qualifications: LLB (Soton)

Dobry *Ms Josephine Carola*
Call Date: Oct 1995 (Inner Temple)
Qualifications: BA (Oxon), MA (Bris)

Dobson *Miss Sally Louise*
Call Date: July 1998 (Lincoln's Inn)
Qualifications: LLB (Hons)(Lond)

Docksey *Christopher* •
Legal Adviser, Legal Service,
Commission of, the European
Communities, Rue de la Loi 200,
B-1049 Brussels, Belgium, Belgium,
32-2-2955717, Fax: 32-2-2965971, Call
Date: July 1976 (Inner Temple)
Qualifications: MA (Cantab), LLM
(Virginia)

Dodd *Miss Philippa Alice May*
Simmons & Simmons, 21 Wilson
Street, London EC2M 2TX, 0171 628
2020, Fax: 0171 628 2070, Call Date:
Oct 1995 (Inner Temple)
Qualifications: LLB (Sheff), LLM
(Lond)

Dodds *Malcolm Douglas*
Secretariat Offices, Court House, Tufton
Street, Ashford, Kent TN23 1QS, 01233
663203, Fax: 01233 663206, Area
Director of Social Services (North
Kent), Call Date: Nov 1984 (Middle
Temple) Qualifications: BA (Kent),
LLM.(Manch), DMS

Dodgshon *Simon Earl*
Deputy Clerk to the Justices, Stockport
Magistrates Court, P.O.Box. 155, Court
House, Edward Street, Stockport
SK1 3NF, 0161 477 2020, Fax: 0161
474 1115, Call Date: July 1986 (Middle
Temple) Qualifications: BA Hons,
D.M.S.

Dodson *Timothy Charles*
Principal Court Clerk, Cardiff
Magistrates Court, Fitzalan Place,
Cardiff CR2 1RZ, 01222 463040, Fax:
01222 456224, Call Date: Jan 1980
(Gray's Inn)

Doggart *Anthony Hamilton*
Finance Director of Robert Fleming
Asset Management Ltd, 23 Ovington
Gardens, London SW3 1LE, 0171 880
3297, Fax: 0171 880 3294, also Inn of
Court L, Call Date: July 1962 (Middle
Temple)

Doggett *John Clayton*
Call Date: May 1941 (Middle Temple)

Doggett *Roderick Alistair Manning*
Recorder, 4 Paper Bldgs, Ground Floor,
Temple, London, EC4Y 7EX, Call Date:
July 1969 (Gray's Inn) Qualifications:
BA (Oxon)

Dogra *Miss Tanyia Anita*
Call Date: Oct 1994 (Gray's Inn)
Qualifications: LLB, LLM

Dogra-Brazell *Ms Julia Marisa*
Call Date: Oct 1995 (Lincoln's Inn)
Qualifications: BA (Hons) , MA (Lond)

Doherty *Miss Faye Maria*
Richards Butler, Beaufort House, 15 St
Botolph Street, London EC3A 7EE,
0171 247 6555, Fax: 0171 247 5091,
Call Date: Nov 1989 (Lincoln's Inn)
Qualifications: LLB (Lond)

Dolby-Stevens *Mrs Wendy Elizabeth*
Visiting Law Lecturer, Call Date: Oct
1996 (Middle Temple) Qualifications:
LLB (Hons)

Dolphin *Miss Kelly Louise*
Call Date: Oct 1996 (Inner Temple)
Qualifications: BA (Oxon), CPE (City)

Don *Andrew George*
Deputy Chairman A.L.T (S.E.)
Examiner (Ecclesiastial Jurisdiction -
Norwich Diocese), The Old Rectory,
Little Dunham, Kings Lynn, Norfolk
PE32 2DG, 01760 722584, Fax: 01760
720709, Call Date: Nov 1960 (Inner
Temple) Qualifications: MA (Cantab)

Donald Keith Malcolm Hamilton •
General Counsel, International Water
Limited, New Zealand House, 10th Floor,
80 Haymarket, London SW1Y 4TE, 0171
766 5100/5160, Fax: 0171 766 5180,
Call Date: July 1978 (Gray's Inn)
Qualifications: LLB (Sheff)

Donaldson Nicholas John
Credit Lyonnais Securities, Broadwalk
House, 5 Appold Street, London
EC2A 2DA, 0171 588 4000, Fax: 0171
588 0278, Call Date: July 1976 (Middle
Temple) Qualifications: LLB (Lond)

Donegan Ms Sally Frances Averill •
Crown Prosecution Service, Crown
Prosecution Service, River Park House,
High Road, London N22, 0181 888 8889,
Fax: 0181 888 0746, Call Date: Oct 1992
(Gray's Inn) Qualifications: LL.B (Lond)

Donelon Miss Anne
Call Date: 1995 (Lincoln's Inn)
Qualifications: LLB (Hons)(Hull)

Donnabella Miss Rosemary
Blythe Liggins Solicitors, Edmund
House, Rugby Road, Leamington Spa
CV32 6EL, 1 Dr Johnson's Bldgs, Ground
Floor, Temple, London, EC4Y 7AX, Call
Date: Feb 1991 (Middle Temple)
Qualifications: LLB

Donnelly Brian
44 Main Street, Ledston, Castleford, W.
Yorkshire WF10 2AB, 01977 516563, Call
Date: July 1976 (Gray's Inn)
Qualifications: LLB, FRICS

Donnelly William Howard •
Prosecution Team Leader, Crown
Prosecution Service, 1st Floor,
Churchgate House, Bolton BL1 1JG,
01204 535202, Fax: 01204 364569, Call
Date: Nov 1981 (Gray's Inn)
Qualifications: BA

Donovan Allan James
LLB Hons, Call Date: Nov 1991 (Middle
Temple)

Donovan Guy Patrick
Call Date: Oct 1998 (Lincoln's Inn)
Qualifications: LLB (Hons)(Dunelm)

Donovan The Hon Hugh Desmond
Call Date: Apr 1959 (Middle Temple)
Qualifications: MA (Oxon)

Doody Richard James
Call Date: Oct 1995 (Inner Temple)
Qualifications: LLB (Huddersfield)

Dookhee Mohamade Ally Noorooddin
Company Director/Secretary, 97 Chase
Road, Southgate, London N14, 0181 351
7189, Fax: 0181 882 7744, Call Date:
Nov 1997 (Middle Temple)
Qualifications: LLB (Hons)

Dootson Iain Stuart
Call Date: Feb 1984 (Gray's Inn)
Qualifications: LLB (Hons Lond)

Doran James Christopher
Beachcroft Stanleys, 20 Furnival Street,
London EC4A 1BN, 0171 242 1011, Fax:
0171 831 6630, Call Date: Oct 1990
(Lincoln's Inn) Qualifications: LLB
(Essex)

Doran Kevin Reginald
Call Date: Nov 1979 (Gray's Inn)
Qualifications: DML

Dorey Robert Graham
Call Date: Nov 1996 (Inner Temple)
Qualifications: LLB (So'ton)

Dorey Thomas Alan
Le Haugard, Rue De Sorel, St John,
Jersey JE3 4AA, 01534 862258, Formerly
Judicial Greffier Formerly Commissioner
of the Royal Court of Jersey Formerly
Police Court Magistrate & Judge of the
Petty Debts Courts. and Member Jersey,
Call Date: May 1958 (Gray's Inn)
Qualifications: MA, PhD

Dorner Miss Irene Mitchell
Chief Operating Officer, HSBC MIDLAND,
Thames Exchange, 10 Queen Street
Place, London EC4R 1BQ, 0171 336
3300, Fax: 0171 336 2738, Call Date:
July 1977 (Middle Temple)
Qualifications: MA (Oxon)

Double Paul Robert Edgar •
Counsel to City Remembrancer (Parl &
Bill drafting work), City Remembrancer's
Office, PO Box 270, London EC2P 2EJ,
0171 332 1207, Fax: 0171 332 1895,
Call Date: July 1981 (Middle Temple)
Qualifications: BSc, LLM

Douer Ariel
Suite 301, 1170 N Federal Hwy, Fort
Lauderdale, Florida 33304, 954-463
1670, 954 761 8280 Residence, Call
Date: Nov 1975 (Lincoln's Inn)
Qualifications: LLB

Dougall Alistair Ross
Call Date: July 1983 (Inner Temple)
Qualifications: LLB (Lond)

Dougall Mrs Anne Louise Borisova
3 Etheldene Avenue, Muswell Hill,
London N10 3QG, 0181 444 9551, Fax:
0181 444 9551, Call Date: Nov 1981
(Inner Temple) Qualifications: LL.B

Douglas Mary
Call Date: July 1976 (Middle Temple)
Qualifications: MBA, LLB

Dourado Mrs Maria Alba Aldonca
Senior Court Clerk, Coventry Magistrates
Court, Little Park Street, Coventry
CVI 2SQ, 01203 630666, Fax: 01203
256513, and Member Kenya Bar, Call
Date: July 1967 (Inner Temple)

Dove-Edwin Bassey Tokumboh
Lehman Brothers, One Broadgate,
London EC2M 7HA, 0171 260 2053, Fax:
0171 260 2207, Call Date: Feb 1995
(Inner Temple) Qualifications: BA
(Notts), ACA

Dow Harold Peter Bourner
Mustow House, Mustow Street, Bury St
Edmunds, Suffolk IP33 1XL, 01284
725093, Fax: 01284 704227, Call Date:
Nov 1946 (Middle Temple)
Qualifications: MA (Cantab)

Dowarris Colin
Call Date: Nov 1998 (Lincoln's Inn)
Qualifications: LLB (Hons)(Staffs)

Dowd Miss Carmen Jane Louise •
Crown Prosecutor, Crown Prosecution
Service, 50 Ludgate Hill, London
EC4M 7EX, 0171 273 8486, Fax: 0171
329 8164, Call Date: July 1989 (Gray's
Inn) Qualifications: BA

Dowell Ms Nita Mary •
Senior Crown Prosecutor, Crown
Prosecution Service, 491 Abergele Road,
Old Colwyn, Colwyn Bay, Clwyd, Call
Date: July 1982 (Gray's Inn)
Qualifications: LLB (L'pool)

Dowling Carl Michael
Call Date: Mar 1998 (Gray's Inn)
Qualifications: LLB (Lond)

Down Miss Sara Lydia
Assistant Ombudsman (Legal), Prisons
Ombudsmans Office, Ashley House, 2
Monck Street, London SW1, 0171 276
2863, Call Date: Oct 1991 (Gray's Inn)
Qualifications: LLB (L'pool)

Downey Mrs Sally-Ann •
Senior Principal Legal Officer, D.S.S.,
Block 2, Spur R, Room 20, Government
Buildings, Honeypot Lane, Stanmore,
Middlesex HA7 1AY, 0171 972 3849, Call
Date: Nov 1985 (Gray's Inn)
Qualifications: BA

Downie Anthony Robert •
Group Secretary & Legal Adviser,
Anglo-Norden Limited, Orwell Terminal,
Duke Street, Ipswich IP3 0AJ, 01473
220120, Fax: 01473 230805, Call Date:
Oct 1995 (Gray's Inn) Qualifications: BA
(L'Pool), MBA (Sheff), Dip Law
(Westminst) , MIMgt

Doyle Mrs Kim Jane •
Crown Prosecutor, Crown Prosecution
Service, 8th Floor, Sunlight House, Quay
Street, Manchester M60 3LU, 0161 908
2611, Fax: 0161 908 2686, Call Date: Apr
1986 (Middle Temple) Qualifications:
B.A

Drabble John William David
Call Date: Nov 1997 (Gray's Inn)
Qualifications: LLB (Sussex)

Drage Mrs Lesley Anne
Legal Adviser, Rochford and Southend,
Magistrates Court, The Court House,
Victoria Avenue, Southend on Sea, Essex
SS2 6EU, 01702 348491, Call Date: Apr
1991 (Middle Temple) Qualifications: BA
(Hons), Cert Ed

Draper *Miss Jeannette* •
Senior Crown Prosecutor, Solar House, 1-9 Romford Road, Stratford, London E15, 0181 534 6601, Fax: 0181 522 1236, Call Date: Oct 1992 (Middle Temple) Qualifications: LL.B (Hons)

Draper *Norman Henry* •
Clerk to the Justices/Justices Chief Executive, Knowsley Magistrates', Courts Committee, The Court House, Lathom Road, Huyton, Merseyside L36 9XY, 0151 481 4400, Fax: 0151 449 2841, Call Date: Nov 1978 (Inner Temple) Qualifications: BA (Hons)

Draycott *Paul Richard*
Tribunal Representative - Employment & Social Security Law., Fulham Legal Advice Centre, 679A Fulham Road, London SW6 5PZ, 0171 731 2401, Fax: 0171 731 6654, Call Date: Nov 1994 (Gray's Inn) Qualifications: LLB (Hull)

Drayton *Fitzroy* •
Prosecution Team Leader, Crown Prosecution Service, Central Confiscation Branch, Central Casework, 50 Ludgate Hill, London EC4M 7EX, 0171 273 1314, Fax: 0171 273 1325, Call Date: July 1983 (Middle Temple) Qualifications: BA

Dreelan *Ian Christopher James*
Call Date: Oct 1995 (Inner Temple) Qualifications: LLB (Sheff)

Drew *Dorian Warrick Sheridan*
Lovell White Durrant, 65 Holborn Viaduct, London EC1A 2DY, Call Date: Oct 1995 (Gray's Inn) Qualifications: LLB (Hons) (Lond)

Drewry *Nigel*
Court Clerk, Bromley Magistrates Court, London Road, Bromley, Kent BR1 1BY, 0181 325 4000, Fax: 0181 325 4006, Call Date: Oct 1991 (Lincoln's Inn) Qualifications: LLB (Hons)

Driscoll *Tristan Laurence*
Call Date: Nov 1998 (Lincoln's Inn) Qualifications: LLB (Hons) (Leics)

Driver *Miss Shirley* •
Senior Crown Prosecutor, Crown Prosecution Service, 8th Floor, Prospect Park, 81 Station Road, Croydon, Surrey CR0 2RD, 0181 251 5430, Call Date: May 1993 (Middle Temple) Qualifications: LLB (Hons)

Drury *Jonathan Michael*
Criminal Clerk, Call Date: Nov 1995 (Lincoln's Inn) Qualifications: LLB (Hons)

Drury *Michael John* •
Lawyer, CESG, M Block, Priors Road, Cheltenham GL52 5AJ, 01242 221 491 x 2349, Call Date: July 1982 (Middle Temple) Qualifications: LLB (Hons), LLM

Drybrough-Smith *Robert Ian* •
Assistant Chief Crown Prosecutor, Crown Prosecution Service, 50 Ludgate Hill, London EC4M 7EX, 0171 273 8000, Call Date: July 1975 (Inner Temple) Qualifications: LLB (Leeds)

Dryden *Miss Bonita*
Call Date: Oct 1998 (Lincoln's Inn) Qualifications: BA (Hons)

Drysdale *John Gillespie*
21 East Common, Harpenden, Hertfordshire AL5 1BJ, 01582 621103, Fax: 01582 621103, and Member Irish Bar, Call Date: July 1965 (Gray's Inn) Qualifications: MA, M.Sc(Oxon)

Drysdale Wilson *Alexander*
C/O 8 New Square, Lincoln's Inn, London WC2A 3QP, Also Inn of Court L, Call Date: July 1981 (Gray's Inn) Qualifications: BSc Eng RMCS

Dubicka *Miss Elizabeth*
Call Date: Feb 1995 (Middle Temple) Qualifications: BA (Hons) (B'ham), MA (Leic), CPE (City)

Dubljevic *Alexander Salvatore* •
Senior Crown Prosecutor, Crown Prosecution Service, Capital Tower, 20th Floor, Greyfriars Road, Cardiff CF1 3PL, 01222 378201, Call Date: July 1979 (Middle Temple) Qualifications: LLB (Cardiff)

Duck *Hywel Ivor*
Kasteelstraat 78, 3090 Overiouse Belgium, 010322 6878270, Fax: 010322 6878270, Call Date: June 1956 (Gray's Inn) Qualifications: MA, Diplome D'Etudes, Superieures , Europeennes

Duckworth *Mrs Margaret Ashworth* •
Senior Crown Prosecutor, Crown Prosecution Service, 2nd Floor, Calder House, St James Street, Burnley, Lancashire BB11 1XG, 01282 412298, Call Date: Feb 1990 (Middle Temple) Qualifications: LLB Hons

Duckworth *Miss Shirley Lynne*
Call Date: Oct 1997 (Gray's Inn) Qualifications: LLB (De Montfort)

Duddington *John Gabriel*
6 Hanbury Park Road, St John's, Worcester WR2 4PB, 01905 423131, Fax: 01905 423131, Call Date: July 1976 (Middle Temple) Qualifications: LLB (Hull)

Dudley *Mrs Julia Jill*
Call Date: Nov 1982 (Middle Temple) Qualifications: Dip Law Poly of, Central London

Duff *Miss Jacki Kim*
Call Date: Nov 1997 (Middle Temple) Qualifications: LLB (Hons)

Duff *Mrs Jayne Peta*
Call Date: Nov 1992 (Inner Temple) Qualifications: LLB

Duffield *Mrs Janet Rachel*
Senior Court Clerk, Calderdale Magistrates Court, PO Box 32, Harrison Road, Halifax, Yorks HX1 2AN, 01422 360695, Fax: 01422 347874, Call Date: Nov 1990 (Middle Temple) Qualifications: LLB (Lancaster)

Duffill *David William*
Call Date: Feb 1973 (Gray's Inn)

Duffus *Howard James* •
Call Date: July 1969 (Gray's Inn)

Duffy *Desmond Joseph* •
Crown Prosecution Service, C/O 50 Ludgate Hill, London EC4M 7EX, Call Date: Nov 1993 (Gray's Inn) Qualifications: BA

Duffy *Simon John* •
Legal Officer, Office of the Solicitor, Room 510, East Wing, Somerset House, London WC2R 1LB, 0171 438 7147, Fax: 0171 438 6246, Call Date: Oct 1996 (Lincoln's Inn) Qualifications: BSc (Hons) (Sheff), CPE (Northumbria), ARICS

Dugan *Humphrey John Aurelius*
Goodwyn House, 12 High Street, Datchet, Berkshire SL3 9EQ, 01753 542904, Fax: 01753 582585, Call Date: Feb 1957 (Gray's Inn) Qualifications: MA, LLB (Cantab)

Dulay *Miss Ranjeet*
Call Date: Mar 1999 (Inner Temple) Qualifications: LLB (B'ham)

Dulwich *David John*
Clerk to the Justices, Wiltshire Magistrates Court, 43-55 Milford Street, Salisbury, Wiltshire SP1 2BP, 0722 333225, Fax: 0722 413395, Call Date: July 1970 (Gray's Inn)

Duma *Alexander Agim*
13 Coulson Street, London SW3, 0171 823 7422, Fax: 0171 581 0982, Call Date: Nov 1969 (Gray's Inn) Qualifications: LLB, FCA

Dumbuya *Ibrahim Pierre Hassan* •
Legal Services Department, London Borough of, Waltham Forest, Sycamore House, Town Hall Complex, Forest Road, London E17 4SY, 0181 925 5258, and Member Sierra Leone Bar, Call Date: Nov 1981 (Gray's Inn) Qualifications: BA (Hons), LLM

Duncan *Ms Denise*
Deputy Chief Clerk, Inner London Magistrates', Courts Service, 65 Romney Street, London SW1P 3RD, 0171 799 3332, Call Date: Nov 1985 (Gray's Inn) Qualifications: LLB

Duncan *Douglas John Stewart*
Legislative Counsel, 86 Cromwell Road, Winchester, Hants S023 4AE, 01962 856048, Fax: 01962 856048, and Member Scottish Bar, Call Date: Nov 1990 (Inner Temple) Qualifications: LLB (Aberdeen)

Duncan Miss Gracie Sharon
Call Date: Feb 1995 (Gray's Inn)
Qualifications: LLB

Duncan Kenneth Stroud
Tax Consultant, Bon Accord, Heath
Drive, Walton on the Hill, Tadworth,
Surrey KT20 7QQ, 01737 813520, Fax:
01737 813520, Call Date: Feb 1976
(Gray's Inn) Qualifications: LLB (Lond),
F.T.I.I, F.C.C.A.

Duncan Mrs Sarah
Call Date: Nov 1996 (Gray's Inn)
Qualifications: LLB

Duncan Simon Ross •
Senior Crown Prosecutor, Crown
Prosecution Service, 7th Floor South,
Royal Liver Building, Pier Head,
Liverpool, Call Date: May 1987
(Lincoln's Inn) Qualifications: LLB

Duncan Miss Susan Elizabeth Ramsay
• Principal Legal Officer, HM Customs &
Excise, New Kings Beam House, 22
Upper Ground, London SE1 9PJ, Call
Date: Nov 1987 (Gray's Inn)
Qualifications: BA (Newc)

Dundas James Frederick Trevor
Director, 16 Norland Square, London
W11 6PX, 0171 727 3781, Fax: 0171 792
1089, Call Date: Nov 1972 (Inner
Temple) Qualifications: BA (Oxon)

Dunk David Frederick •
Senior Crown Prosecutor, Crown
Prosecution Service, New Magistrates
Court Building, Burneside Road, Kendal,
Cumbria LA9 4RT, 01539 728999 Ext 25,
Fax: 01539 725270, Call Date: July 1977
(Middle Temple) Qualifications: LLB
(Sheff)

Dunleavy Miss Ann Geraldine •
Legal Adviser & Company Secretary,
Mace Limited, Atelier House, 64 Pratt
Street, Camden, London NW1 0LF, 0171
554 8000, Fax: 0171 554 8111, Call
Date: Nov 1988 (Inner Temple)
Qualifications: B.Ed (Newc), LLB

Dunlop Garry Bruce
Call Date: Oct 1998 (Lincoln's Inn)
Qualifications: LLB (Hons)(Sussex)

Dunn Philip •
Company Secretary, James Walker Group
Ltd, Lion House, Woking, Surrey
GU22 9LL, 01483 746146, Fax: 01483
746123, Call Date: July 1975 (Gray's
Inn) Qualifications: LLB

Dunn Miss Sarah Patricia Quincey
Call Date: Nov 1998 (Lincoln's Inn)
Qualifications: BA (Hons)(Oxon)

Dunn Timothy Neville
Call Date: 1996 (Inner Temple)
Qualifications: LLB (Hons)(Exon)

Dunne Ms Margaret
Call Date: Nov 1996 (Lincoln's Inn)
Qualifications: LLB (Hons)(Middx)

Dunstan Mrs Tessa Jane •
Legal Advisor, Dept of Trade & Industry,
10 Victoria Street, London SW1E 0NN,
0171 215 3144, Fax: 0171 215 3221,
Call Date: Nov 1967 (Middle Temple)
Qualifications: MA (Oxon)

Dunt Robert John
Call Date: May 1997 (Middle Temple)
Qualifications: BA (Hons)(Bris)

Dupplin The Viscount Charles William
Harley Hay
Partner, Hiscox plc, 1 Great St Helens,
London EC3A 6HX, 0171 448 6000, Fax:
0171 448 6395, Call Date: Oct 1990
(Middle Temple) Qualifications: MA
(Oxon), Dip Law (City)

Durack John Francis •
Special Casework Lawyer, Crown
Prosecution Service, River Park House,
225 High Road, Wood Green, London
N22 4HQ, 0181 888 8889 x 344, Fax:
0181 365 7752, Call Date: Nov 1970
(Middle Temple) Qualifications: MA
(Cantab)

Durance Alexander Christian John
Call Date: Nov 1997 (Middle Temple)
Qualifications: BA (Hons)

During Miss Jacqueline Alison
Call Date: Oct 1996 (Inner Temple)
Qualifications: BA (Lond)

Durnin Martin Laurence •
Clerk to the Justices South East Surrey,
Surrey Magistrates Court, The Law
Courts, Hatchlands Road, Redhill, Surrey
RH1 6DH, 01737 765581, Fax: 01737
764972, Call Date: Nov 1978 (Lincoln's
Inn) Qualifications: BA

Durston Gregory John
Senior Lecturer Kingston Law School,
Kingston Law School, Kingston Hill,
Kingston Upon Thames, Surrey KT2 7LB,
0181 549 1141, Fax: 0181 547 1440,
Also Inn of Court L, Call Date: Nov 1985
(Middle Temple) Qualifications: MA (St
Andrews), Dip Law, LLM (Lond)

Dutnall Julian Richard
Call Date: Oct 1995 (Inner Temple)
Qualifications: LLB (Exon)

Dutton Andrew
Phoenix Chambers, First Floor, Gray's
Inn Chambers, Gray's Inn, London,
WC1R 5JA, Call Date: Oct 1997 (Gray's
Inn) Qualifications: LLB (Manc)

Dutton James Alexander •
Assistant Solicitor, Charity Commission,
St Albans House, 57/60 Haymarket,
London SW1Y 4QX, 0171 210 4406, Fax:
0171 210 4604, Call Date: Nov 1971
(Middle Temple) Qualifications: BA
(Hons)

Dworzak Rudolf John Christopher
Call Date: July 1998 (Middle Temple)
Qualifications: LLB (Hons)(City)

Dwyer John Augustine
Call Date: Nov 1986 (Gray's Inn)
Qualifications: LLB(Lond)

Dwyer Timothy John
Coopers & Lybrand, Hadrian House,
Higham Place, Newcastle Upon Tyne
NE1 8BP, 0191 269 3204, Call Date: Oct
1993 (Inner Temple) Qualifications: LLB
(Hons)

Dyer Mrs Barbara Ann •
Senior Legal Adviser, Texaco Ltd, Legal
Dept, 1 Westferry Circus, Canary Wharf,
London E14 4HA, 0171 719 3402, Fax:
0171 719 5124, Call Date: Nov 1985
(Inner Temple) Qualifications: BA Hons

Dyer Christopher Guy
29 Charnwood Drive, South Woodford,
London E18 1PF, 0181 989 0676, Call
Date: Oct 1993 (Gray's Inn)
Qualifications: LLB

Dyer Miss Sandra Penelope •
Senior Crown Prosecutor, Crown
Prosecution Service, Chartist Tower,
Dock Street, Newport, Gwent, Call Date:
Nov 1983 (Middle Temple)
Qualifications: BA (Hons)

Dymond Anthony Simon
Call Date: Feb 1993 (Inner Temple)
Qualifications: BA

Dyson Robert Frank •
Principal Crown Prosecutor, CPS
(London), 18th Floor, Tolworth Tower,
Surbiton, Surrey KT6 7DS, 0181 399
5171, Fax: 0181 390 3474, Call Date:
Nov 1973 (Lincoln's Inn) Qualifications:
LLB (Lond)

Dyson Mr Stephen John
Deputy Clerk to the Justices,
Northamptonshire Magistrates', Courts,
Regent's Pavillion, Summerhouse Road,
Moulton Park, Northampton NN3 6AS,
01604 497011, Fax: 01604 497010, Call
Date: Feb 1986 (Gray's Inn)
Qualifications: MBA (Bham)

Dzakpasu Lucas Kwami Wenceslav
and Member Ghana, Call Date: Nov 1997
(Middle Temple) Qualifications: LLB
(Hons)(Lond), BA (Ghana)

Eades Christopher Mark
Call Date: July 1998 (Middle Temple)
Qualifications: LLB (Hons)(Sussex)

Eades Christopher Nicholas
Principal Court Clerk, Coventry
Magistrates Court, Little Park Street,
Coventry, West Midlands CV1 2SQ, 01203
630666 Ext 2176, Fax: 01203 256513,
Call Date: Nov 1984 (Lincoln's Inn)
Qualifications: LLB

Eaglestone Dr Frank Nelson
Senior Examiner to the Chartered
Insurance Institute, 5 St Michael's
Avenue, Bramhall, Stockport, Cheshire
SK7 2PT, 0161 439 4628, Call Date: Nov
1972 (Gray's Inn) Qualifications: LLB
(Lond), FCII, FCIArb, PhD

Eames Anthony John
Call Date: July 1981 (Gray's Inn)

Earles *Charles Graham*
Slaughter & May, 35 Basinghall Street, London EC2 3DB, 0171 710 5028, Call Date: Oct 1990 (Lincoln's Inn) Qualifications: MA (Cantab)

Eastham *John*
Call Date: Nov 1998 (Gray's Inn) Qualifications: BA (Sunderland)

Easton *Dr Susan Margaret*
Senior Lecturer, Department of Law, Brunel University, Uxbridge, Middlesex UB8 3PH, 01895 274000, Fax: 01895 810476 (Law Dept), Call Date: Nov 1988 (Inner Temple) Qualifications: BSc (Econ, Wales), LLM (Lond), PhD (Soton), Dip Law (City)

Easton *Miss Tracy* •
Senior Crown Prosecutor, Crown Prosecution Service, 2nd Floor, Froomsgate House, Rupert Street, Bristol BS1 2DJ, 0117 927 3093, Call Date: Nov 1992 (Inner Temple) Qualifications: BA (Hons) , Dip in Law

Eastwood *Mrs Hilary Ann* •
Director of Administration, Liverpool City Magistrates Crt, 107-109 Dale Street, Liverpool L2 2JQ, 0151 243 5672, Fax: 0151 243 5685, Call Date: Feb 1991 (Middle Temple) Qualifications: LLB

Eatwell *Nikolai Jonathan*
Call Date: Nov 1995 (Lincoln's Inn) Qualifications: BA (Hons)

Eberwein *Irving James* •
Trust & Taxation Director, CMI Financial Services Ltd, Narrow Plain, Bristol BS2 0JH, 0181 520 0123, Fax: 0181 520 7501, Associate Fellow of the Society for Advanced Legal Studies, Call Date: Nov 1975 (Inner Temple) Qualifications: LLB, LLM (Lond), TEP

Eble *Keith James* •
Call Date: Oct 1994 (Lincoln's Inn) Qualifications: LLB (Hons)(Wales)

Eborn *Andrew Martin James*
Managing Director, Eborn & Associates Ltd, Law & Buisiness Offices, Sponsorship & Rights Mngment, 195 Euston Road, London NW1 2BN, 0171 383 5884, Fax: 0171 753 8648, Former Solicitor, Call Date: July 1985 (Inner Temple) Qualifications: BA (Dunelm)

Ebulue *Emmanuel Reginald Ordiranachuh* •
Health & Safety Executive, Rose Court, 2 Southwark Bridge, London SE1 9HS, 0171 717 6666, Fax: 0171 717 6661, Call Date: Feb 1979 (Middle Temple) Qualifications: LLB (Lond), MA

Eccles *Alan Michael* •
Clerk to the Justices, Dudley Magistrates' Court, The Inhedge, Dudley, West Midlands DY1 1RY, 01384 211411, Fax: 01384 211415, Call Date: July 1981 (Middle Temple) Qualifications: BA Hons

Eckersley *Basil Stuart*
Call Date: Jan 1949 (Lincoln's Inn) Qualifications: MA (Oxon)

Eckersley *Simon James*
Goldman Sachs International, Limited, 133 Fleet Street, London EC4A 2BB, 0171 774 5275, Fax: 0171 774 1700, Call Date: Nov 1988 (Lincoln's Inn) Qualifications: LLB Hons (LSE), Dip D'Etudes Jur, MBA

Ede *Ronald George* •
Senior Crown Prosecutor, Crown Prosecution Service, Lysnoweth, Infirmary Hill, Truro, Cornwall TRi 2XG, 01872 70127, Fax: 01872 42495, Call Date: July 1981 (Middle Temple) Qualifications: BA, DMS

Eden *Edgar*
8 Woodcote, Maidenhead, Berkshire SL6 4DU, 01628 783678, Call Date: Nov 1950 (Inner Temple) Qualifications: MA (Oxon)

Eden-Shallcross *Mrs Deborah Doreen*
Court Clerk, North Sefton Magistrates'Court, The Law Courts, Albert road, Southport PR9 0LJ, 01704 534141, Fax: 01704 500226, Call Date: Feb 1991 (Middle Temple) Qualifications: LLB (L'pool)

Edgell *Mrs Shobha Goriah*
Magistrates' Court Clerk, Justices' Clerk's Office, The Court House, Civic Centre, St Peter Street, St Albans AL1 3LB, 01727 816823/36, Fax: 01727 816829, Call Date: July 1988 (Inner Temple) Qualifications: LLB (Wales)

Edila *Ms Gifty*
Head of Legal Services, Legal Division, London Borough of Newham, Barking Road, London E6 2RP, 0181 472 1430 x 23003, Fax: 0181 472 0480, and Member Nigerian Bar, Call Date: July 1979 (Inner Temple) Qualifications: LLB,LLM (Lond)

Edlington *Crawford Ian Anthony*
Call Date: Nov 1997 (Middle Temple) Qualifications: LLB (Hons)

Edmonds *Mrs Vanessa Moragh* •
Legal Advisor, Call Date: July 1994 (Lincoln's Inn) Qualifications: LLB (Hons, Bucks)

Edney *Miss Sarah Mary*
Call Date: July 1982 (Inner Temple) Qualifications: MA (Oxon)

Edusei *John Roger* •
Associate at Andrade & Co, Bank Chambers, 48 Onslow Gardens, London SW7 3AH, 0171 581 2871, Fax: 0171 581 0275, Call Date: Oct 1991 (Gray's Inn) Qualifications: LLB (Lond)

Edward Jnr *Fred*
Cain & Abel Law Firm, 239 Missenden, Inville Road, London SE17 2HX, 0171 701 2327, Fax: 0171 201 2327, Call Date: Nov 1996 (Lincoln's Inn) Qualifications: LLB (Hons), LLM (Lond)

Edwards *Miss Anna Charlotte*
Call Date: Nov 1998 (Inner Temple) Qualifications: LLB, LLM (LSE)

Edwards *Miss Benita Ava*
Call Date: Oct 1997 (Middle Temple) Qualifications: LLB (Hons)(Lond)

Edwards *David Charles* •
Senior Lawyer, The Greenalls Group plc, Wilderspool House, Greenalls Avenue, Warrington WA4 6RH, 01925 51234, Fax: 01925 244957, Call Date: Nov 1978 (Gray's Inn) Qualifications: LLB (Nottm)

Edwards *David William* •
Senior Crown Prosecutor, Crown Prosecution Service, River Park House, 225 High Road, London N22 4HQ, 0181 888 8889, Fax: 0181 365 7752, Call Date: July 1988 (Middle Temple) Qualifications: LLB (Hons)

Edwards *Miss Jane Grace Wyn* •
Garretts Law Firm, 180 Strand, London WC2R 2NN, Call Date: Nov 1994 (Lincoln's Inn) Qualifications: BA (Hons)(Belfast), MA (Durham), Dip in Law (City)

Edwards *Jonathan Leighton*
Call Date: Oct 1997 (Gray's Inn) Qualifications: LLB (Wales)

Edwards *Miss Judith Caroline* •
Tax Consultant, Tusons, 29/30 Newbury Street, London EC1A 7HU, 0171 600 0203, Fax: 0171 600 0795, Call Date: Nov 1989 (Inner Temple) Qualifications: BA (Dunelm)

Edwards *Miss Julie*
Call Date: July 1992 (Gray's Inn) Qualifications: LLB (Wales)

Edwards *Mrs Katherine Louise* •
Executive Director & Counsel, Goldman Sachs International, Peterborough Court, 133 Fleet Street, London EC4A 2BB, 0171 774 6354, Fax: 0171 774 1313, Call Date: July 1987 (Inner Temple) Qualifications: BA Sheffield

Edwards *Miss Luisa Francesca*
Theodore Goddard Solicitors, 150 Aldersgate Street, London EC1A 4EJ, 0171 606 8855, Fax: 0171 606 4390, Call Date: Oct 1992 (Lincoln's Inn) Qualifications: MA (Hons) (Oxon), Lic.Spec Dr Eur, (Brussels)

Edwards *Martin Russell*
Court Clerk, Call Date: Nov 1992 (Lincoln's Inn) Qualifications: LLB (Hons)

Edwards *Michael George* •
Crown Prosecution Service, C/O 50
Ludgate Hill, London EC4M 7EX, Call
Date: Feb 1988 (Lincoln's Inn)
Qualifications: LLB (UC Wales)

Edwards *Miss Patricia Anne* •
Legal Director, Office of Fair Trading,
Office of Fair Trading, Field House,
15-25 Bream's Buildings, London
EC4A 1PR, Call Date: July 1967 (Middle
Temple) Qualifications: LLB

Edwards *Peter Alfred Howard* •
Employment Law Consultant, Call Date:
Oct 1996 (Inner Temple) Qualifications:
LLB (Hons)

Edwards *Mrs Sheila Therese Sarah* •
Senior Crown Prosecutor, Crown
Prosecution Service, Chippenham,
Wiltshire SN15 1BN, 01249 443443, Call
Date: Nov 1980 (Gray's Inn)
Qualifications: LLB Hons

Edwards *Steven John* •
Senior Lawyer, Abbey National Treasury,
Services plc, Legal & Documentation,
Abbey House, Baker Street, London
NW1 6XL, 0171 612 4487, Fax: 0171 612
4581, Call Date: Oct 1995 (Inner
Temple) Qualifications: BA, LLB

Edwards *Mrs Susan* •
Assistant Director, Legal Services, Office
of the Solicitor, Dept of Health & Social,
Security, New Court, 48 Carey Street,
London WC2A 2LS, 0171 412 1402, Call
Date: Nov 1972 (Gray's Inn)
Qualifications: LLB (Lond)

Edwards *Miss Teresa Louise*
Call Date: Oct 1996 (Lincoln's Inn)
Qualifications: LLB (Hons)(L'pool)

Efstathiou *Miss Antigoni*
Call Date: May 1995 (Inner Temple)
Qualifications: LLB (Wales)

Eidinow *John Allan Lindsay*
68 North Road, London N6, 0181 340
0835, Call Date: May 1961 (Middle
Temple) Qualifications: MA, LLM
(Cantab)

Eimer *Mrs Vivien Ruth*
Call Date: Nov 1969 (Gray's Inn)
Qualifications: LLB (Hons)(Leeds)

Ejindu *Mrs Virginia Obiageli* •
Senior Crown Prosecutor, Crown
Prosecution Service, Youth Branch, The
Cooperage, Gainsford Street, London
SE1 2NG, Call Date: July 1987 (Lincoln's
Inn) Qualifications: LLB Hons [Lond],
BL Hons [Nigeria]

Ekwere *Augustine Udo*
Call Date: Oct 1997 (Middle Temple)
Qualifications: LLB (Hons)(Lond)

Elahi *Rizwan* •
Crown Prosecution Service, Horseferry
Road & Thames Branc, 4th Floor, 50
Ludgate Hill, London EC4M 7EX, 0171
273 8000, Fax: 0171 273 1488, Call
Date: May 1990 (Middle Temple)
Qualifications: LLB (Hons)

Elcock *Julian Edward* •
Senior Crown Prosecutor, St George's
House, Lever Street, Wolverhampton,
West Midlands, 01902 870900, Call Date:
Oct 1992 (Middle Temple)
Qualifications: LLB (Hons)

Eldridge *Mark Graham*
Justices' Chief Executive & Joint Justices'
Clerk, Warwickshire Magistrates', Courts
Committee, PO Box 16, Leamington Spa,
Warwickshire CV32 4XG, 01926 883350,
Fax: 01926 335051, Call Date: Nov 1975
(Gray's Inn) Qualifications: LLB

Eliot Smith *Ms Valerie* •
Senior Crown Prosecutor, Crown
Prosecution Service, River Park House,
8th Floor, 225 High Road, Wood Green,
London N22, 1181 888 8889, Call Date:
Nov 1987 (Gray's Inn) Qualifications: BA
(Lond), Dip Law

Elkeles *Mrs Arran*
11 Askew Road, Moor Park, Northwood,
Middlesex HA6 2JE, 01923 827341, Call
Date: July 1969 (Gray's Inn)
Qualifications: MA, MIPD

Elkin *Alexander*
70 Apsley House, Finchley Road, St
John's Wood, London NW8 ONZ, 0171
483 2475, Call Date: June 1937 (Middle
Temple) Qualifications: LLM (Lond) Dr
jur, (Kiel)

Elkington *Mrs Annabel Louise*
Lecturer, Call Date: Oct 1996 (Gray's
Inn) Qualifications: MA (Edinburgh),
Dip Law

Elles *Baroness Diana Louie*
3 Verulam Buildings, London, WC1R
5NT, Call Date: June 1956 (Lincoln's
Inn) Qualifications: BA (Lond)

Ellinas *Miss Evanthia*
Call Date: Nov 1995 (Inner Temple)
Qualifications: LLB (Lond)

Elliott *Miss Catherine* •
Call Date: Nov 1990 (Lincoln's Inn)
Qualifications: LLB (B'ham)

Elliott *John Mark* •
Principal Crown Prosecutor, Crown
Prosecution Service, Justian House,
Spitfire Close, Ermine Business Park,
Huntingdon Cambs, 01480 432333, Call
Date: Nov 1978 (Gray's Inn)
Qualifications: BA (Keele)

Elliott *Miss Tracey Ann*
Call Date: July 1986 (Gray's Inn)
Qualifications: LLB Birmingham

Ellis *David Leon*
Head of Product Development, Gartmore
Investment Management, 16-18
Monument Street, London EC3R 8AJ,
Call Date: July 1981 (Gray's Inn)
Qualifications: MA (Cantab), LLM (Lond)

Ellis *Edward David*
Attorney in Guyana Attorney in New York,
and Member Guyana Bar New York Bar,
Call Date: July 1979 (Lincoln's Inn)
Qualifications: BA

Ellis *Mrs Edwina Francesca* •
Principal Legal Advisor, Stratford
Magistrates' Court, The Courthouse,
389-397 High Street, Stratford, London
E15 4SB, 0181 522 5000, Fax: 0181 519
9214, Call Date: Nov 1984 (Middle
Temple) Qualifications: BA (Hons)

Ellis *Professor Evelyn Daphne* •
Professor of Public Law, Faculty of Law,
University of Birmingham, Edgbaston,
Birmingham B15 2TT, 0121 414 6306,
Call Date: Nov 1972 (Middle Temple)
Qualifications: MA, LLM, PhD

Ellis *Patrick John Cleverly*
Call Date: May 1965 (Gray's Inn)
Qualifications: MA (Oxon)

Ellis *Paul David d'Andria*
Senior Court Clerk, Ealing Magistrates
Court, The Court House, Green Man
Lane, West Ealing, London W13 OSD,
0181 579 9311, Fax: 0181 579 2935,
Call Date: Nov 1990 (Inner Temple)
Qualifications: LLB (Lond)

Ellis *Ralph Lewis*
Nettle Beds, Old Alresford, Hants
SO24 9RF, 01962 734761, Call Date: July
1972 (Middle Temple) Qualifications:
LLB, FCIArb, MILDM, FCIPS

Ellis *Miss Rebecca Lisa* •
Law Commission, Conquest House, 37/
38 John Street, Theobalds Road, London
WC1N, 0171 453 1221, Fax: 0171 453
1297, Call Date: Nov 1992 (Inner
Temple) Qualifications: BA (Oxon), BCL

Ellis *William Rowland* •
Managing Director, Temple Lectures Ltd,
Charter House, Bexhill-on-Sea, East
Sussex TN40 1JA, 01424 212021, Fax:
01424 730074, Call Date: Nov 1976
(Gray's Inn) Qualifications: LLB Lond

Ellison *Ms Alice Louise*
Call Date: Oct 1994 (Gray's Inn)
Qualifications: LLB (Manch)

Ellison *John Anthony*
c/o Conyers Dill & Pearman, Clarendon
House, Church Street, Hamilton HM CX,
441 295-1422, Fax: 441 292-4720, and
Member Bahamas Bar Bermuda Bar,
Call Date: 1957 (Inner Temple)
Qualifications: MA

Elliston *Miss Sarah Joanne*
Lecturer in Medical Law, Medical Law
Unit, School of Law, Stair Building,
University of Glasgow, Glasgow G12 8QQ,
0141 339 8855 x 3528/2966, Fax: 0141
330 4698, Call Date: Feb 1993 (Lincoln's
Inn) Qualifications: MA (Hons), LLM

Elphick *Timothy*
Publisher, 23 Lilyville Road, London
SW6 5DP, 0171 371 8532, Call Date: Nov
1988 (Middle Temple) Qualifications:
MA (Cantab)

Elphicke *Brett Charles Anthony*
Wilde Sapte, 1 Fleet Street, London, 0171
246 7676, Fax: 0171 246 7777, Call
Date: Nov 1994 (Middle Temple)
Qualifications: LLB (Hons)

Elsey *Derek William* •
Head of Legal Services, Division of
Legal Services, Secretriat, University of
Teesside, Middlesbrough, Cleveland,
01642 218121 X2027/342027, Fax:
01642 342067 or 342071, Call Date:
July 1980 (Middle Temple)
Qualifications: LLB(Hons) (Wales)

Ely *Jonathan Michael Charles*
Call Date: Apr 1991 (Gray's Inn)
Qualifications: LLB

Emanuel *Miss Justina Omowunmi*
Call Date: Nov 1990 (Inner Temple)
Qualifications: BA (Kent)

Emberton *Miss Judith Elizabeth* •
Call Date: Oct 1992 (Middle Temple)
Qualifications: LL.B (Hons, Nott'm)

Emerson *Mrs Emerson Tina Mary*
Emilestream, Henfield Road, Upper
Beeding, West Sussex BN44 3TF, 01903
813729, Fax: 01903 813729, Call Date:
July 1992 (Lincoln's Inn)
Qualifications: LLB (Hons) (Lond)

Emerton *Lieutenant Commander Mark
Simon* •
Naval Officer Advocate, DNSC, Room
215, Victory Building, H M Naval Base,
Portsmouth PO1 3LS, 01705 727246,
Fax: 01705 727175, Call Date: Oct
1991 (Gray's Inn) Qualifications: MA
(Oxon), Dip Law (City), MIMgt, FRGS

Emeruwa *John* •
Legal Advisor, Department of Trade &
Industry, Ashdown House, 123 Victoria
Street, London SW1E 6RB, 0171 215
6979, Call Date: July 1989 (Inner
Temple) Qualifications: LLM (S'ton)

Emmanuel *Ms Christine Lorna*
Call Date: July 1995 (Lincoln's Inn)
Qualifications: LLB (Hons)

Emmanuel *Miss Eileen Elizabeth*
Call Date: Nov 1990 (Gray's Inn)
Qualifications: LLB (Bristol)

Emodi *Miss Rosemary*
Call Date: Feb 1994 (Inner Temple)
Qualifications: LLB, LLM (Lond)

Empson *Gordon Everett*
28A Herschell Square, Walmer, Kent
CT14 7SF, 01304 239335, Call Date:
Nov 1948 (Middle Temple)

Emson *Raymond Neal*
Call Date: Nov 1994 (Middle Temple)
Qualifications: B.Sc (Hons), LLB
(Hons)

Endicott *David Nigel*
Call Date: Feb 1994 (Lincoln's Inn)
Qualifications: LLB (Hons, Bucks)

England *James* •
Branch Crown Prosecutor, Central
Casework, Crown Prosecution Service,
50 Ludgate Hill, London EC4M 7EX,
Call Date: July 1981 (Gray's Inn)
Qualifications: LLB (Lond)

English *Ms Helen Warnock*
32 Ellington Street, London N7 8PL,
0171 607 1628, Fax: 0171 609 6451,
Phi Beta Kappa and Member New York
Bar (Called 1979), Call Date: May 1988
(Middle Temple) Qualifications: BA,
Juris Doctor (US), Dip Law (City)

English *Miss Katherine Louise*
Call Date: Oct 1994 (Gray's Inn)
Qualifications: LLB (Manch)

English *Lawrence James* •
Prosecution Team Leader, Crown
Prosecution Service, Level 3, Beaumont
House, Cliftonville, Northampton
NN1 5PE, 01604 230220 x 136, Fax:
01604 232081, Call Date: Nov 1988
(Lincoln's Inn) Qualifications: LLB
(Nott'm)

English *Ms Rosalind Catherine*
Part-time BBC Presenter Lecturer in
Law, Merton College, Oxford, 15
Fentiman Road, London SW8 1LF,
0171 582 7592, Fax: 0171 793 8741,
Former Solicitor, Call Date: July 1993
(Gray's Inn) Qualifications: MA, LLM

Enright *Guy Thomas*
Call Date: Nov 1993 (Middle Temple)
Qualifications: BA (Hons) (Oxon)

Entwistle *Miss Janet Anne Catherine* •
Call Date: July 1984 (Gray's Inn)
Qualifications: BA (Keele), LLM (Lond)

Entwistle *John Reid*
Call Date: Nov 1995 (Gray's Inn)
Qualifications: LLB

Entwistle *Robert Mark*
Call Date: May 1997 (Lincoln's Inn)
Qualifications: LLB (Hons) (Lond),
B.Tech, FRICS, FCIOB, FCIArb, FFB

Envis *Gary*
Eastern Caribbean, Call Date: Nov 1992
(Inner Temple) Qualifications: LLB

Erdeljan *Branislav*
Call Date: Oct 1991 (Inner Temple)
Qualifications: LLB, LLM (Lond)

Ershad *Miss Jennifer*
Call Date: Oct 1994 (Middle Temple)
Qualifications: LLB (Hons) (Lond)

Ershad *Sheikh Monsore Habib*
Deputy Chief Clerk, Inner London
Magistrates', Courts Service, 3rd Floor,
North West Wing, Bush House,
Aldwych, London WC2B 4PJ, Call Date:
Nov 1988 (Middle Temple)
Qualifications: LLB

Erskine *Alexander Jude*
Assistant Director (Legal &
Compliance) Deputy Company
Secretary, Call Date: Nov 1996 (Inner
Temple) Qualifications: LLB (Wales)

Esmail *Miss Lubna*
Call Date: Mar 1997 (Inner Temple)
Qualifications: BA

Esparon *Miss Nichole Denise*
Call Date: Nov 1998 (Lincoln's Inn)
Qualifications: LLB (Hons) (Middx)

Espiner *Miss Claire Anne*
Call Date: Oct 1995 (Middle Temple)
Qualifications: BA (Hons)

Essayan *Michael*
Also Inn of Court L, Call Date: Feb 1957
(Middle Temple) Qualifications: MA
(Oxon)

Essien *Carl Anthony Ekong*
Leasehold Advisor, Leasehold
Enfranchisement, Advisory Service, 8
Maddox Street, London W1R 9PN, 0171
493 3116, Fax: 0171 493 4318, Call
Date: Oct 1991 (Gray's Inn)
Qualifications: LLB (Bucks), LLM
(Lond)

Essien *Mrs Olive* •
Call Date: July 1990 (Gray's Inn)
Qualifications: LLB

Etherton *Michael Robert*
Call Date: July 1996 (Middle Temple)
Qualifications: BA (Hons) (Oxon), LTCL

Eubank *Miss Nicole Ruth*
Call Date: Oct 1997 (Middle Temple)
Qualifications: LLB (Hons) (Lond)

Evans *Alastair Mackenzie*
Manager, International Affairs, Lloyd's
of London, 1 Lime Street, London
EC3M 7HA, 0171 327 6682, Fax: 0171
327 5255, Call Date: Feb 1995 (Inner
Temple) Qualifications: MA (Oxon),
LLB (Lond), A.C.I.S., A.C.I.I.

Evans *Miss Alison* •
Senior Legal Adviser, West Glamorgan
Magistrates', Courts Committee, West
Wales, Call Date: Nov 1991 (Gray's Inn)
Qualifications: LLB

Evans *Mrs Carole Patricia* •
CPS (Birmingham), Colmore Gate, 2
Colmore Row, Birmingham B3 2QA,
0121 629 7200, Call Date: Oct 1997
(Gray's Inn) Qualifications: BA
(Middx), LLB (Anglia)

Evans *Christian William Philip Roe*
Call Date: May 1996 (Gray's Inn)
Qualifications: LLB (Hull)

Evans *Edward Owen* •
Legal Officer, University of Salford,
Salford M5 4WT, 0161 295 5035, Fax:
0161 295 5016, Call Date: May 1987
(Lincoln's Inn) Qualifications: LLB
(Lond), LLM (Lond), FCIS, ACIArb

Evans *Miss Gwawr*
Call Date: Mar 1996 (Inner Temple)
Qualifications: LLB (Wales)

Evans *Gwilym Thomas*
18 The Rath, Milford Haven, Dyfed
SA73 2QA, Call Date: Feb 1973 (Middle
Temple) Qualifications: Extra Master,
(Mariner)

Evans *Ian Michael Probyn*
Bridge Farm House, Chelsworth,
Ipswich, Suffolk IP7 7HX, Call Date:
Feb 1955 (Inner Temple)
Qualifications: BCL, MA (Oxon)

Evans *James Martin Crispin* •
Director of Legal & Business Affairs,
Polygram International Music,
Publishing Ltd, 8 St James Square,
London SW1Y 4JU, 0171 747 4000, Fax:
0171 747 4467, Call Date: July 1977
(Inner Temple) Qualifications: B.A.

Evans *Jeremy Mark*
Call Date: Nov 1998 (Lincoln's Inn)
Qualifications: LLB (Hons)(Leics)

Evans *Jeremy Roger*
10 Barbara Nard Court, Brockway Close,
Leytonstone, London E11 4TF, 0181 539
3316, Call Date: Nov 1997 (Middle
Temple) Qualifications: BSc
(Hons)(Sheff)

Evans *Jonathan Dominic David*
46/48 Essex Street, London, WC2R 3GH,
Call Date: Oct 1990 (Gray's Inn)
Qualifications: LLB

Evans *Mrs Judith Anne*
Addleshaw Booth & Co, Sovereign House,
P.O.Box 8, Sovereign Street, Leeds
LS1 1HQ, 0113 209 2000, Fax: 0113 209
2060, Call Date: July 1998 (Gray's Inn)
Qualifications: LLB (N'castle)

Evans *Nicholas John*
Call Date: Nov 1997 (Gray's Inn)
Qualifications: LLB, LLM (Warw)

Evans *Miss Penelope Caroline* •
Legal Advisor, BBC, British Broadcasting,
Corporation, 201 Wood Lane, London
W12 7TS, 0181 752 5734, Fax: 0181 752
5080, Call Date: July 1987 (Gray's Inn)
Qualifications: BA (Durham)

Evans *Mrs Penelope Susan*
Senior Court Clerk, The Court House,
Oldbury Ringway, Oldbury, Warley, West
Midlands B69 4JN, 0121 511 2222, Fax:
0121 544 8492, Call Date: Feb 1993
(Gray's Inn) Qualifications: LLB
(B'ham)

Evans *Peter Norman*
01703 252667, Fax: 01703 252667, and
Member New York Bar, Call Date: May
1963 (Gray's Inn) Qualifications: MA
(Oxon)

Evans *Peter William* •
Legal Services, Department of Trade &
Industry, 10 Victoria Street, London
SW1H 0NN, 0171 215 3176, Fax: 0171
215 3221, Call Date: Nov 1994 (Middle
Temple) Qualifications: BA (Hons)

Evans *Robert James Francis*
Call Date: Nov 1975 (Middle Temple)
Qualifications: LLB

Evans *Mrs Sally Anne* •
Deputy Legal Adviser, The Home Office,
50 Queen Anne's Gate, London
SW1H 9AT, Call Date: Feb 1971 (Gray's
Inn) Qualifications: LLB

Evans *Miss Sian Amanda*
Call Date: Oct 1997 (Lincoln's Inn)
Qualifications: LLB (Hons)(Greenwic),
LLM (Lond)

Evans *Miss Susan*
Call Date: Nov 1992 (Inner Temple)
Qualifications: LLB (Hull)

Evans *William James*
Attridges Solicitors, 436 High Road,
Tottenham, London N17 9JB, Call Date:
Nov 1988 (Middle Temple)
Qualifications: LLB (L'pool)

Evans *Sir (William) Vincent John*
4 Bedford Road, Moor Park, Northwood,
Middlesex HA6 2BB, 01923 824085, Call
Date: June 1939 (Lincoln's Inn)
Qualifications: MA, BCL (Hons)

Evans-Lombe *Miss Sarah Frances*
Call Date: Nov 1992 (Inner Temple)
Qualifications: LLB (Bris)

Everett *Henry Wentworth*
Call Date: Mar 1996 (Gray's Inn)
Qualifications: BA (Reading)

Everington *Dr Anthony Herbert*
GP, Stepney, London, 28 Rhondda Grove,
London E3 5AP, 0181 981 6996, Call
Date: July 1978 (Gray's Inn)
Qualifications: MB, BS, MRCGP

Everson *Mrs Susan Lilian*
2 Fernsdale Cottages, Rays Lane, Tylers
Green Common, Penn, Bucks
HP10 8LH, 0149 481 4637, Call Date:
July 1988 (Middle Temple)
Qualifications: LLB (Hons)

Eveson *Trevor John*
Call Date: Feb 1986 (Gray's Inn)

Ewen *Mrs Lorna Sylvia* •
Principal Crown Prosecutor (part time),
Crown Prosecution Service, 1st Floor,
The Cooperage, 8 Gainsford Street,
London SE1 2NE, 0171 357 7010, Fax:
0171 962 0906, Call Date: Nov 1983
(Gray's Inn) Qualifications: BA, LLB

Ewing *Ms Michelle* •
Treasury Solicitor, Queen Anne's
Chambers, 28 Broadway, London
SW1H 9JS, 0171 210 3382, Fax: 0171
210 3132, Call Date: Oct 1994 (Middle
Temple) Qualifications: BA
(Hons)(Oxon), LLM (Canada)

Exton *Miss Lesley Mary*
Call Date: Oct 1992 (Middle Temple)
Qualifications: BA(Oxon), LLB(Lond)

Eyeington *Miss Louise Rebecca* •
Legal Adviser, Dept of Environment,
Transport, & the Regions, 76 Marsham
Street, London SW1, 0171 271 4421,
Fax: 0171 271 4496, Call Date: Nov 1993
(Inner Temple) Qualifications: LLB
(Warw)

Eyles *Alan James* •
C/O CPS Headquarters, 50 Ludgate Hill,
London EC4M 7EX, 0171 273 8000, Call
Date: Feb 1989 (Gray's Inn)
Qualifications: LLB

Eyre *Edward*
1 Serjeants' Inn, 5th Floor, Fleet Street,
Temple, London, EC4Y 1LH, Call Date:
July 1957 (Inner Temple) Qualifications:
LLB (Harvard)

Eyre *Philip James*
Call Date: Nov 1994 (Middle Temple)
Qualifications: LLB (Hons), ARICS

Eyres *Raymond John* •
Director & Company Secretary,
Cummins Engine Co Ltd, 46-50 Coombe
Rd, New Malden, Surrey KT3 4QL, 0181
700 6920, Fax: 0181 949 5604, Call
Date: Nov 1973 (Inner Temple)
Qualifications: LLB, MA, MBA

Eze *Miss Ugoji Adanma*
and Member Nigerian Bar, Call Date: Oct
1994 (Gray's Inn) Qualifications: BA

Ezekiel *Solomon Jonathan*
Call Date: Nov 1993 (Lincoln's Inn)
Qualifications: LLB (Hons)

Fadden *Dr Kathleen*
0171 367 3000, Fax: 0171 367 2000,
Call Date: Oct 1993 (Inner Temple)
Qualifications: BSc, PhD, LLB

Fahy *Ms Sheila Catherine Elise*
Call Date: Nov 1994 (Inner Temple)
Qualifications: LLB (Lond)

Faiers *Andrew Clive* •
Lawyer, Crown Prosecution Service, 50
Ludgate Hill, London EC4, Call Date: July
1976 (Gray's Inn)

Fainer *Miss Geraldine*
Room W234, Royal Courts of Justice,
Strand, London WC2, Law Reporter, Call
Date: Nov 1985 (Middle Temple)
Qualifications: LLB

Fairclough *Murray Simon Charles* •
General Manager of Legal Services, Abbey
Legal Protection Limited, 17 Lansdowne
Road, Croyson, Surrey CR0 2BX, 0181
730 6000, Fax: 0181 730 6001, Call
Date: Nov 1993 (Inner Temple)
Qualifications: LLB, LLM

Fairman *Miss Johanna Kirsty Abegail*
Call Date: Oct 1996 (Lincoln's Inn)
Qualifications: LLB (Hons)(Lond)

Fais *Robert Ismail*
Call Date: Nov 1997 (Gray's Inn)
Qualifications: BA (Exon)

Falconer of Thoroton *Lord*
Recorder, Fountain Court, Temple,
London, EC4Y 9DH, Call Date: July 1974
(Inner Temple) Qualifications: MA
(Cantab)

Falk *Andrew Michael Pope* •
Solicitor to the Metropolitan, Police, New
Scotland, Broadway, London SW1, Call
Date: Nov 1977 (Inner Temple)
Qualifications: MA (Cantab)

Faloon *Miss Nicola Jane*
Call Date: July 1998 (Lincoln's Inn)
Qualifications: BA (Hons)

Falsafi *Miss Laya*
Legal Associate, Pullig & Co Solicitors,
Bridewell House, 9 Bridewell Place,
London EC4V 6AP, 0171 353 0505, Call
Date: Feb 1991 (Lincoln's Inn)
Qualifications: LLB (Buck'ham)

Falshaw *William Fredrick* •
Senior Crown Prosecutor, Crown
Prosecution Service, Level 3, Beaumont
House, Cliftonville, Northampton
NN1 5BN, 01604 230220, Fax: 01604
232081, Call Date: July 1987 (Inner
Temple) Qualifications: Dip Law (City),
BA (Hons)

Fanner *Roger Martin*
Deputy Clerk to the Justices, The Court
House, Homer Road, Solihull B91 3RD,
0121 705 8101, Fax: 0121 711 2045,
Call Date: July 1978 (Gray's Inn)

Fanning *Miss Claire Elizabeth* •
Call Date: Oct 1993 (Lincoln's Inn)
Qualifications: BA (Hons)(Lond), CPE
(Lond)

Faraway *Michael John David*
Call Date: Nov 1971 (Middle Temple)

Farazi *Shahin*
Call Date: Mar 1997 (Lincoln's Inn)
Qualifications: BA (Hons)(L'pool), MA,
MPhil (Kent), CPE (Lond)

Farley *Peter John* •
Legal Director & Company Secretary,
Fiat Auto (UK) Ltd, Fiat House, 266
Bath Road, Slough, Berks SL1 4HJ,
01753 511431, Fax: 01753 511506,
Call Date: July 1982 (Middle Temple)
Qualifications: BA (Hons), LLM (Lond)

Farmer *David George*
Call Date: Oct 1996 (Middle Temple)
Qualifications: LLB (Hons) (Leics)

Farmiloe *Mrs Collette Marie* •
Assistant Group Legal Advisor Burton
Group Plc, The Burton Group Plc, 214
Oxford Street, London W1N 9DF, Call
Date: Nov 1990 (Middle Temple)
Qualifications: BA (PCL)

Farnsworth *Miss Joanne*
Professional Support Lawyer, 59 St
Martin's Lane, London WC2N 4JS, 0171
379 4441, Fax: 0171 240 3982, and
Member Canadian Bar, Call Date: May
1983 (Middle Temple) Qualifications:
BA (Hons), LLB, LLM (Lond)

Farooq *Mohammed Khan* •
Senior Lawyer, Dudley Metropolitan
Borough, Council, Legal & Property
Services, 3 St James Road, Dudley
DY1 1HL, 01384 815333, Fax: 01384
815325, Call Date: Oct 1993 (Lincoln's
Inn) Qualifications: LLB (Hons)(Warw)

Farr *Adam Rufus*
Call Date: Oct 1997 (Middle Temple)
Qualifications: BA (Hons)(Loughbor),
CPE (Middx)

Farr *Alastair Richard*
Trett Consulting, Cap House, 9-12 Long
Lane, London EC1A 9HA, 0171 600
2211, Fax: 0171 600 3818, Call Date:
Oct 1995 (Middle Temple)
Qualifications: LLB (Hons)

Farr *Sebastian Charles Arthur David* •
Legal Adviser, Office of
Telecommunications, 50 Ludgate Hill,
London, Belgium EC4M 7JJ, 02 511
7270, Fax: 02 513 4220, Call Date: July
1981 (Gray's Inn) Qualifications: BA

Farran *Ms Denise Margaret*
Call Date: Mar 1996 (Gray's Inn)
Qualifications: B.Soc.Sci, MA, PhD,
(Manch)

Farrar *John Jewell*
22 Sylvan Way, West Wickham, Kent
BR4 9HB, Call Date: July 1970 (Gray's
Inn) Qualifications: Chartered Chemist,
Fellow, Royal Soc of, Chemistry &
Royal, Soc of Arts

Farren *Brendan Martin* •
Citibank International plc, St Martin's
House, 1 Grove Road, Hammersmith,
London W6 0NY, 0171 500 3814, Call
Date: Nov 1988 (Middle Temple)
Qualifications: LLB (Warwick)

Farren *Joseph Michael* •
Executive, Corporate Finance, Robert
Fleming & Co Limited, 25 Copthall
Avenue, London EC2R 7DR, 0171 382
8224, Fax: 0171 638 9110, Call Date:
Mar 1997 (Lincoln's Inn)
Qualifications: BA (Hons) (Oxon)

Farrer *Miss Angela Jane*
Call Date: Oct 1998 (Inner Temple)
Qualifications: BA (Oxon), CPE (City)

Farrington *Ms Gemma* •
Kent County Council, Legal Services, 27
Castle Street, Canterbury CT1 2PZ,
01227 767020, Fax: 01227 780671,
Call Date: Oct 1994 (Gray's Inn)
Qualifications: BA

Farthing *Richard Bruce Crosby*
Commander Royal Norwegian Order of
Merit, 44 St George's Drive, London
SW1V 4BT, 0171 834 1211, Fax: 0171
834 1211, Call Date: Feb 1954 (Inner
Temple) Qualifications: MA (Cantab) ,
FIMgt

Fateh *Anatul*
General Counsel, KAFCO Limited
Dhaka, Consultant, Beale and
Company, London, KAFCO Limited,
GPO Box 3049, Uttara Bank Building,
15th F, 90-91 Motijeel Commercial
Area, Dhaka 1000, 00 880 2 956 5055/
56, Fax: 00 880 2 956 5060, and
Member Bangladesh Bar, Call Date:
Feb 1983 (Lincoln's Inn)
Qualifications: BSc (Econ)(LSE), Dip
Law (City)

Faulkner *Miss Angela Elizabeth* •
Legal Services Manager, CGU Life, 2
Rougier Street, York YO1 1HR, 01904
452403, Fax: 01904 452422, Call Date:
Nov 1988 (Middle Temple)
Qualifications: LLB (L'pool)

Faulkner *Robert Michael*
Call Date: Oct 1997 (Lincoln's Inn)
Qualifications: LLB (Hons)(B'ham)

Faulkner *Mrs Sabrina Louise* •
Official Solicitor of, The Supreme
Court, 81 Chancery Lane, London
WC2A 1DD, 0171 911 7124, Fax: 0171
911 7105, Call Date: July 1974 (Gray's
Inn)

Fawcett *Miss Alison Jane*
Call Date: Nov 1992 (Lincoln's Inn)
Qualifications: BA (Hons)(Wales)

Fawcett *Miss Donna Marie*
Customer Services Manager/ Board
Secretary, Lincolnshire Health
Authority, Cross O'Cliff, Bracebridge
Heath, Lincolnshire LN4 2HN, 01522
515326, Call Date: Feb 1994 (Gray's
Inn) Qualifications: LLB

Fayers *Roger Darley*
UK Delegate on Uncitral Working
Group, 16 Grove Way, Esher, Surrey
KT10 8HL, 0181 398 4744, Fax: 0181
398 8284, Call Date: July 1966 (Middle
Temple) Qualifications: LLB

Feargrieve *Matthew Adam*
Call Date: Oct 1998 (Lincoln's Inn)
Qualifications: BA (Hons)

Feaster *Miss Trudy Dawn* •
Eversheds, Cloth Hall Court, Infirmary
Street, Leeds LS1 2JB, 0113 243 0391,
Fax: 0113 245 6188, Call Date: Oct
1993 (Inner Temple) Qualifications:
LLB (Warw), Diplome Special en, Droit

Feather *Miss Janet*
Call Date: Nov 1990 (Middle Temple)
Qualifications: LLB (Leic), LLM
(Florence)

Fedrick *Mrs Janet* •
Prosecutor for the Environment
Agency, King Meadows House, Kings
Meadow Road, Reading, Berks
RG1 8DQ, Call Date: Nov 1974 (Gray's
Inn)

Feely *Miss Teresa Mary* •
Senior Crown Prosecutor, Unigate
Centre, Lords Walk, Preston,
Lancashire, 0151 236 7575, Call Date:
Nov 1989 (Gray's Inn) Qualifications:
LLB

Feeney *Thomas Francis Patrick*
Call Date: Nov 1992 (Lincoln's Inn)
Qualifications: LLB (Hons)

Fellas *Miss Thekla Rebecca*
Call Date: Oct 1992 (Middle Temple)
Qualifications: LLB (Hons)

Fellingham *Paul*
Clerk to the Justices, Hertfordshire
Magistrates Crt, Bayley House, Sish
Lane, Stevenage SG1 3SS, 01438
730430, Fax: 01438 730413, Call Date:
Nov 1982 (Middle Temple)
Qualifications: Dip Mag Law

Fenwick *Daniel Fitzgerald*
Call Date: Oct 1993 (Lincoln's Inn)
Qualifications: BA (Hons)(Manc), CPE
(Manc)

Ferguson *Francis John* •
Senior Crown Prosecutor, Crown
Prosecution Service, Haldin House, Old
Bank of England Court, Queen Street,
Norwich NR2 4SX, 01603 666491, Fax:
01603 617989, Call Date: Nov 1992
(Gray's Inn) Qualifications: BA (Hons)

Ferguson *Gerald Patrick*
Court Clerk/Legal Adviser, Bedfordshire
Magistrates Court, St Paul's Square,
Shire Hall, Bedford MK40 1SQ, 01234
359426, Fax: 01234 210607, Call Date:
Nov 1991 (Gray's Inn) Qualifications: BA
(Dub), LLB (Lond)

Ferguson *Gregor James*
Call Date: Nov 1995 (Lincoln's Inn)
Qualifications: BA (Hons), LLM
(Canada), LLM

Ferley *Mrs Joyce Mary*
6 Arran Mews, Crosslands Ave, Ealing,
London W5 3PY, 0181 993 4968, Call
Date: Feb 1964 (Gray's Inn)

Fernandes *John Piedade Amaranto
Lorencio*
Call Date: Nov 1979 (Middle Temple)
Qualifications: LLB, LLM, FT11

Fernandes *Miss Joy Agnes*
Call Date: Oct 1997 (Gray's Inn)
Qualifications: LLB (Lond)

Fernandes *Nicholas John Damian* •
Lawyer, Ministry of Agriculture,,
Fisheries & Food, Legal Dept, 55
Whitehall, London SW1A 2EY, 0171 270
8093, Fax: 0171 270 8096, Call Date:
Nov 1984 (Lincoln's Inn) Qualifications:
LLM, BA, Dip French, Law

Fernando *Hemaka*
Third Floor, 46 Balcombe Street, London
NW1 6ND, 0171 724 1973, Fax: 0171
723 1940, Call Date: July 1983 (Gray's
Inn) Qualifications: LLB (Lond), LLM
(Lond)

Ferrari *Cesare Maria Primo* •
Senior Crown Prosecutor, Crown
Prosecution Service, Bow Street/
Clerkenwell Branch, 4th Floor, 50
Ludgate Hill, London EC4M 7EX, 0171
273 8238, Call Date: Feb 1979 (Middle
Temple) Qualifications: BA (Oxon)

Ferreira *Clive Joaquim* •
Medley, Kingston Hill,
Kingston-Upon-Thames, Surrey KT2 7IU,
Call Date: Nov 1985 (Gray's Inn)
Qualifications: LLB - Hons (Brunel)

Ferrer *Peter Andrew*
Call Date: Oct 1998 (Inner Temple)
Qualifications: BA (Wales), CPE (City)

Field *Mrs Frances Myra*
10 Thornton Way, London NW11 6RY,
Call Date: Nov 1970 (Gray's Inn)

Field *Miss Sally Ann* •
Company Secretary, De La Rue Plc, De
La Rue House, Jays Close, Viables,
Basingstoke, Hampshire RG22 4BS,
01256 329122, Fax: 01256 467106, Call
Date: July 1970 (Gray's Inn)
Qualifications: MA (Cantab)

Field *Terence Robert* •
Legal Advisor, Brown & Root Limited,
Hill Park Court, Springfield Drive,
Leatherhead, Surrey KT24 7NL, 0181
544 5000, Fax: 0181 544 4400, Call
Date: July 1973 (Gray's Inn)
Qualifications: BA (Hons) (Lond)

Field-Fisher *Thomas Gilbert*
Chairman Police Disciplinary Appeal
Tribunal, 2 King's Bench Walk, Temple,
London EC4Y 7DE, 0171 736 4627, 2
King's Bench Walk, Ground Floor,
Temple, London, EC4Y 7DE, Call Date:
Nov 1942 (Middle Temple)
Qualifications: MA (Cantab)

Fielding *Janick Raphael Alexander*
Call Date: Oct 1997 (Inner Temple)
Qualifications: BA (LSE)

Fife *Richard Ian Macduff*
Senior Court Clerk, Nottinghamshire
Magistrates', Carrington Street,
Nottingham NG2 1EE, 0115 955 8111,
Fax: 0115 955 8131, Call Date: July 1973
(Inner Temple)

Figgest *Lee*
Call Date: May 1996 (Lincoln's Inn)
Qualifications: LLB (Hons) (Dunelm)

Finch *Michael Anthony*
Call Date: Nov 1971 (Gray's Inn)
Qualifications: LLB

Findlay *John Harley Sefton Max*
3 Lainson Street, London SW18 5RS,
0181 870 0466, Call Date: Nov 1974
(Middle Temple) Qualifications: MA
(Oxon)

Findlay *Miss Lorna Anne*
Call Date: July 1987 (Middle Temple)
Qualifications: LLB (Edin)

Fine *Miss Pamela Margaret*
Call Date: Nov 1983 (Lincoln's Inn)
Qualifications: LLB (Bristol)

Fine *Mrs Suzanne Joy*
Senior Lecturer, The College of Law, 50/
52 Chancery Lane, London WC2A 1SX,
Queen Elizabeth Bldg, Ground Floor,
Temple, London, EC4Y 9BS, Call Date:
July 1976 (Middle Temple)
Qualifications: BSc (Lond)

Finlason *Dr Elizabeth Wynne* •
The Law Commission, Conquest House,
37-38 John Street, Theobalds Road,
London WC1N 2BQ, 0171 453 1220, Fax:
0171 453 1297, Call Date: July 1978
(Inner Temple) Qualifications: LLB
(Hons), LLM , (Wales),Ph.D (Wales)

Finlay *Fabian John Adam*
Audley House, 9 North Audley Street,
London W1Y 1WF, 0171 629 7821, Fax:
0171 408 1581, Lincoln's Inn Ad
Eundem Jan 1978, Call Date: July 1976
(Middle Temple) Qualifications: LLB,
FCA

Finn *Miss Sally Frances* •
Call Date: Nov 1972 (Gray's Inn)
Qualifications: BA, LLM

Finn *Sean Brendan* •
Call Date: May 1996 (Lincoln's Inn)
Qualifications: LLB (Hons) (L'pool), LLM
(Manc)

Finnegan *Ms Lorna Ann*
Call Date: Feb 1994 (Inner Temple)
Qualifications: BA, LLB (Ireland)

Finney *John Stephen*
Call Date: July 1970 (Middle Temple)
Qualifications: MA (Oxon), Dip Ed

Finney *Mark Matyas Veszy* •
Head of Legal Department Assistant
Director, J Henry Schroder & Co Limited,
Senator House, 85 Queen Victoria Street,
London EC4V 4EJ, 0171 658 3425, Fax:
0171 658 4997, Call Date: Nov 1983
(Gray's Inn) Qualifications: LLB
(Reading)

Finnigan *John Anthony*
Justices' Chief Executive,
Gloucestershire, Magistrates Courts
Committee, The Court House, Gander
Lane, Tewksbury, Gloucestershire
GL20 5TR, 01684 294632, Fax: 01684
274596, Call Date: July 1970 (Gray's
Inn) Qualifications: FIMgt

Firman *Miss Avril Mary*
Call Date: May 1987 (Middle Temple)
Qualifications: LLB, ACIS

Firth *Ms Sarah Maria Eileen*
Call Date: Oct 1997 (Inner Temple)
Qualifications: BA (Essex), CPE

Firth *Miss Sheila Ruth* •
Barnet Magistrates Court, 7c High Street,
Barnet, Herts, Call Date: Nov 1996
(Lincoln's Inn) Qualifications: LLB
(Hons) (Hull)

Fish *James Andrew*
Trade Mark Agent, Page White Farrer, 54
Doughty Street, London WC1N 2LS, 0171
831 7929, Fax: 0171 831 8040, Call
Date: Nov 1996 (Inner Temple)
Qualifications: LLB (Huddersfield), LLM
(Manch)

Fisher *Miss Brigitte Jane*
Call Date: Nov 1991 (Inner Temple)
Qualifications: LLB, LLM

Fisher *Charles Nicholas*
and Member New Mexico Bar 4 Brick
Court, Ground Floor, Temple, London,
EC4Y 9AD, Call Date: Nov 1973 (Middle
Temple) Qualifications: BA (Oxon)

Fisher *John Charles*
Call Date: Nov 1995 (Inner Temple)
Qualifications: BA (Kent)

Fitzgerald *Miss Elizabeth Anne* •
Call Date: July 1982 (Inner Temple)
Qualifications: LLB (Hull), LLM (Lond)

FitzGerald *John William*
Call Date: Oct 1998 (Inner Temple)
Qualifications: BA (Lond), CPE
(W'Minster)

Fitzgibbon *Terence*
Executive Director, James R Knowles,
43 The Parade, Roath, Cardiff CF2 3AB,
01222 471144, Fax: 01222 471658,
Call Date: Nov 1995 (Lincoln's Inn)
Qualifications: LLB (Hons) (Wales),
BSc (Hons) (Aston), ARICS , FCI Arb

Fitzlyon *Ms Anastasia Catya*
Call Date: Nov 1982 (Gray's Inn)
Qualifications: LLB (Lond)

Fitzpatrick *Desmond Christopher* •
Corporation of Lloyds, 1 Lime Street,
London EC3M 7HA, Call Date: July
1983 (Inner Temple) Qualifications:
BA (York), Dip in law , Post-graduate
Dip in, Law (Lond)

Fitzpatrick *John Anthony* •
Legal Adviser, Legal Services Dept,
International Stock Exchange, The
Tower, Old Broad Street, London
EC2N 1HP, Call Date: Nov 1983 (Gray's
Inn) Qualifications: BA, LLB

Fitzpatrick *Ross Antony*
Call Date: July 1972 (Middle Temple)

Fitzsimmons *Roy Dunsmore* •
Sales & Marketing Director, William
Ransom & Son plc, Bancroft, Hitchin,
Herts SG5 1LY, 01462 437615, Fax:
01462 420528, Call Date: Nov 1982
(Lincoln's Inn) Qualifications: B
Pharm (Brad) , LLB (Lond), MR
Pharm , LLM (Wales), MCIM, MIM

Fitzsimons *Miss Melanie Ann*
Call Date: Nov 1994 (Middle Temple)
Qualifications: LLB (Hons)

Flaherty *Michael Francis*
Adams Blair Cox Solicitors, 29/31
Guildhall Walk, Portsmouth PO1 2RU,
01705 296705, Call Date: Oct 1995
(Inner Temple) Qualifications: LLB

Flanagan *Commander John* •
Royal Navy Officer, Fleet Legal &,
Personnel Officer, Office of
Commander-in-Chief, Northwood,
Middlesex HA6 3HP, 01923 837157,
Fax: 01923 837090, Call Date: Oct
1991 (Middle Temple) Qualifications:
BA Hons (Dunelm), Dip Law

Flattery *Miss Amanda Nichole* •
Lancashire County Council, Call Date:
Oct 1993 (Lincoln's Inn)
Qualifications: BA (Hons) (Lancaster),
MA (York), CPE

Fleay *Miss Amanda Louise*
South Wales, Call Date: July 1998
(Middle Temple) Qualifications: LLB
(Hons) (Exon)

Fleming *Ms Annabel Clare* •
Call Date: Oct 1995 (Middle Temple)
Qualifications: BA (Hons)

Fleming *Martin Dominic* •
Crown Prosecutor, Crown Prosecution
Service, 8th Floor, Sunlight House,
Quay Street, Manchester M60 3LU,
0161 837 7402, Fax: 0161 835 2663,
Call Date: July 1983 (Inner Temple)

Fleming *Peter James* •
72 Leybourne Road, Leytonstone,
London E11 3BT, 0181 530 2515, Call
Date: July 1988 (Middle Temple)
Qualifications: LLB (Hons)

Fletcher *Alan Philip*
26 Hollies Close, Royston, Herts
SG8 7DZ, 01763 248580, Call Date:
Nov 1940 (Inner Temple)
Qualifications: MA

Fletcher *Clifford Daniel St Quentin*
42A Cyncoed Road, Cardiff CF2 6BH,
01222 464790, Call Date: July 1946
(Gray's Inn) Qualifications: LLB

Fletcher *Miss Elizabeth*
Call Date: Oct 1998 (Inner Temple)
Qualifications: BA (Keele), CPE (City)

Fletcher Rogers *Mrs Helen Susan* •
European Legal Director, Kodak Ltd,
Kodak Hse, Station Rd, Hemel
Hempstead, Herts HP1 1JU, 01442
844413, Fax: 01442 844807, Call Date:
July 1965 (Gray's Inn) Qualifications:
LLB (Hons) (Lond)

Fletcher-Cooke *Sir Charles Fletcher*
Gray's Inn Chambers, Gray's Inn Road,
London WC1R 5JA, 0171 404 1111,
Fax: 0171 430 1522, DATO of Sovereign
of Brunei and Member Gambia &
Sierra Leone Bars Gray's Inn
Chambers, 5th Floor, Gray's Inn,
London, WC1R 5JA, Call Date: Nov 1938
(Lincoln's Inn) Qualifications: MA
A.R.I.Arb

Flood *John* •
Senior Civil Service, Solicitor's Office, H
M Customs & Excise, 22 Upper Ground,
London SE1 9PJ, 0171 865 5530, Fax:
0171 865 5022, Call Date: July 1975
(Middle Temple) Qualifications: LLB

Florendine *Matthew David*
North Wales, Call Date: Nov 1998
(Inner Temple) Qualifications: LLB

Florendine *Miss Sarah Ann* •
Legal Advisor, RAC Legal Services,
P.O.Box 700, Bristol, Avon, 0345 300
400, Call Date: July 1996 (Gray's Inn)
Qualifications: LLB (West of England)

Florin *Miss Catherine France*
Call Date: Feb 1995 (Middle Temple)
Qualifications: BA (Hons) (Cantab)

Flower *Philip Harvey*
Police Superintendent, 0171 321 8801,
Call Date: Nov 1995 (Inner Temple)
Qualifications: LLB (Lond)

Flowitt *Mrs Nicola* •
Court Clerk/Legal Advisor, Justices'
Clerk's Office, Shire Hall, Bury St
Edmunds IP33 1HF, 01284 352300,
Fax: 01284 352345, Call Date: Nov
1986 (Inner Temple) Qualifications:
LLB

Floy *Geoffrey Alan*
Old Farmhouse, Whitlenge Lane,
Hartlebury, Worcestershire DY10 4HD,
01299 251643, Call Date: July 1974
(Gray's Inn) Qualifications: LLB, BA,
M.PHIL

Fluker *Miss Christine Louise* •
Senior Legal Adviser, Jays Close,
Viables, Basingstoke, Hampshire
RG22 4BS, 01256 329122, Fax: 01256
467106, Call Date: Nov 1976 (Gray's
Inn) Qualifications: MA [Cantab], LLB
(Cantab)

Flynn *Mr. Paul Francis*
Call Date: Oct 1994 (Middle Temple)
Qualifications: BSc (Lond), LLB
(Hons) (Lond)

Foakes *Ms Joanne Sarah* •
Legal Counsellor, Legal Department,
Foreign & Commonwealth Office, King
Charles Street, London SW1A 2AH,
0171 270 3075/01580 754710, Fax:
0171 270 2767/01580 754710, Call
Date: July 1979 (Inner Temple)
Qualifications: MA (Oxon)

Fodor *Dr Neil Harris* •
Crown Prosecution Service, 3rd Floor,
Benton House, Sandyford Road,
Newcastle on Tyne NE2 1QE, Call Date:
Nov 1991 (Inner Temple)
Qualifications: MA (Dundee), PHD
(Glas), Dip Law

Foggitt *Eben Robin* •
Joint Managing Director, Ardent
Productions Limited, Ariel House, 74a
Charlotte Street, London W1P 2DA,
0171 636 5010, Fax: 0171 636 5574,
Call Date: July 1978 (Gray's Inn)
Qualifications: BA

Foley *Benedict James* •
The Post Office, Legal Services, Impact
House, 2 Edridge Road, Croydon
CR9 1PJ, 0181 681 9473, Fax: 0181
681 9135, Call Date: Mar 1996 (Gray's
Inn) Qualifications: BA (Wales)

Foley *John Sheldon*
Deputy Clerk to the Justices, Stockport
Magistrates, Courts Committee,
Courthouse, Edward Street, Stockport
SK1 3NF, 0161 477 2020, Call Date:
July 1981 (Lincoln's Inn)
Qualifications: LLB

Foley *Michael Timothy*
Call Date: Nov 1970 (Gray's Inn)
Qualifications: BSc [Eng] (Lond),
C.Eng, F.I.C.E, F Cons E

Folland *David James*
Clerk to the Justices, Dyfed Magistrates'
Crts Comm, 4/5 Quay Street,
Carmarthen, Dyfed SA31 3JT, 01267
221658, Fax: 01267 221812, Call Date:
Oct 1976 (Lincoln's Inn) Qualifications:
BSc

Follows *Terence John*
Lecturer, Call Date: July 1992 (Middle
Temple) Qualifications: LLB (Hons)
(Leeds), FCIArb

Foo *Frederick Kong Tuck*
Solicitor, Ince & Co, Knollys House, 11
Byward Street, London EC3R JEN,
Singapore 2057, 0171 623 2011, Fax:
0171 623 3225, Call Date: July 1996
(Lincoln's Inn) Qualifications: LLB
(Hons)(Lond)

Foo *Yoke Yan* •
M & A Commercial Lawyer, British
Telecommunications plc, Group Legal
Services, BT Centre, 81 Newgate Street,
London EC1A 7AJ, 0171 356 5545, Fax:
0171 356 4012, Call Date: July 1989
(Lincoln's Inn) Qualifications: BSc
(Keele)

Footring *Mrs Marika Everdina*
01206 825310, Call Date: Nov 1985
(Inner Temple) Qualifications:
LLB(Essex)

Forbes *Miss Janet*
115 Bedfont Close, Bedfont, Middlesex
TW14 8LH, Call Date: July 1998 (Middle
Temple) Qualifications: BH
(Hons)(Lond), PG Dip Law

Ford *Miss Margo*
Barrister of Ireland, Call Date: July 1991
(Middle Temple) Qualifications: LLB
(Hons) (Galway)

Ford *Miss Patricia Ann* •
Legal Adviser, Young & Rubicam Group
Limited, Greater London House,
Hampstead Road, London NW1 7QP,
0171 611 6835, Fax: 0171 611 6915,
Call Date: Oct 1995 (Middle Temple)
Qualifications: LLB (Hons)

Ford *Richard Andrew* •
In House Lawyer, Call Date: Oct 1993
(Middle Temple) Qualifications: BSc
Econ (Hons)

Forde *Patrick Bernard*
Brook Hse, Moreton Morrell, Warwicks
CV35 9AN, 01926 651733, Irish Bar
1951, Call Date: July 1966 (Gray's Inn)
Qualifications: BCom (Dub)

Forder *Kenneth John*
Freeman of the City of London, Napier
Cottage, 2a Napier Avenue, Hurlingham,
London SW6 3NJ, 0171 736 3958,
Former Registrar of UK Architects, Call
Date: May 1963 (Gray's Inn)
Qualifications: MA (Oxon), BA (Cantab)

Fordjour *Oscar*
Call Date: Nov 1994 (Middle Temple)
Qualifications: BA (Hons), LLB (Hons)

Foreman *Frederick Christopher* •
Senior Legal Advisor, Legal & General
Assurance, Society Limited, Legal &
General House, Kingsworth,Tadworth,
Surrey KT20 6EU, 01737 376129, Fax:
01737 376144, Call Date: Feb 1991
(Inner Temple) Qualifications: LLB

Forer *Lt Cdr Timothy John* •
Staff Legal Advisor, Flag Officer Surface
Flotilla, HM Naval Base, Portsmouth,
Hants PO1 3NB, 01705 726519, Fax:
01705 726614, Call Date: Oct 1993
(Gray's Inn) Qualifications: BA
(Dunelm)

Forgaard *Ms Alexandra Katherine*
Call Date: Nov 1997 (Inner Temple)
Qualifications: BA (Bris)

Forman *Ian Douglas* •
DTI Legal Services Directorate, D2, 10
Victoria Street, London SW1H 0NN, 0171
215 6740, Fax: 0171 215 3223, and
Member Northern Ireland, Gibraltar, Call
Date: Nov 1984 (Middle Temple)
Qualifications: LLB (Lond)

Forman *John Wilson* •
Chase House, Scarletts Chase, West
Bergholt, Essex CO6 3DH, 01206
240300, Call Date: Nov 1970 (Lincoln's
Inn) Qualifications: ACI.Arb MCIT

Forrest *Ms Gabrielle*
Call Date: Nov 1993 (Gray's Inn)
Qualifications: MA (Oxon)

Forrester *Stephen Kenneth*
Company Secretary, Call Date: Nov 1993
(Lincoln's Inn) Qualifications: BA
(Hons), MA

Forsdike *Ms Clare Louise*
Court Clerk, Justices' Clerk's Office,
Magistrates' Courthouse, North Quay,
Great Yarmouth, Norfolk NR30 1PW, Call
Date: Oct 1997 (Inner Temple)
Qualifications: LLB (Luton)

Forster *Brian Howard*
Justices' Chief Executive, Gwent
Magistrates' Court Comm, 2nd Floor,
Gwent House, Gwent Square, Cwmbran,
Gwent NP44 IPL, 01633 645000, Fax:
01633 645015, Call Date: July 1966
(Middle Temple) Qualifications: MA
(Oxon), M I Mgt

Forsyth *Anthony Stewart Karl*
Call Date: Nov 1995 (Lincoln's Inn)
Qualifications: LLB (Hons)

Forsyth *Dr Christopher Forbes*
Fellow of Robinson College Lecturer
Cambridge University, 0171 583 1111,
Fax: 0171 353 3978, Advocate of the
Supreme Court of South Africa, Call
Date: May 1987 (Inner Temple)
Qualifications: BSc, LLB, LLB, PhD

Fortunato *Miss Karen* •
Company Secretary, Abbey National
Treasury Services plc, Abbey National
Treasury, Services plc, Abbey House,
Baker Street, London NW1 6XL, 0171
612 4677, Fax: 0171 612 4319, and
Member Gibraltar Bar, Call Date: July
1986 (Lincoln's Inn) Qualifications: LLB
(Lond)

Forward *Michael Edmond*
Call Date: Nov 1984 (Inner Temple)
Qualifications: BA (Hons)

Forwood *Miss Victoria Clare* •
Legal Officer, Treasury Solicitors
Department, Queen Anne's Chambers,
28 Broadway, London SW1, 0171 210
3332, Fax: 0171 210 3232, Call Date: Oct
1997 (Gray's Inn) Qualifications: BA,
LLM

Foster *Adrian Gavin* •
Senior Crown Prosecutor, Crown
Prosecution Service, West London
Branch, 3rd Floor, 50 Ludgate Hill,
London EC4M 7EX, 0171 273 8422, Fax:
0171 273 8042, Call Date: Oct 1993
(Inner Temple) Qualifications: LLB

Foster *Colin Joseph Kenneth*
Call Date: Nov 1998 (Lincoln's Inn)
Qualifications: LLB (Hons), LLM

Foster *David Christopher*
Litigation Lawyer, Samuels Solicitors,
196 Alexandra Road, Barnstaple, Devon
EX32 8BA, 01271 343457, Fax: 01271
322187, Call Date: Oct 1992 (Inner
Temple) Qualifications: LLB (Warwick),
Dip in Enviromental, Health

Foster *Desmond Roy* •
The Legal Aid Board, 85 Gray's Inn Road,
London WC1X 8AA, 0171 813 1000, Fax:
0171 813 8658, Call Date: Oct 1996
(Lincoln's Inn) Qualifications: BSc
(Hons)(W.Indies), LLB (Hons)(Warw)

Foster *Miss Elizabeth Anne*
Assistant Solicitor, Clifford Chance, 200
Aldersgate Street, London EC2A 4JJ, 0171
600 1000, Fax: 0171 600 5555, Call
Date: Oct 1992 (Middle Temple)
Qualifications: LLB (Hons, Leic)

Foster *Guy Robert*
Simmons & Simmons, 21 Wilson Street,
London EC2M 2TX, 0171 628 2020, Fax:
0171 628 2070, Call Date: Oct 1995
(Inner Temple) Qualifications: LLB
(Lond)

Foster *Jonathan Robert Melville*
0181 670 4754, Fax: 0181 670 4754,
Call Date: Feb 1978 (Middle Temple)
Qualifications: BA

Fotherby *Gordon*
Senior Civil Service (Formerly Grade 3),
HM Customs & Excise, Solicitor's Office,
New King's Beam House, Upper Ground,
London SE1, 0171 865 5124, Fax: 0171
865 4820, Call Date: Nov 1973 (Inner
Temple) Qualifications: LLB

Fotheringham *Mrs Emma Clark*
Major Crime Support Analyst, Kent
Police Authority, Police Headquarters,
Sutton Road, Maidstone, Kent
ME14 9BZ, 01622 654682, Call Date:
Nov 1992 (Gray's Inn) Qualifications:
LLB

Foucar *Antony Emile*
Call Date: Jan 1949 (Middle Temple)

Foudy *Ms Denise* •
Group Legal Advisor & Company
Secretary, Isode Ltd, The Dome, The
Square, Richmond, Surrey TW9 1DT,
0181 332 9091, Fax: 0181 332 9019,
Call Date: July 1983 (Gray's Inn)
Qualifications: BSc (Bath), Dip Law

Foulkes *Dyfed Charles*
Justices' Clerk, The Law Courts, Alfred
Gelder Street, Kingston Upon Hull
HU1 2AD, 01482 328914, Call Date:
July 1986 (Gray's Inn) Qualifications:
LLB, Dip.Mgt (Open),, MIMgt, Assoc
IPD

Fountain *David Charles*
P O Box 3213, Palm Springs, California
92263, 760 866 7103, Fax: 760 323
8742, Call Date: Mar 1997 (Middle
Temple) Qualifications: LLB
(Hons)(Lancs)

Fountain *Jonathan William*
The Smith Partnership, 25 Wardwick,
Derby DE1 1HA, 01332 346084, Fax:
01332 292183, Call Date: May 1994
(Middle Temple) Qualifications: BSc
(Hons, Dunelm)

Fovargue *Ms Sara Jane*
Call Date: Oct 1994 (Lincoln's Inn)
Qualifications: LLB (Hons)(Leic)

Fowell *Eoin Maurice*
Foot & Bowden Solicitors, The Foot &
Bowden Building, 21 Derry's Cross,
Plymouth, Devon PL1 2SW, 01752
675000, Fax: 01752 671802, Call Date:
Oct 1996 (Inner Temple)
Qualifications: BSc (L'pool), CPE
(Middx)

Fowler *Adrian Paul Brian*
Call Date: Nov 1998 (Gray's Inn)
Qualifications: LLB (Exon)

Fowler *Christopher Allan*
Call Date: Nov 1998 (Middle Temple)
Qualifications: LLB (Hons)(Wales)

Fowler *Christopher Stephen* •
Legal Assistant, Volkswagen Financial
Services, (UK) Limited, Yeomans Drive,
Blakelands, Milton Keynes MK14 5AN,
01908 601452, Fax: 01908 601873,
Call Date: Feb 1994 (Lincoln's Inn)
Qualifications: LLB (Hons)

Fowler *Geoffrey Alan*
Justices Chief Executive, Derbyshire
Magistrates' Court, West Bank House,
Albion Road, Chesterfield, Derby,
01246 220008, Call Date: Nov 1977
(Gray's Inn) Qualifications: LLB (Lond)

Fowler *Ian*
Deputy Traffic Commissioner, 6 Dence
Park, Herne Bay, Kent CT6 6BG, 01227
375530, Call Date: July 1957 (Gray's
Inn) Qualifications: MA (Oxon)

Fox *Mrs Celia Janet Clough*
Call Date: Nov 1969 (Lincoln's Inn)

Fox *Miss Claire Louise*
Legal Advisor, Southend & Rochford,
Magistrates' Court, 80 Victoria Avenue,,
Southend-on-Sea, Essex SS2 6EU,
01702 348491, Call Date: Oct 1993
(Lincoln's Inn) Qualifications: LLB
(Hons), MSC

Fox *Martin George* •
Senior Crown Prosecutor, Crown
Prosecution Service, 17th Floor,
Tolworth Tower, Surbiton, Surrey
KT6 7DS, 0181 399 5171, Call Date:
July 1981 (Middle Temple)
Qualifications: LLB

Fox *Nicholas Russell Philip*
Call Date: Oct 1994 (Lincoln's Inn)
Qualifications: BA (Hons)

Fox *Ms Victoria Charlotte* •
Principal Legal Officer, Department of
Social Security, 48 Carey Street, London
WC2A 2LS, 0171 962 8000, Call Date:
Nov 1995 (Middle Temple)
Qualifications: LLB (Hons), LLM

Foxall-Smedley *Miss Diana*
Call Date: Nov 1972 (Gray's Inn)
Qualifications: MA (TCD)

Frame *Stuart James*
Call Date: May 1997 (Gray's Inn)
Qualifications: LLB (Kingston), MA
(Brunel)

Francis *Ms Angela Pamela*
Former Solicitor, Call Date: Feb 1995
(Middle Temple) Qualifications: BA
(Hons)(Kent)

Francis *Ms Angela Valerie*
Insurance Ombudsman - Executive
Officer, Insurance Ombudsman
Bureau, City Gate One, 135 Park Street,
London SE1 9EA, 0171 902 8100, Fax:
0171 902 8197, Call Date: Nov 1989
(Middle Temple) Qualifications: LLM,
LLB

Francis *Ms Claire Louise* •
Senior Legal Officer, Solicitors Office,
Somerset House, London, 0171 438
7410, Call Date: Nov 1987 (Inner
Temple) Qualifications: BA, BCL
(Oxon)

Francis *Hollis Eustace*
Call Date: July 1998 (Inner Temple)
Qualifications: LLB (Wolves)

Francis *Ms Margaret Ayodele*
21 Holywell Close, London SE16 3EF,
0171 231 6883, Call Date: Oct 1997
(Inner Temple) Qualifications: BSc
(Nigeria), MSc, MBA (Nigeria), CPE

Francis *Michael Anthony*
Call Date: Oct 1996 (Gray's Inn)
Qualifications: LLB

Francombe *Miss Susan Jane*
Construction Lawyer, Hammond
Suddards Solicitors, 7 Devonshire
Square, Cutlers Gardens, London
EC2M 4YH, 0171 655 1157, Fax: 0171
655 1001, Call Date: May 1997 (Inner
Temple) Qualifications: BSc (Wales),
C.Eng, MICE, LLDip

Frankham *David Mark*
Deputy Justices Clerk, Devon and
Cornwall Magistrates, Courts
Committee, North Quay House, Sutton
Harbour, Plymouth PL4 1RA, 01271
388461, Call Date: Feb 1988 (Gray's
Inn)

Frankl *Dr Anna Maria*
102 East Sheen Avenue, London
SW14 8AU, 0181 876 6108, Call Date:
Feb 1956 (Lincoln's Inn)
Qualifications: LLD (Prague), LLB
(Wales)

Franklin *Mrs Helen Jane* •
Counsel, Mobil North Sea Ltd, Mobil
Court, 3 Clements Inn, London
WC2A 2GB, 0171 412 2517, Fax: 0171
404 0035, Call Date: July 1985
(Lincoln's Inn) Qualifications: BA
(Law), Dip Pet, Law (Dundee)

Franks *Mrs Deborah*
Call Date: Mar 1997 (Gray's Inn)
Qualifications: BA (B'ham), LL Dip

Fraser *Anthony Kenneth* •
Grade 6, Treasury Solicitor's Dept,
Queen Anne's Chambers, 28 Broadway,
London SW1H 9JS, 0171 210 3000,
Fax: 0171 222 6006, and Member
British Columbia Bar, Call Date: Nov
1986 (Lincoln's Inn) Qualifications: BA
(Victoria), LLB (Brit Columbia), BA
(Oxon)

Fraser *Commander Robert William* •
DNSD, Ministry of Defence, Whitehall,
London SW1A 2HB, 0171 218 3079,
Fax: 0171 218 4207, Call Date: July
1984 (Gray's Inn) Qualifications: LLB

Frazer *Ms Onike Letitia*
Holborn College, 200 Greyhound Road,
London W14 9RY, 0171 385 3377, Fax:
0171 381 3377, and Member Sierra
Leone, Call Date: Nov 1995 (Middle
Temple) Qualifications: LLB (Hons)

Freeland *Sir John Redvers*
Judge, European Crt of Human Rights,
Also Inn of Court M, Call Date: Feb
1952 (Lincoln's Inn) Qualifications:
MA

Freeland *Richard Daniel*
Call Date: May 1997 (Gray's Inn)
Qualifications: BA (Lond)

Freeman *Mrs Elizabeth Mary*
College Lecturer, Clare College,
Cambridge CB2 1TL, 01223 333200,
Call Date: Nov 1970 (Middle Temple)
Qualifications: MA, LLB, LLM, Lic en,
droit europeen

• Barrister in employment

Freeman *Miss Lucy Mekhala Catherine* and Member Republic of Ireland, Call Date: Oct 1990 (Middle Temple) Qualifications: BA (Oxon), Dip Law

Freemantle *Clive James Francis* • Senior Crown Prosecutor, Crown Prosecution Service, 3rd Floor, Cuthbert House, All Saints Office Centre, Newcastle upon Tyne NE1 2DW, 0191 232 6602, Call Date: July 1982 (Inner Temple) Qualifications: BA Hons

Freij *Miss Deema Mounir* Call Date: Nov 1996 (Lincoln's Inn) Qualifications: BA (Hons)

French *Alan Van* • Senior Crown Prosecutor, Crown Prosecution Service, St George's House, Lever Street, Wolverhampton WV2 1EZ, 01902 870900, Call Date: July 1984 (Middle Temple) Qualifications: LLB

French *John* Councillor, Legal Advisor for Royal & Sun Alliance plc, 35 Hinckley Road, Stoke Golding, Warks CV13 6DU, (01455) 212359, Call Date: July 1996 (Lincoln's Inn) Qualifications: LLB (Hons)

French *Michael Alan* • Prosecution Team Leader, Crown Prosecution Service, St Andrew's Court, 12 St Andrew's Street, Plymouth PL1 2AH, 01752 668700, Call Date: Nov 1986 (Middle Temple) Qualifications: LLB (Nott'm)

French *Richard Anthony Lister* • Xerox Limited, Parkway, Marlow, Bucks SL7 17L, Call Date: Nov 1995 (Gray's Inn) Qualifications: B.Eng (Exon)

Frend *Captain David Peter* • Call Date: Nov 1994 (Inner Temple) Qualifications: BA (Keele)

Frias *Miss Cristina Samanta Hustwait* Portugal, Call Date: Mar 1997 (Middle Temple) Qualifications: BA (Hons)

Friend *Alasdair James Christopher* • Call Date: Oct 1993 (Lincoln's Inn) Qualifications: MA (Cantab), Dip Law

Frisby *Roger Harry Kilbourne* Call Date: Jan 1950 (Lincoln's Inn) Qualifications: MA (Oxon), LLB (Lond

Fritchie *Andrew Peel* • Group Counsel-Head of Legal Affairs, Company Secretary, Marlborough Stirling, 16 Imperial Square, Cheltenham, Gloucestershire GL50 1QZ, 01242 221973, Fax: 01242 520329, Call Date: July 1988 (Inner Temple) Qualifications: LLB (Wales)

Frith *Miss Alexandra Jane* Call Date: Oct 1997 (Middle Temple) Qualifications: LLB (Hons)(Lond)

Frost *Frank Reginald* Call Date: Apr 1951 (Middle Temple)

Frost *Peter* • Principal Crown Prosecutor, CPS, St Mark House, 2 Conway Street, Birkenhead, Merseyside L41 6QD, 0151 647 4681, Call Date: Feb 1985 (Gray's Inn) Qualifications: DML

Frudd *Mrs Stephanie Julia* Deputy Justices' Chief Executive, 19 Lime Tree Walk, Virginia Park, Virginia Water, Surrey GU25 4SW, 01344 844 654, Call Date: Nov 1981 (Gray's Inn) Qualifications: LLB (Hons)

Fry *Laurence Frederick* • Legal Manager, Monument Exploration and, Production Limited, Kierran Cross, 11 Strand, London WC2N 5HR, 0171 891 2294, Fax: 0171 891 2222, and Member California Bar, Call Date: Nov 1989 (Middle Temple) Qualifications: LLB Hons (Nott'm)

Fulbrook *Dr Julian George Holder* London School of Economics &, Political Science, Houghton Street, London WC2A 2AE, 0171 955 7244, Fax: 0171 955 7366, Call Date: July 1977 (Inner Temple) Qualifications: PhD (Cantab)

Fullalove *Mrs Elizabeth Anne* Call Date: Oct 1995 (Inner Temple) Qualifications: BA (Oxon)

Fullarton *Patrick James John* Director, Pegasus Commmercial & Property, Consultants Plc, 38 The Ropewalk, Nottingham NG1 5DW, 0115 959 0834, Call Date: Nov 1979 (Gray's Inn) Qualifications: BSc (Wales)

Fullbrook *Ms Suzanne Dorothy* 35a Silvester Road, East Dulwich, London SE22 9PB, 0181 299 3928, Fax: 0181 299 2522, Call Date: Nov 1994 (Middle Temple) Qualifications: LLB (Hons) , M.Phil, RGN

Fuller *Graham Francis* • Senior Legal Advisor, 31 Seawalls Road, Sneyd Park, Bristol, Avon BS9 1PG, 01179 688103, Fax: 01179 626690, Call Date: July 1969 (Gray's Inn) Qualifications: LLB

Fuller *Peter Anthony* Call Date: Oct 1998 (Middle Temple) Qualifications: LLB (Hons)(Plymouth)

Fullman *Peter Michael* 47 London Road, Canterbury, Kent CT2 8LF, 01227 456352, Call Date: Nov 1997 (Middle Temple) Qualifications: MB.BS., FRCS (Ed),, FRCOG (Royal Lond., Hosp. Med. School), LLB (Hons)(Lond), LLM (Wales)

Fulton *Mrs Kathryn Mary* • Chief Counsel, Young & Rubicam Group Ltd, Greater London House, Hampstead Road, London NW1 7QP, 0171 611 6374, Fax: 0171 611 6915, Call Date: July 1987 (Inner Temple) Qualifications: LLB (Lond)(Hons)

Fung *Leonard Shui-Kei* Call Date: Nov 1995 (Gray's Inn) Qualifications: BA

Fung *Miss Nora Yin Ling* Commercial & Legal Adviser, HVCA, Esca House, 34 Palace Court, Bayswater, London W2 4JG, 0171 313 4921, Fax: 0171 727 9268, and Member Malaysia Bar, Call Date: Nov 1993 (Gray's Inn) Qualifications: LLB (Lond), ACIArb

Furlonger *Miss Lesley Margaret* Stocks Farm, New Road, Rayne, Essex CM7 8SY, (0376) 61109, Call Date: July 1968 (Inner Temple)

Furness *Clive William* 11 Fisher Street, London E16 4DS, 0171 474 5262, Call Date: Feb 1995 (Gray's Inn) Qualifications: LLB (Sheff), D.M.S.

Fussell *Charles Edward Roger* Call Date: Nov 1994 (Lincoln's Inn) Qualifications: BA (Hons)(Exon), Dip in Law

Futerman *Samuel* Call Date: Nov 1996 (Middle Temple) Qualifications: LLB (Hons)(Manch)

Gabathuler *David* Call Date: Nov 1996 (Inner Temple) Qualifications: LLB (Nott'm), LLM (Lond)

Gabbert *Dale* • J P Morgan Investment Mngment, 28 King Street, London SW1Y 6XA, 0171 451 8000, Fax: 0171 451 8693, Call Date: Oct 1993 (Inner Temple) Qualifications: LLB, LLM

Gabisi *Naurajudin* Call Date: Oct 1998 (Middle Temple) Qualifications: BSc (Hons)(Lond), CPE

Gabriel *Mrs Wendy Alicia* Company Secretary, Call Date: Oct 1995 (Lincoln's Inn) Qualifications: BA (Hons)

Gabrielczyk *Mrs Maria Genowefa* Principal Court Clerk, Mansfield Magistrates Court, Rosemary Street, Mansfield, Nottinghamshire NG19 6EE, 01623 451500, Fax: 01623 451648, Call Date: Nov 1975 (Gray's Inn) Qualifications: MA

Gadd *Miss Suzanne Heather* Deputy Clerk to the Justices, North & East Hertfordshire, Magistrates' Court, Bayley House, Sish Lane, Stevenage SG1 3S8, 01438 730431, Fax: 01438 730413, Call Date: July 1984 (Lincoln's Inn) Qualifications: LLB

Gadras *Mrs Susan Elizabeth* Court Clerk, West Hertfordshire Magistrates, Court, The Court House, Clarendon Road, Watford, Herts WD1 1ST, 01923 297500, Fax: 01923 297528, Call Date: July 1989 (Inner Temple) Qualifications: LLB

Gafoor *Anthony David Jalil* •
Legal Adviser, Dept of Trade & Industry,
Solicitor's Office, Room 114, 10 Victoria
Street, London SW1H 0NN, 0171 215
3412, Fax: 0171 215 3479, Member of
the Inter Bar Association. Member of
BACFI. Member of the Administrative
Bar Association and Member Trinidad
& Tobago, Call Date: July 1987 (Gray's
Inn) Qualifications: LLB (UWI),LLM
(Lond), MA, Dip Commercial, Law, Dip
European, Community Law (Lond),
Cert in Air Law, Cert in Corporate &,
Investment Law, Dip Copyright Law &,
Related rights

Gagg *Mrs Lesley Florence*
Deputy Clerk to the Justices, Somerset
Magistrates Court, The Courthouse,
Northgate, Bridgwater, Somerset
TA6 3EU, 01278 452182, Fax: 01278
453667, Call Date: Nov 1984 (Inner
Temple) Qualifications: M.Soc.Sc

Gairdner *Ms Margaret Christine*
Call Date: Mar 1998 (Inner Temple)
Qualifications: LLB (Sussex)

Galgani *Padraig*
Call Date: Nov 1997 (Middle Temple)
Qualifications: BA (Buck), LLB, MA,
LLM

Gallagher *David Leslie* •
Occupational Pensions, Regulatory
Authority, Invicta House, Trafalgar
Place, Brighton BN1 4DW, 01273
627600, Fax: 01273 627631, Call Date:
Oct 1992 (Gray's Inn) Qualifications:
BA (Hons)(Cantab)

Gallagher *Dr Margaret Sutherland* •
Treasury Solicitors Chambers, Queen
Anne's Chambers, Broadway, London
SW1, 0171 210 3390, Call Date: July
1989 (Inner Temple) Qualifications:
LLB (Glas), D Phil (Oxon)

Gallagher *Ms Maria Theresa* •
Treasury Solicitors Department, Call
Date: Nov 1997 (Inner Temple)
Qualifications: LLB (L'pool)

Gallagher *Mrs Sarah Jane* •
Principal Crown Prosecutor
Prosecution Team Leader, Crown
Prosecution Service, St Andrews Court,
12 St Andrew Street, Plymouth, Devon
PL1 2AH, 01752 668700, Call Date: July
1976 (Inner Temple) Qualifications:
B.A. (Dunelm)

Gallagher *Mrs Susan Wendy*
Lecturer in Law, Call Date: Nov 1994
(Lincoln's Inn) Qualifications: LLB
(Hons)(Sheff)

Galliford *Leslie Bertram*
Coppinside, 11 Kenwith Road, Raleigh,
Bideford, Devon EX39 3NW, Call Date:
Feb 1952 (Lincoln's Inn)
Qualifications: LLB

Galligan *Denis James*
Call Date: July 1996 (Gray's Inn)
Qualifications: LLB (Queensland), BCL,
MA (Oxon)

Gallimore *Patrick James*
Inns of Court, School of Law, 4 Gray's
Inn Place, Gray's Inn, London
WC1R 5DX, Call Date: Oct 1992 (Middle
Temple) Qualifications: LLB (Hons)
(Lond), LLM (Lond)

Galloway *Miss Natasha Clare*
Call Date: Feb 1993 (Middle Temple)
Qualifications: BA (Hons)(Oxon), Dip
in Law (City)

Gamble *Miss Helen Louise*
Call Date: Nov 1998 (Inner Temple)
Qualifications: LLB (Hull)

Gammanpila *Miss Dakshina Kumudu*
Tutor in Criminology, Centre for
Criminal Justice, Studies, University of
Leeds, West Yorkshire, Undertaking
Firensic Medicine PhD, Call Date: Oct
1992 (Inner Temple) Qualifications:
LLB (Hons) , MA

Gammon *Jonathan Michael Hugh*
Team Leader, Court House, Bishops
Road, Highgate, London N6 4HS, 0181
340 3472, Fax: 0181 348 3343, Call
Date: Oct 1990 (Middle Temple)
Qualifications: LLB (Bris)

Gan *Miss Jui Fui*
Call Date: July 1997 (Gray's Inn)
Qualifications: LLB (Notts)

Ganatra *Hargovind Gorhandas*
'Vrindavan', 1 Wentworth Avenue,
Elstree, Herts WD6 3PX, 0181 207
4231, Call Date: July 1967 (Lincoln's
Inn)

Ganchi *Kasam Bhai*
Call Date: Nov 1998 (Middle Temple)
Qualifications: LLB (Hons)(Lancs)

Gandham *Bopinder Paul Singh*
Call Date: Nov 1997 (Lincoln's Inn)
Qualifications: LLB

Gandolfi *Mrs Joan*
Call Date: May 1997 (Lincoln's Inn)
Qualifications: LLB (Hons)

Gandy *Geoffrey Harold*
Vice President, Montell Polyolefins
Intellectual Property, Call Date: Feb
1963 (Inner Temple) Qualifications:
MA, LLM (Cantab)

Gannon *Miss Catherine*
Legal Advisor, Baker & McKenzie
Solicitors, 100 New Bridge Street,
London EC4V 6JA, 0171 919 1000, Fax:
0171 919 1999, Member of Chartered
Institute of Taxation, Call Date: Feb
1994 (Lincoln's Inn) Qualifications:
LLB (Hons), ATII

Gans-Lartey *Joseph Kojo* •
Principal Crown Prosecutor
(Prosecution Team Leader), Crown
Prosecution Service, Croydon Branch,
Prospect West, 8th Floor, 81 Station
Road, Croydon CR0 2RD, 0181 251
5479, Fax: 0181 251 5454, and
Member Bar of Trinidad & Tobago, Call
Date: July 1983 (Lincoln's Inn)
Qualifications: LLB, LLM (Lond)

Gardam *David Hill*
Call Date: Nov 1949 (Inner Temple)
Qualifications: MA (Oxon)

Gardiner *Miss Jennifer Anne Victoria*
Call Date: Oct 1998 (Inner Temple)
Qualifications: MA (St Andrews), CPE
(City)

Gardiner *Miss Joanna Marie*
Call Date: Oct 1996 (Middle Temple)
Qualifications: LLB (Hons)(Kent)

Gardner *Alan George*
23 The Daedings, Deddington,
Banbury, Oxon OX15 0RT, 01869
338138, Call Date: Nov 1973 (Middle
Temple) Qualifications: LLB, ACIS

Gardner *Miss Angela*
Call Date: Nov 1998 (Middle Temple)
Qualifications: BA (Hons)(Sheff)

Gardner *Carl Martin* •
Call Date: Nov 1993 (Gray's Inn)
Qualifications: BA

Gardner *David Andrew* •
Call Date: Oct 1992 (Middle Temple)
Qualifications: BA(Hons) & MA (Exen)

Gardner *Dr John Blair*
Reader in Legal Philosophy in the
University of London, School of Law,
King's College London, Strand, London
WC2R 2LS, 0171 873 2203, Call Date:
July 1988 (Inner Temple)
Qualifications: MA, BCL (Oxon), D.Phil

Gardner *John Willoughby*
Rowancroft, Upton Grey, Hants
RG25 2RJ, 01256 862476, Call Date:
Apr 1964 (Middle Temple)

Gardner *Michael Anthony Graham*
Call Date: Nov 1959 (Middle Temple)

Gardner *Mrs Pamela Jeannette Noall*
Call Date: Nov 1974 (Inner Temple)

Gardner-Bougaard *Paul Frederick
Francis*
Managing Director, Cornerstone, Abbey
National Estate Agents, Abbey House,
Baker Street, London NW1 6XL, 0171
486 5555, Fax: 0171 486 8822, Call
Date: July 1972 (Middle Temple)
Qualifications: LLB, LLM

Garen *Edgar*
The Thames Chambers, Wickham
House, 10 Cleveland Way, London, E1
4TR, Call Date: May 1994 (Inner
Temple)

Garland *Gary John Richard* •
Senior Crown Prosecutor, CPS Tyneside
Branch, 3rd Floor, Cuthbert House, All
Saints Office, Newcastle-upon-Tyne,
Call Date: Nov 1989 (Inner Temple)
Qualifications: LLB (Hons), F.T.C.

Garland *Stuart* •
Legal Adviser, Call Date: Feb 1992
(Lincoln's Inn) Qualifications: BA
(Hons) (Oxon)

Garland-Collins *Francis*
Deputy Justices Clerk, Inner London
Magistrates', Courts Committee,
Camberwell Green Magistrates, Court, 15
D'Eynsford Road, London SE5, 0171 703
0909, Fax: 0171 277 2014, Call Date:
July 1974 (Middle Temple)

Garlick *Mrs Helen Mary* •
Serious Fraud Office, Elm House, 10-16
Elm Street, London WC1X 0BJ, Call Date:
Nov 1974 (Middle Temple)
Qualifications: LLB

Garlick *Neil Harvey*
9 Windsor Road, Gee Cross, Hyde,
Cheshire SK14 5JB, 0161 367 7663, Call
Date: Nov 1983 (Middle Temple)
Qualifications: BA, ALCM

Garmon-Jones *Richard* •
The Citibank Private Bank, 41 Berkeley
Square, London W1X 6NA, 0171 409
5000, Call Date: Feb 1993 (Middle
Temple) Qualifications: LLB
(Hons)(Lond), ACIB

Garner *Miss Margaret Theresa* •
Head of Group Legal Services (London),
Legal Dept, Credit Agricole Indosuez, 122
Leadenhall Street, London EC3V 4QH,
0171 971 4000, Fax: 0171 971 4407,
Call Date: Nov 1968 (Gray's Inn)

Garnett *David Michael* •
Senior Crown Prosecutor, Crown
Prosecution Service, The Ryedale
Building, 60 Piccadilly, York, 01904
610726, Fax: 01904 610394, Call Date:
July 1981 (Gray's Inn) Qualifications:
LLB

Garratt *Basil Sanders*
Call Date: Feb 1971 (Gray's Inn)
Qualifications: LLB

Garraway *Colonel Charles Henry Barre* •
Legal Officer in Armed Forces,
Directorate of Army Legal, Services (ALS
2), Metropole Building, Northumberland
Avenue, London WC2N 5BL, 0171 218
4766, Fax: 0171 218 9944, Call Date:
July 1972 (Inner Temple) Qualifications:
MA (Cantab)

Garside *John-Paul*
Kingsley Napley Solicitors, St Johns Lane,
London EC1, Call Date: Oct 1996 (Inner
Temple) Qualifications: LLB (Lond)

Garvey *Ms Sarah* •
Allen & Overy, One New Change, London,
Call Date: Oct 1994 (Gray's Inn)
Qualifications: BA

Garvin *Peter Nigel*
Call Date: Nov 1998 (Lincoln's Inn)
Qualifications: LLB (Hons)(Derby)

Gaskell *Mrs Vera Norma*
Call Date: Nov 1985 (Gray's Inn)

Gasper *Michael Charles Kinahan* •
Senior Lawyer Employed by the Solicitor
for Customs & Excise, Solicitor's Office,
HM Customs & Excise, New King's Beam
House, 22 Upper Ground, London
SE1 9PJ, 0171 865 5201, Fax: 0171 865
5194, Call Date: Feb 1964 (Gray's Inn)

Gasson *John Gustav Haycraft*
The White House, Candys Lane,
Blandford Road, Shillingstone Road,
Dorset DT11 0SF, 01258 861690, Call
Date: Feb 1957 (Gray's Inn)
Qualifications: BA (Cape Town), MA, BCL
(Oxford)

Gates *Harvey Stuart*
Call Date: Oct 1998 (Inner Temple)
Qualifications: LLB (Lanc)

Gates *Peter Leslie*
94 St Margarets, Stevenage, Herts
SG2 8RE, Call Date: Feb 1987 (Gray's
Inn) Qualifications: LLB (E Anglia)

Gaunt *Stephen Alistair*
Ford & Warren Solicitors, Westgate Point,
Westgate, Leeds LS1 2AX, 0113 243
6601, Fax: 0113 242 0905, Solicitor, Call
Date: Nov 1995 (Gray's Inn)
Qualifications: BA (Manc)

Gautama *Miss Nisha*
Deputy Justices Clerk, Church End, 448
High Road, Willesden, London
NW10 2DZ, 0181 451 7111, Fax: 0181
451 2040, Call Date: Nov 1988 (Middle
Temple) Qualifications: LLB (B'ham)

Gavin *Alastair Douglas*
2 Phillimore Terrace, Allen Street,
London W8, Call Date: Nov 1957 (Inner
Temple) Qualifications: BA

Gavin *Miss Georgia Henrietta Bulkely*
Call Date: Nov 1989 (Inner Temple)
Qualifications: BA (Manch), Dip Law

Gavin *Jake Alfred Bulkeley*
Call Date: Oct 1993 (Inner Temple)
Qualifications: BA, CPE

Gawne *Miss Anne Maria*
Call Date: Oct 1990 (Middle Temple)
Qualifications: LLB (Lond)

Gaymer *Mrs Vivien Murray* •
Company Secretary, Enterprise Oil Plc,
Grand Buildings, Trafalgar Square,
London WC2N 5EJ, 0171 925 4194, Fax:
0171 925 4606, Call Date: Feb 1971
(Middle Temple) Qualifications: LLB
Hons

Gbondo *Joseph Dominic Andrew* •
Principal Contracts Lawyer, London
Borough of Islington, The Town Hall,
Upper Street, Islington, London N1 2UD,
0171 477 3314, Call Date: Nov 1983
(Gray's Inn) Qualifications: BA
Dip.Construction, Law & Arbitration ,
(Kings College Lon)

Geater *Miss Sara Kate*
119 Tottenham Road, London N1 4EA,
Call Date: Mar 1998 (Middle Temple)
Qualifications: LLB (Hons)

Gebbie *Mrs Sarah Jane*
Call Date: Oct 1992 (Middle Temple)
Qualifications: LL.B (Hons, Brunel)

Gee *Mrs Peta Marie*
2 Paper Bldgs, Temple, London, EC4Y
7ET, Call Date: Nov 1973 (Gray's Inn)
Qualifications: BA (Hons), Dip Ed

Geering *Philip James* •
Legal Adviser, Legal Secretariat to the
Law, Officers, Attorney General's
Chambers, 9 Buckingham Gate, London
SW1E 6JP, Call Date: July 1984 (Middle
Temple) Qualifications: LLB (Hons)

Gelber *Christopher Julian Neil*
McFarlanes Solcitors, Former Solicitor,
Call Date: Nov 1997 (Middle Temple)
Qualifications: LLB (Hons)(Sydney),
LLM (Cantab)

Gemmell *Mrs Marie Cecile*
28 A Simpson Street, London SW11 3HN,
0171 585 2530, Fax: 0171 585 2530,
Call Date: Oct 1994 (Gray's Inn)
Qualifications: LLB

Gent *Matthew Thomas*
Call Date: Nov 1998 (Gray's Inn)
Qualifications: BA (Cantab)

George *Dr Carlisle Eldwidge*
Lecturer, University of Northumbria at
Newcastle, c/o Dept of Computing &,
Mathematics, University of Northumbria
at Newcastle, Ellison Building,Ellison
Place, Newcastle Upon Tyne NE1 8ST,
West Indies, 0956 839 542/0191 281
8734, and Member St Lucia, Call Date:
July 1998 (Lincoln's Inn) Qualifications:
BSc (West Indies), PhD (Lond), PGDip
(Law)(Nott'm)

George *Gareth Richard Llewellyn*
9 Park Place, Cardiff, CF1 3DP, Call Date:
Nov 1977 (Middle Temple)
Qualifications: MA (Oxon)

George *Mrs Judy Ava*
Assistant Director (Strategy & Support
Services), Social Services Department,
Corporation of London, Milton Court,
Moor Lane, London EC2Y 9BL, 0171 332
1211, Fax: 0171 588 9173, Call Date:
May 1977 (Middle Temple)
Qualifications: BA (Hons)

George *Laurence Christopher Tyacke*
LAG 844, PO Box 289, Weybridge, Surrey
KT13 8WJ, Admitted as a Solicitor of
England & Wales, Call Date: Nov 1976
(Middle Temple) Qualifications: LLB,MA

Georghiadou *Miss Chrysso Souli*
Company Secretary/Legal Advise, Call
Date: July 1983 (Middle Temple)
Qualifications: BA

Georgiou *Ms Angela Kyriacos*
Call Date: Oct 1997 (Inner Temple)
Qualifications: LLB (Sheffield)

Georgulas *Miss Efrocynne*
Call Date: Nov 1995 (Gray's Inn)
Qualifications: BA, LLB (City)

Geraghty *Miss Sarah Margret*
Call Date: Oct 1994 (Lincoln's Inn)
Qualifications: BA (Hons)

Geraghty *Miss Toni* •
Lincolnshire County Council, Lincoln,
01522 552222, Fax: 01522 552138,
Call Date: Oct 1993 (Middle Temple)
Qualifications: LLB (Hons) (Lond)

Germain *Mrs Jadwiga Anne Teresa*
ILMCS, 65 Romney Street, London
SW1P 3RD, Call Date: July 1966 (Inner
Temple) Qualifications: LLB

Germany *Mrs Alison* •
Court Clerk, Call Date: Nov 1985
(Gray's Inn) Qualifications: LLB

Gerrard *Stephen*
Call Date: Mar 1997 (Gray's Inn)
Qualifications: LLB (Manch)

Gethin *Mrs Susan Jane* •
Senior Crown Prosecutor, Crown
Prosecution Service, Froomsgate
House, 1st Floor, Rupert Street, Bristol
BS1 2QJ, Call Date: Oct 1990 (Inner
Temple) Qualifications: LLB (Hons)

Gething *Daniel Robert*
Call Date: Nov 1997 (Lincoln's Inn)
Qualifications: LLB (Hons) (B'ham)

Getley *Miss Kate Ann Cameron*
Mount Pleasant Farm, Andrew Hill
Lane, Hedgerley, Bucks SL2 3UW,
01753 648255, Fax: 01753 648256,
Call Date: Feb 1988 (Inner Temple)
Qualifications: BA (Oxon)

Gettleson *Michael Francis*
17 Bedford Row, London, WC1R 4EB,
Call Date: July 1952 (Middle Temple)
Qualifications: MA, BCL

Ghaleigh *Navraj Singh*
Call Date: Nov 1996 (Middle Temple)
Qualifications: LLB (Hons) (Lond)

Ghandour *Miss Zeina*
The Morroccan Information and,
Advice Centre, 61 Golborne Road,
London W10, Call Date: Nov 1990
(Inner Temple) Qualifications: BA, LLM
(Kent)

Gheera *Ms Manjit*
Call Date: Oct 1997 (Inner Temple)
Qualifications: LLB (Reading)

Ghosh *Miss Fiona* •
Weil Gotshal & Manges, Call Date: Nov
1997 (Middle Temple) Qualifications:
BA (Hons) (Oxon)

Ghosh *Matilal*
7F Sandridge Court, 10 Queen's Drive,
London N4 2XA, and Member Calcutta
High Court, Call Date: Nov 1975 (Inner
Temple) Qualifications: MA (Calcutta)

Ghows-Retnam *Jiva*
Call Date: July 1989 (Middle Temple)
Qualifications: LLB (Newc)

Ghumman *Mohammed-Khurram*
Call Date: Nov 1997 (Lincoln's Inn)
Qualifications: BA, LLM (Punjab), LLM
(Lond)

Giaquinto *Martino John*
Call Date: Oct 1996 (Lincoln's Inn)
Qualifications: BSc (Hons) (Aston)

Gibb *Jeremy Roderick* •
Immigration Advisor, Tower Hamlets
Law Centre, 341 Commercial Road,
London E1 2PS, 0171 791 0741, Fax:
0171 702 7301, Call Date: July 1989
(Middle Temple) Qualifications: BA
(Oxon) MST(Oxon), Dip Law

Gibbard-Jones *David Mark*
Call Date: Oct 1993 (Middle Temple)
Qualifications: LLB (Hons, B'ham)

Gibbins *Brian Richard* •
Senior Crown Prosecutor, London
Branch 2, CPS Central Casework, 50
Ludgate Hill, London EC4M 7EX, 0171
273 1250, Fax: 0171 329 8164, and
Member Northern Ireland Bar, Call
Date: Nov 1986 (Middle Temple)
Qualifications: LLB(Hons) London,
Assoc of Inst of, Linguists

Gibbons *Miss Dorn Ellen*
Call Date: Oct 1998 (Middle Temple)
Qualifications: BA (Hons) (Sussex),
MSc(Lond), CPE (City)

Gibbons *Miss Linda Marie*
Call Date: Oct 1996 (Inner Temple)
Qualifications: LLB (L'pool)

Gibbons *Miss Mary Regina*
Call Date: Mar 1999 (Lincoln's Inn)
Qualifications: Dip Law

Gibbs *David*
Clerk to the Justices, Justices' Clerk's
Office, The Court House, Civic Centre,
St Peter's Street, St Albans AL1 3LB,
01727 816822, Fax: 01727 816829,
Call Date: Nov 1984 (Gray's Inn)
Qualifications: DML, DMS

Gibbs *Nigel James* •
Senior Crown Prosecutor, Crown
Prosecution Service, 5th Floor, River
Park House, High Road, Wood Green,
London N22, Call Date: July 1985
(Inner Temple) Qualifications: LLB
(Brunel)

Gibbs *Simon Thomas Bernard*
Negotiations Manager, Legal Costs
Negotiators Ltd, 56 Marsh Wall, London
E14, 0171 510 2345, Fax: 0171 515
5000, Call Date: Oct 1995 (Middle
Temple) Qualifications: LLB (Hons)

Gibson *Bryan Donald*
Waterside, Domum Road, Winchester
SO23 9NN, 01256 882250, Fax: 01256
882250, Call Date: July 1976 (Gray's
Inn) Qualifications: BA (Hons)

Gibson *John Philip Robson*
Information Services Team, Dibb
Lupton Alsop, Liverpool, 0345 262728,
Lecturer part time within the
Department of Law, Crosby Adult
Education Centre, 53 Cambridge Road,
Crosby, L21 1E7, Call Date: July 1990
(Inner Temple) Qualifications: LL.M,
MA, BA (Hons),, pg.Dip (Adult & H.Ed,
& ALA Barrister

Gibson *Miss Ruth Mary*
Call Date: Oct 1998 (Lincoln's Inn)
Qualifications: LLB (Hons) (B'ham)

Gibson *Mrs Sally Ann Safeena*
Kiln Wood, Huntsland Drive, Crawley
Down, West Sussex RH10 4HB, 01342
716 790 (0589 156 061 Mobile), Fax:
01342 717 533, Call Date: Nov 1979
(Lincoln's Inn) Qualifications: BA
(Hons)

Gibson *Scott William*
Call Date: Oct 1996 (Gray's Inn)
Qualifications: LLB (Wales)

Gibson *Miss Susan Eile*
Wilde Sapte, 1 Fleet Place, London
EC4M 7WS, 0171 246 7168, Fax: 0171
246 7000, Call Date: Oct 1995
(Lincoln's Inn) Qualifications: LLB
(Hons) (Lond), ACIS, AGSM

Giglioli *George*
P.O.Box 1316, George Town, Grand
Cayman, Cayman Islands, 12 New
Square, Ground Floor, Lincoln's Inn,
London, WC2A 3SW, Call Date: July
1982 (Lincoln's Inn) Qualifications:
BSc (Exon),Dip Law

Gilbert *Carl St. John* •
United Bank of Kuwait, 7 Baker Street,
London W1M 1AB, 0171 487 6591, Call
Date: Oct 1996 (Middle Temple)
Qualifications: BA (Hons) (Exon), CPE
(Notts)

Gilbert *David Richard*
Consultant/Secretary of Horizon IJUC
Ltd, Little Orchard, Littlewick Green,
Berks SL6 3RA, 01628 828462, Fax:
01628 828462, Call Date: Feb 1957
(Middle Temple) Qualifications: MA,
LLM

Gilbert *Mrs Jeanine Bryony*
Lecturer in Law, University of Exeter,
Faculty of Law, Amory Building, Rennes
Drive, Exeter EX4 4RJ, 01392 263263,
Call Date: Nov 1987 (Lincoln's Inn)
Qualifications: BD (Hons) (Lond),, Dip
Law, AKC, LLM (Leic)

Gilbert *Robert Greenway*
5 Orchid Avenue, Kingsteignton,
Newton Abbot, Devon TQ12 3HG,
016263 61718, Call Date: Nov 1950
(Lincoln's Inn) Qualifications: MA

Giles *Derryck Peter Fitzgibbon*
Suttons Hospital in Charter, House,
Chartrhouse Square, London
EC1M 6AN, 0171 336 7212, Call Date:
July 1954 (Gray's Inn) Qualifications:
LLB

Gilhespy *Mrs Sonia* •
Senior Crown Prosecutor, Crown
Prosecution Service, York House, 34
Princes Street, Leicester LE1 5TU, 0116
254 9333, Call Date: Oct 1990 (Gray's
Inn) Qualifications: LLB (Newc)

• Barrister in employment

Giliker *Ms Paula Rosalind*
Queen Mary & Westfield College, Faculty of Laws, 330 Mile End Road, London E1 4NS, Call Date: Oct 1994 (Gray's Inn) Qualifications: MA (Oxon), BCL (Oxon), PHD (Cantab)

Gilks *Matthew Christopher*
Call Date: July 1997 (Lincoln's Inn) Qualifications: BA (Hons)(Warw)

Gill *David Edwin*
Call Date: July 1983 (Middle Temple) Qualifications: BA(Cantab), Dip Law

Gill *Mrs Elizabeth Jane*
Principal Legal Adviser, Basildon Magistrates' Court, Great Oaks, Basildon, Essex, 01268 293129, Fax: 01268 293187, Call Date: Feb 1987 (Middle Temple) Qualifications: BA (Hons), Dip MLaw

Gill *Ian Charles*
Clerk to the Magistrates, N.E. Essex Magistrates Courts, Stanwell House, Stanwell Street, Colchester, Essex CO2 7DL, 01206 563057, Fax: 01206 563694, Call Date: May 1984 (Middle Temple) Qualifications: Dip MLaw

Gill *Julian Clive* •
Prosecution Team Leader, Crown Prosecution Service, 5th Floor, St Peters House, Gowers Street, Derby, 01332 621600, Call Date: July 1987 (Gray's Inn) Qualifications: LLB

Gill *Maninder Singh*
Company Legal Adviser, Legal Department, Northern & Shell Plc, Northern & Shell Tower, City Harbour, London N14 9GL, 0171 308 5268, Fax: 0171 308 5077, Call Date: Nov 1992 (Gray's Inn) Qualifications: LLB (Bris), LLM (Lond)

Gill *Mrs Naranderjit*
Litigation Manager, First National Bank Plc, First National House, College Road, Harrow, Middlesex HA1 1FB, Call Date: Nov 1988 (Inner Temple) Qualifications: LLM (Lond), LLB

Gill *Stephen Courtney Ray*
Arthur Anderson, Chartered Accountants, 5th Floor, 17 Lansdowne Road, Croydon CR9 2PL, 0181 666 9081, Fax: 0181 666 9090, Call Date: July 1975 (Middle Temple) Qualifications: LLB (Hons)(Lond)

Gill *Miss Susan Eveline*
Deputy Chief Clerk, Inner London Magistrates', Courts Service, 65 Romney Street, London SW1P 3RD, 0171 799 3332, Fax: 0171 799 3072, Call Date: Nov 1987 (Gray's Inn) Qualifications: BA

Gill *Mrs Susan Li-Tseng*
Legal Advisor, OMLX, The London Securities &, Derivatives Exchange, 107 Cannon Street, London EC4N 5AD, 0171 283 0678, Fax: 0171 815 8508, Call Date: Nov 1993 (Gray's Inn) Qualifications: LLB, LLM

Gillanders *Roderick Colin Fabian* •
Senior Advisory Lawyer, Senior Fraud Office, Serious Fraud Office, Elm House, 10-16 Elm Street, London WC1X 0BJ, 0171 239 7106, Fax: 0171 833 5475, Call Date: July 1976 (Middle Temple) Qualifications: LLB (Lond)

Gillespie *Alisdair Allan*
Call Date: Oct 1996 (Middle Temple) Qualifications: LLB (Hons)

Gillett *Ms Tonia Jane*
Call Date: Oct 1997 (Inner Temple) Qualifications: LLB (Birmingham)

Gilliland *David Jeremy*
Eversheds, Sun Alliance House, 35 Mosley Street, Newcastle-upon-Tyne NE1 1XX, 0191 261 1661, Fax: 0191 261 8270, Call Date: Oct 1994 (Gray's Inn) Qualifications: BSc, MSc, CEng, MIChem E

Gilling *Simon Jolyon* •
Legal Adviser & Partnership Secretary & Legal Director, Mercury Personal Communication, T/A One to One, Imperial Place, Maxwell Road, Borehamwood, Herts WD6 1EA, 0181 214 2310, Fax: 0181 214 3441, Call Date: July 1981 (Middle Temple) Qualifications: BSc, Dip Law

Gilmore *Stephen*
University Lecturer, Call Date: Nov 1993 (Lincoln's Inn) Qualifications: LLB (Hons, Leic), LLM

Gilpin *Matthew Thomas Diarmuid*
Assistant, Securities Group, Corporate Finance Department, S J Berwin & Co, 222 Gray's Inn Road, London WC1X 8HB, 0171 533 2222, Fax: 0171 533 2000, Call Date: Nov 1993 (Middle Temple) Qualifications: MA (Hons)(Oxon),AMSI

Gilthorpe *Miss Charlotte Emma Tiffany* •
Head of Competition Policy, Cable & Wireless Communication, 26 Red Lion Square, London WC1R 4HQ, 0171 528 3712, Fax: 0171 528 2163, Call Date: July 1996 (Middle Temple) Qualifications: BSc (Hons)

Gingell *Miss Melanie Ann*
Mitre House Chambers, Mitre House, 44 Fleet Street, London, EC4Y 1BN, Call Date: Nov 1988 (Middle Temple) Qualifications: LLB (Hons Lond)

Gingell *Miss Virginia Carol*
Call Date: Nov 1990 (Inner Temple) Qualifications: LLB

Ginn *Mrs Adeline-Marie Odile Claude*
Solicitor, Call Date: Nov 1994 (Inner Temple) Qualifications: LLB (Warw), LLM (Canada)

Ginn *Michael Anthony*
Barlow Lyde & Gilbert Sols, Call Date: Nov 1994 (Inner Temple) Qualifications: BA (E.Anglia), M.Phil (Oxon)

Gittens *Miss Chrystine Louise* •
London Borough of Newham, 0181 472 1430, Call Date: Feb 1994 (Inner Temple) Qualifications: BA (Lond), CPE

Gittens *Ms Janet Dianne*
Court Clerk, Bexley Magistrates Court, Norwich Place, Bexleyheath, Kent DA5 7NB, 0181 304 5211, Fax: 0181 303 6849, Call Date: Nov 1989 (Gray's Inn) Qualifications: LLB

Gittings *David Howard*
Director, Regulation, Lloyd's of London, Lloyd's of London, One Lime Street, London EC3, 0171 327 5355, Fax: 0171 327 6606, Call Date: July 1977 (Middle Temple) Qualifications: LLB Hons (Lond)

Gittins *David James* •
Senior Crown Prosecutor, Crown Prosecution Service, Plymouth Branch Office, St Andrews Court, 12 St Andrews Street, Plymouth PL1 2AH, 01752 668700, Fax: 01752 672093, Call Date: July 1971 (Inner Temple) Qualifications: MA (Cantab)

Gladwell *David John* •
Head of Civil Justice Division, Lord Chancellor's Department, Selborne House, 54-60 Victoria Street, London SW1E 6QW, 0171 210 8789, Fax: 0171 210 0682, Call Date: July 1972 (Gray's Inn) Qualifications: LLM (Exon), Dip IP Law (Lond), CEDR , Accredited Mediator

Glanvill *Dr Michael Edward*
Jocelyn Mews, 18A High Street, Chard, Somerset TA20 1QL, 01460 63348, Call Date: Nov 1956 (Middle Temple) Qualifications: BA, MRCS, LRCP,, MRCGP, DMJ

Gleave *Edward Ernest James*
31 Winston Drive, Nocturum, Birkenhead, Wirral, Liverpool L43 9RU, 0151 678 4030, Call Date: July 1968 (Lincoln's Inn) Qualifications: BCom

Gleave *Miss Justina Louise* •
Trogan Television Limited, Queen Anne House, Charlotte Street, Bath BA1 2NE, 01795 536969, Call Date: May 1988 (Gray's Inn) Qualifications: LLB (SOAS)

Gledhill *Orlando John*
1 Essex Court, Ground Floor, Temple, London, EC4Y 9AR, Call Date: Oct 1998 (Inner Temple) Qualifications: BA (Canada), MPhil (Oxon), CPE (City)

Gleeson *Donough Patrick*
and Member Irish Bar, Call Date: July 1963 (Gray's Inn) Qualifications: BA

Gleeson *Mark Anthony John* •
Office of the Solicitor, Dept of Social Security, New Court, 48 Carey Street, London WC2A 2LS, 0171 962 8000, Call Date: Oct 1995 (Middle Temple) Qualifications: B.Sc (Hons) (Manch)

Gleeson *Michael Joseph*
Call Date: Nov 1998 (Gray's Inn) Qualifications: BA (Glamorgan)

Glenister *Richard Edwin* •
Lawyer Central Casework, Crown
Prosecution Service, 50 Ludgate Hill,
London EC4M 7EX, 0171 273 1227,
Fax: 0171 329 8164, Call Date: July
1972 (Gray's Inn) Qualifications: MA
(Oxon)_

Glenn *Miss Angela Veronica*
Messrs Leonard & Swain Sols, Solent
House, 121 Shirley Road, Southampton
SO15 3FF, 01703 234433, Call Date:
Nov 1981 (Gray's Inn) Qualifications:
BA

Glenn *Miss Christine Mary*
Justices' Chief Executive, Inner London
Magistrates' Crts, Committee, 65
Romney Street, London SW1P 3RD,
0171 799 3332, Fax: 0171 799 3072,
Call Date: July 1980 (Gray's Inn)
Qualifications: BA (L'pool)

Glenn *Miss Nicola Louise* •
Principal Legal Officer, H M Customs &
Excise, New Kings Beam House, 22
Upper Ground, London SE1, 0171 865
5247, Call Date: Nov 1992 (Lincoln's
Inn) Qualifications: LLB (Hons)

Glover *Mrs Audrey Frances* •
Legal Counsellor, Call Date: Feb 1961
(Gray's Inn)

Glover *Miss Hannah Rebecca*
Call Date: July 1998 (Middle Temple)
Qualifications: BSc (Hons)(Salford),
Dip Law

Glover *Miss Justine Rebecca* •
Dept of Social Security, New Court,
Carey Street, London WC2A 2LS, Call
Date: Oct 1991 (Inner Temple)
Qualifications: LLB (Hull)

Glover *Kevin Peter*
London Borough of Islington, 222 Uper
Street, London N1, Call Date: Nov 1980
(Inner Temple) Qualifications: BA

Glover *Nigel David*
Call Date: July 1985 (Gray's Inn)
Qualifications: BA (Cantab)

Glyde-Coleman *Kenneth Shane*
Call Date: July 1970 (Gray's Inn)
Qualifications: LLB

Goad *Ms Donna Elizabeth*
Call Date: Nov 1995 (Inner Temple)
Qualifications: LLB

Gobir *Nuhu Garba*
Call Date: Oct 1998 (Middle Temple)
Qualifications: LLB (Hons)(Wales),
LLM (Warwick)

Goddard *Ian Lester*
Call Date: July 1974 (Gray's Inn)
Qualifications: BA Oxon

Godding *John Peter*
15 Sunbury Avenue, London
SW14 8RA, 0181 876 5064, Fax: 0181
876 5064, Call Date: Nov 1978 (Gray's
Inn) Qualifications: ACII

Godfrey *Mrs Julie Maria*
Rose Cottage, 1 Church Way, Alconbury
Weston, Huntingdon PE17 5JB, Call
Date: Oct 1998 (Middle Temple)
Qualifications: BA (Hons)(Oxon)

Godfrey *Timothy Andrew Ellinger*
Call Date: Oct 1997 (Middle Temple)
Qualifications: LLB (Hons)(Sheff)

Goggins *Michael Eugene*
Call Date: Feb 1995 (Gray's Inn)
Qualifications: LLB (Coventry)

Gogo *Emmanuel Markwei Kofi* •
Senior Assistant Solicitor, Legal Services
Division, Newham Borough Council,
Town Hall, East Ham, London E6 2RP,
0181 472 1430 ext 23069, Fax: 0181
472 0480, Call Date: July 1984 (Middle
Temple) Qualifications: LL.B, LL.M

Goh *Miss Susan Guat Eng*
Call Date: Mar 1997 (Gray's Inn)
Qualifications: LLB (L'pool)

Gold *William Duncan*
30 Oakwood Drive, Fulwood, Preston,
Lancs PR2 3LY, Call Date: Nov 1964
(Gray's Inn) Qualifications: LLM
(Lond), A.C.I.S

Goldberg *Ms Joy Paula*
Call Date: Nov 1994 (Middle Temple)
Qualifications: BA (Hons)

Goldberg *Mrs Rhoda Joyce*
Chair of Independent Review Panel for
North Thames N.H.S., Call Date: Oct
1997 (Middle Temple) Qualifications:
BA (Hons)(Boston), MA (Chicago), LLB
(Hons)(Lond)

Golden *Mrs Aviva*
Call Date: Nov 1969 (Middle Temple)
Qualifications: BA (S.Africa)

Goldie *Charles William Homan*
2 Myddylton Place, Saffron Walden,
Essex CB10 1BB, 01799 521417, Fax:
01799 520387, Call Date: Nov 1965
(Middle Temple) Qualifications: MA,
LLB

Golding *Timothy John*
Call Date: July 1994 (Gray's Inn)
Qualifications: LLB (Wolv)

Goldman *James Simon Mark*
Call Date: Nov 1994 (Middle Temple)
Qualifications: B.Sc

Goldring *Mrs Judith Ann*
Managing Director, Clark Goldring &
Page Ltd, Beech House, St Swithun
Street, Winchester, Hampshire
SO23 9HU, 01962 842726, Fax: 01962
842726, Call Date: Nov 1979 (Gray's
Inn) Qualifications: LLB

Goldsbrough *Ms Felicity* •
Legal Costs Negotiators, Call Date: May
1997 (Inner Temple) Qualifications:
BA (Humberside)

Goldsmith *Mrs Joy*
7 Hanover Terrace, Regents Park,
London NW1 4RJ, Call Date: July 1973
(Lincoln's Inn) Qualifications: BA
(Hons), LLB, LLM

Goldspink *Justin Stephen*
Call Date: Nov 1994 (Inner Temple)
Qualifications: BA (Oxon), LLM (Notts)

Goldsworth *John Graham*
Goldsworth Chambers, 1st Floor, 11
Gray's Inn Square, London, WC1R 5JD,
Call Date: Nov 1965 (Middle Temple)

Goldsworthy *Ian Francis*
Recorder, 23 Essex Street, London,
WC2R 3AS, Call Date: Nov 1968 (Inner
Temple)

Goldsworthy *Lt Peter Jarvis* •
11 Orme Lane, Bayswater, London
W2 4RR, Call Date: July 1993 (Inner
Temple) Qualifications: B Eng (Hons,
Bris)

Golley *Omrie Michael*
Legal Advisor, Call Date: Nov 1983
(Inner Temple) Qualifications: BA
(Hull)

Gomez *David Jide* •
Legal Officer, Treasury Solicitor's Dept,
Queen Anne's Chambers, 28 Broadway,
London SW1H 9JS, 0171 210 3273,
Fax: 0171 210 3143, Call Date: Oct
1995 (Lincoln's Inn) Qualifications:
MA (Hons)(Oxon), LLM, Dip in Law

Gomez *Dax Stuart*
Call Date: July 1998 (Middle Temple)
Qualifications: LLB (Hons)(L'pool)

Gondal *Miss Sofia Bashir*
Powell & Co Solicitors, 77 Woolwich
New Road, Woolwich, London
SE18 6ED, 0181 854 9131, Fax: 0181
855 4174, Call Date: Nov 1994 (Middle
Temple) Qualifications: LLB (Hons),
LLM

Gooch *Ian Edward* •
A Bilbrough & Co, 50 Leman Street,
London E1 8HQ, 0171 772 8000, Fax:
0171 772 8200, Call Date: Nov 1989
(Inner Temple) Qualifications: LLB

Goodchild *Graham Stuart* •
Head of Legal Section (Northern
Office), Charity Commission, Northern
Office, 20 Kings Parade, Queens Dock,
Liverpool L3 4DQ, 0151 703 1538, Call
Date: July 1966 (Lincoln's Inn)

Goodchild *John Cadbury*
Call Date: July 1973 (Middle Temple)
Qualifications: BA (Hons) Law,
Southampton

Goodier *John Stuart* •
Senior Crown Prosecutor, Call Date: Oct
1992 (Middle Temple) Qualifications:
MA (Oxon)

Goodman David Roderick
Deputy Clerk to the Justices, Stafford Magistrates Court, The Court House, South Walls, Stafford ST16 3DW, 01785 223144, Fax: 01785 58508, Call Date: Nov 1983 (Gray's Inn) Qualifications: DML

Goodyear Damon John
Thurleigh MK44 2DB, 01234 771983, Call Date: May 1997 (Middle Temple) Qualifications: BSc (Hons)(Denelm), MSc

Goom Ms Sarah Louise •
Grade 7 Lawyer, Lord Chancellor's Department, Royal Courts of Justice, Strand, London, 0171 936 6517, Fax: 0171 936 6900, Call Date: Nov 1992 (Inner Temple) Qualifications: BA (Kent), MPhil (Cantab)

Gopaul Miss Dorothea Mohinee
Call Date: July 1990 (Lincoln's Inn) Qualifications: LLB

Gordon Alexander George
Clifford Chance, 200 Aldersgate Street, London EC1A 4JJ, Call Date: Feb 1995 (Lincoln's Inn) Qualifications: BA (Hons)

Gordon Andrew
Fellow of the Royal Institution of Chartered Surveyors, Call Date: Oct 1998 (Inner Temple) Qualifications: BSc, MBA (Hong Kong), CPE (Manch)

Gordon Asher Karleel •
Office of the Building Society, Ombudsman, Millbank Tower, Millbank, London SW1P 4XS, 0171 931 0044, Fax: 0171 931 8485, Call Date: Feb 1989 (Middle Temple) Qualifications: LLM (Wales), BA

Gordon Ashley •
Head of Legal and Compliance, The Bank of Tokyo-Mitsubishi, Limted, 12-15 Finsbury Circus, London EC2M 7BT, 0171 577 1295, Fax: 0171 577 1299, Call Date: Feb 1988 (Inner Temple) Qualifications: BSc, Dip Law (City)

Gordon David •
Halifax Plc, Trinity Road, Halifax, West Yorkshire HX1 2RG, 01422 333333 Ext 33238, Fax: 01422 333453, Call Date: July 1984 (Middle Temple) Qualifications: LLB [Manc] , M Phil [Manc]

Gordon Duncan Silvester
Call Date: Nov 1957 (Gray's Inn) Qualifications: MA (Oxon)

Gordon Graeme Andrew
Eversheds, Cloth Hall Court, Leeds, 0113 2430391, Call Date: July 1984 (Gray's Inn) Qualifications: MA (Oxon), LLM

Gordon Ian Jason
Simmons & Simmons, 21 Wilson Street, London, 0171 825 4765, Call Date: Oct 1994 (Lincoln's Inn) Qualifications: MA, BCL

Gordon Joseph Isaac
1 Beech Drive, Borehamwood, Herts WD6 4QU, 0181 207 3533, Call Date: July 1957 (Gray's Inn) Qualifications: LLB, FCIArb

Gordon Mrs Sophia Ira Geraldine
Mayer, Brown & Platt, Bucklersbury House, 3 Queen Victoria Street, London EC4N 8EL, 0171 246 6249, Fax: 0171 329 4465, and Member India (West Bengal) Bar, Call Date: Nov 1994 (Inner Temple) Qualifications: AB (Wellesley), MA (Cantab)

Gordon Miss Tracy Jane
Call Date: Nov 1998 (Inner Temple) Qualifications: BA (Staffs), LLM (Lancs)

Gordon Mrs Vanessa Maria Juliet Maxine
7 Edwardes Square, London W8 6HE, Call Date: July 1970 (Gray's Inn) Qualifications: LLB (Hons)(Lond) , A.K.C.

Gore Mark
Call Date: July 1947 (Inner Temple) Qualifications: MA (Oxon), FCIArb

Gorman Mark
Call Date: Nov 1996 (Gray's Inn) Qualifications: LLB

Gornall Mark Andrew •
Crown Prosecutor, Crown Prosecution Service, 2nd Floor, Prudential House, Topping Street, Blackpool FY1 3AB, Call Date: July 1987 (Middle Temple) Qualifications: LLB (Hons) Lancaster

Gornall Paul
Call Date: July 1991 (Middle Temple) Qualifications: BSC (Edin), Dip Law

Gorner Jason
Call Date: Oct 1994 (Gray's Inn) Qualifications: LLB (Hons) (Law with, French Law) (Leeds)

Gorringe Mathew David •
Tax Consultant at Eversheds, Eversheds, Cloth Hall Court, Infirmary Street, Leeds LS1 2JB, 0113 200 4111, Call Date: Feb 1995 (Middle Temple) Qualifications: BSc (Hons)(E.Anglia), MSc (Kent), CPE (Coventry)

Gort Miss Jill Christina •
p/t Chairman of VAT Tribunal Commission, Member Criminal Cases Review Commission, Criminal Case Review, Commission, Alpha Tower, Birmingham B1 1TT, 0121 633 1800, Call Date: July 1977 (Gray's Inn) Qualifications: BA (Sussex)

Gosalia Miss Amita Ashok
Enron Europe Limited, Four Millbank, London SW1P 3ET, 0171 316 5466, Call Date: Oct 1991 (Inner Temple) Qualifications: LLB (Lond)

Gosland Daniel Emrys •
Call Date: Mar 1996 (Gray's Inn) Qualifications: MA

Goss Kenneth Jack •
Principal Crown Prosecutor, Priory Gate, Union Street, Maidstone, Kent, 01622 686425, Call Date: Nov 1985 (Gray's Inn)

Goswell Joseph Ahosu
Call Date: Nov 1997 (Middle Temple) Qualifications: LLB (Hons)(Lond)

Goudie William Henry
24 Nimala Street, Rosny, Tasmania 7018, 0102 442326, Formerly Solicitor England (1938) Barrister & Solicitor Tasmania (1972), Call Date: July 1952 (Gray's Inn)

Gough Mark
Call Date: Oct 1997 (Lincoln's Inn) Qualifications: LLB (Hons)(Luton)

Goulandris Miss Atalanta Eugenia
13 King's Bench Walk, 1st Floor, Temple, London, EC4Y 7EN, Call Date: Nov 1985 (Middle Temple) Qualifications: BA (Lond), Dip law

Gould Miss Ciaran Amy
Palser Grossman Solicitors, Discovery House, Scotts Harbour, Cardiff bay CF1 5PJ, 01222 452770, Call Date: Nov 1996 (Gray's Inn) Qualifications: LLB (Wales), PGC PGD (Social Sc)

Gould Mrs Helen Patricia Mary
Franklins Solcitors, 14 Castiliam Street, Northampton NN1 1JX, 01604 828282, Fax: 01604 250208, Currently practising as a Solciitor, Call Date: Nov 1990 (Inner Temple) Qualifications: LLB (Hons)(Lond)

Govindasamy Paul Elangovan •
Senior Crown Prosecutor, CPS (London), Solar House, 1-9 Romford Road, Stratford, London E15 4LJ, and Member Singapore Bar, Call Date: July 1983 (Lincoln's Inn) Qualifications: BA,LLM

Grady Paul Damien
District Auditor, Audit Commission, Nicholson House, Lime Kiln Close, Stoke Gifford, Bristol BS12 6SU, 0117 923 6757, Fax: 0117 979 4100, Call Date: Nov 1996 (Lincoln's Inn) Qualifications: LLB (Hons)(Warw)

Graffy Miss Colleen Patricia
Director of Pepperdine Univ, 9 Gough Square, London, EC4A 3DE, Call Date: 1991 (Middle Temple) Qualifications: BA, MA, Dip Law

Graham Miss Adena Rozanne
Call Date: Nov 1994 (Gray's Inn) Qualifications: LLB

Graham Alexander Donald •
Head of Legal Services, CGU Life Services Ltd, Wellington Road, York YO90 1WR, 01904 452400, Fax: 01904 452696, Call Date: Feb 1975 (Inner Temple) Qualifications: LLB

Graham *Miss Ann Marie*
Court Clerk, Chesterfield Magistrates
Court, c/o The Court House, West Bars,
Chesterfield S40 1AE, Call Date: Nov
1991 (Middle Temple) Qualifications:
LLB Hons (Cardiff)

Graham *Jeremy John Mason* •
Deputy Clerk to the Justices (Legal)
Gateshead Magistrates' Court, Call
Date: Nov 1984 (Gray's Inn)
Qualifications: LLB (Manch)

Graham *Stewart David*
6 Grosvenor Lodge, Dennis Lane,
Stanmore, Middlesex HA7 4JE, 0181
954 3783, Call Date: Feb 1957 (Middle
Temple)

Graham *Mrs Susan Elizabeth*
Principal Court Clerk, Kingston
Magistrates Court, 19 High Street,
Kingston upon Thames, Surrey
KT1 1JW, 0181 546 5603, Fax: 0181
547 3551, Call Date: Feb 1985 (Gray's
Inn)

Graham *Mrs Veronica Joo Lee*
Thrings and Long Solicitors, Midland
Bridge, Bath BA1 2HQ, Fax: 01225
448494, Call Date: Nov 1994 (Gray's
Inn) Qualifications: LLB

Graham-Dixon *Anthony Philip*
Masketts Manor, Nutley, East Sussex
TN22 3HD, 01825 712010, Fax: 01825
712241, Call Date: Feb 1956 (Inner
Temple) Qualifications: MA (Oxon)

Graham-Wells *Miss Alison Christine* •
Solicitor's Office, H M Customs &
Excise, Manchester HQ, Ralli Quay
(West), 3 Stanley Street, Salford
M60 9LB, 0161 827 0507, Fax: 0161
827 0550, Call Date: July 1992 (Inner
Temple)

Grainger *John Andrew* •
Assistant Legal Adviser, Foreign &
Commonwealth Office, Legal Advisers,
King Charles Street, London SW1A 2AH,
Call Date: July 1981 (Lincoln's Inn)
Qualifications: BA (Cantab), BA, BCL
(Oxon)

Grand *David Anthony*
Call Date: Nov 1984 (Middle Temple)
Qualifications: BA (Hons)

Grange *Miss Katherine Elizabeth*
Call Date: Nov 1998 (Middle Temple)
Qualifications: BA (Hons)(Cantab)

Grange-Bennett *Derek Francis Dupre* •
Legal Adviser, Glenburn, Insurance
Brokers, Oaks House, 16-22 West
Street, Epsom, Surrey KT18 7RQ,
01372 727271, Fax: 01372 747574,
Call Date: June 1949 (Inner Temple)
Qualifications: MA (Oxon)

Grant *Andrew*
J.P., White Lodge, Courtenay Avenue,
London N6 4LR, 0181 348 1555, Call
Date: Nov 1968 (Inner Temple)

Grant *Miss Angela Marie*
Call Date: Nov 1997 (Lincoln's Inn)
Qualifications: LLB (Hons)(Dunelm)

Grant *Miss Berenice Anne*
Call Date: July 1990 (Inner Temple)
Qualifications: LLB (Warw)

Grant *David Ericson*
Call Date: Mar 1999 (Inner Temple)
Qualifications: BA, BCL (Oxon)

Grant *Edward Alexander Gordon*
Scotland, Call Date: Nov 1991 (Inner
Temple) Qualifications: LLB (So'ton)

Grant *Ian Edward*
Call Date: May 1994 (Middle Temple)
Qualifications: LLB (Hons)

Grant *James Alexander*
Spring Bank, Sutton Valence, Nr
Maidstone, Kent ME17 3BT, Call Date:
Nov 1979 (Inner Temple)
Qualifications: MA (Cantab), RIBA,,
FCIArb.

Grant *Miss Julie*
Call Date: Nov 1991 (Middle Temple)
Qualifications: BSc Hons (Manch), MA,
Dip Law

Grant *Nicolas Stuart* •
Legal Adviser, J Sainsbury plc, Stamford
House, Stamford Street, London
SE1 9LL, 0171 695 6000, Call Date:
Nov 1995 (Inner Temple)
Qualifications: BA (York), MSc (Lond),
Dip Law (City)

Grant-Whyte *Graham Denoon*
and Member South Africa, Call Date:
July 1963 (Gray's Inn) Qualifications:
MA, LLB (Cantab)

Grantham *David Adrian*
Call Date: Feb 1994 (Gray's Inn)
Qualifications: LLB (Lond)

Graves *Mrs Sheila May* •
Company Secretary, Urenco Limited, 18
Oxford Road, Marlow, Bucks SL7 2NL,
01628 486941, Fax: 01628 475867,
Call Date: July 1988 (Inner Temple)
Qualifications: LLB (Hons)

Gray *James Richard*
Call Date: Nov 1997 (Middle Temple)
Qualifications: LLB (Hons)(Kent), BA
(Hons)(Liverpool)

Gray *Mrs Jennifer Jane*
2 Temple Gardens, Temple, London,
EC4Y 9AY, Call Date: Nov 1988 (Middle
Temple) Qualifications: BA (Manch),
Dip Law (City)

Gray *John Christopher*
9 Gough Square, London, EC4A 3DE,
Call Date: Nov 1970 (Gray's Inn)
Qualifications: LLB

Gray *Professor Kevin John*
Professor of Law, University of
Cambridge. Fellow of Trinity College,
Cambridge, Trinity College, Cambridge
CB2 1TQ, (0223) 338400, Fax: (0223)
338564, Call Date: July 1993 (Middle
Temple) Qualifications: MA, Ph.D &
LL.D, (Cantab), DCL (Oxon)

Gray *Miss Pauline Alison*
Hardwicke Building, New Square,
Lincoln's Inn, London, WC2A 3SB, Call
Date: July 1980 (Inner Temple)
Qualifications: LLB (Soton)

Gray *Dr Peter*
11 The Street, Newnham, Nr
Sittingbourne, Kent ME9 0LQ, 01795
890162, Fax: 01795 890162, Call Date:
Oct 1992 (Middle Temple)
Qualifications: B.Sc (St Andrews), MB,
Ch.B (Manch), Diploma in Law,
MRCGP

Gray *Lt Cdr Robert Stanley* •
A/Sec to Second Sea Lord, Room 247,
Victory Building, HM Naval Base,
Portsmouth, Hants, 01705 727002,
Fax: 01705 727009, Call Date: Oct
1992 (Middle Temple) Qualifications:
BSc (Econ)(Wales), Common
Professional , Examination

Grayson *Mrs Myra Wendy* •
p/t Chairman Social Security Disability
Appeal Tribunals, 3rd Floor Flat, 1
Brick Court, Temple, London
EC4Y 9BY, 0171 583 6207, Also Inn of
Court Middle (1961)., Call Date: Feb
1952 (Gray's Inn) Qualifications: LLB

Grayson *Mrs Shamini Nainappan* •
Senior Crown Prosecutor, Call Date:
Nov 1988 (Middle Temple)
Qualifications: LLB (Leeds)

Grayson *Stephen Arthur* •
Senior Principal Legal Officer, DTI
Solicitors Office, LS D2, 10 Victoria
Street, London SW1H 0NN, 0171 215
3150, Fax: 0171 215 3235, Call Date:
Nov 1990 (Inner Temple)
Qualifications: BA

Grazebrook *Donald McDonald Dennis
Durley*
Honorary Life President International
Nuclear Law Association (AIDN/INLA),
Call Date: Feb 1952 (Lincoln's Inn)
Qualifications: LLB (Lond)

Greaves *Miss Simone Janette* •
Law Reporter, Messrs Allen & Overy,
One New Change, London EC4M 9QQ,
Call Date: Oct 1991 (Lincoln's Inn)
Qualifications: LLB (Hons), LLM
(Lond)

Grech *Leslie Francis*
Villa Grech-Mifsud, Mosta, Malta
MST 06, 432071 243946, Fax: 414458,
and Member Malta Bar, Call Date: June
1944 (Gray's Inn)

Green *Andrew William Nightingale* •
Legal & Administration Director,
Amalgamated Metal Corporation plc, 55
Bishopsgate, London EC2N 3AH, 0171
626 4521, Fax: 0171 623 6015, Call
Date: Feb 1960 (Gray's Inn)

Green *Christopher Steven*
Call Date: July 1998 (Middle Temple)
Qualifications: LLB (Hons)(Lond)

Green *Cyril*
44 High Haden Road, Cradley Heath,
West Midlands B64 7PJ, 0121 550 1099,
Call Date: Feb 1958 (Middle Temple)
Qualifications: LLB, FCIS

Green *David Allen Taylor*
Call Date: Mar 1999 (Lincoln's Inn)
Qualifications: MA (Oxon), Dip Law
(B'ham)

Green *David Michael* •
Legal Counsel, Klesch & Company
Limited, 6 Queen Street, Mayfair,
London W1X 7PH, 0171 493 4300, Fax:
0171 493 2525, Call Date: Nov 1987
(Middle Temple) Qualifications: LLB
(Hons)

Green *Graham Andrew*
Call Date: Mar 1999 (Inner Temple)
Qualifications: BA (Dunelm), CPE (City)

Green *Mrs Miranda Odofuorkor*
Senior Court Clerk, Victoria Law Courts,
Corporation Street, Birmingham, West
Midlands B4 6QA, 0121 235 4798, Fax:
0121 236 7837, Call Date: Nov 1983
(Gray's Inn) Qualifications: BA

Green *Robert Alan*
Call Date: Nov 1990 (Gray's Inn)
Qualifications: BSc (Econ) (Cardiff)

Green *William Henry Duncan*
Call Date: July 1998 (Middle Temple)
Qualifications: LLB (Hons)(Wolves)

Green *Mrs Yvonne*
and Member New York Bar 4 Field Court,
Gray's Inn, London, WC1R 5EA, Call
Date: July 1982 (Inner Temple)
Qualifications: LLB (Lond)

Greenald *Miss Miriam Ruth*
Call Date: Oct 1996 (Inner Temple)
Qualifications: LLB (Dunelm), MA in
Legal Studies

Greenald *Timothy Alexander* •
Lawyer, Crown Prosecution Service, C/O
50 Ludgate Hill, London EC4M 7EX, Call
Date: Mar 1996 (Middle Temple)
Qualifications: LLB (Hons)

Greenberg *Daniel Isaac* •
Senior Assistant Parliamentary Counsel,
Office of the Parliamentary, Counsel, 36
Whitehall, London SW1, 0171 210 3000,
Call Date: July 1987 (Lincoln's Inn)
Qualifications: BA (Cantab)

Greene *Richard Joseph Eugene*
Northern Ireland, and Member Northern
Ireland, Call Date: Nov 1990 (Middle
Temple) Qualifications: MA (Cantab)

Greenhalgh *Stephen John Edwin* •
Legal Team Leader, Personal Investment
Authority, 1 Canada Square, Canary
Wharf, London E14 5AZ, 0171 538 8860,
Fax: 0171 418 9300, Call Date: July 1977
(Inner Temple) Qualifications: LLB
(London)

Greenhill *John William*
Call Date: Nov 1972 (Middle Temple)

Greenland *Mrs Sheridan Dawn*
Deputy Clerk to the Justices, Surrey
Magistrates Court Comm, Chief
Executive's Office, Court House, London
Road, Dorking, Surrey RH4 1SX, 01306
885544, Fax: 01306 877447, Call Date:
July 1982 (Inner Temple) Qualifications:
LLB

Greenrod *Mrs Barbara* •
Senior Solicitor, Hampshire County
Council, The Castle, Winchester
SO23 8UJ, 01962 847377, Call Date: Feb
1974 (Inner Temple) Qualifications: LLB

Greensmith *David*
Clerk to the Justices, The Courthouse, P
O Box 8, Town Meadows, Rochdale
OL16 1AR, 01706 352442, Call Date: July
1981 (Gray's Inn) Qualifications: BA,
D.M.S, MIMgt,, MIPD, MBA

Greenway *Mrs Doreen Susan*
Call Date: Oct 1992 (Lincoln's Inn)
Qualifications: LLB(Hons)

Greenwood *Miss Fiona Caroline*
10 King's Bench Walk, Ground Floor,
Temple, London, EC4Y 7EB, Call Date:
Nov 1986 (Gray's Inn) Qualifications:
LLB, Dip in Law

Greenwood *Geoffrey William* •
Crown Prosecutor, Crown Prosecution
Service, Heron House, Houghoumont
Avenue, Crosby, Merseyside, Call Date:
July 1979 (Lincoln's Inn) Qualifications:
BA (Nottm)

Greenwood *George Edward*
39 Bell Lane, London E1 7LU, Call Date:
July 1973 (Inner Temple) Qualifications:
LLB

Greenwood *Mrs Sarah Elizabeth Ewule* •
Assistant Solicitor, West Lancashire
District, Council, P O Box 16, 52 Derby
Street, Ormskirk, Lancashire L39 2DF,
01695 585026, Fax: 01695 585082, Call
Date: July 1975 (Lincoln's Inn)
Qualifications: BA (Hons)

Greeves *Miss Susan Patricia* •
Crown Prosecutor, Crown Prosecution
Service, 4/5 South Parade, Wakefield
WF1 1LR, Call Date: Oct 1990 (Inner
Temple) Qualifications: LLB

Gregory *Rupert Giles Conal*
Call Date: July 1998 (Lincoln's Inn)
Qualifications: LLB (Hons)

Gregory *Miss Sarah Jane*
Call Date: Nov 1998 (Gray's Inn)
Qualifications: BA (Leics)

Gretason *The Reverend Mark Nicholas*
Eldon Chambers, Fourth Floor, 30/32
Fleet Street, London, EC4Y 1AA, Call
Date: May 1992 (Lincoln's Inn)
Qualifications: BA, MTA, AKC

Grew *Miss Michelle Robyn* •
Director of Compliance (Europe),
Lehman Brothers, One Broadgate,
London EC2M 7HA, 0171 260 2057, Call
Date: Oct 1991 (Middle Temple)
Qualifications: LLB (Hons)

Grewal *Jarnel Singh*
66 Gunnersbury Avenue, Ealing, London
W5 4HA, Call Date: Nov 1981 (Gray's
Inn) Qualifications: BA, ATII, ACCA

Grey *John Egerton*
51 St Peter's Road, West Mersea,
Colchester, Essex CO5 8LL, 01206
383007, Call Date: June 1954 (Inner
Temple) Qualifications: MA. BCL

Grey *The Hon Jolyon Kenneth Alnwick*
Consultant & p/t Adjudicator,
Immigration Appeals, Messrs Sedgwick,
Detert,, Moran & Arnold, 5 Lloyds
Avenue, London EC3N 3AE, 0171 929
1829, Fax: 0171 929 1808, Call Date:
Nov 1968 (Inner Temple) Qualifications:
MA (Cantab)

Grief *Professor Nicholas John*
Head of School of Finance & Law,
Bournemouth University, Dorset House,
Talbot Campus, Fern Barrow, Poole,
Dorset BH12 5BB, 01202 595428, Fax:
01202 595261, Call Date: Mar 1996
(Gray's Inn) Qualifications: BA, PhD
(Kent)

Grier *Warren*
Court Clerk, Sunderland Magistrates
Court, Gilbridge Avenue, Sunderland
SR1 3AP, 0191 5141621, Fax: 0191
5658564, Call Date: Nov 1989 (Inner
Temple) Qualifications: LLB (Newc)

Grieve *Dr Susan Jane*
Oriel Cottage, Broomhill Road,
Tunbridge Wells, Kent TN3 0TD, 01892
579365, Fax: 01892 579365, Call Date:
July 1998 (Inner Temple) Qualifications:
BSc (Manch), PhD (Lond), Dip.Law

Griffin *Miss Charlotte Louise*
Masons Solicitors, 30 Aylesbury Street,
London EC1R 0ER, 0171 490 4000, Fax:
0171 490 2545, Call Date: Oct 1995
(Lincoln's Inn) Qualifications: BA
(Hons), B.Arch (Manc), CPE (Manc)

Griffin *Miss Jacqueline*
Call Date: Nov 1998 (Inner Temple)
Qualifications: LLB

Griffith *Dr Gavan*
QC Australia, Australia, and Member
Victoria Bar Essex Court Chambers, 24
Lincoln's Inn Fields, London, WC2A
3ED, Call Date: Nov 1969 (Lincoln's Inn)
Qualifications: LLB (Mel)

Griffith *Shelley Raphael Walsh*
Call Date: Nov 1998 (Middle Temple)
Qualifications: BSc (Hons)(Kingston)

E

Griffiths *Bryn Lloyd*
Fleet Chambers, Mitre House, 44-46
Fleet Street, London, EC4Y 1BN, Call
Date: Apr 1989 (Inner Temple)
Qualifications: LLB

Griffiths *David Huw*
Call Date: May 1997 (Gray's Inn)
Qualifications: LLB (Exon)

Griffiths *Mr Huw David*
Compliance Consultant, Flat 3, 26
Woodstock Road, Croydon, Surrey
CR0 1JR, 0181 680 8614, Call Date:
Nov 1992 (Inner Temple)
Qualifications: LLB

Griffiths *Jonathan Morris*
Compliance, Director, Betting &
Gaming, Ladbroke Group PLC, 71
Queensway, London W2 4QH, 0171
313 7061, Fax: 0171 313 7003, Call
Date: July 1975 (Middle Temple)
Qualifications: LLB(Lond)

Griffiths *Ms Judith*
Call Date: Nov 1995 (Gray's Inn)
Qualifications: LLB (Wales)

Griffiths *Lawrence*
Former Recorder, Former Prosecution
Counsel to C & E and Inland Revenue
Iscoed Chambers, 86 St Helen's Road,
Swansea, SA1 4BQ, Call Date: Nov 1957
(Inner Temple) Qualifications: MA
(Cantab)

Griffiths *Mark Peter*
Call Date: Nov 1986 (Lincoln's Inn)
Qualifications: LLB (Leeds)

Griffiths *Matthew Stephen*
Call Date: July 1998 (Middle Temple)
Qualifications: LLB (Hons) (Bris)

Griffiths *Michael David* •
Principal Legal Adviser (Civil),
Staffordshire Police HQ, Cannock Road,
Stafford ST17 0QG, 01785 232153, Fax:
01785 232313, Call Date: May 1993
(Middle Temple) Qualifications: LLB
(Hons) (Cardiff)

Griffiths *Robert Norton* •
Senior Crown Prosecutor, Crown
Prosecution Service, First Floor, Oxford
House, Oxford Road, Bournemouth,
Dorset BH8 8HA, 01202 296917, Fax:
01202 556513, Call Date: July 1988
(Middle Temple) Qualifications: LLB
(Hons) (Reading)

Griffiths *Robert Ray*
Call Date: Oct 1995 (Lincoln's Inn)
Qualifications: LLB (Hons) (Leeds)

Griffiths *Miss Sarah-Jane*
Call Date: July 1998 (Lincoln's Inn)
Qualifications: LLB (Hons)

Griggs *Mrs Cecile Beatrice Jeanne*
Court Clerk, Croydon Magistrates'
Court, Barclay Road, Croydon, Surrey
CR9 3NG, 0181 686 8680, Fax: 0181
680 9801, Call Date: Nov 1988
(Lincoln's Inn) Qualifications: BA
(Sydney), LLB (Lond), MA

Grimshaw *David* •
Senior Legal Adviser, Conoco (UK)
Limited, Park House, 116 Park Street,
London W1Y 4NN, 0171 408 6527, Fax:
0171 408 6466, Call Date: Nov 1975
(Middle Temple) Qualifications: BA
(Cantab) MA, (Business Law), MBA

Grindrod *Mark Adrian*
Call Date: July 1987 (Lincoln's Inn)
Qualifications: BA (Sussex) Dip Law

Griswood *Miss Lisa Claire*
Healthcare Consultant, Hogg Robinson
Financial Services, 110 Fenchurch
Street, London EC3M 5JJ, Call Date: Oct
1995 (Middle Temple) Qualifications:
LLB (Hons)

Groombridge *Duncan James*
Call Date: July 1998 (Gray's Inn)
Qualifications: LLB (Huddersfield)

Grose *Robert John*
Call Date: Apr 1991 (Middle Temple)
Qualifications: LLB (Hons)

Grounds *Christopher Malcolm*
501 Man Yee Bldg, 60-68 Des Voeux
Road, Central, Hong Kong, and Member
Hong Kong Bar 1 Gray's Inn Square,
Ground Floor, London, WC1R 5AA, Call
Date: Feb 1977 (Inner Temple)
Qualifications: LLB

Groves *Ms Veronica Nadia*
Call Date: Feb 1990 (Lincoln's Inn)
Qualifications: B.ScEcon Hons ,
[Cardiff]

Grundy *Ms Stephanie Christine* •
Legal Advisor, H M Treasury,
Parliament Street, London SW1, Call
Date: July 1983 (Middle Temple)
Qualifications: MA, BCL

Gubbay *Mrs Joyce Bolissa*
Call Date: July 1972 (Middle Temple)
Qualifications: BA

Guedes *Lawrence*
Legal Advisor (Computer Law/
Commercial/Corporate), Call Date: Oct
1992 (Gray's Inn) Qualifications: LLB,
LLM

Guiloff *Miss Carolina Adela*
Call Date: Oct 1996 (Middle Temple)
Qualifications: LLB (Hons) (Kent)

Gujadhur *Tikanand*
Mauritius, Call Date: Oct 1997 (Middle
Temple) Qualifications: BA (Hons),
LLM (Cantab)

Gulleford *Dr Kenneth Arnold*
Company Secretary Professional
Solutions & Services Ltd, 26 Wakelin
Chase, Ingatestone, Essex CM4 9HH,
Formerly Senior Lecturer in Law, Call
Date: Nov 1991 (Lincoln's Inn)
Qualifications: LLB (Hons) (Birm),
PhD (Birm)

Gulliford *Jonathan Robert*
Call Date: Nov 1992 (Middle Temple)
Qualifications: LLB (Hons), LLM

Gulliver *Miss Heather Dawn Mia*
Call Date: Oct 1998 (Inner Temple)
Qualifications: LLB (Kent)

Gumbel *Rev Nicholas Glyn Paul*
Call Date: July 1977 (Middle Temple)
Qualifications: MA (Cantab) MA(Oxon)

Gunasekera *Miss Geshni Lankabhimani*
Call Date: July 1998 (Lincoln's Inn)
Qualifications: BA (Hons) (Lond)

Gunning *Alastair John Alan Bond*
and Member Bermuda Bar, Call Date:
Nov 1961 (Lincoln's Inn)
Qualifications: MA (Oxon)

Gunning *James John*
Alnor House, 23-25 The Green, Wye, Nr
Ashford, Kent TN25 5AJ, 01233 812
771, Fax: 01233 812 771, Call Date:
June 1956 (Inner Temple)
Qualifications: MA

Gupta *Ms Rajita Sharma*
Slaughter and May, 35 Basinghall
Street, London EC2V 5DB, 0171 710
4016/6001200, Fax: 0171 620 0289,
Member of the Bombay Bar Association
and Member Indian Bar, Call Date: July
1992 (Inner Temple) Qualifications:
BSc (Bombay), LLB (Bombay), LLM
(London)

Gustafson *Timothy Kaj*
Call Date: Nov 1998 (Middle Temple)
Qualifications: BA (Hons) (Middx), MSc
(LSE)

Guy *Ian Leslie* •
Senior Lawyer, Legal Services
Department, Neath Port Talbot, County
Borough Council, Civic Centre, Port
Talbot SA13 1PJ, 01639 763365, Fax:
01639 763370, Call Date: Nov 1988
(Gray's Inn) Qualifications: BA (Hons),
FRSA

Haddock *Glen Neil*
Senior Lecturer in Law (BVC),
University of Northumbria, School of
Law, Sutherland Building, Newcastle
Upon Tyne NE1 8ST, 0151 933 1334/
0191 227 3833, Fax: 0191 227 4557,
Call Date: Mar 1996 (Inner Temple)
Qualifications: LLB, LLM (L'pool)

Haddock *Miss Julie Angela*
Call Date: July 1998 (Lincoln's Inn)
Qualifications: LLB (Hons) (Nott'm)

Hadik *Andrew John William Michael* •
Branch Crown Prosecutor, Crown
Prosecution Service, Camberwell
Branch, 2nd Floor, The Cooperage,
Gainsford Street, London SE1 2NG,
0171 357 7010, Fax: 0171 962 0902,
Call Date: Nov 1980 (Middle Temple)
Qualifications: BA, MA (Lond)

Hadjisimou *Miss Androulla Sotiris*
Call Date: Mar 1998 (Inner Temple)
Qualifications: LLB (Keele)

Haffenden *Mrs Rebekah Ruth* •
Senior Lawyer, HM Customs & Excise,
New King's Beam House, 22 Upper
Ground, London SE1 9PJ, Call Date: July
1987 (Lincoln's Inn) Qualifications: LLB

Hage *Joseph*
Call Date: Oct 1991 (Lincoln's Inn)
Qualifications: BA (York)

Hagenmeyer *Moritz Wilhelm*
4 Paper Bldgs, Ground Floor, Temple,
London, EC4Y 7EX, Call Date: July 1995
(Inner Temple) Qualifications: Doctorate
in Law , (Hamburg), CPE (City)

Haigh *John* •
Group Corporate Lawyer & Company
Secretary, Kalon Group Plc, Huddersfield
Road, Birstall, Batley, W Yorks
WF17 9XA, 01924 477201, Fax: 01924
470950, Call Date: Nov 1976 (Lincoln's
Inn) Qualifications: BA Hons

Hailes *Ms Susan Dulcie Luisa*
Call Date: Oct 1995 (Inner Temple)
Qualifications: MA (Cantab), CPE

Haines *William Michael*
Old School House, Colwinston,
Cowbridge, Vale of Glamorgan CF71 7NL,
01656 654330, Call Date: Feb 1960
(Gray's Inn) Qualifications: MA (Oxon)

Haithwaite *Mrs Emily Pia*
Le Quatorze, 14 Gorey Pier, St Martin,
Jersey JE3 6EW, 01534 853392, Fax:
01534 853392, Call Date: Oct 1996
(Gray's Inn) Qualifications: BA (Keele),
LLM

Haitink *Mrs Patricia*
Call Date: Nov 1995 (Middle Temple)
Qualifications: BA (Hons)

Hajjar *Miss Fountoun Taj*
Legal Advisor, Sookias & Sookias Sol, 3rd
Floor, Clarebell House, 6 Cork Street,
London W1X 1PB, 0171 465 8000, Fax:
0171 465 8001, Call Date: Nov 1993
(Inner Temple) Qualifications: BA
(Washington), BA (Cantab)

Haldane *Mrs Sally Anne* •
Principal Crown Prosecutor, Crown
Prosecution Service, St Georges House,
Lever Street, Wolverhamton, 01902
870900, Fax: 01902 352017, Also Inn of
Court L, Call Date: July 1983 (Inner
Temple) Qualifications: BA (Hons)

Hale *Miss Catherine Margaret*
Call Date: Feb 1995 (Middle Temple)
Qualifications: LLB (Hons)(Warws)

Hale *Mrs Diane*
Call Date: Apr 1964 (Middle Temple)
Qualifications: LLB

Hales *Christopher James* •
Lawyer Grade 7, Treasury Solicitor's,
Queen Anne's Chambers, 28 Broadway,
London SW1H 9JS, 0171 210 3000, Fax:
0171 222 6006, Call Date: Nov 1979
(Gray's Inn) Qualifications: BA

Halhead *Thomas Edmund*
Call Date: Nov 1960 (Lincoln's Inn)

Hall *Amory Jocelyn Arnold*
Legal Advisor, Huddersfield Magistrates
Court, Justice Clerks Office, The Court
House, P.O.Box B37, Civic Centre,
Huddersfield HD1 2NH, 01 484 423552,
Call Date: Nov 1992 (Inner Temple)
Qualifications: LLB (Lancs)

Hall *Douglas Peter*
Bircham & Co, 1 Dean Farrar Street,
London SW1H 0DY, 0171 222 9458, Fax:
0171 222 0650, Call Date: Oct 1996
(Lincoln's Inn) Qualifications: BA
(Hons)(Oxon), Dip in Legal Studies

Hall *Edmund Charles Douglas* •
Crown Prosecution Service, Highbury
Branch, 1-9 Romford Road, Stratford,
London E15 4LJ, 0181 534 6601, Call
Date: Oct 1993 (Middle Temple)
Qualifications: BA (Hons)(Newc), CPE
(City)

Hall *Eric Michael* •
Principal Crown Prosecutor Prosecution
Team Leader, Crown Prosecution
Service, City of London Team, 1st Floor,
8 Gainsford Street, London SE1 2NE,
0171 962 2659, Call Date: Nov 1986
(Lincoln's Inn) Qualifications: Dip Mag
Law

Hall *Miss Janet Marie* •
Assistant Legal Counsel, Shanks &
McEwan Limited, Southern Waster
Services, Dunedin House, Auckland
Park, Mount Farm, Milton Keynes, Bucks
MK1 1BU, 01908 650 560, Call Date: Oct
1997 (Inner Temple) Qualifications: LLB
(Middlesex)

Hall *Leo John*
Call Date: Nov 1998 (Gray's Inn)
Qualifications: LLB (Brunel)

Hall *mrs Lorraine Mary*
Senior Court Clerk, Mansfield Magistrates
Court, Rosemary Street, Mansfield,
Nottinghamshire NG19 6EE, 01623
451500, Fax: 01623 451648, Call Date:
Feb 1988 (Gray's Inn) Qualifications:
Diploma in Magister-, ial Law, Diploma
Law

Hall *Miss Margaret Anne*
Call Date: July 1982 (Inner Temple)
Qualifications: BA

Hall *Mark Kevin*
Solicitor, Call Date: Nov 1990 (Lincoln's
Inn) Qualifications: LLB (Hons), BCL

Hall *Matthew Ronald Vickery*
Call Date: Oct 1990 (Middle Temple)
Qualifications: BA (Oxon)

Hall *Mrs Rosemary*
Call Date: June 1964 (Inner Temple)

Hall *Stephen* •
Call Date: July 1983 (Lincoln's Inn)
Qualifications: BA(Cardiff)

Hall *Miss Victoria Jayne*
Call Date: Mar 1996 (Gray's Inn)
Qualifications: LLB (Leeds)

Hall-Paterson *Wayne*
Call Date: Mar 1998 (Gray's Inn)
Qualifications: LLB

Hallam *Nigel Edwin*
Clerk to the Justices, Derby and South
Derbyshire, Magistrates Court, The Court
House, Derwent Street, Derby DE1 2EP,
01332 292 100, Fax: 01332 293 459,
Call Date: July 1987 (Gray's Inn)
Qualifications: Diploma Magistrate's,
Court Law, DMS,, MIMgt, MCI NVQ Level,
5 in Senior Mgmnt

Hallam *Mrs Susan*
Part-time Court Clerk, Bolton
Magistrates', Courts Committee, PO Box
24, Civic Centre, Bolton BL1 1QX, 01204
522244, Fax: 01204 364373, Call Date:
Feb 1987 (Lincoln's Inn) Qualifications:
Dip M Law, (Manchester)

Halliday *Christopher Martin Jonathan*
7 Thorn Grove, Ladybarn, Manchester,
Eire, 0161 224 4015, Call Date: Nov
1997 (Gray's Inn) Qualifications: LLB,
LLM (Nott'm)

Halpern *Leonard Isaac*
Linwood, Warren Rd, Fairlight, Hastings,
E Sussex TN35 4AN, 01424 813424, Call
Date: Apr 1947 (Middle Temple)
Qualifications: LLB (Lond)

Hambley *Ms Elizabeth* •
Treasury Solicitor, H M Treasury,
Parliament Street, London SW1P 3AG,
0171 270 5000, Call Date: Nov 1992
(Inner Temple) Qualifications: LLB
(Warw)

Hamblin *Miss Susan Caroline* •
Senior Publishing Editor, John Wiley &
Sons LTD, 42 Leinster Gardens, London
W2 3AN, 0171 298 3832, Fax: 0171 262
5093, Call Date: Nov 1990 (Lincoln's
Inn) Qualifications: LLB (Wales)

Hambly *Hedley Maurice*
Call Date: Nov 1960 (Gray's Inn)

Hambrook *Ronald Vivian*
136 Waxwell Lane, Pinner, Middlesex
HA5 3ES, Also Member of M, Call Date:
Nov 1953 (Gray's Inn) Qualifications:
LLB, DGA

Hamed *Joseph Mohamed Joseph*
1 Crown Office Row, Ground Floor,
Temple, London, EC4Y 7HH, Call Date:
July 1982 (Middle Temple)
Qualifications: LLB (Lond), BA

Hamid *Miss Simea*
Call Date: Nov 1997 (Lincoln's Inn)
Qualifications: LLB (HOns)

Hamill *Miss Elaine* •
Call Date: July 1979 (Gray's Inn)
Qualifications: LLB (L'pool), A.C.I.B

Hamill *Michael Garvin* •
Senior Legal Adviser - Legal
Deparmtment - Training & Derivatives,
Deutsche Bank AG, 133 Houndsditch,
London EC3A 7DX, 0171 545 4061,
Fax: 0171 545 1999, Call Date: Nov
1989 (Inner Temple) Qualifications:
LLB (Hons)

Hamilton *James Frederick Hume*
Acting Chairman,Kenya Law Reform
Commission, Kenya Law Reform
Commission, Maendeleo House, 8th
Floor, Monrovia Street,, PO Box 34999,
Nairobi Kenya, Nairobi 220888/9, and
Member Kenya Bar, Call Date: Jan 1938
(Gray's Inn) Qualifications: MA
(Cantab)

Hamilton *Miss Laura*
Slaughter & May, 35 Basinghall Street,
London EC2V 5DB, 0171 600 1200,
Call Date: Nov 1987 (Lincoln's Inn)
Qualifications: BA (Lond) Dip Law,
(City)

Hamilton *Patrick Joseph Martin*
Clerk to the Justices Justices Chief
Executive, Uxbridge Magistrates Court,
The Court House, Harefield Road,
Uxbridge, Middlesex UB8 1PQ, 01895
208401, Fax: 01895 274280, Call Date:
July 1980 (Gray's Inn) Qualifications:
MA (Oxon)

Hamilton *Mrs Penelope Ann*
Chartered Tax Adviser Partner, Indirect
Tax Division, Pricewaterhouse Coopers,
1 Embankment Place, London
WC2N 6NN, 0171 213 5855, Fax: 0171
213 4607, Call Date: July 1972 (Gray's
Inn) Qualifications: LLB (Hons)
(Bristol), FTII

Hamilton *Simon Austin*
Call Date: Oct 1992 (Lincoln's Inn)
Qualifications: BA(Hons), LLM

Hamilton Sugden *Miss Meredith
Theresa* •
Managing Director, Hamilton Advisory
Services Ltd, 7th Floor, Sir John
Moores' Building, 100 Old Hall Street,
Liverpool L3 9QJ, 0151 236 0510, Fax:
0151 255 0675, Call Date: Nov 1969
(Gray's Inn)

Hamlyn Williams *Philip Leslie Anstee* •
Diocesan Secretary, The Lincoln
Diocesan Trust and, Board of Finance
Ltd, The Old Palace, Lincoln LN2 1PU,
01522 529241, Fax: 01522 512717,
Call Date: Apr 1978 (Lincoln's Inn)
Qualifications: FCA, ATII

Hamm *Roderick Norman Lewis*
p/t Chairman: Lancashire Valuation
Tribunal, Call Date: Feb 1954
(Lincoln's Inn) Qualifications: MA

Hammersley *Bryan James* •
Legal Adviser, Department of the
Environment,, Transport and the
Regions, 76 Marsham Street, London
SW1, 0171 890 6480, Call Date: June
1970 (Middle Temple)

Hammerton *Ms Gillian Margaret Felicity*
1 Pump Court, Lower Ground Floor,
Temple, London, EC4Y 7AB, Call Date:
Nov 1973 (Gray's Inn) Qualifications:
BSc,LLB

Hammond *Miss Karen Ann* •
3 Gray's Inn Square, Ground Floor,
London, WC1R 5AH, Call Date: July
1985 (Middle Temple) Qualifications:
LLB(Notts)

Hammond *Michael John* •
Senior Crown Prosecutor, Crown
Prosecution Service, 50 Ludgate Hill,
London EC4M 7EX, Call Date: Oct 1991
(Inner Temple) Qualifications: BSc,
CPE

Hammond *Miss Tracey Ann*
Deputy Chief Clerk, Inner London
Magistrates, Courts Service, SW
Magistrates' Court, Lavender Hill,
London SW11, Call Date: Feb 1989
(Gray's Inn) Qualifications: LLB (Lond)

Hamon *Kenneth George*
Woodside, Shinfield Roadn, Shinfield,
Reading, Berks RG2 9BE, Call Date:
July 1972 (Gray's Inn)

Hamper *Andrew John Paul*
Call Date: Oct 1991 (Middle Temple)
Qualifications: LLB Hons (B'ham)

Hampshire *Mrs Ann Christine* •
Principal Crown Prosecutor, Crown
Prosecution Service, Hawkins House,
Pynes Hill, Rydon Lane, Exeter, Devon
EX2 5SS, 01392 422555, Fax: 01392
422111, Call Date: Nov 1983 (Gray's
Inn) Qualifications: LLB (Sheff)

Hampson *Professor Francoise Jane*
Professor of Law, Department of Law &
Human, Rights Centre, University of
Essex, Wivenhoe Park, Colchester,
Essex CO4 3SQ, 01206 872564, Fax:
01206 873428, Call Date: Nov 1996
(Lincoln's Inn) Qualifications: LLB
(Hons)

Hampson *Michael David* •
Company Secretary, RMC Group plc,
RMC House, Coldharbour Lane,
Thorpe, Egham, Surry TW20 8TD,
01932 568833, Fax: 01932 568933,
Call Date: July 1985 (Middle Temple)
Qualifications: LLB (Cardiff)

Hampson *Rodney*
Clerk to the Justices, Sefton
Magistrates, Courts Committee, The
Law Courts, Albert Road, Southport
PR9 0LJ, 01704 534141, Fax: 01704
500226, Call Date: Nov 1982 (Gray's
Inn) Qualifications: LLB (Lond)

Hampton *John*
Recorder Formerly Deputy Traffic
Commissioner. Deputy Chairman
Agricultural Land Tribunal (Yorkshire
& Humberside)., 37 Park Square,
Leeds LS1 2NY, 0113 243 9422, Fax:
0113 242 4229, 37 Park Square, Leeds,
LS1 2NY, Call Date: July 1952 (Inner
Temple) Qualifications: LLB

Hamzah *Miss Nor Raviah Adliza*
Call Date: Oct 1996 (Lincoln's Inn)
Qualifications: LLB (Hons)

Hancock *Miss Claire*
Call Date: Nov 1998 (Lincoln's Inn)
Qualifications: LLB (Hons)(Manch)

Hands *Mrs Maryvonne Edith*
Tax Consultant General Commissioner
of Taxation, Browne Jacobson, 44
Castle Gate, Nottingham NG1 6EA, 0115
9500055, Fax: 0115 9475246, Call
Date: July 1974 (Inner Temple)
Qualifications: MA (Oxon), ATII

Hankers *Miss Julia Anne*
Principal Legal Advisor, Bedfordshire
Magistrates Court, The Court House,
Stuart Street, Luton, Beds LU1 5BL,
01582 402333, Fax: 01582 24852, Call
Date: Jan 1985 (Gray's Inn)

Hanlon *Keith George*
33 Bedford Row, London, WC1R 4JH,
Call Date: Nov 1979 (Gray's Inn)
Qualifications: LLB, MSc, BSc,
F.I.Mech.E, FIEE,C.Eng A.C.I.Arb

Hanna *Ms Elizabeth Colette* •
Call Date: Feb 1994 (Lincoln's Inn)
Qualifications: LLB (Hons)

Hannibal *Martin Charles* •
School of Law, Staffordshire University,
College Road, Stoke on Trent ST4 2DE,
01782 573407, Fax: 01782 294335,
Call Date: May 1988 (Lincoln's Inn)
Qualifications: BA (Hons) , LLM

Hanratty *Miss Judith Christine* •
Company Secretary, The British
Petroleum Company plc, The British
Petroleum Co plc, Britannic House, 1
Finsbury Circus, London EC2M 7BA,
0171 496 4244, Fax: 0171 496 4678,
and Member Victoria Bar New Zealand
Bar, Call Date: Feb 1987 (Inner
Temple) Qualifications: LLB, LLM

Hanson *Derrick George*
Tower House, Grange Lane, Formby,
Merseyside L37 7BR, 01704 874040,
Fax: 01704 831731, Call Date: July
1952 (Lincoln's Inn) Qualifications:
LLM, FCIB, MPhil

Hanson *Ian Lawrence* •
Executive Vice President, EMI Records
Limited, 43 Brook Green, London
W6 7EF, 0171 605 5407, Fax: 0171 605
5069, Call Date: Feb 1989 (Inner
Temple) Qualifications: LLB, MBA

Happe *Dominic Peter Alexander*
Call Date: 1993 (Gray's Inn)
Qualifications: BA

Happold *Matthew Charles Edmund*
Call Date: Nov 1995 (Middle Temple)
Qualifications: BA (Hons), MSc, MA
(Oxon)

Haq *Mahmoodul*
Call Date: Feb 1981 (Middle Temple)
Qualifications: BA, LLB

Haque *Md Nizamul*
Legal Adviser, 4 Carpenter House,
Burgess Street, London E14 7BB, 0171
515 0400/0181 687 1948/0181 543
3111, Fax: 0181 543 0033, and Member
Bangladesh Bar, Call Date: Mar 1997
(Lincoln's Inn) Qualifications: LLB
(Hons)(Dhaka), LLB (Hons), LLM,
(Lond)

Harakis *Michael Joseph*
Call Date: Nov 1998 (Lincoln's Inn)
Qualifications: BSc (Hons), LLM,
(So'ton)

Harbert *Ms Anna Katherine* •
Legal Adviser, Imperial Chemical
Industries, Plc, Wexham Road, Slough,
Berks, 01753 877338, Call Date: July
1980 (Inner Temple) Qualifications: BA
(Hons), Diploma in , Intellectural,
Property Law

Hardcastle *Ian Martin*
Legal Advisor ; Senior Lecture in Law,
01604 591272, Fax: 01604 591941, Call
Date: Nov 1995 (Gray's Inn)
Qualifications: LLB (Leeds), LLM,
(Lond), MBA, (Bradford)

Harding *Edward James*
Clerk to the Justices, Gwent Magistrates
Court, 2nd Floor, Gwent House, Gwent
Square, Cwnbran, Gwent NP44 1PL,
01633 862112, Fax: 01633 868944, Call
Date: Nov 1984 (Middle Temple)
Qualifications: Dip Law

Harding *Geoffrey Nathaniel Augustine A*
Call Date: July 1994 (Lincoln's Inn)
Qualifications: BA (Hons)

Harding *Kenneth*
01423 886380, Call Date: Nov 1970
(Gray's Inn)

Harding *Malvin Adebayo Julian*
Legal Consultant, Harding & Co, Legal
Consultants, South Bank House, Black
Prince Road, London SE1 7SJ, 0171 582
9708/735 8171, Fax: 0171 735 1555,
Call Date: Oct 1990 (Middle Temple)
Qualifications: LLB (Hons) (Lond), BSc
(Econ) (Hons)

Harding *Simon John*
Call Date: Oct 1998 (Middle Temple)
Qualifications: BA (Hons)(York), CPE
(Sussex)

Hardman *Miss Eryl Wendy*
Call Date: Oct 1997 (Middle Temple)
Qualifications: LLB (Hons)(B'ham)

Hardwick *Malcolm Rodger*
Arbitrator (Civil Actions), Supreme Court
of New South Wales (1990-95), Australia,
QC NSW & ACT Bar and Member
Barrister and Solicitor for Supreme Ct
Papua New Guinea, Call Date: Nov 1950
(Inner Temple) Qualifications: MA
(Oxon)

Hardy *Benedict*
Call Date: Oct 1995 (Inner Temple)
Qualifications: BA (Keele), MA (Bris)

Hardy *David Peter*
Deputy Chief Clerk, Clerkenwell
Magistrates Court, 78 King's Cross Road,
London WC1X 5QS, 0171 278 6571, Fax:
0171 633 3662, Call Date: Nov 1987
(Gray's Inn)

Hardy *Richard Evelyn Whittelle*
Japonica Cottage, 205 Stanley Road,
Twickenham TW2 5NW, 0181 977 5611,
Call Date: July 1974 (Inner Temple)
Qualifications: BA, MSc (Lond), FCA,
MBA

Hare *Ivan Charles*
Fellow & Director of Studies in Law,
Trinity College, Cambridge CB2 1TQ,
01223 338420, Fax: 01223 338564, Call
Date: Oct 1991 (Inner Temple)
Qualifications: LLB (Lond), BCL (Oxon),
LLM (Harvard), MA (Cantab)

Harffey *Robert*
18 Victoria Drive, Eastbourne, East
Sussex BN20 8JX, 0831 728245, Call
Date: Nov 1986 (Middle Temple)
Qualifications: BA

Harington *Sir Nicholas John* •
Legal Adviser ECGD, ECGD, 2 Exchange
Tower, Harbour Exchange Square,
London E14 9GS, 0171 512 7862, Fax:
0171 572 7052, Call Date: July 1969
(Inner Temple) Qualifications: MA
(Oxon)

Harley *David William* •
Senior Crown Prosecutor, Crown
Prosecution Service, Seaton House, 62
Wellington Street, Stockport, Cheshire,
Call Date: July 1988 (Middle Temple)
Qualifications: LLB (Hons)

Harling *Peter John*
Clerk to the Justices, Lancashire
Magistrates Courts, Commitee, Penine
Magistrates Courts, P O Box 64, Burnley
BB10 2NQ, 01282 610032, Fax: 01282
610034, Call Date: July 1980 (Gray's
Inn) Qualifications: Dip Law

Harling *Russell James* •
Thomas R Miller & Sons, International
House, Creechurch Lane, London
EC3A 5BA, 0171 283 4646, Call Date: Apr
1991 (Gray's Inn) Qualifications: BA
(Oxford)

Harlow *Mrs Irma Sylvia*
Call Date: Nov 1971 (Lincoln's Inn)
Qualifications: BA, Dip Ed(Leeds)

Harlow *Mrs Nirmala*
Call Date: Nov 1974 (Lincoln's Inn)

Harman *Andrew Michael* •
Casework Lawyer, Crown Prosecution
Service, 50 Ludgate Hill, London EC4,
0171 273 1230, Fax: 0171 329 8171,
Call Date: July 1983 (Gray's Inn)
Qualifications: BA

Harman *Lady Katherine Frances Goddard*
Call Date: July 1960 (Inner Temple)

Harmer *Donald Leonard*
Apartado 901, 04638 Mojacar, Almeria,
950 472864, Fax: 950 472864, Call Date:
Nov 1979 (Lincoln's Inn) Qualifications:
Dip Arch (Leics), RIBA

Harmes *Stephen Douglas* •
Senior Crown Prosecutor, CPS Cardiff,
Pearl Assurance House, Greyfriars Road,
Cardiff CF1 3PL, 01222 378201 Ext 168,
Fax: 01222 373596, Call Date: Oct 1993
(Gray's Inn) Qualifications: B.Sc (Econ,
Wales)

Harms *Anthony David*
60 Lordship Park, London N16 5UA,
0181 800 5735, Fax: 0181 800 5735,
Call Date: Nov 1997 (Middle Temple)
Qualifications: BA (Hons)(Manch), LLB
(Hons)(City)

Harold *Miss Caroline Grace* •
Lawyer, The Office of the Solicitor, Dept
of Social Security, London South Area
Lawyers, Office, Sutherland House,
29-37 Brighton Road, Sutton SM2 5AN,
0181 652 6500, Call Date: July 1993
(Inner Temple) Qualifications: LLB

Harold *Fergus Dougal*
Call Date: Oct 1996 (Gray's Inn)
Qualifications: BA (Dunelm)

Harper *Mrs Belinda Margaret*
Call Date: Oct 1993 (Lincoln's Inn)
Qualifications: BSc (Hons)(Leeds),
Zoology, Dip Law, (B'ham)

Harper *Miss Lisa-Jane*
Tax Consultant, KPMG, 1-2 Dorset Rise,
London EC4, 0171 311 1000, Call Date:
Oct 1996 (Lincoln's Inn) Qualifications:
BSc (Hons)(St Andr) , Dip in Law (City)

Harper *Mrs Sandra Elizabeth Lillian*
Call Date: July 1985 (Middle Temple)
Qualifications: BA (Soton)

Harper *Mrs Vivian* •
Senior Crown Prosecutor, Crown
Prosecution Service, 1st Floor, Coniston
House, District 4, Washington, Tyne &
Wear NE38 7RN, Call Date: Oct 1990
(Gray's Inn) Qualifications: BA

Harries *Miss Janet Mary*
Principal Court Clerk, Magistrates Court,
Fitzalan Place, Cardiff, South Glamorgan
CF2 1RZ, 01222 463040, Fax: 01222
460264, Call Date: July 1978 (Gray's
Inn) Qualifications: LLB (Hons), MBA

Harrigan *Patrick Bernard*
Human Resources Advisor, School Croft,
off Church Lane, ADEL, Leeds LS16 8DE,
Call Date: Nov 1982 (Gray's Inn)
Qualifications: LLB

Harrington *Miss Clare Stephanie*
Call Date: Oct 1998 (Lincoln's Inn)
Qualifications: LLB (Hons)(Lond)

Harrington *Mrs Elaine* •
Commercial Manager, CSC Comouter
Sciences Limited, Drakes Court, 302
Alcester Road, Wythall, Birmingham
B47 6JR, 01564 821169, Fax: 01564
821001, Call Date: Nov 1996 (Gray's
Inn) Qualifications: LLB, ACIS

Harris *Mrs Alyson* •
Senior Crown Prosecutor, Crown
Prosecution Service, Froomsgate
House, Rupert Street, Bristol, Avon
BS1 2PS, 0117 9273093, and Member
Hong Kong Bar, Call Date: July 1979
(Middle Temple) Qualifications: LLB
(B'ham)

Harris *Miss Claire-Louise*
Call Date: Oct 1998 (Lincoln's Inn)
Qualifications: BA (Hons)(B'ham), CPE

Harris *Colin*
3 St Leonards Terrace, London
SW3 4QA, 0171 730 8746, Fax: 0171
824 8320, Call Date: June 1956 (Inner
Temple) Qualifications: MA (Cantab)

Harris *Daniel Alexander*
and Member Cayman Islands, Call
Date: Oct 1995 (Lincoln's Inn)
Qualifications: LLB (Hons)(Sussex)

Harris *Miss Elizabeth Mary*
Call Date: Mar 1996 (Inner Temple)
Qualifications: LLB

Harris *Graham Anthony*
Crown Prosecutor Hong Kong 7 Stone
Bldgs, 1st Floor, Lincoln's Inn, London,
WC2A 3SZ, Call Date: Nov 1975 (Middle
Temple) Qualifications: LLB

Harris *John David* •
Senior Crown Prosecutor, Crown
Prosecution Service, Provincial House,
140 Victoria Street, Grimsby, Call Date:
Nov 1981 (Inner Temple)
Qualifications: LLB

Harris *Martin John*
Legal Advisor, Essex Magiatrates' Court
Cmtte, The Court House, Victoria
Avenue, Southend on Sea, Essex
SS2 6EU, 01702 348491, Call Date: July
1984 (Lincoln's Inn) Qualifications: BA

Harris *Michael Joseph George*
Formerly a Solicitor, Call Date: July
1970 (Middle Temple) Qualifications:
MA (Oxon)

Harris *Neil Charles* •
Head of Legal Affairs Company
Secretary, Shire Pharmaceuticals
Group, plc,, East Anton, Andover, Hants
SP1D 5RG, 01264 333455, Fax: 01264
334657, Call Date: July 1984 (Middle
Temple) Qualifications: BA (Hons)

Harris *Professor Neville Stuart*
Professor of Law, School of Law,
Liverpool John Moores, University,
Liverpool, 0151 231 2000, Fax: 0151
231 3935, Call Date: Feb 1993 (Gray's
Inn) Qualifications: LLB, LLM, Ph.D
(Sheff)

Harris *Paul*
1 Gray's Inn Square, 1st Floor, London,
WC1R 5AG, Call Date: Feb 1976
(Lincoln's Inn) Qualifications: MA
Hons [Oxon]

Harris *Peter Graham* •
Head of Family Law & Procedure
Division, Lord Chancellor's
Department, Trevelyan House, Great
Peter Street, London SW1, Call Date:
Nov 1973 (Inner Temple)

Harris *Peter Michael* •
Official Solicitor to the Supreme Court,
The Official Solicitor, 81 Chancery
Lane, London WC2A 1DD, 0171 911
7116, Fax: 0171 911 7105, Call Date:
Nov 1971 (Gray's Inn)

Harris *Rupert William* •
Steamship Mutual Underwriting,
Association Limited, 39 Bell Lane,
Aquatical House, London E1 7LU, 0171
247 5490 Ext 463, Fax: 0171 377 2912,
Call Date: Oct 1993 (Lincoln's Inn)
Qualifications: LLB (Hons)(Bris)

Harris *Miss Sally Fiona* •
Principal Legal Officer, Office of the
Solicitor, Dept of Social Security, Dept,
of Health, 48 Carey Street, London
WC2A 2LS, 0171 412 1262, Fax: 0171
412 1499, Call Date: July 1986 (Inner
Temple) Qualifications: LLB (Hull)

Harris *Miss Sarah Katharine Holtby*
Indigo Events Limited, 32-34 Great
Marlborough Street, London W1V 1HA,
Call Date: Nov 1989 (Middle Temple)
Qualifications: BA (Hons) , Dip.Law

Harris *William Barclay*
Moatlands, Vowels Lane, East
Grinstead, Sussex RH19 4LL, 01342
810 228, Call Date: Jan 1937 (Inner
Temple) Qualifications: MA (Cantab)

Harrison *Mrs Angela Marjorie*
South Lawn, Eastcote High Rd, Pinner,
Middx HA5 2HJ, 0181 866 5416, Call
Date: Nov 1961 (Gray's Inn)

Harrison *Ms Anne Denise* •
Advisory Counsel, Environment Agency,
King's Meadow House, King's Meadow
Road, Reading RG1 8DQ, 0118 953
5000, Fax: 0118 950 9440, Call Date:
May 1992 (Inner Temple)
Qualifications: LLB

Harrison *Mrs Caroline Anne*
Court Clerk, Norwich Magistrates Court,
Bishopsgate, Norwich NR3 1UP, 01603
632421, Fax: 01603 663263, Call Date:
Oct 1992 (Lincoln's Inn)
Qualifications: LLB(Hons)

Harrison *Christopher Robert* •
Lawyer, Ministry of Agriculture,,
Fisheries and Food, 55 Whitehall,
London SW1A 2EY, 0171 270 8312, Call
Date: July 1975 (Middle Temple)
Qualifications: LLB (Hons)

Harrison *Clive Osler*
c/o Acceptar Corporation Ltd, 12th
Floor, Ruttonjee House, 11 Duddell
Street, (852) 2521 3661, Fax: (852)
2845 9198, Call Date: Mar 1997 (Inner
Temple) Qualifications: LLB (Wales)

Harrison *Mrs Hazel Kathleen* •
Lawyer, Ministry of Agriculture,,
Fisheries and Food, 55 Whitehall,
London SW1A 2EY, 0171 270 8337, Call
Date: July 1981 (Lincoln's Inn)
Qualifications: LLB (Hons)

Harrison *Miss Jane Emily*
Call Date: Nov 1996 (Inner Temple)
Qualifications: BSc (L'pool)

Harrison *Miss Karen Anne*
Call Date: Oct 1998 (Lincoln's Inn)
Qualifications: LLB (Hons)(Wales)

Harrison *Michael John* •
Assistant Legal Advisor, Ministry of
Defence, Room 0182, Main Building,
White Hall, London SW1A 2HB, 0171
218 1933, Call Date: Oct 1994 (Middle
Temple) Qualifications: MA
(Hons)(Cantab)

Harrison *Neil Richard*
Call Date: Nov 1997 (Lincoln's Inn)
Qualifications: LLB (Hons)(Leics)

Harrison *Nigel Jeffrey* •
Crown Prosecutor, Crown Prosecution
Service, 2nd Floor, Calder House, St
James Street, Burnley, Lancashire
BB11 1XG, Call Date: Nov 1985 (Gray's
Inn) Qualifications: LLB(Sheffield)

Harrison *Mrs Rosalynde Victoria* •
Commercial Legal Support Ltd, 103 St
Kilda Road, West Ealing, London
W13 9DF, 0181 840 5930, Fax: 0181
568 4082, Call Date: July 1981 (Middle
Temple) Qualifications: BA

Harrison *Rupert Knight*
12 Clarendon Road, London W11 3AB,
0171 491 0491, Call Date: July 1982
(Middle Temple) Qualifications: LLB
(Lond), LLM (Lond)

Harrison *Mrs Teresa Frances Helen* •
Assistant Solicitor, Town Hall, The
Burroughs, Hendon, London NW4 4BG,
Fax: 0181 359 2680, Call Date: Nov
1992 (Middle Temple) Qualifications:
LLB (Hons)

Harrison *Thomas Gwyn*
Call Date: Oct 1998 (Lincoln's Inn)
Qualifications: BA (Bris), BArch (Bris),
LLB (Hons)

Harrison *Trevor Kenneth* •
Group Legal Adviser, Tramp Group Ltd,
Wells House, 15-17 Elmfield Road,
Bromley, Kent BR1 1LT, 0181 315
7779, Fax: 0181 315 7788, Call Date:
July 1978 (Inner Temple)
Qualifications: LLB

Harrison-Hall *Rupert Andrew James*
44a Hazelbourne Road, London
SW12 9NS, 0181 675 6648, Call Date:
Oct 1991 (Inner Temple) Qualifications:
LLB (Bucks), Dip Agriculture , (MRAC)

Harrold *Nicholas James*
Call Date: Mar 1998 (Lincoln's Inn)
Qualifications: LLB (Hons)(Leics)

Harsham *Joseph Amin*
3 Briar Road, Pollards Hill, Norbury,
London SW16 4LT, 0181 764 5480, and
Member Guyana Bar, Call Date: July
1969 (Inner Temple) Qualifications: LLB
Lond, MBIM

Hart *John Richard Samuel*
Manchester House, Bramdean, Alresford,
Hampshire SO24 0LW, 01962 771091,
Fax: 01962 771034, Call Date: June 1955
(Middle Temple) Qualifications: FCIS

Hart *Peter Martin* •
Deputy Insurance Ombudsman,
Insurance Ombudsman Bureau, City
Gate One, 135 Park Street, London
SE1 9EA, 0171 902 8151, Fax: 0171 902
8198, Call Date: Nov 1975 (Lincoln's
Inn) Qualifications: BA (Cantab)

Hart *Robert William*
Call Date: June 1961 (Inner Temple)
Qualifications: BA (Cantab)

Hart *William*
Call Date: Oct 1998 (Inner Temple)
Qualifications: BA (Leeds), CPE

Hartley *Christopher John* •
Prosecution Team Leader, Crown
Prosecution Service, Humber, Greenfield
House, 32 Scotland Street, Sheffield
S3 7DQ, Call Date: July 1987 (Inner
Temple) Qualifications: BA (Hons)
(Kent)

Hartridge *Miss Juliet Claire* •
Principal Legal Officer, Treasury
Solicitor's, Queen Anne's Chambers, 28
Broadway, London SW1H 9JS, 0171 210
3363, Fax: 0171 210 3001, Call Date: Oct
1993 (Lincoln's Inn) Qualifications: LLB
(Hons)(Lond)

Hartshorne *John Trevor*
Lecturer in Law, University of Leicester,
Faculty of Law, University Road, Leicester
LE1 7RH, 0116 252 2363, Fax: 0116 252
5023, Call Date: Oct 1993 (Inner
Temple) Qualifications: LLB (Exon),
LLM (Leics)

Harty *Mrs Eily Imogen Mary*
Part-time Chairman Social Security
Appeal Tribunals, The Thatched House,
Littlewarth Avenue, Esher, Surrey
KT10 9PB, Call Date: Nov 1977 (Middle
Temple) Qualifications: MA (Oxon)

Harty *Martin John* •
European Compliance Director, Citibank
N.A., 336 Syrand, London WC2R 1HB,
0171 500 0454, Fax: 0171 500 7219,
Call Date: July 1976 (Middle Temple)
Qualifications: MA (Oxon), ACIArb

Harvey *Ms Alison Roma*
Call Date: Nov 1994 (Inner Temple)
Qualifications: BA (Oxon), M.Litt/D.Phil
(Oxon), MA (Leic)

Harvey *Miss Jayne Denise* •
Head of Legal Affairs, Global Reach Ltd,
New Loom House, 101 Back Church
Lane, London E1 1LU, 0171 423 0613,
Call Date: Feb 1992 (Middle Temple)
Qualifications: LLB (Hons), LLM (Lond)

Harvey *Mrs Leah*
28 Rodway Road, London SW15 5DS,
0181 788 9778, Justice of the Peace,
Inner London, South Central Division
1965-1989, Call Date: July 1972 (Gray's
Inn) Qualifications: Dip Criminology

Harvey *Peter*
Call Date: June 1948 (Lincoln's Inn)
Qualifications: MA, BCL (Oxon)

Harvey *Richard Derek* •
Region Manager, Legal (Europe Russia,
Africa, Middle East), BHP Petroleum
Limited, Devonshire House, Picadilly,
London W1X 6AQ, 0171 408 7055, Fax:
0171 408 7095, Call Date: July 1976
(Lincoln's Inn) Qualifications: BSc, MSc,
CEng MIChem E

Harvey Wood *Andrew James*
Camp Lodge, The Camp, Near Stroud,
Gloucs GL6 7EW, Call Date: Nov 1965
(Inner Temple)

Harwick *Ms Elizabeth Adams*
Call Date: Mar 1999 (Lincoln's Inn)
Qualifications: BA (USA)

Harwood *Mrs Lesley Jean*
Call Date: Mar 1999 (Lincoln's Inn)
Qualifications: BA (Hons)(Open), CPE
(Manch)

Harwood *Matthew Nicholas*
Call Date: July 1974 (Gray's Inn)
Qualifications: LLB

Harwood *Miss Susan Mary Josephine* •
Grade 7 Lawyer, Department of Trade &
Industry, Legal Services, D2, 10 Victoria
Street, London SW1H 0NN, 0171 215
3168, Fax: 0171 215 3235, Call Date:
Nov 1988 (Middle Temple)
Qualifications: BA (Keele)

Hasan *Miss Jamila Zehra*
Freelance Journalist, Call Date: May 1993
(Inner Temple) Qualifications: LLB
(Southbank), LLM (Lond)

Hashim *Mohamed Zuraish Hifaz*
Call Date: Nov 1998 (Middle Temple)
Qualifications: LLB (Hons)(Wolves)

Haslam *Miss Emily*
Lecturer, Centre for Legal Studies,
University of Sussex, Falmer, Brighton
BN1 9QN, 01273 606755, Fax: 01273
678466, Call Date: Nov 1995 (Middle
Temple) Qualifications: LLB (Hons),
LLM

Hassan *Miss Fleur Judith Sol*
Gibraltar, Call Date: Nov 1996 (Middle
Temple) Qualifications: LLB (Hons)

Hassan *Robin Anthony* •
Junior Counsel, British Sky Broadcasting
Ltd, Grant Way, Isleworth, Middlesex
TW7 5QD, 0171 705 3387, Fax: 0171
705 3254, Call Date: Nov 1994 (Inner
Temple) Qualifications: LLB (Essex)

Hassan *Toper*
Call Date: July 1989 (Middle Temple)
Qualifications: BA (Sussex), LLM (Lond)

Hatcher *Mark*
Head of Public Affairs Consultancy, Head
of Public Affairs,
PricewaterhouseCoopers,
PricewaterhouseCooper, 1 Embankment
Place, London WC2N 6NN, 0171 213
4714, Fax: 0171 213 4409, Also L 1982
Inns of Court, Call Date: Nov 1978
(Middle Temple) Qualifications: MA
(Oxon), FRSA

Hatfield *Mrs Linda*
Call Date: July 1974 (Middle Temple)
Qualifications: MA (Cantab)

Hattersley *Lt Cdr Jonathan Peter
George* •
Call Date: Nov 1984 (Gray's Inn)
Qualifications: LLB (Hons)

Hatton *Miss Theresa Jacqueline*
Call Date: Mar 1998 (Lincoln's Inn)
Qualifications: LLB (Hons)(Derby)

Haugstad *Miss Annelise Charlotte*
Call Date: Nov 1996 (Lincoln's Inn)
Qualifications: BA (Hons)(Keele)

Havard *Dr John David Jayne*
1 Wilton Square, London N1 3DL, 0171
383 6095, Fax: 0171 383 6195, Hon Sec
Commonwealth Medical Assoc Secretary
BMA 1979-89, Call Date: July 1954
(Middle Temple) Qualifications: MA, MD,
LLM (Cantab), FRCP (Lond), FRCGP,
(Hons)

Havard *Nigel George* •
Service Manager - Property Team Legal &
Committee Services, Council of the City
& County, of Swansea, County Hall,
Oystermouth Road, Swansea SA1 3SN,
01792 636291, Call Date: Mar 1998
(Gray's Inn) Qualifications: BA

Havelock *Martin John*
Group Personnel Director: Oxford
University Press, Oxford University Press,
Great Clarendon Street, Oxon OX2 6DP,
01865 267611, Fax: 01865 267612, Call
Date: Nov 1977 (Gray's Inn)
Qualifications: MA (Oxon)

Havers *John Kingsley*
QC Belize (1966) QC Gibraltar (1972),
The Glebe Cottage, Woolfardisworthy, Nr
Crediton, Devon EX17 4RX, 01363
866484, Senior Magistrate British Indian
Ocean Territory, Call Date: Feb 1952
(Inner Temple) Qualifications: MA,BCL

Haw Smalley *Mrs Judith Mary* •
Springwell House,
Shipton-By-Beningbrough, York
YO30 1AB, 01904 470522, Call Date: July
1973 (Gray's Inn)

E

Haward *Mrs Linda Ruth*
Jacksons Solicitors, Queens Square, Middlesbrough, Call Date: July 1994 (Lincoln's Inn) Qualifications: LLB (Hons) (Essex)

Hawe *Miss Cathleen Margaret* •
Senior Principal Legal Officer, HM Customs & Excise, New King's Beam House, 22 Upper Ground, London SE1 9PJ, 0171 865 5135, Fax: 0171 865 5248, Call Date: Nov 1972 (Gray's Inn)

Hawken *Simon Charles*
Lovell White Durrant, 65 Holborn Viaduct, London EC1A 2DY, 0171 236 0066, Fax: 0171 248 4212, Call Date: July 1977 (Middle Temple) Qualifications: MA

Hawker *Miss Susan Rachel Louise*
Beachcroft Stanleys, 20 Furnival Street, Call Date: Nov 1994 (Lincoln's Inn) Qualifications: MA (Oxon), CPE (Sussex)

Hawkes *Miss Audrey* •
Principal Crown Prosecutor, Crown Prosecution Service, 50 Ludgate Hill, London EC4M 7EX, 0171 273 8000, Call Date: July 1983 (Inner Temple) Qualifications: LLB (Lond)

Hawkes *Ms Gillian*
Call Date: Oct 1997 (Gray's Inn) Qualifications: LLB (Lond)

Hawkes *Terence Arthur*
8 Dale Drive, Holmer, Hereford HR4 9RF, Call Date: July 1962 (Gray's Inn)

Hawkins *Miss Alison*
Call Date: Nov 1978 (Gray's Inn) Qualifications: BA

Hawkins *Andrew Stehen Lindsay*
Director of Policy & PR, London Chamber of Commerce, & Industry, 33 Queen Street, London EC4P 1AP, 0171 203 1898, Fax: 0171 203 1920, Call Date: July 1995 (Gray's Inn) Qualifications: MA (St Andrews)

Hawkins *Nicholas John*
Parliamentary Private Secretary MOD, then DNH, House of Commons, Westminster, London SW1A 0AA, 0171 219 6329, Fax: 0171 219 2754/2693, Verulam Chambers, Peer House, 8-14 Verulam Street, Gray's Inn, London, WC1X 8LZ, Call Date: Nov 1979 (Middle Temple) Qualifications: MA (Oxon),ACIArb,, Assoc IPS

Hawkins *Commander Nicholas Simon* •
Naval Prosecuting Authority, Jervis Block, HMS Nelson, Queen Street, Portsmouth, Hants PO1 3HH, 01705 726218, Call Date: Oct 1991 (Inner Temple) Qualifications: MA (Oxon), Dip Law

Hawkins *Richard George Plume*
International Environment Consultant, Eden Hall, Kelso, Roxburghshire TD5 7QD, 01890 830666, Fax: 01890 830667, Call Date: Nov 1954 (Inner Temple) Qualifications: MA (Oxon)

Hawkins *Mrs Sandra Jane Henderson* •
Sidley & Austin, 1 Threadneedle Street, London EC2R 8AW, 0171 360 3600, Call Date: Oct 1997 (Gray's Inn) Qualifications: BSc (Bris), LLB (Lond)

Hawks *James Edward*
Call Date: Nov 1996 (Gray's Inn) Qualifications: LLB (Bris)

Haworth *Paul George* •
Senior Crown Prosecutor, Crown Prosecution Service, 2nd Floor, Solar House, 1-9 Romford Road, Stratford, London E15 4LJ, 0181 534 6601, Fax: 0181 519 5479, Call Date: May 1985 (Lincoln's Inn) Qualifications: BA (Hons)

Haworth *Thomas*
Senior Court Clerk, Hull Magistrates Court, 31 Lairgate, Beverley, North Humberside, 01482 881264, Call Date: Feb 1991 (Gray's Inn) Qualifications: LLB (Hull)

Hawthorne *Mrs Caroline Jane*
Call Date: Oct 1994 (Lincoln's Inn) Qualifications: LLB (Hons)

Hawthorne *Michael Eliot*
Call Date: Nov 1994 (Lincoln's Inn) Qualifications: LLB (Hons)(Lond)

Hawtin *Ian Alexander* •
Company Secretary, The Boots Company Plc, Head Office, 1 Thane Road West, Nottingham NG2 3AA, 0115 9687092, Fax: 0115 9687152, Call Date: July 1967 (Gray's Inn) Qualifications: MA (Oxon)

Hay *Miss Eleanor Frances Margaret*
Call Date: Nov 1996 (Lincoln's Inn) Qualifications: LLB (Hons)

Haycock *Mrs Anne* •
Legal Adviser to Social Services,Berkshire, Member of the Joint Legal Team for Berkshire Unitary Authorities, Call Date: Nov 1986 (Gray's Inn) Qualifications: Dip.Mag.Law

Haycock *Jonathan Allan*
Call Date: Oct 1996 (Middle Temple) Qualifications: B.Sc. (Hons)

Hayden *Matthew Simon*
Call Date: Oct 1994 (Gray's Inn) Qualifications: LLB

Haydock *James William*
Clerk to the Justices, Wigan Magistrates' Court, Darlington Street, Wigan WN1 1DW, 01942 405405, Fax: 01942 405444, Call Date: Feb 1984 (Inner Temple) Qualifications: DML

Haydon *Hilary Risdon*
Also Inn of Court I, Call Date: June 1961 (Gray's Inn) Qualifications: MA (Cantab)

Haye *Miss Cinderella*
Call Date: Nov 1982 (Lincoln's Inn) Qualifications: BA (Hons)

Hayes *John Patrick* •
Bracher Rawlins Solicitors, 180 Fleet Street, London EC4A 2LL, Call Date: Nov 1993 (Inner Temple) Qualifications: BA

Hayes *Julian Michael*
Call Date: Oct 1995 (Gray's Inn) Qualifications: BA (Kent)

Hayes *Miss Susan Mary*
Call Date: Oct 1990 (Inner Temple) Qualifications: LLB (Lond)

Hayes *Timothy Patrick*
Call Date: July 1998 (Inner Temple) Qualifications: BSc (Lond), MBA (Hawaii), CPE (Lond)

Hayford *Miss Jane Helene*
Call Date: Oct 1997 (Gray's Inn) Qualifications: LLB (Bucks)

Hayley *Mrs Angela Judith*
and Member Brunei Bar 1975, Call Date: July 1973 (Inner Temple) Qualifications: LLB Hons (Bristol)

Haynes *Gregory Laurence Warwick*
Call Date: Nov 1997 (Inner Temple) Qualifications: LLB (Wales)

Haynes *Miss Karen La Verne*
Wade's Gardens, Basseterre, St Kitts, Call Date: July 1998 (Middle Temple) Qualifications: BA (Hons)(W. Indies), LLB (Hons)(Lond), CPE (Wolves)

Hayward *Peter Allan*
St Peter's College, Oxford OX1 2DL, Call Date: Nov 1958 (Lincoln's Inn) Qualifications: MA (Cantab) MA, (Oxon)

Haywood *Keith Brett*
Call Date: Oct 1996 (Gray's Inn) Qualifications: LLB (Anglia)

Haywood Crouch *Kevin*
Call Date: Oct 1996 (Middle Temple) Qualifications: BA (Hons)(Lanc), CPE (Northumbria)

Hayzelden *John Eastcott*
Ofwat Thames Customer Service Committee, Panel Chairman, Uplands, 39 Mortimer Hill, Tring, Herts HP23 5JB, Call Date: Nov 1968 (Middle Temple) Qualifications: MA

Hazarika *Loona*
Campaign Manager, Burton Group., London Correspondent The Sentinel, Burton Group (Home Shopping), 32 Haymarket, London SW1Y 4TP, Call Date: Mar 1997 (Inner Temple) Qualifications: MA (Cantab)

Hazelden *John Winston*
Director & Legal Counsel Compliance, The Risk Advisory Group Ltd, Russell Square, 10-12 Russell Square, London WC1B 5EH, 0171 578 0000, Fax: 0171 578 7855, Call Date: July 1975 (Middle Temple)

Hazell *Dirk Nicholas Downing* •
6 Deepdale, Wimbledon Common,
London SW19 5EZ, 0181 946 8486, Fax:
0181 946 8486, Call Date: July 1978
(Middle Temple) Qualifications: MA
(Cantab)

Hazell *Laurence Paul*
York Chambers, 14 Toft Green, York,
YO1 6JT, Call Date: Nov 1984 (Gray's
Inn) Qualifications: BA Hons PhD
(Dunelm)

Hazewindus *Frank Sieger* •
Intellectual Property Lawyer, Shell
International Petroleum Co Ltd, Shell
Centre, London SE1 7NA, 0171 934
4379, Fax: 0171 934 6627, and Member
Holland Bar, Call Date: Nov 1982
(Middle Temple) Qualifications: LLB
(Utrecht) , LLM (Univ Chicago) , Dip Law
(City)

Head *David Mark*
Call Date: Oct 1990 (Lincoln's Inn)
Qualifications: BSC (Hons) (Essex), MSC
(Reading), Dip Law (City)

Head *John Kenneth*
1 Woodfield Gardens, Highcliffe,
Christchurch, Dorset BH23 4QA, 01425
273594, Call Date: Feb 1965 (Lincoln's
Inn) Qualifications: LLB (Lond)

Head *John Sebastian*
Foot & Bowden Solicitors, The Foot &
Bowden Building, 21 Derry's Cross,
Plymouth, Devon PL1 2SW, 01752
675000, Fax: 01752 671802, Call Date:
Nov 1987 (Gray's Inn) Qualifications: MA
(Cantab)

Headen *Miss Margaret Bernice*
Clerk to the Justices, Clerk to the
Justices', Barbican Way, Bearland,
Gloucester GL1 2JH, 01452 426152, Call
Date: Nov 1970 (Gray's Inn)

Heagney *Ms Caroline Ann*
Call Date: Oct 1995 (Gray's Inn)
Qualifications: LLB

Heal *James Arthur David*
Consultant in Judicial Administration
Associate Fellow of the Society for
Advanced Legal Studies, Wroxham, 12
Oakfield Road, Ashtead, Surrey
KT21 2RE, 01372 274003, Fax: 01372
278369, Call Date: Jan 1951 (Middle
Temple) Qualifications: LLB (Lond)

Healing *William Michael Christian*
Dawson Cornwell & Co, Solicitors, 16
Red Lion Square, London WC1R 4QT,
0171 242 2556, Fax: 0171 831 0478,
Call Date: Mar 1997 (Gray's Inn)
Qualifications: BA (Oxon)

Healy *Miss Angela Maria*
Call Date: Mar 1997 (Lincoln's Inn)
Qualifications: LLB (Hons)

Healy *Antony Julian*
11 Boardman Close, Barnet, Herts
EN5 2NA, 0181 447 1471, Call Date: July
1998 (Middle Temple) Qualifications:
LLB (Hons) (W'minster

Healy *Ms Margaret Virginia*
Call Date: Nov 1996 (Gray's Inn)
Qualifications: BA (Open), MA (Sussex)

Healy-Pratt *James Simon* •
Legal Adviser U.S. Attorney, British
Aviation Insurance Grp, Fitzwilliam
House, 10 St Mary Avenue, London
EC3A 8EQ, 0171 369 2244, Fax: 0171
369 2820, and Member New York, Call
Date: Oct 1991 (Gray's Inn)
Qualifications: BA (Durham), LLM
(Lond UCL), Cert. Air Law

Heap *Michael James*
Justices' Chief Executive, South Wales,
Committee Offices, 47 Charles Street,
Cardiff CF1 4ED, 01222 300250, Fax:
01222 300240, Call Date: July 1975
(Middle Temple) Qualifications: MBA

Hearn *Steven Maxwell* •
Crown Prosecutor, Crown Prosecution
Service, King's Road, Kymberley Road,
Harrow, Middlesex HA1 1YH, 0181 424
8688, Fax: 0181 424 9134, Call Date:
Nov 1992 (Inner Temple) Qualifications:
LLB, LLM

Hearne *Mrs Jennifer Christina*
Call Date: Nov 1977 (Inner Temple)

Hearsey *Miss Rebecca Elizabeth*
Call Date: Nov 1998 (Lincoln's Inn)
Qualifications: LLB (Hons)

Heath *Philip James*
Deputy District Secretary, Local & Public
Authority Unit, Lawrence Graham
Solicitors, 190 Strand, London
WC2R 1JN, 0171 379 0000, Fax: 0171
379 6854, Call Date: Nov 1988 (Gray's
Inn) Qualifications: LLB, MA

Heather *Miss Catherine Ann* •
Senior Crown Prosecutor, Crown
Prosecution Service, Fox Talbot House,
Bellinger Close, Malmesbury Road,
Chippenham, Wiltshire ON15 1BN,
01249 443 443, Fax: 01249 440 800,
Call Date: Oct 1992 (Gray's Inn)
Qualifications: BA (Dunlem)

Heatley *Richard Jonathon* •
Prosecution Team Leader, Crown
Prosecution Service, 18th Floor,
Tolworth Tower, Tolworth, Surbiton,
0181 399 5171, Call Date: Nov 1989
(Inner Temple) Qualifications: LLB
(Oxon), LLM (Lond)

Heaton *Richard Nicholas* •
Grade 6 Lawyer, Home Office, 50 Queen
Anne's Gate, London SW1H 9AT, 0171
273 2217, Call Date: July 1988 (Inner
Temple) Qualifications: BA (Oxon)

Hebblethwaite *Ms Sandra Louise* •
Acting Branch Crown Prosecutor, Crown
Prosecution Service, 2-4 City Gates,
Southgate, Chichester, West Sussex
PO19 2DJ, 01243 776851, Fax: 01243
784316, Call Date: Nov 1986 (Gray's
Inn) Qualifications: LLB (Brunel)

Hedge *Leslie Joseph*
5 Evendons Lane, Wokingham, Berks
RG41 4AA, Call Date: June 1955 (Gray's
Inn) Qualifications: LLB (Lond)

Hedley-Dent *Mrs Gloria* •
Senior Civil Service, Legal Dept,
Department of the, Environment,
Transport and, the Regions, Eland
House, 2 Bressenden Place, London
SW1E 5DU, 0171 890 4819, Call Date:
July 1970 (Inner Temple) Qualifications:
BA (Dunelm)

Hee *Rev Kim San Vincent*
53 Ember Court, White Acre, Colindale,
London NW9 5FX, 0181 200 4370, Call
Date: Nov 1989 (Gray's Inn)
Qualifications: LLB (Lond), GG (USA),
FGA (GB), LLM (Lond)

Heenan *Miss Rachael Ann Georgina*
Wansbroughs Willey Hargrave, Solicitors,
241 Glossop Road, Sheffield S10 2GZ,
0114 272 7485, Call Date: Nov 1995
(Middle Temple) Qualifications: LLB
(Hons), LLM

Heffernan *John Francis*
City Editor, Yorkshire Post 1985/93,
Prime Warden 1996/97 Worshipful
Company of Basketmakers. President,
City Livery Club 1997/8, 1 Fern Dene,
Templewood, London W13 8AN, 0181
997 6868, Call Date: Nov 1954 (Inner
Temple) Qualifications: BCom (Hons)

Heggs *Oliver Geoffrey*
Call Date: Nov 1987 (Middle Temple)
Qualifications: LLB (Lond), MBA (Lond)

Heginbotham *Iaford*
Valenciennes, Thurston Clough Road,
Dobcross, Oldham, Lancashire OL3 5RE,
Call Date: Oct 1998 (Inner Temple)
Qualifications: LLB (Essex), LLM
(Netherlands)

Heim *Mathew Jacques*
Honorary Research Fellow, Centre of
European Studies, Exeter University.
Francis Taylor Bldg, 3rd Floor, Temple,
London, EC4Y 7BY, Call Date: Oct 1993
(Lincoln's Inn) Qualifications: BA
(Hons)(Bris), MA (Exon), CPE (Stafford)

Hein *Raymond Marie Marc*
Thomas More Chambers, 52 Carey
Street, Lincoln's Inn, London, WC2A 2JB,
Call Date: July 1979 (Gray's Inn)

Heine *Ms Eleanor Louise*
Sedgwick, Detert, Moran &, Arnold, 5
Lloyds Avenue, London EC3N 3AX, 0171
929 1829, Fax: 0171 929 1808, and
Member New York Bar, Call Date: Nov
1995 (Inner Temple) Qualifications: BA
(Pennsylvania), LLB

Heinz *Volker Gustav Stefan*
, Rechtsanwalt & Notar, Barrister at
Law, 'Private & Confidential',
Haarmann, Hemmelrath & Partner,
Budapester Strasse 40 A, D-10787
Berlin, and Member German Bar
Berlin 3 Verulam Buildings, London
WC1R 5NT, Call Date: Nov 1989 (Inner
Temple) Qualifications: Dip Law, First
& Second German Legal State
Examinations

Hellens *Matthew James*
Sarjeant & Sheppard, 150 Friar Street,
Reading, Berks RG1 1HE, 0118 957
3425, Fax: 0118 959 7302, Solicitor,
Call Date: Oct 1992 (Lincoln's Inn)
Qualifications: MA (Cantab)

Heller *Miss Claire Andrea*
6 Cascade Avenue, London N10 3PU,
0181 883 1041, Call Date: Nov 1992
(Inner Temple) Qualifications: BA
(Exon), CPE

Heller *Richard Marc*
Call Date: Oct 1998 (Lincoln's Inn)
Qualifications: BA (Hons) (Herts), CPE

Hellier *Ms Sarah Jane Elizabeth*
Call Date: Nov 1994 (Inner Temple)
Qualifications: BA, CPE (City)

Hellings *Ms Suzan Marion* •
Hellings Morgan Associates, House No
5, Bisney View, 47-49 Bisney Road,
Pokfulam, Hong Kong, Hong Kong,
2855 1428, Fax: 2855 1510, Call Date:
July 1981 (Middle Temple)
Qualifications: LLB (Hons), FCIArb

Hemingway *Ian Thomas*
Call Date: Oct 1998 (Inner Temple)
Qualifications: LLB (Sheff)

Hemming *Martin John* •
Ministry of Defence Legal Adviser,
Ministry of Defence, Metropole
Building, Northumberland Building,
London WC2 5BL, 0171 218 0723, Fax:
0171 218 9451, Call Date: July 1972
(Gray's Inn) Qualifications: MA
(Cantab), LLM (Lond)

Hemming *Miss Susan Jane* •
Acting Principal Crown Prosecutor,
Crown Prosecution Service, Justinian
House, Spitfire Way, Ermine Business
Park, Huntingdon Cambs PE18 6XY,
01480 432333, Fax: 01480 432404,
Call Date: July 1988 (Middle Temple)
Qualifications: LLB (Hons) (Wales)

Hemmings *Liam*
Call Date: Nov 1996 (Inner Temple)
Qualifications: LLB (Huddersfield)

Hendrickson *Miss Christine*
Call Date: Nov 1982 (Inner Temple)
Qualifications: LLB (UCL)

Hendry *Ian Duncan* •
Legal Counsellor, Foreign &
Commonwealth Office, King Charles
Street, London SW1A 2AH, 0171 270
3041, Call Date: July 1971 (Gray's Inn)
Qualifications: LLB, LLM

Hendy *Robert James*
Call Date: Nov 1996 (Inner Temple)
Qualifications: LLB (Lond), BCL
(Oxon)

Heneghan *Patrick Michael*
Call Date: Nov 1997 (Middle Temple)
Qualifications: BA (Hons) (Cantab),,
BCL (Oxon)

Henley *Mrs Margaret Edith Mary*
Court Clerk, Walsall Magistrates Court,
Stafford Street, Walsall, West Midlands
WS2 8HA, 01922 638222, Fax: 01922
635657, Call Date: Oct 1990 (Middle
Temple) Qualifications: BSc (Hons)

Henley *Mark Simon*
Call Date: Oct 1996 (Middle Temple)
Qualifications: BA (Hons) (Oxon)

Henley-Price *Julian Kendall* •
Legal Counsel, Rothmans of Pall Mall,
(International Limited), Oxford Road,
Aylesbury, Bucks WD1 1QH, 01296
335000, Fax: 01296 335985, Call Date:
Feb 1994 (Gray's Inn) Qualifications:
LLB (Lond), Maitrise de Droit , Prive
(Paris)

Henning *Miss Caroline Ann*
Hill Dickenson Davis Campbell, Pearl
Assurance House, Derby Square,
Liverpool L2 9XL, 0151 236 5400, Fax:
0151 236 2175, Call Date: Nov 1993
(Middle Temple) Qualifications: BA
(Hons) (Oxon), CPE, MA (Oxon)

Hennity *Paul Martin*
Call Date: Nov 1998 (Inner Temple)
Qualifications: LLB (Wolves)

Henriques *Cecil Quixano*
Call Date: June 1936 (Inner Temple)
Qualifications: MA, BCL (Oxon)

Henry *Mrs Carole Anne* •
Senior Crown Prosecutor, Crown
Prosecution Service, 32 Scotland Street,
Sheffield S3 7DQ, 0114 2912000, Call
Date: Oct 1993 (Inner Temple)
Qualifications: LLB (Hons) (Leic)

Henry *Ian Leroy* •
Employment Lawyer Part-time
Chairman, Employment Tribunal,
London Borough of Hackney, Legal
Trading Unit, 183-187 Stoke
Newington, High Street, London N16,
0181 356 6186, Fax: 0181 356 6193,
and Member Jamaica Bar, Call Date:
Nov 1983 (Middle Temple)
Qualifications: BA

Henry *Philip Ivan* •
Assistant Director, Serious Fraud Office,
Elm House, 10-16 Elm Street, London
WC1X 0BJ, and Member Antigua Bar
Northern Ireland Bar, Call Date: Nov
1979 (Gray's Inn) Qualifications: BA

Henry *Miss Winsome Hyacinth*
Appointed Stipendary Magistrate,
Montego Bay, Jamaica. Staple Inn
Chambers, 1st Floor, 9 Staple Inn ,
Holborn, London, WC1V 7QH, Call
Date: Nov 1979 (Middle Temple)
Qualifications: BA

Heppel *Kenneth Henry*
The Cottage, Bishops Itchington,
Leamington Spa, Warks CV33 0QB,
01926 612463, Fax: 01926 612463,
Call Date: Nov 1960 (Middle Temple)
Qualifications: LLB, LLM

Heptonstall *Miss Emma Victoria*
Call Date: Nov 1997 (Gray's Inn)
Qualifications: LLB (Keele)

Herbert *Piers Marinel*
also Inn of Court G, Call Date: Feb 1960
(Inner Temple) Qualifications: MA
(Oxon)

Herbert Young *Nicholas Anthony*
Denton Hall, Five Chancery Lane,
Cliffords Inn, London EC4A 1BU, Call
Date: May 1988 (Middle Temple)
Qualifications: LLB (Hons) Lond , LLM
(Hons) Lond

Herbst *Jonathan Raymond Selbey* •
Call Date: Nov 1992 (Gray's Inn)
Qualifications: BA (Exon)

Heritage *John Langdon*
Director, Chesham Bldg Society, C/O
Chesham Building Society, 12 Market
Square, Chesham, Bucks HP5 1ER,
01494 72 5165, Fax: 01494 72 5165,
Call Date: Feb 1956 (Middle Temple)
Qualifications: MA (Oxon)

Herling *Dr David Andrew*
Law Department, City University,
Northampton Square, London
EC1V 0HB, 0171 477 8301, Fax: 0171
477 8578, Call Date: Oct 1991 (Gray's
Inn) Qualifications: BA,
MA,D.Phil(Oxon)

Hermele *Daniel Stephen*
Call Date: Oct 1994 (Lincoln's Inn)
Qualifications: BSc (Hons), MA (Bris)

Hermon *Richard Alexander Gower* •
Senior Legal Assistant, Lord
Chancellor's Department, Selborne
House, 54/60 Victoria Street, London
SW1E 6QB, Call Date: Nov 1977 (Inner
Temple) Qualifications: MA

Heron *Ronald*
Call Date: July 1957 (Middle Temple)
Qualifications: MA (Cantab)

Heron *Ms Sarah Katherine* •
Ministry of Agriculture, Fisheries &
Food, 55 Whitehall, London SW1A 2EY,
0171 270 8727, Fax: 0171 270 8096,
Call Date: Oct 1991 (Middle Temple)
Qualifications: BSc Hons (Manch), Dip
Law

Herring *Richard Alan*
Call Date: Nov 1998 (Middle Temple)
Qualifications: BA (Hons) (Wales)

Herrity *Peter*
Honorary Legal Adviser,British
Performing Arts Medicine Trust
Honorary Legal Adviser,British
Association for Performing Arts
Medicine, 15 Manstone Road, London
NW2 3XH, 0181 452 2197, Fax: 0181
208 3328, Call Date: July 1982
(Lincoln's Inn) Qualifications: BSc
(Social Science,, Lond)

Hesford *Stephen*
38 Young Street, Manchester, M3 3FT,
Call Date: Nov 1981 (Gray's Inn)
Qualifications: BSc (Bradford)

Hession *Martin Niall*
Call Date: Nov 1991 (Lincoln's Inn)
Qualifications: LLB (Hons) (Dublin),
LLM

Hesslewood *Mrs Josephine Florence*
Call Date: Mar 1996 (Gray's Inn)
Qualifications: LLB (Lond)

Hetherington *Sir Thomas Chalmers*
Rosemount, Mount Pleasant Road,
Lingfield, Surrey RH7 6BH, 01342
833923, Call Date: Nov 1952 (Inner
Temple)

Hewitson *Miss Melanie Jayne*
Call Date: Oct 1996 (Middle Temple)
Qualifications: LLB (Hons) (Lond)

Hewitt *John Allan*
Call Date: Feb 1993 (Middle Temple)
Qualifications: BA (Hons), LLM

Hewitt *Miss Monica Diane*
Call Date: Nov 1994 (Inner Temple)
Qualifications: LLB (Lond)

Hext *Christopher John Richard* •
Senior Crown Prosecutor, Crown
Prosecution Service, County House,
County Square, 100 New London Road,
Chelmsford, Essex CM2 0RG, 01245
252939, Fax: 01245 494710, Call Date:
July 1986 (Lincoln's Inn) Qualifications:
LLB

Hey *Peter Wilson*
59 Rue Porte Poitevine, 37600 Loches,
02 47 59 10 04, Call Date: June 1948
(Inner Temple) Qualifications: MA, LLB
(Cantab)

Heybrook *Miss Rose Catherine*
Call Date: Oct 1993 (Inner Temple)
Qualifications: MA (Cantab)

Heycock *David Huw* •
CPS Inter-Agency Projects Manager,
Crown Prosecution Service, 50 Ludgate
Hill, London EC4M 7EX, 0171 273 8058,
Fax: 0171 329 8167, Call Date: Feb 1982
(Middle Temple) Qualifications: LLB
(Lond) , MPhil (Cantab), Dip Psyc
(Wales)

Heywood *Eric* •
Senior Crown Prosecutor, CPS
(G.Manchester Area), PO Box 377, 8th
Floor,Sunlight House, Quay Street,
Manchester M60 3LU, 0161 837 7402,
Call Date: Feb 1988 (Gray's Inn)

Heywood *Dr Linda Jane*
Family Planning, Instructing Doctor,
Fornham End, Sheepwash Bridge,
Fornham All Saints, Bury St Edmunds,
Suffolk IP28 6JJ, 01284 769772, Call
Date: Oct 1993 (Inner Temple)
Qualifications: MB, ChB (University, of
Leeds Medical, School), CPE, MFFP

Hibbert *Arthur John* •
Principal Crown Prosecutor, Crown
Prosecution Service, Greenfield House,
32 Scotland Street, Sheffield, South
Yorkshire S3 7DQ, 0114 2912000, Call
Date: May 1984 (Middle Temple)
Qualifications: BA (Manch)

Hickey *Desmond Paul*
Call Date: Mar 1998 (Gray's Inn)
Qualifications: BA (Dublin)

Hickman *Ms Jane* •
Principal Legal Officer, Metropolitan
Police Sols Dept, Wellington House,
67-73 Buckingham Gate, London SW1,
Call Date: Nov 1983 (Gray's Inn)
Qualifications: BA (Lond), Dip Law

Hicks *Ms Barbara Helen*
Chairman of the Welsh Consumer
Council., Call Date: July 1995 (Gray's
Inn) Qualifications: LLB (Glamorgan)

Hicks *Miss Lisa Marie*
HW In-House Legal, 52-54 High Holborn,
London WC1V 6RL, 0171 405 0151, Fax:
0171 831 6498, Call Date: Nov 1991
(Inner Temple) Qualifications: LLB
(So'ton)

Hickson *Miss Fabiola Annaliese Amelia* •
Call Date: Nov 1992 (Inner Temple)
Qualifications: LLB

Higgins *Gary*
Call Date: July 1998 (Gray's Inn)
Qualifications: LLB (Wales)

Higgins *Kevin*
Call Date: Oct 1990 (Inner Temple)
Qualifications: LLB (Hons)

Higgins *Richard* •
Legal Consultant, OFTEL, 50 Ludgate
Hill, London EC4M 7JJ, Call Date: Nov
1955 (Inner Temple) Qualifications:
B.C.L., MA

Higgins *Dame Rosalyn*
Member of the International Court of
Justice, The Hague, International Court
of Justice, Peace Palace, 2517 KJ The
Hague, (31 70) 3022415, Fax: (31 70)
3022409, Bencher of the Inner Temple
(1989), Counsel for the International Tin
Council in a series of cases in the United
Kingdom, President, tribunal of the
International Centre for Settlement of
Investment Disputes., Call Date: Nov
1975 (Inner Temple) Qualifications: MA
LLB (Cantab), JSD, (Yale), LLM, LLD,
(Hons) (Paris)

Higham *Cdr Michael Bernard Shepley*
Grand Secretary, United Grand Lodge of
England 1980-98, Call Date: July 1968
(Middle Temple)

Highman *Mark Gideon*
Call Date: Feb 1993 (Gray's Inn)
Qualifications: BA

Hill *Alastair Malcolm*
Recorder Lawyer part-time Panel
Member of the Criminal Injuries
Compensation Appeals Panel., Crown
Prosecution Service, Police Division, 10
Furnival Street, London EC4A 1PE, Call
Date: May 1961 (Gray's Inn)
Qualifications: BA (Oxon)

Hill *Miss Catherine Mary*
Lecturer, 2 Paper Bldgs, 1st Floor,
Temple, London, EC4Y 7ET, Call Date:
Nov 1991 (Inner Temple) Qualifications:
BA (Newc), Dip Law

Hill *David Lewis* •
Legal Adviser, General Counsel's
Department, Bristol & West plc, P.O.Box
27, Broad Quay, Bristol BS99 7AX, 0117
943 2395, Fax: 0117 929 1115, Call
Date: Oct 1992 (Middle Temple)
Qualifications: MA (Cantab)

Hill *Jeffrey Paul*
Call Date: Mar 1997 (Gray's Inn)
Qualifications: LLB (Staff)

Hill *Richard Aubrey*
Legal Assistant, McKenna & Co, Mitre
House, 160 Aldersgate Street, London
EC1A 4DD, 0171 606 9000, Fax: 0171
606 9100, Call Date: Nov 1992 (Middle
Temple) Qualifications: BA (Hons), Dip
in Law

Hill *Richard David*
Associate, Dispute Resolution Baker &
McKenzie, Call Date: Oct 1996 (Gray's
Inn) Qualifications: BA (Cantab)

Hill *Miss Susan Enid Clare* •
Principal Legal Officer, Office of the
Solicitor DHSS, SOL A1, Room [492],
New Court, 48 Carey Street, London
WC2A 2LS, 0171 412 1260, Fax: 0171
412 1394, Call Date: Oct 1992 (Gray's
Inn) Qualifications: MA (Oxon)

Hillas *Miss Samantha*
Call Date: Oct 1996 (Inner Temple)
Qualifications: LLB (Hull)

Hillier *Gerald Cyril* •
Crown Prosecution Service, Winston
Churchill Avenue, Portsmouth PO1 2PJ,
Call Date: July 1978 (Middle Temple)
Qualifications: BA (Manch), LLB (Lond)

Hillman *Michael John Timothy*
Call Date: Nov 1995 (Inner Temple)
Qualifications: LLB

Hilton *George* •
Company Secretary, Lloyd Thompson
Group Plc, Beaufort House, 15 St
Botolph Street, London EC3A 7LT, 0171
247 2345, Fax: 0171 247 4488, Call
Date: July 1976 (Inner Temple)
Qualifications: BA

Hinchliffe *Peter Michael* •
Legal & Commercial Director, GPT Ltd,
New Century Park, P.O.Box 53,
Coventry CV3 1HS, 01203 563930, Fax:
01203 562295, Call Date: July 1982
(Lincoln's Inn) Qualifications: LLB

Hind *Mrs Nirmala*
Tax Advisor, Brebner, Allen & Trapp,
180 Wardour Street, London W1H 4LB,
0171 734 2244, Fax: 0171 287 5315,
Call Date: July 1994 (Lincoln's Inn)
Qualifications: LLB (Hons), ATT

Hindley *Mrs Brenda Mary*
Part-time Chairman Tribunals, 6
Longworth Drive, Maidenhead, Berks
SL6 8XA, 01628 777668, Fax: 01628
630167, Call Date: Nov 1962 (Lincoln's
Inn) Qualifications: LLB

Hine *Miss Ruth Alison* •
Competition Lawyer, OFTEL, 50
Ludgate Hill, London EC4M 7JJ, 0171
634 8700, Fax: 0171 634 8943, Call
Date: Oct 1992 (Gray's Inn)
Qualifications: LLB

Hinton *Ian Hughes*
25 Glebelands, Bidborough, Tunbridge
Wells, Kent TN3 0UQ, 01892 529604,
Call Date: May 1957 (Gray's Inn)
Qualifications: MA (Oxon) , MIMgt

Hinton *Richard John*
Call Date: Nov 1998 (Lincoln's Inn)
Qualifications: LLB (Hons) (Anglia)

Hippe *Ms Birgit*
Call Date: Oct 1994 (Middle Temple)
Qualifications: LLB (Hons) (Lond)

Hirst *Martin Lewis*
Call Date: Nov 1998 (Lincoln's Inn)
Qualifications: BSc (Hons) (Leeds),
Dip Law

Hirst *Richard Dodsworth* •
A T & T (UK) Ltd, Norfolk House, 31 St
James's Square, London SW1Y 4JR, Call
Date: Nov 1981 (Middle Temple)
Qualifications: MA (Oxon)

Hirtenstein *Anthony Trevor* •
Senior Legal Assistant, Department of
the Environment, Transport and the
Regions, 8/H9, Eland House,
Bressenden Place, London SW1E 5DU,
0171 890 4755, Fax: 0171 890 4782,
Call Date: July 1969 (Gray's Inn)
Qualifications: MA (Oxon)

Hiscock *Miss Olive Gladys*
Call Date: July 1985 (Inner Temple)
Qualifications: Dip Law

Hitchings *Paul Barrington Knowles* •
Group Legal Adviser, Eagle Star
Holdings Plc, 60 St Mary Axe, London
EC3A 8JQ, 0171 929 1111, Fax: 0171
626 0311, Call Date: July 1968 (Gray's
Inn) Qualifications: BA (Oxon)

Hoare *John Michael*
Cuylers, Little Thurlow, Nr Haverhill,
Suffolk CB9 7LA, 01440 783251, Fax:
01440 783028, Call Date: Feb 1955
(Inner Temple) Qualifications: MA
[Cantab]

Hoare *Robin William*
Call Date: Mar 1999 (Middle Temple)
Qualifications: LLB (Hons) (Lond)

Hoare Temple *Piers Howard*
3 Serjeants Inn, London, EC4Y 1BQ,
Call Date: July 1972 (Middle Temple)

Hobbs *Miss Patricia Joan*
Call Date: Nov 1995 (Inner Temple)
Qualifications: LLB (Kent)

Hobday *Miss Natasha Anne*
First Telecom plc, One Harbour
Exchange Square, London E14 9GB,
0171 572 7700, Fax: 0171 572 7701,
Call Date: Oct 1991 (Middle Temple)
Qualifications: LLB Hons (Exon)

Hockey *Gordon Andrew* •
Secretary to the Statutory Committee of
the Pharmaceutica Society, Royal
Pharmaceutical Society, of Great
Britain, 1 Lambeth High Street, London
SE1 7JN, 0171 735 9141, Fax: 0171
735 7629, Call Date: Feb 1995
(Lincoln's Inn) Qualifications: BSc
(Manc)

Hocking *Stephen John*
Call Date: Nov 1994 (Inner Temple)
Qualifications: BA (Oxon), CPE (City)

Hockman *David Philip*
Polygram International, Music
Publishing Limited, 8 St James's
Square, London SW1Y 4JU, 0171 747
4000, Fax: 0171 747 4467, Call Date:
May 1972 (Inner Temple)
Qualifications: LLB

Hodges *Mark Cameron*
RAC Legal Services, P.O.Box 700, Great
Park Road, Almondsbury, Bristol
BS12 4QP, 0117 9441515, Call Date:
Nov 1992 (Lincoln's Inn)
Qualifications: LLB (Hons)

Hodgetts *Glen*
Call Date: Nov 1995 (Inner Temple)
Qualifications: LLB (Lancs)

Hodgson *John James*
Toynbee Itall Legal Advice Centre,
Voluntary Panel, 44 Cephas Avenue,
London E1 4AT, 0171 791 3594, Call
Date: June 1955 (Gray's Inn)
Qualifications: MA,Law Society Final

Hodgson *Miss Lisa*
Call Date: Oct 1998 (Lincoln's Inn)
Qualifications: LLB (Hons) (Leeds)

Hodgson *Mrs Margaret* •
Deputy Registrar of Court of Appeal
(Civil Division)., Legal Secretary to the
Master of the Rolls, Lord Chancellor's
Department, Royal Courts of Justice,
Strand, London WC2A 2LL, 0171 936
7171, Call Date: July 1978 (Gray's Inn)
Qualifications: BA

Hodgson *Nicholas* •
Grade 6 (Legal), Lord Chancellor's
Department, Selborne House, 54-60
Victoria Street, London SW1E 6QW,
0171 210 0714, Fax: 0171 210 0746,
Call Date: July 1976 (Middle Temple)
Qualifications: MA (Oxon)

Hodson *Miss Loveday Cerys*
Call Date: July 1997 (Gray's Inn)
Qualifications: LLB (Warwick)

Hoffman *David John* •
General Counsel, Oracle Corporation
UK Limited, Oracle Centre, The Ring,
Bracknell, Berkshire RG12 1BW, Call
Date: Feb 1991 (Inner Temple)
Qualifications: LLB (Manch)

Hoffman *Timothy Mark*
Call Date: Oct 1998 (Inner Temple)
Qualifications: LLB (Bris)

Hogan *Miss Catherine Anne*
Call Date: Nov 1997 (Gray's Inn)
Qualifications: LLB (L'pool), LLM
(L'pool)

Hogarth *Adrian John* •
Deputy Parliamentary Counsel, Office
of the Parliamentary, Counsel, 36
Whitehall, London SW1A 2AY, 0171 210
6646, Call Date: July 1983 (Inner
Temple) Qualifications: IT, MA, LLM
(Cantab)

Hohler *Miss Camilla Clare* •
47 Sutton Square, Urswick Road,
London E9 6EQ, Call Date: Nov 1994
(Middle Temple) Qualifications: BA
(Hons)

Holden *Dr Hazel Diane*
Call Date: Feb 1995 (Gray's Inn)
Qualifications: B.Sc (St Andrews), Ph.D
(St Andrews)

Holden *Richard Thomas*
South Acre, Barlow, Blaydon on Tyne,
Tyne & Wear NE21 6JU, 01207 544331,
Call Date: Nov 1978 (Lincoln's Inn)
Qualifications: BSc, MSc (Dunelm),,
LLB (Lond), MA, Dip Ed (Dunelm),
C.Chem,MRSC, C.Phy, M.Inst.P

Holder *Jonathan Alfred* •
Head of Legal/Company Secretary, BBC
Worldwide Limited, Wood Lane,
London W12 0TT, 0181 576 2308, Call
Date: July 1980 (Middle Temple)
Qualifications: BA Leeds

Holderness *David Alan* •
Crown Prosecutor, Crown Prosecution
Service, 4-5 South Parade, Wakefield,
West Yorkshire WF1 1LR, 01924
290620, Call Date: Nov 1991 (Lincoln's
Inn) Qualifications: BA (Hons)

Holdsworth *Robert Drewry*
Part time President of Mental Health
Review Tribunal, Call Date: July 1979
(Gray's Inn) Qualifications: MA
(Cantab)

• Barrister in employment

Holiday *Ms Yewa Sarah-Jane*
Case Review Manager, Criminal Cases
Review Comm., Alpha Tower, Suffolk
Street, Queensway, Birmingham, 0121
633 1800, Fax: 0121 633 1823, Call
Date: Nov 1996 (Middle Temple)
Qualifications: BA (Hons) (Cantab), LLM
(Cantab)

Holland *Miss Charlotte Claire*
Call Date: Oct 1998 (Inner Temple)
Qualifications: BA (Lincs)

Holland *Damian Paul* •
Principal Crown Prosecutor, Crown
Prosecution Service, Sceptre House, 7-9
Castle Street, Luton, Beds, 01582
404808, Fax: 01582 400642, Call Date:
Nov 1986 (Middle Temple)
Qualifications: LLB (Manch)

Holland *David Henry Bramwell*
Call Date: Feb 1979 (Gray's Inn)

Holland *Richard David* •
Legal Manager, Crewe Magistrates Court,
Civic Centre, Crewe, Cheshire CW1 2DT,
01270 256221, Fax: 01270 589357, Call
Date: Nov 1987 (Gray's Inn)
Qualifications: Dip Magisteral Law,
Common Professional, Examination Law

Holland *Miss Susanne*
Call Date: Oct 1998 (Gray's Inn)
Qualifications: LLB (Wales)

Holland-Elliott *Dr Kevin*
Chief Medical Adviser, The Chaucer
Hospital, Knackington Roasd,
Canterbury, Kent CT4 7AR, 01227
455466, Health & Safety/Medico-Legal
Opinion, Call Date: May 1996 (Middle
Temple) Qualifications: MB.ChB, MFOM,
MRCGP, MIOSH

Holleyhead *James Collis*
Call Date: Nov 1998 (Inner Temple)
Qualifications: MA (Oxon)

Hollick *Cllr Peter Nugent*
Bedfordshire Police Authority
Bedfordshire Probation Board, 1 Carlisle
Close, Dunstable, Beds LU6 3PH, 01582
662821, Fax: 01582 476619, Call Date:
July 1973 (Middle Temple)
Qualifications: JP,LLB (Hons) (B'ham),
MEd,FCollP

Hollins *Lt Cdr Rupert Patrick* •
Naval Barrister, 01329 832047, Call
Date: Oct 1995 (Gray's Inn)
Qualifications: MA (Oxon)

Hollis *Daniel Ayrton*
Call Date: Nov 1949 (Middle Temple)
Qualifications: MA (Oxon)

Holloway *Brian Spencer Charles*
Legal Adviser, Brewer Consulting, 95-97
High Street, Esher, Surrey KT10 9QE,
01733 263991, Fax: 01733 331533, Call
Date: Nov 1987 (Gray's Inn)
Qualifications: LLB (Lond), CEng, FICE,
FCIArb, MSc (Const Law)

Holloway *Ms Jean*
Court Clerk, Richmond Upon Thames
Mag Crt, Richmond Magistrates Court,
Parkshot, Richmond, Surrey TW9 2RF,
0181 948 2101, Fax: 0181 322 2628,
Call Date: July 1983 (Gray's Inn)
Qualifications: BA (Hons)

Holmes *Carl Stanley* •
Principal Crown Prosecutor, Crown
Prosecution Service, 1-9 Romford Road,
Stratford, 0181 534 6601 Ext 215, Call
Date: July 1986 (Lincoln's Inn)
Qualifications: B.A.

Holmes *Paul Cyril*
p/t Industrial Tribunal Chairman,
Perkins & Co Solicitors, 1 Kign Street,
Manchester M2 6AW, 0161 834 7770,
Fax: 0161 834 8399, Call Date: July 1979
(Gray's Inn) Qualifications: MA (Cantab)

Holt *Jason Brian*
Accredited Police Station Representative,
Stevens Solicitors, Fitzgerald House,
Sutherland Road, Longton, Stoke on
Trent, Staffordshire ST3 1HH, 01782
343353, Fax: 01782 599321, Call Date:
Oct 1996 (Middle Temple)
Qualifications: LLB (Hons) (B'ham)

Holt *Peter Alexander*
C/O Langley & Co, 199 Bishopsgate,
London EC2M 3TY, 0171 814 6637, Fax:
0171 814 6604, Call Date: Mar 1996
(Inner Temple) Qualifications: LLB
(Teeside)

Holter *Michael Rolf*
Wilmer, Cutler & Pickering, 4 Carlton
Gardens, Pall Mall, London SW1Y 5AA,
0171 872 1000, Fax: 0171 839 3537,
Call Date: Nov 1988 (Lincoln's Inn)
Qualifications: BA Hons (Cantab)

Honey *Damian James Bartholemew*
Holman Fenwick & Willan, Marlow
House, Lloyds Avenue, London
EC3N 3AL, 0171 488 2300, Fax: 0171
481 0316, Call Date: Nov 1994 (Inner
Temple) Qualifications: LLB (Sheff)

Honeyball *Dr Simon Eric*
Head of Department of Law, University of
Exeter 1993-1995 Senior Lecturer in
Law, Chilton Barton, Chilton, Stockleigh
Pomeroy, Nr Crediton EX17 4AQ, 01363
866198, Fax: 01363 263196, Call Date:
July 1996 (Middle Temple)
Qualifications: LLB (Hons), PhD
(B'ham), ARCM

Hood *Ms Rachel Dene Serena*
and Member Attorney at Law, California,
Call Date: July 1976 (Middle Temple)
Qualifications: MA Hons [Cantab]

Hood *Miss Rosalind Emily* •
Court Clerk, Secretariat Offices, Court
House, London Road, Dorking, Surrey,
01306 885544, Call Date: Nov 1986
(Gray's Inn)

Hoodless *Neil Gordon* •
Senior Crown Prosecutor, Crown
Prosecution Service, 5th Floor, St Peters
House, Gower Street, Derby DE1, 01332
621600, Call Date: Nov 1989 (Middle
Temple) Qualifications:
LLB (Hons) (Essex)

Hooker *Miss Louise Jane*
Solicitor, Call Date: Nov 1993 (Gray's
Inn) Qualifications: LLB

Hoon *Geoffrey William*
House of Commons, King Charles House,
Standard Hill, Nottingham, NG1 6FX, Call
Date: July 1978 (Gray's Inn)
Qualifications: MA (Cantab)

Hooper *Brian Michael* •
Grade 6 Senior Principal, Dept of Trade
& Industry, 10-18 Victoria Street, London
SW1H 0NN, 0171 215 3020, Call Date:
July 1971 (Middle Temple)

Hooper *Graham Boucher*
Clerk to the Justices, Nottinghamshire
Magistrates', Court, The Court House,
Carrington Street, Nottingham NG2 1EE,
0115 955 8102, Fax: 0115 955 8104,
Call Date: July 1984 (Lincoln's Inn)
Qualifications: LLB

Hooper *Ms Louise*
Call Date: Nov 1997 (Gray's Inn)
Qualifications: BA (Lond)

Hope *Jacques Derek*
Call Date: Nov 1952 (Gray's Inn)
Qualifications: LLB (Manch)

Hope *John Richard*
Deputy Clerk to the Justices, Chief
Executive Wiltshire MCC, 43/55 Milford
Street, Salisbury SP1 2BP, 0722 333225,
Fax: 0722 413395, Call Date: Nov 1980
(Gray's Inn)

Hope *Ms Karen Andrea*
Call Date: Nov 1997 (Gray's Inn)
Qualifications: BA

Hopkin *Ms Jean Winifred*
01298 872327, and Member Hong Kong
Bar, Call Date: July 1987 (Lincoln's Inn)
Qualifications: BA

Hopkins *Anthony*
Call Date: Oct 1997 (Middle Temple)
Qualifications: LLB (Hons) (Kingston)

Hopkins *Christopher Neil* •
Call Date: Oct 1995 (Gray's Inn)
Qualifications: BA

Hopkins *Nicholas Martin*
Call Date: July 1984 (Middle Temple)
Qualifications: LLB (Bucks)

Hopper *Martyn John* •
The Securities & Investments, Board,
Gavrelle House, 2-14 Bunhill Row,
London EC1Y 8RA, 0171 638 1240, Fax:
0171 382 5997, Call Date: Nov 1991
(Middle Temple) Qualifications: BA Hons
(Oxon), LLM (Lond)

Hopwell *Mark David*
Call Date: Oct 1997 (Lincoln's Inn)
Qualifications: LLB (Hons) (Derby)

Hopwood *Miss Sandra Margaret*
Call Date: July 1985 (Gray's Inn)
Qualifications: LLB

Hoque *Iftekar Ahmed*
Call Date: Nov 1998 (Lincoln's Inn)
Qualifications: LLB (Hons) (Lond)

Horan *Shaun Patrick Robert*
Call Date: Nov 1995 (Inner Temple)
Qualifications: LLB (Soton)

Hormaeche *Miss Alejandra*
Call Date: Oct 1998 (Middle Temple)
Qualifications: LLB (Hons) (Manc)

Horn *Mark Phillip Malcolm* ●
International Aluminium and Steel
Analyst, T Hoare & Co, 4th Floor,
Cannon Bridge, 25 Dowgate Hill,
London EC4R 2YA, 0171 220 7001,
Fax: 0171 929 1836, Call Date: Nov
1993 (Lincoln's Inn) Qualifications:
BA, BA (Hons) & MA, (Rhodes S.A.),
LLB, (Lond), Dip in Bus, Admin, MSI
(Dip)

Horn *Miss Shirley Ann*
Senior Legal Adviser, Secretariat
Offices, The Court House, Tufton Street,
Ashford, Kent TN23 1QS, 01233
663706, Fax: 01233 663206, Call Date:
Feb 1987 (Middle Temple)
Qualifications: BA (Hons) (Kent)

Hornby *Mrs Elizabeth Jane*
Consultant, Elizabeth Hornby &
Associates, 30 Welford Place,
Wimbledon, London SW19 5AJ, 0181
944 1004, Fax: 0181 944 1004, Call
Date: July 1988 (Gray's Inn)
Qualifications: LLB (Notts), M.Phil
(Cantab)

Horne *Brian Joseph* ●
Principal Crown Prosecutor, Crown
Prosecution Service, 2nd Floor,
Portland House, Stag Place, Victoria,
London SW1E 5BH, Call Date: Nov
1986 (Inner Temple) Qualifications:
LLB (PCL), LLM (Lond)

Horne *John Newport*
Senior Executive, The General Council
of the Bar, 3 Bedford Row, London
WC1R 4DB, 0171 242 0082, Fax: 0171
831 9217, Call Date: Nov 1972 (Gray's
Inn) Qualifications: BCL

Horsford *Cyril Edward Sheehan*
Clerk to Bar Disciplinary Tribunal
(1990-1998), 32 Prairie Street, London
SW8 3PP, Call Date: Feb 1953 (Inner
Temple) Qualifications: MA (Cantab)

Horsington *Simon* ●
Fidelity Investments Services, Oakhill
House, 130 Tonbridge Road,
Hildenborough, Tonbridge, Kent
TN11 9DZ, 01732 777473, 20 Britton
Street, 1st Floor, London, EC1M 5NQ,
Call Date: July 1978 (Gray's Inn)

Horton *Daniel Edmund*
Level 62, MCL Centre, Martin's Place,
Sydney, NSW 2000 Australia, QC Sydney
Brick Court Chambers, 7-8 Essex
Street, London, WC2R 3LD, Call Date:
July 1985 (Middle Temple)
Qualifications: LLB (Sydney)

Hosein *Miss Aisling Tara Philomena* ●
Crown Prosecution Service, 50 Ludgate
Hill, LondoN EC4M 7EX, Call Date: Nov
1990 (Middle Temple) Qualifications:
LLB (W Indies)

Hosking *Emile John*
London Rent Assessment Panel, 99
Priory Road, London NW6 3NL, Call
Date: Nov 1976 (Lincoln's Inn)
Qualifications: LLB, LLM (Lond), MSc,
FCIArb ARICS

Hossain *Mohammed Monwar*
50 Howard Road, Walthamstow,
London E17 4SJ, 0181 520 8224, Call
Date: July 1998 (Lincoln's Inn)
Qualifications: LLB (Hons), M.Com
(Mgment)

Hotchen *Miss Jennifer Marie Anne*
Deputy Chief Clerk, Inner London
Magistrates', Courts Service, 65
Romney Street, London SW1 3RD, Call
Date: July 1985 (Middle Temple)
Qualifications: BA (Keele)

Hotham *Anthony*
Call Date: Nov 1971 (Middle Temple)

Hough *Mrs Alison Jayne*
Willaston House, 3 Slough Road,
Datchet, Berks SL3 9AP, 01753
541286, Call Date: July 1997 (Lincoln's
Inn) Qualifications: LLB (Hons) (Lond)

Houghton *Edward John Willoughby*
Justices' Clerk, Fixed Penalty Clerk for
Inner London. London Parking
Adjudicator, Marylebone Magistrates
Court, 181 Marylebone Road, London
NW1 5QS, 0171 706 1261, Fax: 0171
724 9884, Call Date: July 1975 (Gray's
Inn) Qualifications: MA (Cantab)

Houghton *Timothy James*
Call Date: Oct 1997 (Inner Temple)
Qualifications: BA (Oxon), CPE (City)

Houghton-Jones *Mrs Gaynor*
Justices Clerk, Inner London
Magistrates', Courts Service, 65
Romney Street, London SW1P 3RD,
0171 799 3072, Call Date: Nov 1971
(Gray's Inn) Qualifications: LLB
(Wales)

House *Christopher* ●
Assistant Treasury Solicitor, Dept of
Education/Employment, Queen Anne's
Chambers, 28 Broadway, London
SW1H 9JS, Call Date: Nov 1976
(Lincoln's Inn) Qualifications: LLB
(Lond)

Housego *Nigel William*
Manager, Legal Dept, Hambro Legal
Protection Ltd, Stephenson Road,
Colchester, Essex CO4 4QR, 0990
234500, Fax: 0990 234508, Call Date:
Nov 1989 (Lincoln's Inn)
Qualifications: LLB

Houseley *William John*
Call Date: Mar 1999 (Lincoln's Inn)
Qualifications: LLB (Hons) (Reading),
LLM (Lond)

Howard *David*
Call Date: Mar 1996 (Gray's Inn)
Qualifications: LLB (Wales)

Howard *Ian David*
Call Date: Nov 1998 (Inner Temple)
Qualifications: LLB (Sheff)

Howard *Miss Jane Anna*
Call Date: Mar 1998 (Middle Temple)
Qualifications: LLB (Hons)

Howard *Michael*
Recorder, 4 Breams Buildings, London,
EC4A 1AQ, Call Date: Nov 1964 (Inner
Temple) Qualifications: BA, LLB
(Cantab)

Howard *Ms Rebecca Alexandra*
Employment Litigator, Irwin Mitchell, 9
Arkwright Road, Hampstead, London
NW3 6AB, Call Date: Oct 1991 (Middle
Temple) Qualifications: BSc

Howard *Robin Ivan*
Call Date: July 1976 (Gray's Inn)
Qualifications: Associate of the , ICAEW

Howard *Dr Timothy John*
Call Date: May 1996 (Gray's Inn)
Qualifications: B.Med.Sci, B.M.B.S,
(Nottingham)

Howe *Peter Charles* ●
Company Secretary, Zurich Financial
Services, UK Life Limited, Allied
Dunbar Centre, Station Road, Swindon
SN1 1EL, 01793 514514, Fax: 01793
513076, Call Date: July 1974 (Gray's
Inn) Qualifications: LLB

Howe of Aberavon *Lord*
House of Lords, London SW1A 0PW,
0171 236 0137, Call Date: Feb 1952
(Middle Temple) Qualifications: MA,
LLB (Cantab)

Howells *Ian David* ●
Commercial Contracts Business
Manager, British Telecommunications
plc, Group Commercial Contracts, pp
3c2, 5 Brindley Place, Birmingham
B1 2BL, 0121 230 4966, Fax: 0121 230
4961, Call Date: July 1989 (Middle
Temple) Qualifications: LLB

Howes *Miss Pamela Ann*
Call Date: Mar 1999 (Lincoln's Inn)
Qualifications: LLB (Hons) (Sussex)

Howse *Miss Lindsey Anne*
Call Date: Oct 1998 (Gray's Inn)
Qualifications: LLB (Wales), LLM
(L'pool)

Howse *Miss Patricia Geraldine* •
Financial Services Authority, 25 The
North Colonnade, Canary Wharf, London
E14 5HS, 0171 676 1000, Call Date: Nov
1972 (Gray's Inn) Qualifications: LLB

Hoyle *Dr Robert*
8 Tyndale Road, Oxford OX4 1JL, 01865
727929, Fax: 07070 621731, Diploma in
Advanced Studies in Law (Oxford
Brookes) Oxford City Councillor, Call
Date: Nov 1996 (Inner Temple)
Qualifications: MA (Cantab), MSc (Bris),
MA, DPhil (Oxon)

Hubbard *Miss Rosemary Sylvia* •
Legal Adviser, The Brewers & Licensed,
Retailers Association, 42 Portman
Square, London W1H 0BB, 0171 486
4831, Fax: 0171 935 3991, Call Date:
July 1974 (Inner Temple) Qualifications:
LLB

Hubbick *Mrs Elizabeth Anne*
Associate, Bacon & Woodrow, St Olaf
House, London Bridge City, London
SE1 2PE, 0171 716 7434, Fax: 0171 716
7144, Call Date: July 1986 (Lincoln's
Inn) Qualifications: BA (Dunelm), Dip
Law (PCL)

Hudgson *Ms Fiona Jane*
Ashurst Morris Crisp, Sols, Broadwalk
House, 5 Appold Street, London
EC2A 2HA, 0171 638 1111, Fax: 0171
972 7990, Former Solicitor, Call Date:
Feb 1995 (Middle Temple)
Qualifications: LLB, BSc (Melbourne)

Hudson *Alastair Scott*
Lecturer in Law, Queen Mary & Westfield
College, University of London, Legal
Affairs. Policy Adviser Labour Party,
Faculty of Law, Queen Mary & Westfield
College, Mile End Road, London E1 4NS,
0171 775 3164, Fax: 0181 981 8733,
Call Date: Oct 1991 (Lincoln's Inn)
Qualifications: LLB (Hons) (Lond), LLM
(Hons) (Lond)

Hudson *Ms Eleanor Jane* •
Department of the Environment,
Transport & the Regions, Eland House,
Bressenden Place, London, Call Date:
Oct 1997 (Inner Temple) Qualifications:
BA (Cantab)

Hudson *Miss Emma Ceril* •
Community Care Lawyer Senior Lawyer,
London Borough of Lewisham, Call Date:
Nov 1992 (Inner Temple) Qualifications:
LLB (Hons)

Hudson *Miss Esther*
Call Date: Nov 1998 (Inner Temple)
Qualifications: LLB (De Montfort)

Hudson *Frank Michael Stanislaus*
Former Recorder of the Crown Court,
Call Date: June 1961 (Middle Temple)
Qualifications: BA

Hudson Davies *Gwilym Ednyfed*
2 King's Bench Walk, 1st Floor, Temple,
London, EC4Y 7DE, Call Date: 1975
(Gray's Inn) Qualifications: MA (Oxon)

Huebner *Michael Denis* •
Head of Judicial Appointments, Lord
Chancellor's Department, Deputy Clerk
of Crown in Chancery, Lord Chancellor's
Department, Selborne House, 54-60
Victoria Street, London SW1E 6QW, Call
Date: Nov 1965 (Gray's Inn)
Qualifications: BA

Huggett *Miss Clare Lesley*
Call Date: Nov 1987 (Lincoln's Inn)
Qualifications: LLB (Bristol)

Huggett *Sean Dolan*
Call Date: Oct 1998 (Middle Temple)
Qualifications: BA (Hons) (Manc), CPE

Huggins *Anthony Arthur*
Hayes Barton, Betchworth, Surrey
RH3 7DF, 01737 842648, Call Date: Feb
1959 (Middle Temple)

Huggins *Toby James*
Call Date: Nov 1998 (Middle Temple)
Qualifications: BSc (Hons) (Bris)

Hugh-Jones *Michael Gwyn*
141 Were Street, Brighton, Victoria,
Australia, Barrister & Solicitor, High
Court of Australia & Supreme Court of
Victoria. and Member Victoria Bar, Call
Date: July 1970 (Lincoln's Inn)

Hughes *Alan John* •
Head of Prosecutions (Manchester), H M
Customs & Excise, Solicitor's Office, Ralli
Quays West, 3 Stanley Street, Salford
M60 9LB, 0161 827 0553, Fax: 0161 827
0550, Call Date: Nov 1971 (Middle
Temple)

Hughes *Anthony Pelham Cotton*
PricewaterhouseCoopers, 1
Embankment Place, London WC2N 6NN,
0171 213 5466, Fax: 0171 213 2418,
Call Date: Nov 1975 (Inner Temple)
Qualifications: MA, ATII

Hughes *Barry Michael* •
Assistant Chief Crown Prosecuter, Crown
Prosecution Service, 50 Ludgate Hill,
Stag Place, London EC4M 7EX, 0171 273
1141, Call Date: Nov 1983 (Middle
Temple) Qualifications: LLB (Sheff)

Hughes *Charles Michael*
Yewlands, Penton Grafton, Nr Andover,
Hants SP11 0RR, 01264 772330, Call
Date: Jan 1937 (Middle Temple)

Hughes *Clarence Albert Fitzgerald*
and Member Guyana & Grenada Bars
Cloisters, 1st Floor, Temple, London,
EC4Y 7AA, Call Date: Feb 1958 (Inner
Temple) Qualifications: LLB

Hughes *David Gordon*
Call Date: Oct 1997 (Middle Temple)
Qualifications: BA (Hons) (Wolves), CPE
(Glamorgan)

Hughes *David Martin* •
Senior Crown Prosecutor, Crown
Prosecution Service, 4 Artillery Row,
London SW1, Call Date: Nov 1984
(Gray's Inn) Qualifications: LLB

Hughes *Gareth Bryn* •
Chief Advocate - City of Westminster,
Westminster City Council, City Hall, 64
Victoria Street, London SW1E 6QP, 0171
641 6000, Call Date: Nov 1984 (Lincoln's
Inn) Qualifications: LLB (Wales)

Hughes *Geoffrey Tudor*
Call Date: May 1955 (Gray's Inn)
Qualifications: MA (Oxon)

Hughes *Miss Gwyneth Elizabeth* •
Grade 7 Lawyer, Treasury Solicitor's
Dept, 28 Broadway, London SW1H 9JS,
Call Date: Nov 1992 (Lincoln's Inn)
Qualifications: BA (Hons)

Hughes *MrS Helen Sian* •
Senior Crown Prosecutor, Crown
Prosecution Service, 1-9 Romford Road,
Stratford, London E15, 0181 534 6601,
Fax: 0181 519 9690, Call Date: Oct 1993
(Inner Temple) Qualifications: BSc
(Lond), CPE

Hughes *Mrs Merril* •
Principal Crown Prosecutor, Crown
Prosecution Service, 4-6 Prebendal
Court, Oxford Road, Aylesbury,
Buckinghamshire, Call Date: July 1984
(Lincoln's Inn) Qualifications: LLB

Hughes *Miss Olwen Catherine*
Principle Assistant, Wrexham
Magistrates' Court, Bodhyfryd, Wrexham,
Clwyd, 01978 291855, Fax: 01978
358213, Call Date: Feb 1988 (Gray's
Inn) Qualifications: LLB (Wales)

Hughes *Paul Laurence*
Call Date: Oct 1995 (Middle Temple)
Qualifications: LLB (Hons)

Hughes *Miss Sally Catherine*
Solicitor, Scott-Moncrieff, Harbour &,
Sinclair, 49/51 Farringdon Road, London
EC1M 3JB, 0171 242 4114, Fax: 0171
242 3605, Call Date: Oct 1992 (Middle
Temple) Qualifications: BA(Hons) (Lond)

Hughes *Simon Henry Ward*
13 King's Bench Walk, 1st Floor, Temple,
London, EC4Y 7EN, Call Date: July 1974
(Inner Temple) Qualifications: BA
(Cantab)

Hughes *Miss Susan Ann* •
Senior Crown Prosecutor Part Time
Lecturer in Adult Education, Crown
Prosecution Service, Cambia House,
Merthyd Tydfil Industrial, Estate,
Pentrebach, Merthyd Tydfil CF48 4X, Call
Date: Nov 1982 (Gray's Inn)
Qualifications: LLB (Leeds)

Hughes *Miss Suzy Belinda* •
European Legal Counsel, Central &
Eastern Europe, Newcourt Financial
Limited, 66 Buckingham Gate, London
SW1E 6AU, 0171 411 4800, Fax: 0171
411 5032, Call Date: Nov 1991 (Lincoln's
Inn) Qualifications: LLB (Hons)
(Manch)

Hughes-O'Flanagan *Mrs Margaret Winifred* •
Legal Advisor, Bank of Ireland, 36 Queen Street, London EC4R 1BN, 0171 236 2000, Fax: 0171 634 3102, Call Date: Feb 1981 (Lincoln's Inn) Qualifications: MA, LLB (Dublin), DEA (Paris)

Hugill *Miss Cheryl Dawn* •
Senior Principal Legal Officer, Solicitors Office, HM Customs & Excise, New Kings Beam House, 22 Upper Ground, London SE1 9PJ, 0171 865 5187, Call Date: Nov 1979 (Gray's Inn) Qualifications: LLB (Lond)

Hugill *John*
Recorder (retired 1996) Member Criminal Injuries Compensation Board., 45 Hardman Street, Manchester M3 3HA, 01260 224 368, Fax: 01260 224 703, Call Date: Feb 1954 (Middle Temple) Qualifications: MA (Cantab)

Huka *Mrs Geraldine Oghenenyorbe*
Call Date: July 1981 (Middle Temple) Qualifications: LLB, LLM

Hulme *Mrs Susan Anne*
Pioneered Pupillage in a Law Centre, Call Date: Oct 1994 (Middle Temple) Qualifications: BSc (Hons) , ARCS (Lond), LLB (Hons)

Humberstone *Miss Sarah Georgina*
Call Date: Nov 1984 (Gray's Inn) Qualifications: LLB (Bristol)

Humby *Lee Richard*
Call Date: Mar 1997 (Middle Temple) Qualifications: LLB (Hons)

Hume *Miss Elizabeth Anna* •
Legal Officer, Welsh Office, Crown Buildings, Cathays Park, Cardiff CF1 3NQ, Call Date: Nov 1983 (Gray's Inn) Qualifications: LL.B (Wales)

Humphrey *Captain David Roger* •
Chief Naval Judge Advocate/ Recorder, Call Date: July 1975 (Middle Temple)

Humphreys *David Charlton*
P/t Chairman Property Investment Company, Call Date: Jan 1948 (Inner Temple) Qualifications: MA (Oxon)

Humphreys *Nicholas Bruce*
Bower Cotton, 36 Whitefriars Street, London EC4Y 8DH, 0171 353 3040, Call Date: Oct 1994 (Lincoln's Inn) Qualifications: LLB (Hons), LLM (Lond)

Humphries *Neil Thomas*
Call Date: Nov 1993 (Lincoln's Inn) Qualifications: LLB (Hons)

Hungerford-Welch *Peter John* •
Senior Lecturer (I.C.S.L.), Inns of Court school of Law, 4 Gray's Inn Place, London WC1R 5DX, 0171 404 5787, Fax: 0171 831 4188, Call Date: July 1984 (Inner Temple) Qualifications: LLB (Hull)

Hunt *Mrs Melinda Rose*
Justices Clerks Assistant, The Courthouse, Victoria AvenuE, Southend-on-Sea Essex, 01702 3488491, Call Date: Nov 1994 (Middle Temple) Qualifications: LLB (Hons), Dip Law

Hunt *Paul David*
Harvey Ingram Ouston, Solicitors, 20 New Walk, Leicester LE1 6TX, Call Date: July 1985 (Lincoln's Inn) Qualifications: BA

Hunt *Peter John*
165 Verulam Road, St Albans, Herts AL3 4DW, 01727 851428, also Inn of Court I, Call Date: Nov 1964 (Lincoln's Inn) Qualifications: MA (Cantab)

Hunt *Ronald Frank*
25 Worlds View, Abelia Street, Somerset West 7130, Cape, 8553860, Call Date: July 1967 (Inner Temple)

Hunt *Miss Victoria Katharine*
Call Date: Nov 1995 (Gray's Inn) Qualifications: BA

Hunt *Miss Victoria Mary*
Brethertons Solicitors, 16 Church Street, Rugby, Warwickshire, 01788 579579, Fax: 01788 570947, Solicitor, Call Date: Oct 1993 (Middle Temple) Qualifications: BA (Hons))Leic

Hunt *Wilfred*
20 Britton Street, 1st Floor, London, EC1M 5NQ, Call Date: July 1979 (Gray's Inn) Qualifications: LLB (Lond)

Hunter *Mrs Johanis Mariam* •
Lawyer Grade 7, Court of Criminal appeal, Royal Court of Justice, The Strand, London, 0171 936 6098, Call Date: Oct 1990 (Lincoln's Inn) Qualifications: LLB (Brunel)

Hunter *Timothy Charles*
Call Date: Oct 1998 (Inner Temple) Qualifications: BA (Bris), CPE

Huque *Mrs Daliah Shah*
In House Barrister, J H Nathan & Co, 21 Dudden Hill Lane, London NW10, Call Date: Feb 1974 (Lincoln's Inn)

Hurley *Michael James Le Mesurier* •
Moving Edge Limited, Challenge House, 52-54 Holton Road, Barry, South Glamorgan CF63 4HE, +44 (0)1446 749111, Fax: +44 (0)1446 730370, Call Date: July 1966 (Middle Temple)

Hurrell *Mrs Nicola Hilda*
Call Date: Oct 1998 (Middle Temple) Qualifications: LLB (Hons)(Oxon)

Husain *Farrukh Najeeb*
Immigration & Nationality Adviser, Watford Council Community, Services, Rights & Advice Unit, Town Hall, Watford WD1 3EX, 01923 226400, Fax: 01923 232381, Call Date: July 1996 (Inner Temple) Qualifications: LLB, LLM (Lond)

Husain *Maqbool Asker* •
Senior Crown Prosecutor, Crown Prosecution Service, 8th Floor, Prospect House, 81 Station Road, Croydon, Call Date: Nov 1985 (Lincoln's Inn) Qualifications: BA

Husain-Naviatti *Miss Robina*
Call Date: Nov 1997 (Lincoln's Inn) Qualifications: BA (Hons)

Huskinson *Mrs Pennant Elfrida Lascelles*
11 Glebe Place, Chelsea, London SW3 5LB, Former Solcitor of the Supreme Court (1967-1972), Call Date: May 1972 (Inner Temple)

Hussain *Asam*
Call Date: Nov 1996 (Lincoln's Inn) Qualifications: Bsc (Hons)(City)

Hussain *Ghulam*
Call Date: Oct 1998 (Inner Temple) Qualifications: LLB (Leeds)

Hussain *Karamat*
Call Date: July 1996 (Lincoln's Inn) Qualifications: LLB (Hons)

Hussain *Muhammad Altaf*
Cambridge House Legal Centre, 137 Camberwell Road, London SE5 0HF, Call Date: July 1970 (Middle Temple) Qualifications: BA MA LLB

Hussain *Tariq Parvez*
Legal Advisor/Advocate, Alan Petherbridge & Co, Solicitors/Advocates, 1st Floor, 10 Piece Hallyard, Bradford, 01274 724114, Fax: 01274 724161, Call Date: Nov 1991 (Lincoln's Inn) Qualifications: LLB (Hons)

Hutchinson *Andrew Richard*
Call Date: Oct 1998 (Lincoln's Inn) Qualifications: BA (Hons)

Hutchinson of Lullington *Lord*
House of Lords, London SW1, Call Date: June 1939 (Middle Temple) Qualifications: MA (Oxon)

Hutley *Robert Neil*
Justices' Chief Executive (Devon and Cornwall), Justices' Chief Executive's, Headquarters, Ground Floor, North Quay House, Sutton Harbour, Plymouth PL4 0RA, 01752 222522, Fax: 01752 222520, Call Date: Feb 1976 (Middle Temple) Qualifications: LLB (Lond)

Huxtable *Mrs Alison Jane* •
Executive Manager Corporate & Commercial Services, Amerada Hess Limited, 33 Grosvenor Place, London SW7 1HX, Call Date: July 1983 (Gray's Inn) Qualifications: LLB Hons (Manc)

Hyams *David Ian* •
Corporate Vice President, Commercial & Legal Affairs & Company Secretary, Fujitsu Computers (Europe) Ltd, Lovelace Road, Bracknell, Berks RG12 8SN, 01344 475000, Call Date: July 1981 (Middle Temple) Qualifications: LLB [Lond]

Hyams Miss Natalie Anne
Call Date: Oct 1998 (Lincoln's Inn)
Qualifications: BA (Hons)(Westmin),
CPE

Hyde David Austin
Flat 4, 15 Nevern Place, London
SW5 9NP, 0171 373 5992, Fax: 0171
633562, Call Date: Nov 1997 (Lincoln's
Inn) Qualifications: BA (Hons)(Lancs),
MBA (City), Dip Law, (Nth Lond)

Hyder Stuart Henry •
Senior Counsel, Chevron UK Ltd, 2
Portman Street, London W1H 0AN, 0171
487 8828, Fax: 0171 487 8905, Call
Date: July 1974 (Lincoln's Inn)
Qualifications: MA (Cantab) MBA

Hynes Dermott Francis
Brandon Lodge, New Ross, Co Wexford,
0151 425005, Call Date: July 1963
(Inner Temple) Qualifications: LLM, LLB
(Lond)

Ibrahim Sarfraz •
Senior Crown Prosecutor, Crown
Prosecution Service, Froomsgate House,
Rupert Street, Bristol, Avon BS1 2PS,
0117 9273093, Fax: 0117 9230697, Call
Date: July 1982 (Gray's Inn)
Qualifications: LLB (Lond)

Idan Lionel
Call Date: Mar 1996 (Middle Temple)
Qualifications: LLB (Hons)

Idris Miss Kemi Rashida •
Office of the Solicitor, Call Date: Feb
1995 (Lincoln's Inn) Qualifications: LLB
(Hons)(Bris)

Iles Colin John
Clerk to the Justices, Secretariat Offices,
The Courthouse, Tufton Street, Ashford,
Kent TN23 1QS, 01233 663203, Fax:
01233 663206, Call Date: Nov 1984
(Middle Temple)

Iles Trevor Anthony
4 Lansdown Close, Banbury, Oxon
OX16 9LH, 01295 254345, Call Date: Nov
1983 (Middle Temple) Qualifications:
M.Soc.Sc, DML, Dip, Law

Illingworth Graham
16 Bromwich House, 45 Howson
Terrace, Richmond Hill, Richmond,
Surrey TW10 6RU, 0181 940 4655, Call
Date: Feb 1964 (Gray's Inn)

Ilyas Daud •
Legal Advisor, European Bank for
Reconstruction & Development, 5
Whittingstall Road, London SW6 4EA,
0171 736 5137, Fax: 0171 371 7242,
Advocate, Supreme Court of Pakistan,
Call Date: Nov 1959 (Gray's Inn)
Qualifications: BCL, MA (Oxon)

Ilyas Gheias Uddin Azam
Call Date: Mar 1996 (Middle Temple)
Qualifications: B.Sc (Hons)(Leeds)

Impey Gerald Lawrence
Nigerian Bar Council (1964) Chief Editor
Lawtel, The Ashlish, 2 Close Famman,
Port Erin, Isle of Man IM9 6BJ, 01624
835548/833550, Fax: 01624 624344/
835551/834022, and Member Nigerian
Bar, Call Date: July 1954 (Middle
Temple)

Ina Miss Eucharia Asari •
Legal Adviser, DAS Legal Expenses
Insurance, Company Limited, DAS
House, Quay Side, Temple Back, Bristol
BS1 6NH, Call Date: Nov 1992 (Inner
Temple) Qualifications: LLB (E. Lond),
LLM (Cantab)

Ing Noel Denis
37 Anthony Close, Colchester CO4 4LD,
Call Date: June 1958 (Lincoln's Inn)
Qualifications: MA (Oxon)

Ingham Charles Neill •
Assistant Chief Crown Prosecutor CPS
Anglia Part-time Industrial Tribunal
Chairman (London North Region),
Crown Prosecution Service, Queen's
House, 58 Victoria Street, St Albans,
Herts AL1 3HZ, 01727 818104, Fax:
01727 833144, and Member Hong Kong
Bar, Call Date: Nov 1972 (Inner Temple)
Qualifications: BA (Lond)

Ingle Norman
Call Date: Nov 1977 (Lincoln's Inn)
Qualifications: DMA

Inglese Anthony Michael Christopher •
Deputy Treasury Solicitor, Treasury
Solicitors Dept, Queen Annes Chambers,
28 Broadway, London SW1H 9JS, Call
Date: Nov 1976 (Gray's Inn)
Qualifications: MA, LLB

Inglewood The Rt Hon Lord
Hutton-in-the Forest, Penrith, Cumbria
CA11 9TH, 017684 84500, Fax: 017684
84571, Call Date: July 1975 (Lincoln's
Inn) Qualifications: MA (Cantab), ARICS

Inglis George Grant Gordon Otto
Refugee Legal Centre, Call Date: Oct
1991 (Inner Temple) Qualifications: BSc
(Dunelm), LLB (Bucks)

Ingman Miss Ruth Margaret
Call Date: Feb 1992 (Inner Temple)
Qualifications: LLB

Ingram Jamie Andrew •
Business Affairs Executive, Sony
Psygnosis, Napier Court, Stephenson
Way, Wavetree Technology Park,
Liverpool L13 1HD, 0151 2823000, Fax:
0151 2823001, Call Date: Oct 1994
(Middle Temple) Qualifications: LLB
(Hons)

Ingram Philip John
Call Date: Nov 1996 (Lincoln's Inn)
Qualifications: LLB (Hons)

Innes Miss Jane
Bristows, 3 Lincoln's Inn Fields, London
WC2A 3AA, 0171 400 8000, Call Date:
Nov 1994 (Lincoln's Inn) Qualifications:
LB (Hons)(B'ham)

Innes Thomas John Stanley
64 Monnow Street, Monmouth, Gwent
NP5 3EN, 01600 2372, Call Date: Nov
1982 (Middle Temple) Qualifications: BA
(Oxon)

Insole Roy William
The Garden House, Smeeth, Ashford,
Kent TN25 6SP, 0130 381 3011, Fax:
0130 381 4313, Call Date: Nov 1974
(Inner Temple)

Ireland Sidney Harold
01753 663684, Call Date: Nov 1979
(Middle Temple) Qualifications: B Com
(Hons), BSC (Hons)

Irvine Norman Forrest
11 Upland Park Road, Oxford OX2 7RU,
01865 513570, Formerly a
Solicitor,Scotland, Call Date: Nov 1955
(Gray's Inn) Qualifications: BL
(Glasgow)

Irving Edward
Call Date: Feb 1976 (Inner Temple)
Qualifications: BA (Oxon)

Isaacs Miss Deborah Jane •
Contoller of Legal Services, London
Weekend Television Ltd, South Bank
Television Centre, London SE1 9LT,
0171 261 3586, Fax: 0171 928 7825,
Call Date: Nov 1987 (Lincoln's Inn)
Qualifications: MA (Oxon) Dip Law

Ishaque Miss Shabnam
Call Date: Oct 1996 (Lincoln's Inn)
Qualifications: BSc (Hons)(Lond), CPE

Isherwood John Denys
Director of Development, PT Fajar
Surashakti, Samudera Indonesia
Building, Jalan Let.S. Parman Kav 35,
Jakarta 11480, Jakarta 5307877, Fax:
Jakarta 5482567, Call Date: Nov 1986
(Gray's Inn) Qualifications: Bsc(Eng)
MBA, CEng, Eur Ing, FICE, FIArb

Isherwood Malcolm Oliver •
Principal Crown Prosecutor, Crown
Prosecution Service, Prudential House,
Topping Street, Blackpool, Lancashire
FY1 3AB, 01253 299822, Call Date: Nov
1980 (Gray's Inn) Qualifications: BA

Islam Abdul Kashem Muhammad Fakrul
Call Date: May 1997 (Gray's Inn)
Qualifications: BSS, MSS (Dhaka), LLB
(Hertfordshire)

Islam Misbahul
5 Nottingwood House, Clarendon Road,
London W11, Call Date: Nov 1977
(Lincoln's Inn) Qualifications: MA, MSc,
Dip M, DIA

Islam Zaglul •
Inland Revenue, East Wing, Somerset
House, Strand, London WC2R 1LB, 0171
438 6881, Fax: 0171 438 6246, Call
Date: Nov 1995 (Lincoln's Inn)
Qualifications: BSc (Hons) (Wales), Dip
Law (Lond)

Ismail *Miss Bilkis*
Tax Consultant, KPMG, St James'
Square, Manchester M2 6DS, 0161 838
4000 Ext 4389, Call Date: Oct 1998
(Lincoln's Inn) Qualifications: LLB
(Hons)

Ismail *Miss Shahin*
Call Date: Nov 1993 (Lincoln's Inn)
Qualifications: LLB (Hons)

Ispahani *Mrs Sabina*
Call Date: Nov 1986 (Middle Temple)
Qualifications: BA [Kent]

Ivamy *Mrs Christine Ann Frances*
7 Egliston Mews, London SW15 1AP,
0181 785 6718, Call Date: Nov 1968
(Gray's Inn) Qualifications: MA (Hons)

Ives *Terence John*
Superintendent, Hertfordshire
Constabulary, County H.Q., Welwyn
Garden City, Herts, 01707 331177, Call
Date: July 1990 (Middle Temple)
Qualifications: MA (Cantab)

Iyer *Miss Shobana*
Call Date: July 1998 (Gray's Inn)
Qualifications: BSc (King's), LLB,
(Brunel)

Jabbar *Miss Sk. Jenwfa Khanom*
Call Date: Mar 1997 (Lincoln's Inn)
Qualifications: LLB (Hons) (Lond)

Jackson *Andrew Richard* •
European Legal Counsel, Kroll
Associates UK Limited, 25 Saville Row,
London W1X 0AL, 0171 396 0000, Fax:
0171 396 9966, Call Date: July 1987
(Gray's Inn) Qualifications: LLB
(Warwick)

Jackson *Calvin Leigh Raphael*
Head of Strategic Compensation
Consulting, Watson Wyatt Partners, 21
Tothill Street, London SW1H 9LL, 0171
222 8033, Fax: 0171 222 9182, Call
Date: July 1975 (Lincoln's Inn)
Qualifications: LLB,LLM (Lon) , MPhil
[Cantab]

Jackson *Ms Carol* •
Crown Prosecution Service, 'D'
Division, Manchester, 0161 908 2682,
Call Date: Oct 1994 (Inner Temple)
Qualifications: BA (Essex), CPE (Lond)

Jackson *Professor David Cooper*
Call Date: Feb 1957 (Inner Temple)

Jackson *Edward Oliver*
23 Lyndale Avenue, London NW2 2QB,
0171 794 5090, Room 716, Royal
Courts of Justice Tel: 01-405 4248, Call
Date: June 1951 (Inner Temple)
Qualifications: MA, BSc

Jackson *Lee Anthony*
Caseworker, Refugee Legal Centre,
Sussex House, 39-45 Bermondsey
Street, London SE1 3XF, 0171 827
5362, Fax: 0171 378 1979, Call Date:
Oct 1995 (Lincoln's Inn)
Qualifications: LLB (Hons) (Lond)

Jackson *Ms Madeleine Annette* •
Acquisition Editor, Sweet and Maxwell
Ltd, South Quay Plaza, 183 Marsh Wall,
London E14 9FT, 0171 538 8686, Fax:
0171 538 8625, and Member Israel
Bar, Call Date: Nov 1983 (Middle
Temple) Qualifications: BA Hons Law
(Nott'm)

Jackson *Marc Richard Steen* •
Call Date: Nov 1992 (Middle Temple)
Qualifications: LLB (Hons)(Hull)

Jackson *Mark Adrian* •
Dentmaster Holdings plc, Grosvenor
House, Hollinswood Road, Central
Park, Telford TF2 9TW, Call Date: July
1986 (Lincoln's Inn) Qualifications:
LLB

Jackson *Philip Andrew*
Call Date: July 1998 (Middle Temple)
Qualifications: BA (Hons)(Sheff)

Jackson *Philip David Martin*
Lecturer in Law, Commercial Dispute
Mediator, Flat 2, 73 Shooters Hill Road,
Blackheath, London SE3 7HU, 0181
293 4210, Call Date: Nov 1995 (Inner
Temple) Qualifications: BSc (York),
CPE (Lond)

Jackson *Miss Samantha Jane*
Call Date: Nov 1996 (Middle Temple)
Qualifications: LLB (Hons), LLM

Jackson *Stephen Malcolm*
Bristol Claims & Property, Consultants,
27 Westbury Road, Westbury-On-Trym,
Bristol BS9 3AX, 0117 9624665, Fax:
0117 9744701, Call Date: July 1975
(Gray's Inn) Qualifications: LLB

Jackson *Mrs Tara Veronica* •
Company Secretary, Call Date: July
1988 (Middle Temple) Qualifications:
LLB

Jackson *Warner*
Call Date: Feb 1991 (Lincoln's Inn)
Qualifications: LLB

Jacob *Miss Cynty*
Call Date: Oct 1995 (Middle Temple)
Qualifications: LLB (Hons)

Jacob *George Ramkissoon*
Call Date: July 1994 (Lincoln's Inn)

Jacob *Peter Leo* •
Lord Chancellor's Dept, Southside, 105
Victoria Street, London SW1E 6QT, Call
Date: July 1974 (Middle Temple)

Jacobs *Miss Leonie Kathleen Jennie
T'Sahai*
and Member St Vincent & The
Grenadines Bar, Call Date: July 1995
(Middle Temple) Qualifications: LLB
(Hons)

Jacobs *Miss Susan Jane* •
Crown Prosecutor, Crown Prosecution
Service, The Cooperage, 8 Gainsford
Street, London SE1 2NG, Call Date: Nov
1988 (Gray's Inn) Qualifications: BA

Jacobs *Timothy Julian*
Call Date: Oct 1995 (Middle Temple)
Qualifications: BA (Hons)

Jacobsen *Miss Anne Marie Elisabeth*
Ledbury Cottage, Lebury Road, Reigate,
Surrey RH2 9HN, 01737 249100,
Former Deputy Charity Commissioner,
Call Date: Nov 1950 (Gray's Inn)
Qualifications: BA (Hons) (Cantab)

Jacobson *Miss Rivka*
Call Date: Nov 1998 (Inner Temple)
Qualifications: BA (Israel)

Jacomb *Sir Martin Wakefield*
142 Holborn Bars, London EC1N 2NH,
Call Date: Nov 1955 (Inner Temple)
Qualifications: MA

Jaffer *Miss Masooma*
Call Date: Nov 1998 (Middle Temple)
Qualifications: LLB (Hons)(Bucks)

Jagatheeson *Miss Premelaa*
Call Date: July 1997 (Gray's Inn)
Qualifications: BA

Jaggers *Desmond* •
Principal Crown Prosecutor, Crown
Prosecution Service, Birmingham
Branch 1, Colmore Gate, 2 Colmore
Row, Birmingham B3 2QA, 0121 629
7200, Fax: 0121 629 7335, Call Date:
July 1974 (Inner Temple)
Qualifications: LLB

Jaggi *Deepak* •
Senior Legal Officer, Revenue Solicitor's
Office, Somerset House (East Wing),
The Strand, London WC2R 1LB, 0171
438 7259, Fax: 0171 438 6246, Call
Date: Nov 1977 (Middle Temple)
Qualifications: BA (Oxon)

Jagmohan *Ms Judith*
Call Date: Nov 1993 (Middle Temple)
Qualifications: BA (Hons)(Keele), LLM
(Nott'm)

Jago *Miss Catherine Jane*
Call Date: Oct 1998 (Inner Temple)
Qualifications: BSc (Surrey), CPE (W.
of England)

Jalleh *Ms Mayleen Ann*
Law Lecturer LLM (Cantab), University
of the West of, England, Frenchay
Campus, Coldharbour Lane, Bristol
BS16 1QY, 0117 9656261, and Member
Malaysia Bar New York Bar, Call Date:
July 1986 (Lincoln's Inn)
Qualifications: LLB (Hons) Warwick

Jamal *Miss Damaris Dorothy* •
Crown Prosecutor, Crown Prosecution
Service, 2nd Floor, Kings House,
Kymberley Road, Harrow, Middlesex,
0181 424 8688, Call Date: July 1989
(Gray's Inn) Qualifications: BA
[Dunelm]

James *Andrew John* •
Marconi Communications Limited,
Edge Lane, Liverpool L7 9NW, 0151
254 4340, Fax: 0151 254 3326, Call
Date: July 1983 (Gray's Inn)
Qualifications: BA

James *Mrs Anita Mary* •
Senior Principal Legal Officer, Solicitor &
Legal Adviser's, Officer, Department of
the, Environment, Transport & the,
Regions, Eland House, Bressender Place,
London SW1E 5DU, 0171 890 4756, Fax:
0171 890 4752, Call Date: July 1974
(Middle Temple) Qualifications: BA Hons

James *Arnold Victor* •
Office of the Social Security,
Commissioners, Harp House, 83
farringdon Street, London EC4A 4DH,
0171 395 3330, Call Date: Nov 1991
(Inner Temple) Qualifications: BSc, Dip
Law

James *Basil*
Presiding Special Commissioner of
Income Tax 1983, Call Date: June 1940
(Lincoln's Inn) Qualifications: MA
(Cantab)

James *Brian Wardell*
Call Date: Feb 1961 (Middle Temple)
Qualifications: LLB (Lond)

James *Mrs Clare Louise* •
Alliance & Leicester PLC, Customer
Service Centre, Carlton Park,
Narborough, Leicester LE9 5XX, 0116
200 3527, Fax: 0116 200 3549, Call
Date: Mar 1996 (Lincoln's Inn)
Qualifications: LLB (Hons)(Leics)

James *David John*
Call Date: May 1996 (Gray's Inn)
Qualifications: LLB

James *David Madoc* •
Legal Adviser (Grade 6), Dept of Trade &
Industry, 10-18 Victoria Street, London
SW1H 0NN, 0171 215 3050, Fax: 0171
215 3141, Call Date: July 1973
(Lincoln's Inn)

James *Frederick Nicholas* •
Group Legal Adviser, Burnah Castrol
Plc, Burmah Castrol House, Pipers Way,
Wiltshire SN3 1RE, 01793 452500, Fax:
01793 618162, Call Date: July 1977
(Inner Temple)

James *John Maxwell*
11 Broadmead Green, Thorpe End,
Norwich, Norfolk NR13 5DE, Call Date:
June 1948 (Lincoln's Inn)
Qualifications: LLB (Lond)

James *Ms Julie* •
Head of Legal and Committee Services.,
City & County of Swansea, County Hall,
Swansea SA1 3SN, 01792 636012, Fax:
01792 637120, Call Date: July 1983
(Gray's Inn) Qualifications: BA Sussex,
Dip Law

James *Leslie*
Call Date: Nov 1951 (Gray's Inn)
Qualifications: BA, LLB, FCIT

James *Mark David*
Lecturer, Manchester Metropiltan Uni.,
School of Law, Hatersage Road,
Manchester M13 0JA, 0161 247 2432,
Fax: 0161 224 0893, Call Date: Nov 1994
(Lincoln's Inn) Qualifications: LLB
(Hons)(Leeds)

James *Mark Stephen*
Call Date: Nov 1998 (Middle Temple)
Qualifications: BSc (Hons)(Lond)

James *Roger Ivor Rendall*
Baker & McKenzie, 100 New Bridge
Street, London EC4V 6JA, and Member
New York Bar (1990), Call Date: July
1988 (Lincoln's Inn) Qualifications: LLB
(Hons)

James *Miss Suzanne Margaret*
17 Downs Court Road, Purley, Surrey
CR8 1BE, Call Date: July 1985 (Gray's
Inn) Qualifications: BA (Cantab), BA
(Lond)

Jameson *Commander Andrew Charles* •
Royal Naval Officer, NPA, Jervis Block,
Third Floor, HMS Nelson, Queen Street,
Portsmouth PO1 3HH, 0181 858 2154,
Call Date: Oct 1993 (Middle Temple)
Qualifications: LLB (Hons)(Newc)

Jameson *Gary Antony*
Call Date: Mar 1997 (Lincoln's Inn)
Qualifications: LLB (Hons)

Jamieson *Andrew* •
Legal Adviser/Director, I.T.I.M. Ltd,
International House, 26 Creechurch
Lane, London EC3A 5BA, 0171 338
0150, Fax: 0171 338 0151, Call Date:
July 1985 (Middle Temple)
Qualifications: BA (Lond), Dip Law, ACI
Arb

Jamieson *Mrs Cara*
Call Date: Oct 1994 (Lincoln's Inn)
Qualifications: LLB (Hons)(Lond)

Jamieson *Miss Debra Audrey*
Call Date: Nov 1996 (Inner Temple)
Qualifications: LLB (So'ton)

Jamil-Nordin *Miss Ida Nurbayatuty*
Call Date: July 1998 (Lincoln's Inn)
Qualifications: LLB (Hons)

Jani *Miss Jamie*
Call Date: Oct 1995 (Inner Temple)
Qualifications: LLB (Lond)

Janner of Braunstone *Lord*
Chairman, Parliamentary Employment
Select Committee 1992-96, House of
Lords, London SW1A 2PW, 0171 222
2863, Fax: 0171 222 2864, Call Date:
July 1954 (Middle Temple)
Qualifications: MA (Cantab), PhD (Hon)

Janusz *Mrs Frances Miriam* •
Principal Crown Prosecutor, Crown
Prosecution Service, C/O 50 Ludgate Hill,
London EC4M 7EX, Call Date: July 1979
(Lincoln's Inn) Qualifications: BA
(Reading)

Jap *Ms Chee Miau*
Call Date: Nov 1971 (Gray's Inn)
Qualifications: LLB (Lond)

Jardine *Dr Francis Stephen John* •
Deputy Company Secretary, Enterprise
Oil Plc, Grand Buildings, Trafalgar
Square, London WC2N 5EJ, 0171 925
4236, Call Date: July 1996 (Gray's Inn)
Qualifications: BSc, D.Phil (Sussex),
LLB, LLM (London), C Eng, MIM, ACIS,
FCCA, MIM, MIMgt

Jarman *David A E*
Justice of the Peace, West Sussex, Call
Date: July 1969 (Inner Temple)

Jarratt *William Frederic Seaton*
Call Date: July 1998 (Gray's Inn)
Qualifications: MA (St Andrews)

Jarrett *Mrs Evelyne Blake Chinedum*
Legal Officer, 10 Springett House, St
Matthews Road, Brixton Hill, London
SW2 1NG, Call Date: Mar 1996 (Middle
Temple) Qualifications: BA (Nigeria),
LLB (Hons) (Lond), MA (B'ham)

Jarvis *Julian Ross*
Call Date: Oct 1995 (Inner Temple)
Qualifications: LLB (Sussex)

Jeddere-Fisher *Arthur Joseph*
Call Date: June 1949 (Inner Temple)

Jee *Mrs Jane Angela*
Division Manager, Mondex International
Ltd, 47-53 Cannon Street, London
EC4M 5SQ, 0171 557 5129, Fax: 0171
557 5329, nee HAZLEWOOD, Call Date:
July 1977 (Inner Temple) Qualifications:
LLB Hons (Exon), Dip (Indus Relat & ,
Personnel Manag)

Jeffrey *David Abbott*
Business Consultant, Cahill, Foxton,
Alnwick, Northumberland NE66 3BB,
01665 830553, Call Date: July 1960
(Lincoln's Inn) Qualifications: LLB,
FCIS, C.Inst.M

Jeffrey *Mrs Elisabeth* •
Crown Prosection Service, Sunlight
House, Manchester, Call Date: Oct 1990
(Middle Temple) Qualifications: LLB
(Nott'm)(Hons)

Jeffrey *Sean Peter*
Call Date: July 1995 (Middle Temple)
Qualifications: BA (Hons) (Oxon)

Jeffreys *Mrs Michelle Joy*
Senior Court Clerk, Nottingham
Magistrates' Court, Carrington Street,
Nottingham NG2 1EE, 0115 955 8111,
Fax: 0115 955 8131, Call Date: July 1980
(Gray's Inn) Qualifications: LLB
(B'ham)

Jeffreys *Miss Rosemary Anne* •
Legal Adviser. Consitution Secretariat,
Cabinet Office, 70 Whitehall, London
SW1A 2AS, 0171 270 6093, Call Date:
July 1978 (Gray's Inn) Qualifications:
LLB(Bristol), LLM [Lond]

Jeffries *William Anthony*
Chief Executive, Victoria Law Courts,
Corporation Street, Birmingham, 0121
212 6612, Fax: 0121 212 6766, Call
Date: Nov 1979 (Gray's Inn)
Qualifications: MBA

Jelf *Simon Edward*
Call Date: Oct 1996 (Gray's Inn)
Qualifications: LLB (E.Anglia)

Jellie *Miss Violet Hilary*
Call Date: Nov 1958 (Gray's Inn)

Jelly *Fullerton McWilliam*
Call Date: July 1984 (Middle Temple)
Qualifications: BSc (Belfast),CEng ,
MICE, FIMgt

Jenking-Rees *Mark* •
Principal Legal Officer, Department of
Social Security, New Court, 48 Carey
Street, London WC2, Call Date: May
1987 (Lincoln's Inn) Qualifications:
LLB

Jenkins *Arthur Bernard*
46 Court Hill, Sanderstead, Surrey
CR2 9NA, Call Date: Nov 1959
(Lincoln's Inn) Qualifications: LLB,
FCII

Jenkins *Miss Glynys Ceri* •
Senior Principal Legal Officer, HM
Customs & Excise, 22 Upper Ground,
London SE1 9PJ, 0171 865 5210, Fax:
0171 865 5022, Call Date: July 1974
(Gray's Inn) Qualifications: LLB

Jenkins *Mark Anthony*
Call Date: Nov 1998 (Lincoln's Inn)
Qualifications: Dip Law (Wolves)

Jenkins *Paul Christopher* •
The Legal Adviser, Lord Chancellor's
Department, Lord Chancellors' Dept,
Selborne House, 54-60 Victoria Street,
London SW1E 6QW, 0171 210 0711,
Fax: 0171 210 0746, Call Date: July
1977 (Middle Temple) Qualifications:
LLB

Jenkins *Philip Dunsford*
Call Date: Nov 1970 (Lincoln's Inn)
Qualifications: LLB (Lond)

Jenkins *Miss Sarah Valerie*
Call Date: Oct 1994 (Middle Temple)
Qualifications: LLB (Hons) (Leeds)

Jenkinson *Daniel Thomas*
Compliance Officer, Natwest Life,
Trinity Quay, Avon Street, Bristol
B52 OYY, 0117 9404715, Fax: 0117
9404807, Call Date: July 1981 (Middle
Temple) Qualifications: BA Hons

Jennings *Mrs Caroline Patricia*
Deputy Clerk to the Justices Assistant
Training Officer, Northamptonshire
Magistrates, Court, Regents Pavillion,
Summerhouse Road, Moulton Park,
Northampton NN3 1AS, 01604 497036,
Fax: 01604 497010, Call Date: July
1989 (Middle Temple) Qualifications:
Dip Law, Dip Mag Law, Dip
Management Stud

Jennings *Mrs Gina Anne*
Freshfields, 65 Fleet Street, London
EC4Y 1HS, 0171 832 7202, Fax: 0171
832 7518, Call Date: July 1980 (Gray's
Inn) Qualifications: LLB (Bris)

Jennings *Mark*
25 Waldgrave Road, Wavertree,
Liverpool L15 7JL, 0151 722 9806, Call
Date: Oct 1995 (Gray's Inn)
Qualifications: LLB

Jennings *Michael Stuart* •
Call Date: Oct 1994 (Gray's Inn)
Qualifications: BA

Jennings *Ms Sally Jane* •
Zeneca Limited, Fernhurst, Haslemere,
Surrey GU27 3JE, 01428 655905, Fax:
01428 655679, Call Date: Oct 1991
(Middle Temple) Qualifications: BA
Hons , Dip Law, LLM (Lond)

Jensen *Paul*
Registered Arbitrator, Paul Jensen
Associates, 61B Gerard Street, Ashton
in Makerfield, Wigan WN4 9AG, 01942
715001, Fax: 01942 715100, Call Date:
July 1979 (Lincoln's Inn)
Qualifications: FRICS, FCIArb

Jerram *Nelson Richard Joseph*
Paterson & Co Solicitors, Clent
Chambers, Barnsley Hall Drive,
Birmingham Road, Bromsgrove,
Worcestershire B61 0ED, 01527
577715, Fax: 01527 577716, Call Date:
Nov 1980 (Gray's Inn) Qualifications:
Dip Law

Jessel *Robin Richard*
Call Date: June 1953 (Lincoln's Inn)

Jeyaretnam *Philip Antony*
11 King's Bench Walk, Temple,
London, EC4Y 7EQ, Call Date: July
1987 (Gray's Inn)

Jhowry *Miss Anjali*
Call Date: July 1998 (Middle Temple)
Qualifications: LLB (Hons)

Jimdar *Roger Michael* •
Principal Legal Officer, HM Customs &
Excise, New King's Beam House, 22
Upper Ground, London SE1 9PJ, 0171
865 5983, and Member Trinidad &
Tobago Bar, Call Date: Nov 1986
(Lincoln's Inn) Qualifications: LLB
(Lond)

Jinadu *Mr Justice Yaya Abiodun
Olatunde*
Formerly; Deputy Town Clerk of Lagos;
Crown Counsel, Treasury Counsel,
Deputy Solicitor- General of Nigeria, 2
Redwoods, Alton Road, Roehampton,
London SW15 4NL, 0181 788 3192,
High Court Judge, formerly of Lagos
State, Call Date: July 1954 (Middle
Temple) Qualifications: LLB (Lond)

Joad *Miss Nicola Ward* •
Senior Principal Legal Officer, HM
Customs & Excise, New Kings Beam
House, 22 Upper Ground, London
SE1 9PJ, Call Date: Nov 1983 (Middle
Temple) Qualifications: LLB (Lond)

Jobanputra *Sandip Mukund*
Call Date: Oct 1996 (Gray's Inn)
Qualifications: BA (Oxon)

Jobes *Mrs Jharna* •
Crown Prosecution Service, 50 Ludgate
Hill, London EC4M 7EX, Call Date: July
1982 (Middle Temple) Qualifications:
BA

Joel *Dan*
Advocate & Notary, Joel & Joel, P.O.B.
1671, Tel Aviv 61015, 4 Rothschild
Boulevard, 66881 Tel-Aviv, Israel,
Israel, 013 65 8317, and Member
Israeli Bar Blackstone Chambers,
Blackstone House, Temple, London,
EC4Y 9BW, Call Date: Nov 1967 (Inner
Temple)

Joels *Harold*
11A Arkwright Road, Hampstead,
London NW3 6AA, 0171 794 9683, Fax:
0171 794 2042, Also Inn of Court I, Call
Date: Nov 1954 (Gray's Inn)
Qualifications: MA LLB (Cantab)

Joelson *Stephen Laurance Robert*
and Member California Bar Hardwicke
Building, New Square, Lincoln's Inn,
London, WC2A 3SB, Call Date: Nov
1980 (Gray's Inn) Qualifications: LLB
(Reading)

Johal *Inderjit Singh*
Call Date: Oct 1998 (Inner Temple)
Qualifications: LLB (De Montfort)

Johal *Sudeep Singh*
Call Date: Oct 1996 (Gray's Inn)
Qualifications: LLB (Lond)

Johansen *Piers Charles Christian*
Call Date: Nov 1995 (Middle Temple)
Qualifications: BA (Hons)(Dunelm)

John *Miss Lisa*
Call Date: Nov 1998 (Gray's Inn)
Qualifications: LLB (Glamorgan), LLM
(Bris)

John *Miss Louise*
Clifford Chance, 200 Aldersgate Street,
London EC1A 4JJ, 0171 600 1000, Fax:
0171 600 5555, Call Date: July 1989
(Inner Temple) Qualifications: LLB

John-Charles *Lee* •
Lawyer, Treasury Solicitors, Queen
Anne's Chambers, 28 Broadway,
London SW1H 9JS, 0171 210 3446,
Fax: 0171 210 3250, Call Date: Nov
1985 (Lincoln's Inn) Qualifications:
LLB (Hons)

Johnson *Ms Alexia Maud Ann*
Call Date: Oct 1997 (Inner Temple)
Qualifications: LLB (Birmingham)

Johnson *Ms Annette Rose-Marie*
Tax Specialist, Call Date: Nov 1988
(Inner Temple) Qualifications: LLB (W
Indies), LLM (York Uni Can)

Johnson *Babatunde* •
Commercial Director, Adecco, Adecco
House, Elstree Way, Borehamwood,
Herfordshire WD6 1HY, 0181 236
5346, Fax: 0181 905 2541, Call Date:
July 1989 (Inner Temple)
Qualifications: BA, Dip Law

E

Johnson *Miss Busola*
Call Date: Nov 1998 (Inner Temple)
Qualifications: BA (Lond), BA (Cantab)

Johnson *Mrs Catherine Anne*
Call Date: Feb 1978 (Lincoln's Inn)
Qualifications: BA,MA (Oxon)

Johnson *Craig Rothwell*
Legal Officer, The Engineering
Employers, Federation (East Midlands
Ass), Barleythorpe, Oakham, Rutland
LE15 7ED, 01572 723711, Fax: 01572
757657, Call Date: Nov 1995 (Gray's
Inn) Qualifications: BSc (Hons), Dip
Law, PGCE

Johnson *Miss Debra Ann*
Call Date: July 1998 (Inner Temple)
Qualifications: LLB (Hull)

Johnson *Ms Diana Ruth*
North Lewisham Law Centre, 28
Deptford High Street, London SE8 4AF,
0181 692 5355, Fax: 0181 694 2516,
Call Date: Nov 1991 (Middle Temple)
Qualifications: LLB Hons (Lond)

Johnson *Edward Thomas Darren*
Call Date: Nov 1995 (Inner Temple)
Qualifications: LLB (L'pool)

Johnson *Miss Gillian Sheila* •
Legal Adviser, DSS, Solicitor's Office, New
Court, 48 Carey Street, London
WC2A 2LS, Call Date: July 1965 (Gray's
Inn) Qualifications: LLB

Johnson *Gregory Thomas*
Call Date: Oct 1998 (Inner Temple)
Qualifications: LLB (Sussex)

Johnson *Lindsay Charles Whitley*
Research Scholar at Nottingham
University, Call Date: Oct 1997 (Inner
Temple) Qualifications: BSc (Brunel),
MA (London)

Johnson *Matthew Stuart* •
Lawyer, Solicitor's Office, H M Customs
& Excise, New King's Beam House, 22
Upper Ground, London SE1 9PJ, Call
Date: Oct 1995 (Lincoln's Inn)
Qualifications: LLB (Hons) (Leic)

Johnson *Miss Melanie Jane*
Call Date: Oct 1993 (Middle Temple)
Qualifications: MA (Hons) (Oxon), CPE
(City)

Johnson *Miss Nancy Alexander Miller*
Call Date: July 1993 (Middle Temple)
Qualifications: LLB (Hons)

Johnson *Dr Nicholas Francis*
Call Date: July 1998 (Middle Temple)
Qualifications: MBBS (Lond), Dip Law,
FRACGP

Johnson *Nicholas Guy*
Call Date: Nov 1993 (Inner Temple)
Qualifications: MA (Oxon), CPE

Johnson *Ms Nicola Lorraine*
Call Date: Oct 1997 (Gray's Inn)
Qualifications: BSc (Manc)

Johnson *Richard Francis*
Call Date: Oct 1996 (Gray's Inn)
Qualifications: LLB (Lond)

Johnson *Mrs Sandra*
Bridge Gap, Main Street, Linton,
Wetherby, W Yorks LS22 4HT, Call Date:
Feb 1977 (Middle Temple)
Qualifications: LLB, MA

Johnston *Dr Alexandra Kate* •
Board Advocates, Criminal Injuries
Board, Morley House, 26-30 Holborn
Viaduct, London EC1A 2JQ, Call Date: Oct
1993 (Inner Temple) Qualifications: MB
ChB (University , of Leicester Medical,
School), Specialist, Diploma in Tort, CPE

Johnston *David Ian*
Call Date: Oct 1994 (Lincoln's Inn)
Qualifications: LLB (Hons) (Leeds)

Johnston *Frank* •
Legal Advisor, Leeds City Council, Call
Date: Oct 1995 (Inner Temple)
Qualifications: LLB (Sheff)

Johnston *James Scott* •
Legal Services Manager, Dept of Central
Services, Legal Services Division,
Darlington Borough Council, Town Hall,
Darlington DL1 5QT, 01325 388232,
Fax: 01325 388333, Call Date: Oct 1990
(Lincoln's Inn) Qualifications: LLB
(Hons)

Johnston *John Douglas Hartley*
Assistant Editor, Simon's Tax Cases,
Butterworths, Halsbury House, 35
Chancery Lane, London WC2A 1EL, 0171
400 2500, Call Date: July 1962
(Lincoln's Inn) Qualifications: MA, LLB,
LLM (Harvard), PHD (Cambridge)

Johnston *John Leslie Kerr*
de Zoete & Bevan Ltd, Ebbgate House, 2
Swan Lane, London EC4R 3TS, 0171 623
2323, Call Date: Nov 1980 (Lincoln's
Inn) Qualifications: LLB (Lond)

Johnston *Lindsay Alexander McLennan*
Legal Advisor, 46 Cedars Drive, Walton,
Stone, Staffordshire ST15 0BB, 01785
819202, Fax: 01785 819202, Call Date:
Nov 1996 (Lincoln's Inn) Qualifications:
LLB (Hons), LLM, BSc, ACIArb

Johnston *Paul Charles*
Construction & Engineering Grp, Pinsent
Curtis, 3 Colmore Circus, Birmingham
B4 6BH, 0121 200 1050, Fax: 0121 626
1040, Call Date: Nov 1998 (Middle
Temple) Qualifications: BSc (Hons),
ARICS, ACIarb

Johnstone *James Burke*
Treleaver, Coverack, Cornwall TR12 6SF,
0374 44 5020, Call Date: Nov 1994
(Lincoln's Inn) Qualifications: BA
(Hons)

Jones *Adrian Richard Hope* •
Steamship Mutual Underwriting,
Association (Bermuda) Limited, Call
Date: Nov 1994 (Inner Temple)
Qualifications: BA (Durham), MA (York),
CPE (Lond)

Jones *Anthony Charles Frederick Norm*
Call Date: July 1970 (Inner Temple)
Qualifications: BA

Jones *Mrs Beverley Lynne*
Call Date: Nov 1998 (Middle Temple)
Qualifications: LLB (Hons) (Wales)

Jones *Mrs Carmel Margaret Anne*
Principal Legal Advisor, Ealing
Magistrates' Court, Green Man Lane,
West Ealing, London W13, 0181 579
9311, Call Date: Nov 1970 (Inner
Temple)

Jones *Miss Catherine Sian*
Call Date: Oct 1998 (Gray's Inn)
Qualifications: LLB

Jones *Ms Catrin Helen* •
Litigation Lawyer, London Borough of
Richmond, Legal Services, Civic Centre,
44 York Street, Twickenham TW1 3BZ,
0181 891 7142, Call Date: Nov 1994
(Lincoln's Inn) Qualifications: LLB
(Hons) (Lanc)

Jones *Daniel Owen Malcolm* •
Legal Affairs/ Contracts Officer, Matsusita
Communication, Industrial UK Limited,
Daytona Drive, Colthrop, Thacham,
Berkshire RG19 4ZD, 01635 871466,
Fax: 01635 873638, Call Date: Nov 1995
(Middle Temple) Qualifications: BA
(Hons), LLM

Jones *Darius Wilmoth*
East Caribbean Supreme Court
(Dominica) 1998, Call Date: July 1997
(Lincoln's Inn) Qualifications: LLB
(Hons) (Lond), LEC (West Indies)

Jones *David Elwyn*
Call Date: Oct 1996 (Inner Temple)
Qualifications: BA (E.Ang), CPE

Jones *Dominic Clive*
Morgan Stanley & Co, International, 25
Cabot Square, London E14 4QA, 0171
425 8689, Fax: 0171 425 8971, and
Member French Bar, Call Date: July 1987
(Middle Temple) Qualifications: LLB
(Bristol)

Jones *Mrs Doris Jean*
56 Grove Park Terrace, Chiswick,
London W4 3QE, 0181 994 2241, Call
Date: Jan 1948 (Lincoln's Inn)
Qualifications: MA (Oxon)

Jones *Edward John*
Clerk to the Justices, Jutices Chief
Secretary to Walsall Committee of Lord
Chancellor, The Court House, Stafford
Street, Walsall, West Midlands WS2 8HA,
01922 638222, Fax: 01922 35657, Call
Date: July 1982 (Gray's Inn)
Qualifications: Dip Law

Jones *Gareth Alun*
Litigation Support, Legal Technologies,
126-134 Baker Street, LondoN WC1,
Wales, 0171 935 8242, Call Date: Oct
1997 (Middle Temple) Qualifications:
LLB (Hons) (Lond)

Jones *Graham Bennett Ap Aled*
Call Date: Oct 1998 (Gray's Inn)
Qualifications: LLB (Wales)

• Barrister in employment

Jones *Grant Meredith*
Beaumont & Son Solicitors, Lloyds
Chambers, 1 Portsoken Street, London
E1 8AW, 0181 481 3100, Fax: 0181 481
3353, and Member US Federal
(Southern District of Manhattan) New
York, Call Date: Nov 1996 (Middle
Temple) Qualifications: LLB, LLM, FCA,
FCCA, FSPI, FCIArb

Jones *Haydn Peter*
Bankers Trust Limited, 1 Appold Street,
Broadgate, London EC1, 0171 885
1019, Fax: 0171 885 8566, Call Date:
Oct 1995 (Inner Temple)
Qualifications: M.Eng (Manc), CPE
(City), AMIEE

Jones *Miss Hilary Jean*
Silwood House, Runnymede Close,
Gateacre, Woolton, Liverpool L25 5JU,
Call Date: June 1951 (Middle Temple)
Qualifications: LLB

Jones *Huw Gruffydd*
Hopkins Williams Shaw, 110
Kennington Road, London SE11 6RE,
0171 582 4662, Fax: 0171 735 0719,
Call Date: Nov 1993 (Middle Temple)
Qualifications: BA (Hons)(Kent), MA,
(Lond), CPE

Jones *Ian Harvey* •
Asst Director of Resources (Legal &
Admin) Oadby & Wigston B.C., Oadby &
Wigston Brgh Council, Council Offices,
Station Road, Wigston, Leicestershire
LE18 2DR, 0116 288 8961, Fax: 0116
288 7828, Call Date: Oct 1993 (Inner
Temple) Qualifications: MA (Oxon)

Jones *Miss Jacqueline Margarete*
Call Date: Feb 1995 (Gray's Inn)
Qualifications: B.Sc, LLB (Wales),
M.Phil (Wales)

Jones *James William* •
Legal Manager Production Sales &
Marketing, Powergen PLC, Westwood
Business Park, Coventry CV4 8LG,
01203 424000, Fax: 01203 425248,
Call Date: Feb 1989 (Middle Temple)
Qualifications: LLB

Jones *Mrs Jane Margaret*
Call Date: July 1980 (Inner Temple)
Qualifications: MA (Cantab), LL.M

Jones *The Hon Jeffrey Richard*
Chief Justice, Bradley Cottage, Holt,
Wilts BA14 6QE, 01225 782004, and
Member Kiribati Nigerian Bar, Call
Date: July 1954 (Middle Temple)
Qualifications: MA Oxon

Jones *Miss Joanne Claire* •
Legal Advisor, Lancashire Magistrates
Court, Preston, Call Date: July 1997
(Middle Temple) Qualifications: LLB
(Hons)

Jones *John Edward*
Assistant Solicitor, Call Date: July 1973
(Middle Temple) Qualifications: LL.B
[Lond]

Jones *John Nicholas*
Justices' Chief Exec/Justices' Clerk,
Justices' Chief Executive's, Office, The
Courthouse, Worcester Road, Ledbury,
Hertfordshire HR8 3QL, 01531 634658,
Call Date: July 1977 (Gray's Inn)
Qualifications: LLB, MIPD

Jones *Jonathan Guy* •
HM Treasury, Parliament Street,
London SW1P 3AG, 0171 270 1664,
Fax: 0171 270 1668, Call Date: July
1985 (Middle Temple) Qualifications:
BA (Durham)

Jones *Mrs Jorina Mary* •
Dept of Trade & Industry, Investigations
& Enforcement, Room 425, 10 Victoria
Street, London SW1, 0171 215 5000,
Call Date: July 1986 (Middle Temple)
Qualifications: BA (Hons)

Jones *Ms Karen Jane* •
Legal Advisor, DVLA, Longview Road,
Swansea SA6 7JL, 01792 782335, Fax:
01792 783567, and Member Ontario,
Canada, Call Date: July 1998 (Gray's
Inn) Qualifications: BA (Canada), LLB
(Canada)

Jones *Dr Karen Patricia Nievergelt* •
Legal Adviser, Country Landowners'
Assoc., 16 Belgrave Square, London
SW1X 8PX, 0171 460 7952, Call Date:
Nov 1995 (Middle Temple)
Qualifications: BSc (Hons)(Wales),
Ph.D (Cantab)

Jones *Ms Kathrine Margaret* •
Legal Advisor, Leeds City Council, Civic
Hall, Leeds LS1 1UR, 0113 224 3263,
Fax: 0113 247 4729, Call Date: Nov
1995 (Gray's Inn) Qualifications: BA
(Hons)

Jones *Miss Kathryn Anne* •
Senior Crown Prosecutor, Crown
Prosecution Service, Cae Banc,
Tanerdy, Carmarthen, Dyfed, 01267
237779, Call Date: July 1992 (Middle
Temple) Qualifications: LLB (Hons)

Jones *Miss Kathy*
Call Date: Nov 1998 (Gray's Inn)
Qualifications: BA (De Montfort)

Jones *Kelvin McAllister*
Call Date: Oct 1995 (Inner Temple)
Qualifications: LLB

Jones *Miss Kristin Francesca Deirdre* •
Lawyer, Legal Secretariat to the Law,
Offices, Attorney Generals, Chambers, 9
Buckingham Gate, London SW1E 6JP,
0171 271 2414, Fax: 0171 271 2434,
Call Date: July 1984 (Inner Temple)
Qualifications: LLB (Nottm)

Jones *Marc Paul*
Call Date: Mar 1997 (Gray's Inn)
Qualifications: BA (Oxon)

Jones *Michael Scott*
Advocates Library, Parliament House,
Edinburgh EH1 1RF, 0131 226 5071,
Fax: 0131 226 3642, Queen's Counsel
in Scotland (1989) and Member
Scottish Bar, Call Date: July 1987
(Lincoln's Inn) Qualifications: LLB
(Dundee)

Jones *Lieutenant Colonel Neil James
Henry* •
SO1 Prosecutions Germany, Army
Prosecuting Authority, (Germany),
Block 3, Rochdale Barracks, BFPO 39,
0049 521 9254 469/0049 521 2399
243, Fax: 0049 521 9254 472, Call
Date: Nov 1978 (Gray's Inn)
Qualifications: LLB Newc

Jones *Oliver Egerton*
Call Date: Nov 1998 (Inner Temple)
Qualifications: LLB (Lond)

Jones *Paul*
Call Date: Oct 1994 (Gray's Inn)
Qualifications: BA (Manch)

Jones *Peter Michael*
Legal Manager, Warrington Magistrates'
Court, Winmarleigh Street, Warrington
WA1 1PB, 01925 253136, Call Date:
Nov 1987 (Middle Temple)
Qualifications: LLB

Jones *Philip*
Call Date: Nov 1993 (Lincoln's Inn)
Qualifications: MA (Cantab)

Jones *Miss Philippa Nancy Hudson*
Call Date: Oct 1992 (Gray's Inn)
Qualifications: LLB

Jones *Reginald Lewis*
69 Ashley Gdns, Ambrosden Avenue,
London SW1P IQG, Call Date: June
1948 (Lincoln's Inn)

Jones *Rhys Matthew*
Call Date: Nov 1998 (Gray's Inn)
Qualifications: LLB (Wales)

Jones *Roger Kenneth*
41 Townscliffe Lane, Marple Bridge,
Stockport SK6 5AP, Call Date: Feb 1977
(Gray's Inn) Qualifications: BA Hons
(Econ)

Jones *Miss Sarah Elizabeth*
Personal Injury Bar Association 9 Park
Place, Cardiff, CF1 3DP, Call Date: July
1989 (Gray's Inn) Qualifications: BA
(Exon), MA (Cantab)

Jones *Ms Sharon Maria* •
Principal Legal Adviser, Call Date: July
1981 (Middle Temple) Qualifications:
LLB(Lond)

Jones *Ms Sian Elizabeth*
Deputy Clerk to the Justices, Wrexham
Maelor & Flintshire, Magistrates Court,
Law Courts, Bodhyfrd, Wrexham, Clwyd
LL12 7BP, 01978 291855, Fax: 01978
358213, Call Date: July 1981 (Lincoln's
Inn) Qualifications: LLB (Hons), DMS

Jones *Simon Alexander*
Call Date: Nov 1994 (Inner Temple)
Qualifications: BSC (Bris), Dip Law
(Lond)

Jones *Simon David* •
Legal Adviser, Royal Borough of
Kensington &, Chelsea, The Town Hall,
London W8 7NX, 0171 361 2194, Fax:
0171 361 3488, Call Date: Nov 1985
(Gray's Inn) Qualifications: LLB
(Sheffield)

Jones *Miss Susan Ann*
Legal Advisor, Call Date: July 1987
(Lincoln's Inn) Qualifications: LLB
(Hons)

Jones *Mrs Susan Eleanor*
Principal Court Clerk Deputy Stipendiary
Magistrate, Victoria Law Courts,
Corporation Street, Birmingham, West
Midlands, 0121 212 6676, Fax: 0121 212
6613, Call Date: July 1972 (Lincoln's
Inn) Qualifications: LLB (Sheff)

Jones *Miss Susan Heather*
Senior Court Clerk, Hertfordshire
Magistrates', Courts Committee, The
Register Office Block, County Hall,
Hertford, Hertfordshire SG13 8DF,
01727 816823, Fax: 01727 816829, Call
Date: Nov 1985 (Lincoln's Inn)
Qualifications: BA

Jones *Timothy Leighton*
Solicitor, Call Date: Nov 1997 (Lincoln's
Inn) Qualifications: LLB (Hons) (Wales)

Jones *Mrs Vanessa* •
Manager, Capital Corporation PLC, 7
Down Street, London W1Y 7DS, 0171
317 6889, Fax: 0171 629 6440, Call
Date: Nov 1984 (Gray's Inn)
Qualifications: LLB (Hons), ACSA

Jones *Miss Verity Gill*
Part time Parking Adjudicator, 71
Mapledene Road, London E8 3JW, 0171
275 8327, Call Date: July 1986 (Inner
Temple) Qualifications: LLB London

Joo *Miss Connie Mei Ling*
Legal Adviser, and Member Malaysia Bar,
Call Date: Nov 1990 (Middle Temple)
Qualifications: LLB (Lond)

Joomratty *Mohammud Massood*
Call Date: Nov 1995 (Gray's Inn)
Qualifications: LLB

Jopling *Norman*
Call Date: Nov 1978 (Middle Temple)
Qualifications: LLB (Lond), ACIS

Jordan *Christopher Nigel*
Head of Legal Services, Ealing
Magistrates Court Cmtte, Green Man
Lane, London W13 9EN, 0181 579 9311,
Fax: 0181 840 9492, Call Date: July 1978
(Middle Temple) Qualifications: MA
(Oxon)

Jordan *Miss Elizabeth Irene*
Call Date: Oct 1998 (Gray's Inn)
Qualifications: LLB (Manchester)

Jordan *Ms Fiona Clare*
Call Date: Oct 1991 (Gray's Inn)
Qualifications: LLB (Hons, Lond)

Jordan *Mark Gareth*
Call Date: Nov 1998 (Inner Temple)
Qualifications: LLB (So'ton)

Jordan *Nigel Alan* •
Legal Adviser, Griffin Services Limited,
Royton House, 14 George Road,
Edgbaston, Birmingham B15 1NT, 0121
455 2732, Fax: 0121 455 2770, Call
Date: July 1982 (Gray's Inn)
Qualifications: LLB (Lond), ACIB

Jordan *Miss Sarah Louise* •
Call Date: Nov 1995 (Inner Temple)
Qualifications: LLB (Notts)

Jordan *Victor Charles*
43 Cornwall Road, Cheam, Surrey
SM2 6DU, 0181 642 2635, Call Date:
June 1959 (Gray's Inn) Qualifications:
LLB , F.I.O.S.H.

Jordan *Victor Frederick John*
8 Gresham Way, Wimbledon Park,
London SW19 8ED, Call Date: Feb 1968
(Middle Temple) Qualifications: MA,
LLM (Cantab)

Jorro *Peter Antonio Raimo*
Call Date: Nov 1986 (Lincoln's Inn)
Qualifications: LLB (Hons) (LSE)

Joseph *Leslie*
Devereux Chambers, Devereux Court,
London, WC2R 3JJ, Call Date: Nov 1952
(Middle Temple) Qualifications: LLB

Joseph *Miss Sandradee Theresa*
Call Date: July 1998 (Inner Temple)
Qualifications: LLB (Thames)

Joseph *Miss Susanne* •
Call Date: Nov 1995 (Middle Temple)
Qualifications: LLB (Hons)

Joshi *Rajendra Jugatray* •
Crown Prosecution Service,
Headquarters, 50 Ludgate Hill, London
EC4M 7EX, 0171 273 8318, Fax: 0171
329 8165, Diplome de l'Institut
International de Droits de l'Homme, Call
Date: Nov 1983 (Inner Temple)
Qualifications: BA (Hons)

Joshi *Sunit Kishor*
Call Date: Nov 1997 (Lincoln's Inn)
Qualifications: LLB (Hons) (Nott'm)

Joshua *Julian Mathic* •
Directorate-General for Competition,
Commission of the, European
Communities, 200 Rue de la Loi, 1049
Brussels, 295 5519, Fax: 299 0880, Call
Date: Nov 1969 (Middle Temple)
Qualifications: MA (Cantab)

Joshua *Ms Susan Mary* •
Call Date: May 1993 (Gray's Inn)
Qualifications: MA

Joslin *Mrs Elizabeth Anne* •
Principal Crown Prosecutor, Crown
Prosecution Service, Solar House, 1-9
Romford Road, Stratford, London
E15 4LJ, 0181 534 6601, Call Date: July
1984 (Lincoln's Inn) Qualifications: LLB
(Hons) (Lond),, AKC

Jouanneau *Mrs Angela* •
Senior Crown Prosecutor, Crown
Prosecution Service, Priory Gate, 29
Union Gate, Maidstone, Call Date: Nov
1987 (Gray's Inn)

Jouhal *Sukhraj* •
Litigation Co-ordinator, GE Capital Anglo,
Capital House, Bond Street, Bristol
BS1 3LA, 0117 946 3612, Fax: 0117 946
3664, Call Date: Nov 1996 (Inner
Temple) Qualifications: LLB (Lond)

Jowett *Edward Ian* •
Director of Legal Affairs, European Credit
Operations, Ford of Europe Inc, The
Drive, Warley, Brentwood, Essex
CM13 3AR, 01277 224400, Call Date:
Nov 1955 (Middle Temple)
Qualifications: MA, BCL

Jowitt *Justin Samuel*
Allen & Overy, 1 New Change, London
EC4N 9QQ, Call Date: Nov 1993 (Middle
Temple) Qualifications: BA
(Hons) (Oxford)

Joyce *Mrs Eva Margaret Bridget*
Anglia Polytechnic University, Dept of
Law, Victoria Road South, Chelmsford
CM1 1LL, 01245 493131, Call Date: Oct
1990 (Lincoln's Inn) Qualifications: BA
(Kent)

Joyce *John Gerald McEwan*
Ballaig Hse, Comrie, Crieff, Perthshire
PH7 4JX, 017646 70261, Call Date: Nov
1964 (Inner Temple) Qualifications: BL

Joynes *Matthew Robert*
Pinsent Curtis Solicitors, 41 Park Square,
Leeds LS1 2NS, 0113 244 5000, Call
Date: Oct 1994 (Inner Temple)
Qualifications: BSc (Hon) (Econ), MA
(Belgium)

Judge *Mrs Ruth Patricia*
Lecturer, BPP Law School, 128
Theobalds Road, London WC1X 8RL, Call
Date: Oct 1993 (Gray's Inn)
Qualifications: BA (Leic), MA (Cantab)

Judge *Ms Sophie Tallulah* •
Senior Crown Prosecutor, Crown
Prosecution Service, 17th Floor,
Tolworth Tower, Ewell Road, Surbiton,
Surrey KT6 7DS, 0181 399 5171, Fax:
0181 390 3474, Call Date: Nov 1990
(Inner Temple) Qualifications: LLB

Judson *Steven Newell*
Call Date: Oct 1998 (Inner Temple)
Qualifications: LLB (Keele)

Julian *Gareth Wynn* •
Lawyer, Crown Prosecution Service, 50
Ludgate Hill, London EC4Y 7EX, Call
Date: July 1980 (Gray's Inn)
Qualifications: LLB (Warw), FRSA

E

Jump *Michael Edward Pearson*
Formerly a Solicitor, Malta, Formerly
24 Old Bldgs, Lincoln's Inn, Call Date:
June 1964 (Lincoln's Inn)

Jupe *Mrs Patricia Lorna*
Call Date: July 1958 (Gray's Inn)

Kaim-Caudle *Peter Robert*
Emeritus Professor of Social Policy,
Beechwood, Princes Street, Durham
DH1 4RP, 0191 3864768, Fax: 0191
3744743, Call Date: Nov 1956
(Lincoln's Inn)

Kainyah *Miss Rosalind Nana Emela*
0171 465 7344, Fax: 0171 465 7320,
Call Date: July 1988 (Gray's Inn)
Qualifications: BA (Ghana), LLB
(Lond), LLM (Lond)

Kale *Samuel Meano* •
Senior Legal Adviser, Bank of Scotland,
Legal Services, 1st Floor, 55 Old Broad
Street, London EC2P 2HL, 0171 601
6718, Fax: 0171 601 6713, Call Date:
July 1987 (Lincoln's Inn)
Qualifications: LLB (L'pool)

Kaleniuk *Nicholas George*
Call Date: Nov 1992 (Inner Temple)
Qualifications: LLB (L'pool)

Kalirai *Amerjit Singh*
Call Date: Nov 1997 (Lincoln's Inn)
Qualifications: LLB (Hons)(Manch)

Kalis *Dirk Hems*
14 Westfield Road, Lymington,
Hampshire SO41 3PY, 01590 679542,
Fax: 01590 679486, Call Date: Nov
1968 (Inner Temple) Qualifications:
MA (Cantab)

Kalra *Kasturi*
Kalra & Co, 304 High Road, Leyton,
London E10 5PW, 0181 539 0123, Fax:
0181 558 4243, Call Date: Nov 1985
(Lincoln's Inn) Qualifications: MA, LLB

Kamara *Miss Lanla Fatma*
Basma & Macaulay Solicitors, 21
Charlotte Street, P O Box 83, Freetown,
232 22 222798, Fax: 232 22 224248,
Call Date: July 1995 (Lincoln's Inn)
Qualifications: LLB (Hons), LLM
(Sheff)

Kamber *Louis*
Call Date: July 1998 (Middle Temple)
Qualifications: LLB (Hons), LLM (LSE)

Kandola *Miss Gurinder*
Senior Court Clerk, Walsall Magistrates
Court, Stafford Street, Walsall WS2 8HA,
01922 38222, Fax: 01922 35657, Call
Date: May 1984 (Middle Temple)

Kanfer *George Thomas*
GM Industrial Supply Co Ltd, Victoria
Hse, Bloomsbury Sq, London
WC1B 4DH, 0171 242 7553, Fax: 0171
242 5850, Call Date: Feb 1981
(Lincoln's Inn) Qualifications: MA
(Cantab), MSc MBA

Kanu *Allieu Ibrahim Badara*
Call Date: May 1984 (Middle Temple)
Qualifications: BA (Ealing), MA
(Prague), MSc (Southampton)

Karaa *Ms Radhia* •
Call Date: Nov 1995 (Inner Temple)
Qualifications: BA (Wales), CPE
(Wales)

Karan-Appukutten *Shubakaran* •
Senior Crown Prosecutor, Crown
Prosecution Service, Richmond &
Kingston Branch, 18th Floor, Tolworth
Tower, Surbiton KT6 7DS, 0181 399
5171, Call Date: Feb 1991 (Lincoln's
Inn) Qualifications: LLB (Warw)

Karia *Binoy*
Call Date: Nov 1998 (Inner Temple)
Qualifications: LLB (Kent), LLM (Lond)

Karim *Faizal*
Call Date: Mar 1997 (Inner Temple)
Qualifications: LLB

Karim *Khurram*
Call Date: May 1997 (Lincoln's Inn)
Qualifications: LLB (Hons)

Karlin *Ms Fiona Elizabeth Joy*
Fiona Karlin Corporate, Services,
Sheraton House, Castle Park,
Cambridge CB3 OAX, 01223 300960,
Fax: 01223 300942, Call Date: July
1982 (Gray's Inn) Qualifications: MA
(Cantab), FCIArb

Karpinski *(Charles) Jan* •
Head of Legal & Compliance, Bristol &
West plc, PO Box 27, Broad Quay,
Bristol, Avon BS99 7AX, 0117 9432553,
Fax: 0117 9291115, Call Date: Nov
1976 (Middle Temple) Qualifications:
BA. [Oxon]

Karume *Miss Fatma Amani*
Call Date: Nov 1998 (Middle Temple)
Qualifications: LLB (Hons), LLM,
(Sussex)

Karuppen *Miss Nagesvary*
Call Date: Oct 1996 (Gray's Inn)
Qualifications: LLB (Lond)

Kassim *Ms Shishila Surya*
01245 514489, and Member Malaysia
Bar, Call Date: Feb 1993 (Gray's Inn)
Qualifications: LLB (Nott')

Katan *Miss Deborah Rachel* •
HM Customs & Excise, Solicitors Office,
22 Upper Ground, London SE1 9PJ,
0171 620 1313, Call Date: Nov 1983
(Middle Temple) Qualifications: BA
Hons

Kathriaratchi *Miss Shaminka*
Tax Graduate, Coutts & Co, Strand.
London, Call Date: Nov 1997 (Lincoln's
Inn) Qualifications: LLB (Hons)(Keele)

Katsapaou *Miss Chrystalla*
Call Date: May 1995 (Inner Temple)
Qualifications: LLB (Sussex)

Kaur *Miss Har Sharon*
Call Date: July 1990 (Middle Temple)
Qualifications: LLB (Lond)

Kaur *Miss Jagdish* •
Senior Crown Prosecutor, Crown
Prosecution Service, 8th Floor,
Prospect West, 81 Station Road,
Croydon CR0 2RD, 0181 251 5410, Call
Date: Nov 1988 (Middle Temple)
Qualifications: LLB (L'pool)

Kaur *Miss Kulwinder* •
Legal Officer, Salisbury District Council,
The Council Offices, Bourne Hill,
Salisbury SP1 3UZ, 01722 434233, Call
Date: July 1984 (Middle Temple)
Qualifications: BA Dip Law

Kaur *Miss Mejindarpal*
Call Date: July 1989 (Lincoln's Inn)
Qualifications: LLB (Lond), LLM
(Lond)

Kaur *Miss Ravinder*
Call Date: Oct 1994 (Lincoln's Inn)
Qualifications: LLB (Hons)(Bucks)

Kaur *Miss Sangreet*
Call Date: July 1990 (Lincoln's Inn)
Qualifications: LLB (Wales)

Kavanagh *Daniel Antony* •
Call Date: Nov 1988 (Lincoln's Inn)
Qualifications: BA Hons, Dip Law

Kavanagh *Giles Wilfred Conor* •
Barlow Lyde & Gilbert, Beaufort House,
15 Botolph Street, London EC3A 7NJ,
0171 247 2277, Fax: 0171 782 8500,
Call Date: Feb 1984 (Middle Temple)
Qualifications: MA,LLM (Cantab)

Kavanagh *Kevin* •
Principal Crown Prosecutor, Crown
Prosecution Service, King Edward
Court, King Edward Street, Nottingham,
0115 9480480, Call Date: July 1983
(Gray's Inn) Qualifications: B.A.

Kay *Graham* •
Principal Court Clerk, Hereford &
Worcester, Magistrates' Courts
Committee, Call Date: Nov 1985 (Gray's
Inn) Qualifications: BA

Kay *John Lawrence* •
Manager - Business Legal Services,
Imperial Chemical Industries, PLC, PO
Box 90, Wilton, Middlesborough,
Cleveland TS90 8JE, 01642 454144,
Fax: 01642 432971, Call Date: July
1973 (Middle Temple) Qualifications:
LLB, LLM (Lond)

Kay *Ms Sylvia Mary* •
Legal Adviser, UK, Call Date: Nov 1969
(Gray's Inn) Qualifications: LLB
(B'ham)

Kaya *Hussein Ahmet* •
Senior Principal Legal Officer,
Department of Trade & Industry,
Solicitors Office, 10-18 Victoria Street,
London SW1H 0NN, 0171 215 3444,
Fax: 0171 215 3141, Call Date: July
1977 (Gray's Inn) Qualifications: LLB
(Lond), LLM (Lond)

Kaye *David Grahame*
Legal Adviser Principal Assistant,
Scunthorpe Magistrates Court, Justices
Clerks Office, Corporation Road,
Scunthorpe, North Lincolnshire
DN15 6QB, 01724 281100, Fax: 01724
281890, Call Date: Nov 1989 (Gray's
Inn) Qualifications: DML

Kaye *Jeremy Robin* •
Company Secretary, Secure Trust
Banking Group Plc, Royex House,
Aldermanbury Square, London
EC2V 7HR, 0171 600 3831, Fax: 0171
626 7041, Call Date: July 1962 (Inner
Temple) Qualifications: MA (Oxon), FCIS

Kaye *Professor Peter*
Department of Law, University of Wales
Swansea, Singleton Park, Swansea
SA2 8PP, 01792 295831/3, Fax: 01792
295855, Call Date: Oct 1994 (Gray's Inn)
Qualifications: LLB, AKC, LLM, Ph.D,
(Lond)

Kaye *Ms Siana*
Call Date: Nov 1994 (Inner Temple)
Qualifications: BA (Lond), CPE (City)

Kaza *Miss Ajanta*
Call Date: Nov 1998 (Lincoln's Inn)
Qualifications: LLB (Hons)

Kazzora *John Wycliffer*
and Member Uganda Bar Chancery
Chambers, 1st Floor Offices, 70/72
Chancery Lane, London, WC2A 1AB, Call
Date: June 1958 (Middle Temple)

Kearns *James Anthony*
Call Date: July 1997 (Middle Temple)
Qualifications: BA (Hons), Dip Law

Kearns *Kevin Patrick*
Call Date: July 1992 (Lincoln's Inn)
Qualifications: BA (L'Pool), LLB, (Lond),
MA (S'field)

Kedge *Miss Natalie Louise*
Call Date: Oct 1993 (Middle Temple)
Qualifications: BA (Hons)(Lond), CPE

Kee *Chuin Liang Alvyn*
Call Date: Nov 1997 (Lincoln's Inn)
Qualifications: LLB (Hons), (Wolver'ton)

Kee *Peter William*
and Member Papua New Guinea, Call
Date: July 1983 (Middle Temple)
Qualifications: BA (Oxon), LLM
(Leicester)

Keegan *Joseph David*
Call Date: July 1998 (Middle Temple)
Qualifications: LLB (Hons0(L'pool)

Keen *Mrs Patricia*
'Laujan', Ashton Road, Siddington,
Cirencester, Glos GL7 6HD, 01285
654978, Call Date: July 1985 (Gray's
Inn) Qualifications: Dip Law

Keenan *Miss Claudia Louise* •
General Counsel & Company Secretary,
Premier Oil plc, 23 Lower Belgrave
Street, London SW1W 0NR, 0171 730
1111, Fax: 0171 730 4696, Call Date:
July 1986 (Middle Temple)
Qualifications: LLB

Keene *Gareth John* •
Director/International Counsel, GAMIDA
for Life BV, Marten Meesweg 51, 3068 AV
Rotterdam, The Netherlands, 010 31 20
5497777, Fax: 010 31 20 6610654, Call
Date: May 1966 (Gray's Inn)
Qualifications: MA, LLM (Cantab)

Keeton *Darren*
Call Date: Oct 1994 (Lincoln's Inn)
Qualifications: LLB (Hons)(E.Ang)

Keigwin *Richard Skarratt*
Constant & Constant Solicitors, Sea
Containers House, 20 Upper Ground,
Blackfriars Bridge, London SE1 9QT,
0171 261 0006, Fax: 0171 401 2161,
Call Date: Oct 1996 (Inner Temple)
Qualifications: LLB (Exon)

Keir *James Dewar*
Chairman Professional Committee, Royal
College of Speech & Language
Therapists, The Crossways, 1 High Street,
Dormansland, Lingfield, Surrey
RH7 6PU, 01342 834621, Call Date: Nov
1949 (Inner Temple) Qualifications: MA

Kellam *James Antony Plenderleith* •
Senior Crown Prosecutor, CPS (Thames
Branch), 50 Ludgate Hill, London EC4,
0171 273 8000, Fax: 0171 273 1499,
Call Date: Nov 1991 (Inner Temple)
Qualifications: LLB (South)

Kelleher *Miss Catherine*
Call Date: July 1979 (Middle Temple)
Qualifications: BA, M Phil(Lond)

Kelley *Simon Sukhdeep*
Call Date: Nov 1996 (Lincoln's Inn)
Qualifications: LLB (Hons)(Cardiff), LLM
(Tulane), Dip. (Ship) Law, (Lond)

Kellock *James Donald* •
Grade 5 Lawyer, Serious Fraud Office,
Elm House, 10-16 Elm Street, London
WC1X 0BJ, Fax: 0717 239 7115, Call
Date: Nov 1979 (Inner Temple)
Qualifications: MA (Cantab)

Kellow *Ian Robert* •
Managing Director and General Counsel,
ING Barings, 60 London Wall, London
EC2M 5TQ, 0171 767 6060, Fax: 0171
767 7076, Call Date: July 1982 (Inner
Temple) Qualifications: MBA, LLB

Kelly *Andrew Mark* •
Prosecuting Solicitor, HM Customs &
Excise, New King's Beam House, 22
Upper Ground, London SE1, Call Date:
July 1985 (Inner Temple) Qualifications:
LLB

Kelly *Bernard Anthony*
Part Time Chairman of Industrial
Tribunals, Northbrook, 32 Fairmile
Lane, Cobham, Surrey KT11 2DQ, 01932
867811, Fax: 01932 867811, Call Date:
July 1957 (Gray's Inn) Qualifications: MA
(Cantab)

Kelly *Mrs Carys Lindsay*
Deputy Chief Clerk, Inner London
Magistrates', Courts Service, 65 Romney
Street, London SW1P 3RD, Call Date: July
1982 (Gray's Inn) Qualifications: LLB
(B'ham)

Kelly *Christopher Andrew*
Pinsent Curtis, 3 Colmore Circus,
Birmingham B3, 0121 200 1050, Fax:
0121 626 1040, Call Date: Nov 1993
(Middle Temple) Qualifications: LLB
(Hons)(Lond)

Kelly *Mrs Henrietta* •
Chairman,London Rent Assessment
Panel,Chairman Leashold Valuation
Tribunal, Call Date: Feb 1960 (Middle
Temple) Qualifications: LLB

Kelly *James*
Call Date: Nov 1981 (Gray's Inn)
Qualifications: LLB (Lond)

Kelly *John Denis Ryan*
Director, United Nations, 23 Avenue de
Bude, CH-1202 Geneva, Geneva
733-79-13, Call Date: Jan 1943 (Inner
Temple) Qualifications: MA (Oxon)

Kelly *Mark Frank*
Call Date: Nov 1997 (Gray's Inn)
Qualifications: LLB

Kelly *Miss Mary Josephine* •
Senior Crown Prosecutor, Crown
Prosecution Service, South Parade,
Wakefield WF1 1LR, Wakefield 290620,
Call Date: Nov 1986 (Gray's Inn)
Qualifications: BSc, Dip Law

Kelly *Mrs Maureen Elizabeth*
Deputy Chief Clerk, Inner London
Magistrates', Courts Service, 65 Romney
Street, London SW1P 3RD, Call Date: Nov
1988 (Gray's Inn) Qualifications: BA
(Lond)

Kelly *Miss Sheron*
Call Date: Nov 1982 (Middle Temple)
Qualifications: BA

Kelly *Ms Tara Jane*
Legal Advisor, Derby & South Derbyshire,
Magistrates' Court, The Court House,
Derwent Street, Derby DE1 2EP, (01332)
292100, Fax: (01332) 293459, Call Date:
Oct 1992 (Gray's Inn) Qualifications:
LLB, LLM

Kelly *Miss Teresa Josephine*
Call Date: Nov 1998 (Gray's Inn)
Qualifications: LLB (Thames)

Kelso *Donald Iain Junor*
Call Date: Nov 1995 (Lincoln's Inn)
Qualifications: BA (Hons)

Kelvin *Carl George Leslie Steven* •
Senior Crown Prosecutor, Crown
Prosecution Service, Southern Branch,
The Cooperage, Gainsford Street, London
SE1 2NG, Call Date: Nov 1988 (Middle
Temple) Qualifications: LLB (Hons),
LLM (Lond)

Kemp *David Ashton McIntyre*
and Member Hong Kong, Gibraltar,
Malaysia & Kenya Bars Monckton
Chambers, 4 Raymond Buildings,
Gray's Inn, London, WC1R 5BP, Call
Date: Nov 1948 (Inner Temple)
Qualifications: BA (Cantab), FCIArb

Kendall *Mark Noel* •
Principal Crown Prosecutor, Call Date:
Nov 1987 (Inner Temple)
Qualifications: LLB (So'ton)

Kendrew *Miss Elizabeth Anne Hamilton*
Call Date: July 1997 (Middle Temple)
Qualifications: BA (Hons)(Cantab)

Kennedy *Andrew George* •
Legal Advisor, Lloyds Registrar of
Shipping, 71 Fenchurch Street, London
EC3M 4BS, 0171 423 2439, Fax: 0171
709 9166, Call Date: July 1987 (Middle
Temple) Qualifications: BA (Kent)

Kennedy *Ian McColl*
University College, Department of Law,
London, Blackstone Chambers,
Blackstone House, Temple, London,
EC4Y 9BW, Call Date: July 1974 (Inner
Temple) Qualifications: LLB, LLM

Kennedy *John Brendan* •
Crown Prosecutor, Crown Prosecution
Service, Trafalgar House, 2 Bedford
Park, Croydon, Surrey, Call Date: July
1987 (Lincoln's Inn) Qualifications:
LLB (B'ham)

Kennedy *Michael Joseph*
Call Date: Nov 1991 (Middle Temple)
Qualifications: LLB Hons (Manch)

Kennedy *Paul Gilbert* •
Financial Services Authority, 25 The
North Colonnade, Canary Wharf,
London EC14 5HS, 0171 676 3320,
Qualified Actuary - Examiner, Call Date:
Nov 1991 (Lincoln's Inn)
Qualifications: MA (Cantab), FIA, FCII,
ACCA

Kennon *Andrew Rowland*
Parliamentary Adviser, Cabinet Office,
Cabinet Office, 70 Whitehall, London
SW1A 2AS, Call Date: July 1979 (Gray's
Inn) Qualifications: MA (Cantab)

Kenny *Miss Bernadette Joan* •
Lord Chancellors Department,
Trevelyan House, 30 Great Peter Street,
London SW1P 2BY, Call Date: July 1979
(Lincoln's Inn) Qualifications: LLB
(Hons)

Kent *Gordon Peter Selim Mehmet*
Call Date: Feb 1995 (Gray's Inn)
Qualifications: LLB (Lond)

Kent *Graham Edward* •
Legal Adviser, BFI, Benefit Fraud
Inspectorate, Dept of Social Security,
8th Floor, Victory House, 30-34
Kingsway, London WC2B 6EW, Call
Date: July 1975 (Gray's Inn)
Qualifications: MA (Oxon) ,
M.Jur[Man]

Kent *Mr. Graham Gregory*
International Securities & Capital
Markets, Simmons & Simmons, 21
Wilson Street, London EC2M 2TX, 0171
628 2020, Fax: 0171 628 2070, Call
Date: Oct 1995 (Gray's Inn)
Qualifications: LLB

Kent *Philip Anthony* •
Lawyer (Grade 5), Ministry of
Agriculture,, Fisheries and Food, 55
Whitehall, London SW1A 2EY, 0171 270
8399, Fax: 0171 270 8270, Call Date:
July 1977 (Gray's Inn) Qualifications:
LLB (Lond)

Kenton *Simon Timothy*
26 Melina Road, London W12 9HZ,
0181 749 8658, Call Date: Feb 1993
(Gray's Inn) Qualifications: LLB

Kenyon-Jackson *Mrs Carolyn*
Call Date: July 1990 (Middle Temple)
Qualifications: BA (Hons), CPE

Keogh *Andrew William* •
Call Date: Nov 1994 (Inner Temple)
Qualifications: LLB (Sheff)

Keogh *Miss Sonia Elizabeth*
Call Date: July 1995 (Gray's Inn)
Qualifications: LLB (Lond)

Kerr *Ms Clare Patricia* •
Criminal Appeal Office, Royal Courts of
Justice, London WC1R, 0171 936 6725,
Call Date: Nov 1995 (Middle Temple)
Qualifications: BA (Hons), MA (Cantab)

Kerr *Miss Elizabeth Ann Scott*
Call Date: Mar 1997 (Lincoln's Inn)
Qualifications: LLB (Hons)(L'pool)

Kerr *Miss Joanne Lesley*
Call Date: Oct 1998 (Inner Temple)
Qualifications: LLB (Lond)

Kerrigan *Mrs Greer Sandra* •
Legal Director, Solicitor's Office, Dept
of, Social Security,Dept of Health, New
Court, 48 Carey Street, London
WC2A 2LS, 0171 412 1341, Fax: 0171
412 1583, and Member Trinidad &
Tobago, Call Date: July 1971 (Middle
Temple)

Kerrigan *Peter Francis*
Peter Kerrigan Associates, 4 Abbots
Quay, Monks Ferry, Birkenhead,
Merseyside L41 5LH, 0151 647 8862,
Fax: 0151 647 8863, Chartered
Quantity Surveyor, Call Date: Nov 1986
(Lincoln's Inn) Qualifications: LLB
(Hons)(L'pool), FRICS, ACIArb

Kershaw *Dr Steven*
Call Date: Oct 1997 (Lincoln's Inn)
Qualifications: BSc (Hons)(Bris)

Kessel *Ms Joanna Nicolle*
Television Reporter/Director, Call Date:
Oct 1993 (Middle Temple)
Qualifications: BA (Hons)(Sussex)

Kesselman *Rabbi Neville* •
Senior Crown Prosecutor, London Area,
Kings House, Kymberley Road, Harrow,
Middlesex HA1 1YH, 0181 424 8688,
Fax: 0181 424 9134, Formerly a
Solicitor, Call Date: July 1970 (Gray's
Inn)

Kew *Michael Deslie*
Call Date: Nov 1967 (Inner Temple)
Qualifications: LLB (Lond)

Kewley *Miss Sarah Helen*
Wansbroughs Solicitors, 5 Imperial
Road, Edgerton, Huddersfield, West
Yorkshire HD3 3AF, 01484 544484,
Call Date: Nov 1994 (Lincoln's Inn)
Qualifications: BA (Hons)(B'ham), Dip
in Law (City)

Keymer *Robert Michael*
Call Date: Nov 1995 (Inner Temple)
Qualifications: LLB (Lancs)

Khakhar *Miss Ketki*
Call Date: Nov 1975 (Middle Temple)
Qualifications: BA

Khambatta *Sam Pirosha*
5 St Margaret's Close, Horstead, Norfolk
NR12 7ER, Also Inn of Court G
International Law Assoc 1952-1987 and
Member India Bar Nigeria Bar, Call
Date: June 1929 (Middle Temple)

Khan *Abdul Shakoor*
Call Date: Nov 1997 (Lincoln's Inn)
Qualifications: BA (Peshawar), LLB
(Hons) (Leeds)

Khan *Ms Amira Farhat* •
Call Date: Nov 1994 (Inner Temple)
Qualifications: BA (Middx), CPE (Lond)

Khan *Miss Anbreen Sakina*
VAT Consultant, Deloitte & Touche, Hill
House, 1 Little New Street, London
EC4A 3TR, 0171 303 4041, Fax: 0171
583 8517, Call Date: Nov 1993
(Lincoln's Inn) Qualifications: BA
(Hons), CPE

Khan *Miss Anika Praveen*
Call Date: Nov 1987 (Gray's Inn)
Qualifications: LLB (Manch)

Khan *Averroes Aldeboran Karam* •
Principal Legal Officer, HM Customs &
Excise, New Kings Beam House, 22
Upper Ground, London SE1 9PJ, and
Member Trinidad & Tobago Bar, Call
Date: Nov 1986 (Lincoln's Inn)
Qualifications: MA (Cantab)

Khan *Inayat Ullah* •
Director, and Member Punjab Bar
Council, Call Date: Nov 1980 (Lincoln's
Inn) Qualifications: LLB (Leeds), BA,
Dip in Law

Khan *(Karimulla Hyat) Akbar*
Legal Attache to the United Nations,
United Nations Office at, Geneva, 1511
Villa la Pelouse, Geneva, Verulam
Chambers, Peer House, 8-14 Verulam
Street, Gray's Inn, London, WC1X 8LZ,
Call Date: Oct 1990 (Middle Temple)
Qualifications: LLB (Hons) Reading, LLM
(Cambs), Postgrad Cert in , Human
Rights

Khan *Mohamed Amjad*
Call Date: May 1992 (Lincoln's Inn)
Qualifications: LLB (Hons)

Khan *Miss Nadine Miriam*
Call Date: May 1995 (Lincoln's Inn)
Qualifications: LLB (Hons)

Khan *Ms Naseem Akbar*
Paddington Law Centre, 346 Harrow
Road, London W10 4RE, 0181 960 3155,
Fax: 0181 968 0417, Immigration Case
Worker, Call Date: Nov 1973 (Inner
Temple)

Khan *Nicholas Paul* •
Legal Adviser, Legal Service, Commission
of European Communities, 200 Rue de
la Loi, 1049 Brussels, Belgium, Belgium,
010 322 295 4137, Fax: 010 322 296
5965, Call Date: July 1983 (Inner
Temple) Qualifications: LLB Soton

Khan *Miss Noshaba Sarfaraz*
Call Date: Nov 1997 (Middle Temple)
Qualifications: LLB (Hons)(Lond)

Khan *Miss Roshan Ara*
Call Date: Feb 1994 (Middle Temple)
Qualifications: LLB (Hons)(Lond)

Khan *Tariq*
Call Date: Mar 1999 (Lincoln's Inn)
Qualifications: LLB (Hons)

Khan *Tariq Ali*
Call Date: Nov 1996 (Lincoln's Inn)
Qualifications: LLB (Hons)

Khan *Miss Yasmin*
Call Date: Oct 1996 (Lincoln's Inn)
Qualifications: LLB (Hons)(Lond)

Khan *Miss Zoe Yasmin* •
5 King Street Cloisters, Clifton Walk,
London W6 0GY, Call Date: Oct 1993
(Middle Temple) Qualifications: MA
(Cantab)

Kharran *Miss Devi Samantha*
Call Date: July 1994 (Lincoln's Inn)
Qualifications: LLB (Hons)

Khasru *Najrul Islam*
Court Clerk, Waltham Forest
Magistrates', Court, 1 Farnan Avenue,
Walthamstow E17 4NX, 0181 527 8000,
Fax: 0181 527 9063, Call Date: July 1988
(Inner Temple) Qualifications: LLB

Khattak *Aurang Zeb* •
Senior Crown Prosecutor, Crown
Prosecution Service, Dale House, Dale
End, Birmingham B5, 233-3133, Call
Date: Apr 1989 (Gray's Inn)
Qualifications: LLB (Hons)

Khaw *Ms Claire Kuen Hui*
Call Date: Nov 1997 (Gray's Inn)
Qualifications: LLB (Kingston)

Khawar *Mansur Ata*
Call Date: Nov 1996 (Inner Temple)
Qualifications: BA (Oxon), CPE (Manch)

Khoo *Hong Aun*
Call Date: Nov 1998 (Lincoln's Inn)
Qualifications: LLB (Hons)(Lond)

Khubchand-Daswani *Miss Karina
Krishna*
Marrache & Co, 5 Cannon Lane, 350
79918, Fax: 350 73315, and Member
Gibraltar Bar, Call Date: May 1996
(Middle Temple) Qualifications: LLB
(Hons)(Manch)

Kiddle *John Otto*
Keeper's Cottage, Privett, Alton, Hants
GU34 3PF, Privett 217, Call Date: Feb
1958 (Lincoln's Inn)

Kidwell *Raymond Incledon*
Recorder, Call Date: Nov 1951 (Gray's
Inn) Qualifications: MA, BCL (Oxon)

Kiellor *Miss Kirsty-Ann*
Call Date: Oct 1998 (Lincoln's Inn)
Qualifications: LLB (Hons)(Westmin)

Kilby *Edwin Philip*
Grade 6 (Legal), Lord Chancellor's Dept,
Selborne House, 54-60 Victoria Street,
London SW1E 6QW, 0171 210 0740, Fax:
0171 210 0746, Call Date: July 1980
(Inner Temple)

Kilby *James Richard* •
Lawyer, Charity Commission, The Deane,
Tangier, Taunton, Somerset TA1 4A, Call
Date: Nov 1979 (Inner Temple)
Qualifications: MA (Hons) (Oxon)

Kilgarriff *Patrick Herbert* •
Treasury Solicitor's Dept, Queen Anne's
Chambers, 28 Broadway, London
SW1H 9JS, Call Date: Nov 1986 (Gray's
Inn) Qualifications: BSc, Dip Law

Killick *James Richard McFadyen*
Call Date: Oct 1996 (Middle Temple)
Qualifications: BA (Hons) (Camb), LLM
(Edinburgh)

Killick *Marcus Charles* •
Director, KPMG, 1 The Embankment,
Neville Street, Leeds LS1 4DW, 0113 231
3000, Fax: 0113 231 3139, and Member
New York Bar, Call Date: July 1989
(Gray's Inn) Qualifications: LLB (Leeds)

Kilpatrick *Miss Lisa*
Call Date: Nov 1995 (Gray's Inn)
Qualifications: BA (Manch)

Kim *Theodore Joseph*
37 Store Street, London WC1E 7BS, Fax:
(44) 171 681 1506, Call Date: Nov 1995
(Lincoln's Inn) Qualifications: BSc
(Hons)(Econ), MSc (Econ)

Kinahan *Mrs Ann*
Joint Manager of Bromley Citizens Advice
Bureau, 83 Tweedy Road, Bromley
BR1 1RG, 0181 464 0599, Call Date: Nov
1981 (Inner Temple) Qualifications: LLB

Kinch *Alec Anthony*
36 Greenways, Beckenham, Kent
BR3 3NG, 0181 658 2298, Fax: 0181 663
0737, Call Date: Nov 1951 (Middle
Temple) Qualifications: MA (Oxon)

Kindell *James William*
Company Secretary, Company Secretarial
Department, PriceWaterhouseCoopers,
No 1 London Bridge, London SE1 9QL,
0171 939 3000/939 5019, Fax: 0171 403
5265/939 4173, Call Date: Nov 1992
(Middle Temple) Qualifications: B.Sc
(Hons, City), Dip in Law, LLM (Surrey),
GRADICSA

Kindred *Frank Paul* •
26 Offley Road, London SW9, 0171 735
1444, Call Date: July 1985 (Gray's Inn)
Qualifications: BSc (Lond), MSc,
(Dunelm)

King *Miss Barbara Maxine*
3 Dr Johnson's Bldgs, Ground Floor,
Temple, London, EC4Y 7BA, Call Date:
Nov 1980 (Gray's Inn) Qualifications: BA
(Hons)

King *Ms Deborah*
Hillingdon Legal Resource Cent, 12
Harold Avenue, Hayes, Middlesex
UB3 4QW, 0181 561 9400, Fax: 0181
756 0837, Call Date: Nov 1986 (Gray's
Inn) Qualifications: LLB(Brunel), LLM

King *Frank Rowland*
Cherries, 26 Druid Stoke Avenue, Stoke
Bishop, Bristol BS9 1DD, Call Date: July
1970 (Gray's Inn) Qualifications: LLB
(Lond)

King *Geoffrey William*
Company Secretary, Financial Services
Authority, 25 The North Colonnade,
Canary Wharf, London E14 5HS, 0171
676 1000, Fax: 0171 676 1099, Call
Date: May 1968 (Gray's Inn)
Qualifications: LLB, AKC, FCIS, FInst M

King *Henry George John*
Call Date: Nov 1998 (Inner Temple)
Qualifications: BA (Oxon)

King *Miss Jacqueline Doreen*
Court Clerk, Call Date: Feb 1983 (Middle
Temple)

King *James Charles*
Call Date: Oct 1996 (Inner Temple)
Qualifications: LLB (Soton)

King *Mrs Joyce Belinda*
Deputy Clerk to the Justices, Wiltshire
Magistrates Court, 43-55 Milford Street,
Salisbury SP1 2BP, 01722 333225, Fax:
01722 413395, Call Date: July 1985
(Gray's Inn)

King *Miss Juliet Ann*
Call Date: Feb 1995 (Inner Temple)
Qualifications: LLB (Soton)

King *Mark Courtney Dilke*
Call Date: Oct 1997 (Inner Temple)
Qualifications: BSc (London), CPE
(Thames Valley)

E

King *Michael Bruce*
1 Gray's Inn Square, 1st Floor, London, WC1R 5AG, Call Date: July 1971 (Gray's Inn)

King *Robert George Cecil*
Call Date: Nov 1965 (Lincoln's Inn)

King *Simon David* •
Claims Executive, A Bilbrough & Co Ltd, 50 Leman Street, London E1 8HQ, 0171 772 8000, Fax: 0171 772 8200, Call Date: Oct 1991 (Inner Temple) Qualifications: BA (Dunelm), CPE

Kingsbury *Miss Carol Jayne*
Allen & Overy Solicitors, One New Change, London EC4M 9QQ, 0171 330 3000, Fax: 0171 330 9999, Call Date: July 1984 (Middle Temple) Qualifications: MA (Cantab)

Kingsbury *Lt Cdr James Arthur Timothy* •
Directorate of Defence Programming, Defence programmes - CP5a, Ministry of Defence, Room 4304, Main Building, Whitehall, London SW1A 2HB, Call Date: July 1989 (Middle Temple) Qualifications: BSc , Dip Law

Kingsbury *Simon Anthony*
Call Date: Nov 1996 (Gray's Inn) Qualifications: LLB (Sussex)

Kingsdown *Lord*
Torry Hill, Sittingbourne, Kent ME9 0SP, 01795 830 258, Fax: 01795 830 243, Call Date: July 1954 (Inner Temple)

Kingsmill *Miss Elizabeth* •
Lord Chancellor's Department, Criminal Appeal Office, Royal Courts of Justice, The Strand, London WC2A 2LL, 0171 936 6070, Fax: 0171 936 6900, Call Date: July 1985 (Lincoln's Inn) Qualifications: LLB(Lond)

Kinnell *Ian* •
Arbitrator, Woodside House, The Maypole, Monmouth NP5 3QH, 01600 713077, Fax: 01600 772880, Call Date: July 1967 (Gray's Inn)

Kinsman *Ms Fiona Jane* •
Legal Adviser, Equal Opportunities Unit DG5, European Commission, Rue de la Loi 200, Belgium, 32 2 299 59 28, Fax: 32 2 296 35 62, Call Date: July 1989 (Lincoln's Inn) Qualifications: BA (Kent), Dip French Law, LLM (Lond)

Kiralfy *Professor Albert Roland*
Retired Professor of Law, c/o School of Law, King's College, Strand, London, Call Date: Jan 1947 (Gray's Inn) Qualifications: PhD, LLM, LLB

Kirk *Alexander Frederick*
Bailache Labesse Trustees Ltd, Piermont House, 33-35 Pier Road, St Helier, Jersey JE1 1BD, Channel Islands, (44) 534 818444, Fax: (44) 534 818445, Call Date: June 1949 (Middle Temple) Qualifications: MA (Oxon)

Kirkham *Miss Karen Lesley* •
Acting Director of Legal Affairs, Building Employers, Confederation, 82 New Cavendish Street, London W1M 8AD, 0171 580 5588, Call Date: Nov 1988 (Middle Temple) Qualifications: MA (Oxon)

Kirkham *Keith* •
Principal Crown Prosecutor, Crown Prosecution Service, Unicentre, Lords Walk, Preston, Lancashire PR1 1DH, 01772 555015, Call Date: Feb 1985 (Middle Temple)

Kirkham-Smith *Mrs Marjorie Anne* •
Senior Crown Prosecutor, CPS, 4-12 Queen Anne's Gate, London SW1H 9AZ, Call Date: July 1981 (Middle Temple) Qualifications: BA (Hons)

Kirkman *Patrick John* •
Legal Advisor, The West of England Ship, Owners Insurance Services Ltd, 224-226 Tower Bridge Road, London SE1 2UP, 0171 716 6015, Fax: 0171 716 6111, Call Date: Nov 1990 (Middle Temple) Qualifications: MA (St Andrew's), Dip Law (City)

Kirkpatrick *Gavin Waring* •
Crown Prosecution Service, 10 Furnival St, London EC4A 1PE, Call Date: Nov 1981 (Middle Temple) Qualifications: BA (Hons)

Kirsop *Ms Sara Jane*
Call Date: Nov 1997 (Inner Temple) Qualifications: BSc (So'ton)

Kitchin *Ms Hilary Judith*
Local Government Information, Unit, 1-5 Bath Street, London EC1V 9QQ, 0171 608 1051, Former Solicitor 4 Brick Court, Ground Floor, Temple, London, EC4Y 9AD, Call Date: Nov 1987 (Lincoln's Inn) Qualifications: BA (Sussex)

Klausner *Isidor* •
Stancroft Trust Limited, Bride House, 20 Bride Lane, London EC4Y 8DX, 0171 583 3808, Fax: 0171 583 5912, Call Date: Nov 1981 (Middle Temple) Qualifications: LLM, DRS EC [Rotterdam]

Klein *Miss Miriam-Xenia*
Financial Advisor, City Financial Partners, Russell Square House, London WC1B 5EH, 0171 323 2828, Fax: 0171 436 0304, Call Date: July 1997 (Lincoln's Inn) Qualifications: LLB (Hons), LLM

Klein *Silviu Thomas Rudolf* •
Director of Legal Affairs, Specialist Engineering, Contractors Group, ESCA House, 34 Palace Court, Bayswater,London W2 4JG, 0171 229 2488, Fax: 0171 727 9268, Call Date: Nov 1979 (Middle Temple) Qualifications: LLB (Hons) (Lond)

Klouda *Thomas Joseph* •
Senior Crown Prosecutor, Crown Prosecution Service, CPS Yorkshire, Wakefield Branch Office, 4-5 South Parade, Wakefield WF1 1LR, Call Date: Nov 1980 (Middle Temple) Qualifications: BA, LLB (Leeds)

Knapman *Mrs Lynne Geraldine* •
Head of Crown Office and Deputy Registrar of Criminal Appeals, Lord Chancellor's Department, Crown Office/Criminal Appeal, Royal Courts of Justice, The Strand, London WC2A, 0171 936 6454, Fax: 0171 936 6276, Call Date: July 1973 (Middle Temple) Qualifications: LLB (Hons) Lond

Knapper *Don* •
Crown Prosectution Service, Blackburn House, Midway, Newcastle-under-Lyme, Staffordshire, Call Date: Oct 1992 (Gray's Inn) Qualifications: B.Sc

Kneller *Sir Alister Alister Walter Arthur Ernest*
15 Summersdale Court, The Drive, Lavant Road, Chichester, West Sussex PO19 4RF, 01243 528408, Knight Bachelor, Call Date: June 1953 (Gray's Inn) Qualifications: MA (Hons) (Cantab), LLM (Hons) (Cantab)

Kneller *Miss Karen Belinda* •
Crown Prosecutor, Crown Prosecution Service, Crown House, Winston Churchill Avenue, Portsmouth, 01705 752004, Fax: 01705 753390, Call Date: Nov 1993 (Inner Temple) Qualifications: BA (L'pool), LLB (Lond)

Knight *Miss Amanda*
26C Browning Street, London SE17 1LU, 0171 703 1178, Call Date: Oct 1994 (Gray's Inn) Qualifications: BA

Knight *David Alan*
Chairman of Barnsbury Housing Association, Member of Member Investment Property Forum Investment Property Forum, Member of British Property Forum European Forum, Lovell White Durrant, 65 Holborn Viaduct, London EC1A 2DY, 0171 236 0066, Fax: 0171 248 4212, Call Date: Nov 1983 (Inner Temple) Qualifications: BA (Hons)

Knight *Nigel Merley* •
Principal Team Leader, Crown Prosecution Service, PO Box 229, Horsham, West Sussex RH12 1YB, 01403 272923, Call Date: July 1984 (Gray's Inn) Qualifications: LLB (E Anglia)

Knight *Miss Sarah Elizabeth*
Call Date: Oct 1998 (Lincoln's Inn) Qualifications: BA (Hons)

Knight *Miss Suzanne Catherine*
Call Date: Nov 1998 (Inner Temple) Qualifications: LLB (So'ton)

Knorpel *Henry*
Conway, 32 Sunnybank, Epsom, Surrey
KT18 7DX, 01372 721394, Call Date: Jan
1947 (Inner Temple) Qualifications:
BCL, MA (Oxon)

Knott *Miss Judith Mary* •
Principal Crown Prosecutor, Crown
Prosecution Service, 8th Floor, Sunlight
House, Quay Street, Manchester
M60 3LU, 0161 626 6238, Fax: 0161 835
2663, Call Date: July 1980 (Inner
Temple) Qualifications: LL.B. (Hull)

Knowles *James Roger*
53 Bedford Square, London WC1B 3DP,
0171 580 3536, Fax: 0171 436 4860,
Call Date: Nov 1971 (Lincoln's Inn)
Qualifications: FRICS,FCIArb

Knowles *Mrs Patricia Katharine* •
Grade 6, Department of the
Environment, 2 Marsham Street, London
SW1P 3EB, Call Date: Oct 1971 (Gray's
Inn)

Knowles *Peter Francis Arnold* •
Parliamentary Counsel, Parlimentary
Counsel Office, 36 Whitehall, London
SW1A 2AY, Call Date: July 1971 (Gray's
Inn) Qualifications: MA (Oxon)

Knowles *Philip Jonathan*
Justices' Clerk, Buckingham Magistrates
Courts, Service, The Magistrates Court,
Wlton Street, Aylesbury, Bucks
HP21 7QZ, 01296 338959, Fax: 01296
338960, Call Date: July 1982 (Gray's
Inn) Qualifications: LLB (Lond), DMS

Knox *Miss Heather Elizabeth* •
Legal Adviser, Premier Consolidated,
Oilfields plc, 23 Lower Belgrave Street,
London SW1W 0NR, Call Date: Nov 1976
(Gray's Inn)

Knox *Terry Daniel*
Call Date: Oct 1996 (Middle Temple)
Qualifications: LLB (Hons) (Lond)

Knox-Hooke *Zaccheaus Aubrey*
Call Date: Oct 1991 (Inner Temple)
Qualifications: BSc, LLB (Lond), LLM
(Lond)

Kobani *Kenneth Bie*
Call Date: Nov 1994 (Inner Temple)
Qualifications: BA, MA (Keele)

Koenig *Michel*
Legal Adviser to French Embassy &
Consulate General, 4 Essex Court,
Temple, London, EC4Y 9AJ, Call Date:
Nov 1953 (Middle Temple)

Koenigsberger *Carl Wolfgang*
Call Date: Feb 1958 (Gray's Inn)
Qualifications: BA

Kohl *Miss Sarah Jane*
Call Date: Nov 1998 (Inner Temple)
Qualifications: BA (Manch)

Konecki *Andrew Anthony*
Legal Advisor, Company Director, Call
Date: Nov 1991 (Lincoln's Inn)
Qualifications: LLB (Hons), MA (Lond)

Konstam *Michael John*
Legal Adviser, A & L Goodbody Solicitors,
Pinnacle House, 23-26 St Dunstan's Hill,
London EC3R 8HN, 0171 929 2425, Fax:
0171 489 9677, Call Date: July 1981
(Gray's Inn) Qualifications: MA (Cantab)

Koo *John*
Call Date: Feb 1993 (Lincoln's Inn)
Qualifications: LLB (Hons)

Koroma *Saidu Abdulai* •
Senior Crown Prosecuter, Crown
Prosecution Service, 50 Ludgate Hill,
(3rd Floor) Marylebone Section, London
EC4M 7EX, 0171 273 8303, Call Date:
Feb 1987 (Gray's Inn) Qualifications:
BSc Econ Hons (Lond), Dip Law

Kotun *Chief Lateef Olakunle*
Legal Adviser & Consultant, 14
Westhorpe Gardens, Hendon, London
NW4 1TU, 0181 203 5053, and Member
Nigerian Bar, Call Date: Feb 1962 (Inner
Temple)

Kotwal *Ebrahim Mohammad*
Call Date: Feb 1962 (Middle Temple)

Koul *Ms Priyanka*
Call Date: Nov 1997 (Inner Temple)
Qualifications: LLB (Kent)

Kowlessur *Miss Nita*
4 Temple Road, Epsom, Surrey
KT19 8HA, Call Date: July 1995 (Gray's
Inn) Qualifications: BA (Keele), Dip Law

Kramer *Ian Lewis*
and Member California Bar, Call Date:
Nov 1996 (Lincoln's Inn) Qualifications:
BA, MA (Oxon), JD (Columbia)

Kratz *Peter Charles*
Call Date: Feb 1952 (Gray's Inn)

Kreisberger *Miss Ronit Charlotte*
Call Date: Mar 1999 (Middle Temple)
Qualifications: BA (Hons), BCL(Oxon)

Kreling *Paul Alexander Julian* •
Senior Legal Officer, Inland Revenue,
Solicitors' Office, Somerset House,
Strand, London WC2R 1LB, 0171 438
6747, Fax: 0171 438 6246, Call Date:
Nov 1989 (Inner Temple) Qualifications:
LLB (Exon)

Krishnan *Miss Usha Devi*
0171 263 7517, and Member Malaysian
Bar, Call Date: Nov 1986 (Middle
Temple) Qualifications: LLB
(Hons) (Lond)

Krofah *Miss Rosemary*
44 Clifton Road, Finchley, London
N3 2AR, Call Date: July 1995 (Middle
Temple) Qualifications: LLB (Hons)

Kron *Michael* •
Head of Rules of Court & Regulations
Division. Joint Secretary to Lord Woolfs
Inquiry, Lord Chancellors Department,
Selborne House, 54-60 Victoria Street,
London SW1E 6QT, 0171 210 0729, Fax:
0171 210 0725, Call Date: July 1975
(Lincoln's Inn)

Kucharczyk *Dr Wojciech Andrzej Jerzy*
General Medical Pratitioner. Medical
Member Disability Appeals Tribunal.
Medical Assessor Social Security Appeals
Tribunal., 01484 607072, Member of the
Royal College of Surgeons Licentiate of
the Royal College of Phsicians, Call Date:
Nov 1996 (Inner Temple) Qualifications:
CPE (Huddersfield), LRCP (Lond), MRCS
(Eng), Dip Law, Cert FPA, Cert.Med.Law
(Glas), Associate Chartered , Institute of ,
Arbitrators.

Kudiabor *Cyril Fui*
0181 858 2776, Call Date: Nov 1996
(Inner Temple) Qualifications: BA
(Kent), LLM (Lond)

Kullar *Mrs Richenda Margaret*
Senior Assistant Lawyer, Alliance &
Leicester plc, Carlton Park, Narborough,
Leicester LE9 5XX, 0116 200 4149, Call
Date: Feb 1993 (Gray's Inn)
Qualifications: LLB

Kumar *Vivek Raj*
Call Date: Oct 1997 (Middle Temple)
Qualifications: BA (Hons) (Cantab), CPE
(City)

Kunzlik *Professor Peter Forster*
The Nottingham Law School, The
Nottingham Trent Universit, Burton
Street, Nottingham, Bradford NG1 4BU,
0115 948 8418, Paradise Square
Chambers, 26 Paradise Square,
Sheffield, S1 2DE, Call Date: July 1983
(Inner Temple) Qualifications: MA, LLM
(Cantab)

Kurdi *Miss Suzan*
Call Date: Nov 1998 (Gray's Inn)
Qualifications: LLB (LSE)

Kuzmicki *Marcin Dominic*
Call Date: Nov 1998 (Inner Temple)
Qualifications: BA (Cantab)

Ky *Ms Tania Kim*
Call Date: July 1977 (Middle Temple)
Qualifications: LLB (Lond)

Kyle *David William* •
Call Date: July 1973 (Inner Temple)
Qualifications: BA (Cantab)

Kyle *Miss Samantha Ann Wilcock*
Call Date: Oct 1995 (Inner Temple)
Qualifications: BA (Dunelm)

Kyriacou *Kyriacos Philippou*
Call Date: Feb 1994 (Lincoln's Inn)
Qualifications: LLB (Hons)

La Niece *Jeremy Peter Babington* •
Head of SFA Litigation, The Securities
and Futures, Authority Limited, 25 The
North Colonnade, Canary Wharf, London
E14 5HS, 0171 676 1328, Fax: 0171 676
1329, Call Date: Nov 1973 (Middle
Temple) Qualifications: LLB

Lack *Paul Vernon*
Call Date: Oct 1993 (Lincoln's Inn)
Qualifications: LLB (Hons)

Ladimeji *Waliu Dele*
Call Date: Nov 1995 (Middle Temple)
Qualifications: BA (Hons) (Anglia), MA
(Cantab)

Ladlow *Mrs Loraine Lesley*
Principal Court Clerk, Justices Clerks
Office, Huntingdon Magistrates Court,
Market Hill, Huntingdon PE18 6PG,
01480 451118, Fax: 01480 434228,
Call Date: Nov 1993 (Gray's Inn)
Qualifications: BA, DMS

Lai *Miss Amy Hur-Ling*
Call Date: July 1995 (Lincoln's Inn)
Qualifications: LLB (Hons), LLM
(Lond)

Lai *Miss Iy Lee*
Court Clerk, Cambridgeshire
Magistrates', Courts Committee, Bridge
Street, Peterborough, Cambs PE1 1ED,
01733 63971, Fax: 01733 313749, Call
Date: July 1989 (Middle Temple)
Qualifications: BSoc Sci [Keele]

Lai *Philippe*
Call Date: July 1997 (Lincoln's Inn)
Qualifications: MSc, CPE

Lai *Stanley Tze Chang*
Lee & Lee, Level UIC Building, No 5
Shenton Way Singapore, Republic of
Singapore, 65 2200666, Fax: Z, and
Member Singapore Bar, Call Date: Nov
1993 (Lincoln's Inn) Qualifications:
LLB (Hons, Leic), LLM (Hons) (Cantab)

Lai Pat Fong *Miss Josee*
Tax Adviser, and Member Mauritian
Bar, Call Date: Nov 1987 (Gray's Inn)
Qualifications: LLB (Lond), AKC, ACA ,
ATII

Laidlaw *Stuart Robert* •
Crown Prosecutor, Crown Prosecution
Service, Croydon Branch, Trafalgar
House, 2 Bedford Prk, Croydon, Call
Date: Feb 1989 (Inner Temple)
Qualifications: LLB (B'ham)

Laing *Adrian Charles* •
Director of Legal Affairs, Harper-Collins
Publishers, 77/85 Fulham Palace Road,
Hammersmith, London W6 8JB, 0181
307 4665, Fax: 0181 307 4668, Call
Date: Nov 1979 (Inner Temple)
Qualifications: LLB (Exon)

Laing *Hugh Charles Desmond*
11 Great Oak Court, Great Yeldam,
Halstead, Essex CO9 4PZ, 01787 237
924, Call Date: Nov 1976 (Inner
Temple)

Lake *Andrew Peter*
Call Date: Nov 1995 (Inner Temple)
Qualifications: BA (York), CPE (City)

Laken *Mrs Elaine Anne*
Clerk to the North Avon Justices, Avon
Magistrates Court, C/O Bristol
Magistrates Court, Nelson Street,
Bristol, 01454 310505, Call Date: July
1978 (Inner Temple)

Lakin *Mrs Deborah Rachel*
Court Clerk, Kingston Magistrates
Court, 19-23 High Street, Kingston,
Surrey KT1 1JW, 0181 546 5603, Fax:
0181 547 3551, Call Date: Nov 1992
(Inner Temple) Qualifications: LLB
(Hons)

Lakin *Mark Anthony* •
Crown Prosecutor, Crown Prosecution
Service, Gemini Centre, 88 New London
Road, Chelmsford, Essex CM2 0BR,
01245 252939, Fax: 01245 490476,
Call Date: July 1986 (Gray's Inn)
Qualifications: LLB

Lalani *Mrs Salma Hedeeda*
Call Date: Oct 1998 (Middle Temple)
Qualifications: BA (Hons), LLB (City)

Lamba *Sanjay*
Call Date: Nov 1994 (Gray's Inn)
Qualifications: LLB (Bris)

Lambert *Nigel Acheson Drummond* •
Head of Division, Legal B4, MAFF,
Room 36A, 55 Whitehall, London
SW1A 2EY, 0171 270 8409, Fax: 0171
270 8353, Call Date: July 1975 (Middle
Temple) Qualifications: LLB (Belfast),
LLM (Lond)

Lambie *Donald Goodwyn*
Call Date: July 1978 (Lincoln's Inn)
Qualifications: LLB (Lond)

Lampard *Miss Kathryn Felice*
1 New Square, Ground Floor, Lincoln's
Inn, London WC2A 3SA, 0171 405
0884, 1 New Square, Ground Floor,
Lincoln's Inn, London, WC2A 3SA, Call
Date: Nov 1984 (Middle Temple)
Qualifications: BA (Exon),, Dip Law
(City)

Lanch *David*
Langdale, Regal Way, Kenton, Harrow,
Middlesex HA3 0RX, 0181 907 9388,
Call Date: July 1987 (Lincoln's Inn)
Qualifications: BA, MA M.LITT (Oxon),
FCA, Dip Law

Landau *Frederic Moses*
Ex-Chairman, Sunday Trading Trib, 5
Langford Close, London NW8 0LN,
0171 328 1145, Rights and Duties,
Transport Undertakings (Pitmans), Call
Date: May 1928 (Gray's Inn)
Qualifications: LLB (Lond)

Landau *Lady Pamela Ann*
Call Date: Nov 1985 (Gray's Inn)
Qualifications: LLB (Lond)

Landman *Rowland Harold*
Director of Companies, 17 Harley
Street, London WIN IDA, 0171 935
0106, Fax: 0171 255 1039, Call Date:
May 1936 (Middle Temple)
Qualifications: MA (Cantab)

Lane *Mrs Alison Joy* •
Legal Adviser, Galileo International,
Galileo Centre Europe, Windmill Hill,
Swindon, Wilts SN5 6PH, 01793
888116, Fax: 01798 886 190, Call Date:
Nov 1993 (Inner Temple)
Qualifications: MA (Cantab)

Lane *Nicholas John Graham*
Call Date: Mar 1997 (Gray's Inn)
Qualifications: BA (Cantab)

Lane *Miss Nyree Victoria* •
First American Title Insurance,
Company (UK) plc, Broxbournebury
Mansion, White Stubbs Lane,
Broxbourne, Herfordshire EN10 7AF,
01992 479200, Fax: 01992 479299,
Call Date: Oct 1994 (Middle Temple)
Qualifications: LLB (Hons) (Bucks)

Lane *Paul Timothy*
Legal Adviser, Eastbourne & Hailsham
Mags Crt, Old Orchard Road,
Eastbourne BN21 4UN, 01323 727518,
Call Date: Oct 1993 (Inner Temple)
Qualifications: LLB

Lane *William*
87 New Henry House, 10 Ice House
Street, Hong Kong, Channel Islands,
522 5494, 22 Old Bldgs, Lincoln's Inn,
London, WC2A 3UJ, Call Date: July
1971 (Gray's Inn) Qualifications:
FRICS, FCIArb., QC Hong Kong

Lanfear *Paul Simon*
Call Date: Oct 1998 (Lincoln's Inn)
Qualifications: LLB (Hons) (Huddes)

Langat *Ronald*
Call Date: Nov 1998 (Gray's Inn)
Qualifications: LLB (Leeds), LLM (LSE)

Langdon *Miss Penelope Jane*
Acting Senior Deputy Chief Clerk, Inner
London Magistrates', Courts Service, 65
Romney Street, London W1, Call Date:
May 1981 (Inner Temple)
Qualifications: LLB (Cardiff)

Lange *Dr Kezia Jane De Haviland*
Call Date: July 1998 (Lincoln's Inn)
Qualifications: MBBCh (Witwatersrand),
BA (Hons)

Langley *Mrs Patricia Virginia* •
Head of Legal Services, National
Heritage Memorial, Fund, Heritage
Lottery Fund, 7 Holbein Place, London
SW1W 8NR, 0171 591 6000, Fax: 0171
591 6276, Call Date: July 1978 (Gray's
Inn) Qualifications: LLB (Wales), LLM
(Lond)

Langrish *Mrs Sally* •
Assistant Legal Adviser, Foreign &
Commonwealth Office, King Charles
Street, London SW1, 0171 270 1478,
Fax: 0171 270 2280, Call Date: Apr
1991 (Middle Temple) Qualifications:
LLB (Hons)

Langsdale *Miss Jane*
Call Date: Nov 1989 (Inner Temple)
Qualifications: BA, Dip Law (City)

Langton *Miss Sara Louise* •
Head of Legal & Business Affairs,
Concorgence Productions Ltd, 10-12
Crown Street, London W3 8SB, 0181
993 3666, Call Date: Nov 1997 (Middle
Temple) Qualifications: BA (Hons)

• **Barrister in employment**

Lannigan *Miss Philippa Jane*
Call Date: July 1998 (Lincoln's Inn)
Qualifications: LLB (Hons)(Keele)

Lapaz *Miss Annie*
Call Date: Oct 1998 (Inner Temple)
Qualifications: LLB (Brunel)

Larkin *James Alan* •
Managing Director, Aon Trade Finance,
13 Grosvenor Place, London SW1X 7HH,
0171 253 3550, Fax: 0171 235 4397,
Call Date: Nov 1974 (Middle Temple)
Qualifications: BA

Lass *Jonathan Marc*
Call Date: Mar 1998 (Gray's Inn)
Qualifications: LLB (Lond)

Last *Peter Raymond*
35A Fitzwilliam Road, Clapham, London
SW4 0DP, 0171 627 2189, Fax: 0171 627
2189, Call Date: Oct 1995 (Lincoln's
Inn) Qualifications: LLB (Hons)(Lond),
LLM (Lond)

Latham *Matthew John Richard*
Call Date: Nov 1997 (Lincoln's Inn)
Qualifications: LLB (Hons)(Leics)

Latimer *Miss Karen Elaine* •
Senior Crown Prosecutor, Solar House,
1-9 Romford Road, Stratford, London
E15, and Member New Zealand Bar, Call
Date: Nov 1990 (Inner Temple)
Qualifications: LLB

Lau *Miss Mei Lyn*
Solicitor and Member Malaysian Bar,
Call Date: July 1994 (Middle Temple)
Qualifications: LLB (Hons)(Kent)

Laubi *Anthony Henry Alfred*
Flat 4, 52 Onslow Gardens, London
SW7 3QA, 0171 373 0533, Fax: 0171 982
2256, Call Date: July 1988 (Gray's Inn)
Qualifications: LLB

Laughton *Denis Sidney*
The Red Hse, Sandpits Lane, Penn, High
Wycombe, Bucks HP10 8HD, 01494
813182, Call Date: June 1949 (Gray's
Inn) Qualifications: MA, LLB (Cantab)

Laughton *Miss Victoria Jane*
Call Date: Oct 1998 (Lincoln's Inn)
Qualifications: LLB (Hons)(Leic)

Laurance *Miss Julie Astrid Marina
Salicath*
Investment Insurance Int'l, AON Group
LTD, 109-117 Middlesex Street, London
E1 7JF, 0171 668 9368, Fax: 0171 301
4170, Call Date: Nov 1995 (Gray's Inn)
Qualifications: LLB (Bucks)

Lavender *Michael David* •
Legal Adviser, Lombard Tricity Finance
Ltd, 284 Southbury Road, 116
Cockfosters Road, Enfield, 0181 344
6572, Fax: 0181 344 6591, Call Date:
Nov 1986 (Lincoln's Inn) Qualifications:
LLB (Birmingham)

Lavers *Professor Anthony Philip*
Call Date: July 1997 (Lincoln's Inn)
Qualifications: LLB (Hons)(Lond), MPhil
(S'ton), Phd (Singapore)

Lavin *Miss Mary Mandie Jane* •
Director of Professional Conduct at
UKCC, UKCC, 23 Portland Place, London
W1N 4JT, 0171 333 6548, Fax: 0171 333
6536, Call Date: Oct 1993 (Middle
Temple) Qualifications: LLB
(Hons)(Lond), MA

Lavin *Miss Sarah Joy*
Call Date: Nov 1996 (Gray's Inn)
Qualifications: BA (Keele)

Law *Robert*
Office of the Minister of, State for Justice
&, Constitutional Affairs, P O Box 7272,
Kampala, 430431, 3 Temple Gardens,
2nd Floor, Temple, London, EC4Y 9AU,
Call Date: July 1987 (Middle Temple)
Qualifications: BA, Dip Law, FRGS

Lawless *Ms Jacqueline*
Call Date: Mar 1997 (Inner Temple)
Qualifications: BA (Westminster), Dip In
Law (City)

Lawrence *Miss Ceri Jane*
Call Date: Oct 1998 (Middle Temple)
Qualifications: BA (Hons)(Oxon)

Lawrence *Eloghosa Stephen*
Call Date: Feb 1994 (Middle Temple)
Qualifications: LLB (Hons)(Lond)

Lawrence *Miss Ruth Isabel*
Call Date: July 1980 (Middle Temple)
Qualifications: MA (Cantab)

Lawrence *Stuart John* •
Principal Legal Officer in Customs
International Advisory Division, H M
Customs & Excise, New King's Beam
House, 22 Upper Ground, London
SE1 9PJ, 0171 865 5170, Fax: 0171 865
5248, Call Date: Nov 1994 (Inner
Temple) Qualifications: BSc (Swansea),
CPE (Bournemouth)

Lawrey *Keith*
Justice of Peace Member Social Security
Appeals Tribunal Panel, Foundation for
Science &, Technology, Buckingham
Court, 78 Buckingham Gate, London
SW1E 6PE, 0171 222 1222, Fax: 0171
222 1225, Call Date: July 1972 (Gray's
Inn) Qualifications: JP, LLB, MA MSc
Econ, FCIS, FCOLLP

Laws *Stephen Charles* •
Parliamentary Counsel, Office of the
Parliamentary, Counsel, 36 Whitehall,
London SW1, 0171 210 6639, Fax: 0171
210 6632, Call Date: Feb 1973 (Middle
Temple) Qualifications: LLB

Lawson *Martin Jeffery*
Legal Advisor, Hambro Legal Protection
Ltd, Hambro House, Stephenson Road,
Colchester, Essex CO4 4QR, 0990
234500, Fax: 0990 234508, Call Date:
Feb 1994 (Lincoln's Inn) Qualifications:
LLB (Hons, Essex), DMS

Lawson *Miss Nicola Jane* •
Assistant Group Chief Legal Adviser,
Lloyds TSB Group plc, Legal Dept, 71
Lombard St, London EC3P 3BS, 0171
356 1200, Fax: 0171 929 1654, Call
Date: July 1978 (Middle Temple)
Qualifications: BA (Oxon)

Lawton *(John) Philip*
Formerly a Solicitor, 12 Abbotts, 129
Kings Road, Brighton, Sussex BN1 2FA,
Call Date: May 1971 (Lincoln's Inn)
Qualifications: MA, LLM (Cantab)

Lawumi *Miss Deborah Eniola*
31 Russell Avenue, Wood Green, London
N22 6QB, 0181 889 2652, Call Date: Nov
1993 (Inner Temple) Qualifications: LLB
(Lond), P.N.L.

Lawunmi *Miss Doyin Margaret* •
Legal Adviser, Department of Trade &
Industry, 10 Victoria Street, London
SW1H 0NN, Call Date: Nov 1984 (Inner
Temple) Qualifications: BA, LLM

Lay *Mrs Teresa Christine*
Call Date: Nov 1993 (Inner Temple)
Qualifications: LLB (So'ton)

Laycock *Miss Ann*
The Corn Exchange, 5th Floor, Fenwick
Street, Liverpool, L2 7QS, Call Date: July
1980 (Gray's Inn) Qualifications: LLB
(L'pool)

Layman *Mrs Anne Valaire* •
Acting Senior Solicitor, London Borough
of Camden, Legal Services, Town Hall,
Euston Road, London NW1 2RU, 0171
860 5588, Fax: 0171 860 5649, and
Member Trinidad & Tobago Bar, Call
Date: Nov 1987 (Middle Temple)
Qualifications: LLB (LSE)

Layne *Miss Beverley Joanna*
Call Date: Nov 1998 (Lincoln's Inn)
Qualifications: BA (Hons)

Layton *Mr John Michael George*
94 The Broadway, Thorpe Bay, Southend
On Sea, Essex SS1 3HH, 01702 587834,
Fax: 01702 587834, Call Date: Nov 1978
(Middle Temple) Qualifications: BSC
(Dunelm) , BA (Lond)

Le Cras *Miss Karen Michelle*
Barlow Lyde & Gilbert, Solicitors,
Beaufort House, 15 St Botolph Street,
London EC31 7NJ, Call Date: Nov 1995
(Middle Temple) Qualifications: LLB
(Hons)

Le Faye *Kenneth*
Californian State Bar (Former Member),
Call Date: July 1952 (Gray's Inn)
Qualifications: BA (Oxon)

Le Feuvre *Miss Dorothy Mary*
Deputy Clerk to the Justices,
Cambridgeshire Magistrates Crt, Windsor
House, Anderson Centre, Spitfire Close,
Huntingdon PE18 6XY, 01480 414455,
Fax: 01480 123220, Call Date: Feb 1987
(Gray's Inn) Qualifications: LLB

Le Marchant *Piers Alfred* •
Legal Counsel, Lehman Brothers Int
(Europe), 1 Broadgate, London EC3,
0171 260 2944, Call Date: Nov 1987
(Inner Temple) Qualifications: LLB
(Lond)

Le Sueur *Andrew Philip*
Reader in Laws, University College
London, Faculty of Laws, University
College London, Bentham House,
Endsleigh Gardens, London
WC1H OEG, 0171 391 1417, Fax: 0171
387 9597, Call Date: July 1987 (Middle
Temple) Qualifications: LLB (Lond)

Lea *Lady Gerry Valerie* •
Senior Court Clerk, West Suffolk
Magistrates' Crt, Shire Hall, Honey Hill,
Bury St Edmunds, Suffolk IP33 1HF,
01284 352300, Fax: 01284 352345,
Call Date: Nov 1969 (Gray's Inn)

Leach *Miss Judith Vanessa*
Call Date: Nov 1994 (Inner Temple)
Qualifications: LLB

Leach *Miss Sandra Elizabeth*
Secretariat Offices, The Courthouse,
Tufton Street, Ashford, Kent, 01233
663203, Magistrates' Clerk, West kent
Magistrates Court, Call Date: Apr 1986
(Middle Temple) Qualifications: LLB
(Hons)

Leach-Smith *Mrs Caryn Gail* •
Senior Crown Prosecutor, Crown
Prosecution Service, St Georges House,
Lever Street, Wolverhampton WV2 1EZ,
01902 870900, Call Date: July 1988
(Lincoln's Inn) Qualifications: LLB
(Hons)

Leader *Peter George Frederick*
Tankards, Ockham, Woking, Surrey
GU23 6NQ, 01483 225178, Fax: 01483
211505, Barrister and Solicitor of the
Supreme Court of New Zealand, Call
Date: July 1954 (Lincoln's Inn)

Leamy *Miss Claire Elizabeth*
Call Date: Oct 1997 (Lincoln's Inn)
Qualifications: LLB (Hons)(Hull)

Lean *Vincent Edward*
Case Review Manager, CCRC, Alpha
Tower, Suffolk Street, Queensway,
Birmingham B1 1TT, 0121 6331853,
Call Date: Oct 1992 (Lincoln's Inn)
Qualifications: LLB(Hons)(Leeds)

Leasor *Miss Julia*
Call Date: Mar 1997 (Lincoln's Inn)
Qualifications: LLB (Hons)

Leat *Ian Ralph*
Call Date: Oct 1993 (Middle Temple)
Qualifications: BSc (Hons)

Leathem *Ms Patricia Elton*
Call Date: Nov 1979 (Inner Temple)
Qualifications: AB Magna Cum Laude,
MSc, LLM

Lebus *Timothy Andrew*
BT Alex Brown International, 1 Appold
Street, Broadgate, London EC2A 2HE,
0171 982 2500, Fax: 0171 982 2251,
and Member New York State Bar, Call
Date: Nov 1973 (Gray's Inn)
Qualifications: MA (Cantab)

Ledwidge *Francis Andrew*
Call Date: Oct 1990 (Gray's Inn)
Qualifications: MA (Oxon)

Lee *Audley Martin Dowell*
Call Date: July 1968 (Gray's Inn)
Qualifications: MA, ACII

Lee *Chee Hong*
Call Date: Nov 1996 (Middle Temple)
Qualifications: LLB (Hons)(Lond)

Lee *Daniel Lawson*
Call Date: Nov 1995 (Middle Temple)
Qualifications: BA (Hons)

Lee *Edward Adam Michael*
Consultant and Trust Coordinator Non
Executive Director, Crediton Minerals
Plc Secretary, Inverforth Charitable
Trust, Matthews Wrightson, Charitable
Trust, The Farm, Northington,
Alresford, Hampshire SO24 9TH, 01962
73 2205, Fax: 01962 73 2205, Call
Date: June 1964 (Middle Temple)
Qualifications: MA (Oxon), FCIB

Lee *Gordon*
Call Date: Nov 1998 (Middle Temple)
Qualifications: LLB (Hons)(Kingston)

Lee *Mrs Helen*
Call Date: Nov 1992 (Lincoln's Inn)
Qualifications: LLB (Hons)

Lee *Jonathan Joshua* •
Manager, Legal Affairs, Enterprise Oil
plc, Grand Buildings, Trafalgar Square,
London WC2N 5EJ, 0171 925 4000,
Fax: 0171 925 4606, Call Date: July
1974 (Middle Temple) Qualifications:
LLB

Lee *Martin John* •
Principal Assistant - Family, Leeds
Magistrates' Court, P O Box 97,
Westgate, Leeds LS1 3JP, 0113 245
9653, Fax: 0113 244 7400, Call Date:
Nov 1987 (Lincoln's Inn)
Qualifications: LLB (Hons)(Manc),
DMS, Assoc I.P.D.

Lee *Miss Pamela Wing Haan*
1E Villa Monte Rosa, 12/F, 41A Stubbs
Road, and Member Hong Kong Bar
Melbourne, Call Date: July 1966 (Inner
Temple)

Lee *Paul Richard* •
Senior Attorney - AT&T Uk, Basking
Ridge, Kettlewell Close, Horsell,
Woking, Surrey GU21 4HY, 01483
715359, Fax: 01483 727412, Call Date:
Feb 1990 (Gray's Inn) Qualifications:
LLB [Lanc]

Lee *Richard Ian Jeremy*
Call Date: Nov 1995 (Inner Temple)
Qualifications: LLB (L'pool), LLM
(Dunelm)

Lee *Mrs Siew See* •
Director of Legal Affairs, Zepter
International (UK) Ltd, 4th Floor, Great
West House, Great West Road,
Brentford, Middlesex TW8 9DF, 0181
213 7100, Fax: 0181 232 8518, Call
Date: July 1993 (Gray's Inn)
Qualifications: LLB (Hons)

Lee *Miss Vanessa Jayne*
Call Date: Oct 1995 (Inner Temple)
Qualifications: LLB (Huddersfield)

Lee *Miss Victoria Jane* •
Commissioning Editor - Law, Oxford
University Press, Great Clarendon
Street, Oxford OX2 6DP, 01865 556767,
Call Date: Nov 1994 (Lincoln's Inn)
Qualifications: LLB (Hons)(Lond)

Leece *Patrick Richard James*
Cameron McKenna, Mitre House, 160
Aldersgate Street, London EC1A 4DD,
Call Date: Oct 1993 (Lincoln's Inn)
Qualifications: LLB (Hons)(Leic)

Leeder *Miss Lynne Angela* •
Senior Legal Officer (B1), Tax
Simplication Project Team, South West
Bush House, The Strand, London
WC2B 4RO, 0171 438 7568, Fax: 0171
438 7959, Call Date: July 1985
(Lincoln's Inn) Qualifications: MA
[Cantab]

Lees *Alan James*
Call Date: Nov 1952 (Gray's Inn)
Qualifications: MA, LLB (Edin)

Lees *Alastair Richard*
Call Date: Feb 1995 (Inner Temple)
Qualifications: BA (Durham)

Lees *David Slater*
BSL, Clinton House, P.O.Box 900,
Kenilworth, Warwickshire CV8 1ZA,
01926 852200, Call Date: July 1984
(Middle Temple) Qualifications: BA

Lees *Gordon Clifford*
Clerk to the Justices, North Yorkshire
Magistrates', Courts Committee, The
Law Courts, Clifford Street, York
YO1 1RE, 01904 615200, Fax: 01904
615201, Call Date: July 1979 (Gray's
Inn) Qualifications: BA, Dip Law

Lees *Rear Admiral Rodney Burnett* •
Defence Services Secretary, MOD, 0171
218 6186, Call Date: July 1976 (Gray's
Inn)

Lefcoe *Miss Karen Vivian*
Call Date: Oct 1997 (Middle Temple)
Qualifications: LLB (Hons)(City)

Lefton *Nigel Spencer* •
Assistant Solicitor, Attorney General's
Chambers, 9 Buckingham Gate,
London SW1, 828 1553, Call Date: Nov
1979 (Inner Temple)

Legair *Isaac Naaman*
and Member St Vincent & The
Grenadines Bar (December 1977), Call
Date: Oct 1997 (Lincoln's Inn)
Qualifications: FCCA, LLDip, MA

Legg *Miss Christina Marie*
Legal Assistant, GE Capital Equipment
Finance, Limited, Capital House, Bond
Street, Bristol BS1 3LA, 0117 946 3615,
Fax: 0117 946 3539, Call Date: Oct 1997
(Middle Temple) Qualifications: LLB
(Hons)(Bournem)

Leigh *Miss Camilla Anne*
Call Date: July 1984 (Lincoln's Inn)
Qualifications: MA (Cantab)

Leigh *Geoffrey*
14 Gresley Court, Little Heath, Potters
Bar, Herts EN6 1LF, 01707 647162, Call
Date: Nov 1959 (Gray's Inn)
Qualifications: MA, FCIS

Leigh-Smith *Alfred Nicholas Hardstaff*
Clerk to the Justices, Cambridgeshire
Magistrates' Ct, The Court House, Lion
Yard, Cambridge CB2 3NA, 01223
314311, Fax: 01223 355237, Call Date:
Nov 1976 (Lincoln's Inn) Qualifications:
LLB (Leeds)

Leighton *Miss Alison Margaret*
Compensation Manager, Dresdner
Kleinwort Benson, 20 Fenchurch Street,
London EC3P 3DB, 0171 623 8000, Call
Date: Oct 1990 (Middle Temple)
Qualifications: LLB, LLM (Tax Law), ATT
ATII

Leighton *Paul Robert*
Senior Quantity Surveyor. Legal Advisor.,
Turner & Townsend Contract, Services, 1
Clinton Terrace, Derby Road, Nottingham
NG7 1LY, 0115 947 0997, Fax: 0115 947
5679, Call Date: July 1997 (Middle
Temple) Qualifications: BSc (Hons),
ARICS, ACIArb

Leith *Daniel*
Call Date: Nov 1995 (Inner Temple)
Qualifications: LLB (Exon)

Lekic *Milo*
5 Septembra 68, Surdulica 17530, Serbia
Yugoslavia, 38 1 17 85 22 1, Call Date:
Nov 1975 (Gray's Inn) Qualifications:
LLB (Belgrade), LLB (Exon)

Lemkey *Miss Jennifer Anne*
Call Date: July 1987 (Middle Temple)
Qualifications: MA (Cantab)

Lemon *Guy Robert* •
Assistant Legal Adviser to Chief
Constable, Thames Valley Police HQ,
Oxford Road, Kidlington, Oxford
OX5 2NX, 01865 846676, Call Date: Nov
1995 (Inner Temple) Qualifications: LLB
(B'ham)

Leng *Mrs Jacqueline Mary*
Call Date: Nov 1996 (Middle Temple)
Qualifications: LLB (Hons)

Lenihan *Martin* •
Legal Adviser, Legal Dept, John Laing
PLC, Page Street, Mill Hill, London
NW7 2ER, Call Date: July 1983 (Middle
Temple) Qualifications: BA, LL.M
[Lond], ACI Arb

Lenygon *Mr Bryan Norman*
Company Director General Comm of
Income Tax, Highfield, Bells Yew Green,
East Sussex TN3 9AP, 01892 750343,
Fax: 01892 750609, Call Date: Nov 1976
(Gray's Inn) Qualifications: MA, LLB,
FCA, FCIS,, ATII

Leonard *Ms Catherine Martine* •
Senior Crown Prosecutor, Crown
Prosecution Service, Central Casework,
50 Ludgate Hill, London EC4, 0171 273
8078, Call Date: Nov 1990 (Middle
Temple) Qualifications: BA (Oxon)

Leonard-Morgan *Scott*
Call Date: Oct 1996 (Middle Temple)
Qualifications: LLB (Hons)(Lond)

Leone *Miss Sidonie Lisa Maria*
Call Date: Feb 1991 (Lincoln's Inn)
Qualifications: Diploma in Law (PCL)

Leong *Andrew Seng Poh*
Call Date: Oct 1998 (Middle Temple)
Qualifications: LLB (Hons)(Bris)

Leong *Gary Tat Hau* •
Senior Crown Prosecutor, Crown
Prosecution Service, 50 Ludgate Hill,
London EC4, Call Date: July 1990 (Gray's
Inn) Qualifications: LLB (Lond)

Leppik *Miss Heidi* •
Principal Crown Prosecutor &
Prosecution Team Leader, Crown
Prosecution Service, Central Casework,
United House, Piccadilly, York, 01904
450070, Fax: 01904 456577, Call Date:
July 1980 (Gray's Inn) Qualifications: BA
(Hons)(Sheff)

Leskin *Ian Paul* •
Assistant, Call Date: Feb 1991 (Inner
Temple) Qualifications: BA (Lanc), Dip
Law (PCL)

Leslie *Craig Raymond*
Call Date: Oct 1996 (Middle Temple)
Qualifications: LLB (Hons)(Lond)

Lesser *Miss Janis Erica*
Deputy Justices' Clerk, Inner London
Magistrates', Courts Service, 65 Romney
Street, London SW1, Call Date: Nov 1970
(Inner Temple)

Lester *Alan Nicholas* •
Employment Lawyer, John Lewis plc, 171
Victoria Street, London SW1E 5NN, 0171
592 6287, Fax: 0171 592 6566, Call
Date: July 1984 (Inner Temple)
Qualifications: MA (Oxon)

Lester *Lady Catherine Elizabeth Debora*
Immigration Adjudicator, Special
Adjudicator, 38 Half Moon Lane, London
SE24 9HU, 0171 733 2964, Fax: 0171
737 7282, Call Date: Nov 1969 (Lincoln's
Inn) Qualifications: MA, LLB (Cantab),
LLM (Harvard)

Letemendia *Dr Miren Argi* •
Legal Adviser, Dept of the Environment,
Transport & the Regions, Great Minster
House, 76 Marsham Street, London
SW1P 4DR, 0171 890 6491, Fax: 0171
676 2226, Call Date: Nov 1973 (Middle
Temple) Qualifications: MA ,
Lic.spec.dr.eur, LLD

Levene *Mordecai*
1 Temple Gardens, London EC4, 0181
203 2234, Fax: 0181 203 2234, Call
Date: Jan 1937 (Lincoln's Inn)
Qualifications: LLB

Levene *Richard William Osborne* •
Principal Team Leader, Crown
Prosecution Service, 2nd Floor'
Froomsgate House, Rupert Street,
Bristol, Avon BS1 2PS, 0117 9273093
x350, Fax: 0117 9230697, Call Date: July
1982 (Gray's Inn) Qualifications: BA
(Law) Kent

Levin *Andrew Paul* •
Principal Crown Prosecutor Prosecution
Team Leader, Crown Prosecution
Service, 3rd Floor, King's House,
Kymberley Road, Harrow, Middlesex
HA1 1YH, 0181 424 8688 X 287, Fax:
0181 424 9157, Call Date: July 1984
(Middle Temple) Qualifications: BA
(Hons)

Levine *Ms Iona Jayne* •
Senior Legal Adviser, Hammond
Suddards Solicitors, 7 Devonshire
Square, Cutlers Gardens, London
EC2M 4YH, 0171 655 1000, Fax: 0171
655 1001, Call Date: Feb 1982 (Lincoln's
Inn)

Levine *Joshua Mark*
Call Date: Nov 1994 (Inner Temple)
Qualifications: LLB (Soton), LLM (Lond)

Levine *Sydney*
Retired Recorder, Call Date: Nov 1952
(Inner Temple) Qualifications: LLB

Levins *Thomas Arthur* •
Senior Crown Prosec utor, Crown
Prosecution Service, Harrow Branch,
2nd Floor, Kings House, Kymberley
Road, Harrow, Middlesex HA1 1YH, 0181
424 8688, Fax: 0181 424 9134, Call
Date: Nov 1988 (Middle Temple)
Qualifications: LLB

Levitt *Matthew Charles*
Call Date: Feb 1992 (Middle Temple)
Qualifications: BA (Hon), BCL (Oxon)

Levy *Nicholas*
Call Date: Nov 1997 (Lincoln's Inn)
Qualifications: BA (Hons)(Oxon)

Lew *Miss Chen Chen*
Call Date: July 1996 (Lincoln's Inn)
Qualifications: LLB (Hons)

Lewer *Ms Helen Jeannette*
Deputy Clerk to the Justices, Brent
Magistrates Court, Church End, 448 High
Road, London NW10 2DZ, 0181 451
7111, Call Date: Nov 1993 (Inner
Temple) Qualifications: BA (Lond), CPE
(City)

E

Lewin *Miss Maurine Joy*
Senior Deputy Chief Clerk, Inner
London Magistrates', Courts Service, 65
Romnay Street, London SW1P 3RD,
0171 706 1261 x 6678, Fax: 0171 724
9884, Call Date: July 1982 (Middle
Temple) Qualifications: MA (Sheffield),
BA (Hons)

Lewis *Alexandre Xavier Pierre* •
Legal Service, European Commission,
Rue de la Loi, 200, 1049 Brussels,
Belgium, Belgium, and Member Paris
Bar, Call Date: July 1983 (Middle
Temple) Qualifications: LLB (Lond),
Maitrise en Droit, DEA Droit Prive

Lewis *Alun Kynric*
Recorder, Call Date: Nov 1954 (Middle
Temple) Qualifications: B.Sc, LLB

Lewis *Miss Ann Molyneux*
Secretary & Registrar Royal
Pharmaceutical Society of Great
Britain, Past President 1994/6, Royal
Pharmaceutical Society, of Great
Britain, 1 Lambeth High Street, London
SE1 7JN, 0171 735 9141, Fax: 0171
582 3401, Call Date: July 1980 (Gray's
Inn) Qualifications: LLB (Lond) Hon
DSc, FRPharmS

Lewis *Mrs Anne Morag*
Advertising Manager, British Airways,
Waterside, Harmondsworth UB7 0GB,
Call Date: Nov 1994 (Gray's Inn)
Qualifications: LLB

Lewis *The Hon Antony Thomas*
Chairman: Powys Health Care NHS
Trust, The Skreen, Erwood, Builth
Wells, Powys LD2 3SJ, Call Date: Nov
1971 (Inner Temple) Qualifications:
LLM

Lewis *Brandon Keith*
Windermere, 3 Roundwood Lake,
Hutton Mount, Brentwood, Essex
CM13 2NJ, 01277 260575, Fax: 0277
264205, Call Date: Oct 1997 (Inner
Temple) Qualifications: LLB
(Buckingham), BSc (Bucks)

Lewis *Miss Caroline Daphne*
Training Officer, Inner London
Magistrates', Courts Service, 65
Romney Street, London SW1P 3RD,
0171 799 3332, Call Date: Nov 1975
(Middle Temple) Qualifications: MA
(Oxon)

Lewis *Miss Caroline Susannah*
Call Date: July 1988 (Middle Temple)
Qualifications: BA (Oxon)

Lewis *Ms Catrin Eluned* •
Hackney Law Centre, 236-238 Mare
Street, London E8 1HE, Call Date: Nov
1991 (Middle Temple) Qualifications:
BA (Hons)(Lond), Dip Law

Lewis *Cenio Elwin* •
Legal Officer, High Commission for
Eastern, Caibbean States, 10
Kensington Court, London W8 5DL,
0171 937 9522, Fax: 0171 937 5514,
Call Date: Apr 1978 (Lincoln's Inn)
Qualifications: LLB, LLM (Lond), MA

Lewis *Charles Eliot* •
Legal Adviser, Department of Trade &
Industry, Room 118, 10 Victoria Street,
London SW1H 0NN, 0171 215 5000,
Call Date: Nov 1986 (Gray's Inn)
Qualifications: MA, PhD(Cantab)

Lewis *Christopher David*
Call Date: July 1998 (Lincoln's Inn)
Qualifications: BSc (Hons)(Brighton),
LLDip (Holborn)

Lewis *Mrs Clare*
Deputy Chief Court Clerk, Camberwell
Green Magistrates, D'Eynsford Road,
London SE5, 0171 7030 0909, Call
Date: July 1988 (Lincoln's Inn)
Qualifications: LLB (Hons) (Lond), BA
(Hons)

Lewis *David Vaughan*
Call Date: Mar 1999 (Gray's Inn)
Qualifications: LLB (Lond)

Lewis *Duncan Iain*
Call Date: Nov 1998 (Gray's Inn)
Qualifications: LLB (E.Anglia)

Lewis *Miss Jacqueline Ann*
Clifford Chance, 200 Aldersgate Street,
London EC1A 4JJ, 0171 600 1000 Ext
8697, Fax: 0171 600 5555, Call Date:
Oct 1992 (Lincoln's Inn)
Qualifications: BSc(Hons)(Bris), Dip
Law

Lewis *Mrs Lesley*
38 Whitelands Hse, Cheltenham
Terrace, London SW3 4QY, Call Date:
Nov 1956 (Lincoln's Inn)
Qualifications: MA [Lond]

Lewis *Mrs Pauline Grace*
Legal Adviser, McDonald's Restaurants
Limited, 11-59 High Road, East
Finchley, London N2 8AW, 0181 883
6400, Fax: 0181 442 1379, Call Date:
Nov 1984 (Lincoln's Inn)
Qualifications: LLB (Hons)

Lewis *Philip Stephen* •
Serious Fraud Office, Elm House,
10-16 Elm Street, London WC1X 0BI,
Call Date: July 1981 (Gray's Inn)
Qualifications: BA, MA Dip L

Lewis *Robyn*
Former Solicitor, Call Date: Nov 1997
(Gray's Inn) Qualifications: LLB
(Wales)

Lewis *Lieutenant Colonel Roger David* •
Legal Officer, Army Prosecution
Authority, RAF Uxbridge, Middlesex
UB10 0XE, Call Date: Nov 1983
(Lincoln's Inn) Qualifications: LLB
Lond

Lewis *Miss Sara Michelle*
Call Date: Oct 1996 (Inner Temple)
Qualifications: MA (Aberdeen), CPE
(York)

Lewis *Stephen John*
Call Date: Feb 1992 (Lincoln's Inn)
Qualifications: LLB (Hons), ACIArb,
LLM (L'pool)

Lewis *Miss Susan Ann*
Call Date: July 1997 (Lincoln's Inn)
Qualifications: LLB (Hons)(L'pool),
LLM (L'Pool)

Lewis *Wayne Anthony*
Wayne Lewis Associates, 97 Avenue
Road, Swiss Cottage, London NW3 5EJ,
0171 722 7778, Fax: 0171 586 9879,
Call Date: Nov 1982 (Lincoln's Inn)
Qualifications: LLB

Lewis-Jones *Robert Kevin*
Call Date: Oct 1996 (Middle Temple)
Qualifications: BA (Hons) (Kingston),
Dip Law

Lewis-Nunn *Howard*
Capsticks Solicitors, 77-83 Upper
Richmond Road, London SW15 2TT,
Call Date: Nov 1994 (Inner Temple)
Qualifications: LLB (E.Anglia)

Lewis-Ruttley *Miss Hilary Jane* •
Jt Director of Studies (Int & Prof
Training Unit) and Research Fellow,
Inst of Advanced Legal Studies (Lond),
Institute of Advanced, Legal Studies,
Charles Clore House, 17 Russell
Square, London WC1B 5DR, 0171 637
1731, Fax: 0171 580 9613 or 436
8824, Call Date: July 1980 (Inner
Temple) Qualifications: BA

Leyland *Mrs Sheila Margaret*
Call Date: Nov 1970 (Inner Temple)
Qualifications: LLB

Lian *Miss Alice Meng Li*
Call Date: July 1996 (Lincoln's Inn)
Qualifications: LLB (Hons)(Herts)

Libbish *Simon Lyndsey Darren* •
High Risk Unit, Credit & Risk, First
Direct, 40 Wakefield Road, Stourton,
Leeds LS98 1FD, 0113 2766729, Fax:
0113 2766531, Call Date: Nov 1993
(Inner Temple) Qualifications: LLB

Licata *Joseph*
Bench Legal Adviser, Northampton
Magistrates Court3, Regents Pavilion,
Summerhouse Road, Moulton Park,
Northampton NN3 1AS, 01604 497000,
Fax: 01604 497010; 497020, Call Date:
July 1981 (Middle Temple)
Qualifications: BA (Hons), MBA

Licht *Mrs Judith*
56 Egerton Crescent, Chelsea, London
SW3 2ED, Call Date: Nov 1971
(Lincoln's Inn)

Lidher *Miss Raminder Kaur*
Call Date: July 1998 (Middle Temple)
Qualifications: LLB (Hons)(Wolves)

Liew-Mouawad *Mrs Joyce Huey*
Lecturer, Holborn College, Holborn College, 200 Greyhound Road, London W14 9RY, 0171 385 3377, Fax: 0171 381 3377, Call Date: May 1995 (Middle Temple) Qualifications: LLB (Hons) (Lond)

Lightfoot *Miss Kathryn Louise*
Call Date: Feb 1991 (Middle Temple) Qualifications: LLB (Manch)

Lillycrop *David Peter* •
Main Board Director & General Counsel, TI Group plc, TI Group plc, Lambourn Court, Abingdon, Oxon OX14 1UH, 01235 555570/01235 540133, Fax: 01235 555818/01235 554216, Call Date: July 1978 (Middle Temple) Qualifications: LLB (Exon), FIMgt

Lillywhite *David Victor* •
Legal Advisor and Compliance Manager, National Provident Institution, 55 Calverley Road, Tunbridge Wells, Kent TN1 2UE, 01892 705314, Fax: 01892 705614, Call Date: Nov 1980 (Middle Temple) Qualifications: LLB

Lim *Karl Adrian*
Call Date: Oct 1995 (Inner Temple) Qualifications: LLB (Exon)

Lim *Ms Nyuk Yun*
Call Date: July 1997 (Inner Temple) Qualifications: BSc

Lim *Miss Ping*
Call Date: Nov 1997 (Lincoln's Inn) Qualifications: LLB (Hons) (Lond)

Lim *Miss Siew Peng*
Cain & Abel Law Firm, 239 Missenden, Inville Road, London SE17 2HX, Singapore 730035, 0171 701 2327, Fax: 0171 701 2327, Call Date: July 1996 (Lincoln's Inn) Qualifications: BA (Hons) (Keele)

Lindblom *Mrs Fiona Margaret* •
N M Rothschild & Sons, New Court, St Swithins Lane, London EC4P 4DU, 0171 280 5000, Fax: 0171 929 5239, Also Inn of Court L, Call Date: July 1989 (Inner Temple) Qualifications: BA (Oxon)

Lindemann *Michael Jurgen*
Call Date: Nov 1998 (Lincoln's Inn) Qualifications: LLB (Hons) (Leics)

Lindsay *Alistair David*
Allen & Overy Solicitors, Call Date: Oct 1993 (Inner Temple) Qualifications: BA

Lindsay *Ronald Blennerhassett*
Kings Inns (Dublin) 1969 Westgate Chambers, 144 High Street, Lewes, East Sussex, BN7 1XT, Call Date: Nov 1975 (Gray's Inn) Qualifications: BA, LLB (TCD)

Line *Matthew*
Call Date: Oct 1997 (Lincoln's Inn) Qualifications: LLB (Hons) (L'pool)

Lines *Paul Francis*
Managing Director, Widney plc, Willowbank House, Oxford Road, Uxbridge, Middlesex UB 1UL, 01895 819340, Fax: 01895 819341, Call Date: Nov 1969 (Middle Temple) Qualifications: LLB (So'ton)

Lines *Richard* •
Highways Agency, Room 11/19, St Christopher House, Southwark Street, London SE1 0TE, 0171 921 4658, Fax: 0171 921 4060, Call Date: Feb 1965 (Gray's Inn) Qualifications: MA (Oxon)

Ling *Ms Sharon Hea Mei*
Call Date: Oct 1997 (Inner Temple) Qualifications: LLB (Brunel)

Ling *Miss Victoria Jane*
Call Date: Oct 1998 (Middle Temple) Qualifications: LLB (Hons) (Notts)

Linkins *Mark Harold* •
Principal Crown Prosecutor, Crown Prosecution Service, Mayfield House, Mayfield Drive, London Road, Shrewsbury SY2 6PE, 01743 234700, Fax: 01743 234749, Call Date: Nov 1986 (Gray's Inn)

Linnett *Mrs Lynn Marie*
Court Clerk, Northampton Magistrates Court, Regents Pavilion, Summerhouse Road, Moulton Park, Northampton NN3 1AS, 01604 497000, Fax: 01604 497010, Call Date: Nov 1986 (Gray's Inn) Qualifications: Dip Law

Linsey *Mrs Pamela Christine* •
The Lord Chancellor's Dept, Selborne House, Victoria Street, London SW1, Call Date: July 1988 (Lincoln's Inn) Qualifications: LLB (Hons) (Essex)

Linton *Miss Georgina Charmaine* •
Corporate Counsel European Region, Jacobs Engineering Ltd, Croydon, Surrey, 0181 688 4477, Fax: 0181 667 0852, Call Date: July 1985 (Middle Temple) Qualifications: LLB (Hons)

Linton *Miss Sara Geraldine* •
SCS, HM Customs & Excise, The Solicitor's Office, New Kings Beam House, 22 Upper Ground, London SE1 9PJ, Call Date: Nov 1970 (Inner Temple)

Lippell *Miss Sabrina Rose*
Management & Training Consultant. Business Development Consultant to the Institute of Personnel & Development., 01705 631574, Fax: 01705 631574, Call Date: Oct 1994 (Lincoln's Inn) Qualifications: BSc (Hons) (Soton), CPE (Lond)

Lipscomb *Mrs Marina Lynn* •
Group Solicitor Public Relations Officer. Bar Association for Local Government and the Public Service, Milton Keynes Council, Civic Offices, 1 Saxon Gate East, Milton Keynes MK9 3HG, 01908 252478, Fax: 01908 252600, Call Date: Nov 1987 (Gray's Inn) Qualifications: BSc Econ (Hons), Dip Law

Lipskier-Curtis *Mrs Sylvie*
Call Date: Oct 1990 (Gray's Inn) Qualifications: BA (Kent), MA (France)

Lipworth *Sir Sydney*
Master of the Bench Deputy Chairman, National Westminster Bank PLC Chairman, Zeneca Group Plc Chairman Financial Reporting Council, 41 Lothbury, London EC2P 2BP, 0171 726 1225, Fax: 0171 726 1038, and Member South Africa Bar, Call Date: Oct 1991 (Inner Temple) Qualifications: B.Com LLB

Lis *Miss Jacqueline Mary* •
Crown Prosecutor, Call Date: July 1985 (Lincoln's Inn) Qualifications: BA, Dip Law

Lisk *Mrs Ida Elvira Pauline*
Legal Advisor, 53 Elton Avenue, Greenford, Middlesex UB6 0PP, 0181 422 2584, and Member Sierra Leone Bar, Call Date: Nov 1975 (Inner Temple) Qualifications: LLB, Dip Law, LLM

Lister *Ms Theresa Ann Alice* •
Senior Crown Prosecutor, Crown Prosecution Service, 5-6 Prebendal Court, Oxford Road, Aylesbury HP19 3EY, 01296 436441, Call Date: May 1990 (Lincoln's Inn) Qualifications: LLB (Hons)

Litchfield *Miss Sarah Kate* •
Dept of Trade & Industry, Queen Anne's Chambers, 28 Broadway, London SW1H 9JS, Call Date: Feb 1992 (Gray's Inn) Qualifications: BA (Oxon)

Litherland *Miss Rebecca Jane*
Call Date: July 1987 (Middle Temple) Qualifications: LLB (Bham)

Little *Andrew Paul*
Call Date: July 1996 (Middle Temple) Qualifications: LLB (Hons)

Little *Miss Claire*
Call Date: Oct 1997 (Gray's Inn) Qualifications: LLB (Hull)

Little *Robert Edward*
Little Heavegate, Crowborough, East Sussex TN6 1TU, 01892 652035, Call Date: Feb 1955 (Gray's Inn) Qualifications: LLM, FCIS

Littlewood *Mrs Helen Elizabeth*
Deputy Clerk to the Justices, Harrow Magistrates', Courts Committee, PO Box 164, Rosslyn Crescent, Harrow HA1 2JY, 0181 427 5146, Call Date: July 1980 (Gray's Inn) Qualifications: BA (Nott'm)

Litvin *Mark Ian*
Call Date: Feb 1993 (Middle Temple) Qualifications: BA (Hons) (Oxon)

Livesey *Miss Julia Mary*
Stipendiary Magistrate in Hong Kong, Hong Kong, 2 King's Bench Walk, 1st Floor, Temple, London, EC4Y 7DE, Call Date: 1974 (Gray's Inn) Qualifications: BA

E

Livingstone *Reuben*
Call Date: Nov 1995 (Inner Temple)
Qualifications: BA, MA (Lond), LLB
(Lond), LLM (Lond)

Llewellyn *David Alexander Wilson*
Senior Legal Adviser, The British
Petroleum Co. plc, Sunbury Research &
Engineering, Centre, Chertsey Road,
Sunbury on Thames, Middlesex
TW16 7LN, 01932 762395, Fax: 01932
762381, Call Date: Mar 1998 (Inner
Temple) Qualifications: MA (Cantab)

Llewellyn *Howard Neil* •
Legal Adviser to Chief Constable and
Director of Legal Services,
Cambridgeshire Constabulary,
Headquarters, Hinchingbrooke Park,
Huntingdon PE18 8NP, 01480 456111,
Fax: 01480 422297, Call Date: July
1982 (Middle Temple) Qualifications:
BA (Hons)(Law)

LLewellyn-Evans *Ms Audrey*
Call Date: Oct 1997 (Middle Temple)
Qualifications: LLB (Hons)(Wales)

Llewellyn-Lloyd *Edward John*
Chief Executive, Close Brothers
Corporate, Finance Limited, 12 Appold
Street, London EC2A 2AA, Call Date:
Nov 1984 (Inner Temple)
Qualifications: BA (Oxon)

Lloyd *Daniel Rhys*
Call Date: Nov 1996 (Inner Temple)
Qualifications: BA (Wales)

Lloyd *David Gareth Beechey*
Call Date: Mar 1996 (Gray's Inn)
Qualifications: BA (Dunelm)

Lloyd *Mrs Eirlys Morven Sheena Lloyd*
Part Time Chairman Social Security
Appeal Tribunal, Disabilties Tribunal,
Advocates Library, Parliament House,
Parliament Square, Edinburgh,
Scotland, 0131 226 5071, Scottish
Advocate, Call Date: Apr 1991 (Middle
Temple) Qualifications: LLB (Edin)

Lloyd *John Desmond* •
Senior Crown Prosecutor, Crown
Prosecution Service, South Glamorgan
Branch, 19th,20th & 21st Floor, Pearl
Assurance House, Greyfriars Road,
Cardiff CF1 3PL, Call Date: Nov 1987
(Gray's Inn) Qualifications: LLB
(Wales)

Lloyd *Miss Marisa Rachel*
Ford & Warren Solicitors, Westgate
Point, Westgate, Leeds LS1 2AX, 0113
243 6601, Call Date: Nov 1994 (Inner
Temple) Qualifications: BA (Essex),
CPE (Glamorgan)

Lloyd *Reginald William* •
Legal Advisor, Hambro Assistance,
Hambro House, Stephenson Road,
Colchester Business Park, Colchester,
Essex, Call Date: Nov 1993 (Lincoln's
Inn) Qualifications: CPE, LLM (Wales)

Lloyd *Rupert Charles*
26 Lancaster Mews, London W2, Call
Date: Nov 1990 (Lincoln's Inn)
Qualifications: MA (Oxon), Dip Law
(PCL)

Lloyd *Mrs Susan Helen* •
President of the London Rent
Assessment Panel Member of the
Broadcasting Standards Commission.
Governor of the Expert Witness
Institute, London Rent Assessment
Panel, Whittington House, 19-30 Alfred
Place, London WC1E 7LR, 0171 637
1250, Fax: 0171 637 1250, Call Date:
July 1965 (Middle Temple)

Lloyd-Nesling *Miss Tracey Norma
Beatrice* •
Senior Crown Prosecutor, Crown
Prosecution Service, Lakeside House,
Holsworth Park, Bicton Heath,
Shrewsbury SY3 5HJ, 01743 234700,
Fax: 01743 234749, Call Date: July
1988 (Middle Temple) Qualifications:
LLB (Hons) (Bucks)

Lloyd-Williams *Miss Mairwen Cecelia*
148 Sutton Court, Sutton Court Road,
Chiswick, London W4 3EF, 0181 747
3217, Fax: 0181 747 9671, Call Date:
Oct 1995 (Lincoln's Inn)
Qualifications: LLB (Hons)(Lond), BSc
(Hons)

Lobo *Anthony Finton*
8 Jaquets Court, North Cray Rd, Bexley,
Kent DA5 3NF, 01322 524436, Call
Date: Nov 1958 (Lincoln's Inn)
Qualifications: BA, LLB, Dip Law,
(International)

Lobo *Matthew Joseph Edwin* •
Autonomy Systems Ltd, St John's
Innovation Centre, Cowley Road,
Cambridge CB4 4WS, Call Date: Oct
1995 (Middle Temple) Qualifications:
BA (Hons) (Cantab)

Lock *Alex Richard*
Call Date: Oct 1996 (Inner Temple)
Qualifications: LLB (Wales)

Lock *David Anthony*
St Philip's Chambers, Fountain Court,
Steelhouse Lane, Birmingham, B4
6DR, Call Date: 1985 (Gray's Inn)
Qualifications: MA (Cantab), DipL

Locke *Geoffrey Norman Wanstall*
Deputy Stipendiary Magistrate, Call
Date: Nov 1970 (Gray's Inn)

Lockey *Mrs Barbara Louise*
8 The Ridgeway, Radlett, Herts
WD7 8PR, 01923 859380, Call Date:
July 1987 (Lincoln's Inn)
Qualifications: LLB (Hons)

Lockley *Peter Jonathan* •
Legal Adviser, Leicestershire
Magistrates', Courts' Committee, 674
Melton Road, Thurmaston, Leicester,
0116 2640920, Call Date: Mar 1998
(Lincoln's Inn) Qualifications: BA
(Hons)(Oxon)

Lockley *Miss Victoria Jean*
Call Date: Nov 1998 (Middle Temple)
Qualifications: LLB (Hons)

Loebl *Ms Daphne Miriam*
Wilde Sapte, 1 Fleet Place, London
EC4M 7WS, 0171 46 7000, Call Date:
July 1985 (Middle Temple)
Qualifications: MA (Cantab)

Loft *Laurence*
Clerk to the Justices, P O Box No 717
Weind House, Park Hill Road, Garstang,
Lancashire PR3 1EY, 01995 601596,
Fax: 01995 601776, Call Date: July
1981 (Gray's Inn)

Logan *Cecil Corbett Malcolm*
Galleries, Harewood End, Hereford
HR2 8JT, 01989 730226, Call Date: Nov
1934 (Gray's Inn) Qualifications: TD,
MA (Oxon)

Lomax *Ian Stuart*
Clerk to the Justices/ Justices' Chief
Executive Acting Stipendary Magistrate,
City Magistrate'sCourt, Crown Square,
Manchester M60 1PR, 0161 832 7272,
Fax: 061 834 2198, Call Date: May
1977 (Gray's Inn) Qualifications:
MSoc.Sc., LLB, FIMgt, FIPD

Loney *Keith Edward*
Institute of Advanced Legal, Studies,
University of London, London
WC1B 5DR, 0171 637 1731, Fax: 0171
580 9613, Call Date: Nov 1972
(Lincoln's Inn) Qualifications: LLM
(Lond), FCA

Long *Miss Lorinda Joanne* •
Legal Adviser, International Finance &
Legal, Dept, Paribas, 10 Harewood
Avenue, London NW1 6AA, 0171 595
2438, Fax: 0171 595 5094, Call Date:
Nov 1988 (Middle Temple)
Qualifications: LLB, Dip in Pet Law

Long *Marc Steven*
Call Date: Oct 1995 (Gray's Inn)
Qualifications: LLB

Looker *Roger Frank William*
Director, Rea Brothers ltd Chairman,
RPS Plc Member Financial Reporting
Review Panel, Norwood Farmhouse,
Cobham, Surrey KT11 1BS, 01932
862531, Call Date: Feb 1978 (Lincoln's
Inn) Qualifications: LLB

Lopez *Carlos Ramon*
Linder Myers Solicitors, Phoenix
House, 45 Cross Street, Manchester
M2 4JF, Call Date: Nov 1995 (Lincoln's
Inn) Qualifications: BA (Hons)

Lord *Nicholas Jeffrey*
Deputy Clerk to the Justices, Cornwall
Magistrates', Courts Committee,
Justices' Clerks' Office, Tremorvah
Wood Lane, Mitchell Hill, Truro
TR1 3HQ, 01872 274075, Fax: 01872
276227, Call Date: Feb 1986 (Gray's
Inn) Qualifications: Dip Law

• Barrister in employment

Lothian *Miss Lisa Amanda* •
Tax Accountant, Coopers & Lybrand,
Central Business Exchange, Midsummer
Boulevard, Central Milton Keynes
MK9 2DF, 01908 690064, Call Date: Oct
1997 (Lincoln's Inn) Qualifications: LLB
(Hons)(Keele)

Loughlin *Ms Paula Mary*
Call Date: Nov 1988 (Lincoln's Inn)
Qualifications: LLB Hons (Lond), LLM
(Lond)

Loughrey *James Terence John* •
Legal Adviser, Siemens Group Services
Limited, Siemens House, Oldbury,
Bracknell, Berkshire RG12 8FZ, 01344
396104, Call Date: July 1979 (Inner
Temple) Qualifications: LLB (Hull)

Louis *Miss Adele Havlynn*
Call Date: Mar 1999 (Inner Temple)
Qualifications: LLB (E.Anglia)

Lourdes *Louis Joseph*
Call Date: Nov 1998 (Lincoln's Inn)
Qualifications: LLB (Hons)(Thames)

Loustau-Lalanne *Bernard Michel*
and Member Member Seychelles Bar,
Call Date: July 1969 (Middle Temple)

Love *Miss Kathy Lee* •
Senior Legal Adviser, Shell International
B.V., LSOP/1 Postbus 162, NL-2501 AN
The Hague, 00 31 70 377 47 96, Fax: 00
31 70 377 67 90, and Member
California, US Federal, Call Date: Nov
1977 (Gray's Inn) Qualifications: BA,
LLM [Cantab]

Lovejoy *Edward Iain Graham*
Call Date: Mar 1996 (Lincoln's Inn)
Qualifications: BA (Hons)

Lovelock *Christopher Thomas*
Call Date: Oct 1998 (Lincoln's Inn)
Qualifications: LLB (Hons)(Notts)

Lovett *Miss Linda Marie* •
Area Lawyer, D.S.S., Sutherland House,
29-37 Brighton Road, Sutton, Surrey,
0181 652 6504, Call Date: Nov 1994
(Inner Temple) Qualifications: LLB
(Westminster)

Low *Mrs Cheng Mooi* •
Senior Crown Prosecutor, Call Date: Nov
1990 (Lincoln's Inn) Qualifications: LLB
(Buck'ham)

Low *Ms Polly Ann* •
Principal Lawyer, Islington Council, Chief
Executive's Department, Town Hall,
Upper Street, London N1 2UD, 0171 477
1234, Fax: 0171 477 3243, Call Date:
Nov 1990 (Middle Temple)
Qualifications: LLB (Cardiff)

Lowans *Benjamin Anthony*
Call Date: Mar 1997 (Gray's Inn)
Qualifications: LLB (Sheff)

Lowdon *Christopher Ian*
Call Date: Oct 1994 (Lincoln's Inn)
Qualifications: LLB (Hons)(Plymouth)

Lowe *Mrs Jane*
Legal Adviser, Basingstoke Magistrates
Court, Court House, London Street,
Basingstoke, 01252 366000, Call Date:
Oct 1992 (Gray's Inn) Qualifications: BA
(Kent)

Lowe *Professor Nigel Vaughan*
St John's Chambers, Small Street,
Bristol, BS1 1DW, Call Date: Nov 1972
(Inner Temple) Qualifications: LLB

Lowe *Philip Raymond* •
Senior Crown Prosecutor, Crown
Prosecution Service, Lakeside House,
Holsworth Park, Bicton Heath,
Shrewsbury SY3 5HJ, 01743 234700,
Fax: 01743 234747, Call Date: July 1986
(Middle Temple) Qualifications: LLB
Wolverhampton

Lowe *Roger*
15 Winckley Square, Preston, PR1 3JJ,
Call Date: July 1984 (Inner Temple)
Qualifications: LLB (Sheff)

Loweth *Chris Richard* •
Programme Lawyer, Live TV, Edinburgh
Live, Easter Road Stadium, South Stand,
Albion Road, Edinburgh EH7 5QY,
Scotland, 0131 622 1818, Fax: 0131 622
7701, Call Date: Oct 1996 (Lincoln's
Inn) Qualifications: LLB (Hons)(Lond)

Lowndes *Miss Joanna Bridin*
Northern Ireland, Call Date: Mar 1997
(Gray's Inn) Qualifications: BA (Manch)

Lowndes *Ms Melanie Louise Anne* •
Head of World Service Legal, BBC World
Service Legal Dept, Bush House, G21
NW, P O Box 76, Strand, London
WC2B 4PH, 0171 557 2697, Fax: 0171
240 6254, Call Date: July 1988 (Inner
Temple) Qualifications: BA (Sussex)

Lowndes *William David* •
Goldman Sachs International, Limited,
140 Fleet Street, London EC4A 2BJ, 0171
774 5018, Fax: 0171 774 1475, Call
Date: July 1985 (Middle Temple)
Qualifications: BA (Lond)

Lowry *Benjamin Blair*
Call Date: July 1998 (Gray's Inn)
Qualifications: BA (Sussex)

Lowther *Ms Joanna Clayre*
Patent & Trade Mark Agent, Marks &
Clerk, 57-60 Lincoln's Inn Fields,
London WC2A 3LS, 0171 400 3044, Call
Date: July 1996 (Lincoln's Inn)
Qualifications: BSc (Hons)(Lond), ARCS
, Dip in Law, Cert of , Intellectural,
Property.

Lowther *Mrs Samantha Sarah-Anne*
and Member Irish Bar, Call Date: July
1995 (Lincoln's Inn) Qualifications:
BCL, BL

Lowy *Mrs Julienne Katrine*
United States of America, 24 Old Bldgs,
Ground Floor, Lincoln's Inn, London,
WC2A 3UJ, Call Date: July 1986 (Middle
Temple) Qualifications: BA (Oxon) Dip
Law, (City)

Loyal *Mrs Jasbir* •
Director of Legal/HR Services, PPP/
Columbia Healthcare Ltd, 4 Connaught
Place, London W2 2ET, 0171 616 4848,
Fax: 0171 616 4866, Call Date: July 1984
(Inner Temple) Qualifications: LLB, LLM

Loynes *Mrs Kate Julia* •
Lawyer (Legal Services, Social Services
Team), Kent County Council, County
Hall, Maidstone, Kent ME14 1XQ, 01622
694413, Fax: 01622 694266, Call Date:
Oct 1994 (Lincoln's Inn) Qualifications:
LLB (Hons)

Lubin *Dean Jonathon*
Call Date: Oct 1994 (Gray's Inn)
Qualifications: BA

Lucie *Gary Allan* •
Lawyer, West Sussex County Council,
County Hall, Chichester, West Sussex
PO19 1RQ, 01243 777925, Fax: 01243
777952, Call Date: Oct 1994 (Middle
Temple) Qualifications: LLB
(Hons)(Manc)

Luck *John Michael*
Call Date: Mar 1998 (Gray's Inn)
Qualifications: LLB (Kingston), LLM

Luckham *Kai Anthony*
Teacher of Law, Shena Simon College,
Whitworth Street, Manchester M1 3HB,
0161 236 3418, Call Date: Nov 1991
(Inner Temple) Qualifications: LLB

Lumb *Keith Simon Martin* •
Crown Prosecutor, Crown Prosecution
Service, 3rd Floor, Beaumont House,
Cliftonville, Northampton NN1 5BE, Call
Date: Nov 1979 (Gray's Inn)

Lumm *David*
Assistant Deputy Justices' Clerk,
Magistrates' Courts Brent, Church End,
448 High Road, London NW10 2DZ,
0181 451 7111, Fax: 0181 451 2040,
Call Date: Nov 1987 (Gray's Inn)

Lung *Dr Francois Ka-Kui*
Director, Call Date: Nov 1992 (Inner
Temple) Qualifications: Bsc (Hong
Kong), DPhil (Leeds),Master, in Mgtmt,
LLB (Lond)

Lunn *Miss Christine Nicola*
Court Clerk, Wimbledon Magistrates'
Court, The Law Courts, Alexandra Road,
Wimbledon, London SW19 7JP, 0181
946 8622, Call Date: Nov 1992 (Lincoln's
Inn) Qualifications: LLB (Hons)

Lunn *Christopher Simon* •
Specialist Derivatives Lawyer, J.P.Morgan
Securties Limited, P.O.Box 161, 60
Victoria Embankment, London EC4Y 0JP,
0171 325 4384, Fax: 0171 325 8205,
Call Date: Nov 1995 (Gray's Inn)
Qualifications: LLB (Lond)

Lunt *Mark Antony* •
Senior Crown Prosecutor, Crown
Prosecution Service, (Staffordshire &
Warwickshire), Newbold Terrace,
Leamington Spa, Warwickshire, 01926
450131, Call Date: Nov 1984 (Inner
Temple) Qualifications: LLB
(Manchester)

Lupton *Charles Stephen Douglas* •
Vice President, Legal Services, AGCO
Ltd, P.O.Box 62, Banner Lane, Coventry
CV4 9GF, 01203 531285, Fax: 01203
531398, Call Date: July 1970 (Gray's
Inn) Qualifications: LLB

Lutter *Mrs Susan*
Acting Justices Clerk, Chief Executive &
Clerk to MCC, Berkeley House, Walton
Street, Aylesbury, Bucks HP21 7QG,
01296 383058, Fax: 01296 383436,
Call Date: July 1978 (Gray's Inn)
Qualifications: LLB, DMS

Luttrell *Dr Steven Richard Rankin*
Church Cottage, Grovely Wood, Great
Wishford, Salisbury, Wiltshire SP3 4SQ,
Call Date: Oct 1992 (Lincoln's Inn)
Qualifications: MB ChB BSc(Glas), Dip
Law, MRCP

Lydiate *Peter William Henry*
Clerk to the Justices, Magistrates Courts
Brent, Church End, 448 High Road,
London NW10 2DZ, 0181 451 7111,
Fax: 0181 451 2040, Call Date: July
1974 (Middle Temple) Qualifications:
LLB

Lynch *Dermot Michael* •
Call Date: Nov 1994 (Gray's Inn)
Qualifications: LLB (Kent)

Lynch *Michael John*
Lecturer and Researcher, 9 Suckling
Green Lane, Codsall, Wolverhampton
WV8 2BL, 01902 843471, Fax: 01902
843471, Call Date: Nov 1994 (Middle
Temple) Qualifications: MA, LLB

Lynch *Miss Selena Ruth*
Full-time Coroner, Former Solicitor,
Call Date: May 1992 (Middle Temple)

Lyne *Godfrey John* •
Assistant Parliamentary Counsel, Office
of the Parliamentary, Counsel, 36
Whitehall, London SW1A 2AY, 0171 210
6626, Fax: 0171 210 6632, Call Date:
July 1987 (Middle Temple)
Qualifications: MA (Cantab)

Lyon *Mrs Jacqueline Anne* •
Call Date: Feb 1988 (Inner Temple)
Qualifications: LLB (Hons)

Lyons *Mrs Anne Rebecca*
27 Manor Crescent, Surbiton, Surrey
KT5 8LG, 0181 399 1452, Call Date:
June 1964 (Gray's Inn) Qualifications:
LLB

Lyons *Edward*
Recorder, 4 Primley Park Lane, Leeds
LS17 7JR, Call Date: Nov 1952
(Lincoln's Inn) Qualifications:
LLB(Hons)

Lyons *Mrs Ruth* •
Lawyer Grade 6, Dept of Trade &
Industry, 10-18 Victoria Street, London
SW1, 0171 215 3523, Call Date: Nov
1981 (Middle Temple)

Lyster *Miss Grania Mary*
Call Date: Nov 1992 (Inner Temple)
Qualifications: MA (Cantab), Dip Law

Lythgoe *Stuart Graham Silvester* •
Call Date: July 1982 (Gray's Inn)
Qualifications: LLB (Bristol)

Ma *Geoffrey Tao-Li*
Temple Chambers, Unit 1607-1612,
One Pacific Place, 88 Queensway, 5-2
32003, Fax: 5-8 100302, and Member
Hong Kong Bar Brick Court Chambers,
7-8 Essex Street, London, WC2R 3LD,
Call Date: July 1978 (Gray's Inn)
Qualifications: LLB(Birmingham)

Ma *Dr Siu Yung Alan*
Odebrecht - SLP Engineering, c/o
Tenenge (UK) Holdings Ltd, 197
Knightsbridge, London SW7 1RB, 0171
225 3393, Fax: 0171 225 3133, Call
Date: Nov 1993 (Lincoln's Inn)
Qualifications: BSc (Hons, Warw), PhD
(Warw), CEng,, MICE, MBCS, FCIArb

MacArthur *Ian Stewart*
Call Date: Nov 1995 (Inner Temple)
Qualifications: B.Acc (Glasgow), CPE
(Lond)

Macaulay *Neil David* •
Principal Legal Officer, 0171 865
5044, Fax: 0171 865 4875, Call Date:
Nov 1990 (Lincoln's Inn)
Qualifications: LLB

Macaulay *Roderick Hugh Russell* •
Senior Crown Prosecutor, Crown
Prosecution Service, Headquarters, 50
Ludgate Hill, London EC4, Call Date:
July 1989 (Inner Temple)
Qualifications: BA, Dip Law

Maccartie *Miss Peta*
Call Date: July 1998 (Middle Temple)
Qualifications: LLB (Hons)

MacCormick *Prof Donald Neil*
Regius Professor of Public Law,
Littleton Chambers, 3 King's Bench
Walk North, Temple, London, EC4Y
7HR, Call Date: 1971 (Inner Temple)
Qualifications: Jur Dr Lc (Uppsala),
LLD (Edinburgh), MA, (Oxon), MA
(Glasgow)

MacCrindle *Robert Alexander*
and Member Hong Kong Bar Essex
Court Chambers, 24 Lincoln's Inn
Fields, London, WC2A 3ED, Call Date:
Feb 1952 (Gray's Inn) Qualifications:
LLB (Cantab) LLB, (Lond)

MacCrone *Miss Roberta*
Part Time Chairman of Tribunal, Call
Date: Nov 1975 (Inner Temple)
Qualifications: LLB, MBA

MacDaid *Miss Moira Majella*
Call Date: July 1985 (Gray's Inn)
Qualifications: BA (Hons)

Macdonald *Alasdair Neil Gray*
Call Date: Oct 1994 (Gray's Inn)
Qualifications: BA (Cantab)

Macdonald *Donald Gordon*
Call Date: Oct 1995 (Lincoln's Inn)
Qualifications: BA (Hons)(Lond)

Macdonald *Miss Janet Ann*
Call Date: July 1998 (Gray's Inn)
Qualifications: BA (Glasgow)

Macdonald *Miss Morag*
Company Secretary, Ardshiel, Gwydyr
Road, Crieff, Perthshire PH7 4BS, Call
Date: July 1974 (Inner Temple)
Qualifications: LLB (Hons), BA

Macdonald *Miss Patricia Margaret Jean*
Thomas More Chambers, 52 Carey
Street, Lincoln's Inn, London, WC2A
2JB, Call Date: Nov 1979 (Inner
Temple) Qualifications: LLB (Hull)

MacDonald *Ms Sarah Jane*
Call Date: Nov 1994 (Inner Temple)
Qualifications: BA (Lond), CPE (Lond)

Mace *Andrew James*
Call Date: Oct 1997 (Lincoln's Inn)
Qualifications: LLB (Hons)(Wales)

MacEvilly *Conn Jeremy*
Call Date: Oct 1997 (Inner Temple)
Qualifications: LLB (Dublin), LLM
(LSE)

Macfarlane *Mrs Alison Jane*
Eversheds Solicitors, 1 Royal Standard
Place, Nottingham NG1 6FZ, Call Date:
Oct 1993 (Middle Temple)
Qualifications: LLB (Hons, Nott'm)

Macfarlane *Miss Tabitha Lucy*
Call Date: Nov 1998 (Inner Temple)
Qualifications: BA (Greenwich)

Maciejowski *Mrs Mara Georgina* •
Senior Crown Prosecutor, Call Date:
Nov 1990 (Inner Temple)
Qualifications: BA , MA (Lond)

MacInnes *Colin Charles* •
Senior Crown Prosecutor, Crown
Prosecution Service, County House,
New London Road, Chelmsford, Essex,
Call Date: Nov 1989 (Inner Temple)
Qualifications: LLB

MacIver *Anthony Digby Duffus*
Faculty of Advocates, Advocates Library,
Parliament House, Edinburgh
EH1 1RF, 0131 226 2881, Fax: 0131
225 3642, Standing Junior Counsel for
Scottish Charities Office and Member
Scottish Bar, Call Date: Apr 1991
(Lincoln's Inn) Qualifications: LLB
(Hons) (Edin)

MacKean *Ms Sarah Sutton*
Call Date: Nov 1992 (Inner Temple)
Qualifications: MA (Oxon), Dip in Law
(City)

Mackelvie Jutsum *Miss Jane Margaret Louise*
47 Moreton Place, London SW1V 2NL, 0171 821 6410, Fax: 0171 828 0021, Call Date: Oct 1995 (Gray's Inn) Qualifications: B.Sc (Wales), MSc (Lond), DIC, Dip Law, FGS

Mackender *Richard Philip*
Call Date: Oct 1997 (Gray's Inn) Qualifications: LLB (Wales)

MacKenzie *Miss Judith-Anne* •
Head of Railways Division, 1/08 Great Minster House, 76 Marsham Street, 10 Victoria Street, London SW1P 4DR, 0171 890 6130, Fax: 0171 890 2226, Call Date: July 1987 (Lincoln's Inn) Qualifications: LLB, LLM (Univ Lond), AKC

Mackenzie *Robert Sutherland*
308 Windsor Road, Oldham, Lancashire OL8 4HA, 0161 624 2698, Call Date: Mar 1996 (Gray's Inn) Qualifications: BA (Hons)(U.C.L.), M.S.I. (Dip)

Mackenzie of Mornish *Captain John Hugh Munro*
President of SEET plc, Mortlake Hse, Vicarage Rd, London SW14 8RU, 0171 580 7557, Fax: 0181 878 1065, Harmsworth Law, Call Date: June 1950 (Middle Temple) Qualifications: MA (Hons, Oxon), FRSA, CBIM

Mackenzie-Williams *Barry James George*
'Wenlock Edge', 6 Earlsdon Road, St Johns, Worcester WR2 4PF, 01905 748 018, Call Date: Feb 1994 (Inner Temple) Qualifications: BA, MA (Cantab), Ceng, MIEE

Mackesy *Ms Tertia Elizabeth* •
Senior Crown Prosecutor, Crown Prosecution Service, The Cooperage, Gainsford Street, London SE1 2NG, 0171 962 2626, Fax: 0171 962 0906, Call Date: Nov 1993 (Inner Temple) Qualifications: BA, CPE (City)

Mackey *Miss Sarah Margaret*
Call Date: Oct 1997 (Lincoln's Inn) Qualifications: BA (Hons)

Mackiggan *Keith Sinclair* •
Principal Legal Officer, H M Customs & Excise, New King's Beam House, 22 Upper Ground, London SE1 9PJ, 0171 865 4840, Fax: 0171 865 5989, Call Date: Oct 1996 (Lincoln's Inn) Qualifications: BA (Hons)(Cantab)

Mackintosh *Andrew Stuart* •
Crown Prosecution Service, Oxford House, Oxford Row, Leeds, 0113 245 4590, Fax: 0113 242 1302, Call Date: Nov 1990 (Middle Temple) Qualifications: BA (Keele), MPhil (Cantab)

Mackley *David John*
Call Date: Oct 1997 (Lincoln's Inn) Qualifications: BA (Hons)(Wales)

Maclean *Andrew Donald*
Call Date: Nov 1995 (Inner Temple) Qualifications: LLB (B'ham), M.St (Oxon)

Maclean *Cameron Hugh*
Call Date: Mar 1999 (Middle Temple) Qualifications: LLB (Hons)

MacLean *Miss Corryne Yvonne*
Call Date: Oct 1998 (Inner Temple) Qualifications: LLB (Thames)

Maclennan *John Gordon*
Call Date: Oct 1995 (Lincoln's Inn) Qualifications: LLB (Hons)(Newc)

Maclennan *The Rt Hon Robert Adam Ross*
House of Commons, London SW1A 0AA, 0171 219 6553, Fax: 0171 219 4846, Call Date: May 1962 (Gray's Inn) Qualifications: MA (Oxon), LLB (Cantab)

Macleod *Francis Roderick* •
Chief Executive, Foundation, 55/57 Owen Street, Hereford HR1 2JQ, 01432 264777, Fax: 01432 264888, Call Date: Nov 1978 (Inner Temple) Qualifications: MA (Oxon)

MacNamara *Miss Jillian* •
Principal Crown Prosecutor, CPS Ealing Hounslow Branch, 2nd Floor, Kings House, Kymberley Road, Harrow, Middlesex HA1 1YH, 0181 424 8688, Call Date: Feb 1987 (Gray's Inn) Qualifications: LLB (Nott)

Macnaughton *Alistair David* •
Gartmore Investment Ltd, 16-18 Monument Street, London EC3R 8AJ, 0171 782 2359, Call Date: Nov 1986 (Middle Temple) Qualifications: BSc (Wales), MA

Macrae *Mrs Anne Glover* •
Jacobs Engineering Limited, Knollys House, 17 Addiscombe Road, Croydon, Surrey CR0 6SR, 0181 688 4477, Fax: 0181 681 3869, Call Date: Nov 1989 (Inner Temple) Qualifications: B.Arch (Glas), Dip Law (City), R.I.B.A, ACIArb

Maddan *Archie Gracie* •
London Borough of Enfield, Call Date: Nov 1993 (Gray's Inn) Qualifications: BA (Dunelm)

Madnani *Ms Veena*
Call Date: Nov 1980 (Lincoln's Inn) Qualifications: MA (Bus.Law)

Magee *Miss Rosemary*
Call Date: May 1997 (Lincoln's Inn) Qualifications: BA (Hons)

Maggs *Ian Lorne*
Apt 1, 28 Lampard Grove, Stoke Newington, London N16 0XB, 0181 442 4458, Fax: 0181 442 4458, Call Date: Nov 1996 (Inner Temple) Qualifications: BSc (York), Dip Law (City)

Maggs *Patrick Terence*
Call Date: Oct 1996 (Inner Temple) Qualifications: BA (Exon), CPE (Lond)

Maggs *Stuart Peter*
Call Date: May 1997 (Lincoln's Inn) Qualifications: LLB (Hons)(Lond)

Magne *Dominic Loic Christopher*
Call Date: Mar 1996 (Gray's Inn) Qualifications: BA

Maguire *Dermot Gerard*
Call Date: Nov 1995 (Gray's Inn) Qualifications: BSc, LLB

Maguire *Miss Lindsay Jane* •
County Secretary's Dept(Legal), West Sussex County Council, County Hall, Chichester, West Sussex PO19 1RH, Call Date: Nov 1981 (Gray's Inn) Qualifications: BA (Hons)

Maguire *Patrick Robert* •
Group Company Secretary, Atrium Cockell Group Limited, Room 790, Lloyds, Lime Street, London EC3M 7DQ, 0171 327 3487, Fax: 0171 327 4878, Call Date: July 1973 (Inner Temple) Qualifications: MA (Cantab), FCII

Maguire *Richard*
Northern Ireland, Call Date: Oct 1998 (Middle Temple) Qualifications: LLB (Hons)(Wales)

Maguire *Richmond Edmund*
Call Date: Nov 1978 (Inner Temple) Qualifications: BA

Magyar *Nicholas* •
Legal Adviser, The Treasury Solicitor, Queen Anne's Chambers, 28 Broadway, London SW1H 9JS, Call Date: July 1986 (Inner Temple) Qualifications: LLB (So'ton)

Mahalingam *Miss Jayanthi*
Call Date: Mar 1999 (Gray's Inn) Qualifications: LLB

Mahan *Anil Kumar*
Call Date: Nov 1992 (Inner Temple) Qualifications: LLB (B'ham)

Maharaj *Miss Saveeta*
Call Date: Oct 1993 (Inner Temple) Qualifications: BA, LLM

Mahendra *Dr Bala*
37 Jessel House, Judd Street, London WC1H 9NU, 0171 833 8321, Fax: 0171 833 8321, Call Date: Oct 1993 (Gray's Inn) Qualifications: LLB (Lond)

Mahendra *Sabanayagam*
Call Date: May 1957 (Middle Temple) Qualifications: BSc (Wales)

Mahmood *Asad*
Call Date: Mar 1996 (Lincoln's Inn) Qualifications: LLB (Hons)

Mahmood *Eida Khan*
Call Date: Nov 1994 (Lincoln's Inn) Qualifications: LLB (Hons)(Wolves)

Mahmood *Miss Nayyera*
Call Date: Nov 1998 (Middle Temple) Qualifications: LLB (Hons), (De Montfort)

Mahmood Miss Samira
Call Date: Nov 1995 (Lincoln's Inn)
Qualifications: LLB (Hons)

Mahmood Shiraz
Call Date: Nov 1992 (Middle Temple)
Qualifications: BA (Hons, Herts)

Mahomed Ismail
Doughty Street Chambers, 11 Doughty
Street, London, WC1N 2PG, Call Date:
July 1984 (Gray's Inn)

Mahoney Paul John •
Deputy Registrar, European Court of
Human Rights, Council of Europe, 67
075 Strasbourg Cedex, 03 88 41 23 93,
Fax: 03 88 41 27 91, Call Date: Nov
1971 (Inner Temple) Qualifications:
MA, LLM

Mahoney Miss Sarah Ann
Call Date: Oct 1996 (Middle Temple)
Qualifications: LLB (Hons) (Wales)

Mahy Ms Helen Margaret •
Group General Counsel & Commercial
Manager, Babcock International Group,
PLC, Badminton Court, Church Street,
Amersham, Bucks HP7 0DD, 01494
727296, Fax: 01494 721909, Call Date:
July 1982 (Middle Temple)
Qualifications: LLB (Hons) (Manch)

Maiden Andrew Simon Kelly
Call Date: Oct 1996 (Middle Temple)
Qualifications: LLB (Hons) (Lond)

Main Ms Angela Patricia
Lloyds TSB, IT Legal Department, Red
Lion Court, 46-48 Park Street, London
SE1 9EQ, 0171 463 1754, Fax: 0171
232 3730, Call Date: July 1997
(Lincoln's Inn) Qualifications: BA, MA
(Auckland), Dip in Journalism,
(Cantab), Dip in Law

Maione Antonino
2 Harrogate Court, Langley, Slough,
Berks SL3 8JR, (01753) 543574, Call
Date: July 1998 (Inner Temple)
Qualifications: LLB, LLM (Warw0

Mair Mrs Margaret Mary Plowden •
Lawyer, Dept of Social Security, New
Court, Carey Street, London WC2, Call
Date: Nov 1977 (Inner Temple)
Qualifications: MA (Oxon)

Maitland Richard John
Call Date: Mar 1997 (Gray's Inn)
Qualifications: LLB (L'pool)

Maitland Roger Dundas •
Senior Legal Assistant, Lord
Chancellor's Department, The Law
Commission, Conquest House, 37-38
John Street, London WC1N 2BQ, Call
Date: Nov 1965 (Gray's Inn)

Maizels Miss Heather Jill
Barclays Private Bank Limited,
Executive Director, Barclays Private
Bank Limited, 43 Brook Street, London
W1Y 2PB, 0171 487 2000, Fax: 0171
487 2042, Call Date: July 1977 (Inner
Temple) Qualifications: MA (Cantab)

Majid Dr Amir Ali
Part time Immigration Adjudicator
Reader in Law Member of the Disability
Appeal Tribunal, Dept of Law, London
Guildhall University, 84 Moorgate,
London EC2M 6SQ, 0171 320 1507,
Fax: 0181 925 9577, Call Date: Nov
1980 (Lincoln's Inn) Qualifications:
BA, LLB,LLM (Lond), DCL

Majumdar Soumya Kanti •
Senior Crown Prosecutor, Crown
Prosecution Service, Central Casework,
50 Ludgate Hill, London EC4M 7EX,
0171 273 1310, Fax: 0171 273 1325,
Call Date: Nov 1988 (Lincoln's Inn)
Qualifications: LLB Hons

Maka Ishaq
Call Date: Oct 1998 (Lincoln's Inn)
Qualifications: LLB (Hons) (Manc)

Makele Ibrahim Daniel •
Legal Counsel - International, Financial
Insurance Group Ltd, Vantage West,
Great West Road, Brentford, Middlesex
TW8 9AG, 0181 380 3064, Fax: 0181
380 3065, Call Date: Nov 1992 (Inner
Temple) Qualifications: BA (Sussex),
LLM (Bris)

Makkan Shamshuddin •
Senior Crown Prosecutor, Crown
Prosecution Service, Sunlight House,
8th Floor, Quay Street, Manchester
M60 3LU, 0161 837 7402/908 2600,
Fax: 0161 835 2663, Call Date: Feb
1987 (Lincoln's Inn) Qualifications:
LLB Hons

Maland David
Call Date: Nov 1986 (Gray's Inn)
Qualifications: MA(Oxon)

Male Christopher
'Conifers', 34 Morview Road, Widegates,
Nr Looe, Cornwall PL13 1QE, (01503)
240525, Part time President of Mental
Health Review Tribunal, Part Time
Chairman Social Security Appeals
Tribunal, Call Date: July 1979 (Gray's
Inn) Qualifications: DML

Male Kevin
Call Date: Nov 1998 (Lincoln's Inn)
Qualifications: LLB (Hons) (Staffs)

Malik Ahmed Yar
Call Date: Nov 1987 (Gray's Inn)
Qualifications: BA (Keele)

Malik Ijaz Ahamed •
Crown Prosecution Service, C/O 50
Ludgate Hill, London EC4M 7EX, Call
Date: Nov 1982 (Gray's Inn)
Qualifications: LLB

Malik Sajid Mehmood
Messrs Sehgal & Co Solicitors, 456
Stratford Road, Sparkhill, Birmingham
B11 4AE, Call Date: July 1989
(Lincoln's Inn) Qualifications: LLB
(Warw)

Malik Tahir
and Member Advocate of the Kenyan
Bar, Call Date: June 1951 (Gray's Inn)
Qualifications: MAE

Malins Stephen John
Deputy Clerk to the Justices, The Court
House, Friars Walk, Lewes, East Sussex
BN7 2PG, 01273 486455, Fax: 01273
486470, Call Date: Nov 1981 (Middle
Temple) Qualifications: LLB(Lond)

Malkin Captain Henry Charles
West Cottage, Cromer, Norfolk
NR27 9EF, 01263 513335, Call Date:
Jan 1950 (Inner Temple)
Qualifications: MA

Malley Brian Malcolm •
Legal Advisor, Flyde Clerkship, P.O.Box
27, Chapel Street, Blackpool FY1 5RH,
01253 757000, Fax: 01253 757024,
Call Date: May 1983 (Gray's Inn)

Mallia Steven Joseph
The Times, 341 St Paul Str, Valletta,
00356 224483, Fax: 00356 247901,
Call Date: Nov 1996 (Inner Temple)
Qualifications: BA (Nott'm)

Malone Gerald Fergus
Call Date: Nov 1998 (Inner Temple)
Qualifications: LLB (Hull)

Malpass Roger Ernest •
Principal Crown Prosecutor., Crown
Prosecution Service, St George's House,
Lever Street, Wolverhampton WV2 1EZ,
01384 230471, Fax: 01384 236301,
Call Date: Feb 1983 (Middle Temple)
Qualifications: BA, Dip Mag Law

Maltz Ben Daniel
Call Date: Oct 1998 (Lincoln's Inn)
Qualifications: LLB (Lond)

Mandal Paritosh
Ireland, and Member Southern Ireland
Bar, Call Date: June 1941 (Middle
Temple)

Mandal Miss Ruma •
Legal Consultant with United Nations
High Commission for Refugees,
Geneva/London, Call Date: Oct 1994
(Inner Temple) Qualifications: MA
(Cantab)

Mander Ms Verinder Kaur
Call Date: Nov 1996 (Middle Temple)
Qualifications: LLB (Hons)

Mangat Arvinder Singh
Call Date: Nov 1996 (Inner Temple)
Qualifications: BA (Oxon)

Mann Peter •
Crown Prosecutor, Crown Prosecution
Service, Kingston Branch, Tolworth
Tower, Surbiton, Surrey KT6 7DS, 0181
399 5171, Fax: 0181 390 3474, Call
Date: July 1986 (Middle Temple)
Qualifications: LLB (Manch)

Manning James Robert
Call Date: Nov 1993 (Gray's Inn)
Qualifications: B.Sc (Bris)

Manning Paul Jonathan
Call Date: Nov 1997 (Lincoln's Inn)
Qualifications: BA (Hons) (Oxon)

Manning *Mrs Sharon Ann* •
Deputy Clerk to the Justices, Secretariat
Offices, The Court House, London Road,
Dorking RG64 1SX, Call Date: May 1988
(Gray's Inn)

Mannish *Martin*
Call Date: July 1996 (Lincoln's Inn)
Qualifications: BA (Hons)

Mansell *Mrs Deborah Anne*
Technical Advisor to the Institute of
Credit Management (Pro Bono), Call
Date: Nov 1994 (Middle Temple)
Qualifications: BA (Hons), MICM (Grad)

Mansell *Jason Francis Guy* •
Senior Crown Prosecutor, Crown
Prosecution Service, Central Casework,
CPS National HQ, Ludgate Hill, London,
0171 273 8000, Call Date: Oct 1991
(Lincoln's Inn) Qualifications: LLB
(Hons) (Birm)

Mansfield *The Earl of*
Call Date: Feb 1958 (Inner Temple)

Mansi *Miss Luisa Margaret*
Call Date: Oct 1997 (Lincoln's Inn)
Qualifications: LLB (Hons) (Oxon)

Mansoori *Miss Sara Louise*
Call Date: 1997 (Lincoln's Inn)
Qualifications: LLB (Hons) (Leeds)

Maples *John Craddock*
Economic Secretary to the Treasury (90/
92) Shadow Secretary of State for
Defence 97-, House of Commons,
London SW1A 0AA, 0171 219 5495,
Former MP (83/92) MP for Stratford on
Avon 97-, Call Date: July 1965 (Inner
Temple) Qualifications: MA (Cantab)

Maqsood *Miss Kalsoom Akhtar*
Call Date: Oct 1998 (Middle Temple)
Qualifications: LLB (Hons) (Notts)

Marballie *Anthony*
Magistrates Clerk, Inner London
Magistrates Court, Horseferry Road,
Magistrates Court, 70 Horseferry Road,
London SW1P 2AX, 0171 233 2000, Call
Date: Nov 1994 (Lincoln's Inn)
Qualifications: LLB (Hons) (Lond)

Marchant *Percy Faredoon*
Ex Local Councillor 1990-94 London
Borough of Merton, 0171 521 2658, Fax:
0171 521 2551, and Member India Bar,
Call Date: July 1988 (Lincoln's Inn)
Qualifications: LLB (Hons) (LSE)

Marcus *Miss Michelle*
Call Date: Nov 1976 (Gray's Inn)

Marenah *Miss Kirsten Tiyana Clare*
Call Date: Nov 1997 (Middle Temple)
Qualifications: LLB (Hons) (B'ham)

Marett *Dr Warwick Paul*
20 Barrington Road, Stoneygate,
Leicester LE2 2RA, 0116 2703392, Call
Date: July 1993 (Gray's Inn)
Qualifications: BA (Bris), BA (CNAA), MA
(Cantab), BScEcon, (Lond), BCom
(Lond), PhD (Lond), FCIArb

Markey *Miss Eileen Elizabeth*
Call Date: Nov 1994 (Lincoln's Inn)
Qualifications: LLB (Hons) (Warw)

Markey *Mrs Mo Lan Maureen*
14 Greenwich House, 10-12 Chesterfield
Road, Eastbourne, East Sussex
BN20 7NU, 01323 411828, Fax: 01323
411828, and Member Hong Kong Bar,
Call Date: Nov 1988 (Gray's Inn)
Qualifications: BSocSc, MSocSc, LLB
(Lond)

Marks *Miss Clementine Medina*
46/48 Essex Street, London, WC2R 3GH,
Call Date: Oct 1992 (Middle Temple)
Qualifications: BA (Hons), Diploma in
Law

Marks *Miss Katharine Anne*
Call Date: Oct 1998 (Middle Temple)
Qualifications: LLB (Hons) (Leeds)

Marks *Stuart David* •
Assistant Legal Adviser, Legal Dept, Office
of the Rail Regulator, 1 Waterhouse
Square, 138-142 Holborn, London
EC1N 2ST, 0171 282 2146, Fax: 0171
282 2040, Call Date: July 1982 (Gray's
Inn) Qualifications: LLB (Lond)

Marland *Ross Crispian* •
Consultant, Maxwell Marland &
Associates, 84 East Hill, Wandsworth,
London SW18 2HG, 0181 874 5964, Fax:
0181 488 7487, Call Date: Nov 1975
(Inner Temple) Qualifications: LLM
(Lond), MRAes,, AIA, MRIN, Dip Air Law

Marreco *Anthony*
Call Date: Jan 1941 (Inner Temple)

Marriner *Mrs Elaine*
Assistant Company Secretary, The
Morgan Crucible Company, plc, Morgan
House, Madeira Walk, Windsor,
Berkshire SL4 1EP, 01753 837000, Fax:
01753 868194, Call Date: Feb 1992
(Middle Temple) Qualifications: LLB
(Hons), FCIS

Marriott *Ian Leslie* •
Local Authority Lawyer, C/O City
Secretary's Dept, Coventry City Council,
Council House, Coventry CV1 1NH,
01203 833085, Fax: 01203 833070, Call
Date: Nov 1984 (Middle Temple)
Qualifications: LLB (Nott'm)

Marsden *Jonathan Patrick*
Call Date: July 1998 (Gray's Inn)
Qualifications: LLB (Sheff)

Marsden *Miss Marion Jean*
Call Date: Nov 1996 (Gray's Inn)
Qualifications: BA (Leeds)

Marsh *Norman Stayner*
Law Commissioner 1965-78, Wren
House, 13 North Side, Clapham
Common, London SW4, 0171 622 2865,
Call Date: Apr 1937 (Middle Temple)
Qualifications: MA BCL (Oxon)

Marsh *Miss Susan Amanda*
Call Date: Oct 1998 (Inner Temple)
Qualifications: LLB

Marsh *Toby Neil Alan*
Call Date: Oct 1998 (Inner Temple)
Qualifications: LLB (Lond)

Marshall *Adam*
Pitmans Solicitors, 47 Castle Street,
Reading, Berkshire RG1 7SR, 0118 958
0224, Call Date: Nov 1995 (Lincoln's
Inn) Qualifications: LLB (Hons)

Marshall *Albert Simon Obiri*
Call Date: Nov 1995 (Middle Temple)
Qualifications: LLB (Hons), LLM

Marshall *Mrs Alison Jean*
Principal Legal Adviser, Derbyshire
County Council, Clerk to the Justices,
Derwent Street, Derby, 01332 292100,
Fax: 01332 293459, Call Date: Nov 1987
(Inner Temple) Qualifications: LLB
(Leic)

Marshall *Andrew Francis*
11 Moore Road, Church, Crookham,
Hampshire GU13 0JB, Call Date: May
1996 (Gray's Inn) Qualifications: BA
(L'pool)

Marshall *Andrew George*
Clerk to the Justices, Justices Clerk's
Office, 55 Wade Street, Lichfield, Staffs
WS13 6HW, 01543 264124, Fax: 01543
258701, Call Date: July 1978 (Gray's
Inn)

Marshall *Christopher Allen*
Call Date: Nov 1968 (Inner Temple)
Qualifications: MA, LLB (Cantab)

Marshall *Miss Hannah Louise*
Call Date: Oct 1998 (Gray's Inn)
Qualifications: LLB

Marshall *Ms Joanna Tamar*
Legal Adviser, Norton Rose, Kempson
House, Camomile Street, London
EC3A 7AN, 0171 444 2531, Call Date:
Nov 1990 (Middle Temple)
Qualifications: BA (Cantab), Dip
European Law,, Bruges

Marshall *Mrs Katherine Jane*
Legal Team Manager, Berkshire &
Oxfordshire, Magistrates Courts
Committee, Easby House, Northfield
End, Henley, Oxon RG9 2NB, 01491
412720, Fax: 01491 412762, Call Date:
July 1983 (Inner Temple) Qualifications:
D.M.S.

Marshall *Miss Nicola Jane*
Call Date: Oct 1991 (Middle Temple)

Marshall *Sir Roy*
Kirk House, Kirk Croft, Cottingham, East
Yorkshire HU16 4AU, 01482 847413,
Fax: 01482 847413, and Member
Barbados Bar Jamaican Bar, Call Date:
Jan 1947 (Inner Temple) Qualifications:
MA, PhD, LLD (Hon), D.Litt (Hon)

Marshall *Ms Susan Elizabeth*
Bursar, Exeter College, Oxford OX1 3DP,
01865 279649, Fax: 01865 279630, Call
Date: Nov 1978 (Middle Temple)
Qualifications: MA

Marshall Bain Miss Lydia Esther
Call Date: Mar 1998 (Lincoln's Inn)
Qualifications: LLB (Hons)

Marson Mrs Patricia Ann
Stocks Tree, Preston Wynne,
Herefordshire HR1 3PB, Call Date: Nov
1980 (Middle Temple) Qualifications:
LLB (Leeds)

Marston Dr Geoffrey
Fellow of Sidney Sussex CollegeLecturer
in Law, University of Cambridge, Sidney
Sussex College, Cambridge CB2 3HU,
01223 338800, Fax: 01223 338884,
Call Date: July 1993 (Middle Temple)
Qualifications: LLB (Hons), LLM &,
Ph.D

Marston-Parchment Ms Murziline
Call Date: Nov 1989 (Inner Temple)
Qualifications: LLB (So'ton)

Martin Miss Abie Margaret
Call Date: Oct 1996 (Lincoln's Inn)
Qualifications: LLB (Hons) (Leic)

Martin Sir Bruce
Call Date: Feb 1960 (Middle Temple)
Qualifications: LLB (L'pool)

Martin Christopher Leonard •
Company Secretary, Avon Rubber Plc,
Manvers House, Kingston Road,
Bradford-on-Avon, Wilts BA15 1AA,
01225 861100, Fax: 01225 861195,
Call Date: Feb 1967 (Gray's Inn)
Qualifications: LLB (Nott'm)

Martin Dennis James
Justices' Chief Executive, 15 Newland,
Lincoln LN1 1XE, 01522 514200, Call
Date: Nov 1978 (Gray's Inn)
Qualifications: B.A.

Martin Edward James
Call Date: July 1983 (Lincoln's Inn)

Martin Mrs Elizabeth Anne •
Principal Crown Prosecutor, Crown
Prosecution Service, CPS Humber,
Greenfield House, 39 Scotland Street,
Sheffield S3 7DQ, 0114 291 2000, Call
Date: Nov 1984 (Middle Temple)
Qualifications: LLB (Hons)

Martin Gerard •
Senior Crown Prosecutor, Crown
Prosecution Service, Solar House, 1-9
Romford House, Stratford, London
E15 4LJ, 0181 534 6601, Fax: 0181
522 1236, Call Date: July 1986 (Gray's
Inn) Qualifications: LLB (Lond)

Martin Henry
3 Westmount Park, Newtownards,
Northern Ireland BT23 4BP, Northern
Ireland, 01247 819809, Call Date: July
1971 (Inner Temple) Qualifications:
LLB, FCA

Martin Miss Rachael Christina
Kirkpatrick Solcitiors, 24B High Street,
Huntingdon, Cambs, 01480 459531,
Solicitor (1998), Call Date: Nov 1991
(Inner Temple) Qualifications: BA
(Sussex)

Martin Robert Marshall
Call Date: July 1978 (Gray's Inn)

Martin Miss Susannah Nicole •
Legal Officer, Treasury Solicitor's Dept,
Queen Anne's Chambers, 28 Broadway,
London SW1H 9JS, 0171 210 3197,
Fax: 0171 210 3433, Call Date: Oct
1996 (Inner Temple) Qualifications:
LLB (Bris)

Martin Mrs Thelma Lynne
Call Date: July 1976 (Inner Temple)

Martin Thomas John
Call Date: July 1998 (Lincoln's Inn)
Qualifications: LLB (Hons)

Martin Captain Timothy Frederick
Wilkins •
Cdr RNSS, HMS Raleigh, Torpoint,
Cornwall PL11 2PD, Call Date: July
1985 (Gray's Inn) Qualifications: LLB
(Cardiff)

Martindale Peter Edward
Call Date: Oct 1997 (Middle Temple)
Qualifications: BA (Hons) (Lond), CPE
(Sussex)

Martine Giselle Clare
Shearsby House, Shearsby,
Leicestershire LE17 6PN, 0116
2478644, Fax: 0116 2478057, Call
Date: July 1977 (Middle Temple)
Qualifications: BA

Martyn Peter Leyshon
Call Date: Nov 1950 (Lincoln's Inn)
Qualifications: LLB (Lond)

Martyn Tristram Ralph
Pauntley, 13 Upland Rd, Eastbourne,
East Sussex BN20 8EN, 01323 723642,
Hon.Fellow, College of Estate
Management, Call Date: Nov 1965
(Middle Temple) Qualifications: LLB,
DipEd (Lond)

Maryan-Green Neville Ayton
77 bis Avenue de Bieteul, 75015 Paris,
France, and Member Paris Bar 17
Bedford Row, London, WC1R 4EB, Call
Date: Nov 1963 (Middle Temple)
Qualifications: BA LLB (Cantab)

Mascarenhas Clarence Wilfred
Call Date: June 1958 (Lincoln's Inn)

Mashhadi Ahsan Hussain
Lecturer in Law, City & Islington
College, 45 Courtney Road, Colliers
Wood, London SW19 2EE, 0181 544
0347, Call Date: July 1980 (Lincoln's
Inn) Qualifications: LLB (Hons),, LLM
(Lond), Cert Ed (Dist)

Mason James Stephen •
Counsel to the Speaker, House of
Commons, London SW1A OAA, 0171
219 3776, Call Date: Oct 1958 (Middle
Temple) Qualifications: MA, BCL

Mason Revd. Nigel James
The Church Flat, Wilbury Road, Hove,
East Sussex BN3 3PB, Call Date: Nov
1987 (Inner Temple) Qualifications:
Dip Law

Mason Philip Jude •
Assistant Director (Legal), Norwich City
Council, St Peters Street, Norwich,
Norfolk, Call Date: July 1975 (Gray's
Inn) Qualifications: BA

Mason Stephen Charles Winston
Director, Legal Education, Ivel Meads
Legal Services Ltd, 19A Church Street,
Langford, Biggleswade, Bedfordshire
SG18 9QT, 01462 701098, Fax: 01462
701098, Call Date: Nov 1988 (Middle
Temple) Qualifications: BA (Hons), MA,
LLM, PGCE (FE)

Massam Arthur David Wright •
80a Westbury Road, Finchley, London
N12 7PD, 0181 446 1037, Call Date:
Nov 1968 (Inner Temple)
Qualifications: LLB (Lond), FRPharmS

Massey Peregrine Tatton Eyre
Director, Thomas Miller & Co Ltd,
Thomas Miller & Co Ltd, International
House, 26 Creechurch Lane, London
EC3A 5BA, 0171 283 4646, Fax: 0171
621 1782, Call Date: Nov 1975 (Middle
Temple) Qualifications: MA (Cantab)

Matharu Jitinder Singh •
Principal Crown Prosecutor, Crown
Prosecution Service, Colmore Gate, 2
Colmore Row, Birmingham B3 2QA,
0121 629 7200, Fax: 0121 629 7335,
Call Date: July 1981 (Inner Temple)

Mather Miss Alison Elisabeth
Call Date: Oct 1997 (Lincoln's Inn)
Qualifications: BA (Hons)

Mather Steven James
Kingston Law School, Kingston
University, Kingston Hill, Kingston
Upon Thames, Surrey KT2 7LB, 0181
547 7324, Fax: 0181 547 7038, Call
Date: Oct 1997 (Middle Temple)
Qualifications: B.Ed (Hull), Dip Law
(Kingston)

Matin Miss Tahamina
Call Date: Oct 1996 (Lincoln's Inn)
Qualifications: LLB (Hons) (Lond)

Matthews Charles Howard •
Woodhouse, Idsworth, Horndean,
Hampshire, PO8 OAN, 01705 413276,
and Member Supreme Court of New
South Wales, Call Date: July 1976
(Middle Temple) Qualifications: BSc
(Eng), C Eng, MIEE

Matthews Mrs Emma Elizabeth •
The Lord Chancellor's Dept, Selborne
House, 54-60 Victoria Street, London
SW1E 6QW, Call Date: Nov 1987 (Inner
Temple) Qualifications: BA (Cantab)

Matthews Miss Keirumetse Seipelo
Thandeka •
Call Date: July 1982 (Middle Temple)
Qualifications: BA

Matthews Mrs Margaret Louise
Lecturer, Exeter College, Call Date: July
1988 (Middle Temple) Qualifications:
LLB (Hons) (Lond)

Matthews *Paul Justin*
Call Date: Nov 1993 (Gray's Inn)
Qualifications: BA (Sheff)

Matthews *Paul William*
Call Date: Nov 1996 (Lincoln's Inn)
Qualifications: LLB (Hons)(L'pool)

Matthias *Mrs Sarah Elizabeth*
Call Date: Nov 1988 (Middle Temple)
Qualifications: MA (Oxon)

Maurice *Jack* •
Head of Ethics & Legal Services, Institute
of Chartered, Accountants in England &
Wales, Gloucester House, 399 Silbury
Boulevard, Central Milton Keynes
MK9 2HL, 01908 546283, Fax: 01908
546271, Call Date: May 1957 (Gray's
Inn) Qualifications: MA (Cantab)

Maurice-Williams *Miss Harriet Elizabeth*
Anne
Call Date: Nov 1997 (Middle Temple)
Qualifications: BA (Hons)(Lond)

Maxted *Timothy Paul*
Call Date: Mar 1999 (Lincoln's Inn)
Qualifications: LLB (Hons)(Leics)

Maxwell-Scott *Miss Annabel Jane*
Call Date: Oct 1996 (Inner Temple)
Qualifications: BSc (Bris), CPE (Lond)

Maxwell-Smith *Miss Shelley Louise*
Call Date: July 1998 (Inner Temple)
Qualifications: BA (Dunelm)

May *James Nicholas Welby*
Director General, UK Offshore Operators
Assoc, 30 Buckingham Gate, London
SW1E 6NN, 0171 802 2400, Fax: 0171
802 2401, Call Date: July 1974
(Lincoln's Inn) Qualifications: BSc

Maycock *Miss Tania Jane*
Call Date: Nov 1993 (Inner Temple)
Qualifications: BA, CPE

Maydon *Gary*
Masons Solicitors, 30 Aylesbury
Solicitors, London EC1R 0ER, 0171 490
6207, Fax: 0171 490 2545, Partnership
Secretary, Masons Solicitors, Call Date:
July 1996 (Middle Temple)
Qualifications: LLB (Hons)(Lond), FCIS,
FCIB, FFA

Mayer *Alexander Timothy*
Call Date: 1997 (Gray's Inn)
Qualifications: BA, BCL (Oxon)

Mayer *Mrs Jane Carolyn Stafford* •
Principal Crown Prosecutor, Crown
Prosecution Service, 2nd Floor,
Blackburn House, The Midway,
Newcastle-U-Lyme, Staffs, Call Date: Nov
1966 (Lincoln's Inn) Qualifications: LLB
(B'ham)

Mayer *Mrs Nancy Elaine* •
Senior Lawyer, HM Customs & Excise,
Ralli Quays West, Stanley Street, Salford,
Manchester M60 9LB, 0161 839 7839,
Call Date: Nov 1983 (Middle Temple)
Qualifications: LLB (Nott'm)

Mayhew of Twysden *The Rt Hon Lord*
House of Lords, London SW1A 0PW,
0171 219 3000, 1 Temple Gardens, 1st
Floor, Temple, London, EC4Y 9BB, Call
Date: June 1955 (Middle Temple)
Qualifications: MA (Oxon)

Mayhew-Arnold *Michael Charles John* •
Director, Henry Ansbacker & Co Limited,
One Mitre Square, London EC3A 5AN,
0171 283 2500, Fax: 0171 626 5372,
Call Date: Nov 1983 (Inner Temple)
Qualifications: LLB (Hons) (So'ton)

Maynard *Mrs Jane Anne*
House Editor, Butterworths, 52 Linwood
Close, Grove Park, London SE5 8UU, Call
Date: Oct 1994 (Inner Temple)
Qualifications: BA (Hons)(Keele)

Maynard *Michael John* •
Senior Principal Legal Officer, Treasury
Solicitors Dept, Queen Anne's Chambers,
28 Broadway, London, 0171 210 3041,
Call Date: July 1984 (Middle Temple)
Qualifications: BA (Hons)

Mayne *Miss Caroline Margaret* •
Head of Litigation Team, Lloyds of
London, 1 Lime Street, London EC3,
0171 327 6955, Fax: 0171 327 5502,
Call Date: Nov 1984 (Inner Temple)
Qualifications: LLB Hons (Leics)

Mazzawi *Prof Musa Elias*
Lane House, Mortimer, Reading, Berks
RG7 3PP, 01189 332897, Fax: 01189
331501, Call Date: Nov 1950 (Gray's
Inn) Qualifications: LLM, PhD (Lond)

McAleer *Dominic Alphonsus*
Call Date: Nov 1989 (Gray's Inn)
Qualifications: BA [Oxon]

McArdle *Kevin Edward* •
Legal Officer, Merck Sharp & Dohme
Limited, Hertford Road, Hoddesdon,
Hertfordshire EN11 9BU, 01992 452509,
Fax: 01992 470189, Call Date: Nov 1989
(Middle Temple) Qualifications: BSc,
LLB

McAvock *Captain Gabrielle* •
55 Temple Chambers, Temple Avenue,
London, EC4Y 0HP, Call Date: Oct 1994
(Lincoln's Inn) Qualifications: LLB
(Hons)(Lond)

McBride *Martin Peter*
Call Date: Oct 1994 (Lincoln's Inn)
Qualifications: LLB (Hons)(Plymouth)

McCabe *Adrian Thomas*
Call Date: May 1994 (Inner Temple)
Qualifications: BA, LLB

McCabe *Matthew Mel* •
Acting Assistant Branch Crown
Prosecutor, Crown Prosecution Service,
3rd Floor, Government Blgs, Bromyard
Avenue, Acton, London W3 7AY, Call
Date: Nov 1973 (Lincoln's Inn)
Qualifications: LLB (Cantab)

McCabe *Robert Stuart*
Sony, 25 Golden Square, London
W1R 6LU, 0171 533 1481, Fax: 0171 533
1488, Vice President Finance Group -
Sony Corporation of America, Call Date:
Nov 1988 (Inner Temple) Qualifications:
BA (Dunelm), ACA, ATII

McCahon *David John* •
Senior Legal Assistant, Consumer and
Retail Finance Group, Cameron
McKenna, Mitre House, 160 Aldersgate
Street, London EC1A 4DD, 0171 367
3000, Fax: 0171 367 2000, Call Date:
July 1988 (Middle Temple)
Qualifications: LLB (Hons) (Reading),
LLM (Cantab)

McCall *Miss Lynnsey Jane*
Call Date: Nov 1996 (Gray's Inn)
Qualifications: LLB (Leeds)

McCance *John Neill*
Brook Farm, Bramley Road, Silchester,
Reading, Berks RG7 2LJ, 01256 881383,
Fax: 01256 880985, Call Date: July 1952
(Inner Temple) Qualifications: MA
(Oxon)

McCandlish *John Gordon*
Former Solicitor, Call Date: Oct 1995
(Gray's Inn)

McCann *Miss Mary Brigid*
Call Date: July 1995 (Gray's Inn)
Qualifications: BA (Middx)

McCarroll *John Michael*
Call Date: Oct 1997 (Gray's Inn)
Qualifications: LLB (Wales)

McCarthy *Miss Mary Patricia Nodlaig*
Irish Barrister, and Member Southern
Ireland Bar, Call Date: Feb 1988 (Inner
Temple) Qualifications: BL, LLB
(Dublin)

McCartin *John*
Call Date: Nov 1989 (Inner Temple)
Qualifications: BA (Kent)

McCleave *Miss Ingrid Anne*
Call Date: Oct 1995 (Lincoln's Inn)
Qualifications: LLB (Hons)

McClellan *Anthony*
Formerly Principal Legal Advisor,
European Commission, Brussels., Call
Date: Nov 1958 (Inner Temple)

McClelland *Ms Sara Louise* •
The Home Office, 50 Queen Anne's Gate,
London SW1H 9AT, Call Date: Nov 1992
(Middle Temple) Qualifications: BA
(Hons) & BCL, (Oxon)

McCloskey *Conor Martin*
Call Date: Oct 1996 (Inner Temple)
Qualifications: LLB (N. Lond)

McCombie-Lawrence *Miss Alison Maria*
Call Date: Nov 1993 (Inner Temple)
Qualifications: LLB

McConochie *Mark Lea*
Call Date: Nov 1996 (Middle Temple)
Qualifications: BPharm (Hons)

McConomy *Paul*
Call Date: July 1997 (Inner Temple)
Qualifications: LLB (Leics)

McCormac *Kevin Francis*
Justices' Chief Executive, West Sussex
Magistrates, West Sussex Magistrates
Courts, Sussex Chambers, 5 Liverpool
Terrace, Worthing, West Sussex
BN11 1TA, 01903 232218, Fax: 01903
214778, Call Date: July 1974 (Gray's
Inn) Qualifications: MA (Oxon)

McCorry *Miss Helen Joanne*
Call Date: Oct 1997 (Lincoln's Inn)
Qualifications: LLB (Hons)(Lond)

McCrory *Miss Amanda Jayne*
Call Date: May 1996 (Inner Temple)
Qualifications: LLB

McCrudden *Dr John Christopher*
Fellow, Lincoln College, Oxford Reader
in Law, Oxford University, Lincoln
College, Oxford OX1 3DR, (01865)
279772, Fax: (01865) 279802, Call
Date: May 1996 (Gray's Inn)
Qualifications: LLB (Belfast), LLM
(Yale), MA (Oxon), D.Phil (Oxon)

McDermott *Norman*
Call Date: Oct 1998 (Lincoln's Inn)
Qualifications: LLB (Hons)(Teesside)

McDonagh *Peter Martin Michael* •
Prosecution Team Leader, Crown
Prosecution Service, Leicestershire
Branch, Princes Court, 34 York Road,
Leicester LE1 5TU, 0116 2549333, Call
Date: July 1981 (Inner Temple)
Qualifications: LLB

McDonald *Adrian Clive*
Call Date: Feb 1995 (Inner Temple)
Qualifications: BA, LLM (Edin)

McDonald *David*
Deputy Clerk to the Justices, Bedford
Magistrates Court, Shire Hall, St Paul's
Square, Bedford MK40 1SQ, 01234
359422, Fax: 01234 354515, Call Date:
Nov 1985 (Gray's Inn) Qualifications:
Diploma Mag Law, Diploma in ,
Management Studies

McDonald *David*
Call Date: Nov 1998 (Lincoln's Inn)
Qualifications: LLB (Hons)(Middx)

McDonald *Miss Eileen Rebecca*
Call Date: Feb 1993 (Inner Temple)
Qualifications: LLB (Wolver'ton)

McDonald *Miss Gail Marie*
Osborne Clarke, 50 Queen Charlotte
Street, Bristol BS1 4HE, 0117 984
5300, Fax: 0117 925 9798, Call Date:
July 1986 (Middle Temple)
Qualifications: LLB (B'ham)

McDonald *Miss Julie Anne Marie*
Welfare Advisor, Benefits Section,
Elmbridge Borough Council, Civic
Centre, High Street, Esher, Surrey
KT10 9SD, 01372 474292, Fax: 01372
474936, Call Date: Nov 1996 (Gray's
Inn) Qualifications: LLB (Kent)

McDonald *Junior Lloyd*
Call Date: Nov 1998 (Middle Temple)
Qualifications: LLB (Hons)(Lond)

McDonald *Lawrence Patrick*
Call Date: Oct 1996 (Inner Temple)
Qualifications: LLB (Lond)

McDonald *Ms Susan Michelle* •
Legal Advisor, Sun Life Assurance
Society, 107 Cheapside, London
EC2V 0DU, 0171 606 7788, Call Date:
Nov 1993 (Lincoln's Inn)
Qualifications: BA (Hons), LLM

McDonnell *Martin James*
Call Date: Oct 1997 (Middle Temple)
Qualifications: LLB (Hons)(Lond)

McDonnell *Captain Scott* •
Legal Officer, Directorate of Army Legal,
Services, Trenchard Lines, Upavon,
Pewsey, Wiltshire SN9 6BE, Call Date:
Oct 1994 (Middle Temple)
Qualifications: BA (Hons), CPE
(Bournemouth)

McDougall *Jamie*
Call Date: Mar 1999 (Inner Temple)
Qualifications: BA (Exon), CPE (City)

McElhatton *Miss Ita Louise Patricia*
10 Foxes Dale, Blackheath, London
SE3 9BA, Call Date: Nov 1993 (Gray's
Inn) Qualifications: B.Sc (Salford)

McElroy *Miss Josephine Ann*
Call Date: Feb 1995 (Inner Temple)
Qualifications: BSc (Ulster), CPE
(Middx)

McEneny *Greg Martin*
Freshfields, 65 Fleet Street, London
EC4Y 1HS, 0171 832 7285, Fax: 0171
832 7001, Call Date: Nov 1995 (Middle
Temple) Qualifications: BA
(Hons)(Sheff), Dip Law

McEntee *Francis Richard* •
Senior Crown Prosecutor, Crown
Prosecution Service, Calder House, St
James's Street, Burnley, Lancashire,
Call Date: July 1987 (Inner Temple)
Qualifications: LLB

McEntegart *Francis Lee*
Call Date: Nov 1998 (Gray's Inn)
Qualifications: LLB (L'pool)

McEvedy *Miss Flora Helen*
Call Date: Oct 1995 (Inner Temple)
Qualifications: LLB (City), BA (Oxon)

McEwen *Miss Ruth Elizabeth* •
Legal Adviser Grade 7, DSS, New Court,
48 Carey Street, London WC2A 2LS,
0171 412 1492, Fax: 0171 412 1523,
Call Date: Oct 1992 (Middle Temple)
Qualifications: MA (Hons, St.Andrews,
Diploma in Law(City)

McFarlane *Miss Marcia Pamela* •
Lawyer, Call Date: Feb 1990 (Lincoln's
Inn) Qualifications: LLB Hons

McGee *Professor Andrew*
Professor of Law, Call Date: Nov 1998
(Lincoln's Inn) Qualifications: BA, BCL
(Oxon)

McGee *Miss Kathryn C* •
Oxfordshire County Council, New Road,
Oxford, Call Date: Nov 1978 (Middle
Temple) Qualifications: BA (Sussex)

McGee *Terence Alfred Francis*
2 Frensham Way, Pewsey, Wiltshire
SN9 5HA, 01672 564641, Fax: 01672
564631, Call Date: Nov 1959 (Gray's
Inn) Qualifications: LLB, FCIS

McGibbon *Eric John Wallace* •
Legal Adviser, The Post Office, Legal
Services, Impact House, 2 Edridge
Road, Croydon CR9 1PJ, 0181 681
9025, Fax: 0181 681 9334, Call Date:
July 1978 (Gray's Inn) Qualifications:
LLB (Lond)

McGibbon *Miss Susanna Justine* •
Legal Adviser, Call Date: Nov 1990
(Lincoln's Inn) Qualifications: LLB
(Sheff)

McGill *John Gerard Antony*
Call Date: July 1992 (Lincoln's Inn)
Qualifications: LLB (Hons), Bsc ACIArb

McGinty *Kevin Charles Patrick* •
Legal Adviser, Legal Secretariat to the
Law, Officers, 9 Buckingham Gate,
London SW1E 6JP, 0171 271 2412,
Fax: 0171 271 2434, and Member
Northern Ireland Bar, Call Date: July
1982 (Gray's Inn) Qualifications: BA

McGirl *Barry John* •
Lawyer, CPS (Midlands), St George's
House, Lever Street, Wolverhampton
WV2 1EZ, 01902 870900, Fax: 01902
871570, Call Date: July 1974 (Gray's
Inn) Qualifications: BA (Oxon)

McGirr *Eoin*
Call Date: Nov 1997 (Gray's Inn)
Qualifications: BA (Nott'm)

McGlyne *John Edward*
Call Date: May 1993 (Gray's Inn)
Qualifications: LLB (Lond)

McGonigal *Miss Rachel*
Call Date: Oct 1991 (Lincoln's Inn)
Qualifications: BA (Hons), Dip Law

McGowan *James*
Call Date: July 1998 (Middle Temple)
Qualifications: LLB (Hons)(L'pool)

McGrath *Simon James*
Holman Fenwick & Willan Sols, Call
Date: Oct 1995 (Inner Temple)
Qualifications: MA (Edinburgh), CPE
(City)

McGrath *Miss Siobhan Evelyn* •
P/T Chair, Social Security Appeals
Tribunal, Arden Chambers, 27 John
Street, London, WC1N 2BL, Call Date:
July 1982 (Middle Temple)
Qualifications: BA (Sussex)

McGuinness *Robin Michael*
Call Date: Oct 1995 (Gray's Inn)
Qualifications: B.Sc

• Barrister in employment

McHaffie *Malcolm Bruce* •
Senior Crown Prosecutor, Crown
Prosecution Service, Bow Street Branch,
4th Floor, 50 Ludgate Hill, London
SW1E 5BH, 0171 273 8000, Fax: 0171
915 5850, Call Date: Oct 1991 (Lincoln's
Inn) Qualifications: LLB (Hons) (Birm)

McHale *Henry*
Call Date: Nov 1969 (Inner Temple)
Qualifications: MA (Cantab)

McHenry *Brian Edward* •
Senior Civil Service Lawyer., Currently
Solicitor to the the BSE Inquiry, Treasury
Solicitors Department, Queen Anne's
Chambers, 28 Broadway, London SW1,
0171 210 3000, Call Date: July 1976
(Middle Temple) Qualifications: MA
(Oxon)

McHugo *Christopher Benedict* •
Head of Taxation, Assoc of British
Insurers, 51 Gresham Street, London
EC2V 7HQ, 0171 216 7620, Fax: 0171
696 8997, Call Date: Nov 1978 (Middle
Temple) Qualifications: MA (Oxon),FCA

McIlroy *Mrs Rosemary* •
Senior Crown Prosecutor, Crown
Prosecution Service, 1-2 York Place,
Scarborough, North Yorkshire, 01723
500206, Call Date: July 1981 (Lincoln's
Inn) Qualifications: LLB (Hons) (Leeds)

McInnes *Richard Bishop*
24 Heritage Way, Cleveleys FY5 3BD, Call
Date: July 1971 (Middle Temple)
Qualifications: MA

McIntosh *Milton Pyxlie*
Members of RICS Practice Panel on
Dilapidations, Call Date: Nov 1994
(Lincoln's Inn) Qualifications: BSc
(Hons), ARICS, ACIArb

McIntyre *David John Christopher* •
Assistant Solicitor, HM Customs &
Excise, New King's Beam House, Upper
Ground, London SE1, Call Date: July
1976 (Gray's Inn) Qualifications: LLB
(Lond)

McKee *Miss Katherine*
Call Date: Nov 1998 (Middle Temple)
Qualifications: BA (Hons) (Nott'm), MA
(Essex), Dip Law

McKee *Richard Anthony*
Imigration Advisory Service, Tribunal
Unit, Third Floor, County House, 190
Great Dover Street, London SE1 4YB,
0171 967 1227, Eldon Chambers, Fourth
Floor, 30/32 Fleet Street, London, EC4Y
1AA, Call Date: Oct 1991 (Inner Temple)
Qualifications: MA (Cantab), MA (Lond)

McKenna *Mrs Alison Jayne* •
Mental Health Act Commissioner, Charity
Commission, Woodfield House, Tanger,
Taunton, Somerset TA1 4BL, 01823
345000, Fax: 01823 345002, Call Date:
July 1988 (Middle Temple)
Qualifications: LLB

McKenna *Ms Mariead Maria* •
Legal Director, Cendant Business
Answers, (Europe) PLC, PHH Centre,
Windmill Hill, Whitehill Way, Swindon
SN5 9YT, 01793 884706, Fax: 01793
886056, Irish Barrister and Member
Ireland, Call Date: July 1992 (Gray's Inn)
Qualifications: BCL

McKenny *Simon Edward*
James R Knowles, Wardle House, King
Street, Knutsford, Cheshire WA16 6PD,
01565 654666, Fax: 01565 755009, Call
Date: Feb 1991 (Lincoln's Inn)
Qualifications: BSc , LLB (Lond), ARICS,
ACIArb

McKenzie *Mrs Dulcibel Edna Jenkins*
89 Cornwall Gardens, London SW7 4AX,
0171 5847674/01243 512411, Fax: 0171
5847674, Call Date: July 1967 (Lincoln's
Inn) Qualifications: BA, DIP Ed (Lond)

McKeon *Ms Caroline*
1 Pump Court, Lower Ground Floor,
Temple, London, EC4Y 7AB, Call Date:
Nov 1983 (Inner Temple) Qualifications:
BA

McKeown *Miss Jennifer*
Call Date: Oct 1994 (Gray's Inn)
Qualifications: LLB, LLM

McKevitt *Miss Una Frances*
Legal Adviser, McCann Fitzgerald
Solicitors, St Michael's House, 1 George
Yard, Lombard Street, London
EC3U 9DH, 0171 621 1000, Fax: 0171
621 9000, Call Date: Oct 1995 (Inner
Temple) Qualifications: LLB (Manc)

McKibbin *Robert*
29 Brookfield, Weald Hall Lane,
Thornwood, Epping, Essex CM16 6NG,
01992 560 348, Chartered Architect, Call
Date: July 1997 (Middle Temple)
Qualifications: BSc (Belfast), MSc
(Lond), RIBA, FCIArb

McKie *Miss Suzanne Elizabeth*
Fox Williams, City Gate House, 39-45
Finsbury Square, London EC2A 1UU,
0171 628 2000, Fax: 0171 628 2100,
Call Date: Nov 1991 (Inner Temple)
Qualifications: LLB (Notts)

McLachlan *Ewan* •
Senior Crown Prosecutor, Crown
Prosecution Service, Windsor House, 10
Manchester Road, Bradford, 01274
742530, Call Date: July 1984 (Gray's
Inn) Qualifications: LLB (Leeds)

McLachlan *Paul Robert*
Call Date: Oct 1996 (Middle Temple)
Qualifications: BA (Hons) (Oxon), CPE
(Westminster)

McLachlan *Stuart Munro* •
Senior Crown Prosecutor, 2 Bedford
Park, Croydon CR0 2AP, 9 King's Bench
Walk, Ground Floor, Temple, London,
EC4Y 7DX, Call Date: July 1982 (Gray's
Inn) Qualifications: LL.B (Nottingham)

McLean *Mrs Helen Lavinia Freda Allen*
The Gnomon, Cuttinglye Rd, Crawley
Down, West Sussex RH10 4LR, 01342
712432, Call Date: Nov 1951 (Middle
Temple) Qualifications: MA (Oxon)

McLean *Ms Isabella*
Call Date: Nov 1997 (Lincoln's Inn)
Qualifications: LLB (Hons), LLM,
(Essex)

McLean *Mrs Joanne Mary*
Former Solicitor, Call Date: July 1996
(Inner Temple) Qualifications: BSc

McLean *Miss Suzanne Victoria* •
Director of legal Affairs and Company
Secretary, Biocompatibles International,
PLC, Frensham House, Farnham
Business Park, Weydon Lane ,Farnham
Surrey, 01252 732640, Fax: 01252
732699, Call Date: July 1979 (Gray's
Inn) Qualifications: BA

McLeish *Ms Jennifer Kerr*
Call Date: Oct 1993 (Gray's Inn)
Qualifications: BA

McLeod *Ms Geraldine Fiona*
Call Date: July 1981 (Inner Temple)
Qualifications: BSc, MA

McLoughlin *Miss Catherine Mary* •
Office of the Solicitor, DSS/DH, New
Court, 48 Carey Street, London
WC2A 2LS, 0171 962 8000, Fax: 0171
412 1227, Call Date: Nov 1994 (Middle
Temple) Qualifications: BA (Oxon),
M.Phil (Cantab)

McLoughlin *Ms Joan* •
Grade 6, Health and Safety Executive,
Rose Court, 2 Southwark Bridge, London
SE1 9HS, 0171 717 6000, Call Date: Nov
1984 (Middle Temple) Qualifications:
BSc,MSc, Dip Law

McLoughlin *Sean Francis*
Call Date: Oct 1996 (Gray's Inn)
Qualifications: BSc (Lond)

McLusky *Nigel John Cooper*
Recorder, Kerris Vean, Old Church Road,
Mawnan, Falmouth TR11 5HX, Call Date:
Nov 1960 (Middle Temple)
Qualifications: LLB

McLusky *Torquil Corbett*
Call Date: Nov 1994 (Inner Temple)
Qualifications: BA (Lond), CPE
(Wolverhampton)

McMahon *Miss Andrea Elizabeth*
Call Date: Mar 1998 (Middle Temple)
Qualifications: LLB (Hons)

McMahon *Andrew Neil McIntyre*
Call Date: Nov 1998 (Middle Temple)
Qualifications: LLB (Hons) (Lond)

McMahon *Miss Jacynta Elizabeth Mary*
Call Date: Nov 1994 (Middle Temple)
Qualifications: BA (Hons)

McMahon *Miss Kathleen Mary*
Call Date: Nov 1998 (Inner Temple)
Qualifications: LLB (East Anglia)

McMath *Miss Clare Mary Astrid*
Deloitte & Touche, Hill House, 1 Little
New Street, London EC4A 3TR, 0171
303 4195, Fax: 0171 583 8517, Call
Date: Oct 1992 (Lincoln's Inn)
Qualifications: BA (Hons) ATII

McMenemy *Simon John*
Assistant, Allen & Overy Solicitors, One
New Change, London EC4M 9QQ, 0171
330 3000, Call Date: Oct 1995 (Inner
Temple) Qualifications: LLB (Lond)

McMillan *Robert Edward*
Call Date: Nov 1998 (Middle Temple)
Qualifications: LLB (Hons) (W'minster

McMinnies *Stephen Mark*
1B Cloudesley Place, Islington, London
N1 0JA, 0171 833 9382 Mobile
telephone 0956 104517, Call Date: Nov
1996 (Gray's Inn) Qualifications: LLB
(Hons) (Lond)

McMorrow *Ms Grainne*
and Member Irish Bar July 1985 New
South Wales Australia, Sydney, Call
Date: July 1989 (Middle Temple)
Qualifications: BA (Hons), LLB (Hons),
BL

McMullan *Miss Adele Maree*
Legal Clerk, Levi & Co Solicitors, First
Floor Deacon House, Seacroft Avenue,
Leeds LS14, Call Date: Nov 1996
(Middle Temple) Qualifications: LLB
(Hons) (Lancs)

McMurray *Edward*
Call Date: Oct 1998 (Middle Temple)
Qualifications: LLB (Kent)

McNally *Joseph George*
Call Date: July 1998 (Middle Temple)
Qualifications: MBA (Aston)

McNamara *Rosemary Cardus*
Call Date: Oct 1994 (Gray's Inn)
Qualifications: BA

McNaught *Peter Godfrey* •
Crown Prosecution Service, 4th Floor,
PO Box 28, Sunlight House, Quay
Street, Manchester M60 3PP, 0161 908
2820, Fax: 0161 908 2784, Call Date:
July 1982 (Middle Temple)
Qualifications: LL.B (B'ham)

McNeely *Gerard Martin*
Call Date: Nov 1998 (Lincoln's Inn)
Qualifications: LLB (Hons) (Sheff)

McNeill *George Kenneth*
Project Manager, Hornagold & Hills,
29-31 Kingston Road, Staines,
Middlesex TW18 4QS, 01784 469930,
Call Date: Oct 1997 (Inner Temple)
Qualifications: LLB (Middlesex),
MCIOB

McNerney *Kevin John* •
Royal College of Nursing, Raven House,
81 Clarendon Road, Leeds LS2 9PJ,
0113 244 4725, Fax: 0113 234 3641,
Call Date: Nov 1992 (Inner Temple)
Qualifications: BA, Dip in Law

McNicholas *Christopher John*
13 Dingle Gardens, Poplar, London
E14 0DN, 0171 538 4339, Fax: 0171
615 2533, Securities Associate-Royal
Bank of Scotland, Call Date: Nov 1995
(Lincoln's Inn) Qualifications: LLB
(Hons), ACIB

McQuaid *Miss Paula*
Call Date: Oct 1993 (Middle Temple)
Qualifications: LLB (Hons)

McRobb *Martin Frederick David* •
Rochdale CPS, 4th Floor, Newgate
House, Newgate, Rochdale OL16 1XA,
01706 352 434, Call Date: Oct 1994
(Gray's Inn) Qualifications: LLB
(Hons)

McShane *Miss Anne*
Call Date: Oct 1992 (Middle Temple)
Qualifications: LLB (Hons, Leic)

McVey *Ms Najma* •
Legal Officer, HM Customs & Excise,
New Kings Beam House, 22 Upper
Ground, London SE1 9PJ, 0171 865
5820, Fax: 0171 865 5502, Call Date:
July 1993 (Lincoln's Inn)
Qualifications: BSc (Glasgow), LLB
(Hons)

McVitie *Miss Justine*
Call Date: Nov 1995 (Inner Temple)
Qualifications: LLB (Lond)

McWilliams *Sir Francis*
Chairman C.E.B.R., Bartlett House,
9-12 Basinghall Street, London
EC2V 5NS, 0171 600 6661, Fax: 0171
600 6671, 1 Atkin Building, Gray's Inn,
London, WC1R 5AT, Call Date: July
1978 (Lincoln's Inn) Qualifications:
BSc Eng, C. (Eng), FICE

Meachem *Stephen John*
Kingsland Chambers, 539b Kingsland
Road, London E8 4AR, 0171 241 6606,
Fax: 0171 241 6606, Affiliate Member
of the Institute of Export, Call Date: July
1993 (Lincoln's Inn) Qualifications:
European Community, Law & Human
Rights, Bar Examination., BA (Hons),
MSc Econ., Diploma in Law

Meacher *Miss Alsion Meryl*
Call Date: Nov 1998 (Lincoln's Inn)
Qualifications: LLB (Jnt Hons) (Wales)

Mead *Geoffrey Hugh*
Call Date: Nov 1993 (Lincoln's Inn)
Qualifications: BA (Hons), BCL

Mead *Larry Frederick*
57 Cavendish Way, Mickleover, Derby,
Derbyshire DE3 5BL, 01332 518397,
Call Date: July 1977 (Lincoln's Inn)
Qualifications: LLB (Lond)

Mead *Miss Vanessa June*
Call Date: Oct 1997 (Middle Temple)
Qualifications: LLB (Hons) (Lond)

Meade *Stephen John*
Call Date: Nov 1997 (Middle Temple)
Qualifications: LLB (Hons) (Manch)

Meadows *Ian James*
Call Date: Mar 1996 (Lincoln's Inn)
Qualifications: LLB (Hons), LLM,
(E.Anglia)

Meager *Miss Karen Margaret* •
Crown Prosecution Service, The
Cooperage, 8 Gainsford Street, London
SE1 2NE, 0171 962 2646, Fax: 0171
378 7539, Call Date: Oct 1992 (Inner
Temple) Qualifications: MA (Cantab),
CPE

Meah *Ashook*
Call Date: May 1997 (Gray's Inn)
Qualifications: BA (Lond), MA (Essex)

Mear *Miss Lynn* •
Legal Adviser, Solicitor's Office, Dept of
Tade & Industry, 10 Victoria Street,
London SW1H 0NN, 0171 215 3000,
Call Date: July 1981 (Gray's Inn)
Qualifications: LLB, DEJF (Limoges)

Medcalf *Jonathan Paul*
Call Date: Nov 1994 (Inner Temple)
Qualifications: LLB (Soton)

Medlock *Andrew Hewitt*
Company Director, 52 Tanbridge Park,
Horsham, West Sussex RH12 1SZ,
01403 257112, Call Date: Nov 1969
(Middle Temple) Qualifications: LLB

Medwynter *Philip Edward* •
Prosecution Team Leader, c/o Crown
Prosecution Service, Marylebone West
London Branch, 50 Ludgate Hill,
London EC4M 7EX, Call Date: Nov 1982
(Middle Temple) Qualifications: LLB
(Hons)

Meechan *Hugh Lawrence*
10 Barnsdale Close, Gt. Easton
LE16 8SQ, Call Date: July 1984 (Inner
Temple) Qualifications: BA (Lond) Dip
Law

Meek *Ian Kingsley*
Winding Wood House, Kintbury,
Hungerford, Berkshire RG17 9RN,
01488 658957, and Member Malaysia
Bar Singapore Bar, Call Date: Jan 1950
(Inner Temple) Qualifications: MA
(Oxon)

Meeke *Colin Wilson* •
Senior Crown Prosecutor, Crown
Prosecution Service, Fox Talbot House,
Bellinger Close, Malmesbury Road,
Chippenham SN15 1BN, 01249
443443, Fax: 01249 440800, Call Date:
July 1983 (Gray's Inn) Qualifications:
BA Leics

Meeres *Mrs Nicola Jane*
Call Date: Nov 1988 (Gray's Inn)
Qualifications: BA

Meeson *Michael Anthony* •
Partnership Secretary, Rowe & Maw,
0171 248 4282, Fax: 0171 248 4282,
Call Date: Nov 1978 (Middle Temple)
Qualifications: MBIM, MBA

Mehta *Ismail*
Head of Legal & Compliance
Department., Call Date: Nov 1984
(Gray's Inn) Qualifications: LLB
(Hons)(Lond)

Mehta *Dr Khurram Alex*
Call Date: Mar 1998 (Lincoln's Inn)
Qualifications: BA (Hons)(Oxon), D.Phil
(Oxon)

Mehta *Mrs Krushavali*
Team Leader, Legal Advisers Team,
Trafford Magistrates' Court, P O Box 13,
Ashton Lane, Sale M33 1UP, 0161 976
3333, Fax: 0161 962 4333, Call Date:
July 1980 (Gray's Inn) Qualifications:
B.A.

Mehta *Sharad Navnitlal*
Call Date: Nov 1959 (Middle Temple)

Mehta *Mrs Smita Durgesh*
Call Date: Nov 1982 (Gray's Inn)
Qualifications: BA

Meigh *Andrew Patrick*
Call Date: Oct 1995 (Lincoln's Inn)
Qualifications: BA (Hons)(Leeds), Dip in
Law (Covent)

Melhuish-Hancock *Simon* •
Senior Legal Adviser, British Steel plc, 15
Marylebone Road, London NW1 5JD,
0171 314 5517, Fax: 0171 314 5622,
Call Date: July 1981 (Gray's Inn)
Qualifications: LLB

Mellish *George Harvey*
Call Date: Oct 1995 (Gray's Inn)
Qualifications: B.Sc

Mello *Michael Joseph*
Justice of Supreme Court of Bermuda,
QC Bermuda (1990) and Member
Bermuda Bar 10 Old Square, Ground
Floor, Lincoln's Inn, London, WC2A 3SU,
Call Date: July 1972 (Gray's Inn)
Qualifications: BA

Mellows *Julian Harvey*
Call Date: Nov 1998 (Lincoln's Inn)
Qualifications: LLB (Hons)(Nott'm)

Melnick *Miss Judith Ann*
Deputy Justices Clerk, Bow Street,
Magistrates Court, 28 Bow Street,
London WC2E 7AS, 0171 379 4713, Call
Date: July 1979 (Middle Temple)
Qualifications: LLB (Lond)

Melville-Brown *Ms Penelope Gillian*
Call Date: July 1989 (Gray's Inn)
Qualifications: BA, DipLaw, PGCE

Melvin *James Warren*
Call Date: Nov 1997 (Inner Temple)
Qualifications: LLB (South Bank)

Mendonca *Mrs Judith Mary*
Call Date: Nov 1989 (Middle Temple)
Qualifications: LLB

Menon *Miss Sumytra*
Call Date: Nov 1993 (Lincoln's Inn)
Qualifications: LLB (Hons, B'ham)

Mensah *Miss Helyn*
Call Date: Oct 1998 (Lincoln's Inn)
Qualifications: LLB (Hons)(Kingston)

Mensah *Miss Lorraine Sonia Louise*
Call Date: Oct 1997 (Gray's Inn)
Qualifications: LLB (L'pool)

Menzies *Robert Anthony*
Corporate Legal Adviser, Greystones, 1
North Court, Nettleham, Lincoln
LN2 2XJ, 01522 754287, Fax: 01522
595515, Call Date: July 1978 (Middle
Temple) Qualifications: F.C.I.S, F.C.IArb

Mercer *Ms Amanda* •
Senior Crown Prosecutor, Crown
Prosecution Service, Tolworth Tower,
Surbiton, Surrey KT6 7DS, Call Date: July
1986 (Inner Temple) Qualifications: LLB

Mercer *Anthony Michael*
Senior Court Clerk, Ashton Under Lyne
Mag Crt, Henry Square, Ashton-u-Lyne,
Manchester OL6 7TP, 0161 330 2023,
Fax: 0161 343 1498, Call Date: Feb 1989
(Middle Temple) Qualifications: LLB
(Hons), DMS

Mercer *Nicholas John*
Incorporated Council of Law, Reporting,
Staple Inn Chambers, 1st Floor, 9 Staple
Inn , Holborn, London, WC1V 7QH, Call
Date: 1994 (Lincoln's Inn)
Qualifications: BA (Hons)(Lond), CPE
(Sussex)

Merchant *Miss Fauzia*
Call Date: Nov 1998 (Lincoln's Inn)
Qualifications: LLB (Hons)(Bucks)

Merchant *Liaquat Habib*
Call Date: Nov 1991 (Gray's Inn)
Qualifications: BA, LLB (Bombay)

Meredith *Stephen Paul*
Call Date: Oct 1995 (Lincoln's Inn)
Qualifications: LLB (Hons)(Wales)

Meredith-Hardy *Michael Francis*
Chairman - Immigration Adjud
Chairman Appeal Board High Court
Examiner. Tribunal Chairman., Radwell
Mill, Baldock, Herts SG7 5ET, Call Date:
Nov 1951 (Inner Temple)

Merrick *Scott Jonathan*
Call Date: Oct 1992 (Lincoln's Inn)
Qualifications: LLB(Hons)

Merrills *Jon Vernon*
Parkdale House, Peveril Drive, The Park,
Nottingham, Call Date: Feb 1986 (Middle
Temple) Qualifications: B.Pharm; BA,
BA(Law)

Merriman *Huw William* •
Legal Advisor, Legal Department, Natwest
Global Financial Mkts, 135 Bishopsgate,
London EC2M 3UR, 0171 375 6378, Call
Date: Oct 1996 (Inner Temple)
Qualifications: BA (Dunelm)

Merritt *Miss Hazel Anne*
Call Date: Oct 1992 (Gray's Inn)
Qualifications: BA

Mertcan *Erol*
Call Date: Nov 1996 (Gray's Inn)
Qualifications: LLB, LLM (LSE)

Messeter *Paul Geoffrey*
ILMCS, 65 Romney Street, London
SW1P 3RD, Call Date: July 1982 (Gray's
Inn) Qualifications: BA

Messeter *Mrs Ulanta Ann*
Court Clerk, Bromley Magistrates Court,
Court House, South Street, Bromley,
Kent BR1 3RD, 0181 4666621, Fax: 0181
4666214, Call Date: Apr 1991 (Gray's
Inn) Qualifications: LLB , B.Ed

Metcalf *Richard James*
Call Date: Nov 1992 (Lincoln's Inn)
Qualifications: LLB (Hons)

Metcalf *Robert Edward* •
Group Legal Adviser, Vision Holdings
(UK) Limited, Albemarle House, 1
Albemarle Street, Mayfair, London
W1X 3HF, 0171 491 9200, Call Date: July
1998 (Lincoln's Inn) Qualifications: BA
(Hons)

Metcalfe *Miss Jacqueline Nellie*
Granby, 27 Godstone Road, Purley,
Surrey CR8 2AN, 0181 660 4588, Call
Date: June 1948 (Inner Temple)

Metcalfe *Noel Percy*
Law Reporter,Editor Criminal Appeal
Reports, 4 Field Court, Gray's Inn,
London, WC1R 5EA, Call Date: July 1952
(Inner Temple) Qualifications: MA
(Cantab)

Metson *Nicholas Richard*
Call Date: Oct 1996 (Inner Temple)
Qualifications: LLB (Dunelm)

Meyrick *George William Owen*
Clifford Chance Solicitors, 200 Aldersgate
Street, London EC1A 4JJ, 0171 600 1000,
Fax: 0171 600 5555, Call Date: Mar 1997
(Lincoln's Inn) Qualifications: BA
(Hons)

Miah *Ahmed*
Call Date: Oct 1998 (Middle Temple)
Qualifications: LLB (Hons)(Lond)

Miah *Anawar Babul*
Raj Bari, Whistlets Close, West Hunsbury,
Northampton NN4 9XB, Call Date: July
1998 (Lincoln's Inn) Qualifications: LLB
(Hons)(Middx)

Miah *Miss Jusna Begum*
Call Date: Nov 1998 (Lincoln's Inn)
Qualifications: LLB (Hons)

Mian *Ms Sminah*
Pinsent Curtis, Dashwood House, 69 Old
Broad Street, London EC2M 1NR, 0171
418 7000, Fax: 0171 418 7050, Call
Date: Oct 1995 (Inner Temple)
Qualifications: LLB (Newcastle)

Michael *Michael* •
Senior Civil Servant, H.M. Customs and
Excise, Solicitor's Office, New King's
Beam House, 22 Upper Ground, London
SE1 9PJ, 0171 865 5205, Fax: 0171 865
5194, Call Date: Nov 1969 (Inner
Temple)

Michaelson *Justin Barrie*
Call Date: 1997 (Lincoln's Inn)
Qualifications: LLB (Hons)(Leeds)

Michell *Charles Henry Wroughton*
1 Gray's Inn Square, 1st Floor, London, WC1R 5AG, Call Date: July 1978 (Lincoln's Inn)

Middleton *Christopher Edward*
Call Date: Oct 1997 (Middle Temple) Qualifications: BSc (Hons) (Kingston), MA (Lond), CPE (Lond)

Middleton *Miss Emma Louise*
Call Date: Nov 1996 (Lincoln's Inn) Qualifications: BA(Jnt Hons) (Dunelm)

Middleton *Timothy John* •
Deputy Legal Adviser, Home Office, 50 Queen Anne's Gate, London SW1H 9AT, 0171 273 3098, Fax: 0171 273 4075, Call Date: July 1977 (Gray's Inn) Qualifications: MA (Oxon)

Midha *Om Parkash*
Call Date: July 1967 (Inner Temple)

Mifsud *Miss Gabrielle Marie*
Call Date: Nov 1997 (Middle Temple) Qualifications: BA (Hons)

Miles *Miss Alice Cecile Vernor*
Call Date: Nov 1994 (Inner Temple) Qualifications: BA (Soton), CPE (City)

Miles *Eric Charles*
Thornhill, Redlands Lane, Ewshot, Farnham, Surrey GU10 5AS, Call Date: Nov 1962 (Gray's Inn) Qualifications: FRAeS

Miles *William Frank*
Clerk to the Justices, Berkshire & Oxfordshire, Magistrates Courts Committee, Easby House, Northfield End, Henley, Oxon RG9 2NB, 01491 412720, Fax: 01491 412762, Call Date: July 1976 (Gray's Inn) Qualifications: LLB (Lond)

Millar *Alexander David Wharton*
Call Date: Nov 1995 (Inner Temple) Qualifications: BA (Cantab), LLM (Illinois, USA)

Millar *Ms Alison Mary*
Call Date: Nov 1995 (Inner Temple) Qualifications: BA (Cantab)

Millar *David Bruce*
Call Date: Nov 1975 (Inner Temple) Qualifications: MA (Oxon)

Millar-Parker *Miss Yvonne*
Call Date: May 1993 (Inner Temple) Qualifications: LLB (Reading)

Millarini *Miss Lucrezia Gaia*
Call Date: Oct 1998 (Inner Temple) Qualifications: LLB (Bris)

Millbrook *Miss Alexandra Maria* •
Legal Manager, Intervention Board Executive, Agency, Kings House, 33 Kings Road, Reading RG1 3BV, 0118 953 1216, Fax: 0118 953 1230, Call Date: July 1987 (Middle Temple) Qualifications: BA (Hons) (Oxon), Dip Law

Milledge *Peter Neil* •
Assistant Director of Legal Services, Solicitor's Office DHSS, New Court, 48 Carey Street, London WC2A 2LS, 0171 412 1343, Fax: 0171 412 1394, Call Date: July 1977 (Middle Temple) Qualifications: LLB (Lond)

Miller *Andrew Paul*
Macfarlanes Solicitors, 10 Norwich Street, London EC4Y 1BD, Solicitor, Call Date: Nov 1995 (Inner Temple) Qualifications: MA (Oxon)

Miller *Miss Anna Belinda*
Call Date: Nov 1996 (Inner Temple) Qualifications: BA (Sussex)

Miller *Anthony Frederick Charles*
31 Cotsford Avenue, New Malden, Surrey KT3 5EU, Call Date: June 1956 (Gray's Inn) Qualifications: BSc, LLB

Miller *Christopher Albert*
Call Date: Oct 1998 (Lincoln's Inn) Qualifications: LLB (Hons) (Sheff)

Miller *Mrs Diana Susan* •
Company Legal Adviser Director (Compliance), Legal & General Assurance, Society Ltd, Legal & General House, St Monica's Road, Kingswood, Tadworth, Surrey KT20 6EU, 01737 370370, Fax: 01737 376240, Call Date: July 1980 (Gray's Inn) Qualifications: LLB

Miller *Miss Jaine Caroline* •
Senior Legal Adviser, Lasmo Plc, 101 Bishopsgate, London EC2M 3XH, 0171 892 9711, Fax: 0171 892 9262, Call Date: Mar 1996 (Lincoln's Inn) Qualifications: LLB (Hons)

Miller *James Edward*
Call Date: Oct 1995 (Middle Temple) Qualifications: LLB (Hons) (Bris), LLM

Miller *John William*
30 Bolent Way, Alverstoke, Gosport, Hants PO12 2NS, 01705 526829, Fax: 01705 366159, Call Date: July 1976 (Middle Temple)

Miller *Mrs Lynne*
Barrister of South Africa, Call Date: Apr 1991 (Middle Temple) Qualifications: BA (South Africa), LLb (South Africa)

Miller *Mrs Maureen Patricia*
Call Date: Oct 1997 (Middle Temple) Qualifications: BA (Hons) (Lond), LLB (Hons) (Lond)

Miller *Nathaniel Thomas*
Call Date: Oct 1994 (Middle Temple) Qualifications: BA (Hons) (Cantab)

Miller *Ronald Kinsman*
Part-time Chairman of VAT & Duties Tribunals, 4 Liskeard Close, Chislehurst, Kent BR7 6RT, Call Date: Nov 1953 (Gray's Inn)

Miller *Stephen David*
Call Date: Oct 1996 (Gray's Inn) Qualifications: LLB (Staffs), MA (Keele)

Millhouse *Mrs Susan Mary*
Call Date: Nov 1996 (Gray's Inn) Qualifications: BA (N.Wales), LLB (E. Anglia)

Milligan *Scott Gregor* •
Dept of Trade and Industry, 10 Victoria Street, London SW1H 0NN, 0171 215 5000, Fax: 0171 215 3221, Call Date: July 1975 (Middle Temple) Qualifications: MA (Oxon)

Millin *Mrs Leslie Marilyn*
Capsticks, 77/83 Upper Richmond Road, London SW15 2TT, 0181 780 2211, Fax: 0181 780 1141, Call Date: Nov 1988 (Gray's Inn) Qualifications: LLB (Reading)

Millington *Trevor John* •
Senior Principal Legal Officer, HM Customs & Excise, New King's Beam House, 22 Upper Ground, London SE1 9PJ, 0171 865 5819, Fax: 0171 865 5902, Call Date: July 1981 (Middle Temple) Qualifications: LLB (Wales)

Mills *Miss Andrea Elaine Susan* •
Call Date: Oct 1991 (Lincoln's Inn) Qualifications: LLB (Hons)

Mills *Dame Barbara Jean Lyon*
72 Albert Street, London NW1 7NR, 0171 388 9206, Fax: 0171 388 3454, QC, Northern Ireland, Call Date: July 1963 (Middle Temple) Qualifications: MA (Oxon)

Mills *George Arthur Charles* •
Case Controller, Serious Fraud Office, Serious Fraud Office, Elm House, 10-16 Elm Street, London WC1X 0BJ, 0171 239 7061, Fax: 0171 833 2443, Call Date: Nov 1987 (Inner Temple) Qualifications: LLB (So'ton), LLM (Lond), M.Phil (Cantab)

Mills *Ms Janet*
Call Date: Mar 1996 (Inner Temple) Qualifications: LLM (Harvard, USA), BA (Hons)

Mills *Mrs Julie Ann* •
Deputy Clerk to the Justices, Bath & Wansdyke Magistrates', Court,, North Parade Road, Bath, Avon BA1 5AF, 01225 463281, Fax: 01225 420255, Call Date: July 1986 (Inner Temple)

Mills *Michael John Patrick*
Hatten Asplin Glenny, 90 Orsett Road, Grays, Essex RM17 5ER, 01375 374851, Fax: 01375 374332, Solicitor of the Supreme Court of England & Wales, Call Date: Oct 1992 (Inner Temple) Qualifications: BA (Hons)

Mills *Peter John*
Manager of Legal & Corporate Services, The Court House, Lichfield Road, Sutton Coldfield B74 2NS, 0121 354 7777, Fax: 0121 355 0547, Call Date: Nov 1983 (Gray's Inn) Qualifications: BA

Mills *Richard Sinclair*
EC Harris, 7-12 Tavistock Square, London WC1H 9LX, 0171 387 8431, Fax: 0171 380 0493, Call Date: July 1994 (Lincoln's Inn) Qualifications: LLB (Hons), BSc,, FRICS

Mills *Miss Sarah Jane*
Call Date: Oct 1995 (Lincoln's Inn) Qualifications: LLB (Hons)(Leic)

Mills *Miss Susan Elizabeth*
Call Date: Mar 1998 (Lincoln's Inn) Qualifications: LLB (Hons)(L'pool)

Millward *Kevin Philip*
Call Date: Oct 1998 (Lincoln's Inn) Qualifications: LLB (Hons)(Derby)

Millward *Mrs Lisa Sarah Liat*
Toad Hall, Marshall's Lane, Sacombe Green, Hertfordshire SG12 0JQ, 01727 868686/ 01920 438877, Fax: 01920 438999, Call Date: Nov 1996 (Lincoln's Inn) Qualifications: LLB (Hons)(Lond)

Milner *Miss Lesley* •
17th Floor, Tolworth Tower, Surbiton, Surrey KT6 7DS, 399-5171, Fax: 390-3474, Call Date: Feb 1992 (Middle Temple) Qualifications: BA (Hon) (Lond), LLB (Hons) (Lond)

Milner *Nicholas Emmanuel*
Call Date: Mar 1996 (Gray's Inn) Qualifications: MA (Edinburgh)

Milner *Ms Victoria Sylvia*
Call Date: Oct 1996 (Gray's Inn) Qualifications: BA (Cantab)

Miltiadou *Miss Frosso*
Call Date: Mar 1996 (Inner Temple) Qualifications: LLB (Manch)

Mimmack *Andrew Elstob*
Clerk to the Justices, East Devon Magistrates', Courts, Exeter Trust House, Blackboy Road, Exeter EX4 6TZ, 01392 270081, Fax: 01392 421525, Call Date: July 1973 (Inner Temple) Qualifications: LLB, MSc

Minchin *Brian Patrick John*
Call Date: June 1959 (Gray's Inn) Qualifications: MA (Cantab)

Minichiello *Miss Andrea Rose*
Call Date: July 1988 (Inner Temple) Qualifications: BA (Wales)

Minns *Miss Tracy Jane*
Assistant Director - Case & Legal Work, Acton for Victims of Medical, Accidents, 44 High Street, Croydon CR0 1YB, 0181 688 9555, Call Date: Nov 1991 (Gray's Inn) Qualifications: MA (Oxon)

Mirrielees *Miss Esther Margaret*
Call Date: Oct 1998 (Inner Temple) Qualifications: LLB (Lond)

Mistlin *Trevor*
Former Solicitor, Call Date: Nov 1996 (Lincoln's Inn) Qualifications: BSc (Hons)(Notts)

Mistry *Mrs Chandraprabha* •
Senior Crown Prosecutor, Crown Prosecution Service, St Albans Branch, Queens House, 58 Victoria Street, St Albans AL1 3HZ, Call Date: July 1976 (Inner Temple)

Mitcalf *Richard James* •
Principal Crown Prosecutor Prosecution Team Leader, Crown Prosecution Service, 7th Floor South, Royal Liver Buildings, Water Street, Liverpool L3 1HN, 01282 412298, Fax: 01282 458097, Call Date: July 1983 (Gray's Inn) Qualifications: BA (Hons)

Mitchell *Anthony Geoffrey Fulton*
Call Date: Feb 1959 (Gray's Inn) Qualifications: LLB

Mitchell *Harry*
Part-time Immigration Adjudicator Trustee, The Migraine Trust Chairman, Sarsen Housing Assoc, The Mount, Brook Street, Great Bedwyn, Marlborough, Wilts SN8 3LZ, 01672 870898, Call Date: July 1968 (Gray's Inn) Qualifications: BA,FCIS

Mitchell *Ian Marcus*
Call Date: Nov 1995 (Lincoln's Inn) Qualifications: B.Eng (Hons)

Mitchell *John Winterburn* •
Principal Crown Prosecutor, Crown Prosecution Service, Crosstrend House, 10A Newport, Loncoln LN1 3DF, 01522 889800, Fax: 01522 889700, Call Date: Nov 1984 (Gray's Inn)

Mitchell *Mrs Karen Joy*
Principle Assistant - Legal, Bolton Magistrates Court, P O Box 24, The Courts, Civic Centre, Bolton BL1 1QX, 01204 522244, Fax: 01204 364373, Call Date: Nov 1982 (Gray's Inn)

Mitchell *Miss Kirsty Ellen*
245 Stanford Road, London SW16 4QH, 0181 679 0915, Call Date: July 1998 (Middle Temple) Qualifications: LLB (Hons)(Teeside)

Mitchell *Paul Martin Selby*
Deputy Clerk to the Justices, The Secretariat, The Court House, Friars Walk, Lewes, East Sussex BN7 2PE, 01273 486455, Call Date: Nov 1986 (Gray's Inn)

Mitchell *Mrs Sally* •
Assistant to the Head of Legal, UKAEA, Marshall Building, B.521 Downs Way, Harwell, Didcot, Oxfordshire OX11 0RA, Counsels' Chambers, 2nd Floor, 10-11 Gray's Inn Square, London, WC1R 5JD, Call Date: Oct 1990 (Inner Temple) Qualifications: LLB

Mitchell *Mrs (Sarah) Felicity Jane* •
Adjudicator, The Office of the Banking, Ombudsman, 70 Gray's Inn Road, London WC1, 0171 404 9944, Call Date: Oct 1992 (Middle Temple) Qualifications: BA (Hons), Dip in Law

Mitchels *David Lloyd*
The Legal Department, U.N.R.A.W., Vienna International Centre, A-1400 Vienna, Austria, and Member Seychelles Bar 14 Tooks Court, Cursitor St, London, EC4A 1LB, Call Date: Nov 1970 (Lincoln's Inn) Qualifications: LLB (Lond)

Mitchiner *James Patrick*
Call Date: Oct 1996 (Middle Temple) Qualifications: BSc (Hons)(Lond), Dip in Law (Notts)

Mitchinson *Mr Robert Charles*
Glovers, Whites Lane, Little Leighs, Chelmsford CM3 1PA, 01245 362472, Fax: 01245 362472, Call Date: Nov 1969 (Gray's Inn) Qualifications: ACIS, FIMgt

Mittelholzer *Neville Arthur*
Call Date: Nov 1967 (Middle Temple)

Miyajima *Miss Mitsue*
8 Welbeck Street, London W1M 7PB, Call Date: July 1997 (Lincoln's Inn) Qualifications: BA (Japan), ACIB, LLDip (Wolves)

Mobsby *Mrs Sheilah Innes*
Call Date: Feb 1965 (Middle Temple) Qualifications: LLB (Exon)

Mochun *Dr Wolodymyr*
11 Seely Road, Nottingham NG7 7NU, Pharmacist, Call Date: Nov 1992 (Inner Temple) Qualifications: BSc, LLB, PhD, MSc, (M.I.P.L), LLM

Mockett *Graham Andrew*
Principal Court Clerk, Feltham Magistrates Court, Hanworth Road, Feltham, Middlesex TW13 5AG, 0181 751 3727, Fax: 0181 844 1779, Call Date: July 1989 (Middle Temple) Qualifications: Dip Law, Dip Mag Law, Diploma in , Management Studies, (DMS)

Moerman *Dr Ellen Ruth*
Call Date: July 1998 (Middle Temple) Qualifications: Licence de Universit, Paul Valery

Moffat *Alexander Peter*
Call Date: Nov 1985 (Lincoln's Inn)

Mohamed *Miss Fathima Shaheeda*
Call Date: Oct 1997 (Gray's Inn) Qualifications: LLB

Mohamedi *Miss Reena* •
Ince & Co, Knollys House, 11 Byward Street, London EC3R 5EN, 0171 623 2011, Fax: 0171 623 3225, Call Date: July 1987 (Middle Temple) Qualifications: BA (Cantab) BS (USA), Georgetown Uni

Mohammed *Asif*
Call Date: July 1997 (Lincoln's Inn) Qualifications: BA (Hons)(Swansea)

Mohammed Razaq *Nawaz*
Call Date: Nov 1998 (Lincoln's Inn) Qualifications: LLB (Hons)(Hull)

Mohindra *Dr Raj Kumar*
Currently Practising Doctor, 89 Albion
Road, Hounslow, Middlesex TW3 3RS,
Call Date: Oct 1991 (Inner Temple)
Qualifications: MA (Cantab), BM Bch
(Oxon), MRCP (UK)

Mohipp *H. Anthony*
Senior Magistrate - Judiciary, 10 Morley
Crescent East, Stanmore, Middlesex
HA7 2LH, and Member Trinidad &
Tobago Bar, Call Date: July 1957
(Middle Temple) Qualifications: LLB

Mokhtiar *Baldev Singh*
Call Date: Nov 1995 (Middle Temple)
Qualifications: LLB (Hons) (Keele)

Molla *Abdur Razzaq*
and Member Bangladesh Bar, Call
Date: Nov 1970 (Inner Temple)
Qualifications: BA, LLB

Molloy *Colin Vincent* •
Principal Crown Prosecutor, Crown
Prosecution Service, St Johns House,
Union Street, Dudley DY2 8PP, 01384
230471, Call Date: Feb 1985 (Middle
Temple) Qualifications: BA (Hons)

Moloney *Miss Louise Claire*
Marlebone Magistrates Court, 181
Marylebone Road, London NW1 5QJ,
Call Date: Nov 1988 (Gray's Inn)
Qualifications: BA

Monaghan *Peter John*
Bench Legal Adviser, Dorset
Magistrates' Court, The Law Courts,
Park Road, Poole, Dorset BH15 2RH,
01305 783891, Call Date: Feb 1986
(Middle Temple) Qualifications: Dip
Mag Law, DMS MIMgt

Monaghan *Miss Sarah Jane*
Call Date: Feb 1995 (Inner Temple)
Qualifications: BA (Keele), CPE

Monah *Miss Helen Anne*
Call Date: Nov 1996 (Lincoln's Inn)
Qualifications: LLB (Hons) (Lond)

Monekosso *Miss Silo Gladys*
Call Date: Nov 1998 (Lincoln's Inn)
Qualifications: LLB (Hons) (Bucks)

Monk *Miss Sheryl Jane* •
Call Date: Nov 1996 (Gray's Inn)
Qualifications: BA (Nott'm)

Monk *Thomas John* •
Legal Adviser, Railpart (UK) Limited, P
O Box 159, Denison House, Doncaster,
South Yorkshire DN4 0DB, Call Date:
July 1976 (Middle Temple)
Qualifications: LLB

Monnington *Bruce Gilbert*
Country Landowners Assoc., 16
Belgrave Square, London SW1X 8PQ,
0171 235 0511, Call Date: July 1989
(Inner Temple) Qualifications: MA
(City), Dip EU Law (Lond)

Monro *Miss Vijaya* •
Senior Crown Prosecutor, Crown
Prosecution Service, St Peter's House,
Gower Street, Derby, 01332 621600,
Call Date: May 1990 (Lincoln's Inn)
Qualifications: BA (Hons)

Montador *Adrien Francis*
Legal Advisor, The Court House,
Elmleigh Road, Havant PO9 2AL, 01252
366083, Fax: 01256 811447, Call Date:
May 1987 (Lincoln's Inn)
Qualifications: LLB (Dundee)

Montague *Major John Charles*
Peamore Cottage, Alphington, Exeter
EX2 9SJ, 01392 832606, Call Date: Nov
1972 (Inner Temple) Qualifications:
AMICE

Montaz-McGowan *Ms Yves-Chantelle*
Call Date: Oct 1998 (Lincoln's Inn)
Qualifications: LLB (Hons) (Lond)

Montgomery *Miss Katrina Lisette*
Call Date: Oct 1998 (Middle Temple)
Qualifications: LLB (Hons) (Lond)

Montgomery *Ms Laura Louise* •
Company Secretary, L L Briggs Limited,
Three Mill Island, Three Mill Lane,
London E3 3DZ, 0181 980 3000, Fax:
0181 980 4544, Call Date: Nov 1992
(Gray's Inn) Qualifications: LLB
(Westminster)

Moody *Miss Joanne Elizabeth*
Call Date: Oct 1998 (Lincoln's Inn)
Qualifications: LLB (Hons) (Leeds)

Moody *John David*
Trainee Solicitor, Simons & Simons, 21
Wilson Street, London, 0171 825 3530,
Call Date: Oct 1996 (Middle Temple)
Qualifications: BA (Hons), LLM (Lond)

Moolla *Umer Faruque*
Call Date: Nov 1994 (Gray's Inn)
Qualifications: LLB

Moorby *Idris James*
Justices' Chief Executive, Weind House
P O Box 717, Parkhill Road, Garstang,
Lancs PR3 1EY, 01995 601596, Fax:
01995 601776, Call Date: Nov 1979
(Gray's Inn) Qualifications: BA, MBA

Moore *Alan*
Justices' Clerk, Justices' Clerk's Office,
Corporation Road, Scunthorpe
DN15 6QB, 01724 281100, Call Date:
Nov 1981 (Inner Temple)

Moore *Miss Caroline Mary Phyllis*
Accredited CEDR Mediator, Lovell White
Durrant, 65 Holborn Viaduct, London
EC1A 2DY, 0171 236 0066, Fax: 0171
248 4212, Call Date: July 1977 (Middle
Temple) Qualifications: BA (Oxon)

Moore *Christopher Peter John* •
Assistant Lawyer, Bridge Information
Systems, Winchmore House, 15 Fetter
Lane, London EC4A 1BW, 44 171 832
9506, Fax: 44 171 583 3900, Call Date:
Oct 1995 (Middle Temple)
Qualifications: B.Sc (Hons) (Dunelm),
Grad Inst P

Moore *Colin*
28 Orchard Court, St Chad's Road,
Leeds LS16 5QS, 0113 274 0900, Fax:
0113 274 0900, Call Date: Nov 1967
(Gray's Inn)

Moore *Derek Edmund*
20 Sussex Street, London SW1V 4RW,
0171 834 5286, Call Date: July 1957
(Gray's Inn) Qualifications: MA

Moore *Dominique Jean* •
Legal Officer, Treasury Solicitor, Queen
Anne's Chambers, 28 Broadway,
London SW1H 9JS, 0171 210 3370,
Fax: 0171 310 3433, Call Date: Oct
1996 (Inner Temple) Qualifications:
BA (Cantab)

Moore *Dudley John*
Law Lecturer, Bellerbys College, 44
Cromwell Road, Hove, Sussex, 01273
723911, Call Date: Oct 1996 (Middle
Temple) Qualifications: BA
(Hons) (Sussex), LLM

Moore *Eric Frank*
Senior Crown Prosecutor (Retired), Call
Date: Nov 1976 (Lincoln's Inn)
Qualifications: LLB (Lond)

Moore *Geoffrey*
Call Date: July 1965 (Gray's Inn)

Moore *Mrs Gillian Patricia*
Court Clerk, The Law Courts, Alexandra
Road, Wimbledon, London SW19 7JP,
0181 946 8622, Fax: 0181 946 7030,
Call Date: Nov 1982 (Gray's Inn)

Moore *Mrs Karen Marie* •
Southwark Council, Strategic Services
Department, Southwark Town Hall, 31
Peckham Road, London SE5 8UB, 0171
525 5000, Call Date: Nov 1992 (Middle
Temple) Qualifications: LLB (Hons)

Moore *Kevin Ryland* •
Redbridge Magistrates Court, The Court
House, 850 Cranbrook Road, Ilford,
Essex IG6 1HW, 0181 551 4461, Call
Date: July 1983 (Lincoln's Inn)
Qualifications: Dip Law (Mag), Adv.Dip
P.T.D., M.I.Mgt

Moore *Matthew James* •
Bureau LEO 5A53, Legal Service,
European Parliamemt, 89-113 Rue
Belliard, B-1047 Bruxelles, Belgium,
Call Date: Nov 1989 (Inner Temple)
Qualifications: BA (Kent)

Moore *Miss Nicola Jean* •
Flight Lieutenant - RAF, RAF Innsworth,
Gloucestershire, Call Date: Nov 1993
(Lincoln's Inn) Qualifications: LLB
(Hons, Bris)

Moore *Mrs Patricia Margaret Waring*
Kirklands, West Street, Odiham, Hook,
Hants RG29 1NT, 01256 703085, Call
Date: May 1953 (Inner Temple)
Qualifications: LLB

Moore *Philip Anthony* •
Senior Crown Prosecutor, Crown
Prosecution Service, The Cooperage, 6
Gainsford Street, London SE1 2NS, Call
Date: July 1971 (Gray's Inn)
Qualifications: BA

Moore *Philton*
Call Date: Nov 1998 (Inner Temple)
Qualifications: LLB (Greenwich)

Moore *Richard John*
Call Date: Oct 1992 (Lincoln's Inn)
Qualifications: BA(Hons)

Moore *Robert Dennis* •
International Legal Manager, Enterprise
Oil Plc, Grand Buildings, Trafalgar
Square, London WC2N 5EJ, 0171 925
4000, Fax: 0171 925 4606, Call Date:
July 1981 (Middle Temple)
Qualifications: BA (Hons)

Moore *Rowland Peter*
Kirklands, West Street, Odiham, Hook,
Hants RG29 1NT, 01256 703085, Call
Date: July 1952 (Lincoln's Inn)
Qualifications: LLB

Moore-Williams *Miss Anne Elizabeth* •
Lawyer (Company & Commercial Team),
Law Commission, Conquest House, 37/
38 John Street, Theobalds Road, London
WC1N 2BQ, 0171 453 1220, Fax: 0171
453 1297, and Member Czech Republic
Bar, Call Date: Oct 1992 (Inner Temple)
Qualifications: BA (Keele), LLM (Lond)

Moorhouse *Brendon Scott* •
Senior Crown Prosecutor, Crown
Prosecution Service, 2nd Floor,
Froomsgate House, Rupert Street, Bristol
BS1 2QS, 0117 9273093, Fax: 0117
9230697, Call Date: Nov 1992 (Middle
Temple) Qualifications: LLB (Hons)

Moosajee *Mrs Aliya Khanum*
Call Date: July 1987 (Middle Temple)
Qualifications: LLB (Lond), LLM (LSE)

Moran *Ms Elena Roberta*
Call Date: Nov 1989 (Inner Temple)
Qualifications: LLB, LLM (UCL)

Moran *Mr. John Michael* •
Regulatory Lawyer, BBC, Call Date: Nov
1995 (Inner Temple) Qualifications: BA
(Oxon), LLM (Berkeley, USA)

Moran *Patrick Michael*
Herbert Smith, Exchange House,
Primrose Street, London EC2A 2HS,
0171 374 8000, Fax: 0171 374 0888,
Call Date: Oct 1997 (Inner Temple)
Qualifications: LLB (Birmingham)

More *Ms Gillian Catherine* •
Visiting Fellow, London School of
Economics, Office of the Solicitor,
Department of Health/DSS, New Court,
48 Carey Street, London WC2A 2LS, Call
Date: Nov 1996 (Middle Temple)
Qualifications: BA (Hons)(Kent), LLM
(Canada)

Moreno *Mrs Yvonne Laraine* •
Principal Crown Prosecutor Team
Leader, Crown Prosecution Service, Kings
House, 3rd Floor, Kymberley Road,
Harrow on the Hill, Middlesex HA1 1YH,
0181 424 8688 Ext 301, Call Date: Nov
1974 (Gray's Inn) Qualifications: LLB
(Hons), M/C , Dip in Criminology,
(Cantab)

Moreton *Mrs Kirsty Leigh*
Call Date: Nov 1996 (Gray's Inn)
Qualifications: LLB (Wales)

Morey *Mrs Deborah Ann*
Call Date: Oct 1997 (Middle Temple)
Qualifications: LLB (Hons)(Lond), LLM
(UCL)

Morgan *Andreww Philip*
Call Date: Oct 1998 (Gray's Inn)
Qualifications: LLB (Wales)

Morgan *Ceri Richards*
18 Bowham Avenue, Bridgend, Mid
Glamorgan CF31 3PA, 01656 667294,
Call Date: Nov 1982 (Gray's Inn)
Qualifications: LLB (Lond), M.C.I.E.H.,
M.I.O.S.H.

Morgan *Charles Lawrence* •
Legal & Negotiations Manager, LASMO
Plc, 101 Liverpool Street, London EC2,
0171 892 9707, and Member California,
USA, Call Date: Feb 1977 (Middle
Temple) Qualifications: MA (Oxon)

Morgan *Miss Diana Mary*
Call Date: Nov 1976 (Gray's Inn)
Qualifications: BA (Hons), Post-,
Graduate Diploma in, Language Studies

Morgan *Glyn James*
Call Date: Nov 1947 (Middle Temple)
Qualifications: MA (Cantab)

Morgan *Miss Gwyneth Anne Rhoda*
Call Date: July 1977 (Gray's Inn)
Qualifications: BA [Oxon]

Morgan *John Vincent Lyndon*
Orchard House, The Way, Reigate, Surrey
RH2 0LB, 01737 247071, Call Date: Feb
1960 (Gray's Inn) Qualifications: MA
(Oxon)

Morgan *Mrs Marilynne Ann* •
The Solicitor to the Dept of Social
Security & the Dept of Health., Dept of
Social security, Dept of Health, New
Court, 48 Carey Street, London
WC2A 2LS, 0171 412 1404, Fax: 0171
412 1501, Call Date: Nov 1972 (Middle
Temple) Qualifications: BA (Lond)

Morgan *Miss Marlene Marilyn* •
Legal Officer, Inland Revenue, Solicitors
Office, Somerset House, The Strand,
London WC2R 1LB, 0171 438 6669, Call
Date: July 1989 (Lincoln's Inn)
Qualifications: LLB, LLM

Morgan *Rhys Gareth*
Call Date: Nov 1995 (Inner Temple)
Qualifications: BA (Swansea), CPE
(Wolves)

Morgan *Richard James Nicholas*
Call Date: Nov 1997 (Gray's Inn)
Qualifications: BA (Hons)

Morgan *Robert James Marcello* •
Senior Consultant, Hellings Morgan
Associates, No 5, Bisney View, 47-49
Bisney Road, Pokfulam, Hong Kong,
Hong Kong, +852 2855 1428/2819
5792, Fax: +852 2855 1510, Call Date:
Feb 1980 (Gray's Inn) Qualifications: BA
(Hons), LLM, FCIArb, FHKIArb, FSIArb,
AMAE

Morgan *Miss Shelagh Elizabeth*
Call Date: June 1964 (Middle Temple)
Qualifications: LLB

Morgan *Simon Halvor*
Call Date: Feb 1995 (Lincoln's Inn)
Qualifications: LLB (Hons)

Morgan *Mrs Tina Jane* •
Company Secretary, Autoglass Ltd, 1
Priory Business Park, Cardington,
Bedford MK44 3US, 01234 273636, Fax:
01234 831100, Call Date: Oct 1995
(Middle Temple) Qualifications: LLB
(Hons)

Morkel *Richard Pierre*
Call Date: Nov 1994 (Gray's Inn)
Qualifications: LLB (Bris)

Morley *Alistair Eric* •
Call Date: Nov 1991 (Middle Temple)
Qualifications: BA Hons (Lond), MPhil
(Oxon)

Morley *Miss Joanne Louise* •
Lawyer (Prosecutions), Solicitors Office,
H M Customs & Excise, New Kings Beam
House, 22 Upper Ground, London SE1,
0171 620 1313, Call Date: Feb 1995
(Inner Temple) Qualifications: BA
(Oxon)

Morrell *Neil Edward Sheperd*
Call Date: Nov 1995 (Lincoln's Inn)
Qualifications: LLB (Hons)

Morris *Mrs Helen Elizabeth* •
Crown Prosecution Service, 7th Floor,
Liver Building, Pier Head, Liverpool,
Former Solicitor, Call Date: Nov 1996
(Gray's Inn) Qualifications: LLB (Lond)

Morris *Jeremy James* •
Eastleigh Housing Assoc Ltd, Charlotte
Yonge House, Tollgate, Chandlers Ford,
Eastleigh, Hants SO53 3WQ, 01703
684307, Call Date: Mar 1997 (Lincoln's
Inn) Qualifications: LLB (Hons)(Leeds)

Morris *The Rt Hon John* •
Attorney General Recorder, Privy
Councillor, and Member Northern
Ireland Bar (June 1997) 3 Hare Court, 1
Little Essex Street, London, WC2R 3LD,
Call Date: Feb 1954 (Gray's Inn)
Qualifications: LLM

Morris *Nicholas Guy Ussher*
Woodfield House, Oxford Road, Clifton,
Hampden, Oxon OX14 3EW, 01865
407149, Fax: 01865 407149, Call Date:
July 1970 (Middle Temple)
Qualifications: MA (Oxon)

Morris *Paul Derek*
Call Date: Oct 1996 (Inner Temple)
Qualifications: LLB (Lancs)

Morris *Paul Xavier* •
Legal Adviser, Lloyds of London, Legal
Services Department, 1958 Building,
Lime Street, London EC3M 7HA, 0171
327 6672, Fax: 0171 327 5502, Call
Date: Nov 1993 (Middle Temple)
Qualifications: MA (Cantab)

Morris *Richard Gideon*
Call Date: July 1998 (Gray's Inn)
Qualifications: LLB (Derby)

Morris *William John* •
Commercial Union Assurance,
Company plc, Room 113, Institute of
London, Underwriters, 49 Leadenhall
St, London EC3A 2BE, 0171 283 7500,
Call Date: May 1996 (Middle Temple)
Qualifications: LLB (Hons), LLM
(Dunelm)

Morris-Marsham *Mrs Margaret Lindelia*
Legal Adviser, ABAS Accounting
Technical, PricewaterhouseCoopers, 1
Embankment Place, London
WC2N 6NN, 0171 583 5000, Fax: 0171
213 2463, Call Date: Nov 1967
(Lincoln's Inn)

Morrison *Philip William*
Call Date: Nov 1956 (Gray's Inn)
Qualifications: LLB

Morse *Miss Beverley Anne*
Justices' Clerk, Inner London
Magistrates', Courts Service, 65
Romney Street, London SW1P 3RD,
0171 799 3332, Fax: 0171 799 3072,
Call Date: July 1978 (Gray's Inn)
Qualifications: LLM (Cantab), Cert
Crim (Lond)

Morse *Nicholas Stephen*
Call Date: Oct 1997 (Lincoln's Inn)
Qualifications: LLB (Hons)(Lond)

Mortimer *John Clifford*
1 Dr Johnson's Bldgs, Ground Floor,
Temple, London, EC4Y 7AX, Call Date:
Jan 1948 (Inner Temple)
Qualifications: BA

Mortimer *Jonathan* •
Chairman's Research Assistant at the
Law Commission, Call Date: Oct 1996
(Gray's Inn) Qualifications: BA
(Dunelm), LLM (Cantab)

Morton *Michael Quentin*
Deputy Clerk to the Justices', The Court
House, Tufton Street, Ashford, Kent
TN23 1QS, 01233 663204, Fax: 01233
663206, Call Date: July 1979 (Lincoln's
Inn) Qualifications: BA (Lond), DMS

Morton *Mrs Sheelagh Alice* •
Prosecution Team Leader, CPS
(Derby), 5th Floor, St Peter's House,
Gower Street, Derbyshire DE1 1SB,
01332 621 600, Call Date: Nov 1980
(Inner Temple) Qualifications: LLB
(Hull),MA

Morton *Thomas*
Call Date: Oct 1995 (Inner Temple)
Qualifications: BSc (Lond), CPE

Moscrop *Dr John James* •
Senior Crown Prosecutor, Crown
Prosecution Service, 8th Floor, Sunlight
House, Quay Street, Manchester, 0161
908 2600, Fax: 0161 908 2608, Call
Date: July 1983 (Middle Temple)
Qualifications: BA (Manch) LLB(Hull),
M Phil (Salford), Dip Lib Studs (Bel),
PhD (Leic), FRSA

Moses *Eric George Rufus*
Broome Cottage, Castle Hill, Nether
Stowey, Bridgwater, Somerset TA5 1NB,
Call Date: Jan 1938 (Middle Temple)

Moss *Jeremy Paul*
Senior Court Lawyer, Cambridge
Magistrates Court, The Court House,
Lion Yard, Cambridge CB2 3NA, 01223
314311, Fax: 01223 355237, Call Date:
Nov 1989 (Inner Temple)
Qualifications: LLB

Moss *Mitchell James* •
VAT Consultant, Ernest & Young,
Becket House, 1 Lambeth Palace Road,
London SE1, 0171 931 4394, Fax: 0171
931 4055, Call Date: Feb 1992 (Gray's
Inn) Qualifications: BA (Oxon)

Moss *Mrs Sandra Marie* •
Competition Consultant, C. I. P. F. A, 27
Queen Anne's Gate, London
SW1H 9BU, 0181 667 1144/01245
400476, Call Date: Oct 1993 (Gray's
Inn) Qualifications: LLB (Anglia)

Mott *Matthew John Spencer* •
Company Secretary & Legal Adviser,
William Hill Organization, Greenside
House, 50 Station Road, Wood Green,
London N22 4TP, 0181 918 3600, Fax:
0181 918 3726, Call Date: July 1983
(Gray's Inn) Qualifications: LLB FCIS

Mottram *Paul Richard* •
Legal Advisor to the Sunday Mirror,
MGN Ltd, 1 Canada Square, Canary
Wharf, London E14 5AP, 0171 293
3934, Call Date: Nov 1995 (Middle
Temple) Qualifications: LLB (Hons)

Motts *Miss Kirsteen*
Call Date: Nov 1996 (Lincoln's Inn)
Qualifications: BA (Hons)

Moulden *Simon Peter*
Call Date: Oct 1995 (Inner Temple)
Qualifications: LLB (Leic)

Mount *David Richard* •
Legal Advisor/Head of Claims, Tamoil
Shipping Limited, Leconfield House,
Curzon Street, London W1Y 7FB, 0171
344 5650, Call Date: Nov 1973 (Inner
Temple)

Mount *Harry Francis Gregory*
Call Date: Mar 1999 (Middle Temple)
Qualifications: BA (Hons)(Oxon)

Mouton *Marc Phillippe*
Call Date: Oct 1995 (Inner Temple)
Qualifications: LLB (Exon)

Mowbray *Anthony Leighton* •
Senior Crown Prosecutor, Crown
Prosecution Service, Heritage House,
Fishermans Wharf, Grimsby DN31 1SY,
01472 240170, Fax: 01472 240756,
Call Date: Nov 1983 (Middle Temple)
Qualifications: LLB (Wales)

Moxom *John Matthew Cameron*
'Pannells', Sudbury, Belchamp St Paul,
Suffolk CO10 7BS, 01787 277410, Also
Inn of Court G, Call Date: July 1968
(Inner Temple) Qualifications: MA
(Cantab)

Moylan *Ms Pauline Mary* •
61 Fairburn Drive, Garforth, Leeds,
Yorkshire LS25 2AR, 0113 232 0779,
and Member New South Wales, Call
Date: Nov 1995 (Gray's Inn)
Qualifications: LLB

Mpanga *David Frederick Kisitu*
Five Paper Bldgs, 1st Floor, Five Paper
Blgs, Temple, London, EC4Y 7HB, Call
Date: Nov 1993 (Middle Temple)
Qualifications: LLB (Hons)(Exon)

Muehl *Miss Ruth Anna*
Untere Feldstrasse 2, 81675 Munchen,
Germany, Germany, 089 475707, Call
Date: Feb 1960 (Gray's Inn)

Mufti *Sohail Imran*
Call Date: Nov 1995 (Inner Temple)
Qualifications: LLB (Lond)

Mughal *Mrs Sahzadi Bilqiis*
Legal Adviser & Assistant, 135
Mornington Crescent, Cranford,
Hounslow, Middlesex TW8 9SU, 0181
759 2003, Fax: 0181 759 2005, Call
Date: Nov 1995 (Lincoln's Inn)
Qualifications: LLB (Hons)

Mukherjee *Abhijeet*
Call Date: Feb 1995 (Middle Temple)
Qualifications: LLB (Hons)(Lond)

Mukherjee *Mihir Kumar*
Tottenham Law Centre, 15 West Green
Road, London N15 5BX, 0181 802
0911, and Member Indian Bar, Call
Date: Nov 1975 (Lincoln's Inn)
Qualifications: MA LLB DJ (Cal) LLM,
(Lond)

Mukhi *Miss Anna-Kumkum*
The Penthouse, Flat 18, 65 Ladbroke
Grove, London W11 2PD, 0171 243
4670, Fax: 0171 727 8867, Call Date:
Feb 1994 (Gray's Inn) Qualifications:
BA (Bris)

Mulhern *John Joseph*
Justices' Clerk, Inner London
Magistrates', Courts Service, 65
Romney Street, London SW1P 3RD, Call
Date: July 1974 (Middle Temple)
Qualifications: LLB (Lond)

• Barrister in employment

Mulholland *John Peter Patrick*
New Cottage, Painswick, Gloucestershire
GL6 6UA, 01452 812960, Fax: 01452
812960, also Inn of Court L and Member
Irish Republic Bar, Call Date: Nov 1969
(Middle Temple) Qualifications: BA,
ACIArb, MRAC

Mulholland *Michael Joseph*
Call Date: Nov 1997 (Inner Temple)
Qualifications: BA (Hull)

Mullan *James Anthony* •
Business Affairs Manager, EMI Records
Ltd., EMI Records Ltd, EMI House, 43
Brook Green, London W6 7EF, 0171 605
5233, Fax: 0171 605 5140, and Member
Northern Ireland Bar, Call Date: Feb
1995 (Lincoln's Inn) Qualifications: MA
(Cantab)

Mullarkey *Miss Claire Marie*
Call Date: July 1998 (Inner Temple)
Qualifications: LLB (East Lond)

Mullen *Miss Emily-Jane*
Call Date: Oct 1997 (Gray's Inn)
Qualifications: BA

Mullins *Miss Lorraine Pamela* •
Team Leader, IMRO, Broadwalk House,
6 Appold Street, London EC2A 2AA, Call
Date: July 1981 (Gray's Inn)
Qualifications: BA (Oxon)

Mulreany *James Vivian*
Deputy Justices' Clerk Acting Stipendiary
Magistrate, Inner London Magistrates',
Courts Service, 65 Romney Street,
London SW1 3RD, 0171 799 3332, Fax:
0171 799 3072, Call Date: Nov 1974
(Gray's Inn) Qualifications: MA (Oxon)

Mulvenna *Ms Glenis Beverley* •
Senior Legal Advisor, Glaxo Wellcome
PLC, Glaxo Wellcome House, Berkeley
Avenue, Greenford, Middlesex UB6 0NN,
0171 493 4060, Call Date: July 1983
(Inner Temple) Qualifications: LLB
(Bris)

Munden *Paul Alexanda*
Business Adviser Justice of the Peace, 15
Woodlands Avenue, Wanstead, London
E11 3RA, 0171 354 6400, Fax: 0171 704
2565, Call Date: Oct 1996 (Inner
Temple) Qualifications: LLB (Lond)

Munro *Christopher Hamish*
Call Date: Oct 1997 (Gray's Inn)
Qualifications: BA

Munro *Miss Fiona Caroline*
Also Inn of Court I Queen Elizabeth Bldg,
Ground Floor, Temple, London, EC4Y
9BS, Call Date: July 1986 (Lincoln's Inn)
Qualifications: LLB

Munro *Ranald Torquil Ian* •
Counsel UK & Ireland, Chubb Insurance
Company of, Europe, 106 Fenchurch
Street, London EC3M 5JB, 0171 867
5555, Solicitor, Call Date: July 1986
(Gray's Inn) Qualifications: BA (Hons),
Dip Law

Munsaf *Waheed*
Call Date: Nov 1996 (Lincoln's Inn)
Qualifications: LLB (Hons)

Munshi *Muhammed Biplob Islam*
Call Date: July 1997 (Lincoln's Inn)
Qualifications: LLB (Hons) (Middx)

Munton *Miss Jean Margaret*
Deputy clerk to the Justices for the Isle of
Wight, Magistrate's Clerk's Office, Quay
Street, Isle of Wight PO30 5BB, 01983
524244, Call Date: July 1983 (Middle
Temple) Qualifications: BA (Hons) ,
DMS

Munu *Miss Neneh Hawa*
Call Date: July 1997 (Inner Temple)
Qualifications: LLB (Leeds), LLM (LSE)

Muquit *Mohammed Shuyeb*
Call Date: July 1998 (Inner Temple)
Qualifications: BSc (LSE)

Murdie *Alan David*
Call Date: Nov 1988 (Lincoln's Inn)
Qualifications: LLB

Murdoch *Miss Janet*
Call Date: Nov 1996 (Lincoln's Inn)
Qualifications: BA (Hons)(York)

Murdoch-De Silva *Mrs Constance
Arlene* •
Senior Crown Prosecutor, Crown
Prosecution Service, Marylebone/West
London Branch, 50 Ludgate Hill, London
EC4M 7EX, 0171 273 1167, Fax: 0171
273 8039, Call Date: Nov 1989 (Middle
Temple) Qualifications: BA, LLB (Lond)

Murgatroyd *Christopher George*
Call Date: Nov 1989 (Middle Temple)
Qualifications: BA Hons (Oxon)

Murley *Ms Jenny* •
Officer - Enforcement, Lloyds Chambers,
1 Portsoken Street, London E1 8BT,
0171 390 5515, Fax: 0171 480 5846,
Call Date: July 1982 (Lincoln's Inn)
Qualifications: BA (Hons), LLM

Murphie *Ian Richard*
Call Date: Oct 1995 (Lincoln's Inn)
Qualifications: BA, LLB (Cape Town)

Murphy *Francis Patrick* •
Senior Crown Prosecutor, Crown
Prosecution Service, Fox Talbot House,
Bellington Close, Malmesbury Road,
Chippenham, Wilts SN15 1BN, 01249
443 443, Call Date: Nov 1976 (Middle
Temple) Qualifications: BA

Murray *Archibald Russell*
38 Gallow Hill, Peebles, Borders
EH45 9BG, 01721 721095, Call Date:
Feb 1963 (Lincoln's Inn) Qualifications:
BA (Dunelm)

Murray *Miss Christine Maria*
Principal Assistant, Buckinghamshire
Magistrates', Court Committee, Berkeley
House, Walton Street, Aylesbury,
Buckinghamshire HP21 7QG, 01296
82371, Fax: 01296 26347, Call Date: Oct
1992 (Gray's Inn) Qualifications: LL.B

Murray *Miss Fiona Mary*
Call Date: Nov 1995 (Middle Temple)
Qualifications: LLB (Hons)

Murray *Iain Patrick Joseph*
Automobile Association Legal Advisor, A
A Legal Dept, Lambert House, Stockport
Road, Cheadle, Cheshire SK8 2DY, 0161
488 7505, Fax: 0161 488 7260, Call
Date: Nov 1993 (Middle Temple)
Qualifications: LLB (Hons)

Murray *Miss Jean Lennox* •
Principal Legal Officer, The Treasury
Solicitor, Queen Anne's Chambers, 28
Broadway, London SW1H 9JS, Call Date:
Oct 1992 (Middle Temple)
Qualifications: LL.B (Hons, Lond)

Murray *Michael*
1 Denbigh Close, Chislehurst, Kent
BR7 5EB, Call Date: June 1953 (Gray's
Inn)

Murray *Richard Kennett*
Deputy Coroner,City of L'pool, Flat 10,
The Outlook, Riverside, Hightown,
Merseyside L38 OBU, 0151 929 2282,
Call Date: June 1950 (Middle Temple)
Qualifications: LLB (Lond)

Murray *Richard Petrocokino Dalrymple*
Call Date: Oct 1993 (Inner Temple)
Qualifications: BA, CPE

Murray-Walker *Miss Lynette Ruth*
Call Date: Oct 1994 (Lincoln's Inn)
Qualifications: LLB (Hons)(Leic)

Murrin *Mrs Denise Selby* •
Magistrates Court Clerk, Magistrates
Court, 7c High Street, Barnet, Herts
EN5 5UE, Call Date: Nov 1993 (Inner
Temple) Qualifications: LLB (So'ton)

Murugason *Ranjit*
Investment Banker, 0171 286 4387, Fax:
0171 286 4387, Call Date: July 1989
(Middle Temple) Qualifications: LLB
(Lond), BCL, (Oxon)

Musaret *Miss Shaheen* •
Legal Advisor, Lancashire County
Council, Trading Standards Dept, 55
Guildhall Street, Preson PR1 3NU,
(01772) 263574, Mayoress of Hyndburn,
Call Date: Nov 1991 (Lincoln's Inn)
Qualifications: LLB (Hons)

Musselwhite *Harry Thomas*
College Secretary & Registrar, King's
College London, Waterloo Bridge House,
Waterloo Road, London SE1 8WA, 0171
872 3435/6, Fax: 0171 872 3437, Call
Date: July 1983 (Gray's Inn)
Qualifications: BA (Lond) , FKC

Musson *Anthony Joseph*
University Lecturer, School of Law,
University of Exeter, Amory Building,
Rennes Drive, Exeter EX4 4RJ, 01392
263362, Fax: 01392 263196, Call Date:
Oct 1997 (Middle Temple)
Qualifications: MA, Mus.B (Cantab), LLM
(Lancs), Ph.D (Cantab)

Mustakas *Dr George*
150 Minories, London EC3N 1LS, 0171
264 2110, Fax: 0171 264 2107,
Attorney & Counselor at Law (USA) and
Member Louisiana Bar, Federal Bar
(USA), Call Date: Oct 1994 (Middle
Temple) Qualifications: BA
(Louisiana), JD (Tulane), LLM (Europa
, Institute Edinburgh)

Muston *Miss Ester Philippa*
Call Date: Oct 1998 (Inner Temple)
Qualifications: BA (Cantab), CPE

Muttitt *Andrew*
Call Date: Nov 1994 (Lincoln's Inn)
Qualifications: BA (Hons)(Leeds), Dip
Law (City), LLM (Nottingham)

Muttukumaru *Christopher Peter
Jayantha* •
Assistant Treasury Solicitor Appointed
the Secretary to the Lord Justice Scott's
Inquiry into the Export of Defence
Equipment & Dual use Goods to Iraq:
November 1992, Deputy Legal Adviser,
(General & International), Ministry of
Defence, Room 3/37, Metropole
Building, Nortumbeeland Avenue
WC2N 5BL, 0171 218 9451, Call Date:
Nov 1974 (Gray's Inn) Qualifications:
MA (Oxon)

Mutucumarara *Mrs Liyange
Sugunawathi*
7 Balmuir Gardens, London SW15,
0181 788 9311, Call Date: June 1964
(Gray's Inn)

Myers *Miss Elayne* •
Crown Prosecution Service, Ludgate
Hill, London, Call Date: Oct 1997
(Middle Temple) Qualifications: LLB
(Hons)

Myers *John Richard*
001 212 558 3971, Fax: 001 212 558
3588, Call Date: Oct 1996 (Gray's Inn)
Qualifications: BA (Cantab), LLM
(Harvard), DESS (Paris I)

Myers *Stephen Paul* •
Grade 6 Lawyer, Serious Fraud Office,
Elm House, 10-16 Elm Street, London
WC1X 0BJ, Call Date: July 1980 (Middle
Temple) Qualifications: BA (Essex)

Myles *Charles Rory*
Call Date: May 1996 (Gray's Inn)
Qualifications: BA (Bris)

Mylvaganam *(Miceal) Joseph
(Tharmasothy)* •
Head of Legal Affairs, Channel One T.V.
Ltd, 60 Charlotte Street, London
W1P 2AX, and Member Hong Kong Bar,
Call Date: July 1989 (Inner Temple)
Qualifications: BSc (Hons)(E.Ang), Dip
Law, LLM (Lond)(I.P)

N'dow *Saidou Abdoulie*
Call Date: Mar 1998 (Inner Temple)
Qualifications: LLB (Middx)

N'Jai *Miss Safiya*
Call Date: July 1998 (Middle Temple)
Qualifications: LLB (Hons)(Thames)

Nabi *Muhammed Ghulam*
Call Date: July 1971 (Lincoln's Inn)
Qualifications: BA, LLB

Nadarajah *Ranjan Errol*
Param & Co Solicitors, 221 Edgware
Road, Colindale, London NW9 6LP, Call
Date: Nov 1995 (Inner Temple)
Qualifications: LLB (Lond)

Nadarajah *Mrs Tapashi* •
Senior Crown Prosecutor, Crown
Prosecution Service, Queen's House, 58
Victoria Street, St Albans AL1 3HZ,
01727 818100, Fax: 01727 833144,
Call Date: Nov 1989 (Inner Temple)
Qualifications: LLB

Nagel *William*
10 Ely Place, London EC1N 6TY, 0171
242 9636, Fax: 0171 430 0990, Call
Date: June 1949 (Lincoln's Inn)
Qualifications: LLB (Hons)

Nagra *Kashmir*
Call Date: Oct 1994 (Gray's Inn)
Qualifications: BSc

Nainappan *Shane*
Lot 2224/18, Taman Tanjung Gemuk,
71000 Port Dickson, Negeri Semilan,
Malaysia, and Member Malaysia Bar,
Call Date: Nov 1994 (Middle Temple)
Qualifications: LLB (Hons)

Nainby-Luxmoore *James Victor Chave*
Call Date: July 1985 (Gray's Inn)
Qualifications: BA

Naismith *Dr William Edwin Fraser*
Call Date: July 1978 (Middle Temple)
Qualifications: BSc, PhD (Glas),

Namakula *Ms Ritah Harriet*
Call Date: Nov 1997 (Inner Temple)
Qualifications: LLB (Lond)

Napal *Raj*
20 Britton Street, 1st Floor, London,
EC1M 5NQ, Call Date: Nov 1981
(Middle Temple) Qualifications: LLB
(Hons)(Leeds)

Napper *Miss Miranda Fleur* •
Lawyer, H M Customs & Excise, New
King's Beam House, 22 Upper Ground,
London SE1 9PJ, 0171 865 5165, Fax:
0171 865 5197, Call Date: Oct 1993
(Lincoln's Inn) Qualifications: LLB
(Hons)(B'ham)

Naqvi *Ms Syeda Shazia Haider*
Call Date: Mar 1998 (Gray's Inn)
Qualifications: LLB (LSE)

Narayan *Miss Janise*
Call Date: Nov 1989 (Middle Temple)
Qualifications: LLB

Nardi *Riccardo Angelo* •
Head of Legal Services/Company
Secretary, The Association of British,
Travel Agents, 68-71 Newman Street,
London W1P 4AH, 0171 307 1910, Fax:
0171 631 4623, Call Date: Nov 1989
(Middle Temple) Qualifications: LLB
(Lanc)

Narwal *Miss Jaswant Kaur* •
Senior Crown Prosecutor, Crown
Prosection Service, 50 Ludgate Hill,
London EC4M 7EX, 0171 273 8401,
Fax: 0171 273 8039, Call Date: Nov
1993 (Inner Temple) Qualifications:
BA (Lancs), CPE

Nash *Matthew Roger*
Call Date: Nov 1997 (Middle Temple)
Qualifications: LLB (Hons)(Exon)

Nash *Ms Susan Joyce*
14 Tooks Court, Cursitor St, London,
EC4A 1LB, Call Date: July 1979 (Gray's
Inn) Qualifications: B Ed (Sussex) LLM

Nasir *Khaled Jahal Nasir*
Call Date: Nov 1991 (Lincoln's Inn)
Qualifications: BA (Hons) (Cambs)

Nasser *Ms Amatul-Shafi* •
Grade 7 (Lawyer), The Treasury
Solicitor, Queen Anne's Chambers, 28
Broadway, London SW1H 9JS, 0171
210 3501, Call Date: Nov 1988
(Lincoln's Inn) Qualifications: LLB
Hons

Nasser *Mrs Anne Kathleen*
Legal Adviser/Court Clerk, Barking
Magistrates' Court, East Street, Barking,
Essex IG11 8EW, 0181 594 5311, Fax:
0181 594 4297, Call Date: July 1990
(Middle Temple) Qualifications: LLB,
LLM (Lond)

Nath *Rakesh* •
Legal Adviser & Secretary, BBC
Resources, Room 2672, White City,
Wood Lane, London W12 7TS, and
Member Mauritius Bar, Call Date: July
1985 (Inner Temple) Qualifications:
LLB (Lond)

Naughten *John Peter*
Call Date: Oct 1995 (Lincoln's Inn)
Qualifications: LLB (Hons)(Lond)

Naughton *Miss Regina Marian* •
Principal Crown Prosecutor, Crown
Prosecution Service, 4th Floor, Ludgate
Hill, London EC4M 7EX, 0171 273
8000, Fax: 0171 273 1488, Call Date:
July 1980 (Gray's Inn) Qualifications:
LLB (Brunel)

Nawbatt *Lalchand*
Lawyer/Supervisor, 10 Victoria Street,
London SW1H 0NN, 0171 215 3174,
and Member Guyana Bar, Call Date:
July 1972 (Middle Temple)
Qualifications: LLB (Hons)(Lond)

Nayee *Mrs Manjula Dullabhbhai* •
Call Date: Nov 1988 (Gray's Inn)
Qualifications: LLB (Lond)

Nazeer *Malik Mohammed*
Arbitrator, Khair Court, 67 Inverness
Terrace, Bayswater, London W2 3JT,
and Member Pakistan Bar, Call Date:
May 1993 (Lincoln's Inn)
Qualifications: LLB (Hons)

Ncube *Ms Elizabeth Betty*
Managing Director, Global Legal
Immigration, Consultancy, Suite 114,
Queensway House, 275-281 High Street,
Stratford, London E15 2TF, 0181 534
2229, Fax: 0181 534 2229, Call Date: Oct
1994 (Lincoln's Inn) Qualifications: BA
(Hons), LLB (Lond)

Neafsey *Giles Edward*
Call Date: Oct 1995 (Gray's Inn)
Qualifications: LLB (Wales)

Nebhrajani *Miss Mel* •
Charity Commission, St Albans House,
57-60 Haymarket, London SW1Y 4QX,
Call Date: Nov 1994 (Middle Temple)
Qualifications: BA (Hons) (Dunelm),
Dip Law (City)

Needham *Christopher Eric* •
Senior Legal Adviser Group Legal
Department, Royal & Sun Alliance
Insurance, Group., P O Box 30, New Hall
Place, Old Hall Street, Liverpool
L69 3HS, 0151 239 4170, Fax: 0151 239
3342, Call Date: Nov 1974 (Middle
Temple) Qualifications: LLB

Neenan *Miss Lesley*
Call Date: Nov 1990 (Inner Temple)
Qualifications: LLB (Hons)

Neil *Miss Susan Deborah* •
Senior Principle Legal Officer, HM
Customs & Excise, New King's Beam
House, 22 Upper Ground, London
SE1 9PJ, 0171 865 5930, Fax: 0171 865
5022, Call Date: Nov 1986 (Inner
Temple) Qualifications: LLB (Soton)

Neilly *Miss Heather Robina*
Cayman Islands Law School, 12 Farley
Copse, Binfield, Bracknell, Berks
RG42 1BF, Call Date: Oct 1990 (Middle
Temple) Qualifications: BSc (Aston),
LLB (Lond), MPhil (Ulster)

Neilson *Robert Rowan Cochrane*
Call Date: Nov 1947 (Inner Temple)
Qualifications: MA (Cantab)

Nell *Adam Edward O'Neill*
11A Storefield Street, Islington, London
N1 0HW, 0171 837 1715, Fax: 0171 837
1718, Call Date: Nov 1995 (Gray's Inn)
Qualifications: BA

Nelson *Desmond Montague*
Call Date: Nov 1975 (Gray's Inn)
Qualifications: LLB

Nelson *Mrs Paula Miriam* •
Company Secretary & Head of Legal &
Pensions Department, Nestle UK Ltd, St
George's House, Croydon, Surrey
CR9 1NR, 0181 667 5648, Fax: 0181 667
5775, Solicitor Nigeria and Member
Nigerian Bar, Call Date: July 1973 (Gray's
Inn) Qualifications: LLB

Nelson *Robert Charles James*
Deputy Chairman, Bushfield Alloys
Limited, Chairman, Britannic Group
PLC, Director Armourglass Limited,
Chairman Ionian Ltd, Room 77, London
Fruit Exchange, BrushField Street,
London E1 6EP, 0171 377 9784, Fax:
0171 377 9839, Call Date: June 1959
(Middle Temple) Qualifications: BA
juris(Oxon)

Nelson *Robin Stuart* •
Principal Crown Prosecutor, Crown
Prosecution Service, 2nd Floor, Portland
House, Stag Place, Victoria, London
SW1E 5BH, 0171 915 5797, Fax: 0171
915 5811, Call Date: Nov 1983 (Middle
Temple) Qualifications: BA, LLM

Neofytou *Thomas*
Call Date: Oct 1996 (Lincoln's Inn)
Qualifications: LLB (Hons) (Hudders)

Neoh *Anthony Francis*
13th Floor, 10 Queen's Road, Central,
Hong Kong, 5 2 23365, Fax: 810 1872,
QC Hong Kong 1990 and Member Hong
Kong Bar 2 Mitre Ct Bldgs, 2nd Floor,
Temple, London, EC4Y 7BX, Call Date:
July 1976 (Gray's Inn)

Nesbitt *Alexander Owain Peter*
Betesh Fox & Co Solicitors, 16-17 Ralli
Courts, West Riverside, Manchester
M3 5FT, 0161 832 6131, Call Date: Oct
1995 (Lincoln's Inn) Qualifications: BA
(Hons)(Oxon)

Nesbitt *Lawrence Kenneth*
South Wales, Call Date: Oct 1996 (Gray's
Inn) Qualifications: LLB

Nettelton *John Marcus* •
Manager Commercial, Hardy Oil & Gas
plc, 10 Great George Street, London
SW1P 3AE, 0171 470 2262, Fax: 0171
470 2300, Call Date: Nov 1986 (Middle
Temple) Qualifications: BA

Neville *James Richard*
Specialist Reports (Editor), Butterworths
& Co, Halsbury House, 35 Chancery
Lane, London WC2A 1EL, 0171 400
2500, Fax: 0171 400 2559, and Member
Southern Ireland, Call Date: Nov 1991
(Lincoln's Inn) Qualifications: BCL
(Cork), BL (Dublin)

Neville *Miss Karen Wendy*
Call Date: Nov 1986 (Inner Temple)
Qualifications: LLB

Nevshehir-Owen *Miss Carolyn
Elisabeth* •
Director, NDN Owen Ltd, 39A Smallgate,
Beccles, Suffolk NR34 9AE, 01508
548613, Fax: 01508 548613, Call Date:
Nov 1990 (Inner Temple) Qualifications:
BA, ACIArb, FLAND Inst

Newbold *Dr Anne Lorraine Elsie* •
Legal Director,, Rabobank International,
108 Cannon Street, London EC4N 6RN,
0171 280 3000, Fax: 0171 283 4446,
Call Date: Nov 1990 (Lincoln's Inn)
Qualifications: LLB, PhD (Lond)

Newbold *Ronald Edgar*
Former Recorder St Philip's Chambers,
Fountain Court, Steelhouse Lane,
Birmingham, B4 6DR, Call Date: July
1965 (Inner Temple) Qualifications: MA
(Oxon), DIP.ED

Newcombe *Richard Allan* •
Branch Crown Prosecutor, Crown
Prosecution Service, Ealing/Hounsow
Branch, 2nd Floor, Kings House,
Kymberley Road, Harrow, Middlesex
HA3 1YH, 0181 424 8688, Fax: 0181 424
9134, Call Date: July 1979 (Middle
Temple) Qualifications: LLB (Bris)

Newcombe *Robert William*
Call Date: May 1996 (Lincoln's Inn)
Qualifications: LLB (Hons)

Newell *Christopher William Paul* •
Director of Casework Evaluation and
Chief Inspector, Crown Prosecution
Service, 50 Ludgate Hill, London
EC4M 7EX, 0171 273 1226, Fax: 0171
329 8167, Call Date: July 1973 (Middle
Temple) Qualifications: LLB

Newey *Miss Rachel Anne*
Senior Legal Adviser, Berkshire &
Oxfordshire, Magistrates Court's
Committee, Easby House, Northfield
End, Henley-on-Thames, 01491 412720,
Fax: 01491 412762, Call Date: Oct 1993
(Middle Temple) Qualifications: LLB
(Hons)(Lanc)

Newman *Miss Erica Rachel*
Warner Cranston Solicitors, Pickfords
Wharf, Clink Street, London SE1 9DG,
0171 403 2900, Fax: 0171 403 4221,
Call Date: Nov 1994 (Inner Temple)
Qualifications: BA (Oxon)

Newman *Paul*
Accredited Adjudicator RIBA,
Construction Industry Council, Edwards
Geldard, Dumfries House, Dumfries
Place, Cardiff CF1 4YF, 01222 238239,
Fax: 01222 237268, Call Date: Nov 1982
(Gray's Inn) Qualifications: MA
(Cantab), Dip Law, (City), ACIArb

Newman *Paul*
Call Date: Nov 1990 (Middle Temple)
Qualifications: BA

Newman *Peter David*
Call Date: Nov 1995 (Middle Temple)
Qualifications: LLB (Hons) (Essex)

Newman *Miss Susan Alexandra*
Court Clerk, Cambridgeshire
Magistrates', Courts, The Court House,
Lion Yard, Cambridge CB2 3NA, 01223
314311, Fax: 01223 355237, Call Date:
July 1980 (Lincoln's Inn)

Newman *Mrs Veronica*
University of Glamorgan, Pontypridd,
Mid Glamorgan CF37 1DL, Call Date: Nov
1984 (Gray's Inn) Qualifications: BA
DipLaw

Newman-Chalk Geoffrey
101 Mount View Road, Hornsey,
London, N4 4JH, 0181 340 1649, Call
Date: Oct 1992 (Gray's Inn)
Qualifications: BA, ATC, Post Cert, RA,
Dip Law , FRSA

Newton Andrew Charles •
In-House Barrister, First Assist Group
Limited, Marshall's Court, Sutton,
Surrey SM1 4DU, 0181 652 1313, Call
Date: Nov 1997 (Inner Temple)
Qualifications: LLB (Hons) (Lancs)

Newton Clive Trevor
Call Date: Nov 1969 (Middle Temple)
Qualifications: LLB, FCCA

Newton Miss Heather Campbell
Call Date: July 1998 (Middle Temple)
Qualifications: BA (Hons) (Hull), MSc
(LSE), Dip Law (BPP)

Newton Miss Jessica Clare •
Assistant Parliamentary Counsel,
Parliamentary Counsel Office, 36
Whitehall, London SW1A 2AU, 0171
210 6631, Fax: 0171 210 6632, Call
Date: Oct 1994 (Gray's Inn)
Qualifications: BA (Bris)

Niblett Ramon John
Call Date: Nov 1979 (Gray's Inn)

Nicholas Arthur Leary
14 Elmete Drive, Roundhay, Leeds,
West Yorks LS8 2LA, Call Date: Nov
1956 (Middle Temple) Qualifications:
MA (Oxon), DipEd

Nicholas Ms Christina Michalina de
Weld
Call Date: Nov 1997 (Inner Temple)
Qualifications: BA (Warsaw, Poland)

Nicholls James William
Freshfields Solicitors, 65 Fleet Street,
London EC4Y 1HS, 0171 832 7529,
Fax: 0171 732 7001, Call Date: Nov
1997 (Middle Temple) Qualifications:
BA (Hons) (Kent)

Nicholls Michael John •
Principal Crown Prosecutor, Crown
Prosecution Service, Sedgemore House,
Deane Gate Avenue, Taunton, Somerset
TA1 2UH, 01823 442422, Call Date:
July 1978 (Gray's Inn) Qualifications:
LLB (Nott'm)

Nicholls Miss Suzanna Elizabeth
Call Date: Oct 1998 (Middle Temple)
Qualifications: LLB (Hons) (Sussex)

Nicholson Andrew David
Director of Legal Services, Wimbledon
Magistrates' Court, The Law Courts,
Alexandra Road, London SW19 7JP,
0181 946 8622, Call Date: July 1987
(Inner Temple) Qualifications: BA
(Oxon)

Nicholson Edward Graves
Call Date: Nov 1993 (Middle Temple)
Qualifications: BA (Hons) (Lanc), CPE

Nicholson John •
Manches & Co, Aldwych House, 81
Aldwych, London WC2B 4RP, 0171 404
4433, Fax: 0171 404 1838, Call Date:
Nov 1994 (Middle Temple)
Qualifications: MA

Nicholson Paul Andrew
Eatons Solicitors, The Old Library, 34A
Darley Street, Bradford, BD1 3LH,
01274 728 327, Fax: 01274 305 056,
Call Date: Oct 1992 (Lincoln's Inn)
Qualifications: LLB (Hons)

Nicholson Miss Susan
Call Date: Oct 1995 (Inner Temple)
Qualifications: BSc (Bradford), CPE
(Northumbria)

Nicks Marvin •
Legal Manager, Intervention Board,
Kings House, 33 Kings Road, Reading
RG1 3YD, 01734 531522, Fax: 01734
531230, Call Date: May 1971 (Gray's
Inn) Qualifications: MA (Oxon)

Nicoletti Gian-Lorenzo
10 Hillside Avenue, Exeter EX4 4NW,
Call Date: July 1994 (Inner Temple)
Qualifications: LLB (Warwick)

Nicolle Jason Paul St John
Channel Islands, Call Date: Nov 1995
(Inner Temple) Qualifications: BA
(Oxon), CPE

Niekirk Paul Henry
40 Rectory Avenue, High Wycombe,
Bucks HP13 6HW, 01494 527200, Call
Date: June 1956 (Gray's Inn)
Qualifications: MA

Nield Jason Paul
Call Date: Oct 1996 (Lincoln's Inn)

Nightingale Andrew John
Call Date: Nov 1987 (Inner Temple)
Qualifications: LLB (Lond)

Nightingale Revd John Stuart
Catholic Priest (Archdiocese of
Birmingham), 20 Beaumont Buildings,
Oxford OX1 2LL, 01865 553536, Call
Date: Nov 1985 (Middle Temple)
Qualifications: BA (Lond)

Nijabat Miss Reedah Zahra
Director - ArRUM Ltd, Call Date: Nov
1997 (Lincoln's Inn) Qualifications:
LLB (Hons), LLM (Lond).

Nimmo Smith Miss Harriet Louise Hilda
Call Date: Nov 1996 (Lincoln's Inn)
Qualifications: BA (Hons)

Niven Laurence
Tax Partner, 36 Main Street, Great Glen,
Leicester LE8 9GG, 0116 259 3349,
Fax: 0116 259 3349, Call Date: July
1975 (Gray's Inn) Qualifications: LLB,
ACA

Nixon Miss Abigail Lisa Barbara •
Crown Prosecutor, Crown Prosecution
Service, Buckinghamshire Branch,
4,5,6 & 7 Prebendal Court, Oxford
Road, Aylesbury, Bucks HP19 3EY, Call
Date: Oct 1991 (Inner Temple)
Qualifications: BA (Dunelm)

Nixon Anthony Michael
The Warwick Partnership, 70 Warwick
Road, St Albans, Hertfordshire
AL1 4DL, 01727 835826, Fax: 01727
810885, Call Date: July 1979 (Middle
Temple) Qualifications: MA
(Cantab),FCIArb, CEDR Accredited ,
Mediator, DipICArb

Niyazi Ihsan
Principal Legal Adviser, Haringey
Magistrates Court, The Court house,
Bishops Road, Archway Road, Highgate,
London N6 4HS, 0181 340 3472, Fax:
0181 348 3343, Call Date: July 1973
(Middle Temple)

Noakes Christopher
Part Time Chairman of Tribunal, Call
Date: Nov 1972 (Gray's Inn)

Noble David Jonathan •
Attorney General's Chambers, 9
Buckingham Gate, London SW1E 6JP,
0171 271 2411, Fax: 0171 271 2434,
Legal Secretariat to the Law Officers,
Call Date: July 1981 (Gray's Inn)
Qualifications: M.Soc.Sci., LLB

Noble-Mathews Dr Priscilla Mary
Lovehill Cottage, Trotton, Petersfield,
Hampshire GU31 5ER, 01730 816583,
Fax: 01730 816583, Call Date: Feb
1953 (Middle Temple) Qualifications:
BM (Soton), Dip PALL MED, Dip IMC
(RCS ED)

Nock Reginald Stanley
Deloitte & Touche, Stonecutter Court, 1
Stonecutter Street, London EC4A 4TR,
0171 936 3000, Fax: 0171 583 1198,
Call Date: Nov 1968 (Lincoln's Inn)
Qualifications: LLB, LLM (Lond), FTII

Noel Lynton Cosmas
Call Date: Nov 1976 (Middle Temple)
Qualifications: LLB (Lond)

Norcross Miss Sarah Ann
Call Date: Oct 1990 (Gray's Inn)
Qualifications: LLB (Lond)

Norfolk Miss Bridget Jane •
Crown Prosecutor, Crown Prosecution
Service, 3 Clifton Mews, Clifton Hill,
Brighton, East Sussex BN1 3HR, Call
Date: July 1989 (Middle Temple)
Qualifications: LLB [Leic]

Norman Mrs Helen Elizabeth
Senior Lecturer in Law, Faculty of Law,
University of Bristol, Wills Memorial
Building, Queens Road, Bristol
BS8 1RJ, 0117 9288245, Fax: 0117
9251870, Call Date: Nov 1973 (Gray's
Inn) Qualifications: LLB,LLM

Norrell Gregory Gordon
Call Date: July 1980 (Middle Temple)
Qualifications: LLB

Norris Charles John •
Legal Adviser (Range 11), Solicitors
Office, Dept of Trade & Industry, 10
Victoria Street, London SW1, 0171 215
3259, Call Date: July 1986 (Lincoln's
Inn) Qualifications: LLB, LLM (Wales)

Norris *Graham Kenneth* •
Clerk to the Justices & Justices Chief
Executive, Stratford Magistrates' Court,
The Court House, 389-397 High Street,
Stratford, London E15 4SB, 0181 522
5000, Fax: 0181 519 9214, Call Date:
Nov 1974 (Gray's Inn) Qualifications:
B.Tech (Hons)

Norris *Dr James Alfred*
Non-Executive Director, Dist Health
Commission 1990-96; Norfolk County
Councillor 1997, 25 West End,
Northwold, Norfolk IP26 5LE, 01366
728296, Fax: 01366 728059, Call Date:
July 1975 (Middle Temple)
Qualifications: MA, PhD (Cantab)

North *David Michael* •
Assistant Solicitor, HM Customs &
Excise, New King's Beam House, 22
Upper Ground, London SE1, 0171 865
5235, Call Date: July 1974 (Middle
Temple)

North *Sir Peter Machin*
Principal of Jesus College, Oxford Master
of the Bench, Jesus College, Oxford
OX1 3DW, 01865 279701, Fax: 01865
279696, Call Date: May 1992 (Inner
Temple) Qualifications: BA (Oxon), MA
(Oxon), BCL (Oxon), DCL (Oxon)

North *Simon Timothy* •
Principal Crown Prosecutor, Crown
Prosecution Service, Sceptre House, 7-9
Castle Street, Luton, Beds LU1 3AJ,
01582 404808, Fax: 01582 400642, Call
Date: Nov 1984 (Gray's Inn)
Qualifications: BA

Northage *Mark Jason*
Barrister & Solicitor Australia, Call Date:
Nov 1992 (Gray's Inn) Qualifications:
LLB , BSc Econ (Australia)

Northover *Jonathan Ashley James*
Call Date: Oct 1998 (Middle Temple)
Qualifications: LLB (Hons)(Lond)

Northway *Ms Nicola Jane*
Allen & Overy Solicitors, 9 Cheapside,
London EC2V 6AD, Call Date: Nov 1989
(Middle Temple) Qualifications: LLB
(Hons), LLM

Norton *Paul Andrew James Edward* •
Deputy Chief Clerk, Inner London
Magistrates', Courts Service, Old Street
Magistrates' Court, 335 Old Street,
London EC1, Call Date: Apr 1989 (Inner
Temple) Qualifications: LLB (Leeds)

Norton *Mrs Roswitha*
Call Date: July 1979 (Lincoln's Inn)
Qualifications: LLB (Lond)

Nottidge *Oliver Richard*
Deputy Director, Recruitment &
Placement Division - UN United Nations
Secretariat 1988-92, Apt 5D, 176 E.71st
Street, New York, NY 10021-5159, (212)
936 0565, Call Date: Feb 1958 (Middle
Temple) Qualifications: BA, MA (Cantab)

Nottridge *Robin Ernest*
Director of Training for Justices and
Legal Staff, Leicestershire Magistrates',
Courts Committee, 674 Melton Road,
Thurmaston, Leicester LE4 8BB, 0116
264 0922, Fax: 0116 269 2369, Call
Date: June 1961 (Middle Temple)
Qualifications: BA

Nowak *Miss Karen Elizabeth*
Call Date: Nov 1976 (Inner Temple)
Qualifications: LLB

Nunkoo *Miss Shani*
Call Date: Nov 1989 (Inner Temple)
Qualifications: LLB, LLM (LSE)

Nunns *Malcolm Reeve Mark*
Garden Chambers, 5th Floor, 10 Queen's
Road Central, Hong Kong, 2525 0221,
Fax: 2845 2441, and Member Hong Kong
Bar, Call Date: July 1969 (Middle
Temple) Qualifications: LLB (Exon),
F.C.I.Arb

Nursaw *Sir James* •
Call Date: Nov 1955 (Middle Temple)
Qualifications: MA, LLB (Cantab)

Nursimloo *Kumaraswamy*
Call Date: Nov 1993 (Lincoln's Inn)
Qualifications: LLB (Hons)

Nussle *Miss Sophie Juliette Suzanne*
Call Date: Feb 1994 (Middle Temple)
Qualifications: BA (Hons)(Oxon), CPE
(City)

Nutley *Dr Peter Graham*
Bishops Park Health Centre, Bishops
Stortford, Herts CM23 4DA, 01279
755057, Call Date: July 1984 (Middle
Temple) Qualifications: BA, MB, BS,
LRCP, MRCS,DCH, DRCOG,MFPM

Nwanodi *Antony Chidi Kojo Ezihuo* •
Grade 7 (L) Principal Legal Officer,
Treasury Solicitors Department, Queen
Anne's Chambers, 28 Broadway, London
SW1H 9JS, Call Date: Nov 1987 (Gray's
Inn) Qualifications: BA (Keele), LLB,
(Buck)

Nwosu *Dominic Chukwuneke* •
Legal Consultant, Call Date: Nov 1987
(Inner Temple) Qualifications: LLB
(Essex)

Nyhan *Miss Norah Maria*
Call Date: Mar 1996 (Lincoln's Inn)
Qualifications: LLB (Hons)(Sheff)

Nylander *Leslie Arthur*
Call Date: Oct 1992 (Gray's Inn)
Qualifications: LLB, LLM

Nylander *Miss Margaret Olatokunboh
Alexandra*
Wandsworth Law Centre, 246-248
Lavender Hill, Wandsworth, London
SW11, Call Date: July 1991 (Gray's Inn)
Qualifications: BA, MA (So'ton), Nigerian
Bar

O'Brien *Paul Anthony* •
Company Secretary, 20 Parkfield Road
South, Didsbury, Manchester M20 0DH,
0161 434 9721, Call Date: July 1981
(Inner Temple) Qualifications: MA
(Oxon)

O'Brien *Peter Arthur*
18a Carlisle Avenue, St Albans, Herts
AL3 5LU, 01727 851941, Fax: 01727
851941, Call Date: Nov 1992 (Inner
Temple) Qualifications: BA (New
Zealand), Dip in Law

O'Brien *William Anthony Patrick*
Call Date: Nov 1994 (Gray's Inn)
Qualifications: BA

O'Callaghan *John Anthony*
Call Date: Nov 1988 (Gray's Inn)
Qualifications: LLB (Lond)

O'Connell *David James Oliver* •
Senior Crown Prosecutor, Crown
Prosecution Service, 4 Artillery Row,
London SW1, 0171 976 5699, Call Date:
July 1988 (Gray's Inn)

O'Connell *Eamon Francis*
Call Date: Nov 1977 (Middle Temple)
Qualifications: LLB (Warwick), LLM
(Lond)

O'Connor *Miss Julie Elizabeth*
Call Date: July 1980 (Gray's Inn)
Qualifications: BA

O'Connor *Michael Patrick* •
Deputy Master QBD. High Court
Arbitrator, The Questor Consultancy
Group, Tailours, Windmill Way, Much
Haddham, Herts SG10 6BH, 01279
842721, Fax: 01279 842721, Call Date:
Nov 1973 (Middle Temple)
Qualifications: LLB (Lond), FCIArb

O'Connor *Mrs Sharon Noelle*
Call Date: Nov 1995 (Lincoln's Inn)
Qualifications: BSc (Hons)

O'Connor *Stephen Robert William* •
Police Officer, Metropolitan Police, New
Scotland Yard, London SW1P 4AN, 0171
230 1212, Call Date: Nov 1996 (Inner
Temple) Qualifications: BSc (L'pool)

O'Dair *David Richard Frazer*
Lecturer, University College of London,
Bentham House, 4-8 Endsleigh Gardens,
London WC1H 0EG, 0171 387 8057, Fax:
0171 387 8057, Call Date: Nov 1987
(Gray's Inn) Qualifications: MA, BCL
(Oxon)

O'Donnell *Peter John* •
Senior Crown Prosecutor, Wales, Call
Date: July 1983 (Middle Temple)
Qualifications: BA (Hons)

O'Donnell *Mrs Sara Jean* •
Crown Prosecutor, Crown Prosecution
Service, Guildford Branch, One Onslow
Street, Guildford, Call Date: July 1985
(Middle Temple) Qualifications: LLB
(Lond)

O'Donoghue *Miss Margaret Mary* •
Call Date: Nov 1986 (Gray's Inn)
Qualifications: MA (London), BA
(Sheffield)

O'Donoghue *Michael Gerard* •
Paddington Law Centre, 439 Harrow
Road, London W10 4RE, 0181 960
3155, Fax: 0181 968 0417, Call Date:
July 1993 (Lincoln's Inn)
Qualifications: LLM, BA

O'Donoghue *Robert Peter*
Bruxelles, Call Date: Nov 1996
(Lincoln's Inn) Qualifications: LLB
(Hons), LLM (Bris)

O'Donovan *Morgan Teige Gerald*
Farrer & Company Solicitors, 66
Lincoln's Inn Fields, London
WC2A 3LH, 0171 242 2022, Fax: 0171
831 9748, Call Date: Nov 1985 (Middle
Temple) Qualifications: MA (Cantab)

O'Donovan *Patrick Anthony Hopkins*
Maritime Arbitrator, Churcham House,
1 Bridgeman Road, Teddington,
Middlesex TW11 8DR, 0181 977 3666,
Fax: 0181 977 3052, Call Date: Nov
1976 (Middle Temple) Qualifications:
MA (Cantab), FCI Arb

O'Driscoll *Denis Patrick*
Call Date: Nov 1997 (Inner Temple)
Qualifications: BSc (L'pool), LLB
(Lond), ARICS

O'Flynn *Miss Elisabeth Nuala* •
Legal Director, Dept of Trade &
Industry, 10 Victoria Street, London
SW1H ONN, 0171 215 3473, Fax: 0171
215 3471, Call Date: Feb 1965 (Inner
Temple) Qualifications: LLB (Lond)

O'Grady *Miss Eileen Joyce* •
Editor, Law Reporter Managing Editor,
Thomson Tax Ltd, 51 Wicket Road,
Greenford, Middlesex UB6 8YJ, 01865
261 430, Fax: 01865 261 404/0181 998
0501, Call Date: Nov 1976 (Lincoln's
Inn) Qualifications: LLB

O'Halloran *Mark Anthony*
General Counsel, Tokyo Electron
Europe Ltd, Premiere House, Betts
Way, Crawley, West Sussex RH10 2GB,
01293 655897, Fax: 01293 655854,
Call Date: Nov 1995 (Inner Temple)
Qualifications: LLB (Essex)

O'Hare *Miss Jane Anne Josephine Mary*
Deputy Chairman Oxfordshire Health
Authority Discipline Committee (Part
Time), Call Date: Nov 1977 (Gray's
Inn) Qualifications: LLB (Newc)

O'Kane *Michael Colin* •
Call Date: Nov 1992 (Middle Temple)
Qualifications: LLB (Hons)

O'Kelly *Donal Francis*
'Different Strokes', Sir Walter Scott
House, 2 Broadway Market, London
E8 4QJ, 0171 249 6645, Fax: 0171 249
6645, Criminal Bar Association Family
Law Bar Association, Call Date: July
1973 (Inner Temple) Qualifications:
LLB

O'Leary *Miss Carol-Ann*
Call Date: July 1982 (Middle Temple)
Qualifications: LLB (Lond)

O'Leary *Miss Fiona Kieran Margaret*
Call Date: Apr 1978 (Inner Temple)

O'Leary *Shaun Vincent Patrick* •
Assistant Director Chartered Insurer,
Allied Dunbar, Allied Dunbar Centre,
Station Road, Swindon, Wilts SN6 1EL,
01793 514 514, Call Date: July 1979
(Inner Temple) Qualifications: LLB
(Manch), A.C.I.I

O'Mahony *Declan Liam*
Call Date: July 1980 (Inner Temple)
Qualifications: BA (Hons, Hull), Dip
Law, FCIArb

O'Malley *Eamon Augustine*
Call Date: Mar 1997 (Middle Temple)

O'Neill *Ms Elizabeth Helen* •
Lord Chancellor's Department,
Criminal Appeal Office, Royal Courts of
Justice, The Strand, London WC2, Call
Date: Nov 1984 (Middle Temple)

O'Neill *Miss Elizabeth Marie*
Freshfields, 65 Fleet Street, London
EC4Y 1HS, 0171 936 4000, Fax: 0171
832 7001, Call Date: Nov 1996 (Middle
Temple) Qualifications: LLB
(Hons)(Dublin), BCL (Oxon)

O'Neill *Mrs Joanne*
U.S.D.A.W., 188 Wilmslow Road,
Fallowfield, Manchester M14 6LJ, 0161
224 2804 Ext 256, Call Date: Feb 1995
(Lincoln's Inn) Qualifications: LLB
(Hons)(L'pool)

O'Neill *Paul Gerard*
Call Date: Oct 1994 (Gray's Inn)
Qualifications: LLB (Leeds)

O'Reilly *Michael Anthony Joseph* •
Legal Advisor, Kvaerner Construction
Group Lt, Maple Cross House, Denham
Way, Maple Cross, Rickmansworth,
Herts WD3 2SW, 01923 776666, Call
Date: Oct 1997 (Inner Temple)
Qualifications: BSc, CPE

O'Riordan *Miss Catherine Nuala* •
Assistant Parliamentary Counsel,
Parliamentary Counsel Office, 36
Whitehall, London SW1, Call Date: Nov
1989 (Middle Temple) Qualifications:
MA (Oxon),BCL

O'Riordan *Dennis Thomas Delcaron* •
Associate General Counsel, The
Republic National Bank of, New York,
30 Monument Street, London
EC3R 8NB, 0171 860 3332, Fax: 0171
860 3289, and Member New York, Call
Date: Oct 1993 (Inner Temple)
Qualifications: LLB (Hons), MA (Lon)

O'Rourke *Thomas*
British Telecom, 5 Brindley Place,
Bir *ham, 0121 230 4970, Fax: 0121
230 4961, Call Date: Nov 1991
(Lincoln's Inn) Qualifications: BA
(Hons) (Cardiff), LLB (Hons)*

O'Shea *Carl David*
Call Date: Nov 1998 (Middle Temple)
Qualifications: BA (Hons)(Essex)

O'Sullivan *Patrick John*
Property Adviser, Assignments
International Ltd, 14 Old Square,
Lincoln's Inn, London WC2A 3UB,
0171 447 1278, Fax: 0171 447 1279,
Call Date: July 1982 (Lincoln's Inn)
Qualifications: BA

O'Sullivan *Miss Rosalind Mary*
Call Date: Mar 1998 (Middle Temple)
Qualifications: LLB (Hons)(Lond)

O'Sullivan *Sean Denis*
Call Date: Oct 1995 (Middle Temple)
Qualifications: B.Sc (Hons)(Wales), Dip
in Law

O'Toole *Miss Ellie*
Call Date: Mar 1998 (Gray's Inn)
Qualifications: LLB (Not'ham)

Oakes *Miss Sheila Gwendoline*
Principal Legal Adviser, Derbyshire
Magistrates, Courts Committee, West
Bank House, Albion Road, Chesterfield,
Derbyshire S40 1UQ, 01246 220008,
Fax: 01246 231196, Call Date: July
1990 (Middle Temple) Qualifications:
LLB

Oakley *Miss Jemima Jane* •
Two Garden Court, 1st Floor, Middle
Temple, London, EC4Y 9BL, Call Date:
Nov 1992 (Inner Temple)
Qualifications: BA (Oxon)

Oakley-White *Olivier Philip*
Call Date: Feb 1995 (Gray's Inn)
Qualifications: BA (Oxon)

Oates *Laurence Campbell* •
Director, Lord Chancellor's Magistrates'
Courts Group, Lord Chancellor's Dept,
Selborne House, 54-60 Victoria Street,
London SW1E 6QW, 0171 210 8809,
Call Date: July 1968 (Middle Temple)
Qualifications: LLB

Obi *Onyeabo C*
Call Date: Nov 1962 (Gray's Inn)

Obonyo *Miss Caroline Amony*
Call Date: Oct 1996 (Middle Temple)
Qualifications: LLB (Hons)(Anglia)

Oddie *Ms Rosamund Juliet*
Call Date: Oct 1990 (Middle Temple)
Qualifications: BA (Oxon), Dip Law

Oderberg *Keith John*
South China Chambers, Room 1101,
16 Harcourt Road, 01852 5282378,
Fax: 01852 5201512, and Member
Hong Kong Bar Victorian Bar 2 King's
Bench Walk, 1st Floor, Temple,
London, EC4Y 7DE, Call Date: July
1990 (Middle Temple) Qualifications:
LLB, BA (Melbourne)

Odilibe *Miss Amanda Ifeoma*
Call Date: Nov 1992 (Middle Temple)
Qualifications: LLB (Hons)

Odim *Edward Usim*
Call Date: Nov 1995 (Middle Temple)
Qualifications: BA (Hons), Dip in, Law

Odlum *Miss Che Georgia*
Call Date: Oct 1998 (Lincoln's Inn)
Qualifications: BA (Hons)

Oduba *Olujimi Olajide*
and Member Nigerian Bar, Call Date: Nov
1971 (Gray's Inn) Qualifications: LLB
Hons (Lond)

Ofokansi *Emmanuel Nwalie*
Member - Inst of Professional Managers
and Specialists, Formerly Deputy Chief
Clerk to the Justices - Inner London
Magistrates' Court Service., Call Date:
July 1967 (Lincoln's Inn)

Ogborne *Nigel John* •
Prosecution Team Leader, CPS,
Prebendal Court, 4-7 Oxford Road,
Aylesbury, Bucks HP19 3EY, 01296
436441, Fax: 01296 88664, Call Date:
Nov 1985 (Gray's Inn) Qualifications: BA

Ogilvie-Graham *Dr Thomas Syme*
Call Date: Oct 1998 (Gray's Inn)
Qualifications: BVM & S.,DVM & S.,,
(Royal College of, Veterinary Surgeons),
(Edinburgh), Msc (Reading)

Ogle *Michael Burton*
Skerraton, Buckfastleigh, Devon
TQ11 0NB, 01364 642232, Fax: 01364
644282, Call Date: Feb 1956 (Inner
Temple) Qualifications: MA

Ohene-Kontoh *Kenneth*
Lecturer in Law, 111 Knoll Drive,
Styvechale, Coventry CV3 5DE, Call Date:
Nov 1975 (Middle Temple)
Qualifications: LLB (Lond), MBIM

Ohonbamu *Miss Fleur Izogie Carmen*
Call Date: Nov 1997 (Lincoln's Inn)
Qualifications: LLB (Hons)(Lond)

Ojo *Chief Samuel Ladosu*
Bowland Court, 230 Elvate Crescent,
Manchester M8 8DH, 0161 8634 8172,
Fax: 0161 819 2904, Hon Citizen of
Louisville, Kentucky State, U.S.A. and
Member Nigerian Bar, Call Date: Nov
1962 (Lincoln's Inn) Qualifications:
MSc, LLB (Lond), LLM (Leic)

Ojukwu *Mrs Mary Ada* •
Housing Advice Lawyer - London
Borough of Lambeth, Call Date: Oct
1993 (Lincoln's Inn) Qualifications: BA
(Hons) , MSc

Okara *Kemela Oduoboye Olisaeloka* •
Solicitor & Advocate, 0181 731 9393,
Fax: 0181 731 9393, and Member
Nigeria, Call Date: Feb 1989 (Gray's Inn)
Qualifications: LLB

Okaru *Paul Newton Chinedu*
Call Date: Nov 1996 (Lincoln's Inn)
Qualifications: LLB (Hons)(LSE)

Okereke *Mrs Florence Chinyere*
Legal Assistant - Litigation Commercial
II, Dental Hall, 5 Chancery Lane,
London, 0171 320 6961, and Member
Nigeria Bar, Call Date: Oct 1996 (Middle
Temple) Qualifications: LLB (Hons)
(Bucks)

Okezue *Miss Ifeoma Chicka*
Call Date: Mar 1996 (Lincoln's Inn)
Qualifications: LLB (Hons)

Okhai *Miss Zeenat Kassam*
Watson, Farley & Williams, 15 Appold
Street, London EC2A 2HB, 0171 814
8000, Fax: 0181 814 8141/2, Call Date:
Oct 1996 (Gray's Inn) Qualifications:
LLB (Kent), LLM (Cantab)

Okine *Miss Julie Anne*
Call Date: Oct 1996 (Lincoln's Inn)
Qualifications: LLB (Hons)(Lond)

Okorefe *Miss Nancy Emuobo*
Call Date: Nov 1992 (Middle Temple)
Qualifications: LLB (Hons)

Okoro *James Derek*
Call Date: Oct 1997 (Gray's Inn)
Qualifications: LLB (Lond)

Okosi *Miss Felicia Nkechi Bernadette*
Mildred & Beaumont Solicitors, 299B
Lavender Hill, London SW11 1LN, Call
Date: Feb 1994 (Inner Temple)
Qualifications: LLB (Wales)

Okosi *Miss Frances Chineze*
Call Date: Oct 1995 (Gray's Inn)
Qualifications: LLB

Okpaluba *Johnson Chukwuemeka*
Call Date: Nov 1992 (Inner Temple)
Qualifications: LLB, LLM (Lond)

Okubajo *Miss Olufunmilayo Olukemi* •
Senior Crown Prosecutor, Crown
Prosecutor Service, 50 Ludgate Hill,
London EC4M, 0171 273 8427, Fax:
0171 273 8042, Call Date: Oct 1994
(Gray's Inn) Qualifications: BA (Nigeria),
CPE (Middx)

Okunlola *Oluwaremilekun Oluwatoyin*
Deputy Chief Clerk, Student of the New
York State Bar, Call Date: July 1989
(Lincoln's Inn) Qualifications: LLB
(Hons)

Okunnu *Miss Lateefa Abisola*
Head of Chambers, Femi Okunnu & Co
(legal Prac), 3 Karimu Kotun Street,
Victoria Island, Lagos, 01 261
5010;615009, Fax: 01 615025, Member
Nigerian Bar Association and Member
Nigerian Bar, Call Date: July 1987 (Gray's
Inn) Qualifications: LLB (LSE)

Olabode *Adewale*
Call Date: July 1998 (Middle Temple)
Qualifications: BSc (Hons), MPA, (Lagos)

Olaide *Fatai Adeleke*
38 Lynn Road, Clapham South, London
SW12 9LA, 0171 498 0467 or 0958 317
233, Call Date: Nov 1996 (Inner Temple)
Qualifications: LLB

Old-Hall *Mrs Rachaelle Catherine*
Call Date: July 1998 (Lincoln's Inn)
Qualifications: BA (Hons)

Oldfield *Ian John Frank Robert*
Call Date: Nov 1996 (Inner Temple)
Qualifications: LLB (Bris)

Oldknow *Christopher James*
Legal Associate at Microsoft, 0118 404
3186, Fax: 0118 404 6767, Call Date: Oct
1995 (Middle Temple) Qualifications:
B.Sc (Hons), Dip Law, LLM

Olhausen *Rev William Paul*
Greyfriars Church, 26 Prospect Street,
Reading RG1 7YG, Call Date: Nov 1993
(Middle Temple)

Oliver *Mrs Judy Dorothy*
'Appledene', 8 Woodruff Close,
Upchurch, Rainham/Gillingham, Kent
ME8 7XQ, 01634 268707, Fax: 01474
331674, Freelance Consultant, Call Date:
Feb 1980 (Lincoln's Inn) Qualifications:
BA, FIPM

Oliver *Miss Lindsey Frances*
Call Date: July 1977 (Middle Temple)
Qualifications: BA

Oliver *Mrs Marcia Frances* •
Britvic Soft Drinks Limited, Britvic
House, Broomfield Road, Chelmsford
CM1 1TU, (01245) 261871, Fax:
(01245) 346983, Call Date: Nov 1984
(Middle Temple) Qualifications: LLB
(Hons)(Lond)

Oliver *Dr Peter John* •
Member, Legal Service, Legal Service,
European Commission, Rue de Loi 200,
1049 Brussels, 296 63 39, Fax: 296 43
08, Call Date: Nov 1977 (Middle Temple)
Qualifications: BA (Cantab), Licence
Speciale, en Droit Europeen, (Brussels),
PhD [Cantab]

Ollerenshaw *Michael Frederic*
Eighteen Carlton Crescent,
Southampton, SO15 2XR, Call Date:
1969 (Gray's Inn)

Olphin *Albert Edward Laurence*
Foxes Meadow, 12 Daisy Lane, Alrewas,
Staffs DE13 7EW, 01283 790185, Call
Date: May 1958 (Lincoln's Inn)
Qualifications: LLB

Olsen *Mrs Jeraine Dickin* •
p/t Commissioner on the Mental Health
Act Commission, Call Date: July 1969
(Gray's Inn)

Olver *Graham Dudley* •
Legal & Contracts Director, Alstom UK
Ltd, Investment Projects Depart, P O Box
115, Mill Road, Rugby CV21 1ZN, 01788
545300, Fax: 01788 535305, Call Date:
Nov 1985 (Gray's Inn) Qualifications: BA
(Warw)

Omar *Paul Johan*
Flat 3, 25 Holland Road, Hove, Sussex
BN3 1JF, (01273) 739921, and Member
Malaysia Bar, Call Date: Oct 1990 (Gray's
Inn) Qualifications: LLB (Exeter), LLM
(Sussex)

Omezie *Anthony Nwabudike*
Chancery Chambers, 1st Floor Offices, 70/72 Chancery Lane, London, WC2A 1AB, Call Date: Nov 1991 (Lincoln's Inn) Qualifications: LLB (Hons), LLM

Omotosho *Mrs Olalekan Kuburat*
Deputy Chief Clerk, Inner London Magistrates', Courts Service, 3rd Floor, North West Wing, Bush House, Aldwych, London SE15 5QF, Call Date: Nov 1989 (Gray's Inn) Qualifications: LLB Hons (Lond), Post.Dip. Management, Studies

Onafowokan *Miss Oluwayinka Taiwo*
Call Date: Nov 1994 (Middle Temple) Qualifications: LLB (Hons)

Onalo *Miss Jacqueline Wedube*
Call Date: Nov 1998 (Inner Temple) Qualifications: LLB (Wolves)

Ong *Chee Kiam*
Deputy Chief Clerk, Inner London Magistrates', Courts Service, 65 Romney Street, London SW1P 3RD, Call Date: July 1988 (Lincoln's Inn) Qualifications: LLB (Hons) (Lond), MA (City)

Ong *Miss Sharon Si Hsien* •
Counsel, EDS, EDS Park, Stonehill Road, Ottershaw, Chertsey KT16 0AX, 01932 897160, Call Date: July 1987 (Middle Temple) Qualifications: BSc, MSc (Lond) , Dip Law (City)

Ong *Miss Su Mei*
Call Date: Oct 1996 (Middle Temple) Qualifications: LLB (Hons) (Notts), LLM (Lond)

Onuma-Elliott *Mrs Nkolika Anne* •
Senior Crown Prosecutor, Kings House, Kymberly Road, Harrow, Middlesex HA1, 0181 424 8688, and Member Law School Nigeria, Call Date: Oct 1992 (Inner Temple) Qualifications: LLB, LLM (Lond)

Oogarah *Jason Rishi*
Call Date: Nov 1998 (Inner Temple) Qualifications: LLB (Sheff)

Oppenheimer *Mrs Nicola Anne* •
Principal Establishment & Finance Officer, Call Date: July 1972 (Middle Temple) Qualifications: LLB

Opstad *Christopher Thorleif*
Call Date: July 1975 (Lincoln's Inn) Qualifications: MA (Oxon) MPhil, (Lond)

Oram *Miss Deborah Ruth*
Legal Advisor, Wragge & Co Solicitors, 55 Colmore Row, Birmingham B3 2AS, 0121 233 1000, Fax: 0171 210 3171, Call Date: Oct 1991 (Lincoln's Inn) Qualifications: LLB (Hons)

Orange *John Robert Wellwood*
Chief Executive, Manor House, Tot Hill, Fornham All Saints, Bury St Edmunds, Suffolk IP28 6LD, Call Date: Nov 1966 (Gray's Inn) Qualifications: BA Hons (Dublin)

Orange *Stephen Michael*
160 Aldersgate Street, LondoN EC1A 4DD, 0171 367 3000, Fax: 0171 367 2000, Call Date: Mar 1997 (Inner Temple) Qualifications: LLB (Nott'm)

Ordish *Mrs Judith*
Senior Court Clerk, Nottinghamshire Mags Court, Carrington Street, Nottingham NG2 1EE, 0115 955 8111, Fax: 0115 955 8131, Call Date: Nov 1983 (Inner Temple) Qualifications: BA, MBA

Orgill *Mrs Deborah Jean*
Call Date: Oct 1997 (Lincoln's Inn) Qualifications: LLB (Hons) (B'Ham)

Orkin *Edmond Leonard*
41 Elliot Road, London NW4 3DS, 0181 203 7077, Fax: 0181 202 7077, Call Date: Nov 1950 (Middle Temple) Qualifications: LLB (Lond)

Orme *Simon Timothy* •
Senior Crown Prosecutor, Crown Prosecution Service, United House, Piccadilly, York YO1 1SQ, 01904 456684, Call Date: July 1986 (Inner Temple) Qualifications: BSc (Econ)

Ormsby *Miss Carol-Anne Rose*
Call Date: Nov 1993 (Middle Temple) Qualifications: LLB (Natal), CPE (Bris)

Orphanou *Vrahimis Antoniou*
34 Parkgate Avenue, Hadley Wood, Herts EN4 0NR, 0181 364 9544, and Member Cyprus, Call Date: Nov 1971 (Lincoln's Inn)

Orr *Miss Patricia*
Call Date: Nov 1995 (Lincoln's Inn) Qualifications: BA (Hons)

Orrell *John Edward*
Call Date: Nov 1957 (Gray's Inn) Qualifications: BA (Oxon)

Osammor *Edward*
Call Date: Mar 1999 (Gray's Inn) Qualifications: BSc (Econ), LLB

Osborne *Andrew James* •
Group Legal Adviser & Deputy Company Secretary, Camelot Group Plc, Tolpits Lane, Watford WD1 8RN, 01923 425104, Fax: 01923 425006, Call Date: Feb 1984 (Gray's Inn) Qualifications: LLB (Reading)

Osborne *Miss Antoinette Marie-Therese*
Legal Advisor, Abbey Legal Protection Limited, 17 Lansdowne Road, Croydon, Surrey CR0 2BX, 0181 730 6119, Fax: 0181 730 6001, Call Date: Nov 1996 (Inner Temple) Qualifications: BA (Lond), LLB (Lond)

Osborne *Miss Christine Louise* •
Professional Services, (Life & Pensions) Limited, Allied Dunbar Centre, Swindon SN1 1EL, 01793 514514, Call Date: Nov 1995 (Gray's Inn) Qualifications: B.Comm (B'ham)

Osborne *Ms Clare Elizabeth Ann* •
Legal Advisor, Zurich Financial Services, UK Life Limited, Allied Dunbar Centre, Swindon SN1 1EL, 01793 505796, Call Date: Nov 1994 (Middle Temple) Qualifications: BA (Hons)

Osborne *Clive Maxwell Lawton* •
Legal Director, Department of Trade & Industry, 10 Victoria Street, London SW1, 0171 215 3263, Fax: 0171 215 3242, Call Date: Nov 1978 (Gray's Inn) Qualifications: MA (Oxon)

Osborne *Miss Jennifer Janet* •
Joint Council for the Welfare, 115 Old Street, London EC1V 9JR, 0171 251 8708, Fax: 0171 251 8707, Call Date: Nov 1992 (Lincoln's Inn) Qualifications: LLB (Hons)

Osborne *Miss Nicola Frances* •
Solicitor's Office, East Wing, Somerset House, Strand, London WC2R 1LB, 0171 438 6111, Fax: 0171 438 6246, Call Date: Nov 1994 (Lincoln's Inn) Qualifications: LLB (Hons) (Anglia)

Osiecki *Desmond*
Call Date: Nov 1996 (Middle Temple) Qualifications: LLB (Hons)

Osner *Nigel Ralph* •
Judicial Appointments Group, Lord Chancellor's Department, Selborne House, 54-60 Victoria Street, London SW1E 6QW, 0171 210 8860, Call Date: July 1971 (Inner Temple) Qualifications: LLB

Ossei *Mrs Vida Afua Sarpong*
Call Date: July 1996 (Inner Temple) Qualifications: LLB

Oster *Norman Howard*
7 Etzion Street, Ramat Gan 52383, 03 5743834, Fax: 03 6776942, 9 Gough Square, London, EC4A 3DE, Call Date: Feb 1954 (Middle Temple)

Otieno *John Rowland* •
Principal Legal Officer, The Solicitor's Office, Health & Safety Executive, Rose Court, 2 Southwark Bridge, London SE1 9NS, 0171 717 6912, Fax: 0171 717 6661, Call Date: July 1979 (Lincoln's Inn) Qualifications: LLB (Hons),, LLM (Lond)

Ottaway *Bradley John Charles*
53 Carew Road, London N17 9BA, 0181 808 1826, Call Date: Feb 1994 (Lincoln's Inn) Qualifications: BA (Hons, Toronto), MA (Lond), LLB (Hons, Lond)

Otty *Neville John*
Corporate Pensions Technical Manager, 74 Elm Grove Road, Barnes, London SW13 0BS, 0181 878 1646, Member of Association of Persian Lawyers, Call Date: Nov 1962 (Gray's Inn) Qualifications: APMI

Oultram *Jonathan Richard Gerard* •
Senior Crown Prosecutor, Crown
Prosecution Service, Windsor House, 10
Manchester Road, Bradford, BD5 0QH,
Fax: 01274 870640, Call Date: Nov 1988
(Middle Temple) Qualifications: LLB

Outhwaite *Brian* •
Senior Crown Prosecutor, Call Date: Nov
1988 (Lincoln's Inn) Qualifications: LLB
Hons (Leeds)

Oven *Patrick Jerome* •
Principal Crown Prosecutor, Crown
Prosecution Service, One Onslow Street,
Guildford GU1 4YA, 01483 882600, Fax:
01483 882603/4, Call Date: Nov 1984
(Gray's Inn) Qualifications: LLB
(Manch)

Overton *Martin John* •
Company/Commercial Lawyer, Ernst &
Young, Becket House, 1 Lambeth Palace
road, London SE1 7EU, Call Date: July
1987 (Lincoln's Inn) Qualifications:
LLB.

Owen *Christopher Henry*
Call Date: Feb 1963 (Inner Temple)

Owen *David Paul*
Head of Legal Services, Trafford
Magistrates' Court, The Court House,
Ashton Lane, Sale M33 1UP, 0161 976
3333, Fax: 0161 962 4333, Call Date:
Nov 1983 (Gray's Inn) Qualifications: BA

Owen *Ms Elen Mai* •
Senior Crown Prosecutor, Crown
Prosecution Service, Haes y Ffynon,
Penrhos Road, Bangor, North Wales,
01248 373151, Fax: 01248 373150, Call
Date: Nov 1985 (Gray's Inn)
Qualifications: LLB (Lond)

Owen *Miss Elizabeth Jane* •
Group Legal Adviser, Aon UK Holdings
Ltd, Law Division, 8 Devonshire Square,
London EC2M 4PL, 0171 623 5500, Fax:
0171 972 9862, Call Date: July 1978
(Middle Temple) Qualifications: MA
(Oxon)

Owen *Gerald Victor*
also Inn of Court I 1969, Call Date: June
1949 (Gray's Inn) Qualifications: MA
(Cantab) LLB, (Lond)

Owen *James Alexander Dalziel*
Call Date: Mar 1996 (Gray's Inn)
Qualifications: BA (Dunelm)

Owen *Mrs Mary Lisa Hacon* •
Senior Commercial Lawyer Cadbury
Schweppes plc and Company Secretary
Trebor Bassett Ltd, Cadbury Schweppes
Plc, Legal Department, Franklin House,
Bournville Lane, Birmingham B30 2NB,
0121 698 4813, Fax: 0121 459 0383,
Call Date: July 1972 (Gray's Inn)

Owen *Paul* •
Legal Advisor, Knowsley Magistrates
Court, The Court House, Lathom Road,
Huyton, Merseyside L36 9XY, 0151 481
4418, Call Date: July 1998 (Inner
Temple) Qualifications: LLB

Owen *Miss Susanna Wynne*
Lecturer in Law, Law School, University
of East London, 0181 590 7722 Ext
2192, Fax: 0181 599 5122, Call Date:
July 1988 (Lincoln's Inn) Qualifications:
BA (Hons) (Oxon), Dip Law

Owen *Mrs Tracy Rebecca* •
Senior Legal Adviser, Company Secretary
(CACS), Institute of Chartered,
Accountants, Silbury Boulevard, Central
Milton Keynes MK9 2HL, 01908 546289,
Fax: 01908 691165, Call Date: July 1984
(Middle Temple) Qualifications: LLB

Owen *William John*
Neuadd Deg, 31 Bronwydd Road,
Carmarthen, Dyfed SA31 2AL, 01267
236437, Fax: 01267 236437, Call Date:
June 1949 (Lincoln's Inn)

Owen Hughes *Archibald*
First National Building, 2nd Floor, 24
Fenwick Street, Liverpool, L2 7NE, Call
Date: Nov 1940 (Gray's Inn)
Qualifications: LLM

Owens *Gareth Richard* •
Principal Legal Officer, West Wiltshire
District, Council, Bradley Road,
Trowbridge, Wiltshire BA14 ORD, 01225
770310, Fax: 01225 761053, Call Date:
Nov 1993 (Gray's Inn) Qualifications:
LLB (Wales)

Owusu-Afriyie *John*
Advisor, and Member Ghana Bar, Call
Date: July 1963 (Inner Temple)
Qualifications: BL

Owusu-Afriyie *Samuel Osei* •
Nimoh & Co Solicitors, 92 Coldharbour
Lane, London SE5 9PU, Call Date: Nov
1992 (Middle Temple) Qualifications:
LLB (Hons, Lond)

Owusu-Akyaw *Miss Jennifer*
Call Date: Oct 1998 (Gray's Inn)
Qualifications: LLB (Wales)

Owusu-Tevie *Ms Alberta Elizabeth* •
Chief Solicitor, Town Hall, The
Burroughs, Hendon NW4 4BG, 0181 359
2517, Fax: 0181 359 2680, Call Date:
July 1984 (Inner Temple) Qualifications:
BA

Oyediji *Chief Ademola Olushola*
New Tower Centre, 181 Tower Bridge
Road, London SE1 2EU, 0171 357 0445/
0171 378 9506, Fax: 0171 357 0288,
and Member Nigeria, Call Date: July
1997 (Lincoln's Inn) Qualifications: LLB
(Hons)(Lond), LLM (Lagos), BL

Pacifico *Adam Louis*
Call Date: Nov 1991 (Inner Temple)
Qualifications: LLB

Pacifico *Miss Stephanie Lizbeth*
Call Date: July 1982 (Gray's Inn)
Qualifications: BA

Paddock *Richard Christopher*
Solicitor, Call Date: July 1979 (Lincoln's
Inn) Qualifications: LLB (Manch)

Padfield *Guy Lawrence Notton*
Call Date: Oct 1995 (Inner Temple)
Qualifications: MA (Cantab), M.Phil
(Oxon), CPE

Page *Matthew Charles* •
Legal Services Manager, Financial
Services Authority, 25 North Colonnade,
Canary Wharf, London E14 5HS, 0171
676 1392, Fax: 0171 676 1393, Call
Date: Feb 1986 (Middle Temple)
Qualifications: MA (Oxon), MSc , ACI Arb

Page *Miss Melinda*
Call Date: Nov 1996 (Middle Temple)
Qualifications: LLB (Hons)(Manch)

Page *Miss Sarah Elizabeth* •
Senior Crown Prosecutor, CPS
(Oxfordshire Branch), The Courtyard,
Lombard Street, Abingdon, Oxon
OX14 5SE, 01235 555678, Call Date: July
1989 (Inner Temple) Qualifications: LLB
(Hons)

Paget-Brown *Ian*
West Wind Building, Harbour Drive, Box
2197, Grand Cayman, 809-949-4904,
Fax: 809-949-7920, and Member
Washington, Virginia, Colorado Bar
Cayman Islands Bar 5 Paper Bldgs,
Ground Floor, Temple, London, EC4Y
7HB, Call Date: July 1968 (Lincoln's
Inn) Qualifications: LLB (Lond)

Pain *Kevin Mark*
Call Date: Oct 1995 (Gray's Inn)
Qualifications: BA

Pakenham-Walsh *John* •
Standing Counsel to the General Synod of
the Church of England, Crinken,
Weydown Road, Haslemere, Surrey
GU27 1DS, 01428 642033, Call Date:
June 1951 (Lincoln's Inn)
Qualifications: MA (Oxon)

Pal *Partha Sarathi*
and Member India Bar, Call Date: May
1994 (Gray's Inn) Qualifications: BA
(Cantab)

Palin *Henry* •
Regional Lawyer, Department of Social
Security, Government Buildings, St Agnes
Road, Galbalfa, Cardiff, 01222 586749,
Fax: 01222 586080, Call Date: Nov 1971
(Gray's Inn) Qualifications: LLB

Pallister *Neil* •
Senior Crown Prosecutor, Crown
Prosecution Service, A, 136 Sandyford
Road, Newcastle Upon Tyne, Tyne &
Wear, Call Date: July 1982 (Lincoln's
Inn) Qualifications: LLB (Hull)

Pallot *Lieutenant Marcus Louis
Alexander* •
ACNJA, Royal Naval College, Greenwich,
London SE10 9NN, Royal Naval Officer,
Call Date: Oct 1997 (Middle Temple)
Qualifications: LLB (Hons)(B'ham)

Palmer *Mrs Ann*
Senior Legal Adviser, Leicester
Magistrates' Court, 674 Melton Road,
Thurmaston, Leicester LE4 8BB, 0116
2692369, Call Date: July 1988 (Middle
Temple) Qualifications: BA (Hons) ,
Assoc IPD

Palmer *Martin James* •
Corporate Tax Analyst, Arthur
Anderson, Abbots House, Abbey Street,
Reading RG1 3BD, 0118 950 8141, Call
Date: Nov 1998 (Middle Temple)
Qualifications: LLB (Hons) (L'pool)

Palmer *Dr Roy Newberry*
Medico-Legal Consultant (1989-1998),
57 Kennington Road, London SE1 7PZ,
0171 401 9158, Fax: 0171 401 9158,
Call Date: Feb 1977 (Middle Temple)
Qualifications: MB, BS, MRCS, LRCP,
DObstRCOG, LLB

Palmer *Miss Tara Marie*
Call Date: July 1998 (Gray's Inn)
Qualifications: LLB (L'pool)

Palmes *Peter Manfred Jerome*
Call Date: Jan 1948 (Inner Temple)

Palser *Miss Rebecca*
Call Date: Oct 1998 (Inner Temple)
Qualifications: BA (E. Anglia)

Panayides *Ioannis*
Finance & Legal Advisor, P O Box 4682,
3726 Limassol, 00 357 5 586876, Call
Date: Nov 1992 (Middle Temple)
Qualifications: LLB (Hons) (Lond),
M.I.C.S., F.C.M.A.

Pandey *Reuben Vrijendra Kumar
Marcus*
Call Date: Nov 1996 (Lincoln's Inn)
Qualifications: BA (Hons), BCL

Pang *Chesper-Joghne*
Houghie & Co, 18 Fairlie Court,
Stroudley Walk, London E3 9HG, Call
Date: Mar 1997 (Lincoln's Inn)
Qualifications: LLB (Hons) (Lond)

Pang *Wai-Cheung*
Winstan & Co Solicitors, 72/74 Notting
Hill Gate, London W11 3HT, 0171 727
5675, Fax: 0171 221 1211, Call Date:
May 1992 (Lincoln's Inn)
Qualifications: BSc (Hon), Dip
Associateship, Dip Law

Paonessa *Miss Laura Alexandria*
Call Date: Oct 1993 (Middle Temple)
Qualifications: BA (Hons) (Manc)

Papadopulos *Nicholas Charles*
Call Date: Oct 1990 (Middle Temple)
Qualifications: BA (Cantab), Dip Law
(City)

Paradysz *Roger John* •
Principal Crown Procurator, Crown
Prosecution Service, 50 Ludgate Hill,
London EC4, Call Date: Nov 1985
(Gray's Inn) Qualifications: BA (Hons)
(Trent)

Parasie *Ms Gudrun*
European Legal Advice (ELA) Service,
0181 888 0216, President of the
Employed & Non-practising Bar
Assocication (ENPBA), Call Date: Oct
1994 (Middle Temple) Qualifications:
LLB (Hons) (Lond)

Parasram *Miss Isabelle Amanda* •
Group Legal Adviser, Hambro
Countrywide PLC, Kingsgate, 1 King
Edward Road, Brentwood, Essex
CM14 4HG, 01277 264466, Fax: 01277
217916, Call Date: Oct 1995 (Gray's
Inn) Qualifications: LLB (Hons) (Lond)

Parchment *Nollis Reginald*
and Member Jamaica Trinidad &
Tobago Bars, Call Date: Nov 1974
(Lincoln's Inn) Qualifications: LLB
(Lond)

Parfitt *Mrs Ifeyinwa Maureen*
65 Worcester Road, Walthamstow,
London E17 5QR, 0181 923 2187, and
Member Nigeria, Call Date: July 1983
(Lincoln's Inn) Qualifications: BA

Parikh *Romesh Chandra*
8 Shackleton Road, Southall, Middlesex
UB1 2JA, Call Date: Nov 1975 (Middle
Temple)

Paris *Mrs Susan Jill*
Call Date: Nov 1979 (Lincoln's Inn)
Qualifications: BA (Hons)

Park *Mrs Deborah Jane*
32 Birchwood Avenue, London
N10 3BE, Call Date: Nov 1994 (Inner
Temple) Qualifications: BA (Lond),
CPE (Middx)

Parker *Christopher Ian* •
Director, Legal Services, Digital
Equipment Co Ltd, Digital Park,
Imperial Way, Worton Grange, Reading
RG2 0TL, 01734 203850, Fax: 01734
202390, Call Date: July 1977 (Gray's
Inn) Qualifications: LLB

Parker *Christopher John Gorrill*
Talltrees, 197 Newport, Lincoln
LN1 3DX, 01522 526534, Call Date:
July 1984 (Inner Temple)
Qualifications: LLB (Newcastle)

Parker *Miss Emma-Louise*
Call Date: July 1998 (Lincoln's Inn)
Qualifications: LLB (Hons)

Parker *Miss Fern*
Call Date: Oct 1995 (Lincoln's Inn)
Qualifications: BA (Hons) (Bris), Dip in
Law (City)

Parker *George Brian*
alos Inn of Court L, Call Date: Nov 1934
(Middle Temple) Qualifications: MA,
LLB (Cantab)

Parker *Miss Janice Teresa*
Deputy Chief Clerk, Inner London &
City Family, Proceedings Court, 59-65
Wells Street, London W1A 3AE, Call
Date: July 1981 (Lincoln's Inn)
Qualifications: LLB (Lond)

Parker *Mark Laurence*
Call Date: July 1983 (Inner Temple)
Qualifications: MA (Hons) (Cantab)

Parker *Nigel Denis* •
Assistant Legal Adviser, Foreign &
Commonwealth Office, King Charles
Street, London SW1A 2AH, 0171 270
2576, Fax: 0171 270 2767, Call Date:
July 1985 (Middle Temple)
Qualifications: MA (Cantab)

Parker *Oliver John* •
Lord Chancellor's Department,
Trevelyan House, Great Peter Street,
London SW1, Call Date: Nov 1977
(Inner Temple)

Parker *Robert Stewart* •
Parliamentary Counsel, Office of The
Parliamentary Counsel, 36 Whitehall,
London SW1A 2AY, 0171 210 6611,
also Inn of Court L, Call Date: July 1975
(Middle Temple) Qualifications: MA
(Oxon), M.I.Mgt

Parker *Stephen Albert* •
The Home Office, Room 806, Queen
Annes's Gate, London SW1H 9AD, 0171
273 2768, Call Date: July 1982
(Lincoln's Inn) Qualifications: MA, LLB
(Cantab)

Parkes *Bruce Winfield*
Company Secretary, 'Littlefields', Lea
Lane, Little Braxted, Witham, Essex
CM8 3XA, Call Date: Nov 1953 (Middle
Temple) Qualifications: LLB (Lond)

Parkes *David John*
Call Date: Nov 1969 (Middle Temple)

Parkin *Ms Victoria Howell*
Sweet & Maxwell, 100 Avenue Road,
London NW3 3PF, 0171 393 7000, Fax:
0171 393 7010, Call Date: Nov 1994
(Inner Temple) Qualifications: LLB
(Soton)

Parkins *Miss Diane Julie* •
Barrister, Bedfordshire County Council,
County Hall, Bedford MK42 9AP, 01234
228802, Fax: 01234 228125, Call Date:
Feb 1986 (Gray's Inn)

Parkinson *Mrs Dorren Patricia* •
Lord Chancellor's Department,
Criminal Appeal Office, Royal Courts of
Justice, The Strand, London WC2A 2LL,
Call Date: Feb 1973 (Inner Temple)

Parkinson *Stephen Lindsay* •
Queen Anne's Chambers, 28 Broadway,
London SW1, 0171 210 3233, Head of
Company/Chancery Litigation, Treasury
Solicitors Department, Call Date: July
1980 (Lincoln's Inn) Qualifications:
LLB (Lond)

Parks *Miss Fiona Catherine*
Call Date: Oct 1996 (Gray's Inn)
Qualifications: BA (Dunelm), MSc
(Sheff)

Parnell *Mrs Charlotte Angela*
Call Date: July 1983 (Gray's Inn)
Qualifications: BA

Parnell *Christopher Charles* •
Director, The Lantern Corporation.,
Adviser to the Russian Securities
Commission Securities Markets
Arbitrator, 52 Addington Square, London
SE5 7LB, 0171 701 8315, Fax: 0171 703
4209, Call Date: Nov 1979 (Lincoln's
Inn) Qualifications: LLB (Hons)

Parnell *Mrs Michele Donna* •
Financial Services Authority, 25 The
North Colonnade, Canary Wharf, London
E14 5HS, 0171 676 1218, Fax: 0171 676
1025, Call Date: Nov 1980 (Lincoln's
Inn) Qualifications: LLB (Hons), FCIArb

Parr-Ferris *Benedict Joseph George*
Call Date: Nov 1996 (Middle Temple)
Qualifications: LLB (Hons)

Parrack *Miss Jane Elizabeth*
Call Date: July 1978 (Lincoln's Inn)
Qualifications: LLB (Lond)

Parrish *Mrs Melanie Jane* •
Crown Prosecution Service, Portland
House, London SW1, Call Date: Nov 1992
(Middle Temple) Qualifications: BA
(Hons)

Parry *Dr Anthony*
Director, British Aerospace, 227 Rue De
La Loi, 1040 Brussels, Belgium, 010 322
2800300, Fax: 010 322 2800375, Call
Date: Feb 1971 (Middle Temple)
Qualifications: BA (Cantab), MA, PhD

Parry *Mrs Deborah* •
Legal Advisor, Preston Magistrates' Court,
Lawson Street, Preston, 01772 208000,
Call Date: Feb 1994 (Inner Temple)
Qualifications: LLB (Lancs)

Parry *Miss Hannah Jane*
Call Date: Nov 1997 (Inner Temple)
Qualifications: LLB (Wales)

Parry *Hubert Brian*
Call Date: Nov 1997 (Middle Temple)
Qualifications: LLB (Hons)(Lond), BA
(Hons) (Lond)

Parry *Jacques Henri* •
Head of Criminal Law Team, Law
Commission, Conquest House, 37-38
John Street, Theobalds Road, London
WC1N 2BQ, Call Date: July 1975 (Middle
Temple) Qualifications: BCL,MA

Parry *Miss Margaret Helen*
Justices' Clerk & Clerk to the Licensing
Justices, Thames Division Justice's
Clerkto the Inner London Youth Courts.,
West London Magistrates' Court, 181
Talgarth Road, London W6 8DN, 0181
741 1234, Fax: 0181 741 0808, Call
Date: July 1974 (Gray's Inn)
Qualifications: LLB (Lond)

Parry *Philip Christopher*
Russell & Russell Solicitors, 7-13 Wood
Street, Bolton BL1 1EE, 01204 399299,
Fax: 01204 389223, Solicitor, Call Date:
Oct 1995 (Lincoln's Inn) Qualifications:
LLB (Hons)(Sheff)

Parry *Richard Gwynedd* •
Carmarthenshire County Council, County
Hall, Carmarthen SA31 1JP, 01267
224012, Fax: 01267 230848, Call Date:
Oct 1993 (Gray's Inn) Qualifications:
LLB (Hons)(Wales)

Parry *Stuart David*
Legal Assistant, 2 Bracken Road,
Atherton, Manchester M46 9BF, 01942
884493, Call Date: July 1998 (Lincoln's
Inn) Qualifications: LLB (Hons)(Sheff)

Parsell *Richard Alan* •
Senior Crown Prosecutor, Crown
Prosecution Service, Teeside Branch,
Crown House, Linthorpe Road,
Middlesborough, Cleveland TS1 1TX,
01642 230444, Fax: 01642 253224, Call
Date: July 1975 (Gray's Inn)
Qualifications: LLB (B'ham)

Parsey *Richard Leveson Moreland*
40 Eastbury Avenue, Northwood,
Middlesex HA6 3LN, 01923 821484, Call
Date: Nov 1954 (Inner Temple)
Qualifications: M.A.

Parson *Peter John* •
Principal Crown Prosecutor, Crown
Prosecution Service, Artillery House,
Heritage Way, Droitwich, Worcestershire,
Call Date: Nov 1976 (Middle Temple)
Qualifications: BA (Oxon)

Parsons *David Robert Kingdon*
Lovell White Durrant Solicitor, 65
Holborn Viaduct, London EC1A 2DY,
0171 236 0066, Fax: 0171 248 4212,
Call Date: July 1985 (Middle Temple)
Qualifications: MA (Cantab)

Parsons *Mrs Kathryn Louise*
Call Date: Oct 1992 (Lincoln's Inn)
Qualifications: LLB(Hons)

Parsons *Thomas Alan*
Part Time Chairman of Tribunal, 11
Northiam Street, Pennethorne Place,
London E9 7HX, 0181 986 0930, Call
Date: Jan 1950 (Middle Temple)
Qualifications: LLB

Partridge *Ms Elizabeth Ann* •
Senior Court Clerk, West Glamorgan
Magistrates', Courts Committee, Grove
Place, Swansea, West Glamorgan
SA1 5DB, 01792 655171, Fax: 01792
651066, Call Date: July 1989 (Gray's
Inn) Qualifications: LLB [So'ton]

Partridge *Graham David* •
Senior Crown Prosecutor, Crown
Prosecution Service, London Branch,
Prospect West, Croydon, Surrey, Call
Date: Feb 1991 (Gray's Inn)
Qualifications: LLB (Lond)

Partridge *Richard Jack*
Call Date: Oct 1997 (Inner Temple)
Qualifications: LLB (Manchester)

Partridge *William George*
Deputy Clerk to the Justices, Berkshire &
Oxfordshire, Magistrates' Court Service,
Easby House, Henley, Oxon, Call Date:
Feb 1984 (Middle Temple)
Qualifications: Dip in Magisteral , Law
(Bris), M.Soc.Sci

Paschalides *Philip Andrew Stewart*
Call Date: Oct 1997 (Inner Temple)
Qualifications: MA (St Andrews), CPE
(City)

Pascoe *Eric Kenneth*
Calenick House, Calenick, Truro,
Cornwall TR3 6AA, 01872 272128, Call
Date: Nov 1958 (Middle Temple)
Qualifications: FCIB

Pascoe *Michael Peter*
Justice's Clerk, West Central Division of
Inner London, Inner London
Magistrates', Courts Service, Clerkenwell
Magistrates' Court, 78 King's Cross Road,
London WC1X 9QJ, 0171 278 6541, Fax:
0171 837 4526, Call Date: Oct 1966
(Middle Temple)

Passfield *Miss Zoe Victoria*
Call Date: Nov 1995 (Inner Temple)
Qualifications: LLB (Lancs)

Passi *Pradeep Kumar*
Freelance Researcher/Employed, 01772
254527, Call Date: Nov 1993 (Inner
Temple) Qualifications: LLB (Manch),
LLM (Lancs)

Patel *Alpesh Bipin*
Company Director, Melina Court, Melina
Place, St John's Wood, Lonodn NW8 9SB,
0171 286 6718, Fax: 0171 286 6718,
Call Date: Nov 1993 (Lincoln's Inn)
Qualifications: LLB (Hons), A.K.C., BA
(Oxford)

Patel *Miss Mannisha*
Call Date: Nov 1998 (Middle Temple)
Qualifications: LLB (Hons)(Sheff)

Patel *Mayoor* •
Legal Advisor, Lombard Bank Limited,
Lombard House, 339 Southbury Road,
Enfield, Middlesex EN1 1TW, 0181 344
5811, Fax: 0181 344 5601, Call Date:
Feb 1989 (Inner Temple) Qualifications:
LLM (Lond), LLB (Hons)

Patel *Pravin Mahendra*
Call Date: July 1978 (Middle Temple)
Qualifications: BA

Patel *Sheriyar*
Call Date: Oct 1996 (Gray's Inn)
Qualifications: B.Sc (City), LLB

Paterson *Alex Norman*
Company Secretary & Lawyer, Oscar
Faber Plc, Marlborough House, Upper
Marlborough Road, St Albans, Herts
AL1 3UT, 0181 784 5784, Call Date: Feb
1958 (Gray's Inn) Qualifications: LLB

Paterson *Gerald Dudley*
Former Chairman of a European Patent
Office Board of Appeal, 11 South
Square, 2nd Floor, Gray's Inn, London,
WC1R 5EU, Call Date: July 1966 (Gray's
Inn) Qualifications: MA (Oxon)

Paterson *Richard Christopher* •
Crown Prosecutor, Crown Prosecution
Service, Essex South Branch, County
House, 100 New London Road,
Chelmsford, Essex CM2 0RG, 01245
252 939, Call Date: Nov 1994 (Middle
Temple) Qualifications: BA
(Hons)(Lancs)

Patra *Biswa Nath*
MA, BCom, 1-5 Nant Road, London
NW2 2AL, 0181 209 1112, Fax: 0181
458 3207, Call Date: July 1965 (Inner
Temple)

Patrick *Miss Joanne Penelope* •
Crown Prosecution Service, Princes
Court, 34 York Street, Leicester
LE1 5TU, 0116 2549333, Fax: 0116
2550855, Call Date: July 1992 (Middle
Temple) Qualifications: BA (Hons), Dip
Law

Patten *Mrs Mary Lavender St Leger*
Call Date: Feb 1969 (Gray's Inn)
Qualifications: BA (Oxon)

Patterson *Brent James* •
Forbes & Partners Solicitors, 73
Northgate, Blackburn BB2 1AA, 01254
580000, Fax: 01254 682392, Call Date:
Nov 1991 (Inner Temple)
Qualifications: LLB

Patterson *Miss Carina Jane*
Call Date: Nov 1997 (Gray's Inn)
Qualifications: LLB (Derby)

Patterson *Lloyd Roy*
Call Date: Mar 1997 (Lincoln's Inn)
Qualifications: LLB (Hons)

Patterson *Miss Margaret Elizabeth*
The Legal Adviser, Home Office, Call
Date: July 1973 (Middle Temple)
Qualifications: LLB (lond)

Patterson *Ms Nicole* •
Dibb Lupton Alsop, 6 Dowgate Hill,
London EC4R 2SS, 0171 796 6821,
Fax: 0171 489 8102, Call Date: Nov
1995 (Middle Temple) Qualifications:
LLB (Hons)

Pattie *The Rt Hon Sir Geoffrey Edwin*
GEC PLC, 1 Bruzon Street, London
W1X 7AQ, 0171 493 8484, Call Date:
Nov 1964 (Gray's Inn) Qualifications:
MA

Pattinson *John Ernest* •
Principal Legal Officer, HM Customs &
Excise, The Solicitors Office, 22 Upper
Ground, London SE1, 0171 865 5189,
Fax: 0171 865 5987, Also Inn of Court
I, Call Date: Nov 1983 (Middle Temple)
Qualifications: LLB

Paul *Miss Jennifer Margaret* •
Call Date: Nov 1988 (Middle Temple)
Qualifications: LLB (Hons)

Pawson *Kenneth Vernon Frank*
Haggas Hall, Weeton, Nr Leeds, North
Yorkshire LS17 0BH, 01423 734200,
Fax: 01423 734731, Call Date: June
1949 (Gray's Inn) Qualifications: MA

Paxton *Paul*
Partner,Stewarts Solicitors, Stewarts, 63
Lincoln's Inn Fields, London
WC2A 3LW, 0171 242 6462, Fax: 0171
831 6843, Call Date: Nov 1993 (Middle
Temple) Qualifications: BSc
(Hons)(Lough)

Payne *Miss Helen Margaret* •
Senior Vice President - Law &
Contracts, Kvaerner Oil & Gas Limited,
Trafalgar HOuse, Hareness Road,
Altens, Aberdeens AB12 3RB, 01224
400042, Fax: 01224 402700, Call Date:
July 1987 (Gray's Inn) Qualifications:
LLB, MSc

Payne *Ms Joanne Margaret* •
Barlow Lyde & Gilbert, Beaufort House,
15 St Botolph Street, London EC3A 7NJ,
0171 247 2277, Call Date: Oct 1997
(Inner Temple) Qualifications: LLB
(Essex), BCL (Oxford)

Payne *Jonathan Edward*
Call Date: Oct 1997 (Gray's Inn)
Qualifications: BSc (Wales)

Payton *Miss Keima*
Solicitor, Payton & Partners, 97 Fleet
Street, London EC4Y 1DH, 0171 353
4999, Fax: 0171 353 5269, Senior
Partner at Payton & Partners, Call Date:
Nov 1994 (Lincoln's Inn)
Qualifications: LLB (Hons)

Peach *Neville Eric*
4 Pondfield Road, Hayes, Kent
BR2 7HS, 0181 462 4745, Call Date:
Feb 1960 (Gray's Inn) Qualifications:
ACII

Peacock *Kenneth Samuel*
Call Date: May 1994 (Middle Temple)
Qualifications: LLB (Hons)

Peacock *Miss Natasha Valerie* •
Legal Services Manager, National
Mutual Life, Assurance Society, The
Priory, Hitchin, Herts SG5 2DW, 01462
439332, Call Date: Oct 1995 (Gray's
Inn) Qualifications: LLB (Hons)

Peaker *Marcus Timothy George*
Meis Limited, 34 Paradise Road,
Richmond upon Thames, Surrey
TW9 1SE, 0181 332 7171, Fax: 0181
332 7210, Call Date: July 1994
(Lincoln's Inn) Qualifications: MA

Pearl *Bernard* •
4 Kidderpoor Avenue, London
NW3 7SP, 0171 435 1081, 7 New
Square, Lincoln's Inn, London, WC2A
3QS, Call Date: Nov 1970 (Gray's Inn)
Qualifications: BDS (Lond), LDS. RCS,
ENG., BA (OU), Dip, Soc (Lond), Dip
F.O.

Pearn *Ms Shirley Linda* •
Call Date: Nov 1997 (Inner Temple)
Qualifications: LLB (Kent)

Pearse *Miss Christine Anne*
Director, ABS Riste Management Price
Waterhouse, Price Waterhouse, 32
London Bridge Street, London SE1 9SY,
0171 939 3934, Fax: 0171 939 3276,
Call Date: Oct 1996 (Inner Temple)
Qualifications: LLB (L'pool), ACA

Pearson *Edward Stuart*
Visiting Professor - Cranfield University,
20 Cyprss Avenue, Osborne Park,
Welwyn Garden City, Herts AL7 1HN,
01707 326085, Call Date: July 1965
(Gray's Inn) Qualifications: BA (Hons),
B.SC, (Econ), LLM, Ph.D

Pearson *Glen*
Call Date: Oct 1998 (Gray's Inn)
Qualifications: BA (Keele)

Pearson *Peter Roderick Prescott* •
Crown Prosecutor, Crown Prosecution
Service, C/O 50 Ludgate Hill, LondoN
EC4M 7EX, Call Date: July 1972 (Middle
Temple) Qualifications: LLB (Lond)

Pearson *Mrs Vivienne Mary* •
Senior Crown Prosecutor, Crown
Prosecution Service, Priory Gate, Starne
Court, Union Street, Maidstone, Kent,
01622 686425, Call Date: July 1982
(Middle Temple) Qualifications: B.A.

Pearson *Mrs Wendy*
Call Date: Nov 1996 (Lincoln's Inn)
Qualifications: LLB (Hons)(Lancs)

Peat *Richard Colin* •
Enforcement Counsel, Financial
Services Authority, 25 The North
Colonnade, Canary Wharf, London
E14 5HS, 0171 676 1268, Call Date:
Oct 1993 (Gray's Inn) Qualifications:
BA

Peckham *Stephen John*
Clerk to the Justices, South Devon
Magistrates Court, The Court House,
Union Street, Torquay TQ1 4BP, 01803
202202, Fax: 01803 202200, Call Date:
July 1989 (Gray's Inn) Qualifications:
DML, Cert Mgmt

Peddie *Jonathan Peter*
Corporate & Industrial Litigation
Department of Clifford Chance, Clifford
Chance, 200 Aldersgate Street, London
EC1A 4JJ, 0171 600 1000, Fax: 0171
600 5555, Call Date: Nov 1994 (Inner
Temple) Qualifications: BA (Soton),
CPE (City)

Pedlar *Samuel James*
Woodley, 7 Wychbury, Fox Hollies
Road, Sutton Coldfield, West Midlands
B76 1BY, 0121 351 7124, Fax: 0121
351 7124, Call Date: July 1952
(Lincoln's Inn) Qualifications: MA

Pedropillai *Ms Corinne Damayanthi*
Call Date: Oct 1992 (Gray's Inn)
Qualifications: LL.B (Leic)

Peel *Mrs Victoria Sarah*
Call Date: Nov 1990 (Inner Temple)
Qualifications: BSc (Edin), Dip Law
(City)

• Barrister in employment

Peers *Benedict Giles Frederick*
Call Date: Mar 1998 (Middle Temple)
Qualifications: BA (Hons)(Exon)

Pegg *Captain Jason Geoffrey*
SO3 Legal, HQ 4th Division, Legal
Branch, Aldershot, Hants, 01252
347346, Call Date: Oct 1994 (Gray's Inn)
Qualifications: LLB (Anglia)

Pegler *Miss Michelle Ruth*
DAS Legal Expenses Insurance,
Non-Motor Claims Department, DAS
House, Quayside, Temple Back, Bristol
BS1 6NH, 0117 9342000, Call Date: Oct
1998 (Gray's Inn) Qualifications: LLB
(West England)

Pelham *Paul Nicolas David*
Manor Farm House, Manningford
Bohune, Pewsey, Wiltshire SN9 6JR,
01980 630036, Fax: 01980 630058, Also
Lincoln's Inn May 1971, Call Date: July
1969 (Gray's Inn) Qualifications: MA
(Oxon)

Pendley *Mrs Beryl Elizabeth*
0171 370 6955, Fax: 0171 244 7596,
Call Date: Nov 1994 (Inner Temple)
Qualifications: LLB

Pendley *James Ian*
KPMG Corporate Finance, 8 Salisbury
Square, London EC4Y 8BB, 0171 311
8539, Fax: 0171 311 8252, Call Date: Oct
1992 (Inner Temple) Qualifications: BSc
(Finance), MA (Law)

Pendower *John Edward Hicks*
Rosemary, Promenade de Verdun,
Purley, Surrey CR8 3LN, Call Date: July
1972 (Inner Temple) Qualifications: MB,
BS, FRCS

Penfold *Ronald Dean*
4 Livingstone Court, Christchurch Lane,
Barnet, Herts EN5 4PL, 0181 449 6854,
Call Date: Nov 1949 (Lincoln's Inn)
Qualifications: LLB (Lond)

Penhale *Ms Deborah Jane*
Court Clerk, Cardiff Magistrate's Court,
Fitzalan Place, Cardiff, 01222 463040,
Call Date: Feb 1994 (Inner Temple)
Qualifications: BA (Kent)

Penketh *Steven James*
Call Date: Nov 1995 (Inner Temple)
Qualifications: BA (Lond), CPE

Pennell *Mrs Lindsay Alexandra*
Call Date: Nov 1994 (Inner Temple)
Qualifications: LLB (Wales)

Pennels *Mrs Caroline Jane*
Call Date: Mar 1998 (Middle Temple)
Qualifications: BSc (Hons)(Lond), MSc
(City)

Pennycook *Ms Margaret Corrigan*
Call Date: Nov 1992 (Middle Temple)
Qualifications: BA (Hons)

Penry *John Richard Phelps*
01795 886 213, Scholar of Worcester
College, Call Date: July 1960 (Inner
Temple) Qualifications: MA (Oxon)

Pera *Mrs Mary*
Boxted Hall, Colchester, Essex CO4 5TJ,
Call Date: Jan 1948 (Lincoln's Inn)

Percival *Richard Allighan* •
Special Cases/Research Lawyer, Criminal
Appeal Office, Royal Courts of Justice,
Strand, London WC2A 2LL, 0171 936
5070, Fax: 0171 936 6900, Call Date: Oct
1992 (Gray's Inn) Qualifications: MA
(Oxon)

Perez *Ms Rachel Anne* •
Dept of Social Security, Room 407, New
Court, 48 Carey Street, London
WC2A 2LS, 0171 412 1359, Fax: 0171
412 1394, Call Date: Oct 1992 (Gray's
Inn) Qualifications: BA Dual Hons
(Sheff)

Perkins *John Beaumont*
21 Crossby Close, Alkrington, Middleton,
Manchester M24 1NU, Call Date: July
1968 (Gray's Inn) Qualifications: LLB
(Lond)

Perkins *Michael*
Call Date: Oct 1994 (Gray's Inn)
Qualifications: BA, MA (Keele)

Perkins *Richard Charles* •
Legal Director, Department of Trade &
Industry, 10 Victoria Street, London
SW1H 0NN, 0171 215 3257, Fax: 0171
215 3503, Call Date: Nov 1972 (Inner
Temple) Qualifications: MA (Oxon)

Perrett *Anthony James* •
Legal Advisor & Assistant Registrar of
Friendly Societies, Registry of Friendly
Societies, Victory House, 30-34 Kingsway,
London WC2B 6ES, 0171 663 5000/
5180, Fax: 0171 269 9820, Legal Advisor
Building and Friendly Societies
Commissions, Call Date: July 1972
(Lincoln's Inn) Qualifications: CEng,
MIEE, BA Hons

Perrins *Mrs Victoria Patricia*
Call Date: Oct 1996 (Lincoln's Inn)
Qualifications: LLB (Hons)

Perry *Miss Angela Jane*
Call Date: Nov 1996 (Middle Temple)
Qualifications: LLB (Hons)(Brunel)

Perry *Gary Stephen* •
Principal Crown Prosecutor, Crown
Prosecution Service, 27 St Leonards
Road, Eastbourne, East Sussex
BN21 3NN, Call Date: July 1989 (Middle
Temple) Qualifications: LLB (Leic)

Perry *Hugh Stanley*
Elm House, Coxwold, York YO6 4AB,
01347 868354, Fax: 01347 868390, Call
Date: July 1957 (Gray's Inn)
Qualifications: BA, LLB

Perry *Miss Susan Eluned*
Call Date: Oct 1998 (Inner Temple)
Qualifications: BA (Oxon)

Perryer *Miss Charlotte Lindsay*
Call Date: Oct 1993 (Gray's Inn)
Qualifications: BA

Pert *Mrs Vivien Victoria* •
Branch Crown Prosecutor, Call Date: Nov
1970 (Gray's Inn) Qualifications: LLB

Perveen *Ms Usmat*
Call Date: Nov 1995 (Lincoln's Inn)
Qualifications: BSc (Hons)

Peters *David Edward Oluremi*
Senior Court Clerk, Berkeley House,
Walton Street, Aylesbury, Bucks
HP21 7QG, 0126 383058, Fax: 01296
383436, Call Date: Apr 1978 (Lincoln's
Inn)

Peters *Mrs Emma-Kate* •
Legal Officer, Army Prosecuting
Authority, RAF Uxbridge, Middlesex, Call
Date: Oct 1991 (Lincoln's Inn)
Qualifications: LLB (Hons)

Peters *Francis Raymond*
Residinza Platani, Via G Di Vittorio 4,
27020 Travaco, Siccomario Pv, 382
499827, Fax: 382 499827, Call Date: Feb
1955 (Inner Temple) Qualifications: MA
(Oxon)

Peters *Miss Sarah Leanne*
South Wales, Call Date: Mar 1999 (Gray's
Inn) Qualifications: LLB (Wales)

Pettican *Kevin*
Wilmer Cutler & Pickering, 4 Carlton
Gardens, London SW1Y 5AA, 0171 872
1000, Fax: 0171 839 3537, Call Date:
Nov 1994 (Inner Temple) Qualifications:
BA, BCL (Oxon)

Pettinger *Stephen James*
Call Date: Nov 1997 (Gray's Inn)
Qualifications: BA

Pettit *Ms Victoria Clare*
Call Date: Oct 1997 (Inner Temple)
Qualifications: BA (E.Anglia), CPE, LLB
(London)

Petty *Christopher Roger William* •
Legal Director, Zeneca Pharmaceuticals,
Alderley Park, Macclesfield, Cheshire
SK10 4TF, 01625 512591, Fax: 01625
585618, Call Date: Nov 1976 (Middle
Temple) Qualifications: MA (Cantab)

Phelan *Miss Patricia Jean*
Threeburnford, Oxon, Lauder,
Berwickshire TD2 6PU, 01578 750615,
Call Date: July 1977 (Gray's Inn)
Qualifications: MA (Cantab)

Phillipps *Miss Karen Shirley*
2 King's Bench Walk, 1st Floor, Temple,
London, EC4Y 7DE, Call Date: July 1980
(Gray's Inn) Qualifications: BA

Phillips *Alfred William*
Call Date: Nov 1998 (Inner Temple)
Qualifications: BA (Open Uni), LLB

Phillips *Mrs Anne Margaret* •
Senior Crown Prosecutor, Crown
Prosecution Service, Woolwich/Bexley
Branch, The Cooperage, 8 Gainsford
Street, London SE1 2NG, 0171 357 7010,
Fax: 0171 962 0903, Call Date: July 1988
(Middle Temple) Qualifications: LLB
(Hons), LLM

• Barrister in employment

Phillips *Bleddyn Glynne Leyshon*
Clifford Chance (Solicitors), 200
Aldersgate Street, London EC1, 0171
600 1000, Fax: 0171 600 5555, Call
Date: July 1978 (Gray's Inn)
Qualifications: BCL, LLB, AKC

Phillips *Miss Claudette* •
Senior Crown Prosecutor, Crown
Prosecution Service, Ealing/Hounslow
Branch, 2nd Floor, King's House,
Kimberley Road, Harrow, Middlesex
HA1 1YH, 0181 424 8688, Fax: 0181
424 9134, Call Date: Nov 1991 (Middle
Temple) Qualifications: BA Hons
(Kent)

Phillips *Colin Andrew* •
VAT Consultant, Price Waterhouse, No 1
London Bridge, London SE1 9QL, 0171
939 3000, Call Date: Nov 1995 (Gray's
Inn) Qualifications: LLB (Wales)

Phillips *Mrs Elaine Margaret*
Call Date: Oct 1997 (Gray's Inn)
Qualifications: BA

Phillips *Fraser Guy* •
Legal Advisor, Computercenter (Uk)
Limited, Link House, Colonial Way,
Watford WD2 4HZ, 01923 478764, Fax:
01923 478848, Call Date: Nov 1996
(Gray's Inn) Qualifications: LLB
(Swansea)

Phillips *Lady Hazel Bradbury*
Fountain Court, Temple, London
EC4Y 9DH, 0171 353 7356/1878, Also
Inn of Court G, Call Date: June 1948
(Inner Temple) Qualifications: LLB

Phillips *Howard Michael* •
Crown Prosecutor, Crown Prosecution
Service, Oxford House, Leeds, Call
Date: Nov 1991 (Inner Temple)
Qualifications: LLB (Reading)

Phillips *Miss Lisa Rochelle*
Call Date: Mar 1997 (Inner Temple)
Qualifications: LLB

Phillips *Mark David* •
Crown Prosecutor, Call Date: Apr 1991
(Middle Temple) Qualifications: BSc
Econ (Hons)

Phillips *Michael Roland* •
Call Date: Oct 1994 (Lincoln's Inn)
Qualifications: LLB (Hons)

Phillips *Norman Robert*
The White Cottage, 26 Stirling Road,
Burley in Wharfedale, Ilkley, West
Yorkshire LS29 7LH, 01943 864 818,
Call Date: July 1965 (Gray's Inn)
Qualifications: LLB (Lond)

Phillips *Rhodri Jonathan Humphrey V*
Company Secretary, 3 Coopers Lane,
Cowbridge, South Glamorgan, 01446
774861, Call Date: Feb 1990 (Inner
Temple) Qualifications: MA (Cantab)

Phillips *Roger Michael*
Non Executive Director, Thameside
Community Healthcare NHS Trust.,
Thurrock Community Hospital, Long
Lane, Grays RM16 2PX, 01375 390044,
Fax: 01375 364468, Call Date: Nov
1983 (Gray's Inn) Qualifications: BA

Phillips *Miss Rowena Jane*
Senior Legal Adviser, Berkshire
Magistrates' Crt, Easby House,
Northfield End, Henley on Thames,
Oxon RG9 2NB, 01491 412720, Fax:
01491 412762, Call Date: Nov 1989
(Gray's Inn)

Philliskirk *Ian* •
The Solicitor's Office, Welsh Office,
Cathays Park, Cardiff CF1 3NQ, Call
Date: Nov 1993 (Lincoln's Inn)
Qualifications: LLB

Phillp *Ms Sara*
Call Date: Mar 1999 (Gray's Inn)
Qualifications: BA (Oxon)

Philp *David Hugh* •
36 Ashbury Road, London SW11 5UN,
0171 350 1494, Fax: 0171 350 1494,
Call Date: July 1973 (Middle Temple)
Qualifications: MA (Oxon)

Philpott *Mrs Deirdre Patricia Mary* •
Senior Crown Prosecutor, Crown
Prosecution Service, Eaton Court,
Oxford Road, Reading, Call Date: July
1976 (Gray's Inn) Qualifications: LLB
(Lond)

Philpott *John Philip*
Call Date: Oct 1997 (Lincoln's Inn)
Qualifications: LLB (Hons)(Westmins)

Phipps *Matthew Llewelyn*
Eversheds, Fitzalan House, Fitzalan
Road, Cardiff CF2 1XZ, 01222 471147,
Call Date: May 1992 (Lincoln's Inn)
Qualifications: BA (Hons) (Reading),
Dip Law

Phipps *Piers Anthony Constantine H*
Managing Director of Hoopoe Finance
Limited, Trerose Manor, Mawnan,
Falmouth, Cornwall, 0171 292 5420,
Fax: 0171 292 5435, Call Date: Apr
1986 (Inner Temple)

Photis *Andrew David*
21 Linden Rise, Warley, Brentwood,
Essex CM14 5UB, 01277 220439,
Former DC to J, Call Date: July 1982
(Middle Temple) Qualifications: Dip
Law (Lond), DMS

Phull *Miss Tarjinder Kaur*
Call Date: Nov 1998 (Lincoln's Inn)
Qualifications: LLB (Hons)

Piatt *Andrew*
Associate, Dibb Lupton Alsop Solicitors,
101 Barbirolli Square, Manchester
M2 3DL, 0161 235 4024, Fax: 0161
235 4125, Solicitor, Call Date: July
1987 (Gray's Inn) Qualifications: LLB
(Soton) (Hons)

Piccolo *Vaughan*
Call Date: Nov 1994 (Inner Temple)
Qualifications: BA (Cantab)

Pickard *Henry Francis*
17 Grangewood Court, Otley Road,
Leeds LS16 6ED, Call Date: Feb 1973
(Gray's Inn) Qualifications: LLB, MA
(Cantab), M.S.I.

Pickering *Mrs Jane Margaret* •
Grade 7 Legal, Lord Chancellor's
Department, Criminal Appeal Office,
Royal Courts of Justice, Strand
WC2A 2LL, 0171 936 7406, Call Date:
July 1971 (Inner Temple)

Pickering *Miss Lorna Blanche* •
Senior Crown Prosecutor, Crown
Prosecution Service, Inner London
Branch, Call Date: Nov 1990 (Inner
Temple) Qualifications: BA (Hons)
(L'pool), Dip Law (City)

Pickering *Robert*
Call Date: July 1983 (Inner Temple)
Qualifications: LLB (Soton)

Pickett *Ian Jeffrey*
Former Police Officer, Call Date: Oct
1997 (Middle Temple) Qualifications:
BA (Hons)(Salford), CPE (Lond)

Pickett *Mrs Jennifer Wynne* •
Trade Marks Manager, Chanel Limited,
Queens Way, Croydon, Surrey CR9 4DL,
0181 688 7131, Fax: 0181 688 0012,
Call Date: July 1985 (Inner Temple)
Qualifications: LLB (Cardiff)

Pickup *David Francis William* •
Solicitor for the Customs & Excise, New
Kings Beam House, 22 Upper GroundD,
London SE1 9PJ, 0171 865 5121, Fax:
0171 865 4820, and Member Gibraltar,
Call Date: Nov 1976 (Lincoln's Inn)
Qualifications: LLB (Lond)

Pierpoint *Mrs Louise Marie* •
Senior Crown Prosecutor, Crown
Prosecution Service, Rossmore House,
10 Newbold Terrace, Leamington Spa,
Call Date: July 1979 (Gray's Inn)
Qualifications: LLB (Leic)

Pigford *Jonathan Robert*
Call Date: Nov 1995 (Middle Temple)
Qualifications: LLB (Hons)

Pigott *Mrs Margaret Louise* •
Head of Judicial Appointments Division
1(Job Share) Grade 5, Lord
Chancellor's Department, Selborne
House, 54/60 Victoria Street, London
SW1E 6QB, Call Date: Nov 1973
(Middle Temple) Qualifications: MA

Pigott *Miss Sarah-Jane*
International Criminal Tribunal for the
former Yugoslavia The Haque,
Netherlands - General Assistant to the
President, Call Date: July 1998 (Inner
Temple) Qualifications: LLB (Lond)

Pikett *Christopher* •
Company Secretary General Manager
Legal Affairs, 3M United Kingdom PLC,
3M House, PO Box No 1, Bracknell,
Berkshire RG12 1JU, 01344 858565, Fax:
01344 858553, Call Date: Nov 1975
(Middle Temple) Qualifications: LLB
(Hons, Soton)

Pilcher *Ms Rebecca Charlotte*
C/O The Garden House, Steventon,
Basingstoke, Hampshire, and Member
Northern Ireland Bar, Call Date: Nov
1994 (Middle Temple) Qualifications:
MA

Pilcher *Miss Sara Kate* •
Crown Prosecutor, Crown Prosecution
Service, Yorkshire Area Office, 6th Floor,
Ryedale Building, Piccadilly, York
YO1 1NS, Call Date: Nov 1996 (Gray's
Inn) Qualifications: LLB (Brunel)

Pilkington *Aubrey Alfred St John*
Justices Clerk, PDSs of Elloes Grantham,
Sleaford & Bourne and Stamford,
Lincolnshire Magistrates', Courts
Committee, 15 Newland, Lincoln
LN1 1XG, 01522 514200, Fax: 01522
514200, Call Date: Nov 1982 (Middle
Temple) Qualifications: LLB (Brunel),
DMS (Notts)

Pilkington *Lionel Alexander* •
Senior Crown Prosecutor, Crown
Prosecution Service, The Cooperage, 8
Gainsford Street, London SE1 2NE, 0171
357 7010/962 2785, Fax: 0171 962
0902, Call Date: Nov 1974 (Inner
Temple) Qualifications: BA

Pillai *Ms Smeetha* •
Crown Prosecution Service, Kings House,
Kymberley Road, Harrow, Middlesex,
Malaysia, Call Date: July 1988 (Gray's
Inn) Qualifications: LLB (London)

Pillans *Mrs Diana Kerin*
Associate Director College of Graduate &
Professional Studies, Thames Valley
University, St Mary's Road, Ealing,
London W5, 0181 579 5000, Fax: 0181
231 2307, Call Date: July 1985 (Gray's
Inn) Qualifications: BSc (Lond), LL.B

Pilling *Miss Cynthia Dorothy*
Call Date: Nov 1959 (Gray's Inn)
Qualifications: LLB (Hons)

Pilling *David James*
33b Willoughby Park Road, Tottenham,
London N17 0RR, 0181 801 7950, Call
Date: Feb 1992 (Gray's Inn)
Qualifications: LLB

Pimm *Geoffrey Leonard*
Royal Courts of Justice, Strand, London
WC2A 2LL, South Africa, Goldsworth
Chambers, 1st Floor, 11 Gray's Inn
Square, London, WC1R 5JD, Call Date:
Feb 1952 (Gray's Inn)

Pincher *Richard Andrew*
Coopers & Lybrand, Erskine House,
68-73 Queen Street, Edinburgh
EH2 3NH, 0131 226 4488, Call Date: Nov
1985 (Middle Temple) Qualifications:
LLB (B'ham)

Pincott *Mrs Antoinette Jean Marie*
Chartered Accountant, Grant Thornton,
Grant Thornton House, Melton Street,
Euston Square, London NW1 2EP, 0171
728 2672, Fax: 0171 353 4035, Call
Date: Feb 1991 (Middle Temple)
Qualifications: LLB (Reading), ACA

Pinfold *Martin Franks* •
The Serious Fraud Office, Elm House,
10-16 Elm Street, London WC1X 0BJ,
Call Date: July 1981 (Middle Temple)
Qualifications: LLB (London)

Pinion *Mrs Deborah*
Call Date: Oct 1992 (Gray's Inn)
Qualifications: LLB (Lancs)

Pinnell *Ellis Anthony*
Call Date: Oct 1998 (Lincoln's Inn)
Qualifications: LLB (Hons)

Pinson *Barry*
804 Hood House, Dolphin Square,
London SW1V 3NL, 0171 798 8450, Fax:
0171 834 9881, Call Date: Nov 1949
(Gray's Inn) Qualifications: LLB

Pinto *Timothy John*
Call Date: Oct 1996 (Inner Temple)
Qualifications: BA (Lond), CPE (Lond)

Pirbhai Zamin *Miss Iram*
Call Date: May 1997 (Middle Temple)
Qualifications: LLB (Hons)

Pitblado *Alastair Bruce* •
Department of Trade & Industry, Legal
Services Directorate B, 10 Victoria Street,
London SW1H 0NN, 0171 215 3433, Fax:
0171 215 3520, Call Date: July 1974
(Middle Temple)

Pitt *Miss Andrea Elaine* •
Call Date: July 1987 (Inner Temple)
Qualifications: LLB

Pitt *Daniel Crawford* •
Wandsworth Borough Council, London
SW18 2PU, Call Date: Oct 1995 (Inner
Temple) Qualifications: BSc (Bath) , CPE

Pitt *Mrs Georgina*
Senior Court Clerk, Law Courts, North
Street, Wolverhampton WV1 1RA, 01902
773151, Fax: 01902 27875, Call Date:
Nov 1984 (Gray's Inn) Qualifications: BA
(Joint Hons)

Plant *Dr Glen*
Sweden, 20 Essex Street, London, WC2R
3AL, Call Date: July 1985 (Inner Temple)
Qualifications: MA (Oxon), Ph.D (Lond),
MA (USA)

Platt *Robert Fetherston*
Curtis Davis Garrard Solicitor, Lancaster
House, Northumberland House, Staines
TW19 7LN, 0181 400 2400, Fax: 0181
400 2420, Currently a Solicitor, Call
Date: Oct 1993 (Lincoln's Inn)
Qualifications: MA (Oxon)

Platt *Steven*
Clerk to the Justices, Clerk to the
Justices, Justices Clerks Office, Northern
Clerkship, The Courthouse, Woodgate,
Loughborough, Leicestershire LE11 2XB,
01509215715, Fax: 01509 261714, Call
Date: Feb 1986 (Middle Temple)
Qualifications: BA, DML

Platt *Terence Frederick* •
Legal Advisor, Kent County Council, Legal
Services Department, County Hall,
Maidstone, Kent ME14 1XQ, 01622
671411, Fax: 01622 694266, Call Date:
Nov 1977 (Middle Temple)
Qualifications: LLB

Platten *Ty*
Call Date: Mar 1999 (Middle Temple)
Qualifications: BA (Hons)

Pledge *Miss Emma Louise*
Call Date: Mar 1999 (Gray's Inn)
Qualifications: LLB (B'ham)

Pliskin *Miss Melanie Clare* •
Prosecution Team Leader, Crown
Prosecution Service, 3rd Floor, Black
Horse House, Leigh Road,
Eastleigh,Hants, Call Date: Nov 1985
(Lincoln's Inn) Qualifications: BA, LLM
(S'oton), MA (S'oton)

Plume *John Trevor*
Call Date: June 1936 (Gray's Inn)
Qualifications: LAM, RTPI

Plummer *Paul* •
Crown Prosecution Service, Eaton Court,
112 Oxford Road, Reading RG1 7LL, Call
Date: Feb 1986 (Middle Temple)
Qualifications: Dip Mag Law, Dip Law

Plumptre *Miss Jane Constance*
Call Date: July 1975 (Inner Temple)
Qualifications: BA

Plunkett *Oliver*
Call Date: Nov 1997 (Middle Temple)
Qualifications: LLB (Hons) (Kingston)

Pocock *Louis John*
Call Date: Oct 1997 (Gray's Inn)
Qualifications: BSc , Msc, MBA (Cape
Town)

Polaine *Martin Daniel* •
Senior Case Lawyer, Crown Prosecution
Service, 50 Ludgate Hill, London
EC4M 7EX, 0171 273 8333, Call Date:
July 1988 (Gray's Inn) Qualifications: BA
(Manc), DIP.LAW (The City, Univ)

Polding *Richard John* •
Director, Business & Legal Affairs, V2
Music Group Limited, 131 Holland Park
Avenue, London W11 4UT, 0171 471
3644, Fax: 0171 471 3606, Call Date:
July 1985 (Inner Temple) Qualifications:
LLB Hons (L'pool)

Poles *George Christian Harry*
Call Date: Nov 1991 (Middle Temple)
Qualifications: BA Hons (Oxon)

Pollard *Bernard* •
Clerk to the Commissioners, General
Commissioners, of Income Tax,
(Blackheath Division), Call Date: July
1968 (Middle Temple) Qualifications:
BA, BSC Econ

Pollard *Carl Andrew*
Call Date: Mar 1999 (Inner Temple)
Qualifications: BSc, CPE, FRICS

Pollard *Mrs Lynn Annette* •
Crown Prosecutor, CPS (Coventry
Branch), Hertford House, Hertford
Street, Coventry, Warwickshire CV1 1LS,
Call Date: July 1967 (Lincoln's Inn)

Polledri *Miss Elisabetta* •
Legal Adviser, Treasury Solicitors
Department, Queen Anne's Chambers,
28 The Broadway, London SW1H 9JS,
0171 218 0714, Call Date: July 1989
(Lincoln's Inn) Qualifications: LLB

Pollock *Adam Alexander Brewis*
113 Moore Park Road, London
SW6 4PS, 0171 885 6529, Fax: 0171
885 8307, Call Date: July 1982 (Gray's
Inn) Qualifications: LLB (Hons)

Pollock *Desmond Thomas Campbell*
Call Date: Feb 1952 (Inner Temple)
Qualifications: LLB Hons (Lond)

Pollock *Miss Julia Mary* •
Legal Adviser, Country Landowners
Association, 16 Belgrave Square,
London SW1X 8PQ, 0171 235 0511,
Fax: 0171 235 4696, Call Date: Nov
1984 (Lincoln's Inn) Qualifications:
LLB (Hons)

Polsom-Jenkins *Keith* •
Commercial Union Plc, 13th Floor, St
Helens, 1 Undershaft, London
EC3P 3DQ, 0171 283 7500, Call Date:
July 1971 (Inner Temple)
Qualifications: LLB

Pomson *David Seymour*
16 Prothero Gardens, London
NW4 3SL, 0181 203 3364, Fax: 0181
203 7651, Call Date: Nov 1955 (Middle
Temple) Qualifications: MA (Oxon)

Pond *James Oswin*
Paralegal, Freshfields, 65 Fleet Street,
London EC4Y 1HS, 0171 716 4243,
Fax: 0171 353 4952, Call Date: July
1998 (Inner Temple) Qualifications:
BA (Oxon), LLM (Cantab)

Poole *Frederick Thomas*
The Old Rectory, Landbeach,
Cambridge CB4 4ED, 01223 861408,
Fax: 01223 441276, Call Date: July
1966 (Lincoln's Inn) Qualifications:
MA, LLB(Cantab)

Poole *Mrs Jill*
Law Lecturer, Cardiff Law School,
Cardiff University, Cardiff, PO Box 427
Museum Avenue, Cardiff CF1 1XD,
01222 874367, Fax: 01222 874097,
Call Date: Feb 1992 (Lincoln's Inn)
Qualifications: LLB (Hons) (Reading),
LLM (Bristol), Commercial Law, ACIArb

Poole *Michael George*
David & Levene & Co, Ashley House,
235-239 High Road, Wood Green,
London N22, 0181 881 7777, Fax:
0181 889 6395, Call Date: Nov 1993
(Inner Temple) Qualifications: LLB
(Notts)

Poostchi *Miss Banafsheh*
Call Date: Nov 1996 (Lincoln's Inn)
Qualifications: BA (Hons)(Oxon)

Pope *George Philip*
6 Chyngton Way, Seaford, E Sussex
BN25 4JA, 01323 898 603, Call Date:
July 1970 (Gray's Inn) Qualifications:
DMA

Pope *Jeremy David*
New Zealand Solicitor (1963), 42
madrid Road, London SW13 9PG, 0181
748 7405, and Member New Zealand
Bar, Call Date: Nov 1993 (Inner
Temple) Qualifications: LLB
(N.Zealand)

Pope *Miss Lucy Anne*
Trade Marks Adviser, Clifford Chance,
200 Aldersgate Street, London EC1A 4JJ,
0171 600 1000, Call Date: Nov 1992
(Middle Temple) Qualifications: LLB
(Hons, B'ham)

Pope *William David Longfield*
Call Date: Nov 1995 (Lincoln's Inn)
Qualifications: MA (Oxon)

Porta *Miss Angela Teresa*
S J Berwin & Co, 322 Gray's Inn Road,
London WC1X 8HB, Call Date: Nov
1994 (Inner Temple) Qualifications:
BA (Oxon), CPE

Porteous *Miss Janette* •
University of Lincolnshire &,
Humberside, Brayford Pool, Lincoln
LN6 7TS, 01522 882 000, Call Date:
Nov 1986 (Lincoln's Inn)
Qualifications: LLB (Hons)

Porter *Miss Elaine Margaret* •
Legal Adviser, UBS Asset Management
London, Ltd, 14 Triton Court, London,
0171 901 5257, Call Date: July 1987
(Middle Temple) Qualifications: LLB

Porter *Gordon John*
9 Bromham Mill, Giffard Park, Milton
Keynes MK14 5QP, 01908 612 892, Call
Date: Nov 1962 (Gray's Inn)
Qualifications: LLB (Lond)

Porter *Miss Jane Elizabeth*
Court Clerk, Manchester City
Magistrates', Court, Crown Square,
Manchester M60 1PR, 0161 832 7272,
Fax: 0161 832 5421, Call Date: Nov
1988 (Middle Temple) Qualifications:
BA Hons

Porter *Mark Alexander* •
Sema Group UK Limited, Norcliffe
House, Station Road, Wilmslow,
Cheshire SK9 1BU, Call Date: July 1982
(Lincoln's Inn) Qualifications: LLB
(Hons)

Porter *Stephen David* •
Legal Adviser, British Telecom, 2-12
Gresham Street, London EC2V 7AG,
0171 356 8488, Fax: 0171 356 3719,
Call Date: Feb 1992 (Lincoln's Inn)
Qualifications: LLB (Hons)

Posner *Robert* •
Assistant Controller of Legal Services.
Hon Sec. Assoc for Barristers in local
Govt and Public Service, London
Borough of Bexley, Bexley Civic Offices,
Broadway, Bexleyheath, Kent DA6 7LB,
0181 303 7777, Fax: 0181 301 2661,
and Member Victoria Bar Queensland
Bar, Call Date: July 1981 (Lincoln's
Inn) Qualifications: BA (Hons)

Pote *Mrs Tracey Ann Candlish* •
Court Clerk, Ipswich Magistrates Court,
Elm Street, Ipswich, Suffolk IP1 2AP,
01473 217261, Fax: 01473 231249,
Call Date: Nov 1991 (Gray's Inn)
Qualifications: BA (Hons)

Potel *Ronnie Xerxes*
Call Date: Oct 1998 (Lincoln's Inn)
Qualifications: LLB (Hons)(Newc)

Potter *Miss Alison Lisa*
4 Pump Court, Temple, London, EC4Y
7AN, Call Date: Feb 1987 (Middle
Temple) Qualifications: MA (Oxon)

Potter *Donald Charles*
Pump Court Tax Chambers, 16 Bedford
Row, London WC1R 4ED, 0171 414
8080, also Inn of Court L and Member
Northern Ireland Bar Pump Court Tax
Chambers, 16 Bedford Row, London,
WC1R 4EB, Call Date: Nov 1948
(Middle Temple) Qualifications: LLB

Potter *Miss Felicite*
Gapperies, West Porlock, Somerset
TA24 8NX, 01643 862497, Call Date:
June 1951 (Lincoln's Inn)

Potter *Raymond*
p/t President, South Western Rent
Assessment Panel, Call Date: Nov 1971
(Inner Temple)

Potts *Miss Nicola Michelle*
Call Date: Oct 1998 (Gray's Inn)
Qualifications: LLB (Newcastle)

Potts *Richard Vivian*
Corporate Finance - Associate Director,
Panmure Gordon & Co Limited, New
Broad Street House, 35 New Broad
Street, London EC2M 1SQ, 0171 638
4010, Fax: 0171 588 5297, Call Date:
July 1982 (Middle Temple)
Qualifications: BA, MSI

Povey *Jonathan Micheal*
Assistant Counsel, Coutts Group, Trust
& Fiduciary Services, Talstrasse 59, CH
80222, Zurich, 00 41 (0) 1 214 5277,
Fax: 00 41 (0) 1 214 5563, Call Date:
Oct 1996 (Gray's Inn) Qualifications:
LLB (Wales), LLM (Cantab)

Powar *Mrs Sabina Ayesha*
Legal Adviser, The Law Courts, Alexandra
Road, London SW19 7JP, 0181 946
8622, Call Date: Nov 1986 (Middle
Temple) Qualifications: LLB

Powell *Miss Alison Louise*
Call Date: July 1982 (Inner Temple)
Qualifications: LLB (Manch)

Powell *Glyn Stephen* •
Crown Prosecutor, Crown Prosecution
Service, 2nd Floor, Kings House,
Kymberley Road, Harrow, Middlesex
HA1 1YH, 0181 424 8688, Fax: 0181 429
9134, Call Date: Oct 1993 (Middle
Temple) Qualifications: LLB
(Hons)(Lond)

Powell *Ian George* •
Legal Adviser, Bass plc, 20 North Audley
Street, London W1Y 1WE, 0171 409
8419, Fax: 0171 409 8526, Call Date:
July 1983 (Inner Temple) Qualifications:
LLB (Sheff)

Powell *Mrs Josephine* •
Crown Prosecutor, Crown Prosecution
Service, Fylde & North Lancs, Prudential
House, Topping Street, Blackpool,
Lancaster PR1 1ER, 01772 556886, Call
Date: Nov 1987 (Middle Temple)
Qualifications: LLB (UCL), M.Phil

Powell *Michael*
Call Date: July 1998 (Middle Temple)
Qualifications: BA (Hons)(Ports'm)

Powell *Richard Arthur Gayler*
Court Clerk, Exeter & E Devon
Magistrates, The Court House, Heavitree
Road, Exeter, Devon, 01392 270081,
Fax: 01392 420913, Call Date: July 1989
(Middle Temple) Qualifications: LLB
(Hons), LLM

Powell *Miss Tracey Ann* •
Crown Prosecutor, Crown Prosecution
Service, The Courtyard, Lombard Street,
Abingdon, Oxfordshire OX14 5SE, 01235
555678, Fax: 01235 554144, Call Date:
Nov 1989 (Middle Temple)
Qualifications: BA (Hons) (Sheff), Dip in
Law

Power *Ms Alexia Clare* •
Senior Crown Prosecutor, Crown
Prosecution Service, Tower Hill & City,
Branch Office, The Cooperage, 8
Gainsford St, London SE1 2NG, 0171 357
7010, Fax: 0171 962 0905, Call Date: Oct
1992 (Gray's Inn) Qualifications: BSc
(Hons)(Surrey)

Power *Miss Kathryn Mary* •
Call Date: Oct 1991 (Inner Temple)
Qualifications: LLB (Exon)

Powick *Miss Anna* •
Call Date: Oct 1997 (Middle Temple)
Qualifications: LLB (Hons)(Leeds)

Poxon *Philip Edward* •
Senios Counsel, Halliburton Company,
Wellheads Place, Wellheads Industrial
Estate, Dyce, Aberdeen AB21 7GB,
Scotland, 01244 778332, Fax: 01224
777744, Call Date: July 1985 (Lincoln's
Inn) Qualifications: LLB (Newc)

Prabhu *Miss Warsha Rewati Sudhakar*
Call Date: Nov 1997 (Lincoln's Inn)
Qualifications: BA (Hons)(Cantab)

Prasad *Henry Durga*
90 Ingleton Road, London N18 2RT,
0181 292 9984, and Member Guyana,
Bermuda, Call Date: July 1965 (Middle
Temple)

Pratt *Derek Norman* •
Senior Civil Servant, HM Customs &
Excise, Solicitor's Office, New King's
Beam House, London SE1 9PJ, 0171 865
5530, Fax: 0171 865 5989, Call Date:
July 1971 (Gray's Inn) Qualifications:
LLB

Pratt *Simon Derek* •
Financial Director Group Company
Secretary, Aureus Leisure Group Ltd, 22
High Street, Leicester LE1 5YN, 0116
2511229, Call Date: July 1981 (Lincoln's
Inn) Qualifications: BA Hons (Durham),
M.B.A [Leics]

Pratt *Timothy Jean Geoffrey*
Old Vicarage, Radwinter, Saffron Waldon,
Essex CB10 2SN, 01799 599507, Call
Date: Feb 1959 (Middle Temple)
Qualifications: MA

Precious *Stephen Michael*
Call Date: Oct 1998 (Lincoln's Inn)
Qualifications: LLB (Hons)(Staffs)

Prendiville *Rice Irwin* •
Legal Advisor, Old Mutual International
Ltd, 2 Bartley Way, Hook, Hampshire
RG27 9XA, 01256 768 888, Fax: 01256
768 804, Call Date: July 1981 (Gray's
Inn)

Prentice *Ms Dorothy May* •
Crown Prosecutor, Crown Prosecution
Service, First Floor, Oxford House,
Oxford Road, Bournemouth BH8 8HA,
Call Date: 1983 (Lincoln's Inn)
Qualifications: BA

Prentis *Mrs Victoria Mary Boswell* •
Legal Officer, The Treasury Solicitor,
Queen Anne's Chambers, 28 Broadway,
London SW1H 9JS, 0171 210 3090, Call
Date: Oct 1995 (Middle Temple)
Qualifications: MA (Hons)

Press *Barry*
Call Date: July 1975 (Inner Temple)
Qualifications: BA, MSc (Oxon)

Preston *Alan David* •
Financial Services Authority, 25 The
North Colonnade, Canary Wharf, London
E14 5HS, 0171 676 1000, Fax: 0171 676
1099, Call Date: May 1972 (Gray's Inn)
Qualifications: LLM

Preston *Geoffrey Averill*
Call Date: June 1950 (Gray's Inn)

Prew *James Martin*
Enviromental Claims Manager, CGU Plc,
St Helens, 1 Undershaft, London
EC3P 3DQ, 0171 283 7500, Fax: 0171
662 1025, Call Date: Nov 1976 (Lincoln's
Inn) Qualifications: LLB (Lond), FCII

Price *Anthony John* •
Group Legal Director Secretary, Bartle
Bogle Hegarty Ltd, 60 Kingly Street,
London W1R 3DS, 0171 734 1677, Fax:
0171 437 3666, Call Date: July 1983
(Gray's Inn) Qualifications: BA Hons

Price *Mrs Caroline Sarah* •
Legal Adviser Grade 5, The Home Office,
50 Queen Anne's Gate, London
SW1H 9AT, Call Date: July 1970 (Gray's
Inn) Qualifications: LLB

Price *David Allan*
Managing Director - International
Division, 21 Hallside Park, Knutsford,
Cheshire WA16 8NQ, Call Date: Feb 1991
(Lincoln's Inn) Qualifications: BSc
(Hons), LLB, FRICS, Dip Arb, FCIArb

Price *Mrs Huma Sabih*
Call Date: Nov 1991 (Inner Temple)
Qualifications: LLB

Price *John Philip*
Company Secretary, Express Dairies plc,
Express House, Meridian East, Meridian
Business Park, Leicester LE3 2TP, 0116
281 6281, Fax: 0116 281 6282, Call
Date: July 1974 (Inner Temple)
Qualifications: MA, B Phil (Oxon)

Price *Jonathan Nicholas*
Deputy Clerk to the Justices,
Northampton Magistrates' Court, Regents
Pavillion, Summerhouse Road, Moulton
Park, Northampton NN3 6AS, 01604
497033, Fax: 01604 497010, Call Date:
Nov 1989 (Inner Temple) Qualifications:
LLB (B'ham), MBA (B'ham)

Price *Ms Kim Elizabeth* •
Senior Lawyer, Cheltenham & Gloucester
Plc, Barnet Way, Barnwood, Gloucester
GL4 7RL, 01452 375547, Fax: 01452
375570, Call Date: Nov 1982 (Gray's
Inn) Qualifications: LLB

Price *Miss Pauline Beryl* •
Senior Crown Prosecutor, Crown
Prosecution Service, St John's House,
Union Street, Dudley, W Midlands, 01384
230471, Call Date: Nov 1985 (Middle
Temple) Qualifications: BA (Hons)

Price *Thomas Leolin Alfred*
Call Date: Oct 1994 (Middle Temple)
Qualifications: BA (Hons)(Oxon)

Price *Toby David*
Call Date: Mar 1997 (Lincoln's Inn)
Qualifications: LLB (Hons)(Warw)

Price *Miss Victoria*
In-House Counsel, Linder Myers
Solicitors, 45 Cross Street, Manchester,
0161 832 6972, Fax: 0161 834 0718,
Call Date: Oct 1993 (Gray's Inn)
Qualifications: BA (Sussex), Dip Law
(Staff)

Pridham *Miss Laura Rebecca*
Wales, Call Date: Oct 1997 (Gray's Inn)
Qualifications: LLB (Glamorgan)

Priest *Andrew Jonathan*
Call Date: Nov 1994 (Inner Temple)
Qualifications: BA (Oxon)

Priest *Mrs Jacqueline Ann*
York Chambers, 14 Toft Green, York,
YO1 6JT, Call Date: July 1973 (Inner
Temple) Qualifications: LLB

Priestley *Richard William Marshall*
Call Date: July 1998 (Middle Temple)
Qualifications: LLB (Hons) (Leeds)

Prince *Oscar Peter* •
Company Lawyer, RMC Group plc, RMC
House, Coldharbour Lane, Thorpe,
Egham, Surrey TW20 8TD, 01932
568833, Fax: 01932 568933, Call Date:
Nov 1966 (Gray's Inn)

Prince *Raymond Andrew* •
Department of Law, London Borough
of Harrow, PO Box 2, Civic Centre,
Station Road,, Harrow, Middlesex
HA1 2UH, Call Date: July 1985
(Lincoln's Inn) Qualifications: BA

Prinn *Edmund Charles*
Call Date: Oct 1997 (Middle Temple)
Qualifications: BA , LLB (City)

Pritchard *Anthony Paul*
Call Date: Nov 1992 (Inner Temple)
Qualifications: LLB

Pritchard *Miss Cecilia Mary*
Call Date: July 1998 (Middle Temple)
Qualifications: LLB (Hons)

Pritchard *Mr. John Bertram*
Admitted as a Solicitor 1998, Call Date:
Oct 1995 (Inner Temple)
Qualifications: LLB (Kent)

Procter *Miss Diana Elizabeth Cecil*
45 Tredegar Square, London E3, Call
Date: July 1973 (Lincoln's Inn)
Qualifications: BA (Lond)

Proctor *Adrian Francis*
Financial Advisor, 0161 236 7885, Call
Date: Mar 1996 (Inner Temple)
Qualifications: BA (Honours)

Proctor *Miss Carmel Gail* •
BUPA, Anchorage Quay, Salford Quay,
Manchester M5 2XL, 0161 931 5586,
Call Date: Oct 1997 (Lincoln's Inn)
Qualifications: LLB (Hons) (Manc)

Proctor *Charles Robert*
Cumbria Social Services, 3 Victoria
Place, Carlisle, Cumbria CA1 1EH,
01228 607162, Call Date: July 1980
(Lincoln's Inn) Qualifications: BA
(Dunelm), MA (Hull)

Prosser *John Rogers*
Editor - Accounting & Business, ACCA,
29 Lincoln's Inn Fields, London
WC2A 3EE, 0171 396 5734, Fax: 0171
396 5741, Call Date: July 1975 (Middle
Temple) Qualifications: LLB

Pryer *David*
Clerk to the Justices Justices' Chief
Executive, Northumberland
Magistrates', Courts Committee, PO
Box 16, Law Courts, Bedlington,
Northumberland NE22 5PQ, 01670
531100, Fax: 01665 510247, Call Date:
Nov 1982 (Gray's Inn) Qualifications:
MIMgt

Pryer *Eric John*
Hon Assc Member RICS, 'Sprangewell',
Poles Lane, Ware, Herts SG12 0SQ,
01920 462595, Fax: 01920 462212,
Call Date: Nov 1957 (Gray's Inn)
Qualifications: BA Hons, Hon Assc
Member RICS

Pryer *Mrs Julia Mary* •
Crown Prosecution Service, (Leics/
Northants), 50 Ludgate Hill, London
EC4M 7EX, Call Date: Feb 1986 (Middle
Temple) Qualifications: BA

Pugh *Clive Anthony*
Call Date: Oct 1994 (Lincoln's Inn)
Qualifications: LLB (Hons) (Lond)

Pugh *Denzil Anthony* •
Barrier House, Barrier Road, Chatham,
Kent ME4 4SG, Call Date: July 1980
(Gray's Inn)

Pullin *Miss Samantha Joan*
Sub Editor for Halsbury's Laws of
England, Butterworths plc, Halsbury
House, Chancery Lane, London WC1,
Call Date: Oct 1996 (Middle Temple)
Qualifications: LLB (Hons) (Wales)

Pulsford-Harris *Miss Dorothy Ann* •
Senior Crown Prosecutor, Crown
Prosecution Service, Haldin House, Old
Bank of England Court, Queen Street,
Norwich, Norfolk NR2 4SX, 01603
666491, Fax: 01603 617989, Call Date:
Nov 1988 (Middle Temple)
Qualifications: LLB (E Anglia) (Hons)

Pumphrey *Mrs Lyn Susan*
Hounslow Magistrates' Court, Justices'
Clerk's Office, Market Place, Brentford,
Middlesex TW8 8EN, 0181 568 9811,
Legal Adviser (Magistrates), Call Date:
May 1994 (Lincoln's Inn)
Qualifications: BA (Hons, Hull), LLB
(Hons), Dip Ed

Purcell *John Thomas*
Senior Lecturer in Law, School of Law,
University of Westminster, 4-12 Little
Titchfield Street, London W1P 7FW,
0171 911 5000 ext 2513, Fax: 0171
911 5152, Call Date: July 1987
(Lincoln's Inn) Qualifications: LLB

Purcell *William Ware*
Call Date: Oct 1996 (Middle Temple)
Qualifications: BA (Hons) (York), LLB
(Hons) (Leeds)

Purnell *Christopher Arthur*
Plumstead Community Law Centre,
105 Plumstead High Street, London
SE18 1SB, 0181 244 4958, Call Date:
July 1980 (Gray's Inn) Qualifications:
BA (OXON)

Purnell *Miss Marcia Ann*
Call Date: Nov 1983 (Gray's Inn)
Qualifications: BA LLM PhD

Purse *Alfred Turnbull*
8 Wellesford Close, Banstead, Surrey
SM7 2HL, 01737 355804, Call Date:
Nov 1942 (Gray's Inn) Qualifications:
LLB, FCIS

Purse *Hugh Robert Leslie*
Part Time Chairman of Industrial
Tribunals, The Industrial Tribunal, 44
Broadway, Stratford, London E15 1XH,
Call Date: Feb 1964 (Gray's Inn)
Qualifications: LLB (Lond)

Purves *Michael Neil* •
Principal Officer, HM Customs &
Excise, Solicitors Office, 22 Upper
Ground, London SE1 9PJ, 0171 865
5153, Fax: 0171 865 5194, Call Date:
July 1989 (Inner Temple)
Qualifications: LLB (Lond)

Purves *Robert Frederick*
Australia, and Member New South
Wales Bar 36 Bedford Row, London,
WC1R 4JH, Call Date: July 1973 (Middle
Temple) Qualifications: BA, LLB

Purvis *Andrew John* •
Compliance Officer, Call Date: Feb
1993 (Gray's Inn) Qualifications: Bsc
(Econ) (Wales), FCII

Purvis *Ian Bremmer*
Senior Legal Adviser & General
Counsel, Age Concern England, Astral
House, 1268 London Road, London
SW16 4ER, 0181 679 8000, Fax: 0181
679 6069, Call Date: Nov 1960 (Inner
Temple) Qualifications: BA (Law)
(So'ton)

Purvis *Julian*
Call Date: Nov 1997 (Lincoln's Inn)
Qualifications: BA (Hons), MA (Oxon),
LLB (Hons)

Purvis *Stephen Harald* •
Manager, North of England Protecting
&, Indemnity Association Ltd, The
Quayside, Newcastle Upon Tyne
NE1 3DU, 0191 232 5221, Fax: 0191
261 0540, Call Date: Nov 1984 (Middle
Temple) Qualifications: BA

Pustam *Miss Helen Denise*
Senior Court Clerk, Berkeley House,
Walton Street, Aylesbury, Bucks
HP21 7QG, 01296 383058, Fax: 01296
383436, Call Date: Oct 1992 (Lincoln's
Inn) Qualifications: LLB(Hons)

Puxon *Mrs Christine Margaret*
Medical Legal Consultant, 19 Clarence
Gate Gardens, London NW1 6AY, 0171
723 7922, Fax: 0171 258 1038, also
Gray's Inn 1965, Call Date: Feb 1954
(Inner Temple) Qualifications: MB,
CHB, MRCS,, LRCP, MD, FRCOG

     • Barrister in employment

Pye *James Edward Kensey* •
Group Legal Adviser, Vendome Luxury
Group, 27 Knightsbridge, London
SW1X 7YB, 0171 838 8500, Fax: 0171
838 8555, Call Date: July 1972 (Gray's
Inn) Qualifications: LLB

Pym *Michael John* •
In-house Counsel, Cognos Limited,
Westerly Point, Market Street, Bracknell,
Berkshire RG12 1QB, 01344 707 789,
Fax: 01344 707 703, Call Date: Nov 1986
(Gray's Inn) Qualifications: LLB(Sheff)

Qadri *Adnan Abdullah Shafqat*
Call Date: July 1995 (Middle Temple)
Qualifications: LLB (Hons)

Quaife *Ramsay Justin Malin*
Lawtel, 50 Poland Street, London
W1V 4AX, 0171 970 4632, Fax: 0171 970
4694, Editor- Crown Office Court of
Appeal Criminal Division, Call Date: Oct
1995 (Middle Temple) Qualifications: BA
(Hons), Dip Law

Quashie *Ms Juliet Sharon* •
Lawyer, Hammond Suddards, 7
Devonshire Square, Cutlers Gardens,
London EC2M 4YH, 0171 655 1000, Fax:
0171 655 1001, Call Date: Mar 1998
(Inner Temple) Qualifications: BA
(Toronto), LLB (Lond), BA (Hons)

Quenby *Richard Alan*
Call Date: July 1985 (Inner Temple)
Qualifications: BA

Quickfall *Frank*
Call Date: Nov 1959 (Gray's Inn)
Qualifications: LLB

Quinlan *Henry Charles Raymond*
Call Date: Oct 1998 (Inner Temple)
Qualifications: BA (Oxon), CPE (City)

Quinlan *Kevin Joseph* •
Senior Legal Advisor, Securities &
Futures Authority, Cottons Centre,
Cottons Lane, London SE1 2QB, 0171
378 9000, Call Date: Feb 1995 (Gray's
Inn) Qualifications: LLB (L'pool)

Quinlan *Michael John Maxwell*
Director of Stamp Duty, Pricewaterhouse
Coopers, 1 Embankment Place, London
WC2N 6NN, 0171 213 5836, Fax: 0171
213 2440, and Member Australia Bar,
Call Date: July 1992 (Middle Temple)
Qualifications: LLB, LLM

Quinn *Stuart John* •
Cleveland Magistrates Courts,
Committee, Teeside Law Courts, Victoria
Square, Middlesborough, Cleveland
TS1 2AS, 01642 240301, Fax: 01642
224010, Call Date: Oct 1990 (Gray's Inn)
Qualifications: BSc, LLM

Quinn *Miss Tamara Jane*
Call Date: Oct 1995 (Lincoln's Inn)
Qualifications: BA (Hons)(Lond)

Quinn-Smith *Duncan Niall*
Call Date: Oct 1995 (Inner Temple)
Qualifications: LLB (Bris)

Qureshi *Adnan Aslam*
Call Date: Nov 1994 (Gray's Inn)
Qualifications: LLB (Middx)

Qureshi *Azra Perveen* •
Crown Prosecutor, Crown Prosecution
Service, Queen's House, 58 Victoria
Street, St Albans, Herts Al1 3HZ, and
Member Pakistan Bar, Call Date: Nov
1983 (Lincoln's Inn) Qualifications: LLB
(Hons)

Qureshi *Miss Yasmin* •
Senior Crown Prosecutor, Crown
Prosecution Service, Kings House, 2nd
Floor, Kymberley Road, Harrow,
Middlesex HA1 1YH, 0181 424 8688 X
204, Call Date: Nov 1985 (Lincoln's Inn)
Qualifications: BA (Hons) (Lond), LLM
(Lond)

Rabin *Anthony Leon Philip*
Call Date: July 1978 (Middle Temple)
Qualifications: LLB, FCA

Raby *Edward Menashi*
01865 341694, Call Date: Nov 1967
(Inner Temple) Qualifications: BA

Rackow *Patrick Joseph William*
Call Date: Nov 1992 (Inner Temple)
Qualifications: MA (St.Andrews), Dip in
Law

Radcliffe *George Whiteley*
18 Bladon Drive, Belfast BT9 5JL, Call
Date: July 1985 (Inner Temple)
Qualifications: MA (Oxon), FCA

Radcliffe *Miss Penelope Jane*
Capsticks, 77/83 Upper Richmond Road,
London SW15 2TT, 0181 780 4716, Fax:
0181 780 4728, Call Date: Oct 1992
(Middle Temple) Qualifications: BA
(Hons, Dumelm), Diploma in Law(City)

Radford *Patrick Vaughan*
Langford Hall, Newark, Notts NG23 7RS,
01636 610825, Fax: 01636 613029, Call
Date: Nov 1954 (Gray's Inn)
Qualifications: FCIS

Radon *Mrs Joyce*
Flat 2, 188 Kennington Lane, (Entrance
Cardigan Street), London SE11 5DL,
0171 735 1574, Call Date: July 1976
(Inner Temple)

Radstone *Graham Michael*
Call Date: July 1979 (Inner Temple)
Qualifications: BA (Cantab)

Radway *Jonathan Mark*
Justices' Chief Executive, Justices' Chief
Executive, Hertfordshire Magistrates,
Court Service, Register Office Block,
County Hall, Hertford SG13 8DF, 01992
556544, Call Date: July 1977 (Middle
Temple) Qualifications: LLB (Lond),
MIMgt

Rae *Alexander* •
Senior Principal Legal Officer, Legal
Department, Ministry of Agriculture, 55
Whitehall, London SW1A 2EY, 0171 270
8227, Fax: 0171 270 8295, Call Date:
July 1978 (Inner Temple) Qualifications:
BA (Dunelm)

Rae *Ian Andrew* •
Legal Advisor, Provident Mutual Life,
Assurance Association, Six Hills Way,
Stevenage, Herts SG1 2ST, 01438
732755, Fax: 01438 732415, Call Date:
Nov 1986 (Middle Temple)
Qualifications: LLB, MBA, DIC

Rafiq *Nabil*
Khan Solicitors, 235 Manningham Lane,
Bradford, West Yorkshire, Call Date: Mar
1998 (Middle Temple) Qualifications:
LLB (Hons) (Brunel)

Rafn *Jamie George*
Call Date: Oct 1996 (Lincoln's Inn)
Qualifications: BA (Hons) (Oxon)

Ragnauth *Mrs Janet*
Call Date: July 1991 (Lincoln's Inn)
Qualifications: LLB (Hons)

Ragnauth *Miss Portia Uranie* •
Crown Prosecutor, Crown Prosecution
Service, 23rd Floor, Portland House, Stag
Place, London SW1E 5BH, Call Date: July
1985 (Lincoln's Inn) Qualifications: LLB

Rahaman *S M Atikur*
Call Date: Mar 1999 (Lincoln's Inn)
Qualifications: LLB (Hons) (Lond)

Rahman *Imran*
and Member Sierra Leone Bar, Call Date:
July 1974 (Middle Temple)

Rahman *Leo Ferhanur*
and Member Bangladesh Bar, Call Date:
July 1998 (Lincoln's Inn) Qualifications:
BA (Hons) (Keele), LLM (Sussex)

Rahman *Qazi Abdur* •
Almizan Law Offices, 54 Edgware Road,
Marble Arch, London W2 2EH, 0171 724
4977, Fax: 0171 706 2988, Call Date:
Nov 1977 (Gray's Inn) Qualifications:
BA, BL MA Business Law

Rahul *Miss Sunita Devi*
Call Date: Nov 1998 (Middle Temple)
Qualifications: BA (Hons), (De Montfort)

Rai *Yogesh Kumar*
Call Date: Nov 1995 (Middle Temple)
Qualifications: BA (Hons)

Rainbird *Johann Pieter* •
Paralegal, Clifford Chance, 200
Aldersgate Street, London EC1A 4JJ, 0171
600 1000, Call Date: Nov 1998 (Middle
Temple) Qualifications: LLB
(Hons) (Thames)

Rainford *David* •
Employed Barrister Specialisin in
Intellectual Property Law, Taylor Vinters,
Merlin Place, Milton Road, Cambridge
CB4 4DP, 01223 423444 x 2288, Call
Date: Oct 1997 (Inner Temple)
Qualifications: BSc (London), PhD
(London), CPE (City)

Raja *Anil Jayantilal* •
Express Dairies plc, Express House,
Meridan East, Meridan Business Park,
Leicester LE3 2TP, 0116 281 6281, Fax:
0116 281 6371, Call Date: Mar 1996
(Gray's Inn) Qualifications: LLB (Lond)

Raja *Miss Fozia Naz* •
In-house Lawyer, MDIS Limited,
Boundary Way, Hemel Hempstead,
Herts HP2 7HU, Call Date: Nov 1994
(Inner Temple) Qualifications: LLB
(Hull)

Rajanathan *John Victor Stanislaus*
28 Cromer Road, Leyton, London
E10 6JA, 0181 539 5140, Call Date: Nov
1970 (Middle Temple) Qualifications:
BSc Econ(Lond)

Rajasingham *Rajanathan*
18 Cunningham Avenue, Guildford,
Surrey GU1 2PE, 01483 562852, QC
(Belize) and Member Sri Lankan Bar,
Call Date: July 1957 (Lincoln's Inn)
Qualifications: MA, LLB (Cantab)

Ralph *Nicholas Stuart* •
Crown Prosecutor, Crown Prosecution
Service, Teesside Branch, Crown
House, Linthorpe Road,
Middlesbrough, Cleveland TS1 1TX,
01642 230444, Fax: 01642 253224,
Call Date: Oct 1997 (Inner Temple)
Qualifications: LLB (Durham)

Ralston *Peter Saintjohn*
Call Date: May 1997 (Gray's Inn)
Qualifications: LLB (Liverpool)

Rama *Miss Vivien*
Call Date: Oct 1996 (Lincoln's Inn)
Qualifications: LLB (Hons)(Brunel)

Ramachandran *Ms Aruna*
2 Paper Bldgs, 1st Floor, Temple,
London, EC4Y 7ET, Call Date: July 1985
(Gray's Inn) Qualifications: LLB (Lond)

Ramanathan *Miss Shamini*
W3 6DG, Call Date: Nov 1994
(Lincoln's Inn) Qualifications: LLB
(Hons)(Lond)

Rambridge *Rene Charles*
Call Date: Nov 1997 (Middle Temple)
Qualifications: LLB (Hons)

Ramful *Jugdeo* •
Assistant Solicitor, and Member
Mauritius Bar, Call Date: Nov 1984
(Lincoln's Inn) Qualifications: BA

Ramnarace *William Taij Bhowan* •
Principal Crown Prosecutor, Crown
Prosecution Service, 3rd Floor,
Kymberley Road, Harrow, Middlesex,
0181 248 5738, Call Date: Nov 1979
(Lincoln's Inn) Qualifications: BA
(Hons) LAW

Ramsahoye *Fenton Harcourt Wilworth*
Doughty Street Chambers, 11 Doughty
Street, London, WC1N 2PG, Call Date:
Feb 1953 (Lincoln's Inn)

Ramsay *Miss Cheryl Diana*
Call Date: Oct 1997 (Inner Temple)
Qualifications: LLB, MA (Brunel)

Ramsay *Jonathan Michael*
Northern Ireland, Call Date: July 1998
(Middle Temple) Qualifications: LLB
(Hons)(Dunelm)

Ramsden *Dr William Michael* •
Whitehead Woodwards & Co, 26 Talbot
Road, Blackpool, Lancashire BT1 1NJ,
Call Date: Oct 1992 (Lincoln's Inn)
Qualifications: LLB(Hons), Ph.D,LL.D

Ramsey *Miss Jane* •
Head of Law and Public Service, Legal
Services, London Borough of Islington,
Town Hall, Upper Street, London
N1 2UD, 0171 477 3174, Fax: 0171 477
3267, Call Date: July 1989 (Middle
Temple) Qualifications: BA Hons, MSc

Ramshaw *Anthony Kevin*
Call Date: Nov 1998 (Middle Temple)
Qualifications: LLB (Hons)(Luton)

Ranasinha *Mrs Ranmini Manisha*
Call Date: July 1993 (Middle Temple)
Qualifications: MA (Hons)(Oxon), LLM
(Lond)

Randall *Sean Gustavo*
1 Trenance, Woking, Surrey GU21 3LR,
01483 836338, Fax: 01483 757516,
Call Date: Nov 1997 (Inner Temple)
Qualifications: LLB (So'ton)

Randle *Alexander Toby*
Call Date: Nov 1994 (Lincoln's Inn)
Qualifications: BA (Hons)(Lond)

Rankin *Glynn* •
Principal Crown Prosecutor, Crown
Prosecution Service, 2nd Floor,
Windsor Hse, Pepper Street, Chester
CH1 1TD, Call Date: Feb 1983 (Middle
Temple) Qualifications: LLB

Rapley *Clifford*
Call Date: Nov 1998 (Inner Temple)
Qualifications: BSc

Rapson *Ms Isabel Frances* •
London Borough of Hounslow,
Borough Solicitor's Dept, Civic Centre,
Lampton Road, Hounslow TW3 4DN,
0181 862 5763, Fax: 0181 862 5008,
Call Date: Oct 1995 (Gray's Inn)
Qualifications: BA (Hull), MA (UEA),,
Dip Law

Rasaiah *Ms Santha Geraldine* •
Head of Legal and Regulatory Affairs,
The Newspaper Society, Bloomsbury
House, Bloomsbury Square, 74-77
Great Russell Street, London
WC1B 3DA, 0171 636 7014, Fax: 0171
631 5119, Call Date: July 1983 (Middle
Temple) Qualifications: BA (Oxon)

Rashid *Miss Fozia Anjum*
Call Date: Nov 1998 (Lincoln's Inn)
Qualifications: LLB (Hons)(Oxon)

Rashid *Miss Parveen Akhtar* •
Crown Prosecution Service, Essex South
Branch, County House, New London
Road, Chelmsford, Essex, Call Date: Oct
1992 (Lincoln's Inn) Qualifications:
LLB(Hons)

Rashid *Miss Yasmin*
Call Date: Mar 1996 (Lincoln's Inn)
Qualifications: LLB (Hons)

Ratcliffe *Simon Timothy James*
Call Date: Oct 1997 (Gray's Inn)
Qualifications: BA (Anglia)

Ratcliffe *Steven James* •
Lincolnshire County Council, (Legal
Division), 13 The Avenue, Lincoln,
Lincs LN1 1YP, 01522 552114, Fax:
01522 552138, Call Date: Nov 1984
(Gray's Inn) Qualifications: LLB
(Hons), Warwick

Ratnayake *Miss Nimali Anusha*
Call Date: July 1998 (Inner Temple)
Qualifications: LLB (Wolves)

Ratti *Ms Alison Julie*
Oakleigh, Wernffrwd, Gower, Swansea
SA4 3TY, 01792 851599, Fax: 01792
850056, Call Date: Nov 1991 (Gray's
Inn) Qualifications: BA (Oxon)

Rattray *Ms Frances Mary Howick*
Call Date: Oct 1998 (Inner Temple)
Qualifications: LLB (Kingston)

Raut *Viveka*
Call Date: May 1994 (Inner Temple)
Qualifications: LLB, MSc

Raval *AnilKumar Harish* •
Legal Advisor, Morgan Stanley UK
Group, 25 Cabot Square, Canary Wharf,
London E14 4QA, 0171 425 6379, Fax:
0171 425 8971, Call Date: Oct 1991
(Lincoln's Inn) Qualifications: MA
(Hons) (Cantab)

Rawat *Mrs Ismet Parveen* •
Crown Prosecutor, Crown Prosecution
Service, The Cooperage, Gainsford
Street, London SE1, 0171 962 2701,
Call Date: Nov 1992 (Inner Temple)
Qualifications: BA (Hons)

Rawat *Miss Saheema Dawood*
Call Date: Nov 1998 (Lincoln's Inn)
Qualifications: BA (Hons)(LSE)

Rawlings *David William*
Call Date: Nov 1995 (Gray's Inn)
Qualifications: LLB (Lond)

Rawlins *Christopher Stuart*
Assistant Recorder, 01454 313230, Fax:
01454 313230, Call Date: Feb 1957
(Gray's Inn)

Rawlins *Jeremy John* •
Senior Crown Prosecutor, CPS, 2 King
Edward Street, Nottingham NG1 1EL,
Call Date: Nov 1982 (Middle Temple)
Qualifications: LLB (Hons)

Rawlinson *Jonathan James Charles*
Call Date: Oct 1997 (Lincoln's Inn)
Qualifications: BA (Hons)(Leeds)

Rawlinson *William*
11 King's Bench Walk, Temple, London
EC4Y 7EQ, 0171 632 8500/0171 583
0610, Fax: 0171 583 9123/3690, 11
King's Bench Walk, Temple, London,
EC4Y 7EQ, Call Date: Jan 1939 (Inner
Temple) Qualifications: MA

Rawlinson of Ewell *The Rt Hon Lord* Honorary Recorder Kingston-upon-Thames Hon Fellow US College of Trial Lawyers, House of Lords, London SW1, Hon Fellow Christ's College Cambridge QC Northern Ireland (1971) and Member American Bar, Call Date: Nov 1946 (Inner Temple)

Rawnsley *Miss Collette Lianne* Call Date: Nov 1998 (Middle Temple) Qualifications: LLB (Hons)(Bucks)

Ray *John Betson* 'Pond Acre', Malthouse Lane, West Ashling, Chichester, West Sussex PO18 8DX, Call Date: Feb 1956 (Inner Temple) Qualifications: MA (Oxon)

Rayne *Jason Edward* Call Date: July 1997 (Gray's Inn) Qualifications: LLB (Middx)

Rayner *Christopher Glenn* Senior Legal Adviser, Colchester Magistrates' Court, Stanwell House, Stanwell Street, Colchester CO2 7DL, 01206 563057, Fax: 01206 42933, Call Date: Feb 1977 (Middle Temple) Qualifications: LLB

Rayner *Miss Donna Frances* ● Principal Crown Prosecutor, Crown Prosecution Service, Riverpark House, 225 High Road, Wood Green, London N22, 0181 888 8889, Fax: 0181 888 0746, Call Date: Nov 1988 (Gray's Inn) Qualifications: BA (Hons)

Rayner *Miss Jacqueline* Senior Court Clerk, Sutton Coldfield Mag Court, The Court House, Lichfield Road, Sutton Coldfield B74 2NG, 0121 354 7777, Fax: 0121 355 0547, Call Date: Nov 1991 (Gray's Inn) Qualifications: LLB

Raywood *Caleb* Clyde & Co, 51 Eastcheap, London EC3M 1JP, 0171 623 1244, Fax: 0171 623 5427, Call Date: Oct 1995 (Inner Temple) Qualifications: LLB (Essex), LLM (Netherlands)

Razi *Akhtar Abdul Waheed* Call Date: June 1959 (Lincoln's Inn) Qualifications: MA

Rea *James* ● Police Legal Adviser, Devon & Cornwall Constabulary, Police Headquarters, Middlemoor, Exeter, Devon EX2 7HQ, 01392 52101 Ext 22863, Fax: 01392 452765, Call Date: July 1978 (Gray's Inn) Qualifications: BA

Read *Miss Pauline Anne* Call Date: May 1979 (Inner Temple) Qualifications: LLB (Hons) (Leeds),, Dip Public Admin, (Manch)

Reading *Timothy Mark Lucas* ● Manager, Legal BP Shipping Ltd, BP Shipping Limited, Breakspear Park, Breakspear Way, Hemel Hempstead, Herts HP2 4UL, 01442 225536, Fax: 01442 225855, Call Date: July 1981 (Lincoln's Inn) Qualifications: MA (Oxon)

Record *Miss Suzannah Jane* Call Date: Nov 1997 (Gray's Inn) Qualifications: BSc (Kent)

Reddin *Lieutenant Colonel David Gordon* ● Directorate of Army Legal Svcs, Ministry of Defence, Trenchard Lines, Upavon, Wiltshire SN9 6BE, Call Date: Nov 1982 (Gray's Inn) Qualifications: LLB (Hons) (L'pool)

Reddy *Miss Challa Anudita* ● Legal Officer, H M Customs & Excise, New Kings Beam House, 22 Upper Ground, London SE1, 0171 865 5109, Fax: 0171 865 5197, Call Date: Nov 1993 (Inner Temple) Qualifications: BSc (Lond), CPE (City)

Redfearn *Charles* ● Legal Adviser, General Counsel's Office, Export Credits Guarantee Dept, P.O.Box 2200, 2 Exchange Tower, Harbour Exchange Square, London E14 9GS, 0171 512 7177, Fax: 0171 512 7052, Call Date: Nov 1986 (Lincoln's Inn) Qualifications: BA , Dip Law

Redman *Graham Frederick* Assistant Grand Secretary United Grand Lodge of England, 60 Great Queen Street, London WC2B 5AZ, 0171 831 9811, Fax: 0171 831 6021, Call Date: July 1974 (Middle Temple) Qualifications: MA (Oxon)

Redman *Martin David* Legal Adviser, Old School, Piddinghoe, Newhaven, Sussex BN9 9AP, 01273 514768, Call Date: Nov 1969 (Inner Temple)

Redman *Paul Darren* ● Havering Magistrates Court, The Court House, Main Road, Romford, Essex RM1 3BH, Call Date: July 1994 (Lincoln's Inn) Qualifications: MA

Redman *Stephen Michael* ● Unum Limited, Milton Court, Dorking, Surrey RH4 3LZ, 01306 887766, Fax: 01306 887504, Call Date: July 1986 (Lincoln's Inn) Qualifications: BA

Redpath *John Scott* Hammond Suddards Solicitors, 7 Devonshire Square, Cutlers Gardens, London EC2M 4YH, 0171 655 1000, Call Date: Oct 1996 (Middle Temple) Qualifications: BA (Hons) MA (Hons), (Lond)

Redpath *Ms Lara Catherine* ● Senior Crown Prosecutor, Crown Prosecution Service, Brent Section, 3rd Floor, King's House, Kymberly Road, Harrow HA1 1YH, 0181 424 8688 Ext 270, Call Date: Feb 1994 (Lincoln's Inn) Qualifications: BA (Hons)(Oxon)

Reece *Alan Charles* ● Director of Negotiations, Kerr McGee Oil (UK) PLC, 75 Davies Street, London W1Y 1FA, 0171 872 9778, Fax: 0171 493 2672, Call Date: July 1974 (Lincoln's Inn)

Reed *Ms Jane Elizabeth* ● Call Date: Nov 1986 (Middle Temple) Qualifications: BA (Oxon) DipLing,, Dip Law

Reed *Mrs Marie Gabrielle* ● Principal Crown Prosecutor Prosecution Team Leader, Crown Prosecution Service, Kings House, Kymberley Road, Harrow, Middlesex HA1 1YH, 0181 424 8688, Fax: 0181 424 9134, Call Date: Nov 1972 (Gray's Inn) Qualifications: LLB

Reed *Philip James William* Messrs Norton Rose, Kempson House, Camomile Street, London EC3N 7AN, 0171 283 6000, Fax: 0171 283 6500, Call Date: July 1985 (Lincoln's Inn) Qualifications: MA (Oxon)

Rees *Daneil Simon James* Wales, Call Date: Oct 1998 (Inner Temple) Qualifications: LLB (Herts)

Rees *Gareth* Call Date: Mar 1999 (Gray's Inn) Qualifications: LLB (Cardiff)

Rees *Mrs Patricia Anne* Call Date: Oct 1995 (Inner Temple) Qualifications: BSc (Australia), CPE (Lond)

Rees *Miss Penelope* ● Senior Crown Prosecutor, Crown Prosecution Service, 2-4 South Gate, Chichester CF1 3PL, 01222 378201, Call Date: July 1985 (Gray's Inn) Qualifications: BA (Hons)(E.Anglia)

Rees *The Rt Hon Lord Peter Wynford Innes* Call Date: Feb 1953 (Inner Temple) Qualifications: MA (Hons)(Oxon)

Rees *Roland Vaughan* 4 The Close, Richmond, Surrey TW9 4QW, 0181 876 2948, Call Date: Nov 1966 (Middle Temple) Qualifications: LLB

Rees *Thomas Lionel* ● Lord Chancellor's Department, Criminal Appeal Office, Law Courts, The Strand, London WC2A 2LL, 0171 936 6606, Call Date: Nov 1968 (Middle Temple) Qualifications: MA, LLM (Cantab)

E

E

Rees *William Patrick Charles*
Deputy Justice's Clerk, Inner London
Magistrates', Courts Service, 65
Romney Street, London SW1, Call Date:
Nov 1974 (Middle Temple)
Qualifications: LLB (Lond)

Reese *Dr Alan John Morris*
9 Hopping Lane, Canonbury, London
N1 2NU, 0171 226 2088, Call Date: Nov
1955 (Middle Temple) Qualifications:
MD (Lond), FRCPath

Reeve *Robert Arthur*
Call Date: Nov 1975 (Middle Temple)
Qualifications: BA, FCIS

Reeves *Christopher David*
Lecturer (BVC), The College of Law,
50-52 Chancery Lane, London
WC2A 1SX, 0171 969 3146, Fax: 0171
969 3150, Call Date: Oct 1992
(Lincoln's Inn) Qualifications:
LLB(Hons)(Sheff)

Reeves *Christopher Patrick*
Call Date: July 1993 (Inner Temple)
Qualifications: BA (E. Anglia), Dip. in
Law

Reeves *Mrs Mary* •
Civil Servant Senior Crown Prosecutor,
Call Date: Oct 1994 (Middle Temple)
Qualifications: BA (Hons), CPE (Middx)

Regan *Gerald Thomas* •
Prinicpal Legal Officer, H M Customs &
Excise, New King's Beam House, 22
Upper Ground, London, 0171 865
5149, Fax: 0171 865 5194, Call Date:
Nov 1993 (Middle Temple)
Qualifications: BA (Hons)(Leeds), CPE
(City)

Regan *Matthew James*
I T & Management Consultant
Company Director, Metro Consulting,
17 Queen Anne's Gate, London
SW1H 9BU, 0171 222 2526, Fax: 0171
222 2527, Call Date: Mar 1996 (Middle
Temple) Qualifications: BA (Hons)

Reggiori *Miss Brenda Clare* •
Inspector, Crown Prosecution Service,
CPS Inspectorate, 50 Ludgate Hill,
London EC4M 7EX, 0171 273 1286,
Fax: 0171 273 8194, Call Date: Nov
1970 (Middle Temple) Qualifications:
LLB (Lond), LLM

Regis *Simon Trevor Andrew* •
Call Date: Oct 1997 (Inner Temple)
Qualifications: BA (Warwick)

Regnart *Horace*
Call Date: July 1985 (Gray's Inn)
Qualifications: LLB (Newc)

Rehman *Miss Ghulam Sakina*
Call Date: July 1994 (Lincoln's Inn)
Qualifications: LLB (Hons)

Reid *Ms Claire Fiona*
Call Date: July 1995 (Inner Temple)
Qualifications: LLB (Lond)

Reid *Dr George Alan* •
Senior Bursar, St John's College,
Cambridge CB2 1TP, 01223 338627,
Fax: 01223 338762, Call Date: July
1972 (Lincoln's Inn) Qualifications:
MA, Ph.D (Cantab)

Reid *James Gordon*
Standing Junior Scottish Office,
Environment Dept 1986 to 1993,
Advocatess Library, Parliament House,
Edinburtgh, Scotland EH1 1RF, 031
226 5071, Fax: 031 225 3642, QC
Scotland 1993 and Member Scottish
Bar 1 Atkin Building, Gray's Inn,
London, WC1R 5AT, Call Date: Apr
1991 (Inner Temple) Qualifications:
LLB (Edin), F.C.I.Arb

Reid *Kiron John Cuchulain*
Lecturer in Law, Faculty of Law,
University of Liverpool, Liverpool
L69 3BX, 0151 794 2801, Fax: 0151
794 2884, Call Date: Nov 1994 (Inner
Temple) Qualifications: LLB (Bris)

Reid *Mrs Mary Helene Theresa* •
Team Leader, Crown Prosecution
Service, One Onslow Street, Guildford,
Surrey GU1 4YA, 01483 882600, Fax:
01483 882603/4, Call Date: Nov 1982
(Middle Temple) Qualifications: LLB
(Hons)

Reihill *Mark*
Call Date: Nov 1996 (Gray's Inn)
Qualifications: MA (St. Andrews)

Reilly *Miss Clare* •
Associate, Financial Services Authority,
25 The North Colonnade, Canary
Wharf, London E14 5HS, Call Date: Feb
1988 (Inner Temple) Qualifications:
MA, LLM

Reilly *Thomas Edward Martin*
Call Date: Nov 1996 (Lincoln's Inn)
Qualifications: LLB (Hons)

Rein *Dr Andrew Paul* •
Legal Officer, Inland Revenue,
Somerset House, London, 0171 438
7079, Call Date: Nov 1992 (Middle
Temple) Qualifications: BA (Hons), MA,
B.Phil & D.Phil

Relan *Vershal*
Call Date: Oct 1997 (Gray's Inn)
Qualifications: LLB (L'pool)

Rendell *Antoine Mark John*
Principal Court Clerk, Bristol
Magistrates Court, P O Box 107, Nelson
Street, Bristol, Avon BS99 7BJ, 0117
9435100, Call Date: Nov 1987 (Gray's
Inn) Qualifications: LLB (Reading)

Rendell-Reynolds *Charles James
Samuel*
Call Date: Mar 1997 (Lincoln's Inn)
Qualifications: LLB (Hons)

Rene *Mrs Karen Anne* •
Call Date: Oct 1992 (Lincoln's Inn)
Qualifications: LLB(Hons)

Rennell *Nigel John Nicholas* •
Bench Legal Adviser, The Law Courts,
Park Road, Poole, Dorset BH15 2RH,
01202 721650, Fax: 01202 745309,
Call Date: Nov 1990 (Lincoln's Inn)
Qualifications: BA (Hons)

Rennie *Mrs Brenda Dawn*
Call Date: July 1985 (Inner Temple)
Qualifications: LLB (Lond)

Renton *The Rt Hon Lord*
Bencher. Treasurer 1979. Chairman,
Committee on Preparation of
Legislation. President, Statute Law
Society Recorder of Rochester 1963-68.
Recorder of Guildford 1968-71. Deputy
Speaker House of Lords 1982-88, 16
Old Bldgs, Lincoln's Inn, London
WC2A 3TL, 0171 242 8986, Hon.Fellow:
Univ.College,Oxon Member of Royal
Commission on the Constitution
1971-73, Call Date: Jan 1933 (Lincoln's
Inn) Qualifications: MA, BCL

Renton *David Malcolm Alexander*
Call Date: Nov 1997 (Gray's Inn)
Qualifications: LLB

Renwick *John* •
Call Date: Feb 1987 (Middle Temple)
Qualifications: LLB

Revell *Marcus John* •
Nominated Officer, Office of the Social
Security, and Child Support
Commissioner, Hapr House, 83-86
Farringdon Street, London EC4A 4DH,
0171 395 3328, Call Date: Nov 1992
(Middle Temple) Qualifications: BA
(Hons, Kent), LLB (Hons)

Reyes *Stephen Edward* •
Magistrates' Clerk, Call Date: Nov 1991
(Gray's Inn) Qualifications: BA

Reynolds *Basil John*
50 The Avenue, Cheam, Sutton, Surrey
SM2 7QE, 0181 642 2324, Call Date:
Nov 1953 (Gray's Inn)

Reynolds *John Adam*
Call Date: Oct 1998 (Gray's Inn)
Qualifications: BA

Reynolds *Steven*
Call Date: Feb 1981 (Middle Temple)
Qualifications: LLB (Hull), MBA, Dip M

Rhodes *Richard William*
12 Avenue Peschier, 1206 Geneva,
(022) 3463775, Call Date: Feb 1958
(Inner Temple) Qualifications: MA
(Oxon)

Rhodes *Steven Marc* •
Liberty RE, Corn Exchange, 55 Mark
Lane, London EC3R 7NE, 0171 661
9000, Fax: 0171 903 7720, Call Date:
Oct 1991 (Lincoln's Inn)
Qualifications: BD , AKC , Dip L

Rhone-Adrien *Miss Paula Christina*
Call Date: Oct 1998 (Inner Temple)
Qualifications: LLB (East London)

• Barrister in employment

Ribeiro *Roberto Alexandre Vieira*
Member Hong Kong Law Reform
Commission Member Operations Review
Committee, Independent Commision
Against Corruption., Temple Chambers,
16th Floor, One Pacific Place, 88
Queensway, 00 852 5232033/25263263,
Fax: 00 852 5232033/281003021, QC
Hong Kong 1990 and Member Hong
Kong Bar Singapore Bar 4 Essex Court,
Temple, London, EC4Y 9AJ, Call Date:
1978 (Inner Temple) Qualifications:
LLM (Lond) LLB

Rich *Gordon Ian* •
Musicians' Union, 60/62 Clapham Road,
London SW9 0JJ, 0171 582 5566, Fax:
0171 582 9805, Call Date: Nov 1960
(Gray's Inn) Qualifications: MA

Rich *Mrs Marion Constance* •
Director of Legal & Contractual Affairs
and Company Secretary, The British
Constructional, Steelwork Association
Limited, 4 Whitehall, Westminster,
London SW1A 2ES, 0171 839 8566, Fax:
0171 976 1634, Call Date: Nov 1978
(Middle Temple) Qualifications: MSc

Richard *Solomon Asoka*
Call Date: July 1994 (Lincoln's Inn)
Qualifications: BA (Econs), MA (Econs),
LLB (Wales)

Richards *Alun*
Deputy Clerk to the Justices,
Cambridgeshire Magistrates' Ct, Lion
Yard, Cambridge CB2 3NA, 01223
314311, Fax: 01223 355237, Call Date:
Nov 1985 (Middle Temple)
Qualifications: LLB

Richards *Huw Joseph*
Principal Court Clerk, Waltham Forest
Magistrates Crt, The Court House, 1
Farnan Avenue, Walthamstow, London
E17 4NX, 0181 531 3121, Fax: 0181 527
9063, Call Date: Nov 1986 (Gray's Inn)

Richards *Jefry Loyd*
01902 750497, Call Date: July 1978
(Gray's Inn) Qualifications: LLB, MBA

Richards *John Hesketh Rigby* •
Deputy Head of Unit, DGI, European
Commission, European Commission,
CHAR 13/149, B-1049 Brussels, 010322
2354397, Call Date: July 1974 (Gray's
Inn) Qualifications: LLB

Richards *Keith David* •
Head of Consumer Affairs, ABTA, 68-71
Newman Street, London W1P 4AH, 0171
637 2444, Fax: 0171 631 4623, Call
Date: July 1985 (Middle Temple)
Qualifications: BA (Kent)

Richards *Quinton Clive*
Call Date: Oct 1996 (Inner Temple)
Qualifications: BSc (Wales), CPE
(Sussex)

Richardson *Frank Cameron* •
Principal Crown Prosecutor, Crown
Prosecution Service, Black Horse House,
8-10 Leigh Road, Eastleigh, Hants
SO50 4FH, 01703 614622, Call Date: July
1981 (Inner Temple) Qualifications: BSc
(Hons), Dip Law

Richardson *Miss Penelope Iona*
Call Date: Mar 1999 (Lincoln's Inn)
Qualifications: BA (Hons)(Edinburgh)

Richardson *Philip Martin* •
Legal Services Manager, Rugby Borough
Council, Town Hall, Rugby CV21 2LB,
01788 533533, Fax: 01788 533577, Call
Date: July 1988 (Lincoln's Inn)
Qualifications: LLB (Hons) (Leics)

Richardson *Professor Sam Scruton*
Law Revision Commissioner, Northern
States of Nigeria. Vice President Britain
Australia Society., The Malt Hse, Wylye,
Warminster, Wilts BA12 0QP, 01985 248
348, Call Date: May 1960 (Lincoln's Inn)
Qualifications: MA, LLD

Richardson *Miss Sheila Frances*
Accredited CEDR Mediator, The Warwick
Partnership, 70 Warwick Road, St Albans,
Hertfordshire AL1 4DL, 01727 835826,
Fax: 01727 810885, Call Date: July 1979
(Middle Temple) Qualifications: MA
(Cantab)

Richardson *Miss Shelagh Barbara*
Call Date: Oct 1996 (Middle Temple)
Qualifications: LLB (Hons) (Manch)

Richer *Mark*
Call Date: Nov 1998 (Middle Temple)
Qualifications: B.Vet.Med (Royal,
Vetinary College)

Richmond *Daniel Henry*
Call Date: Oct 1998 (Lincoln's Inn)
Qualifications: LLB (Hons)(Leeds)

Richmond *David Andrew*
Court Clerk, Legal Team Manager, West
Riding Metropolitan, Magistrates' Court
Committee, The Court House, P.O.Box
B37, Civic Centre, Huddersfield, West
Yorkshire HD1 2NH, 01484 423552, Fax:
01484 430085, Call Date: Nov 1992
(Inner Temple) Qualifications: LLB

Richmond *Paul Anthony Oliffe*
Call Date: Oct 1998 (Inner Temple)
Qualifications: LLB (Soton)

Richter *Ryan Robert* •
Paralegal, Freshfields Solicitors, 65 Fleet
Street, London EC4Y 1HS, 0171 832
7033, Call Date: Oct 1998 (Lincoln's
Inn) Qualifications: BA (Hons)

Ricketts *Pascal John*
Call Date: Feb 1962 (Inner Temple)
Qualifications: MA, FCIS

Rideout *Dr Roger William*
255 Chipstead Way, Woodmansterne,
Surrey SM7 3JW, 01737 52033, Call
Date: Apr 1964 (Gray's Inn)
Qualifications: LLB, Ph.D

Rider *Professor Barry Alexander Kenneth*
Professor of Law and Director of the
Institute of Advanced Legal Studies,
University of London & Fellow of Jesus
College, Cambridge, Fellow in Law, Jesus
College, Cambridge CB5 8BL, 01223
339339, Call Date: Feb 1979 (Inner
Temple) Qualifications: LLB, PhD
(Lond), MA, PhD (Cantab), LLD

Ridgeway *Giles Mansel*
Call Date: Nov 1998 (Gray's Inn)
Qualifications: LLB

Ridgway *Philip* •
Deloitte & Touche, 1 Little New Street,
London EC4A 3TR, 0171 303 3434, Fax:
0171 303 4778, Principal, Deloitte &
Touche, Chairman London Branch,
Chartered Institute of Taxation, Call
Date: July 1986 (Middle Temple)
Qualifications: BA, LLM(Cantab)

Rigby *Miss Charity Elizabeth*
Call Date: 1993 (Lincoln's Inn)
Qualifications: LLB (Hons) (Leic)

Riggs *Miss Rachel*
Assistant Solicitor, Nelsons Solicitors,
Pennine House, 8 Stanford Street,
Nottingham, 0115 958 6262, Call Date:
Oct 1994 (Lincoln's Inn) Qualifications:
LLB (Hons) (Leic)

Riglia *Enzo* •
Senior Court Clerk, Barnet, 13 Calder
Avenue, Perivale, Greenford, Middlesex
UB6 8JQ, 0181 997 5027, Call Date: May
1990 (Inner Temple) Qualifications: LLB

Riley *Mrs Alison Claire* •
Principal Crown Prosecutor, Crown
Prosecution Service, 50 Ludgate Hill,
London EC4M 7EX, 0171 273 1240, Fax:
0171 329 8164, Call Date: July 1981
(Middle Temple) Qualifications: BA
(Hons)

Riley *James Edward*
Call Date: Nov 1995 (Inner Temple)
Qualifications: LLB

Riley *Philip Duncan* •
Senior Crown Prosecutor, Crown
Prosecution Service, 2 Aalborg Square,
Lancaster LA1 1GG, 01524 847676, Call
Date: July 1981 (Inner Temple)
Qualifications: BA

Riley *Richard Patrick*
Call Date: Oct 1997 (Gray's Inn)
Qualifications: BA (Kent)

Riley *Mrs Susan Peta Lonsdale* •
Legal Advisor, Call Date: Nov 1976
(Middle Temple) Qualifications: LLB
(London)

Ring *Thomas Joseph*
Clerk to the Justices, Call Date: Nov 1987
(Inner Temple) Qualifications: LLB

Ringguth *John Stephen* •
Assistant Chief Crown Prosecutor,
Central Casework, Call Date: July 1974
(Gray's Inn) Qualifications: LLB

E

Rioda *Carlo Mark*
Call Date: May 1993 (Middle Temple)
Qualifications: LLB (Hons)(B'ham)

Ripman *Peter Hugo*
Call Date: June 1947 (Inner Temple)
Qualifications: MA (Cantab)

Rippengal *Derek* •
Counsel to the Chairman of
Committees, Call Date: June 1953
(Middle Temple) Qualifications: MA

Rippon *Simon John*
Call Date: Nov 1996 (Gray's Inn)
Qualifications: BA (Lond)

Rivlin *Paul Denis*
6 Bishopsgate, London EC2N 4DA,
0171 545 2111, Fax: 0171 545 2092,
Call Date: Nov 1995 (Middle Temple)
Qualifications: BA (Hons), FCMA, MCT

Riza *Ms Sheila Shule Antoinette* •
Legal Officer, Claims Manager, M.E
Warrington & Others, Syndicate 1239,
84 Fenchurch Street, London
EC3M 4BY, 0171 661 5512, Fax: 0171
481 1631, Call Date: July 1982 (Gray's
Inn) Qualifications: BA Law, A.C.I.I

Roath *Mrs Josephine Elizabeth Mary*
Lincolns, Boyatt Lane, Eastleigh,
Hampshire SO50 4LJ, 01703 252727,
Call Date: July 1981 (Middle Temple)
Qualifications: LLB (Hons), MA

Robb *Ms Cairo Anne Reyner*
Research Fellow at the Lauterpacht
Research Centre for International Law,
Cambridge, Editor, Int'l Environmental
Law Reports (CUP), Call Date: Oct 1993
(Middle Temple) Qualifications: MA
(Cantab), LIC.Spec.Dr Eur, (Brussels)

Robb *John Edmund Boulton*
Call Date: Mar 1998 (Gray's Inn)
Qualifications: BA (Oxon)

Robb *Lt Cdr RN Louis Joseph*
Scotland, Scottish Advocate, Call Date:
June 1964 (Inner Temple)

Robbins *Miss Emelita Ann*
12 Clarence Road, London N15 5BB,
0181 245 4839, Call Date: Oct 1995
(Middle Temple) Qualifications: LLB
(Hons)

Robbins *Ms Kelly*
Call Date: Nov 1995 (Middle Temple)
Qualifications: BA (Hons)

Roberts *Miss Andrea*
Call Date: Oct 1994 (Middle Temple)
Qualifications: BA (Hons)(Oxon)

Roberts *Mrs Anne P*
Call Date: July 1982 (Gray's Inn)
Qualifications: BA (Hons), Dip Droit
Francais

Roberts *Christopher Andrew*
Clerk to the Justices, Justices' Clerk's
Office, The Court House, College Lane,
King's Lynn, Norfolk PE30 1PQ, 01553
763341, Fax: 01553 775098, Call Date:
July 1980 (Gray's Inn)

Roberts *Colin*
HM Diplomatic Service, Call Date: Nov
1986 (Inner Temple) Qualifications:
MA (Cantab), Dip Law (City), ACIArb

Roberts *Craig* •
Home Office Presenting Officer, Home
Office Presenting, Officers Unit, 3rd &
4th Floors, Feltham Green, 21-47 High
St, Feltham, Middlesex TW13 4AG,
0181 957 3228, Fax: 0181 957 3259,
Call Date: Nov 1994 (Lincoln's Inn)
Qualifications: LLB (Hons), LLM,
(Lond), MRIN

Roberts *Dafydd Owen*
Call Date: Oct 1998 (Gray's Inn)
Qualifications: BA (Wales)

Roberts *Miss Emma Charlotte* •
Cazenove & Co, 12 TokenHouse Yard,
London, 0171 588 2828, Call Date: Nov
1996 (Middle Temple) Qualifications:
BA (Hons)(Manch)

Roberts *Graham Martin*
Senior Lecturer, Dept of Management
&, Professional Development, London
Guildhall University, 84 Moorgate,
London EC2M 6SQ, 0171 320 1581,
Fax: 0171 320 1585, Call Date: July
1982 (Middle Temple) Qualifications:
BA (Kent)

Roberts *Howard Vincent* •
Senior Principal Legal Officer,
Department of Social Security, New
Court, 48 Carey Street, London
WC2A 2LS, 0171 412 1591, Fax: 0171
412 1440, Call Date: July 1972 (Middle
Temple) Qualifications: LLB

Roberts *Jack*
Call Date: Nov 1998 (Middle Temple)
Qualifications: BA (Hons)(Manch), LLB
(John Moores)

Roberts *Mrs Jane Carol*
Call Date: Nov 1996 (Inner Temple)
Qualifications: BA (Oxon), MA (Kent),
LLB (City)

Roberts *Mrs Marian*
Assistant Director (Professional
Practice & Training), National Family
Mediator, NFM, 9 Tavistock Place,
London WC1H 9SN, 0171 383 5993,
Fax: 0171 383 5994, Call Date: July
1979 (Gray's Inn) Qualifications: BA,
PGrad.Dip, (Social Studies)

Roberts *Miss Sarah*
Call Date: Oct 1991 (Middle Temple)
Qualifications: LLB (Hons)

Roberts *Miss Stella*
Justices' Chief Executive, Berkshire &
Oxfordshire, Magistrates' Courts'
Committee, Easby House, Northfield
End, Henley on Thames, Oxon
RG9 2NB, 01491 412720, Fax: 01491
412762, Call Date: Feb 1984 (Lincoln's
Inn) Qualifications: MIPD, MIMgt

Roberts *Stephen Gwilym*
Court Clerk, North Wales Magistrates
Court, 11 Rhiw Road, Colwyn Bay,
Conwy LL29 7TE, 01492 534 550, Call
Date: Nov 1987 (Gray's Inn)
Qualifications: LL.B.(Cardiff)

Robertshaw *Alan Stuart*
Call Date: Oct 1997 (Middle Temple)
Qualifications: LLB (Lond)

Robertson *Mrs Elaine Emmett*
Appletree House, Burnthouse Lane,
Whickham NE16 5AS, 0191 488 6027,
Fax: 0191 496 1685, and Member
Hong Kong Bar Dec 1987, Call Date:
Nov 1977 (Gray's Inn) Qualifications:
BA (Hon)

Robertson *John*
44 Willoughby Road, London NW3 1RU,
0171 435 4907, Call Date: Nov 1961
(Lincoln's Inn) Qualifications: LLB

Robertson *Miss Rachel Dawn*
Call Date: Oct 1998 (Inner Temple)
Qualifications: LLB (Soton)

Robertson *Miss Victoria*
Call Date: Mar 1999 (Inner Temple)
Qualifications: LLB (East Anglia)

Robins *Mrs Charlotte Elizabeth*
ILMCS, 65 Romney Street, London
SW1P 3RD, Call Date: Nov 1975
(Middle Temple)

Robinson *David Edward* •
Crown Prosecution Service, Crown
Prosecution Service, The Court Yard,
Lombard Street, Abingdon, Oxon
OX14 5SE, 01235 555678, Call Date:
Oct 1993 (Gray's Inn) Qualifications:
BSc (So'ton)

Robinson *David Francis* •
Director & Secretary, Robinson & Sons
Ltd, Wheat Bridge, Chesterfield,
Derbyshire S40 1YE, 01246 220022,
Fax: 01246 209517, Call Date: Nov
1963 (Inner Temple) Qualifications:
BA [Oxon]

Robinson *Miss Deirdre Maura*
Call Date: Mar 1999 (Gray's Inn)
Qualifications: LLB

Robinson *Miss Emma Millicent* •
Principal Legal Officer, Lord
Chancellor's Department, Drafting
Services Division, Legal Adviser's
Group, Selbourne House, 54-60
Victoria Street, London SW1E 6QW,
0171 210 0605, Fax: 0171 210 0725,
Call Date: May 1995 (Inner Temple)
Qualifications: BA, CPE

Robinson *Miss Justine Victoria*
Partner in Private Practice, Messrs
Marron Dodds Solicitors, 32 Friar Lane,
Leicester LE1 5RA, 0116 2628596, Fax:
0116 2518322, Call Date: Nov 1990
(Middle Temple) Qualifications: BA
(Hons)(Kent), M Phil (Cantab)

Robinson *Mrs Letchumy*
Call Date: July 1975 (Inner Temple)

Robinson *Mrs Maura Frances*
Call Date: Oct 1992 (Lincoln's Inn)
Qualifications: BA , LLB (Hons)

Robinson *Paul Anthony* •
Principle Crown Prosecutor, Crown
Prosecution Service, Headquarters, 50
Ludgate Hill, London EC4M 7EX, 0171
273 1288, Fax: 0171 273 1325, Call
Date: Nov 1985 (Middle Temple)
Qualifications: LLB

Robinson *Miss Penelope Therese*
Call Date: Nov 1986 (Gray's Inn)
Qualifications: BSc (Cardiff)

Robinson *Raymund Francis*
Call Date: Nov 1968 (Gray's Inn)

Robinson *Steven Andrew* •
Inspector, CPS Inspectorate, Crown
Prosecution Service HQ, 50 Ludgate Hill,
London EC4, 0171 273 8157, Call Date:
Nov 1985 (Gray's Inn) Qualifications: BA

Robinson *Miss Tina* •
Legal Adviser, Ministry of Defence, Room
4107, Main Building, Whitehall, London
SW1A 2HB, Call Date: July 1989 (Inner
Temple) Qualifications: LLB (Lanc),
LLM (Leics)

Robinson *Warren John*
Call Date: Mar 1996 (Lincoln's Inn)
Qualifications: LLB (Hons) (Leeds)

Robson *Andrew John* •
General Counsel and Company Secretary,
Research Machines plc, New Mill House,
183 Milton Park, Abingdon Oxon, Call
Date: July 1985 (Inner Temple)
Qualifications: LLB(Nott'm)

Robson *Cameron James Elliot*
Call Date: Oct 1993 (Lincoln's Inn)
Qualifications: LLB (Hons) (Wolver), BA
(Oxon), LLM (L'pool)

Robson *John Christian* •
Prosecution Team Leader, Crown
Prosecution Service, First Floor, The
Cooperage, Gainsford Street, London
SE1, 0171 962 2625, Fax: 0171 962
0906, Call Date: Nov 1987 (Inner
Temple) Qualifications: MA [Carleton],
BA [Lond], Dip in Law

Roche *Mrs Barbara Maureen*
Member of Parliament, House of
Commons, London SW1, 0171 219
3000, Call Date: July 1977 (Middle
Temple) Qualifications: BA (Oxon)

Roche *Michael Anthony* •
Assistant Land Registrar H M Land
Registry, Telford District Land Registry,
Parkside Court, Hall Park Way, Telford,
Shropshire TF3 4LR, 01952 290355, Call
Date: July 1973 (Gray's Inn)

Rodaway *Miss Deborah Jackson*
Martin Murray & Associates, Solicitors,
138 High Street, Yiewsley, West DraytoN,
Middlesex UB7 7BD, 01895 431332, Call
Date: July 1997 (Gray's Inn)
Qualifications: BSc (Lond)

Roe *Jeremy James*
Downe Farm, Hartland, Woking,
Bideford, North Devon EX39 6DA, 01237
441210, Fax: 01237 441881, Call Date:
July 1972 (Lincoln's Inn) Qualifications:
LLB, AIB

Rogers *Christopher John Edwin* •
Hungerford House, Hungerford,
Fordingbridge, Hampshire SP6 2QG,
01425 652116, Call Date: Nov 1981
(Gray's Inn) Qualifications: MA (Cantab)

Rogers *Mrs Deborah Elizabeth* •
Principal Crown Prosecutor, Crown
Prosecution Service, Pearl Assurance
House, 20th Floor, Greyfriars Road,
Cardiff CF1 3PL, Call Date: July 1983
(Lincoln's Inn) Qualifications: BA

Rogers *Ms Francesca*
Legal Assistant, Shearman & Sterling,
199 Bishopsgate, London EC2, Call Date:
Nov 1996 (Inner Temple) Qualifications:
BA (Lond)

Rogers *Miss Glenda Mary*
Call Date: Mar 1999 (Gray's Inn)
Qualifications: LLB (L'pool)

Rogers *Kevin Patrick* •
Prosecution Team Leader, Crown
Prosecution Service, 8th Floor, Sunlight
House, Quay Street, Manchester
M60 3PT, Call Date: Nov 1985 (Middle
Temple)

Rogers *Michael* •
Legal Director, Harrods Limited, 85-137
Brompton Road, Knightsbridge, London
SW1X 7XL, 0171 225 5735, Fax: 0171
225 5906, Call Date: Nov 1974 (Gray's
Inn) Qualifications: LLB

Rogers *Raymond Alexander*
Deputy Clerk to the Justices, Doncaster
Magistrates' Court, PO Box 49, The Law
Courts, College Road, Doncaster
DN1 3HT, 01302 366711, Fax: 01302
340323, Call Date: Nov 1978 (Gray's
Inn) Qualifications: BA

Rogers *Richard John*
Call Date: Nov 1994 (Lincoln's Inn)
Qualifications: LLB (Hons) (Sheff)

Rogers *Simon John* •
Principal Legal Officer, Office of the
Solicitor, Dept of Health & Social,
Security, New Court, 48 Carey Street,
London3 WC2A 2LS, 0171 412 1475, Call
Date: May 1994 (Gray's Inn)
Qualifications: BA

Rogers *Stephen Thomas*
Law Lecturer (Freelance), Call Date: Nov
1968 (Gray's Inn) Qualifications: LLB

Rogers *Stephen Urban*
Legal Adviser, 15 Warren Road,
Wanstead, London E11 2LX, Call Date:
May 1988 (Gray's Inn) Qualifications:
BSc (Leeds), M Jur (B'ham)

Rogerson *Paul* •
Chief Legal Officer, Leeds City Council,
Legal Services, Civic Hall, Leeds LS1 1UR,
0113 2474414, Fax: 0113 2474651, Call
Date: Feb 1971 (Gray's Inn)
Qualifications: LLB, MA (Econ)

Rokison *Kenneth Stuart*
20 Essex Street, London, WC2R 3AL, Call
Date: Feb 1961 (Gray's Inn)
Qualifications: BA (Cantab)

Rolls *Richard Michael*
Call Date: Mar 1999 (Middle Temple)
Qualifications: LLB (Hons) (Thames),
LLM (Lond)

Ronan *Michael Marc*
Call Date: Mar 1998 (Lincoln's Inn)
Qualifications: LLB (Hons) (Thames)

Rook *Ms Susanne Elizabeth*
Call Date: May 1994 (Lincoln's Inn)
Qualifications: LLB (Hons)

Roopra *Ravinder Singh* •
Legal Adviser, Hambro Legal Protection
Ltd, Hambro House, Stephenson Road,
Colchester, Essex CO4 4QR, 0990
234500, Fax: 0990 234508, Call Date:
Oct 1996 (Lincoln's Inn) Qualifications:
LLB (Hons) (Wolves)

Roper *Frank Spencer Duncan* •
Senior Legal Adviser, BG plc, Transco
Legal Services, St Martin's House, 2nd
Floor, 140 Tottenham Court Road,
London W1P 9LN, 0171 387 7527, Fax:
0171 387 7009, Call Date: Nov 1975
(Middle Temple) Qualifications: LLB

Roper *Miss Sophia*
Call Date: Oct 1990 (Middle Temple)
Qualifications: MA (Cantab), BCL (Oxon)

Roscoe *John Gareth*
Legal Adviser, 18 College Gardens,
Dulwich, London SE21 7BE, 0181 693
5680, Fax: 0181 693 9858, Call Date:
Nov 1972 (Gray's Inn) Qualifications:
LLB(Lond)

Roscoe *Nicholas Charles Marshall* •
Legal Adviser, Sedgwick, Sedgwick House,
Sedgwick Centre, London E1 8DX, 0171
377 3456, Fax: 0171 377 3199, Call
Date: Nov 1990 (Middle Temple)
Qualifications: BA (Manch), Dip Law
(City)

Rose *Andrew Wyness*
Call Date: Nov 1968 (Gray's Inn)
Qualifications: MA, LLB (Cantab)

Rose *Craig Mark*
Legal Editor of Commerical Lawyer, Call
Date: Nov 1994 (Lincoln's Inn)
Qualifications: BA (Hons) (Bris), Ph.D

Rose *Martin John* •
Group Legal & Compliance Director,
Smith & Williamson Investment,
Management Limited, No 1 Riding House
Street, London W1A 3AS, 0171 637 5377,
Fax: 0171 631 0741, Call Date: July 1979
(Middle Temple) Qualifications: LLB

Rose *Martyn Craig*
Call Date: July 1972 (Inner Temple)

E

Rose *Miss Vivien Judith* •
Lawyer (Grade 6), Tresurer's Solicitor's
Dept, Queen Anne's Chambers, 28
Broadway, London SW1H 9JS, Call
Date: July 1984 (Gray's Inn)
Qualifications: MA (Cantab) BCL Oxon

Rosell *Mrs Tracey Allison Grosser* •
Director(Expatriate Services), Anglo St
James House, Southgate Street,
Winchester, Hampshire SO23 9EH,
01962 850888, Fax: 01962 851777,
Call Date: Nov 1987 (Middle Temple)
Qualifications: LLB, ATT, Assoc IPD

Rosen *Jonathan Leon*
Co-ordinating Court Reporter, Lawtel,
St Giles House, 50 Poland Street,
London W1V 4AX, 0171 970 4632, Fax:
0171 970 4694, Call Date: Nov 1996
(Gray's Inn) Qualifications: BSc, LLB
(Lond)

Rosenberg *Robert Alan*
Call Date: July 1983 (Gray's Inn)
Qualifications: BA (Hons), MSc, MICM,
CeMAP

Ross *Ms Alison*
Senior Legal Advisor, Ealing
Magistrates' Court, Green Man Lane,
Ealing, London W13 OSD, 0181 579
9311, Fax: 0181 579 2985, Call Date:
July 1982 (Middle Temple)
Qualifications: BA (Hons)

Ross *Miss Alison Mary*
Call Date: Nov 1992 (Middle Temple)
Qualifications: LLB (Hons)

Ross *David*
Director, Company Secretary, Call Date:
Mar 1996 (Gray's Inn) Qualifications:
BA (York), ACIS

Ross *John*
Call Date: Oct 1997 (Middle Temple)
Qualifications: LLB (Hons)(Lond)

Ross *Martin Christopher Jude* •
Principal Court Clerk, North East &
Surrey Mag's Crt, The Law Courts,
Knowle Green, Staines, Middlesex
TW18 1XR, 01784 459261, Fax: 01784
466257, Call Date: Nov 1976 (Gray's
Inn)

Ross *Ms Nicola Jane*
Call Date: Oct 1992 (Middle Temple)
Qualifications: BA (Hons)

Ross *Stephen David*
Senior Legal Adviser, Staffordshire
Magistrates Crt, P O Box 428, Leek,
Staffordshire ST13 5ST, 01538 372858,
Call Date: Nov 1990 (Inner Temple)
Qualifications: LLB

Ross *Miss Susan Janet* •
Legal Adviser, Treasury Solicitors Dept.,
Queen Annes Chambers, 28 Broadway,
London SW1, 0171 210 3243, Fax:
0171 210 3410, Call Date: July 1985
(Middle Temple) Qualifications: LLB
(Warwick)

Rossiter *Derek Trevor*
Hon.President of P.T.M.G, The Wall
House, 31a Cottenham Park Road,
London SW20 0RX, 0181 946 8564,
Fax: 0181 944 0062, Call Date: Nov
1968 (Middle Temple) Qualifications:
BA

Rought-Brooks *Miss Hannah Mildred*
Call Date: Mar 1999 (Middle Temple)
Qualifications: LLB (Hons)(B'ham)

Rowan *Michael Anthony* •
Principal Lawyer, North Somerset
Council, Town Hall, Legal Dept,
Weston-super-Mare, North Somerset
BS23 4XE, 01934 634946, Fax: 01934
418194, Call Date: Nov 1992 (Inner
Temple) Qualifications: LLB

Rowbottom *Jacob Hartley*
Call Date: Nov 1997 (Gray's Inn)
Qualifications: BA

Rowbottom *Stephen Peter*
Clerk to the Gateshead Justices Justices'
Chief Executive to Gateshead
Magistrates' Court., Gateshead
Magistrates, Courts Committee, P O
Box 26, Warwick Street, Gateshead,
Tyne & Wear NE8 1DT, 0191 477 5821,
Fax: 0191 478 7825, Call Date: Feb
1983 (Gray's Inn) Qualifications: LLB,
MBA

Rowland *Edward Anthony Powys Lance*
25a Holland Park Gardens, London
W11, 0171 912 0952, Fax: 0171 912
0952, Call Date: May 1992 (Middle
Temple) Qualifications: BA (Durham),
MA (Durham), Dip Law, LLM (Lond)

Rowland *Mrs Marjorie Susan*
Hollywood, Tokers Green, S Oxon
RG4 9EB, 01734 723107, Call Date:
Nov 1975 (Inner Temple)

Rowland *Robert Todd*
Part-time Chairman, Value Added Tax
Tribunals, The Periwinkle, 25 Back
Lane, South Luffenham, Rutland
LE15 8NQ, 01780 721 520, QC. N
Ireland Retired County Court Judge in
Northern Ireland and Member
Northern Ireland Bar, Call Date: July
1989 (Lincoln's Inn) Qualifications:
LLB (Belfast)

Rowlands *Ian Richard*
Call Date: Nov 1986 (Middle Temple)
Qualifications: BSc (Econ)(Hons)

Rowlands *Oscar Thomas* •
Legal Adviser, Group Technology &
Operations, Standard Chartered Bank,
1 Aldermanbury Square, London
EC1M 4DB, 0171 280 7500, Call Date:
Nov 1990 (Inner Temple)
Qualifications: MSc (Wales)

Rowley *Mrs Adrienne Lindsay*
Call Date: July 1998 (Lincoln's Inn)
Qualifications: LLB (Hons)(Leics)

Rowley-Fox *Ms Rachael*
Call Date: July 1998 (Gray's Inn)
Qualifications: BA (Hull)

Roy *John Scott* •
Legal Adviser, Royal Bank of Scotland,
29 Gresham Street, London EC2V 7HM,
0171 615 5588, Fax: 0171 726 2338,
Call Date: Feb 1991 (Inner Temple)
Qualifications: LLB (Lond)

Roy *Ms Shapna*
Lawyer, Lovell White Durrant, 65
Holborn Viaduct, London EC1A 2DY,
0171 236 0066, Fax: 0171 248 4212,
and Member Malaysian Bar, Call Date:
Nov 1995 (Lincoln's Inn)
Qualifications: LLB (Hons), CLP

Royce *Mrs Rosemary Elizabeth*
Call Date: Nov 1976 (Lincoln's Inn)

Royce-Lewis *Ms Christine Alison* •
Vice President Senior Legal Adviser,
Visa International Service, Association,
PO Box 253, London W8 5TE, 0171 937
8111, Fax: 0171 937 3390, Call Date:
Nov 1982 (Middle Temple)
Qualifications: BA MSc (Wales)

Roycroft *Andrew Alan*
Call Date: Nov 1993 (Gray's Inn)
Qualifications: LLB (Bris)

Royle *Charles Fanshawe*
Call Date: Oct 1997 (Lincoln's Inn)
Qualifications: BSc (Hons), Dip in law
(City)

Royle *John Hardy Layton*
24 Beaconsfield Road, Claygate, Esher,
Surrey KT10 0PW, Call Date: June 1937
(Inner Temple) Qualifications: MA
(Cantab)

Ruane *James FitzGerald*
0171 832 7255, Fax: 0171 832 7001,
Call Date: Nov 1994 (Middle Temple)
Qualifications: BA (Hons)

Ruck Keene *Benjamin Charles*
Bursar-Corpus Christi College Oxford JP
(Oxfordshire), Mill Hill, Brandsby, York
YO6 4RQ, Call Date: July 1971 (Gray's
Inn) Qualifications: BA (York), MA
(Oxon)

Rudd *David Eric*
Legal Services Manager, Salford
Magistrates Court, The Court House,
Bexley Square, Salford M3 6DJ, 0161
834 9457, Fax: 0161 839 1806, Call
Date: July 1981 (Inner Temple)
Qualifications: LLB (Hull)

Rudeloff *Walter*
4 King's Bench Walk, Ground/First
Floor, Temple, London, EC4Y 7DL, Call
Date: Oct 1990 (Middle Temple)
Qualifications: BA , LLM (Lond)

Rudoff *Stephen Frederick* •
Business Affairs Executive, Call Date:
July 1979 (Middle Temple)
Qualifications: LLB (B'ham)

• Barrister in employment

Rudralingham *Miss Sharadamani*
Legal Executive, Electronic Data
Interchange (M) SDN BHD, 15 Jalan
Telok Gadon G, 41200 Kelang, Selangor,
(603) 2536676, Fax: (603) 2537767,
and Member Malaysia, Call Date: Nov
1992 (Inner Temple) Qualifications:
LLB, LLM (Lond)

Ruff *Ms Anne Russell*
Principal Lecturer in Law Part-Time
Chairman - Social Security Appeals
Tribunals, Middlesex University, The
Burroughs, London NW4 4BT, 0181 362
5000, Fax: 0181 202 1539, Call Date:
July 1989 (Gray's Inn) Qualifications:
LLB (Lond), LLM (Lond)

Ruffin *William Haywood*
Attorney of the United States and
Member Pennsylvania, New York & North
Carolina Bars 9 Stone Buildings, 9 Stone
Bldgs, Lincoln's Inn, London, WC2A
3NN, Call Date: July 1972 (Inner
Temple) Qualifications: BA, JD

Rufford *John George* •
Investigator, The Financial Services
Auth., 9th Floor, 25 The North
Colonnade, Canary Wharf, London
E14 5HS, 0171 676 1000, Fax: 0171 676
1099, Call Date: Nov 1986 (Middle
Temple) Qualifications: LLB (Leeds)

Rufus-Isaacs *The Lord Alexander Gerald*
Recorder, Rosenfeld, Meyer & Susman,
9601 Wilshire Boulevard, Fourth Floor,
Beverly Hills, California 90210 - 5288, 1
Gray's Inn Square, Ground Floor,
London, WC1R 5AA, Call Date: Nov 1982
(Middle Temple) Qualifications: BA
(Oxon)

Rumgay *Peter Nicholas*
Senior Quantity Surveyor, 199 West Park
Drive West, Roundhay, Leeds, Yorks
LS8 2BE, Call Date: Mar 1996 (Gray's
Inn) Qualifications: B.Sc, Dip Law, ARICS

Rundle *Mrs Christina Marie*
Call Date: Nov 1994 (Lincoln's Inn)
Qualifications: BSc (Hons)(Exon), CPE
(Bournemouth)

Rundle *Simon Maurice*
Call Date: Nov 1998 (Middle Temple)
Qualifications: BA (Open), Dip Law

Rush *Anthony John*
Call Date: Feb 1993 (Lincoln's Inn)
Qualifications: BCL

Rushford *Anthony Redfern*
46 Lower Sloane Street, London
SW1W 8BP, 0171 730 4714, Formerly a
Solicitor (1944-57), Call Date: Nov 1983
(Inner Temple) Qualifications: MA, LLM
(Cantab)

Rushton *Ms Elizabeth Lisa*
Call Date: Nov 1991 (Inner Temple)
Qualifications: LLB

Rushton *Jonathon Barker*
Call Date: Nov 1997 (Inner Temple)
Qualifications: LLB (Middx)

Rushton *Miss Marilyn*
4a Carey Mansions, Rutherford Street,
Westminster, London SW1P 2LT, 0171
828 3954, Call Date: Nov 1992 (Inner
Temple) Qualifications: MSC, LLB, MA

Rushton-Turner *John Martin* •
Legal Advisor, Nat West Capital Markets,
135 Bishopsgate, London EC2M, 0171
375 5454, Fax: 0171 334 1004, and
Member New York Bar, Call Date: Oct
1991 (Middle Temple) Qualifications:
LLB Hons, ACA

Russell *Miss Carron-Ann*
0956 545448, Fax: 0181 240 0908,
Opinion Writing & Drafting in Contract
Law, Cavendish Press 1996. and Member
Jamaican Bar, Call Date: July 1986
(Middle Temple) Qualifications: LLB
(Hons)(W.Indies), LLM (Hons)(Lond),
BA (Hons)(Sussex), PGCE (Oxon)

Russell *Christopher Corbet*
Assistant Recorder, 20 Essex Street,
London, WC2R 3AL, Call Date: July 1973
(Middle Temple) Qualifications: MA
(Oxon)

Russell *Mrs Elizabeth Ann Millicent R* •
Senior Prinicipal Legal Officer, HM
Customs & Excise, New Kings Beam
House, 22 Upper Ground, London
SE1 9PJ, 0171 620 1313, Fax: 0171 865
5243, Call Date: Nov 1983 (Middle
Temple) Qualifications: BA (Hons)

Russell *Mrs Fiona McLean* •
Principal Crown Prosecutor, CPS,
Headquarters, 50 Ludgate Hill, London
EC4M 7EX, 0171 273 8000, Call Date:
Nov 1978 (Gray's Inn) Qualifications: BA

Russell *Geoffrey David* •
Legal Advisor, Nottinghamshire County
Council, Loughborough Road, West
Bridgford, Nottingham NG2 7QP, 01159
773111, Fax: 01159 9455131, Call Date:
July 1997 (Inner Temple) Qualifications:
LLB (Nott'm)

Russell *Mrs Gillian*
Senior Court Clerk, Milton Keynes
Magistrates' Crt, 301 Silbury Boulevard,
Witan Gate East, Milton Keynes, Bucks
MK9 2AJ, 01908 684901, Fax: 01908
684904, Call Date: July 1986 (Gray's
Inn) Qualifications: BA (Hons)

Russell *Nicholas Ogilvy Hunter*
Call Date: Nov 1996 (Gray's Inn)
Qualifications: LLB (Sussex)

Russell *Miss Susan McCarrison*
3 Serjeants Inn, London, EC4Y 1BQ,
0171 353 5537, Call Date: Nov 1972
(Middle Temple)

Russell *Miss Veena Maya* •
Legal Advisor, CSO Valuations AG, 17
Charterhouse Street, London EC1N 6RA,
0171 404 4444/430 3040, Fax: 0171 430
3445, Call Date: July 1976 (Gray's Inn)
Qualifications: LLB (Lond)

Russell-Hargreaves *Barry* •
Call Date: Nov 1988 (Middle Temple)
Qualifications: LLB

Rutherford *Mrs Hazel Linda*
Call Date: Oct 1997 (Gray's Inn)
Qualifications: BA

Ryan *Alexander Cameron Cranston*
Call Date: July 1972 (Inner Temple)
Qualifications: BA

Ryan *Miss Catherine Mary*
Call Date: Oct 1997 (Middle Temple)
Qualifications: LLB (Hons)(Lond)

Ryan *Miss Hilary Margaret* •
Crown Prosecution Service, Trafalgar
House, 2 Bedford Park, Croydon
CR0 2AP, 0181 686 6033, Call Date: Feb
1990 (Inner Temple) Qualifications: LLB
(Hons)

Ryan *Mark Richard*
Associate Lecturer in Law, 64 Cliffe Way,
Warwick, Warwickshire CV34 5JG, Call
Date: Feb 1993 (Gray's Inn)
Qualifications: BA (Ulster), MA (City),
Cert Ed (Cardiff)

Ryan *Martin Philip* •
Principal Crown Prosecutor T.L., Crown
Prosecution Service, The Cooperage, 8
Gainsford Street, London SE1, 0171 357
7010, Fax: 0171 962 0905, Call Date:
Feb 1978 (Lincoln's Inn) Qualifications:
BA Hons

Ryan *William Charles* •
81 Antrim Mansions, Antrim Road,
London NW3 4XL, 0171 722 7492, Call
Date: July 1989 (Lincoln's Inn)
Qualifications: LLB (Dub)

Ryb *Miss Samantha Danielle* •
Call Date: Oct 1993 (Middle Temple)
Qualifications: LLB (Hons)(Lond)

Ryder *Derek* •
2 Kimbrose Way, Gloucester G4 2DB,
Call Date: May 1988 (Gray's Inn)

Rylands *Keith William* •
Principal Crown Prosecutor, Crown
Prosecution Service, County House,
County Square, 100 New London Road,
Chelmsford, Essex CM2 0BR, 01245
252939, Fax: 01245 490476, Call Date:
July 1979 (Middle Temple)
Qualifications: LL.B (Lond)

Sabben-Clare *Mrs Geraldine Mary*
Part-time Teacher of Law at Winchester
College, General Commissioner for
Income Tax, Witham Close, 62 Kingsgate
Street, Winchester, Hants SO23 9PF,
01962 865832, Independent Director
Winchester & Eastleigh Healthcare NHS
Trust, Call Date: July 1966 (Gray's Inn)
Qualifications: LLB (Lond)

Sabene *Lupus Emiliano Paolo*
Call Date: Oct 1998 (Middle Temple)
Qualifications: LLB (Hons)(Soton)

Sachdeva *Akash*
Call Date: Mar 1997 (Lincoln's Inn)
Qualifications: LLB (Hons)

Sachdeva *Sanjiv*
Business Consultant, Governor Wyggeston & Queen Elizabeth I Sixth Form College, Leicester, 758 Hanworth Road, Richmond, Middlesex TW4 5NU, 0171 971 8845, Call Date: Nov 1991 (Inner Temple) Qualifications: LLB (Lond)(Hons)

Sachs *Mrs Anne Marie* •
Department of Trade & Industry, Solicitors Department, 10-18 Victoria Street, London SW1H 0NN, Call Date: July 1978 (Gray's Inn) Qualifications: MA (Cantab), LLM (Lond)

Sadd *Robert Clive* •
Crown Prosecutor, CPS Suffolk Branch, Saxon House, 1 Cromwell Square, Ipswich IP1 1TS, 01473 230332, Call Date: Oct 1990 (Inner Temple) Qualifications: LLB (Reading)

Sadheura *Dr Mohinder Kumar*
Call Date: Mar 1998 (Middle Temple) Qualifications: BSc (Hons), MBBS MRCGP (Royal London, Hospital Medical, College)

Saffian *Ms Leah Susan*
and Member California Bar, Call Date: July 1992 (Gray's Inn) Qualifications: BA, JD, LLM

Sagar *Miss Nadia*
Call Date: Nov 1997 (Middle Temple) Qualifications: LLB (Hons)

Sagayam *Miss Selina Shanti*
Simmons & Simmons, 21 Wilson Street, London EC2M 2TX, 0171 628 2020, Fax: 0171 628 2070, Call Date: Oct 1993 (Gray's Inn) Qualifications: LLB (Hons), LLM (Lond)

Sage *Miss Melanie Jane* •
Senor Crown Prosecutor, Queens House, 58 Victoria Street, St Albans, Hertfordshire AL1 3HZ, 01727 818 100, Call Date: July 1984 (Lincoln's Inn) Qualifications: LLB (Hons) (B'ham)

Sainer *Alan Philip* •
Senior Legal Officer, Solicitor's Office, Inland Revenue, Somerset House, Strand, London WC2R 1LB, 0171 438 6765, Call Date: Nov 1974 (Lincoln's Inn) Qualifications: MA (Cantab)

Sajid *Ahmer*
Call Date: Nov 1998 (Lincoln's Inn) Qualifications: LLB (Hons)(Wolves)

Sale *Martin Ronald*
Justices Chief Executive, Norfolk Magistrates Court, Service, 4 Barton Way, Carrow Road, Norwich NR1 1DL, 01603 219223, Fax: 01603 219227, Call Date: Nov 1982 (Gray's Inn) Qualifications: DML

Sales *Harry Brimelow*
Four Winds, Mousehole Lane, Paul, Penzance, Cornwall TR19 6TY, 01736 731997, Fax: 01736 731997, Formerly a Solicitor, Call Date: Apr 1975 (Inner Temple) Qualifications: LLM (Manch)

Salisbury *Derek John Brian*
Lower Wickton, Stoke Prior, Ledminster, Herefordshire HR6 0LN, Call Date: Feb 1957 (Gray's Inn) Qualifications: MA (Cantab)

Salmon *Ms Christine* •
Assistant Secretary, The Committee & Standards in, Public Life, Horse Guards Road, London SW1P 2AL, 0171 270 5869, Call Date: Nov 1989 (Gray's Inn) Qualifications: MA (Oxon) Dip Law

Salmon *Richard Mark*
Call Date: Oct 1997 (Inner Temple) Qualifications: BA (Manchester), CPE

Salmon *Rudolf Archibald*
PO Box 143, 50 Main Street, St Anne's Bay, Jamaica, 0101 809 972 2423, and Member Jamaican Bar Southsea Chambers, PO Box 148, Southsea, Portsmouth, Hampshire, PO5 2TU, Call Date: Nov 1965 (Lincoln's Inn)

Salmond *Giles Menzies*
Garretts, 180 Strand, London WC2R 2NN, 0171 344 0344, Fax: 0171 438 2518, Solicitor, Call Date: Oct 1992 (Inner Temple) Qualifications: LLB (Hull)

Salmons *Miss Caroline Louise*
Call Date: Nov 1995 (Middle Temple) Qualifications: BA (Hons) (Kent)

Salomon *William Henry*
Chairman, Rea Brothers Group Plc, Rea Brothers Group Plc, Alderman's House, Alderman's Walk, London EC2M 3XR, 0171 816 6872, Fax: 0171 626 3446, Call Date: July 1986 (Inner Temple) Qualifications: MA, LLB

Saltissi *Miss Kathleen Dorothy* •
Principal Legal Officer, HM Customs & Excise, New King's Beam House, 22 Upper Ground, London SE1, Call Date: July 1985 (Inner Temple) Qualifications: BA, MSR, SRR

Salvi *Miss Sharmila Vijay*
Call Date: Nov 1997 (Lincoln's Inn) Qualifications: BSc (Hons)(Lond)

Sambei *Miss Arvinder Kaur* •
Principal Crown Prosecutor, Crown Prosecution Service, 50 Ludgate Hill, London EC4M 7EX, Call Date: July 1985 (Gray's Inn) Qualifications: BA (Kent)

Samiloff *Julian*
Call Date: July 1988 (Inner Temple) Qualifications: BSc, Dip Law

Sammon *Miss Sarah Bridget*
Nicholas Street Chambers, 22 Nicholas Street, Chester, CH1 2NX, Call Date: Oct 1991 (Middle Temple) Qualifications: BA (Hons), Dip Law

Samnadda *Ms Julie Karen* •
Grade 7 Lawyer, D.T.I., 10-18 Victoria Street, London SW1H ONN, Call Date: Nov 1986 (Middle Temple)

Sample *Miss Jacquelyn* •
Crown Prosecutor, Crown Prosecution Service, Yorkshire Area Office, 6th Floor, Ryedale Building, Piccadilly, York YO1 1NS, 01904 610726, Fax: 01904 610394, Call Date: Feb 1994 (Inner Temple) Qualifications: BA, CPE

Sampson *Alistair Hubert*
103 Clifton Hill, London NW8, 0171 624 6483, Call Date: June 1955 (Gray's Inn) Qualifications: BA (Cantab)

Sampson *Jonathan Charles Hiaulme*
Call Date: Oct 1996 (Inner Temple) Qualifications: BA (Herts)

Sampson *William Stuart* •
London Area Grade 6 Special Casework Lawyer, Bow Street & Clerkenwell Brch, 4th Floor, 50 Ludgate Hill, London, London EC4M 7EX, 0171 273 8236, Fax: 0171 273 8268, Call Date: July 1974 (Inner Temple) Qualifications: LLB

Samuel *Adam Wilfred*
14C Adamson Road, London NW3 3HR, 0171 586 1938, Fax: 0171 586 1938, and Member New York, Call Date: July 1983 (Inner Temple) Qualifications: BA (Oxon), LLM (Boston), ACI Arb, FPC

Samuel *Edwin Douglas Lincoln*
Call Date: Mar 1998 (Inner Temple) Qualifications: BA (Oxon)

Samuel *Ms Katja Lilian Hamilton*
Call Date: Oct 1997 (Gray's Inn) Qualifications: BA (Dunelm)

Samuels *Miss Carla Simone*
Call Date: Oct 1996 (Lincoln's Inn) Qualifications: BA (Hons)(Oxon)

Samuels *Darren Scott* •
Board Advocate, Criminal Injuries Compensation, Board, Morley House, 26-30 Holborn Viaduct, London EC1A 2JQ, 0171 842 6800, Call Date: Oct 1992 (Middle Temple) Qualifications: BA (Hons)(York), Dip Law

Samuelson *Neville Anthony Wylie*
The Manor Hse, Totteridge, London N20, 0181 445 1330, Fax: 0181 446 0944, Call Date: Nov 1950 (Inner Temple)

Samupfonda *Ms Evis* •
London Borough of Southwark, Call Date: Nov 1992 (Inner Temple) Qualifications: LLB

Samwell-Smith *Mrs Rosemary Sheila* •
Law Lecturer, Special Adjudicator (Part Time), Council of Legal Education, The Inns of Court, School of Law, Gray's Inn PLace, London WC1R 5DX, Call Date: Nov 1986 (Gray's Inn) Qualifications: LLB, LLM (Lond)

Sandelson *Neville Devonshire*
Dep Circuit Judge & Asst Recorder 1977-1985, Call Date: Nov 1946 (Inner Temple) Qualifications: MA (Cantab)

Sanders *Daniel Simon*
Call Date: May 1997 (Middle Temple)
Qualifications: LLB (Manch)

Sanders *Oliver Tschanz* •
Home Office, Legal Adviser's Bramch,
London, 0171 273 3197, Call Date: July
1995 (Inner Temple) Qualifications: LLB
(Lond), BCL (Oxon)

Sanderson *Mrs Bronwen Jane*
Call Date: Nov 1996 (Lincoln's Inn)
Qualifications: LLB (Hons) (Manch)

Sanderson *Miss Katie Alison*
Call Date: Nov 1996 (Gray's Inn)
Qualifications: LLB (Sheff)

Sandford *Miss Amanada Janes*
Call Date: Nov 1998 (Middle Temple)
Qualifications: BA (Hons) (Wales)

Sandhu *Miss Sandip*
Call Date: Nov 1997 (Gray's Inn)
Qualifications: LLB (East Lond)

Sandiford *David Charles*
Call Date: Oct 1995 (Gray's Inn)
Qualifications: BA

Sandiford-Austin *Miss Allison Joanne*
Call Date: Mar 1996 (Middle Temple)
Qualifications: B.Sc (Hons)

Sandilands *Richard James* •
Company Secretary, Abbey National
Treasury, Services plc, Abbey House,
Baker Street, London NW1 6XL, 0171
204 1000, Fax: 0171 612 4581, Call
Date: July 1995 (Lincoln's Inn)
Qualifications: BA (Hons)

Sandys *Michael Lawrence*
Cobbetts Solicitors, Ship Canal House,
King Street, Manchester M2 4WB, 0161
833 3333, Fax: 0161 833 3030, Call
Date: Nov 1991 (Middle Temple)
Qualifications: LLB Hons (Lond), LLM
(L'pool)

Sangam *Paul Stephen Jason* •
Head of Legal Affairs, ETT Records
Limited, 42-46 St Lukes Mews, London
W11 1DG, 0171 211 5101, Fax: 0171
211 3374, Call Date: Oct 1996 (Inner
Temple) Qualifications: LLB
(Westminster)

Sanitt *Adam Franklin* •
Associate, Bucklersbury House, 3 Queen
Victoria Street, London EC4N 8EL, 0171
246 6200, Fax: 0171 329 4465, Call
Date: Oct 1995 (Lincoln's Inn)
Qualifications: MA (Cantab), BCL (Oxon)

Sankar *Ramphal*
Principal Court Clerk, Enfield
Magistrates' Court, Lordship Lane,
Tottenham, London N17 6RT, 0181 808
5411, Call Date: Nov 1971 (Lincoln's
Inn)

Sansam *Miss Heather Rosemary*
Senior Legal Manager, Warley Magistrates
Court, Oldbury Ringway, Oldbury, Warley
B69 4JN, 0121 511 2222, Fax: 0121
5448492, Call Date: July 1981 (Gray's
Inn) Qualifications: LLB

Sansom *Nicholas* •
Thomas Miller & Co, International
House, 26 Creechurch Lane, London
EC3, 0171 283 4646, Call Date: Nov
1978 (Inner Temple) Qualifications: LLB
(Lond)

Sarai *Miss Mandeep Kaur*
Call Date: Nov 1997 (Lincoln's Inn)
Qualifications: BA (Hons)

Sargeant *Mrs Mary Bernadette*
Call Date: Oct 1998 (Middle Temple)
Qualifications: LLB (Hons) (Bris)

Sarkar *Rakhal Chandra*
50 Cleveleys Road, Hackney, London
E5 9JN, 0181 806 7027, Call Date: Nov
1978 (Inner Temple) Qualifications: MA

Sarkaria *Mrs Neelam* •
Senior Crown Prosecutor, Crown
Prosecution Service, Harrow Branch,
Kings House, Kymberley Road, Harrow,
Middlesex, 0181 424 8688, Fax: 0181
424 9157, Call Date: Nov 1988 (Gray's
Inn) Qualifications: BA Hons

Sarwar *Ms Firdus Akhtar*
Call Date: Nov 1997 (Lincoln's Inn)
Qualifications: LLB (Hons) (Derby)

Sasegbon *Daniel Afolabi Olanrewaju*
Call Date: Nov 1996 (Gray's Inn)
Qualifications: LLB (Lond), LLM (Lond),
MPhil (Lond)

Satkuru-Granzella *Mrs Sheamala*
Project/Research Officer, The Malaysian
Timber Council, 24 Old Queen Street,
London SW1H 9HP, 0171 222 8188, Fax:
0171 222 8884, Call Date: July 1993
(Inner Temple) Qualifications: LLB, LLM

Saujani *Vijesh*
Call Date: May 1997 (Lincoln's Inn)
Qualifications: LLB (Hons)

Saul *Anthony Joseph* •
Senior Legal Adviser, Statoil (UK)
Limited, Statoil House, 11 Regent Street,
London SW1Y 4ST, Call Date: Feb 1989
(Middle Temple) Qualifications: LLB

Saul *Anthony Mark*
Call Date: Mar 1999 (Lincoln's Inn)
Qualifications: LLB (Hons) (Leeds)

Saul *Guy Patrick Selwyn* •
Crown Prosecutor, Crown Proseution
Service, North London Area, 2nd
Floor,Kings House, Kymberley Road,
Harrow,Middlesex HA1 1YH, 0181 424
8688 Ext 286, Fax: 0181 424 9157, Call
Date: Nov 1980 (Lincoln's Inn)
Qualifications: BA

Saunders *Mrs Alison Margaret* •
Grade 6 Inspector, Crown Prosecution
Service, 50 Ludgate Hill, London
EC4M 7EX, 0171 273 8171, Fax: 0171
329 8166, Call Date: Nov 1983 (Inner
Temple) Qualifications: LLB (Leeds)

Saunders *Denis*
Company Director, TI Group plc, 50
Curzon Street, London W1Y 7PN, 0171
499 9131, Fax: 0171 493 6533, Call
Date: Feb 1958 (Gray's Inn)
Qualifications: MA, LLM

Saunders *Edward Philip Morton*
Call Date: Nov 1992 (Middle Temple)
Qualifications: B.Mus (Hons)

Saunders *Miss Emma Charlotte*
Appeals Caseworker, Arden Chambers,
27 John Street, London, WC1N 2BL, Call
Date: Nov 1994 (Gray's Inn)
Qualifications: BA (Sheff), CPE (Manch)

Saunders *Miss Harriet Mary Elizabeth*
Solicitor, Call Date: Oct 1995 (Gray's
Inn) Qualifications: LLB

Saunders *Philip George*
Call Date: Oct 1997 (Lincoln's Inn)
Qualifications: LLB (Hons) (Brunel)

Saunt *Ms Linda Patricia* •
Legal Adviser, Dept of Trade & Industry,
10 Victoria Street, London SW1H 0NN,
0171 215 3345, Fax: 0171 215 3221,
Call Date: Nov 1986 (Inner Temple)
Qualifications: MA (Cantab)

Savage *Dr Andrew William George*
Medical Pratitioner, Minstrel Cottage,
Westmill, Herts SG9 9LL, 01763 271636,
Call Date: Nov 1993 (Lincoln's Inn)
Qualifications: MBBS (Medicine), Dip
Law

Savage *David James*
17 St Andrew's Wharf, 12 Shad Thames,
London SE1 2YN, 0171 403 2416, Fax:
0171 403 2416, Call Date: Nov 1994
(Middle Temple) Qualifications: BA
(Hons)

Savage *Miss Mai-Ling Carmen*
Call Date: Oct 1998 (Inner Temple)
Qualifications: BDiv (Lond), CPE

Savage *Stephen Richard*
Clerk to the Justices, Maidstone
Sevenoaks, Tonbridge & Malling,
Tunbridge Wells & Cranbrook, Kent
Magistrates Court, The Court House,
Tufton Street, Ashford, Kent TN23 1QS,
01233 663204, Call Date: Nov 1976
(Middle Temple) Qualifications: LLB,
MBA

Savin *Charles Timothy*
Call Date: Nov 1962 (Gray's Inn)
Qualifications: BSc, FRSC, C.Chem,,
MIPD

Saw *Miss Lily* •
Crown Prosecution Service, 4 Artillery
Row, Victoria, London SW1P 1RZ, 0171
976 5699, Call Date: Feb 1987 (Middle
Temple) Qualifications: LLB (Newc),
LLM

Sawtell-Fearn *Ms Jane Elizabeth*
Call Date: Oct 1997 (Gray's Inn)
Qualifications: LLB (De Montfort)

Sawyer *Ms Katrine Mary* •
Legal Officer, Treasury Solicitor, Queen
Anne's Chambers, 28 Broadway,
London SW1H 9JS, 0171 210 3522,
Fax: 0171 210 3143, Call Date: 1996
(Middle Temple) Qualifications: BA
(Hons)(Oxon)

Saxton *Ian Sanders*
23 Melcombe Ct, Dorset Sq, London,
NW1, Call Date: July 1973 (Gray's Inn)

Sayal *Miss Meena Kumari* •
Trade Marks Manager, United Distillers
& Vinters, Kingsley House, 1A Wimpole
Street, London W1M 8DB, 0171 927
4170, Fax: 0171 927 5041, Call Date:
Nov 1990 (Lincoln's Inn)
Qualifications: LLB (Hons)

Sayed *Miss Rubina*
Call Date: Mar 1999 (Inner Temple)
Qualifications: LLB (Sussex)

Sayers *Michael Warwick* •
The Secretary, Law Commission,
Conquest House, 37/38 John Street,
Theobalds Road, London WC1N 2BQ,
0171 411 1250, Fax: 0171 411 1297,
Call Date: July 1967 (Middle Temple)

Scarborough *Dominic Philip*
Call Date: Nov 1995 (Middle Temple)
Qualifications: BA (Hons)

Sceeny *Mark David* •
Insurance Ombudsman Bureau, 135
Park Street, London SE1 9EA, 0171 928
7600, Call Date: Oct 1995 (Gray's Inn)
Qualifications: LLB

Schapira *Lawrence*
0171 267 3925, Call Date: Nov 1984
(Gray's Inn) Qualifications: BA (Keele)

Schenck *Mrs Susan Jean* •
Senior Crown Prosecutor, Crown
Prosecution Service, 7th Floor, Liver
Buildings, Liverpool, Merseyside, Call
Date: July 1981 (Gray's Inn)
Qualifications: BA (Hons)

Schepes *Miss Luisa*
Call Date: Nov 1992 (Middle Temple)
Qualifications: LLB (Hons), LLM

Scheurer *Vincent Stuart* •
Company Lawyer, Europress Software
Limited, Europa House, Adlington
Park, Macclesfield SK10 4NP, 01625
855000, Fax: 01625 855111, Call Date:
Nov 1994 (Lincoln's Inn)
Qualifications: BA (Hons)(Oxon)

Schiess *Guy Thomas*
Call Date: Feb 1992 (Middle Temple)
Qualifications: LLB (Hons) (Lond)

Schmiegelow *Ian Lunn*
46 Catherine Place, London SW1E 6HL,
0171 233 7440, Fax: 0171 233 7442,
Call Date: July 1967 (Inner Temple)
Qualifications: MA (Cantab)

Schofield *Miss Kathrine Lucy*
Call Date: Oct 1998 (Inner Temple)
Qualifications: BA (Leeds), CPE

Schofield *Peter Graham* •
Head of Legal Affairs, EEF, Broadway
House, Tothill Street, London
SW1H 9NQ, 0171 222 7777, Fax: 0171
222 1877, Call Date: Feb 1988
(Lincoln's Inn) Qualifications: BA
(Hons) Durham

Scholefield *Miss Jane Elizabeth* •
Senior Crown Prosecutor, Crown
Prosecution Service, 17th Floor,
Tolworth Tower, Ewell Road, Surbiton,
Surrey KT6 7DS, 399 5171, Call Date:
Oct 1991 (Middle Temple)
Qualifications: BSc, Dip Law

Schooling *Simon John*
Call Date: Nov 1995 (Lincoln's Inn)
Qualifications: BA (Hons)

Schroder *Miss Hildegard Katharina* •
Law Lecturer, Colchester Institute,
Sheepen Road, Colchester, Call Date:
Nov 1983 (Inner Temple)
Qualifications: BA

Schwarzschild *Maimon*
1 Gray's Inn Square, 1st Floor, London,
WC1R 5AG, Call Date: May 1987
(Lincoln's Inn) Qualifications: BA, JD
Columbia Univ

Schymyck *Nicholas Michael*
Call Date: Nov 1998 (Middle Temple)
Qualifications: BA (Hons)(Warw)

Science *Benjamin David*
12 Morritt Avenue, Halton, Leeds,
Yorkshire LS15 7EP, 0113 2946805,
Call Date: Oct 1993 (Gray's Inn)
Qualifications: LLB (Leeds), MSc

Sciolti *Giles David*
Call Date: July 1998 (Inner Temple)
Qualifications: BSc (Newcastle Upon,
Tyne)

Scipio *Miss Mona Kathleen*
Deputy Chief Clerk, Inner London
Magistrates', Courts Service, Highbury
Magistrtates' Court, 51 Holloway Road,
London N7, Call Date: Nov 1970
(Middle Temple) Qualifications: LLB
(Lond)

Scoon *Leo Rennie* •
Principal Legal Officer, Office of the
Solicitor, Department of Social Security,
New Court, 48 Carey Street, London
WC2A 2LS, 0171 412 1498, Fax: 0171
412 1220, Call Date: Feb 1986 (Inner
Temple) Qualifications: LL.B.

Scott *The Revd Adam*
Senior Research Fellow, School of
Social Sciences, University of St
Andrews, 19 Blackheath Park,
Blackheath, London SE3 9RW, 0181
852 3286, Fax: 0181 852 6247, Call
Date: Nov 1972 (Inner Temple)
Qualifications: MA (Oxon), MSc, (City),
CEng, FIEE, FRSA

Scott *David Gidley*
High Court Bankruptcy Registrar
(1984-96), 45 Benslow Lane, Hitchin,
Herts SG4 9RE, 01462 434391, also
Inn of Court L, Call Date: June 1951
(Middle Temple) Qualifications: MA,
LLM (Cantab)

Scott *Mrs Fusun*
Call Date: Nov 1988 (Inner Temple)
Qualifications: BA (Lond), Dip in Law

Scott *Howard David Ashley*
Call Date: May 1996 (Lincoln's Inn)
Qualifications: BA (Hons)

Scott *Professor Ian Richard*
Barber Professor of Law, University of
Birmingham, Faculty of Law, University
of Birmingham, Birmingham B15 2TT,
0121 414 6291, Call Date: Nov 1995
(Gray's Inn) Qualifications: LLB
(Melbourne), PhD (Lond)

Scott *Miss Josephine Sarah*
Call Date: May 1997 (Middle Temple)
Qualifications: LLB (Hons), LLM
(Lond)

Scott *Miss Karen*
Legal Advisor/Senior Consultant., E C
Harris, Lynton House, 7-12 Tavistock
Square, London WC1H 9LX, 0171 391
2583, Fax: 0171 383 2481, Call Date:
Nov 1997 (Middle Temple)
Qualifications: BSc (Hons)(Reading),
LLB (Hons)(Westmin) , ARICS

Scott *Kenneth Leslie*
K L Scott Associates, Chartered Quantity
Surveyors, Central Chambers, Eldon
Street, Barnsley S Yorks, 01226
201342, Fax: 01226 294632, Call Date:
May 1988 (Middle Temple)
Qualifications: LLB (Hons), Dip.Arb,
FRICS, FCIOB, FCIArb

Scott *Miss Kristine*
Employment Advisor, Rickerby
Watterson Solicitors, Ellenborough
House, Wellington Street, Cheltenham
GL50 1YO, 01242 224422, Fax: 01242
518428, Call Date: Nov 1992 (Inner
Temple) Qualifications: LLB

Scott *Miss Rachael Elizabeth* •
Senior Crown Prosecutor, Crown
Prosecution Service, Second Floor,
Froomsgate House, Rupert Streey,
Bristol, Avon BS1 2QJ, 0117 9273093,
Call Date: July 1989 (Inner Temple)
Qualifications: LLB(Hons)

Scott *Mrs Sandra Louise*
Call Date: July 1997 (Gray's Inn)
Qualifications: LLB (Lanc), BEd, MEd,,
BA (Hons)

Scott *Stuart*
Call Date: Nov 1998 (Inner Temple)
Qualifications: LLB (Lond)

Scott *Trevor Pierre* •
Slough Borough Council, Call Date: Oct
1996 (Gray's Inn) Qualifications: LLB
(Anglia)

Scott-Wilson *Christopher John* •
Principal Legal Adviser, Guinness Plc, 39
Portman Square, London W1H 9HB,
0171 486 0288, Fax: 0171 486 0279,
Call Date: July 1982 (Middle Temple)
Qualifications: BSc

Scowen *Clive Richard*
69 Brooke Avenue, Roxeth, Harrow,
Middlesex, HA2 0ND, Call Date: July
1981 (Inner Temple) Qualifications: LLB
(Bris)

Scrantom *Timothy Dillon*
United States of America, Goldsworth
Chambers, 1st Floor, 11 Gray's Inn
Square, London, WC1R 5JD, Call Date:
Feb 1995 (Gray's Inn) Qualifications: BA
(Stetson, USA), JD (Georgia, USA), LLM

Scrase *Thomas Davis*
24 Castle Street, Buckingham MK18 1BP,
01280 823073, Fax: 01280 823774, Call
Date: Feb 1953 (Middle Temple)
Qualifications: LLB (Lond)

Scruton *Professor Roger Vernon*
Call Date: Feb 1978 (Inner Temple)

Scudder *Mrs Laura Jean* •
Senior Court Clerk (part time), Havering
Magistrates', Courts Committee, The
Courthouse,Main Raod, Romford, Essex
RM1 3BH, 01708 771771, Fax: 01708
771777, Call Date: Nov 1984 (Gray's
Inn)

Scudder *Peter Alan* •
Court Clerk, Redbridge Magistrates',
Court Committee, 850 Cranbrook Road,
Barkingside, Essex IG6 1HW, 0181 551
4461, Call Date: July 1983 (Gray's Inn)
Qualifications: LLB

Scully *Miss Barbara Louise* •
Call Date: Nov 1985 (Middle Temple)
Qualifications: B Soc Sci (Keele)

Seagroatt *Conrad*
Formerly Solicitor of the Supreme Court.
3 Fountain Court, Steelhouse Lane,
Birmingham, B4 6DR, Call Date: Apr
1970 (Gray's Inn) Qualifications: MA
(Oxon)

Sealy *Richard Campbell* •
Crown Prosecutor, Crown Prosecution
Service, No 3 Bankside, Crosfield Street,
Warrington, Cheshire, Call Date: July
1981 (Lincoln's Inn) Qualifications: BA
(Hons)

Searle *Ms Frances Anne*
Deputy Chief Clerk, Inner London Mag
Crt Service, 65 Romney Street, London
SW1P 3RD, 0171 799 3332, Call Date:
Nov 1979 (Gray's Inn) Qualifications: BA
(Hons) (Lond)

Searle *Jason Ario Xavier*
Advocate, Bullivant Jones & Co Solicitor,
State House, 22 Dale Street, Liverpool
L2 4UR, Call Date: Oct 1993 (Middle
Temple) Qualifications: LLB (Hons)

Searle *Miss Lyndsey Anne* •
Tax and VAT & Litigator, Deloitte &
Touche, Hill House, 1 Little New Street,
London EC4A 3TR, 0171 303 3565, Fax:
0171 303 4780, Call Date: Oct 1995
(Middle Temple) Qualifications: B.Sc

Searle *Richard Nathan* •
Call Date: Oct 1995 (Middle Temple)
Qualifications: BA (Hons)

Sears *John Russell* •
Legal Advisor, Suffolk Magistrates' Crt
Comm, The Magistrates' Court, Shire
Hall, Bury St Edmunds, Suffolk
IP33 1HF, 01284 352300, Fax: 01284
352343, Call Date: Nov 1976 (Lincoln's
Inn)

Seaton *Ian Christopher Norman*
Director, Citigate Communications Ltd,
26 Finsbury Square, London EC2, 0171
282 8000, Fax: 0171 282 8010, Call
Date: Apr 1975 (Middle Temple)
Qualifications: LLB (Hons) (Bris)

Sebastos *George* •
Legal Counsel, CEDEL International,
42nd Floor, 1 Canada Square, London
E14 5DR, Call Date: Oct 1994 (Lincoln's
Inn) Qualifications: LLB (Hons)(Lond)

Seben *Ivan Michael*
35 Church Street, Saffron Walden, Essex
CB10 1JQ, 01799 522576, Fax: 01799
513067, Call Date: May 1953 (Inner
Temple)

Seculer *Mrs Joy Rosina* •
Lawyer, Welsh Office Office, Welsh Office,
Civic Centre, Cardiff CF1, Call Date: Nov
1983 (Middle Temple)

Seculer-Faber *Anthony Roy*
Clerk to the Justices, Vale of Glamorgan
Magistrates, Court, Thompson Street,
Barry CF63 4SX, 01268 293129, Fax:
01268 293187, Call Date: Nov 1985
(Middle Temple) Qualifications: B.Sc
(Cardiff)

Seely *Richard Evelyn*
33 Upper Park Road, London NW3 2UL,
Call Date: Nov 1961 (Gray's Inn)

Seenath Dass *Rajkumar*
Call Date: July 1976 (Lincoln's Inn)

Seepersad *Mark Robert*
Call Date: Mar 1999 (Inner Temple)
Qualifications: LLB, LLM (Lond)

Seevaratnam *Harichandran*
0181 445 9101, Call Date: May 1960
(Gray's Inn)

Seevaratnam *Miss Nathalie Mallikai*
Call Date: Oct 1994 (Inner Temple)
Qualifications: LLB (Bucks)

Sefton *Miss Claire Louise*
Call Date: Oct 1997 (Inner Temple)
Qualifications: BA (London), CPE

Sefton *David Graeme Fennick* •
Call Date: Nov 1995 (Middle Temple)
Qualifications: BA (Hons), BCL

Segal *Mrs Jill Patricia*
2 Cinnamon Row, Plantation Wharf,
London SW11 3TW, 0171 738 0017, Fax:
07070 603710, Call Date: July 1974
(Gray's Inn)

Segbefia *Alex Percival* •
Senior Crown Prosecutor, Crown
Prosecution Service, 2nd Floor, Kings
House, Kimberley Road, Harrow, Middx
HA1 1YH, 0181 424 8688, Fax: 0181 424
9157, Call Date: Nov 1988 (Inner
Temple) Qualifications: LLB (Essex)

Segovia *Christopher John*
Call Date: July 1998 (Inner Temple)
Qualifications: BSc (Hons),
(Northumbria), PgDipLaw, PgDip, (BVC)

Sehmi *Mandeep Singh*
Call Date: Oct 1997 (Lincoln's Inn)
Qualifications: LLB (Hons)(Greenwic)

Sehrawat *Sahib Ram* •
District Land Registrar, Portsmouth
District Land, Registry, St Andrews
Court,, St Michaels Rd, Portsmouth,
Hants PO1 2JH, 01705 768800, Fax:
01705 768768, and Member India Bar,
Call Date: July 1979 (Middle Temple)
Qualifications: BA, LLB

Sekhon *Gurmit Singh*
Call Date: Nov 1988 (Lincoln's Inn)
Qualifications: LLB Hons

Sellers *Geoffrey Bernard* •
Parliamentary Counsel, Parliamentary
Counsel Office, 36 Whitehall, London
SW1A 2AY, Call Date: July 1971 (Gray's
Inn) Qualifications: MA, BCL

Sells *Peter Charles*
c/o Azema Sells, Aldwych House, 81
Aldwych, London WC2B 4HN, 0171 836
7993, Fax: 0171 836 3882, and Member
Avocat a la Cour de Paris, Call Date: Nov
1976 (Inner Temple) Qualifications: MA
(Cantab), A.C.I.,Arb

Selvaratnam *Joseph* •
Crown Prosecution Service, Ealing/
Hounslow, 2nd Floor, King's House,
Kymberley Road, Harrow on the Hill,
0181 424 8688, Call Date: Nov 1990
(Gray's Inn) Qualifications: LLB
(Bristol), LLM (Lond)

Selwyn *Norman*
Chairman SSAT, Immigration Adjudictor,
14 Blythe Way, Solihull, West Midlands
B91 3EY, 0121 705 3330, Call Date: Feb
1961 (Gray's Inn) Qualifications: LLM,
Dip Econ (Oxon)

Semega-Janneh *Miss Ebironke*
Call Date: Nov 1998 (Inner Temple)
Qualifications: LLB (Hull)

Sen *Ms Lisa*
34 Church Street, Leatherhead, Surrey
KT22 8DW, 01372 375144, Fax: 01372
360292, and Member India Bar, Call
Date: July 1995 (Gray's Inn)
Qualifications: BA, MA (New York), LLB
(Lond)

Sen *Miss Sheila Ruth*
Call Date: July 1974 (Inner Temple)
Qualifications: LLB (Lond) , MJur
(Manc)

Sentance *Joseph Richard Pattison* •
Crown Prosecutor, Crown Prosecution
Service, 1st Floor, The Cooperage,
Gainsford Street, London SE1 2NG, Call
Date: Nov 1986 (Inner Temple)
Qualifications: BA(Cantab)

Serjeant *David John* •
Assistant Legal Adviser, BBC, British
Broadcasting Corp., Room 1055,
Broadcasting House, Portland Place,
London W1A 1AA, Call Date: Nov 1973
(Middle Temple) Qualifications: LLB

Sessions *Paul Mark*
Thomas Miller & Co Ltd, International
House, 26 Creechurch Lane, London
EC3A 5BA, 0171 204 2211, Fax: 0171
204 2102, Call Date: Feb 1991 (Inner
Temple) Qualifications: BA (Lond),
LLM

Seth *Mrs Prabha*
Call Date: July 1993 (Middle Temple)
Qualifications: LLB (Hons)(Lond)

Seward *Guy William*
Stocking Lane Cottage, Ayot St
Lawrence, Welwyn, Herts AL6 9BW,
01438 820 259, Call Date: June 1956
(Inner Temple)

Seward *Robert Canton* •
47 Kingstown Street, London NW1 8JP,
Call Date: July 1971 (Inner Temple)
Qualifications: MA (Oxon)

Sewell *Miss Emma*
Call Date: Oct 1998 (Gray's Inn)
Qualifications: BA

Seyan *Balbir* •
Aylesbury Crown Pros Service, 4,5 and
6 Prebendal Court, Oxford Road,
Aylesbury, Buckinghamshire HP19 3EY,
01296 436441, Fax: 01296 88664, Call
Date: July 1984 (Inner Temple)
Qualifications: BA

Seymour *Christopher Roger*
Justices Chief Executive & Clerk to the
Justices, Wolverhampton Magistrates',
Courts, Law Courts, North Street,
Wolverhampton WV1 1RA, 01902
773151, Fax: 01902 27875, Call Date:
July 1972 (Gray's Inn)

Seymour *David* •
Legal Secretary to the Law Offices,
Attorney General Chambers, 9
Buckingham Gate, London SW1E 6JP,
0171 271 2401, Fax: 0171 271 2431,
and Member Northern Ireland 1997,
Call Date: July 1975 (Gray's Inn)
Qualifications: MA (Oxon), LLB
(Cantab)

Seymour *Miss Judit Emese Agnes* •
Moody's Investors Service Ltd, 2
Minster Court, Mincing Lane, London
EC3R 7XB, 0171 621 9068, Call Date:
Oct 1990 (Inner Temple)
Qualifications: LLB (Lond), LLM
(Lond)

Shafiq *Mohammad*
Call Date: Nov 1996 (Lincoln's Inn)
Qualifications: LLB (Hons)(Lond)

Shah *Ms Fatima* •
Head of Legal Affairs, Gotaas-Larsen
Ltd, 105 Vctoria Street, London
SW1E 6QJ, 0171 828 7822, Fax: 0171
834 2259, Call Date: Nov 1987 (Gray's
Inn) Qualifications: LLB (Hons)

Shah *Miss Rukhsana Anjum* •
Senior Lawyer, HM Customs & Excise,
New King's Beam House, Upper
Ground, London SE1, Call Date: July
1976 (Middle Temple)

Shah *Sattar* •
Senior Crown Prosecutor, Crown
Prosecution Service, Special Casework
Unit, Portland House, Stag Place,
Victoria, London SW1, Call Date: Nov
1989 (Lincoln's Inn) Qualifications:
LLB (B'ham), B.Ed, MBA

Shah *Miss Sheena*
Call Date: Nov 1993 (Inner Temple)
Qualifications: LLB (Hons)(Lond)

Shah *Miss Sheilja Harsukhlal* •
Legal Advisor, Department of Trade &
Industry, 10 Victoria Street, London
SW1H 0NN, 0171 215 5000, Call Date:
Oct 1994 (Middle Temple)
Qualifications: LLB (Hons), LLM
(Lond)

Shah *Miss Shilpa* •
Paralegal - Employment & Pensions,
Freshfields, 65 Fleet Street, London
EC4Y 1HS, 0171 936 4000, Call Date:
July 1998 (Lincoln's Inn)
Qualifications: LLB (Hons)(Brunel)

Shah *Shuaib Mohammed* •
Legal Counsel, Citibank, N.A, 41
Berkeley Square, Mayfiar, London
W1X 6NA, 0171 508 8045, Fax: 0171
508 8472, Call Date: Nov 1994 (Inner
Temple) Qualifications: BA (Lond)

Shah *Tajamal Hussain* •
Legal Adviser, Call Date: Nov 1989
(Lincoln's Inn) Qualifications: LLB,
LLM

Shah *Zawar Hussain*
Call Date: July 1998 (Lincoln's Inn)
Qualifications: BA (Hons)(Derby), Dip
Law

Shah-Kazemi *Mrs Sonia Nourin Gul*
Senior Lecturer in Law, University of
Westminster, Faculty of Law, 4 Little
Titchfield Street, London W1P 7FH,
0171 911 5000, Call Date: Nov 1988
(Lincoln's Inn) Qualifications: LLB
Hons

Shahar-Martin *Mrs Norshila* •
Senior Crown Prosecutor, Crown
Prosecution Service, 5th Floor, River
Park House, 225 High Road, Wood
Green, London N22 4HQ, 0181 888
8889, Fax: 0181 888 0746, Call Date:
Nov 1988 (Lincoln's Inn)
Qualifications: LLB (Lond)

Shahjahan *Abul Monsur*
Call Date: Mar 1999 (Lincoln's Inn)
Qualifications: LLB (Hons)(Wolves)

Shahrim *Ms Azlina*
Call Date: Nov 1996 (Gray's Inn)
Qualifications: LLB (Warw), LLM
(Cantab)

Shakesby *David John*
Call Date: Oct 1996 (Inner Temple)
Qualifications: LLB

Sham *Ms Rachel Fung-Ying* •
Solicitor, Redbridge Magistrates Court,
850 Cranbrook Road, Barkingside,
Essex IG6 1HW, 0181 551 4461, Call
Date: Nov 1986 (Lincoln's Inn)
Qualifications: LLB (Hons)

Shamel *Ms Linda Jusuf Zain* •
Principal Crown Prosecutor, Crown
Prosecution Service, Bow Street/
Clerkenwell Section, Fourth Floor,
Ludgate Hill, London EC4M 7EX, 0171
273 8000, Call Date: Nov 1984 (Middle
Temple) Qualifications: LLB (Hons),
MA (Jurisprudence)

Shamsuddin *Mrs Heidi*
Call Date: Nov 1997 (Lincoln's Inn)
Qualifications: LLB (Hons)(Nott'm),
MA (Leeds), LLM, (LSE)

Shamsuddin *Shamsuflan B* •
Legal Adviser, Shell UK Limited,
Shell-Mex House, Strand, London
WC2R 0DX, 0171 257 3539, Fax: 0171
257 3441, Call Date: July 1990 (Middle
Temple) Qualifications: LLB (B'ham)

Shankland *Matthew*
Call Date: Oct 1997 (Inner Temple)
Qualifications: LLB

Shanmugaguru *Miss Shanthini*
Call Date: Oct 1997 (Gray's Inn)
Qualifications: LLB (Lond)

Shannon *Simon Joseph*
Call Date: Mar 1999 (Inner Temple)
Qualifications: BA (Oxon), CPE

Sharif *Raja* •
In House Counsel, Guardian iT PLC,
Benchmark House, St George's
Business Centre, 203 Brooklands Road,
Weybridge, Surrey KT13 0RH, Call Date:
Nov 1992 (Gray's Inn) Qualifications:
LLB (Hull), LLM (Notts)

Shariff *Navroz*
Call Date: May 1990 (Inner Temple)
Qualifications: LL.B. (Lond)

Sharifi *Ms Neda*
Call Date: Nov 1991 (Lincoln's Inn)
Qualifications: LLB (Hons) (Lond)

• Barrister in employment

Sharma *Miss Aneeta*
Call Date: Nov 1991 (Lincoln's Inn)
Qualifications: LLB (Hons)

Sharp *Ms Deborah Anne*
PricewaterhouseCoopers, 1
Embankment Place, London WC2N 6NN,
0171 213 5618, Fax: 0171 213 4607,
Call Date: July 1982 (Gray's Inn)
Qualifications: BA (Kent)

Sharpe *Jonathan Naylor*
Call Date: Mar 1999 (Gray's Inn)
Qualifications: BA (Newcastle)

Sharpe *Mrs Susan Elizabeth* •
Director of Legal Services, Royal
Pharmaceutical Society, of Great Britain
(RPSGB), 1 Lambeth High Street,
London SE1 7JN, 0171 735 9141, Fax:
0171 735 7629, Call Date: Nov 1972
(Gray's Inn) Qualifications: LLB

Sharples *Ignatius Brian*
Chartered Surveyor, Francis Taylor Bldg,
3rd Floor, Temple, London, EC4Y 7BY,
Call Date: Nov 1986 (Lincoln's Inn)
Qualifications: LLB (Hons, E.Anglia)

Sharples *John Michael*
Call Date: Nov 1992 (Inner Temple)
Qualifications: LLB (Hons)

Sharples *Miss Lesley-Anne*
Call Date: Oct 1997 (Lincoln's Inn)
Qualifications: LLB (Hons)

Sharples *Paul James*
Call Date: Feb 1994 (Middle Temple)
Qualifications: BA (Hons)(Oxon), MA

Sharples *Simon Andrew*
Call Date: July 1987 (Inner Temple)
Qualifications: BA (Kent), Dip Law, LLM

Sharpling *Miss Drusilla Hope* •
Chief Crown Prosecutor, Central
Casework, Crown Prosecution Service, 50
Ludgate Hill, London EC4M 7EX, Call
Date: July 1987 (Gray's Inn)
Qualifications: LLB (B'ham)

Shatz *Anthony* •
S J Berwin & Co, 222 Gray's Inn Road,
London WC1X 8HB, 0171 533 2064, Fax:
0171 533 2000, Call Date: Oct 1995
(Lincoln's Inn) Qualifications: LLB
(Hons)(Lond)

Shaw *Dr Gordon Wallace*
206 Nelson House, Dolphin Square,
London SW1V 3LX, 0171 798 5742, and
Member American Bar Association, Call
Date: Nov 1955 (Gray's Inn)
Qualifications: PhD, LLB , FCII

Shaw *Ian Douglas* •
Senior Crown Prosecutor, Crown
Prosecution Service, St Peters House,
Gower Street, Derby DE1 1SB, 01332
621615, Fax: 01332 621698, Call Date:
Nov 1991 (Middle Temple)
Qualifications: BSc (Hons)

Shaw *Mrs Irene Marcia*
Call Date: July 1998 (Middle Temple)
Qualifications: BSc (Hons)

Shaw *John Martin* •
Legal Adviser, NPI, National Provident
House, Tunbridge Wells, Kent TN1 2UE,
01892 515151, Fax: 01892 705843, Call
Date: Nov 1992 (Lincoln's Inn)
Qualifications: LLB (Hons

Shaw *Justin Edward Magnus*
Call Date: Nov 1992 (Lincoln's Inn)
Qualifications: BA (Hons), Dip in Law

Shaw *Mrs Lesley Margaret*
Law Lecturer in Chester Contracts
Manager, WorldCom, Call Date: Oct 1998
(Gray's Inn) Qualifications: BA
(E.Anglia)

Shaw *Peter Vernon Hugh*
Call Date: Nov 1993 (Lincoln's Inn)
Qualifications: BA (Hons)

Shaw *Mrs Sandra Nan Demby* •
General Manager, Commercial & Legal,
LASMO North Sea PLC, 101 Bishopsgate,
London EC2M 3XH, 0171 892 9712, Fax:
0171 892 9793, and Member Florida
Bar, Call Date: Nov 1987 (Gray's Inn)
Qualifications: BA (New Orleans), Juris
Doctorate, (Florida)

Shaw *Terence John* •
Legal Correspondent, Daily Telegraph, 1
Canada Square, London E14 5DT, 0171
538 5000 DL 6498, Fax: 0171 538 6268,
Call Date: Nov 1961 (Gray's Inn)
Qualifications: MA (Cantab)

Shawcross *Rt Hon Lord*
60 Victoria Embankment, London
EC4Y OJP, 0171 325 5127, Fax: 0171
325 8195, Honorary Chairman of the
Bar Council., Call Date: May 1925
(Gray's Inn) Qualifications: LLM,LLD

Shawkat *Miss Tasnim* •
Senior Lawyer, Surrey County Council,
County Hall, Kingston Upon Thames
KT1 2DN, 0181 541 9259, Fax: 0181 541
9005, Call Date: Oct 1991 (Inner
Temple) Qualifications: LLB (Brunel)

Shea *Nicholas James*
Call Date: Oct 1993 (Middle Temple)
Qualifications: BA (Hons)(Oxon), Dip in
Law (City)

Shea *Paul William*
Call Date: Nov 1998 (Middle Temple)
Qualifications: LLB (Hons)(Herts)

Shear *Elliot Marc*
Call Date: Oct 1996 (Inner Temple)
Qualifications: LLB (Hons)(Leeds)

Shedden *Colonel Robert Charles*
Chief Clerk, Clerkenwell Magistrates
Court, 78 King's Cross Road, London
WC1X 9QJ, 0171 278 6541, Fax: 0171
833 3662, Call Date: July 1979 (Gray's
Inn)

Sheehan *Mrs Jayne Mary*
Senior Legal Adviser, Harlow Magistrates
Court, South Gate, The High, Harlow,
Essex CM20 1HH, 01279 425108, Fax:
01279 450522, Call Date: July 1989
(Middle Temple) Qualifications: LLB
Hons

Sheehan *Richard Anthony Padraig*
Director; HSBC Gibbs Ltd Chairman:
GHC Financial Institutions Insurance
Services Ltd, 50 Cadogan Place, London
SW1X 9RT, 0171 247 5433, Call Date:
July 1973 (Gray's Inn) Qualifications:
MA, A.C.I.I

Sheinfield *Miss Anne Harriet* •
Manager, Legal Affairs, Sony Music
Entertainment (UK), Ltd, 10 Great
MarlborougH Street, LondoN W1V 2LP,
Call Date: Nov 1990 (Middle Temple)
Qualifications: Dip Law (City), MA
(Cantab)

Shek *Tristan Randy Shu-Ming*
Call Date: Oct 1998 (Middle Temple)
Qualifications: LLB (Hons)(Warwick)

Sheldrick *Benjamin Charles Patrick*
D J Webb & Co, 43 Berkeley Square,
Mayfair, London W1X 5DB, 0171 499
3009, Fax: 0171 499 3004, Call Date: Oct
1994 (Lincoln's Inn) Qualifications: BA
(Hons)(Lond)

Shell *Ms Sally Louise* •
Head of Business Affairs, Wall to Wall
Television Ltd, 8-9 Spring Place, Kentish
Town, London NW5 3ER, 0171 485
7424, Fax: 0171 267 5292, Call Date:
July 1989 (Gray's Inn) Qualifications:
LLB (Lanc)

Shelley *Ms Catherine Jean*
Social Concerns Officer, RC Diocese of
Arundel & Brighton, Call Date: Oct 1990
(Lincoln's Inn) Qualifications: LLM
(Cantab), MA (Cantab)

Shelley *Dr Frederick Charles*
7-27 Heathside, Avalon, Poole, Dorset
BH14 8HT, 01202 707510, Call Date:
Nov 1976 (Gray's Inn) Qualifications:
MB BS FRCA DA

Shelton-Agar *Charles Wedderburn
Shelton*
Call Date: July 1965 (Gray's Inn)
Qualifications: BA (Cantab)

Shenstone-Davies *Russell*
Call Date: Nov 1998 (Gray's Inn)
Qualifications: LLB (Glamorgan)

Shenton *Alan Newman*
Partner, c/o Ernst & Young, Apex Plaza,
Reading RG1 1YE, 01189 500611, Fax:
01189 507744, Call Date: Nov 1985
(Gray's Inn) Qualifications:
LLB(Warwick), FCA, ATII

Shenyuz *Alkan Tarik*
Clifford Chance, (Securities
Department), 200 Aldersgate Street,
London EC1A 4JJ, Call Date: Nov 1997
(Lincoln's Inn) Qualifications: LLB
(Hons)(Sussex), LLM

Shephard *Mrs Carole* •
Company Secretary, Xerox Ltd, The
Parkway, Marlow, Bucks SL7 1YL, 01628
890000, and Member New York Bar, Call
Date: July 1979 (Middle Temple)
Qualifications: LLB (Lond)

E

Shephard *Ms Judith Catherine* •
Crown Prosecution Service, Severn/
Thames Area, Buckinghamshire
Branch, 4-7 Prebendal Court, Oxford
Rd, Aylesbury, Bucks HP19 3EY, 0296
436441, Call Date: July 1989 (Gray's
Inn) Qualifications: LLB [Lond], AKC
[Lond]

Shepherd *Mrs Amanda Robin*
Call Date: Nov 1992 (Middle Temple)
Qualifications: LLB (Hons)

Shepherd *Miss Johanna Kate*
Public Relations Consultant, Declavy
Public Relations, 3 Northington Street,
London WC1N 2JE, 0171 404 3244,
Fax: 0171 404 3233, Call Date: Oct
1995 (Lincoln's Inn) Qualifications:
LLB (Hons)(Lond)

Shepherd *Ms Judith Elizabeth*
Call Date: Oct 1996 (Lincoln's Inn)
Qualifications: LLB (Hons)(Derby)

Shepherd *Mark Andrew*
Call Date: Oct 1996 (Middle Temple)
Qualifications: LLB (Hons)(Manc)

Sheppard *Miss Caroline Diana Burnell* •
Chief Adjudicator, Chief Adjudicator,
Parking Appeals Service, New Zealand
House, 80 Haymarket, London
SW1Y 4TE, 0171 747 4700, Fax: 0171
747 4848, Call Date: Nov 1974 (Gray's
Inn)

Sheppard *Samuel Edward Hugh* •
Senior Crown Prosecutor, CPS
(London), Bow Street/Clerkenwell
Branch, Portland House 3rd Floor, Stag
Place, London SW1E 5BH, 0171 915
5700, Fax: 0171 915 5850, Call Date:
July 1976 (Gray's Inn)

Sheppard *Miss Susannah George
Fullerton* •
Lawyer, Call Date: Nov 1994 (Lincoln's
Inn) Qualifications: BA (Hons)(Oxon)

Sher *Christopher* •
12A High Street, Slough, Berkshire
SL1 1EE, 01753 535577, Fax: 01753
535770, Call Date: Nov 1993 (Gray's
Inn) Qualifications: BA

Sher *Miss Shamim Akhtar* •
Call Date: May 1995 (Lincoln's Inn)
Qualifications: LLB (Hons)

Shergill *Miss Usha Sita* •
Senior Crown Prosecutor, Crown
Prosecution Service, North London
Area, Harrow Branch 2nd Floor, Kings
House,Kymberley Road,
Harrow,Middlesex HA1 1YH, 0181 424
8688, Fax: 0181 424 9134, Call Date:
July 1984 (Gray's Inn) Qualifications:
BA (Hons)(Law)

Sheridan *Brian Dominic George*
Call Date: Oct 1994 (Inner Temple)
Qualifications: LLB (Lond), LLM
(Lond)

Sherlock *Peter Anthony*
Clerk to the Justices/Justices Chief
Executive, Calderdale P.S.D., Justices'
Clerk's Office, PO Box 32, Harrison
Road, Halifax HX1 2AN, 01422 360695,
Fax: 01422 347874, Call Date: Apr
1986 (Middle Temple) Qualifications:
Dip in Magisterial, Law

Sherrard *Michael David*
Director of Middle Temple Advocacy,
0171 427 4816, Fax: 0171 427 4817,
Also Inn of Court I Treasurer Middle
Temple 1996, Call Date: June 1949
(Middle Temple) Qualifications: LLB
(Lond), F.R.S.A.

Sherratt *Peter Robert* •
Legal Director, Board Director &
Company Secretary, Lehman Brothers
Group, 1 Broadgate, London
EC2M 7HA, 0171 260 3132, Fax: 0171
260 2882, Call Date: July 1985 (Inner
Temple) Qualifications: BA (Oxon),
LLM (Cantab)

Sheth *Pranlal*
Company Secretary Executive Director -
Legal Div, 70 Howberry Road, Edgware,
Middlesex HA8 6SY, 0181 952 2413,
Fax: 0181 952 5332, Former Advocate
High Court of Kenya, Call Date: July
1962 (Lincoln's Inn) Qualifications:
F.Inst.M., F.Inst.D.

Shewaram *Ms Harsha* •
Lawyer, Office of Fair Trading, Field
House, Breams Buildings, London
EC4A 1PR, 0171 211 8577, Fax: 0171
211 8830, Call Date: Nov 1995 (Middle
Temple) Qualifications: BA
(Hons)(Manch)

Shi *Miss Xiao-Cong*
Legal Assistant, Call Date: July 1994
(Lincoln's Inn) Qualifications: LLB
(Hons), BA (Hons)

Shields *Leslie Stuart*
Recorder, Devereux Chambers,
Devereux Court, London, WC2R 3JJ,
Call Date: Jan 1948 (Middle Temple)
Qualifications: BA (Oxon)

Shilson *Stuart James*
Call Date: Oct 1992 (Middle Temple)
Qualifications: BA (Hons) (Oxon), MSc
(Oxon), MPhil (Cantab)

Shiner *David Colin*
Legal Advisor, Suffolk County Council,
St Helen Court, County Hall, Ipswich
IP4 2JS, 01473 264147, Fax: 01473
214549, Call Date: Nov 1990 (Middle
Temple) Qualifications: BSc (Hons)

Shipsey *Miss Helen Judith* •
Country Landowners Association, 16
Belgrave Square, London SW1X 8PQ,
0171 235 0511, Fax: 0171 235 4696,
Call Date: Nov 1991 (Inner Temple)
Qualifications: LLB (Hons)(Lond)

Shivaprasad *Suvarna Sudarshan*
5 South Side, Stamford Brook, London
W6 0XY, Attorney at Law, Republic of
Trinidad & Tobago and Member
Trinidad & Tobago Bar, Call Date: Nov
1987 (Lincoln's Inn) Qualifications: BA
(Canada), LLB (Lond), LLM (Lond)

Shoderu *Ms Aderonke Olayinka*
Senior Lecturer Commercial & Int'l
Law, The Business School, Stapleton
House, University of North London,
277-281 Holloway Road, London
N7 8HN, 0171 607 2789, Fax: 0171 852
8871, Call Date: July 1997 (Lincoln's
Inn) Qualifications: BA (Hons)

Short *Mrs Amanda Noreen* •
Grade 7, Dept of the Environment,,
Transport & the Regions, Eland House,
Floor 8/F6, Bressenden Place, London
SW1E 5DU, Call Date: July 1983 (Gray's
Inn) Qualifications: LLB (Hons)
(Warw)

Short *Miss Hannah Louise*
Call Date: Nov 1997 (Middle Temple)
Qualifications: BA (Hons)(Oxon)

Shorts *Edwin Michael*
Call Date: Nov 1989 (Lincoln's Inn)
Qualifications: MA (Dub), Dip Law

Shoulders *Paul*
Deputy Clerk to the Justices,
Lincolnshire Magistrates Court, 358
High Street, Lincoln LN5 7QA, 01522
528218, Fax: 01522 560139, Call Date:
Feb 1988 (Middle Temple)
Qualifications: Dip Mag Law, Dip Law,
Dip in Management, Studies, MBA

Shour *Miss Rima Fouad*
47 Eaton Place, London SW1X 8DE,
0171 235 9009, Call Date: July 1988
(Gray's Inn) Qualifications: LLB (LSE)

Shrieves-Yeates *Robert*
Call Date: Nov 1998 (Inner Temple)
Qualifications: LLB (Brunel)

Shrimplin *Miss Katherine Anne* •
Grade 6, Dept of Trade & Industry,
Solicitor's Office, Legal Services:
Prosecutions, Room 423, 10-18
Victoria Street, London SW1H 0NN,
0171 215 3203, Fax: 0171 215 3235,
Call Date: July 1984 (Middle Temple)
Qualifications: LLB (Lond)

Shroff *Cyrus* •
Principal Crown Prosecutor, Crown
Prosecution Service, 1st Floor, County
House, 100 New London Road,
Chelmsford, Essex CM2 0RG, 01245
252939, Fax: 01245 490476, Call Date:
July 1983 (Gray's Inn) Qualifications:
BA

Shroff *Mrs Kaiser Deepak*
P O Box 250, Penta Court,
Borehamwood, Herts WD6 1DW, Call
Date: July 1988 (Lincoln's Inn)
Qualifications: LLB, LLM (Hons),
Bombay, BSc (Hons) Baroda

Shropshire *Miss Alison Elizabeth Mary* •
Employment Law & Policy Adviser, BAA
Plc, Group Personnel Dept, Heathrow
Point, 234 Bath Road, Harlington,
Middlesex UB3 5AP, 0181 745 7342, Call
Date: Nov 1979 (Lincoln's Inn)
Qualifications: BA (CNAA),LLM (Lond)

Shucksmith *Thomas Sykes*
Shucksmith & Co., Consulting Actuaries,
Lincoln House, Nutley Lane, Reigate,
Surrey RH2 9HP, 01737 222011, Fax:
01737 222130, Call Date: July 1977
(Lincoln's Inn) Qualifications: MA
(Cantab), FIA, F.P.M.I

Shulman *Mark Bernard* •
Litigation Group Leader, Legal &
Secretariat, Kent County Council, County
Hall, Maidstone, Kent ME14 1XQ, 01622
694394, Fax: 01622 694498, Call Date:
July 1981 (Middle Temple)

Shuster *Robert Anthony* •
Senior Crown Prosecutor (p/t) Senior
Lecturer Inns of Court School of law
Independent Member Central Rail Users
Consultative Committee, Crown
Prosecution Service, Beaumont House,
Cliftonville, Northampton NN1 5BE,
01604 230220, Fax: 01604 232081,
Council of Legal Education, Inns of Court
School of Law, 39 Eagle Street, London,
0171 404 5787, Call Date: July 1988
(Middle Temple) Qualifications: LLB
(Hons), BA

Shuttleworth *Mrs Julie Dawn*
Ribb Lupton Alsop, 125 London Wall,
London EC2Y 5AE, Call Date: Oct 1995
(Gray's Inn) Qualifications: BA (Warw),
LLB

Siani *Paul Anthony* •
Company Director, 304 St Pauls Road,
London N1 2LH, 0171 359 3669, Call
Date: May 1997 (Inner Temple)
Qualifications: LLB (Wales)

Siaw *Jacob Aning Kwadwo*
Call Date: July 1976 (Lincoln's Inn)

Sibbles *Miss Geraldine Jane* •
Legal Team Manager, Bradford
Magistrates' Court, City Courts, The Tyrls,
Bradford, W Yorkshire BD1 1JL, 01274
390111, Fax: 01274 391731, Call Date:
Nov 1979 (Gray's Inn)

Sidhu *Ms Citra Sheila Sarjit*
Call Date: Nov 1994 (Gray's Inn)
Qualifications: LLB

Sidhu *Ravi* •
Senior Crown Prosecutor, Crown
Prosecution Service, Eaton Court, Oxford
Road, Reading, Berkshire, Call Date: Feb
1988 (Inner Temple) Qualifications: LLB
(Lancaster)

Sillis *Ms Louise Ann* •
Call Date: Nov 1994 (Middle Temple)
Qualifications: MA (Cantab)

Silman *Stephen Anthony*
Director, Barclays Private Bank Limited,
43 Brook Street, London W1Y 2PB, 0171
487 2000, Fax: 0171 487 1010, Call
Date: Nov 1974 (Middle Temple)
Qualifications: MA (Oxon)

Silver *Richard Norman*
Legal Advisor, Alway Associates, 196a
High Street, Epping, Essex CM16 4AQ,
01992 576440, Fax: 01992 576445, Call
Date: July 1997 (Gray's Inn)
Qualifications: LLB (Lond), ADBM,
MCIOB

Simmance *Alan James Francis*
Route De Mucelle, 01630 Challex, 04
(50) 563511, and Member Kenya Bar,
Call Date: July 1957 (Inner Temple)
Qualifications: BA, FCIS, FIM

Simmonds *Andrew John* •
Arthur Young, Rolls House, 7 Rolls
Buildings, Fetter Lane, London
EC4A 1NH, 0171 831 7130, Fax: 0171
405 2147, Call Date: Nov 1986 (Gray's
Inn) Qualifications: LLB(Hons)

Simmonds *John Andrew*
Court Clerk, Manchester City Magistrates,
Court, Crown Square, Manchester
M60 1PR, 0161 832 7272, Fax: 0161 832
5421, Call Date: Nov 1991 (Inner
Temple) Qualifications: LLB (Manch)

Simmons *Mrs Patterson Carr*
Principal Lecturer in Law, Middlesex
University, The Burroughs, London
NW4 4BT, 0181 362 5000, Fax: 0181 202
1539, Call Date: July 1983 (Gray's Inn)
Qualifications: MA, LLB, LLM

Simmons *Ronald*
Burley Gate, 54 Coggeshall Road, Earls
Colne, Essex CO6 2JR, 01787 222715,
Call Date: July 1966 (Inner Temple)
Qualifications: LLB, FCII

Simon *Miss Dale Inez* •
Crown Prosecutor, Crown Prosecution
Service, 1/9 Romford Road, Stratford,
London E15, 0181 534 6601, Call Date:
Nov 1986 (Inner Temple) Qualifications:
LLB

Simons *Charles*
Flat 8, 16 THe Ridgeway, Enfield,
Middlesex EN2 8QH, 0181 367 5731, Call
Date: Nov 1950 (Inner Temple)
Qualifications: PH.D,BSc

Simons *Gary Peter*
Call Date: Nov 1995 (Gray's Inn)
Qualifications: BA (Keele),MA (Lond),
MA (E.Anglia)

Simpson *Professor Alfred William Brian*
36 High Street, Wingham, Canterbury,
Kent CT3 1AB, 01227 720 979, Call Date:
Oct 1994 (Gray's Inn) Qualifications:
MA, F.B.A., F.A.A.A.S., DCL

Simpson *Brian Adam*
Call Date: Mar 1998 (Middle Temple)
Qualifications: LLB (Hons)(Essex)

Simpson *Miss Carol Monica*
Stewart & Co, 76 West Green Road,
Tottenham, London N15 5NS, 0181 802
6037, Fax: 0181 802 3092, Call Date:
Mar 1998 (Gray's Inn) Qualifications:
LLB (Thames)

Simpson *Charles James Geraint*
C/O J A Hassan & Partners, 57-63 Line
Wall Road, 00 350 79000, Fax: 00 350
79166, and Member Gibraltar Bar, Call
Date: Oct 1996 (Middle Temple)
Qualifications: BA (Hons)(B'ham), CPE
(Westminster)

Simpson *Mrs Christine Ffoulkes* •
Legal Advisor & Company Secretary,
POINT Group Limited, 25-26 Ivor Place,
London NW1 6HR, 0171 616 8100, Fax:
0171 616 8105, Call Date: Nov 1993
(Inner Temple) Qualifications: LLB
(Hons)

Simpson *Miss Lydia Caron*
Call Date: Feb 1993 (Lincoln's Inn)
Qualifications: LLB , A.T.I.I.

Simpson *Mark Banner*
Call Date: July 1994 (Inner Temple)
Qualifications: LLB (Manch)

Simpson *Robert Laver* •
Hewlett-Packard Limited, Cain Road,
Bracknell, Berkshire RG12 1HN, 01 344
362214, Fax: 01 344 362224, Call Date:
July 1974 (Middle Temple)
Qualifications: LLB (Hons)

Simpson *Robert Thompson* •
Crown Prosecution Service, 1-9 Romford
Road, Stratford, London E15, Call Date:
Nov 1986 (Inner Temple) Qualifications:
LLB (Manch)

Simpson *Robin Muschamp Garry*
Call Date: June 1951 (Middle Temple)
Qualifications: MA (Cantab)

Simpson *William Peter*
and Member Advocat of Royal Court of
Guernsey 11 King's Bench Walk, 1st
Floor, Temple, London, EC4Y 7EQ, Call
Date: July 1980 (Lincoln's Inn)
Qualifications: LLB (Leeds)

Sinai *Ali Reza*
Call Date: July 1997 (Gray's Inn)
Qualifications: LLB, LLM, Diplome
d'Etudes , Juridiques (Strasbo)

Sinanan *Travers Selden* •
88 Fotherington Road, Enfield, EN1 1QG,
0181 888 8889, Fax: 0181 888 0746,
Now a Solicitor of the Supreme Court
and Member Trinidad & Tobago Bar
Association, Call Date: Nov 1982
(Lincoln's Inn) Qualifications: BA Hons

Sinclair *Duncan Edward MacCallum* •
Government Legal Service, 48 Carey
Street, London, 0171 412 1541, Call
Date: Oct 1996 (Lincoln's Inn)
Qualifications: BA (Hons), LLM (Cantab)

E

Singh *Andel*
Messrs Pictons, 13 Town Square,
Stevenage, Herts SG1 1BP, 01438
350711, Fax: 01438 359255, Call Date:
July 1987 (Middle Temple)
Qualifications: LLB

Singh *Mrs Anjali*
Call Date: July 1994 (Gray's Inn)
Qualifications: LLB (Bucks)

Singh *Ms Ann-Marie Valerie* •
Asprey Plc, 165-169 New Bond Street,
London W1Y 0AR, 0171 493 6767, Fax:
0171 918 8086, Call Date: July 1986
(Gray's Inn) Qualifications: LLB

Singh *David Hardatt* •
18 Sydney Road, West Ealing, London
W13 9EY, 0181 840 0083, Call Date:
Feb 1965 (Lincoln's Inn)

Singh *Jagjit Richard* •
Legal Counsel, Lehman Brothers
Limited, 1 Broadgate, London
EC2M 7HA, 0171 260 2748, Fax: 0171
260 2882, Call Date: Nov 1994 (Gray's
Inn) Qualifications: BA

Singh *Mrs Kumud* •
Senior Crown Prosecutor, Crown
Prosection Service, Priory Gate,
Maidstone, Call Date: Nov 1987 (Inner
Temple) Qualifications: LLB (Hons),
LLM

Singh *Raj Kumar*
Beresford Chambers, 21 King Street,
Luton, Bedfordshire, LU1 2DW, Call
Date: May 1992 (Gray's Inn)
Qualifications: LLB

Singh *Rajesh Kumar*
Freshfields, 65 Fleet Street, London
EC4Y 1HS, 0171 936 4000, Fax: 0171
832 7001, Call Date: Nov 1996 (Gray's
Inn) Qualifications: MA (Cantab)

Sinha *Ms Monica Smirta*
Call Date: Mar 1997 (Gray's Inn)
Qualifications: LLB

Siohn *Daniel Asher*
Call Date: May 1997 (Inner Temple)
Qualifications: BA, LLM, MA (Leeds)

Sisson-Pell *Mrs Jane Alison* •
Senior Crown Prosecutor, Crown
Prosecution Service, 4-5 South Parade,
Wakefield, 01924 290620, Fax: 01924
369360, Call Date: July 1984 (Lincoln's
Inn) Qualifications: BA (Hons)

Sivell *Colin Peter* •
Head of Legal Services, Chief Executive,
Brentwood Council Offices, Brentwood,
Essex CM15 8AY, Call Date: July 1979
(Inner Temple)

Skeen *Colin Jeffrey* •
Managing Director, Member Services,
The Automobile Association, Norfolk
House, Priestley Road, Basingstoke,
Hants RG24 9NY, 01256 493060, Call
Date: July 1975 (Inner Temple)
Qualifications: LLB (Lond)

Skelcher *Gary Stephen* •
Corporate Commercial Adviser, Thames
Water PLC, Commercial Services
Group, Blake House, Manor Farm,
Reading, 01734 236689, Call Date: Mar
1996 (Middle Temple) Qualifications:
LLB (Hons)

Skellett *Rupert William Nicholas*
Call Date: Nov 1996 (Gray's Inn)
Qualifications: BA (Cantab), LLB (City)

Skelly *Stephen Thomas* •
Chief Fiduciary Services Director,
Barclays Private Banking, 49 Grosvenor
Street, London W1X 9FH, 0171 487
2128, Fax: 0171 487 2044, Call Date:
July 1983 (Middle Temple)
Qualifications: LLB (Hons)(E.Angl)

Skemp *Mrs Sandra Pauline*
997 Finchley Road, London NW11 7HB,
0181 455 7335, Fax: 0181 458 2164,
Call Date: June 1964 (Middle Temple)
Qualifications: MA, BCL

Skinner *Conor William Richard* •
Senior Legal Adviser, B G plc
(International, Downstream), 100
Thames Valley Park Drive, Reading,
Berkshire RG6 1PT, 0118 929 3697,
Pepys' Chambers, 17 Fleet Street,
London, EC4Y 1AA, Call Date: Nov 1979
(Gray's Inn) Qualifications: MA

Skinner *Miss Sarah Caroline*
Call Date: Oct 1998 (Inner Temple)
Qualifications: LLB (Hull)

Skyrme *Sir Thomas Charles*
Call Date: Jan 1935 (Inner Temple)
Qualifications: MA

Slack *Jason*
Colemans Solicitors, Elisabeth House,
16 St Peter's Square, Manchester
M2 3DF, 0161 228 7393, Fax: 0161
228 7509, Call Date: Oct 1995
(Lincoln's Inn) Qualifications: LLB
(Hons)(Anglia)

Slade *Miss Shelagh Patricia* •
Associate General, Counsel Europe
Middle East and Africa Divison, Oracle
Corporation UK Limited, Oracle
Parkway, Thames Valley Park, Reading,
Berkshire RG6 1RA, 0118924 0000,
Fax: 0118924 3717, Call Date: Nov
1985 (Inner Temple) Qualifications:
LLB (Lond), LLM (Can

Sladen *Michael*
10 Little Lane, Ely, Cambridge
CB6 1AZ, Call Date: Feb 1963
(Lincoln's Inn) Qualifications: LLB,
FCIB

Slaney *Miss Louise Pauline* •
Wiltshire County Council, Chief
Executive's Office, County Hall,
Trowbridge, Wiltshire BA14 8JN, 01225
713062, Call Date: Nov 1990 (Inner
Temple) Qualifications: LLB (Exon)

Slater *Miss Sarah Helen*
Call Date: Oct 1996 (Gray's Inn)
Qualifications: LLB (Sussex) (Hons)

Slattery *Peter Anthony*
6 Wonford House, Heath Drive, Walton
on the Hill, Tadworth, Surrey
KT20 7QL, 01737 814086, Fax: 01737
814086, Call Date: July 1957 (Middle
Temple)

Slaughter *Miss Ingrid Elizabeth* •
Assistant Legal Adviser, General Synod
of the Church of, England, Church
House, Great Smith Street, London
SW1P 3NZ, 0171 340 0208, Fax: 0171
233 2660, Call Date: July 1969 (Gray's
Inn) Qualifications: LLB (Lond)

Slegg *Kevin Andrew* •
Quantity Surveyor, Project Manager,
Drake & Reynolds, The Old Mill, Mill
Lane, Godalming, Surrey GU7 1EY,
01483 425744, Fax: 01483 426936,
Call Date: Nov 1996 (Middle Temple)
Qualifications: BSc , LLB (Hons), ARICS

Sleight *Nigel*
Call Date: Oct 1998 (Lincoln's Inn)
Qualifications: LLB (Hons)(Hull)

Sleightholme *Alexander James*
Call Date: Oct 1998 (Lincoln's Inn)
Qualifications: LLB (Hons)(Notts)

Sloma *Albert Abraham*
PO Box 555, Gibraltar, Gibraltar, 350
79385, Fax: 350 79385, Call Date: July
1963 (Gray's Inn) Qualifications: B.Sc
(Eng), FICE, LMRTPI, FGIS

Small *Miss Elizabeth Anne*
Taylor Joynson Garrett, Carmelite, 50
Victoria Embankment, London
EC4Y 0DX, 0171 353 1234, Call Date:
Feb 1991 (Lincoln's Inn)
Qualifications: LLB

Smallwood *Miss Laura Jane*
Guildford Chambers, Stoke House,
Leapale Lane, Guildford, Surrey, GU1
4LY, Call Date: July 1987 (Middle
Temple) Qualifications: MA (Cantab),
Dip Law (City)

Smals *Rufus Alexander Ogilvie* •
Head of Legal Dept., Chairman CBI
Competition Panel, GKN plc, P.O. Box
55, Ipsley House, Ipsley Church Lane,
Redditch, Worcs B98 OTL, 01527
517715, Fax: 01527 533470, Call Date:
Nov 1973 (Middle Temple)
Qualifications: MA (Cantab) Dip Euro,
Integration, (Amsterdam)

Smart *Neil Alexander*
Call Date: July 1998 (Lincoln's Inn)
Qualifications: BSc (Hons)(Sheff)

Smedley *George Roscoe Relph Boleyne*
Garden House, Whorlton, Barnard
Castle, Co Durham DL12 8XQ, 01833
627381, also Inn of Court L, Call Date:
May 1965 (Inner Temple)
Qualifications: LLB (Lond)

Smedley *Nicholas Keith*
North Yorkshire Police, Police Station,
North Park Road, Harrogate, North
Yorkshire, (0423) 505541, Fax: (0423)
539313, Call Date: Nov 1990 (Inner
Temple) Qualifications: LLB (Lond)

Smele *Jeffrey Stephen*
External Affairs Executive, Rio Tinto plc, 6 St. James's Square, London SW1Y 4LD, 0171 753 2458, Fax: 0171 753 2309, Call Date: July 1995 (Middle Temple) Qualifications: B.Met (Hons), C.Eng, LLB (Hons), M.I.M

Smith *Miss Abigail Jill*
Call Date: Oct 1996 (Inner Temple) Qualifications: LLB (City)

Smith *Alexander Gordon*
334 Walton Road, East Molesey, Surrey KT8 2JD, Call Date: July 1980 (Gray's Inn) Qualifications: BSc, PhD, FGS

Smith *Miss Alison Dawn*
Call Date: Nov 1998 (Middle Temple) Qualifications: LLB (Hons) (Thames)

Smith *Miss Amelie Jane* •
ATC Contracts Manager, Raytheon Systems Limited, The Pinnacles, Harlow, Essex CM19 5BB, 01279 426862, Fax: 01279 410413, Call Date: Nov 1992 (Lincoln's Inn) Qualifications: LLB (Hons) (B'ham)

Smith *Mrs Angela Rosemary*
Senior Court Clerk, Grimsby Magistrates' Court, The Law Courts, Victoria Street, Grimsby, North East Lincs DN31 1RD, 01472 320444, Fax: 01472 320440, Call Date: July 1986 (Middle Temple) Qualifications: BA (Dunelm)

Smith *Professor Anthony Terry Hanmer*
Professor of Criminal and Public Laws, Gonville & Caius College, Cambridge CB2 1TA, 01223 332 449, Fax: 01223 332 456, Fellow of Gonville & Caius College, Cambridge and Member New Zealand Bar, Call Date: May 1992 (Middle Temple) Qualifications: PhD (Cantab), LLM (Cantuar) (New, Zealand)

Smith *Benjamin Michael*
Call Date: Oct 1997 (Inner Temple) Qualifications: LLB (Bristol)

Smith *Carl Neville* •
Health Safety & Environmental Advisor, P & O Trans European Ltd, Peninsular House, 11/13 Lower Brook Street, Ipswich IP4 1AQ, 01642 394715, Fax: 01642 394701, Call Date: Nov 1990 (Inner Temple) Qualifications: LLB

Smith *Ms Carol Marie*
Call Date: Nov 1997 (Inner Temple) Qualifications: LLB (Lond)

Smith *Cornelius Leo*
Legal Assistant, 14 Fairholme Road, West Kensington, London W14 9JX, 0171 381 8083, Call Date: July 1974 (Inner Temple) Qualifications: BCL

Smith *Miss Damask Mary*
Call Date: July 1997 (Middle Temple) Qualifications: LLB (Hons)

Smith *David Martin*
Director, Jacob White (Packaging) Ltd, Unit F, Riverside Industrial, Estate, Riverside Way, Dartford, Kent DA1 5BY, Call Date: July 1981 (Inner Temple) Qualifications: LLB (Wales), ACIS

Smith *David McLeod*
Call Date: Oct 1996 (Inner Temple) Qualifications: LLB (City)

Smith *Ms Deana Kay*
Call Date: Nov 1998 (Gray's Inn) Qualifications: BSc (Lond), MSc (Lond)

Smith *Derek Owen*
7 Dartmouth Row, London SE10 8AW, 0181 692 1463, Call Date: Nov 1962 (Inner Temple) Qualifications: MA (Cantab)

Smith *Duncan Graeme* •
Recorder Case Controller, Serious Fraud House, 3rd Floor, Elm House, 10-16 Elm Street, London WC1X OBJ, 0171 239 7355, Fax: 0171 713 7708, Call Date: July 1989 (Gray's Inn) Qualifications: LLB (Hons) (Lanc), Dip E.I. (Amsterdam)

Smith *Graham Stuart*
Deputy Clerk to the Justices, Tameside Magistrates' Courts, Henry Square, Ashton under Lyne, Tameside OL6 7TP, 0161 330 2023, Fax: 0161 343 1498, Call Date: July 1973 (Gray's Inn) Qualifications: LLB (Lond), DMS, MA

Smith *Grant Ian Graham*
Call Date: Mar 1998 (Gray's Inn) Qualifications: LLB (Leeds)

Smith *Dr Harry*
65 Meriden Road, Hampton in Arden, Solihull, West Midlands B92 OBS, and Member Victoria Bar, Call Date: Nov 1957 (Gray's Inn) Qualifications: BA, LLB, MA, PhD

Smith *James Arthur*
Chartered Accountant, Robert Fleming & Co, 25 Copthall Avenue, London, 0171 814 2623, Call Date: Oct 1994 (Lincoln's Inn) Qualifications: LLB (Hons) (E.Ang)

Smith *Miss Jane*
Call Date: Oct 1998 (Inner Temple) Qualifications: LLB (L'pool)

Smith *Jeffrey Prowse*
37 Alderbrook Road, Solihull, W Midlands B91 1NW, Call Date: June 1951 (Inner Temple) Qualifications: MA

Smith *Jeremy James Russell*
Director, Local Government International, Bureau, 35 Great Smith Street, London SW1P 3BJ, 0171 664 3100, Fax: 0171 664 3128, Call Date: July 1969 (Lincoln's Inn) Qualifications: BA (Cantab)

Smith *Miss Jessica Clare* •
Employed Barrister, Advises the Chief,Adjudication Officer, Dept of Health & Social, Security, New Court, 48 Carey Street, London WC2A 2LS, 0171 412 1372, Fax: 0171 412 1220, Call Date: Oct 1992 (Middle Temple) Qualifications: BA (Hons, Dunelm), Diploma in Law

Smith *Julian Robert*
Call Date: Mar 1998 (Lincoln's Inn) Qualifications: LLB (Hons) (LSE)

Smith *Miss Lorna Marie*
Call Date: Oct 1997 (Middle Temple) Qualifications: BA (Hons) (Lond), CPE (Manc)

Smith *Mark Andrew*
Call Date: Feb 1995 (Lincoln's Inn) Qualifications: BSc (Salford), LLB (Hons) (Manc)

Smith *Mark Winton* •
Legal Adviser to the Certification Officer for Trade Unions & Employers' Associations, Solicitor's Office, Department of Trade & Industry, 10 Victoria Street, London SW1H ONN, 0171 215 3326, Fax: 0171 215 3308, Call Date: July 1982 (Middle Temple) Qualifications: BA (Dunelm)

Smith *Martin Lloyd*
Solicitor, Rowe & Maw, 20 Blackfriars Lane, London EC4V 6HD, 0171 248 4282, Call Date: Oct 1996 (Middle Temple) Qualifications: BA (Hons) (Oxon)

Smith *Mrs Mary Edwina Elizabeth*
Call Date: July 1980 (Lincoln's Inn) Qualifications: LLB

Smith *Miss Mary-Emma* •
Call Date: Nov 1991 (Inner Temple) Qualifications: MA (Cantab), Dip Law

Smith *Matthew James* •
Barlow, Lyde & Gilbert, 0171 782 8471, Fax: 0171 782 8450, Call Date: Oct 1993 (Middle Temple) Qualifications: BA (Hons) (Oxon)

Smith *Miss Megan Emma*
Call Date: Oct 1994 (Lincoln's Inn) Qualifications: LLB (Hons) (Wales)

Smith *Michael Steven*
Immigration Lawyer, BCL Immigration Services, 11-14 Grafton Street, Mayfair, London W1X 4NP, 0171 495 3999, Fax: 0171 495 3991, Call Date: Oct 1995 (Middle Temple) Qualifications: BA (Hons)

Smith *Miss Monica Frances*
Call Date: Oct 1996 (Inner Temple) Qualifications: LLB (Lond)

Smith *Murray Lorne*
Essex Court Chambers, 24 Lincoln's Inn Fields, London, WC2A 3ED, Call Date: May 1990 (Middle Temple) Qualifications: LL.B., LL.M.

Smith *Mr. Neal Trevor*
Call Date: Oct 1996 (Inner Temple) Qualifications: LLB (Buck'ham)

Smith *Dr Peter Michael*
Faculty of Law, Amory Building, Rennes Drive, Exeter EX4 4RJ, 0392 263263, Fax: 0392 263196, Call Date: Feb 1993 (Lincoln's Inn) Qualifications: LLB & Ph.D (Sheff)

Smith *Peter Stanley* •
Consultant, Old Gold Script Services, An Cala House, 10 Kingsfold Close, Billingshurst, West Sussex RH14 9HG, 01403 782853, Fax: 01403 782796, Call Date: July 1980 (Middle Temple) Qualifications: LLB (Hons)

Smith *Peter Vivian Henworth*
Likabula, 14 St Albans Road, Clacton on Sea, Essex CO15 6BA, 01255 422053, Call Date: Feb 1953 (Lincoln's Inn) Qualifications: MA, BCL (Oxon)

Smith *Ralph Clovis Henniker*
Call Date: Jan 1949 (Gray's Inn) Qualifications: MA

Smith *Richard Vernon*
Director of Marketing (UK) Ltd, Onyx UK Ltd, Onyx House, Mile End Road, London E3, 0181 983 1000, Call Date: Nov 1977 (Middle Temple) Qualifications: BSc Econ

Smith *Roger Paul Radford*
Chairman, Who Cares? Trust Chairman, Hounslow Police Consultative Committee Financial Correspondent Counsel Magazine Since 1996, Radford Smith Financial, Services Limited, 46 Chiswick High Road, London W4 1SZ, 0181 995 8351, Fax: 0181 995 2488, Resident Financial Correspondent in Counsel Magazine, Call Date: July 1975 (Middle Temple) Qualifications: LLB (Lond)

Smith *Mrs Sara Margaret* •
Senior Crown Prosecutor, 7 Denwick Terrace, Tynemouth, Tyne & Wear NE30 2SG, 0191 296 3489, Call Date: Nov 1982 (Gray's Inn) Qualifications: BA

Smith *Sean Michael*
Call Date: Oct 1994 (Gray's Inn) Qualifications: LLB

Smith *Stephen Vernon* •
Branch Crown Prosecutor, Crown Prosecution Service, 2nd Floor, Blackburn House, Midway, Newcastle-under Lyme ST5 1TB, Call Date: Nov 1969 (Inner Temple) Qualifications: LLB (Lond)

Smith *Timothy Paul*
Deputy Chief Clerk, Inner London Magistrates', Courts Service, Greenwich Magistrates Court, 9-10 Blackheath Road, London SE10 8PG, Call Date: July 1983 (Middle Temple) Qualifications: BA (Lond) BSc, (Hull) Dip Law, LLM (Lond), MSC (Lond)

Smith-Hughes *Miss Alexandra Marika Niki* •
Senior Legal Assistant, Crown Prosecution Service, 50 Ludgate Hill, London EC4M 7EX, 0171 273 8361, Fax: 0171 273 8450, Call Date: July 1975 (Inner Temple) Qualifications: LLB (Leeds)

Smith-Jones *John Anthony* •
Clerk to the Justices, Dyfed Magistrates Courts, 4/5 Quay Street, Carmathen, Dyfed SA31 3JT, 01267 221658, Fax: 01267 221812, Call Date: Feb 1987 (Gray's Inn)

Smithard *Ms Jane Caroline Grantham* •
Company Secretary & Legal Counsel, Micro Focus Ltd, 26 West St, Newbury, Berks, 01635 32646, Fax: 01635 33966, Call Date: July 1982 (Middle Temple) Qualifications: BA Hons, FCI Arb

Smithburn *Professor John Eric*
Notre Dame Law School, Notre Dame, Indiana 46556, U.S.A, United States of America, 219 631 5865, and Member Indiana Bar, USA 1 Mitre Ct Bldgs, Ground Floor, Temple, London, EC4Y 7BS, Call Date: July 1989 (Middle Temple) Qualifications: BS, MA, JD

Smithies *Miss Emma Claire*
Call Date: Nov 1997 (Middle Temple) Qualifications: BSc (Hons) (Herts)

Smout *Mrs Ann Susan*
Call Date: July 1988 (Gray's Inn) Qualifications: BA (Lond)

Smyth *Mrs Philippa Jane*
Kersey's Solicitors, 32 Lloyd Avenue, Ipswich, Suffolk IP1 3HD, 01473 213311, Fax: 01473 257739, Call Date: May 1995 (Lincoln's Inn) Qualifications: LLB (Hons)

Snell *John Bernard*
Managing Director, Romney Hythe &, Dymchurch Railway, New Romney, Kent TN28 8PL, 01797 362353, Fax: 01797 363591, Call Date: Nov 1971 (Lincoln's Inn) Qualifications: BA (Oxon)

Snowdon *Peter David*
Call Date: Oct 1997 (Inner Temple) Qualifications: LLB (Westminster), LLM (London)

Soanes *Marcus Robert*
Senior Lecturer at the ICSL, Call Date: Oct 1991 (Lincoln's Inn) Qualifications: BA (Hons), MA (Lond), Dip Law

Soar *Miss Rebecca Jane*
Call Date: Nov 1996 (Gray's Inn) Qualifications: LLB (Nott'm)

Sobowale *Olumide*
Call Date: Oct 1998 (Inner Temple) Qualifications: LLB (De Montfort)

Sodha *Babubhai Nanjibhai* •
Senior Court Clerk, Bradford Magistrates' Cts Comm, The Tyrls, Bradford, W Yorkshire BD1 1JL, 01274 390111, Fax: 01274 391731, Call Date: Nov 1964 (Inner Temple)

Sofat *Sushil Kumar Baburam* •
Regulatory Control Consultant Legal Adviser BPCA. Legal Advisor SOFHT, 44 Greenacres, Leverstock Green, Hemel Hempstead, Herts HP2 4NA, 01442 257579, Fax: 01442 257579, Call Date: July 1960 (Lincoln's Inn) Qualifications: BSc Hons, BSc Tech, C.Chem, F.R.S.C

Sofowora *Mrs Paula Bolanle*
Call Date: Oct 1993 (Inner Temple) Qualifications: BA (Nigeria), LLB (Lond)

Solomon *Miss Carolyn Astrid Louise*
Call Date: Nov 1998 (Middle Temple) Qualifications: LLB (Hons) (Lond)

Solomon *Daniel Iestyn* •
Crown Prosecution Service, River Park House, 225 High Road, Woodgreen, London N22 4HQ, Call Date: Oct 1996 (Gray's Inn) Qualifications: BA (Oxon)

Solomon *Miss Stella*
Call Date: July 1965 (Gray's Inn) Qualifications: LLB

Solomon *Steven Jack Sido Feller*
3 Briary Close, Fellows Road, London NW3 3JZ, 0171 586 8156, Call Date: July 1978 (Gray's Inn) Qualifications: LLB (Belfast) MSc, (Lond), MSI

Somerville *Andrew Alexander*
KPMG Peat Marwick, 1 Puddle Dock, Blackfriars, London EC4V, 0171 311 2583, Fax: 0171 311 2902, Call Date: Oct 1993 (Lincoln's Inn) Qualifications: MA (Hons) (Edin), Dip in Law (Lond)

Somerville *Miss Rachel*
Call Date: Mar 1996 (Lincoln's Inn) Qualifications: LLB (Hons)

Soosai *Joseph Arokianathan* •
Senior Court Clerk, Havering Magistrates' Court, The Court House, Main Road, Romford, Essex RM1 3BH, 01708 771741, Fax: 01708 47947, Call Date: July 1987 (Lincoln's Inn) Qualifications: BA (Hons)

Soquar *Miss Ruta Woldehaimanot*
Call Date: July 1997 (Inner Temple) Qualifications: LLB (Dunelm)

Sotunde *Miss Marie-Therese Olufunmilayo Ngo* •
Associate Director, Tokyo-Mitsubishi Intl plc, 6 Broadgate, London EC2M 2AA, 0171 577 2813, Fax: 0171 577 2872, Call Date: July 1988 (Middle Temple) Qualifications: BA (Hons) (Essex)

Southcombe *Alan Melville*
Call Date: July 1983 (Gray's Inn) Qualifications: BA (Leic), LLM (Exon)

Southern *Raymond Joseph*
31 Ellington Road, Hounslow, Middlesex
TW3 4HX, Call Date: Oct 1997 (Middle
Temple) Qualifications: LLB
(Hons)(Keele)

Southworth *Miss Jean May*
Part Time Chairman, Police Discipline &
Misuse of Drugs Act Appeal Committee,
Call Date: Feb 1954 (Gray's Inn)
Qualifications: MA (Oxon)

Sower *Mrs Patricia Ann* •
Crown Prosecutor, Crown Prosecution
Service, St Georges House, Lever Road,
Wolverhampton, West Midlands, Call
Date: Nov 1986 (Middle Temple)
Qualifications: LLB (Wolv)

Sowerby *Ms Helen Jane*
Temple & Bargh Gatey Heelis, 01539
723757, Call Date: Nov 1994 (Middle
Temple) Qualifications: BA (Hons), Dip
Law

Sparkes *Duncan Alistair*
Call Date: Oct 1996 (Middle Temple)
Qualifications: BA (Hons)(Sheff), CPE

Sparks *Miss Jocelyn Margaret*
Hollis Whiteman Chambers, 3rd/4th
Floor, Queen Elizabeth Bldg, Temple,
London, EC4Y 9BS, Call Date: Nov 1987
(Inner Temple) Qualifications: LLB

Sparks *Ms Paula Denise*
Call Date: Oct 1994 (Gray's Inn)
Qualifications: LLB

Speak *Richard Gibson* •
Legal Negotiator, Barclays De Zoete
Wedd, Legal Ebbgate House, 2 Swan
Lane, London EC3R 3TS, 0171 775
6752, Call Date: Nov 1992 (Inner
Temple) Qualifications: LLB

Speck *Christopher John* •
BT Group Commercial Contracts,
Telecom House, 91 London Road,
Manchester M60 1HQ, 0161 600 2551,
Fax: 0161 236 4269, Call Date: Oct 1996
(Lincoln's Inn) Qualifications: BSc
(Hons)(Manc)

Speed *David Mervyn*
Clerk to the Justices, Bristol Magistrates'
Court, P.O.Box 107, Nelson Street,
Bristol BS99 7BJ, 0117 943 5100, Call
Date: Nov 1976 (Middle Temple)
Qualifications: MA (Oxon)

Speed *Sir Robert*
6 Upper Culham, Wargrave, Reading,
Berkshire RG10 8NR, 01491 574271,
Call Date: Jan 1928 (Inner Temple)
Qualifications: MA

Spence *Lt Cdr Andrei Barry* •
Royal Naval Officer, SLA to FOST,
Grenville Block, HMS Drake, Devonport,
Plymouth PL2 2BG, Call Date: Oct 1993
(Middle Temple) Qualifications: BSc
(Hons)(Aston), CPE (Lond)

Spence *Joseph Desmond*
51 Stradbroke Grove, Buckhurst Hill,
Essex IG9 5PE, Call Date: Nov 1982
(Middle Temple) Qualifications: LLB

Spencer *Miss Alison Heather*
Mills & Reeves Solicitors, Francis House,
112 Hills Road, Cambridge CB2 1PH,
01223 364422, Fax: 01223 355848, Call
Date: Nov 1995 (Middle Temple)
Qualifications: BA (Hons)(York), MA
(York)

Spencer *Antony Francis Newman*
Call Date: Oct 1993 (Middle Temple)
Qualifications: BSc (Hons)(Newc)

Spencer *Barry Michael*
Call Date: Nov 1989 (Gray's Inn)
Qualifications: LLB

Spencer *Miss Francoise Mary* •
Departmetn of Trade & Industry, Legal
Services Directorate B3, (EC & Trade
Law), 10 Victoria Street (R227), London
SW1H 0NN, 0171 215 3413, Fax: 0171
215 3182, Call Date: Feb 1993 (Gray's
Inn) Qualifications: LLB, Diplome de
Hautes, Etudes Europeannes, (Droit),
Bruges

Spencer *George Charles Wellesley*
Call Date: Mar 1999 (Gray's Inn)
Qualifications: BSc (Lond), DPhil
(Oxon), BA (Cantab)

Spencer *Mrs Geraldine Erica* •
Senior Crown Prosecutor, Crown
Prosecution Service, The Cooperage,
Gainsford Street, London SE1 2NG, Call
Date: Nov 1968 (Gray's Inn)

Spencer *Miss Janet Elizabeth*
Deputy Clerk to the Justices Part Time
Chairman I.T.S., North Sefton
Magistrates Court, The Law Courts, Albert
Road, Southport PR9 OLJ, 01704
534141, Fax: 01704 500226, Call Date:
July 1983 (Gray's Inn) Qualifications:
D.M.L., D.M.S.

Spencer *John Richard*
Call Date: July 1988 (Lincoln's Inn)
Qualifications: BA (Hons) (Oxon), Dip
Law

Spencer *Mrs Maureen Patricia*
Senior Lecturer in Law, School of Law,
The Burrows, Hendon, London
NW4 4BT, Call Date: July 1989 (Inner
Temple) Qualifications: BA (Oxon), Dip
Law, LLM (Lond)

Spencer *Mrs Sheela Kumari Ann Marie*
Call Date: Nov 1996 (Middle Temple)
Qualifications: LLB (Hons)(Lond)

Spicer *David Leslie* •
Assistant Head of Legal Services,
Nottinghamshire County Council, Legal
Services Division, Friary Chambers, 26/
34 Friar Lane, Nottingham NG1 6DQ,
0115 9243010, Fax: 0115 9243020, Call
Date: July 1973 (Gray's Inn)
Qualifications: LLB

Spier *Miss Sian*
10 King's Bench Walk, Ground Floor,
Temple, London, EC4Y 7EB, Call Date:
Nov 1989 (Inner Temple) Qualifications:
LLB (Buck)

Spilsbury *Miss Jane Helen* •
Principle Legal Officer, New King's Beam
House, 22 Upper Ground, London SE1,
Call Date: Nov 1984 (Gray's Inn)
Qualifications: BA Hons

Spina *Miss Naomi Angela*
Call Date: Nov 1994 (Middle Temple)
Qualifications: BA (Hons)

Spink *Jonathan Howard*
Fagus House, Castlegate, Pickering,
North Yorkshire YO18 7AX, 01751
473413, Call Date: Nov 1991 (Gray's
Inn) Qualifications: BSc (Lond), MSc
(Lond), PGCE (Lond)

Spokes *John Arthur Clayton*
p/t Chairman Data Protn Trib, Call Date:
June 1955 (Gray's Inn)

Spong *Alan Michael* •
Branch Crown Prosecutor, Crown
Prosecution Service, Riding Gate House,
37 Old Dover Road, Canterbury, Kent
CT1 3JG, 01227 451144, Fax: 01227
456368, Call Date: July 1979 (Lincoln's
Inn) Qualifications: LLB (Lond)

Spooner *Mrs Karen Margaret*
Clerk to the Justices, North
Worcestershire Mag's Crt, Grove Street,
Redditch, Worcs B98 8DB, 01527
591035, Fax: 01527 64580, Call Date:
Nov 1984 (Middle Temple)
Qualifications: LLB

Sprigge *William Liddon* •
Director of Legal Services, Office of Gas
Supply, Stockley House, 130 Wilton
Road, London SW1V 1LQ, 0171 932
1670, Fax: 0171 932 1600, Call Date:
July 1976 (Lincoln's Inn) Qualifications:
BSc, ACIS

Spring *Anthony John*
4 Worcester Court, 5 Worcester Road,
Sutton, Surrey SM2 6PE, Call Date: Nov
1963 (Gray's Inn)

Spring *Miss Linda*
Call Date: July 1998 (Middle Temple)
Qualifications: LLB (Hons)(LSE)

Squire *Stuart James*
Winchester House School, Brackley,
Northants NN13 7AZ, 01280 700750, Call
Date: Nov 1994 (Middle Temple)
Qualifications: BA (Hons), Dip Law,
PGCE

Sram *Iqbal Singh*
Call Date: Oct 1996 (Lincoln's Inn)
Qualifications: M.B, CH.B (Manc), CPE

Stadnik *Miss Nina*
Principal Court Clerk, Leicestershire
Magistrates' Ct, The Court House,
Woodgate, Loughborough, 01509
215715, Call Date: Nov 1986 (Inner
Temple) Qualifications: BA

Staheli *Mrs Rebecca* •
Legal Advisor, Office of Fair Trading,
Field House, 15-22 Breams Buildings,
London EC4A 1PR, 0171 269 8896,
Fax: 0171 269 8830, Call Date: Nov
1989 (Middle Temple) Qualifications:
BA (Cantab)

Staley *Miss Helen Elizabeth*
Call Date: Mar 1997 (Lincoln's Inn)
Qualifications: LLB (Hons)(Hull)

Stalker *Miss Monica*
Call Date: July 1967 (Gray's Inn)
Qualifications: LLB (Manch)

Stallebrass *Paul*
Call Date: Oct 1991 (Inner Temple)
Qualifications: BA (Cantab)

Stanbrook *Dr Ivor Robert*
Call Date: May 1960 (Inner Temple)
Qualifications: BSc (Econ), Ph.D.

Stancliffe *David*
Call Date: Nov 1995 (Middle Temple)
Qualifications: LLB (Hons)(Kent)

Stanek *Mrs Susan Alexandra*
Woodperry Farm, Woodperry, Oxford
OX33 1AH, Call Date: Nov 1972 (Middle
Temple)

Stanley *Dr Christopher John*
Quintin Hogg Research Fellow in Law &
Social Theory, School of Law, University
of Westminster, 4 Red Lion Square,
London WC1R 4AR, 0171 911 5000,
Call Date: Apr 1986 (Gray's Inn)
Qualifications: LLB, Ph.D

Stanley *Giles Adam*
Call Date: Mar 1999 (Middle Temple)
Qualifications: BA (Hons)(Lond)

Stanley *Oliver Duncan*
Company Chairman, 5 The Park,
London NW11 7SR, Call Date: Nov 1963
(Middle Temple) Qualifications: MA
(Oxon)

Stanley *Simon Hugh Francis*
Corporate Public Affairs Consultant.
Former Legal Policy Assistant to Paul
Boateng M.P., Councillor Royal
Borough of Kensington & Chelsea,
Bruce Naughton Wade, Public Affairs
Management, Consultants, Enterprise
House, 59/65 Upper Ground, London
SE1 9PQ, 0171 620 1113, Fax: 0171
401 8319, Call Date: Nov 1993
(Lincoln's Inn) Qualifications: BA
(Hons)(Dunelm), Dip in Law (City)

Stanley *Miss Sybella Jane*
Call Date: Nov 1984 (Lincoln's Inn)
Qualifications: MA (Oxon)

Stannard *Grady Jon*
Call Date: Nov 1998 (Inner Temple)
Qualifications: LLB

Stanojlovic *Miss Mara Ellena*
Call Date: Nov 1992 (Inner Temple)
Qualifications: LLB (Lond)

Stansfield *Miss Jane* •
Principle Crown Prosecutor, Crown
Prosecution Service, 3-5 Lumley
Avenue, Skegness, Call Date: July 1986
(Lincoln's Inn) Qualifications: LLB
Business Law

Stansfield *Robert Harvey*
Bexhill Citizens Advice Bureau, 38
Sackville Road, Bexhill-on-Sea, East
Sussex TN39 3JE, 01424 215055, Call
Date: Nov 1991 (Inner Temple)
Qualifications: BSc (Eng), Dip Law

Stanton *Miss Alexandra Victoria*
Assistant, Simmons & Simmons, 21
Wilson Street, London EC2M 2TX, 0171
628 2020, Fax: 0171 628 2070, Call
Date: Nov 1993 (Middle Temple)
Qualifications: BA (Hons)(Cantab) MA,
Licence Speciale Eu, Droit Europeen,
(Bruxelles)

Stanton *Miss Margaret Judith*
Westbourne, 21 Station Rd, Princes
Risborough, Aylesbury, Bucks
HP27 9DE, Call Date: July 1966 (Gray's
Inn) Qualifications: BA (Hons)

Stanway-Mayers *Martin Victor James* •
BP Exploration, Gas Int'l, D'Arcy
House, 146 Queen Victoria Street,
London EC4V BY, 0171 579 7504, Fax:
0171 579 7776, Call Date: July 1976
(Middle Temple) Qualifications: LLB
(Lond)

Stapleton *David Alan*
Call Date: Nov 1997 (Inner Temple)
Qualifications: BSc

Starling *Keith*
Tewkesbury Magistrates' Court, Gander
Lane, Tewkesbury, Gloucestershire
GL20 5TR, 01684 294632, Fax: 01684
274596, Deputy Clerk to the Justices,
West Gloucestershire Clerkship, Call
Date: Nov 1983 (Gray's Inn)
Qualifications: LLB,Dip Law

Steadman *Mark John*
The Faculty Office of the, Archbishop of
Canterbury, Lee Bolton & Lee, 1 The
Santuary, Westminster, London
SW1P 3JT, 0171 222 5381, Fax: 0171
222 7502, Call Date: Oct 1996 (Inner
Temple) Qualifications: LLB (Soton)

Stearns *Dr Elizabeth Jane Elford*
H.M.Coroner - Eastern District of
Greater London, Call Date: Oct 1997
(Inner Temple) Qualifications: BDS,
MBBS, CPE (London)

Stedman *Aryan John*
Call Date: Nov 1997 (Middle Temple)
Qualifications: LLB (Hons)(Kent)

Steel *Commander David George* •
Commander, Royal Navy. Commander,
Supply HMS Invincible BFPO 308,
Supply Officer, HMS Invincible
BFPO 308, Call Date: July 1988 (Middle
Temple) Qualifications: BA (Hons)
(Dunelm)

Steel *Henry*
Call Date: June 1951 (Lincoln's Inn)
Qualifications: BA (Oxon)

Steel *Mrs Marianne Valentine*
Swindon Hall, Swindon Village,
Cheltenham, Glos GL51 9QR, Call Date:
June 1950 (Gray's Inn) Qualifications:
LLB (Wales)

Steel *Nicholas Peter Robin*
Call Date: Oct 1993 (Middle Temple)
Qualifications: BA (Hons)

Steel *Stephen Paul* •
Crown Prosecution Service, C/O 50
Ludgate Hill, London EC4M 7EX, Call
Date: Nov 1985 (Lincoln's Inn)
Qualifications: BSc, Dip Law

Steen *Anthony David*
Blackstone Chambers, Blackstone
House, Temple, London, EC4Y 9BW,
Call Date: May 1962 (Gray's Inn)

Steer *Miss Joanne Monica* •
Legal Advisor, Retail Motor Industry
Fed., 201 Great Portland Street, London
W1N 0AB, Call Date: Oct 1995
(Lincoln's Inn) Qualifications: LLB
(Hons)(Exon)

Steiner *William Anthony Frederick Paul*
27 Cavendish Avenue, Cambridge
CB1 7UP, 01223 247131, Call Date:
Nov 1942 (Gray's Inn) Qualifications:
MA (Cantab), LLM (Lond), FLA,
Dipl.Kons

Stephens *James Ross*
Beachcroft Stanleys, 20 Furnival Street,
London EC4A 1BN, Call Date: Nov 1994
(Middle Temple) Qualifications: BA
(Hons)

Stephens *Mark Timothy Edwin*
Call Date: Nov 1998 (Middle Temple)
Qualifications: BA (Hons)(Manch), Dip
Law

Stephens *Ms Stella Chinweoke*
Call Date: July 1998 (Lincoln's Inn)
Qualifications: BSC (Nigeria), MBA
(Paris), Dip in Law (Lond)

Stephenson *Miss Stephanie Joy*
Call Date: July 1970 (Gray's Inn)
Qualifications: LLB,AKC

Stephenson *Sydney Dingaan*
Call Date: Nov 1996 (Middle Temple)
Qualifications: LLB (Hons)(Lond)

Stephenson *Thomas* •
Town Clerk, Leicester City Council, New
Walk Centre, Welford Place, Leicester
LE1 6ZG, 0116 252 6300, Fax: 0116
254 3668, Call Date: July 1976 (Middle
Temple) Qualifications: BSc, Cert. Ed

Stephenson-Burton *Ian*
Call Date: Oct 1994 (Inner Temple)
Qualifications: BSc (Sheff), MPhil
(Cantab), CPE (Lond)

Stern *George Jerome Albert*
6 Eton Court, Shepherds Hill, London
N6 5AF, 0181 340 0214, Fax: 0181 348
6586, Call Date: Nov 1994 (Middle
Temple) Qualifications: MA, BSc, Msc,
F.S.S.

Stern *Ronald Dougas* •
Legal Advisor, Region Counsel for
Cadbury Schweppes Beverages, Africa,
India, Middle East and Europe Region.
Company Secretary : Schweppes
International Limited Cadbury Bevarages
Limited. Director : Schweppes Limited, L
Rose & Co Limited., CSB House, 28
Clarendon Road, Watford WD1 1JJ, +44
(0) 1923 412983, Fax: +44 (0) 1923
230157, Call Date: Nov 1972 (Middle
Temple)

Stevens *Clyde Robert*
Call Date: July 1978 (Middle Temple)
Qualifications: LLB (Hons) Leicester,
ADPTD (Homerton)

Stevens *Mark Nicholas*
Call Date: Nov 1998 (Inner Temple)
Qualifications: LLB (N.Lond), LLM
(Lond)

Stevens *Robert Bocking*
Essex Court Chambers, 24 Lincoln's Inn
Fields, London, WC2A 3ED, Call Date:
Feb 1956 (Gray's Inn) Qualifications:
MA, BCL (Oxon), LLM

Stevens *Robert Hedley*
Fellow & Tutor in Law, Lady Margaret
Hall, Oxford OX2 6QA, 01865 274289,
Call Date: Nov 1992 (Gray's Inn)
Qualifications: BA (Oxon), BCL (Oxon)

Stevens *Miss Sussannah Rachel*
Call Date: Oct 1997 (Middle Temple)
Qualifications: LLB (Hons)(Manc)

Stevenson *Heon Lindsay Stuart*
C/O 12 Fern Road, Storrington, West
Sussex RH20 4LW, Call Date: May 1994
(Gray's Inn) Qualifications: MA

Stevenson *John Michael*
Tower Bridge Court, 224 Tower Bridge
Road, London SE1 2UP, 0171 716 6000,
Fax: 0171 716 6104, Call Date: July 1967
(Middle Temple)

Stevenson *Mark Jonathan Blane*
Call Date: Oct 1998 (Inner Temple)
Qualifications: LLB (Hull)

Steward *Derek John*
Little Thatch, Mill Lane, Bradford Abbas,
Sherborne, Dorset DT9 6RH, 01935
427111, Call Date: Feb 1973 (Inner
Temple) Qualifications: LDSRCS, DDPH

Stewart *Andrew William* •
Range 11, Solicitor's Office, Dept of
Trade & Industry, 10-18 Victoria Street,
London SW1H 0NN, 0171 215 3446, Fax:
0171 215 3182, Call Date: July 1983
(Middle Temple) Qualifications: BA Hons
{Oxon}

Stewart *Robin Milton*
Recorder, Call Date: Feb 1963 (Middle
Temple) Qualifications: MA (Oxon)

Stewart *Mrs Victoria Joy*
Capsticks Solicitors, 77-83 Upper
Richmond Road, London SW15 2TT,
0181 780 2211, Fax: 0181 780 1141,
Solicitor, Call Date: Feb 1990 (Inner
Temple) Qualifications: LLB

Stewart-Richardson *Alastair Lucas
Graham*
General Commissioner for Income Tax,
Call Date: Nov 1952 (Inner Temple)
Qualifications: MA (Cantab)

Stibbs *Michael John Parker*
Senior Court Clerk, Solihull Magistrates
Court, Homer Road, Solihull,
Birmingham B91 3RD, 0121 705 8101,
Fax: 0121 711 2045, Call Date: Nov 1982
(Middle Temple) Qualifications: BA

Stickings *Miss Sian Rosemary*
Devereux Chambers, Devereux Court,
London, WC2R 3JJ, Call Date: Nov 1983
(Inner Temple) Qualifications: MA
(Oxon)

Stirling *Andrew Fraser* •
Senior Crown Prosecutor, Crown
Prosecution Service, 2nd Floor, King
Willam House, Market Place, Kingston
upon Hull, Call Date: July 1985
(Lincoln's Inn) Qualifications: LLB
(Hons) (B'ham)

Stock *Robert Alexander*
Call Date: Oct 1998 (Inner Temple)
Qualifications: BA (Oxon)

Stockdale *James Arthur Fitzroy*
Call Date: July 1972 (Gray's Inn)

Stocks *Neil Richard* •
Managing Director, Head of Legal &
Compliance, UBS AG, Private Banking, 1
Curzon Street, London W1Y 7FN, 0171
567 2804, Fax: 0171 567 4260, Call
Date: July 1978 (Middle Temple)
Qualifications: B.Sc (Lond)

Stockton *Miss Fay*
Call Date: July 1976 (Lincoln's Inn)
Qualifications: LLB

Stockton *John Paul* •
Director of Tribunal Operations, The
Court Service, 48/49 Chancery Lane,
London WC2A 1JR, 0171 936 7199, Fax:
0171 736 7187, Call Date: Nov 1974
(Middle Temple) Qualifications: BA
(Oxon)

Stockwell *Matthew Charles*
Call Date: Oct 1998 (Gray's Inn)
Qualifications: LLB (L'pool)

Stokes *Dylan Daniel* •
Legal/Compliance Officer, Deutsche
Bank, 133 Houndsditch, 5th Floor,
Global Markets Compliance, London
EC3A 7DX, 0171 547 6796, Call Date:
Nov 1998 (Inner Temple) Qualifications:
BA (Dunelm)

Stokes *Stanley William*
Clerk to the Justices/Justices Chief
Executive, Doncaster Magistrates', Courts
Committee, P O Box 49, College Road,
Doncaster DN1 3HT, 01302 366711, Fax:
01302 340323, Call Date: Nov 1985
(Gray's Inn)

Stoll *James Andrew*
Call Date: Nov 1994 (Inner Temple)
Qualifications: LLB (Hons)(Soton)

Stomberg *Miss Christina-Caroline*
Call Date: Oct 1992 (Gray's Inn)
Qualifications: MA (St.Andrews Scot)

Stone *Andrew Mark*
Call Date: May 1997 (Lincoln's Inn)
Qualifications: LLB (Hons)(Derby)

Stone *Ms Frances Julia*
School of Health, University of
Greenwich, Avery Hill Campus,
Southwood Site, Avery Hill Road, London
SE9 2UG, 0181 331 8239, Lecturer in
Healthcare Law & Ethnics, Call Date: July
1987 (Middle Temple) Qualifications:
LLB(Hons) (Manc), MA

Stone *Miss Gillian*
Call Date: July 1997 (Middle Temple)
Qualifications: LLB (Nott'm)

Stone *Julian Anthony*
Call Date: July 1997 (Gray's Inn)
Qualifications: LLB

Stone *Miss Penelope Helen* •
Call Date: Nov 1984 (Gray's Inn)

Stone *Professor Richard Thomas Horner*
Prinicipal, Inns of Court School of Law,
Inns of Court School of Law, 4 Gray's Inn
Place, Gray's Inn, London WC1R 5DX,
0171 400 3601, Fax: 0171 831 4188,
Call Date: July 1998 (Gray's Inn)
Qualifications: LLB (So'ton), LLM (Hull)

Stonecliffe *Miss Heidi Lorraine*
Call Date: Oct 1996 (Inner Temple)
Qualifications: LLB (LSE)

Stoplar *David Jonathan Aron* •
Assistant Legal Adviser, Civil Aviation
Authority, CAA House, 45-59 Kingsway,
London WC2B 6TE, 0171 832 5417, Fax:
0171 832 6635, Call Date: July 1982
(Gray's Inn) Qualifications: LLB (Lond)

Storey *Mrs Bernadette* •
Senior Crown Prosecutor, Crown
Prosecution Service, Crown House,
Winston Churchill Avenue, Portsmouth,
Hampshire PO12 2PJ, 01705 752004,
Call Date: Feb 1990 (Lincoln's Inn)
Qualifications: LLB Hons

Storey *Ms Elizabeth Anne* •
Legal Officer, Call Date: Apr 1991 (Gray's
Inn) Qualifications: BA (Sydney), LLB

Storey *Steven David*
Regional Director - Engineering Division,
James R Knowles, Suite 39, Langford
House, 40 Friar Lane, Nottingham
NG1 6DQ, 0115 941 9595, Fax: 0115
950 2062, Call Date: July 1998
(Lincoln's Inn) Qualifications: LLB
(Hons)(Sheff), BSc (Hons)(Nott'm)

Storr *Philip Leonard*
Crown Counsel to the Government of Bermuda, P.O.Box HM 2653, Hamilton, HMKX, Bermuda, Bermuda, (809) 296 1807, Fax: (809) 292 3608, Former Solicitor (1958) and Member Bermuda 46/48 Essex Street, London, WC2R 3GH, Call Date: 1990 (Inner Temple) Qualifications: MA

Storrs-Fox *Jonathan Storrs*
Former Solicitor, Call Date: Feb 1993 (Gray's Inn) Qualifications: LLB (Hull)

Stout *Geoffrey Hamer*
4 Greenlands, Tattenhall, Chester CH3 9QY, 01829 70461, Call Date: Nov 1982 (Gray's Inn) Qualifications: LLB (Lond), LDS (Man

Strachan *Jeremy Alan Watkin* •
Executive Director, Glaxo Wellcome plc, Glaxo Wellcome House, Berkeley Avenue, Greenford, Middlesex UB6 0NN, 0171 493 4060, Fax: 0181 966 8330, Call Date: Nov 1969 (Inner Temple) Qualifications: MA (Cantab), LLM

Strachan *Ms Mary Jane*
Call Date: Nov 1991 (Inner Temple) Qualifications: LLB (Hons)

Stranaghan *Miss Patricia Ann* •
Legal Advisor, G E Capital Equipment Finance, Limited, Capital House, 3 Bond Street, Bristol BS1 3LA, 0117 946 3301, Call Date: Nov 1984 (Lincoln's Inn) Qualifications: LLB (Hons)

Strauss *Dr Herman*
New Zealand Barrister & Solicitor, Flat 2A, 88A Salamanca Road, Wellington 5, 4727455, Call Date: Nov 1951 (Lincoln's Inn)

Straw *The Rt.Hon John Whitaker*
MP for Blackburn, House Of Commons, London, SW1, 0171 219 5477, Fax: 0171 219 6694, Inner Temple Bencher 1997, Call Date: July 1972 (Inner Temple) Qualifications: LLB

Straw *Miss Louise Victoria*
Burton Copeland Solicitors, Royal London House, 196 Deansgate, Manchester M3 3NE, 0161 834 7374, Call Date: Nov 1987 (Gray's Inn) Qualifications: LLB (L'pool)

Stripp *Ian Robert*
Police Officer Detective Superintendent, Leicestershire Constabulary, Police Headquarters, St Johns, Enderby, PO Box 999, Leicestershire, 0116 2482511, Fax: 0116 2484127, Call Date: Nov 1993 (Middle Temple) Qualifications: LLB (Hons)

Strong *Richard Neville*
Solicitors Law Stationery, Society Ltd, Oyez House, PO Box 55, 7 Spa Road, London SE16 3QQ, Call Date: July 1991 (Inner Temple) Qualifications: LLM (Lond), LLB, DMS

Strong *Samuel Jonathan*
Call Date: Feb 1995 (Middle Temple) Qualifications: LLB (Hons) (Bucks)

Struggles *Jonathan Michael*
Call Date: Oct 1997 (Gray's Inn) Qualifications: LLB (Bris)

Stuart *Mrs Margaret Ann*
Call Date: Nov 1990 (Lincoln's Inn) Qualifications: LLB (Essex)

Stubbs *Matthew James* •
Grade 7 Lawyer, Health & Safety Executive, Rose Court, 2 Southwark Bridge, London SE1 9HS, 0171 717 6668, Call Date: July 1989 (Inner Temple) Qualifications: LLB [Exon]

Stuckey *Derek Richard*
3 Dr Johnson's Bldgs, Ground Floor, Temple, London, EC4Y 7BA, Call Date: May 1949 (Gray's Inn) Qualifications: MA, BCL (Oxon)

Stutt *Colin Richard Hamilton* •
Legal Adviser, Legal Aid Board Head Office, 85 Gray's Inn Road, London WC1X 8AA, 0171 813 1000, Fax: 0171 813 8631, Call Date: July 1985 (Inner Temple) Qualifications: MA (Cantab)

Styles *Peter Richard* •
Vice-President, European Government Affairs, Enron Europe, Four Millbank, London SW1P 3ET, 0171 316 5480, Fax: 0171 316 5391, 1996-7 Chairman of Bar Association for Commerce Finance & Industry Member of the Bar Council, Call Date: July 1978 (Inner Temple) Qualifications: MA (Cantab)

Styles *Timothy Charles*
Call Date: Nov 1998 (Middle Temple) Qualifications: LLB (Hons) (Plymouth)

Subramaniam *Bhaskar S*
In House Barrister, Mathis Solicitors, 231-232 Elephant & Castle, Shopping Centre, London SE1 6TE, 0171 277 0306, Fax: 0171 277 0313, Call Date: July 1997 (Middle Temple) Qualifications: LLB (Hons) (Lond), MA (Lond)

Suddaby *John Andrew* •
Call Date: Nov 1990 (Inner Temple) Qualifications: BA (Hons), Dip Law

Sugden *Richard Alexander*
Call Date: Oct 1997 (Gray's Inn) Qualifications: BSc (Middx)

Sugrue *Miss Clare Veronica* •
Director, Legal & Business Affairs, Islands Records Ltd, 22 St Peters Square, London W6 9NW, 0181 910 3287, Fax: 0181 910 3218, Call Date: Nov 1985 (Middle Temple) Qualifications: LLB (Lond)

Sukul *Ganesh Shankar*
G & S Law Offices, Suite 24, 28 Cathedral Road, Cardiff, South Wales CF1 9LJ, 01222 660163, Fax: 01222 664891, Call Date: July 1982 (Gray's Inn) Qualifications: BA

Sukul *Ms Kheemelia*
Trainee Inspector of Taxes, Inland Revenue, Streatham District, Radnor House, London Road, Norbury, London SW16 4DU, 0181 679 2341, Fax: 0181 679 6058, Call Date: Oct 1997 (Inner Temple) Qualifications: LLB (Lond)

Sukul *Mrs Sitalakshmi*
G & S Law Offices, Suite 24, 28 Cathedral Road, Cardiff, South Wales CF1 9LJ, 01222 660163, Fax: 01222 664891, Call Date: Nov 1982 (Lincoln's Inn) Qualifications: BA (Hons)

Sulehria *Mrs Carol Joan*
Principal Legal Adviser, Ealing Magistrates' Court, Green Man Lane, London W13 0SD, 0181 579 9311, Fax: 0181 579 2985, Call Date: Nov 1974 (Middle Temple) Qualifications: LLB (Lond)

Sulek *Ms Joanna Elizabeth Maria*
Call Date: Oct 1994 (Gray's Inn) Qualifications: MA, LLB (Leeds)

Sullivan *David Douglas Hooper*
Call Date: Nov 1951 (Inner Temple) Qualifications: MA, BCL

Sullivan *Mrs Debra* •
Trade Marks Adviser, BATMark Limited, Export House, Cawsey Way, Woking, Surrey GU21 1YB, 01483 792967, Fax: 01483 759982, Call Date: July 1988 (Lincoln's Inn) Qualifications: LLB (Hons) (Lond), Maitrise En Droit, (Sorbonne)

Summerfield *Henry Jacob Isidore*
Camden Mediation Services Management Committee Member, 38 Hillfield Court, London NW3 4BJ, 0171 209 1379, Also Inn of Court I, Call Date: Apr 1948 (Gray's Inn) Qualifications: BA (Cantab), ACIArb

Summerlin *Mrs Sara Hill* •
Senior Crown Prosecutor, Crown Prosecution Service, Hull Branch Office, King William House, Market Place, Kingston Upon Hull HU1 1RS, 01482 228816, Fax: 01482 587275, Call Date: Oct 1993 (Gray's Inn) Qualifications: B.Sc (Hons)

Summers *Gary*
Magrath & Co, 52/54 Maddox Street, London W1R 9PA, 0171 495 3003, Call Date: Nov 1985 (Gray's Inn) Qualifications: BA

Sundram-Selvadurai *Mrs Naomi* •
Head of Claims, Medical Protection Society, 33 Cavendish Square, London W1M 0PS, 0171 399 1379, Fax: 0171 399 1377, Call Date: Oct 1990 (Lincoln's Inn) Qualifications: LLB

Sunkin *Maurice Simon*
1 Pump Court, Lower Ground Floor, Temple, London, EC4Y 7AB, Call Date: July 1975 (Middle Temple) Qualifications: LLM

• Barrister in employment

Sunnassee *Atmanand*
Lecturer, Call Date: Nov 1988 (Lincoln's Inn) Qualifications: MSc (LSE), BA, Dip Law

Sunner *Navtej Singh*
Call Date: Oct 1994 (Lincoln's Inn) Qualifications: LLB (Hons) (Wolves)

Sunner *Miss Sundip Kaur*
Call Date: Nov 1997 (Middle Temple) Qualifications: LLB (Hons) (Hull)

Supramaniam *Ramesh*
Call Date: July 1996 (Middle Temple) Qualifications: LLB (Hons) (Lond)

Surman *Peter John*
Fiji, Judge of the Supreme Court, Fiji 1 Temple Gardens, 1st Floor, Temple, London, EC4Y 9BB, Call Date: July 1974 (Gray's Inn)

Surridge *Mr. Robert Conway*
Litigation Executive, Silverbeck Rymer, Heywood Building, Brunswick Street, Liverpool, 0151 236 2164, Fax: 0151 236 7926, Call Date: Mar 1996 (Gray's Inn) Qualifications: LLB

Sutcliffe *Miss Katrina Jane Stuart*
Senior Recruitment Consultant for In-house Legal Appointments QD group., 37-41 Bedford Row, London WC1R 4JH, 0171 405 6062, Fax: 0171 831 6394, Call Date: Nov 1994 (Lincoln's Inn) Qualifications: LLB (Hons) (Kingston)

Sutherland *Miss Alison Jane Benham* •
Local Government Association, 26 Chapter Street, London SW1P 4ND, 0171 664 3246, Fax: 0171 664 3232, Call Date: Nov 1981 (Gray's Inn) Qualifications: MA (Cantab), Dip Law

Sutherland *Mrs Jill Beatrice*
Call Date: July 1989 (Lincoln's Inn) Qualifications: BA (Kent)

Sutherland *Robert David*
Inner London Magistrates', Courts Service, 65 Romney Street, London SW1P 3RD, Deputy Assistant Justices' Clerk (Licensing), Call Date: July 1985 (Lincoln's Inn) Qualifications: LLB

Sutherland *Miss Victoria Jane*
Call Date: Nov 1997 (Lincoln's Inn) Qualifications: BA (Hons)

Sutton *Andre John*
Call Date: Nov 1994 (Middle Temple) Qualifications: LLB (Hons)

Sutton *Paul Edmund*
Call Date: July 1973 (Middle Temple) Qualifications: LLB (Lond)

Suzin *Adam Anthony*
Call Date: Mar 1999 (Gray's Inn) Qualifications: BA, LLM (Sussex)

Swabey *John Charles Merttins*
Legal Advisor/Company Secretary, JJB Consultancy Services Ltd, 27 High Street, Shaftesbury, Dorset S77 7JE, 0171 792 1618, Call Date: Nov 1974 (Gray's Inn)

Swain *Barry* •
Senior Crown Prosecutor, Crown Prosecution Service, 32 Scotland Street, Sheffield S3 7DQ, 0114 291 2062, Fax: 0114 291 2050, Call Date: July 1989 (Inner Temple) Qualifications: LLB (Hons) (Sheff)

Swainson *Mrs Jill Marguerite* •
Principal Legal Officer, Department of Social Security, New Court, 48 Carey Street, London WC2A 2LS, Call Date: Feb 1970 (Gray's Inn) Qualifications: BA

Swainson *John Honeyman* •
Grade 5, Solicitor's Office, DSS, New Court, Carey Street, London WC2A 2LS, 0171 412 1355, Fax: 0171 412 1513, Call Date: July 1966 (Lincoln's Inn) Qualifications: BA (Hull)

Swan *Ms Pauline Mary*
Call Date: Mar 1998 (Gray's Inn) Qualifications: LLB (Lond)

Swan *Stephen Andrew John* •
Barrister, Advisory & Drafting, Health & Safety Executive, Solicitor's Office, Room 842, Rose Court, 2 Southwark Bridge, London SE1 9HS, 0171 717 6659, Fax: 0171 717 6661, Call Date: July 1983 (Lincoln's Inn) Qualifications: LLB (Hons) (Lond), LLM (Lond)

Swan *Rev Thomas Hugh Winfield*
24 Chiefs Street, Ely, Cambridge CB6 1AT, 01353 668452, Call Date: June 1951 (Lincoln's Inn) Qualifications: MA (Oxon)

Swannell *Robert William Ashburnham*
Vice-Chairman - J Henry Schroder & Co Limited, 120 Cheapside, London EC2V 6DS, 0171 658 6000, Fax: 0171 658 6459, Call Date: Nov 1976 (Lincoln's Inn) Qualifications: FCA

Swayne *Christopher David George*
Call Date: Feb 1983 (Inner Temple) Qualifications: MA (Oxon)

Sweeney *James Peter*
Eversheds, Sun Alliance House, 35 Mosley Street, Newcastle upon Tyne NE1 1XX, 0191 261 1661, Fax: 0191 261 8270, Call Date: 1989 (Inner Temple) Qualifications: LLB (Hons)

Sweeney *Thomas Gerard* •
Principal Crown Prosecutor, CPS (G.Manchester Area), PO Box 377, 8th Floor,Sunlight House, Quay Street, Manchester M60 3LU, 0161 837 7402, Call Date: Feb 1988 (Gray's Inn)

Sweeney-Baird *Mrs Magarita*
Lecturer, Birmingham Business School, University of Birmingham (p/t) & Queen Mary & Westfield College Law School University of London (p/t), 225 Leigh Hunt Drive, Southgate, London N14 6DS, 0181 447 9392, Call Date: July 1989 (Middle Temple) Qualifications: LLB [Glas], LLM [Harvard]

Sweeting *Miss Cheryl Tonia*
Call Date: July 1998 (Lincoln's Inn) Qualifications: LLB (Hons)

Sweeting *Miss Valerie Frances*
Edwin Coe Solicitors, 2 Stone Buildings, Lincoln's Inn, London WC2A 3TH, Call Date: Mar 1998 (Lincoln's Inn) Qualifications: BA (Econ) (Canada), Dip Law (Westmister)

Swift *Christopher Richard* •
Legal Adviser, Office of Fair Trading, Field House, 15-25 Bream's Buildings, London EC4A 1PR, Call Date: Nov 1972 (Middle Temple) Qualifications: MA, LLB (Cantab)

Swift *David Bernard*
44 Jacksons Lane, Highgate, London N6 5SX, 0181 348 2154, Fax: 0181 348 4287, Call Date: Nov 1955 (Gray's Inn) Qualifications: MA (Cantab)

Swinhoe *Luke Francis* •
Darlington Borpough Council, Central Services Department, Town Hall, Darlington DL1 5QT, 01325 388337, Call Date: Nov 1987 (Inner Temple) Qualifications: BA (Hons), LLM

Syed *Abdur Razzaque*
77 Cecil Avenue, Barking, Essex IG11 9TG, 0181 220 9479, Call Date: July 1971 (Inner Temple) Qualifications: BA, LLB

Syed *Mohammed Hussain*
3rd Floor,ZAB Centre, 5-A Constitution Avenue, F-5/1 Islamabad, (+9251) 279739, Fax: (+9251) 279776, and Member Pakistan Bar, Call Date: Nov 1989 (Lincoln's Inn) Qualifications: BA (Oxon), Dip Law (City)

Syed *Nayleem Ahmed* •
Legal & Business Affairs Manager, Coalition Recordings/Warner, Music International, Electric Lighting Station, 46 Kensington Court, London W8 5DP, 0171 591 5900, Fax: 0171 591 5999, Call Date: May 1995 (Lincoln's Inn) Qualifications: LLB (Hons), LLM, Dip Law

Sykes *Martin Howard*
129 Millgate, Selby, N Yorkshire YO8 3LL, 01757 702826, Call Date: May 1973 (Middle Temple) Qualifications: MA (Oxon)

Sylvester *Ms Alison Mary*
Call Date: Feb 1993 (Inner Temple) Qualifications: BA, MA (Oxon), Diploma in Law

Symes *Ms Mary Elizabeth*
Call Date: July 1977 (Lincoln's Inn)

Symington *Noel Ian*
1 Asserton Cottages, Berwick St James, Salisbury, Wilts SP3 4TY, 01722 790785, Fax: 01722 782356, Call Date: Nov 1993 (Inner Temple) Qualifications: BA, CPE

Symonds *Robert Stephen*
Call Date: Nov 1995 (Gray's Inn) Qualifications: LLB (Warw)

E

Symons *Miss April Naomi Wallace*
120 Grove End Gardens, London
NW8 9LR, Call Date: June 1953 (Inner
Temple) Qualifications: MA (Oxon)

Synmoie *Ms Lorrayne* •
Crown Prosecutor, Rossmore House,
10 Newbold Terrace, Leamington Spa
CV32 4EA, 01926 450277, Call Date:
July 1991 (Lincoln's Inn)
Qualifications: LLB (Hons) (Hull)

Synnott *Terence James*
Director & Group Secretary at DSR
Group Director/Company Secretary
Keele Consultants, Bank House, 21
Market Street, Edenfield, Via Bury,
Lancashire BL0 0JQ, 01706 821990,
Fax: 01604 702558, Consultant to
Warren-Thomas Corporate Solicitors,
Call Date: July 1989 (Lincoln's Inn)
Qualifications: BA Hons (Keele)

Szagun *Miss Teresa Ewa*
Clerk to the Magistrates, Justices
Training Office & Legal Trainer Essex,
Magistrates' Courts, Basildon
Magistrates' Court, Great Oaks,
Basildon, Essex SS14 1EH, 01268
293129, Fax: 01268 293187, Call Date:
Nov 1985 (Middle Temple)
Qualifications: BA (Hons) , Dip Law

Szatter *Miss Patricia*
Call Date: Oct 1998 (Inner Temple)
Qualifications: BA (Stirling), LLB
(Nott'm)

Szell *Patrick John* •
Head of the International
Environmental Law Division, Dept of
the Environment,, Transport and the
Regions, Eland House, Bressenden
Place, London SW1E 5DU, 0171 890
4820, Fax: 0171 890 4804, Call Date:
Nov 1966 (Inner Temple)
Qualifications: MA, LLB (Dub)

Tabbush *Simon James* •
Lord Chancellor's Department,
Selborne House, 54-60 Victoria Street,
London SW1E 6QW, 0171 210 0734,
Fax: 0171 210 0725, Call Date: July
1979 (Middle Temple) Qualifications:
MA (Oxon)

Tack *Geoffrey Joel* •
Principal Legal Officer, Solicitor's
Office, HM Customs and Exise, New
King's Beam House, 22 Upper Ground,
London SE1 9PJ, 0171 620 1313, Call
Date: Feb 1989 (Lincoln's Inn)
Qualifications: LLB(Hons)

Tackie *Abraham Nokwei*
Senior Lecturer, Middlesex University,
Faculty of Business Studies, and
Management, Middlesex, Business
School, Law School, The Burroughs,
London NW4 4BT, 0181 362 5000, Fax:
0181 202 1539, Call Date: Nov 1983
(Middle Temple) Qualifications: BA
(Hons) (Law), LLM, RMN

Tagg *Gavin Kenneth* •
Contracts Manager, Gatton Volt Group,
Gatton Place, St Matthews Road,
Redhill, Surrey RH1 1TA, Call Date: Oct
1995 (Middle Temple) Qualifications:
LLB (Hons) (Wales)

Taggart *Anthony Francis*
Call Date: June 1955 (Lincoln's Inn)
Qualifications: LLB (Lond)

Tague *Miss Estelle* •
Trainee Tax Consultant, KPMG, 1 The
Embankment, Neville Street, Leeds
LS1 4DW, 0113 231 3000, Call Date:
July 1998 (Lincoln's Inn)
Qualifications: LLB (Hons) (Sheff)

Tailby *Christopher Russell*
Price Waterhouse Coopers, Cornwall
Court, 19 Cornwall Street, Birmingham
B3 2DT, 0121 200 3000, Fax: 0121 200
2464, Call Date: Nov 1971 (Inner
Temple)

Tait *Ms Helen*
Call Date: Oct 1997 (Inner Temple)
Qualifications: BA (Wolverhampton),
CPE

Takla *Miss Joanna Antoine*
Call Date: Oct 1997 (Inner Temple)
Qualifications: BA (Westminster)

Talbot *Lawrence Keith*
Call Date: Oct 1998 (Lincoln's Inn)
Qualifications: LLB (Hons) (Kingston)

Tallents *Anthony Alan* •
Senior Legal Adviser, British Steel plc,
15 Marylebone Road, London NW1 5JD,
0171 314 5518, Fax: 0171 314 5614,
Call Date: Nov 1970 (Gray's Inn)
Qualifications: LLB Hons, MBA

Tam *Miss Winnie Wan-Chi*
Hong Kong, and Member Hong Kong
Bar Australia Bar 8 New Square,
Lincoln's Inn, London, WC2A 3QP, Call
Date: Feb 1988 (Middle Temple)
Qualifications: LLB (Hons) Hong Kong

Tamlyn *Alexander*
Dibb Lupton Alsop, 125 London Wall,
London EC2Y 5AE, 0171 796 6185,
Fax: 0171 600 1727, Call Date: July
1988 (Lincoln's Inn) Qualifications:
LLB (Hons) (Cardiff)

Tampion *Andrew Neil* •
Call Date: May 1988 (Lincoln's Inn)
Qualifications: BA (Hons) Keele

Tan *Boon Chiang*
Director of General Magnetics Ltd.;
Member, Committee of Experts on the
Application of Conventions and
Recommendations, International
Labour Office, Geneva, 75 Shelford
Road, 4622914, Fax: 4622924, Call
Date: Nov 1954 (Lincoln's Inn)
Qualifications: LL.B, Dip.Arts

Tan *Miss Esther* •
Magistrates' Court Clerk, Norwich
Magistrates' Court, Bishopgate,
Norwich, Norfolk NR3 1UP, 01603
679548, Fax: 01603 663263, Call Date:
Nov 1990 (Middle Temple)
Qualifications: LLB (Buck'ham)

Tan *Miss Jeannie*
and Member Singapore Bar, Call Date:
July 1993 (Lincoln's Inn)
Qualifications: LLB (Hons)

Tan *Kay Kian*
Sinclair Roche & Temperley, Royex
House, 5 Aldermanbury Square,
London EC2V 7LE, Singapore 1128,
Call Date: July 1995 (Middle Temple)
Qualifications: LLB (Hons)

Tan *Miss Oi Peng*
Call Date: Nov 1994 (Inner Temple)
Qualifications: LLB (Kent)

Tan *Tee Poon*
Unit 12, Blue Bay Apartments, Valley
Road, Halls Head WA 6210, Australia,
Call Date: Feb 1963 (Middle Temple)
Qualifications: BDS (Malaya)

Tan *Woon Chay*
Figueiredo & Co Solicitors, Berkeley
House, 3rd Floor, 73 Upper Richmond
Road, Putney, London SW15 2SZ, 0181
877 3844, Fax: 0181 877 0556, Call
Date: July 1991 (Inner Temple)
Qualifications: BA (Kent)

Tan *Miss Ying Hui*
Call Date: Nov 1978 (Gray's Inn)
Qualifications: BA, (Lond)

Tanaka *Ms Diana Tei*
0171 286 7089, and Member Eastern &
Southern Districts of New York
(Federal) USA, First Circuit (Federal)
USA, Massachusetts District Court
(Federal) USA, New York Washington
DC & Massachusetts State Bar (USA),
Call Date: Nov 1988 (Middle Temple)
Qualifications: BA [Harvard], JD
[Harvard], LLM [Georgetown]

Tank *Rajnikant*
Head of Legal Department, Firstassist
Limited, Legal Department, Wheatfield
Way, Hinckley, Leicestershire
LE10 1YG, 01455 251500, Fax: 01455
251112, Call Date: Mar 1996 (Inner
Temple) Qualifications: LLB (LSE)

Tankel *David*
Director, New Bridge Street
Consultants, 20 Little Britain, London
EC1A 7DH, 0171 282 3030, Fax: 0171
282 0011, Call Date: July 1983 (Middle
Temple) Qualifications: BA (Manch),
Dip Law

Tanner *Ms Liz Anne* •
Company Lawyer, Cendent Business
Answers, (Europe) PLC, PHH Centre,
Windmill Hill, Swindon SN5 1PH,
01793 884424, Fax: 01793 886056,
Call Date: Nov 1994 (Inner Temple)
Qualifications: LLB (Swansea)

Tanner *Dr Mark*
Consultant Psychiatrist, Hertford County Hospital, North Road, Hertford, Call Date: Nov 1986 (Middle Temple) Qualifications: MB, BCh, Dip Law, MRC Psych

Tanner *Peter Christopher*
5 West View Close, Colchester CO4 4SP, 01206 844577, Fax: 01206 665831, Call Date: Feb 1990 (Gray's Inn) Qualifications: LLB [Essex]

Tanner *Miss Rachel Jane*
Call Date: Mar 1997 (Gray's Inn) Qualifications: LLB (Lond)

Tantam *Mark Andrew Howard*
Partner, Fraud Management, Deloitte & Touche, Chartered Accountants, Hill House, 1 Little New Street, London EC4A 3TR, 0171 936 3000, Fax: 0171 936 2638, Call Date: July 1982 (Inner Temple) Qualifications: MA (Oxon)

Tapiero *Ms Elena* •
Legal Advisor/Assistant, British Aviation Insurance, Group (Technical Services) Ltd, Fitzwilliam House, 10 St Mary Axe, London EC3A 8EQ, 0171 369 2244, Fax: 0171 369 2800, Call Date: Nov 1996 (Inner Temple) Qualifications: LLB (Lond), Maitrise in French, Law (Paris)

Tappin *Douglas Owen* •
Island Records Limited, 22 St Peters Square, London W6 9NW, Call Date: Oct 1993 (Lincoln's Inn) Qualifications: LLB (Hons)(Lond)

Tarling *Mrs Angela Bernadette Hardie*
Call Date: Oct 1990 (Gray's Inn) Qualifications: LLB (Hons), MA

Tarling *Miss Karen Joan* •
Essex County Council, Legal Services, County Hall, Chelmsford, Essex CM1 1LX, 01245 492211 Ext 20422, Fax: 01245 346994, Call Date: July 1991 (Gray's Inn) Qualifications: LLB

Tarling *Richard David* •
Assistant Director, EULER Trade Indemnity plc, 1 Canada Square, London E14 5DX, 0171 860 2753, Fax: 0171 729 7682, Call Date: Nov 1976 (Gray's Inn) Qualifications: LLB, ACIS.

Tarran *Ms Emma Rachel*
Call Date: July 1997 (Gray's Inn) Qualifications: LLB

Tate *William John* •
Legal Secretary, PO Box 18031, London EC3V 9JB, 0171 464 8767, Fax: 0171 464 8753, Call Date: July 1974 (Gray's Inn) Qualifications: LLB

Tatham *Allan Francis*
Call Date: Oct 1992 (Gray's Inn) Qualifications: BA (Dunelm), BCL (Dunelm)

Tattersall *Bruce*
Call Date: Oct 1997 (Middle Temple) Qualifications: MA (Edinburgh), CPE (Westminster)

Tausz *Mrs Dilys Kim*
Call Date: July 1974 (Inner Temple) Qualifications: LLB

Tawiah *James Kofi* •
Legal Adviser, 8 Bernwood House, Seven Sister Road, Woodbery Down, London N4 2RU, 0181 802 4065, Fax: 0171 690 5404, and Member Ghana Bar, Call Date: May 1960 (Lincoln's Inn) Qualifications: LLB(London)

Tayler *Mrs Keri* •
Southampton City Council, Southbrook Rise, 4-8 Millbrook Road East, Southampton SO15 1YG, 01703 833213, Fax: 01703 833217, Call Date: Feb 1995 (Inner Temple) Qualifications: LLB (Soton)

Taylerson *Anthony William Finlay*
Call Date: Apr 1951 (Lincoln's Inn) Qualifications: MA (Oxon)

Taylor *Adrian*
Former Lecturer in Law University of Hull, University of Kent, Call Date: July 1977 (Inner Temple) Qualifications: MA, LLB (Cantab)

Taylor *Miss Anne Bridget*
Deputy Chief Clerk, Inner London & City Family, Proceedings Court, 59/65 Wells Street, London W1A 3AE, 0171 323 1649, Fax: 0171 636 0617, Call Date: July 1976 (Middle Temple) Qualifications: LLB

Taylor *Arthur Rodney* •
Senior Pensions Lawyer, CGU Life, Pensions Legal, Six Hills Way, Stevenage, Herts SG1 2ST, 01438 732716, Call Date: Nov 1966 (Middle Temple)

Taylor *Christopher Paul* •
Litigation Counsel, Enviroment Agency, Kingfisher House, Goldhay Way, Orton Goldhay, Peterborough PE2 5ZR, 01733 464434, Fax: 01733 464487, 7 New Square, Lincoln's Inn, London, WC2A 3QS, Call Date: Oct 1990 (Lincoln's Inn) Qualifications: LLB (Hons)

Taylor *Dale James*
7 Birch Street, Hightown, Wrexham LL13 7AN, Call Date: July 1998 (Lincoln's Inn) Qualifications: LLB (Hons)(Keele)

Taylor *David Christopher*
Call Date: Oct 1998 (Lincoln's Inn) Qualifications: LLB (Hons)(L'pool)

Taylor *Miss Diana Folland*
Allen & Overy Solicitors, One New Change, London EC4M 9QQ, Call Date: Nov 1970 (Gray's Inn)

Taylor *Miss Helga June*
Call Date: Nov 1952 (Gray's Inn) Qualifications: LLB (L'pool)

Taylor *Howard*
Bench Legal Adviser, Northamptonshire Mags Court, Magistrates Court Office, Regents Pavilion, Summerhouse Road, Moulton Park, Northampton NN3 6AS, 01604 497001, Call Date: May 1988 (Gray's Inn)

Taylor *Howard Robert Frank*
Call Date: Nov 1995 (Inner Temple) Qualifications: LLB (Lond)

Taylor *Ian Russell* •
Group Barrister, Chequepoint, 85 Cromwell Road, London SW7 5BW, 0171 373 0111, Call Date: Mar 1998 (Gray's Inn) Qualifications: MA (Cantab)

Taylor *James Edward*
R D Black & Co, 31 Old Jewry, London EC2R 8DQ, 0171 600 8282, Fax: 0171 600 8228, and Member Bar of Western Australia, Call Date: July 1986 (Inner Temple) Qualifications: LLB Nottingham

Taylor *Mrs Jean Margaret*
Call Date: July 1998 (Gray's Inn) Qualifications: LLB (Manch)

Taylor *Ms Judith Hannah*
Call Date: Nov 1994 (Inner Temple) Qualifications: LLB (Lond), LLB (Hons)

Taylor *Julian Mark* •
Simmons & Simmons, 21 Wilson Street, London EC2M 2TX, Call Date: Oct 1994 (Gray's Inn) Qualifications: BA, Dip Law

Taylor *Miss Louise Alexandra Keats*
Text Editor, Butterworths, Call Date: Oct 1998 (Inner Temple) Qualifications: LLB (Sheff)

Taylor *Mark*
Call Date: Oct 1998 (Lincoln's Inn) Qualifications: LLB (Hons)(Leic), BSc

Taylor *Michael John* •
Deputy General Counsel, 1 Queen Caroline Street, London W6 9BN, 0181 600 1010, Fax: 0181 741 0851, Call Date: Feb 1986 (Gray's Inn) Qualifications: BA

Taylor *Michael John*
Call Date: Nov 1998 (Inner Temple) Qualifications: BA (Newcastle Upon, Tyne)

Taylor *Michael Joseph Fitz*
Kemp & Co, Sadlers House, Gutter Lane, London EC2V 6BR, 0171 710 1614, Fax: 0171 600 8989, Call Date: Nov 1996 (Middle Temple) Qualifications: BA ((Ons))

Taylor *Neil*
Recorder, Call Date: Jan 1949 (Inner Temple) Qualifications: MA (Oxon)

Taylor *Peter John Bernard*
Dearden Associates Limited, The Tower Trinity Centre, Bimport, Shaftesbury, Dorset SP7 8BW, 01747 854141, Call Date: Nov 1997 (Inner Temple) Qualifications: MBE, FICE, FCIArb,, CE

Taylor *Peter John Frederick*
Consultant & Construction Law Advisor, McCullers Zola, 28 Great Pulteney Street, Bath BA2 4BU, 01225 483583, Fax: 01225 315164, Included on FIDIC & ICE List of Arbitrators, Call Date: Nov 1979 (Middle Temple) Qualifications: C.Eng, FIStrE.FHKIE, FCIArb

Taylor *Peter William Edward*
also Lincoln's Inn, Call Date: Nov 1946
(Inner Temple) Qualifications: MA

Taylor *Richard Graham*
Call Date: Oct 1992 (Gray's Inn)
Qualifications: BA (Hons), MBA, Dip
Law

Taylor *Ross Clyde*
Call Date: July 1984 (Gray's Inn)
Qualifications: LLB (Lond)

Taylor *Simon Mark* •
Legal Advisor, Cable & Wireless
Communication, 26 Red Lion Square,
London WC1R 4HQ, 0171 528 2167,
Fax: 0171 528 2039, Call Date: Nov
1987 (Gray's Inn) Qualifications: BA
(Oxon), License Speciale en , droit
Europeen, (Brussels)

Taylor *Lieutenant Commander Stephen
John* •
Staff Legal Adviser, Flag Officer
Scotland,Northern, England, &
Northern Ireland, Bonaventure
Building, HM Naval Base Clyde
G84 8HL, Call Date: Oct 1996 (Middle
Temple) Qualifications: BA (Hons)
(York)

Taylor *Miss Susan Mary Edith* •
Branch Crown Prosecution, Crown
Prosecution Service, Central Casework,
50 Ludgate Hill, London EC4M 7EX,
0171 273 1232, Fax: 0171 329 8171,
Call Date: July 1980 (Middle Temple)
Qualifications: LLB (Leeds)

Taylor *Miss Teresa Dawn*
Call Date: Nov 1994 (Gray's Inn)
Qualifications: LLB

Taylor *Timothy John*
Call Date: Nov 1953 (Gray's Inn)

Taylor of Warwick *Lord*
9 Gough Square, London, EC4A 3DE,
Call Date: Feb 1978 (Gray's Inn)
Qualifications: BA (Hons)(Keele)

Teah *Mrs Jacqueline Mooi Hua* •
Call Date: Feb 1992 (Lincoln's Inn)
Qualifications: LLB (Hons) , LLM

Teasdale *Jonathan Paul*
Public Law Consultant, Bunkers
Solicitors, 7 The Drive, Hove, East
Sussex BN3 3JS, 01273 329797, Fax:
01273 324082, Past Vice Chairman Bar
Assoc for Local Govt & the Public
Service. Past Chairman Joint Practice
Management Working Party. Member
Administrative Law Bar Association.,
Call Date: July 1977 (Inner Temple)
Qualifications: LLB, ACIArb, FRSA,
Legal Associate RTPI

Teather *Mrs Maureen*
Legal Advisor, Derbyshire Magistrates'
Court, P O Box 11, The Court House,
West Bars, Chesterfield S40 1AE, 01246
278171, Fax: 01246 276344, Call Date:
May 1992 (Inner Temple)
Qualifications: LLB

Tegally *Mrs Assila Bibi*
Call Date: Oct 1992 (Lincoln's Inn)
Qualifications: LLB(Hons)

Tehal *Tanvir*
Call Date: Nov 1996 (Middle Temple)
Qualifications: LLB (Hons)

Telfer *Miss Fredelinda Jane*
Project Manager, Call Date: Feb 1995
(Middle Temple) Qualifications: Dip in
Stage , Management, LLB
(Hons)(Lond)

Telling *Arthur Edward*
Call Date: June 1949 (Inner Temple)
Qualifications: MA (Oxon)

Tempest *Alistair Mark*
Call Date: Oct 1997 (Middle Temple)
Qualifications: LLB (Hons)(Lond)

Tempest *Leonard*
Deputy Clerk to the Justices for
Leicestershire's Northern Divisions,
Leicestershire Magistrates Crt, 674
Melton Road, Thurmaston, Leicester
LE4 8BB, 01162 640920, Fax: 01162
692369, Call Date: Feb 1987 (Gray's
Inn) Qualifications: DML, DMS,
M.A.(Mgmt), 0

Temple *Matthew*
0171 388 2525, Call Date: Nov 1992
(Inner Temple) Qualifications: LLB
(Hons)

Teo *Miss Deav-Tieng*
Call Date: Nov 1995 (Middle Temple)
Qualifications: LLB (Hons)(Lond)

Teo *Miss May May* •
Lawyer (Grade 7), Office of the Social
Security, & Child Support
Commissioners, Harp House, 83-86
Farringdon Street, London EC4A 4DH,
0171 353 5145, Fax: 0171 936 2171,
Call Date: July 1989 (Middle Temple)
Qualifications: LLB

Terry *James* •
Principal Crown Prosecutor, Crown
Prosecution Service, Saxon House, 1
Cromwell Square, Ipswich, Suffolk
IP1 1TS, 01473 230332, Fax: 01473
231 377, Call Date: Nov 1981 (Gray's
Inn) Qualifications: LLB

Terry *Mrs Jennifer* •
Principal Crown Prosecutor, Crown
Prosecution Service, 50 Ludgate Hill,
London EC4, 0171 273 8305, Fax:
0171 329 8166, Call Date: Nov 1973
(Inner Temple) Qualifications: MSc,
LLB, Dip Soc Ad

Tester *John William Nielson* •
Assistant Secretary (Legal), Solicitors
Office, HM Customs & Excise, New
King's Beam House, 22 Upper Ground,
London SE1 9PJ, 0171 865 5212, Fax:
0171 865 5022, Call Date: July 1980
(Gray's Inn) Qualifications: LLB
(B'ham)

Tetsola *Miss Augustina* •
Crown Prosecutor, Crown Prosecution
Service, 3 Clifton Mews, Clifton Hill,
Brighton, East Sussex, Call Date: July
1988 (Lincoln's Inn) Qualifications:
LLB (Hons) (Essex)

Teuten *Miss Julie Helen* •
Assistant Counsel, Coutts & Co, 440
Strand, London WC2R 0QS, 0171 753
1820, Fax: 0171 957 2244, Call Date:
Nov 1990 (Middle Temple)
Qualifications: LLB

Tevlin *Aidan Matthew* •
Prosecution Team Leader, Crown
Prosecution Service, Justinian House,
Spitfire Close, Ermine Business Park,
Huntingdon Cambs PE18 6XY, 01480
432333, Call Date: July 1980 (Gray's
Inn) Qualifications: LLB (Leic),MA,
MPhil (CNAA)

Tew *Lieutenant Commander John
Philip* •
Command Legal Adviser, Flag Officer
Naval Aviation, Command Legal
Adviser, Flag Officer Naval Aviation,
FONA HQ, Yeovil, Somerset BA22 8HL,
01935 455503, Fax: 01935 455844,
Call Date: Oct 1993 (Lincoln's Inn)
Qualifications: BA (Hons), LLM

Thain *Derek Anthony Teague*
Hon Director, European Union Council
Secretariat, Woodlands, Bishop's Down
Park Rd, Tunbridge Wells, Kent
TN4 8XR, 01892 526372, Fax: 01892
538408, Call Date: Nov 1963 (Inner
Temple)

Thakkar *Mrs Sapna Niranjan*
Veja & Co Solicitors, Point West, Suite
503, 1040 Uxbridge Road, Hayes,
Middlesex UB4 0RJ, Call Date: Oct 1993
(Middle Temple) Qualifications: LLB
(Hons)

Thakrar *Miss Bijal*
Call Date: July 1996 (Middle Temple)
Qualifications: LLB (Hons)(Lond), LLM
(Keele)

Thalben-Ball *John Michael*
51 Lodge Close, Stoke D'Abernon,
Cobham, Surrey KT11 2SQ, 01932
863995, Call Date: Nov 1958 (Middle
Temple) Qualifications: MA (Cantab)

Thanki *Mrs Catherine Jane Margaret*
Call Date: Nov 1988 (Lincoln's Inn)
Qualifications: BA (Durham)

Thatcher *Miss Nichola Jane* •
Principal Legal Officer, Metropolitan
Police Service, New Scotland Yard,
Broadway, London SW1H 0BG, 0171
230 7339, Fax: 0171 230 7209, Call
Date: Nov 1992 (Inner Temple)
Qualifications: LLB (Hons)

Thatcher *Roger Francis* •
Senior Crown Prosecutor, Formerly a
solicitor, Call Date: Feb 1977 (Gray's
Inn) Qualifications: Dip Criminology

                      • Barrister in employment

Thavalou *Rajah Kulan*
Call Date: Nov 1996 (Middle Temple)
Qualifications: LLB (Hons) (Lond), MA
(Guildhall)

Theaker *Mrs Michele Lorraine* •
Legal Counsel, Genesys
Telecommunications, Laboratories
Europe Limited, Genesys House,
Mulberry, Business Park, Fishponds
Road, Wokingham, Berks RG41 2GY,
0118 974 7000, Fax: 0118 974 7001,
Call Date: Oct 1997 (Inner Temple)
Qualifications: LLB (Reading)

Thew *Mrs Stephanie Mary* •
Clerk to the Justices, The Magistrates
Court, Elm Street, Ipswich, Suffolk
IP1 2AP, 01473 217261, Fax: 01473
231249, Call Date: July 1973 (Middle
Temple) Qualifications: LLB

Thomas *Alan David*
Call Date: Oct 1996 (Inner Temple)
Qualifications: LLB (Lancs)

Thomas *Ms Belinda Jane* •
Government Lawyer, Investigations &
Enforcement Directorate, Dept. Trade &
Industry, Dept of Trade & Industry, 419
Victoria Buildings, 10 Victoria Street,
London SW1H 0NN, 0171 215 3214, Call
Date: Oct 1991 (Middle Temple)
Qualifications: BA Hons (B'ham), Dip
Law

Thomas *Miss Christina* •
Portsmouth City Council, Call Date: Feb
1994 (Inner Temple) Qualifications: LLB
(Wales)

Thomas *Miss Christine Margaret Mary*
Law Lecturer, Mitre House Chambers,
Mitre House, 44 Fleet Street, London,
EC4Y 1BN, Call Date: 1991 (Inner
Temple) Qualifications: LLB (Hons)

Thomas *David John*
Call Date: Nov 1996 (Gray's Inn)
Qualifications: BA, MPhil (Nott'm)

Thomas *Miss Deirdre Elizabeth Alice*
Call Date: July 1998 (Lincoln's Inn)
Qualifications: LLB (Hons) (Leics), BSc
(Hons)

Thomas *Hugh Vivian* •
Senior Attorney, Merrill Lynch Europe
Plc, Ropemaker Place, 25 Ropemaker
Street, London EC2Y 9LY, 0171 867
4451, Fax: 0171 867 4818, Call Date:
Nov 1986 (Lincoln's Inn) Qualifications:
LLB

Thomas *Ian Geoffrey*
Aviation Insurance Underwriter, Robert
Malatier Limited, 8-11 Lime Street,
London EC3M 7AA, 0171 623 4524, Fax:
0171 623 3648, Call Date: Nov 1991
(Middle Temple) Qualifications:
LLB,(Lond) FCII , ACIS

Thomas *Miss Janet Elfrida* •
Patterson Sebastian & Co Sols, Suite
226-227, 1 Olympic Way, Wembley,
Middlesex HA9 0NP, 0181 286 9430/
07971 755 059, Fax: 0181 286 9430,
Call Date: 1994 (Gray's Inn)
Qualifications: BA (Lancs)

Thomas *Jason Richard* •
Call Date: Oct 1996 (Lincoln's Inn)
Qualifications: BA (Hons) (Lond), LLB
(Hons) (City)

Thomas *Norman Edgar*
Sun Holm, 51 Cranford Avenue,
Littleham Cross, Exmouth, Devon
EX8 2QF, 01395 264802, Call Date: Nov
1956 (Lincoln's Inn) Qualifications:
BSc[Eng],MIEE, CEng

Thomas *Robert Gregory*
Guildhall Chambers, 23 Broad Street,
Bristol, BS1 2HG, Call Date: Apr 1991
(Gray's Inn) Qualifications: LLB

Thomason *Miss Ernitia Eileen*
Call Date: Oct 1998 (Inner Temple)
Qualifications: LLB (Reading)

Thomasson *Miss Claire Margaret Mary* •
Senior Crown Prosecutor, Crown
Prosecution Service, Cuthbert House, All
Saints Office Centre, Newcastle Upon
Tyne, 0191 232 6602, Call Date: Oct
1991 (Gray's Inn) Qualifications: BA
(Hons)

Thomlinson *Peter Robert* •
Legal Advisor, Mitsubishi Electric Europe
B.V, Travellers Lane, Hatfield, Herts
AL10 8XB, 01707 276100, Fax: 01707
278525, and Member Northern Ireland
Bar, Call Date: July 1981 (Lincoln's Inn)
Qualifications: BA, LLM

Thompson *Andrew Graham* •
Legal Technologies Limited, 126-134
Baker Street, London W1M 1FH, 0171
935 8242, Call Date: July 1998
(Lincoln's Inn) Qualifications: LLB
(Hons) (Anglia)

Thompson *Dennis*
8 Rue des Belles Filles, 1299 Crans, 022
7761687, Fax: 022 7767303, LI (ad
eundem), Call Date: Jan 1939 (Inner
Temple) Qualifications: MA (Cantab) ,
FCIArb (Ret'd)

Thompson *Miss Elizabeth*
Call Date: Mar 1997 (Middle Temple)
Qualifications: LLB (Hons) (E.Lond)

Thompson *Miss Elizabeth Joyce*
Call Date: July 1968 (Middle Temple)
Qualifications: BA (Hons)

Thompson *Mrs Paula Mary*
Call Date: July 1989 (Middle Temple)
Qualifications: LLB [Lond]

Thompson *Miss Pauline Sonita*
Call Date: July 1998 (Middle Temple)
Qualifications: LLB (Hons)

Thompson *Peter Kenneth James*
Call Date: Feb 1961 (Lincoln's Inn)
Qualifications: MA, LLB

Thompson *Ryan Jerome*
Call Date: Mar 1999 (Lincoln's Inn)
Qualifications: LLB (Hons) (Leeds)

Thompson *Miss Sharyn Anne* •
Senior Crown Prosecutor, Crown
Prosecution Service, Hawkins House,
Pynes Hill, Exeter, Devon EX2 5SS,
01392 422555, Fax: 01392 422111, Call
Date: July 1975 (Inner Temple)
Qualifications: LLB

Thompson *Stephen Julian*
Call Date: July 1998 (Gray's Inn)
Qualifications: LLB (Staffs)

Thompson *Thomas*
Construction disputes Consultant/
Arbitrator, Garth House, Evening Hill,
Thursby, Carlisle CA5 6PU, 01228
710688, Call Date: June 1958 (Middle
Temple) Qualifications: MA (Oxon),
ACIArb

Thomson *Eric Matheson*
Call Date: Feb 1957 (Gray's Inn)
Qualifications: BA

Thomson *Malcolm George*
Chairman Natioanl Health Services
Tribunal (Scotland) Member of Scottish
Legal Aid Board, 12 Succoth Avenue,
Edinburgh EH12 6BT, Scotland, 0131
337 4911, Fax: 0131 337 9100, QC
Scotland, Call Date: Apr 1991 (Lincoln's
Inn) Qualifications: LLB (Edin)

Thomson *Peter*
Church View, 1 Bullfield Close,
Greetham, Oakham, Rutland LE15 7NY,
01572 813132, Fax: 01572 813132, Call
Date: May 1966 (Middle Temple)
Qualifications: MA (Oxon)

Thomson *Ronald Christopher*
Call Date: Apr 1986 (Gray's Inn)
Qualifications: BA (Hons), FRICS,
ACIArb.

Thong *Miss Yen Hwa*
Court Clerk, Court House, Oldbury
Ringway, Oldbury, Warley, West Midlands
B69 4JN, 0121 511 2222, Fax: 0121 544
8492, and Member Malaysia Bar, Call
Date: July 1982 (Lincoln's Inn)
Qualifications: LLB (Law)

Thorley *Giles Alexander* •
Chief Executive, Retaillink Management
Limited, Mill House, Aylesbury Road,
Thame, Oxon OX9 3AT, 01844 262000,
Fax: 01864 261320, Call Date: Oct 1990
(Inner Temple) Qualifications: LLB
(Lond)

Thorn *Miss Sheryl Lorraine* •
Court Clerk, Norwich Magistrates Court,
The Court House, Bishopgate, Norwich,
Norfolk NR3 1UP, 01603 679500, Fax:
01603 663263, Call Date: Oct 1994
(Inner Temple) Qualifications: LLB
(E.Anglia)

Thorndycraft *Mr. Jason Victor Francis*
Call Date: July 1995 (Inner Temple)
Qualifications: LLB, LLM

Thorne-Johnson *Mrs Mary Ann*
Call Date: Nov 1987 (Lincoln's Inn)
Qualifications: LLB (Hons) (Lond)

Thornton *Alexander*
Call Date: Oct 1996 (Lincoln's Inn)
Qualifications: BA (Hons) (Cantab), MA
(Yale), Dip in Law (City)

Thornton *Miss Justine*
Simmons & Simmons, 21 Wilson
Street, London EC2M 2TX, 0171 628
2020, Call Date: Feb 1994 (Lincoln's
Inn) Qualifications: BA (Hons)

Thornton *Ms Sara Dawn* •
Call Date: Oct 1996 (Middle Temple)
Qualifications: BA (Hons) (Cantab),
CPE (City)

Thorpe *Harry* •
Legal Adviser Managing Director,
Juriscommerce Securities Ltd, 32-36
Bath Road, Hounslow TW3 3EF, 0114
233 2683, Fax: 0114 233 2683, Call
Date: Feb 1965 (Middle Temple)
Qualifications: MA (Oxon)

Thorpe *The Rt Hon John Jeremy*
2 Orme Square, London W2 4RS, 0171
727 8175, Fax: 0171 792 5950, Call
Date: Feb 1954 (Inner Temple)
Qualifications: MA (Oxon), LLB
(Hons) (Exon)

Thorpe *Richard David*
Call Date: Nov 1997 (Lincoln's Inn)
Qualifications: LLB (Hons) (Nott'm)

Thrower *Miss Alexandra Katherine*
Wales, Call Date: Oct 1997 (Middle
Temple) Qualifications: LLB
(Hons) (Keele)

Tibbitts *Mrs Susan Lesley Marilyn* •
Senior Attorney, Hewlett Packard Ltd,
Cain Road, Amen Corner, Bracknell,
Berkshire, 01344 362212, Fax: 01344
362224, Call Date: Nov 1977 (Lincoln's
Inn) Qualifications: LLB

Tickner *Ms Karen Sara* •
Hammersmith & Fulham, Legal
Services, Town Hall, King Street,
Hammersmith W6 9JU, 0181 748
3020, and Member New York, Call
Date: Nov 1992 (Middle Temple)
Qualifications: LLB (Hons, Manch),
BCL (Oxon)

Tilley *Miss Tina Suzanne*
Call Date: Nov 1997 (Lincoln's Inn)
Qualifications: LLB (Hons) (Lond)

Tillson *Mrs Judith Anne*
Call Date: Nov 1994 (Lincoln's Inn)
Qualifications: BA (Hons) (York), CPE
(Notts)

Timms *Howard Maurice Wainwright*
Swepstone Walsh, 9 Lincoln's Inn
Fields, London, Call Date: Nov 1992
(Inner Temple) Qualifications: LLB
(So'ton)

Timson *Corin James*
Call Date: Nov 1994 (Inner Temple)
Qualifications: BA (B'ham), CPE (City)

Tincey *Miss Nasreeen Akhter*
Call Date: Mar 1999 (Middle Temple)
Qualifications: LLB (Hons) (Herts)

Tingle *John Harold*
Reader in Health Law, Nottingham Law
School, Nottingham Trent University,
Burton Street, Nottingham NG8 5AY,
0115 9486045, Call Date: Nov 1979
(Gray's Inn) Qualifications: BA, Cert
Ed., MEd

Tippet *Vice Admiral Sir Anthony Sanders*
Chairman, Funding Agency for
Schools., Meadow Court, 95 Morton
Lane, East Morton, Keighley, West
Yorkshire BD20 5RP, 01274 510712,
Fax: 01274 510 807, Call Date: Apr
1959 (Gray's Inn) Qualifications: Hon
FICH, Hon FSBU

Tippet *Simon John* •
Manager, Corporate Affairs, Renault UK
Limited, Denham Lock, Widewater
Place, Moorhall Road, Harefield,
Middlesex UB9 6RT, 01895 827660,
Fax: 01895 827681, Call Date: July
1989 (Gray's Inn) Qualifications: BA
(Hull), Dip Law (CLP)

Tipping *John Alfred*
Call Date: Nov 1992 (Lincoln's Inn)
Qualifications: BSc (Lond), LLB
(Hons), FCA

Titchener *Alan John* •
Legal Advisor, Willis Corroon Group Plc,
Ten Trinity Square, London EC3P 3AX,
0171 488 8259, Fax: 0171 488 8882,
Call Date: Feb 1990 (Lincoln's Inn)
Qualifications: LLB Hons [Leeds]

Toal *Kieran Michael*
L'Attitude Sports Consultancy, Ltd, Lock
Keeper's Cottage, 9 Century Street,
Whitworth St West, Manchester
M3 4QL, 0161 832 3131, Fax: 0161
832 2333, Call Date: Mar 1998 (Gray's
Inn) Qualifications: LLB (Sheff)

Tobitt *Ms Linda Jean*
Contracts Advisor, Villiers House, Haven
Green, Ealing, London W5, 0181 231
9633, Call Date: Oct 1997 (Inner
Temple) Qualifications: LLB
(Wolverhampton)

Todd *Miss Bridget Louise*
Call Date: Oct 1996 (Gray's Inn)
Qualifications: LLB (Leeds)

Todd *Mrs (Joan) Hilary*
Court Clerk, Surrey Magistrates Courts
Comm, Secretariat Offices, Court
House, London Road, Dorking, Surrey
RH4 1SX, 01306 885544, Call Date: Nov
1967 (Middle Temple)

Todd *Miss Judith Ann*
Senior Lawyer, Call Date: Feb 1960
(Gray's Inn) Qualifications: LLB

Todhunter *Stephen Edward*
ILMCS, 65 Romney Street, London
SW1P 3RD, Call Date: Apr 1989
(Lincoln's Inn) Qualifications: LLB
(Lanc)

Toft *Nigel Timothy* •
Law Department, London Guildhall
University, 84 Moorgate, London EC2,
0171 320 1000, Call Date: Nov 1974
(Inner Temple) Qualifications: LL.M
(Lond)

Tolan *Anthony* •
General Manager, Legal Services
Department, Hitachi Europe Limited,
Whitebrook Park, Lower Cookham
Road, Maidenhead, Berkshire SL6 8YA,
01628 585000, Fax: 01628 585380,
Call Date: Nov 1974 (Lincoln's Inn)
Qualifications: BA

Tolland *Ms Anne Marie*
Senior Court Clerk, South Somerset
Magistrates Crt, Law Courts, Petters
Way, Yeovil, Somerset BA20 1SW,
01935 426281, Fax: 01935 431022,
Call Date: July 1988 (Lincoln's Inn)
Qualifications: LLB (Hons) Sheffield

Toman *Mrs Maria* •
Assistant Company Secretary Member
of Board of Visitors, HM YOI/RC
Reading, YWCA of Great Britain,
Clarendon House, 52 Cornmarket
Street, Oxford OX1 3EJ, Fax: 01865
204805, Call Date: Nov 1972 (Inner
Temple) Qualifications: LLB, MA

Toman *Vincent* •
Robin Thompson & Partners,
Wentworth House, Eastern Avenue,
Gantshill, Ilford, Essex IG2 6NH, 0181
554 2263, Fax: 0181 518 4819, Call
Date: Nov 1988 (Inner Temple)
Qualifications: LLB (Shef)

Tomkyns *Miss Patricia Yvonne*
Call Date: Oct 1998 (Lincoln's Inn)
Qualifications: BSc (Hons) (Surrey),
CPE (Middx)

Tomlin *Miss Adele Lisa*
Call Date: Oct 1996 (Inner Temple)
Qualifications: LLB (Warw)

Tomlinson *Bernard Thomas Bertram*
33 Palatine Road, London N16, Call
Date: Nov 1954 (Inner Temple)
Qualifications: MSc (Lond), ARCS

Tomlinson *Mark James*
Call Date: Oct 1998 (Lincoln's Inn)
Qualifications: LLB (Hons) (Keele)

Tompkinson *Miss Catherine Mary* •
Senior Principal Legal Officer, HM
Customs & Excise, Solicitor's Office,
New King's Beam House, 22 Upper
Ground, London SE1 9PJ, Call Date:
Feb 1985 (Middle Temple)
Qualifications: BA (Hons) (Lond) , Dip
Law

Tong *Ronny Ka Wah*
16th Floor, Temple Chambers, One
Pacific Place, 88 Queensway, Hong
Kong, 00 852 5232033, Fax: 00 852
8100302, QC Hong Kong and Member
Singapore Bar 4 Essex Court, Temple,
London, EC4Y 9AJ, Call Date: Nov 1974
(Middle Temple) Qualifications: BCL
(Oxon) LLB (HK)

Tong *Miss Tricia Min Wei*
43 Nim Green, and Member Singapore Bar, Call Date: July 1996 (Lincoln's Inn) Qualifications: LLB (Hons)(Lond)

Tonge *Andrew*
Commercial Litigation Lawyer, Horwich Farrelly, National House, St Ann Street, Manchester, 0161 834 3585, Fax: 0161 834 3630, Call Date: Oct 1995 (Inner Temple) Qualifications: LLB (Sheff)

Tooley *Michael Philip* •
Senior Crown Prosecutor, Crown Prosecution Service, 32 Scotland Street, Sheffield S1 2EH, 0114 291 2000, Fax: 0114 291 2050, Call Date: Nov 1982 (Gray's Inn) Qualifications: LLB (Reading)

Toon *Anthony Douglas*
Deputy Clerk to the Justices, Hampshire Magistrates Court, The Court House, Elmleigh Road, Havant, Hampshire PO9 2AL, 01705 492024, Fax: 01705 475356, Call Date: Nov 1982 (Gray's Inn) Qualifications: D.M.S.

Torrance *Guy*
Court Clerk, Chairman of Opera by Charabanc trading as 'Opera by Charabanc' Limited, Stockport Magistrates' Courts Committee, Edward Street, PO Box 155, Stockport SK1 3NF, 0161 477 2020, Fax: 0161 474 1115, Call Date: Nov 1988 (Middle Temple) Qualifications: LLB (LSE)

Torrington *John Raymond Lyon*
7 Hythe Place, New Gate Park, Sandwich, Kent CT13 0RB, 01304 615076, Call Date: Nov 1962 (Gray's Inn)

Towler *Lt Cdr Alison* •
Supply Officer, Supply Officer, HMS Norfolk, Call Date: Oct 1995 (Gray's Inn) Qualifications: B.Sc (Wales)

Townley *Miss Lynne*
Call Date: Oct 1996 (Middle Temple) Qualifications: LLB (Hons), LLM (B'ham)

Townsend *Miss Amanda Jane* •
Legal Advisor, The Legal Dept, Legal & General Assurance Grp, Legal & General House, Kingswood, Tadworth, Surrey KT20 6EU, Call Date: July 1995 (Lincoln's Inn) Qualifications: LLB (Hons)

Townsend *Peter Maurice*
Clerk to the Justices, Powys Magistrates' Court Comm, The Court House, Back Lane, Newtown, Powys SY16 2NJ, 01686 627150, Fax: 01686 628304, Call Date: July 1980 (Gray's Inn)

Townsend *Miss Stephanie Holly Bligh*
Call Date: Oct 1998 (Inner Temple) Qualifications: LLB

Tozzi *Miss Sarah*
Call Date: Oct 1998 (Inner Temple) Qualifications: LLB (Reading)

Tracey *Simon William*
Litigation Department, Titmuss Sainer Dechert, 2 Serjeant's Inn, London EC4Y 1LT, 0171 583 5353, Fax: 0171 353 3683, Call Date: Mar 1996 (Middle Temple) Qualifications: BA (Hons), MA (Cantab)

Tramboo *Abdul Majid*
Tramboo Partnership, 168a High Street, Hounslow, Middlesex TW3 1BQ, Scotland, 0181 570 6659, Fax: 0181 814 0862, Call Date: Nov 1980 (Lincoln's Inn)

Tranter *Gavin Andrew*
Call Date: Oct 1996 (Middle Temple) Qualifications: BA (Hons) (Cantab)

Travers *Michael Garry* •
Senior Crown Prosecutor, Crown Prosecution Service, Calder House, St James Street, Burnley, Lancashire, Call Date: July 1985 (Middle Temple) Qualifications: LLB (L'pool)

Travis *Ms Kendal*
Call Date: Oct 1997 (Gray's Inn) Qualifications: LLB (Lond)

Traynor *Miss Julie*
3200 Northwood Drive, [H]207-4, Concord, California 94520, Call Date: Nov 1993 (Lincoln's Inn) Qualifications: BSC (Cmnd), LLB, ARICS, ACIArb

Treanor *Stephen John*
Call Date: Oct 1997 (Gray's Inn) Qualifications: BSc (Notts)

Trefgarne *The Hon Mary Elizabeth* •
Assistant Director (Legal), Office of the Solicitor to the, the Departments of Health, and Social Security, New Court, Carey Street, London WC2A 2LS, 0171 412 1371, Fax: 0171 412 1440, Call Date: Nov 1971 (Gray's Inn)

Treherne *Miss Victoria Margaret* •
Deputy Company Secretary, Abbey National Treasury, Services plc, Abbey House, Baker Street, London NW1 6XL, 0171 612 4451, Fax: 0171 612 4319, Call Date: July 1979 (Gray's Inn) Qualifications: LLB (Hons)

Tremlett *Mrs Iona Alison*
35 Brockenhurst Gardens, Mill Hill, London NW7 2JY, 0181 959 0400, Call Date: Jan 1950 (Gray's Inn) Qualifications: BA, LLB (Manch), LLM (Lond)

Trenhaile *John Stevens*
Call Date: July 1972 (Middle Temple) Qualifications: MA (Oxon)

Trenton *Anthony Eric*
Associate, Solcitor Advocate (Higher Courts - Civil), Taylor Joynson Garrett, Carmelite, 50 Victoria Embankment, Blackfriars, London EC4Y 0DX, 0171 353 1234, Fax: 0171 936 2666, Solicitor, Call Date: Oct 1993 (Inner Temple) Qualifications: MA, CPE, Dip. in, Intellectual, Property

Treuherz *Timothy Daniel*
124 Kyverdale Road, London N16 6PR, 0181 806 1868, Call Date: Mar 1997 (Middle Temple) Qualifications: BSc (Hons)

Trew *John Alistair*
Call Date: Nov 1997 (Inner Temple) Qualifications: BA (Leeds), MICS, (Lond)

Trinder *Jeremy Alexander*
Solicitor, Lovell White Durrant, 65 Holborn Viaduct, London EC1A 2DY, 0171 236 0066, Fax: 0171 248 4212, Call Date: Oct 1996 (Lincoln's Inn) Qualifications: LLB (Hons)(Lond)

Trivess-Smith *Mrs Veronica*
Call Date: Oct 1995 (Middle Temple) Qualifications: LLB (Hons)

Trotman *Paul Edward*
Hugh James Solicitors, Merthyr Tydfil, Call Date: July 1988 (Gray's Inn) Qualifications: LLB (Cardiff)

Trounson *Richard Noy*
Lawyer, Dibb Lupton Alsop, 125 London Wall, London EC2Y 5AE, 0171 796 6318, Fax: 0171 796 6588, Call Date: Nov 1975 (Lincoln's Inn) Qualifications: MA (Oxon)

Trueman *Scott Andrew*
Call Date: Oct 1996 (Middle Temple) Qualifications: LLB (Hons)(Manc)

Trupke *Miss Isabella* •
UBS, Warburg Dhillon Reed, 1 Finsbury Avenue, London EC2M 2PG, Italy, Call Date: July 1998 (Inner Temple) Qualifications: LLB with German Law, (LSE)

Truscott *Miss Caroline*
Call Date: Nov 1998 (Lincoln's Inn) Qualifications: LLB (Hons)(LSE), BCL (Oxon)

Truss *Mrs Maureen* •
Principal Crown Prosecutor, Crown Prosecution Service, 10th Floor, Grosvenor House, Basing View, Basingstoke RG21 4RD, 01256 466722, Fax: 01256 840268, Call Date: July 1975 (Inner Temple)

Tsang *Dr Lincoln Ling Hong*
Principal Officer, Medicines Control Agency, Department of Health, 1 Nine Elms Lane, London SW8 5NQ, 0171 273 0465, Fax: 0171 273 0062, Call Date: Nov 1995 (Inner Temple) Qualifications: B.Pharm (Lond), PhD (B'ham), LLB (Lond)

Tubb *Mrs Elizabeth Janet Mary* •
Group Legal Adviser, Legal & General Group Plc, Temple Court, 11 Queen Victoria Street, London EC4N 4TP, 0171 528 6375, Fax: 0171 528 6220, Call Date: Nov 1989 (Middle Temple) Qualifications: LLB (Hons)

Tuck *Gordon Charles*
Call Date: Feb 1955 (Gray's Inn) Qualifications: LLB

Tucker *Miss Clare Elizabeth* •
Principal Crown Prosecutor, Crown
Prosecution Service, The Courtyard,
Lombard Street, Abingdon, Oxon
OX13 5SE, 01235 555678, Call Date:
July 1982 (Gray's Inn) Qualifications:
LLB

Tucker *Mrs Lorraine Jean* •
Principal Crown Prosecutor, Crown
Prosecution Service, Haldin House, Old
Bank Of, England Crt, Queen Street,
Norwich, Norfolk NR2 4SX, 01603
666491, Fax: 01603 617989, Call Date:
Nov 1982 (Middle Temple)
Qualifications: BA

Tudor *Anthony David* •
The Chartered Insurance, Institute, 20
Aldermanbury, London EC2V 7HY,
0171 606 3835, Fax: 0171 726 0131,
Call Date: Feb 1983 (Lincoln's Inn)
Qualifications: BA (Exon), LLB (Lond)

Tudor *Miss Carol*
Call Date: Oct 1996 (Inner Temple)
Qualifications: LLB (Manc)

Tueje *Miss Patricia*
Call Date: Mar 1999 (Inner Temple)
Qualifications: BSc (So'ton), CPE (City)

Tullo *Mrs Carol*
Controller, Her Majesty's Stationery
Office. Queen's Printer. Deputy
Director, Cabinet Office., St Clements
House, 2-16 Colegate, Norwich
NR3 1BQ, 01603 723012, Fax: 01603
723018, Call Date: July 1977 (Inner
Temple) Qualifications: LLB (Hons)

Tulloch *Mrs Gloria Veronica* •
Court Clerk, Bexley Magistrates Court,
Norwich Place, Bexleyheath, Kent
DA6 7NB, 0181 304 5211 X 128, Call
Date: Nov 1987 (Middle Temple)
Qualifications: LLB (London)

Tully *John James*
Call Date: Oct 1995 (Middle Temple)
Qualifications: LLB (Hons)

Tun *Alan* •
Compliance Officer, Paribas,
Compliance Department, 10 Harewood
Avenue, London NW1 6AA, 0171 595
2000, Fax: 0171 595 5093, Call Date:
July 1984 (Inner Temple)
Qualifications: BSc (Notts), LLB (Lond)

Tupper *Stephen Charles Preiswerk*
and Member New York Bar, Call Date:
Nov 1982 (Middle Temple)
Qualifications: LLB

Turfitt *Richard James Grenville* •
Legal Officer, Treasury Solicitor, Queen
Anne's Chambers, 28 Broadwayy,
London SW1, 0171 210 3283, Fax:
0171 210 3250, Call Date: Oct 1993
(Middle Temple) Qualifications: LLB
(Hons) (Kingston)

Turnbull *Miss Glenda* •
Magistrates Court Clerk (Trainee),
South East Northumberland,
Magistrates, The Law Courts,
Bedlington, Northumberland
NE22 7LX, 01670 531100, Fax: 01670
820133, Call Date: July 1998 (Gray's
Inn) Qualifications: LLB (Luton)

Turnbull *Graham Walter*
Forbes Chambers, 185 Elizabeth Street,
Sydney 2000, Australia, 02-93907777,
Formerly a Solicitor of the Supreme
Court of New South Wales and Member
New South Wales Bar 3 Hare Court, 1
Little Essex Street, London, WC2R 3LD,
Call Date: July 1990 (Gray's Inn)
Qualifications: BA, LLB

Turnbull *Mrs Linda Angela*
Call Date: Mar 1998 (Lincoln's Inn)
Qualifications: LLB (Northumbria)

Turner *Alan Richard* •
Legal Adviser, The British Petroleum Co
Plc, Britannic House, Finsbury Circus,
London EC2M 7BA, 01932 762887,
Fax: 01932 762381, Call Date: July
1992 (Inner Temple) Qualifications:
LLB (Hons) (Lond), BSc (Hons)
(Wales)

Turner *Christopher*
Call Date: Nov 1992 (Inner Temple)
Qualifications: LLB, LLM

Turner *Ms Deborah*
Legal Consultant, Hope House,
Maidford, Towcester, Northants
NN12 8HU, 01327 860997, Fax: 01327
860997, Call Date: Feb 1964 (Gray's
Inn) Qualifications: MA (Hons)
(Cantab), LLM (Warwick)

Turner *John Charles*
4 Brookside Manor, 240 Leigh Road,
Wimborne, Dorset BH21 2BZ, 01202
840502, Call Date: Nov 1989 (Gray's
Inn) Qualifications: LLB [Lond], DPA

Turner *Joseph Seymour Hume* •
Deputy Fleet Legal & Personnel Officer,
Commander in Chief Fleet, Eastbury
Park, Northwood, Middlesex HA6 3HP,
01923 837138, Fax: 01923 837090,
Call Date: Oct 1997 (Gray's Inn)
Qualifications: MA (Edin), Dip Law

Turner *Ms Nicola Gail*
Chubb Bulleid, 6 Farm Road, Street,
Somerset BA16 0EL, 01749 836100,
Call Date: Nov 1995 (Gray's Inn)
Qualifications: LLB (L'pool)

Turner *Nigel Stuart*
Call Date: Nov 1990 (Gray's Inn)
Qualifications: LLB (Hons) (B'ham)

Turner *Paul Antony*
Call Date: Nov 1998 (Lincoln's Inn)
Qualifications: LLB (Hons) (Sussex)

Turner *Miss Rowena M* •
Legal Manager, Panasonic UK Limited,
Panasonic House, Willoughby Road,
Bracknell, Berkshire RG12 8FP, 01344
853599, Fax: 01344 853727, Call Date:
Nov 1996 (Lincoln's Inn)
Qualifications: LLB (Hons) (Lond), LLM
(Wolv)

Turner *Mrs Shalimar Wilhelmina Varuna*
Scotland, and Member Trinidad &
Tobago Bar, Call Date: July 1985
(Lincoln's Inn) Qualifications: BSc
Zoology (Lond) , Dip Law, Graduate,
ICSA

Turner *Stephen Anthony John*
Call Date: Oct 1997 (Inner Temple)
Qualifications: LLB (Lond)

Turner-Samuels *David Jessel*
1A Arawak, The Towers, Westmoorings,
Trinidad, Trinidad, 0171 353 7613/00
1 868 632 4720, Fax: 0171 353 7613/
00 1 868 632 4720, and Member
Trinidad & Tobago Bar Antigua Bar
Cloisters, 1st Floor, Temple, London,
EC4Y 7AA, Call Date: May 1939 (Middle
Temple)

Turnill *James Lindsay* •
Crown Prosecutor, Crown Prosecution
Service, London Area, Horseferry Road
Branch, Portland House, Stag Place,
London SW1E 5BH, Call Date: Nov
1989 (Middle Temple) Qualifications:
BA Hons [York], Dip in Law

Turquet *Mrs Susan Jane*
Part-Time Chairman SSAT Tribunal,
Parking Adjudicator, Member of the
Parole Board, Call Date: July 1966
(Inner Temple) Qualifications: LLB,
AKC

Tuxford *Miss Emma-Jane* •
Senior Crown Prosecutor, Crown
Prosecution Service, Burnley Branch
Office, 2nd Floor, Calder House, St
James Street, Burnley, Lancashire
BB11 1XC, 01282 412298 X 172, Fax:
01282 458097, Call Date: Nov 1991
(Middle Temple) Qualifications: LLB
(Hons)

Tweeddale *Andrew Gavin*
Corbett & Co, Churcham House, 1
Bridgeman Road, Teddington,
Middlesex TW11 9AJ, 0181 943 9885,
Fax: 0181 977 3122, Call Date: Feb
1992 (Inner Temple) Qualifications:
LLB (Reading), MSc, Dip Arb, FCIArb

Tweeddale *Mrs Keren Danielle*
Eldon Chambers, Fourth Floor, 30/32
Fleet Street, London, EC4Y 1AA, Call
Date: Oct 1991 (Lincoln's Inn)
Qualifications: BA (Hons) (Lond)

Twort *Alastair Crampton* •
Senior Principal Legal Officer, Lord
Chancellor's Department, Royal Courts
of Justice, The Strand, London
WC2A 2LL, Call Date: July 1971 (Inner
Temple) Qualifications: LLB

Twycross-Hills *Ms Lorna Jane*
31 Eagle Heights, The Falcons, Battersea, London SW11 2LJ, Call Date: Feb 1991 (Gray's Inn) Qualifications: BA (Lond), LLB (Warw), ALCM

Tyler *Christopher Robin* •
Special Verications Assistant (Trade Marks), BAT, Export House, Cawsey Way, Woking, Surrey GU21 1YB, 01483 792385, Fax: 01483 792581, Call Date: Oct 1994 (Middle Temple) Qualifications: LLB (Hons) , M.Sc (Lond), MBCS

Tyler *Ms Elizabeth Osyth Eyre* •
Assistant Union Solicitor, National Union Students, Nelson Mandela House, 461 Holloway Road, London N7 6LJ, 0171 272 8900, Fax: 0171 263 5713, Call Date: Oct 1997 (Inner Temple) Qualifications: BA (York), CPE (De Montford)

Tyrer *Mrs Monica Jane*
Senior Lecturer in Law Thames Valley University, Randall's Cottage, Lower Road, Loosley Row, Princes Risborough, Bucks HP27 ONU, Call Date: Nov 1973 (Inner Temple) Qualifications: LLB, MA

Tyrrell *Simon James Walter* •
Legal Adviser, Lloyd's of London, One Lime Street, London EC3M 7HA, 0171 623 7100, Fax: 0171 623 8236, Call Date: Feb 1989 (Middle Temple) Qualifications: BA (Hons)

Uddin *Syed Afsor Hasan*
Call Date: May 1997 (Lincoln's Inn) Qualifications: LLB (Hons)(Lond)

Udeze *Ufondu Karuiki* •
Call Date: Oct 1995 (Inner Temple) Qualifications: LLB (Plymouth)

Uff *Keith* •
Assistant Director of the Legal Office of the University of Birmingham., Faculty of Law, Univ of Birmingham, PO Box 363, Birmingham, B15 2TT, 0121 414 3344, Fax: 0121 414 3971, Call Date: Nov 1969 (Gray's Inn) Qualifications: MA, BCL (Oxon)

Uhlmann *Miss Maria Anna* •
Principal Solicitor, London Borough of Newham, Legal Services, Town Hall, Barking Road, East Ham, London E6 2RP, Call Date: Nov 1982 (Lincoln's Inn) Qualifications: LLB

Umoren *Ms Aniekan* •
Call Date: July 1983 (Lincoln's Inn) Qualifications: BA (Hons) Law, MA

Underhill *Miss Caroline Patricia*
Legal Adviser, Avon & Bristol Law Centre, 2 Moon Street, Stokes Croft, Bristol BS2 8QE, 0117 924 8662, Fax: 0117 924 8020, Call Date: July 1982 (Gray's Inn) Qualifications: BSc (Hons)(Bris)

Underhill *Gareth Adam* •
Grade 7 Lawyer, Criminal Appeal Office, Royal Courts of Justice, Strand, London WC2A 2LL, 0171 936 6098, Fax: 0171 936 6900, Call Date: Oct 1995 (Lincoln's Inn) Qualifications: LLB (Hons)(Huddersf)

Unerman *Ms Sandra Diane* •
Grade 3, Department of the Environment,, Transport & the Regions, Great Minster House 1/06, 76 Marsham Street, London SW1, Call Date: July 1973 (Inner Temple) Qualifications: BA

Unwin *Paul Charles*
Thailand 20260, Call Date: July 1968 (Middle Temple) Qualifications: LLB (Hons)

Urquhart *Miss Jane Abigail*
Maxwell Batley, 27 Chancery Lane, London WC2A 1PA, Call Date: Nov 1994 (Middle Temple) Qualifications: BA (Hons)

Urquhart *Miss Mhairi Christine* •
Principal Crown Prosecutor, Crown Prosecution Service, The Cooperage, 8 Gainsford Street, Bermondsey, London SE1 1NG, 0171 962 2761, Fax: 0171 962 0902, Call Date: Nov 1984 (Gray's Inn) Qualifications: LLB (B'ham)

Usher *Richard Ian* •
Head of Group Legal Dept., A Meredith Jones & Co Ltd, Yorkshire House, 18 Chapel Street, Liverpool L3 9AG, 0151 236 3563, Fax: 0151 236 6699, Call Date: Oct 1996 (Gray's Inn) Qualifications: LLB (Hons), LLM (Sheff)

Uttley *Stephen Edward* •
Senior Crown Prosecutor, Crown Prosecution Service, Windsor House, 10 Manchester Road, Bradford BD5 0QH, 01274 742530, Call Date: Apr 1986 (Inner Temple) Qualifications: BA (Hons)

Uwemedimo *David Brian Okuma*
Campbell Hooper, 35 Old Queen Street, London SW1H 9JD, 0171 222 9070, Fax: 0171 222 5591, Call Date: July 1986 (Lincoln's Inn) Qualifications: BA, LLB

Vacy-Ash *Charles Gilbert* •
Manager Legal Affairs, Europe Ford Motor Company Limited Assistant Company Secretary; Ford Motor Company Limited Senior Attorney, Office of the General Counsel; Jaguar Cars Limited, Ford Motor Company Ltd, Eagle Way, Brentwood, Essex CM13 3BW, 01277 253000, Fax: 01277 252676, Jaguar Cars Limited, Browns Lane, Allesley, Coventry CV5 9DR Tel. 01203 202114 Fax. 01203 407150, Call Date: Nov 1972 (Middle Temple) Qualifications: Dip, Management , Studies

Vahey *Philip Thomas Anthony*
Clerk to the Justices, The Law Courts, P O Box 199, Christchurch Road, West Sussex BN11 1JE, 01903 534801, Fax: 01903 820074, Call Date: Nov 1986 (Inner Temple) Qualifications: MBA

Vaines *Peter Stephen*
J.P., Brebner Allen & Trapp, Chartered Accountants, The Quadrangle, 180 Wardour Street, London W1V 3AA, 0171 734 2244, Fax: 0171 287 5315, Call Date: July 1989 (Middle Temple) Qualifications: FCA, ATII

Vaizey *The Hon Edward Henry Butler*
Call Date: Oct 1993 (Middle Temple) Qualifications: BA (Hons)(Oxon), CPE (City)

Valansot *Miss Christiane* •
Legal Advisor, First Boston, Credit Suisse, One Cabot Square, London E14 4QR, 0171 888 8939, Fax: 0171 888 4251, Call Date: Nov 1989 (Middle Temple) Qualifications: BA

Valera *Miss Elizabeth* •
Senior Crown Prosecutor, Crown Prosecution Service, 1-9 Romford Road, Solar House, Stratford, London E8, 0181 534 6601, Fax: 0181 519 9690, Call Date: Oct 1991 (Middle Temple) Qualifications: BA Hons (Kent)

Vallat *Sir Francis Aime*
Call Date: Jan 1935 (Gray's Inn) Qualifications: BA,LLB (Cantab)

Vallera *Giovanni*
Call Date: Oct 1996 (Lincoln's Inn) Qualifications: LLB (Hons)(Cardiff)

Valley *Stanley John*
11 Park Row, Farnham, Surrey GU9 7JH, 01252 715840, Call Date: July 1966 (Middle Temple)

Valton *Miss Vernishia*
Call Date: Nov 1998 (Lincoln's Inn) Qualifications: LLB (Hons)(Warw)

Van Der Wal *Dominic Piet* •
Legal Officer, The Office of the Solicitor, DHSS, Sutherland House, 29-37 Brighton Road, Sutton, Surrey SM2 5AN, 0181 652 6184, Fax: 0181 652 6400, Call Date: Oct 1996 (Lincoln's Inn) Qualifications: LLB (Hons)(Lond)

Vantyghem *Julien Darren*
Senior Legal Adviser to the Justices, Birmingham District, Magistrates' Court, Victoria Law Courts, Birmingham, 0121 212 6600, Fax: 0121 212 6661, Call Date: Oct 1992 (Inner Temple) Qualifications: LLB

Varela *Miss Anna*
Call Date: Nov 1996 (Middle Temple) Qualifications: BA (Hons), Dip Law

Varley *Miss Lisa*
Call Date: Nov 1998 (Lincoln's Inn) Qualifications: LLB (Hons)(Teeside)

Varma *Satya Narayan*
44 Alanthus Close, Lee Green, London
SE12 8RE, 0181 852 0317, Call Date:
Feb 1963 (Gray's Inn) Qualifications:
ACIArb, Cert Ed

Varney *Philip*
Call Date: Oct 1996 (Middle Temple)
Qualifications: B.Ed (Brighton), M.Sc
(Staffs)

Vassis *Mrs Stacy Gemma Mary*
Call Date: Nov 1986 (Middle Temple)
Qualifications: BA, DipEd. (W. Aust),
Dip Law

Vaughan-Davies *Geoffrey*
'Ardmore', 13 Norfolk Avenue,
Sanderstead, South Croydon, Surrey
CR2 8AT, 0181 657 1449, Call Date:
June 1953 (Inner Temple)
Qualifications: MA (Cantab)

Vaz *Keith Anthony Standish*
144 Uppingham Road, Leicester
LE5 OQF, 0116 2122020, Fax: 0116
2122121, Former Solicitor, Call Date:
Nov 1990 (Gray's Inn) Qualifications:
MA (Cantab)

Vaz *Ms Maria Dolores*
Call Date: Oct 1998 (Gray's Inn)
Qualifications: BA (Warwick), LLB
(Lond)

Veen *Andrew Tavis*
In-House Counsel (Commercial
Litigation), Fenwick & Co, 125 High
Holborn, London WC1V 6QA, 0171 404
5474, Fax: 0171 831 5695, Call Date:
Nov 1993 (Middle Temple)
Qualifications: BA (Jnt Hons)

Veits *Peter John*
Clerk to the Justices, Lincolnshire
Magistrates Crt, The Court House, 358
High Street, Lincoln LN5 7QA, 01522
528218, Fax: 01522 560139, Call Date:
Oct 1985 (Gray's Inn)

Veljovic *Mark*
Call Date: Nov 1996 (Middle Temple)
Qualifications: LLB (Hons)(Lond)

Vencatachellum *Ms Glenda Roxande*
Call Date: Oct 1996 (Middle Temple)
Qualifications: LLB (Hons) (Keele)

Vening-Richards *Mrs Hilary Jane* •
Senior Crown Prosecutor, Crown
Prosecution Service, Princes Court,
York Road, Leicester, 0116 2549333,
Call Date: Nov 1990 (Middle Temple)
Qualifications: BA

Venkatasami *Kris* •
Senior Crown Prosecutor, Crown
Prosecution Service, Horseferry Road/
Thames Branch, 50 Ludgate Hill,
London EC4M 7EX, 0171 273 8028,
Call Date: July 1989 (Lincoln's Inn)
Qualifications: LLB (Hons) , MA

Venn *Mark Austin* •
Lawyer, Credit Suisse Financial Produc,
One Cabot Square, London E14 4QS,
0171 888 2000, Fax: 0171 888 2772,
Call Date: Nov 1991 (Middle Temple)
Qualifications: MA Hons (Cantab)

Venn *Robert Denis*
Call Date: July 1983 (Middle Temple)
Qualifications: LLB Lond

Venne *Roger Andre* •
Deputy Secretary of Commissions, Lord
Chancellor's Department, Selbourne
House, 54-60 Victoria Street, London
SW1E 6QW, 0171 210 8986, Fax: 0171
210 0660, Call Date: July 1972 (Gray's
Inn)

Ventrella *Antonio* •
Director of Legal Services, Concorde
House, Trinity Park, Bickenhill Lane,
Birmingham B37 7ES, 0121 782 2073,
Fax: 0121 782 2079, Call Date: July
1978 (Lincoln's Inn) Qualifications:
LLB (Sheff), MA (Lond)

Venturi *Gary Anthony*
Call Date: Oct 1996 (Middle Temple)
Qualifications: LLB (Hons)(City)

Venturino *Ms Anna Maria Alfonsina*
Call Date: Mar 1998 (Middle Temple)
Qualifications: BA (Hons), Dip Law

Vercoe *John Christopher William*
Baker & McKenzie, 8th Floor, 155 Abai
Avenue, Almaty, Call Date: Nov 1973
(Gray's Inn) Qualifications: LLB(Lond)

Verghese-Dipple *Mrs Mary*
In-House Lawyer, European Bank for,
Reconstruction & Development, One
Exchange Square, London EC2A 2EH,
Call Date: Nov 1991 (Lincoln's Inn)
Qualifications: LLB (Hons), MA
Business Law

Verghis *Mrs Kathryn Mary*
Principal Court Clerk, Justices' Clerks
Office, Hanworth Road, Feltham,
Middlesex TW13 5AG, 0181 890 4811,
Fax: 0181 844 1779, Call Date: Nov
1985 (Inner Temple) Qualifications:
LLB

Verghis *Mathew* •
Senior Legal Officer, The Inland
Revenue, Solicitor's Office, Somerset
House, The Strand, London WC2R 1LB,
0171 438 7083, Fax: 0171 438 6246,
and Member Malaysia Bar, Call Date:
Nov 1984 (Inner Temple)
Qualifications: LLB

Vernon *Ms Helen Sara Jane*
Call Date: Oct 1995 (Inner Temple)
Qualifications: BA , CPE

Vernor-Miles *Mrs Georgina Mary* •
Contracts Lawyer, International
Management Group, (UK) Ltd, Pier
House, Strand on the Green, Chiswick
W4 3NN, Call Date: Mar 1996 (Inner
Temple) Qualifications: BSc (Manch)

Vessey *Miss Gloria Clare*
Call Date: Oct 1996 (Middle Temple)
Qualifications: BA, MA (Lond), CPE

Vethanayagam *Maria Stanislas*
Call Date: Nov 1996 (Middle Temple)
Qualifications: LLB (Hons)(Lond)

Vickers *Andrew Robert*
Clerk to the Justices Justices Chief
Executive Kingston Upon Thames Petty
Sessions Area., Kingston Upon Thames
Court, 19 High Street, Kingston Upon
Thames, Surrey KT1 1JW, 0181 546
5603, Fax: 0181 974 5612, Call Date:
Nov 1987 (Gray's Inn) Qualifications:
BA (Lond)

Vickers *Paul Andrew* •
Company Secretary and Group Legal
Director, Mirror Group PLC, One
Canada Square, Canary Wharf, London
E14 5AP, 0171 293 3359, Fax: 0171
293 3360, Call Date: July 1983 (Inner
Temple) Qualifications: LLB (soton)

Vickery *Mrs Maeve Teresa* •
Group Employment Advisor, United
news & Media plc, Ludgate House, 245
Blackfriars Road, London SE1 9UY,
0171 921 5000, Call Date: Oct 1994
(Middle Temple) Qualifications: BA
(Hons)(B'ham), Dip in Law (City)

Victor-Mazeli *Miss Jacqueline*
0181 889 4967, Call Date: Nov 1997
(Middle Temple) Qualifications: LLB
(Hons)(Leeds), BA (Hons)

Vigar *Miss Amanda Adele*
Ernst & Young, Cambridge, Call Date:
Nov 1987 (Inner Temple)
Qualifications: LLB (Reading), ACA,
ATII

Vijh *Naveen Kumar*
Group Legal Adviser, Berwin Leighton,
Adelaide House, London Bridge,
London EC4R 9HA, 0171 623 3144,
Fax: 0171 623 4416, Call Date: Nov
1995 (Inner Temple) Qualifications:
LLB (Lond)

Villiers *Miss Theresa Anne*
Lecturer, King's College London,
Strand, London WC2R 2LS, 0171 836
5454, Fax: 0171 873 2465, 5 New
Square, 1st Floor, Lincoln's Inn,
London, WC2A 3RJ, Call Date: Nov 1992
(Inner Temple) Qualifications: LLB
(Hons, Bris), BCL (Oxon)

Vincent *Miss Claire*
Call Date: Nov 1993 (Middle Temple)
Qualifications: LLB (Hons)(Lond)

Vincent *Keith*
Call Date: Nov 1998 (Inner Temple)
Qualifications: LLB (LSE)

Vincent-Emery *Ms Bobbie Maureen
Mary* •
Senior Crown Prosecutor, Youth
Branch, CPS, The Cooperage, Gainsford
St, London SE1 2NG, 0171 962 2369,
Call Date: July 1984 (Middle Temple)
Qualifications: BA

Vinestock *Mrs Jacqueline Marion*
Call Date: Oct 1995 (Lincoln's Inn)
Qualifications: MA (Edinburgh), CPE (Notts)

Vitiello *Fabio Angelo-Giuseppe*
48 Beavers Lane, hounslow, Middlesex TW4 6EL, Call Date: Oct 1995 (Inner Temple) Qualifications: Dr Jur (Naples), CPE (Lond)

Vizard *Miss Diana Jane* •
Head of Commercial Legal Department, British Broadcasting Corp, Room 3664, White City, 201 Wood Lane, London W12 7TS, 0181 752 5523/5742, Fax: 0181 752 4750, Call Date: Nov 1977 (Middle Temple)

Von Achten *Miss Susan Jane*
Call Date: Oct 1992 (Lincoln's Inn)
Qualifications: LLB (Hons)(Sheff)

Von Pokorny *Thomas Laszlo*
01905 355221, and Member New Zealand Hong Kong Bar, Call Date: Feb 1959 (Middle Temple) Qualifications: LLB

Vos *Andrew Mitchell* •
UK Group Legal Adviser, Sema Group UK Ltd, Fulcrum House, 2 Killick Street, London N1 9AZ, 0171 830 4213, Fax: 0171 830 4206, Call Date: July 1978 (Gray's Inn) Qualifications: MA Hons (Cantab)

Vose *Martin*
Principal Court Clerk, City of London Magistrates', Courts Committee, No.1 Queen Victoria Street, London EC4M 4XY, 0171 260 1185, Fax: 0171 260 1493, Call Date: July 1983 (Inner Temple) Qualifications: LLB(Hons) Kings Coll, London

Waddington *Lord*
Recorder, 2 Pump Court, 1st Floor, Temple, London, EC4Y 7AH, Call Date: June 1951 (Gray's Inn) Qualifications: BA

Wade *David Anthony*
Arbitrator: Insurance, Financial Services, Solicitors Panels, Professional Negligence, SFA & ABTA, Roman Way, Benenden, Kent TN17 4ES, 01580 241873, Call Date: Feb 1959 (Inner Temple) Qualifications: FCI Arb

Wade *Mrs Vyvienne Yvonne Alexandra* •
Group Legal Director, Jardine Lloyd Thompson Group, Plc, Jardine House, 6 Crutched Friars, London EC3N 2HT, 0171 528 4151, Fax: 0171 528 4432, Call Date: July 1984 (Inner Temple) Qualifications: LLB (Hons)(Reading)

Wadham *Vivian Anthony*
p/t Chairman of Social Security Appeals Tribunals, Rose Farm, Barton, Malpas, Cheshire SY14 7HU, 01829 782 396, Fax: 01829 782 107, and Member Barrister & Solicitor, Victoria, Australia Advocate of Brunei Darus Salam, Call Date: June 1955 (Gray's Inn) Qualifications: MA (Oxon)

Wadhams *Matthew Lee*
Call Date: Nov 1997 (Lincoln's Inn)
Qualifications: BA (Hons)

Wagner *Miss Juliette Gabrielle*
Call Date: Mar 1996 (Gray's Inn)
Qualifications: LLB

Wagstaff *David St John Rivers*
Call Date: July 1954 (Lincoln's Inn)
Qualifications: MA, LLB (Cantab)

Wagstaff *Matthew Edward* •
Legal Officer, H M Customs & Excise, New Kings Beam House, 22 Upper Ground, London SE1 9PJ, 0171 865 5427, Fax: 0171 865 5461, Call Date: Oct 1993 (Lincoln's Inn) Qualifications: LLB (Hons)(E.Ang)

Wain *Miss Clare Louise*
Call Date: July 1998 (Gray's Inn)
Qualifications: BA (Coventry)

Waite *William Francis* •
European Regional Counsel and Head of Corporate Investigations Board Member - American Corporate Counsel Association - Europe, Kroll Associates UK Ltd, 25 Saville Row, London W1X 0AL, 0171 396 0000, Fax: 0171 396 9966, Call Date: Nov 1984 (Middle Temple) Qualifications: LLB (E Anglia), LLM

Wakefield *Gavin Jonathan* •
Legal Advisor, Dun & Bradstreet Ltd, Holmers Farm Way, High Wycombe, Bucks HP12 4UL, 01494 423413, Fax: 01494 423551, Call Date: Oct 1992 (Inner Temple) Qualifications: LLB (Warw)

Wakefield *James Alan George* •
The Lawyers Christian, Fellowship, 97 High Road, Beeston, Nottingham NG9 2LH, 0115 9255335, Fax: 0115 9431222, Call Date: Nov 1993 (Lincoln's Inn) Qualifications: BA (Hons, Keele)

Wakeford *Geoffrey Michael Montgomery*
Call Date: Feb 1961 (Gray's Inn)
Qualifications: MA, LLB (Cantab)

Wakeham *Mrs Jane Elizabeth*
Managing Director, Surrey Roll Leaf Ltd, Castleham Road, St Leonards on Sea, East Sussex TN38 9NS, 01424 775769, Fax: 01424 775769, Call Date: Nov 1984 (Middle Temple) Qualifications: LLB (Lond)

Walcott *Stephen John*
Call Date: Oct 1998 (Middle Temple)
Qualifications: BSc (Hons)(Herts)

Walder *Kenneth James Mowbray* •
Directorr of Operations and Chief Legal Adviser BAIG (Technical Services) Ltd, 109a Onslow Square, London SW7 3LU, 0171 369 2731, Fax: 0171 369 2800, Call Date: July 1966 (Gray's Inn)

Waldon *Bernard Samuel*
Call Date: July 1966 (Gray's Inn)
Qualifications: MA [Cantab]

Waldron *Miss Kay* •
Legal Adviser/Representive, West Glamorgan County Council, County Hall, Swansea, 01792 471111, Call Date: Nov 1989 (Inner Temple) Qualifications: LLB

Walford *Justin Hugh* •
Legal Advisor, Legal Department, Express Newspapers Plc, 245 Blackfriars Road, London SE1 9UX, 0171 922 7785, Fax: 0171 922 7967, Call Date: July 1981 (Inner Temple) Qualifications: BA Hons (Sussex)

Walker *Andrew Viersen* •
Crown Prosecution Service, Brighton, Sussex, Call Date: Nov 1987 (Inner Temple) Qualifications: BA, Dip Law (City)

Walker *Miss Charlotte Louise*
Call Date: Oct 1998 (Middle Temple)
Qualifications: BA (Hons)(York)

Walker *Miss Debra Dorothy*
Deputy Chief Clerk, Inner London Magistrates', Courts Service, 65 Romney Street, London SW1P 3RD, 0171 799 3332, Call Date: May 1990 (Inner Temple) Qualifications: LLB

Walker *Miss Diana Kate*
Call Date: Nov 1998 (Middle Temple)
Qualifications: LLB (Hons)(Sheff)

Walker *Miss Hazel Louise* •
Company Secretary & Director of Legal Services, Southern Electric plc, Southern Electric House, Westacott Way, Littlewick Green, Maidenhead, Berks SL6 3QB, 01628 822166, Call Date: Nov 1982 (Gray's Inn) Qualifications: BA (Hons)

Walker *Miss Jill Christine Vezey* •
Senior Legal Assistant, Lord Chancellor's Department, Office of Social Security, Commissioners, Harp House, 83-86 Farringdon Street, London EC4A 4BL, 0171 353 5145, Fax: 0171 936 2171, Call Date: Nov 1970 (Middle Temple) Qualifications: LLB (Hons, Lond)

Walker *Matthew Robert Michael* •
Canary Wharf Contractors Ltd, 1 Canada Square, Canary Wharf, London E14 5AB, 0171 418 2000, Fax: 0171 418 2222, Call Date: Oct 1997 (Lincoln's Inn) Qualifications: LLB (Hons)(Lond)

Walker *Miss Muriel Maud Florence Goldsmith*
10 The Meadows, West Rainton, Houghton-Le-Spring, Tyne & Wear DH4 6NP, Call Date: May 1936 (Lincoln's Inn)

Walker *Murray*
Assistant Branch Secretary & Compliance Officer, Assicurazioni Generali Spa, United Kingdom Branch, 117 Fenchurch Street, London EC3M 5DY, 0171 488 0733, Fax: 0171 481 0745, Call Date: Nov 1985 (Lincoln's Inn) Qualifications: LLB Hons [Reading]

E

Walker *Peter Maxwell* •
Vice President-Finance, E.C. Datacom
Limited, Linburn House, 342 Kilburn
High Road, London NW6 2QJ, 0171 624
6054, Fax: 0171 372 7087, Call Date:
July 1977 (Lincoln's Inn)
Qualifications: LLB (Lond), FFA, FIAB,
MISM

Walker *Robert Greenhalgh*
12 Wilfred Street, Hamilton, Call Date:
July 1972 (Lincoln's Inn)

Walker *Miss Suzanne Jayne*
Call Date: July 1998 (Lincoln's Inn)
Qualifications: LLB (Hons)(Bris)

Walker *Mrs Wei Hong*
14 Claremont Park, Finchley, London
N3 1TH, 0181 522 5000, Fax: 0181 519
9214, Call Date: July 1988 (Lincoln's
Inn) Qualifications: BA (Hons)
Newcastle, Dip Law

Walker *William Henry*
Call Date: Feb 1961 (Gray's Inn)
Qualifications: LLB (Lond)

Walklate *Mrs Rebecca Christine* •
Legal Advisor, Messrs Hibbert Durrad
Davies, 25 Barker Street, Nantwich,
Cheshire CW5 5EN, 01270 624225,
Fax: 01270 628065, Call Date: July
1995 (Inner Temple) Qualifications:
LLB (Staffs)

Walkling *Miss Helen Kay* •
HM Customs & Excise, Call Date: Nov
1995 (Lincoln's Inn) Qualifications:
LLB (Hons)

Wall *Ian Laurence*
Call Date: Nov 1994 (Inner Temple)
Qualifications: LLB

Wallace *Alasdair Willaim McKinnon* •
Head of International & Common Law
Services Division, Lord Chancellor's
Department, Legal Adviser's Group,
Selborne House, London SW1E 6QW,
Call Date: July 1985 (Gray's Inn)
Qualifications: MA, LLM

Wallace *Derek Earl*
Call Date: Mar 1999 (Gray's Inn)
Qualifications: LLB (Warw)

Wallace *Miss Janet Mary* •
6 Agar Street, London WC2N 4HR, Call
Date: Nov 1963 (Middle Temple)

Wallace *John Francis Newlyn* •
Court Clerk, Richmond Magistrates
Court, Parkshot, Richmond, Surrey,
0181 948 2101, Call Date: July 1989
(Gray's Inn) Qualifications: BA (Hons)
Law

Wallace *Philip Christopher* •
Investment Management, Regulatory
Organisation, Lloyds Chambers, 1
Portsoken Street, London E1 8BT, 0171
390 5717, Fax: 0171 480 5846, Call
Date: Nov 1994 (Gray's Inn)
Qualifications: BA (Exon)

Wallbank *Gerhard Henry Anthony*
and Member New Zealand, Call Date:
Nov 1990 (Lincoln's Inn)
Qualifications: LLB, LLM (UCL)

Walledge *Christopher Rowan*
The Magistrates' Court, Union Street,
Torquay, Devon TQ1 2BP, 01803
202202, Fax: 01803 202200, Call Date:
Feb 1995 (Inner Temple)
Qualifications: LLB (Exeter)

Waller *Miss Katherine Wendy Ann*
Cheltenham District Citizens, Advice
Bureau, Legal Sus, 14 Royal Crescent,
Cheltenham GL50 3DA, 01242 583028,
Fax: 01242 228801, Call Date: July
1998 (Middle Temple) Qualifications:
BA (Hons), Dip Law

Wallington *Andrew David* •
Senior Crown Prosecutor, Crown
Prosecution Service, Bristol Branch,
2nd Floor, Froomsgate House, Rupert
Street, Bristol BS1 2QJ, 0117 9273093,
Call Date: Nov 1993 (Inner Temple)
Qualifications: BA, CPE

Wallis *Dominic Laurence Carden*
Call Date: Nov 1992 (Gray's Inn)
Qualifications: BA

Wallis *Mrs Sarah Elizabeth*
Call Date: Nov 1997 (Middle Temple)
Qualifications: BA (Hons)

Wallis *Timothy James*
Director (Designate), Bachmann Trust
Co UK Ltd, Grenville Court, Britwell
Road, Burnham, Bucks SL1 8DF,
01628 666916, Fax: 01628 661532,
Call Date: July 1979 (Gray's Inn)
Qualifications: BA

Walmsley *Keith*
The Mentor Partnership, Vulcan House,
Restmor Way, Hackbridge, Surrey
EC4Y 0HP, 0181 773 8123, Call Date:
July 1972 (Gray's Inn) Qualifications:
LLB (Lond), FCIS

Walmsley *Peter Matthew*
Call Date: Nov 1995 (Middle Temple)
Qualifications: LLB (Hons)

Walsh *Bernard David James*
The Old Rectory, Burgate, Diss, Norfolk
IP22 1QD, 01379 783278, Call Date:
Nov 1952 (Inner Temple)

Walsh *Darren Stephen*
Call Date: Oct 1997 (Inner Temple)
Qualifications: LLB (Staffordshire)

Walsh *Ms Elizabeth* •
Legal Adviser, Office of
Telecommunications, 50 Ludgate Hill,
London EC4M 7JJ, 0171 634 8856, Fax:
0171 634 8975, Call Date: July 1987
(Gray's Inn) Qualifications: BA
(Hons)(Cantab), LLM

Walsh *Francis*
Carraroe, 1 Polefield Road, Blackley,
Manchester M9 6FN, 0161 740 5788,
Call Date: July 1972 (Lincoln's Inn)
Qualifications: LLB, LLM (Lond), FCA,
FCCA, FCMA, FCIS, FTII

Walsh *Graham*
Call Date: Nov 1992 (Inner Temple)
Qualifications: BChD LDS (Leeds), LLB
(Leeds)

Walsh *Gregory Francis Andrew* •
Legal Adviser, Royal Insurance plc,
P.O.Box 30, New Hall Place, Liverpool
L69 3HS, 0151 239 4775, Fax: 0151
239 3360, Call Date: Feb 1991
(Lincoln's Inn) Qualifications: LLB
(L'pool)

Walsh *Ms Greta Margaret Breda* •
C/O Crown Prosecution Service, 50
Ludgate Hill, London EC4M 7EX, Call
Date: Nov 1986 (Middle Temple)
Qualifications: BCL (Dub)

Walter *Philip Lewis*
2 Field Court, Gray's Inn, London,
WC1R 5BB, Call Date: July 1975 (Inner
Temple) Qualifications: MA (Cantab)

Walters *Miss Dinah Mary* •
Crown Prosecution Service, County
House, County Square, New London
Road, Chelmsford, Essex CM2 0RG,
01245 252939, Fax: 01245 490476,
Call Date: Nov 1981 (Gray's Inn)
Qualifications: LLB (B'ham)

Walters *Sir Donald*
Chairman Council of Welsh Library and
Information Services, 120 Cyncoed
Road, Cardiff CF2 6BL, 01222 753166,
Fax: 01222 759515, Call Date: Nov
1946 (Inner Temple) Qualifications:
LLB

Walters *Mrs Kathryn Ann* •
p/t Court Clerk, Call Date: Nov 1981
(Gray's Inn) Qualifications: BSc

Walters *Kevin Frank*
Magnolia House, Winchester Hill,
Romsey, Hamshire S051 7NL, 01794
512710, Call Date: July 1975 (Inner
Temple) Qualifications: MA FCIS FIPD

Walters *Richard Fraser* •
Assistant Solicitor of Inland Revenue,
The Inland Revenue, Solicitor's Office,
Somerset House (East Wing), The
Strand, London WC2R 1LB, 0171 438
7286, Fax: 0171 438 7550, Call Date:
Nov 1977 (Inner Temple)
Qualifications: LLB (Hons), MA, Dip in
EC Law

Walters-James *Leigh Martin*
Call Date: Oct 1996 (Lincoln's Inn)
Qualifications: BA (Hons)(Lond), CPE

Walton *Andrew David* •
Vice President & Legal Counsel, Morgan
Stanley, 25 Cabot Square, London
E14 4QA, 0171 425 8908, Fax: 0171
425 8971, Call Date: Nov 1986 (Inner
Temple) Qualifications: BA,LLM

Walton *Derek Antony Ruffel* •
Assistant Legal Adviser, Switzerland,
Call Date: Nov 1989 (Lincoln's Inn)
Qualifications: MA, LLM (Cantab)

Walton *John Lawson* •
Evington Corporation, Ltd, Evington House, Smalldale, Bradwell, Hope Valley S33 9JQ, 01433 621599, Fax: 01433 621544, Call Date: Nov 1970 (Gray's Inn)

Wan *Mrs Sally Elizabeth*
Lawyer, Call Date: Oct 1991 (Middle Temple) Qualifications: BSc (Brunel) (Hons), MBA, DipM

Wanduragala *Miss Louise-Marie Randini*
21 Holden Road, North Finchley, London N12 8HP, 0181 445 4614, and Member Gibraltar Bar, Call Date: Nov 1984 (Gray's Inn) Qualifications: LLB (Aberystwyth)

Warburton *John Kenneth*
35 Hampshire Drive, Birmingham B15 3NY, 0121 454 6764, Formerly Director General, Birmingham Chamber of Commerce & Industry, Call Date: Feb 1977 (Gray's Inn) Qualifications: MA, Cedr Accredited , Mediator

Warburton *Paul Richard*
Call Date: Mar 1998 (Lincoln's Inn) Qualifications: LLB (Hons)

Ward *Anthony Desborough*
Call Date: Oct 1994 (Gray's Inn) Qualifications: MA, MSc

Ward *Benjamin William*
Editor in Chief. American Language Review. Publisher Arch Law., 8383 Wilshire Boulevard, Suite 360, Beverley Hills, California 90211, 213 658 7620, Fax: 213 658 7530, Call Date: Nov 1994 (Gray's Inn) Qualifications: BA (Manch), MA (Lond)

Ward *Mr Brian Stanley*
Nottingham Law School, Nottingham Trent University, Nottingham, 0115 9418418, Fax: 0115 9486489, Call Date: Feb 1988 (Lincoln's Inn) Qualifications: BA (Hons) Keele, PGCE

Ward *Miss Claire* •
Principal Crown Prosecutor, Call Date: July 1985 (Lincoln's Inn) Qualifications: LLB (Hons)

Ward *George Arthur*
38 Arlington Square, London N1 7DP, Call Date: July 1973 (Inner Temple) Qualifications: BA

Ward *Ian Robert*
Legal Adviser, Ministry of Defence, Room 4107, Main Building, Whitehall, London SW1A 2HB, Call Date: Nov 1981 (Middle Temple) Qualifications: BA LLB (Cantab), LLM (UBC)

Ward *Squadron Leader John Harold*
Half Acre, Ampney Crucis, Cirencester, Glos GL7 5RY, 01285 851323, Call Date: July 1946 (Inner Temple)

Ward *Marcus Daniel Wright* •
Business Development Manager, The Princes Trust Volunteers, 18 Park Square East, London NW1 4LH, 0171 251 2696 ext 107, Call Date: Oct 1996 (Lincoln's Inn) Qualifications: LLB (Hons)(Newc)

Ward *Ms Orla Mary*
Call Date: Oct 1996 (Gray's Inn) Qualifications: BA (Cantab)

Ward *Peter Graham*
Director of Corporate Services, Victoria Law Courts, Corporation Street, Birmingham B4 6QA, 0121 212 6622, Fax: 0121 236 7837, Call Date: Nov 1987 (Lincoln's Inn) Qualifications: LLB, DMS

Ward *Russell* •
Elf Aquitaine Gas UK Ltd, 59 Markham Street, Chelsea, London SW3 3NR, Call Date: Oct 1992 (Middle Temple) Qualifications: B.Sc (Hons,Bradford), MA (Hons, Cantab)

Ward *Ms Susan Mary* •
General Counsel P/t Immigration Appeals Adjudicator & Special Adjudicator, APACS, Mercury House, Triton Court, 14 Finsbury Square, London EC2A 1BR, 0171 711 6216, Fax: 0171 711 6276, Barrister of NSW & High Court of Australia and Member New South Wales Bar, Call Date: July 1976 (Inner Temple) Qualifications: LLB (Bristol) (Hons), Dip M

Ward *Vincent*
Lecturer in Law, University of Northumbria at, Newcastle, Sutherland Building, Newcastle Upon Tyne NE1 8ST, 0191 227 4494, Fax: 0191 227 4557, Call Date: July 1998 (Middle Temple) Qualifications: LLB (HOns)(N'castle)

Ware *Michael John*
Chairman, Meat Hygiene Appeals Tribunal for England & Wales, 12 Hill Road, Haslemere, Surrey GU27 2JN, 01428 644699, Call Date: Feb 1955 (Middle Temple) Qualifications: BA, LLB

Wareham *Gerard* •
Crown Prosecutor, Crown Prosecution Service, Portland House, Stag Place, Victoria, London SW1E 5BH, Call Date: July 1988 (Gray's Inn) Qualifications: BA

Wareham *Mrs Tracey Anne* •
Prosecution Team Leader, Crown Prosecution Service, Queen's House, Victoria Street, St Albans AL1, 01727 818100, Call Date: Nov 1987 (Gray's Inn) Qualifications: LLB (Wales)

Warhurst *Keith*
Call Date: July 1996 (Gray's Inn) Qualifications: LLB

Waring *Thomas*
Legal Affairs Adviser to H M Government of Brunei Darussalam, Call Date: Feb 1965 (Gray's Inn)

Warland *Christian Geoffery Lougheed*
Clifford Chance, 200 Aldersgate Street, London EC1A 4JJ, 0171 600 1000, Fax: 0171 600 5555, Call Date: Nov 1993 (Middle Temple) Qualifications: BA (Hons)(Exon), CPE

Warman *Andrew Cecil James* •
Senior Crown Prosecutor, Crown Prosecution Service, Bromfield House, Ellice Way, Wrexham Technology Park, Wrexham, Clwyd, 01978 312002, Fax: 01978 311960, Call Date: Feb 1994 (Inner Temple) Qualifications: BSc (Wales), CPE

Warnford-Davis *John David*
Hill Barn, Hailey, Ipsden, Wallingford, Oxon OX10 6AD, 01491 681655, Fax: 01491 681203, Call Date: Nov 1954 (Gray's Inn)

Warnsby *Grant Darren*
Call Date: May 1997 (Lincoln's Inn) Qualifications: BA (Hons)(Keele)

Warren *James*
Call Date: Nov 1996 (Middle Temple) Qualifications: BSc (Econ)(Wales)

Warren *John Benton* •
Principal Crown Prosecutor, Crown Prosecution Service, Fifth Floor, Chartist Tower, Dock Street, Newport, Gwent NP9 1DW, Call Date: Nov 1978 (Gray's Inn) Qualifications: LLB (Soton)

Warrick *Paul Terence Philip* •
Law Office of Paul Warrick, 7 Hobury Street, London SW10 0JD, 0171 795 1122, Fax: 0171 823 3007, Call Date: July 1972 (Inner Temple) Qualifications: BL

Wasley *Julian Mark*
Call Date: Oct 1996 (Lincoln's Inn) Qualifications: LLB (Hons)(Wales)

Wass *Andrew Paul*
Call Date: July 1986 (Middle Temple) Qualifications: BA (Notts) Dip Law, (City)

Wasserson *Rodney Bernard*
Deputy Chief Clerk, Inner London Magistrates', Courts Service, 65 Romney Street, London SW1P 3RD, Call Date: Nov 1970 (Lincoln's Inn) Qualifications: BA (Rhodes), LLB (Edin)

Wasunna *Miss Karen Jane*
Call Date: Oct 1998 (Gray's Inn) Qualifications: LLB (London)

Waters *Conrad Alexis*
Senior Credit Analyst, Bank of Tokyo - Mitsubishi, The Bank of Tokyo - Mitsubishi, limited, Finsbury Circus House, 12-15 Finsbury Circus, London EC2M 7BT, 0171 577 1228, Fax: 0171 577 1234, Call Date: Nov 1989 (Gray's Inn) Qualifications: LLB (L'pool), ACIB

Waters *Jonathan Roy* •
UK Legal Advisor Queens Moat House plc., Employment Law Consul., Law Lecturer, Queens Moat Houses plc, Queens Court, 9-17 Eastern Road, Romford, Essex RM1 3NG, 01708 730522, Fax: 01708 737998, Association of Law Teachers Employment Lawyers Association, Call Date: Nov 1990 (Lincoln's Inn) Qualifications: LLB (Hons), ACIarb, LLM

Waterson *Roger Stephen* •
Assistant Solicitor, The Inland Revenue, Solicitor's Office, Somerset House, The Strand, London WC2R 1LB, 0171 438 7118, Fax: 0171 438 6246, Call Date: Nov 1968 (Gray's Inn) Qualifications: BA, BCL {oxon}

Watherston *John Anthony Charles* •
Registrar of the Judicial Committee of the Privy Council, Privy Council Office, Downing Street, London SW1A 2AJ, Call Date: Nov 1967 (Inner Temple) Qualifications: MA

Watkin *Tegwyn Thomas Herbert*
Gwynda, Ffordd Henllan, Nr Trefnant, St Asaph, Clwyd LL17 OBT, 01745 730342, Call Date: Nov 1968 (Lincoln's Inn) Qualifications: ACIB

Watkins *Mrs Beverley Anne* •
Senior Crown Prosecutor, Crown Prosecution Service, 10th Floor, Grosvenor House, Basing View, Basingstoke, Call Date: July 1982 (Gray's Inn) Qualifications: BA

Watkins *Dr Owen David* •
Securities & Investments Board, Gavrelle House, 2-14 Bunhill Row, London EC1Y 8RA, 0171 638 1240, Fax: 0171 382 5900, Call Date: July 1986 (Lincoln's Inn) Qualifications: MA, D.Phil (Oxon) , MA (City)

Watkins *Paul John* •
Head of Regulation, European Repo Exchange, 245 Blackfriars Road, London SE1 9UY, 0171 579 4468, Fax: 0171 579 4478, Call Date: Nov 1986 (Middle Temple) Qualifications: LLB (Manc)

Watkinson *Miss Sasha Louise*
Call Date: Oct 1998 (Lincoln's Inn) Qualifications: LLB (Hons) (L'pool)

Watson *Andrew Robert James*
Call Date: Nov 1982 (Lincoln's Inn) Qualifications: LLB MA (Sheffield), Dip Soc Admin

Watson *Andrew Simon*
Call Date: Oct 1997 (Lincoln's Inn) Qualifications: BA (Hons) (Leeds), CPE (Northumbria)

Watson *Anthony*
Associate, Institute of Investment Management and Research, Cedar Hse, 50 The Street, Manuden, Bishop's Stortford, Herts CM23 1DJ, Call Date: Nov 1976 (Lincoln's Inn) Qualifications: BSc (Econ)

Watson *Bernard Gerald* •
Police Inspector, Surrey Police, Mount Brown, Sandy Lane, Guildford GU3 1HG, 01483 482484, Head of Fraud & Financial Investigation, Call Date: Oct 1997 (Middle Temple) Qualifications: BA (Hons) (Kingston)

Watson *Miss Deborah Jane* •
Crown Prosecution Service, Essex Area Office, 2nd Floor, County House, 100 New London Road, Chelmsford, Essex CM2 0RG, 01245 252939, Call Date: Oct 1992 (Inner Temple) Qualifications: LLB

Watson *Ms Deidre Mary Watson* •
Company Secretary, Lancaster plc, Charter Court, Colchester, Essex C04 4TG, 01206 224547, Fax: 01206 845460, Call Date: Nov 1996 (Inner Temple) Qualifications: BA (Lond), MBA, FCIS

Watson *Duncan Allen*
Call Date: Oct 1997 (Inner Temple) Qualifications: BA (Wales), CPE

Watson *Ms Isobel Mary* •
Senior Principal Legal Officer, Department of the Environment, Transport and the Regions, Eland House, Bressenden Place, London SW1E 5DU, Call Date: July 1975 (Middle Temple) Qualifications: LLB

Watson *James*
Call Date: Nov 1996 (Lincoln's Inn) Qualifications: BA (Hons) (Sheff)

Watson *John Brook Carr*
9-13 Cursitor Street, London EC4A 1LL, 0171 831 6664, Fax: 0171 404 1098, NSW Bar 1972 Assistant Editor, Weekly Law Reports, Call Date: Nov 1979 (Lincoln's Inn)

Watson *Nicholas Bruce*
Clerk to the Justices, Leicester Magistrates' Ct, P.O.Box 1, Pocklingtons Walk, Leicester LE1 9BE, 0116 255 3666, Fax: 0116 254581, Call Date: July 1986 (Gray's Inn) Qualifications: LLB, LLM

Watson *Roy Stuart*
Senior Legal Adviser, Berkshire Magistrates' Court, Easby House, Northfield End, Henley-on-Thames, Oxon RG9 2NB, 01491 412720, Fax: 01491 412762, Call Date: Feb 1993 (Gray's Inn) Qualifications: BA

Watson *Miss Zillah Mary*
Call Date: Nov 1994 (Gray's Inn) Qualifications: BA

Watt *James Muir*
47 Fort Street, Ayr KA7 1DH, 01292 203102, Call Date: Jan 1935 (Inner Temple) Qualifications: MA (Oxon), MA (Glas), Hon Assoc RICS, FAAV

Watters *Charles Patrick*
Group Secretary and General Counsel, Call Date: July 1981 (Middle Temple) Qualifications: LLB (Hons)

Watts *Mrs Alison*
Clerk to the Justices, Derbyshire Magistrates' Court, The Court House, West Bars, Chesterfield, Derbyshire S40 1AE, 01246 278171, Fax: 01246 276344, Call Date: July 1984 (Inner Temple)

Watts *Ronald*
79 Great King Street, Edinburgh, Scotland EH3 6RN, 0131 557 4474, Call Date: June 1964 (Gray's Inn) Qualifications: LLB (Nott), LLM (Cantab), BD (Edin)

Wayman *Mrs Anne Elizabeth* •
Principal Court Clerk, Sutton Magistrates Court, Shotfield, Wallington, Surrey SM6 0JA, 0181 770 5939, Fax: 0181 770 5959, Call Date: Nov 1987 (Gray's Inn) Qualifications: D.M.L.

Wayman *Miss Caroline Ann*
13 Dowgate Close, Tonbridge, Kent TN9 2EH, Call Date: Mar 1998 (Middle Temple) Qualifications: LLB (Hons)

Weaver *Oliver*
also Inn of Court L Erskine Chambers, 30 Lincoln's Inn Fields, Lincoln's Inn, London, WC2A 3PF, Call Date: Feb 1965 (Middle Temple) Qualifications: MA, LLM (Cantab)

Weaver *Miss Ouida Marjorie*
Human Resources Manager, Manpower plc, International House, 66 Chiltern Street, London W1M 1PR, 0171 224 6688, Fax: 0171 935 6611, Call Date: July 1983 (Lincoln's Inn) Qualifications: BA (Washington) LLB, (Lond)

Weaver *Mrs Valerie June*
Call Date: Nov 1979 (Middle Temple) Qualifications: BA

Webb *David Royston* •
Consultant, Harrods Holdings Plc, 13 Buckingham Hse, Courtlands, Sheen Road, Richmond, Surrey TW10 5AX, 0171 409 2963, Fax: 0171 491 2472, Call Date: May 1973 (Lincoln's Inn) Qualifications: LLB, ACIS

Webb *Ian Christopher*
Justices' Chief Executive, Call Date: July 1979 (Gray's Inn) Qualifications: BA

Webb *Malcolm George John*
Kelsters Cottage, Hugus, Near Truro, Cornwall TR3 6EQ, (01872) 560696, Call Date: July 1972 (Middle Temple) Qualifications: FFA,ACIS

Webb *Mark Colin*
The Bank, Braybrooke Road, Little Bowden, Market Harborough, Leicestershire LE16 8AD, Call Date: Oct 1998 (Lincoln's Inn) Qualifications: LLB (Hons) (L'pool)

Webb *Robert Craig* •
Assistant Legal Counsel, Lazard Brothers & Co Limited, 21 Moorfields, London EC2P 2HT, Call Date: Oct 1993 (Lincoln's Inn) Qualifications: BA (Hons) (Notts)

Webb *Robert Stopford* •
Recorder, General Counsel, British Airways, Legal Department (HBA3), PO Box 365, Harmondsworth UB7 0GB, Also Inn of Court L, Call Date: July 1971 (Inner Temple) Qualifications: LLB

Webb *Mrs Susan Pamela*
14 Hanson Close, London SW14 7SH, 0181 392 2801, Fax: 0181 392 2801, Call Date: Oct 1995 (Middle Temple) Qualifications: LLB (Hons)

Webber *Andrew John*
Call Date: Feb 1994 (Middle Temple) Qualifications: LLB (Hons) (Lond)

Webber *David Malcolm*
Part Time Chairman of Medical Appeal Tribunal and Disability Appeal Tribunal, Call Date: Nov 1955 (Gray's Inn) Qualifications: MA (Cantab)

Webster *Colin Peter*
Legal Team Manager, The Court House, Speedwell Street, Oxford OX1 1RZ, 01865 815092/815938 (direct line), Fax: 01865 243730, Call Date: Nov 1987 (Middle Temple) Qualifications: Dip Mag Law, DMS, IOSH

Webster *Ms Gail Louise*
4 Brick Court, Ground Floor, Temple, London, EC4Y 9AD, Call Date: July 1981 (Gray's Inn)

Webster *Miss Helen Louise*
Call Date: July 1998 (Gray's Inn) Qualifications: LLB (Teeside)

Webster *Ms Mandy Patricia*
Call Date: May 1993 (Lincoln's Inn) Qualifications: BA (Hons, Keele), ACIS

Webster *Peter*
Call Date: Nov 1994 (Lincoln's Inn) Qualifications: LLB (Hons)

Wedderburn *Miss Kim* •
UK Legal Counsel, J.D.Edwards (UK) Limited, Oxford Road, Stokenchurch, High Wycombe, Bucks HP14 3AD, 01494 682700, Fax: 01494 682699, Call Date: Nov 1991 (Middle Temple) Qualifications: LLB (Hons)

Wee *Miss Nicole Fiona Sue-Ren*
Call Date: July 1995 (Lincoln's Inn) Qualifications: LLB (Hons)

Weeden-Padgham *Miss Louise Anne* •
Senior Crown Prosecutor, Crown Prosecution Service, Saxon House, 1 Cromwell Square, Ipswich, Suffolk IP1 1TS, 01473 230332, Fax: 01473 231377, Call Date: Nov 1987 (Inner Temple) Qualifications: LLB

Weedon *Simon John*
Call Date: Oct 1994 (Gray's Inn) Qualifications: LLB

Weeks *Stephen Thomas* •
Company Secretary, Freemans PLC, 139 Clapham Road, London SW99 0HR, 0171 820 2336, Fax: 0171 820 2796, Call Date: July 1978 (Lincoln's Inn) Qualifications: MA (Cantab)

Wehlau *Mrs Caroline Ann*
Call Date: July 1983 (Inner Temple) Qualifications: LLB (Soton)

Weinberg *Mrs Jose Letitia*
Special Adjudicator Immigration p/t, Elm Green Cottage, Drinkstone, Nr Bury St Edmunds, Suffolk IP30 9TN, 01449 737 640, Call Date: July 1963 (Middle Temple)

Weir *Miss Heather Anne* •
Senior Crown Prosecutor, Crown Prosecution Service, Windsor House, 10 Manchester Road, Bradford BD5 0QH, 01274 742 530 EXT 149, Call Date: July 1989 (Gray's Inn) Qualifications: LLB Hons

Weir *Ms Rachel Sian Shapland*
Call Date: Nov 1991 (Inner Temple) Qualifications: MA(Cantab)

Weir *Richard Stanton*
10 Fort Gate, Newhaven, East Sussex BN9 9DR, 01273 516851, Call Date: Nov 1957 (Inner Temple) Qualifications: MA (Oxon)

Weisberger *Marc Oliver*
Call Date: Oct 1998 (Gray's Inn) Qualifications: BA (Cantab)

Weitzman *Peter*
Member of Criminal Injuries Compensation Board, 21 St James's Gardens, London W11 4RE, 0171 603 4476, Call Date: July 1952 (Gray's Inn) Qualifications: MA (Oxon)

Welch *Bryan James* •
Legal Director, Department of Trade and Industry, Dept of Trade & Industry, Room 201, 10 Victoria Street, London SW1H 0NN, 0171 215 3460, Fax: 0171 215 3520, Call Date: July 1975 (Inner Temple) Qualifications: MA (Cantab)

Welch *Nicholas Randall*
Call Date: Oct 1994 (Gray's Inn) Qualifications: BA, LLB

Welling *Robert David* •
Senior Crown Prosecutor, Crown Prosecution Service, Avonbridge House, Bath Road, Chippenham, Wiltshire SN15 2BB, 01249 659622, Fax: 01249 659722, Call Date: Nov 1989 (Lincoln's Inn) Qualifications: LLB

Wells *Anthony Francis Michael* •
Senior Crown Prosecutor, Crown Prosecution Service, Princes Court, 34 York Road, Leicester LE1 5TU, 0116 2549333, Fax: 0116 2550855, Call Date: Nov 1968 (Gray's Inn) Qualifications: MA (Oxon)

Wells *Ronald Michael* •
North Herts College, Cambridge Road, Hitchin, Herts, 01462 422882, Call Date: Apr 1989 (Gray's Inn) Qualifications: BA, LLB (Lond), LLM

Wells *Ms Stephanie Jane*
David Truex & Co, Solicitors, 212 Strand, London WC2R 1AP, 0171 583 5040, Fax: 0171 583 5151, Call Date: Nov 1997 (Inner Temple) Qualifications: BA (La Trobe,, Australia), LLB , (Reading)

Wells-Thorpe *Rupert Sebastian*
Call Date: Nov 1997 (Inner Temple) Qualifications: LLB (Wolver'ton)

Welsh *Miss Amanda Jane*
Call Date: Nov 1992 (Gray's Inn) Qualifications: LLB (Leeds)

Welsh *Malcolm James MacGregor*
Call Date: Oct 1996 (Gray's Inn) Qualifications: BSc (Lond)

Wendon *John Mark* •
Divisional Director Area Counsel Europe, Letterland Limited, 33 New Road, Barton, Cambridgeshire CB3 7AY, 01223 26 2781, Fax: 01223 26 4126, Call Date: Nov 1975 (Middle Temple) Qualifications: MA (Cantab)

Werbicki *Mrs Anne Vivien* •
Grade 6 Lawyer, Ministry of Agriculture,, Fisheries and Food, Legal Dept, 55 Whitehall, London SW1A 2EY, 0171 270 8257, Fax: 0171 270 8096, and Member Gibraltar Bar, Call Date: Feb 1981 (Gray's Inn) Qualifications: LLB (Bris)

Werhun *John* •
Senior Crown Prosecutor, Crown Prosecution Service, Sunlight House, 5th Floor, Quay Street, Manchester, 0161 908 2696, Fax: 0161 869 2663, Call Date: July 1982 (Gray's Inn) Qualifications: BA (Law)

Werrett *Miss Melanie Gertrude* •
Principal Crown Prosecutor, Crown Proecution Service, Gemini Centre, 88 New London Road, Chelmsford, Essex CM2 0BR, 01245 252939, Fax: 01245 490476, Call Date: July 1979 (Gray's Inn)

Wesel *Thomas*
Call Date: Nov 1993 (Middle Temple) Qualifications: LLB (Hons) (Lond)

Wessels *Mattheus Hendrikus*
Iustitia Chambers, Aliwal Street,
Bloemfontein 9301, Republic of South
Africa, Republic of South Africa, 051
303567, Fax: 051 474228, Senior
Counsel, South Africa Member: Orange
Free State Society of Advocates and
Member South African Bar Lesotho Bar
28 St John Street, Manchester, M3 4DJ,
Call Date: Oct 1993 (Gray's Inn)
Qualifications: B.Iuris, LLB

West *Andrew Peter* •
Crown Prosecutor, Crown Prosecution
Service, 4th Floor, 50 Ludgate Hill,
London EC4M 7EX, 0171 273 1461,
Fax: 0171 273 1499, Call Date: Nov
1995 (Gray's Inn) Qualifications: BA
(Hons)

West *Christopher John* •
Solicitor to HM Land Registry, HM Land
Registry, 32 Lincoln's Inn Fields,
London WC2A 3PH, 0171 917 5994,
Fax: 0171 917 5966, Call Date: July
1966 (Lincoln's Inn)

West *David John Courtney* •
Head of Legal Services, Atomic
Weapons Establishment, Aldermaston,
Reading RG7 4PR, 0118 982 5095, Fax:
0118 981 0772, Call Date: July 1977
(Middle Temple) Qualifications: LLB
(Hons)

West *Mrs Julie Amanda* •
Sedgwick Noble Lowndes Ltd, P.O.Box
144, Norfolk House, Wellesley Road,
Croydon CR3 3EB, 0181 686 2466, Fax:
0181 681 1458, Call Date: Nov 1984
(Middle Temple) Qualifications: BA
(Hons)

Westbrook *Miss Clara Nieves*
Call Date: Nov 1998 (Lincoln's Inn)
Qualifications: LLB (Hons)

Westcott *Richard Henry*
Deputy Chairman, Fairview New Homes
plc, Call Date: July 1978 (Lincoln's
Inn) Qualifications: FCA,FTII,ACIB

Westlake *George Alan*
Call Date: Oct 1992 (Lincoln's Inn)
Qualifications: BA(Hons) (Bris), Dip in
Law

Weston *Miss Sarah Dawn* •
Bench Legal Adviser, Dorset Magistrates
Courts, Law Courts, Park Road, Poole,
Dorset BH15 2RJ, 0202 743309, Fax:
0202 711999, Call Date: July 1985
(Gray's Inn) Qualifications: LLB
(Manchester), DMS, MBA

Wetherfield *Ms Alison Clare*
Associate, Warner Cranston, Warner
Cranston, Pickfords'Wharf, Clink Street,
London SE1 9DG, 0171 403 2900, Fax:
0171 403 4221, and Member New
York, Call Date: May 1996 (Middle
Temple) Qualifications: BA
(Hons) (Cantab), LLM (Harvard)

Weyers *Jacek Witold*
Juris Angliae Scientia, Warsaw
University, The White House,
Gotherington Lane, Cheltenham,
Gloucester GL52 4EN, 01242 678283,
Fax: 01242 678283, Call Date: Nov
1956 (Gray's Inn) Qualifications: LLB,
MIWSP

Whale *Stephen John Trehane*
Clerk to the Justices, Brecknock and
Radnorshire, Magistrates' Clerks Office,
Captains Walk, Brecon, Powys
LD3 7HS, 01874 622993, Fax: 01874
622441, Call Date: Feb 1986 (Gray's
Inn) Qualifications: MBA, Dip (Mag
Law)

Wharam *Alan Neville*
Call Date: Nov 1953 (Inner Temple)
Qualifications: MA (Cantab)

Whatham *Stephen Benjamin* •
Senor Crown Prosecutor, Heron House,
Houghamont Avenue, Crosby,
Merseyside L22 0LL, Call Date: Nov
1990 (Inner Temple) Qualifications:
LLB

Whattam *Charles Barrie*
Call Date: Oct 1996 (Lincoln's Inn)
Qualifications: BA (Hons) (Portsm), Dip
in Law (Westmin)

Wheater *Miss Jennifer Clare*
Call Date: Nov 1995 (Inner Temple)
Qualifications: BA (Dunelm)

Wheatley *Derek Peter Francis* •
Chairman, Manorgate (UK) Ltd,
Communications House, Cricklewood
Business Centre, Cricklewood
Broadway, London NW2 1ET, 0181 208
8900, Fax: 0181 830 5455, Call Date:
Apr 1951 (Middle Temple)
Qualifications: MA (Oxon)

Wheeldon *Stuart Lawrence Verner* •
Principal Crown Prosecutor, CPS, 4-12
Queen Anne's Gate, London SW1H 9AZ,
Call Date: Feb 1988 (Lincoln's Inn)
Qualifications: LLB

Wheldon *Miss Caroline Anne*
Call Date: Nov 1992 (Inner Temple)
Qualifications: BA, Dip in Law (City)

Wheldon *Miss Juliet Louise* •
Legal Administrator to the Home Office,
Home Office, 4-12 Queen Anne's Gate,
London SW1, 0171 273 2681, Call
Date: July 1975 (Gray's Inn)
Qualifications: MA (Oxon)

Whetcombe *Timothy Howard Arundel* •
Legal Adviser, Lloyds Bank Plc, Private
Banking & Financial, Services Division,
Capital Hse, 1/5 Perrymount Rd,
Haywards Heath W.Sussex, 01444
459144, Call Date: July 1987 (Lincoln's
Inn) Qualifications: LLB (Lond)

Whincup *Miss Catherine Elizabeth* •
Senior Crown Prosecutor, C/O CPS
Headquarters, 50 Ludgate Hill, London
EC4M 7EX, 0171 357 7010, Call Date:
Nov 1987 (Middle Temple)
Qualifications: LLB

Whipham *Thomas Henry Martin*
Also Inn of Court M, Call Date: Jan
1949 (Lincoln's Inn)

Whipp *Roger Donald* •
Legal Adviser, British Airways Plc,
Waterside (HB13), P.O.Box 365,
Harmondsworth UB7 09B, 0181 738
6885, Fax: 0181 738 9962, Call Date:
July 1987 (Lincoln's Inn)
Qualifications: LLB (Hons)

Whisson-Eastwick *Kevin Paul* •
CPS (Norfolk Branch), Haldin House,
Old Bank of England Court, Queen
Street, Norwich, Norfolk NR2 4SX, Call
Date: Nov 1989 (Middle Temple)
Qualifications: BA Hons, Dip in Law

Whiston *Ms Teresa*
Call Date: July 1997 (Inner Temple)
Qualifications: LLB

Whitaker *Anthony Cowburn* •
36 Doddington Grove, Kennington,
London SE17 3TT, Fax: 0171 793 8851,
Call Date: June 1958 (Gray's Inn)
Qualifications: BA

White *Alistair Sinclair* •
Newcourt Credit Limited, 66
Buckingham gate, London SW1E 6AU,
Call Date: July 1989 (Middle Temple)
Qualifications: LLB

White *Miss Amanda Ashley*
Call Date: Nov 1995 (Inner Temple)
Qualifications: LLB (Middx)

White *Andrew Mark*
Court Clerk, The Law Courts, Northway,
Scarborough YO12 7AE, 01723 354258,
Fax: 01723 353250, Call Date: Nov
1986 (Gray's Inn) Qualifications: BA
(Kent)

White *Miss Catherine Rose*
Deputy Clerk to the Justices, 4/5 Quay
Street, Carmarthen, Dyfed SA31 3JT,
01267 221658, Fax: 01267 221812,
Call Date: July 1977 (Gray's Inn)
Qualifications: LLB

White *Charles David* •
Crown Prosecutor, Crown Prosecution
Service, Queens House, 58 Victoria
Street, St Albans AL1 3HQ, 01727
818100, Fax: 01727 851080, Call Date:
May 1988 (Inner Temple)
Qualifications: LLB (Hull)

White *Christopher Bevis Eve*
Call Date: Nov 1972 (Inner Temple)
Qualifications: MA

White *David John* •
Senior Crown Prosecutor, 4 Highbury
Crescent, London N5, 0171 609 9151,
Fax: 0171 607 4793, Call Date: Nov
1978 (Gray's Inn) Qualifications: LLB

White *David Malcolm*
Clerk to the Justices & Chief Executive,
Sheffield Magistrates' Court, Castle
Street, Sheffield S3 8LU, 0114 276
0760, Fax: 0114 272 0129, Call Date:
July 1976 (Middle Temple)
Qualifications: LLB, MSc MIMgt

• Barrister in employment

White *Miss Esther Ceridwen* •
Call Date: Nov 1991 (Gray's Inn)
Qualifications: MA (Oxon)

White *Giles Alistair*
Call Date: Oct 1997 (Inner Temple)
Qualifications: LLB (London)

White *Graham Allen*
and Member Zambia Bar, Call Date: Nov
1967 (Gray's Inn) Qualifications: BA, MA
(1967)

White *Iain Charles* •
Senior Crown Prosecutor, Crown
Prosecution Service, Avon Office, Level 1,
Froomsgate House, Rupert Street, Bristol
BS1 2QJ, Call Date: July 1986 (Middle
Temple) Qualifications: MA (Hons)
(Cantab)

White *Ian Robert* •
Company Secretary/In House Lawyer,
Gartmore Investment Management,
Gartmore House, 16-18 Monument
Street, London EC3R 8AJ, 0171 940
5743, Fax: 0171 638 3468, Call Date:
Nov 1989 (Inner Temple) Qualifications:
BA (Bris), Dip Law (City)

White *Ms Jennifer Susan* •
Legal Adviser, The Electricity Association,
30 Millbank, London, SW1P 4RD, 0171
963 5932, Fax: 0171 630 6186, Call
Date: July 1970 (Middle Temple)
Qualifications: LLB

White *Jeremy Barry* •
Senior Lawyer, KPMG Tax Advisers,
P.O.Box 486, 1 Puddle Dock, London
EC4V 3PD, 0171 311 1000, Fax: 0171
311 2943, Call Date: July 1976 (Gray's
Inn) Qualifications: LLB

White *Miss Julia Anne Springett*
Call Date: Oct 1998 (Inner Temple)
Qualifications: BA (Lond)

White *Martin Stephen* •
Call Date: July 1973 (Middle Temple)
Qualifications: BA (Cantab)

White *Miss Michele Karen Marie*
Legal Counsel, Call Date: Nov 1978
(Middle Temple) Qualifications: LLB
(Lond), CFE (LBS)

White *Paul Murray*
11 King's Bench Walk, 1st Floor, Temple,
London, EC4Y 7EQ, Call Date: July 1975
(Lincoln's Inn) Qualifications: BA
(Cantab)

White *Miss Rachel*
Watson Wyatt Partners, Park Gate, 21
Tothill Street, London SW1H 9LL, 0171
222 8033, Fax: 0171 222 9182, Call
Date: July 1974 (Gray's Inn)

White *Richard Charles* •
Call Date: Nov 1983 (Gray's Inn)
Qualifications: BA

Whitehead *Miss Claire Helen* •
Hammond Suddards Solicitors, Call
Date: May 1997 (Lincoln's Inn)
Qualifications: MA (Hons), Dip Law

Whitehouse *Miss Helen Louise*
Call Date: Mar 1999 (Middle Temple)
Qualifications: LLB (Hons)(Plymouth)

Whitehouse *John Frederic*
Woodstock, Marlow Road, Abbotsbrook,
Bourne End, Bucks SL8 5NU, 01628
522898, Call Date: Nov 1958 (Inner
Temple) Qualifications: LLB

Whitehouse *Martin* •
Principal Crown Prosecutor, Crown
Prosecution Service, 5th Floor, River
Park House, 225 High Road, Woodgreen,
London N22 4HQ, 0181 888 8889, Fax:
0181 365 7752, Call Date: Feb 1985
(Middle Temple) Qualifications: LLB

Whiteley *Miss Karen Lorraine*
Call Date: Nov 1998 (Middle Temple)
Qualifications: LLB (Hons)

Whiteley *Miss Miranda Blyth*
Mills & Reeve Solicitors, Francis House,
112 Hills Road, Cambridge CB2 1PH,
Call Date: Nov 1985 (Middle Temple)
Qualifications: MA (Cantab)

Whiteside *Miss Nilkanthi Maharanee*
Legal Advisor, City of Salford Magistrates
Ct, The Court House, Bexley Square,
Salford M3 6DJ, 0161 834 9457, Fax:
0161 839 1806, Call Date: Feb 1990
(Middle Temple) Qualifications: LLB
Hons

Whitesides *Keith Robert*
Director (Investor Relations), The Boots
Company Plc, Nottingham NG2 3AA,
(0115) 9687031, Fax: (0115) 9687212,
Call Date: Nov 1972 (Gray's Inn)
Qualifications: MPhil, LLB ACII

Whiting *David Justin* •
In-House Legal, THe BPA Group, 18-20
St John Street, London EC1M 4AY, 0171
251 5657, Fax: 0171 251 5658, Call
Date: May 1995 (Lincoln's Inn)
Qualifications: BA (Hons), CPE

Whiting *Richard James*
Newport Chambers, 12 Clytha Park Road,
Newport, Gwent, NP9 47L, Call Date: July
1976 (Middle Temple)

Whitney *David Roy*
Call Date: Mar 1998 (Gray's Inn)
Qualifications: LLB (W'hampton)

Whittaker *Brian Paul* •
Branch Crown Prosecutor, Branch
Crown Prosecutor, Bromfield House,
Wrexham Technology Park, Wrexham,
Clwyd LL13 7YW, 01978 312002 X 301,
Fax: 01978 311960, Call Date: July 1977
(Gray's Inn) Qualifications: BA Hons

Whittaker *Ian Dorien Geoffrey* •
H M Customs & Excise, Solicitor's Office,
New Kings Beam House, 22 Upper
Ground, London SE1 9PJ, 0171 865
5332, Fax: 0171 865 5248, Call Date: Oct
1994 (Inner Temple) Qualifications: MA
(Oxon), CPE

Whittaker *Rodney Martin* •
Associate General Counsel, SmithKline
Beecham plc, One New Horizons Court,
Brentford, Middlesex TW8 9EP, 0181 975
2052, Fax: 0181 975 2070, Call Date:
July 1971 (Inner Temple) Qualifications:
MA (Oxon)

Whittaker *Dr Simon John*
Fellow, St John's College, Oxford, St
John's College, Oxford OX1 3JP, 01865
277300, Fax: 01865 277435, Call Date:
Nov 1987 (Lincoln's Inn) Qualifications:
BCL MA DPhil (Oxon)

Whitting *Mrs Emma Elizabeth* •
Call Date: Nov 1991 (Inner Temple)
Qualifications: MA (Oxon), Dip Law

Whitworth *Peter Ernest*
Dorchester House, 5 Dorchester Drive,
London SE24 0DQ, 0171 733 2978, Also
L & I Inns Court, Call Date: July 1946
(Middle Temple) Qualifications: BA

Whitworth *Simon William Battams*
Legal Consultant, O'Higgins 1085,
(1686) Hurlingham, Provincia Buenos
Aires, 54 1 662 8216, Fax: 54 1 662
8216, Call Date: July 1974 (Inner
Temple) Qualifications: MA (Cantab)

Whomersley *Christopher Adrian* •
Legal Counsellor, Foreign &
Commonwealth Office, King Charles
Street, London SW1, Call Date: Nov 1980
(Middle Temple) Qualifications: LLB
(LSE), LLM (Cantab)

Whyatt *Bernard Anthony*
Call Date: Oct 1996 (Middle Temple)
Qualifications: BA (Hons)(Leeds), LLB
(Hons)

Wicken *Ronald Edward* •
Principal Assistant, Dudley Magistrates
Court, The Inhedge, Dudley, West
Midlands, 01384 455200, Call Date: Nov
1984 (Inner Temple)

Wickrama-Sekera *Miss Yasoda*
Legal Officer, Department of Fair
Trading, 1 Fitzwilliam Street, New South
Wales 2150, 02 9895 0643, Fax: 02 9635
5247, and Member New South Wales Bar
Australia Bar, Call Date: Oct 1994
(Lincoln's Inn) Qualifications: LLB
(Hons)(Lond), MA (Brunel)

Wickremasinghe *Mrs Jayanthi
Abhayaratne*
Crown Prosecution Service, Priory Gate,
29 Union Street, Maidstone, Kent, 01622
686425, Call Date: July 1975 (Lincoln's
Inn) Qualifications: BA

Wicks *Raymond*
Call Date: Oct 1997 (Inner Temple)
Qualifications: BSc (Reading), MBA, CPE
(Middlesex)

Wield *Miss Sally Anne*
Call Date: July 1998 (Middle Temple)
Qualifications: BSc (Hons)(So'ton)

E

Wienholdt *Barry*
Well Bank Cottage, Over Peover, Knutsford, Cheshire WA16 8UW, 01625 861488, Call Date: July 1970 (Gray's Inn)

Wightman *Paul Edward*
Call Date: May 1996 (Middle Temple) Qualifications: LLB (Hons)

Wightwick *Ian Richard*
49 Molyneux Street, London W1H 5HW, 0171 262 9085, Fax: 0171 262 9085, Call Date: June 1959 (Inner Temple) Qualifications: MA

Wignall *Julian David*
Chief Executive, City of London Magistrates', Courts, 1 Queen Victoria Street, London EC4N 4XY, 0171 332 1820/1828, Fax: 0171 332 1493, Call Date: July 1975 (Middle Temple) Qualifications: LLB, M.B.A.

Wignall *Miss Natalie Elizabeth* •
Legal Adviser, Legal Department, Marconi Communications Limited, Edge Lane, Liverpool L7 9NW, 0151 254 3769, Fax: 0151 254 3326, Call Date: Oct 1992 (Lincoln's Inn) Qualifications: LLB(Hons)

Wigoder *Lord*
Call Date: Nov 1946 (Gray's Inn) Qualifications: MA (Oxon)

Wijeyaratne *Miss Sonali Arundhini* •
Head of Legal & Business Affairs, Pathe Distribution & Pathe, Production Limited, Kent House, 14-17 Market Place, Great Titchfield Street, London W1N 8AR, 0171 323 5151, Fax: 0171 462 4417, Call Date: Nov 1986 (Middle Temple) Qualifications: BA (Oxon)

Wikeley *Professor Nicholas John*
p/t Chairman,Social Security Appeal Tribunals & Disability Appeal Tribunals, Faculty of Law, The University, Highfield, Southampton SO17 1BJ, 01703 593416, Fax: 01703 593024, Call Date: July 1981 (Gray's Inn) Qualifications: MA (Cantab)

Wilbraham *Miss Stephanie Jane*
Call Date: July 1998 (Inner Temple) Qualifications: BA (Humberside), MA (Hull), LLM (Leeds)

Wilchcombe *Miss Sarah Diana*
Call Date: July 1998 (Lincoln's Inn) Qualifications: LLB (Hons)

Wilcox *Stephen John* •
Senior Principal, Lord Chancellor's Department, Selborne House, 54-60 Victoria Street, London SW1E 6QW, 0171 210 0718, Fax: 0171 210 0725, Call Date: July 1972 (Gray's Inn) Qualifications: LLB

Wilde *James Richard*
Call Date: Jan 1935 (Middle Temple)

Wilde *Ralph Garfield*
Corpus Christi College, Cambridge CB2 1RH, Call Date: Oct 1997 (Middle Temple) Qualifications: BSc (Econ) (LSE), CPE (City)

Wiles *Philip George* •
Group Legal Adviser, Sun Life Assurance Society Plc, 107 Cheapside, London EC2V 6DU, 0171 606 7788, Fax: 0171 378 1865, Call Date: Nov 1982 (Gray's Inn)

Wilfred Jr *Bode*
Call Date: Nov 1997 (Middle Temple) Qualifications: LLB (Hons) (Sheff), LLM (Dundee)

Wilkes *Miss Jayne Denise* •
Crown Prosecution Service, The Old Barracks, Sandon Road, Grantham NG32 9AS, (01476) 70585, Fax: (01476) 590857, Call Date: Nov 1991 (Inner Temple) Qualifications: LLB

Wilkins *Adrian Mark*
Call Date: Oct 1992 (Gray's Inn) Qualifications: LL.B (L'pool), MSc (Stirling)

Wilkins *Nigel Granville* •
Principal Crown Prosecutor, Crown Prosecution Service, Friars House, Manor House Drive, Coventry CV1 2TE, Call Date: Feb 1974 (Inner Temple) Qualifications: LLB

Wilkins *Richard Leslie*
Call Date: Mar 1996 (Middle Temple) Qualifications: BA (Hons)

Wilkinson *Mrs Ann Elizabeth* •
Call Date: July 1988 (Inner Temple) Qualifications: LLB (Soton)

Wilkinson *James Leo* •
Senior Counsel, Smithkline Beecham Plc, One New Horizons Court, Brentford, Middlesex TW8 9EP, 0181 975 2058, Fax: 0181 975 2071, Call Date: July 1972 (Middle Temple) Qualifications: MR Pharm S

Wilks *Miss Elizabeth*
Call Date: Nov 1997 (Gray's Inn) Qualifications: LLB

Wilks *Ian*
Call Date: Oct 1996 (Middle Temple) Qualifications: LLB (Hons) (Sheff)

Willey *Stuart Christopher* •
Financial Services Authority, 25 The North Colonade, Canary Wharf, London, Canary Wharf E14 5HS, 0171 676 3330, Chief Counsel-Investment Business, Call Date: May 1979 (Middle Temple) Qualifications: B.A. (York)

Williams *Alexander Steuart*
Call Date: Oct 1994 (Lincoln's Inn) Qualifications: BA (Hons) (Oxon), Dip in Law (City)

Williams *Mrs Annie Yoke Yean Chew*
Call Date: Nov 1992 (Middle Temple) Qualifications: LLB (Hons)

Williams *Mrs Beverley*
Senior Court Clerk - Part time, Victoria Law Courts, Corporation Street, Birmingham B4 6QA, 0121 212 6612, Fax: 0121 212 6766, Call Date: Feb 1985 (Middle Temple) Qualifications: BA

Williams *Carl David*
Call Date: Nov 1994 (Inner Temple) Qualifications: LLB (Essex)

Williams *Charles Edouard Vaughan* •
Directorate General for, Competition, Commission of the European, Communities, Rue de la loi 200, B-1049, Belgium, Call Date: Nov 1990 (Middle Temple) Qualifications: BA (Oxon), DAES (Bruges)

Williams *Ms China*
Call Date: Nov 1994 (Inner Temple) Qualifications: MA (Edinburgh), CPE (City)

Williams *David Edward Huw*
Legal Consultant, 7 Hertford Street, London W1Y 8LP, 0171 355 1886, Fax: 0171 355 1887, Call Date: Nov 1977 (Lincoln's Inn)

Williams *David John*
10e Thorney Crescent, Morgans Walk, London SW11 3TR, 0171 223 9059, Call Date: Jan 1939 (Inner Temple) Qualifications: MA (Oxon)

Williams *David Michael* •
Lawyer Fraud London Division, Crown Prosecution Service, Headquarters, 50 Ludgate Hill, London EC4M 7EX, 0171 273 1338, Call Date: July 1972 (Inner Temple) Qualifications: LLB (Manch), MBA

Williams *Miss Elaine Denise* •
Director, Transferry Shipping Co Ltd, Transferry House, Southend Arterial Road, Hornchurch, Essex RM11 3UT, 01708 452500, Fax: 01708 456218, Call Date: July 1982 (Gray's Inn) Qualifications: BA (Kent), LLM (Lond, M.B.A (Warw), F.Inst.D.

Williams *Francis Joseph*
Call Date: Nov 1984 (Inner Temple) Qualifications: BA, PGCE

Williams *Huw David* •
The Environment Agency, Rio House, Waterside Drive, Aztec West, Almondsbury, Bristol BS12 4UD, 01454 624022, Fax: 01454 624010, Call Date: July 1988 (Inner Temple) Qualifications: BA (Cantab), Dip Law

Williams *Miss Kathleen Anne* •
Bechtel Limited, 245 Hammersmith Road, London W6 8DP, Former Solicitor, Call Date: July 1998 (Middle Temple) Qualifications: BA (Hons) (Oxon)

Williams *Leon Norman*
1 Mitre Ct Bldgs, Ground Floor, Temple, London, EC4Y 7BS, Call Date: May 1943 (Gray's Inn)

Williams *Llewelyn Jones*
4 Raphael Avenue, Brackla, Bridgend
CF31 2AU, 01656 647477, Call Date: July
1983 (Gray's Inn)

Williams *Miss Natasha Louise* •
Company Lawyer, JC Decaux UK Ltd,
Uniti Goldhawk Ind Est, 2A Brackenbury
Road, London W6 0BA, 0181 746 1000,
Fax: 0181 749 2046, Call Date: Oct 1995
(Gray's Inn) Qualifications: LLB

Williams *Paul Richard* •
Legal Advisor, Banque Nationale de
Paris, London Branch, 8-13 King William
Street, London EC4P 4HS, 0171 548
9511, Fax: 0171 548 9387, Call Date:
Nov 1984 (Middle Temple)
Qualifications: BA (Hons)(B'ham), Dip
Law (Lond)

Williams *The Hon Miss Rebecca Clare*
Call Date: Feb 1995 (Inner Temple)
Qualifications: MA (Oxon), M.Phil
(Cantab)

Williams *Richard Mark St.John*
Call Date: Oct 1997 (Gray's Inn)
Qualifications: BA (Dunelm)

Williams *Robert Charles*
Call Date: July 1973 (Inner Temple)
Qualifications: MA (Oxon)

Williams *Commander Robert Evan* •
DNSC/C2, Room 215a, Victory Building,
HM Naval Base, Portsmouth PO1 3LR,
01705 727252, Fax: 01705 727112, Call
Date: July 1981 (Gray's Inn)
Qualifications: LLB

Williams *Miss Rosemarie Maud
Josephine* •
and Member Attorney at Law, Guyana,
Call Date: July 1978 (Middle Temple)
Qualifications: BA (Kent), LLM (Lond)

Williams *Ms Rowan Elaine*
Bench Legal Adviser, Eastbourne &
Hailsham, Magistrates Court, The Law
Courts, Old Orchard Road, Eastbourne,
East Sussex BN21 4UN, 01323 727518,
Fax: 01323 649372, Call Date: July 1981
(Middle Temple)

Williams *Miss Samantha* •
Senior Crown Prosecutor, Crown
Prosecution Service, Brighton, Call Date:
Oct 1992 (Lincoln's Inn) Qualifications:
LLB(Hons)(Wales)

Williams *Ms Samantha Tracey*
Call Date: Nov 1997 (Lincoln's Inn)
Qualifications: LLB (Hons)(Middx)

Williams *Miss Sara*
Call Date: Oct 1996 (Lincoln's Inn)
Qualifications: LLB (Hons)(Wales)

Williams *Dr Sheridan Petrea* •
Senior Medico-Legal Adviser, The
Medical Protection Society, 33 Cavendish
Square, London W1M 0PS, 0171 399
1300, MFPHM (Member Faculty Public
Health Medicine (Royal College of
Physicians)), Call Date: July 1998
(Middle Temple) Qualifications: MBBS
(Middx Hosp), Dip Law

Williams *Simon David*
Norton Rose Solicitors, Kempson House,
Camomile Street, London EC3A 7AN,
0171 283 6000, Call Date: Oct 1996
(Gray's Inn) Qualifications: BA (Oxon)

Williams *Simon Peter* •
Lawyer, HM Customs & Excise, Solicitors
Office, 2nd Floor, New Kings Beam
House, 22 Upper Ground, London
SE1 9PJ, 0171 865 5547, Fax: 0171 865
5989, Call Date: Nov 1993 (Lincoln's
Inn) Qualifications: LLB (Hons)

Williams *Stephen John*
Call Date: Nov 1977 (Middle Temple)
Qualifications: LLB (Hons)(Lond)

Williams *Terence John*
Call Date: Nov 1992 (Gray's Inn)

Williams *Thomas Anthony John* •
Senior Crown Prosecutor, Crown
Prosecution Service, Seven Thames Area,
Berkshire Branch Office, Eaton Court,
112 Oxford Road, Reading RG1 7LL,
01734 503771, Fax: 01734 508192, Call
Date: Nov 1983 (Gray's Inn)
Qualifications: LLB (wales)

Williams *Timothy Ifor*
Call Date: July 1998 (Inner Temple)
Qualifications: BA (Cantab), PGCE
(Oxon), PhD (Wales), CPE (Glamorgan)

Williams *Miss Victoria Anna*
Call Date: Mar 1998 (Middle Temple)
Qualifications: BSc (Hons)(Lond)

Williams *William Gwynn* •
Legal Advisor, Laura Ashley Holdings plc,
Third Floor, The Chambers, Chelsea
Harbour, London, Call Date: July 1996
(Gray's Inn) Qualifications: LLB
(Wolverhampton)

Williams of Mostyn *Lord*
Recorder Deputy High Court Judge, also
Inns of Court I & L and Member
Northern Ireland Bar Irish Bar, Call
Date: Feb 1965 (Gray's Inn)
Qualifications: MA, LLM(Cantab)

Williamson *Ms Jacqueline*
Scotland, and Member Scottish Bar, Call
Date: Feb 1995 (Inner Temple)
Qualifications: LLB , LLM (Lond)

Williamson *Mrs Judith Nicola*
Grove House, Semley, Shaftesbury,
Dorset SP7 9AP, 01747 830389, Call
Date: Nov 1978 (Inner Temple)

Williamson *Miss Rosemary Anne* •
Court Clerk, Buckinghamshire County
Council, County Hall, Aylesbury, Bucks,
0296 82371, Fax: 0296 26347, Call Date:
Feb 1979 (Middle Temple)
Qualifications: BA (Lond)

Williamson *Stephen Ellis*
The Corner, 1a Glen Iris Ave, Canterbury,
Kent CT2 8HW, Call Date: Jan 1951
(Inner Temple) Qualifications: MA
(Cantab)LLB

Willis-Jones *William Mark* •
Deputy General Counsel - International,
Armstrong World Industries, Armstrong
House, 38 Market Square, Uxbridge,
Middlesex UB8 1NG, 01895 202045, Fax:
01895 256869, Call Date: Nov 1982
(Middle Temple) Qualifications: BSc
(Lond) Dip Law

Willits *Ms Joanne Cresswell*
Matthew Wilkinson Solicitors, 39 Albert
Road, Law Department, Middlesbrough
TS1 1NX, 01642 218888, Fax: 01642
221222, Call Date: Nov 1993 (Gray's
Inn) Qualifications: LLB (L'pool)

Willmer *John Franklin*
Arbitrator: Wreck Commissioner,
Non-Practising Member of the Midland &
Oxford Circuit 7 King's Bench Walk,
Ground Floor, Temple, London, EC4Y
7DS, Call Date: Feb 1955 (Inner Temple)
Qualifications: MA (Oxon)

Willmer *Paul Richard*
Principal Court Clerk, Humberside
Magistrates Court, 31 Lairgate, Beverley
HU17 8EP, 01482 881264, Call Date: Feb
1989 (Gray's Inn) Qualifications: LLB
(Hull)

Willmin *Mrs Rosalind Dawn* •
Senior Crown Prosecutor, Crown
Prosecution Service, 4/6 Prebendal
Court, Oxford Road, Aylesbury,
Buckinghamshire, 01296 436441, Call
Date: Nov 1984 (Middle Temple)
Qualifications: Dip Magisterial Law

Willmore *Ms Christine Joan*
3 Church Farm Close, Yate, Bristol
BS17 5BZ, 01454 311777, Fax: 01454
311777, Call Date: July 1979 (Inner
Temple) Qualifications: LLB (Bris)

Wills *Jeffrey*
Court Clerk, Manchester City,
Magistrates' Court, Crown Square,
Manchester M60 1PR, 0161 832 7272,
Fax: 0161 832 5421, Call Date: Nov 1991
(Gray's Inn) Qualifications: Dip Law,
CPE, Cert , in Training & , Development,
Dip., Nebs.M.

Willson *John* •
Legal Adviser, The Yasuda Trust &
Banking, Company Limited, 1 Liverpool
Street, London EC2M 7NH, 0171 628
5721, Call Date: July 1978 (Lincoln's
Inn)

Wilne *Richard James*
Call Date: July 1996 (Middle Temple)
Qualifications: BA (Hons)(Durham)

Wilson *Adam Richard*
SFA (Registered Representive), Teather &
Greenwood, 12-20 Camomile Street,
London EC3A 7NN, 0171 426 9510, Fax:
0171 929 0900, Private Client
Stockbroker, Call Date: Nov 1994 (Gray's
Inn) Qualifications: BA (Essex), Dip Law,
Dip Fin ALLMR, MSI

Wilson *Alan Paul*
Senior Law Lecturer Consumer &
Contract Law, University of East
London, Longbridge Road, Dagenham,
London, Essex RM8 2AS, 0181 590
7722, Fax: 0181 590 7799, Formerly of
the Consumers Association, Call Date:
May 1983 (Gray's Inn) Qualifications:
LLB (L'pool), LLM (Lond)

Wilson *Miss Anne Christine* •
Senior Legal Adviser, 3i plc, 91
Waterloo Road, London SE1 8XP, 0171
928 3131, Call Date: Nov 1970 (Gray's
Inn) Qualifications: LL.B

Wilson *Arthur William Darragh*
Call Date: July 1957 (Inner Temple)
Qualifications: MA (Cantab)

Wilson *Miss Caroline Ann*
Systems Administrator at SmithKline
Beecham, SmithKline Beecham, Stoke
Poges Lane, Slough, 01753 502354,
Fax: 01753 502001, Call Date: Oct
1993 (Inner Temple) Qualifications:
LLB (Northumbria)

Wilson *Charles Jonathan*
Call Date: Oct 1995 (Gray's Inn)
Qualifications: BA (Wales), LLB
(Lond), LLM (Cantab)

Wilson *Mrs Christine Elisabeth*
Legal Team Manager, Berkshire &
Oxfordshire Mag's, Court's Committee,
Easby House, Northfield End, Henley
on Thames, Oxfordshire RG9 2NB,
01491 412720, Fax: 01491 412762,
and Member Singapore Bar, Call Date:
July 1974 (Inner Temple)
Qualifications: LLB

Wilson *Mrs Faye Claudette* •
Crown Prosecutor, Crown Prosecution
Service, 8th Floor, Prospect West, 81
Station Road, Croydon, Surrey, Call
Date: Nov 1983 (Lincoln's Inn)
Qualifications: BSc.Soc, LLB (W
Indies), LLM (Lond)

Wilson *Gareth William*
Solicitor, J R Jones Solicitors, 56a The
Mall, Ealing Broadway, London W5 3TA,
0181 566 2595, Fax: 0181 579 4288,
Call Date: Feb 1986 (Lincoln's Inn)
Qualifications: LLM (Cantab), BA

Wilson *Gavin Bruce*
2/12 Abercorn Place, London NW8 9XP,
0171 286 3045, Call Date: Nov 1976
(Gray's Inn) Qualifications: BSc (Hons)
, C.Eng,MICE

Wilson *Miss Hilary Margaret* •
Legal Adviser, Kvaerner Construction
Group Lt, Maple Cross House, Denham
Way, Maple Cross, Rickmansworth,
Herts WD3 2SW, 01923 776666, Fax:
01923 423864, Call Date: Nov 1974
(Gray's Inn) Qualifications: MA
(Cantab)

Wilson *Mrs Hilda*
7 Acacia Gardens, London NW8 6AH,
0171 722 7809, Fax: 0171 722 7809,
also Inn of Court M & L, Call Date: Nov
1953 (Gray's Inn) Qualifications: BA

Wilson *James Mason*
Call Date: Nov 1991 (Inner Temple)
Qualifications: LLB (Hons)(Leeds)

Wilson *Julian* •
Lawyer, Durham County Council,
County Hall, Durham DH1 5UL, (0191)
386 4411, Call Date: Oct 1994 (Middle
Temple) Qualifications: BSc
(Hons)(York), CPE (Northumbria)

Wilson *Mrs Katy-Marie*
Clifford Chance, 200 Aldersgate Street,
London EC1A 4JJ, 0171 600 1000, Fax:
0171 600 5555, Call Date: Oct 1993
(Gray's Inn) Qualifications: LLB
(B'ham)

Wilson *Kenneth*
42 Hawthylands Road, Hailsham, East
Sussex BN27 1EY, 01323 840966, Call
Date: Nov 1957 (Middle Temple)
Qualifications: LLB

Wilson *Leslie Arnold*
Call Date: Nov 1974 (Inner Temple)
Qualifications: BA

Wilson *Mark John* •
Senior Principal Legal Officer,
Department of Social Security,
Department of Health, New Court, 48
Carey Street, London WC2A 2LS, 0171
412 1234, Fax: 0171 412 1227, Call
Date: Apr 1991 (Lincoln's Inn)
Qualifications: LLB (Hons)

Wilson *Michael Alexander*
Editor, Butterworth, Halsbury House,
35 Chancery Lane, London WC2A 1EL,
0171 400 2688, Call Date: Oct 1994
(Inner Temple) Qualifications: BA, CPE
(Coventry)

Wilson *Michael J. H.*
Clerk to the Justices, Huddersfield
Magistrates' Crt, Civic Centre,
Huddersfield, 01484 423552, Call Date:
Nov 1975 (Inner Temple)
Qualifications: LLM

Wilson *Mrs Shelley Anne* •
Senior Crown Prosecutor, Crown
Prosecution Service, Justinian House,
Spitfire Close, Ermine Bus Pk,
Huntington, Cambs, Call Date: Nov
1987 (Inner Temple) Qualifications:
BA (Kent)

Wilson *Terence John* •
Head of Legal Department, Mansfield
District Council, Civic Centre,
Chesterfield Road South, Mansfield,
Notts NG19 7BH, 01623 463226, Call
Date: Nov 1982 (Lincoln's Inn)
Qualifications: LLB (Leics)

Wilson *Miss Vanessa Gay*
Legal & Business Affairs Executive,
United Broadcasting &, Enertainment,
Ludgate House, 245 Blackfriars Road,
London SE1 9UY, 0171 579 4418, Fax:
0171 579 4438, Call Date: Oct 1992
(Middle Temple) Qualifications: LLB
(Hons)

Wilson *Ms Victoria Anne* •
Legal Services, London Borough of
Camden, Town Hall, Judd Street,
London WC1H 9LP, 0171 278 4444,
Fax: 0171 860 5671, Call Date: Nov
1994 (Inner Temple) Qualifications:
BA, CPE (Notts)

Wilson *The Hon William Edward
Alexander* •
Dept of Environment Transport & the
Regions, Legal Dept Harkness
Fellowship 1, 9/J10 Eland House,
Bressenden Place, London SW1E 5DU,
0171 890 4809, Fax: 0171 890 4804,
Call Date: Nov 1978 (Middle Temple)
Qualifications: LLM

Wilson jr. *John*
365 Dam Street, Colombo 12, 94 1
324579 or 94 1 446954, Fax: 94 1
446954, Call Date: Oct 1996 (Lincoln's
Inn) Qualifications: LLB
(Hons)(Lond), Maitrise en Droit,
Francais (Paris)

Wilson *Thomas Robert*
Senior Consultant, Legal and
Regulatory, InterConnect
Communications, Merlin House
Ltd, Station Road, Chepstow,
Monmouthshire NP6 5PB, 44 (0) 1291
620425, Fax: 44 (0) 1291 627119, Call
Date: July 1977 (Inner Temple)
Qualifications: BSc (Hons)

Wilton *Stephen Barsley* •
Senior Court Clerk, Magistrates' Courts,
PO Box 97, Westgate, Leeds LS1 3JP,
0113 2459653, Fax: 0113 2444700,
Call Date: May 1976 (Middle Temple)
Qualifications: LLB (Lond)

Winch *Mrs Jennifer Lynn*
Call Date: July 1966 (Inner Temple)
Qualifications: LLB (Lond)

Winckley *Peter Frederick*
J Chandler & Co (Buckfast) Ltd, Abbey
House, Peterborough Road, London
SW6 3BP, 0171 736 2185, Fax: 0171
736 4503, Call Date: July 1989 (Gray's
Inn) Qualifications: LLB [Wales]

Windsor *Miss Ann Victoria*
Call Date: Nov 1969 (Inner Temple)
Qualifications: LLB (Lond), LLM
(Lond)

Winfield *Miss Georgina Mary* •
Senior Crown Prosecutor, Crown
Prosecution Service, 17th Floor,
Tolworth Tower, Surbiton, Surrey
KT6 7DS, Call Date: Nov 1989 (Middle
Temple) Qualifications: LLB Hons

• Barrister in employment

Winfield *Miss Sarah* •
Legal Officer, Metropolitian Police,
Solicitor's Department, New Scotland
Yard, Broadway, London SW1H 0BG,
0171 230 7242, Fax: 0171 230 7209,
Call Date: Oct 1990 (Inner Temple)
Qualifications: LLB (Hons)(Exon)

Wingfield-Digby *Kenelm Edward*
Call Date: Oct 1996 (Inner Temple)
Qualifications: BSc (City), CPE
(Westminster)

Wingrove *Roderick Stephen Fontannaz*
73 Elgin Crescent, London W11 2JE,
0171 727 5722, Fax: 0171 229 8907,
Call Date: Nov 1973 (Middle Temple)
Qualifications: MA (Cantab)

Winkley *Julian Patrick* •
Senior Lawyer, HM Customs & Excise,
Solicitor's Office, Ralli Quays, 3 Stanley
Street, Salford M60 9LB, 0161 827 0500,
Fax: 0161 827 0551, Call Date: Nov 1983
(Middle Temple) Qualifications: BA

Winn-Jones *Ms Elizabeth Margaret*
Call Date: July 1985 (Lincoln's Inn)
Qualifications: BA (Colombia), BA
(Cantab)

Winship *Peter Thomas* •
Principal Crown Prosecutor (Team
Leader), Crown Prosecution Service,
Windsor House, 10 Manchester Road,
Bradford, West Yorks BD5 0QH, Call
Date: Nov 1988 (Gray's Inn)
Qualifications: MA (St Andrews)

Winter *Rex Alexander*
Call Date: Oct 1997 (Lincoln's Inn)
Qualifications: CPE (Northumbria)

Winter *Mrs Tracy-Ellen* •
Employment Law Advisor, The British
Dental Association, 64 Wimpole Street,
London W1M 8AL, 0171 735 0875, Call
Date: Oct 1998 (Middle Temple)
Qualifications: LLB (Hons)(Kent)

Wise *Curt Nicolas* •
Principal Crown Prosecutor, Crown
Prosecution Service, 50 Ludgate Hill,
London EC4M 7EX, 0171 273 8120, Call
Date: Nov 1983 (Middle Temple)
Qualifications: BA, LLM

Witcombe *Richard Joshua*
Call Date: Oct 1997 (Lincoln's Inn)
Qualifications: LLB (Hons)(Coventry),
LLM (Lond)

Witham *Simon* •
Senior Legal Adviser, Gallaher Limited,
Member's Hill, Brooklands Road,
Weybridge, Surrey, 01932 859777, Fax:
01932 832570, Call Date: Nov 1987
(Gray's Inn) Qualifications: LLB

Withey *Richard Leslie*
Call Date: Oct 1996 (Inner Temple)
Qualifications: LLB

Withington *Neil Robert* •
Deputy General Counsel, British
American Tobacco, Globe House, 4
Temple Place, London WC2R 2PG, 0171
845 1000, Fax: 0171 240 0555, Call
Date: July 1981 (Middle Temple)
Qualifications: MA (Oxon) B.C.L.

Wittering *Robin*
Herbert Smith, Exchange House,
Primrose Street, London EC2A 2HS,
0171 374 8000, Fax: 0171 374 8000,
Call Date: Nov 1995 (Lincoln's Inn)
Qualifications: BA, LLM, MA

Wolfin *Jolyon Howard*
Call Date: Oct 1992 (Middle Temple)
Qualifications: BA (Hons)

Woloski *Miss Lindsey Isobel* •
Office of the Insurance, Ombudsman,
135 Park Street, London SE1 9EA, 0171
902 8185, Call Date: Nov 1988 (Gray's
Inn) Qualifications: LLB

Womersley *Walter Giro*
41 Tennyson Avenue, Harrogate, North
Yorkshire HG1 3LE, 01423 563442, Call
Date: Nov 1994 (Gray's Inn)
Qualifications: LLB (Warw)

Womersley-Smith *Howard Anthony* •
Legal Advisor, Colt Telecommunications,
0171 390 3006, Fax: 0171 390 3750,
Call Date: Nov 1996 (Inner Temple)
Qualifications: LLB (Plymouth)

Wong *Chin Wun Wilfred*
Call Date: Oct 1992 (Middle Temple)
Qualifications: LLB(Hons), LLM(Lond)

Wong *Joseph Tai Nang*
Call Date: July 1984 (Gray's Inn)
Qualifications: LLB, MA (Social, Science)

Wong *Ronny Fook*
SC Hong Kong and Member Hong Kong
Bar 3 Verulam Buildings, London, WC1R
5NT, Call Date: Nov 1970 (Lincoln's Inn)
Qualifications: LLB (Hull)

Wong *Tsu Sien*
Call Date: Nov 1996 (Middle Temple)
Qualifications: LLB (Hons)(Lond)

Wong *Wai Ip*
17 Gerrard Street, London W1V 8HB, 44
0171 301 8881, Fax: 44 0171 301 8807,
and Member Hong Kong, Call Date: July
1997 (Lincoln's Inn) Qualifications: LLB
(Hons)BSc (Hons), MSc, MScDP, MA,
ACCA, FCIArb, ACIB, MCIPS, MCIM,
MIMgt, MACS, MIEEE

Wong *Miss Weng Ho*
Trade Mark Associate, D Young & Co, 10
Staple Inn, London WC1, Call Date: July
1987 (Gray's Inn) Qualifications: LLB
(Lond), LLM (Lond)

Wong *Miss Weng Yuen* •
Senior Crown Prosecutor, Crown
Prosecution Service, 3rd Floor, King's
House, Kymberley Road, Harrow,
Middlesex, 0181 424 8688, Fax: 0181
424 9157, Call Date: July 1990 (Middle
Temple) Qualifications: LLB (Brunel)

Wong *Miss Yoke Sum*
Call Date: Nov 1992 (Middle Temple)
Qualifications: LLB

Wood *Allan William*
Arbitrator, Adjudicator, James R Knowles,
Wardle House, King Street, Knutsford,
Cheshire WA16 6PD, 01565 654666, Fax:
01565 755009, Call Date: Mar 1996
(Lincoln's Inn) Qualifications: BSc
(Sheff), Dip Law, C Eng, FICE, FCIArb

Wood *Andrew Nigel Marquis* •
Principal Court Clerk, Barnet Magistrates
Court, 7c High Street, Barnet, Herts,
0181 441 9042, Call Date: Nov 1991
(Lincoln's Inn) Qualifications: LLB
(Hons) (Hull)

Wood *Miss Caroline Sarah* •
Call Date: Mar 1998 (Gray's Inn)
Qualifications: LLB (W'hampton)

Wood *Christopher Douglas*
Garretts, 1 Victoria Square, Birmingham
B1 1BD, 0121 698 9000, Fax: 0121 698
9050, Call Date: May 1997 (Lincoln's
Inn) Qualifications: BSc (Hons), Dip
Law, MSc, ARICS, MCIOB,, ACIArb

Wood *Christopher Martin*
Call Date: Oct 1997 (Gray's Inn)
Qualifications: BSc (L'pool)

Wood *Wing Commander Christopher
Nigel Wiley* •
Legal Services, RAF Prosecuting
Authority, HQ PTC RAF Innsworth,
Gloucester GL3 1EZ, 01452 712612, Fax:
01452 510829, Call Date: July 1977
(Middle Temple) Qualifications: MA
(Cantab)

Wood *Miss Emily Bridget Ellen*
Call Date: Mar 1998 (Lincoln's Inn)
Qualifications: LLB (Hons)(Wales)

Wood *Miss Gaynor Ellen* •
Legal Adviser, Banque Nationale de Paris,
Interest rate Derivatives, Legal
Department, 8-13 King William Street,
London EC4P 4HS, 0171 548 9413, Fax:
0171 772 9655, Call Date: Nov 1994
(Gray's Inn) Qualifications: LLB

Wood *James Maitland* •
Crown Prosecution Service, Crown
Prosecution Service, Colemore Gate, 2
Colemore Row, Birmingham B3 2QA,
0121 629 7200, Call Date: Nov 1989
(Lincoln's Inn) Qualifications: LLB
(Wales)

Wood *Mrs Janine Suzanne Dean* •
CPS Midlands, 12th Floor, Colmore Gate,
2 Colmore Row, Birmingham B3 2QA,
Call Date: July 1983 (Inner Temple)
Qualifications: BA

Wood *Sir John Crossley*
Judicial Studies Board (Tribunals
Committee), Queen's Chambers, 5 John
Dalton Street, Manchester, M2 6ET, Call
Date: June 1950 (Gray's Inn)
Qualifications: LLB, LLM (Manch)

E

Wood *Karl Bradwell*
Call Date: Feb 1994 (Middle Temple)
Qualifications: LLB (Hons) (Anglia)

Wood *Kelvin John* •
Principal Crown Prosecutor, Crown
Prosecution Service, Crown House,
Winston Churchill Avenue, Portsmouth,
Hants, 01705 752004, Call Date: Nov
1985 (Middle Temple) Qualifications:
MA (Cantab)

Wood *Michael Charles* •
Deputy Legal Adviser at the Foreign &
Commonwealth Office, Foreign &
Commonwealth Office, Legal Advisers,
King Charles Street, London SW1A 2AH,
0171 270 3061, Fax: 0171 270 2280,
Call Date: Nov 1968 (Gray's Inn)
Qualifications: MA, LLB

Wood *Miss Priscilla Jane*
Call Date: Nov 1973 (Middle Temple)
Qualifications: BA, MLitt (Edin)

Wood *Richley William* •
Senior Crown Prosecutor, Crown
Prosecution Service, Westway House,
Westway Road, Weymouth, Dorset, Call
Date: Nov 1980 (Lincoln's Inn)
Qualifications: BA (Hons)

Wood *Robert*
Call Date: Oct 1997 (Gray's Inn)
Qualifications: BA (Durham)

Wood *Mrs Sarah Ann* •
Director/Company Secretary Re-Waste
Group plc Director,ECO Europe
Director/Co Secretary Sear Green Cone
Ltd, Cockshoot Farm, West Wycombe,
High Wycombe, Buckinghamshire
HP14 3AR, 01494 443329 or 01 494
564004, Fax: 01494 442194, Call Date:
July 1989 (Inner Temple)
Qualifications: BA, MI Infsci, F InstD,
M.Inst WM

Wood *Stephen Paul*
Call Date: Nov 1998 (Gray's Inn)
Qualifications: LLB (Brunel)

Woodford *Miss Clare Judith*
Call Date: Mar 1999 (Gray's Inn)
Qualifications: BA (Nott'm)

Woodhead *Mrs Sarah Elizabeth*
Foster Solicitors, 60 London Street,
Norwich NR2 1JY, 01603 620508, Fax:
01603 624090, Call Date: Nov 1991
(Inner Temple) Qualifications: LLB

Woodhead *Simon Andrew*
Eversheds, Holland Court, The Close,
Norwich NR1 4DX, 01603 272727, Fax:
01603 610535, Call Date: Oct 1990
(Lincoln's Inn) Qualifications: LLB
(E.Anglia)

Woodhouse *Antony James*
D J Freeman, 43 Fetter Lane, London
EC4A IJU, 0171 583 4055, Fax: 0171
353 7377, Call Date: Oct 1993
(Lincoln's Inn) Qualifications: BA
(Hons)

Woodhouse *John Sidney Lister*
Brooklyn, Kelsall, Tarporley, Cheshire
CW6 OQB, 01829 751462, Call Date:
June 1949 (Gray's Inn) Qualifications:
MA (Cantab)

Woodhouse *Richard Francis* •
H.M.Senior Planning Inspector,
Department of the Environment,
Tollgate House, Houlton Street, Bristol
BS2 9DJ, Call Date: July 1962 (Inner
Temple) Qualifications: MA (Cantab)

Woodhull *Miss Anuita*
Llewelyn Zietman Solicitors, Temple
Bar House, 23-28 Fleet Street, London
EC4Y 1AA, 0171 842 5400, Fax: 0171
842 5463, Call Date: May 1997 (Inner
Temple) Qualifications: LLB (Lond)

Wooding *Mrs Anne Marie*
Call Date: Mar 1997 (Gray's Inn)
Qualifications: LLB (Nott'm)

Woodings *David Jon* •
Senior Crown Prosecutor, Call Date: Oct
1992 (Lincoln's Inn) Qualifications:
BA(Hons) (Lancaster),
LLB(Hons) (Lond), LLM (Sussex)

Woodman *Paul Norman* •
Legal Adviser with the Ministry of
Defence, MOD (Commercial)Legal
Advisers, Poplat [H] 120, MOD Abbey
Wood, Bristol BS34 8JH, 0117 91
32641, Fax: 0117 91 30965, Call Date:
Oct 1991 (Inner Temple)
Qualifications: LLB (Hull)

Woods *Alex*
'Nightingales', Birch, Colchesterr, Essex
CO2 0NA, 01206 330325, Call Date:
July 1996 (Inner Temple)
Qualifications: BA (Lond), CPE

Woods *Miss Lynn*
Call Date: Feb 1965 (Middle Temple)
Qualifications: MA (Oxon)

Woods *Sidney Wilfred*
Bramley Mill, Mill Lane, Bramley,
Guildford, Surrey GU5 0HW, Call Date:
June 1951 (Gray's Inn) Qualifications:
LLB, BCom (Hons)

Woodward *Mrs Georgina*
Legal Adviser, Hampshire Magistrates
Court, The Court house, Elmleigh
Road, Havant, Hants PO9 2AL, 01705
492024, Fax: 01705 475356, Call Date:
May 1983 (Gray's Inn) Qualifications:
LLB (Manch)

Woodward *Jeremy Paul* •
Legal Adviser, James R Knowles
Limited, Langdale House, Gadbrook
Business Centre, Rudheath, Northwich,
Cheshire CW9 7UL, 01606 814720, Call
Date: Oct 1996 (Inner Temple)
Qualifications: LLB (Leics)

Woodward *Mrs Sarah Elizabeth Ann*
Legal Adviser, Bedfordshire Mag Crts
Comm, Shire Hall, 3 St Paul's Square,
Bedford, 01234 359422, Call Date: Nov
1988 (Gray's Inn) Qualifications: BA

Woodyatt *Mrs Valerie Anne*
Call Date: Nov 1972 (Inner Temple)
Qualifications: LLM

Woogara *Ranjitsingh*
Call Date: Nov 1994 (Middle Temple)
Qualifications: BA, LLB

Wooler *Stephen John* •
Deputy Legal Secretary to the Law
Officers, Legal Secretariat to the Law,
Officers, Attorney General's Chambers,
9 Buckingham Gate, London SW1 6JP,
0171 271 2403, Fax: 0171 271 2433,
Call Date: Nov 1969 (Gray's Inn)
Qualifications: LLB (Lond)

Woolf *John Moss*
West Lodge, 113 Marsh Lane,
Stanmore, Middx HA7 4TH, 0181 952
1373, Call Date: June 1948 (Lincoln's
Inn)

Woolfe *Steven Marcus*
Associate Corporate Department
Financial Services Law., Taylor Joynson
Garrett, Carmelite, 50 Victoria
Embankment, Blackfriars, LondoN
EC4Y 0DK, 0171 353 1234, Fax: 0171
936 2666, Call Date: Oct 1992 (Inner
Temple) Qualifications: LLB (Hons)

Woolgar *Paul Justin*
Call Date: Mar 1998 (Middle Temple)
Qualifications: LLB (Hons) (Essex)

Woolhouse *Ms Sarita Patil*
Herbert Smith, Exchange House,
Primrose Street, London EC2A 2HS,
0171 374 8000, Fax: 0171 374 0888,
Solicitor and Member India Bar, Call
Date: Nov 1994 (Inner Temple)
Qualifications: M.Phil (Cantab)

Woolich *Mrs Sara Jayne* •
London Borough of Lewisham, Town
Hall, London SE6 4RU, 0181 695 6000,
Call Date: Oct 1990 (Inner Temple)
Qualifications: LLB (So'ton)

Woollcombe *James Humphrey George*
Call Date: Feb 1955 (Inner Temple)
Qualifications: MA, BCL Hons [Oxon]

Woolley *David John Llewellyn*
Call Date: May 1987 (Gray's Inn)
Qualifications: LLB, FCII, FTII

Woolley *Mrs Diana Rosemary* •
Group Company Secretary, Diversified
Agency, Services Limited, 239 Old
Marylebone Road, London NW1 5QT,
0171 298 7000, Fax: 0171 724 8292,
Call Date: July 1962 (Gray's Inn)
Qualifications: LLB

Wootton *Miss Nicola Jane Dawn*
Oxford Magisttrates Court, Speedwell
Street, Oxford, Call Date: July 1995
(Middle Temple) Qualifications: BA
(Hons)

Workman *Andrew John*
Senior Principal Court Clerk, Liverpool
Magistrates Court, Committee, Liverpool
Magistrates Court, 107 Dale Street,
Liverpool L2 2JQ, 0151 236 5871, Fax:
0151 231 5594, Call Date: Feb 1994
(Gray's Inn) Qualifications: LLB

Workman *Andrew Jonathan*
Call Date: Oct 1998 (Lincoln's Inn)
Qualifications: BA (Kent)

Wormald-Cripps *Darren William* •
Legal Counsel (Fixed Income Capital
Markets Division), Lehman Brothers
International, One Broadgate, Broadgate
Circle, London EC2M 7HA, 0171 260
2085, Fax: 0171 260 2882, Call Date:
Nov 1995 (Lincoln's Inn) Qualifications:
LLB (Hons)(Essex)

Worrell *Gavin Jon Francis* •
Legal Advisor, Vine House, 184 Staines
Road East, Sunbury on Thames,
Middlesex TW16 5AY, Call Date: Nov
1994 (Middle Temple) Qualifications: BA
(Hons)

Worsfold *Miss Priscilla Anne* •
Principal Crown Prosecutor (Team
Leader), Crown Prosecution Service,
Broadlands House, Staplers Road,
Newport, Isle of Wight PO30 2HY, 01983
528309, Fax: 01983 521808, Call Date:
July 1975 (Gray's Inn)

Worsley *Miss Jane Fay*
97 East Hill, London SW18 2QD, 0181
875 0781, Call Date: Feb 1995 (Inner
Temple) Qualifications: CPE (Middx),
FIBMS

Worsley *John Bertrand*
Furlong Hse, West Furlong Lane,
Hurstpierpoint, Sussex BN6 9QA, 01273
833320, Call Date: July 1954 (Inner
Temple) Qualifications: MA, LLB
(Cantab)

Worthington *Robert Edward*
Call Date: Oct 1996 (Gray's Inn)
Qualifications: BSc (Leeds)

Wragg *Jonathan Robert* •
Deputy Principal Civil Litigation
Barrister, Legal Services Department,
The Town Hall, King Street,
Hammersmith, London, 0181 576 5304,
Call Date: Nov 1995 (Gray's Inn)
Qualifications: BMUS (Hull), Dip Law

Wreford *John Bertram*
01732 456439, Call Date: July 1954
(Gray's Inn) Qualifications: FCII

Wrench *Benjamin James* •
Compliance Assistant, Refco Overseas
Limited, Trinity Tower, 9 Thomas Moore
Street, London EC1 9YN, Call Date: Nov
1995 (Lincoln's Inn) Qualifications: LLB
(Hons)(Exon)

Wright *Alistair Charles*
Solicitor, Call Date: Nov 1992 (Gray's
Inn) Qualifications: LLB (Hons)

Wright *Mrs Angela* •
Librarian & Information Officer,
Fishburn Boxer, 60 Strand, London
WC2N 5LR, 0171 925 2884, Fax: 0171
486 3256, Call Date: Oct 1993 (Inner
Temple) Qualifications: MA (Cantab)

Wright *Brendan Paul*
Call Date: Feb 1995 (Gray's Inn)
Qualifications: MA (Cantab)

Wright *Miss Charlotte Helen Mary*
Legal Adviser, Call Date: Nov 1991
(Middle Temple) Qualifications: LLB
Hons (Leic)

Wright *Desmond Garforth*
Call Date: Jan 1950 (Lincoln's Inn)
Qualifications: MA (Oxon)

Wright *Miss Emma Louise*
Call Date: Oct 1998 (Lincoln's Inn)
Qualifications: LLB (Hons)(Leeds)

Wright *Gerard Henry*
Call Date: Feb 1954 (Gray's Inn)
Qualifications: BCL, BA (Oxon)

Wright *Miss Gwendolyn Patricia*
Call Date: Nov 1998 (Lincoln's Inn)
Qualifications: LLB (Hons)

Wright *Mrs Lesley Ann*
Legal Adviser, The Court House, Tufton
Street, Ashford, Kent TN23 1QS, 01233
663203, Fax: 01233 663206, Call Date:
Nov 1986 (Lincoln's Inn) Qualifications:
BA

Wright *Mark John*
Call Date: Oct 1997 (Middle Temple)
Qualifications: LLB (Hons)(Lond), LLM
(Sussex)

Wright *Mrs Moira Elynwy*
Faculty of Law, University of
Birmingham, Edgbaston, Birmingham
B15 2TT, Call Date: July 1989 (Gray's
Inn) Qualifications: LLB [Wales], BCL
[Oxon]

Wright *Paul* •
Lord Chancellor's Dept, Selborne House,
54/60 Victoria Street, London
SW1E 6QW, 0171 210 1300, Call Date:
Oct 1993 (Inner Temple) Qualifications:
BA (Manch), CPE

Wright *Robert Anthony Kent*
Call Date: Jan 1949 (Lincoln's Inn)
Qualifications: MA (Oxon)

Wright *Robert Pickering* •
Lord Chancellor's Department,
Headquarters, Selborne House, 54-60
Victoria Street, London SW1E 6QW, 0171
210 8810, Call Date: Nov 1986 (Lincoln's
Inn) Qualifications: LLB

Wright *Robin*
Clerk to the Justices & Justices Chief
Executive, Barking & Dagenham
Magistrates, Courts Committee, The
Court House, East Street, Barking,Essex
IG11 8EW, 0181 594 5311, Fax: 0181
594 4297, Call Date: July 1980 (Gray's
Inn) Qualifications: DML, DMS

Wright *Mrs Rosalind* •
Director, Serious Fraud Office, Elm
House, 10-16 Elm Street, London
WC1X 0BJ, 0171 239 7272, Fax: 0171
837 1689, Member International Bar
Association, Call Date: June 1964
(Middle Temple) Qualifications: LLB
(Hons)

Wright *Lt Cdr Stuart Hugh* •
Supply Officer, HMS Nottingham, Call
Date: Oct 1995 (Middle Temple)
Qualifications: BA (Hons)

Wright *Ms Teresa Jane*
Call Date: Nov 1996 (Lincoln's Inn)
Qualifications: LLB (Hons)(Herts)

Wrobel *Brian John Robert Karen*
0171 243 8105, Also Inn of Court G.,
Honorary Legal Adviser, Parliamentary
Human Rights Group and Member Atty
at Law California, USA Supreme Court
Bar, Call Date: Nov 1973 (Lincoln's Inn)
Qualifications: LLM (Lond)

Wrzesien *Thomas James*
Call Date: Oct 1995 (Lincoln's Inn)
Qualifications: LLB (Lond)

Wyatt *Murat William* •
Legal Advisor to Legal Costs Negotiators
Limited, 18 Sheridan Lodge, Chase Side,
Southgate, London N14 4PJ, Call Date:
Oct 1996 (Lincoln's Inn) Qualifications:
LLB (Hons)(Lond)

Wyles *Miss Rhona Irene*
Managing Director, Director: IBC Group
plc, IBC UK Conferences Limited,
Gilmoora House, 57-61 Mortimer Street,
London W1N 8JX, 0171 637 4383, Fax:
0171 631 3214, Call Date: July 1973
(Inner Temple) Qualifications: BA (Jt
Hons)

Wylie *Alexander Featherstonhaugh*
Advocates Library, Parliament House,
Edinburgh, Lothian EH1 1RF, 0131 226
2881 (Clerk), Fax: 0131 225 3642, QC,
Formerly a Scottish Solicitor and
Member Scottish Bar, Call Date: Nov
1990 (Lincoln's Inn) Qualifications: LLB
(Edin), FCI Arb

Wyllie *Alistair*
Simmons & Simmons, 71 Connell
Crescent, Ealing, London W5 3BH, 0171
628 2020, Fax: 0171 628 2070, Call
Date: Feb 1989 (Inner Temple)
Qualifications: LLB (Dundee), LLM
(Cantab)

Wynn Davies *Arthur Geraint* •
Legal Manager, Telegraph Group
Limited, 1 Canada Square, Canary Wharf,
London E14 5DT, 0171 538 6220, Fax:
0171 538 7838, Call Date: Nov 1971
(Middle Temple) Qualifications: LLB
(Wales)

Wynne *Michael Williams*
Call Date: July 1979 (Gray's Inn)
Qualifications: MA (Cantab)

Wynne-Griffiths *David Peter*
Group Legal Auditor, ARC Ltd, Ivy
Cottage, Kingsdown, Corsham, Wilts
SN13 8AZ, 01225 742904, Fax: 01225
742904, Call Date: Feb 1955 (Gray's
Inn) Qualifications: MA (Cantab)

Yale *Andrew Charles John* •
BACFI Executive Committee, 29 Colville
Road, Notting Hill, London W11 2BT,
0171 4602633, Call Date: Mar 1998
(Inner Temple) Qualifications: BA
(Kingston), MA (Washington), CPE
(Lond)

Yap *Richard Hoong Keng* •
Senior Crown Prosecutor, Crown
Prosecution Service, Queen's House, 58
Victoria Street, St Albans, Herts
AL1 3HZ, 01727 818100, Fax: 01727
851080, Call Date: July 1985 (Lincoln's
Inn) Qualifications: BA

Yap *Yew Inn*
Call Date: July 1995 (Gray's Inn)
Qualifications: LLB (Lond)

Yardley *Robert Huw* •
Senior Crown Prosecutor, Crown
Prosecution Service, 5th Floor, Chartist
Tower, Upper Dock Street, Newport,
Gwent NP9 1DW, 01633 241024, Fax:
01633 842953, Call Date: Oct 1990
(Gray's Inn) Qualifications: LLB

Yardy *Keith Stuart* •
Senior Crown Prosecutor, Crown
Prosecution Service, Priory Gate, 29
Union Street, Maidstone, Kent
ME14 1PT, 01622 686425, Call Date:
July 1988 (Inner Temple)
Qualifications: LLB (Lond)

Yassin *Miss Aishah Saleema*
Call Date: Nov 1993 (Inner Temple)
Qualifications: LLB (Hons), LLM
(Notts)

Yates *Miss Lindsay Anne*
The Vicarage, 292 Thorney Leys,
Witney, Oxon OX8 7YP, 01993 773281,
Call Date: Nov 1992 (Inner Temple)
Qualifications: MA (Cantab), Dip Th

Yeates *Stephen Robert* •
Crown Prosecuter, Crown Prosecution
Service, 2nd Floor, Froomsgate House,
Rupert Street, Bristol BS1 2QJ, 0117
9273093, Call Date: Nov 1992 (Middle
Temple) Qualifications: BA (Hons,
Wales)

Yelloly *Christopher John*
Part-time Immigration Appeals
Ajudicator, Call Date: Nov 1964 (Middle
Temple)

Yeo *Clayton Jack* •
Senior Crown Prosecutor, Crown
Prosecution Service, 29th Floor,
Portland House, Stag Place, London
SW1E 5BH, Call Date: Nov 1988 (Gray's
Inn) Qualifications: BA, MA
(Manitoba), LLB (Lond)

Yeoh *Miss Grace Chee Leng*
Advocate and Solcitor, High Court of
Malaya and Member Malaysia Bar, Call
Date: Nov 1990 (Lincoln's Inn)
Qualifications: LLB (East Anglia)

Yeoman *Howard Victor*
Associate Lecturer in Law - Open
University, Call Date: Nov 1995 (Gray's
Inn) Qualifications: BA, Dip Law

Yerrell *Miss Nicola Jane* •
Legal Service, European Commission,
Avenue des Nerviens, 105, B-1040
Bruxelles, Belgium, +32 2 295 1969,
Fax: +32 2 296 5972, Call Date: Oct
1993 (Middle Temple) Qualifications:
BA (Hons) (Oxon), Licence Special en,
Droit Europeen Brussels

Yew *Andrew*
Call Date: Mar 1997 (Lincoln's Inn)
Qualifications: LLB

Yilman *Hussein Djahit*
11 Mahmout Pasha Street, PO Box 556,
Lefkosa, Mersin 10, 90392-2271646/
2272406, Fax: 90392-2288154, Retired
District Court President Overseas
Expert on Turkish Law and Member
Cyprus Bar, Call Date: Feb 1962 (Gray's
Inn) Qualifications: LLB (Istanbul)

Yip *Mrs Aik Hooi* •
Principle Legal Adviser, Newham
Magistrates', Court Committee,
389-397 High Street, Stratford, London
E15 4SB, 0181 522 5000, Fax: 0181
519 9214, Call Date: July 1985
(Lincoln's Inn) Qualifications: BA
(Sussex)

Yip *Allan Kai-Lun*
Call Date: Oct 1995 (Middle Temple)
Qualifications: BA (Hons)

Yip *Vincent*
Call Date: July 1998 (Gray's Inn)
Qualifications: BA (De Montefort)

Yonge *William James George Rowley*
Titmuss Sainer Dechert, 2 Serjeants
Inn, London EC4Y 1LT, 0171 583 5353,
Fax: 0171 353 3683, Call Date: July
1989 (Middle Temple) Qualifications:
BA Hons (Dunelm), AMSI

Youell *Christopher James* •
Senior Crown Prosecutor, Crown
Prosecution Service, Haldin House,
Queen Street, Norwich, Norfolk
NR2 4SX, 01603 666491, Call Date: Feb
1991 (Gray's Inn) Qualifications: LLB

Young *Mr Andrew David*
Crown Prosecution Service, 11A Princes
Street, Stafford ST16 2EU, 01785
223511, Fax: 01785 223577, Call Date:
Jul 1986 (Gray's Inn) Qualifications:
MA (Cantab)

Young *Andrew Paul*
Head of Legal Services, Deloitte &
Touche, Customs/Inland Revenue,
Litigation and Advisory, Hill House, 1
Little New Street, London EC4A 3TR,
0171 303 3398, Fax: 0171 303 4780,
Call Date: Oct 1992 (Lincoln's Inn)
Qualifications: LLB(Hons), BSc

Young *Barry* •
The Red House, Heckington, Lincs
NG34 9QU, 01529 460205, Fax: 01529
461144, Call Date: Nov 1968 (Inner
Temple) Qualifications: F.P.M.I

Young *Dr David Reginald*
Managing Director Oxford Analytica,
Oxford Analytica, 5 Alfred Street, Oxford
OX1 4EH, 01865 343202, Fax: 01865
242018, and Member New York and
District of Columbia, USA, US Supreme
Court, Call Date: July 1965 (Inner
Temple) Qualifications: BA (Oxon), MA
(Oxon), D.Phil (Oxon), LLB, (Cornell),
BS, (Wheaton)

Young *Edward William*
Call Date: Nov 1988 (Gray's Inn)
Qualifications: LLB (Manch)

Young *Edwin Briden John*
Consultant, Call Date: Nov 1977
(Lincoln's Inn) Qualifications: MA
(Cantab)

Young *Jeffrey Sinclair*
Justices' Chief Executive Justices Clerk,
Magistrates' Courts, Market Street,
Newcastle Upon Tyne NE1 6UR, 0191
232 7326, Fax: 0191 221 0025, Call
Date: Feb 1973 (Middle Temple)
Qualifications: LLB

Young *Michael James*
Call Date: Oct 1994 (Inner Temple)
Qualifications: MA (Cantab), BCL
(Oxon)

Young *Mrs Patricia Nuckchin*
Barrister - Family Law Dept, Neve
Solicitors, 8 George Street West, Luton,
Beds LU1 2DA, 01582 725311, Fax:
01582 400972, Call Date: May 1997
(Lincoln's Inn) Qualifications: LLB
(Hons) (Lond)

Young *Peter John* •
and Member New York, Call Date: Oct
1995 (Lincoln's Inn) Qualifications:
LLB (Hons) (Bucks), LLM (Cantab)

Younger *Ms Brynn Leadbitter*
25 Rainbow Street, London SE5 7TB,
Call Date: Nov 1994 (Gray's Inn)
Qualifications: BA (Hons) (Dunelm),
Dip Law

Youngman *Brian John*
Orchard Rise, Priory Close, East
Budleigh, Devon EX9 7EZ, 01395
444015, Fax: 01395 444015, Call Date:
June 1953 (Gray's Inn) Qualifications:
LLB (Lond)

Yousef *Mrs Naseem*
Call Date: Mar 1997 (Lincoln's Inn)
Qualifications: LLB (Hons)

Youssef *Ragi Anthony*
Call Date: July 1998 (Middle Temple)
Qualifications: LLB (Hons)

Yousuf *Miss Farah*
Assistant Deputy Justices Clerk,
Magistrates' Courts Brent, Church End,
448 High Road, London NW10 2DZ,
0181 451 7111, Fax: 0181 451 2040,
Call Date: July 1985 (Lincoln's Inn)
Qualifications: BA

Yusuf *Ismail*
Call Date: Nov 1992 (Lincoln's Inn)
Qualifications: LLB (Hons)

Zabihi *Miss Tanya* •
Lawyer, Legal Services Division, County
Hall, Surrey County Council, Kingston
upon Thames, 0181 541 9125, Fax:
0181 541 9005, Call Date: Nov 1988
(Gray's Inn) Qualifications: LLB

Zacharias *Dr Peter Lindsay*
Consultant Occupational Physician, 88
Rodney Street, Liverpool L1 9AR, 0151
707 0733, Call Date: July 1973 (Middle
Temple) Qualifications: MA, MB, ChB,
MFOM, DIH

Zackon *Israel Terence* •
Secretary to Lord Chancellor's Advisory
Committee On Legal Education and
Conduct, Lord Chancellor's Advisory,
Committee on Legal Education, and
Conduct, 8th Floor, Millbank Tower,
Millbank SW1P 4QU, 0171 217 4296,
Call Date: Nov 1978 (Inner Temple)
Qualifications: BA (Oxon)

Zafar *Ms Yasmeen*
Wakefields, Thames House, 58
Southwark Bridge Road, London
SE1 0AZ, 0171 654 0200, Fax: 0171 654
0221, Call Date: Nov 1993 (Lincoln's
Inn) Qualifications: MA (Oxon), LLM

Zaki *Ms Sara*
Credit Lyonnais Rouse Ltd, Broadwalk
House, 5 Appold Street, London
EC2A 2DA, 0171 214 6586, Fax: 0171
638 0401, Call Date: May 1997
(Lincoln's Inn) Qualifications: BA
(Hons)(Lond)

Zakir *Mohammad*
Call Date: Nov 1998 (Lincoln's Inn)
Qualifications: LLB (Hons)(Herts)

Zaman *Miss Parvin*
Call Date: July 1998 (Inner Temple)
Qualifications: LLB (Newcastle Upon,
Tyne)

Zaman *Mrs Sajada* •
Senior Solicitor, Stockport Metropolitan,
Borough Council, Town Hall, Edward
Street, Stockport, Cheshire, 0161 474
3247, Call Date: Nov 1985 (Lincoln's
Inn) Qualifications: BA

Zeb *Miss Emma Sabeena*
Call Date: Oct 1998 (Inner Temple)
Qualifications: LLB (Lond)

Zeffman *Michael* •
Senior Principal Legal Officer, HM
Customs & Excise, Solicitor's Office, New
King's Beam House, 22 Upper Ground,
London SE1 9PJ, Call Date: July 1977
(Gray's Inn) Qualifications: LLB (Lond)

Zellick *Professor Graham John*
Emeritus, Professor of Law,
Vice-Chancellor, 3 Verulam Buildings,
London, WC1R 5NT, Call Date: Nov 1992
(Middle Temple) Qualifications: BA
(Hons), MA & PhD, (Cantab),
CIMgt,FRSA, FInstD, FRSM, FICPD, Hon
FSALS

Zinner *Peter Anthony* •
Principal Crown Prosecutor, Crown
Prosecution Service, London Area, 4th
Floor, Portland House, London
SW1E 5BH, 0171 915 5700, Roll of
Solicitors for England and Wales, Call
Date: Nov 1983 (Middle Temple)
Qualifications: BA (Hons)

Zollner *Roland Louis* •
Senior Crown Prosecutor, CPS Mersey
North, Heron House, Hougoumont
Avenue, Crosby, Merseyside L22 0LL,
0151 920 8711, Fax: 0151 920 8233,
Call Date: July 1978 (Middle Temple)
Qualifications: BA

Zombory-Moldovan *Peter Paul*
Squire & Co, 49-52 St John's Street,
London EC1V 4JL, 0171 490 3444, Fax:
0171 250 4087, Call Date: Oct 1995
(Middle Temple) Qualifications: BA
(Hons), MA, Dip Law

Zoumaras *Miss Anna*
Channel Islands, Call Date: Oct 1997
(Gray's Inn) Qualifications: LLB (Sheff)

Zugg *Julian Michael*
Call Date: July 1996 (Inner Temple)
Qualifications: LLB (Bucks)

Zwennes *Charles William Leopold Bartel*
Call Date: Nov 1995 (Gray's Inn)
Qualifications: LLB (Kent)

Zymanczyk-Tedder *Miss Bozenna Zofia
Zuzanna*
Senior Court Clerk, Nottingham
Magistrates' Court, Carrington Street,
Nottingham NG2 1EE, 0115 955 8111,
Fax: 0115 955 8139, Call Date: July 1982
(Middle Temple) Qualifications: BSc
(Lond)

Zysman *Lawrence Irvin*
Call Date: July 1974 (Middle Temple)
Qualifications: LLB, LLM (Lond)

E

Individual Barristers Overseas

This section lists barristers who are based overseas. Barristers are listed alphabetically by surname and details include their membership of other Bars where appropriate, date of call to the Bar, their Inn of Court and academic qualifications.

F

F

Ab-Rahman *Miss Laura Anne*
1422 Lrg Tmn Sabariah, Jun Peng,
Chepa 15400, Kotabharu, Kelantan,
Malaysia, Malaysia, 00 60-9-7749348,
Fax: 00 60-9-7749348, and Member
Malaysia Bar, Call Date: July 1998
(Lincoln's Inn) Qualifications: LLB
(Hons)(Nott'm)

Abbasi *Mrs Saadia*
Pakistan, Call Date: Oct 1998
(Lincoln's Inn) Qualifications: MA
(Boston), Dip in Law

Abdul Ghafor *Miss Siti Norishan*
51 Jalan Madewa, Jalan Tutong, Bandar
Seri Begawan 2688, Brunei, 00673 (2)
651732, Legal Advisor, Brunei Attorney
General's Chamber, Call Date: July
1996 (Lincoln's Inn) Qualifications:
LLB (Hons) (LSE)

Abdul Hamid *Miss Muslin*
Malaysia, Call Date: July 1993 (Middle
Temple) Qualifications: LLB (Hons,
Warw)

Abdul Jabid *Miss Soraya*
Malaysia, Call Date: Nov 1995
(Lincoln's Inn) Qualifications: LLB
(Hons)

Abdul Kadir *Rizal*
Shell Malaysia Ltd, Legal Department,
Bangunan Shell, Off Jalan Semantan,
P.O.Box 11027, 50732 Kuala Lumpur,
Malaysia, 60 - 3 - 2512891, Fax: 60 - 3
- 2512732, Legal Adviser, Call Date: Nov
1993 (Lincoln's Inn) Qualifications:
LLB (Hons, Leic)

Abdul Karim *Miss Yasmeen*
Singapore 529892, Call Date: July 1997
(Lincoln's Inn) Qualifications: LLB
(Hons)(Lond)

Abdul Khalid *Taufiq*
Malaysia, Call Date: July 1998
(Lincoln's Inn) Qualifications: LLB
(Hons)(Leeds)

Abdul Malek *Faisal Ramza*
Malaysia, Call Date: July 1995 (Middle
Temple) Qualifications: LLB (Hons)

Abdul Rahim *Miss Katina Nurani*
Malaysia, Call Date: Oct 1998
(Lincoln's Inn) Qualifications: LLB
(Hons)(Notts)

Abdul Rahman *Mrs Ramzidah*
Judicial Department, Supreme Court,
Jalan Tutong, Bandar Seri Begawan,
Brunei BA 1910, Brunei Darussalam,
(673)(2) 243939, Registrar of the
Supreme Court Brunei, Magistrate,
Deputy Official Reciever and Deputy
Probate Officer, Call Date: Mar 1998
(Lincoln's Inn) Qualifications: LLB
(Hons)

Abdul Rashid *Miss Zaidatul Mazwin*
Malaysia, Call Date: Nov 1996
(Lincoln's Inn) Qualifications: LLB
(Hons)(Manch)

Abdul Shukor *Miss Shazwan*
Malaysia, Call Date: July 1996
(Lincoln's Inn) Qualifications: LLB
(Hons)(Sheff)

Abdullah *Arshad*
BAP 35-C, Cantonment Plaza, Sadmar
Road, Peshawar, N W F P, Pakistan, 00
92 91 285 277, Fax: 00 92 91 285 277,
Advocate, and Member Pakistan, Call
Date: Nov 1996 (Lincoln's Inn)
Qualifications: LLM (Staff), MA
(Pakistan)

Abdullah *Miss Azleena*
Malaysia, Call Date: Nov 1997 (Gray's
Inn) Qualifications: LLB (Bris)

Abdullah *Miss Hajah Pauziah*
Darussalam, Call Date: July 1996
(Lincoln's Inn) Qualifications: LLB
(Hons)(Kent)

Abdulrahim *Miss Nor Rejina*
Commerce - BT Unit Trust,
Management Berhad, Level 18, Menara
Dato Onn, Putra World Trade Centre,
45 Jalan Tun Ismail, 50480, Malaysia,
(603) 469 7177, Fax: (603) 469 4832,
Compliance Manager, Call Date: July
1997 (Lincoln's Inn) Qualifications:
LLB (Hons)(Kent)

Abedi *Ali Abbas Welayat Husain*
Abbas F.Ghazzawi Law Firm, P O Box
2335, Jeddah 21451, (+9662)
6654646, Fax: (+9662) 6659155, and
Member New York, Call Date: Nov 1988
(Middle Temple) Qualifications: LLB
(Lond), LLM (NY)

Abu Bakar *Mustaffa*
Singapore 460119, Call Date: July 1996
(Lincoln's Inn) Qualifications: LLB
(Hons)(L'pool)

Abu Bakar *Miss Nor'ain Binte*
Singapore 520298, Call Date: July 1996
(Middle Temple) Qualifications: LLB
(Hons)(Lond)

Ackland *Miss Sacha Marie*
Call Date: Oct 1998 (Inner Temple)
Qualifications: BA (Lond), CPE (Lond)

Acton-Bond *Jonathan Edward*
Hong Kong, and Member Hong Kong
Bar, Call Date: July 1971 (Gray's Inn)
Qualifications: BA

Adaikalasamy *Miss Jeyanthy*
Singapore 560102, Call Date: Nov 1997
(Lincoln's Inn) Qualifications: LLB
(Hons)(N'Castle)

Adam *Syed Nasirudin*
Malaysia, Call Date: Nov 1998
(Lincoln's Inn) Qualifications: LLB
(Hons)(Hull)

Adamidou *Miss Effie*
P.O.Box 1211, Nicosia, Cyprus, Greece,
357 2 31899\5, Fax: 357 2 314869,
Legal Advisor, and Member Cyprus Bar,
Call Date: Feb 1993 (Middle Temple)
Qualifications: LLB (Hons)(Leic), Dip
in Shipping Law, (UCL)

Adderley *Miss Paula Anne Lilith*
Graham Thompson & Co, P O Box
N272, Nassau, Bahamas, 242 322
4130, Fax: 242 328 1069, and Member
Bahamas Bar, Call Date: July 1997
(Middle Temple) Qualifications: BA
(Hons)

Adimoolam *Anpualagan*
Singapore 1232, Call Date: July 1996
(Middle Temple) Qualifications: LLB
(Hons)(Lond)

Advani *Ajay Jiwat*
Singapore 259711, Call Date: July 1997
(Middle Temple) Qualifications: LLB
(Hons)(Nott'm)

Aepli *Peter Andrew*
16 A, Chemin du Grand Communal,
CH-1222 Vesenaz, Geneva, (41 22) 855
07 23, Fax: (41 22) 855 07 24, Call
Date: July 1974 (Inner Temple)

Aghadiuno *Miss Patricia Nnonye*
Singapore 289252, and Member
Nigerian Bar, Call Date: July 1993
(Gray's Inn) Qualifications: LLB, LLM

Ahmad *Azlin*
Malaysia, Call Date: July 1996 (Gray's
Inn) Qualifications: LLB (Warwick)

Ahmad *Mrs Sahia*
P.O.Box 3251, Dubai, United Arab
Emirates, 9714 323190, Fax: 9714
323192, Legal Advisor, Call Date: Nov
1994 (Lincoln's Inn) Qualifications:
LLB (Hons)(Lond)

Ahmad *Miss Sakinah*
Singapore 258590, Call Date: Nov 1997
(Middle Temple) Qualifications: LLB
(Hons)(Lond)

Ahmed *Miss Ayla*
Rizvi, Isa & Co, 517/518 Clifton Centre,
DC - 1, Block 5, Clifton, Karachi 75600,
Pakistan, (92)(21) 570727/5836308/
5872879/5865198, Fax: (92)(21)
5865107/5870014, Associate, Call Date:
July 1997 (Lincoln's Inn)
Qualifications: LLB (Hons)(Lond), LLM
(Cantab)

Ahmed *Sultan Tanvir*
Pakistan, and Member Punjab Bar, Call
Date: Nov 1996 (Lincoln's Inn)
Qualifications: BA (Punjab), LLB
(Bucks)

Ahyow *Miss Dorothee Paola Cathie*
Mauritius, and Member Mauritian Bar,
Call Date: Nov 1996 (Lincoln's Inn)
Qualifications: BSc (Hons)(Wales), Dip
Law

Aiken *Nigel Alexander Carlisle*
9 Bedford Row, London, WC1R 4AZ,
Call Date: 1974 (Inner Temple)
Qualifications: BA

Akand *Shahnawaz*
Bangladesh, 008802 822497, Fax:
008802 9669122, and Member
Bangladesh Bar Council, Call Date: Nov
1996 (Lincoln's Inn) Qualifications:
LLB (Hons)(Lond)

Akel *Richard Livingstone*
Weitz & Luxemberg, 180 Maiden Lane, 17th Floor, NY, NY 10038, United States of America, 212 558 5617, Royal New Zealand Infantry (Hon. Discharge), American Trial Lawyers Association, Trial Lawyers' Associations of Washington DC & California & South Carolina American Bar Association. International Bar Association U.S.Supreme Court, U.S. Courts of Appeal for District of Columbia and 3rd, 4th, 5th, Call Date: July 1992 (Lincoln's Inn) Qualifications: LLB (Hons, N.Z.), LLM (Cantab), Dip., of Trial Advocacy , (U.S.)

Akosile *Adeleke Jacob*
Nigeria, Call Date: Mar 1997 (Lincoln's Inn) Qualifications: LLB (Hons)

Al-Jaraf *Mulham Bashir*
P.O.Box 2222, Muscat. PC 112, Sultanate of Oman, + 968 9346911, Fax: + 968 604200, Legal Researcher, Call Date: July 1998 (Gray's Inn) Qualifications: BBA (Marymount, USA), Dip Law

Alam *Kazi Mohammad Tanjibul*
Bangladesh, Call Date: Nov 1997 (Lincoln's Inn) Qualifications: LLB (Hons) (Lond)

Alexandrou *Miss Maria*
Cyprus, Call Date: Mar 1996 (Gray's Inn) Qualifications: LLB (East Anglia)

Ali *Md Hyder*
Bangladesh, Call Date: Nov 1998 (Lincoln's Inn) Qualifications: LLB (Hons) (Wolves)

Ali *Muhammad Imman*
2 Nawratan Heights, New Baily Road, Dhaka - 1000, Advocate of the Supreme Court of Bangladesh, High Court Division and Appellate Divisio Deputy Attorney General, and Member Dhaka Supreme Court Bar, Call Date: July 1978 (Inner Temple) Qualifications: BA, LLM

Aling *Miss Jenny Li Ting Chin*
West Malaysia, Call Date: July 1995 (Middle Temple) Qualifications: LLB (Hons)

Alizai *Taha*
Pakistan, Call Date: Nov 1998 (Lincoln's Inn) Qualifications: LLB (Hons) (Bucks)

Allan *Blair Robert*
1780 Mirador Drive, Azusa, California 91702, United States of America, Staff Lawyer - American Corporation, Call Date: Oct 1991 (Gray's Inn) Qualifications: BSc (California), LLB (East Anglia)

Allen *Andrew Clifford*
Bahamas, Call Date: Nov 1996 (Gray's Inn) Qualifications: LLB (Hull)

Allen *Miss Nicole Natacha*
West Indies, Call Date: Mar 1999 (Gray's Inn) Qualifications: LLB (City), BA (Econ) (Florida)

Allen *Miss Tawanna Cherrel*
Bahamas, Call Date: July 1995 (Gray's Inn) Qualifications: BA (Ottawa), LLB (Hull)

Allgrove *Jeffrey William*
Unilever United States, 390 Park Avenue, New York, NY 10022 USA, United States of America, Vice President - Finance, Call Date: July 1976 (Lincoln's Inn) Qualifications: LLB, FCCA

Ameen *Mahmud Riad*
Sri Lanka, Call Date: Mar 1998 (Lincoln's Inn) Qualifications: LLB (Hons) (Lond)

Ameer *Mohammed Ameen Chezard*
Sri Lanka, Call Date: July 1996 (Middle Temple) Qualifications: LLB (Hons) (Lond)

Amin *Omar Kemal Shaikh Mohamed*
Nairobi Hilton, Mama Ngina Street, P O Box 25241, Nairobi, Kenya, East Africa, 254 (2) 334000/242443, Fax: 254 (2) 227794, Advocate of the High Court of Kenya, and Member Kenya Bar, Call Date: Nov 1991 (Lincoln's Inn) Qualifications: LLB (Hons) (Bucks)

Amin *Salah-El-Din Mohamed*
First Floor, Nairobi Hilton Building, P O Box 25241, Nairobi, East Africa, 254-2-242443/254-2-48453, Advocate of the High Court of Kenya, Call Date: Oct 1993 (Lincoln's Inn) Qualifications: LLB (Hons) (Bucks)

Anamalai *Saravanan*
Malaysia, Call Date: July 1998 (Lincoln's Inn) Qualifications: LLB (Hons) (Thames)

Ananda *Miss Roshni Rekha*
Malaysia, Call Date: July 1998 (Gray's Inn) Qualifications: LLB (Bris)

Anandakrishna *Thiagu*
West Malaysia, Call Date: Nov 1997 (Middle Temple) Qualifications: LLB (Hons) (Manch)

Anastassiou *Miss Maria Andreas*
Cyprus, Call Date: July 1997 (Gray's Inn) Qualifications: LLB (Lond)

Anderson *Mrs Maxanne Javita*
Appleby Spurling & Kempe, Barristers & Attorneys, Cedar House,41 Cedar Avenue, Hamilton, Bermuda, (441) 295-2244, Fax: (441) 292-8666, Call Date: May 1997 (Lincoln's Inn) Qualifications: LLB (Hons) (Kent), BA (Atlanta)

Anderson *Peter Lawrence*
54 Glen Shian Lane, Mount Eliza, Victoria 3930, and Member New York, Call Date: July 1970 (Gray's Inn) Qualifications: FCCA

Andreou *Andreas*
8 Rigas Fereos Str, Libra Chambers, 3095 Limassol, Cyprus, 00357 5 363154, Fax: 00357 5 342887, and Member Cyprus Bar, Call Date: Nov 1995 (Lincoln's Inn) Qualifications: LLB (Hons) (Leic)

Andrews *Robert Craig*
Admiralty centre, 1405 Tower 2, 18 Harcourt Road, Hong Kong, 00852 25273082, Fax: 00852 25298226, Chairman, Appeal Tribunal (Buildings), and Member Hong Kong Bar, Call Date: May 1971 (Middle Temple) Qualifications: BA

Ang *Miss Alexia Hui Tsun*
Canada, Call Date: July 1997 (Middle Temple) Qualifications: LLB (Hons)

Ang *Andrew Lye Whatt*
Singapore 457707, Call Date: July 1996 (Middle Temple) Qualifications: LLB (Hons) (Leic)

Ang *Cheng Yong*
10 Brooke Road, [H]13-04, Singapore 1851, 3467807, Fax: 3467807, Legal Assistant, and Member Singapore Bar, Call Date: July 1991 (Gray's Inn) Qualifications: LLB (Hons) (Lond), ACII, LM(Lond)

Ang *Khoon Cheong*
c/o Messrs C P Ang & Co, 18 Lebuh Kampung Benggali, 12000 Butterworth, Penang, Malaysia, 04 3313009, Fax: 04 3328115, and Member Malaysia, Call Date: July 1995 (Middle Temple) Qualifications: LLB (Hons) (Wales)

Ang *Miss Kim Noi*
Singapore 2368, Call Date: July 1995 (Middle Temple) Qualifications: LLB (Hons)

Ang *Miss Ru-Lin*
Singapore 269673, Call Date: July 1997 (Middle Temple) Qualifications: LLB (Hons) (Nott'm)

Ang *Miss Sue Khoon*
Malaysia, and Member Malaysia Bar, Call Date: July 1994 (Middle Temple) Qualifications: LLB (Hons) (Bris)

Ang *Wen Po Andrew*
Singapore 118155, Call Date: July 1997 (Gray's Inn) Qualifications: LLB (Notts)

Ang *Woon Kherk*
Singapore 440012, Call Date: July 1996 (Lincoln's Inn) Qualifications: LLB (Hons)

Angelides *Savvas*
Cyprus, Call Date: Nov 1997 (Gray's Inn) Qualifications: LLB

Annanth *Mrs Parvathi*
Singapore 809645, Call Date: Nov 1996 (Middle Temple) Qualifications: LLB (Hons)

Ansah-Twum *Miss Wonta Nana Asuaa*
Call Date: Oct 1998 (Middle Temple) Qualifications: LLB (Hons) (Kingston)

Antao *Mrs Alexia Gertrude*
355b Romford Road, Forest Gate, London E7 8AA, Seychelles, 0181 519 8658, Barrister & Attorney at Law in La Poudriere Law of Comsultancy Chambers (Legal Advisor, Litigation etc), and Member Seychelles Bar, Call Date: May 1996 (Inner Temple) Qualifications: LLB (Hons)(Lond), LLM (LSE)

Anuar *Miss Ifa Mutiara*
Malaysia, Call Date: Nov 1997 (Lincoln's Inn) Qualifications: LLB (Hons)(Nott'm)

Anuar *Miss Zeti Azita*
4288 Jalan Kampung Gajah, 12200 Butterworth, Penang, Malaysia, and Member High Court of Malaya, Malaysia, Call Date: Nov 1997 (Lincoln's Inn) Qualifications: LLB (Hons)(Warw)

Anwar *Miss Fatema*
Bangladesh, Call Date: Nov 1997 (Lincoln's Inn) Qualifications: LLB (Hons) (Lond)

Apostolou *Evangelos Christopher*
Christos Pourgourides & Co, Law Office., P.O.Box 4137, Limassol, Cyprus, 00 3575 346634, Advocate, Call Date: Mar 1998 (Lincoln's Inn) Qualifications: BA (Hons) (Lond)

Appaduray *Miss Nina Urmilla*
West Malaysia, Call Date: July 1996 (Middle Temple) Qualifications: LLB (Hons)(Lond)

Arashan *Miss Shabnam*
Singapore 1953, Call Date: Nov 1998 (Middle Temple) Qualifications: LLB (Hons)(Hull)

Archer *Miss Tara*
NP Bahamas, Call Date: Oct 1998 (Lincoln's Inn) Qualifications: LLB (Hons)(Essex)

Armstrong *Henry Napier*
Northern Ireland, Adv High Ct Kenya Chairman Legal & Commercial Committee. Ulster Farmers Union, Call Date: June 1961 (Inner Temple) Qualifications: BA

Armstrong *Ronald Grieve*
Hong Kong, Call Date: Nov 1998 (Middle Temple) Qualifications: MA (Glasgow)

Arrowsmith *Christopher John*
Mann & Partners, 20 Finch Road, Douglas, Isle of Man IM1 2PS, Isle of Man, 01624 622221, Fax: 01624 627222, Advocate, Partner and Member Manx Bar, Call Date: Oct 1990 (Gray's Inn) Qualifications: LLB (Hons) (Brunel)

Asher *Peter John*
5 Garth Road, Kingston 8, Jamaica, West Indies, West Indies, 876 960 6978, Fax: 876 960 6979, and Member Jamaican Bar, Call Date: July 1994 (Lincoln's Inn) Qualifications: LLB (Hons), BA

Ashhab *Bazul*
Singapore 731891, Call Date: July 1997 (Lincoln's Inn) Qualifications: LLB (Hons)(Lond)

Ashraf *Ms Leila*
Singapore 0923, Call Date: July 1995 (Gray's Inn) Qualifications: LLB (E.Anglia)

Ashraf *Miss Nida*
Pakistan, Call Date: July 1996 (Lincoln's Inn) Qualifications: BA (Hons)(Kent)

Aslam *Miss Sharen*
Block 554, [H] 11-219, Bedok North Street 3, Singapore 460554, Singapore 1955, 2436057, Call Date: July 1995 (Middle Temple) Qualifications: LLB (Hons)

Asnani *Shankar Ram Pohumall*
East Malaysia, Call Date: July 1995 (Middle Temple) Qualifications: LLB (Hons) (Wales)

Astaphan *Mrs Jennifer*
West Indies, Call Date: July 1998 (Lincoln's Inn) Qualifications: LLB (Hons)(Bucks)

Attard *Professor David Joseph*
Malta, Call Date: Nov 1998 (Middle Temple) Qualifications: LLB (Malta), DPhil (Oxon)

Attaur-Rehman *Ahmad*
Orr Dignam & Co Advocates, 3 Street 32 F-8/1, Islamabad, 260517/253086/ 260518, Fax: 260653, and Member Lahore High Court Bar, Call Date: Nov 1993 (Lincoln's Inn) Qualifications: LLB (Hons), LLM

Attygalle *Miss Amila Sita*
Sri Lanka, Call Date: July 1996 (Lincoln's Inn) Qualifications: LLB (Hons)(LSE)

Au *Cheen Kuan*
Malaysia, Call Date: July 1995 (Middle Temple) Qualifications: LLB (Hons)

Au *Seng Heng*
Malaysia, Call Date: Mar 1996 (Middle Temple) Qualifications: LLB (Hons)

Au *Tony Thye Chuen*
111 North Bridge Road, [H]22-04, Singapore 0617, Singapore 2260, 4338102, Fax: 3395436, Call Date: July 1995 (Lincoln's Inn) Qualifications: LLB (Hons)

Au Yong *Miss Pei Yi*
Malaysia, and Member Malaysia, Call Date: July 1996 (Lincoln's Inn) Qualifications: LLB (Hons)(Sheff)

Aussant *Mrs Jill Amaryllis*
Council of the European Union, Legal Dept, Rue de la Loi 175, 1049 Bruxelles, Belgium, Belgium, 02 285 7919, Fax: 285 6743, Legal Adviser, Call Date: Nov 1966 (Inner Temple) Qualifications: MA (Cantab), LLB

Austin *Christopher Bound*
Bedell & Cristin, Advocates & Notaries Public, P.O.Box 75, One The Forum, Grenville Street, St Helier, Jersey JE4 8PP, Channel Islands, 01534 814814, Fax: 01534 814815, Call Date: May 1996 (Inner Temple) Qualifications: LLB (Hons)

Avraamides *Nicos*
10 Mylinae Str, Off 22, Nicosia, Cyprus, 766156 or 766157, Fax: 766123, Call Date: Nov 1995 (Middle Temple) Qualifications: LLB (Hons)(Hull)

Aw *Dominic Kian-Wee*
DKH Management & Sdn Bhd, 20th Floor, Mewara Multi, Purpose, 8 Jalan Munshi Abdullah, 50100 Kuala Lumpur, Malaysia, 603 2982611, Fax: 603 2928112, Assistant General Manager, and Member Malaysia Bar, Call Date: July 1992 (Middle Temple) Qualifications: LLB (Hons) (Hull)

Ayaduray *Jeyapalan*
Singapore 118863, Call Date: July 1997 (Lincoln's Inn) Qualifications: LLB (Hons)(Lond)

Ayres *Andrew John*
Manor Place, St Peter Port, Guernsey, Channel Islands, Channel Islands, (01481) 723191, Fax: (01481) 700171, and Member Guernsey Bar, Call Date: Nov 1992 (Inner Temple) Qualifications: LLB (Warw)

Aziz *Imran*
Pakistan, Call Date: July 1997 (Lincoln's Inn) Qualifications: LLB (Lond), LLM (Lond)

Aziz *Miss Miriam*
Mommsentrabe 47, 10629 Berlin, Call Date: July 1994 (Inner Temple) Qualifications: LLB (Manch)

Aziz *Munir Mydin Abdul*
8 Jalan Desa Ria, Taman Desa, 58100 Kuala Lumpur, Malaysia, 00 603 7803766, Call Date: July 1997 (Lincoln's Inn) Qualifications: BA (Hons)

Aziz *Miss Noraini*
Khattar Wong & Partners, 80 Raffles Place [H]25-01, Plaza 1, Advocate & Solcitor, and Member Singapore, Call Date: Nov 1993 (Gray's Inn) Qualifications: LLB, LLM

Aziz *Miss Tengku Azrina Bt Raja Abdul*
Malaysia, Call Date: July 1997 (Lincoln's Inn) Qualifications: BA (Hons)

Azlan *Miss Nor Azrini*
Malaysia, Call Date: July 1995
(Lincoln's Inn) Qualifications: BA
(Hons)

Azopardi *The Hon Keith*
213 Rosia Plaza, Rosia Bay, Gibraltar,
(350) 50294/48184, Fax: (350) 71143,
Minister for the Environment & Health,
Government of Gibraltar. Member of
the House of Assembly, and Member
Gibraltar Bar, Call Date: Nov 1990
(Middle Temple) Qualifications: BA
(Keele)

Babalola *Chief Emmanuel Afe*
Nigeria, and Member Nigerian Bar, Call
Date: July 1963 (Lincoln's Inn)
Qualifications: B.Sc (Econ)(Lond), LLB
(Hons)(Lond), B.L

Bacik *Ms Ivana Catherine Alexis*
Law School, Trinity College, Dublin 6,
Republic of Ireland, 608 2299, Fax: 677
0449, Reid Professor of Criminal Law
and Criminology, Trinity College
Dublin, Member of King's Inns, Dublin
and Member Southern Ireland Bar, Call
Date: Nov 1992 (Middle Temple)
Qualifications: LLB , LLM

Badaruddin *Nabil Daraina*
Attorney General's Chambers, Jalan
Tutong, Bandar Seri, Begawan BA 1910,
Brunei, Darussalam, (673)(2)244872,
Deputy Public Prosecutor Counsel, Call
Date: Nov 1996 (Lincoln's Inn)
Qualifications: LLB (Hons)(Bucks)

Bahadursingh *Ravi Ananta*
2 Main Street, New Amsterdam,
Berbice, Barbados, (592) 3 2841, and
Member Guyana Bar, Call Date: Nov
1995 (Gray's Inn) Qualifications: LLB
(Dublin)

Bahrin *Awangku Izad-Ryan*
Skrine & Co, 303B Wisma Jaya, 406A
Jalan Pemancha, Bandar Seri Begawan
2085, Brunei, Brunei, 23 29 46/48,
Fax: 23 29 49, and Member Brunei
Darussalam, Call Date: Nov 1994
(Lincoln's Inn) Qualifications: BA
(Hons)(Keele), LLM

Bahrin *Miss Dayangku Nina Jasmine*
Brunei Darussalam, Call Date: Mar
1998 (Lincoln's Inn) Qualifications:
LLB (Hons)(E.Anglia)

Bailey *Miss Samantha Joanne*
Channel islands, Call Date: Oct 1998
(Inner Temple) Qualifications: LLB
(Warw)

Bainbridge *Garth Tristan Athelstan*
Ozannes, 1 Le Marchant St, St Peter
Port, Guernsey, Channel Islands, 01481
723466, Fax: 01481 727935/720378,
and Member Guernsey Bar, Call Date:
Nov 1978 (Gray's Inn) Qualifications:
LLB

Bajaj *Harpal Singh*
Singapore 460072, Call Date: Nov 1997
(Middle Temple) Qualifications: LLB
(Hons)(Lond)

Bajwa *Dr Farooq Naseem*
Pakistan, Call Date: July 1998 (Middle
Temple) Qualifications: BA
(Hons)(Lond), PhD (LSE)

Bakar *Miss Falisa Abu*
Zaid Ibrahim & Co, Tingkat 12, Menara
Bank, Pembangunlan, Jalan Sultan,
Ismail, 50250 Kuala Lumpur, Malaysia,
6 03 2926688, Legal Assistant, Call
Date: July 1996 (Gray's Inn)
Qualifications: LLB (Manchester)

Bakar *Mohamad Husini*
Brunei Shell Petroleum Company,
Sendirian Berhad, Seria 7082, Brunei,
Darussalam, Darussalam, 673 3
373375, Fax: 673 3 373996, Assistant
Legal Adviser & Assistant Company
Secretary, and Member Supreme Court
of Brunei, Call Date: July 1994
(Lincoln's Inn) Qualifications: BA
(Hons) (Keele)

Bal *Miss Karen Kaur*
Malaysia, Call Date: July 1995 (Inner
Temple) Qualifications: LLB
(Northumbria)

Balakrishnan *Miss Mahaletchumi*
Malaysia, Call Date: Oct 1998
(Lincoln's Inn) Qualifications: LLB
(Hons)(Bris)

Balendra *Miss Natasha Thiruni Jayasekara*
Sri Lanka, Call Date: July 1994
(Lincoln's Inn) Qualifications: LLB
(Hons)

Balfour *James Selby*
France, Call Date: Nov 1997 (Inner
Temple) Qualifications: BA

Balgobin *Miss Priscilla*
Mauritius, Call Date: Oct 1998 (Middle
Temple) Qualifications: LLB (Hons)

Balia *Miss Sabwati Shukrin*
Malaysia, Call Date: July 1996
(Lincoln's Inn) Qualifications: LLB
(Hons)(Soton)

Bandali *Miss Noorjehan Murtaza*
Kenya, Call Date: Nov 1998 (Lincoln's
Inn) Qualifications: LLB (Hons)(Lond)

Barit *Ms Georgette De Stefanis*
Appleby, Spurling & Kempe, 41 Cedar
Avenue, Hamilton, 441 295 7563, and
Member Bermuda Bar, Call Date: Feb
1995 (Middle Temple) Qualifications:
MBA, BA, CPE (City), Dip Law

Baron *Miss Francis Althea*
Commonwealth of Dominica, Call Date:
July 1995 (Middle Temple)
Qualifications: LLB (Hons)

Barrett *Paul Nicholas*
Hong Kong, Call Date: Nov 1998
(Middle Temple) Qualifications: LLB
(Hons)(Lond)

Barrett *Richard*
Republic of Ireland, Second Legal
Assistant in the Office of the Attorney
General Dublin, and Member Northern
Ireland Bar Southern Ireland Bar, Call
Date: Feb 1988 (Middle Temple)
Qualifications: BCL, LLB (Ireland),
LLM (Lond)

Barretto *Ruy Octavio*
Temple Chambers, 16/F One Pacific
Place, 88 Queensway, 25232003, Fax:
28100302, Part-Time Chairman,
Pollution Control Appeal Boards,
Member (Part Time) Legal Aid Services
Council, Director (Part Time) Kadoorie
Farm & Botanic Garden, and Member
New South Wales Bar Hong Kong Bar,
Call Date: Nov 1974 (Middle Temple)
Qualifications: LLB (Lond), AKC

Barrow *Miss Michelle Cathendi*
West Indies, Call Date: Nov 1998
(Gray's Inn) Qualifications: LLB
(Wolves)

Basah *Miss Nashah*
Malaysia, Call Date: Mar 1998 (Middle
Temple) Qualifications: LLB
(Hons)(Staffs)

Basaran Eronen *Ms Gonul*
Supreme Court, PO Box 61, Lefkosa,
Turkish Republic of Northern, Cyprus,
Mersin 10, Turkey, Fax:
90-392-2285265, Supreme Court
Judge, Call Date: Nov 1975 (Gray's Inn)

Basheer-Ahmad *Sheikh Mohd Eusoff*
Singapore 470729, Call Date: July 1998
(Middle Temple) Qualifications: LLB
(Hons)(Hull)

Bastos G Martin *Philip John*
Dorsey & Whitney LLP, 35 Square de
Meeus, B-1000 Brussels, (32-2)
5044611, Fax: (32-2) 5044646, and
Member Brussels, Call Date: Nov 1993
(Gray's Inn) Qualifications: LLB
(Essex), DEA (France)

Baudains *Martyn*
Babbe Le Poidevin Allez, Hirzel Court,
P.O.Box 612, St Peter Port, Guernsey
GY1 4NZ, Channel Islands, 01481
710585, Fax: 0181 712245, Call Date:
Mar 1998 (Gray's Inn) Qualifications:
LLB (W'hampton)

Bauer *Christian Rudolf Johann*
University of Passau, Faculty of Law,
Inn - Sh 40, 94032 Passau, Germany,
Lecturer in Law, Call Date: Oct 1996
(Lincoln's Inn) Qualifications: LLB
(Hons)(Lond), Dipl German Law

Bay *Miss Chern Chieh*
Singapore 2057, Call Date: July 1995
(Middle Temple) Qualifications: LLB
(Hons)

Beel *Robert William Trevor*
Hong Kong, Call Date: May 1996
(Gray's Inn) Qualifications: LLB (Lond)

Belle *Mrs Berthalee Louise*
Turks & Caicos Islands, and Member
Turks & Caicos Bar, Call Date: Oct 1997
(Gray's Inn) Qualifications: BA
(Denison), LLB (Leeds)

Benest *David John*
Baillache Labesse, 14/16 Hill Street, St
Helier, Jersey JE1 1BD, Channel
Islands, 01534 888777, Fax: 01534
888778, Advocate of the Royal Court of
Jersey, Call Date: Nov 1995 (Inner
Temple) Qualifications: BA (Sussex)

Benest *Frederick John*
Benest & Syvret, Royal Court
Chambers, 10 Hill Street, St Helier,
Jersey JE2 4UA, Channel Islands, 01534
875875, Fax: 01534 875885, Partner,
and Member Jersey, Call Date: July
1996 (Middle Temple)

Benest *Miss Nina Sophie Hacquoil*
Benest & Syvret, Royal Court
Chambers, 10 Hill Street, St Helier,
Jersey JE2 4UA, Channel Islands, 01534
875875, Fax: 01534 875885, Call Date:
July 1996 (Middle Temple)
Qualifications: LLB (Hons) (Kent)

Beng *Miss Li-Sher*
Singapore 258993, Call Date: July 1996
(Middle Temple) Qualifications: BA
(Hons) (Notts)

Bennett *Miss Dawn Marie*
Canada, Call Date: Oct 1998 (Lincoln's
Inn) Qualifications: LLB (Hons) (Bris),
HBA (Ontario), HBComm (Ontario)

Bensadon *Mrs Janine Yvette*
Gibraltar, and Member Gibraltar Bar,
Call Date: Oct 1994 (Lincoln's Inn)
Qualifications: LLB (Hons) (Hudders)

Bentick-Owens *Ms Pia Anne Maria*
South Australia, Call Date: July 1997
(Gray's Inn) Qualifications: ACIS, LL
Dip

Benzaquen *Joseph Pinhas*
Gibraltar, 350 78534, Fax: 350 73201/
46562, and Member Gibraltar Bar, Call
Date: July 1992 (Middle Temple)
Qualifications: LLB (Hons)

Benzaquen *Rafael Jacob*
Legislation Support Unit, 13 Town
Range, Gibraltar, + (350) 41821, Fax:
+ (350) 41822, Law Draftsman, Call
Date: July 1995 (Middle Temple)
Qualifications: LLB (Hons), Maitre en
Droit , (Paris)

Bernacchi *Brook Antony*
1103 Prince's Building, Central, 5 2
20066, Fax: 8 450851, Arbitration
Panel Hong Kong, QC, Hong Kong, Call
Date: Jan 1943 (Middle Temple)
Qualifications: FCIArb

Best *Harold Alexander*
Northern Ireland, Call Date: Nov 1998
(Middle Temple) Qualifications: BA
(Hons) (Ulster)

Bethell *Reno Terrance Richardo*
Bahamas, Call Date: Nov 1998
(Lincoln's Inn) Qualifications: LLB
(Hons) (Wales)

Bhar *Miss Sherina*
Malaysia, Call Date: Nov 1997
(Lincoln's Inn) Qualifications: LLB
(Hons)

Bhima *Miss Preety Sharmila*
Mauritius, Call Date: July 1998
(Lincoln's Inn) Qualifications: LLB
(Hons) (Reading)

Bhimjee *Anwar Ali*
244 Juanita Way, San Francisco,
California 94127, (415) 242 1734,
Chartered Accountant, Call Date: July
1965 (Lincoln's Inn) Qualifications:
MA, FCA, LLB

Bhola *Miss Susan*
West Indies, and Member Supreme
Court of Trinidad & Tobago, Call Date:
Nov 1993 (Lincoln's Inn)
Qualifications: LLB (Hons, Buck'ham)

Biesmans *John Robert*
European Parliament, Rue Belliard 97,
1040 Brussels, 02 284 30 26, Fax: 02
231 11 83/ 02 284 9877, Deputy
Secretary General, Call Date: July 1979
(Middle Temple) Qualifications: MA
(Oxon) , LLB (Cantab) LLM

Binder *Miss Naveen Kaur*
Malaysia, Call Date: July 1995 (Middle
Temple) Qualifications: LLB (Hons)

Binet *Miss Francoise Charlotte*
Channel Islands, Call Date: Mar 1998
(Lincoln's Inn) Qualifications: LLB
(Hons), LLM, (Bucks)

Birt *Michael Cameron St John*
Law Officer's Department, Morier
House, St Helier, Jersey JE1 1DD, 0534
502200, Fax: 0534 502299, H M
Attorney General of Jersey, QC 1995
and Member Jersey Bar 9 Bedford Row,
London, WC1R 4AZ, Call Date: 1970
(Middle Temple) Qualifications: MA
(Cantab)

Birtwistle *Daniel James*
Channel Islands, Call Date: July 1996
(Middle Temple) Qualifications: LLB
(Hons) (Wales)

Bishop *Miss Anne-Marie*
West Indies, Call Date: July 1998
(Lincoln's Inn) Qualifications: LLB
(Hons)

Black *James Walter*
Edmund Barton Chambers, Level 44
MLC Centre, Martin Place, Sydney
2000, Australia, 02 9220 6100, Fax: 02
9232 3949, and Member Australian
Capitol Territory New South Wales Bar,
Call Date: Feb 1964 (Middle Temple)
Qualifications: MA (Cantab)

Black *Julian Neil*
Northern Ireland, Call Date: Oct 1995
(Lincoln's Inn) Qualifications: LLB
(Hons) (De, Montfort)

Blackburn *Mrs Diana Jeanette*
P.O.Box 539, Mornington, Victoria
3931, Australia, 03 59751031, and
Member New Zealand Bar, Call Date:
Nov 1991 (Middle Temple)
Qualifications: BA Hons (Kent), ACIArb
, AArbInz

Blackman *Colin*
Wharf Cable, 8/F Wharf Cable Tower, 9
Hoi Shing Road, Tsuen Wan, Hong
Kong, 2112 6222, Fax: 2112 7824, M
Inst P, Call Date: July 1988 (Gray's Inn)
Qualifications: BSc (Lond), MSc
(Reading), C Phys

Blackshaw *Miss Gail*
Gibraltar, Call Date: Oct 1997 (Middle
Temple) Qualifications: BSc
(Hons) (Bris), CPE

Blake *Miss Una*
Ireland, Call Date: Oct 1998 (Middle
Temple) Qualifications: LLB
(Hons) (Wales)

Boal *Ms Kathleen Lindsay*
Bar Library, Royal Courts of Justice,
Chichester Street, Belfast BT1 3JP,
Northern Ireland, 01232 562444, Fax:
01232 231850, and Member Northern
Ireland, Call Date: Oct 1997 (Inner
Temple) Qualifications: LLB (Belfast)

Boal *Mrs Lay Bee*
Messrs Shahriza,Varegheeses &,
Chandran, No 119a Jalan Gasing, 1st
Floor, Petaling Jaya 46000, Selangor,
United States of America, 03 7565299/
177, Fax: 03 7572655, and Member
Malaysia Bar, Call Date: July 1992
(Inner Temple) Qualifications: LLB

Bodden *Miss Joannah Lurline*
P O Box 1347G, Grand Cayman,
Cayman Islands, 345.949.7508,
Attorney, Call Date: July 1998
(Lincoln's Inn) Qualifications: LLB
(Hons) (Exon)

Bodden *Truman Murray*
Truman Bodden & Co, P O Box 1796,
Anderson Square Building, Grand
Cayman, British West Indies, British
West Indies, 809 949 7555, Fax: 809
949 8492, and Member Cayman
Islands, Call Date: July 1969 (Inner
Temple) Qualifications: ACIB, FFA,
FICM, FCI, MBIM, ACIArB, FBSC, LLB
(Hons) (Lond)

Bodruddoza *Md*
Hall Room, No 3, Supreme Court Bar
Association, Building, Dhaka-1000,
Bangladesh, Chamber 45/Kha, New
Eskaton 2nd Floor, Dhaka, India,
88-02-9340080, and Member
Bangladesh Bar Council Dhaka Bar,
Call Date: Nov 1995 (Lincoln's Inn)
Qualifications: LLB (Hons) (Lond), LLB
(Hons) (Banglade), LLM (Bangladesh)

F

Bogaert *Peter Willy Luc*
Kunstlaan 44, 1040 Brussel, Belgium, 32-2-5495230, Fax: 32-2-5021598, and Member Brussels Bar, Call Date: May 1995 (Gray's Inn) Qualifications: Licenciaat in de, Rechten, BA

Boh *Miss Wah Boon*
Singapore 521113, Call Date: July 1996 (Middle Temple) Qualifications: LLB (Hons) (Glamorg)

Bolton *Miss Sally Margaret*
Isle of Man, and Member Manx Bar, Call Date: July 1988 (Gray's Inn) Qualifications: BA (E Anglia), Dip Law

Bon *Edmund*
Malaysia, Call Date: July 1997 (Lincoln's Inn) Qualifications: LLB (Hons) (Lond)

Bong *Miss Ping Chong Eunice*
Malaysia, Call Date: Oct 1998 (Lincoln's Inn) Qualifications: LLB (Hons) (Leic)

Boo *Moh Cheh*
Singapore 1955, Call Date: July 1994 (Lincoln's Inn) Qualifications: LLB (Hons)

Borge *Paul Louis Anthony*
Budhrani & Co, Suite 1, 62 Main Street, Gibraltar, (00-350) 73521, Fax: (00-350) 79895, and Member Gibraltar Bar, Call Date: Mar 1998 (Gray's Inn) Qualifications: BA (Derby)

Boss *Miss Bernadette Carmel*
Dept of Defence - Army, Defence Centre Melbourne, Victoria Barracks, St Kilda Road, Melbourne 3006, Australia 3028, 00 617 364 4455, Senior Legal Officer, and Member Queensland Bar, Call Date: Oct 1992 (Middle Temple) Qualifications: B.Sc (Hons, Lond), Diploma in Law

Bossino *Damon James*
Suite C, 2nd Floor, Regal House, Queensway, Gibraltar, 010 350 79423, Fax: 010 350 71405, and Member Gibraltar, Call Date: Nov 1995 (Middle Temple) Qualifications: LLB (Hons)

Bossino *Stephen Richard*
5 Secretary's Lane, P.O.Box 659, Gibraltar, Gibraltar, 74998/73316, Fax: 73074, and Member Gibraltar, Call Date: Oct 1994 (Lincoln's Inn) Qualifications: LLB (Hons) (Leic)

Bostwick *Ms Janet Lissette Racquel*
Bostwick & Bostwick, Attorneys at Law, 50 George Street, PO Box N-1605, Nassau N.P., Bahamas, (242) 322 2039/2038, Fax: (242) 328 2521, and Member Bahamas Bar Association, Call Date: July 1996 (Gray's Inn) Qualifications: BA (McGill, Canada), LLB (Buckingham)

Bostwick *John Henry*
Bostwick & Bostwick, 50 George Street, P O Box N-1605, Nassau, Bahamas, (242) 322 2038, Fax: (242) 328 2521, and Member Bahamas Bar, Call Date: Nov 1995 (Gray's Inn) Qualifications: BA (Keele)

Boucly *Miss Nathalie*
Call Date: Nov 1996 (Middle Temple) Qualifications: LLB (Hons) (LSE)

Boustouler *Andrew Peter*
Whiteley Chambers, Don Street, St Helier, Jersey JE4 9WG, Channel Islands, 01534 504000, Fax: 01534 35328, Call Date: July 1998 (Lincoln's Inn) Qualifications: BA (Herts), Post Graduate, Diploma in Law

Bowers *Miss Deborah*
Alberton Richelieu & Associate, P.O.Box 2130, Gros-Islet, St Lucia, St Lucia, 001 758 4524515, Fax: 001 758 4523329, and Member St Lucia, Call Date: July 1997 (Middle Temple) Qualifications: LLB (Hons) (Lond)

Boyle *Miss Jane Kerr*
Via Roma 51, 35122 Padua, 049/654058, Call Date: Feb 1992 (Middle Temple) Qualifications: MA (Lond), LLB (Hons)

Boyle *Dr John Charles*
Kvaerner PLC, 55/F Central Plaza, 18 Harbour Road, Wanchai, (852) 28681100, Fax: (852) 28681522, Legal Adviser, Call Date: July 1974 (Lincoln's Inn) Qualifications: B.Sc, PhD, C.Eng, M.I.C.E

Boyton *David Rex*
Queen's Square Chambers, Level 1, 235 Macquarie Street, Sydney, New South Wales 2000, Hong Kong, (832) 2521 5544, Fax: (832) 2524 4951, and Member Hong Kong, Call Date: July 1997 (Gray's Inn) Qualifications: BA (Newc), LLB (Lond), LLM (Lond)

Bradley *Michael James*
British West Indies, Call Date: Mar 1999 (Gray's Inn) Qualifications: BA (Oxon)

Brady *Kevin Joseph*
47 Hervey Close, Finchley, London N3 06H, Northern Ireland, Lecturer in Law, Call Date: July 1984 (Gray's Inn) Qualifications: BA (Belfast) LLB, (Lond)

Brady *Scott*
Scotland, Scottish Advocate, and Member Scotland, Call Date: July 1998 (Middle Temple) Qualifications: LLB (Edinburgh)

Brandon *Michael*
P O Box 200, 1291 Commugny, Vaud, 0041 22 776 14 00/776 15 00, Fax: 0041 22 776 55 18, Call Date: Nov 1952 (Inner Temple) Qualifications: MA, LLM (Cantab), MA (Yale), FCIArb

Brankin *Sean-Paul*
Belgium, Call Date: Oct 1993 (Lincoln's Inn) Qualifications: BA (Hons), LLM (Virginia)

Brewer *Miss Michelle Louise*
Call Date: Mar 1999 (Inner Temple) Qualifications: LLB

Bridge *Mrs Anabelle Jane*
Le Haugard, La Ville de l'Eglise, St Ouen, Jersey JE3 2LR, Channel Islands, 01534 482671, Fax: 01534 481675, Call Date: Nov 1981 (Gray's Inn) Qualifications: LLB (Nott'm)

Bridge *Mark David*
3395 Cadboro Bay Road, Victoria, BC, Canada V8R 5K4, Canada, 604-592 9457, Professor of Taxation, University of Victoria, Canada, and Member British Columbia, Call Date: July 1992 (Lincoln's Inn) Qualifications: LLB (Canada), BSc (Canada), LLM (Lond)

Bridgeford *William Andrew Macrae*
Crills, 44 The Esplanade, St Helier, Jersey, Channel Islands, Channel Islands, 01534 873521, Advocate of the Royal Court of Jersey, Call Date: July 1986 (Middle Temple) Qualifications: LLB (Dundee) MPhil, (Cantab)

Bristol *Anthony Fitzgerald Le Varrie*
West Indies, Call Date: Oct 1997 (Gray's Inn) Qualifications: BSc (West Indies)

Bristol *James Anthony Louis*
Henry, Henry & Bristol, P.O.Box 386, St. Georges, Grenada, 473 440 2500/2809, Fax: 473 440 4128, Chairman, Air Transport & Licensing Board, and Member Grenada, Trinidad & Tobago, St Lucia, Barbados, Call Date: July 1989 (Middle Temple) Qualifications: LLB

Britton *His Honour Judge Ian Robert*
The Law Courts, Harbour Road, Wan Chai, 5824106, District Judge, Formerly a Solicitor admitted 1965, Call Date: May 1977 (Inner Temple)

Brodie *Philip Hope*
Advocates Library, Parliament House, Edinburgh, Scotland EH1 1RF, Scotland, 031 226 5071, Fax: 031 225 3642, Scottish Advocate Queens Counsel, Scotland, Call Date: Nov 1991 (Lincoln's Inn) Qualifications: LLB (Hons) (Edin), LLM Virginia

Brown *Eric Crichton*
Advocate's Library, Parliament House, Edinburgh, Scotland EH1 1RF, Scotland, 0131 226 5071, Fax: 0131 225 3642, and Member Scottish Bar, Call Date: Nov 1990 (Lincoln's Inn) Qualifications: LLB (Hons) (Edin)

Brown *Miss Pamela Lucean*
Bahamas, Call Date: Nov 1998 (Middle Temple) Qualifications: LLB (Hons) (L'pool)

Brunton *Captain Ian Arthur Joseph*
6 La Boiselle Road, La Baja, St Joseph,
Trinidad, West Indies, West Indies,
868-645 5693, Fax: 868-662 4822,
Airline Captain/Private Law practice
Rep of Trinidad & Tobago., and
Member Trinidad & Tobago Bar Antigua
Bar Bermuda Bar, Call Date: July 1990
(Lincoln's Inn) Qualifications: LLB
(Lond)

Buchanan *Mrs Charissa Siew-Fong*
Messrs Rodyk & Davidson, 9 Raffles
Place [H]55-01, Republic Plaza,
Singapore 048619, Republic of
Singapore, (65) 5399247/22552626,
Fax: (65) 2251838 & 2257511, and
Member Singapore Bar, Call Date: July
1993 (Inner Temple) Qualifications:
LLB (Hons)(Notts)

Buchanan *Mark Philip*
Singapore 1026, Call Date: Nov 1991
(Inner Temple) Qualifications: LLB

Bukhari *Syed Mustafa Ali*
Pakistan, Call Date: July 1997
(Lincoln's Inn) Qualifications: LLB
(Hons)(Lond)

Bull *Cavinder*
Drew & Napier, 20 Raffles Place, Ocean
Towers [H]17-00, Singapore 048620,
(65) 531 2416, Fax: (65) 532 7149,
and Member Singapore Bar, New York,
Call Date: July 1993 (Gray's Inn)
Qualifications: BA (Oxon),, LLM (Harv)

Bunting *Michael Robert Daniel*
Temple Chambers, 16th Floor, 1 Pacific
Place, 88 Queensway, 5-2 32003, Fax:
5-8 400711, and Member Hong Kong
Bar, Call Date: Nov 1972 (Middle
Temple) Qualifications: MA (Oxon)

Burch *Miss Rosalyn*
France, Call Date: Oct 1997 (Middle
Temple) Qualifications: BA
(Hons)(Keele)

Burger *Schalk Frederick*
621 Innes Chambers, Pritchard Street,
Johannesburg, 11-333 8903, Fax:
11-333 0626, Practising Advocate,
South Africa, Botswana & Namibia, and
Member Johannesburg Bar; Senior
Counsel Cape Town; Senior Counsel,
Call Date: Feb 1974 (Lincoln's Inn)
Qualifications: B.Comm, LLB,
(Stellenbosch), LLM (Lond)

Burke *John Stewart*
Ireland, Call Date: Oct 1994 (Gray's
Inn) Qualifications: BA

Burney *Ali Hasan*
3404 Rosendale Road, Nisskayuna, NY
12309, U.S.A., (518) 785 2742, Call
Date: Nov 1997 (Lincoln's Inn)
Qualifications: BA (Hons)(Tennessee)

Burrell *The Hon Mr Justice Michael
Peter*
Supreme Court, Queensway, Hong
Kong, Hong Kong, 28254316, Fax:
28495494, District Court Judge 1991
High Court Judge 1995 (HK), and
Member Hong Kong Bar, Call Date: July
1971 (Inner Temple) Qualifications:
MA (Cantab)

Burriss *Rhys*
West Indies, 0191 383 1641/001 664
491 4056, Senior Magistrate,
Montserrat West Indies, Member
Institute of Management, Call Date:
May 1979 (Gray's Inn) Qualifications:
BA (Oxon), Dip Uni Lisbon

Burrows *Miss Tameka Shevone*
Attorney Generals Office, P.O.Box
N3007, Nassau N.P., Bahamas, Attorney
at Law, and Member Bahamas, Call
Date: July 1997 (Middle Temple)
Qualifications: LLB (Hons)

Burton *Ralph Dennis*
Ascoli & Weil, Tte. Gral. Juan D Peron
328, 4th Floor, 1038 Buenos Aires,
Argentina, 00 54 1 342 0081, Fax: 00
54 1 331 7150, Call Date: Nov 1985
(Inner Temple) Qualifications: BA
(Hons)(Oxon)

Bury *Miss Claire Louise*
Rue de la Loi 200, 1040 Brussels,
Belgium, 00 32 2 296 0499, Fax: 00 32
2 295 2483, Member of the Legal
Service of the European Commission,
Call Date: July 1988 (Middle Temple)
Qualifications: LLB (Hons) (Lond)

Butler *Miss Bernadette Mae Evelyn*
Bahamas, Call Date: July 1995
(Lincoln's Inn) Qualifications: LLB
(Hons)

Butler *Miss Jacinda Pomona*
Bahamas, Call Date: Nov 1995 (Gray's
Inn) Qualifications: LLB (Lond)

Butler *Truman Kirkland*
Bahamas, Call Date: July 1996 (Middle
Temple) Qualifications: LLB
(Hons)(Wolves)

Butterfield *Toby Michael John*
Kay Collyer & Boose LLP, One Dag
Hammarskjold Plaza, New York, NY
10017-2299, USA, United States of
America, (212) 940 8369, Fax: (212)
755 0921, Secretary, Cemorc Ltd, and
Member New York, Call Date: July 1989
(Lincoln's Inn) Qualifications: BA
(Oxon), LLM (Int'l)

Butterworth *Miss Pamela*
Isle of Man, Call Date: Nov 1995
(Middle Temple) Qualifications: LLB
(Hons)(Dundee)

Cahalan *Michael James*
Northern Ireland, and Member
Northern Ireland Bar, Call Date: July
1996 (Middle Temple) Qualifications:
CPE, B.S.Sc, M.Sc (Belfast)

Caldwell *Miss Marion Allan*
Advocates' Library, Parliament, House,
Parliament Square, Edinburgh
EH1 1RF, Scotland, 0131 226 5071,
Standing Junior to the Accountant of
Court, Scottish Advocate, Call Date: July
1991 (Inner Temple) Qualifications:
LLB (Aberdeen), Dip Law P (Glasgow)

Callaghan *Valentine Edward*
Guillermo Golding Abogados S.L,
Bethencourt Alfonso, 33-3o, 38002
Santa Cruz De Tenerife, 24 12 85/38 40
17, Fax: 24 25 27/37 03 78, Legal
Advisor, King's Inns, Call Date: Nov
1979 (Lincoln's Inn) Qualifications:
MA, BCL (Dub), Post Grad Dip Eu Law

Callender *Jason Colin*
Callenders & Co, One Millars Court, PO
Box N-7117, Nassau, Bahamas, 809
322 2511, Fax: 809 326 7666, and
Member Bahamas Bar (1996), Call
Date: July 1996 (Middle Temple)
Qualifications: LLB (Hons)(Soton)

Calvert-Lee *Miss Georgina Eliza Jane*
Sonnenschein, Nath & Rosenthal, 8000
Sears Tower, Chicago, Illinois 60606,
(USA) 312 876 8964, Fax: (USA) 312
876 7934, Call Date: Oct 1993 (Middle
Temple) Qualifications: MA
(Hons)(Oxon), CPE (City)

Campbell *Charles Grigor Gordon*
45 Avenue Montaigne, 75008 Paris,
0147-23-64-82, Fax: 0147-23-37-74,
Avocat in France and Member Paris
Bar, Call Date: Feb 1965 (Gray's Inn)
Qualifications: BA (Cantab), Cert
Comm Mkt Law, (Paris)

Campbell *Miss Michelle Yvonne*
P.O. Box N-9180, Nassau, Bahamas,
(809) 393 5551, Fax: (809) 393 5116,
and Member Member of the Bar of the
Commonwealth of The Bahamas, Call
Date: July 1996 (Inner Temple)
Qualifications: LLB (Lond)

Campbell *Miss Susanne Allison*
West Indies, Call Date: Oct 1995
(Middle Temple) Qualifications: BA
(Canada)

Campos *Miss Pamela Jennifer*
Singapore 277546, Call Date: Nov 1996
(Middle Temple) Qualifications: LLB
(Hons)(Wales)

Canepa *James Silvio*
Gibraltar, Call Date: May 1996 (Inner
Temple) Qualifications: LLB (Lond)

Cargill *Miss Marie*
P O Box SS-5569, Nassau, Bahamas,
Bahamas, Call Date: Nov 1993 (Gray's
Inn) Qualifications: BA , MBA , LLB

Cariou *Marcel Robert*
Les Queux, Ruette Des Effards, Castel,
Guernsey, Channel Islands, Call Date:
Nov 1987 (Gray's Inn) Qualifications:
LLB(Hons)

F

Carr *Miss Chelon Marie*
Lennox Paton, Devonshire House,
Queens Street, P O Box N-4875,
Nassau, Bahamas, (809) 328 0563,
Fax: (809) 328 0566, Associate, and
Member Bahamas Bar, Call Date: July
1996 (Lincoln's Inn) Qualifications:
LLB (Hons) (Leeds)

Carter *Miss Allison Clara*
Channel Islands, Call Date: Oct 1998
(Middle Temple) Qualifications: BSc
(Hons) (Plymouth), CPE

Carter *Robert James*
Shell International B.V., Carel Van
Bylandtlaan 30, 2501 An The Hague,
The Netherlands, 31 (0)70 377 1822,
Fax: 31 (0) 70 377 6141, Licensing
Lawyer, Call Date: July 1995 (Inner
Temple) Qualifications: BSc (Leeds),
CPE (Notts)

Casey *Miss Niamh Ann*
France, Call Date: Nov 1993 (Middle
Temple) Qualifications: BCL, LLM

Ch'ng *Frank Eng Hing*
Malaysia, Call Date: July 1995 (Middle
Temple) Qualifications: LLB (Hons)

Ch'ng *Miss Li-Ling*
Singapore 239566, Call Date: July 1996
(Lincoln's Inn) Qualifications: LLB
(Hons) (Lond)

Chadwick *Neville*
Attorney General's Chambers, Private
Bag 62, Francistown, 212 342, Fax: 213
402, Principal State Counsel, Advocate
of the High Court of Botswana, Call
Date: July 1972 (Middle Temple)
Qualifications: BA, LLM (Lond)

Chai *Hean Leong*
Malaysia, Call Date: July 1996
(Lincoln's Inn) Qualifications: LLB
(Hons) (Lond)

Chai *Mrs Karen Um-Chai Hui Lin*
Oversea-Chinese Banking, Corporation
Limited, 65 China Street, [H]29-02/04,
OCBC Centre, Singapore 459732,
5306143, Fax: 5352335, Legal Officer,
Call Date: Nov 1995 (Middle Temple)
Qualifications: LLB (Hons)

Chai *Miss Yoke Peng*
Singapore 1232, Call Date: July 1995
(Lincoln's Inn) Qualifications: LLB
(Hons)

Chair *Yong Huang Adrian*
162D Jalan Limau Gedong, off Jalan
Meru, 41050 Klang, Malaysia, 603-254
8111, Fax: 603-254 3211, Legal
Assistant, and Member Malaya Bar, Call
Date: July 1996 (Gray's Inn)
Qualifications: LLB (Leicester)

Chan *Allan Chun Hwee*
Singapore 760326, Call Date: July 1996
(Middle Temple) Qualifications: LLB
(Hons) (Lond)

Chan *Miss Amanda Yuk Ying*
Hong Kong, Call Date: July 1996
(Middle Temple) Qualifications: LLB
(Hons) (Wolves)

Chan *Bo Ching*
Room 18, 1/F, New Henry House, 10
Ice House Street, Central, Hong Kong,
852 2869 8399, Fax: 852 2537 8363,
and Member Hong Kong, Call Date: July
1995 (Gray's Inn) Qualifications: LLB,
LLM (Lond), MBA, ACIB

Chan *Ms Charmaine Poh Meng*
Singapore 574327, Call Date: July 1997
(Gray's Inn) Qualifications: LLB (Notts)

Chan *Che Bun Anderson*
Hong Kong, and Member Hong Kong
Bar, Call Date: Nov 1997 (Gray's Inn)
Qualifications: LLB, LLM (Lond),, LLM
(Deakin Australia), ARICS, DipProjMan

Chan *Chee Choong*
Malaysia, Call Date: Nov 1997
(Lincoln's Inn) Qualifications: LLB
(Hons)

Chan *Miss Ching Fan*
Suites 1108-1109, 1517-1522, Two
Pacific Place, 88 Queensway, (852)
2810 7222, Fax: (852) 2526 8201, and
Member Hong Kong Bar, Call Date: July
1996 (Middle Temple) Qualifications:
BA (Hons) (Hong Kong), CPE (Manc)

Chan *David Ming Onn*
Singapore 288866, Call Date: July 1996
(Middle Temple) Qualifications: LLB
(Hons) (Lond)

Chan *Mrs Dora Kit Ho*
Hong Kong, and Member Hong Kong,
Call Date: July 1996 (Middle Temple)
Qualifications: BSc (Hons) (Lond), MSc
(City), CPE (Manc)

Chan *Eu Gene*
Malaysia, Call Date: Nov 1996 (Middle
Temple) Qualifications: LLB (Hons)

Chan *Miss Fiona Foong Ling*
Singapore 439816, Call Date: July 1996
(Lincoln's Inn) Qualifications: LLB
(Hons) (Leics)

Chan *Fu Kit Brian*
Hong Kong, and Member Hong Kong
Bar, Call Date: July 1996 (Gray's Inn)
Qualifications: LLB (Wolverhampton)

Chan *Hing Wai*
Hong Kong, and Member Hong Kong
Bar, Call Date: July 1990 (Gray's Inn)
Qualifications: B.Pharm (Brad),
MRPharmS, LLB (Lond)

Chan *Hon Wan Edwin*
Department of Building & Real, Estate,
Hong Kong Polytechnic Uni, Hung
Hom, Kowloon, Hong Kong, Hong Kong,
(HK) 27665800, Fax: (HK) 27645131,
and Member Hong Kong Bar, Call Date:
July 1993 (Inner Temple)
Qualifications: BA, Dip. Arch., MA, LLB,
RIBA, ACIArb, Pg.D PRC law

Chan *Ms Ifan*
Temple Chambers, 1607-1612 One
Pacific Place, 88 Queensway, Hong
Kong, 852 25232003, Fax: 852
28179326, Publisher, Hong Kong
Transit Publishing Co Ltd, and Member
Hong Kong Bar, Call Date: July 1996
(Inner Temple) Qualifications: BA ,
CPE

Chan *Ka Sing Louise*
Hong Kong, Call Date: Nov 1997 (Inner
Temple) Qualifications: LLB, LLM

Chan *Miss Keng Yean*
Malaysia, Call Date: Nov 1997
(Lincoln's Inn) Qualifications: LLB
(Hons) (L'pool)

Chan *Kia Khuang*
Singapore 289435, Call Date: July 1996
(Middle Temple) Qualifications: LLB
(Hons) (Bris)

Chan *Kong Meng Lawrence*
Messrs Drew & Napier, 20 Raffles Place,
[H]17-00 Ocean Towers, Singapore
310164, 5314148, Fax: 5354864, Legal
Assistant, and Member Singapore, Call
Date: July 1997 (Middle Temple)
Qualifications: LLB (Hons) (Keele)

Chan *Kwok-Chun*
Hong Kong, Call Date: Nov 1997 (Gray's
Inn) Qualifications: LLB (Lond), BSc,
MSc, (Hong Kong)

Chan *Miss Lin Wai Ruth*
Singapore 1026, Call Date: July 1995
(Gray's Inn) Qualifications: LLB (Bris)

Chan *Miss Lin-Mei*
Singapore 229952, Call Date: July 1996
(Lincoln's Inn) Qualifications: LLB
(Hons) (Lond)

Chan *LLoyd Kah Seng*
Singapore 289274, Call Date: July 1996
(Middle Temple) Qualifications: LLB
(Hons) (Lond)

Chan *Miss Michelle Geraldine Chui-Wah*
10 Collyer Quay, 08-02 Ocean Building,
Singapore 118642, (65) 534 0195, Fax:
(65) 534 5864, and Member Singapore
Bar, Call Date: Nov 1993 (Middle
Temple) Qualifications: LLB
(Hons) (B'ham)

Chan *Ming-Ki*
Hong Kong, and Member Barrister,
Supreme Court of Hong Kong, Call
Date: Oct 1995 (Middle Temple)
Qualifications: LLB (Hons), LLM

Chan *Miss Ngai Fung*
Malaysia, Call Date: July 1998
(Lincoln's Inn) Qualifications: LLB
(Hons) (Lond)

Chan *Nicholas Kei Cheong*
Orrick, Herrington & Sutcliffe, 10
Collyer Quay, [H]23-08 Ocean
Building, Singapore 049315, Singapore
1026, (65) 538 6116, Fax: (65) 538
0606, and Member Singapore Bar, Call
Date: Feb 1993 (Inner Temple)
Qualifications: MA (Cantab)

Chan *Pat Lun*
Des Voeux Chambers, 10th Floor, Bank
of East Asia Building, 10 Des Voeux
Road, Central, (852) 2526 3071, Fax:
(852) 2810 5287, and Member Hong
Kong Bar, Call Date: July 1994
(Lincoln's Inn) Qualifications: BA
(Hons)

Chan *Peter Chi-Kwan*
604 Cosmos Bldg, 8-11 Lan Kwai Fong,
D'Aguilar St, 852 25230858, Fax: 852
28684673, Fellow of the Chartered
Institute of Arbitrators, and Member
Hong Kong Bar, Call Date: Nov 1965
(Middle Temple)

Chan *Miss Pik Dzee*
Malaysia, Call Date: July 1995 (Middle
Temple) Qualifications: LLB (Hons)

Chan *Miss Shui Ping Peggy*
Hong Kong, 23480435, and Member
Hong Kong, Call Date: July 1997
(Middle Temple) Qualifications: LLB
(Hons)(Lond)

Chan *Siu Lun*
Hong Kong, Call Date: July 1998
(Middle Temple) Qualifications: BSc
(Hong Kong)

Chan *Miss Suk-Wai Winsome*
Room 649, High Block, Queensway
Government Offices, Admiralty, Hong
Kong, (852) 28672303, Fax: (852)
25368423, Call Date: Nov 1994 (Gray's
Inn) Qualifications: BA (Hong Kong)

Chan *Tak Pun*
Hong Kong, Call Date: Nov 1997 (Gray's
Inn) Qualifications: BSc (Hong Kong)

Chan *Dr Yee Kwong*
Hong Kong Polytechnic Uni.,
Department of Business Studies, Hung
Hom, Kowloon, Hong Kong, (852) 2766
7110, Fax: (852) 2765 0611, Assistant
Professor, Call Date: Mar 1998 (Middle
Temple) Qualifications: LLB
(Hons)(Lond), LLM (Lond), PhD,
(Chinese Uni of HK)

Chan *Yoong Heng*
Malaysia, Call Date: July 1997
(Lincoln's Inn) Qualifications: LLB
(Hons)(Lond)

Chandrakesan *Prabakaran*
West Malaysia, Advocate and Solicitor of
the High Court of Malaya and Member
Malaysian Bar, Call Date: Mar 1998
(Middle Temple) Qualifications: LLB
(Hons)

Chandran *Ramesh N P*
21 Lorong Kemaris Dua, Bukit
Bandaraya, 59100 Kuala Lumpur,
Malaysia, 60 03 2561198, Fax: 60 03
2521932, Call Date: July 1998 (Middle
Temple) Qualifications: LLB
(Hons)(Warw), LLM (So'ton), FRSA,,
MMIArbs, MISM

Chandranayagam *Daniel Masillamaney*
Malaysia 47300, and Member
Malaysian Bar, Call Date: July 1997
(Gray's Inn) Qualifications: LLB
(Glamorgan)

Chang *Miss Jo-Anne*
Singapore 1024, Call Date: Nov 1996
(Lincoln's Inn) Qualifications: LLB
(Hons)(Lond), AKC Diploma

Chang *Kin Hui*
Brunei, Call Date: Nov 1995 (Middle
Temple) Qualifications: BA (Hons)

Changaroth *Anil M*
Lim & Lim, 63 Market Street,
[H]13-03/05, Tat Lee Bank Building,
Singapore 550225, 5358626, Fax:
5356736, Legal Assistant, and Member
Singapore Bar, Call Date: Nov 1993
(Middle Temple) Qualifications: LLB
(Hons)(Bucks)

Chao *Bernard Wee Chun*
Chung Tan & Partners, 1 North Bridge
Road, [H]13-05 High Street Centre,
Singapore 2158, 065 339 8048, Fax:
065 334 7933, and Member Singapore,
Call Date: July 1993 (Lincoln's Inn)
Qualifications: LLB (Hons)

Chao *Miss Elaine Wen Su*
Drew & Napier, 20 Raffles Place,
[H]17-00, Ocean Towers, Singapore
269352, (65) 531 2496, Fax: (65) 532
7149, and Member Singapore, Call
Date: July 1996 (Middle Temple)
Qualifications: LLB (Hons)(Lond)

Chapman *Christopher Scott*
Buddle Findlay, P O Box 2694, 1 Willis
Street, Wellington, 00 644 499 4242,
Fax: 00 644 499 4141, Barrister &
Solicitor, High Court of New Zealand
(1983) Formerly a solicitor of the
Supreme court and Member New
Zealand Bar, Call Date: July 1980
(Inner Temple) Qualifications: BSc,
LLM (Vic, Wellington)

Chapman *James Charles*
Begg-Hempton
P O Box 1234 GT, Grand Cayman, 345
949 9876, Fax: 345 949 9877, and
Member Cayman Islands, Call Date:
Nov 1987 (Inner Temple)
Qualifications: LLM, MA (Cantab), BSc,
BA

Chapman *Richard Kenneth*
2 Route De La Cascade, 78110 Le
Vesinet, 00 33 1 34801234, Fax: 00 33
1 34801263, Call Date: Nov 1976
(Lincoln's Inn) Qualifications: FCA

Charalambous *Andreas*
Cyprus, Call Date: Nov 1997 (Gray's
Inn) Qualifications: LLB (Sheff)

Charalambous *Miss Christina*
Cyprus, Call Date: Nov 1998 (Gray's
Inn) Qualifications: LLB (Lond)

Charitonos *Miss Panayiota Costa*
Cyprus, Call Date: Nov 1995 (Middle
Temple) Qualifications: LLB (Hons)

Chau *Miss Catherine Siew Ping*
40 Luyang Phase 4, Jalan Kijang, 88100
Koya Kinabalu, Sabah, and Member
Advocate, Sabah Bar, Call Date: Nov
1991 (Gray's Inn) Qualifications: BA
(Hons) (Kent), LLM (Lond)

Chau *Kwok Leung Raymond*
Hong Kong, Projext Engineer, and
Member Hong Kong SAR, Call Date: Oct
1997 (Middle Temple) Qualifications:
BSc (Hons)(Lond)

Chau *Philip*
Pacific Chambers, Room 901 Dina
House, 11 Duddell Street, Central,
2521 5544, Fax: 2524 5912, and
Member Hong Kong Bar, Call Date: May
1995 (Inner Temple) Qualifications:
LLB

Chaudhri *Ferhan Munir*
East Africa, Call Date: Nov 1995
(Lincoln's Inn) Qualifications: LLB
(Hons)(Warw)

Chaudhry *Muhammad Alfaz*
Pakistan, Call Date: Nov 1997
(Lincoln's Inn) Qualifications: BA, LLB
(Punjab), LLM (Lond)

Chay *Miss Kum Yoon*
Block 68, Dakota Crescent [H]12-600,
Singapore 390068, 346 2990, Call Date:
July 1996 (Middle Temple)
Qualifications: LLB (Hons)(Leeds)

Che *Shu Fai*
Hong Kong, Call Date: Nov 1992
(Lincoln's Inn) Qualifications: LLB
(Hons)

Cheah *Peng Kun*
Malaysia, Call Date: July 1995 (Middle
Temple) Qualifications: LLB (Hons)
(Wales)

Cheah *Sau Voon*
Messrs Mohd Noor & SY Lee, Room
110, 1st Floor, Asia Life Building, 45-B
Jalan Tun Sambanthan, 30000 Ipoh,
Perak, Malaysia, 05 2543589/9823,
Fax: 05 2542611, and Member
Malaysia, Call Date: Nov 1995 (Middle
Temple) Qualifications: LLB (Hons)

Cheah *Soo Chuan*
Malaysia, Call Date: July 1995
(Lincoln's Inn) Qualifications: LLB
(Hons)

Cheah *Tien Eu*
Malaysia, Call Date: July 1996
(Lincoln's Inn) Qualifications: LLB
(Hons)(Leeds)

Cheah *Mrs Wai Mun*
Singapore 1027, and Member
Singapore Bar, Call Date: July 1986
(Lincoln's Inn) Qualifications: BA
(Kent)

Cheam *Miss Phaik Ling*
Nordin Hamid & Co, 9th Floor,
Campbell Complex, Jalan DanG Wangi,
50100 Kuala Lumpur, Malaysia,
03-2944677, Fax: 03-2944418, and
Member Malaysia Bar, Call Date: July
1992 (Middle Temple) Qualifications:
LLB (Hons) (Leics)

Chechatwala *Shabbir Ismail*
Messrs Edmond Pereira & Prtns, 111
North Bridge Road, [H]18-02/03/04,
Peninsula Plaza, Singapore 1542, 65
336 2122, Fax: 65 336 3433, Legal
Assistant, and Member Singapore, Call
Date: July 1997 (Middle Temple)
Qualifications: LLB (Hons) (Keele)

Chedumbarum Pillay *Neil
Radhakrishna*
Mauritius, Call Date: July 1997 (Middle
Temple) Qualifications: LLB
(Hons) (Wales)

Chee *Miss Diane Sui-Yen*
Singapore 259449, Call Date: July 1998
(Middle Temple) Qualifications: BA
(Hons) (Exon)

Chee *Miss Julie Suk-Yuen*
Malaysia, Call Date: Nov 1996 (Gray's
Inn) Qualifications: LLB (LSE), MA
(Lond)

Chee *Miss Le Anne*
Malaysia, Call Date: July 1998 (Middle
Temple) Qualifications: LLB
(Hons) (Nott'm)

Chee *Yew Chung*
Chong Chja & Lim, 20 Maxwell House,
03-01E/F Maxwell House, Singapore
120611, Int + + (65) 2246696, Fax:
Int + + (65) 2241294, and Member
Singapore Bar, Call Date: July 1996
(Inner Temple) Qualifications: LLB
(Hull)

Cheesman *William James*
Call Date: Nov 1990 (Lincoln's Inn)
Qualifications: LLB (Lond)

Chellam *Miss Gwendolyn Mae*
Singapore 308231, Call Date: July 1998
(Gray's Inn) Qualifications: LLB
(Leeds)

Chelliah *Kumarendran*
Singapore 1955, Call Date: July 1995
(Middle Temple) Qualifications: LLB
(Hons)

Chen *Mian Kuang*
Messrs Raja, Darryl & Loh, 18th Floor,
Wisma Sime Darby, Jalan Raja Laut,
50350, Kuala Lumpur, Malaysia,
(Malaysia) 03 2949999, and Member
Malaysia Bar, Call Date: July 1995
(Lincoln's Inn) Qualifications: LLB
(Hons)

Cheng *Alvin Sun Cheok*
2 Handy Road, [H]10-02, Cathay
Building, Singapore 308381, 3366533,
Fax: 3370906, Legal Assistant, and
Member Singapore Bar, Call Date: Nov
1993 (Lincoln's Inn) Qualifications:
LLB (Hons)

Cheng *Miss Angelina Tan*
Malaysia, Call Date: July 1996 (Middle
Temple) Qualifications: LLB
(Hons) (Kent)

Cheng *Glenn Li Huei*
Singapore 592001, Call Date: Nov 1995
(Middle Temple) Qualifications: LLB
(Hons) (Wales)

Cheng *Hock Hua*
Singapore 1852, Call Date: Oct 1993
(Middle Temple) Qualifications: LLB
(Hons) (Lond)

Cheng *Kim Kuan*
Billy Ng Chua & Partners, Advocates &
Solicitors, No 17 Upper Circular Road,
[H]02-01, Singapore 380060, 5366382,
Fax: 5366387, Advocate & Solicitor, and
Member Singapore, Call Date: July
1996 (Middle Temple) Qualifications:
BA (Hons) (Keele)

Cheng *Miss Kitty Kit Yee*
c/o Legal Service Division, Legislative
Council Secretaria, 8 Jackson Road,
Central, Hong Kong, Hong Kong,
8699209, Fax: 8775029, Assistant Legal
Adviser, and Member Hong Kong Bar
Australian Capital Territory Bar, Call
Date: Apr 1991 (Gray's Inn)
Qualifications: LLB, PCLL, MIL

Cheng *Miss Mai*
Measat Broadcast Network SDN, BHD,
All Asia Broadcast Centre, Lebuhraya
Puchong - SG Besi, Bukit Jalil, Kuala
Lumpur, Malaysia, 603-5836688, Fax:
603-5836872, and Member Malaysia
Bar, Call Date: July 1993 (Middle
Temple) Qualifications: LLB
(Hons) (Lond)

Cheng *Miss Patricia May Li*
M/S C C Choo & Co, Suite D33 & D34,
3rd Floor, Pekeliling Plaza, Jalan Tun
Razak, 50400 Kuala Lumour, Malaysia,
603 4411481, Fax: 603 4411481,
Advocate & Solicitor, and Member
Malaysia Bar, Call Date: July 1995
(Middle Temple) Qualifications: LLB
(Hons)

Cheng *Peter Ong Lip*
Singapore 520255, and Member
Malaysia Bar, Call Date: Nov 1995
(Inner Temple) Qualifications: LLB
(Lond)

Cheng *Tak Ying*
Hong Kong, Call Date: Nov 1996
(Middle Temple) Qualifications: LLB
(Hons)

Cheng *Miss Teresa Chin Pei*
West Malaysia, Call Date: July 1994
(Middle Temple) Qualifications: LLB
(Hons) (Sheff)

Cheng *Miss Wei Lin*
Toh Tan & Partners, Advocates &
Solicitors, 79 Robinson Road, [H]
21-03, CPF Building, Singapore, 225
6446, Fax: 225 2356, Legal Assistant,
and Member Singapore Bar, Call Date:
July 1993 (Lincoln's Inn)
Qualifications: LLB (Hons, Bris)

Cheng *Miss Wei Min*
C/O Linklaters & Paines, 14th Floor,
Alexandra House, Chater Road, Central,
Singapore 0923, Call Date: Nov 1995
(Middle Temple) Qualifications: LLB
(Hons)

Cheng *Miss Yen Lin*
Singapore 0923, and Member
Singapore Bar, Call Date: July 1993
(Lincoln's Inn) Qualifications: LLB
(Hons, L'pool)

Cheng *Miss Yvonne Wai Sum*
16th Floor, Temple Chambers, One
Pacific Place, 88 Queensway, Hong
Kong, 2840 1131, Fax: 2810 0302, and
Member Hong Kong Bar, Call Date: July
1996 (Gray's Inn) Qualifications: BA
(Oxon)

Cheok *Robin Van Kee*
Abrahams, Davidson & Co, Room 516,
5th Floor, Plaza Athirah, Jalan Kubah
Makam Diraja, Bandar Seri Begawan,
Brunei Darussala, Brunei 2180, 673 2
242840, Fax: 673 2 242836, and
Member Brunei Darussalam, Call Date:
July 1995 (Inner Temple)
Qualifications: LLB (Essex)

Cheong *Chin Min*
Singapore 533015, Call Date: July 1996
(Middle Temple) Qualifications: LLB
(Hons) (Lond)

Cheong *Goh Boon Wilfred*
Apt Block 111, Whampoa Road
[H]07-29, Singapore 321111, Republic
of Singapore, 5365334/96787826/
96810380, Fax: 5365134, Barrister/
Arbitrator Advocate & Solicitor, and
Member Supreme Court of Australian
Capital Territory, Supreme Court of
Brunei Darrussalam Singapore Bar
Supreme Court of Singapore, Call Date:
Nov 1990 (Lincoln's Inn)
Qualifications: LLb (Lond) (Hons)

Cheong *Miss Seok Wah*
7500 Beach Road, [H] 07-301 The
Plaza, Singapore 199591, 65 2985755,
Fax: 65 2988390, and Member
Singapore Bar, Call Date: July 1993
(Middle Temple) Qualifications: LLB
(Hons, Bris)

Cheong *Miss Whye Mun*
Malaysia, Call Date: July 1995
(Lincoln's Inn) Qualifications: LLB
(Hons)

Cheong *Yuk Leung*
Malaysia, and Member Malaysian Bar,
Call Date: July 1996 (Lincoln's Inn)
Qualifications: LLB (Hons) (Warw)

F

Chern *Aik Hua*
Singapore 510419, and Member
Singapore Bar, Call Date: July 1992
(Lincoln's Inn) Qualifications: LLB
(Hons) (Lond)

Chern *Miss Chyi Ching*
15 Tagore Avenue, Singapore 787650,
Republic of Singapore, Singapore 2678,
and Member Singapore Bar, Call Date:
July 1994 (Lincoln's Inn)
Qualifications: LLB (Hons)

Chesney *George Cecil*
Bar Library, Royal Courts of Justice,
Chichester Street, Belfast, N Ireland,
Northern Ireland, 0232 241523, Fax:
0232 231850, Chairman, Pensions
Appeal Tribunal, and Member Northern
Ireland Bar, Call Date: May 1988
(Middle Temple) Qualifications: LLB
(Hons) Bristol, BA

Cheuk *Yiu Ming*
Hong Kong, Call Date: Nov 1998
(Middle Temple) Qualifications: LLB
(Hons) (Lond)

Cheung *Adonis Kam Wing*
Suite 405, Printing House, 6 Duddell
Street, Central, 852 2526 5222, Fax:
852 2801 5883, and Member Hong
Kong Bar, Call Date: July 1994 (Inner
Temple) Qualifications: LLB

Cheung *K-John*
7208 Queenston Court, Burnaby, B.C.
V5A 3M4, (604) 299 8193, Fax: (604)
299 8365, and Member British
Columbia Law Society (Canada),
Canada, Hong Kong & Victoria
(Austraila) Bars Hong Kong Bar, Call
Date: July 1973 (Lincoln's Inn)
Qualifications: BSc, LLB, JD Dip Comp
Law , Dip Ch Law

Cheung *Miss Man Ching*
Hong Kong, Call Date: Nov 1996
(Lincoln's Inn) Qualifications: LLB
(Hons)

Cheung *Man To Raymond*
Suite 1319-1320, Prince's Building, 10
Chater Road, Central, Hong Kong,
(852) 2869 6253, Fax: (852) 2869
6375, and Member Hong Kong Bar, Call
Date: Nov 1997 (Lincoln's Inn)
Qualifications: Postgraduate Diploma,
In Law

Cheung *Sir Oswald Victor*
New Henry House, 10th Floor, 10 Ice
House Street, 2524-2156, Fax:
2810-5656, QC Hong Kong, Call Date:
Jan 1950 (Lincoln's Inn)
Qualifications: MA (Oxon)

Cheung *Phei Chiet*
Singapore 1545, and Member
Singapore Bar, Call Date: July 1994
(Gray's Inn) Qualifications: BA , LLM

Cheung *Tai Yau*
Hong Kong, 25941438, and Member
Hong Kong SAR,PRC, Call Date: July
1998 (Lincoln's Inn) Qualifications:
LLB (Lond), BSC (QS) (HKPU),
ACCA,AHKSA,AciArb

Cheung *Miss Tania Su Li*
Singapore 2678, Call Date: July 1995
(Lincoln's Inn) Qualifications: LLB
(Hons)

Chew *Miss Chin Yean*
Singapore 2159, Call Date: Nov 1996
(Lincoln's Inn) Qualifications: LLB
(Hons) (Kent)

Chew *Miss Eng Cheng*
Malaysia, Call Date: Nov 1998
(Lincoln's Inn) Qualifications: LLB
(Hons) (Thames)

Chew *Eng Ghee*
Messrs P S Ranjan & Co, Advocates &
Solicitors, 12th Floor MUI Plaza, Jalan P
Ramlee, 50250 Kuala Lumpur, 03
2489200, Fax: 03 2423758, and
Member Malaysia Bar, Call Date: Nov
1992 (Lincoln's Inn) Qualifications:
LLB (Hons)

Chew *Hew Wearn*
Malaysia, Call Date: Nov 1997
(Lincoln's Inn) Qualifications: LLB
(Hons) (Sheff)

Chew *Kei-Jin*
9 Battery Road, Straits Trading
Building, [H]15-00, Singapore 049910,
Singapore 1025, 65 5322271, Fax: 65
5352975, Legal Assistant, and Member
Singapore Bar, Call Date: July 1993
(Middle Temple) Qualifications: BA
(Cantab), MA (Cantab)

Chew *Kok Liang*
2 Jalan SS 20/22, Damansara Utama,
47400 Petaling Jaya, Selangor,
Malaysia, Malaysia, 03 7180095, and
Member Malaysia Bar, Call Date: July
1991 (Inner Temple) Qualifications:
BSc Econ (Wales), LLM (Leic), Dip in
Shariah Law &, Practice (IIU)

Chew *Kok Wye*
Singapore 457595, Call Date: Nov 1997
(Middle Temple) Qualifications: LLB
(Hons) (Kent)

Chew *Kwee-San*
Singapore 0922, Advocate & Solicitor of
the Supreme Court in Singapore, Call
Date: July 1994 (Middle Temple)
Qualifications: LLB (Hons) (Notts)

Chew *Miss Lynette Mei Lin*
79 Robinson Road, [H]24-01 CPF
Building, Singapore 1544, 223 3227,
Fax: 223 0003, Legal Assistant, and
Member Singapore, Call Date: July
1995 (Lincoln's Inn) Qualifications:
LLB (Hons)

Chew *Miss Mong Fei Vivian*
Singapore 310030, Call Date: Nov 1997
(Middle Temple) Qualifications: LLB
(Hons) (Lond)

Chew *Miss Pitt Har*
Malaysia, and Member Malaysia Bar,
Call Date: July 1992 (Lincoln's Inn)
Qualifications: LLB (Hons) (Lanc)

Chew *Miss Soo San*
Messrs Tang & Yoges, 8b Jalan Raja
Haroun, 43000 Kajang, Selangor Darul
Ehsan, Malaysia, 60-3-8376510, Fax:
60-3-8376515, and Member Malaysia
Bar, Call Date: July 1992 (Middle
Temple) Qualifications: LLB (Hons)
(Warw)

Chew *Yee Teck Eric*
Blk 113, Clementi Street 13, [H]06-25,
269158 Singapore, 8728562, Call Date:
July 1997 (Gray's Inn) Qualifications:
LLB (Sheff), ACIArb

Chhabra *Vinit*
Singapore 130026, Call Date: July 1996
(Middle Temple) Qualifications: LLB
(Hons) (Lond)

Chia *Miss Angela Sharon See Kim*
64 Porchester Avenue, Singapore
556346, 05 280 351, Call Date: July
1998 (Middle Temple) Qualifications:
LLB (Hons) (Wales)

Chia *Miss Chwee Imm Helen*
Singapore 640919, 0065 791 0028, Call
Date: July 1998 (Middle Temple)
Qualifications: LLB (Hons) (Wolves)

Chia *Miss En-Lin*
151 Cavenagh Road, [H]09-159,
229628 Singapore, 0065 7340697/
7384245, Call Date: Nov 1996 (Gray's
Inn) Qualifications: LLB (Nott'm)

Chia *Miss Gillian Hsu-Lien*
Singapore 268163, Call Date: July 1997
(Gray's Inn) Qualifications: LLB (Bris)

Chia *Miss Jeanette Shau Ken*
Malaysia, Call Date: July 1996
(Lincoln's Inn) Qualifications: LLB
(Hons) (Leeds)

Chia *Soo Michael*
Messrs Rajah & Tan, 9 Battery Road
08-03/12, Straits Trading Building,
Singapore 730034, (65) 535 3600, Fax:
(65) 538 8598, Advocate & Solicitor
(Supreme Court of Singapore), Call
Date: July 1997 (Middle Temple)
Qualifications: LLB (Hons),
DipS11,AffA11, MSIArb

Chiah *Miss Yoke Li*
Malaysia, Call Date: July 1997
(Lincoln's Inn) Qualifications: LLB
(Hons) (Wales)

Chiang *Pak Chien*
17 Goldhill Drive, Singapore 1130, (65)
3520821, Legal Assistant, and Member
Singapore, Call Date: Nov 1995 (Middle
Temple) Qualifications: LLB (Hons)

Chiang *Wee Sean*
Singapore 2573, Call Date: July 1995
(Middle Temple) Qualifications: LLB
(Hons)

F

Chiang *Miss Wen-Shan*
Singapore 1335, and Member
Singapore Bar, Call Date: July 1990
(Gray's Inn) Qualifications: LLB (Leic)

Chien *Hoe Yong*
Henco & Associates Limited, 2502 First
Pacific Bank Centre, 51-57 Gloucester
Road, Wanchai, Hong Kong, 25289228,
Group Managing Director, Call Date:
Nov 1988 (Middle Temple)
Qualifications: LLB (Lanc), ACA, HKSA

Chieng *Miss Stephanie Lun Tying*
Awang Lai & Co Advocates, Lots 432 &
434, 2nd Floor, Jalan Bendahara,
98000 Miri, Sarawak, Malaysia,
Malaysia, 085-416688, Fax:
085-416684, and Member Sarawak
Bar, Call Date: July 1995 (Inner
Temple) Qualifications: LLB (Kent)

Chiew *Ean Vooi*
Malaysia, Call Date: July 1997 (Middle
Temple) Qualifications: LLB
(Hons)(Leeds)

Chijner *David*
Weil Gotshal & Manges LLP, 81 Avenue
Louise, Box 9-10, 1050 Brussels, (32
2) 543 7460, Fax: (32 2) 543 7489,
Call Date: Oct 1993 (Inner Temple)
Qualifications: Diplome de Droit,
Francais (Paris) BA (Kent) , LLM
(European , University Institut)

Chin *Chee Chien*
No 20 Jalan SS 21/32, Damansara
Utama, 47400 Petaling Jaya, Selangor
Darul Ehsan, Malaysia, 603-716-9285,
Fax: 603-716-9287, and Member
Malaysian Bar, Call Date: Nov 1993
(Gray's Inn) Qualifications: LLB

Chin *Hein Choong*
Malaysia, Call Date: July 1995
(Lincoln's Inn) Qualifications: LLB
(Hons)

Chin *Miss Jia Huey*
7-4 Lorong Teratai 4, Off Jalan Haji
Jaib, 84000 Muar, Johor, Malaysia,
Malaysia, 06 921367, Fax: 03 2301768,
and Member Malaysia Bar, Call Date:
July 1992 (Lincoln's Inn)
Qualifications: LLB (Hons), LLM

Chin *Julian Ye-Fung*
Asia Pulp & Paper Co Ltd, 1 Maritime
Square, [H]10-01 (Lobby B), World
Trade Centre, Singapore 558693, (65)
3749284, Fax: (65) 3749388, Legal
Counsel, and Member Singapore Bar,
Call Date: July 1992 (Middle Temple)
Qualifications: LLB (Hons) (Leics)

Chin *Keith Hsiun*
c/o Yong Wong & Chin Advocates, 1st
Floor, Bangunan Chin Fook, Lot 382
South Yu Seng Road, P O Box 736
98007 Miri, Sarawak, 085 414348, Fax:
085 415602, Sarawak Advocates
Association,High Court of Sabah
Sarawak and Member Brunei
Darrusalam (High Court of Brunei)
Malaya (Kuala Lumpur Bar), Call Date:
July 1995 (Lincoln's Inn)
Qualifications: LLB (Hons) (Sheff)

Chin *Miss Mye-Ling*
Western Australia 6027, and Member
High Court of Malaya, Call Date: Nov
1994 (Middle Temple) Qualifications:
LLB

Chin *Miss Oi Jean*
123 Jalan SS22/37, Damansara Jaya,
47400 Petaling Jaya, Selangor,
Malaysia, (60)(3) 7189 232, Call Date:
Nov 1995 (Lincoln's Inn)
Qualifications: LLB (Hons), LLM

Chin *Miss Pheik Lin Elaine*
Malaysia, Call Date: Nov 1997
(Lincoln's Inn) Qualifications: LLB
(Hons)

Chin *Miss Pik Khiun*
M/S Kean Chye & Sivalingam, 42 Jalan
Medan Ipoh 6, Bandar Baru Medan
Ipoh, 31400 Ipoh, Perak, Malaysia,
05-545 6010, Fax: 05-545 6359, Legal
Assistant, and Member High Court of
Malaya, Call Date: July 1995 (Lincoln's
Inn) Qualifications: LLB (Hons)

Chin *Miss Tze Jin*
Malaysia, Call Date: July 1996
(Lincoln's Inn) Qualifications: LLB
(Hons) (Kent)

Chin *Tze Jone*
Malaysia, Call Date: July 1995 (Middle
Temple) Qualifications: LLB (Hons)

Chin *Yuen Fong*
Malaysia, Call Date: Nov 1995 (Middle
Temple) Qualifications: BA
(Hons)(Keele)

Chin *Miss Yvonne Mei Oy*
Malaysia, Call Date: Nov 1989
(Lincoln's Inn) Qualifications: LLB,
LLM (Lond)

Ching *Miss Fiona Pui Yeng*
Singapore 1025, and Member
Singapore, Call Date: July 1994 (Middle
Temple) Qualifications: LLB
(Hons)(Notts)

Ching *Leonard Tchi Pang*
Singapore 2057, Call Date: Nov 1994
(Middle Temple) Qualifications: LLB
(Hons)

Chionh *Miss Mavis Sze-Chyi*
Singapore 574281, Call Date: July 1993
(Middle Temple) Qualifications: BA
(Hons)

Chisholm *Miss Marcela*
Glasgow Caledonian University, Dept of
Law and Public Admin, Cowcaddens
Road, Glasgow G4 OBA, Scotland, 0141
331 3427, Fax: 0141 331 3798, Senior
Lecturer in Law, Call Date: July 1991
(Gray's Inn) Qualifications: JUDr
(Prague), LLM (Manch)

Chitthu *Arut*
Singapore 2368, Call Date: July 1995
(Middle Temple) Qualifications: LLB
(Hons)

Chiu *Hsu-Hwee*
Singapore 2057, and Member
Singapore, Call Date: July 1995 (Middle
Temple) Qualifications: LLB (Hons)
(Hull)

Chiu *Kwok Kit*
C/O Hong Kong Inland Revenue,
Appeals Section, 36/F Wanchai Tower 3,
5 Gloucester Road, Hong Kong, Hong
Kong, 852 2594 5038, Fax: 852 2877
1131, Senior Assessor (Appeals
Section), Call Date: Nov 1990
(Lincoln's Inn) Qualifications: LLB
(Lond), LLM, (Lond), LLB (Peking),
MCom, FCCA, AHKSA,, CPA (Aust),
Graduate, Diploma in Taxation

Chiu *Michael Kai Ting*
Flat B, Block 1, Littleton Garden, 17
Lyttelton Road, Hong Kong, (852) 2559
0736, and Member Hong Kong, Call
Date: Nov 1996 (Middle Temple)
Qualifications: LLB (Hons), MA (Hull)

Chiu *Paul Hung Shun*
16th Floor, Chuang's Tower, 30-32
Connaught Road Central, Hong Kong,
(852) 2522 9168, Fax: (852) 2845
2072, F.I.S.M., Barrister & Solicitor
Supreme Court and High Court of
Australian Capital Territory and
Barrister of High Court of Hong Kong
and Member Australian Bar Hong Kong
Bar, Call Date: Nov 1971 (Middle
Temple)

Chiu *Ms Yong Yong*
Singapore 640498, Call Date: July 1997
(Lincoln's Inn) Qualifications: LLB
(Hons)(Lond)

Chng *Miss Angeline Kim-Ann*
3 Astrid Hill, Singapore 269926,
Singapore 269926, 65-4697011, Fax:
65-4697012, and Member Singapore,
Call Date: July 1995 (Middle Temple)
Qualifications: LLB (Hons), LLM

Cho *Chi-kong*
10/F, 2 Murray Road, Central, Hong
Kong, Hong Kong, 28264397, Fax:
25626912, Barrister Supreme Court of
Hong Kong and Member Canberra,
Australia, Call Date: Nov 1989
(Lincoln's Inn) Qualifications: LLB
(Lond)

Choa *Brendon Sn-Yien*
133 New Bridge Road, Chinatown Point
[H]15-09, Singapore, 5382687, Fax:
5380287, Partner, Advocate & Solicitor
Supreme Court of Singapore and
Member Singapore, Call Date: July
1991 (Inner Temple) Qualifications:
BA (Sussex)

Choi *Sheung Kong*
Hong Kong, Call Date: Nov 1997
(Lincoln's Inn) Qualifications: LLB
(Hons)(Lond)

Chok *Miss Ketty Li Ket*
Ronny Cham & Co, P.O.Bix No 13121,
88835 Kota Kinabalu, Sabah, Malaysia,
088 231111, Fax: 088 233122, Legal
Advisor, Call Date: July 1997 (Middle
Temple) Qualifications: LLB
(Hons)(Wales)

Chong *Miss Angie Siew Lin*
Malaysia, Call Date: Nov 1998
(Lincoln's Inn) Qualifications: LLB
(Hons)(Staffs)

Chong *Miss Ann Ching*
Malaysia, Call Date: July 1997 (Middle
Temple) Qualifications: LLB
(Hons)(Leics)

Chong *Avery Soon Yong*
Singapore 669837, Call Date: July 1996
(Inner Temple) Qualifications: LLB
(Warwick)

Chong *Miss Boon Chin*
Malaysia, Call Date: July 1997
(Lincoln's Inn) Qualifications: LLB
(Hons)(Leics)

Chong *Chi On*
Malaysia, Call Date: Nov 1997
(Lincoln's Inn) Qualifications: LLB
(Hons)

Chong *Miss Fiona Yeo-Peen*
Malaysia, Call Date: July 1993
(Lincoln's Inn) Qualifications: LLB
(Hons)

Chong *Gerald Siak Yen*
20 Malacca Street [H]05-00, Malacca
Centre, Singapore 048979, Singapore
459667, (65) 536 5369, Fax: (65) 536
5811, and Member Singapore Bar, Call
Date: Nov 1994 (Middle Temple)
Qualifications: BA (Joint Hons)

Chong *Miss Jia Ling*
Malaysia, Call Date: July 1996
(Lincoln's Inn) Qualifications: LLB
(Hons)

Chong *Kah Heng*
Malaysia, Legal Assistant, and Member
Malaysian Bar, Call Date: July 1996
(Gray's Inn) Qualifications: LLB
(Leicester)

Chong *Kenneth Yun Kien*
c/o Chin Lau Wong & Foo, A818, 8th
Floor, Wisma Merdeka, 88000 Kota
Kinablau, Sabah, Malaysia, 088
238111, Fax: 088 238222, and Member
Sabah, Call Date: July 1993 (Lincoln's
Inn) Qualifications: LLB (Hons, Leeds)

Chong *Kuok Peng*
Messrs Zaid Ibahim & Co, Tingkat 12,
Menara Bank Pembangunan, Jalan
sultan Ismail, 50250 Kuala Lumpur,
Malaysia, 603-292 6688, Fax: 603-298
1632, Associate, and Member
Malaysian Bar, Call Date: July 1997
(Lincoln's Inn) Qualifications: LLB
(Hons)(Exon)

Chong *Miss Mae Shan*
35 Jelutong Villas, Lorong Jelutong
Kanan, Damansara Heights, 50490
Kuala Lumpur, 254 8111, Call Date:
July 1996 (Middle Temple)
Qualifications: BA (Hons)(Cantab)

Chong *Mark Choong Weng*
Singapore 469978, Call Date: July 1996
(Lincoln's Inn) Qualifications: LLB
(Hons)(Lond)

Chong *Miss May Yean*
Malaysia, Call Date: July 1996
(Lincoln's Inn) Qualifications: LLB
(Hons)(Wales)

Chong *Michael Wai Yen*
Singapore 459667, Call Date: Mar 1998
(Middle Temple) Qualifications: LLB
(Hons)(Keele)

Chong *Miss Shin Yih*
Singapore 416877, Call Date: Mar 1999
(Lincoln's Inn) Qualifications: LLB
(Nott'm)

Chong *Miss Su Ping Cecilia*
M/S Kenneth Koh & Co, 1 Colombo
Court [H]06-02, Singapore 308930,
(65) 336 7377, Fax: (65) 338 7077,
and Member Singapore Bar, Call Date:
July 1997 (Middle Temple)
Qualifications: LLB (Hons)(Hull)

Chong *Victor Thien Loi*
Malaysia, Call Date: July 1995 (Middle
Temple) Qualifications: BA (Hons)
(Keele)

Choo *Miss Audrey Pao Lin*
Malaysia 59100, Call Date: Nov 1997
(Lincoln's Inn) Qualifications: LLB
(Nott'm)

Choo *Jeremy Yinn Hsin*
Singapore 570155, Call Date: Mar 1999
(Lincoln's Inn) Qualifications: LLB
(Hons)(Bris)

Choo *Miss Josephine Poh Hua*
Singapore 530133, Call Date: Nov 1996
(Middle Temple) Qualifications: LLB
(Hons)(Lond)

Choo *Raymond Choon Sheng*
Singapore 1544, and Member
Singapore, Call Date: Nov 1995 (Middle
Temple) Qualifications: LLB
(Hons)(Hull), LLM (King's College,
Lond)

Choo *Miss Yuin*
Malaysia, Call Date: July 1996
(Lincoln's Inn) Qualifications: LLB
(Hons)(Leeds)

Choong *Allen Ching Yet*
Malaysia, Call Date: Nov 1997
(Lincoln's Inn) Qualifications: LLB
(Hons)(Lond)

Choong *Miss Kartina Abdullah*
Malaysia, Call Date: July 1995
(Lincoln's Inn) Qualifications: LLB
(Hons)

Choong *Miss Pek Yoke*
Singapore 648927, Call Date: July 1998
(Lincoln's Inn) Qualifications: LLB
(Hons)(Leeds)

Chou *Sean Yu*
Messrs Wong Partnership, 80 Raffles
Place, [H]58-01, UOB Plaza 1,
Singapore 0106, Singapore 229670,
532 7488, Fax: (65) 532 5722, and
Member Singapore Bar, Call Date: July
1993 (Middle Temple) Qualifications:
LLB (Hons, Bris)

Chow *Miss Fung Kwan*
Hong Kong, Call Date: Oct 1997
(Middle Temple) Qualifications: BSc
(Hong Kong), CPE (Hong Kong), BSSC
(Hong Kong), CPE

Chow *Kelvin Yok Yeen*
Malaysia, Call Date: July 1998 (Middle
Temple) Qualifications: LLB
(Hons)(Wales), LLM (Wolves)

Chow *Kenneth Charn Ki*
22/F On Hing Building, 1-9 On Hing
Terrace, Central, Hong Kong,
25212555, Fax: 28691527, Formerly
Solicitor, Call Date: May 1988 (Middle
Temple) Qualifications: LLB (Hons),,
LLM (London)

Chow *Kenneth Kok Wee*
Malaysia, Call Date: July 1995
(Lincoln's Inn) Qualifications: LLB
(Hons)

Chow *Kenny Yin Wo*
Flat 12h, Braemar Terrace, 1 Pak Fuk
Road, Hong Kong, 28950025, Fax:
28950025, Superintendent, Hong Kong
Police Force, and Member Supreme
Court of the Australia Capital Territory,
Call Date: July 1990 (Gray's Inn)
Qualifications: LLB (Lond)

Chow *Miss Letty Yu Shu*
Hong Kong, and Member Hong Kong
Bar, Call Date: Nov 1985 (Lincoln's
Inn) Qualifications: LLB

Chow *Miss Min Wei*
Singapore 1129, Call Date: July 1995
(Middle Temple) Qualifications: LLB
(Hons) (Hull)

Chow *Miss Nona Swee Li*
Malaysia, Call Date: Nov 1997
(Lincoln's Inn) Qualifications: LLB
(Hons)(Wales)

Chow *Wai Lun*
Hong Kong, Call Date: Nov 1997 (Gray's
Inn) Qualifications: BSc (Eng)(Hong
Kong), Diplome d'ingenieur, (Ecole
Nationale des, Travaux Publics), CEng,
MICE, MIStruct E, P.Eng

Chowdhury *Khaled Hamid*
Asfia House, Road 36, House 13,
Ghulshan, Dhaka 1212, Bangladesh,
880 2 885872/017525542, Fax: 880 2
885736, and Member Dhaka,
Bangladesh, Call Date: July 1995
(Lincoln's Inn) Qualifications: LLB
(Hons), MA (Legal Studies), LLM (Int'l
Bus Law), (KCL)

Chowdhury *Mohammad Mehedi Hasan*
Bangladesh, Call Date: July 1998
(Lincoln's Inn) Qualifications: LLB
(Hons)

Choy *Montague Wing Kin*
Singapore 268162, Call Date: July 1997
(Lincoln's Inn) Qualifications: LLB
(Hons) (L'pool)

Christofides *Miss Etta*
Cyprus, Call Date: Feb 1993 (Gray's
Inn) Qualifications: LLB (Anglia), LLM

Christopher *Craig-Eliot Marcus*
West Indies, Call Date: Oct 1998
(Middle Temple) Qualifications: LLB
(Hons) (Lond)

Chrysanthou *Nicos*
4 Demosthenes Str, P.O.Box 1762,
1513 Nicosia, Cyprus, (3572) 677443,
Fax: (3572) 672075, Partner, and
Member Cyprus, Call Date: Nov 1996
(Inner Temple) Qualifications: LLB
(Lond), LLM (So'ton)

Chrysostomides *Mrs Eleni*
Dr K Chrysostomides & Co, PO Box
2119, 1 Lambousa Street, Nicosia, 777
000, Fax: 02 77 99 39, Call Date: Nov
1973 (Gray's Inn) Qualifications: LLB

Chu *Chung Keung*
Hong Kong, Call Date: Nov 1996
(Middle Temple) Qualifications: LLB
(Hons)

Chu *Miss Yuen Yee*
Hong Kong, Call Date: July 1995
(Middle Temple) Qualifications: LLB
(Hons)

Chua *Miss Cynthia Cher Lan*
Hong Kong, and Member Singapore
Bar, Call Date: July 1995 (Middle
Temple) Qualifications: LLB (Hons)

Chua *Miss Geok Hong*
Singapore 520229, Call Date: Nov 1995
(Middle Temple) Qualifications: LLB
(Hons)

Chua *Miss Grace Hwee Bin*
Malaysia, and Member Malaysia Bar,
Call Date: Nov 1992 (Lincoln's Inn)
Qualifications: LLB (Hons) (Wales)

Chua *Miss Huey Sian*
M/S Chooi & Company, Penthouse,
Ming Building PH-01, Jalan Bukit
Nanas, 50200 Kuala Lumpur, Malaysia,
03 2327344, Legal Assistant, and
Member Malaysia, Call Date: July 1996
(Lincoln's Inn) Qualifications: LLB
(Hons) (Sheff)

Chua *Miss Hui Peng*
Malaysia, and Member Malaysian Bar,
Call Date: July 1995 (Middle Temple)
Qualifications: LLB (Hons)

Chua *Kok Wan*
Singapore 1130, Call Date: July 1995
(Middle Temple) Qualifications: B.Ec,
LLB

Chua *Miss Lay Kuang*
Hong Kong, Call Date: Nov 1994
(Middle Temple) Qualifications:
B.Pharm (Hons)

Chua *Miss Lucianna Mei Ling*
2 Ridgewood Close, [H]05-02, Himiko
Court, Singapore 276693, and Member
Singapore, Call Date: July 1996 (Middle
Temple) Qualifications: LLB
(Hons) (Sheff)

Chua *Miss Siew Gaik*
Malaysia, Call Date: July 1996
(Lincoln's Inn) Qualifications: BA
(Hons)

Chua *Miss Soo Fon*
Malaysia, Call Date: July 1995
(Lincoln's Inn) Qualifications: LLB
(Hons)

Chua *Sui Tong*
Singapore 259548, Call Date: Oct 1998
(Middle Temple) Qualifications: LLB
(Hons) (Notts)

Chua *Miss Suzanie May-Li*
Ernst & Young Tower, P.O.Box 251, 222
Bay Street, Toronto-Dominion Centre
M5K 1J7, Canada, (416) 943 2145, Fax:
(416) 943 3796, Chartered Accountant
(ICAEW), Honorary Legal Scholar
(Centre for Int'l Legal Studies) and
Member Singapore Bar Law Society of
british Columbia, Canada, Call Date:
July 1988 (Gray's Inn) Qualifications:
LLB Hons (Bris)

Chua *Tze Wei*
Singapore 1128, Call Date: July 1990
(Gray's Inn) Qualifications: LLB (Bris),
BCL (Oxon)

Chua *Miss Yak Hoon*
15 N Kang Choo Bin Road, Singapore
548285, Singapore 548 285, Call Date:
July 1991 (Middle Temple)
Qualifications: LLB (Hons) (Lond)

Chuah *Miss Hooi Bien*
Malaysia, Call Date: July 1997 (Middle
Temple) Qualifications: LLB
(Hons) (Leics)

Chuah *Jern Ern*
Shearn Delamore & Co, 7th Floor,
Wisma Hamzah, Kwong-Hing, 2 Leboh
Ampang, 50100 Kuala Lumpur,
Malaysia, 2300644 (0603), Fax:
2386525, Legal Associate, and Member
Malaysia Bar, Call Date: July 1993
(Lincoln's Inn) Qualifications: LLB
(Hons, N'ham)

Chuah *Miss Sheena Sze Ching*
Malaysia, Call Date: July 1997 (Middle
Temple) Qualifications: LLB (Hons)

Chuah *Miss Yean Ping*
Messrs Shook Lin & Bok, Advocates &
Solicitors, 20th Floor, Arab - Malaysian,
Building, 55 Jalan Raja Chulan, 50200
Kuala Lumpur, Malaysia, 03 2011788,
Fax: 03 2011778/779/775, Legal
Assistant, and Member Malaysia, Call
Date: July 1996 (Lincoln's Inn)
Qualifications: LLB (Hons) (Leics)

Chuang *Miss Effie Twan Phey*
Singapore 2776, Call Date: Nov 1997
(Lincoln's Inn) Qualifications: LLB
(Hons) (Leeds)

Chuang *Keng Chiew*
2 Hanoy Road, Cathay Building,
[H]10-02, Singapore 140021, 3366533,
Fax: 3370906, and Member Singapore
Bar, Call Date: July 1996 (Middle
Temple) Qualifications: LLB
(Hons) (Lond)

Chui *Miss Yee Mei Ivy*
Hong Kong, Call Date: July 1996
(Middle Temple) Qualifications: LLB
(Hons) (Wales)

Chularojmontri *Prathan*
Thailand, Call Date: July 1995 (Gray's
Inn) Qualifications: LLB (Wales)

Chun *Lim Whei*
Malaysia, Call Date: Nov 1997 (Inner
Temple) Qualifications: LLB (Lond)

Chung *Domminick*
Hong Kong, Call Date: Nov 1998
(Middle Temple) Qualifications: LLB
(Hons) (Wolves)

Chung *Kee Ying*
Hong Kong, and Member Hong Kong
Bar Supreme Court of the Australian
Capital Territory, Call Date: Nov 1990
(Gray's Inn) Qualifications: LLB (Lond)

Chung *Miss Rebecca Wan-Yi*
20 Jalan Jun Tan, 836 6366, Fax: 836
6266, and Member Singapore Bar, Call
Date: Nov 1992 (Middle Temple)
Qualifications: LLB (Hons, Hull)

Chung *Yiu Ming*
26d South Bay Towers, 59 South Bay
Road, (852) 25769090, and Member
Hong Kong Bar, Call Date: July 1991
(Lincoln's Inn) Qualifications: BSc
(Hons) , Dip Law (City Uni), ACIArb,
FRICS, FHKIS

Chwee *Han Sin*
Singapore 1130, Call Date: Nov 1995
(Middle Temple) Qualifications: LLB
(Hons)

Cirillo *Mrs Angela*
Republic of Ireland, Barrister of
Ireland, Call Date: July 1998 (Middle
Temple) Qualifications: LLB
(Hons) (Dublin), BL (King's Inn)

Clark *Dr Margaret Lynda*
Advocates Library, Parliament Square, Edinburgh, Scotland, Scotland, 031 226 2881, MP, QC Scotland and Member Scottish Bar, Call Date: July 1988 (Inner Temple) Qualifications: PhD (Edinburgh), LLB (St Andrews)

Clarke *Dominic Tobias*
40 King Street West, Suite 2100, Toronto M5H 3C2, Canada, (416) 869 5300, Fax: (416) 360 8877, and Member Ontario Bar, Call Date: July 1988 (Middle Temple) Qualifications: MA, LLM (Cantab)

Clarke *Mrs Maria Anne*
11a Craigleith Drive, Edinburgh EH4 3HR, and Member Scottish Bar, Call Date: Apr 1991 (Inner Temple) Qualifications: LLB (Glasgow), BA (Hons) Open

Clasper *Stephen Reid*
c/o The Whitney Group, 3007, 30th Floor, The Exchange Square, Central, and Member California, USA, Call Date: July 1971 (Gray's Inn) Qualifications: MA (Cantab)

Cleare *Miss Camille Amanda*
Harry B Sands and Company Cha, Shirley House, 50 Shirley Street, P.O.Box N 624, Nassau, Bahamas, 242 322 2670, Fax: 242 323 8914, and Member Bahamas Bar, Call Date: Nov 1997 (Gray's Inn) Qualifications: LLB (Kent)

Clifford *Nigel Robert Leslie*
Hunter & Hunter, P.O.Box 190, Gt Grand Cayman, Cayman Islands, 345 949 4900, Fax: 345 949 2575, Admitted as Attorney-at-Law Cayman Islands, Call Date: July 1973 (Middle Temple) Qualifications: LLB (Hons)

Coast-Powell *Mrs Susan Mary*
Cater Allen Trust Co Ltd, Channel Islands, 01534 828000, Legal Advisor, Director, Call Date: Nov 1994 (Middle Temple) Qualifications: LLB (Hons), TEP

Codrai *Christian Augustus*
Legal Services, I.F.A.D. of the United Nations, 107 Via Del Serafico, 00142 Roma, Italy, (39) 065459 2457, Fax: (39) 06504-3463, Senior Counsel, International Fund for Agricultural Development (IFAD), Call Date: Nov 1979 (Inner Temple) Qualifications: LLB,LLM

Coelho *Oswaldo Gerardo*
Pta A H Batte 22-R/C Fte, PO Box 91, 8600 Lagos, 82 762408, Fax: 82 767266, and Member Portugal, Call Date: Nov 1979 (Lincoln's Inn) Qualifications: MA (Hons) (Bombay),, Licentiate in Law, (Lisbon)

Coffey *Paul Michael Matthew*
Law Library, Four Courts, Dublin, Republic of Ireland, Republic of Ireland, 720622, Fax: 722254, King's Inns (Dublin) and Member Southern Ireland Bar, Call Date: Feb 1988 (Middle Temple) Qualifications: BCL (Ireland), LLM (Dublin

Cohen *Ms Susan Elizabeth*
Polygram Pty Ltd, 3 Munn Reserve, Millers Point, Sydney 2000, N.S.W. Australia, Australia, (02) 9207 0519, Fax: (02) 9241 1497, Director of Legal & Business Affairs, Call Date: July 1981 (Gray's Inn) Qualifications: LLB (B'ham),MA

Colclough *Mrs Leslie Ann*
Lobosky & Lobosky, P O Box N-7123, Nassau, Bahamas, (242) 323 1317, Fax: (242) 323 1318, and Member Bahamas Bar, Call Date: Nov 1996 (Lincoln's Inn) Qualifications: LLB (Hons)(Bucks)

Colebrook *Miss Ashlar Shikell*
Bahamas, Trust Officer, and Member Bahamas Bar, Sept 1996, Call Date: July 1996 (Lincoln's Inn) Qualifications: BBA (Miami), MA (Bris)

Colgan *Jeremy Spencer*
Gide Loyvette Nouel, 26 Cours Albert 1er, Paris 75008, 00 331 40752980, Fax: 00 331 40753719, Call Date: Oct 1996 (Inner Temple) Qualifications: LLB (Queens , University Bristol)

Collie *Ellison Isaac*
Michael A Dean & Co, 94 Dowdeswell Street, P O Box N7521, Nassau, Bahamas, 809 322 3997, Fax: 809 325 3345, Counsel and Attorney-at-Law and Member Bahamas Bar Association, Call Date: July 1996 (Lincoln's Inn) Qualifications: CPE (City)

Collie *Miss Inell*
Bahamas, Call Date: July 1998 (Middle Temple) Qualifications: LLB (Hons)(Keele)

Collins *Ruaidhri Jolyon McCracken*
Northern Ireland, Call Date: Oct 1994 (Middle Temple) Qualifications: BA (Hons)(Cantab), LLM (Lond)

Collins *Miss Sara Jane*
W S Walker & Co, P O Box 26SGT, Grand Cayman, British West Indies, 1-809-949-0100, Fax: 1-809-949-7886, and Member Cayman Islands Bar, Call Date: July 1995 (Lincoln's Inn) Qualifications: LLB (Hons)

Collu *Miss Melissa*
Italy, Call Date: Oct 1997 (Middle Temple) Qualifications: BA (Hons)(Notts), CPE (Lond)

Colombo *Kevin Joseph*
Gibraltar, Call Date: Mar 1996 (Gray's Inn) Qualifications: LLB

Colquitt *Robert Ian*
Cains Advocates, 15-19 Athol Street, Douglas IM1 1LB, Isle of Man, 01624 638300, Fax: 01624 638345, Manx Advocate, and Member Isle of Man, Call Date: July 1995 (Inner Temple) Qualifications: LLB

Colunday *Shummoogum*
Mauritius, Call Date: Nov 1998 (Lincoln's Inn) Qualifications: LLB (Hons)(Lond), MA (E.Lond)

Commissiong *Miss Mira Elisabet*
Commissiong & Commissiong, Equity Chambers, Halifax Street, Kingstown, The Grenadines, (809) 457 1293, Fax: (809) 456 2696, Call Date: July 1997 (Lincoln's Inn) Qualifications: LLB (Hons)(City)

Compton *Petrus*
Attorney General's Chambers, Block D, Waterfront Building, Castries, St Lucia, 758 45 23622/23772, Fax: 758 45 36315, Honourable Attorney General, Eastern Caribbean Supreme Court, Call Date: July 1992 (Gray's Inn) Qualifications: BA, LLB, LLM (Lond)

Concisom *Miss Audry*
Concisom & Co, 2 Jalan Seenivasagam, 30450 Ipoh, Perak, Legal Adviser, and Member Malaysia Bar, Call Date: Nov 1996 (Middle Temple) Qualifications: LLB (Hons)

Conlon *Benjamin Vincenzo Rosario*
P.O.Box 924, Davidson, Lake Norman, North Carolina 28036, United States of America, 00 1 (704) 662 7994, Fax: 00 1 (704) 662 7994, Arbitrator to US District Court for the Northern District of New York, US. Supreme Court, US. Court of Appeals for 2nd, 3rd and 9th Circuits, US. District Courts for Northern, Southern, Eastern and Western Districts of New York. US. District Court of Vermont, US. Tax Court, US Court of International Trade and Member New, Call Date: Nov 1975 (Gray's Inn) Qualifications: LLB (Hons)

Conlon *Mrs Loraine*
Conlon Law Offices, Keene Road, Elizabethtown, New York 12932-0937, United States of America, (518) 873 6887, Fax: (518) 873 6897, Member of Committee for Special Education, Member of Committee for Pre-School Special Education, Member of Shared Decision Making Team, Essex County Bar Assoc 2-4 Tudor Street, London, EC4Y 0AA, Call Date: Nov 1977 (Gray's Inn)

Constantinidou *Ms Eleni Adoni*
P.O.Box 897, Larnaca, Cyprus, Cyprus, 04-620400, Fax: 04-620860, Legal Advisor of Offshore Company, and Member Cyprus Bar, Call Date: July 1992 (Lincoln's Inn) Qualifications: LLB (Hons) (Leics)

Constantinou *Miss Maria*
Cyprus, Call Date: Feb 1994 (Lincoln's
Inn) Qualifications: LLB (Hons)

Conti *John Patrick*
Conti, 17 Circular Road, Douglas, Isle
of Man IM1 1AF, Isle of Man, 01624
670003, Fax: 01624 612281, Member
International Bar Association and
Member Isle of Man Bar, Call Date: Nov
1988 (Inner Temple) Qualifications:
LLB (Wales)

Coope *Simon Paul*
20 Market Street, Cold Spring, NY
10516, 914 265 5367, and Member
New York State Bar, Call Date: Oct 1991
(Middle Temple) Qualifications: LLB
Hons

Coriat *Christopher Archibald*
Coriats Trustees, Bristol House, PO Box
171, Providenciales, Turks & Caicos
Islands, British West Indies, +1 649
946 4800, Fax: +1 649 946 4850,
Attorney at Law, Turks & Caicos Islands
and Member Turks & Caicos Islands,
Call Date: July 1977 (Lincoln's Inn)
Qualifications: TEP

Corke *Donald Stevenson*
Advocates Library, Parliament House,
Edinburgh EH1 1RF, Scotland, 0131
226 5071, Fax: 0131 225 3642,
Part-time Special Adjudicator
(Immigration Appeals), and Member
Scottish Bar, Call Date: July 1995
(Middle Temple) Qualifications: BA
(Cape Town), LLB (Witwatersrand)

Coroneos *Miss Georgina*
B Logothetidis 23, Athens 115-24,
Greece, 6928040, Fax: 6928040, Call
Date: Oct 1996 (Middle Temple)
Qualifications: BA (Hons) (Keele)

Corrigan *Anthony John*
15/F Printing House, 6 Duddell Street,
Central, 25212 616, Fax: 28450260,
Call Date: July 1962 (Gray's Inn)
Qualifications: LLB

Cort *Dr Leon Errol*
Chambers, 44 Church Street, PO Box
260, St John's, Antigua, West Indies,
809 462 5232, Fax: 809 462 5234,
Adviser to Government of Antigua &
Barbuda Chairman of the St John's
Development Corporation, Eastern
Caribbean, Call Date: Nov 1990 (Middle
Temple) Qualifications: B Comm, MA,
PhD (Canada), MA (Oxon)

Cort *Miss Sharon May*
West Indies, Call Date: Nov 1997
(Middle Temple) Qualifications: LLB
(Hons)

Cosma *Miss Maria*
Cyprus, Call Date: Oct 1994 (Middle
Temple) Qualifications: LLB
(Hons) (Reading)

Cotsen *Stuart Hugh*
15/F Printing House, 6 Duddell Street,
Central, Hong Kong, Hong Kong,
25212616, Fax: 28450260, Formerly
Solicitor of the Supreme Court of
England & Wales and Member Australia
Bar Hong Kong Bar Victoria Bar New
South Wales Bar, Call Date: Apr 1986
(Middle Temple)

Coucouni *Miss Dimitria*
Cyprus, Call Date: Mar 1996 (Lincoln's
Inn) Qualifications: LLB (Hons) (Leics)

Coucounis *Tasos Andrea*
Cyprus, Call Date: Nov 1998 (Gray's
Inn) Qualifications: LLB (Lond)

Course *Ms Lindy*
New Zealand, and Member Hong Kong
Bar, Call Date: July 1994 (Middle
Temple) Qualifications: BA
(Hons) (Lanc), CPE (Manc)

Coutts *Thomas Gordon*
6 Heriot Row, Edinburgh, Scotland
EH3 6HU, Scotland, 0131 556 3042,
Fax: 0131 556 3042, Part-time
Chairman Industrial Tribunals 1972-
M.A.T., 1984 Temporary Judge, Court of
Session 1991. Vice President (Scot) VAT
& Duties Tribunals 1996. Special
Commission Income Tax., A Scottish
Advocate and Member Scottish Bar, Call
Date: July 1995 (Lincoln's Inn)
Qualifications: MA, LLB, FCI(Arb)

Cox *Miss Cherise Felicia Vanessa*
Higgs & Johnson Chambers, 83
Sandringham House, Shirley Street,
Nassau, Bahamas, Bahamas,
1-809-32-28571-9, Fax:
1-809-32-87727, and Member
Bahamas Bar, Call Date: July 1991
(Lincoln's Inn) Qualifications: BA
(Hons) (Cant), LLM (Lond)

Cox *David Rupert Fenwick*
Avenue des Cormorans 16, 1150
Brussels, Belgium, 32 2 771 68 14, Call
Date: July 1970 (Middle Temple)
Qualifications: MA

Cox *Ms Iona Maxine*
Callenders & Co, One Millars Court,
P.O.Box N 7117, Nassau, Bahamas, 242
322 2511, Fax: 242 326 7666, and
Member Bahamas, Call Date: Nov 1997
(Lincoln's Inn) Qualifications: LLB
(Hons)

Crabbe *The Hon Mr Justice Vincent
Cyril Richard Arthur C*
Faculty of Law, University of The West
Indies, Cave Hill Campus, Bridgetown,
(246) 417 4236, Fax: (246) 424 1788,
Professor of Legislative Drafting,
Director, Legislative Drafting
Programme, Call Date: Feb 1955
(Inner Temple) Qualifications: LLD

Crean *Ms Catherine*
Law Library, P.O. Box 2424, Four
Courts, Dublin 7, 3531 8174999/353
872889558, Fax: 3531 8174999, and
Member Irish Bar, Call Date: May 1982
(Middle Temple) Qualifications: BA,
HDE, LLB, ALCM, MA, LLM, FLSM, Dip.,
Soc.Sc

Crichlow *Carl Ulrick*
Middle Chambers, Cr Crichlow's Alley &
Maidens, Lane, Roebuck Street,
Bridgetown, Barbados W I, West Indies,
246 427 8191, Fax: 246 427 8213, and
Member Barbados Bar
Association,Barbados,West Indies, Call
Date: July 1987 (Middle Temple)
Qualifications: BSc (Boston), LLB,
(Lond), FCCA, LLM (Lond)

Crichton-Gold *Peter Leonard*
USA, Call Date: July 1972 (Gray's Inn)
Qualifications: LLB (Lond), FCIArb

Crivon *Mrs Louise Anne*
Republic of Ireland, Barrister of
Ireland, Call Date: July 1998 (Middle
Temple) Qualifications: BL (King's Inn)

Crossley *Anthony Dominic*
Reinsurance Australia Corp Ltd, Level
41, Tower Building, Australia Square,
264 George Street, Sydney 2000, New
South Wales, Australia, Australia, 9247
6565, Fax: 9252 1614, Chief Operating
Officer Director, Call Date: Nov 1977
(Lincoln's Inn) Qualifications: LLB
(Lond), ACA

Crowley *Dale Michael*
Maples & Calder, P O Box 309, Cayman
Islands, British West Indies, (345) 949
8066, Fax: (345) 949 8080, and
Member Attorney-at-Law, Cayman
Islands, Call Date: July 1996 (Middle
Temple) Qualifications: LLB
(Hons) (L'pool)

Cubbon *John Edward*
Legal Adviser, United Nations Mission
in Bosnia & Herzegovina, Call Date: Oct
1993 (Middle Temple) Qualifications:
BA (Hons) (Oxon), MSc , B Phil

Cubitt Sowden *Patrick Flinn*
PO Box 72, 44 The Esplanade, St
Helier, Jersey JE4 8PN, 01534 871415,
Fax: 01534 872699, Advocate of Royal
Court of Jersey Notary Public and
Member Jersey Bar, Call Date: Nov
1960 (Middle Temple)

Cucchi *Frederick*
Via F. Civinini, 111, 00197 Rome,
39-6-8085460, Fax: 39-6-8072793, Call
Date: Nov 1978 (Middle Temple)
Qualifications: MA (Oxon)

Culbard *Ms Karen Cecilia*
Inn Chambers, Inga Lodge, Pinfold
Street, Bridgetown, Barbados, (246)
427-7192, Fax: (246) 429-2771, and
Member Barbados Bar, Call Date: Nov
1994 (Inner Temple) Qualifications:
LLB (W. Indies), LLM (Lond), CPE
(Lond)

Cumberbatch *Miss Sherrylyn Kathlean*
Bahamas, Call Date: July 1997 (Middle
Temple) Qualifications: LLB (Hons)

Cushen *Mrs Helen Margaret*
Crills, 44 Esplanade, St Helier, Jersey
JE4 8PZ, Channel Islands, (0) 534
611055, Fax: (0) 534 611066, and
Member Jersey Bar, Call Date: Nov
1993 (Middle Temple) Qualifications:
BA (Hons) (Lond), MA (Kent), CPE
(City)

Cushen *Peter Roy*
Crills, P.O. Box No 72, 44 Esplanade, St
Helier, Jersey JE4 8PN, 01534 611055,
Fax: 01534 611066, Advocate, Admitted
to the Jersey Bar (Oct 1984) and
Member Jersey Bar, Call Date: July
1981 (Inner Temple) Qualifications:
LLB (Soton)

Dalton *Nicholas David*
NomoS, Societe d'Avocats, 13 rue
Alphonse de Neuville, 75017 Paris,
France, 00 331 43 18 55 00, Legal &
Business Affairs Manager, Call Date:
Oct 1993 (Lincoln's Inn)
Qualifications: BA (Hons) (Exon), Dip
in Law (Lond)

Dang *Miss Lee Boon*
2, 2nd Floor, Jalan Pinggir, Off Jalan
Kolam Air, (Jalan Ipoh), 51200 Kuala
Lumpur, Malaysia, 603-4444133, Fax:
603-4444233, and Member Malaysian
Bar, Call Date: July 1997 (Middle
Temple) Qualifications: LLB (Hons)

Dangerfield *Jeremy George Bubb*
3P-300 Roslyn Road, Winnipeg,
Manituba R3L0H4, (204) 453-8340, QC
Canada and Member Manituba Bar,
Call Date: Nov 1983 (Gray's Inn)
Qualifications: BSc,LLM (Manitoba)

Daniel *Andy Glenn*
St Lucia, Call Date: Nov 1998 (Middle
Temple) Qualifications: LLB
(Hons) (Wolves)

Daniel *Miss Delia*
West Indies, Call Date: July 1998
(Middle Temple) Qualifications: LLB
(Hons) (Wolves)

Danker *Miss Geralyn Germaine*
34 Jalan Chelagi, Singapore 1750, 542
6684, Call Date: July 1995 (Middle
Temple) Qualifications: LLB (Hons)

Dann *Miss Tiffany*
Callenders & Co, P O Box F-40132,
Freeport, Grand Bahama, Bahamas,
242-352-7458, Fax: 242-352-4000, and
Member Bahamas Bar, Call Date: July
1998 (Lincoln's Inn) Qualifications:
LLB (Hons), LLM

Danou *Miss Georgia*
The Cyprus Popular Bank Ltd, Popular
Bank Building, 154 Limassol Avenue, P
O Box 2032 CY-1598, Nicosia, Cyprus,
02 81 1187, Fax: 02 81 1492, Assistant
Legal Advisor, The Cyprus Popular
Bank Ltd, and Member Cyprus Bar, Call
Date: Feb 1991 (Lincoln's Inn)
Qualifications: LLB (Leic), LLM (Lond)

Darley *Miss Gillian Elizabeth Anne*
Jan Van Ruusbroeclaan 24, 3080
Tervuren, Belgium, (0032) 2 768 15
65, Call Date: July 1981 (Inner
Temple) Qualifications: LLB (Lond),
AKC

Darr *Miss Amber*
Pakistan, Call Date: July 1997
(Lincoln's Inn) Qualifications: BA
(Pennsylvania)

Darville *Miss Camille Diane*
Bahamas, Call Date: July 1995 (Gray's
Inn) Qualifications: BA (Soc) (Ontario),
LLB (Leeds)

Darwyne *Michael Thurston*
P.O.Box 38, Peel IM5 1RL, Isle of Man,
01624 844 908, Fax: 01624 845 038,
and Member Hong Kong Bar, Fiji Bar,
New York Bar, Call Date: July 1969
(Inner Temple) Qualifications: MA,
BCL (Oxon),, LLM (Harvard)

Dato Hj Abdul Rahman *Mohd
Rozaiman*
Attorney General Chambers, Ministry of
Law, B.S.B., Brunei, Darussalam 2016,
Darussalam 2016, 6732 244872 Ext
174, Fax: 6732 222720, Legal Counsel,
and Member Brunei Bar, Call Date: July
1995 (Lincoln's Inn) Qualifications:
LLB (Hons), LLM (Exeter)

Dato Hj Zaidan *Miss Hanariza*
Malaysia, Call Date: Nov 1997
(Lincoln's Inn) Qualifications: LLB
(Hons) (Wales)

David *Paul Wilson*
Russell McVeagh McKenzie, Bartlett &
Co, The Shortland Centre, 51-53
Shortland Street, P O Box 8, Auckland,
00649 3098539, Fax: 00649 3678592,
Barrister & Solicitor of New Zealand
1990, Call Date: Nov 1981 (Inner
Temple) Qualifications: BA,LLM
(Cantab)

Davidson *Alasdair Michael*
West Murdieston, Thornhill, Stirling
FK8 3QE, Attorney at Law, and Member
Turks & Caicos Islands, Call Date: Oct
1992 (Gray's Inn) Qualifications: LL.B
(Newc)

Davidson *Neil Forbes*
Advocates' Library, Parliament House,
Edinburgh EH1 1RF, Scotland, 031 226
5071, Fax: 031 220 4440, Director-City
Disputes Panel, QC (Scotland) and
Member Scottish Bar, Call Date: May
1990 (Inner Temple) Qualifications:
B.A. (Stirl), M.Sc. (Brad), LL.B.& LL.M.
(Edin)

Davies *Dr Gillian*
European Patent Office, DG III,
Erhardtstrasse 27, D-80298 Munich,
Germany, Germany, 4989 2399 3230,
Fax: 4989 2399 3014, Hon. Professor,
University of Wales, Aberystwyth,
Chairman, Technical Board of Appeal
and Member, Enlarged Board of
Appeal, EPO, Call Date: Nov 1961
(Lincoln's Inn) Qualifications: Ph.D

Davis *Andrew Raj*
Malaysia, Call Date: July 1997
(Lincoln's Inn) Qualifications: LLB
(Hons) (Nott'm), LLM (Nott'm)

Davis *Peter Andrew*
S G Archibald, Archibald Andersen
Association, d'Avocats, 41 rue Ybry,
92576 Neuilly-sur-Seine Cedex, France,
331 55 61 12 69, Fax: 331 55 61 15 15,
Call Date: Oct 1994 (Lincoln's Inn)
Qualifications: LLB (Hons) (Leic)

Davis *Miss Susan Lynn*
Bermuda, Call Date: Mar 1998 (Gray's
Inn) Qualifications: LLB (Bucks)

Dawes *Gordon Stephen Knight*
Ozannes, P O Box 186, 1 Le Marchant
Street, St Peter Port, Guernsey
GY1 4HP, Call Date: July 1989 (Middle
Temple) Qualifications: MA [Oxon],
Dip Law

Dawson *Miss Anne Diana*
Malaysia, Call Date: July 1996 (Middle
Temple) Qualifications: LLB
(Hons) (Lond)

Daya-Winterbottom *Trevor*
Chapman Tripp Sheffield Young, Level
35, Coopers & Lybrand Tower, 23-29
Albert Street, Auckland, 00 64 9 357
9000, Fax: 00 64 9 357 9099, Senior
Solicitor, and Member Barrister &
Solicitor of the High Court of New
Zealand (Admitted November 1996),
Call Date: Nov 1985 (Lincoln's Inn)
Qualifications: BA (Hons),Diplome de,
Droit International, et De Droit
Compares, des Droits de , l'Homme,
MA, Legal, Associate of the, Royal Town
Planning, Institute. FRSA, Affiliate
Member of, the New Zealand , Planning
Institute

De Berti *Giovanni*
De Berti,Jacchia,Perno & Assc., Foro
Buonaparte 20, 20121 Milano, 39-
2-725541, Fax: 39- 2-72554600, and
Member Italy Bar, Call Date: Nov 1970
(Gray's Inn)

de Bruir *Rory*
Law Library, Four Courts, Dublin 7,
045 521881, Fax: 045 521881, and
Member Southern Ireland Bar
Northern Ireland Bar, Call Date: Oct
1992 (Middle Temple) Qualifications:
Diploma in Legal , Studies (Kings
Inns), Dip US Army Command, &
General Staff , College, Commission,
Irish Army, BL, FCIArb

F

De Cruz *Miss Clares*
24 Raffles Place, [H]18-00 Clifford
Centre, Singapore 1544, 533 2323, Fax:
533 1579, Advocate & Solicitor, and
Member Singapore Bar, Call Date: July
1995 (Middle Temple) Qualifications:
LLB (Hons), BA (Singapore)

De Rozario *Miss Lynette Rita*
Singapore 1545, Call Date: Nov 1992
(Middle Temple) Qualifications: BA
(Hons, Kent)

De Saram *Savantha Rishad Sproule*
Sri Lanka, Call Date: Nov 1998
(Lincoln's Inn) Qualifications: LLB
(Hons)(Wolves)

De Silva *Miss Natasha Esther*
Singapore 807361, Call Date: July 1997
(Middle Temple) Qualifications: LLB
(Hons)(Warw)

De Silva *Suren Charitha*
Sri Lanka, Call Date: July 1996 (Gray's
Inn) Qualifications: LLB (Wales)

De Souza *Miss Vanessa-Anne*
Straits Tradine Building, 9 Battery
Road, [H]15-00, Singapore 597138,
(65) 5322271, Fax: (65) 5352475, and
Member Singapore, Call Date: July
1996 (Middle Temple) Qualifications:
LLB (Hons)(Leeds)

De Ste Croix *Miss Emma Rebecca*
Ogier & Le Masurier, P O Box 404,
Whiteley Chambers, Don Street, St
Helier, Jersey, Channel Islands, 01534
504000, Fax: 01534 35328, Call Date:
May 1995 (Inner Temple)
Qualifications: LLB

Dean *Ms Margaret*
B-1050 Brussels, Call Date: Nov 1992
(Middle Temple) Qualifications: B.Sc
(Hons, Wales)

Deeny *Donnell Justin*
Bar Library, Royal Courts of Justice,
Belfast, 0232 241523/323243, Fax:
0232 231850, QC Northern Ireland
Senior Counsel Republic of Ireland and
Member Northern Ireland Bar, Call
Date: July 1986 (Middle Temple)
Qualifications: BA Dublin

Delaney *Barry Douglas*
P O Box 36, Orchasrd Point, Singapore
9123, Call Date: Oct 1993 (Inner
Temple) Qualifications: LLB (Lond)

Delip Singh *Tara Singh*
Malaysia, Call Date: Nov 1995
(Lincoln's Inn) Qualifications: LLB
(Hons)

Demetriou *Antonis*
Cyprus, Call Date: Oct 1996 (Gray's
Inn) Qualifications: LLB (Kent)

Demetriou *Miss Elina*
Cyprus, Call Date: Nov 1995 (Lincoln's
Inn) Qualifications: LLB (Hons)
(So'ton)

Dendroff *Jason Peter*
Singapore 1646, Call Date: Nov 1993
(Middle Temple) Qualifications: LLB
(Hons)(Lond)

Deo *Jagdeep Singh*
C/O Karpal Singh & Co, 17 Green Hall,
10200 Penang, Malaysia, Malaysia, 04
2638543/2639558, Fax: 04 2630461,
Legal Assistant, and Member Malaysia
Bar, Call Date: July 1993 (Gray's Inn)
Qualifications: LLB (Warw)

DeSilva *Miss Joanne*
Morgan, Lewis & Badans LLP, 80
Raffles Place, [H]14-20 UOB Plaza 2,
Singapore 2880, (010) (65) 438 2188,
Fax: (010) (65) 230 7100, Associate,
and Member Singapore Bar, Call Date:
Oct 1992 (Gray's Inn) Qualifications:
BA

Dessain *Anthony James*
Bedell & Cristin, P.O. Box 75, One the
Forum, Grenville Street, St Helier,Jersey
JE4 8PP, 01534 814814, Fax: 01534
814815, Advocate, Notary Public, Crown
Advocate, Call Date: July 1974 (Middle
Temple) Qualifications: LLB

Devendarajah *Vivekananda*
Singapore 2056, Call Date: July 1995
(Middle Temple) Qualifications: LLB
(Hons)(Wales)

Deverell *William Shirley*
Kaplan & Stratton, Advocates, PO Box
40111, Nairobi, Kenya, 335 333, Fax:
340 827, and Member Advocate of the
High Court of Kenya, Call Date: Nov
1961 (Gray's Inn) Qualifications: BA

Dhaniram *Mahendranath*
5 Gordon Street (North), San
Fernando, Trinidad, West Indies, (809)
652 6806, Fax: (809) 652 6806, and
Member Trinidad & Tobago Bar, Call
Date: Feb 1994 (Gray's Inn)
Qualifications: LLB (Lond), LLM
(Lond), LEC (Trinidad &, Tobago)

Dharsan *Miss Kiranjit Kaur*
Singapore 760288, Call Date: July 1997
(Middle Temple) Qualifications: LLB
(Hons)(Lond)

Dhillon *Gurmit Singh*
Singapore 0409, Call Date: Nov 1996
(Lincoln's Inn) Qualifications: LLB
(Hons)

Dhillon *Gursharan Singh*
Malaysia, Call Date: Nov 1996 (Middle
Temple) Qualifications: LLB
(Hons)(Leeds)

Dhillon *Surinder Singh*
Chua Dhillon Tan & Partners, 71
Robinson Road, [H]03-03, Singapore
0409, 32332320, Fax: 2213211, and
Member Singapore Bar, Call Date: Nov
1991 (Lincoln's Inn) Qualifications:
LLB (Hons) (Lond)

Dilbert *Miss Sophia Armanda*
Maples & Calder, PO Box 309, Ugland
House, George Town, Grand Cayman,
British West Indies, (345) 9498066,
Fax: (345) 9498080, Cayman Islands
Attorney at Law and Member Cayman
Islands Bar, Call Date: July 1996
(Middle Temple) Qualifications: LLB
(Hons)(L'pool)

Dixon *Keith Owen*
Ogier & Le Masurier, Pirouet House,
Union Street, St Helier, Jersey, Channel
Islands, Channel Islands, 01534
504000, Fax: 01534 35238, and
Member Jersey Bar, Call Date: May
1994 (Middle Temple) Qualifications:
MA (Hons)

Dodin *Aldo Bruno Didier*
33 Prince Charles Avenue, Rose Hill,
Mauritius, Call Date: July 1998 (Middle
Temple) Qualifications: LLB
(Hons)(Lond)

Doherty *John*
Republic of Ireland, Barrister of
Ireland, Call Date: Nov 1995 (Middle
Temple) Qualifications: BL (King's Inn)

Don *Brendan Robert*
Singapore 1025, Call Date: July 1994
(Middle Temple) Qualifications: LLB
(Hons)(Leic), LLM (Boston)

Dorai Raj *Dinesh Pragasam*
Singapore 570213, Call Date: Nov 1995
(Middle Temple) Qualifications: LLB
(Hons)(Wales)

Doraisamy *Raghunath Ramachandran*
Singapore 449032, Call Date: Nov 1997
(Middle Temple) Qualifications: LLB
(Hons)(Nott'm)

Dorey *Sir Graham Martyn*
The Bailiff's Chambers, Royal Court,
Guernsey, Channel Islands, 01481
726161, Fax: 01481 713861, Bailiff of
Guernsey, President Guernsey Court of
Appeal, Former Solicitor and Member
Member of the Jersey Court of Appeal,
Call Date: Feb 1992 (Gray's Inn)
Qualifications: BA (Bristol)

Dorsett *Kenred Michael Ansara*
Providence Consulting Group, P.O.Box
N-1527, Nassau, Bahamas, (240) 394
0886, Fax: (240) 394 0573, Executive
Director, and Member Bahamas Bar,
Call Date: July 1995 (Middle Temple)
Qualifications: BA (Hons) (Keele)

Dougan *Miss Carla Nyan*
West Indies, Call Date: Oct 1998 (Inner
Temple) Qualifications: LLB (Kent)

Drahaman *Ms Cirami Mastura*
Malaysia, Call Date: Nov 1996 (Gray's
Inn) Qualifications: LLB (Lond)

Drui McNaught *Mrs Sera Palu*
Australia, Legal Officer, and Member
The Fiji Bar, Call Date: July 1995
(Inner Temple) Qualifications: LLB
(Wolverhampton)

F

Dudley *Anthony Edward*
Gibraltar, Call Date: Nov 1989 (Middle Temple) Qualifications: LLB Hons [Hull]

Duffett *Peter Lionel*
c/o Allianz Shanghai, Representative Office, 707 Office Complex, Hotel Equatorial Shangai, 65 Yanan Xi Lu, Shanghai 2000040, 0086 21 6248 8148, Fax: 0086 21 6248 8240, Actuary, Call Date: Feb 1980 (Middle Temple) Qualifications: MA, FIA, FCCA, FCII

Dukes *Christopher James Noel*
Yolaw Trust & Corporate, Services Limited, P O Box 415, Templar House, Don Road, St Helier, Jersey JE4 8WH, Channel Islands, 01534 500419, Fax: 01534 500450, Call Date: July 1983 (Middle Temple) Qualifications: LLB

Duncan *Benjamin Paul*
Hill and Knowlton, 118 Avenue de Carenburg, B-1040, Belgium, Call Date: Oct 1990 (Lincoln's Inn) Qualifications: LLB (Lanc), LLM (Edin)

Duncan *Delroy*
Messrs Trott & Duncan, 1st Floor, Sea Venture, Building 19, Parliament Street, Hamilton, 441 295 7444, Fax: 441 295 6600, and Member Bermuda, Call Date: Nov 1984 (Gray's Inn) Qualifications: MA, LLB, FCIArb

Duncan *Miss Marjorie Camille*
Jamaica, Call Date: Mar 1996 (Gray's Inn) Qualifications: BA (West Indies), LLB (Lond)

Duncanson *Beryn Sigurd*
British West Indies, Call Date: Mar 1997 (Gray's Inn) Qualifications: BA (Toronto), LLB (Bucks)

Dunham *Michael John*
29 Spring Street, Sandringham, Victoria 3191, 9 336 1917, Fax: 9 320 4178, and Member Australia Bar, Call Date: Nov 1980 (Middle Temple) Qualifications: Master Mariner

Dunn *John Christie*
The Cloisters Apartment, The Elms, Weston Park West, Bath BA1 4AR, 01225 483412, and Member Hong Kong Bar, Call Date: July 1989 (Inner Temple) Qualifications: LLB (Lond), M.SocSc

Dunnett *Denzil Roderick Rawcliffe*
L-2950 Luxembourg, Luxembourg, 352 43791, Fax: 352 437704, Assistant General Counsel, European Investment Bank, Call Date: Nov 1970 (Middle Temple) Qualifications: MA (Oxon)

Duraipandi *Miss Ganaselvarani*
M.N.Swami & Yap, No 1 North Bridge Road, [H]18-05 High Street Centre, Singapore 0410, 3361677, Fax: 3371737, and Member Singapore Bar, Call Date: Feb 1994 (Lincoln's Inn) Qualifications: LLB (Hons, Lond)

Dusun *Marcus*
Malaysia, Call Date: Nov 1996 (Lincoln's Inn) Qualifications: LLB (Hons)(Lond)

Dwan *Francis Eugene*
The Law Library, The Four Courts, Inns Quay, Dublin 7, Republic of Ireland, 00 353 1 817 3925, Fax: 00 353 1 817 2769, Barrister of Ireland, Call Date: Mar 1996 (Middle Temple) Qualifications: BA (Hons), BL (Kings Inn)

Dykes *Philip John*
Suites 1517-1522, Two Pacific Place, Queensway, 2810 7222, Fax: 2845 0439, Queen's Counsel (Hong Kong 1997), Senior Counsel, (1997) and Member Hong Kong Bar, Call Date: July 1977 (Lincoln's Inn) Qualifications: BA (Oxon)

Edgar *Effrem Owen*
Edgar & Co Chambers, P.O.Box 500, Castries, St Lucia, 758 452 2405, Fax: 758 451 8979, and Member East Caribbean Supreme Court (St Lucia), Call Date: July 1995 (Lincoln's Inn) Qualifications: BA (Hons), LLM

Edmonds *Mrs Mary Xue-Ying*
Al Hussieu & Co, [H]04-00 Pkms Bldg, Changi Road, Singapore 150008, 344 5738, and Member Singapore, Call Date: Nov 1996 (Lincoln's Inn) Qualifications: LLB (Hons)(Lond)

Edmondson *James Douglas*
The Bar Library, Royal Courts of Justice, Belfast BT1 3JP, Northern Ireland, 01232 562449, Fax: 01232 231850, and Member Northern Ireland, Call Date: Oct 1997 (Gray's Inn) Qualifications: BA, MBA (Belfast)

Ee *Miss Annie Yeok Leng*
Malaysia, Call Date: Mar 1998 (Lincoln's Inn) Qualifications: LLB (Hons)(Keele)

Efrem *Mrs Eleni Andreas*
District Court of Larnaca, Larnaca, Cyprus, 04 630531, District Court Judge, Call Date: July 1990 (Gray's Inn) Qualifications: LLB (E Ang), LLM (Lond)

Ehamparam *Santhirasegaram*
Canada, Call Date: July 1995 (Inner Temple) Qualifications: LLB

Ekins *Charles Wareing*
Montserrat, Assistant Recorder, H.M. Attorney General for Montserrat Sovereign Chambers, 25 Park Square, Leeds, LS1 2PW, Call Date: July 1980 (Gray's Inn) Qualifications: LLB (Leeds)

El Hassan *HRH Princess Badiya*
Jordan, Call Date: Oct 1998 (Lincoln's Inn) Qualifications: BA (Hons), Dip in Law

Elkinson *Jeffrey Philip*
Conyers Dill & Pearman, Clarendon House, Church Street, Hamilton HM CX, 809 295 1422, Fax: 809 292 4720, and Member Southern Ireland (1978) Hong Kong (1985), New South Wales, Australia (1985), New York (1987), Bermuda (1989) New York (1987) and Bermuda (1989) Bars, Call Date: Feb 1982 (Middle Temple) Qualifications: BL, MA, LLB, FCIArb

Elliott *Sebastion Michael Garcia*
United States of America, Call Date: Oct 1996 (Lincoln's Inn) Qualifications: BA (Hons)(Essex), Dip in Law (City)

Ellul *Marc Xavier*
Suite 7, Hadfield House, Library Street, Gibraltar, 00 (350) 70921, Fax: 00 (350) 74969, and Member Gibratar, Call Date: Nov 1993 (Inner Temple) Qualifications: BA (Hons)(Cardiff)

Emsellem *Miss Catherine Marie*
France, Call Date: Oct 1998 (Middle Temple) Qualifications: LLB (Hons)

Enser *Miss Juliette Corinne*
Weil, Gotshal and Manges LLP, 81 Avenue Louise, P.O.Box 9-10, 1050 Brussels, Belgium, 00 32 2 543 7484, Call Date: Oct 1991 (Inner Temple) Qualifications: BA (Oxon), Dip EC LAW

Ephraim *Miss Pamela*
Messrs Zaman & Associates, Suite 04-06 & 04-07, Wisma Maria, Jalan Ngee Heng, Johor Bahru, Johor, Malaysia, 07-2229788/89, Fax: 07-2238073, and Member Malaysia Bar, Call Date: July 1997 (Middle Temple) Qualifications: LLB (Hons)(Lond)

Er *Miss Joanna Wuan Sher*
Singapore 1646, Call Date: July 1995 (Lincoln's Inn) Qualifications: LLB (Hons)

Ern *Lai Daryl Chee*
Singapore 46001, Call Date: July 1997 (Inner Temple) Qualifications: LLB (Lond)

Erotocritou *Miss Electra*
Cyprus, Call Date: Nov 1998 (Gray's Inn) Qualifications: LLB (Kent)

Erotocritou *Miss Elena*
Cyprus, Call Date: Nov 1996 (Lincoln's Inn) Qualifications: LLB (Hons)(Leics)

Erotokritou *Miss Christianna A*
A.P.Erotokritou & Co, Advocates Legal Consultants, Offices 502-504, Augusta, Building, 10 Stasadrou Street, P.O.Box 2154, Nicosia, Cyprus, 357 2 764466, Fax: 357 2 758566, and Member Cyprus, Call Date: Nov 1997 (Lincoln's Inn) Qualifications: LLB (Hons)

Erriah *Ramdeo*
Mauritius, Call Date: Nov 1995 (Gray's Inn) Qualifications: LLB (Lond)

F

Erskine *Thomas Ralph*
Office of the Legislative Csl., Parliament Bldgs, Stormont, Belfast, Northern Ireland BT4 3SW, Northern Ireland, Call Date: Feb 1962 (Gray's Inn) Qualifications: LLB

Eshun *Yaw Fenyi*
West Africa, Call Date: July 1995 (Lincoln's Inn) Qualifications: BA (Hons) (Ghana)

Etican *Ramsay Roy*
Malaysia, Call Date: July 1997 (Lincoln's Inn) Qualifications: LLB (Hons) (Hull)

Evangelou *Miss Theano Alexandros*
Cyprus, Call Date: July 1995 (Gray's Inn) Qualifications: LLB (Lond)

Evans *Guy St John*
World Trade Organisation, Geneva, France, Legal Affairs Officer, Call Date: Nov 1992 (Inner Temple) Qualifications: BA (Hons) (Kent), MA (Bruges)

Everett-Heath *Miss Catharine Rose*
Italy, Call Date: Nov 1989 (Lincoln's Inn) Qualifications: MA (Cantab)

Evie *Mrs Georgiou Antoniou*
Attorney General's Office, Nicosia, Cyprus, 02-469159, Attorney to the Republic of Cyprus, and Member Cyprus Bar, Call Date: Nov 1995 (Gray's Inn) Qualifications: LLB (Leic), LLM

Eyles *Keith*
Venus Shipping Company S.A., 19 Avenue de la Costa, Monte Carlo 98000, Monaco, 00377 93 15 71 71, Fax: 00377 93 15 71 99, Legal Adviser, Call Date: July 1983 (Inner Temple) Qualifications: BA (Keele)

Faherty *Miss Mary*
Law Library, Four Courts, Dublin 7, Ireland, Chairperson, Empoyment Appeals Tribunal, and Member Irish Bar, Call Date: Nov 1996 (Middle Temple) Qualifications: BA, LLB (Galway), BL (King's Inn), Dip.Arb, Dip.Antl., Arb, ACIArb

Fair *James Dale*
29154 Jefferson Ct, St Clair Shores, Michigan 48081, 810 447 8093, Fax: 810 447 8546, and Member State of Kansas USA, Call Date: Nov 1980 (Lincoln's Inn) Qualifications: AB (Princeton), MA, (Oxon) JD (Stanford)

Fairclough *Sara*
Smith-Hughes, Raworth & McKenzie, Sea Meadow House, P O Box 173, Road Town, Tortola, British Virgin Islands, Company Director/Mental Health Manager, Call Date: Oct 1992 (ERROR) Qualifications: LLB Hons

Fairey *Hamish Webster*
New Zealand, Call Date: Nov 1997 (Lincoln's Inn) Qualifications: LLB (Hons)

Fan *Edward*
and Member Hong Kong, Call Date: July 1997 (Inner Temple) Qualifications: BDS (Lond), MGDSRCS (Edinburgh), Dip.F.Od (LHMC), LLB (Westminster), ACIArb

Fan *Miss Yuen Chi Edwina*
Singapore 049910, Call Date: July 1995 (Middle Temple) Qualifications: LLB (Hons)

Farid *Ms Fuzet*
2 Lorong Abang Haji Openg 3, Taman Tun Dr Ismail, 60000 Kuala Lumpur, Malaysia, 603-718 2198, Fax: 603-201 4257, Fellow of Cambridge Commonwealth Society Annotated Statutesof Malaysia: Carriage of Goods by Sea Act, 1950 and Member Malaysia Bar, Call Date: July 1993 (Middle Temple) Qualifications: BA (Hons), LLM

Fear *Richard David*
British West Indies, Chartered Accountant, Call Date: July 1998 (Middle Temple) Qualifications: LLB (Hons) (L'pool), LLM (Cantab)

Fennelly *Nial (Michael Patrick)*
84 Rue de Kirchberg, L-1858, Republic of Ireland, Advocate General, European Court, Senior Counsel, Ireland (1978) and Member Southern Ireland Bar Northern Ireland Bar, Call Date: July 1988 (Middle Temple) Qualifications: MA (Dublin)

Ferguson *Miss Joyann Louise*
Bahamas, Call Date: Nov 1997 (Gray's Inn) Qualifications: BA, MA (Morgan State,) LLB (Bucks)

Ferguson *Samuel William*
Northern Ireland, Barrister in N Ireland Employed barrister, Call Date: July 1991 (Gray's Inn) Qualifications: LLB (Belfast)

Fernandez *James*
Brunei, Call Date: July 1996 (Lincoln's Inn) Qualifications: LLB (Hons) (Lond)

Fernandez *Johann Christian*
Gibraltar, Call Date: Oct 1998 (Middle Temple) Qualifications: LLB (Hons) (Essex)

Ferry *John Edward*
France, Call Date: Feb 1956 (Gray's Inn) Qualifications: MA (Oxon)

Fields *Mrs Fiona Catharine*
Lowlands, Ville Au Bas, St Ouen, Jersey JE3 2LT, Channel Islands, 01534 484315, Fax: 01534 484312, Call Date: Nov 1984 (Middle Temple) Qualifications: BA (Kent)

Finch *Paul John*
Australia, (612) 9331 0364, Fax: (612) 9368 1403, and Member Australia, California and New York Bars 2 Field Court, Gray's Inn, London, WC1R 5BB, Call Date: Nov 1990 (Lincoln's Inn) Qualifications: LLB, B.Comm (NSW)

Findlay *The Hon Mr Justice James Kerr*
High Court, Queensway, 2825 4325, Fax: 2523 4253, Judge of the High Court Hong Kong, Formerly a Solicitor (Scotland) QC Hong Kong and Member Zimbabwe Bar Victoria Bar Hong Kong Bar, Call Date: May 1985 (Inner Temple) Qualifications: LLB (Lond), FCIA

Finigan *John Patrick*
Qatar National Bank SAQ, P O Box 1000, Doha, 00974 430240, Fax: 00974 438349, Chief Executive, Call Date: July 1980 (Lincoln's Inn) Qualifications: FCIB, ACIS, FRSA, MSI

Finnegan *Joseph Gerald*
Ardara, Killarney Road, Bray, Co Wicklow, Republic of Ireland, 2868 108, Fax: 2867 306, Senior Counsel,Republic of Ireland, Call Date: Nov 1986 (Middle Temple) Qualifications: BCL LLB (Dublin)

Fisher *Michael John*
Hong Kong, Call Date: July 1992 (Gray's Inn) Qualifications: LLB (Manch), MA (Brunel)

Fitzgerald *Tyrone Leon Easton*
Bahamas, Call Date: July 1995 (Lincoln's Inn) Qualifications: LLB (Hons)

Fitzpatrick *David*
Room 3507-8 Tower One, Lippo Centre, 89 Queensway, Hong Kong, 852 2866 8233, Fax: 852 2866 7858, Barrister of Hong Kong Barrister & Solicitor of Supreme Court of Victoria, Call Date: July 1992 (Middle Temple) Qualifications: MA (Cambs)

Fitzpatrick *Mark John*
Scotland, Scottish Advocate, Call Date: July 1991 (Lincoln's Inn) Qualifications: BA (Oxon), MA (Oxon)

Fitzsimons *Eoghan Patrick*
Law Library, Four Courts, Dublin 7, Ireland, Republic of Ireland, 01 8174944, Fax: 01 8720455, S.C.(Ireland) and Member Southern Ireland Bar New South Wales Bar, Call Date: Feb 1986 (Middle Temple) Qualifications: BCL (U C Dublin), LLM (Yale), Doct de l'Univ, (Paris)

Fletcher *Peter Grey*
Charlotte House Nassau, P.O.Box N3950, Nassau NP, Bahamas, 809 322 2871, Fax: 809 322 2874, and Member Commonwealth of the Bahamas, Call Date: Nov 1992 (Lincoln's Inn) Qualifications: LLB (Hons) (E Anglia)

Flood *Miss Sarah-Lucy*
West Indies, 1 809 453 6966, Fax: 1 809 452 5655, Minister for Health, Human Services Family Affairs, Women's Affairs, Call Date: July 1995 (Lincoln's Inn) Qualifications: LLB (Hons), MP

Floyd *Robert Hamilton*
22-24 Boulevard Alexander 111, 06400
Cannes, 00 334 93 43 93 55, Fax: 00
334 93 43 40 26, Avocat Au Barreau De
Grasse 06 France, Call Date: Nov 1971
(Middle Temple) Qualifications: LLM
(Lond)

Fock *Miss Yin Ling*
Singapore 259718, Call Date: July 1996
(Middle Temple) Qualifications: LLB
(Hons) (Bris)

Fogarty *Kenneth Christopher*
Ireland, Barrister of Ireland, Call Date:
Mar 1999 (Middle Temple)
Qualifications: BL (King's Inn)

Fogarty *Paul*
The Bar Library, Four Courts, Dublin 7,
Ireland, Republic of Ireland, 283 3513/
677 8373, Fax: 677 8375, and Member
Southern Ireland Bar, Call Date: May
1988 (Middle Temple) Qualifications:
BCL (Dublin), BA, BL (Kings Inn),
ACIArb

Foggin *Miss Erica*
Alexiou, Knowles & Co, P O Box
F42531, Freeport, Grand Bahama,
Bahamas, 001 242 351 7371, Fax: 001
242 351 7505, Call Date: July 1980
(Middle Temple) Qualifications: MA
(Oxon)

Fong *Miss Cornelia Siew Ping*
13 Crichton Close, Singapore 557990,
Singapore 557990, 0065 2888365,
Legal Assistant, and Member Singapore
Bar, Call Date: July 1994 (Inner
Temple) Qualifications: LLB (Nott'm)

Fong *Miss Gwendolyn Teen-Li*
Messrs Shook Lin & Bok, 1 Robinson
Road, AIA Tower, [H]18-00, Singapore
2260, Company Secretary, and Member
Singapore, Call Date: July 1995 (Middle
Temple) Qualifications: LLB
(Hons) (Hull)

Fong *Kelvin Kai Tong*
325k Bukit Timah Road, Singapore
259714, Singapore 259174, (65)
2355120, Fax: (65) 2353500, Call
Date: July 1996 (Middle Temple)
Qualifications: LLB (Hons) (Newc)

Fong *Min Yong*
Singapore 807937, Call Date: Nov 1998
(Middle Temple) Qualifications: LLB
(Hons) (Bucks)

Fong *Ms Shin Ni*
Malaysia, Call Date: Nov 1997
(Lincoln's Inn) Qualifications: LLB
(Hons) (Sheff)

Fong *Miss Yuke Ching*
Singapore 0314, Call Date: July 1994
(Lincoln's Inn) Qualifications: LLB
(Hons)

Foo *Ms Chiew Eng*
479 River Valley Road, [H]13-07, Valley
Park, Call Date: July 1996 (Inner
Temple) Qualifications: LLB (Lond)

Foo *Miss Fiona Wei Ling*
Singapore 570408, and Member
Singapore, Call Date: July 1997
(Lincoln's Inn) Qualifications: LLB
(Lond)

Foo *Miss Jick Liang*
Malaysia, Call Date: July 1998
(Lincoln's Inn) Qualifications: LLB
(Hons)

Foo *Miss Jon-Hui Amanda*
Khattar Wong & Partners, 80 Raffles
Place, [H]25-01 UOB Plaza 1,
Singapore 048624, Singapore, 535
6844, Fax: 533 0585, and Member
Singapore Bar, Call Date: Oct 1990
(Gray's Inn) Qualifications: LLB
(Lond), LLM (Lond), AKC

Foo *Ms Li Mei*
27 Jalan Telawi 8, Bangsar Baru, 59100
Kuala Lumpur, Malaysia, 09 7474 653,
Call Date: July 1996 (Lincoln's Inn)
Qualifications: LLB (Hons) (Cardiff)

Foo *Miss Michele Li-Ming*
Singapore 259704, Call Date: July 1998
(Middle Temple) Qualifications: LLB
(Hons) (Wales)

Foo *Say Tun*
Messrs Wee, Tay and Limners,
Advocates & Solicitors, 133 New bridge
Road, [H]19-09/10 Chinatown Point,
Singapore 669559, 65 533 2228, Fax:
65 535 7813, and Member Malaysia
Bar Singapore Bar, Call Date: Nov 1991
(Middle Temple) Qualifications: LLB
Hons (E Ang)

Foo *Yong Teng*
Malaysia, Call Date: Nov 1995
(Lincoln's Inn) Qualifications: LLB
(Hons)

Foon *Miss Su Li Shirley*
Malaysia, Call Date: Nov 1998
(Lincoln's Inn) Qualifications: LLB
(Hons) (Staffs)

Forbes *Miss Jacqueline Roann*
Bahamas, Call Date: Nov 1998 (Gray's
Inn) Qualifications: BA (Kent)

Forde *Dr Michael Patrick*
33 Mountainview Rd, Dublin 6, 00353
14 978349, Fax: 00353 14 966835,
King's Inn, Dublin (1984), Senior
Counsel (1995) and Member Bar of
Ireland, Call Date: Nov 1987 (Middle
Temple) Qualifications: BA, LLB
(Dublin),, LLM (Brussels), PhD
(Cantab)

Foreman *Mrs Marguerite Alyce*
Seaton & Foreman, Chambers P O Box
82, Central Street, Basseterre, St Kitts,
West Indies, (809) 465 9292, Fax:
(809) 465 7373, Saint Christopher &
Nevis (Eastern Caribbean Supreme
Court), and Member Saint Christopher
& Nevis, Call Date: Oct 1991 (Inner
Temple) Qualifications: MA (Edin),
LLB (Hons), D.M.S.

Forsyth *Alistair James Menteith*
Ethie Castle, By Arbroath, Angus
DD11 5SP, Scotland, 01241 830458,
Fax: 01241 830477,
Director,Hargreaves,Reiss & Quinn Ltd,
Also Inn of Court L and Member
Scottish Bar, Call Date: July 1990
(Inner Temple) Qualifications: MTh (St
Andrews), LLB (Buck), LLB,
(Edinburgh),FSA.Scot, DipLp
(Edinburgh), ACII, Chartered,
Insurance Practiner

Forsyth *Iain Grant*
C.P.V.O., PO Box 2141, F-40921 Angers,
Cedex 02, Paris, 33 0241 36 84 74, Fax:
33 0241 36 84 60, Legal Advisor to the
Community Plant Variety Office, Call
Date: Feb 1988 (Inner Temple)
Qualifications: LLB (Notts)

Foy *Miss Agnes*
Ireland, Barrister of Ireland, Call Date:
Nov 1996 (Middle Temple)
Qualifications: BA (Dublin), BL (King's
Inn)

Francis *Benedict Peter Beauchamp*
7002 Hillcrest Pl, Chevy Chase,
Maryland 20815, USA, and Member
New York, Call Date: Nov 1989
(Lincoln's Inn) Qualifications: MA
(Edin), Dip Law (City), LLM (USA)

Francis *Miss Bridget Cecile*
Bahamas, Call Date: Nov 1997 (Gray's
Inn) Qualifications: LLB (Lond), LLM

Francis *Ms Charmaine*
Singapore 2057, Call Date: July 1995
(Middle Temple) Qualifications: LLB
(Hons)

Francis *Derek Roy Lebert*
Advocates' Library, Parliament House,
Edinburgh, Scotland, Scottish Advocate,
Call Date: Feb 1991 (Lincoln's Inn)
Qualifications: LLB (Edin)

Francis *Miss Kenrah Nicole Philippa*
Chancery Law Associates, P.O.Box
N-8199, Nassau, Bahamas, 1-242 356
6108, Fax: 1-242 356 6109, Associate,
and Member Bahamas, Call Date: July
1996 (Lincoln's Inn) Qualifications:
LLB (Hons) (Reading)

Freminot *Sammy Antoine*
Republic of Seychelles, Call Date: Nov
1998 (Gray's Inn) Qualifications: LLB
(Bucks), BSc (Mauritius)

Frida *Miss Samantha*
Australia, Call Date: July 1996
(Lincoln's Inn) Qualifications: LLB
(Hons) (Leeds)

Froomkin *Saul Morten*
Mello,Hollis,Jones & Martin, Reid
House, 31 Church Street, PO Box HM
1564, Hamilton,Bermuda, Bermuda,
441-292 1345, Fax: 441-292 2277,
Senior Litigation Partner, QC (Canada
& Bermuda) and Member Canada,
Bermuda, Anguilla, Call Date: Apr 1989
(Middle Temple) Qualifications: LLB,
LLM (Manitoba), FCIArb, F.S.A.L.S.

F

Fuchs *Miss Iris*
Germany, Call Date: Oct 1997 (Middle
Temple) Qualifications: LLB
(Hons)(Lond), BA (New York)

Fuller *Nicolas Alan*
West Indies, Call Date: July 1995
(Middle Temple) Qualifications: LLB
(Hons)

Fulthorpe *Mrs Elizabeth Clare*
Sutton Associates, 60 Avenue de
Wagram, 75017 Paris, 331 4440 0232/
46681 0159, Fax: 331 4440 0232/
46681 0159, Call Date: Nov 1974
(Gray's Inn) Qualifications: LLB Hons

Fung *Miss Catherine Shuk Yin*
Department of Justice, Queensway Govt
Offices, 66 Queensway, Hong Kong,
28672356, Fax: 28690236, Senior
Crown Counsel, and Member
Australian Capital Territory, 1988 &
Northern Territory, Australia 1991
Australia Bar Hong Kong Bar, Call Date:
July 1987 (Middle Temple)
Qualifications: BA (Manitoba) LLB,
(Bucks)

Fung *Daniel Richard*
4th Floor, High Block, 10/F Bank of
East Asia, Bldg 10 Des Voeux Road
Central, (852) 252 63071, Fax: (852)
281 05287, Member of China
International Economic & Trade
Arbitration Commission, Q.C., S.C.,
Hong Kong and Member Victoria,
Australian Capital Territory Bar Hong
Kong Bar, Call Date: Nov 1975 (Middle
Temple) Qualifications: LLB LLM

Fung *Eugene Ting Sek*
Temple Chambers, 16/F One Pacific
Place, 88 Queensway, (852) 2523
2003, Fax: (852) 2810 0302, and
Member Hong Kong, Call Date: Mar
1997 (Lincoln's Inn) Qualifications:
MA (Cantab), LLM, (Cantab)

Fung *Miss Lucille Yun Sim*
A2-19 Evergreen Villa, 43 Stubbs Road,
and Member Brunei, and Victoria Bars
Hong Kong Bar New South Wales, Call
Date: July 1960 (Middle Temple)
Qualifications: BA, MCI Arb

Fung *Patrick Chee Yuen*
Singapore 0316, and Member
Singapore Bar, Call Date: July 1992
(Middle Temple) Qualifications: LLB
(Hons) (Leics)

Fung *Patrick Pak-Tung*
10/F, New Henry House, 10 Ice House
Street, Central, (852) 2524 2156, Fax:
(852) 2810 5656, Queen's Counsel
1995 (Hong Kong) and Member Hong
Kong Bar, Call Date: Nov 1968 (Inner
Temple) Qualifications: LLB (Lond),
FCI Arb

Gaik *Miss Anne Ooi*
Malaysia, Call Date: July 1994 (Middle
Temple) Qualifications: LLB
(Hons)(Sheff)

Gajadhar *Jerome*
West Indies, 868 668 3783, Call Date:
Nov 1996 (Lincoln's Inn)
Qualifications: BA, MA (Ontario), LLM
(Leeds)

Gallagher *Miss Grace Marie Walsh*
Southern Ireland, Call Date: Nov 1997
(Lincoln's Inn) Qualifications: BA, LLB
(Galway), BL (King's Inn)

Gallagher *Martin John*
No 1 Arran Square, Arran Quay, Dublin
7, 872 5908, Fax: 872 8963, Senior
Counsel, Call Date: Nov 1981 (Middle
Temple) Qualifications: BA, FCIArb

Gan *Gerry Kian Koon*
Singapore 329977, Call Date: July 1997
(Middle Temple) Qualifications: LLB
(Hons)

Gan *Miss Huey Piin*
C/O M/S Gulam & Wong, Advocates &
Solicitors, Suite 1103-1106, 11th Floor,
15 Jalan Gereja, 80100 Johor, West
Malaysia, Malaysia, 07-2246851/2
2245963, Fax: 07-2246854 2245460,
Call Date: July 1994 (Lincoln's Inn)
Qualifications: LLB

Gan *Miss Jui Chui*
Malaysia, Call Date: July 1995
(Lincoln's Inn) Qualifications: LLB
(Hons)

Gan *Kah Loon*
Malaysia, Call Date: July 1998
(Lincoln's Inn) Qualifications: LLB
(Hons) (L'pool)

Gan *Ping Wan*
Malaysia, Call Date: Oct 1998
(Lincoln's Inn) Qualifications: LLB
(Hons) (Leeds)

Gan *Miss Sye Ni*
Malaysia, Call Date: July 1997
(Lincoln's Inn) Qualifications: LLB
(Hons) (Wales)

Gan *Miss Yee Min*
Sidley & Austin, One First National
Plaza, Chicago, Illinois 60611,
Malaysia, 1 (312) 853 2063, Fax: 1
(312) 863 7036, Currently an Attorney
at Law in the State of New York and
Member New York, Malaysia, Call Date:
July 1995 (Middle Temple)
Qualifications: LLB (Hons), LLM
(Northwestern, Uni)

Gan *Miss Yvonne Ai Wah*
Malaysia, Call Date: Nov 1998
(Lincoln's Inn) Qualifications: LLB
(Hons) (Wolves)

Ganesan *Anandan*
Malaysia, Call Date: July 1996 (Middle
Temple) Qualifications: LLB
(Hons) (Bris)

Ganesan *Miss Susila*
Singapore 0410, Call Date: July 1995
(Lincoln's Inn) Qualifications: LLB
(Hons)

Ganeson *Miss Visahini*
Malaysia, Call Date: July 1995
(Lincoln's Inn) Qualifications: LLB
(Hons)

Gangadharan *Miss Prasanna Devi*
Singapore 440035, Call Date: Nov 1996
(Middle Temple) Qualifications: LLB
(Hons) (Lond)

Garfield *Scott Kennedy*
Nomura International (Hong, Kong)
Ltd, 20/F Asia Pacific Finance Towe,
Citibank Plaza, 3 Garden Road, Central,
Hong Kong, 00 852 2536 1426, Fax: 00
852 2536 1593, In-House Counsel, Call
Date: Nov 1996 (Middle Temple)
Qualifications: LLB (Hons), LLM
(Lond)

Garland *Peter William*
1501, Two Pacific Place, 88 Queensway,
852-28401130, Fax: 852-28100612, QC
(Hong Kong 1995), SC (Hong Kong
1997), Supreme Court of the Australian
Capital Territory, High Court of
Australia and Member Hong Kong Bar,
Call Date: Nov 1978 (Middle Temple)

Gau *Miss Susan*
Malaysia, Call Date: July 1996
(Lincoln's Inn) Qualifications: LLB
(Hons)(Hull)

Gaudin *James Harman*
Channel Islands, Call Date: Nov 1996
(Middle Temple) Qualifications: LLB
(Hons)

Gauntlett *Jeremy John*
1114 Huguenot Chambers, 40 Queen
Victoria St, Cape Town, South Africa,
South Africa, 4249340, Fax: 4245666,
Acting Judge, Cape Supreme Court
(1991 & 1994) Judge of Appeal,
Kingdom of Lesotho, Senior Counsel,
South Africa, Lesotho & Namibia, Call
Date: May 1994 (Gray's Inn)
Qualifications: BA, LLB, BCL

Gavaloo *Miss Vedna*
Mauritius, Call Date: Nov 1995
(Lincoln's Inn) Qualifications: LLB
(Hons)

Geer *David John Granville*
Delegation of the European,
Commission in Georgia, C/O
Diplomatic Pouch, 1 Rue de Geneve,
B-1140 Brussels, Belgium B-1000, 995
32 999 602, Fax: 995 32 990 833, Call
Date: Nov 1988 (Middle Temple)
Qualifications: BA (Cantab), Dip Law,
LLM

Genkatharan *Mrs Kala Malar*
Singapore 538361, Call Date: Mar 1998
(Middle Temple) Qualifications: LLB
(Hons) (Lond)

George *Miss Caroline Mary*
Malaysia, Call Date: Nov 1996
(Lincoln's Inn) Qualifications: LLB
(Hons)

George *Rynholdt*
Group 500, Innes Chambers, P.O.Box 1073, Johannesburg 2000, (2711) 337 4355, Fax: (2711) 333 1602, Advocate of Supreme Court of South Africa, and Member Johannesburg Bar, Call Date: July 1996 (Lincoln's Inn) Qualifications: LLB (Hons), BA(Hon), (Oxon)

Georgiadis *Byron Nicholas*
P.O.Box 42851, Nairobi, Kenya, Nairobi 882319/884037, Fax: 884037, Arbitrator, and Member Kenya Bar Seychelles Bar, Call Date: Nov 1951 (Inner Temple) Qualifications: MA (Oxon), MCA Arb

Georgiou *Miss Chloe*
Cyprus, Call Date: Nov 1997 (Gray's Inn) Qualifications: LLB (Leics)

Georgis Taylor *Miss Vivian*
Peter I Foster & Associates, 35 Jeremie Street, Castries, West Indies, 758 4531100, Fax: 758 4524940, and Member St Lucia, Call Date: Nov 1995 (Middle Temple) Qualifications: LLB (Hons)

Gevisser *Advocate Antony James*
12 Montrose Road, Hurlingham, Sandton 2196, South Africa, South Africa, 0171 730 9371, Fax: 011 7831317, Part Time Commissioner at Commission for Conciliation Arbitration and Mediator C Johannesburg, Arbitrator (Arbitration Foundation of SA), and Member Johannesburg Bar, Call Date: Nov 1993 (Gray's Inn) Qualifications: BA, LLB (Cape), HDipARb

Ghandinesen *Kanarasan*
Malaysia, Call Date: July 1995 (Lincoln's Inn) Qualifications: LLB (Hons)

Ghani *Ahmad Shukri Abdul*
Malaysia, Call Date: Nov 1997 (Gray's Inn) Qualifications: LLB (Wales)

Ghani *Miss Marianne Antoinette*
P.O.Box 13799, 88843 Kota Kinabalu, Sabah, Malaysia, 00 60 88 218667/ 218663, Fax: 00 60 88 239627, and Member Sabah & Sarawak, Malaysia, Call Date: Oct 1995 (Gray's Inn) Qualifications: LLB

Ghosh *Dhruba*
India 700026, Call Date: July 1995 (Lincoln's Inn) Qualifications: LLB (Hons)

Gibbons *John Thomas*
Law Library, Four Courts, Inns Quay, Dublin 7, Ireland, 01 872 0622, Barrister of Ireland and Member Kings Inn, Dublin, Call Date: Nov 1991 (Middle Temple) Qualifications: BL (Dublin), BE, (NUI), DIP. LScEng,, FIEI, FCIArb, LAM, RTPI

Gibson *Mrs Mavis Dorothy*
Zimbabwe, Call Date: Nov 1965 (Lincoln's Inn)

Gilbert *Miss Dionne*
Crill Canavan, 40 Don Street, St Helier, Jersey, Channel Islands, 01534 601700, Fax: 01534 601701, Call Date: July 1996 (Inner Temple) Qualifications: LLB (Bucks)

Gill *The Honourable Lord*
Court of Session, Parliament House, Edinburgh EH1 1RQ, Scotland, 0131 225 2595, Fax: 0131 225 8213, Senator of the College of Justice in Scotland. Chairman, Scottish Law Commission., Call Date: Apr 1991 (Lincoln's Inn) Qualifications: MA (Glas), LLB (Glas), PH.D (Edinburgh), LLD (Hon:Glas)

Gill *Amarick Singh*
Singapore 320102, Call Date: Mar 1998 (Middle Temple) Qualifications: LLB (Hons)

Gill *Miss Harminder Kaur*
Malaysia, Call Date: Oct 1998 (Middle Temple) Qualifications: LLB (Hons) (Wales)

Gill *Jagjit Singh*
Chinese Chambers of Commerce, & Industry Building, 47 Hill Street, [H]04-03, Singapore 530310, 3382622, Fax: 3392386, Advocate & Solicitor, Legal Assistant, and Member Singapore, Call Date: July 1996 (Lincoln's Inn) Qualifications: LLB (Hons) (Lond)

Gill *Zaminder Singh*
No 87 Beach Road, [H]04-01 Chye Sing Building, Singapore 550312, 3387225, Fax: 3388815, and Member Singapore, Call Date: Nov 1993 (Middle Temple) Qualifications: LLB (Hons) (Lanc)

Gillard *The Hon Mr Justice Eugene William*
Judges' Chambers, Supreme Court of Victoria, 210 William Street, Melbourne, Vic.3000, (03) 9603 6222, Fax: (03) 9670 8408, Chairman; Victorian Bar Council 1988-1990. President; Australian Bar Association 1989-1990. Justice of the Supreme Court of Victoria, QC (Australia) and Member Victorian, Tasmania, New South Wales, Queensland 4 Stone Bldgs, Ground Floor, Lincoln's Inn, London, WC2A 3XT, Call Date: Feb 1991 (Gray's Inn) Qualifications: LLB (Melbourne)

Gillespie *Brian David*
2 Glenvar Park, Blackrock, Co. Dublin, 2882887, Fax: 8720455, and Member Southern Ireland Bar, Call Date: July 1989 (Middle Temple) Qualifications: MA [Dub], MAI [Dub], B Comm [Dub], FIEE

Gilpin *Miss Roma Elizabeth*
Scotland, Call Date: Nov 1993 (Middle Temple) Qualifications: BA (Hons) (Oxon)

Gittings *Daniel John*
South China Morning Post, 29/F Dorset House, 979 King's Road, Hong Kong, + 852 28653584, Fax: + 852 28653464, Associate Editor, and Member High Court of Hong Kong, Call Date: July 1997 (Gray's Inn) Qualifications: MA

Glinton *Dwight Donald*
Bahamas, Call Date: Nov 1998 (Inner Temple) Qualifications: LLB (Herts)

Glitzenhirn-Augustin *Mrs Natalie Elaine*
P O Box 1695, Castries, Fax: (758) 451 8409, and Member St Lucia Bar Association, Call Date: July 1996 (Middle Temple) Qualifications: BA (Hons) (Warw), CPE

Gnanapragasam *Miss Christina Olivia*
Malaysia, Call Date: Nov 1997 (Middle Temple) Qualifications: LLB (Hons) (Wales)

Go *Tiong Siew*
Go Tiong Sie & Associates, Peguambela & Peguamcara, Advocates & Solicitors, 1-11 Jalan PM 3, Mahkota Square, 75000 Melaka, Malaysia, 06 2862201, Fax: 06 2862202, Pracitsing as a Sole Proprietor, and Member Malaysia, Call Date: July 1997 (Lincoln's Inn) Qualifications: LLB (Hons)

Goddard *David John*
Chapman Tripp Sheffield Young, Barristers & Solicitors, P O Box 993, Wellington, 64 4 499 5999, Fax: 64 4 472 7111, Barrister & Solicitor of the High Court of New Zealand, Call Date: July 1988 (Lincoln's Inn) Qualifications: BA (Hons) (Victoria), BA (Oxon)

Goddard *Peter Andrew George*
ATC Trustees (BVI) Limited, P O Box 933, Road Town Tortola, British West Indies, (809) 494 6122, Fax: (809) 494 6124, Managing Director of ATC Trustees (BVI) Limited, Formerly a solicitor, Call Date: Nov 1987 (Middle Temple) Qualifications: LLB (Wales)

Goh *Boon Yee*
Malaysia, Call Date: July 1996 (Middle Temple) Qualifications: LLB (Hons) (Lond)

Goh *Choon Hian Leonard*
Call Date: July 1991 (Lincoln's Inn) Qualifications: BA (Hons) (Cambs)

Goh *Miss Christina Choy Boon*
Block 7, Teck Whye Ave [H]04-102, Singapore 680007, Singapore 2368, 7647753, Call Date: July 1995 (Middle Temple) Qualifications: LLB (Hons) (Lond), BSC (Est Mg+) (Hons)

Goh *Chuan Huat*
Singapore 548443, Call Date: July 1996 (Middle Temple) Qualifications: LLB (Hons) (Lond)

Goh *Gavin Soon Chye*
Singapore 650216, Call Date: July 1998
(Lincoln's Inn) Qualifications: LLB
(Buck'ham)

Goh *Hoon Huar*
Malaysia, Call Date: July 1996 (Middle
Temple) Qualifications: LLB
(Hons)(Notts)

Goh *Miss Hui Nee*
Singapore 2264, Call Date: Nov 1996
(Lincoln's Inn) Qualifications: BA
(Hons)(Keele)

Goh *Miss Joan Penn Nee*
Malaysia, Call Date: July 1996
(Lincoln's Inn) Qualifications: LLB
(Hons)(Wales)

Goh *Miss Justine Soo Hsien*
Malaysia, Call Date: Nov 1997 (Gray's
Inn) Qualifications: LLB (LSE)

Goh *Kien Ping*
Lot 864, 1st Floor, Jalan Permaisuri,
98000 Miri, Malaysia, 085 437600/
438600, Fax: 085 439600, Managing
Pertner of Ting Goh & Associates, and
Member Malaysia, Call Date: Nov 1993
(Lincoln's Inn) Qualifications: LLB
(Hons)

Goh *Laurence Eng Yau*
47 Saraca Road, Singapore 807392,
Republic of Singapore, Singapore
807392, 4822285/ 3240727, Fax:
4841060/ 3240703, Legal Advisor,
Company Secretary, Advocate &
Solicitor, Singapore and Member
Singapore Bar, Call Date: July 1989
(Lincoln's Inn) Qualifications: LLB
(Hons)(Lond)

Goh *Miss Li Peen*
546 Ang Mo Kio Avenue 10,
[H]03-2252, Singapore 560546,
Singapore 560546, 65 4578225, and
Member Singapore Bar, Call Date: July
1994 (Gray's Inn) Qualifications: LLB
(Lond)

Goh *Miss Li Yen*
17 Thomson View, Singapore 2057,
Singapore 2057, (65) 455 4883,
Associate, and Member Singapore Bar,
Call Date: July 1994 (Middle Temple)
Qualifications: BA (Hons)(Oxon)

Goh *Miss Maxine Whui Min*
West Malaysia, Call Date: Nov 1995
(Middle Temple) Qualifications: LLB
(Hons)(Hull)

Goh *Miss Pricilla May Lih*
2175-J Taman Tunku Habsah, 05100,
Alor Setar, Kedah, Malaysia, 04
7317154, Fax: 04 7311375, Legal
Assistant, and Member Malaysia Bar,
Call Date: July 1995 (Lincoln's Inn)
Qualifications: LLB (Hons)

Goh *Miss Sen Fong*
Malaysia, Call Date: July 1995
(Lincoln's Inn) Qualifications: BA
(Hons)

Goh *Seng Leong Christopher*
Harry Elias & Partners, 9 Raffles Place,
[H]12-00 Republic Plaza, Singapore
298265, 535 0550, Fax: 438 0550, and
Member Singapore, Call Date: July
1996 (Middle Temple) Qualifications:
LLB (Hons)(Lond)

Goh *Miss Susan Hui San*
Singapore 598435, Call Date: July 1992
(Lincoln's Inn) Qualifications: LLB
(Hons)(Notts)

Goh *Miss Swee Hua Phylina*
Singapore 576472, Call Date: July 1997
(Middle Temple) Qualifications: LLB
(Hons)(Lond)

Goh *Miss Yolande Hui Lynn*
Singapore 468337, Call Date: July 1996
(Lincoln's Inn) Qualifications: LLB
(Hons)

Goins *Ms Debra Lynn*
Bermuda Monetary Authority, Burnaby
House, 26 Burnaby Street, Hamilton,
SN01 Bermuda, 441 295 5278, Fax:
441 292 7471, Legal Analyst, and
Member Bermuda, Call Date: Nov 1996
(Inner Temple) Qualifications: LLB
(Lond)

Golamaully *Abdus Samad*
Mauritius, Call Date: Nov 1995
(Lincoln's Inn) Qualifications: LLB
(Hons)

Goldie *Gainneos Jacob*
Messrs Yusoff Shamsuddin &, Partners,
5th Floor, Straits Trading, Building No
4 Lebow Pasar, Besar 50050, Kuala
Lumpur Malaysia, Malaysia, 03
2938244, Fax: 03 2938381, and
Member Malaysia Bar, Call Date: Nov
1992 (Middle Temple) Qualifications:
LLB (Hons)

Golding *Ms Jane Lindsey*
Taylor Joynson Garrett, Rue Montoyer
14, B-1000 Brussels, Italy, 00 322 514
0402, Fax: 00 322 514 0088, Call Date:
Nov 1989 (Lincoln's Inn)
Qualifications: LLB (Lond), Maitrise
(Paris)

Goldsmith *Immanuel*
Smart & Biggar, 438 University Avenue,
Suite 1500, Box 111, Toronto, Ontario
M5G 2K8, Canada M4V 2L1, 416 593
5514, Fax: 416 591 1690, QC Canada,
and Member Ontario Bar, Call Date:
Jan 1950 (Middle Temple)
Qualifications: LLB

Gollop *Advocate Julian Clive*
Crills, PO Box 72, 44 Esplanade, St
Helier, Jersey, C I JE4 8PN, Channel
Islands, 01534 611055, Fax: 01534
611066, Advocate Royal Ct Jersey &
Crown Advocate, Call Date: July 1983
(Gray's Inn) Qualifications: BA (Hons)

Golt *Miss Samantha Noelle*
Gibraltar, Call Date: Nov 1998 (Middle
Temple) Qualifications: LLB
(Hons)(Kent)

Gomez *Miss Monique Vanessa Ann*
Office of Attorney General, 4th, 5th &
6th Floors, Post Office Building, East
Hill Street,P.O.Box N3007, Nassau, N.P.
Bahamas, Bahamas, 809 32221141,
Fax: 809 3222555, and Member
Bahamas Bar, Call Date: July 1988
(Lincoln's Inn) Qualifications: LLB
(Hons) (Lond)

Gomez *Miss Tracy Donna*
West Malaysia, Call Date: July 1998
(Inner Temple) Qualifications: LLB
(Newcastle Upon, Tyne)

Goncalves *Miss Elaine Laura*
Isola & Isola, Suite 23, Portland House,
Glacis Road, Gibraltar, 78363, Fax:
78699, and Member Gibraltar Bar, Call
Date: Nov 1995 (Middle Temple)
Qualifications: LLB (Hons)

Gong *Chin Nam*
Singapore 1026, Call Date: July 1995
(Middle Temple) Qualifications: LLB
(Hons) (Hull)

Gonsalves-Sabola *Miss Mary Margaret*
McKinney, Bancroft & Hughes, Counsel
& Attorneys-at-Law, PO Box N-3937, No
4 George Street, Mareva House Nassau,
Bahamas, (242) 322 4195, Fax: (242)
328 2520, Registered Associate,
McKinney Bancroft & Hughes, Nassau,
Bahamas, and Member Jamaica,
Antigua & Barbuda Bars, Call Date: Nov
1994 (Gray's Inn) Qualifications: LLB,
LLM

Goodwill *John Francis*
Schwarzerdweg, Postfach 67, 9204
Andwil, Switzerland, Also Inn of Court
G, Call Date: Nov 1974 (Lincoln's Inn)
Qualifications: MA (Hons)(Oxon)

Gooi *Hsiao-Leung*
Malaysia, Call Date: July 1995
(Lincoln's Inn) Qualifications: LLB
(Hons)

Gopalakrishnan *Dinagaran*
Singapore 2057, Call Date: Nov 1996
(Lincoln's Inn) Qualifications: LLB
(Hons)(Lond)

Gordon *Miss Veronica Tamae*
Bermuda, Call Date: Nov 1998 (Gray's
Inn) Qualifications: LLB, LLM (Bucks)

Gour *Miss Bharati*
Singapore 570101, Call Date: July 1996
(Lincoln's Inn) Qualifications: LLB
(Hons)(Lond)

Gouthro *William Christopher*
McKinney, Bancroft, & Hughes,
Chambers, Mareva House, 4 George
Street, P.O.Box N3937 Nassau,
Bahamas, 809 322 4195, Fax: 809 356
2713, Associate, and Member
Bahamas, Call Date: July 1996 (Middle
Temple) Qualifications: LLB
(Hons)(Lond)

Govindan *Sathees Kumar*
Malaysia, Call Date: July 1996
(Lincoln's Inn) Qualifications: LLB
(Hons)(E.Lond)

Gowings *James Richard Humphrey*
France, Call Date: Nov 1973 (Lincoln's Inn) Qualifications: MA (Oxon)

Goyder *Miss Joanna Ruth*
Linklaters & Alliance, Rue Brederode 13A, 1000 Brussels, 32 2 505 0211, Fax: 32 2 502 2644, Barrister working for Linklaters & Alliance,Brussels, and Member Flemish Bar of Brussels, Call Date: Nov 1987 (Lincoln's Inn) Qualifications: MA (Cantab), Licence Speciale, (Brussels), LLM (Florence)

Gracie *Malcolm Reeves*
12th Floor, Wentworth Chambers, 180 Phillip Street, Sydney, New South Wales 2000, 61 29 232 4293, Fax: 61 29 221 7183, and Member New South Wales, Victoria, Queensland, Northern Territory, Australian Capital Territory. New South Wales Bar, Call Date: July 1992 (Lincoln's Inn) Qualifications: BA, LLB (Hons)

Graham *Sir Peter*
Le Petit Chateau, La Vallette, 87190 Magnac Level, Consultant to J Hassan & Partners, Gibraltar, Also Inn of Court L, Call Date: June 1958 (Gray's Inn) Qualifications: MA, LLM (Cantab)

Grant *Professor Alan*
Fraser Grant Associates, P O Box 275, Eureka, Nova Scotia Bok 1BO, 902-923-2866, Fax: 902-923-2755, Chair, First Nations Resources Negotiations Ontario, and Member Ontario Bar, Call Date: Nov 1970 (Inner Temple) Qualifications: LLB (Lond)

Granville *Steven James*
Chambers Defoe S.L, Avda Severo Ochoa 28, Edificio Marina Marbella 6-A, 29600 Marbella, (34) 952820339, Fax: (34) 952821114, Call Date: Nov 1991 (Gray's Inn) Qualifications: LLB (Leics)

Greaves *David William*
SITA, 26 Chemin de Joinville, 1216 Cointrin, Geneva, 41.22.710.0112, Fax: 41.22.710.0166, Legal Counsel, Call Date: Feb 1990 (Gray's Inn) Qualifications: LLB (So'ton)

Grech *Miss Maria Penelope Christine*
Gibraltar, Call Date: July 1996 (Inner Temple) Qualifications: LLB (Wolverhampton)

Green *Miss Carol Laura Nancy*
Mauritius, Call Date: Nov 1994 (Lincoln's Inn) Qualifications: LLB (Hons)(Bucks)

Green *Jason Brian*
Advocates Collas Day & Rowland, Manor Place, St Peter Port, Guernsey GY1 4EW, Channel Islands, 01481 723191, Fax: 01481 711880, and Member Guernsey Bar, Call Date: July 1996 (Inner Temple) Qualifications: LLB (W.Eng)

Green *Mrs Karen Patricia*
Box 1460, Mendocino, CA 95460, U.S.A., United States of America, 707 937 3960, Fax: 707 937 5861, and Member California, USA, Call Date: May 1990 (Middle Temple) Qualifications: LLB (Cardiff)

Greenidge *Douglas Burton*
Bonnetts, Brittons Hill, St Michael, Barbados, Barbados, 4360001, Attorney-at-Law, Barbados and the West Indies, and Member Barbados Bar Association, Call Date: Nov 1982 (Gray's Inn) Qualifications: LLB (Lond)

Grierson *Robert James*
Messrs Maples & Calder, Ugland House, P O Box 309GT, South Church Street, George Town, Cayman Islands, British West Indies, 1 345 949 8066, Fax: 1 345 949 8080. Also Inn of Court L and Member Cayman Islands, Call Date: Oct 1991 (Middle Temple) Qualifications: MA, LLM (Cantab)

Griffiths *Miss Dawn Christine*
Conyers Dill & Pearman, Clarendon House, Church Street, Hamilton HM 11, (441) 295 1422, Fax: (441) 292 4720, Associate, and Member Bermuda Bar, Call Date: May 1995 (Lincoln's Inn) Qualifications: LLB (Hons)

Griffiths *John Calvert*
Des Voeux Chambers, 10/F Bank of East Asia Bldg, 10 Des Voeux Road Central, 2526-3071, Fax: 2810-5287, Recorder, and Member Brunei Bars Hong Kong Bar Brick Court Chambers, 7-8 Essex Street, London, WC2R 3LD, Call Date: June 1956 (Middle Temple) Qualifications: MA (Cantab)

Grohs *Miss Sibylle Dietlinde*
Brussels, Call Date: Feb 1993 (Middle Temple) Qualifications: LLB (Hons)(Lond)

Gross *Richard Stephen*
Kibbutz, GVAT, Israel, 972 5 1234 349, Part time Chairman of Tribunal Company Secretary, Legal Advisor, Mediator, and Member Israel, Call Date: Oct 1992 (Middle Temple) Qualifications: LL.B (Hons)

Ground *The Hon Mr Justice Richard William*
The Chief Justice, Courts Office, Grand Turk, Turks & Caicos Islands, (649) 946 2114, Fax: (649) 946 2720, Chief Justice, QC Cayman Islands and Member Turks & Caicos Islands, Call Date: July 1975 (Gray's Inn) Qualifications: BA (Oxon)

Guch *Miss Karen Anne*
Wong and Partners, Faber Imperial Court, Suite 12-A, Jalan Sultan Ismail, 50250 Kuala Lumpur, Malaysia, 00 603 2558596/4011888, Fax: 00 603 2555673/4603880, and Member Malaysia, Call Date: Nov 1996 (Lincoln's Inn) Qualifications: LLB (Hons)(Lond), LLM (Hons)(Cantab)

Guha Thakurta *Sujoy*
Singapore 579361, Call Date: Nov 1996 (Middle Temple) Qualifications: LLB (Hons)(Hull)

Gujadhur *Anand Kumar*
Morcellement, GIDC, Floreal, Indian Ocean, (00230) 6860080, Call Date: July 1998 (Middle Temple) Qualifications: LLB (Hons)(Wales)

Gunasekera *Miss Kuda Liyanage Don Manuja*
286 Bullers Road, Colombo 7, Sri Lanka, Sri Lanka, 716011, Call Date: Feb 1994 (Lincoln's Inn) Qualifications: LLB (Hons), LLM, Dip Business , Administration

Gupta *Ranadhir*
Singapore 510579, Call Date: Nov 1998 (Lincoln's Inn) Qualifications: LLB (Hons)(Lond)

Guttman *Professor Egon*
930 Clintwood Drive,, Silver Spring, Maryland, 20902, USA, United States of America, 301 649 5739/202 274 4213, Fax: 202 274 4130, American University Washington US Dept of State Advisory Com. on Private International Law. American Law Institute. American Bar Association. American Federal Bar Association., Call Date: May 1952 (Middle Temple) Qualifications: LLM

Gwee *Boon Kim*
11 Lothian Terrace, Singapore 456784, Republic of Singapore, Singapore 456784, 4424652, and Member Singapore Bar, Call Date: July 1994 (Middle Temple) Qualifications: LLB (Hons)(L'pool)

Haberbeck *Andreas*
Abbas F.Ghazzawi Law Firm, P.O.Box 2335, Jeddah 21451, 966 2 6654646, Fax: 966 2 6659155, Call Date: Nov 1981 (Gray's Inn) Qualifications: LLB, LLM

Hadjimanoli *Miss Marina*
P O Box 1358, Limassol, Cyprus, 05-587535, Fax: 05-584072, Lawyer, and Member Cyprus Bar, Call Date: Nov 1995 (Lincoln's Inn) Qualifications: LLB (Hons)

Hadjipetrou *Leonidas*
Cyprus, 00-357-2-510165/660297, Fax: 00-357-2-510181, and Member Cyprus Bar, Call Date: Nov 1995 (Lincoln's Inn) Qualifications: LLB (Hons), LLM (Lond)

Haines *Michael John*
6 Priory Farm, Inner Road, St Clements, Jersey JE2 6GP, Channel Islands, 01534 854412, Call Date: July 1995 (Gray's Inn) Qualifications: LLB

Hajamaideen *Shamim Fyaz Bin*
Malaysia, Call Date: July 1997 (Middle Temple) Qualifications: LLB (Hons)

F

Hajarnis *Miss Aditi*
Seychelles, Call Date: July 1995
(Lincoln's Inn) Qualifications: LLB
(Hons)

Haji Abdul Hamid *Muhammad Zainidi*
Brunei, and Member Brunei Bar, Call
Date: July 1996 (Lincoln's Inn)
Qualifications: LLB (Hons) (Manch)

Haji Anuar *Fathan*
Attorney General's Chambers, Ministry
of Law, Bandar Seri Begawan, Brunei
2690, 2690 Brunei, (6732) 244872,
Fax: (6732) 223100, Legal Counsel,
Call Date: July 1995 (Lincoln's Inn)
Qualifications: LLB (Hons)

Haji Ismail *Miss Norismizan*
Darussalam, Call Date: Nov 1996
(Lincoln's Inn) Qualifications: LLB
(Hons)

Haji Mohammed *Miss Mazlin Haslinda*
Malaysia, Call Date: Nov 1995
(Lincoln's Inn) Qualifications: LLB
(Hons)

Haji Sahlan *Miss Shahida*
Malaysia, Call Date: Nov 1995
(Lincoln's Inn) Qualifications: LLB
(Hons)

Hakimi *Miss Hasrina*
Malaysia, Call Date: Oct 1997 (Gray's
Inn) Qualifications: LLB (Notts)

Halliday *David Ross*
Northern Ireland, Call Date: Mar 1996
(Inner Temple) Qualifications: LLB
(Wolverhampton)

Hamon *Francis Charles*
La Maison Du Sud, Rue De La Piece
Mauger, Trinity, Jersey JE3 5HW, 01534
863199, Deputy Bailiff Royal Court of
Jersey, and Member Jersey, Call Date:
Nov 1966 (Middle Temple)

Hampson *Graham William*
c/o Quin & Hampson, Barristers &
Attorneys at Law, PO Box 1348
Georgetown, Grand Cayman, Cayman
Islands, British West Indies, 809
9494123, Fax: 809 9494647, Former
solicitor and Member Cayman Islands
Bar, Call Date: Feb 1992 (Middle
Temple) Qualifications: LLB (Hon)
(Notts)

Hamzah *Miss Hanim*
Malaysia, Call Date: July 1998
(Lincoln's Inn) Qualifications: LLB
(Hons) (Sheff)

Hamzah *Miss Hazleena*
Malaysia, Call Date: Nov 1996
(Lincoln's Inn) Qualifications: LLB
(Hons) (Bris)

Han *Miss Chin June*
Malaysia, Call Date: Mar 1997
(Lincoln's Inn) Qualifications: BSc
(Hons), CPE

Han *Miss Chin May*
Malaysia, Call Date: July 1996
(Lincoln's Inn) Qualifications: LLB
(Hons) (Sheff)

Han *Hean Juan*
Singapore 140165, Call Date: July 1996
(Inner Temple) Qualifications: LLB
(Lond)

Han *Teck Kwong*
Singapore 2776, Call Date: July 1995
(Middle Temple) Qualifications: LLB
(Hons)

Hanam *Andrew John*
Blk 350, Woodlands Ave 3, 11-99, Call
Date: Nov 1996 (Middle Temple)
Qualifications: LLB (Hons)

Handmaker *Jeffrey David*
Lawyers for Human Rights, 730 Van
Erkom Bldg, 217 Pretorius St, Pretoria
0002, United States of America, +27
12 21 21 35, Fax: +27 12 32 56 318,
Call Date: July 1995 (Inner Temple)
Qualifications: LLB (Newc), LLM
(Lond)

Hangchi *Kevin*
Singapore 266812, Call Date: July 1997
(Middle Temple) Qualifications: BSc
(Hons)

Haq *Miss Tasneem Rehana*
20 Oei Tiong Ham Park, Singapore
267025, and Member Singapore, Call
Date: Nov 1996 (Middle Temple)
Qualifications: BA (Hons) (Keele)

Haque *Mohammad Aneek Rushd*
Bangladesh, Call Date: Oct 1998
(Gray's Inn) Qualifications: LLB

Haque *Mohammed Azharul*
Bangladesh, Call Date: 1997 (Inner
Temple) Qualifications: B.Com
(Bangladesh), LLB (Lond)

Harben *Paul Ralph*
Crill Canavan, 40 Don Road, St Helier
JE1 4XD, Channel Islands, 01534
601700, Fax: 01534 601702, Jersey
Solicitor, Call Date: Oct 1993 (Middle
Temple) Qualifications: LLB
(Hons) (Kingston)

Harding *Miss Patricia Yvette*
Hodges Chambers, The Valley, P.O.Box
840, Anguilla, 264 497 3793, Fax: 264
497 2863, and Member Anguilla Bar
(Eastern Caribbean States), Call Date:
July 1980 (Middle Temple)
Qualifications: BA

Hariri *Arham Rahimy*
Malaysia, Call Date: Nov 1997
(Lincoln's Inn) Qualifications: LLB
(Hons) (L'pool)

Haris *Mrs Shazlin*
Messrs Shahrizat & Tan, Advocates &
Solicitors, Loteise2, Level 4, Block E
South, Pusat Bandar, Damansara,
50490 Kuala Lumpur, Malaysia, 603
2541755, Fax: 603 2549755, Advocate
& Solicitor, and Member Malaysia, Call
Date: July 1995 (Lincoln's Inn)
Qualifications: LLB (Hons)

Harkins *Mrs Sheila*
Malaysia, Call Date: Nov 1995
(Lincoln's Inn) Qualifications: LLB
(Hons) (Wales)

Haron *Miss Hidayati*
Malaysia, Call Date: Nov 1997
(Lincoln's Inn) Qualifications: LLB
(Hons)

Haron Kamar *Miss Haslinda*
Malaysia, Managing Director, and
Member Malaysia, Call Date: July 1996
(Lincoln's Inn) Qualifications: LLB
(Hons) (Notts)

Haroon *Miss Sony Sadaf*
Bangladesh, Call Date: July 1998
(Lincoln's Inn) Qualifications: LLB
(Hons)

Harraj *Mohammad Raza Hayat*
Pakistan, Call Date: Nov 1995
(Lincoln's Inn) Qualifications: BA
(Hons), LLB (Hons) (Leics)

Harre *Mr George Elliott*
Les Rousses, St Paul Le Jeune, (33)
475 398791, Fax: (33) 475 398513,
Chief Justice (Retired), Call Date: Feb
1954 (Middle Temple) Qualifications:
MA

Harshaw *Paul Andrew*
Suite 349, 48 Par-la-Ville Road,
Hamilton HM 11, Bermuda, +441
295 1422, Fax: +441 292 4720, and
Member Bermuda Bar, Call Date: May
1997 (Lincoln's Inn) Qualifications:
LLB (Hons)

Hart *Timothy George*
Bailhache Labesse, Advocates &
Solicitors, 14/16 Hill Street, St Helier,
Jersey, Channel Islands, 01534 888777,
Fax: 01534 888778, Solicitor, and
Member Jersey Bar, Call Date: Feb
1995 (Gray's Inn) Qualifications: BA
(Oxon)

Harvey *Christopher*
Russell & DuMoulin, 2100-1075 W
Georgia St, Vancouver V6E 3G2, 604
631 4822, Fax: 604 631 3232, QC
British Columbia Bar and Member
British Columbia Bar, Call Date: July
1968 (Middle Temple) Qualifications:
BA (Mcgill), Dip Law, LLM, PhD (Lond)

Hasan *Mohammed Ziaul*
Bangladesh, Call Date: Mar 1997
(Gray's Inn) Qualifications: LLB (Lond)

Hashim *Miss Zaheera*
M/S Haq & Namazie Partnership, 20
Cecil Street, [H]22-03, Singapore 1545,
(65) 4386604, Fax: (65) 4387383,
Legal Assistant, and Member Singapore
Bar, Call Date: July 1995 (Middle
Temple) Qualifications: LLB (Hons),
BA

F

Haskins *Mrs Felicity Jane*
F Haskins & Co, College Chambers, 3 St James' Street, St Peter Port, Guernsey, Channel Islands, 01481 721316, Fax: 01481 721317, Partner, Advocate of Royal Court of Guernsey, Call Date: Nov 1989 (Inner Temple) Qualifications: LLB (Lond)

Hassan *Miss Haslina*
Malaysia, Call Date: July 1995 (Middle Temple) Qualifications: LLB (Hons) (Kent)

Hassett *Professor Patricia*
Syracuse College of Law, Syracuse, New York 13244, United States of America, 315 443 2535, Fax: 315 443 4141, US Supreme Court and Member New York Bar, Call Date: Nov 1992 (Inner Temple) Qualifications: BA, LLB, LLM , Proff at Law

Hatfield-Hadjiioannou *Mrs Ruth Elizabeth*
Christos M Georgiades &, Telemachos M Georgiades Advoc., 22 25th March Street, P.O.Box 85, Paphos, and Member Cyprus Bar, Call Date: Nov 1986 (Gray's Inn) Qualifications: LLB (Nott'm)

Hawa *Miss Nayla*
Al Tamimi & Company, P.O.Box 9275, Dubai, United Arab Emirates, 009714 317090, Fax: 009714 3613177, Call Date: Oct 1994 (Middle Temple) Qualifications: LLB (Hons) (Lond)

Healy *John Pascal*
Tara, Waterfall Road, Bishoptown, Cork, 353 21 371562, Fax: 353 21 371562, Arbitrator, Kings Inn, Dublin and Member Southern Ireland Bar, Call Date: Feb 1982 (Middle Temple) Qualifications: ACIArb

Hee *Miss Cher Sun*
7 Jalan Cahaya 6, Taman Salak Selatan, 57100 Kuala Lumpur, Malaysia, (603) 957 3693, Fax: (603) 957 3695, Call Date: July 1995 (Middle Temple) Qualifications: LLB (Hons)

Helfrecht *William John*
Boxalls, CIBC Financial Centre, P O Box 1234, George Town, Grand Cayman, Cayman Islands, (345) 949 9876, Fax: (345) 949 9877, Partner (Litigation), and Member Cayman Islands, Call Date: Nov 1978 (Middle Temple) Qualifications: MA (Oxon)

Hellman *Stephen Geoffrey*
Paget-Brown, Quin & Hampson, Harbour Centre, Third Floor, P.O.Box 1348, Grand Cayman, Cayman Islands, 00 1 809 949 4123, Fax: 00 1 809 949 4647, Call Date: July 1988 (Inner Temple) Qualifications: BA (Oxon), Dip Law

Heng *Clive Boon Howe*
17 Leedon Road, Wilmer Park, 3244 553, Fax: 65 3244 552, Managing Director of an Investment Holding Company, and Member Singapore Bar, Call Date: July 1976 (Lincoln's Inn) Qualifications: LLB (Hons) (Lond)

Heng *Hui Tek*
Heng & Co, 1 Colombo Court, [H]09-06B, Singapore 1026, 336 0800, Fax: 334 6678, Commissioner for Oaths, Advocate & Solicitor, Singapore and Member Singapore Bar, Call Date: July 1984 (Lincoln's Inn) Qualifications: LLB (Warwick) M.Phil (Cantab)

Hernandez *Christian*
Gibraltar, Call Date: Nov 1995 (Middle Temple) Qualifications: LLB (Hons)

Hesse-Djabatey *Mrs Leonora Akousa Kwakua*
P.O.Box 128, Tradefair Site, Accra, Ghana, 665915, and Member Ghana, Call Date: Nov 1988 (Gray's Inn) Qualifications: LLB (Lond)

Hiew *Miss Fatimah Yen Won*
Malaysia, Call Date: Mar 1998 (Lincoln's Inn) Qualifications: LLB (Hons)

Higgs *Conrad Clephane*
South School Lane, Back Salina, Grand Turk, Turks & Caicos Islands, British West Indies, (809) 946 1320, and Member Turks & Caicos Bar, Call Date: Nov 1995 (Middle Temple) Qualifications: BA (Hons) (W.Indies), MSc (B'ham)

Hingorani *Jeevan*
Pacific Chambers, 1301 Dina House, 11 Duddell Street, Central, 521 5544, Fax: 524 5912, and Member West Indies Bar, Call Date: Feb 1977 (Gray's Inn) Qualifications: BA (Hons)

Hirst *Alastair John*
72 Northumberland Street, Edinburgh EH3 6JG, Scotland, 031 556 5324, Fax: 031 557 5338, Arbitrator, and Member Sultanate of Oman, Call Date: Nov 1971 (Inner Temple) Qualifications: MA (Cantab), FCIArb

Hj Mat *Yaackub*
Batu 34, Kampong Baru Myalas, 77100 Asahan, Melaka, Malaysia, 06-5229689, Legal Advisor, Call Date: Mar 1997 (Lincoln's Inn) Qualifications: LLB (Hons), LLM (Wales)

Hj Md Noor *Zulkhairi*
Brunei, Call Date: Nov 1996 (Lincoln's Inn) Qualifications: LLB (Hons)

Ho *Ms Adaline See Yin*
Singapore 360012, 2805759 (Home), and Member Singapore, Call Date: July 1997 (Inner Temple) Qualifications: LLB (Lond)

Ho *Kam Tim*
Hong Kong, Call Date: Nov 1993 (Lincoln's Inn) Qualifications: LLB (Hons, Lond)

Ho *Kenneth Boon Kuan*
Singapore 428319, Call Date: July 1996 (Lincoln's Inn) Qualifications: LLB (Hons) (Notts)

Ho *Miss Kim Foong*
Sim Hill Tan & Wong, 4 Shenton Way, 14-07/12, Shing Kwan House, Singapore 0106, Singapore 2057, 65 2200035, Fax: 65 2240693, and Member Singapore Bar, Call Date: July 1994 (Middle Temple) Qualifications: BA (Hons) (Keele)

Ho *Miss Mary May Ling*
Malaysia, Call Date: July 1998 (Lincoln's Inn) Qualifications: LLB (Hons)

Ho *Sammy Wai Chuen*
16/F, Malahon Centre, 10-12 Stanley Street, Central, Hong Kong, (852) 2522 7330/9677 6077, Fax: (852) 2801 4729, and Member Hong Kong, Call Date: Nov 1997 (Inner Temple) Qualifications: BSc (Hong Kong), LLB (Lond)

Ho *Shi King*
Hong Kong, Call Date: Oct 1996 (Middle Temple) Qualifications: LLB (Hons)

Ho *Thiam Huat*
Singapore 550135, Call Date: Nov 1998 (Middle Temple) Qualifications: LLB (Hons) (Wolves)

Hock *Lee Kay*
Malaysia, Call Date: July 1991 (Gray's Inn) Qualifications: B.Soc.Sci (Keele)

Hodder *Andrew Charles*
France, Call Date: Oct 1997 (Gray's Inn) Qualifications: LLB (Wales), MBA (Lond)

Hoe *Cheah Seng*
Malaysia, Legal Assistant, and Member Malaysia, Call Date: Nov 1996 (Lincoln's Inn) Qualifications: LLB (Hons) (Sheff)

Hoe *Miss Chee May*
Singapore 436668, Call Date: July 1997 (Middle Temple) Qualifications: LLB (Hons), LLM, (L'pool)

Hoh *Miss Gigi Anne*
Singapore 1543, 3451308, Fax: 3451182, Call Date: July 1995 (Middle Temple) Qualifications: LLB (Hons)

Holmback *Dr Ulf Aake Olof*
Svartmangatan 27, S-111 29 Stockholm, 0046 8218129, and Member Sweden Bar, Call Date: July 1979 (Gray's Inn) Qualifications: JUR DR (Uppsala)

Holmberg *Miss Loretta Vanessa*
Singapore 120325, Call Date: July 1996 (Middle Temple) Qualifications: LLB (Hons) (Wales)

Hon *Chi Keung*
Hong Kong, Call Date: Nov 1994 (Middle Temple) Qualifications: LLB (Hons)

F

Hon *Omar Adam*
12 Lorong Dungun, Damansara
Heights, 50490, Kuala Lumpur,
Malaysia, 603-2530078, Fax:
603-2541750, Legal Assistant, Advocate
& Solicitor and Member Malaysia Bar,
Call Date: Nov 1996 (Middle Temple)
Qualifications: LLB (Hons)

Hong *Aeron Yea Chun*
Malaysia, (60) 3 7743063, and Member
Malaysian Bar, Call Date: Oct 1995
(Middle Temple) Qualifications: LLB
(Hons)

Hoo *Alan*
16th Floor, Malahon Centre, 10-12
Stanley Street, Central, 852-28686155,
Fax: 852-28106795, Queen's Counsel
in Hong Kong and Member Hong Kong
Bar, Call Date: Nov 1973 (Middle
Temple) Qualifications: LLB (Lond)

Hoo *Miss Lina*
Malaysia, Call Date: Nov 1997
(Lincoln's Inn) Qualifications: LLB
(Hons) (L'pool)

Hoo *Miss Sheau Peng*
Singapore 1953, Call Date: Oct 1993
(Middle Temple) Qualifications: BA
(Hons)

Hoosen *Abdul Aziz*
South China Chambers, 904 Tower
Two, Lippo Centre, 89 Queensway,
2528 2378, Fax: 2520 1512, and
Member Hong Kong Bar, Call Date: Nov
1974 (Gray's Inn) Qualifications: BA
(McGill)

Horne *Miss Zhinga Arlette*
Phillips & Williams, Middle Street, P O
Box 262, St Vincent, West Indies, (784)
456 1390, Fax: (784) 456 2344, Legal
Advisor, and Member St Vincent & the
Grenadines Bar, Call Date: Oct 1995
(Middle Temple) Qualifications: LLB
(Hons), LLM (Cantab), LLM
(IMLI,Malta)

Horspool *Anthony Bernard Graeme*
Hardwicke Building, New Square,
Lincoln's Inn, London, WC2A 3SB, Call
Date: Nov 1991 (Middle Temple)
Qualifications: MA Hons (Oxon), Dip
Law

Horton-Strachan *Mrs Arlean Patricia*
Bahamas, Call Date: Nov 1995 (Gray's
Inn) Qualifications: BSc (W.Indies),
LLB (Lond)

Hosein *Faarees Fayaz*
39 Richmond Street, PO Box 1003, Port
of Spain, Trinidad W.I., West Indies,
623-2695/8303, Fax: 623-8303,
Attorney-at-Law, Supreme Court of
Trinidad & Tobago (Admitted October
1988), Attorney-at-Law, Supreme Court
of Barbados (Admitted May 1991), Call
Date: July 1988 (Lincoln's Inn)
Qualifications: LLB (Hons) (Dundee)

Hoskins *Nicholas John*
46 Par-La-Ville Road, Hamilton HM11,
Bermuda, Bermuda, (441) 296 0253,
Fax: (441) 296 0809, and Member
Bermuda, Call Date: Nov 1992 (Middle
Temple) Qualifications: LLB (Hons,
Bucks)

Hossain *Ms Lolita Lamis*
P.O.Drawer 1734, Atlanta, GA 30301,
and Member New York, Dhaka, Call
Date: July 1997 (Lincoln's Inn)
Qualifications: LLB (Hons) (LSE), LLM
(Harvard)

Houghton *Anthony Kenneth*
Des Voeux Chambers, 10/F Bank of
East Asia Bldg, 10 Des Voeux Road
Central, Hong Kong, 2526-3071, Fax:
2810 5287/5309/0274, and Member
Hong Kong Bar, Call Date: Nov 1988
(Gray's Inn) Qualifications: LLB
(Lond), ARICS, AHKIS,FCI Arb

Hourican *James Kevin*
District Attorney Office, Los Angeles
County, 18000 Criminal Courts
Building, 210 West Temple Street, Los
Angeles CA 90012, United States of
America, 011 1 818 5003593, Fax: 011
1 818 548 1392, Deputy District
Attorney, Los Angeles County,
California USA., Major, United States
Marine Corps Reserve and Member
Pennsylvania Bar California Bar, Call
Date: Feb 1994 (Gray's Inn)
Qualifications: BA JD (Pittsburgh)

How *Chi Hoong Nicholas*
Singapore 328105, Call Date: July 1996
(Middle Temple) Qualifications: LLB
(Hons) (Bris)

How *Miss Su Fen*
Malaysia, Call Date: July 1997
(Lincoln's Inn) Qualifications: LLB
(Hons) (Wales), LLM (Lond)

Howard *Nicholas William*
Gibraltar, Call Date: Oct 1998
(Lincoln's Inn) Qualifications: LLB
(Hons) (Leeds)

Howell *Lt Col David Malcom*
Hong Kong, Chief Military Legal Advisor
GOC Hong Kong, Call Date: July 1973
(Lincoln's Inn) Qualifications: LLB
(Hons)

Huang *Miss Lianne*
JP Morgan, 259660 Singapore, (65)
320 9243, Investment Banker, Call
Date: July 1997 (Gray's Inn)
Qualifications: LLB (Bristol)

Huggins *Adrian Armstrong*
Temple Chambers, 16th Floor, One
Pacific Place, 88 Queensway, 852 2523
2003, Fax: 852 2523 6343, QC (Hong
Kong) and Member Hong Kong Bar,
Call Date: Nov 1975 (Gray's Inn)
Qualifications: MA (Cantab), LLM

Hughes *Jonathan Patrick*
Solomon, Zauderer, Ellenhorn,, Frisher
& Sharp, 45 Rockefeller Plaza, New
York, NY 10111, (212) 424 0728, Fax:
(212) 956 4068, Partner, and Member
New York Bar, Call Date: Nov 1983
(Middle Temple) Qualifications: LLB
(Sheff)

Hughes *Mrs Julie*
Channel Islands, Call Date: July 1998
(Lincoln's Inn) Qualifications: BA
(Hons) (Manch), LLB (Hons) (Lond)

Hughes Ferrari *Mrs Margaret Hazell*
Hughes & Cummings, P.O. Box 32,
Saint Vincent & The Grenadines, 809
456 1954/1711, Fax: 809 457 2768,
and Member Saint Vincent and The
Grenadines Bar, Call Date: July 1990
(Lincoln's Inn) Qualifications: LLB
(Lond)

Hui *Wai Chun Sammy*
1318 Princes Building, Chater Road,
Central, Hong Kong, 2526 8128, Fax:
2526 8500, and Member Hong Kong
Bar, Call Date: July 1991 (Lincoln's
Inn) Qualifications: LLB (Hons)

Hui *Miss Ying Ying*
Hong Kong, Call Date: Nov 1996 (Gray's
Inn) Qualifications: LLB

Humphreys *Gordon David Thomas*
21 Boulevard Pierre Dupont, L-1430
Luxembourg, Luxembourg, 352 44 65
64, Fax: 352 44 65 64, and Member
Belgium Bar, Call Date: Nov 1986
(Middle Temple) Qualifications: LLB
(Bucks), LLM (UWIST), Licence
speciale en , droit Economique, (Univ
de Liege)

Hung *Miss Veron Mei-Ying*
Hong Kong, and Member New York,
Call Date: July 1998 (Middle Temple)
Qualifications: LLB (Hons) (HongKong),
LLM (America)

Huq *Faheemul*
Huq & Company, 47/1 Purana Paltan,
Dhaka, Bangladesh, 880-2-955-5953/
880-2-955-2196, Fax: 880-2-956-2434,
Advocate, Supreme Court of Bagladesh
Bangladesh Supreme Court Bar
Association, Call Date: Nov 1997
(Lincoln's Inn) Qualifications: LLB
(Hons) , (Wolverhampton) &,
(Dhaka,Bangladesh)

Huq *Rafique-ul*
Huq & Company, 47/1 Purana Paltan,
Dhaka, Bangladesh, 880 2 955 5953/
880 2 955 2196, Fax: 880 2 956 2434,
Head of Chambers, Senior Advocate,
Supreme Court of Bangladesh and
Member Bangladesh Supreme Court
Bar Association, Call Date: Nov 1962
(Lincoln's Inn) Qualifications: MA, LLB

Hurhangee *Ashley*
Mauritius, Call Date: Mar 1997
(Lincoln's Inn) Qualifications: LLB
(Hons)

Husain *Rehan*
Bangladesh, Call Date: Nov 1996
(Lincoln's Inn) Qualifications: LLB
(Hons) (Leeds)

Hussain *Miss Dheena*
Republic of Maldives, Call Date: July
1997 (Lincoln's Inn) Qualifications:
LLB (Hons)

Hutton *Miss Louise Mary*
Northern Ireland, Call Date: Oct 1998
(Inner Temple) Qualifications: BA
(Oxon)

Iacovides *Petros*
Libra Housa, 21 P Catelaris Str, P O Box
5001, Nicosia, Cyprus, Cyprus, 02 46
67 66, Fax: 02 44 87 77, and Member
Cyprus Bar, Call Date: Feb 1994 (Gray's
Inn) Qualifications: B.Soc.Sc (Keele)

Ian *Lim Teck Soon*
Blk 24 (Ruby), Semei Street 1,
[H]05-10, Singapore 529946, (65)
7832080, Call Date: Nov 1997 (Inner
Temple) Qualifications: LLB (Lond),
ACII

Ibbotson *David James*
Bedell & Cristin, Normandy House,
Grenville Street, St Helier, Jersey,
Channel Islands, 814814, Fax: 814815,
Call Date: Mar 1996 (Middle Temple)
Qualifications: LLB (Hons) (Wales)

Ibrahim *Miss Hasnah*
Attorney General's Chambers, Bandar
Seri Begawan, 2016 Negara, Brunei,
Darussalam, Darussalam, Legal
Counselor, DPP at the Attorney
General's Chambers of law, Brunei,
Darussalam, Call Date: July 1994
(Lincoln's Inn) Qualifications: LLB
(Hons)

Ibrahim s/o Mohamed Yakub
Mohamed
Block 3, Toa Payoh Lorong 7, 03-79,
3530784, and Member Singapore Bar,
Call Date: July 1996 (Middle Temple)
Qualifications: LLB (Hons) (Lond)

Idrees *Rasheed*
Haidermota & Co, 303-305 Kashif
Centre, Sharea Faisal, Karachi 75530,
519226/5662589/5133714, Fax:
5662583/58770761, Advocate, and
Member Pakistan Bar, Call Date: Nov
1994 (Inner Temple) Qualifications:
LLB (Lond)

Ioannides *Mrs Eleni*
Chr.Sozou 2, Flat 206, Nicosia, 357 2
473558/ 474533, Fax: 357 2 475692,
and Member Cyprus Bar, Call Date: Nov
1961 (Middle Temple)

Ip *Tak Keung*
603 Ruttonjee House, 11 Duddell
Street, Central, 2868 1249, Fax: 2868
0368, and Member Hong Kong Bar
Singapore Bar Barrister of the
Australian Capital Terrritory Australian
Capital Territory Bar, Call Date: July
1985 (Gray's Inn) Qualifications: LLB
(Bucks) B.Soc.Sc, LLM (LSE),ACIArb,
Dip (Chinese Law)

Irani *Miss Simone*
3 Pandan Valley, [H] 16-313, Singapore
597627, 4699286/4677276, Fax:
4633209, Legal Associate (Hewlett-
Packard, Singapore), Call Date: Nov
1995 (Middle Temple) Qualifications:
LLB (Hons)

Irving *Ms Frances Margaret*
7 Mount Nicholson, 103 Mount
Nicholson Road, Hong Kong,
28955332, Fax: 28955175, and
Member Hong Kong Bar, Call Date: July
1996 (Gray's Inn) Qualifications: MA
(Edinburgh)

Isa *Amir Yahaya*
Malaysia, Call Date: July 1997 (Middle
Temple) Qualifications: BA
(Hons) (Keele)

Isaac *Miss Elma Gene*
West Indies, Call Date: Nov 1997
(Lincoln's Inn) Qualifications: LLB
(Hons)

Isaac *Tito Shane*
No. 38C Circular Road, Singapore
470704, (065) 533 0288, Fax: (065)
533 8802, Member of the panel of
Mediators, and Member Singapore Bar,
Call Date: Nov 1994 (Gray's Inn)
Qualifications: LLB (Leeds)

Ishak *Miss Irma Norris*
Malaysia, Call Date: Nov 1997
(Lincoln's Inn) Qualifications: LLB
(Hons) (Wales)

Ismail *Miss Zarina*
Malaysia, Call Date: Nov 1997 (Middle
Temple) Qualifications: LLB (Hons)

Issa *Khoda-Baksh Mahmood Ibreh*
Mauritius (Indian Ocean), Call Date:
Nov 1996 (Inner Temple)
Qualifications: LLB (Lond)

Iyer *Mrs Rukmani Tiru Krishna*
114A Newlands Road, Newlands,
Wellington, New Zealand, (64-4)
4773191, Fax: (64-4) 4773191,
Barrister and Solicitor and Member
Wellington, New Zealand, Call Date:
July 1995 (Gray's Inn) Qualifications:
LLB (Lond), Master, of Business
Studies

Izzuddin *Miss Izzaty*
Malaysia, Call Date: July 1995 (Inner
Temple) Qualifications: LLB (Sheff)

Jaafar *Miss Jafisah*
Malaysia 40000, Call Date: July 1992
(Lincoln's Inn) Qualifications: BA
(Hons) (Kent)

Jaafar *Sallehudin*
Messrs Yeow & Salleh, Suite 6.02, 6th
Floor, Wisma MCA, Jalan Ampang,
50450 Kuala Lumpur, Malaysia, 03
2623833, Fax: 03 2613833, and
Member Malaysia Bar, Call Date: Nov
1992 (Lincoln's Inn) Qualifications:
LLB (Hons) (Sheff)

Jaafar-Thani *Dzuhairi*
Malaysia, Call Date: Nov 1996 (Middle
Temple) Qualifications: LLB (Nott'm)

Jack *Mrs Juliana Marie*
Mello,Hollis,Jones & Martin, Reid
House, 31 Church Street, Hamilton,
Bermuda, (441) 292 1345, Fax: (441)
292 2277, Education Committee,
Bermuda Bar Association, Treatment of
Offenders Board, and Member
Bermuda Bar, Call Date: Oct 1994
(Inner Temple) Qualifications: BA
(California), BA (Oxon)

Jackson *His Honour Peter Brierley*
Magistrate's Chambers, Judicial
Department, P.O. Box 495, George
Town, Grand Cayman,
1-345-949-3823/4296, Fax:
1-345-949-9856, Dep Chief Clerk
ILMCS 1980-89 Registrar of Court of
Appeal & Chief Clerk of the Grand Court
1989-93, Stipendiary Magistrate 1993 to
date., Call Date: July 1979 (Gray's Inn)
Qualifications: MA (Cantab), Dip in
Crim.[Lond], FBIM, Teaching Cert in
F.E

Jackson *Ronald*
Geologistics Corporation, 13952 Denver
West Parkway, Golden, Colorado 8041,
United States of America, 303 704
4426, Fax: 303 704 4410, V.P.and
General Counsel, Call Date: July 1975
(Gray's Inn) Qualifications: LLB (Lond)

Jackson-Lipkin *The Hon Mr Justice*
Miles Henry
Hong Kong, (852) 2838 1838, Fax:
(852) 2891 6993, Arbitrator and
Consultant M.L.C.I.A., and Member
Hong Kong Bar New South Wales Bar,
Call Date: June 1951 (Middle Temple)
Qualifications: FCIArb, CArb (Canada)

Jaffu *Miss Fiona Atupele*
Central Africa, Call Date: July 1998
(Gray's Inn) Qualifications: LLB
(Leeds)

Jaganathan *Miss Chamundeeswari*
Malaysia, Call Date: July 1998 (Gray's
Inn) Qualifications: LLB (Warw)

Jaganathan *Jagan Persath s/o*
Malaysia, Call Date: Nov 1996
(Lincoln's Inn) Qualifications: LLB
(Hons) (Wolv'ton)

Jaganathan *Miss Shanti*
Singapore 460042, Call Date: Nov 1996
(Lincoln's Inn) Qualifications: LLB
(Hons) (Leics)

F

Jalan *Prateek*
7th Floor, 233/5 Acharya J.C. Bose
Road, Calcutta 700020, India, India,
(91-33) 2475990/402549, Fax: (91-33)
401727, and Member India Bar, Call
Date: July 1993 (Inner Temple)
Qualifications: BA (Delhi), BA
(Cantab), LLM (Michigan)

Jamaludin *Miss Aini Hayati*
Messrs Lee Hishammuddin, Advocate &
Solicitors, 16th Floor, Wisma Hla,
Jalan Raja Chulan, 50200 Kuala
Lumpur, Malaysia, (6-03) 2011681,
Fax: (6-03) 2011714/2011746,
Advocate & Solicitor, High Court of
Malaya, and Member Malaysia Bar, Call
Date: July 1995 (Inner Temple)
Qualifications: LLB (Nott)

James *Miss Gloria Magdalen*
Blk 170, [H]02-865, Yishun Ave 7,
Singapore 760170, pgr: 93062380/
7530014, and Member Singapore, Call
Date: July 1995 (Lincoln's Inn)
Qualifications: LLB (Hons)

James *Miss Jacquelinne Agnes*
Gomez Building, High Street, St John's,
P O Box 1519, Antigua, 268 462 4468/
9, Fax: 268 462 0327, and Member
Antigua Bar Barbuda Bar, Call Date:
Nov 1995 (Lincoln's Inn)
Qualifications: LLB (Hons)(Leeds)

James *Miss Mabel Nirmala*
64 Jalan 2/27C, Section 5, Wangsa
MAJU, 53300 Kuala Lumpur, Malaysia,
03-4118391, Legal Assistant Advocate &
Solicitor, and Member Malaysia, Call
Date: July 1996 (Lincoln's Inn)
Qualifications: LLB (Hons), LLM
(Wolves)

Jamieson *Maurice*
Scotland, Assigned Defence Counsel to
the International Tribunal on war
crimes in the former Yugoslavia., and
Member Scotland, Call Date: July 1997
(Middle Temple) Qualifications: LLB
(Hons)

Jamil *Zahid Usman*
Pakistan, Call Date: July 1997 (Gray's
Inn) Qualifications: LLB (Lond)

Jarraw *Colin Tarang*
Battenberg & Talma Advocates, 1st
Floor, No 4, Song Thian, Cheok Road,
93100 Kuching, Sarawak, East
Malaysia, (082) 253277/253827/
428882/428380, Fax: (082)420430,
and Member Sarawak, Malaysia, Call
Date: July 1996 (Inner Temple)
Qualifications: LLB (Northumbria),
M.Phil (Cantab)

Jarrett *Miss Stephanie Ann*
Switzerland, Call Date: Oct 1990
(Lincoln's Inn) Qualifications: LLB
(Lond)

Jat *Sew Tong*
Temple Chambers, 1607 One Pacific
Place, 88 Queensway, Hong Kong, Hong
Kong, 852 2523 2003, Fax: 852 2810
0302, and Member Hong Kong
Singapore Bar, Call Date: July 1988
(Gray's Inn) Qualifications: LLB
(LSE),BCL(Oxon)

Javali *Kirit Sharat*
India, Call Date: Oct 1996 (Gray's Inn)
Qualifications: BA (Delhi), LLB (Leeds)

Jayadevan *Jayaperakash*
M/S Reginald Vallipuram & Co, Suite 1,
23rd Floor, Tun Abdul Razak Complex,
Jalan Wong Ah Fook, 80000 Johor
Bahru, Malaysia, 07-22212677/7, Fax:
07-2241939, and Member Malaysia
Bar, Call Date: Nov 1997 (Lincoln's
Inn) Qualifications: LLB (Hons)

Jayakumar *Miss Shalita*
Singapore 1025, and Member
Singapore Bar, Call Date: July 1995
(Middle Temple) Qualifications: LLB
(Hons)

Jee *Fabian Soo Chen*
183269 Singapore, Call Date: Nov 1996
(Gray's Inn) Qualifications: BA (Keele)

Jeganathan *Miss Michelle Frances*
21 Shangri La Walk, Singapore 568198,
65 452 1733, Fax: 65 458 5486, and
Member Singapore Bar, Call Date: July
1996 (Inner Temple) Qualifications:
LLB (Hull)

Jeganathan *Nadarajah*
Malaysia, Call Date: Nov 1998 (Middle
Temple) Qualifications: LLB
(Hons)(Lond)

Jhogasundram *Miss Jayanthi*
Singapore 0316, Call Date: July 1995
(Lincoln's Inn) Qualifications: LLB
(Hons)

Jinu *Ms Feona*
33B-13-8 Villa Putera, Condominiums,
Jalan Tun Ismail, 50480 Kuala
Lumpur, Malaysia, and Member
Borneo Bar, Call Date: May 1990
(Gray's Inn) Qualifications: LL.B., LLM

Joethy *Jeeva Arul*
Singapore 298817, Call Date: Oct 1998
(Middle Temple) Qualifications: LLB
(Hons)(Lond)

Johar *Mrs Upbinder Sunita*
14 Mules Place, Macarthur ACT 2904,
Singapore, Australia,
(061)(02)62919971, and Member
Singapore, Call Date: July 1994 (Middle
Temple) Qualifications: LLB
(Hons)(Newc)

Johari *Miss Lindahyni*
Malaysia, Call Date: July 1997
(Lincoln's Inn) Qualifications: LLB
(Hons)(L'pool)

John *Jeevan Noel*
Singapore 538172, Call Date: Nov 1997
(Middle Temple) Qualifications: BA
(Hons)(Keele)

John *Jeffrey*
Malaysia, Call Date: July 1996
(Lincoln's Inn) Qualifications: LLB
(Hons)

John *Vincent*
Singapore 310217, Call Date: July 1998
(Middle Temple) Qualifications: LLB
(Hons)(L'pool)

Johnatty *Malcom*
P.O.Box 146, Port of Spain, Trinidad &
Tobago, Trinidad & Tobago,
1-809-665-6173, and Member Trinidad
& Tobago Bar, Call Date: July 1994
(Inner Temple) Qualifications: BSc
(West Indies), LLB (Lond)

Johns *Alain*
c/o Messrs John & Co, No 7500A Beech
Road, [H]14-302 The Plaza, Singapore
2366, 294 3150/ 296 2975, Fax: 291
4662, and Member Singapore, Call
Date: July 1995 (Middle Temple)
Qualifications: LLB (Hons)

Johnson *Anthony Lesroy*
West Indies, Call Date: July 1995
(Lincoln's Inn) Qualifications: LLB
(Hons)

Johnson *Lenworth Walter*
55 Newgate Street, St John's, Antigua,
West Indies, 268 460 9714, Fax: 268
460 9715, and Member Antigua &
Barbuda, Call Date: Nov 1996 (Inner
Temple) Qualifications: LLB
(Wolverh'ton)

Johnston *Kenneth Barry*
Level 3, Landcorp House, 101 Lambton
Quay, P.O.Box 5058, Wellington, New
Zealand, 471 2727, Fax: 499 4620, and
Member New Zealand Bar, Call Date:
May 1988 (Middle Temple)
Qualifications: LLB, DIP H.R.M.

Johnston *Mark*
Rue De L'Epargne 10 BTE 7,
1000-Bruxelles, Belgium, Republic of
Ireland, 00 322 223 2785, Member of
King's Inn, Dublin and Member
Southern Ireland Bar, Call Date: July
1988 (Middle Temple) Qualifications:
BCL (U.C.D), BL (Kings Inns)

Jones *Andrew John*
Maples and Calder, P.O. Box 309 GT,
Grand Cayman, Cayman Islands, 345
949 8066, Fax: 345 949 8080, Attorney
at Law, Cayman Is Panel member,
American Arbitration Association, and
Member Cayman Islands, Call Date:
Nov 1973 (Inner Temple)
Qualifications: MA (Cantab)

Jones *Mrs Anjette Nadine*
20 Queensway Quay, Gibraltar, 00 350
40730, Fax: 00 350 73315, and
Member Gibraltar Bar, Call Date: Oct
1992 (Inner Temple) Qualifications:
LLB

Jones-Crawford *Mrs Shaaron*
179 Dawlish Avenue, Toronto, Ontario
M4N1H6, Canada, 416 485 3410, Fax:
416 485 3329, Call Date: July 1990
(Lincoln's Inn) Qualifications: LLB

Jong *Miss Ling*
Malaysia, Call Date: Nov 1996
(Lincoln's Inn) Qualifications: LLB
(Hons)(Hull)

Joof *Miss Amie*
Gambia, Call Date: Nov 1997 (Lincoln's
Inn) Qualifications: LLB (Hons)(Warw)

Joon *Ms Loy Siew*
Singapore 2264, Call Date: Nov 1996
(Inner Temple) Qualifications: LLB
(Lond)

Joseph *Eugene Roy*
Shook Lin & Bok, 20th Floor,
Arab-Malaysian Building, 55 Jalan Raja
Chulan, 50200 Kuala Lumpur,
Malaysia, 03 2011788, Fax: 03 201175/
8/9, and Member Malaysia Bar, Call
Date: July 1996 (Lincoln's Inn)
Qualifications: LLB (Hons)(Lond)

Joseph *Miss Margaret Mary*
Malaysia, Advocate & Solcitor, and
Member Malaya, Call Date: July 1996
(Middle Temple) Qualifications: LLB
(Hons)(Lond)

Joseph *Vincent*
Malaysia, Call Date: July 1996
(Lincoln's Inn) Qualifications: LLB
(Hons)(Lond)

Josephson *Ms Diana Hayward*
1000 Navy Pentagon, Washington D.C.
20350-1000, United States of America,
703 693 4527, Principal Deputy
Assistant Secretary of the Navy (
Installations and Environment) US
Department of Defense, and Member
District of Columbia Bar, Call Date:
June 1959 (Gray's Inn) Qualifications:
BA,MA (Hons) (Oxon), M Comp.

Jospeh Xavier *Annou Anselm*
Malaysia, Call Date: Nov 1996
(Lincoln's Inn) Qualifications: LLB
(HOns)(Lond)

Jublee *Cilve Clive*
P.O.Box 21206, 88769 Luyang, Sabah,
Malaysia, 088 231111, Fax: 088
233122, and Member Advocate &
Solcitor, Sabah, Call Date: July 1995
(Middle Temple) Qualifications: LLB
(Hons)(Warw)

Juggeet Singh *Rabinder Singh s/o*
West Malaysia, Call Date: Oct 1998
(Middle Temple) Qualifications: LLB
(Hons)(Lond)

Jung *Moo-Kyung*
Republic of Korea, Call Date: July 1996
(Middle Temple) Qualifications: BA
(Hons)(Seoul), LLM (Warw), CPE
(B'ham)

Kaburise *Professor John Bonaventure
Kubongpwa*
Department of Public Law, Faculty of
Law, University of Durban-Westville,
Private Bag X54001, Durban 4000,
(031) 820 9111, Fax: (031) 820 2848,
Professorship of Public Law, Solicitor
Papua New Guinea and Member Papua
New Guinea Bar, Call Date: July 1988
(Middle Temple) Qualifications: LLB
(Hons) (Ghana), LLM (Pennsylvannia)

Kahar Bador *Rizal*
Malaysia, Call Date: Nov 1997
(Lincoln's Inn) Qualifications: BA
(Hons)(Oxon)

Kam *Aubeck Tse Tsuen*
Singapore 680602, Call Date: July 1993
(Lincoln's Inn) Qualifications: LLB
(Hons)

Kam-Chuen *Cheung*
Hong Kong, and Member Hong Kong
Bar, Call Date: July 1996 (Inner
Temple) Qualifications: LLB
(Wolverhampton), MBA (Leic), LLM
(Wolves)

Kamalanathan *Selva Kumaran*
Malaysia, and Member Malaysia Bar,
Call Date: July 1994 (Lincoln's Inn)
Qualifications: LLB (Hons), LLM
(Malaya)

Kamaruddin *Kamarul Hisham*
Malaysia, Call Date: May 1995 (Gray's
Inn) Qualifications: LLB

Kamil *Mrs Nik Mariah Zainab*
S G Lingham & Co, Suite 502, 5th
Floor, Bangunan Loke Yew, Jalan
Mahkamah Persekutuan, 50050 Kuala
Lumpur, Malaysia, 603-2982833, Fax:
603-2982876, Fellow, Institute of Legal
Executives and Member Malaysian Bar,
Call Date: July 1971 (Lincoln's Inn)
Qualifications: LLB

Kammitsi *Miss Lefkothea*
C/O George L Savvides & Co, 1 Glafkos
Str, 1085 Nicosia, Cyprus, 02-422355,
Fax: 02-421819, Associate, and
Member Cyprus Bar, Call Date: July
1990 (Middle Temple) Qualifications:
BSocSc (Keele)

Kan *Miss Caroline Yuen Oi*
M/s Harry Elias & Partners, 79
Robinson Road [H]16-03, CPF
Building, Singapore 0106, Singapore
9117, Call Date: Nov 1987 (Middle
Temple) Qualifications: LLB(Hons)
London, BA(Hons) McMaster

Kanagarajan *Veluthevar*
The Ministry of Foreign Affairs, Raffles
City 06-00, 250 North Bridge Road,
Singapore, 179101, Singapore 0922,
336 1177, Fax: 339 4330, Ambassador,
Call Date: Nov 1977 (Lincoln's Inn)
Qualifications: LLB (Lond)

Kanagavijayan *Nadarajan*
Singapore 806109, Call Date: Nov 1996
(Inner Temple) Qualifications: BA
(Singpaore), LLB, LLM (Lond)

Kang *Colin Seng Kok*
Singapore 530533, Call Date: Nov 1997
(Middle Temple) Qualifications: LLB
(Hons)(Bucks)

Kang *Miss June Karjun*
28 Ewart Park, Singapore 278730, Call
Date: July 1998 (Middle Temple)
Qualifications: BA (Melbourne), LLB
(Hons)(So'ton)

Kangeson *Miss Gowri R.*
Malaysia, Call Date: Oct 1997 (Gray's
Inn) Qualifications: LLB (Glamorgan)

Kanthosamy *Rajendran*
Singapore 527230, Call Date: July 1996
(Middle Temple) Qualifications: LLB
(Hons)(Lond)

Kanyerezi *Timothy Masembe*
Mugerwa & Matovu Advocates, 3rd
Floor, Diamond Trust Bldg, Plot 17/19
Kampala Road, PO Box 7166, Kampala,
256 41 343859,259920,255431, Fax:
256 41 259992, and Member Ugandan
Bar, Call Date: July 1992 (Inner
Temple) Qualifications: LLB (Lond)

Kapetaniou *Miss Phani*
Cyprus, Call Date: Mar 1996 (Lincoln's
Inn) Qualifications: LLB (Hons)(Leics)

Kaplan *Neil*
Suite 1106, Kinwick Centre, 32
Hollywood Road, Central, Hong Kong
S.A.R, (852) 2869 6301, Fax: (852)
2869 6372, Arbitrator, QC (Hong Kong)
and Member Hong Kong & New York
Bars Victoria Bar Victoria Australia
Essex Court Chambers, 24 Lincoln's
Inn Fields, London, WC2A 3ED, Call
Date: Feb 1965 (Inner Temple)
Qualifications: LLB (Lond) FCIArb

Kapri *Miss Zuhra Jabeen*
Kenya, Call Date: Nov 1996 (Lincoln's
Inn) Qualifications: LLB (Hons)

Kapur *Ravi Krishan*
India, Call Date: July 1997 (Lincoln's
Inn) Qualifications: B.Com (Hons),
(Calcutta), LLB, (Hons)(Leeds)

Karia *Chirag*
Gray Cary Ware & Freidenrich, 400
Hamilton Avenue, Palo Alto, CA
94301-1825, United States of America,
(650) 833 2147, Fax: (650) 327 3699,
and Member The State Bar of
California, Call Date: Nov 1988
(Lincoln's Inn) Qualifications: BA
(Hons)(Cantab), MA (Hons)(Cantab),
LLM (UC Berkeley)

Karim *Shaikh Saleem*
Malaysia, Call Date: Oct 1996 (Middle
Temple) Qualifications: LLB
(Hons)(Essex)

Karupiah *Jegathesean*
Malaysia, Call Date: Oct 1995 (Gray's
Inn) Qualifications: BA

Karuppiah *Kalidass s/o*
Singapore 080107, Call Date: Nov 1996
(Inner Temple) Qualifications: LLB
(Lond)

Karuppiah *Sathinathan*
Tan Lian Ker & Company, 2 Havelock
Road [H] 07-10, Apollo Centre,
Singapore 550545, 65 532 7117, Legal
Assistant, Call Date: July 1996
(Lincoln's Inn) Qualifications: LLB
(Hons), LLM (Sussex)

Karydes *Marios Andrea*
P.O.Box 77086, GR 175, 10 Athens,
Greece, 01-4116942, Fax: 01-4179221,
and Member Piraeus Bar Association,
Call Date: July 1971 (Inner Temple)
Qualifications: Athens University, Law
Degree

Kasim *Ms Siti Zabedah*
Malaysia, Call Date: Nov 1997 (Gray's
Inn) Qualifications: LLB

Kassim *Miss Noor Sukhairiyani*
Attorney General's Chambers, The Law
Building, Jalan Tutong, Bandar Seri
Begawan, BA 1910, Negara Brunei,
Darussalam, (673 - 2) 244876, Legal
Adviser (Counsel), Call Date: Nov 1997
(Lincoln's Inn) Qualifications: LLB
(Hons)(B'ham)

Kattan *William Victor*
Attorney General's Chambers, G Pobal
House, 43 Church Street, Hamilton
HM12, (441) 297 7421/292 2463, Fax:
(809)946 2588, Parliamentary
Counsel, Call Date: May 1973 (Gray's
Inn) Qualifications: LLB,LLM (Lond)

Kaur *Miss Balbir*
Singapore 2775, Call Date: July 1995
(Middle Temple) Qualifications: LLB
(Hons) (Lond)

Kaur *Miss Baltej*
Singapore 600317, Advocate & Solicitor
in Singapore, Call Date: July 1995
(Middle Temple) Qualifications: LLB
(Hons)

Kaur *Miss Daljit*
Malaysia, Call Date: July 1997
(Lincoln's Inn) Qualifications: LLB
(Hons)

Kaur *Miss Devinder*
Malaysia, Call Date: July 1995
(Lincoln's Inn) Qualifications: LLB
(Hons)

Kaur *Miss Harshinder*
Malaysia, Call Date: July 1998 (Middle
Temple) Qualifications: LLB
(Hons)(Wales)

Kaur *Miss Jasvendar*
Singapore 1336, Call Date: July 1995
(Middle Temple) Qualifications: LLB
(Hons)

Kaur *Miss Kiren*
Singapore 270007, Call Date: July 1998
(Middle Temple) Qualifications: LLB
(Hons)(Lond)

Kaur *Mrs Paramjit*
Singapore 320105, Call Date: July 1996
(Lincoln's Inn) Qualifications: LLB
(Hons)(Lond)

Kaur *Miss Sharanjit*
Singapore 0315, and Member
Singapore Bar, Call Date: July 1995
(Middle Temple) Qualifications: LLB
(Hons)

Kaur Jaswant Singh *Miss Sharan*
Malaysia, Call Date: July 1997 (Middle
Temple) Qualifications: LLB
(Hons)(Wales)_

Kawa *Miss Lois Anita*
West Africa, Call Date: Nov 1997
(Lincoln's Inn) Qualifications: BA
(Hons)(Luton)

Kawaley *Ian Rowe Chukudinka*
c/o Milligan Whyte & Smith, Richmond
House, 12 Par la Ville Road, Hamilton
HM11, (441) 295 4294, Fax: (441) 295
1348, Head of Insolvency and
Corporate Rescue, Justice of the Peace,
Member of the Bermuda Bar Council
(1992) and Member Bermuda Bar, Call
Date: July 1978 (Middle Temple)
Qualifications: LLB (Liverpool), LLM
(LSE)

Kazantzis *Ms Miranda Elizabeth*
44 Leamington Road Villas, London
W11 1HT, 0171 243 2549, Fax: 0171
243 2549, Call Date: Feb 1993 (Middle
Temple) Qualifications: BA (Hons)
(Oxon), MA, Dip in Law

Kearsey *Miss Jane*
Aicatel - Compagnie Financiere, 54 Rue
de la Boetie, Paris 75008, France, 00
33 1 30 54 49 73, Assistant European
Affairs, Call Date: Oct 1998 (Middle
Temple) Qualifications: LLB
(Hons)(Wales)

Keegan *Brian McMurrough*
Northern Ireland, Call Date: Mar 1998
(Lincoln's Inn) Qualifications: LLB
(Hons)(Leics)

Keery *Neil William*
Northern Ireland, and Member
Northern Ireland Bar, Call Date: Oct
1997 (Gray's Inn) Qualifications: LLB
(Belfast)

Kelaart *Ms Jennifer Rosanne Sabina*
12/2A Tickell Road, Colombo 8, Sri
Lanka, (94-1) 696623, Fax: (94-1)
422768, Lecturer in Law - University of
Colombo - Sri Lanka, Call Date: Nov
1995 (Inner Temple) Qualifications:
LLB (Lond), LLM (Syd)

Kelleher *Dr John Daniel*
Olsen Backhurst & Dorey, Eaton
House, 9 Seaton Place, St Helier, Jersey
JE2 3QL, 01534 888900, Fax: 01534
887744, Partner, Advocate of the Royal
Court of Jersey (1995). Jersey Law
Society. and Member Jersey Bar, Call
Date: Oct 1991 (Middle Temple)
Qualifications: BA Hons (Warw), Dip
Law (Lond), PhD (Warw), Certificat De
, Juridiques Francaise

Kelly *Philip James*
Ireland, Barrister of Ireland, Call Date:
May 1996 (Middle Temple)
Qualifications: BA, MSc (Dublin)

Kelly *Miss Sandra Marie*
Norton Rose Consultants O.E., 126
Kolokotroni Street, 185 35 Piraeus, 30
1 428 0202, Former Solicitor, Call
Date: Nov 1992 (Inner Temple)
Qualifications: LLB (Hons) (Glas), Dip
in Higher, European Studies,, College of
Europe

Kennedy *Hugh Paul*
Bar Library, Royal Courts of Justice,
Chichester Street, Belfast, Northern
Ireland, 0232 241523, Fax: 0232
231850, Bencher Inn of Court N
Ireland Past Chairman Bar Council of
N.I., Past Treasurer, Inn of Court of
N.I., Member Supreme Court Rules
Committee., Council of Law Reporting
(NI), QC (N Ireland) SC Republic of
Ireland, Call Date: Nov 1990 (Gray's
Inn) Qualifications: BA,LLB (Belfast)

Kennedy *Thomas Alastair Plunkett*
Court of Justice of the, European
Communities, L 2925, 352-4303 3355,
Fax: 352-4303 2500, Principal
Administration Press and Information
Division, Call Date: Nov 1975 (Gray's
Inn) Qualifications: LLB (Hons)

Kenny *Judge Harvey*
Yorkville, York Hill, Cork City, Ireland,
021 551125, Fax: 021 504406, Judge of
the Western Circuit Court, and Member
Southern Ireland Bar, Call Date: Feb
1982 (Middle Temple) Qualifications:
BCL (Nat Univ, Ireland), ACIArB

Kentish *Mrs Louise Anne*
J A Hassan & Partners, 57/63 Line Wall
Road, Spain, 00 350 79000, Fax: 00
350 71966, Associate, and Member
Gibraltar, Call Date: Nov 1996 (Middle
Temple) Qualifications: BA (Hons)

Keoy *Soo Khim*
Singapore 0511, Call Date: July 1997
(Gray's Inn) Qualifications: LLB

Kershaw *Nicholas John*
Ogier & Le Masurier, Pirouet House,
Union Street, St Helier, Jersey, Channel
Islands, Channel Islands, 01534
504000, Fax: 01534 35328, and
Member New South Wales Bar Jersey
Bar, Call Date: May 1988 (Middle
Temple) Qualifications: LLB (Hons)
London

Kesavapany *Muralitherapany*
Singapore 1027, Call Date: Nov 1995
(Middle Temple) Qualifications: LLB
(Hons)(Lond)

Khairuddin *Miss Fateh Hanum*
Malaysia, Call Date: July 1996
(Lincoln's Inn) Qualifications: BA
(Hons)(Keele)

Khan *Karim Asad Ahmad*
Office of the Prosecutor, United Nations, International, Criminal Tribunal, 1 Churchill Plein, 2517JA, Den Haag, 0031 70 4165353, Fax: 0031 70 4165325, Legal Advisor, Call Date: Oct 1992 (Lincoln's Inn) Qualifications: LLB(Hons)(Lond), AKC (Lond), Dip Int Rel (Nice)

Khan *Miss Mahreen Aziz*
Pakistan, Call Date: Nov 1994 (Inner Temple) Qualifications: MA (Cantab), MPP (Harvard)

Khan *Mirazul Hossain*
Bangladesh, Call Date: Nov 1997 (Lincoln's Inn) Qualifications: LLB (Hons)(Lond)

Khan *Muhammad Zaffarullah*
Pakistan, Call Date: Oct 1998 (Lincoln's Inn) Qualifications: LLB (Hons)(City)

Khan *Muhammed Mustafizur Rahman*
Bangladesh, Call Date: Nov 1997 (Lincoln's Inn) Qualifications: BSS (Hons)(Dhaka), LLB (Hons)

Khanna *Nechal Chand*
Malaysia, Call Date: July 1997 (Middle Temple) Qualifications: LLB (Hons)

Khaw *Miss Gim Hong*
27 Jalan Bijaksana, Taman Century, 80250 Johor Bahru, Johor, Malaysia, Malaysia, 07 3327351, and Member Singapore Bar, Call Date: July 1994 (Middle Temple) Qualifications: LLB (Hons), ACCA

Khaw *Kenneth Jin Teck*
Malaysia, Call Date: July 1993 (Middle Temple) Qualifications: LLB (Hons, Bris), ACA

Khaw *Oliver Kar Heng*
Malaysia, and Member Malaysian Bar, Call Date: July 1997 (Middle Temple) Qualifications: LLB (Hons)

Khera *Darshan Singh*
Messrs Darshan Singh & Co, No 18-A Lebuh Pantai, First Floor, 10300 Penang, Malaysia, 0106 04 2611820, Fax: 0106 04 2627476, Partner, Call Date: July 1971 (Lincoln's Inn)

Khong *Miss Gilliam Li Shen*
Singapore 239277, Call Date: July 1997 (Middle Temple) Qualifications: LLB (Hons)(Nott'm)

Khoo *Gavin Lay Keong*
Singapore 238619, Call Date: July 1997 (Middle Temple) Qualifications: LLB (Hons)(Wales)

Khoo *Kay Kwan*
Malaysia, Call Date: Nov 1997 (Lincoln's Inn) Qualifications: LLB (Hons)(Wales)

Khoo *Melvin Lay Jin*
Singapore 0923, Call Date: Nov 1993 (Middle Temple) Qualifications: LLB (Hons)(Bucks)

Khoo *Miss Selkie*
Malaysia, Call Date: Nov 1997 (Middle Temple) Qualifications: LLB (Hons)(Leics)

Khoo *Miss Su Sen*
Malaysia, Call Date: July 1996 (Middle Temple) Qualifications: LLB (Hons)(Glamorg)

Khor *Wee Siong*
Singapore 089934, and Member Singapore Bar, Call Date: July 1996 (Lincoln's Inn) Qualifications: LLB (Hons)(Hull)

Khosa *Muhammad Yousef Khan*
Pakistan, Call Date: July 1998 (Lincoln's Inn) Qualifications: LLB (Hons)(Wales)

Kieran *Brian Laurence*
P.O.Box 2071, General Post Office, (852) 2501 0471, Fax: (852) 2592 7086, and Member Jamaica Bar Hong Kong Bar, Call Date: July 1968 (Gray's Inn) Qualifications: LLB, DIP Air, FBIS

Killerby *Miss Joan Margaret*
Council of Europe, Strasbourg Cedex, F-67075, France, 03 88 41 22 10, Fax: 03 88 41 27 94, Head of the Private Law Division, Call Date: Nov 1967 (Inner Temple) Qualifications: doc de Univ d'Aix-, Marseille

King *Paul John*
Graham Thompson & Co, Sasson House, Shirley Street, Victoria Avenue, P.O.Box N272, Nassau, Bahamas, (242) 322 4130, Fax: (242) 328 1069, and Member Bahamas, Call Date: July 1996 (Middle Temple) Qualifications: LLB (Hons)(Soton), BA (Hons)(Miami)

King *Peter Andrew*
Bar Library, Royal Courts of Justice, P O Box 414, Chichester Street, Belfast BT1 3JP, 01232 562354, Fax: 01232 231850, and Member Northern Ireland Bar, Call Date: Nov 1993 (Gray's Inn) Qualifications: LLB (Manch)

Kinnear *David Thomas Alexander*
212 325 7029, Fax: 212 325 9177, Director Credit Suisse, First Boston Corporation, Call Date: July 1989 (Middle Temple) Qualifications: LLB (Manch)

Kinoshi *John Ayoola*
5 Kinoshi St, Abeokuta, Nigeria, Nigeria, Legal Advisor (Legal Private Practitioner), Also Inn of Court I and Member Nigerian Bar, Call Date: Nov 1972 (Lincoln's Inn)

Kiplagat *Miss Betty Jepkoech*
East Africa, Call Date: Nov 1996 (Middle Temple) Qualifications: LLB (Hons)

Kishan *Pratap*
Singapore 518687, Call Date: July 1998 (Middle Temple) Qualifications: LLB (Hons)(Lond)

Knight *Miss Tracey Ann*
Misick and Stanbrook, Attorneys at Law, P.O.Box 127, Providenciales, (1) 649 946 4732, Fax: (1) 649 946 4734, and Member Turks & Caicos Islands, Call Date: Oct 1997 (Lincoln's Inn) Qualifications: LLB (Hons)(Oxon), LLM (E.Anglia)

Knowles *Miss Adrianna Desiree*
Bahamas, and Member Bahamas Bar, Call Date: July 1997 (Lincoln's Inn) Qualifications: LLB (Hons), LLM

Knowles *Edwin Leroy*
Bahamas, Call Date: Nov 1998 (Lincoln's Inn) Qualifications: LLB (Hons)(Wales)

Knowles *Miss Samantha Sophia*
Bahamas, and Member Bahamas, Call Date: July 1998 (Inner Temple) Qualifications: LLB (Wolves)

Ko *Hiu Fung*
6g Fu Wai Court, Fortress Garden, 32 Fortress Hill Road, North Point, Hong Kong, (852) 250 33598, Fax: (852) 280 61302, and Member Hong Kong Bar Association, Call Date: Nov 1997 (Lincoln's Inn) Qualifications: LLB (Hons)

Ko *Justin King Sau*
806 Wheelock House, 20 Pedder Street, Central, Hong Kong, Hong Kong, 852 25220209, Fax: 852 28450720, and Member Hong-Kong Bar, Call Date: July 1993 (Lincoln's Inn) Qualifications: LLB (Hons, B'ham)

Koe *Miss Kian Fei*
36 Robinson Road, [H]07-01, City House, Singapore 618650, 2239009, Fax: 2256914, Legal Assistant, and Member Singapore, Call Date: July 1996 (Middle Temple) Qualifications: LLB (Hons)(Lond)

Koh *Miss Aileen Geok Pin*
Singapore 2264, Call Date: July 1995 (Middle Temple) Qualifications: LLB (Hons)

Koh *Chia Ling*
Singapore 100051, and Member Singapore, Call Date: July 1997 (Middle Temple) Qualifications: LLB (Hons)(Lond)

Koh *Darren Ngiap Thiam*
United Nations Compensation, Commission, Villa la Pelouse, Palais des Nations, Ch - 1211 Geneva 10, Japan, 41 22 907 6074, Fax: 41 22 917 0315, Call Date: July 1989 (Lincoln's Inn) Qualifications: LLB (Buck), ACA, ATII

Koh *Gerald Teck Hock*
Singapore 309892, Call Date: Mar 1996 (Middle Temple) Qualifications: LLB (Hons)

Koh *Glen Teck Beng*
Singapore 269939, Call Date: Oct 1998 (Middle Temple) Qualifications: LLB (Hons)(Lond)

Koh *Miss Jean Bee Khim*
Singapore 679556, Call Date: Oct 1996
(Middle Temple) Qualifications: LLB
(Hons)(Lond), LLM (Shipping Law)

Koh *Miss Joanna Wei Ser*
C/O 9 Battery Road, [H]15-00, Straits
Trading, Building, Singapore 427233,
(65) 539 1681, Fax: (65) 532 2271,
and Member Singapore Bar, Call Date:
July 1997 (Middle Temple)
Qualifications: LLB (Hons)(Exon)

Koh *Kok Shen*
Singapore 1026, Call Date: Oct 1995
(Middle Temple) Qualifications: LLB
(Hons)

Koh *Miss Lee Tze*
Singapore 0512, Call Date: July 1995
(Lincoln's Inn) Qualifications: LLB
(Hons)

Koh *Miss Maisie Su-Mei*
Singapore 1545, and Member
Singapore, Call Date: July 1995 (Middle
Temple) Qualifications: LLB (Hons)

Koh *Sam Mong Poo*
Block 817, Tampines Street 81, [H]
04-588, Singapore 520817, 65
7892048, and Member Member of the
Singapore Bar, Call Date: July 1996
(Middle Temple) Qualifications: LLB
(Hons)(Wolves), M.Inst A.M (dip)(UK),
M.I.S.M.(dip)(UK)

Koh *Miss Selena Lay Na*
Singapore 0923, and Member
Singapore, Call Date: Nov 1996 (Middle
Temple) Qualifications: LLB
(Hons)(Bucks)

Koh *Siew Hui*
Malaysia, Call Date: July 1995
(Lincoln's Inn) Qualifications: LLB
(Hons)

Koh *Sim Teck*
Singapore 1648, Call Date: May 1994
(Middle Temple) Qualifications: LLB
(Hons)

Koh *Terence Kah Hoe*
Malaysia, Call Date: Oct 1995 (Middle
Temple) Qualifications: LLB (Hons)

Koh *Terence Sebastian Ker Siang*
Singapore 2880, Call Date: July 1996
(Middle Temple) Qualifications: LLB
(Hons)(Bris)

Kok *Miss Aik Wan*
Malaysia, Call Date: Nov 1996
(Lincoln's Inn) Qualifications: LLB
(Hons)(So'ton)

Kok *Miss Meng Wei*
Malaysia, Call Date: July 1995
(Lincoln's Inn) Qualifications: LLB
(Hons)(Leeds)

Kok *Ms Yoke Kieng*
Singapore, Call Date: Nov 1996 (Gray's
Inn) Qualifications: LLB

Kong *Chi Man*
Hong Kong, Call Date: Nov 1997
(Middle Temple) Qualifications:
B.Soc.Sci (Hong Kong

Kong *Miss Jennifer Lee Jean*
Malaysia, Advocate & Solicitor in a Legal
Firm, and Member Sabah Bar Malaysia
Bar, Call Date: Nov 1992 (Lincoln's
Inn) Qualifications: BA (Hons)(Nott'm)

Kong *Kelvin Wen Wai*
Malaysia, Call Date: July 1989
(Lincoln's Inn) Qualifications: LLB
(Newc)

Kong *Miss Seh Ping*
Malaysia, Call Date: July 1995 (Middle
Temple) Qualifications: LLB (Hons)

Konotey-Ahulu *Dawid Konotey-Adade*
Natwest Markets Ltd, 135 Bishopsgate,
London EC2M 3UR, Singapore 258427,
0171 334 1780, Fax: 0171 375 5060,
Director, Call Date: Nov 1987
(Lincoln's Inn) Qualifications: LLB
Hons

Kooi *Tock Ken*
Malaysia, Call Date: July 1996
(Lincoln's Inn) Qualifications: LLB
(Hons)(Lond)

Koon *Keen Hoong*
Malaysia, Call Date: July 1996 (Gray's
Inn) Qualifications: LLB (Exeter)

Kor *Darren Yit Meng*
Malaysia, Call Date: July 1996
(Lincoln's Inn) Qualifications: LLB
(Hons)(Warw)

Kor *Don Shiang Hua*
Malaysia, and Member Malaysia Bar,
Call Date: July 1994 (Middle Temple)
Qualifications: BA (Hons)(Manc)

Koudounari *Miss Evelina*
Cyprus, Call Date: Nov 1998 (Inner
Temple) Qualifications: BA (Keele)

Koy *Andy Kwan Loong*
Malaysia, Call Date: Nov 1998
(Lincoln's Inn) Qualifications: LLB
(Hons)(Lond)

Kremner *Jonathan*
8721 Bay Pointe Drive, Tampa, Florida
33615, USA 813 884 8841, Fax: USA
813 885 2846, and Member New York,
Call Date: July 1984 (Inner Temple)
Qualifications: MA (Law), BA (Hons),
Dip Law

Krishna *Miss Maheswari Rani*
Singapore 2057, and Member Malaysia,
Call Date: July 1995 (Lincoln's Inn)
Qualifications: LLB (Hons)

Krishnan *Elengovan*
Block 661, Buffalo Road, 11-29
Singapore 210661, Singapore 210661,
Call Date: July 1993 (Middle Temple)
Qualifications: LLB (Hons, Hull)

Krishnan *Miss Shubhaa*
Malaysia, Call Date: Nov 1997
(Lincoln's Inn) Qualifications: LLB
(Hons)(Lond)

Krishnasamy *Miss Anuthara*
Malaysia, Call Date: Nov 1998
(Lincoln's Inn) Qualifications: LLB
(Hons)(Leeds)

Krishnasamy *Siva Sambo*
S Bala & Associates, Advocates &
Solicitors, 135 Cecil Street, [H]08-02,
LKN Building, Singapore 456338, 225
5277, Fax: 225 2498, and Member
Singapore Bar, Call Date: July 1995
(Lincoln's Inn) Qualifications: LLB
(Hons)

Krrishnan *Ms Seethalkshmi P S*
Singapore 151126, Call Date: July 1997
(Lincoln's Inn) Qualifications: LLB
(Hons)(Lond)

Ku *Miss Pui Fong*
Hong Kong, and Member Hong Kong
Bar, Call Date: Nov 1991 (Gray's Inn)
Qualifications: LLB (Lond)(Hon) ,
A.C.I.S.

Kua *Miss Lay Theng*
Messrs Skrine & Co, Unit No 50-8-1,
8th Floor, Wisma Uoa Damansara, 50
Jalan Dungan, Damansara, Heights.
50490 Kuala Lumpur, Malaysia, 03
2548111, Fax: 03 2543211, and
Member Malaysia, Call Date: July 1997
(Middle Temple) Qualifications: LLB
(Hons)(Leics)

Kuan *Anthony Chee Kee*
Malaysia, Call Date: Nov 1996
(Lincoln's Inn) Qualifications: LLB
(Hons)

Kudjawu *Miss Magdalen Sena*
Ghana, Call Date: Oct 1998 (Middle
Temple) Qualifications: LLB
(Hons)(Warwick)

Kuen *Paul Yong Wei*
Singapore 1231, Call Date: July 1995
(Inner Temple) Qualifications: LLB
(Lond)

Kumalae *Mrs Quinell Maria*
Bermuda Monetary Authority, Burnaby
House, 26 Burnaby Street, Hamilton
HM11, Bermuda, (441) 295 5278, Fax:
(441) 292 7474, and Member
Bermuda, Call Date: Nov 1997
(Lincoln's Inn) Qualifications: LLB
(Hons)

Kumar *Miss Neeta*
596 Taman Asean, Jalan Malim, 75250
Melaka, Malaysia, 00 606 3358814, Call
Date: July 1998 (Middle Temple)
Qualifications: LLB (Hons)

Kumar *Rajesh*
Malaysia, Call Date: Nov 1997 (Middle
Temple) Qualifications: LLB
(Hons)(Newcas)

Kumar *Miss Sharika*
Malaysia, Call Date: July 1996
(Lincoln's Inn) Qualifications: LLB
(Hons)(Lond)

F

Kumar *Vishnu*
Malaysia, Advocate & Solicitor of the
High Court of Malaya and Member
Maylaysian Bar, Call Date: July 1995
(Middle Temple) Qualifications: LLB
(Hons), LLM (Lond)

Kumarasamy *Pathmanathan*
West Malaysia, Call Date: Nov 1996
(Gray's Inn) Qualifications: LLB
(Wales)

Kung *Kenny Yong Jin*
Malaysia, Call Date: July 1998
(Lincoln's Inn) Qualifications: BA
(Singapore), LLB (Hons)(Lond)

Kunjuraman *Dharmendra*
Singapore 310126, Call Date: Nov 1996
(Middle Temple) Qualifications: LLB
(Hons)(Nott'm)

Kunjuraman *Miss Previtha*
Singapore 1231, Call Date: July 1996
(Middle Temple) Qualifications: LLB
(Hons)(Wolves)

Kuok *David Han Peh*
54A Tekam Road, 96000 Sibu, Sarawak,
Malaysia, 00 60 843 11279, Advocate,
and Member Malaysia, Call Date: July
1997 (Lincoln's Inn) Qualifications:
LLB (Hons)(Wales)

Kuok *Miss Pearl Ming Yew*
Allen & Gledhill, 36 Robinson Road
[H]18-01, City House, Singaopre 0106,
Singapore 118174, 65 2251611, Fax:
65 2233787, Legal Advisor, and
Member Singapore Bar, Call Date: July
1992 (Middle Temple) Qualifications:
LLB (Hons) (Lond)

Kuppusamy *Miss Kalaichelvi M*
Singapore 650136, Call Date: July 1998
(Middle Temple) Qualifications: LLB
(Hons)(Lond)

Kuppusamy *Mahendran*
Block 136, Bukit Batok West Avenue 6,
[H]08-509, 5690464, Call Date: July
1996 (Middle Temple) Qualifications:
LLB (Hons)(Lond), LLM (Lond)

Kwa *Miss Su-Lin*
Western Australia, and Member
Western Australia Bar, Call Date: July
1995 (Inner Temple) Qualifications:
LLB (Lond)

Kwan *Pang Moon*
Hong Kong, Call Date: Mar 1998
(Gray's Inn) Qualifications: LLB (Lond)

Kwan Pang *Mrs Maying*
Republic of Mauritius, Call Date: Nov
1996 (Lincoln's Inn) Qualifications:
LLB (Hons)(Wales)

Kwan Tat *Dick Jeremy*
Mauritius, Call Date: Nov 1998 (Middle
Temple) Qualifications: LLB (Hons)

Kwek *Julian Choon Yeow*
24 Raffles Place, Clifford Centre
[H]18-00, Singapore 2159,
65-5332323, Fax: 65-5337029, Legal
Assistant, Haridas Ho & Partners, and
Member Singapore Bar, Call Date: July
1995 (Middle Temple) Qualifications:
LLB (Hons)

Kwok *Lester Chi-Hang*
30th Floor, Wing On House, 71 Des
Voeux Road, Central, (852) 2523 4091,
Fax: (852) 2868 0118, Associate
Member of the Hong Kong Bar
Association, Call Date: Nov 1975
(Gray's Inn) Qualifications: BA
(Stanford)

Kwok *Peter Chi Yeung*
Hong Kong, Call Date: Nov 1998
(Middle Temple) Qualifications: MB,
BS (Hong Kong)

Kyprianou *Menelaos Michael*
Law Office of Michael, Kyprianou &
Associates, P.O.Box 8765, Stassinos
Court, Stassinos Avenue, Nicosia,
Cyprus, 02 360800, Fax: 02 467880,
and Member Cyprus Bar, Call Date: Nov
1994 (Middle Temple) Qualifications:
LLB (Hons)

Labesse *Advocate Jacques Pierre*
Piermont Hse, 33 Pier Rd, St Helier,
Jersey, 0534 888777, Fax: 0534
888778, Call Date: July 1957 (Inner
Temple) Qualifications: MA (Oxon)

Lack *Daniel*
Ziegler, Poncet et Grumbach, 14 Cours
des Bastions, CP.18, CH-1211 Geneve
12, (41-22) 311 00 10, Fax: (41-22)
311 00 20, Consultant (of Counsel),
Registered as Foreign Lawyer Geneva
Bar, Call Date: Nov 1955 (Middle
Temple) Qualifications: MA (Oxon)

Lack *Jeremy*
Becton Dickinson Europe, 5 Chemin
Des Sources, B.P.37, 38241 Meylan
Cedex, (+33) 7641 6801, Fax: (+33)
7641 6800, Attorney, Admitted to
various US Federal Courts & the US
CAFC Registered U.S. Patent Attorney,
Reg No 35, 813 and Member New York
State Bar (1990), Call Date: Nov 1989
(Middle Temple) Qualifications: MA
(Oxon), Jurisprudence &, Physiological,
Sciences

Lai *Miss Fui Sim*
16 Lorong Kemaris 4, Bukit Bandaraya,
Bangsar, 59100 Kuala Lumpur,
Malaysia, 03 2561243, Call Date: July
1995 (Lincoln's Inn) Qualifications:
LLB (Hons)

Lai *Kwok Seng*
Singapore 1544, Call Date: Nov 1995
(Lincoln's Inn) Qualifications: LLB
(Hons)

Lai *Miss Sheau Wei*
Malaysia, Call Date: July 1997 (Middle
Temple) Qualifications: LLB
(Hons)(Hull)

Lai *Soo Hua*
Malaysia, Call Date: July 1998
(Lincoln's Inn) Qualifications: LLB
(Hons)(Hull)

Lakeman *Advocate Christopher Gerard
Pellow*
Olsen Backhurst & Dorey, Eaton
House, 9 Seaton Place, St Helier, Jersey
JE2 3QL, +44 (0) 01534 888900, Fax:
+44 (0) 01534 887744/55, Formerly
Ecrivain (Jersey 1994) Advocate of the
Royal Court of Jersey (1995) Jersey Law
Society and Member Jersey Bar, Call
Date: Nov 1991 (Middle Temple)
Qualifications: BA Hons (Kent),
Diplome de Droit, Francais (Paris XI)

Lall *Tersaim*
Shariz Sdn BHD, No 39B Jalan SS 3/29,
Taman University, 47300 Petaling Jaya,
Selangor Darul, Ehsan, 00 603
7761641, Fax: 00 603 7766818,
Chartered Management Accountan, and
Member Malaysia, Call Date: July 1996
(Gray's Inn) Qualifications: Dip Law

Lam *Ms Che-Mai*
Malaysia, Call Date: July 1998
(Lincoln's Inn) Qualifications: LLB
(Hons)(Lond)

Lam *Chee On*
Singapore 568205, Call Date: July 1997
(Lincoln's Inn) Qualifications: LLB
(Hons)(Lond)

Lam *Edward Chung Weng*
Alban Tay Mahtani & de Silva, 105 Cecil
Street, [H]13-00 The Octagon,
Singapore 118174, 65-534 5266, Fax:
65-223 8762, Legal Assistant, and
Member Singapore Bar, Call Date: July
1992 (Middle Temple) Qualifications:
LLB (Hons) (E.Ang)

Lam *Jen Yii*
Malaysia, Call Date: July 1996 (Middle
Temple) Qualifications: LLB
(Hons)(Warw)

Lam *Ken Chung Simon*
1103 Prince's Building, Central, Hong
Kong, 25220066, Fax: 28450851, and
Member Australian Capital Territory
Hong Kong Bar, Call Date: July 1989
(Middle Temple) Qualifications: BSc,
LLB (Buck)

Lam *Osmond Kwok Fai*
Hong Kong, and Member Hong Kong
Bar, Call Date: 1988 (Inner Temple)
Qualifications: LLB (Manch), LLM
(Lond)

Lam *Ms Shiao-Ning*
M/S Arfat Selvam & Gunasingham, 30
Raffles Place, [H] 12-00 Caltex House,
Singapore 1543, Legal Associate, and
Member Singapore Bar, Call Date: July
1996 (Inner Temple) Qualifications:
LLB (Hull)

F

Lam *Stephen Sui Lung*
4th Floor, High Block, Queensway
Government Offices, 66 Queensway,
Hong Kong, 2867 2160, Fax: 2869
0720, Director of Administration &
Development, Department of Justice,
Hong Kong, Call Date: Feb 1986 (Gray's
Inn) Qualifications: BSocSc, LLB

Lam *Steven Kuet Keng*
Apt Blk 121, [H] 01-81, Bishan St 12, S
570121, Singapore, Singapore 2057,
2587480(H)/97370110/2999500, Fax:
3330455, Lecturer at Law/Tutor
Singapore Institute of Commerc
Advocate & Solicitor at M/S Kamppan
Chettiar & Partners, and Member
Singapore, Call Date: July 1995 (Middle
Temple) Qualifications: LLB (Hons)

Lam *Tin Sing*
Hong Kong, Call Date: Nov 1994
(Middle Temple) Qualifications: LLB
(Hons)

Lam *Miss Tse-Yi*
Singapore 276663, Call Date: July 1998
(Gray's Inn) Qualifications: LLB
(Wales)

Lammy *David Lindon*
Howard Rice, Nemerovski, Canady, Falk
& Rabkin, Three Embarcadero Center,
7th Floor, San Francisco 941114065,
001 415 434 1600, and Member
California Bar, Call Date: Feb 1995
(Lincoln's Inn) Qualifications: LLB
(Hons)(Lond)

Lan *Ms Sin Cynthia Mei*
Malaysia, Call Date: Nov 1997 (Inner
Temple) Qualifications: BA (LSE)

Lancaster *Kenneth Alan*
The Netherlands, Call Date: July 1995
(Lincoln's Inn) Qualifications: LLM
(Lond), FCA,, ACIArb

Landick *Pierre Stanley*
Ogier & Le Masurier, Whiteley
Chambers, Don Street, St Helier, Jersey
JE4 9WG, Channel Islands, 01534
504000, Fax: 01534 35328, and
Member Advocate of the Royal Court of
Jersey, Call Date: Feb 1989 (Lincoln's
Inn) Qualifications: LLB

Lane *John Robert Benjamin*
Frommer Lawrence & Haug LLP, 745
Fifth Avenue, New York, NY 10151,
United States of America, 212 588
0800, Fax: 212 588 0500, and Member
New York Bar Washington DC Bar, Call
Date: Nov 1989 (Middle Temple)
Qualifications: BA

Lang *Lawrence Fatt Khim*
Singapore 520360, Call Date: July 1996
(Middle Temple) Qualifications: LLB
(Hons)(Wolves)

Langridge *Ms Natalie Katherine*
Estudio Interjuridico S.L., Estudio Legal
y Tributario, Edificio IVC, Arturo Soria,
245, 28033 Madrid, Spain, (341) 359
7679, Fax: (341) 345 5373, and
Member Madrid-Spain Bar, Call Date:
Nov 1992 (Middle Temple)
Qualifications: BA (Hons, Kent),
Diplome de Droit, Francais (Paris XI),,
European Law Diploma, (Bruges,
Belgium)

Langwaller *David Johann Herbert*
Ireland, and Member Irish Bar, Call
Date: Feb 1993 (Gray's Inn)
Qualifications: BA (Law Trinity,
Dublin), LLM (LSE), BL (King's Inn,
Dublin), LLM , (Harvard)

Larder *Graham Charles*
Thomas Howell Group(S.A.)(PTY), GF
Office Park, Grosvenor Road,
Bryanston, 2021, Republic of South
Africa, (011) 463 5900, Fax: (011) 463
5920, Loss Adjuster, Call Date: Nov
1974 (Middle Temple) Qualifications:
LLB

Latimer *Mrs Ai-Yuen*
5/61 Wyralla Avenue, Epping 2121,
Sydney NSW, Australia, 02 9868 5773,
Fax: 02 9868 5771, and Member
Malaysia, Call Date: July 1994 (Middle
Temple) Qualifications: LLB
(Hons)(Reading)

Latimer *Raymond Raj*
5/61 Wyralla Avenue, Epping 2121,
Sydney NSW, Australia, 02 9868 5773,
Fax: 02 9868 5771, and Member
Malaysia, Call Date: July 1994 (Middle
Temple) Qualifications: LLB
(Hons)(Reading)

Lau *Cecil Ning Kiang*
Malaysia, Call Date: July 1995
(Lincoln's Inn) Qualifications: LLB
(Hons)

Lau *Miss Cheh Meng Patricia*
Malaysia, Call Date: July 1995 (Middle
Temple) Qualifications: LLB (Hons)

Lau *Miss Chew Mee*
Malaysia, Call Date: Nov 1996
(Lincoln's Inn) Qualifications: LLB
(Hons)(L'pool)

Lau *Dennis Yee Meng*
Bong & Co Advocates, Lot 954, 1st
Floor, Mayflower Commercial Building,
Jalan Kwang Tung, 98008 Miri, Sarawak
Malaysia, Malaysia, 60 85 439969, Fax:
60 85 435313, and Member High Court
of Malaya High Court of Sabah and
Sarawak, Call Date: July 1995
(Lincoln's Inn) Qualifications: LLB
(Hons)

Lau *Dr James Chi Wang*
Flat 3A, Block 8 29, Braemar Hill Road,
Hong Kong, Hong Kong, 852-8930332,
Fax: 852-8380011, Call Date: July 1992
(Gray's Inn) Qualifications: LLB
(Lond), PhD (Lond), MSc (Manch),
LLM (Hong Kong), MSc (Econ)(Lond),
MBA, MICE, FIStructE, Ceng, FHKIE

Lau *Miss Jean Aye Lin*
Singapore 2158, Call Date: July 1996
(Lincoln's Inn) Qualifications: LLB
(Hons)

Lau *Lee Sing Edward*
See Hua Daily News/The Borneo, Post/
Sinhua Evening News, PO Box 20,
96007 Sibu,Sarawak, E Malaysia,
Malaysia, 084 332055, Fax: 084
321255, Legal Adviser/Assistant General
Manager, and Member Sarawak Bar
Malaysia Bar, Call Date: July 1988
(Lincoln's Inn) Qualifications: LLB
(Hons) (Manch), LLM (Hons) (Lond)

Lau *Miss Man Sai*
[H]07-07 Derby Court, 5 Derbyshire
Road, Singapore 1130, (65) 355 1507,
Fax: (65) 222 2521, and Member
Singapore Bar, Call Date: Oct 1995
(Middle Temple) Qualifications: LLB
(Hons)

Lau *Robert Chun Keong*
M/S Rashid & Lee, 6th Floor, 56 Jalan
Tuanku, Abdul Rahman, 50100 Kuala
Lumpur, Malaysia, 60 3 2938155 Ext
333, Fax: 60-3-2939566, and Member
Malaysia Bar, Call Date: Oct 1991
(Gray's Inn) Qualifications: LLB
(Warwick)

Lau *Teik Soon*
Singapore 588333, Call Date: July 1996
(Lincoln's Inn) Qualifications: LLB
(Hons)(Lond)

Lau *Tiew Kung*
Malaysia, Call Date: July 1996
(Lincoln's Inn) Qualifications: LLB
(Hons)(Lond)

Lau *Wai Hin*
Hong Kong, Call Date: Nov 1997
(Lincoln's Inn) Qualifications: BSc
(eng)(Hons)(Hong, Kong), CPE
(Manch)

Lau *Miss Wei Shieong*
Malaysia, Call Date: Oct 1998
(Lincoln's Inn) Qualifications: LLB
(Leic)

Lau *William John*
Hong Kong, Investment Banker, and
Member Hong Kong Bar, Call Date: July
1990 (Lincoln's Inn) Qualifications:
LLB (B'ham), ACCA, AHKSA

Lau *Miss Winnie Yee Wan*
Hong Kong, Call Date: Nov 1997
(Middle Temple) Qualifications: BSc
(Hons)(Lond)

Lau *Ms Yin Fong*
Hong Kong, Call Date: Nov 1997
(Middle Temple) Qualifications: LLB
(Hons)(Lond), BA (Hons) (HKU)

Laurence Wee Ewe Lay *John*
No 2 Ewart Park, 65 5345155, Fax: 65
5342622, Advocate & Solicitor of the
Supreme Court of Singapore, Call Date:
July 1982 (Middle Temple)
Qualifications: LLB (Hons)

Law *Ms Cheok Yin*
Top Floor, See Woh Building, 90 Jalan Pudu, 55100 Kuala Lumpur, Malaysia, (603) 2381231, Fax: (603) 2329430, and Member Malaysian Bar, Call Date: July 1993 (Middle Temple) Qualifications: BA (Hons)(Cantab)

Law *Chun Keat*
Malaysia, Call Date: July 1997 (Middle Temple) Qualifications: LLB (Hons)

Law *Miss Jee Wei*
Singapore 577491, Call Date: July 1996 (Middle Temple) Qualifications: LLB (Hons)(Lond)

Law *Miss Yuk-Ching*
Hong Kong, and Member Hong Kong Bar, Call Date: Nov 1997 (Middle Temple) Qualifications: BA (Hons)

Lawrence *Bernard Hilary*
Malaysia, Call Date: Nov 1996 (Gray's Inn) Qualifications: LLB (Warw)

Lawrence *Miss Kerry Joy*
Ogier & Le Masurier, P O Box 404, Pirouet House, Union Street, St Helier, Jersey JE4 9WG, Channel Islands, 01534 504000, Fax: 01534 35328, Advocate of the Royal Court of Jersey, Call Date: Nov 1995 (Inner Temple) Qualifications: MA (Oxon), CPE (Lond), BA (Hons)

Le Cocq *Timothy John*
Ogier & Le Masurier, P O Box 404, Whiteley Chambers, Don Street, St Helier JE4 8WZ, Channel Islands, 01534 504370, Fax: 01534 35328, Partner - Litigation Group, Advocate of the Royal Court of Jersey and Member Jersey Bar, Call Date: July 1981 (Inner Temple) Qualifications: BA (Hons)(Keele)

Le Pichon *Mrs Doreen*
High Court, 38 Queensway, Hong Kong, (852) 2825 4430, Fax: (852) 2523 3387, Judge of the High Court, and Member Hong Kong Bar New York Bar, Call Date: Nov 1969 (Lincoln's Inn) Qualifications: BA, BCL (Oxon)

Le Poidevin *Nicholas*
Advocates Babbe Le Poidevin, Allez P O Box 612, Hirzel Court, St Peter Port, Guernsey, Channel Islands, Channel Islands, 01481 710585, Fax: 01481 712245, and Member Royal Court of Guernsey, Call Date: Nov 1986 (Gray's Inn) Qualifications: MA (Oxon) , PhD (RVC Lond), C.Biol

Le Quesne *David Fisher*
Vibert & Valpy, 8 Duhamel Place, St Helier, Jersey JE1 3WF, 0534 888666, Fax: 0534 888555, Advocate of the Royal Ct of Jersey., Call Date: Nov 1976 (Inner Temple) Qualifications: LLB

Leck *Andy Kwang Hwee*
c/o Messrs Baker & McKenzie, 1 Temasek Avenue 27-01, Millenia Tower, 65 338 1888, Fax: 65 337 5100, and Member Singapore Bar, Call Date: July 1992 (Gray's Inn) Qualifications: LLB (Bristol)

Lee *Brian Ying Wah*
51 Sixth Crescent, Singapore 276453, 65 4690892, Fax: 65 4697554, Company Secretary, and Member Advocate & Solicitor Singapore, Call Date: July 1995 (Middle Temple) Qualifications: LLB (Hons)

Lee *Chau Ee*
Singapore 1953, Call Date: July 1995 (Middle Temple) Qualifications: LLB (Hons)

Lee *Chau Yee*
M/S Chor Pee Anwarul & Co, Unit 10.01, Level 10, Wisma LKN, 49 Jalan Wong Ah Fook, 80000 Johor Bahru, Malaysia, 607 2234733, Fax: 607 2234734, and Member Malaysia Bar, Call Date: July 1995 (Lincoln's Inn) Qualifications: LLB (Hons)

Lee *Miss Cheryl Siew Fung*
Singapore 2057, Call Date: July 1995 (Middle Temple) Qualifications: LLB (Hons) (Hull)

Lee *Miss Chiek Chuin*
West Malaysia, Call Date: July 1996 (Middle Temple) Qualifications: LLB (Hons)(Notts)

Lee *Miss Chin Theng*
No 74, Jalan 11/3N, Subang Jaya, 47620 Petaling Jaya, Selangor, Malaysia, 03-737 6846, Legal Officer, and Member Malaysian Bar, Call Date: July 1996 (Lincoln's Inn) Qualifications: LLB (Hons)(Lond)

Lee *Chong Ting*
Hong Kong, Call Date: Nov 1998 (Middle Temple) Qualifications: MBA (East Asia)

Lee *David Ken Hwa*
Malaysia, Call Date: July 1997 (Middle Temple) Qualifications: LLB (Hons)

Lee *Miss Deanna Maria*
West Indies, Call Date: Mar 1997 (Middle Temple) Qualifications: BSc (Florida), LLB (Hons) (L'pool)

Lee *Dennis Preston*
7 Canna Road, Victoria Gardens North, Diego Martin, Trinidad, (868) 633 5344, Fax: (868) 633 5361, E.V.P. Clico Investment Bank Limited, and Member Jamaica Trinidad & Tobago Bar, Call Date: July 1988 (Lincoln's Inn) Qualifications: BSc (Hons) (Lond), MBA (California)

Lee *Desmond Boon Teck*
Singapore 258068, Call Date: July 1996 (Lincoln's Inn) Qualifications: LLB (Hons)(Leeds)

Lee *Miss Elaine Yu Lian*
Singapore 299584, Call Date: July 1997 (Lincoln's Inn) Qualifications: LLB (Hons)(Lond), LLM (Lond)

Lee *Eng Seng*
Chew, Tan & Lim, Advocates & Solicitors, 51-20 A Menara BHL Bank, 10050 Penang, Malaysia, 04-2281998, Fax: 04-2281367 & 04-2285521, and Member Malaysia Bar, Call Date: July 1995 (Lincoln's Inn) Qualifications: LLB (Hons)

Lee *Eugene*
Malaysia, Call Date: July 1997 (Lincoln's Inn) Qualifications: LLB (Hons)

Lee *George Swee Seng*
Malaysia, Call Date: Nov 1998 (Lincoln's Inn) Qualifications: LLB (Hons)

Lee *Han Meng*
Malaysia, Call Date: July 1996 (Lincoln's Inn) Qualifications: LLB (Hons)(Lond)

Lee *Dr Helen Ho-Yan*
Securities and Futures Comm, 12/F Edinburgh Tower, The Landmark, 15 Queen's Road Central, Hong Kong, 28409246, Fax: 25217929, Hong Kong Barrister, Call Date: Nov 1989 (Middle Temple) Qualifications: LLB, LLM M Soc Sc, PhD

Lee *Miss Hong*
84 Jalan Daud, [H]12-03 Windy Heights, Singapore 1441, Singapore 1441, 7465086, Fax: 7465973, Call Date: July 1995 (Lincoln's Inn) Qualifications: LLB (Hons) (Wales)

Lee *James*
1323A Prince's Building, 10 Chater Road, Central, Hong Kong, Hong Kong, (852) 252-66182, Fax: (852) 252-66011, Reg Architect (Hong Kong) Chief Inspector Ryl Hong Kong Aux Police Force.Personal Asst to Commandant of Ryl Hong Kong Aux Police. Div Vice-President St John's Ambulance Brigade. Vice-President Director & Hon Sec of Lions Club. Dist Gov of Interact CI, and Member Hong Kong Bar, Call Date: Feb 1992 (Gray's Inn) Qualifications: B.Arch (Hong Kong), BA (Arch Studies), (HK) , RIBA, ARAIA, HKIA, ACIArb, AHKCIArb, Dip in, Chinese Law, LLB (China) , LLB (Hons)(Lond)

Lee *Jonathan Kuan Yee*
591200 Malaysia, 60-3-2823916, Fax: 60-3-2825687, Call Date: July 1996 (Middle Temple) Qualifications: LLB (Hons)(Bris)

F

Lee *Miss Joyce Cheng Lye*
Cy-Handee Rubber Mouldings, SDN.
BHD, 2nd Floor, Lot 2.08B Choo Plaz,
41 Aboo Sittee Lane, 10400 Penang,
Malaysia, 60-4 2296141, Fax: 60-4
2291336, Executive Director, Call Date:
Nov 1998 (Lincoln's Inn)
Qualifications: LLB (Hons) (Wolves)

Lee *Miss June Hsiao Tsun*
Hong Kong, Call Date: Nov 1992
(Middle Temple) Qualifications: LLB
(Hons, Hull)

Lee *Keat Chee*
Hong Kong, Call Date: Oct 1996
(Lincoln's Inn) Qualifications: LLB
(Hons) (L'pool)

Lee *Khai*
256 Jalan Utara, 11700 Gelugor,
Penang, Malaysia, Malaysia, 04
6579757, and Member Malaysia Bar,
Call Date: July 1993 (Lincoln's Inn)
Qualifications: LLB (Hons, N'ham)

Lee *Kim Meng David*
Malaysia, Call Date: July 1997 (Gray's
Inn) Qualifications: LLB (Notts)

Lee *Kok Chew*
Malaysia, Call Date: July 1997
(Lincoln's Inn) Qualifications: LLB
(Hons) (LSE)

Lee *Ms Kuan Wei*
Malaysia, Call Date: July 1997 (Gray's
Inn) Qualifications: LLB (Sheff)

Lee *Miss Lai Lee Lily*
Malaysia, Call Date: Nov 1996 (Gray's
Inn) Qualifications: LLB

Lee *Miss Lucy*
Canada, Call Date: Oct 1998 (Middle
Temple) Qualifications: BA (Ontario),
LLB

Lee *Miss Mary Chung Ching*
Szetu & Associates, 95 Lorong Ikan
Lais, off Jalan Mat Salleh, 88100
Tanjung Aru, P.O.Box 319, 88858
Tanjung Aru, Kota Kinaba, Malaysia,
088 221125/233558, Fax: 088 237543,
Advocate of the High Court in Sabah &
Sarawak in the State of Sabah
(Malaysia), Call Date: July 1996
(Lincoln's Inn) Qualifications: BSc
(Hons), MSc (Hons) (Leeds), Dip in
Law

Lee *Miss Melanie Anne*
Singapore 358660, Call Date: July 1997
(Middle Temple) Qualifications: LLB
(Hons)

Lee *Min Kin*
8 Nim Drive, Seletar Hills, Singapore
2880, Singapore 28800, 00 65
4812024, Call Date: July 1993 (Inner
Temple) Qualifications: LLB (Warw)

Lee *Miss Noushi*
Messrs Gideon Tan Razali Zaini, No 314
Block A., Kelana Business Centre, Jln
SS7/2, 47301 Petaling Jaya, Selangor
Darul Ehsan, Malaysia, 603-5820016,
Fax: 603-5820015, and Member
Malaysia Bar, Call Date: July 1997
(Lincoln's Inn) Qualifications: LLB
(Hons) (Leeds)

Lee *Miss Nyet Fah Alyssa*
Messrs Lim & Gopalan, 20 Maxwell
Road, [H]05-11/15 Maxwell House,
Singapore 069113, Singapore 320098,
220 2344, Fax: 225 9503, and Member
Singapore Bar, Call Date: July 1996
(Middle Temple) Qualifications: LLB
(Hons) (Lond)

Lee *Pak Chau*
Hong Kong, Call Date: Mar 1997
(Middle Temple) Qualifications: BSc
(Hons) (L'pool), MSc (B'ham)

Lee *Miss Patricia Suk Kee*
White & Case Solicitors, 9th Floor,
Gloucester Tower, The Landmark, 11
Pedder Street, Central, Hong Kong,
(852) 2822 8762/2822 8700, Fax:
(852) 2845 9070, Legal Assistant, Call
Date: July 1998 (Middle Temple)
Qualifications: LLB (Hons) (Lond)

Lee *Miss Pauline Aileen*
Malaysia, and Member Malaysia Bar,
Call Date: July 1995 (Middle Temple)
Qualifications: LLB (Hons) (Wales)

Lee *Peter Kong Chung*
c/o Messrs Lee & Associates, Advocates
& Solicitors, P.O. Box 12604, 88829
Kota Kinaban, Sabah, 088 215262,
Fax: 088 217892, Sabah Bar, The
Sabah Law Association, Call Date: July
1988 (Lincoln's Inn) Qualifications:
LLB (Hons) (Bucks)

Lee *Miss Pin Pin*
Malaysia, Call Date: Nov 1995 (Middle
Temple) Qualifications: LLB (Hons)

Lee *Richard Teck-Soon*
Malaysia, Call Date: Nov 1997 (Inner
Temple) Qualifications: LLB (Lond)

Lee *Miss Seow Ser*
Singapore 458659, Call Date: July 1996
(Middle Temple) Qualifications: LLB
(Hons) (Leeds)

Lee *Miss Siew Mui*
Singapore 330047, Call Date: July 1996
(Lincoln's Inn) Qualifications: LLB
(Hons) (Lond)

Lee *Miss Siew Peng*
Malaysia, Call Date: Feb 1995 (Middle
Temple) Qualifications: LLB
(Hons) (Lond)

Lee *Miss Simone*
Malaysia, Call Date: July 1995 (Middle
Temple) Qualifications: LLB (Hons)
(Bris)

Lee *Miss Su Fern*
Singapore 298818, Call Date: July 1998
(Middle Temple) Qualifications: LLB
(Hons) (Lond)

Lee *Miss Sue Chien*
Malaysia, Call Date: July 1997 (Middle
Temple) Qualifications: LLB
(Hons) (Warw)

Lee *Teck Hock*
Malaysia, Call Date: Mar 1998
(Lincoln's Inn) Qualifications: LLB
(Hons) (Leics)

Lee *Tin Yan*
Hong Kong, Call Date: July 1994
(Middle Temple) Qualifications: LLB
(Hons) (Lond)

Lee *Towk Boon*
Malaysia, Call Date: July 1995
(Lincoln's Inn) Qualifications: LLB
(Hons)

Lee *Tzu Voon*
P O Box 20269, Pejabat Pos Luyang,
88759 Kota Kinabal, Sabah, Malaysia,
6 088 224820, Fax: 6 088 219046, Call
Date: Nov 1994 (Lincoln's Inn)
Qualifications: LLB (Hons) (Lond)

Lee *Wei Chiang*
Malaysia, Call Date: Oct 1997 (Gray's
Inn) Qualifications: LLB (Lancs)

Lee *Wei Yung*
B 873 Yishun St 81, 03-167, 535 0550,
Fax: 438 0550, Senior Investigating
Officer, Legal Assistant (Litigation -
Insurance, Contract, Shipping) Senior
Officer, Singapore Police Force (PNS),
and Member Singapore Bar, Call Date:
July 1991 (Middle Temple)
Qualifications: LLB (Hons) (Warw)

Lee *Miss Wendy Hsiao Wen*
Singapore 1544, and Member
Singapore Bar, Call Date: July 1993
(Middle Temple) Qualifications: LLB
(Hons)

Lee *Mrs Wendy Su Lin*
Singapore 438073, Company Secretary,
and Member Singapore (1996), Call
Date: July 1995 (Middle Temple)
Qualifications: LLB (Hons) (Hull)

Lee *Yi Chung*
Malaysia, Call Date: Nov 1996 (Middle
Temple) Qualifications: LLB
(Hons) (Hull)

Lee *Yih Leang*
Malaysia, Call Date: July 1995
(Lincoln's Inn) Qualifications: LLB
(Hons)

Lee *Mr Yuen Wai*
16 Raffles Quay, [H]36-00, Singapore
2057, (65) 322 1479, Fax: (65) 234
2621, and Member Singapore Bar, Call
Date: July 1993 (Lincoln's Inn)
Qualifications: LLB (Hons, Sheff)

Leigh-Morgan *Miss Tonia Lesley Winson*
Channel Islands, Call Date: Nov 1996 (Lincoln's Inn) Qualifications: LLB (Hons)

Leng *Chua Kee*
Malaysia, Call Date: Nov 1997 (Inner Temple) Qualifications: B.Acc (Singapore), LLB (Lond)

Leng *Miss Lai Yoke*
Zaid Ibrahim & Co, 12th Floor, Menara Bank, Pembangunan, Jalan Sultan Ismail, 50250 Kuala Lumpur, Malaysia, 603 2926688, Fax: 603 2981632, Associate, and Member Bar of Malaysia, Call Date: July 1993 (Inner Temple) Qualifications: LLB (Nott'm)

Lenny *Lenny Matthew*
Northern Ireland, Call Date: July 1998 (Gray's Inn) Qualifications: BSc (Ulster), LLB (Belfast)

Leon *Kwong Wing*
35 Dunearn Close, Singapore 299595, (65) 466 0285, Fax: (65) 466 0285, and Member Singapore, Call Date: Nov 1995 (Gray's Inn) Qualifications: LLB (Wales)

Leon *Miss Le Lyn*
Singapore 1129, Call Date: Nov 1995 (Gray's Inn) Qualifications: LLB (Wales)

Leonard *Eamonn Benedict Knightley*
E102, Hermann-Ehlers-Hans, Martinsburg 29, 49078 Osnabrück, Germany (0541) 41599, Call Date: Nov 1992 (Inner Temple) Qualifications: BA (Dunelm), LLM (Osnabruck)

Leonard *Hywel*
One Harbour Place, P.O. Box 3239, Tampa, Florida 33601, 813 223 7000, Fax: 813 229 4133, and Member Florida, Call Date: July 1974 (Gray's Inn) Qualifications: LLB (Wales) , JD [Florida State]

Leonard *Miss Julia Adella*
British Virgin Islands, Call Date: Nov 1996 (Gray's Inn) Qualifications: BBA (Puerto Rico), LLM (Manch)

Leong *Miss Bik Yoke*
Malaysia, Call Date: July 1994 (Lincoln's Inn) Qualifications: LLB (Hons, Leic)

Leong *Miss Chee Wei*
Singapore 2880, Call Date: Nov 1995 (Middle Temple) Qualifications: LLB (Hons) (Hull)

Leong *Miss Cherly Suet Mei*
Malaysia, and Member Malaysia, Call Date: Nov 1997 (Lincoln's Inn) Qualifications: LLB (Hons) (Leics)

Leong *Miss Constance Choy Leng*
Singapore 599700, and Member Singapore, Call Date: July 1996 (Middle Temple) Qualifications: LLB (Hons) (Lond), BA (Singapore)

Leong *Miss Isabelle May Yue*
Singapore 271009, Call Date: July 1997 (Middle Temple) Qualifications: LLB (Hons) (Sheff)

Leong *Miss Jacqueline Pamela*
1531 Prince's Building, Chater Road, (852) 2523-2899, Fax: (852) 2840-0786, QC Hong Kong and Member Hong Kong, Victoria, New South Wales Singapore Bar, Call Date: July 1970 (Inner Temple)

Leong *Miss Joycelyn Wai Keng*
Malaysia, Call Date: July 1991 (Lincoln's Inn) Qualifications: LLB (Hons) (East An)

Leong *Kee Han*
Malaysia, Call Date: Nov 1996 (Lincoln's Inn) Qualifications: LLB (Hons)

Leong *Miss Kit Wan*
Singapore 809760, Call Date: July 1998 (Middle Temple) Qualifications: LLB (Hons) (Hull)

Leong *Kwok Yan*
12th Floor, Menara Bank Pembangunan, Jalan Sultan Ismail, 50250 Kuala Lumpur, Malaysia, 03 292 6688, Fax: 07 298 1632, and Member Malaysia, Call Date: July 1992 (Lincoln's Inn) Qualifications: LLB (Hons) (Lond)

Leong *Miss Li Lian*
Singapore 1334, Call Date: Nov 1995 (Gray's Inn) Qualifications: LLB

Leong *Michael Kim Seng*
Singapore 610151, Call Date: Nov 1997 (Middle Temple) Qualifications: BA (Singapore), LLB (Hons) (Lond)

Leong *Miss Nu-Yen Mireille*
161027 Singapore, Call Date: Nov 1997 (Lincoln's Inn) Qualifications: LLB (Hons) (Leeds)

Leong *Miss Pat Lynn*
Singapore 1545, Call Date: July 1992 (Lincoln's Inn) Qualifications: LLB (Hons) (Exon)

Leong *Miss Sue Lynn*
Singapore 456478, Call Date: Nov 1995 (Middle Temple) Qualifications: BA (Hons) (Keele)

Leong *Why Kong*
Braddell Brothers, 1 Colombo Court, [H]06-30, Singapore 648602, (65) 3366032, Fax: (65) 3366042, and Member Singapore, Call Date: July 1995 (Gray's Inn) Qualifications: LLB (Lond)

Leow *Miss Fui Fui*
Malaysia, Call Date: July 1995 (Middle Temple) Qualifications: LLB (Hons) (Wales)

Leow *Michael Yung Fuong*
Robert W H Wang & Woo, 9 Temasek Boulevard [H]14-01, Suntec Tower 2, Singapore 269294, 336 0123, Fax: 332 1480, and Member Singapore Bar, Call Date: July 1992 (Gray's Inn) Qualifications: LLB, LLM (Lond)

Leung *Michael Hung Kuk*
1002 Chekiang First Bank, 1 Duddell Street, Central, Hong Kong, 2521 7317, Fax: 2845 0654, and Member Hong Kong Bar, Call Date: Nov 1993 (Gray's Inn) Qualifications: LLB (Lond)

Leung *Paul Hei Ming*
Hong Kong, Call Date: Nov 1997 (Middle Temple) Qualifications: B.Eng (Hons) (NSW,, Australia)

Leung *Richard Wai-Keung*
Des Voeux Chambers, 10/F Bank of East Asia, Building, 10 Des Voeux Road, Central, Hong Kong, 852 2526 3071, Fax: 852 2810 5287, and Member Hong Kong Bar, Call Date: July 1994 (Inner Temple) Qualifications: MA (Lancs), LLB

Leung *Siu Ying*
Hong Kong, and Member Hong Kong Bar, Call Date: Nov 1992 (Gray's Inn) Qualifications: B Arch (Newc), LLB (Lond)

Leung *Sun So*
Hong Kong, Call Date: Nov 1989 (Gray's Inn) Qualifications: LLB [Lond]

Leung *Tak Yin*
Hong Kong, and Member Hong Kong Bar, Call Date: July 1995 (Middle Temple) Qualifications: LLB (Hons)

Leung *Wai Man R*
Temple Chambers, 16th Floor, One Pacific Place, 88 Queensway, 2523 2003, Fax: 2810 0302, and Member Hong Kong Bar, Call Date: Feb 1992 (Gray's Inn) Qualifications: BA (Hong Kong), LLB (Lond)

Leung *Yew Kwong*
Inland Revenue Authority of, Singapore Law Division, 55 Newtown Road, Revenue House, Singapore 1646, 00656 3512022, Fax: 00656 3512077, Chief Legal Officer, Advocate & Solicitor (Singapore), Call Date: Nov 1989 (Lincoln's Inn) Qualifications: LLB, BSc (Lond), MSc (Reading), MBA (Singapore)

Leung *Miss Yuet Ngor*
Hong Kong, Call Date: Oct 1996 (Middle Temple) Qualifications: BSc (Hons) (HongKong), CPE (Manc)

Lever *Mrs Andrina Gay Richards*
Suite 2308, 965 Bay Street, Toronto, Ontario M55 2A3, 416 920 5114, Fax: 416 920 6764, Managing Director, and Member Victoria Bar Australia Bar, Call Date: July 1980 (Gray's Inn) Qualifications: BA, BA (Hons)

F

Levin *David Samuel*
Owen Dixon Chambers, 205 William St, Melbourne 3000, 61 39608 7043, Fax: 61 39608 8186, Advocate Member Legal Profession Tribunal (Vic), QC (Victoria) and Member Victoria, Australian Capital Territory, Tasmania, New South Wales, Northern Territory, South Australia New South Wales Bar South Australia Bar, Call Date: July 1972 (Middle Temple) Qualifications: MA (Cantab)

Lewin *Miss Megan Karola*
Cox, Hallett & Wilkinson, Milner House, 18 Parliament Street, Hamilton, Bermuda, (441) 295 4630, Fax: (441) 292 7880, and Member Bermuda, Call Date: Mar 1997 (Lincoln's Inn) Qualifications: LLB (Hons) (B'ham)

Lewis *Edwin*
C/O Lee Hishammuddin, 16th Floor, Wisma HLA, Jalan Raja Chulan, 50200 Kuala Lumpur, Malaysia, 603-2011681, 2018415 Ext 185, Fax: 603-2011746, 2011714, Legal Assistant, Advocate & Solicitor (West Malaysia) and Member West Malaysia Bar, Call Date: Nov 1997 (Lincoln's Inn) Qualifications: LLB (Hons)

Lewis *Miss Kadian Elaine*
West Indies, Call Date: Oct 1998 (Gray's Inn) Qualifications: LLB

Lewis *Miss Linda Catherine*
Germany, Call Date: Feb 1990 (Inner Temple) Qualifications: BSc (Surrey), LLM

Lewis *Linton Aron*
P.O.Box 1407, Queen's Drive, St Vincent & The Grenadines, 1 809 456 2577, Fax: 1 809 456 5372, Offshore Finance Inspector, and Member St VIncent & The Grenadines, Call Date: July 1996 (Gray's Inn) Qualifications: MA (Bristol), ACCA

Li *Ms Cynthia Sun-Ming*
1318 Prince's Building, 10 Chater Road, Central, Hong Kong, Hong Kong, (852) 2526 8128, Fax: (852) 2526 8500, and Member Hong Kong Bar, Call Date: July 1994 (Inner Temple) Qualifications: BA (Canada), LLB

Li *Miss Gladys Veronica*
2507 Edinburgh Tower, The Landmark, 15 Queen's Road Central, 25-2 17188, Fax: 2810 1823, SC (Hong Kong) and Member Hong Kong Bar, Call Date: 1971 (Lincoln's Inn) Qualifications: MA (Cantab)

Liao *(Cheung-Sing)Andrew*
Hong Kong, Call Date: July 1974 (Lincoln's Inn)

Liao *Martin Cheung-Kong*
61 New Henry House, 10 Ice House Street, Central, Hong Kong, Hong Kong, 2522 5121, and Member Hong Kong Bar Singapore Bar, Call Date: July 1984 (Lincoln's Inn) Qualifications: BSc (Econ), LLM , Dip Law

Liew *Bernard Jin Yang*
Neptune Orient Lines Limited, 456 Alexandra Road [H]06-00, Nol Building, Singapore 119962, Singapore 1545, (65) 3715381, Fax: (65) 2731697, Assistant Manager, and Member Singapore Bar, Call Date: July 1989 (Gray's Inn) Qualifications: LLB (Bucks)

Liew *Miss Lan-Hing*
Singapore 2880, Call Date: July 1995 (Middle Temple) Qualifications: B.Sc (Hons), LLB (Hons)

Liew *Miss Siew Ling*
Malaysia, Call Date: July 1997 (Lincoln's Inn) Qualifications: LLB (Hons)

Liew *Sunny Siew Pang*
Liew Hazalina, Suite 708, Block E, Phileo Damansara I, Jalan Damansara, 46350 Petaling Jaya, Selangor, Malaysia, (603) 460 7668, Fax: (603) 460 8166, and Member Malaysia Bar, Call Date: July 1993 (Gray's Inn) Qualifications: LLB (Brunel)

Lightbourn *Miss Sandra Jean*
Bahamas, Call Date: July 1997 (Lincoln's Inn) Qualifications: LLB (Hons)

Lim *Miss Ai Leen*
Malaysian Derivatives Clearing, House, 5th Floor, Citypoint, Dayabumi Complex, 50050 Kuala Lumpur, 60 3 294 5070, Fax: 60 3 294 5040, Legal Executive Officer, and Member Malaysia Bar, Call Date: Oct 1992 (Middle Temple) Qualifications: LL.B (Hons, B'ham)

Lim *Miss Choi Ming*
Singapore 2367, and Member Singapore Bar, Call Date: July 1995 (Middle Temple) Qualifications: LLB (Hons)

Lim *Chong Fong*
Azman Davidson & Co, Advocates & Solicitors, Suite 13.03, Menara Tan & Tan, 207 Jalan Tun Razak, 50400 Kuala Lumpur Malaysia, Malaysia, 603 264 0200, Fax: 603 264 0280, Partner, and Member Malaysia Bar, Call Date: July 1995 (Middle Temple) Qualifications: LLB (Hons), BSc, (Bldg) (Hons), ARICS,, ACIArb

Lim *Choon How*
Singapore 120413, Call Date: Nov 1996 (Lincoln's Inn) Qualifications: LLB (Hons) (Lond)

Lim *Christopher Su Heng*
Suite 16.01, 16th Floor, Wisma Nusantara, Jalan Punchak, 50050 Kuala Lumpur, Malaysia, 0603 202 3541, Fax: 0603 202 3542, Legal Assistant (Corporate Affairs), and Member Malaysia Bar, Call Date: July 1996 (Lincoln's Inn) Qualifications: LLB (Hons) (Bris), BCL (Oxon)

Lim *Miss Cynthia Siew Leng*
Messrs Iza Ng Yeoh & Kit, Suite 13.08, 13th Floor, Plaza 138, No 138 Jalan Ampang, 50450 Kuala Lumpur, Malaysia, 4694888, Fax: 4694848, Legal Assistant, and Member Malaysia Bar, Call Date: July 1992 (Lincoln's Inn) Qualifications: LLB (Hons) (Lond)

Lim *Fung Peen*
Singapore 449029, Call Date: Nov 1995 (Middle Temple) Qualifications: LLB (Hons)

Lim *Miss Gek Hoon*
Singapore 530018, Call Date: July 1996 (Lincoln's Inn) Qualifications: LLB (Hons) (Lond)

Lim *George Chee Huat*
Singapore 530144, Call Date: July 1997 (Middle Temple) Qualifications: LLB (Hons) (Lond)

Lim *Ms Goon Lwee*
Singapore 288601, 065-545 9918, Fax: 065-545 9908, Chief Financial Officer, Call Date: July 1996 (Inner Temple) Qualifications: LLB (Lond), FCMA, FCIS, B.Acc, CPA

Lim *Miss Grace Siew Hua*
Sime Darby Bhd, 2187 Floor, Wisma Sime Darby, Jalan Raja Laut, 50350 Kuala Lumpur, Malaysia, 603 2914122, Fax: 603 2935030, Legal Advisor, and Member Malaysia, Call Date: July 1994 (Lincoln's Inn) Qualifications: LLB (Hons)

Lim *Miss Helen Bek Yun*
P.O.Box 2773, 90731 Sandakan, Sabah, Malaysia, (089) 222188, Advocate of the High Court in Sabah & Sarawak, Malaysia Advocate of the Supreme Court of Brunei Darussalam, Call Date: July 1995 (Lincoln's Inn) Qualifications: LLB (Hons) (Leeds)

Lim *Miss Heliz Hsien Ling*
Malaysia, Call Date: Nov 1997 (Lincoln's Inn) Qualifications: LLB (Hons) (E.Lond)

Lim *Miss Hui Min*
51 Dyson Road, Singapore 309392, 2551868, Fax: 2519078, Call Date: July 1996 (Lincoln's Inn) Qualifications: BA (Oxon), BCL

Lim *Miss Hui Ting*
Malaysia, Legal Assistant Assistant Bulletin Editor of Rotary Club of Kulai, and Member Malaya Bar, Call Date: Nov 1996 (Lincoln's Inn) Qualifications: LLB (Hons) (Sheff)

Lim *Miss Hwee Bin*
Malaysia, Call Date: July 1996 (Lincoln's Inn) Qualifications: LLB (Hons)

Lim *Miss Jacqueline Hui Erh*
9F Three Exchange Square, 8
Connaught Place, Central, 852 2840
1282, Fax: 852 2840 0515, Call Date:
Oct 1994 (Middle Temple)
Qualifications: LLB (Hons) (Bris), LLM
(Bris)

Lim *Miss Jane Chen*
Lot 309-311 (2nd Floor), Forever
Building, Abell Road, 93100 Kuching,
Sarawak, Malaysia, (006) (082)415902/
412062/259548, Fax:
(006) (082)240302, chambering
student/pupil (1/12/97-1/12/98), Call
Date: Nov 1997 (Lincoln's Inn)
Qualifications: LLB (Hons) (Bucks)

Lim *Miss Jeanne Tsze Ye*
Singapore 2057, Call Date: Nov 1992
(Middle Temple) Qualifications: LLB
(Hons, Lond)

Lim *Miss Jessica Hai Ean*
Malaysia, Call Date: July 1997
(Lincoln's Inn) Qualifications: LLB
(Hons)

Lim *Miss Julie Siu Yen*
Singapore 650252, Call Date: July 1997
(Middle Temple) Qualifications: LLB
(Hons) (Lond)

Lim *Miss Kay Li Deborah*
Singapore 556655, Call Date: July 1997
(Middle Temple) Qualifications: LLB
(Hons) (Nott'm)

Lim *Kevin Tzee-Yung*
Singapore 669561, Call Date: July 1998
(Middle Temple) Qualifications: LLB
(Hons) (Lond)

Lim *Kong Yuk*
Malaysia, Call Date: Nov 1996 (Middle
Temple) Qualifications: LLB
(Hons) (Wales)

Lim *Kuok Sim Edwin*
42 Jalan Permai, Robson Heights, Kuala
Lumpur 50460, (603) 2742234, Legal
Advisor, Call Date: Nov 1995 (Gray's
Inn) Qualifications: LLB (Wales), LLM
(Bris)

Lim *Lay Hor*
Lim Lay Hor & Associates, No 3A, Jalan
Samudra barat, Taman Perindustrian
Samudra, 68100 Batu Caves, Selangor
Darul Ehsan, Malaysia, 03 687 2799,
Fax: 03 687 0799, Call Date: July 1997
(Middle Temple) Qualifications: LLB
(Hons) (Lond)

Lim *Miss Lee Hoon*
Malaysia, Call Date: July 1995
(Lincoln's Inn) Qualifications: LLB
(Hons)

Lim *Miss Li Lian*
Singapore 2880, and Member
Singapore Bar, Call Date: Nov 1992
(Middle Temple) Qualifications: LLB
(Hons, Sheff)

Lim *Miss Li Lin*
Malaysia, Call Date: July 1996 (Middle
Temple) Qualifications: LLB
(Hons) (Lanc)

Lim *Miss Li Yen*
Malaysia, Call Date: Oct 1998 (Inner
Temple) Qualifications: LLB (Notts)

Lim *Miss Liau Yan*
Brunei Darussalam, Call Date: July
1997 (Lincoln's Inn) Qualifications:
LLB (Hons) (Kent)

Lim *Lionel Soon Yee*
Singapore 277315, Call Date: July 1998
(Middle Temple) Qualifications: LLB
(Hons) (Kent)

Lim *Mark Chin Hian*
Malaysia, Call Date: Nov 1996 (Middle
Temple) Qualifications: BA (Hons)

Lim *Miss Michele Hwee Ling*
Singapore 0512, Call Date: July 1995
(Middle Temple) Qualifications: LLB
(Hons) (Hull)

Lim *Miss Michele Kythe Beng Sze*
Malaysia, Call Date: Nov 1992 (Middle
Temple) Qualifications: LLB (Hons)

Lim *Miss Pui Keng*
Malaysia, Call Date: July 1997
(Lincoln's Inn) Qualifications: LLB
(Hons) (Leics)

Lim *Ralph Howard U Wei*
Singapore 1128, Call Date: July 1995
(Lincoln's Inn) Qualifications: LLB
(Hons)

Lim *Raymond Kuan Yew*
Blk 34 [H]02-218, Jalan Bahagia,
Singapore 320034, Singapore 1232,
2547821, and Member Singapore Bar,
Call Date: July 1995 (Lincoln's Inn)
Qualifications: LLB (Hons)

Lim *Richard Teck Hock*
81 Kampong Bahru Road, Singapore
0315, 2277668 169378, Advocate &
Solicitor of the Supreme Court of
Singapore, and Member Singapore, Call
Date: July 1995 (Lincoln's Inn)
Qualifications: LLB (Hons)

Lim *Miss Say Fang*
Singapore 271012, Call Date: July 1998
(Lincoln's Inn) Qualifications: LLB
(Hons) (Sheff), ACIS

Lim *Seng Sheoh*
Singapore 1129, Call Date: Nov 1994
(Middle Temple) Qualifications: BA
(Hons) (Kent)

Lim *Miss Sharon Yen Li*
Chooi & Company, Penthouse, Ming
Building, Jalan Bukit Nanas, 50250
Kuala Lumpur, Malaysia, (603) 232
7344, Fax: (603) 238 2915, and
Member Malaysia, Call Date: July 1995
(Lincoln's Inn) Qualifications: LLB
(Hons)

Lim *Miss Siew Ming*
Malaysia, Call Date: July 1996
(Lincoln's Inn) Qualifications: LLB
(Hons) (Sheff)

Lim *Miss Siew Symn*
c/o Messrs Abdullah,Ooi & Chan, Suite
17-03, 17th Floor, MCB Plaza, 6
Cangkat Raja Chulan, 50200 Kuala
Lumpur Malaysia, Malaysia, 603
2324293, Fax: 603 2301644, Advocate
& Solicitor of the High Court of Malaya,
Call Date: Nov 1992 (Gray's Inn)
Qualifications: LLB (So'ton)

Lim *Miss Sim Yi*
Republic of Singapore, Call Date: July
1995 (Gray's Inn) Qualifications: LLB

Lim *Siu Yin Jeffrey*
455307 Singapore, Call Date: July 1997
(Gray's Inn) Qualifications: LLB (Bris)

Lim *Song Chia*
Singapore 596700, (65) 439 5680, Fax:
(65) 532 0206, First Vice President, PT
Bank Ekspor Impor Indonesia(Persero
Singapore Branch, Call Date: Nov 1996
(Lincoln's Inn) Qualifications: LLB
(Hons) (Lond)

Lim *Stephen Yew Huat*
15th/16th Floors, Bank of China
Building, 4 Battery Road, Singapore,
535 3600, Fax: 538 8598, Advocate &
Solicitor of Supreme Court of Singapore
and Member Singapore, Call Date: July
1992 (Middle Temple) Qualifications:
LLB (Hons) LSe, LLM (Columbia)

Lim *Miss Su-ching*
Messrs Ramdas & Wong, 6 Shenton
Way, [H] 25-06 DBS Building Tower 2,
Singapore 068809, Singapore 669559,
65 220 1121, Fax: 65 225 9152/65 225
9153, and Member Singapore Bar, Call
Date: July 1992 (Middle Temple)
Qualifications: LLB (Hons) (E.Ang)

Lim *Miss Su-Fen*
Drew & Napier, 20 Raffles Place,
[H]17-00 Ocean Towers, Singapore
048620, Singapore 267041, (65) 535
0733, Fax: (65) 535 4864, and Member
Singapore Bar, Call Date: Nov 1994
(Middle Temple) Qualifications: LLB
(Hons)

Lim *Miss Su-Lynn*
Drew & Napier, 20 Raffles Place, [H]
17.00 Ocean Towers, Singapore 2880,
535 0733, Fax: 532 7149, and Member
Singapore Bar, Call Date: July 1995
(Middle Temple) Qualifications: LLB
(Hons) (Hull)

Lim *Swee Tee*
Singapore 330068, Call Date: July 1996
(Middle Temple) Qualifications: BSc
(Singapore), LLB (Hons) (Wolves)

F

Lim *Tanguy Yuteck*
Chor Pee & Partners, 9 Penang Road
[H] 11-08, Parl Mall, Singapore 2159,
332 9555, Fax: 336 2282, Advocate &
Solicitor, and Member Singapore, Call
Date: Nov 1993 (Middle Temple)
Qualifications: LLB (Hons)(Wales)

Lim *Tchuang Cheio Tchwonyoson*
Sembawang Shipyard Pte Ltd, Admiralty
Road West, Singapore 2057, 65 752
2222, Fax: 65 758 1025, Legal Counsel,
and Member Singapore Bar, Call Date:
July 1993 (Middle Temple)
Qualifications: LLB (Hons)(Lond)

Lim *Tiong-Piow*
Malaysia, Call Date: July 1995
(Lincoln's Inn) Qualifications: LLB
(Hons)

Lim *Tuck Sum*
Malaysia, Call Date: July 1996
(Lincoln's Inn) Qualifications: LLB
(Hons)(Lond)

Lim *Wye Hon*
58000 Malaysia, Call Date: July 1996
(Middle Temple) Qualifications: LLB
(Hons)(Leic)

Lim *Yang Hsing Leslie*
Singapore 530448, Call Date: July 1995
(Middle Temple) Qualifications: LLB
(Hons)(Kent)

Lim *Yek Lai*
Malaysia, Call Date: July 1996
(Lincoln's Inn) Qualifications: LLB
(Hons)

Lim *Miss Yen-Hui*
No 50, Jalan 37/70A, Desa Sri
Hartamas, 50480 - Kuala Lumpur,
Malaysia, and Member Malaysia Bar,
Call Date: July 1997 (Gray's Inn)
Qualifications: LLB (Bristol)

Lim *Miss Yoon Cheng Audrey*
Supreme Court, St Andrew's Road,
Singapore 0617, Malaysia, 3323918,
Fax: 3379450, Justices' Law Clerk -
Supreme Court of Singapore, Assistant
Registrar - Supreme Court of
Singapore, and Member Singapore, Call
Date: July 1994 (Middle Temple)
Qualifications: BA (Hons)(Cantab)

Lim *Miss Yuh-Sze Esther*
Singapore 520264, Call Date: July 1998
(Middle Temple) Qualifications: LLB
(Hons)(Wales)

Lin *Miss Diaan-Yi*
Malaysia, Call Date: July 1996
(Lincoln's Inn) Qualifications: BA
(Hons)

Lin *Feng*
Hong Kong, Call Date: Nov 1997
(Middle Temple) Qualifications: LLB
(Fudan), LLM (Victoria)

Lindsay *Miss Alison*
Ireland, Barrister of Ireland, Call Date:
May 1996 (Middle Temple)
Qualifications: BA (Hons)(Dublin), BL
(King's Inn)

Ling *Miss Carolyn Dora Li-Hsing*
Singapore 679389, Call Date: Nov 1989
(Middle Temple) Qualifications: LLB
(Newc), LLM (Lond)

Ling *Chun Wai*
Temple Chambers, 16/F One Pacific
Place, 88 Queensway, Hong Kong,
(852) 2523 2003, Fax: (852) 2810
0302, and Member Hong Kong, Call
Date: July 1996 (Lincoln's Inn)
Qualifications: LLB (Hons)(Lond), LLM
(Cantab)

Ling *Clarence Louis Li-Tien*
Alban Tay Mahtani & de Silva, 39
Robinson Road, [H] 07-01, Robinson
Point, Singapore 2367, (65) 5345266,
Fax: (65) 2238762, and Member
Singapore, Call Date: Nov 1995
(Lincoln's Inn) Qualifications: LLB
(Hons) (Leics), BSc (Chem.emph,
Biochem)

Ling *Hee Keat*
54 Jalan Setiabakti 8, Bukit
Damansara, 50490 Kuala Lumpur,
Malaysia, Malaysia, 03 2535949, Fax:
03 2533580, Call Date: July 1995
(Lincoln's Inn) Qualifications: LLB
(Hons)

Ling *Miss Jing Jinn*
Ting Goh & Associates Advocate, 117,
Lot 156, 1st Floor, Lorong 7, Jalan Ang
Cheng Ho, 93100 Kuching, Sarawak,
Singapore 2366, 082 248008/258008,
Fax: 082 422008, Advocate & Solicitor
of Singapore Advocate of Sarawak, Call
Date: July 1994 (Middle Temple)
Qualifications: LLB (Hons)(Manc)

Ling *Miss Jocettta Ching Tse*
Malaysia, Call Date: July 1995
(Lincoln's Inn) Qualifications: LLB
(Hons)

Ling *Leong Hui*
Singapore 570444, Call Date: July 1996
(Inner Temple) Qualifications: LLB
(Lond)

Ling *Peter Liong Ing*
BP Asia Pacific Pte. Ltd, 396 Alexandra
Road, [H]18-01, BP Tower, (65) 371
8701, Fax: (65) 371 8797, Regional
General Counsel, Call Date: Nov 1969
(Lincoln's Inn)

Ling *Tien Wah*
M/S Helen Yeo & Partners, 11 Collyer
Quay [H]12-01, The Arcade, Singapore
486850, 2251400, Fax: 2221345,
Partner, and Member Singapore Bar
Malaysia Bar, Call Date: Nov 1990
(Lincoln's Inn) Qualifications: LLB
(Leeds)

Ling *Miss Wei Lin*
Malaysia, Call Date: July 1996
(Lincoln's Inn) Qualifications: LLB
(Hons)(Leeds)

Lio *Chee Yeong*
Malaysia, Call Date: Nov 1996 (Middle
Temple) Qualifications: LLB
(Hons)(Lond)

Litton *Henry Denis*
Court of Final Appeal, 1 Battery Path,
Hong Kong, 852-2123-0012, Fax:
852-2524-3991, Permanent Judge of
the Court of Final Appeal, Hong Kong
QC, Call Date: June 1959 (Gray's Inn)
Qualifications: MA (Oxon)

Liu *Kee Yong*
Singapore 0316, Call Date: July 1996
(Middle Temple) Qualifications: LLB
(Hons)(Hull)

Liu *Owen Heng Su*
Taiwan, Call Date: Nov 1997 (Lincoln's
Inn) Qualifications: LLB
(Hons)(Manch)

Liu *Sern Yang*
127660 Singapore, Call Date: Nov 1996
(Gray's Inn) Qualifications: LLB

Liu *Zhipeng*
Singapore 0513, Call Date: July 1996
(Middle Temple) Qualifications: LLB
(Hons)(Notts)

Lloren *Matthew Alviar*
United States of America, Call Date:
Mar 1999 (Lincoln's Inn)
Qualifications: MA (Bris), BA (Stirling)

Lloyd *Michael Gordon*
Rua do Norte 18,20, 1200 Lisbon, 00
351 1 343 3762, Fax: 00 351 1 343
3762, Call Date: Nov 1967 (Gray's Inn)
Qualifications: MA (Oxon)

Lo *Miss Phyllis Set Fui*
East Malaysia, Call Date: July 1996
(Middle Temple) Qualifications: LLB
(Hons)(Bris)

Lo *Pui Yin*
3507-3508 Tower One, Lippo Centre,
89 Queensway, Hong Kong, (852) 2866
8233, Fax: (852) 2866 3932, and
Member Hong Kong Bar, Call Date: July
1992 (Inner Temple) Qualifications:
LLB (LSE)

Locke *William George*
Office of the Public Defender, Alameda
County Court House, 1225 Fallon
Street, Oakland, California 94612
U.S.A., United States of America, 1 510
272 6600, Fax: 1 510 272 6610,
Assistant Public Defender, and Member
California, USA Bar, US District Court,
Northern District of California Bar, Call
Date: Nov 1989 (Inner Temple)
Qualifications: BA (Notre Dame), MA
(Indiana), JD (California)

Logan *David Preston*
Department of Justice, Queensway
Government Offices, 66 Queensway,
852 2867 2366, Fax: 852 2869 0062,
Senior Government Counsel -
Department of Justice, Appearing on
behalf of the Hong Kong Special
Administrative Region of China in the
Hong Kong Courts, International Law
Division, Mutual Legal Assistance Unit
and Member Hong Kong Bar, Call Date:
July 1983 (Inner Temple)
Qualifications: LLB (Sheff)

F

Loh *Miss Annabelle Li Kien*
Singapore 560109, Call Date: July 1997
(Middle Temple) Qualifications: LLB
(Hons)(Lond)

Loh *Benjamin Tse Min*
K T Lim & Company, 101 Cecil Street,
Tong Eng Building, [H]25-06,
Singapore 467493, (65) 324 0822, Fax:
(65) 324 0922, and Member
Singapore, Call Date: July 1996 (Middle
Temple) Qualifications: LLB
(Hons)(Hull)

Loh *Miss Christina Huey Shya*
Singapore 080105, Call Date: July 1997
(Lincoln's Inn) Qualifications: LLB
(Hons)(Leeds)

Loh *Lik Peng*
Singapore 457996, Call Date: July 1997
(Middle Temple) Qualifications: LLB
(Hons)(Sheff)

Loh *Ms Lynette Moon Lan*
Malaysia, Call Date: Nov 1997 (Inner
Temple) Qualifications: LLB (Leics)

Loh *Miss May*
Supreme Court, St Andrew's Road,
Singapore 267774, (65) 332 4026, Fax:
(65) 337 9450, Justices' Law Clerk, and
Member Singapore Bar, Call Date: July
1996 (Middle Temple) Qualifications:
LLB (Hons)(Kent)

Loh *Miss Melissa Yuet Meng*
Malaysia, Call Date: Nov 1997
(Lincoln's Inn) Qualifications: LLB
(Hons)

Loh *Miss Mui Leng*
Malaysia, Call Date: Nov 1993 (Gray's
Inn) Qualifications: LLB

Loh *Nigel Lin Kwang*
Darussalam, Call Date: July 1995
(Middle Temple) Qualifications: LLB
(Hons) (Leic)

Loh *Shu Hon*
Singapore 1130, Call Date: July 1993
(Middle Temple) Qualifications: LLB
(Hons)

Loh *Miss Siau Joe*
Malaysia, Call Date: July 1996 (Gray's
Inn) Qualifications: LLB (West of
England

Loh *Ms Yee Mun*
Italy, and Member Malaysian Bar, Call
Date: July 1994 (Lincoln's Inn)
Qualifications: LLB (Hons, Warw), LLM
(Warw)

Loh *Ms Yun Ping*
Malaysia 56100, Graduate Trainee in
DCB Bank, Call Date: July 1995 (Gray's
Inn) Qualifications: B.Soc.Sci (Keele)

Loi *Dhillon Chia Wei*
Singapore 1334, Fax: 065 280 4930,
Call Date: July 1996 (Lincoln's Inn)
Qualifications: LLB (Hons)

Loke *Adrian Weng Hong*
Messrs Rodyk & Davidson, 9 Raffles
Place, Republic Plaza, [H]55-01 &
[H]56-01, Singapore 1543, 225 2626,
Fax: 225 1838, Legal Assistant, Call
Date: July 1995 (Middle Temple)
Qualifications: LLB (Hons), LLM
(Lond)

Loke *Miss Moon Cee*
Malaysia, Call Date: July 1997
(Lincoln's Inn) Qualifications: LLB
(Hons)(Manch)

Loke *Siew Meng*
42 Everton Road [H]17-02, Asia
Gardens, Singapore 0208, Singapore
0208, 2204980, Fax: 5364748, Partner,
and Member Singapore Bar, Call Date:
Nov 1990 (Lincoln's Inn)
Qualifications: LLB (Lond), AIBA,, LLM
(Lond), CDAF,, B.Sc (Est Man) Hons,
(S'pore)

Loming *James Ih-wuen*
No 37 (1st Floor), BDA- Shahida
Centre, Abang Galau Road, 97000
Bintulu, Sarawak, Malaysia, 086
331991, Fax: 086 338339, and Member
Sabah Bar Sarawak Bar, Call Date: Oct
1992 (Middle Temple) Qualifications:
LL.B (Hons)

Long *Mervyn Tan Chye*
Singapore 2159, Call Date: July 1994
(Inner Temple) Qualifications: LLB
(Lond)

Long *Patrick*
Law Library, Four Courts, Dublin 7,
Ireland, Ireland, 8214397, Fax:
8215297, United Nations Consultant
Fellow of Irish Institute of Secretaries
(FIIS), Barrister of King's Inn, Dublin,
Call Date: Nov 1994 (Middle Temple)
Qualifications: Dip Law

Longley *His Honour Judge*
District Judge's Chambers, Wan Chai
Law Courts, Wan Chai Tower 1, 12
Harbour Road, 2582 4425, Fax: 2824
1641, and Member Hong Kong Bar, Call
Date: Nov 1970 (Lincoln's Inn)
Qualifications: MA (Oxon)

Loo *Miss Bernice Ming Nee*
Singapore 1129, and Member
Singapore Bar, Call Date: July 1995
(Lincoln's Inn) Qualifications: LLB
(Hons)

Loo *Miss Ee-Ling*
c/o Messrs Raja, Darryl & Loh, 18th
Floor, Wisma Sime Darby, Jalan Raja
Laut, 50350 Kuala Lumpur, Malaysia,
03 294 9999, Fax: 03 298 4759/293
8028/3823, and Member Malaysia, Call
Date: July 1997 (Lincoln's Inn)
Qualifications: LLB (Hons)

Loo *Miss Hwee Fang*
Singapore, Call Date: July 1997 (Gray's
Inn) Qualifications: LLB (Sheff)

Loo *Miss Peggy Chee Hoon*
Malaysia, and Member Malaysia Bar,
Call Date: Nov 1990 (Gray's Inn)
Qualifications: LLB (Lond)

Loo *Miss Peh Fern*
Malaysia, Call Date: Nov 1997
(Lincoln's Inn) Qualifications: LLB
(Hons)(Warw)

Lord *Simon John*
Canada T2G 4T8, Call Date: July 1976
(Middle Temple)

Lourdesamy *Gerard Samuel Vijayan*
No 546 Jalan 17/15, 46400 Petaling
Jaya, Selangor, and Member Malaysia
Bar, Call Date: July 1992 (Lincoln's
Inn) Qualifications: LLB (Hons)
(Leeds)

Lovell *Harold Earl Edmund*
P O Box 20, 29 Redcliffe Street, St
John's, 268 462 1136, Fax: 268 462
8980, Notary Public (Antigua &
Barbuda), and Member Antigua Bar
Monserrat Bar Barbuda Bar, Call Date:
July 1987 (Middle Temple)
Qualifications: BA (W.Indies), LLB
(Thames Valley), M.Jur (B'ham)

Low *Miss Anisah Suyuti*
50490 Malaysia, Call Date: July 1995
(Lincoln's Inn) Qualifications: LLB
(Hons)

Low *Dr Cheng Teong*
111 Taman Sia Her Yam, 85000
Segamat Johor, Malaysia, 07 931 2042,
Fax: 07 931 2042, Oral Surgeon, Call
Date: Nov 1996 (Lincoln's Inn)
Qualifications: LLB (Hons)(Lond), BDS
(Singapore)

Low *Miss Chi Cheng*
Lim Kian Leong & Co, Suite 1802 18th
Floor, Wisma Hamzah-Kwong Hing, No
1 Leboh Ampang, 50100 Kuala
Lumpur, Malaysia, 2301440, 2301441,
Fax: 2388039, Advocate & Solicitor, and
Member Malaysia Bar, Call Date: July
1991 (Middle Temple) Qualifications:
LLB (Hons) (Leics)

Low *Chwan Yiing Dennis*
Singapore 369082, Call Date: Nov 1996
(Lincoln's Inn) Qualifications: LLB
(Nott'm)

Low *Denis Kheng Yin*
Zaid Ibrahaim & Co, 12th Floor,
Menara Bank, Pembangunan, Jalan
Sultan Ismail, 50250 Kuala Lumpur,
Malaysia, 603 2926688, Fax: 6 03
2981632, Call Date: Nov 1997 (Middle
Temple) Qualifications: LLB (Hons),
LLM (Cantab)

Low *Miss Geok Ping*
Malaysia, Call Date: July 1997
(Lincoln's Inn) Qualifications: LLB
(Hons)

F

Low *Hun Kiat*
Hanlow Holdings Sdn.Bhd, 1002B, 10th Floor, Wisma Pahlawan, Jalan Sultan Sulaiman, 50000 Kuala Lumpur, Malaysia, 603 2738139, Fax: 603 2743432, Director, Advocate & Solicitor of High Court of Malaya, Call Date: July 1995 (Middle Temple) Qualifications: LLB (Hons), MBA

Low *Jeng Kiat Timothy Aeron*
Singapore 1024, Call Date: July 1996 (Middle Temple) Qualifications: LLB (Hons) (Wolves)

Low *Keng Siong*
Malaysia, Call Date: Nov 1997 (Lincoln's Inn) Qualifications: LLB (Hons) (Lond)

Low *Miss Lynette*
c/o M/S Allen & Gledhill, [H] 18-01 City House, 36 Robinson Road, Singapore, Singapore 2158, (65) 4207964, Fax: (65) 2254950/2250062, Legal Assistant, and Member Singapore Bar, Call Date: Nov 1993 (Middle Temple) Qualifications: LLB (Hons)

Low *Miss Peck Yin*
Malaysia, Call Date: July 1996 (Lincoln's Inn) Qualifications: LLB (Hons)

Low *Miss Peng Peng*
Malaysia, Call Date: July 1996 (Lincoln's Inn) Qualifications: LLB (Hons) (Wales)

Low *Reginald Heng Chuan*
Singapore 558725, Call Date: Nov 1997 (Middle Temple) Qualifications: LLB (Hons) (Leics)

Low *Wan Kwong*
Block 125, BT Batok Central, [H]12-399, Singapore 650157, 561 6334, Fax: 569 9715, Advocate & Solcitor, and Member Singapore, Call Date: Nov 1996 (Middle Temple) Qualifications: LLB (Hons)

Low *Miss Wee Jee*
Singapore 0314, Call Date: July 1995 (Lincoln's Inn) Qualifications: LLB (Hons)

Low *Willin*
S(538921) Singapore, Call Date: July 1997 (Gray's Inn) Qualifications: LLB (Notts)

Lu *Miss Su Lian*
Malaysia, Call Date: July 1996 (Middle Temple) Qualifications: BA (Hons) (Cantab)

Lucey *John Joseph*
Ireland, Call Date: May 1996 (Middle Temple) Qualifications: BCL (Cork), LLM, (Cork), BL (King's, Inn)

Lugar-Mawson *His Hon Judge Gareth John*
High Court, 38 Queensway, Hong Kong, 852 2825 4336, Fax: 852 2869 0640, Deputy Chairman, Town Planning Appeal Board (Hong Kong) Honorary Lecturer in the Department of Professional Legal Education, University of Hong Kong & Consultant to the Faculty of Law in Advocacy Member of the Board of the Hong Kong Law School, City, Former Solicitor (England & Wales and Hong Kong) Judge of the District Court of Hong Kong and Deputy Judge of the High Court of Hong Kong and Member Hong Kong Bar, Call Date: July 1985 (Middle Temple) Qualifications: LLB (Lond), FCIArb, FHKIArb

Lui *Simon Kin Man*
Ground Floor, 189 Sai Wan Ho Street, Shaukeiwan, Hong Kong, and Member Hong Kong, Call Date: Nov 1997 (Gray's Inn) Qualifications: BSc (Hong Kong), ARICS

Luis *Gerard Andrew*
Dell Asia Pacific SDN, Plot P27, Bayan Lepas Industrial Zone, Phase IV, 11900 Bayan Lepas, Penang, Malaysia, 60 4 810 4768, Fax: 60 4 810 4148, Contracts Executive, Advocate & Solicitor (Malaysia), Call Date: July 1991 (Lincoln's Inn) Qualifications: LLB (Hons) (Lond), LLM (Lond)

Luk *King Yip*
Hong Kong, Call Date: Nov 1997 (Middle Temple) Qualifications: BS.Sc (Hons) (Hong, Kong)

Lum *Miss May Lee Chan*
10 Kensington Park Drive, [H] 18-03, Singapore 1955, 2857352, Call Date: July 1995 (Middle Temple) Qualifications: BA (Hons) (Keele), LLM (Lond)

Lum *Michael Kah Heng*
Malaysia, Call Date: Oct 1998 (Middle Temple) Qualifications: LLB (Hons) (Notts)

Luthi *Charles Christian Rolf*
c/o Conyers, Dill & Pearman, Clarendon House, Church Street, Hamilton, Bermuda, Bermuda, (441) 295 1422, Fax: (441) 295 4720, Secretary, Chartered Institute of Arbitrators Bermuda Branch, and Member Bermuda, Call Date: Feb 1993 (Middle Temple) Qualifications: BA (Hons) (Oxon)

Lynch *Bernard Gerard*
B und P, Bavcoordination UND, Projektsteuerung GMBH, Hauptstrasse 24, 48712 Gescher, 02542 5099, Project Manager, Call Date: Nov 1995 (Lincoln's Inn) Qualifications: LLB (Hons) (Lond)

M'Bai *Ousman*
The Gambia, Call Date: Oct 1996 (Lincoln's Inn) Qualifications: LLB (Hons) (Leeds)

Ma *Miss Pin Yen*
Malaysia, Call Date: Nov 1997 (Lincoln's Inn) Qualifications: LLB (Hons) (Leeds)

Maarof *Miss Norzaimah*
Malaysia, Call Date: Nov 1993 (Inner Temple) Qualifications: LLB (So'ton)

MacDiarmid *Ross*
ING Bank, 15 Kiseleff Boulevard, Sector 1, Bucharest, 00 401 222 1600, Fax: 00 401 222 1401, Senior Relationship Manager, Call Date: Nov 1982 (Inner Temple) Qualifications: BSc (Reading) Hons, ARICS, Dip Law

Macdonald *Duncan Hamish*
'Sitio Santa Cruz', MG 060 - No 3850, Santa Afonso, Betim, Minas Gerais, Brazil CEP 325000, 00 55 31 799 2828, and Member Gibraltar Bar, St Helena, Call Date: Oct 1992 (Middle Temple) Qualifications: LL. B (Hons)

Macdonald *Roderick Francis*
6A Lennox Street, Edinburgh EH4 1QA, Scotland, 0131 332 7240, Fax: 0131 332 7240, Member of the Criminal Injuries Compensation Board, Member of the Criminal Injuries Compensations Appeals Panel, QC of Scotland and Member Scotland, Call Date: July 1997 (Inner Temple) Qualifications: LLB (Glasgow)

Machado *Miss Thushani Vincentia Michele*
Sri Lanka, Call Date: Nov 1997 (Lincoln's Inn) Qualifications: LLB (Lond)

MacKenzie *Miss Cailin Catriona Elizabeth*
Belgium, Call Date: Nov 1992 (Lincoln's Inn) Qualifications: LLB (Hons) (Lond), Maitrise (Paris)

MacKenzie *Ross David*
South China Chambers, 904 Tower Two, Lippo Centre, 89 Queensway, 852 2528 2378, Fax: 852 2520 1512, and Member Hong Kong, SAR China Victoria (Australia), Call Date: Nov 1962 (Gray's Inn) Qualifications: MA (Cantab)

Madhani *Mohamed Ali Kassamali*
Mohamed Madhani & Co Advocates, P O Box 48539, Nairobi, Kenya, East Africa, 254 2 228255/229233, Fax: 254 2 230896, and Member Kenya, Call Date: July 1980 (Lincoln's Inn) Qualifications: LLB, FCII

Madhub *Oomeshwarnath Beny*
Mauritius, Call Date: July 1991 (Middle Temple) Qualifications: LLB (Hons) (Warw)

Madigan *Mrs Patricia Josephine*
Southern Ireland, Barrister of Ireland, Call Date: Nov 1995 (Middle Temple) Qualifications: BL (King's Inn)

Magennis *Bernard James Joseph*
Rossglass, Downpatrick, Co Down,
Republic of Ireland, 01396 842082,
and Member Southern Ireland Bar, Call
Date: Oct 1994 (Middle Temple)
Qualifications: BA, BL

Magimay *Miss Anita Shoba*
Malaysia, and Member Malaysian Bar,
Call Date: July 1996 (Lincoln's Inn)
Qualifications: LLB (Hons)

Mah *Miss Catherine Siok Hean*
Singapore 308954, Call Date: July 1988
(Gray's Inn) Qualifications: LLB
(Bristol)

Mah *Cheong Fatt*
Singapore 680203, Call Date: July 1997
(Middle Temple) Qualifications: LLB
(Hons) (Lond)

Maharaj *Miss Lou-Ann*
Jamaica, Call Date: Nov 1991 (Gray's
Inn) Qualifications: LLB (W Indies),
LLM

Mahatantila *Duleep Rohan*
Sri Lanka, Executive, Development
Finance Corporation of Ceylon, Call
Date: Nov 1988 (Middle Temple)
Qualifications: BA, Dip Law

Mahendran *Miss Jyeshta*
Malaysia, Call Date: Nov 1995
(Lincoln's Inn) Qualifications: BSc
(Hons) (Keele)

Mahendran *Miss Sonia*
West Malaysia, Call Date: July 1995
(Middle Temple) Qualifications: LLB
(Hons) (Warw)

Mahmood *Mario Bin*
Malaysia, Call Date: Nov 1996 (Middle
Temple) Qualifications: LLB (Hons)

Mahmud *Mrs Ishrat*
Legal Rehedy, Ispahani Building (1st
Floor), 14-15 Motijheel Commercial,
Area, Dhaka 1000, Bangladesh, 955
0645/414224, Fax: 00 88 02 918161,
Councillor Education of the Law Tutors,
Dhaka Bangladesh, and Member
Bangladesh, Call Date: Mar 1997
(Lincoln's Inn) Qualifications: LLB
(Hons)

Mahmud *Ms Sahia*
Pakistan, Call Date: July 1996
(Lincoln's Inn)

Maidment *Richard John Haylock*
c/o Clerk B, Owen Dixon Chambers,
205 William Street, Melbourne, Victoria
3000, 039 608 7049, Fax: 039 608
8485, and Member Victorian Bar New
South Wales Bar, Call Date: Nov 1971
(Gray's Inn) Qualifications: LLM

Maillis II *Alexander Pericles*
Bahamas, and Member Bahamas, Call
Date: July 1997 (Lincoln's Inn)
Qualifications: LLB (Hons) (Wales)

Majiyagbe *Jonathan Babatunde*
J B Majiyagbe & Co, Barristers Solicitors
&, Notaries Public, 4 Human Rights
Avenue, P.O.Box 726, Kano, 064
631261/064 644171, Fax: 064 647146,
Senior Advocate of Nigeria and Member
Nigerian Bar, Call Date: Nov 1964
(Middle Temple) Qualifications: LLB
(Lond)

Mak *Andrew Yip Shing*
Room 1432, Prince's Building, Central,
Hong Kong, 25 2 40151, Fax: 28
101731, and Member Hong Kong,
Australia, Singapore, Call Date: July
1988 (Lincoln's Inn) Qualifications:
BSc, MBA (Hong Kong), LLB, LLM
(Lond) ACIS, Dip Dev Studies,
(Cantab), ACIArb

Mak *Chi Biu*
Flat 3B, Block 29, Greenwood Terrace,
26-28 Sui Wo Road, Sha Tin, Hong
Kong, 852 2601 6587, Fax: 852 2577
3562, Contract Advisor, and Member
Hong Kong Bar, Call Date: Nov 1992
(Gray's Inn) Qualifications: BSc
(Eng) (Hong Kong), LLB (Lond), MICE,,
MIStructE, FCIArb

Mak *Miss Mabel Min-Theng*
535352 Singapore, Call Date: July 1997
(Gray's Inn) Qualifications: LLB (Bris)

Mak *Miss Rosanna Tsui Shan*
Singapore 650222, Call Date: Nov 1997
(Gray's Inn) Qualifications: LLB (Lond)

Malaiyandi Chettiar *Kamalarajan*
36 Robinson Road, [H] 18-01 City
House, Singapore 0821, 420 7841, Fax:
420 7592, and Member Singapore Bar,
Call Date: Nov 1995 (Middle Temple)
Qualifications: LLB (Hons)

Mallett *Laurence Edwin*
BP Oil Europe, Legal Department, Les
Quatre, Bras, Chaussee de Malines 455,
1950 Kraainem, 32 2 766 3849 or
3020, Fax: 32 2 766 3476, Legal
Adviser, Call Date: May 1969 (Middle
Temple) Qualifications: LLB

Mamun *Abdullah Al*
Admiralty Chambers, Barristers,
Advocates &, Notaries, 53 Dit Extension
Rd, Naya Paltan, Mothijheel,
Bangladesh, 834327 (W) 319870 (H),
and Member Bangladesh Bar, Call
Date: July 1994 (Lincoln's Inn)
Qualifications: LLB (Hons), BA (Hons),
MA

Manecksha *Ms Ferina Pervez*
IT Publications SDN BHD, Balai Berita
Level 2, 31 Jalan Riong, 59000 Kuala
Lumpur, West Malaysia, 603 282 2022
x 118, Fax: 603 282 0097/8214,
Editorial Executive,Computimes, Call
Date: July 1995 (Inner Temple)
Qualifications: LLB (Northumbria)

Mani *Somasuraeisan*
Malaysia, Call Date: July 1998 (Middle
Temple) Qualifications: LLB (Hons)

Manickam *Ms Kasturibai*
Singapore 271004, Call Date: July 1997
(Lincoln's Inn) Qualifications: LLB
(Hons)

Manickam *Vengetraman*
34 Jalan Dinding, Lim Garden, 30100
Ipoh, Perak Malaysia, Malaysia, 05
5275305, and Member Malaysia, Call
Date: July 1995 (Lincoln's Inn)
Qualifications: LLB (Hons)

Manishagaran *Miss Chitra*
Singapore 120311, Call Date: Oct 1998
(Middle Temple) Qualifications: LLB
(Hons) (Lond)

Mapondera *Miss Dulcie Tsitsi*
Switzerland, Call Date: Nov 1987
(Middle Temple) Qualifications: LLB,
LLM (LSE), MBA (Warwick)

Marcou *Miss Mary-Ann*
The Law Office of the Republic, of
Cyprus, Apellis Str, Nicosia, Cyprus,
Counsel for the Republic of Cyprus,
Attorney General's Attorney Office,
Nicosia, Cyprus, and Member Cyprus
Bar, Call Date: Nov 1993 (Gray's Inn)
Qualifications: LLB (Sheff), LLM
(Cantab)

Mariappan *Mogan*
Nor'Ain Mogan & Manoharan, 72B Ting
1, Jalan Melati, 28400 Mentakab,
Pahang Darulmakmur, Malaysia,
09-2782290/2784131, Fax:
09-2782293, and Member Malaysia
Bar, Call Date: July 1993 (Inner
Temple) Qualifications: LLB (Lancs),
AFF.A.I.I.

Marican *Abdul Rahim*
Singapore 1648, Call Date: May 1996
(Lincoln's Inn) Qualifications: LLB
(Hons) (Lond)

Marican *Mrs Bee Bee Sultan*
Singapore 1749, Call Date: July 1995
(Lincoln's Inn) Qualifications: LLB
(Hons)

Marimuthu *Jeeva Kumar*
Malaysia, Call Date: Nov 1997
(Lincoln's Inn) Qualifications: LLB
(Hons)

Marimuthu *Miss Meera*
Malaysia, Call Date: Nov 1997
(Lincoln's Inn) Qualifications: LLB
(Hons) (Herts)

Marimuttu *Jeyan T M*
Messrs Teo Marimuttu & Ptnrs, P O
Box No 10869, 88809 Kota Kinabalu,
Sabah, Malaysia, Malaysia, 088 252997/
252998, Fax: 088 252889, and Member
Malaysia Bar, Call Date: Nov 1992
(Gray's Inn) Qualifications: LLB
(Buckingham), MI Mgt

Markar *Mrs Fathima Faiza*
Sri Lanka, Call Date: Mar 1998
(Lincoln's Inn) Qualifications: LLB
(Lond)

F

Markey *Ms Anne King*
United States of America, Call Date: July 1995 (Inner Temple) Qualifications: LLB

Marlor *Richard James Darwen*
John Street Chambers, 44 John Street, Stanley, Falkland Islands, Falkland Islands, (00500) 22765, Fax: (00500) 22639, Barrister and Legal Practitioner, Call Date: July 1998 (Middle Temple) Qualifications: LLB (Hons) (Leeds)

Marrache *Benjamin John Samuel*
Fortress House, Gibraltar, Gibraltar, 00 350 79918/74901, Fax: 00 350 74042/73315, Call Date: Nov 1988 (Inner Temple) Qualifications: LLB, LLM (LSE)

Marshall *William Roberts*
Department of Justice, Queensway Government Office, 3rd Floor, High Block, 66 Queensway, Hong Kong, Hong Kong, 852 2867 2092, Fax: 852 2869 0670, Legal Consultant, Hong Kong SAR Government of China, and Member Hong Kong Bar Victoria Bar, Call Date: Nov 1968 (Inner Temple) Qualifications: MA (Glas) LLB (Lond)

Martin *Jason Alexander*
West Indies, Call Date: Oct 1998 (Middle Temple) Qualifications: LLB (Hons) (Notts)

Martin *Nigel Gregory*
Bar Library, Royal Courts of Justice, Chichester Street, Belfast, Northern Ireland, (01232) 562263, Fax: (01232) 231850, Chairperson; The Family Bar Association (N.Z.) 1997 to date, Barrister of Northern Ireland, Call Date: May 1994 (Middle Temple) Qualifications: LLB (Hons), CPLS

Martin *Peter David Acheson*
Mello Hollis Jones & Martin, Reid House, 31 Church Street, Hamilton HM 13, (809) 292 1345, Fax: (809) 292 9151, Legal Adviser, and Member Bermuda Bar, Call Date: Nov 1983 (Gray's Inn) Qualifications: LLB (Manch)

Masemola *Nathaniel Mashilo*
P.O.Box 576, Gallo Manor 2052, Sandton, Johannesburg, South Africa, (011) 804 5341, Fax: (011) 804 3579, and Member Botswana & Zambia Bars South Africa Bar, Call Date: June 1964 (Gray's Inn) Qualifications: BA LLB (SA) , LLB (Lond), UED (Rhodes) , FILGAZ (Zambia)

Masood *Syed Aaamir*
Pakistan, Call Date: Nov 1997 (Lincoln's Inn) Qualifications: BSc (Hons) (LSE)

Massias *Isaac Clive*
Massias & Partners, 117 Main Street, P.O.Box 213, 40888, Fax: 40999, and Member Gibraltar Bar, Call Date: Nov 1986 (Middle Temple) Qualifications: LLB (Hons)

Massias *Miss Victoria Stella*
Massias & Partners, 117 Main Street, P.O.Box 213, Gibraltar, 40888, Fax: 40999, and Member Gibraltar Bar, Call Date: Nov 1989 (Middle Temple) Qualifications: LLB Hons (Lond), LLM (Lond)

Mathialahan *K*
Singapore 1438, Call Date: July 1996 (Middle Temple) Qualifications: LLB (Hons) (Leic)

Mathiavaranam *Rueben*
Azman, Davidson & Co, Suite 13-03 13th Floor, Menara Tan & Tan, 207 Jalan Tun Razak, 50400 Kuala Lumpur Malaysia, Malaysia, (03) 2640200, Fax: (03) 2640280, and Member Malaysia Bar Australia Bar, Call Date: Nov 1989 (Lincoln's Inn) Qualifications: BA (Kent)

Maxwell *Anthony Michael Lockhart*
Gesnaire, Le Petit Val, Alderney GY9 3UX, Channel Islands, 01481 823889, Fax: 01481 824319, Call Date: Nov 1985 (Middle Temple) Qualifications: LLB (Lond),MRIN, MRAeS , Cert Air & Space Law, (UCL)

Maxwell *Christopher Murray*
Owen Dixon Chambers West, 205 William Street, Melbourne, 3000 Victoria, Australia, (03) 9608 8163, Fax: (03) 9608 8248, Call Date: Nov 1978 (Lincoln's Inn) Qualifications: BA (Melbourne) , LLB (Victoria)

Mayers *Miss Maferne Telene*
West Indies, Call Date: Nov 1997 (Gray's Inn) Qualifications: LLB (Wolver'ton)

Mazlan *Azri Sani*
Malaysia 20400, Call Date: Nov 1995 (Gray's Inn) Qualifications: LLB (Wales)

Mbanefo *Thomas Chuba*
Adiebo Chambers, Baico Plaza, 12 Abibu Oki Street, 6th Floor, Lagos, 2663616, Fax: 2663445, Managing Partner, Mbanefo & Mbanefo, Legal Practitioners, and Member Nigerian Bar, Call Date: July 1988 (Gray's Inn) Qualifications: LLB (Warwick), LLM (Lond), BL (Nigeria)

Mbiti *John Maithya*
414 w 44 Street Apt 1E, New York, Ny 10036, Call Date: Oct 1996 (Lincoln's Inn) Qualifications: LLB (Hons) (Lond)

McAleer *James Joseph*
Northern Ireland, 01232 643920, Fax: 01232 643879, Former Police Officer and Member Northern Ireland Bar, Call Date: Oct 1997 (Middle Temple) Qualifications: MA (Hons) (Oxon)

McArdle *Eamonn Terence*
The Bar Library, Royal Courts of Justice, Chichester Street, Belfast BT1 3JP, Northern Ireland, 01232 241523, Fax: 01232 231850, and Member Northern Ireland, Call Date: Oct 1996 (Inner Temple) Qualifications: BA (East Anglia), CALS (Belfast)

McCartney, *Miss Clarise Yvette*
Yvette McCartney Chambers, Wilmacs Pharmacy Building, No 55 Collins Avenue, P.O.Box G.T. 2830, Nassau, N.P., Bahamas, 242 328 6725/326 4620, Fax: 242 328 6725, and Member Bahamas, Call Date: Nov 1992 (Inner Temple) Qualifications: LLB (Wales)

McCartney *Miss Tanya Cecile*
Bahamas, Call Date: July 1995 (Lincoln's Inn) Qualifications: LLB (Hons)

McCullough *Miss Denise Susanne*
6 Ballycastle Road, Newtownards, Co.Down, N.Ireland BT22 2AY, Northern Ireland, 01247 815737, Member of the Honorable Society of the Inn of Court of Northern Ireland and Member Northern Ireland Bar, Call Date: Nov 1992 (Lincoln's Inn) Qualifications: BA (Hons) (Belfast), CPE

McCully *Alvin Jeffrey*
Singapore 257910, Call Date: July 1997 (Middle Temple) Qualifications: LLB (Hons)

McDowell *Major Thomas Bleakley*
St Thomas, Whitechurch, County Dublin 16, Chairman The Irish Times Ltd, and Member Southern Ireland Bar, Call Date: June 1951 (Gray's Inn) Qualifications: LLB

McGovern *Edmond Terence*
Call Date: Nov 1966 (Middle Temple) Qualifications: LLB (B'ham)

McGowan *James Hugh Menzies*
Admiralty Chambers, 1405 Tower 11, Admiralty Centre, (852) 2527 3082, Fax: (852) 2529 8226, and Member Hong Kong Bar, Call Date: July 1979 (Middle Temple) Qualifications: BA (Nott'm), Dip Comm Law (HK)

McGrath *John Thomas*
L7, 233 Macquarie Street, Sydney, New South Wales 2000, Australia, +61 2 9221 1199, Fax: +61 416 990 405, Part Time University Lecturer, Commercial Mediator, NSW Supreme Court and Member New South Wales Bar, Call Date: Apr 1991 (Lincoln's Inn) Qualifications: BA, LLB, BEc (Sydney), LLM, (Euro Law) (Lond)

McGrath *Ms Sarah Linda*
Deloitte Touche Tohmatsu, 26th Floor, Wing on Centre, 111 Connaught Road, Hong Kong, (852) 28521095, Fax: (852) 25434647, Tax Partner, Deloitte Touche Tohmatsu, Call Date: Feb 1990 (Lincoln's Inn) Qualifications: B.Soc.Sc [Hong Kong], LLB Hons [Lond]

McGrenaghan *Aidan Edward*
57 Wynchurch Road, Belfast BT6 0JH,
Northern Ireland, 01232 705065, Call
Date: July 1997 (Lincoln's Inn)
Qualifications: LLB (Hons)(Lond)

McLaughlin *Richard*
Bar Library, P.O.Box 414, Royal Courts
of Justice, Chichester Street, Belfast
BT1 3JP, Northern Ireland, 01232
660283, Fax: 01232 667399,
Chairman, Bar Council (NI)
1994-1996, QC 1985
(N.Ireland)(Called 1971) and Member
Bar of N.Ireland (1971) King's
Inn,Dublin (1978) and Bar of N.S.W.
Australia 1992, Call Date: Nov 1974
(Gray's Inn) Qualifications: LLB, LLM,
F.C.I.Arb

McLeish *Robin*
Office of the Privacy, Commissioner for
Personal Data, Unit 2001, 20/F Office
Tower, Convention Plaza, 1 Harbour
Rd, Wanchai, Hong Kong, (852) 2877
7128, Fax: (852) 2877 7026, Deputy
Provacy Commissioner for Personal
Data, and Member Hong Kong, Call
Date: Oct 1997 (Gray's Inn)
Qualifications: MA

McMahon *Richard James*
St James' Chambers, Guernsey
GY1 2PA, Channel Islands, 01481
723355, Fax: 01481 725439, Legislative
Draftsman, States of Guernsey, and
Member Guernsey (1998), Call Date:
Nov 1986 (Middle Temple)
Qualifications: LLB (L'pool), LLM
(Cantab)

McManus *Miss Mairin*
Ireland, and Member Ireland, Call
Date: Nov 1998 (Middle Temple)
Qualifications: BL (King's Inn)

McRandal *Mrs Pauline Mary*
10 Fairlawns, Saval Park Road, Dalkey,
Co Dublin, 2856078, Fax: 2856078,
and Member Southern Ireland Bar, Call
Date: July 1988 (Middle Temple)
Qualifications: BL (Kings Inns)

Mcshane *Ms Anne Mary Sylvia*
University College, Dublin, Republic of
Ireland, Call Date: July 1989 (Gray's
Inn) Qualifications: BA

Meade *Barrie Norman*
A S & K Services Limtied, Cedar House,
41 Cedar Avenue, Hamilton HM 12,
Bermuda, Bermuda, 441 295 2244,
Fax: 441 292 8666, Compliance Officer,
Commander Brother of the Order of St
John Queens Counsel (Bermuda 1996)
and Member Bermuda, Call Date: July
1981 (Inner Temple) Qualifications:
LLB (Lond), FCIArb

Meakin *Ian Leonard*
Byrne-Sutton, Bonnard Lawson,
Meakin & Associes, 11 Rue General
Dufour, 1204 Geneva, Switzerland,
0041 22 328 6393, Fax: 0041 22 781
1340, Arbitrator, Call Date: Oct 1991
(Gray's Inn) Qualifications: BD, AKC,
Dip Law, ACIArb

Meharia *Miss Vineeta*
57A Block D, New Alipore, Calcutta
700053, India, Call Date: July 1997
(Gray's Inn) Qualifications: LLB (Lond)

Mehdi *Mrs Wajiha Maryam*
Pakistan, Call Date: July 1998
(Lincoln's Inn) Qualifications: BA
(Hons)

Melling *Gerard Philip*
Tombo Aviation Inc, 3780 Kilroy Airport
Way, [H]700, Long Beach 90806,
California, 1 562 997 3256, Fax: 1 562
988 2694, VP Legal, Tombo Aviation
Inc, Call Date: Nov 1980 (Gray's Inn)
Qualifications: LLB (Lond), Dip Eur Int
, (Amsterdam)

Menell *Dr Emma Jeanne*
300 Innes Chambers, 84 Pritchard
Street, Johannesburg 2001, South
Africa, +27 11 337 2370, Fax: +27 11
333 8425, and Member Johannesburg
Bar, Call Date: Nov 1995 (Middle
Temple) Qualifications: BA, M.Phil,
D.Phil

Menezes *Justin Carl*
Wilmer, Cutler & Pickering, Rue de la
Loi 15, B-1040 Brussels, Brussels, (32)
(2) 2854900, Fax: (32) (2) 2854949,
and Member Belgium, Call Date: Oct
1995 (Lincoln's Inn) Qualifications:
LLB (Hons)(Sheff)

Meng *Miss Lovie Genevieve Chua Geok
Meng*
Singapore 560620, Call Date: July 1998
(Gray's Inn) Qualifications: LLB
(Wolves)

Menon *Mrs Deborah Damayanthi*
Malaysia, Call Date: Nov 1995 (Inner
Temple) Qualifications: LLB (Herts)

Menon *Sree Govind*
Singapore 467484, Call Date: July 1996
(Lincoln's Inn) Qualifications: LLB
(Hons)(Lond)

Mensah *Mrs Grace*
West Africa, 00 233 21 22 4260, Fax: 00
233 21 23 2262, Call Date: Nov 1995
(Lincoln's Inn) Qualifications: LLB
(Hons)(Lond)

Meredith *Jack Edward*
Scotland, Call Date: Nov 1996
(Lincoln's Inn) Qualifications: LLB
(Hons)(Herts)

Merican *Megat Suffian*
Malaysia, Call Date: July 1996
(Lincoln's Inn) Qualifications: LLB
(Hons)

Merrien *Alan Martin*
Ozanne Van Leuven Perrot &, Evans, 1
Le Marchant Street, St Peter Port,
Guernsey, Channel Islands, Channel
Islands, 0481 723466, Fax: 0481
727935, Litigation Assistant, and
Member Guernsey Bar, Call Date: Feb
1992 (Inner Temple) Qualifications:
LLB (So'ton)

Merrigan *Thomas Joseph*
Harney, Westwood & Riegels, Craigmur
Chambers, P.O.Box 71, Road Town,
Tortola, British Virgin Islands, 00 284
494 2233 x 242, Call Date: July 1998
(Lincoln's Inn) Qualifications: Post
Graduate Dip, in Law

Mesenas *Miss May Lucia*
Attorney General's Chambers, 1
Coleman Street, [H]10-00 The Adelphi,
Singapore 1130, (65) 3325940, Fax:
(65) 3390286/4355100, Deputy Public
Prosecutor State Counsel (Singapore),
Call Date: July 1995 (Middle Temple)
Qualifications: LLB (Hons)

Michaelides *Miss Christiana Kyriacou*
Kyriacos Th Michaelides Law, Offices, P
O Box 1548, Crete Str 2, Nicosia 1510,
Cyprus, 02 763751/750995, Fax: 02
761878, and Member Cyprus Bar, Call
Date: Nov 1992 (Middle Temple)
Qualifications: LLB (Hons, Lond)

Michaelides *Miss Dina*
Chrysses Demetriades & Co, Fortuna
Court, Block B, 2nd F, 284 Arch.
Makarios III Avenue, P.O.Box 50132,
Limasol 3601, Cyprus, 00357 5
582424, Fax: 00357 5 588055, Legal
Advisor in the Shipping Finance
Department, and Member Cyprus, Call
Date: Nov 1996 (Middle Temple)
Qualifications: LLB (Hons)(Warw),
LLM (So'ton)

Michaelides *Nicos R.*
P O Box 86, 3600 Limassol, Cyprus,
00357 5363742, and Member Cyprus
Bar, Call Date: Nov 1995 (Middle
Temple) Qualifications: LLB (Hons)

Michaelides *Renos Kyriacou*
Crete Street No2, PO Box 1548, Nicosia,
Cyprus, Cyprus, 357-2 763751/750995,
Fax: 357-2 761878, Advocate & Legal
Advisor, and Member Cyprus Bar, Call
Date: Nov 1988 (Middle Temple)
Qualifications: LLB (Lond)

Middleton *Miss Anne*
610 North 32nd Avenue, Hollywood,
Florida 33021, Call Date: July 1970
(Gray's Inn)

Mifsud *Simon Paul*
S Mifsu & Sons Ltd, 311 Republic
Street, Valletta - VLT 04, Malta, 00 356
232211, Fax: 00 356 240097, Legal
Advisor, Call Date: Nov 1992 (Inner
Temple) Qualifications: LLB,
LLM(Buckingham)

Milford *Mark Geoffrey*
Bank for International, Settlements, Centralbahnplatz 2, CH-4002 Basle, 41 61 2809736, Fax: 41 61 2809112, and Member New York, Call Date: Oct 1991 (Lincoln's Inn) Qualifications: LLB (Hons) (Lond), Maitrise (Paris)

Millard *Ian Robert*
Legal Consultant, and Member New York Bar, Call Date: Nov 1991 (Lincoln's Inn) Qualifications: LLB (Hons)

Miller *Michael Christopher*
Bahamas, Call Date: Nov 1995 (Middle Temple) Qualifications: LLB (Hons) (Leeds)

Miller *Mrs Yvonne Ann*
9 Cassia Drive, 65 466 5470, Fax: 65 466 2792, Legal Advisor, Call Date: Nov 1985 (Inner Temple) Qualifications: LLB(B'ham), LLM (Cantab)

Millett *Timothy Patrick*
European Parliament, rue Wirtz, B-1047, (00352) 284 3313, Fax: (00352) 284 99870, Head of Division, Legal Service, Call Date: Nov 1975 (Gray's Inn) Qualifications: MA (Oxon)

Mills *Leopold Nathaniel*
PO Box HM 287, Hamilton HMAX, 441 292 5501, Fax: 441 292 8397, Secretary to the Cabinet, and Member Bermuda Bar, Call Date: Nov 1988 (Middle Temple) Qualifications: LLB (Bucks)

Minta *Ms Lucia*
Darshan Singh & Co, No 18-A, Lebuh Pantai, (Beach Street), 10300 Pulau Pinang, Malaysia, 0106 04 2611820, Fax: 0106 04 2627476, Master in Tropical Health of the University of Queensland, Australia, Call Date: July 1997 (Lincoln's Inn) Qualifications: BSc (Hons) (Salford)

Mirpuri *Miss Sunita*
Hong Kong, Former Solicitor, Call Date: Nov 1996 (Inner Temple) Qualifications: BA (Kent)

Misick *Miss Yvette Denise*
McLean Mcnally, McLean Building, P O Box 62, 2001 Leeward Highway, Providenciales, West Indies, 809 946 4277, Call Date: July 1996 (Lincoln's Inn) Qualifications: LLB (Hons) (Leeds)

Mitchell *Miss Sarah Louise*
West Indies, Call Date: Oct 1998 (Inner Temple) Qualifications: LLB (Manc)

Mitha *Abdulsultan Alibhai*
32 Hawkwood Place NW, Calgary Alberta T3G 1X6, 403 239 7427, Fax: 403 277 3117, Call Date: July 1972 (Inner Temple) Qualifications: MA

Mitra *Siddhartha*
India, Call Date: July 1991 (Lincoln's Inn) Qualifications: LLB (Hons)

Mittelstadt *David Joseph*
The Thompson Corporation, Metro Center, One Staton Place, Stamford CT 06902, (203) 328 9457, and Member Massachusettss (USA) US Tax Court, Call Date: Feb 1989 (Lincoln's Inn) Qualifications: MA (Cantab), JD (Chicago)

Mockett *Judge John Vere Brooke*
Supreme Court, Gibraltar, Judge and Stipendiary Magistrate, and Member Gibraltar, Call Date: Feb 1958 (Gray's Inn) Qualifications: MA (Oxon)

Moe *Mr Justice Henry Stanley Rawle*
High Court of Justice, Antigua & Barbuda, P.O.Box 1722, St John's, Antigua, 462 0039, Justice of the Supreme Court, Eastern Caribbean, Attorney at Law, Barbados and Member Barbados, Call Date: Nov 1970 (Lincoln's Inn) Qualifications: BA (Hons) Durham, PG Dip Ed, FCI, MBIM, ACIS, LLM (Leic)

Moh Yong *Alan Chee Chuen*
Singapore 600116, Call Date: Nov 1995 (Middle Temple) Qualifications: LLB (Hons)

Mohamad Faiz *Miss Noor Alina*
Malaysia, Call Date: July 1998 (Middle Temple) Qualifications: LLB (Hons) (Leics)

Mohamad Hashim *Miss Haslinda*
Malaysia, Call Date: Oct 1998 (Lincoln's Inn) Qualifications: LLB (Hons) (Notts)

Mohamad Salleh *Miss Aldila*
Attorney's General Chambers, Law Building, Jalan Tutong, Brunei, Darussalam 2016, Darussalam 3680, 673-2244872/2225919, Fax: 672-2222720, Deputy Public Prosecutor, Call Date: Oct 1994 (Middle Temple) Qualifications: LLB (Hons) (Bris)

Mohamed Haniffa *Seeni Syed Ahamed Kabeer*
Singapore 640953, Call Date: July 1996 (Middle Temple) Qualifications: LLB (Hons) (Lond)

Mohamed Hashim *Abdul Rasheed*
Blk 602, Yishun St 61, [H]06-359, Singapore 2776, 06-359 Singapore, 0065 7523574, Legal Advisor, Advocate & Solicitor of the Supreme Court of Singapore, Call Date: July 1993 (Lincoln's Inn) Qualifications: LLB (Hons)

Mohammad Taha *Zamri*
Df Abang Zen, Advocates & Sols, 4th Floor, Wisma Hallah Fatima, 22/23 Jalan Sultan, P.O.Box 2822, Bandar Seri, Begawan 1928, Brunei, 02 221877/02 236680/02 236681, Fax: 673 2 224351, and Member Brunei, Call Date: July 1997 (Lincoln's Inn) Qualifications: LLB (Hons)

Mohammed *Miss Mardzlinda*
Malaysia, Call Date: May 1995 (Lincoln's Inn) Qualifications: LLB (Hons)

Mohd Ali *Miss Nor Hasliza*
Mohd Ali & Co, Advocates & Solicitors, No 105 Jalan Telawi, Bangsar Baru, 59100 Kuala Lumpur, Malaysia, 00 603 2842276, Fax: 00 603 2842273, Legal Assistant, and Member Malaysia Bar, Call Date: July 1995 (Lincoln's Inn) Qualifications: LLB (Hons)

Mohd Ibrahim Zain *Miss Rosdena*
Malaysia, Call Date: July 1997 (Middle Temple) Qualifications: LLB (Hons) (Nott'm)

Mohd Kalok *Miss Azlina Yati*
Malaysia, Call Date: July 1996 (Lincoln's Inn) Qualifications: LLB (Hons) (Notts)

Mohd Khalil *Miss Mas Aryani*
Malaysia, Call Date: July 1996 (Middle Temple) Qualifications: LLB (Hons) (Keele), BA (Hons) (Keele)

Mohd Naim *Miss Farah Wahidah*
Wan Haron Sukri & Nordin, Advocates & Solcitors, No 64-2 Jalan 2A/27A, Seksyen 1, Bandar Baru Wangsa, Maju, 53300 Setapak, Kuala Lumpur, Malaysia, 603 4112611, Fax: 603 4112622, Advocate & Solicitor (Malaysia) and Member Malaysia Bar, Call Date: July 1993 (Lincoln's Inn) Qualifications: LLB (Hons), LLM (Lond)

Mohd Radzi *Miss Nonee Ashirin*
Malaysia, Call Date: July 1997 (Lincoln's Inn) Qualifications: LLB (Hons)

Mohd Saffian *Miss Azlin*
Heng & Moran, No 8 Lorong Maarof, Bangsar Park, 59000 Kuala Lumpur, Malaysia, 603-2842828, Fax: 603-2840728, Legal Assistant, and Member Malaysia Bar, Call Date: July 1996 (Lincoln's Inn) Qualifications: LLB (Hons)

Mohd Said *Miss Norhafiza*
Messrs 12a Ng Yeoh & Kit, 19th Floor, Bangunan Dato, Zainal 23 Jalan Melaka 50100 Kuala Lumpur, Malaysia, 01-06-03 2986066, Fax: 01-06-03-2982593, Legal Assistant, and Member Malaysian Bar, Call Date: July 1995 (Middle Temple) Qualifications: LLB (Hons) (Wales)

Mok *Miss Ida Yin Leng*
Malaysia, Call Date: Nov 1995 (Middle Temple) Qualifications: LLB (Hons)

Mok *Ignatius Yann Shi*
16 Jalan ATI-ATI, Taman Perdana, 83000 Batu Pahat, Johor, Malaysia, 00-6007-4318694, Fax: 00-6007-4320588, and Member Malaysia Bar, Call Date: July 1996 (Lincoln's Inn) Qualifications: LLB (Hons) (Lond)

Mok *Miss Karen Yu-Yen*
Singapore 598506, Call Date: July 1996
(Inner Temple) Qualifications: LLB
(Hull)

Mok *Shao Pern*
Singapore 518517, Call Date: July 1998
(Middle Temple) Qualifications: LLB
(Hons)(Lond)

Mok *Miss Wai Mun*
56-H King's Road, Singapore 268118,
Singapore 278210, 466 1703, Advocate
& Solicitor of the Supreme Court of
Singapore, Call Date: July 1994 (Middle
Temple) Qualifications: LLB
(Hons)(B'ham)

Mok *Yick-Fan Danny*
c/o Works Branch, 11/F Murray
Building, Garden Road, Hong Kong,
Hong Kong, (852) 28482045, Fax:
(852) 28108502, Chief Engineer, Hong
Kong Government, Call Date: Feb 1994
(Gray's Inn) Qualifications: BSc (Eng) ,
MBA (CUHK), MSocSc (Hong Kong),
LLB (Lond), LLM (Lond)

Mok *Yiu Fai*
Hong Kong, Call Date: July 1995 (Gray's
Inn) Qualifications: LLB (Wales)

Mokal *Sardar Rizwaan Jameel*
103 Judd Street, London WC1H 9NE,
Pakistan, and Member Lahore, Call
Date: Nov 1997 (Gray's Inn)
Qualifications: BSc (Punjab), LLB
(Lond), BCL (Oxon)

Mokty *Miss Mazita*
Malaysia, Call Date: July 1995
(Lincoln's Inn) Qualifications: LLB
(Hons)

Mollah *Mohammed Salauddin*
India, Call Date: Nov 1998 (Lincoln's
Inn) Qualifications: LLB
(Hons)(Lond), LLM (L'pool)

Molloy *Ms Karen Rose*
Northern Ireland, Call Date: May 1996
(Gray's Inn) Qualifications: LLB
(Belfast)

Monteil *Dr Rene Leon*
The National Gas Company of, Trinidad
& Tobago, Goodrich Bay Road, Point
Lisas, Trinidad, 1-809 636
4662, Fax: 1-809 636 2905, Former
Lecturer at the University of the West
Indies, Call Date: July 1987 (Middle
Temple) Qualifications: BSc, PhD
(Lond), MA (Law) (City), FRSC,
C.Chem

Monteiro *James Patrick*
Malaysia, Call Date: Nov 1995
(Lincoln's Inn) Qualifications: LLB
(Hons)

Moo *Chee Leong*
No 18-1 Changkat Bukit Bintang,
(Hicks Road), 50200 Kuala lumpur,
West Malaysia, 2432128, Fax: 2433919,
and Member Malaya Bar, Call Date: July
1995 (Middle Temple) Qualifications:
LLB (Hons) (Lond)

Moore *George Crawford Jackson*
Citzens Building, Suite 812, 105 S.
Narcissus Avenue, West Palm Beach,
Florida 33401, United States of
America, (561) 833 9000, Fax: (561)
833 9990, Attorney, and Member
Florida, Jamaica, Turks & Caicos
Islands, British Virgin Islands, Grenada,
Montserrat, St Lucia and Antigua, Call
Date: July 1970 (Inner Temple)
Qualifications: BA, BPhil, MA, (Cantab),
LLM

Moosdeen *Miss Munira*
2108 Melbourne Plaza, No 33 Queen's
Road Central, 25239775, Fax:
28452464, Call Date: July 1984
(Lincoln's Inn) Qualifications: LLB,
PCLL

Moreira *John Robert*
Channel Islands, Call Date: Nov 1997
(Gray's Inn) Qualifications: BA

Moriarty *Andrew Joseph*
The Bar Library, The Royal Courts of
Justice, Chichestr Street, Belfast,
Northern Ireland, 01232 241523, Fax:
01232 231850, and Member Northern
Ireland, Call Date: July 1998 (Middle
Temple) Qualifications: LLB (Hons)

Morris *Sheriff John Cameron*
Queens Counsel, Advocates Library,
Parliament House, Edinburgh,
Scotland, 0131 226 5071, Scottish
Advocate, Sheriff (Scotland) Queen's
Counsel (Scotland), Call Date: July
1990 (Inner Temple) Qualifications:
LLB (Strathclyde)

Morris *Ms Karen Anne*
Chubb Insurance Company of, Europe
S.A., 16 Avenue de Matignan, Paris,
331/45.61.73.67, Fax: 331/
45.61.41.62, European Counsel- Vice
President, Call Date: Nov 1986 (Gray's
Inn) Qualifications: MA (Edin), Dip
Law, (City), LLM (Univ of, Lond)

Morrison *Sheriff Nigel Murray Paton*
9 India Street, Edinburgh EH3 6HA,
031 225 2807, Fax: 031 225 5688,
Sheriff of Lothian and Borders at
Edinburgh, and Member Scottish Bar,
Call Date: Nov 1972 (Inner Temple)

Morsingh *Miss Wern Li*
Malaysia, Call Date: July 1996 (Gray's
Inn) Qualifications: LLB (London)

Mosko *Nicholas Terry*
Bahamas, Call Date: Nov 1995 (Middle
Temple) Qualifications: LLB (Hons)

Moss *Paul David*
P O Box N-9932, Nassau, Bahamas,
1-242 32-65084, Fax: 1-242 32-80541,
Legal Adviser, Estate Planner, and
Member Bahamas Bar, Call Date: July
1995 (Lincoln's Inn) Qualifications:
LLB (Hons), BA, TEP

Moushouttas *Michael*
Cyprus, Call Date: July 1998 (Gray's
Inn) Qualifications: LLB (Lond)

Moustras *Andrew Thomas*
Moore Stephens, P O Box 236, First
island Holbe, St Helier, Jersey, Channel
Islands, 01534 880088, Senior Legal
Administrator to Trust and Company
Secretarial Department, Call Date: Nov
1995 (Inner Temple) Qualifications:
BA (Wales)

Moutou *Lewis Toussaint*
10 Georges Guibert Street, Port-Louis,
Mauritius, 230 2085153, Fax: 230
28338678/230 210 7888, and Member
Mauritius Bar, Call Date: Apr 1975
(Middle Temple)

Mubarak *Syed*
Malaysia, 03-2981128/2986036, Fax:
603-2913816, Call Date: Nov 1995
(Lincoln's Inn) Qualifications: LLB
(Hons), LLM, (Lond), FCCA, FCIS

Muhammad *Nor Hisham Haji*
Ram Reza & Muhammad, Advocates &
Solicitors, 20-2 Jalan 2/50C, Genting
Crt, Taman Setapak indah Jaya, Off
Jalan Genting Klang, Malaysia 75460,
03 4229277/4229377, Fax: 03
4223477, Malaysian Bar, Call Date: Nov
1995 (Gray's Inn) Qualifications: LLB
(Sheff), LLM

Mulcahy *Michael Edward Joseph Ruben*
Ireland, and Member King's Inn, Call
Date: Mar 1998 (Middle Temple)
Qualifications: BA (Dublin)

Mullins *Bruce Ashley*
P O Box 200, Jewel Beach, Postal Code
134, Muscat, Sultanate of Oman,
Sultanate of Oman, (968) 607725, Fax:
(968) 607724, Registered Foreign
Resident Lawyer, and Member Hong
Kong Bar Ministry of Justice, Awqaf &
Islamic Affairs, Sultanate of Oman., Call
Date: July 1980 (Lincoln's Inn)
Qualifications: B.Sc (Hons)(Wales)

Muniandy *Ms Anjalli*
Singapore 330057, Call Date: July 1996
(Inner Temple) Qualifications: LLB
(Lond)

Munroe *Miss Miranda Melissa*
Bahamas, Call Date: July 1998 (Gray's
Inn) Qualifications: LLB (Hull)

Muntakim *Mohammad Abdul*
Bangladesh, Call Date: Nov 1996
(Lincoln's Inn) Qualifications: LLB
(Wolv'ton)

Mure *Kenneth Nisbet*
Advocates Library, Parliament House,
Edinburgh EH1 1RF, 0131 226 5071,
QC in Scotland Temporary Sheriff
(Scotland), Call Date: July 1990 (Gray's
Inn) Qualifications: LLB (Glas), MA
(Glas), F.T.I.I.

F

Murphy *Professor Peter William*
Professor of Law, South Texas College
of Law, 1303 San Jacinto, Houston,
Texas 77002, 713-646 1849, Fax: 713
659 2217, Trustee of the American
Inns of Court Foundation, Master of
Bench, American Inn of Court XV and
Member California Bar Texas Bar, Call
Date: July 1968 (Middle Temple)
Qualifications: MA, LLB

Murphy *Pierre Eric*
Law Offices of Pierre Murphy, Suite
260, 2445 M Street N.W., Washington
D.C. 20037, (202) 872 1679, Fax:
(202) 872 1725, and Member District
of Columbia, Wisconsin, Call Date: July
1979 (Lincoln's Inn) Qualifications:
LLB, JD

Murray *Keiron James*
Cains, Advocates & Solicitors, 15-19
Thol Street, Douglas IM1 1LB, Isle of
Man, 01624 628303, Call Date: Oct
1997 (Middle Temple) Qualifications:
LLB (Hons) (Sheff)

Murray *Miss Virginia Louise*
C/O Professor I K Rokas, 25
Boukourestiou St, Athens, and Member
Athens Bar 9 Bedford Row, London,
WC1R 4AZ, Call Date: 1991 (Middle
Temple) Qualifications: MA Hons
(Cantab)

Murugasu *Miss Chitrakala*
Malaysia, Call Date: July 1995 (Middle
Temple) Qualifications: LLB (Hons)

Musariri *Miss Blessing Concilia
Ropafadzo*
P.O.Box 1795, Harare, Zimbabwe,
739772-6/698047, Fax: 739002, Legal
Advisor, Public Relations Officer, Call
Date: July 1997 (Middle Temple)
Qualifications: LLB (Hons) (Wolv'ton),
MA

Mussenden *Larry Devron*
PO Box HM 2186, Hamilton HMJX,
Bermuda, and Member Bermuda Bar,
Call Date: Oct 1995 (Gray's Inn)
Qualifications: B.Sc (Canada), MA
(USA), LLB (Kent)

Muthu *Muthuraman*
Malaysia, Call Date: Oct 1996 (Gray's
Inn) Qualifications: LLB (Sheff)

Muthupalaniyappan *Yegappan*
Macquarie University, School of Law,
NSW 2109, Australia, 61 2 98507069/
97753468, Fax: 61 2 98507686,
Advocate & Solicitor of the High Court
of Malaya and Member Malaysia, Call
Date: Oct 1996 (Lincoln's Inn)
Qualifications: LLB (Hons), LLM
(Staffs), UPg.Dip (Staffs)

Muthusamy *Panirselvam s/o*
Singapore 806524, Call Date: July 1997
(Lincoln's Inn) Qualifications: LLB
(Hons) (Lond)

Muthusamy *Ms Santhi*
West Malaysia, Call Date: Nov 1995
(Inner Temple) Qualifications: LLB
(Bucks)

Mylona *Miss Sofi C*
Cyprus, Legal Advisor, and Member
Cyprus Bar Association, Call Date: Nov
1996 (Lincoln's Inn) Qualifications:
LLB (Hons) (Leics)

Nabi *Miss Nighat Sultana*
Ground Fllor, House [H] 375, Lane [H]
28, New D.O.H.S., Mohakhali, Dhaka
1206, Bangladesh, 880 02 607710/ 880
02 9660301, and Member Bangladesh,
Call Date: Nov 1997 (Lincoln's Inn)
Qualifications: LLB (Hons) (Lond)

Nadarajah *Miss Sumithra*
Malaysia, Call Date: July 1997
(Lincoln's Inn) Qualifications: LLB
(Hons) (L'pool)

Nadarajan *Mrs Kanakavalli*
Malaysia, Call Date: July 1997
(Lincoln's Inn) Qualifications: LLB
(Hons)

Nadasan *Dinesh*
25 Telok Blangah Crescent, [H]06-77,
Singapore 090025, 2739619, Call Date:
July 1996 (Middle Temple)
Qualifications: LLB (Hons) (Lond)

Nadchatiram *Thiruchelva Segaram*
Malaysia, Call Date: July 1996 (Inner
Temple) Qualifications: LLM (Cantab),
LLB (Lond)

Nagaraja *Maniam*
Singapore 090041, Call Date: July 1997
(Middle Temple) Qualifications: LLB
(Hons) (Lond)

Nagaraw *Samyraw*
Malaysia, Call Date: Nov 1997
(Lincoln's Inn) Qualifications: LLB
(Hons)

Nagreh *Miss Ranmeet Kaur*
Malaysia, and Member Malaysian, Call
Date: July 1996 (Lincoln's Inn)
Qualifications: LLB (Hons) (Sheff)

Nahar *Miss Lutfun*
Bangladesh, Call Date: Nov 1997
(Lincoln's Inn) Qualifications: LLB
(Hons) (Lond)

Naidu *Kuppusamy Jayakumar*
Singapore 730840, Call Date: Nov 1998
(Inner Temple) Qualifications: LLB
(Lond)

Nair *Miss Heama Latha*
Malaysia, Call Date: Nov 1996
(Lincoln's Inn) Qualifications: LLB
(Hons) (Lond)

Nair *Kesavan*
M P D Nair & Co, [H]12-15
International Plaza, 10 Anson Road,
Singapore 0207, Singapore 1024,
2218800, Fax: 2240667, Partner,
Supreme Court of Singapore and
Member Canberra, Australian Capital
Territory, Call Date: Nov 1990 (Middle
Temple) Qualifications: LLB M.S.I.Arb

Nair *Miss Maala*
Block 209, Tampines Street 21,
[H]08-1335, Singapore 520209,
Singapore 1852, and Member
Singapore, Call Date: July 1995 (Middle
Temple) Qualifications: LLB (Hons)

Nair *Miss Namarath Sudha*
Malaysia, and Member Singapore Bar,
Malaysian Bar, Call Date: Feb 1994
(Lincoln's Inn) Qualifications: LLB
(Hons, Lond)

Nair *Prakesh*
Singapore 560204, Call Date: July 1996
(Middle Temple) Qualifications: LLB
(Hons) (Lond)

Nair *Miss Sharmila*
M P D Nair & Co, [H]12-15
International Plaza, 10 Anson Road,
Singapore 1024, 221-8800, Fax:
224-0667, and Member Singapore Bar,
Call Date: July 1995 (Middle Temple)
Qualifications: LLB (Hons)

Nair *Miss Sulojana*
Malaysia, Call Date: Oct 1997 (Middle
Temple) Qualifications: LLB (Hons)
(Lond)

Nalpon *Zero Geraldo Mario*
Singapore 460081, Call Date: Feb 1993
(Gray's Inn) Qualifications: LLB (Hull)

Namasivayam *Ramesh*
Malaysia, Call Date: July 1996
(Lincoln's Inn) Qualifications: LLB
(Hons) (Lond)

Namasivayam *Srinivasan s/o*
Singapore 577106, Call Date: July 1997
(Lincoln's Inn) Qualifications: LLB
(Hons) (Lond)

Nanaykkara *Harshana Jayabahu
Wickramathilak*
Sri Lanka, Call Date: Nov 1998
(Lincoln's Inn) Qualifications: LLB
(Hons) (Sheff)

Nandwani *Manoj Prakash*
[H]19-02 Peach Garden, Meyer Road,
Singapore 437606, 2353536, Fax:
7351210, Advocate & Solicitor, and
Member Singapore Bar, Call Date: July
1996 (Middle Temple) Qualifications:
LLB (Hons) (Lond)

Narayanan *Nicholas Jeyaraj*
Singapore 217570, Call Date: July 1997
(Inner Temple) Qualifications: LLB

Narayanan *Palaniappan*
India, Call Date: May 1996 (Inner
Temple) Qualifications: BA (Madras,
India), LLM (Lond)

Narayanasamy *Miss Subashini d/o*
Block 152, Lorong 2, Toa Payoh,
[H]11-450, Singapore 310152,
3531272, Call Date: Nov 1996
(Lincoln's Inn) Qualifications: LLB
(Hons) (Lond)

Naritomi *Nobukata*
Naritomi Office, 12-17 Shiroganedai
4-Chome, Minato-ku, Tokyo 108-0071,
81 3 3441 0567, Fax: 81 3 5447 5305,
and Member Daiichi Tokyo Bar
Association, Call Date: July 1972
(Lincoln's Inn) Qualifications: LL.B
(Tokyo)

Nasir *Syed Azfar Ali*
Pakistan, Call Date: July 1997
(Lincoln's Inn) Qualifications: LLB
(Hons)

Nathan *Dr Kathirgamar Veeragathy
Sinnath*
Studio Legale Nathan, Viale Mazzini 12,
35035 Mestrino (PD), 049 9002326,
Fax: 049 9002313, Int Comm Lawyer/
Arbitrator, Call Date: July 1971 (Middle
Temple) Qualifications: EurIng BSc
BSc (Eng), LLB (Leeds)LLM(Kent),
Phd in Law, (Lond)

Natverlal *Deepak*
Apt Blk 117, [H]05-523, Pasir Ris
Street 11, Singapore 510117, 3393303,
Fax: 3321101, and Member Singapore
Bar, Call Date: July 1995 (Lincoln's
Inn) Qualifications: LLB (Hons), LLM
(Lond)

Naughton *John Stuart*
Information Economies Dept, Deloitte
& Touche, Berkenlaan 6, 1831 Diegem,
Belgium, 32 2 718 9397, Fax: 32 2 718
9692, Legal Adviser, Call Date: Oct
1993 (Gray's Inn) Qualifications: LLB
(Hons)(Wales)

Navaratnam *Sivarajan*
Malaysia, Call Date: July 1997
(Lincoln's Inn) Qualifications: LLB
(Hons)

Navaratnam *Miss Vijaylakshumi*
Malaysia, Call Date: Nov 1998
(Lincoln's Inn) Qualifications: LLB
(Hons)(Wolves)

Nayar *David*
Singapore 510463, and Member
Singapore Bar, Call Date: July 1992
(Gray's Inn) Qualifications: LLB (Lond)

Nazar *Boaz*
M/S Laycock & Ong, 41 Bukit Pasoh
Road, Singapore 470620, 533 9115,
Fax: 533 2206, and Member Singapore
Bar, Call Date: July 1993 (Lincoln's
Inn) Qualifications: LLB (Hons)

Nazar *Mrs Claire*
Singapore 730036, Call Date: Nov 1998
(Lincoln's Inn) Qualifications: LLB
(Hons)(Leics)

Nazmi *Saiful*
Malaysia, Call Date: July 1996
(Lincoln's Inn) Qualifications: LLB
(Hons)(Notts)

Nemchand *Radhakrishan*
Mauritius, Call Date: Nov 1998
(Lincoln's Inn) Qualifications: LLB
(Hons)(Wolves)

Neo *Miss Shien Ching*
Malaysia, Call Date: Mar 1998
(Lincoln's Inn) Qualifications: LLB
(Hons)(Lond)

Neocleous *Elias Andrea*
Neocleous House, 199 Makarios III
Avenue, P.O.Box 613, Limassol, Cyprus,
357 5 362818, Fax: 357 5 359262, and
Member Cyprus Bar, Call Date: May
1993 (Inner Temple) Qualifications:
BA (Oxon)

Neocleous *Ms Olympia*
Cyprus, Call Date: Nov 1997 (Inner
Temple) Qualifications: LLB (Lond),
MSc, (Lond)

Neoh *Ang Wei*
Messrs Mohd Noor & S Y Lee, Room
110, First Floor,, Asia Life Building,
45-B Jalan Tun Sambanthan, 30000
Ipoh, Perak, Malaysia, (05) 2543589,
Fax: (05) 2542611, and Member
Malaya Bar, Call Date: July 1995
(Lincoln's Inn) Qualifications: LLB
(Hons), LLM (Lond)

Neoh *Miss Hong Sean*
Malaysia, and Member Malaysia Bar,
Call Date: July 1996 (Lincoln's Inn)
Qualifications: LLB (Hons)(Leeds)

Neoh *Ms Sue Lynn*
Philips Electronics Asia, Pacific
Limited, 1 Temasek Avenue, [H]
23-01/03 Millenia Tower, Singapore
600302, Regional Legal Counsel, and
Member Singapore Bar, Call Date: Oct
1990 (Gray's Inn) Qualifications: LLB
LLM

Nesbitt *Richard Law*
2 Arran Square, Arran Quay, Dublin 7,
8733344, Fax: 8733737, Member of the
Committee on Court Practice and
Procedure in Ireland, Senior Counsel,
The Bar of Ireland Oct 1993 and
Member Northern Ireland Bar Bar of
Ireland, Call Date: May 1987 (Middle
Temple) Qualifications: TCD

Newell *Michael Harold Banks*
Michael Newell & Co, Barristers
Solicitors & Notaries, 225 Oxford Street,
Leederville WA 6007, 61 8 94432888,
Fax: 61 8 94441871, Commissioner for
Affidavits, Notary Public, Migration
Agent, Barrister and Solicitor W
Australia 1980 Member of the
Administrative Law and Native Title
Committees Barrister and Solicitor
High Court of Australia 1984, Call Date:
July 1965 (Middle Temple)
Qualifications: LLB

Ng *Miss Ann Gie*
Malaysia, Call Date: July 1998
(Lincoln's Inn) Qualifications: LLB
(Hons)

Ng *Miss Audrey Su Yin*
Malaysia, Call Date: July 1997
(Lincoln's Inn) Qualifications: LLB
(Hons)(Lond)

Ng *Bock Hoh*
Singapore 1953, Call Date: Nov 1991
(Gray's Inn) Qualifications: LLB (E
Ang)

Ng *Miss Chiunga*
Hong Hong, Call Date: Oct 1998
(Lincoln's Inn) Qualifications: LLB
(Hons)(Belfast)

Ng *Daryll Richard*
United Arab Emirates, Call Date: July
1996 (Middle Temple) Qualifications:
LLB (Hons)(Notts)

Ng *David Wai Cheong*
Singapore S141026, Call Date: Mar
1998 (Lincoln's Inn) Qualifications:
LLB (Hons)(Lond)

Ng *Desmond Tiong Keng*
Singapore 266880, Call Date: Nov 1997
(Middle Temple) Qualifications: LLB
(Hons)(Hull)

Ng *Miss Eileen*
Singapore 2678, Call Date: July 1995
(Lincoln's Inn) Qualifications: LLB
(Hons)

Ng *Miss Hwee Lee*
Singapore 128945, Call Date: Nov 1995
(Middle Temple) Qualifications: LLB
(Hons)(Kent)

Ng *Kenneth Lien Shen*
Singapore 577204, Call Date: July 1995
(Middle Temple) Qualifications: LLB
(Hons)(Hull)

Ng *Kim Tean*
Blk 331, [H]14-225 Bukit Batok, Street
33, Singapore 2365, 65 9 6651538,
Fax: 65 5614891, Legal Counsel, and
Member Singapore Bar, Call Date: July
1995 (Middle Temple) Qualifications:
LLB (Hons), B.Eng

Ng *Miss Lee Chin*
Malaysia, Call Date: July 1998
(Lincoln's Inn) Qualifications: LLB
(Hons)(L'pool)

Ng *Miss Ling Li*
John Koh & Co, 8 Robinson Road,
[H]12-00 Casco Building, Malaysia,
(65) 5389880, Fax: (65) 5382221,
Legal Assistant, and Member Malaysia
Bar, Call Date: July 1992 (Lincoln's
Inn) Qualifications: LLB (Hons)
(Lond), LLM (Lond)

Ng *Miss Lyn*
Singapore 1024, Call Date: July 1992
(Middle Temple) Qualifications: BA
(Hons) (Oxon)

Ng *Miss Pei Chun*
Malaysia, Call Date: July 1997 (Middle
Temple) Qualifications: LLB
(Hons)(Leics)

Ng *Robert Chee Siong*
17 Mt. Cameron Road, The Peak, (852)
2734-8383, Fax: 2369 8471, Call Date:
July 1975 (Middle Temple)

F

Ng *Seng Chan*
Alexander Lee & Associates, P O Box
90943 AMSC, Auckland, New Zealand,
3600478, Fax: 3608478, New Zealand
Bar, Call Date: July 1996 (Inner
Temple) Qualifications: LLB
(Hons) (Lond), BSocSC (Hons), BA
(Lond)

Ng *Ser Chiang*
Singapore 440032, Call Date: Nov 1998
(Middle Temple) Qualifications: LLB
(Hons) (Wolves)

Ng *Miss Shan Shan*
Nashir Johal & Co, Suite A13, 11th
Floor, Bangunan Angkasa Raya, Jalan
Ampang, 50450 Kuala Lumpur,
Malaysia, 03-7755539, Fax:
03-7189235, Call Date: July 1998
(Lincoln's Inn) Qualifications: LLB
(Hons) (Wales)

Ng *Miss Shoo Cheng*
Singapore 535943, Call Date: Nov 1996
(Lincoln's Inn) Qualifications: LLB
(Hons) (Lond)

Ng *Siew Hoong*
Singapore 460140, Call Date: July 1997
(Middle Temple) Qualifications: LLB
(Hons) (Lond)

Ng *Miss Sonia Win-Yen*
Malaysia, Call Date: July 1996
(Lincoln's Inn) Qualifications: LLB
(Hons) (So'ton)

Ng *Stephen Shiu Chi*
Hong Kong, Call Date: July 1997
(Middle Temple) Qualifications: LLB
(Hons)

Ng *Miss Su Chin*
Singapore 429451, Call Date: Nov 1998
(Lincoln's Inn) Qualifications: LLB
(Hons(Lond), BSc(Hons) (Singapore)

Ng *Miss Su Hing*
Malaysia, Call Date: Nov 1997
(Lincoln's Inn) Qualifications: LLB
(Hons)

Ng *Sze Meng*
Singapore 769678, Call Date: July 1996
(Middle Temple) Qualifications: LLB
(Hons) (Lond)

Ng *Timothy Wai Keong*
Singapore 1027, Call Date: Nov 1995
(Gray's Inn) Qualifications: LLB
(Bucks)

Ng *Wai Chiu*
Singapore 787153, Call Date: July 1998
(Inner Temple) Qualifications: LLB
(Hull)

Ng *Miss Wendy Yee Cheng*
Singapore 268920, Call Date: July 1996
(Inner Temple) Qualifications: LLB
(Bristol)

Ng *Miss Yee Yung*
Singapore, Call Date: Nov 1993 (Gray's
Inn) Qualifications: B.Sc, B.Com,
(Melbourne), LLB, (Lond)

Ng *Miss Yuet Lai*
West Malaysia, Call Date: Nov 1998
(Middle Temple) Qualifications: LLB
(Hons) (Lond)

Ng *Yushan*
Singapore 467198, Call Date: Oct 1998
(Lincoln's Inn) Qualifications: BA
(Hons)

Ngeh *Anthony Koh Seh*
East Malaysia, Call Date: July 1997
(Lincoln's Inn) Qualifications: LLB
(Hons) (Wales)

Ngooi *Chiu-Ing*
Baker & Mckenzie, 1 Temasek Avenue
[H] 27-01, Millenia Tower, Singapore
0511, 65 338 1888, Fax: 65 337 5100,
Associate, and Member Australian
Capital Territory Malaysia Bar, Call
Date: July 1991 (Lincoln's Inn)
Qualifications: BA (Oxford)

Nicolaou *Miss Athena Maria*
P.L.Cacoyannis & Co, Libra Chambers,
8 Rigas Fereos Str, Limassol 3095,
Cyprus, 00 357 5 363154, Fax: 00 357
5 342887, Advocate, and Member
Cyprus, Call Date: Nov 1995 (Middle
Temple) Qualifications: LLB (Hons),
LLM

Niehorster *James William*
Hong Kong, Call Date: Nov 1998 (Gray's
Inn) Qualifications: BSc, MSc

Nijar *Miss Belinder Kaur*
Singapore 640835, Call Date: July 1997
(Middle Temple) Qualifications: LLB
(Hons) (Lond)

Niklas *Miss Elizabeth Anne*
Office of Corporate Counsel, Charles
Schwab & Co.,Inc., 101 Montgomery
Street, San Francisco, CA 94104, United
States of America, (415) 363 1417, Fax:
(415) 363 1366, Legal Advisor, Call
Date: Nov 1995 (Middle Temple)
Qualifications: BA (Cincinnati), Dip in
Law

Niraiselvan *Kumaravellu*
Singapore 059214, Call Date: July 1995
(Lincoln's Inn) Qualifications: LLB
(Hons)

Nisbett *Mrs Belva Lenis*
P.O.Box 517, Charlestown, Nevis, West
Indies, 869 469 1913, Fax: 869 469
5806, Call Date: July 1998 (Lincoln's
Inn) Qualifications: LLB (Hons)

Nixon *Miss Paulette Pamela*
Bahamas, Call Date: July 1997
(Lincoln's Inn) Qualifications: LLB
(Hons)

Njie *Omar Momodou Musa*
78 Wellington Street, Banjul, The
Gambia, The Gambia, 00 220 2?9819,
Fax: 00 220 229347, and Member
Gambia Bar, Call Date: Oct 1991
(Middle Temple) Qualifications: BA
Hons (E Anglia)

Njonjo *Miss Waringa*
Kenya, Call Date: Nov 1998 (Middle
Temple) Qualifications: BSc Econ
(Hons), (Wales)

Nordin *Norazali Bin*
Malaysia, Call Date: Nov 1997
(Lincoln's Inn) Qualifications: LLB
(Hons) (Nott'm)

Norris *Richard*
Logica Inc., 32 Hartwell Avenue,
Lexington, MA 01273, United States of
America, 00 1 617 476 8132, Fax: 00 1
617 476 8010, Director, Customer Care
Solutions, Call Date: July 1979 (Inner
Temple) Qualifications: LLB (So'ton),
ACMA

Nottage *D. Sean*
Graham Thompson & Co, Sassoon
House, P.O.Box N272, Nassau, The
Bahamas, (809) 322 4130, Fax: (809)
328 1069, Associate, Graham,
Thompson & Co, and Member
Massachusetts, Commonwealth of the
Bahamas, Call Date: Nov 1993 (Middle
Temple) Qualifications: LLB
(Hons) (Bucks), JD (Suffolk Uni, Law,
School, Boston, Massachusetts)

Nurse *Lewitt Carter*
U.S.A., Call Date: Oct 1990 (Inner
Temple) Qualifications: LLB (W
Indies), LLM (Lond)

O'Brien *James Gerard*
P O Box 2424, Law Library, Four
Courts, Dublin 7, Republic of Ireland,
8720622, Fax: 8720455, and Member
Southern Ireland Bar, Call Date: July
1988 (Middle Temple) Qualifications:
BL (King's Inn), LLM

O'Culachain *Maoiliosa Seosamh*
Telecom Eirann PLC, St Stephen's
Green West, Dublin 2, Republic of
Ireland, 00 3531 701 6230, Fax: 00
3531 671 4255, ESOP Manager, Call
Date: Feb 1995 (Lincoln's Inn)
Qualifications: BA (Hons), LLB
(Hons) (Galway)

O'Donnell *Everard Jeffrey Echlin*
United States of America, Call Date: July
1976 (Gray's Inn) Qualifications: MSc

O'Donovan *Sean*
Republic of Ireland, Barrister of
Ireland, Call Date: May 1996 (Middle
Temple) Qualifications: BA (Cork), BL
(King's Inn)

O'Driscoll *Miss Karen Margaret Helen*
Courthouse Chambers, 27/29
Washington Street, Cork, Ireland, 00
353 21 275151, Fax: 00 353 21
272821, Barrister of Ireland, Call Date:
May 1997 (Middle Temple)
Qualifications: BCL (Cork), M.Litt
(Dublin)

O'Dubhghaill *Feargal Padraig*
Republic of Ireland, Barrister of
Ireland, Call Date: May 1996 (Middle
Temple) Qualifications: BCL (Cork), BL
(King's Inn)

O'Gorman *Patrick Kieran*
Republic of Ireland, Barrister of
Ireland, Call Date: July 1998 (Middle
Temple) Qualifications: BA
(Hons) (Galway)

O'Neill *Aidan Mark*
ADvocates Library, Parliament House,
Edinburgh EH1 1RF, Scotland, 0131
226 5071, Fax: 0131 225 3642,
Member of the Faculty of Advocates,
Scotland (July 1987) and Member
Scotland Bar, Call Date: July 1996
(Inner Temple) Qualifications: LLB
(Edinburgh), LLM (Sydney), LLM
(Florence)

O'Neill *Ms Heather June*
77 Jane Street, New York, United States
of America, and Member New York
State Bar, Call Date: Oct 1992 (Inner
Temple) Qualifications: LLB(Hons)

O'Neill *Miss June*
Simcocks Advocates, Ridgway House,
Ridgway Street, Douglas IM99 1OY, Isle
of Man, 01624 620821, Fax: 01624
620994, Call Date: Nov 1997 (Lincoln's
Inn) Qualifications: LLB (Hons) (Lond)

O'Riordan *Mrs Miriam Bernadette*
'Courthouse Chambers, 27-9
Washington Street, Cork, (021)
277563, Fax: (021) 277563, Member
Cork & Munster Circuit, Republic of
Ireland Barrister at Law, Kings Inn
Dublin Member Hepatitis C
Compensation Tribunal and Member
Southern Ireland Bar, Call Date: Feb
1982 (Middle Temple) Qualifications:
BCL Cork

O'Rourke *Raymond John*
Stanbrook & Hooper, European
Community Lawyers, Rue du Taciturne
42, 1000 Brussels, Belgium, (32-2)
230 50 59, Fax: (32-2) 230 57 13, Call
Date: Nov 1995 (Gray's Inn)
Qualifications: BA, MA (Dublin), LLB
(Lond)

O'Shea *Kevin Brendan*
Ireland, Call Date: Nov 1998 (Middle
Temple) Qualifications: LLB
(Hons) (Wales)

O'Sullivan *Miss Lorraine Anne*
Courthouse Chambers, 27/29
Washington Street, Cork, Republic of
Ireland, 0044 353 21 276186, Fax:
(021) 272821, Barrister of Ireland, Call
Date: May 1996 (Middle Temple)
Qualifications: BCL (Cork), BL (King's
Inn)

Oei *Miss Carolyn Jane*
81 Langford Court, Langford Place, 22
Abbey Road, London NW8 9DP,
Singapore 2880, and Member
Singapore Bar, Call Date: July 1995
(Gray's Inn) Qualifications: LLB (Lond)

Oei *Miss Joanne Jacinta*
Malaysia, Call Date: July 1998 (Middle
Temple) Qualifications: LLB
(Hons) (L'pool)

Oei *Miss Mona*
Singapore 0923, Call Date: Nov 1993
(Lincoln's Inn) Qualifications: LLB
(Hons)

Oei *Su Chi Ian*
Singapore 449291, Call Date: July 1997
(Middle Temple) Qualifications: LLB
(Hons) (Lond)

Oh *Miss Carolyn Li Lin*
Ghazi & Lim, 19th Floor, Plaza House,
No 8 Farquhar Street, 10200 Penang,
Malaysia 10250, 01 06 04 2633 688,
Fax: 01 06 04 2633 188, and Member
Malaysia Bar, Call Date: July 1994
(Middle Temple) Qualifications: LLB
(Hons) (Kent)

Oh *Douglas Kim Chuan*
Malaysia, Call Date: July 1996
(Lincoln's Inn) Qualifications: LLB
(Hons) (Lond)

Ohiullah *Muhammad*
Orr, Dignam & Co, 80, Motijheel
Commercial Area, (1st Floor), Dhaka -
1000, 880-2-9563950/880-2-9563946,
Fax: 880-2-9560257/880-2-9559887,
Bangladesh Supreme Court Bar
Association Advocate, Supreme Court of
Bangladesh, Call Date: July 1997 (Inner
Temple) Qualifications: LLB (So'ton)

Ollivry *Guy Marie*
105 Chancery House, Port-Louis,
Mauritius, Mauritius, (230) 2123083/
2129906, Fax: (203) 2128799, QC
Mauritius 1987 and Member Mauritius
Bar, Call Date: July 1957 (Gray's Inn)

Omar *Muhammad Shahjahan*
Bangladesh, Call Date: Nov 1998
(Lincoln's Inn) Qualifications: LLB
(Hons) (Wolves)

Ong *Basil Kah Liang*
Madhavan Louis & Partners, 2
Finlayson Green, [H]11-07 Asia
Insurance Building, Singapore 2880,
2255111, Fax: 2243594, and Member
Singapore Bar, Call Date: July 1993
(Middle Temple) Qualifications: LLB
(Hons) (Lond)

Ong *Chee Huan*
32 Jalan Setiabakti 8, Bukit
Damansara, 50490 Kuala Lumpur,
Malaysia, 010 60 3 2541842, Legal
Assistant, and Member Malaysia Bar,
Call Date: July 1995 (Lincoln's Inn)
Qualifications: LLB (Hons)

Ong *Miss Chih-Ching*
Singapore 2880, and Member
Singapore Bar, Call Date: Nov 1992
(Gray's Inn) Qualifications: LLB
(Buckingham)

Ong *Dr Colin Yee Cheng*
Brunei, (006732) 420913, Fax:
(006732) 420911, Visiting Fellow,
QMW College, University of London,
and Member Brunei Bar Essex Court
Chambers, 24 Lincoln's Inn Fields,
London, WC2A 3ED, Call Date: Nov
1991 (Inner Temple) Qualifications:
LLB (Sheff), LLM, PhD (Lond), ACIArb

Ong *Eben Eng Tuan*
Loh Eben Ong & Partners, 112 Middle
Road [H] 07-00, Midland House, (65)
338 1810, Fax: (65) 338 7678, and
Member Singapore Bar, Call Date: July
1991 (Gray's Inn) Qualifications: LLB

Ong *Miss Ellen Mei Luan*
Malaysia, Call Date: July 1997 (Middle
Temple) Qualifications: LLB (Hons)

Ong *Hean Jin*
Singapore 119165, Call Date: Nov 1998
(Lincoln's Inn) Qualifications: LLB
(Hons), LLM, (Lond)

Ong *Ivan Ban Phing*
Hamzah & Ong Advocates, 13, 1st
Floor, Jalan P Ramlee, 93400 Kuching,
P.O.Box 1543, 93730 Kuching,
Malaysia, 082 246876, Fax: 082
247217, Call Date: July 1989 (Middle
Temple) Qualifications: LLB [Essex]

Ong *Miss Janaine Jo Lin*
Singapore 228576, Call Date: July 1997
(Middle Temple) Qualifications: LLB
(Hons) (Hull)

Ong *Miss Jo-Ann Wei-Syn*
Singapore 259617, Call Date: July 1997
(Lincoln's Inn) Qualifications: LLB
(Hons) (Sheff)

Ong *Kenneth Heng Heng*
Singapore 267422, Call Date: Nov 1996
(Middle Temple) Qualifications: LLB
(Hons) (Bucks)

Ong *Kingsley Tze-Wei*
Republic of Singapore, Call Date: Oct
1998 (Inner Temple) Qualifications:
LLB (Hull)

Ong *Lee Woei*
Singapore 534648, Call Date: Nov 1993
(Lincoln's Inn) Qualifications: LLB
(Hons), LLM (Exon)

Ong *Ms May Anne*
United States of America, Call Date: July
1994 (Middle Temple) Qualifications:
BA (Hons) (Cantab)

Ong *Miss May Li Karen*
Malaysia, Call Date: July 1997 (Middle
Temple) Qualifications: LLB
(Hons) (Kent)

Ong *Miss Melita Sue Chen*
20 Ford Avenue, Singapore 268700,
Singapore 1026, 00 65 4622176, and
Member Singapore Bar, Call Date: July
1997 (Lincoln's Inn) Qualifications:
LLB (Hons)

Ong *Miss Ming Suan*
Messrs Raja Eleena,Siew,Ang &,
Associates, Suite 20.03 20th Floor,
Plaza See Hoy Chan, Jalan Raja,
Chulan, 50200 Kuala Lumpur Malaysia,
Malaysia, 03 2322411, Fax: 03
2301613, and Member Malaysia Bar,
Call Date: July 1991 (Lincoln's Inn)
Qualifications: LLB (Hons) (Warwick)

Ong *Peng Boon*
Singapore 150129, (65) 3232202, Fax:
(65) 3232252, Partner, and Member
Singapore Bar, Call Date: Feb 1994
(Middle Temple) Qualifications: LLB
(Hons) (Lond)

Ong *Seng Hoong*
Malaysia, Call Date: July 1994
(Lincoln's Inn) Qualifications: LLB
(Hons)

Ong *Miss Sharon Get-Jin*
Singapore 1130, Call Date: July 1993
(Inner Temple) Qualifications: BA

Ong *Miss Shirley*
Singapore 1544, Call Date: July 1994
(Lincoln's Inn) Qualifications: LLB
(Hons)

Ong *Sim Ho*
Inland Revenue Authority of, Singapore,
Fullerton Building, Singapore,
Singapore 1852, 065-7856932, Senior
Officer (Tax Interpretations & Treaties),
Bachelor of Accountancy Co-Author,
Goods & Services Tax-Law & Practice,
Butterworths 1995., Call Date: July
1995 (Lincoln's Inn) Qualifications:
LLB (Hons), BAcc (Hons) (S'pore)

Ong *Sin Qui*
P.O.Box 2670, Robinson Road, (65)
5339115, Fax: (65) 5332206, Member
Criminal Law Advisory Committee,
Advocate & Solicitor, Singapore and
Member Singapore Bar, Call Date: Nov
1974 (Middle Temple) Qualifications:
MA (Cantab)

Ong *Miss Su-Lin Vivienne*
Singapore 309041, Call Date: Nov 1996
(Middle Temple) Qualifications: LLB
(Hons) (Kent)

Ong *Miss Sue Fen*
Brunei, Call Date: July 1996 (Middle
Temple) Qualifications: LLB
(Hons) (Notts)

Ong *Miss Suzanna Ann-Francesca*
Singapore 5807550, Call Date: July
1996 (Lincoln's Inn) Qualifications:
LLB (Hons) (Bris)

Ong *Teng Kok*
Singapore 600123, Call Date: July 1997
(Lincoln's Inn) Qualifications: LLB
(Hons)

Ong *Teng Ping*
Paul Ong & Associates, 7th Floor,
Bangunan Yee Seng, No 15 Jalan Raja
Chulan, 50200 Kuala Lumpur,
Malaysia, 03 2321562, Fax: 603
2327260, Public Accountant of
Malaysian Institute of Accountants, and
Member Malaysian Bar, Call Date: July
1995 (Lincoln's Inn) Qualifications:
LLB (Hons), FCCA, ATII, PA

Ong *Theng Soon*
Malaysia, Call Date: July 1997
(Lincoln's Inn) Qualifications: LLB
(Hons) (Leeds)

Ong *Miss Wee En*
Malaysia, Call Date: July 1997
(Lincoln's Inn) Qualifications: LLB
(Hons) (Wales)

Ong *Miss Yin Ee*
Abu Talib Shahrom & Zahari, Advocates
& Solicitors, 43-1 Jalan Desa, 58100
Kuala Lumpur, Malaysia, (603) 780
4494, Fax: (603) 784 5434, Call Date:
July 1997 (Middle Temple)
Qualifications: LLB (Hons)

Ong *Yu En*
Singapore 807221, and Member
Singapore Bar, Call Date: July 1994
(Middle Temple) Qualifications: LLB
(Hons) (Hull)

Ooi *Huey Miin*
Malaysia, Call Date: Oct 1998 (Middle
Temple) Qualifications: LLB
(Hons) (Sheff)

Ooi *Peng Cuan*
Malaysia, Call Date: July 1996
(Lincoln's Inn) Qualifications: LLB
(Hons) (Lond)

Ooi *Miss Shu-Mei*
Malaysia, Call Date: Oct 1998 (Gray's
Inn) Qualifications: LLB (Leeds)

Oon *Miss Diana Bee Lin*
Malaysia, Call Date: July 1995 (Middle
Temple) Qualifications: BA (Hons)

Oon *Wee Phing*
Singapore 310179, Call Date: Nov 1996
(Middle Temple) Qualifications: LLB
(Hons) (Lond)

Ortega *Mark Benjamin*
12 Jalan Anak Patong, Singapore
489328, Singapore 489328, (65)
4458691, and Member Singapore Bar,
Call Date: July 1995 (Middle Temple)
Qualifications: LLB (Hons)

Osman *Miss Nishet*
SW15 3NZ, Call Date: July 1995 (Middle
Temple) Qualifications: LLB (Hons)

Osofsky *Mrs Lisa Kate*
United States of America, American
Attorney, Call Date: Nov 1997 (Middle
Temple) Qualifications: BA (Amherst),
JD (Harvard)

Osoria *Miss Paulette Barbara*
The Grand Bahama Port, Authority
Limited, P O Box F.42666, Freeport,
Grand Bahama, Bahamas, 242 352
6611 Ext 2242, Fax: 242 352 4568, Call
Date: July 1997 (Gray's Inn)
Qualifications: BSc (Ontario), LLB
(Bucks)

Ouzounian *Dickran Aram*
Dickran Ouzounian & Co Ltd, PO Box
1567, Nicosia, Cyprus, Cyprus, 02
353053, Fax: 02 350536, General
Manager, Call Date: Nov 1988 (Inner
Temple) Qualifications: LLB

Ow *Tan Cheng*
Malaysia, Call Date: Nov 1996
(Lincoln's Inn) Qualifications: LLB
(Hons) (Lond)

Owaisi *Asaduddin*
India, Call Date: May 1995 (Lincoln's
Inn) Qualifications: LLB (Hons)

Oxley *Miss Denise Eudene*
Apt 411, Cabrillo Square, 1399 Ninth
Avenue, San Diego, California 92101,
United States of America, (619) 231
4113, Call Date: Oct 1993 (Lincoln's
Inn) Qualifications: LLB (Hons) (Lond)

Paglar *Miss Constance Margaret*
Singapore 310028, Call Date: Nov 1996
(Inner Temple) Qualifications: LLB
(Lond)

Pah *Miss Yvonne Li-Ean*
Bustaman & Co, Lot C9-3, Jalan
Selaman 1, Dataran Palma, Jalan
Ampang, 68000 Ampang, Selangor,
Malaysia, and Member Malaysian Bar,
Call Date: July 1995 (Middle Temple)
Qualifications: LLB (Hons), LLM

Palaniyappan *Allagarsamy s/o*
Singapore 530720, Call Date: Nov 1996
(Lincoln's Inn) Qualifications: LLB
(Hons) (Lond)

Palar *Miss Sharlini*
Malaysia, Call Date: Mar 1999
(Lincoln's Inn) Qualifications: LLB
(Hons) (Lond), LLM (Bris)

Palas *Miss Esme*
Cyprus, Call Date: Nov 1996 (Gray's
Inn) Qualifications: LLB (Bris)

Palmer *Adrian Jeremy*
18 Heads Road, Donvale 3111,
Melbourne, Victoria, 61 3 873 5650,
Call Date: Nov 1978 (Middle Temple)
Qualifications: MA, LLM, Dip Comp, Sci
(Cantab)

Pan *Wai Liong*
Blk 704 [H]11-137, Pasir Ris Drive 10,
Singapore 510704, 5842476, Call Date:
July 1996 (Middle Temple)
Qualifications: LLB (Hons) (Wolves)

Panaech *Dave Jeet Singh*
Singapore 455060, Call Date: July 1998
(Inner Temple) Qualifications: LLB
(So'ton), LLM (Lond)

Panagopoulos *Dr Panayotis Constantinou*
8 Merlin Steet No 8, 10671 Athens, 362 3 930, Fax: 30- 1-3628.566, and Member Athens Bar, Call Date: Nov 1951 (Gray's Inn) Qualifications: LLB, BSc, LLD , (Athens)

Pang *Kong Seng*
Malaysia, Call Date: July 1998 (Lincoln's Inn) Qualifications: LLB (Hons)

Pannirselvam *Miss Priya*
Singapore 437410, Call Date: Nov 1997 (Lincoln's Inn) Qualifications: LLB (Hons)(Nott'm)

Panoo *Sunil Singh*
Singapore 461033, Call Date: July 1996 (Middle Temple) Qualifications: LLB (Hons)(Lond)

Pao *Felix Ho Ming*
87 New Henry House, 10 Ice House Street, Hong Kong, Hong Kong, 2522 5494, Fax: 2810 4677, Consultant Editor of the Hong Kong Law Digest, and Member Hong Kong Bar Australia Bar, Call Date: Apr 1991 (Gray's Inn) Qualifications: LLB, PCLL

Papachan *Gopalan Krishnan*
Malaysia, Call Date: Nov 1990 (Gray's Inn) Qualifications: BSc, Dip Law

Papacosta *Miss Ismini Andrea*
Cyprus, Call Date: Nov 1996 (Gray's Inn) Qualifications: LLB (Lond), LLM (E.Anglia)

Paphiti *Anthony Steven*
Commander, Army Prosecuting Authority, (Germany), Rochdale Barracks, British Forces Post Office 39, 00 49 521 9254 3468, Fax: 00 49 521 9254 3472, Chief Legal Officer, Call Date: Nov 1975 (Inner Temple) Qualifications: LLB (Leeds)

Parameswaran *Kiran Anthony*
Malaysia, Call Date: July 1998 (Lincoln's Inn) Qualifications: LLB (Hons)

Parhar *Miss Sunita Sonya*
Fourth Floor, 6 Temasek Boulevard, Suntec Tower Four, Singapore 570257, 2201911, Fax: 2244118, Kelvin Chia Partnership and Member Singapore Bar, Call Date: Nov 1995 (Lincoln's Inn) Qualifications: LLB (Hons)(Lond)

Parker *Miss Danya Larissa*
Bahamas, Call Date: July 1997 (Middle Temple) Qualifications: LLB (Hons)

Parmar *Karam Singh*
Lee & Lee, Level 19, UIC Building, 5 Shenton Way, 00 65 22 00 666, Fax: 00 65 22 19 712, Legal Associate, and Member Singapore Bar, Call Date: Nov 1992 (Middle Temple) Qualifications: B.Eng (Singapore), LLB (Hons, Lond), ACIArb, MSc (Lond)

Parnell King *Mrs Sarah Lorraine*
Bahamas, Call Date: July 1996 (Middle Temple) Qualifications: LLB (Hons)(Soton)

Parslow *Carl Geoffrey*
Ogier & Le Masurier, Advocates & Solicitors, P.O.Box 404, Whiteley Chambers, Don Street, St Helier, Jersey, Channel Islands, 01534 504000, Fax: 01534 35328, Call Date: Oct 1996 (Middle Temple) Qualifications: LLB (Hons)(Plymouth)

Parwani *Miss Sharon Sheela*
Singapore 440031, Call Date: Nov 1995 (Lincoln's Inn) Qualifications: LLB (Hons)(Lond)

Pasha *Miss Dua Sultan*
United Arab Emirates, Call Date: July 1996 (Lincoln's Inn) Qualifications: LLB (Hons)

Patel *Miss Rujuta*
Kenya, Call Date: Oct 1998 (Lincoln's Inn) Qualifications: LLB (Hons)(Bris)

Pathumanathan *Miss Kaushala*
Malaysia, Call Date: Nov 1996 (Lincoln's Inn) Qualifications: LLB (Hons)(Leics)

Patmore *Miss Janet Adelza*
Supreme Court of Judicature of, Jamaica, Public Building E, 134 Tower Street, Kingston, Jamaica, (809) 922 8300, Fax: (809) 967 0669, Deputy Registrar, Supreme Court of Jamaica, and Member Jamaica, Call Date: July 1992 (Middle Temple) Qualifications: LLB (Hons)

Paton *Michael Lennox*
Devonshire House, Queen Street, P.O.Box N4875, Nassau, Bahamas, 242 328 0563, Fax: 242 328 0566, and Member Bahamas Bar, Call Date: July 1991 (Lincoln's Inn) Qualifications: BSc (USA), Dip Law, CPA (USA)

Patrick *Sheriff Gail*
ADVOCATE, 13 Succoth Place, EDINBURGH EH12 6BJ, Scotland, 031 346 1883, Fax: 031 346 0004, Sheriff, Kirkcaldy, Fife, and Member Scottish Bar, Call Date: Nov 1990 (Lincoln's Inn) Qualifications: MA (St A's), LLB (Edin)

Paul *Miss Cynthia*
Malaysia, Call Date: July 1997 (Lincoln's Inn) Qualifications: LLB (Hons)(Reading)

Pearmain *Advocate Susan Ann*
Bedell & Cristin, PO Box 75, One the Forum, Grenville Street, St Helier, Jersey JE4 8PP, 01534 814814, Fax: 01534 814815, Consultant Advocate with Bedell & Cristin Notary Public Former Acting Batonnier, and Member Jersey, Call Date: Nov 1971 (Middle Temple)

Pearman *Miss Jo-Dina Michelle*
Gwendolyn House Chambers, P.O.Box N 3928, Nassau, Bermuda, (242) 356 2038, Fax: (242) 356 2039, Crown Counsel, Attorney General's Chambers, Call Date: July 1994 (Lincoln's Inn) Qualifications: BA, LLB (Hons)

Pearman *Peter Appleby Scott*
Conyers Dill & Pearman, Clarendon House, Church Street, Hamilton, Bermuda, 441 295 1422, Fax: 441 292 4720, Associate, and Member Bermuda Bar, Call Date: July 1995 (Middle Temple) Qualifications: LLB (Hons), BA

Peh *Khaik Kew*
96 Jalan Gasing, 46000 Petaling Jaya, Selangor, Malaysia, 03-7568752, Legal Assistant, Advocate & Solicitor of the High Court of Malaya and Member Malaysia Bar, Call Date: Nov 1996 (Lincoln's Inn) Qualifications: LLB (Hons)(Warw)

Peh *Miss Natalie Suan Wan*
6 Jalan SS 19/4, Subang Jaya, 47500 Selangor, Malaysia, 03 7365308, and Member Malaysia, Call Date: July 1995 (Gray's Inn) Qualifications: LLB (Bris), LLM (Lond)

Peh *Miss Xiao-Shan*
46 Siglap Hill, Singapore 456096, Legal Associate, and Member Singapore, Call Date: July 1996 (Lincoln's Inn) Qualifications: LLB (Hons)(LSE)

Pek *Miss Chin-Choo*
Malaysia, Call Date: July 1996 (Lincoln's Inn) Qualifications: LLB (Hons)(Sheff)

Pelekanos *Michalis*
Pelekanos & Co, Advocate & Legal Consultants, P.O.Box 2124, Larnaca, Cyprus, 4 657272, Fax: 4 653531, and Member Cyprus, Call Date: Nov 1996 (Gray's Inn) Qualifications: LLB (Kent)

Pelekanou Loizou *Mrs Elena*
Evagorou & Arch Makarios 111, Ave, Mitsis Building 3, 1st Floor Office 111, P O Box 1633, Nicosia, 1511, Cyprus, 00-357-2753400, Fax: 00-357-2753939, and Member Cyprus Bar, Call Date: Nov 1995 (Lincoln's Inn) Qualifications: LLB (Hons)(So'ton)

Pengiran Tengah *Miss Dayangku Siti Nurbani*
Brunei, Call Date: Nov 1994 (Lincoln's Inn) Qualifications: LLB (Hons)(Lond)

Peralta *Paul Charles Philip*
Gibraltar, and Member Gibraltar Bar, Call Date: Oct 1994 (Middle Temple) Qualifications: LLB (Hons)(Lond)

Perceval-Price *Mrs Mayo*
Northern Ireland, Vice President Industrial Tribunals, and Member Northern Ireland, Call Date: July 1998 (Middle Temple) Qualifications: LLB (Hons)(Dublin), MA (Dublin)

F

Perera *Miss Menaka Ramani*
83/6 Buthgamuisa Road, Kalapaluwave,
Rajagiriya, Sri Lanka, 0094 1 86626,
Call Date: July 1998 (Lincoln's Inn)
Qualifications: BA (Hons), Dip in Law

Permanand *Miss Radha*
West Indies, Call Date: July 1996
(Lincoln's Inn) Qualifications: LLB
(Hons)(LSE)

Perrot *Roger Allen*
Ozanne's, 1 Le Marchant Street, St
Peter Port, Guernsey CI, Channel
Islands, 0481723466, Fax:
0481727935, and Member Guernsey
Bar, Call Date: Nov 1974 (Inner
Temple) Qualifications: BSc (Lond),
FCIArb

Perumal *Miss Krisna Kumari*
Singapore 499397, Call Date: Nov 1996
(Middle Temple) Qualifications: LLB
(Hons)(Lond)

Perumal *Vasantha Kumar*
Singapore 0512, Call Date: Nov 1993
(Gray's Inn) Qualifications: LLB (Lond)

Petasis *Andreas*
Karides, Karides & Georghiades,
Tribune House, 10 Scopa Street,
CY-1075, Nicosia, P O Box 4736,
CY-1303 Nicosia, Cyprus, +357 2
767515, Fax: +357 2 761542, and
Member Cyprus Bar, Call Date: Nov
1997 (Inner Temple) Qualifications:
LLB (Lancs)

Petri-Kassapi *Mrs Rona Vrahimi*
89 Kennedy Avenue, Off 201, P O Box
6624, Nicosia, Cyprus, Cyprus,
357-2-379210, Fax: 357-2-379212,
Legal Advisor, and Member Cyprus Bar,
Call Date: May 1993 (Gray's Inn)
Qualifications: LLB (E.Anglia), LLM
(Lond)

Petty *George Oliver*
843 Arlington Avenue, Berkeley, CA
94707, United States of America, (510)
528-1721, Fax: (510) 528-9180, and
Member State Bar of California, Call
Date: Apr 1986 (Middle Temple)
Qualifications: BA, LLB (U, California)

Pg Hj Mohammad *Miss Dk Hajah Siti
Rahmah*
Brunei, Call Date: Nov 1995 (Lincoln's
Inn) Qualifications: LLB (Hons)

Phan *Miss Catherine Pui Lin*
Singapore 510414, Call Date: Nov 1997
(Lincoln's Inn) Qualifications: LLB
(Hons)(Lond)

Phelan *Diarmuid Rossa*
Ireland, and Member Ireland, Call
Date: Nov 1998 (Lincoln's Inn)
Qualifications: BCL (Dublin), LLM
(California), PhD (European Uni. ,
Institute), BL , (King's Inn, Dublin)

Phelan *Ms Kristina Claudia*
Walch & Schurti, Zollstrasse 9, 9490
Vaduz, Liechtenstein, Lawyer, Call Date:
Oct 1995 (Middle Temple)
Qualifications: BA (Hons), Dip Law

Philcox *Miss Barbara Anne*
Australia, Queen Elizabeth Bldg,
Ground Floor, Temple, London, EC4Y
9BS, Call Date: July 1988 (Inner
Temple) Qualifications: LLB (Soton)

Phillips *Mrs Henrike Deborah*
Africa, Call Date: Oct 1992 (Lincoln's
Inn) Qualifications: LLB(Hons)

Phua *Chung Ann Robert*
Singapore 268202, Call Date: July 1997
(Lincoln's Inn) Qualifications: LLB
(Hons)(Leeds)

Phua *Miss Karen Jin Sim*
Malaysia, Call Date: July 1996 (Middle
Temple) Qualifications: LLB
(Hons)(Warw)

Phua *Pao Ann*
Malaysia, Call Date: July 1996 (Middle
Temple) Qualifications: BA
(Hons)(Cantab)

Pierce *Raymond John Joseph*
Flat D, 10/F, University Heights, 42-44
Kotewell Road, (0852) 2813 7827, Fax:
(0852) 9106 0054, and Member Hong
Kong Bar, Call Date: Feb 1995 (Gray's
Inn) Qualifications: LLB (Lond)

Pikis *Michael G*
12 Promitheos Str, Pelekanos Court 21,
Office 401, 1065 Nicosia Cyprus,
Cyprus, 02 476838, Fax: 02 476631,
and Member Cyprus Bar, Call Date: Nov
1994 (Gray's Inn) Qualifications: LLB
(Hons)

Pilbrow *David Gordon*
15/F Printing House, 6 Duddell Street,
Hong Kong, Hong Kong, 852 25212616,
Fax: 852 28450260, Former Solicitor
and Member Hong Kong Bar, Call Date:
July 1989 (Middle Temple)
Qualifications: BA [Oxon]

Pilcher *William Edgar*
Bahamas, Call Date: Nov 1996
(Lincoln's Inn) Qualifications: LLB
(Hons)(Bucks)

Pillai *Gopinath*
Singapore 2573, Call Date: July 1995
(Lincoln's Inn) Qualifications: LLB
(Hons)

Pillai *Pradeep G*
Singapore 600118, Call Date: July 1997
(Middle Temple) Qualifications: LLB
(Hons)

Pillai *Prakash*
Singapore 2158, Call Date: July 1995
(Middle Temple) Qualifications: LLB
(Hons)

Pillai *Miss Sharmini*
Messrs Tan Eng Choong & Co, Jalan
Yap Ahloy, Kuala Lumpur, Malaysia,
and Member Malaysian Bar (July
1995), Call Date: July 1994 (Middle
Temple) Qualifications: LLB
(Hons)(Lond)

Ping *Miss Lim Yoke*
37 Jalan 5/66, Bukit Gasing 46000,
Petaling Jaya, Selangor, 03-7958833,
Fax: 03-7928833, Legal Assistant, and
Member Malaysia Bar, Call Date: July
1993 (Inner Temple) Qualifications:
LLB (Nott'm)

Pinsolle *Philippe*
c/o Shearman & Sterling, 114 avenue
des Champs Elysees, 75008 Paris,
France, France, (33) 1 53 89 70 00,
Fax: (33) 1 53 89 70 70, and Member
Paris Bar, Call Date: July 1995 (Gray's
Inn) Qualifications: Maitrise En Droit ,
(Paris) , M.Juris (Oxon),Essec

Pirie *Nicholas Frederick Francis*
Garden Chambers, 5th Floor, 10
Queen's Road Central, 2525-0221, Fax:
2845-2441, Fellow of the Chartered
Institute of Arbitrators, and Member
Hong Kong Bar 2-3 Gray's Inn Square,
Gray's Inn, London, WC1R 5JH, Call
Date: Nov 1971 (Inner Temple)
Qualifications: LLB (Hons)

Pirzada *Syed Sharifuddin*
Press Centre, Sharah-e-Kamal Ataturk4,
Karachi, 2635151-5874439, Fax:
5862552, Ex Secy. General OIC, Ex Law
Minister & Ex Foreign Minister of
Pakistan, Ex Attorney General,
(Honorary) Ambassasdor at large, with
status of Fed.Minister and Member
Pakistan Bar Senior Advocate Supreme
Court of Pakistan, Call Date: Feb 1981
(Lincoln's Inn)

Pishias *Yiannis*
Cyprus, Call Date: Nov 1997 (Lincoln's
Inn) Qualifications: LLB (Hons)(Warw)

Pisias *Leandros*
Cyprus, Call Date: Nov 1998 (Lincoln's
Inn) Qualifications: LLB (Hons)(Warw)

Pitman *Miss Frances Mary*
Mourant Du Feu & Jeune, Advocates,
Solicitors &, Notaries Public, 22
Grenville Street, St Helier, Jersey
JE4 8PX, Channel Islands, 01534
609000, Fax: 01534 609333, Call Date:
Oct 1995 (Lincoln's Inn)
Qualifications: LLB (Hons)(Bucks)

Pitto *Charles John*
Attorney General's Chambers, 17 Town
Range, Gibraltar, Gibraltar, (010350)
70723, and Member Gibraltar Bar, Call
Date: Nov 1994 (Inner Temple)
Qualifications: CPE (Wolverhampton),
BA (Newc)

Platt *The Hon Mr Justice Harold Grant*
Supreme Court of Uganda, P O Box
6679, Kampala, 270 362/3, Justice of
the Sup CT,Uganda, Call Date: Feb 1952
(Middle Temple)

Png *Cheong-Ann*
Institute of Advanced Legal, Studies, University of London, Charles Clore House, 17 Russell Square, London WC1H 2AB, Singapore 090024, Advocate & Solicitor Supreme Court of Singapore, Call Date: July 1996 (Gray's Inn) Qualifications: LLB (London)

Poh *Ban Chuan*
Malaysia, Call Date: July 1993 (Lincoln's Inn) Qualifications: LLB (Hons)

Pohjola *Ms Satu Heidi*
Rovastintie, 1 20 c, 03400 Vihti, Finland, 358 9 2247699, Fax: 358 9 2249041, Call Date: Oct 1995 (Middle Temple) Qualifications: LLB (Hons), MAG.IUR

Pok *Miss Abby Say Lin*
Malaysia, Call Date: Nov 1996 (Middle Temple) Qualifications: LLB (Hons) (Leics)

Pok *John Li-Wen*
Singapore 2159, Call Date: Nov 1993 (Middle Temple) Qualifications: LLB (Hons) (Lond)

Pokkan Vasu *Rakesh*
Singapore 760742, Call Date: July 1996 (Middle Temple) Qualifications: LLB (Hons) (Lond)

Ponnambalam *Gajendrakumar Gangaser*
Sri Lanka, Call Date: Nov 1997 (Lincoln's Inn) Qualifications: LLB (Hons) (Lond)

Ponnusamy *Miss Grace Malathy d/o*
Singapore 640828, Call Date: July 1997 (Lincoln's Inn) Qualifications: LLB (Hons) (Lond)

Pool *Mrs Lucie Antoinette*
Dept of Legal Affairs, P O Box 58, National House, Victoria, Mahe, Seychelles, 00 248 38300, Fax: 225063, State Counsel, Call Date: Nov 1995 (Lincoln's Inn) Qualifications: LLB (Hons)

Poon *Mr Lik Hang Herman*
801 Yip Fung Building, 2-12 D'Aguilar Street, Central, Hong Kong, Hong Kong, and Member Hong Kong Bar, Call Date: Nov 1992 (Inner Temple) Qualifications: LLB (Reading)

Poopalaratnam *Miss Shamini d/o*
Malaysia, Call Date: Nov 1996 (Lincoln's Inn) Qualifications: LLB (Hons) (Lond)

Pooran *Miss Priya Nandita*
119 Eastern Main Road, St Augustine, Trinidad, West Indies, 868 662 9792, Fax: 868 662 9792, Call Date: Nov 1997 (Gray's Inn) Qualifications: LLB, LLM (LSE)

Poots *Laurence James*
Flat A, 25th Floor, Belmont Garden, 15 Arbuthnot Road, Central, Hong Kong, 26666033, Fax: 26677662, and Member Hong Kong Bar Australia Bar, Call Date: Nov 1990 (Gray's Inn) Qualifications: LLB (Lond), MIMgt

Portland *Miss Brender*
West Indies, Call Date: Nov 1997 (Middle Temple) Qualifications: LLB (Hons)

Portwood *Timothy Gordon*
France, Call Date: Nov 1988 (Gray's Inn) Qualifications: BA (Cantab)

Pourgourides *Evangelos*
P.O.Box 4137, Limassol, Cyprus, (00357) 5 346634, Fax: (00357) 5 346633, Practising Barrister in Cyprus and Member Cyprus, Call Date: July 1997 (Lincoln's Inn) Qualifications: LLB (Hons) (Leics)

Povall *Ms Kathryn Elizabeth*
Allen & overy, One New Change, London EC4M 9QQ, Hong Kong, 9714 282296, Fax: 9714 212860, Legal Consultant, Dubai, Call Date: Oct 1991 (Lincoln's Inn) Qualifications: LLB (Hons) (New)

Powell *Guy Storer*
Bedell & Cristin, Normandy House, Grenville Street, St Helier, Jersey, Channel Islands, 01534 872949, Call Date: Nov 1982 (Middle Temple) Qualifications: LLB

Prabhakaran *Miss Prasanna T.V.*
Singapore 140111, Call Date: July 1996 (Middle Temple) Qualifications: LLB (Hons) (Lond)

Pratt *Miss Chinique Elmega*
Bahamas, Call Date: Nov 1997 (Gray's Inn) Qualifications: BA (Windsor, Canada), LLB (Kent)

Pratt *Miss Olivia Deloris*
Bahamas, and Member Bahamas, Call Date: Nov 1996 (Gray's Inn) Qualifications: LLB (Buckingham)

Premaraj *Belden*
Sivananthan, Suite 253-4, 4th Floor, 253 Jalan Tun Sambanthan, 50470 Kuala Lumpur, Malaysia, 2738273, Fax: 2739273, and Member Malaysia Bar, Call Date: Nov 1993 (Lincoln's Inn) Qualifications: LLB (Hons, L'pool)

Prentice *Edward Arthur Gerald*
Ozannes Advocates, 1 le Marchant Street, St Peter Port, Guernsey, 01481 723466, Fax: 01481 714571, Advocate of Royal Court of Guernsey, Notary Public Notary Public, Call Date: Nov 1983 (Inner Temple) Qualifications: LLB (Lond)

Priddis *Simon James*
Cleary, Gottlieb, Steen &, Hamilton, Rue de la Loi, 1040 Bruxelles, 00 32 2 287 21 74, Fax: 00 32 2 231 16 61, Legal Officer, and Member Brussels, Call Date: Oct 1995 (Lincoln's Inn) Qualifications: MA (Hons), LLM

Pringle *Robert Henry Becker*
Barristers' Chambers, Allendale Square, 77 St George's Terrace, Perth WA 6000, (08) 9220 0444, Fax: (08) 9325 9008/9111, QC Western Australia, Call Date: Nov 1978 (Gray's Inn) Qualifications: BA, LLB

Psaila *Ms Tara Antonia Maria*
Southern Ireland, Call Date: Mar 1998 (Gray's Inn) Qualifications: LLB., BCL (Cork), LLM (Lond)

Pung *Miss So Ken*
NO 68 Jalan Seri Cheras 6A, Taman Seri Cheras, BT 9 1/2 Cheras, 43200 BT 9 Cheras, Selangor Malaysia, Malaysia, Call Date: July 1995 (Inner Temple) Qualifications: LLB

Pushparasah *Miss Thevarani*
Malaysia, Advocate & Solicitor of the High Court of Malaya and Member Malaysian Bar, Call Date: July 1996 (Lincoln's Inn) Qualifications: LLB (Hons)

Pyfrom *Basil Lorraine*
Bahamas, Call Date: July 1997 (Inner Temple) Qualifications: LLB (Dunelm)

Pyrgou *Mrs Melina*
Kinanis - Pyrgou & Co, Annis Komninis 29A, P.O.Box 2303, Nicosia, Cyprus, Cyprus, 00357 2 762888, Fax: 00357 2 759777, Partner, and Member Cyprus Bar Association, Call Date: Nov 1995 (Gray's Inn) Qualifications: B.Soc.Sci (Keele)

Qayyum *Abdul*
Village Bhuttian Mohra, Tehsil-Gujar-Khan, Dist, Rawalpindi, Call Date: May 1982 (Gray's Inn) Qualifications: BA, LLb

Qazi *Faysal Ali*
Pakistan, Call Date: Mar 1997 (Lincoln's Inn) Qualifications: LLB (Hons)

Quek *Miss Bee Choo*
1 Park Road, [H] 04-04 People's Park Complex, Singapore 1852, 5336077, Fax: 5342339, and Member Singapore Bar, Call Date: Nov 1995 (Lincoln's Inn) Qualifications: LLB (Hons)

Quek *Miss Gwang Hwa*
Singapore 550329, Call Date: July 1996 (Lincoln's Inn) Qualifications: LLB (Hons)

Quek *Miss Karen Chia-Huei*
36 Robinson Road, [H] 18-01, City
House, Singapore 597629, 065 420
7653, Fax: 065 224 8210, Legal
Assistant, Company Secretary, and
Member Singapore Bar, Call Date: July
1995 (Lincoln's Inn) Qualifications:
LLB (Hons)

Quek *Miss Karen Tzun Tjin*
597270 Singapore, Call Date: July 1997
(Gray's Inn) Qualifications: LLB

Quek *Miss Sue Yian*
Malaysia, Call Date: Oct 1997 (Middle
Temple) Qualifications: LLB
(Hons)(Brunel)

Quinn *Anthony Michael*
Channel Islands, Call Date: Mar 1999
(Lincoln's Inn) Qualifications: BA
(Hons)(Staffs)

Quinn *Anthony Paschal*
Law Library, Four Courts, Dublin 7,
Ireland, Republic of Ireland, 0001
8720622/2854811, Fax: 0001
8721455/720031, Barrister, Kings Inn
Dublin Also Inn of Court M and
Member Northern Ireland Bar, Call
Date: July 1990 (Lincoln's Inn)
Qualifications: MA, DipPbl, ADM (Dub,
Dip Lgl Studies, (Kings Inns), FCIArb,
Dip Intnl Arb, Dip Arb Law, B.COMM,
FCIS

Qureshi *Ms Zainab Bilal*
Pakistan, Call Date: July 1997 (Inner
Temple) Qualifications: BA (Sussex)

Radin *Alang Iskandar*
32 Jalan Tun Mhd, Fuad 2, Taman Tun,
Dr Ismail, 60000, Kuala Lumpur,
Malaysia 46200, 03 7179193/4577602,
Fax: 03 7175193, and Member
Malaysia, Call Date: Oct 1995 (Middle
Temple) Qualifications: BA (Hons)

Rahim *Miss Anisah Binte Abdul*
55 Market Street, Sinsov Building,
[H]08-01, Singapore 1646,
65-5383177, Advocate & Solicitor, and
Member Singapore Bar, Call Date: July
1995 (Middle Temple) Qualifications:
LLB (Hons)

Rahman *Andaleeve*
Bangladesh, Call Date: Mar 1998
(Lincoln's Inn) Qualifications: LLB
(Hons)(Wolv'ton)

Rahming *Andre Joseph*
Bahamas, Call Date: July 1995 (Gray's
Inn) Qualifications: LLB (Lond)

Raina *Miss Simran*
Malaysia, Call Date: Nov 1998
(Lincoln's Inn) Qualifications: LLB
(Hons)(Bris)

Raja *Nomaam Akram*
Pakistan 54600, Call Date: July 1997
(Gray's Inn) Qualifications: LLB

Raja Abdul Rashid *Miss Raja Rozmin*
Malaysia, Call Date: Nov 1996 (Middle
Temple) Qualifications:
LLB(Hons)(Glamorgan)

Raja Alang Petra *Miss Raja Nor Azwa*
Land & General Berhad, 1st Floor,
Rumah Rohas, 61 Jalan Raja Abdullah,
50300 Kuala Lumpur, Malaysia, 603
2941344 (T), Fax: 603 2927711 (F),
Corporate Counsel, and Member
Malaysia, Call Date: July 1995 (Gray's
Inn) Qualifications: LLB (Kent)

Rajah *Tharuma*
Malaysia, Call Date: July 1993
(Lincoln's Inn) Qualifications: LLB
(Hons)

Rajan *Sanjiv Kumar*
M/S Allen & Gledhill, 36 Robinson
Road, [H]18-00, City House, Singapore
449291, 2251611, Fax: 2258557, and
Member Singapore, Call Date: July
1997 (Middle Temple) Qualifications:
LLB (Hons)(Leics)

Rajaratnam *Miss Indira*
Malaysia, and Member Advocate &
Solicitor of the High Court of Malaya,
Call Date: Nov 1995 (Lincoln's Inn)
Qualifications: BA (Hons)(Kent)

Rajendra *Miss Rayvathi*
Malaysia, Call Date: Mar 1999
(Lincoln's Inn) Qualifications: LLB
(Hons)(Nott'm)

Rajendran *Miss Kalyani*
Australia, Call Date: July 1997 (Middle
Temple) Qualifications: LLB
(Hons)(Leics)

Rajendran *Kumaresan*
Singapore 320085, Call Date: July 1996
(Middle Temple) Qualifications: LLB
(Hons)(Lond)

Rajendran *M S*
Singapore 180013, Call Date: Nov 1997
(Lincoln's Inn) Qualifications: LLB
(Hons)(Lond)

Rajvinder Singh
53 Jalan Air Duson, Setapak, 53200
Kuala Lumpur, Legal Assistant, and
Member Malaysia Bar, Call Date: July
1994 (Lincoln's Inn) Qualifications:
LLB (Hons, Lond)

Rajwani *Ms Vandana*
Flat 2-B Kam Fai Mansions, 68a
Macdonnell Road, Hong Kong, (852)
28575089, Fax: (852) 28681652, and
Member Hong Kong Bar, Call Date: July
1996 (Lincoln's Inn) Qualifications: BA

Ram Chandra *Ramesh*
Singapore 530145, Call Date: Nov 1998
(Lincoln's Inn) Qualifications: LLB
(Hons)(Wolves)

Ramachandran *A J*
Apt Block 49, Telok Blangah Dr,
[H]04-03, Singapore 100049, Republic
of Singapore, Singapore 100049, 535
3600, Fax: 536 1335, and Member
Singapore Bar, Call Date: July 1994
(Lincoln's Inn) Qualifications: LLB
(Hons), B.Sc (Singapore)

Ramachandran *Miss Deepa*
Malaysia, Call Date: Nov 1997
(Lincoln's Inn) Qualifications: LLB
(Hons)(Nott'm)

Ramachandran *Sathish*
No 6 Tepian Tunku, Bukit Tunku,
50480 Kuala Lumpur, Malaysia, 603
6512989, Fax: 603 6510850, and
Member Malaysia, Call Date: July 1993
(Middle Temple) Qualifications: LLB
(Hons)(Kent)

Ramalingam *Paramasivam*
Singapore 560521, Call Date: July 1996
(Lincoln's Inn) Qualifications: LLB
(Hons)(Lond)

Ramanathan *Miss Sharmila*
Malaysia, Call Date: Nov 1998
(Lincoln's Inn) Qualifications: LLB
(Hons)(Wolves)

Ramason *Raji*
Ms Tan Rajah & Cheah, Straits Trading
Building, 9 Battery Road, [H]15-00,
Singapore 297880, 5391652, Fax:
5352475, and Member Singapore, Call
Date: July 1996 (Middle Temple)
Qualifications: LLB (Hons)(Wolves)

Ramiah *Sivaraja*
Malaysia, Call Date: July 1996
(Lincoln's Inn) Qualifications: LLB
(Hons)(Lond)

Ramlogan *Anand*
113 Ben-Lomond Village, Williamsville
P.O., Trinidad, West Indies,
809-650-0536, Fax: 809 658 0350, and
Member Trinidad & Tobago, Call Date:
July 1995 (Middle Temple)
Qualifications: LLB (West Indies), LLM
(Lond), Dip (Law), LEC

Rampersad *Miss Nalini Cindy*
West Indies, Call Date: Nov 1998
(Lincoln's Inn) Qualifications: LLB
(Hons)(Wolves)

Ramphul *Shaheel Kumar Joy*
9 Buswell Avenue, Quatre Bornes,
Mauritius, (230) 4540559, and
Member Mauritian Bar, Call Date: July
1998 (Middle Temple) Qualifications:
LLB (Hons)(Wales)

Ramsewak *Miss Premila*
Mauritius, Call Date: July 1996
(Lincoln's Inn) Qualifications: LLB
(Hons)

Ranai *Ashok Kimar Mahadev*
Skrine & Co, No 4, Leboh Pasar Besar,
Straits Trading Building, 50050 Kuala
Lumpur, Malaysia, 603 2945111, Fax:
603 2934327, Advocate & Solicitor,
High Court of Malaya and Member
Malaysian Bar, Call Date: Nov 1995
(Gray's Inn) Qualifications: LLB
(Wales)

Randhawa *Miss Anit Kaur*
Malaysia, Call Date: Nov 1998
(Lincoln's Inn) Qualifications: LLB
(Hons)(Bris)

Randhawa *Ravinderpal Singh*
Bernard, Rada, Barker and, Pauline
Chen, Advocates & Solicitors, 1
Colombo Court, [H]07-30, Singapore
2573, 336 1717, Fax: 339 9782/339
4991, and Member Singapore, Call
Date: July 1995 (Middle Temple)
Qualifications: LLB (Hons) (Wales)

Rasa-Ratnam *Lambert Thuraisingham*
16th Floor, Wisma HLA, Jalan Raja
Chulan, 50200 Kuala Lumpur,
Malaysia, 603 2011681, Fax: 603
2011746/2011714, and Member
Malaysia, Call Date: Nov 1983
(Lincoln's Inn) Qualifications: BA
(Hons)

Rasanayagam *Miss Marlene Sunita*
Singapore 298044, Call Date: July 1996
(Middle Temple) Qualifications: LLB
(Hons) (Bucks)

Rashid *Khurram*
Pakistan, Call Date: Nov 1997
(Lincoln's Inn) Qualifications: LLB
(Hons)

Rasiah *Sanjeev Kumar*
Serine & Co, (Advocates & Solicitors),
No % Leboh Pasar Besar, 50050 Kuala
Lumpur, Malaysia, Malaysia, and
Member Malaysia Bar, Call Date: July
1994 (Middle Temple) Qualifications:
LLB (Hons) (Hull)

Ratliff *John Harrison*
Stanbrook & Henderson, Rue du
Taciturne 42, B 1040 Brussels,
Belgium, (02) 230 5059, Fax: (02) 230
5713, Call Date: July 1980 (Middle
Temple) Qualifications: BA (Oxon),
Diploma in European, Intergration
(NDR), (Amsterdam)

Ratnasingham *Rajasingham*
Malaysia, Call Date: July 1996
(Lincoln's Inn) Qualifications: LLB
(Hons)

Rauf *Miss Neetasha*
Malaysia, Call Date: July 1995
(Lincoln's Inn) Qualifications: LLB
(Hons), LLM

Ravi *Arumugam*
Block 551, Pasir Ris Street 51,
[H]08-97, and Member Singapore Bar,
Call Date: July 1995 (Lincoln's Inn)
Qualifications: LLB (Hons)

Ravidass *Ambalavanar*
Singapore 640407, Call Date: July 1998
(Middle Temple) Qualifications: LLB
(Hons) (Lond)

Rawlinson *Iain David*
P.O.Box 25011, Awali, Bahrain, 973
756565, Fax: 973 756057, Call Date:
Oct 1994 (Lincoln's Inn)
Qualifications: BA (Hons) (Durham)

Ray *Gaur Gopal*
SANG Health Affairs, King Fahad
National Guard, Hospital, P.O. Box
22490, Riyadh 11426, (KSA) 1 252
0088 Ext.3738, Fax: (KSA) 1 252 0088
Ext.3744, Legal Consultant Legal
Advisor/Evaluator, Advocate, Supreme
Court of India and Member West
Bengal Bar, Call Date: July 1973
(Lincoln's Inn) Qualifications: BCom,
FCIArb

Ray *Miss Lapita*
India, Call Date: July 1997 (Lincoln's
Inn) Qualifications: LLB
(Hons) (Leeds)

Raza *Khurram*
Pakistan, Call Date: Nov 1995
(Lincoln's Inn) Qualifications: LLB
(Hons)

Razzaque *Miss Jona*
Bangladesh, Call Date: Nov 1997
(Lincoln's Inn) Qualifications: LLM
(Lond)

Rea *Luigi Orlando Anthony*
Garden Flat, 14 Grantham Street,
Dublin 8, 0001 4781105, Fax: 0001
4781105, and Member Southern
Ireland Bar, Call Date: July 1982
(Middle Temple) Qualifications: BA
(Dublin)

Rea *Robert Kevin*
The Bar Library, Royal Courts of
Justice, Chichester Street, Belfast,
Northern Ireland, (01232) 562438, and
Member Northern Ireland, Call Date:
Mar 1996 (Gray's Inn) Qualifications:
LLB, LLM (Int'l &, European)

Regal *Richard Neill*
International Federation of,
Accountants, 535 Fifth Avenue, 26th
Floor, New York 10017, 001 212 286
9344, Fax: 001 212 286 9570,
Technical Manager, Call Date: July
1997 (Inner Temple) Qualifications:
BA (L'pool), MBA (Kingston), FCA, ATII

Renganathan *Nandakumar*
1 Colombo Court, [H]09-05, Singapore
2776, 3362626, Fax: 3388001, Legal
Associate, and Member Singapore, Call
Date: Nov 1993 (Lincoln's Inn)
Qualifications: LLB (Hons, Sheff)

Rengasamy *Rama Krishnan*
Malaysia, Call Date: July 1997
(Lincoln's Inn) Qualifications: LLB
(Hons)

Renouf *Mark Philip*
22 Grenville Street, St Helier, Jersey
JE4 8PX, Channel Islands, (01534)
609000, Call Date: Oct 1994 (Middle
Temple) Qualifications: LLB
(Hons) (Lond)

Rentrop *Timm Ulrich Wilhelm*
Square Marguerite 1/49, B-1000
Bruxelles, 322 733 1236, Call Date: Nov
1991 (Inner Temple) Qualifications:
MA (Oxon), Licence Speciale en, Droit
Europeen

Rethinasamy *Rameson*
Malaysia, Call Date: Nov 1998
(Lincoln's Inn) Qualifications: LLB
(Hons) (Warw)

Reyes *Dr Anselnio Francisco Trinidad*
Hong Kong, and Member Hong Kong
Bar, Call Date: Nov 1985 (Inner
Temple) Qualifications: MA, LLM,
PhD(Cantab), BA (Harv)

Reyes *John Bernard*
Government of Gibraltar, Legislation
Support Unit, 13 Town Range,
Gibraltar, 00350 45925, Fax: 00350
41822, and Member Gibraltar, Call
Date: Nov 1996 (Middle Temple)
Qualifications: BA (Hons)

Reza *Abu Mohammad Manzur Ahsan*
India, Call Date: Nov 1995 (Lincoln's
Inn) Qualifications: LLB
(Hons) (Dhaka), LLM (Dhaka), LLM
(Lond)

Riaz *Zahir*
Pakistan, Call Date: Mar 1997 (Gray's
Inn) Qualifications: LLB (LSE), LLB
(Cantab)

Rich *Christopher Paul Donald*
Barings (Guernsey) Ltd, Arnold House,
St Julians Avenue, St Peter Port,
Guernsey, Advocate, Supreme Court of
the Northern Territory, Australia and
Member Royal Court of Guernsey, Call
Date: Nov 1988 (Gray's Inn)
Qualifications: LLB (Soton)

Richings *Francis Gordon*
908 Salmon Grove Chambers, 407
Smith Street, Durban 4001, South
Africa, (031)3018694, Fax:
(031)3056420, Advocate of South
Africa and Member Lesotho Bar, Call
Date: May 1992 (Middle Temple)
Qualifications: BA,LLB (Cape Town), M
Phil (Cantab)

Richmond *Martyn*
Hong Kong, Call Date: Nov 1997 (Gray's
Inn) Qualifications: BA (Newcastle),
LLB (Lond)

Riegels *Colin David*
Harney Westwood & Riegels, Craigmuir
Chambers, P.O.Box 71, Road Town,
Tortola, (284) 494 2233, Fax: (284)
494 3547, Call Date: Oct 1996
(Lincoln's Inn) Qualifications: LLB
(Hons) (Bris), BCL (Oxon)

Rigby *Gareth Andrew*
Mourant Du Feu & Jeune, P.O.Box 87,
22 Grenville Street, St Helier, Jersey
JE4 8PX, Channel Islands, 01534
609000, Legal Assistant, Call Date: Oct
1998 (Middle Temple) Qualifications:
BSc (Hons) (Plymouth), CPE

Rigby *Jonathan David*
Mourant de Feu & Jeune, Jersey,
Channel Islands, Legal Associate, Call
Date: Oct 1995 (Middle Temple)
Qualifications: BA (Hons)

Rigby *Raynard Sherman*
McKinney, Bancroft & Hughes, Mareva House, 4 George Street, P.O.Box N 3937, Nassau, Bahamas, Call Date: July 1995 (Gray's Inn) Qualifications: BA (Ontario), LLB (Leeds)

Robert *Leslie Gregory*
47 Jalan Sajak, Singapore 2776, 257 7255, and Member Singapore Bar, Call Date: July 1995 (Lincoln's Inn) Qualifications: LLB (Hons)

Roberts *Simon David*
Shanks & Herbert, 1033 N.Fairfax Street, Suite 306, Alexandria VA 22314, 703-683-3600, Fax: 703-683-9875, and Member New York State Bar US Patent Bar, Call Date: Nov 1991 (Gray's Inn) Qualifications: BSc, BA (Exon)

Robertson *Miss Samantha Veronica*
West Indies, Call Date: July 1998 (Inner Temple) Qualifications: BA (West Indies), LLB (Wolves)

Robinson *Miss Genell Kendra*
Bahamas, Call Date: July 1998 (Lincoln's Inn) Qualifications: LLB (Hons)(Leeds)

Robinson *Wendel Glenroy*
West Indies, (1) 268 4622380/12684 628901, Fax: 268 4622385/1268 46299492, Inspector of Police Legal Advisor to the Commissioner of Police, Call Date: Nov 1997 (Inner Temple) Qualifications: LLB (Lond)

Rocca *Terence Joseph*
Attorney-General's Chambers, 17 Town Range, Gibraltar, Gibraltar, 010 350 78882, Fax: 010 350 79891, and Member Gibraltar Bar, Call Date: Oct 1993 (Middle Temple) Qualifications: LLB (Hons)(Kingston)

Rochat-Spechter *Mrs Alison Jean*
Secretan, Troyanov and Partners, 2 Rue Charles - Bonnet, P.O.Box 189, 1211 Geneva 12, Switzerland, Switzerland, (41) 22 789 7000, Fax: (41) 22 789 7070, Associate (Foreign Lawyer), Call Date: Oct 1993 (Gray's Inn) Qualifications: LLB (Buck'm)

Rochester *Miss Oonagh Bahia*
Bermuda, Call Date: July 1998 (Middle Temple) Qualifications: LLB (Hons)(Staffs)

Rodgers *Dywan Arnold-George Roy*
Bahamas, Call Date: July 1998 (Lincoln's Inn) Qualifications: LLB (Hons)(Essex)

Rodrigo *Jayanath Avindra Gian*
Sri Lanka, (94) 1-328493/(94) 722 54344, Fax: (94) 1 330387, and Member Sri Lanka, Call Date: Feb 1994 (Gray's Inn) Qualifications: LLB (Warwick)

Rodriguez *Stuart James*
Gibraltar, Call Date: Mar 1997 (Middle Temple) Qualifications: LLB (Hons), MA (Leeds)

Rogers *Anthony Gerrard Vernede*
11th Floor, Southern Cross Building, cnr Victoria St East & High St, Auckland 1, New Zealand, 093733 196, Fax: 09 3774850, PO Box 1771, Auckland, New Zealand and Member New Zealand Bar New South Wales Bar 6 King's Bench Walk, Ground Floor, Temple, London, EC4Y 7DR, Call Date: Feb 1986 (Inner Temple) Qualifications: LLM (Hons), (U Auckland)

Rogers *Anthony Gordon*
Supreme Court, Queensway, 852 2825 4306, Fax: 852 2552 3327, Judge of Court of Appeal, Hong Kong, Former Chairman Hong Kong Bar Association, QC Hong Kong Bar Association, Call Date: Nov 1969 (Gray's Inn)

Rogers *Michael Richard*
Law Chambers, World Trade Centre, P.O.Box 896, 1215 Geneva 15, +44 22 788 0551, Fax: +44 22 788 1502, Call Date: Feb 1972 (Inner Temple) Qualifications: F.C.I.S., A.C.I.I

Rooney *John*
Republic of Ireland, Call Date: Nov 1998 (Inner Temple) Qualifications: LLB (Wolves), LLM (Lond)

Rose *Dr Christopher Philip*
Cayman Islands, Call Date: Oct 1995 (Gray's Inn) Qualifications: B.Sc, MD (Canada), MA (Oxon), FRCP (c), CFA, ACIArb

Ross *Keith James*
10 Roper Place, Chifley ACT 2606, 0262 816748, Tutor, University of Canberra Law School, and Member Barrister & Solicitor Papau New Guinea, Australian Capital Territory, Federal Court, Solicitor, New South Wales New South Wales Bar Solicitor, New South Wales, Call Date: July 1967 (Lincoln's Inn) Qualifications: LLB

Rover *Jan-Hendrik Manfred*
Franz-Joseph - Str 44, 80801 Munich, Germany, Visiting Fellow, King's College London, Centre of European Law, and Member Munich Bar, Call Date: Mar 1996 (Middle Temple) Qualifications: LLM (LSE)

Rozain *Miss Roz Mawar*
54 Setiabakit 9, Bukit Damansara, 50490 Kuala Lumpur, Malaysia, 00603 2551179, and Member Malaysian Bar, Call Date: July 1995 (Lincoln's Inn) Qualifications: LLB (Hons)

Rozain *Miss Roz Yanti*
Malaysia, Call Date: Oct 1998 (Lincoln's Inn) Qualifications: LLB (Bris)

Ruane *Miss Mairead Mary*
Southern Ireland, Call Date: Nov 1991 (Gray's Inn) Qualifications: BCL (Dub)

Rubin *Mohideen M P Haja*
Singapore 0617, Member of Appeal Board Singapore Syariah Court, Call Date: July 1987 (Middle Temple) Qualifications: LLB

Rubin Mohideen *Miss Rasina*
Singapore 248792, Call Date: Mar 1999 (Middle Temple) Qualifications: LLB (Hons)(Bris)

Rugarabamu *Ms Donata Mary*
Ground Floor Flat, 36 Sinclair Road, London W14 0NH, Switzerland, 0171 603 5025, Fax: 0171 603 5025, Associate Legal Officer, Call Date: July 1992 (Lincoln's Inn) Qualifications: MA (Hons)

Rupasinghe *Miss Anouchka Charmini*
Sri Lanka, and Member Sri Lanka, Call Date: Nov 1996 (Lincoln's Inn) Qualifications: LLB (Hons)(E.Anglia)

Ryan *William Fabian*
Southern Ireland, Associate of the Royal Institution of Chartered Surveyors, Call Date: Mar 1998 (Inner Temple) Qualifications: BSc (Dublin), Dip Law (Thames)

Ryde *Richard Alexander*
16 rue de Naples, 75007 Paris, 00 331 4294 8264, Fax: 00 331 4294 1404, and Member Paris Bar, Call Date: July 1986 (Middle Temple) Qualifications: BA (Hons) (Oxon)

Rynd *Dr Aaron James*
Spier Harben, Barristers & Solicitors, Suite 1000, Dominion House, 665-8 Street S.W., Calgary, Alberta T2P 3K7, 403 263 5130, Fax: 403 264 9600, and Member Alberta, Canada, Call Date: July 1976 (Lincoln's Inn) Qualifications: BA, PHd

Ryou *Miss Ji Youn*
Republic of Korea, Call Date: Nov 1998 (Middle Temple) Qualifications: LLB (Hons)(Anglia)

Saadi *Mir Abdul Wares*
Bangladesh, Call Date: Nov 1996 (Lincoln's Inn) Qualifications: LLB (Hons)(Lond)

Sadanandan *Miss Kalpana*
Singapore 520925, Call Date: July 1998 (Middle Temple) Qualifications: LLB (Hons)(Wolves)

Sadat *Omar*
Bangladesh, Call Date: Nov 1997 (Lincoln's Inn) Qualifications: LLB (Hons)(Lond), LLM (Cantab)

Sadhwani *Kamlesh Arjan*
Room 1405, Tower II, Admiralty Centre, 18 Harcourt Road, Hong Kong, 25273082, Fax: 25298226, and Member Hong Kong Bar, Call Date: July 1995 (Lincoln's Inn) Qualifications: BA (Hons)

Sadjadi-Nourani *Mrs Leila*
Law Offices of Foley & Lardner, 2029
Century Park East, 35th Floor, Los
Angeles, CA 90067, 310-975 7853, Fax:
310-557 8475, and Member California
Bar, Call Date: Nov 1990 (Gray's Inn)
Qualifications: LLB (Hons)

Said *Miss Farah Shireen Mohamed*
Malaysia, Call Date: July 1997 (Gray's
Inn) Qualifications: LLB (Lond)

Said *Yousaf Zalme*
Pakistan, Call Date: Nov 1998
(Lincoln's Inn) Qualifications: LLB
(Hons) (Lond)

Sakhrani *Miss Anisha*
Hong Kong, Call Date: July 1996
(Lincoln's Inn) Qualifications: LLB
(Hons)

Sakhrani *Sanjay Arjan*
Temple Chambers, 16/F One Pacific
Place, 88 Quennsway, Hong Kong,
Hong Kong, 2523 2003, Fax: 2810
0302, and Member Hong Kong Bar, Call
Date: July 1995 (Lincoln's Inn)
Qualifications: BA, LLB (Hons) (Lond)

Salehkon *Ramli Bin*
Kertar & Co, Advocates & Solicitors, 133
New Bridge Road, [H] 17-04,
Chinatown Point, Singapore 520424,
(65) 5366266, Fax: (65) 5366533, Call
Date: Nov 1995 (Middle Temple)
Qualifications: LLB (Hons)(Lond), BA
(Singapore)

Sallehuddin *Mohamed Nasri*
Malaysia, Call Date: July 1995 (Gray's
Inn) Qualifications: LLB (Wales)

Sam *Miss Lisa Hui Min*
Messrs Donaldson & Burkinshaw, 24
Raffles Place [H] 15-00, Clifford Centre,
Singapore 519691, 5339422, Fax:
5337806/5330809, Legal Assistant, and
Member Singapore Bar, Call Date: July
1996 (Inner Temple) Qualifications:
LLB (Kent)

Saminathan *Miss Vignaswari*
Malaysia, Call Date: Nov 1995 (Middle
Temple) Qualifications: LLB
(Hons) (Sheff)

Samnakay *Mrs Minaxi Saeed*
East Africa, and Member Kenyan Bar,
Call Date: Nov 1989 (Inner Temple)
Qualifications: BA (Nairobi), LLB

Samuel *Miss Shanti Loraine*
Singapore 579978, Call Date: Nov 1996
(Inner Temple) Qualifications: LLB
(Hull)

Samuel *Mrs Vimala*
Singapore 1026, Call Date: Nov 1990
(Lincoln's Inn) Qualifications: LLB
(Lond)

Sanchez *Mrs Karin Louise*
Management & Service Co Ltd, P.O.Box
F 42544, Freeport, Bahamas, 242 352
7063, Fax: 242 352 3932, and Member
Bahamas, Call Date: July 1996
(Lincoln's Inn) Qualifications: LLB
(Hons)

Sandhu *Sarbrinder Singh*
Singapore 1545, Call Date: July 1994
(Middle Temple) Qualifications: LLB
(Hons) (Wales)

Sandhu *Miss Viviene Kaur*
M/S Kumar & Loh, Advocates &
Solicitors, 51 Anson Road [H] 10-53,
Anson Centre, Singapore 130012, 225
6362, Fax: 225 9690, and Member
Singapore, Call Date: Nov 1996 (Middle
Temple) Qualifications: LLB
(Hons) (L'pool)

Sands *Miss Christel Claudette*
Bahamas, Call Date: Oct 1998 (Middle
Temple) Qualifications: LLB
(Hons) (Reading)

Sangha *Ranbir Singh*
Malaysia 98000, Call Date: July 1995
(Lincoln's Inn) Qualifications: BA
(Hons)

Sankaran *Chandrakandan*
Malaysia, Call Date: July 1995
(Lincoln's Inn) Qualifications: LLB
(Hons)

Sarfraz *Miss Ayesha*
Pakistan, Call Date: Nov 1995 (Gray's
Inn) Qualifications: BA (Punjab), LLB
(Dunelm)

Sarkar *Shib Sankar*
21/2 Gora Chand Road,
Calcutta-700014, India,
009133-244-8778, Senior Advocate of
the Supreme Court of India, Call Date:
May 1997 (Lincoln's Inn)
Qualifications: MA, LLB (Calcutta), FCI
Arb (Lond)

Sarvananthan *Ganendran*
Malaysia, Call Date: July 1998
(Lincoln's Inn) Qualifications: LLB
(Hons) (Lond)

Sathiasingam *Miss Lynette Shakunthala*
Singapore 2880, (65) 481 3113, Call
Date: July 1995 (Middle Temple)
Qualifications: LLB (Hons)

Saveriades *Marios Kyriacou*
Iris House, John Kennedy Str, Office
740B, Limassol, Cyprus, Cyprus, (05)
366767, Fax: 4745 JUSTLAW, and
Member Cyprus Bar, Call Date: Feb
1995 (Lincoln's Inn) Qualifications:
LLB (Hons) (Leic)

Savvides *George Loukis*
1st, 2nd & 4th Floor, Omega Court, 4
Rigas Fereos Street, P.O.Box 4098,
3720 Limmassol, Cyprus, 357 5
376886, Fax: 357 5 374930, Managing
Partner, Call Date: July 1983 (Middle
Temple) Qualifications: LLB
(Hons) (Exon), ACIArb

Saw *Miss Hooi Lee*
Malaysia, Call Date: July 1997
(Lincoln's Inn) Qualifications: LLB
(Hons) (Wales)

Saw *Leon Eng Tiong*
Malaysia, Call Date: July 1995
(Lincoln's Inn) Qualifications: LLB
(Hons)

Saw *Seang Kuan*
5 Shenton Way, [H]19-00 UIC Building,
Singapore 068808, Singapore 1129,
2200666, Fax: 2219712, and Member
Singapore Bar, Call Date: July 1996
(Middle Temple) Qualifications: BA
(Hons) (Cantab)

Say *Miss Caryne Sue Lynn*
Malaysia, Call Date: Mar 1999 (Middle
Temple) Qualifications: LLB
(Hons) (Nott'm)

Sayers *Ms Veronica Margaret*
Law Officers' Department, Morier
House, St Helier, Jersey JE1 1DD,
Channel Islands, 01534 502200, Fax:
01534 502299, Legal Assistant, Call
Date: Nov 1997 (Inner Temple)
Qualifications: BSc (Open Uni), LLB
(So'ton)

Schinis *Miss Theodoti A*
P.L.Cacoyannis & Co, B, Rigas Feros
Street, Libra Chambers, Limassol, P.O.
Box 122, Cyprus, (357) 5 363154,
Assiciate Advocate, Call Date: Nov 1997
(Lincoln's Inn) Qualifications: LLB
(Hons) (Leics)

Schoneveld *Frank Robert*
Chief General Legal Division, UNRWA,
HQ (Gaza), P O Box 338, IL-78100
Ashqelon, + 972 7 677 7716, Fax: +
972 7 677 7696, Counsel
(International), and Member Australia
Bar 2 Harcourt Bldgs, Ground Floor/
Left, Temple, London, EC4Y 9DB, Call
Date: May 1992 (Inner Temple)
Qualifications: B.Jurisprudence, LLB
(Australia), Dip Eur Law (Neth)

Schwartzman *Ivor Walter*
300 Innes Chambers, Johannesburg,
South Africa, South Africa, Supreme
Court Judge, and Member South Africa
Bar Swaziland Bar, Call Date: May 1988
(Lincoln's Inn) Qualifications: BA, LLB
(Rand)

Schwarz *Dr Heinz*
P O Box 3089, Parklands 2121, (2711)
286 1115, Fax: (2711) 784 9976,
Former Ambassador of South Africa to
the United States of America, Dr of
Humane Letters (Honoris Causa), Call
Date: Nov 1961 (Inner Temple)
Qualifications: BA, LLB, D.Phil, (Hon
Causa),

Scordis *Kyriacos*
P O Box 533, 30 Karpenisi Street, The
Business Forum, Nicosia, Cyprus,
(357) 2 843000, Fax: (357) 2 375227,
and Member Cyprus Bar, Call Date: Nov
1994 (Lincoln's Inn) Qualifications:
LLB (Hons), LLM (Lond)

Scott *Miss Charlene Annette*
Attorney General's Chambers, Global
House, 43 Church Street, Hamilton HM
12, Bermuda, 441 292 2463, Fax: 441
292 3608, Crown Counsel (Criminal),
Call Date: Nov 1986 (Inner Temple)
Qualifications: BA, MSc (New York),
LLB (Essex)

Scudamore *Jeremy Richard*
Mejia Lequerica 7, 1 dcha, 28004
Madrid, +34 91 457 72 63, Fax: +34
619 29 09 86, and Member Madrid
Bar, Call Date: Nov 1982 (Middle
Temple) Qualifications: BA (Hons)
(Exeter)

Scully *Gerard*
17 Mulgrave terrace, Dun Laoghaire,
County Dublin, Call Date: Nov 1996
(Middle Temple) Qualifications: BA
(Dublin), MA (Lond)

Seah *Miss Chui Ling Engelyn*
Singapore 575415, Call Date: July 1994
(Middle Temple) Qualifications: LLB
(Hons)(Lond)

Seah *Miss Hwee Ying Melina*
Singapore 1232, Call Date: Nov 1995
(Middle Temple) Qualifications: LLB
(Hons)

Seah *Miss Lu Sean*
Malaysia, Call Date: July 1996 (Gray's
Inn) Qualifications: LLB (Warwick)

Seah *Miss Suat Eng*
Malaysia, and Member Singapore Bar,
Call Date: July 1994 (Lincoln's Inn)
Qualifications: BSc (Econ) (Hons)

Sears *The Hon Mr Justice*
The High Court, 38 Queensway, Hong
Kong, 8254433, Fax: 8690640,
Commioner of the Supreme Crt of
Brunei, Justice of the High Court of
Hong Kong, Call Date: Feb 1957 (Gray's
Inn) Qualifications: MA (Cantab)

Sebom *Polycarp Teo*
East Malaysia, and Member Sarawak
Bar, Call Date: Oct 1991 (Inner
Temple) Qualifications: BA, LLB (Hull),
ACIS, ATII

See *Ben Sin*
Malaysia, Call Date: July 1997
(Lincoln's Inn) Qualifications: LLB
(Hons)(Lond)

See *David Thiam Soon*
Singapore 099779, Call Date: Nov 1997
(Middle Temple) Qualifications: LLB
(Hons)(Reading)

See *Eng Teong*
Malaysia, Call Date: July 1996
(Lincoln's Inn) Qualifications: LLB
(Hons)(Lond)

See *Ms Esther Lay Lin*
Messrs Cheang & Ariff, 39 Court, 39
Jalan Yap Kwan Seng, 50450 Kuala
Lumpur, Malaysia, 03 2610803, Fax:
03 2614475, Legal Adviser, and
Member Malaysia, Call Date: July 1995
(Middle Temple) Qualifications: LLB
(Hons)

See *Miss Guat Har*
Messrs Shearn Delamore & Co, 6th
Floor,Wisma Penang Gdn, No.42 Jalan
Sultan Ahmad Shah, 10050 Penang
Malaysia, Malaysia, 04-2267062/
2264899, Fax: 04-2275166, Senior
Assistant, and Member Malaysia Bar,
Call Date: July 1989 (Middle Temple)
Qualifications: BA, LLB (Bucks)

See Tho *Miss Ving Mei*
Singapore 1025, Call Date: July 1995
(Middle Temple) Qualifications: LLB
(Hons) (Hull)

Sefton *Peter Stewart*
Northern Ireland, and Member
Northern Ireland, Call Date: Nov 1998
(Inner Temple) Qualifications: LLB
(Belfast), FCIArb

Sekarajasekaran *Miss Sharmila*
Malaysia, Call Date: Nov 1996 (Middle
Temple) Qualifications: BA
(Hons)(Keele)

Seligman *Edgar*
Harry B. Sands & Co, Chambers, 50
Shirley Street, P O Box N-624, Nassau,
Bahamas, Bahamas, 1-242-322 2670,
Fax: 1-242-323 8914, and Member
Bahamas, Call Date: Oct 1992 (Gray's
Inn) Qualifications: MA (Dublin), Dip
Law

Seller *Timothy John*
Call Date: May 1997 (Lincoln's Inn)
Qualifications: BA (Hons)(Dunelm)

Selvakumar *MIss Shiela*
Malaysia, Call Date: July 1997
(Lincoln's Inn) Qualifications: LLB
(Hons)

Selvan *Kaniamuthan s/o Thiruvida*
Malaysia, Call Date: Nov 1997
(Lincoln's Inn) Qualifications: LLB
(Hons)

Selvaraj *Steven*
West Malaysia, Call Date: Nov 1996
(Gray's Inn) Qualifications: LLB (Lond)

Selvarajah *Miss Pushpaleela*
Malaysia, Call Date: Feb 1995
(Lincoln's Inn) Qualifications: LLB
(Hons)(Lond)

Selvarajan *Balamurugan*
Singapore 730123, Call Date: Nov 1997
(Lincoln's Inn) Qualifications: LLB
(Hons)(Wolv)

Sen *Raj Ratna*
149/IC Rash Behari Avenue, Calcutta,
700029, India, (033) 464-3601/464
2651, Call Date: July 1994 (Gray's Inn)
Qualifications: BA (Calcutta), LLB
(Leeds)

Sengupta *Miss Amgana*
India, Call Date: July 1995 (Inner
Temple) Qualifications: LLB (Lond)

Seow *John Hwang Seng*
Singapore 1231, Call Date: July 1995
(Middle Temple) Qualifications: LLB
(Hons)

Serghides *Miss Lydia Gabrielle*
Cyprus, Call Date: July 1997 (Gray's
Inn) Qualifications: LLB (Kent)

Sevasamy *Shankar Angammah*
Singapore 560131, Call Date: July 1996
(Middle Temple) Qualifications: LLB
(Hons)(Lond)

Sewpal *Pranay*
Mauritius, Call Date: Nov 1998
(Lincoln's Inn) Qualifications: LLB
(Hons)(Wolves)

Seymour *Dr Colin Brian*
Republic of Ireland, and Member
King's Inn (Dublin), Call Date: May
1996 (Lincoln's Inn) Qualifications:
PhD (Dublin)

Shadid *Miss Lina Ali*
Afridi & Angell, Legal Consultants,
P.O.Box 9371, Dubai, United Arab
Emirates, 00971 4 883900, Fax: 00971
4 883979, Call Date: July 1996
(Lincoln's Inn) Qualifications: LLB
(Hons)(Lond)

Shafiq *Imran*
Pakistan, Call Date: Nov 1997
(Lincoln's Inn) Qualifications: LLB
(Hons), LLM (Georgetown)

Shah *Ms Bhavini Jayakant*
Singapore 1542, Call Date: July 1994
(Middle Temple) Qualifications: LLB
(Hons)(Lond)

Shahrom *Abdul Razak*
Malaysia, Call Date: July 1998
(Lincoln's Inn) Qualifications: LLB
(Hons)(Wales)

Shaik Hussain *Miss Khatijah*
Messrs Isharidah, Ho, Chong &,
Menon, Advocates & Solicitors, Unit
A11-1 & 2, Megan Phileo, Promanade,
No 189 Jalan Tun, Razak, 50400 Kuala
Lumpur, Malaysia, 03 4602299/
4602901/4602909, Fax: 03 4602266,
and Member Malaysian Bar, Call Date:
July 1993 (Lincoln's Inn)
Qualifications: LLB (Hons, Manch)

Shaikh *Zaher Abduz*
Bangladesh, Call Date: Nov 1997
(Gray's Inn) Qualifications: B.Com
(Bangladesh), LLB

Sham *Chun Hung*
Hong Kong, and Member Hong Kong
Bar, Call Date: Feb 1992 (Gray's Inn)
Qualifications: BSc (Hong Kong), LLB
(Lond), C.Biol (UK)

Shankar *Renganathan*
Singapore 2776, Call Date: July 1995
(Middle Temple) Qualifications: LLB
(Hons)

Shanmuga *Kanesalingham*
Malaysia, Call Date: Oct 1998
(Lincoln's Inn) Qualifications: LLB
(Hons)(Lond)

Shanmuganathan *Indran*
Malaysia, Call Date: July 1996
(Lincoln's Inn) Qualifications: LLB
(Hons)(Leics)

Sharif *Hussain Nawaz*
Pakistan, Call Date: Nov 1996
(Lincoln's Inn) Qualifications: LLB
(Hons)(LSE)

Sharma *Miss Jyoti*
Malaysia, Call Date: July 1996 (Gray's
Inn) Qualifications: LLB (Wales), LLM

Sharpe *Mrs Sally*
Law Officers' Department, Morier
House, St Helier, Jersey JE1 1DD,
Channel Islands, 01534 502200, Fax:
01534 502299, Crown Advocate,
Advocate of the Royal Court of Jersey
(1992), Call Date: July 1988 (Middle
Temple) Qualifications: BA (OU), LLB
(Hons) (Lond)

Sharpe *Miss Susan Clare*
Law Officers' Department, Royal Court
House, Royal Square, Jersey JE1 1DD,
Channel Islands, 01534 502200, Fax:
01534 502299, Call Date: Oct 1992
(Middle Temple) Qualifications: BA
(Hons)

Shaw *Jonathan Leonard Maukes*
Des Voeux Chambers, 10F Bank of East
Asia Building, 10 Des Voeux Road,
Central, Hong Kong, 2845 1909/2526/
3071, Fax: 2877 8634/2810/5867, and
Member Hong Kong Bar, Call Date: Nov
1978 (Gray's Inn) Qualifications:
FCIArb, LLM

Sheldrick *Andrew William*
3 Radford Court, Princeton Junction,
New Jersey, 08550-2218, 609 799
5719, Fax: 609 799 9170, and Member
New York Bar, Call Date: July 1979
(Gray's Inn) Qualifications: MA
(Cantab), MCL(George, Washington
Univ)

Shepheard *Huw Owen*
Insinger Trust (Jersey) Ltd, P O Box
546, 28-30 The Parade, St Helier, Jersey
JE4 8XY, 01534 636211, Fax: 01534
636215, Compliance Manager, Call
Date: July 1982 (Gray's Inn)
Qualifications: LLB (Hons)

Sherlock *Miss Samatha Frances*
Pollonais, Blanc,De La Bastide, &
Jacelon, 62 Sackville Street, Port of
Spain, Trindad, Trinidad, 623-5461,
Fax: 625-8415, and Member Trinidad &
Tobago Bar, Call Date: July 1995
(Gray's Inn) Qualifications: LLB
(Warks)

Shiacolas *Mrs Galatia*
Cyprus, Call Date: Nov 1995 (Lincoln's
Inn) Qualifications: LLB (Hons) (Kent)

Shiacolas *Menelaos*
Cyprus, Call Date: Nov 1995 (Lincoln's
Inn) Qualifications: LLB (Hons)(Kent),
LLM

Shields *Mrs Janice Rhian*
Isle of Man, and Member Isle of Man,
Call Date: Oct 1993 (Inner Temple)
Qualifications: LLB (Manch)

Shine *Miss Clare Camilla*
37 Rue Erlanger, 75016 Paris, France,
France, (33 1) 46 51 90 11, Fax: (33 1)
46 51 90 11, Call Date: Nov 1988
(Middle Temple) Qualifications: BA
(Oxon), Dip Law (Central), D.E.A.
(Paris)

Shooter *Mrs Louise Anne*
KPMG, Heritage Court, 41 Athol Street,
Douglas, Isle of Man, 01624 681000,
Fax: 01624 681098, Tax Manager, Call
Date: Nov 1994 (Lincoln's Inn)
Qualifications: LLB (Hons)

Shum *Cheuk Yum*
24th Floor, Shum Tower, 268 Des
Voeux Road, Sheung Wan, (852)2805
2730, Fax: (852)2851 2266, and
Member Hong Kong Bar, Call Date:
June 1959 (Middle Temple)
Qualifications: LLB (Lond)

Shum *Ka Hei*
Hong Kong, Call Date: July 1996
(Middle Temple) Qualifications: BSSc
(Hons) , (Hong Kong), CPE (Staffs)

Sia *Edmund Wei Keong*
Malaysia, Call Date: July 1996
(Lincoln's Inn) Qualifications: LLB
(Hons)(Warw)

Sia *Miss Pebble Huei-Chieh*
Singapore 309502, Call Date: July 1996
(Middle Temple) Qualifications: LLB
(Hons)(Lond)

Siah *Miss Karen Wei Kuan*
Singapore 149002, Call Date: Nov 1996
(Middle Temple) Qualifications: LLB
(Hons)(Sheff)

Siddondo *Miss Camilla Dorothy
Adhiambo*
East Africa, Call Date: July 1995
(Lincoln's Inn) Qualifications: LLB
(Hons)

Sidhu *Miss Anup Kaur*
Malaysia, Call Date: Mar 1998
(Lincoln's Inn) Qualifications: B.Econ
(Australia), LLB (Hons)(Lond), LLM
(Lond)

Sidhu *Mr Daljit Singh*
M/S Y H Goh & Co, 101 Upper Cross
Street, [H]05-40 People's Park Centre,
Singapore 0105, Singapore 2057, 535
9022/535 6641, Fax: 538 4313, and
Member Singapore Bar, Call Date: July
1990 (Middle Temple) Qualifications:
LLB (Lond)

Sidhu *Sarjeet Singh*
Messrs Gill & Tang, 130-A Jalan Choo
Cheng Khay, 50460 Kuala Lumpur
Malaysia, Malaysia, 03 2440266, Fax:
03 2410413, and Member Malaysian
Bar, Call Date: Nov 1992 (Gray's Inn)
Qualifications: LLB (So'ton)

Siew *Miss Anne Eee Peng*
Malaysia, Call Date: Nov 1995
(Lincoln's Inn) Qualifications: LLLB
(Hons), LLM (Dunelm)

Siew *Miss Li-Lian*
M/S K M Chye & Partners, Advocates &
Solicitors, 6th Floor, UBN Tower, Letter
Box 163, Jalan P Ramlee, 50250 Kuala
Lumpur, Malaysia, (603) 2388055,
Fax: (603) 2019300, Legal Advisor, and
Member Malaysia, Call Date: July 1995
(Lincoln's Inn) Qualifications: BCL

Siew *Miss Yvonne*
Malaysia, Call Date: Nov 1997
(Lincoln's Inn) Qualifications: LLB
(Hons)(Wales)

Silvera *Wayne Delano*
Clayton Morgan & Co, 59 Church Street,
Kingston, Montego Bay, (876) 952
1800/979 1733, Fax: (876) 952 1514,
and Member Jamaican, Call Date: July
1996 (Lincoln's Inn) Qualifications:
LLB (Hons), BSc (Lond)

Silvester *John Darragh Mostyn*
Lenana Forest Centre, Ngong Road, P O
Box 24397, Nairobi, 254 2 567251/
577374-81, Fax: 254 2 564945,
Advocate of High Court - Kenya, Uganda
& Tanzania, Call Date: June 1958
(Inner Temple) Qualifications: MA
(Hons) (Oxon), ACIA (Lond)

Silwaraju *Miss Hemalatha*
Singapore 679038, Call Date: July 1997
(Middle Temple) Qualifications: LLB
(Hons)(Wales)

Sim *Miss Annabelle Seu Cheun*
Malaysia, Call Date: July 1997
(Lincoln's Inn) Qualifications: LLB
(Hons)(Leics)

Sim *Chee Siong*
Singapore 099308, Call Date: Nov 1995
(Middle Temple) Qualifications: LLB
(Hons)

Sim *Miss Christina Choy Jing*
Singapore 579205, Call Date: July 1998
(Middle Temple) Qualifications: BA
(Hons)(Exon)

Sim *Geoffrey Poh Leong*
c/o Messrs. Sandhu & Co, Suites 6, 7 &
8, 5th Floor, Badiah Complex, Kin 2,
Jalan Tutong, BA 2112, Darussalam,
673 2 220783, Fax: 673 2 241237, Call
Date: July 1993 (Lincoln's Inn)
Qualifications: LLB (Hons)

Sim *Miss Hwee Ai*
Singapore 1545, Call Date: July 1994
(Middle Temple) Qualifications: LLB
(Hons)(Lond)

Sim *Miss Sok Nee*
Malaysia, Call Date: Nov 1997
(Lincoln's Inn) Qualifications: LLB
(Hons)(Wales)

Simmons *Everard Barclay*
Bermuda, Call Date: Mar 1997 (Gray's
Inn) Qualifications: LLB (Kent)

Simpson *Anthony Maurice Herbert*
Avenue Michel-Ange 57, 1000 Brussels,
Belgium, Belgium, (00 322) 7364219,
Fax: (00 322) 7339404, European Civil
Servant, Call Date: Feb 1961 (Inner
Temple) Qualifications: MA , LLM

Sin *Miss Charlotte Minng Minng*
Singapore 2057, Call Date: July 1996
(Middle Temple) Qualifications: LLB
(Hons)(Hull)

Sin *Miss Li Lian*
Malaysia, Call Date: July 1996
(Lincoln's Inn) Qualifications: LLB
(Hons)(Sheff)

Sin *Pui Wah*
Hong Kong, Call Date: Nov 1997
(Middle Temple) Qualifications: BSSc
(Hong Kong), MPA (Hong Kong)

Singh *Ajinderpal*
Singapore 2366, Call Date: July 1996
(Middle Temple) Qualifications: LLB
(Hons)(Leeds)

Singh *Bhajanvir*
Singapore 559686, and Member
Singapore Bar, Call Date: July 1994
(Lincoln's Inn) Qualifications: LLB
(Sheff)

Singh *Gurcharanjit Dewan*
Singapore 0409, Call Date: July 1996
(Lincoln's Inn) Qualifications: LLB
(Hons)(Lond)

Singh *Herbans*
Singapore 520940, Call Date: Nov 1997
(Lincoln's Inn) Qualifications: LLB
(Hons)(Lond)

Singh *Jispal*
08-25 Singapore 600404, Call Date:
July 1997 (Lincoln's Inn)
Qualifications: LLB (Hons)(Lond)

Singh *Kertar*
Singapore 1438, Call Date: Feb 1994
(Middle Temple) Qualifications: LLB
(Hons)(Wolves)

Singh *Kirindeep*
Singapore 2366, Call Date: July 1996
(Middle Temple) Qualifications: LLB
(Leeds)

Singh *Kuldip*
Winston Low & Partners, 1 Colombo
Court, [H] 05-05, Singapore 090028,
65 3383722, Fax: 65 3376122, and
Member Singapore Bar, Call Date: Nov
1995 (Middle Temple) Qualifications:
LLB (Hons)(Lond)

Singh *Mohan s/o Gurdial Singh*
Block 52, Apt No 04-299, Lengkok
Bahru, Singapore 150052, Singapore
0315, 4727479, Call Date: July 1995
(Lincoln's Inn) Qualifications: LLB
(Hons)

Singh *Mohan s/o Kernal Singh*
Malaysia, Call Date: Nov 1995
(Lincoln's Inn) Qualifications: LLB
(Hons)(Lond)

Singh *Ranjit*
Singapore 1953, Call Date: July 1993
(Middle Temple) Qualifications: LLB
(Hons)

Singh *Sarindar*
Singapore 950033, Call Date: Nov 1996
(Lincoln's Inn) Qualifications: LLB
(Hons)

Singh *Sarjeet*
Singapore 1646, Call Date: July 1992
(Middle Temple) Qualifications: LLB
(Hons)(Lond)

Singh Deo *Gobind*
Malaysia, Call Date: July 1995
(Lincoln's Inn) Qualifications: LLB
(Hons)

Sinnapaan *Doraraj*
Singapore 578311, Call Date: Mar 1999
(Lincoln's Inn) Qualifications: LLB
(Hons)(Lond)

Siow *Miss Hua Lin*
Singapore 1128, Call Date: Nov 1995
(Middle Temple) Qualifications: LLB
(Hons)(Hull)

Siow *Kim Leong*
Malaysia, Call Date: Nov 1996 (Middle
Temple) Qualifications: LLB (Hons)

Siraj *Miss Sarawat*
Bangladesh, Call Date: Nov 1998
(Lincoln's Inn) Qualifications: LLB
(Hons)(Herts)

Sircar *Muhammad Jamiruddin*
Supreme Court Bar, Room 41, Dhaka,
Bangladesh, Bangladesh, 8802 896883,
Senior Counsel, Member of Parliament
Bangladesh Formerly Minister for
Education Formerly Minister for Law,
Justice & Parliamentary Affairs. and
Member Supreme Court of Bangladesh,
Call Date: Nov 1967 (Lincoln's Inn)
Qualifications: MA, LL.B

Sissoho *Edrisa Mansajang*
Department of State for, Justice (The
Gambia), Attorney General's Chambers,
Marina Parade, Banjul, West Africa, 220
228181, Fax: 220 225352, State
Counsel, Member of the Gambia Bar
Association, Call Date: Mar 1998
(Lincoln's Inn) Qualifications: LLB
(Hons)

Sithawalla *Moiz Haider*
Singapore 289448, Call Date: Nov 1998
(Middle Temple) Qualifications: LLB
(Hons)(Nott'm)

Sivagnanam *Rutheran*
Shearn Delamore & Co, No 2 Benteng,
50050 Kuala Lumpur, Malaysia,
2300644, Fax: 2385625, and Member
Malaysia, Call Date: Nov 1994
(Lincoln's Inn) Qualifications: LLB
(Hons)(Leeds)

Sivagnanaratnam *Sivananthan*
Messrs Drew & Napier, 20 Raffles Place,
[H]17-00 Ocean Towers, Singapore
048620, Singapore 2057, 65 5350733,
Fax: 65 5330694/5330693, Partner
(Since 1/7/97), Advocate & Solicitor in
Singapore (May 1992)0 and Member
Singapore Bar, Call Date: July 1991
(Middle Temple) Qualifications: LLB
(Hons) (Lond)

Sivalingam *Miss Seetha*
Singapore 557460, Call Date: Nov 1996
(Middle Temple) Qualifications: LLB
(Hons)(Lond)

Sivaloganathan *Miss Damita Devi*
Singapore 0719, Call Date: July 1995
(Lincoln's Inn) Qualifications: LLB
(Hons)

Sivapiragasam *Miss Rani Christina*
Pernas Otis Elevator Co, Son BHD, 2
Medan Setia 2, Plaza Damansara, Bukit
Damansara, 50490, Malaysia, 03
2554811, Fax: 03 2559684, and
Member Malaysia Bar, Call Date: Feb
1993 (Lincoln's Inn) Qualifications:
LLB (Buck'ham), LLM (Buck'ham)

Sivasankar *Chelliah*
42 Jalan Bintang, Taman Westpool,
Ipoh, Perak, Malaysia, 05-5489451,
Fax: 05-5497311, Advocate and
Solicitor, High Court of Malaya and
Member Malaysian Bar, Call Date: Nov
1993 (Gray's Inn) Qualifications: LLB

Sivasubramaniam *Miss Kavitha*
Sri Lanka, Call Date: Nov 1997
(Lincoln's Inn) Qualifications: LLB
(Hons)

Sivasubramaniam *Sivaruban*
Malaysia, Call Date: July 1996
(Lincoln's Inn) Qualifications: LLB
(Hons)

Sivgnasundram *Arulchelvan*
Singapore 531007, Call Date: July 1998
(Middle Temple) Qualifications: LLB
(Hons)(Wales)

Skinner *Miss Sarah Elizabeth*
Bermuda, Call Date: Nov 1994
(Lincoln's Inn) Qualifications: LLB
(Hons)(Lond)

Skordis *Christos*
Scordis; Papapetrou & Co, 30 Karpenisi
Street, PO Box 533, 1660 Nicosia,
Cyprus, 00 357 2 843000, Fax: 00 357
2 375227, and Member Cyprus Bar,
Call Date: July 1998 (Lincoln's Inn)
Qualifications: LLB (Hons), LLM

Smagh *Jerrinder Singh*
Singapore 550117, Call Date: Nov 1997
(Middle Temple) Qualifications: LLB
(Hons)

Smith *Miss Allison L*
Bermuda, Call Date: July 1998 (Middle Temple) Qualifications: LLB (Hons)(Buck'm)

Smith *Miss Charmaine Natasha*
Bahamas, Call Date: July 1997 (Gray's Inn) Qualifications: BA (Canada), LLB (Lond)

Smith *Geoffrey*
BP13, 78113 Bourdonne, France, 134871746, Fax: 134871751, Arbitrator Expert Witness Adjudicator, Conciliator, Call Date: Feb 1995 (Middle Temple) Qualifications: BSc (Loughborough), LLDip, CDipAF , CEng, FICE, ACIArb

Smith *Leroy Neville*
P.O.Box CB 13537, New Providence, Bahamas, (242) 322 1881, and Member Bahamas, Call Date: July 1998 (Lincoln's Inn) Qualifications: LLB (Hons)(So'ton)

Smith *Marcus Andrew Charles*
Call Date: July 1998 (Lincoln's Inn) Qualifications: LLB (Hons)

Smith *The Hon Mr Justice Neville Leroy*
Bahamas, Member of Bars of Barbados and the Bahamas Justice of the Supreme Court of the Bahamas Formerly a solicitor of England and of Barbados, Call Date: July 1991 (Lincoln's Inn)

Smithers *Miss Amelia Frances Otway*
CH-6921 Vico Morcote, Switzerland, Switzerland, 41-91-9961973, Fax: 41-91-9961692, and Member Turks & Caicos Islands Bar, Call Date: Oct 1991 (Inner Temple) Qualifications: BA (Lond), Dip Law

Smouha *Derrick Maurice*
32 Chemin des Crets-de-Champel, 1206 Geneva, (00) 41 22/347 05 18, Fax: (00) 41 22/346 15 16, Call Date: Nov 1962 (Lincoln's Inn) Qualifications: MA (Cantab)

Smyth *John Jackson*
PO Box CH 210, Chisipite, Harare, 490561, Fax: 494127, Director of Zambesi Ministries, Call Date: July 1965 (Inner Temple) Qualifications: MA, LLB (Cantab)

Soh *Miss Diana Wei Yi*
Singapore 2159, Call Date: July 1995 (Middle Temple) Qualifications: LLB (Hons)(Warw)

Somen *Michael Lewis*
Hamilton Harrison & Matthews, ICEA Building, Kenyatta Avenue, P.O. Box 30333, Nairobi Kenya, 254 2 330870, Fax: 254 2 222318, Commissioner for Oaths Notary Public, Advocate High Court of Kenya and Member Kenya, Call Date: Feb 1961 (Gray's Inn) Qualifications: MA (Oxon)

Somu *Retana Vellu Palani*
Singapore 1231, Call Date: July 1995 (Gray's Inn) Qualifications: LLB (Lond)

Soo *Kok Loong*
P.O.Box 378, 90704 Sandakan, Sabah, Malaysia, (089) 222188, and Member Advocate of the High Court in Sabah & Sarawak, Malaysia Advocate of the Supreme Court in Brunei, Darussalam, Call Date: Nov 1992 (Inner Temple) Qualifications: BA (Keele)

Soo *Kwok Leung*
1320 Prince's Building, Central, Hong Kong, Hong Kong, and Member Hong Kong Bar, Call Date: July 1995 (Gray's Inn) Qualifications: BSc (Hong Kong), LLB (Lond), C.Eng, MIStractE, MICE, MHKIE, RPE, ACIArb, MIQA, AHKIArb

Soo *Miss Li Yian*
Malaysia, Call Date: Nov 1998 (Gray's Inn) Qualifications: LLB (Sheff)

Soo *Ms Sheagan*
Messrs Soo Thien Ming &, Nashrah, No 1, 1st Floor, Jalan SS2/55, 47300 Petaling, Jaya, Malaysia, 03-7748763, Fax: 03-7744314, Call Date: July 1995 (Gray's Inn) Qualifications: LLB (Middx)

Soo *Miss Wai Leng*
Malaysia, Call Date: July 1995 (Lincoln's Inn) Qualifications: LLB (Hons)

Soo *Miss Wee Loon*
Malaysia 80200, Call Date: July 1998 (Lincoln's Inn) Qualifications: LLB (Hons)(L'pool)

Soon *Eric Boon Teck*
Malaysia, Call Date: July 1994 (Lincoln's Inn) Qualifications: LLB (Hons)

Soon *Miss Vivienne Wen Pin*
Singapore 249963, Call Date: July 1995 (Lincoln's Inn) Qualifications: LLB (Hons)

Spear *Christopher Mark*
201-140 King Street, Peterborough, Ontario, Canada K93 728, Canada, 705-7412144, Fax: 705-7412712, and Member Ontario, Canada, Call Date: July 1981 (Middle Temple) Qualifications: BA, Dip Law, LLB

Speck *Jonathan Paul*
Messrs Mourant du Feu & Jeune, Advocates & Solicitors, 22 Grenville Street, St Helier, Jersey JE4 8PX, Channel Islands, 01534 609000, Fax: 01534 609333, and Member Jersey Eighteen Carlton Crescent, Southampton, SO15 2XR, Call Date: 1990 (Middle Temple) Qualifications: LLB (Exon)

Spencer *Mrs Margaret Elizabeth*
Bachmann & Co Limited, Frances House, Sir William Place, Guernsey GY1 4HQ, Channel Islands, 01481 723573, Fax: 01481 711353, President of Guernsey International Legal Ass., Call Date: Feb 1989 (Gray's Inn)

Spencer *Miss Maureen Cecilia*
Patton Boggs LLP, 2550 M Street NW, Washington DC 20037, 001 202 457 6000, Fax: 001 202 457 6315, Law Clerk, Call Date: Oct 1994 (Gray's Inn) Qualifications: BA, LLM

Spicer *Rupert Nicholas Bullen*
15th Fl Printing House, 6 Duddell Street, Central, 852 2 5 212616, Fax: 852 2 8 450260, and Member Hong Kong Bar, Call Date: Nov 1980 (Lincoln's Inn) Qualifications: BSc (Dunelm), Diplaw

Spyrou *George Andrew Rankin*
12 Richmond Hill Road, Greenwich CT 06831, 203 625 0071, Fax: 203 625 0065, Chairman, Airship Management Services Ltd, Call Date: Nov 1980 (Inner Temple) Qualifications: AB (Harvard), MA LLB (Cantab)

Sreenevasan *Gopal*
Malaysia, and Member Malaysia, Call Date: Nov 1993 (Middle Temple) Qualifications: LLB (Hons)(Warwick)

Sreenivasan *Rajesh*
94 Jalan Angin Laut, Singapore 1648, Singapore 1648, 00 65 5453851, and Member Singapore Bar, Call Date: July 1993 (Middle Temple) Qualifications: LLB (Hons)

Staff *Marcus Richard*
Brunschwig Wittmer, 13, Quai de L'ile, 1211 Geneva 11, Switzerland, 4122 781 33 22, Fax: 4122 781 31 00, Employed Barrister, International Commercial Law, Call Date: 1994 (Inner Temple) Qualifications: BA (York)

Steel *Simon Arthur*
Simpson. Thacher & Bartlett, 425 Lexington Avenue, New York, NY 10017-3954, United States of America, 001 212 455 3789, Fax: 001 212 455 2502, and Member New York, Call Date: Feb 1992 (Lincoln's Inn) Qualifications: MA (Hons) (Cambs), LLM (Chicago)

Steinke *Gerald Rolf*
Germany, Call Date: Oct 1997 (Gray's Inn) Qualifications: LLB, LLM (Bucks)

Stephens-Ofner *John Alfred*
Lersnerstrasse 5 A, 85579 Neubiberg, Judge on the Board of Appeals of the European Patent Organ. Organisation, Call Date: Nov 1966 (Middle Temple) Qualifications: MA (Oxon)

Stesin *Mrs Vasantha*
6 Amber Close, Brighton, Victoria 3186, (03) 9596 0697, Fax: (03) 9596 0747, Solicitor, and Member Australian Capital Territory, Victoria, Singapore Bar, Call Date: Nov 1990 (Lincoln's Inn) Qualifications: LLB (Wales), LLM (Lond)

Steves *Bernhard*
Shato Roa 3003, Maginu 1904-1
Miyamae-Ku, Kawasaki, Japan 216,
Japan, 81-3 3479 3768, Fax: 81-33470
3152, Call Date: Nov 1987 (Lincoln's
Inn) Qualifications: BA (SOAS), Dip
Law (City)

Stivadoros *Paul George*
5 Loukis Akritas Avenue, CY-1100
Nicosia, Cyprus, 00357-2-772501, Fax:
00357-2-773170, and Member Cyprus
Bar, Call Date: Nov 1962 (Gray's Inn)
Qualifications: LLB (Lond)

Stoneham *Ms Nicole Holly Marie*
Attorney General's Chambers, Global
House, 43 Church Street, Hamilton HM
12, (441) 292 2463, Fax: (441) 292
3608, Crown Counsel, and Member
Bermuda Bar, Call Date: Nov 1992
(Gray's Inn) Qualifications: BA, LLB

Stratford *Jonathan Charles*
First Executive, York Chambers, York
Street, St Helier, Jersey JE2 3RQ,
Channel Islands, 01534 631636, and
Member Jersey Bar, Call Date: Oct 1995
(Gray's Inn) Qualifications: LLB

Stuart-Moore *The Hon. Mr Justice
Michael*
Court of Appeal, High Court, 38
Queensway, Hong Kong, Justice of
Appeal of the High Court, Hong Kong,
Call Date: July 1966 (Middle Temple)

Stubbs *Michael James*
DreamWorks, 10 Universal City Plaza,
Building 10, Universal City, California
91608 U.S.A, United States of America,
818 7336000, Fax: 818 7336194,
Business Affairs Attorney, Call Date: Oct
1993 (Gray's Inn) Qualifications: LLB
(Buck'ham)

Stylianou *Miss Eleni Byron*
Cyprus, Call Date: Nov 1994 (Gray's
Inn) Qualifications: LLB (Lond)

Subraa
Singapore 578286, Call Date: Nov 1996
(Lincoln's Inn) Qualifications: LLB
(Hons)

Subramaniam *Miss Pushpakantha*
Level 40, Menara Lion, No 165 Jalan
Ampang, P O Box 12485, 50780 Kuala
Lumpur, Malaysia, 03-4677868, Fax:
03-4666546, Legal Officer/Advisor, and
Member Malaysia Bar, Call Date: Nov
1994 (Inner Temple) Qualifications:
LLB (Hons)(Lond)

Subramaniam *Rethinakumar*
Malaysia, Call Date: Nov 1998 (Middle
Temple) Qualifications: LLB
(Hons)(E.Lond)

Subramaniam *Miss Sumitra R*
West Malaysia, Call Date: July 1996
(Middle Temple) Qualifications: LLB
(Hons)(Wales)

Subramaniam Eliatamby *Nathan*
Malaysia, Call Date: July 1995 (Middle
Temple) Qualifications: LLB (Hons),
LLM

Sudin *Miss Suhana*
Darussalam, Call Date: Nov 1995
(Lincoln's Inn) Qualifications: LLB
(Hons)

Sugden *Paul Birkby*
Olsen Backhurst & Dorey, Eaton
House, Seaton Place, St Helier, Jersey
JE4 3QL, Channel Islands, 44 (0) 1534
888900, Fax: 44 (0) 1534 887744, and
Member Jersey Bar, Call Date: July
1983 (Lincoln's Inn) Qualifications:
BA,ACIB

Suhara *Miss Binte Mohd Said*
Malaysia, 603 9583857, Fax: 603
9583859, Call Date: Nov 1996
(Lincoln's Inn) Qualifications: LLB
(Hons)(Lond)

Sujore *Soobeeraj*
No 1, Cretin Lane, Boundary, Rose-Hill,
Mauritius, Mauritius, (00230) 465
8393, Fax: (00230) 465 6349, Call
Date: July 1998 (Middle Temple)
Qualifications: LLB (Hons)(Wolves)

Suleman *Miss Nigar*
Pakistan, Call Date: July 1998
(Lincoln's Inn) Qualifications: LLB
(Hons)

Sum *Chin Liang*
Malaysia, Call Date: July 1995
(Lincoln's Inn) Qualifications: LLB
(Hons)

Sumner *Miss Michaela Simone*
Graham Thompson & Co, P.O.Box
N272, Nassau N.P, Bahamas, 00 1 242
322 4130, Fax: 00 1 242 328 1069,
Associate, and Member Bahamas, Call
Date: July 1997 (Middle Temple)
Qualifications: LLB (Hons)

Sumputh *Miss Vijaya Kumaree*
Mauritius, Call Date: Nov 1998
(Lincoln's Inn) Qualifications: LLB
(Hons)(Wolves)

Sundaram *Subramanian*
Singapore 30341, Advocate & Solicitor
in the Republic of Singapore, Call Date:
Nov 1993 (Middle Temple)
Qualifications: LLB (Hons)(Lond)

Sundararaj *Miss Aneeta Rajah*
Malaysia, 60 4 7310049, Legal Assistant
Advocate and Solicitor of the High Court
of Malaya, Call Date: Nov 1996 (Middle
Temple) Qualifications: LLB
(Hons)(Wales), LLM (Wales)

Suntharalingam *Miss Rajita*
Malaysia, Call Date: July 1998
(Lincoln's Inn) Qualifications: LLB
(Hons)(N'castle)

Supaiyah *Dravida Maran*
Apt Blk 31, Dover Road, 02-109,
Singapore 130031, Call Date: Mar 1998
(Lincoln's Inn) Qualifications: LLB
(Hons)

Suppayan *Miss Malarkodi*
Singapore 1851, Call Date: Nov 1995
(Lincoln's Inn) Qualifications: LLB
(Hons)

Suppayya *Gogulakannan s/o*
Singapore 310014, Call Date: July 1997
(Lincoln's Inn) Qualifications: LLB
(Hons)(Lond)

Suppiah *Arul*
Singapore 141168, Call Date: Nov 1997
(Middle Temple) Qualifications: LLB
(Hons)(Lond)

Suppiah *Krishnamurthi*
Singapore 310257, Call Date: July 1996
(Middle Temple) Qualifications: LLB
(Hons)(Lond)

Suppiah *Sarasvathy*
Singapore 120427, Call Date: July 1997
(Lincoln's Inn) Qualifications: LLB
(Hons)(Leeds)

Supramaniam *Rajan*
Singapore 310037, Call Date: Nov 1998
(Lincoln's Inn) Qualifications: LLB
(Hons)(Lond)

Sureshan *T. Kulasingam*
Singapore 808012, Call Date: July 1996
(Middle Temple) Qualifications: LLB
(Hons)(Lond)

Surjit *Miss Belinda Kaur*
Malaysia, Call Date: Nov 1997
(Lincoln's Inn) Qualifications: LLB
(Hons)(Thames)

Sussex *Charles Anthony*
Des Voeux Chambers, 10th Floor Bank
of East Asia, Building, 10 Des Voeux
Road Central, 00 852 2526 3071, Fax:
00 852 2810 5287, Formerly a Solicitor
and Member Hong Kong & New South
Wales Bars, Call Date: May 1982
(Middle Temple) Qualifications: LLB
(Lond)

Suttill *Brian*
Law Draftsman's Office, States Greffe,
Jersey JE1 1DD, Channel Islands,
01534 502006, Fax: 01534 502098,
Assistant Law Draftsman, Member LCIA
(London Court of International
Arbitration) and Member Hong Kong
Bar York Chambers, 14 Toft Green,
York, YO1 6JT, Call Date: Nov 1970
(Gray's Inn) Qualifications: LLB
(Leeds), Dip L.D. (Ottawa)

Sutton *Mrs Joyah Junella*
P.O.Box 534, Main Street, Charlestown,
Nevis, West Indies, 00 1 869 469 5158/
1326, Fax: 00 1 869 469 5834, and
Member St Kitts & Nevis, Call Date: July
1993 (Middle Temple) Qualifications:
LLB (Hons), BA, LEC, ACIArb

Svoboda *Marek John Julian*
Neklanova 14, 128 00 Prague 2, Czech
Republic, 0042 2 21664401, Fax: 0042
2 21664402, and Member Czech Bar,
Call Date: July 1986 (Lincoln's Inn)
Qualifications: MA (Cantab), MSc
(Lond)

Swain *Miss Hadassah Annette*
Bain & Co, P O Box F-44533, Freeport, Grand Bahama, Bahamas, (242) 352 5971, Fax: (242) 352 6075, and Member Bahamas Bar, Call Date: July 1997 (Gray's Inn) Qualifications: LLB (Lond)

Swami *Miss Sobana*
7 Surin Lane, Singapore 1953, and Member Singapore, Call Date: July 1996 (Middle Temple) Qualifications: LLB (Hons)

Swartz *Bruce Carlton*
Shea & Gardner, 1800 Massachusetts Avenue N.W, Washington DC 20036, United States of America, 202-828 2023, Fax: 202-828 2195, Call Date: July 1997 (Middle Temple) Qualifications: BA, JD (Yale)

Swee *Colin Lay Keong*
24 Jalan Ladang, Palm Grove, Klang, Selangor 41200, Malaysia, Malaysia, 60 3 3326200, and Member Malaysia Bar, Call Date: Nov 1993 (Lincoln's Inn) Qualifications: LLB (Hons, Sheff)

Sweeting *Roy William Mark*
Bahamas, Call Date: Nov 1997 (Lincoln's Inn) Qualifications: LLB (Hons)

Swetenham *Richard Clement*
European Commission, L-2920, Luxembourg, 00 352 4301 32400, Fax: 00 352 4301 33190, Call Date: Nov 1974 (Middle Temple) Qualifications: BA (Oxon)

Sy *Choon Yen*
W Malaysia, Call Date: July 1996 (Inner Temple) Qualifications: LLB (Manchester)

Syed *Yahya*
26 Maria Avenue, Singapore 456757, 241 1883/5338188, Fax: 533 6100, Advocate & Solicitor, Supreme Court, Singapore Commissioner for Oaths and Member Singapore Bar, Call Date: July 1981 (Inner Temple)

Syed Abu Bakar *Miss Sharifah Mazwin*
Malaysia, Call Date: July 1993 (Lincoln's Inn) Qualifications: BA (Hons)

Syed-Mohamed *Miss Sharifah Saeedah*
Khairuddin, Ngiam & Tan, Advocates & Solicitors, Lot 16.03, 16th Floor, Wisma, Nusantara, Jalan Punchak off, Jalan P Ramlee, 50250 Kuala Lumpur, Malaysia, 6 03 2382388/2305081, Fax: 6 03 2301994, and Member Malaysia Bar, Call Date: July 1995 (Gray's Inn) Qualifications: LLB (E.Anglia)

Sykes *Richard John Davies*
Nestle S.A., Avenue Nestle 55, 1800 Vevey, Switzerland, Switzerland, 021 924 3429, Legal Adviser, Call Date: July 1981 (Gray's Inn) Qualifications: BA, LLM

Symeonidou *Miss Eleni*
Cyprus, Call Date: Nov 1997 (Lincoln's Inn) Qualifications: LLB (Hons) (Lond)

Sze *Ge Pek*
Singapore 680354, Assistant Superintendent of Police, Call Date: Nov 1996 (Middle Temple) Qualifications: LLB (Hons) (Lond), Postgraduate PLC

Sze-Ling *Miss Shum*
Singapore 2159, Call Date: Nov 1993 (Inner Temple) Qualifications: LLB, LLM

Szeto *Benjamin*
Singapore, Call Date: July 1997 (Lincoln's Inn) Qualifications: LLB (Hons)

Sziklai *Mrs Siew Fong*
738 S.E. 8th St, Ocala FL 34471, United States of America, (352) 620 8033, Call Date: July 1995 (Middle Temple) Qualifications: LLB (Hons)

Taggart *Patrick Joseph*
Bar Library, Royal Courts of Justice, Chichester Street, Belfast, Northern Ireland, 01232 241523, Fax: 01232 231850, and Member Northern Ireland Bar, Call Date: Mar 1997 (Gray's Inn) Qualifications: LLB

Tai *Cheh Seak*
Malaysia, Call Date: July 1997 (Lincoln's Inn) Qualifications: LLB (Hons) (Lond)

Tait *Ms Arabella Elizabeth Connel Cargill*
Faculty of Advocates, Advocates Library, Parliament House, Edinburgh, Scotland EH1, Scotland, 0131 226 5071, and Member Scottish Bar, Call Date: Oct 1993 (Inner Temple) Qualifications: BA, LLM

Talib *Miss Muna Mohamad*
Singapore 579720, Call Date: Nov 1996 (Lincoln's Inn) Qualifications: LLB (Hons) (Lond)

Tam *Chee Jack*
Rajinder Singh Veriah & Co, Advocates & Solcitors, No 17 & 19 Jalan Tun H S Lee, 50000 Kualal Lumpur, Malaysia, 03 2386899, Fax: 03 2386901, Advocate & Solicitor, and Member Malaya, Call Date: Nov 1997 (Lincoln's Inn) Qualifications: LLB (Hons) (Lond)

Tam *Yue Shing*
Hong Kong, Call Date: Nov 1998 (Middle Temple) Qualifications: B.Eng (Hong Kong)

Tan *Adrian Chong Jin*
Singapore 1027, Call Date: July 1995 (Middle Temple) Qualifications: LLB (Hons)

Tan *Miss Ai Ling Joanna*
Singapore 438354, Call Date: July 1996 (Middle Temple) Qualifications: LLB (Hons) (Kent)

Tan *Miss Ai Tin*
Singapore 789077, Call Date: Nov 1996 (Lincoln's Inn) Qualifications: LLB (Hons) (Lond)

Tan *Miss Alison Geck-Chin*
c/o Procter & Gamble Asia Ltd, 150 Beach Road, 29-00 The Gateway West, Singapore 189720, Singapore 2158, 65 390 5877, Fax: 65 390 5889, Legal Assistant, Trademarks Counsel (Asia) and Member Singapore Bar, Call Date: July 1994 (Lincoln's Inn) Qualifications: BA (Hons)

Tan *Ms Anastasia Pei Pei*
Chew, Tan & Lim, Asia Insurance Building, No 1 China Street, 10200 Penang, West Malaysia, West Malaysia, and Member Malaysia Bar, Call Date: July 1994 (Gray's Inn) Qualifications: LLB (Lond)

Tan *Aylwin Wee En*
45 Trevose Crescent, Singapore 1129, 065 2543513, Fax: 065 6732327, and Member Singapore Bar, Call Date: July 1997 (Middle Temple) Qualifications: BA (Hons) (Kent)

Tan *Bak Leng*
Singapore 535412, Call Date: July 1997 (Lincoln's Inn) Qualifications: LLB (Hons) (Leics)

Tan *Beng Lok Edwin*
Sembawang Marine & Logistics, Ltd, Singapore 160088, 6639244, Legal Counsel, and Member Singapore Bar, Call Date: July 1995 (Middle Temple) Qualifications: LLB (Hons) (Lond)

Tan *Bernard E Wei*
Joseph Tan Jude Benny, 2 Mistri Road, [H]14-00 HMC BUilding, Singapore 460406, (65) 2209388, Fax: (65) 2257827, Legal Assistant, Advocate & Solicitor, and Member Singapore, Call Date: July 1997 (Lincoln's Inn) Qualifications: LLB (Hons)

Tan *Boon Khai*
10 Palm Drive, Singapore 456490, Singapore 456490, 4483600, Justices's Law Clerk, Supreme Court, Singapore, Call Date: July 1996 (Lincoln's Inn) Qualifications: LLB (Hons) (Notts)

Tan *Brian Yang Seng*
Singapore 410639, Call Date: Nov 1996 (Middle Temple) Qualifications: LLB (Hons) (Lond)

Tan *Miss Cheng Cheng*
Malaysia, Call Date: July 1998 (Lincoln's Inn) Qualifications: LLB (Hons)

Tan *Miss Cheng Foong*
Malaysia, Call Date: July 1996 (Middle Temple) Qualifications: LLB (Hons) (Leic)

Tan *Miss Chin Chin*
Malaysia, Call Date: July 1997 (Middle Temple) Qualifications: LLB (Hons) (Wales)

Tan *Chin Tee*
Singapore 2264, Call Date: July 1996
(Middle Temple) Qualifications: LLB
(Hons)(Sheff)

Tan *Choo Teck*
Kington & Tan, Advocates & Solicitors,
Suite 6, 4th Floor, Wisma Ann Koai, 67
Jalan Ampang, Kuala Lumpur 50450,
Malaysia, 03 238 2128, Fax: 03 201
2272, Dato (Malaysian Royal Honour)
and Member Malaysia Bar, Call Date:
Nov 1992 (Lincoln's Inn)
Qualifications: LLB (Hons)(Lond)

Tan *Miss Christine Mai Yean*
Malaysia, Call Date: July 1997
(Lincoln's Inn) Qualifications: LLB
(Hons)(Wales)

Tan *Chuan Thye*
M/S Allen & Gledhill, 36 Robinson Road
[H]18-01, City House, Singapore
068877, Singapore 2057, 225 1611,
Fax: 224 8210, Hon Secretary,
Committee on Legal Education &
Studies, Singapore Academy of Law,
and Member Singapore Bar, Call Date:
July 1990 (Middle Temple)
Qualifications: BA (Oxon)

Tan *Chun Hou*
Malaysia, Call Date: July 1997
(Lincoln's Inn) Qualifications: LLB
(Hons)(Lond)

Tan *Clarence Keng Loon*
Singapore 0512, and Member
Singapore, Call Date: Nov 1995
(Lincoln's Inn) Qualifications: LLB
(Hons) (Leeds)

Tan *Colin Teck-Ee*
Singapore 576193, Call Date: July 1997
(Middle Temple) Qualifications: BA
(Hons)

Tan *Dennis Lip Fong*
80 Raffles Place, [H]25-00, UOB Plaza
1, Singapore 427917, 5356844, Fax:
5351606, and Member Singapore, Call
Date: July 1996 (Middle Temple)
Qualifications: LLB (Hons)(Notts)

Tan *Miss Diana Mei-Ying*
Singapore 1231, Advocate & Solicitor of
Singapore, Call Date: July 1992
(Lincoln's Inn) Qualifications: LLB
(Hons)

Tan *Dominic Dwayne Kok Heng*
9 Penang Road, [H]11-08 Park Mall,
Singapore, 332 9555, Fax: 336 2282,
and Member Singapore Bar, Call Date:
July 1992 (Lincoln's Inn)
Qualifications: LLB (Hons) (Bucks),
LLM (London)

Tan *Miss E-Laine*
Singapore 424224, Call Date: Oct 1998
(Middle Temple) Qualifications: LL.3
(Hons)(Hull)

Tan *Edmund Yen Kuan*
N M Rothschild & Sons Ltd, The
Exchange, 20 Cecil Street, [H]09-00,
Singapore 0104, Malaysia, 65 535
8311, Fax: 65 535 9109, Merchant
Banker, Project Finance, Call Date: Nov
1992 (Middle Temple) Qualifications:
LLB (Hons, Lond), MBA (City)

Tan *Miss Emily Jee Neo*
Malaysia, and Member Malaysia, Call
Date: July 1996 (Lincoln's Inn)
Qualifications: LLB (Hons), BEc
(Hons), MBA (Hons), LLM (Hons)

Tan *Eu Gin*
Singapore 559236, Call Date: July 1996
(Middle Temple) Qualifications: LLB
(Hons)(Hull)

Tan *Freddie Kuok Lin*
Malaysia, Call Date: Nov 1998
(Lincoln's Inn) Qualifications: LLB
(Hons)(LSE)

Tan *Miss Gek Sim*
Singapore 277856, Call Date: July 1998
(Middle Temple) Qualifications: LLB
(Hons)(Warw)

Tan *Hee Liang*
Tan See Swan & Co, Advocates &
Solicitors, No 1 Park Road [H]04-49,
People's Park Complex, Singapore
0105, Singapore 457023, 5351442/
5323265/5344252, Fax: 5333609, and
Member Singapore Bar, Call Date: July
1988 (Inner Temple) Qualifications: B
Soc Sc (Keele), LLM (Singapore)

Tan *Hock Boon David*
Block 718, Hougang Avenue 2,
[H]04-313, 530718 Singapore,
65-2886011, Call Date: Nov 1996
(Gray's Inn) Qualifications: LLB

Tan *Miss Hsiao Ling*
Malaysia, Call Date: July 1996 (Middle
Temple) Qualifications: LLB
(Hons)(Warw)

Tan *Miss Hui Mei*
M/S Drew & Napier, 20 Raffles Place
[H]17-00, Ocean Towers, Singapore
546024, 2803136 (Resid), Fax:
2803958, Legal Assistant, and Member
Singapore Bar, Call Date: July 1995
(Middle Temple) Qualifications: LLB
(Hons)

Tan *Miss Hui Tsing*
Singapore 1027, Call Date: July 1995
(Middle Temple) Qualifications: LLB
(Hons)

Tan *Miss Ivy*
26 Sennett Avenue, S 467034, (S1953)
Singapore, (065) 2448556, Call Date:
July 1997 (Gray's Inn) Qualifications:
LLB

Tan *Miss Jacqueline*
Singapore 288262, Call Date: Nov 1996
(Middle Temple) Qualifications: LLB
(Hons)(Sheff)

Tan *James Chee Hau*
C/O HSBC Investment Bank Asia, Level
15, 1 Q.R.C., Hong kong SAR, Justices'
Law Clerk, Singapore Supreme Court,
and Member Singapore Bar, Call Date:
July 1993 (Middle Temple)
Qualifications: BA (Hons)

Tan *Jonanthan See Leh*
Singapore 425061, Call Date: July 1996
(Lincoln's Inn) Qualifications: LLB
(Hons)(Lond)

Tan *Kee Tay*
Malaysia, Call Date: Nov 1997
(Lincoln's Inn) Qualifications: LLB
(Hons)(Lond)

Tan *Kelvin David Sia Khoon*
Singapore 259281, Call Date: Nov 1996
(Middle Temple) Qualifications: LLB
(Hons)(Hull)

Tan *Kelvin Miang Ser*
180 Tai Keng Gardens, Singapore
535446, Magistrate, Deputy Registrar
and Coroner of The Subordinate Courts
of the Republic of Singapore, Call Date:
July 1996 (Lincoln's Inn)
Qualifications: LLB (Hons)(Leeds),
ACIArb, MSIArb

Tan *Kheng-Guan*
465 Lorong 17/13A, 46400 Petaling
Jaya, Selangor, Malaysia, 03 7573081,
and Member Malaysia, Call Date: Nov
1996 (Middle Temple) Qualifications:
BA (Hons)(Keele)

Tan *Kian Yuap*
Malaysia, and Member Malaysia, Call
Date: July 1996 (Lincoln's Inn)
Qualifications: LLB (Hons)(Lond)

Tan *Kiley Ban Teong*
56 Midlans Drive, Pulau Tikus, 10250
Penang, Malaysia, 604 229 8595, Call
Date: July 1998 (Lincoln's Inn)
Qualifications: LLB (Hons)

Tan *Miss Kim Suan*
Singapore 310001, Call Date: Nov 1996
(Middle Temple) Qualifications: LLB
(Hons)(Lond)

Tan *Kok Siang*
Singapore 1025, and Member
Singapore Bar, Call Date: Apr 1991
(Gray's Inn) Qualifications: LLB,
MSIArb

Tan *Kong Yam*
Kadir, Tan & Ramli, 8th Floor, Sqfuan
Tower, 80 Jalan Ampang, 50450 Kuala
Lumpur, Malaysia, 6 03 2382888, Fax:
6 03 2388431, Advocate & Solicitor
High Court of Malaya and Member
Malaysia Bar, Call Date: July 1996
(Lincoln's Inn) Qualifications: LLB
(Hons), LLM (LSE)

Tan *Kwong Ming Gerald*
Singapore 1335, Call Date: Nov 1994
(Lincoln's Inn) Qualifications: LLB
(Hons)(Lond)

Tan *Lai An*
C/O Tan & Lee, Advocates & Solicitors,
Suite 2.04 2nd Level, Wisma MBF 37c
Jalan Meldrum, 80000 Johor Bahru,
Johor, (607) 2239259, Fax: (607)
2239142, and Member Malaysia Bar,
Call Date: July 1989 (Lincoln's Inn)
Qualifications: LLB (Lond)

Tan *Miss Lai Tee*
Malaysia, Call Date: Nov 1997
(Lincoln's Inn) Qualifications: LLB
(Hons)(Leeds)

Tan *Dr Lauren Guet Lan*
Philips Consumer Communication,
Asia Pacific Pte Ltd, 620A, Lorong 1,
Toa Payoh TP1, Legal Department,
Singapore 1438, (65) 351 7160, Fax:
(65) 256 2694, Regional Legal Counsel,
and Member Singapore Bar, Call Date:
Nov 1993 (Middle Temple)
Qualifications: LLB (Hons), PH.D
(B'ham)

Tan *Miss Lay Keng*
Hong Kong, Call Date: Feb 1994 (Inner
Temple) Qualifications: LLB (Essex)

Tan *Miss Lay Khim*
Singapore 276523, Call Date: July 1996
(Middle Temple) Qualifications: LLB
(Hons)(Bris)

Tan *Leroy Kok Heng*
Singapore 568760, Call Date: Nov 1996
(Middle Temple) Qualifications: LLB
(Hons)

Tan *Miss Lip Sim*
Malaysia, Call Date: July 1997 (Middle
Temple) Qualifications: LLB
(Hons)(Lond)

Tan *Miss Lu Gim*
Allen & Gledhill, 36 Robinson Road
[H]18-01, City House, Singapore 0106,
Singapore 268828, 2251611, Fax:
2254950, and Member Singapore Bar,
Call Date: Nov 1991 (Lincoln's Inn)
Qualifications: BA (Hons) (Kent)

Tan *Lye Huat*
Singapore 460547, Call Date: Nov 1997
(Middle Temple) Qualifications: LLB
(Hons)(Lond)

Tan *Miss Marissa Anne*
Singapore 1543, Call Date: Nov 1998
(Lincoln's Inn) Qualifications: LLB
(Hons)(Sheff)

Tan *Mark Chai Ming*
Singapore 268209, Call Date: Oct 1998
(Middle Temple) Qualifications: LLB
(Hons)(Notts)

Tan *Mark Jin Leong*
Western Australia 6062, LLB
(Hons)(Notts), Call Date: July 1996
(Middle Temple)

Tan *Miss May Yee*
Singapore 439852, Call Date: Nov 1997
(Middle Temple) Qualifications: LLB
(Hons)

Tan *Miss Mei-Yen*
Malaysia, Call Date: July 1995 (Middle
Temple) Qualifications: LLB (Hons)
(Warw)

Tan *Miss Michelle Ai Ling*
Singapore 579036, and Member
Singapore Bar, Call Date: Mar 1997
(Middle Temple) Qualifications: LLB
(Hons)(Bris)

Tan *Ms Michelle Su May*
Singapore 1130, Call Date: July 1995
(Middle Temple) Qualifications: LLB
(Hons)

Tan *Miss Peck Yen*
Malaysia, Call Date: July 1997
(Lincoln's Inn) Qualifications: LLB
(Hons) (Lond)

Tan *Miss Ping Ying*
Malaysia, and Member Malaysia, Call
Date: July 1996 (Inner Temple)
Qualifications: LLB (Wolverhampton),
MA

Tan *Miss Poh Hua*
Malaysia, Call Date: July 1995
(Lincoln's Inn) Qualifications: LLB
(Hons)

Tan *Miss Reina Chui-Lin*
Malaysia, Call Date: Nov 1997 (Gray's
Inn) Qualifications: LLB (Nott'm)

Tan *Richard Seng Chew*
Singapore 590004, and Member
Singapore, Call Date: Nov 1996 (Inner
Temple) Qualifications: LLB (Lond)

Tan *Miss Sandra Mei Yee*
Malaysia, Call Date: Nov 1998
(Lincoln's Inn) Qualifications: LLB
(Hons)(Sheff)

Tan *Miss Selene Ling Ling*
c/o Allen & Gledhill, 36 Robinson Road,
[H]18-01 City House, Singapore
319771, 4207632, Fax: 2241574, and
Member Singapore, Call Date: July
1994 (Middle Temple) Qualifications:
LLB (Hons)(B'ham)

Tan *Miss Sharon Suyin*
Messrs Zaid Ibrahim & Co, 12th Floor,
Menara Bank, Pembangunan, Jalan
Sultan, Ismail, Kuala Lumpur 50250,
Malaysia, 603 292 6688, Fax: 603 292
1638, Legal Assistant, and Member
Malaysia, Call Date: July 1996
(Lincoln's Inn) Qualifications: LLB
(Hons)(Lond)

Tan *Miss Sheh-Lynn*
Malaysia, and Member Malaysia Bar,
Call Date: July 1991 (Middle Temple)
Qualifications: LLB (Hons) (Wales)

Tan *Miss Sherain Ai Seok*
c/o Winston Chen & Partners, 5
Shenton Way, [H]31-01 UIC Building,
Singapore 538970, (65) 220 6888, Fax:
(65) 223 1736, Legal Assistant, and
Member Singapore, Call Date: Mar
1997 (Lincoln's Inn) Qualifications:
LLB (Hons)(Lond)

Tan *Miss Siew Siew*
Malaysia, and Member Malaysian Bar,
Call Date: July 1997 (Gray's Inn)
Qualifications: LLB (Bris)

Tan *Miss Siew Wai*
Singapore 1027, and Member
Singapore Bar, Call Date: July 1992
(Lincoln's Inn) Qualifications: LLB
(Hons) (Bucks)

Tan *Miss Siew Yung*
Malaysia, Call Date: July 1997
(Lincoln's Inn) Qualifications: LLB
(Hons)

Tan *Sin Oon*
Supreme Court of Singapore, St
Andrews Road, Singapore 178957,
Singapore 048692, 65-5320151, Fax:
65-5323101, Attorney, Formerley a
Justices' Law Clerk at the Supreme
Court of Singapore and Member
Singapore Bar, Call Date: July 1995
(Middle Temple) Qualifications: LLB
(Hons) (Bris)

Tan *Miss Sin Yee*
Malaysia, Call Date: Oct 1998
(Lincoln's Inn) Qualifications: LLB
(Hons)(Notts)

Tan *Miss Soek Phee*
West Malaysia, Call Date: July 1996
(Middle Temple) Qualifications: LLB
(Hons) (Wales)

Tan *Miss Spring*
Singapore 458829, Call Date: Nov 1998
(Middle Temple) Qualifications: LLB
(Hons)(Lond)

Tan *Stanley Richard Sia Kong*
Singapore 269497, Call Date: July 1995
(Inner Temple) Qualifications: LLB

Tan *Su Shong Shawn*
Singapore, Call Date: Nov 1998
(Lincoln's Inn) Qualifications: LLB
(Hons)(Sheff)

Tan *Miss Sue Ann*
Malaysia, Call Date: July 1997
(Lincoln's Inn) Qualifications:
LLB(Hons)(Wales)

Tan *Ms Sui Lin*
Singapore 1027, and Member
Singapore Bar, Call Date: July 1991
(Middle Temple) Qualifications: BA
(Hons) (Cambs)

Tan *Miss Suzanne Sie Gek*
Singapore, Call Date: Nov 1996
(Lincoln's Inn) Qualifications: LLB
(Hons)(Bucks)

Tan *Miss Swee Lin Corrine*
Brunei, Call Date: July 1997 (Gray's
Inn) Qualifications: LLB (Bristol)

Tan *Miss Tammy*
Singapore 248470, Call Date: July 1996
(Middle Temple) Qualifications: LLB
(Hons)(Lond)

Tan *Teck Kiong*
Malaysia, Call Date: Nov 1997
(Lincoln's Inn) Qualifications: LLB
(Hons) (Thames.V)

Tan *Teng Ta Benedict*
Singapore 760351, Call Date: July 1997
(Middle Temple) Qualifications: LLB
(Hons)

Tan *Terence Li-Chern*
Messrs Wong Partnership, 80 Raffles
Place, [H] 58-01 UOB Plaza 1,
Singapore 0923, (65) 539 7503, Fax:
(65) 532 5722, and Member Singapore
Bar, Call Date: July 1995 (Inner
Temple) Qualifications: LLB (Kent)

Tan *Tian Luh*
11 Collyer Quay, [H] 12-01 The Arcade,
Singapore 597159, and Member
Singapore Bar, Call Date: July 1996
(Lincoln's Inn) Qualifications: LLB
(Hons) (B'ham)

Tan *Tuan Wee*
Singapore 0208, Call Date: Nov 1995
(Middle Temple) Qualifications: LLB
(Hons)

Tan *Miss Valerie Whei Tet*
Singapore 1026, Call Date: July 1995
(Middle Temple) Qualifications: BA
(Hons)

Tan *Miss Wei Mann Germaine*
Malaysia, Call Date: Nov 1997
(Lincoln's Inn) Qualifications: LLB
(Hons)

Tan *Miss Wei-Lyn*
Singapore 1027, Call Date: July 1995
(Middle Temple) Qualifications: LLB
(Hons)

Tan *Winston Kheng Huang*
Malaysia, Call Date: July 1997
(Lincoln's Inn) Qualifications: LLB
(Hons)

Tan *Yew Hwee*
Singapore 560156, Call Date: Nov 1997
(Middle Temple) Qualifications:
B.Soc.Sc (Hons), (Singapore), LLB,
(Lond)

Tan *Yew Teck*
Singapore 460045, Call Date: Mar 1998
(Gray's Inn) Qualifications: LLB (Lond)

Tan *Miss Ying Wee*
Singapore 1543, Call Date: July 1995
(Middle Temple) Qualifications: LLB
(Hons)

Tang *Miss Ai Leen*
Malaysia, Call Date: Mar 1998 (Middle
Temple) Qualifications: LLB
(Hons) (B'ham)

Tang *Alvin Wye Keet*
Malaysia, Call Date: Oct 1998
(Lincoln's Inn) Qualifications: LLB
(Hons) (Leic)

Tang *Edmund Ming-Wai*
Hong Kong, Call Date: Nov 1994 (Gray's
Inn) Qualifications: LLB (Lond)

Tang *Ms Fong Har*
Hong Kong, Advocate & Solicitor of the
Supreme Court of Singapore and
Member Singapore Bar, Call Date: July
1990 (Inner Temple) Qualifications:
LLB (Hons) Singapore

Tang *Jay Son*
Malaysia, and Member Malaysia, Call
Date: July 1997 (Lincoln's Inn)
Qualifications: LLB (Hons) (Lond)

Tang *Kwong Leung*
Hong Kong, and Member Hong Kong
Bar, Call Date: Feb 1992 (Gray's Inn)
Qualifications: B.Soc.Sc (Hong Kong),
MSW (Hong Kong), MSc (LSE),LLB
(Lond), LLM (Cantab), Ph.D (Berkley)

Tang *Michael Vee Mun*
Malaysia, Advocate & Solicitor, and
Member Malaysia, Call Date: July 1995
(Lincoln's Inn) Qualifications: LLB
(Hons)

Tang *Quin Choy*
Singapore 210043, Call Date: July 1997
(Middle Temple) Qualifications: LLB
(Hons) (Lond)

Tang *Ms Suet Yean*
Malaysia, and Member Malaysia, Call
Date: July 1993 (Lincoln's Inn)
Qualifications: LLB (Hons)

Tangavellu *Resebalingam*
Malaysia, Call Date: July 1995
(Lincoln's Inn) Qualifications: LLB
(Hons)

Taposh *Sheikh Fazle Noor*
Bangladesh, Call Date: Nov 1997
(Lincoln's Inn) Qualifications: LLB
(Hons)

Tay *Ms April Glenys*
Singapore 557206, and Member
Singapore Bar, Call Date: Nov 1996
(Lincoln's Inn) Qualifications: LLB
(Hons) (Lond)

Tay *Miss Elaine Ling Yan*
Singapore 650250, Call Date: July 1997
(Middle Temple) Qualifications: LLB
(Hons)

Tay *Francis Chien Thuan*
Deutsche Bank AG, 6 Shenton Way
[H] 13-00, Singapore 1129, 65
4236023, Fax: 65 2257825, Legal
Counsel Asia, and Member Singapore,
Call Date: Oct 1994 (Middle Temple)
Qualifications: LLB (Hons) (Kent)

Tay *Miss Hwee Hua*
Singapore 0923, and Member
Singapore Bar, Call Date: Nov 1995
(Middle Temple) Qualifications: LLB
(Lond)

Tay *Miss Jin Keng*
Singapore 429925, Call Date: Nov 1995
(Middle Temple) Qualifications: LLB
(Hons) (Lond)

Tay *Lai Eng*
Malaysia, Call Date: Nov 1996
(Lincoln's Inn) Qualifications: LLB
(Hons)

Tay *Miss Li Shing*
789997 Singapore, Call Date: July 1997
(Gray's Inn) Qualifications: LLB (Bris)

Tay *Miss Sock Kheng*
Singapore 428648, Call Date: July 1996
(Lincoln's Inn) Qualifications: LLB
(Hons) (Lond)

Tay *Miss Yien Ling Daisy*
Singapore 1955, Call Date: July 1994
(Middle Temple) Qualifications: LLB
(Hons) (Lond)

Tay *Yu Jin*
Call Date: Oct 1998 (Gray's Inn)
Qualifications: LLB, LLM (Lond)

Taye *Miss Lynette Wei Ching*
Malaysia, Call Date: July 1997
(Lincoln's Inn) Qualifications: LLB
(Hons) (Nott'm)

Taylor *Ms Wendy Rutledge*
Risk Enterprise Management Ltd, 59
Maiden Lane, New York, New York
10038, United States of America, 212
5306944, Fax: 212 5306997, Associate
Reinsurance Counsel, and Member
State of New Jersey Bar, Call Date: July
1987 (Lincoln's Inn) Qualifications:
BA, H.Dip. Pers.Man, Dip Law, JD

Taylor *Winston Donald*
Isle of Man, Call Date: Oct 1998
(Middle Temple) Qualifications: CPE

Taylor-Carroll De Mueller *Mrs Athena
Robina*
2904 Viceroy Avenue, Forestville,
Maryland 20747-3215, General
Counsel, Action on Smoking & Health,
Washington D.C.1984-1996; Trustee
Emirita 1997, and Member US Sup Ct,
US Ct of App(DC Cir),US Dist Ct (DC),
Dist of Columbia Ct of Appeals, Call
Date: July 1952 (Lincoln's Inn)
Qualifications: MA,LLB (Cantab), JD,
LLM (Miami)

Tee *Miss Clare Antoinette*
Channel Islands, and Member
Guernsey Bar, Call Date: Nov 1995
(Inner Temple) Qualifications: LLB
(Manc)

Tee *Miss Dawn Pei Sze*
Singapore 0410, Call Date: July 1996
(Lincoln's Inn) Qualifications: LLB
(Hons) (Notts)

Tee *Miss En Peng*
Malaysia, Call Date: July 1997
(Lincoln's Inn) Qualifications: LLB
(Hons) (Lond)

Tee *Ling Zhi*
Singapore, Call Date: Nov 1997
(Lincoln's Inn) Qualifications: LLB
(Hons)

Teh *Chin Lam*
Malaysia, Call Date: July 1998
(Lincoln's Inn) Qualifications: LLB
(Hons) (Leeds)

Teh *Miss Ee-Von*
Singapore 808804, Call Date: July 1997
(Middle Temple) Qualifications: LLB
(Hons)(Leics)

Teh *Miss Hong Koon*
B C Teh & Yeoh, Advocates & Solicitors,
Unit 3 & 4, 4th & 5th Floor, Canton
Square, 56 Cantonment Road, 10250
Penang, Malaysia, 00 604 228 0133,
Fax: 00 604 286 0740, and Member
Malaysian, Call Date: Nov 1997
(Lincoln's Inn) Qualifications: LLB
(Hons)(E.Lond)

Teh *John Teong Beng*
Malaysia, Call Date: Nov 1995 (Middle
Temple) Qualifications: LLB
(Hons)(Wales)

Teh *Ms Julie Chooi Gan*
Dorairaj, Low & Teh, Wisman AMGM,
1st Floor, No 57 Jalan Hang Lekiu,
50100 Kuala Lumpur, Malaysia, 03
2011136, Fax: 03 2010113, Partner,
and Member Malaysia Bar, Call Date:
Nov 1992 (Gray's Inn) Qualifications:
LLB (Lond)

Teh *Khang Suon*
c/o Azalina Chan & Chia, Advocates &
Solicitors, Lot 716, 7th Floor, Wisma,
Cosway, 88 Jalan Raja Chulan, 50200
Kuala Lumpur, Malaysia, 603 2488625,
Fax: 603 2411913, Legal Assistant
(Practising Lawyer), Call Date: Nov
1996 (Gray's Inn) Qualifications: LLB
(Sheff)

Teh *Lawrence Kee Wee*
C/O Rodyk & Davidson, 9 Raffles Place,
[H]55-00 Republic Plaza, Singapore
048619, 65 225 2626, Fax: 65 225
1838, and Member Singapore Bar, Call
Date: Nov 1992 (Inner Temple)
Qualifications: LLB (Lond)

Teh *Miss Wee Tee*
Malaysia, Call Date: July 1995 (Middle
Temple) Qualifications: LLB (Hons)
(Wales)

Teh *Miss Yuen Ting*
Singapore 436882, Call Date: July 1997
(Lincoln's Inn) Qualifications: LLB
(Hons)(Nott'm)

Telemaque *Marc Timothy*
Bermuda, Call Date: May 1993 (Gray's
Inn) Qualifications: LLB
(Buckinghamshi)

Teng *Hin Fatt*
Block 128, Lorong Ah Soo, [H]12-314,
Singapore 1953, Singapore 1953, Call
Date: Nov 1993 (Lincoln's Inn)
Qualifications: LLB (Hons, Lond)

Teng *Miss Joanna*
Salina, Lim Kim Chuan & Co, Advocates
& Solciters, No 28-c Lorong Abu Siti,
10400 Penang, Malaysia, 228 2089,
Fax: 228 2093, Legal Assistant, and
Member Malaysia, Call Date: July 1995
(Lincoln's Inn) Qualifications: LLB
(Hons)

Tengara *Miss Mestika*
11 Barker Road, 2511685, Assistant
Manager (Property), Call Date: Nov
1996 (Lincoln's Inn) Qualifications:
LLB (Hons)(Kent)

Tengku Ismail *Miss Tengku Ida Adura*
Lloyd Fernando & Razak, Suite 1203,
12th Floor, Wisma Hangsam, No 1
Jalan Hang Lekir, 50000 Kuala
Lumpur, Malaysia, 603 2308036, Fax:
603 2320312, Legal Assistant (Advocate
& Solicitor), and Member High Court of
Malaya, Call Date: July 1996 (Lincoln's
Inn) Qualifications: LLB (Hons)(Notts)

Teo *Miss Bee Leay*
99 Sunset Way, Singapore 2159,
Singapore 2159, 4691221, Fax:
4663583, and Member New York State
Bar, Call Date: July 1993 (Middle
Temple) Qualifications: LLB (Hons,
Kent), LLM (Boston, USA)

Teo *Eng Thye*
Singapore 592001, Call Date: Nov 1998
(Middle Temple) Qualifications: LLB
(Hons)(Lond), LLM (Wolves)

Teo *Eu Jin Nicholas*
Singapore 787322, Call Date: July 1996
(Middle Temple) Qualifications: LLB
(Hons)(Leic)

Teo *Eugene Weng Kuan*
Supreme Court, City Hall, St Andrews
Road, Singapore 535423, Assistant
Registrar, Call Date: July 1995 (Middle
Temple) Qualifications: LLB (Hons)
(Hull)

Teo *Francis Teng Siu*
Singapore 456974, Call Date: Nov 1996
(Lincoln's Inn) Qualifications: BSc,
ARICS, LLB (Hons)(Lond)

Teo *Miss Josephine Siew Ing*
Malaysia, Call Date: July 1995 (Middle
Temple) Qualifications: LLB (Hons)
(Hull)

Teo *Miss Yi-Ling*
c/o 111 North Bridge Road, [H]22-01,
Peninsula Plaza, Singapore 1545, and
Member Singapore, Call Date: Nov
1996 (Middle Temple) Qualifications:
LLB (Hons)(L'pool)

Teoh *Ms Gim See*
Malaysia, Call Date: Nov 1996
(Lincoln's Inn) Qualifications: BA
(Hons)(E.Anglia)

Tey *Tsun Hang*
Malaysia, Call Date: July 1995 (Gray's
Inn) Qualifications: LLB

Thacker *Charles Malcom Belford*
Messrs Vibert & Valpy, Advocates, 8
Duhamel Place, St Helier, Jersey
JE2 4XA, 0534 888666, Fax: 0534
888555, Notary Public, and Member
Jersey Bar, Call Date: Nov 1970
(Lincoln's Inn) Qualifications: MA
(Hons)

Thai *Jiin Peir*
No 46B Lorong Ismail, 81000 Kulai,
Johor, Malaysia, 07 6624732/3/
6625057, Fax: 07 6624639, and
Member Malaysia Bar, Call Date: Nov
1993 (Lincoln's Inn) Qualifications:
LLB (Hons)

Thakar *Miss Rina Rajendra*
Kenya, Call Date: July 1997 (Gray's
Inn) Qualifications: LLB (Warwick)

Tham *Miss Melissa Lyn-li*
Singapore 1646, Call Date: July 1995
(Middle Temple) Qualifications: LLB
(Hons)

Tham *Soong Meng Edwin*
Allen & Overy Legal Services, Moscow,
Dmitrovskiy Pereulok, 9, 103031
Moscow, Singapore 1027, 7 501 725
7900, Fax: 7 501 725 7949, Associate,
and Member New York Bar, Call Date:
July 1989 (Middle Temple)
Qualifications: LLB [Nott'm]

Tham *Miss Swee Hiong*
Overseas Chinese Banking Corp, 65
Chulia Street, Singapore 270009,
5357222/5302929, Fax: 5340559,
Senior Planner, Call Date: July 1995
(Middle Temple) Qualifications: LLB
(Hons)

Thampuran *Miss Sandhia*
Singapore 2056, and Member
Singapore Bar, Call Date: July 1995
(Middle Temple) Qualifications: LLB
(Hons)

The *Miss Diana Hui Ling*
20 Malacca Street, [H]08-00, Malacca
Centre, Singapore 787409, (065)
4566501/2253838, Fax: (065)
5335388, Legal Assistant Advocate &
Solictor, and Member Singapore, Call
Date: July 1996 (Middle Temple)
Qualifications: LLB (Hons)(Bris)

Theodorides *Miss Melita-Despina*
Cyprus, Call Date: Mar 1997 (Lincoln's
Inn) Qualifications: LLB (Leics)

Theseira *Joseph Dominic*
Palakrishnan & Partners, Advocates &
Solicitors, 1 Colombo Court, [H]07-13/
14/15a, Republic of Singapore,
3382294, Fax: 3391400, and Member
Singapore Bar, Call Date: Nov 1991
(Middle Temple) Qualifications: LLB
(Hons) (Lond)

Thiagarajah *Miss Thanuja*
Singapore 0314, Call Date: July 1996
(Lincoln's Inn) Qualifications: LLB
(Hons)(Lond)

Thiagarajan *Anand*
Anand and Bala Partnership, No 1
North Bridge Road, [H]14-01 High
Street Centre, Singapore 1953, 65 333
4424, Fax: 65 334 2344, Court
Mediator, and Member Singapore Bar,
Call Date: July 1995 (Lincoln's Inn)
Qualifications: LLB (Hons)

Thinathayalan *Suppiah*
Singapore 141168, and Member
Singapore, Call Date: July 1996 (Inner
Temple) Qualifications: LLB,LLM
(Lond)

Thio *Miss Jean Puay Jin*
Singapore 249262, Call Date: July 1997
(Lincoln's Inn) Qualifications: LLB
(Hons)(Lond)

Thirumaney *Miss Manimala*
Malaysia, Call Date: Nov 1996
(Lincoln's Inn) Qualifications: LLB
(Hons)

Thng *Miss Hwei Lin*
Singapore 2260, Call Date: July 1993
(Middle Temple) Qualifications: LLB
(Hons)

Thomas *Andreas*
Cyprus, Call Date: Mar 1999 (Gray's
Inn) Qualifications: BSc (Lond)

Thomas *Ms Cheryl Diane*
Bar Library, The Royal Courts of
Justice, Chichester Street, Belfast
BT9 6DW, 01232 224269, and Member
Northern Ireland, Call Date: Oct 1997
(Inner Temple) Qualifications: LLB
(Hull)

Thomas *Christopher James*
Rue Franz Merjay 97, B-1050
Bruxelles, Referendaire, Court of First
Instance of the European
Communities, Call Date: Oct 1990
(Middle Temple) Qualifications: MA
(Cantab), LLM (College of , Europe)

Thomas *John*
34B Bayshore Road, The Bayshore,
Tower 2b [H]18-02, Singapore 469976,
65-2452040, Law Society of Singapore,
Call Date: Oct 1993 (Gray's Inn)
Qualifications: BA, B.Soc.Sci (Hons),
(Singapore), LLB, (Manch)

Thompson *Mrs Diana Elizabeth*
La Hure, Rue des Cambrees, Torteral,
Guerney GY8 0LD, Channel Islands,
0481 65831, Fax: 0481 66160, and
Member Royal Court of Guernsey, Call
Date: Nov 1990 (Inner Temple)
Qualifications: LLB

Thompson *Gilbert Anselm*
McKinney, Bancroft & Hughes, P.O. Box
F-40437, Freeport, Bahamas, (242)
352 7425-7, Fax: (242) 352 7214, and
Member Bahamas Bar (September
1996), Call Date: July 1996 (Gray's
Inn) Qualifications: BA (Canada), LLB
(Buck)

Thompson *James Kwasi*
James R Thompson & Company, Suite
31A, Kipling Building, P.O.Box F 42912,
Freeport, GB, Bahamas, Bahamas,
(242) 352 7451 2, Fax: (242) 352
7453, Associate Attorney, and Member
Bahamas, Call Date: July 1997 (Middle
Temple) Qualifications: LLB (Hons)

Thompson *John David*
Ballyrawer House, Carrowdore, Co
Down BT22 2HZ, Northern Ireland,
01247 861478, Fax: 01247 861095,
Inspector into suspected insider
dealing under Financial Services Act
1986, QC (Northern Ireland) and
Member Northern Ireland Bar Republic
of Ireland Bar, Call Date: Nov 1992
(Gray's Inn) Qualifications: LLB
(Belfast)

Thompson *Miss Lillian Amorella
Elizabeth*
42 Rockford Ave, Daly City, CA 94015,
U.S.A., United States of America, Call
Date: Nov 1993 (Inner Temple)
Qualifications: LLB (Lond)

Thomson *James Smith*
Gilt Chambers, Room 1001, Far East
Finance Centre, 16 Harcourt Road,
Central Hong Kong, Hong Kong, 866
8233, Fax: 866 3932, and Member
Hong Kong Bar, Call Date: July 1983
(Lincoln's Inn) Qualifications: BA
(Kent)

Thomson *Neil Clarke*
Des Voeux Chambers, 10/F Bank of
East Asia Bldg, 10 Des Voeux Road,
Central, Hong Hong, Hong Kong, 2526
3071, Fax: 2810 5287, and Member
Hong Kong Bar, Call Date: Nov 1994
(Gray's Inn) Qualifications: BA, LLM,
FTIHK, ACIArb

Thong *Ms Jessie Yuen Siew*
Dave, Shahn, Patel & Jim, 158 Cecil
Street, [H]09-03, Singapore 466760,
3230030, Fax: 3230032, Partner, and
Member Singapore Bar, Call Date: Apr
1991 (Gray's Inn) Qualifications: BA,
LLM

Tiah *Miss Ee Laine*
Lee Hishammuddin, Advocates &
Solicitors, 16th Floor, Wisma HLA,
50200 Kuala Lumpur, Canada, 03
2011681, Fax: 03 2011714, Advocate &
Solcitor, and Member Malaysia, Call
Date: July 1996 (Middle Temple)
Qualifications: LLB (Hons)(Kent)

Tiang *Michael Ming Tee*
Malaysia, Call Date: July 1997 (Middle
Temple) Qualifications: LLB
(Hons)(Wales)

Tibbo *Miss Heather Dorothy*
Messrs Ogier & Le Masurier, P O Box
404, Whiteley Chambers, Don Street, St
Helier, Jersey JE4 9WG, Channel
Islands, 01534 504000, Fax: 01534
35328, Associate, and Member
Advocate of the Royal Court of Jersey,
Call Date: Nov 1989 (Middle Temple)
Qualifications: LLB

Timms *Neil Richard Frederick Charles*
Maples & Calder, PO Box 309, George
Town, Grand Cayman, 001 809949
8066, Fax: 001 809949 8080, and
Member Cayman Bar, Call Date: Nov
1974 (Inner Temple) Qualifications:
MA (Cantab)

Timothis *Miss Alison*
Cyprus, Call Date: Nov 1995 (Lincoln's
Inn) Qualifications: LLB (Hons)

Timothy *Miss Sonia Agnes*
P.O.Box N3007, Bahamas, (242) 322
1141, Fax: (242) 356 9277, Crown
Counsel Commonwealth of the
Bahamas, and Member Bahamas Bar,
Call Date: July 1996 (Lincoln's Inn)
Qualifications: LLB (Hons)

Ting *Ping Kiong*
Malaysia, Call Date: Nov 1998 (Middle
Temple) Qualifications: LLB
(Hons)(Warw)

Ting *Shu Kiong*
Malaysia, Call Date: July 1997
(Lincoln's Inn) Qualifications: LLB
(Hons)(Leeds)

Ting *Shu Leong*
Messrs Jayasuriya Kah & Co, Room 207,
2nd Floor, Wisma Sabah, P.O.Box
11350, 88815 Kota Kinabalu, Sabah,
Malaysia, 088 242311 (W)/ 211742
(H), Fax: 088 231250, Legal Adviser,
and Member Sabah, Call Date: July
1995 (Lincoln's Inn) Qualifications:
LLB (Hons)

Ting *Ms Sui Ing*
Malaysia, Call Date: July 1996
(Lincoln's Inn) Qualifications: LLB
(Hons)

Tiong *Hok Chiun*
Malaysia, and Member Advocate of the
High Court in Sabah & Sarawak,
Malaysia, Call Date: July 1996
(Lincoln's Inn) Qualifications: LLB
(Hons)(Leeds)

Tiwari *Rama Shankar*
Singapore 427954, Call Date: July 1998
(Middle Temple) Qualifications: LLB
(Hons)

Tiwary *Miss Anuradha*
Singapore 1953, Call Date: July 1996
(Lincoln's Inn) Qualifications: LLB
(Hons) (Lond)

Tobias *Douglas Guedella*
South Africa, South Africa 031 301
1196, Fax: South Africa 031 301 2138,
Barrister of South Africa, Call Date: July
1991 (Middle Temple) Qualifications:
B Com (Cape Town), Dip Juris
(Witwaters, -rand), LLB (Natal), LLM
(Natal)

Todd *Arnold James III*
Bermuda, Call Date: Mar 1998 (Gray's
Inn) Qualifications: BA (Ontario), LLB
(Lond)

Toh *Miss Beng Suan*
Malaysia, Call Date: July 1995
(Lincoln's Inn) Qualifications: LLB
(Hons)

Toh *Lean Seng*
Malaysia, Call Date: July 1997
(Lincoln's Inn) Qualifications: LLB
(Hons) (Lond)

F

Toh *Miss May Ching Jenny*
Messrs Toh Chin & Co, Advocates &
Solicitors, No 21, 1st Floor, Jalan Dato,
Abdul Rahman, 70000 Seremban,
N.Sembilan, Malaysia, (06) 7635058/
5059, Fax: (06) 7624308, and Member
Malaysia, Call Date: Oct 1996
(Lincoln's Inn) Qualifications: LLB
(Hons)(Leic)

Toh *Miss Su Fen*
Singapore 348670, Call Date: July 1996
(Lincoln's Inn) Qualifications: LLB
(Hons)(Lond)

Tok *Miss Julie Chwee Hwei*
Singapore 0314, Call Date: July 1995
(Lincoln's Inn) Qualifications: LLB
(Hons)

Tokunbo *Khamisi Mawuli*
Attorney General's Chambers, Global
House, 43 Church Street, Hamilton
5-24, 809 292 2463, Fax: 809 292
3608, Principal Crown Counsel, Call
Date: Nov 1988 (Inner Temple)
Qualifications: BA (Ohio), LLB (Lond)

Tolia *Miss Dina Arun*
East Africa, Call Date: July 1996
(Lincoln's Inn) Qualifications: BA
(Hons)(Warw)

Tong *Mrs Ah Pooi*
Fin d'Elez, 1261 Le Muids, (022) 366
4606, Fax: (022) 366 4606, Call Date:
Nov 1988 (Lincoln's Inn)
Qualifications: LLB (Lond)

Tong *Kington Kum Loong*
Suite 6, 4th Floor, Wisma Ann Koai, 67
Jalan Ampang, 50450 Kuala Lumpur,
West Malaysia, 03-2382128, Fax:
03-2012272, Partner, and Member
Malaysian Bar, Call Date: July 1992
(Gray's Inn) Qualifications: LLB (Lond)

Tong *Raymond Wei Min*
C/O Shook Lin & Bok, 1 Robinson
Road, [H]18-00 A1A Tower, Singapore
1024, 65-4394895, Fax: 65-5358577,
and Member Singapore Bar, Call Date:
Nov 1991 (Middle Temple)
Qualifications: LLB Hons (Nott'm)

Torode *Mark Andrew*
Channel Islands, Call Date: Oct 1995
(Inner Temple) Qualifications: LLB
(Sussex)

Torrens *Barry Ian*
Call Date: Mar 1999 (Lincoln's Inn)
Qualifications: BA (Hons)(Edinburgh)

Touche Arends *Mrs Susan Ruth*
Steraloids Inc, P O Box 689, Newport,
Rhode Island 02840, 02840 USA, 401
848 5422, Fax: 401 848 5638, Call
Date: Nov 1991 (Gray's Inn)
Qualifications: BFA (Canada), Dip in,
Law, Professional, Certification ,
(Education)

Tracey *Ms Gerardine Anne*
Northern Ireland, Call Date: Oct 1992
(Lincoln's Inn) Qualifications:
LLB(Hons)

Trenado *Dairon Francis*
Gibraltar, Call Date: Nov 1998 (Middle
Temple) Qualifications: LLB
(Hons)(Greenwich

Triay *Louis Bernard*
Louis W Triay & Partners, Suite C, 2nd
Floor, Regal House, Queensway, 00 350
79423, Fax: 00 350 71405, and
Member Gibraltar Bar, Call Date: July
1989 (Middle Temple) Qualifications:
LLB [Lond]

Tsang *David Kwok Kei*
Des Voeux Chambers, 10/F Bank of
East Asia Bldg, 10 Des Voeux Road
Central, Hong Kong, Hong Kong, (852)
2526 3071, Fax: (852) 2810 5287, and
Member Hong Kong Bar Attorney at
Law of the Peoples Republic of China,
Call Date: July 1994 (Middle Temple)
Qualifications: BSc(Hons)(Hong Kong),
CPE (Manc), FRICS, ACIArb

Tsang *Miss Jennifer Chiu Chun*
1501 Two Pacific Place, 88 Queensway,
Hong Kong, Hong Kong, (852) 2840
1130, Fax: (852) 2810 0612, and
Member Hong Kong Bar, Call Date: July
1994 (Middle Temple) Qualifications:
LLB (Hons)(Bris)

Tsang *Ms Ka Lai*
Hong Kong, Call Date: Nov 1997 (Inner
Temple) Qualifications: BA (Hong
Kong), LLB (Lond)

Tsang *Siu Wah*
Mei Foo Sun Chuen, 99c Broadway, 6/
F, Kowloon, (852) 2378 6297, Fax:
(852) 2716 1309, and Member
Ontario, Call Date: Nov 1988 (Middle
Temple) Qualifications: LLB (Lond)

Tse *Hayson Ka Sze*
Hong Kong Government, Department of
Justice, Queensway Government Office,
Queensway, Hong Kong, Hong Kong,
2867 2378, Government Counsel, and
Member Hong Kong Bar, Call Date: July
1995 (Lincoln's Inn) Qualifications:
LLB (Hons), Dip Chinese Law

Tse *Sammy Lai*
Hong Kong, Member of the Hong Kong
Bar Association, Call Date: Nov 1997
(Middle Temple) Qualifications: LLB
(Hons)

Tselingas *Charalambos Christophorou*
Cyprus, Call Date: Nov 1997 (Lincoln's
Inn) Qualifications: LLB (Hons)(Leics)

Tsirides *Alexandros*
Panavides Building, 2nd Floor, Grivas
Digens Str, Limassol 3305, P.O.Box
56250, Cyprus, 00 357 5 365090, Fax:
00 357 5 359772, and Member Cyprus,
Call Date: Nov 1997 (Lincoln's Inn)
Qualifications: LLB (Hons), llm (Hons)

Tsui *Chi Keung Wilfred*
Hong Kong, Call Date: May 1996
(Gray's Inn) Qualifications: BSc
(Lond), MBA (Hong Kong), MHA(New
South Wales)

Tsui *Cho Man*
Hong Kong, Call Date: Mar 1998
(Middle Temple) Qualifications: BSc
(Hons)(HongKong)

Tsui *Chung Man*
Hong Kong, Call Date: July 1998
(Middle Temple) Qualifications: B.Eng
(Hons) (Lond)

Tuite *Michael Donald*
The Law Library, The Four Courts, Inns
Quay, Dublin 7, Ireland, 00 353 1
8174792, Fax: 00 353 1 8724901,
Barrister of Ireland and Member
Ireland Bar New York Bar Littman
Chambers, 12 Gray's Inn Square,
London, WC1R 5JP, Call Date: Nov 1996
(Lincoln's Inn) Qualifications: BCL
(Dublin), LLM (Cantab)

Tung *Dr Wai Kit*
Hong Kong, M.B.B.S.(Hong Kong), and
Member Hong Kong Bar, Call Date: July
1992 (Gray's Inn) Qualifications:
M.B.BS, LLB (Lond), FRCS
(Edinburgh)

Tung *Yau Ming*
James R Knowles (Hong Kong)Ltd,
1001-3 Wing On Centre, 111
Connaught Road Central, Hong Kong,
(852) 25422818, Fax: (852) 25414648,
Director, Chartered Quantity Surveyor
and Member Hong Kong Bar, Call Date:
July 1992 (Middle Temple)
Qualifications: BSc (QS) (Hons), LLM,
ARICS, AHKIS, ACIArb, MA Cost E

Turner *Miss Amber Nicole*
Gibraltar, Call Date: Nov 1998 (Middle
Temple) Qualifications: BSc (Hons),
Dip Law

Turner *Marcus Philip Robert*
Roadrunner International BV, Bijdorp
2, 1181 MZ, Amsterdam, + + 31 20
65 66 670, Fax: + + 31 20 64 06 126,
Head of Legal Affairs, Amsterdam based
Record & Music Publishing Co, Call
Date: Nov 1991 (Middle Temple)
Qualifications: LLB Hons (Lond)

Typographou *Martinos*
Cyprus, Call Date: Nov 1998 (Gray's
Inn) Qualifications: LLB (Hull)

Uddin *Syed Afzal Hasan*
Syed Ishtiaq Ahmed e'Associate, Walson
Towers (First Floor), 21-23 Kazi Nazrul
Islam Ave, Dhaka, (00) 880 2 966
9878, Fax: (00) 880 2 966 5354, Call
Date: Mar 1996 (Lincoln's Inn)
Qualifications: LLB (Hons)

Ullaganathan *Krishnasamy Velu Archary*
Singapore 1027, Call Date: July 1993
(Lincoln's Inn) Qualifications: LLB
(Hons)

Umar *Miss Hajh Sarimah Haji*
Abrahams, Davidson & Co, Room 516,
5th Floor Plaza, Athirah, Jln Kubah
Makan, Diraja, B.S.B. 2682, Brunei,
Brunei, Legal Assistant, Call Date: Nov
1993 (Gray's Inn) Qualifications: LLB

F

Underwood *Geoffrey Edward*
Sixth Floor, Wentworth Selborne
Chambers, 180 Phillip Street, Sydney
NSW 2000, Australia, (0011) 612 9235
0140, Fax: (0011) 612 9221 5604,
Former Solicitor and Member Victoria
Bar, Queensland Bar, Northern
Territory Bar Australian Capital
Territory Bar, Western Australia Bar
New South Wales Bar, Call Date: July
1995 (Middle Temple) Qualifications:
B.Comm (Queensland), LLB
(Queensland), LLM (London)

Ung *Eu-Chung*
Duval & Stachenfeld LLP, 405
Lexington Avenue, 32nd Floor, New
York, NY 10174, United States of
America, (212) 605 0104, Fax: (212)
883 8883, and Member New York
(1994), Call Date: July 1990 (Lincoln's
Inn) Qualifications: LLB (Lond) 1989,
LLM (Fordham) 1991, JD
(Georgetown) 1994

Ung *Miss Monin*
Clifford Chance, 30th Floor, Jardine
House, One Connaught Place, (852)
28258809, Fax: (852) 28690067, and
Member Singapore Bar Hong Kong Law
Society, Call Date: July 1993 (Gray's
Inn) Qualifications: LLB (Brunel)

Upadhyaya *Miss Kanaklata Bhaskerrai*
Malaysia, Call Date: Oct 1997 (Middle
Temple) Qualifications: LLB
(Hons)(Lond)

Usher *Professor John Anthony*
Scotland, Call Date: Nov 1993
(Lincoln's Inn) Qualifications: LLB
(Hons)

Uthayachanran *B*
Singapore 1953, Call Date: July 1993
(Middle Temple) Qualifications: LLB
(Hons)(Lond)

Vagg *Ms Irene Juliette*
Isle of Wight, Call Date: Oct 1995
(Gray's Inn) Qualifications: BA
(Ghana)

Van Der Stoep *David Floris*
Le Panorama, 57 Rue Grimaldi,
MC-98000, Moaco, 377 9310 6311,
Fax: 377 9310 6313, Call Date: Nov
1970 (Gray's Inn) Qualifications: Dip
Law

Van Hagen *Anthony Frederick William*
Cabinet Van Hagen, 6 Avenue George V,
Paris 75008, 01 47200064, Fax: 01
47202509, Avocat a la Cour, and
Member French Bar, Call Date: Nov
1975 (Lincoln's Inn) Qualifications: BA
(Hons) Law

van Leuven *Advocate John Nikolas*
Ozannes, 1 Le Marchant Street, St Peter
Port, Guernsey, 0481 723466, Fax:
0481 727935/714571/714653, Call
Date: Nov 1970 (Inner Temple)
Qualifications: MA (Cantab), ACIArb

Varghese *Joseph*
Varghese & Co, 112 East Coast Road,
[H] 03-33 Katong Mall, Singapore
460096, 3444989, Fax: 3444419, and
Member Singapore Bar, Call Date: July
1994 (Lincoln's Inn) Qualifications:
LLB (Hons)

Varughese *Miss Sucy*
9 Dilali Road, City Beach, Western
Australia WA 6015, Western Australia,
(09) 385 9552, Call Date: Oct 1993
(Lincoln's Inn) Qualifications: LLB
(Hons)(Bucks)

Vasu *Rajasekharan*
Singapore 520925, Call Date: Nov 1996
(Middle Temple) Qualifications: LLB
(Hons)

Vasudevan *Dhanaraj*
Malaysia, Call Date: July 1996 (Middle
Temple) Qualifications: LLB
(Hons)(Lond)

Vaswani *Mrs Honey*
Singapore 437147, and Member
Singapore, Call Date: Nov 1995 (Middle
Temple) Qualifications: LLB (Hons)

Vaughan *Beverley Seymour Tyrone*
Australia, Call Date: July 1978 (Gray's
Inn) Qualifications: MA, tcd

Veerasamy *Miss Sarojini Muthusamy*
Darussalam, Call Date: Nov 1997
(Lincoln's Inn) Qualifications: LLB
(Hons), LLM

Vellani *Badaruddin Fatehali*
Vellani & Vellani, 148, 18th East Street,
Phase 1, Defence Officers' Housing,
Authority, Karachi 75500, (92) (21)
580 1000, Fax: (92) (21) 580 1020,
Call Date: July 1982 (Middle Temple)
Qualifications: BSc Diplaw

Vellani *Fatehali Walimohammad*
Vellani & Vellani, 148 18th East Street,
Phase 1, Defence Officers' Housing,
Authority, Karachi 75500, (92) (21)
580 1000, Fax: (92) (21) 580 1020,
Call Date: Feb 1956 (Middle Temple)

Vengadasalam *Mrs Pakkia Letchumi*
Fuji Xerox Asia Pacific Pte, Ltd, 2nd
Floor, Plaza See Hoy Chan, Jalan Raja
Chulan, 50200 Kuala Lumpur,
Malaysia, 03-238 6600 Ext 297, Fax:
03-238 6631, Legal Affairs Manager,
and Member Malaysia Bar, Call Date:
Nov 1995 (Lincoln's Inn)
Qualifications: LLB (Hons)

Vengadesan *Miss Joanne Jayanti*
Malaysia, Call Date: July 1996 (Middle
Temple) Qualifications: LLB (Notts)

Venkata Rajoo *Miss Sheila Devi*
Malaysia, Call Date: Nov 1995
(Lincoln's Inn) Qualifications: LLB
(Hons)

Venn *John Kenneth*
124 Young Street, Hamilton, Ontario,
Canada L8N 1V6, Canada, (905) 522
9116, Fax: 9905) 529 5112, and
Member Upper Canada, Call Date: July
1971 (Middle Temple) Qualifications:
M.A (Oxon), M.B.A (Warwick)

Venugopal *Vijayan*
Shearn Delamore & Co, 7th Floor,
Wisma Hamzah Kwong - Hing, No 1
Leboh Ampang, 50100 Kuala Lumpur,
Malaysia, 03 2300644, Fax: 03
2385625, and Member Malaysia Bar,
Call Date: July 1993 (Middle Temple)
Qualifications: LLB (Hons)

Vesin-Samnadda *Mrs Indrani Veronica*
Credit Suisse Private Banking, P O Box
500, CH-1211 Geneva, Switzerland, 41
22 391 34 66, Fax: 41 22 391 38 77,
Entitled to practice in Caricom States
Currently practising in Switzerland. and
Member Trinidad and Tobago Bar, Call
Date: July 1992 (Middle Temple)
Qualifications: LLB (Hons) (Exeter)

Vibert *Miss Rebecca Louise*
Channel Islands, Call Date: Nov 1998
(Middle Temple) Qualifications: LLB
(Hons)(Bucks)

Vij *Arvind Kumar*
Milbank, Tweed, Hadley &, McClay, 1
Chase Manhattan Plaza, New York, NY
10005-1413, Singapore 0922, (212)
530-5000, Fax: (212) 530-5219,
Associate, and Member Singapore Bar,
Call Date: July 1995 (Middle Temple)
Qualifications: LLB (Hons), BBA
(Hons)

Vijayaratnam *Mohan Das*
Singapore 538091, Call Date: July 1998
(Middle Temple) Qualifications: LLB
(Hons)(Wales)

Voliotis *Dr Seraphim*
Rizariou 3, Chalandri 152 33, Athens,
Greece, 00 30 1 6853320/1/2, Fax: 00
30 1 6857530, Call Date: Oct 1995
(Lincoln's Inn) Qualifications: BA
(Hons), MA, PhD (Cantab)

Voo *Miss Mui Ching Cheryl*
7 Pemimpin Place, Singapore 576005,
65-2581213, Fax: 65-4539160, Legal
Assistant, and Member Singapore, Call
Date: July 1997 (Gray's Inn)
Qualifications: LLB (Lond)

Voon *Miss Meng Lye*
Blk 66 [H]02-339, Commonwealth
Drive, Singapore 140066, Singapore
0314, 4730146, Call Date: July 1995
(Lincoln's Inn) Qualifications: LLB
(Hons)

Voon *Richard Chee Fatt*
Malaysia, Call Date: Nov 1996
(Lincoln's Inn) Qualifications: LLB
(Hons)(Bucks)

Vung *Peter Yin Sing*
Malaysia, Call Date: July 1996 (Middle
Temple) Qualifications: BA
(Hons)(Keele)

F

Wahi *Miss Shelina Razaly*
Malaysia, Call Date: July 1996
(Lincoln's Inn) Qualifications: LLB
(Hons) (Bris)

Wahyuni *Faizal*
Singapore 600272, Call Date: July 1994
(Lincoln's Inn) Qualifications: LLB
(Hons)

Wainwright *Richard Barry*
Commission of the European
Communities, 200 Rue de La Loi, 1049
Brussels, Belgium, 02 295 3807, Fax:
02 295 2486, Principal Legal Adviser,
Call Date: July 1965 (Middle Temple)
Qualifications: BA (Oxon)

Wakerley *John Charles*
SmithKline Beecham Corporation, One
Franklin Plaza, P O Box 7929,
Philadelphia, PA 19101-7929, (215)
751 5844, Fax: (215) 751 5132, Senior
Vice President, Director & General
Counsel - USA, and Member New York
Bar, Call Date: May 1960 (Gray's Inn)
Qualifications: LLB

Wako *Julius*
Kenya, Call Date: Nov 1998 (Lincoln's
Inn) Qualifications: LLB (Hons) (Warw)

Walker *William Stuart*
W S Walker & Company, P O Box 265G,
Walker House, Grand Cayman,
(345)949-0100, Fax: (345)949-7886,
Chairman; Cayman Islands Planning
Appeals Tribunal, Chairman;
Caledonian Bank & Trust Company Ltd,
Dep. Chairman; British Caymanian
Insurance Company Ltd, Member of
Financial Secretary's Private Sector
Consultative Committee,
Attorney-at-Law Cayman Islands Notary
Public, Cayman Islands, Call Date: June
1950 (Inner Temple) Qualifications:
MA (Cantab)

Walsh *Mrs Margaret Josephine*
91 Whitebarn Road, Churchtown,
Dublin 14, 00 3531 2981346, Barrister
of Ireland, Call Date: May 1995 (Middle
Temple) Qualifications: BL (King's Inn)

Walters *Jeannot-Michel*
West Indies, Call Date: Nov 1997
(Middle Temple) Qualifications: LLB
(Hons)

Walton *Jeremy Paul*
Hunter & Hunter, Attorneys at Law,
P.O.Box 190, Grand Cayman, 001 345
949 4900, Fax: 001 345 949 2575,
Contributor to Atkin's Court Forms,
and Member Cayman Islands Bar, Call
Date: Nov 1995 (Lincoln's Inn)
Qualifications: BA (Hons)

Wan *Azli Kuzaini*
Malaysia, Call Date: Nov 1995
(Lincoln's Inn) Qualifications: LLB
(Hons)

Wan *Kai Chee*
43 Jalan Desa Seputeh 4, Taman Desa
Lumpur, 58000 Kuala Lumpur,
Malaysia, 00 609 319 7465, Fax: 00
603 274 9481, Call Date: July 1997
(Lincoln's Inn) Qualifications: LLB
(Hons) (Lond)

Wan *Ms Shuk Fong Polly*
6/F High Block, Queensway
Government Offices, 66 Queensway,
Hong Kong, 28672302, Fax: 28451609,
Senior Government Counsel,
Department of Justice, Hong Kong, and
Member Hong Kong Bar, Call Date: Nov
1993 (Gray's Inn) Qualifications: LLB

Wan *Miss Teh Leok*
2193-A Lorong Kampung Pisang, Alor
Setar, 05100 Kedah, Malaysia, Malaysia,
0604 7330837, and Member Malaysia
Bar, Call Date: July 1995 (Inner
Temple) Qualifications: LLB (Soton)

Wan Hussin *Wan Fairuz*
Singapore 2880, Call Date: July 1995
(Middle Temple) Qualifications: BA
(Hons) (Keele)

Wan Mohd Noor *Wan Annuar*
Malaysia, Call Date: Nov 1995
(Lincoln's Inn) Qualifications: LLB
(Hons)

Wang *John Shing Chun*
52 Kampong Chantek, Singapore, (65)
4668928, Call Date: July 1996 (Middle
Temple) Qualifications: BA
(Hons) (Cantab)

Wang *Peter Kai-Hung*
Canada, Call Date: July 1995 (Middle
Temple) Qualifications: B.Sc, M.Sc
(Toronto), LLB (Hons), LLM, (Wales)

Wang *Sui Sang*
Malaysia, Call Date: Nov 1991
(Lincoln's Inn) Qualifications: LLB
(Hons) (L'Pool)

Ward *Andrew Robert*
Cleary, Goitlieb, Steen and, Hamilton,
Avenue de la Loi, 23, Brussels 1040, 00
32 2 287 2000, Call Date: Oct 1997
(Lincoln's Inn) Qualifications: BA
(Hons)

Ward *Eoin Francis*
Kindle Banking Systems, East Point
Business Park, Dublin 3 Ireland,
Ireland, 353 1 68554555, Fax: 353 1
8554550, Company Lawyer, and
Member Irish Bar (King's Inn), Call
Date: July 1988 (Middle Temple)
Qualifications: BCL (Dublin), AITI,
(Dublin), Dip , European Law(Dublin)

Warne *Francis*
Gibraltar, Call Date: Oct 1998 (Middle
Temple) Qualifications: LLB
(Hons) (Wales)

Warwick *Kevin*
Gibraltar, Call Date: Oct 1995 (Middle
Temple) Qualifications: LLB (Hons)

Watt *John Gillie McArthur*
Advocates Library, Parliament House,
Edinburgh, United States of America,
303 456 1548, Fax: 303 456 1548,
Temporary Sheriff, Scottish Advocate,
QC Scotland 1992 and Member
Colorado Bar, Call Date: Feb 1992
(Middle Temple) Qualifications: LLB
(Edin)

Watters *Simon Barry*
P O Box X 2291, Perth, Western
Australia 6001, 08-9321-8531, Fax:
08-9322-6953, Practitioner - Federal &
High Court of Australia, Former
Solicitor and Member Western Australia
Bar, Federal & High Court of Australia
Tasmania Bar, Call Date: July 1992
(Gray's Inn) Qualifications: BA, LLB

Watts *Trevor Robert*
Chateau Du Seuil, Cerons 33720,
France, France, 00 33 56271156, Fax:
00 33 56272879, Call Date: Nov 1979
(Lincoln's Inn) Qualifications: FRVA,
FSVA, Winemaker

Wazir *Miss Bushra*
Karachi 74800, Pakistan, Call Date: Oct
1998 (Lincoln's Inn) Qualifications:
LLB (Hons)(Keele)

Weatherhead *Miss Louise*
Bar Library, Royal Courts of Justice,
Chichester Street, Belfast BT1 3JP,
01232 562234, and Member Northern
Ireland, Call Date: Oct 1997 (Lincoln's
Inn) Qualifications: BA (Hons) (Sheff)

Wee *Miss Adeline Ai Lin*
Singapore 1445, Call Date: July 1995
(Middle Temple) Qualifications: BA
(Hons) (Keele)

Wee *Aloysius Meng Seng*
105 Cecil Street, [H] 10-02 The
Octagon, Singapore 350117, 5352077,
Fax: 5333969, and Member Singapore
Bar, Call Date: Oct 1994 (Middle
Temple) Qualifications: BA
(Hons) (Kent)

Wee *Desmond Guan Oei*
Singapore 1024, Call Date: July 1995
(Middle Temple) Qualifications: LLB
(Hons)

Wee *Gerald Martin Ee Ming*
Singapore 440028, Call Date: Nov 1996
(Middle Temple) Qualifications: LLB
(Hons) (L'pool)

Wee *Miss Majorie Chiu Yeh*
Singapore 229769, Call Date: July 1998
(Lincoln's Inn) Qualifications: LLB
(Hons) (Buck'm)

Wee *Miss Ying Ling Beverly*
Singapore 1024, Call Date: July 1995
(Gray's Inn) Qualifications: LLB

Wee Inn *The Hon. Mr Roland Sagrah*
M/S David Allan Sagah & Teng,
Advocates, Lot 196, Sublot 4, 1st Floor,
Jalan Kulas, Satok CDT 3045, 93990
Kuching, Malaysia, 082-232739, Fax:
082-251831, State Assemblyman,
State Legislative Assembly Sarawak,
Malaysia, Advocate & Solicitor of the
High Court of Sabah & Sarawak
Malaysia. and Member Sarawak Bar,
Call Date: July 1980 (Gray's Inn)
Qualifications: LLB (Hons Lond)

Wei *Miss Hui Yen*
Malaysia, Call Date: July 1996 (Gray's
Inn) Qualifications: BA (Keele), MBA
(London)

Weiner *Sharise Erica*
South Africa, South African Pratitioner,
Call Date: Mar 1999 (Gray's Inn)
Qualifications: BA, LLB, (Witwatersand)

Weir *Alan Anthony*
Northern Ireland, Northern Ireland
Barrister, Call Date: Nov 1996 (Gray's
Inn) Qualifications: BSc, MSc (Belfast)

Weir *Robert Angus Alexander*
New Zealand, and Member New
Zealand Bar, Call Date: Oct 1998
(Gray's Inn) Qualifications: LLB
(Auckland)

Wells *Commander Anthony Roland*
P.O. Box 2102, Middleburg 20118,
Virginia, 703-253 5048, Fax: 703-253
5049, Call Date: Nov 1980 (Lincoln's
Inn) Qualifications: MA (Dunelm),
MSc, PhD (Lond)

Westbrook *Simon Nicholas*
Des Voeux Chambers, 10/F Bank of
East Asia Bldg, 10 Des Voeux Road
Central, (852) 2526 3071, Fax: (852)
2810 5287, and Member Hong Kong
Bar, Call Date: July 1973 (Inner
Temple) Qualifications: LLB, FCIArb

Whatnell *Mrs Helen Mary*
1407 Azalea Bend, Sugar Land TX
77479, United States of America, 281
343 7569, Fax: 281 343 6019, Call
Date: Nov 1993 (Inner Temple)
Qualifications: LLB

Wheeler *John Gerald Patrick*
Le Gallais & Luce, 6 Hill Street, St
Helier, Jersey JE4 8YX, Channel Islands,
0534 875544, Fax: 0534 878118,
Advocate of the Royal Court of Jersey,
Call Date: July 1978 (Inner Temple)
Qualifications: BA

Wheeler *Miss Philippa Ruth*
Hewlett Packard GMBH, Postfach 1430,
D 71003 Boeblingen, Germany, 49
7031 14 3169, Fax: 49 7031 14 3812,
European Trade Mark Attorney, Call
Date: July 1988 (Inner Temple)
Qualifications: LLB

Whitford *Richard Henry*
Whitford & Co, P.O.Box 370, Town
Mills, Trinity Square, St Peter Port,
Guernsey GY1 3YN, Channel Islands,
01481 712020, Fax: 01481 712271,
Call Date: Nov 1970 (Gray's Inn)
Qualifications: LLB (Lond), ACIB

Willers *Peter Alan*
Ballagawne Farm, Baldrine, 0624
661662, Fax: 0624 661663, Legal
Director, Call Date: Nov 1973 (Middle
Temple) Qualifications: MA (Cantab)

Williams *Miss Ameeta Chandra*
Singapore 2057, Call Date: Nov 1995
(Middle Temple) Qualifications: LLB
(Hons)(Sheff)

Williams *Miss April Nicole*
NP Bahamas, Call Date: Nov 1996
(Inner Temple) Qualifications: BA
(Canada), BA (Keele)

Williams *Ms Caroline*
5 Cool Na Mara, Marine Terrace,
Dunlaoghaire, Co Dublin, Republic of
Ireland, 00353 12842770, Fax: 00353
12842770, Barrister of King's Inn, Call
Date: Nov 1994 (Middle Temple)

Williams *Cecil Alfred*
St Vincent & the Grenadines, Call Date:
July 1997 (Gray's Inn) Qualifications:
BA (West Indies), MSc (Bradford), LLB
(Lond)

Williams *Judge Jonathan Steuart*
Judges Chambers, District Court of
NSW, P.O.Box K1026, Haymarket, NSW
2000, Australia, 02 9287 7446, Fax: 02
9287 7493, Senior Crown Prosecutor
Magistrate of the NSW Local Court, and
Member Australian Capital Territory
New South Wales Bar, Call Date: May
1990 (Lincoln's Inn) Qualifications:
Dip Law, Dip Crim, LLM

Williams *Richard David*
Maples & Calder, P O Box 309, Ugland
House, Grand Cayman, Call Date: Oct
1993 (Gray's Inn) Qualifications: MA

Williamson *Kris*
Daniel & CIA, AV.Republica Do Chile,
230/6o - Centro, Rio De Janeiro
20031-170, 00552l 224 4212, Fax:
005521 224 3344, Legal Adviser, Call
Date: Nov 1993 (Middle Temple)
Qualifications: BA (Hons)(Leic), LLB
(Hons)(Lond)

Williamson *Mrs Romi Wai Ming*
1 Highlands, 35 Plantation Road, Hong
Kong, 25222884, and Member Hong
Kong Bar, Call Date: Nov 1994 (Middle
Temple) Qualifications: BA
(Econ)(Australia)

Willimsky *Miss Sonya Margaret*
Haarmann, Hemmelrath & Partner,
Maximillan Str.35, 40212 Dusseldorf,
80539 Munich, Germany, 00 49 89
216360, Fax: 00 49 89 21636-133,
Corporate/Commercial Lawyer, Call
Date: Nov 1996 (Lincoln's Inn)
Qualifications: LLB (Hons)(Lond)

Wilmott *Eric Leroy*
Bahamas, Call Date: Nov 1998 (Middle
Temple) Qualifications: LLB
(Hons)(Keele)

Wilson *Graham James*
Wilson Associates-Luxembourg, PO Box
742, 00352 252740, Fax: 00352
252741, Gray's Inn Tax Chambers, 3rd
Floor, Gray's Inn Chambers, Gray's
Inn, London, WC1R 5JA, Call Date: July
1975 (Gray's Inn) Qualifications: LLB
(Lond)

Wilson *John Frederick*
C/O Parliamentary Counsel, Office,
Parliament Buildings, Suva, Fiji
Islands, (679) 305811, Fax: (679)
305325, First Parliamentary Counsel,
Call Date: July 1966 (Inner Temple)
Qualifications: BA (Oxon)

Wilson *Miss Sharlyn Rondel*
P.O.Box N3739, Nassau, Bahamas,
(242) 324 6403, Fax: (242) 394 0019,
and Member The Bahamas, Call Date:
July 1998 (Middle Temple)
Qualifications: LLB (Hons)(Reading)

Wilson Appukuttan *Joy*
Messrs Kitson Foong &, Associates, No
75B Jalan Dato Haji Eusoff, Damai
Complex, Off Jalan Ipoh, 50400 Kuala
Lumpur, West Malaysia, 603 4436797/
603-4428411, Fax: 603-4429297,
Advocate & Solicitor and Member
Malaysia Bar Singapore Bar, Call Date:
Nov 1989 (Middle Temple)
Qualifications: LLB Hons (Lond)

Winckless *Michael Louis John*
1430 Prince's Building, Central, Hong
Kong, (852) 2525 7388, Fax: (852)
2525 3930, ACIArb, and Member Hong
Kong Bar, Call Date: July 1994 (Middle
Temple) Qualifications: BSc (Hons) ,
MBA

Winny *Ms Elspeth Margaret*
Hong Kong, Call Date: Nov 1996
(Lincoln's Inn) Qualifications: LLB
(Hons)(Lond)

Wiseheart *Malcolm Boyd*
2840 Southwest Third Avenue, Miami,
Florida 33129, 305 285 1222, Fax: 305
858 4864, Special Master, Property
Appraisal Adjustment Board, and
Member Florida & Washington DC Bars
Jamaica & Trinidad & Tobago Bars, Call
Date: Feb 1970 (Gray's Inn)
Qualifications: MA (Cantab) JD,
(Florida) BA (Yale)

Wong *Aaron Kang Way*
Malaysia, Call Date: Mar 1999
(Lincoln's Inn) Qualifications: LLB
(Hons)(Sheff)

Wong *Adrian Kwai Ming*
Brunei, Call Date: July 1997 (Lincoln's
Inn) Qualifications: LLB
(Hons)(Leeds)

Wong *Alex Li Kok*
Malaysia, Call Date: July 1997 (Middle
Temple) Qualifications: LLB (Hons)

Wong *Miss Angela Mo Yen*
2056 Singapore, Call Date: Nov 1996
(Gray's Inn) Qualifications: LLB

Wong *Annie Sook Cheng*
Singapore 440033, Call Date: Nov 1997
(Middle Temple) Qualifications: LLB
(Hons)(Lond)

Wong *Chak Yan*
Hong Kong, Call Date: Nov 1997
(Middle Temple) Qualifications: BSc
(Hons,Hong Kong)

Wong *Chao-Wai*
CNAC Group Building, 13th Flr, 10
Queens Road C, Central, Hong Kong,
Hong Kong, 28101008, Fax: 25960945,
Associate, Hong Kong Institute of
Arbitrators Ltd, and Member Hong
Kong Bar, Call Date: Nov 1991 (Inner
Temple) Qualifications: LLB, LLM, MA,
MIL , ACIArb (Hong Kong)

Wong *Miss Cheryl Pooi Leng*
Malaysia, Call Date: July 1996
(Lincoln's Inn) Qualifications: LLB
(Hons)(Lond)

Wong *Chi Wing John*
Hong Kong, Call Date: Nov 1997
(Middle Temple) Qualifications: LLB
(Hons)

Wong *Miss Denise Chin Wuen*
Malaysia, Call Date: July 1996
(Lincoln's Inn) Qualifications: LLB
(Hons)(Bris)

Wong *Eden Yi Dung*
Hong Kong, Call Date: Nov 1997 (Gray's
Inn) Qualifications: B.Com
(Melbourne), LLB (Lond)

Wong *Mrs Fung Kwai*
Singapore 2365, 065 5660812, Call
Date: July 1995 (Middle Temple)
Qualifications: LLB (Hons)

Wong *Miss Grace Teck Lian*
Singapore 1545, Call Date: July 1996
(Lincoln's Inn) Qualifications: LLB
(Hons)(Leics)

Wong *Hong Wai*
c/o Cheang & Ariff, Advocates &
Solicitors, 39 Court, No 39 Jalan Yap
Kwan, Seng, 50450, Kuala Lumpur
Malaysia, Malaysia, 03 2610803, Fax:
03 2614475, Legal Assistant, Call Date:
Nov 1992 (Gray's Inn) Qualifications:
LLB (Hull)

Wong *James Seow Boon*
Singapore 417055, Call Date: Nov 1996
(Middle Temple) Qualifications: LLB
(Hons)(Bucks), LLM (USA)

Wong *James Yuen Weng*
Singapore 597559, Call Date: July 1996
(Lincoln's Inn) Qualifications: LLB
(Hons)(Nott's)

Wong *John Sing Kiu*
Racal Survey (S) Pte Ltd, 45 Joo Koon
Circle, Singapore 159954, (65)
8610878/(65) 8687224, Fax: (65)
8618939, Commercial Manager (Far
East Region), Call Date: Nov 1994
(Middle Temple) Qualifications: B.Sc,
LLB (Hons), ARICS, MSISV

Wong *Jonathan*
Hong Kong, Call Date: July 1998 (Inner
Temple) Qualifications: BA (Canada),
CPE (Manch)

Wong *Kah Hui*
Malaysia, Call Date: Nov 1995
(Lincoln's Inn) Qualifications: LLB
(Hons)

Wong *Kean Li*
Malaysia, Call Date: July 1995 (Middle
Temple) Qualifications: BA (Hons)

Wong *Kee Them*
Malaysia, Call Date: Nov 1997
(Lincoln's Inn) Qualifications: LLB
(Hons)

Wong *Kelvin Weng Wah*
Singapore 1953, and Member
Singapore Bar, Call Date: July 1995
(Middle Temple) Qualifications: LLB
(Hons), ACIArb

Wong *Miss Ket Yee*
Malaysia, Call Date: July 1997 (Middle
Temple) Qualifications: LLB
(Hons)(B'ham)

Wong *Kwee Hoi*
Malaysia, Call Date: Nov 1997
(Lincoln's Inn) Qualifications: LLB
(Hons)

Wong *Kwok Fai*
Hong Kong, Call Date: Nov 1996
(Middle Temple) Qualifications: LLB
(Hons)(Lond)

Wong *Miss Li Chien*
c/o Albar Zulkifly & Yap, Suite 17.01,
17th Floor, Menara Panglobal, 8
Lorong P Ramlee, 50200 Kuala
Lumpur, Malaysia, Fax: 03 2041917,
Legal Assistant, and Member Malaysia,
Call Date: Nov 1996 (Middle Temple)
Qualifications: BA (Hons)(Kent)

Wong *Li Fei*
Malaysia, Call Date: July 1997
(Lincoln's Inn) Qualifications: LLB
(Hons)

Wong *Mark Kuan Meng*
P.K.Wong & Advani, 20 Raffles Place,
[H]12-03 Ocean Towers, Singapore
0104, Singapore 577533, 65 5381822,
Fax: 65 5381838, and Member
Singapore Bar, Call Date: Nov 1992
(Middle Temple) Qualifications: LLB
(Hons, Hull)

Wong *Dr Melvin*
Hong Kong, Fax: (852) 26987403, and
Member Hong Kong Bar, Call Date: July
1997 (Gray's Inn) Qualifications:
Pharm.D, LLB (Lond)

Wong *Ming Fung*
Hong Kong, Call Date: July 1997
(Middle Temple) Qualifications: BA
(Hons)

Wong *Nai Chee*
No 25 Lorong Hang Jebat, 75200
Melaka, Malaysia, 010606 2825105,
Fax: 010606 2848004, and Member
Malaysia Bar, Call Date: July 1994
(Middle Temple) Qualifications: LLB
(Hons)(Hull)

Wong *Pak Heung*
3rd Floor, Fook Shing Court, 50
Wyndham Street, 852 2523 3450, and
Member Supreme Court of Hong Kong
Supreme Court of Australian Capital
Territory, Call Date: July 1966 (Inner
Temple)

Wong *Miss Pei-Ling*
37 Lorong Maa'rof, Bangsar Park,
59000 Kuala Lumpur, Malaysia, 03
2836193, Call Date: July 1996
(Lincoln's Inn) Qualifications: LLB
(Hons)

Wong *Raymond Kwai Sang*
Hong Kong, Call Date: Nov 1996
(Middle Temple) Qualifications: LLB
(Hons)(HongKong)

Wong *Richard T W*
Room 1205-6 New World Tower, Tower
1, 16-18 Queens Road Central, Central,
25211388, Fax: 28451738, Barrister of
the Supreme Court of the Australian
Capital Territory(Dec 1990) and
Member Hong Kong Bar, Call Date: Nov
1986 (Inner Temple) Qualifications:
LLB (Lond), PCLL (HK)

Wong *Miss Rita Kee Ning*
Malaysia, Call Date: July 1996
(Lincoln's Inn)

Wong *Miss Rosaline Wing Yue*
Hong Kong, and Member Hong Kong,
Call Date: July 1993 (Middle Temple)
Qualifications: LLB (Hons)(Lond)

Wong *Miss Shou Ning*
Malaysia, Call Date: Nov 1996 (Middle
Temple) Qualifications: LLB
(Hons)(Kent)

Wong *Ms Shou Sien*
Wong & Partners, Suite 12-1A, Faber
Imperial Court, Jln Sultan Ismail,
50250 Kuala Lumpur, Malaysia, 603
4611888, Fax: 603 4603880, and
Member Malaysia Bar, Call Date: Feb
1994 (Middle Temple) Qualifications:
LLB (Hons)(Kent), LLM (Lond)

Wong *Miss Siew Mei*
Malaysia, Call Date: July 1997 (Middle
Temple) Qualifications: LLB
(Hons)(Wales)

Wong *Miss Sook Ling*
Shooklin & Bok, Advocates & Solicitors,
1 Robinson Road, [H]18-00 AIA Tower,
Singapore 099310, Singapore 0409,
(65) 535 1944, Fax: (65) 535 8577,
and Member Singapore Bar, Call Date:
July 1994 (Inner Temple)
Qualifications: LLB

Wong *Ms Soon Chee*
Malaysia, Call Date: July 1997
(Lincoln's Inn) Qualifications: LLB
(Hons)(Lond)

Wong *Sow Wei*
Malaysia, and Member Advocate &
Solicitor of the High Court of Malaya,
Call Date: July 1996 (Lincoln's Inn)

Wong *Miss Su-Mene*
Malaysia, Call Date: July 1995 (Middle
Temple) Qualifications: LLB (Hons)

Wong *Miss Sui Ching Janet*
Hong Kong, Call Date: Nov 1997
(Middle Temple) Qualifications: BA
(Hons)(Hong Kong)

Wong *Wai Keong*
Malaysia, and Member Malaysia, Call
Date: Nov 1995 (Lincoln's Inn)
Qualifications: LLB (Hons)(Lond)

Wong *Wee Kok*
Malaysia, Call Date: Nov 1996
(Lincoln's Inn) Qualifications: LLB
(Hons)(Wales)

Wong *Winston Paul Chi-Huang*
Suite 12-02, 12th Floor, Menara
Pelangi, Jalan Kuning, 80400 Johor
Bahru, Johor Malaysia, Malaysia, 010
60 7 3342266, Fax: 010 60 7 3344708,
Legal Assistant, and Member Malaysia
Bar, Call Date: Nov 1994 (Middle
Temple) Qualifications: BA (Hons),
LLM, (Singapore)

Wong *Yew Kit*
Singapore 0512, and Member
Singapore, Call Date: July 1995 (Middle
Temple) Qualifications: LLB (Hons)

Wong *Yun Wah Gordon*
Pacific Chambers, 901 Dina House,
Ruttonjee Centre, 11 Duddell Street,
Central, Hong Kong, (852) 2521 5544,
Fax: (852) 2524 5912, and Member
Hong Kong Bar, Call Date: July 1996
(Lincoln's Inn) Qualifications: LLB
(Hons)(Leeds)

Woo *Hubert Iu-Kwok*
New World Tower, Room 602, 18
Queen's Road Central, Hong Kong,
Hong Kong, 2525 7007, Fax: 2845
2001, and Member Hong Kong Bar, Call
Date: Feb 1992 (Gray's Inn)
Qualifications: BSc (Hong Kong), LLB
(Lond), MICE,FCIArb

Woo *Miss Siew Khim*
Blk 623, Bukit Batok Central,
[H]03-680, Singapore 650623,
7786740, Senior Bank Officer, Call
Date: Nov 1993 (Middle Temple)
Qualifications: LLB (Hons)(Lond)

Woo *Wei Kwang*
Malaysia, Call Date: July 1997
(Lincoln's Inn) Qualifications: LLB
(Hons)(Leeds)

Woodworth *Miss Michelle Elizabeth*
Singapore 321021, Call Date: July 1996
(Middle Temple) Qualifications: LLB
(Hons)(Lond)

Woolley *Edward Timothy Starbuck*
c/o The Court of Final Appeal, 1 Battery
Path, 2123 0017, Fax: 2121 0312,
Registrar, Court of Final Appeal and
Member Hong Kong Bar, Australian
Bar, Call Date: July 1968 (Middle
Temple)

Wrightson *Mrs Sandra Anne*
De Cotta McKenna y Santafe, C Com
Valdepinos 1 y 3a, Urb Calipso, Mijas
Costa, Malaga 29647, Spainish Lawyer,
Call Date: Nov 1997 (Middle Temple)
Qualifications: BA (Open), LLB(Hons),
(Lond)

Wu *Chi Sing*
Hong Kong, Call Date: Nov 1995 (Gray's
Inn) Qualifications: LLB (Lond)

Wu *Chun Shing*
Flat A, 3/F, Block 6, Metro City, 1 Wan
Hang Road, Tseung Kwan O, N.T., (00
852) 2695 0252, Fax: (00 852) 2695
0252, and Member Hong Kong, Call
Date: Nov 1996 (Gray's Inn)
Qualifications: LLB (Lond)

Wu *Mrs Lorna Shui Wan*
1002 Chekiang Bank Centre, 1 Duddell
Street, Hong Kong, 5 25217317, Fax:
852 5 28450654, p/t Small Claims
Adjudicator of Hong Kong Judiciary,
and Member Hong Kong & Singapore
Bars, Call Date: Nov 1982 (Inner
Temple) Qualifications: LLB, Dip in
Chinese Law, ACIArb

Wun *Rizwi*
Singapore 787057, Company Secretary.
Sembawang Engineering &
Construction PTE Ltd, and Member
Singapore, Call Date: July 1992 (Gray's
Inn) Qualifications: LLB (Lond)

Wylie-Otte *Ms Regan*
3 Um Kallek, L-5369 Schuttrange,
Senior Counsel, Call Date: Feb 1978
(Middle Temple) Qualifications: MA,
LLM

Xu *Daniel Atticus*
100 Jalan Sultan, [H]08-16 Sultan
Plaza, Singapore 560344, (65)
2941010, Fax: (65) 2969992, Call
Date: Nov 1997 (Middle Temple)
Qualifications: LLB (Hons)(Lond)

Yam *Jeffrey Pei Tseng*
Messrs Rodyk & Davidson, 9 Raffles
Place, [H]55-01, Republic Plaza,
Singapore 266800, 65 5399254, Fax:
65 2251838, Call Date: July 1996
(Middle Temple) Qualifications: LLB
(Hons)(Wales)

Yang *Miss Carol*
Singapore 109258,

Yang *Joe-Hynn*
Malaysia, Call Date: Oct 1998 (Gray's
Inn) Qualifications: BA (Oxon)

Yap *Ms Adeline Bee-Yen*
Azri Chuah & Yap, No 72A (1st Floor),
Jalan Padang Belia, Brickfields, 50470
Kuala Lumpur, Malaysia, 603 2746014/
2746018/2746019, Fax: 603 2748207,
Partner, and Member Malaysia Bar,
Call Date: July 1992 (Middle Temple)
Qualifications: LLB (Hons) (Manch)

Yap *Benjamin Soon Tat*
Natsteel Limited, 22 Tanjong Kling
Road, Singapore 809476, (065)
6607833, Fax: 2664338, Legal Officer,
and Member Singapore, Call Date: Nov
1994 (Middle Temple) Qualifications:
LLB (Hons)

Yap *Miss Camilla Tee Neo*
Malaysia, Call Date: Nov 1995
(Lincoln's Inn) Qualifications: LLB
(Hons)

Yap *Miss Hsu-Lyn*
Malaysia, Call Date: July 1997
(Lincoln's Inn) Qualifications: LLB
(Hons)(Nott'm)

Yap *Miss Huey Hoong*
Malaysia, Call Date: July 1996
(Lincoln's Inn) Qualifications: LLB
(Hons)

Yap *Miss Janice Bee Hong*
Malaysia, Call Date: July 1997
(Lincoln's Inn) Qualifications: LLB
(Hons)(Leeds)

Yap *Ms Juliana Chin Choo*
B-3258, Taman Tunas, 25300 Kuantan,
Pahang Darulmakmur, Malaysia,
Malaysia, and Member Singapore Bar,
Call Date: July 1995 (Inner Temple)
Qualifications: LLB (Lond), LLM
(Singapore)

Yap *Keng Siong*
Suite 7-05, 7th Floor, Wisma Equity,
150 Jlana Ampang, 50450 Kuala
Lumpur, Malaysia, 603 2610677, Fax:
603 2613787, Legal Assitant, and
Member Malaysia, Call Date: July 1996
(Lincoln's Inn) Qualifications: LLB
(Hons)

Yap *Miss Lai-Lian*
Malaysia, Call Date: Nov 1996
(Lincoln's Inn) Qualifications: LLB
(Hons)(Herts)

Yap *Miss Lareina Chu Han*
[H]02-01, Amica Block, The
Beaumont, 147 Devonshire Road,
733-9923, Legal Assistant, and Member
Supreme Court of Brunei Darussalam
Singapore Bar, Call Date: Nov 1988
(Middle Temple) Qualifications: LLB
(Brunel), LLM (Lond)

Yap *Miss Lay Kuan*
Malaysia, and Member Malaysian Bar,
Call Date: Nov 1997 (Middle Temple)
Qualifications: LLB (Hons), MBA

Yap *Miss Lisa*
Malaysia, Call Date: Nov 1996 (Middle Temple) Qualifications: LLB (Hons)(Kent)

Yap *Miss Lynette*
Singapore 429690, Call Date: Nov 1996 (Lincoln's Inn) Qualifications: LLB (Hons)(Lond)

Yap *Miss Pett Chin*
Singapore 281125, Call Date: Nov 1996 (Lincoln's Inn) Qualifications: LLB (Hons)(Leics)

Yap *Miss Rhoda Jin Lyn*
Malaysia, Call Date: Oct 1998 (Lincoln's Inn) Qualifications: LLB (Hons)(Lond)

Yap *Miss Shirley Mae-Yen*
Singapore 456781, Call Date: July 1996 (Lincoln's Inn) Qualifications: LLB (Hons)

Yap *Miss Vicky Lan Hiang*
Singapore 1026, Call Date: July 1995 (Inner Temple) Qualifications: LLB (Warw)

Yap *Vincent Leng Khim*
Chooi & Company, Advocates & Solicitors, Penthouse, Bangunan Ming, Jalan Bukit Nanas, 50250 Kuala Lumpur, Malaysia, 03 2327344, Fax: 03 2382915/2308708, Advocate & Solicitor, and Member Malaysia, Call Date: July 1997 (Lincoln's Inn) Qualifications: LLB (Hons)

Yasin *Saladin Mohd.*
No 3 Jalan 4/3F, 40000 Shah Alam, Selangor, Malaysia, Malaysia, Call Date: July 1993 (Gray's Inn) Qualifications: LLB

Yau *Wai-Leong*
Chan & Associates, Standard Chartered Bank Chamb., 21-27 Jalan Dato Maharaja Lela, 30000 Ipoh, Malaysia, 605 2545293, Fax: 605 2534091, Advocate & Solicitor, and Member Malaysia, Call Date: July 1996 (Lincoln's Inn) Qualifications: LLB (Hons)(Leeds)

Yeap *Chin Pho*
Malaysia, Call Date: July 1998 (Lincoln's Inn) Qualifications: CPE (Nth London), LLM (Buck'ham)

Yearwood *Martin Edmund*
31 La Estancia Drive, PO Box 3239, Diego Martin, Trinidad, West Indies, 632-8223, Call Date: Nov 1971 (Lincoln's Inn) Qualifications: BSc

Yeats *Liam James*
Stagnetto & Co, 186 Main Street, Gibraltar, and Member Gibraltar, Call Date: Mar 1997 (Middle Temple) Qualifications: LLB (Hons)

Yee *Miss Eileen Khor Kit*
Singapore 2057, Call Date: July 1995 (Middle Temple) Qualifications: LLB (Hons)

Yee *Jackie Keen Meng*
Malaysia, Call Date: July 1995 (Lincoln's Inn) Qualifications: LLB (Hons)

Yee *Mei Ken*
Shearn Delamore & Co, 7th Floor, Wisma Hamzah Kwong, No 1 Leboh Ampang, 50100 Kuala Lumpur, Malaysia, 06 03 230 0644, Fax: 06 03 204 2763, and Member Malaysia Bar, Call Date: July 1997 (Lincoln's Inn) Qualifications: LLB (Hons)(Wales)

Yeen *Chong Foo*
Lim Seong Chun & Co, No 11, Jalan Panglima, 30000 Ipoh, Perak, Malaysia, (05) 2413655, Fax: (05) 2550194, Call Date: July 1997 (Inner Temple) Qualifications: LLB (Sheff)

Yen *Heng Teng*
West Malaysia, Call Date: Nov 1996 (Middle Temple) Qualifications: LLB (Hons)(Hull)

Yen-Yen *Ms Lee Amelia*
Western Malaysia, Call Date: Nov 1997 (Inner Temple) Qualifications: LLB, LLM (Lond)

Yeo *Miss Chiew Pin*
Malaysia, Call Date: Nov 1997 (Lincoln's Inn) Qualifications: LLB (Hons)(Wales)

Yeo *Jih Shian*
Singapore 187958, Call Date: July 1993 (Gray's Inn) Qualifications: BA

Yeo *Ms Marianne Mei-Lin*
5B Sea & Sky Court, 92 Stanley Main Street, Stanley, 852 28131788, Fax: 852 28132086, and Member Malaysia Bar, Call Date: July 1982 (Inner Temple) Qualifications: BSc (Manch), Diplaw

Yeo *Raymond Khee Chye*
Singapore 808014, Call Date: July 1996 (Lincoln's Inn) Qualifications: LLB (Hons)(Lond)

Yeo *Ronald*
Malaysia, Call Date: Feb 1993 (Lincoln's Inn) Qualifications: LLB (Hons)

Yeo *Seng Hong*
Singapore 470736, Call Date: Mar 1999 (Middle Temple) Qualifications: LLB (Hons)(Lond)

Yeo *Sia Eng*
Malaysia, Call Date: Oct 1997 (Middle Temple) Qualifications: LLB (Hons)(Lond)

Yeo *Miss Siok Kiang Fiona*
Singapore 400413, Criminal Case Review Manager CCRC, Call Date: July 1996 (Middle Temple) Qualifications: LLB (Hons)(Hull)

Yeo *Willie Sie Keng*
Singapore 059413, and Member Singapore Bar, Call Date: July 1995 (Lincoln's Inn) Qualifications: LLB (Hons)

Yeo *Miss Yee Ling*
Malaysia, Call Date: July 1997 (Gray's Inn)

Yeoh *Miss Daryl*
Chan & Associates, Advocates & Solicitors, Standard Chartered Bk Chambers, 21-27 Jalan Dato Maharja Lela, 30000 Ipoh, Perak Malaysia, Malaysia, Call Date: July 1995 (Lincoln's Inn) Qualifications: LLB (Hons)

Yeoh *Gary Cheng Lee*
7th Floor, Bangunan Kassim Chan, 3 Cangkat Raja Chulan, P O Box 11151, 50736 Kuala Lumpur, Malaysia, 2320711, Fax: 2300585, Legal Advisor, and Member Malaysia Bar, Call Date: May 1994 (Lincoln's Inn) Qualifications: LLB (Hons)

Yeoh *Miss Geraldine Poh Im*
7th Floor, 3 Changkat Raja Chulan, 50200 Kuala Lumpur, P.O.Box 11151, 50736 Kuala Lumpur Malaysia, Malaysia, 03 2320711, Fax: 03 2304746/2300585, Advocate & Solicitor, and Member Malaysia Bar, Call Date: Nov 1991 (Lincoln's Inn) Qualifications: LLB (Hons)(Reading), LLM

Yeoh *Miss Huei-Keng*
Malaysia, Call Date: July 1997 (Lincoln's Inn) Qualifications: LLB (Hons)

Yeoh *Leonard Soon Beng*
Malaysia, Call Date: July 1995 (Lincoln's Inn) Qualifications: LLB (Hons)

Yeoh *Miss Melissa Ann Lin*
Malaysia, Call Date: Nov 1997 (Middle Temple) Qualifications: LLB (Hons)(Nott'm)

Yeoh *Nigel Lian Chuan*
Singapore 1026, Call Date: July 1993 (Lincoln's Inn) Qualifications: LLB (Hons)

Yeoh *Miss Wai Ling*
Malaysia, Call Date: July 1996 (Lincoln's Inn) Qualifications: LLB (Hons)(Warw)

Yeow *Miss Ping Lin*
Attorney General's Chambers, 1 Coleman Street [H]10-00, The Aldelphi, Singapore 0617, Singapore 1026, 3361411 (065), Fax: 3390286, State Counsel, and Member Singapore Bar, Call Date: July 1993 (Middle Temple) Qualifications: BA (Hons, Bris)

Yeung *Miss Lai Sheung*
Hong Kong, and Member Hong Kong Bar, Call Date: May 1994 (Middle Temple) Qualifications: LLB (Hons)

F

Yeung *Sunny Kwong*
C2 8F, YY Mansions, 96 Pokfulam Road, Hong Kong, 892-2118-8230 892-2816 6946, Fax: 892-2118-8084 892-2816 7762, and Member Hong Kong Bar, Call Date: Nov 1997 (Inner Temple) Qualifications: FRAIA

Yeung *Yiu Wing*
Hong Kong, Call Date: Nov 1995 (Middle Temple) Qualifications: BSc, MSc & MBA, (Hong Kong)

Yew *Mrs Lily*
Hong Kong, Call Date: July 1985 (Lincoln's Inn) Qualifications: BSc (Detroit) LLB, (Lond)

Yik *Miss Sara Synn Yi*
Jurong Town Corporation, 301 Jurong Town Hall Road, Singapore 591001, Singapore 591301, 65 5688293, Fax: 65 5651977, Legal Counsel, and Member Singapore Bar, Call Date: July 1995 (Middle Temple) Qualifications: LLB (Hons)

Yin *Michael Chi-Ming*
10/F New Henry House, 10 Ice House Street, and Member Hong Kong, Call Date: Nov 1993 (Lincoln's Inn) Qualifications: LLB (Hons)(Bris), LLM (Bris)

Ying *Wan Chong*
Flat 20G, Fu Dat Court, 32 Fortress Hill Road, 887 8552, Fax: 858 4575, Call Date: Nov 1990 (Gray's Inn) Qualifications: BScEng (HK), MSc (LSE), LLB (Lond)

Yip *Kwok Ching*
Official Receiver's Office, 11/F1 Queensway Government, Offices, 66 Queensway, Hong Kong, Senior Solicitor, Official Receiver's Office, Hong Kong Government, and Member Hong Kong Bar, Call Date: Nov 1988 (Gray's Inn) Qualifications: LLB (Lond), BSocSc, MSocSc (Hong Kong), ACIS, MCIT

Yip *Marcus Tai Meng*
Republic of Singapore, Call Date: Oct 1998 (Gray's Inn) Qualifications: LLB (Lond)

Yip *Shee Yin*
70 St Thomas Walk, [H] 07-70 Pheonix Court, Singapore 238139, 732 0758, and Member Singapore, Call Date: Nov 1996 (Inner Temple) Qualifications: BA (Dunelm)

Yiu *Kam Hung*
Hong Kong, Call Date: Nov 1994 (Middle Temple) Qualifications: B.Soc.Sc (Hons)

Yo-Hann *Tan*
Singapore 440029, Call Date: July 1997 (Inner Temple) Qualifications: LLB (Kent), LLM (Lond)

Yong *Alvin Sze Lung*
Malaysia, Call Date: Nov 1996 (Gray's Inn) Qualifications: LLB

Yong *Miss Fook-Tai*
Malaysia, and Member Malaysian Bar, Call Date: Nov 1995 (Middle Temple) Qualifications: LLB (Hons)

Yong *Miss Janet Hway Ming*
Shook Lin & Bok, 20th Floor, Arab-Malaysian Bld, 55 Jalan Raja Chulan, 50200 Kuala Lumpur, Malaysia, (03) 2011788, Legal Assistant, and Member Malaya Bar, Call Date: July 1995 (Lincoln's Inn) Qualifications: LLB (Hons), LLM

Yong *Miss Jocelyn*
Singapore 2057, Call Date: Nov 1992 (Lincoln's Inn) Qualifications: LLB (Hons)(Lond)

Yong *Sek-Cheong*
Malayan Law Journal, 3rd Floor, Wisma Bandar, No 18, Jalan Tuanku Abdul, Rahman, Kuala Lumpur 50100, Malaysia, 291 7273, Fax: 291 6440, and Member Malaysia Bar, Call Date: Oct 1992 (Gray's Inn) Qualifications: BA (Kent)

Yong *Miss Siew Lee Magdalene*
Blk 408, [H]12-433, Pasir Ris Drive 6, Singapore 510408, Singapore 1851, 5820103, Call Date: July 1995 (Middle Temple) Qualifications: LLB (Hons)

Yong *Vincent Wai Bun*
Singapore 2880, Call Date: July 1996 (Lincoln's Inn) Qualifications: LLB (Hons)

Yongo *Thomas*
United Nations Environment, Programme, Secretariat of the, Convention on Biological, Diversity, 393 St-Jacques, Suite 300,Montreal,Quebec H2Y IN9, (514) 288 2220, Fax: (514) 288 6588, Associate Legal Officer, Call Date: Nov 1994 (Gray's Inn) Qualifications: BA (Michigan), Diploma(Cantab), LLB (Kent), LLM (Lond)

Yoon *Ming Sun*
10 Lorong Derumun, Damansara Heights, 50490 Kuala Lumpur, Malaysia, 03 255 8307, Fax: 03 255 8307, Legal Assistant (Advocate & Solicitor), and Member Malaysia, Call Date: Nov 1995 (Middle Temple) Qualifications: LLB (Hons), MSc (So'ton)

Yoong *Weng Leong*
21 Jalan 5/4, 46000 Petaling Jaya, Selangor, West Malaysia, Malaysia, and Member Malaysia Bar, Call Date: Nov 1992 (Lincoln's Inn) Qualifications: BA (Hons)(Keele)

Yoshinaga *Junichiro*
General Manager, Sony Corp, 6-7-35 Kitashinagawa, Shinagawa, Tokyo 141, Japan, 03 5448 2315, Fax: 03 5448 7492, General Manager, Trade Affairs & Export Administration Dept Corp, Call Date: July 1994 (Lincoln's Inn) Qualifications: BA (Econ) (Hons), Dip Law

You *Miss Lou Yuh*
Malaysia, Call Date: July 1997 (Lincoln's Inn) Qualifications: LLB (Hons)(Lond)

Young *Miss Ai Peng*
Messrs Shareena Abdullah & Lim, No 92 Jalan Nakhoda 12, Taman Ungku Tun Aminah, 81300 Skudai, Johor Bahru, Johor, 07 5575268, Legal Assistant, Call Date: Nov 1997 (Lincoln's Inn) Qualifications: LLB (Hons)

Young *Simon Jonathan*
Bedell & Cristin, One the Forum, St Helier, Jersey JE4 8PP, 01534 814814, Fax: 01534 814815, Civil & Commercial Litigation, and Member Jersey Bar, Call Date: Oct 1991 (Middle Temple) Qualifications: LLB Hons (Buck'ham), F.I.B.M.S.

Young *Stuart Richard*
M.Hamel-Smith & Co, 19 St Vincent Street, Port of Spain, P.O.Box 219, Trinidad, West Indies, (868) 623 4237, Fax: (868) 625 0601, Associate at Law Firm, and Member Trinidad & Tobago, Call Date: July 1997 (Gray's Inn) Qualifications: LLB (Notts)

Yu *Denis Gordon Quok Chung*
Hong Kong, Call Date: July 1982 (Lincoln's Inn) Qualifications: BA (Oxon)

Yu-Min *Ms Ng Adeline*
Singapore 467018, Call Date: July 1997 (Inner Temple) Qualifications: LLB (LSE)

Yue *Jonathan Tin-Kong*
Gilt Chambers, Room 3507, Tower I, Lippo Centre, 89 Queensway, Hong Kong, 2866 8233, Fax: 2866 7858, Hong Kong Special Administration Region, Supreme Court of Hong Kong and Member Hong Kong, Call Date: Nov 1994 (Middle Temple) Qualifications: BA (Hons)

Yung *Shing Jit*
M/S Haridass Ho & Partners, 24 Raffles Place, [H]18-00 Clifford Centre, Singapore, 048621, Singapore 289509, 65-5332323, Fax: 65-5331579, Partner, and Member Singapore Bar, Call Date: July 1990 (Middle Temple) Qualifications: LLB (Hull)

Yusoff *Yusrin Faidz*
34 Jalan SS21/44, Damansara Utama, 47400 Petaling Jaya, Selangor, Malaysia, 03 7171210, Legal Assistant, and Member Malaysia, Call Date: July 1996 (Lincoln's Inn) Qualifications: LLB (Hons), MBA

Yusuf *Miss Kartini*
17-27-1 Majestic Tower, Mont' Kiara Palma, Jln Mont Kiara, Jln 1/40c, 50480 Kuala Lumpur, Malaysia, (03) 2533127, Call Date: May 1995 (Lincoln's Inn) Qualifications: BA (Hons), LLB (Hons), LLM

Zachariadou *Miss Anthie Philippou*
14 Mnasiadou Street, Nicosia, Cyprus,
003572 475047, Fax: 003572 467532,
Call Date: Feb 1995 (Lincoln's Inn)
Qualifications: LLB (Hons)(Lond)

Zadra-Symes *Mrs Lynda Julie*
Knobbe Martens Olson & Bear, 620
Newport Center Drive, Newport Beach
CA 92660, 00 1 714 760 0404, Fax: 00
1 714 760 9502, and Member
California Bar, Call Date: Nov 1989
(Inner Temple) Qualifications: LLB

Zafer *Mohammed Abu*
Bangladesh, Call Date: Mar 1997
(Gray's Inn) Qualifications: MCom
(Dhaka), LLB (Lond)

Zaharudin *Miss Faten Aina*
Malaysia, Call Date: July 1997
(Lincoln's Inn) Qualifications: LLB
(Hons)(Nott'm)

Zainal *Ms Suriawati*
Malaysia, Call Date: July 1994
(Lincoln's Inn) Qualifications: LLB
(Hons)

Zam Zam *Mrs Asiah*
101 Upper Cross Street, [H]06-18
People's Park, Centre, Singapore
710579, 5338188, Fax: 5336100, Legal
Assistant, Call Date: Nov 1996
(Lincoln's Inn) Qualifications: LLB
(Hons)(Lond)

Zambarta *Miss Myrto*
Cyprus, Call Date: Oct 1998 (Middle
Temple) Qualifications: BA
(Hons)(Cantab)

Zawoda-Martin *Justin Raphael*
Coutts Group, Talstrasse 59, P O Box
CH-8022, Zurich, Switzerland, +41 1
214 5580, Fax: +41 1 214 5563, Chief
of Staff, Call Date: Oct 1994 (Middle
Temple) Qualifications: BA
(Hons)(Lond), CPE (City)

Zornoza *Simon*
Legal Division - Securities Op, State
Street Bank & Trust Co, 1776 Heritage
Drive, North Quincy, MA 02171, United
States of America, (617) 985 9271, Fax:
(617) 985 4000, Vice President and
Counsel, and Member New York Bar,
District of Columbia Bar, Call Date: July
1983 (Inner Temple) Qualifications:
LLB (B'ham), Diplome, d'Etudes
Juridiques, Francaises

Zuberi *Miss Danish*
Pakistan, Call Date: Nov 1995 (Gray's
Inn) Qualifications: LLB (Wales)

Zulkifli *Miss Zurisafina*
Malaysia, Legal Assistant, and Member
Malaysia, Call Date: July 1997
(Lincoln's Inn) Qualifications: LLB
(Hons)

a watchful eye

T he Royal Air Forces Association helps over 50,000 serving and retired RAF men and women and their dependants each year.

We rely totally on donations and legacies to fund our work - please help us to watch over those in need of our care.

For further information or a FREE copy of our Guide to Making a Will please contact:

RAFA
THE ROYAL AIR FORCES ASSOCIATION

Charity Registration No. 226686

The Direct Fundraising Co-ordinator
The Royal Air Forces Association • Dept BARD/2000
FREEPOST W4 3BR • 43 Grove Park Road • London • WR14 1BR
Telephone: 0181 994 8504 Facsimile: 0181 742 1927

Photo courtesy of Rolls Royce Plc.

Cancer
stopped my life
One in four people die from it

"My life stopped when I was diagnosed with breast cancer. I needed a break from the endless round of tests and treatments. So I agreed to attend the Paul Bevan Hospice. Therapies helped ease the pain and sharing how I felt, helped me to cope with the turmoil that cancer brings." Paul Bevan patient.

A time comes in all our lives when it may not be possible to care for ourselves. No one to share the experience with. No one to tell about the loneliness, the pain and loss of independence one feels. We help them through this painful experience providing comforting care, in a loving environment, where they can communicate with other patients. We support their families and carers, providing respite and counselling at a traumatic stage of life.

The Paul Bevan Day Hospice is a registered charity that provides for 3,750 patients a year. We receive no money from the government. We rely entirely on compassionate people who care about those with terminal illness.

Our special care is free to all patients. But care is not cheap. Donations, Legacies and Covenants are a vital source of income to continue our work. When it comes to making a Will, your recommendation is important. Please ask your clients to leave a legacy of hope.

Make us your 1st Choice
Caring for the ones you love

Paul Bevan Day Hospice, Paul Bevan House,
King's Ride, Ascot SL5 7RD
Tel 01344 877877 Fax 01344 877878

REGISTERED CHARITY NO. 1027496

THE
PAUL BEVAN
DAY HOSPICE

Caring for the ones you love

Index of Languages Spoken

This section provides an index of all languages spoken by chambers and individual barristers. The languages are listed alphabetically, as are chambers and individuals.

All chambers in this section have an expanded entry in *Part C Chambers by Location* and all individual barristers in this section have an expanded entry in *Part D Individual Barristers in Private Practice.*

G

AFRIKAANS

Fountain Court
Two Garden Court
Littman Chambers
Oriel Chambers
Tselentis, Michael

ARABIC

One Essex Court
Foster, Charles Andrew
One Hare Court
Hossain, Ajmalul
Keating Chambers
2 Paper Buildings
3 Paper Buildings
3 Raymond Buildings

BENGALI

8 Fountain Court
Hossain, Ajmalul
1 Middle Temple Lane

BRITISH SIGN LANGUAGE

Doughty Street Chambers
Chambers of Ian Macdonald QC
  (In Association with Two
  Garden Court, Temple,
  London)

BULGARIAN

1 Pump Court

CANTONESE

One Essex Court
Guildford Chambers
13 King's Bench Walk
2 Paper Buildings

CHINESE

Essex Court Chambers

CZECH

Sovereign Chambers

DANISH

Chambers of Ian Macdonald QC
  (In Association with Two
  Garden Court, Temple,
  London)
4 Paper Buildings

DUTCH

Blackstone Chambers
Chancery House Chambers
4 Essex Court
Two Garden Court
3 Hare Court
Lamb Building
Littman Chambers
Monckton Chambers
Old Square Chambers
4 Paper Buildings
1 Pump Court
3 Raymond Buildings
2-4 Tudor Street
Turner, James Michael

FARSI

Hardwicke Building
Mitre House Chambers

FINNISH

Blackstone Chambers

FRENCH

Anderson, Miss Julie
Arden Chambers
Beaumont, Marc Clifford
Becket Chambers
Chambers of Michael Pert QC
9-12 Bell Yard
Blackstone Chambers
4 Breams Buildings
4 Brick Court
4 Brick Court, Chambers of
  Anne Rafferty QC
Cakebread, Stuart Alan Charles
17 Carlton Crescent
Catchpole, Stuart Paul
Central Chambers
Chancery House Chambers
Cobden House Chambers
College Chambers
Conlon, Michael Anthony
Chambers of Mr Peter Crampin
  QC
1 Crown Office Row
Two Crown Office Row
Devereux Chambers
Doughty Street Chambers
3 Dr Johnson's Buildings
Dr Johnson's Chambers
Eighteen Carlton Crescent
Elleray, Anthony John
Enterprise Chambers
One Essex Court
One Essex Court
4 Essex Court
Essex Court Chambers
20 Essex Street
35 Essex Street
39 Essex Street
Exchange Chambers
Farrar's Building
Chambers of Norman Palmer
4 Field Court
Foster, Charles Andrew
Fountain Court
3 Fountain Court
5 Fountain Court
2nd Floor, Francis Taylor
  Building
Furnival Chambers
Two Garden Court
Goldsmith Building
9 Gough Square
Gough Square Chambers
Gray's Inn Chambers, The
  Chambers of Norman
  Patterson
2-3 Gray's Inn Square
4-5 Gray's Inn Square
Guildford Chambers
1 Harcourt Buildings
2 Harcourt Buildings
2 Harcourt Buildings
Harcourt Chambers
Hardwicke Building

1 Hare Court
One Hare Court
3 Hare Court
Harrow on the Hill Chambers
Hendy, John Giles
Hockman, Stephen Alexander
Hodgkinson, Tristram Patrick
1 Inner Temple Lane
Jones, Timothy Arthur
Keating Chambers
40 King Street
One King's Bench Walk
4 King's Bench Walk
6 King's Bench Walk
11 King's Bench Walk
12 King's Bench Walk
13 King's Bench Walk
Kolodziej, Andrzej Jozef
Kramer, Stephen Ernest
Lamb Building
Littleton Chambers
Littman Chambers
Chambers of Ian Macdonald QC
  (In Association with Two
  Garden Court, Temple,
  London)
Maidstone Chambers
Malecka, Dr Mary Margaret
McMullen, Jeremy John
McNeill, Miss Elizabeth Jane
Melville, Richard David
Mercer, Hugh Charles
Merchant Chambers
Michael, Simon Laurence
1 Middle Temple Lane
Mitre Court Chambers
Mitre House Chambers
Monckton Chambers
New Court
New Court Chambers
1 New Square
Chambers of John L Powell QC
8 New Square
12 New Square
Newman, Miss Catherine Mary
Oakley, Anthony James
22 Old Buildings
Twenty-Four Old Buildings
9 Old Square
11 Old Square
Old Square Chambers
Oriel Chambers
2 Paper Buildings
3 Paper Buildings
4 Paper Buildings
5 Paper Buildings
Park Court Chambers
30 Park Square
37 Park Square Chambers
Parkin, Jonathan
Persey, Lionel Edward
Pitt-Payne, Timothy Sheridan
Plender, Richard Owen
Portsmouth Barristers'
  Chambers
1 Pump Court
Pump Court Chambers
4 Pump Court
5 Pump Court
Queen Elizabeth Building
Hollis Whiteman Chambers

Queen's Chambers
3 Raymond Buildings
5 Raymond Buildings
3 Serjeants' Inn
Serle Court Chambers
Sheridan, Maurice Bernard
  Gerard
3/4 South Square
11 South Square
Southall, Richard Anthony
Southern, David Boardman
Sovereign Chambers
St James's Chambers
28 St John Street
St Paul's House
St Philip's Chambers
Stanbrook & Henderson
Sternberg, Michael Vivian
3 Stone Buildings
5 Stone Buildings
9 Stone Buildings
Stone, Gregory
199 Strand
1 Temple Gardens
2 Temple Gardens
3 Temple Gardens
Thomas More Chambers
14 Tooks Court
Trace, Anthony John
2-4 Tudor Street
Turner, James Michael
Turner, Jonathan David Chattyn
West, Mark
Wilberforce Chambers
Wilson, Alastair James Drysdale
Windsor Chambers
9 Woodhouse Square
York Chambers

GAELIC

5 Paper Buildings

GERMAN

Chambers of Michael Pert QC
9-12 Bell Yard
Blackstone Chambers
Central Chambers
Chancery House Chambers
Chambers of Mr Peter Crampin
  QC
Devereux Chambers
Doughty Street Chambers
Eighteen Carlton Crescent
Enterprise Chambers
One Essex Court
4 Essex Court
Essex Court Chambers
20 Essex Street
35 Essex Street
39 Essex Street
Chambers of Norman Palmer
4 Field Court
Fountain Court
3 Fountain Court
5 Fountain Court
Furnival Chambers
Two Garden Court
Gray's Inn Chambers, The
  Chambers of Norman
  Patterson
2-3 Gray's Inn Square

4-5 Gray's Inn Square
1 Harcourt Buildings
2 Harcourt Buildings
Harcourt Chambers
Hardwicke Building
3 Hare Court
1 Inner Temple Lane
Keating Chambers
40 King Street
One King's Bench Walk
4 King's Bench Walk
6 King's Bench Walk
Lamb Building
Littleton Chambers
Littman Chambers
Chambers of Ian Macdonald QC
    (In Association with Two
    Garden Court, Temple,
    London)
Mercer, Hugh Charles
1 Middle Temple Lane
Mitre Court Chambers
Mitre House Chambers
Monckton Chambers
New Court
New Court Chambers
Chambers of John L Powell QC
8 New Square
12 New Square
9 Old Square
Oriel Chambers
2 Paper Buildings
3 Paper Buildings
4 Paper Buildings
4 Paper Buildings
5 Paper Buildings
Park Court Chambers
30 Park Square
37 Park Square Chambers
Portsmouth Barristers'
    Chambers
1 Pump Court
Pump Court Chambers
4 Pump Court
5 Pump Court
Hollis Whiteman Chambers
3 Raymond Buildings
5 Raymond Buildings
Rowe, John Jermyn
3 Serjeants' Inn
Serle Court Chambers
3/4 South Square
11 South Square
Southern, David Boardman
Sovereign Chambers
St James's Chambers
St Philip's Chambers
199 Strand
1 Temple Gardens
2 Temple Gardens
3 Temple Gardens
14 Tooks Court
2-4 Tudor Street
Turner, James Michael
Wilberforce Chambers
9 Woodhouse Square
York Chambers

GREEK

4 Brick Court
Doughty Street Chambers
4 Essex Court

Fountain Court
Furnival Chambers
2-3 Gray's Inn Square
4-5 Gray's Inn Square
Hardwicke Building
1 Hare Court
1 Inner Temple Lane
Littleton Chambers
2 Paper Buildings
3 Paper Buildings
5 Pump Court
Hollis Whiteman Chambers

GUJARATI

39 Essex Street
Harrow on the Hill Chambers
1 Pump Court

HEBREW

4 Brick Court
Central Chambers
Doughty Street Chambers
One Essex Court
Chambers of Norman Palmer
9 Gough Square
Gray's Inn Chambers, The
    Chambers of Norman
    Patterson
3 Hare Court
One King's Bench Walk
Lamb Building
Littleton Chambers
Chambers of Ian Macdonald QC
    (In Association with Two
    Garden Court, Temple,
    London)
Merchant Chambers
New Court Chambers
4 Paper Buildings
37 Park Square Chambers
Serle Court Chambers
199 Strand
2-4 Tudor Street

HINDI

Ali, Zafar
9-12 Bell Yard
Blackstone Chambers
4 Brick Court
4 Brick Court, Chambers of
    Anne Rafferty QC
Central Chambers
8 Fountain Court
Two Garden Court
Gray's Inn Chambers, The
    Chambers of Norman
    Patterson
Hardwicke Building
1 Hare Court
Harrow on the Hill Chambers
Hossain, Ajmalul
Chambers of Ian Macdonald QC
    (In Association with Two
    Garden Court, Temple,
    London)
Mitre House Chambers
New Court Chambers
Chambers of John L Powell QC
2 Paper Buildings
Park Court Chambers
1 Pump Court

5 Pump Court
Queen Elizabeth Building
St Paul's House

IBO

Old Square Chambers

ICELANDIC

30 Park Square

ITALIAN

9-12 Bell Yard
Blackstone Chambers
4 Brick Court
4 Brick Court, Chambers of
    Anne Rafferty QC
17 Carlton Crescent
Chambers of Mr Peter Crampin
    QC
Two Crown Office Row
Doughty Street Chambers
Enterprise Chambers
One Essex Court
4 Essex Court
Essex Court Chambers
20 Essex Street
35 Essex Street
39 Essex Street
Chambers of Norman Palmer
4 Field Court
Fountain Court
Furnival Chambers
Gray's Inn Chambers, The
    Chambers of Norman
    Patterson
2-3 Gray's Inn Square
2 Harcourt Buildings
Hardwicke Building
3 Hare Court
1 Inner Temple Lane
Jones, Timothy Arthur
6 King's Bench Walk
11 King's Bench Walk
12 King's Bench Walk
13 King's Bench Walk
Lamb Building
Littleton Chambers
Chambers of Ian Macdonald QC
    (In Association with Two
    Garden Court, Temple,
    London)
Maidstone Chambers
McNeill, Miss Elizabeth Jane
Mercer, Hugh Charles
Mitre House Chambers
New Court
Chambers of John L Powell QC
8 New Square
Nuvoloni, Stefano Vincenzo
22 Old Buildings
Twenty-Four Old Buildings
Old Square Chambers
2 Paper Buildings
4 Paper Buildings
5 Paper Buildings
4 Pump Court
5 Pump Court
Hollis Whiteman Chambers
3 Raymond Buildings
5 Raymond Buildings

Sheridan, Maurice Bernard
    Gerard
3/4 South Square
Sovereign Chambers
St Paul's House
St Philip's Chambers
Stanbrook & Henderson
5 Stone Buildings
2 Temple Gardens
14 Tooks Court
2-4 Tudor Street
Windsor Chambers

JAPANESE

Blackstone Chambers
2 Harcourt Buildings
4 King's Bench Walk
Monckton Chambers
3 New Square
30 Park Square
Stanbrook & Henderson
199 Strand

KRIO (SIERRA LEONE)

3 Hare Court

MALAY

Guildford Chambers

MANDARIN CHINESE

4 Brick Court
Chambers of Norman Palmer
Littleton Chambers
3/4 South Square
199 Strand

MARATHI

2 Paper Buildings

NEPALI

New Court Chambers

NORWEGIAN

Blackstone Chambers
40 King Street

PERSIAN

4 Field Court

POLISH

Chambers of Michael Pert QC
Kolodziej, Andrzej Jozef
Littman Chambers
Malecka, Dr Mary Margaret
Merchant Chambers
2 Paper Buildings
5 Raymond Buildings

PORTUGUESE

Blackstone Chambers
Enterprise Chambers
4 Essex Court
Furnival Chambers
Hardwicke Building
One King's Bench Walk
12 King's Bench Walk
13 King's Bench Walk

Chambers of Ian Macdonald QC
  (In Association with Two
  Garden Court, Temple,
  London)
4 Paper Buildings
Stanbrook & Henderson
3 Stone Buildings
2-4 Tudor Street

PUNJABI

Ali, Zafar
8 Fountain Court
Hardwicke Building
Chambers of Ian Macdonald QC
  (In Association with Two
  Garden Court, Temple,
  London)
5 Paper Buildings
1 Pump Court
Sovereign Chambers
St Philip's Chambers

RUSSIAN

9-12 Bell Yard
Blackstone Chambers
4 Brick Court
Doughty Street Chambers
Chambers of Norman Palmer
Fountain Court
Littman Chambers
Malecka, Dr Mary Margaret
New Court
4 Paper Buildings
Hollis Whiteman Chambers
Sovereign Chambers
St James's Chambers

SERBO-CROAT

Chambers of Michael Pert QC
Chambers of Norman Palmer
Furnival Chambers
3 Hare Court
Mitre Court Chambers

SINHALA

Two Garden Court
Mitre House Chambers

SPANISH

Chambers of Michael Pert QC
9-12 Bell Yard
Blackstone Chambers
4 Brick Court
4 Brick Court, Chambers of
  Anne Rafferty QC
1 Crown Office Row
Doughty Street Chambers
Dr Johnson's Chambers
Enterprise Chambers
One Essex Court
4 Essex Court
Essex Court Chambers
20 Essex Street
39 Essex Street
Chambers of Norman Palmer
5 Fountain Court
Furnival Chambers
Two Garden Court

Gray's Inn Chambers, The
  Chambers of Norman
  Patterson
4-5 Gray's Inn Square
1 Harcourt Buildings
2 Harcourt Buildings
Hardwicke Building
1 Hare Court
Keating Chambers
One King's Bench Walk
4 King's Bench Walk
6 King's Bench Walk
11 King's Bench Walk
12 King's Bench Walk
Lamb Building
Littman Chambers
Chambers of Ian Macdonald QC
  (In Association with Two
  Garden Court, Temple,
  London)
Mercer, Hugh Charles
Merchant Chambers
Mitre Court Chambers
Mitre House Chambers
Chambers of John L Powell QC
8 New Square
Oakley, Anthony James
Twenty-Four Old Buildings
9 Old Square
11 Old Square
Old Square Chambers
Oriel Chambers
2 Paper Buildings
3 Paper Buildings
4 Paper Buildings
4 Paper Buildings
5 Paper Buildings
Plender, Richard Owen
1 Pump Court
4 Pump Court
Queen Elizabeth Building
Hollis Whiteman Chambers
3 Raymond Buildings
3/4 South Square
Sovereign Chambers
St James's Chambers
28 St John Street
St Philip's Chambers
Stanbrook & Henderson
3 Stone Buildings
5 Stone Buildings
7 Stone Buildings
1 Temple Gardens
2 Temple Gardens
Thomas More Chambers
14 Tooks Court
2-4 Tudor Street
9 Woodhouse Square

SWAHILI

Trace, Anthony John

SWEDISH

Blackstone Chambers

TURKISH

One Essex Court
4 King's Bench Walk
Mitre House Chambers
14 Tooks Court

URDU

Ali, Zafar
Chambers of Michael Pert QC
9-12 Bell Yard
Blackstone Chambers
Central Chambers
3 Dr Johnson's Buildings
4 Field Court
8 Fountain Court
Two Garden Court
Gray's Inn Chambers, The
  Chambers of Norman
  Patterson
Hardwicke Building
1 Hare Court
Hossain, Ajmalul
40 King Street
Chambers of Ian Macdonald QC
  (In Association with Two
  Garden Court, Temple,
  London)
Park Court Chambers
1 Pump Court
5 Pump Court
St Paul's House
Thomas More Chambers
14 Tooks Court

WELSH

Chambers of Ian Macdonald QC
  (In Association with Two
  Garden Court, Temple,
  London)
3 Paper Buildings
St Philip's Chambers
Windsor Chambers

YORUBA

Gray's Inn Chambers, The
  Chambers of Norman
  Patterson

Qualified Members of the Institute of Barristers' Clerks

This section lists all qualified members of the Institute of Barristers' Clerks. The listings are divided into four sections: Senior Clerks, Junior Clerks, Senior Associates and Junior Associates. The information in Part H was supplied by the Institute of Barristers' Clerks. The year of qualification, if supplied, is shown in brackets. Management Committee Members and Executive Committee Members are identified by the following symbols:

* Management Committee Members
** Executive Committee Members

SENIOR CLERKS

Alden, Philip (1990)
Colleton Chambers, Colleton Crescent, Exeter EX2 4DG, DX:8330, Tel: 01392 274898

Aldridge, Kevin (1979)
3 Temple Gardens, Temple, EC4Y 9AU, LDE 485, Tel: 0171 353 9297

Appleyard, Neil
Broadway House Chambers, 9 Bank Street, Bradford BD1 1TW, DX 11746 Bradford, Tel: 01274 722560

Armstrong, Gordon (1978)
4 Essex Court, Temple, EC4Y 9AP, LDE 292, Tel: 0171 797 7970

Arter, John
2 Pump Court, Temple, EC4Y 7AH, LDE 290, Tel: 0171 353 5597

Austin Alan, (1983)
9 Stone Buildings, Lincoln's Inn, WC2A 3NN, LDE 314, Tel: 0171 404 5055

Austin, David (1976)
Rope Walk Chambers, Nottingham, DX 10060, Tel: 01159 472581

Austin, M. (Trevor)
Verulam Chambers, Peer House, 8/14 Verulam Street, WC1X 8LZ, LDE 436, Tel: 0171 813 2400

Ballard, Paul (1979)
1 Hare Court, Temple, EC4Y 7BE, LDE 0065, Tel: 0171 353 3171

Barrow, Adrian (1979)
6 Pump Court, Temple, EC4Y 7AR, LDE 409, Tel: 0171 583 6013

Bayliss, Richard
3 New Square, Lincoln's Inn, WC2A 3RS, LDE 384, Tel: 0171 405 5577

Beazley, Roy
8 New Square, Lincoln's Inn, WC2A 3QP, LDE 311, Tel: 0171 306 0102

Berry, Christopher
11 Stone Buildings, Lincoln's Inn, WC2A 3TG, LDE 1022 Tel: 0171 831 6381

Blaney, Arthur
11 King's Bench Walk, Temple, EC4Y 7EQ, LDE 389, Tel: 0171 353 3337

Brewer, Alan
22 Old Buildings, Lincoln's Inn, WC2A 3UJ, LDE 201, Tel: 0171 831 0222

Bridgman, Barry
10 Essex Street, Outer Temple, WC2R 3AA, LDE 1045, Tel: 0171 240 6981

Brinning, David
32 Park Place, Cardiff, CF1 3BA, DX 50769, Tel: 01222 397364

Brooks, Norman (1976)
4 King's Bench Walk, Temple, EC4Y 7DL, LDE 383, Tel: 0171 353 6832

Brown, William (1978)
40 King Street, Manchester, M2 6BA, DX 718188 MAN 3, Tel: 0161 832 9082

Bryant, Stuart
5 Paper Buildings, Temple, EC4Y 7HB, LDE 365, Tel: 0171 583 6117

Burton, Russell (1995)
Albion Chambers, 22 Albion Place, Northampton, NN1 1UD, DX 12464 Northampton, Tel: 01604 36271

Butchard, Robin
10 Park Square, Leeds, LS1 2LH, DX 26412 Leeds, Tel: 0113 245 5438

Broom, Christopher (1987)
2/3 Gray's Inn Square, WC1R 5JH, LDE 316, Tel: 0171 242 4986

Butler, Deryk
1 Hare Court, Temple, EC4Y 7BE, LDE 444, Tel: 0171 353 3982

Calver, Neil

Call, John
8, New Square, Lincoln's Inn, WC2A 3QP, LDE 379, Tel: 0171 405 4321

Charlick, John
3 Paper Buildings, Temple, EC4Y 7EU, LDE 1024, Tel: 0171 583 8055

Chessis, Clark
1 Serjeants' Inn, London, EC4Y 1LL, LDE 364, Tel: 0171 353 9901

Clark, Michael
2 Field Court, Gray's Inn, WC1R 5BB, LDE 457, Tel: 0171 405 6114

Clark, Stephen
Lorne Park Chambers, 20, Lorne Park Road, Bournemouth, BH1 1JN, DX 7612 Bournemouth, Tel: 01202 292102

**Clayton, Barry
9 Old Square, Lincoln's Inn, WC2A 3SR, LDE 301, Tel: 0171 405 9471 (Chancery Secretary)

Clewley, Mark
Falcon Chambers, Falcon Court, EC4Y 1AA, LDE 408, Tel: 0171 353 2484

Collier, Alan
2 Harcourt Buildings, Temple, EC4Y 9DB, LDE 402, Tel: 0171 353 8415

Collins, Ian (1977)
3, Raymond Buildings, Gray's Inn,WC1R 5BH, LDE 237, Tel: 0171 831 3833

Collison, Peter
25 Byron Street, Manchester, M3 4PF, DX 718156 MAN 3, Tel: 0161 829 2100

Conner, Alan
King's Bench Walk Chambers, Wellington House, 175 Holdenhurst Road, Bournemouth, BH8 8DQ, DX 7617 Bournemouth, Tel: 01202 250025

Conner, William
New Court Chambers, 5 Verulam Buildings, WC1R 5LY, LDE 363, Tel: 0171 831 9500

Cook, Colin
2 Garden Court, Temple, EC4Y 9BL, LDE 34, Tel: 0171 353 1633

Coomber, Simon
New Court, Temple, EC4Y 9BE, LDE 420, Tel: 0171 797 8999

Corrigan, Michael
4th Floor, 4 Brick Court, Temple, EC4Y 9AD, LDE 491, Tel: 0171 797 8910

*Creathorn, Teresa
Deans Court Chambers, Manchester, M3 3HA, DX 18155, Tel: 0161 834 4097

Davies, Hugh (1988)
30 Park Place, Cardiff, CF1 3BA, DX 50756, Tel: 01222 398421

Dean, Michael (1988)
5 Essex Court, Temple, EC4Y 9AH, LDE 1048, Tel: 0171 583 2825

Dear, David (1988)
1 King's Bench Walk, Temple, EC4Y 7DB, LDE 20, Tel: 0171 583 6266

Diggles, S
68 Quay Street, Manchester, M3 3BL, DX 14350, Tel: 0161 834 7000

Dixon, Christopher (1987)
25 Park Square, Leeds LS1 2PW, DX 26408, Tel: 0113 2457841

Doe, Christopher
1, Essex Court, Temple, EC4Y 9AR, LDE 371, Tel: 0171 936 3030

Driscoll, Robin
2 Paper Buildings, Temple, EC4, LDE 494, Tel: 0171 936 2611

Duane, Patrick
2 Dr Johnson's Buildings, Temple, EC4Y 7BY, LDE 429, Tel: 0171 353 4716

Elder, Malcolm (1976)

Edmiston, James

Effeny, Wayne (1984)
2/3 College Place, Southampton, SO1 2FB, DX 38533, Tel: 01703 230338

Ellis, Barry
1 Hare Court, Temple, EC4Y 7BE, LDE 0065, Tel: 0171 353 3171

English, Stephen
46/48, Essex Street, WC2R 3GH, LDE 1014, Tel: 0171 583 8800

Eves, Michael (1975)
4 Brick Court, 1st Floor, Temple, EC4Y 9AD, LDE 453, Tel: 0171 583 8455

Farrell, Michael (1978)

Flanagan, Paul (1988)
20/23 Holborn, EC1N 2JD, LDE 336, Tel: 0171 242 8508

Foss, Marc (1984)
8 King's Bench Walk, Temple, EC4Y 7DU, LDE 195, Tel: 0171 797 8888

Gallogly, Lawrence (1976)
Phoenix Chambers, 47A, Bedford Row, WC1R 4LR, LDE 78, Tel: 0171 404 7888

Garstang, David
6 King's Bench Walk, Temple, EC4Y 7DR, LDE 26, Tel: 0171 583 0410

Gibbs, Michael (1988)
11 New Square, Lincoln's Inn, WC2A 3QB, LDE 319, Tel: 0171 831 0081

Gilbert, Richard
Tindall Chambers, 3, Waxhouse Gate, St. Albans, Hertfordshire, AL5 4DU, DX 6116 St Albans, Tel: 01727 843383

**Goddard, David (1976)
4 Stone Buildings, Lincoln's Inn, WC2A 3XT, LDE 385, Tel: 0171 242 5524 **(Chairman)**

Goldsmith, Stuart (1976)
1 Atkin Building, Gray's Inn, WC1R 5BQ, DX 1033, Tel: 0171 404 0102

Goodger, Gary (1980)
Lamb Buildings, Temple, EC4, LDE 1038, Tel: 0171 797 7788

Graham, Stephen
4 Breams Buildings, London, EC4A 1AQ, LDE 1042, Tel: 0171 353 5835

Green, Paul (1982)
Tindall Chambers, Chelmsford, CM1 1SW, DX 3358, Tel: 01245 267742

Greenaway, Michael
Queen Elizabeth Building, Temple, EC4Y 9BS, LDE 482, Tel: 0171 583 5766

Grief, David (1976)
Essex Court Chambers, EC4Y 9AJ, LDE 320, Tel: 0171 813 8000

**Griffiths, Martin (1978)
199 Strand, London, WC2R 1DR, LDE 322, Tel: 0171 379 9779

Grisdale, Neil (1976)
20 North John Street, Liverpool, L2 9RL, DX 14220, Tel: 0151 236 6757

**Gutteridge, John (1983)
32, Furnival Street, EC4A 1JQ, LDE 72, Tel: 0171 405 3232

Hallett, C J
Thomas More Chambers, 51/52 Carey Street, WC2A 2JB, LDE 90, Tel: 0171 404 7000

**Hannibal, Michael (1977)
Erskine Chambers, 30 Lincoln's Inn Fields, WC2A 3PF, LDE 308, Tel: 0171 242 5532 **(Treasurer)**

Harwood, John

Hawes, Julian
Brick Court Chambers, Devereaux Court, WC2, LDE 302, Tel:0171 583 0777

Hayfield, C
1 Fountain Court, Birmingham, B4 6DR, DX 16077 Birmingham, Tel: 0121 236 5721

Hogg, Ian (1991)
Hamilton House, 1, Temple Avenue, EC4Y 0HA, LDE 416, Tel: 0171 353 4212

Hopgood, Nicholas
23 Essex Street, London, WC2 3AS, LDE 148, Tel: 0171 413 0353

Hoskins, Peter
14, Gray's Inn Square, WC1R 5JP, LDE 399, Tel: 0171 242 0858

Hyatt, Bernie (1988)
7 King's Bench Walk, Temple, EC4Y 7DS, LDE 239, Tel: 0171 583 0404

Hyde, Nicholas
St. John's Chambers, Small Street, Bristol, BS1 1DW, DX 78138, Tel: 0117 921 3456

James, Christopher (1988)

Jeffery, Gary (1988)
6 King's Bench Walk, Temple, EC4Y 7EQ, LDE 471, Tel: 0171 353 4931

Jenkins, Derek (1988)
35, Essex Street, Temple, WC2R 3AR, LDE 351, Tel: 0171 353 6381

Jennings, Paul (1986)
5, Stone Buildings, Lincoln's Inn, WC2, LDE 304, Tel: 0171 242 6201

Jones, Michael
15 Winkley Square, Preston, PR1 3JJ, DX 17110, Tel: 01772 252828

Kaplan, Michael
4/5 Gray's Inn Square, WC1R, LDE 1029, Tel: 0171 404 5252

Kay, Jonathan
3 East Pallant, Chichester, PO19 1TR, DX 30303, Tel: 01243 784538

Kennedy, John
Wilberforce Chambers, Kingston upon Hull, HU1 1PA, DX 11940, Tel: 01482 323264

Kilbey, Alan
Farrars Building, Temple, EC4Y 7DB, LDE 406, Tel: 0171 583 9241

* Management Committee Members, ** Executive Committee Members

King, Robert
Peel House, 5/7 Harrington Street, Liverpool, L2 9QA, DX 14225, Tel: 0151 236 4321

Knight, Lynda
17 Carlton Crescent, Southampton SO9 5AL, DX 49663, Tel: 01703 639001

Laking, John

Lee, Warren
1 New Square, Lincoln's Inn, WC2A 3SA, LDE 295, Tel: 0171 405 0884

Lister, Graham
4 Raymond Buildings, Gray's Inn, WC1R 5BP, LDE 257, Tel: 0171 405 7211

*Lister, John
11 Bolt Court, London, EC4A 3DQ, LDE 0022, Tel: 0171 353 2300

Logan, Graeme
36, Bedford Row, WC1R 4JH, LDE 360, Tel: 0171 421 8000

Luff, Alan
8, Stone Buildings, WC2A 3TA, LDE 216, Tel: 0171 831 9881

Madden, Barry
Tindal Chambers, 3/5 New St, Chelsmford, CM1 1NT, DX 3358, Tel: 01245 267742

Maloney, Miss C
8 Fountain Court, Birmingham, B4 6DR, DX 16078 Birmingham, Tel: 0121 236 5514

Markham, John
2 Mitre Court, Temple, EC4Y 7BX, LDE 0023, Tel: 0171 353 1353

Markham, Timothy
5 Pump Court, Temple, EC4Y 7AP, LDE 497, Tel: 0171 353 2532.

Martin, Michael

Maryon, Elton
Devereux Chambers, Devereux Court, Temple, WC2R 3JJ, LDE 349, Tel: 0171 353 7534

*Maskew, Jonathan (1988)
3 Fountain Court, Birmingham, B4 6DR, DX 16079, Tel: 0121 236 2286

McCombe, Carolyn
4 Pump Court, Temple, EC4Y 7AN, LDE 303, Tel: 0171 353 2656

McDaid, Anthony (1988)
5 Fountain Court, Birmingham, B4 6DR, DX 16705, Tel: 0121 236 5771

McLaren, Fraser
East Anglian Chambers, Colchester, CO1 1PY, DX 361, Tel: 01206 573401

Merry-Price, Roger
3 Verulam Buildings, WC1R 5NT, LDE 331, Tel: 0171 831 8441

Milsom, Dennis
Albion Chambers, Broad St, Bristol BS1 1DR, DX 7822 Bristol, Tel: 0117 927 2144

Monham, Philip
11 King's Bench Walk, Temple, EC4Y 7EQ, LDE 368, Tel: 0171 583 0610

**Monksfield, Celia
Goldsmith Chambers, Temple EC4Y 7BL, LDE 376, Tel: 0171 353 6802(Common Law Secretary)

Moore, John
13 Old Square, Lincoln's Inn, WC2A 3UA, LDE 326, Tel: 0171 404 4800

Moore, Kevin (1979)
Francis Taylor Building, Temple, EC4Y 7BY, LDE 211, Tel: 0171 353 9942

*Moore, Richard
Guildford Chambers, Guildford, GU1 4LY, DX 97863, Tel: 01483 539131

Neeld, Rodney
4 Fountain Court, Birmingham, B4 6DR, DX 16074, Tel: 0121 236 3476

Nicholls, Martyn (1980)
11 South Square, Gray's Inn, WC1, LDE 433, Tel: 0171 405 1222

*Nixon, Peter
Assize Court Chambers, Bristol, BS1 1DE, DX 78134, Tel: 0117 926 4587

**Odiam, Alan (1990)
3 Paper Buildings, Temple, EC4, LDE 1024, Tel: 0171-583-8055 (Education Secretary)

Owen, Christopher
9, Bedford Row, WC1R 4AZ, LDE 347, Tel: 0171 242 3555

Palmer, Neil (1984)
20 Essex Street, London, WC2R 3AL, LDE 0009, Tel: 0171 583 9294

Parker, David
Rougemont Chambers, 8 Colleton Crescent, Exeter, Devon, EX2 4DG, DX 8396 Exeter 1, Tel: 01392 208484

Payne, John
Park Lane Chambers, 19, Westgate, Leeds, LS1 2RD, DX 26404 Leeds Park Square, Tel: 0113 228 5000

Petchey, Clive (1984)
12 New Square, Lincoln's Inn, WC2A 3SW, LDE 366, Tel: 0171 405 3808

Pithers, Jason
3-4 South Square, Gray's Inn, WC1R 5HP, LDE 338, Tel: 0171 696 9900

Phipps, John
1 Crown Office Row, Temple, EC4Y 7HH, LDE 226, Tel: 0171 797 7111

Pickles, Jack
28 St. John Street Chambers, Manchester, M3 4DJ, DX 728861, Tel: 0161 834 8418

*Poulter, Martin
36, Bedford Row, London, WC1R 4JH, LDE 360, Tel: 0171 421 8000

**Price, Michael
Queen Elizabeth Building, Temple, EC4Y 9BS, LDE 340, Tel: 0171 353 7181

Pyne, John (1991)
1 Middle Temple Lane, Temple, EC4, LDE 464, Tel: 0171 583 0659

Ralphs, Robert
1 Essex Court, Temple, EC4Y 9AR, LDE 430, Tel: 0171 583 2000

Rayner, Howard 1988)
1 Garden Court, Temple, EC4, LDE 1034, Tel: 0171 797 7900

*Redmond, Declan (1987)
8, New Square, Lincoln's Inn, WC2A 3QS, LDE 311, Tel: 0171 306 0102

Reed Gary (1980)
9/12 Bell Yard, WC2N 3ED, LDE 390, Tel: 0171 400 1800

Regan, John
Gray's Inn Chambers, London, WC1R 5JA, LDE 352, Tel: 0171 242 2642

---

* Management Committee Members, ** Executive Committee Members

Rogers, Graham
Crown Square Chambers,
Manchester, M3 3HA, DX 14326,
Tel: 0161 833 9801

Riley, Hugh

Rugg, John
Gray's Inn Chambers, Gray's Inn,
WC1R 5JA, LDE 0074, Tel: 0171
404 1111

Ryan, Michael
27 New Walk, Leicester, LE1 6TE,
DX 10872, Tel: 01162 559144

*Salt, Nicholas (1977)
3 Serjeants' Inn, London, EC4Y
1BQ, LDE 421, Tel: 0171 353 5537

Sampson, Paul
4, Brick Court, Temple, EC4Y 9AD,
LDE 404, Tel: 0171 797 7766

Segal Robert
29 Bedford Row, London, WC1R
4HE, LDE 1044, Tel: 0171 831
2626

Shrubsall, Paul
1 Essex Street, Temple, EC4Y 9AR,
LDE 430, Tel: 0171 583 2000

Slater, Stephen (1983)
25 Park Square (West), Leeds, LS1
2PW, DX 16408, Tel: 0113 245
1841

Smith, Alan
5 Fountain Court, Steelhouse Lane,
Birmingham, B4 6DR, DX 16075
Birmingham, Tel: 0121 606 0500

**Smith, Martin
Blackstone Chambers, Temple,
EC4Y, LDE 281, Tel: 0171 583 1770

Stammers, Alan
5 Paper Buildings, Temple, EC4Y
7HB, LDE 415, Tel: 0171 583 9275

Stinton, Linda (1984)

Strong, Michael

Taylor, John
Old Square Chambers, 1 Verulam
Buildings, Gray's Inn, LDE 1046,
Tel: 0171 831 0801

Terry, Neil (1995)
Barton Mill House, Canterbury, CT1
1BP, DX 5342, Tel: 01227 764899

Thomas, Joanne (1992)
2, Paper Buildings, Temple, EC4Y
7ET, LDE 210, Tel: 0171 936 2613

Townsend, Gregory
17 Carlton Crescent, Southampton,
SO9 5AL, DX 49663, Tel: 01703
320320

Tracy Andrea

Treherne, Ivor
Queen Elizabeth Building, Temple,
EC4Y 9BS, LDE 339, Tel: 0171 797
7837

Ward, Stephen
South Western Chambers, Taunton,
TA1 1SH, DX 32146, Tel: 01823
331919

Watts, Michael
2 Harcourt Buildings, Temple,
EC44Y 9DB, LDE 489, Tel: 0171
353 2112

Weaver, Andrew
Lincoln House, Manchester, M2
5EL, DX 14338, Tel: 0161 832 5701

*Whinnett, Robin
21 Whitefriars, Chester CH1 1NJ,
DX 19979, Tel: 01244 323070

White, John
2 Harcourt Buildings, Temple,
EC4Y 9DB, LDE 1039, Tel: 0171
583 9020

Whitman, Peter
8 King Street, Manchester, M2 6AQ,
DX 14354, Tel: 0161 834 9560

Wilson, David
50 High Pavement, Nottingham,
NG1 1HN, DX 10036, Tel: 01602
503503

Woods, Robert (1984)
2 Mitre Court Buildings, Temple,
EC4Y 7BX, LDE 0032, Tel: 0171
583 1380

Wright, Peter
Young Street Chambers, 38 Young
St. Manchester, M3 3FT, DX 25583
Man. 5, Tel: 0161 835 3938

JUNIOR CLERKS

Allen, Elizabeth (1976)
Gray's Inn Chambers, Gray's Inn,
WC1, LDE 352, Tel: 0171 242 2642

Allen, Perry (1992)
9, Bedford Row, WC1R, LDE 347,
Tel: 0171 242 3555

Ansell, Richard (1988)
3 Gray's Inn Place, Gray's Inn,
WC1, LDE 331, Tel: 0171 831 8441

Barker, Tracy (1992)
3 Serjeants' Inn, London EC4, LDE
421, Tel: 0171 353 5537

Barnes, Andrew (1979)
6 King's Bench Walk, Temple, EC4,
LDE 26, Tel: 0171 583 0410

Barnes, David
1 Atkin Building, Gray's Inn, WC1,
LDE 1033, Tel: 0171 404 0201

Bateman, Garfield
3 Stone Buildings, Lincoln's Inn,
WC2, LDE 317, Tel: 0171 242 4937

Belford, Carol
10 King's Bench Walk, Temple,
EC4, LDE 294, Tel: 0171 353 2501

Bennett, Mark
18 Red Lion Court, London, EC4A
3EB, LDE 478, Tel: 0171 520 6000

Biggerstaff, Sam
Essex Court Chambers, 24
Lincoln's Inn Fields, WC2A 3ED,
LDE 320, Tel: 0171 813 8000

Bocock, Robert (1994)
Old Square Chambers, 1 Verulam
Buildings, WC1R 5LQ, LDE 1046,
Tel: 0171 831 0801

Boutwood, Simon (1994)
2 Harcourt Buildings, Temple, EC4,
LDE 1039, Tel: 0171 583 9020

Branchflower, Rich.(1993)
Blackstone Chambers, Temple,
EC4Y, LDE 281, Tel: 0171 583 1770

Burnell, Philip (1992)
4 King's Bench Walk, Temple, EC4,
LDE 1050, Tel: 0171 353 3581

Butler, David
5 Stone Buildings, Lincoln's Inn,
WC2A 3XT, LDE 304, Tel: 0171 242
6201

Clark, Janet
Francis Taylor Building, Temple,
EC4Y 7BY, LDE 441, Tel: 0171 353
7768

Clark, Nick (1995)
1 Atkin Buildings, Gray's Inn, WC1R
5BQ, LDE 1033, Tel: 0171 404
0102

Connor, Paul (1992)
Gray's Inn Chambers, Gray's Inn,
WC1, LDE 352, Tel: 0171 242 2642

Cornell, Mark (1988)
1 Paper Buildings, Temple, EC4,
LDE 332, Tel: 0171 353 3728

Coyne, Alistair (1990)
Littleton Chambers, Temple, EC4, LDE 1047, Tel: 0171 797 8600

Davis, Spencer
1, Raymond Buildings, Gray's Inn, WC1R 5BZ, LDE 16, Tel: 0171 430 1234

Downey, Alan
11 Old Square, Lincoln's Inn, WC2A 3TS, LDE 1031, Tel: 0171 430 0341

Doyle, Jason (1990)
4 Stone Buildings, Lincoln's Inn, WC2, LDE 385, Tel: 0171 242 5524

Easton, Andrew (1987)
Park Court Chambers, Leeds, LS1 2QH, DX 26401, Tel: 0113 433277

Fantham, Danny (1988)
3 Pump Court, Temple, EC4, LDE 362, Tel: 0171 353 0711

Farrell, Chris (1990)
Farrars Building, Temple, EC4, LDE 406, Tel: 0171 585 9241

Ferrigno, Joe (1987)
24, Lincoln's Inn Fields, WC1A 3ED, LDE 320, Tel: 0171 813 8000

Fleming, Matthew (1988)
7, Fountain Court, Birmingham, B4 6DR, DX 16073, Tel: 0121 233 3282

Frewin, Gregory
2 Crown Office Row, Temple, EC4Y 7HJ, LDE 344, Tel: 0171 797 8100

Gant, Judy (1991)
35,Essex Street, WC2R 3AR, LDE 351, Tel: 0171 353 6381

Garrett, Neil
12 New Square, Lincoln's Inn, WC2, LDE 366, Tel: 0171 405 3808

Gibbons, Matthew
Deans Court Chambers, Manchester, DX 718155, Tel: 0161 834 4097

Ginty, Jacqueline (1994)
1 Essex Court, Temple, EC4, LDE 430, Tel: 0171 583 2000

Goldsmith, Philip (1980)
10 Essex Street, Outer Temple, WC2, LDE 1045, Tel: 0171 240 6981

Gray, Mary (1978)
1 Essex Court, Temple, EC4, LDE 430, Tel: 0171 583 2000

Gray, Michael
Oriel Chambers, 14 Water St. Liverpool, L2 8TD, DX 14106, Tel: 01151 236 7191

Griffin, Colin (1988)
40 King Street, Manchester, M2 6BA, DX 718188, Tel: 0161 832 9082

Grove, Tom (1987)
2 Temple Gardens, Temple, EC4, LDE 134, Tel: 0171 583 6041

Haigh, Joanne
2, Pump Court, Temple, EC4Y 7AH, LDE 290, Tel: 0171 353 5597

Hall, Andrew
5, Paper Building, EC4Y 7HB, LDE 415, Tel: 0171 583 9275

**Hall, Stuart
10 Kings Bench Walk, Temple, EC4Y 7EB, LDE 294, Tel: 0171 353 2501

Hamilton, Nicholas (1990)
2 Crown Office Row, Temple, EC4, LDE 344, Tel: 0171 797 8100

Hawes, Adrian (1990)
Lamb Building, Temple, EC4Y 7AS, LDE 418, Tel: 0171 797 8300

Hewitt, David (1988)
Hollins Chambers, 64 Bridge Street, Manchester, M3 3BA, DX 14327, Tel: 0161 835 3451

*Hill, Nicholas (1991)
Essex Court Chambers, Lincoln's Inn Fields, LDE 320, Tel: 0171 813 8000

Hobbs, Russell
King Charles House, Standard Hill, Nottingham, DX10042 Tel: 0121 236 5771

Hodkinson, Denise

Holland, Clifford (1992)
Devereux Chambers, Devereux Court, WC2, LDE 349, Tel: 0171 353 7534

Housden, Jason (1992)
Hardwicke Building, 3 New Square, Lincoln's Inn, WC2, LDE 393, Tel: 0171 242 2523

Johnson, Lee
3 Serjeants' Inn, London, EC4Y 1BQ, LDE 421, Tel: 0171 353 5537

Jones, Matthew
2 Garden Court, Temple, EC4Y 9BL, LDE 34, Tel: 0171 353 1633

Jones, Nigel (1988)
Essex Court Chambers, Lincoln's Inn, WC1A 3ED, LDE 320, Tel: 0171 813 8000

Kilbey, Michael
4 Paper Buildings, Temple, EC4Y 7EX, LDE 1036, Tel: 0171 353 3366

Land, Lynne (1984)
199 Strand, London, WC2, LDE 322, Tel: 0171 379 9770

Lay, Michael (1992)
4 Paper Buildings, Temple, EC4Y 7EX, LDE 1035, Tel: 0171 583 0816

Lee, Brian (1980)
20 Essex Court, Temple, EC4, LDE 0009, Tel: 0171 583 9294

Livesey, Graham
9, St. Johns Street, Manchester, M3 3HA, DX 14326, Tel: 0161 955 9000

Lombardi, Franco (1994)
24 Old Buildings, Lincoln's Inn, WC2, LDE 386, Tel: 0171 242 2744

Madden, Timothy
1 King's Bench Walk, Temple, EC4Y 7DB, LDE 360, Tel: 0171 353 8436

*Makepeace, Emma
10, Kings Bench Walk, Temple, EC4Y 7EB, LDE 294, Tel: 0171 353 2501

Marquis, Peter
Queen Elizabeth Building, Temple, EC4, LDE 482, Tel: 0171 583 5766

Macdonald, Brian
Hamilton House, Temple, EC4Y, Tel: 0171 353 6336

McCarron-Child, Nicholas
10 Essex Street, Outer Temple, WC2, LDE 1045, Tel: 0171 240 6981

Mitchell, Kevin
Hardwicke Buildings, 3 New Square, Lincoln's Inn, WC2, LDE 393, Tel: 0171 242 2523

Miller, Jonathan
2 Crown Office Row, Temple, EC4Y 7HJ, LDE 344, Tel: 0171 797 8100

Moore, Andrew (1988)
4 Raymond Buildings, Gray's Inn, WC1, LDE 257, Tel: 0171 405 7211

Morley, Stephen (1988)
Queen Elizabeth Building, Temple, EC4, LDE 339, Tel: 0171 797 7837

Munday, Paul (1984)
2 Harcourt Buildings, Temple, EC4, LDE 402, Tel: 0171 353 8415

Munton, John (1997)
10 Essex Street, London, WC2R 3AA, LDE 1045, Tel: 0171 240 6981

Nicholls, Clive (1987)
5 New Square, Lincoln's Inn, WC2, LDE 272, Tel: 0171 404 0404

Norton, Gary (1988)
1 Harcourt Buildings, Temple, EC4, LDE 417, Tel: 0171 353 9421

Oliver, Gary
Blackstone Chambers, Temple, EC4Y, LDE 281, Tel: 0171 583 1770

Oliver, Michael (1979)
1 Crown Office Row, Temple, EC4, LDE 212, Tel: 0171 583 9292

O'Mullane, Paul (1988)
Lamb Building, Temple, EC4Y 7AB, LDE 418, Tel: 0171 797 8300

Ozga, Nicholas
11 Stone Buildings, Lincoln's Inn, WC2A 3TG, LDE 1022, Tel: 0171 831 6381

Parkinson, Nick (1994)
5, King's Bench Walk, Temple, EC4Y 7DN, LDE 478, Tel: 0171 797 7600

Partridge, David (1988)
2 Fountain Court, Birmingham B4 6DR, DX 16071, Tel: 0121 236-3882

Perry, Ben
Essex Court Chambers, 24 Lincoln's Inn Fields, WC2A 3ED, LDE 320, Tel: 0171 813 8000

Perry, Simon

Phelan, Sean (1975)
Phoenix Chambers, 47A, Bedford Row, WC1R 4LR, Tel: 0171 404 7888

Phipps, Matthew (1988)
1 Crown Office Row, Temple, EC4, LDE 1020, Tel: 0171 797 7500

Phipps, Michael (1988)
39, Essex Street, London, WC2R 3AT, LDE 298, Tel: 0171 583 1111

Piner, Gregory
Hardwicke Buildings, New Square, Lincoln's Inn, WC2, LDE 393, Tel: 0171 242 2523

Powell, Haydn (1982)
1 New Square, Lincoln's Inn, WC2, LDE 295, Tel: 0171 405 0884

Price, Stephen (1978)
33 Park Place, Cardiff, CF1 3BA, DX 50755 Cardiff 2, Tel: 01222 233313

Price Stephen
25, Byrom Street, Manchester, M3 4PF, DX 718156, Tel: 0161 829 2100

Rankin, Louis (1991)
Fenners Chambers, 3 Madingley Road, Cambridge, CB3 0EE, DX 5809 Cambridge 1, Tel: 01223 368761

Read, Paul (1988)
New Court Chambers, 5 Verulam Buildings, WC1R 5LY, LDE 363, Tel: 0171 831 9500

Reade, Christopher (1988)
Erskine Chambers, 30 Lincoln's Inn Fields, WC2, LDE 308, Tel: 0171 242 5532

Reece, Paul (1991)
4 Stone Buildings, Lincoln's Inn, WC2, LDE 385, Tel: 0171 242 5524

Ridley, Clive (1995)
6, Fountain Court, Steelhouse Lane, Birmingham, DX 16076, Tel: 0121 233 3282

Riordan, Matthew
1 Harcourt Buildings, EC4Y, LDE 417, Tel: 0171 353 9421

Robson, Hadyn (1988)
3 Temple Gardens, Temple, EC4, LDE 485, Tel: 0171 353 9297

Ronan, Christopher (1988)
28 St. John Street, Manchester, M3 4EA, DX 72886, Tel: 0161 834 8418

Rowe, Maureen (1993)
St. John's Chambers, Bristol, BS1 1DW, DX 78138, Tel: 01272 213456

Sabini, Dominic (1993)
2 Crown Office Row, EC4Y 7HJ, LDE 1041, Tel: 0171 797 8000

Sale, Matthew (1992)
11 Stone Buildings, Lincoln's Inn, WC2, LDE 314, Tel: 0171 404 5055

Scothern, David
2, Dyers Buildings, EC1, LDE 175, Tel: 0171 404 1881

Shiakallis, A
11 Stone Buildings, Lincoln's Inn, WC2A 3TG, LDE 1022, Tel: 0171 831 6381

Simpkin, Mark (1991)
Brick Court Chambers, 15-19 Devereux Court, WC2R 3JJ, LDE 302, Tel: 0171 583 0777

Smith, David (1991)
39 Essex Street, London WC2, LDE 298, Tel: 0171 583 1111

Smith, Francis
11 South Square, Gray's Inn, WC1, LDE 433, Tel: 0171 405 1222

Smith, Lloyd (1975)
Hardwicke Buildings, New Square, Lincoln's Inn, WC2A, LDE 393, Tel: 0171 242 2523

Southworth, Helen
Peel House, Harrington Street, Liverpool 2, DX 14227, Tel: 0151 236 0718

Strong, Clifford (1992)
1 Middle Temple Lane, Temple, EC4, LDE 464, Tel: 0171 583 0659

Stubbs, Michael (1988)
40 King Street, Manchester B2 6BA, DX 718188, Tel: 0161 832 9082

Stubbs, Susan (1988)
Manchester House Chambers, 18-22 Bridge Street, Manchester, DX 718153 Manchester 3, Tel: 0161 834 7007

Swallow, Mark (1983)
Erskine Chambers, 30 Lincoln's Inn Fields, WC2, LDE 308, Tel: 0171 242 5532

Taylor, Judith (1988)
Assize Court Chambers, Bristol, BS1 1DE, DX 78134, Tel: 0117 926 4587

Thompson, Paul (1980)
14 Water Street, Liverpool, L2 8TD, DX 14106, Tel: 0151 236 7191

Walker, John (1992)
4, Essex Court, Temple, EC4Y 9AJ, LDE 292, Tel: 0171 797 7970

Wall, Stephen (1979)
1 Hare Court, Temple, EC4, LDE 444, Tel: 0171 353 5324

* Management Committee Members, ** Executive Committee Members

Walter, Mark (1987)
1 Paper Buildings, Temple, EC4, LDE 80, Tel: 0171 583 7355

West Samantha (1995)
1, Mitre Court, Temple, EC4Y 7BS, LDE 342, Tel: 0171 797 7070

Winders Ann (1990)
1 Serjeants Inn, Fleet Street, London EC4, LDE 364, Tel: 0171 353 9901

SENIOR CLERK ASSOCIATED MEMBERS

Acton Meriel,
26, Waterloo Rd, Wolverhampton, WV1 4BL, DX 722200 Wolverhampton 15, Tel: 01902 426222

Ashford, Samantha
9 Woodhouse Square, Leeds, LS3 1AD, DX 26406 Leeds Park Square, Tel: 0113 2451986

Ashton, Steven (1987)
1, Gray's Inn Square, WC1R 5AA, LDE 238, Tel: 0171 405 8946

Ayles, Russell
5, King's Bench Walk, Temple, EC4Y 7D, LDE 367, Tel: 0171 353 5638

Barber David
3, Pump Court, Temple, EC4, LDE 362, Tel: 0171 353 0711

Barrett, Graham
33 Park Place, Cardiff, CF1 3BA, DX 50755 Cardiff 2, Tel: 01222 233313

Beams, F.R.
1 Mitre Court Building, Temple, EC4Y 7BS, LDE 342, Tel: 0171 797 7070

Beaumont, Kevin
14 Toft Green, York, YD1 1JT, DX 61517, Tel: 01904 620048

Bell, Brian
33 Broad Chare, Newcastle Upon Tyne, NE1 3DQ, DX 61001, Tel: 0191 232 0541

Biswas, Savanah
New Bailey Chambers, Preston, PR1 2QT, DX 710050, Tel: 01772 258087

Boardman Ian
17 Bedford Row, WC1R 4EB, LDE 370, Tel: 0171 353 0711

Boye-Anawomah, Philip
Acre Lane Neighbourhood Chambers, 30A Acre Lane, Brixton, SW2 5SG, DX 58782 Brixton, Tel: 0171 274 4400

Bromage, Philip
15 North Church Street Chambers, Sheffield, S1 2DH, DX 10629 Sheffield, Tel: 0114 275 9708

Brown, Kim J
Lion Court, Chancery Lane, WC2A 1SJ, LDE 98, Tel: 0171 404 6565

Burgess, Jonathan
Solent Chambers, 2nd Floor, Coronation House, 1 Kings Terrace, Portsmouth, PO5 3AR, DX 2280 Portsmouth, Tel: 01705 821818

Burrow, Ian
2 Pump Court, Temple, EC4Y 9AB, LDE 109, Tel: 0171 353 4341

Campbell, Alastair
Merchant Chambers, 1 North Parade, Parsonage Gardens, Manchester, M3 2NH, DX 14319 Manchester 1, Tel: 0161 839 7070

Cavanagh, Sarah
Oriel Chambers, 5 Covent Garden, Liverpool, L2 8UD, DX 14106 Liverpool, 0151 236 7191

Chilton, Deborah
Bank House Chambers, Old Bank House, Hartshead, Sheffield, S1 2EL DX 10522 Sheffield, Tel: 0114 275 1223

Clarke, Lisa
177, Corporation Street, Birmingham, DX 23520 Birmingham 3, Tel: 0121 236 9900

Collins, Tim
6, Park Square, Leeds, LS1 2LW, DX 26402 Leeds Park Sqare, Tel: 0113 245 9763

Connor, Jennifer
19, Castle Street, Liverpool, L2 4SX, DX 14193 Liverpool, Tel: 0151 236 9402

Connor, Nigel
39 Essex Street, London, WC2R 3AT, LDE 298, Tel: 0171 583 1111

Constable, Richard
6, Pump Court, Temple, EC4Y 7AR, LDE 293, Tel: 0171 797 8400

Cooke, Paul
17 Charlton Crescent, Southampton, SO15 2XR, DX 96877, Tel: 01703 639001

Coveney, Paul
4 Field Court, Gray's Inn, WC1R 5EA, LDE 483, Tel: 0171 440 6900

Cubley, Colin
2nd Floor, Chavasse Court, Liverpool, L2 1TA, DX 14223, Tel: 0151 707 1191

Curtis, Alan
10 King's Bench Walk, EC4Y 7EB, LDE 24, Tel: 0171 353 7742

Cutler Lee
12 Gray's Inn Square, London, WC1R 5JP, LDE 0055, Tel: 0171 404 4866

Cuttle, Karen
Parsonage Chambers, 3, The Parsonage, Manchester, M3 2HW, Tel: 0161 833 1996, DX 718183 Manchester 3

Daniell, Joy
33 Southernhay East, Exeter, EX1 1NX, DX 8353, Tel: 01392 55777

Davies Andrew
Chartland Chambers, Cherry Tree Lane, Great Houghton, Northants, NN4 7AT, DX 12408 Northampton 1, Tel: 01604 700524

Davis, Robert
Maidstone Chambers, 33 Earl Street, Maidstone, ME14 1PF, DX 51982 Maidstone 2, Tel: 01622 688592

Day, Anthony

De Rose, Ann
3 Temple Gardens, Temple, EC4Y 9AU, Tel: 0171 353 7884

Dewar, Stewart
9, Old Steine, Brighton, BN1 1FJ, DX 2724 Brighton 1, Tel: 01273 607953

Doe, Christopher
Walnut House, 63, St David's Hill, Exeter, EX4 4DW, DX115582 Exeter St. David's, Tel: 01392 79751

Donovan, James
1, Crown Office Row, Temple, EC4, LDE 212, Tel: 0171 583 9292

Dooley, Leslie
33 King Street Chambers, Manchester, M3 3PW, DX 18160, Tel: 0161 834 4364

Douglas, David
Littleton Chambers, 3 Kings Bench Walk, EC4Y 7HR, LDE 1047, Tel: 0171 797 8600

Dring, Margaret
9, Woodhouse Square, Leeds, LS3 1AD, DX 26406 Leeds Park Square, Tel: 0113 2451986

Duncan, Adrian
3 Temple Gardens, EC4Y, LDE 0064, Tel: 0171 583 1155

Duric, David
1 High Pavement, Nottingham, NG1 1HF, DX 10168, Tel: 0115 941 8218

Edmonds, Shelley
Peel Court Chambers, 45 Hardman Street, Manchester, M3 3HA, DX 14320 Manchester 1, Tel: 0161 832 3791

Evers, Stephen

Farrow, Peter
15, Hyde Gardens, Eastbourne, BN21 4PR, DX 6925, Tel: 01323 642102

Finney, Roy
Exchange Chambers, Pearl Assurance House, Derby Square, Liverpool, L2 9XX, DX 14207, Tel: 0151 236 7747

Freeman, Stephen
All Saints Chambers, Bristol, BS1 2HP, DX 7870 Bristol, Tel: 0117 921 1966

Grant Trace,

Green, David
Francis Taylor Buildings, Temple, EC4Y 7BX, LDE 441, Tel: 0171 353 7768

Grimmer, John
1 Little Essex Street, WC2R 3LD, LDE 17, Tel: 0171 395 2000

Grimshaw, C
St. Pauls House, 25, Park Square, Leeds, LS1 2ND, DX 26410, Tel: 0113 245 5866

Grimwood, Rachel
9 Baker Street, Middlesbrough, DX 60591 Middlesbrough, Tel: 01642 873873

Gunner Mary
Earl Street Chambers, Broughton House, 33 Earl Street, Maidstone, ME14 1PF, DX 4844 Maidstone 1, Tel: 01622 671222

Handley, Thomas
Exchange Chambers, Derby Square Liverpool, L2 9XX, DX 14207, Tel: 0151 236 7747

Hands, Colin
9-12 Trinity Chase, Newcastle Upon Tyne, DX 61185, Tel: 0191 232 1927

Harding, Paul
3 Temple Gardens, Temple, EC4Y 9AU, LDE 427, Tel: 0171 353 0832

Harris, Michael
6, Fountain Court, Birmingham, B4 6DR, DX 16076, Tel: 0121 233 3282

Hart, Martin
2 Grays Inn Square, London, WC1R 5JH, LDE 316, Tel: 0171 242 4986

Hewitt, Dorothy
Pump Court Chambers, 5, Temple Street, Swindon, SN1 1SQ, DX 38639 Swindon 2, Tel: 01793 539899

Hopkins, Annie

Hubbard, John
3 Dr Johnson's Building, Temple, EC4Y 7BA, LDE 1009, Tel: 0171 353 4854

Hughes, Francis
New Court Chambers, 3 Broad Chare, Newcastle upon Tyne, NE1 3DQ, DX 61012 Newcastle 1, Tel: 0191 232 1980

Hutchins, Andrew
Goldsworth Chambers, 10/11 Gray's Inn Square, WC1R 5JD, LDE 1057, Tel: 0171 405 7117

Hutt, Carey
2, New Street, Leicester, LE1 5NA, DX 10849 Leicester l, Tel: 0116 262 5906

Islin, Graham
2 Dyers Buildings, EC1N 2JT, LDE 175, Tel: 0171 404 1881

Jackson, Edward
98 Mariners Wharf, Liverpool, L3 4DH, DX 14101 Liverpool 1, Tel: 0151 707 1752

Janes, Mrs Kim
5, Raymond Buildings, Gray's Inn, WC1R 5BP, LDE 1054, Tel: 0171 242 2902

Jeavons, Craig
St. Ives Chambers, 9 Fountain Court, Steelhouse Lane, Birmingham, B4 6DR, DX 16072 Birmingham, Tel: 0121 236 0863

Jones, Stuart
14 Castle Street, Liverpool, L2 YLS, DX 14176, Tel: 0151 236 4421

Kelly, Peter
Lamb Buldings, Temple, EC4Y 7AS, LDE 418, Tel: 0171 797 8300

Kemp, Roy
Park Court Chambers, Leeds, LS1 2QH, DX 26401, Tel: 0113 243 3277

Kettle, Graham
16 Bedford Row, London, WC1R 4EB, LDE 312, Tel: 0171 414 8080

Kilgallon, John
Martins Buildings, Liverpool, L2 3SP, DX 14232, Tel: 0151 236 4919

Landa, Barry
Arden Chambers, 27 John Street, WC1N 2BL, LDE 29, Tel: 0171 242 4244

Lewis, Julie
Becket Chambers, 17 New Dover Road, Canterbury, DX 5330, Tel: 01227 786331

McSweeney, Christopher
9 Old Square, WC2A, LDE 305, Tel: 0171 405 4682

Marsh, Anthony
7 Stone Buildings, Lincoln's Inn, WC2A 3SZ, LDE 335, Tel: 0171 405 3886

Marsh, Iain
Windsor Chambers, 2 Penuel Lane, Pontypridd, South Wales, CF37 4UF, DX 44354 Pontypridd, Tel: 01443 402067

May, Kay
4 Paper Buildings, Temple, EC4Y 7EX, LDE 1035, Tel: 0171 583 0816

Maynard, William
Coleridge Chambers, Birmingham, B4 6RG, DX 23503, Tel: 0121 233 3303

* Management Committee Members, ** Executive Committee Members

Moore, Keith

Morgan, Gary
9, King's Bench Walk, Temple, EC4Y 7DX, LDE 472, Tel: 0171 353 7202

Morrison Jacq,
Victory House, 7 Belle Vue Terrace, Portsmouth, PO5 3AT, DX 2239 Tel: 01705 831292

Moss, Robert
Peel House, 5-7 Harrington Street, Liverpool, L2 9XN, DX 14227, Tel: 0151 236 0718

Mylchreest, Terry
5 John Dalton Street, Manchester, M2 6ET, DX 18182, Tel: 0161 834 6875

Nagle, Keith
11 Old Square, Lincoln's Inn, WC2A 3TS, LDE 1031, Tel: 0171 430 0341

O'Connor, Sandra
Lancaster Buildings, 77 Deansgate, Manchester, M3 2BW, DX 14488 Manchester 2, Tel: 0161 661 4444

Palmer, Andrew
3 Stone Buildings, Lincolns Inn, WC2A 3XL, LDE 317, Tel: 0171 242 4937

Plowman, Keith
10 Old Square, Lincolns Inn, WC2A 3SU, LDE 306, Tel: 0171 405 0758

Poulton, Joanna
9, Gough Square, EC4A 3DE, LDE 439, Tel: 0171 353 5371

Rainbird, Walter
86 St. Helens Road, Swansea, SA1 4BQ, DX 39554, Tel: 01792 652988

Rotherham, Geoffrey
King Charles House, Standard Hill, Notts, DX 10042, Tel: 0115 941 8851

Salter, John

Simpson, Michelle
Doughty Street Chambers, 11 Doughty Street, London, WC1N 3PG, LDE 223, Tel: 0171 404 1313

Smith, Hilary
Lloyds House Chambers, 3rd Floor, 18, Lloyd Street, Manchester, M2 5WA, DX 14388 Manchester 1, Tel: 0161 839 3371

Smith, Stephen
4 Paper Buildings, Temple, EC4Y 7EB, LDE 1036, Tel: 0171 353 3366

Springham, Mark
3 Madingley Road, Cambridge, CB3 0EE, DX 5809, Tel: 01223 68761

Stapley, Joanne
25-27 Castle Street, Liverpool, L2 4TA, DX 14224, Tel: 0151 227 5661

Summerell, Zena
Theatre House, Percival Road, Clifton, Bristol, BS8 3LE, Tel: 0117 974 1553

Thiele, Teresa
Manchester House Chambers, 18-22 Bridge Street, Manchester, M3 3BZ, DX 718153 Manchester 3, Tel: 0161 834 7007

Thorne, Jeremy

Thwaites Tristan
Guildhall Chambers, Portsmouth, PO1 2DE, DX 2225, Tel: 01705 75240

Trotter, Andrew
Equity Chambers, Suite 110, Gazette Building, 168 Corporation Street, Birmingham, B4 6TF, DX 23531 Birmingham 3, Tel: 0121 233 2100

Watts, Chris
11 Old Square, Lincoln's Inn, WC2A 3TS, LDE 164, Tel: 0171 242 5022

Wells, Anthony
4/5, Gray's Inn Square, WC1R 5AY, LDE 1029, Tel: 0171 404 5252

Weekes, Bob
6-7 Gough Square, London, EC4A 3DE, LDE 476, Tel: 0171 353 0924

Weston, Allan
Derby Square Chambers, Liverpool, L2 1TS, DX 14213, Tel: 0151 709 4222

Wheeler, Brian
2 Harcourt Buildings, Temple, EC4Y 9DB, LDE 373, Tel: 0171 353 6961

Willmore, Keith
Trinity Chambers, 140 New London Road, Chelmsford, CM2 0AW, DX 89725 Chelmsford 2, Tel: 01245 605040

Winschief, Sandra
Veritas Chambers, 33 Corn Street, Bristol, BS1 1HT, DX 133602 Bristol 1, Tel: 0117 930 8802

Woodcock, John
1 Brick Court, Temple, EC4Y 9BY, LDE 468, Tel: 0171 353 8845

Wright, Paul
Regency Chambers, 18, Cowgate, Peterborough, PE1 1NA, DX 12349 Peterborough 1, Tel: 01733 315215

JUNIOR CLERK ASSOCIATED MEMBERS

Abdo, Elizabeth
95A, Chancery Lane, London, WC2A 1DT, LDE 275, Tel: 0171 242 2440

Ackerley, Neville
2 Paper Buildings, Temple, EC4Y 7ET, LDE 286, Tel: 0171 353 0933

Addis, Frances
Blackstone Chambers, Temple, EC4Y, LDE 281, Tel: 0171 583 1770

Adlam, Andrew
3 Raymond Buildings, Gray's Inn, WC1, LDE 237, Tel: 0171 831 3833

Albon, Casta
1 Crown Office Row, Temple, EC4Y 7HH, LDE 1020, Tel: 0171 797 7500

Alexander Michael
Arden Chambers, 59 Fleet Street, EC4Y 1JU, LDE 29, Tel: 0171 353 3132

Allen, Justin
199 Strand, WC2R 1DR, LDE 322, Tel: 0171 379 9779

Ambrose, Daphne
5 Paper Buildings, Temple, EC4, LDE 415, Tel: 0171 583 9275

Anderson, Deborah
Littleton Chambers, Temple, EC4, LDE 1047, Tel: 0171 797 8600

Armstrong, Anthony
Enterprise Chambers, 9, Old Square, WC2A 3SR, LDE 301, Tel: 0171 405 4682

Armstrong, S K
20 Essex Street, WC2R 3AL, LDE 0009, Tel: 0171 583 9294

Archer, Matthew
22, Old Buildings, Lincoln's Inn, WC2A 3UJ, LDE 201, Tel: 0171 831 0222

Arthur, Louise
7 Stone Buildings, Lincoln's Inn, WC2A 3SZ, LDE 1007, Tel: 0171 242 0961

Ashton, Lucy
Westgate Chambers, 144 High Street, Lewes, East Sussex, BN7 1XT, DX 50250 Lewes 2, Tel: 01275 480510

Atkins, Tony
Francis Taylor Buildings, Temple, EC4Y 7BY, LDE 46, Tel: 0171 797 7250

Baldwin, Scott
Hollins Chambers, 64A Bridge St, M3 3BA, DX 14327 Manchester, Tel: 0161 835 3451

Barnes, Jayne
4 King's Bench Walk, Temple, EC4, LDE 1050, Tel: 0171 353 3581

Barrow, David
199 Strand, WC2R 1DR, LDE 322, Tel: 0171 379 9779

Barrow, Kevin
2/3 Gray's Inn Square, WC1R 5JH, LDE 316, Tel: 0171 242 4986

Barrow, Ryan
6, Pump Court, Temple, EC4Y 7AR, LDE 293, Tel: 0171 797 8000

Bartlett, Ryan
Francis Taylor Building, EC4Y 7BY, LDE 211, Tel: 0171 353 9942

Bear, Daniel
16, Bedford Row, London, WC1R 4EB, LDE 312, Tel: 0171 414 8080

Beard, Christopher
15-19, Devereux Court, WC2R 3JJ, LDE 302, Tel: 0171 583 0777

Bennett, Paul
24, Old Buildings, Lincoln's Inn, WC2A LDE 307, Tel: 0171 404 0946

Bennett, Peter
5 Paper Buildings, Temple, EC4Y 7HB, LDE 415, Tel: 0171 583 9275

Bennetts, Angharad
36, Bedford Row, London, WC1R 4JH, LDE 360, Tel: 0171 421 8000

Bester, Yvonne
Gray's Inn Chambers, London, WC1R 5JA, LDE 0074, Tel: 0171 404 1111

Bingham, David
3 New Square, WC2A 3RS, LDE 384, Tel: 0171 405 5577

Binnie, Mark
3, Gray's Inn Place, WC1R 5EA, LDE 331, Tel: 0171 831 8441

Birkbeck, Katherine
6, Park Square, Leeds, LS1 2LW, DX 26402 Leeds Park Square, Tel: 0113 245 9763

Bisland John
13 Old Square, Lincoln's Inn, WC2, LDE 326, Tel: 0171 404 4800

Borrow, Jonathan
15, Winckley Square, Preston, PR1 3JJ, DX 17110 Preston l, Tel: 01772 252828

Braithwaite, Denise
3, Temple Gardens, Temple, EC4Y 9AU, LDE 0064, Tel: 0171 583 1155

Breingan, Damien
19, Castle Street, Liverpool, L2 4SX, DX 14193 Liverpool, Tel: 0151 236 9402

Bridger, Thomas
24, Lincoln's Inn Fields, WC1R, LDE 320, Tel: 0171 813 8000

Briggs, Graham
Francis Taylor Buildings, Temple, EC4Y 7BY, LDE 211, Tel: 0171 353 9924

Brindley, Christina
8 King Street, Manchester, M2 6AQ, DX 14354 Manchester 1, Tel: 0161 834 9560

Briton, Andrew
2 Harcourt Buildings, Temple, EC4Y 9DB, LDE 489, Tel: 0171 353 8339

Broadbent, Matthew
8 New Square, Lincoln's Inn, WC2A, LDE 311, Tel: 0171 306 0102

Broom, Stephen
Essex Court Chambers, 24 Lincoln's Inn Fields, WC2A 3ED, LDE 320, Tel: 0171 813 8000

Brown, Alexander
3 Fountain Court, Birmingham, B4 6DR, DX 16079, Birmingham 4, Tel: 0121 236 5854

Brown, Justin
1 New Square, Lincoln's Inn, WC2, LDE 295, Tel: 0171 405 0884

Bryant, Gary Bryant, Robert
4, King's Bench Walk, Temple, EC4Y 7DL, LDE 1050, Tel: 0171 353 3581

Bunting, Paul
Hardwicke Buildings, Lincoln's Inn, WC2A 3SB, LDE 393, Tel: 0171 242 2523

Burgess, Tony
2/3 Gray's Inn Square, WC1R 5JM, LDE 316, Tel: 0171 242 4986

Burrows, Andrew
5 Verulam Buildings, Grays Inn, WC2R 5NT, LDE 363, Tel: 0171 831 9500

Butchard, Matthew
3, Gray's Inn Square, London, WC1R 5AH, LDE 1043, Tel: 0171 831 2311

Butcher, Sophie
2, Crown Office Row, Temple, EC4Y 7HJ, LDE 1041, Tel: 0171 797 8000

Byrne, Michael
Goldsmith Chambers, Temple, EC4Y 7BL, LDE 435, Tel: 0171 353 6802

Cade, Richard
36, Bedford Row, London, WC1R 4JH, LDE 360, Tel: 0171 421 8000

Cadwallader, Lee
1st Floor, Refuge Association House, Derby Square, Liverpool, L2 1TS, DX 14213, Tel: 0151 709 4222

Call, Andrew
1, New Square, Lincoln's Inn, WC2A, LDE 295, Tel: 0171 405 0884

Carter, Vincent
11, Old Square, Lincoln's Inn, WC2A 3TS, LDE 1031, Tel: 0171 430 0341

Carter, Andrea
Godolphin Chambers, 50 Castle Street, Truro, TR1 3AF, DX 81233, Tel: 01872 76312

Caswell, David

Charlick, Anthony
Cloisters, 1 Pump Court, EC4Y, LDE 452, Tel: 0171 827 4048

Chapman, Michael
1 Gray's Inn Square, WC1R 5AA, LDE 1013, Tel: 0171 405 8946

Christie, Susan
7, Stone Buildings, WC2A 3SZ, LDE 1007, Tel: 0171 242 0961

Clarke, Addeline
2, New Street, Leicester, LE1 5NA, DX 17404 Leicester 3, Tel: 0116 262 5906

Clark, Michael
11 New Square, Lincoln's Inn, WC2A 3QB, LDE 319, Tel: 0171 831 0081

Clarke, Paul
40 King Street, Manchester, M2 6BA, DX 718188 Manchester 3, Tel: 0161 832 9082

Clay, Daniel
13, King's Bench Walk, Temple, EC4Y, LDE 359, Tel: 0171 353 7204

Clayton, Andrew
8, New Square, Lincoln's Inn, WC2A, LDE 379, Tel: 0171 405 4321

Clayton, David
11, Stone Buildings, Lincoln's Inn, WC2A 3TG, LDE 314, Tel: 0171 404 5055

Clent, Victoria
Northampton Chambers, NN1 1UD, DX 12464 Northampton 1, Tel: 01604 36271

Cole, Elaine
St. Johns Chambers, Small Street, Bristol, BS1 1DW, DX 78138 Bristol, Tel: 0117 921 3456

Colley Martin
13 Old Square, Lincoln's Inn, WC2A 3UA, LDE 326, Tel: 0171 404 4800

Collings, Janet
18 Red Lion Court, London, EC4, LDE 478, Tel: 0171 520 6000

Colloff, Graham
6, Pump Court, Temple, EC4Y 7AR, LDE 293, Tel: 0171 797 8400

Conway, Kirstie
2, Mitre Court Buildings, Temple, EC4Y, LDE 0032, Tel: 0171 583 1380

Cooklin Paul
3 Verulam Buildings, WC1R 5NT, LDE 331, Tel: 0171 831 8441

Cooper John
12, Kings Bench Walk, Temple, EC4Y 97E, LDE 1037, Tel: 0171 583 0811

Coote, Daniel
Falcon Chambers, Temple, EC4Y 1AA, LDE 408, Tel: 0171 353 2484

Costa, James
3/4, South Square, Gray's Inn, WC1R 5HP, DX 338, Tel: 0171 696 9900

Cote, Helen
East Anglian Chambers, 52 North Hill, Colchester, CO1 1PY, DX 3611 Colchester, Tel: 01206 572756

Cowling C
St. Paul's Chambers, 23 Park Square South, Leeds, LS1 2ND, DX 26410 Tel: 0113 245 5866

Cowup, Julie
Furnival Chambers, 32 Furnival Street, EC4A 1TQ, LDE 72, Tel: 0171 405 3232

Creighton, David
29 Bedford Row, London, WC1R 4HE, LDE 1044, Tel: 0171 831 2626

Croke, Robert
199 Strand, London, WC2R 1DR, LDE 322, Tel: 0171 379 9779

Cue, Jonathan
14, Gray's Inn Square, WC1R 5JP, LDE 399, Tel: 0171 242 0858

Darvell, Mark
Gray's Inn Chambers, 5th Floor, WC1R 5JA, LDE 0074, Tel: 0171 404 1111

Davis, Glenn
3, Temple Gardens, Lower Ground Floor, Temple, EC4Y 9AU, LDE 485, Tel: 0171 353 3102

Day, Ann
4, Breams Buildings, EC4A 1AQ, LDE 1042, Tel: 0171 353 5835

Davidson, Alastair
1 Essex Court, Temple, EC4Y 9AR, LDE 430, Tel: 0171 583 2000

Dear, Christopher

Denney, Jay
East Anglian Chambers, 52 North Hill, Colchester, CO1 1PY, DX 3611 Colchester, Tel: 01206 572756

Dibsdall, Katherine
9 Bedford Row, WC1R 4AZ, LDE 347, Tel: 0171 242 3555

Digby, Wayne
Old Bank Chambers, Old Bank House, Hartshead, Sheffield, S1 2EL, DX 10522 Sheffield, Tel: 0114 275 1223

Donaghey, Sylvia
1 & 2 Plowden Buildings, Temple, EC4Y 9BU, LDE 0020, Tel: 0171 583 0808

Douglas, Marie
35 Essex Street, WC2R 3AR, LDE 351, Tel: 0171 353 6381

Drakesford, Jason
29 Bedford Row, London, WC1R 4HE, LDE 1044, Tel: 0171 831 2626

Driscoll, Sarah

Duckett, Andrew
Farrars Buildings, Temple, EC4Y 7BD, LDE 406, Tel: 0171 583 9241

Dyer, Justin
1, Gray's Inn Square, Gray's Inn, WC1R 5AA, LDE 1013, Tel: 0171 405 8946

Eadie, Christine
5, King's Bench Walk, Temple, EC4Y 7, LDE 367, Tel: 0171 353 5638

East, Nigel
7 Park Place, Cardiff, CF1 3TN, DX 50757, Tel: 01222 382731

Eaton, Paul
2 Harcourt Buildings, Temple, EC4Y 9DB, LDE 1039, Tel: 0171 583 9020

Ecclestone, Andrea
New Court Chambers, 3 Broad Street, Newcastle upon Tyne, NE1 3DQ, DX 61012 Newcastle 1, Tel: 0191 232 1980

Edwards, Elizabeth
Angel Chambers, 94 Walter Road, Swansea, SM1 5QA, DX 39566 Swansea, Tel: 01792 464623

Eeles, Paul
8, Stone Buildings, Lincoln's Inn, WC2A 3TA, LDE 216, Tel: 0171 831 9881

Emmings, Christopher
6, King's Bench Walk, EC4Y 7DR, LDE 26, Tel: 0171 583 0410

Essex, Mark
6 King's Bench Walk, Temple, EC4Y 7DR, LDE 26, Tel: 0171 583 0410

Essex, Michael
2 King's Bench Walk, Temple, EC4Y 7DE, LDE 1032, Tel: 0171 353 1746

Evans, Jeffrey
Iscoed Chambers, 86 St.Helen's Road, Swansea, SA1 4BQ, DX 39554, Tel: 01792 652988

Evans, Nicholas
12 King's Bench Walk, Temple, EC4Y 7EL, LDE 1037, Tel: 0171 583 0811

Fairbanks, Davie

Fairburn Timothy
3, New Square, Lincoln's Inn, WC2A 3RS, LDE 454, Tel: 0171 405 1111

Falconer, Charlotte
1 Atkin Building, Gray's Inn, WC1R 5AT, LDE 1033, Tel: 0171 404 0102

Farrow, Garry
9, Gough Square, EC4A 3DE, DX 439 Chancery Lane, Tel: 0171 353 5371

Fawole, Dele
Suite 1, 2nd Floor, Gray's Inn Chambers, WC1R, LDE 442, Tel: 0171 405 7011

Ferrison, Chris
1 Garden Court, Temple, EC4Y 9BL, LDE 1034, Tel: 0171 797 7900

Field, Adam
39, Essex Street, London, WC2A 3AT, LDE 298, Tel: 0171 832 1111

Filby, Martin
2, Pump Court, Temple, EC4Y 7AH, LDE 290, Tel: 0171 353 5597

Finney, Roy
Exchange Chambers, Pearl Assurance House, Derby Square, Liverpool, L2 9XX DX 14207 Liverpool, Tel: 0151 236 7747

Fletcher, Paul
Guildhall Chambers, 23 Broad Street, Bristol, BS1 2HG, DX 7823 Tel: 0117 927 3366

Foreman, Dean

Foster, Elly
Doughty Street Chambers, 11 Doughty Street, WC1N 2PG, LDE 223, Tel: 0171 404 1313

Foweraker, Chris
15, Winckley Square, Preston PR1 3JJ, DX 17110 Preston 1, Tel: 01772 252828

Fowler, Richard
7, Fountain Court, Birmingham, DX 16073 Birmingham, Tel: 0121 236 8531

Francis, Stephen
Falcon Chambers, Falcon Court, EC4Y 1AA, LDE 408, Tel: 0171 353 2484

Frankland, Andrew
Devereux Chambers, London, WC2R 3JJ, LDE 349, Tel: 0171 353 7534

Friend, P W
Farrars Building, Temple, EC4Y 7BD, LDE 406, Tel: 0171 583 9241

Friend, Kara Fullilove S (Jay)
4, Breams Buildings, EC4A 2AQ, LDE 1042, Tel: 0171 430 1221

Gallagher, Nathan
5, Fountain Court, Steelhouse Lane, Birmingham, B4 6DR, DX 16075, Tel: 0121 606 0500

Garnham, Jacqueline
5 Raymond Buildings, WC1R 5BP, LDE 1054, Tel: 0171 242 2902

Gibbs, Stewart
4, Pump Court, Temple, EC4Y 7AN, LDE 303, Tel: 0171 353 2656

Gidaree, Sandra
2 Crown Office Row, Temple, EC4Y 7HJ, LDE 344, Tel: 0171 797 8100

Gilbert, Michelle
5 Stone Buildings, Lincoln's Inn, WC2A, LDE 304, Tel: 0171 242 6201

Gillespie-Bell, Sylvia
King Charles House, Nottingham, NG1 6FX, DX 10042, Tel: 0115 941 8851

Gilson, John
2, Harcourt Buildings, Temple, EC4, LDE 1039, Tel: 0171 583 9020

Goddard, Marc
4 Paper Buildings, Temple, EC4Y 7EX, LDE 1036, Tel: 0171 353 3366

Goggin, Claire
Wilberforce Chambers, 8 New Square, WC2A 3QP, LDE 311, Tel: 0171 306 0102

Goodrham, Jayne
5 Pump Court, Temple, EC4Y 7AP, LDE 497, Tel: 0171 353 2532

Goodridge, Michael
2 Gray's Inn Square, WC1R 5AA, LDE 43, Tel: 0171 242 0328

Gould, Sean
Westgate Chambers, 144 High Street, Lewes, BN7 1XT, DX 50250 Lewis 2, Tel: 01273 480510

Gray, Joanna
3 Madingley Rd, Cambridge, CB2 0EE, DX 5809 Cambridge, Tel: 01223 368761

Griggs, Pauline
Francis Taylor Building, Temple, EC4Y 7BY, LDE 46, Tel: 0171 797 7250

Guzder, Robert
7, Fountain Court, Steelhouse Lane, Birmingham, B4 6DR, DX 16073 Birmingham, Tel: 0121 236 8531

Haley, David
Peel Court Chambers, 45 Hardman Street, M3 3PL, DX 14320 Manchester 2, Tel: 0161 8323791

Haley, Nicholas
15 Winkley Square, Preston, PR1 3JJ, DX 17110, Tel: 01772 252828

Hammond, John
18, St. John Street, Manchester, M3 4EA, DX 728854, Tel: 0161 834 9843

Hammond, Paul
Lamb Building, Temple, EC4Y 7AS, LDE 1038, Tel: 0171 797 7788

Harding, Mark
4 Brick Court, Temple, EC4Y 9AD, LDE 453, Tel: 0171 583 8455

Harding Michael
Albion Chambers, Broad Street, Bristol, BS1 1DR, DX 7822, Tel: 0117 927 2144

Harris, Lian
50 High Pavement, Nottingham, NG1 1HW, DX 10036, Tel: 0115 959 3503

Harris, Paul
1 Garden Court, Temple, EC4Y 9BL, LDE 1034, Tel: 0171 797 7900

Harrison, Mark
17 Carlton Crescent, Southampton, SO9 5AL, DX 96875, Tel: 01703 320320

Hart, James
9, Stone Buildings, Lincoln's Inn, WC2A 3NN, LDE 314, Tel: 0171 404 5055

Hawkey, Jonathan
Regency Chambers, Cathedral Square, Peterborough, PE1 1XW, DX 12349 Peterborough 1, Tel: 01733 315215

Haws, Kevin
First Floor, 1 Essex Court, Temple, EC4Y 9AR, LDE 371, Tel: 0171 936 3030

Hayns, Deborah

Heath, Mark
3, Verulam Buildings, WC1R 5NT, LDE 331, Tel: 0171 831 8441

Heep, Andrew
Peel House, 5/7 Harrington Street, Liverpool, L2 9QA, DX 14225 Liverpool 2, Tel: 0151 236 4321

Henshaw, David
13, King's Bench Walk, Temple, EC4Y 7EN, LDE 359, Tel: 0171 353 7204

Herron, Alistair

Heyhirst, Bridget
St. Paul's House, 23 Park Square South, Leeds, LS1 2ND, DX 26410, Tel: 0113 245 5866

Hill, Anthony
Ropewalk Chambers, 24 The Ropewalk, Nottingham, NG1 5EF, DX 10060 Nottingham 17, Tel: 0115 947 2581

Hockney, David
4 Raymond Buildings, Gray's Inn, WC1R 5BP, LDE 257, Tel: 0171 405 7211

Hockney, Nicholas
1 Hare Court, Temple, EC4Y 7BE, LDE 0065, Tel: 0171 353 3171

Hodges, Kelly
27 New Walk, Leicester, LE1, DX 10872 Leicester 1, Tel: 0116 255 9144

Hogg, David
Bracton Chambers, 95A, Chancery Lane, WC2A 1DT, LDE 416, Tel: 0171 242 4248

Hoile, Darren
5th Floor, Gray's Inn Chambers, WC1R 5JA, LDE 0074, Tel: 0171 404 1111

Holcombe, Julie
2, Crown Office Row, Temple, EC4Y 7HJ, LDE 344, Tel: 0171 797 8100

Holden, Pauline
Lincoln House Chambers, 1 Brazenose Street, Deansgate, Manchester, M3, DX 14338 Manchester 1, Tel: 0161 832 5301

Holland, Edward
4, King's Bench Walk, EC4, LDE 422, Tel: 0171 353 0478

Homersham, Sarah
2, Paper Buildings, EC4Y 7ET, LDE 210, Tel: 0171 936 2613

Hood, Clare
1 Hare Court, Temple, EC4Y 7BE, LDE 0065, Tel: 0171 353 3171

Hooson, Stacey
Refuge House, Derby Square, Lord Street, Liverpool, DX 14213, Tel: 0151 709 4222

Hotchin, James
Lancaster Buildings Chambers, Manchester, M3 2BW, DX 14488 Manchester 2, Tel: 0161 661 4444

Houchin, Terry
Francis Taylor Building, EC4Y 7BY, LDE 441, Tel: 0171 353 7768

Howdle, Colin
1, Fountain Court, Steelhouse Lane, Birmingham, DX 16077, Tel: 0121 236 5721

Hughes, Paul
2 Gray's Inn Square Chambers, WC1R 5AA, LDE 43, Tel: 0171 242 0328

Hughton, Michelle
14 Tooks Court, Cursitor Street, EC4A 1JY, LDE 68, Tel: 0171 405 8828

Hugo, Catherine
East Anglian Chambers, 52 North Hill, Colchester, CO1 1PY, DX 3611 Colchester, Tel: 01206 572756

Hunt, Mary
5 King's Bench Walk, Temple, EC4Y 7DN, LDE 478, Tel: 0171 797 7600

Hunt, Carl
5, Fountain Court, Steelhouse Lane, Birmingham, DX 16075, Tel: 0121 606 0500

Hurst, Muriel

Hyde, Janet
33, Broad Chare, Newcastle Upon Tyne, NE1 3OQ, DX 61001, Tel: 0191 232 0541

Irons, Luke
Wilberforce Chambers, 8 New Square, Lincoln's Inn, WC2A 3QS, LDE 311, Tel: 0171 306 0102

Jarvis, Neil
2, Crown Office Row, Temple, EC4YU 7HJ, LDE 1041, Tel: 0171 797 8000

Jennings, Marc
2, Paper Buildings, Temple, EC4Y 7ET, LDE 494, Tel: 0171 936 2611

Johns, Eddie
7, Kings Bench Walk, Temple, EC4Y 7DS, LDE 239, Tel: 0171 583 0404

Johnson, Graham
199, Strand, London, WC2R 1DR, LDE 322, Tel: 0171 379 9778

Johnson, Susan
199, Strand, London, WC2R 1DR, LDE 322, Tel: 0171 379 9778

Jones, Dale
5 Paper Buildings, Temple, EC4Y 7HB, LDE 365, Tel: 0171 583 6117

Jones, Daniel
1 Atkin Building, Gray's Inn, WC1R 5AT, LDE 1033, Tel: 0171 404 1033

Jones, Georgina
6,Fountain Court, Steelhouse Lane, Birmingham, B4 6DR, DX 16076, Tel: 0121 233 3282

Kansley, Nicole
23, Essex Street, WC2R 3AS, LDE 148, Tel: 0171 413 0353

Kelley, Nicola
9 King's Bench Walk, Temple, EC4Y, LDE 472, Tel: 0171 353 7202

Kelly, Kevin
13 King's Bench Walk, Temple, EC4Y 7EN, LDE 359, Tel: 0171 353 7204

Kelly, Shona
7 Stone Buildings, Lincoln's Inn, WC2A 3SZ, LDE 335, Tel: 0171 405 3886

Kelly, Lisa
St. John's Chambers, Small Street, Bristol, BS1 1DW, DX 78138, Tel: 0117 921 3456

Kempston, Julie
2 Mitre Court Buildings, Temple,
EC4Y 7BX, LDE 0023, Tel: 0171
353 1353

Kesbey, Jack
9 Bedford Row, London, WC1R 4AZ,
LDE 347, Tel: 0171 242 3555

Kesby, Matthew
24, Lincoln's Inn Fields, WC1A
3ED, LDE 320, Tel: 0171 813 8000

Kilsby, Angela
Northampton Chambers, 22 Albion
Place, Northampton, NN1, DX
12464 Northampton, Tel: 01604
636271

Kitchen, Ian
5, New Square, Lincoln's Inn, WC2A
3RJ, LDE 272, Tel: 0171 404 0404

Krogulec, Anthony
King Charles House, Standard Hill,
Nottingham, DX 10042, Tel: 0115
947 2581

Lamba, Raj Krishan
3 Verulam Buildings, WC1R 5NT,
LDE 33, Tel: 0171 831 8441

Lane, Christopher
24 Old Buildings, WC2A 3UJ, LDE
307, Tel: 0171 404 0946

Lane, Wendy
4, Brick Court, Temple, EC4Y 9AD,
LDE 491, Tel: 0171 797 8910

Laverty, Paul
28 St. John Street, Manchester, M3
4DJ, DX 728861, Tel: 0161 834
8418

Lawrence, Stephen
12, Gray's Inn Square, WR1R 5JP,
LDE 0055, Tel: 0171 404 4866

Laws, Rebecca
36, Bedford Row, London, WC1R
4JH, LDE 360, Tel: 0171 421 8000

Layzell, Christopher
2 Field Court, Gray's Inn, WC1R
5BB, LDE 457, Tel: 0171 405 6114

Lea, David
8, King Street, Manchester, M2 6AQ,
DX 14354 Manchester, Tel: 0161
834 9560

Lea, Janet
1, St. Ignatius Square, Preston, PR1
1TT, DX, Tel: 01772 558778

Leahy, Paul
New Court, Temple, EC4Y 9BE, LDE
0018, Tel: 0171 583 5123

Lee, Terence
10 King's Bench Walk, EC4Y 7EB,
LDE 24, Tel: 0171 353 7742

Leech, Martin
8, King Street, Manchester, M2 6AQ,
DX 14354 Manchester, Tel: 0161
834 9560

Lashmar Ben
4 Stone Buildings, Lincoln's Inn,
WC2A, LDE 385, Tel: 0171 242
5524

Lewis, Jenny
Crown Office Row Chambers,
Brighton, BN1 1WH, DX 36670, Tel:
01273 625626

Liddon, Anthony
8, New Square, Lincoln's Inn, WC2A
3QP, LDE 379, Tel: 0171 405 4321

Longhurst, Dominic
18, St. John Street, Manchester, M3
4EA, DX 728854 Manchester 4, Tel:
0161 278 1800

Love, Andrew
5 Raymond Buildings, Gray's Inn,
WC1R, LDE 1054, Tel: 0171 242
2902

Loxton, Stephen
5 Fountain Court, Birmingham,
B46 DR, DX 16075 Birmingham,
Tel: 0121 606 0500

Luckman, Justin
3 Fountain Court, Steelhouse Lane,
Birmingham, B4 6DR, DX 16079,
Tel:0121 236 5854

Lucas, Samantha

Mace, David
1 Brick Court, Temple, EC4Y 9BY,
LDE 468, Tel: 0171 353 8845

Malcolmson, Ang
40, King Street, Chester, CH1 2AH,
DX 22154 Chester, Tel: 01244
323886

Maloney Rosemary 8
Fountain Court, Birmingham, DX
15078, Tel: 0121 236 5514

Mansell, Mark
4 Fountain Court, Birmingham, B4
6DR, DX 16074, Tel: 0121 236
3476

Margrett, Bruce
Westgate Chambers, 144, High
Street, Lewes, East Sussex, BN7
1XT, DX 50250 Lewes 2, Tel: 01273
480510

Maguire, Isabelle
Acre Lane Chambers, 30A, Acre
Lane, Brixton, SW2 5SG, DX 58782
Brixton, Tel: 0171 274 4400

Marsh, Darin
32 Furnival Street, EC4A 1JQ, LDE
72, Tel: 0171 405 3232

Marshall, Lisa
24 The Ropewalk, Nottingham, NG1
5EF, DX 10060 Nottingham 17, Tel:
0115 947 2581

Martin, Kenneth
6 King's Bench Walk, Temple, EC4Y
7DR, LDE 26, Tel: 0171 842 0406

Mason, Natasha
Devereux Chambers, Devereux
Court, WC2R 3JJ, LDE 349, Tel:
0171 353 7534

McBlain, Alexis
29 Bedford Row, London, WC1R
4HE, LDE 1044, Tel: 0171 831
2626

McBlain, Tiffany
Holborn Chambers, 6 Gate Street,
WC2A 3HP, LDE 159, Tel: 0171 242
6060

McCarthy, Kevin
3 Temple Gardens, EC4Y, LDE
0008, Tel: 0171 353 0853

McCourt, Kevin
1 Paper Buildings, Temple, EC4Y
7EP, LDE 80, Tel: 0171 583 7355

McCrone, Steven
1 Mitre Court Buildings, Temple,
EC4Y 7BS, LDE 342, Tel: 0171 797
7070

McDermott, Gail
Peel Court Chambers, 45 Hardman
Street, Manchester, M3 3HH, DX
14320 Manchester 2, Tel: 0161 832
3791

McDonald, David
1 King's Bench Walk, Temple, EC4Y
7DB, LDE 20, Tel: 0171 583 6266

McGrath, Michelle
33, Bedford Row, London, WC1R
4JH, LDE 75, Tel: 0171 242 6476

McHugh, Neil
3rd Floor, Peel House, 5-7 Harrington Street, Liverpool, L2 9NX, DX 14227 Liverpool, Tel: 0151 234 0718

McKay, Ben
8, King Street, Manchester, M2 6AQ, DX 14354 Manchester 1, Tel: 0161 834 9560

McKay, Fiona
Young Street Chambers, 38 Young Street, Manchester, M3 3FT, DX 25583 Manchester 5, Tel: 0161 833 0489

McKenna, Toni
4, Field Court, Gray's Inn, WC1R, LDE 483, Tel: 0171 440 6900

McKenzie, Errol
2, Mitre Court Buildings, Temple, EC4Y 7BX, LDE 0032, Tel: 0171 583 1380

McKimm, William
3 Temple Gardens, Temple, EC4Y 9AU, LDE 0073, Tel: 0171 583 0010

McQuade, Sam
3 Serjeants Inn, Temple, EC4Y, LDE 421, Tel: 0171 353 5377

Meade, William
Old Square Chambers, 3 Verulam Buildings, WC1R 5LQ, LDE 1046, Tel: 0171 831 0801

Meikle, Elizabeth
10-11, Gray's Inn Square, WC1R 5JD, LDE 484, Tel: 0171 405 2576

Melli Yvonne
All Saints Chambers, Bristol, DX 7870 Bristol, Tel: 0117 921 1966

Messenger, Paul
6/7 Gough Square, London, EC4A 3DE, LDE 476, Tel: 0171 353 0924

Milsom, Pavel
2 Crown Office Row, EC4Y 7HJ, LDE 1041, Tel: 0171 797 8000

Milton, Daren
23 Essex Street, WC2R 3AS, LDE 148, Tel: 0171 413 0353

Mo, George
4, Brick Court, Temple, EC4Y 9AD, LDE 404, Tel: 0171 797 7766

Moles, Annette
St John's Chbs, Small Street, Bristol, BS1 1DW, DX 78138 Bristol, Tel: 0117 921 3456

Monaghan, Daniel
Cobden House, 19 Quay Street, Manchester, M3 3HN, DX 14327 Manchester 3, Tel: 0161 833 6000

Monks, John
1 Atkin Buildings, WC1R 5BQ, LDE 1033, Tel: 0171 404 0102

Money Moira
Park Court Chambers, 40 Park Court Street, Leeds, LS1 2QH, DX 26401, Tel: 0113 243 3277

Morecroft, Paul
9 St. John Street, Manchester, M3 4DN, DX 14326 Manchester, Tel: 0161 955 9000

Morrissey, Anthony
9 St. John Street, Manchester, M3 4DN, DX 14326 Manchester, Tel: 0161 955 9000

Mott, Stanley
1 Middle Temple Lane, EC4Y 9AA, LDE 464, Tel: 0171 583 0659

Mumford-Lloyd, Jennifer
Byrom Street Chambers, 25, Byrom Street, Manchester, M3 4PF, DX 718156 Manchester 3, Tel: 0161 829 2100

Neil, Donna

Nettleton, Andrea
6 Park Square, Leeds, LS1 2LW, DX 26402 Leeds Park Square, Tel: 0113 245 9783

Newman, Nicholas
Queen Elizabeth Building, EC4Y 9BS, LDE 482, Tel: 0171 583 5766

Newton, Mark
7 Stone Buildings, Lincoln's Inn, WC2A 3SZ, LDE 335, Tel: 0171 405 3886

Nicholas, James
1 Mitre Court, Temple, EC4Y 7BS, LDE 342, Tel: 0171 797 7070

Nicholl, Vincent
5 Paper Buildings, Temple, EC4Y 7HB, LDE 365, Tel: 0171 583 6117

Nickless, Julia

Norman, Daniel
East Anglian Chambers, 52 North Hill, Colchester, CO1 1PY, DX 3611, Tel: 01206 572756

Nunn, Alex
Goldsmith Chambers, Goldsmith Buildings, EC4Y 7BL, LDE 376, Tel: 0171 353 6802

O'Brien D
Goldsmith Building, Temple, EC4Y 7BL, LDE 435, Tel: 0171 353 7881

Opoku, Kofi
12, Old Square, Lincoln's Inn, WC2A 3TX, LDE 130, Tel: 0171 404 0875

O'Sullivan, Orla
1 Crown Office Row, Temple, EC4Y 7HH, LDE 226, Tel: 0171 797 7111

O'Sullivan, Geraldine
16, Bedford Row, WC1R 4EB, LDE 312, Tel: 0171 414 8080

Outen, Paul
4 Brick Court, 1st Floor, Temple, EC4Y 9AD, LDE 453, Tel: 0171 583 8455

Owen, Carla
2 King's Bench Walk, Temple, EC4Y 7DE, LDE 477, Tel: 0171 353 9276

Parham, Donna
55 Temple Chambers, Temple Avenue, EC4Y, LDE 260, Tel: 0171 353 7400

Parr, Steven
Thomas More Chambers, 51/52 Carey Street, WC2A 2JB, LDE 90, Tel: 0171 404 7000

Passmore Bonita
Albion Chambers, Broad Street, Bristol, BS1 1DR, DX 7822, Tel: 0117 927 2144

Patrick Richard
39, Essex Street, London, WC2R 3AT, LDE 298, Tel: 0171 583 1111

Peck Dennis
2 Crown Office Row, Temple, EC4Y 7HJ, LDE 1041, Tel: 0171 797 8000

Penfold, Teresa
Eastborne Chambers, 15, Hyde Gardens, Eastbourne, DX 6925 Eastbourne, Tel: 01323 642102

Penson, David
Blackstone Chambers, Temple, EC4Y, LDE 281, Tel: 0171 583 1770

Penson Stephen
11 King's Bench Walk, Temple, EC4Y 7EQ, LDE 368, Tel: 0171 583 0610

Peters, Brian
3 Temple Gardens, Temple, EC4Y 9AU, LDE 0008, Tel: 0171 353 0853

Peto, Nicholas
31/33 Broad Chare Chambers, Newcastle-Under-Tyne, NE1 3DQ, DX 61001, Tel: 0191 232 0541

Phillips, David
1st Floor, 3 Paper Buildings, EC4Y 7EU, LDE 1024, Tel: 0171 583 8055

Phillips-Griffiths, Phil
30, Park Place, Cardiff, CF1 3BA, DX 50756, Tel: 01222 398421

**Pickersgill, Joanne
36, Bedford Row, London, WC1R 4JH, LDE 360, Tel: 0171 421 8000

Pike, James
5 Bell Yard, London, WC2, LDE 400, Tel: 0171 333 8811

Pocock, Susie
9, Bedford Row, WC1R 4DB, LDE 347, Tel: 0171 242 3555

Portch, David
Old Square Chambers, 1 Verulam Buildings, WC1R 5LQ, LDE 1046, Tel: 0171 831 0801

Poyser, A
13, Old Square, Lincoln's Inn, WC2A 3UA, LDE 1025, Tel: 0171 242 6105

Poyser, David
5 Verulam Buildings, WC1R, LDE 363, Tel: 0171 831 9500

Preston, Richard
3rd Floor Francis Taylor Building, EC4Y 7BY, LDE 46, Tel: 0171 797 7250

Price, Steven J
2/3, College Place, London Road, SO1 2FB, DX 38533, Tel: 01703 230338

Pringle, Stuart
4 St. Peter Street, Winchester, SO23 8BW, DX 2507, Tel: 01962 868884

Pullam, Stuart
2-3 Gray's Inn Square, WC1H 5JH, LDE 316, Tel: 0171 242 4986

Rankin, Lewis
Blackstone Chambers, Temple, EC4Y, LDE 281,Tel: 0171 583 1770

Raszka, Maria
15 North Church Street Chambers, Sheffield, S1 2DH, DX 10629 Sheffield, Tel: 0114 275 9708

Ratcliffe, Christopher
Suite 1, 2nd Floor, Gray's Inn Chambers, WC1R, LDE 442, Tel: 0171 405 7011

Raymond, Karen
Littman Chambers, 12 Gray's Inn Square, WC1R 5JP, LDE 0055, Tel: 0171 404 4866

Reding, S
2 Gray's Inn Square, Gray's Inn, WC1R 5AA, LDE 43, Tel: 0171 242 0328

Reeves, Andrew
18, St. John Street, Manchester, DX 728854 Manchester 4, Tel: 0161 278 1800

Regan, Mark
4/5 Gray's Inn Square, Gray's Inn, WC1R 5AY, LDE 1029, Tel: 0171 404 5252

Reynolds, Conrad
Deans Court Chambers, Crown Square, Manchester, M3 3HA, DX 718155, Tel: 0161 834 4097

Ritchie, Stuart
39 Essex Street, London, WC2, LDE 298, Tel: 0171 583 1111

Robinson, Mark
21 Whitefriars, Chester, CH1 1NZ, DX 19979, Tel: 01244 323070

Robinson, Francis
1 Little Essex Street, EC2R 3LD, LDE 17, Tel: 0171 395 2000

Robinson, Jonathan
24-26, Lincoln's Inn Fields, WC2A 3ED, LDE 320, Tel: 0171 813 8000

Robinson, Simon
19 Old Buildings, Lincoln's Inn, WC2, LDE 397, Tel: 0171 405 2001

Robson, Sharon
New Court Chbs, 3 Broad Chare, Newcastle upon Tyne, NE1 3DQ DX 61012 Newcastle 1, Tel: 0191 232 1980

Rogers, Lisa
40, King Street, Manchester, M, DX 718188 Manchester 3, Tel: 0161 832 9082

Rogers, Maxine
Queen Elizabeth Building, EC4Y, LDE 340, Tel: 0171 353 7181

Rogers, Janet
Redhill Chambers, Seloduct House, Station Road, Redhill, RH1 1NF, DX 100203 Redhill, Tel: 01737 780781

Rose, Nick
4 Paper Buildings, Temple, EC4Y 7EX, LDE 1036, Tel: 0171 353 3366

Roukin, Jason
4, Essex Court, Temple, EC4Y 9AJ, LDE 292, Tel: 0171 797 7970

Royal, Leigh
Deans Court Chambers, Manchester, M3 3HA, DX 718188 Manchester 3, Tel: 0161 834 4097

Ruben, David
11 King's Bench Walk, Temple, EC4Y 7EQ, LDE 368, Tel: 0171 632 8500

Rycroft, Timothy
Essex Court Chambers, 24 Lincoln's Inn Fields, WC2A 3ED, LDE 320, Tel: 0171 813 8000

Sams, James
4 Stone Buildings, Lincoln's Inn, WC2A 3XT, LDE 385, Tel: 0171 242 5524

Sansom, Carol
50 High Pavement, Nottingham, NG1 1HW, DX 10036, Tel: 0115 950 3503

Savage, Jason
2, Temple Gardens, EC4Y 9AY, LDE 134, Tel: 0171 583 6041

Schofield, Marc
10 Old Square, Lincoln's Inn, WC2A 3SU, LDE 306, Tel: 0171 405 0758

Schultz, Jean P
4, Field Court, Gray's Inn, WC1R 5EA, LDE 483, Tel: 0171 440 6900

Secrett, Martin
Queen Elizabeth Building, EC4, LDE 340, Tel: 0171 353 7181

Sellen, Stuart
Thomas More Building, 51/2,Carey Street, Lincoln's Inn, LDE 90, Tel: 0171 404 7000

Shaw, James
33 Earl Street, Maidstone, ME14 1PF, DX 51982 Maidstone 2, Tel: 01622 688592

Sherriff, Pippa
Guildford Chambers, Stoke House, Leapale Lane, Guildford, GU1 4LY, DX 97863 Guildford 5, Tel: 01483 539131

Shortall, James
1 Serjeants' Inn, EC4Y 1LL, LDE 364, Tel: 0171 415 6666

Shrubsall, William
11 Stone Buildings, Lincoln's Inn, WC2A 3TG, LDE 1022, Tel: 0171 831 6381

Silverman, Philip
5, Pump Court, Temple, EC4Y 7AP, LDE 497, Tel: 0171 353 2532

Sizer, John
5, Raymond Buildings, Gray's Inn, WC1R 5BP, LDE 1054, Tel: 0171 242 2902

Slade, Melanie
Littman Chambers, 12 Gray's Inn Square, WC1R 5JP, LDE 0055, Tel: 0171 404 4866

Slattery, Simon
4, Pump Court, Temple, EC4Y 7AN, LDE 303, Tel: 0171 353 2656

Smillie, Danny
Wilberforce Chambers, 8 New Square, WC2A 3QP, LDE 311, Tel: 0171 306 0102

Smith, Ann
Park Court Chambers, 40 Park Cross Street, Leeds, LS1 2QH, DX 26401,Tel: 0113 243 3277

Smith, Gary
5 Fountain Court, Birmingham, B46DR, DX 16075 Birmingham, Tel: 0121 606 0500

Smith, Stuart
5 Fountain Court, Birmingham, B4 6DR, DX 16075 Birmingham, Tel: 0121 606 0500

Snith, Sandra
39, Essex Street, London, WC2A 3AT, LDE 298, Tel: 0171 832 1111

Smith, Tom
11, Stone Buildings, Lincoln's Inn, WC2A 3TG, LDE 1022, Tel: 0171 831 6381

Sommerville, Stephen
6 Pump Court, Temple, EC4Y 7AR, LDE 409, Tel: 0171 583 6013

Speller, Gregory
South-Western Chambers, 12 Middle Street, Taunton, DX 32146, Tel: 01823 331919

Spencer, Ian
Fenners Chambers, 3 Madingley Rd, CB3OEE, DX 5809 Cambridge, Tel: 01223 368761

Squires, Kevin
1 Serjeants Inn, Temple, EC4Y 1NH, LDE 440, Tel: 0171 583 1355

Stammers, James
New Court, Temple, EC4Y 9BE, LDE 0018, Tel: 0171 583 5123

Stanhope, Darren
Francis Taylor Building, Temple, EC4Y 7BY, LDE 441, Tel: 0171 797 8999

Stewart, John
New Bailey Chambers, 10 Lawson Street, Preston, PR1 2QS, DX 710050 Preston 10, Tel: 01772 258087

Stickels, Gareth
40 King Street, Chester, DX 22154 Chester Northgate, Tel: 01244 323886

Storer, Alison
Refuge House, Derby Square, Liverpool 2, DX 14213, Tel: 0151 709 4222

Strachan, Thomas
Claremont Chambers, 26 Walterloo Street, Wolverhampton, WV1 4BL, DX 10455 Wolverhampton 1, Tel: 01902 426222

Street, Gary
13, Old Square, Lincoln's Inn, WC2A 3UA, LDE 326, Tel: 0171 404 4800

Street, Tommy
4 Brick Court, Temple, EC4Y 9AD, LDE 453, Tel: 0171 583 8455

Streeting, Carl
3 Fountain Court, Birmingham, B4 6DR, DX 16079 Birmingham, Tel: 0121 236 5854

Summers, Bruce
New Court Chambers, 3 Broad Chare, Newcastle upon Tyne, NE1 3DQ, DX 61012 Newcastle 1, Tel: 0191 232 1980

Sundborg, Benjamin
Farrars Building, EC4Y, LDE 406, Tel: 0171 583 9241

Swann, Christopher
Trinity Chambers, 9-12, Trinity Chare, Quayside, Newcastle upon Tyne, NE1 3DF, DX 61185 Newcastle, Tel: 0191 232 1927

Swile, Robert
5th Floor, Gray's Inn Chambers, Gray's Inn, WC1R 5JA, LDE 0074, Tel: 0171 404 1111

Taghi, Louise
2, Temple Gardens, Temple, EC4Y 9AY, LDE 134, Tel: 0171 583 6041

Tansley, Philip
2, Field Court, Gray's Inn, WC1R 5BB, LDE 457, Tel: 0171 405 6114

Tidiman, Cheri
Littleton Chambers, 3, KBW, EC4Y 7HR, LDE 1047, Tel: 0171 797 8600

Tindale, Eleanore
1 Little Essex Street, WC2R 3LD, LDE 17, Tel: 0171 395 2000

Thorne, Kris
Iscoed Chambers, 86 St.Helen's Road, Swansea, DX 39554 Swansea 1, Tel: 01792 652988

Thornton, Kathryn
2nd Floor, Francis Taylor Building, Temple, EC4Y 7BY, LDE 211, Tel: 0171 353 9942

Tolman, Dean
2, Harcourt Buildings, Temple, EC4Y 7HJ, LDE 1039, Tel: 0171 583 9020

Tong, Tanya
2-3 Gray's Inn Square, Gray's Inn, WC1R 5JH, LDE 316, Tel: 0171 242 4986

Townsend, Mark
17, Bedford Row, WC1R 4EB, LDE 370, Tel: 0171 831 7314

Tulett, Peter
4 Breams Buildings, London, EC4A 1AQ, LDE 1042, Tel: 0171 353 5835

Turner, Danielle
Furnival Chambers, 32 Furnival Street, EC4A 1JQ, LDE 72, Tel: 0171 405 3232

H

Turner, E
5th Floor, Gray's Inn Chambers,
WC1A 5JA, LDE 0074, Tel: 0171 404
1111

Turner, James
23 Broad Street, Bristol, BS1 2HG,
DX 7823 Bristol, Tel: 0117 927
3366

Vella, Rita
7 Stone Buildings, 1st Floor,
Lincoln's Inn, WC2A 3SZ, LDE
1007, Tel: 0171 242 0961

Venables, Duncan
Lamb Building, Temple, EC4Y 7AS,
LDE 418, Tel: 0171 797 8300

Venables, Paul
5, Kings Bench Walk, Temple, EC4Y
7, LDE 367, Tel: 0171 353 5638

Ventura, Gary
11 New Square, Lincoln's Inn,
WC2A 3QB, LDE 319, Tel: 0171 831
0081

Vile, Richard
1 Middle Temple Lane, Temple,
EC4Y 9AA, LDE 464, Tel: 0171 583
0659

Wadden, Clair
14, Small Street, Bristol, BS1 1DE,
DX 78134 Bristol, Tel: 0117 926
4587

Wakeling, Lee
14, Tooks Court, Cursitor Street,
EC4A 1LB, DX 68, Tel: 0171 405
8828

Walker, Julia
31, Southgate Street, Winchester,
SO23 9EE, DX 2514 Winchester,
Tel: 01962 868161

Walker, Scott
5 Fountain Court, Birmingham,
B4 6DR, DX 16075 Birmingham,
Tel: 0121 606 0500

Wall, Carl
4, Pump Court, Temple, EC4Y 7AN,
LDE 303, Tel: 0171 353 2656

Wallis, Daniel
1, Pump Court, Temple, EC4Y 7AB,
LDE 109, Tel: 0171 353 4341

Ward David

Watson, Sarah

Wedderburn Everton
36, Bedford Row, WC1R, LDE 360,
Tel: 0171 421 8000

Wells, Karen
2 Harcourt Buildings, Temple,
EC4Y 9DB, LDE 402, Tel: 0171 353
8145

Wheeler, Timothy
2, Harcourt Buildings, Temple,
EC4Y, 9DB, LDE 373, Tel: 0171 353
6961

Whitaker, Steven
13 Old Square, Lincoln's Inn, WC2A
3UA, LDE 1025, Tel: 0171 242
6105

Whitford, William
Queen Elizabeth Building, Temple,
EC4Y 9BS, LDE 482, Tel: 0171 583
5766

Wigley, Simon
4 Paper Buildings, Temple, EC4Y
7EX, LDE 1036, Tel: 0171 353 3
366

Wiggs, Robert
1, Atkin Buildings, Gray's Inn,
WC1R 5BQ, LDE 1033, Tel: 0171
404 0102

Wildish, Matthew
Francis Taylor Buildings, EC4Y 9BY,
LDE 46, Tel: 0171 797 7250

Wilkes, Emma
1st Floor, 1 Brick Court, Temple,
EC4Y 9BY, LDE 468, Tel: 0171 353
8845

Wilkinson, Danny
Fountain Court, Temple, EC4Y
9DH, LDE 5, Tel: 0171 583 3335

Williams, Emlyn

Williams Alister J
3 New Square, Lincoln's Inn, WC2A
3RS, LDE 384, Tel: 0171 405 5577

Williams, Gary
1 Fountain Court, Steelhouse Lane,
Birmingham, B4 6DR, DX 16077,
Tel: 0121 236 5721

Williams Guy
3, Gray's Inn Square, WC1R 5AH,
LDE 1043, Tel: 0171 520 5600

Williams, A. Keith Williams Martin
8 New Square, Lincoln's Inn, WC2A
3QP, LDE 379, Tel: 0171 405 4321

Williams, Paula
1, Temple Gardens, EC4Y 9BB, LDE
382, Tel: 0171 583 1315

Williams Sandra
33 Park Place, Cardiff, CF1 3BA, DX
50755 Cardiff 2, Tel: 01222 233313

Willicombe, Laurence
5 Paper Buildings, Temple, EC4Y 7,
LDE 415, Tel: 0171 583 9275

Willicombe, Richard
1 Middle Temple Lane, EC4Y 9AA,
LDE 464, Tel: 0171 583 0659

Winrow, Mark
Brick Court Chambers, 7/8 Essex
Street, WC2R 3LD, LDE 302, Tel:
0171 379 3550

Wood, Debbie
10 Old Square, Lincoln's Inn, WC2A
3SU, LDE 306, Tel: 0171 405 0758

Woodbridge, Daniel
3 Serjeants Inn, EC4Y 1BQ, LDE
421, Tel: 0171 353 5537

Woods, Danny
4 Brick Court, Temple, EC4Y LDE
453, Tel: 0171 583 8455

Wragg, Nigel
1 High Pavement, Nottingham, NG1
1HF, DX 10168 Nottingham, Tel:
0115 941 8218

Wright, Seb

Wright, Clare
2, Dr Johnson's Buildings, Temple,
EC4Y 7BA, LDE 429, Tel: 0171 353
4716

Wright, David
Kenworthy Chambers, 83 Bridge
Street, Manchester, M3 2RF, DX
718200 Manchester 3, Tel: 0161
832 4036

Wright, Sarah
Kenworthy Chambers, 83, Bridge
Street, Manchester, M3 2RF, DX
718200 Manchester 3, Tel: 0161
832 4036

Yacoub, Susan
Francis Taylor Building, 2nd Floor,
EC4Y 7BY, LDE 211, Tel: 0171 353
9942

PART I

A-Z Index of Chambers

This section lists all the chambers from *Part C Chambers by Location* alphabetically with the Part C page reference.

A

A K Chambers 19 Headlands Drive, Hessle, Hull HU13 0JP
01482 641180 .... C22

Abbey Chambers PO Box 47, 47 Ashurst Drive, Shepperton,
Middlesex TW17 0LD 01932 560913 .... C192

ACHMA Chambers 44 Yarnfield Square, Clayton Road, London
SE15 5JD 0171 639 7817/0171 635 7904 .... C37

Acre Lane Neighbourhood Chambers 30A Acre Lane, London
SW2 5SG 0171 274 4400 .... C37

Advolex Chambers 70 Coulsdon Road, Coulsdon, Surrey
CR5 2LB 0181 763 2345 .... C19

3 Aisby Drive Rossington, Doncaster DN11 0YY
01302 866495 .... C19

Alban Chambers 27 Old Gloucester Street, London WC1N 3XX
0171 419 5051 .... C37

Albany Chambers 91 Kentish Town Road, London NW1 8NY
0171 485 5736/5758 .... C37

Albion Chambers Broad Street, Bristol BS1 1DR
0117 9272144 .... C11

Alexandra Chambers 163 Albert Road, London N22 7AQ
0181 881 8523 .... C37

Amhurst Chambers 76 Amhurst Park, London N16 5AR
0181 800 5817 .... C37

Chambers of Andrew Campbell QC 10 Park Square, Leeds
LS1 2LH 0113 2455438 .... C24

Chambers of Gamini Angammana 'Woodcroft', 13 Woodend,
Upper Norwood, London SE19 3NU 0181 240 7476 .... C37

Angel Chambers 94 Walter Road, Swansea, West Glamorgan
SA1 5QA 01792 464623/464648 .... C194

54 Anne Way Ilford, Essex IG6 2RL 0181 501 4311 .... C23

Chambers of James Apea 11 Helix Road, London SW2 2JR
0181 244 5545 .... C38

Arbitration Chambers 22 Willes Road, London NW5 3DS
020 7267 2137 .... C38

Arcadia Chambers P O Box 16674, 18 Kensington Court,
London W8 5DW 0171 938 1285 .... C38

Arden Chambers 27 John Street, London WC1N 2BL
020 7242 4244 .... C39

Arlington Chambers 5 Park Crescent Mews East, Great
Portland Street, London W1N 5HB 0171 580 9188 .... C39

Chambers of Dr Michael Arnheim 101 Queen Alexandra
Mansions, Judd Street, London WC1H 9DP 0171 833 5093 C39

6 Ascot Road Shotley Bridge, Consett, County Durham
DH8 0NU 01207 507785 .... C19

Assize Court Chambers 14 Small Street, Bristol BS1 1DE
0117 9264587 .... C11

3 Atkin Street Douglas, Isle of Man 01624 897 420 .... C19

Atkin Chambers 1 Atkin Building, Gray's Inn, London
WC1R 5AT 020 7404 0102 .... C39

Avondale Chambers 2 Avondale Avenue, London N12 8EJ
0181 445 9984 .... C40

B

Number Ten Baker Street 10 Baker Street, Middlesbrough
TS1 2LH 01642 220332 .... C177

Baker Street Chambers 9 Baker Street, Middlesbrough
TS1 2LF 01642 873873 .... C177

Balham Chambers 82 Balham High Road, London SW12 9AG
0181 675 4609 .... C40

47 Banbury House Banbury Road, London E9 7EB
0181 985 8716 .... C40

Bank House Chambers Old Bank House, Hartshead, Sheffield
S1 2EL 0114 2751223 .... C191

Barclay Chambers 2a Barclay Road, Leytonstone, London
E11 3DG 0181 558 2289/925 0688 .... C40

Barnard's Inn Chambers 6th Floor, Halton House, 20-23
Holborn, London EC1N 2JD 0171 369 6969 .... C40

Barristers' Common Law Chambers 57 Whitechapel Road,
Aldgate East, London E1 1DU 0171 375 3012 .... C40

Becket Chambers 17 New Dover Road, Canterbury, Kent
CT1 3AS 01227 786331 .... C14

Bedford Chambers 2 Park Hill, Ampthill, Bedford MK45 2LW
0870 7337333 .... C3

9 Bedford Row London WC1R 4AZ 0171 242 3555 .... C40

17 Bedford Row London WC1R 4EB 0171 831 7314 ...... C41

33 Bedford Row London WC1R 4JH 0171 242 6476 .... C41

Chambers of Michael Pert QC 36 Bedford Row, London
WC1R 4JH 0171 421 8000 .... C41

48 Bedford Row London WC1R 4LR 0171 430 2005 ...... C43

29 Bedford Row Chambers London WC1R 4HE
0171 831 2626 .... C43

9-12 Bell Yard London WC2A 2LF 0171 400 1800 .... C43

Bell Yard Chambers 116/118 Chancery Lane, London
WC2A 1PP 0171 306 9292 .... C44

Belmarsh Chambers 20 Warland Road, London SE18 2EU
0181 316 7322 .... C44

Beresford Chambers 21 King Street, Luton, Bedfordshire
LU1 2DW 01582 429111 .... C165

Berkeley Chambers 1st Floor, 52 High Street, Henley-in-Arden,
Warwickshire B95 5AN 01564 795546 .... C22

4 Bingham Place London W1M 3FF 0171 486 5347/
071 487 5910 .... C44

Blackstone Chambers Blackstone House, Temple, London
EC4Y 9BW 0171 583 1770 .... C44

11 Bolt Court (also at 7 Stone Buildings - 1st Floor) London
EC4A 3DQ 0171 353 2300 .... C46

Bond Street Chambers Standbrook House, 2-5 Old Bond
Street, Mayfair, London W1X 3TB 01932 342951 .... C46

23 Bracken Gardens Barnes, London SW13 9HW
0181 748 4924 .... C46

Bracton Chambers 95a Chancery Lane, London WC2A 1DT
0171 242 4248 .... C46

4 Breams Buildings London EC4A 1AQ 0171 353 5835/
430 1221 .... C46

Brentwood Chambers Denton, North Yorkshire LS29 0HE
01943 817230 .... C19

1 Brick Court 1st Floor, Temple, London EC4Y 9BY
0171 353 8845 .... C47

4 Brick Court Temple, London EC4Y 9AD 0171 797 8910 C48

4 Brick Court Ground Floor, Temple, London EC4Y 9AD
0171 797 7766 .... C48

4 Brick Court, Chambers of Anne Rafferty QC 1st Floor,
Temple, London EC4Y 9AD 0171 583 8455 .... C48

Brick Court Chambers 7-8 Essex Street, London WC2R 3LD
0171 379 3550 .... C49

Bridewell Chambers 2 Bridewell Place, London EC4V 6AP
020 7797 8800 .... C49

Britton Street Chambers 1st Floor, 20 Britton Street, London
EC1M 5NQ 0171 608 3765 .... C50

Broad Chare 33 Broad Chare, Newcastle upon Tyne NE1 3DQ
0191 232 0541 .... C178

Broadway House Chambers Broadway House, 9 Bank Street,
Bradford, West Yorkshire BD1 1TW 01274 722560 .... C10

Broadway House Chambers 31 Park Square West, Leeds
LS1 2PF 0113 246 2600 .... C24

Bromley Chambers 39 Durham Road, Bromley, Kent BR2 0SN
0181 325 0863 .... C14

517 Bunyan Court Barbican, London EC2Y 8DH
0171 638 5076 .... C50

Chambers of Martin Burr Fourth Floor, Eldon Chambers,
30/32 Fleet Street, London EC4Y 1AA 0171 353 4636 .... C50

Byrom Street Chambers Byrom Street, Manchester M3 4PF
0161 829 2100 .... C167

C

Camberwell Chambers 66 Grove Park, Camberwell, London
SE5 8LF 0171 274 0830 .... C50

16a Campden Hill Court Campden Hill Road, London W8 7HS
0171 937 3492 .... C50

Cardinal Chambers 4 Old Mitre Court, 4th Floor, Temple,
London EC4Y 7BP 020 7353 2622 .... C50

17 Carlton Crescent Southampton SO15 2XR 023 8032 0320/
0823 2003 .... C192

Carmarthen Chambers 30 Spilman Street, Carmarthen, Dyfed
SA31 1LQ 01267 234410 .... C16

146 Carshalton Park Road Carshalton, Surrey SM5 3SG
0181 773 0531 .... C16

25-27 Castle Street 1st Floor, Liverpool L2 4TA
0151 227 5661/051 236 5072 .... C32

19 Castle Street Chambers Liverpool L2 4SX
0151 236 9402 .... C32

Castle Street Chambers 2nd Floor, 42 Castle Street, Liverpool
L2 7LD 0151 242 0500 .... C33

Cathedral Chambers Milburn House, Dean Street, Newcastle
upon Tyne NE1 1LE 0191 232 1311 .... C178

Cathedral Chambers, Ely P O Box 24, Ely, Cambridgeshire
CB6 1SL 01353 666775 .... C20

**Cathedral Chambers (Jan Wood Independent Barristers'
Clerk)** 1 Maple Road, Exeter, Devon EX4 1BN
01392 210900 .... C20

55B Cavendish Road Brondesbury, London NW2 3TN
0181 830 1495 .... C50

Central Chambers 89 Princess Street, Manchester M1 4HT
0161 236 1133 .... C168

39 Windsor Road London N3 3SN 0181 349 9194 .... C50

Chancery Chambers 1st Floor Offices, 70/72 Chancery Lane,
London WC2A 1AB 0171 405 6879/6870 .... C51

Chancery House Chambers 7 Lisbon Square, Leeds LS1 4LY
0113 244 6691 .... C24

74 Chancery Lane First Floor, London WC2A 1AA
0171 430 0667 .... C51

95A Chancery Lane London WC2A 1DT
0171 405 3101 .... C51

70 Charlecote Drive Wollaton, Nottingham NG8 2SB
0115 928 8901 .... C182

Chartlands Chambers 3 St Giles Terrace, Northampton
NN1 2BN 01604 603322 .... C180

Chavasse Court Chambers 2nd Floor, Chavasse Court, 24 Lord
Street, Liverpool L2 1TA 0151 707 1191 .... C33

19 Chestnut Drive Pinner, Middlesex HA5 1LX 0181 866 7603/
933 2382 .... C186

Chichester Chambers 12 North Pallant, Chichester, West
Sussex PO19 1TQ 01243 784538 .... C18

140 Cholmeley Road Reading, Berkshire RG1 3LR
01189 665174 .... C189

Clapham Chambers 21-25 Bedford Road, Clapham North,
London SW4 7SH 0171 978 8482/642 5777 .... C51

Claremont Chambers 26 Waterloo Road, Wolverhampton
WV1 4BL 01902 426222 .... C198

Clock Chambers 78 Darlington Street, Wolverhampton
WV1 4LY 01902 313444 .... C198

Cloisters 1 Pump Court, Temple, London EC4Y 7AA
0171 827 4000 .... C51

The Clove Hitch High Street, Iron Acton, Bristol BS37 9UG
01454 228243 .... C12

Cobden House Chambers 19 Quay Street, Manchester M3 3HN
0161 833 6000 .... C168

Coleridge Chambers Citadel, 190 Corporation Street,
Birmingham B4 6QD 0121 233 8500 .... C3

College Chambers 19 Carlton Cresent, Southampton
SO15 2ET 01703 230338 .... C193

Colleton Chambers Colleton Crescent, Exeter, Devon EX2 4DG
01392 274898/9 .... C20

Colleton Chambers Powlett House, 34 High Street, Taunton,
Somerset TA1 3PN 01823 324252 .... C196

Commonwealth Chambers 354 Moseley Road, Birmingham
B12 9AZ 0121 446 5732 .... C3

Corn Exchange Chambers 5th Floor, Fenwick Street, Liverpool
L2 7QS 0151 227 1081/5009 .... C33

62 Cortworth Road Ecclesall, Sheffield S11 9LP
0114 236 0988 .... C191

Chambers of Mr Peter Crampin QC Ground Floor, 11 New
Square, Lincoln's Inn, London WC2A 3QB
020 7831 0081 .... C51

21 Craven Road Kingston-Upon-Thames, Surrey KT2 6LW
0181 974 6799 .... C23

Crawford Chambers 7 Gerrard House, 23-25 Crawford Place,
London W1H 1HY 0171 724 0835 .... C52

Crayshott House Woodlands Road, West Byfleet, Surrey
KT14 6JW 01932 342951 .... C197

Cromwell-Ayeh-Kumi Chambers 1st Floor Suite, 119
Cricklewood Broadway, London NW2 3JG
0181 450 6620 .... C52

1 Crown Office Row Ground Floor, Temple, London EC4Y 7HH
0171 797 7500 .... C52

1 Crown Office Row 3rd Floor, Temple, London EC4Y 7HH
0171 583 9292 .... C53

Two Crown Office Row Ground Floor, Temple, London
EC4Y 7HJ 020 7797 8100 .... C53

Crown Office Row Chambers Blenheim House, 120 Church
Street, Brighton, Sussex BN1 1WH 01273 625625 .... C11

Crystal Chambers 25A Cintra Park, London SE19 2LH
0181 402 5801 .... C54

D

De Montfort Chambers 95 Princess Road East, Leicester
LE1 7DQ 0116 254 8686 .... C31

Deal Chambers 60 Moordown, Shooters Hill, London
SE18 3NG 0181 856 8738 .... C54

Deans Court Chambers 24 St John Street, Manchester M3 4DF
0161 214 6000 .... C169

Deans Court Chambers 41-43 Market Place, Preston PR1 1AH
01772 555163 .... C188

334 Deansgate Manchester M3 4LY 0161 834 3767 ...... C169

Derby Square Chambers Merchants Court, Derby Square,
Liverpool L2 1TS 0151 709 4222 .... C34

Design Chambers 30 Fleet Street, London EC4Y 1AA
0171 353 0747 .... C54

Devereux Chambers Devereux Court, London WC2R 3JJ
0171 353 7534 .... C54

Devizes Chambers 11 High Street, Potterne, Devizes, Wiltshire
SN10 5PY 01380 724896 .... C19

Devon Chambers 3 St Andrew Street, Plymouth PL1 2AH
01752 661659 .... C186

Doughty Street Chambers 11 Doughty Street, London
WC1N 2PG 0171 404 1313 .... C56

1 Dr Johnson's Buildings Ground Floor, Temple, London
EC4Y 7AX 0171 353 9328 .... C57

3 Dr Johnson's Buildings Ground Floor, Temple, London
EC4Y 7BA 0171 353 4854 .... C57

Dr Johnson's Chambers Two Dr Johnson's Buildings, Temple,
London EC4Y 7AY 0171 353 4716 .... C58

Dr Johnson's Chambers The Atrium Court, Apex Plaza,
Reading, Berkshire RG1 1AX 01734 254221 .... C189

Chambers of Dominic Dudkowski 7 White Street, Brighton,
Sussex BN2 2JH 0973 314252 .... C11

Durham Barristers' Chambers 27 Old Elvet, Durham
DH1 3HN 0191 386 9199 .... C19

2 Dyers Buildings London EC1N 2JT 0171 404 1881 .... C58

E

Earl Street Chambers 47 Earl Street, Maidstone, Kent
ME14 1PD 01622 671222 .... C165

East Anglian Chambers 52 North Hill, Colchester, Essex
CO1 1PY 01206 572756 .... C18

East Anglian Chambers Gresham House, 5 Museum Street,
Ipswich, Suffolk IP1 1HQ 01473 214481 .... C23

East Anglian Chambers 57 London Street, Norwich NR2 1HL
01603 617351 .... C182

Eastbourne Chambers 15 Hyde Gardens, Eastbourne, East
Sussex BN21 4PR 01323 642102 .... C20

Eastern Chambers Badgers Bottom, Dysons Wood Lane,
Tokers Green, Oxford RG4 9EY 0118 972 3722 .... C183

Eaton House 1st Floor, 4 Eaton Road, Branksome Park, Poole,
Dorset BH13 6DG 01202 766301/768068 .... C186

43 Eglantine Road London SW18 2DE 0181 874 3469 .... C58

Eighteen Carlton Crescent Southampton SO15 2XR
01703 639001 .... C193

38 Eldon Chambers 30 Fleet Street, London EC4Y 1AA
0171 353 8822 .... C59

197 Ellesmere Road London NW10 1LG
0181 208 1663 .... C59

61 Elm Grove Sutton, Surrey SM1 4EX 0181 643 9714 .. C194

Emmanuel Chambers 259 Gray's Inn Road, London WC1X 8QT
0171 713 7772 .... C59

Enfield Chambers First Floor, Refuge House, 9-10 River Front,
Enfield, Middlesex EN1 3SZ 0181 364 5627 .... C20

Enterprise Chambers 9 Old Square, Lincoln's Inn, London
WC2A 3SR 0171 405 9471 .... C59

Enterprise Chambers 38 Park Square, Leeds LS1 2PA
0113 246 0391 .... C25

Enterprise Chambers 65 Quayside, Newcastle upon Tyne
NE1 3DS 0191 222 3344 .... C179

Equity Barristers' Chambers Temple Chambers, Second Floor
rooms 152-153, 3-7 Temple Avenue, London EC4Y 0NP
0181 558 8336 .... C59

Equity Chambers 3rd Floor, 153a Corporation Street,
Birmingham B4 6PH 0121 233 2100 .... C4

Erimus Chambers P.O.Box 458, Brixworth, Northampton
NN6 9ZT 01604 882942 .... C181

Erskine Chambers 30 Lincoln's Inn Fields, Lincoln's Inn,
London WC2A 3PF 0171 242 5532 .... C60

One Essex Court Ground Floor, Temple, London EC4Y 9AR
020 7583 2000 .... C60

One Essex Court 1st Floor, Temple, London EC4Y 9AR
0171 936 3030 .... C61

4 Essex Court Temple, London EC4Y 9AJ
020 7797 7970 .... C62

5 Essex Court 1st Floor, Temple, London EC4Y 9AH
0171 410 2000 .... C62

Essex Court Chambers 24 Lincoln's Inn Fields, London
WC2A 3ED 0171 813 8000 .... C63

Essex House Chambers Unit 6 (Part 2nd Floor South),
Stratford Office Village, 14-30 Romford Road, London E15 4BZ
0181 536 1077 .... C64

20 Essex Street London WC2R 3AL 0171 583 9294 .... C64

23 Essex Street London WC2R 3AS 0171 413 0353/
836 8366 .... C65

35 Essex Street Temple, London WC2R 3AR
0171 353 6381 .... C65

39 Essex Street London WC2R 3AT 0171 832 1111 .... C66

Chambers of Geoffrey Hawker 46/48 Essex Street, London
WC2R 3GH 0171 583 8899 .... C67

Eurolawyer Chambers PO Box 3621, London N7 0BQ
0171 607 0075 .... C67

Everest Twin Firs, PO Box 32, Talygarn, Pontyclun, Cardiff
CF72 9BY 01443 229850 .... C186

Exchange Chambers Pearl Assurance House, Derby Square,
Liverpool L2 9XX 0151 236 7747 .... C34

F

16 Fairhazel Gardens London NW6 3SJ
0171 328 5486 .... C67

Falcon Chambers Falcon Court, London EC4Y 1AA
0171 353 2484 .... C67

3 & 4 Farnham Hall Farnham, Saxmundham, Suffolk
IP17 1LB 01728 602758 .... C191

Farrar's Building Temple, London EC4Y 7BD
0171 583 9241 .... C68

Fenners Chambers 3 Madingley Road, Cambridge CB3 0EE
01223 368761 .... C14

Fenners Chambers 8-12 Priestgate, Peterborough PE1 1JA
01733 562030 .... C185

Chambers of Norman Palmer 2 Field Court, Gray's Inn,
London WC1R 5BB 0171 405 6114 .... C69

4 Field Court Gray's Inn, London WC1R 5EA
0171 440 6900 .... C69

Field Court Chambers 2nd Floor, 3 Field Court, Gray's Inn,
London WC1R 5EP 0171 404 7474 .... C70

First National Chambers 2nd Floor, First National Building,
24 Fenwick Street, Liverpool L2 7NE 0151 236 2098 .... C35

Fleet Chambers Mitre House, 44-46 Fleet Street, London
EC4Y 1BN 0171 936 3707 .... C70

Forest House Chambers 15 Granville Road, Walthamstow,
London E17 9BS 0181 925 2240 .... C71

Chambers of Wilfred Forster-Jones New Court, 1st Floor
South, Temple, London EC4Y 9BE 0171 353 0853/
4/7222 .... C71

Fountain Chambers Cleveland Business Centre, 1 Watson
Street, Middlesbrough TS1 2RQ 01642 804040 .... C177

Fountain Court Temple, London EC4Y 9DH
0171 583 3335 .... C71

1 Fountain Court Steelhouse Lane, Birmingham B4 6DR
0121 236 5721 .... C4

3 Fountain Court Steelhouse Lane, Birmingham B4 6DR
0121 236 5854 .... C4

4 Fountain Court Steelhouse Lane, Birmingham B4 6DR
0121 236 3476 .... C5

5 Fountain Court Steelhouse Lane, Birmingham B4 6DR
0121 606 0500 .... C5

6 Fountain Court Steelhouse Lane, Birmingham B4 6DR
0121 233 3282 .... C6

8 Fountain Court Steelhouse Lane, Birmingham B4 6DR
0121 236 5514/5 .... C7

9 Fountains Way Pinders Heath, Wakefield, West Yorkshire
WF1 4TQ 01924 378631 .... C196

Francis Taylor Building Ground Floor, Temple, London
EC4Y 7BY 0171 353 7768/7769/2711 .... C72

2nd Floor, Francis Taylor Building Temple, London EC4Y 7BY
0171 353 9942/3157 .... C72

Francis Taylor Building 3rd Floor, Temple, London EC4Y 7BY
0171 797 7250 .... C72

Chambers of Herbert Francois 62 St James Road, Mitcham,
Surrey CR4 2DB 0181 640 4529 .... C178

Frederick Place Chambers 9 Frederick Place, Clifton, Bristol
BS8 1AS 0117 9738667 .... C12

55 Frith Road Leytonstone, London E11 4EX C73

Furnival Chambers 32 Furnival Street, London EC4A 1JQ
0171 405 3232 .... C73

Fyfield Chambers Field Cottage, Fyfield, Southrop,
Gloucestershire GL7 3NT 01367 850304 .... C194

G

Chambers of Davina Gammon Ground Floor, 103 Walter
Road, Swansea, West Glamorgan SA1 5QF 01792 480770   C195

One Garden Court Family Law Chambers Ground Floor,
Temple, London EC4Y 9BJ 0171 797 7900 .... C74

Two Garden Court 1st Floor, Middle Temple, London EC4Y 9BL
0171 353 1633 .... C74

The Garden House 14 New Square, Lincoln's Inn, London
WC2A 3SH 0171 404 6150 .... C75

1 Garfield Road Battersea, London SW11 5PL
0171 228 1137 .... C75

159 Gleneagle Road Streatham, London SW16 6AZ
0181 769 3063 .... C75

Godolphin Chambers 50 Castle Street, Truro, Cornwall
TR1 3AF 01872 276312 .... C196

2 Goldingham Avenue Loughton, Essex IG10 2JF
0181 502 4247 .... C165

Goldsmith Building 1st Floor, Temple, London EC4Y 7BL
0171 353 7881 .... C75

Goldsmith Chambers Ground Floor, Goldsmith Building,
Temple, London EC4Y 7BL 0171 353 6802/3/4/5 .... C76

Goldsworth Chambers 1st Floor, 11 Gray's Inn Square,
London WC1R 5JD 0171 405 7117 .... C77

Goodwin Chambers Goodwin Cottage, 14 Doddington Road,
Wellingborough, Northamptonshire NN8 2JG
01933 222790 .... C197

Gosforth Chambers 2 Lansdowne Place, Gosforth, Newcastle
upon Tyne NE3 1HR 0191 285 4664 .... C179

9 Gough Square London EC4A 3DE 020 7832 0500 .... C77

Gough Square Chambers 6-7 Gough Square, London
EC4A 3DE 0171 353 0924 .... C79

Granary Chambers 4 Glenleigh Park Road, Bexhill-On-Sea,
East Sussex TN39 4EH 01424 733008 .... C3

Gray's Inn Chambers, The Chambers of Norman Patterson
First Floor, Gray's Inn Chambers, Gray's Inn, London WC1R 5JA
0171 831 5344 .... C79

Gray's Inn Chambers Chambers of Nigel Ley (2nd Floor),
Gray's Inn, London WC1R 5JA 0171 831 7888 (Chambers)/
0171 831 7904 (Mr M Ullah) C80

Gray's Inn Chambers 5th Floor, Gray's Inn, London WC1R 5JA
0171 404 1111 .... C80

96 Gray's Inn Road London WC1X 8AL 0171 405 0585 ... C80

**1 Gray's Inn Square, Chambers of the Baroness Scotland of
Asthal QC** 1st Floor, London WC1R 5AG 0171 405 3000 .. C80

1 Gray's Inn Square Ground Floor, London WC1R 5AA
0171 405 8946/7/8 .... C80

2-3 Gray's Inn Square Gray's Inn, London WC1R 5JH
0171 242 4986 .... C80

2 Gray's Inn Square Chambers 2nd Floor, Gray's Inn, London
WC1R 5AA 020 7242 0328 .... C82

3 Gray's Inn Square Ground Floor, London WC1R 5AH
0171 520 5600 .... C82

4-5 Gray's Inn Square Ground Floor, Gray's Inn, London
WC1R 5JP 0171 404 5252 .... C83

6 Gray's Inn Square Ground Floor, Gray's Inn, London
WC1R 5AZ 0171 242 1052 .... C85

8 Gray's Inn Square Gray's Inn, London WC1R 5AZ
0171 242 3529 .... C85

Counsels' Chambers 2nd Floor, 10-11 Gray's Inn Square,
London WC1R 5JD 0171 405 2576 .... C86

14 Gray's Inn Square Gray's Inn, London WC1R 5JP
0171 242 0858 .... C86

Gray's Inn Tax Chambers 3rd Floor, Gray's Inn Chambers,
Gray's Inn, London WC1R 5JA 0171 242 2642 .... C86

100e Great Portland Street London W1N 5PD
0171 636 6323 .... C86

Greenway Sonning Lane, Sonning-on-Thames, Berkshire
RG4 6ST 0118 969 2484 .... C192

45 Greenway Frinton-on-Sea, Essex CO13 9AJ
01255 670699 .... C21

Chambers of Helen Grindrod QC 4th Floor, 15-19 Devereux
Court, London WC2R 3JJ 0171 583 2792 .... C87

Guildford Chambers Stoke House, Leapale Lane, Guildford,
Surrey GU1 4LY 01483 539131 .... C21

Guildhall Chambers 22-26 Broad Street, Bristol BS1 2HG
0117 9273366 .... C12

Guildhall Chambers Portsmouth Prudential Buildings, 16
Guildhall Walk, Portsmouth, Hampshire PO1 2DE
01705 752400 .... C187

Chambers of Beverley Gutteridge 36 Dunmore Road,
Wimbledon, London SW20 8TN 0181 947 0717 .... C87

H

Hampshire Chambers Malton House, 24 Hampshire Terrace,
Portsmouth, Hampshire PO1 2QF 01705 826636/
826426 .... C187

Chambers of John Hand QC 9 St John Street, Manchester
M3 4DN 0161 955 9000 .... C169

Harbour Court Chambers 11 William Price Gardens, Fareham,
Hampshire PO16 7PD 01329 827828 .... C21

1 Harcourt Buildings 2nd Floor, Temple, London EC4Y 9DA
0171 353 9421/0375 .... C87

2 Harcourt Buildings Ground Floor/Left, Temple, London
EC4Y 9DB 0171 583 9020 .... C88

2 Harcourt Buildings 1st Floor, Temple, London EC4Y 9DB
020 7353 2112 .... C89

2 Harcourt Buildings 2nd Floor, Temple, London EC4Y 9DB
020 7353 8415 .... C89

Harcourt Chambers Churchill House, 3 St Aldate's Courtyard,
St Aldate's, Oxford OX1 1BN 01865 791559 .... C183

Harcourt Chambers 1st Floor, 2 Harcourt Buildings, Temple,
London EC4Y 9DB 0171 353 6961 .... C90

Hardwicke Building New Square, Lincoln's Inn, London
WC2A 3SB 020 7242 2523 .... C91

1 Hare Court Ground Floor, Temple, London EC4Y 7BE
0171 353 3982/5324 .... C93

One Hare Court 1st Floor, Temple, London EC4Y 7BE
020 7353 3171 .... C93

3 Hare Court 1 Little Essex Street, London WC2R 3LD
0171 395 2000 .... C95

Chambers of Harjit Singh Ground Floor, 2 Middle Temple
Lane, Temple, London EC4Y 9AA 0171 353 1356 (4 Lines) C96

Chambers of Alan Harle 19 Summerhouse Farm, East
Rainton, Houghton-le-Spring, Tyne & Wear DH5 9QQ
0191 5844604 .... C22

23 Harries Road Hayes, Middlesex UB4 9DD
0181 841 8236 .... C22

Chambers of Averil Harrison 7 King George Street, Greenwich,
London SE10 8QJ 0181 692 4949 .... C96

Harrow on the Hill Chambers 60 High Street, Harrow-on-the-
Hill, Middlesex HA1 3LL 0181 423 7444 .... C96

Helions Chambers Pilgrims' Way, Camps Road, Helions
Bumpstead, Haverhill, Suffolk CB9 7AS 01440 730523 ...... C22

Herons Rest Parkham Lane, Brixham, Devon TQ5 9JR
01803 882293 .... C13

Hickstead Cottage Brighton Road, Hickstead, West Sussex
RH17 5NU 01444 881182 .... C22

High Pavement Chambers 1 High Pavement, Nottingham
NG1 1HF 0115 9418218 .... C182

High Street Chambers 102 High Street, Godalming, Surrey
GU7 1DS 01483 861170 .... C21

Higher Combe Hawkcombe, Porlock, Minehead, Somerset
TA24 8LP 01643 862722 .... C178

10 Highlever Road North Kensington, London W10 6PS
0181 969 8514 .... C97

Chambers of Paul Hogben 199 Kingsworth Road, Ashford,
Kent TN23 6NB 01233 645805 .... C3

Holborn Chambers 6 Gate Street, Lincoln's Inn Fields, London
WC2A 3HP 0171 242 6060 .... C97

Horizon Chambers 95a Chancery Lane, London WC2A 1DT
0171 242 2440 .... C97

Chambers of Michael Pert QC 24 Albion Place, Northampton
NN1 1UD 01604 602333 .... C181

Chambers of Michael Pert QC 104 New Walk, Leicester
LE1 7EA 0116 249 2020 .... C31

I

India Buildings Chambers Water Street, Liverpool L2 0XG
0151 243 6000 .... C35

1 Inner Temple Lane Temple, London EC4Y 1AF
020 7353 0933 .... C97

International Law Chambers ILC House, 77/79 Chepstow
Road, Bayswater, London W2 5QR 0171 221 5684/5/4840 C97

Iscoed Chambers 86 St Helen's Road, Swansea, West
Glamorgan SA1 4BQ 01792 652988/9/330 .... C195

J

John Pugh's Chambers 3rd Floor, 14 Castle Street, Liverpool
L2 0NE 0151 236 5415 .... C35

John Street Chambers 2 John Street, London WC1N 2HJ
0171 242 1911 .... C97

Justice Court Chambers 75 Kendal Road, Willesden Green,
London NW10 1JE 0181 830 7786 .... C98

K

Merriemore Cottage Sawbridge, Nr Rugby, Warwickshire
CV23 8BB 01788 891832 .... C190

Keating Chambers 10 Essex Street, Outer Temple, London
WC2R 3AA 0171 544 2600 .... C98

Kenworthy's Chambers 83 Bridge Street, Manchester M3 2RF
0161 832 4036/834 6954 .... C170

King Charles House Standard Hill, Nottingham NG1 6FX
0115 9418851 .... C183

40 King Street Manchester M2 6BA 0161 832 9082 ...... C170

65-67 King Street Leicester LE1 6RP 0116 2547710 ...... C32

8 King Street Chambers 8 King Street, Manchester M2 6AQ
0161 834 9560 .... C171

58 King Street Chambers 1st Floor, Kingsgate House, 51-53
South King Street, Manchester M2 6DE 0161 831 7477 ... C172

King's Bench Chambers 115 North Hill, Plymouth PL4 8JY
01752 221551 .... C186

King's Bench Chambers 32 Beaumont Street, Oxford OX1 2NP
01865 311066 .... C184

King's Bench Chambers Wellington House, 175 Holdenhurst
Road, Bournemouth, Dorset BH8 8DQ 01202 250025 ...... C10

One King's Bench Walk 1st Floor, Temple, London EC4Y 7DB
0171 936 1500 .... C99

2 King's Bench Walk Ground Floor, Temple, London EC4Y 7DE
0171 353 1746 .... C99

4 King's Bench Walk Ground/First Floor/Basement, Temple,
London EC4Y 7DL 0171 822 8822 .... C100

4 King's Bench Walk 2nd Floor, Temple, London EC4Y 7DL
020 7353 3581 .... C101

5 King's Bench Walk Temple, London EC4Y 7DN
0171 353 5638 .... C101

6 King's Bench Walk Ground Floor, Temple, London
EC4Y 7DR 0171 583 0410 .... C101

6 King's Bench Walk Ground, Third & Fourth Floors, Temple,
London EC4Y 7DR 0171 353 4931/583 0695 .... C102

S Tomlinson QC 7 King's Bench Walk, Temple, London
EC4Y 7DS 0171 583 0404 .... C102

8 King's Bench Walk 2nd Floor, Temple, London EC4Y 7DU
0171 797 8888 .... C102

9 King's Bench Walk Ground Floor, Temple, London EC4Y 7DX
0171 353 7202/3909 .... C103

The Chambers of Mr Ali Mohammed Azhar Basement, 9
King's Bench Walk, Temple, London EC4Y 7DX
0171 353 9564 .... C103

10 King's Bench Walk Ground Floor, Temple, London
EC4Y 7EB 0171 353 7742 .... C103

10 King's Bench Walk 1st Floor, Temple, London EC4Y 7EB
0171 353 2501 .... C103

11 King's Bench Walk 3 Park Court, Park Cross Street, Leeds
LS1 2QH 0113 297 1200 .... C25

11 King's Bench Walk Temple, London EC4Y 7EQ
0171 632 8500/583 0610 .... C104

11 King's Bench Walk 1st Floor, Temple, London EC4Y 7EQ
0171 353 3337 .... C104

12 King's Bench Walk Temple, London EC4Y 7EL
0171 583 0811 .... C105

13 King's Bench Walk 1st Floor, Temple, London EC4Y 7EN
0171 353 7204 .... C106

2 King's Bench Walk Chambers 1st Floor, 2 King's Bench
Walk, Temple, London EC4Y 7DE 020 7353 9276 .... C106

8 King's Bench Walk North 1 Park Square East, Leeds LS1 2NE
0113 2439797 .... C25

King's Chambers 5a Gildredge Road, Eastbourne, East Sussex
BN21 4RB 01323 416053 .... C20

King's Chambers 49a Broadway, Stratford, London
E15 4BW C107

10 Kingsfield Avenue Harrow, Middlesex HA2 6AH
0181 427 8709/081 248 4943 .... C22

Kingsway Chambers 88 Kingsway, Holborn, London
WC2B 6AA 07000 653529 .... C107

L

Lamb Building Ground Floor, Temple, London EC4Y 7AS
020 7797 7788 .... C107

Lamb Chambers Lamb Building, Temple, London EC4Y 7AS
020 7797 8300 .... C108

8 Lambert Jones Mews Barbican, London EC2Y 8DP
0171 638 8804 .... C108

29a Lambs Conduit Street Holborn, London WC1N 3NG
0171 831 9907 .... C108

Lancaster Building 77 Deansgate, Manchester M3 2BW
0161 661 4444/0171 649 9872 .... C172

21 Lauderdale Tower Barbican, London EC2Y 8BY
0171 920 9308 .... C108

10 Launceston Avenue Caversham Park Village, Reading,
Berkshire RG4 6SW 01189 479548 .... C189

Lavenham Chambers Rookery Farm, Near Lavenham, Suffolk
CO10 0BJ 01787 248247 .... C178

Law Chambers 2nd Floor, 5 Cardiff Road, Luton, Bedfordshire
LU1 1PP 01582 431352 or 0958 674785 .... C165

Leone Chambers 72 Evelyn Avenue, Kingsbury, London
NW9 0JH 0181 200 4020 .... C108

Chambers of Stuart Lightwing Tudor Court, Church Lane,
Nunthorpe, Middlesbrough TS7 0PD 01642 315000 .... C177

Lincoln House Chambers 5th Floor, Lincoln House, 1
Brazennose Street, Manchester M2 5EL 0161 832 5701 ... C172

Lion Court Chancery House, 53-64 Chancery Lane, London
WC2A 1SJ 0171 404 6565 .... C108

Littleton Chambers 3 King's Bench Walk North, Temple,
London EC4Y 7HR 0171 797 8600 .... C109

Littman Chambers 12 Gray's Inn Square, London WC1R 5JP
020 7404 4866 .... C110

114 Liverpool Road Islington, London N1 0RE 0171 226 9863
C110

Lloyds House Chambers 3rd Floor, 18 Lloyds House, Lloyd
Street, Manchester M2 5WA 0161 839 3371 .... C173

235 London Road Twickenham, London TW1 1ES
0181 892 5947 .... C111

Luton Bedford Chambers C/O Mr Alex Reid, 92 Holly Park
Road, Friern Barnet, London N11 3HB 0181 361 9024/
0181 444 6337 .... C111

Adrian Lyon's Chambers 14 Castle Street, Liverpool L2 0NE
0151 236 4421/8240 .... C35

M

**Chambers of Ian Macdonald QC (In Association with Two
Garden Court, Temple, London)** Waldorf House, 5 Cooper
Street, Manchester M2 2FW 0161 236 1840 .... C173

Maidstone Chambers 33 Earl Street, Maidstone, Kent
ME14 1PF 01622 688592 .... C166

Manchester House Chambers 18-22 Bridge Street,
Manchester M3 3BZ 0161 834 7007 .... C173

5 Marney Road Battersea, London SW11 1ES
0171 978 4492 .... C111

Martins Building 2nd Floor, No 4 Water Street, Liverpool
L2 3SP 0151 236 5818/4919 .... C35

Melbury House 55 Manor Road, Oadby, Leicester LE2 2LL
0116 2711848 .... C32

22 Melcombe Regis Court Weymouth Street, London
W1N 3LG 0171 487 5589 .... C111

Mendhir Chambers 38 Priest Avenue, Wokingham, Berkshire
RG40 2LX 0118 9771274 .... C198

Merchant Chambers 1 North Parade, Parsonage Gardens,
Manchester M3 2NH 0161 839 7070 .... C173

Mercury Chambers Mercury House, 33-35 Clarendon Road,
Leeds LS2 9NZ 0113 234 2265 .... C26

1 Middle Temple Lane Temple, London EC4Y 1LT
0171 583 0659 (12 Lines) C111

1a Middle Temple Lane Ground Floor, Temple, London
EC4Y 9AA 0171 353 8815 .... C111

2 Middle Temple Lane 3rd Floor, Temple, London EC4Y 9AA
0171 583 4540 .... C111

Middlesex Chambers Suite 3 & 4 Stanley House, Stanley
Avenue, Wembley, Middlesex HA0 4SB 0181 902 1499 .... C197

Milburn House Chambers 'A' Floor, Milburn House, Dean
Street, Newcastle upon Tyne NE1 1LE 0191 230 5511 ...... C179

6-8 Mill Street Maidstone, Kent ME15 6XH
01622 688094 .... C166

10 Millfields Road London E5 0SB 0181 986 8059 .... C112

Milton Keynes Chambers 61 London Road, Loughton, Milton
Keynes, Buckinghamshire MK5 8AF 01908 664 128 .... C177

Chambers of Lesley Mitchell Stapleton Lodge, 71 Hamilton
Road, Brentford, Middlesex TW8 0QJ 0181 568 2164 .... C11

1 Mitre Court Buildings Temple, London EC4Y 7BS
0171 797 7070 .... C112

2 Mitre Court Buildings 1st Floor, Temple, London EC4Y 7BX
0171 353 1353 .... C112

2 Mitre Court Buildings 2nd Floor, Temple, London EC4Y 7BX
0171 583 1380 .... C112

Mitre Court Chambers 3rd Floor, Temple, London EC4Y 7BP
0171 353 9394 .... C113

Mitre House Chambers 15-19 Devereux Court, London
WC2R 3JJ 0171 583 8233 .... C113

Monckton Chambers 4 Raymond Buildings, Gray's Inn,
London WC1R 5BP 0171 405 7211 .... C114

26 Morley Avenue Ashgate, Chesterfield S40 4DA
01246 234790/01298 871350 .... C18

Chambers of Christopher J Morrison 2 Brook Mead, Ewell
Court, Epsom, Surrey KT19 0BD 0181 393 8376 .... C20

Mottingham Barrister's Chambers 43 West Park, London
SE9 4RZ 0181 857 5565 .... C115

Chambers of Janaki Mylvaganam 8B Aristole Road, London
SW4 2HZ 0171 627 4006 .... C115

N

Chambers of Dr Jamal Nasir 1st Floor, Lincoln's Inn, London
WC2A 3RH 0171 405 3818/9 .... C115

Neston Home Chambers 42 Greenhill, Neston, Corsham,
Wiltshire SN13 9SQ 01225 811909 .... C195

New Bailey Chambers 10 Lawson Street, Preston PR1 2QT
01772 258087 .... C188

New Chambers 3 Sadleir Road, St Albans, Herts AL1 2BL
0966 212126 .... C190

New Court Temple, London EC4Y 9BE 0171 583 5123/
0510 .... C115

New Court Chambers 5 Verulam Buildings, Gray's Inn, London
WC1R 5LY 0171 831 9500 .... C116

New Court Chambers Gazette Building, 168 Corporation
Street, Birmingham B4 6TZ 0121 693 6656 .... C7

New Court Chambers 3 Broad Chare, Newcastle upon Tyne
NE1 3DQ 0191 232 1980 .... C179

1 New Square Ground Floor, Lincoln's Inn, London WC2A 3SA
0171 405 0884/5/6/7 .... C116

Chambers of Lord Goodhart QC Ground Floor, 3 New Square,
Lincoln's Inn, London WC2A 3RS 0171 405 5577 .... C118

3 New Square Lincoln's Inn, London WC2A 3RS
0171 405 1111 .... C118

Chambers of John L Powell QC Four New Square, Lincoln's
Inn, London WC2A 3RJ 0171 797 8000 .... C118

5 New Square Ground Floor, Lincoln's Inn, London WC2A 3RJ
020 7404 0404 .... C119

7 New Square Lincoln's Inn, London WC2A 3QS
0171 430 1660 .... C120

7 New Square 1st Floor, Lincoln's Inn, London WC2A 3QS
020 7404 5484 .... C120

8 New Square Lincoln's Inn, London WC2A 3QP
0171 405 4321 .... C120

Chambers of John Gardiner QC 1st Floor, 11 New Square,
Lincoln's Inn, London WC2A 3QB 0171 242 4017 .... C121

12 New Square Lincoln's Inn, London WC2A 3SW
0171 419 1212 .... C121

2 New Street Leicester LE1 5NA 0116 2625906 .... C32

New Walk Chambers 27 New Walk, Leicester LE1 6TE
0116 2559144 .... C32

Newport Chambers 12 Clytha Park Road, Newport, Gwent
NP9 4TL 01633 267403/255855 .... C180

Nicholas Street Chambers 22 Nicholas Street, Chester
CH1 2NX 01244 323886 .... C17

No. 6 6 Park Square, Leeds LS1 2LW 0113 2459763 .... C26

15 North Church Street Chambers 15 North Church Street,
Sheffield S1 2DH 0114 2759708/2738380 .... C191

North London Chambers 14 Keyes Road, London NW2 3XA
0181 208 4651 .... C122

Northampton Chambers 22 Albion Place, Northampton
NN1 1UD 01604 636271 .... C181

O

Octagon House 19 Colegate, Norwich NR3 1AT
01603 623186 .... C182

Odogor Chambers 14 Cairns Road, Battersea, London
SW11 1ES C122

Chambers of Joy Okoye Suite 1, 2nd Floor Gray's Inn
Chambers, Gray's Inn, London WC1R 5JA 0171 405 7011 C122

19 Old Buildings Lincoln's Inn, London WC2A 3UP
0171 405 2001 .... C123

22 Old Buildings Lincoln's Inn, London WC2A 3UJ
0171 831 0222 .... C123

Twenty-Four Old Buildings Ground Floor, Lincoln's Inn,
London WC2A 3UP 0171 404 0946 .... C124

24 Old Buildings First Floor, Lincoln's Inn, London WC2A 3UP
020 7242 2744 .... C125

Old Colony House 6 South King Street, Manchester M2 6DQ
0161 834 4364 .... C174

9 Old Square Ground Floor, Lincoln's Inn, London WC2A 3SR
0171 405 4682 .... C125

The Chambers of Leolin Price CBE, QC 10 Old Square,
Lincoln's Inn, London WC2A 3SU 0171 405 0758 .... C126

11 Old Square Ground Floor, Lincoln's Inn, London WC2A 3TS
0171 242 5022/405 1074 .... C126

11 Old Square Ground Floor, Lincoln's Inn, London WC2A 3TS
020 7430 0341 .... C126

12 Old Square 1st Floor, Lincoln's Inn, London WC2A 3TX
0171 404 0875 .... C127

13 Old Square Ground Floor, Lincoln's Inn, London WC2A 3UA
0171 404 4800 .... C128

Old Square Chambers 1 Verulam Buildings, Gray's Inn,
London WC1R 5LQ 0171 269 0300 .... C128

Old Square Chambers Hanover House, 47 Corn Street, Bristol
BS1 1HT 0117 9277111 .... C12

Oriel Chambers 14 Water Street, Liverpool L2 8TD
0151 236 7191/236 4321 .... C36

Chambers of Thelma Osborne-Halsey North Eastern
Chambers, 19 Augustus Drive, Alcester, Warwickshire B49 5HH
01789 766206 .... C3

The Outer Temple Room 26, 222/225 Strand, London
WC2R 1BQ 0171 353 4647 .... C129

4 Overdale Road Knighton, Leicester LE2 3YH
0116 2883930 .... C32

90 Overstrand Mansions Prince of Wales Drive, London
SW11 4EU 0171 622 7415 .... C129

P

12 Page Court Ely, Cambridgeshire CB7 4SD
01353 669213 .... C20

One Paper Buildings Ground Floor, Temple, London EC4Y 7EP
0171 583 7355 .... C129

1 Paper Buildings 1st Floor, Temple, London EC4Y 7EP
0171 353 3728/4953 .... C130

2 Paper Buildings 1st Floor, Temple, London EC4Y 7ET
020 7556 5500 .... C130

2 Paper Buildings, Basement North Temple, London
EC4Y 7ET 0171 936 2613 .... C131

3 Paper Buildings Ground Floor, Temple, London EC4Y 7EU
0171 797 7000 .... C131

3 Paper Buildings Temple, London EC4Y 7EU
020 7583 8055 .... C131

4 Paper Buildings Ground Floor, Temple, London EC4Y 7EX
0171 353 3366/583 7155 .... C132

4 Paper Buildings 1st Floor, Temple, London EC4Y 7EX
0171 583 0816/353 1131 .... C133

5 Paper Buildings Ground Floor, Temple, London EC4Y 7HB
0171 583 9275/583 4555 .... C134

Five Paper Buildings 1st Floor, Five Paper Bldgs, Temple,
London EC4Y 7HB 0171 583 6117 .... C134

3 Paper Buildings (Bournemouth) 20 Lorne Park Road,
Bournemouth, Dorset BH1 1JN 01202 292102 .... C10

3 Paper Buildings (Oxford) 1 Alfred Street, High Street, Oxford
OX1 4EH 01865 793736 .... C184

3 Paper Buildings (Winchester) 4 St Peter Street, Winchester
SO23 8BW 01962 868884 .... C197

Paradise Chambers 26 Paradise Square, Sheffield S1 2DE
0114 2738951 .... C192

39 Park Avenue Mitcham, Surrey CR4 2ER
0181 648 1684 .... C178

Park Court Chambers 16 Park Place, Leeds LS1 2SJ
0113 2433277 .... C26

Park Lane Chambers 19 Westgate, Leeds LS1 2RD
0113 2285000 .... C27

The Chambers of Philip Raynor QC 5 Park Place, Leeds
LS1 2RU 0113 242 1123 .... C27

9 Park Place Cardiff CF1 3DP 01222 382731 .... C15

30 Park Place Cardiff CF1 3BA 01222 398421 .... C15

32 Park Place Cardiff CF1 3BA 01222 397364 .... C15

33 Park Place Cardiff CF1 3BA 02920 233313 .... C16

30 Park Square Leeds LS1 2PF 0113 2436388 .... C28

39 Park Square Leeds LS1 2NU 0113 2456633 .... C28

37 Park Square Chambers 37 Park Square, Leeds LS1 2NY
0113 2439422 .... C28

Parsonage Chambers 5th Floor, 3 The Parsonage, Manchester
M3 2HW 0161 833 1996 .... C174

12 Paxton Close Kew Gardens, Richmond-upon-Thames,
Surrey TW9 2AW 0181 940 5895 .... C190

Peel Court Chambers 45 Hardman Street, Manchester M3 3PL
0161 832 3791 .... C174

Pembroke House 18 The Crescent, Leatherhead, Surrey
KT22 8EE 01372 376160/376493 .... C23

Pendragon Chambers 124 Walter Road, Swansea, West
Glamorgan SA1 5RG 01792 411188 .... C195

Pepys' Chambers 17 Fleet Street, London EC4Y 1AA
0171 936 2710 .... C135

Perivale Chambers 15 Colwyn Avenue, Perivale, Middlesex
UB6 8JY 0181 998 1935/081 248 0246 .... C185

Phoenix Chambers First Floor, Gray's Inn Chambers, Gray's
Inn, London WC1R 5JA 0171 404 7888 .... C135

Phydeaux Chambers Dunelm, Mount Pleasant Road,
Camborne, Cornwall TR14 7RJ 01209 715285 .... C14

Plowden Buildings 2nd Floor, 2 Plowden Buildings, Middle
Temple Lane, London EC4Y 9BU 0171 583 0808 .... C135

Plowden Buildings 1 Jesmond Dene Terrace, Newcastle upon
Tyne NE2 2ET 0191 281 2096 .... C179

Point House Spooner Row, Wymondham, Norfolk NR18 9LQ
01953 606965 .... C199

21 Portland Road Clarendon Park, Leicester LE2 3AB
0116 2706235 .... C32

Portsmouth Barristers' Chambers Victory House, 7 Bellevue
Terrace, Portsmouth, Hampshire PO5 3AT 023 92 831292/
811811 .... C187

Portsmouth Barristers' Chambers Winchester Annexe, First
Floor, 28 St Stephens Road, Winchester SO22 6DE
01962 863222 .... C197

Portsmouth Barristers' Chambers Isle of Wight Annexe, 35
Alpine Road, Ventnor, Isle of Wight PO38 1BU
01983 855 666 .... C196

Primrose Chambers 5 Primrose Way, Alperton, Middlesex
HA0 1DS 0181 998 1806 .... C3

Prince Henry's Chamber 109 Grosvenor Road, Westminster,
London SW1V 3LG 0171 834 2572 .... C135

Prince Henry's Chambers 2 Tamar House, 12 Tavistock Place,
London WC1H 9RA 0171 713 0376 .... C136

Pulteney Chambers 14 Johnstone Street, Bath BA2 4DH
01225 723987 .... C3

1 Pump Court Lower Ground Floor, Temple, London EC4Y 7AB
0171 583 2012/353 4341 .... C136

2 Pump Court 1st Floor, Temple, London EC4Y 7AH
0171 353 5597 .... C137

Pump Court Chambers Upper Ground Floor, 3 Pump Court,
Temple, London EC4Y 7AJ 0171 353 0711 .... C137

4 Pump Court Temple, London EC4Y 7AN
020 7842 5555 .... C138

5 Pump Court Ground Floor, Temple, London EC4Y 7AP
020 7353 2532 .... C139

Chambers of Kieran Coonan QC Ground Floor, 6 Pump Court,
Temple, London EC4Y 7AR 0171 583 6013/2510 .... C140

6 Pump Court 1st Floor, Temple, London EC4Y 7AR
0171 797 8400 .... C141

Pump Court Chambers 31 Southgate Street, Winchester
SO23 9EE 01962 868161 .... C198

Pump Court Chambers 5 Temple Chambers, Temple Street,
Swindon SN1 1SQ 01793 539899 .... C195

Pump Court Tax Chambers 16 Bedford Row, London
WC1R 4EB 0171 414 8080 .... C141

Q

Queen Elizabeth Building Ground Floor, Temple, London
EC4Y 9BS 0171 353 7181 (12 Lines) C141

Hollis Whiteman Chambers 3rd Floor, Queen Elizabeth Bldg,
Temple, London EC4Y 9BS 020 7583 5766 .... C142

Queen Elizabeth Building 2nd Floor, Temple, London
EC4Y 9BS 0171 797 7837 .... C142

Queen Square Chambers 56 Queen Square, Bristol BS1 4PR
0117 921 1966 .... C13

Queen's Chambers 5 John Dalton Street, Manchester M2 6ET
0161 834 6875/4738 .... C174

Queens Chambers 4 Camden Place, Preston PR1 3JL
01772 828300 .... C188

R

The Ralek 66 Carshalton Park Road, Carshalton, Surrey
SM5 3SS 0181 669 1777 .... C17

189 Randolph Avenue London W9 1DJ
0171 624 9139 .... C143

One Raymond Buildings Gray's Inn, London WC1R 5BH
0171 430 1234 .... C143

3 Raymond Buildings Gray's Inn, London WC1R 5BH
020 7831 3833 .... C143

5 Raymond Buildings 1st Floor, Gray's Inn, London WC1R 5BP
0171 242 2902 .... C143

18 Red Lion Court (Off Fleet Street), London EC4A 3EB
0171 520 6000 .... C144

Redhill Chambers Seloduct House, 30 Station Road, Redhill,
Surrey RH1 1NF 01737 780781 .... C190

Regency Chambers Sheraton House, Castle Park, Cambridge
CB3 0AX 01223 301517 .... C14

Regency Chambers Cathedral Square, Peterborough PE1 1XW
01733 315215 .... C185

Regent Chambers 8 Pall Mall, Hanley, Stoke On Trent ST1 1ER
01782 286666 .... C194

Resolution Chambers Oak Lodge, 55 Poolbrook Road,
Malvern, Worcestershire WR14 3JN 01684 561279 .... C166

Richmond Green Chambers Greyhound House, 23-24 George
Street, Richmond-upon-Thames, Surrey TW9 1HY
0181 940 1841 .... C190

20 Richmond Way 1st Floor, London W12 8LY
0181 749 2004 .... C144

Ridgeway Chambers 6 The Ridgeway, Golders Green, London
NW11 8TB 0181 455 2939 .... C145

Roehampton Chambers 30 Stoughton Close, Roehampton,
London SW15 4LS 0181 788 1238 .... C145

Ropewalk Chambers 24 The Ropewalk, Nottingham NG1 5EF
0115 9472581 .... C183

27 Rose Grove Bury, Greater Manchester BL8 2UJ
0161 763 4739 .... C14

Rosemont Chambers 26 Rosemont Court, Rosemont Road,
London W3 9LS 0181 992 1100 .... C145

Rougemont Chambers 8 Colleton Crescent, Exeter, Devon
EX1 1RR 01392 208484 .... C20

Rowchester Chambers 4 Rowchester Court, Whittall Street,
Birmingham B4 6DH 0121 233 2327/2361951 .... C7

S

Sackville Chambers Sackville Place, 44-48 Magdalen Street,
Norwich NR3 1JU 01603 613516/616221 .... C182

2 Salvia Gardens Perivale, Middlesex UB6 7PG
0181 997 9905 .... C185

Sedan House Stanley Place, Chester CH1 2LU
01244 320480/348282 .... C17

No. 1 Serjeants' Inn 5th Floor Fleet Street, Temple, London
EC4Y 1LH 0171 415 6666 .... C145

1 Serjeants' Inn 4th Floor, Temple, London EC4Y 1NH
0171 583 1355 .... C145

3 Serjeants' Inn London EC4Y 1BQ 0171 353 5537 .... C145

Serle Court Chambers 6 New Square, Lincoln's Inn, London
WC2A 3QS 0171 242 6105 .... C146

20 Sewardstone Gardens Chingford, London E4 7QE
0181 524 3054 .... C147

26 Shaftesbury Road Earlsdon, Coventry, Warwickshire
CV5 6FN 01203 677337 .... C19

Chambers of Pavan Sharma 286 Overdown Road, Tilehurst,
Reading, Berkshire RG31 6PP 0118 9625 832 .... C189

Slough Chamber 11 St Bernards Road, Slough, Berkshire
SL3 7NT 01753 553806/817989 .... C192

Chambers of Robert Smith 16 Wilson Road, Chessington,
Surrey KT9 2HE 0181 288 2594 .... C17

Solent Chambers 2nd Floor, Coronation House, 1 King's
Terrace, Portsmouth, Hampshire PO5 3AR
01705 821818 .... C187

Somersett Chambers 25 Bedford Row, London WC1R 4HE
0171 404 6701 .... C148

2 South Avenue Cleverley, Lancashire C18

3/4 South Square Gray's Inn, London WC1R 5HP
0171 696 9900 .... C148

11 South Square 2nd Floor, Gray's Inn, London WC1R 5EU
0171 405 1222 (24hr messaging service) C149

South Western Chambers Melville House, 12 Middle Street,
Taunton, Somerset TA1 1SH 01823 331919 (24 hrs) C196

Southernhay Chambers 33 Southernhay East, Exeter, Devon
EX1 1NX 01392 255777 .... C21

Southsea Chambers PO Box 148, Southsea, Portsmouth,
Hampshire PO5 2TU 01705 291261 .... C188

Sovereign Chambers 25 Park Square, Leeds LS1 2PW
0113 2451841/2/3 .... C29

Spon Chambers 13 Spon Street, Coventry, Warwickshire
CV1 3BA 01203 632977 .... C19

85 Springfield Road King's Heath, Birmingham B14 7DU
0121 444 2818 .... C8

St Albans Chambers Dolphin Lodge, Dolphin Yard, Holywell
Hill, St Albans, Herts AL1 1EX 01727 843383 .... C191

St David's Chambers 10 Calvert Terrace, Swansea, West
Glamorgan SA1 5AR C195

St Ive's Chambers Whittall Street, Birmingham B4 6DH
0121 236 0863/5720 .... C8

St James's Chambers 68 Quay Street, Manchester M3 3EJ
0161 834 7000 .... C175

18 St John Street Manchester M3 4EA
0161 278 1800 .... C175

24a St John Street Manchester M3 4DF
0161 833 9628 .... C175

28 St John Street Manchester M3 4DJ 0161 834 8418 .. C176

St John's Chambers Small Street, Bristol BS1 1DW
0117 9213456/298514 .... C13

St John's Chambers 2 St John's Street, Manchester M3 4DT
0161 832 1633 .... C176

St John's Chambers One High Elm Drive, Hale Barns, Cheshire
WA15 0JD 0161 980 7379 .... C22

St Mary's Chambers 50 High Pavement, Lace Market,
Nottingham NG1 1HW 0115 9503503 .... C183

St Paul's House 5th Floor, St Paul's House, 23 Park Square
South, Leeds LS1 2ND 0113 2455866 .... C30

St Philip's Chambers Fountain Court, Steelhouse Lane,
Birmingham B4 6DR 0121 246 7000 .... C8

Stanbrook & Henderson Ground Floor, 2 Harcourt Bldgs,
Temple, London EC4Y 9DB 0171 353 0101 .... C149

Staple Inn Chambers 1st Floor, 9 Staple Inn, Holborn Bars,
London WC1V 7QH 0171 242 5240 .... C150

Chambers of Michael Stephen 118 Kennington Road, London
SE11 6RE 07071 780690 .... C151

Chambers of Elizabeth Steventon 50 Firle Road, Brighton,
Sussex BN2 2YH 01273 670394 .... C11

Chambers of Mr G B Stewart Ridge Hall, Ridge Lane, Staithes,
Saltburn-by-the-Sea, Cleveland TS13 5DX 01947 840511 . C191

3 Stone Buildings Lincoln's Inn, London WC2A 3XL
0171 242 4937 .... C151

4 Stone Buildings Ground Floor, Lincoln's Inn, London
WC2A 3XT 0171 242 5524 .... C152

5 Stone Buildings Lincoln's Inn, London WC2A 3XT
0171 242 6201 .... C152

7 Stone Buildings Ground Floor, Lincoln's Inn, London
WC2A 3SZ 0171 405 3886/242 3546 .... C153

7 Stone Buildings (also at 11 Bolt Court) 1st Floor, Lincoln's
Inn, London WC2A 3SZ 0171 242 0961 .... C153

8 Stone Buildings Lincoln's Inn, London WC2A 3TA
0171 831 9881 .... C154

9 Stone Buildings Lincoln's Inn, London WC2A 3NN
0171 404 5055 .... C154

11 Stone Buildings Lincoln's Inn, London WC2A 3TG
+44 (0)207 831 6381 .... C154

Stour Chambers Barton Mill House, Barton Mill Road,
Canterbury, Kent CT1 1BP 01227 764899 .... C15

199 Strand London WC2R 1DR 0171 379 9779 .... C155

Sussex Chambers 9 Old Steine, Brighton, Sussex BN1 1FJ
01273 607953 .... C11

Swan House PO Box 8749, London W13 8ZX
0181 998 3035 .... C156

T

Temple Chamber Suite 241, 4th Floor 3-7 Temple Avenue,
London EC4Y 0HP 0171 353 4461 .... C156

Temple Chambers Rooms 111/112, 3/7 Temple Avenue,
London EC4Y 0HP 0171 583 1001 (2 lines) C156

55 Temple Chambers Temple Avenue, London EC4Y 0HP
0171 353 7400 .... C156

169 Temple Chambers Temple Avenue, London EC4Y 0DA
0171 583 7644 .... C156

Temple Fields Hamilton House, 1 Temple Avenue, London
EC4Y 0HA 0171 353 4212 .... C156

1 Temple Gardens 1st Floor, Temple, London EC4Y 9BB
0171 583 1315/353 0407 .... C157

2 Temple Gardens Temple, London EC4Y 9AY
0171 583 6041 .... C157

3 Temple Gardens Lower Ground Floor, Temple, London
EC4Y 9AU 0171 353 3102/5/9297 .... C158

3 Temple Gardens 2nd Floor, Temple, London EC4Y 9AU
0171 583 1155 .... C159

3 Temple Gardens 3rd Floor, Temple, London EC4Y 9AU
0171 353 0832 .... C159

3 Temple Gardens 3rd Floor, Temple, London EC4Y 9AU
0171 583 0010 .... C159

Temple Gardens Tax Chambers 1st Floor, 3 Temple Gardens,
Temple, London EC4Y 9AU 0171 353 7884/5 8982/3 ..... C159

The Thames Chambers Wickham House, 10 Cleveland Way,
London E1 4TR 0171 366 6655/790 2424 X390 .... C159

Theatre House Percival Road, Clifton, Bristol BS8 3LE
0117 974 1553 .... C13

Thetford Lodge Farm Santon Downham, Brandon, Suffolk
IP27 0TU 01842 813132 .... C11

Thomas More Chambers 52 Carey Street, Lincoln's Inn, London WC2A 2JB 0171 404 7000 ...... C159

Chambers of Robert Thoresby 37 Redbridge Lane West, Wanstead, London E11 2JX 0181 530 5267 ...... C160

29 Gwilliam Street Bristol BS3 4LT 0117 966 8997 ...... C13

Thornwood House 102 New London Road, Chelmsford, Essex CM2 0RG 01245 280880 ...... C17

Tindal Chambers 3/5 New Street, Chelmsford, Essex CM1 1NT 01245 267742 ...... C17

Tollgate Mews Chambers 113 Tollgate Road, Tollgate Mews, North Beckton, London E6 5JY 0171 511 1838 ...... C160

14 Tooks Court Cursitor St, London EC4A 1LB 0171 405 8828 ...... C160

58 Topham Square Tottenham, London N17 7HL 0181 365 1918 ...... C161

Tower Hamlets Barristers Chambers First Floor, 45 Brick Lane, London E1 6PU 0171 247 9825 ...... C161

Tower Hamlets Barristers Chambers 37B Princelet Street, London E1 5LP 0171 377 8090 ...... C161

Trafalgar Chambers 53 Fleet Street, London EC4Y 1BE 0171 583 5858 ...... C161

Trinity Chambers 9-12 Trinity Chare, Quayside, Newcastle upon Tyne NE1 3DF 0191 232 1927 ...... C180

Trinity Chambers 140 New London Road, Chelmsford, Essex CM2 0AW 01245 605040 ...... C17

2-4 Tudor Street London EC4Y 0AA 0171 797 7111 ...... C161

U

Chambers of Mohammed Hasmot Ullah 1st Floor, 72 Brick Lane, London E1 6RL 0171 377 0119 ...... C162

45 Ullswater Crescent Kingston Vale, London SW15 3RG 0181 546 9284 ...... C162

V

Veritas Chambers 33 Corn Street, Bristol BS1 1HT 0117 930 8802 ...... C13

3 Verulam Buildings London WC1R 5NT 0171 831 8441 ...... C162

Verulam Chambers Peer House, 8-14 Verulam Street, Gray's Inn, London WC1X 8LZ 0171 813 2400 ...... C162

Victoria Chambers 3rd Floor, 177 Corporation Street, Birmingham B4 6RG 0121 236 9900 ...... C9

Virtual Chambers (accepting briefs soon), London 07071 244 944 ...... C163

W

Walnut House 63 St David's Hill, Exeter, Devon EX4 4DW 01392 279751 ...... C21

23 Warham Road Otford, Sevenoaks, Kent TN14 5PF 01959 522325 ...... C191

Warwick House Chambers 8 Warwick Court, Gray's Inn, London WC1R 5DJ 0171 430 2323 ...... C163

Warwick Square London SW1V 2AJ 0171 630 6237 ...... C163

Watford Chambers 74 Mildred Avenue, Watford, Hertfordshire WD1 7DX 01923 220553 ...... C196

3 Wellington Road Poole, Dorset BH14 9LF 07771 905671 (Mobile) C187

Chambers of Paschal J Welsh 11 Carlisle House, 105 Old Church Street, London SW3 6DS C163

52 Wembley Park Drive Wembley, Middlesex HA9 8HB 0181 902 5629 ...... C197

1 Wensley Avenue Woodford Green, Essex IG8 9HE 0181 505 9259 ...... C198

Wessex Chambers 48 Queens Road, Reading, Berkshire RG1 4BD 0118 956 8856 ...... C189

West Lodge Farm Wrotham Road, Meopham, Kent DA13 0QG 01474 812280 ...... C177

243 Westbourne Grove London W11 2SE 0171 229 3819 ...... C163

1c Westbourne Terrace Road London W2 6NG C163

28 Western Road Oxford OX1 4LG 01865 204911 ...... C185

Westgate Chambers 144 High Street, Lewes, East Sussex BN7 1XT 01273 480510 ...... C32

Westgate Chambers 67a Westgate Road, Newcastle upon Tyne NE1 1SG 0191 261 4407/2329785 ...... C180

Westgate Chambers 16-17 Wellington Square, Hastings, East Sussex TN34 1PB 01424 432105 ...... C22

Westgate Chambers 4 Copse Close, Northwood, Middlesex HA6 2XG 01923 823671 ...... C181

Westleigh Chambers Westleigh Wiltown, Curry Rivel, Langport, Somerset TA10 0JE 01458 251261 ...... C23

7 Westmeath Avenue Evington, Leicester LE5 6SS 0116 2412003 ...... C32

Westminster Chambers 3 Crosshall Street, Liverpool L1 6DQ 0151 236 4774 ...... C37

Chambers of Paul Wetton 16 Pont Street, London SW1X 9EN 0171 235 8485 ...... C164

103 Wexham Close Luton, Bedfordshire LU3 3TX 01582 598394 ...... C165

White Friars Chambers 21 White Friars, Chester CH1 1NZ 01244 323070 ...... C18

Chambers of Geoffrey White 9 The Finches, Sandy, Bedfordshire SG19 2UL 01767 692782 ...... C191

Wilberforce Chambers 8 New Square, Lincoln's Inn, London WC2A 3QP 0171 306 0102 ...... C164

Wilberforce Chambers 7 Bishop Lane, Hull, East Yorkshire HU1 1PA 01482 323264 ...... C22

Chambers of Derek Willmott 8 Links Crescent, St Marys Bay, Romney Marsh, Kent TN29 0RS 01303 87 3899 ...... C190

7 Wilton Road Redhill, Surrey RH1 6QR 01737 760264 ...... C190

15 Winckley Square Preston PR1 3JJ 01772 252828 ...... C189

Windsor Barristers' Chambers Windsor 01753 648899 ...... C198

Windsor Chambers 2 Penuel Lane, Pontypridd, South Wales CF37 4UF 01443 402067 ...... C186

10 Winterbourne Grove Weybridge, Surrey KT13 0PP 0181 941 3939 ...... C197

9 Woodhouse Square Leeds LS3 1AD 0113 2451986 ...... C30

66 Worthington Road Surbiton, Kingston-Upon-Thames, Surrey KT6 ...... C23

Wynne Chambers 1 Wynne Road, London SW9 0BB 0181 961 6144 ...... C165

Y

York Chambers 14 Toft Green, York YO1 6JT 01904 620048 ...... C199

Young Street Chambers 38 Young Street, Manchester M3 3FT 0161 833 0489 ...... C176

F.M.A.

- Mediator Training
- Member Support Services
- Independent Training
  in Mediator/ ADR Skills
- Working with Family Breakdown
- Supervisor Consultants
- Consulting Services

CPD Courses 1999

- 25 November
- 3 December
- 6 December

Drafting Summaries
Competence Assessment
Domestic Violence Screening

Courses cost £120 and carry 8 CPD points.
All courses in Central London location.

Foundation Training Programme 2000

Four 8 day courses during the year

Course one: 26-28 January, 16-18 February, 18, 19 May
Course two: 5-7 April, 17-19 April, 20,21 July
Course three: 7-9 June, 28-30 June, 28, 29 September
Course four: 20-22 September, 18-20 October, 19, 20 January 2001

Courses cost £1675 and carry 52 CPD points.
All courses in Central London location.

For further information, please contact:
Family Mediators Association, 46 Grosvenor Gardens, London SW1W 0EB
Tel: 0171 881 9400 Fax: 0171 881 9401

E-mail:fmassoc@globalnet.co.uk   *Internet:www.familymediators.co.uk*

Pleased to be co-founders of the UK College

Registered Charity No. 1002971
Company Limited by Guarantee
Registered in England and Wales No. 3780128